U0928329

中国金融统计（1949—2005 年）

China Financial Statistics（1949—2005）

（上册）

主　编　苏　宁

Editor - in - chief　Su Ning

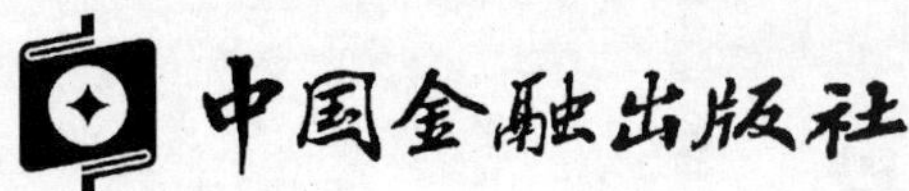

责任编辑：黄海清
责任校对：孙 蕊
责任印制：裴 刚

图书在版编目（CIP）数据

中国金融统计.1949—2005年（Zhongguo Jinrong Tongji）/苏宁主编.—北京：中国金融出版社，2007.6
ISBN 978-7-5049-4384-2

Ⅰ.中… Ⅱ.苏… Ⅲ.金融—统计资料—中国—1949～2005 Ⅳ.F832-66

中国版本图书馆CIP数据核字（2007）第055220号

出版
发行 中国金融出版社
社址 北京市广安门外小红庙南里3号
市场开发部 （010）63272190，66070804（传真）
网上书店 http://www.chinafph.com
（010）63286832，63365686（传真）
读者服务部 （010）66070833，82672183
邮编 100055
经销 新华书店
印刷 北京盛通彩色印刷有限公司
尺寸 185毫米×260毫米
印张 87
字数 2438千
版次 2007年6月第1版
印次 2007年6月第1次印刷
定价 198.00元（上下册）
ISBN 978-7-5049-4384-2/F.3944

中国金融统计（1949—2005年）

China Financial Statistics（1949—2005）

主　　编　苏　宁

Editor - in - Chief　Su Ning

副 主 编　唐思宁

Associate Editor - in - Chief　Tang Sining

编写人员

Editorial Staff

才宏远 Cai Hongyuan	李海龙 Li Hailong	郭永强 Guo Yongqiang	李　红 Li Hong	李瑞芳 Li Ruifang
王东妮 Wang Dongni	王新华 Wang Xinhua	岳　丹 Yue Dan	计　茜 Ji Qian	毛奇正 Mao Qizheng
刘　珂 Liu Ke	马松林 Ma Songlin	李　媛 Li Yuan	丁林润 Ding Linrun	冯仲坡 Feng Zhongpo
常宝玺 Chang Baoxi	周　婷 Zhou Ting	邹　炜 Zou Wei	于建新 Yu Jianxin	郑洪斌 Zheng Hongbin
廖　毅 Liao Yi	王　匀 Wang Yun	许加宏 Xu Jiahong	刘在榕 Liu Zairong	杨秀红 Yang Xiuhong
梁景宗 Liang Jingzong				

序

《中国金融统计（1949—2005年）》终于和大家见面了，我由衷地感到高兴。

金融统计是国家统计体系中的一个重要组成部分，是中国人民银行的一项重要基础工作。从新中国成立至今，五十多年来，金融统计始终围绕我国金融工作的中心服务，以其综合、灵敏、及时的特点，提供了准确可靠的金融统计资料，在国家宏观调控中发挥了重要作用。

近年来，中国金融业发生了深刻的变化，成立了许多新的金融机构，金融业务不断创新，新的金融工具相继涌现，金融对外交流与开放步伐加快，金融体制改革日益深入，金融业经营管理水平不断提高，中央银行在宏观调控和金融稳定方面的职能持续强化，这些工作都对金融统计工作提出了新的要求和挑战。面对市场经济体制改革的深化和金融业的改革创新与发展，中国人民银行的统计工作者不断地对金融统计制度进行改革和完善，以适应金融体系运行中的各种变化。几年来的实践表明，金融统计各项制度的改革，基本上实现了金融统计从服务于计划经济向服务于社会主义市场经济的转变，较好地满足了党中央、国务院领导和中央银行货币政策、金融稳定及相关部门对金融统计信息的需求，同时为金融机构自身的经营管理提供了必要的决策依据。

统计信息来源于社会公众，应为社会公众所利用，同时信息披露也是一个国家文明、开放程度的重要标志。随着我国社会主义市场经济体制的建立，特别是我国加入世界贸易组织和GDDS（国际货币基金组织发布的“数据公布通用系统”）以来，社会公众对金融统计信息的关注度越来越高，金融信息已成为社会公众经济生活中不可缺少的一部分。为了方便社会公众了解金融运行情况和有效利用金融统计数据，中国人民银行调查统计司陆续编辑出版了《中国金融统计（1952—1991年）》、《中国金融统计（1952—1996年）》、《中国金融统计（1997—1999年）》，这次编辑出版的《中国金融统计（1949—2005年）》，不仅汇集了2000—2005年最新的统计数据，同时还发掘增补了1949—1951年的统计数据。此前出版的统计资料，最早起始年份都是1952年，均未包括1949—1951年的金融统计数据，此次出版填补了这个空白。因此，本书能够更加全面、真实、连贯地记录和反映中国金融的发展进程和改革成果。此次出版的内容主要包括信贷收支统计、现金收支统计、货币统计三部分，其中，货币统计是按照国际通行的原则和方法编制的，包括货币供应量统计、货币概览、银行概览等数据，其中的大部分从未在以往出版的资料中完整、系统地披露过。为满足读者的传统阅读习惯，该书总体沿用以往书籍中“资金平衡表”的模式，将金融机构资金来源方和资金运用方的主要统计项目分别列示。为便于读者开展研究，采用以往出版的书籍中未采用过的“时间序列表（包括年度时序与月度时序）”的形式列示重要金融统计指标，这些指标包括存款、贷款、货币供应量、外汇储备等总量指标，反映全社会资金总量及供求情况。读者可在宏观上把握金融业的发展轨迹及货币供应总量状况，也可以进行时间序列研究和横向区域比较分析。为保证数据的可比性、增强金融统计的科学性和严谨性，此书还增加了数据诠释的内容，即对金融统计制度、方法或指标上的一些重大的调整和变化作出阶段性说明，以便于统一数据使用者对数据内涵的理解以及进行可比性分析。此书的出版为分析、研究金融改革与发展提供了十分专业、翔实、系统和权威的数据平台，是分析、研究中国金融改革和发展的一部很有价值的大型资料性、历史性的金融工具书。

二十一世纪是信息经济时代，金融业的改革与和谐发展离不开数据平台的建设和支撑，希望此书能为从事金融事业的人们提供帮助，促进中国金融事业的发展。

苏宁

二〇〇六年十二月

FOREWORD

I am very pleased at the publication of the *China Financial Statistics* (*1949—2005*).

Financial statistics is an important part of China's national statistical system, and collecting and compiling financial statistical data is a key and basic responsibility of the People's Bank of China. Financial statistics has well served the development of China's financial sector by providing comprehensive, timely, accurate and reliable financial data, thus playing an important role in the process of macroeconomic management.

In recent years, China's financial system has been undergoing profound changes as marked by the emergence of new financial institutions and new financial instruments, the innovation of financial businesses, accelerated pace of financial opening – up, deepening of the financial system reform, improvement in the operation and management of the financial sector, and the strengthened role of the central bank in conducting macroeconomic management and promoting financial stability. All these have brought new requirements and challenges to financial statistics. Against the background of deepened market economic system reform as well as the innovation and development of the financial sector, the People's Bank of China has continuously reformed aod improved the financial statistical system in an effort to respond to the changes in the financial system. Experiences in the past years have shown that, with various reform measures, the financial statistics system has been transformed from serving the planned economy to serving the socialist market economy, and financial statistics has well served the needs of state leaders and government departments for financial statistical information, assisted the central bank in formulating and implementing monetary policy and promoting financial stability, and provided a sound basis for the decision – making of the financial institutions.

Statistical information originates from the general public and is used by the general public. Information disclosure is also an important indicator of a country's degree of civilization and openness. As China established the socialist market economy, and in particular since China became a member of the WTO and participated in the General Data Dissemination System of the IMF, the public has paid closer attention to the financial statistical information, and financial information has become an indispensable part of the economic life of the public. To make the public informed of the operation of the financial sector and to help them make effective use of the financial statistical data, the Financial Survey and Statistics Department of the People's Bank of China complied and published progressively the *China Financial Statistics* (*1952—1991*), *China Financial Statistics* (*1952—1996*), and *China Financial Statistics* (*1997—1999*). This issue of the *China Financial Statistics* (*1949—2005*) contains not only the latest statistical data from 2000 to 2005 but also those from 1949 to

1951. The financial statistical information published previously all start from 1952, not covering the period from 1949 to 1951. The *China Financial Statistics* (*1949—2005*) fills this gap, thus records and reflects the development and reform of China's financial system in a more comprehensive, accurate and consistent way. This issue of the *China Financial Statistics* is comprised of three key parts, namely, credit statistics, cash statistics and monetary statistics. The monetary statistics, which has been compiled in accordance with internationally accepted principles and methodologies, includes money supply statistics, monetary survey and banking survey, most of which have never been completely and systematically disclosed in any previous statistical publications. In consideration of the readers' habit, this book basically follows the pattern of "balance sheet of funds" that is used in the previous publications, separately listing the major statistical items for the sources of fund and uses of fund. To facilitate the readers' research activities, this book arranges key financial indicators in time series tables, including annual series and monthly series, reflecting total amount as well as the supply and demand of funds. These key indicators include deposits, loans, money supply, foreign exchange reserves, financial assets, etc. Presenting these indicators with time series tables will enable the readers not only to keep breast of the development of the financial sector and money supply at a macro level, but also to make time series and cross – regional analysis. To make the financial statistical data more comparable and accurate, and to present these data in a more scientific way, the book also contains metadata to explain the major changes in the financial statistical system, methodologies and indicators. The metadata will enable the readers to better understand the concepts of the data and to conduct comparison analysis. This book provides a professional, comprehensive, systematic and authoritative data platform for the analysis and research of financial reform and development. Containing large amount of historic data and materials, it also serves as valuable reference book for the above research and analysis.

The 21st Century is the age of information economy. Reform and harmonious development of the financial sector depend on well – developed financial statistical data. It's my sincere wish that this book will assist the people engaging in the financial industry and promote the development of China's financial sector.

苏宁

December 2006

目　录

第一部分　各年度金融统计情况

第二部分 金融统计主要指标时间序列表

CONTENTS

Part Ⅰ: Financial Statistics for Each Year

Part Ⅱ: Time Series of Major Financial Indicators

第一部分
Part Ⅰ

各年度金融统计情况
Financial Statistics for Each Year

编制说明

一、编制的基本原则

在第一部分资料的编辑过程中，编者坚持“真实、完整、科学”的基本原则，即：真实反映各历史时期统计指标的设置和数据原貌，完整再现金融统计体系中各类金融机构相关业务的统计数据，按照金融机构及其业务产生的先后顺序，科学组织各类金融机构在不同历史时期的金融统计数据。同时，准确解释主要统计指标含义，说明金融统计制度变化以及金融机构的变迁，使本资料更加实用。该部分资料以机构为主线、时间为辅线谋篇布局，反映信贷收支统计、现金收支统计等各年度情况。

二、金融统计的发展背景演变

在不同的历史时期、不同的经济社会背景下，金融统计管理体系、金融统计指标设置、统计框架、指标含义和统计口径等发生着不同程度的变化，并渐趋科学和完善。

1949—1952 年，新中国成立后的这三年时间，是国民经济恢复时期。通过整顿、改造、改组、撤并、接管、取消等有效手段，使私营银行、公私合营银行为当时的国民经济恢复、支持经济重建作出了积极贡献。此时，金融业务相对单一，信贷政策的主要内容是大力积聚资金，积极支持国营经济及合作社经济的发展并坚持“先工后商”的原则。金融统计指标比较单一，只有对公、对私的存贷款和储蓄存款等。

1953—1978 年，我国处于计划经济时期，实行高度集中的金融组织体系和金融管理体制。国家逐步将公私合营银行纳入中国人民银行体系，成立了农村信用合作社，成为人民银行开展农村金融工作的有力助手。在国家集中统一的计划经济管理体制下，银行信贷业务坚持“统存统贷”的原则，信贷收支统计报表成为执行国民经济计划的主要形式和手段之一。

1979—1996 年，我国处于改革开放新时期。实现了人民银行的中央银行业务与商业（专业）银行业务的分离，确立了人民银行作为中央银行的地位、职能等基本框架，成立政策性银行，明确要把国家专业银行办成国有商业银行。积极发展股份制商业银行和城市合作银行。逐步实现了金融机构多样化、职能专业化，金融机构体系进一步丰富。与之相适应，在金融统计体系中出现了政策性银行、其他商业银行、财务公司、信托投资公司、金融租赁公司等汇总类的信贷收支表。

1997 年以后，随着我国金融体制改革的深入推进，金融体系不断丰富、金融业务得到充分发展，金融统计制度也得到进一步的完善。中国人民银行于 1997 年建立、实施了金融统计“全科目上报”体系。“全科目上报”统计体系在指标的设置、统计项目的归属和统计数据的质量控制等方面凸显出规范、统一、高效等优越性。1997 年以后的金融统计数据来源于“全科目上报”指标体系，以及在此基础上进行的各种数据加工处理。

三、金融统计制度各年度主要调整说明

- **1949—1951** 年　新中国成立伊始，金融机构和金融业务单一，金融统计项目设置比较简单，只有公存款、私存款、对公贷款、对私贷款和储蓄存款等项目。

● **1952—1977**年　采用平衡表的形式将资金来源与资金运用分别列示，细化各项存、贷款项下的分类项目，用以反映不同行业、不同形式的存、贷款业务。

● **1978**年　新增“部队存款”项目，将其数据从“机关团体存款”中调出；对各项贷款项下的分类项目进行了较大调整。

● **1985**年　停用“基本建设存款”项目，其数据并入“企业存款”中。

● **1988**年　增设“金融债券”指标，将其数据从“其他类存款”中调出；将“乡镇企业贷款”数据从“农业贷款”项下调至“流动资金贷款”项下；合并“机关团体存款”与“部队存款”项目为“机关团体部队存款”。

● **1990**年　将邮政储蓄存款纳入“城镇储蓄存款”中。

● **1994**年　1993年7月，财政部、中国人民银行颁发了《金融企业会计制度》，自1994年起按照此制度对原有会计制度进行了调整，同时以会计科目为基础的统计项目归属内容也进行了调整，因此，1994年的统计指标和口径与以前年度相比差异较大。其中：“农业存款”项目不再包括农村信用社转存款及缴存准备金存款；“其他存款”指标中的某些项目调入“企业存款”等指标内。

● **1997**年　（1）扩大了统计范围，将各商业银行所属房地产信贷部、国际业务部和信用卡部等部门数据并入表中。（2）将“部队存款”从“机关团体存款”中调出。（3）拆分“信托类存款”项目为“信托存款”和“委托存款”两项。（4）“金融债券”仅反映金融机构所发行的被金融系统以外各部门所持有的金融债券数值。（5）调整“有价证券及投资”归属：一是将金融机构之间交叉持有的有价证券投资数据轧差反映，二是将非银行金融机构的信托投资、自营证券部分并入。

● **1998**年　（1）自3月起，财政预算外存款被列为一般性存款，因此，在金融机构、国家银行信贷收支表中，将“财政预算外存款”从“财政存款”项下调出。银行类信贷收支表中，将“财政预算外存款”、“机关团体存款”从“财政存款”项下调至“其他存款”项内。（2）自4月起，金融机构、国家银行、国有商业银行信贷收支表中，“保函垫款”从“其他”项中调至“其他短期贷款”内。（3）中国工商银行“申购新股冻结款”自本年起从“活期储蓄”中调入“同业存放”项内。

● **1999**年　（1）按照《关于商业银行账外账并账问题的通知》（银发［1999］303号）要求：各行于1999年12月31日前完成并账。共计并入存款43.2亿元，贷款160.5亿元。（2）金融机构信贷收支表中的“各项存款”项目增加财务、信托、租赁公司的“租赁保证金”数据。（3）根据财政部有关规定，自1999年3月起，将“中央及地方基建、地质勘探资金”作为一般性存款，故在中国建设银行信贷收支表中，该类存款余额由“代理性财政存款”调入“其他存款”。（4）年末，中国工商银行、中国银行、中国建设银行、国家开发银行进行不良资产剥离和划转。相关报表的“余额”为剥离后的实际数据，“比年初增减额”为“本年余额增减数”与“本年剥离数”之和。

● **2000**年　（1）广东省的全部城市信用社于1999年12月关闭，河南、湖北、江苏等省的部分城市信用社更名为农村信用社，新成立呼和浩特、孝感市城市商业银行，致使城市商业银行、农村信用社、城市信用社数据发生变化。（2）从2月起，各省的部分农村基金会并入农村信用社。（3）工商银行将在“储蓄存款”中的“证券清算资金”自2000年1月1日起改为归入“同业存放”项下的“证券公司存放”。（4）中国工商银行、中国农业银行、中国银行、中国建设银行、国家开发银行的不良资产剥离和划转工作继续进行，相关报表的“余额”为剥离后的实际数据，“比年初增减额”为“本年余额增减数”与“本年剥离数”之和。

● **2001** 年 (1) 将交通银行和中信实业银行数据从国家银行数据调入其他商业银行数据中。(2) 将“贴现”从“短期贷款”中调出，调入到新增设项目“票据融资”中。(3) 将“各项垫款”从“短期贷款”中调出，调至新增设项目“各项垫款”中，同时将个人贷款划分为“个人短期消费贷款”与“个人长期消费贷款”。(4) 取消“逾期类贷款”项目，并按其来源将数据分别返还到“各项贷款”的分类项目中。(5) 银行类报表中，新增“机关团体存款”指标，其数据从“其他存款”中调出。

● **2002** 年 (1) 从本年开始，将外资银行纳入金融统计体系中。(2) 在金融机构和国家银行信贷收支表中，表内机构的“贴现及转贴现”与人民银行的“再贴现”数据加总后反映在“票据融资”项目中，计入“各项贷款”。(3) 由于中国建设银行和中国工商银行进行了会计制度改革，该机构在报送年初结转数时，2001 年年末数据与 2002 年年初数据差异较大。其中：“技术改造贷款”不含中国工商银行数据，其数据调入“其他中长期贷款”与“基本建设贷款”中。(4) 考虑到信托投资公司的市场退出因素，相关信贷收支表中余额数据为剔除市场退出机构后的实际数据，增减额数据为包含退出机构的可比数据。

● **2003** 年 (1) 将“证券公司股票质押贷款”从“其他类短期贷款”中调至“拆放同业”项下，这一调整引起各金融机构信贷收支表中“各项贷款”与“同业往来”数据同时变动。(2) 表中“金融债券”为中国人民银行和政策性银行发行的被非并表机构（证券公司、保险公司、基金管理公司、资产管理公司）持有的金融债券总额。(3) 由于中国工商银行和中国建设银行政策性住房委托贷款并账，引起“各项贷款”与“同业往来”数据变动。(4) 农村信用社自本年起细化投资类会计科目，在金融机构信贷收支表中，将投资其他金融机构的金融性债券数据轧差。

● **2004** 年 (1)“票据融资”，其中：“贴现”项目仅反映各金融机构直贴的票据和从其他金融机构买入的买断式转贴现票据，不再扣减“再贴现”。(2) 在国有商业银行、政策性银行和农村信用社信贷收支表中，“邮政储汇局定期存款”计入“各项存款”内。(3) 在金融机构和国家银行信贷收支表中，将“财政预算外存款”计入“各项存款”下的财政存款项目，在其余各信贷收支表中“财政预算外存款”不再计入“各项存款”，而计入“代理财政性存款”项目。(4) 中国建设银行将财政预算内基本建设资金地质勘探费存款从“财政预算外存款”调至“企业活期存款”中，将土地储备贷款自“房地产开发企业流动资金贷款”调入“其他地产开发贷款”，致使“建筑业贷款”和“基本建设贷款”数据变化。(5) 6 月，中国银行、中国建设银行和交通银行进行了不良贷款剥离和划转，凡是涉及三个机构相关报表的贷款余额为真实数据，比较数为可比口径数据。

● **2005** 年 (1) 终止“其他长期负债”项下的“住房公积金存款”，将其纳入“其他存款”项下。(2) 5 月、6 月，中国工商银行进行了不良贷款剥离和划转，农村信用合作社进行了票据置换，凡是涉及这两个机构相关报表的贷款余额为真实数据，比较数为可比口径数据。(3) 本年有 53 家农村信用社改制为农村商业银行或者农村合作银行，导致相关数据有较大变动。

四、数据的机构范围

各报表所包含的机构涵盖范围详见相关报表的注释。

五、其他说明

在信贷收支表中，设置“余额”和“比年初增减额”两种属性。

● 余额：为存量概念，反映该统计指标年末的数据存量。

- 比年初增减额：为流量概念，反映该统计指标当年的变化情况。

1993 年之前，金融统计制度中尚未采用“结转数”[①] 的概念，本书中 1993 年之前各年末的“比年初增减额”即为本年年末余额减去上年年末余额。对于由于年度间金融统计制度变化引起的项目变化或者项目内涵变化，如果无法进行可比口径调整，则在比较数栏的相应位置以“—”代替，表示不可比。

1993 年起，采用“结转数”的概念，“比年初增减额”即为本年末余额减去本年初结转数余额。

① 结转数，指金融机构将上年年末（上年 12 月 31 日）数据按照当年的统计口径重新归并之后以当年 1 月 1 日名义报送的数据，以此作为当年各期数据“比年初”的基准。除了年度金融统计制度调整的因素之外，结转数与上年年末数之间的差异还包括各金融机构根据自身会计制度和业务情况的变化自行调整某些归属以及统计机构范围的变化。

项目注释

本项目注释针对第一部分资料中信贷收支统计、现金收支统计部分的主要统计指标的含义和数据属性给予解释。

一、信贷收支统计

- 各项存款：金融机构资金来源的主要项目，包括企业存款、财政存款、储蓄存款、农业存款、其他存款等。
- 企业存款：金融机构吸收的各种所有制形式、各行业企业单位的存款，有活期存款与定期存款之分。
- 财政存款：中国人民银行和金融机构代理的各项财政预算内存款。
- 储蓄存款：金融机构吸收的城镇居民和农户的个人储蓄存款，有活期储蓄存款与定期储蓄存款之分。
- 机关团体存款：中国人民银行和金融机构办理的各项机关团体存款。
- 农村（业）存款：农村集体单位、乡镇企业、各种专业户和承包户的生产周转金、积累基金等，主要是中国农业银行和农村信用社吸收的农业企业存款。
- 信托存款：根据存款单位或个人的申请，委托代营或运营的资金。
- 其他类存款：表中各项存款项下列示各类存款以外的存款，如部队存款、保证金存款、应解汇款及临时性存款、财政预算外存款、保险公司存放款项、非银行金融机构租赁保证金等。
- 金融债券：非金融机构持有的金融机构发行的各类金融债券。
- 流通中货币：由中国人民银行发行的，扣除金融机构库存现金之外的全部流通中纸币、硬币之和。
- 各项贷款：金融机构资金运用的主要项目，包括短期贷款、中长期贷款、信托贷款、票据融资和各项垫款等。
- 短期贷款：金融机构发放的期限在1年以下（含1年 ）的用于流动资金的贷款，包括工业贷款、商业贷款、建筑业贷款、农业贷款、乡镇企业贷款、私营企业及个体贷款、其他短期贷款等。
- 中长期贷款：金融机构发放的期限在1年以上用于基本建设、技术改造等的贷款，包括基本建设贷款、住房开发贷款，以及技术改造贷款和其他中长期贷款。
- 票据融资：商业票据的贴现和转贴现形成的资金运用。
- 有价证券及投资：金融机构购买的以生息为目的的各类有价证券，如自营投资、信托投资、长期投资等。
- 外汇占款：金融机构购买外汇而占用的人民币资金，包括结售汇人民币资金、兑换和外汇占款 。
- 贴现：反映金融机构为客户办理未到期商业票据贴现扣除金融机构再贴现与转贴现之后的余额。
- 中期流动资金贷款：期限在1~3年（含3年）的流动资金贷款。

二、现金收支统计

● 商品销售收入：在银行开立账户的国有企事业单位、集体企事业单位、股份制合作企业、联营企业、有限责任公司、股份有限公司、私营企业、外资企业及其他单位销售商品收入的现金。

● 服务业收入：在银行开立账户的国有企事业单位、集体企事业单位、股份制合作企业、联营企业、有限责任公司、股份有限公司、私营企业、外商投资企业及服务单位通过提供服务收入的现金。

● 税款收入：中央、地方财政部门各项现金收入，包括税金收入、罚款收入等。

● 城乡个体经营收入（支出）：在银行开立结算账户的城乡个体工商户、农村各种专业户的各种现金收入（支出）。

● 储蓄存款收入（支出）：银行办理储蓄业务收入（支出）的现金。

● 其他金融机构收入（支出）：其他金融机构如信托投资公司、财务公司、租赁公司、证券公司、保险公司的现金收入中除保险公司的保费收入、有价证券收入（支出）以外，所有存入银行或从银行支取的经营性现金收入和现金支出。

● 居民归还贷款收入：城乡居民归还银行、信用社贷款的现金收入（含利息）。

● 汇兑收入（支出）：邮局向银行交存（支取）的汇兑款。

● 有价证券收入（支出）：个人或单位购买各类有价证券的现金支出（收入），以及其他金融机构办理的所有发行、代理发行、买卖、兑付有价证券业务发生的现金收支。

● 工资性支出：在银行开户单位的所有工资、奖金支出及对个人其他支出。

● 农副产品采购支出：国有企事业单位、集体企事业单位、联营企业、有限责任公司、股份有限公司、私营企业、外资企业等采购农、林、牧、副、渔产品的现金支出。

● 工矿及其他产品采购支出：国有企事业单位、集体企事业单位、股份制合作企业、联营企业、有限责任公司、股份有限公司、私营企业、外资企业采购的工矿产品、手工业产品及其他商品的现金支出。

● 行政企业管理费支出：国有企事业单位、集体企事业单位、股份制合作企业、联营企业、有限责任公司、股份有限公司、私营企业、外资企业从行政费、企业管理费、商品流通费等各项费用中支付的非商品性支出的现金。

● 居民提取贷款支出：城乡居民在银行、信用社提取贷款的现金支出。

三、城乡储蓄存款统计和分地区存贷款统计

● 农户储蓄存款：农信社吸收的各类储蓄存款。

● 总行：总行直接吸收的存款和发放的贷款，这部分存款或者贷款由总行直接管理并负责。

Compilation Instructions

1. Basic Principles

Throughout the compilation process, the basic principles of accurate, comprehensive and sound data has always been followed; in other words, we aim at presenting the statistical data of all historical periods accurately, providing statistics on relevant businesses of all categories of financial institutions of the financial system comprehensively, and organizing statistics of all categories of financial institutions in different historical periods soundly in order of their creation and establishment. Meanwhile, major indicators are defined accurately. Changes in financial statistics framework and evolution of financial institutions are explained to make the data more usable. We presents the sources and uses of credit funds and cash receipts and expenditures firstly by financial institutions and secondly by time sequence.

2. Evolution of Financial Statistics

Against different socio – economic backgrounds at different historical periods, the mangement of financial statistics and their coverage have evolved and become more scientific, including the relevant financial statistics being collected, key indicators, definitions and framework.

The years from 1949 to 1952, the first three years of the People's Republic of China, witnessed the recovery of the national economy. Through a series of measures, such as reorganization, consolidation, take – over and merger, etc., private banks and jointly – owned banks contributed a lot to the economic recovery and rebuilding. At this time, businesses of financial institutions were relatively simple, and the major task of credit policy was to collect funds to support the public sector and the cooperatives, in the principle of the industrial sector coming first and the commercial sector second. This situation resulted in a relatively simple set of financial indicators being collected, including deposits by public sector, deposits by private sector, loans to public sector, loans to private sector, and savings deposits, etc.

The years from 1953 to 1978 witnessed a planned economic system in China. During these years, the financial system and its management were highly centralized. Step by step, the jointly – owned banks were merged into the People's Bank of China, and rural credit cooperatives were established as a complement to People's Bank of China in developing financial services in rural areas. During this period, with the central government acting as the master planner, deposits taking & lending quota were centrally planned at the headquarters of each specialized bank, and the statement of sources and uses of credit funds became the primary instrument in carrying out national economic plans.

The years from 1979 to 1996 witnessed the opening – up and reform of the Chinese economy. The central bank business of the People's Bank of China was separated from the commercial (specialized) banking business. The central bank status and responsibility were established for the People's Bank of China. Policy banks were set up. The state specialized banks were to become the state – owned commercial banks. Meanwhile, the joint –

stock commercial banks and urban cooperative banks were developed. The diversification of financial institutions and specialization of responsibilities enriched financial institution system. At the same time, the statements sources and uses of credit funds of policy banks, other commercial banks, finance companies, trust and investment companies and financial leasing companies were brought into the financial statistical system.

With the further advance of financial system reform, diversification of financial system and development of financial businesses, the financial statistical system was improved in late 1990s. The People's Bank of China established the All Account financial statistical framework in 1997. This framework has superior advantage in setting up and classifying statistical data as well as controlling data quality. Since 1997, all financial statistics were obtained from this All Account framework, and further processed.

3. Major Adjustments in the Financial Statistical Framework

● 1949—1951 In the early years of the People's Republic of China, both financial institutions and their businesses were simple. There were only a limited number of financial statistical indicators, including deposits by public sector, deposits by private sector, loans to public sector, loans to private sector, and savings deposits.

● 1952—1977 Sources of credit funds and uses of credit funds were listed separately in a balance sheet format, with detailed items under deposits and loans reflecting deposit and lending businesses to various sectors and in varied forms.

● 1978 Deposits by the army became a separated item, which were previously part of deposits by government agencies and organizations; a comprehensive adjustment was made to items under the category of total loans.

● 1985 Capital construction deposits were removed, which became part of deposits by enterprises.

● 1988 Financial bonds became a separate item, which were previously part of other deposits; loans to village and township enterprises were removed from loans to agricultural sector to working capital loans; deposits by government agencies and organizations and deposits by the army were merged and became the deposits by government agencies, organizations and army.

● 1990 Post savings deposits began to be included in urban savings deposits.

● 1994 Financial Enterprise Accounting Standards, jointly issued by the Ministry of Finance and the People's Bank of China in July 1993, was implemented in 1994. Following the new accounting standards on financial enterprises, financial statistics were adjusted accordingly. Such adjustments accounted for the differences in the statistics and their coverage in 1994 from those of previous years. Among the adjustments: (i) re – deposits and required reserves by rural credit cooperatives were excluded from deposits by agricultural sector; (ii) some components of other deposits were reclassified into deposits by enterprises and others.

● 1997 (i) the coverage of data collection was extended to include data of real estate credit businesses, international businesses, credit card businesses and other businesses of commercial banks; (ii) deposits by the army became separated from deposits by government agencies and organizations; (iii) trust deposits were split into trust deposits and designated deposits; (iv) financial bonds only reflected bonds issued by financial institutions and held by non – financial sectors; (v) securities and investments were adjusted to reflect the net position of securities cross – held among financial institutions and trust investments and proprietary securities held by non – bank financial institutions.

- 1998 (i) As of March, extra – budgetary fiscal deposits were treated as ordinary deposits. Therefore, in the statement of sources and uses of credit funds of state banks and the statement of sources and uses of credit funds of financial institutions, extra – budgetary fiscal deposits were separated from fiscal deposits since March, 1998. In the statement of sources and uses of credit funds of banking institutions, extra – budgetary deposit and deposits by government agencies and organizations were transferred from fiscal deposits to other deposits; (ii) in the statements of sources and uses of credit funds of financial institutions, sources and uses of credit funds of state banks and sources and uses of credit funds of state – owned commercial banks, advance under letter of guarantee were transferred from other loans to other short – term loans since April, 1998; (iii) in the reporting form of Industrial and Commercial Bank of China, deposits frozen for new shares application were transferred from demand deposits to due to banks and other financial institutions since 1998.

- 1999 (i) As required by the Notice of Issues on the Consolidation of Out of Account Accounts of Commercial Banks (PBC Document No. 303 [1999]), all banks should finish the consolidation before December 31, 1999. The consolidation resulted in 4.32 billion yuan increase in total deposits and 16.05 billion yuan increase in total loans; (ii) in the statement of sources and uses of credit funds of financial institutions, security deposits for leases of finance corporations, trust and investment companies and financial leasing companies were included in total deposits; (iii) according to the regulations of the Ministry of Finance, capital construction and geological exploration fund of central and local governments should be treated as ordinary deposits since March, 1999. Therefore, in the statement of sources and uses of credit funds of Construction Bank of China, such deposits were transferred from agency fiscal deposits to other deposits; (iv) the non – performing assets of the Industrial and Commercial Bank of China, Bank of China, Construction Bank of China and State Development Bank were transferred to asset management companies at the end of 1999. The balances in the reporting forms of these institutions reflected the balances remaining after the NPLs transfer, while the amount in the changes within the year reflected the sum of actual movement in the balances and the NPLs transferred.

- 2000 (i) All urban credit cooperatives in Guangdong Province were closed in December 1999. Some Urban credit cooperatives in Henan Province, Hubei Province and Jiangsu Province were renamed as rural credit cooperatives, and city commercial banks were newly established in Huhhot and Xiaogan. Such changes led to corresponding changes in the statistics of city commercial banks, rural credit cooperatives and urban credit cooperatives; (ii) for all the provinces, some of local cooperative foundations were merged into rural credit cooperatives since February, 2000; (iii) as of January 1, 2000, the Industrial and Commercial Bank of China reclassified security clearing fund, which was formerly under savings deposits, into deposits by security companies, a sub – item of due to banks and other financial institutions; (iv) the transfer of non – performing assets in the Industrial and Commercial Bank of China, Agricultural Bank of China, Bank of China, China Construction Bank and State Development Bank continued. The balances in the reporting forms of these institutions were the balances after the NPLs transfer, while the amount in the changes within the year reflected the sum of actual movement in the balances and NPLs transferred.

- 2001 (i) Bank of Communications and CITIC Industrial Bank were reclassified from state banks to other commercial banks, with their data being adjusted and classified accordingly; (ii) discount was transferred out of short – term loans into the newly established paper financing; (iii) total advances were transferred out of short – term loans into total advances, which were newly established; loans to individuals were further categorized into two sub – items, short – term consumer credit and long – term consumer credit; (iv) over – due loans were abolished as a separate item, and reclassified into the sub – item under total loans; (v) in the reporting forms of banking institutions, deposits by government agencies and organizations were established as a separate item, previously included in other deposits.

- 2002 (i) Since this year, data of foreign – funded banks were included in the financial statistical framework; (ii) in the statement of sources and uses of credit funds of financial institutions and the statement of sources and uses of credit funds of state banks, the sum of discount and rediscount of financial institutions and rediscount of the People's Bank of China, were included in paper financing, a sub – item under total loans; (iii) China Construction Bank and Industrial and Commercial Bank of China reformed their accounting systems, leading to large variances between the data on December 31, 2001 and on January 1, 2002. In particular: technical improvement loans on January 1, 2002 did not include that of Industrial and Commercial Bank of China; technical improvement loans of Industrial and Commercial Bank of China on January 1, 2002 were included in other medium and long – term loans and capital construction loans respectively; (iv) given the market exit of some trust and investment companies, balances in the related statements of sources and uses of credit funds did not include the liquidated trust and investment companies, while the changes within the year included liquidated the exiting institutions and were, therefore, comparable with previous years.

- 2003 (i) Stock collateralized loans to securities firms were transferred from other short – term loans to placements with banks and other financial institutions, which resulted in variances in total loans and inter – bank transactions in the statement of sources and uses of credit funds of various financial institutions; (ii) financial bonds were the sum of financial bonds issued by the People's Bank of China and policy banks and held by non – consolidated financial institutions, such as securities companies, insurance companies, fund management companies and asset management companies; (iii) the consolidation of policy designated loans on housing held by the Industrial and Commercial Bank of China and China Construction Bank led to changes in total loans and inter – bank transactions; (iv) since this year, detailed accounting items of investments were adopted by rural credit cooperatives, and the balance of investments on financial bonds issued by other financial institutions was netted in the statement of sources and uses of credit funds of financial institutions.

- 2004 (i) Discount and paper financing only included commercial paper discounted by financial institutions and outright purchase of discounted commercial paper from other financial institutions, and rediscount was no longer deducted; (ii) in the statements of sources and uses of credit funds of state – owned commercial banks, policy banks and rural credit cooperatives, time deposits of postal savings bureau was included in total deposits; (iii) in the statement of sources and uses of credit funds of state banks and the statement of sources and uses of credit funds of financial institutions , extra – budgetary fiscal deposits were included in fiscal deposits under total deposits, while for other institutions, they were no longer included in total deposits, but in agency fiscal deposits; (iv) China Construction Bank transferred budgetary appropriation of capital construction funds for funding geological explorations from extra – budgetary deposits to demand deposits by enterprises, and transferred loans for land reserve from working capital loans of real estate development firms to other real estate development loans, leading to changes in loans to construction sector and in capital construction loans; (v) the non – performing loans in Bank of China, China Construction Bank and Bank of Communication were transferred in June, and the balances of total loans in various statements of the above three banks excluded the transferred amount, while the changes within the year were comparable with previous years.

- 2005 (i) Deposits by housing provident funds, which were previously included in other long – term liabilities, were abolished, and related data were included in other deposits; (ii) the non – performing loans in the Industrial and Commercial Bank of China were transferred in May and June, and qualified rural credit cooperatives conducted an asset swap of non – performing loans with the central bank. Therefore, the balances of total loans reported by ICBC and the qualified rural credit cooperatives excluded the NPLs transferred while the changes within the year were comparable with previous years; (iii) fifty – three rural credit cooperatives were restructured into rural commercial banks or rural cooperative banks. Such changes have led to the changes of relative data.

4. Institutional Coverage of Data

Please refer to notes attached to each statement for detailed information on institutions covered.

5. Other Matters

Items in this part are captured in two dimensions, balance and changes within the year.

- Balance: stock data, measuring the end – of – year amount of each indicator.

- Changes within the Year: flow data, measuring changes in the amount of the indicator during the year.

- The concept of opening balances[①] was not adopted until 1993. Changes within the year prior to 1993 were measured as the difference between the year – end balances of two sequential years; for the variances in items or in the definition of items caused by adjustment in financial statistical system, if we could not conduct the adjustments on comparable basis, the changes within the year were substituted by symbol "—", meaning that it was not comparable.

From 1993 on, the concept of opening balances was introduced. Changes within the year measured the difference between the year – end balances and the opening balances at the beginning of the year.

---

① Opening balances refer to statistical data reported by financial institutions. The data was based upon year – end balances of the previous financial year, but was adjusted and re – classified on a basis consistent with the requirements of the financial statistical framework applicable in the year. Except for adjustments to the statistical system, other factors, changes in accounting regulations and the business activities of financial institutions, as well as the changes in institutional coverage, could also cause the differences between the opening balances and the year – end amount.

Compilation Notes on Major Indicators

Compilation explanation is given to assist in gaining a general understanding of the meaning and coverage of major indicators reported in the sources and uses of credit funds statistics and cash statistics.

1. Major Indicators in Sources and Uses of Credit Funds Statistics

- Total Deposits: Important in sources of credit funds for financial institutions, including deposits by enterprises, fiscal deposits, savings deposits, deposits by agricultural sector, other deposits, etc.

- Deposits by Enterprises: Deposits with financial institutions by enterprises regardless of their ownership and industries, further divided into demand deposits and time deposits.

- Fiscal Deposits: Deposits held by government sector with the People's Bank of China and other financial institutions acting as agents.

- Savings Deposits: Deposits with financial institutions by urban and rural individuals, further divided into demand deposits and time deposits.

- Deposits by Government agencies and organizations: Designated deposits with the People's Bank of China and other financial institutions by government agencies and organizations.

- Rural Deposits/ Deposits by Agricultural Sector: Deposits by rural collectives, township & village enterprises and rural households. Such deposits are used for providing working capital or part of accumulated funds from operations. The majority of such deposits are deposits by agricultural enterprises in Agricultural Bank of China and rural credit cooperatives.

- Trust Deposits: Deposits from organizations and individuals. The funds are designated for certain usage as expressed in the depositor's application. The financial institutions holding such liabilities act as agents of the depositors.

- Other Deposits: Deposits not categorized previously within other sub - items if total deposits, includes but not limited to deposits by the army, margins, remittance and temporary deposits, extra - budgetary fiscal deposits, deposits by insurance companies, security deposits for lease from non - bank financial institutions, etc.

- Financial Bonds: Bonds issued by financial institutions and held by non - financial institutions.

- Currency in Circulation: The sum of notes and coins issued by the People's Bank of China, excluding the amount of cash in vault held by financial institutions.

- Total Loans: Important in uses of credit funds by financial institutions, including short - term loans, medium and long - term loans, trust loans, paper financing and total advances.

- Short – term Loans: Working capital loans issued by financial institutions with maturity equal to or less than one year, including loans to industrial sector, loans to commercial sector, loans to construction sector, loans to agricultural sector, loans to township & village enterprises, loans to privately – run enterprises and self – employed businesses, other short – term loans, etc.

- Medium and Long – term Loans: Loans issued by financial institutions with maturity longer than one year, for capital construction, and technology upgrading, etc, including capital construction loans, housing development loans, technical improvement loans and other medium and long – term loans.

- Paper Financing: Funds used for discounting and re – discounting of commercial papers.

- Securities and Investments: Securities held by financial institutions for interest earning, including proprietary investments, trust investments, long – term investments, etc.

- Positions for Foreign Exchanges Purchase: Funds used by financial institutions to purchase foreign exchanges, including RMB funds for foreign exchange transactions with clients at bank counters, for currency exchanges and funds for foreign exchanges.

- Discount: the amount of undue commercial papers discounted by financial institutions for its costumers minus the amount of re – discount with another financial institution and the central bank.

- Medium – term Working Capital Loans: Working capital loans with maturity longer than one year but with a maximum maturity of three years.

2. Major Indicators in Statistics on Savings in Urban and Rural Areas and Statistics on Regional Deposits and Loans

Rural Savings Deposits: Savings deposits with rural credit cooperatives.

Headquarters: Deposits directly deposited with headquarters and loans directly issued by headquarters. These deposits and loans are directly managed by headquarters.

3. Major Indicators in Cash Receipt and Expenditure Statistics

- Commodity Sales Receipts: Cash receipts from the sales of goods by entities including state – owned enterprises, collectively owned enterprises and organizations, joint ventures, limited companies, joint – stock limited companies, private firms, foreign funded enterprises and other organizations.

- Service Receipts: Cash receipts from services provided by entities, which including state owned enterprises, collectively owned enterprises and organizations, joint ventures, limited liability companies, joint – stock limited companies, private firms, foreign funded enterprises and other organizations.

- Tax Receipts: Receipts of central and local governments, including tax payment, fines and confiscations.

- Receipts (Expenditures) of Self – employed Entities: Cash receipts or expenditures of self – employed entities in urban and rural areas.

● Receipts (Expenditures) of Savings Deposits: Cash receipts or expenditures of banks relating to deposit business.

● Receipts (Expenditures) of Other Financial Institutions: Cash receipts or expenditures other than premium incomes for insurance companies and securities incomes or expenditures of other financial institutions. Other financial institutions include trust and investment companies, finance companies, leasing companies, securities companies and insurance companies, etc.

● Receipts of Paying Back Loans by Households: Cash receipts from loan repayments (including interests) by rural and urban residents to banks and credit cooperatives.

● Remittance Receipts (Expenditures): Remittance from post offices to banks or remittance drawn by post offices from banks.

● Receipts (Expenditures) of /on Securities (purchase): Includes (i) cash expenditures or receipts of individuals and organizations from securities transactions, and (ii) cash receipts or expenditures of other financial institutions for the sales, agent sales, trading and redemption of securities.

● Wages Payments: Salaries, bonuses and all other cash payments to individuals that are reflected in the bank account of an organization.

● Expenditures on Agricultural Products: Cash expenditures for purchasing agricultural, forestry, animal husbandry and fishery products and goods by entities including state – owned enterprises, collectively – owned enterprises and organizations, joint ventures, limited companies, joint – stock limited companies, private firms, foreign – funded enterprises and other organizations.

● Expenditures on Industrial and Other Products: Cash expenditures for purchasing industrial, mineral and other products by entities including state owned enterprises, collectively owned enterprises and organizations, joint – stock companies, joint ventures, limited companies, joint – stock limited companies, private firms, foreign funded enterprises and other organizations.

● Administrative Expenditures of Public Institutions and Enterprises: Cash expenditures for administrative, corporate management and selling purposes of entities including state owned enterprises, collectively owned enterprises and organizations, joint ventures, limited companies, joint – stock limited companies, private firms, foreign – funded enterprises and other organizations.

● Withdrawing of Loans by Households: Cash payments incurred when a bank or a rural credit cooperative disburses loans to urban or rural residents.

一、信贷收支统计
Sources and Uses of Credit Funds

（一）人民币信贷收支统计
Sources and Uses of Credit Funds（RMB）

1. 金融机构人民币信贷收支表* （1949—2005 年）
Sources and Uses of Credit Funds of Financial Institutions（RMB）（1949—2005）

金融机构人民币存贷款情况表

Deposits and Loans of Financial Institutions（RMB）

（1949 年末）

（Year－end of 1949）

单位：亿元（旧币）

Unit：100 Million Yuan（Old RMB）

项　目 Items	余　额 Balance	项　目 Items	余　额 Balance
存款总额 Total Deposits	14856.00	放款总额 Total Loans	10395.00
公存款 Deposits by Public Sector	11304.00	对公放款 Loans to Public Sector	7033.00
私存款 Deposits by Private Sector	3552.00	对私放款 Loans to Private Sector	3362.00
储蓄存款 Savings Deposits	—		

注：1. 旧币 1 万元＝人民币 1 元。

2. 公存款包括企业结算、机关往来、基本建设基金监理、合作事业、金库等类型的存款；私存款包括工商业、金融业存款。

3. 对公放款包括对公营企业（含中央企业、地方企业、机关生产）和合作事业的放款；对私放款包括对工商业、金融业、农村的放款。

Notes：

1. Old RMB is the first version of RMB，Which circulated from 1948 to 1955. The first version of RMB 100 thousands yuan equals to the second version of RMB 1 yuan.

2. Deposits by public sector include deposits for enterprises settlement，government agencies transactions，Surveillance on funds for capital construction，cooperatives，state treasury and soon. Deposits by private sector include deposits by industrial and commercial enterprises and deposits by financial institution.

3. Loans to public sector include loans to public－operated enterprises，Which include enterprises owned by the central government or by local government，government agencies production and cooperatives. Loans to private sector include loans to industrial and commercial enterprises，financial institutions and rural area.

* 本表机构包括中国人民银行（1949—2005年）①、私营银行（1949—1951年）、合营银行（1950—1952年）、农村信用合作社（1953—2005年）、中国农业银行（1978—2005年）、中国银行（1978—2005年）、中国工商银行（1984—2005年）、中国建设银行（1985—2005年）、城市信用合作社（1986—2005年）、交通银行（1988—2005年）、中信实业银行（1988—2005年，2005年更名为中信银行）、信托投资公司（1988—2005年）、邮政储汇局（1990—2005年）、中国光大银行（1993—2005年）、华夏银行（1993—2005年）、广东发展银行（1993—2005年）、深圳发展银行（1993—2005年）、招商银行（1993—2005年）、上海浦东发展银行（1993—2005年）、福建兴业银行（1993—2005年，2003年更名为兴业银行）、烟台住房储蓄银行（1993—2005年，2003年更名为恒丰银行）、蚌埠住房储蓄银行（1993—2005年，2001年改制为城市商业银行）、财务公司（1993—2005年）、中国农业发展银行（1994—2005年）、中国投资银行（1995—1998年）、海南发展银行（1995—1997年）、国家开发银行（1995—2005年）、中国进出口银行（1995—2005年）、中国民生银行（1996—2005年）、城市合作银行（1997—1998年）、金融租赁公司（1997—2005年）、城市商业银行（1999—2005年）、外资银行②（2002—2005年）、农村商业银行（2002—2005年）、浙商银行（2004—2005年）、农村合作银行（2005年）。

* Financial institutions of this statement include the People' s Bank of China（1949—2005）①，Private－operated Banks（1949—1951），Public－private Joint Venture Banks（1950—1952），Rural Credit Cooperatives（1953—2005），Agricultural Bank of China（1978—2005），Bank of China（1978—2005），Industrial and Commercial Bank of China（1984—2005），China Construction Bank（1985—2005），Urban Credit Cooperatives（1986—2005），Bank of Communications（1988—2005），CITIC Industrial Bank（Included in this statement Since 1988 and renamed as China CITIC Bank in 2005），Trust and Investment Companies（1988—2005），Postal Savings Bureau（1990—2005），China Everbright Bank（1993—2005），Huaxia Bank（1993—2005），Guangdong Development Bank（1993—2005），Shenzhen Development Bank（1993—2005），China Merchants Bank（1993—2005），Shanghai Pudong Development Bank（1993—2005），Fujian Industrial Bank（Included in this statement from 1993 to 2005 and renamed as Industrial Bank in 2003），Yantai Housing and Savings Bank（Included in this statement from 1993 to 2005 and re－organized and renamed as Evergrowing Bank in 2003），Bengbu Housing and Savings Bank（Included in this statement from 1993 to 2005 and re－organized to be a city commercial bank in 2001），Finance Companies（1993—2005），Agricultural Development Bank of China（1994—2005），China Investment Bank（1995—1998），Hainan Development Bank（1995—1997），China Development Bank（1995—2005），the Export－Import Bank of China（1995—2005），China Minsheng Banking Corporation（1996—2005），Urban Cooperative Banks（1997—1998），Financial Leasing Companies（1997—2005），City Commercial Banks（1999—2005），Foreign－funded Banks②（2002—2005），Rural Commercial Banks（2002—2005），China Zheshang Bank（2004—2005）and Rural Cooperative Banks（2005）.

注①：括号中的年份为此机构并入本表的起止年份（下同）。

Note①：The figures in the bracket refer to the time period during which the data of the institution were covered in this statement（the same applies hereinafter）.

注②：外资银行包括外国银行分行、外资独资银行、合资银行、外资独资财务公司和合资财务公司。

Note②：Foreign－funded Banks include foreign bank branches，solely－foreign funded banks，joint－equity banks，solely－foreign funded finance companies and joint－equity finance companies.

金融机构人民币存贷款情况表
Deposits and Loans of Financial Institutions（RMB）

（1950年末）

（Year - end of 1950）

单位：亿元（旧币）

Unit：100 Million Yuan（Old RMB）

项　目 Items	余　额 Balance	比年初增减额 Changes within the Year	项　目 Items	余　额 Balance	比年初增减额 Changes within the Year
存款总额 Total Deposits	264456.00	249600.00	放款总额 Total Loans	186353.00	175958.00
公存款 Deposits by Public Sector	216633.00	205329.00	对公放款 Loans to Public Sector	170478.00	163445.00
私存款 Deposits by Private Sector	34653.00	31101.00	对私放款 Loans to Private Sector	15875.00	12513.00
储蓄存款 Savings Deposits	13170.00	13170.00			

金融机构人民币存贷款情况表

Deposits and Loans of Financial Institutions（RMB）

（1951年末）

（Year－end of 1951）

单位：亿元（旧币）

Unit：100 Million Yuan（Old RMB）

项　目 Items	余　额 Balance	比年初增减额 Changes within the Year	项　目 Items	余　额 Balance	比年初增减额 Changes within the Year
存款总额 Total Deposits	659768.00	395312.00	放款总额 Total Loans	657666.00	471313.00
公存款 Deposits by Public Sector	493332.00	276699.00	对公放款 Loans to Public Sector	607830.00	437352.00
私存款 Deposits by Private Sector	111586.00	76933.00	对私放款 Loans to Private Sector	49836.00	33961.00
储蓄存款 Savings Deposits	54850.00	41680.00			

金融机构人民币信贷收支表

Sources and Uses of Credit Funds of Financial Institutions (RMB)

（1952 年末）

(Year - end of 1952)

单位：亿元

Unit: 100 Million Yuan

项目 Items	余额 Balance	比年初增减额 Changes within the Year	项目 Items	余额 Balance	比年初增减额 Changes within the Year
一、各项存款 Total Deposits	93.30	27.32	一、各项贷款 Total Loans	108.00	42.23
1. 企业存款 Deposits by Enterprises	33.00	—	1. 工业生产企业贷款 Loans to Industrial Production Enterprises	9.50	—
2. 财政存款 Fiscal Deposits	19.50	—	2. 商业企业贷款 Loans to Commercial Enterprises	93.80	—
3. 基本建设存款 Capital Construction Deposits	4.10	—	3. 城镇集体企业贷款 Loans to Urban Collective Enterprises	0.50	—
4. 机关团体存款 Deposits by Government Agencies and Social Organizations	28.10	—	4. 农业贷款 Loans to Agricultural Sectors	4.20	—
5. 城镇储蓄存款 Urban Savings Deposits	8.60	—	二、黄金占款 Position for Bullion and Silver Purchase	4.80	—
6. 农村存款 Rural Deposits			三、外汇占款 Position for Foreign Exchange Purchase	6.00	—
二、流通中货币 Currency in Circulation	27.50	—			
三、银行自有资金 Own Capital	11.00	—			
四、其他 Others	-13.00	—			
资金来源总计 Total Sources	**118.80**	—	**资金运用总计 Total Uses**	**118.80**	—

金融机构人民币信贷收支表

Sources and Uses of Credit Funds of Financial Institutions（RMB）

（1953 年末）

（Year - end of 1953）

单位：亿元

Unit：100 Million Yuan

项目 Items	余额 Balance	比年初增减额 Changes within the Year	项目 Items	余额 Balance	比年初增减额 Changes within the Year
一、各项存款 Total Deposits	107.70	14.40	一、各项贷款 Total Loans	134.80	26.80
1. 企业存款 Deposits by Enterprises	31.80	-1.20	1. 工业生产企业贷款 Loans to Industrial Production Enterprises	13.00	3.50
2. 财政存款 Fiscal Deposits	33.30	13.80	2. 商业企业贷款 Loans to Commercial Enterprises	114.30	20.50
3. 基本建设存款 Capital Construction Deposits	6.70	2.60	3. 城镇集体企业贷款 Loans to Urban Collective Enterprises	0.70	0.20
4. 机关团体存款 Deposits by Government Agencies and Social Organizations	22.50	-5.60	4. 农业贷款 Loans to Agricultural Sector	6.80	2.60
5. 城镇储蓄存款 Urban Savings Deposits	12.20	3.60	二、黄金占款 Position for Bullion and Silver Purchase	4.80	
6. 农户储蓄存款 Savings Deposits by Rrual Households	0.10	0.10	三、外汇占款 Position for Foreign Exchange Purchase	5.30	-0.70
7. 农村存款 Rural Deposits	1.10	1.10			
二、流通中货币 Currency in Circulation	39.40	11.90			
三、银行自有资金 Own Capital	15.90	4.90			
四、其他 Others	-18.10	-5.10			
资金来源总计 Total Sources	**144.90**	**26.10**	**资金运用总计 Total Uses**	**144.90**	**26.10**

金融机构人民币信贷收支表

Sources and Uses of Credit Funds of Financial Institutions (RMB)

(1954年末)

(Year - end of 1954)

单位：亿元

Unit: 100 Million Yuan

项目 Items	余额 Balance	比年初增减额 Changes within the Year	项目 Items	余额 Balance	比年初增减额 Changes within the Year
一、各项存款 Total Deposits	154.10	46.40	一、各项贷款 Total Loans	185.80	51.00
1. 企业存款 Deposits by Enterprises	34.40	2.60	1. 工业生产企业贷款 Loans to Industrial Production Enterprises	14.60	1.60
2. 财政存款 Fiscal Deposits	61.30	28.00	2. 商业企业贷款 Loans to Commercial Enterprises	161.80	47.50
3. 基本建设存款 Capital Construction Deposits	7.50	0.80	3. 城镇集体企业贷款 Loans to Urban Collective Enterprises	0.60	-0.10
4. 机关团体存款 Deposits by Government Agencies and Social Organizations	30.70	8.20	4. 农业贷款 Loans to Agricultural Sector	8.80	2.00
5. 城镇储蓄存款 Urban Savings Deposits	14.30	2.10	二、黄金占款 Position for Bullion and Silver Purchase	4.80	
6. 农户储蓄存款 Savings Deposits by Rural Households	1.60	1.50	三、外汇占款 Position for Foreign Exchange Purchase	9.40	4.10
7. 农村存款 Rural Deposits	4.30	3.20			
二、流通中货币 Currency in Circulation	41.20	1.80			
三、银行自有资金 Own Capital	21.00	5.10			
四、其他 Others	-16.30	1.80			
资金来源总计 Total Sources	**200.00**	**55.10**	**资金运用总计 Total Uses**	**200.00**	**55.10**

金融机构人民币信贷收支表

Sources and Uses of Credit Funds of Financial Institutions（RMB）

（1955 年末）

（Year - end of 1955）

单位：亿元

Unit：100 Million Yuan

项目 Items	余额 Balance	比年初增减额 Changes within the Year	项目 Items	余额 Balance	比年初增减额 Changes within the Year
一、各项存款 Total Deposits	141.90	-12.20	一、各项贷款 Total Loans	206.60	20.80
1. 企业存款 Deposits by Enterprises	32.40	-2.00	1. 工业生产企业贷款 Loans to Industrial Production Enterprises	18.10	3.50
2. 财政存款 Fiscal Deposits	36.10	-25.20	2. 商业企业贷款 Loans to Commercial Enterprises	175.30	13.50
3. 基本建设存款 Capital Construction Deposits	8.00	0.50	3. 城镇集体企业贷款 Loans to Urban Collective Enterprises	0.80	0.20
4. 机关团体存款 Deposits by Government Agencies and Social Organizations	42.20	11.50	4. 农业贷款 Loans to Agricultural Sector	12.40	3.60
5. 城镇储蓄存款 Urban Savings Deposits	16.90	2.60	二、黄金占款 Position for Bullion and Silver Purchase	4.80	
6. 农户储蓄存款 Savings Deposits by Rural Households	3.00	1.40	三、外汇占款 Position for Foreign Exchange Purchase	9.70	0.30
7. 农村存款 Rural Deposits	3.30	-1.00			
二、流通中货币 Currency in Circulation	40.30	-0.90			
三、银行自有资金 Own Capital	25.90	4.90			
四、其他 Others	13.00	29.30			
资金来源总计 Total Sources	**221.10**	**21.10**	**资金运用总计 Total Uses**	**221.10**	**21.10**

金融机构人民币信贷收支表

Sources and Uses of Credit Funds of Financial Institutions (RMB)

(1956年末)

(Year - end of 1956)

单位：亿元

Unit: 100 Million Yuan

项目 Items	余额 Balance	比年初增减额 Changes within the Year	项目 Items	余额 Balance	比年初增减额 Changes within the Year
一、各项存款 Total Deposits	136.80	-5.10	一、各项贷款 Total Loans	239.20	32.60
1. 企业存款 Deposits by Enterprises	45.00	12.60	1. 工业生产企业贷款 Loans to Industrial Production Enterprises	27.90	9.80
2. 财政存款 Fiscal Deposits	16.40	-19.70	2. 商业企业贷款 Loans to Commercial Enterprises	172.60	-2.70
3. 基本建设存款 Capital Construction Deposits	3.20	-4.80	3. 城镇集体企业贷款 Loans to Urban Collective Enterprises	3.20	2.40
4. 机关团体存款 Deposits by Government Agencies and Social Organizations	39.10	-3.10	4. 农业贷款 Loans to Agricultural Sector	35.50	23.10
5. 城镇储蓄存款 Urban Savings Deposits	22.40	5.50	二、黄金占款 Position for Bullion and Silver Purchase	4.80	
6. 农户储蓄存款 Savings Deposits by Rural Households	4.30	1.30	三、外汇占款 Position for Foreign Exchange Purchase	3.50	-6.20
7. 农村存款 Rural Deposits	6.40	3.10			
二、流通中货币 Currency in Circulation	57.30	17.00			
三、银行自有资金 Own Capital	38.10	12.20			
四、其他 Others	15.30	2.30			
资金来源总计 Total Sources	**247.50**	**26.40**	**资金运用总计 Total Uses**	**247.50**	**26.40**

金融机构人民币信贷收支表

Sources and Uses of Credit Funds of Financial Institutions（RMB）

（1957 年末）

（Year－end of 1957）

单位：亿元

Unit：100 Million Yuan

项　目 Items	余　额 Balance	比年初增减额 Changes within the Year	项　目 Items	余　额 Balance	比年初增减额 Changes within the Year
一、各项存款 Total Deposits	168.30	31.50	一、各项贷款 Total Loans	283.00	43.80
1. 企业存款 Deposits by Enterprises	39.70	－5.30	1. 工业生产企业贷款 Loans to Industrial Production Enterprises	30.30	2.40
2. 财政存款 Fiscal Deposits	20.60	4.20	2. 商业企业贷款 Loans to Commercial Enterprises	216.40	43.80
3. 基本建设存款 Capital Construction Deposits	10.10	6.90	3. 城镇集体企业贷款 Loans to Urban Collective Enterprises	3.10	－0.10
4. 机关团体存款 Deposits by Government Agencies and Social Organizations	49.30	10.20	4. 农业贷款 Loans to Agricultural Sector	33.20	－2.30
5. 城镇储蓄存款 Urban Savings Deposits	27.90	5.50	二、黄金占款 Position for Bullion and Silver Purchase	4.80	
6. 农户储蓄存款 Savings Deposits by Rural Households	7.30	3.00	三、外汇占款 Position for Foreign Exchange Purchase	3.30	－0.20
7. 农村存款 Rural Deposits	13.40	7.00			
二、流通中货币 Currency in Circulation	52.80	－4.50			
三、银行自有资金 Own Capital	54.30	16.20			
四、其他 Others	15.70	0.40			
资金来源总计 Total Sources	**291.10**	**43.60**	**资金运用总计 Total Uses**	**291.10**	**43.60**

金融机构人民币信贷收支表

Sources and Uses of Credit Funds of Financial Institutions (RMB)

(1958年末)

(Year - end of 1958)

单位：亿元

Unit: 100 Million Yuan

项 目 Items	余 额 Balance	比年初增减额 Changes within the Year	项 目 Items	余 额 Balance	比年初增减额 Changes within the Year
一、各项存款 Total Deposits	304.00	135.70	一、各项贷款 Total Loans	498.15	215.15
1. 企业存款 Deposits by Enterprises	77.60	37.90	1. 工业生产企业贷款 Loans to Industrial Production Enterprises	89.20	58.90
2. 财政存款 Fiscal Deposits	49.90	29.30	2. 商业企业贷款 Loans to Commercial Enterprises	342.40	126.00
3. 基本建设存款 Capital Construction Deposits	20.10	10.00	3. 城镇集体企业贷款 Loans to Urban Collective Enterprises	2.70	-0.40
4. 机关团体存款 Deposits by Government Agencies and Social Organizations	84.80	35.50	4. 农业贷款 Loans to Agricultural Sector	63.85	30.65
5. 城镇储蓄存款 Urban Savings Deposits	35.10	7.20	二、黄金占款 Position for Bullion and Silver Purchase	4.80	
6. 农户储蓄存款 Savings Deposits by Rural Households	20.10	12.80	三、外汇占款 Position for Foreign Exchange Purchase	2.70	-0.60
7. 农村存款 Rural Deposits	16.40	3.00			
二、流通中货币 Currency in Circulation	67.80	15.00			
三、银行自有资金 Own Capital	96.90	42.60			
四、其他 Others	36.95	21.25			
资金来源总计 Total Sources	**505.65**	**214.55**	**资金运用总计 Total Uses**	**505.65**	**214.55**

金融机构人民币信贷收支表

Sources and Uses of Credit Funds of Financial Institutions（RMB）

（1959年末）

（Year－end of 1959）

单位：亿元

Unit：100 Million Yuan

项 目 Items	余 额 Balance	比年初增减额 Changes within the Year	项 目 Items	余 额 Balance	比年初增减额 Changes within the Year
一、各项存款 Total Deposits	407.50	103.50	一、各项贷款 Total Loans	814.70	316.55
1. 企业存款 Deposits by Enterprises	70.00	－7.60	1. 工业生产企业贷款 Loans to Industrial Production Enterprises	254.80	165.60
2. 财政存款 Fiscal Deposits	82.10	32.20	2. 商业企业贷款 Loans to Commercial Enterprises	495.30	152.90
3. 基本建设存款 Capital Construction Deposits	40.10	20.00	3. 城镇集体企业贷款 Loans to Urban Collective Enterprises	3.50	0.80
4. 机关团体存款 Deposits by Government Agencies and Social Organizations	111.00	26.20	4. 农业贷款 Loans to Agricultural Sector	61.10	－2.75
5. 城镇储蓄存款 Urban Savings Deposits	47.30	12.20	二、黄金占款 Position for Bullion and Silver Purchase	3.80	－1.00
6. 农户储蓄存款 Savings Deposits by Rural Households	21.00	0.90	三、外汇占款 Position for Foreign Exchange Purchase	－2.20	－4.90
7. 农村存款 Rural Deposits	36.00	19.60			
二、流通中货币 Currency in Circulation	75.10	7.30			
三、银行自有资金 Own Capital	293.80	196.90			
四、其他 Others	39.90	2.95			
资金来源总计 Total Sources	**816.30**	**310.65**	**资金运用总计 Total Uses**	**816.30**	**310.65**

金融机构人民币信贷收支表

Sources and Uses of Credit Funds of Financial Institutions（RMB）

（1960 年末）

（Year－end of 1960）

单位：亿元

Unit：100 Million Yuan

项　目 Items	余　额 Balance	比年初增减额 Changes within the Year	项　目 Items	余　额 Balance	比年初增减额 Changes within the Year
一、各项存款 Total Deposits	468.50	61.00	一、各项贷款 Total Loans	983.90	169.20
1. 企业存款 Deposits by Enterprises	86.00	16.00	1. 工业生产企业贷款 Loans to Industrial Production Enterprises	362.80	108.00
2. 财政存款 Fiscal Deposits	146.60	64.50	2. 物资供销企业贷款 Loans to Material Supply and Sale Enterprises	30.80	30.80
3. 基本建设存款 Capital Construction Deposits	29.60	－10.50	3. 商业企业贷款 Loans to Commercial Enterprises	506.30	11.00
4. 机关团体存款 Deposits by Government Agencies and Social Organizations	96.60	－14.40	4. 城镇集体企业贷款 Loans to Urban Collective Enterprises	6.50	3.00
5. 城镇储蓄存款 Urban Savings Deposits	51.10	3.80	5. 农业贷款 Loans to Agricultural Sector	77.50	16.40
6. 农户储蓄存款 Savings Depostis by Rural Households	15.20	－5.80	二、黄金占款 Position for Bullion and Silver Purchase	3.80	
7. 农村存款 Rural Deposits	43.40	7.40	三、外汇占款 Position for Foreign Exchange Purchase	－12.30	－10.10
二、流通中货币 Currency in Circulation	95.90	20.80			
三、银行自有资金 Own Capital	369.90	76.10			
四、其他 Others	41.10	1.20			
资金来源总计 Total Sources	**975.40**	**159.10**	**资金运用总计 Total Uses**	**975.40**	**159.10**

金融机构人民币信贷收支表

Sources and Uses of Credit Funds of Financial Institutions（RMB）

（1961年末）

（Year - end of 1961）

单位：亿元

Unit：100 Million Yuan

项　目 Items	余　额 Balance	比年初增减额 Changes within the Year	项　目 Items	余　额 Balance	比年初增减额 Changes within the Year
一、各项存款 Total Deposits	491.10	22.60	一、各项贷款 Total Loans	814.80	- 169.10
1. 企业存款 Deposits by Enterprises	116.10	30.10	1. 工业生产企业贷款 Loans to Industrial Production Enterprises	167.10	- 195.70
2. 财政存款 Fiscal Deposits	174.60	28.00	2. 物资供销企业贷款 Loans to Material Supply and Sale Enterprises	25.30	- 5.50
3. 基本建设存款 Capital Construction Deposits	30.30	0.70			
4. 机关团体存款 Deposits by Government Agencies and Social Organizations	72.30	- 24.30	3. 商业企业贷款 Loans to Commercial Enterprises	537.50	31.20
			4. 城镇集体企业贷款 Loans to Urban Collective Enterprises	9.90	3.40
5. 城镇储蓄存款 Urban Savings Deposits	39.20	- 11.90	5. 农业贷款 Loans to Agricultural Sector	75.00	- 2.50
6. 农户储蓄存款 Savings Deposits by Rural Households	16.20	1.00	二、黄金占款 Position for Bullion and Silver Purchase	3.80	
7. 农村存款 Rural Deposits	42.40	- 1.00	三、外汇占款 Position for Foreign Exchange Purchase	- 10.20	2.10
二、流通中货币 Currency in Circulation	125.70	29.80			
三、银行自有资金 Own Capital	183.30	- 186.60			
四、其他 Others	8.30	- 32.80			
资金来源总计 Total Sources	**808.40**	**- 167.00**	**资金运用总计 Total Uses**	**808.40**	**- 167.00**

金融机构人民币信贷收支表

Sources and Uses of Credit Funds of Financial Institutions (RMB)

(1962 年末)

(Year - end of 1962)

单位：亿元

Unit: 100 Million Yuan

项目 Items	余额 Balance	比年初增减额 Changes within the Year	项目 Items	余额 Balance	比年初增减额 Changes within the Year
一、各项存款 Total Deposits	411.80	-79.30	一、各项贷款 Total Loans	691.70	-123.10
1. 企业存款 Deposits by Enterprises	152.30	36.20	1. 工业生产企业贷款 Loans to Industrial Production Enterprises	119.80	-47.30
2. 财政存款 Fiscal Deposits	79.90	-94.70	2. 物资供销企业贷款 Loans to Material Supply and Sale Enterprises	27.00	1.70
3. 基本建设存款 Capital Construction Deposits	44.70	14.40	3. 商业企业贷款 Loans to Commercial Enterprises	459.00	-78.50
4. 机关团体存款 Deposits by Government Agencies and Social Organizations	69.70	-2.60	4. 城镇集体企业贷款 Loans to Urban Collective Enterprises	9.60	-0.30
5. 城镇储蓄存款 Urban Savings Deposits	31.40	-7.80	5. 农业贷款 Loans to Agricultural Sector	76.30	1.30
6. 农户储蓄存款 Savings Deposits by Rural Households	9.80	-6.40	二、黄金占款 Position for Bullion and Silver Purchase	3.80	
7. 农村存款 Rural Deposits	24.00	-18.40	三、外汇占款 Position for Foreign Exchange Purchase	-5.90	4.30
二、流通中货币 Currency in Circulation	106.50	-19.20			
三、银行自有资金 Own Capital	201.30	18.00			
四、其他 Others	-30.00	-38.30			
资金来源总计 Total Sources	**689.60**	**-118.80**	**资金运用总计 Total Uses**	**689.60**	**-118.80**

金融机构人民币信贷收支表

Sources and Uses of Credit Funds of Financial Institutions（RMB）

（1963 年末）

（Year－end of 1963）

单位：亿元

Unit：100 Million Yuan

项　目 Items	余　额 Balance	比年初增减额 Changes within the Year	项　目 Items	余　额 Balance	比年初增减额 Changes within the Year
一、各项存款 Total Deposits	414.90	3.10	一、各项贷款 Total Loans	576.50	－115.20
1. 企业存款 Deposits by Enterprises	176.80	24.50	1. 工业生产企业贷款 Loans to Industrial Production Enterprises	76.90	－42.90
2. 财政存款 Fiscal Deposits	67.30	－12.60	2. 物资供销企业贷款 Loans to Material Supply and Sale Enterprises	31.50	4.50
3. 基本建设存款 Capital Construction Deposits	43.00	－1.70			
4. 机关团体存款 Deposits by Government Agencies and Social Organizations	56.70	－13.00	3. 商业企业贷款 Loans to Commercial Enterprises	384.40	－74.60
			4. 城镇集体企业贷款 Loans to Urban Collective Enterprises	4.40	－5.20
5. 城镇储蓄存款 Urban Savings Deposits	35.60	4.20	5. 农业贷款 Loans to Agricultural Sector	79.30	3.00
6. 农户储蓄存款 Savings Deposits by Rural Households	10.10	0.30	二、黄金占款 Position for Bullion and Silver Purchase	3.80	
7. 农村存款 Rural Deposits	25.40	1.40	三、外汇占款 Position for Foreign Exchange Purchase	2.40	8.30
二、流通中货币 Currency in Circulation	89.90	－16.60			
三、银行自有资金 Own Capital	229.70	28.40			
四、其他 Others	－151.80	－121.80			
资金来源总计 Total Sources	**582.70**	**－106.90**	**资金运用总计 Total Uses**	**582.70**	**－106.90**

金融机构人民币信贷收支表
Sources and Uses of Credit Funds of Financial Institutions（RMB）

（1964 年末）

（Year - end of 1964）

单位：亿元

Unit：100 Million Yuan

项　目 Items	余　额 Balance	比年初增减额 Changes within the Year	项　目 Items	余　额 Balance	比年初增减额 Changes within the Year
一、各项存款 Total Deposits	439.34	24.44	一、各项贷款 Total Loans	588.75	12.25
1. 企业存款 Deposits by Enterprises	156.10	- 20.70	1. 工业生产企业贷款 Loans to Industrial Production Enterprises	76.00	- 0.90
2. 财政存款 Fiscal Deposits	84.80	17.50	2. 物资供销企业贷款 Loans to Material Supply and Sale Enterprises	31.60	0.10
3. 基本建设存款 Capital Construction Deposits	38.60	- 4.40	3. 商业企业贷款 Loans to Commercial Enterprises	396.60	12.20
4. 机关团体存款 Deposits by Government Agencies and Social Organizations	69.60	12.90	4. 城镇集体企业贷款 Loans to Urban Collective Enterprises	3.20	- 1.20
5. 城镇储蓄存款 Urban Savings Deposits	44.80	9.20	5. 农业贷款 Loans to Agricultural Sector	81.35	2.05
6. 农户储蓄存款 Savings Deposits by Rural Households	10.70	0.60	二、黄金占款 Position for Bullion and Silver Purchase	3.80	
7. 农村存款 Rural Deposits	34.74	9.34	三、外汇占款 Position for Foreign Exchange Purchase	10.90	8.50
二、流通中货币 Currency in Circulation	80.00	- 9.90			
三、银行自有资金 Own Capital	102.70	- 127.00			
四、其他 Others	- 18.59	133.21			
资金来源总计 Total Sources	**603.45**	**20.75**	**资金运用总计 Total Uses**	**603.45**	**20.75**

金融机构人民币信贷收支表

Sources and Uses of Credit Funds of Financial Institutions（RMB)

（1965 年末）

（Year - end of 1965）

单位：亿元

Unit：100 Million Yuan

项 目 Items	余 额 Balance	比年初增减额 Changes within the Year	项 目 Items	余 额 Balance	比年初增减额 Changes within the Year
一、各项存款 Total Deposits	481.65	42.31	一、各项贷款 Total Loans	656.65	67.90
1. 企业存款 Deposits by Enterprises	181.90	25.80	1. 工业生产企业贷款 Loans to Industrial Production Enterprises	93.20	17.20
2. 财政存款 Fiscal Deposits	74.20	- 10.60	2. 物资供销企业贷款 Loans to Material Supply and Sale Enterprises	41.30	9.70
3. 基本建设存款 Capital Construction Deposits	41.70	3.10			
4. 机关团体存款 Deposits by Government Agencies and Social Organizations	80.80	11.20	3. 商业企业贷款 Loans to Commercial Enterprises	431.30	34.70
			4. 城镇集体企业贷款 Loans to Urban Collective Enterprises	3.40	0.20
5. 城镇储蓄存款 Urban Savings Deposits	52.30	7.50	5. 农业贷款 Loans to Agricultural Sector	87.45	6.10
6. 农户储蓄存款 Savings Deposits by Rural Households	12.90	2.20	二、黄金占款 Position for Bullion and Silver Purchase	4.80	1.00
7. 农村存款 Rural Deposits	37.85	3.11	三、外汇占款 Position for Foreign Exchange Purchase	10.00	- 0.90
二、流通中货币 Currency in Circulation	90.80	10.80			
三、银行自有资金 Own Capital	106.50	3.80			
四、其他 Others	- 7.50	11.09			
资金来源总计 Total Sources	**671.45**	**68.00**	**资金运用总计 Total Uses**	**671.45**	**68.00**

金融机构人民币信贷收支表

Sources and Uses of Credit Funds of Financial Institutions (RMB)

(1966 年末)

(Year - end of 1966)

单位：亿元

Unit: 100 Million Yuan

项 目 Items	余 额 Balance	比年初增减额 Changes within the Year	项 目 Items	余 额 Balance	比年初增减额 Changes within the Year
一、各项存款 Total Deposits	554.75	73.10	一、各项贷款 Total Loans	766.85	110.20
1. 企业存款 Deposits by Enterprises	185.00	3.10	1. 工业生产企业贷款 Loans to Industrial Production Enterprises	122.30	29.10
2. 财政存款 Fiscal Deposits	95.80	21.60	2. 物资供销企业贷款 Loans to Material Supply and Sale Enterprises	52.20	10.90
3. 基本建设存款 Capital Construction Deposits	51.60	9.90	3. 商业企业贷款 Loans to Commercial Enterprises	498.60	67.30
4. 机关团体存款 Deposits by Government Agencies and Social Organizations	100.60	19.80	4. 城镇集体企业贷款 Loans to Urban Collective Enterprises	5.10	1.70
5. 城镇储蓄存款 Urban Savings Deposits	57.70	5.40	5. 农业贷款 Loans to Agricultural Sector	88.65	1.20
6. 农户储蓄存款 Savings Deposits by Rural Households	14.60	1.70	二、黄金占款 Position for Bullion and Silver Purchase	4.80	
7. 农村存款 Rural Deposits	49.45	11.60	三、外汇占款 Position for Foreign Exchange Purchase	9.80	-0.20
二、流通中货币 Currency in Circulation	108.50	17.70			
三、银行自有资金 Own Capital	124.30	17.80			
四、其他 Others	-6.10	1.40			
资金来源总计 Total Sources	**781.45**	**110.00**	**资金运用总计 Total Uses**	**781.45**	**110.00**

金融机构人民币信贷收支表

Sources and Uses of Credit Funds of Financial Institutions（RMB）

（1967 年末）

（Year – end of 1967）

单位：亿元

Unit：100 Million Yuan

项　目 Items	余　额 Balance	比年初增减额 Changes within the Year	项　目 Items	余　额 Balance	比年初增减额 Changes within the Year
一、各项存款 Total Deposits	582.46	27.71	一、各项贷款 Total Loans	806.95	40.10
1. 企业存款 Deposits by Enterprises	199.40	14.40	1. 工业生产企业贷款 Loans to Industrial Production Enterprises	173.60	51.30
2. 财政存款 Fiscal Deposits	67.30	– 28.50	2. 物资供销企业贷款 Loans to Material Supply and Sale Enterprises	51.80	– 0.40
3. 基本建设存款 Capital Construction Deposits	49.30	– 2.30			
4. 机关团体存款 Deposits by Government Agencies and Social Organizations	130.00	29.40	3. 商业企业贷款 Loans to Commercial Enterprises	483.00	– 15.60
			4. 城镇集体企业贷款 Loans to Urban Collective Enterprises	6.80	1.70
5. 城镇储蓄存款 Urban Savings Deposits	59.80	2.10	5. 农业贷款 Loans to Agricultural Sector	91.75	3.10
6. 农户储蓄存款 Savings Deposits by Rural Households	14.00	– 0.60	二、黄金占款 Position for Bullion and Silver Purchase	4.80	
7. 农村存款 Rural Deposits	62.66	13.21	三、外汇占款 Position for Foreign Exchange Purchase	9.20	– 0.60
二、流通中货币 Currency in Circulation	121.90	13.40			
三、银行自有资金 Own Capital	145.40	21.10			
四、其他 Others	– 28.81	– 22.71			
资金来源总计 Total Sources	**820.95**	**39.50**	**资金运用总计 Total Uses**	**820.95**	**39.50**

金融机构人民币信贷收支表

Sources and Uses of Credit Funds of Financial Institutions (RMB)

(1968年末)

(Year-end of 1968)

单位：亿元

Unit: 100 Million Yuan

项目 Items	余额 Balance	比年初增减额 Changes within the Year	项目 Items	余额 Balance	比年初增减额 Changes within the Year
一、各项存款 Total Deposits	621.62	39.16	一、各项贷款 Total Loans	902.55	95.60
1. 企业存款 Deposits by Enterprises	211.80	12.40	1. 工业生产企业贷款 Loans to Industrial Production Enterprises	213.10	39.50
2. 财政存款 Fiscal Deposits	92.30	25.00	2. 物资供销企业贷款 Loans to Material Supply and Sale Enterprises	62.50	10.70
3. 基本建设存款 Capital Construction Deposits	31.70	-17.60	3. 商业企业贷款 Loans to Commercial Enterprises	525.00	42.00
4. 机关团体存款 Deposits by Government Agencies and Social Organizations	143.70	13.70	4. 城镇集体企业贷款 Loans to Urban Collective Enterprises	8.50	1.70
5. 城镇储蓄存款 Urban Savings Deposits	62.30	2.50	5. 农业贷款 Loans to Agricultural Sector	93.45	1.70
6. 农户储蓄存款 Savings Deposits by Rural Households	16.00	2.00	二、黄金占款 Position for Bullion and Silver Purchase	6.70	1.90
7. 农村存款 Rural Deposits	63.82	1.16	三、外汇占款 Position for Foreign Exchange Purchase	8.00	-1.20
二、流通中货币 Currency in Circulation	134.10	12.20			
三、银行自有资金 Own Capital	166.60	21.20			
四、其他 Others	-5.07	23.74			
资金来源总计 Total Sources	**917.25**	**96.30**	**资金运用总计 Total Uses**	**917.25**	**96.30**

金融机构人民币信贷收支表

Sources and Uses of Credit Funds of Financial Institutions（RMB）

（1969年末）

（Year - end of 1969）

单位：亿元

Unit：100 Million Yuan

项　目 Items	余　额 Balance	比年初增减额 Changes within the Year	项　目 Items	余　额 Balance	比年初增减额 Changes within the Year
一、各项存款 Total Deposits	641.19	19.57	一、各项贷款 Total Loans	959.05	56.50
1. 企业存款 Deposits by Enterprises	215.50	3.70	1. 工业生产企业贷款 Loans to Industrial Production Enterprises	234.00	20.90
2. 财政存款 Fiscal Deposits	119.60	27.30	2. 物资供销企业贷款 Loans to Material Supply and Sale Enterprises	69.10	6.60
3. 基本建设存款 Capital Construction Deposits	16.20	-15.50	3. 商业企业贷款 Loans to Commercial Enterprises	547.50	22.50
4. 机关团体存款 Deposits by Government Agencies and Social Organizations	151.00	7.30	4. 城镇集体企业贷款 Loans to Urban Collective Enterprises	10.90	2.40
5. 城镇储蓄存款 Urban Savings Deposits	61.00	-1.30	5. 农业贷款 Loans to Agricultural Sector	97.55	4.10
6. 农户储蓄存款 Savings Deposits by Rural Households	14.90	-1.10	二、黄金占款 Position for Bullion and Silver Purchase	6.70	
7. 农村存款 Rural Deposits	62.99	-0.83	三、外汇占款 Position for Foreign Exchange Purchase	16.30	8.30
二、流通中货币 Currency in Circulation	137.10	3.00			
三、银行自有资金 Own Capital	193.10	26.50			
四、其他 Others	10.66	15.73			
资金来源总计 Total Sources	**982.05**	**64.80**	**资金运用总计 Total Uses**	**982.05**	**64.80**

金融机构人民币信贷收支表

Sources and Uses of Credit Funds of Financial Institutions (RMB)

(1970年末)

(Year-end of 1970)

单位：亿元

Unit: 100 Million Yuan

项目 Items	余额 Balance	比年初增减额 Changes within the Year	项目 Items	余额 Balance	比年初增减额 Changes within the Year
一、各项存款 Total Deposits	702.40	61.21	一、各项贷款 Total Loans	1047.95	88.90
1. 企业存款 Deposits by Enterprises	226.10	10.60	1. 工业生产企业贷款 Loans to Industrial Production Enterprises	241.40	7.40
2. 财政存款 Fiscal Deposits	176.80	57.20	2. 物资供销企业贷款 Loans to Material Supply and Sale Enterprises	67.40	-1.70
3. 基本建设存款 Capital Construction Deposits	12.20	-4.00	3. 商业企业贷款 Loans to Commercial Enterprises	626.60	79.10
4. 机关团体存款 Deposits by Government Agencies and Social Organizations	141.40	-9.60	4. 城镇集体企业贷款 Loans to Urban Collective Enterprises	12.90	2.00
5. 城镇储蓄存款 Urban Savings Deposits	64.50	3.50	5. 农业贷款 Loans to Agricultural Sector	99.65	2.10
6. 农户储蓄存款 Savings Deposits by Rural Households	15.00	0.10	二、黄金占款 Position for Bullion and Silver Purchase	6.70	
7. 农村存款 Rural Deposits	66.40	3.41	三、外汇占款 Position for Foreign Exchange Purchase	6.50	-9.80
二、流通中货币 Currency in Circulation	123.60	-13.50			
三、银行自有资金 Own Capital	220.30	27.20			
四、其他 Others	14.85	4.19			
资金来源总计 Total Sources	**1061.15**	**79.10**	**资金运用总计 Total Uses**	**1061.15**	**79.10**

金融机构人民币信贷收支表

Sources and Uses of Credit Funds of Financial Institutions（RMB）

（1971年末）

（Year - end of 1971）

单位：亿元

Unit：100 Million Yuan

项目 Items	余额 Balance	比年初增减额 Changes within the Year	项目 Items	余额 Balance	比年初增减额 Changes within the Year
一、各项存款 Total Deposits	770.24	67.84	一、各项贷款 Total Loans	1130.76	82.81
1. 企业存款 Deposits by Enterprises	226.80	0.70	1. 工业生产企业贷款 Loans to Industrial Production Enterprises	251.90	10.50
2. 财政存款 Fiscal Deposits	188.90	12.10	2. 物资供销企业贷款 Loans to Material Supply and Sale Enterprises	126.00	58.60
3. 基本建设存款 Capital Construction Deposits	24.00	11.80	3. 商业企业贷款 Loans to Commercial Enterprises	667.20	40.60
4. 机关团体存款 Deposits by Government Agencies and Social Organizations	161.10	19.70	4. 城镇集体企业贷款 Loans to Urban Collective Enterprises	17.20	4.30
5. 城镇储蓄存款 Urban Savings Deposits	73.30	8.80	5. 农业贷款 Loans to Agricultural Sector	68.46	-31.19
6. 农户储蓄存款 Savings Deposits by Rural Households	17.00	2.00	二、黄金占款 Position for Bullion and Silver Purchase	8.60	1.90
7. 农村存款 Rural Deposits	79.14	12.74	三、外汇占款 Position for Foreign Exchange Purchase	4.90	-1.60
二、流通中货币 Currency in Circulation	136.20	12.60			
三、银行自有资金 Own Capital	152.30	-68.00			
四、其他 Others	85.52	70.67			
资金来源总计 Total Sources	**1144.26**	**83.11**	**资金运用总计 Total Uses**	**1144.26**	**83.11**

金融机构人民币信贷收支表
Sources and Uses of Credit Funds of Financial Institutions (RMB)

(1972年末)

(Year-end of 1972)

单位：亿元

Unit: 100 Million Yuan

项目 Items	余额 Balance	比年初增减额 Changes within the Year	项目 Items	余额 Balance	比年初增减额 Changes within the Year
一、各项存款 Total Deposits	781.60	11.36	一、各项贷款 Total Loans	1163.76	33.00
1. 企业存款 Deposits by Enterprises	239.00	12.20	1. 工业生产企业贷款 Loans to Industrial Production Enterprises	224.30	-27.60
2. 财政存款 Fiscal Deposits	172.60	-16.30	2. 物资供销企业贷款 Loans to Material Supply and Sale Enterprises	151.30	25.30
3. 基本建设存款 Capital Construction Deposits	34.30	10.30	3. 商业企业贷款 Loans to Commercial Enterprises	693.80	26.60
4. 机关团体存款 Deposits by Government Agencies and Social Organizations	153.90	-7.20	4. 城镇集体企业贷款 Loans to Urban Collective Enterprises	19.60	2.40
5. 城镇储蓄存款 Urban Savings Deposits	85.10	11.80	5. 农业贷款 Loans to Agricultural Sector	74.76	6.30
6. 农户储蓄存款 Savings Deposits by Rural Households	20.10	3.10	二、黄金占款 Position for Bullion and Silver Purchase	8.60	
7. 农村存款 Rural Deposits	76.60	-2.54	三、外汇占款 Position for Foreign Exchange Purchase	8.70	3.80
二、流通中货币 Currency in Circulation	151.20	15.00			
三、银行自有资金 Own Capital	138.90	-13.40			
四、其他 Others	109.36	23.84			
资金来源总计 Total Sources	**1181.06**	**36.80**	**资金运用总计 Total Uses**	**1181.06**	**36.80**

金融机构人民币信贷收支表

Sources and Uses of Credit Funds of Financial Institutions（RMB）

（1973年末）

（Year－end of 1973）

单位：亿元

Unit：100 Million Yuan

项目 Items	余额 Balance	比年初增减额 Changes within the Year	项目 Items	余额 Balance	比年初增减额 Changes within the Year
一、各项存款 Total Deposits	869.05	87.45	一、各项贷款 Total Loans	1287.06	123.30
1.企业存款 Deposits by Enterprises	279.00	40.00	1.工业生产企业贷款 Loans to Industrial Production Enterprises	231.10	6.80
2.财政存款 Fiscal Deposits	160.80	－11.80	2.物资供销企业贷款 Loans to Material Supply and Sale Enterprises	179.60	28.30
3.基本建设存款 Capital Construction Deposits	51.30	17.00			
4.机关团体存款 Deposits by Government Agencies and Social Organizations	172.50	18.60	3.商业企业贷款 Loans to Commercial Enterprises	776.90	83.10
			4.城镇集体企业贷款 Loans to Urban Collective Enterprises	22.60	3.00
5.城镇储蓄存款 Urban Savings Deposits	94.10	9.00	5.农业贷款 Loans to Agricultural Sector	76.86	2.10
6.农户储蓄存款 Savings Deposits by Rural Households	27.10	7.00	二、黄金占款 Position for Bullion and Silver Purchase	8.60	
7.农村存款 Rural Deposits	84.25	7.65	三、外汇占款 Position for Foreign Exchange Purchase	5.90	－2.80
二、流通中货币 Currency in Circulation	166.10	14.90			
三、银行自有资金 Own Capital	183.10	44.20			
四、其他 Others	83.31	－26.05			
资金来源总计 Total Sources	**1301.56**	**120.50**	**资金运用总计 Total Uses**	**1301.56**	**120.50**

金融机构人民币信贷收支表
Sources and Uses of Credit Funds of Financial Institutions (RMB)

(1974年末)

(Year - end of 1974)

单位：亿元

Unit: 100 Million Yuan

项 目 Items	余 额 Balance	比年初增减额 Changes within the Year	项 目 Items	余 额 Balance	比年初增减额 Changes within the Year
一、各项存款 Total Deposits	903.09	34.04	一、各项贷款 Total Loans	1373.26	86.20
1. 企业存款 Deposits by Enterprises	324.80	45.80	1. 工业生产企业贷款 Loans to Industrial Production Enterprises	266.70	35.60
2. 财政存款 Fiscal Deposits	137.30	-23.50	2. 物资供销企业贷款 Loans to Material Supply and Sale Enterprises	179.60	
3. 基本建设存款 Capital Construction Deposits	53.80	2.50	3. 商业企业贷款 Loans to Commercial Enterprises	815.00	38.10
4. 机关团体存款 Deposits by Government Agencies and Social Organizations	152.40	-20.10	4. 城镇集体企业贷款 Loans to Urban Collective Enterprises	28.20	5.60
5. 城镇储蓄存款 Urban Savings Deposits	105.80	11.70	5. 农业贷款 Loans to Agricultural Sector	83.76	6.90
6. 农户储蓄存款 Savings Deposits by Rural Households	30.60	3.50	二、黄金占款 Position for Bullion and Silver Purchase	12.20	3.60
7. 农村存款 Rural Deposits	98.39	14.14	三、外汇占款 Position for Foreign Exchange Purchase	10.20	4.30
二、流通中货币 Currency in Circulation	176.60	10.50			
三、银行自有资金 Own Capital	222.60	39.50			
四、其他 Others	93.37	10.06			
资金来源总计 Total Sources	**1395.66**	**94.10**	**资金运用总计 Total Uses**	**1395.66**	**94.10**

金融机构人民币信贷收支表

Sources and Uses of Credit Funds of Financial Institutions（RMB）

（1975 年末）

（Year – end of 1975）

单位：亿元

Unit：100 Million Yuan

项　目 Items	余　额 Balance	比年初增减额 Changes within the Year	项　目 Items	余　额 Balance	比年初增减额 Changes within the Year
一、各项存款 Total Deposits	982.50	79.41	一、各项贷款 Total Loans	1486.98	113.72
1. 企业存款 Deposits by Enterprises	362.70	37.90	1. 工业生产企业贷款 Loans to Industrial Production Enterprises	293.50	26.80
2. 财政存款 Fiscal Deposits	140.20	2.90	2. 物资供销企业贷款 Loans to Material Supply and Sale Enterprises	179.10	-0.50
3. 基本建设存款 Capital Construction Deposits	63.20	9.40	3. 商业企业贷款 Loans to Commercial Enterprises	884.70	69.70
4. 机关团体存款 Deposits by Government Agencies and Social Organizations	157.50	5.10	4. 城镇集体企业贷款 Loans to Urban Collective Enterprises	33.00	4.80
5. 城镇储蓄存款 Urban Savings Deposits	114.60	8.80	5. 农业贷款 Loans to Agricultural Sector	96.68	12.92
6. 农户储蓄存款 Savings Deposits by Rural Households	35.10	4.50	二、黄金占款 Position for Bullion and Silver Purchase	12.20	
7. 农村存款 Rural Deposits	109.20	10.81	三、外汇占款 Position for Foreign Exchange Purchase	9.80	-0.40
二、流通中货币 Currency in Circulation	182.60	6.00			
三、银行自有资金 Own Capital	258.10	35.50			
四、其他 Others	85.78	-7.59			
资金来源总计 Total Sources	**1508.98**	**113.32**	**资金运用总计 Total Uses**	**1508.98**	**113.32**

金融机构人民币信贷收支表

Sources and Uses of Credit Funds of Financial Institutions（RMB）

（1976 年末）

（Year – end of 1976）

单位：亿元

Unit：100 Million Yuan

项 目 Items	余 额 Balance	比年初增减额 Changes within the Year	项 目 Items	余 额 Balance	比年初增减额 Changes within the Year
一、各项存款 Total Deposits	993.16	10.66	一、各项贷款 Total Loans	1574.14	87.16
1. 企业存款 Deposits by Enterprises	389.80	27.10	1. 工业生产企业贷款 Loans to Industrial Production Enterprises	329.40	35.90
2. 财政存款 Fiscal Deposits	97.90	-42.30	2. 物资供销企业贷款 Loans to Material Supply and Sale Enterprises	173.30	-5.80
3. 基本建设存款 Capital Construction Deposits	65.80	2.60	3. 商业企业贷款 Loans to Commercial Enterprises	908.00	23.30
4. 机关团体存款 Deposits by Government Agencies and Social Organizations	166.10	8.60	4. 城镇集体企业贷款 Loans to Urban Collective Enterprises	40.70	7.70
5. 城镇储蓄存款 Urban Savings Deposits	122.20	7.60	5. 农业贷款 Loans to Agricultural Sector	122.74	26.06
6. 农户储蓄存款 Savings Deposits by Rural Households	36.90	1.80	二、黄金占款 Position for Bullion and Silver Purchase	12.20	
7. 农村存款 Rural Deposits	114.46	5.26	三、外汇占款 Position for Foreign Exchange Purchase	12.30	2.50
二、流通中货币 Currency in Circulation	204.00	21.40			
三、银行自有资金 Own Capital	303.00	44.90			
四、其他 Others	98.48	12.70			
资金来源总计 Total Sources	**1598.64**	**89.66**	**资金运用总计 Total Uses**	**1598.64**	**89.66**

金融机构人民币信贷收支表

Sources and Uses of Credit Funds of Financial Institutions（RMB）

（1977 年末）

（Year – end of 1977）

单位：亿元

Unit：100 Million Yuan

项目 Items	余额 Balance	比年初增减额 Changes within the Year	项目 Items	余额 Balance	比年初增减额 Changes within the Year
一、各项存款 Total Deposits	1080.44	87.28	一、各项贷款 Total Loans	1699.54	125.40
1. 企业存款 Deposits by Enterprises	384.70	–5.10	1. 工业生产企业贷款 Loans to Industrial Production Enterprises	334.20	4.80
2. 财政存款 Fiscal Deposits	151.90	54.00	2. 物资供销企业贷款 Loans to Material Supply and Sale Enterprises	187.90	14.60
3. 基本建设存款 Capital Construction Deposits	77.50	11.70	3. 商业企业贷款 Loans to Commercial Enterprises	996.90	88.90
4. 机关团体存款 Deposits by Government Agencies and Social Organizations	171.40	5.30	4. 城镇集体企业贷款 Loans to Urban Collective Enterprises	46.00	5.30
5. 城镇储蓄存款 Urban Savings Deposits	135.10	12.90	5. 农业贷款 Loans to Agricultural Sector	134.54	11.80
6. 农户储蓄存款 Savings Deposits by Rural Households	46.50	9.60	二、黄金占款 Position for Bullion and Silver Purchase	12.20	
7. 农村存款 Rural Deposits	113.34	–1.12	三、外汇占款 Position for Foreign Exchange Purchase	23.80	11.50
二、流通中货币 Currency in Circulation	195.40	–8.60			
三、银行自有资金 Own Capital	359.90	56.90			
四、其他 Others	99.80	1.32			
资金来源总计 Total Sources	**1735.54**	**136.90**	**资金运用总计 Total Uses**	**1735.54**	**136.90**

金融机构人民币信贷收支表
Sources and Uses of Credit Funds of Financial Institutions (RMB)
(1978 年末)
(Year - end of 1978)

单位：亿元
Unit: 100 Million Yuan

项目 Items	余额 Balance	比年初增减额 Changes within the Year	项目 Items	余额 Balance	比年初增减额 Changes within the Year
一、企业存款 Deposits by Enterprises	368.43	-16.27	一、工业贷款 Loans to Industrial Sector	616.83	—
二、财政存款 Fiscal Deposits	187.35	35.45	二、中短期设备贷款 Short and Medium - term Equipment Loans		
三、基本建设存款 Capital Construction Deposits	109.63	32.13	三、基本建设投资贷款 Capital Construction Investment Loans		
四、机关团体存款 Deposits by Government Agencies and Social Organizations	89.52	—	四、商业贷款 Loans to Commercial Sector	1117.65	—
五、部队存款 Deposits by Army	70.31	—	五、个体工商业贷款 Loans to Self - employed Entities		
六、储蓄存款 Savings Deposits	154.91	19.81	六、预购订金贷款 Loans for Advance Payment on Future Purchase	7.15	—
七、社员个人存款 Deposits by Associators	55.70	9.20	七、国营农业贷款 Loans to State Agricultural Enterprises	6.35	—
八、农村存款 Rural Deposits	119.16	5.82	八、社队农业贷款 Loans to Agricultural Communities	142.44	—
存款合计 Total Deposits	**1155.01**	**74.57**	**贷款合计 Total Loans**	**1890.42**	**190.88**
九、汇兑在途资金 Remittance in Transit	94.16	—	九、金银库存占款 Position for Bullion and Silver Purchase	12.20	
十、流通中货币 Currency in Circulation	212.00	16.60	十、外汇库存占款 Position for Foreign Exchange Purchase	14.34	-9.46
十一、自有资金 Own Capital	421.90	62.00	十一、上缴利润和税金 Payment of Profits and Taxes	13.61	13.61
十二、当年结益 Net Earnings	67.55	67.55			
十三、其他 Others	-20.05	—			
资金来源总计 Total Sources	**1930.57**	—	**资金运用总计 Total Uses**	**1930.57**	—

金融机构人民币信贷收支表

Sources and Uses of Credit Funds of Financial Institutions（RMB）

（1979 年末）

（Year - end of 1979）

单位：亿元

Unit：100 Million Yuan

项　目 Items	余　额 Balance	比年初增减额 Changes within the Year	项　目 Items	余　额 Balance	比年初增减额 Changes within the Year
一、企业存款 Deposits by Enterprises	468.91	100.48	一、工业贷款 Loans to Industrial Sector	670.64	53.81
二、财政存款 Fisal Deposits	148.68	- 38.67	二、中短期设备贷款 Short and Medium - term Equipment Loans		
三、基本建设存款 Capital Construction Depotits	131.30	21.67	三、基本建设投资贷款 Capital Construction Investment Loans		
四、机关团体存款 Deposits by Government Agencies and Social Organizations	110.80	21.28	四、商业贷款 Loans to Commercial Sector	1232.25	114.60
			五、个体工商业贷款 Loans to Self - employed Entities		
五、部队存款 Deposits by Army	74.08	3.77			
			六、预购订金贷款 Loans for Advance Payment on Future Purchase	6.98	- 0.17
六、储蓄存款 Savings Deposits	202.56	47.65			
七、社员个人存款 Deposits by Associators	78.40	22.70	七、国营农业贷款 Loans to State Agricultural Enterprises	6.86	0.51
八、农村存款 Rural Deposits	147.83	28.67	八、社队农业贷款 Loans to Agricultural Communities	165.74	23.30
其中：社队集体存款 Of Which：Deposits by Collectives of Communities	108.63	—	**贷款合计 Total Loans**	**2082.47**	**192.05**
社队企事业存款 Deposits by Enterprises and Establishments of Communities	21.90	—	九、金银库存占款 Position for Bullion and Silver Purchase	12.20	
			十、外汇库存占款 Position for Foreign Exchange Purchase	20.58	6.24
存款合计 Total Deposits	**1362.56**	**207.55**	十一、上缴利润和税金 Payment of Profits and Taxes	12.52	12.52
九、汇兑在途资金 Remittance in Transit	93.31	- 0.85			
十、流通中货币 Currency in Circulation	267.70	55.70			
十一、自有资金 Own Capital	471.10	49.20			
十二、当年结益 Net Earnings	61.75	61.75			
十三、其他 Others	- 128.65	- 162.54			
资金来源总计 Total Sources	**2127.77**	**210.81**	**资金运用总计 Total Uses**	**2127.77**	**210.81**

金融机构人民币信贷收支表

Sources and Uses of Credit Funds of Financial Institutions（RMB）

（1980年末）

（Year－end of 1980）

单位：亿元

Unit：100 Million Yuan

项　目 Items	余　额 Balance	比年初增减额 Changes within the Year	项　目 Items	余　额 Balance	比年初增减额 Changes within the Year
一、企业存款 Deposits by Enterprises	561.01	92.10	一、工业贷款 Loans to Industrial Sector	743.76	73.12
二、财政存款 Fiscal Deposits	160.68	12.00	二、中短期设备贷款 Short and Medium－term Equipment Loans	47.51	47.51
三、基本建设存款 Capital Construction Deposits	173.37	42.07	三、基本建设投资贷款 Capital Construction Investment Loans		
四、机关团体存款 Deposits by Government Agencies and Social Organizations	146.94	36.14	四、商业贷款 Loans to Commercial Sector	1437.14	204.89
			五、个体工商业贷款 Loans to Self－employed Entities		
五、部队存款 Deposits by Army	81.95	7.87	六、预购订金贷款 Loans for Advance Payment on Future Purchase	7.87	0.89
六、储蓄存款 Savings Deposits	278.77	76.21			
七、社员个人存款 Deposits by Associators	117.03	38.63	七、国营农业贷款 Loans to State Agricultural Enterprises	9.41	2.55
八、农村存款 Rural Deposits	169.91	22.08	八、社队农业贷款 Loans to Agricultural Communities	232.39	66.65
其中：社队集体存款 Of Which：Deposits by Collectives of Communities	120.11	11.48	**贷款合计 Total Loans**	**2478.08**	**395.61**
社队企事业存款 Deposits by Enterprises and Establishment of Communities	29.50	7.60	九、金银库存占款 Position for Bullion and Silver Purchase	12.20	
			十、外汇库存占款 Position for Foreign Exchange Purchase	－8.34	－28.92
存款合计 Total Deposits	**1689.66**	**327.10**	十一、上缴利润和税金 Payment of Profits and Taxes	32.00	32.00
九、汇兑在途资金 Remittance in Transit	105.71	12.40	十二、财政透支和借款 Overdraft by State Finance	170.20	
十、流通中货币 Currency in Circulation	346.20	78.50			
十一、自有资金 Own Capital	496.90	25.80			
十二、当年结益 Net Earnings	51.78	51.78			
十三、其他 Others	－6.11	－96.89			
资金来源总计 Total Sources	**2684.14**	**398.69**	**资金运用总计 Total Uses**	**2684.14**	**398.69**

金融机构人民币信贷收支表

Sources and Uses of Credit Funds of Financial Institutions（RMB）

（1981 年末）

（Year - end of 1981）

单位：亿元

Unit：100 Million Yuan

项目 Items	余额 Balance	比年初增减额 Changes within the Year	项目 Items	余额 Balance	比年初增减额 Changes within the Year
一、企业存款 Deposits by Enterprises	676.96	115.95	一、工业贷款 Loans to Industrial Sector	839.13	95.37
二、财政存款 Fiscal Deposits	194.29	33.61	二、中短期设备贷款 Short and Medium - term Equipment Loans	83.74	36.23
三、基本建设存款 Capital Construction Deposits	228.88	55.51	三、基本建设投资贷款 Capital Construction Investment Loans		
四、机关团体存款 Deposits by Government Agencies and Social Organizations	183.81	36.87	四、商业贷款 Loans to Commercial Sector	1639.21	202.07
			五、个体工商业贷款 Loans to Self - employed Entities	0.47	0.47
五、部队存款 Deposits by Army	90.91	8.96	六、预购订金贷款 Loans for Advance Payment on Future Purchase	7.39	-0.48
六、储蓄存款 Savings Deposits	353.80	75.03			
七、社员个人存款 Deposits by Associators	169.55	52.52	七、国营农业贷款 Loans to State Agricultural Enterprises	16.82	7.41
八、农村存款 Rural Deposits	174.44	4.53	八、社队农业贷款 Loans to Agricultural Communities	256.78	24.39
其中：社队集体存款 Of Which：Deposits by Collectives of Communities	137.64	17.53	九、信托及其他贷款 Trust and Other Loans	9.75	9.75
			贷款合计 Total Loans	**2853.29**	**375.21**
社队企事业存款 Deposits by Enterprises and Establishment of Communities	29.70	0.20	十、金银库存占款 Position for Bullion and Silver Purchase	12.00	-0.20
九、信托及其他存款 Trust and Other Deposits	24.55	24.55	十一、外汇库存占款 Position for Foreign Exchange Purchase	89.60	97.94
存款合计 Total Deposits	**2097.19**	**407.53**	十二、上缴利润和税金 Payment of Profits and Taxes	32.00	32.00
十、汇兑在途资金 Remittance in Transit	129.73	24.02	十三、财政透支和借款 Overdraft by State Finance	170.20	
十一、流通中货币 Currency in Circulation	396.34	50.14			
十二、自有资金 Own Capital	497.05	0.15			
十三、当年结益 Net Earnings	50.66	50.66			
十四、其他 Others	-13.88	-27.55			
资金来源总计 Total Sources	**3157.09**	**504.95**	**资金运用总计 Total Uses**	**3157.09**	**504.95**

金融机构人民币信贷收支表

Sources and Uses of Credit Funds of Financial Institutions（RMB）

（1982 年末）

（Year - end of 1982）

单位：亿元

Unit：100 Million Yuan

项　目 Items	余　额 Balance	比年初增减额 Changes within the Year	项　目 Items	余　额 Balance	比年初增减额 Changes within the Year
一、企业存款 Deposits by Enterprises	761.64	84.68	一、工业贷款 Loans to Industrial Sector	866.58	27.45
二、财政存款 Fiscal Deposits	175.76	- 18.53	二、中短期设备贷款 Short and Medium - term Equipment Loans	138.62	54.88
三、基本建设存款 Capital Construction Deposits	284.80	55.92	三、基本建设投资贷款 Capital Construction Investment Loans	13.36	13.36
四、机关团体存款 Deposits by Government Agencies and Social Organizations	218.24	34.43	四、商业贷款 Loans to Commercial Sector	1806.60	167.39
			五、个体工商业贷款 Loans to Self - employed Entities	0.55	0.08
五、部队存款 Deposits by Army	113.19	22.28	六、预购订金贷款 Loans for Advance Payment on Future Purchase	7.43	0.04
六、储蓄存款 Savings Deposits	447.33	93.53			
七、社员个人存款 Deposits by Associators	228.11	58.56	七、国营农业贷款 Loans to State Agricultural Enterprises	19.81	2.99
八、农村存款 Rural Deposits	188.84	14.40	八、社队农业贷款 Loans to Agricultural Communities	295.64	38.86
其中：社队集体存款 Of Which: Deposits by Collectives of Communities	148.14	10.50	九、信托及其他贷款 Trust and Other Loans	14.11	4.36
			贷款合计 Total Loans	**3162.70**	**309.41**
社队企事业存款 Deposits by Enterprises and Establishment of Communities	33.70	4.00	十、金银库存占款 Position for Bullion and Silver Purchase	12.00	
九、信托及其他存款 Trust and Other Deposits	31.14	6.59	十一、外汇库存占款 Position for Foreign Exchange Purchase	217.70	128.10
存款合计 Total Deposits	**2449.05**	**351.86**	十二、上缴利润和税金 Payment of Profits and Taxes	67.10	67.10
十、汇兑在途资金 Remittance in Transit	139.64	9.91	十三、财政透支和借款 Overdraft by State Finance	170.20	
十一、流通中货币 Currency in Circulation	439.12	42.78			
十二、自有资金 Own Capital	518.29	21.24			
十三、当年结益 Net Earnings	103.78	103.78			
十四、其他 Others	- 20.18	- 24.96			
资金来源总计 Total Sources	**3629.70**	**504.61**	**资金运用总计 Total Uses**	**3629.70**	**504.61**

金融机构人民币信贷收支表

Sources and Uses of Credit Funds of Financial Institutions（RMB）

（1983 年末）

（Year - end of 1983）

单位：亿元

Unit：100 Million Yuan

项 目 Items	余 额 Balance	比年初增减额 Changes within the Year	项 目 Items	余 额 Balance	比年初增减额 Changes within the Year
一、企业存款 Deposits by Enterprises	864.99	103.35	一、工业贷款 Loans to Industrial Sector	973.53	106.95
二、财政存款 Fiscal Deposits	229.89	54.13	二、中短期设备贷款 Short and Medium - term Equipment Loans	163.83	25.21
三、基本建设存款 Capital Construction Deposits	299.67	14.87	三、基本建设投资贷款 Capital Construction Investment Loans	28.26	14.90
四、机关团体存款 Deposits by Government Agencies and Social Organizations	253.42	35.18	四、商业贷款 Loans to Commercial Sector	2003.11	196.51
			五、个体工商业贷款 Loans to Self - employed Entities	1.50	0.95
五、部队存款 Deposits by Army	118.27	5.08	六、预购订金贷款 Loans for Advance Payment on Future Purchase	6.71	- 0.72
六、储蓄存款 Savings Deposits	572.60	125.27			
七、社员个人存款 Deposits by Associators	320.33	92.22	七、国营农业贷款 Loans to State Agricultural Enterprises	25.47	5.66
八、农村存款 Rural Deposits	190.06	1.22	八、社队农业贷款 Loans to Agricultural Communities	346.73	51.09
其中：社队集体存款 Of Which：Deposits by Collectives of Communities	119.07	- 29.07	其中：社队生产费用、设备贷款 Of Which：Loans to Communitiey for Expenses of Production & Equipment Purchase	112.71	—
社队企事业存款 Deposits by Enterprises and Establishment of Communities	62.71	29.01	其中：社队生产费用贷款 Of Which：Loans to Communities for Expenses of Production		
九、信托及其他存款 Trust and Other Deposits	34.09	2.95	社队生产设备贷款 Loans to Communities for Equipment Purchase		
存款合计 **Total Deposits**	**2883.32**	**434.27**			
十、汇兑在途资金 Remittance in Transit	147.89	8.25	社队企业贷款 Loans to Enterprises of Communities	140.73	—
十一、流通中货币 Currency in Circulation	529.78	90.66	社员贷款 Loans to Associators	93.29	—
十二、自有资金 Own Capital	547.36	29.07	九、信托及其他贷款 Trust and Other Loans	17.42	3.31
十三、当年结益 Net Earnings	120.60	120.60	**贷款合计** **Total Loans**	**3566.56**	**403.86**
十四、其他 Others	- 87.66	- 133.56	十、金银库存占款 Position for Bullion and Silver Purchase	12.00	
			十一、外汇库存占款 Foreign Exchange Purchase	266.10	48.40
			十二、上缴利润和税金 Payment of Profits and Taxes	97.03	97.03
			十三、财政透支和借款 Overdraft by State Finance	199.60	
资金来源总计 **Total Sources**	**4141.29**	**549.29**	**资金运用总计** **Total Uses**	**4141.29**	**549.29**

金融机构人民币信贷收支表
Sources and Uses of Credit Funds of Financial Institutions (RMB)

(1984 年末)

(Year – end of 1984)

单位：亿元

Unit: 100 Million Yuan

项目 Items	余额 Balance	比年初增减额 Changes within the Year	项目 Items	余额 Balance	比年初增减额 Changes within the Year
一、企业存款 Deposits by Enterprises	1251.79	386.80	一、流动资金贷款 Working Capital Loans	3763.04	767.48
二、财政存款 Fiscal Deposits	210.93	– 18.96	1. 工业贷款 Loans to Industrial Sector	1316.88	343.35
三、基本建设存款 Capital Construction Deposits	335.67	36.00	2. 商业贷款 Loans to Commercial Sector	2346.53	343.42
四、机关团体存款 Deposits by Government Agencies and Social Organizations	282.22	28.80	3. 个体工商业贷款 Loans to Self – employed Entities	10.62	9.12
			4. 信托及其他贷款 Trust and Other Loans	89.01	71.59
五、部队存款 Deposits by Army	91.79	– 26.48			
			二、固定资产贷款 Fixed Asset Loans	294.03	101.94
六、储蓄存款 Savings Deposits	776.58	203.98	1. 技术改造贷款 Technical Improvement Loans	229.37	65.54
七、社员个人存款 Deposits by Associators	438.12	117.79	2. 基本建设贷款 Capital Construction Loans	52.98	24.72
八、农村存款 Rural Deposits	228.76	38.70	3. 发展少数民族经济贷款 Loans to Ethnic Minority Regions	5.47	5.47
九、信托及其他存款 Trust and Other Deposits	119.47	85.38	4. 特种外汇兑换 Special Foreign Exchange	6.21	6.21
存款合计 Total Deposits	**3735.33**	**852.01**	三、农业贷款 Loans to Agricultural Sector	689.73	310.82
十、汇兑在途资金 Remittance in Transit	324.76	176.87	其中：社队农业贷款 Of Which: Loans to Agricultural Communities	632.24	285.51
十一、流通中货币 Currency in Circulation	792.11	262.33			
十二、自有资金 Own Capital	573.17	25.81	**贷款合计 Total Loans**	**4746.80**	**1180.24**
十三、当年结益 Net Earnings	124.49	124.49	四、金银库存占款 Position for Bullion and Silver Purchase	12.00	
十四、其他 Others	– 105.95	– 41.86	五、外汇库存占款 Position for Foreign Exchange Purchase	263.60	– 2.50
			六、上缴财政利润和税金 Payment of Profits and Taxes to Government Finance	105.53	105.53
			七、财政透支和借款 Overdraft by State Finance	260.80	61.20
			八、待核销机电产品贷款损失 Mechanical and Electrical Products Loan Loss to be Written – off	55.18	55.18
资金来源总计 Total Sources	**5443.91**	**1399.65**	**资金运用总计 Total Uses**	**5443.91**	**1399.65**

金融机构人民币信贷收支表

Sources and Uses of Credit Funds of Financial Institutions（RMB）

（1985年末）

（Year - end of 1985）

单位：亿元

Unit：100 Million Yuan

项　目 Items	余　额 Balance	比年初增减额 Changes within the Year	项　目 Items	余　额 Balance	比年初增减额 Changes within the Year
一、企业存款 Deposits by Enterprises	1735.89	484.10	一、流动资金贷款 Working Capital Loans	4554.19	791.15
二、财政存款 Fiscal Deposits	404.10	193.17	1. 工业贷款 Loans to Industrial Sector	1609.96	293.08
三、基本建设存款 Capital Construction Deposits	249.70	- 32.52	2. 商业贷款 Loans to Commercial Sector	2723.49	376.96
四、机关团体存款 Deposits by Government Agencies and Social Organizations	76.44	- 15.35	3. 建筑企业流动资金贷款 Working Capital Loans to Construction Enterprises	93.56	93.56
五、部队存款 Deposits by Army	1057.76	281.18	4. 个体工商业贷款 Loans to Self - employed Entities	10.65	0.03
六、储蓄存款 Savings Deposits	564.81	126.69	5. 信托贷款 Trust Loans	97.83	—
七、社员个人存款 Deposits by Associators	199.51	- 29.25	6. 其他贷款 Other Loans	18.70	—
八、农村存款 Rural Deposits	118.41	—	二、农业贷款 Loans to Agricultural Sector	775.57	85.84
九、信托及其他存款 Trust and Other Deposits	153.33	33.86	其中：集体农业贷款 Of Which：Loans to Agricultural Collectives	711.61	79.37
存款合计 Total Deposits	**4559.95**	**824.62**	三、固定资产贷款 Fixed Asset Loans	686.25	392.22
十、汇兑在途资金 Remittance in Transit	366.74	41.98	1. 技术改造贷款 Technical Improvement Loans	417.55	188.18
十一、流通中货币 Currency in Circulation	987.83	195.72	2. 基本建设贷款 Capital Construction Loans	213.14	160.16
十二、自有资金 Own Capital	738.31	165.14	3. 发展少数民族经济贷款 Loans to Ethnic Minority Regions	12.54	7.07
十三、当年结益 Net Earnings	207.58	207.58	4. 开发性贷款 Development Loans	43.02	43.02
十四、其他 Others	- 93.27	—	5. 特种外汇兑换 Special Foreign Exchange	0.00	- 6.21
			四、购买外汇额度人民币专项贷款 Earmarked Loans for the Purchase of Foreign Exchange Quota	30.57	30.57
			五、其他专项贷款 Other Earmarked Loans	151.80	151.80
			贷款合计 Total Loans	**6198.38**	**1451.58**

续表
Continued

项　目 Items	余　额 Balance	比年初增减额 Changes within the Year	项　目 Items	余　额 Balance	比年初增减额 Changes within the Year
			六、金银库存占款 Position for Bullion and Silver Purchase	12.00	
			七、外汇库存占款 Position for Foreign Exchange Purchase	93.10	—
			八、上缴财政利润和税金 Payment of Profits and Taxes to Government Finance	132.18	132.18
			九、财政透支和借款 Overdraft by State Finance	275.10	14.30
			十、待核销商品贷款损失 Commodity Loan Loss to be Written－off	56.38	1.20
资金来源总计 Total Sources	**6767.14**	—	**资金运用总计 Total Uses**	**6767.14**	—

金融机构人民币信贷收支表

Sources and Uses of Credit Funds of Financial Institutions（RMB）

（1986 年末）

（Year - end of 1986）

单位：亿元

Unit：100 Million Yuan

项　目 Items	余　额 Balance	比年初增减额 Changes within the Year	项　目 Items	余　额 Balance	比年初增减额 Changes within the Year
一、企业存款 Deposits by Enterprises	2265.94	530.05	一、流动资金贷款 Working Capital Loans	5650.99	1194.63
二、财政存款 Fiscal Deposits	348.61	-55.49	1. 工业贷款 Loans to Industrial Sector	2232.34	622.38
三、机关团体存款 Deposits by Government Agencies and Social Organizations	310.27	60.57	2. 商业贷款 Loans to Commercial Sector	3188.14	464.65
			3. 建筑企业流动资金贷款 Working Capital Loans to Construction Enterprises	132.06	38.50
四、部队存款 Deposits by Army	78.85	2.41			
五、城镇储蓄存款 Urban Savings Deposits	1471.67	413.91	4. 个体工商业贷款 Loans to Self - employed Entities	13.12	2.47
六、农户储蓄存款 Savings Deposits by Rural Households	766.14	201.33	5. 其他贷款 Other Loans	85.33	66.63
七、农村集体存款 Deposits by Collectives of Rural	252.75	53.24	二、农业贷款 Loans to Agricultural Sector	1095.60	320.03
八、信托存款 Trust Deposits	204.86	86.45	其中：集体农业贷款 Of Which：Loans to Agricultural Collectives	1002.61	291.00
九、其他存款 Other Deposits	234.79	81.46			
			三、固定资产贷款 Fixed Asset Loans	975.97	289.72
存款合计 Total Deposits	**5933.88**	**1373.93**			
			1. 技术改造贷款 Technical Improvement Loans	585.87	168.32
十、汇兑在途资金 Remittance in Transit	428.98	62.24			
			2. 基本建设贷款 Capital Construction Loans	297.89	84.75
十一、流通中货币 Currency in Circulation	1218.36	230.53			
			3. 发展少数民族经济贷款 Loans to Ethnic Minority Regions	20.16	7.62
十二、自有资金 Own Capital	780.69	42.38			
			4. 开发性贷款 Development Loans	72.05	29.03
十三、当年结益 Net Earnings	259.54	259.54			
			四、购买外汇额度人民币专项贷款 Earmarked Loans for the Purchase of Foreign Exchange Quota	43.21	12.64
十四、其他 Others	202.19	220.06			
			五、其他专项贷款 Other Earmarked Loans	203.24	51.44
			六、信托贷款 Trust Loans	173.71	75.88
			贷款合计 Total Loans	**8142.72**	**1944.34**
			七、金银库存占款 Position for Bullion and Silver Purchase	12.00	

续表
Continued

项　目 Items	余　额 Balance	比年初增减额 Changes within the Year	项　目 Items	余　额 Balance	比年初增减额 Changes within the Year
			八、外汇库存占款 Position for Foreign Exchange Purchase	38.10	-55.00
			九、上缴财政利润和税金 Payment of Profits and Taxes to Government Finance	177.10	177.10
			十、财政透支和借款 Overdraft by State Finance	370.10	95.00
			十一、待核销商品贷款损失 Commodity Loan Loss to be Written - off	83.62	27.24
资金来源总计 Total Sources	**8823.64**	**2188.68**	**资金运用总计 Total Uses**	**8823.64**	**2188.68**

金融机构人民币信贷收支表

Sources and Uses of Credit Funds of Financial Institutions（RMB）

（1987 年末）

（Year - end of 1987）

单位：亿元

Unit：100 Million Yuan

项目 Items	余额 Balance	比年初增减额 Changes within the Year	项目 Items	余额 Balance	比年初增减额 Changes within the Year
一、企业存款 Deposits by Enterprises	2701.12	435.18	一、流动资金贷款 Working Capital Loans	6669.55	1018.56
二、财政存款 Fiscal Deposits	331.98	- 16.63	1. 工业贷款 Loans to Industrial Sector	2639.84	407.50
三、机关团体存款 Deposits by Government Agencies and Social Organizations	347.18	36.91	2. 商业贷款 Loans to Commercial Sector	3632.30	444.16
			3. 建筑企业流动资金贷款 Working Capital Loans to Construction Enterprises	170.56	38.50
四、部队存款 Deposits by Army	101.51	22.66			
五、城镇储蓄存款 Urban Savings Deposits	2075.51	603.84	4. 个体工商业贷款 Loans to Self - employed Entities	22.31	9.19
六、农户储蓄存款 Savings Deposits by Rural Households	1007.90	241.76	5. 其他贷款 Other Loans	204.54	119.21
七、农村集体存款 Deposits by Collectives of Rural	289.60	36.85	二、农业贷款 Loans to Agricultural Sector	1427.70	332.10
八、信托存款 Trust Deposits	162.52	- 42.34	其中：集体农业贷款 Of Which：Loans to Agricultural Collectives	1311.11	308.50
九、其他存款 Other Deposits	375.08	140.29			
			三、固定资产贷款 Fixed Asset Loans	1221.61	245.64
存款合计 Total Deposits	**7392.40**	**1458.52**			
			1. 技术改造贷款 Technical Improvement Loans	696.22	110.35
十、汇兑在途资金 Remittance in Transit	229.07	- 199.91	2. 基本建设贷款 Capital Construction Loans	418.84	120.95
十一、流通中货币 Currency in Circulation	1454.48	236.12	3. 发展少数民族经济贷款 Loans to Ethnic Minority Regions	29.31	9.15
十二、自有资金 Own Capital	830.92	50.23			
			4. 开发性贷款 Development Loans	77.24	5.19
十三、当年结益 Net Earnings	292.88	292.88			
			四、购买外汇额度人民币专项贷款 Earmarked Loans for the Purchase of Foreign Exchange Quota	60.53	17.32
十四、其他 Others	513.55	228.92			
			五、其他专项贷款 Other Earmarked Loans	285.53	82.29
			六、信托贷款 Trust Loans	149.17	- 24.54
			贷款合计 Total Loans	**9814.09**	**1671.37**
			七、金银库存占款 Position for Bullion and Silver Purchase	12.00	

续表
Continued

项　目 Items	余　额 Balance	比年初增减额 Changes within the Year	项　目 Items	余　额 Balance	比年初增减额 Changes within the Year
			八、外汇库存占款 Position for Foreign Exchange Purchase	132.10	94.00
			九、上缴财政利润和税金 Payment of Profits and Taxes to Government Finance	183.38	183.38
			十、财政透支和借款 Overdraft by State Finance	515.80	145.70
			十一、待核销商品贷款损失 Commodity Loan Loss to be Written – off	55.93	–27.69
资金来源总计 Total Sources	**10713.30**	**2066.76**	**资金运用总计 Total Uses**	**10713.30**	**2066.76**

金融机构人民币信贷收支表

Sources and Uses of Credit Funds of Financial Institutions（RMB）

（1988年末）

（Year - end of 1988）

单位：亿元

Unit：100 Million Yuan

项目 Items	余额 Balance	比年初增减额 Changes within the Year	项目 Items	余额 Balance	比年初增减额 Changes within the Year
一、各项存款 Total Deposits	8810.36	1417.96	一、各项贷款 Total Loans	11964.25	2150.16
1. 企业存款 Deposits by Enterprises	3010.26	309.14	1. 流动资金贷款 Working Capital Loans	8026.14	1356.59
2. 财政存款 Fiscal Deposits	294.10	-37.88	（1）工业贷款 Loans to Industrial Sector	3163.42	523.58
3. 机关团体部队存款 Deposits by Government Agencies, Social Organizations and Army	392.68	-56.01	（2）商业贷款 Loans to Commercial Sector	4264.98	632.68
			（3）建筑业贷款 Loans to Construction Sector	252.64	82.08
4. 城镇储蓄存款 Urban Savings Deposits	2679.85	604.34	（4）个体工商业贷款 Loans to Self - employed Entities	31.53	9.21
5. 农户储蓄存款 Savings Deposits by Rural Households	1139.24	131.34	（5）乡镇企业贷款 Loans to Village and Township Enterprises	313.57	—
6. 农村存款 Rural Deposits	349.56	59.96			
7. 信托类存款 Trust Deposits	175.33	12.81	2. 农业贷款 Loans to Agricultural Sector	1277.59	-150.11
8. 其他类存款 Other Deposits	769.34	394.26	3. 固定资产贷款 Fixed Asset Loans	1558.20	336.59
二、金融债券 Financial Bonds	80.41	—	（1）基本建设贷款 Capital Construction Loans	501.17	82.33
三、代理发行债券 Agency Bond Issue	5.56	—	（2）技术改造贷款 Technical Improvement Loans	892.93	196.71
四、流通中货币 Currency in Circulation	2134.03	679.55	（3）老少边穷经济贷款 Loans to Former - revolutionary Base Areas, Areas Inhabited by Minority Nationalities, Remote and Border Areas and Poverty - stricken Areas for Economic Development	39.09	—
五、信贷基金及自有资金 Credit Funds and Own Capital	1133.26	302.34			
六、当年结益 Net Earnings	672.60	672.60			
七、汇兑在途资金 Remittance in Transit	218.37	-10.70	（4）地方经济开发贷款 Loans for Local Economic Development	125.01	—
八、其他 Others	56.63	-602.26			
			4. 信托类贷款 Trust Loans	281.20	132.03
			5. 其他类贷款 Other Loans	821.12	475.06
			二、购买债券 Bond Purchase	121.81	
			三、金银占款 Position for Bullion and Silver Purchase	12.00	

续表
Continued

项　目 Items	余　额 Balance	比年初增减额 Changes within the Year	项　目 Items	余　额 Balance	比年初增减额 Changes within the Year
			四、外汇占款 Position for Foreign Exchange Purchase	158.40	26.30
			五、上缴财政税利 Payment of Profits and Taxes to Government Finance	222.33	222.33
			六、财政透支和借款 Overdraft by State Finance	576.50	60.70
			七、待核销贷款损失 Loan Loss to be Written - off	55.93	
资金来源总计 Total Sources	**13111.22**	**2459.49**	**资金运用总计 Total Uses**	**13111.22**	**2459.49**

金融机构人民币信贷收支表

Sources and Uses of Credit Funds of Financial Institutions（RMB）

（1989 年末）

（Year - end of 1989）

单位：亿元

Unit：100 Million Yuan

项目 Items	余额 Balance	比年初增减额 Changes within the Year	项目 Items	余额 Balance	比年初增减额 Changes within the Year
一、各项存款 Total Deposits	10709.57	1899.21	一、各项贷款 Total Loans	14248.81	2284.56
1. 企业存款 Deposits by Enterprises	3174.11	163.85	1. 流动资金贷款 Working Capital Loans	10178.55	2152.41
2. 财政存款 Fiscal Deposits	460.79	166.69	（1）工业贷款 Loans to Industrial Sector	3888.14	724.72
3. 机关团体部队存款 Deposits by Government Agencies, Social Organizations and Army	482.20	89.52	（2）商业贷款 Loans to Commercial Sector	5010.55	745.57
			（3）建筑业贷款 Loans to Construction Sector	283.69	31.05
4. 城镇储蓄存款 Urban Savings Deposits	3780.36	1100.51	（4）个体工商业贷款 Loans to Self - employed Entities	32.75	1.23
5. 农户储蓄存款 Savings Deposits by Rural Households	1404.10	264.86	（5）乡镇企业贷款 Loans to Village and Township Enterprises	963.42	649.84
6. 农村存款 Rural Deposits	331.37	- 18.19			
7. 信托类存款 Trust Deposits	122.25	- 53.08	2. 农业贷款 Loans to Agricultural Sector	984.19	- 293.40
8. 其他类存款 Other Deposits	954.39	185.05	3. 固定资产贷款 Fixed Asset Loans	1780.18	221.98
二、金融债券 Financial Bonds	74.38	- 6.03	（1）基本建设贷款 Capital Construction Loans	581.42	80.25
三、代理发行债券 Agency Bond Issue	6.23	0.67	（2）技术改造贷款 Technical Improvement Loans	1003.11	110.18
四、流通中货币 Currency in Circulation	2344.02	209.99	（3）老少边穷经济贷款 Loans to Former - revolutionary Base Areas, Areas Inhabited by Minority Nationalities, Remote and Border Areas and Poverty - stricken Areas for Economic Development	50.13	11.04
五、信贷基金及自有资金 Credit Funds and Own Capital	1380.03	246.77			
六、当年结益 Net Earnings	500.79	500.79			
七、汇兑在途资金 Remittance in Transit		- 218.37	（4）地方经济开发贷款 Loans for Local Economic Development	145.52	20.51
八、其他 Others	658.10	151.20			
			4. 信托类贷款 Trust Loans	282.95	1.75
			5. 其他类贷款 Other Loans	1022.94	201.82
			二、购买债券 Bond Purchase	135.51	13.70
			三、金银占款 Position for Bullion and Silver Purchase	12.00	

续表
Continued

项 目 Items	余 额 Balance	比年初增减额 Changes within the Year	项 目 Items	余 额 Balance	比年初增减额 Changes within the Year
			四、外汇占款 Position for Foreign Exchange Purchase	264.50	106.10
			五、上缴财政税利 Payment of Profits and Taxes to Government Finance	271.77	271.77
			六、财政透支和借款 Overdraft by State Finance	684.60	108.10
			七、待核销贷款损失 Loan Loss to be Written – off	55.93	
资金来源总计 Total Sources	**15673.12**	**2784.23**	**资金运用总计 Total Uses**	**15673.12**	**2784.23**

金融机构人民币信贷收支表

Sources and Uses of Credit Funds of Financial Institutions（RMB）

（1990 年末）

（Year－end of 1990）

单位：亿元

Unit：100 Million Yuan

项　目 Items	余　额 Balance	比年初增减额 Changes within the Year	项　目 Items	余　额 Balance	比年初增减额 Changes within the Year
一、各项存款 Total Deposits	13942.94	3233.37	一、各项贷款 Total Loans	17511.02	3262.21
1. 企业存款 Deposits by Enterprises	4063.90	889.79	1. 流动资金贷款 Working Capital Loans	12480.42	2301.87
2. 财政存款 Fiscal Deposits	427.11	－33.68	（1）工业贷款 Loans to Industrial Sector	4990.17	1102.03
3. 机关团体部队存款 Deposits by Government Agencies，Social Organizations and Army	597.02	114.82	（2）商业贷款 Loans to Commercial Sector	5966.59	956.04
			其中：收购农副产品 Of Which：Loans for the Purchase of Farm Products	2315.57	—
4. 城镇储蓄存款 Urban Savings Deposits	5278.56	1498.20			
5. 农户储蓄存款 Savings Deposits by Rural Households	1841.00	436.90	（3）建筑业贷款 Loans to Construction Sector	316.77	33.08
6. 农村存款 Rural Deposits	393.58	62.21	（4）个体工商业贷款 Loans to Self－employed Entities	40.03	7.28
7. 信托类存款 Trust Deposits	176.18	53.93	（5）乡镇企业贷款 Loans to Village and Township Enterprises	1166.86	203.44
8. 其他类存款 Other Deposits	1165.59	211.20	2. 农业贷款 Loans to Agricultural Sector	1244.09	259.90
二、金融债券 Financial Bonds	96.44	22.06	3. 固定资产贷款 Fixed Asset Loans	2214.89	434.71
三、代理发行债券 Agency Bond Issue	11.80	5.57	（1）基本建设贷款 Capital Construction Loans	818.29	236.87
四、流通中货币 Currency in Circulation	2644.87	300.85	（2）技术改造贷款 Technical Improvement Loans	1163.80	160.69
五、信贷基金及自有资金 Credit Funds and Own Capital	1552.28	172.25	（3）老少边穷经济贷款 Loans to Former－revolutionary Base Areas，Areas inhabited by Minority Nationalities，Remote and Border Areas and Poverty－stricken Areas for Economic Development	59.98	9.85
六、当年结益 Net Earnings	395.68	395.68			
七、其他 Others	845.55	－41.57			
			（4）地方经济开发贷款 Loans for Local Economic Development	172.82	27.30
			4. 信托类贷款 Trust Loans	319.43	36.48
			5. 其他类贷款 Other Loans	1252.19	229.25

续表
Continued

项　目 Items	余　额 Balance	比年初增减额 Changes within the Year	项　目 Items	余　额 Balance	比年初增减额 Changes within the Year
			二、购买债券 Bond Purchase	206.15	70.64
			三、金银占款 Position for Bullion and Silver Purchase	12.00	
			四、外汇占款 Position for Foreign Exchange Purchase	599.40	334.90
			五、上缴财政税利 Payment of Profits and Taxes to Government Finance	303.97	303.97
			六、财政透支和借款 Overdraft by State Finance	801.10	116.50
			七、待核销贷款损失 Loan Loss to be Written－off	55.92	－0.01
资金来源总计 Total Sources	**19489.56**	**4088.21**	**总计 Total Uses**	**19489.56**	**4088.21**

金融机构人民币信贷收支表

Sources and Uses of Credit Funds of Financial Institutions（RMB）

（1991年末）

（Year – end of 1991）

单位：亿元

Unit：100 Million Yuan

项　目 Items	余　额 Balance	比年初增减额 Changes within the Year	项　目 Items	余　额 Balance	比年初增减额 Changes within the Year
一、各项存款 Total Deposits	17972.84	4029.90	一、各项贷款 Total Loans	21116.39	3605.37
1. 企业存款 Deposits by Enterprises	5215.29	1151.39	1. 流动资金贷款 Working Capital Loans	14624.69	2144.27
2. 财政存款 Fiscal Deposits	504.29	77.18	（1）工业贷款 Loans to Industrial Sector	5916.78	926.61
3. 机关团体部队存款 Deposits by Government Agencies, Social Organizations and Army	753.35	156.33	（2）商业贷款 Loans to Commercial Sector	6845.38	878.79
			其中：收购农副产品 Of Which：Loans for the Purchase of Farm Products	2973.03	657.46
4. 城镇储蓄存款 Urban Savings Deposits	6925.48	1646.92			
5. 农户储蓄存款 Savings Deposits by Rural Households	2319.36	478.36	（3）建筑业贷款 Loans to Construction Sector	363.62	46.85
6. 农村存款 Rural Deposits	506.82	113.24	（4）个体工商业贷款 Loans to Self – employed Entities	49.16	9.13
7. 信托类存款 Trust Deposits	168.05	– 8.13	（5）乡镇企业贷款 Loans to Village and Township Enterprises	1449.75	282.89
8. 其他类存款 Other Deposits	1580.20	414.61			
			2. 农业贷款 Loans to Agricultural Sector	1562.37	318.28
二、金融债券 Financial Bonds	119.54	23.10			
			3. 固定资产贷款 Fixed Asset Loans	3046.14	831.25
三、代理发行债券 Agency Bond Issue	29.34	17.54	（1）基本建设贷款 Capital Construction Loans	1259.11	440.82
四、流通中货币 Currency in Circulation	3177.80	532.93	（2）技术改造贷款 Technical Improvement Loans	1519.95	356.15
五、信贷基金及自有资金 Credit Funds and Own Capital	1737.68	185.40	（3）老少边穷经济贷款 Loans to Former – revolutionary Base Areas, Areas Inhabited by Minority Nationalities, Remote and Border Areas and Poverty – stricken Areas for Economic Development	80.54	20.56
六、当年结益 Net Earnings	499.88	499.88			
七、其他 Others	542.76	– 394.50			
			（4）地方经济开发贷款 Loans for Local Economic Development	186.54	13.72
			4. 信托类贷款 Trust Loans	301.03	– 18.40
			5. 其他类贷款 Other Loans	1582.16	329.97

续表
Continued

项 目 Items	余 额 Balance	比年初增减额 Changes within the Year	项 目 Items	余 额 Balance	比年初增减额 Changes within the Year
			二、购买债券 Bond Purchase	337.63	131.48
			三、金银占款 Position for Bullion and Silver Purchase	12.00	
			四、外汇占款 Position for Foreign Exchange Purchase	1228.10	628.70
			五、上缴财政税利 Payment of Profits and Taxes to Government Finance	262.00	262.00
			六、财政透支和借款 Overdraft by State Finance	1067.80	266.70
			七、待核销贷款损失 Loan Loss to be Written – off	55.92	
资金来源总计 Total Sources	**24079.84**	**4894.25**	**资金运用总计 Total Uses**	**24079.84**	**4894.24**

金融机构人民币信贷收支表

Sources and Uses of Credit Funds of Financial Institutions（RMB）

（1992 年末）

（Year - end of 1992）

单位：亿元

Unit：100 Million Yuan

项 目 Items	余 额 Balance	比年初增减额 Changes within the Year	项 目 Items	余 额 Balance	比年初增减额 Changes within the Year
一、各项存款 Total Deposits	23143.81	5170.97	一、各项贷款 Total Loans	25742.81	4626.42
1. 企业存款 Deposits by Enterprises	7074.94	1859.65	1. 流动资金贷款 Working Capital Loans	17258.08	2633.39
2. 财政存款 Fiscal Deposits	250.16	- 254.13	（1）工业贷款 Loans to Industrial Sector	6862.60	945.82
3. 机关团体部队存款 Deposits by Government Agencies, Social Organizations and Army	687.12	- 66.23	（2）商业贷款 Loans to Commercial Sector	8007.63	1162.25
			其中：收购农副产品 Of Which：Loans for the Purchase of Farm Products	3191.26	218.23
4. 城镇储蓄存款 Urban Savings Deposits	8889.87	1964.39			
5. 农户储蓄存款 Savings Deposits by Rural Households	2867.41	548.05	（3）建筑业贷款 Loans to Construction Sector	436.22	72.60
6. 农村存款 Rural Deposits	948.84	442.02	（4）个体工商业贷款 Loans to Self - employed Entities	67.32	18.16
7. 信托类存款 Trust Deposits	201.42	33.37	（5）乡镇企业贷款 Loans to Village and Township Enterprises	1884.31	434.56
8. 其他类存款 Other Deposits	2224.05	643.85			
			2. 农业贷款 Loans to Agricultural Sector	1984.15	421.78
二、发行及代理发行证券 Securities Issue and Agency Securities Issue	177.02	177.02	3. 固定资产贷款 Fixed Asset Loans	3924.02	877.88
三、国家投资债券 State Investment Bonds	122.68	122.68	（1）基本建设贷款 Capital Construction Loans	1685.73	426.62
四、流通中货币 Currency in Circulation	4336.00	1158.20	（2）技术改造贷款 Technical Improvement Loans	1927.82	407.87
五、信贷基金及自有资金 Credit Funds and Own Capital	1943.31	205.63	（3）老少边穷经济贷款 Loans to Former - revolutionary Base Areas, Areas Inhabited by Minority Nationalities, Remote and Border Areas and Poverty - stricken Areas for Economic Development	94.64	14.10
六、当年结益 Net Earnings	424.58	424.58			
七、其他 Others	- 988.22	- 1917.74			
			（4）地方经济开发贷款 Loans for Local Economic Development	215.83	29.29
			4. 信托类贷款 Trust Loans	220.61	- 80.42
			5. 其他类贷款 Other Loans	2355.95	773.79

续表
Continued

项 目 Items	余 额 Balance	比年初增减额 Changes within the Year	项 目 Items	余 额 Balance	比年初增减额 Changes within the Year
			二、购买债券 Bond Purchase	587.13	249.50
			三、国家投资债券贷款 Loans Related to State Investment Bonds	156.82	156.82
			四、金银占款 Position for Bullion and Silver Purchase	12.00	
			五、外汇占款 Position for Foreign Exchange Purchase	1102.00	-126.10
			六、上缴财政税利 Payment of Profits and Taxes to Government Finance	261.40	261.40
			七、财政透支和借款 Overdraft by State Finance	1241.10	173.30
			八、待核销贷款损失 Loan Loss to be Written - off	55.92	
资金来源总计 Total Sources	**29159.18**	**5341.34**	**资金运用总计 Total Uses**	**29159.18**	**5341.34**

金融机构人民币信贷收支表

Sources and Uses of Credit Funds of Financial Institutions（RMB）

（1993 年末）

（Year - end of 1993）

单位：亿元

Unit：100 Million Yuan

项目 Items	余额 Balance	比年初增减额 Changes within the Year	项目 Items	余额 Balance	比年初增减额 Changes within the Year
一、各项存款 Total Deposits	29645.99	5876.92	一、各项贷款 Total Loans	32955.83	6335.40
1. 企业存款 Deposits by Enterprises	8673.77	1254.97	1. 流动资金贷款 Working Capital Loans	21370.60	3815.17
2. 财政存款 Fiscal Deposits	502.34	256.62	（1）工业贷款 Loans to Industrial Sector	8451.93	1511.07
3. 机关团体部队存款 Deposits by Government Agencies, Social Organizations and Army	717.10	25.52	（2）商业贷款 Loans to Commercial Sector	9625.24	1554.57
			（3）建筑业贷款 Loans to Construction Sector	527.19	90.31
4. 城镇储蓄存款 Urban Savings Deposits	11627.30	2700.76	（4）个体工商业贷款 Loans to Self - employed Entities	108.57	38.96
5. 农户储蓄存款 Savings Deposits by Rural Households	3576.24	708.96	（5）乡镇企业贷款 Loans to Village and Township Enterprises	2437.74	554.05
6. 农村存款 Rural Deposits	1073.56	121.74			
7. 信托类存款 Trust Deposits	1591.42	323.66	（6）其他流动资金贷款 Other Working Capital Loans	219.93	66.21
8. 其他类存款 Other Deposits	1884.26	484.69	2. 农业贷款 Loans to Agricultural Sector	2401.28	410.97
二、发行及代理发行证券 Securities Issue and Agency Securities Issue	196.17	- 57.88	3. 固定资产贷款 Fixed Asset Loans	5197.21	1245.84
			4. 信托类贷款 Trust Loans	1660.98	334.67
三、国家投资债券 State Investment Bonds	126.60	3.85	5. 其他类贷款 Other Loans	2325.76	528.75
四、流通中货币 Currency in Circulation	5864.70	1528.72	二、有价证券 Securities	863.09	197.47
五、信贷基金及自有资金 Credit Funds and Own Capital	2688.79	189.83	三、国家投资债券贷款 Loans Related to State Investment Bonds	157.72	0.90
六、当年结益 Net Earnings	541.50	541.50	四、金银占款 Position for Bullion and Silver Purchase	12.00	
七、其他 Others	- 1673.00	- 490.16	五、外汇占款 Position for Foreign Exchange Purchase	1431.80	329.80
			六、上缴财政税利 Payment of Profits and Taxes to Government Finance	388.21	388.21
			七、财政借款及透支 Overdraft by State Finance	1582.10	341.00
资金来源总计 Total Sources	**37390.75**	**7592.78**	**资金运用总计 Total Uses**	**37390.75**	**7592.78**

金融机构人民币信贷收支表

Sources and Uses of Credit Funds of Financial Institutions (RMB)

(1994 年末)

(Year - end of 1994)

单位：亿元

Unit: 100 Million Yuan

项目 Items	余额 Balance	比年初增减额 Changes within the Year	项目 Items	余额 Balance	比年初增减额 Changes within the Year
一、各项存款 Total Deposits	40502.54	11269.29	一、各项贷款 Total Loans	39975.99	7216.62
1. 企业存款 Deposits by Enterprises	13278.98	3498.64	1. 短期贷款 Short - term Loans	26948.70	4942.93
其中：单位定期存款 Of Which: Time Deposits	1387.38	628.05	(1) 工业贷款 Loans to Industrial Sector	9948.26	1463.20
2. 财政存款 Fiscal Deposits	862.26	368.74	(2) 商业贷款 Loans to Commercial Sector	10509.84	1991.52
3. 机关团体部队存款 Deposits by Government Agencies, Social Organizations and Army	857.79	141.59	其中：收购农采贷款 Of Which: Loans for the Purchase of Farm Products	3826.02	1037.40
4. 城镇储蓄存款 Urban Savings Deposits	16702.77	5075.27	(3) 建筑企业贷款 Loans to Construction Enterprises	617.21	87.92
5. 农户储蓄存款 Savings Deposits by Rural Households	4816.02	1239.99	(4) 农业贷款 Loans to Agricultural Sector	1143.85	299.47
6. 农业存款 Deposits by Agricultural Sector	1063.19	162.22	(5) 乡镇企业贷款 Loans to Village and Township Enterprises	2002.38	544.01
7. 信托类存款 Trust Deposits	2360.05	676.89	(6) 个体工商业贷款 Loans to Self - employed Entities	155.86	66.60
8. 其他类存款 Other Deposits	561.48	105.95	(7) 三资企业贷款 Loans to Foreign Investment Enterprises and Ventures	792.32	258.35
二、金融债券 Financial Bonds	93.51	-43.80			
三、国家投资债券 State Investment Bonds	120.01	-0.01	(8) 其他短期贷款 Other Short - term Loans	1778.98	231.86
四、流通中货币 Currency in Circulation	7288.60	1423.90	2. 中长期贷款 Medium and Long - term Loans	7774.92	1199.01
五、所有者权益 Owner's Equity	3698.26	293.06	3. 信托类贷款 Trust Loans	2110.03	516.12
其中：实收资本 Of Which: Paid - in Capital	3526.51	283.61	4. 其他类贷款 Other Loans	3142.34	558.56
六、当年结益 Net Earnings	381.85	381.85	二、有价证券及投资 Securities and Investments	2462.42	1174.35
七、其他 Others	-2844.31	-1827.37	三、国家投资债券贷款 Loans Related to State Investment Bonds	89.31	-30.44
			四、金银占款 Position for Bullion and Silver Purchase	12.00	
			五、外汇占款 Position for Foreign Exchange Purchase	4503.90	3072.10
			六、库存现金 Cash in Vault	614.74	64.29
			七、财政借款及透支 Overdraft by State Finance	1582.10	
资金来源总计 Total Sources	**49240.46**	**11496.92**	**资金运用总计 Total Uses**	**49240.46**	**11496.92**

金融机构人民币信贷收支表

Sources and Uses of Credit Funds of Financial Institutions（RMB）

（1995年末）

（Year－end of 1995）

单位：亿元

Unit：100 Million Yuan

项目 Items	余额 Balance	比年初增减额 Changes within the Year	项目 Items	余额 Balance	比年初增减额 Changes within the Year
一、各项存款 Total Deposits	53882.10	12956.69	一、各项贷款 Total Loans	50544.09	9339.82
1. 企业存款 Deposits by Enterprises	17323.82	3885.09	1. 短期贷款 Short－term Loans	33371.97	5933.82
其中：单位定期存款 Of Which：Time Deposits	2670.41	1230.67	（1）工业贷款 Loans to Industrial Sector	11774.70	1761.48
2. 财政存款 Fiscal Deposits	1005.40	139.32	（2）商业贷款 Loans to Commercial Sector	12837.13	2222.25
3. 机关团体部队存款 Deposits by Government Agencies, Social Organizations and Army	917.28	73.44	其中：收购农采贷款 Of Which：Loans for the Purchase of Farm Products	5445.06	1187.74
4. 城镇储蓄存款 Urban Savings Deposits	23466.69	6738.85	（3）建筑企业贷款 Loans to Construction Enterprises	799.34	165.33
5. 农户储蓄存款 Savings Deposits by Rural Households	6195.56	1387.27	（4）农业贷款 Loans to Agricultural Sector	1544.79	398.54
6. 农业存款 Deposits by Agricultural Sector	1196.22	137.92	（5）乡镇企业贷款 Loans to Village and Township Enterprises	2514.85	516.99
7. 信托类存款 Trust Deposits	3051.50	451.11	（6）个体工商业贷款 Loans to Self－employed Entities	196.18	76.08
8. 其他类存款 Other Deposits	725.63	143.69	（7）三资企业贷款 Loans to Foreign Investment Enterprises and Ventures	999.12	249.48
二、金融债券 Financial Bonds	1683.83	836.36			
三、国家投资债券 State Investment Bonds	116.74	－7.19	（8）其他短期贷款 Other Short－term Loans	2705.86	543.67
四、流通中货币 Currency in Circulation	7885.34	596.74	2. 中长期贷款 Medium and Long－term Loans	10699.32	2020.06
五、所有者权益 Owner's Equity	4113.37	439.68	3. 信托类贷款 Trust Loans	2643.20	371.78
其中：实收资本 Of Which：Paid－in Capital	3657.20	282.07	4. 其他类贷款 Other Loans	3829.60	1014.16
六、当年结益 Net Earnings	187.73	187.73	二、有价证券及投资 Securities and Investments	4215.72	1364.61
七、其他 Others	－3943.89	－1913.89	三、国家投资债券贷款 Loans Related to State Investment Bonds	75.52	－13.79
			四、金银占款 Position for Bullion and Silver Purchase	12.00	
			五、外汇占款 Position for Foreign Exchange Purchase	6774.45	2302.85
			六、库存现金 Cash in Vault	721.34	102.63
			七、财政借款及透支 Overdraft by State Finance	1582.10	
资金来源总计 Total Sources	**63925.22**	**13096.12**	**资金运用总计 Total Uses**	**63925.22**	**13096.12**

金融机构人民币信贷收支表
Sources and Uses of Credit Funds of Financial Institutions (RMB)

(1996年末)

(Year - end of 1996)

单位：亿元

Unit: 100 Million Yuan

项　目 Items	余　额 Balance	比年初增减额 Changes within the Year	项　目 Items	余　额 Balance	比年初增减额 Changes within the Year
一、各项存款 Total Deposits	68595.59	14792.36	一、各项贷款 Total Loans	61156.55	10683.33
1. 企业存款 Deposits by Enterprises	22450.17	5026.29	1. 短期贷款 Short - term Loans	40210.01	6653.34
其中：单位定期存款 Of Which: Time Deposits	4224.88	1462.15	(1) 工业贷款 Loans to Industrial Sector	14213.27	2422.86
2. 财政存款 Fiscal Deposits	1274.16	273.93	(2) 商业贷款 Loans to Commercial Sector	15332.64	2540.49
3. 机关团体部队存款 Deposits by Government Agencies, Social Organizations and Army	968.95	52.51	其中：收购农采贷款 Of Which: Loans for the Purchase of Farm Products	6870.77	1564.69
4. 城镇储蓄存款 Urban Savings Deposits	30850.23	7331.16	(3) 建筑企业贷款 Loans to Construction Enterprises	973.79	171.52
5. 农户储蓄存款 Savings Deposits by Rural Households	7670.61	1474.31	(4) 农业贷款 Loans to Agricultural Sector	1919.12	378.08
6. 农业存款 Deposits by Agricultural Sector	1364.09	168.62	(5) 乡镇企业贷款 Loans to Village and Township Enterprises	2821.88	308.65
7. 信托类存款 Trust Deposits	3179.11	305.99	(6) 个体工商业贷款 Loans to Self - employed Entities	279.78	83.50
8. 其他类存款 Other Deposits	838.27	159.55	(7) 三资企业贷款 Loans to Foreign Investment Enterprises and Ventures	1346.30	345.07
二、金融债券 Financial Bonds	2484.24	806.53			
三、国家投资债券 State Investment Bonds	120.17	-0.25	(8) 其他短期贷款 Other Short - term Loans	3323.23	403.17
四、流通中货币 Currency in Circulation	8802.01	916.67	2. 中长期贷款 Medium and Long - term Loans	12672.59	2041.25
五、所有者权益 Owner's Equity	4480.48	371.18	3. 信托类贷款 Trust Loans	2819.54	333.36
其中：实收资本 Of Which: Paid - in Capital	3918.05	270.27	4. 其他类贷款 Other Loans	5454.41	1655.38
六、当年结益 Net Earnings	-31.05	-31.05	二、有价证券及投资 Securities and Investments	5644.85	1510.61
七、其他 Others	-5746.57	-1961.15	三、国家投资债券贷款 Loans Related to State Investment Bonds	69.10	-6.66
			四、金银占款 Position for Bullion and Silver Purchase	12.00	
			五、外汇占款 Position for Foreign Exchange Purchase	9578.68	2764.59
			六、库存现金 Cash in Vault	661.59	-57.58
			七、财政借款及透支 Overdraft by State Finance	1582.10	
资金来源总计 Total Sources	**78704.87**	**14894.29**	**资金运用总计 Total Uses**	**78704.87**	**14894.29**

金融机构人民币信贷收支表

Sources and Uses of Credit Funds of Financial Institutions（RMB）

（1997 年末）

（Year - end of 1997）

单位：亿元

Unit：100 Million Yuan

项　目 Items	余　额 Balance	比年初增减额 Changes within the Year	项　目 Items	余　额 Balance	比年初增减额 Changes within the Year
一、各项存款 Total Deposits	82392.79	12940.82	一、各项贷款 Total Loans	74914.07	10702.97
1. 企业存款 Deposits by Enterprises	28656.25	4449.47	1. 短期贷款 Short - term Loans	55418.27	7754.06
（1）活期存款 Demand Deposits	21917.71	3184.45	（1）工业贷款 Loans to Industrial Sector	16526.63	2120.19
（2）定期存款 Time Deposits	6738.54	1265.02	（2）商业贷款 Loans to Commercial Sector	18356.61	2452.00
2. 财政存款 Fiscal Deposits	1574.90	184.46	其中：农副产品贷款 Of Which：Loans for the Purchase of Farm Products	8501.74	1666.40
3. 机关团体存款 Deposits by Government Agencies and Social Organizations	858.57	39.59	（3）建筑业贷款 Loans to Construction Sector	1591.06	171.96
4. 储蓄存款 Savings Deposits	46279.80	7498.89	（4）农业贷款 Loans to Agricultural Sector	3314.64	659.02
（1）活期储蓄 Demand Deposits	10053.06	2376.12	（5）乡镇企业贷款 Loans to Village and Township Enterprises	5035.80	710.49
（2）定期储蓄 Time Deposits	36226.74	5122.77	（6）三资企业贷款 Loans to Foreign Investment Enterprises and Ventures	1890.96	444.62
5. 农业存款 Deposits by Agricultural Sector	1532.99	283.76	（7）私营企业及个体贷款 Loans to Privately - run Enterprises and Self - employed Entities	386.65	47.53
6. 信托存款 Trust Deposits	723.36	97.77	（8）其他短期贷款 Other Short - term Loans	8315.92	1148.25
7. 委托存款 Designated Deposits	1911.31	216.45	2. 中长期贷款 Medium and Long - term Loans	15468.65	1849.38
8. 其他存款 Other Deposits	855.61	170.43	（1）基本建设贷款 Capital Construction Loans	7693.07	1137.50
二、金融债券 Financial Bonds	29.89	- 45.30	（2）技术改造贷款 Technical Improvement Loans	4886.00	409.80
三、国家投资债券 State Investment Bonds	81.59	- 38.71	（3）其他中长期贷款 Other Medium and Long - term Loans	2889.58	302.08
四、证券业务款项 Securities Business Funds	425.47	59.60	3. 信托贷款 Trust Loans	606.88	94.67
五、流通中货币 Currency in Circulation	10177.61	1375.60	4. 融资租赁 Financing Leases	81.08	- 1.94
六、所有者权益 Owner's Equity	4517.75	2.65	5. 委托贷款 Designated Loans	1634.16	195.26
其中：实收资本 Of Which：Paid - in Capital	4661.81	455.30			
当年结益 Net Earnings	- 166.63	- 166.63			

续表
Continued

项 目 Items	余 额 Balance	比年初增减额 Changes within the Year	项 目 Items	余 额 Balance	比年初增减额 Changes within the Year
七、其他 Others	-1098.23	-994.77	6. 逾期类贷款 Overdue Loans	1705.03	811.54
			二、国家投资债券贷款 Loans Related to State Investment Bonds	43.32	-25.78
			三、有价证券及投资 Securities and Investments	3671.74	-444.62
			四、证券业务占款 Funding of Securities Purchase	340.74	35.14
			五、委托投资 Designated Investments	1669.06	-151.97
			六、金银占款 Position for Bullion and Silver Purchase	12.04	0.04
			七、外汇占款 Position for Foreign Exchange Purchase	13467.20	3027.15
			八、库存现金 Cash in Vault	826.64	157.00
			九、财政借款 Overdraft by State Finance	1582.06	-0.04
资金来源总计 **Total Sources**	**96526.87**	**13299.89**	**资金运用总计** **Total Uses**	**96526.87**	**13299.89**

注：逾期类贷款不含中国工商银行、中国农业银行、中国银行、中国建设银行的数据。

Note: The data of overdue loans don't include the data of Industrial and Commercial Bank of China, Agricultural Bank of China, Bank of China, China Construction Bank.

金融机构人民币信贷收支表

Sources and Uses of Credit Funds of Financial Institutions（RMB）

（1998年末）

（Year－end of 1998）

单位：亿元

Unit：100 Million Yuan

项目 Items	余额 Balance	比年初增减额 Changes within the Year	项目 Items	余额 Balance	比年初增减额 Changes within the Year
一、各项存款 Total Deposits	95697.94	13402.05	一、各项贷款 Total Loans	86524.13	11490.94
1. 企业存款 Deposits by Enterprises	32486.63	3900.48	1. 短期贷款 Short－term Loans	60613.22	5953.02
（1）活期存款 Demand Deposits	24184.72	2338.06	（1）工业贷款 Loans to Industrial Sector	17821.47	1479.17
（2）定期存款 Time Deposits	8301.91	1562.42	（2）商业贷款 Loans to Commercial Sector	19752.43	1469.98
2. 财政存款 Fiscal Deposits	2187.89	636.19	其中：农副产品贷款 Of Which：Loans for the Purchase of Farm Products	7657.95	－811.44
3. 机关团体存款 Deposits by Government Agencies and Social Organizations	1285.37	404.42	（3）建筑业贷款 Loans to Construction Sector	1628.73	158.74
4. 储蓄存款 Savings Deposits	53407.47	7615.39	（4）农业贷款 Loans to Agricultural Sector	4444.24	635.96
（1）活期储蓄 Demand Deposits	11615.90	2141.67	（5）乡镇企业贷款 Loans to Village and Township Enterprises	5580.04	649.38
（2）定期储蓄 Time Deposits	41791.57	5473.72	（6）三资企业贷款 Loans to Foreign Investment Enterprises and Ventures	2487.52	598.90
5. 农业存款 Deposits by Agricultural Sector	1748.01	237.20			
6. 信托存款 Trust Deposits	799.57	7.10	（7）私营企业及个体贷款 Loans to Privately－run Enterprises and Self－employed Entities	471.64	90.55
7. 委托存款 Designated Deposits	2086.85	134.95	（8）其他短期贷款 Other Short－term Loans	8427.15	870.34
8. 其他存款 Other Deposits	1696.15	466.32	2. 中期流动资金贷款 Medium－term Working Capital Loans	1773.27	1371.25
二、金融债券 Financial Bonds	56.20	25.57	3. 中长期贷款 Medium and Long－term Loans	18944.51	3068.52
三、国家投资债券 State Investment Bonds	80.26	－1.34	（1）基本建设贷款 Capital Construction Loans	10442.75	2364.56
四、证券业务款项 Securities Business Funds	609.63	163.10	（2）技术改造贷款 Technical Improvement Loans	5118.22	235.52
五、流通中货币 Currency in Circulation	11204.15	1026.54	（3）其他中长期贷款 Other Medium and Long－term Loans	3383.54	468.44
六、所有者权益 Owner's Equity	6943.11	2293.55			
其中：实收资本 Of Which：Paid－in Capital	7560.10	2877.01	4. 信托贷款 Trust Loans	660.51	41.47
当年结益 Net Earnings	－454.86	－454.86	5. 融资租赁 Financing Leases	68.13	－0.23

续表
Continued

项　　目 Items	余　额 Balance	比年初增减额 Changes within the Year	项　　目 Items	余　额 Balance	比年初增减额 Changes within the Year
七、其他 Others	-2195.01	-1185.74	6.委托贷款 Designated Loans	1792.64	179.08
			7.逾期类贷款 Overdue Loans	2671.85	877.83
			二、国家投资债券贷款 Loans Related to State Investment Bonds	37.84	-5.48
			三、有价证券及投资 Securities and Investments	8112.24	4426.46
			四、证券业务占款 Funding of Securities Purchase	376.46	33.33
			五、委托投资 Designated Investments	1134.31	-531.72
			六、金银占款 Position for Bullion and Silver Purchase	12.04	
			七、外汇占款 Position for Foreign Exchange Purchase	13728.28	255.55
			八、库存现金 Cash in Vault	888.92	54.65
			九、财政借款 Overdraft by State Finance	1582.06	
资金来源总计 Total Sources	**112396.28**	**15723.73**	**资金运用总计 Total Uses**	**112396.28**	**15723.73**

注：逾期类贷款不含中国工商银行、中国农业银行、中国银行、中国建设银行、农村信用合作社的数据。

Note: The data of overdue loans don't include the data of Industrial and Commercial Bank of China, Agricultural Bank of China, Bank of China, China Construction Bank, Rural Credit Cooperatives.

金融机构人民币信贷收支表

Sources and Uses of Credit Funds of Financial Institutions（RMB）

（1999 年末）

（Year - end of 1999）

单位：亿元

Unit：100 Million Yuan

项　目 Items	余　额 Balance	比年初增减额 Changes within the Year	项　目 Items	余　额 Balance	比年初增减额 Changes within the Year
一、各项存款 Total Deposits	108778.94	13162.45	一、各项贷款 Total Loans	93734.28	10846.36
1. 企业存款 Deposits by Enterprises	37182.36	4724.86	1. 短期贷款 Short - term Loans	63887.55	5245.58
（1）活期存款 Demand Deposits	27705.52	3580.38	（1）工业贷款 Loans to Industrial Sector	17948.87	1128.61
（2）定期存款 Time Deposits	9476.84	1144.48	（2）商业贷款 Loans to Commercial Sector	19890.86	405.03
2. 财政存款 Fiscal Deposits	2128.06	- 57.28	其中：农副产品贷款 Of Which：Loans for the Purchase of Farm Products	8349.45	8.65
3. 机关团体存款 Deposits by Government Agencies and Social Organizations	1814.46	529.49	（3）建筑业贷款 Loans to Construction Sector	1476.86	240.71
4. 储蓄存款 Savings Deposits	59621.83	6253.03	（4）农业贷款 Loans to Agricultural Sector	4792.39	348.32
（1）活期储蓄 Demand Deposits	14666.72	3054.48	（5）乡镇企业贷款 Loans to Village and Township Enterprises	6161.26	558.04
（2）定期储蓄 Time Deposits	44955.11	3198.55	（6）三资企业贷款 Loans to Foreign Investment Enterprises and Ventures	2985.82	505.99
5. 农业存款 Deposits by Agricultural Sector	2126.33	379.05			
6. 信托存款 Trust Deposits	930.31	129.50	（7）私营企业及个体贷款 Loans to Privately - run Enterprises and Self - employed Entities	579.08	108.29
7. 委托存款 Designated Deposits	2141.86	56.56	（8）其他短期贷款 Other Short - term Loans	10052.41	1950.59
8. 其他存款 Other Deposits	2833.73	1147.24	2. 中期流动资金贷款 Medium - term Working Capital Loans	2989.09	1321.41
二、金融债券 Financial Bonds	39.47	- 4.68	3. 中长期贷款 Medium and Long - term Loans	20979.23	3489.49
三、国家投资债券 State Investment Bonds	0.21	- 80.04	（1）基本建设贷款 Capital Construction Loans	11840.11	2434.37
四、证券业务款 Securities Business Funds	787.28	214.30	（2）技术改造贷款 Technical Improvement Loans	5025.87	215.01
五、流通中货币 Currency in Circulation	13455.49	2251.34	（3）其他中长期贷款 Other Medium and Long - term Loans	4113.25	840.11
六、所有者权益 Owner's Equity	6674.89	- 216.28			
其中：实收资本 Of Which：Paid - in Capital	7643.15	98.54	4. 信托贷款 Trust Loans	645.48	- 9.36
当年结益 Net Earnings	- 399.13	- 399.13	5. 融资租赁 Financing Leases	64.84	- 2.50

续表
Continued

项 目 Items	余 额 Balance	比年初增减额 Changes within the Year	项 目 Items	余 额 Balance	比年初增减额 Changes within the Year
七、其他 Others	-4323.68	1380.72	6. 委托贷款 Designated Loans	1794.27	0.32
			7. 逾期类贷款 Overdue Loans	3373.82	801.42
			二、国家投资债券贷款 Loans Related to State Investment Bonds	34.11	-2.25
			三、有价证券及投资 Securities and Investments	12505.79	4407.18
			四、证券业务占款 Funding of Securities Purchase	284.85	-77.65
			五、委托投资 Designated Investments	825.85	-309.28
			六、金银占款 Position for Bullion and Silver Purchase	12.04	
			七、外汇占款 Position for Foreign Exchange Purchase	14792.35	1090.47
			八、库存现金 Cash in Vault	1641.27	752.98
			九、财政借款 Overdraft by State Finance	1582.06	
资金来源总计 Total Sources	**125412.60**	**16707.81**	**资金运用总计 Total Uses**	**125412.60**	**16707.81**

注：逾期类贷款不含中国工商银行、中国农业银行、中国银行、中国建设银行、农村信用合作社的数据。

Note：The data of overdue loans don't include the data of Industrial and Commercial Bank of China，the Agricultural Bank of China，Bank of China，China Construction Bank，Rural Credit Cooperatives.

金融机构人民币信贷收支表

Sources and Uses of Credit Funds of Financial Institutions（RMB）

（2000 年末）

（Year – end of 2000）

单位：亿元

Unit：100 Million Yuan

项目 Items	余额 Balance	比年初增减额 Changes within the Year	项目 Items	余额 Balance	比年初增减额 Changes within the Year
一、各项存款 Total Deposits	123804.35	15411.94	一、各项贷款 Total Loans	99371.07	13346.61
1. 企业存款 Deposits by Enterprises	44093.73	6998.52	1. 短期贷款 Short – term Loans	65748.07	7874.58
（1）活期存款 Demand Deposits	32832.65	5197.78	（1）工业贷款 Loans to Industrial Sector	17019.33	738.18
（2）定期存款 Time Deposits	11261.08	1800.74	（2）商业贷款 Loans to Commercial Sector	17868.50	417.10
2. 财政存款 Fiscal Deposits	3508.09	1384.37	其中：农副产品贷款 Of Which：Loans for the Purchase of Farm Products	8064.33	29.78
3. 机关团体存款 Deposits by Government Agencies and Social Organizations	2224.27	430.88	（3）建筑业贷款 Loans to Construction Enterprises	1617.05	127.66
4. 储蓄存款 Urban Savings Deposits	64332.38	4976.69	（4）农业贷款 Loans to Agricultural Sector	4888.99	538.36
（1）活期储蓄 Demand Deposits	18190.72	3666.35	（5）乡镇企业贷款 Loans to Village and Township Enterprises	6060.78	484.07
（2）定期储蓄 Time Deposits	46141.66	1310.34	（6）三资企业贷款 Loans to Foreign Investment Enterprises and Ventures	3049.79	254.77
5. 农业存款 Deposits by Agricultural Sector	2642.86	507.79	（7）私营企业及个体贷款 Loans to Privately – run Enterprises and Self – employed Entities	654.60	95.01
6. 信托存款 Trust Deposits	767.32	– 155.79	（8）其他短期贷款 Other Short – term Loans	14589.03	5219.43
7. 委托存款 Designated Deposits	2106.31	– 28.68	2. 中期流动资金贷款 Medium – term Working Capital Loans	4385.22	1605.20
8. 其他存款 Other Deposits	4129.39	1298.16	3. 中长期贷款 Medium and Long – term Loans	23545.97	3792.73
二、金融债券 Financial Bonds	30.19	– 8.98	（1）基本建设贷款 Capital Construction Loans	13742.22	2380.13
三、国家投资债券 State Investment Bonds	0.25	0.04	（2）技术改造贷款 Technical Improvement Loans	4861.07	395.85
四、证券业务款项 Securities Business Funds	948.70	153.89	（3）其他中长期贷款 Other Medium and Long – term Loans	4942.68	1016.75
五、流通中货币 Currency in Circulation	14652.65	1197.16	4. 信托贷款 Trust Loans	547.23	– 80.92
六、所有者权益 Owner's Equity	6694.87	23.12	5. 融资租赁 Financing Leases	69.19	4.28
其中：实收资本 Of Which：Paid – in Capital	7753.49	122.82			
当年结益 Net Earnings	– 207.29	– 207.29			

续表
Continued

项 目 Items	余 额 Balance	比年初增减额 Changes within the Year	项 目 Items	余 额 Balance	比年初增减额 Changes within the Year
七、其他 Others	-8796.58	2862.01	6. 委托贷款 Designated Loans	1793.29	5.43
			7. 逾期类贷款 Overdue Loans	3282.10	145.31
			二、国家投资债券贷款 Loans Related to State Investment Bonds	32.55	-2.05
			三、有价证券及投资 Securities and Investments	19651.07	7152.80
			四、证券业务占款 Funding of Securities Purchase	324.31	39.48
			五、委托投资 Designated Investments	764.09	-62.10
			六、金银占款 Position for Bullion and Silver Purchase	12.04	
			七、外汇占款 Position for Foreign Exchange Purchase	14291.14	-501.58
			八、库存现金 Cash in Vault	1306.10	-333.98
			九、财政借款 Overdraft by State Finance	1582.06	
资金来源总计 Total Sources	**137334.43**	**19639.18**	**资金运用总计 Total Uses**	**137334.43**	**19639.18**

注：逾期类贷款不含中国工商银行、中国农业银行、中国银行、中国建设银行、农村信用合作社的数据。

Note: The data of overdue loans don't include the data of the Industrial and Commercial Bank of China, Agricultural Bank of China, Bank of China, China Construction Bank, Rural Credit Cooperatives.

金融机构人民币信贷收支表

Sources and Uses of Credit Funds of Financial Institutions（RMB）

（2001年末）

（Year - end of 2001）

单位：亿元

Unit：100 Million Yuan

项目 Items	余额 Balance	比年初增减额 Changes within the Year	项目 Items	余额 Balance	比年初增减额 Changes within the Year
一、各项存款 Total Deposits	143617.17	20117.72	一、各项贷款 Total Loans	112314.70	12912.85
1. 企业存款 Deposits by Enterprises	51546.63	7199.47	1. 短期贷款 Short - term Loans	67327.23	4488.81
（1）活期存款 Demand Deposits	37366.49	4550.50	（1）工业贷款 Loans to Industrial Sector	18636.68	996.08
（2）定期存款 Time Deposits	14180.14	2648.97	（2）商业贷款 Loans to Commercial Sector	18563.41	28.90
2. 财政存款 Fiscal Deposits	3369.75	- 135.94	其中：农副产品贷款 Of Which：Loans for the Purchase of Farm Products	7984.23	- 80.48
3. 机关团体存款 Deposits by Government Agencies and Social Organizations	2852.82	632.30	（3）建筑业贷款 Loans to Construction Sector	2099.58	359.21
4. 储蓄存款 Savings Deposits	73762.43	9457.64	（4）农业贷款 Loans to Agricultural Sector	5711.48	789.12
（1）活期储蓄 Demand Deposits	22327.57	4144.48	（5）乡镇企业贷款 Loans to Village and Township Enterprises	6412.99	290.05
（2）定期储蓄 Time Deposits	51434.86	5313.16	（6）三资企业贷款 Loans to Foreign Investment Enterprises and Ventures	3263.48	60.12
5. 农业存款 Deposits by Agricultural Sector	3083.26	425.67	（7）私营企业及个体贷款 Loans to Privately - run Enterprises and Self - employed Entities	918.04	170.33
6. 信托存款 Trust Deposits	317.99	- 79.16	（8）其他短期贷款 Other Short - term Loans	11721.57	1795.00
7. 委托存款 Designated Deposits	2371.76	329.50	其中：个人短期消费贷款 Of Which：Short - term Consumer Credit	556.09	106.82
8. 其他存款 Other Deposits	6312.53	2288.24	2. 中期流动资金贷款 Medium - term Working Capital Loans	4965.58	588.13
二、金融债券 Financial Bonds	51.38	23.69	3. 中长期贷款 Medium and Long - term Loans	34272.50	5960.34
三、应付及暂收款 Account Payable and Receipts on Account	4049.36	- 328.53	（1）基本建设贷款 Capital Construction Loans	16270.78	2279.32
其中：应付及预收利息 Of Which：Interest Payable and Received in Advance	1428.65	- 138.01	（2）技术改造贷款 Technical Improvement Loans	5000.68	177.11
四、流通中货币 Currency in Circulation	15688.80	1036.15	（3）其他中长期贷款 Other Medium and Long - term Loans	13001.04	3503.91
五、各项准备 Total Provisions	1294.29	503.44			

续表
Continued

项　目 Items	余　额 Balance	比年初增减额 Changes within the Year	项　目 Items	余　额 Balance	比年初增减额 Changes within the Year
其中：贷款呆账准备金 Of Which: Provisions for Bad Loans	1234.43	488.11	其中：个人中长期消费贷款 Of Which: Medium and Long－term Consumer Credit	6434.16	2648.41
六、所有者权益 Owner's Equity	6713.10	－219.07	4. 信托贷款 Trust Loans	411.48	－103.05
其中：实收资本 Of Which: Paid－in Capital	8014.97	259.19	5. 融资租赁 Financing Leases	79.60	20.77
当年结益 Net Earnings	－152.37	－152.37	6. 委托贷款 Designated Loans	2086.07	334.97
七、其他 Others	－9710.37	－4056.92	7. 票据融资 Paper Financing	2814.04	1551.14
			其中：贴现 Of Which: Discount	2814.04	1551.14
			8. 各项垫款 Total Advances	358.20	71.74
			二、有价证券及投资 Securities and Investments	23112.65	3009.00
			三、应收及预付款 Accounts Receivable and Advance Payments	4696.43	－2676.32
			其中：应收利息 Of Which: Interest Receivable	2130.28	－250.82
			四、委托投资 Designated Investments	685.94	－68.41
			五、金银占款 Position for Bullion and Silver Purchase	256.00	243.96
			六、外汇占款 Position for Foreign Exchange Purchase	17856.43	3763.62
			七、库存现金 Cash in Vault	1199.52	－108.22
			八、财政借款 Overdraft by State Finance	1582.06	
资金来源总计 Total Sources	**161703.73**	**17076.48**	**资金运用总计 Total Uses**	**161703.73**	**17076.48**

金融机构人民币信贷收支表

Sources and Uses of Credit Funds of Financial Institutions（RMB）

（2002 年末）

（Year - end of 2002）

单位：亿元

Unit：100 Million Yuan

项　目 Items	余　额 Balance	比年初增减额 Changes within the Year	项　目 Items	余　额 Balance	比年初增减额 Changes within the Year
一、各项存款 Total Deposits	170917.40	27789.70	一、各项贷款 Total Loans	131293.93	18475.01
1. 企业存款 Deposits by Enterprises	60028.57	9534.86	1. 短期贷款 Short - term Loans	74247.90	7755.31
（1）活期存款 Demand Deposits	43594.73	6382.35	（1）工业贷款 Loans to Industrial Sector	20190.47	2712.58
（2）定期存款 Time Deposits	16433.84	3152.51	（2）商业贷款 Loans to Commercial Sector	17973.12	- 638.54
2. 财政存款 Fiscal Deposits	3481.90	128.76	其中：农副产品贷款 Of Which：Loans for the Purchase of Farm Products	7818.19	- 121.19
3. 机关团体存款 Deposits by Government Agencies and Social Organizations	5184.48	1508.72	（3）建筑业贷款 Loans to Construction Sector	2747.99	884.16
4. 储蓄存款 Savings Deposits	86910.65	13233.08	（4）农业贷款 Loans to Agricultural Sector	6884.58	1177.44
（1）活期储蓄 Demand Deposits	28121.71	5801.14	（5）乡镇企业贷款 Loans to Village and Township Enterprises	6812.26	386.59
（2）定期储蓄 Time Deposits	58788.94	7431.94	（6）三资企业贷款 Loans to Foreign Investment Enterprises and Ventures	2697.35	- 407.04
5. 农业存款 Deposits by Agricultural Sector	3764.24	674.12			
6. 信托存款 Trust Deposits	220.72	- 27.37	（7）私营企业及个体贷款 Loans to Privately - run Enterprises and Self - employed Entities	1058.77	318.97
7. 委托存款 Designated Deposits	2193.65	63.68	（8）其他短期贷款 Other Short - term Loans	15883.36	3321.15
8. 其他存款 Other Deposits	9133.19	2673.85	其中：个人短期消费贷款 Of Which：Short - term Consumer Credit	802.16	174.20
二、金融债券 Financial Bonds	90.34	44.26			
三、应付及暂收款 Account Payable and Receipts on Account	3326.94	- 256.13	2. 中期流动资金贷款 Medium - term Working Capital Loans	6189.68	274.28
			3. 中长期贷款 Medium and Long - term Loans	42452.36	8163.68
其中：应付及预收利息 Of Which：Interest Payable and Received in Advance	1387.04	- 29.70	（1）基本建设贷款 Capital Construction Loans	22434.61	3174.71
四、流通中货币 Currency in Circulation	17278.03	1589.23	（2）技术改造贷款 Technical Improvement Loans	2029.78	64.91
五、各项准备 Total Provisions	2071.94	758.03	（3）其他中长期贷款 Other Medium and Long - term Loans	17987.97	4924.06

续表
Continued

项目 Items	余额 Balance	比年初增减额 Changes within the Year	项目 Items	余额 Balance	比年初增减额 Changes within the Year
其中：贷款呆账准备金 Of Which: Provisions for Bad Loans	1678.21	422.35	其中：个人中长期消费贷款 Of Which: Medium and Long-term Consumer Credit	9869.95	3519.86
六、所有者权益 Owner's Equity	7293.50	457.38	4. 信托贷款 Trust Loans	224.87	-56.35
其中：实收资本 Of Which: Paid-in Capital	7150.66	-373.92	5. 融资租赁 Financing Leases	98.44	26.96
当年结益 Net Earnings	749.01	749.01	6. 委托贷款 Designated Loans	1945.44	66.19
七、其他 Others	-12198.18	-3168.95	7. 票据融资 Paper Financing	5752.02	2231.97
			其中：贴现 Of Which: Discount	5752.02	2231.97
			8. 各项垫款 Total Advances	383.22	12.97
			二、有价证券及投资 Securities and Investments	26789.73	3305.71
			三、应收及预付款 Accounts Receivable and Advance Payments	3582.10	-538.98
			其中：应收利息 Of Which: Interest Receivable	1672.36	-429.75
			四、委托投资 Designated Investments	637.75	-50.68
			五、金银占款 Position for Bullion and Silver Purchase	337.24	81.24
			六、外汇占款 Position for Foreign Exchange Purchase	23223.34	5812.09
			七、库存现金 Cash in Vault	1333.82	129.13
			八、财政借款 Overdraft by State Finance	1582.06	
资金来源总计 Total Sources	**188779.97**	**27213.52**	**资金运用总计 Total Uses**	**188779.97**	**27213.52**

金融机构人民币信贷收支表

Sources and Uses of Credit Funds of Financial Institutions（RMB）

（2003年末）

（Year - end of 2003）

单位：亿元

Unit：100 Million Yuan

项　目 Items	余　额 Balance	比年初增减额 Changes within the Year	项　目 Items	余　额 Balance	比年初增减额 Changes within the Year
一、各项存款 Total Deposits	208055.59	37188.44	一、各项贷款 Total Loans	158996.23	27651.67
1. 企业存款 Deposits by Enterprises	72487.05	12548.10	1. 短期贷款 Short - term Loans	83661.15	9496.33
（1）活期存款 Demand Deposits	51546.27	8127.63	（1）工业贷款 Loans to Industrial Sector	22756.00	2574.09
（2）定期存款 Time Deposits	20940.78	4420.47	（2）商业贷款 Loans to Commercial Sector	17994.41	39.75
2. 财政存款 Fiscal Deposits	5126.94	1656.73	其中：农副产品贷款 Of Which：Loans for the Purchase of Farm Products	7282.86	-535.36
3. 机关团体存款 Deposits by Government Agencies and Social Organizations	6727.65	1544.00	（3）建筑业贷款 Loans to Construction Sector	3002.14	248.53
4. 储蓄存款 Savings Deposits	103617.65	16631.90	（4）农业贷款 Loans to Agricultural Sector	8411.35	1531.13
（1）活期储蓄 Demand Deposits	35118.98	6957.38	（5）乡镇企业贷款 Loans to Village and Township Enterprises	7661.55	849.67
（2）定期储蓄 Time Deposits	68498.67	9674.52	（6）三资企业贷款 Loans to Foreign Investment Enterprises and Ventures	2569.41	-130.97
5. 农业存款 Deposits by Agricultural Sector	4898.33	1132.76	（7）私营企业及个体贷款 Loans to Privately - run Enterprises and Self - employed Entities	1461.59	401.96
6. 信托存款 Trust Deposits	239.38	12.57	（8）其他短期贷款 Other Short - term Loans	19804.70	3982.17
7. 委托存款 Designated Deposits	2218.72	55.62	其中：个人短期消费贷款 Of Which：Short - term Consumer Credit	1076.16	306.52
8. 其他存款 Other Deposits	12739.87	3606.76	2. 中期流动资金贷款 Medium - term Working Capital Loans	6591.50	403.91
二、金融债券 Financial Bonds	2226.27	301.86	3. 中长期贷款 Medium and Long - term Loans	56809.90	14203.36
三、应付及暂收款 Account Payable and Receipts on Account	3865.27	561.22	（1）基本建设贷款 Capital Construction Loans	28857.12	6373.43
其中：应付及预收利息 Of Which：Interest Payable and Received in Advance	1437.03	53.74	（2）技术改造贷款 Technical Improvement Loans	2208.75	178.39
四、同业往来 Inter - bank Transactions	4419.76	-519.04	（3）其他中长期贷款 Other Medium and Long - term Loans	25744.03	7651.54
五、流通中货币 Currency in Circulation	19745.99	2467.96			

续表
Continued

项 目 Items	余 额 Balance	比年初增减额 Changes within the Year	项 目 Items	余 额 Balance	比年初增减额 Changes within the Year
六、各项准备 Total Provisions	3378.41	1169.95	其中：个人中长期消费贷款 Of Which: Medium and Long - term Consumer Credit	14659.55	4784.48
其中：贷款损失准备 Of Which: Provisions for Loan Losses	2696.45	903.84	4. 信托贷款 Trust Loans	252.94	42.40
七、所有者权益 Owner's Equity	7869.97	1089.21	5. 融资租赁 Financing Leases	140.01	41.63
其中：实收资本 Of Which: Paid - in Capital	8196.85	1086.86	6. 委托贷款 Designated Loans	2028.38	101.72
当年结益 Net Earnings	516.20	516.20	7. 票据融资 Paper Financing	9170.73	3403.08
八、其他 Others	- 11783.37	- 4618.18	其中：贴现 Of Which: Discount	9156.27	3389.73
			8. 各项垫款 Total Advances	341.62	- 40.76
			二、有价证券及投资 Securities and Investments	30259.47	3832.82
			三、应收及预付款 Accounts Recceivable and Advane Payments	2977.92	- 552.84
			其中：应收利息 Of Which: Interest Receivable	1127.62	- 542.02
			四、同业往来 Inter - bank Transactions	884.73	48.49
			五、人行对资产管理公司再贷款 Loans to the Asset Management Companies by the Central Bank	6057.37	
			六、委托投资 Designated Investments	864.51	228.01
			七、金银占款 Position for Bullion and Silver Purchase	337.24	
			八、外汇占款 Position for Foreign Exchange Purchase	31122.40	7872.02
			九、固定资产 Fixed Asset	4768.80	- 32.58
			十、库存现金 Cash in Vault	1509.22	175.89
			十一、财政借款 Overdraft by State Finance		- 1582.06
资金来源总计 Total Sources	**237777.89**	**37641.42**	**资金运用总计 Total Uses**	**237777.89**	**37641.42**

金融机构人民币信贷收支表

Sources and Uses of Credit Funds of Financial Institutions（RMB）

（2004年末）

（Year－end of 2004）

单位：亿元

Unit：100 Million Yuan

项　目 Items	余　额 Balance	比年初增减额 Changes within the Year	项　目 Items	余　额 Balance	比年初增减额 Changes within the Year
一、各项存款 Total Deposits	241424.32	33405.60	一、各项贷款 Total Loans	178197.78	22673.28
1.企业存款 Deposits by Enterprises	84669.47	11646.09	1.短期贷款 Short－term Loans	86840.60	6500.44
（1）活期存款 Demand Deposits	59286.91	6991.94	（1）工业贷款 Loans to Industrial Sector	23896.61	1676.79
（2）定期存款 Time Deposits	25382.56	4654.15	（2）商业贷款 Loans to Commercial Sector	17074.11	－96.35
2.财政存款 Fiscal Deposits	6236.17	563.64	其中：农副产品贷款 Of Which：Loans for the Purchase of Farm Products	7523.16	240.21
3.机关团体存款 Deposits by Government Agencies and Social Organizations	8152.39	1362.64			
			（3）建筑业贷款 Loans to Construction Sector	2780.13	43.41
4.储蓄存款 Savings Deposits	119555.39	15929.42	（4）农业贷款 Loans to Agricultural Sector	9843.11	1588.94
（1）活期储蓄 Demand Deposits	41416.53	6288.86	（5）乡镇企业贷款 Loans to Village and Township Enterprises	8069.22	520.25
（2）定期储蓄 Time Deposits	78138.86	9640.56			
			（6）三资企业贷款 Loans to Foreign Investment Enterprises and Ventures	2198.37	－149.91
5.农业存款 Deposits by Agricultural Sector	5526.32	627.80			
6.信托存款 Trust Deposits	256.57	16.11	（7）私营企业及个体贷款 Loans to Privately－run Enterprises and Self－employed Entities	2081.59	285.05
7.委托存款 Designated Deposits	2752.04	547.00			
			（8）其他短期贷款 Other Short－term Loans	20897.46	2632.26
8.其他存款 Other Deposits	14275.97	2712.90			
			其中：个人短期消费贷款 Of Which：Short－term Consumer Credit	1254.23	173.32
二、金融债券 Financial Bonds	3954.76	2108.89			
三、应付及暂收款 Account Payable and Receipts on Account	4256.08	469.31	2.中期流动资金贷款 Medium－term Working Capital Loans	6361.49	－111.12
			3.中长期贷款 Medium and Long－term Loans	70341.39	13698.80
其中：应付及预收利息 Of Which：Interest Payable and Received in Advance	1681.63	268.62			
			（1）基本建设贷款 Capital Construction Loans	35050.64	6267.87
四、同业往来 Inter－bank Transactions	3538.81	－825.02	（2）技术改造贷款 Technical Improvement Loans	2312.67	229.78
五、流通中货币 Currency in Circulation	21468.30	1722.31	（3）其他中长期贷款 Other Medium and Long－term Loans	32978.08	7201.15

续表
Continued

项目 Items	余额 Balance	比年初增减额 Changes within the Year	项目 Items	余额 Balance	比年初增减额 Changes within the Year
六、各项准备 Total Provisions	4007.98	633.44	其中：个人中长期消费贷款 Of Which: Medium and Long－term Consumer Credit	18627.82	4154.16
其中：贷款损失准备 Of Which: Provisions for Loan Losses	3205.38	543.45	4. 信托贷款 Trust Loans	215.55	25.69
七、所有者权益 Owner's Equity	8799.03	1085.32	5. 融资租赁 Financing Leases	127.94	－3.95
其中：实收资本 Of Which: Paid－in Capital	11223.43	3110.30	6. 委托贷款 Designated Loans	2505.62	501.32
当年结益 Net Earnings	481.51	481.51	7. 票据融资 Paper Financing	11521.45	2026.00
八、其他 Others	－9392.49	1857.77	其中：贴现 Of Which: Discount	11502.83	2025.67
			8. 各项垫款 Total Advances	283.74	36.10
			二、有价证券及投资 Securities and Investments	30931.01	962.99
			三、应收及预付款 Accounts Receivable and Advance Payments	3634.52	740.73
			其中：应收利息 Of Which: Interest Receivable	1170.20	－200.23
			四、同业往来 Inter－bank Transactions	746.10	－35.75
			五、人行对资产管理公司再供款 Loans to the Asset Management Companies by the Central Bank	7673.74	1616.37
			六、委托投资 Designated Investments	924.48	64.86
			七、金银占款 Position for Bullion and Silver Purchase	337.24	
			八、外汇占款 Position for Foreign Exchange Purchase	48866.50	14138.17
			九、固定资产 Fixed Asset	4943.44	117.81
			十、库存现金 Cash in Vault	1801.98	179.16
资金来源总计 Total Sources	**278056.79**	**40457.62**	**资金运用总计 Total Uses**	**278056.79**	**40457.62**

金融机构人民币信贷收支表

Sources and Uses of Credit Funds of Financial Institutions（RMB）

（2005 年末）

（Year – end of 2005）

单位：亿元

Unit：100 Million Yuan

项　目 Items	余　额 Balance	比年初增减额 Changes within the Year	项　目 Items	余　额 Balance	比年初增减额 Changes within the Year
一、各项存款 Total Deposits	287169.52	43918.07	一、各项贷款 Total Loans	194690.39	23543.82
1. 企业存款 Deposits by Enterprises	96143.74	11358.96	1. 短期贷款 Short – term Loans	87449.16	6509.24
（1）活期存款 Demand Deposits	63042.76	3652.92	（1）工业贷款 Loans to Industrial Sector	22516.66	1579.88
（2）定期存款 Time Deposits	33100.98	7706.04	（2）商业贷款 Loans to Commercial Sector	16447.55	765.27
2. 财政存款 Fiscal Deposits	7996.26	1758.41	其中：农副产品贷款 Of Which：Loans for the Purchase of Farm Products	8055.13	531.96
3. 机关团体存款 Deposits by Government Agencies and Social Organizations	12052.33	3868.02	（3）建筑业贷款 Loans to Construction Sector	2983.72	204.12
4. 储蓄存款 Savings Deposits	141050.99	21496.77	（4）农业贷款 Loans to Agricultural Sector	11529.93	1786.74
（1）活期储蓄 Demand Deposits	48787.45	7369.60	（5）乡镇企业贷款 Loans to Village and Township Enterprises	7901.76	496.93
（2）定期储蓄 Time Deposits	92263.54	14127.17			
			（6）三资企业贷款 Loans to Foreign Investment Enterprises and Ventures	1975.31	– 90.56
5. 农业存款 Deposits by Agricultural Sector	6203.78	676.63			
6. 信托存款 Trust Deposits	441.39	128.15	（7）私营企业及个体贷款 Loans to Privately – run Enterprises and Self – employed Entities	2180.75	124.30
7. 委托存款 Designated Deposits	3020.37	268.48			
			（8）其他短期贷款 Other Short – term Loans	21913.48	1642.56
8. 其他存款 Other Deposits	20260.66	4362.65			
			其中：个人短期消费贷款 Of Which：Short – term Consumer Credit	1277.54	11.70
二、金融债券 Financial Bonds	5672.79	999.64			
三、应付及暂收款 Account Payable and Receipts on Account	5847.95	1556.56	2. 中期流动资金贷款 Medium – term Working Capital Loans	6090.88	– 84.59
			3. 中长期贷款 Medium and Long – term Loans	81369.54	11972.40
其中：应付及预收利息 Of Which：Interest Payable and Received in Advance	2245.71	569.67			
			（1）基本建设贷款 Capital Construction Loans	40336.50	6174.62
四、同业往来 Inter – bank Transactions	4345.39	1028.15	（2）技术改造贷款 Technical Improvement Loans	2361.05	59.13
五、流通中货币 Currency in Circulation	24031.67	2563.37	（3）其他中长期贷款 Other Medium and Long – term Loans	38671.99	5738.65

续表
Continued

项目 Items	余额 Balance	比年初增减额 Changes within the Year	项目 Items	余额 Balance	比年初增减额 Changes within the Year
六、各项准备 Total Provisions	4739.21	807.51	其中：个人中长期消费贷款 Of Which: Medium and Long - term Consumer Credit	20673.67	1984.55
其中：贷款损失准备 Of Which: Provisions for Loan Losses	4194.01	997.55	4. 信托贷款 Trust Loans	401.27	117.12
七、所有者权益 Owner's Equity	16205.79	6758.45	5. 融资租赁 Financing Leases	197.63	69.74
其中：实收资本 Of Which: Paid - in Capital	12269.40	893.51	6. 委托贷款 Designated Loans	2724.90	211.31
当年结益 Net Earnings	3867.50	3867.50	7. 票据融资 Paper Financing	16231.18	4711.48
八、其他 Others	-25794.56	-7181.73	其中：贴现 Of Which: Discount	16175.18	4674.10
			8. 各项垫款 Total Advances	225.83	37.12
			二、有价证券及投资 Securities and Investments	34942.14	4083.24
			三、应收及预付款 Accounts Receivable and Advance Payments	6623.78	3691.81
			其中：应收利息 Of Which: Interest Receivable	1051.45	-141.21
			四、同业往来 Inter - bank Transactions	1310.40	575.62
			五、人行对资产管理公司再贷款 Loans to the Asset Management Companies by the Central Bank	12146.38	4472.64
			六、委托投资 Designated Investments	546.35	-46.69
			七、金银占款 Position for Bullion and Silver Purchase	337.24	
			八、外汇占款 Position for Foreign Exchange Purchase	66245.12	13652.85
			九、固定资产 Fixed Asset	5375.96	476.73
资金来源总计 Total Sources	**322217.76**	**50450.02**	**资金运用总计 Total Uses**	**322217.76**	**50450.02**

2. 国家银行人民币信贷收支表*（1949—2005 年）
Sources and Uses of Credit Funds of State Banks（RMB）（1949—2005）

国家银行人民币存贷款情况表
Deposits and Loans of State Banks in RMB

（1949 年末）

（Year - end of 1949）

单位：亿元（旧币）

Unit：100 Million Yuan（Old RMB）

项 目 Items	余 额 Balance	项 目 Items	余 额 Balance
存款总额 Total Deposits	11304.00	放款总额 Total Loans	7033.00
公存款 Deposits by Public Sector	11304.00	对公放款 Loans to Public Sector	7033.00
私存款 Deposits by Private Sector	—	对私放款 Loans to Private Sector	—
储蓄存款 Savings Deposits	—		

* 本表机构包括中国人民银行（1949—2005 年）、私营银行（1949—1951 年）、合营银行（1950—1952 年）、中国农业银行（1978—2005 年）、中国银行（1978—2005 年）、中国工商银行（1984—2005 年）、中国建设银行（1985—2005 年）、交通银行（1988—2000 年）、中信实业银行（1988—2000 年）、邮政储汇局（1990—2005 年）、中国农业发展银行（1997—2005 年）、国家开发银行（1997—2005 年）、中国进出口银行（1997—2005 年）。

* State Banks of this statement include the People's Bank of China（1949—2005），Private - operated Banks（1949—1951），Public - private Joint Venture Banks（1950—1952），Agricultural Bank of China（1978—2005），Bank of China（1978—2005），Industrial and Commercial Bank of China（1984—2005），China Construction Bank（1985—2005），Bank of Communications（1988—2000），CITIC Industrial Bank（1988—2000），Postal Savings Bureau（1990—2005），Agricultural Development Bank of China（1997—2005），China Development Bank（1997—2005）and the Export - Import Bank of China（1997—2005）.

国家银行人民币信贷收支表

Sources and Uses of Credit Funds of State Banks (RMB)

(1950 年末)

(Year – end of 1950)

单位：亿元（旧币）

Unit: 100 Million Yuan (Old RMB)

项　目 Items	余　额 Balance	比年初增减额 Changes within the Year	项　目 Items	余　额 Balance	比年初增减额 Changes within the Year
一、存款总额 Total Deposits	243398.00	232094.00	一、放款总额 Total Loans	182363.00	175330.00
1. 财政性存款 Fiscal Deposits	122957.00	—	1. 国营企业及合作放款 Loans to State Enterprises and Cooperatives	170278.00	—
中央金库款 Central Government Treasury Deposits	19245.00	—	国营工业放款 Loans to State Industrial Enterprises	15059.00	—
地方金库款 Local Government Treasury Deposits	6493.00	—	国营林业放款 Loans to State Forestry Enterprises	787.00	—
机关团体存款 Deposits by Government Agencies and Social Organizations	90115.00	—	国营贸易放款 Loans to State Trade Enterprises	146550.00	—
特种存款 Special Deposits			国营商业放款 Loans to State Commercial Enterprises		
基本建设存款 Capital Construction Deposits	4340.00	—	国营外贸放款 Loans to State Foreign Trade Enterprises		
保险公司存款 Deposits by Insurance Companies	2764.00	—	国营粮食放款 Loans to State Food Supply Enterprises		
2. 国营企业及合作存款 Deposits by State Enterprises and Cooperatives	96050.00	—	国营交通邮电放款 Loans to State Transportation, Posts and Telecommunications Enterprises	319.00	—
国营工业存款 Deposits by State Industrial Enterprises	20835.00	—	国营其他企业放款 Loans to Other State Enterprises	1693.00	—
国营贸易存款 Deposits by State Trade Enterprises	31592.00	—	地方国营企业放款 Loans to Local State Enterprises	3442.00	—
国营商业存款 Deposits by State Commercial Enterprises			地方工业放款 Loans to Local Industrial Enterprises	1822.00	—
国营外贸存款 Deposits by State Foreign Trade Enterprises			地方商业放款 Loans to Local Commercial Enterprises	614.00	—
国营粮食存款 Deposits by State Food Supply Enterprises			地方其他企业放款 Loans to Other Local Enterprises	1006.00	—
国营交通邮电存款 Deposits by State Transportation, Posts and Telecommunications Enterprises	13347.00	—	合作放款 Loans to Cooperatives	2428.00	—
国营农林水利存款 Deposits by State Agriculture, Forestry and Water Conservancy Enterprises	2035.00	—	供销合作放款 Loans to Supply and Marketing Cooperatives	2310.00	—

续表
Continued

项目 Items	余额 Balance	比年初增减额 Changes within the Year	项目 Items	余额 Balance	比年初增减额 Changes within the Year
国营其他企业存款 Deposits by Other State Enterprises	9418.00	—	其他合作放款 Loans to Other Cooperatives	118.00	—
地方国营企业存款 Deposits by Local State Enterprises	15966.00	—	2. 合私营企业放款 Loans to Joint Venture and Private Enerprises	4045.00	—
合作存款 Deposits by Cooperatives	2857.00	—	合营企业放款 Loans to Joint Venture Enerprises	507.00	—
供销合作存款 Deposits by Supply and Marketing Cooperatives			私营企业放款 Loans to Private Enerprises	3353.00	—
其他合作存款 Deposits by Other Cooperatives			城市手工业放款 Loans to Urban Handicraft Industry	185.00	—
3. 合私营企业存款 Deposits by Joint Venture and Private Enerprises	10321.00	—	3. 农业放款 Loans to Agricultural Sector	8040.00	—
合营企业存款 Deposits by Joint Venture Enerprises	1375.00	—	国营农业水利放款 Loans to State Agriculture, Forestry and Water Conservancy Enterprises	1562.00	—
私营企业存款 Deposits by Private Enerprises	8946.00	—	农村放款 Loans to Rural Area	6478.00	—
4. 合营银行往来 Inter - joint Venture Banks Transactions	900.00	—	二、代理地方放款 Agency Loans for Local States		
5. 储蓄存款 Savings Deposits	13170.00	—	三、库存现金 Cash in Vault	30011.00	—
城市储蓄 Urban Savings Deposits			四、外汇占款 Position for Foreign Exchange Purchase	109148.00	—
农村储蓄 Rural Savings Deposits			五、金银占款 Position for Bullion and Silver Purchase	12364.00	—
6. 农村存款 Rural Deposits			六、其他支出 Other Expenditures	68745.00	—
信用合作存款 Deposits by Credit Cooperatives					
农业生产合作存款 Deposits by Agricultural Production Cooperatives					
二、地方托放款项 Deposits by Local Entrust Lending	3438.00	—			
三、占用汇款 Cash Remittance in Transit	97234.00	—			
四、自有资金及盈余累积 Own Capital & Surplus Accumulation	5694.00	—			
五、其他收入 Other Incomes	52867.00	—			
资金来源总计 Total Sources	**402631.00**	**—**	**资金运用总计 Total Uses**	**402631.00**	**—**

国家银行人民币信贷收支表
Sources and Uses of Credit Funds of State Banks (RMB)

(1951 年末)

(Year – end of 1951)

单位：亿元（旧币）

Unit: 100 Million Yuan (Old RMB)

项目 Items	余额 Balance	比年初增减额 Changes within the Year	项目 Items	余额 Balance	比年初增减额 Changes within the Year
一、存款总额 Total Deposits	587865.00	344467.00	一、放款总额 Total Loans	638874.00	456511.00
1. 财政性存款 Fiscal Deposits	324824.00	201867.00	1. 国营企业及合作放款 Loans to State Enterprises and Cooperatives	602793.00	432515.00
中央金库款 Central Government Treasury Deposits	61198.00	41953.00	国营工业放款 Loans to State Industrial Enterprises	10537.00	–4522.00
地方金库款 Local Government Treasury Deposits	31221.00	24728.00	国营林业放款 Loans to State Forestry Enterprises	265.00	–522.00
机关团体存款 Deposits by Government Agencies and Social Organizations	195636.00	105521.00	国营贸易放款 Loans to State Trade Enterprises	481563.00	335013.00
特种存款 Special Deposits			国营商业放款 Loans to State Commercial Enterprises		
基本建设存款 Capital Construction Deposits	26557.00	22217.00	国营外贸放款 Loans to State Foreign Trade Enterprises		
保险公司存款 Deposits by Insurance Companies	10212.00	7448.00	国营粮食放款 Loans to State Food Supply Enterprises		
2. 国营企业及合作存款 Deposits by State Enterprises and Cooperatives	170662.00	74612.00	国营交通邮电放款 Loans to State Transportation, Posts and Telecommunications Enterprises	2037.00	1718.00
国营工业存款 Deposits by State Industrial Enterprises	43007.00	22172.00	国营其他企业放款 Loans to Other State Enterprises	55771.00	54078.00
国营贸易存款 Deposits by State Trade Enterprises	25434.00	–6158.00	地方国营企业放款 Loans to Local State Enterprises	21526.00	18084.00
国营商业存款 Deposits by State Commercial Enterprises			地方工业放款 Loans to Local Industrial Enterprises	10082.00	8260.00
国营外贸存款 Deposits by State Foreign Trade Enterprises			地方商业放款 Loans to Local Commercial Enterprises	7730.00	7116.00
国营粮食存款 Deposits by State Food Supplies Enterprises			地方其他企业放款 Loans to Other Local Enterprises	3714.00	2708.00
国营交通邮电存款 Deposits by State Transportation, Posts and Telecommunications Enterprises	34967.00	21620.00	合作放款 Loans to Cooperatives	31094.00	28666.00
国营农林水利存款 Deposits by State Agriculture, Forestry and Water Conservancy Enterprises	3761.00	1726.00	供销合作放款 Loans to Supply and Marketing Cooperatives	30209.00	27899.00

续表
Continued

项　目 Items	余　额 Balance	比年初增减额 Changes within the Year	项　目 Items	余　额 Balance	比年初增减额 Changes within the Year
国营其他企业存款 Deposits by Other State Enterprises	18927.00	9509.00	其他合作放款 Loans to Other Cooperatives	885.00	767.00
地方国营企业存款 Deposits by Local State Enterprises	34686.00	18720.00	2. 合私营企业放款 Loans to Joint Venture and Private Enerprises	15487.00	11442.00
合作存款 Deposits by Cooperatives	9880.00	7023.00	合营企业放款 Loans to Joint Venture Enerprises	2809.00	2302.00
供销合作存款 Deposits by Supply and Marketing Cooperatives			私营企业放款 Loans to Private Enerprises	11627.00	8274.00
其他合作存款 Deposits by Other Cooperatives			城市手工业放款 Loans to Urban Handicraft Industry	1051.00	866.00
3. 合私营企业存款 Deposits by Joint Venture and Private Enerprises	33842.00	23521.00	3. 农业放款 Loans to Agricultural Sector	20594.00	12554.00
			国营农业水利放款 Loans to State Agriculture，Forestry and Water Conservancy Enterprises	5299.00	3737.00
合营企业存款 Deposits by Joint Venture Enerprises	9912.00	8537.00			
私营企业存款 Deposits by Private Enerprises	23930.00	14984.00	农村放款 Loans to Rural Area	15295.00	8817.00
4. 合营银行往来 Inter－joint Venture Banks Transactions	3687.00	2787.00	二、代理地方放款 Agency Loans for Local States		
			三、库存现金 Cash in Vault	35243.00	5232.00
5. 储蓄存款 Savings Deposits	54850.00	41680.00	四、外汇占款 Position for Foreign Exchange Purchase	24038.00	－85110.00
城市储蓄 Urban Savings Deposits			五、金银占款 Position for Bullion and Silver Purchase	31837.00	19473.00
农村储蓄 Rural Savings Deposits			六、其他支出 Other Expenditures	93173.00	24428.00
6. 农村存款 Rural Deposits					
信用合作存款 Deposits by Credit Cooperatives					
农业生产合作存款 Deposits by Agricultural Production Cooperatives					
二、地方托放款项 Deposits by Local Entrust Lending	3213.00	－225.00			
三、占用汇款 Cash Remittance in Transit	74109.00	－23125.00			
四、自有资金及盈余累积 Own Capital and Surplus Accumulation	39620.00	33926.00			
五、其他收入 Other Incomes	118358.00	65491.00			
资金来源总计 Total Sources	**823165.00**	**420534.00**	**资金运用总计 Total Uses**	**823165.00**	**420534.00**

国家银行人民币信贷收支表
Sources and Uses of Credit Funds of State Banks（RMB）

（1952 年末）

（Year – end of 1952）

单位：亿元

Unit：100 Million Yuan

项　目 Items	余　额 Balance	比年初增减额 Changes within the Year	项　目 Items	余　额 Balance	比年初增减额 Changes within the Year
一、各项存款 Total Deposits	93.30	34.51	一、各项贷款 Total Loans	108.00	44.11
1. 企业存款 Deposits by Enterprises	33.00	—	1. 工业生产企业贷款 Loans to Industrial Production Enterprises	9.50	—
2. 财政存款 Fiscal Deposits	19.50	—	2. 商业企业贷款 Loans to Commercial Enterprises	93.80	—
3. 基本建设存款 Capital Construction Deposits	4.10	—	3. 城镇集体企业贷款 Loans to Urban Collective Enterprises	0.50	—
4. 机关团体存款 Deposits by Government Agencies and Social Organizations	28.10	—	4. 农业贷款 Loans to Agricultural Sector	4.20	—
5. 城镇储蓄存款 Urban Savings Deposits	8.60	—	二、黄金占款 Position for Bullion and Silver Purchase	4.80	—
6. 农村存款 Rural Deposits			三、外汇占款 Position for Foreign Exchange Purchase	6.00	—
二、流通中货币 Currency in Circulation	27.50	—			
三、银行自有资金 Own Capital	11.00	—			
四、其他 Others	- 13.00	—			
资金来源总计 Total Sources	**118.80**	—	**资金运用总计 Total Uses**	**118.80**	—

国家银行人民币信贷收支表

Sources and Uses of Credit Funds of State Banks（RMB）

（1953 年末）

（Year - end of 1953）

单位：亿元

Unit：100 Million Yuan

项目 Items	余额 Balance	比年初增减额 Changes within the Year	项目 Items	余额 Balance	比年初增减额 Changes within the Year
一、各项存款 Total Deposits	107.60	14.30	一、各项贷款 Total Loans	134.60	26.60
1. 企业存款 Deposits by Enterprises	31.80	-1.20	1. 工业生产企业贷款 Loans to Industrial Production Enterprises	13.00	3.50
2. 财政存款 Fiscal Deposits	33.30	13.80	2. 商业企业贷款 Loans to Commercial Enterprises	114.30	20.50
3. 基本建设存款 Capital Construction Deposits	6.70	2.60	3. 城镇集体企业贷款 Loans to Urban Collective Enterprises	0.70	0.20
4. 机关团体存款 Deposits by Government Agencies and Social Organizations	22.50	-5.60	4. 农业贷款 Loans to Agricultural Sector	6.60	2.40
5. 城镇储蓄 Urban Savings Deposits	12.20	3.60	二、黄金占款 Position for Bullion and Silver Purchase	4.80	
6. 农村存款 Rural Deposits	1.10	1.10	三、外汇占款 Position for Foreign Exchange Purchase	5.30	-0.70
二、流通中货币 Currency in Circulation	39.40	11.90			
三、银行自有资金 Own Capital	15.90	4.90			
四、其他 Others	-18.20	-5.20			
资金来源总计 Total Sources	**144.70**	**25.90**	**资金运用总计 Total Uses**	**144.70**	**25.90**

国家银行人民币信贷收支表
Sources and Uses of Credit Funds of State Banks (RMB)

(1954 年末)

(Year - end of 1954)

单位：亿元

Unit: 100 Million Yuan

项　目 Items	余　额 Balance	比年初增减额 Changes within the Year	项　目 Items	余　额 Balance	比年初增减额 Changes within the Year
一、各项存款 Total Deposits	152.50	44.90	一、各项贷款 Total Loans	184.60	50.00
1. 企业存款 Deposits by Enterprises	34.40	2.60	1. 工业生产企业贷款 Loans to Industrial Production Enterprises	14.60	1.60
2. 财政存款 Fiscal Deposits	61.30	28.00	2. 商业企业贷款 Loans to Commercial Enterprises	161.80	47.50
3. 基本建设存款 Capital Construction Deposits	7.50	0.80	3. 城镇集体企业贷款 Loans to Urban Collective Enterprises	0.60	-0.10
4. 机关团体存款 Deposits by Government Agencies and Social Organizations	30.70	8.20	4. 农业贷款 Loans to Agricultural Sector	7.60	1.00
5. 城镇储蓄 Urban Savings Deposits	14.30	2.10	二、黄金占款 Position for Bullion and Silver Purchase	4.80	
6. 农村存款 Rural Deposits	4.30	3.20	三、外汇占款 Position for Foreign Exchange Purchase	9.40	4.10
二、流通中货币 Currency in Circulation	41.20	1.80			
三、银行自有资金 Own Capital	21.00	5.10			
四、其他 Others	-15.90	2.30			
资金来源总计 Total Sources	**198.80**	**54.10**	**资金运用总计 Total Uses**	**198.80**	**54.10**

国家银行人民币信贷收支表
Sources and Uses of Credit Funds of State Banks（RMB）

（1955年末）

（Year－end of 1955）

单位：亿元

Unit：100 Million Yuan

项目 Items	余额 Balance	比年初增减额 Changes within the Year	项目 Items	余额 Balance	比年初增减额 Changes within the Year
一、各项存款 Total Deposits	141.70	－10.80	一、各项贷款 Total Loans	204.20	19.60
1. 企业存款 Deposits by Enterprises	32.40	－2.00	1. 工业生产企业贷款 Loans to Industrial Production Enterprises	18.10	3.50
2. 财政存款 Fiscal Deposits	36.10	－25.20	2. 商业企业贷款 Loans to Commercial Enterprises	175.30	13.50
3. 基本建设存款 Capital Construction Deposits	8.00	0.50	3. 城镇集体企业贷款 Loans to Urban Collective Enterprises	0.80	0.20
4. 机关团体存款 Deposits by Government Agencies and Social Organizations	42.20	11.50	4. 农业贷款 Loans to Agricultural Sector	10.00	2.40
5. 城镇储蓄 Urban Savings Deposits	16.90	2.60	二、黄金占款 Position for Bullion and Silver Purchase	4.80	
6. 农村存款 Rural Deposits	6.10	1.80	三、外汇占款 Position for Foreign Exchange Purchase	9.70	0.30
二、流通中货币 Currency in Circulation	40.30	－0.90			
三、银行自有资金 Own Capital	25.90	4.90			
四、其他 Others	10.80	26.70			
资金来源总计 Total Sources	**218.70**	**19.90**	**资金运用总计 Total Uses**	**218.70**	**19.90**

国家银行人民币信贷收支表
Sources and Uses of Credit Funds of State Banks (RMB)

(1956年末)

(Year - end of 1956)

单位：亿元

Unit: 100 Million Yuan

项目 Items	余额 Balance	比年初增减额 Changes within the Year	项目 Items	余额 Balance	比年初增减额 Changes within the Year
一、各项存款 Total Deposits	134.10	-7.60	一、各项贷款 Total Loans	233.90	29.70
1. 企业存款 Deposits by Enterprises	45.00	12.60	1. 工业生产企业贷款 Loans to Industrial Production Enterprises	27.90	9.80
2. 财政存款 Fiscal Deposits	16.40	-19.70	2. 商业企业贷款 Loans to Commercial Enterprises	172.60	-2.70
3. 基本建设存款 Capital Construction Deposits	3.20	-4.80	3. 城镇集体企业贷款 Loans to Urban Collective Enterprises	3.20	2.40
4. 机关团体存款 Deposits by Government Agencies and Social Organizations	39.10	-3.10	4. 农业贷款 Loans to Agricultural Sector	30.20	20.20
5. 城镇储蓄 Urban Savings Deposits	22.40	5.50	二、黄金占款 Position for Bullion and Silver Purchase	4.80	
6. 农村存款 Rural Deposits	8.00	1.90	三、外汇占款 Position for Foreign Exchange Purchase	3.50	-6.20
二、流通中货币 Currency in Circulation	57.30	17.00			
三、银行自有资金 Own Capital	38.10	12.20			
四、其他 Others	12.70	1.90			
资金来源总计 Total Sources	**242.20**	**23.50**	**资金运用总计 Total Uses**	**242.20**	**23.50**

国家银行人民币信贷收支表

Sources and Uses of Credit Funds of State Banks（RMB）

（1957年末）

（Year - end of 1957）

单位：亿元

Unit：100 Million Yuan

项　目 Items	余　额 Balance	比年初增减额 Changes within the Year	项　目 Items	余　额 Balance	比年初增减额 Changes within the Year
一、各项存款 Total Deposits	165.50	31.40	一、各项贷款 Total Loans	277.50	43.60
1. 企业存款 Deposits by Enterprises	39.70	-5.30	1. 工业生产企业贷款 Loans to Industrial Production Enterprises	30.30	2.40
2. 财政存款 Fiscal Deposits	20.60	4.20	2. 商业企业贷款 Loans to Commercial Enterprises	216.40	43.80
3. 基本建设存款 Capital Construction Deposits	10.10	6.90	3. 城镇集体企业贷款 Loans to Urban Collective Enterprises	3.10	-0.10
4. 机关团体存款 Deposits by Government Agencies and Social Organizations	49.30	10.20	4. 农业贷款 Loans to Agricultural Sector	27.70	-2.50
5. 城镇储蓄 Urban Savings Deposits	27.90	5.50	二、黄金占款 Position for Bullion and Silver Purchase	4.80	
6. 农村存款 Rural Deposits	17.90	9.90	三、外汇占款 Position for Foreign Exchange Purchase	3.30	-0.20
二、流通中货币 Currency in Circulation	52.80	-4.50			
三、银行自有资金 Own Capital	54.30	16.20			
四、其他 Others	13.00	0.30			
资金来源总计 Total Sources	**285.60**	**43.40**	**资金运用总计 Total Uses**	**285.60**	**43.40**

国家银行人民币信贷收支表
Sources and Uses of Credit Funds of State Banks（RMB）

（1958年末）

（Year－end of 1958）

单位：亿元

Unit：100 Million Yuan

项　目 Items	余　额 Balance	比年初增减额 Changes within the Year	项　目 Items	余　额 Balance	比年初增减额 Changes within the Year
一、各项存款 Total Deposits	295.30	129.80	一、各项贷款 Total Loans	477.70	200.20
1. 企业存款 Deposits by Enterprises	77.60	37.90	1. 工业生产企业贷款 Loans to Industrial Production Enterprises	89.20	58.90
2. 财政存款 Fiscal Deposits	49.90	29.30	2. 商业企业贷款 Loans to Commercial Enterprises	342.40	126.00
3. 基本建设存款 Capital Construction Deposits	20.10	10.00	3. 城镇集体企业贷款 Loans to Urban Collective Enterprises	2.70	－0.40
4. 机关团体存款 Deposits by Government Agencies and Social Organizations	84.80	35.50	4. 农业贷款 Loans to Agricultural Sector	43.40	15.70
5. 城镇储蓄存款 Urban Savings Deposits	35.10	7.20	二、黄金占款 Position for Bullion and Silver Purchase	4.80	
6. 农村存款 Rural Deposits	27.80	9.90	三、外汇占款 Position for Foreign Exchange Purchase	2.70	－0.60
二、流通中货币 Currency in Circulation	67.80	15.00			
三、银行自有资金 Own Capital	96.90	42.60			
四、其他 Others	25.20	12.20			
资金来源总计 Total Sources	**485.20**	**199.60**	**资金运用总计 Total Uses**	**485.20**	**199.60**

国家银行人民币信贷收支表
Sources and Uses of Credit Funds of State Banks（RMB）

（1959 年末）

（Year - end of 1959）

单位：亿元

Unit：100 Million Yuan

项目 Items	余额 Balance	比年初增减额 Changes within the Year	项目 Items	余额 Balance	比年初增减额 Changes within the Year
一、各项存款 Total Deposits	398.70	103.40	一、各项贷款 Total Loans	798.10	320.40
1. 企业存款 Deposits by Enterprises	70.00	-7.60	1. 工业生产企业贷款 Loans to Industrial Production Enterprises	254.80	165.60
2. 财政存款 Fiscal Deposits	82.10	32.20	2. 商业企业贷款 Loans to Commercial Enterprises	495.30	152.90
3. 基本建设存款 Capital Construction Deposits	40.10	20.00	3. 城镇集体企业贷款 Loans to Urban Collective Enterprises	3.50	0.80
4. 机关团体存款 Deposits by Government Agencies and Social Organizations	111.00	26.20	4. 农业贷款 Loans to Agricultural Sector	44.50	1.10
5. 城镇储蓄存款 Urban Savings Deposits	47.30	12.20	二、黄金占款 Position for Bullion and Silver Purchase	3.80	-1.00
6. 农村存款 Rural Deposits	48.20	20.40	三、外汇占款 Position for Foreign Exchange Purchase	-2.20	-4.90
二、流通中货币 Currency in Circulation	75.10	7.30			
三、银行自有资金 Own Capital	293.80	196.90			
四、其他 Others	32.10	6.90			
资金来源总计 Total Sources	**799.70**	**314.50**	**资金运用总计 Total Uses**	**799.70**	**314.50**

国家银行人民币信贷收支表
Sources and Uses of Credit Funds of State Banks (RMB)

(1960年末)

(Year – end of 1960)

单位：亿元

Unit：100 Million Yuan

项目 Items	余额 Balance	比年初增减额 Changes within the Year	项目 Items	余额 Balance	比年初增减额 Changes within the Year
一、各项存款 Total Deposits	459.80	61.10	一、各项贷款 Total Loans	969.20	171.10
1. 企业存款 Deposits by Enterprises	86.00	16.00	1. 工业生产企贷款 Loans to Industrial Production Enterprises	362.80	108.00
2. 财政存款 Fiscal Deposits	146.60	64.50	2. 物资供销企业贷款 Loans to Material Supply and Sale Enterprises	30.80	30.80
3. 基本建设存款 Capital Construction Deposits	29.60	– 10.50	3. 商业企业贷款 Loans to Commercial Enterprises	506.30	11.00
4. 机关团体存款 Deposits by Government Agencies and Social Organizations	96.60	– 14.40	4. 城镇集体企业贷款 Loans to Urban Collective Enterprises	6.50	3.00
5. 城镇储蓄存款 Urban Savings Deposits	51.10	3.80	5. 农业贷款 Loans to Agricultural Sector	62.80	18.30
6. 农村存款 Rural Deposits	49.90	1.70	二、黄金占款 Position for Bullion and Silver Purchase	3.80	
二、流通中货币 Currency in Circulation	95.90	20.80	三、外汇占款 Position for Foreign Exchange Purchase	– 12.30	– 10.10
三、银行自有资金 Own Capital	369.90	76.10			
四、其他 Others	35.10	3.00			
资金来源总计 Total Sources	**960.70**	**161.00**	**资金运用总计 Total Uses**	**960.70**	**161.00**

国家银行人民币信贷收支表

Sources and Uses of Credit Funds of State Banks（RMB）

（1961 年末）

（Year - end of 1961）

单位：亿元

Unit：100 Million Yuan

项　目 Items	余 额 Balance	比年初增减额 Changes within the Year	项　目 Items	余 额 Balance	比年初增减额 Changes within the Year
一、各项存款 Total Deposits	488.70	28.90	一、各项贷款 Total Loans	803.50	- 165.70
1. 企业存款 Deposits by Enterprises	116.10	30.10	1. 工业生产企业贷款 Loans to Industrial Production Enterprises	167.10	- 195.70
2. 财政存款 Fiscal Deposits	174.60	28.00	2. 物资供销企业贷款 Loans to Material Supply and Sale Enterprises	25.30	- 5.50
3. 基本建设存款 Capital Construction Deposits	30.30	0.70	3. 商业企业贷款 Loans to Commercial Enterprises	537.50	31.20
4. 机关团体存款 Deposits by Government Agencies and Social Organizations	72.30	- 24.30	4. 城镇集体企业贷款 Loans to Urban Collective Enterprises	9.90	3.40
5. 城镇储蓄存款 Urban Savings Deposits	39.20	- 11.90	5. 农业贷款 Loans to Agricultural Sector	63.70	0.90
6. 农村存款 Rural Deposits	56.20	6.30	二、黄金占款 Position for Bullion and Silver Purchase	3.80	
二、流通中货币 Currency in Circulation	125.70	29.80	三、外汇占款 Position for Foreign Exchange Purchase	- 10.20	2.10
三、银行自有资金 Own Capital	183.30	- 186.60			
四、其他 Others	- 0.60	- 35.70			
资金来源总计 Total Sources	**797.10**	**- 163.60**	**资金运用总计 Total Uses**	**797.10**	**- 163.60**

国家银行人民币信贷收支表
Sources and Uses of Credit Funds of State Banks (RMB)

(1962 年末)

(Year - end of 1962)

单位：亿元
Unit: 100 Million Yuan

项　目 Items	余　额 Balance	比年初增减额 Changes within the Year	项　目 Items	余　额 Balance	比年初增减额 Changes within the Year
一、各项存款 Total Deposits	409.60	-79.10	一、各项贷款 Total Loans	682.10	-121.40
1. 企业存款 Deposits by Enterprises	152.30	36.20	1. 工业生产企业贷款 Loans to Industrial Production Enterprises	119.80	-47.30
2. 财政存款 Fiscal Deposits	79.90	-94.70	2. 物资供销企业贷款 Loans to Material Supply and Sale Enterprises	27.00	1.70
3. 基本建设存款 Capital Construction Deposits	44.70	14.40	3. 商业企业贷款 Loans to Commercial Enterprises	459.00	-78.50
4. 机关团体存款 Deposits by Government Agencies and Social Organizations	69.70	-2.60	4. 城镇集体企业贷款 Loans to Urban Collective Enterprises	9.60	-0.30
5. 城镇储蓄存款 Urban Savings Deposits	31.40	-7.80	5. 农业贷款 Loans to Agricultural Sector	66.70	3.00
6. 农村存款 Rural Deposits	31.60	-24.60	二、黄金占款 Position for Bullion and Silver Purchase	3.80	
二、流通中货币 Currency in Circulation	106.50	-19.20	三、外汇占款 Position for Foreign Exchange Purchase	-5.90	4.30
三、银行自有资金 Own Capital	201.30	18.00			
四、其他 Others	-37.40	-36.80			
资金来源总计 Total Sources	**680.00**	**-117.10**	**资金运用总计 Total Uses**	**680.00**	**-117.10**

国家银行人民币信贷收支表
Sources and Uses of Credit Funds of State Banks（RMB）

（1963 年末）

（Year - end of 1963）

单位：亿元

Unit：100 Million Yuan

项　目 Items	余　额 Balance	比年初增减额 Changes within the Year	项　目 Items	余　额 Balance	比年初增减额 Changes within the Year
一、各项存款 Total Deposits	414.00	4.40	一、各项贷款 Total Loans	568.00	- 114.10
1. 企业存款 Deposits by Enterprises	176.80	24.50	1. 工业生产企业贷款 Loans to Industrial Production Enterprises	76.90	- 42.90
2. 财政存款 Fiscal Deposits	67.30	- 12.60	2. 物资供销企业贷款 Loans to Material Supply and Sale Enterprises	31.50	4.50
3. 基本建设存款 Capital Construction Deposits	43.00	- 1.70			
4. 机关团体存款 Deposits by Government Agencies and Social Organizations	56.70	- 13.00	3. 商业企业贷款 Loans to Commercial Enterprises	384.40	- 74.60
			4. 城镇集体企业贷款 Loans to Urban Collective Enterprises	4.40	- 5.20
5. 城镇储蓄存款 Urban Savings Deposits	35.60	4.20	5. 农业贷款 Loans to Agricultural Sector	70.80	4.10
6. 农村存款 Rural Deposits	34.60	3.00	二、黄金占款 Position for Bullion and Silver Purchase	3.80	
二、流通中货币 Currency in Circulation	89.90	- 16.60	三、外汇占款 Position for Foreign Exchange Purchase	2.40	8.30
三、银行自有资金 Own Capital	229.70	28.40			
四、其他 Others	- 159.40	- 122.00			
资金来源总计 Total Sources	**574.20**	**- 105.80**	**资金运用总计 Total Uses**	**574.20**	**- 105.80**

国家银行人民币信贷收支表
Sources and Uses of Credit Funds of State Banks（RMB）

（1964 年末）

（Year – end of 1964）

单位：亿元

Unit：100 Million Yuan

项目 Items	余额 Balance	比年初增减额 Changes within the Year	项目 Items	余额 Balance	比年初增减额 Changes within the Year
一、各项存款 Total Deposits	439.50	25.50	一、各项贷款 Total Loans	578.90	10.90
1. 企业存款 Deposits by Enterprises	156.10	– 20.70	1. 工业生产企业贷款 Loans to Industrial Production Enterprises	76.00	– 0.90
2. 财政存款 Fiscal Deposits	84.80	17.50	2. 物资供销企业贷款 Loans to Material Supply and Sale Enterprises	31.60	0.10
3. 基本建设存款 Capital Construction Deposits	38.60	– 4.40	3. 商业企业贷款 Loans to Commercial Enterprises	396.60	12.20
4. 机关团体存款 Deposits by Government Agencies and Social Organizations	69.60	12.90	4. 城镇集体企业贷款 Loans to Urban Collective Enterprises	3.20	– 1.20
5. 城镇储蓄存款 Urban Savings Deposits	44.80	9.20	5. 农业贷款 Loans to Agricultural Sector	71.50	0.70
6. 农村存款 Rural Deposits	45.60	11.00	二、黄金占款 Position for Bullion and Silver Purchase	3.80	
二、流通中货币 Currency in Circulation	80.00	– 9.90	三、外汇占款 Position for Foreign Exchange Purchase	10.90	8.50
三、银行自有资金 Own Capital	102.70	– 127.00			
四、其他 Others	– 28.60	130.80			
资金来源总计 Total Sources	**593.60**	**19.40**	**资金运用总计 Total Uses**	**593.60**	**19.40**

国家银行人民币信贷收支表

Sources and Uses of Credit Funds of State Banks（RMB）

（1965年末）

（Year－end of 1965）

单位：亿元

Unit：100 Million Yuan

项　目 Items	余　额 Balance	比年初增减额 Changes within the Year	项　目 Items	余　额 Balance	比年初增减额 Changes within the Year
一、各项存款 Total Deposits	481.00	41.50	一、各项贷款 Total Loans	647.40	68.50
1. 企业存款 Deposits by Enterprises	181.90	25.80	1. 工业生产企业贷款 Loans to Industrial Production Enterprises	93.20	17.20
2. 财政存款 Fiscal Deposits	74.20	－10.60	2. 物资供销企业贷款 Loans to Material Supply and Sale Enterprises	41.30	9.70
3. 基本建设存款 Capital Construction Deposits	41.70	3.10	3. 商业企业贷款 Loans to Commercial Enterprises	431.30	34.70
4. 机关团体存款 Deposits by Government Agencies and Social Organizations	80.80	11.20	4. 城镇集体企业贷款 Loans to Urban Collective Enterprises	3.40	0.20
5. 城镇储蓄存款 Urban Savings Deposits	52.30	7.50	5. 农业贷款 Loans to Agricultural Sector	78.20	6.70
6. 农村存款 Rural Deposits	50.10	4.50	二、黄金占款 Position for Bullion and Silver Purchase	4.80	1.00
二、流通中货币 Currency in Circulation	90.80	10.80	三、外汇占款 Position for Foreign Exchange Purchase	10.00	－0.90
三、银行自有资金 Own Capital	106.50	3.80			
四、其他 Others	－16.10	12.50			
资金来源总计 Total Sources	**662.20**	**68.60**	**资金运用总计 Total Uses**	**662.20**	**68.60**

国家银行人民币信贷收支表

Sources and Uses of Credit Funds of State Banks (RMB)

(1966年末)

(Year-end of 1966)

单位：亿元

Unit: 100 Million Yuan

项目 Items	余额 Balance	比年初增减额 Changes within the Year	项目 Items	余额 Balance	比年初增减额 Changes within the Year
一、各项存款 Total Deposits	553.60	72.60	一、各项贷款 Total Loans	755.90	108.50
1. 企业存款 Deposits by Enterprises	185.00	3.10	1. 工业生产企业贷款 Loans to Industrial Production Enterprises	122.30	29.10
2. 财政存款 Fiscal Deposits	95.80	21.60	2. 物资供销企业贷款 Loans to Material Supply and Sale Enterprises	52.20	10.90
3. 基本建设存款 Capital Construction Deposits	51.60	9.90	3. 商业企业贷款 Loans to Commercial Enterprises	498.60	67.30
4. 机关团体存款 Deposits by Government Agencies and Social Organizations	100.60	19.80	4. 城镇集体企业贷款 Loans to Urban Collective Enterprises	5.10	1.70
5. 城镇储蓄存款 Urban Savings Deposits	57.70	5.40	5. 农业贷款 Loans to Agricultural Sector	77.70	-0.50
6. 农村存款 Rural Deposits	62.90	12.80	二、黄金占款 Position for Bullion and Silver Purchase	4.80	
二、流通中货币 Currency in Circulation	108.50	17.70	三、外汇占款 Position for Foreign Exchange Purchase	9.80	-0.20
三、银行自有资金 Own Capital	124.30	17.80			
四、其他 Others	-15.90	0.20			
资金来源总计 Total Sources	**770.50**	**108.30**	**资金运用总计 Total Uses**	**770.50**	**108.30**

国家银行人民币信贷收支表

Sources and Uses of Credit Funds of State Banks（RMB）

（1967 年末）

（Year - end of 1967）

单位：亿元

Unit：100 Million Yuan

项　目 Items	余　额 Balance	比年初增减额 Changes within the Year	项　目 Items	余　额 Balance	比年初增减额 Changes within the Year
一、各项存款 Total Deposits	575.10	21.50	一、各项贷款 Total Loans	796.60	40.70
1. 企业存款 Deposits by Enterprises	199.40	14.40	1. 工业生产企业贷款 Loans to Industrial Production Enterprises	173.60	51.30
2. 财政存款 Fiscal Deposits	67.30	- 28.50	2. 物资供销企业贷款 Loans to Material Supply and Sale Enterprises	51.80	- 0.40
3. 基本建设存款 Capital Construction Deposits	49.30	- 2.30	3. 商业企业贷款 Loans to Commercial Enterprises	483.00	- 15.60
4. 机关团体存款 Deposits by Government Agencies and Social Organizations	130.00	29.40	4. 城镇集体企业贷款 Loans to Urban Collective Enterprises	6.80	1.70
5. 城镇储蓄存款 Urban Savings Deposits	59.80	2.10	5. 农业贷款 Loans to Agricultural Sector	81.40	3.70
6. 农村存款 Rural Deposits	69.30	6.40	二、黄金占款 Position for Bullion and Silver Purchase	4.80	
二、流通中货币 Currency in Circulation	121.90	13.40	三、外汇占款 Position for Foreign Exchange Purchase	9.20	- 0.60
三、银行自有资金 Own Capital	145.40	21.10			
四、其他 Others	- 31.80	- 15.90			
资金来源总计 **Total Sources**	**810.60**	**40.10**	**资金运用总计** **Total Uses**	**810.60**	**40.10**

国家银行人民币信贷收支表

Sources and Uses of Credit Funds of State Banks (RMB)

(1968年末)

(Year - end of 1968)

单位：亿元

Unit: 100 Million Yuan

项目 Items	余额 Balance	比年初增减额 Changes within the Year	项目 Items	余额 Balance	比年初增减额 Changes within the Year
一、各项存款 Total Deposits	625.10	50.00	一、各项贷款 Total Loans	890.30	93.70
1. 企业存款 Deposits by Enterprises	211.80	12.40	1. 工业生产企业贷款 Loans to Industrial Production Enterprises	213.10	39.50
2. 财政存款 Fiscal Deposits	92.30	25.00	2. 物资供销企业贷款 Loans to Material Supply and Sale Enterprises	62.50	10.70
3. 基本建设存款 Capital Construction Deposits	31.70	- 17.60	3. 商业企业贷款 Loans to Commercial Enterprises	525.00	42.00
4. 机关团体存款 Deposits by Government Agencies and Social Organizations	143.70	13.70	4. 城镇集体企业贷款 Loans to Urban Collective Enterprises	8.50	1.70
5. 城镇储蓄存款 Urban Savings Deposits	62.30	2.50	5. 农业贷款 Loans to Agricultural Sector	81.20	- 0.20
6. 农村存款 Rural Deposits	83.30	14.00	二、黄金占款 Position for Bullion and Silver Purchase	6.70	1.90
二、流通中货币 Currency in Circulation	134.10	12.20	三、外汇占款 Position for Foreign Exchange Purchase	8.00	- 1.20
三、银行自有资金 Own Capital	166.60	21.20			
四、其他 Others	- 20.80	11.00			
资金来源总计 Total Sources	**905.00**	**94.40**	**资金运用总计 Total Uses**	**905.00**	**94.40**

国家银行人民币信贷收支表

Sources and Uses of Credit Funds of State Banks（RMB）

（1969年末）

（Year - end of 1969）

单位：亿元

Unit：100 Million Yuan

项　目 Items	余　额 Balance	比年初增减额 Changes within the Year	项　目 Items	余　额 Balance	比年初增减额 Changes within the Year
一、各项存款 Total Deposits	641.70	16.60	一、各项贷款 Total Loans	945.50	55.20
1. 企业存款 Deposits by Enterprises	215.50	3.70	1. 工业生产企业贷款 Loans to Industrial Production Enterprises	234.00	20.90
2. 财政存款 Fiscal Deposits	119.60	27.30	2. 物资供销企业贷款 Loans to Material Supply and Sale Enterprises	69.10	6.60
3. 基本建设存款 Capital Construction Deposits	16.20	-15.50	3. 商业企业贷款 Loans to Commercial Enterprises	547.50	22.50
4. 机关团体存款 Deposits by Government Agencies and Social Organizations	151.00	7.30	4. 城镇集体企业贷款 Loans to Urban Collective Enterprises	10.90	2.40
5. 城镇储蓄存款 Urban Savings Deposits	61.00	-1.30	5. 农业贷款 Loans to Agricultural Sector	84.00	2.80
6. 农村存款 Rural Deposits	78.40	-4.90	二、黄金占款 Position for Bullion and Silver Purchase	6.70	
二、流通中货币 Currency in Circulation	137.10	3.00	三、外汇占款 Position for Foreign Exchange Purchase	16.30	8.30
三、银行自有资金 Own Capital	193.10	26.50			
四、其他 Others	-3.40	17.40			
资金来源总计 Total Sources	**968.50**	**63.50**	**资金运用总计 Total Uses**	**968.50**	**63.50**

国家银行人民币信贷收支表

Sources and Uses of Credit Funds of State Banks (RMB)

(1970年末)

(Year - end of 1970)

单位：亿元

Unit: 100 Million Yuan

项　目 Items	余　额 Balance	比年初增减额 Changes within the Year	项　目 Items	余　额 Balance	比年初增减额 Changes within the Year
一、各项存款 Total Deposits	704.30	62.60	一、各项贷款 Total Loans	1033.40	87.90
1. 企业存款 Deposits by Enterprises	226.10	10.60	1. 工业生产企业贷款 Loans to Industrial Production Enterprises	241.40	7.40
2. 财政存款 Fiscal Deposits	176.80	57.20	2. 物资供销企业贷款 Loans to Material Supply and Sale Enterprises	67.40	-1.70
3. 基本建设存款 Capital Construction Deposits	12.20	-4.00			
4. 机关团体存款 Deposits by Government Agencies and Social Organizations	141.40	-9.60	3. 商业企业贷款 Loans to Commercial Enterprises	626.60	79.10
			4. 城镇集体企业贷款 Loans to Urban Collective Enterprises	12.90	2.00
5. 城镇储蓄存款 Urban Savings Deposits	64.50	3.50	5. 农业贷款 Loans to Agricultural Sector	85.10	1.10
6. 农村存款 Rural Deposits	83.30	4.90	二、黄金占款 Position for Bullion and Silver Purchase	6.70	
二、流通中货币 Currency in Circulation	123.60	-13.50	三、外汇占款 Position for Foreign Exchange Purchase	6.50	-9.80
三、银行自有资金 Own Capital	220.30	27.20			
四、其他 Others	-1.60	1.80			
资金来源总计 Total Sources	**1046.60**	**78.10**	**资金运用总计 Total Uses**	**1046.60**	**78.10**

国家银行人民币信贷收支表

Sources and Uses of Credit Funds of State Banks（RMB）

（1971 年末）

（Year－end of 1971）

单位：亿元

Unit：100 Million Yuan

项目 Items	余额 Balance	比年初增减额 Changes within the Year	项目 Items	余额 Balance	比年初增减额 Changes within the Year
一、各项存款 Total Deposits	767.60	63.30	一、各项贷款 Total Loans	1113.90	80.50
1. 企业存款 Deposits by Enterprises	226.80	0.70	1. 工业生产企业贷款 Loans to Industrial Production Enterprises	251.90	10.50
2. 财政存款 Fiscal Deposits	188.90	12.10	2. 物资供销企业贷款 Loans to Material Supply and Sale Enterprises	126.00	58.60
3. 基本建设存款 Capital Construction Deposits	24.00	11.80	3. 商业企业贷款 Loans to Commercial Enterprises	667.20	40.60
4. 机关团体存款 Deposits by Government Agencies and Social Organizations	161.10	19.70	4. 城镇集体企业贷款 Loans to Urban Collective Enterprises	17.20	4.30
5. 城镇储蓄存款 Urban Savings Deposits	73.30	8.80	5. 农业贷款 Loans to Agricultural Sector	51.60	－33.50
6. 农村存款 Rural Deposits	93.50	10.20	二、黄金占款 Position for Bullion and Silver Purchase	8.60	1.90
二、流通中货币 Currency in Circulation	136.20	12.60	三、外汇占款 Position for Foreign Exchange Purchase	4.90	－1.60
三、银行自有资金 Own Capital	152.30	－68.00			
四、其他 Others	71.30	72.90			
资金来源总计 Total Sources	**1127.40**	**80.80**	**资金运用总计 Total Uses**	**1127.40**	**80.80**

国家银行人民币信贷收支表
Sources and Uses of Credit Funds of State Banks (RMB)

(1972年末)

(Year - end of 1972)

单位：亿元

Unit: 100 Million Yuan

项 目 Items	余 额 Balance	比年初增减额 Changes within the Year	项 目 Items	余 额 Balance	比年初增减额 Changes within the Year
一、各项存款 Total Deposits	776.30	8.70	一、各项贷款 Total Loans	1145.60	31.70
1. 企业存款 Deposits by Enterprises	239.00	12.20	1. 工业生产企业贷款 Loans to Industrial Production Enterprises	224.30	-27.60
2. 财政存款 Fiscal Deposits	172.60	-16.30	2. 物资供销企业贷款 Loans to Material Supply and Sale Enterprises	151.30	25.30
3. 基本建设存款 Capital Construction Deposits	34.30	10.30	3. 商业企业贷款 Loans to Commercial Enterprises	693.80	26.60
4. 机关团体存款 Deposits by Government Agencies and Social Organizations	153.90	-7.20	4. 城镇集体企业贷款 Loans to Urban Collective Enterprises	19.60	2.40
5. 城镇储蓄存款 Urban Savings Deposits	85.10	11.80	5. 农业贷款 Loans to Agricultural Sector	56.60	5.00
6. 农村存款 Rural Deposits	91.40	-2.10	二、黄金占款 Position for Bullion and Silver Purchase	8.60	
二、流通中货币 Currency in Circulation	151.20	15.00	三、外汇占款 Position for Foreign Exchange Purchase	8.70	3.80
三、银行自有资金 Own Capital	138.90	-13.40			
四、其他 Others	96.50	25.20			
资金来源总计 Total Sources	**1162.90**	**35.50**	**资金运用总计 Total Uses**	**1162.90**	**35.50**

国家银行人民币信贷收支表

Sources and Uses of Credit Funds of State Banks（RMB）

（1973 年末）

（Year - end of 1973）

单位：亿元

Unit：100 Million Yuan

项　　目 Items	余　额 Balance	比年初增减额 Changes within the Year	项　　目 Items	余　额 Balance	比年初增减额 Changes within the Year
一、各项存款 Total Deposits	865.00	88.70	一、各项贷款 Total Loans	1269.00	123.40
1. 企业存款 Deposits by Enterprises	279.00	40.00	1. 工业生产企业贷款 Loans to Industrial Production Enterprises	231.10	6.80
2. 财政存款 Fiscal Deposits	160.80	-11.80	2. 物资供销企业贷款 Loans to Material Supply and Sale Enterprises	179.60	28.30
3. 基本建设存款 Capital Construction Deposits	51.30	17.00	3. 商业企业贷款 Loans to Commercial Enterprises	776.90	83.10
4. 机关团体存款 Deposits by Government Agencies and Social Organizations	172.50	18.60	4. 城镇集体企业贷款 Loans to Urban Collective Enterprises	22.60	3.00
5. 城镇储蓄存款 Urban Savings Deposits	94.10	9.00	5. 农业贷款 Loans to Agricultural Sector	58.80	2.20
6. 农村存款 Rural Deposits	107.30	15.90	二、黄金占款 Position for Bullion and Silver Purchase	8.60	
二、流通中货币 Currency in Circulation	166.10	14.90	三、外汇占款 Position for Foreign Exchange Purchase	5.90	-2.80
三、银行自有资金 Own Capital	183.10	44.20			
四、其他 Others	69.30	-27.20			
资金来源总计 Total Sources	**1283.50**	**120.60**	**资金运用总计 Total Uses**	**1283.50**	**120.60**

国家银行人民币信贷收支表
Sources and Uses of Credit Funds of State Banks (RMB)

(1974年末)

(Year－end of 1974)

单位：亿元

Unit: 100 Million Yuan

项目 Items	余额 Balance	比年初增减额 Changes within the Year	项目 Items	余额 Balance	比年初增减额 Changes within the Year
一、各项存款 Total Deposits	897.50	32.50	一、各项贷款 Total Loans	1353.50	84.50
1. 企业存款 Deposits by Enterprises	324.80	45.80	1. 工业生产企业贷款 Loans to Industrial Production Enterprises	266.70	35.60
2. 财政存款 Fiscal Deposits	137.30	－23.50	2. 物资供销企业贷款 Loans to Material Supply and Sale Enterprises	179.60	
3. 基本建设存款 Capital Construction Deposits	53.80	2.50	3. 商业企业贷款 Loans to Commercial Enterprises	815.00	38.10
4. 机关团体存款 Deposits by Government Agencies and Social Organizations	152.40	－20.10	4. 城镇集体企业贷款 Loans to Urban Collective Enterprises	28.20	5.60
5. 城镇储蓄存款 Urban Savings Deposits	105.80	11.70	5. 农业贷款 Loans to Agricultural Sector	64.00	5.20
6. 农村存款 Rural Deposits	123.40	16.10	二、黄金占款 Position for Bullion and Silver Purchase	12.20	3.60
二、流通中货币 Currency in Circulation	176.60	10.50	三、外汇占款 Position for Foreign Exchange Purchase	10.20	4.30
三、银行自有资金 Own Capital	222.60	39.50			
四、其他 Others	79.20	9.90			
资金来源总计 Total Sources	**1375.90**	**92.40**	**资金运用总计 Total Uses**	**1375.90**	**92.40**

国家银行人民币信贷收支表

Sources and Uses of Credit Funds of State Banks（RMB）

（1975 年末）

（Year－end of 1975）

单位：亿元

Unit：100 Million Yuan

项　目 Items	余　额 Balance	比年初增减额 Changes within the Year	项　目 Items	余　额 Balance	比年初增减额 Changes within the Year
一、各项存款 Total Deposits	975.10	77.60	一、各项贷款 Total Loans	1462.70	109.20
1. 企业存款 Deposits by Enterprises	362.70	37.90	1. 工业生产企业贷款 Loans to Industrial Production Enterprises	293.50	26.80
2. 财政存款 Fiscal Deposits	140.20	2.90	2. 物资供销企业贷款 Loans to Material Supply and Sale Enterprises	179.10	－0.50
3. 基本建设存款 Capital Construction Deposits	63.20	9.40	3. 商业企业贷款 Loans to Commercial Enterprises	884.70	69.70
4. 机关团体存款 Deposits by Government Agencies and Social Organizations	157.50	5.10	4. 城镇集体企业贷款 Loans to Urban Collective Enterprises	33.00	4.80
5. 城镇储蓄存款 Urban Savings Deposits	114.60	8.80	5. 农业贷款 Loans to Agricultural Sector	72.40	8.40
6. 农村存款 Rural Deposits	136.90	13.50	二、黄金占款 Position for Bullion and Silver Purchase	12.20	
二、流通中货币 Currency in Circulation	182.60	6.00	三、外汇占款 Position for Foreign Exchange Purchase	9.80	－0.40
三、银行自有资金 Own Capital	258.10	35.50			
四、其他 Others	68.90	－10.30			
资金来源总计 Total Sources	**1484.70**	**108.80**	**资金运用总计 Total Uses**	**1484.70**	**108.80**

国家银行人民币信贷收支表
Sources and Uses of Credit Funds of State Banks (RMB)

(1976年末)

(Year - end of 1976)

单位：亿元

Unit: 100 Million Yuan

项目 Items	余额 Balance	比年初增减额 Changes within the Year	项目 Items	余额 Balance	比年初增减额 Changes within the Year
一、各项存款 Total Deposits	978.50	3.40	一、各项贷款 Total Loans	1541.80	79.10
1. 企业存款 Deposits by Enterprises	389.80	27.10	1. 工业生产企业贷款 Loans to Industrial Production Enterprises	329.40	35.90
2. 财政存款 Fiscal Deposits	97.90	-42.30	2. 物资供销企业贷款 Loans to Material Supply and Sale Enterprises	173.30	-5.80
3. 基本建设存款 Capital Construction Deposits	65.80	2.60	3. 商业企业贷款 Loans to Commercial Enterprises	908.00	23.30
4. 机关团体存款 Deposits by Government Agencies and Social Organizations	166.10	8.60	4. 城镇集体企业贷款 Loans to Urban Collective Enterprises	40.70	7.70
5. 城镇储蓄存款 Urban Savings Deposits	122.20	7.60	5. 农业贷款 Loans to Agricultural Sector	90.40	18.00
6. 农村存款 Rural Deposits	136.70	-0.20	二、黄金占款 Position for Bullion and Silver Purchase	12.20	
二、流通中货币 Currency in Circulation	204.00	21.40	三、外汇占款 Position for Foreign Exchange Purchase	12.30	2.50
三、银行自有资金 Own Capital	303.00	44.90			
四、其他 Others	80.80	11.90			
资金来源总计 Total Sources	**1566.30**	**81.60**	**资金运用总计 Total Uses**	**1566.30**	**81.60**

国家银行人民币信贷收支表

Sources and Uses of Credit Funds of State Banks（RMB）

（1977年末）

（Year - end of 1977）

单位：亿元

Unit：100 Million Yuan

项　目 Items	余　额 Balance	比年初增减额 Changes within the Year	项　目 Items	余　额 Balance	比年初增减额 Changes within the Year
一、各项存款 Total Deposits	1063.80	85.30	一、各项贷款 Total Loans	1663.30	121.50
1. 企业存款 Deposits by Enterprises	384.70	-5.10	1. 工业生产企业贷款 Loans to Industrial Production Enterprises	334.20	4.80
2. 财政存款 Fiscal Deposits	151.90	54.00	2. 物资供销企业贷款 Loans to Material Supply and Sale Enterprises	187.90	14.60
3. 基本建设存款 Capital Construction Deposits	77.50	11.70	3. 商业企业贷款 Loans to Commercial Enterprises	996.90	88.90
4. 机关团体存款 Deposits by Government Agencies and Social Organizations	171.40	5.30	4. 城镇集体企业贷款 Loans to Urban Collective Enterprises	46.00	5.30
5. 城镇储蓄存款 Urban Savings Deposits	135.10	12.90	5. 农业贷款 Loans to Agricultural Sector	98.30	7.90
6. 农村存款 Rural Deposits	143.20	6.50	二、黄金占款 Position for Bullion and Silver Purchase	12.20	
二、流通中货币 Currency in Circulation	195.40	-8.60	三、外汇占款 Position for Foreign Exchange Purchase	23.80	11.50
三、银行自有资金 Own Capital	359.90	56.90			
四、其他 Others	80.20	-0.60			
资金来源总计 Total Sources	**1699.30**	**133.00**	**资金运用总计 Total Uses**	**1699.30**	**133.00**

国家银行人民币信贷收支表
Sources and Uses of Credit Funds of State Banks (RMB)

(1978年末)

(Year – end of 1978)

单位：亿元

Unit：100 Million Yuan

项目 Items	余额 Balance	比年初增减额 Changes within the Year	项目 Items	余额 Balance	比年初增减额 Changes within the Year
一、企业存款 Deposits by Enterprises	368.43	– 16.27	一、工业贷款 Loans to Industrial Sector	616.83	—
其中：工业存款 Of Which：Industrial Deposits	185.91	—	1. 工业生产企业贷款 Loans to Industrial Production Enterprises	322.67	—
专用基金存款 Special Fund Deposits	41.09	—	2. 工业供销企业贷款 Loans to Industrial Supply and Marketing Enterprises	125.17	—
二、财政存款 Fiscal Deposits	187.35	35.45			
1. 中央财政存款 Central Fiscal Deposits	72.60	—	其中：中央供销企业贷款 Of Which：Loans to Central Supply and Marketing Enterprises	64.58	—
2. 地方财政存款 Local Fiscal Deposits	86.16	—			
3. 地方财政预算外存款 Local Extra – budgetary Fiscal Deposits	28.59	—	3. 物资部门贷款 Loans to Materials Sector	90.38	—
三、基本建设存款 Capital Construction Deposits	109.63	32.13	其中：中央物资部门贷款 Of Which：Central Loans to Materials Sector	10.93	—
四、机关团体及部队存款 Deposits by Government Agencies, Social Organizations and Army	159.83	– 11.57	4. 集体工业贷款 Loans to Industrial Collective Enterprises	49.77	—
1. 机关团体存款 Deposits by Government Agencies and Social Organizations	89.52	—	5. 工业结算贷款 Industrial Settlement Loans	28.84	—
			二、商业贷款合计 Total Loans to Commercial Sector	1117.65	—
2. 部队存款 Deposits by Army	70.31	—	1. 商业贷款 Loans to Commercial Enterprises	488.77	—
五、城镇储蓄存款 Urban Savings Deposits	154.91	19.81	2. 供销合作贷款 Loans to Supply and Marketing Cooperatives	221.70	—
六、农村存款 Rural Deposits	154.41	11.21			
存款合计 Total Deposits	**1134.56**	**70.76**	3. 粮食贷款 Grain Loans	152.59	—
七、汇兑在途资金 Remittance in Transit	94.16	—	4. 外贸贷款 Loans to Foreign Trade Enterprises	200.73	—
八、财政增拨信贷资金 Additional Credit Funds from State Treasury	8.00	—	5. 其他商业贷款 Loans to Other Commercial Enterprises	53.86	—
			三、预购订金贷款 Loans for Advance Payment on Future Purchase	7.15	—
九、结益 Net Earnings	67.55	67.55			
十、流通中货币 Currency in Circulation	212.00	16.60	四、国营农业贷款 Loans to State Agricultural Enterprises	6.35	—
十一、银行自有资金 Own Capital	421.90	62.00	五、社队农业贷款 Loans to Agricultural Communities	101.98	—

续表
Continued

项　目 Items	余　额 Balance	比年初增减额 Changes within the Year	项　目 Items	余　额 Balance	比年初增减额 Changes within the Year
十二、其他 Others	-48.06	—	**贷款合计 Total Loans**	**1849.96**	**186.66**
			六、购买金银用款 Position for Bullion and Silver Purchase	12.20	
			七、购买外汇用款 Position for Foreign Exchange Purchase	14.34	-9.46
			八、上缴财政 Payment to Government Finance	13.61	13.61
资金来源总计 Total Sources	**1890.11**	—	**资金运用总计 Total Uses**	**1890.11**	—

国家银行人民币信贷收支表
Sources and Uses of Credit Funds of State Banks（RMB）
（1979 年末）
（Year – end of 1979）

单位：亿元
Unit：100 Million Yuan

项　目 Items	余　额 Balance	比年初增减额 Changes within the Year
一、企业存款 Deposits by Enterprises	468.91	100.48
二、财政存款 Fiscal Deposits	148.68	– 38.67
1. 中央财政存款 Central Fiscal Deposits	23.33	– 49.27
2. 地方财政存款 Local Fiscal Deposits	85.66	– 0.50
3. 地方财政预算外存款 Local Extra – budgetary Fiscal Deposits	39.69	11.10
三、基本建设存款 Capital Construction Deposits	131.30	21.67
四、机关团体及部队存款 Deposits by Government Agencies, Social Organizations and Army	184.88	25.05
1. 机关团体存款 Deposits by Government Agencies and Social Organizations	110.80	21.28
2. 部队存款 Deposits by Army	74.08	3.77
五、城镇储蓄存款 Urban Savings Deposits	202.56	47.65
六、农村存款 Rural Deposits	203.71	49.30
存款合计 Total Deposits	**1340.04**	**205.48**
七、汇兑在途资金 Remittance in Transit	93.31	– 0.85
八、财政增拨信贷资金 Additional Credit Funds from State Treasury	6.00	– 2.00
九、结益 Net Earnings	61.75	61.75
十、流通中货币 Currency in Circulation	267.70	55.70
十一、银行自有资金 Own Capital	471.10	49.20
十二、其他 Others	– 64.77	– 70.65
资金来源总计 Total Sources	**2175.13**	**298.63**

项　目 Items	余　额 Balance	比年初增减额 Changes within the Year
一、工业贷款 Loans to Industrial Sector	670.64	53.81
1. 工业生产企业贷款 Loans to Industrial Production Enterprises	344.49	21.82
2. 工业供销企业贷款 Loans to Industrial Supply and Marketing Enterprises	135.33	10.16
3. 物资部门贷款 Loans to Materials Sector	106.79	16.41
4. 集体工业贷款 Loans to Industrial Collective Enterprises	57.51	7.74
5. 工业结算贷款 Industrial Settlement Loans	26.52	– 2.32
二、商业贷款合计 Total Loans to Commercial Sector	1232.25	114.60
1. 商业贷款 Loans to Commercial Enterprises	512.91	24.14
2. 供销合作贷款 Loans to Supply and Marketing Cooperatives	229.35	7.65
3. 粮食贷款 Grain Loans	216.32	63.73
4. 外贸贷款 Loans to Foreign Trade Enterprises	219.56	18.83
5. 其他商业贷款 Loans to Other Commercial Enterprises	54.11	0.25
三、预购订金贷款 Loans for Advance Payment on Future Purchase	6.98	– 0.17
四、国营农业贷款 Loans to State Agricultural Enterprises	6.86	0.51
五、社队农业贷款 Loans to Agricultural Communities	122.90	20.92
贷款合计 Total Loans	**2039.63**	**189.67**
六、购买金银用款 Position for Bullion and Silver Purchase	12.20	
七、购买外汇用款 Position for Foreign Exchange Purchase	20.58	6.24
八、上缴财政 Payment to Government Finance	12.52	12.52
九、财政透支和借款 Overdraft by State Finance	90.20	90.20
资金运用总计 Total Uses	**2175.13**	**298.63**

国家银行人民币信贷收支表

Sources and Uses of Credit Funds of State Banks（RMB）

（1980 年末）

（Year – end of 1980）

单位：亿元

Unit：100 Million Yuan

项目 Items	余额 Balance	比年初增减额 Changes within the Year
一、企业存款 Deposits by Enterprises	561.01	92.10
二、财政存款 Fiscal Deposits	160.68	12.00
1. 中央财政存款 Central Fiscal Deposits	26.40	3.07
2. 地方财政存款 Local Fiscal Deposits	92.54	6.88
3. 地方财政预算外存款 Local Extra – budgetary Fiscal Deposits	41.74	2.05
三、基本建设存款 Capital Construction Deposits	173.37	42.07
四、机关团体存款 Deposits by Government Agencies and Social Organizations	146.94	36.14
五、部队存款 Deposits by Army	81.95	7.87
六、城镇储蓄存款 Urban Savings Deposits	278.77	76.21
1. 城镇储蓄存款 Urban Savings Deposits	249.57	—
2. 集镇储蓄存款 Market Town Savings Deposits	27.64	—
3. 华侨通讯存款 Overseas Chinese Communication Deposits	1.56	—
七、农村存款 Rural Deposits	241.82	38.11
存款合计 **Total Deposits**	**1644.54**	**304.50**
八、汇兑在途资金 Remittance in Transit	105.71	12.40
九、财政增拨信贷资金 Additional Credit Funds from State Treasury		- 6.00
十、结益 Net Earnings	51.78	51.78
十一、流通中货币 Currency in Circulation	346.20	78.50
十二、银行自有资金 Own Capital	477.93	6.83

项目 Items	余额 Balance	比年初增减额 Changes within the Year
一、工业贷款 Loans to Industrial Sector	743.76	73.12
1. 工业生产企业贷款 Loans to Industrial Production Enterprises	401.35	56.86
2. 工业供销企业贷款 Loans to Industrial Supply and Marketing Enterprises	138.59	3.26
3. 物资部门贷款 Loans to Materials Sector	97.40	- 9.39
4. 集体工业贷款 Loans to Industrial Collective Enterprises	86.31	28.80
5. 工业结算贷款 Industrial Settlement Loans	20.11	- 6.41
二、中短期设备贷款 Short and Medium – term Equipment Loans	47.51	47.51
三、商业贷款合计 Total Loans to Commercial Sector	1437.14	204.89
1. 商业贷款 Loans to Commercial Enterprises	544.38	31.47
2. 供销合作贷款 Loans to Supply and Marketing Cooperatives	278.66	49.31
3. 粮食贷款 Grain Loans	246.69	30.37
4. 外贸贷款 Loans to Foreign Trade Enterprises	308.63	89.07
5. 其他商业贷款 Loans to Other Commercial Enterprises	58.78	4.67
四、预购订金贷款 Loans for Advance Payment on Future Purchase	7.87	0.89
五、国营农业贷款 Loans to State Agricultural Enterprises	9.41	2.55
六、社队农业贷款 Loans to Agricultural Communities	154.80	31.90
贷款合计 **Total Loans**	**2400.49**	**360.86**
七、购买金银用款 Position for Bullion and Silver Purchase	12.20	

续表
Continued

项 目 Items	余 额 Balance	比年初增减额 Changes within the Year	项 目 Items	余 额 Balance	比年初增减额 Changes within the Year
十三、其他 Others	-19.61	-4.07	八、购买外汇用款 Position for Foreign Exchange Purchase	-8.34	-28.92
			九、上缴财政 Payment to Government Finance	32.00	32.00
			十、中央财政透支及借支 Overdraft by State Finance	170.20	80.00
资金来源总计 Total Sources	**2606.55**	**443.94**	**资金运用总计 Total Uses**	**2606.55**	**443.94**

国家银行人民币信贷收支表

Sources and Uses of Credit Funds of State Banks（RMB）

（1981 年末）

（Year - end of 1981）

单位：亿元

Unit：100 Million Yuan

项 目 Items	余 额 Balance	比年初增减额 Changes within the Year	项 目 Items	余 额 Balance	比年初增减额 Changes within the Year
一、企业存款 Deposits by Enterprises	676.96	115.95	一、工业贷款 Loans to Industrial Sector	839.13	95.37
二、财政存款 Fiscal Deposits	194.29	33.61	1. 工业生产企业贷款 Loans to Industrial Production Enterprises	479.49	78.14
1. 中央财政存款 Central Fiscal Deposits	37.05	10.65	2. 工业供销企业贷款 Loans to Industrial Supply and Marketing Enterprises	152.38	13.79
2. 地方财政存款 Local Fiscal Deposits	111.11	18.57	3. 物资部门贷款 Loans to Materials Sector	88.86	-8.54
3. 地方财政预算外存款 Local Extra - budgetary Fiscal Deposits	46.13	4.39	4. 集体工业贷款 Loans to Industrial Collective Enterprises	98.71	12.40
三、基本建设存款 Capital Construction Deposits	228.88	55.51	5. 工业结算贷款 Industrial Settlement Loans	19.69	-0.42
四、机关团体存款 Deposits by Government Agencies and Social Organizations	183.81	36.87	二、中短期设备贷款 Short and Medium - term Equipment Loans	83.74	36.23
五、部队存款 Deposits by Army	90.91	8.96	三、商业贷款合计 Total Loans to Commercial Sector	1639.21	202.07
六、城镇储蓄存款 Urban Savings Deposits	353.80	75.03	1. 商业贷款 Loans to Commercial Enterprises	539.89	-4.49
1. 城镇储蓄存款 Urban Savings Deposits	309.94	60.37	2. 供销合作贷款 Loans to Supply and Marketing Cooperatives	316.08	37.42
2. 集镇储蓄存款 Market Town Savings Deposits	42.22	14.58	3. 粮食贷款 Grain Loans	298.31	51.62
3. 华侨通讯存款 Overseas Chinese Communication Deposits	1.64	0.08	4. 外贸贷款 Loans to Foreign Trade Enterprises	356.89	48.26
七、农村存款 Rural Deposits	278.47	36.65	5. 其他商业贷款 Loans to Other Commercial Enterprises	128.04	69.26
八、其他存款 Other Deposits	24.55	24.55	四、个体工商贷款 Loans to Self - employed Eatities	0.47	0.47
存款合计 Total Deposits	**2031.67**	**387.13**	五、预购订金贷款 Loans for Advance Payment on Future Purchase	7.39	-0.48
九、汇兑在途资金 Remittance in Transit	129.73	24.02	六、国营农业贷款 Loans to State Agricultural Enterprises	16.82	7.41
十、流通中货币 Currency in Circulation	396.34	50.10	七、社队农业贷款 Loans to Agricultural Communities	168.34	13.54
十一、银行自有资金 Own Capital	497.05	19.12	八、其他贷款 Other Loans	9.75	9.75
十二、当年结益 Net Earnings	50.66	50.66			
十三、其他 Others	-36.80	-36.93			

续表
Continued

项 目 Items	余 额 Balance	比年初增减额 Changes within the Year	项 目 Items	余 额 Balance	比年初增减额 Changes within the Year
			贷款合计 **Total Loans**	**2764.85**	**364.36**
			九、金银库存占款 Position for Bullion and Silver Purchase	12.00	-0.20
			十、外汇库存占款 Position for Foreign Exchange Purchase	89.60	97.94
			十一、上缴财政 Payment to Government Finance	32.00	32.00
			十二、中央财政透支 Overdraft by State Finance	170.20	
资金来源总计 **Total Sources**	**3068.65**	**494.10**	**资金运用总计** **Total Uses**	**3068.65**	**494.10**

国家银行人民币信贷收支表

Sources and Uses of Credit Funds of State Banks（RMB）

（1982 年末）

（Year - end of 1982）

单位：亿元

Unit：100 Million Yuan

项目 Items	余额 Balance	比年初增减额 Changes within the Year	项目 Items	余额 Balance	比年初增减额 Changes within the Year
一、企业存款 Deposits by Enterprises	761.64	84.68	一、工业贷款 Loans to Industrial Sector	866.58	27.45
二、财政存款 Fiscal Deposits	175.76	- 18.53	1. 工业生产企业贷款 Loans to Industrial Production Enterprises	492.66	13.17
1. 中央财政存款 Central Fiscal Deposits	27.62	- 9.43	2. 物资供销企业贷款 Loans to Material Supply and Sale Enterprises	239.85	—
2. 地方财政存款 Local Fiscal Deposits	99.58	- 11.53	3. 集体工业贷款 Loans to Industrial Collective Enterprises	102.13	3.42
3. 地方财政预算外存款 Local Extra - budgetary Fiscal Deposits	48.56	2.43	4. 工业结算贷款 Industrial Settlement Loans	19.95	0.26
三、基本建设存款 Capital Construction Deposits	284.80	55.92	5. 小额贷款 Petty Loans	11.99	—
四、机关团体存款 Deposits by Government Agencies and Social Organizations	218.24	34.43	二、中短期设备贷款 Short and Medium - term Equipment Loans	138.62	54.88
五、部队存款 Deposits by Army	113.19	22.28	三、基建贷款 Capital Construction Investment Loans	13.36	13.36
六、储蓄存款 Savings Deposits	447.33	93.53	四、商业贷款合计 Total Loans to Commercial Sector	1806.60	167.39
1. 城镇储蓄存款 Urban Savings Deposits	391.64	81.70	1. 商业贷款 Loans to Commercial Enterprises	553.02	13.13
2. 集镇储蓄存款 Market Town Savings Deposits	53.76	11.54	2. 供销合作贷款 Loans to Supply and Marketing Cooperatives	346.76	30.68
3. 华侨通讯存款 Overseas Chinese Communication Deposits	1.93	0.29	3. 粮食贷款 Grain Loans	349.65	51.34
七、农村存款 Rural Deposits	329.94	51.47	4. 外贸贷款 Loans to Foreign Trade Enterprises	403.03	46.14
八、信托及其他存款 Trust and Other Deposits	31.14	6.59	5. 其他商业贷款 Loans to Other Commercial Enterprises	154.14	26.10
存款合计 Total Deposits	**2362.04**	**330.37**	五、个体工商贷款 Loans to Self - employed Entities	0.55	0.08
九、汇兑在途资金 Remittance in Transit	139.64	9.91	六、预购订金贷款 Loans for Advance Payment on Future Purchase	7.43	0.04
十、流通中货币 Currency in Circulation	439.12	42.78	七、国营农业贷款 Loans to State Agricultural Enterprises	19.81	2.99
十一、银行自有资金 Own Capital	518.29	21.24	八、社队农业贷款 Loans to Agricultural Communities	185.21	16.87
十二、当年结益 Net Earnings	103.78	103.78			

续表
Continued

项　目 Items	余　额 Balance	比年初增减额 Changes within the Year	项　目 Items	余　额 Balance	比年初增减额 Changes within the Year
十三、其他 Others	-43.60	-25.46	九、信托及其他贷款 Trust and Other Loans	14.11	4.36
			贷款合计 **Total Loans**	**3052.27**	**287.42**
			十、金银库存占款 Position for Bullion and Silver Purchase	12.00	
			十一、外汇库存占款 Position for Foreign Exchange Purchase	217.70	128.10
			十二、上缴利润和税金 Payment of Profits and Taxes	67.10	67.10
			十三、财政透支和借款 Overdraft by State Finance	170.20	
资金来源总计 **Total Sources**	**3519.27**	**482.62**	**资金运用总计** **Total Uses**	**3519.27**	**482.62**

国家银行人民币信贷收支表

Sources and Uses of Credit Funds of State Banks（RMB）

（1983年末）

（Year - end of 1983）

单位：亿元

Unit：100 Million Yuan

项　目 Items	余额 Balance	比年初增减额 Changes within the Year	项　目 Items	余额 Balance	比年初增减额 Changes within the Year
一、企业存款 Deposits by Enterprises	864.99	103.35	一、工业贷款 Loans to Industrial Sector	973.53	106.95
二、财政存款 Fiscal Deposits	229.89	54.13	1. 工业生产企业贷款 Loans to Industrial Production Enterprises	545.72	53.06
1. 中央财政存款 Central Fiscal Deposits	51.39	23.77	2. 物资供销企业贷款 Loans to Material Supply and Sale Enterprises	268.79	28.94
2. 地方财政存款 Local Fiscal Deposits	125.23	25.65	3. 集体工业贷款 Loans to Industrial Collective Enterprises	120.93	18.80
3. 地方财政预算外存款 Local Extra - budgetary Fiscal Deposits	53.27	4.71	4. 工业结算贷款 Industrial Settlement Loans	22.66	2.71
三、基本建设存款 Capital Construction Deposits	299.67	14.87	5. 小额贷款 Petty Loans	15.43	3.44
四、机关团体存款 Deposits by Government Agencies and Social Organizations	253.42	35.18	二、中短期设备贷款 Short and Medium - term Equipment Loans	163.83	25.21
五、部队存款 Deposits by Army	118.27	5.08	三、基建贷款 Capital Construction Loans	28.26	14.90
六、储蓄存款 Savings Deposits	572.60	125.27	四、商业贷款合计 Total Loans to Commercial Sector	2003.11	196.51
1. 城镇储蓄存款 Urban Savings Deposits	502.70	111.06	1. 商业贷款 Loans to Commercial Enterprises	556.20	3.18
2. 集镇储蓄存款 Market Town Savings Deposits	66.96	13.20	2. 供销合作贷款 Loans to Supply and Marketing Cooperatives	419.45	72.69
3. 华侨通讯存款 Overseas Chinese Communication Deposits	2.94	1.01	3. 粮食贷款 Grain Loans	445.02	95.37
七、农村存款 Rural Deposits	391.31	61.37	4. 外贸贷款 Loans to Foreign Trade Enterprises	410.32	7.29
八、信托及其他存款 Trust and Other Deposits	34.09	2.95	5. 其他商业贷款 Loans to Other Commercial Enterprises	172.12	17.98
存款合计 Total Deposits	**2764.24**	**402.20**	五、个体工商贷款 Loans to Self - employed Entities	1.50	0.95
九、汇兑在途资金 Remittance in Transit	147.89	8.25	六、预购订金贷款 Loans for Advance Payment on Future Purchase	6.71	-0.72
十、流通中货币 Currency in Circulation	529.78	90.66	七、国营农业贷款 Loans to State Agricultural Enterprises	25.47	5.66
十一、银行自有资金 Own Capital	547.36	29.07	八、社队农业贷款 Loans to Agricultural Communities	199.34	14.13
十二、当年结益 Net Earnings	120.60	120.60			

续表
Continued

项 目 Items	余 额 Balance	比年初增减额 Changes within the Year	项 目 Items	余 额 Balance	比年初增减额 Changes within the Year
十三、其他 Others	-115.97	-109.05	九、信托及其他贷款 Trust and Other Loans	17.42	3.31
			贷款合计 **Total Loans**	**3419.17**	**366.90**
			十、金银库存占款 Position for Bullion and Silver Purchase	12.00	
			十一、外汇库存占款 Position for Foreign Exchange Purchase	266.10	48.40
			十二、上缴利润和税金 Payment of Profits and Taxes	97.03	97.03
			十三、财政透支和借款 Overdraft by State Finance	199.60	29.40
资金来源总计 **Total Sources**	**3993.90**	**541.73**	**资金运用总计** **Total Uses**	**3993.90**	**541.73**

国家银行人民币信贷收支表

Sources and Uses of Credit Funds of State Banks（RMB）

（1984 年末）

（Year – end of 1984）

单位：亿元

Unit：100 Million Yuan

项　目 Items	余　额 Balance	比年初增减额 Changes within the Year	项　目 Items	余　额 Balance	比年初增减额 Changes within the Year
一、企业存款 Deposits by Enterprises	1251.79	386.80	一、流动资金贷款 Loans for Circulation Funds	3763.04	—
二、财政存款 Fiscal Deposits	210.93	– 18.96	1. 工业贷款 Loans to Industrial Sector	1316.88	—
1. 中央财政存款 Central Fiscal Deposits	52.80	1.41	2. 商业贷款 Loans to Commercial Sector	2346.53	—
2. 地方财政存款 Local Fiscal Deposits	105.09	– 20.14	3. 个体工商业贷款 Loans to Self – employed Entities	10.62	—
3. 地方财政预算外存款 Local Extra – budgetary Fiscal Deposits	53.04	– 0.23	4. 信托及其他贷款 Trust and Other Loans	89.01	—
三、基本建设存款 Capital Construction Deposits	335.67	36.00	二、固定资产贷款 Fixed Asset Loans	294.03	—
四、机关团体存款 Deposits by Government Agencies and Social Organizations	282.22	28.80	1. 技术改造贷款 Technical Improvement Loans	229.37	—
			2. 基本建设贷款 Capital Construction Loans	52.98	—
五、部队存款 Deposits by Army	91.79	– 26.48	3. 发展少数民族经济贷款 Loans to Ethnic Minority Regions	5.47	—
六、城镇储蓄存款 Urban Savings Deposits	776.58	203.98	4. 特种外汇兑换 Special Exchange for Foreign Exchage	6.21	—
七、农村存款 Rural Deposits	370.21	– 21.10	三、农业贷款 Loans to Agricultural Sectors	366.54	—
八、信托及其他存款 Trust and Other Deposits	119.47	85.38	其中：社队农业贷款 Of Which：Loans to Agricultural Communities	309.05	—
存款合计 **Total Deposits**	**3438.66**	**674.42**			
九、汇兑在途资金 Remittance in Transit	324.76	176.87	**贷款合计** **Total Loans**	**4423.61**	**1004.44**
十、流通中货币 Currency in Circulation	792.11	262.33	四、金银库存占款 Position for Bullion and Silver Purchase	12.00	
十一、银行自有资金 Own Capital	573.17	25.81	五、外汇库存占款 Position for Foreign Exchange Purchase	263.60	– 2.50
十二、当年结益 Net Earnings	124.49	124.49	六、上缴财政利润和税金 Payment of Profits and Taxes to Government Finance	105.53	105.53
十三、其他 Others	– 132.47	– 40.07	七、财政透支和借款 Overdraft by State Finance	260.80	61.20
			八、待核销机电产品贷款损失 Mechanical and Electrical Products Loan Loss to be Written – off	55.18	55.18
资金来源总计 **Total Sources**	**5120.72**	**1223.85**	**资金运用总计** **Total Uses**	**5120.72**	**1223.85**

国家银行人民币信贷收支表

Sources and Uses of Credit Funds of State Banks (RMB)

(1985 年末)

(Year - end of 1985)

单位：亿元

Unit: 100 Million Yuan

项目 Items	余额 Balance	比年初增减额 Changes within the Year	项目 Items	余额 Balance	比年初增减额 Changes within the Year
一、企业存款 Deposits by Enterprises	1735.89	484.10	一、流动资金贷款 Loans for Circulation Funds	4554.19	791.15
二、财政存款 Fiscal Deposits	404.10	193.17	1. 工业贷款 Loans to Industrial Sector	1609.96	293.08
1. 中央财政存款 Central Fiscal Deposits	138.98	86.18	2. 商业贷款 Loans to Commercial Sector	2723.49	376.96
2. 地方财政存款 Local Fiscal Deposits	159.95	54.86	3. 建筑企业流动资金贷款 Working Capital Loans to Construction Enterprises	93.56	93.56
3. 地方财政预算外存款 Local Extra - budgetary Fiscal Deposits	50.57	- 2.47	4. 个体工商业贷款 Loans to Self - employed Entities	10.65	0.03
4. 建行财政存款 Fiscal Deposits by Construction Bank	54.60	54.60	5. 信托贷款 Trust Loans	97.83	—
三、基本建设存款 Capital Construction Deposits		- 335.67	6. 其他贷款 Other Loans	18.70	—
四、机关团体存款 Deposits by Government Agencies and Social Organizations	249.70	- 32.52	二、农业贷款 Loans to Agricultural Sector	409.23	42.69
五、部队存款 Deposits by Army	76.44	- 15.35	其中：集体农业贷款 Of Which: Loans to Agricultural Collectives	345.27	36.02
六、城镇储蓄存款 Urban Savings Deposits	1057.76	281.18	三、固定资产贷款 Fixed Asset Loans	686.25	392.22
七、农村存款 Rural Deposits	449.10	78.89	1. 技术改造贷款 Technical Improvement Loans	417.55	188.18
八、信托存款 Trust Deposits	118.41	—	2. 基本建设贷款 Capital Construction Loans	213.14	160.16
九、其他存款 Other Deposits	153.33	—	3. 发展少数民族经济贷款 Loans to Ethnic Minority Regions	12.54	7.07
存款合计 Total Deposits	**4244.73**	**806.07**	4. 开发性低息贷款 Cheap Money for Development	43.02	43.02
十、汇兑在途资金 Remittance in Transit	366.74	41.98	5. 特种外汇兑换 Special Foreign Exchange		- 6.21
十一、流通中货币 Currency in Circulation	987.83	195.72	四、购买外汇额度人民币专项贷款额度 Earmarked Loans for the Purchase of Foreign Exchange Quota	30.57	30.57
十二、银行自有资金 Own Capital	738.31	165.14	五、其他专项贷款 Other Earmarked Loans	151.80	151.80
十三、当年结益 Net Earnings	207.58	207.58	**贷款合计 Total Loans**	**5832.04**	**1408.43**
十四、其他 Others	- 144.39	- 30.88	六、金银库存占款 Position for Bullion and Silver Purchase	12.00	

续表
Continued

项 目 Items	余 额 Balance	比年初增减额 Changes within the Year	项 目 Items	余 额 Balance	比年初增减额 Changes within the Year
			七、外汇库存占款 Position for Foreign Exchange Purchase	93.10	-170.50
			八、上缴财政税利 Payment of Profits and Taxes to Government Finance	132.18	132.18
			九、财政透支和借款 Overdraft by State Finance	275.10	14.30
			十、待核销商品贷款损失 Commodity Loan Loss to be Written - off	56.38	1.20
资金来源总计 Total Sources	**6400.80**	**1385.61**	**资金运用总计 Total Uses**	**6400.80**	**1385.61**

国家银行人民币信贷收支表

Sources and Uses of Credit Funds of State Banks (RMB)

(1986年末)

(Year-end of 1986)

单位：亿元

Unit: 100 Million Yuan

项目 Items	余额 Balance	比年初增减额 Changes within the Year	项目 Items	余额 Balance	比年初增减额 Changes within the Year
一、企业存款 Deposits by Enterprises	2244.94	509.05	一、流动资金贷款 Loans for Circulation Funds	5631.49	1175.13
二、财政存款 Fiscal Deposits	348.61	-55.49	1. 工业贷款 Loans to Industrial Sector	2225.14	615.18
1. 中央财政存款 Central Fiscal Deposits	136.84	-2.14	2. 商业贷款 Loans to Commercial Sector	3182.04	458.55
2. 地方财政存款 Local Fiscal Deposits	120.48	-39.47	3. 建筑企业流动资金贷款 Working Capital Loans to Construction Enterprises	132.06	38.50
3. 地方财政预算外存款 Local Extra-budgetary Fiscal Deposits	64.45	13.88	4. 个体工商业贷款 Loans to Self-employed Entities	10.82	0.17
4. 建行财政存款 Fiscal Deposits by Construction Bank	26.84	-27.76	5. 其他贷款 Other Loans	81.43	62.73
三、机关团体存款 Deposits by Government Agencies and Social Organizations	310.27	60.57	二、农业贷款 Loans to Agricultural Sector	570.13	160.90
四、部队存款 Deposits by Army	78.85	2.41	其中：集体农业贷款 Of Which: Loans to Agricultural Collectives	477.14	131.87
五、城镇储蓄存款 Urban Savings Deposits	1470.77	413.01	三、固定资产贷款 Fixed Asset Loans	975.97	289.72
六、农村存款 Rural Deposits	560.80	111.70	1. 技术改造贷款 Technical Improvement Loans	585.87	168.32
七、信托存款 Trust Deposits	204.86	86.45	2. 基本建设贷款 Capital Construction Loans	297.89	84.75
八、其他存款 Other Deposits	227.19	73.86	3. 发展少数民族经济贷款 Loans to Ethnic Minority Regions	20.16	7.62
存款合计 Total Deposits	**5446.29**	**1201.56**	4. 开发性低息贷款 Cheap Money for Development	72.05	29.03
九、汇兑在途资金 Remittance in Transit	428.98	62.24	四、购买外汇额度人民币专项贷款额度 Earmarked Loans for the Purchase of Foreign Exchange Quota	43.21	12.64
十、流通中货币 Currency in Circulation	1218.36	230.53	五、其他专项贷款 Other Earmarked Loans	203.24	51.44
十一、银行自有资金 Own Capital	779.29	40.98	六、信托贷款 Trust Loans	173.71	75.88
十二、当年结益 Net Earnings	259.54	259.54	**贷款合计 Total Loans**	**7597.75**	**1765.71**
十三、其他 Others	146.21	215.20	七、金银库存占款 Position for Bullion and Silver Purchase	12.00	
			八、外汇库存占款 Position for Foreign Exchange Purchase	38.10	-55.00

续表
Continued

项 目 Items	余 额 Balance	比年初增减额 Changes within the Year	项 目 Items	余 额 Balance	比年初增减额 Changes within the Year
			九、上缴财政税利 Payment of Profits and Taxes to Government Finance	177.10	177.10
			十、财政透支和借款 Overdraft by State Finance	370.10	95.00
			十一、待核销商品贷款损失 Commodity Loan Loss to be Written - off	83.62	27.24
资金来源总计 Total Sources	**8278.67**	**2010.05**	**资金运用总计 Total Uses**	**8278.67**	**2010.05**

国家银行人民币信贷收支表

Sources and Uses of Credit Funds of State Banks (RMB)

(1987年末)

(Year - end of 1987)

单位：亿元

Unit: 100 Million Yuan

项目 Items	余额 Balance	比年初增减额 Changes within the Year	项目 Items	余额 Balance	比年初增减额 Changes within the Year
一、企业存款 Deposits by Enterprises	2660.52	415.58	一、流动资金贷款 Loans for Circulation Funds	6606.15	974.66
二、财政存款 Fiscal Deposits	331.98	-16.63	1. 工业贷款 Loans to Industrial Sector	2615.94	390.80
1. 中央财政存款 Central Fiscal Deposits	116.56	-20.28	2. 商业贷款 Loans to Commercial Sector	3614.60	432.56
2. 地方财政存款 Local Fiscal Deposits	144.66	24.18	3. 建筑企业流动资金贷款 Working Capital Loans to Construction Enterprises	170.56	38.50
3. 地方财政预算外存款 Local Extra - budgetary Fiscal Deposits	54.57	-9.88	4. 个体工商业贷款 Loans to Self - employed Entities	15.51	4.69
4. 建行财政存款 Fiscal Deposits by Construction Bank	16.19	-10.65	5. 其他贷款 Other Loans	189.54	108.11
三、机关团体存款 Deposits by Government Agencies and Social Organizations	347.18	36.91	二、农业贷款 Loans to Agricultural Sector	691.11	120.98
四、部队存款 Deposits by Army	101.51	22.66	其中：集体农业贷款 Of Which: Loans to Agricultural Collectives	574.52	97.38
五、城镇储蓄存款 Urban Savings Deposits	2067.41	596.64	三、固定资产贷款 Fixed Asset Loans	1221.61	245.64
六、农村存款 Rural Deposits	631.95	71.15	1. 技术改造贷款 Technical Improvement Loans	696.22	110.35
七、信托存款 Trust Deposits	162.52	-42.34	2. 基本建设贷款 Capital Construction Loans	418.84	120.95
八、其他存款 Other Deposits	348.18	120.99	3. 发展少数民族经济贷款 Loans to Ethnic Minority Regions	29.31	9.15
存款合计 Total Deposits	**6651.25**	**1204.96**	4. 开发性低息贷款 Cheap Money for Development	77.24	5.19
九、汇兑在途资金 Remittance in Transit	229.07	-199.91	四、购买外汇额度人民币专项贷款额度 Earmarked Loans for the Purchase of Foreign Exchange Quota	60.53	17.32
十、流通中货币 Currency in Circulation	1454.48	236.12	五、其他专项贷款 Other Earmarked Loans	285.53	82.29
十一、银行自有资金 Own Capital	828.12	48.83	六、信托贷款 Trust Loans	149.17	-24.54
十二、当年结益 Net Earnings	292.88	292.88	**贷款合计 Total Loans**	**9014.10**	**1416.35**
十三、其他 Others	457.51	228.86	七、金银库存占款 Position for Bullion and Silver Purchase	12.00	
			八、外汇库存占款 Position for Foreign Exchange Purchase	132.10	94.00

续表
Continued

项 目 Items	余 额 Balance	比年初增减额 Changes within the Year	项 目 Items	余 额 Balance	比年初增减额 Changes within the Year
			九、上缴财政税利 Payment of Profits and Taxes to Government Finance	183.38	183.38
			十、财政透支和借款 Overdraft by State Finance	515.80	145.70
			十一、待核销商品贷款损失 Commodity Loan Loss to be Written - off	55.93	-27.69
资金来源总计 Total Sources	**9913.31**	**1811.74**	**资金运用总计 Total Uses**	**9913.31**	**1811.74**

国家银行人民币信贷收支表
Sources and Uses of Credit Funds of State Banks (RMB)
(1988年末)
(Year-end of 1988)

单位：亿元
Unit: 100 Million Yuan

项 目 Items	余 额 Balance	比年初增减额 Changes within the Year	项 目 Items	余 额 Balance	比年初增减额 Changes within the Year
一、各项存款 Total Deposits	7448.82	797.57	一、各项贷款 Total Loans	10551.35	1537.25
1. 企业存款 Deposits by Enterprises	2936.58	276.06	1. 流动资金贷款 Loans for Circulation Funds	8026.14	1419.99
2. 财政存款 Fiscal Deposits	294.10	-37.88	(1) 工业贷款 Loans to Industrial Sector	3118.75	502.81
(1) 中央财政存款 Central Fiscal Deposits	53.19	-63.37	(2) 商业贷款 Loans to Commercial Sector	4224.82	610.22
(2) 地方财政存款 Local Fiscal Deposits	169.08	24.42	(3) 建筑业贷款 Loans to Construction Sector	252.64	82.08
(3) 财政预算外存款 Local Extra-budgetary Fiscal Deposits	55.68	1.11	(4) 个体工商业贷款 Loans to Self-employed Entities	19.32	3.81
			(5) 乡镇企业贷款 Loans to Village and Township Enterprises	410.61	—
(4) 建行财政存款 Fiscal Deposits by Construction Bank	8.50	-7.69			
(5) 财政性定期存款 Fiscal Time Deposits	7.65	7.65	2. 农业贷款 Loans to Agricultural Sector	403.61	-287.50
3. 机关团体部队存款 Deposits by Government Agencies, Social Organizations and Army	392.68	-56.01	3. 固定资产贷款 Fixed Asset Loans	1558.20	336.59
			(1) 基本建设贷款 Capital Construction Loans	501.17	82.33
4. 城镇储蓄存款 Urban Savings Deposits	2659.16	591.75	(2) 技术改造贷款 Technical Improvement Loans	892.93	196.71
其中：定期 Of Which: Time Deposits	2045.16	—	(3) 老少边穷经济贷款 Loans to Former-revolutionary Base Areas, Areas Inhabited by Minority Nationalities, Remote and Border Areas and Poverty-stricken Areas for Economic Development	39.09	—
5. 农村存款 Rural Deposits	669.53	37.58			
6. 信托类存款 Trust Deposits	115.24	-47.28			
7. 其他类存款 Other Deposits	381.53	33.35	(4) 地方经济开发贷款 Loans for Local Economic Development	125.01	—
二、金融债券 Financial Bonds	75.55	—			
三、代理发行债券 Agency Bonds Issue	0.02	—	4. 信托类贷款 Trust Loans	96.03	-53.14
四、流通中货币 Currency in Circulation	2134.03	679.55	5. 其他类贷款 Other Loans	467.37	—
五、信贷基金 Credit Funds	961.93	—	二、购买债券 Bond Purchase	110.38	—
六、当年结益 Net Earnings	362.86	362.86	三、金银占款 Position for Bullion and Silver Purchase	12.00	

续表
Continued

项　目 Items	余　额 Balance	比年初增减额 Changes within the Year	项　目 Items	余　额 Balance	比年初增减额 Changes within the Year
七、汇兑在途资金 Remittance in Transit	218.37	－10.70	四、外汇占款 Position for Foreign Exchange Purchase	158.40	26.30
八、其他 Others	590.35	—	五、库存现金 Cash in Vault	105.04	—
			六、上缴财政税利 Payment of Profits and Taxes to Government Finance	222.33	222.33
			七、财政透支和借款 Overdraft by State Finance	576.50	60.70
			八、待核销贷款损失 Loan Loss to be Written－off	55.93	
资金来源总计 Total Sources	**11791.93**	**—**	**资金运用总计 Total Uses**	**11791.93**	**—**

国家银行人民币信贷收支表
Sources and Uses of Credit Funds of State Banks（RMB）

（1989 年末）

（Year－end of 1989）

单位：亿元

Unit：100 Million Yuan

项　目 Items	余　额 Balance	比年初增减额 Changes within the Year	项　目 Items	余　额 Balance	比年初增减额 Changes within the Year
一、各项存款 Total Deposits	9027.03	1578.21	一、各项贷款 Total Loans	12402.85	1851.50
1. 企业存款 Deposits by Enterprises	3085.36	148.78	1. 流动资金贷款 Loans for Circulation Funds	9493.41	1467.27
2. 财政存款 Fiscal Deposits	460.79	166.69	（1）工业贷款 Loans to Industrial Sector	3817.92	699.17
（1）中央财政存款 Central Fiscal Deposits	114.97	61.78	（2）商业贷款 Loans to Commercial Sector	4952.86	728.04
（2）地方财政存款 Local Fiscal Deposits	227.38	58.30	（3）建筑业贷款 Loans to Construction Sector	283.69	31.05
（3）财政预算外存款 Local Extra-budgetary Fiscal Deposits	67.98	12.30	（4）个体工商业贷款 Loans to Self－employed Entities	15.39	－3.93
			（5）乡镇企业贷款 Loans to Village and Township Enterprises	423.55	12.94
（4）建行财政存款 Fiscal Deposits by Construction Bank	46.36	37.86			
（5）财政性定期存款 Fiscal Time Deposits	4.10	－3.55	2. 农业贷款 Loans to Agricultural Sector	470.55	66.94
3. 机关团体部队存款 Deposits by Government Agencies，Social Organizations and Army	482.20	89.52	3. 固定资产贷款 Fixed Asset Loans	1780.18	221.98
			（1）基本建设贷款 Capital Construction Loans	581.42	80.25
4. 城镇储蓄存款 Urban Savings Deposits	3730.88	1071.72	（2）技术改造贷款 Technical Improvement Loans	1003.11	110.18
其中：定期 Of Which：Time Deposits	3098.52	1053.36	（3）老少边穷经济贷款 Loans to Former-revolutionary Base Areas，Areas Inhabited by Minority Nationalities，Remote and Border Areas and Poverty-stricken Areas for Economic Development	50.13	11.04
5. 农村存款 Rural Deposits	715.87	46.34			
6. 信托类存款 Trust Deposits	97.07	－18.17			
7. 其他类存款 Other Deposits	454.86	73.33	（4）地方经济开发贷款 Loans for Local Economic Development	145.52	20.51
二、金融债券 Financial Bonds	69.55	－6.00			
三、代理发行债券 Agency Bonds Issue	0.18	0.16	4. 信托类贷款 Trust Loans	76.31	－19.72
四、流通中货币 Currency in Circulation	2344.02	209.99	5. 其他类贷款 Other Loans	582.40	115.03
五、信贷基金 Credit Funds	1142.02	180.09	二、购买债券 Bond Purchase	118.58	8.20
六、当年结益 Net Earnings	476.82	476.82	三、金银占款 Position for Bullion and Silver Purchase	12.00	

续表
Continued

项 目 Items	余 额 Balance	比年初增减额 Changes within the Year	项 目 Items	余 额 Balance	比年初增减额 Changes within the Year
七、汇兑在途资金 Remittance in Transit		-218.37	四、外汇占款 Position for Foreign Exchange Purchase	264.50	106.10
八、其他 Others	750.61	124.77	五、上缴财政税利 Payment of Profits and Taxes to Government Finance	271.77	271.77
			六、财政透支和借款 Overdraft by State Finance	684.60	108.10
			七、待核销贷款损失 Loan Loss to be Written - off	55.93	
资金来源总计 Total Sources	**13810.23**	**2345.67**	**资金运用总计 Total Uses**	**13810.23**	**2345.67**

国家银行人民币信贷收支表

Sources and Uses of Credit Funds of State Banks (RMB)

(1990年末)

(Year - end of 1990)

单位：亿元

Unit: 100 Million Yuan

项目 Items	余额 Balance	比年初增减额 Changes within the Year	项目 Items	余额 Balance	比年初增减额 Changes within the Year
一、各项存款 Total Deposits	11653.99	2626.96	一、各项贷款 Total Loans	15140.43	2737.58
1. 企业存款 Deposits by Enterprises	3946.66	861.30	1. 流动资金贷款 Loans for Circulation Funds	11593.98	2100.57
2. 财政存款 Fiscal Deposits	427.11	-33.68	(1) 工业贷款 Loans to Industrial Sector	4899.73	1081.81
(1) 中央财政存款 Central Fiscal Deposits	84.21	-30.76	(2) 商业贷款 Loans to Commercial Sector	5895.57	942.71
(2) 地方财政存款 Local Fiscal Deposits	220.41	-6.97	其中：收购农副产品 Of Which: Loans for the Purchase of Farm Products	2315.57	—
(3) 财政预算外存款 Local Extra - budgetary Fiscal Deposits	89.54	21.56	(3) 建筑业贷款 Loans to Construction Sector	316.77	33.08
(4) 建行财政存款 Fiscal Deposits by Construction Bank	27.94	-18.42	(4) 个体工商业贷款 Loans to Self - employed Entities	15.40	0.01
(5) 财政性定期存款 Fiscal Time Deposits	5.01	0.91	(5) 乡镇企业贷款 Loans to Village and Township Enterprises	466.51	42.96
3. 机关团体部队存款 Deposits by Government Agencies, Social Organizations and Army	597.02	114.82	2. 农业贷款 Loans to Agricultural Sector	571.93	101.38
4. 城镇储蓄存款 Urban Savings Deposits	5192.93	1462.05	3. 固定资产贷款 Fixed Asset Loans	2214.89	434.71
其中：定期 Of Which: Time Deposits	4395.69	1297.17	(1) 基本建设贷款 Capital Construction Loans	818.29	236.87
5. 农村存款 Rural Deposits	844.09	128.22	(2) 技术改造贷款 Technical Improvement Loans	1163.80	160.69
6. 信托类存款 Trust Deposits	107.01	9.94	(3) 老少边穷经济贷款 Loans to Former - revolutionary Base Areas, Areas Inhabited by Minority Nationalities, Remote and Border Areas and Poverty - stricken Areas for Economic Development	59.98	9.85
7. 其他类存款 Other Deposits	539.17	84.31			
二、金融债券 Financial Bonds	91.79	22.24			
三、代理发行债券 Agency Bonds Issue	0.18		(4) 地方经济开发贷款 Loans for Local Economic Development	172.82	27.30
四、流通中货币 Currency in Circulation	2644.37	300.35	4. 信托类贷款 Trust Loans	87.39	11.08
五、信贷基金 Credit Funds	1260.92	118.90	5. 其他类贷款 Other Loans	672.24	89.84
六、当年结益 Net Earnings	371.43	371.43			

续表
Continued

项　目 Items	余　额 Balance	比年初增减额 Changes within the Year	项　目 Items	余　额 Balance	比年初增减额 Changes within the Year
七、其他 Others	1071.39	115.73	二、购买债券 Bond Purchase	181.25	62.67
			三、金银占款 Position for Bullion and Silver Purchase	12.00	
			四、外汇占款 Position for Foreign Exchange Purchase	599.40	334.90
			五、上缴财政税利 Payment of Profits and Taxes to Government Finance	303.97	303.97
			六、财政透支和借款 Overdraft by State Finance	801.10	116.50
			七、待核销贷款损失 Loan Loss to be Written – off	55.92	-0.01
资金来源总计 Total Sources	**17094.07**	**3555.61**	**资金运用总计 Total Uses**	**17094.07**	**3555.61**

国家银行人民币信贷收支表
Sources and Uses of Credit Funds of State Banks (RMB)
(1991 年末)
(Year - end of 1991)

单位：亿元
Unit: 100 Million Yuan

项　目 Items	余　额 Balance	比年初增减额 Changes within the Year	项　目 Items	余　额 Balance	比年初增减额 Changes within the Year
一、各项存款 Total Deposits	14881.59	3227.60	一、各项贷款 Total Loans	18061.42	2920.99
1. 企业存款 Deposits by Enterprises	5058.06	1111.40	1. 流动资金贷款 Loans for Circulation Funds	13476.71	1882.73
2. 财政存款 Fiscal Deposits	504.29	77.18	(1) 工业贷款 Loans to Industrial Sector	5801.99	902.26
(1) 中央财政存款 Central Fiscal Deposits	50.21	- 34.00	(2) 商业贷款 Loans to Commercial Sector	6757.52	861.95
(2) 地方财政存款 Local Fiscal Deposits	242.54	22.13	其中：收购农副产品 Of Which: Loans for the Purchase of Farm Products	2973.03	657.46
(3) 财政预算外存款 Local Extra - budgetary Fiscal Deposits	99.29	9.75	(3) 建筑业贷款 Loans to Construction Sector	363.62	46.85
(4) 建行财政存款 Fiscal Deposits by Construction Bank	105.89	77.95	(4) 个体工商业贷款 Loans to Self - employed Entities	16.54	1.14
(5) 财政性定期存款 Fiscal Time Deposits	6.36	1.35	(5) 乡镇企业贷款 Loans to Village and Township Enterprises	537.04	70.53
3. 机关团体部队存款 Deposits by Government Agencies, Social Organizations and Army	753.35	156.33	2. 农业贷款 Loans to Agricultural Sector	708.72	136.79
4. 城镇储蓄存款 Urban Savings Deposits	6790.90	1597.97	3. 固定资产贷款 Fixed Asset Loans	3046.14	831.25
其中：定期 Of Which: Time Deposits	5715.61	1319.92	(1) 基本建设贷款 Capital Construction Loans	1259.11	440.82
5. 农村存款 Rural Deposits	1031.57	187.48	(2) 技术改造贷款 Technical Improvement Loans	1519.95	356.15
6. 信托类存款 Trust Deposits	65.52	- 41.49	(3) 老少边穷经济贷款 Loans to Former - revolutionary Base Areas, Areas Inhabited by Minority Nationalities, Remote and Border Areas and Poverty - stricken Areas for Economic Development	80.54	20.56
7. 其他类存款 Other Deposits	677.90	138.73			
二、金融债券 Financial Bonds	114.24	22.45			
三、代理发行债券 Agency Bonds Issue		- 0.18	(4) 地方经济开发贷款 Loans for Local Economic Development	186.54	13.72
四、流通中货币 Currency in Circulation	3177.80	533.43	4. 信托类贷款 Trust Loans	58.24	- 29.15
五、信贷基金 Credit Funds	1373.63	112.71	5. 其他类贷款 Other Loans	771.61	99.37
六、当年结益 Net Earnings	470.73	470.73			

续表
Continued

项　目 Items	余　额 Balance	比年初增减额 Changes within the Year	项　目 Items	余　额 Balance	比年初增减额 Changes within the Year
七、其他 Others	941.75	-197.10	二、购买债券 Bond Purchase	272.37	91.12
			三、金银占款 Position for Bullion and Silver Purchase	12.00	
			四、外汇占款 Position for Foreign Exchange Purchase	1228.10	628.70
			五、上缴财政税利 Payment of Profits and Taxes to Government Finance	262.13	262.13
			六、财政透支和借款 Overdraft by State Finance	1067.80	266.70
			七、待核销贷款损失 Loan Loss to be Written-off	55.92	
资金来源总计 Total Sources	**20959.74**	**4169.64**	**资金运用总计 Total Uses**	**20959.74**	**4169.64**

国家银行人民币信贷收支表
Sources and Uses of Credit Funds of State Banks (RMB)

(1992 年末)

(Year - end of 1992)

单位：亿元

Unit: 100 Million Yuan

项目 Items	余额 Balance	比年初增减额 Changes within the Year	项目 Items	余额 Balance	比年初增减额 Changes within the Year
一、各项存款 Total Deposits	18907.80	4026.21	一、各项贷款 Total Loans	21570.02	3508.60
1. 企业存款 Deposits by Enterprises	6822.62	1764.56	1. 流动资金贷款 Loans for Circulation Funds	15634.84	2158.13
2. 财政存款 Fiscal Deposits	250.17	-254.12	(1) 工业贷款 Loans to Industrial Sector	6709.89	907.90
(1) 中央财政存款 Central Fiscal Deposits	-2.21	-52.42	(2) 商业贷款 Loans to Commercial Sector	7876.51	1118.99
(2) 地方财政存款 Local Fiscal Deposits	167.68	-74.86	其中：收购农副产品 Of Which: Loans for the Purchase of Farm Products	3191.26	218.23
(3) 财政预算外存款 Local Extra - budgetary Fiscal Deposits	74.62	-24.67	(3) 建筑业贷款 Loans to Construction Sector	436.22	72.60
(4) 建行财政存款 Fiscal Deposits by Construction Bank	3.27	-102.62	(4) 个体工商业贷款 Loans to Self - employed Entities	22.60	6.06
(5) 财政性定期存款 Fiscal Time Deposits	6.81	0.45	(5) 乡镇企业贷款 Loans to Village and Township Enterprises	589.62	52.58
3. 机关团体部队存款 Deposits by Government Agencies, Social Organizations and Army	687.12	-66.23	2. 农业贷款 Loans to Agricultural Sector	859.55	150.83
4. 城镇储蓄存款 Urban Savings Deposits	8677.29	1886.39	3. 固定资产贷款 Fixed Asset Loans	3924.02	877.88
其中：定期 Of Which: Time Deposits	7035.35	1319.74	(1) 基本建设贷款 Capital Construction Loans	1685.73	426.62
5. 农村存款 Rural Deposits	1409.46	377.89	(2) 技术改造贷款 Technical Improvement Loans	1927.82	407.87
6. 信托类存款 Trust Deposits	79.10	13.58	(3) 老少边穷经济贷款 Loans to Former - revolutionary Base Areas, Areas Inhabited by Minority Nationalities, Remote and Border Areas and Poverty - stricken Areas for Economic Development	94.64	14.10
7. 其他类存款 Other Deposits	982.04	304.13			
二、金融债券 Financial Bonds	162.58	48.34			
三、国家投资债券 State Investment Bonds	122.68	122.68	(4) 地方经济开发贷款 Loans for Local Economic Development	215.83	29.29
四、流通中货币 Currency in Circulation	4336.00	1158.20	4. 信托类贷款 Trust Loans	83.92	25.68
五、信贷基金 Credit Funds	1497.63	124.00	5. 其他类贷款 Other Loans	1067.69	296.08
六、当年结益 Net Earnings	382.93	382.93			

续表
Continued

项 目 Items	余 额 Balance	比年初增减额 Changes within the Year	项 目 Items	余 额 Balance	比年初增减额 Changes within the Year
七、其他 Others	-553.40	-1703.75	二、购买债券 Bond Purchase	456.96	184.59
			三、国家投资债券贷款 Loans Related to State Investment Bonds	156.82	156.82
			四、金银占款 Position for Bullion and Silver Purchase	12.00	
			五、外汇占款 Position for Foreign Exchange Purchase	1102.00	-126.10
			六、上缴财政税利 Payment of Profits and Taxes to Government Finance	261.40	261.40
			七、财政透支和借款 Overdraft by State Finance	1241.10	173.30
			八、待核销贷款损失 Loan Loss to be Written-off	55.92	
资金来源总计 Total Sources	**24856.22**	**4158.61**	**资金运用总计 Total Uses**	**24856.22**	**4158.61**

国家银行人民币信贷收支表

Sources and Uses of Credit Funds of State Banks（RMB）

（1993 年末）

（Year - end of 1993）

单位：亿元

Unit: 100 Million Yuan

项 目 Items	余 额 Balance	比年初增减额 Changes within the Year	项 目 Items	余 额 Balance	比年初增减额 Changes within the Year
一、各项存款 Total Deposits	23245.36	4339.27	一、各项贷款 Total Loans	26461.14	4845.61
1. 企业存款 Deposits by Enterprises	7671.62	855.85	1. 流动资金贷款 Loans for Circulation Funds	18688.70	3045.48
2. 财政存款 Fiscal Deposits	502.34	256.63	(1) 工业贷款 Loans to Industrial Sector	8110.02	1397.58
(1) 中央财政存款 Central Fiscal Deposits	49.55	51.76	(2) 商业贷款 Loans to Commercial Sector	9314.15	1430.43
(2) 地方财政存款 Local Fiscal Deposits	300.93	133.44	其中：收购农副产品 Of Which: Loans for the Purchase of Farm Products	3563.94	386.82
(3) 财政预算外存款 Local Extra - budgetary Fiscal Deposits	96.18	21.73	(3) 建筑业贷款 Loans to Construction Sector	523.66	88.93
(4) 建行财政存款 Fiscal Deposits by Construction Bank	53.40	54.75	(4) 个体工商业贷款 Loans to Self - employed Entities	34.02	11.13
(5) 财政性定期存款 Fiscal Time Deposits	2.28	-5.05	(5) 乡镇企业贷款 Loans to Village and Township Enterprises	706.85	117.41
3. 机关团体部队存款 Deposits by Government Agencies, Social Organizations and Army	713.10	25.64	2. 农业贷款 Loans to Agricultural Sector	1013.38	154.10
4. 城镇储蓄存款 Urban Savings Deposits	11187.58	2509.49	3. 固定资产贷款 Fixed Asset Loans	5170.53	1245.98
其中：定期 Of Which: Time Deposits	8855.06	1841.83	(1) 基本建设贷款 Capital Construction Loans	2419.83	734.83
5. 农村存款 Rural Deposits	1752.85	343.43	(2) 技术改造贷款 Technical Improvement Loans	2391.39	461.68
6. 信托类存款 Trust Deposits	93.53	14.48	(3) 老少边穷经济贷款 Loans to Former - revolutionary Base Areas, Areas Inhabited by Minority Nationalities, Remote and Border Areas and Poverty - stricken Areas for Economic Development	113.81	19.35
7. 其他类存款 Other Deposits	1324.34	333.75			
二、金融债券 Financial Bonds	98.63	-64.07			
三、国家投资债券 State Investment Bonds	126.60	3.85	(4) 地方经济开发贷款 Loans for Local Economic Development	245.50	30.12
四、流通中货币 Currency in Circulation	5864.70	1528.72	4. 信托类贷款 Trust Loans	138.28	32.03
五、同业往来 Inter - bank Transactions	3781.06	1252.19	5. 其他类贷款 Other Loans	1450.25	368.02

续表
Continued

项 目 Items	余 额 Balance	比年初增减额 Changes within the Year	项 目 Items	余 额 Balance	比年初增减额 Changes within the Year
其中：拆入资金 Of Which: Placements from Banks and Other Financial Institutions	2831.60	978.45	二、购买债券 Bond Purchase	604.13	146.45
			三、国家投资债券贷款 Loans Related to State Investment Bonds	157.72	0.90
六、信贷基金 Credit Funds	1644.16		四、金银占款 Position for Bullion and Silver Purchase	12.00	
七、当年结益 Net Earnings	460.53	460.53	五、外汇占款 Position for Foreign Exchange Purchase	1431.80	329.80
八、其他 Others	226.87	-623.90	六、上缴财政税利 Payment of Profits and Taxes to Government Finance	388.21	388.21
			七、财政透支和借款 Overdraft by State Finance	1582.10	341.00
			八、同业往来 Inter-bank Transactions	4322.89	657.62
			其中：拆出资金 Of Which: Placements with Banks and Other Financial Institutions	3385.66	473.23
			九、库存现金 Cash in Vault	432.00	187.00
			十、待核销贷款损失 Loan Loss to be Written-off	55.92	
资金来源总计 Total Sources	**35447.91**	**6896.59**	**资金运用总计 Total Uses**	**35447.91**	**6896.59**

国家银行人民币信贷收支表

Sources and Uses of Credit Funds of State Banks (RMB)

(1994 年末)

(Year - end of 1994)

单位：亿元

Unit: 100 Million Yuan

项　目 Items	余　额 Balance	比年初增减额 Changes within the Year	项　目 Items	余　额 Balance	比年初增减额 Changes within the Year
一、各项存款 Total Deposits	29356.75	7951.90	一、各项贷款 Total Loans	31602.90	5161.00
1. 企业存款 Deposits by Enterprises	11466.58	2733.31	1. 短期贷款 Short - term Loans	23427.77	3786.57
其中：定期存款 Of Which: Time Deposits	1052.85	412.60	(1) 工业贷款 Loans to Industrial Sector	9368.01	1301.33
2. 财政存款 Fiscal Deposits	862.24	368.72	(2) 商业贷款 Loans to Commercial Sector	10052.72	1828.16
(1) 中央财政存款 Central Fiscal Deposits	164.05	121.95	其中：农副产品采购贷款 Of Which: Loans for the Purchase of Farm Products	3826.02	1037.40
(2) 地方财政存款 Local Fiscal Deposits	447.68	141.45	(3) 建筑业贷款 Loans to Construction Sector	612.53	86.50
(3) 财政预算外存款 Local Extra - budgetary Fiscal Deposits	151.93	51.28	(4) 农业贷款 Loans to Agricultural Sector	755.80	163.75
(4) 建行财政存款 Fiscal Deposits by Construction Bank	97.16	54.61	(5) 乡镇企业贷款 Loans to Village and Township Enterprises	798.27	167.66
(5) 财政性定期存款 Fiscal Time Deposits	1.42	- 0.57	(6) 个体工商业贷款 Loans to Self - employed Entities	53.54	31.09
3. 机关团体部队存款 Deposits by Government Agencies, Social Organizations and Army	853.53	141.34	(7) 三资企业贷款 Loans to Foreign Investment Enterprises and Ventures	737.01	236.11
4. 城镇储蓄存款 Urban Savings Deposits	15844.46	3629.74	(8) 其他短期贷款 Other Short - term Loans	1049.89	- 28.03
其中：定期 Of Which: Time Deposits	12469.72	3629.74	2. 中长期贷款 Medium and Long - term Loans	7172.93	1195.24
5. 农业存款 Deposits by Agricultural Sector	195.11	18.57	(1) 基本建设贷款 Capital Construction Loans	2766.21	345.02
6. 信托类存款 Trust Deposits	134.83	31.86	(2) 技术改造贷款 Technical Improvement Loans	2985.18	665.20
二、金融债券 Financial Bonds	73.74	- 34.96	(3) 其他中长期贷款 Other Medium and Long - term Loans	1421.54	185.02
三、国家投资债券 State Investment Bonds	120.01	- 0.01			
四、流通中货币 Currency in Circulation	7288.60	1423.90	3. 信托类贷款 Trust Loans	11.87	5.52
五、同业往来 Inter - bank Transactions	7605.34	4441.08	4. 其他类贷款 Other Loans	990.33	173.67

续表
Continued

项目 Items	余额 Balance	比年初增减额 Changes within the Year	项目 Items	余额 Balance	比年初增减额 Changes within the Year
其中：拆入资金 Of Which：Placements from Banks and Other Financial Institutions	412.94	-8.10	二、有价证券及投资 Securities and Investments	1802.91	962.42
			三、国家投资债券贷款 Loans Related to State Investment Bonds	89.31	-30.44
六、所有者权益 Owner's Equity	2260.93	126.80	四、同业往来 Inter-bank Transactions	5821.09	3840.09
其中：实收资本 Of Which：Paid-in Capital	2195.66	32.19	其中：拆出资金 Of Which：Placements from Banks and Other Financial Institutions	1111.83	130.79
七、当年结益 Net Earnings	362.01	362.01			
八、其他 Others	-1151.19	-1252.60	五、金银占款 Position for Bullion and Silver Purchase	12.00	
			六、外汇占款 Position for Foreign Exchange Purchase	4503.90	3072.10
			七、库存现金 Cash in Vault	446.06	12.95
			八、财政透支和借款 Overdraft by State Finance	1582.10	
			九、待核销贷款损失 Loan Loss to be Written-off	55.92	
资金来源总计 Total Sources	**45916.19**	**13018.12**	**资金运用总计 Total Uses**	**45916.19**	**13018.12**

国家银行人民币信贷收支表
Sources and Uses of Credit Funds of State Banks (RMB)

(1995 年末)

(Year - end of 1995)

单位：亿元

Unit: 100 Million Yuan

项 目 Items	余 额 Balance	比年初增减额 Changes within the Year	项 目 Items	余 额 Balance	比年初增减额 Changes within the Year
一、各项存款 Total Deposits	38784.83	9375.48	一、各项贷款 Total Loans	39393.40	6915.45
1. 企业存款 Deposits by Enterprises	14519.63	3004.13	1. 短期贷款 Short - term Loans	28477.49	4648.53
其中：单位定期存款 Of Which: Time Deposits	1910.13	848.94	(1) 工业贷款 Loans to Industrial Sector	10918.99	1525.69
2. 财政存款 Fiscal Deposits	1005.40	139.32	(2) 商业贷款 Loans to Commercial Sector	12163.33	2025.03
3. 机关团体部队存款 Deposits by Government Agencies, Social Organizations and Army	899.81	64.74	其中：农副产品采购贷款 Of Which: Loans for the Purchase of Farm Products	5445.06	1187.74
4. 城镇储蓄存款 Urban Savings Deposits	21941.03	6087.70	(3) 建筑业贷款 Loans to Construction Sector	785.45	167.06
5. 农业存款 Deposits by Agricultural Sector	216.83	22.06	(4) 农业贷款 Loans to Agricultural Sector	962.42	197.39
6. 信托类存款 Trust Deposits	202.13	57.53	(5) 乡镇企业贷款 Loans to Village and Township Enterprises	959.13	164.75
二、金融债券 Financial Bonds	1664.41	839.02	(6) 个体工商业贷款 Loans to Self - employed Entities	34.06	16.17
三、国家投资债券 State Investment Bonds	116.74	-7.19	(7) 三资企业贷款 Loans to Foreign Investment Enterprises and Ventures	899.97	226.92
四、流通中货币 Currency in Circulation	7885.34	596.74	(8) 其他短期贷款 Other Short - term Loans	1754.14	325.52
五、所有者权益 Owner's Equity	2540.53	360.02	2. 中长期贷款 Medium and Long - term Loans	10025.58	2024.25
其中：实收资本 Of Which: Paid - in Capital	2534.39	212.24	3. 信托类贷款 Trust Loans	13.39	1.80
六、当年结益 Net Earnings	210.75	210.75	4. 其他类贷款 Other Loans	876.94	240.87
七、其他 Others	201.18	-947.96	二、有价证券及投资 Securities and Investments	3064.19	1198.33
			三、国家投资债券贷款 Loans Related to State Investment Bonds	75.52	-13.79
			四、金银占款 Position for Bullion and Silver Purchase	12.00	
			五、外汇占款 Position for Foreign Exchange Purchase	6774.45	2270.55
			六、库存现金 Cash in Vault	502.12	56.32
			七、财政透支和借款 Overdraft by State Finance	1582.10	
资金来源总计 Total Sources	**51403.78**	**10426.86**	**资金运用总计 Total Uses**	**51403.78**	**10426.86**

国家银行人民币信贷收支表

Sources and Uses of Credit Funds of State Banks（RMB）

（1996年末）

（Year - end of 1996）

单位：亿元

Unit：100 Million Yuan

项目 Items	余额 Balance	比年初增减额 Changes within the Year	项目 Items	余额 Balance	比年初增减额 Changes within the Year
一、各项存款 Total Deposits	49596.52	10709.55	一、各项贷款 Total Loans	47434.52	7937.75
1. 企业存款 Deposits by Enterprises	18496.82	3876.63	1. 短期贷款 Short - term Loans	34432.84	5759.97
其中：单位定期存款 Of Which：Time Deposits	3032.24	1028.74	（1）工业贷款 Loans to Industrial Sector	13099.96	2154.51
2. 财政存款 Fiscal Deposits	1274.16	273.93	（2）商业贷款 Loans to Commercial Sector	14417.12	2305.60
3. 机关团体部队存款 Deposits by Government Agencies，Social Organizations and Army	947.71	48.75	其中：收购贷款 Of Which：Loans for the Purchase of Farm Products	6870.77	1564.69
4. 城镇储蓄存款 Urban Savings Deposits	28524.16	6538.38	（3）建筑业贷款 Loans to Construction Sector	949.42	161.16
5. 农业存款 Deposits by Agricultural Sector	238.74	21.95	（4）农业贷款 Loans to Agricultural Sectors	1209.61	247.21
6. 信托类存款 Trust Deposits	114.93	- 50.09	（5）乡镇企业贷款 Loans to Village and Township Enterprises	1158.16	199.16
二、金融债券 Financial Bonds	2465.07	800.65	（6）个体工商业贷款 Loans to Self - employed Entities	53.76	19.37
三、国家投资债券 State Investment Bonds	120.17	- 0.25	（7）三资企业贷款 Loans to Foreign Investment Enterprises and Ventures	1217.28	315.34
四、流通中货币 Currency in Circulation	8802.01	916.67	（8）其他短期贷款 Other Short - term Loans	2327.53	357.62
五、所有者权益 Owner's Equity	2901.95	385.03	2. 中长期贷款 Medium and Long - term Loans	12034.17	2045.90
其中：实收资本 Of Which：Paid - in Capital	2745.53	210.46	3. 信托类贷款 Trust Loans	7.37	- 5.87
六、当年结益 Net Earnings	51.68	51.68	4. 其他类贷款 Other Loans	960.14	137.75
七、其他 Others	- 717.79	- 1117.89	二、有价证券及投资 Securities and Investments	4097.80	1066.95
			三、国家投资债券贷款 Loans Related to State Investment Bonds	69.10	- 6.66
			四、金银占款 Position for Bullion and Silver Purchase	12.00	
			五、外汇占款 Position for Foreign Exchange Purchase	9578.40	2803.90
			六、库存现金 Cash in Vault	445.69	- 56.50
			七、财政透支和借款 Overdraft by State Finance	1582.10	
资金来源总计 Total Sources	**63219.61**	**11745.44**	**资金运用总计 Total Uses**	**63219.61**	**11745.44**

国家银行人民币信贷收支表

Sources and Uses of Credit Funds of State Banks (RMB)

(1997年末)

(Year-end of 1997)

单位：亿元

Unit: 100 Million Yuan

项　目 Items	余　额 Balance	比年初增减额 Changes within the Year	项　目 Items	余　额 Balance	比年初增减额 Changes within the Year
一、各项存款 Total Deposits	60005.43	9056.90	一、各项贷款 Total Loans	59317.50	8142.59
1. 企业存款 Deposits by Enterprises	22590.89	3255.31	1. 短期贷款 Short-term Loans	44259.19	6250.62
(1) 活期存款 Demand Deposits	17595.50	2292.99	(1) 工业贷款 Loans to Industrial Sector	15434.02	2010.77
(2) 定期存款 Time Deposits	4995.39	962.32	(2) 商业贷款 Loans to Commercial Sector	17410.52	2490.39
2. 财政存款 Fiscal Deposits	1534.78	236.66	其中：农副产品贷款 Of Which: Loans for the Purchase of Farm Products	8501.02	1666.44
3. 机关团体存款 Deposits by Government Agencies and Social Organizations	848.10	56.49	(3) 建筑业贷款 Loans to Construction Sector	1507.59	150.80
4. 储蓄存款 Savings Deposits	34190.33	5393.18	(4) 农业贷款 Loans to Agricultural Sector	1536.29	294.62
(1) 活期储蓄 Demand Deposits	7647.79	1966.36	(5) 乡镇企业贷款 Loans to Village and Township Enterprises	1527.14	231.64
(2) 定期储蓄 Time Deposits	26542.54	3426.82	(6) 三资企业贷款 Loans to Foreign Investment Enterprises and Ventures	1716.17	403.19
5. 农业存款 Deposits by Agricultural Sector	263.99	25.04			
6. 信托存款 Trust Deposits	29.54	-30.85	(7) 私营企业及个体贷款 Loans to Privately-run Enterprises and Self-employed Entities	161.44	17.40
7. 其他存款 Other Deposits	547.80	121.07	(8) 其他短期贷款 Other Short-term Loans	4966.02	651.81
二、委托存款及投资基金 Designated Deposits and Designated Investment Funds	259.10	-78.46	2. 中长期贷款 Medium and Long-term Loans	14724.63	1813.58
三、金融债券 Financial Bonds	2.23	-60.71	(1) 基本建设贷款 Capital Construction Loans	7574.47	1090.58
四、国家投资债券 State Investment Bonds	81.58	-38.72	(2) 技术改造贷款 Technical Improvement Loans	4851.98	397.57
五、同业往来 Inter-bank Transactions	1911.11	807.79	(3) 其他中长期贷款 Other Medium and Long-term Loans	2298.18	325.43
1. 同业存放 Due to Banks and Other Financial Institutions	1722.10	790.99	3. 信托贷款 Trust Loans	36.33	-2.01
2. 同业拆借 Placements from Banks and Other Financial Institutions	189.01	16.80	4. 逾期类贷款 Overdue Loans	297.35	80.40

续表
Continued

项目 Items	余额 Balance	比年初增减额 Changes within the Year	项目 Items	余额 Balance	比年初增减额 Changes within the Year
六、流通中货币 Currency in Circulation	10177.61	1375.60	二、国家投资债券贷款 Loans Related to State Investment Bonds	43.32	-25.78
七、所有者权益 Owner's Equity	2992.03	-70.67	三、有价证券及投资 Securities and Investments	2180.12	-660.25
其中：实收资本 Of Which: Paid-in Capital	3072.54	312.23	四、同业往来 Inter-bank Transactions	773.87	-98.56
当年结益 Net Earnings	-220.85	-220.85	1. 存放同业 Due from Banks and Other Financial Institutions	106.43	-33.37
八、其他 Others	2454.68	-509.72			
			2. 拆放同业 Placements with Banks and Other Financial Institutions	667.44	-65.19
			五、金银占款 Position for Bullion and Silver Purchase	12.04	0.04
			六、外汇占款 Position for Foreign Exchange Purchase	13431.94	3031.69
			七、库存现金 Cash in Vault	542.92	92.32
			八、财政借款 Overdraft by State Finance	1582.06	-0.04
资金来源总计 Total Sources	**77883.77**	**10482.01**	**资金运用总计 Total Uses**	**77883.77**	**10482.01**

注：逾期类贷款不含中国工商银行、中国农业银行、中国银行、中国建设银行的数据。

Note: The date of overdue loans don't include the data of Industrial and Commercial Bank of China, Agricultural Bank of China, Bank of China and China Construction Bank.

国家银行人民币信贷收支表

Sources and Uses of Credit Funds of State Banks (RMB)

(1998年末)

(Year - end of 1998)

单位：亿元

Unit: 100 Million Yuan

项目 Items	余额 Balance	比年初增减额 Changes within the Year	项目 Items	余额 Balance	比年初增减额 Changes within the Year
一、各项存款 Total Deposits	69782.21	10106.03	一、各项贷款 Total Loans	68442.11	9100.39
1. 企业存款 Deposits by Enterprises	25249.11	2669.85	1. 短期贷款 Short - term Loans	48105.68	4600.27
(1) 活期存款 Demand Deposits	19146.10	1556.56	(1) 工业贷款 Loans to Industrial Sector	16664.06	1400.66
(2) 定期存款 Time Deposits	6103.01	1113.29	(2) 商业贷款 Loans to Commercial Sector	18746.74	1389.41
2. 财政存款 Fiscal Deposits	2169.60	656.44	其中：农副产品贷款 Of Which: Loans for the Purchase of Farm Products	7656.84	- 811.75
3. 机关团体存款 Deposits by Government Agencies and Social Organizations	1215.56	366.21	(3) 建筑业贷款 Loans to Construction Sector	1512.36	125.96
4. 储蓄存款 Savings Deposits	39560.98	5968.08	(4) 农业贷款 Loans to Agricultural Sector	1781.63	244.66
(1) 活期储蓄 Demand Deposits	8722.20	1674.69	(5) 乡镇企业贷款 Loans to Village and Township Enterprises	1754.92	232.54
(2) 定期储蓄 Time Deposits	30838.78	4293.39	(6) 三资企业贷款 Loans to Foreign Investment Enterprises and Ventures	2226.92	511.20
5. 农业存款 Deposits by Agricultural Sector	300.62	36.64	(7) 私营企业及个体贷款 Loans to Privately - run Enterprises and Self - employed Entities	208.27	49.95
6. 信托存款 Trust Deposits	10.05	- 19.49	(8) 其他短期贷款 Other Short - term Loans	5210.78	645.89
7. 其他存款 Other Deposits	1276.29	428.30	2. 中期流动资金贷款 Medium - term Working Capital Loans	1642.54	1277.00
二、委托存款及投资基金 Designated Deposits and Designated Investment Funds	127.34	- 136.25	3. 中长期贷款 Medium and Long - term Loans	18101.75	2964.32
三、金融债券 Financial Bonds	1.69	- 0.57	(1) 基本建设贷款 Capital Construction Loans	10267.76	2307.91
四、国家投资债券 State Investment Bonds	80.26	- 1.33	(2) 技术改造贷款 Technical Improvement Loans	5088.64	235.56
五、同业往来 Inter - bank Transactions	2705.99	368.72	(3) 其他中长期贷款 Other Medium and Long - term Loans	2745.35	420.85
1. 同业存放 Due to Banks and Other Financial Institutions	2676.50	528.28	4. 信托贷款 Trust Loans	28.46	- 7.53
2. 同业拆借 Placements from Banks and Other Financial Institutions	29.49	- 159.56			

续表
Continued

项目 Items	余额 Balance	比年初增减额 Changes within the Year	项目 Items	余额 Balance	比年初增减额 Changes within the Year
六、流通中货币 Currency in Circulation	11204.15	1026.54	5. 逾期类贷款 Overdue Loans	563.68	266.33
七、所有者权益 Owner's Equity	5491.64	2380.44	二、国家投资债券贷款 Loans Related to State Investment Bonds	37.84	-5.48
其中：实收资本 Of Which: Paid - in Capital	5838.36	2766.76	三、有价证券及投资 Securities and Investments	6037.62	3863.85
当年结益 Net Earnings	-345.11	-345.11	四、同业往来 Inter - bank Transactions	669.56	-107.09
八、其他 Others	1623.90	-637.58	1. 存放同业 Due from Banks and Other Financial Institutions	86.12	-22.77
			2. 拆放同业 Placements with Banks and Other Financial Institutions	583.44	-84.32
			五、金银占款 Position for Bullion and Silver Purchase	12.04	
			六、外汇占款 Position for Foreign Exchange Purchase	13660.57	225.96
			七、库存现金 Cash in Vault	575.38	28.37
			八、财政借款 Overdraft by State Finance	1582.06	
资金来源总计 Total Sources	**91017.18**	**13106.00**	**资金运用总计 Total Uses**	**91017.18**	**13106.00**

注：逾期类贷款不含中国工商银行、中国农业银行、中国银行、中国建设银行的数据。

Note: The data of overdue loans don't include the data of Industrial and Commercial Bank of China and Agricultural Bank of China, Bank of China and China Construction Bank.

国家银行人民币信贷收支表

Sources and Uses of Credit Funds of State Banks（RMB）

（1999年末）

（Year – end of 1999）

单位：亿元

Unit：100 Million Yuan

项　目 Items	余　额 Balance	比年初增减额 Changes within the Year	项　目 Items	余　额 Balance	比年初增减额 Changes within the Year
一、各项存款 Total Deposits	79973.51	10212.30	一、各项贷款 Total Loans	73695.85	8742.41
1. 企业存款 Deposits by Enterprises	28733.07	3481.22	1. 短期贷款 Short – term Loans	50113.23	3913.59
（1）活期存款 Demand Deposits	21810.36	2700.35	（1）工业贷款 Loans to Industrial Sector	16786.51	1122.36
（2）定期存款 Time Deposits	6922.71	780.87	（2）商业贷款 Loans to Commercial Sector	18989.51	508.03
2. 财政存款 Fiscal Deposits	2106.33	– 58.69	其中：农副产品贷款 Of Which：Loans for the Purchase of Farm Products	8348.92	9.12
3. 机关团体存款 Deposits by Government Agencies and Social Organizations	1720.34	503.18	（3）建筑业贷款 Loans to Construction Sector	1322.84	216.78
4. 储蓄存款 Savings Deposits	44827.99	5264.95	（4）农业贷款 Loans to Agricultural Sector	1744.63	– 32.82
（1）活期储蓄 Demand Deposits	11225.32	2501.01	（5）乡镇企业贷款 Loans to Village and Township Enterprises	1905.36	151.99
（2）定期储蓄 Time Deposits	33602.67	2763.94	（6）三资企业贷款 Loans to Foreign Investment Enterprises and Ventures	2675.46	456.44
5. 农业存款 Deposits by Agricultural Sector	342.09	41.47	（7）私营企业及个体贷款 Loans to Privately – run Enterprises and Self – employed Entities	301.01	93.24
6. 信托存款 Trust Deposits	6.72	– 3.33	（8）其他短期贷款 Other Short – term Loans	6387.91	1397.57
7. 其他存款 Other Deposits	2236.97	983.50	2. 中期流动资金贷款 Medium – term Working Capital Loans	2821.74	1287.70
二、委托存款及投资基金 Designated Deposits and Designated Investment Funds	80.95	– 46.32	3. 中长期贷款 Medium and Long – term Loans	19970.02	3259.61
三、金融债券 Financial Bonds	1.39	– 0.28	（1）基本建设贷款 Capital Construction Loans	11635.79	2384.75
四、国家投资债券 State Investment Bonds	0.21	– 80.04	（2）技术改造贷款 Technical Improvement Loans	4981.52	198.82
五、同业往来 Inter – bank Transactions	3137.80	303.14	（3）其他中长期贷款 Other Medium and Long – term Loans	3352.71	676.04
1. 同业存放 Due to Banks and Other Financial Institutions	3120.49	373.24	4. 信托贷款 Trust Loans	24.08	– 4.38
2. 同业拆借 Placements from Banks and Other Financial Institutions	17.31	– 70.10			

续表
Continued

项目 Items	余额 Balance	比年初增减额 Changes within the Year	项目 Items	余额 Balance	比年初增减额 Changes within the Year
六、流通中货币 Currency in Circulation	13455.49	2251.34	5. 逾期类贷款 Overdue Loans	766.78	285.89
七、所有者权益 Owner's Equity	5353.28	-107.59	二、国家投资债券贷款 Loans Related to State Investment Bonds	34.04	-2.32
其中：实收资本 Of Which: Paid-in Capital	5830.39	-6.70	三、有价证券及投资 Securities and Investments	9675.01	3946.55
当年结益 Net Earnings	-195.17	-195.17	四、同业往来 Inter-bank Transactions	928.06	211.51
八、其他 Others	-226.99	1997.67	1. 存放同业 Due from Banks and Other Financial Institutions	243.60	153.46
			2. 拆放同业 Placements with Banks and Other Financial Institutions	684.46	58.05
			五、金银占款 Position for Bullion and Silver Purchase	12.04	
			六、外汇占款 Position for Foreign Exchange Purchase	14671.91	1030.13
			七、库存现金 Cash in Vault	1176.67	601.94
			八、财政借款 Overdraft by State Finance	1582.06	
资金来源总计 Total Sources	**101775.64**	**14530.22**	**资金运用总计 Total Uses**	**101775.64**	**14530.22**

注：逾期类贷款不含中国工商银行、中国农业银行、中国银行、中国建设银行的数据。

Note: The data of overdue loans don't include the data of Industrial and Commercial Bank of China, Agricultural Bank of China, Bank of China and China Construction Bank.

国家银行人民币信贷收支表

Sources and Uses of Credit Funds of State Banks（RMB）

（2000年末）

（Year - end of 2000）

单位：亿元

Unit：100 Million Yuan

项　目 Items	余　额 Balance	比年初增减额 Changes within the Year	项　目 Items	余　额 Balance	比年初增减额 Changes within the Year
一、各项存款 Total Deposits	90892.70	11010.89	一、各项贷款 Total Loans	76393.75	10074.02
1. 企业存款 Deposits by Enterprises	33337.57	4606.39	1. 短期贷款 Short - term Loans	49242.11	5035.10
（1）活期存款 Demand Deposits	25585.35	3776.91	（1）工业贷款 Loans to Industrial Sector	15657.66	524.30
（2）定期存款 Time Deposits	7752.22	829.48	（2）商业贷款 Loans to Commercial Sector	16958.48	371.60
2. 财政存款 Fiscal Deposits	3477.25	1374.79	其中：农副产品贷款 Of Which：Loans for the Purchase of Farm Products	8064.05	29.83
3. 机关团体存款 Deposits by Government Agencies and Social Organizations	2079.43	379.88	（3）建筑业贷款 Loans to Construction Sector	1425.61	88.85
4. 储蓄存款 Savings Deposits	48626.81	3856.83	（4）农业贷款 Loans to Agricultural Sector	1289.42	-26.29
（1）活期储蓄 Demand Deposits	14043.86	2879.49	（5）乡镇企业贷款 Loans to Village and Township Enterprises	1415.30	73.92
（2）定期储蓄 Time Deposits	34582.95	977.34	（6）三资企业贷款 Loans to Foreign Investment Enterprises and Ventures	2678.33	194.57
5. 农业存款 Deposits by Agricultural Sector	372.03	29.92	（7）私营企业及个体贷款 Loans to Privately - run Enterprises and Self - employed Entities	354.38	61.41
6. 信托存款 Trust Deposits	1.17	-0.84	（8）其他短期贷款 Other Short - term Loans	9462.93	3746.74
7. 其他存款 Other Deposits	2998.44	763.92	2. 中期流动资金贷款 Medium - term Working Capital Loans	4179.94	1562.53
二、委托存款及投资基金 Designated Deposits and Designated Investment Funds	70.88	-10.13	3. 中长期贷款 Medium and Long - term Loans	22226.15	3453.64
三、金融债券 Financial Bonds	1.01	-0.06	（1）基本建设贷款 Capital Construction Loans	13454.76	2298.19
四、国家投资债券 State Investment Bonds	0.25	0.04	（2）技术改造贷款 Technical Improvement Loans	4811.09	388.89
五、同业往来 Inter - bank Transactions	6141.02	2742.83	（3）其他中长期贷款 Other Medium and Long - term Loans	3960.30	766.56
1. 同业存放 Due to Banks and Other Financial Institutions	5400.76	2019.89	4. 信托贷款 Trust Loans	15.90	3.97
2. 同业拆借 Placements from Banks and Other Financial Institutions	740.26	722.94			

续表
Continued

项　目 Items	余　额 Balance	比年初增减额 Changes within the Year	项　目 Items	余　额 Balance	比年初增减额 Changes within the Year
六、流通中货币 Currency in Circulation	14652.65	1197.16	5. 逾期类贷款 Overdue Loans	729.65	18.78
七、所有者权益 Owner's Equity	5413.05	68.31	二、国家投资债券贷款 Loans Related to State Investment Bonds	32.55	－1.98
其中：实收资本 Of Which：Paid－in Capital	5862.27	31.81	三、有价证券及投资 Securities and Investments	16419.43	6698.57
当年结益 Net Earnings	－131.86	－131.86	四、同业往来 Inter－bank Transactions	941.58	44.63
八、其他 Others	－6744.17	1003.76	1. 存放同业 Due from Banks and Other Financial Institutions	106.65	－108.46
			2. 拆放同业 Placements with Banks and Other Financial Institutions	834.93	153.09
			五、金银占款 Position for Bullion and Silver Purchase	12.04	
			六、外汇占款 Position for Foreign Exchange Purchase	14203.46	－468.37
			七、库存现金 Cash in Vault	842.52	－334.07
			八、财政借款 Overdraft by State Finance	1582.06	
资金来源总计 Total Sources	**110427.39**	**16012.80**	**资金运用总计 Total Uses**	**110427.39**	**16012.80**

注：逾期类贷款不含中国工商银行、中国农业银行、中国银行、中国建设银行数据。

Note：The data of overdue loans don't include data of Industrial and Commercial Bank of China，Agricultural Bank of China，Bank of China and China Construction Bank.

国家银行人民币信贷收支表

Sources and Uses of Credit Funds of State Banks (RMB)

(2001 年末)

(Year - end of 2001)

单位：亿元

Unit: 100 Million Yuan

项　目 Items	余　额 Balance	比年初增减额 Changes within the Year	项　目 Items	余　额 Balance	比年初增减额 Changes within the Year
一、各项存款 Total Deposits	97346.93	11798.29	一、各项贷款 Total Loans	80077.59	7290.20
1. 企业存款 Deposits by Enterprises	33081.29	3370.61	1. 短期贷款 Short - term Loans	43679.83	1479.92
(1) 活期存款 Demand Deposits	25192.77	2238.84	(1) 工业贷款 Loans to Industrial Sector	15763.21	638.85
(2) 定期存款 Time Deposits	7888.52	1131.77	(2) 商业贷款 Loans to Commercial Sector	16463.49	- 106.73
2. 财政存款 Fiscal Deposits	3330.60	- 143.93	其中：农副产品贷款 Of Which: Loans for the Purchase of Farm Products	7983.63	- 80.43
3. 机关团体存款 Deposits by Government Agencies and Social Organizations	2493.60	493.37	(3) 建筑业贷款 Loans to Construction Sector	1684.81	234.48
4. 储蓄存款 Savings Deposits	54306.87	6994.49	(4) 农业贷款 Loans to Agricultural Sector	1272.27	- 15.56
(1) 活期储蓄 Demand Deposits	16626.64	3004.75	(5) 乡镇企业贷款 Loans to Village and Township Enterprises	1450.54	36.79
(2) 定期储蓄 Time Deposits	37680.23	3989.74	(6) 三资企业贷款 Loans to Foreign Investment Enterprises and Ventures	2392.16	- 0.19
5. 农业存款 Deposits by Agricultural Sector	409.74	37.78	(7) 私营企业及个体贷款 Loans to Privately - run Enterprises and Self - employed Entities	425.94	86.60
6. 其他存款 Other Deposits	3724.83	1045.97	(8) 其他短期贷款 Other Short - term Loans	4227.41	605.68
二、委托存款及委托投资基金 Designated Deposits and Designated Investment Funds	60.89	0.24	其中：个人短期消费贷款 Of Which: Short - term Consumer Credit	391.31	68.54
三、金融债券 Financial Bonds	0.84	0.03	2. 中期流动资金贷款 Medium - term Working Capital Loans	4342.76	344.85
四、应付及暂收款 Account Payable and Receipts on Account	2172.91	- 492.69	3. 中长期贷款 Medium and Long - term Loans	30652.92	4760.01
其中：应付及预收利息 Of Which: Interest Payable and Received in Advance	975.83	- 138.94	(1) 基本建设贷款 Capital Construction Loans	15495.17	2043.43
五、同业往来 Inter - bank Transactions	5870.87	900.05	(2) 技术改造贷款 Technical Improvement Loans	4816.66	149.25
1. 同业存放 Due to Banks and Other Financial Institutions	5812.69	857.00	(3) 其他中长期贷款 Other Medium and Long - term Loans	10341.09	2567.33

续表
Continued

项　目 Items	余　额 Balance	比年初增减额 Changes within the Year	项　目 Items	余　额 Balance	比年初增减额 Changes within the Year
2. 同业拆借 Placements from Banks and Other Financial Institutions	58.18	43.05	其中：个人中长期消费贷款 Of Which：Medium and Long－term Consumer Credit	5787.37	2265.86
六、流通中货币 Currency in Circulation	15688.80	1036.15	4. 票据融资 Paper Financing	1087.99	647.81
七、各项准备 Total Provisions	743.49	258.55	其中：贴现 Of Which：Discount	1087.99	647.81
其中：贷款呆账准备金 Of Which：Provisions for Bad Loans	714.35	251.77	5. 各项垫款 Total Advances	314.09	57.61
八、所有者权益 Owner's Equity	4866.45	－374.96	二、有价证券及投资 Securities and Investments	17913.39	634.71
其中：实收资本 Of Which：Paid－in Capital	5676.76	－8.68	三、应收及预付款 Accounts Receivable and Advance Payments	2779.43	－2704.24
当年结益 Net Earnings	－135.17	－135.17	其中：应收利息 Of Which：Interest Receivable	1625.81	－190.33
九、其他 Others	－4594.58	－3773.40	四、同业往来 Inter－bank Transactions	1153.67	255.44
			1. 存放同业 Due from Banks and Other Financial Institutions	61.62	－41.07
			2. 拆放同业 Placements with Banks and Other Financial Institutions	1092.05	296.51
			五、金银占款 Position for Bullion and Silver Purchase	256.00	243.96
			六、外汇占款 Position for Foreign Exchange Purchase	17687.32	3717.84
			七、库存现金 Cash in Vault	707.14	－85.65
			八、财政借款 Overdraft by State Finance	1582.06	
资金来源总计 Total Sources	**122156.60**	**9352.26**	**资金运用总计 Total Uses**	**122156.60**	**9352.26**

国家银行人民币信贷收支表
Sources and Uses of Credit Funds of State Banks (RMB)

(2002年末)

(Year-end of 2002)

单位：亿元

Unit: 100 Million Yuan

项 目 Items	余 额 Balance	比年初增减额 Changes within the Year	项 目 Items	余 额 Balance	比年初增减额 Changes within the Year
一、各项存款 Total Deposits	113452.28	16120.72	一、各项贷款 Total Loans	90892.63	10476.60
1. 企业存款 Deposits by Enterprises	35980.06	3880.69	1. 短期贷款 Short-term Loans	45800.67	3174.84
(1) 活期存款 Demand Deposits	27546.94	2541.47	(1) 工业贷款 Loans to Industrial Sector	16745.38	2088.46
(2) 定期存款 Time Deposits	8433.12	1339.22	(2) 商业贷款 Loans to Commercial Sector	15760.12	-785.24
2. 财政存款 Fiscal Deposits	3447.90	126.85	其中：农副产品贷款 Of Which: Loans for the Purchase of Farm Products	7817.58	-121.34
3. 机关团体存款 Deposits by Government Agencies and Social Organizations	4610.00	1292.82	(3) 建筑业贷款 Loans to Construction Sector	2168.03	718.09
4. 储蓄存款 Savings Deposits	64024.46	9716.36	(4) 农业贷款 Loans to Agricultural Sector	1286.04	6.62
(1) 活期储蓄 Demand Deposits	20893.90	4256.73	(5) 乡镇企业贷款 Loans to Village and Township Enterprises	1542.61	92.15
(2) 定期储蓄 Time Deposits	43130.56	5459.63	(6) 三资企业贷款 Loans to Foreign Investment Enterprises and Ventures	1723.46	-515.55
5. 农业存款 Deposits by Agricultural Sector	465.72	55.34	(7) 私营企业及个体贷款 Loans to Privately-run Enterprises and Self-employed Entities	392.42	139.28
6. 其他存款 Other Deposits	4924.14	1048.66	(8) 其他短期贷款 Other Short-term Loans	6182.61	1431.03
二、委托存款及委托投资基金 Designated Deposits and Designated Investment Funds	66.52	15.53	其中：个人短期消费贷款 Of Which: Short-term Consumer Credit	553.92	107.04
三、金融债券 Financial Bonds	0.47	-0.37	2. 中期流动资金贷款 Medium-term Working Capital Loans	5183.80	-108.53
四、应付及暂收款 Account Payable and Receipts on Account	1857.59	-340.78	3. 中长期贷款 Medium and Long-term Loans	37133.41	6377.90
其中：应付及预收利息 Of Which: Interest Payable and Received in Advance	897.35	-88.46	(1) 基本建设贷款 Capital Construction Loans	21370.27	2883.75
五、同业往来 Inter-bank Transactions	5055.76	-498.56	(2) 技术改造贷款 Technical Improvement Loans	1811.42	31.05
1. 同业存放 Due to Banks and Other Financial Institutions	4944.75	-552.32	(3) 其他中长期贷款 Other Medium and Long-term Loans	13951.72	3463.10

续表
Continued

项　目 Items	余　额 Balance	比年初增减额 Changes within the Year	项　目 Items	余　额 Balance	比年初增减额 Changes within the Year
2.同业拆借 Placements from Banks and Other Financial Institutions	111.01	53.76	其中：个人中长期消费贷款 Of Which：Medium and Long－term Consumer Credit	8611.03	2892.12
六、流通中货币 Currency in Circulation	17278.03	1589.23	4.票据融资 Paper Financing	2458.77	1035.55
七、各项准备 Total Provisions	1387.57	603.71	其中：贴现 Of Which：Discount	2458.77	1035.55
其中：贷款呆账准备金 Of Which：Provisions for Bad Loan	1029.08	274.35	5.各项垫款 Total Advances	315.98	－3.16
八、所有者权益 Owner's Equity	5234.58	154.60	二、有价证券及投资 Securities and Investments	19488.39	1094.64
其中：实收资本 Of Which：Paid－in Capital	5011.98	－664.77	三、应收及预付款 Accounts Recceivable and Advance Payments	2262.99	－537.30
当年结益 Net Earnings	637.21	637.21	其中：应收利息 Of Which：Interest Receivable	1319.49	－306.11
九、其他 Others	－4915.94	－812.39	四、同业往来 Inter－bank Transactions	1060.85	－111.74
			1.存放同业 Due to Banks and Other Financial Institutions	105.63	31.31
			2.拆放同业 Placements with Banks and Other Financial Institutions	955.22	－143.05
			五、金银占款 Position for Bullion and Silver Purchase	337.24	81.24
			六、外汇占款 Position for Foreign Exchange Purchase	23014.07	5763.85
			七、库存现金 Cash in Vault	778.63	64.40
			八、财政借款 Overdraft by State Finance	1582.06	
资金来源总计 Total Sources	**139416.86**	**16831.69**	**资金运用总计 Total Uses**	**139416.86**	**16831.69**

国家银行人民币信贷收支表
Sources and Uses of Credit Funds of State Banks (RMB)

(2003年末)

(Year - end of 2003)

单位：亿元

Unit: 100 Million Yuan

项　目 Items	余　额 Balance	比年初增减额 Changes within the Year	项　目 Items	余　额 Balance	比年初增减额 Changes within the Year
一、各项存款 Total Deposits	134650.27	21212.00	一、各项贷款 Total Loans	106155.93	15107.86
1. 企业存款 Deposits by Enterprises	41594.94	5698.99	1. 短期贷款 Short - term Loans	47987.46	2183.06
(1) 活期存款 Demand Deposits	31504.35	4133.75	(1) 工业贷款 Loans to Industrial Sector	17639.07	891.89
(2) 定期存款 Time Deposits	10090.59	1565.24	(2) 商业贷款 Loans to Commercial Sector	15168.83	-574.48
2. 财政存款 Fiscal Deposits	5083.45	1647.25	其中：农副产品贷款 Of Which: Loans for the Purchase of Farm Products	7282.62	-534.99
3. 机关团体存款 Deposits by Government Agencies and Social Organizations	5593.99	985.90	(3) 建筑业贷款 Loans to Construction Sector	1938.17	-233.76
4. 储蓄存款 Savings Deposits	75834.83	11727.32	(4) 农业贷款 Loans to Agricultural Sector	1271.81	-10.20
(1) 活期储蓄 Demand Deposits	25944.22	5008.00	(5) 乡镇企业贷款 Loans to Village and Township Enterprises	1680.49	137.87
(2) 定期储蓄 Time Deposits	49890.61	6719.32	(6) 三资企业贷款 Loans to Foreign Investment Enterprises and Ventures	1679.67	-46.75
5. 农业存款 Deposits by Agricultural Sector	463.28	-3.07	(7) 私营企业及个体贷款 Loans to Privately - run Enterprises and Self - employed Entities	539.70	144.98
6. 其他存款 Other Deposits	6079.78	1155.61	(8) 其他短期贷款 Other Short - term Loans	8069.72	1873.51
二、委托存款及委托投资基金 Designated Deposits and Designated Investment Funds	32.30	-34.61	其中：个人短期消费贷款 Of Which: Short - term Consumer Credit	754.95	189.66
三、金融债券 Financial Bonds	5429.75	1108.41	2. 中期流动资金贷款 Medium - term Working Capital Loans	5329.92	145.61
四、应付及暂收款 Account Payable and Receipts on Account	2300.77	447.16	3. 中长期贷款 Medium and Long - term Loans	47811.23	10525.83
其中：应付及预收利息 Of Which: Interest Payable and Received in Advance	877.68	-19.68	(1) 基本建设贷款 Capital Construction Loans	27184.87	5769.01
五、卖出回购证券 Repo	27.52	-214.02	(2) 技术改造贷款 Technical Improvement Loans	1904.42	93.05
六、同业往来 Inter - bank Transactions	4757.27	-433.21	(3) 其他中长期贷款 Other Medium and Long - term Loans	18721.94	4663.77

续表
Continued

项　目 Items	余　额 Balance	比年初增减额 Changes within the Year	项　目 Items	余　额 Balance	比年初增减额 Changes within the Year
1. 同业存放 Due to Banks and Other Financial Institutions	4711.56	-370.95	其中：个人中长期消费贷款 Of Which: Medium and Long-term Consumer Credit	12181.83	3571.99
2. 同业拆借 Placements from Banks and Other Financial Institutions	45.71	-62.26	4. 票据融资 Paper Financing	4751.74	2292.92
			其中：贴现 Of Which: Discount	4740.54	2281.72
七、流通中货币 Currency in Circulation	19745.99	2467.96	5. 各项垫款 Total Advances	275.58	-39.56
八、各项准备 Total Provisions	2492.33	966.14	二、有价证券及投资 Securities and Investments	21860.55	2371.48
其中：贷款损失准备 Of Which: Provisions for Loan Losses	1859.39	707.75	三、应收及预付款 Accounts Receivable and Advance Payments	1794.98	-462.10
九、所有者权益 Owner's Equity	5705.15	973.43	其中：应收利息 Of Which: Interest Receivable	857.51	-462.92
其中：实收资本 Of Which: Paid-in Capital	5675.07	663.22	四、买入返售证券 Reverse Repo	1142.29	117.77
当年结益 Net Earnings	308.61	308.61	五、同业往来 Inter-bank Transactions	731.53	-356.60
十、其他 Others	-11427.72	-3398.84	1. 存放同业 Due to Banks and Other Financial Institutions	155.97	50.44
			2. 拆放同业 Placements with Banks and Other Financial Institutions	575.56	-407.04
			六、金银占款 Position for Bullion and Silver Purchase	337.24	
			七、外汇占款 Position for Foreign Exchange Purchase	30840.72	7826.36
			八、库存现金 Cash in Vault	850.39	71.71
			九、财政借款 Overdraft by State Finance		-1582.06
资金来源总计 Total Sources	**163713.63**	**23094.42**	**资金运用总计 Total Uses**	**163713.63**	**23094.42**

国家银行人民币信贷收支表

Sources and Uses of Credit Funds of State Banks（RMB）

（2004 年末）

（Year－end of 2004）

单位：亿元

Unit：100 Million Yuan

项目 Items	余额 Balance	比年初增减额 Changes within the Year	项目 Items	余额 Balance	比年初增减额 Changes within the Year
一、各项存款 Total Deposits	153556.60	18902.71	一、各项贷款 Total Loans	116050.92	12863.39
1. 企业存款 Deposits by Enterprises	48491.87	6123.93	1. 短期贷款 Short－term Loans	46164.00	672.37
（1）活期存款 Demand Deposits	35964.82	3687.48	（1）工业贷款 Loans to Industrial Sector	17400.71	338.55
（2）定期存款 Time Deposits	12527.05	2436.45	（2）商业贷款 Loans to Commercial Sector	14079.90	－284.59
2. 财政存款 Fiscal Deposits	6105.73	667.86	其中：农副产品贷款 Of Which：Loans for the Purchase of Farm Products	7523.01	240.39
3. 机关团体存款 Deposits by Government Agencies and Social Organizations	6589.89	995.86	（3）建筑业贷款 Loans to Construction Sector	1210.80	－410.15
4. 储蓄存款 Savings Deposits	86469.56	10627.26	（4）农业贷款 Loans to Agricultural Sector	1296.59	27.79
（1）活期储蓄 Demand Deposits	30205.96	4256.73	（5）乡镇企业贷款 Loans to Village and Township Enterprises	1786.88	107.25
（2）定期储蓄 Time Deposits	56263.60	6370.53	（6）三资企业贷款 Loans to Foreign Investment Enterprises and Ventures	1352.50	－97.43
5. 农业存款 Deposits by Agricultural Sector	484.99	21.68	（7）私营企业及个体贷款 Loans to Privately－run Enterprises and Self－employed Entities	741.51	76.79
6. 其他存款 Other Deposits	5414.56	466.12	（8）其他短期贷款 Other Short－term Loans	8295.11	914.16
二、委托存款及委托投资基金 Designated Deposits and Designated Investment Funds	36.73	4.60	其中：个人短期消费贷款 Of Which：Short－term Consumer Credit	691.37	－17.21
三、金融债券 Financial Bonds	10094.96	4808.55	2. 中期流动资金贷款 Medium－term Working Capital Loans	4711.06	－441.53
四、应付及暂收款 Account Payable and Receipts on Account	2556.12	263.83	3. 中长期贷款 Medium and Long－term Loans	57579.23	9907.70
其中：应付及预收利息 Of Which：Interest Payable and Received in Advance	996.29	132.87	（1）基本建设贷款 Capital Construction Loans	32586.45	5511.59
五、卖出回购资产 Assets Repo（Including Securities）	144.51	38.85	（2）技术改造贷款 Technical Improvement Loans	1906.26	121.05
六、同业往来 Inter－bank Transactions	4318.54	－380.03	（3）其他中长期贷款 Other Medium and Long－term Loans	23086.52	4275.06

续表
Continued

项　　目 Items	余　额 Balance	比年初增减额 Changes within the Year	项　　目 Items	余　额 Balance	比年初增减额 Changes within the Year
1. 同业存放 Due to Banks and Other Financial Institutions	4295.18	-357.68	其中：个人中长期消费贷款 Of Which：Medium and Long-term Consumer Credit	14517.76	2615.38
2. 同业拆借 Placements from Banks and Other Financial Institutions	23.36	-22.35	4. 票据融资 Paper Financing	7391.21	2713.06
			其中：贴现 Of Which：Discount	7380.06	2713.11
七、流通中货币 Currency in Circulation	21468.30	1722.31	5. 各项垫款 Total Advances	205.42	11.79
八、各项准备 Total Provisions	2810.25	317.90	二、有价证券及投资 Securities and Investments	22494.86	563.11
其中：贷款损失准备 Of Which：Provisions for Loan Losses	2094.11	263.83	三、应收及预付款 Accounts Receivable and Advance Payments	2554.57	748.80
九、所有者权益 Owner's Equity	5156.10	-126.81	其中：应收利息 Of Which：Interest Receivable	903.31	-181.91
其中：实收资本 Of Which：Paid-in Capital	7596.36	1921.29	四、买入返售资产 Assets Reverse Repo（Including Securities）	1226.76	-129.03
当年结益 Net Earnings	321.57	321.57	五、同业往来 Inter-bank Transactions	1505.36	723.31
十、其他 Others	-6168.85	3492.03	1. 存放同业 Due to Banks and Other Financial Institutions	1053.14	846.67
			2. 拆放同业 Placements with Banks and Other Financial Institutions	452.22	-123.36
			六、金银占款 Position for Bullion and Silver Purchase	337.24	
			七、外汇占款 Position for Foreign Exchange Purchase	48747.02	14181.87
			八、库存现金 Cash in Vault	1056.53	92.49
资金来源总计 Total Sources	**193973.26**	**29043.94**	**资金运用总计 Total Uses**	**193973.26**	**29043.94**

国家银行人民币信贷收支表

Sources and Uses of Credit Funds of State Banks（RMB）

（2005 年末）

（Year－end of 2005）

单位：亿元

Unit：100 Million Yuan

项 目 Items	余 额 Balance	比年初增减额 Changes within the Year	项 目 Items	余 额 Balance	比年初增减额 Changes within the Year
一、各项存款 Total Deposits	181120.65	25794.16	一、各项贷款 Total Loans	120851.06	10931.75
1. 企业存款 Deposits by Enterprises	53490.49	4839.43	1. 短期贷款 Short－term Loans	42045.65	816.51
（1）活期存款 Demand Deposits	36708.39	624.48	（1）工业贷款 Loans to Industrial Sector	14693.21	250.80
（2）定期存款 Time Deposits	16782.10	4214.95	（2）商业贷款 Loans to Commercial Sector	13198.71	513.56
2. 财政存款 Fiscal Deposits	7822.19	1716.27	其中：农副产品贷款 Of Which：Loans for the Purchase of Farm Products	8054.48	531.47
3. 机关团体存款 Deposits by Government Agencies and Social Organizations	10128.69	3504.73	（3）建筑业贷款 Loans to Construction Sector	1012.47	－198.28
4. 储蓄存款 Savings Deposits	100633.26	14163.89	（4）农业贷款 Loans to Agricultural Sector	1384.22	96.34
（1）活期储蓄 Demand Deposits	35158.26	4952.66	（5）乡镇企业贷款 Loans to Village and Township Enterprises	1726.53	－60.35
（2）定期储蓄 Time Deposits	65475.00	9211.23	（6）三资企业贷款 Loans to Foreign Investment Enterprises and Ventures	1211.36	－4.94
5. 农业存款 Deposits by Agricultural Sector	424.19	－60.82	（7）私营企业及个体贷款 Loans to Privately－run Enterprises and Self－employed Entities	706.22	－17.23
6. 其他存款 Other Deposits	8621.83	1630.66	（8）其他短期贷款 Other Short－term Loans	8112.93	236.61
二、委托存款及委托投资基金 Designated Deposits and Designated Investment Funds	34.58	7.11	其中：个人短期消费贷款 Of Which：Short－term Consumer Credit	650.12	－30.30
三、金融债券 Financial Bonds	14384.90	3588.43	2. 中期流动资金贷款 Medium－term Working Capital Loans	4115.29	－396.73
四、应付及暂收款 Account Payable and Receipts on Account	3611.58	1057.68	3. 中长期贷款 Medium and Long－term Loans	64991.15	8310.04
其中：应付及预收利息 Of Which：Interest Payable and Received in Advance	1394.65	403.80	（1）基本建设贷款 Capital Construction Loans	37016.03	5320.55
五、卖出回购资产 Assets Repo（Including Securities）	4275.26	4130.75	（2）技术改造贷款 Technical Improvement Loans	1911.66	23.19
六、同业往来 Inter－bank Transactions	5542.97	1440.25	（3）其他中长期贷款 Other Medium and Long－term Loans	26063.46	2966.30

续表
Continued

项目 Items	余额 Balance	比年初增减额 Changes within the Year	项目 Items	余额 Balance	比年初增减额 Changes within the Year
1. 同业存放 Due to Banks and Other Financial Institutions	5488.88	1409.52	其中：个人中长期消费贷款 Of Which: Medium and Long - term Consumer Credit	15532.03	1005.47
2. 同业拆借 Placements from Banks and Other Financial Institutions	54.09	30.73	4. 票据融资 Paper Financing	9574.68	2184.59
七、流通中货币 Currency in Circulation	24884.39	2671.44	其中：贴现 Of Which: Discount	9525.05	2146.11
八、各项准备 Total Provisions	3170.60	443.04	5. 各项垫款 Total Advances	124.29	17.34
其中：贷款损失准备 Of Which: Provisions for Loan Losses	2794.11	700.02	二、有价证券及投资 Securities and Investments	25067.51	2668.14
九、所有者权益 Owner's Equity	10745.71	4931.03	三、应收及预付款 Accounts Receivable and Advance Payments	5340.13	3528.41
其中：实收资本 Of Which: Paid - in Capital	7712.20	111.69	其中：应收利息 Of Which: Interest Receivable	814.68	- 112.52
当年结益 Net Earnings	3207.27	3207.27	四、买入返售资产 Assets Reverse Repo (Including Securities)	1744.81	517.94
十、其他 Others	- 26572.37	- 12527.26	五、同业往来 Inter - bank Transactions	1730.38	234.70
			1. 存放同业 Due to Banks and Other Financial Institutions	1427.95	374.81
			2. 拆放同业 Placements with Banks and Other Financial Institutions	302.43	- 140.11
			六、金银占款 Position for Bullion and Silver Purchase	337.24	
			七、外汇占款 Position for Foreign Exchange Purchase	66127.14	13655.69
资金来源总计 Total Sources	**221198.27**	**31536.63**	**资金运用总计 Total Uses**	**221198.27**	**31536.63**

3. 政策性银行人民币信贷收支表* （1997—2005 年）
Sources and Uses of Credit Funds of Policy Banks（RMB）（1997—2005）

政策性银行人民币信贷收支表
Sources and Uses of Credit Funds of Policy Banks（RMB）

（1997 年末）

（Year－end of 1997）

单位：亿元

Unit：100 Million Yuan

项　目 Items	余　额 Balance	比年初增减额 Changes within the Year	项　目 Items	余　额 Balance	比年初增减额 Changes within the Year
一、各项存款 Total Deposits	366.21	73.30	一、各项贷款 Total Loans	12124.08	3331.31
1. 企业存款 Deposits by Enterprises	347.15	63.61	1. 短期贷款 Short－term Loans	7328.86	1616.22
（1）活期存款 Demand Deposits	345.85	62.54	（1）工业贷款 Loans to Industrial Sector		
（2）定期存款 Time Deposits	1.30	1.07	（2）商业贷款 Loans to Commercial Sector	7246.12	1606.85
2. 城镇储蓄存款 Urban Savings Deposits			其中：收购贷款 Of Which：Loans for the Purchase of Farm Products	6914.94	1548.69
（1）活期储蓄 Demand Deposits			（3）建筑业贷款 Loans to Construction Sector		
（2）定期储蓄 Time Deposits			（4）农业贷款 Loans to Agricultural Sector		
3. 农业存款 Deposits by Agricultural Sector			（5）乡镇企业贷款 Loans to Village and Township Enterprises		
4. 信托存款 Trust Deposits					
5. 其他存款 Other Deposits	19.06	9.69	（6）三资企业贷款 Loans to Foreign Investment Enterprises and Ventures		
二、代理财政性存款 Agency Fiscal Deposits	107.33	2.02	（7）私营企业及个体贷款 Loans to Privately－run Enterprises and Self－employed Entities		
三、发行金融债券 Financial Bonds Issue	3509.58	1104.98			
其中：发行政策性金融债券 Of Which：Policy Financial Bonds Issue	3509.58	1104.98	（8）贴现 Discount		
			（9）其他短期贷款 Other Short－term Loans	82.74	9.37
四、国家投资债券 State Investment Bonds			2. 中长期贷款 Medium and Long－term Loans	4792.62	1713.43
五、卖出回购证券 Repo			（1）基本建设贷款 Capital Construction Loans	3454.28	1175.79

* 本表机构包括国家开发银行、中国进出口银行、中国农业发展银行。

Policy Banks of this statement include China Development Bank，The Export－Import Bank of China and Agricultural Development Bank of China.

续表
Continued

项目 Items	余额 Balance	比年初增减额 Changes within the Year
六、向中央银行借款 Borrowings from the Central Bank	8167.79	2070.88
七、同业往来 Inter - bank Transactions	8.19	- 37.38
1. 同业存放 Due to Banks and Other Financial Institutions	8.19	- 37.38
2. 同业拆借 Placements from Banks and Other Financial Institutions		
八、委托存款及委托投资基金 Designated Deposits and Designated Investment Funds	0.03	0.03
1. 委托存款 Designated Deposits	0.03	0.03
2. 委托投资基金 Designated Investment Funds		
九、代理金融机构委托贷款基金 Designated Loan Funds on Behalf of Financial Institutions		
其中：中央银行委托贷款基金 Of Which: Loan Funds Designated by the Central Bank		
十、所有者权益 Owner's Equity	604.47	132.27
其中：实收资本 Of Which: Paid - in Capital	604.67	154.28
当年结益 Net Earnings	- 18.08	- 18.08
十一、其他 Others	- 194.54	- 68.39
资金来源总计 Total Sources	**12569.06**	**3277.71**

项目 Items	余额 Balance	比年初增减额 Changes within the Year
（2）技术改造贷款 Technical Improvement Loans	118.69	- 1.60
（3）其他中长期贷款 Other Medium and Long - term Loans	1219.65	539.24
3. 信托贷款 Trust Loans		
4. 逾期类贷款 Overdue Loans	2.60	1.66
二、国家投资债券贷款 Loans Related to State Investment Bonds		
三、有价证券及投资 Securities and Investments	1.02	- 5.50
四、缴存人行准备金 Reserves with the Central Bank	34.48	11.78
五、在人行存款 Deposits with the Central Bank	282.16	- 45.57
六、存放中央银行特种存款 Special Deposits with the Central Bank		
七、存放中央银行财政性存款 Fiscal Deposits with Central Bank		
八、同业往来 Inter - bank Transactions	123.69	- 16.19
1. 存放同业 Due from Banks and Other Financial Institutions	123.69	- 3.86
2. 拆放同业 Placements with Banks and Other Financial Institutions		- 12.33
九、代理金融机构贷款 Lending on Behalf of Financial Institutions		
其中：代理人行专项贷款 Of Which: Agency Earmarked Loans of the Central Bank		
十、库存现金 Cash in Vault	3.09	1.56
十一、外汇占款 Position for Foreign Exchange Purchase	0.54	0.32
资金运用总计 Total Uses	**12569.06**	**3277.71**

政策性银行人民币信贷收支表

Sources and Uses of Credit Funds of Policy Banks（RMB）

（1998 年末）

（Year-end of 1998）

单位：亿元

Unit：100 Million Yuan

项　目 Items	余　额 Balance	比年初增减额 Changes within the Year	项　目 Items	余　额 Balance	比年初增减额 Changes within the Year
一、各项存款 Total Deposits	205.34	-164.65	一、各项贷款 Total Loans	12119.04	-8.87
1. 企业存款 Deposits by Enterprises	190.66	-156.99	1. 短期贷款 Short-term Loans	7053.64	-256.27
（1）活期存款 Demand Deposits	190.17	-156.18	（1）工业贷款 Loans to Industrial Sector		
（2）定期存款 Time Deposits	0.49	-0.81	（2）商业贷款 Loans to Commercial Sector	6971.71	-246.00
2. 城镇储蓄存款 Urban Savings Deposits			其中：收购贷款 Of Which：Loans for the Purchase of Farm Products	6262.28	-623.78
（1）活期储蓄 Demand Deposits			（3）建筑业贷款 Loans to Construction Sector		
（2）定期储蓄 Time Deposits			（4）农业贷款 Loans to Agricultural Sector		
3. 农业存款 Deposits by Agricultural Sector			（5）乡镇企业贷款 Loans to Village and Township Enterprises		
4. 信托存款 Trust Deposits			（6）三资企业贷款 Loans to Foreign Investment Enterprises and Ventures		
5. 其他存款 Other Deposits	14.68	-7.66	（7）私营企业及个体贷款 Loans to Privately-run Enterprises and Self-employed Entities		
二、代理财政性存款 Agency Fiscal Deposits	191.14	83.75	（8）贴现 Discount		
三、发行金融债券 Financial Bonds Issue	5145.11	1635.52	（9）其他短期贷款 Other Short-term Loans	81.93	-10.27
其中：发行政策性金融债券 Of Which：Policy Financial Bonds Issue	5145.11	1635.52	2. 中长期贷款 Medium and Long-term Loans	4954.90	139.52
四、国家投资债券 State Investment Bonds			（1）基本建设贷款 Capital Construction Loans	4410.61	952.69
五、卖出回购证券 Repo			（2）技术改造贷款 Technical Improvement Loans	143.78	25.09
六、向中央银行借款 Borrowings from the Central Bank	6573.76	-1593.97	（3）其他中长期贷款 Other Medium and Long-term Loans	400.51	-838.26
七、同业往来 Inter-bank Transactions	2.35	-7.33	3. 信托贷款 Trust Loans		
1. 同业存放 Due to Banks and Other Financial Institutions	2.35	-7.33	4. 逾期类贷款 Overdue Loans	110.50	107.88
2. 同业拆借 Placements from Banks and Other Financial Institutions					

续表
Continued

项目 Items	余额 Balance	比年初增减额 Changes within the Year	项目 Items	余额 Balance	比年初增减额 Changes within the Year
八、委托存款及委托投资基金 Designated Deposits and Designated Investment Funds		-0.31	二、国家投资债券贷款 Loans Related to State Investment Bonds		
1. 委托存款 Designated Deposits		-0.31	三、有价证券及投资 Securities and Investments	0.36	-0.66
2. 委托投资基金 Designated Investment Funds			四、缴存人行准备金 Reserves with the Central Bank		
九、代理金融机构委托贷款基金 Designated Loan Funds on Behalf of Financial Institutions			五、缴存准备金存款 Reserve Deposits with the Central Bank	270.63	-41.94
其中：中央银行委托贷款基金 Of Which: Loan Funds Designated by the Central Bank			六、存放中央银行特种存款 Special Deposits with the Central Bank		
十、所有者权益 Owner's Equity	590.08	-47.12	七、存放中央银行财政性存款 Fiscal Deposits with the Central Bank		
其中：实收资本 Of Which: Paid-in Capital	611.01	6.26	八、同业往来 Inter-bank Transactions	115.93	-7.37
当年结益 Net Earnings	-31.88	-31.88	1. 存放同业 Due from Banks and Other Financial Institutions	107.93	-15.37
十一、其他 Others	-197.88	35.58	2. 拆放同业 Placements with Banks and Other Financial Institutions	8.00	8.00
			九、代理金融机构贷款 Lending on Behalf of Financial Institutions		
			其中：代理人行专项贷款 Of Which: Agency Earmarked Loans of the Central Bank		
			十、库存现金 Cash in Vault	4.00	0.91
			十一、外汇占款 Position for Foreign Exchange Purchase	-0.06	-0.60
资金来源总计 Total Sources	**12509.90**	**-58.53**	**资金运用总计 Total Uses**	**12509.90**	**-58.53**

政策性银行人民币信贷收支表
Sources and Uses of Credit Funds of Policy Banks（RMB）

（1999 年末）

（Year – end of 1999）

单位：亿元

Unit：100 Million Yuan

项 目 Items	余 额 Balance	比年初增减额 Changes within the Year	项 目 Items	余 额 Balance	比年初增减额 Changes within the Year
一、各项存款 Total Deposits	376.36	176.64	一、各项贷款 Total Loans	13094.82	1460.07
1. 企业存款 Deposits by Enterprises	368.06	182.70	1. 短期贷款 Short – term Loans	7295.98	249.59
（1）活期存款 Demand Deposits	366.35	181.53	（1）工业贷款 Loans to Industrial Sector		
（2）定期存款 Time Deposits	1.71	1.17	（2）商业贷款 Loans to Commercial Sector	7188.09	205.68
2. 城镇储蓄存款 Urban Savings Deposits			其中：收购贷款 Of Which：Loans for the Purchase of Farm Products	7174.89	206.52
（1）活期储蓄 Demand Deposits			（3）建筑业贷款 Loans to Construction Sector		
（2）定期储蓄 Time Deposits			（4）农业贷款 Loans to Agricultural Sector		
3. 农业存款 Deposits by Agricultural Sector			（5）乡镇企业贷款 Loans to Village and Township Enterprises		
4. 信托存款 Trust Deposits					
5. 其他存款 Other Deposits	8.30	–6.06	（6）三资企业贷款 Loans to Foreign Investment Enterprises and Ventures		
二、代理财政性存款 Agency Fiscal Deposits	186.40	–4.90	（7）私营企业及个体贷款 Loans to Privately – run Enterprises and Self – employed Entities		
三、发行金融债券 Financial Bonds Issue	6311.74	1166.63	（8）贴现 Discount		
其中：发行政策性金融债券 Of Which：Policy Financial Bonds Issue	6311.74	1166.63	（9）其他短期贷款 Other Short – term Loans	107.89	43.91
四、国家投资债券 State Investment Bonds			2. 中长期贷款 Medium and Long – term Loans	5646.51	1085.86
五、卖出回购证券 Repo			（1）基本建设贷款 Capital Construction Loans	5052.53	1024.20
六、向中央银行借款 Borrowings from the Central Bank	6794.23	220.47	（2）技术改造贷款 Technical Improvement Loans	113.92	–10.64
七、同业往来 Inter – bank Transactions	15.28	7.23	（3）其他中长期贷款 Other Medium and Long – term Loans	480.06	72.30
1. 同业存放 Due to Banks and Other Financial Institutions	15.28	7.23	3. 信托贷款 Trust Loans		
2. 同业拆借 Placements from Banks and Other Financial Institutions			4. 逾期类贷款 Overdue Loans	152.33	124.62

续表
Continued

项目 Items	余额 Balance	比年初增减额 Changes within the Year	项目 Items	余额 Balance	比年初增减额 Changes within the Year
八、委托存款及委托投资基金 Designated Deposits and Designated Investment Funds			二、国家投资债券贷款 Loans Related to State Investment Bonds		
			三、有价证券及投资 Securities and Investments	0.36	
1. 委托存款 Designated Deposits			四、缴存准备金存款 Reserves Deposits with the Central Bank	317.41	43.46
2. 委托投资基金 Designated Investment Funds			五、存放中央银行特种存款 Special Deposits with the Central Bank		
九、代理金融机构委托贷款基金 Designated Loan Funds on Behalf of Financial Institutions			六、存放中央银行财政性存款 Fiscal Deposits with the Central Bank		
其中：中央银行委托贷款基金 Of Which: Loan Funds Designated by the Central Bank			七、同业往来 Inter-bank Transactions	119.70	5.48
			1. 存放同业 Due from Banks and Other Financial Institutions	69.70	-36.52
十、所有者权益 Owner's Equity	703.47	113.43			
其中：实收资本 Of Which: Paid-in Capital	660.56	49.56	2. 拆放同业 Placements with Banks and Other Financial Institutions	50.00	42.00
当年结益 Net Earnings	5.62	5.62			
十一、其他 Others	-852.57	-171.81	八、代理金融机构贷款 Lending on Behalf of Financial Institutions		
			其中：代理人行专项贷款 Of Which: Agency Earmarked Loans of the Central Bank		
			九、库存现金 Cash in Vault	2.62	-1.38
			十、外汇占款 Position for Foreign Exchange Purchase		0.06
资金来源总计 Total Sources	**13534.91**	**1507.69**	**资金运用总计 Total Uses**	**13534.91**	**1507.69**

政策性银行人民币信贷收支表
Sources and Uses of Credit Funds of Policy Banks (RMB)

(2000年末)

(Year - end of 2000)

单位：亿元

Unit: 100 Million Yuan

项 目 Items	余 额 Balance	比年初增减额 Changes within the Year	项 目 Items	余 额 Balance	比年初增减额 Changes within the Year
一、各项存款 Total Deposits	531.56	155.22	一、各项贷款 Total Loans	14149.87	1315.83
1. 企业存款 Deposits by Enterprises	526.59	158.55	1. 短期贷款 Short - term Loans	7374.57	78.60
(1) 活期存款 Demand Deposits	523.17	156.84	(1) 工业贷款 Loans to Industrial Sector		
(2) 定期存款 Time Deposits	3.42	1.71	(2) 商业贷款 Loans to Commercial Sector	7303.69	115.51
2. 城镇储蓄存款 Urban Savings Deposits			其中：收购贷款 Of Which: Loans for the Purchase of Farm Products	7289.75	114.86
(1) 活期储蓄 Demand Deposits			(3) 建筑业贷款 Loans to Construction Sector		
(2) 定期储蓄 Time Deposits			(4) 农业贷款 Loans to Agricultural Sector		
3. 农业存款 Deposits by Agricultural Sector			(5) 乡镇企业贷款 Loans to Village and Township Enterprises		
4. 信托存款 Trust Deposits			(6) 三资企业贷款 Loans to Foreign Investment Enterprises and Ventures		
5. 其他存款 Other Deposits	4.97	- 3.33	(7) 私营企业及个体贷款 Loans to Privately - run Enterprises and Self - employed Entities		
二、代理财政性存款 Agency Fiscal Deposits	211.57	25.17	(8) 贴现 Discount		
三、发行金融债券 Financial Bonds Issue	7395.35	1083.61	(9) 其他短期贷款 Other Short - term Loans	70.88	- 36.91
其中：发行政策性金融债券 Of Which: Policy Financial Bonds Issue	7395.35	1083.61	2. 中长期贷款 Medium and Long - term Loans	6668.95	1227.29
四、国家投资债券 State Investment Bonds			(1) 基本建设贷款 Capital Construction Loans	5956.25	1098.96
五、卖出回购证券 Repo			(2) 技术改造贷款 Technical Improvement Loans	117.08	12.77
六、向中央银行借款 Borrowings from the Central Bank	6705.65	- 88.58	(3) 其他中长期贷款 Other Medium and Long - term Loans	595.62	115.56
七、同业往来 Inter - bank Transactions	14.51	- 0.81	3. 信托贷款 Trust Loans		
1. 同业存放 Due to Banks and Other Financial Institutions	14.51	- 0.81	4. 逾期类贷款 Overdue Loans	106.35	9.94
2. 同业拆借 Placements from Banks and Other Financial Institutions					

续表
Continued

项 目 Items	余 额 Balance	比年初增减额 Changes within the Year	项 目 Items	余 额 Balance	比年初增减额 Changes within the Year
八、委托存款及委托投资基金 Designated Deposits and Designated Investment Funds	0.53	0.53	二、国家投资债券贷款 Loans Related to State Investment Bonds		
			三、有价证券及投资 Securities and Investments	52.43	4.47
1. 委托存款 Designated Deposits	0.53	0.53	四、缴存准备金存款 Reserve Deposits with the Central Bank	216.43	－100.99
2. 委托投资基金 Designated Investment Funds			五、存放中央银行特种存款 Special Deposits with the Central Bank		
九、代理金融机构委托贷款基金 Designated Loan Funds on Behalf of Financial Institutions			六、存放中央银行财政性存款 Fiscal Deposits with the Central Bank		
其中：中央银行委托贷款基金 Of Which: Loan Funds Designated by the Central Bank			七、同业往来 Inter－bank Transactions	172.33	52.51
			1. 存放同业 Due from Banks and Other Financial Institutions	52.63	－17.19
十、所有者权益 Owner's Equity	763.82	57.47			
其中：实收资本 Of Which: Paid－in Capital	691.93	31.29	2. 拆放同业 Placements with Banks and Other Financial Institutions	119.70	69.70
当年结益 Net Earnings	32.29	32.29	八、代理金融机构贷款 Lending on Behalf of Financial Institutions		
十一、其他 Others	－1017.03	51.50	其中：代理人行专项贷款 Of Which: Agency Earmarked Loans of the Central Bank		
			九、库存现金 Cash in Vault	2.05	－0.56
			十、外汇占款 Position for Foreign Exchange Purchase	12.85	12.85
资金来源总计 Total Sources	**14605.96**	**1284.11**	**资金运用总计 Total Uses**	**14605.96**	**1284.11**

政策性银行人民币信贷收支表
Sources and Uses of Credit Funds of Policy Banks (RMB)

(2001 年末)

(Year－end of 2001)

单位：亿元

Unit: 100 Million Yuan

项　目 Items	余　额 Balance	比年初增减额 Changes within the Year	项　目 Items	余　额 Balance	比年初增减额 Changes within the Year
一、各项存款 Total Deposits	552.38	20.83	一、各项贷款 Total Loans	15218.91	910.66
1. 企业存款 Deposits by Enterprises	549.27	22.70	1. 短期贷款 Short－term Loans	7431.85	55.60
(1) 活期存款 Demand Deposits	544.00	37.85	(1) 工业贷款 Loans to Industrial Sector		
(2) 定期存款 Time Deposits	5.27	－15.15	(2) 商业贷款 Loans to Commercial Sector	7301.40	－2.56
2. 机关团体存款 Deposits by Government Agencies and Social Organizations			其中：收购贷款 Of Which: Loans for the Purchase of Farm Products	7288.28	－1.75
3. 储蓄存款 Urban Savings Deposits			(3) 建筑业贷款 Loans to Construction Sector		
(1) 活期储蓄 Demand Deposits			(4) 农业贷款 Loans to Agricultural Sector		
(2) 定期储蓄 Time Deposits			(5) 乡镇企业贷款 Loans to Village and Township Enterprises		
4. 农业存款 Deposits by Agricultural Sector			(6) 三资企业贷款 Loans to Foreign Investment Enterprises and Ventures		
5. 其他存款 Other Deposits	3.11	－1.87			
二、代理财政性存款 Agency Fiscal Deposits	277.41	65.80	(7) 私营企业及个体贷款 Loans to Privately－run Enterprises and Self－employed Entities		
三、金融债券 Financial Bonds	8393.28	997.93	(8) 其他短期贷款 Other Short－term Loans	130.45	58.16
其中：政策性金融债券 Of Which: Policy Financial Bonds	8393.28	997.93	其中：个人短期消费贷款 Of Which: Short－term Consumer Credit		
四、应付及暂收款 Accounts Payable and Receipts on Account	552.17	－14.66			
			2. 中期流动资金贷款 Medium－term Working Capital Loans		
其中：应付及预提利息 Of Which: Interest Payable and Accrued	374.69	－11.69	3. 中长期贷款 Medium and Long－term Loans	7787.06	866.53
五、卖出回购证券 Repo			(1) 基本建设贷款 Capital Construction Loans	6766.48	751.33
六、向中央银行借款 Borrowings from the Central Bank	6749.65	44.00	(2) 技术改造贷款 Technical Improvement Loans	119.21	－5.88
七、同业往来 Inter－bank Transactions	42.19	15.15	(3) 其他中长期贷款 Other Medium and Long－term Loans	901.37	121.08

续表
Continued

项　目 Items	余　额 Balance	比年初增减额 Changes within the Year	项　目 Items	余　额 Balance	比年初增减额 Changes within the Year
1. 同业存放 Due to Banks and Other Financial Institutions	12.19	-14.85	其中：个人中长期消费贷款 Of Which: Medium and Long-term Consumer Credit		
2. 同业拆借 Placements from Banks and Other Financial Institutions	30.00	30.00	4. 票据融资 Paper Financing		
八、委托存款及委托投资基金（净） Designated Deposits and Designated Investment Funds (Net)	0.40	-0.13	其中：贴现 Of Which: Discount		
			5. 各项垫款 Total Advances		-11.47
1. 委托存款及委托投资基金 Designated Deposits and Designated Investment Funds	13.35	2.08	二、有价证券及投资 Securities and Investments	1369.31	1316.88
			三、应收及预付款 Accounts Receivable and Advance Payments	411.71	-1037.77
2. 减：委托贷款及委托投资 Minus: Designated Loans and Designated Investments	12.95	2.21	其中：应收利息 Of Which: Interest Receivable	262.02	-49.39
九、代理金融机构委托贷款基金 Designated Loan Funds on Behalf of Financial Institutions			四、买入返售证券 Reverse Repo	43.90	43.90
			五、存放中央银行准备金存款 Reserve Deposits with the Central Bank	185.19	-31.32
其中：中央银行委托贷款基金 Of Which: Loan Funds Designated by the Central Bank			六、存放中央银行特种存款 Special Deposits with the Central Bank		
十、各项准备 Total Provisions	206.21	97.78	七、缴存中央银行财政性存款 Fiscal Deposits with the Central Bank		
其中：贷款呆账准备金 Of Which: Provisions for Bad Loans	206.21	98.50	八、同业往来 Inter-bank Transactions	94.60	-78.04
十一、所有者权益 Owner's Equity	770.02	7.41	1. 存放同业 Due from Banks and Other Financial Institutions	53.60	0.66
其中：实收资本 Of Which: Paid-in Capital	659.67	-32.26	2. 拆放同业 Placements with Banks and Other Financial Institutions	41.00	-78.70
当年结益 Net Earnings	48.81	48.81			
十二、其他 Others	-135.47	-40.08	九、代理金融机构贷款 Lending on Behalf of Financial Institutions		
			其中：代理人行专项贷款 Of Which: Agency Earmarked Loans of the Central Bank		
			十、库存现金 Cash in Vault	1.65	-0.40
			十一、外汇占款 Position for Foreign Exchange Purchase	82.97	70.12
资金来源总计 Total Sources	**17408.24**	**1194.03**	**资金运用总计 Total Uses**	**17408.24**	**1194.03**

政策性银行人民币信贷收支表

Sources and Uses of Credit Funds of Policy Banks (RMB)

(2002 年末)

(Year - end of 2002)

单位：亿元

Unit: 100 Million Yuan

项　目 Items	余　额 Balance	比年初增减额 Changes within the Year	项　目 Items	余　额 Balance	比年初增减额 Changes within the Year
一、各项存款 Total Deposits	711.26	158.80	一、各项贷款 Total Loans	16605.94	1374.08
1. 企业存款 Deposits by Enterprises	706.08	156.77	1. 短期贷款 Short - term Loans	7496.42	64.57
(1) 活期存款 Demand Deposits	688.90	151.06	(1) 工业贷款 Loans to Industrial Sector		
(2) 定期存款 Time Deposits	17.18	5.71	(2) 商业贷款 Loans to Commercial Sector	7212.18	- 75.43
2. 机关团体存款 Deposits by Government Agencies and Social Organizations			其中：收购贷款 Of Which: Loans for the Purchase of Farm Products	7201.00	- 74.02
3. 储蓄存款 Savings Deposits			(3) 建筑业贷款 Loans to Construction Sector		
(1) 活期储蓄 Demand Deposits			(4) 农业贷款 Loans to Agricultural Sector		
(2) 定期储蓄 Time Deposits			(5) 乡镇企业贷款 Loans to Village and Township Enterprises		
4. 农业存款 Deposits by Agricultural Sector			(6) 三资企业贷款 Loans to Foreign Investment Enterprises and Ventures		
5. 其他存款 Other Deposits	5.18	2.03	(7) 私营企业及个体贷款 Loans to Privately - run Enterprises and Self - employed Entities		
二、代理财政性存款 Agency Fiscal Deposits	411.78	134.40	(8) 其他短期贷款 Other Short - term Loans	284.24	140.00
三、金融债券 Financial Bonds	9685.02	1301.61	其中：个人短期消费贷款 Of Which: Short - term Consumer Credit		
其中：政策性金融债券 Of Which: Policy Financial Bonds	9685.02	1301.61	2. 中期流动资金贷款 Medium - term Working Capital Loans		
四、应付及暂收款 Accounts Payable and Receipts on Account	301.63	- 260.25	3. 中长期贷款 Medium and Long - term Loans	9109.52	1309.51
其中：应付及预提利息 Of Which: Interest Payable and Accrued	243.83	- 140.60	(1) 基本建设贷款 Capital Construction Loans	7979.69	1213.21
五、卖出回购证券 Repo			(2) 技术改造贷款 Technical Improvement Loans	156.17	36.96
六、向中央银行借款 Borrowings from the Central Bank	6501.65	- 248.00	(3) 其他中长期贷款 Other Medium and Long - term Loans	973.66	59.34
七、同业往来 Inter - bank Transactions	57.89	15.72			

续表
Continued

项　目 Items	余　额 Balance	比年初增减额 Changes within the Year
1. 同业存放 Due to Banks and Other Financial Institutions	17.89	5.72
2. 同业拆借 Placements from Banks and Other Financial Institutions	40.00	10.00
八、委托存款及委托投资基金（净） Designated Deposits and Designated Investment Funds（Net）		
1. 委托存款及委托投资基金 Designated Deposits and Designated Investment Funds		
2. 减：委托贷款及委托投资 Minus：Designated Loans and Designated Investments		
九、代理金融机构委托贷款基金 Designated Loan Funds on Behalf of Financial Institutions		
其中：中央银行委托贷款基金 Of Which：Loan Funds Designated by the Central Bank		
十、各项准备 Total Provisions	347.71	141.50
其中：贷款呆账准备金 Of Which：Provisions for Bad Loans	347.71	141.50
十一、所有者权益 Owner's Equity	954.49	184.59
其中：实收资本 Of Which：Paid－in Capital	684.13	24.46
当年结益 Net Earnings	223.67	223.67
十二、其他 Others	－129.51	－6.91
资金来源总计 Total Sources	**18841.92**	**1421.46**

项　目 Items	余　额 Balance	比年初增减额 Changes within the Year
其中：个人中长期消费贷款 Of Which：Medium and Long－term Consumer Credit		
4. 票据融资 Paper Financing		
其中：贴现 Of Which：Discount		
5. 各项垫款 Total Advances		
二、有价证券及投资 Securities and Investments	1412.90	43.59
三、应收及预付款 Accounts Receivable and Advance Payments	209.62	－201.33
其中：应收利息 Of Which：Interest Receivable	197.72	－64.35
四、买入返售证券 Reverse Repo	98.13	54.23
五、存放中央银行准备金存款 Reserve Deposits with the Central Bank	275.22	90.00
六、存放中央银行特种存款 Special Deposits with the Central Bank		
七、缴存中央银行财政性存款 Fiscal Deposits with the Central Bank		
八、同业往来 Inter－bank Transactions	69.62	－24.98
1. 存放同业 Due from Banks and Other Financial Institutions	32.62	－20.98
2. 拆放同业 Placements with Banks and Other Financial Institutions	37.00	－4.00
九、代理金融机构贷款 Lending on Behalf of Financial Institutions		
其中：代理人行专项贷款 Of Which：Agency Earmarked Loans of the Central Bank		
十、库存现金 Cash in Vault	1.99	0.34
十一、外汇占款 Position for Foreign Exchange Purchase	168.50	85.53
资金运用总计 Total Uses	**18841.92**	**1421.46**

政策性银行人民币信贷收支表

Sources and Uses of Credit Funds of Policy Banks（RMB）

（2003 年末）

（Year - end of 2003）

单位：亿元

Unit：100 Million Yuan

项目 Items	余额 Balance	比年初增减额 Changes within the Year	项目 Items	余额 Balance	比年初增减额 Changes within the Year
一、各项存款 Total Deposits	948.83	237.56	一、各项贷款 Total Loans	18489.81	1883.86
1. 企业存款 Deposits by Enterprises	939.45	233.41	1. 短期贷款 Short - term Loans	7243.38	- 253.05
（1）活期存款 Demand Deposits	887.11	198.25	（1）工业贷款 Loans to Industrial Sector		
（2）定期存款 Time Deposits	52.34	35.16	（2）商业贷款 Loans to Commercial Sector	6747.48	- 464.71
2. 机关团体存款 Deposits by Government Agencies and Social Organizations			其中：收购贷款 Of Which：Loans for the Purchase of Farm Products	6737.41	- 463.60
3. 储蓄存款 Savings Deposits			（3）建筑业贷款 Loans to Construction Sector		
（1）活期储蓄 Demand Deposits			（4）农业贷款 Loans to Agricultural Sector		
（2）定期储蓄 Time Deposits			（5）乡镇企业贷款 Loans to Village and Township Enterprises		
4. 农业存款 Deposits by Agricultural Sector			（6）三资企业贷款 Loans to Foreign Investment Enterprises and Ventures		
5. 其他存款 Other Deposits	9.38	4.15	（7）私营企业及个体贷款 Loans to Privately - run Enterprises and Self employed Entities		
二、代理财政性存款 Agency Fiscal Deposits	308.85	- 102.93	（8）其他短期贷款 Other Short - term Loans	495.90	211.66
三、金融债券 Financial Bonds	11410.31	1725.29	其中：个人短期消费贷款 Of Which：Short - term Consumer Credit		
其中：政策性金融债券 Of Which：Policy Financial Bonds	11410.31	1725.29	2. 中期流动资金贷款 Medium - term Working Capital Loans		
四、应付及暂收款 Accounts Payable and Receipts on Account	158.46	- 143.02	3. 中长期贷款 Medium and Long - term Loans	11246.32	2136.80
其中：应付及预提利息 Of Which：Interest Payable and Accrued	122.43	- 121.40	（1）基本建设贷款 Capital Construction Loans	9584.14	1604.45
五、卖出回购证券 Repo			（2）技术改造贷款 Technical Improvement Loans	182.20	26.03
六、向中央银行借款 Borrowings from the Central Bank	6507.00	5.35	（3）其他中长期贷款 Other Medium and Long - term Loans	1479.98	506.32
七、同业往来 Inter - bank Transactions	48.73	- 9.16			

续表
Continued

项目 Items	余额 Balance	比年初增减额 Changes within the Year	项目 Items	余额 Balance	比年初增减额 Changes within the Year
1. 同业存放 Due to Banks and Other Financial Institutions	13.73	-4.16	其中：个人中长期消费贷款 Of Which: Medium and Long-term Consumer Credit		
2. 同业拆借 Placements from Banks and Other Financial Institutions	35.00	-5.00	4. 票据融资 Paper Financing	0.11	0.11
八、委托存款及委托投资基金（净） Designated Deposits and Designated Investment Funds (Net)			其中：贴现 Of Which: Discount	0.11	0.11
			5. 各项垫款 Total Advances		
1. 委托存款及委托投资基金 Designated Deposits and Designated Investment Funds			二、有价证券及投资 Securities and Investments	1350.50	-62.40
			三、应收及预付款 Accounts Receivable and Advance Payments	48.45	-161.02
2. 减：委托贷款及委托投资 Minus: Designated Loans and Designated Investments			其中：应收利息 Of Which: Interest Receivable	40.84	-156.88
九、代理金融机构委托贷款基金 Designated Loan Funds on Behalf of Financial Institutions			四、买入返售证券 Reverse Repo		-98.13
			五、存放中央银行准备金 Reserve Deposits with the Central Bank	521.21	245.98
其中：中央银行委托贷款基金 Of Which: Loan Funds Designated by the Central Bank			六、存放中央银行特种存款 Special Deposits with the Central Bank		
十、各项准备 Total Provisions	508.93	161.22	七、缴存中央银行财政性存款 Fiscal Deposits with the Central Bank		
其中：贷款损失准备 Of Which: Provisions for Loan Losses	418.93	71.22	八、同业往来 Inter-bank Transactions	53.06	-16.48
十一、所有者权益 Owner's Equity	932.93	-21.57	1. 存放同业 Due from Banks and Other Financial Institutions	34.06	1.52
其中：实收资本 Of Which: Paid-in Capital	693.83	9.82			
当年结益 Net Earnings	101.16	101.16	2. 拆放同业 Placements with Banks and Other Financial Institutions	19.00	-18.00
十二、其他 Others	-151.33	-21.74	九、代理金融机构贷款 Lending on Behalf of Financial Institutions		
			其中：代理人行专项贷款 Of Which: Agency Earmarked Loans of the Central Bank		
			十、库存现金 Cash in Vault	1.57	-0.42
			十一、外汇占款 Position for Foreign Exchange Purchase	208.11	39.61
资金来源总计 Total Sources	**20672.71**	**1831.00**	**资金运用总计 Total Uses**	**20672.71**	**1831.00**

政策性银行人民币信贷收支表

Sources and Uses of Credit Funds of Policy Banks（RMB）

（2004 年末）

（Year - end of 2004）

单位：亿元

Unit：100 Million Yuan

项　目 Items	余　额 Balance	比年初增减额 Changes within the Year	项　目 Items	余　额 Balance	比年初增减额 Changes within the Year
一、各项存款 Total Deposits	1250.48	301.42	一、各项贷款 Total Loans	21201.42	2711.61
1. 企业存款 Deposits by Enterprises	1248.30	308.85	1. 短期贷款 Short - term Loans	7754.59	511.21
（1）活期存款 Demand Deposits	1128.32	241.21	（1）工业贷款 Loans to Industrial Sector		
（2）定期存款 Time Deposits	119.98	67.64	（2）商业贷款 Loans to Commercial Sector	7019.02	271.54
2. 机关团体存款 Deposits by Government Agencies and Social Organizations			其中：收购贷款 Of Which：Loans for the Purchase of Farm Products	7009.11	271.70
3. 储蓄存款 Savings Deposits			（3）建筑业贷款 Loans to Construction Sector		
（1）活期储蓄 Demand Deposits			（4）农业贷款 Loans to Agricultural Sector		
（2）定期储蓄 Time Deposits			（5）乡镇企业贷款 Loans to Village and Township Enterprises		
4. 农业存款 Deposits by Agricultural Sector			（6）三资企业贷款 Loans to Foreign Investment Enterprises and Ventures		
5. 其他存款 Other Deposits	2.18	-7.43			
二、代理财政性存款 Agency Fiscal Deposits	463.61	154.76	（7）私营企业及个体贷款 Loans to Privately - run Enterprises and Self - employed Entities		
三、金融债券 Financial Bonds	13939.84	2529.53	（8）其他短期贷款 Other Short - term Loans	735.57	239.67
其中：政策性金融债券 Of Which：Policy Financial Bonds	13939.84	2529.53	其中：个人短期消费贷款 Of Which：Short - term Consumer Credit		
四、应付及暂收款 Accounts Payable and Receipts on Account	185.95	27.89	2. 中期流动资金贷款 Medium - term Working Capital Loans		
其中：应付及预提利息 Of Which：Interest Payable and Accrued	155.02	32.59	3. 中长期贷款 Medium and Long - term Loans	13446.17	2199.85
五、卖出回购资产 Assets Repo（Including Securities）	30.05	30.05	（1）基本建设贷款 Capital Construction Loans	11186.87	1602.73
六、向中央银行借款 Borrowings from the Central Bank	6099.00	-408.00	（2）技术改造贷款 Technical Improvement Loans	183.65	1.45
七、同业往来 Inter - bank Transactions	27.69	-21.04	（3）其他中长期贷款 Other Medium and Long - term Loans	2075.65	595.67

续表
Continued

项　目 Items	余　额 Balance	比年初增减额 Changes within the Year	项　目 Items	余　额 Balance	比年初增减额 Changes within the Year
1. 同业存放 Due to Banks and Other Financial Institutions	7.69	-6.04	其中：个人中长期消费贷款 Of Which: Medium and Long-term Consumer Credit	9.99	9.99
2. 同业拆借 Placements from Banks and Other Financial Institutions	20.00	-15.00	4. 票据融资 Paper Financing	0.66	0.55
八、委托存款及委托投资基金（净） Designated Deposits and Designated Investment Funds (Net)			其中：贴现 Of Which: Discount	0.66	0.55
1. 委托存款及委托投资基金 Designated Deposits and Designated Investment Funds			5. 各项垫款 Total Advances		
2. 减：委托贷款及委托投资 Minus: Designated Loans and Designated Investments			二、有价证券及投资 Securities and Investments	1444.85	94.35
九、代理金融机构委托贷款基金 Designated Loan Funds on Behalf of Financial Institutions	1.23	1.23	三、应收及预付款 Accounts Receivable and Advance Payments	43.09	-5.18
其中：中央银行委托贷款基金 Of Which: Loan Funds Designated by the Central Bank	1.23	1.23	其中：应收利息 Of Which: Interest Receivable	26.41	-14.42
十、各项准备 Total Provisions	547.22	38.29	四、买入返售资产 Assets Reverse Repo (Including Securities)		
其中：贷款损失准备 Of Which: Provisions for Loan Losses	547.22	128.29	五、存放中央银行准备金 Reserve Deposits with the Central Bank	526.16	4.95
十一、所有者权益 Owner's Equity	1096.22	163.29	六、存放中央银行特种存款 Special Deposits with the Central Bank		
其中：实收资本 Of Which: Paid-in Capital	694.12	0.29	七、缴存中央银行财政性存款 Fiscal Deposits with the Central Bank		
当年结益 Net Earnings	129.68	129.68	八、同业往来 Inter-bank Transactions	39.13	-13.97
十二、其他 Others	-170.96	-19.66	1. 存放同业 Due from Banks and Other Financial Institutions	29.13	-4.97
			2. 拆放同业 Placements with Banks and Other Financial Institutions	10.00	-9.00
			九、代理金融机构贷款 Lending on Behalf of Financial Institutions	1.23	1.23
			其中：代理人行专项贷款 Of Which: Agency Earmarked Loans of the Central Bank	1.23	1.23
			十、库存现金 Cash in Vault	1.72	0.15
			十一、外汇占款 Position for Foreign Exchange Purchase	212.73	4.62
资金来源总计 **Total Sources**	**23470.33**	**2797.76**	**资金运用总计** **Total Uses**	**23470.33**	**2797.76**

政策性银行人民币信贷收支表

Sources and Uses of Credit Funds of Policy Banks (RMB)

(2005 年末)

(Year - end of 2005)

单位：亿元

Unit: 100 Million Yuan

项　目 Items	余　额 Balance	比年初增减额 Changes within the Year	项　目 Items	余　额 Balance	比年初增减额 Changes within the Year
一、各项存款 Total Deposits	1605.40	354.92	一、各项贷款 Total Loans	24580.05	3378.63
1. 企业存款 Deposits by Enterprises	1603.40	355.10	1. 短期贷款 Short - term Loans	8869.19	1114.60
(1) 活期存款 Demand Deposits	1468.70	340.38	(1) 工业贷款 Loans to Industrial Sector		
(2) 定期存款 Time Deposits	134.70	14.72	(2) 商业贷款 Loans to Commercial Sector	7595.17	576.15
2. 机关团体存款 Deposits by Government Agencies and Social Organizations			其中：收购贷款 Of Which: Loans for the Purchase of Farm Products	7585.41	576.30
3. 储蓄存款 Savings Deposits			(3) 建筑业贷款 Loans to Construction Sector		
(1) 活期储蓄 Demand Deposits			(4) 农业贷款 Loans to Agricultural Sector		
(2) 定期储蓄 Time Deposits			(5) 乡镇企业贷款 Loans to Village and Township Enterprises		
4. 农业存款 Deposits by Agricultural Sector			(6) 三资企业贷款 Loans to Foreign Investment Enterprises and Ventures		
5. 其他存款 Other Deposits	2.00	-0.18	(7) 私营企业及个体贷款 Loans to Privately - run Enterprises and Self - employed Entities		
二、代理财政性存款 Agency Fiscal Deposits	485.97	22.36	(8) 其他短期贷款 Other Short - term Loans	1274.02	538.45
三、金融债券 Financial Bonds	17910.24	3970.40	其中：个人短期消费贷款 Of Which: Short - term Consumer Credit		
其中：政策性金融债券 Of Which: Policy Financial Bonds	17508.78	3768.94	2. 中期流动资金贷款 Medium - term Working Capital Loans		
四、应付及暂收款 Accounts Payable and Receipts on Account	260.16	74.21	3. 中长期贷款 Medium and Long - term Loans	15710.28	2264.11
其中：应付及预提利息 Of Which: Interest Payable and Accrued	213.24	58.22	(1) 基本建设贷款 Capital Construction Loans	12359.00	1172.13
五、卖出回购资产 Assets Repo (Including Securities)		-30.05	(2) 技术改造贷款 Technical Improvement Loans	198.76	15.11
六、向中央银行借款 Borrowings from the Central Bank	5230.00	-869.00	(3) 其他中长期贷款 Other Medium and Long - term Loans	3152.52	1076.87
七、同业往来 Inter - bank Transactions	373.10	345.41			

续表
Continued

项目 Items	余额 Balance	比年初增减额 Changes within the Year	项目 Items	余额 Balance	比年初增减额 Changes within the Year
1. 同业存放 Due to Banks and Other Financial Institutions	373.10	365.41	其中：个人中长期消费贷款 Of Which: Medium and Long-term Consumer Credit	15.08	5.09
2. 同业拆借 Placements from Banks and Other Financial Institutions		-20.00	4. 票据融资 Paper Financing	0.58	-0.08
八、委托存款及委托投资基金（净） Designated Deposits and Designated Investment Funds (Net)	0.02	0.02	其中：贴现 Of Which: Discount	0.58	-0.08
1. 委托存款及委托投资基金 Designated Deposits and Designated Investment Funds	65.78	65.78	5. 各项垫款 Total Advances		
2. 减：委托贷款及委托投资 Minus: Designated Loans and Designated Investments	65.76	65.76	二、有价证券及投资 Securities and Investments	1315.29	-129.56
九、代理金融机构委托贷款基金 Designated Loan Funds on Behalf of Financial Institutions	2.41	1.18	三、应收及预付款 Accounts Receivable and Advance Payments	110.08	66.99
其中：中央银行委托贷款基金 Of Which: Loan Funds Designated by the Central Bank	2.21	0.98	其中：应收利息 Of Which: Interest Receivable	44.35	17.94
十、各项准备 Total Provisions	472.02	-75.20	四、买入返售资产 Assets Reverse Repo (Including Securities)	36.00	36.00
其中：贷款损失准备 Of Which: Provisions for Loan Losses	461.19	-86.03	五、存放中央银行准备金 Reserve Deposits with the Central Bank	794.52	268.31
十一、所有者权益 Owner's Equity	1478.52	378.16	六、存放中央银行特种存款 Special Deposits with the Central Bank		
其中：实收资本 Of Which: Paid-in Capital	690.03	-8.23	七、缴存中央银行财政性存款 Fiscal Deposits with the Central Bank		
当年结益 Net Earnings	255.89	255.89	八、同业往来 Inter-bank Transactions	336.61	297.49
十二、其他 Others	-123.73	51.33	1. 存放同业 Due from Banks and Other Financial Institutions	36.61	7.49
			2. 拆放同业 Placements with Banks and Other Financial Institutions	300.00	290.00
			九、代理金融机构贷款 Lending on Behalf of Financial Institutions	2.41	1.18
			其中：代理人行专项贷款 Of Which: Agency Earmarked Loans of the Central Bank	2.21	0.98
			十、库存现金 Cash in Vault	1.90	0.18
			十一、外汇占款 Position for Foreign Exchange Purchase	517.25	304.52
资金来源总计 Total Sources	**27694.11**	**4223.74**	**资金运用总计 Total Uses**	**27694.11**	**4223.74**

4. 国有商业银行人民币信贷收支表*（1997—2005年）
Sources and Uses of Credit Funds of State - owned Commercial Banks（RMB）（1997—2005）

国有商业银行人民币信贷收支表
Sources and Uses of Credit Funds of State - owned Commercial Banks（RMB）

（1997年末）

（Year - end of 1997）

单位：亿元

Unit: 100 Million Yuan

项　目 Items	余　额 Balance	比年初增减额 Changes within the Year	项　目 Items	余　额 Balance	比年初增减额 Changes within the Year
一、各项存款 Total Deposits	51220.53	7610.71	一、各项贷款 Total Loans	44823.69	4940.63
1. 企业存款 Deposits by Enterprises	19701.47	2732.11	1. 短期贷款 Short - term Loans	35168.24	4346.98
（1）活期存款 Demand Deposits	15424.31	1893.13	（1）工业贷款 Loans to Industrial Sector	14904.16	1967.71
（2）定期存款 Time Deposits	4277.16	838.98	（2）商业贷款 Loans to Commercial Sector	9841.45	851.68
2. 城镇储蓄存款 Urban Savings Deposits	30724.21	4768.20	其中：收购贷款 Of Which: Loans for the Purchase of Farm Products	1586.08	117.76
（1）活期储蓄 Demand Deposits	6930.99	1819.25	（3）建筑业贷款 Loans to Construction Sector	1501.86	148.18
（2）定期储蓄 Time Deposits	23793.22	2948.95	（4）农业贷款 Loans to Agricultural Sector	1533.61	300.44
3. 农业存款 Deposits by Agricultural Sector	263.99	25.04	（5）乡镇企业贷款 Loans to Village and Township Enterprises	1522.15	227.28
4. 信托存款 Trust Deposits	23.12	- 19.03			
5. 其他存款 Other Deposits	507.74	104.39	（6）三资企业贷款 Loans to Foreign Investment Enterprises and Ventures	1529.98	345.96
二、代理财政性存款 Agency Fiscal Deposits	748.33	27.00	（7）私营企业及个体贷款 Loans to Privately - run Enterprises and Self - employed Entities	156.92	15.85
三、发行金融债券 Financial Bonds Issue	2.29	- 61.58			
其中：发行政策性金融债券 Of Which: Policy Financial Bonds Issue	0.10	- 0.88	（8）贴现 Discount	363.48	77.96
			（9）其他短期贷款 Other Short - term Loans	3814.63	411.92
四、国家投资债券 State Investment Bonds	81.58	- 38.72	2. 中长期贷款 Medium and Long - term Loans	9619.53	595.24
五、卖出回购证券 Repo	59.34	85.19	（1）基本建设贷款 Capital Construction Loans	4048.86	282.10

* 本表机构包括中国工商银行、中国农业银行、中国银行、中国建设银行。

State - owned Commercial Banks of this statement include Industrial and Commercial Bank of China, Agricultural Bank of China, Bank of China and China Construction Bank.

续表
Continued

项 目 Items	余 额 Balance	比年初增减额 Changes within the Year	项 目 Items	余 额 Balance	比年初增减额 Changes within the Year
六、向中央银行借款 Borrowings from the Central Bank	5717.28	-2248.21	（2）技术改造贷款 Technical Improvement Loans	4608.54	394.00
七、同业往来 Inter-bank Transactions	1823.57	697.52	（3）其他中长期贷款 Other Medium and Long-term Loans	962.13	-80.86
1. 同业存放 Due to Banks and Other Financial Institutions	1636.13	677.25	3. 信托贷款 Trust Loans	35.92	-1.59
2. 同业拆借 Placements from Banks and Other Financial Institutions	187.44	20.27	4. 逾期类贷款 Overdue Loans		
八、委托存款及委托投资基金 Designated Deposits and Designated Investment Funds	216.56	18.53	二、国家投资债券贷款 Loans Related to State Investment Bonds	43.32	-25.78
			三、有价证券及投资 Securities and Investments	2746.63	-225.69
1. 委托存款 Designated Deposits	78.84	-39.46	四、缴存人行准备金 Reserves with the Central Bank	6549.39	1110.36
2. 委托投资基金 Designated Investment Funds	137.72	57.99	五、在人行存款 Deposits with the Central Bank	3567.41	-481.29
九、代理金融机构委托贷款基金 Designated Loan Funds on Behalf of Financial Institutions	3023.25	224.78	六、存放中央银行特种存款 Special Deposits with the Central Bank	0.16	-4.38
			七、存放中央银行财政性存款 Fiscal Deposits with the Central Bank	678.84	-132.25
其中：中央银行委托贷款基金 Of Which: Loan Funds Designated by the Central Bank	76.90	-226.38	八、同业往来 Inter-bank Transactions	710.05	-131.62
十、所有者权益 Owner's Equity	1910.06	-95.31	1. 存放同业 Due from Banks and Other Financial Institutions	88.97	-88.95
其中：实收资本 Of Which: Paid-in Capital	1970.00	154.98	2. 拆放同业 Placements with Banks and Other Financial Institutions	621.08	-42.67
当年结益 Net Earnings	-113.99	-113.99			
十一、其他 Others	-1420.64	-839.38	九、代理金融机构贷款 Lending on Behalf of Financial Institutions	3002.21	267.15
			其中：代理人行专项贷款 Of Which: Agency Earmarked Loans of the Central Bank	79.24	-223.51
			十、库存现金 Cash in Vault	500.00	90.32
			十一、外汇占款 Position for Foreign Exchange Purchase	760.45	-26.92
资金来源总计 Total Sources	**63382.15**	**5380.53**	**资金运用总计 Total Uses**	**63382.15**	**5380.53**

国有商业银行人民币信贷收支表

Sources and Uses of Credit Funds of State - owned Commercial Banks（RMB）

（1998 年末）

（Year - end of 1998）

单位：亿元

Unit：100 Million Yuan

项目 Items	余额 Balance	比年初增减额 Changes within the Year	项目 Items	余额 Balance	比年初增减额 Changes within the Year
一、各项存款 Total Deposits	60378.85	8700.07	一、各项贷款 Total Loans	53611.02	8774.59
1. 企业存款 Deposits by Enterprises	22384.32	2684.51	1. 短期贷款 Short - term Loans	39128.48	4693.64
（1）活期存款 Demand Deposits	17085.75	1663.58	（1）工业贷款 Loans to Industrial Sector	16168.66	1436.83
（2）定期存款 Time Deposits	5298.57	1020.93	（2）商业贷款 Loans to Commercial Sector	11427.53	1610.49
2. 城镇储蓄存款 Urban Savings Deposits	35376.75	5249.95	其中：收购贷款 Of Which：Loans for the Purchase of Farm Products	1394.56	- 187.97
（1）活期储蓄 Demand Deposits	7812.49	1481.76	（3）建筑业贷款 Loans to Construction Sector	1505.85	125.17
（2）定期储蓄 Time Deposits	27564.26	3768.19	（4）农业贷款 Loans to Agricultural Sector	1780.05	247.58
3. 农业存款 Deposits by Agricultural Sector	300.62	36.64	（5）乡镇企业贷款 Loans to Village and Township Enterprises	1751.90	234.28
4. 信托存款 Trust Deposits	9.56	- 13.56	（6）三资企业贷款 Loans to Foreign Investment Enterprises and Ventures	1988.24	458.70
5. 其他存款 Other Deposits	2307.60	742.53	（7）私营企业及个体贷款 Loans to Privately - run Enterprises and Self - employed Entities	202.31	48.75
二、代理财政性存款 Agency Fiscal Deposits	249.81	334.19	（8）贴现 Discount	338.45	- 24.80
三、发行金融债券 Financial Bonds Issue	1.66	- 0.60	（9）其他短期贷款 Other Short - term Loans	3965.49	556.64
其中：发行政策性金融债券 Of Which：Policy Financial Bonds Issue	0.01	- 0.04	2. 中期流动资金贷款 Medium - term Working Capital Loans	1584.36	1220.28
四、国家投资债券 State Investment Bonds	80.26	- 1.33	3. 中长期贷款 Medium and Long - term Loans	12869.92	2867.99
五、卖出回购证券 Repo	180.62	120.88	（1）基本建设贷款 Capital Construction Loans	5789.37	1356.44
六、向中央银行借款 Borrowings from the Central Bank	5293.47	- 423.91	（2）技术改造贷款 Technical Improvement Loans	4810.96	202.29
七、同业往来 Inter - bank Transactions	2565.06	198.08	（3）其他中长期贷款 Other Medium and Long - term Loans	2269.59	1309.26
1. 同业存放 Due to Banks and Other Financial Institutions	2536.23	358.24	4. 信托贷款 Trust Loans	28.26	- 7.32
2. 同业拆借 Placements from Banks and Other Financial Institutions	28.83	- 160.16			

续表
Continued

项目 Items	余额 Balance	比年初增减额 Changes within the Year	项目 Items	余额 Balance	比年初增减额 Changes within the Year
八、委托存款及委托投资基金 Designated Deposits and Designated Investment Funds	115.43	-128.97	5. 逾期类贷款 Overdue Loans		
			二、国家投资债券贷款 Loans Related to State Investment Bonds	37.84	-5.48
1. 委托存款 Designated Deposits	90.83	-14.99	三、有价证券及投资 Securities and Investments	6726.52	3979.81
2. 委托投资基金 Designated Investment Funds	24.60	-113.98	四、缴存人行准备金 Reserves with the Central Bank		
九、代理金融机构委托贷款基金 Designated Loan Funds on Behalf of Financial Institutions	47.42	-2891.53	五、缴存准备金存款 Reserve Deposits with the Central Bank	8933.49	-1177.34
其中：中央银行委托贷款基金 Of Which: Loan Funds Designated by the Central Bank	25.84	-47.91	六、存放中央银行特种存款 Special Deposits with the Central Bank	0.14	-0.02
十、所有者权益 Owner's Equity	4294.91	2416.22	七、存放中央银行财政性存款 Fiscal Deposits with the Central Bank	109.51	-569.26
其中：实收资本 Of Which: Paid-in Capital	4724.98	2755.99	八、同业往来 Inter-bank Transactions	620.10	-94.13
当年结益 Net Earnings	-338.38	-338.38	1. 存放同业 Due from Banks and Other Financial Institutions	76.48	-15.43
十一、其他 Others	-2038.24	-497.92	2. 拆放同业 Placements with Banks and Other Financial Institutions	543.62	-78.70
			九、代理金融机构贷款 Lending on Behalf of Financial Institutions	51.27	-2893.58
			其中：代理人行专项贷款 Of Which: Agency Earmarked Loans of the Central Bank	28.16	-51.09
			十、库存现金 Cash in Vault	521.78	17.90
			十一、外汇占款 Position for Foreign Exchange Purchase	557.58	-207.31
资金来源总计 Total Sources	**71169.25**	**7825.18**	**资金运用总计 Total Uses**	**71169.25**	**7825.18**

国有商业银行人民币信贷收支表

Sources and Uses of Credit Funds of State - owned Commercial Banks (RMB)

(1999年末)

(Year - end of 1999)

单位：亿元

Unit: 100 Million Yuan

项目 Items	余额 Balance	比年初增减额 Changes within the Year	项目 Items	余额 Balance	比年初增减额 Changes within the Year
一、各项存款 Total Deposits	69324.91	8956.84	一、各项贷款 Total Loans	57456.22	6849.57
1. 企业存款 Deposits by Enterprises	25363.69	2971.26	1. 短期贷款 Short - term Loans	40686.99	3457.30
(1) 活期存款 Demand Deposits	19283.99	2228.98	(1) 工业贷款 Loans to Industrial Sector	16287.35	1118.74
(2) 定期存款 Time Deposits	6079.70	742.28	(2) 商业贷款 Loans to Commercial Sector	11466.08	314.50
2. 城镇储蓄存款 Urban Savings Deposits	39885.84	4507.03	其中：收购贷款 Of Which: Loans for the Purchase of Farm Products	1174.03	- 197.40
(1) 活期储蓄 Demand Deposits	10023.01	2208.41	(3) 建筑业贷款 Loans to Construction Sector	1315.79	216.24
(2) 定期储蓄 Time Deposits	29862.83	2298.62	(4) 农业贷款 Loans to Agricultural Sector	1742.61	- 32.97
3. 农业存款 Deposits by Agricultural Sector	342.09	41.47	(5) 乡镇企业贷款 Loans to Village and Township Enterprises	1902.97	152.33
4. 信托存款 Trust Deposits	6.25	- 3.31	(6) 三资企业贷款 Loans to Foreign Investment Enterprises and Ventures	2382.98	402.64
5. 其他存款 Other Deposits	3727.04	1440.39	(7) 私营企业及个体贷款 Loans to Privately - run Enterprises and Self - employed Entities	292.24	90.43
二、代理财政性存款 Agency Fiscal Deposits	133.08	- 116.81	(8) 贴现 Discount	291.15	- 47.80
三、发行金融债券 Financial Bonds Issue	1.36	- 0.28	(9) 其他短期贷款 Other Short - term Loans	5005.82	1243.19
其中：发行政策性金融债券 Of Which: Policy Financial Bonds Issue		- 0.01	2. 中期流动资金贷款 Medium - term Working Capital Loans	2703.27	1227.40
四、国家投资债券 State Investment Bonds	0.21	- 80.04	3. 中长期贷款 Medium and Long - term Loans	14041.88	2169.05
五、卖出回购证券 Repo	1620.94	1440.44	(1) 基本建设贷款 Capital Construction Loans	6510.84	1355.92
六、向中央银行借款 Borrowings from the Central Bank	4922.83	- 370.33	(2) 技术改造贷款 Technical Improvement Loans	4729.30	205.22
七、同业往来 Inter - bank Transactions	2910.04	157.57	(3) 其他中长期贷款 Other Medium and Long - term Loans	2801.74	607.91
1. 同业存放 Due to Banks and Other Financial Institutions	2892.65	227.04	4. 信托贷款 Trust Loans	24.08	- 4.18
2. 同业拆借 Placements from Banks and Other Financial Institutions	17.39	- 69.47			

续表
Continued

项目 Items	余额 Balance	比年初增减额 Changes within the Year	项目 Items	余额 Balance	比年初增减额 Changes within the Year
八、委托存款及委托投资基金 Designated Deposits and Designated Investment Funds	70.26	-45.08	5. 逾期类贷款 Overdue Loans		
			二、国家投资债券贷款 Loans Related to State Investment Bonds	34.04	-2.32
1. 委托存款 Designated Deposits	64.64	-26.09	三、有价证券及投资 Securities and Investments	11039.44	4313.18
2. 委托投资基金 Designated Investment Funds	5.62	-18.99	四、缴存准备金存款 Reserve Deposits with the Central Bank	8844.93	-95.79
九、代理金融机构委托贷款基金 Designated Loan Funds on Behalf of Financial Institutions	41.48	-5.98	五、存放中央银行特种存款 Special Deposits with the Central Bank	0.05	-0.07
其中：中央银行委托贷款基金 Of Which：Loan Funds Designated by the Central Bank	21.81	-4.07	六、存放中央银行财政性存款 Fiscal Deposits with the Central Bank	132.99	23.38
			七、同业往来 Inter-bank Transactions	815.72	150.55
十、所有者权益 Owner's Equity	3943.11	-324.49	1. 存放同业 Due from Banks and Other Financial Institutions	232.77	155.35
其中：实收资本 Of Which：Paid-in Capital	4643.87	-80.20			
当年结益 Net Earnings	-271.10	-271.10	2. 拆放同业 Placements with Banks and Other Financial Institutions	582.95	-4.80
十一、其他 Others	-2916.71	2203.17			
			八、代理金融机构贷款 Lending on Behalf of Financial Institutions	44.55	-6.75
			其中：代理人行专项贷款 Of Which：Agency Earmarked Loans of the Central Bank	23.09	-5.10
			九、库存现金 Cash in Vault	1103.35	581.43
			十、外汇占款 Position for Foreign Exchange Purchase	580.22	1.83
资金来源总计 Total Sources	**80051.11**	**11815.01**	**资金运用总计 Total Uses**	**80051.51**	**11815.01**

国有商业银行人民币信贷收支表
Sources and Uses of Credit Funds of State－owned Commercial Banks（RMB）

（2000年末）

（Year－end of 2000）

单位：亿元

Unit：100 Million Yuan

项目 Items	余额 Balance	比年初增减额 Changes within the Year	项目 Items	余额 Balance	比年初增减额 Changes within the Year
一、各项存款 Total Deposits	76945.23	7708.13	一、各项贷款 Total Loans	58250.69	7910.03
1．企业存款 Deposits by Enterprises	29158.29	3796.46	1．短期贷款 Short－term Loans	39100.38	4319.68
（1）活期存款 Demand Deposits	22421.92	3139.82	（1）工业贷款 Loans to Industrial Sector	15132.53	498.35
（2）定期存款 Time Deposits	6736.37	656.64	（2）商业贷款 Loans to Commercial Sector	9261.65	198.31
2．城镇储蓄存款 Urban Savings Deposits	42734.90	2907.07	其中：收购贷款 Of Which：Loans for the Purchase of Farm Products	774.30	－85.03
（1）活期储蓄 Demand Deposits	12447.96	2485.90	（3）建筑业贷款 Loans to Construction Sector	1418.73	89.03
（2）定期储蓄 Time Deposits	30286.94	421.17	（4）农业贷款 Loans to Agricultural Sector	1287.58	－26.10
3．农业存款 Deposits by Agricultural Sector	372.03	29.92	（5）乡镇企业贷款 Loans to Village and Township Enterprises	1413.56	74.58
4．信托存款 Trust Deposits	1.07	－0.47	（6）三资企业贷款 Loans to Foreign Investment Enterprises and Ventures	2352.68	161.40
5．其他存款 Other Deposits	4678.94	975.15	（7）私营企业及个体贷款 Loans to Privately－run Enterprises and Self－employed Entities	340.80	56.59
二、代理财政性存款 Agency Fiscal Deposits	164.75	31.78	（8）贴现 Discount	441.60	150.42
三、发行金融债券 Financial Bonds Issue	0.98	－0.06	（9）其他短期贷款 Other Short－term Loans	7451.25	3117.10
其中：发行政策性金融债券 Of Which：Policy Financial Bonds Issue			2．中期流动资金贷款 Medium－term Working Capital Loans	3994.18	1495.25
四、国家投资债券 State Investment Bonds	0.25	0.04	3．中长期贷款 Medium and Long－term Loans	15140.23	2091.13
五、卖出回购证券 Repo	－39.73	－1660.75	（1）基本建设贷款 Capital Construction Loans	7380.81	1153.95
六、向中央银行借款 Borrowings from the Central Bank	1571.40	－3351.13	（2）技术改造贷款 Technical Improvement Loans	4541.64	362.05
七、同业往来 Inter－bank Transactions	5835.53	2653.69	（3）其他中长期贷款 Other Medium and Long－term Loans	3217.78	575.13
1．同业存放 Due to Banks and Other Financial Institutions	5069.05	1904.60	4．信托贷款 Trust Loans	15.90	3.97
2．同业拆借 Placements from Banks and Other Financial Institutions	766.48	749.09			

续表
Continued

项目 Items	余额 Balance	比年初增减额 Changes within the Year	项目 Items	余额 Balance	比年初增减额 Changes within the Year
八、委托存款及委托投资基金 Designated Deposits and Designated Investment Funds	61.64	-8.68	5. 逾期类贷款 Overdue Loans		
1. 委托存款 Designated Deposits	56.00	-8.63	二、国家投资债券贷款 Loans Related to State Investment Bonds	32.55	-1.98
2. 委托投资基金 Designated Investment Funds	5.64	-0.05	三、有价证券及投资 Securities and Investments	18309.70	7274.69
九、代理金融机构委托贷款基金 Designated Loan Funds on Behalf of Financial Institutions	40.55	-0.18	四、缴存准备金存款 Reserve Deposits with the Central Bank	8616.12	-229.77
其中：中央银行委托贷款基金 Of Which: Loan Funds Designated by the Central Bank	18.74	-2.52	五、存放中央银行特种存款 Special Deposits with the Central Bank	0.05	-0.05
十、所有者权益 Owner's Equity	4121.97	137.16	六、存放中央银行财政性存款 Fiscal Deposits with the Central Bank	176.85	43.87
其中：实收资本 Of Which: Paid-in Capital	4636.77	-7.08	七、同业往来 Inter-bank Transactions	762.77	-23.24
当年结益 Net Earnings	-25.82	-25.82	1. 存放同业 Due from Banks and Other Financial Institutions	98.37	-106.76
十一、其他 Others	-2394.82	7895.42	2. 拆放同业 Placements with Banks and Other Financial Institutions	664.40	83.52
			八、代理金融机构贷款 Lending on Behalf of Financial Institutions	43.36	-0.35
			其中：代理人行专项贷款 Of Which: Agency Earmarked Loans of the Central Bank	19.78	-2.67
			九、库存现金 Cash in Vault	773.10	-330.20
			十、外汇占款 Position for Foreign Exchange Purchase	-657.44	-1237.58
资金来源总计 Total Sources	**86307.75**	**13405.42**	**资金运用总计 Total Uses**	**86307.75**	**13405.42**

国有商业银行人民币信贷收支表

Sources and Uses of Credit Funds of State - owned Commercial Banks (RMB)

(2001 年末)

(Year - end of 2001)

单位：亿元

Unit: 100 Million Yuan

项　目 Items	余　额 Balance	比年初增减额 Changes within the Year	项　目 Items	余　额 Balance	比年初增减额 Changes within the Year
一、各项存款 Total Deposits	87509.57	10569.44	一、各项贷款 Total Loans	64663.14	6412.91
1. 企业存款 Deposits by Enterprises	32532.03	3347.91	1. 短期贷款 Short - term Loans	36247.97	1424.31
(1) 活期存款 Demand Deposits	24648.77	2200.98	(1) 工业贷款 Loans to Industrial Sector	15763.21	638.85
(2) 定期存款 Time Deposits	7883.26	1146.93	(2) 商业贷款 Loans to Commercial Sector	9162.09	- 104.17
2. 机关团体存款 Deposits by Government Agencies and Social Organizations	2450.86	475.09	其中：收购贷款 Of Which: Loans for the Purchase of Farm Products	695.35	- 78.69
3. 储蓄存款 Urban Savings Deposits	48395.21	5660.82	(3) 建筑业贷款 Loans to Construction Sector	1684.81	234.48
(1) 活期储蓄 Demand Deposits	15108.26	2660.24	(4) 农业贷款 Loans to Agricultural Sector	1272.27	- 15.56
(2) 定期储蓄 Time Deposits	33286.95	3000.58	(5) 乡镇企业贷款 Loans to Village and Township Enterprises	1450.54	36.79
4. 农业存款 Deposits by Agricultural Sector	409.74	37.78	(6) 三资企业贷款 Loans to Foreign Investment Enterprises and Ventures	2392.16	- 0.19
5. 其他存款 Other Deposits	3721.73	1047.84			
二、代理财政性存款 Agency Fiscal Deposits	202.70	39.53	(7) 私营企业及个体贷款 Loans to Privately - run Enterprises and Self - employed Entities	425.94	86.60
三、金融债券 Financial Bonds	0.84	0.04	(8) 其他短期贷款 Other Short - term Loans	4096.95	547.51
其中：政策性金融债券 Of Which: Policy Financial Bonds			其中：个人短期消费贷款 Of Which: Short - term Consumer Credit	391.31	68.54
四、应付及暂收款 Accounts Payable and Receipts on Account	1620.74	- 478.03	2. 中期流动资金贷款 Medium - term Working Capital Loans	4342.76	344.85
其中：应付及预提利息 Of Which: Interest Payable and Accrued	601.15	- 127.24	3. 中长期贷款 Medium and Long - term Loans	22670.33	3926.86
五、卖出回购证券 Repo	573.08	- 857.80	(1) 基本建设贷款 Capital Construction Loans	8728.70	1292.11
六、向中央银行借款 Borrowings from the Central Bank	1765.16	193.76	(2) 技术改造贷款 Technical Improvement Loans	4697.45	155.13
七、同业往来 Inter - bank Transactions	5966.93	920.47	(3) 其他中长期贷款 Other Medium and Long - term Loans	9244.18	2479.62

续表
Continued

项目 Items	余额 Balance	比年初增减额 Changes within the Year	项目 Items	余额 Balance	比年初增减额 Changes within the Year
1. 同业存放 Due to Banks and Other Financial Institutions	5908.56	903.46	其中：个人中长期消费贷款 Of Which：Medium and Long－term Consumer Credit	5787.37	2265.86
2. 同业拆借 Placements from Banks and Other Financial Institutions	58.37	17.01	4. 票据融资 Paper Financing	1087.99	647.81
			其中：贴现 Of Which：Discount	1087.99	647.81
八、委托存款及委托投资基金（净） Designated Deposits and Designated Investment Funds（Net）	60.50	－1.40	5. 各项垫款 Total Advances	314.09	69.08
1. 委托存款及委托投资基金 Designated Deposits and Designated Investment Funds	2448.37	－120.39	二、有价证券及投资 Securities and Investments	18955.48	638.87
			三、应收及预付款 Accounts Receivable and Advance Payments	2367.72	－1666.47
2. 减：委托贷款及委托投资 Minus：Designated Loans and Designated Investments	2387.87	－118.99	其中：应收利息 Of Which：Interest Receivable	1363.79	－140.94
九、代理金融机构委托贷款基金 Designated Loan Funds on Behalf of Financial Institutions	13.91	－2.99	四、买入返售证券 Reverse Repo	455.17	－285.12
			五、存放中央银行准备金存款 Reserve Deposits with the Central Bank	10040.34	1423.68
其中：中央银行委托贷款基金 Of Which：Loan Funds Designated by the Central Bank	13.91	－2.99	六、存放中央银行特种存款 Special Deposits with the Central Bank	0.05	
十、各项准备 Total Provisions	537.27	160.77	七、缴存中央银行财政性存款 Fiscal Deposits with the Central Bank	215.92	39.04
其中：贷款呆账准备金 Of Which：Provisions for Bad Loans	508.14	153.26	八、同业往来 Inter－bank Transactions	1148.54	361.35
十一、所有者权益 Owner's Equity	4031.09	－90.96	1. 存放同业 Due from Banks and Other Financial Institutions	58.84	－40.39
其中：实收资本 Of Which：Paid－in Capital	4661.87	25.10			
当年结益 Net Earnings	105.88	105.88	2. 拆放同业 Placements with Banks and Other Financial Institutions	1089.70	401.74
十二、其他 Others	－4187.81	－3782.65	九、代理金融机构贷款 Lending on Behalf of Financial Institutions	16.39	－3.33
			其中：代理人行专项贷款 Of Which：Agency Earmarked Loans of the Central Bank	14.88	－3.07
			十、库存现金 Cash in Vault	687.42	－85.69
			十一、外汇占款 Position for Foreign Exchange Purchase	－456.19	－165.06
资金来源总计 Total Sources	**98093.98**	**6670.18**	**资金运用总计 Total Uses**	**98093.98**	**6670.18**

国有商业银行人民币信贷收支表

Sources and Uses of Credit Funds of State - owned Commercial Banks（RMB）

（2002 年末）

（Year - end of 2002）

单位：亿元

Unit：100 Million Yuan

项　目 Items	余　额 Balance	比年初增减额 Changes within the Year	项　目 Items	余　额 Balance	比年初增减额 Changes within the Year
一、各项存款 Total Deposits	101882.40	14378.36	一、各项贷款 Total Loans	74078.14	9397.59
1. 企业存款 Deposits by Enterprises	35273.98	3723.93	1. 短期贷款 Short - term Loans	38304.25	3110.28
（1）活期存款 Demand Deposits	26858.04	2390.42	（1）工业贷款 Loans to Industrial Sector	16745.38	2088.46
（2）定期存款 Time Deposits	8415.94	1333.51	（2）商业贷款 Loans to Commercial Sector	8547.94	- 709.80
2. 机关团体存款 Deposits by Government Agencies and Social Organizations	4568.36	1293.54	其中：收购贷款 Of Which：Loans for the Purchase of Farm Products	616.58	- 47.31
3. 储蓄存款 Urban Savings Deposits	56655.38	8258.93	（3）建筑业贷款 Loans to Construction Sector	2168.03	718.09
（1）活期储蓄 Demand Deposits	18890.27	3771.48	（4）农业贷款 Loans to Agricultural Sector	1286.04	6.62
（2）定期储蓄 Time Deposits	37765.11	4487.45	（5）乡镇企业贷款 Loans to Village and Township Enterprises	1542.61	92.15
4. 农业存款 Deposits by Agricultural Sector	465.72	55.34	（6）三资企业贷款 Loans to Foreign Investment Enterprises and Ventures	1723.46	- 515.55
5. 其他存款 Other Deposits	4918.96	1046.62			
二、代理财政性存款 Agency Fiscal Deposits	236.51	33.03	（7）私营企业及个体贷款 Loans to Privately - run Enterprises and Self - employed Entities	392.42	139.28
三、金融债券 Financial Bonds	0.47	- 0.37	（8）其他短期贷款 Other Short - term Loans	5898.37	1291.03
其中：政策性金融债券 Of Which：Policy Financial Bonds			其中：个人短期消费贷款 Of Which：Short - term Consumer Credit	553.92	107.04
四、应付及暂收款 Accounts Payable and Receipts on Account	1555.96	- 80.53	2. 中期流动资金贷款 Medium - term Working Capital Loans	5183.80	- 108.53
其中：应付及预提利息 Of Which：Interest Payable and Accrued	653.51	52.13	3. 中长期贷款 Medium and Long - term Loans	27839.14	5079.19
五、卖出回购证券 Repo	599.83	149.82	（1）基本建设贷款 Capital Construction Loans	13390.58	1670.54
六、向中央银行借款 Borrowings from the Central Bank	1758.12	- 8.01	（2）技术改造贷款 Technical Improvement Loans	1655.25	- 5.90
七、同业往来 Inter - bank Transactions	5120.31	- 512.53	（3）其他中长期贷款 Other Medium and Long - term Loans	12793.31	3414.55

续表
Continued

项　目 Items	余 额 Balance	比年初增减额 Changes within the Year	项　目 Items	余 额 Balance	比年初增减额 Changes within the Year
1. 同业存放 Due to Banks and Other Financial Institutions	5009.28	-565.83	其中：个人中长期消费贷款 Of Which: Medium and Long-term Consumer Credit	8611.03	2892.12
2. 同业拆借 Placements from Banks and Other Financial Institutions	111.03	53.30	4. 票据融资 Paper Financing	2434.97	1319.81
八、委托存款及委托投资基金（净） Designated Deposits and Designated Investment Funds (Net)	66.52	15.53	其中：贴现 Of Which: Discount	2434.97	1319.81
1. 委托存款及委托投资基金 Designated Deposits and Designated Investment Funds	2463.87	32.81	5. 各项垫款 Total Advances	315.98	-3.16
2. 减：委托贷款及委托投资 Minus: Designated Loans and Designated Investments	2397.35	17.28	二、有价证券及投资 Securities and Investments	21515.74	2080.32
九、代理金融机构委托贷款基金 Designated Loan Funds on Behalf of Financial Institutions	13.44	1.20	三、应收及预付款 Accounts Receivable and Advance Payments	2053.37	-335.97
其中：中央银行委托贷款基金 Of Which: Loan Funds Designated by the Central Bank	12.93	0.69	其中：应收利息 Of Which: Interest Receivable	1121.77	-241.76
十、各项准备 Total Provisions	1039.86	462.22	四、买入返售证券 Reverse Repo	1509.99	1199.34
其中：贷款呆账准备金 Of Which: Provisions for Bad Loans	681.38	132.87	五、存放中央银行准备金存款 Reserve Deposits with the Central Bank	10998.24	970.40
十一、所有者权益 Owner's Equity	3696.33	-258.61	六、存放中央银行特种存款 Special Deposits with the Central Bank	0.05	
其中：实收资本 Of Which: Paid-in Capital	4108.10	-553.77	七、缴存中央银行财政性存款 Fiscal Deposits with the Central Bank	274.21	58.17
当年结益 Net Earnings	49.54	49.54	八、同业往来 Inter-bank Transactions	1077.67	-87.57
十二、其他 Others	-2956.86	233.26	1. 存放同业 Due from Banks and Other Financial Institutions	102.20	30.67
			2. 拆放同业 Placements with Banks and Other Financial Institutions	975.47	-118.24
			九、代理金融机构贷款 Lending on Behalf of Financial Institutions	13.38	2.69
			其中：代理人行专项贷款 Of Which: Agency Earmarked Loans of the Central Bank	11.03	1.85
			十、库存现金 Cash in Vault	753.90	59.40
			十一、外汇占款 Position for Foreign Exchange Purchase	738.20	1069.00
资金来源总计 Total Sources	**113012.89**	**14413.37**	**资金运用总计 Total Uses**	**113012.89**	**14413.37**

国有商业银行人民币信贷收支表

Sources and Uses of Credit Funds of State - owned Commercial Banks (RMB)

(2003 年末)

(Year - end of 2003)

单位：亿元

Unit: 100 Million Yuan

项目 Items	余额 Balance	比年初增减额 Changes within the Year	项目 Items	余额 Balance	比年初增减额 Changes within the Year
一、各项存款 Total Deposits	119575.12	17693.13	一、各项贷款 Total Loans	87210.09	12976.52
1. 企业存款 Deposits by Enterprises	40655.49	5465.57	1. 短期贷款 Short - term Loans	40744.08	2436.11
(1) 活期存款 Demand Deposits	30617.24	3935.49	(1) 工业贷款 Loans to Industrial Sector	17639.07	891.89
(2) 定期存款 Time Deposits	10038.25	1530.08	(2) 商业贷款 Loans to Commercial Sector	8421.35	- 109.77
2. 机关团体存款 Deposits by Government Agencies and Social Organizations	5535.58	967.23	其中：收购贷款 Of Which: Loans for the Purchase of Farm Products	545.22	- 71.38
3. 储蓄存款 Urban Savings Deposits	66850.39	10111.96	(3) 建筑业贷款 Loans to Construction Sector	1938.17	- 233.76
(1) 活期储蓄 Demand Deposits	23473.19	4540.60	(4) 农业贷款 Loans to Agricultural Sector	1271.81	- 10.20
(2) 定期储蓄 Time Deposits	43377.20	5571.36	(5) 乡镇企业贷款 Loans to Village and Township Enterprises	1680.49	137.87
4. 农业存款 Deposits by Agricultural Sector	463.28	- 3.07	(6) 三资企业贷款 Loans to Foreign Investment Enterprises and Ventures	1679.67	- 46.75
5. 其他存款 Other Deposits	6070.38	1151.44			
二、代理财政性存款 Agency Fiscal Deposits	248.00	11.47	(7) 私营企业及个体贷款 Loans to Privately - run Enterprises and Self - employed Entities	539.70	144.98
三、金融债券 Financial Bonds	0.37	- 0.08	(8) 其他短期贷款 Other Short - term Loans	7573.82	1661.85
其中：政策性金融债券 Of Which: Policy Financial Bonds			其中：个人短期消费贷款 Of Which: Short - term Consumer Credit	754.95	189.66
四、应付及暂收款 Accounts Payable and Receipts on Account	2142.31	590.18	2. 中期流动资金贷款 Medium - term Working Capital Loans	5329.92	145.61
其中：应付及预提利息 Of Which: Interest Payable and Accrued	755.26	101.74	3. 中长期贷款 Medium and Long - term Loans	36380.48	8389.35
五、卖出回购证券 Repo	28.62	17.08	(1) 基本建设贷款 Capital Construction Loans	17600.73	4164.56
六、向中央银行借款 Borrowings from the Central Bank	1906.68	148.56	(2) 技术改造贷款 Technical Improvement Loans	1722.23	67.03
七、同业往来 Inter - bank Transactions	4747.02	- 508.86	(3) 其他中长期贷款 Other Medium and Long - term Loans	17057.52	4157.76

续表
Continued

项目 Items	余额 Balance	比年初增减额 Changes within the Year	项目 Items	余额 Balance	比年初增减额 Changes within the Year
1. 同业存放 Due to Banks and Other Financial Institutions	4726.30	-421.59	其中：个人中长期消费贷款 Of Which: Medium and Long-term Consumer Credit	12181.83	3571.99
2. 同业拆借 Placements from Banks and Other Financial Institutions	20.72	-87.27	4. 票据融资 Paper Financing	4480.03	2045.01
			其中：贴现 Of Which: Discount	4468.83	2033.81
八、委托存款及委托投资基金（净） Designated Deposits and Designated Investment Funds (Net)	32.30	-34.61	5. 各项垫款 Total Advances	275.58	-39.56
1. 委托存款及委托投资基金 Designated Deposits and Designated Investment Funds	2553.18	137.65	二、有价证券及投资 Securities and Investments	25352.53	3836.81
			三、应收及预付款 Accounts Receivable and Advance Payments	1746.53	-301.08
2. 减：委托贷款及委托投资 Minus: Designated Loans and Designated Investments	2520.88	172.26	其中：应收利息 Of Which: Interest Receivable	816.67	-306.04
九、代理金融机构委托贷款基金 Designated Loan Funds on Behalf of Financial Institutions	11.52	-1.80	四、买入返售证券 Reverse Repo	1142.29	-82.61
			五、存放中央银行准备金存款 Reserve Deposits with the Central Bank	12464.55	1465.98
其中：中央银行委托贷款基金 Of Which: Loan Funds Designated by the Central Bank	11.01	-1.80	六、存放中央银行特种存款 Special Deposits with the Central Bank		-0.05
十、各项准备 Total Provisions	1983.40	804.91	七、缴存中央银行财政性存款 Fiscal Deposits with the Central Bank	408.63	134.41
其中：贷款损失准备 Of Which: Provisions for Loan Losses	1440.46	636.53	八、同业往来 Inter-bank Transactions	706.10	-398.93
十一、所有者权益 Owner's Equity	4131.15	573.68	1. 存放同业 Due from Banks and Other Financial Institutions	148.79	46.61
其中：实收资本 Of Which: Paid-in Capital	4761.49	653.39	2. 拆放同业 Placements with Banks and Other Financial Institutions	557.31	-445.54
当年结益 Net Earnings	-213.87	-213.87			
十二、其他 Others	-4140.47	-1533.11	九、代理金融机构贷款 Lending on Behalf of Financial Institutions	10.39	-2.99
			其中：代理人行专项贷款 Of Which: Agency Earmarked Loans of the Central Bank	8.88	-2.15
			十、库存现金 Cash in Vault	834.09	80.15
			十一、外汇占款 Position for Foreign Exchange Purchase	790.82	52.34
资金来源总计 Total Sources	**130666.02**	**17760.55**	**资金运用总计 Total Uses**	**130666.02**	**17760.55**

国有商业银行人民币信贷收支表

Sources and Uses of Credit Funds of State - owned Commercial Banks（RMB）

（2004年末）

（Year - end of 2004）

单位：亿元

Unit: 100 Million Yuan

项　目 Items	余　额 Balance	比年初增减额 Changes within the Year	项　目 Items	余　额 Balance	比年初增减额 Changes within the Year
一、各项存款 Total Deposits	135487.87	16212.71	一、各项贷款 Total Loans	94734.92	10221.64
1. 企业存款 Deposits by Enterprises	47243.57	5815.09	1. 短期贷款 Short - term Loans	38409.40	161.15
（1）活期存款 Demand Deposits	34836.50	3446.28	（1）工业贷款 Loans to Industrial Sector	17400.71	338.55
（2）定期存款 Time Deposits	12407.07	2368.81	（2）商业贷款 Loans to Commercial Sector	7060.87	- 556.14
2. 机关团体存款 Deposits by Government Agencies and Social Organizations	6510.57	974.97	其中：收购贷款 Of Which: Loans for the Purchase of Farm Products	513.89	- 31.33
3. 储蓄存款 Savings Deposits	75682.31	8831.37	（3）建筑业贷款 Loans to Construction Sector	1210.80	- 410.15
（1）活期储蓄 Demand Deposits	27019.26	3545.53	（4）农业贷款 Loans to Agricultural Sector	1296.59	27.79
（2）定期储蓄 Time Deposits	48663.05	5285.84	（5）乡镇企业贷款 Loans to Village and Township Enterprises	1786.88	107.25
4. 农业存款 Deposits by Agricultural Sector	484.99	21.68	（6）三资企业贷款 Loans to Foreign Investment Enterprises and Ventures	1352.50	- 97.43
5. 其他存款 Other Deposits	5566.43	569.60	（7）私营企业及个体贷款 Loans to Privately - run Enterprises and Self - employed Entities	741.51	76.79
二、代理财政性存款 Agency Fiscal Deposits	430.00	- 176.07	（8）其他短期贷款 Other Short - term Loans	7559.54	674.49
三、金融债券 Financial Bonds	661.07	660.70	其中：个人短期消费贷款 Of Which: Short - term Consumer Credit	691.37	- 17.21
其中：政策性金融债券 Of Which: Policy Financial Bonds			2. 中期流动资金贷款 Medium - term Working Capital Loans	4711.06	- 441.53
四、应付及暂收款 Accounts Payable and Receipts on Account	2344.07	195.59	3. 中长期贷款 Medium and Long - term Loans	44018.49	7777.71
其中：应付及预提利息 Of Which: Interest Payable and Accrued	815.17	59.92	（1）基本建设贷款 Capital Construction Loans	21399.58	3908.86
五、卖出回购资产 Assets Repo（Including Securities）	80.51	- 26.25	（2）技术改造贷款 Technical Improvement Loans	1722.62	119.60
六、向中央银行借款 Borrowings from the Central Bank	1885.98	- 264.19	（3）其他中长期贷款 Other Medium and Long - term Loans	20896.29	3749.25
七、同业往来 Inter - bank Transactions	4331.73	- 356.58			

续表
Continued

项目 Items	余额 Balance	比年初增减额 Changes within the Year	项目 Items	余额 Balance	比年初增减额 Changes within the Year
1. 同业存放 Due to Banks and Other Financial Institutions	4308.36	-359.23	其中：个人中长期消费贷款 Of Which: Medium and Long-term Consumer Credit	14507.77	2605.39
2. 同业拆借 Placements from Banks and Other Financial Institutions	23.37	2.65	4. 票据融资 Paper Financing	7390.55	2712.52
八、委托存款及委托投资基金（净） Designated Deposits and Designated Investment Funds (Net)	36.73	4.61	其中：贴现 Of Which: Discount	7379.40	2712.57
			5. 各项垫款 Total Advances	205.42	11.79
1. 委托存款及委托投资基金 Designated Deposits and Designated Investment Funds	4554.28	1890.56	二、有价证券及投资 Securities and Investments	31991.80	6639.16
			三、应收及预付款 Accounts Receivable and Advance Payments	2485.37	741.03
2. 减：委托贷款及委托投资 Minus: Designated Loans and Designated Investments	4517.55	1885.95	其中：应收利息 Of Which: Interest Receivable	852.96	-180.00
九、代理金融机构委托贷款基金 Designated Loan Funds on Behalf of Financial Institutions	20.01	8.48	四、买入返售资产 Assets Reverse Repo (Including Securities)	1219.49	-47.77
其中：中央银行委托贷款基金 Of Which: Loan Funds Designated by the Central Bank	20.00	8.98	五、存放中央银行准备金存款 Reserve Deposits with the Central Bank	14069.91	1605.33
十、各项准备 Total Provisions	2263.02	279.60	六、存放中央银行特种存款 Special Deposits with the Central Bank		
其中：贷款损失准备 Of Which: Provisions for Loan Losses	1546.88	135.54	七、缴存中央银行财政性存款 Fiscal Deposits with the Central Bank	571.42	162.79
十一、所有者权益 Owner's Equity	3840.13	-290.11	八、同业往来 Inter-bank Transactions	545.73	-160.39
其中：实收资本 Of Which: Paid-in Capital	6682.49	1921.00	1. 存放同业 Due from Banks and Other Financial Institutions	102.90	-45.89
当年结益 Net Earnings	191.90	191.90	2. 拆放同业 Placements with Banks and Other Financial Institutions	442.83	-114.50
十二、其他 Others	-2271.41	4769.40	九、代理金融机构贷款 Lending on Behalf of Financial Institutions	7.39	-2.76
			其中：代理人行专项贷款 Of Which: Agency Earmarked Loans of the Central Bank	7.10	-1.53
			十、库存现金 Cash in Vault	889.38	55.29
			十一、外汇占款 Position for Foreign Exchange Purchase	2594.30	1803.57
资金来源总计 Total Sources	**149109.71**	**21017.89**	**资金运用总计 Total Uses**	**149109.71**	**21017.89**

国有商业银行人民币信贷收支表

Sources and Uses of Credit Funds of State - owned Commercial Banks (RMB)

(2005 年末)

(Year - end of 2005)

单位：亿元

Unit: 100 Million Yuan

项　目 Items	余　额 Balance	比年初增减额 Changes within the Year	项　目 Items	余　额 Balance	比年初增减额 Changes within the Year
一、各项存款 Total Deposits	158178.25	20919.81	一、各项贷款 Total Loans	96223.99	7620.71
1. 企业存款 Deposits by Enterprises	51887.10	4484.35	1. 短期贷款 Short - term Loans	33176.44	-298.09
(1) 活期存款 Demand Deposits	35239.70	284.12	(1) 工业贷款 Loans to Industrial Sector	14693.21	250.80
(2) 定期存款 Time Deposits	16647.40	4200.23	(2) 商业贷款 Loans to Commercial Sector	5603.53	-62.59
2. 机关团体存款 Deposits by Government Agencies and Social Organizations	10030.78	3485.48	其中：收购贷款 Of Which: Loans for the Purchase of Farm Products	469.08	-44.81
3. 储蓄存款 Savings Deposits	87034.23	11351.89	(3) 建筑业贷款 Loans to Construction Sector	1012.47	-198.28
(1) 活期储蓄 Demand Deposits	31074.52	4055.23	(4) 农业贷款 Loans to Agricultural Sector	1384.22	96.34
(2) 定期储蓄 Time Deposits	55959.71	7296.66	(5) 乡镇企业贷款 Loans to Village and Township Enterprises	1726.53	-60.35
4. 农业存款 Deposits by Agricultural Sector	424.19	-60.82	(6) 三资企业贷款 Loans to Foreign Investment Enterprises and Ventures	1211.36	-4.94
5. 其他存款 Other Deposits	8801.95	1658.91			
二、代理财政性存款 Agency Fiscal Deposits	568.23	138.23	(7) 私营企业及个体贷款 Loans to Privately - run Enterprises and Self - employed Entities	706.22	-17.23
三、金融债券 Financial Bonds	1194.88	564.91	(8) 其他短期贷款 Other Short - term Loans	6838.90	-301.84
其中：政策性金融债券 Of Which: Policy Financial Bonds	353.84	353.47	其中：个人短期消费贷款 Of Which: Short - term Consumer Credit	650.12	-30.30
四、应付及暂收款 Accounts Payable and Receipts on Account	3308.66	966.80	2. 中期流动资金贷款 Medium - term Working Capital Loans	4115.29	-396.73
其中：应付及预提利息 Of Which: Interest Payable and Accrued	1138.70	328.95	3. 中长期贷款 Medium and Long - term Loans	49233.87	6113.51
五、卖出回购资产 Assets Repo (Including Securities)	1494.26	1413.75	(1) 基本建设贷款 Capital Construction Loans	24657.03	4148.42
六、向中央银行借款 Borrowings from the Central Bank	1516.07	-369.49	(2) 技术改造贷款 Technical Improvement Loans	1712.91	8.08
七、同业往来 Inter - bank Transactions	5499.07	1383.15	(3) 其他中长期贷款 Other Medium and Long - term Loans	22863.93	1957.01

续表
Continued

项　目 Items	余　额 Balance	比年初增减额 Changes within the Year	项　目 Items	余　额 Balance	比年初增减额 Changes within the Year
1. 同业存放 Due to Banks and Other Financial Institutions	5444.93	1352.38	其中：个人中长期消费贷款 Of Which: Medium and Long – term Consumer Credit	15516.95	1000.37
2. 同业拆借 Placements from Banks and Other Financial Institutions	54.14	30.77	4. 票据融资 Paper Financing	9574.10	2184.68
			其中：贴现 Of Which: Discount	9524.47	2146.20
八、委托存款及委托投资基金（净） Designated Deposits and Designated Investment Funds (Net)	34.55	7.06	5. 各项垫款 Total Advances	124.29	17.34
1. 委托存款及委托投资基金 Designated Deposits and Designated Investment Funds	4326.09	1068.16	二、有价证券及投资 Securities and Investments	50355.01	18444.28
			三、应收及预付款 Accounts Receivable and Advance Payments	5073.73	3331.09
2. 减：委托贷款及委托投资 Minus: Designated Loans and Designated Investments	4291.54	1061.10	其中：应收利息 Of Which: Interest Receivable	614.02	– 262.96
九、代理金融机构委托贷款基金 Designated Loan Funds on Behalf of Financial Institutions	0.21	– 2.47	四、买入返售资产 Assets Reverse Repo (Including Securities)	3619.74	2400.13
其中：中央银行委托贷款基金 Of Which: Loan Funds Designated by the Central Bank	0.20	– 2.47	五、存放中央银行准备金存款 Reserve Deposits with the Central Bank	15164.32	1094.40
			六、存放中央银行特种存款 Special Deposits with the Central Bank		
十、各项准备 Total Provisions	2668.89	488.56			
			七、缴存中央银行财政性存款 Fiscal Deposits with the Central Bank	709.77	138.35
其中：贷款损失准备 Of Which: Provisions for Loan Losses	2303.23	756.37			
			八、同业往来 Inter – bank Transactions	538.42	2.37
十一、所有者权益 Owner's Equity	7170.07	4098.56			
			1. 存放同业 Due from Banks and Other Financial Institutions	235.65	132.75
其中：实收资本 Of Which: Paid – in Capital	6802.42	119.93			
当年结益 Net Earnings	902.40	902.40	2. 拆放同业 Placements with Banks and Other Financial Institutions	302.77	– 130.38
十二、其他 Others	– 5513.33	4371.57			
			九、代理金融机构贷款 Lending on Behalf of Financial Institutions	0.20	– 1.93
			其中：代理人行专项贷款 Of Which: Agency Earmarked Loans of the Central Bank	0.19	– 1.93
			十、库存现金 Cash in Vault	964.69	75.31
			十一、外汇占款 Position for Foreign Exchange Purchase	3469.94	875.73
资金来源总计 Total Sources	**176119.81**	**33980.44**	**资金运用总计 Total Uses**	**176119.81**	**33980.44**

5. 其他商业银行人民币信贷收支表*（1993—2005年）
Sources and Uses of Credit Funds of Other Commercial Banks（RMB）（1993—2005）

其他商业银行人民币信贷收支表
Sources and Uses of Credit Funds of Other Commercial Banks（RMB）

（1993年末）

（Year - end of 1993）

单位：亿元

Unit：100 Million Yuan

项目 Items	余额 Balance	比年初增减额 Changes within the Year	项目 Items	余额 Balance	比年初增减额 Changes within the Year
一、各项存款 Total Deposits	458.60	203.30	一、各项贷款 Total Loans	364.27	136.06
1. 企业存款 Deposits by Enterprises	262.98	123.94	1. 流动资金贷款 Working Capital Loans	217.07	96.07
2. 城镇储蓄存款 Urban Savings Deposits	63.94	29.44	（1）工业贷款 Loans to Industrial Sector	84.71	34.35
其中：定期 Of Which：Time Deposits	32.20	15.50	（2）商业贷款 Loans to Commercial Sector	87.18	40.16
活期 Demand Deposits	31.74	13.94	（3）建筑及基建企业贷款 Loans to Construction and Infrastructure Enterprises	3.54	1.39
3. 农村存款 Rural Deposits	3.26	-0.63	（4）承包及个体户贷款 Loans to Self - employed Entities	6.95	5.67
4. 信托类存款 Trust Deposits	6.31	0.60	（5）三资企业贷款 Loans to Foreign Investment Enterprises and Ventures	34.70	14.50
5. 委托存款 Designated Deposits	82.26	17.77			
6. 其他类存款 Other Deposits	39.85	32.18	2. 农业贷款 Loans to Agricultural Sector	3.94	1.24
二、金融债券 Financial Bonds	2.92	1.13	3. 固定资产贷款 Fixed Asset Loans	18.23	-3.48

* 本表机构包括中国光大银行（1993—2005年）、华夏银行（1993—2005年）、广东发展银行（1993—2005年）、深圳发展银行（1993—2005年）、招商银行（1993—2005年）、上海浦东发展银行（1993—2005年）、福建兴业银行（1993—2005年，2003年更名为兴业银行）、烟台住房储蓄银行（1993—2005年，2003年更名为恒丰银行）、蚌埠住房储蓄银行（1993—2000年，2001年改制为城市商业银行）、中国投资银行（1995—1998年）、海南发展银行（1995—1997年）、中国民生银行（1996—2005年）、交通银行（2001—2005年）、中信实业银行（2001—2005年，2005年更名为中信银行）、浙商银行（2004—2005年）。

* Other Commercial Banks of this statement include China Everbright Bank（1993—2005），Huaxia Bank（1993—2005），Guangdong Development Bank（1993—2005），Shenzhen Development Bank（1993—2005），China Merchants Bank（1993—2005），Shanghai Pudong Development Bank（1993—2005），Fujian Industrial Bank（Included in this statement from 1993 to 2005 and renamed as Industrial Bank in 2003），Yantai Housing and Savings Bank（Included in this statement from 1993 to 2005 and re - organized and renamed as Evergrowing Bank in 2003），Bengbu Housing and Savings Bank（Included in this statement from 1993 to 2000 and re - organized to be a city commercial bank in 2001），China Investment Bank（1995—1998），Hainan Develoment Bank（1995—1997），China Minsheng Banking Corporation（1996—2005），Bank of Communications（2001—2005），CITIC Industrial Bank（Included in this statement from 2001 to 2005 and renamed as China CITIC Bank in 2005），China Zheshang Bank（2004—2005）.

续表
Continued

项目 Items	余额 Balance	比年初增减额 Changes within the Year	项目 Items	余额 Balance	比年初增减额 Changes within the Year
三、代理发行债券 Agency Bonds Issue	2.87	0.73	4. 委托贷款 Designated Loans	72.34	15.79
四、代理发行股票 Agency Share Issue	0.05	0.05	其中：固定资产贷款 Of Which：Fixed Asset Loans		0.00
五、人行拨来专项贷款资金 Earmarked Loan Funds Appropriated by the Central Bank	2.86	1.64	5. 信托贷款 Trust Loans	6.35	0.95
			其中：固定资产贷款 Of Which：Fixed Asset Loans		0.00
六、代理财政性存款 Agency Fiscal Deposits	4.00	-0.12	6. 其他贷款 Other Loans	46.08	25.35
七、向人行借款 Borrowings from the Central Bank	23.54	12.90	7. 贴现 Discount	0.26	0.14
其中：季节性 Of Which：Seasonal	19.67	15.19	二、投资及租赁 Investments and Leases	18.08	1.85
日拆性 Overnight	0.69	-1.61	投资 Investments	15.12	1.52
再贴现 Rediscount		-1.50	租赁 Leases	2.96	0.33
八、同业往来 Inter-bank Transactions	44.19	0.65	三、有价证券 Securities	20.70	12.46
其中：拆入资金 Of Which：Placements from Banks and Other Financial Institutions	21.96	-15.61	其中：政府债券 Of Which：State Bonds	0.35	0.01
			四、外汇业务占款 Position for Foreign Exchange Business	2.18	1.26
九、系统内资金往来 Transactions with Branches	-16.27	-14.41	五、代理人行专项贷款 Agency Earmarked Loans of the Central Bank	2.80	1.70
十、呆账准备金 Provisions for Bad Loans	1.90	0.61			
十一、资本金 Capital	60.60	18.33	六、缴存人行财政性存款 Fiscal Deposits with the Central Bank	3.59	-0.27
十二、当年结益 Net Earnings	12.20	12.20	七、缴存人行存款准备金 Reserves with the Central Bank	42.05	20.67
十三、其他 Others	66.58	23.04	八、在人行存款 Deposits with the Central Bank	79.83	53.19
			九、同业往来 Inter-bank Transactions	55.33	7.71
			其中：拆出资金 Of Which：Placements with Banks and Other Financial Institutions	27.67	-10.20
			十、库存现金 Cash in Vault	5.89	3.82
			十一、其他 Others	69.32	21.64
资金来源总计 Total Sources	**664.04**	**260.07**	**资金运用总计 Total Uses**	**664.04**	**260.07**

其他商业银行人民币信贷收支表

Sources and Uses of Credit Funds of Other Commercial Banks (RMB)

(1994年末)

(Year - end of 1994)

单位：亿元

Unit: 100 Million Yuan

项 目 Items	余 额 Balance	比年初增减额 Changes within the Year	项 目 Items	余 额 Balance	比年初增减额 Changes within the Year
一、各项存款 Total Deposits	827.51	372.19	一、各项贷款 Total Loans	613.63	248.23
1. 企业存款 Deposits by Enterprises	541.56	255.39	1. 短期贷款 Short - term Loans	324.52	120.60
活期存款 Demand Deposits	437.44	174.37	(1) 工业贷款 Loans to Industrial Sector	128.34	35.16
定期存款 Time Deposits	104.12	81.02	(2) 商业贷款 Loans to Commercial Sector	134.31	60.92
2. 城镇储蓄存款 Urban Savings Deposits	124.56	60.59	(3) 建筑及基建企业贷款 Loans to Construction and Infrastructure Enterprises	4.69	1.43
其中：定期 Of Which: Time Deposits	72.60	39.98	(4) 承包及个体户贷款 Loans to Self - employed Entities	1.87	0.85
活期 Demand Deposits	51.96	20.61	(5) 三资企业贷款 Loans to Foreign Investment Enterprises and Ventures	55.31	22.24
3. 农村存款 Rural Deposits	2.95	-0.34	2. 农业贷款 Loans to Agricultural Sector	2.59	-1.34
4. 信托类存款 Trust Deposits	8.10	1.25	3. 中长期贷款 Medium and Long - term Loans	22.88	8.80
5. 委托存款 Designated Deposits	126.75	45.00	4. 委托贷款 Designated Loans	107.91	35.57
6. 其他类存款 Other Deposits	23.59	10.30	5. 信托贷款 Trust Loans	5.25	-1.09
二、金融债券 Financial Bonds	1.87	-0.21	6. 其他贷款 Other Loans	141.61	81.33
三、证券业务款项 Securities Business Funds	6.43	2.52	7. 贴现 Discount	1.45	1.19
四、人行拨来专项贷款资金 Earmarked Loan Funds Appropriated by the Central Bank	4.73	1.85	8. 住房专项贷款 Earmarked Housing Loans	7.42	3.17
五、代理财政性存款 Agency Fiscal Deposits	4.26	0.25	二、投资 Investments	59.78	37.92
六、向人行借款 Borrowings from the Central Bank	39.13	15.59	三、中央银行债券 Central Bank Bonds	0.50	-0.09
再贴现 Rediscount	0.13	0.13	四、租赁 Leases	4.30	0.27
七、同业往来 Inter - bank Transactions	90.46	45.69	五、证券业务占款 Funding of Securities Purchase	27.28	9.84
其中：拆入资金 Of Which: Placements from Banks and Other Financial Institutions	33.69	9.17	六、外汇业务占款 Position for Foreign Exchange Purchase	8.91	4.48

续表
Continued

项目 Items	余额 Balance	比年初增减额 Changes within the Year	项目 Items	余额 Balance	比年初增减额 Changes within the Year
八、系统内资金往来 Transactions with Branches	671.27	448.16	七、代理人行专项贷款 Agency Earmarked Loans of the Central Bank	4.86	2.00
九、呆账准备金 Provisions for Bad Loans	3.16	1.22	八、缴存人行财政性存款 Fiscal Deposits with the Central Bank	3.73	0.14
十、所有者权益 Owner's Equity	95.41	25.15	九、缴存人行存款准备金 Reserves with the Central Bank	78.72	36.70
其中：实收资本 Of Which：Paid - in Capital	56.84	0.76	十、在人行存款 Deposits with the Central Bank	139.25	59.42
十一、当年结益 Net Earnings	11.69	11.69	十一、同业往来 Inter - bank Transactions	96.20	43.95
十二、汇出汇款 Outward Remittance	31.97	28.25	其中：拆出资金 Of Which：Placements with Banks and Other Financial Institutions	47.70	18.52
十三、其他 Others	68.92	7.35	十二、系统内资金往来 Transactions with Branches	689.57	477.18
			十三、库存现金 Cash in Vault	7.58	1.66
			十四、其他 Others	122.50	68.00
资金来源总计 Total Sources	**1856.81**	**959.70**	**资金运用总计 Total Uses**	**1856.81**	**959.70**

其他商业银行人民币信贷收支表

Sources and Uses of Credit Funds of Other Commercial Banks（RMB）

（1995年末）

（Year - end of 1995）

单位：亿元

Unit：100 Million Yuan

项　目 Items	余　额 Balance	比年初增减额 Changes within the Year	项　目 Items	余　额 Balance	比年初增减额 Changes within the Year
一、各项存款 Total Deposits	1530.34	607.84	一、各项贷款 Total Loans	1153.62	389.56
1.企业存款 Deposits by Enterprises	1023.85	402.45	1.短期贷款 Short - term Loans	595.64	180.95
活期存款 Demand Deposits	749.45	269.28	（1）工业贷款 Loans to Industrial Sector	253.64	85.04
定期存款 Time Deposits	274.40	133.17	（2）商业贷款 Loans to Commercial Sector	227.31	75.30
2.城镇储蓄存款 Urban Savings Deposits	254.87	121.67	（3）建筑及基建企业贷款 Loans to Construction and Infrastructure Enterprises	13.89	- 1.73
其中：定期 Of Which：Time Depostis	176.81	98.14	（4）承包及个体户贷款 Loans to Self - employed Entities	5.13	3.06
活期 Demand Deposits	78.06	23.53	（5）三资企业贷款 Loans to Foreign Investment Enterprises and Ventures	95.67	19.08
3.农村存款 Rural Deposits	2.11	- 0.84			
4.信托类存款 Trust Deposits	12.08	3.98	2.农业贷款 Loans to Agricultural Sector	2.74	0.15
5.委托存款 Designated Deposits	188.11	60.54	3.中长期贷款 Medium and Long - term Loans	98.92	22.31
6.其他类存款 Other Deposits	49.32	20.04	4.委托贷款 Designated Loans	166.85	34.64
二、金融债券 Financial Bonds	0.14	- 1.73	5.信托贷款 Trust Loans	13.13	7.88
三、证券业务款项 Securities Business Funds	16.29	8.39	6.其他贷款 Other Loans	256.39	130.65
四、人行拨来专项贷款 Earmarked Loan Funds Appropriated by the Central Bank	4.54	- 0.24	7.贴现 Discount	10.02	8.47
			8.住房专项贷款 Earmarked Housing Loans	9.93	2.51
五、代理财政性存款 Agency Fiscal Deposits	17.47	8.69	二、投资 Investments	130.11	65.13
六、向人行借款 Borrowings from the Central Bank	19.80	- 20.05	三、中央银行债券 Central Bank Bonds	3.00	2.50
再贴现 Rediscount	1.62	1.49	四、租赁 Leases	5.84	1.38
七、同业往来 Inter - bank Transactions	219.42	87.35	五、证券业务占款 Funding of Securities Purchase	29.15	- 4.64
其中：拆入资金 Of Which：Placements from Banks and Other Financial Institutions	89.82	24.83	六、外汇业务占款 Position for Foreign Exchange Purchase	30.94	14.31

续表
Continued

项目 Items	余额 Balance	比年初增减额 Changes within the Year	项目 Items	余额 Balance	比年初增减额 Changes within the Year
八、外汇买卖资金 Funds of Foreign Exchange Transactions	0.51	-4.12	其中：售汇资金 Of Which：Position of Foreign Exchange Sales	42.95	32.08
其中：结售汇 Of Which：Purchase and Sale of Foreign Exchange	63.20	56.16	七、代理人行专项贷款 Agency Earmarked Loans of the Central Bank	4.74	-0.12
九、系统内资金往来 Transactions with Branches	633.20	356.86	八、缴存人行财政性存款 Fiscal Deposits with the Central Bank	4.67	0.93
十、呆账准备金 Provisions for Bad Loans	5.61	2.44	九、缴存人行存款准备金 Reserves with the Central Bank	149.88	67.66
十一、所有者权益 Owner's Equity	116.42	2.62	十、缴存人行特种存款 Special Deposits with the Central Bank	25.30	13.10
其中：实收资本 Of Which：Paid - in Capital	94.69	28.73	十一、在人行存款 Deposits with the Central Bank	209.74	71.61
十二、当年结益 Net Earnings	26.57	26.57	十二、同业往来 Inter - bank Transactions	207.81	73.85
十三、汇出汇款 Outward Remittance	39.66	7.38	其中：拆出资金 Of Which：Placements with Banks and Other Financial Institutions	84.33	26.94
十四、其他 Others	174.10	30.40	十三、系统内资金往来 Transactions with Branches	646.12	360.06
			十四、库存现金 Cash in Vault	12.71	3.57
			十五、其他 Others	190.44	53.50
资金来源总计 Total Sources	**2804.07**	**1112.40**	**资金运用总计 Total Uses**	**2804.07**	**1112.40**

其他商业银行人民币信贷收支表
Sources and Uses of Credit Funds of Other Commercial Banks (RMB)

（1996年末）

（Year - end of 1996）

单位：亿元

Unit: 100 Million Yuan

项目 Items	余额 Balance	比年初增减额 Changes within the Year	项目 Items	余额 Balance	比年初增减额 Changes within the Year
一、各项存款 Total Deposits	2348.82	818.14	一、各项贷款 Total Loans	1638.55	484.94
1. 企业存款 Deposits by Enterprises	1612.14	587.60	1. 短期贷款 Short - term Loans	812.59	220.48
（1）活期存款 Demand Deposits	1082.42	332.33	（1）工业贷款 Loans to Industrial Sector	364.23	119.99
其中：单位信用卡 Of Which: Corporate Credit Cards		-0.04	（2）商业贷款 Loans to Commercial Sector	300.49	67.76
（2）定期存款 Time Deposits	529.72	255.27	（3）建筑及基建企业贷款 Loans to Construction and Infrastructure Enterprises	22.61	8.59
2. 城镇储蓄存款 Urban Savings Deposits	411.40	156.44	（4）承包及个体贷款 Loans to Self - employed Entities	7.44	2.33
（1）定期存款 Time Deposits	280.60	103.80	（5）三资企业贷款 Loans to Foreign Investment Enterprises and Ventures	117.82	21.81
其中：保值储蓄 Of Which: Inflation Proot Savings Deposits	9.50	-3.71	2. 农业贷款 Loans to Agricultural Sector	3.86	1.12
（2）活期存款 Demand Deposits	130.80	52.64	3. 中长期贷款 Medium and Long - term Loans	87.08	30.92
其中：个人信用卡 Of Which: Personal Credit Cards	0.24	0.06	4. 委托贷款 Designated Loans	182.43	14.57
3. 农村存款 Rural Deposits	2.38	0.27	5. 信托贷款 Trust Loans	5.96	-6.16
4. 信托存款 Trust Deposits	1.93	-10.15	6. 其他贷款 Other Loans	477.48	187.59
5. 委托存款 Designated Deposits	192.79	4.68	7. 贴现 Discount	37.64	27.62
6. 其他存款 Other Deposits	128.18	79.30	8. 住房专项贷款 Earmarked Housing Loans	31.51	8.80
二、金融债券 Financial Bonds		-0.14	二、投资 Investments	301.60	170.33
三、证券业务款项 Securities Business Funds	29.70	13.28	三、中央银行债券 Central Bank Bonds	6.00	3.00
四、人行拨来专项贷款资金 Earmarked Loan Funds Appropriated by the Central Bank	4.82	0.28	四、租赁 Leases	3.66	-2.18
五、代理财政性存款 Agency Fiscal Deposits	21.23	3.76	五、证券业务占款 Funding of Securities Purchase	59.86	31.69
六、向人行借款 Borrowings from the Central Bank	53.54	33.65	六、外汇业务占款 Position for Foreign Exchange Purchase	37.90	7.77

续表
Continued

项　目 Items	余　额 Balance	比年初增减额 Changes within the Year	项　目 Items	余　额 Balance	比年初增减额 Changes within the Year
其中：再贴现 Of Which: Rediscount	8.01	6.30	其中：售汇资金 Of Which: Position of Foreign Exchange Sales	26.05	11.69
七、同业往来 Inter－bank Transactions	294.81	75.02	七、代理人行专项贷款 Agency Earmarked Loans of the Central Bank	5.03	0.29
其中：同业拆入 Of Which: Placements from Banks and Other Financial Institutions	91.18	0.98	八、缴存人民银行财政性存款 Fiscal Deposits with the Central Bank	9.89	5.22
八、外汇买卖资金 Funds of Foreign Exchange Transactions	11.43	10.92	九、缴存人行存款准备金 Fiscal Deposits with the Central Bank	235.65	87.27
其中：结售汇 Of Which: Purchase and Sale of Foreign Exchange	153.68	104.96	十、缴存人行特种存款 Special Deposits with the Central Bank	0.72	－24.58
九、系统内资金往来 Transactions with Branches	826.98	192.21	十一、在人行存款 Deposits with the Central Bank	275.27	63.71
十、呆账准备金 Provisions for Bad Loans	13.13	2.13	十二、同业往来 Inter－bank Transactions	289.46	80.90
十一、所有者权益 Owner's Equity	195.13	58.30	其中：同业拆出 Of Which: Placements with Banks and Other Financial Institutions	113.04	27.86
其中：实收资本 Of Which: Paid－in Capital	131.84	37.15	十三、系统内资金往来 Transactions with Branches	863.47	215.17
十二、当年结益 Net Earnings	6.15	6.15	十四、库存现金 Cash in Vault	11.45	－1.27
十三、汇出汇款 Outward Remittance	64.88	25.25	十五、其他 Others	367.06	177.96
十四、其他 Others	234.95	61.27			
资金来源总计 Total Sources	**4105.57**	**1300.22**	**资金运用总计 Total Uses**	**4105.57**	**1300.22**

其他商业银行人民币信贷收支表

Sources and Uses of Credit Funds of Other Commercial Banks（RMB）

（1997 年末）

（Year - end of 1997）

单位：亿元

Unit：100 Million Yuan

项目 Items	余额 Balance	比年初增减额 Changes within the Year	项目 Items	余额 Balance	比年初增减额 Changes within the Year
一、各项存款 Total Deposits	2957.91	829.88	一、各项贷款 Total Loans	1976.71	501.63
1. 企业存款 Deposits by Enterprises	2363.12	707.44	1. 短期贷款 Short - term Loans	1552.11	357.30
（1）活期存款 Demand Deposits	1626.77	507.10	（1）工业贷款 Loans to Industrial Sector	377.66	106.80
（2）定期存款 Time Deposits	736.35	200.34	（2）商业贷款 Loans to Commercial Sector	327.32	35.95
2. 城镇储蓄存款 Urban Savings Deposits	536.20	122.78	其中：收购贷款 Of Which：Loans for the Purchase of Farm Products		
（1）活期储蓄 Demand Deposits	179.42	50.37	（3）建筑业贷款 Loans to Construction Sector	38.91	9.63
（2）定期储蓄 Time Deposits	356.78	72.41	（4）农业贷款 Loans to Agricultural Sector	1.52	- 0.59
3. 农业存款 Deposits by Agricultural Sector	3.23	1.09	（5）乡镇企业贷款 Loans to Village and Township Enterprises	7.51	0.03
4. 信托存款 Trust Deposits	30.34	27.39	（6）三资企业贷款 Loans to Foreign Investment Enterprises and Ventures	137.51	25.69
5. 其他存款 Other Deposits	25.02	- 28.82	（7）私营企业及个体贷款 Loans to Privately - run Enterprises and Self - employed Entities	21.60	13.58
二、代理财政性存款 Agency Fiscal Deposits	6.96	- 14.39	（8）贴现 Discount	50.73	17.93
三、发行金融债券 Financial Bonds Issue	4.88	4.88	（9）其他短期贷款 Other Short - term Loans	589.35	148.28
其中：发行政策性金融债券 Of Which：Policy Financial Bonds Issue			2. 中长期贷款 Medium and Long - term Loans	163.60	57.95
四、国家投资债券 State Investment Bonds			（1）基本建设贷款 Capital Construction Loans	50.95	13.34
五、卖出回购证券 Repo	- 20.39	11.18	（2）技术改造贷款 Technical Improvement Loans	5.54	0.99
六、向中央银行借款 Borrowings from the Central Bank	51.24	5.38	（3）其他中长期贷款 Other Medium and Long - term Loans	107.11	43.62
七、同业往来 Inter - bank Transactions	384.78	163.22	3. 信托贷款 Trust Loans	23.65	17.47
1. 同业存放 Due to Banks and Other Financial Institutions	350.37	208.31	4. 逾期类贷款 Overdue Loans	237.35	68.91
2. 同业拆借 Placements from Banks and Other Financial Institutions	34.41	- 45.09			

续表
Continued

项　目 Items	余　额 Balance	比年初增减额 Changes within the Year	项　目 Items	余　额 Balance	比年初增减额 Changes within the Year
八、委托存款及委托投资基金 Designated Deposits and Designated Investment Funds	-9.79	-30.49	二、国家投资债券贷款 Loans Related to State Investment Bonds		
			三、有价证券及投资 Securities and Investments	406.74	88.79
1. 委托存款 Designated Deposits	6.32	-13.04	四、缴存人行准备金 Reserves with the Central Bank	331.76	95.68
2. 委托投资基金 Designated Investment Funds	-16.11	-17.45	五、在人行存款 Deposits with the Central Bank	530.96	247.99
九、代理金融机构委托贷款基金 Designated Loan Funds on Behalf of Financial Institutions	2.83	-23.57	六、存放中央银行特种存款 Special Deposits with the Central Bank		-0.72
其中：中央银行委托贷款基金 Of Which: Loan Funds Designated by the Central Bank	0.44	-2.99	七、存放中央银行财政性存款 Fiscal Deposits with the Central Bank	8.25	2.51
			八、同业往来 Inter-bank Transactions	241.82	26.55
十、所有者权益 Owner's Equity	285.07	90.26	1. 存放同业 Due from Banks and Other Financial Institutions	112.60	-4.14
其中：实收资本 Of Which: Paid-in Capital	167.01	34.18			
当年结益 Net Earnings	55.14	55.14	2. 拆放同业 Placements with Banks and Other Financial Institutions	129.22	30.69
十一、其他 Others	-134.29	-98.68			
			九、代理金融机构贷款 Lending on Behalf of Financial Institutions	2.74	-20.44
			其中：代理人行专项贷款 Of Which: Agency Earmarked Loans of the Central Bank	0.44	-4.77
			十、库存现金 Cash in Vault	19.37	7.94
			十一、外汇占款 Position for Foreign Exchange Purchase	10.85	-12.26
资金来源总计 Total Sources	**3529.20**	**937.67**	**资金运用总计 Total Uses**	**3529.20**	**937.67**

其他商业银行人民币信贷收支表

Sources and Uses of Credit Funds of Other Commercial Banks（RMB）

（1998 年末）

（Year - end of 1998）

单位：亿元

Unit: 100 Million Yuan

项　目 Items	余　额 Balance	比年初增减额 Changes within the Year	项　目 Items	余　额 Balance	比年初增减额 Changes within the Year
一、各项存款 Total Deposits	3839.99	791.92	一、各项贷款 Total Loans	2608.44	587.79
1. 企业存款 Deposits by Enterprises	2958.36	594.13	1. 短期贷款 Short - term Loans	1886.61	322.60
（1）活期存款 Demand Deposits	2000.85	383.28	（1）工业贷款 Loans to Industrial Sector	411.56	30.60
（2）定期存款 Time Deposits	957.51	210.85	（2）商业贷款 Loans to Commercial Sector	319.52	- 8.76
2. 城镇储蓄存款 Urban Savings Deposits	684.73	120.85	其中：收购贷款 Of Which: Loans for the Purchase of Farm Products	0.11	
（1）活期储蓄 Demand Deposits	247.22	63.79			
			（3）建筑业贷款 Loans to Construction Sector	48.80	7.93
（2）定期储蓄 Time Deposits	437.51	57.06			
			（4）农业贷款 Loans to Agricultural Sector	1.08	- 0.43
3. 农业存款 Deposits by Agricultural Sector	3.05	- 0.21			
			（5）乡镇企业贷款 Loans to Village and Township Enterprises	10.26	2.74
4. 信托存款 Trust Deposits	11.79	- 18.55			
5. 其他存款 Other Deposits	182.06	95.70	（6）三资企业贷款 Loans to Foreign Investment Enterprises and Ventures	202.10	64.82
二、代理财政性存款 Agency Fiscal Deposits	2.89	- 0.97			
			（7）私营企业及个体贷款 Loans to Privately - run Enterprises and Self - employed Entities	37.56	15.95
三、发行金融债券 Financial Bonds Issue	16.38	11.50			
其中：发行政策性金融债券 Of Which: Policy Financial Bonds Issue			（8）贴现 Discount	62.38	11.65
			（9）其他短期贷款 Other Short - term Loans	793.35	198.10
四、国家投资债券 State Investment Bonds					
			2. 中期流动资金贷款 Medium - term Working Capital Loans	83.72	67.01
五、卖出回购证券 Repo	119.41	133.59			
			3. 中长期贷款 Medium and Long - term Loans	206.61	53.16
六、向中央银行借款 Borrowings from the Central Bank	72.30	17.14			
			（1）基本建设贷款 Capital Construction Loans	85.25	30.52
七、同业往来 Inter - bank Transactions	343.73	- 57.56			
			（2）技术改造贷款 Technical Improvement Loans	9.74	4.55
1. 同业存放 Due to Banks and Other Financial Institutions	291.65	- 53.79			
			（3）其他中长期贷款 Other Medium and Long - term Loans	111.62	18.09
2. 同业拆借 Placements from Banks and Other Financial Institutions	52.08	- 3.77	4. 信托贷款 Trust Loans	18.56	- 5.09

续表
Continued

项　目 Items	余　额 Balance	比年初增减额 Changes within the Year	项　目 Items	余　额 Balance	比年初增减额 Changes within the Year
八、委托存款及委托投资基金 Designated Deposits and Designated Investment Funds	8.26	1.05	5. 逾期类贷款 Overdue Loans	412.94	150.11
1. 委托存款 Designated Deposits	7.57	1.15	二、国家投资债券贷款 Loans Related to State Investment Bonds		
2. 委托投资基金 Designated Investment Funds	0.69	-0.10	三、有价证券及投资 Securities and Investments	738.12	328.78
九、代理金融机构委托贷款基金 Designated Loan Funds on Behalf of Financial Institutions	2.15	-0.68	四、缴存人行准备金 Reserves with the Central Bank		
			五、缴存准备金存款 Reserve Deposits with the Central Bank	955.39	85.69
其中：中央银行委托贷款基金 Of Which：Loan Funds Designated by the Central Bank	0.06	-0.38	六、存放中央银行特种存款 Special Deposits with the Central Bank	3.50	3.50
			七、存放中央银行财政性存款 Fiscal Deposits with the Central Bank	1.21	-8.51
十、所有者权益 Owner's Equity	291.98	11.23	八、同业往来 Inter-bank Transactions	140.66	-115.03
其中：实收资本 Of Which：Paid-in Capital	171.27	3.74	1. 存放同业 Due from Banks and Other Financial Institutions	75.27	-37.95
当年结益 Net Earnings	38.16	38.16			
十一、其他 Others	-211.35	-23.36	2. 拆放同业 Placements with Banks and Other Financial Institutions	65.39	-77.08
			九、代理金融机构贷款 Lending on Behalf of Financial Institutions	2.26	-0.61
			其中：代理人行专项贷款 Of Which：Agency Earmarked Loans of the Central Bank	0.06	-0.39
			十、库存现金 Cash in Vault	22.28	1.71
			十一、外汇占款 Position for Foreign Exchange Purchase	13.88	0.54
资金来源总计 Total Sources	**4485.74**	**883.86**	**资金运用总计 Total Uses**	**4485.74**	**883.86**

其他商业银行人民币信贷收支表

Sources and Uses of Credit Funds of Other Commercial Banks（RMB）

（1999 年末）

（Year－end of 1999）

单位：亿元
Unit：100 Million Yuan

项　目 Items	余　额 Balance	比年初增减额 Changes within the Year	项　目 Items	余　额 Balance	比年初增减额 Changes within the Year
一、各项存款 Total Deposits	4669.74	888.11	一、各项贷款 Total Loans	3090.21	559.28
1. 企业存款 Deposits by Enterprises	3607.18	679.97	1. 短期贷款 Short－term Loans	2289.96	379.23
(1) 活期存款 Demand Deposits	2412.61	427.03	(1) 工业贷款 Loans to Industrial Sector	419.61	11.11
(2) 定期存款 Time Deposits	1194.57	252.94	(2) 商业贷款 Loans to Commercial Sector	316.19	3.49
2. 城镇储蓄存款 Urban Savings Deposits	755.41	100.61	其中：收购贷款 Of Which：Loans for the Purchase of Farm Products		
(1) 活期储蓄 Demand Deposits	328.43	85.97	(3) 建筑业贷款 Loans to Construction Sector	66.83	3.86
(2) 定期储蓄 Time Deposits	426.98	14.64	(4) 农业贷款 Loans to Agricultural Sector	0.93	－0.15
3. 农业存款 Deposits by Agricultural Sector	3.99	0.96	(5) 乡镇企业贷款 Loans to Village and Township Enterprises	12.15	1.89
4. 信托存款 Trust Deposits	0.17	－11.60			
5. 其他存款 Other Deposits	302.99	118.17	(6) 三资企业贷款 Loans to Foreign Investment Enterprises and Ventures	255.12	53.47
二、代理财政性存款 Agency Fiscal Deposits	1.36	－1.52	(7) 私营企业及个体贷款 Loans to Privately－run Enterprises and Self－employed Entities	49.94	12.39
三、发行金融债券 Financial Bonds Issue	4.36				
其中：发行政策性金融债券 Of Which：Policy Financial Bonds Issue			(8) 贴现 Discount	69.64	7.26
			(9) 其他短期贷款 Other Short－term Loans	1099.55	285.91
四、国家投资债券 State Investment Bonds			2. 中期流动资金贷款 Medium－term Working Capital Loans	97.09	9.74
五、卖出回购证券 Repo	102.57	－16.44	3. 中长期贷款 Medium and Long－term Loans	192.31	44.17
六、向中央银行借款 Borrowings from the Central Bank	110.24	76.45	(1) 基本建设贷款 Capital Construction Loans	77.36	11.42
七、同业往来 Inter－bank Transactions	600.61	286.30	(2) 技术改造贷款 Technical Improvement Loans	11.41	1.69
1. 同业存放 Due to Banks and Other Financial Institutions	498.53	208.22	(3) 其他中长期贷款 Other Medium and Long－term Loans	103.54	31.06
2. 同业拆借 Placements from Banks and Other Financial Institutions	102.08	78.08	4. 信托贷款 Trust Loans		－17.86

续表
Continued

项目 Items	余额 Balance	比年初增减额 Changes within the Year	项目 Items	余额 Balance	比年初增减额 Changes within the Year
八、委托存款及委托投资基金 Designated Deposits and Designated Investment Funds	34.09	26.46	5. 逾期类贷款 Overdue Loans	510.85	144.00
			二、国家投资债券贷款 Loans Related to State Investment Bonds		
1. 委托存款 Designated Deposits	34.09	26.46	三、有价证券及投资 Securities and Investments	947.96	223.13
2. 委托投资基金 Designated Investment Funds			四、缴存准备金存款 Reserve Deposits with the Central Bank	1356.95	403.12
九、代理金融机构委托贷款基金 Designated Loan Funds on Behalf of Financial Institutions	2.05	0.06	五、存放中央银行特种存款 Special Deposits with the Central Bank	1.85	-1.65
其中：中央银行委托贷款基金 Of Which: Loan Funds Designated by the Central Bank	0.06		六、存放中央银行财政性存款 Fiscal Deposits with the Central Bank	0.81	-0.40
			七、同业往来 Inter-bank Transactions	136.24	13.33
十、所有者权益 Owner's Equity	371.51	82.59	1. 存放同业 Due from Banks and Other Financial Institutions	87.15	14.50
其中：实收资本 Of Which: Paid-in Capital	184.87	28.84			
当年结益 Net Earnings	33.12	33.12	2. 拆放同业 Placements with Banks and Other Financial Institutions	49.09	-1.17
十一、其他 Others	-241.88	-59.83	八、代理金融机构贷款 Lending on Behalf of Financial Institutions	1.91	-0.06
			其中：代理人行专项贷款 Of Which: Agency Earmarked Loans of the Central Bank	0.05	-0.01
			九、库存现金 Cash in Vault	56.60	34.54
			十、外汇占款 Position for Foreign Exchange Purchase	62.12	50.89
资金来源总计 Total Sources	**5654.65**	**1282.18**	**资金运用总计 Total Uses**	**5654.65**	**1282.18**

其他商业银行人民币信贷收支表

Sources and Uses of Credit Funds of Other Commercial Banks（RMB）

（2000 年末）

（Year－end of 2000）

单位：亿元
Unit：100 Million Yuan

项　目 Items	余　额 Balance	比年初增减额 Changes within the Year	项　目 Items	余　额 Balance	比年初增减额 Changes within the Year
一、各项存款 Total Deposits	6685.53	2012.04	一、各项贷款 Total Loans	4534.63	1432.62
1. 企业存款 Deposits by Enterprises	4968.01	1358.81	1. 短期贷款 Short－term Loans	3540.59	1240.02
（1）活期存款 Demand Deposits	3264.65	849.01	（1）工业贷款 Loans to Industrial Sector	556.32	135.86
（2）定期存款 Time Deposits	1703.36	509.80	（2）商业贷款 Loans to Commercial Sector	418.63	109.40
2. 城镇储蓄存款 Urban Savings Deposits	947.04	191.51	其中：收购贷款 Of Which：Loans for the Purchase of Farm Products		
（1）活期储蓄 Demand Deposits	482.55	154.06	（3）建筑业贷款 Loans to Construction Sector	77.84	10.85
（2）定期储蓄 Time Deposits	464.49	37.45	（4）农业贷款 Loans to Agricultural Sector	0.70	－0.23
3. 农业存款 Deposits by Agricultural Sector	3.42	－0.57	（5）乡镇企业贷款 Loans to Village and Township Enterprises	11.42	－0.73
4. 信托存款 Trust Deposits	0.16	－0.01			
5. 其他存款 Other Deposits	766.90	462.30	（6）三资企业贷款 Loans to Foreign Investment Enterprises and Ventures	319.94	63.45
二、代理财政性存款 Agency Fiscal Deposits	5.49	3.84	（7）私营企业及个体贷款 Loans to Privately－run Enterprises and Self－employed Entities	90.79	41.33
三、发行金融债券 Financial Bonds Issue	4.23	－0.13			
其中：发行政策性金融债券 Of Which：Policy Financial Bonds Issue			（8）贴现 Discount	371.60	292.50
			（9）其他短期贷款 Other Short－term Loans	1693.35	587.59
四、国家投资债券 State Investment Bonds			2. 中期流动资金贷款 Medium－term Working Capital Loans	142.79	48.52
五、卖出回购证券 Repo	－85.64	－188.21	3. 中长期贷款 Medium and Long－term Loans	302.35	107.40
六、向中央银行借款 Borrowings from the Central Bank	62.72	－47.52	（1）基本建设贷款 Capital Construction Loans	94.41	15.31
七、同业往来 Inter－bank Transactions	998.64	396.55	（2）技术改造贷款 Technical Improvement Loans	7.84	－3.57
1. 同业存放 Due to Banks and Other Financial Institutions	927.25	427.24	（3）其他中长期贷款 Other Medium and Long－term Loans	200.10	95.66
2. 同业拆借 Placements from Banks and Other Financial Institutions	71.39	－30.69	4. 信托贷款 Trust Loans		

续表
Continued

项目 Items	余额 Balance	比年初增减额 Changes within the Year	项目 Items	余额 Balance	比年初增减额 Changes within the Year
八、委托存款及委托投资基金 Designated Deposits and Designated Investment Funds	16.25	-17.88	5. 逾期类贷款 Overdue Loans	548.90	36.68
			二、国家投资债券贷款 Loans Related to State Investment Bonds		
1. 委托存款 Designated Deposits	16.25	-17.88	三、有价证券及投资 Securities and Investments	1344.01	396.01
2. 委托投资基金 Designated Investment Funds			四、缴存准备金存款 Reserve Deposits with the Central Bank	1620.13	260.58
九、代理金融机构委托贷款基金 Designated Loan Funds on Behalf of Financial Institutions	1.96	-0.05	五、存放中央银行特种存款 Special Deposits with the Central Bank	1.85	
其中：中央银行委托贷款基金 Of Which: Loan Funds Designated by the Central Bank	0.06		六、存放中央银行财政性存款 Fiscal Deposits with the Central Bank	0.71	-0.10
十、所有者权益 Owner's Equity	456.31	91.76	七、同业往来 Inter-bank Transactions	264.70	137.78
其中：实收资本 Of Which: Paid-in Capital	172.01	-12.86	1. 存放同业 Due from Banks and Other Financial Institutions	98.01	20.27
当年结益 Net Earnings	44.57	44.57	2. 拆放同业 Placements with Banks and Other Financial Institutions	166.69	117.51
十一、其他 Others	-279.31	-44.41	八、代理金融机构贷款 Lending on Behalf of Financial Institutions	1.84	-0.06
			其中：代理人行专项贷款 Of Which: Agency Earmarked Loans of the Central Bank	0.05	
			九、库存现金 Cash in Vault	44.70	-11.94
			十、外汇占款 Position for Foreign Exchange Purchase	53.61	-8.90
资金来源总计 Total Sources	**7866.18**	**2205.99**	**资金运用总计 Total Uses**	**7866.18**	**2205.99**

其他商业银行人民币信贷收支表
Sources and Uses of Credit Funds of Other Commercial Banks (RMB)

(2001年末)

(Year - end of 2001)

单位：亿元

Unit: 100 Million Yuan

项目 Items	余额 Balance	比年初增减额 Changes within the Year	项目 Items	余额 Balance	比年初增减额 Changes within the Year
一、各项存款 Total Deposits	16560.89	4540.29	一、各项贷款 Total Loans	11462.17	3035.29
1. 企业存款 Deposits by Enterprises	11117.07	2493.32	1. 短期贷款 Short - term Loans	8084.26	1567.35
(1) 活期存款 Demand Deposits	7421.37	1513.33	(1) 工业贷款 Loans to Industrial Sector	1690.65	447.49
(2) 定期存款 Time Deposits	3695.70	979.99	(2) 商业贷款 Loans to Commercial Sector	1180.56	101.04
2. 机关团体存款 Deposits by Government Agencies and Social Organizations	248.50	90.40	其中：收购贷款 Of Which: Loans for the Purchase of Farm Products		-0.01
3. 储蓄存款 Savings Deposits	3121.56	860.06	(3) 建筑业贷款 Loans to Construction Sector	169.37	65.84
(1) 活期储蓄 Demand Deposits	1397.97	492.85	(4) 农业贷款 Loans to Agricultural Sector	7.09	1.89
(2) 定期储蓄 Time Deposits	1723.59	367.21	(5) 乡镇企业贷款 Loans to Village and Township Enterprises	21.84	2.18
4. 农业存款 Deposits by Agricultural Sector	4.77	1.35	(6) 三资企业贷款 Loans to Foreign Investment Enterprises and Ventures	780.00	46.23
5. 其他存款 Other Deposits	2068.99	1095.16	(7) 私营企业及个体贷款 Loans to Privately - run Enterprises and Self - employed Entities	174.53	60.73
二、代理财政性存款 Agency Fiscal Deposits	3.66	-2.39	(8) 其他短期贷款 Other Short - term Loans	4060.22	841.95
三、金融债券 Financial Bonds	0.03	-1.23	其中：个人短期消费贷款 Of Which: Short - term Consumer Credit	133.48	29.57
其中：政策性金融债券 Of Which: Policy Financial Bonds			2. 中期流动资金贷款 Medium - term Working Capital Loans	527.50	212.54
四、应付及暂收款 Accounts Payable and Receipts on Account	642.94	125.75	3. 中长期贷款 Medium and Long - term Loans	1608.75	629.24
其中：应付及预提利息 Of Which: Interest Payable and Accrued	100.56	-0.97	(1) 基本建设贷款 Capital Construction Loans	369.95	79.94
五、卖出回购证券 Repo	254.58	-5.83	(2) 技术改造贷款 Technical Improvement Loans	108.96	2.43
六、向中央银行借款 Borrowings from the Central Bank	73.26	-23.55	(3) 其他中长期贷款 Other Medium and Long - term Loans	1129.84	546.87
七、同业往来 Inter - bank Transactions	1733.45	79.66			

续表
Continued

项目 Items	余额 Balance	比年初增减额 Changes within the Year	项目 Items	余额 Balance	比年初增减额 Changes within the Year
1. 同业存放 Due to Banks and Other Financial Institutions	1679.60	97.60	其中：个人中长期贷款 Of Which: Medium and Long - term Consumer Credit	438.48	252.36
2. 同业拆借 Placements from Banks and Other Financial Institutions	53.85	-17.94	4. 票据融资 Paper Financing	1202.76	616.97
			其中：贴现 Of Which: Discount	1202.76	616.97
八、委托存款及委托投资基金（净） Designated Deposits and Designated Investment Funds (Net)	27.38	0.64	5. 各项垫款 Total Advances	38.90	9.19
1. 委托存款及委托投资基金 Designated Deposits and Designated Investment Funds	250.69	2.41	二、有价证券及投资 Securities and Investments	2864.61	794.91
			三、应收及预付款 Accounts Receivable and Advance Payments	781.84	159.75
2. 减：委托贷款及委托投资 Minus: Designated Loans and Designated Investments	223.31	1.77	其中：应收利息 Of Which: Interest Receivable	144.84	-4.83
九、代理金融机构委托贷款基金 Designated Loan Funds on Behalf of Financial Institutions	2.39	-0.67	四、买入返售证券 Reverse Repo	627.90	206.30
			五、存放中央银行准备金存款 Reserve Deposits with the Central Bank	3348.43	330.31
其中：中央银行委托贷款基金 Of Which: Loan Funds Designated by the Central Bank	0.22	-0.20	六、存放中央银行特种存款 Special Deposits with the Central Bank	1.85	
十、各项准备 Total Provisions	292.78	180.50	七、缴存中央银行财政性存款 Fiscal Deposits with the Central Bank	1.21	-0.30
其中：贷款呆账准备金 Of Which: Provisions for Bad Loans	279.69	177.90	八、同业往来 Inter - bank Transactions	553.10	167.07
十一、所有者权益 Owner's Equity	861.33	85.57	1. 存放同业 Due from Banks and Other Financial Institutions	190.32	68.94
其中：实收资本 Of Which: Paid - in Capital	389.95	41.13			
当年结益 Net Earnings	87.60	87.60	2. 拆放同业 Placements with Banks and Other Financial Institutions	362.78	98.13
十二、其他 Others	-568.67	-223.36	九、代理金融机构贷款 Lending on Behalf of Financial Institutions	15.01	12.81
			其中：代理人行专项贷款 Of Which: Agency Earmarked Loans of the Central Bank	13.22	12.81
			十、库存现金 Cash in Vault	103.79	9.36
			十一、外汇占款 Position for Foreign Exchange Purchase	124.11	36.88
资金来源总计 Total Sources	**19884.02**	**4752.38**	**资金运用总计 Total Uses**	**19884.02**	**4752.38**

其他商业银行人民币信贷收支表

Sources and Uses of Credit Funds of Other Commercial Banks（RMB）

（2002 年末）

（Year - end of 2002）

单位：亿元

Unit：100 Million Yuan

项　目 Items	余　额 Balance	比年初增减额 Changes within the Year	项　目 Items	余　额 Balance	比年初增减额 Changes within the Year
一、各项存款 Total Deposits	22735.91	6180.50	一、各项贷款 Total Loans	16066.25	4585.97
1. 企业存款 Deposits by Enterprises	14479.70	3418.92	1. 短期贷款 Short - term Loans	10329.04	2229.06
（1）活期存款 Demand Deposits	9729.65	2302.17	（1）工业贷款 Loans to Industrial Sector	2125.50	429.60
（2）定期存款 Time Deposits	4750.05	1116.75	（2）商业贷款 Loans to Commercial Sector	1241.96	59.80
2. 机关团体存款 Deposits by Government Agencies and Social Organizations	388.06	139.56	其中：收购贷款 Of Which: Loans for the Purchase of Farm Products		
3. 储蓄存款 Savings Deposits	4347.15	1223.65	（3）建筑业贷款 Loans to Construction Sector	268.76	99.54
（1）活期储蓄 Demand Deposits	1972.94	573.03	（4）农业贷款 Loans to Agricultural Sector	4.94	-2.15
（2）定期储蓄 Time Deposits	2374.21	650.62	（5）乡镇企业贷款 Loans to Village and Township Enterprises	26.36	5.40
4. 农业存款 Deposits by Agricultural Sector	5.34	0.57			
			（6）三资企业贷款 Loans to Foreign Investment Enterprises and Ventures	882.17	106.97
5. 其他存款 Other Deposits	3515.66	1397.80			
二、代理财政性存款 Agency Fiscal Deposits	4.57	0.91	（7）私营企业及个体贷款 Loans to Privately - run Enterprises and Self - employed Entities	288.58	114.25
三、金融债券 Financial Bonds	0.03				
其中：政策性金融债券 Of Which: Policy Financial Bonds			（8）其他短期贷款 Other Short - term Loans	5490.77	1415.65
			其中：个人短期消费贷款 Of Which: Short - term Consumer Credit	162.50	13.80
四、应付及暂收款 Accounts Payable and Receipts on Account	395.06	95.84			
			2. 中期流动资金贷款 Medium - term Working Capital Loans	809.81	282.52
其中：应付及预提利息 Of Which: Interest Payable and Accrued	129.85	29.35	3. 中长期贷款 Medium and Long - term Loans	2705.93	1119.74
五、卖出回购证券 Repo	258.72	4.14	（1）基本建设贷款 Capital Construction Loans	534.73	163.27
六、向中央银行借款 Borrowings from the Central Bank	34.58	-38.68	（2）技术改造贷款 Technical Improvement Loans	112.14	2.83
七、同业往来 Inter - bank Transactions	1687.71	-35.56	（3）其他中长期贷款 Other Medium and Long - term Loans	2059.06	953.64

续表
Continued

项　目 Items	余　额 Balance	比年初增减额 Changes within the Year	项　目 Items	余　额 Balance	比年初增减额 Changes within the Year
1. 同业存放 Due to Banks and Other Financial Institutions	1635.59	-33.83	其中：个人中长期消费贷款 Of Which: Medium and Long-term Consumer Credit	868.78	452.38
2. 同业拆借 Placements from Banks and Other Financial Institutions	52.12	-1.73	4. 票据融资 Paper Financing	2167.42	946.75
			其中：贴现 Of Which: Discount	2167.42	946.75
八、委托存款及委托投资基金（净） Designated Deposits and Designated Investment Funds (Net)	15.36	0.98	5. 各项垫款 Total Advances	54.05	7.90
1. 委托存款及委托投资基金 Designated Deposits and Designated Investment Funds	340.19	102.50	二、有价证券及投资 Securities and Investments	3976.40	1093.85
			三、应收及预付款 Accounts Receivable and Advance Payments	412.93	9.15
2. 减：委托贷款及委托投资 Minus: Designated Loans and Designated Investments	324.83	101.52	其中：应收利息 Of Which: Interest Receivable	72.20	-73.01
九、代理金融机构委托贷款基金 Designated Loan Funds on Behalf of Financial Institutions	19.66	4.27	四、买入返售证券 Reverse Repo	723.02	113.84
			五、存放中央银行准备金存款 Reserve Deposits with the Central Bank	3643.66	295.23
其中：中央银行委托贷款基金 Of Which: Loan Funds Designated by the Central Bank	17.96	4.74	六、存放中央银行特种存款 Special Deposits with the Central Bank		-1.85
十、各项准备 Total Provisions	395.86	103.16	七、缴存中央银行财政性存款 Fiscal Deposits with the Central Bank	4.62	3.41
其中：贷款呆账准备金 Of Which: Provisions for Bad Loans	374.62	95.05	八、同业往来 Inter-bank Transactions	728.31	179.67
十一、所有者权益 Owner's Equity	940.29	81.35	1. 存放同业 Due from Banks and Other Financial Institutions	287.33	97.54
其中：实收资本 Of Which: Paid-in Capital	432.45	42.50	2. 拆放同业 Placements with Banks and Other Financial Institutions	440.98	82.13
当年结益 Net Earnings	110.61	110.61			
十二、其他 Others	-644.91	-72.94	九、代理金融机构贷款 Lending on Behalf of Financial Institutions	19.67	4.66
			其中：代理人行专项贷款 Of Which: Agency Earmarked Loans of the Central Bank	17.96	4.74
			十、库存现金 Cash in Vault	123.37	19.58
			十一、外汇占款 Position for Foreign Exchange Purchase	144.61	20.46
资金来源总计 Total Sources	**25842.84**	**6323.97**	**资金运用总计 Total Uses**	**25842.84**	**6323.97**

其他商业银行人民币信贷收支表

Sources and Uses of Credit Funds of Other Commercial Banks (RMB)

(2003 年末)

(Year - end of 2003)

单位：亿元

Unit: 100 Million Yuan

项 目 Items	余 额 Balance	比年初增减额 Changes within the Year	项 目 Items	余 额 Balance	比年初增减额 Changes within the Year
一、各项存款 Total Deposits	30621.18	7882.39	一、各项贷款 Total Loans	22367.56	6360.04
1. 企业存款 Deposits by Enterprises	18522.86	4040.47	1. 短期贷款 Short - term Loans	13974.59	3704.66
(1) 活期存款 Demand Deposits	12054.63	2322.00	(1) 工业贷款 Loans to Industrial Sector	3575.32	1449.89
(2) 定期存款 Time Deposits	6468.23	1718.47	(2) 商业贷款 Loans to Commercial Sector	1675.66	433.83
2. 机关团体存款 Deposits by Government Agencies and Social Organizations	833.35	445.29	其中：收购贷款 Of Which: Loans for the Purchase of Farm Products		
3. 储蓄存款 Savings Deposits	5851.47	1504.43	(3) 建筑业贷款 Loans to Construction Sector	662.17	393.23
(1) 活期储蓄 Demand Deposits	2616.84	644.04	(4) 农业贷款 Loans to Agricultural Sector	31.73	26.79
(2) 定期储蓄 Time Deposits	3234.63	860.39	(5) 乡镇企业贷款 Loans to Village and Township Enterprises	19.97	-6.39
4. 农业存款 Deposits by Agricultural Sector	15.93	10.59			
5. 其他存款 Other Deposits	5397.57	1881.61	(6) 三资企业贷款 Loans to Foreign Investment Enterprises and Ventures	798.28	-83.78
二、代理财政性存款 Agency Fiscal Deposits	7.21	2.64	(7) 私营企业及个体贷款 Loans to Privately - run Enterprises and Self - employed Entities	450.57	162.15
三、金融债券 Financial Bonds	39.31	45.88	(8) 其他短期贷款 Other Short - term Loans	6760.89	1328.94
其中：政策性金融债券 Of Which: Policy Financial Bonds			其中：个人短期消费贷款 Of Which: Short - term Consumer Credit	228.00	71.91
四、应付及暂收款 Accounts Payable and Receipts on Account	427.96	36.28	2. 中期流动资金贷款 Medium - term Working Capital Loans	969.15	159.34
其中：应付及预提利息 Of Which: Interest Payable and Accrued	157.01	27.08	3. 中长期贷款 Medium and Long - term Loans	4928.29	2221.98
五、卖出回购证券 Repo	290.08	67.30	(1) 基本建设贷款 Capital Construction Loans	882.65	347.92
六、向中央银行借款 Borrowings from the Central Bank	26.02	-8.56	(2) 技术改造贷款 Technical Improvement Loans	138.80	26.66
七、同业往来 Inter - bank Transactions	1644.53	-40.08	(3) 其他中长期贷款 Other Medium and Long - term Loans	3906.84	1847.40

续表
Continued

项目 Items	余额 Balance	比年初增减额 Changes within the Year	项目 Items	余额 Balance	比年初增减额 Changes within the Year
1. 同业存放 Due to Banks and Other Financial Institutions	1596.13	-36.36	其中：个人中长期消费贷款 Of Which: Medium and Long-term Consumer Credit	1836.98	962.45
2. 同业拆借 Placements from Banks and Other Financial Institutions	48.40	-3.72	4. 票据融资 Paper Financing	2442.53	275.11
			其中：贴现 Of Which: Discount	2442.47	275.05
八、委托存款及委托投资基金（净） Designated Deposits and Designated Investment Funds (Net)	10.44	-4.92	5. 各项垫款 Total Advances	53.00	-1.05
1. 委托存款及委托投资基金 Designated Deposits and Designated Investment Funds	585.88	171.90	二、有价证券及投资 Securities and Investments	5039.76	1069.96
			三、应收及预付款 Accounts Receivable and Advance Payments	388.05	-24.86
2. 减：委托贷款及委托投资 Minus: Designated Loans and Designated Investments	575.44	176.82	其中：应收利息 Of Which: Interest Receivable	48.19	-24.06
九、代理金融机构委托贷款基金 Designated Loan Funds on Behalf of Financial Institutions	17.52	-2.14	四、买入返售证券 Reverse Repo	431.94	-310.60
			五、存放中央银行准备金存款 Reserve Deposits with the Central Bank	4549.42	905.76
其中：中央银行委托贷款基金 Of Which: Loan Funds Designated by the Central Bank	15.53	-2.43	六、存放中央银行特种存款 Special Deposits with the Central Bank		
十、各项准备 Total Provisions	509.41	113.57	七、缴存中央银行财政性存款 Fiscal Deposits with the Central Bank	4.55	-0.07
其中：贷款损失准备 Of Which: Provisions for Loan Losses	480.46	105.57	八、同业往来 Inter-bank Transactions	751.39	17.73
十一、所有者权益 Owner's Equity	1127.12	183.34	1. 存放同业 Due from Banks and Other Financial Institutions	418.30	130.97
其中：实收资本 Of Which: Paid-in Capital	536.46	104.01			
当年结益 Net Earnings	121.22	121.22	2. 拆放同业 Placements with Banks and Other Financial Institutions	333.09	-113.24
十二、其他 Others	-930.09	-287.16	九、代理金融机构贷款 Lending on Behalf of Financial Institutions	16.79	-2.88
			其中：代理人行专项贷款 Of Which: Agency Earmarked Loans of the Central Bank	15.51	-2.45
			十、库存现金 Cash in Vault	144.94	21.57
			十一、外汇占款 Position for Foreign Exchange Purchase	96.29	-48.11
资金来源总计 Total Sources	**33790.69**	**7988.54**	**资金运用总计 Total Uses**	**33790.69**	**7988.54**

其他商业银行人民币信贷收支表
Sources and Uses of Credit Funds of Other Commercial Banks (RMB)

(2004年末)

(Year - end of 2004)

单位：亿元

Unit: 100 Million Yuan

项 目 Items	余 额 Balance	比年初增减额 Changes within the Year	项 目 Items	余 额 Balance	比年初增减额 Changes within the Year
一、各项存款 Total Deposits	38064.97	7502.73	一、各项贷款 Total Loans	27496.99	4690.19
1. 企业存款 Deposits by Enterprises	21847.75	3554.35	1. 短期贷款 Short - term Loans	16182.72	2634.79
(1) 活期存款 Demand Deposits	14076.30	2040.09	(1) 工业贷款 Loans to Industrial Sector	4728.56	1103.48
(2) 定期存款 Time Deposits	7771.45	1514.26	(2) 商业贷款 Loans to Commercial Sector	1895.36	225.08
2. 机关团体存款 Deposits by Government Agencies and Social Organizations	1067.21	166.95	其中：收购贷款 Of Which: Loans for the Purchase of Farm Products		
3. 储蓄存款 Savings Deposits	7458.26	1603.35	(3) 建筑业贷款 Loans to Construction Sector	1147.08	432.72
(1) 活期储蓄 Demand Deposits	3258.01	637.73	(4) 农业贷款 Loans to Agricultural Sector	31.87	9.67
(2) 定期储蓄 Time Deposits	4200.25	965.62	(5) 乡镇企业贷款 Loans to Village and Township Enterprises	14.46	-4.15
4. 农业存款 Deposits by Agricultural Sector	19.98	4.05	(6) 三资企业贷款 Loans to Foreign Investment Enterprises and Ventures	758.77	-48.09
5. 其他存款 Other Deposits	7671.77	2174.03			
二、代理财政性存款 Agency Fiscal Deposits	32.34	-33.74	(7) 私营企业及个体贷款 Loans to Privately - run Enterprises and Self - employed Entities	554.58	61.95
三、金融债券 Financial Bonds	427.78	388.47	(8) 其他短期贷款 Other Short - term Loans	7052.04	854.13
其中：政策性金融债券 Of Which: Policy Financial Bonds			其中：个人短期消费贷款 Of Which: Short - term Consumer Credit	338.57	119.12
四、应付及暂收款 Accounts Payable and Receipts on Account	559.20	121.59	2. 中期流动资金贷款 Medium - term Working Capital Loans	1262.67	233.19
其中：应付及预提利息 Of Which: Interest Payable and Accrued	216.85	59.84	3. 中长期贷款 Medium and Long - term Loans	7330.61	2463.92
五、卖出回购资产 Assets Repo (Including Securities)	310.65	-488.37	(1) 基本建设贷款 Capital Construction Loans	1421.68	546.21
六、向中央银行借款 Borrowings from the Central Bank	15.18	-319.55	(2) 技术改造贷款 Technical Improvement Loans	202.01	70.20
七、同业往来 Inter - bank Transactions	1435.32	-197.39	(3) 其他中长期贷款 Other Medium and Long - term Loans	5706.92	1847.51

续表
Continued

项目 Items	余额 Balance	比年初增减额 Changes within the Year	项目 Items	余额 Balance	比年初增减额 Changes within the Year
1. 同业存放 Due to Banks and Other Financial Institutions	1406.69	-190.98	其中：个人中长期消费贷款 Of Which：Medium and Long-term Consumer Credit	2942.01	1136.76
2. 同业拆借 Placements from Banks and Other Financial Institutions	28.63	-6.41	4. 票据融资 Paper Financing	2659.06	-664.15
八、委托存款及委托投资基金（净） Designated Deposits and Designated Investment Funds（Net）	-19.39	-29.83	其中：贴现 Of Which：Discount	2654.75	-667.29
1. 委托存款及委托投资基金 Designated Deposits and Designated Investment Funds	1238.68	652.80	5. 各项垫款 Total Advances	61.93	22.44
2. 减：委托贷款及委托投资 Minus：Designated Loans and Designated Investments	1258.07	682.63	二、有价证券及投资 Securities and Investments	7128.25	2088.49
九、代理金融机构委托贷款基金 Designated Loan Funds on Behalf of Financial Institutions	13.54	-3.98	三、应收及预付款 Accounts Receivable and Advance Payments	418.33	20.61
其中：中央银行委托贷款基金 Of Which：Loan Funds Designated by the Central Bank	13.23	-2.30	其中：应收利息 Of Which：Interest Receivable	86.69	19.99
十、各项准备 Total Provisions	680.13	171.39	四、买入返售资产 Assets Reverse Repo（Including Securities）	730.30	-14.78
其中：贷款损失准备 Of Which：Provisions for Loan Losses	645.01	165.24	五、存放中央银行准备金存款 Reserve Deposits with the Central Bank	5526.86	977.44
十一、所有者权益 Owner's Equity	1303.97	110.45	六、存放中央银行特种存款 Special Deposits with the Central Bank		
其中：实收资本 Of Which：Paid-in Capital	766.96	230.50	七、缴存中央银行财政性存款 Fiscal Deposits with the Central Bank	8.96	4.41
当年结益 Net Earnings	-80.85	-80.85	八、同业往来 Inter-bank Transactions	468.16	-237.90
十二、其他 Others	-796.04	298.48	1. 存放同业 Due from Banks and Other Financial Institutions	258.87	-159.42
			2. 拆放同业 Placements with Banks and Other Financial Institutions	209.29	-78.48
			九、代理金融机构贷款 Lending on Behalf of Financial Institutions	13.39	-3.40
			其中：代理人行专项贷款 Of Which：Agency Earmarked Loans of the Central Bank	13.21	-2.30
			十、库存现金 Cash in Vault	173.04	28.10
			十一、外汇占款 Position for Foreign Exchange Purchase	63.37	-32.91
资金来源总计 Total Sources	**42027.65**	**7520.25**	**资金运用总计 Total Uses**	**42027.65**	**7520.25**

其他商业银行人民币信贷收支表

Sources and Uses of Credit Funds of Other Commercial Banks (RMB)

(2005 年末)

(Year - end of 2005)

单位：亿元

Unit: 100 Million Yuan

项　目 Items	余　额 Balance	比年初增减额 Changes within the Year	项　目 Items	余　额 Balance	比年初增减额 Changes within the Year
一、各项存款 Total Deposits	46533.61	8461.88	一、各项贷款 Total Loans	33461.99	5964.98
1. 企业存款 Deposits by Enterprises	25491.21	3660.22	1. 短期贷款 Short - term Loans	17958.06	1761.40
(1) 活期存款 Demand Deposits	15509.57	1441.97	(1) 工业贷款 Loans to Industrial Sector	5733.65	1005.75
(2) 定期存款 Time Deposits	9981.64	2218.25	(2) 商业贷款 Loans to Commercial Sector	2099.90	201.91
2. 机关团体存款 Deposits by Government Agencies and Social Organizations	1312.85	245.64	其中：收购贷款 Of Which: Loans for the Purchase of Farm Products		
3. 储蓄存款 Savings Deposits	9982.74	2523.79	(3) 建筑业贷款 Loans to Construction Sector	1430.83	282.43
(1) 活期储蓄 Demand Deposits	3960.89	702.83	(4) 农业贷款 Loans to Agricultural Sector	54.28	22.41
(2) 定期储蓄 Time Deposits	6021.85	1820.96	(5) 乡镇企业贷款 Loans to Village and Township Enterprises	14.90	0.43
4. 农业存款 Deposits by Agricultural Sector	20.84	0.86	(6) 三资企业贷款 Loans to Foreign Investment Enterprises and Ventures	665.00	- 97.29
5. 其他存款 Other Deposits	9725.97	2031.37	(7) 私营企业及个体贷款 Loans to Privately - run Enterprises and Self - employed Entities	591.22	33.13
二、代理财政性存款 Agency Fiscal Deposits	38.48	6.14	(8) 其他短期贷款 Other Short - term Loans	7368.28	312.63
三、金融债券 Financial Bonds	732.20	220.93	其中：个人短期消费贷款 Of Which: Short - term Consumer Credit	350.74	12.23
其中：政策性金融债券 Of Which: Policy Financial Bonds	192.14	192.11	2. 中期流动资金贷款 Medium - term Working Capital Loans	1550.00	285.78
四、应付及暂收款 Accounts Payable and Receipts on Account	811.95	252.52	3. 中长期贷款 Medium and Long - term Loans	9338.36	2025.36
其中：应付及预提利息 Of Which: Interest Payable and Accrued	284.35	67.51	(1) 基本建设贷款 Capital Construction Loans	1877.52	454.84
五、卖出回购资产 Assets Repo (Including Securities)	293.54	- 17.11	(2) 技术改造贷款 Technical Improvement Loans	236.95	35.94
六、向中央银行借款 Borrowings from the Central Bank	12.40	- 2.78	(3) 其他中长期贷款 Other Medium and Long - term Loans	7223.89	1534.58
七、同业往来 Inter - bank Transactions	2300.24	865.87			

续表
Continued

项　目 Items	余　额 Balance	比年初增减额 Changes within the Year	项　目 Items	余　额 Balance	比年初增减额 Changes within the Year
1. 同业存放 Due to Banks and Other Financial Institutions	2300.05	894.31	其中：个人中长期消费贷款 Of Which：Medium and Long－term Consumer Credit	3732.14	790.17
2. 同业拆借 Placements from Banks and Other Financial Institutions	0.19	－28.44	4. 票据融资 Paper Financing	4537.41	1879.02
八、委托存款及委托投资基金（净） Designated Deposits and Designated Investment Funds（Net）	76.40	95.77	其中：贴现 Of Which：Discount	4533.58	1879.50
1. 委托存款及委托投资基金 Designated Deposits and Designated Investment Funds	1809.67	570.98	5. 各项垫款 Total Advances	78.16	13.42
2. 减：委托贷款及委托投资 Minus：Designated Loans and Designated Investments	1733.27	475.21	二、有价证券及投资 Securities and Investments	9362.14	2192.89
九、代理金融机构委托贷款基金 Designated Loan Funds on Behalf of Financial Institutions	12.75	－0.79	三、应收及预付款 Accounts Receivable and Advance Payments	559.74	141.18
其中：中央银行委托贷款基金 Of Which：Loan Funds Designated by the Central Bank	12.36	－0.87	其中：应收利息 Of Which：Interest Receivable	96.39	9.71
十、各项准备 Total Provisions	843.72	163.59	四、买入返售资产 Assets Reverse Repo（Including Securities）	2484.31	1754.01
其中：贷款损失准备 Of Which：Provisions for Loan Losses	785.91	141.97	五、存放中央银行准备金存款 Reserve Deposits with the Central Bank	5526.59	－0.27
十一、所有者权益 Owner's Equity	1791.12	487.07	六、存放中央银行特种存款 Special Deposits with the Central Bank		
其中：实收资本 Of Which：Paid－in Capital	978.98	212.02	七、缴存中央银行财政性存款 Fiscal Deposits with the Central Bank	15.95	6.99
当年结益 Net Earnings	431.19	431.19	八、同业往来 Inter－bank Transactions	922.07	453.03
十二、其他 Others	－840.69	2.84	1. 存放同业 Due from Banks and Other Financial Institutions	689.42	430.00
			2. 拆放同业 Placements with Banks and Other Financial Institutions	232.65	23.03
			九、代理金融机构贷款 Lending on Behalf of Financial Institutions	12.53	－0.86
			其中：代理人行专项贷款 Of Which：Agency Earmarked Loans of the Central Bank	12.35	－0.86
			十、库存现金 Cash in Vault	199.63	26.59
			十一、外汇占款 Position for Foreign Exchange Purchase	60.77	－2.61
资金来源总计 Total Sources	**52605.72**	**10535.93**	**资金运用总计 Total Uses**	**52605.72**	**10535.93**

6. 城市商业银行人民币信贷收支表（1999—2005 年）
Sources and Uses of Credit Funds of City Commercial Banks（RMB）（1999—2005）

城市商业银行人民币信贷收支表
Sources and Uses of Credit Funds of City Commercial Banks（RMB）

（1999 年末）

（Year - end of 1999）

单位：亿元

Unit：100 Million Yuan

项 目 Items	余 额 Balance	比年初增减额 Changes within the Year	项 目 Items	余 额 Balance	比年初增减额 Changes within the Year
一、各项存款 Total Deposits	4387.44	626.90	一、各项贷款 Total Loans	2704.04	422.11
1. 企业存款 Deposits by Enterprises	2923.31	465.69	1. 短期贷款 Short - term Loans	1438.26	127.64
（1）活期存款 Demand Deposits	2338.21	399.48	（1）工业贷款 Loans to Industrial Sector	246.89	24.35
（2）定期存款 Time Deposits	585.10	66.21	（2）商业贷款 Loans to Commercial Sector	405.55	- 44.71
2. 城镇储蓄存款 Urban Savings Deposits	1363.02	142.39	其中：收购贷款 Of Which：Loans for the Purchase of Farm Products	0.16	- 0.11
（1）活期储蓄 Demand Deposits	431.24	91.40	（3）建筑业贷款 Loans to Construction Sector	74.18	20.60
（2）定期储蓄 Time Deposits	931.78	50.99	（4）农业贷款 Loans to Agricultural Sector	3.47	2.05
3. 农业存款 Deposits by Agricultural Sector	2.53	0.22	（5）乡镇企业贷款 Loans to Village and Township Enterprises	37.91	7.76
4. 信托存款 Trust Deposits					
5. 其他存款 Other Deposits	98.58	18.60	（6）三资企业贷款 Loans to Foreign Investment Enterprises and Ventures	54.06	0.39
二、代理财政性存款 Agency Fiscal Deposits	2.77	0.81	（7）私营企业及个体贷款 Loans to Privately - run Enterprises and Self - employed Entities	82.96	10.49
三、发行金融债券 Financial Bonds Issue	0.20	- 0.32			
其中：发行政策性金融债券 Of Which：Policy Financial Bonds Issue			（8）贴现 Discount	19.25	5.06
四、国家投资债券 State Investment Bonds			（9）其他短期贷款 Other Short - term Loans	513.99	101.65
五、卖出回购证券 Repo	75.80	71.37	2. 中期流动资金贷款 Medium - term Working Capital Loans	55.37	18.27
六、向中央银行借款 Borrowings from the Central Bank	114.18	92.30	3. 中长期贷款 Medium and Long - term Loans	294.92	138.39
七、同业往来 Inter - bank Transactions	255.28	38.47	（1）基本建设贷款 Capital Construction Loans	102.66	31.28
			（2）技术改造贷款 Technical Improvement Loans	8.38	4.43

续表
Continued

项 目 Items	余 额 Balance	比年初增减额 Changes within the Year	项 目 Items	余 额 Balance	比年初增减额 Changes within the Year
1. 同业存放 Due to Banks and Other Financial Institutions	172.12	53.78	（3）其他中长期贷款 Other Medium and Long - term Loans	183.88	102.68
2. 同业拆借 Placements from Banks and Other Financial Institutions	83.16	- 15.31	4. 信托贷款 Trust Loans		
			5. 逾期类贷款 Overdue Loans	915.49	137.81
八、委托存款及委托投资 Designated Deposits and Designated Investment Funds	3.74	1.28	二、国家投资债券贷款 Loans Related to State Investment Bonds	0.07	0.07
1. 委托存款 Designated Deposits	4.53	2.50	三、有价证券及投资 Securities and Investments	758.78	200.05
2. 委托投资基金 Designated Investment Funds	- 0.79	- 1.22	四、缴存准备金存款 Reserve Deposits with the Central Bank	670.15	129.88
九、代理金融机构委托贷款基金 Designated Loan Funds on Behalf of Financial Institutions	1.94	0.22	五、存放中央银行特种存款 Special Deposits with the Central Bank	0.15	- 0.05
			六、存放中央银行财政性存款 Fiscal Deposits with the Central Bank	1.06	0.22
其中：中央银行委托贷款基金 Of Which：Loan Funds Designated by the Central Bank	0.95	0.32	七、同业往来 Inter - bank Transactions	316.48	- 26.31
十、所有者权益 Owner's Equity	245.80	21.68	1. 存放同业 Due from Banks and Other Financial Institutions	154.07	- 29.09
其中：实收资本 Of Which：Paid - in Capital	238.38	38.19	2. 拆放同业 Placements with Banks and Other Financial Institutions	162.41	2.78
当年结益 Net Earnings	- 5.77	- 5.77			
十一、其他 Others	- 560.20	- 90.15	八、代理金融机构贷款 Lending on Behalf of Financial Institutions	2.24	0.27
			其中：代理人行专项贷款 Of Which：Agency Earmarked Loans of the Central Bank	1.02	0.35
			九、库存现金 Cash in Vault	67.39	30.62
			十、外汇占款 Position for Foreign Exchange Purchase	6.59	5.70
资金来源总计 Total Sources	**4526.95**	**762.56**	**资金运用总计 Total Uses**	**4526.95**	**762.56**

城市商业银行人民币信贷收支表
Sources and Uses of Credit Funds of City Commercial Banks (RMB)

(2000年末)

(Year - end of 2000)

单位：亿元

Unit: 100 Million Yuan

项目 Items	余额 Balance	比年初增减额 Changes within the Year	项目 Items	余额 Balance	比年初增减额 Changes within the Year
一、各项存款 Total Deposits	5278.63	891.29	一、各项贷款 Total Loans	3469.94	765.92
1. 企业存款 Deposits by Enterprises	3659.83	736.52	1. 短期贷款 Short - term Loans	1831.54	392.87
(1) 活期存款 Demand Deposits	2972.79	634.61	(1) 工业贷款 Loans to Industrial Sector	303.58	56.47
(2) 定期存款 Time Deposits	687.04	101.91	(2) 商业贷款 Loans to Commercial Sector	369.58	-36.60
2. 城镇储蓄存款 Urban Savings Deposits	1471.38	108.36	其中：收购贷款 Of Which: Loans for the Purchase of Farm Products	0.12	-0.04
(1) 活期储蓄 Demand Deposits	562.24	131.04	(3) 建筑业贷款 Loans to Construction Sector	101.26	27.03
(2) 定期储蓄 Time Deposits	909.14	-22.68	(4) 农业贷款 Loans to Agricultural Sector	6.52	3.06
3. 农业存款 Deposits by Agricultural Sector	10.13	7.60	(5) 乡镇企业贷款 Loans to Village and Township Enterprises	51.13	13.07
4. 信托存款 Trust Deposits			(6) 三资企业贷款 Loans to Foreign Investment Enterprises and Ventures	50.62	-3.28
5. 其他存款 Other Deposits	137.29	38.81	(7) 私营企业及个体贷款 Loans to Privately - run Enterprises and Self - employed Entities	106.36	23.18
二、代理财政性存款 Agency Fiscal Deposits	3.93	1.16	(8) 贴现 Discount	126.52	107.27
三、发行金融债券 Financial Bonds Issue		-0.20	(9) 其他短期贷款 Other Short - term Loans	715.97	202.67
其中：发行政策性金融债券 Of Which: Policy Financial Bonds Issue			2. 中期流动资金贷款 Medium - term Working Capital Loans	52.61	-2.63
四、国家投资债券 State Investment Bonds			3. 中长期贷款 Medium and Long - term Loans	522.64	228.03
五、卖出回购证券 Repo	95.44	23.64	(1) 基本建设贷款 Capital Construction Loans	174.99	72.33
六、向中央银行借款 Borrowings from the Central Bank	277.73	162.58	(2) 技术改造贷款 Technical Improvement Loans	17.55	9.17
七、同业往来 Inter - bank Transactions	413.39	158.41	(3) 其他中长期贷款 Other Medium and Long - term Loans	330.10	146.53
1. 同业存放 Due to Banks and Other Financial Institutions	317.24	145.12	4. 信托贷款 Trust Loans		
2. 同业拆借 Placements from Banks and Other Financial Institutions	96.15	13.29			

续表
Continued

项目 Items	余额 Balance	比年初增减额 Changes within the Year	项目 Items	余额 Balance	比年初增减额 Changes within the Year
八、委托存款及委托投资 Designated Deposits and Designated Investment Funds	-17.41	-21.15	5. 逾期类贷款 Overdue Loans	1063.15	147.65
			二、国家投资债券贷款 Loans Related to State Investment Bonds		-0.07
1. 委托存款 Designated Deposits	-18.37	-22.90	三、有价证券及投资 Securities and Investments	1010.83	256.35
2. 委托投资基金 Designated Investment Funds	0.96	1.75	四、缴存准备金存款 Reserve Deposits with the Central Bank	823.14	153.19
九、代理金融机构委托贷款基金 Designated Loan Funds on Behalf of Financial Institutions	83.63	81.69	五、存放中央银行特种存款 Special Deposits with the Central Bank		-0.26
其中：中央银行委托贷款基金 Of Which：Loan Funds Designated by the Central Bank	73.28	72.33	六、存放中央银行财政性存款 Fiscal Deposits with the Central Bank	1.31	0.16
			七、同业往来 Inter-bank Transactions	342.94	26.31
十、所有者权益 Owner's Equity	260.20	13.02	1. 存放同业 Due from Banks and Other Financial Institutions	168.36	14.28
其中：实收资本 Of Which：Paid-in Capital	274.64	36.32			
当年结益 Net Earnings	5.81	5.81	2. 拆放同业 Placements with Banks and Other Financial Institutions	174.58	12.03
十一、其他 Others	-592.51	-30.19	八、代理金融机构贷款 Lending on Behalf of Financial Institutions	84.65	82.41
			其中：代理人行专项贷款 Of Which：Agency Earmarked Loans of the Central Bank	74.40	73.38
			九、库存现金 Cash in Vault	61.29	-6.10
			十、外汇占款 Position for Foreign Exchange Purchase	8.93	2.34
资金来源总计 Total Sources	**5803.03**	**1280.25**	**资金运用总计 Total Uses**	**5803.03**	**1280.25**

城市商业银行人民币信贷收支表

Sources and Uses of Credit Funds of City Commercial Banks (RMB)

(2001 年末)

(Year - end of 2001)

单位：亿元

Unit: 100 Million Yuan

项 目 Items	余 额 Balance	比年初增减额 Changes within the Year	项 目 Items	余 额 Balance	比年初增减额 Changes within the Year
一、各项存款 Total Deposits	6789.90	1458.50	一、各项贷款 Total Loans	4527.42	1020.78
1. 企业存款 Deposits by Enterprises	4575.66	882.64	1. 短期贷款 Short - term Loans	3011.49	469.80
(1) 活期存款 Demand Deposits	3641.93	640.87	(1) 工业贷款 Loans to Industrial Sector	574.86	104.64
(2) 定期存款 Time Deposits	933.73	241.77	(2) 商业贷款 Loans to Commercial Sector	744.95	73.89
2. 机关团体存款 Deposits by Government Agencies and Social Organizations	55.77	39.17	其中：收购贷款 Of Which: Loans for the Purchase of Farm Products	0.36	-0.01
3. 储蓄存款 Savings Deposits	1881.78	392.75	(3) 建筑业贷款 Loans to Construction Sector	204.38	43.30
(1) 活期储蓄 Demand Deposits	743.18	174.43	(4) 农业贷款 Loans to Agricultural Sector	9.07	0.48
(2) 定期储蓄 Time Deposits	1138.60	218.32	(5) 乡镇企业贷款 Loans to Village and Township Enterprises	81.17	7.55
4. 农业存款 Deposits by Agricultural Sector	8.82	-1.31	(6) 三资企业贷款 Loans to Foreign Investment Enterprises and Ventures	88.85	14.61
5. 其他存款 Other Deposits	267.87	145.25			
二、代理财政性存款 Agency Fiscal Deposits	6.60	2.67	(7) 私营企业及个体贷款 Loans to Privately - run Enterprises and Self - employed Entities	217.39	46.43
三、金融债券 Financial Bonds			(8) 其他短期贷款 Other Short - term Loans	1090.82	178.90
其中：政策性金融债券 Of Which: Policy Financial Bonds			其中：个人短期消费贷款 Of Which: Short - term Consumer Credit	23.04	10.64
四、应付及暂收款 Accounts Payable and Receipts on Account	130.66	-2.44	2. 中期流动资金贷款 Medium - term Working Capital Loans	79.33	25.68
其中：应付及预提利息 Of Which: Interest Payable and Accrued	40.11	1.81	3. 中长期贷款 Medium and Long - term Loans	1091.97	307.90
五、卖出回购证券 Repo	455.22	187.36	(1) 基本建设贷款 Capital Construction Loans	251.97	42.37
六、向中央银行借款 Borrowings from the Central Bank	282.71	4.83	(2) 技术改造贷款 Technical Improvement Loans	35.26	15.96
七、同业往来 Inter - bank Transactions	411.08	-6.13	(3) 其他中长期贷款 Other Medium and Long - term Loans	804.74	249.57

续表
Continued

项 目 Items	余 额 Balance	比年初增减额 Changes within the Year	项 目 Items	余 额 Balance	比年初增减额 Changes within the Year
1. 同业存放 Due to Banks and Other Financial Institutions	316.17	-4.74	其中：个人中长期消费贷款 Of Which: Medium and Long-term Consumer Credit	175.22	100.22
2. 同业拆借 Placements from Banks and Other Financial Institutions	94.91	-1.39	4. 票据融资 Paper Financing	340.54	213.33
			其中：贴现 Of Which: Discount	340.54	213.33
八、委托存款及委托投资基金（净） Designated Deposits and Designated Investment Funds (Net)	-16.94		5. 各项垫款 Total Advances	4.09	4.07
1. 委托存款及委托投资基金 Designated Deposits and Designated Investment Funds	62.57	10.54	二、有价证券及投资 Securities and Investments	1497.74	483.30
			三、应收及预付款 Accounts Receivable and Advance Payments	238.78	-45.88
2. 减：委托贷款及委托投资 Minus: Designated Loans and Designated Investments	79.51	10.54	其中：应收利息 Of Which: Interest Receivable	94.99	-9.17
九、代理金融机构委托贷款基金 Designated Loan Funds on Behalf of Financial Institutions	21.89	-61.48	四、买入返售证券 Reverse Repo	268.06	95.04
			五、存放中央银行准备金存款 Reserve Deposits with the Central Bank	831.59	-0.22
其中：中央银行委托贷款基金 Of Which: Loan Funds Designated by the Central Bank	3.61	-69.52	六、存放中央银行特种存款 Special Deposits with the Central Bank		
十、各项准备 Total Provisions	52.97	8.34	七、缴存中央银行财政性存款 Fiscal Deposits with the Central Bank	2.90	1.69
其中：贷款呆账准备金 Of Which: Provisions for Bad Loans	49.16	8.29	八、同业往来 Inter-bank Transactions	446.79	91.95
十一、所有者权益 Owner's Equity	304.42	35.88	1. 存放同业 Due from Banks and Other Financial Institutions	228.78	48.92
其中：实收资本 Of Which: Paid-in Capital	325.47	44.67	2. 拆放同业 Placements with Banks and Other Financial Institutions	218.01	43.03
当年结益 Net Earnings	17.28	17.28			
十二、其他 Others	-540.39	-51.88	九、代理金融机构贷款 Lending on Behalf of Financial Institutions	23.12	-61.60
			其中：代理人行专项贷款 Of Which: Agency Earmarked Loans of the Central Bank	4.17	-70.23
			十、库存现金 Cash in Vault	56.25	-5.95
			十一、外汇占款 Position for Foreign Exchange Purchase	5.47	-3.46
资金来源总计 Total Sources	**7898.12**	**1575.65**	**资金运用总计 Total Uses**	**7898.12**	**1575.65**

城市商业银行人民币信贷收支表
Sources and Uses of Credit Funds of City Commercial Banks (RMB)

(2002 年末)

(Year - end of 2002)

单位：亿元
Unit: 100 Million Yuan

项目 Items	余额 Balance	比年初增减额 Changes within the Year	项目 Items	余额 Balance	比年初增减额 Changes within the Year
一、各项存款 Total Deposits	8890.27	2128.64	一、各项贷款 Total Loans	5893.37	1470.72
1. 企业存款 Deposits by Enterprises	5858.51	1306.72	1. 短期贷款 Short - term Loans	3538.45	549.78
(1) 活期存款 Demand Deposits	4584.90	949.43	(1) 工业贷款 Loans to Industrial Sector	615.94	68.68
(2) 定期存款 Time Deposits	1273.61	357.29	(2) 商业贷款 Loans to Commercial Sector	814.42	72.35
2. 机关团体存款 Deposits by Government Agencies and Social Organizations	114.87	59.04	其中：收购贷款 Of Which: Loans for the Purchase of Farm Products	0.38	0.13
3. 储蓄存款 Savings Deposits	2442.23	565.85	(3) 建筑业贷款 Loans to Construction Sector	272.44	65.57
(1) 活期储蓄 Demand Deposits	976.43	234.05	(4) 农业贷款 Loans to Agricultural Sector	12.42	2.94
(2) 定期储蓄 Time Deposits	1465.80	331.80	(5) 乡镇企业贷款 Loans to Village and Township Enterprises	94.86	5.05
4. 农业存款 Deposits by Agricultural Sector	12.69	3.28	(6) 三资企业贷款 Loans to Foreign Investment Enterprises and Ventures	90.37	1.96
5. 其他存款 Other Deposits	461.97	193.75			
二、代理财政性存款 Agency Fiscal Deposits	8.36	2.35	(7) 私营企业及个体贷款 Loans to Privately - run Enterprises and Self - employed Entities	283.06	56.80
三、金融债券 Financial Bonds			(8) 其他短期贷款 Other Short - term Loans	1354.94	276.43
其中：政策性金融债券 Of Which: Policy Financial Bonds			其中：个人短期消费贷款 Of Which: Short - term Consumer Credit	32.13	8.00
四、应付及暂收款 Accounts Payable and Receipts on Account	139.84	13.45	2. 中期流动资金贷款 Medium - term Working Capital Loans	180.72	101.35
其中：应付及预提利息 Of Which: Interest Payable and Accrued	41.30	2.38	3. 中长期贷款 Medium and Long - term Loans	1377.47	367.51
五、卖出回购证券 Repo	1111.11	659.25	(1) 基本建设贷款 Capital Construction Loans	347.98	98.25
六、向中央银行借款 Borrowings from the Central Bank	165.73	-20.34	(2) 技术改造贷款 Technical Improvement Loans	38.74	3.26
七、同业往来 Inter - bank Transactions	438.62	33.43	(3) 其他中长期贷款 Other Medium and Long - term Loans	990.75	266.00

续表
Continued

项　目 Items	余　额 Balance	比年初增减额 Changes within the Year	项　目 Items	余　额 Balance	比年初增减额 Changes within the Year
1. 同业存放 Due to Banks and Other Financial Institutions	389.86	79.24	其中：个人中长期消费贷款 Of Which：Medium and Long－term Consumer Credit	333.28	153.76
2. 同业拆借 Placements from Banks and Other Financial Institutions	48.76	－45.81	4. 票据融资 Paper Financing	783.80	443.24
			其中：贴现 Of Which：Discount	783.80	443.24
八、委托存款及委托投资基金（净） Designated Deposits and Designated Investment Funds（Net）	－17.30	－0.36	5. 各项垫款 Total Advances	12.93	8.84
1. 委托存款及委托投资基金 Designated Deposits and Designated Investment Funds	92.29	12.35	二、有价证券及投资 Securities and Investments	2303.69	818.15
			三、应收及预付款 Accounts Receivable and Advance Payments	236.69	20.99
2. 减：委托贷款及委托投资 Minus：Designated Loans and Designated Investments	109.59	12.71	其中：应收利息 Of Which：Interest Receivable	75.36	－15.96
九、代理金融机构委托贷款基金 Designated Loan Funds on Behalf of Financial Institutions	4.39	－0.29	四、买入返售证券 Reverse Repo	520.05	251.99
			五、存放中央银行准备金存款 Reserve Deposits with the Central Bank	988.75	159.45
其中：中央银行委托贷款基金 Of Which：Loan Funds Designated by the Central Bank	3.44	－0.17	六、存放中央银行特种存款 Special Deposits with the Central Bank	1.24	1.24
十、各项准备 Total Provisions	65.03	29.55	七、缴存中央银行财政性存款 Fiscal Deposits with the Central Bank	4.33	1.42
其中：贷款呆账准备金 Of Which：Provisions for Bad Loans	64.78	29.69	八、同业往来 Inter－bank Transactions	502.08	52.37
十一、所有者权益 Owner's Equity	401.42	83.43	1. 存放同业 Due from Banks and Other Financial Institutions	344.40	111.47
其中：实收资本 Of Which：Paid－in Capital	357.93	40.46			
当年结益 Net Earnings	35.85	35.85	2. 拆放同业 Placements with Banks and Other Financial Institutions	157.68	－59.10
十二、其他 Others	－670.03	－133.00	九、代理金融机构贷款 Lending on Behalf of Financial Institutions	6.49	0.58
			其中：代理人行专项贷款 Of Which：Agency Earmarked Loans of the Central Bank	5.00	0.83
			十、库存现金 Cash in Vault	71.40	15.41
			十一、外汇占款 Position for Foreign Exchange Purchase	9.35	3.79
资金来源总计 Total Sources	**10537.44**	**2796.11**	**资金运用总计 Total Uses**	**10537.44**	**2796.11**

城市商业银行人民币信贷收支表

Sources and Uses of Credit Funds of City Commercial Banks（RMB）

（2003 年末）

（Year - end of 2003）

单位：亿元

Unit: 100 Million Yuan

项目 Items	余额 Balance	比年初增减额 Changes within the Year	项目 Items	余额 Balance	比年初增减额 Changes within the Year
一、各项存款 Total Deposits	11607.27	2716.99	一、各项贷款 Total Loans	7661.64	1766.77
1. 企业存款 Deposits by Enterprises	7441.02	1584.04	1. 短期贷款 Short - term Loans	4319.69	795.03
(1) 活期存款 Demand Deposits	5707.85	1124.48	(1) 工业贷款 Loans to Industrial Sector	755.88	142.48
(2) 定期存款 Time Deposits	1733.17	459.56	(2) 商业贷款 Loans to Commercial Sector	965.00	150.30
2. 机关团体存款 Deposits by Government Agencies and Social Organizations	199.40	84.53	其中：收购贷款 Of Which: Loans for the Purchase of Farm Products	0.15	-0.23
3. 储蓄存款 Savings Deposits	3105.75	663.52	(3) 建筑业贷款 Loans to Construction Sector	330.01	58.58
(1) 活期储蓄 Demand Deposits	1251.92	275.49	(4) 农业贷款 Loans to Agricultural Sector	28.06	15.64
(2) 定期储蓄 Time Deposits	1853.83	388.03	(5) 乡镇企业贷款 Loans to Village and Township Enterprises	107.74	12.91
4. 农业存款 Deposits by Agricultural Sector	12.33	-0.37	(6) 三资企业贷款 Loans to Foreign Investment Enterprises and Ventures	90.33	-0.22
5. 其他存款 Other Deposits	848.77	385.27			
二、代理财政性存款 Agency Fiscal Deposits	11.11	2.75	(7) 私营企业及个体贷款 Loans to Privately - run Enterprises and Self - employed Entities	342.90	59.45
三、金融债券 Financial Bonds			(8) 其他短期贷款 Other Short - term Loans	1699.77	355.89
其中：政策性金融债券 Of Which: Policy Financial Bonds			其中：个人短期消费贷款 Of Which: Short - term Consumer Credit	68.96	36.87
四、应付及暂收款 Accounts Payable and Receipts on Account	149.74	9.72			
			2. 中期流动资金贷款 Medium - term Working Capital Loans	269.97	91.86
其中：应付及预提利息 Of Which: Interest Payable and Accrued	41.38	0.08	3. 中长期贷款 Medium and Long - term Loans	2245.79	866.03
五、卖出回购证券 Repo	883.87	-50.19	(1) 基本建设贷款 Capital Construction Loans	553.59	204.75
六、向中央银行借款 Borrowings from the Central Bank	177.75	12.02	(2) 技术改造贷款 Technical Improvement Loans	61.65	22.76
七、同业往来 Inter - bank Transactions	565.59	127.22	(3) 其他中长期贷款 Other Medium and Long - term Loans	1630.55	638.52

续表
Continued

项目 Items	余额 Balance	比年初增减额 Changes within the Year	项目 Items	余额 Balance	比年初增减额 Changes within the Year
1. 同业存放 Due to Banks and Other Financial Institutions	489.91	100.11	其中：个人中长期消费贷款 Of Which: Medium and Long - term Consumer Credit	559.17	225.37
2. 同业拆借 Placements from Banks and Other Financial Institutions	75.68	27.11	4. 票据融资 Paper Financing	817.00	17.59
			其中：贴现 Of Which: Discount	813.90	15.50
八、委托存款及委托投资基金（净） Designated Deposits and Designated Investment Funds（Net）	-21.65	-4.30	5. 各项垫款 Total Advances	9.19	-3.74
1. 委托存款及委托投资基金 Designated Deposits and Designated Investment Funds	141.29	48.93	二、有价证券及投资 Securities and Investments	2955.71	651.80
2. 减：委托贷款及委托投资 Minus: Designated Loans and Designated Investments	162.94	53.23	三、应收及预付款 Accounts Receivable and Advance Payments	211.06	-25.48
			其中：应收利息 Of Which: Interest Receivable	51.24	-24.08
九、代理金融机构委托贷款基金 Designated Loan Funds on Behalf of Financial Institutions	5.04	0.65	四、买入返售证券 Reverse Repo	257.46	-97.86
			五、存放中央银行准备金 Reserve Deposits with the Central Bank	1418.87	430.13
其中：中央银行委托贷款基金 Of Which: Loan Funds Designated by the Central Bank	3.32	-0.12	六、存放中央银行特种存款 Special Deposits with the Central Bank		-1.24
十、各项准备 Total Provisions	98.62	33.64	七、缴存中央银行财政性存款 Fiscal Deposits with the Central Bank	9.47	5.14
其中：贷款损失准备 Of Which: Provisions for Loan Losses	96.81	33.36	八、同业往来 Inter - bank Transactions	588.59	86.49
十一、所有者权益 Owner's Equity	471.02	71.35	1. 存放同业 Due from Banks and Other Financial Institutions	415.37	71.01
其中：实收资本 Of Which: Paid - in Capital	407.32	49.39			
当年结益 Net Earnings	47.26	47.26	2. 拆放同业 Placements with Banks and Other Financial Institutions	173.22	15.48
十二、其他 Others	-735.39	-81.25	九、代理金融机构贷款 Lending on Behalf of Financial Institutions	7.23	0.74
			其中：代理人行专项贷款 Of Which: Agency Earmarked Loans of the Central Bank	4.74	-0.26
			十、库存现金 Cash in Vault	86.28	14.89
			十一、外汇占款 Position for Foreign Exchange Purchase	16.66	7.22
资金来源总计 Total Sources	**13212.97**	**2838.60**	**资金运用总计 Total Uses**	**13212.97**	**2838.60**

城市商业银行人民币信贷收支表

Sources and Uses of Credit Funds of City Commercial Banks (RMB)

(2004年末)

(Year - end of 2004)

单位：亿元

Unit: 100 Million Yuan

项 目 Items	余 额 Balance	比年初增减额 Changes within the Year	项 目 Items	余 额 Balance	比年初增减额 Changes within the Year
一、各项存款 Total Deposits	13990.19	2466.13	一、各项贷款 Total Loans	8954.97	1394.19
1. 企业存款 Deposits by Enterprises	8603.10	1164.94	1. 短期贷款 Short - term Loans	4672.97	380.15
(1) 活期存款 Demand Deposits	6433.51	728.52	(1) 工业贷款 Loans to Industrial Sector	878.51	120.89
(2) 定期存款 Time Deposits	2169.59	436.42	(2) 商业贷款 Loans to Commercial Sector	889.57	-65.59
2. 机关团体存款 Deposits by Government Agencies and Social Organizations	344.60	144.15	其中：收购贷款 Of Which: Loans for the Purchase of Farm Products		-0.15
3. 储蓄存款 Savings Deposits	3816.61	709.37	(3) 建筑业贷款 Loans to Construction Sector	338.96	8.52
(1) 活期储蓄 Demand Deposits	1475.15	221.74	(4) 农业贷款 Loans to Agricultural Sector	20.64	-7.42
(2) 定期储蓄 Time Deposits	2341.46	487.63	(5) 乡镇企业贷款 Loans to Village and Township Enterprises	93.38	-14.04
4. 农业存款 Deposits by Agricultural Sector	14.14	1.81			
5. 其他存款 Other Deposits	1211.74	445.86	(6) 三资企业贷款 Loans to Foreign Investment Enterprises and Ventures	82.50	-7.78
二、代理财政性存款 Agency Fiscal Deposits	33.76	-60.35	(7) 私营企业及个体贷款 Loans to Privately - run Enterprises and Self - employed Entities	443.10	55.87
三、金融债券 Financial Bonds	30.00	30.00			
其中：政策性金融债券 Of Which: Policy Financial Bonds			(8) 其他短期贷款 Other Short - term Loans	1926.31	289.70
四、应付及暂收款 Accounts Payable and Receipts on Account	170.54	20.00	其中：个人短期消费贷款 Of Which: Short - term Consumer Credit	88.19	23.39
其中：应付及预提利息 Of Which: Interest Payable and Accrued	52.47	11.02	2. 中期流动资金贷款 Medium - term Working Capital Loans	350.16	82.16
			3. 中长期贷款 Medium and Long - term Loans	3054.53	795.01
五、卖出回购资产 Assets Repo (Including Securities)	982.63	54.07	(1) 基本建设贷款 Capital Construction Loans	767.30	175.74
六、向中央银行借款 Borrowings from the Central Bank	119.30	-88.78	(2) 技术改造贷款 Technical Improvement Loans	81.85	19.90
七、同业往来 Inter - bank Transactions	352.88	-197.71	(3) 其他中长期贷款 Other Medium and Long - term Loans	2205.38	599.37

续表
Continued

项　目 Items	余　额 Balance	比年初增减额 Changes within the Year	项　目 Items	余　额 Balance	比年初增减额 Changes within the Year
1. 同业存放 Due to Banks and Other Financial Institutions	336.23	-153.69	其中：个人中长期消费贷款 Of Which: Medium and Long-term Consumer Credit	820.14	260.02
2. 同业拆借 Placements from Banks and Other Financial Institutions	16.65	-44.02	4. 票据融资 Paper Financing	863.60	132.35
八、委托存款及委托投资基金（净） Designated Deposits and Designated Investment Funds (Net)	6.24	3.99	其中：贴现 Of Which: Discount	863.24	135.11
1. 委托存款及委托投资基金 Designated Deposits and Designated Investment Funds	252.68	87.23	5. 各项垫款 Total Advances	13.71	4.52
2. 减：委托贷款及委托投资 Minus: Designated Loans and Designated Investments	246.44	83.24	二、有价证券及投资 Securities and Investments	3519.09	563.63
九、代理金融机构委托贷款基金 Designated Loan Funds on Behalf of Financial Institutions	7.38	2.34	三、应收及预付款 Accounts Receivable and Advance Payments	178.76	-18.69
其中：中央银行委托贷款基金 Of Which: Loan Funds Designated by the Central Bank	3.02	-0.30	其中：应收利息 Of Which: Interest Receivable	39.34	-13.75
十、各项准备 Total Provisions	165.26	66.64	四、买入返售资产 Assets Reverse Repo (Including Securities)	313.59	-132.00
其中：贷款损失准备 Of Which: Provisions for Loan Losses	162.92	66.12	五、存放中央银行准备金存款 Reserve Deposits with the Central Bank	1962.72	543.85
十一、所有者权益 Owner's Equity	568.19	97.65	六、存放中央银行特种存款 Special Deposits with the Central Bank		
其中：实收资本 Of Which: Paid-in Capital	462.35	55.03	七、缴存中央银行财政性存款 Fiscal Deposits with the Central Bank	25.19	15.72
当年结益 Net Earnings	81.72	81.72	八、同业往来 Inter-bank Transactions	488.67	-98.48
十二、其他 Others	-861.55	-114.90	1. 存放同业 Due from Banks and Other Financial Institutions	371.85	-41.35
			2. 拆放同业 Placements with Banks and Other Financial Institutions	116.82	-57.13
			九、代理金融机构贷款 Lending on Behalf of Financial Institutions	9.70	1.87
			其中：代理人行专项贷款 Of Which: Agency Earmarked Loans of the Central Bank	4.26	-0.48
			十、库存现金 Cash in Vault	94.17	7.90
			十一、外汇占款 Position for Foreign Exchange Purchase	17.96	1.09
资金来源总计 Total Sources	**15564.82**	**2279.08**	**资金运用总计 Total Uses**	**15564.82**	**2279.08**

城市商业银行人民币信贷收支表

Sources and Uses of Credit Funds of City Commercial Banks (RMB)

(2005年末)

(Year - end of 2005)

单位：亿元

Unit: 100 Million Yuan

项目 Items	余额 Balance	比年初增减额 Changes within the Year	项目 Items	余额 Balance	比年初增减额 Changes within the Year
一、各项存款 Total Deposits	17029.20	2998.46	一、各项贷款 Total Loans	10812.67	1831.55
1. 企业存款 Deposits by Enterprises	9913.81	1312.06	1. 短期贷款 Short - term Loans	5326.96	635.87
(1) 活期存款 Demand Deposits	7237.93	812.51	(1) 工业贷款 Loans to Industrial Sector	1048.71	163.37
(2) 定期存款 Time Deposits	2675.88	499.55	(2) 商业贷款 Loans to Commercial Sector	925.39	32.25
2. 机关团体存款 Deposits by Government Agencies and Social Organizations	397.90	53.30	其中：收购贷款 Of Which: Loans for the Purchase of Farm Products	0.41	0.41
3. 储蓄存款 Savings Deposits	4901.86	1076.98	(3) 建筑业贷款 Loans to Construction Sector	435.17	96.92
(1) 活期储蓄 Demand Deposits	1790.63	313.30	(4) 农业贷款 Loans to Agricultural Sector	17.39	-3.25
(2) 定期储蓄 Time Deposits	3111.23	763.68	(5) 乡镇企业贷款 Loans to Village and Township Enterprises	94.79	1.69
4. 农业存款 Deposits by Agricultural Sector	16.35	2.21	(6) 三资企业贷款 Loans to Foreign Investment Enterprises and Ventures	92.25	9.56
5. 其他存款 Other Deposits	1799.28	553.91			
二、代理财政性存款 Agency Fiscal Deposits	32.09	-1.67	(7) 私营企业及个体贷款 Loans to Privately - run Enterprises and Self - employed Entities	494.35	43.69
三、金融债券 Financial Bonds	73.00	43.00			
其中：政策性金融债券 Of Which: Policy Financial Bonds			(8) 其他短期贷款 Other Short - term Loans	2218.91	291.64
四、应付及暂收款 Accounts Payable and Receipts on Account	267.60	95.34	其中：个人短期消费贷款 Of Which: Short - term Consumer Credit	111.83	25.86
其中：应付及预提利息 Of Which: Interest Payable and Accrued	73.18	20.50	2. 中期流动资金贷款 Medium - term Working Capital Loans	361.81	0.19
			3. 中长期贷款 Medium and Long - term Loans	3733.90	683.10
五、卖出回购资产 Assets Repo (Including Securities)	684.80	-299.67	(1) 基本建设贷款 Capital Construction Loans	1048.52	281.20
六、向中央银行借款 Borrowings from the Central Bank	65.36	-54.54	(2) 技术改造贷款 Technical Improvement Loans	90.94	7.16
七、同业往来 Inter - bank Transactions	471.36	117.90	(3) 其他中长期贷款 Other Medium and Long - term Loans	2594.44	394.74

续表
Continued

项　目 Items	余　额 Balance	比年初增减额 Changes within the Year	项　目 Items	余　额 Balance	比年初增减额 Changes within the Year
1. 同业存放 Due to Banks and Other Financial Institutions	463.49	126.68	其中：个人中长期消费贷款 Of Which: Medium and Long - term Consumer Credit	905.05	81.39
2. 同业拆借 Placements from Banks and Other Financial Institutions	7.87	- 8.78	4. 票据融资 Paper Financing	1371.16	507.26
			其中：贴现 Of Which: Discount	1368.68	505.14
八、委托存款及委托投资基金（净） Designated Deposits and Designated Investment Funds (Net)	40.55	34.31	5. 各项垫款 Total Advances	18.84	5.13
1. 委托存款及委托投资基金 Designated Deposits and Designated Investment Funds	400.58	147.90	二、有价证券及投资 Securities and Investments	4103.56	581.53
			三、应收及预付款 Accounts Receivable and Advance Payments	166.40	- 12.45
2. 减：委托贷款及委托投资 Minus: Designated Loans and Designated Investments	360.03	113.59	其中：应收利息 Of Which: Interest Receivable	28.78	- 10.49
九、代理金融机构委托贷款基金 Designated Loan Funds on Behalf of Financial Institutions	7.97	0.59	四、买入返售资产 Assets Reverse Repo (Including Securities)	476.60	162.55
其中：中央银行委托贷款基金 Of Which: Loan Funds Designated by the Central Bank	3.02		五、存放中央银行准备金存款 Reserve Deposits with the Central Bank	2072.37	98.32
			六、存放中央银行特种存款 Special Deposits with the Central Bank		
十、各项准备 Total Provisions	207.71	41.92	七、缴存中央银行财政性存款 Fiscal Deposits with the Central Bank	18.47	- 6.72
其中：贷款损失准备 Of Which: Provisions for Loan Losses	198.16	34.87	八、同业往来 Inter - bank Transactions	820.40	322.56
十一、所有者权益 Owner's Equity	811.58	247.40	1. 存放同业 Due from Banks and Other Financial Institutions	703.03	322.22
其中：实收资本 Of Which: Paid - in Capital	589.94	124.64			
当年结益 Net Earnings	112.87	112.87	2. 拆放同业 Placements with Banks and Other Financial Institutions	117.37	0.34
十二、其他 Others	- 1087.72	- 234.84	九、代理金融机构贷款 Lending on Behalf of Financial Institutions	8.92	- 0.78
			其中：代理人行专项贷款 Of Which: Agency Earmarked Loans of the Central Bank	3.61	- 0.65
			十、库存现金 Cash in Vault	107.05	12.56
			十一、外汇占款 Position for Foreign Exchange Purchase	17.06	- 0.92
资金来源总计 Total Sources	**18603.50**	**2988.20**	**资金运用总计 Total Uses**	**18603.50**	**2988.20**

7. 农村商业银行人民币信贷收支表（2002—2005 年）
Sources and Uses of Credit Funds of Rural Commercial Banks（RMB）（2002—2005）

农村商业银行人民币信贷收支表
Sources and Uses of Credit Funds of Rural Commercial Banks（RMB）

（2002 年末）

（Year－end of 2002）

单位：亿元
Unit：100 Million Yuan

项目 Items	余额 Balance	比年初增减额 Changes within the Year	项目 Items	余额 Balance	比年初增减额 Changes within the Year
一、各项存款 Total Deposits	255.26	58.38	一、各项贷款 Total Loans	145.00	44.87
1. 企业存款 Deposits by Enterprises	30.63	11.45	1. 短期贷款 Short－term Loans	118.90	31.09
（1）活期存款 Demand Deposits			（1）工业贷款 Loans to Industrial Sector		
（2）定期存款 Time Deposits	30.63	11.45	（2）商业贷款 Loans to Commercial Sector		
2. 机关团体存款 Deposits by Government Agencies and Social Organizations	0.01	－0.01	其中：收购贷款 Of Which：Loans for the Purchase of Farm Products		
3. 储蓄存款 Savings Deposits	141.39	21.77	（3）建筑业贷款 Loans to Construction Sector		
（1）活期储蓄 Demand Deposits	34.36	11.12	（4）农业贷款 Loans to Agricultural Sector	15.65	5.72
（2）定期储蓄 Time Deposits	107.03	10.65	（5）乡镇企业贷款 Loans to Village and Township Enterprises	99.86	24.63
4. 农业存款 Deposits by Agricultural Sector	79.97	24.23	（6）三资企业贷款 Loans to Foreign Investment Enterprises and Ventures		
5. 其他存款 Other Deposits	3.26	0.94	（7）私营企业及个体贷款 Loans to Privately－run Enterprises and Self－employed Entities		
二、代理财政性存款 Agency Fiscal Deposits	0.03	0.02	（8）其他短期贷款 Other Short－term Loans	3.39	0.74
三、金融债券 Financial Bonds			其中：个人短期消费贷款 Of Which：Short－term Consumer Credit	1.72	1.72
其中：政策性金融债券 Of Which：Policy Financial Bonds			2. 中期流动资金贷款 Medium－term Working Capital Loans		
四、应付及暂收款 Accounts Payable and Receipts on Account	5.35	－1.67	3. 中长期贷款 Medium and Long－term Loans	6.08	5.01
其中：应付及预提利息 Of Which：Interest Payable and Accrued	3.79		（1）基本建设贷款 Capital Construction Loans		
五、卖出回购证券 Repo			（2）技术改造贷款 Technical Improvement Loans		
六、向中央银行借款 Borrowings from the Central Bank					

续表
Continued

项目 Items	余额 Balance	比年初增减额 Changes within the Year	项目 Items	余额 Balance	比年初增减额 Changes within the Year
七、同业往来 Inter - bank Transactions	30.99	13.76	（3）其他中长期贷款 Other Medium and Long - term Loans	6.08	5.01
1. 同业存放 Due to Banks and Other Financial Institutions	3.58	0.46	其中：个人中长期消费贷款 Of Which：Medium and Long - term Consumer Credit	0.33	0.33
2. 同业拆借 Placements from Banks and Other Financial Institutions	27.41	13.30	4. 票据融资 Paper Financing	20.02	8.77
			其中：贴现 Of Which：Discount	20.02	8.77
八、委托存款及委托投资基金（净） Designated Deposits and Designated Investment Funds（Net）	- 0.03	- 0.03	5. 各项垫款 Total Advances		
1. 委托存款及委托投资基金 Designated Deposits and Designated Investment Funds	0.19		二、有价证券及投资 Securities and Investments	87.38	20.44
			三、应收及预付款 Accounts Receivable and Advance Payments	1.16	0.37
2. 减：委托贷款及委托投资 Minus：Designated Loans and Designated Investments	0.22	0.03	其中：应收利息 Of Which：Interest Receivable	0.01	
九、代理金融机构委托贷款基金 Designated Loan Funds on Behalf of Financial Institutions	0.01	- 0.13	四、买入返售证券 Reverse Repo		
			五、存放中央银行准备金存款 Reserve Deposits with the Central Bank	18.84	- 2.49
其中：中央银行委托贷款基金 Of Which：Loan Funds Designated by the Central Bank			六、存放中央银行特种存款 Special Deposits with the Central Bank	7.50	4.30
十、各项准备 Total Provisions	3.91	- 0.03	七、缴存中央银行财政性存款 Fiscal Deposits with the Central Bank		
其中：贷款呆账准备金 Of Which：Provisions for Bad Loans	3.91	- 0.03	八、同业往来 Inter - bank Transactions	32.76	11.54
十一、所有者权益 Owner's Equity	5.21	1.42	1. 存放同业 Due from Banks and Other Financial Institutions	23.46	9.49
其中：实收资本 Of Which：Paid - in Capital	2.51	- 0.22			
当年结益 Net Earnings	0.55	0.55	2. 拆放同业 Placements with Banks and Other Financial Institutions	9.30	2.05
十二、其他 Others	- 5.95	7.61	九、代理金融机构贷款 Lending on Behalf of Financial Institutions	0.01	
			其中：代理人行专项贷款 Of Which：Agency Earmarked Loans of the Central Bank		
			十、库存现金 Cash in Vault	1.89	0.06
			十一、外汇占款 Position for Foreign Exchange Purchase	0.24	0.24
资金来源总计 Total Sources	**294.78**	**79.33**	**资金运用总计 Total Uses**	**294.78**	**79.33**

农村商业银行人民币信贷收支表

Sources and Uses of Credit Funds of Rural Commercial Banks（RMB）

（2003年末）

（Year - end of 2003）

单位：亿元

Unit：100 Million Yuan

项目 Items	余额 Balance	比年初增减额 Changes within the Year	项目 Items	余额 Balance	比年初增减额 Changes within the Year
一、各项存款 Total Deposits	342.83	87.57	一、各项贷款 Total Loans	205.07	60.07
1. 企业存款 Deposits by Enterprises	50.83	20.20	1. 短期贷款 Short - term Loans	179.95	61.05
（1）活期存款 Demand Deposits			（1）工业贷款 Loans to Industrial Sector		
（2）定期存款 Time Deposits	50.83	20.20	（2）商业贷款 Loans to Commercial Sector		
2. 机关团体存款 Deposits by Government Agencies and Social Organizations	0.01		其中：收购贷款 Of Which：Loans for the Purchase of Farm Products		
3. 储蓄存款 Savings Deposits	172.69	31.30	（3）建筑业贷款 Loans to Construction Sector		
（1）活期储蓄 Demand Deposits	47.94	13.58	（4）农业贷款 Loans to Agricultural Sector	20.94	5.29
（2）定期储蓄 Time Deposits	124.75	17.72	（5）乡镇企业贷款 Loans to Village and Township Enterprises	148.88	49.02
4. 农业存款 Deposits by Agricultural Sector	106.44	26.47	（6）三资企业贷款 Loans to Foreign Investment Enterprises and Ventures		
5. 其他存款 Other Deposits	12.86	9.60	（7）私营企业及个体贷款 Loans to Privately - run Enterprises and Self - employed Entities		
二、代理财政性存款 Agency Fiscal Deposits	0.19	0.16	（8）其他短期贷款 Other Short - term Loans	10.13	6.74
三、金融债券 Financial Bonds			其中：个人短期消费贷款 Of Which：Short - term Consumer Credit	0.13	- 1.59
其中：政策性金融债券 Of Which：Policy Financial Bonds			2. 中期流动资金贷款 Medium - term Working Capital Loans		
四、应付及暂收款 Accounts Payable and Receipts on Account	8.05	2.29	3. 中长期贷款 Medium and Long - term Loans	15.82	9.74
其中：应付及预提利息 Of Which：Interest Payable and Accrued	4.65	0.86	（1）基本建设贷款 Capital Construction Loans		
五、卖出回购证券 Repo			（2）技术改造贷款 Technical Improvement Loans		
六、向中央银行借款 Borrowings from the Central Bank			（3）其他中长期贷款 Other Medium and Long - term Loans	15.82	9.74
七、同业往来 Inter - bank Transactions	11.14	- 19.85			

续表
Continued

项 目 Items	余 额 Balance	比年初增减额 Changes within the Year	项 目 Items	余 额 Balance	比年初增减额 Changes within the Year
1. 同业存放 Due to Banks and Other Financial Institutions	2.62	-0.96	其中：个人中长期消费贷款 Of Which：Medium and Long-term Consumer Credit	1.26	0.93
2. 同业拆借 Placements from Banks and Other Financial Institutions	8.52	-18.89	4. 票据融资 Paper Financing	9.30	-10.72
八、委托存款及委托投资基金（净） Designated Deposits and Designated Investment Funds（Net）	-0.04	-0.01	其中：贴现 Of Which：Discount	9.30	-10.72
			5. 各项垫款 Total Advances		
1. 委托存款及委托投资基金 Designated Deposits and Designated Investment Funds	0.79	0.60	二、有价证券及投资 Securities and Investments	97.28	9.90
			三、应收及预付款 Accounts Receivable and Advance Payments	2.07	0.91
2. 减：委托贷款及委托投资 Minus：Designated Loans and Designated Investments	0.83	0.61	其中：应收利息 Of Which：Interest Receivable	0.01	
九、代理金融机构委托贷款基金 Designated Loan Funds on Behalf of Financial Institutions	0.01		四、买入返售证券 Reverse Repo		
其中：中央银行委托贷款基金 Of Which：Loan Funds Designated by the Central Bank			五、存放中央银行准备金存款 Reserve Deposits with the Central Bank	39.28	20.44
			六、存放中央银行特种存款 Special Deposits with the Central Bank		-7.50
十、各项准备 Total Provisions	8.31	4.40	七、缴存中央银行财政性存款 Fiscal Deposits with the Central Bank		
其中：贷款损失准备 Of Which：Provisions for Loan Losses	8.31	4.40	八、同业往来 Inter-bank Transactions	27.13	-5.63
十一、所有者权益 Owner's Equity	3.14	-1.67	1. 存放同业 Due from Banks and Other Financial Institutions	25.73	2.27
其中：实收资本 Of Which：Paid-in Capital	2.22	-0.25			
当年结益 Net Earnings	0.67	0.67	2. 拆放同业 Placements with Banks and Other Financial Institutions	1.40	-7.90
十二、其他 Others	0.45	6.41	九、代理金融机构贷款 Lending on Behalf of Financial Institutions	0.01	
			其中：代理人行专项贷款 Of Which：Agency Earmarked Loans of the Central Bank		
			十、库存现金 Cash in Vault	2.68	0.79
			十一、外汇占款 Position for Foreign Exchange Purchase	0.56	0.32
资金来源总计 Total Sources	**374.08**	**79.30**	**资金运用总计 Total Uses**	**374.08**	**79.30**

农村商业银行人民币信贷收支表

Sources and Uses of Credit Funds of Rural Commercial Banks（RMB）

（2004年末）

（Year - end of 2004）

单位：亿元

Unit: 100 Million Yuan

项目 Items	余额 Balance	比年初增减额 Changes within the Year	项目 Items	余额 Balance	比年初增减额 Changes within the Year
一、各项存款 Total Deposits	495.64	152.81	一、各项贷款 Total Loans	306.83	102.49
1. 企业存款 Deposits by Enterprises	70.67	19.84	1. 短期贷款 Short - term Loans	264.03	87.30
(1) 活期存款 Demand Deposits			(1) 工业贷款 Loans to Industrial Sector		
(2) 定期存款 Time Deposits	70.67	19.84	(2) 商业贷款 Loans to Commercial Sector		
2. 机关团体存款 Deposits by Government Agencies and Social Organizations	1.43	1.42	其中：收购贷款 Of Which: Loans for the Purchase of Farm Products		
3. 储蓄存款 Savings Deposits	253.50	80.81	(3) 建筑业贷款 Loans to Construction Sector		
(1) 活期储蓄 Demand Deposits	78.66	30.72	(4) 农业贷款 Loans to Agricultural Sector	34.60	15.15
(2) 定期储蓄 Time Deposits	174.84	50.09	(5) 乡镇企业贷款 Loans to Village and Township Enterprises	177.98	30.92
4. 农业存款 Deposits by Agricultural Sector	138.26	31.82	(6) 三资企业贷款 Loans to Foreign Investment Enterprises and Ventures		
5. 其他存款 Other Deposits	31.78	18.92	(7) 私营企业及个体贷款 Loans to Privately - run Enterprises and Self - employed Entities		
二、代理财政性存款 Agency Fiscal Deposits		-0.19	(8) 其他短期贷款 Other Short - term Loans	51.45	41.23
三、金融债券 Financial Bonds			其中：个人短期消费贷款 Of Which: Short - term Consumer Credit	0.55	-0.23
其中：政策性金融债券 Of Which: Policy Financial Bonds			2. 中期流动资金贷款 Medium - term Working Capital Loans		
四、应付及暂收款 Accounts Payable and Receipts on Account	15.24	7.00	3. 中长期贷款 Medium and Long - term Loans	28.70	13.12
其中：应付及预提利息 Of Which: Interest Payable and Accrued	6.95	2.30	(1) 基本建设贷款 Capital Construction Loans		
五、卖出回购资产 Assets Repo（Including Securities）	7.98	4.97	(2) 技术改造贷款 Technical Improvement Loans		
六、向中央银行借款 Borrowings from the Central Bank		-2.73	(3) 其他中长期贷款 Other Medium and Long - term Loans	28.70	13.12
七、同业往来 Inter - bank Transactions	3.44	-4.69			

续表
Continued

项目 Items	余额 Balance	比年初增减额 Changes within the Year	项目 Items	余额 Balance	比年初增减额 Changes within the Year
1. 同业存放 Due to Banks and Other Financial Institutions	3.43	0.81	其中：个人中长期消费贷款 Of Which: Medium and Long - term Consumer Credit	2.97	1.39
2. 同业拆借 Placements from Banks and Other Financial Institutions	0.01	-5.50	4. 票据融资 Paper Financing	14.10	2.07
			其中：贴现 Of Which: Discount	14.10	2.07
八、委托存款及委托投资基金（净） Designated Deposits and Designated Investment Funds（Net）		0.04	5. 各项垫款 Total Advances		
1. 委托存款及委托投资基金 Designated Deposits and Designated Investment Funds	0.94	0.15	二、有价证券及投资 Securities and Investments	110.51	13.23
			三、应收及预付款 Accounts Receivable and Advance Payments	1.37	-0.70
2. 减：委托贷款及委托投资 Minus: Designated Loans and Designated Investments	0.94	0.11	其中：应收利息 Of Which: Interest Receivable		-0.01
九、代理金融机构委托贷款基金 Designated Loan Funds on Behalf of Financial Institutions	0.02	0.01	四、买入返售资产 Assets Reverse Repo（Including Securities）	14.23	13.23
其中：中央银行委托贷款基金 Of Which: Loan Funds Designated by the Central Bank			五、存放中央银行准备金存款 Reserve Deposits with the Central Bank	75.38	36.10
			六、存放中央银行特种存款 Special Deposits with the Central Bank		
十、各项准备 Total Provisions	6.70	-1.61	七、缴存中央银行财政性存款 Fiscal Deposits with the Central Bank	0.04	0.04
其中：贷款损失准备 Of Which: Provisions for Loan Losses	6.70	-1.61	八、同业往来 Inter - bank Transactions	30.67	4.54
十一、所有者权益 Owner's Equity	25.11	21.98	1. 存放同业 Due from Banks and Other Financial Institutions	28.12	2.39
其中：实收资本 Of Which: Paid - in Capital	10.31	8.09			
当年结益 Net Earnings	7.66	7.66	2. 拆放同业 Placements with Banks and Other Financial Institutions	2.55	2.15
十二、其他 Others	-9.82	-6.78	九、代理金融机构贷款 Lending on Behalf of Financial Institutions	0.01	
			其中：代理人行专项贷款 Of Which: Agency Earmarked Loans of the Central Bank		
			十、库存现金 Cash in Vault	4.82	2.14
			十一、外汇占款 Position for Foreign Exchange Purchase	0.45	-0.26
资金来源总计 Total Sources	**544.31**	**170.81**	**资金运用总计 Total Uses**	**544.31**	**170.81**

农村商业银行人民币信贷收支表

Sources and Uses of Credit Funds of Rural Commercial Banks (RMB)

(2005年末)

(Year - end of 2005)

单位：亿元

Unit: 100 Million Yuan

项 目 Items	余 额 Balance	比年初增减额 Changes within the Year	项 目 Items	余 额 Balance	比年初增减额 Changes within the Year
一、各项存款 Total Deposits	2563.61	1708.95	一、各项贷款 Total Loans	1576.28	1036.68
1. 企业存款 Deposits by Enterprises	193.40	84.36	1. 短期贷款 Short - term Loans	1022.19	571.08
(1) 活期存款 Demand Deposits			(1) 工业贷款 Loans to Industrial Sector		
(2) 定期存款 Time Deposits	193.40	84.36	(2) 商业贷款 Loans to Commercial Sector		
2. 机关团体存款 Deposits by Government Agencies and Social Organizations	2.95	1.48	其中：收购贷款 Of Which: Loans for the Purchase of Farm Products		
3. 储蓄存款 Savings Deposits	1312.63	868.80	(3) 建筑业贷款 Loans to Construction Sector		
(1) 活期储蓄 Demand Deposits	409.23	277.82	(4) 农业贷款 Loans to Agricultural Sector	88.61	42.15
(2) 定期储蓄 Time Deposits	903.40	590.98	(5) 乡镇企业贷款 Loans to Village and Township Enterprises	718.87	388.31
4. 农业存款 Deposits by Agricultural Sector	927.66	669.32	(6) 三资企业贷款 Loans to Foreign Investment Enterprises and Ventures		
5. 其他存款 Other Deposits	126.97	84.99	(7) 私营企业及个体贷款 Loans to Privately - run Enterprises and Self - employed Entities		
二、代理财政性存款 Agency Fiscal Deposits	2.85	2.85	(8) 其他短期贷款 Other Short - term Loans	214.71	140.62
三、金融债券 Financial Bonds			其中：个人短期消费贷款 Of Which: Short - term Consumer Credit	15.81	4.47
其中：政策性金融债券 Of Which: Policy Financial Bonds			2. 中期流动资金贷款 Medium - term Working Capital Loans		
四、应付及暂收款 Accounts Payable and Receipts on Account	74.50	46.15	3. 中长期贷款 Medium and Long - term Loans	413.71	350.84
其中：应付及预提利息 Of Which: Interest Payable and Accrued	50.73	38.72	(1) 基本建设贷款 Capital Construction Loans	7.05	7.05
五、卖出回购资产 Assets Repo (Including Securities)	102.31	89.33	(2) 技术改造贷款 Technical Improvement Loans		
六、向中央银行借款 Borrowings from the Central Bank			(3) 其他中长期贷款 Other Medium and Long - term Loans	406.66	343.79
七、同业往来 Inter - bank Transactions	14.46	-0.28			

续表
Continued

项　目 Items	余　额 Balance	比年初增减额 Changes within the Year	项　目 Items	余　额 Balance	比年初增减额 Changes within the Year
1. 同业存放 Due to Banks and Other Financial Institutions	14.40	6.83	其中：个人中长期消费贷款 Of Which: Medium and Long - term Consumer Credit	117.81	113.34
2. 同业拆借 Placements from Banks and Other Financial Institutions	0.06	-7.11	4. 票据融资 Paper Financing	140.36	114.74
			其中：贴现 Of Which: Discount	140.36	114.74
八、委托存款及委托投资基金（净） Designated Deposits and Designated Investment Funds (Net)	-0.35	-0.03	5. 各项垫款 Total Advances	0.02	0.02
1. 委托存款及委托投资基金 Designated Deposits and Designated Investment Funds	17.53	16.24	二、有价证券及投资 Securities and Investments	522.80	352.69
			三、应收及预付款 Accounts Receivable and Advance Payments	27.65	25.31
2. 减：委托贷款及委托投资 Minus: Designated Loans and Designated Investments	17.88	16.27	其中：应收利息 Of Which: Interest Receivable	1.15	1.13
九、代理金融机构委托贷款基金 Designated Loan Funds on Behalf of Financial Institutions	0.20	0.18	四、买入返售资产 Assets Reverse Repo (Including Securities)	116.10	101.87
其中：中央银行委托贷款基金 Of Which: Loan Funds Designated by the Central Bank			五、存放中央银行准备金存款 Reserve Deposits with the Central Bank	265.04	138.85
			六、存放中央银行特种存款 Special Deposits with the Central Bank		
十、各项准备 Total Provisions	40.85	29.69	七、缴存中央银行财政性存款 Fiscal Deposits with the Central Bank	0.22	0.13
其中：贷款损失准备 Of Which: Provisions for Loan Losses	40.85	29.69	八、同业往来 Inter - bank Transactions	363.58	307.44
十一、所有者权益 Owner's Equity	154.54	107.33	1. 存放同业 Due from Banks and Other Financial Institutions	300.79	247.22
其中：实收资本 Of Which: Paid - in Capital	72.48	46.65	2. 拆放同业 Placements with Banks and Other Financial Institutions	62.79	60.22
当年结益 Net Earnings	28.74	28.74			
十二、其他 Others	-53.63	-3.41	九、代理金融机构贷款 Lending on Behalf of Financial Institutions	0.20	0.19
			其中：代理人行专项贷款 Of Which: Agency Earmarked Loans of the Central Bank		
			十、库存现金 Cash in Vault	26.34	17.57
			十一、外汇占款 Position for Foreign Exchange Purchase	1.13	0.03
资金来源总计 Total Sources	**2899.34**	**1980.76**	**资金运用总计 Total Uses**	**2899.34**	**1980.76**

8. 农村合作银行人民币信贷收支表（2005年）
Sources and Uses of Credit Funds of Rural Cooperative Banks (RMB) (2005)

农村合作银行人民币信贷收支表
Sources and Uses of Credit Funds of Rural Cooperative Banks (RMB)

（2005年末）

(Year - end of 2005)

单位：亿元

Unit: 100 Million Yuan

项目 Items	余额 Balance	比年初增减额 Changes within the Year	项目 Items	余额 Balance	比年初增减额 Changes within the Year
一、各项存款 Total Deposits	2404.08	1554.63	一、各项贷款 Total Loans	1743.49	1142.85
1. 企业存款 Deposits by Enterprises	183.36	110.19	1. 短期贷款 Short - term Loans	1624.51	1083.17
(1) 活期存款 Demand Deposits	0.22	0.22	(1) 工业贷款 Loans to Industrial Sector		
(2) 定期存款 Time Deposits	183.14	109.97	(2) 商业贷款 Loans to Commercial Sector		
2. 机关团体存款 Deposits by Government Agencies and Social Organizations	26.96	20.67	其中：收购贷款 Of Which: Loans for the Purchase of Farm Products		
3. 储蓄存款 Savings Deposits	1554.42	1034.33	(3) 建筑业贷款 Loans to Construction Sector		
(1) 活期储蓄 Demand Deposits	573.53	409.84	(4) 农业贷款 Loans to Agricultural Sector	651.54	506.97
(2) 定期储蓄 Time Deposits	980.89	624.49	(5) 乡镇企业贷款 Loans to Village and Township Enterprises	783.21	438.84
4. 农业存款 Deposits by Agricultural Sector	515.40	292.41	(6) 三资企业贷款 Loans to Foreign Investment Enterprises and Ventures		
5. 其他存款 Other Deposits	123.94	97.03			
二、代理财政性存款 Agency Fiscal Deposits	1.44	0.61	(7) 私营企业及个体贷款 Loans to Privately - run Enterprises and Self - employed Entities	1.34	1.33
三、金融债券 Financial Bonds					
其中：政策性金融债券 Of Which: Policy Financial Bonds			(8) 其他短期贷款 Other Short - term Loans	188.42	136.03
			其中：个人短期消费贷款 Of Which: Short - term Consumer Credit	11.35	10.72
四、应付及暂收款 Accounts Payable and Receipts on Account	71.24	47.28	2. 中期流动资金贷款 Medium - term Working Capital Loans		
其中：应付及预提利息 Of Which: Interest Payable and Accrued	41.28	27.46	3. 中长期贷款 Medium and Long - term Loans	60.87	31.85
五、卖出回购资产 Assets Repo (Including Securities)	6.64	-7.93	(1) 基本建设贷款 Capital Construction Loans		
六、向中央银行借款 Borrowings from the Central Bank	12.35	4.89	(2) 技术改造贷款 Technical Improvement Loans		

续表
Continued

项目 Items	余额 Balance	比年初增减额 Changes within the Year
七、同业往来 Inter - bank Transactions	45.20	37.96
1. 同业存放 Due to Banks and Other Financial Institutions	36.40	830.25
2. 同业拆借 Placements from Banks and Other Financial Institutions	8.72	7.71
八、委托存款及委托投资基金(净) Designated Deposits and Designated Investment Funds (Net)	0.68	0.62
1. 委托存款及委托投资基金 Designated Deposits and Designated Investment Funds	5.63	3.59
2. 减：委托贷款及委托投资 Minus: Designated Loans and Designated Investments	4.95	2.97
九、代理金融机构委托贷款基金 Designated Loan Funds on Behalf of Financial Institutions	1.15	0.94
其中：中央银行委托贷款基金 Of Which: Loan Funds Designated by the Central Bank		
十、各项准备 Total Provisions	35.69	26.70
其中：贷款损失准备 Of Which: Provisions for Loan Losses	35.56	26.57
十一、所有者权益 Owner's Equity	175.38	117.67
其中：实收资本 Of Which: Paid - in Capital	78.65	53.41
当年结益 Net Earnings	29.98	29.98
十二、其他 Others	- 197.30	- 119.56
资金来源总计 Total Sources	**2556.55**	**1663.81**

项目 Items	余额 Balance	比年初增减额 Changes within the Year
(3) 其他中长期贷款 Other Medium and Long - term Loans	60.87	31.85
其中：个人中长期消费贷款 Of Which: Medium and Long - term Consumer Credit	3.32	1.92
4. 票据融资 Paper Financing	57.88	27.60
其中：贴现 Of Which: Discount	57.88	27.60
5. 各项垫款 Total Advances	0.23	0.23
二、有价证券及投资 Securities and Investments	189.60	105.50
三、应收及预付款 Accounts Receivable and Advance Payments	6.68	1.89
其中：应收利息 Of Which: Interest Receivable	2.26	0.98
四、买入返售资产 Assets Reverse Repo (Including Securities)	9.81	0.53
五、存放中央银行准备金存款 Reserve Deposits with the Central Bank	301.05	187.17
六、存放中央银行特种存款 Special Deposits with the Central Bank		
七、缴存中央银行财政性存款 Fiscal Deposits with the Central Bank	0.20	0.12
八、同业往来 Inter - bank Transactions	268.46	199.97
1. 存放同业 Due from Banks and Other Financial Institutions	265.51	202.33
2. 拆放同业 Placements with Banks and Other Financial Institutions	2.95	- 2.36
九、代理金融机构贷款 Lending on Behalf of Financial Institutions	1.14	0.94
其中：代理人行专项贷款 Of Which: Agency Earmarked Loans of the Central Bank		
十、库存现金 Cash in Vault	34.98	24.07
十一、外汇占款 Position for Foreign Exchange Purchase	1.14	0.77
资金运用总计 Total Uses	**2556.55**	**1663.81**

9. 城市信用合作社人民币信贷收支表（1986—2005 年）
Sources and Uses of Credit Funds of Urban Credit Cooperatives（RMB）（1986—2005）

城市信用合作社人民币信贷收支表
Sources and Uses of Credit Funds of Urban Credit Cooperatives（RMB）

（1986 年末）

（Year - end of 1986）

单位：亿元

Unit：100 Million Yuan

项目 Items	余额 Balance	比年初增减额 Changes within the Year	项目 Items	余额 Balance	比年初增减额 Changes within the Year
一、集体工业存款 Deposits by Collective Industrial Enterprises	8.10	—	一、集体工业贷款 Loans to Collective Industrial Enterprises	7.20	—
二、集体商业存款 Deposits by Collective Commercial Enterprises	9.40	—	二、集体商业贷款 Loans to Collective Commercial Enterprises	6.10	—
三、个体工商户存款 Deposits by Self - employed Entities	3.50	—	三、个体工商户贷款 Loans to Self - employed Entities	2.30	—
四、居民储蓄存款 Savings Deposits by Resident Sector	0.90	—	四、其他贷款 Other Loans	3.90	—
1. 定期存款 Time Deposits	0.50	—	**贷款合计** **Total Loans**	**19.50**	—
2. 活期存款 Demand Deposits	0.40	—	五、在银行存款 Deposits with Banks	11.00	—
五、其他存款 Other Deposits	7.60	—	六、同业往来 Inter - bank Transactions		
存款合计 **Total Deposits**	**29.50**	—	七、缴存准备金 Reserves with the Central Bank	1.30	—
六、向银行借款 Borrowings from Banks	1.00	—	八、库存现金 Cash in Vault	0.10	—
七、同业往来 Inter - bank Transactions	0.80	—	九、购买债券 Bonds Purchase		
八、自有资金 Own Capital	1.40	—			
九、其他 Others	-0.80	—			
资金来源总计 **Total Sources**	**31.90**	**—**	**资金运用总计** **Total Uses**	**31.90**	**—**

城市信用合作社人民币信贷收支表

Sources and Uses of Credit Funds of Urban Credit Cooperatives（RMB）

（1987年末）

（Year - end of 1987）

单位：亿元

Unit：100 Million Yuan

项　目 Items	余　额 Balance	比年初增减额 Changes within the Year	项　目 Items	余　额 Balance	比年初增减额 Changes within the Year
一、集体工业存款 Deposits by Collective Industrial Enterprises	16.60	8.50	一、集体工业贷款 Loans to Collective Industrial Enterprises	23.90	16.70
二、集体商业存款 Deposits by Collective Commercial Enterprises	17.80	8.40	二、集体商业贷款 Loans to Collective Commercial Enterprises	17.70	11.60
三、个体工商户存款 Deposits by Self - employed Entities	6.20	2.70	三、个体工商户贷款 Loans to Self - employed Entities	6.80	4.50
四、居民储蓄存款 Savings Deposits by Resident Sector	8.10	7.20	四、其他贷款 Other Loans	15.00	11.10
1. 定期存款 Time Deposits	5.00	4.50	**贷款合计 Total Loans**	**63.40**	**43.90**
2. 活期存款 Demand Deposits	3.10	2.70	五、在银行存款 Deposits with Banks	21.70	10.70
五、其他存款 Other Deposits	26.90	19.30	六、同业往来 Inter - bank Transactions		
存款合计 Total Deposits	**75.60**	**46.10**	七、缴存准备金 Reserves with the Central Bank	4.60	3.30
六、向银行借款 Borrowings from Banks	6.90	5.90	八、库存现金 Cash in Vault	0.70	0.60
七、同业往来 Inter - bank Transactions	1.10	0.30	九、购买债券 Bonds Purchase		
八、自有资金 Own Capital	2.80	1.40			
九、其他 Others	4.00	4.80			
资金来源总计 Total Sources	**90.40**	**58.50**	**资金运用总计 Total Uses**	**90.40**	**58.50**

城市信用合作社人民币信贷收支表
Sources and Uses of Credit Funds of Urban Credit Cooperatives (RMB)

(1988年末)

(Year - end of 1988)

单位：亿元

Unit: 100 Million Yuan

项目 Items	余额 Balance	比年初增减额 Changes within the Year	项目 Items	余额 Balance	比年初增减额 Changes within the Year
一、集体工业存款 Deposits by Collective Industrial Enterprises	26.41	9.81	一、集体工业贷款 Loans to Collective Industrial Enterprises	44.67	20.77
二、集体商业存款 Deposits by Collective Commercial Enterprises	37.79	19.99	二、集体商业贷款 Loans to Collective Commercial Enterprises	40.16	22.46
三、个体工商户存款 Deposits by Self - employed Entities	9.48	3.28	三、个体工商户贷款 Loans to Self - employed Entities	12.20	5.40
四、居民储蓄存款 Savings Deposits by Resident Sector	20.69	12.59	四、其他贷款 Other Loans	36.83	21.83
1. 定期存款 Time Deposits	11.74	6.74	**贷款合计 Total Loans**	**133.86**	**70.46**
2. 活期存款 Demand Deposits	8.95	5.85	五、在银行存款 Deposits with Banks	32.17	10.47
五、其他存款 Other Deposits	62.65	35.75	六、同业往来 Inter - bank Transactions	0.00	0.06
存款合计 Total Deposits	**157.02**	**81.42**	七、缴存准备金 Reserves with the Central Bank	14.32	9.72
六、向银行借款 Borrowings from Banks	12.71	5.81	八、库存现金 Cash in Vault	1.76	1.06
七、同业往来 Inter - bank Transactions	0.70	-0.40	九、购买债券 Bonds Purchase	2.95	2.95
八、自有资金 Own Capital	7.10	4.30			
九、其他 Others	3.35	-0.65			
十、结益 Net Earnings	4.18	4.18			
资金来源总计 Total Sources	**185.06**	**94.66**	**资金运用总计 Total Uses**	**185.06**	**94.66**

城市信用合作社人民币信贷收支表

Sources and Uses of Credit Funds of Urban Credit Cooperatives（RMB）

（1989 年末）

（Year - end of 1989）

单位：亿元

Unit：100 Million Yuan

项　目 Items	余　额 Balance	比年初增减额 Changes within the Year	项　目 Items	余　额 Balance	比年初增减额 Changes within the Year
一、集体工业存款 Deposits by Collective Industrial Enterprises	32.75	6.34	一、集体工业贷款 Loans to Collective Industrial Enterprises	70.22	25.55
二、集体商业存款 Deposits by Collective Commercial Enterprises	44.62	6.83	二、集体商业贷款 Loans to Collective Commercial Enterprises	57.69	17.53
三、个体工商户存款 Deposits by Self - employed Entities	11.38	1.90	三、个体工商户贷款 Loans to Self - employed Entities	17.36	5.16
四、居民储蓄存款 Savings Deposits by Resident Sector	49.48	28.79	四、其他贷款 Other Loans	51.03	14.20
1. 定期存款 Time Deposits	33.33	21.59	**贷款合计** **Total Loans**	**196.30**	**62.44**
2. 活期存款 Demand Deposits	16.15	7.20	五、在银行存款 Deposits with Banks	57.12	24.95
五、其他存款 Other Deposits	82.58	19.93	六、缴存准备金 Reserves with the Central Bank	21.8	67.54
存款合计 **Total Deposits**	**220.81**	**63.79**	七、缴存特种存款 Special Deposits with the Central Bank	0.91	—
六、向银行借款 Borrowings from Banks	14.60	1.89	八、购买债券 Bonds Purchase	5.44	2.49
七、同业往来 Inter - bank Transactions	12.55	11.85	九、库存现金 Cash in Vault	2.58	0.82
八、自有资金 Own Capital	18.79	11.69			
九、其他 Others	7.66	4.31			
十、结益 Net Earnings	9.80	9.80			
资金来源总计 **Total Sources**	**284.21**	—	**资金运用总计** **Total Uses**	**284.21**	—

城市信用合作社人民币信贷收支表

Sources and Uses of Credit Funds of Urban Credit Cooperatives (RMB)

(1990年末)

(Year－end of 1990)

单位：亿元

Unit: 100 Million Yuan

项 目 Items	余 额 Balance	比年初增减额 Changes within the Year	项 目 Items	余 额 Balance	比年初增减额 Changes within the Year
一、集体工业存款 Deposits by Collective Industrial Enterprises	41.43	8.68	一、集体工业贷款 Loans to Collective Industrial Enterprises	90.44	20.22
二、集体商业存款 Deposits by Collective Commercial Enterprises	59.03	14.41	二、集体商业贷款 Loans to Collective Commercial Enterprises	71.02	13.33
三、个体工商户存款 Deposits by Self－employed Entities	16.78	5.40	三、个体工商户贷款 Loans to Self－employed Entities	24.63	7.27
四、居民储蓄存款 Savings Deposits by Resident Sector	85.63	36.15	四、其他贷款 Other Loans	62.78	11.75
1. 定期存款 Time Deposits	59.92	26.59	**贷款合计 Total Loans**	**248.87**	**52.57**
2. 活期存款 Demand Deposits	25.71	9.56	五、在银行存款 Deposits with Banks	77.55	20.43
五、其他存款 Other Deposits	106.94	24.36	六、缴存准备金 Reserves with the Central Bank	31.33	9.47
存款合计 Total Deposits	**309.81**	**89.00**	七、缴存特种存款 Special Deposits with the Central Bank	1.03	0.12
六、向银行借款 Borrowings from Banks	14.25	－0.35	八、购买债券 Bonds Purchase	9.61	4.17
七、同业往来 Inter－bank Transactions	1.74	－10.81	九、库存现金 Cash in Vault	3.70	1.12
八、自有资金 Own Capital	28.18	9.39			
九、其他 Others	9.65	1.99			
十、结益 Net Earnings	8.46	8.46			
资金来源总计 Total Sources	**372.09**	**87.88**	**资金运用总计 Total Uses**	**372.09**	**87.88**

城市信用合作社人民币信贷收支表
Sources and Uses of Credit Funds of Urban Credit Cooperatives（RMB）

（1991 年末）

（Year - end of 1991）

单位：亿元

Unit：100 Million Yuan

项目 Items	余额 Balance	比年初增减额 Changes within the Year	项目 Items	余额 Balance	比年初增减额 Changes within the Year
一、集体工业存款 Deposits by Collective Industrial Enterprises	54.21	12.78	一、集体工业贷款 Loans to Collective Industrial Enterprises	114.79	24.35
二、集体商业存款 Deposits by Collective Commercial Enterprises	77.80	18.77	二、集体商业贷款 Loans to Collective Commercial Enterprises	87.86	16.84
三、个体工商户存款 Deposits by Self - employed Entities	25.22	8.44	三、个体工商户贷款 Loans to Self - employed Entities	32.62	7.99
四、居民储蓄存款 Savings Deposits by Resident Sector	134.58	48.95	四、其他贷款 Other Loans	80.90	18.12
1. 定期存款 Time Deposits	93.03	33.11	其中：委托及信托贷款 Of Which：Designated and Trust Loans	4.23	—
2. 活期存款 Demand Deposits	41.55	15.84	投资 Investments	1.24	—
五、其他存款 Other Deposits	155.98	49.04	**贷款合计 Total Loans**	**316.17**	**67.30**
存款合计 Total Deposits	**447.79**	**137.98**	五、在银行存款 Deposits with Banks	107.02	29.47
六、向银行借款 Borrowings from Banks	13.68	-0.57	六、代理人民银行专项贷款 Agency Earmarked Loans of the Central Bank	3.07	—
七、人行拨来专项贷款资金 Earmarked Loan Funds Appropriated by the Central Bank	3.09	—	七、缴存准备金 Reserves with the Central Bank	46.63	15.30
八、同业往来 Inter - bank Transactions	35.22	—	八、缴存特种存款 Special Deposits with the Central Bank	0.63	-0.40
九、自有资金 Own Capital	50.56	22.38	九、同业往来 Inter - bank Transactions	63.11	—
十、其他 Others	4.44	—	十、购买债券 Bonds Purchase	22.05	12.44
十一、结益 Net Earnings	8.89	8.89	十一、库存现金 Cash in Vault	4.99	1.29
资金来源总计 Total Sources	**563.67**	—	**资金运用总计 Total Uses**	**563.67**	—

城市信用合作社人民币信贷收支表

Sources and Uses of Credit Funds of Urban Credit Cooperatives (RMB)

(1992年末)

(Year - end of 1992)

单位：亿元

Unit: 100 Million Yuan

项目 Items	余额 Balance	比年初增减额 Changes within the Year	项目 Items	余额 Balance	比年初增减额 Changes within the Year
一、集体工业存款 Deposits by Collective Industrial Enterprises	77.81	23.60	一、集体工业贷款 Loans to Collective Industrial Enterprises	152.71	37.92
二、集体商业存款 Deposits by Collective Commercial Enterprises	126.97	49.17	二、集体商业贷款 Loans to Collective Commercial Enterprises	131.32	43.46
三、集体其他企业存款 Deposits by Other Collective Enterprises	19.26	—	三、集体其他企业贷款 Loans to Other Collective Enterprises	62.31	—
四、小型国营工商企业存款 Deposits by Small State Industrial and Commercial Enterprises	19.41	—	四、小型国营工商企业贷款 Loans to Small State Industrial and Commercial Enterprises	28.02	—
五、个体工商户存款 Deposits by Self - employed Entities	47.54	22.32	五、个体工商户贷款 Loans to Self - employed Entities	44.72	12.10
六、居民储蓄存款 Savings Deposits by Resident Sector	212.58	78.00	六、抵押贷款 Mortagage Loans	6.86	—
1. 定期存款 Time Deposits	135.67	42.64	七、其他贷款 Other Loans	61.35	—
2. 活期存款 Demand Deposits	76.91	35.36	其中：委托及信托贷款 Of Which: Designated and Trust Loans		-4.23
七、单位定期存款 Time Deposits by Enterprises	38.96	—	投资 Investments		-1.24
八、其他存款 Other Deposits	279.37	—	**贷款合计 Total Loans**	**487.29**	**171.12**
存款合计 Total Deposits	**821.90**	**374.11**	八、在银行存款 Deposits with Banks	177.85	70.83
九、向银行借款 Borrowings from Banks	27.61	13.93	九、代理人民银行专项贷款 Agency Earmarked Loans of the Central Bank	5.67	2.60
十、人行拨来专项贷款资金 Earmarked Loan Funds Appropriated by the Central Bank	5.57	2.48	十、缴存准备金 Reserves with the Central Bank	80.08	33.45
十一、自有资金 Own Capital	47.92	-2.64	十一、缴存特种存款 Special Deposits with the Central Bank	1.76	1.13
十二、同业往来 Inter - bank Transactions	86.01	50.79	十二、同业往来 Inter - bank Transactions	186.41	123.30
十三、联社往来 Transactions with Other Credit Cooperatives	21.25	—	十三、联社往来 Transactions with Other Credit Cooperatives	23.98	—
十四、其他 Others	68.77	—	十四、购买债券 Bonds Purchase	38.23	16.18
十五、结益 Net Earnings	11.91	11.91	十五、库存现金 Cash in Vault	8.76	3.77
			十六、证券买卖 Purchase and Sale of Securities	9.58	—
			十七、其他 Others	71.33	—
资金来源总计 Total Sources	**1090.94**	—	**资金运用总计 Total Uses**	**1090.94**	—

城市信用合作社人民币信贷收支表

Sources and Uses of Credit Funds of Urban Credit Cooperatives（RMB）

（1993年末）

（Year - end of 1993）

单位：亿元

Unit：100 Million Yuan

项　目 Items	余　额 Balance	比年初增减额 Changes within the Year	项　目 Items	余　额 Balance	比年初增减额 Changes within the Year
一、集体工业存款 Deposits by Collective Industrial Enterprises	95.40	17.29	一、集体工业贷款 Loans to Collective Industrial Enterprises	198.26	43.24
二、集体商业存款 Deposits by Collective Commercial Enterprises	193.29	65.60	二、集体商业贷款 Loans to Collective Commercial Enterprises	217.27	82.94
三、集体其他企业存款 Deposits by Other Collective Enterprises	213.06	92.28	三、集体其他企业贷款 Loans to Other Collective Enterprises	121.41	58.25
四、小型国营工商企业存款 Deposits by Small State Industrial and Commercial Enterprises	52.73	32.04	四、小型国营工商企业贷款 Loans to Small State Industrial and Commercial Enterprises	60.55	29.49
五、个体工商户存款 Deposits by Self - employed Entities	67.47	20.11	五、个体工商户贷款 Loans to Self - employed Entities	67.60	22.16
六、居民储蓄存款 Savings Deposits by Resident Sector	375.79	161.83	六、抵押贷款 Mortagage Loans	17.68	10.94
1. 定期存款 Time Deposits	238.53	101.54	七、其他贷款 Other Loans	94.58	32.88
2. 活期存款 Demand Deposits	137.26	60.29	**贷款合计** **Total Loans**	**777.35**	**279.90**
七、单位定期存款 Time Deposits by Enterprises	68.74	28.93	八、在银行存款 Deposits with Banks	296.43	117.49
八、其他存款 Other Deposits	273.23	92.4	其中：在专业银行存款 Of Which: Deposits with Special Banks	125.69	69.26
存款合计 **Total Deposits**	**1339.71**	**510.48**	九、代理人民银行专项贷款 Agency Earmarked Loans of the Central Bank	12.51	6.83
九、向银行借款 Borrowings from Banks	29.35	0.95	十、缴存人民银行准备金 Reserves with the Central Bank	134.25	54.04
其中：向专业银行借款 Of Which: Borrowings from Special Banks	6.34	0.70	十一、缴存特种存款 Special Deposits with the Central Bank	5.64	3.97
十、人行拨来专项贷款资金 Earmarked Loan Funds Appropriated by the Central Bank	12.31	6.69	十二、同业往来 Inter - bank Transactions	274.19	85.13
十一、自有资金 Own Capital	84.05	36.04	其中：同业拆出 Of Which: Placements with Banks and Other Financial Institutions	131.35	73.30
十二、同业往来 Inter - bank Transactions	145.06	54.04	十三、联社往来 Transactions with Other Credit Cooperatives	48.62	25.46
其中：拆入资金 Of Which: Placements from Banks and Other Financial Institutions	36.52	7.28	十四、购买债券 Bonds Purchase	73.79	35.81

续表
Continued

项目 Items	余额 Balance	比年初增减额 Changes within the Year	项目 Items	余额 Balance	比年初增减额 Changes within the Year
十三、联社往来 Transactions with Other Credit Coopera-tives	49.50	28.85	十五、库存现金 Cash in Vault	20.59	11.72
			十六、证券买卖 Purchase and Sale of Securities	17.75	7.14
十四、其他 Others	197.77	116.08	十七、其他 Others	217.35	146.36
十五、结益 Net Earnings	20.72	20.72			
资金来源总计 Total Sources	**1878.47**	**773.85**	**资金运用总计 Total Uses**	**1878.47**	**773.85**

城市信用合作社人民币信贷收支表

Sources and Uses of Credit Funds of Urban Credit Cooperatives（RMB）

（1994 年末）

（Year – end of 1994）

单位：亿元

Unit：100 Million Yuan

项 目 Items	余 额 Balance	比年初增减额 Changes within the Year	项 目 Items	余 额 Balance	比年初增减额 Changes within the Year
一、存款合计 Total Deposits	2353.67	989.66	一、贷款合计 Total Loans	1323.62	512.62
1. 集体工业存款 Deposits by Collective Industrial Enterprises	135.95	35.81	1. 集体工业贷款 Loans to Collective Industrial Enterprises	270.27	70.31
2. 集体商业存款 Deposits by Collective Commercial Enterprises	271.40	79.23	2. 集体商业贷款 Loans to Collective Commercial Enterprises	318.90	104.63
3. 集体其他企业存款 Deposits by Other Collective Enterprises	366.44	144.39	3. 集体其他企业贷款 Loans to Other Collective Enterprises	214.06	87.56
4. 国营工商企业存款 Deposits by State Industrial and Commercial Enterprises	119.27	63.27	4. 国营工商企业贷款 Loans to State Industrial and Commercial Enterprises	126.09	52.09
5. 个体工商户存款 Deposits by Self – employed Entities	106.23	38.22	5. 个体工商户贷款 Loans to Self – employed Entities	100.45	34.66
6. 居民储蓄存款 Savings Deposits by Resident Sector	733.74	356.57	6. 抵押贷款 Mortagage Loans	91.73	69.86
（1）定期存款 Time Deposits	485.77	246.94	7. 委托贷款 Designated Loans	52.74	31.06
（2）活期存款 Demand Deposits	247.97	109.63	8. 其他贷款 Other Loans	149.38	62.45
7. 单位定期存款 Time Deposits by Enterprises	204.40	130.96	二、证券业务占款 Funding of Securities Purchase	15.03	0.08
8. 委托存款 Designated Deposits	42.63	21.64	三、代理人民银行专项贷款 Agency Earmarked Loans of the Central Bank	41.74	– 14.57
9. 其他存款 Other Deposits	373.61	119.57	四、在人民银行存款 Deposits with the Central Bank	168.06	51.16
二、证券业务款项 Securities Business Funds	7.04	2.37	五、缴存人民银行准备金 Reserves with the Central Bank	230.47	102.13
三、向银行借款 Borrowings from Banks	34.72	12.21	六、缴存人民银行特种存款 Special Deposits with the Central Bank	46.37	44.92
其中：再贴现 Of Which：Rediscount	0.38	0.37	七、购买人民银行债券 Central Bank Bonds Purchase	20.15	– 3.17
四、银行机构存款 Deposits by Banks	90.75	44.43	八、存放银行机构 Due from Banks	339.95	156.50
五、拆放银行机构 Placements from Banks	66.49	3.81	九、拆放银行机构 Placements with Banks	154.08	33.61
六、金融性公司存款 Desposits by Financial Corporations	17.60	10.94	十、存放金融性公司 Due from Financial Corporations	15.56	9.68

续表
Continued

项　目 Items	余　额 Balance	比年初增减额 Changes within the Year	项　目 Items	余　额 Balance	比年初增减额 Changes within the Year
七、金融性公司拆放 Placements from Financial Corporations	26.40	9.86	十一、拆放金融性公司 Placements with Financial Corporations	124.00	65.66
八、人行拨来专项贷款资金 Earmarked Loan Funds Appropriated by the Central Bank	16.21	4.69	十二、联社往来 Transactions with Other Credit Cooperatives	173.61	77.75
九、联社往来 Transactions with Other Credit Cooperatives	158.56	78.42	十三、投资 Investments	187.12	119.77
			其中：国家债券 Of Which: Treasury Bonds	67.94	39.49
十、所有者权益 Owner's Equity	161.54	58.88	十四、现金 Cash in Vault	32.96	12.33
其中：实收资本 Of Which: Paid-in Capital	111.05	56.20	十五、其他 Others	299.16	93.06
十一、结益 Net Earnings	12.07	12.07			
十二、贷款呆账准备金 Provisions for Bad Loans	8.76	5.32			
十三、其他 Others	218.07	28.87			
资金来源总计 Total Sources	**3171.88**	**1261.53**	**资金运用总计** Total Uses	**3171.88**	**1261.53**

城市信用合作社人民币信贷收支表

Sources and Uses of Credit Funds of Urban Credit Cooperatives（RMB）

（1995 年末）

（Year - end of 1995）

单位：亿元

Unit：100 Million Yuan

项　目 Items	余　额 Balance	比年初增减额 Changes within the Year	项　目 Items	余　额 Balance	比年初增减额 Changes within the Year
一、存款合计 Total Deposits	3357.45	975.49	一、贷款合计 Total Loans	1929.03	580.82
1. 集体工业存款 Deposits by Collective Industrial Enterprises	148.33	10.56	1. 集体工业贷款 Loans to Collective Industrial Enterprises	339.82	71.64
2. 集体商业存款 Deposits by Collective Commercial Enterprises	296.32	22.32	2. 集体商业贷款 Loans to Collective Commercial Enterprises	429.68	109.57
3. 集体其他企业存款 Deposits by Other Collective Enterprises	426.99	61.20	3. 集体其他企业贷款 Loans to Other Collective Enterprises	310.15	95.54
4. 国营工商企业存款 Deposits by State Industrial and Commercial Enterprises	159.90	38.28	4. 国营工商企业贷款 Loans to State Industrial and Commercial Enterprises	181.52	51.59
5. 个体工商户存款 Deposits by Self - employed Entities	140.94	32.61	5. 个体工商户贷款 Loans to Self - employed Entities	156.17	55.84
6. 居民储蓄存款 Savings Deposits by Resident Sector	1259.46	518.15	6. 中长期贷款 Medium and Long - term Loans	41.43	17.03
（1）定期存款 Time Deposits	904.18	412.77	7. 抵押贷款 Mortagage Loans	224.12	118.56
（2）活期存款 Demand Deposits	355.28	105.38	8. 委托贷款 Designated Loans	33.21	-4.20
7. 单位定期存款 Time Deposits by Enterprises	407.20	200.53	9. 其他贷款 Other Loans	212.93	65.25
8. 委托存款 Designated Deposits	40.90	-5.00	二、租赁 Leases	0.23	-0.21
9. 其他存款 Other Deposits	477.41	96.84	三、委托投资 Designated Investments	0.21	-0.22
二、发行债券 Bonds Issue	0.19	-0.13	四、证券业务占款 Funding of Securities Purchase	16.34	3.87
三、证券业务款项 Securities Business Funds	14.91	8.32	五、代理人民银行专项贷款 Agency Earmarked Loans of the Central Bank	19.60	-0.29
四、向银行借款 Borrowings from Banks	29.72	-6.61	六、在人民银行存款 Deposits with the Central Bank	259.14	66.57
其中：再贴现 Of Which：Rediscount	0.62	0.09	七、缴存人行财政性存款 Fiscal Deposits with the Central Bank	7.50	4.28
五、银行机构存款 Deposits by Banks	170.42	76.23	八、缴存人民银行准备金 Reserves with the Central Bank	332.11	104.20
六、银行机构拆放 Placements from Banks	81.62	12.88	九、缴存人民银行特种存款 Special Deposits with the Central Bank	23.46	-25.73

续表
Continued

项　目 Items	余　额 Balance	比年初增减额 Changes within the Year	项　目 Items	余　额 Balance	比年初增减额 Changes within the Year
七、金融性公司存款 Desposits by Financial Corporations	13.41	-5.09	十、购买人民银行债券 Central Bank Bonds Purchase	20.53	1.50
八、金融性公司拆放 Placements from Financial Corporations	44.24	18.35	十一、存放银行机构 Due from Banks	480.52	143.61
九、长期借款 Long-term Borrowing	8.92	8.34	十二、拆放银行机构 Placements with Banks	238.31	81.89
十、代理人行财政性存款 Agency Fiscal Deposits	2.34	-0.26	十三、存放金融性公司 Due from Financial Corporations	15.10	3.51
十一、人行拨来专项贷款资金 Earmarked Loan Funds Appropriated by the Central Bank	19.56	1.69	十四、拆放金融性公司 Placements with Financial Corporations	174.54	46.49
			十五、银行存款 Deposits with Banks	36.98	26.42
十二、联社往来 Transactions with Other Credit Cooperatives	251.45	90.57	十六、联社往来 Transactions with Other Credit Cooperatives	254.12	77.29
十三、所有者权益 Owner's Equity	200.84	36.20	十七、投资 Investments	237.35	47.59
其中：实收资本 Of Which: Paid-in Capital	135.95	23.19	其中：国家债券 Of Which: Treasury Bonds	98.18	27.85
十四、结益 Net Earnings	13.09	13.04	十八、现金 Cash in Vault	47.99	14.35
十五、贷款呆账准备金 Provisions for Bad Loans	13.70	4.79	十九、其他 Others	451.94	158.42
十六、其他 Others	323.14	100.50			
资金来源总计 Total Sources	**4545.00**	**1334.36**	**资金运用总计 Total Uses**	**4545.00**	**1334.36**

城市信用合作社人民币信贷收支表

Sources and Uses of Credit Funds of Urban Credit Cooperatives（RMB）

（1996年末）

（Year - end of 1996）

单位：亿元

Unit：100 Million Yuan

项目 Items	余额 Balance	比年初增减额 Changes within the Year	项目 Items	余额 Balance	比年初增减额 Changes within the Year
一、存款合计 Total Deposits	3998.22	686.70	一、贷款合计 Total Loans	2445.21	521.57
1. 集体工业存款 Deposits by Collective Industrial Enterprises	140.79	-2.86	1. 集体工业贷款 Loans to Collective Industrial Enterprises	393.87	58.42
2. 集体商业存款 Deposits by Collective Commercial Enterprises	287.00	-4.34	2. 集体商业贷款 Loans to Collective Commercial Enterprises	478.52	50.63
3. 集体其他企业存款 Deposits by Other Collective Enterprises	387.65	-30.54	3. 集体其他企业贷款 Loans to Other Collective Enterprises	343.34	30.87
4. 国营工商企业存款 Deposits by State Industrial and Commercial Enterprises	193.44	34.40	4. 国营工商企业贷款 Loans to State Industrial and Commercial Enterprises	223.28	43.24
5. 个体工商户存款 Deposits by Self - employed Entities	162.95	23.36	5. 个体工商户贷款 Loans to Self - employed Entities	212.65	56.79
6. 居民储蓄存款 Savings Deposits by Resident Sector	1832.97	570.06	6. 中长期贷款 Medium and Long - term Loans	63.41	23.57
其中：定期存款 Of Which：Time Deposits	1357.56	450.33	7. 抵押贷款 Mortagage Loans	312.23	83.64
7. 单位定期存款 Time Deposits by Enterprises	474.63	72.45	其中：中长期贷款 Of Which：Medium and Long - term Loans	7.99	-1.64
8. 委托存款 Designated Deposits	37.09	-4.30	8. 委托贷款 Designated Loans	30.45	-3.00
9. 其他存款 Other Deposits	481.70	28.47	9. 其他贷款 Other Loans	387.46	177.41
二、发行债券 Bonds Issue	0.35	0.12	二、租赁 Leases	0.45	0.24
三、证券业务款项 Securities Business Funds	15.41	0.66	三、委托投资 Designated Investments	0.49	0.31
四、向银行借款 Borrowings from Banks	33.72	3.31	四、证券业务占款 Funding of Securities Purchase	13.60	-3.14
其中：再贴现 Of Which：Rediscount	0.05	-0.57	五、代理人民银行专项贷款 Agency Earmarked Loans of the Central Bank	17.24	-2.63
五、银行机构存款 Deposits by Banks	247.62	82.60	六、在人民银行存款 Deposits with the Central Bank	338.15	89.61
六、银行机构拆放 Placements from Banks	168.76	86.29	七、缴存人行财政性存款 Fiscal Deposits with the Central Bank	4.40	-3.22
七、金融性公司存款 Desposits by Financial Corporations	90.12	77.44	八、缴存人民银行准备金 Reserves with the Central Bank	394.65	67.99

续表
Continued

项　　目 Items	余　额 Balance	比年初增减额 Changes within the Year	项　　目 Items	余　额 Balance	比年初增减额 Changes within the Year
八、金融性公司拆放 Placements from Financial Corporations	87.71	42.74	九、缴存人民银行特种存款 Special Deposits with the Central Bank	3.40	-19.69
九、长期借款 Long-term Borrowing	16.60	7.62	十、购买人民银行债券 Central Bank Bonds Purchase	6.38	-13.91
十、代理人行财政性存款 Agency Fiscal Deposits	3.67	1.31	十一、存放银行机构 Due from Banks	493.38	28.85
十一、人行拨来专项贷款资金 Earmarked Loan Funds Appropriated by the Central Bank	17.54	-2.27	十二、拆放银行机构 Placements with Banks	318.24	87.24
			十三、存放金融性公司 Due from Financial Corporations	24.92	8.86
十二、联社往来 Transactions with Other Credit Cooperatives	304.11	62.71	十四、拆放金融性公司 Placements with Financial Corporations	213.35	40.07
十三、所有者权益 Owner's Equity	211.93	3.91	十五、银行存款 Deposits with Banks	48.39	-37.92
其中：实收资本 Of Which：Paid-in Capital	158.41	17.49	十六、联社往来 Transactions with Other Credit Cooperatives	339.95	139.95
十四、结益 Net Earnings	6.04	6.04			
			十七、投资 Investments	285.26	51.63
十五、贷款呆账准备金 Provisions for Bad Loans	15.88	2.31	其中：国家债券 Of Which：Treasury Bonds	99.38	4.34
十六、其他 Others	436.21	110.77	十八、现金 Cash in Vault	42.73	-3.65
			十九、其他 Others	663.70	220.10
资金来源总计 Total Sources	**5653.89**	**1172.26**	**资金运用总计 Total Uses**	**5653.89**	**1172.26**

城市信用合作社人民币信贷收支表

Sources and Uses of Credit Funds of Urban Credit Cooperatives（RMB）

（1997 年末）

（Year - end of 1997）

单位：亿元

Unit：100 Million Yuan

项　　目 Items	余　额 Balance	比年初增减额 Changes within the Year	项　　目 Items	余　额 Balance	比年初增减额 Changes within the Year
一、各项存款 Total Deposits	2846.70	- 124.26	一、各项贷款 Total Loans	1933.90	- 18.20
1. 企业存款 Deposits by Enterprises	1107.09	- 239.45	1. 短期贷款 Short - term Loans	1302.23	- 252.74
（1）活期存款 Demand Deposits	850.88	- 176.74	（1）工业贷款 Loans to Industrial Sector	351.19	- 60.00
（2）定期存款 Time Deposits	256.21	- 62.71	（2）商业贷款 Loans to Commercial Sector	338.03	- 110.86
2. 城镇储蓄存款 Urban Savings Deposits	1681.66	121.00	其中：收购贷款 Of Which：Loans for the Purchase of Farm Products	0.52	- 0.01
（1）活期储蓄 Demand Deposits	385.51	- 18.09	（3）建筑业贷款 Loans to Construction Sector	11.32	- 1.70
（2）定期储蓄 Time Deposits	1296.15	139.09	（4）农业贷款 Loans to Agricultural Sector	1.06	0.24
3. 农业存款 Deposits by Agricultural Sector	0.43	0.27	（5）乡镇企业贷款 Loans to Village and Township Enterprises	22.42	8.18
4. 信托存款 Trust Deposits	0.57	0.34	（6）三资企业贷款 Loans to Foreign Investment Enterprises and Ventures	3.07	- 2.44
5. 其他存款 Other Deposits	56.95	- 6.42	（7）私营企业及个体贷款 Loans to Privately - run Enterprises and Self - employed Entities	162.55	5.14
二、代理财政性存款 Agency Fiscal Deposits	7.54	- 8.08	（8）贴现 Discount	6.43	- 1.00
三、发行金融债券 Financial Bonds Issue	1.86	0.07	（9）其他短期贷款 Other Short - term Loans	406.16	- 90.30
其中：发行政策性金融债券 Of Which：Policy Financial Bonds Issue		- 0.15	2. 中长期贷款 Medium and Long - term Loans	49.59	- 18.98
四、国家投资债券 State Investment Bonds	0.01	0.01	（1）基本建设贷款 Capital Construction Loans	6.43	- 0.57
五、卖出回购证券 Repo	2.00	- 1.70	（2）技术改造贷款 Technical Improvement Loans	0.63	- 1.77
六、向中央银行借款 Borrowings from the Central Bank	26.97	- 6.32	（3）其他中长期贷款 Other Medium and Long - term Loans	42.53	- 16.64
七、同业往来 Inter - bank Transactions	503.86	16.28	3. 信托贷款 Trust Loans	0.16	0.15
1. 同业存放 Due to Banks and Other Financial Institutions	226.65	- 43.32	4. 逾期类贷款 Overdue Loans	581.92	253.37
2. 同业拆借 Placements from Banks and Other Financial Institutions	277.21	59.60			

续表
Continued

项　　目 Items	余　额 Balance	比年初增减额 Changes within the Year	项　　目 Items	余　额 Balance	比年初增减额 Changes within the Year
八、委托存款及委托投资基金 Designated Deposits and Designated Investment Funds	0.94	-4.81	二、国家投资债券贷款 Loans Related to State Investment Bonds		
			三、有价证券及投资 Securities and Investments	97.47	-58.74
1. 委托存款 Designated Deposits	-2.00	-4.57	四、缴存人行准备金 Reserves with the Central Bank	245.68	-1.30
2. 委托投资基金 Designated Investment Funds	2.94	-0.24	五、缴存准备金存款 Reserves with the Central Bank	254.75	-32.88
九、代理金融机构委托贷款基金 Designated Loan Funds on Behalf of Financial Institutions	7.99	-11.74	六、存放中央银行特种存款 Special Deposits with the Central Bank	2.40	-2.76
其中：中央银行委托贷款基金 Of Which：Loan Funds Designated by the Central Bank	4.39	-6.85	七、存放中央银行财政性存款 Fiscal Deposits with the Central Bank	4.04	0.29
			八、同业往来 Inter-bank Transactions	678.16	-97.38
十、所有者权益 Owner's Equity	92.75	-49.55	1. 存放同业 Due from Banks and Other Financial Institutions	385.31	-65.24
其中：实收资本 Of Which：Paid-in Capital	114.57	1.72			
当年结益 Net Earnings	-23.05	-23.05	2. 拆放同业 Placements with Banks and Other Financial Institutions	292.85	-32.14
十一、其他 Others	-225.04	-29.85			
			九、代理金融机构贷款 Lending on Behalf of Financial Institutions	8.15	-13.60
			其中：代理人行专项贷款 Of Which：Agency Earmarked Loans of the Central Bank	4.55	-8.17
			十、库存现金 Cash in Vault	41.03	4.62
			十一、外汇占款 Position for Foreign Exchange Purchase		
资金来源总计 Total Sources	**3265.58**	**-219.95**	**资金运用总计 Total Uses**	**3265.58**	**-219.95**

城市信用合作社人民币信贷收支表

Sources and Uses of Credit Funds of Urban Credit Cooperatives（RMB）

（1998 年末）

（Year - end of 1998）

单位：亿元

Unit：100 Million Yuan

项目 Items	余额 Balance	比年初增减额 Changes within the Year	项目 Items	余额 Balance	比年初增减额 Changes within the Year
一、各项存款 Total Deposits	2461.86	28.63	一、各项贷款 Total Loans	1689.62	67.85
1. 企业存款 Deposits by Enterprises	866.32	-53.87	1. 短期贷款 Short - term Loans	1049.02	-91.02
（1）活期存款 Demand Deposits	689.09	-23.70	（1）工业贷款 Loans to Industrial Sector	272.93	-44.80
（2）定期存款 Time Deposits	177.23	-30.17	（2）商业贷款 Loans to Commercial Sector	241.44	-53.56
2. 城镇储蓄存款 Urban Savings Deposits	1559.87	100.16	其中：收购贷款 Of Which：Loans for the Purchase of Farm Products	0.73	0.39
（1）活期储蓄 Demand Deposits	374.50	38.62	（3）建筑业贷款 Loans to Construction Sector	10.30	3.94
（2）定期储蓄 Time Deposits	1185.37	61.54	（4）农业贷款 Loans to Aricultural Sector	0.78	-0.13
3. 农业存款 Deposits by Agricultural Sector	1.04	0.20	（5）乡镇企业贷款 Loans to Village and Township Enterprises	24.90	8.71
4. 信托存款 Trust Deposits	0.15	-0.42	（6）三资企业贷款 Loans to Foreign Investment Enterprises and Ventures	6.65	4.44
5. 其他存款 Other Deposits	34.48	-17.44	（7）私营企业及个体贷款 Loans to Privately - run Enterprises and Self - employed Entities	160.94	14.40
二、代理财政性存款 Agency Fiscal Deposits	3.31	-0.14	（8）贴现 Discount	1.84	-1.33
三、发行金融债券 Financial Bonds Issue	0.17	-0.30	（9）其他短期贷款 Other Short - term Loans	329.24	-22.69
其中：发行政策性金融债券 Of Which：Policy Financial Bonds Issue	-0.04	-0.04	2. 中期流动资金贷款 Medium - term Working Capital Loans	3.81	-0.59
四、国家投资债券 State Investment Bonds		-0.01	3. 中长期贷款 Medium and Long - term Loans	45.71	10.36
五、卖出回购证券 Repo	0.79	-0.42	（1）基本建设贷款 Capital Construction Loans	4.82	1.41
六、向中央银行借款 Borrowings from Central Bank	17.81	-1.60	（2）技术改造贷款 Technical Improvement Loans	1.13	0.68
七、同业往来 Inter - bank Transactions	365.89	-25.43	（3）其他中长期贷款 Other Medium and Long - term Loans	39.76	8.27
1. 同业存放 Due to Banks and Other Financial Institutions	167.21	-30.98	4. 信托贷款 Trust Loans	0.23	0.07
2. 同业拆借 Placements from Banks and Other Financial Institutions	198.68	5.55			

续表
Continued

项　　目 Items	余　额 Balance	比年初增减额 Changes within the Year	项　　目 Items	余　额 Balance	比年初增减额 Changes within the Year
八、委托存款及委托投资基金 Designated Deposits and Designated Investment Funds	2.95	2.01	5. 逾期类贷款 Overdue Loans	590.85	149.03
1. 委托存款 Designated Deposits	-0.85	1.67	二、国家投资债券贷款 Loans Related to State Investment Bonds		
2. 委托投资基金 Designated Investment Funds	3.80	0.34	三、有价证券及投资 Securities and Investments	67.23	-12.44
九、代理金融机构委托贷款基金 Designated Loan Funds on Behalf of Financial Institutions	4.87	0.02	四、缴存人行准备金 Reserves with the Central Bank		
其中：中央银行委托贷款基金 Of Which：Loan Funds Designated by the Central Bank	1.29	-1.17	五、缴存准备金存款 Reserves with the Central Bank	384.01	-54.59
十、所有者权益 Owner's Equity	22.21	-52.39	六、存放中央银行特种存款 Special Deposits with the Central Bank	1.12	-1.22
其中：实收资本 Of Which：Paid-in Capital	79.37	-10.33	七、存放中央银行财政性存款 Fiscal Deposits with the Central Bank	0.04	-3.86
当年结益 Net Earnings	-34.20	-34.20	八、同业往来 Inter-bank Transactions	486.30	-80.11
十一、其他 Others	-205.91	-30.18	1. 存放同业 Due from Banks and Other Financial Institutions	311.55	-30.81
			2. 拆放同业 Placements with Banks and Other Financial Institutions	174.75	-49.30
			九、代理金融机构贷款 Lending on Behalf of Financial Institutions	5.92	0.37
			其中：代理人行专项贷款 Of Which：Agency Earmarked Loans of the Central Bank	1.28	-1.46
			十、库存现金 Cash in Vault	39.71	4.19
			十一、外汇占款 Position for Foreign Exchange Purchase		
资金来源总计 Total Sources	**2673.95**	**-79.81**	**资金运用总计 Total Uses**	**2673.95**	**-79.81**

城市信用合作社人民币信贷收支表

Sources and Uses of Credit Funds of Urban Credit Cooperatives（RMB）

（1999年末）

（Year - end of 1999）

单位：亿元

Unit：100 Million Yuan

项 目 Items	余 额 Balance	比年初增减额 Changes within the Year	项 目 Items	余 额 Balance	比年初增减额 Changes within the Year
一、各项存款 Total Deposits	2248.84	-112.36	一、各项贷款 Total Loans	1609.47	-17.88
1. 企业存款 Deposits by Enterprises	753.79	-43.00	1. 短期贷款 Short - term Loans	857.29	-146.08
（1）活期存款 Demand Deposits	610.93	-18.64	（1）工业贷款 Loans to Industrial Sector	211.70	-38.94
（2）定期存款 Time Deposits	142.86	-24.36	（2）商业贷款 Loans to Commercial Sector	172.71	-55.31
2. 城镇储蓄存款 Urban Savings Deposits	1456.91	-72.64	其中：收购贷款 Of Which：Loans for the Purchase of Farm Products	0.37	-0.36
（1）活期储蓄 Demand Deposits	367.70	1.85			
（2）定期储蓄 Time Deposits	1089.21	-74.49	（3）建筑业贷款 Loans to Construction Sector	8.57	-0.68
3. 农业存款 Deposits by Agricultural Sector	10.08	1.33	（4）农业贷款 Loans to Agricultural Sector	3.71	0.52
4. 信托存款 Trust Deposits	0.09	-0.06	（5）乡镇企业贷款 Loans to Village and Township Enterprises	18.56	-14.89
5. 其他存款 Other Deposits	27.97	2.01	（6）三资企业贷款 Loans to Foreign Investment Enterprises and Ventures	1.16	-4.32
二、代理财政性存款 Agency Fiscal Deposits	2.14	-1.11	（7）私营企业及个体贷款 Loans to Privately - run Enterprises and Self - employed Entities	144.18	-8.82
三、发行金融债券 Financial Bonds Issue	0.17	0.01	（8）贴现 Discount	3.12	1.25
其中：发行政策性金融债券 Of Which：Policy Financial Bonds Issue		0.04	（9）其他短期贷款 Other Short - term Loans	293.58	-24.89
四、国家投资债券 State Investment Bonds			2. 中期流动资金贷款 Medium - term Working Capital Loans	3.55	0.30
五、卖出回购证券 Repo	1.33	0.54	3. 中长期贷款 Medium and Long - term Loans	42.58	1.37
六、向中央银行借款 Borrowings from the Central Bank	28.87	10.96	（1）基本建设贷款 Capital Construction Loans	5.98	2.32
七、同业往来 Inter - bank Transactions	181.33	22.98	（2）技术改造贷款 Technical Improvement Loans	1.00	0.54
1. 同业存放 Due to Banks and Other Financial Institutions	28.83	1.40	（3）其他中长期贷款 Other Medium and Long - term Loans	35.60	-1.49
2. 同业拆借 Placements from Banks and Other Financial Institutions	152.50	21.58	4. 信托贷款 Trust Loans	0.29	0.06

续表
Continued

项 目 Items	余 额 Balance	比年初增减额 Changes within the Year	项 目 Items	余 额 Balance	比年初增减额 Changes within the Year
八、委托存款及委托投资基金 Designated Deposits and Designated Investment Funds	-0.41	-3.55	5. 逾期类贷款 Overdue Loans	705.76	126.47
			二、国家投资债券贷款 Loans Related to State Investment Bonds		
1. 委托存款 Designated Deposits	-1.32	-0.61	三、有价证券及投资 Securities and Investments	71.78	13.71
2. 委托投资基金 Designated Investment Funds	0.91	-2.94	四、缴存准备金存款 Reserves with the Central Bank	268.93	-102.34
九、代理金融机构委托贷款基金 Designated Loan Funds on Behalf of Financial Institutions	5.39	0.86	五、存放中央银行特种存款 Special Deposits with the Central Bank	0.36	-1.05
其中：中央银行委托贷款基金 Of Which: Loan Funds Designated by the Central Bank	1.44	0.17	六、存放中央银行财政性存款 Fiscal Deposits with the Central Bank	0.02	-0.02
十、所有者权益 Owner's Equity	-29.06	-43.62	七、同业往来 Inter-bank Transactions	229.87	-21.59
其中：实收资本 Of Which: Paid-in Capital	76.31	0.75	1. 存放同业 Due from Banks and Other Financial Institutions	158.58	-7.47
当年结益 Net Earnings	-39.67	-39.67	2. 拆放同业 Placements with Banks and Other Financial Institutions	71.29	-14.12
十一、其他 Others	-216.25	-5.56	八、代理金融机构贷款 Lending on Behalf of Financial Institutions	5.99	0.40
			其中：代理人行专项贷款 Of Which: Agency Earmarked Loans of the Central Bank	1.19	-0.07
			九、库存现金 Cash in Vault	35.93	-2.08
			十、外汇占款 Position for Foreign Exchange Purchase		
资金来源总计 Total Sources	**2222.35**	**-130.85**	**资金运用总计 Total Uses**	**2222.35**	**-130.85**

城市信用合作社人民币信贷收支表

Sources and Uses of Credit Funds of Urban Credit Cooperatives（RMB）

（2000年末）

（Year－end of 2000）

单位：亿元

Unit：100 Million Yuan

项目 Items	余额 Balance	比年初增减额 Changes within the Year	项目 Items	余额 Balance	比年初增减额 Changes within the Year
一、各项存款 Total Deposits	1529.24	－430.71	一、各项贷款 Total Loans	1056.72	－260.32
1. 企业存款 Deposits by Enterprises	565.59	－96.61	1. 短期贷款 Short－term Loans	568.65	－200.33
（1）活期存款 Demand Deposits	460.37	－80.12	（1）工业贷款 Loans to Industrial Sector	130.05	－70.68
（2）定期存款 Time Deposits	105.22	－16.49	（2）商业贷款 Loans to Commercial Sector	104.77	－37.82
2. 城镇储蓄存款 Urban Savings Deposits	931.91	－329.78	其中：收购贷款 Of Which：Loans for the Purchase of Farm Products	0.16	
（1）活期储蓄 Demand Deposits	238.02	－53.58	（3）建筑业贷款 Loans to Construction Sector	6.49	－0.46
（2）定期储蓄 Time Deposits	693.89	－276.20	（4）农业贷款 Loans to Agricultural Sector	4.38	0.80
3. 农业存款 Deposits by Agricultural Sector	13.17	2.85	（5）乡镇企业贷款 Loans to Village and Township Enterprises	14.06	－2.40
4. 信托存款 Trust Deposits	0.09		（6）三资企业贷款 Loans to Foreign Investment Enterprises and Ventures	0.88	0.01
5. 其他存款 Other Deposits	18.48	－7.17	（7）私营企业及个体贷款 Loans to Privately－run Enterprises and Self－employed Entities	102.53	－31.44
二、代理财政性存款 Agency Fiscal Deposits	1.34	0.06	（8）贴现 Discount	4.98	1.92
三、发行金融债券 Financial Bonds Issue	0.03	－0.17	（9）其他短期贷款 Other Short－term Loans	200.51	－60.26
其中：发行政策性金融债券 Of Which：Policy Financial Bonds Issue			2. 中期流动资金贷款 Medium－term Working Capital Loans	2.01	0.24
四、国家投资债券 State Investment Bonds			3. 中长期贷款 Medium and Long－term Loans	32.64	－0.14
五、卖出回购证券 Repo	0.97	－0.37	（1）基本建设贷款 Capital Construction Loans	7.63	2.18
六、向中央银行借款 Borrowings from the Central Bank	36.61	14.42	（2）技术改造贷款 Technical Improvement Loans	0.90	－0.01
七、同业往来 Inter－bank Transactions	93.76	1.59	（3）其他中长期贷款 Other Medium and Long－term Loans	24.11	－2.31
1. 同业存放 Due to Banks and Other Financial Institutions	21.81	－1.82	4. 信托贷款 Trust Loans	0.29	
2. 同业拆借 Placements from Banks and Other Financial Institutions	71.95	3.41			

续表
Continued

项目 Items	余额 Balance	比年初增减额 Changes within the Year	项目 Items	余额 Balance	比年初增减额 Changes within the Year
八、委托存款及委托投资基金 Designated Deposits and Designated Investment Funds	-0.58	-0.34	5. 逾期类贷款 Overdue Loans	453.13	-60.09
			二、国家投资债券贷款 Loans Related to State Investment Bonds		
1. 委托存款 Designated Deposits	-2.46	-1.39	三、有价证券及投资 Securities and Investments	60.73	-3.45
2. 委托投资基金 Designated Investment Funds	1.88	1.05	四、缴存准备金存款 Reserves with the Central Bank	175.32	-78.90
九、代理金融机构委托贷款基金 Designated Loan Funds on Behalf of Financial Institutions	3.89	-0.50	五、存放中央银行特种存款 Special Deposits with the Central Bank	0.91	0.55
其中：中央银行委托贷款基金 Of Which: Loan Funds Designated by the Central Bank	1.10	-0.13	六、存放中央银行财政性存款 Fiscal Deposits with the Central Bank	0.39	0.36
			七、同业往来 Inter-bank Transactions	155.11	-48.28
十、所有者权益 Owner's Equity	-28.02	-24.15	1. 存放同业 Due from Banks and Other Financial Institutions	121.75	-32.59
其中：实收资本 Of Which: Paid-in Capital	49.42	-17.44			
当年结益 Net Earnings	-18.27	-18.27	2. 拆放同业 Placements with Banks and Other Financial Institutions	33.36	-15.69
十一、其他 Others	-156.31	42.09			
			八、代理金融机构贷款 Lending on Behalf of Financial Institutions	4.15	-1.17
			其中：代理人行专项贷款 Of Which: Agency Earmarked Loans of the Central Bank	0.84	-0.28
			九、库存现金 Cash in Vault	27.60	-6.87
			十、外汇占款 Position for Foreign Exchange Purchase		
资金来源总计 Total Sources	**1480.93**	**-398.08**	**资金运用总计 Total Uses**	**1480.93**	**-398.08**

城市信用合作社人民币信贷收支表

Sources and Uses of Credit Funds of Urban Credit Cooperatives（RMB）

（2001 年末）

（Year - end of 2001）

单位：亿元

Unit：100 Million Yuan

项　目 Items	余　额 Balance	比年初增减额 Changes within the Year	项　目 Items	余　额 Balance	比年初增减额 Changes within the Year
一、各项存款 Total Deposits	1071.35	-240.26	一、各项贷款 Total Loans	725.41	-168.84
1. 企业存款 Deposits by Enterprises	426.64	-73.79	1. 短期贷款 Short - term Loans	630.72	-163.92
（1）活期存款 Demand Deposits	340.30	-69.23	（1）工业贷款 Loans to Industrial Sector	164.21	-48.63
（2）定期存款 Time Deposits	86.34	-4.56	（2）商业贷款 Loans to Commercial Sector	152.92	-30.15
2. 机关团体存款 Deposits by Government Agencies and Social Organizations	2.09	0.80	其中：收购贷款 Of Which：Loans for the Purchase of Farm Products	0.23	-0.02
3. 储蓄存款 Savings Deposits	630.86	-162.42	（3）建筑业贷款 Loans to Construction Sector	15.13	1.50
（1）活期储蓄 Demand Deposits	155.47	-41.22	（4）农业贷款 Loans to Agricultural Sector	5.45	-0.63
（2）定期储蓄 Time Deposits	475.39	-121.20	（5）乡镇企业贷款 Loans to Village and Township Enterprises	15.78	-5.97
4. 农业存款 Deposits by Agricultural Sector	2.15	-1.43	（6）三资企业贷款 Loans to Foreign Investment Enterprises and Ventures	1.66	-0.49
5. 其他存款 Other Deposits	9.61	-3.42	（7）私营企业及个体贷款 Loans to Privately - run Enterprises and Self - employed Entities	99.01	-23.83
二、代理财政性存款 Agency Fiscal Deposits	3.84	2.52	（8）其他短期贷款 Other Short - term Loans	176.56	-55.72
三、金融债券 Financial Bonds	0.10	0.07	其中：个人短期消费贷款 Of Which：Short - term Consumer Credit	7.76	-1.93
其中：政策性金融债券 Of Which：Policy Financial Bonds			2. 中期流动资金贷款 Medium - term Working Capital Loans	1.95	-0.30
四、应付及暂收款 Accounts Payable and Receipts on Account	28.88	-8.95	3. 中长期贷款 Medium and Long - term Loans	84.32	-8.76
其中：应付及预提利息 Of Which：Interest Payable and Accrued	10.87	-4.05	（1）基本建设贷款 Capital Construction Loans	11.12	-3.28
五、卖出回购证券 Repo	1.96	0.08	（2）技术改造贷款 Technical Improvement Loans	2.51	-1.06
六、向中央银行借款 Borrowings from the Central Bank	33.55	0.59	（3）其他中长期贷款 Other Medium and Long - term Loans	70.69	-4.42
七、同业往来 Inter - bank Transactions	63.90	-15.75			

续表
Continued

项　目 Items	余　额 Balance	比年初增减额 Changes within the Year	项　目 Items	余　额 Balance	比年初增减额 Changes within the Year
1. 同业存放 Due to Banks and Other Financial Institutions	13.49	-2.16	其中:个人中长期消费贷款 Of Which: Medium and Long-term Consumer Credit	0.78	0.57
2. 同业拆借 Placements from Banks and Other Financial Institutions	50.41	-13.59	4. 票据融资 Paper Financing	8.39	4.11
			其中: 贴现 Of Which: Discount	8.39	4.11
八、委托存款及委托投资基金(净) Designated Deposits and Designated Investment Funds (Net)	0.70	1.22	5. 各项垫款 Total Advances	0.03	0.03
1. 委托存款及委托投资基金 Designated Deposits and Designated Investment Funds	2.91	-0.35	二、有价证券及投资 Securities and Investments	38.86	-14.47
			三、应收及预付款 Accounts Receivable and Advance Payments	49.65	-16.61
2. 减: 委托贷款及委托投资 Minus: Designated Loans and Designated Investments	2.21	-1.57	其中: 应收利息 Of Which: Interest Receivable	19.79	-8.23
九、代理金融机构委托贷款基金 Designated Loan Funds on Behalf of Financial Institutions	2.07	-1.75	四、买入返售证券 Reverse Repo	0.88	
其中: 中央银行委托贷款基金 Of Which: Loan Funds Designated by the Central Bank	0.41	-0.65	五、存放中央银行准备金存款 Reserve Deposits with the Central Bank	144.05	-10.75
			六、存放中央银行特种存款 Special Deposits with the Central Bank	0.52	-0.32
十、各项准备 Total Provisions	8.66	-1.12	七、缴存中央银行财政性存款 Fiscal Deposits with the Central Bank		-0.17
其中: 贷款呆账准备金 Of Which: Provisions for Bad Loans	8.03	-1.62	八、同业往来 Inter-bank Transactions	108.64	-22.03
十一、所有者权益 Owner's Equity	-25.75	1.21	1. 存放同业 Due from Banks and Other Financial Institutions	89.12	-10.51
其中: 实收资本 Of Which: Paid-in Capital	38.25	-0.90			
当年结益 Net Earnings	-8.32	-8.32	2. 拆放同业 Placements with Banks and Other Financial Institutions	19.52	-11.52
十二、其他 Others	-103.54	18.52	九、代理金融机构贷款 Lending on Behalf of Financial Institutions	2.61	-1.47
			其中: 代理人行专项贷款 Of Which: Agency Earmarked Loans of the Central Bank	0.34	-0.46
			十、库存现金 Cash in Vault	15.10	-8.96
			十一、外汇占款 Position for Foreign Exchange Purchase		
资金来源总计 Total Sources	**1085.72**	**-243.62**	**资金运用总计** Total Uses	**1085.72**	**-243.62**

城市信用合作社人民币信贷收支表

Sources and Uses of Credit Funds of Urban Credit Cooperatives（RMB）

（2002年末）

（Year－end of 2002）

单位：亿元

Unit：100 Million Yuan

项　目 Items	余　额 Balance	比年初增减额 Changes within the Year	项　目 Items	余　额 Balance	比年初增减额 Changes within the Year
一、各项存款 Total Deposits	1010.33	74.12	一、各项贷款 Total Loans	664.42	61.74
1.企业存款 Deposits by Enterprises	429.44	37.99	1.短期贷款 Short－term Loans	555.40	31.34
（1）活期存款 Demand Deposits	326.04	10.05	（1）工业贷款 Loans to Industrial Sector	153.91	17.65
（2）定期存款 Time Deposits	103.40	27.94	（2）商业贷款 Loans to Commercial Sector	117.44	－5.47
2.机关团体存款 Deposits by Government Agencies and Social Organizations	6.87	4.96	其中：收购贷款 Of Which：Loans for the Purchase of Farm Products	0.23	0.02
3.储蓄存款 Savings Deposits	549.53	16.52	（3）建筑业贷款 Loans to Construction Sector	17.35	4.54
（1）活期储蓄 Demand Deposits	141.33	9.54	（4）农业贷款 Loans to Agricultural Sector	1.57	－1.19
（2）定期储蓄 Time Deposits	408.20	6.98	（5）乡镇企业贷款 Loans to Village and Township Enterprises	7.45	－1.83
4.农业存款 Deposits by Agricultural Sector	1.01	－0.60	（6）三资企业贷款 Loans to Foreign Investment Enterprises and Ventures	1.07	0.06
5.其他存款 Other Deposits	23.48	15.25	（7）私营企业及个体贷款 Loans to Privately－run Enterprises and Self－employed Entities	93.25	8.32
二、代理财政性存款 Agency Fiscal Deposits	1.58	－1.93	（8）其他短期贷款 Other Short－term Loans	163.36	9.26
三、金融债券 Financial Bonds	0.02	－0.08	其中：个人短期消费贷款 Of Which：Short－term Consumer Credit	10.14	2.56
其中：政策性金融债券 Of Which：Policy Financial Bonds			2.中期流动资金贷款 Medium－term Working Capital Loans	5.95	4.01
四、应付及暂收款 Accounts Payable and Receipts on Account	26.12	4.01	3.中长期贷款 Medium and Long－term Loans	75.69	7.08
其中：应付及预提利息 Of Which：Interest Payable and Accrued	7.06	－0.42	（1）基本建设贷款 Capital Construction Loans	11.04	0.26
五、卖出回购证券 Repo	10.77	9.83	（2）技术改造贷款 Technical Improvement Loans	1.99	－0.49
六、向中央银行借款 Borrowings from the Central Bank	23.59	－1.48	（3）其他中长期贷款 Other Medium and Long－term Loans	62.66	7.31
七、同业往来 Inter－bank Transactions	40.62	1.15			

续表
Continued

项 目 Items	余 额 Balance	比年初增减额 Changes within the Year	项 目 Items	余 额 Balance	比年初增减额 Changes within the Year
1. 同业存放 Due to Banks and Other Financial Institutions	16.48	5.91	其中：个人中长期消费贷款 Of Which: Medium and Long-term Consumer Credit	1.83	1.29
2. 同业拆借 Placements from Banks and Other Financial Institutions	24.14	-4.76	4. 票据融资 Paper Financing	27.35	19.31
			其中：贴现 Of Which: Discount	27.35	19.31
八、委托存款及委托投资基金(净) Designated Deposits and Designated Investment Funds (Net)	0.22	0.20	5. 各项垫款 Total Advances	0.03	
1. 委托存款及委托投资基金 Designated Deposits and Designated Investment Funds	4.46	2.76	二、有价证券及投资 Securities and Investments	51.93	16.36
2. 减：委托贷款及委托投资 Minus: Designated Loans and Designated Investments	4.24	2.56	三、应收及预付款 Accounts Receivable and Advance Payments	38.08	2.44
			其中：应收利息 Of Which: Interest Receivable	12.82	-2.00
九、代理金融机构委托贷款基金 Designated Loan Funds on Behalf of Financial Institutions	1.04	-0.08	四、买入返售证券 Reverse Repo	2.25	1.54
其中:中央银行委托贷款基金 Of Which: Loan Funds Designated by the Central Bank	0.39	-0.02	五、存放中央银行准备金存款 Reserve Deposits with the Central Bank	147.39	10.93
			六、存放中央银行特种存款 Special Deposits with the Central Bank		-0.19
十、各项准备 Total Provisions	7.30	1.77	七、缴存中央银行财政性存款 Fiscal Deposits with the Central Bank		
其中：贷款呆账准备金 Of Which: Provisions for Bad Loans	7.16	2.23	八、同业往来 Inter-bank Transactions	114.94	17.57
十一、所有者权益 Owner's Equity	-1.39	6.80	1. 存放同业 Due from Banks and Other Financial Institutions	96.65	16.54
其中：实收资本 Of Which: Paid-in Capital	37.88	4.60			
当年结益 Net Earnings	-2.03	-2.03	2. 拆放同业 Placements with Banks and Other Financial Institutions	18.29	1.03
十二、其他 Others	-87.50	14.88	九、代理金融机构贷款 Lending on Behalf of Financial Institutions	1.12	-0.08
			其中：代理人行专项贷款 Of Which: Agency Earmarked Loans of the Central Bank	0.32	-0.02
			十、库存现金 Cash in Vault	12.57	-1.12
			十一、外汇占款 Position for Foreign Exchange Purchase		
资金来源总计 Total Sources	**1032.70**	**109.19**	**资金运用总计 Total Uses**	**1032.70**	**109.19**

城市信用合作社人民币信贷收支表
Sources and Uses of Credit Funds of Urban Credit Cooperatives（RMB）

（2003年末）

（Year - end of 2003）

单位：亿元
Unit：100 Million Yuan

项　目 Items	余　额 Balance	比年初增减额 Changes within the Year	项　目 Items	余　额 Balance	比年初增减额 Changes within the Year
一、各项存款 Total Deposits	1270.59	272.05	一、各项贷款 Total Loans	836.99	183.59
1. 企业存款 Deposits by Enterprises	549.84	123.96	1. 短期贷款 Short - term Loans	678.42	132.56
（1）活期存款 Demand Deposits	423.32	98.64	（1）工业贷款 Loans to Industrial Sector	184.24	33.83
（2）定期存款 Time Deposits	126.52	25.32	（2）商业贷款 Loans to Commercial Sector	133.84	18.20
2. 机关团体存款 Deposits by Government Agencies and Social Organizations	15.16	7.13	其中：收购贷款 Of Which：Loans for the Purchase of Farm Products	0.09	- 0.14
3. 储蓄存款 Savings Deposits	647.58	106.04	（3）建筑业贷款 Loans to Construction Sector	30.50	12.87
（1）活期储蓄 Demand Deposits	162.32	23.92	（4）农业贷款 Loans to Agricultural Sector	1.95	0.36
（2）定期储蓄 Time Deposits	485.26	82.12	（5）乡镇企业贷款 Loans to Village and Township Enterprises	8.34	1.11
4. 农业存款 Deposits by Agricultural Sector	1.81	0.80	（6）三资企业贷款 Loans to Foreign Investment Enterprises and Ventures	1.09	0.02
5. 其他存款 Other Deposits	56.20	34.12	（7）私营企业及个体贷款 Loans to Privately - run Enterprises and Self - employed Entities	127.99	35.32
二、代理财政性存款 Agency Fiscal Deposits	1.29	- 0.23	（8）其他短期贷款 Other Short - term Loans	190.47	30.85
三、金融债券 Financial Bonds		- 0.02	其中：个人短期消费贷款 Of Which：Short - term Consumer Credit	12.55	2.44
其中：政策性金融债券 Of Which：Policy Financial Bonds			2. 中期流动资金贷款 Medium - term Working Capital Loans	10.84	4.89
四、应付及暂收款 Accounts Payable and Receipts on Account	25.22	1.13	3. 中长期贷款 Medium and Long - term Loans	108.86	34.65
其中：应付及预提利息 Of Which：Interest Payable and Accrued	6.86	0.93	（1）基本建设贷款 Capital Construction Loans	16.46	5.31
五、卖出回购证券 Repo	11.11	0.34	（2）技术改造贷款 Technical Improvement Loans	4.83	2.74
六、向中央银行借款 Borrowings from the Central Bank	27.88	8.20	（3）其他中长期贷款 Other Medium and Long - term Loans	87.57	26.60
七、同业往来 Inter - bank Transactions	36.58	- 0.97			

续表
Continued

项　目 Items	余　额 Balance	比年初增减额 Changes within the Year	项　目 Items	余　额 Balance	比年初增减额 Changes within the Year
1. 同业存放 Due to Banks and Other Financial Institutions	14.67	-0.74	其中：个人中长期消费贷款 Of Which: Medium and Long-term Consumer Credit	6.07	4.25
2. 同业拆借 Placements from Banks and Other Financial Institutions	21.91	-0.23	4. 票据融资 Paper Financing	38.84	11.49
			其中：贴现 Of Which: Discount	38.84	11.49
八、委托存款及委托投资基金(净) Designated Deposits and Designated Investment Funds (Net)	0.05	-0.14	5. 各项垫款 Total Advances	0.03	
1. 委托存款及委托投资基金 Designated Deposits and Designated Investment Funds	8.89	4.47	二、有价证券及投资 Securities and Investments	74.41	22.58
			三、应收及预付款 Accounts Receivable and Advance Payments	34.14	-0.77
2. 减：委托贷款及委托投资 Minus: Designated Loans and Designated Investments	8.84	4.61	其中：应收利息 Of Which: Interest Receivable	11.87	-0.51
九、代理金融机构委托贷款基金 Designated Loan Funds on Behalf of Financial Institutions	2.81	1.77	四、买入返售证券 Reverse Repo	3.48	1.23
其中：中央银行委托贷款基金 Of Which: Loan Funds Designated by the Central Bank	0.34	-0.05	五、存放中央银行准备金存款 Reserve Deposits with the Central Bank	186.65	39.37
			六、存放中央银行特种存款 Special Deposits with the Central Bank		
十、各项准备 Total Provisions	8.72	1.67	七、缴存中央银行财政性存款 Fiscal Deposits with the Central Bank		
其中：贷款损失准备 Of Which: Provisions for Loan Losses	7.59	1.28	八、同业往来 Inter-bank Transactions	139.89	25.28
十一、所有者权益 Owner's Equity	3.95	2.12	1. 存放同业 Due from Banks and Other Financial Institutions	119.46	22.88
其中：实收资本 Of Which: Paid-in Capital	38.81	1.65			
当年结益 Net Earnings	0.04	0.04	2. 拆放同业 Placements with Banks and Other Financial Institutions	20.43	2.40
十二、其他 Others	-95.13	-10.38	九、代理金融机构贷款 Lending on Behalf of Financial Institutions	2.95	1.83
			其中：代理人行专项贷款 Of Which: Agency Earmarked Loans of the Central Bank	0.29	-0.03
			十、库存现金 Cash in Vault	14.56	2.43
			十一、外汇占款 Position for Foreign Exchange Purchase		
资金来源总计 Total Sources	**1293.07**	**275.54**	**资金运用总计 Total Uses**	**1293.07**	**275.54**

城市信用合作社人民币信贷收支表

Sources and Uses of Credit Funds of Urban Credit Cooperatives（RMB）

（2004年末）

（Year-end of 2004）

单位：亿元

Unit：100 Million Yuan

项目 Items	余额 Balance	比年初增减额 Changes within the Year	项目 Items	余额 Balance	比年初增减额 Changes within the Year
一、各项存款 Total Deposits	1588.76	330.99	一、各项贷款 Total Loans	1014.54	185.52
1.企业存款 Deposits by Enterprises	691.94	147.93	1.短期贷款 Short-term Loans	782.69	120.75
（1）活期存款 Demand Deposits	521.15	100.42	（1）工业贷款 Loans to Industrial Sector	211.46	33.62
（2）定期存款 Time Deposits	170.79	47.51	（2）商业贷款 Loans to Commercial Sector	147.58	19.60
2.机关团体存款 Deposits by Government Agencies and Social Organizations	32.63	17.49	其中：收购贷款 Of Which：Loans for the Purchase of Farm Products	0.15	0.06
3.储蓄存款 Savings Deposits	791.01	148.90	（3）建筑业贷款 Loans to Construction Sector	38.37	8.41
（1）活期储蓄 Demand Deposits	193.42	32.62	（4）农业贷款 Loans to Agricultural Sector	3.38	1.59
（2）定期储蓄 Time Deposits	597.59	116.28	（5）乡镇企业贷款 Loans to Village and Township Enterprises	7.29	-1.03
4.农业存款 Deposits by Agricultural Sector	1.61	-0.20	（6）三资企业贷款 Loans to Foreign Investment Enterprises and Ventures	1.86	0.70
5.其他存款 Other Deposits	71.57	16.87	（7）私营企业及个体贷款 Loans to Privately-run Enterprises and Self-employed Entities	174.86	24.11
二、代理财政性存款 Agency Fiscal Deposits	5.19	0.20	（8）其他短期贷款 Other Short-term Loans	197.89	33.75
三、金融债券 Financial Bonds			其中：个人短期消费贷款 Of Which：Short-term Consumer Credit	19.47	4.04
其中：政策性金融债券 Of Which：Policy Financial Bonds			2.中期流动资金贷款 Medium-term Working Capital Loans	16.32	5.42
四、应付及暂收款 Accounts Payable and Receipts on Account	25.34	3.32	3.中长期贷款 Medium and Long-term Loans	148.62	44.69
其中：应付及预提利息 Of Which：Interest Payable and Accrued	8.34	2.13	（1）基本建设贷款 Capital Construction Loans	26.20	9.83
五、卖出回购资产 Assets Repo（Including Securities）	19.43	6.64	（2）技术改造贷款 Technical Improvement Loans	6.92	2.09
六、向中央银行借款 Borrowings from the Central Bank	31.12	-7.39	（3）其他中长期贷款 Other Medium and Long-term Loans	115.50	32.77
七、同业往来 Inter-bank Transactions	18.16	-2.29			

续表
Continued

项　目 Items	余　额 Balance	比年初增减额 Changes within the Year	项　目 Items	余　额 Balance	比年初增减额 Changes within the Year
1. 同业存放 Due to Banks and Other Financial Institutions	11.60	2.01	其中：个人中长期消费贷款 Of Which: Medium and Long - term Consumer Credit	11.43	4.14
2. 同业拆借 Placements from Banks and Other Financial Institutions	6.56	-4.30	4. 票据融资 Paper Financing	66.85	14.63
			其中：贴现 Of Which: Discount	66.85	14.63
八、委托存款及委托投资基金(净) Designated Deposits and Designated Investment Funds (Net)	0.09	0.05	5. 各项垫款 Total Advances	0.06	0.03
1. 委托存款及委托投资基金 Designated Deposits and Designated Investment Funds	9.93	1.43	二、有价证券及投资 Securities and Investments	75.33	0.99
2. 减：委托贷款及委托投资 Minus: Designated Loans and Designated Investments	9.84	1.38	三、应收及预付款 Accounts Receivable and Advance Payments	35.39	2.70
			其中：应收利息 Of Which: Interest Receivable	10.66	-0.79
九、代理金融机构委托贷款基金 Designated Loan Funds on Behalf of Financial Institutions	3.90	1.09	四、买入返售资产 Assets Reverse Repo (Including Securities)	24.56	21.04
其中：中央银行委托贷款基金 Of Which: Loan Funds Designated by the Central Bank	0.34		五、存放中央银行准备金存款 Reserve Deposits with the Central Bank	263.96	77.45
十、各项准备 Total Provisions	12.68	4.12	六、存放中央银行特种存款 Special Deposits with the Central Bank		
其中：贷款损失准备 Of Which: Provisions for Loan Losses	11.18	3.67	七、缴存中央银行财政性存款 Fiscal Deposits with the Central Bank	0.17	0.17
十一、所有者权益 Owner's Equity	20.39	12.25	八、同业往来 Inter - bank Transactions	174.11	35.46
其中：实收资本 Of Which: Paid - in Capital	48.53	11.08	1. 存放同业 Due from Banks and Other Financial Institutions	155.95	36.92
当年结益 Net Earnings	3.45	3.45	2. 拆放同业 Placements with Banks and Other Financial Institutions	18.16	-1.46
十二、其他 Others	-115.63	-21.77	九、代理金融机构贷款 Lending on Behalf of Financial Institutions	4.44	1.49
			其中：代理人行专项贷款 Of Which: Agency Earmarked Loans of the Central Bank	0.29	
			十、库存现金 Cash in Vault	16.93	2.39
			十一、外汇占款 Position for Foreign Exchange Purchase		
资金来源总计 Total Sources	**1609.43**	**327.21**	**资金运用总计 Total Uses**	**1609.43**	**327.21**

城市信用合作社人民币信贷收支表

Sources and Uses of Credit Funds of Urban Credit Cooperatives（RMB）

（2005年末）

（Year－end of 2005）

单位：亿元

Unit：100 Million Yuan

项目 Items	余额 Balance	比年初增减额 Changes within the Year	项目 Items	余额 Balance	比年初增减额 Changes within the Year
一、各项存款 Total Deposits	1817.72	271.65	一、各项贷款 Total Loans	1131.14	145.10
1. 企业存款 Deposits by Enterprises	766.26	98.71	1. 短期贷款 Short－term Loans	831.17	72.94
（1）活期存款 Demand Deposits	563.92	52.29	（1）工业贷款 Loans to Industrial Sector	216.04	11.66
（2）定期存款 Time Deposits	202.34	46.42	（2）商业贷款 Loans to Commercial Sector	132.28	－11.96
2. 机关团体存款 Deposits by Government Agencies and Social Organizations	47.02	14.86	其中：收购贷款 Of Which：Loans for the Purchase of Farm Products	0.23	0.07
3. 储蓄存款 Savings Deposits	926.35	146.00	（3）建筑业贷款 Loans to Construction Sector	47.98	10.72
（1）活期储蓄 Demand Deposits	212.75	22.29	（4）农业贷款 Loans to Agricultural Sector	2.56	－0.86
（2）定期储蓄 Time Deposits	713.60	123.71	（5）乡镇企业贷款 Loans to Village and Township Enterprises	8.88	1.52
4. 农业存款 Deposits by Agricultural Sector	2.84	0.87	（6）三资企业贷款 Loans to Foreign Investment Enterprises and Ventures	1.79	－0.07
5. 其他存款 Other Deposits	75.61	11.21			
二、代理财政性存款 Agency Fiscal Deposits	13.20	8.01	（7）私营企业及个体贷款 Loans to Privately－run Enterprises and Self－employed Entities	205.10	34.25
三、金融债券 Financial Bonds			（8）其他短期贷款 Other Short－term Loans	216.54	27.68
其中：政策性金融债券 Of Which：Policy Financial Bonds			其中：个人短期消费贷款 Of Which：Short－term Consumer Credit	17.72	－1.43
四、应付及暂收款 Accounts Payable and Receipts on Account	29.71	5.00	2. 中期流动资金贷款 Medium－term Working Capital Loans	22.86	6.54
其中：应付及预提利息 Of Which：Interest Payable and Accrued	10.79	2.71	3. 中长期贷款 Medium and Long－term Loans	209.65	64.78
五、卖出回购资产 Assets Repo（Including Securities）	31.39	11.96	（1）基本建设贷款 Capital Construction Loans	32.74	7.12
六、向中央银行借款 Borrowings from the Central Bank	16.83	－12.35	（2）技术改造贷款 Technical Improvement Loans	6.93	1.83
七、同业往来 Inter－bank Transactions	17.65	－0.01	（3）其他中长期贷款 Other Medium and Long－term Loans	169.98	55.83

续表
Continued

项　　目 Items	余　额 Balance	比年初增减额 Changes within the Year	项　　目 Items	余　额 Balance	比年初增减额 Changes within the Year
1. 同业存放 Due to Banks and Other Financial Institutions	10.46	-0.76	其中：个人中长期消费贷款 Of Which: Medium and Long-term Consumer Credit	14.96	3.15
2. 同业拆借 Placements from Banks and Other Financial Institutions	7.19	0.75	4. 票据融资 Paper Financing	67.26	0.70
八、委托存款及委托投资基金(净) Designated Deposits and Designated Investment Funds (Net)	0.37	0.29	其中：贴现 Of Which: Discount	67.26	0.70
			5. 各项垫款 Total Advances	0.20	0.14
1. 委托存款及委托投资基金 Designated Deposits and Designated Investment Funds	9.59	-0.33	二、有价证券及投资 Securities and Investments	108.61	35.32
			三、应收及预付款 Accounts Receivable and Advance Payments	26.59	-8.07
2. 减：委托贷款及委托投资 Minus: Designated Loans and Designated Investments	9.22	-0.62	其中：应收利息 Of Which: Interest Receivable	8.80	-1.66
九、代理金融机构委托贷款基金 Designated Loan Funds on Behalf of Financial Institutions	3.64	-0.26	四、买入返售资产 Assets Reverse Repo (Including Securities)	28.87	6.34
其中：中央银行委托贷款基金 Of Which: Loan Funds Designated by the Central Bank	0.29	-0.05	五、存放中央银行准备金存款 Reserve Deposits with the Central Bank	311.34	50.76
			六、存放中央银行特种存款 Special Deposits with the Central Bank		
十、各项准备 Total Provisions	17.87	6.05	七、缴存中央银行财政性存款 Fiscal Deposits with the Central Bank	0.17	-0.24
其中：贷款损失准备 Of Which: Provisions for Loan Losses	16.12	5.45	八、同业往来 Inter-bank Transactions	244.66	79.39
十一、所有者权益 Owner's Equity	31.64	13.90	1. 存放同业 Due from Banks and Other Financial Institutions	233.78	86.41
其中：实收资本 Of Which: Paid-in Capital	52.37	7.08			
当年结益 Net Earnings	9.18	9.18	2. 拆放同业 Placements with Banks and Other Financial Institutions	10.88	-7.02
十二、其他 Others	-105.76	6.15	九、代理金融机构贷款 Lending on Behalf of Financial Institutions	3.79	-0.65
			其中：代理人行专项贷款 Of Which: Agency Earmarked Loans of the Central Bank	0.24	-0.05
			十、库存现金 Cash in Vault	19.09	2.44
			十一、外汇占款 Position for Foreign Exchange Purchase		
资金来源总计 Total Sources	**1874.26**	**310.39**	**资金运用总计 Total Uses**	**1874.26**	**310.39**

10. 农村信用合作社人民币信贷收支表（1953—2005 年）
Sources and Uses of Credit Funds of Rural Credit Cooperatives（RMB）（1953—2005）

农村信用合作社人民币存贷款表
Deposits and Loans of Rural Credit Cooperatives（RMB）

（1953—1960 年）

（Year - end of 1953—1960）

年末余额

Year - end Balance

单位：亿元

Unit：100 Million Yuan

项目 Items	1953	1954	1955	1956	1957	1958	1959	1960
存款合计 Total Deposits	0.10	1.60	6.10	10.80	20.70	40.30	45.00	43.10
集体农业存款 Deposits by Agricultural Collectives			3.10	6.50	13.40	20.20	24.00	27.90
乡镇企业存款 Deposits by Village and Township Enterprises								
农户储蓄存款 Savings Deposits by Rural Households	0.10	1.60	3.00	4.30	7.30	20.10	21.00	15.20
其他存款 Other Deposits								
贷款合计 Total Loans	0.20	1.20	3.00	10.20	9.50	24.70	22.90	22.30
集体农业贷款 Loans to Agricultural Collectives	0.20	1.20	3.00	4.10	4.20	13.60	16.00	12.70
乡镇企业贷款 Loans to Village and Township Enterprises								
农户贷款 Loans to Rural Households				6.10	5.30	11.10	6.90	9.60

比年初增减额

Changes within the Year

单位：亿元

Unit：100 Million Yuan

项目 Items	1953	1954	1955	1956	1957	1958	1959	1960
存款合计 Total Deposits	—	1.50	4.50	4.70	9.90	19.60	4.70	-1.90
集体农业存款 Deposits by Agricultural Collectives	—		3.10	3.40	6.90	6.80	3.80	3.90
乡镇企业存款 Deposits by Village and Township Enterprises	—							
农户储蓄存款 Savings Deposits by Rural Households	—	1.50	1.40	1.30	3.00	12.80	0.90	-5.80
其他存款 Other Deposits	—							
贷款合计 Total Loans	—	1.00	1.80	7.20	-0.70	15.20	-1.80	-0.60
集体农业贷款 Loans to Agricultural Collectives	—	1.00	1.80	1.10	0.10	9.40	2.40	-3.30
乡镇企业贷款 Loans to Village and Township Enterprises	—							
农户贷款 Loans to Rural Households	—			6.10	-0.80	5.80	-4.20	2.70

农村信用合作社人民币存贷款表
Deposits and Loans of Rural Credit Cooperatives (RMB)
(1961—1968年)
(Year - end of 1961—1968)

年末余额
Year - end Balance

单位：亿元
Unit: 100 Million Yuan

项目 Items	1961	1962	1963	1964	1965	1966	1967	1968
存款合计 Total Deposits	47.10	28.20	31.40	42.80	48.00	60.90	73.20	75.70
集体农业存款 Deposits by Agricultural Collectives	30.90	18.40	21.30	32.10	35.10	46.30	59.20	59.70
乡镇企业存款 Deposits by Village and Township Enterprises								
农户储蓄存款 Savings Deposits by Rural Households	16.20	9.80	10.10	10.70	12.90	14.60	14.00	16.00
其他存款 Other Deposits								
贷款合计 Total Loans	17.60	15.60	13.80	14.10	13.50	15.20	14.60	16.50
集体农业贷款 Loans to Agricultural Collectives	9.50	7.90	5.60	4.20	3.10	3.80	3.60	4.00
乡镇企业贷款 Loans to Village and Township Enterprises								
农户贷款 Loans to Rural Households	8.10	7.70	8.20	9.90	10.40	11.40	11.00	12.50

比年初增减额
Changes within the Year

单位：亿元
Unit: 100 Million Yuan

项目 Items	1961	1962	1963	1964	1965	1966	1967	1968
存款合计 Total Deposits	4.00	-18.90	3.20	11.40	5.20	12.90	12.30	2.50
集体农业存款 Deposits by Agricultural Collectives	3.00	-12.50	2.90	10.80	3.00	11.20	12.90	0.50
乡镇企业存款 Deposits by Village and Township Enterprises								
农户储蓄存款 Savings Deposits by Rural Households	1.00	-6.40	0.30	0.60	2.20	1.70	-0.60	2.00
其他存款 Other Deposits								
贷款合计 Total Loans	-4.70	-2.00	-1.80	0.30	-0.60	1.70	-0.60	1.90
集体农业贷款 Loans to Agricultural Collectives	-3.20	-1.60	-2.30	-1.40	-1.10	0.70	-0.20	0.40
乡镇企业贷款 Loans to Village and Township Enterprises								
农户贷款 Loans to Rural Households	-1.50	-0.40	0.50	1.70	0.50	1.00	-0.40	1.50

农村信用合作社人民币存贷款表

Deposits and Loans of Rural Credit Cooperatives（RMB）

（1969—1976 年）

（Year - end of 1969—1976）

年末余额

Year - end Balance

单位：亿元

Unit：100 Million Yuan

项目 Items	1969	1970	1971	1972	1973	1974	1975	1976
存款合计 Total Deposits	73.30	76.40	90.30	90.90	104.80	121.20	135.10	141.20
集体农业存款 Deposits by Agricultural Collectives	58.40	61.40	64.20	61.50	67.30	78.10	85.10	89.40
乡镇企业存款 Deposits by Village and Township Enterprises								
农户储蓄存款 Savings Deposits by Rural Households	14.90	15.00	17.00	20.10	27.10	30.60	35.10	36.90
其他存款 Other Deposits			9.10	9.30	10.40	12.50	14.90	14.90
贷款合计 Total Loans	17.80	18.80	19.40	21.12	0.80	22.00	26.70	35.80
集体农业贷款 Loans to Agricultural Collectives	4.50	5.60	6.00	7.90	7.80	10.70	15.40	17.1
乡镇企业贷款 Loans to Village and Township Enterprises			0.80	1.20	1.50			7.00
农户贷款 Loans to Rural Households	13.30	13.20	12.60	12.00	11.50	11.30	11.30	11.70

比年初增减额

Changes within the Year

单位：亿元

Unit：100 Million Yuan

项目 Items	1969	1970	1971	1972	1973	1974	1975	1976
存款合计 Total Deposits	- 2.40	3.10	13.90	0.60	13.90	16.40	13.90	6.10
集体农业存款 Deposits by Agricultural Collectives	- 1.30	3.00	2.80	- 2.70	5.80	10.80	7.00	4.30
乡镇企业存款 Deposits by Village and Township Enterprises								
农户储蓄存款 Savings Deposits by Rural Households	- 1.10	0.10	2.00	3.10	7.00	3.50	4.50	1.80
其他存款 Other Deposits			9.10	0.20	1.10	2.10	2.40	
贷款合计 Total Loans	1.30	1.00	0.60	1.70	- 0.30	1.20	4.70	9.10
集体农业贷款 Loans to Agricultural Collectives	0.50	1.10	0.40	1.90	- 0.10	2.90	4.70	1.70
乡镇企业贷款 Loans to Village and Township Enterprises			0.80	0.40	0.30	- 1.50		7.00
农户贷款 Loans to Rural Households	0.80	- 0.10	- 0.60	- 0.60	- 0.50	- 0.20		0.40

农村信用合作社人民币存贷款表

Deposits and Loans of Rural Credit Cooperatives (RMB)

(1977—1981 年)

(Year - end of 1977—1981)

年末余额 单位：亿元

Year - end Balance Unit: 100 Million Yuan

项目 Items	1977	1978	1979	1980	1981
存款合计 Total Deposits	151.30	166.00	215.90	272.30	319.60
集体农业存款 Deposits by Agricultural Collectives	89.30	93.80	98.30	105.50	113.20
乡镇企业存款 Deposits by Village and Township Enterprises			21.90	29.50	29.70
农户储蓄存款 Savings Deposits by Rural Households	46.50	55.70	78.40	117.00	169.60
其他存款 Other Deposits	15.50	16.50	17.30	20.30	7.10
贷款合计 Total Loans	39.70	45.10	47.50	81.60	96.40
集体农业贷款 Loans to Agricultural Collectives	18.40	21.80	22.40	34.50	35.70
乡镇企业贷款 Loans to Village and Township Enterprises	9.90	12.10	14.20	31.10	35.50
农户贷款 Loans to Rural Households	11.40	11.20	10.90	16.00	25.20

比年初增减额 单位：亿元

Changes within the Year Unit: 100 Million Yuan

项目 Items	1977	1978	1979	1980	1981
存款合计 Total Deposits	10.10	14.70	49.90	56.40	47.30
集体农业存款 Deposits by Agricultural Collectives	- 0.10	4.50	4.50	7.20	7.70
乡镇企业存款 Deposits by Village and Township Enterprises			21.90	7.60	0.20
农户储蓄存款 Savings Deposits by Rural Households	9.60	9.20	22.70	38.60	52.60
其他存款 Other Deposits	0.60	1.00	0.80	3.00	- 13.20
贷款合计 Total Loans	3.90	5.40	2.40	34.10	14.80
集体农业贷款 Loans to Agricultural Collectives	1.30	3.40	0.60	12.10	1.20
乡镇企业贷款 Loans to Village and Township Enterprises	2.90	2.20	2.10	16.90	4.40
农户贷款 Loans to Rural Households	- 0.30	- 0.20	- 0.30	5.10	9.20

农村信用合作社人民币信贷收支表
Sources and Uses of Credit Funds of Rural Credit Cooperatives（RMB）

（1982 年末）

（Year－end of 1982）

单位：亿元

Unit：100 Million Yuan

项目 Items	余额 Balance	比年初增减额 Changes within the Year	项目 Items	余额 Balance	比年初增减额 Changes within the Year
一、社队集体存款 Deposits by Collectives of Communities	121.06	7.90	一、生产费用贷款 Operating Costs Loans	27.94	—
二、社队企业存款 Deposits by Enterprises of Communities	33.66	4.00	二、生产设备贷款 Equipment Loans	6.82	—
三、社队储蓄存款 Savings Deposits of Communities	228.11	58.51	三、社队企业贷款 Loans to Enterprises of Communities	42.30	6.80
其中：定期 Of Which：Time Deposits	154.08	—	其中：生产费用贷款 Of Which：Operating Costs Loans	32.78	—
活期 Demand Deposits	74.03	—	生产设备贷款 Equipment Loans	9.52	—
四、其他存款 Other Deposits	7.05	—	四、社员贷款 Loans to Associators	44.09	18.90
存款合计 Total Deposits	**389.88**	**70.28**	**贷款合计 Total Loans**	**121.15**	**24.75**
五、自有资金 Own Capital	19.22	—	五、其他占款 Position for Other Funds	53.73	—
六、其他资金收入 Other Capital Revenue	50.02	—	六、转存银行款 Redeposits with Banks	299.58	—
七、当年结益 Net Earnings	4.45	4.45			
八、借入银行款 Borrowings from Banks	10.89	—			
资金来源总计 Total Sources	**474.46**	—	**资金运用总计 Total Uses**	**474.46**	—

农村信用合作社人民币信贷收支表
Sources and Uses of Credit Funds of Rural Credit Cooperatives (RMB)

(1983年末)

(Year-end of 1983)

单位：亿元

Unit: 100 Million Yuan

项目 Items	余额 Balance	比年初增减额 Changes within the Year	项目 Items	余额 Balance	比年初增减额 Changes within the Year
一、社队集体存款 Deposits by Collectives of Communities	113.41	-7.65	一、生产费用贷款 Operating Costs Loans	24.55	-3.39
二、社队企业存款 Deposits by Enterprises of Communities	45.53	11.87	二、生产设备贷款 Equipment Loans	4.25	-2.57
三、社队储蓄存款 Savings Deposits of Communities	320.33	92.22	三、社队企业贷款 Loans to Enterprises of Communities	60.39	18.09
其中：定期 Of Which: Time Deposits	218.46	64.38	其中：生产费用贷款 Of Which: Operating Costs Loans	49.60	16.82
活期 Demand Deposits	101.87	27.84	生产设备贷款 Equipment Loans	10.79	1.27
四、其他存款 Other Deposits	8.28	1.23	四、社员贷款 Loans to Associators	74.45	30.36
存款合计 Total Deposits	**487.55**	**97.67**	**贷款合计 Total Loans**	**163.64**	**42.49**
五、自有资金 Own Capital	23.04	3.82	五、其他占款 Position for Other Funds	73.45	19.72
六、其他资金收入 Other Capital Revenue	71.67	17.20	六、转存银行款 Redeposits with Banks	367.02	67.44
七、当年结益 Net Earnings	5.42	5.42			
八、借入银行款 Borrowings from Banks	16.43	5.54			
资金来源总计 Total Sources	**604.11**	**129.65**	**资金运用总计 Total Uses**	**604.11**	**129.65**

农村信用合作社人民币信贷收支表

Sources and Uses of Credit Funds of Rural Credit Cooperatives（RMB）

（1984 年末）

（Year - end of 1984）

单位：亿元

Unit：100 Million Yuan

项目 Items	余额 Balance	比年初增减额 Changes within the Year	项目 Items	余额 Balance	比年初增减额 Changes within the Year
一、存款合计 Total Deposits	624.99	137.44	一、贷款合计 Total Loans	354.52	190.88
1. 集体存款 Deposits by Collectives	186.87	—	1. 集体农业贷款 Loans to Agricultural Collectives	38.41	—
（1）集体农业存款 Deposits by Agricultural Collectives	90.00	—	（1）种养业贷款 Farming and Breeding Loans	25.40	—
（2）社队企业存款 Deposits by Enterprises of Communities	81.11	—	（2）其他行业贷款 Loans to Other Industries	13.01	—
			2. 社队企业贷款 Loans to Enterprises of Communities	135.02	—
（3）集体定期存款 Time Deposits by Collectives	2.65	—			
（4）其他存款 Other Deposits	13.11	—	其中：工业贷款 Of Which：Loans to Industrial Sector	83.73	—
2. 社员储蓄存款 Savings Deposits by Associators	438.12	117.79	生产设备贷款 Equipment Loans	25.53	—
（1）定期 Time Deposits	285.49	67.03	3. 承包户贷款 Loans to Rural Contractors	181.09	—
（2）活期 Demand Deposits	152.63	50.76	其中：种养业贷款 Of Which：Farming and Breeding Loans	119.74	—
二、自有资金 Own Capital	27.87	4.83	生活贷款 Living Loans	30.81	—
三、其他资金收入 Other Capital Revenue	122.44	45.35	沼气贷款 Firedamp Loans	0.10	—
四、借入银行款 Borrowings from Banks	31.18	14.75	二、其他资金占款 Position for Other Funds	131.41	57.96
五、结益 Net Earnings	6.64	6.64	三、转存银行款 Redeposits with Banks	327.19	-39.83
资金来源总计 Total Sources	**813.12**	**209.01**	**资金运用总计 Total Uses**	**813.12**	**209.01**

农村信用合作社人民币信贷收支表
Sources and Uses of Credit Funds of Rural Credit Cooperatives (RMB)

（1985年末）

(Year－end of 1985)

单位：亿元

Unit: 100 Million Yuan

项　目 Items	余　额 Balance	比年初增减额 Changes within the Year	项　目 Items	余　额 Balance	比年初增减额 Changes within the Year
一、存款合计 Total Deposits	724.90	99.91	一、贷款合计 Total Loans	399.95	45.43
1. 集体存款 Deposits by Collectives	160.09	－26.78	1. 集体农业贷款 Loans to Agricultural Collectives	41.39	2.98
(1) 集体农业存款 Deposits by Agricultural Collectives	71.92	－18.08	(1) 种养业贷款 Farming and Breeding Loans	24.95	－0.45
(2) 乡镇企业存款 Deposits by Village and Township Enterprises	72.13	－8.98	(2) 其他行业贷款 Loans to Other Industries	16.44	3.43
			2. 乡镇企业贷款 Loans to Village and Township Enterprises	164.79	29.77
(3) 集体定期存款 Time Deposits by Collectives	2.27	－0.38			
(4) 其他存款 Other Deposits	13.77	0.66	其中：工业贷款 Of Which: Loans to Industrial Sector	104.36	20.63
2. 农户储蓄存款 Savings Deposits by Rural Households	564.81	126.69	生产设备贷款 Equipment Loans	29.65	4.12
(1) 定期 Time Deposits	383.96	98.47	3. 农户贷款 Loans to Rural Households	193.77	12.68
(2) 活期 Demand Deposits	180.85	28.22	其中：种养业贷款 Of Which: Farming and Breeding Loans	127.56	7.82
二、自有资金 Own Capital	31.53	3.66			
三、其他资金收入 Other Capital Revenue	153.98	24.90	生活贷款 Living Loans	30.22	－0.59
四、借入银行款 Borrowings from Banks	32.85	1.67	沼气贷款 Firedamp Loans	0.08	－0.02
五、结益 Net Earnings	12.45	12.45	二、其他资金占款 Position for Other Funds	154.39	22.98
			三、转存银行款 Redeposits with Banks	401.37	74.18
资金来源总计 Total Sources	**955.71**	**142.59**	**资金运用总计 Total Uses**	**955.71**	**142.59**

农村信用合作社人民币信贷收支表

Sources and Uses of Credit Funds of Rural Credit Cooperatives（RMB）

（1986 年末）

（Year – end of 1986）

单位：亿元

Unit：100 Million Yuan

项目 Items	余额 Balance	比年初增减额 Changes within the Year	项目 Items	余额 Balance	比年初增减额 Changes within the Year
一、存款合计 Total Deposits	962.25	237.35	一、贷款合计 Total Loans	568.33	168.38
1. 集体存款 Deposits by Collectives	196.11	36.02	1. 集体农业贷款 Loans to Agricultural Collectives	44.68	3.29
（1）集体农业存款 Deposits by Agricultural Collectives	82.67	10.75	（1）种养业贷款 Farming and Breeding Loans	28.38	3.43
（2）乡镇企业存款 Deposits by Village and Township Enterprises	92.54	20.41	（2）其他行业贷款 Loans to Other Industries	16.30	－0.14
（3）集体定期存款 Time Deposits by Collectives	2.73	0.46	2. 乡镇企业贷款 Loans to Village and Township Enterprises	265.31	100.52
（4）其他存款 Other Deposits	18.17	4.40	其中：工业贷款 Of Which：Loans to Industrial Sector	173.43	69.07
2. 农户储蓄存款 Savings Deposits by Rural Households	766.14	201.33	生产设备 Equipment Loans	46.89	17.24
（1）定期 Time Deposits	547.42	163.46	3. 农户贷款 Loans to Rural Households	258.34	64.57
（2）活期 Demand Deposits	218.72	37.87	其中：种养业贷款 Of Which：Farming and Breeding Loans	171.08	43.52
二、自有资金 Own Capital	44.34	12.81			
三、其他资金收入 Other Capital Revenue	215.60	49.17	生活贷款 Living Loans	36.12	5.90
四、借入银行款 Borrowings from Banks	41.21	8.36	沼气贷款 Firedamp Loans	0.08	
五、结益 Net Earnings	15.46	15.46	二、其他资金占款 Position for Other Funds	216.26	61.87
			三、转存银行款 Redeposits with Banks	494.27	92.90
资金来源总计 Total Sources	**1278.86**	**323.15**	**资金运用总计 Total Uses**	**1278.86**	**323.15**

农村信用合作社人民币信贷收支表

Sources and Uses of Credit Funds of Rural Credit Cooperatives (RMB)

(1987年末)

(Year - end of 1987)

单位：亿元

Unit: 100 Million Yuan

项目 Items	余额 Balance	比年初增减额 Changes within the Year	项目 Items	余额 Balance	比年初增减额 Changes within the Year
一、存款合计 Total Deposits	1229.16	266.91	一、贷款合计 Total Loans	774.24	205.91
1.集体存款 Deposits by Collectives	221.26	25.15	1.集体农业贷款 Loans to Agricultural Collectives	64.94	20.26
(1) 集体农业存款 Deposits by Agricultural Collectives	89.32	6.65	(1) 种养业贷款 Farming and Breeding Loans	36.78	8.40
(2) 乡镇企业存款 Deposits by Village and Township Enterprises	106.63	14.09	(2) 其他行业贷款 Loans to Other Industries	28.16	11.86
			2.乡镇企业贷款 Loans to Village and Township Enterprises	369.08	103.77
(3) 集体定期存款 Time Deposits by Collectives	3.46	0.73			
(4) 其他存款 Other Deposits	21.85	3.68	其中：工业贷款 Of Which: Loans to Industrial Sector	235.05	61.62
2.农户储蓄存款 Savings Deposits by Rural Households	1007.90	241.76	生产设备贷款 Equipment Loans	72.48	25.59
(1) 定期 Time Deposits	709.92	162.50			
			3.农户贷款 Loans to Rural Households	340.22	81.88
(2) 活期 Demand Deposits	297.98	79.26			
			其中：种养业贷款 Of Which: Farming and Breeding Loans	220.29	49.21
二、自有资金 Own Capital	98.86	54.52			
三、其他资金收入 Other Capital Revenue		—	生活贷款 Living Loans	43.85	7.73
四、借入银行款 Borrowings from Banks	37.70	-3.51	工商业贷款 Industrial and Commercial Loans	35.33	—
五、其他 Others	246.03	—			
			二、缴存银行准备金 Reserves with the Central Bank	262.40	—
六、结益 Net Earnings	13.55	13.55			
			三、其他资金占款 Position for Other Funds		—
			四、转存银行款 Redeposits with Banks	328.93	-165.34
			五、其他 Others	259.73	—
资金来源总计 Total Sources	**1625.30**	**346.44**	**资金运用总计 Total Uses**	**1625.30**	**346.44**

农村信用合作社人民币信贷收支表

Sources and Uses of Credit Funds of Rural Credit Cooperatives（RMB）

（1988年末）

（Year - end of 1988）

单位：亿元

Unit：100 Million Yuan

项　目 Items	余　额 Balance	比年初增减额 Changes within the Year	项　目 Items	余　额 Balance	比年初增减额 Changes within the Year
一、存款合计 Total Deposits	1397.66	168.50	一、贷款合计 Total Loans	910.24	136.00
1. 集体存款 Deposits by Collectives	258.42	37.16	1. 集体农业贷款 Loans to Agricultural Collectives	79.17	14.23
（1）集体农业存款 Deposits by Agricultural Collectives	98.90	9.58	（1）种养业贷款 Farming and Breeding Loans	43.91	7.13
（2）乡镇企业存款 Deposits by Village and Township Enterprises	127.76	21.13	（2）其他行业贷款 Loans to Other Industries	35.26	7.10
			2. 乡镇企业贷款 Loans to Village and Township Enterprises	443.79	74.71
（3）集体定期存款 Time Deposits by Collectives	5.60	2.14			
（4）其他存款 Other Deposits	26.16	4.31	（1）流动资金贷款 Working Capital Loans	352.62	—
2. 农户储蓄存款 Savings Deposits by Rural Households	1139.24	131.34	（2）固定资金贷款 Fixed Fund Loans	91.17	—
（1）定期 Time Deposits	788.30	78.38	（3）其他工商业贷款 Other Industrial and Commercial Loans		—
（2）活期 Demand Deposits	350.94	52.96			
			3. 农户贷款 Loans to Rural Households	371.65	31.43
二、自有资金 Own Capital	131.31	32.45	其中：种养业贷款 Of Which：Farming and Breeding Loans	234.84	14.55
三、其他资金收入 Other Capital Revenue	191.04	191.04			
四、借入银行款 Borrowings from Banks	35.60	-2.10	生活贷款 Living Loans	44.85	1.00
五、其他 Others	168.26	-91.32	工商业贷款 Industrial and Commercial Loans	75.98	40.65
六、结益 Net Earnings	12.46	12.46			
			4. 其他工商业贷款 Loans to Other Industrial and Commercial Sectors	15.63	—
			二、缴存银行准备金 Reserves with the Central Bank	275.97	13.57
			三、转存银行款 Redeposits with Banks	301.46	-27.47
			四、在银行特种存款 Special Deposits with Banks	50.34	—
			五、其他 Others	398.32	—
资金来源总计 Total Sources	**1936.33**	**311.03**	**资金运用总计 Total Uses**	**1936.33**	**311.03**

农村信用合作社人民币信贷收支表

Sources and Uses of Credit Funds of Rural Credit Cooperatives (RMB)

(1989 年末)

(Year - end of 1989)

单位：亿元

Unit: 100 Million Yuan

项目 Items	余额 Balance	比年初增减额 Changes within the Year	项目 Items	余额 Balance	比年初增减额 Changes within the Year
一、存款合计 Total Deposits	1658.99	261.33	一、贷款合计 Total Loans	1088.27	178.03
1. 集体存款 Deposits by Collectives	254.89	- 3.53	1. 集体农业贷款 Loans to Agricultural Collectives	106.37	27.20
(1) 集体农业存款 Deposits by Agricultural Collectives	91.95	- 6.95	(1) 种养业贷款 Farming and Breeding Loans	57.32	13.41
(2) 乡镇企业存款 Deposits by Village and Township Enterprises	125.39	- 2.37	(2) 其他行业贷款 Loans to Other Industries	49.05	13.79
			2. 乡镇企业贷款 Loans to Village and Township Enterprises	539.87	96.08
(3) 集体定期存款 Time Deposits by Collectives	7.93	2.33			
(4) 其他存款 Other Deposits	29.62	3.46	(1) 流动资金贷款 Working Capital Loans	456.25	103.63
2. 农户储蓄存款 Savings Deposits by Rural Households	1404.10	264.86	(2) 固定资金贷款 Fixed Fund Loans	83.62	- 7.55
(1) 定期 Time Deposits	1076.73	288.43	(3) 其他工商业贷款 Other Industrial and Commercial Loans		
(2) 活期 Demand Deposits	327.37	- 23.57			
			3. 农户贷款 Loans to Rural Households	412.51	40.86
二、自有资金 Own Capital	228.20	96.89			
			其中：种养业贷款 Of Which: Farming and Breeding Loans	259.93	25.09
三、其他资金收入 Other Capital Revenue	244.72	53.68			
四、借入银行款 Borrowings from Banks	37.58	1.98	生活贷款 Living Loans	44.93	0.08
五、其他 Others	229.04	48.32	工商业贷款 Industrial and Commercial Loans	48.13	- 27.85
六、结益 Net Earnings	- 11.72	- 11.72			
			4. 其他工商业贷款 Loans to Other Industrial and Commercial Sectors	29.52	13.89
			二、其他资金占用 Position for Other Funds	356.54	—
			三、转存银行款 Redeposits with Banks	651.61	350.15
			四、其他 Others	290.39	—
资金来源总计 Total Sources	**2386.81**	**450.48**	**资金运用总计 Total Uses**	**2386.81**	**450.48**

农村信用合作社人民币信贷收支表

Sources and Uses of Credit Funds of Rural Credit Cooperatives（RMB）

（1990 年末）

（Year - end of 1990）

单位：亿元

Unit：100 Million Yuan

项目 Items	余额 Balance	比年初增减额 Changes within the Year	项目 Items	余额 Balance	比年初增减额 Changes within the Year
一、存款合计 Total Deposits	2144.40	485.41	一、贷款合计 Total Loans	1410.78	322.51
1. 集体存款 Deposits by Collectives	303.40	48.51	1. 集体农业贷款 Loans to Agricultural Collectives	134.05	27.68
（1）集体农业存款 Deposits by Agricultural Collectives	106.57	14.62	（1）种养业贷款 Farming and Breeding Loans	70.73	13.41
（2）乡镇企业存款 Deposits by Village and Township Enterprises	149.85	24.46	（2）其他行业贷款 Loans to Other Industries	63.32	14.27
			2. 乡镇企业贷款 Loans to Village and Township Enterprises	700.35	160.48
（3）集体定期存款 Time Deposits by Collectives	12.48	4.55			
（4）其他存款 Other Deposits	34.50	4.88	（1）流动资金贷款 Working Capital Loans	607.96	151.71
2. 农户储蓄存款 Savings Deposits by Rural Households	1841.00	436.90	（2）固定资金贷款 Fixed Fund Loans	92.39	8.77
（1）定期 Time Deposits	1453.82	377.09	3. 农户贷款 Loans to Rural Households	517.69	105.18
（2）活期 Demand Deposits	387.18	9.81	其中：种养业贷款 Of Which：Farming and Breeding Loans	323.42	63.49
二、自有资金 Own Capital	82.43	-145.77			
			生活贷款 Living Loans	52.60	7.67
三、其他资金收入 Other Capital Revenue	97.20	-147.52	工商业贷款 Industrial and Commercial Loans	63.13	15.00
四、借入银行款 Borrowings from Banks	41.91	4.33			
五、其他 Others	659.03	441.71	4. 其他工商业贷款 Loans to Other Industrial and Commercial Sectors	58.69	29.17
六、结益 Net Earnings	-1.62	-1.62			
			二、其他资金占用 Position for Other Funds	119.81	-236.73
			三、转存银行款 Redeposits with Banks	773.58	121.97
			四、其他 Others	719.18	428.79
资金来源总计 Total Sources	**3023.35**	**636.54**	**资金运用总计 Total Uses**	**3023.35**	**636.54**

农村信用合作社人民币信贷收支表
Sources and Uses of Credit Funds of Rural Credit Cooperatives (RMB)

(1991 年末)

(Year - end of 1991)

单位：亿元

Unit: 100 Million Yuan

项目 Items	余额 Balance	比年初增减额 Changes within the Year	项目 Items	余额 Balance	比年初增减额 Changes within the Year
一、存款合计 Total Deposits	2709.33	564.93	一、贷款合计 Total Loans	1808.69	397.91
1. 集体存款 Deposits by Collectives	389.97	86.57	1. 集体农业贷款 Loans to Agricultural Collectives	168.07	34.02
(1) 集体农业存款 Deposits by Agricultural Collectives	135.71	29.14	(1) 种养业贷款 Farming and Breeding Loans	88.33	17.60
(2) 乡镇企业存款 Deposits by Village and Township Enterprises	191.75	41.90	(2) 其他行业贷款 Loans to Other Industries	79.74	16.42
			(3) 科技兴农贷款 Loans for Agriculture Development by Science Technology		—
(3) 集体定期存款 Time Deposits by Collectives	17.72	5.24			
(4) 其他存款 Other Deposits	44.79	10.29	2. 乡镇企业贷款 Loans to Village and Township Enterprises	912.71	212.36
2. 农户储蓄存款 Savings Deposits by Rural Households	2319.36	478.36	(1) 流动资金贷款 Working Capital Loans	791.60	183.64
(1) 定期存款 Time Deposits	1826.33	372.51	(2) 固定资产货款 Fixed Asset Loans	121.11	28.72
(2) 活期存款 Demand Deposits	493.03	105.85	3. 农户贷款 Loans to Rural Households	632.36	114.67
二、自有资金 Own Capital	109.20	26.77	其中：种养业贷款 Of Which: Farming and Breeding Loans	392.01	68.59
三、其他资金收入 Other Capital Revenue	119.67	22.47	生活贷款 Living Loans	59.87	7.27
四、借入银行款 Borrowings from Banks	50.70	8.79	工商业贷款 Industrial and Commercial Loans	78.34	15.21
五、其他 Others	803.29	145.88	4. 其他工商业贷款 Loans to Other Industrial and Commercial Sectors	95.55	36.86
六、结益 Net Earnings	8.36	8.36	二、其他资金占用 Position for Other Funds	158.55	38.74
			三、转存银行款 Redeposits with Banks	916.06	142.48
			四、其他 Others	917.25	198.07
资金来源总计 Total Sources	**3800.55**	**777.20**	**资金运用总计 Total Uses**	**3800.55**	**777.20**

农村信用合作社人民币信贷收支表

Sources and Uses of Credit Funds of Rural Credit Cooperatives（RMB）

（1992 年末）

（Year - end of 1992）

单位：亿元

Unit：100 Million Yuan

项目 Items	余额 Balance	比年初增减额 Changes within the Year	项目 Items	余额 Balance	比年初增减额 Changes within the Year
一、存款合计 Total Deposits	3478.46	769.13	一、贷款合计 Total Loans	2452.80	644.11
1. 集体存款 Deposits by Collectives	309.20	—	1. 集体农业贷款 Loans to Agricultural Collectives	222.34	54.27
（1）集体农业存款 Deposits by Agricultural Collectives	215.51	79.80	（1）种养业贷款 Farming and Breeding Loans	111.81	23.48
（2）集体定期存款 Time Deposits by Collectives	31.03	13.31	（2）其他行业贷款 Loans to Other Industries	104.49	24.75
（3）其他存款 Other Deposits	62.66	—	（3）科技兴农贷款 Loans for Agriculture Development by Science Technology	6.04	6.04
2. 乡镇企业存款 Deposits by Village and Township Enterprises	301.85	—	2. 乡镇企业贷款 Loans to Village and Township Enterprises	1294.69	381.98
3. 农户储蓄存款 Savings Deposits by Rural Households	2867.41	548.05	（1）流动资金贷款 Working Capital Loans	1100.53	308.93
（1）定期存款 Time Deposits	2273.89	447.56	（2）固定资产贷款 Fixed Asset Loans	194.16	73.05
（2）活期存款 Demand Deposits	593.52	100.49	3. 农户贷款 Loans to Rural Households	757.58	125.22
二、自有资金 Own Capital	357.71	248.51	其中：种养业贷款 Of Which：Farming and Breeding Loans	459.55	67.54
三、其他资金收入 Other Capital Revenue	697.67	578.00	生活贷款 Living Loans	68.07	8.20
四、借入银行款 Borrowings from Banks	59.55	8.85	工商业贷款 Industrial and Commercial Loans	95.87	17.53
五、其他 Others	280.37	-531.28	4. 其他工商业贷款 Loans to Other Industrial and Commercial Sectors	178.19	82.64
六、结益 Net Earnings	10.30	10.30	二、其他资金占用 Position for Other Funds	1007.53	848.98
			三、转存银行款 Redeposits with Banks	1078.69	162.63
			四、其他 Others	345.04	-572.21
资金来源总计 Total Sources	**4884.06**	**1083.51**	**资金运用总计 Total Uses**	**4884.06**	**1083.51**

农村信用合作社人民币信贷收支表

Sources and Uses of Credit Funds of Rural Credit Cooperatives (RMB)

(1993年末)

(Year - end of 1993)

单位：亿元

Unit: 100 Million Yuan

项目 Items	余额 Balance	比年初增减额 Changes within the Year	项目 Items	余额 Balance	比年初增减额 Changes within the Year
一、存款合计 Total Deposits	4297.26	819.60	一、贷款合计 Total Loans	3143.86	689.94
1. 集体存款 Deposits by Collectives	358.90	50.27	1. 集体农业贷款 Loans to Agricultural Collectives	262.12	39.46
(1) 集体农业存款 Deposits by Agricultural Collectives	245.75	30.52	(1) 种养业贷款 Farming and Breeding Loans	127.52	15.63
(2) 集体定期存款 Time Deposits by Collectives	38.81	7.74	(2) 其他行业贷款 Loans to Other Industries	128.02	23.60
(3) 其他存款 Other Deposits	74.34	12.01	(3) 科技兴农贷款 Loans for Agriculture Development by Science Technology	6.58	0.23
2. 乡镇企业存款 Deposits by Village and Township Enterprises	362.12	60.37	2. 乡镇企业贷款 Loans to Village and Township Enterprises	1730.89	436.64
3. 农户储蓄存款 Savings Deposits by Rural Households	3576.24	708.96	(1) 流动资金贷款 Working Capital Loans	1508.06	408.12
(1) 定期存款 Time Deposits	2845.24	570.25	(2) 固定资产贷款 Fixed Asset Loans	222.83	28.52
(2) 活期存款 Demand Deposits	731.00	138.71	3. 农户贷款 Loans to Rural Households	880.57	121.09
二、自有资金 Own Capital	407.82	44.31	其中：种养业贷款 Of Which: Farming and Breeding Loans	516.23	54.90
三、其他资金收入 Other Capital Revenue	908.90	221.09	生活贷款 Living Loans	69.60	1.46
四、借入银行款 Borrowings from Banks	60.29	-0.29	工商业贷款 Industrial and Commercial Loans	117.76	21.77
五、其他 Others	458.13	172.92	4. 其他工商业贷款 Loans to Other Industrial and Commercial Sectors	270.28	92.75
六、结益 Net Earnings	8.81	8.81	二、其他资金占用 Position for Other Funds	1274.58	274.12
			三、转存银行款 Redeposits with Banks	1375.96	295.47
			四、其他 Others	346.81	6.91
资金来源总计 Total Sources	**6141.21**	**1266.44**	**资金运用总计 Total Uses**	**6141.21**	**1266.44**

农村信用合作社人民币信贷收支表

Sources and Uses of Credit Funds of Rural Credit Cooperatives（RMB）

（1994 年末）

（Year – end of 1994）

单位：亿元

Unit：100 Million Yuan

项目 Items	余额 Balance	比年初增减额 Changes within the Year	项目 Items	余额 Balance	比年初增减额 Changes within the Year
一、存款合计 Total Deposits	5681.14	1384.01	一、贷款合计 Total Loans	4168.55	913.54
1. 集体存款小计 Deposits by Collectives	865.12	143.99	1. 农业贷款 Loans to Agricultural Sector	808.38	151.33
（1）活期存款 Demand Deposits	805.43	123.89	（1）短期农业贷款 Short – term Loans to Agricultural Sector	385.45	137.05
（2）定期存款 Time Deposits	59.69	20.10	（2）农业中长期贷款 Medium and Long – term Loans to Agricultural Sector	74.39	3.15
2. 农户储蓄存款 Savings Deposits by Rural Households	4816.02	1240.02			
（1）活期存款 Demand Deposits	1005.47	217.37	（3）农业抵押贷款 Mortagage Loans to Agricultural Sector	35.47	16.53
（2）定期存款 Time Deposits	3810.55	1022.65	（4）农业逾期贷款 Overdue Loans to Agricultural Sector	313.07	– 5.40
二、借入银行款 Borrowings from Banks	68.79	8.02	2. 乡镇企业贷款 Loans to Village and Township Enterprises	2279.42	500.37
三、拆入资金 Placements from Banks and Other Financial Institutions	175.59	75.25	（1）短期乡镇企业贷款 Short – term Loans to Village and Township Enterprises	1204.11	376.35
四、同业存放款项 Due to Banks and Other Financial Institutions		—	（2）中长期乡镇企业贷款 Medium and Long – term Loans to Village and Township Enterprises	342.40	– 6.09
五、委托及代理款项 Designated and Agency Funds	140.58	25.69	（3）乡镇企业抵押贷款 Mortagage Loans to Village and Township Enterprises	108.10	46.49
六、调入调剂资金 Equalization Funds Received	815.48	188.28			
七、应付款项 Accounts Payable	499.61	170.06	（4）乡镇企业逾期贷款 Overdue Loans to Village and Township Enterprises	624.81	83.62
八、其他资金往来 Other Funds Transactions	0.98	– 8.85	3. 其他贷款 Other Loans	1080.75	261.84
九、所有者权益 Owner's Equity	616.91	55.86	（1）其他短期贷款 Other Short – term Loans	511.45	172.48
其中：实收资本 Of Which：Paid – in Capital	694.35	142.07	（2）其他中长期贷款 Other Medium and Long – term Loans	147.60	– 3.31
十、当年结益 Net Earnings	– 27.88	– 27.88			
			（3）其他抵押贷款 Other Mortagage Loans	89.74	47.89
			（4）其他逾期贷款 Other Overdue Loans	331.96	44.78

续表
Continued

项　目 Items	余　额 Balance	比年初增减额 Changes within the Year	项　目 Items	余　额 Balance	比年初增减额 Changes within the Year
			二、存放人行款项 Deposits with the Central Bank	88.41	72.71
			三、存放农业银行款项 Deposits with Agricultural Bank of China	1004.49	139.83
			四、缴存存款准备金 Reserves with the Central Bank	672.11	166.09
			五、拆放资金 Placements with Banks and Other Financial Institutions	103.09	43.50
			六、存放其他同业款项 Due from Banks and Other Financial Institutions	122.58	30.70
			七、信托及代理 Trust and Agency	123.16	30.56
			八、调出调剂资金 Equalization Funds Paid	891.59	234.66
			九、其他资金占用 Position for Other Funds	673.03	203.24
			十、库存现金 Cash in Vault	124.19	35.61
资金来源总计 Total Sources	**7971.20**	**1870.44**	**资金运用总计 Total Uses**	**7971.20**	**1870.44**

农村信用合作社人民币信贷收支表

Sources and Uses of Credit Funds of Rural Credit Cooperatives（RMB）

（1995 年末）

（Year - end of 1995）

单位：亿元

Unit：100 Million Yuan

项　目 Items	余　额 Balance	比年初增减额 Changes within the Year	项　目 Items	余　额 Balance	比年初增减额 Changes within the Year
一、存款合计 Total Deposits	7172.84	1503.98	一、贷款合计 Total Loans	5234.24	1055.66
1. 集体存款小计 Deposits by Collectives	977.28	116.71	1. 农业贷款 Loans to Agricultural Sector	1094.85	290.34
（1）活期存款 Demand Deposits	891.97	88.00	（1）短期农业贷款 Short - term Loans to Agricultural Sector	579.62	200.99
（2）定期存款 Time Deposits	85.31	28.71	（2）农业中长期贷款 Medium and Long - term Loans to Agricultural Sector	76.59	2.95
2. 农户储蓄存款 Savings Deposits by Rural Households	6195.56	1387.27	（3）农业抵押贷款 Mortagage Loans to Agricultural Sector	62.71	28.18
（1）活期存款 Demand Deposits	1182.37	180.12	（4）农业逾期及催收贷款 Overdue and Receivable on Demand Loans to Agricultural Sector	375.93	58.22
（2）定期存款 Time Deposits	5013.19	1207.15	2. 乡镇企业贷款 Loans to Village and Township Enterprises	2779.10	500.83
二、借入银行款 Borrowings from Banks	166.13	97.29	（1）短期乡镇企业贷款 Short - term Loans to Village and Township Enterprises	1555.72	352.24
三、拆入资金 Placements from Banks and Other Financial Institutions	67.59	- 45.49	（2）中长期乡镇企业贷款 Medium and Long - term Loans to Village and Township Enterprises	308.69	- 32.42
四、同业存放款项 Due to Banks and Other Financial Institutions	153.73	68.95	（3）乡镇企业抵押贷款 Mortagage Loans to Village and Township Enterprises	139.33	32.01
五、委托及代理款项 Designated and Agency Funds	131.35	- 9.87	（4）乡镇企业逾期及催收贷款 Overdue and Receivable on Demand Loans to Village and Township Enterprises	775.36	149.00
六、调入调剂资金 Equalization Funds Received	903.41	116.50	3. 其他贷款 Other Loans	1301.87	225.50
七、其他负债 Other Liabilities	718.96	243.81	（1）其他短期贷款 Other Short - term Loans	629.70	119.14
八、其他资金往来 Other Funds Transactions	- 8.03	- 11.91	（2）其他中长期贷款 Other Medium and Long - term Loans	121.48	- 25.99
九、所有者权益 Owner's Equity	631.95	23.04	（3）其他抵押贷款 Other Mortagage Loans	126.07	37.35
其中：实收资本 Of Which：Paid - in Capital	377.70	14.35			
十、当年结益 Net Earnings	- 81.04	- 81.04			

续表
Continued

项 目 Items	余 额 Balance	比年初增减额 Changes within the Year	项 目 Items	余 额 Balance	比年初增减额 Changes within the Year
			(4) 其他逾期及催收贷款 Other Overdue and Receivable on Demand Loans	424.62	95.00
			4. 贴现 Discount	58.42	38.99
			二、投资 Investments	338.46	37.47
			三、存放人行款项 Deposits with the Central Bank	187.79	99.60
			四、存放农业银行款项 Deposits with Agricultural Bank of China	1030.50	24.85
			五、缴存存款准备金 Reserves with the Central Bank	875.37	203.84
			六、拆放资金 Placements with Banks and Other Financial Institutions	94.84	-45.30
			七、存放其他同业款项 Deposits with Other Inter-banks	378.72	255.88
			八、信托及代理 Trust and Agency	107.68	-15.36
			九、调出调剂资金 Equalization Funds Paid	994.18	139.41
			十、其他资产 Other Assets	460.05	120.52
			十一、库存现金 Cash in Vault	155.06	28.69
资金来源总计 Total Sources	**9856.89**	**1905.26**	**资金运用总计 Total Uses**	**9856.89**	**1905.26**

农村信用合作社人民币信贷收支表

Sources and Uses of Credit Funds of Rural Credit Cooperatives（RMB）

（1996 年末）

（Year – end of 1996）

单位：亿元

Unit：100 Million Yuan

项　目 Items	余　额 Balance	比年初增减额 Changes within the Year	项　目 Items	余　额 Balance	比年初增减额 Changes within the Year
一、存款合计 Total Deposits	8793.58	1620.74	一、贷款合计 Total Loans	6364.68	1130.42
1. 集体存款小计 Deposits by Collectives	1122.97	146.40	1. 农业贷款 Loans to Agricultural Sector	1486.61	396.75
（1）活期存款 Demand Deposits	1007.43	115.53	（1）短期农业贷款 Short – term Loans to Agricultural Sector	705.65	129.75
（2）定期存款 Time Deposits	115.54	30.87	（2）中长期农业贷款 Medium and Long – term Loans to Agricultural Sectors	73.23	– 3.21
2. 农户储蓄存款 Savings Deposits by Rural Households	7670.61	1474.31	（3）抵押农业贷款 Mortagage Loans to Agricultural Sector	124.13	61.46
其中：定期存款 Of Which：Time Deposits	6294.38	1279.61	（4）逾期及催收农业贷款 Loans to Village and Township Enterprises	583.60	208.75
保值储蓄 Inflation Proot Savings Deposits	1600.99	636.79	2. 乡镇企业贷款 Loans to Village and Township Enterprises	3264.66	485.04
二、借入银行款 Borrowings from Banks	188.42	21.86	（1）短期乡镇企业贷款 Short – term Loans to Village and Township Enterprises	1663.72	109.49
三、拆入资金 Placements from Banks and Other Financial Institutions	62.75	– 4.78	（2）中长期乡镇企业贷款 Medium and Long – term Loans to Village and Township Enterprises	251.93	– 57.53
四、同业存放款项 Due to Bands and Other Financial Institutions	663.16	525.05	（3）乡镇企业抵押贷款 Mortagage Loans to Village and Township Enterprises	173.96	34.17
五、委托及代理款项 Trust and Agency Funds	124.21	– 7.30	（4）乡镇企业逾期及催收贷款 Overdue and Receivable on Demand Loans to Village and Township Enterprises	1175.05	398.91
六、调入调剂资金 Equalization Funds Received	1051.79	146.14	3. 其他贷款 Other Loans	1538.58	232.23
七、其他负债 Other Liabilities	934.11	326.86	（1）其他短期贷款 Other Short – term Loans	636.73	3.75
八、其他资金往来 Other Funds Transactions	– 680.76	– 669.64	（2）其他中长期贷款 Medium and Long – term Other Loans	97.57	– 23.78
九、所有者权益 Owner's Equity	547.73	– 81.02	（3）其他抵押贷款 Other Mortagage Loans	179.21	53.27
其中：实收资本 Of Which：Paid – in Capital	401.12	25.12			
十、当年结益 Net Earnings	– 111.21	– 111.21			

续表
Continued

项　目 Items	余　额 Balance	比年初增减额 Changes within the Year	项　目 Items	余　额 Balance	比年初增减额 Changes within the Year
			(4) 逾期及催收其他贷款 Other Overdue and Receivable on Demand Loans	625.07	198.99
			4. 贴现 Discount	74.83	16.40
			二、投资 Investments	406.30	68.19
			三、存放人行款项 Deposits with the Central Bank	1066.74	879.40
			四、存放农业银行款项 Deposits with Agricultural Bank of China	426.79	-606.42
			五、缴存存款准备金 Reserves with the Central Bank	711.96	-163.07
			六、拆放资金 Placements with Banks and Other Financial Institutions	132.65	39.22
			七、存放其他同业款项 Due from Banks and Other Financial Institutions	469.51	120.04
			八、信托及代理 Trust and Agency	116.56	8.74
			九、调出调剂资金 Equalization Funds Paid	1128.30	127.89
			十、其他资产 Other Assets	593.36	160.08
			十一、库存现金 Cash in Vault	156.93	2.18
资金来源总计 Total Sources	**11573.78**	**1766.67**	**资金运用总计 Total Uses**	**11573.78**	**1766.67**

农村信用合作社人民币信贷收支表
Sources and Uses of Credit Funds of Rural Credit Cooperatives（RMB）

（1997年末）
（Year－end of 1997）

单位：亿元
Unit：100 Million Yuan

项目 Items	余额 Balance	比年初增减额 Changes within the Year	项目 Items	余额 Balance	比年初增减额 Changes within the Year
一、各项存款 Total Deposits	10624.22	1764.06	一、各项贷款 Total Loans	7326.14	972.81
1. 企业存款 Deposits by Enterprises	158.81	42.50	1. 短期贷款 Short－term Loans	6956.39	1026.58
（1）活期存款 Demand Deposits			（1）工业贷款 Loans to Industrial Sector		
（2）定期存款 Time Deposits	158.81	42.50	（2）商业贷款 Loans to Commercial Sector		
2. 农户储蓄存款 Savings Deposits by Rural Households	9132.17	1473.18	其中：收购贷款 Of Which：Loans for the Purchase of Farm Products		
（1）活期储蓄 Demand Deposits	1636.53	265.73	（3）建筑业贷款 Loans to Construction Sector		
（2）定期储蓄 Time Deposits	7495.64	1207.45	（4）农业贷款 Loans to Agricultural Sector	1774.31	363.41
3. 农业存款 Deposits by Agricultural Sector	1264.77	256.81	（5）乡镇企业贷款 Loans to Village and Township Enterprises	3467.79	464.41
4. 信托存款 Trust Deposits			（6）三资企业贷款 Loans to Foreign Investment Enterprises and Ventures		
5. 其他存款 Other Deposits	68.47	－8.43	（7）私营企业及个体贷款 Loans to Privately－run Enterprises and Self－employed Entities		
二、代理财政性存款 Agency Fiscal Deposits			（8）贴现 Discount	52.92	－21.58
三、发行金融债券 Financial Bonds Issue	0.40	－0.04	（9）其他短期贷款 Other Short－term Loans	1661.37	220.34
其中：发行政策性金融债券 Of Which：Policy Financial Bonds Issue			2. 中长期贷款 Medium and Long－term Loans	369.75	－53.77
四、国家投资债券 State Investment Bonds			（1）基本建设贷款 Capital Construction Loans		
五、卖出回购证券 Repo			（2）技术改造贷款 Technical Improvement Loans		
六、向中央银行借款 Borrowings from the Central Bank	16.42	12.15	（3）其他中长期贷款 Other Medium and Long－term Loans	369.75	－53.77
七、同业往来 Inter－bank Transactions	324.76	－7.17	3. 信托贷款 Trust Loans		
1. 同业存放 Due to Banks and Other Financial Institutions	168.68	41.13	4. 逾期类贷款 Overdue Loans		
2. 同业拆借 Placements from Banks and Other Financial Institutions	156.08	－48.30			

续表
Continued

项　目 Items	余　额 Balance	比年初增减额 Changes within the Year	项　目 Items	余　额 Balance	比年初增减额 Changes within the Year
八、委托存款及委托投资基金 Designated Deposits and Designated Investment Funds	-15.08	-23.40	二、国家投资债券贷款 Loans Related to State Investment Bonds		
1. 委托存款 Designated Deposits	-15.08	-23.40	三、有价证券及投资 Securities and Investments	521.74	117.57
2. 委托投资基金 Designated Investment Funds			四、缴存人行准备金 Reserves with the Central Bank	1246.66	221.17
九、代理金融机构委托贷款基金 Designated Loan Funds on Behalf of Financial Institutions	20.37	-0.24	五、缴存准备金存款 Reserves with the Central Bank	702.97	76.13
其中：中央银行委托贷款基金 Of Which: Loan Funds Designated by the Central Bank	0.23	-0.17	六、存放中央银行特种存款 Special Deposits with the Central Bank	97.82	-33.36
十、所有者权益 Owner's Equity	310.01	-171.42	七、存放中央银行财政性存款 Fiscal Deposits with the Central Bank		
其中：实收资本 Of Which: Paid-in Capital	630.52	-39.86	八、同业往来 Inter-bank Transactions	1149.33	150.23
当年结益 Net Earnings	-63.68	-63.68	1. 存放同业 Due from Banks and Other Financial Institutions	998.41	133.38
十一、其他 Others	-15.69	-34.57	2. 拆放同业 Placements with Banks and Other Financial Institutions	150.92	16.85
			九、代理金融机构贷款 Lending on Behalf of Financial Institutions	25.34	2.65
			其中：代理人行专项贷款 Of Which: Agency Earmarked Loans of the Central Bank	0.15	-0.95
			十、库存现金 Cash in Vault	195.24	32.00
			十一、外汇占款 Position for Foreign Exchange Purchase	0.17	0.17
资金来源总计 Total Sources	**11265.41**	**1539.37**	**资金运用总计 Total Uses**	**11265.41**	**1539.37**

农村信用合作社人民币信贷收支表

Sources and Uses of Credit Funds of Rural Credit Cooperatives（RMB）

（1998年末）

（Year - end of 1998）

单位：亿元

Unit：100 Million Yuan

项目 Items	余额 Balance	比年初增减额 Changes within the Year	项目 Items	余额 Balance	比年初增减额 Changes within the Year
一、各项存款 Total Deposits	12191.47	1465.61	一、各项贷款 Total Loans	8340.18	922.14
1.企业存款 Deposits by Enterprises	211.87	35.45	1.短期贷款 Short - term Loans	7973.42	964.40
（1）活期存款 Demand Deposits	6.73	-2.92	（1）工业贷款 Loans to Industrial Sector		-0.19
（2）定期存款 Time Deposits	205.14	38.37	（2）商业贷款 Loans to Commercial Sector		-0.01
2.城镇储蓄存款 Urban Savings Deposits	10441.03	1234.66	其中：收购贷款 Of Which：Loans for the Purchase of Farm Products		
（1）活期储蓄 Demand Deposits	1948.51	295.27	（3）建筑业贷款 Loans to Construction Sector		
（2）定期储蓄 Time Deposits	8492.52	939.39	（4）农业贷款 Loans to Agricultural Sector	2659.29	393.07
3.农业存款 Deposits by Agricultural Sector	1441.00	198.87	（5）乡镇企业贷款 Loans to Village and Township Enterprises	3761.05	398.99
4.信托存款 Trust Deposits			（6）三资企业贷款 Loans to Foreign Investment Enterprises and Ventures		
5.其他存款 Other Deposits	97.57	-3.37	（7）私营企业及个体贷款 Loans to Privately - run Enterprises and Self - employed Entities		
二、代理财政性存款 Agency Fiscal Deposits	0.18	0.08	（8）贴现 Discount	48.86	-4.78
三、发行金融债券 Financial Bonds Issue	0.07	-0.32	（9）其他短期贷款 Other Short - term Loans	1504.22	177.32
其中：发行政策性金融债券 Of Which：Policy Financial Bonds Issue			2.中期流动资金贷款 Medium - term Working Capital Loans		-6.67
四、国家投资债券 State Investment Bonds			3.中长期贷款 Medium and Long - term Loans	366.76	-35.59
五、卖出回购证券 Repo			（1）基本建设贷款 Capital Construction Loans		
六、向中央银行借款 Borrowings from the Central Bank	41.79	24.73	（2）技术改造贷款 Technical Improvement Loans		
七、同业往来 Inter - bank Transactions	434.38	11.90	（3）其他中长期贷款 Other Medium and Long - term Loans	366.76	-35.59
1.同业存放 Due to Banks and Other Financial Institutions	170.25	-7.06	4.信托贷款 Trust Loans		
2.同业拆借 Placements from Banks and Other Financial Institutions	264.13	18.96			

续表
Continued

项　目 Items	余　额 Balance	比年初增减额 Changes within the Year	项　目 Items	余　额 Balance	比年初增减额 Changes within the Year
八、委托存款及委托投资基金 Designated Deposits and Designated Investment Funds	3.28	-2.21	5. 逾期类贷款 Overdue Loans		
			二、国家投资债券贷款 Loans Related to State Investment Bonds		
1. 委托存款 Designated Deposits	3.28	-1.64	三、有价证券及投资 Securities and Investments	848.91	324.63
2. 委托投资基金 Designated Investment Funds		-0.57	四、缴存人行准备金 Reserves with the Central Bank		
九、代理金融机构委托贷款基金 Designated Loan Funds on Behalf of Financial Institutions	13.98	-4.47	五、缴存准备金存款 Reserves with the Central Bank	1876.24	-81.74
其中：中央银行委托贷款基金 Of Which: Loan Funds Designated by the Central Bank	0.08	-0.17	六、存放中央银行特种存款 Special Deposits with the Central Bank	117.58	12.54
			七、存放中央银行财政性存款 Fiscal Deposits with the Central Bank	1.17	0.74
十、所有者权益 Owner's Equity	151.40	-163.32	八、同业往来 Inter-bank Transactions	1197.81	-52.56
其中：实收资本 Of Which: Paid in Capital	658.08	22.55	1. 存放同业 Due from Banks and Other Financial Institutions	913.23	-89.88
当年结益 Net Earnings	-165.84	-165.84			
十一、其他 Others	-225.44	-221.07	2. 拆放同业 Placements with Banks and Other Financial Institutions	284.58	37.32
			九、代理金融机构贷款 Lending on Behalf of Financial Institutions	15.60	-29.60
			其中：代理人行专项贷款 Of Which: Agency Earmarked Loans of the Central Bank	0.05	-0.12
			十、库存现金 Cash in Vault	213.65	15.01
			十一、外汇占款 Position for Foreign Exchange Purchase	-0.03	-0.23
资金来源总计 Total Sources	**12611.11**	**1110.93**	**资金运用总计 Total Uses**	**12611.11**	**1110.93**

农村信用合作社人民币信贷收支表

Sources and Uses of Credit Funds of Rural Credit Cooperatives（RMB）

（1999 年末）

（Year – end of 1999）

单位：亿元

Unit：100 Million Yuan

项　目 Items	余　额 Balance	比年初增减额 Changes within the Year	项　目 Items	余　额 Balance	比年初增减额 Changes within the Year
一、各项存款 Total Deposits	13358.09	1218.95	一、各项贷款 Total Loans	9225.59	994.99
1. 企业存款 Deposits by Enterprises	265.16	54.29	1. 短期贷款 Short – term Loans	8836.42	971.54
（1）活期存款 Demand Deposits	0.38	– 6.35	（1）工业贷款 Loans to Industrial Sector		
（2）定期存款 Time Deposits	264.78	60.64	（2）商业贷款 Loans to Commercial Sector		
2. 城镇储蓄存款 Urban Savings Deposits	11217.25	817.69	其中：收购贷款 Of Which：Loans for the Purchase of Farm Products		
（1）活期储蓄 Demand Deposits	2314.03	374.25	（3）建筑业贷款 Loans to Construction Sector		
（2）定期储蓄 Time Deposits	8903.22	443.44	（4）农业贷款 Loans to Agricultural Sector	3039.64	378.74
3. 农业存款 Deposits by Agricultural Sector	1767.65	335.09	（5）乡镇企业贷款 Loans to Village and Township Enterprises	4187.29	411.30
4. 信托存款 Trust Deposits			（6）三资企业贷款 Loans to Foreign Investment Enterprises and Ventures		
5. 其他存款 Other Deposits	108.03	11.88	（7）私营企业及个体贷款 Loans to Privately – run Enterprises and Self – employed Entities	0.99	0.99
二、代理财政性存款 Agency Fiscal Deposits	7.32	5.04	（8）贴现 Discount	43.31	– 5.54
三、发行金融债券 Financial Bonds Issue	0.01	– 0.06	（9）其他短期贷款 Other Short – term Loans	1565.19	186.05
其中：发行政策性金融债券 Of Which：Policy Financial Bonds Issue			2. 中期流动资金贷款 Medium – term Working Capital Loans		
四、国家投资债券 State Investment Bonds			3. 中长期贷款 Medium and Long – term Loans	389.17	23.45
五、卖出回购证券 Repo			（1）基本建设贷款 Capital Construction Loans		
六、向中央银行借款 Borrowings from the Central Bank	214.35	173.23	（2）技术改造贷款 Technical Improvement Loans		
七、同业往来 Inter – bank Transactions	354.29	63.14	（3）其他中长期贷款 Other Medium and Long – term Loans	389.17	23.45
1. 同业存放 Due to Banks and Other Financial Institutions	205.52	35.95	4. 信托贷款 Trust Loans		
2. 同业拆借 Placements from Banks and Other Financial Institutions	148.77	27.19			

续表
Continued

项目 Items	余额 Balance	比年初增减额 Changes within the Year	项目 Items	余额 Balance	比年初增减额 Changes within the Year
八、委托存款及委托投资基金 Designated Deposits and Designated Investment Funds	4.24	0.13	5. 逾期类贷款 Overdue Loans		
			二、国家投资债券贷款 Loans Related to State Investment Bonds		
1. 委托存款 Designated Deposits	3.24	-0.87	三、有价证券及投资 Securities and Investments	1005.39	157.32
2. 委托投资基金 Designated Investment Funds	1.00	1.00	四、缴存准备金存款 Reserves with the Central Bank	1738.76	-128.07
九、代理金融机构委托贷款基金 Designated Loan Funds on Behalf of Financial Institutions	19.82	6.05	五、存放中央银行特种存款 Special Deposits with the Central Bank	88.63	-36.62
其中：中央银行委托贷款基金 Of Which: Loan Funds Designated by the Central Bank	0.41	0.06	六、存放中央银行财政性存款 Fiscal Deposits with the Central Bank	0.52	-0.70
十、所有者权益 Owner's Equity	-84.48	-232.70	七、同业往来 Inter-bank Transactions	965.89	-94.31
其中：实收资本 Of Which: Paid-in Capital	653.81	-2.59	1. 存放同业 Due from Banks and Other Financial Institutions	803.83	-105.32
当年结益 Net Earnings	-220.85	-220.85	2. 拆放同业 Placements with Banks and Other Financial Institutions	162.06	11.01
十一、其他 Others	-525.60	-247.72	八、代理金融机构贷款 Lending on Behalf of Financial Institutions	22.13	5.59
			其中：代理人行专项贷款 Of Which: Agency Earmarked Loans of the Central Bank	0.35	0.02
			九、库存现金 Cash in Vault	301.16	87.86
			十、外汇占款 Position for Foreign Exchange Purchase	-0.03	
资金来源总计 Total Sources	**13348.04**	**986.06**	**资金运用总计 Total Uses**	**13348.04**	**986.06**

农村信用合作社人民币信贷收支表

Sources and Uses of Credit Funds of Rural Credit Cooperatives（RMB）

（2000 年末）

（Year - end of 2000）

单位：亿元

Unit：100 Million Yuan

项　目 Items	余　额 Balance	比年初增减额 Changes within the Year	项　目 Items	余　额 Balance	比年初增减额 Changes within the Year
一、各项存款 Total Deposits	15129.43	1772.91	一、各项贷款 Total Loans	10489.29	1304.64
1. 企业存款 Deposits by Enterprises	388.64	122.11	1. 短期贷款 Short - term Loans	10109.36	1296.90
（1）活期存款 Demand Deposits	0.50	0.50	（1）工业贷款 Loans to Industrial Sector		
（2）定期存款 Time Deposits	388.14	121.61	（2）商业贷款 Loans to Commercial Sector		
2. 城镇储蓄存款 Urban Savings Deposits	12355.25	1149.78	其中：收购贷款 Of Which：Loans for the Purchase of Farm Products		
（1）活期储蓄 Demand Deposits	2864.06	555.36	（3）建筑业贷款 Loans to Construction Sector		
（2）定期储蓄 Time Deposits	9491.19	594.42	（4）农业贷款 Loans to Agricultural Sector	3587.98	561.03
3. 农业存款 Deposits by Agricultural Sector	2244.11	467.99	（5）乡镇企业贷款 Loans to Village and Township Enterprises	4568.87	400.20
4. 信托存款 Trust Deposits			（6）三资企业贷款 Loans to Foreign Investment Enterprises and Ventures		
5. 其他存款 Other Deposits	141.43	33.03	（7）私营企业及个体贷款 Loans to Privately - run Enterprises and Self - employed Entities	0.53	0.53
二、代理财政性存款 Agency Fiscal Deposits	11.19	3.77	（8）贴现 Discount	78.28	34.92
三、发行金融债券 Financial Bonds Issue	0.13	0.12	（9）其他短期贷款 Other Short - term Loans	1873.70	300.22
其中：发行政策性金融债券 Of Which：Policy Financial Bonds Issue			2. 中期流动资金贷款 Medium - term Working Capital Loans		
四、国家投资债券 State Investment Bonds			3. 中长期贷款 Medium and Long - term Loans	379.93	7.74
五、卖出回购证券 Repo			（1）基本建设贷款 Capital Construction Loans		
六、向中央银行借款 Borrowings from the Central Bank	399.67	183.52	（2）技术改造贷款 Technical Improvement Loa		
七、同业往来 Inter - bank Transactions	403.10	45.05	（3）其他中长期贷款 Other Medium and Long - term Loans	379.93	7.74
1. 同业存放 Due to Banks and Other Financial Institutions	231.47	23.40	4. 信托贷款 Trust Loans		
2. 同业拆借 Placements from Banks and Other Financial Institutions	171.63	21.65			

续表
Continued

项　目 Items	余　额 Balance	比年初增减额 Changes within the Year	项　目 Items	余　额 Balance	比年初增减额 Changes within the Year
八、委托存款及委托投资基金 Designated Deposits and Designated Investment Funds	-0.50	-3.21	5. 逾期类贷款 Overdue Loans		
			二、国家投资债券贷款 Loans Related to State Investment Bonds		
1. 委托存款 Designated Deposits	-0.50	-2.21	三、有价证券及投资 Securities and Investments	1173.30	166.95
2. 委托投资基金 Designated Investment Funds		-1.00	四、缴存准备金存款 Reserves with the Central Bank	1796.97	58.48
九、代理金融机构委托贷款基金 Designated Loan Funds on Behalf of Financial Institutions	27.32	6.87	五、存放中央银行特种存款 Special Deposits with the Central Bank	108.46	19.62
其中：中央银行委托贷款基金 Of Which: Loan Funds Designated by the Central Bank	0.39	-0.03	六、存放中央银行财政性存款 Fiscal Deposits with the Central Bank	0.82	0.23
十、所有者权益 Owner's Equity	-209.56	-119.51	七、同业往来 Inter-bank Transactions	1174.76	202.55
其中：实收资本 Of Which: Paid-in Capital	716.03	62.76	1. 存放同业 Due from Banks and Other Financial Institutions	971.21	161.88
当年结益 Net Earnings	-160.40	-160.40	2. 拆放同业 Placements with Banks and Other Financial Institutions	203.55	40.67
十一、其他 Others	-662.37	-106.42	八、代理金融机构贷款 Lending on Behalf of Financial Institutions	26.25	3.55
			其中：代理人行专项贷款 Of Which: Agency Earmarked Loans of the Central Bank	0.41	-0.01
			九、库存现金 Cash in Vault	327.12	25.61
			十、外汇占款 Position for Foreign Exchange Purchase	1.44	1.47
资金来源总计 Total Sources	**15098.41**	**1783.10**	**资金运用总计 Total Uses**	**15098.41**	**1783.10**

农村信用合作社人民币信贷收支表

Sources and Uses of Credit Funds of Rural Credit Cooperatives（RMB）

（2001 年末）

（Year - end of 2001）

单位：亿元

Unit：100 Million Yuan

项　目 Items	余　额 Balance	比年初增减额 Changes within the Year	项　目 Items	余　额 Balance	比年初增减额 Changes within the Year
一、各项存款 Total Deposits	17263.45	2008.67	一、各项贷款 Total Loans	11971.16	1395.11
1. 企业存款 Deposits by Enterprises	588.96	193.77	1. 短期贷款 Short - term Loans	11355.21	1237.91
（1）活期存款 Demand Deposits	0.54	- 0.10	（1）工业贷款 Loans to Industrial Sector		
（2）定期存款 Time Deposits	588.42	193.87	（2）商业贷款 Loans to Commercial Sector		
2. 机关团体存款 Deposits by Government Agencies and Social Organizations	52.29	8.25	其中：收购贷款 Of Which：Loans for the Purchase of Farm Products		
3. 储蓄存款 Savings Deposits	13821.36	1372.74	（3）建筑业贷款 Loans to Construction Sector		
（1）活期储蓄 Demand Deposits	3404.31	513.66	（4）农业贷款 Loans to Agricultural Sector	4417.57	802.93
（2）定期储蓄 Time Deposits	10417.05	859.08	（5）乡镇企业贷款 Loans to Village and Township Enterprises	4843.38	249.66
4. 农业存款 Deqosits by Agricultural Sector	2657.77	389.27	（6）三资企业贷款 Loans to Foreign Investmenu Enterprises and Ventures		
5. 其他存款 Otier Deposits	143.07	44.64	（7）私营企业及个体贷款 Loans to Privately - run Enterprises and Self - employed Entities	0.90	0.37
二、代理财政性存款 Agency Fiscal Deposits	14.44	3.27	（8）其他短期贷款 Other Short - term Loans	2093.36	184.95
三、金融债券 Financial Bonds	0.08	- 0.05	其中：个人短期消费贷款 Of Which：Short - term Consumer Credit	0.07	- 0.41
其中：政策性金融债券 Of Which：Policy Financial Bonds Issue			2. 中期流动资金贷款 Medium - term Working Capital Loans		
四、应付及暂收款 Accounts Payable and Receipts on Account	449.88	15.80	3. 中长期贷款 Medium and Long - term Loans	503.38	122.37
其中：应付及预提利息 Of Which：Interest Payable and Accrued	224.18	10.55	（1）基本建设贷款 Capital Construction Loans		
五、卖出回购证券 Repo	15.70	15.70	（2）技术改造贷款 Technical Improvement Loans		
六、向中央银行借款 Borrowings from the Central Bank	685.68	285.61	（3）其他中长期贷款 Other Medium and Long - term Loans	503.38	122.37
七、同业往来 Inter - bank Transactions	652.57	248.19			

续表
Continued

项　目 Items	余　额 Balance	比年初增减额 Changes within the Year	项　目 Items	余　额 Balance	比年初增减额 Changes within the Year
1. 同业存放 Due to Banks and Other Financial Institutions	365.28	133.54	其中：个人中长期消费贷款 Of Which: Medium and Long-term Consumer Credit	32.15	30.49
2. 同业拆借 Placements from Banks and Other Financial Institutions	287.29	114.65	4. 票据融资 Paper Financing	112.57	34.83
			其中：贴现 Of Which: Discount	112.57	34.83
八、委托存款及委托投资基金(净) Designated Deposits and Designated Investment Funds (Net)	9.22	9.69	5. 各项垫款 Total Advances		
1. 委托存款及委托投资基金 Designated Deposits and Designated Investment Funds	107.92	25.20	二、有价证券及投资 Securities and Investments	1517.35	340.48
			三、应收及预付款 Accounts Receivable and Advance Payments	283.32	-24.69
2. 减：委托贷款及委托投资 Minus: Designated Loans and Designated Investments	98.70	15.51			
			其中：应收利息 Of Which: Interest Receivable	172.54	-18.23
九、代理金融机构委托贷款基金 Designated Loan Funds on Behalf of Financial Institutions	28.96	1.56	四、买入返售证券 Reverse Repo		
其中：中央银行委托贷款基金 Of Which: Loan Funds Designated by the Central Bank	1.21	0.82	五、存放中央银行准备金存款 Reserve Deposits with the Central Bank	2092.39	295.05
			六、存放中央银行特种存款 Special Deposits with the Central Bank	175.50	66.51
十、各项准备 Total Provisions	158.69	42.05			
			七、缴存中央银行财政性存款 Fiscal Deposits with the Central Bank	1.79	-4.39
其中：贷款呆账准备金 Of Which: Provisions for Bad Loans	158.69	42.05			
			八、同业往来 Inter-bank Transactions	1498.63	321.41
十一、所有者权益 Owner's Equity	-288.04	-58.08			
			1. 存放同业 Due from Banks and Other Financial Institutions	1303.45	331.66
其中：实收资本 Of Which: Paid-in Capital	787.57	65.49			
当年结益 Net Earnings	-130.27	-130.27	2. 拆放同业 Placements with Banks and Other Financial Institutions	195.18	-10.25
十二、其他 Others	-1097.17	-186.51			
			九、代理金融机构贷款 Lending on Behalf of Financial Institutions	31.31	5.11
			其中：代理人行专项贷款 Of Which: Agency Earmarked Loans of the Central Bank	0.79	0.38
			十、库存现金 Cash in Vault	315.63	-13.50
			十一、外汇占款 Position for Foreign Exchange Purchase	6.38	4.81
资金来源总计 Total Sources	**17893.46**	**2385.90**	**资金运用总计 Total Uses**	**17893.46**	**2385.90**

农村信用合作社人民币信贷收支表

Sources and Uses of Credit Funds of Rural Credit Cooperatives（RMB）

（2002 年末）

（Year - end of 2002）

单位：亿元

Unit：100 Million Yuan

项目 Items	余额 Balance	比年初增减额 Changes within the Year	项目 Items	余额 Balance	比年初增减额 Changes within the Year
一、各项存款 Total Deposits	19620.23	2530.77	一、各项贷款 Total Loans	13792.73	1906.25
1. 企业存款 Deposits by Enterprises	775.84	204.19	1. 短期贷款 Short - term Loans	12894.27	1612.37
（1）活期存款 Demand Deposits	2.70	1.09	（1）工业贷款 Loans to Industrial Sector		- 0.05
（2）定期存款 Time Deposits	773.14	203.10	（2）商业贷款 Loans to Commercial Sector		
2. 机关团体存款 Deposits by Government Agencies and Social Organizations	64.08	12.34	其中：收购贷款 Of Which：Loans for the Purchase of Farm Products		
3. 储蓄存款 Savings Deposits	15405.80	1689.02	（3）建筑业贷款 Loans to Construction Sector		
（1）活期储蓄 Demand Deposits	4102.70	716.74	（4）农业贷款 Loans to Agricultural Sector	5563.64	1165.21
（2）定期储蓄 Time Deposits	11303.10	972.28	（5）乡镇企业贷款 Loans to Village and Township Enterprises	5041.13	261.21
4. 农业存款 Deposits by Agricultural Sector	3199.50	591.28	（6）三资企业贷款 Loans to Foreign Investment Enterprises and Ventures		
5. 其他存款 Other Deposits	175.01	33.94			
二、代理财政性存款 Agency Fiscal Deposits	19.05	4.54	（7）私营企业及个体贷款 Loans to Privately - run Enterprises and Self - employed Entities	1.44	0.32
三、金融债券 Financial Bonds	0.06	- 0.02	（8）其他短期贷款 Other Short - term Loans	2288.06	185.68
其中：政策性金融债券 Of Which：Policy Financial Bonds			其中：个人短期消费贷款 Of Which：Short - term Consumer Credit	40.83	40.71
四、应付及暂收款 Accounts Payable and Receipts on Account	494.22	43.00			
其中：应付及预提利息 Of Which：Interest Payable and Accrued	246.10	25.44	2. 中期流动资金贷款 Medium - term Working Capital Loans		- 1.79
			3. 中长期贷款 Medium and Long - term Loans	717.10	215.63
五、卖出回购证券 Repo	37.80	22.10			
六、向中央银行借款 Borrowings from the Central Bank	946.75	259.48	（1）基本建设贷款 Capital Construction Loans		
七、同业往来 Inter - bank Transactions	886.54	249.70	（2）技术改造贷款 Technical Improvement Loans		
1. 同业存放 Due to Banks and Other Financial Institutions	532.14	169.99	（3）其他中长期贷款 Other Medium and Long - term Loans	717.10	215.63

续表
Continued

项　目 Items	余　额 Balance	比年初增减额 Changes within the Year	项　目 Items	余　额 Balance	比年初增减额 Changes within the Year
2. 同业拆借 Placements from Banks and Other Financial Institutions	354.40	79.71	其中：个人中长期消费贷款 Of Which：Medium and Long－term Consumer Credit	52.17	19.98
八、委托存款及委托投资基金(净) Designated Deposits and Designated Investment Funds (Net)	5.52	0.47	4. 票据融资 Paper Financing	181.36	80.04
			其中：贴现 Of Which：Discount	181.36	80.04
1. 委托存款及委托投资基金 Designated Deposits and Designated Investment Funds	122.24	20.35	5. 各项垫款 Total Advances		
2. 减：委托贷款及委托投资 Minus：Designated Loans and Designated Investments	116.72	19.88	二、有价证券及投资 Securities and Investments	1801.65	350.03
			三、应收及预付款 Accounts Receivable and Advance Payments	260.28	－23.25
九、代理金融机构委托贷款基金 Designated Loan Funds on Behalf of Financial Institutions	30.41	－4.24	其中：应收利息 Of Which：Interest Receivable	145.73	－27.36
其中：中央银行委托贷款基金 Of Which：Loan Funds Designated by the Central Bank	0.63	－0.57	四、买入返售证券 Reverse Repo	2.00	2.00
			五、存放中央银行准备金存款 Reserve Deposits with the Central Bank	2244.60	172.01
十、各项准备 Total Provisions	166.10	11.15	六、存放中央银行特种存款 Special Deposits with the Central Bank	258.00	84.84
其中：贷款呆账准备金 Of Which：Provisions for Bad Loans	166.11	11.16	七、缴存中央银行财政性存款 Fiscal Deposits with the Central Bank	65.44	64.75
十一、所有者权益 Owner's Equity	－279.39	20.72	八、同业往来 Inter－bank Transactions	2015.57	536.10
其中：实收资本 Of Which：Paid－in Capital	480.60	61.73	1. 存放同业 Due from Banks and Other Financial Institutions	1809.59	518.72
当年结益 Net Earnings	－59.47	－59.47			
十二、其他 Others	－1110.55	－22.42	2. 拆放同业 Placements with Banks and Other Financial Institutions	205.98	17.38
			九、代理金融机构贷款 Lending on Behalf of Financial Institutions	27.64	－5.50
			其中：代理人行专项贷款 Of Which：Agency Earmarked Loans of the Central Bank	0.76	－0.05
			十、库存现金 Cash in Vault	345.25	31.10
			十一、外汇占款 Position for Foreign Exchange Purchase	3.58	－3.08
资金来源总计 Total Sources	**20816.74**	**3115.25**	**资金运用总计 Total Uses**	**20816.74**	**3115.25**

农村信用合作社人民币信贷收支表

Sources and Uses of Credit Funds of Rural Credit Cooperatives（RMB）

（2003年末）

（Year - end of 2003）

单位：亿元

Unit：100 Million Yuan

项　目 Items	余　额 Balance	比年初增减额 Changes within the Year	项　目 Items	余　额 Balance	比年初增减额 Changes within the Year
一、各项存款 Total Deposits	23710.20	4090.07	一、各项贷款 Total Loans	16978.69	3185.99
1.企业存款 Deposits by Enterprises	1024.50	249.16	1.短期贷款 Short - term Loans	15440.44	2546.32
（1）活期存款 Demand Deposits	4.75	2.60	（1）工业贷款 Loans to Industrial Sector		
（2）定期存款 Time Deposits	1019.75	246.56	（2）商业贷款 Loans to Commercial Sector		
2.机关团体存款 Deposits by Government Agencies and Social Organizations	84.50	20.50	其中：收购贷款 Of Which：Loans for the Purchase of Farm Products		
3.储蓄存款 Savings Deposits	18004.99	2599.05	（3）建筑业贷款 Loans to Construction Sector		
（1）活期储蓄 Demand Deposits	5095.49	992.16	（4）农业贷款 Loans to Agricultural Sector	7056.38	1493.10
（2）定期储蓄 Time Deposits	12909.50	1606.89	（5）乡镇企业贷款 Loans to Village and Township Enterprises	5696.12	655.16
4.农业存款 Deposits by Agricultural Sector	4298.54	1098.34	（6）三资企业贷款 Loans to Foreign Investment Enterprises and Ventures		
5.其他存款 Other Deposits	297.67	123.02	（7）私营企业及个体贷款 Loans to Privately - run Enterprises and Self - employed Entities	0.42	0.05
二、代理财政性存款 Agency Fiscal Deposits	23.31	4.18	（8）其他短期贷款 Other Short - term Loans	2687.52	398.01
三、金融债券 Financial Bonds	0.05	- 0.01	其中：个人短期消费贷款 Of Which：Short - term Consumer Credit	8.68	5.25
其中：政策性金融债券 Of Which：Policy Financial Bonds			2.中期流动资金贷款 Medium - term Working Capital Loans		
四、应付及暂收款 Accounts Payable and Receipts on Account	582.32	76.66	3.中长期贷款 Medium and Long - term Loans	1097.71	380.45
其中：应付及预提利息 Of Which：Interest Payable and Accrued	290.17	44.44	（1）基本建设贷款 Capital Construction Loans		
五、卖出回购证券 Repo	14.74	- 23.06	（2）技术改造贷款 Technical Improvement Loans		
六、向中央银行借款 Borrowings from the Central Bank	1013.67	67.30	（3）其他中长期贷款 Other Medium and Long - term Loans	1097.71	380.45
七、同业往来 Inter - bank Transactions	1148.04	260.24	其中：个人中长期消费贷款 Of Which：Medium and Long - term Consumer Credit	64.57	12.34
1.同业存放 Due to Banks and Other Financial Institutions	827.24	292.49	4.票据融资 Paper Financing	440.54	259.22
2.同业拆借 Placements from Banks and Other Financial Institutions	320.80	- 32.25			

续表
Continued

项 目 Items	余 额 Balance	比年初增减额 Changes within the Year	项 目 Items	余 额 Balance	比年初增减额 Changes within the Year
八、委托存款及委托投资基金(净) Designated Deposits and Designated Investment Funds(Net)	5.23	-0.94	其中:贴现 Of Which:Discount	440.54	259.22
1. 委托存款及委托投资基金 Designated Deposits and Designated Investment Funds	192.46	71.87	5. 各项垫款 Total Advances		
			二、有价证券及投资 Securities and Investments	2067.55	264.51
2. 减:委托贷款及委托投资 Minus:Designated Loans and Designated Investments	187.23	72.81	三、应收及预付款 Accounts Receivable and Advance Payments	234.58	-24.81
九、代理金融机构委托贷款基金 Designated Loan Funds on Behalf of Financial Institutions	42.70	10.63	其中:应收利息 Of Which:Interest Receivable	117.04	-28.66
			四、买入返售证券 Reverse Repo	1.50	-0.50
其中:中央银行委托贷款基金 Of Which:Loan Funds Designated by the Central Bank	0.53	-0.10	五、存放中央银行准备金存款 Reserve Deposits with the Central Bank	2935.64	691.15
十、各项准备 Total Provisions	202.30	36.11	六、存放中央银行特种存款 Special Deposits with the Central Bank	1.44	-256.86
其中:贷款损失准备 Of Which:Provisions for Loan Losses	201.91	39.61	七、缴存中央银行财政性存款 Fiscal Deposits with the Central Bank	1.63	-63.81
十一、所有者权益 Owner's Equity	-143.48	146.62	八、同业往来 Inter-bank Transactions	2643.06	624.25
其中:实收资本 Of Which:Paid-in Capital	616.51	161.32	1. 存放同业 Due from Banks and Other Financial Institutions	2389.43	576.22
当年结益 Net Earnings	-6.77	-6.77	2. 拆放同业 Placements with Banks and Other Financial Institutions	253.63	48.03
十二、其他 Others	-1279.71	-170.79			
			九、代理金融机构贷款 Lending on Behalf of Financial Institutions	40.72	12.28
			其中:代理人行专项贷款 Of Which:Agency Earmarked Loans of the Central Bank	0.66	-0.10
			十、库存现金 Cash in Vault	409.68	64.43
			十一、外汇占款 Position for Foreign Exchange Purchase	4.88	0.38
资金来源总计 Total Sources	**25319.37**	**4497.01**	**资金运用总计 Total Uses**	**25319.37**	**4497.01**

农村信用合作社人民币信贷收支表

Sources and Uses of Credit Funds of Rural Credit Cooperatives(RMB)

(2004 年末)

(Year - end of 2004)

单位:亿元

Unit:100 Million Yuan

项目 Items	余额 Balance	比年初增减额 Changes within the Year	项目 Items	余额 Balance	比年初增减额 Changes within the Year
一、各项存款 Total Deposits	27289.10	3622.84	一、各项贷款 Total Loans	19237.84	2531.52
1. 企业存款 Deposits by Enterprises	1144.08	120.62	1. 短期贷款 Short - term Loans	17391.74	2299.99
(1)活期存款 Demand Deposits	2.25	-1.52	(1)工业贷款 Loans to Industrial Sector		
(2)定期存款 Time Deposits	1141.83	122.14	(2)商业贷款 Loans to Commercial Sector		
2. 机关团体存款 Deposits by Government Agencies and Social Organizations	116.62	36.79	其中:收购贷款 Of Which:Loans for the Purchase of Farm Products		
3. 储蓄存款 Savings Deposits	20766.17	2759.80	(3)建筑业贷款 Loans to Construction Sector		
(1)活期储蓄 Demand Deposits	6205.12	1109.36	(4)农业贷款 Loans to Agricultural Sector	8455.70	1542.18
(2)定期储蓄 Time Deposits	14561.05	1650.44	(5)乡镇企业贷款 Loans to Village and Township Enterprises	5989.22	401.29
4. 农业存款 Deposits by Agricultural Sector	4867.34	568.64	(6)三资企业贷款 Loans to Foreign Investment Enterprises and Ventures		
5. 其他存款 Other Deposits	394.89	136.99			
二、代理财政性存款 Agency Fiscal Deposits	57.72	-10.13	(7)私营企业及个体贷款 Loans to Privately - run Enterprises and Self - employed Entities	167.14	66.07
三、金融债券 Financial Bonds	0.04	-0.01	(8)其他短期贷款 Other Short - term Loans	2779.68	290.45
其中:政策性金融债券 Of Which:Policy Financial Bonds			其中:个人短期消费贷款 Of Which:Short - term Consumer Credit	114.97	45.99
四、应付及暂收款 Accounts Payable and Receipts on Account	674.31	78.19			
其中:应付及预提利息 Of Which:Interest Payable and Accrued	342.48	52.65	2. 中期流动资金贷款 Medium - term Working Capital Loans		
			3. 中长期贷款 Medium and Long - term Loans	1509.09	366.86
五、卖出回购资产 Assets Repo(Including Securities)	37.12	-12.88	(1)基本建设贷款 Capital Construction Loans	4.57	-0.42
六、向中央银行借款 Borrowings from the Central Bank	991.11	-63.97	(2)技术改造贷款 Technical Improvement Loans		
七、同业往来 Inter - bank Transactions	771.68	-125.07	(3)其他中长期贷款 Other Medium and Long - term Loans	1504.52	367.28
1. 同业存放 Due to Banks and Other Financial Institutions	500.54	-113.31	其中:个人中长期消费贷款 Of Which:Medium and Long - term Consumer Credit	318.50	131.17
2. 同业拆借 Placements from Banks and Other Financial Institutions	271.14	-11.76			

续表
Continued

项目 Items	余额 Balance	比年初增减额 Changes within the Year	项目 Items	余额 Balance	比年初增减额 Changes within the Year
八、委托存款及委托投资基金(净) Designated Deposits and Designated Investment Funds(Net)	-3.75	-12.01	4. 票据融资 Paper Financing	336.80	-135.54
			其中:贴现 Of Which: Discount	336.80	-135.54
1. 委托存款及委托投资基金 Designated Deposits and Designated Investment Funds	170.05	-4.30	5. 各项垫款 Total Advances	0.21	0.21
2. 减:委托贷款及委托投资 Minus: Designated Loans and Designated Investments	173.80	7.71	二、有价证券及投资 Securities and Investments	2380.75	313.03
			三、应收及预付款 Accounts Receivable and Advance Payments	224.74	-9.43
九、代理金融机构委托贷款基金 Designated Loan Funds on Behalf of Financial Institutions	109.25	48.35	其中:应收利息 Of Which: Interest Receivable	96.76	-20.18
其中:中央银行委托贷款基金 Of Which: Loan Funds Designated by the Central Bank	1.23	-0.04	四、买入返售资产 Assets Reverse Repo (Including Securities)	104.79	59.44
十、各项准备 Total Provisions	242.46	40.12	五、存放中央银行准备金存款 Reserve Deposits with the Central Bank	4004.03	1066.37
其中:贷款损失准备 Of Which: Provisions for Loan Losses	236.08	34.24	六、存放中央银行特种存款 Special Deposits with the Central Bank	16.78	16.47
十一、所有者权益 Owner's Equity	725.60	885.14	七、缴存中央银行财政性存款 Fiscal Deposits with the Central Bank	3.60	1.97
其中:实收资本 Of Which: Paid - in Capital	1432.68	802.12	八、同业往来 Inter - bank Transactions	2683.65	72.72
当年结益 Net Earnings	95.23	95.23	1. 存放同业 Due from Banks and Other Financial Institutions	2459.78	69.56
十二、其他 Others	-1690.08	-327.85	2. 拆放同业 Placements with Banks and Other Financial Institutions	223.87	3.16
			九、代理金融机构贷款 Lending on Behalf of Financial Institutions	89.21	27.28
			其中:代理人行专项贷款 Of Which: Agency Earmarked Loans of the Central Bank	2.17	-0.04
			十、库存现金 Cash in Vault	455.64	45.92
			十一、外汇占款 Position for Foreign Exchange Purchase	3.53	-2.57
资金来源总计 Total Sources	**29204.56**	**4122.72**	**资金运用总计 Total Uses**	**29204.56**	**4122.72**

农村信用合作社人民币信贷收支表

Sources and Uses of Credit Funds of Rural Credit Cooperatives(RMB)

（2005 年末）

（Year - end of 2005）

单位:亿元

Unit:100 Million Yuan

项目 Items	余额 Balance	比年初增减额 Changes within the Year	项目 Items	余额 Balance	比年初增减额 Changes within the Year
一、各项存款 Total Deposits	27605.61	1525.16	一、各项贷款 Total Loans	18680.86	1271.76
1. 企业存款 Deposits by Enterprises	1050.86	18.05	1. 短期贷款 Short - term Loans	16805.66	1115.41
(1)活期存款 Demand Deposits	3.26	1.33	(1)工业贷款 Loans to Industrial Sector	0.47	0.47
(2)定期存款 Time Deposits	1047.60	16.72	(2)商业贷款 Loans to Commercial Sector	0.06	0.06
2. 机关团体存款 Deposits by Government Agencies and Social Organizations	135.96	27.35	其中:收购贷款 Of Which: Loans for the Purchase of Farm Products		
3. 储蓄存款 Urban Savings Deposits	21739.33	1682.88	(3)建筑业贷款 Loans to Construction Sector		
(1)活期储蓄 Demand Deposits	6681.94	690.85	(4)农业贷款 Loans to Agricultural Sector	9331.01	1123.00
(2)定期储蓄 Time Deposits	15057.39	992.03	(5)乡镇企业贷款 Loans to Village and Township Enterprises	4554.58	- 273.51
4. 农业存款 Deposits by Agricultural Sector	4296.85	- 228.23	(6)三资企业贷款 Loans to Foreign Investment Enterprises and Ventures	0.09	0.09
5. 其他存款 Other Deposits	382.61	25.11	(7)私营企业及个体贷款 Loans to Privately - run Enterprises and Self - employed Entities	182.20	29.24
二、代理财政性存款 Agency Fiscal Deposits	84.66	26.30	(8)其他短期贷款 Other Short - term Loans	2737.25	236.06
三、金融债券 Financial Bonds	0.04		其中:个人短期消费贷款 Of Which: Short - term Consumer Credit	112.41	- 16.32
其中:政策性金融债券 Of Which: Policy Financial Bonds	0.04		2. 中期流动资金贷款 Medium - term Working Capital Loans	0.04	0.04
四、应付及暂收款 Accounts Payable and Receipts on Account	755.81	89.56	3. 中长期贷款 Medium and Long - term Loans	1556.62	133.68
其中:应付及预提利息 Of Which: Interest Payable and Accrued	351.61	27.73	(1)基本建设贷款 Capital Construction Loans	5.00	- 1.09
五、卖出回购资产 Assets Repo(Including Securities)	193.37	175.82	(2)技术改造贷款 Technical Improvement Loans		
六、向中央银行借款 Borrowings from the Central Bank	637.33	- 346.69	(3)其他中长期贷款 Other Medium and Long - term Loans	1551.62	134.77
七、同业往来 Inter - bank Transactions	614.75	- 108.54	其中:个人中长期消费贷款 Of Which: Medium and Long - term Consumer Credit	344.39	- 20.41
1. 同业存放 Due to Banks and Other Financial Institutions	421.84	- 38.94			
2. 同业拆借 Placements from Banks and Other Financial Institutions	192.91	- 69.60			

续表
Continued

项　目 Items	余　额 Balance	比年初增减额 Changes within the Year	项　目 Items	余　额 Balance	比年初增减额 Changes within the Year
八、委托存款及委托投资基金(净) Designated Deposits and Designated Investment Funds(Net)	19.30	19.24	4. 票据融资 Paper Financing	317.30	22.26
			其中:贴现 Of Which: Discount	317.30	22.26
1. 委托存款及委托投资基金 Designated Deposits and Designated Investment Funds	177.22	20.88	5. 各项垫款 Total Advances	1.24	0.37
2. 减:委托贷款及委托投资 Minus: Designated Loans and Designated Investments	157.92	1.64	二、有价证券及投资 Securities and Investments	2099.87	-167.16
			三、应收及预付款 Accounts Receivable and Advance Payments	302.62	42.56
九、代理金融机构委托贷款基金 Designated Loan Funds on Behalf of Financial Institutions	128.30	7.89	其中:应收利息 Of Which: Interest Receivable	81.89	-13.63
其中:中央银行委托贷款基金 Of Which: Loan Funds Designated by the Central Bank	1.53	-0.14	四、买入返售资产 Assets Reverse Repo (Including Securities)	80.56	-17.73
十、各项准备 Total Provisions	321.49	91.67	五、存放中央银行准备金存款 Reserve Deposits with the Central Bank	4303.62	467.56
其中:贷款损失准备 Of Which: Provisions for Loan Losses	291.01	77.51	六、存放中央银行特种存款 Special Deposits with the Central Bank	9.43	-7.24
十一、所有者权益 Owner's Equity	1318.89	696.79	七、缴存中央银行财政性存款 Fiscal Deposits with the Central Bank	5.84	2.27
其中:实收资本 Of Which: Paid-in Capital	1717.23	207.78	八、同业往来 Inter-bank Transactions	2470.84	-55.68
当年结益 Net Earnings	119.68	119.68	1. 存放同业 Due from Banks and Other Financial Institutions	2371.44	63.14
十二、其他 Others	-3120.02	-583.60	2. 拆放同业 Placements with Banks and Other Financial Institutions	99.40	-118.82
			九、代理金融机构贷款 Lending on Behalf of Financial Institutions	136.40	32.31
			其中:代理人行专项贷款 Of Which: Agency Earmarked Loans of the Central Bank	2.31	-0.27
			十、库存现金 Cash in Vault	465.63	24.84
			十一、外汇占款 Position for Foreign Exchange Purchase	3.86	0.11
资金来源总计 Total Sources	**28559.53**	**1593.60**	**资金运用总计 Total Uses**	**28559.53**	**1593.60**

11. 财务公司人民币信贷收支表（1993—2005 年）
Sources and Uses of Credit Funds of Finance Companies（RMB）（1993—2005）

财务公司人民币信贷收支表
Sources and Uses of Credit Funds of Finance Companies（RMB）

（1993 年末）

（Year - end of 1993）

单位：亿元

Unit：100 Million Yuan

项目 Items	余额 Balance	比年初增减额 Changes within the Year	项目 Items	余额 Balance	比年初增减额 Changes within the Year
一、企业存款 Deposits by Enterprises	48.49	18.94	一、流动资金贷款 Working Capital Loans	68.86	0.91
其中：活期存款 Of Which：Demand Deposits	26.01	8.85	其中：工业贷款 Of Which：Loans to Industrial Sector	58.94	35.89
定期存款 Time Deposits	22.48	10.09	商业贷款 Loans to Commercial Sector	6.65	1.04
二、委托存款 Designated Deposits	64.52	15.16	二、固定资产贷款 Fixed Asset Loans	8.45	3.34
三、保证金存款 Guarantee Deposits	2.37	1.22	基建贷款 Capital Construction Loans	0.02	0.02
四、其他存款 Other Deposits	5.28	- 18.13	三、特种贷款 Special Loans		
存款合计 Total Deposits	**120.66**	**17.19**	四、票据贴现 Paper Discount		
五、人民银行委托贷款资金 Loan Funds Designated by the Central Bank	1.00	- 0.07	五、委托贷款 Designated Loans	75.90	18.73
六、发行金融债券 Financial Bonds Issue	0.45	0.22	委托固定资产贷款 Designated Fixed Asset Loans	15.53	- 4.46
七、代理发行债券 Agency Bonds Issue	2.75	1.98	六、其他贷款 Other Loans	1.96	- 3.49
八、向人行借款 Borrowings from the Central Bank	21.07	- 0.64	**贷款合计 Total Loans**	**155.17**	**19.49**
其中：季节性 Of Which：Seasonal	20.67	0.36	七、投资 Investments	9.37	3.75
日拆性 Overnight			八、委托投资 Designated Investments	1.80	1.75
再贴现 Rediscount			九、融资租赁 Financing Leases	1.76	0.39
九、专业银行往来 Transactions with Special Banks	7.35	- 4.05	十、有价证券 Securities	3.68	0.28
十、其他金融机构往来 Transactions with Other Financial Institutions	5.42	- 3.48	十一、外币占款 Position for Foreign Exchange Purchase	1.84	0.03
十一、同业往来 Inter - bank Transactions	14.21	- 8.01	十二、国家债券 Treasury Bonds	0.26	0.01

续表
Continued

项　目 Items	余　额 Balance	比年初增减额 Changes within the Year	项　目 Items	余　额 Balance	比年初增减额 Changes within the Year
其中：拆入资金 Of Which: Placements from Banks and Other Financial Institutions	10.53	-0.13	十三、在人行存款 Deposits with the Central Bank	4.30	0.95
			十四、缴存人行存款准备金 Reserves with the Central Bank	3.13	-0.22
十二、呆账准备金 Provisions for Bad Loans	2.47	2.07	十五、代理人行专项贷款 Agency Earmarked Loans of the Central Bank	18.50	-1.33
十三、资本金 Capital	32.25	8.82			
			十六、专业银行往来 Transactions with Special Banks	12.02	-5.99
十四、当年结益 Net Earnings	5.97	5.97			
			十七、其他金融机构往来 Transactions with Other Financial Institutions	1.91	-2.44
十五、内部往来 Transactions within the Company	7.72	4.00			
十六、其他 Others	18.91	0.05	十八、同业往来 Inter-bank Transactions	8.34	0.58
			其中：拆出资金 Of Which: Placements with Banks and Other Financial Institutions	6.40	4.91
			十九、内部往来 Transactions within the Company	4.75	0.61
			二十、库存现金 Cash in Vault	0.02	0.02
			二十一、其他 Others	13.38	6.17
资金来源总计 Total Sources	**240.23**	**24.05**	**资金运用总计 Total Uses**	**240.23**	**24.05**

财务公司人民币信贷收支表

Sources and Uses of Credit Funds of Finance Companies（RMB）

（1994 年末）

（Year - end of 1994）

单位：亿元

Unit：100 Million Yuan

项目 Items	余额 Balance	比年初增减额 Changes within the Year	项目 Items	余额 Balance	比年初增减额 Changes within the Year
一、存款合计 Total Deposits	182.95	59.28	一、贷款合计 Total Loans	231.48	64.50
1. 企业存款 Deposits by Enterprises	67.13	18.05	1. 短期贷款 Short - term Loans	63.03	1.95
（1）活期存款 Demand Deposits	41.13	14.58	其中：工业贷款 Of Which：Loans to Industrial Sector	55.56	4.31
（2）定期存款 Time Deposits	26.00	3.47	商业贷款 Loans to Commercial Se - ctor	3.90	- 2.21
2. 委托存款 Designated Deposits	106.23	41.62			
3. 信托存款 Trust Deposits	8.37	3.75	2. 中长期贷款 Medium and Long - term Loans	7.31	- 1.96
4. 保证金存款 Guarantee Deposits	0.29	0.20	3. 委托贷款 Designated Loans	129.17	54.26
5. 其他存款 Other Deposits	0.93	- 4.34	其中：中长期贷款 Of Which：Medium and Long - term Loans	5.98	- 17.93
二、发行债券 Bonds Issue	0.60	0.15			
			4. 信托贷款 Trust Loans	28.79	15.51
三、证券业务款项 Securities Business Funds	3.80	- 1.04			
四、人行委托贷款资金 Loan Funds Designated by the Central Bank	1.03	- 0.09	其中：中长期贷款 Of Which：Medium and Long - term Loans	0.64	- 3.05
			5. 抵押贷款 Mortgage Loans	0.64	0.09
五、向人民银行借款 Borrowings from the Central Bank	7.00	- 14.04	6. 贴现 Discount	0.13	0.13
六、银行机构存款 Deposits by Banks	0.80	- 0.13	7. 租赁 Leases	2.41	0.75
七、拆放银行机构 Placements from Banks	23.26	2.32	8. 其他贷款 Other Loans		- 6.23
八、金融性公司存款 Desposits by Financial Corporations	3.11	2.43	二、委托投资 Designated Investments	5.42	3.62
九、金融性公司拆放 Placements from Financial Corporations	34.66	23.28	三、短期投资 Short - term Investments	2.26	0.99
十、所有者权益 Owner's Equity	49.98	12.10	其中：国家债券 Of Which：Treasury Bonds	0.17	0.12
其中：实收资本 Of Which：Paid - in Capital	43.19	8.87	四、长期投资 Long - term Investments	11.93	3.13
十一、结益 Net Earnings	2.80	2.80	其中：国家债券 Of Which：Treasury Bonds	0.55	- 0.18

续表
Continued

项 目 Items	余 额 Balance	比年初增减额 Changes within the Year	项 目 Items	余 额 Balance	比年初增减额 Changes within the Year
十二、贷款呆账准备金 Provisions for Bad Loans	0.96	0.26	五、证券业务占款 Funding of Securities Purchase	7.33	3.18
十三、投资风险准备 Provisions for Investment Risk	0.08	0.05	六、代理人民银行专项贷款 Agency Earmarked Loans of the Central Bank	0.89	-11.15
十四、其他 Others	33.94	10.96	七、在人民银行存款 Deposits with the Central Bank	3.12	-2.61
			八、缴存人民银行准备金 Reserves with the Central Bank	11.20	7.96
			九、缴存人民银行特种存款 Special Deposits with the Central Bank	0.02	0.02
			十、购买人民银行债券 Central Bank Bonds Purchase		
			十一、存放银行机构 Due from Banks	27.78	12.22
			十二、拆放银行机构 Placements with Banks	5.09	3.20
			十三、存放金融性公司 Due from Financial Corporations	5.04	4.52
			十四、拆放金融性公司 Placements with Financial Corporations	11.96	6.33
			十五、现金 Cash in Vault	0.03	
			十六、外币占款 Position for Foreign Exchange Purchase	0.74	-1.75
			十七、其他 Others	20.68	4.17
资金来源总计 Total Sources	**344.97**	**98.33**	**资金运用总计 Total Uses**	**344.97**	**98.33**

财务公司人民币信贷收支表

Sources and Uses of Credit Funds of Finance Companies（RMB）

（1995 年末）

（Year - end of 1995）

单位：亿元

Unit：100 Million Yuan

项目 Items	余额 Balance	比年初增减额 Changes within the Year	项目 Items	余额 Balance	比年初增减额 Changes within the Year
一、存款合计 Total Deposits	451.22	133.34	一、贷款合计 Total Loans	366.53	95.88
1. 企业存款 Deposits by Enterprises	144.67	57.02	1. 短期贷款 Short - term Loans	88.20	22.12
（1）活期存款 Demand Deposits	93.42	36.41	其中：工业贷款 Of Which：Loans to Industrial Sector	73.21	19.99
（2）定期存款 Time Deposits	51.25	20.61	商业贷款 Loans to Commercial Se - ctor	3.12	- 1.34
2. 委托存款 Designated Deposits	237.35	63.10			
3. 信托存款 Trust Deposits	68.35	13.59	2. 中长期贷款 Medium and Long - term Loans	11.76	4.48
4. 保证金存款 Guarantee Deposits	0.22	- 0.07	3. 委托贷款 Designated Loans	175.17	34.98
5. 其他存款 Other Deposits	0.63	- 0.30	其中：中长期贷款 Of Which：Medium and Long - term Loans	35.07	3.05
二、发行债券 Bonds Issue	0.11	- 0.49	4. 信托贷款 Trust Loans	85.15	31.42
三、证券业务款项 Securities Business Funds	3.82	- 2.07	其中：中长期贷款 Of Which：Medium and Long - term Loans	5.72	4.03
四、人行委托贷款资金 Loan Funds Designated by the Central Bank	0.86	- 0.17	5. 抵押贷款 Mortagage Loans	2.58	1.97
五、向人民银行借款 Borrowings from the Central Bank	5.29	- 1.65	6. 贴现 Discount	2.11	1.71
六、银行机构存款 Deposits by Banks	0.30	- 0.50	7. 租赁 Leases	1.56	- 0.19
七、银行机构拆放 Placements from Banks	12.55	5.31	8. 其他贷款 Other Loans		- 0.61
八、金融性公司存款 Desposits by Financial Corporations	4.67	2.57	二、委托投资 Designated Investments	22.73	14.18
九、金融性公司拆放 Placements from Financial Corporations	48.76	22.00	三、短期投资 Short - term Investments	5.86	2.11
十、长期借款 Long - term Borrowing	0.72	- 0.13	其中：国家债券 Of Which：Treasury Bonds	2.44	2.27
十一、所有者权益 Owner's Equity	67.36	9.53	四、长期投资 Long - term Investments	14.91	1.12
其中：实收资本 Of Which：Paid - in Capital	54.30	4.59	其中：国家债券 Of Which：Treasury Bonds	1.23	0.66

续表
Continued

项　目 Items	余　额 Balance	比年初增减额 Changes within the Year	项　目 Items	余　额 Balance	比年初增减额 Changes within the Year
十二、结益 Net Earnings	6.58	6.58	五、证券业务占款 Funding of Securities Purchase	8.78	2.47
十三、贷款呆账准备金 Provisions for Bad Loans	1.15	0.06	六、代理人民银行专项贷款 Agency Earmarked Loans of the Central Bank	0.95	0.06
十四、投资风险准备 Provisions for Investment Risk	0.12	0.03	七、在人民银行存款 Deposits with the Central Bank	12.74	6.73
十五、其他 Others	77.20	46.26	八、缴存人民银行准备金 Reserves with the Central Bank	26.64	6.93
			九、缴存人民银行特种存款 Special Deposits with the Central Bank	6.00	6.00
			十、购买人民银行债券 Central Bank Bonds Purchase		
			十一、存放银行机构 Due from Banks	55.17	3.82
			十二、拆放银行机构 Placements with Banks	4.05	-4.39
			十三、存放金融性公司 Due from Financial Corporations	9.59	2.23
			十四、拆放金融性公司 Placements with Financial Corporations	24.65	-6.04
			十五、现金 Cash in Vault	0.06	0.03
			十六、银行存款 Deposits with Banks	31.11	22.54
			十七、外币占款 Position for Foreign Exchange Purchase	2.67	1.93
			十八、其他 Others	88.27	65.03
资金来源总计 Total Sources	**680.71**	**220.67**	**资金运用总计 Total Uses**	**680.71**	**220.67**

财务公司人民币信贷收支表

Sources and Uses of Credit Funds of Finance Companies（RMB）

（1996 年末）

（Year - end of 1996）

单位：亿元

Unit：100 Million Yuan

项　目 Items	余　额 Balance	比年初增减额 Changes within the Year	项　目 Items	余　额 Balance	比年初增减额 Changes within the Year
一、存款合计 Total Deposits	818.09	298.20	一、贷款合计 Total Loans	634.87	183.92
1. 企业存款 Deposits by Enterprises	245.65	101.24	1. 短期贷款 Short - term Loans	119.57	36.25
（1）活期存款 Demand Deposits	184.55	88.96	其中：工业贷款 Of Which：Loans to Industrial Sector	99.86	24.18
（2）定期存款 Time Deposits	61.10	12.28	商业贷款 Loans to Commercial Sector	4.09	1.15
2. 委托存款 Designated Deposits	339.65	42.60	2. 中长期贷款 Medium and Long - term Loans	16.26	4.50
3. 信托存款 Trust Deposits	230.85	153.26	3. 委托贷款 Designated Loans	303.38	54.51
4. 保证金存款 Guarantee Deposits	0.59	0.37	其中：中长期贷款 Of Which：Medium and Long - term Loans	93.23	1.70
5. 其他存款 Other Deposits	1.35	0.73			
			4. 信托贷款 Trust Loans	165.31	69.37
二、发行债券 Bonds Issue	0.28	0.17			
			其中：中长期贷款 Of Which：Medium and Long - term Loans	39.43	34.42
三、证券业务款项 Securities Business Funds	7.32	1.24			
四、人行委托贷款资金 Loan Funds Designated by the Central Bank	0.86		5. 抵押贷款 Mortagage Loans	5.96	3.36
			其中：中长期贷款 Of Which：Medium and Long - term Loans	0.74	- 0.26
五、向人行借款 Borrowings from the Central Bank	6.68	1.89			
六、银行机构存款 Deposits by Banks	0.01	- 0.29	6. 贴现 Discount	17.59	15.37
七、银行机构拆放 Placements from Banks	12.59	0.04	7. 租赁 Leases	6.80	0.56
八、金融性公司存款 Desposits by Financial Corporations	11.84	6.82	8. 其他贷款 Other Loans		
九、金融性公司拆放 Placements from Financial Corporations	78.27	26.17	二、委托投资 Designated Investments	10.15	- 12.58
十、长期借款 Long - term Borrowing	5.64	4.75	三、短期投资 Short - term Investments	12.12	6.81
十一、所有者权益 Owner's Equity	98.40	14.03	其中：国家债券 Of Which：Treasury Bonds	5.87	3.44
其中：实收资本 Of Which：Paid - in Capital	77.11	10.25	四、长期投资 Long - term Investments	41.80	27.17

续表
Continued

项　目 Items	余　额 Balance	比年初增减额 Changes within the Year	项　目 Items	余　额 Balance	比年初增减额 Changes within the Year
十二、结益 Net Earnings	10.05	10.05	其中：国家债券 Of Which: Treasury Bonds	24.24	22.96
十三、呆账准备金 Provisions for Bad Loans	2.18	0.97	五、证券业务占款 Funding of Securities Purchase	11.58	0.14
十四、投资风险准备 Provisions for Investment Risk	0.11	-0.01	六、代理人行贷款 Special Lending as an Agency of the Central Bank	1.29	0.43
十五、其他 Others	120.50	33.49	七、在人行存款 Deposits with the Central Bank	12.09	0.50
			八、缴存人行准备金 Reserves with the Central Bank	56.96	30.83
			九、缴存人行特种存款 Special Deposits with the Central Bank	0.06	-5.94
			十、购买人行债券 Central Bank Bonds Purchase		
			十一、存放银行机构 Due from Banks	123.89	56.42
			十二、拆放银行机构 Placements with Banks	11.71	7.23
			十三、存放金融性公司 Due from Financial Corporations	18.91	8.91
			十四、拆放金融性公司 Placements with Financial Corporations	33.11	6.05
			十五、现金 Cash in Vault	0.07	0.03
			十六、银行存款 Deposits with Banks	74.55	43.47
			十七、外币占款 Position for Foreign Exchange Purchase	0.53	0.10
			十八、其他 Others	129.13	44.03
资金来源总计 Total Sources	**1172.82**	**397.52**	**资金运用总计 Total Uses**	**1172.82**	**397.52**

财务公司人民币信贷收支表

Sources and Uses of Credit Funds of Finance Companies（RMB）

（1997 年末）

（Year - end of 1997）

单位：亿元

Unit：100 Million Yuan

项目 Items	余额 Balance	比年初增减额 Changes within the Year	项目 Items	余额 Balance	比年初增减额 Changes within the Year
一、各项存款 Total Deposits	1044.75	225.09	一、各项贷款 Total Loans	807.21	180.28
1. 企业存款 Deposits by Enterprises	457.86	111.27	1. 短期贷款 Short - term Loans	240.94	25.45
（1）活期存款 Demand Deposits	325.71	48.39	（1）工业贷款 Loans to Industrial Sector	213.63	43.34
（2）定期存款 Time Deposits	132.15	62.88	（2）商业贷款 Loans to Commercial Sector	13.78	1.44
2. 委托存款及投资基金 Designated Deposits and Designated Investment Funds	416.59	90.87	（3）其他短期贷款 Other Short - term Loans	13.53	- 19.33
			2. 中长期贷款 Medium and Long - term Loans	37.24	- 0.45
（1）委托存款 Designated Deposits	410.16	84.92	3. 委托贷款 Designated Loans	377.55	74.68
（2）委托投资基金 Designated Investment Funds	6.43	5.95	4. 信托贷款 Trust Loans	109.03	68.23
3. 信托存款 Trust Deposits	169.07	22.30	其中：中长期信托贷款 Of Which：Medium and Long - term Trust Loans	93.88	93.69
4. 保证金存款 Guarantee Deposits	1.23	0.65			
5. 其他存款 Other Deposits			5. 抵押贷款 Mortagage Loans	2.39	- 0.55
二、发行金融债券 Financial Bonds Issue	0.98	0.69	6. 贴现贷款 Discount	8.90	- 8.66
三、长期借款 Long - term Borrowing	6.58	2.19	7. 融资租赁 Financing Leases	2.82	- 4.02
四、证券业务款项 Securities Business Funds	2.57	- 4.62	8. 逾期类贷款 Overdue Loans	28.34	25.59
五、卖出回购证券 Repo	- 10.13	- 6.53	二、委托投资 Designated Investments	18.36	8.41
六、向人民银行借款 Borrowings from the Central Bank	4.04	0.14	三、投资 Investments	75.84	21.28
七、同业往来 Inter - bank Transactions	52.41	- 4.98	1. 短期投资 Short - term Investments	33.19	17.32
1. 同业存放 Due to Banks and Other Financial Institutions	6.16	2.11	2. 长期投资 Long - term Investments	42.65	3.96
			四、证券业务款项 Securities Business Funds	2.90	0.83

续表
Continued

项　目 Items	余　额 Balance	比年初增减额 Changes within the Year	项　目 Items	余　额 Balance	比年初增减额 Changes within the Year
2. 同业拆借 Placements from Banks and Other Financial Institutions	46.25	-7.09	五、经营租赁 Operating Leases		
			六、缴存准备金存款 Reserves with the Central Bank	53.43	24.31
八、代理金融机构贷款基金 Designated Loan Funds on Behalf of Financial Institutions	69.67	9.61	七、缴存人行准备金 Reserves with the Central Bank	50.39	15.69
其中：中央银行委托贷款基金 Of Which: Loan Funds Designated by the Central Bank	0.91	0.05	八、缴存人行特种存款 Special Deposits with the Central Bank	0.36	0.16
			九、同业往来 Inter-bank Transactions	156.03	-13.45
九、各项准备 Total Provisions	3.82	1.48	1. 存放同业 Due from Banks and Other Financial Institutions	140.66	4.41
十、所有者权益 Owner's Equity	161.54	60.41			
其中：实收资本 Of Which: Paid-in Capital	119.21	39.14	2. 拆放同业 Placements with Banks and Other Financial Institutions	15.37	-17.86
当年结益 Net Earnings	22.42	22.42			
			十、代理金融机构贷款 Lending on Behalf of Financial Institutions	69.41	11.15
十一、其他 Others	-100.61	-33.42			
			其中：代理人行专项贷款 Of Which: Agency Earmarked Loans of the Central Bank	0.76	-0.10
			十一、现金 Cash in Vault	0.11	0.05
			十二、外币占款 Position for Foreign Exchange Purchase	1.58	1.35
资金来源总计 Total Sources	**1235.62**	**250.06**	**资金运用总计 Total Uses**	**1235.62**	**250.06**

财务公司人民币信贷收支表

Sources and Uses of Credit Funds of Finance Companies（RMB）

（1998 年末）

（Year - end of 1998）

单位：亿元

Unit：100 Million Yuan

项目 Items	余额 Balance	比年初增减额 Changes within the Year	项目 Items	余额 Balance	比年初增减额 Changes within the Year
一、各项存款 Total Deposits	1366.04	315.40	一、各项贷款 Total Loans	1014.36	204.57
1. 企业存款 Deposits by Enterprises	657.75	194.49	1. 短期贷款 Short - term Loans	281.66	47.46
（1）活期存款 Demand Deposits	378.69	48.71	（1）工业贷款 Loans to Industrial Sector	260.13	51.88
（2）定期存款 Time Deposits	279.06	145.78	（2）商业贷款 Loans to Commercial Sector	9.52	- 2.42
2. 委托存款及投资基金 Designated Deposits and Designated Investment Funds	527.54	110.45	（3）其他短期贷款 Other Short - term Loans	12.01	- 2.00
			2. 中长期贷款 Medium and Long - term Loans	44.54	12.87
（1）委托存款 Designated Deposits	478.89	84.02	3. 委托贷款 Designated Loans	478.96	100.80
（2）委托投资基金 Designated Investment Funds	48.65	26.43	4. 信托贷款 Trust Loans	137.80	29.30
3. 信托存款 Trust Deposits	180.34	11.28	其中：中长期信托贷款 Of Which：Medium and Long - term Trust Loans	44.98	- 48.90
4. 保证金存款 Guarantee Deposits	0.41	- 0.82			
5. 其他存款 Other Deposits			5. 抵押贷款 Mortagage Loans	0.77	- 1.62
二、发行金融债券 Financial Bonds Issue	0.36	- 0.62	6. 贴现贷款 Discount	19.53	10.58
三、长期借款 Long - term Borrowing	6.08	- 0.50	7. 融资租赁 Financing Leases	2.95	0.13
四、证券业务款项 Securities Business Funds	4.30	2.14	8. 逾期类贷款 Overdue Loans	48.15	5.05
五、卖出回购证券 Repo	0.67	10.75	二、委托投资 Designated Investments	23.78	5.65
六、向人民银行借款 Borrowings from the Central Bank	6.65	2.62	三、投资 Investments	82.64	6.72
七、同业往来 Inter - bank Transactions	38.83	- 14.02	1. 短期投资 Short - term Investments	39.15	5.89

续表
Continued

项　目 Items	余　额 Balance	比年初增减额 Changes within the Year	项　目 Items	余　额 Balance	比年初增减额 Changes within the Year
1. 同业存放 Due to Banks and Other Financial Institutions	6.43	0.27	2. 长期投资 Long - term Investments	43.49	0.83
			四、证券业务款项 Securities Business Funds	2.93	0.43
2. 同业拆借 Placements from Banks and Other Financial Institutions	32.40	-14.29	五、经营租赁 Operating Leases		
八、代理金融机构贷款基金 Designated Loan Funds on Behalf of Financial Institutions	5.15	-65.59	六、缴存准备金存款 Reserves with the Central Bank	97.80	-5.93
其中：中央银行委托贷款基金 Of Which: Loan Funds Designated by the Central Bank	0.80	-0.11	七、缴存人行准备金 Reserves with the Central Bank		
			八、缴存人行特种存款 Special Deposits with the Central Bank		-0.36
九、各项准备 Total Provisions	5.93	1.95	九、同业往来 Inter - bank Transactions	208.44	47.21
十、所有者权益 Owner's Equity	172.74	20.02	1. 存放同业 Due from Banks and Other Financial Institutions	197.33	51.98
其中：实收资本 Of Which: Paid - in Capital	122.04	2.95	2. 拆放同业 Placements with Banks and Other Financial Institutions	11.11	-4.77
当年结益 Net Earnings	24.57	24.57			
十一、其他 Others	-170.30	-76.59	十、代理金融机构贷款 Lending on Behalf of Financial Institutions	4.86	-62.74
			其中：代理人行专项贷款 Of Which: Agency Earmarked Loans of the Central Bank	0.68	-0.08
			十一、现金 Cash in Vault	0.07	-0.02
			十二、外币占款 Position for Foreign Exchange Purchase	1.57	0.03
资金来源总计 **Total Sources**	**1436.45**	**195.56**	**资金运用总计** **Total Uses**	**1436.45**	**195.56**

财务公司人民币信贷收支表
Sources and Uses of Credit Funds of Finance Companies（RMB）

（1999年末）

（Year - end of 1999）

单位：亿元

Unit：100 Million Yuan

项　目 Items	余　额 Balance	比年初增减额 Changes within the Year	项　目 Items	余　额 Balance	比年初增减额 Changes within the Year
一、各项存款 Total Deposits	1609.59	239.93	一、各项贷款 Total Loans	1219.06	199.34
1. 企业存款 Deposits by Enterprises	759.45	92.18	1. 短期贷款 Short - term Loans	298.97	10.98
（1）活期存款 Demand Deposits	452.68	70.52	（1）工业贷款 Loans to Industrial Sector	273.95	7.56
（2）定期存款 Time Deposits	306.77	21.66	（2）商业贷款 Loans to Commercial Sector	4.02	-5.53
2. 委托存款及投资基金 Designated Deposits and Designated Investment Funds	579.00	56.43	（3）其他短期贷款 Other Short - term Loans	21.00	8.95
			2. 中长期贷款 Medium and Long - term Loans	71.40	22.55
（1）委托存款 Designated Deposits	571.93	98.01	3. 委托贷款 Designated Loans	526.16	47.43
（2）委托投资基金 Designated Investment Funds	7.07	-41.58	4. 信托贷款 Trust Loans	222.43	84.62
3. 信托存款 Trust Deposits	270.42	91.27	其中：中长期信托贷款 Of Which：Medium and Long - term Trust Loans	63.74	18.76
4. 保证金存款 Guarantee Deposits	0.44	0.03			
5. 其他存款 Other Deposits	0.28	0.02	5. 抵押贷款 Mortagage Loans	0.78	0.01
二、发行金融债券 Financial Bonds Issue	1.52	1.16	6. 贴现贷款 Discount	24.88	5.35
三、长期借款 Long - term Borrowing	4.84	-0.78	7. 融资租赁 Financing Leases	1.95	-1.05
四、证券业务款项 Securities Business Funds	0.34	-3.96	8. 逾期类贷款 Overdue Loans	72.49	29.45
五、卖出回购证券 Repo	-4.68	-6.42	二、委托投资 Designated Investments	13.48	-10.44
六、向人民银行借款 Borrowings from the Central Bank	6.60	-0.05	三、投资 Investments	74.91	-8.63
七、同业往来 Inter - bank Transactions	37.74	-0.98	1. 短期投资 Short - term Investments	31.69	-7.73
1. 同业存放 Due to Banks and Other Financial Institutions	7.76	1.59	2. 长期投资 Long - term Investments	43.22	-0.90

续表
Continued

项 目 Items	余 额 Balance	比年初增减额 Changes within the Year	项 目 Items	余 额 Balance	比年初增减额 Changes within the Year
2. 同业拆借 Placements from Banks and Other Financial Institutions	29.98	-2.57	四、证券业务款项 Securities Business Funds	0.37	-2.55
八、代理金融机构贷款基金 Designated Loan Funds on Behalf of Financial Institutions	0.80	-4.35	五、经营租赁 Operating Leases		
其中：中央银行委托贷款基金 Of Which: Loan Funds Designated by the Central Bank	0.80		六、缴存准备金存款 Reserves with the Central Bank	79.75	-18.08
九、各项准备 Total Provisions	7.53	1.01	七、缴存人行特种存款 Special Deposits with the Central Bank		
十、所有者权益 Owner's Equity	166.62	-0.01	八、同业往来 Inter-bank Transactions	247.55	35.63
其中：实收资本 Of Which: Paid-in Capital	129.59	7.75	1. 存放同业 Due from Banks and Other Financial Institutions	237.75	36.95
当年结益 Net Earnings	11.53	11.53	2. 拆放同业 Placements with Banks and Other Financial Institutions	9.80	-1.32
十一、其他 Others	-194.75	-35.72	九、代理金融机构贷款 Lending on Behalf of Financial Institutions		-4.87
			其中：代理人行专项贷款 Of Which: Agency Earmarked Loans of the Central Bank		-0.68
			十、现金 Cash in Vault	0.10	0.03
			十一、外币占款 Position for Foreign Exchange Purchase	0.93	-0.60
资金来源总计 Total Sources	**1636.15**	**189.83**	**资金运用总计 Total Uses**	**1636.15**	**189.83**

财务公司人民币信贷收支表

Sources and Uses of Credit Funds of Finance Companies（RMB）

（2000 年末）

（Year – end of 2000）

单位：亿元

Unit：100 Million Yuan

项目 Items	余额 Balance	比年初增减额 Changes within the Year	项目 Items	余额 Balance	比年初增减额 Changes within the Year
一、各项存款 Total Deposits	1948.35	342.80	一、各项贷款 Total Loans	1414.34	205.76
1. 企业存款 Deposits by Enterprises	1040.75	278.02	1. 短期贷款 Short – term Loans	402.65	108.42
（1）活期存款 Demand Deposits	479.08	27.34	（1）工业贷款 Loans to Industrial Sector	360.20	90.85
（2）定期存款 Time Deposits	561.67	250.68	（2）商业贷款 Loans to Commercial Sector	12.70	8.85
2. 委托存款及投资基金 Designated Deposits and Designated Investment Funds	646.05	70.80	（3）其他短期贷款 Other Short – term Loans	29.75	8.72
			2. 中长期贷款 Medium and Long – term Loans	63.25	– 5.15
（1）委托存款 Designated Deposits	641.33	73.55	3. 委托贷款 Designated Loans	604.82	82.16
（2）委托投资基金 Designated Investment Funds	4.72	– 2.75	4. 信托贷款 Trust Loans	220.13	– 2.30
3. 信托存款 Trust Deposits	260.34	– 6.51	其中：中长期信托贷款 Of Which：Medium and Long – term Trust Loans	52.21	– 11.53
4. 保证金存款 Guarantee Deposits	0.97	0.53			
5. 其他存款 Other Deposits	0.24	– 0.04	5. 抵押贷款 Mortagage Loans	0.76	– 0.02
二、发行金融债券 Financial Bonds Issue	0.28	– 1.24	6. 贴现贷款 Discount	27.64	2.61
三、长期借款 Long – term Borrowing	7.12	2.28	7. 融资租赁 Financing Leases	1.20	– 0.78
四、证券业务占款 Securities Business Funds	8.17	7.83	8. 逾期类贷款 Overdue Loans	93.89	20.82
五、卖出回购证券 Repo	2.16	6.84	二、委托投资 Designated Investments	19.18	5.31
六、向人民银行借款 Borrowings from the Central Bank	7.30	0.70	三、投资 Investments	100.93	26.90
七、同业往来 Inter – bank Transactions	50.31	12.55	1. 短期投资 Short – term Investments	61.55	31.14
1. 同业存放 Due to Banks and Other Financial Institutions	7.54	– 0.22	2. 长期投资 Long – term Investments	39.38	– 4.24

续表
Continued

项　目 Items	余　额 Balance	比年初增减额 Changes within the Year	项　目 Items	余　额 Balance	比年初增减额 Changes within the Year
2. 同业拆借 Placements from Banks and Other Financial Institutions	42.77	12.77	四、证券业务占款 Securities Business Funds	6.76	6.39
			五、经营租赁 Operating Leases		
八、代理金融机构贷款基金 Designated Loan Funds on Behalf of Financial Institutions		-0.80	六、缴存准备金存款 Reserves with the Central Bank	97.99	20.75
其中：中央银行委托贷款基金 Of Which: Loan Funds Designated by the Central Bank		-0.80	七、缴存人行特种存款 Special Deposits with the Central Bank		
			八、同业往来 Inter-bank Transactions	357.51	110.06
九、各项准备 Total Provisions	9.21	1.59	1. 存放同业 Due from Banks and Other Financial Institutions	347.68	109.90
十、所有者权益 Owner's Equity	190.14	27.50			
其中：实收资本 Of Which: Paid-in Capital	143.62	16.19	2. 拆放同业 Placements with Banks and Other Financial Institutions	9.83	0.16
当年结益 Net Earnings	15.89	15.89	九、代理金融机构贷款 Lending on Behalf of Financial Institutions		
十一、其他 Others	-224.74	-25.55	其中：代理人行专项贷款 Of Which: Agency Earmarked Loans of the Central Bank		
			十、现金 Cash in Vault	0.07	-0.02
			十一、外币占款 Position for Foreign Exchange Purchase	1.52	-0.65
资金来源总计 Total Sources	**1998.30**	**374.50**	**资金运用总计 Total Uses**	**1998.30**	**374.50**

财务公司人民币信贷收支表

Sources and Uses of Credit Funds of Finance Companies（RMB）

（2001 年末）

（Year－end of 2001）

单位：亿元

Unit：100 Million Yuan

项目 Items	余额 Balance	比年初增减额 Changes within the Year	项目 Items	余额 Balance	比年初增减额 Changes within the Year
一、各项存款 Total Deposits	2689.77	744.90	一、各项贷款 Total Loans	1832.35	420.50
1. 企业存款 Deposits by Enterprises	1637.28	345.18	1. 短期贷款 Short－term Loans	506.28	－108.49
（1）活期存款 Demand Deposits	721.55	247.46	（1）工业贷款 Loans to Industrial Sector	428.39	－134.17
（2）定期存款 Time Deposits	915.73	97.72	（2）商业贷款 Loans to Commercial Sector	12.58	－1.11
2. 机关团体存款 Deposits by Government Agencies and Social Organizations			（3）其他短期贷款 Other Short－term Loans	65.31	26.79
			2. 中长期贷款 Medium and Long－term Loans	282.34	158.72
3. 委托存款及投资基金 Designated Deposits and Designated Investment Funds	1041.35	395.11	3. 委托贷款 Designated Loans	961.05	346.53
（1）委托存款 Designated Deposits	976.46	334.99	4. 信托贷款 Trust Loans	16.80	－12.32
（2）委托投资基金 Designated Investment Funds	64.89	60.12	其中：中长期信托贷款 Of Which：Medium and Long－term Trust Loans	0.86	－1.74
4. 信托存款 Trust Deposits	8.94	3.62	5. 抵押贷款 Mortagage Loans	2.13	1.20
5. 保证金存款 Guarantee Deposits	2.12	1.15	6. 贴现贷款 Discount	61.77	34.07
6. 其他存款 Other Deposits	0.08	－0.16	其中：贴现 Of Which：Discount	61.77	34.07
二、金融债券 Financial Bonds	0.05	－0.23	7. 融资租赁 Financing Leases	1.98	0.79
三、应付及暂收款 Accounts Payable and Receipts on Account	123.05	32.21	8. 各项垫款 Total Advances		
其中：应付及预提利息 Of Which：Interest Payable and Accrued	23.06	－4.36	二、委托投资 Designated Investments	64.50	45.27
四、长期借款 Long－term Borrowing	3.12	－4.00	三、投资 Investments	268.92	168.37
五、证券业务款项 Securities Business Funds	4.78	－3.39	1. 短期投资 Short－term Investments	94.80	33.30
六、卖出回购证券 Repo	22.63	12.40	2. 长期投资 Long－term Investments	174.12	135.07
七、向中央银行借款 Borrowings from the Central Bank	7.08	－0.22	四、应收及预付款 Accounts Receivable and Advance Payments	63.77	－12.50

续表
Continued

项　目 Items	余　额 Balance	比年初增减额 Changes within the Year	项　目 Items	余　额 Balance	比年初增减额 Changes within the Year
八、同业往来 Inter-bank Transactions	75.26	24.95	其中：应收利息 Of Which: Interest Receivable	13.05	-3.91
1.同业存放 Due to Banks and Other Financial Institutions	8.98	1.44	五、证券业务款项 Securities Business Funds	7.76	1.00
			六、经营租赁 Operating Leases		
2.同业拆借 Placements from Banks and Other Financial Institutions	66.28	23.51	七、买入返售证券 Reverse Repo	19.95	11.88
九、代理金融机构贷款基金 Designated Loan Funds on Behalf of Financial Institutions	0.05	0.05	八、存放中央银行准备金存款 Reserve Deposits with the Central Bank	132.61	34.61
其中：中央银行委托贷款基金 Of Which: Loan Funds Designated by the Central Bank			九、存放中央银行特种存款 Special Deposits with the Central Bank		
			十、同业往来 Inter-bank Transactions	562.12	206.25
十、各项准备 Total Provisions	15.69	6.52	1.存放同业 Due from Banks and Other Financial Institutions	552.21	206.06
其中：贷款呆账准备金 Of Which: Provisions for Bad Loans	14.15	5.63	2.拆放同业 Placements with Banks and Other Financial Institutions	9.91	0.19
十一、所有者权益 Owner's Equity	232.04	44.11			
其中：实收资本 Of Which: Paid-in Capital	196.09	50.70	十一、代理金融机构贷款 Lending on Behalf of Financial Institutions	0.05	0.05
当年结益 Net Earnings	16.49	16.49			
十二、其他 Others	-224.20	10.76	其中：代理人行专项贷款 Of Which: Agency Earmarked Loans of the Central Bank		
			十二、现金 Cash in Vault	0.07	-3.00
			十三、外币占款 Position for Foreign Exchange Purchase	-2.78	-4.37
资金来源总计 Total Sources	**2949.32**	**868.06**	**资金运用总计 Total Uses**	**2949.32**	**868.06**

财务公司人民币信贷收支表

Sources and Uses of Credit Funds of Finance Companies（RMB）

（2002年末）

（Year - end of 2002）

单位：亿元

Unit：100 Million Yuan

项目 Items	余额 Balance	比年初增减额 Changes within the Year	项目 Items	余额 Balance	比年初增减额 Changes within the Year
一、各项存款 Total Deposits	3319.02	651.70	一、各项贷款 Total Loans	2068.94	255.13
1. 企业存款 Deposits by Enterprises	2215.39	600.82	1. 短期贷款 Short - term Loans	632.31	128.69
（1）活期存款 Demand Deposits	1261.82	531.49	（1）工业贷款 Loans to Industrial Sector	541.09	111.81
（2）定期存款 Time Deposits	953.57	69.33	（2）商业贷款 Loans to Commercial Sector	36.92	24.01
2. 机关团体存款 Deposits by Government Agencies and Social Organizations			（3）其他短期贷款 Other Short - term Loans	54.30	-7.13
			2. 中长期贷款 Medium and Long - term Loans	337.26	59.88
3. 委托存款及投资基金 Designated Deposits and Designated Investment Funds	1089.72	47.94	3. 委托贷款 Designated Loans	1018.61	57.99
（1）委托存款 Designated Deposits	1046.49	68.60	4. 信托贷款 Trust Loans	16.72	-0.08
（2）委托投资基金 Designated Investment Funds	43.23	-20.66	其中：中长期信托贷款 Of Which：Medium and Long - term Trust Loans	0.46	-0.40
4. 信托存款 Trust Deposits	10.31	1.53	5. 抵押贷款 Mortagage Loans	2.04	-0.09
5. 保证金存款 Guarantee Deposits	3.34	1.23	6. 票据融资 Paper Financing	60.24	8.96
6. 其他存款 Other Deposits	0.26	0.18	其中：贴现 Of Which：Discount	60.24	8.96
二、金融债券 Financial Bonds		-0.05	7. 融资租赁 Financing Leases	1.76	-0.22
三、应付及暂收款 Accounts Payable and Receipts on Account	117.15	-10.55	8. 各项垫款 Total Advances		
其中：应付及预提利息 Of Which：Interest Payable and Accrued	23.76	1.71	二、委托投资 Designated Investments	64.30	-0.30
			三、投资 Investments	523.15	249.13
四、长期借款 Long - term Borrowing	2.48	-0.64	1. 短期投资 Short - term Investments	186.13	85.28
五、证券业务款项 Securities Business Funds	22.68	17.90			

续表
Continued

项　目 Items	余　额 Balance	比年初增减额 Changes within the Year	项　目 Items	余　额 Balance	比年初增减额 Changes within the Year
六、卖出回购证券 Repo	72.40	49.78	2. 长期投资 Long - term Investments	337.02	163.85
七、向中央银行借款 Borrowings from the Central Bank	7.06	-0.03	四、应收及预付款 Accounts Receivable and Advance Payments	92.18	27.37
八、同业往来 Inter - bank Transactions	78.98	3.65	其中：应收利息 Of Which: Interest Receivable	10.94	-1.88
1. 同业存放 Due to Banks and Other Financial Institutions	9.31	0.37	五、证券业务款项 Securities Business Funds	3.59	-4.17
2. 同业拆借 Placements from Banks and Other Financial Institutions	69.67	3.28	六、经营租赁 Operating Leases		
			七、买入返售证券 Reverse Repo	154.74	134.82
九、代理金融机构贷款基金 Designated Loan Funds on Behalf of Financial Institutions	1.21	1.16	八、存放中央银行准备金存款 Reserve Deposits with the Central Bank	136.88	17.04
其中：中央银行委托贷款基金 Of Which: Loan Funds Designated by the Central Bank			九、存放中央银行特种存款 Special Deposits with the Central Bank		
			十、同业往来 Inter - bank Transactions	794.54	227.94
十、各项准备 Total Provisions	20.54	4.52	1. 存放同业 Due from Banks and Other Financial Institutions	786.04	229.20
其中：贷款呆账准备金 Of Which: Provisions for Bad Loans	18.29	3.84			
十一、所有者权益 Owner's Equity	290.43	55.22	2. 拆放同业 Placements with Banks and Other Financial Institutions	8.50	-1.26
其中：实收资本 Of Which: Paid - in Capital	247.28	46.27	十一、代理金融机构贷款 Lending on Behalf of Financial Institutions	0.05	
当年结益 Net Earnings	28.37	28.37			
十二、其他 Others	-94.39	135.71	其中：代理人行专项贷款 Of Which: Agency Earmarked Loans of the Central Bank		
			十二、现金 Cash in Vault	0.06	-0.01
			十三、外币占款 Position for Foreign Exchange Purchase	-0.87	1.42
资金来源总计 Total Sources	**3837.56**	**908.37**	**资金运用总计 Total Uses**	**3837.56**	**908.37**

财务公司人民币信贷收支表

Sources and Uses of Credit Funds of Finance Companies（RMB）

（2003 年末）

（Year - end of 2003）

单位：亿元

Unit：100 Million Yuan

项目 Items	余额 Balance	比年初增减额 Changes within the Year	项目 Items	余额 Balance	比年初增减额 Changes within the Year
一、各项存款 Total Deposits	4207.97	893.42	一、各项贷款 Total Loans	2500.98	442.72
1. 企业存款 Deposits by Enterprises	2860.21	643.05	1. 短期贷款 Short - term Loans	726.12	98.27
（1）活期存款 Demand Deposits	1632.87	369.27	（1）工业贷款 Loans to Industrial Sector	595.38	58.67
（2）定期存款 Time Deposits	1227.34	273.78	（2）商业贷款 Loans to Commercial Sector	49.88	13.00
2. 机关团体存款 Deposits by Government Agencies and Social Organizations			（3）其他短期贷款 Other Short - term Loans	80.86	26.60
			2. 中长期贷款 Medium and Long - term Loans	494.38	157.12
3. 委托存款及投资基金 Designated Deposits and Designated Investment Funds	1326.59	243.05	3. 委托贷款 Designated Loans	1097.46	85.02
（1）委托存款 Designated Deposits	1143.60	103.29	4. 信托贷款 Trust Loans	27.23	10.54
（2）委托投资基金 Designated Investment Funds	182.99	139.76	其中：中长期信托贷款 Of Which：Medium and Long - term Trust Loans	1.43	0.97
4. 信托存款 Trust Deposits	15.47	5.16	5. 抵押贷款 Mortagage Loans	1.60	- 0.42
5. 保证金存款 Guarantee Deposits	5.70	2.36	6. 票据融资 Paper Financing	142.58	82.34
6. 其他存款 Other Deposits		- 0.20	其中：贴现 Of Which：Discount	142.58	82.34
二、金融债券 Financial Bonds			7. 融资租赁 Financing Leases	8.01	6.25
三、应付及暂收款 Accounts Payable and Receipts on Account	108.21	- 3.88	8. 各项垫款 Total Advances	3.60	3.60
其中：应付及预提利息 Of Which：Interest Payable and Accrued	24.54	1.05	二、委托投资 Designated Investments	191.52	127.37
			三、投资 Investments	738.51	221.15
四、长期借款 Long - term Borrowing	7.04	4.56	1. 短期投资 Short - term Investments	338.34	153.13
五、证券业务款项 Securities Business Funds	0.17	- 22.51			

续表
Continued

项　目 Items	余　额 Balance	比年初增减额 Changes within the Year	项　目 Items	余　额 Balance	比年初增减额 Changes within the Year
六、卖出回购证券 Repo	118.88	47.25	2. 长期投资 Long - term Investments	400.17	68.02
七、向中央银行借款 Borrowings from the Central Bank	5.62	0.09	四、应收及预付款 Accounts Receivable and Advance Payments	61.25	- 20.33
八、同业往来 Inter - bank Transactions	77.08	3.52	其中：应收利息 Of Which: Interest Receivable	9.52	1.56
1. 同业存放 Due to Banks and Other Financial Institutions	16.27	7.19	五、证券业务款项 Securities Business Funds	3.42	- 0.17
2. 同业拆借 Placements from Banks and Other Financial Institutions	60.81	- 3.67	六、经营租赁 Operating Leases		
			七、买入返售证券 Reverse Repo	189.01	33.55
九、代理金融机构贷款基金 Designated Loan Funds on Behalf of Financial Institutions		- 1.21	八、存放中央银行准备金存款 Reserve Deposits with the Central Bank	206.97	70.14
其中：中央银行委托贷款基金 Of Which: Loan Funds Designated by the Central Bank			九、存放中央银行特种存款 Special Deposits with the Central Bank		
			十、同业往来 Inter - bank Transactions	908.13	114.58
十、各项准备 Total Provisions	30.13	9.83	1. 存放同业 Due from Banks and Other Financial Institutions	902.63	117.13
其中：贷款损失准备 Of Which: Provisions for Loan Losses	24.00	7.91			
十一、所有者权益 Owner's Equity	326.79	41.48	2. 拆放同业 Placements with Banks and Other Financial Institutions	5.50	- 2.55
其中：实收资本 Of Which: Paid - in Capital	267.16	23.80	十一、代理金融机构贷款 Lending on Behalf of Financial Institutions	0.05	
当年结益 Net Earnings	35.16	35.16			
十二、其他 Others	- 82.16	16.21	其中：代理人行专项贷款 Of Which: Agency Earmarked Loans of the Central Bank		
			十二、现金 Cash in Vault	0.06	
			十三、外币占款 Position for Foreign Exchange Purchase	- 0.17	- 0.25
资金来源总计 Total Sources	**4799.73**	**988.76**	**资金运用总计 Total Uses**	**4799.73**	**988.76**

财务公司人民币信贷收支表

Sources and Uses of Credit Funds of Finance Companies（RMB）

（2004年末）

（Year - end of 2004）

单位：亿元

Unit：100 Million Yuan

项目 Items	余额 Balance	比年初增减额 Changes within the Year	项目 Items	余额 Balance	比年初增减额 Changes within the Year
一、各项存款 Total Deposits	4863.56	655.36	一、各项贷款 Total Loans	3031.31	515.00
1. 企业存款 Deposits by Enterprises	3231.30	368.22	1. 短期贷款 Short - term Loans	840.55	120.68
（1）活期存款 Demand Deposits	1978.60	344.44	（1）工业贷款 Loans to Industrial Sector	667.73	76.08
（2）定期存款 Time Deposits	1252.70	23.78	（2）商业贷款 Loans to Commercial Sector	58.22	8.34
2. 机关团体存款 Deposits by Government Agencies and Social Organizations			（3）其他短期贷款 Other Short - term Loans	114.60	36.26
			2. 中长期贷款 Medium and Long - term Loans	589.10	94.49
3. 委托存款及投资基金 Designated Deposits and Designated Investment Funds	1600.53	276.58	3. 委托贷款 Designated Loans	1450.37	353.09
（1）委托存款 Designated Deposits	1527.38	386.34	4. 信托贷款 Trust Loans	18.97	- 8.26
（2）委托投资基金 Designated Investment Funds	73.15	- 109.76	其中：中长期信托贷款 Of Which：Medium and Long - term Trust Loans	0.51	- 0.92
4. 信托存款 Trust Deposits	23.90	8.43	5. 抵押贷款 Mortagage Loans	0.71	- 0.88
5. 保证金存款 Guarantee Deposits	7.82	2.12	6. 票据融资 Paper Financing	113.71	- 48.93
6. 其他存款 Other Deposits	0.01	0.01	其中：贴现 Of Which：Discount	110.91	- 48.92
二、金融债券 Financial Bonds			7. 融资租赁 Financing Leases	15.52	7.52
三、应付及暂收款 Accounts Payable and Receipts on Account	85.15	- 21.81	8. 各项垫款 Total Advances	2.38	- 2.71
其中：应付及预提利息 Of Which：Interest Payable and Accrued	24.59	1.34	二、委托投资 Designated Investments	157.60	- 33.84
			三、投资 Investments	926.20	188.02
四、长期借款 Long - term Borrowing	7.09	0.06	1. 短期投资 Short - term Investments	602.88	264.57
五、证券业务款项 Securities Business Funds	1.24	1.07	2. 长期投资 Long - term Investments	323.32	- 76.55
六、卖出回购资产 Assets Repo（Including Securities）	227.34	30.41	四、应收及预付款 Accounts Receivable and Advance Payments	50.67	- 10.19
七、向中央银行借款 Borrowings from the Central Bank	5.51	- 7.91			

续表
Continued

项　目 Items	余　额 Balance	比年初增减额 Changes within the Year	项　目 Items	余　额 Balance	比年初增减额 Changes within the Year
八、同业往来 Inter – bank Transactions	63.22	-9.50	其中：应收利息 Of Which：Interest Receivable	9.39	0.22
1. 同业存放 Due to Banks and Other Financial Institutions	14.65	-1.62	五、证券业务款项 Securities Business Funds	1.14	-2.28
			六、经营租赁 Operating Leases		
2. 同业拆借 Placements from Banks and Other Financial Institutions	48.57	-7.88	七、买入返售资产 Assets Reverse Repo（Including Securities）	72.85	-115.88
九、代理金融机构贷款基金 Designated Loan Funds on Behalf of Financial Institutions			八、存放中央银行准备金存款 Reserve Deposits with the Central Bank	260.91	53.95
其中：中央银行委托贷款基金 Of Which：Loan Funds Designated by the Central Bank			九、存放中央银行特种存款 Special Deposits with the Central Bank		
			十、同业往来 Inter – bank Transactions	1028.70	118.95
十、各项准备 Total Provisions	45.68	15.42	1. 存放同业 Due from Banks and Other Financial Institutions	1025.20	120.96
其中：贷款损失准备 Of Which：Provisions for Loan Losses	26.77	3.11			
十一、所有者权益 Owner's Equity	380.74	54.14	2. 拆放同业 Placements with Banks and Other Financial Institutions	3.50	-2.01
其中：实收资本 Of Which：Paid – in Capital	300.50	34.46	十一、代理金融机构贷款 Lending on Behalf of Financial Institutions	0.05	
当年结益 Net Earnings	41.26	41.26			
十二、其他 Others	-149.97	-3.56	其中：代理人行专项贷款 Of Which：Agency Earmarked Loans of the Central Bank		
			十二、现金 Cash in Vault	0.06	
			十三、外币占款 Position for Foreign Exchange Purchase	0.07	-0.05
资金来源总计 **Total Sources**	**5529.56**	**713.68**	**资金运用总计** **Total Uses**	**5529.56**	**713.68**

财务公司人民币信贷收支表

Sources and Uses of Credit Funds of Finance Companies（RMB）

（2005年末）

（Year - end of 2005）

单位：亿元

Unit：100 Million Yuan

项目 Items	余额 Balance	比年初增减额 Changes within the Year	项目 Items	余额 Balance	比年初增减额 Changes within the Year
一、各项存款 Total Deposits	6043.12	1179.58	一、各项贷款 Total Loans	3717.34	687.89
1. 企业存款 Deposits by Enterprises	4153.23	922.81	1. 短期贷款 Short - term Loans	1041.47	201.53
（1）活期存款 Demand Deposits	2553.25	562.30	（1）工业贷款 Loans to Industrial Sector	810.64	143.52
（2）定期存款 Time Deposits	1599.98	360.51	（2）商业贷款 Loans to Commercial Sector	88.22	30.00
2. 机关团体存款 Deposits by Government Agencies and Social Organizations			（3）其他短期贷款 Other Short - term Loans	142.61	28.01
			2. 中长期贷款 Medium and Long - term Loans	805.56	216.09
3. 委托存款及投资基金 Designated Deposits and Designated Investment Funds	1847.77	246.09	3. 委托贷款 Designated Loans	1664.69	215.87
（1）委托存款 Designated Deposits	1717.37	188.84	4. 信托贷款 Trust Loans	22.51	3.47
（2）委托投资基金 Designated Investment Funds	130.40	57.25	其中：中长期信托贷款 Of Which：Medium and Long - term Trust Loans	5.80	5.29
4. 信托存款 Trust Deposits	38.23	14.62	5. 抵押贷款 Mortagage Loans	0.53	- 0.18
5. 保证金存款 Guarantee Deposits	3.82	- 4.00	6. 票据融资 Paper Financing	82.93	- 30.81
6. 其他存款 Other Deposits	0.07	0.06	其中：贴现 Of Which：Discount	82.93	- 28.01
二、金融债券 Financial Bonds			7. 融资租赁 Financing Leases	96.85	81.45
三、应付及暂收款 Accounts Payable and Receipts on Account	71.36	- 15.45	8. 各项垫款 Total Advances	2.80	0.47
其中：应付及预提利息 Of Which：Interest Payable and Accrued	29.08	4.46	二、委托投资 Designated Investments	134.83	- 22.75
			三、投资 Investments	833.87	- 92.05
四、长期借款 Long - term Borrowing	6.64	- 0.45	1. 短期投资 Short - term Investments	433.97	- 168.90
五、证券业务款项 Securities Business Funds	0.02	- 1.22	2. 长期投资 Long - term Investments	399.90	76.85
六、卖出回购资产 Assets Repo（Including Securities）	244.41	17.67	四、应收及预付款 Accounts Receivable and Advance Pay - ments	51.95	5.82
七、向中央银行借款 Borrowings from the Central Bank	2.91	- 2.60			

续表
Continued

项　目 Items	余　额 Balance	比年初增减额 Changes within the Year	项　目 Items	余　额 Balance	比年初增减额 Changes within the Year
八、同业往来 Inter - bank Transactions	57.94	-5.28	其中：应收利息 Of Which: Interest Receivable	8.60	0.71
1. 同业存放 Due to Banks and Other Financial Institutions	33.94	19.29	五、证券业务款项 Securities Business Funds	0.01	-1.13
			六、经营租赁 Operating Leases		
2. 同业拆借 Placements from Banks and Other Financial Institutions	24.00	-24.57	七、买入返售资产 Assets Reverse Repo (Including Securities)	103.28	30.43
九、代理金融机构贷款基金 Designated Loan Funds on Behalf of Financial Institutions			八、存放中央银行准备金存款 Reserve Deposits with the Central Bank	323.30	63.31
其中：中央银行委托贷款基金 Of Which: Loan Funds Designated by the Central Bank			九、存放中央银行特种存款 Special Deposits with the Central Bank		
			十、同业往来 Inter - bank Transactions	1575.20	545.76
十、各项准备 Total Provisions	61.81	11.22	1. 存放同业 Due from Banks and Other Financial Institutions	1572.87	546.70
其中：贷款损失准备 Of Which: Provisions for Loan Losses	26.98	-1.69			
十一、所有者权益 Owner's Equity	441.95	68.45	2. 拆放同业 Placements with Banks and Other Financial Institutions	2.33	-0.94
其中：实收资本 Of Which: Paid - in Capital	349.24	47.96	十一、代理金融机构贷款 Lending on Behalf of Financial Institutions	0.05	
当年结益 Net Earnings	59.70	59.70			
十二、其他 Others	-191.47	-35.93	其中：代理人行专项贷款 Of Which: Agency Earmarked Loans of the Central Bank		
			十二、现金 Cash in Vault	0.05	-0.01
			十三、外币占款 Position for Foreign Exchange Purchase	-1.19	-1.28
资金来源总计 Total Sources	**6738.69**	**1215.99**	**资金运用总计 Total Uses**	**6738.69**	**1215.99**

12. 信托投资公司人民币信贷收支表（1988—2005 年）
Sources and Uses of Credit Funds of Trust and Investment Companies（RMB）（1988—2005）

信托投资公司人民币信贷收支表
Sources and Uses of Credit Funds of Trust and Investment Companies（RMB）

（1988 年末）

（Year－end of 1988）

单位：亿元

Unit：100 Million Yuan

项目 Items	余额 Balance	比年初增减额 Changes within the Year	项目 Items	余额 Balance	比年初增减额 Changes within the Year
一、委托存款 Designated Deposits	299.56	—	一、委托贷款 Designated Loans	261.18	—
二、信托存款 Trust Deposits	114.57	—	其中：固定资产贷款 Of Which：Fixed Asset Loans	148.26	—
三、保证金存款 Guarantee Deposits	2.68	—	二、信托贷款 Trust Loans	227.15	—
四、其他存款 Other Deposits	22.92	—	其中：固定资产贷款 Of Which：Fixed Asset Loans	92.17	—
存款合计 Total Deposits	**439.73**	—	三、投资 Investments	29.47	—
五、发行债券 Bonds Issue	4.86	—	四、贴息贷款 Discount Government Loans	1.98	—
六、代理发行债券 Agency Bonds Issue	5.54	—	五、抵押贷款 Mortagage Loans	2.61	—
七、向人民银行借款 Borrowings from the Central Bank	6.33	—	六、票据贴现 Paper Discount	1.86	—
其中：季节性借款 Of Which：Seasonal Borrowing	5.03	—	七、金融租赁 Financial Leases	33.46	—
日拆性借款 Overnight Borrowing	0.03	—	八、其他贷款 Other Loans	15.83	—
再贴现 Rediscount	0.38	—	**贷款合计 Total Loans**	**573.54**	—
八、专业银行往来 Transactions with Special Banks	41.98	—	九、在人民银行存款 Deposits with the Central Bank	21.94	—
九、同业往来 Inter－bank Transactions	41.99	—	十、缴存准备金 Reserves with the Central Bank	20.14	—
十、呆账准备金 Provisions for Bad Loans	1.60	—	十一、专业银行往来 Transactions with Special Banks	54.48	—
十一、自有资金 Own Capital	171.33	—	十二、同业往来 Inter－bank Transactions	46.87	—
十二、其他 Others	6.27	—	十三、购买债券 Bonds Purchase	8.48	—
十三、结益 Net Earnings	10.85	—	十四、外币占款 Position for Foreign Exchange Purchase	5.03	—
资金来源总计 Total Sources	**730.48**	**—**	**资金运用总计 Total Uses**	**730.48**	**—**

信托投资公司人民币信贷收支表
Sources and Uses of Credit Funds of Trust and Investment Companies (RMB)

(1989年末)

(Year - end of 1989)

单位：亿元

Unit: 100 Million Yuan

项　目 Items	余　额 Balance	比年初增减额 Changes within the Year	项　目 Items	余　额 Balance	比年初增减额 Changes within the Year
一、委托存款 Designated Deposits	369.69	70.13	一、委托贷款 Designated Loans	323.37	62.19
二、信托存款 Trust Deposits	104.71	-9.86	其中：固定资产贷款 Of Which: Fixed Asset Loans	162.36	14.10
三、保证金存款 Guarantee Deposits	2.71	0.03	二、信托贷款 Trust Loans	262.79	35.64
四、其他存款 Other Deposits	44.55	21.63	其中：固定资产贷款 Of Which: Fixed Asset Loans	96.58	4.41
存款合计 Total Deposits	**521.66**	**81.93**	三、投资 Investments	42.06	12.59
五、发行债券 Bonds Issue	4.83	-0.03	四、贴息贷款 Discount Government Loans	1.14	-0.84
六、代理发行债券 Agency Bonds Issue	6.05	0.51	五、抵押贷款 Mortagage Loans	5.10	2.49
七、人行拨来委托贷款基金 Designated Loan Funds Appropriated by the Central Bank	3.91	—	六、票据贴现 Paper Discount	2.17	0.31
			七、金融租赁 Financial Leases	32.73	-0.73
八、向人民银行借款 Borrowings from the Central Bank	12.36	6.03	八、其他贷款 Other Loans	25.00	9.17
其中：季节性借款 Of Which: Seasonal Borrowing	7.03	2.00	**贷款合计 Total Loans**	**694.36**	**120.82**
日拆性借款 Overnight Borrowing	0.15	0.12	九、代理人民银行贷款 Agency Loans of the Central Bank	2.03	—
再贴现 Rediscount	0.10	-0.28	十、在人民银行存款 Deposits with the Central Bank	31.06	9.12
九、专业银行往来 Transactions with Special Banks	56.15	14.17	十一、缴存准备金 Reserves with the Central Bank	16.57	-3.57
十、同业往来 Inter - bank Transactions	58.78	16.79	十二、缴存特种存款 Special Deposits with the Central Bank	6.52	—
十一、呆账准备金 Provisions for Bad Loans	2.13	0.53	十三、专业银行往来 Transactions with Special Banks	79.53	25.05
十二、自有资金 Own Capital	219.22	47.89	十四、同业往来 Inter - bank Transactions	48.33	1.46
十三、结益 Net Earnings	14.17	14.17	十五、购买债券 Bonds Purchase	11.49	3.01
十四、其他 Others	4.97	—	十六、外币占款 Position for Foreign Exchange Purchase	14.34	9.31
资金来源总计 Total Sources	**904.23**	**173.75**	**资金运用总计 Total Uses**	**904.23**	**173.75**

信托投资公司人民币信贷收支表

Sources and Uses of Credit Funds of Trust and Investment Companies（RMB）

（1990 年末）

（Year - end of 1990）

单位：亿元

Unit：100 Million Yuan

项　　目 Items	余　额 Balance	比年初增减额 Changes within the Year	项　　目 Items	余　额 Balance	比年初增减额 Changes within the Year
一、委托存款	456.67	86.98	一、委托贷款	417.05	93.68
Designated Deposits			Designated Loans		
二、信托存款	154.07	49.36	其中：固定资产贷款	164.59	2.23
Trust Deposits			Of Which：Fixed Asset Loans		
三、保证金存款	3.00	0.29	二、信托贷款	320.48	57.69
Guarantee Deposits			Trust Loans		
四、其他存款	59.81	15.26	其中：固定资产贷款	91.50	- 5.08
Other Deposits			Of Which：Fixed Asset Loans		
存款合计	**673.55**	**151.89**	三、投资	52.91	10.85
Total Deposits			Investments		
五、发行债券	4.65	- 0.18	四、贴息贷款	1.17	0.03
Bonds Issue			Discount Government Loans		
六、代理发行债券	11.62	5.57	五、抵押贷款	9.80	4.70
Agency Bonds Issue			Mortagage Loans		
七、人行拨来委托贷款基金	11.33	7.42	六、票据贴现	3.24	1.07
Designated Loan Funds Appropriated by			Paper Discount		
the Central Bank			七、金融租赁	44.59	11.86
八、向人民银行借款	31.73	19.37	Financial Leases		
Borrowings from the Central Bank			八、其他贷款	41.32	16.32
其中：季节性借款	21.62	14.59	Other Loans		
Of Which：Seasonal Borrowing			**贷款合计**	**890.56**	**196.20**
日拆性借款	0.32	0.17	**Total Loans**		
Overnight Borrowing			九、代理人民银行贷款	17.28	15.25
再贴现	6.22	6.12	Agency Loans of the Central Bank		
Rediscount			十、在人民银行存款	53.74	22.68
九、专业银行往来	88.44	32.29	Deposits with the Central Bank		
Transactions with Special Banks			十一、缴存准备金	21.87	5.30
十、同业往来	104.90	46.12	Reserves with the Central Bank		
Inter - bank Transactions			十二、缴存特种存款	0.38	- 6.14
十一、呆账准备金	5.31	3.18	Special Deposits with the Central Bank		
Provisions for Bad Loans			十三、专业银行往来	84.90	5.37
十二、自有资金	263.18	43.96	Transactions with Special Banks		
Own Capital			十四、同业往来	114.86	66.53
十三、结益	15.79	15.79	Inter - bank Transactions		
Net Earnings			十五、购买债券	15.29	3.80
十四、其他	13.93	- 5.21	Bonds Purchase		
Others			十六、外币占款	25.55	11.21
			Position for Foreign Exchange Purchase		
资金来源总计	**1224.43**	**320.20**	**资金运用总计**	**1224.43**	**320.20**
Total Sources			**Total Uses**		

信托投资公司人民币信贷收支表

Sources and Uses of Credit Funds of Trust and Investment Companies (RMB)

(1991 年末)

(Year－end of 1991)

单位：亿元

Unit: 100 Million Yuan

项　目 Items	余　额 Balance	比年初增减额 Changes within the Year	项　目 Items	余　额 Balance	比年初增减额 Changes within the Year
一、委托存款 Designated Deposits	635.83	179.16	一、委托贷款 Designated Loans	555.59	138.54
其中：财政委托存款 Of Which: Fiscal Designated Deposits		—	其中：固定资产贷款 Of Which: Fixed Asset Loans	205.47	40.88
二、信托存款 Trust Deposits	226.96	72.89	二、信托贷款 Trust Loans	388.61	68.13
三、保证金存款 Guarantee Deposits	6.29	3.29	其中：固定资产贷款 Of Which: Fixed Asset Loans	102.09	10.59
四、其他存款 Other Deposits	104.19	44.38	三、投资 Investments	92.78	39.87
存款合计 Total Deposits	**973.27**	**299.72**	四、贴息贷款 Discount Government Loans	1.20	0.03
五、发行债券 Bonds Issue	5.30	0.65	五、抵押贷款 Mortagage Loans	14.61	4.81
六、代理发行债券 Agency Bonds Issue	29.34	17.72	六、票据贴现 Paper Discount	2.45	－0.79
七、人行拨来委托贷款基金 Designated Loan Funds Appropriated by the Central Bank	14.62	3.29	七、租赁 Leases	95.24	50.65
			八、其他贷款 Other Loans	60.56	19.24
八、向人民银行借款 Borrowings from the Central Bank	40.17	8.44	**贷款合计 Total Loans**	**1211.04**	**320.48**
其中：季节性借款 Of Which: Seasonal Borrowing	26.67	5.05	九、代理人民银行贷款 Agency Loans of the Central Bank	25.54	8.26
日拆性借款 Overnight Borrowing	1.27	0.95	十、在人民银行存款 Deposits with the Central Bank	64.05	10.31
再贴现 Rediscount	0.60	－5.62	十一、缴存准备金 Reserves with the Central Bank	33.08	11.21
九、专业银行往来 Transactions with Special Banks	145.82	57.38	十二、缴存特种存款 Special Deposits with the Central Bank	0.50	0.12
十、同业往来 Inter－bank Transactions	217.09	112.19	十三、专业银行往来 Transactions with Special Banks	124.43	39.53
其中：同业拆入 Of Which: Placements from Banks and Other Financial Institutions		—	十四、同业往来 Inter－bank Transactions	198.52	83.66
			其中：同业拆出 Of Which: Placements with Banks and Other Financial Institutions		—
十一、呆账准备金 Provisions for Bad Loans	3.86	－1.45			
十二、自有资金 Own Capital	313.49	50.31	十五、购买债券 Bonds Purchase	43.21	27.92
十三、结益 Net Earnings	20.26	20.26	十六、外币占款 Position for Foreign Exchange Purchase	28.69	3.14
十四、其他 Others	－34.16	－63.88	十七、其他 Others		
资金来源总计 Total Sources	**1729.06**	**504.63**	**资金运用总计 Total Uses**	**1729.06**	**504.63**

信托投资公司人民币信贷收支表

Sources and Uses of Credit Funds of Trust and Investment Companies（RMB）

（1992 年末）

（Year - end of 1992）

单位：亿元

Unit：100 Million Yuan

项　目 Items	余　额 Balance	比年初增减额 Changes within the Year	项　目 Items	余　额 Balance	比年初增减额 Changes within the Year
一、委托存款 Designated Deposits	861.76	225.93	一、委托贷款 Designated Loans	776.08	220.49
其中：财政委托存款 Of Which：Fiscal Designated Deposits			其中：固定资产贷款 Of Which：Fixed Asset Loans	253.26	47.79
二、信托存款 Trust Deposits	292.47	65.51	二、信托贷款 Trust Loans	411.65	23.04
三、保证金存款 Guarantee Deposits	16.52	10.23	其中：固定资产贷款 Of Which：Fixed Asset Loans	88.06	- 14.03
四、其他存款 Other Deposits	184.36	80.17	三、投资 Investments	258.84	166.06
存款合计 Total Deposits	**1355.11**	**381.84**	四、贴息贷款 Discount Government Loans	0.43	- 0.77
五、发行债券 Bonds Issue	14.44	9.14	五、抵押贷款 Mortagage Loans	33.62	19.01
六、代理发行债券 Agency Bonds Issue	60.26	30.92	六、票据贴现 Paper Discount	2.30	- 0.15
七、人行拨来委托贷款基金 Designated Loan Funds Appropriated by the Central Bank	14.14	- 0.48	七、租赁 Leases	173.02	77.78
八、向人民银行借款 Borrowings from the Central Bank	66.69	26.52	八、其他贷款 Other Loans	144.27	83.71
其中：季节性借款 Of Which：Seasonal Borrowing	21.36	- 5.31	**贷款合计 Total Loans**	**1800.21**	**589.17**
日拆性借款 Overnight Borrowing	9.34	8.07	九、代理人民银行贷款 Agency Loans of the Central Bank	25.46	- 0.08
再贴现 Rediscount	0.06	- 0.54	十、在人民银行存款 Deposits with the Central Bank	83.76	19.71
九、专业银行往来 Transactions with Special Banks	274.96	129.14	十一、缴存准备金 Reserves with the Central Bank	44.95	11.87
十、同业往来 Inter - bank Transactions	398.66	181.57	十二、缴存特种存款 Special Deposits with the Central Bank	0.33	- 0.17
其中：同业拆入 Of Which：Placements from Banks and Other Financial Institutions			十三、专业银行往来 Transactions with Special Banks	170.15	45.72
十一、呆账准备金 Provisions for Bad Loans	4.35	0.49	十四、同业往来 Inter - bank Transactions	264.05	65.53
十二、自有资金 Own Capital	397.76	84.27	其中：同业拆出 Of Which：Placements with Banks and Other Financial Institutions		
十三、结益 Net Earnings	29.74	29.74	十五、购买债券 Bonds Purchase	91.94	48.73
十四、其他 Others	- 102.85	- 88.95	十六、外币占款 Position for Foreign Exchange Purchase	32.41	3.72
			十七、其他 Others		
资金来源总计 Total Sources	**2513.26**	**784.20**	**资金运用总计 Total Uses**	**2513.26**	**784.20**

信托投资公司人民币信贷收支表

Sources and Uses of Credit Funds of Trust and Investment Companies (RMB)

(1993 年末)

(Year – end of 1993)

单位：亿元

Unit: 100 Million Yuan

项目 Items	余额 Balance	比年初增减额 Changes within the Year	项目 Items	余额 Balance	比年初增减额 Changes within the Year
一、委托存款 Designated Deposits	1096.53	241.77	一、委托贷款 Designated Loans	988.99	217.50
其中：财政委托存款 Of Which: Fiscal Designated Deposits	148.83	54.17	其中：固定资产贷款 Of Which: Fixed Asset Loans	268.17	22.76
二、信托存款 Trust Deposits	248.26	33.88	二、信托贷款 Trust Loans	379.12	49.67
三、保证金存款 Guarantee Deposits	29.43	12.82	其中：固定资产贷款 Of Which: Fixed Asset Loans	98.59	7.11
四、其他存款 Other Deposits	209.75	30.44	三、投资 Investments	337.61	80.86
存款合计 Total Deposits	**1583.97**	**318.91**	四、贴息贷款 Discount Government Loans	1.64	0.29
五、发行债券 Bonds Issue	19.32	2.67	五、抵押贷款 Mortagage Loans	44.18	11.35
六、代理发行债券 Agency Bonds Issue	58.57	1.00	六、票据贴现 Paper Discount	1.19	–1.20
七、人行拨来委托贷款基金 Designated loan Funds Appropriated by the Central Bank	9.76	3.08	七、租赁 Leases	185.68	14.91
			八、其他贷款 Other Loans	113.62	–19.06
八、向人民银行借款 Borrowings from the Central Bank	35.31	–6.44	**贷款合计 Total Loans**	**2052.03**	**354.32**
其中：季节性借款 Of Which: Seasonal Borrowing	19.88	–4.08	九、代理人民银行贷款 Agency Loans of the Central Bank	8.89	0.39
日拆性借款 Overnight Borrowing	10.20	–0.35	十、在人民银行存款 Deposits with the Central Bank	70.32	–6.64
九、专业银行往来 Transactions with Special Banks	199.54	–65.88	十一、缴存准备金 Reserves with the Central Bank	40.33	4.45
十、同业往来 Inter – bank Transactions	355.16	–48.88	十二、缴存特种存款 Special Deposits with the Central Bank	0.46	0.46
其中：同业拆入 Of Which: Placements from Banks and Other Financial Institutions	161.30	–10.66	十三、专业银行往来 Transactions with Special Banks	165.03	7.23
			十四、同业往来 Inter – bank Transactions	193.66	–67.58
十一、证券买卖 Purchase and Sale of Securities	10.61	–1.58	其中：同业拆出 Of Which: Placements with Banks and Other Financial Institutions	78.62	–8.02
十二、呆账准备金 Provisions for Bad Loans	6.16	–0.01			
十三、自有资金 Own Capital	459.90	82.33	十五、购买债券 Bonds Purchase	48.13	–31.26
十四、结益 Net Earnings	33.27	33.27	十六、证券买卖 Purchase and Sale of Securities	94.65	26.59
十五、其他 Others	240.84	162.26	十七、外币占款 Position for Foreign Exchange Purchase	21.31	–11.59
			十八、其他 Others	317.60	205.28
资金来源总计 Total Sources	**3012.41**	**480.73**	**资金运用总计 Total Uses**	**3012.41**	**480.73**

信托投资公司人民币信贷收支表

Sources and Uses of Credit Funds of Trust and Investment Companies（RMB）

（1994 年末）

（Year - end of 1994）

单位：亿元

Unit：100 Million Yuan

项目 Items	余额 Balance	比年初增减额 Changes within the Year	项目 Items	余额 Balance	比年初增减额 Changes within the Year
一、存款合计 Total Deposits	2096.21	512.01	一、贷款合计 Total Loans	2031.51	316.41
1. 委托存款 Designated Deposits	1479.59	341.39	1. 委托贷款 Designated Loans	1287.33	292.57
其中：财政委托存款 Of Which：Fiscal Designated Deposits	189.65	86.56	其中：中长期贷款 Of Which：Medium and Long - term Loans	275.80	66.91
2. 信托存款 Trust Deposits	453.57	190.42	2. 信托贷款 Trust Loans	486.96	82.70
3. 保证金存款 Guarantee Deposits	20.08	- 2.40	其中：中长期贷款 Of Which：Medium and Long - term Loans	90.63	3.11
4. 其他存款 Other Deposits	142.97	- 17.40	3. 抵押贷款 Mortagage Loans	64.12	13.70
二、发行债券 Bonds Issue	17.30	- 8.79	4. 贴现 Discount	2.86	1.77
三、证券业务款项 Securities Business Funds	201.72	111.55	5. 租赁 Leases	132.10	- 48.75
四、人行委托贷款资金 Loan Funds Designated by the Central Bank	34.57	24.96	6. 其他贷款 Other Loans	58.14	- 25.58
五、向人民银行借款 Borrowings from the Central Bank	27.87	- 10.23	二、委托投资 Designated Investments	78.29	26.06
六、银行机构存款 Deposits by Banks	54.89	- 6.20	三、短期投资 Short - term Investments	103.89	37.47
七、拆放银行机构 Placements from Banks	261.77	- 41.44	其中：国家债券 Of Which：Treasury Bonds	4.60	1.53
八、金融性公司存款 Desposits by Financial Corporations	38.39	15.72	四、长期投资 Long - term Investments	294.52	12.63
九、金融性公司拆放 Placements from Financial Corporations	186.14	22.45	其中：国家债券 Of Which：Treasury Bonds	13.45	2.46
十、所有者权益 Owner's Equity	513.49	14.27	五、证券业务款项 Securities Business Funds	260.43	90.35
其中：实收资本 Of Which：Paid - in Capital	425.42	43.52	六、代理人民银行专项贷款 Agency Earmarked Loans of the Central Loans	21.66	12.79
十一、结益 Net Earnings	21.15	21.15	七、在人民银行存款 Deposits with the Central Bank	99.60	25.16
十二、贷款呆账准备金 Provisions for Bad Loans	6.34	1.22	八、缴存人民银行准备金 Reserves with the Central Bank	64.02	25.91
十三、投资风险准备 Provisions for Investment Risk	2.54	1.12	九、缴存人民银行特种存款 Special Deposits with the Central Bank	0.10	- 0.30

续表
Continued

项　目 Items	余　额 Balance	比年初增减额 Changes within the Year	项　目 Items	余　额 Balance	比年初增减额 Changes within the Year
十四、其他 Others	444.09	126.76	十、购买人民银行债券 Central Bank Bonds Purchase	1.01	-3.20
			十一、存放银行机构 Due from Banks	161.43	26.10
			十二、拆放银行机构 Placements with Banks	50.21	-23.08
			十三、存放金融性公司 Due from Financial Corporations	47.40	15.38
			十四、拆放金融性公司 Placements with Financial Corporations	136.79	30.15
			十五、现金 Cash in Vault	3.92	1.72
			十六、外币占款 Position for Foreign Exchange Purchase	22.48	6.59
			十七、其他 Other	529.21	184.41
资金来源总计 Total Sources	**3906.47**	**784.55**	**资金运用总计 Total Uses**	**3906.47**	**784.55**

信托投资公司人民币信贷收支表

Sources and Uses of Credit Funds of Trust and Investment Companies（RMB）

（1995年末）

（Year - end of 1995）

单位：亿元

Unit：100 Million Yuan

项目 Items	余额 Balance	比年初增减额 Changes within the Year	项目 Items	余额 Balance	比年初增减额 Changes within the Year
一、存款合计 Total Deposits	2498.51	298.57	一、贷款合计 Total Loans	2409.76	255.82
1. 委托存款 Designated Deposits	1676.61	132.01	1. 委托贷款 Designated Loans	1461.77	117.58
其中：财政委托存款 Of Which：Fiscal Designated Deposits	193.86	73.94	其中：中长期贷款 Of Which：Medium and Long - term Loans	198.98	- 1.84
2. 信托存款 Trust Deposits	625.34	137.93	2. 信托贷款 Trust Loans	694.41	150.22
3. 保证金存款 Guarantee Deposits	21.41	1.09	其中：中长期贷款 Of Which：Medium and Long - term Loans	91.54	- 4.80
4. 其他存款 Other Deposits	175.15	27.54	3. 抵押贷款 Mortagage Loans	76.04	5.84
二、发行债券 Bonds Issue	18.98	- 0.84	4. 贴现 Discount	1.92	- 0.12
三、证券业务款项 Securities Business Funds	207.45	- 12.92	5. 租赁 Leases	109.18	- 28.43
四、人行委托贷款资金 Loan Funds Designated by the Central Bank	29.39	- 4.09	6. 其他贷款 Other Loans	66.44	10.73
五、向人民银行借款 Borrowings from the Central Bank	23.86	- 3.93	二、委托投资 Designated Investments	90.05	8.17
六、银行机构存款 Deposits by Banks	49.38	- 8.61	三、短期投资 Short - term Investments	105.46	- 9.61
七、银行机构拆放 Placements from Banks	294.79	28.25	其中：国家债券 Of Which：Treasury Bonds	4.71	0.47
八、金融性公司存款 Desposits by Financial Corporations	79.12	30.39	四、长期投资 Long - term Investments	311.59	5.06
九、金融性公司拆放 Placements from Financial Corporations	223.64	36.18	其中：国家债券 Of Which：Treasury Bonds	11.21	- 4.03
十、长期借款 Long - term Borrowing	89.64	- 9.83	五、证券业务款项 Securities Business Funds	284.13	11.27
十一、所有者权益 Owner's Equity	545.39	- 1.98	六、代理人民银行专项贷款 Agency Earmarked Loans of the Central Loans	18.44	- 3.22
其中：实收资本 Of Which：Paid - in Capital	449.35	- 21.30	七、在人民银行存款 Deposits with the Central Bank	83.34	- 18.08
十二、结益 Net Earnings	10.44	10.44	八、缴存人民银行准备金 Reserves with the Central Bank	79.34	11.09
十三、贷款呆账准备金 Provisions for Bad Loans	8.09	1.31	九、缴存人民银行特种存款 Special Deposits with the Central Bank	0.08	- 0.04

续表
Continued

项　目 Items	余　额 Balance	比年初增减额 Changes within the Year	项　目 Items	余　额 Balance	比年初增减额 Changes within the Year
十四、投资风险准备 Provisions for Investment Risk	2.99	-3.21	十、购买人民银行债券 Central Bank Bonds Purchase	0.02	-0.43
十五、其他 Others	503.97	77.86	十一、存放银行机构 Due from Banks	125.98	-17.71
			十二、拆放银行机构 Placements with Banks	53.05	-3.40
			十三、存放金融性公司 Due from Financial Corporations	59.51	13.77
			十四、拆放金融性公司 Placements with Financial Corporations	154.92	1.91
			十五、现金 Cash in Vault	2.92	-0.56
			十六、外币占款 Position for Foreign Exchange Purchase	40.72	15.84
			十七、银行存款 Deposits with Banks	62.12	-5.07
			十八、其他 Others	704.21	172.78
资金来源总计 Total Sources	**4585.64**	**437.59**	**资金运用总计 Total Uses**	**4585.64**	**437.59**

信托投资公司人民币信贷收支表

Sources and Uses of Credit Funds of Trust and Investment Companies（RMB）

（1996年末）

（Year - end of 1996）

单位：亿元

Unit：100 Million Yuan

项目 Items	余额 Balance	比年初增减额 Changes within the Year	项目 Items	余额 Balance	比年初增减额 Changes within the Year
一、存款合计 Total Deposits	2474.59	211.36	一、贷款合计 Total Loans	2336.90	198.73
1. 委托存款 Designated Deposits	1655.07	83.96	1. 委托贷款 Designated Loans	1440.95	82.13
其中：财政委托存款 Of Which：Fiscal Designated Deposits	198.76	-27.01	其中：中长期贷款 Of Which：Medium and Long - term Loans	229.39	15.05
2. 信托存款 Trust Deposits	604.40	84.27	2. 信托贷款 Trust Loans	682.51	126.75
3. 保证金存款 Guarantee Deposits	37.95	19.03	其中：中长期贷款 Of Which：Medium and Long - term Loans	94.01	5.71
4. 其他存款 Other Deposits	177.17	24.10	3. 抵押贷款 Mortagage Loans	76.11	21.80
二、发行债券 Bonds Issue	11.69	-1.12	其中：中长期贷款 Of Which：Medium and Long - term Loans	5.39	-2.43
三、证券业务款项 Securities Business Funds	227.84	30.38			
四、人行委托贷款资金 Loan Funds Designated by the Central Bank	27.93	-1.03	4. 贴现 Discount	2.17	-2.72
			5. 租赁 Leases	84.72	-19.41
五、向人行借款 Borrowings from the Central Bank	22.81	-0.85	6. 其他贷款 Other Loans	50.44	-9.82
六、银行机构存款 Deposits by Banks	29.83	4.95	二、委托投资 Designated Investments	93.59	3.15
七、银行机构拆放 Placements from Banks	276.55	49.30	三、短期投资 Short - term Investments	90.16	-5.44
八、金融性公司存款 Desposits by Financial Corporations	56.37	-15.36	其中：国家债券 Of Which：Treasury Bonds	6.71	2.33
九、金融性公司拆放 Placements from Financial Corporations	237.00	35.59	四、长期投资 Long - term Investments	297.28	23.71
十、长期借款 Long - term Borrowing	116.10	30.11	其中：国家债券 Of Which：Treasury Bonds	11.96	0.52
十一、所有者权益 Owner's Equity	480.57	-42.52	五、证券业务款项 Securities Business Funds	232.95	3.13
其中：实收资本 Of Which：Paid - in Capital	371.16	-52.20	六、代理人行贷款 Special Lending on Behalf of the Central Bank	16.33	-2.35
十二、结益 Net Earnings	1.25	1.25			
十三、呆账准备金 Provisions for Bad Loans	6.72	-0.44	七、在人行存款 Deposits with the Central Bank	82.59	5.49

续表
Continued

项目 Items	余额 Balance	比年初增减额 Changes within the Year	项目 Items	余额 Balance	比年初增减额 Changes within the Year
十四、投资风险准备 Provisions for Investment Risk	2.51	0.23	八、缴存人行准备金 Reserves with the Central Bank	87.65	16.22
十五、其他 Others	573.86	144.64	九、缴存人行特种存款 Special Deposits with the Central Bank	0.02	-0.10
			十、购买人行债券 Central Bank Bonds Purchase	0.01	-0.01
			十一、存放银行机构 Due from Banks	140.10	10.25
			十二、拆放银行机构 Placements with Banks	33.84	-9.70
			十三、存放金融性公司 Due from Financial Corporations	30.50	-27.12
			十四、拆放金融性公司 Placements with Financial Corporations	152.83	15.27
			十五、现金 Cash in Vault	3.12	0.82
			十六、外币占款 Position for Foreign Exchange Purchase	5.52	-37.83
			十七、银行存款 Deposits with Banks	66.54	25.49
			十八、其他 Others	875.69	226.78
资金来源总计 Total Sources	**4545.62**	**446.49**	**资金运用总计 Total Uses**	**4545.62**	**446.49**

信托投资公司人民币信贷收支表

Sources and Uses of Credit Funds of Trust and Investment Companies（RMB）

（1997 年末）

（Year - end of 1997）

单位：亿元

Unit：100 Million Yuan

项目 Items	余额 Balance	比年初增减额 Changes within the Year	项目 Items	余额 Balance	比年初增减额 Changes within the Year
一、各项存款 Total Deposits	2265.06	239.91	一、各项贷款 Total Loans	1972.15	211.59
1. 信托存款 Trust Deposits	455.60	58.23	1. 信托贷款 Trust Loans	431.98	11.43
2. 委托存款 Designated Deposits	1431.07	174.44	其中：中长期信托贷款 Of Which：Medium and Long - term Loans	79.79	4.29
（1）委托存款 Designated Deposits	1382.44	255.22	2. 委托贷款 Designated Loans	1235.18	114.74
（2）委托投资基金 Designated Investment Funds	48.63	- 80.78	3. 抵押贷款 Mortagage Loans	31.53	- 5.04
3. 保证金存款 Guarantee Deposits	122.69	94.59	4. 贴现贷款 Discount	0.11	- 1.04
4. 其他存款 Other Deposits	255.70	- 87.35	5. 融资租赁 Financing Leases	30.55	- 2.58
二、金融债券 Financial Bonds	15.41	6.56	6. 其他贷款 Other Loans	242.80	94.08
三、长期借款 Long - term Borrowing	133.83	17.88	二、委托投资 Designated Investments	186.72	27.04
四、证券业务款项 Securities Business Funds	266.98	102.45	三、投资 Investments	444.21	42.97
五、卖出回购证券 Repo	5.33	- 5.34	1. 短期投资 Short - term Investments	134.08	- 5.85
六、向中央银行借款 Borrowings from the Central Bank	35.17	7.49	2. 长期投资 Long - term Investments	310.13	48.82
七、同业往来 Inter - bank Transactions	287.71	11.85	四、证券业务款项 Securities Business Funds	105.01	29.24
1. 同业存放 Due to Banks and Other Financial Institutions	29.01	- 9.51	五、经营租赁 Operating Leases	0.88	- 1.07
2. 同业拆借 Placements from Banks and Other Financial Institutions	258.70	21.36	六、在人民银行存款 Deposits with the Central Bank	77.08	77.07
			七、缴存人行准备金 Reserves with the Central Bank	74.73	19.02
八、代理金融机构贷款基金 Designated Loan Funds on Behalf of Financial Institutions	14.91	- 2.58	八、缴存人行特种存款 Special Deposits with the Central Bank	2.74	- 1.80
其中：人行委托专项贷款基金 Of Which：Earmarked Loan Funds Designated by the Central Bank	0.82	- 1.10	九、同业往来 Inter - bank Transactions	274.48	73.73
			1. 存放同业 Due from Banks and Other Financial Institutions	214.64	104.14

续表
Continued

项 目 Items	余 额 Balance	比年初增减额 Changes within the Year	项 目 Items	余 额 Balance	比年初增减额 Changes within the Year
九、各项准备 Total Provisions	10.48	3.38	2. 拆放同业 Placements with Banks and Other Financial Institutions	59.84	-30.41
十、所有者权益 Owner's Equity	477.61	63.84	十、代理金融机构贷款 Lending on Behalf of Financial Institutions	11.83	-45.38
其中：实收资本 Of Which: Paid - in Capital	411.03	52.07	其中：代理人行专项贷款 Of Which: Agency Earmarked Loans of the Central Bank	2.58	-5.19
当年结益 Net Earnings	30.56	30.56	十一、库存现金 Cash in Vault	2.96	2.96
十一、其他 Others	-342.20	-3.48	十二、外币占款 Position for Foreign Exchange Purchase	17.50	6.59
资金来源总计 Total Sources	**3170.29**	**441.96**	**资金运用总计 Total Uses**	**3170.29**	**441.96**

信托投资公司人民币信贷收支表

Sources and Uses of Credit Funds of Trust and Investment Companies（RMB）

（1998年末）

（Year-end of 1998）

单位：亿元

Unit：100 Million Yuan

项目 Items	余额 Balance	比年初增减额 Changes within the Year	项目 Items	余额 Balance	比年初增减额 Changes within the Year
一、各项存款 Total Deposits	2349.28	78.34	一、各项贷款 Total Loans	2139.21	180.25
1.信托存款 Trust Deposits	561.23	37.14	1.信托贷款 Trust Loans	464.04	21.35
2.委托存款 Designated Deposits	1516.02	77.90	其中：中长期信托贷款 Of Which：Medium and Long-term Loans	86.14	11.62
（1）委托存款 Designated Deposits	1455.24	63.03	2.委托贷款 Designated Loans	1284.80	68.87
（2）委托投资基金 Designated Investment Funds	60.78	14.87	3.抵押贷款 Mortagage Loans	21.30	-1.23
3.保证金存款 Guarantee Deposits	115.08	3.42	4.贴现贷款 Discount	0.10	-0.01
4.其他存款 Other Deposits	156.95	-40.12	5.融资租赁 Financing Leases	26.65	-2.78
二、金融债券 Financial Bonds	34.19	18.08	6.其他贷款 Other Loans	342.32	94.05
三、长期借款 Long-term Borrowing	154.52	26.40	二、委托投资 Designated Investments	179.80	-5.65
四、证券业务款项 Securities Business Funds	445.40	158.74	三、投资 Investments	534.11	77.00
五、卖出回购证券 Repo	35.68	36.78	1.短期投资 Short-term Investments	161.93	29.38
六、向中央银行借款 Borrowings from the Central Bank	36.26	1.10	2.长期投资 Long-term Investments	372.18	47.62
七、同业往来 Inter-bank Transactions	252.59	-30.27	四、证券业务款项 Securities Business Funds	156.98	50.17
1.同业存放 Due to Banks and Other Financial Institutions	26.09	-15.09	五、经营租赁 Operating Leases	1.03	0.15
2.同业拆借 Placements from Banks and Other Financial Institutions	226.50	-15.18	六、缴存准备金存款 Reserve Deposits with the Central Bank	93.23	-59.19
八、代理金融机构贷款基金 Designated Loan Funds on Behalf of Financial Institutions	14.21	-1.03	七、缴存人行准备金 Reserves with the Central Bank		
其中：人行委托专项贷款基金 Of Which：Earmarked Loan Funds Designated by the Central Bank	0.44	-0.38	八、缴存人行特种存款 Special Deposits with the Central Bank	0.38	-2.36
			九、同业往来 Inter-bank Transactions	290.40	14.12
			1.存放同业 Due from Banks and Other Financial Institutions	246.12	33.77

续表
Continued

项 目 Items	余 额 Balance	比年初增减额 Changes within the Year	项 目 Items	余 额 Balance	比年初增减额 Changes within the Year
九、各项准备 Total Provisions	11.74	1.12	2. 拆放同业 Placements with Banks and Other Financial Institutions	44.28	-19.65
十、所有者权益 Owner's Equity	585.44	89.48	十、代理金融机构贷款 Lending on Behalf of Financial Institutions	10.37	-19.79
其中：实收资本 Of Which: Paid-in Capital	485.59	58.04			
当年结益 Net Earnings	24.77	24.77	其中：代理人行专项贷款 Of Which: Agency Earmarked Loans of the Central Bank	2.20	-0.38
十一、其他 Others	-463.34	-113.66	十一、库存现金 Cash in Vault	3.41	0.34
			十二、外币占款 Position for Foreign Exchange Purchase	47.05	30.04
资金来源总计 Total Sources	**3455.97**	**265.08**	**资金运用总计 Total Uses**	**3455.97**	**265.08**

信托投资公司人民币信贷收支表

Sources and Uses of Credit Funds of Trust and Investment Companies（RMB）

（1999 年末）

（Year - end of 1999）

单位：亿元

Unit：100 Million Yuan

项　　目 Items	余　额 Balance	比年初增减额 Changes within the Year	项　　目 Items	余　额 Balance	比年初增减额 Changes within the Year
一、各项存款 Total Deposits	2397.82	49.22	一、各项贷款 Total Loans	2105.75	-47.42
1. 信托存款 Trust Deposits	621.13	57.27	1. 信托贷款 Trust Loans	388.68	-70.39
2. 委托存款 Designated Deposits	1475.58	-41.00	其中：中长期信托贷款 Of Which：Medium and Long - term Loans	87.90	3.17
（1）委托存款 Designated Deposits	1420.78	-36.76	2. 委托贷款 Designated Loans	1243.54	-42.88
（2）委托投资基金 Designated Investment Funds	54.80	-4.24	3. 抵押贷款 Mortagage Loans	18.76	-2.54
3. 保证金存款 Guarantee Deposits	150.22	39.84	4. 贴现贷款 Discount	0.30	0.20
4. 其他存款 Other Deposits	150.89	-6.89	5. 融资租赁 Financing Leases	22.68	-3.25
二、金融债券 Financial Bonds	29.78	-1.90	6. 其他贷款 Other Loans	431.79	71.44
三、长期借款 Long - term Borrowing	146.11	-1.09	二、委托投资 Designated Investments	180.00	2.08
四、证券业务款项 Securities Business Funds	630.21	209.77	三、投资 Investments	578.29	48.08
五、卖出回购证券 Repo	21.04	-18.21	1. 短期投资 Short - term Investments	171.31	5.81
六、向中央银行借款 Borrowings from the Central Bank	37.38	1.12	2. 长期投资 Long - term Investments	406.98	42.27
七、同业往来 Inter - bank Transactions	233.27	-13.64	四、证券业务款项 Securities Business Funds	144.35	11.50
1. 同业存放 Due to Banks and Other Financial Institutions	24.68	-0.58	五、经营租赁 Operating Leases	0.65	-0.38
2. 同业拆借 Placements from Banks and Other Financial Institutions	208.59	-13.06	六、缴存准备金存款 Reserve Deposits with the Central Bank	73.31	-19.59
八、代理金融机构贷款基金 Designated Loan Funds on Behalf of Financial Institutions	11.40	-2.74	七、缴存人行特种存款 Special Deposits with the Central Bank	1.26	0.88
			八、同业往来 Inter - bank Transactions	370.95	82.48
其中：人行委托专项贷款基金 Of Which：Earmarked Loan Funds Designated by the Central Bank	0.42	-0.02	1. 存放同业 Due from Banks and Other Financial Institutions	336.38	90.43

续表
Continued

项　目 Items	余　额 Balance	比年初增减额 Changes within the Year	项　目 Items	余　额 Balance	比年初增减额 Changes within the Year
九、各项准备 Total Provisions	16.83	4.59	2. 拆放同业 Placements with Banks and Other Financial Institutions	34.57	-7.95
十、所有者权益 Owner's Equity	643.38	65.44	九、代理金融机构贷款 Lending on Behalf of Financial Institutions	8.84	-1.53
其中：实收资本 Of Which: Paid-in Capital	518.93	32.31			
当年结益 Net Earnings	19.07	19.07	其中：代理人行专项贷款 Of Which: Agency Earmarked Loans of the Central Bank	2.25	0.05
十一、其他 Others	-652.57	-210.65	十、库存现金 Cash in Vault	3.40	0.07
			十一、外币占款 Position for Foreign Exchange Purchase	47.85	5.74
资金来源总计 Total Sources	**3514.65**	**81.91**	**资金运用总计 Total Uses**	**3514.65**	**81.91**

信托投资公司人民币信贷收支表

Sources and Uses of Credit Funds of Trust and Investment Companies（RMB）

（2000 年末）

（Year - end of 2000）

单位：亿元

Unit：100 Million Yuan

项目 Items	余额 Balance	比年初增减额 Changes within the Year	项目 Items	余额 Balance	比年初增减额 Changes within the Year
一、各项存款 Total Deposits	2297.64	- 97.70	一、各项贷款 Total Loans	1924.31	- 179.73
1. 信托存款 Trust Deposits	472.30	- 149.93	1. 信托贷款 Trust Loans	303.02	- 80.48
2. 委托存款 Designated Deposits	1474.32	0.70	其中：中长期信托贷款 Of Which：Medium and Long - term Loans	88.36	- 0.38
（1）委托存款 Designated Deposits	1373.68	- 45.19	2. 委托贷款 Designated Loans	1166.05	- 74.59
（2）委托投资基金 Designated Investment Funds	100.64	45.89	3. 抵押贷款 Mortagage Loans	10.70	- 6.67
3. 保证金存款 Guarantee Deposits	208.55	58.33	4. 贴现贷款 Discount	0.01	- 0.29
4. 其他存款 Other Deposits	142.47	- 6.80	5. 融资租赁 Financing Leases	22.43	- 0.17
二、金融债券 Financial Bonds	23.77	- 6.01	6. 其他贷款 Other Loans	422.10	- 17.53
三、长期借款 Long - term Borrowing	114.51	10.48	二、委托投资 Designated Investments	260.68	80.15
四、证券业务款项 Securities Business Funds	761.05	123.24	三、投资 Investments	538.42	1.27
五、卖出回购证券 Repo	14.22	- 6.41	1. 短期投资 Short - term Investments	132.32	- 39.77
六、向中央银行借款 Borrowings from the Central Bank	37.14	0.09	2. 长期投资 Long - term Investments	406.10	41.04
七、同业往来 Inter - bank Transactions	243.68	11.59	四、证券业务款项 Securities Business Funds	176.75	28.26
1. 同业存放 Due to Banks and Other Financial Institutions	25.46	0.78	五、经营租赁 Operating Leases	1.24	0.59
2. 同业拆借 Placements from Banks and Other Financial Institutions	218.22	10.81	六、缴存准备金存款 Reserve Deposits with the Central Bank	47.40	- 21.61
八、代理金融机构贷款基金 Designated Loan Funds on Behalf of Financial Institutions	11.82	0.19	七、缴存人行特种存款 Special Deposits with the Central Bank	0.12	- 1.14
			八、同业往来 Inter - bank Transactions	336.80	- 44.94
其中：人行委托专项贷款基金 Of Which：Earmarked Loan Funds Designated by the Central Bank	0.34	- 0.08	1. 存放同业 Due from Banks and Other Financial Institutions	308.71	- 39.02

续表
Continued

项　目 Items	余　额 Balance	比年初增减额 Changes within the Year	项　目 Items	余　额 Balance	比年初增减额 Changes within the Year
九、各项准备 Total Provisions	15.17	-1.37	2. 拆放同业 Placements with Banks and Other Financial Institutions	28.09	-5.92
十、所有者权益 Owner's Equity	604.33	-34.36	九、代理金融机构贷款 Lending on Behalf of Financial Institutions	8.91	0.06
其中：实收资本 Of Which: Paid-in Capital	524.63	6.04	其中：代理人行专项贷款 Of Which: Agency Earmarked Loans of the Central Bank	2.10	-0.15
当年结益 Net Earnings	36.88	36.88	十、库存现金 Cash in Vault	2.77	-0.58
十一、其他 Others	-807.63	-165.79	十一、外币占款 Position for Foreign Exchange Purchase	18.30	-28.38
资金来源总计 Total Sources	**3315.70**	**-166.05**	**资金运用总计 Total Uses**	**3315.70**	**-166.05**

信托投资公司人民币信贷收支表

Sources and Uses of Credit Funds of Trust and Investment Companies（RMB）

（2001 年末）

（Year - end of 2001）

单位：亿元

Unit：100 Million Yuan

项　目 Items	余　额 Balance	比年初增减额 Changes within the Year	项　目 Items	余　额 Balance	比年初增减额 Changes within the Year
一、各项存款 Total Deposits	1913.13	-135.36	一、各项贷款 Total Loans	1612.51	-107.53
1. 信托存款 Trust Deposits	301.88	-71.77	1. 信托贷款 Trust Loans	374.18	-87.53
2. 委托存款 Designated Deposits	1400.59	-1.12	其中：中长期信托贷款 Of Which：Medium and Long - term Loans	134.36	-24.34
（1）委托存款 Designated Deposits	1281.24	-28.93	2. 委托贷款 Designated Loans	1098.97	-15.32
（2）委托投资基金 Designated Investment Funds	119.35	27.81	3. 抵押贷款 Mortagage Loans	31.58	19.32
3. 保证金存款 Guarantee Deposits	89.24	-46.76	4. 票据融资 Paper Financing		-0.01
4. 其他存款 Other Deposits	121.42	-15.71	其中：贴现 Of Which：Discount		-0.01
二、金融债券 Financial Bonds	49.34	27.88	5. 融资租赁 Financing Leases	13.80	-1.32
三、应付及暂收款 Accounts Payable and Receipts on Account	482.99	5.08	6. 各项垫款 Receiables Paid in Advance	1.09	0.85
其中：应付及预提利息 Of Which：Interest Payable and Accrued	53.18	-1.43	7. 其他贷款 Other Loans	92.89	-23.52
			二、委托投资 Designated Investments	283.53	34.10
四、长期借款 Long - term Borrowing	170.10	49.87	三、投资 Investments	644.18	62.46
五、证券业务款项 Securities Business Funds	462.90	-231.51	1. 短期投资 Short - term Investments	124.95	7.97
六、卖出回购证券 Repo	24.00	-1.47	2. 长期投资 Long - term Investments	519.23	54.49
七、向中央银行借款 Borrowings from the Central Bank	47.81	0.92	四、应收及预付款 Accounts Receivable and Advance Payments	476.90	-40.26
八、同业往来 Inter - bank Transactions	168.19	4.83	其中：应收利息 Of Which：Interest Receivable	53.58	-16.42
1. 同业存放 Due to Banks and Other Financial Institutions	27.06	6.01	五、证券业务款项 Securities Business Funds	71.42	-97.52
2. 同业拆借 Placements from Banks and Other Financial Institutions	141.13	-1.18	六、经营租赁 Operating Leases	1.17	-0.60

续表
Continued

项　目 Items	余　额 Balance	比年初增减额 Changes within the Year	项　目 Items	余　额 Balance	比年初增减额 Changes within the Year
九、代理金融机构贷款基金 Designated Loan Funds on Behalf of Financial Institutions	9.73	-1.24	七、买入返售证券 Reverse Repo	14.41	-6.82
其中：中央银行委托专项贷款基金 Of Which：Earmarked Loan Funds Designated by the Central Bank	0.18	-0.16	八、存放中央银行准备金存款 Reserve Deposits with the Central Bank	36.03	-7.60
			九、存放中央银行特种存款 Special Deposits with the Central Bank	0.30	0.30
			十、同业往来 Inter-bank Transactions	339.57	44.35
十、各项准备 Total Provisions	21.40	8.37	1.存放同业 Due from Banks and Other Financial Institutions	319.82	46.19
其中：贷款呆账准备金 Of Which：Provisions for Bad Loans	9.86	3.88	2.拆放同业 Placements with Banks and Other Financial Institutions	19.75	-1.84
十一、所有者权益 Owner's Equity	735.26	29.92			
其中：实收资本 Of Which：Paid-in Capital	572.48	50.81	十一、代理金融机构贷款 Lending on Behalf of Financial Institutions	3.79	-1.92
当年结益 Net Earnings	-0.48	-0.48	其中：代理人行专项贷款 Of Which：Agency Earmarked Loans of the Central Bank	0.18	-0.16
十二、其他 Others	-565.64	132.90	十二、库存现金 Cash in Vault	1.50	-0.53
			十三、外币占款 Position for Foreign Exchange Purchase	33.90	11.76
资金来源总计 Total Sources	**3519.21**	**-109.81**	**资金运用总计 Total Uses**	**3519.21**	**-109.81**

信托投资公司人民币信贷收支表

Sources and Uses of Credit Funds of Trust and Investment Companies（RMB）

（2002 年末）

（Year - end of 2002）

单位：亿元

Unit：100 Million Yuan

项　目 Items	余　额 Balance	比年初增减额 Changes within the Year	项　目 Items	余　额 Balance	比年初增减额 Changes within the Year
一、各项存款 Total Deposits	1450.23	- 51.68	一、各项贷款 Total Loans	1210.99	- 34.64
1. 信托存款 Trust Deposits	207.06	- 26.89	1. 信托贷款 Trust Loans	203.44	- 54.44
2. 委托存款 Designated Deposits	1191.80	- 1.04	其中：中长期信托贷款 Of Which：Medium and Long - term Loans	69.27	- 30.64
（1）委托存款 Designated Deposits	1046.13	- 20.62	2. 委托贷款 Designated Loans	903.22	7.82
（2）委托投资基金 Designated Investment Funds	145.67	19.58	3. 抵押贷款 Mortagage Loans	23.71	- 0.89
3. 保证金存款 Guarantee Deposits	6.61	- 28.43	4. 票据融资 Paper Financing		
4. 其他存款 Other Deposits	44.76	4.68	其中：贴现 Of Which：Discount		
二、金融债券 Financial Bonds	89.57	44.79	5. 融资租赁 Financing Leases	7.24	- 1.43
三、应付及暂收款 Accounts Payable and Receipts on Account	274.99	- 51.97	6. 各项垫款 Total Advances	0.24	- 0.61
其中：应付及预提利息 Of Which：Interest Payable and Accrued	36.06	0.25	7. 其他贷款 Other Loans	73.14	14.91
四、长期借款 Long - term Borrowing	167.20	34.69	二、委托投资 Designated Investments	269.38	4.62
五、证券业务款项 Securities Business Funds	43.75	- 280.85	三、投资 Investments	593.92	97.32
六、卖出回购证券 Repo	21.70	10.35	1. 短期投资 Short - term Investments	164.59	54.46
七、向中央银行借款 Borrowings from the Central Bank	30.09	- 0.42	2. 长期投资 Long - term Investments	429.33	42.86
八、同业往来 Inter - bank Transactions	112.96	- 4.39	四、应收及预付款 Accounts Receivable and Advance Payments	257.95	- 44.17
1. 同业存放 Due to Banks and Other Financial Institutions	11.69	3.05	其中：应收利息 Of Which：Interest Receivable	33.45	- 3.39
2. 同业拆借 Placements from Banks and Other Financial Institutions	101.27	- 7.44	五、证券业务款项 Securities Business Funds	15.11	- 37.77
			六、经营租赁 Operating Leases	1.25	0.09

续表
Continued

项　目 Items	余　额 Balance	比年初增减额 Changes within the Year	项　目 Items	余　额 Balance	比年初增减额 Changes within the Year
九、代理金融机构贷款基金 Designated Loan Funds on Behalf of Financial Institutions	2.39	1.86	七、买入返售证券 Reverse Repo	11.48	3.83
其中：中央银行委托专项贷款基金 Of Which: Earmarked Loan Funds Designated by the Central Bank	0.17		八、存放中央银行准备金存款 Reserve Deposits with the Central Bank	15.75	-9.20
			九、存放中央银行特种存款 Special Deposits with the Central Bank		-0.02
			十、同业往来 Inter-bank Transactions	76.72	-200.27
十、各项准备 Total Provisions	20.39	2.22	1. 存放同业 Due from Banks and Other Financial Institutions	65.04	-198.24
其中：贷款呆账准备金 Of Which: Provisions for Bad Loans	9.15	1.40	2. 拆放同业 Placements with Banks and Other Financial Institutions	11.68	-2.03
十一、所有者权益 Owner's Equity	591.22	-12.68			
其中：实收资本 Of Which: Paid-in Capital	471.38	31.06	十一、代理金融机构贷款 Lending on Behalf of Financial Institutions	0.74	-0.18
当年结益 Net Earnings	-5.54	-5.54	其中：代理人行专项贷款 Of Which: Agency Earmarked Loans of the Central Bank	0.17	
十二、其他 Others	-300.29	113.06			
			十二、库存现金 Cash in Vault	0.36	-0.46
			十三、外币占款 Position for Foreign Exchange Purchase	50.55	25.83
资金来源总计 Total Sources	**2504.20**	**-195.02**	**资金运用总计 Total Uses**	**2504.20**	**-195.02**

信托投资公司人民币信贷收支表

Sources and Uses of Credit Funds of Trust and Investment Companies（RMB）

（2003年末）

（Year - end of 2003）

单位：亿元

Unit：100 Million Yuan

项目 Items	余额 Balance	比年初增减额 Changes within the Year	项目 Items	余额 Balance	比年初增减额 Changes within the Year
一、各项存款 Total Deposits	1579.76	142.76	一、各项贷款 Total Loans	1209.54	24.19
1.信托存款 Trust Deposits	220.83	5.95	1.信托贷款 Trust Loans	212.19	22.87
2.委托存款 Designated Deposits	1300.70	125.45	其中：中长期信托贷款 Of Which：Medium and Long - term Loans	72.44	7.48
（1）委托存款 Designated Deposits	1013.06	-7.63	2.委托贷款 Designated Loans	904.84	14.23
（2）委托投资基金 Designated Investment Funds	287.64	133.08	3.抵押贷款 Mortagage Loans	25.23	5.79
3.保证金存款 Guarantee Deposits	1.60	-4.87	4.票据融资 Paper Financing	0.10	
4.其他存款 Other Deposits	56.63	16.23	其中：贴现 Of Which：Discount		
二、金融债券 Financial Bonds	188.33	99.73	5.融资租赁 Financing Leases	6.16	-0.99
三、应付及暂收款 Accounts Payable and Receipts on Account	236.51	-18.69	6.各项垫款 Total Advances	0.21	-0.03
其中：应付及预提利息 Of Which：Interest Payable and Accrued	28.54	-5.47	7.其他贷款 Other Loans	60.81	-17.68
四、长期借款 Long - term Borrowing	149.83	-17.14	二、委托投资 Designated Investments	456.62	171.12
五、证券业务款项 Securities Business Funds	25.34	-12.06	三、投资 Investments	673.38	89.59
六、卖出回购证券 Repo	32.10	11.40	1.短期投资 Short - term Investments	233.51	70.47
七、向中央银行借款 Borrowings from the Central Bank	15.12	-13.65	2.长期投资 Long - term Investments	439.87	19.12
八、同业往来 Inter - bank Transactions	121.63	13.74	四、应收及预付款 Accounts Receivable and Advance Payments	231.13	2.36
1.同业存放 Due to Banks and Other Financial Institutions	13.34	3.51	其中：应收利息 Of Which：Interest Receivable	30.00	-3.23
2.同业拆借 Placements from Banks and Other Financial Institutions	108.29	10.23	五、证券业务款项 Securities Business Funds	9.19	-4.69
九、代理金融机构贷款基金 Designated Loan Funds on Behalf of Financial Institutions		-2.39	六、经营租赁 Operating Leases	1.21	-0.04
			七、买入返售证券 Reverse Repo	24.87	13.74

续表
Continued

项 目 Items	余 额 Balance	比年初增减额 Changes within the Year	项 目 Items	余 额 Balance	比年初增减额 Changes within the Year
其中：中央银行委托专项贷款基金 Of Which: Earmarked Loan Funds Designated by the Central Bank		-0.17	八、存放中央银行准备金存款 Reserve Deposits with the Central Bank	11.03	-4.07
			九、存放中央银行特种存款 Special Deposits with the Central Bank		
			十、同业往来 Inter-bank Transactions	95.26	17.85
十、各项准备 Total Provisions	23.52	4.77	1. 存放同业 Due from Banks and Other Financial Institutions	86.07	17.70
其中：贷款损失准备 Of Which: Provisions for Loan Losses	14.06	4.43			
十一、所有者权益 Owner's Equity	655.28	62.10	2. 拆放同业 Placements with Banks and Other Financial Institutions	9.19	0.15
其中：实收资本 Of Which: Paid-in Capital	517.30	55.97	十一、代理金融机构贷款 Lending on Behalf of Financial Institutions	0.02	-0.24
当年结益 Net Earnings	3.57	3.57			
十二、其他 Others	-153.77	124.84	其中：代理人行专项贷款 Of Which: Agency Earmarked Loans of the Central Bank		-0.17
			十二、库存现金 Cash in Vault	0.21	-0.05
			十三、外币占款 Position for Foreign Exchange Purchase	161.19	85.65
资金来源总计 Total Sources	**2873.65**	**395.41**	**资金运用总计 Total Uses**	**2873.65**	**395.41**

信托投资公司人民币信贷收支表

Sources and Uses of Credit Funds of Trust and Investment Companies（RMB）

（2004 年末）

（Year - end of 2004）

单位：亿元

Unit：100 Million Yuan

项　目 Items	余　额 Balance	比年初增减额 Changes within the Year	项　目 Items	余　额 Balance	比年初增减额 Changes within the Year
一、各项存款 Total Deposits	1715.33	175.20	一、各项贷款 Total Loans	1286.08	186.67
1. 信托存款 Trust Deposits	227.94	6.02	1. 信托贷款 Trust Loans	194.39	36.72
2. 委托存款 Designated Deposits	1448.47	186.53	其中：中长期信托贷款 Of Which：Medium and Long - term Loans	53.81	15.03
（1）委托存款 Designated Deposits	1150.17	172.63	2. 委托贷款 Designated Loans	1020.74	147.05
（2）委托投资基金 Designated Investment Funds	298.30	13.90	3. 抵押贷款 Mortagage Loans	2.45	- 0.32
3. 保证金存款 Guarantee Deposits	1.45	- 0.08	4. 票据融资 Paper Financing		
4. 其他存款 Other Deposits	37.47	- 17.27	其中：贴现 Of Which：Discount		
二、金融债券 Financial Bonds			5. 融资租赁 Financing Leases	5.32	0.15
三、应付及暂收款 Accounts Payable and Receipts on Account	134.60	- 11.58	6. 各项垫款 Total Advances	0.04	- 0.17
其中：应付及预提利息 Of Which：Interest Payable and Accrued	26.87	1.20	7. 其他贷款 Other Loans	63.14	3.24
			二、委托投资 Designated Investments	505.33	48.76
四、长期借款 Long - term Borrowing	56.08	- 8.48	三、投资 Investments	310.99	- 44.18
五、证券业务款项 Securities Business Funds	6.20	- 6.87	1. 短期投资 Short - term Investments	98.82	- 26.52
六、卖出回购资产 Assets Repo（Including Securities）	40.07	- 2.87	2. 长期投资 Long - term Investments	212.17	- 17.66
七、向中央银行借款 Borrowings from the Central Bank	0.90	- 0.05	四、应收及预付款 Accounts Receivable and Advance Payments	142.98	0.47
八、同业往来 Inter - bank Transactions	79.26	- 30.58			
1. 同业存放 Due to Banks and Other Financial Institutions	9.50	- 6.14	其中：应收利息 Of Which：Interest Receivable	20.65	- 5.06
			五、证券业务款项 Securities Business Funds	1.07	- 4.65
2. 同业拆借 Placements from Banks and Other Financial Institutions	69.76	- 24.44	六、经营租赁 Operating Leases	0.71	- 0.50
九、代理金融机构贷款基金 Designated Loan Funds on Behalf of Financial Institutions			七、买入返售资产 Assets Reverse Repo（Including Securities）	3.31	- 21.06

续表
Continued

项 目 Items	余 额 Balance	比年初增减额 Changes within the Year	项 目 Items	余 额 Balance	比年初增减额 Changes within the Year
其中：中央银行委托专项贷款基金 Of Which: Earmarked Loan Funds Designated by the Central Bank			八、存放中央银行准备金存款 Reserve Deposits with the Central Bank	5.50	-4.67
			九、存放中央银行特种存款 Special Deposits with the Central Bank		
			十、同业往来 Inter-bank Transactions	79.30	-10.45
十、各项准备 Total Provisions	35.13	14.81	1. 存放同业 Due from Banks and Other Financial Institutions	77.08	-7.31
其中：贷款损失准备 Of Which: Provisions for Loan Losses	15.65	5.86			
十一、所有者权益 Owner's Equity	440.97	-5.59	2. 拆放同业 Placements with Banks and Other Financial Institutions	2.22	-3.14
其中：实收资本 Of Which: Paid-in Capital	429.88	7.87			
当年结益 Net Earnings	5.13	5.13	十一、代理金融机构贷款 Lending on Behalf of Financial Institutions	0.02	
十二、其他 Others	-137.45	21.24	其中：代理人行专项贷款 Of Which: Agency Earmarked Loans of the Central Bank		
			十二、库存现金 Cash in Vault	0.17	0.01
			十三、外币占款 Position for Foreign Exchange Purchase	35.63	-5.17
资金来源总计 Total Sources	**2371.09**	**145.23**	**资金运用总计 Total Uses**	**2371.09**	**145.23**

信托投资公司人民币信贷收支表

Sources and Uses of Credit Funds of Trust and Investment Companies（RMB）

（2005 年末）

（Year - end of 2005）

单位：亿元

Unit：100 Million Yuan

项目 Items	余额 Balance	比年初增减额 Changes within the Year	项目 Items	余额 Balance	比年初增减额 Changes within the Year
一、各项存款 Total Deposits	1828.41	51.94	一、各项贷款 Total Loans	1500.21	134.19
1. 信托存款 Trust Deposits	398.14	113.24	1. 信托贷款 Trust Loans	376.96	114.01
2. 委托存款 Designated Deposits	1381.67	- 72.13	其中：中长期信托贷款 Of Which：Medium and Long - term Loans	149.89	56.80
（1）委托存款 Designated Deposits	1090.29	- 57.05	2. 委托贷款 Designated Loans	1037.56	7.30
（2）委托投资基金 Designated Investment Funds	291.38	- 15.08	3. 抵押贷款 Mortagage Loans	1.63	- 1.00
3. 保证金存款 Guarantee Deposits	1.41	- 0.04	4. 票据融资 Paper Financing	0.05	0.05
4. 其他存款 Other Deposits	47.19	10.87	其中：贴现 Of Which：Discount		
二、金融债券 Financial Bonds			5. 融资租赁 Financing Leases	4.50	- 0.89
三、应付及暂收款 Accounts Payable and Receipts on Account	110.37	- 31.16	6. 各项垫款 Total Advances	0.04	
其中：应付及预提利息 Of Which：Interest Payable and Accrued	5.10	- 21.34	7. 其他贷款 Other Loans	79.47	14.72
			二、委托投资 Designated Investments	515.99	10.34
四、长期借款 Long - term Borrowing	49.75	- 5.39	三、投资 Investments	296.63	- 23.34
五、证券业务款项 Securities Business Funds	3.31	- 2.27	1. 短期投资 Short - term Investments	78.95	- 31.33
六、卖出回购资产 Assets Repo（Including Securities）	35.77	- 2.30	2. 长期投资 Long - term Investments	217.68	7.99
七、向中央银行借款 Borrowings from the Central Bank	0.84	- 0.01	四、应收及预付款 Accounts Receivable and Advance Payments	102.77	- 44.91
八、同业往来 Inter - bank Transactions	62.06	- 20.66	其中：应收利息 Of Which：Interest Receivable	3.83	- 17.08
1. 同业存放 Due to Banks and Other Financial Institutions	1.86	- 7.64	五、证券业务款项 Securities Business Funds	0.44	- 0.01
2. 同业拆借 Placements from Banks and Other Financial Institutions	60.20	- 13.02	六、经营租赁 Operating Leases	0.70	0.01
九、代理金融机构贷款基金 Designated Loan Funds on Behalf of Financial Institutions			七、买入返售资产 Assets Reverse Repo（Including Securities）	0.85	- 2.65

续表
Continued

项　目 Items	余　额 Balance	比年初增减额 Changes within the Year	项　目 Items	余　额 Balance	比年初增减额 Changes within the Year
其中：中央银行委托专项贷款基金 Of Which: Earmarked Loan Funds Designated by the Central Bank			八、存放中央银行准备金存款 Reserve Deposits with the Central Bank	3.44	-2.22
			九、存放中央银行特种存款 Special Deposits with the Central Bank		
十、各项准备 Total Provisions	37.38	1.41	十、同业往来 Inter-bank Transactions	94.34	13.35
其中：贷款损失准备 Of Which: Provisions for Loan Losses	13.52	-1.65	1. 存放同业 Due from Banks and Other Financial Institutions	92.89	14.52
十一、所有者权益 Owner's Equity	480.08	12.74	2. 拆放同业 Placements with Banks and Other Financial Institutions	1.45	-1.17
其中：实收资本 Of Which: Paid-in Capital	487.70	28.86	十一、代理金融机构贷款 Lending on Behalf of Financial Institutions		-0.02
当年结益 Net Earnings	0.76	0.76	其中：代理人行专项贷款 Of Which: Agency Earmarked Loans of the Central Bank		
十二、其他 Others	-55.24	81.33	十二、库存现金 Cash in Vault	1.13	0.27
			十三、外币占款 Position for Foreign Exchange Purchase	36.23	0.62
资金来源总计 Total Sources	**2552.73**	**85.63**	**资金运用总计 Total Uses**	**2552.73**	**85.63**

13. 金融租赁公司人民币信贷收支表（1997—2005 年）
Sources and Uses of Credit Funds of Financial Leasing Companies（RMB）（1997—2005）

金融租赁公司人民币信贷收支表
Sources and Uses of Credit Funds of Financial Leasing Companies（RMB）

（1997 年末）

（Year－end of 1997）

单位：亿元

Unit：100 Million Yuan

项目 Items	余额 Balance	比年初增减额 Changes within the Year	项目 Items	余额 Balance	比年初增减额 Changes within the Year
一、各项存款 Total Deposits	71.58	18.08	一、各项贷款 Total Loans	77.39	9.85
1. 信托存款 Trust Deposits	38.25	20.36	1. 信托贷款 Trust Loans	5.72	－0.59
2. 委托存款 Designated Deposits	29.14	1.96	其中：中长期信托贷款 Of Which：Medium and Long－term Trust Loans	1.10	0.06
（1）委托存款 Designated Deposits	29.07	2.20	2. 委托贷款 Designated Loans	21.43	5.85
（2）委托投资基金 Designated Investment Funds	0.07	－0.24	3. 抵押贷款 Mortagage Loans	2.32	2.26
3. 保证金存款 Guarantee Deposits	2.19	0.58	4. 贴现贷款 Discount		
4. 其他存款 Other Deposits	2.00	－4.82	5. 融资租赁 Financing Leases	35.88	6.79
二、金融债券 Financial Bonds	5.58	4.58	6. 其他贷款 Other Loans	12.04	－4.46
三、长期借款 Long－term Borrowing	5.43	－0.76	二、委托投资 Designated Investments	0.15	0.12
四、证券业务款项 Securities Business Funds	2.53	0.16	三、投资 Investments	12.99	7.61
五、卖出回购证券 Repo	1.75	－2.36	1. 短期投资 Short－term Investments	8.60	7.43
六、向中央银行借款 Borrowings from the Central Bank	0.38	－0.02	2. 长期投资 Long－term Investments	4.39	0.18
七、同业往来 Inter－bank Transactions	24.26	1.36	四、证券业务款项 Securities Business Funds	0.31	0.20
1. 同业存放 Due to Banks and Other Financial Institutions	5.61	2.71	五、经营租赁 Operating Leases	0.81	0.48
2. 同业拆借 Placements from Banks and Other Financial Institutions	18.65	－1.35	六、在人民银行存款 Deposits with the Central Bank	1.23	0.33
			七、缴存人行准备金 Reserves with the Central Bank	2.20	1.28
八、代理金融机构贷款基金 Loan Funds on Behalf of Financial Institutions	4.59	1.75	八、缴存人行特种存款 Special Deposits with the Central Bank	0.14	0.14

续表
Continued

项　　目 Items	余　额 Balance	比年初增减额 Changes within the Year	项　　目 Items	余　额 Balance	比年初增减额 Changes within the Year
其中：人行委托专项贷款基金 Of Which：Earmarked Loan Funds Designated by the Central Bank			九、同业往来 Inter - bank Transactions	12.45	4.83
			1. 存放同业 Due from Banks and Other Financial Institutions	5.45	3.43
九、各项准备 Total Provisions	0.36				
			2. 拆放同业 Placements with Banks and Other Financial Institutions	7.00	1.40
十、所有者权益 Owner's Equity	10.69	-0.11			
其中：实收资本 Of Which：Paid - in Capital	8.89	1.14	十、代理金融机构贷款 Lending on Behalf of Financial Institutions	3.63	0.20
当年结益 Net Earnings	-0.50	-0.50			
			其中：代理人行专项贷款 Of Which：Agency Earmarked Loans of the Central Bank		
十一、其他 Others	-10.66	1.97			
			十一、库存现金 Cash in Vault	0.03	-0.01
			十二、外币占款 Position for Foreign Exchange Purchase	5.16	-0.38
资金来源总计 Total Sources	**116.49**	**24.65**	**资金运用总计 Total Uses**	**116.49**	**24.65**

金融租赁公司人民币信贷收支表

Sources and Uses of Credit Funds of Financial Leasing Companies（RMB）

（1998 年末）

（Year - end of 1998）

单位：亿元
Unit：100 Million Yuan

项目 Items	余额 Balance	比年初增减额 Changes within the Year	项目 Items	余额 Balance	比年初增减额 Changes within the Year
一、各项存款 Total Deposits	75.50	3.93	一、各项贷款 Total Loans	91.02	13.41
1. 信托存款 Trust Deposits	36.02	-2.85	1. 信托贷款 Trust Loans	11.41	3.38
2. 委托存款 Designated Deposits	37.32	8.20	其中：中长期信托贷款 Of Which：Medium and Long - term Trust Loans	1.09	-0.02
（1）委托存款 Designated Deposits	36.40	7.35	2. 委托贷款 Designated Loans	28.88	9.41
（2）委托投资基金 Designated Investment Funds	0.92	0.85	3. 抵押贷款 Mortagage Loans	2.36	0.41
3. 保证金存款 Guarantee Deposits	2.09	-0.10	4. 贴现贷款 Discount		
4. 其他存款 Other Deposits	0.07	-1.32	5. 融资租赁 Financing Leases	38.53	2.42
二、金融债券 Financial Bonds	5.29	-0.29	6. 其他贷款 Other Loans	9.84	-2.21
三、长期借款 Long - term Borrowing	6.03	0.60	二、委托投资 Designated Investments	1.72	1.57
四、证券业务款项 Securities Business Funds	0.73	-1.72	三、投资 Investments	16.12	3.13
五、卖出回购证券 Repo	2.09	0.33	1. 短期投资 Short - term Investments	11.72	3.12
六、向中央银行借款 Borrowings from the Central Bank	1.09	0.71	2. 长期投资 Long - term Investments	4.40	0.01
七、同业往来 Inter - bank Transactions	26.49	2.27	四、证券业务款项 Securities Business Funds	0.16	-0.15
1. 同业存放 Due to Banks and Other Financial Institutions	4.70	-0.91	五、经营租赁 Operating Leases	1.86	1.05
2. 同业拆借 Placements from Banks and Other Financial Institutions	21.79	3.18	六、缴存准备金存款 Reserve Deposits with the Central Bank	1.37	-2.06
八、代理金融机构贷款基金 Loan Funds on Behalf of Financial Institutions	6.32	1.74	七、缴存人行准备金 Reserves with the Central Bank		
其中：人行委托专项贷款基金 Of Which：Earmarked Loan Funds Designated by the Central Bank			八、缴存人行特种存款 Special Deposits with the Central Bank		-0.14
			九、同业往来 Inter - bank Transactions	8.38	-3.47

续表
Continued

项　目 Items	余　额 Balance	比年初增减额 Changes within the Year	项　目 Items	余　额 Balance	比年初增减额 Changes within the Year
九、各项准备 Total Provisions	0.43	0.06	1. 存放同业 Due from Banks and Other Financial Institutions	1.58	-3.49
十、所有者权益 Owner's Equity	9.87	-1.72	2. 拆放同业 Placements with Banks and Other Financial Institutions	6.80	0.02
其中：实收资本 Of Which: Paid-in Capital	10.88	1.98			
当年结益 Net Earnings	-2.55	-2.55	十、代理金融机构贷款 Lending on Behalf of Financial Institutions	3.78	0.16
十一、其他 Others	-5.04	6.79	其中：代理人行专项贷款 Of Which: Agency Earmarked Loans of the Central Bank		
			十一、库存现金 Cash in Vault	0.03	
			十二、外币占款 Position for Foreign Exchange Purchase	4.36	-0.80
资金来源总计 Total Sources	**128.80**	**12.70**	**资金运用总计 Total Uses**	**128.80**	**12.70**

金融租赁公司人民币信贷收支表
Sources and Uses of Credit Funds of Financial Leasing Companies（RMB）

（1999 年末）

（Year - end of 1999）

单位：亿元

Unit：100 Million Yuan

项　目 Items	余　额 Balance	比年初增减额 Changes within the Year	项　目 Items	余　额 Balance	比年初增减额 Changes within the Year
一、各项存款 Total Deposits	66.33	-9.19	一、各项贷款 Total Loans	84.35	-6.37
1. 信托存款 Trust Deposits	31.78	-4.05	1. 信托贷款 Trust Loans	10.00	-1.41
2. 委托存款 Designated Deposits	33.32	-4.22	其中：中长期信托贷款 Of Which：Medium and Long - term Trust Loans	1.09	
（1）委托存款 Designated Deposits	31.49	-5.13	2. 委托贷款 Designated Loans	24.57	-4.23
（2）委托投资基金 Designated Investment Funds	1.83	0.91	3. 抵押贷款 Mortagage Loans	0.93	-1.43
3. 保证金存款 Guarantee Deposits	1.18	-0.91	4. 贴现贷款 Discount		
4. 其他存款 Other Deposits	0.05	-0.01	5. 融资租赁 Financing Leases	40.21	1.80
二、金融债券 Financial Bonds	5.40	0.11	6. 其他贷款 Other Loans	8.64	-1.10
三、长期借款 Long - term Borrowing	7.06	1.03	二、委托投资 Designated Investments	2.80	1.08
四、证券业务款项 Securities Business Funds	0.47	-0.27	三、投资 Investments	16.15	0.02
五、卖出回购证券 Repo	2.08		1. 短期投资 Short - term Investments	10.00	-1.73
六、向中央银行借款 Borrowings from the Central Bank	2.08	0.99	2. 长期投资 Long - term Investments	6.15	1.75
七、同业往来 Inter - bank Transactions	23.98	-2.38	四、证券业务款项 Securities Business Funds		-0.16
1. 同业存放 Due to Banks and Other Financial Institutions	4.85	0.15	五、经营租赁 Operating Leases	1.78	-0.08
2. 同业拆借 Placements from Banks and Other Financial Institutions	19.13	-2.53	六、缴存准备金存款 Reserve Deposits with the Central Bank	1.03	-0.35
			七、缴存人行特种存款 Special Deposits with the Central Bank		
八、代理金融机构贷款基金 Loan Funds on Behalf of Financial Institutions	5.44	-0.88	八、同业往来 Inter - bank Transactions	6.77	-1.26
其中：人行委托专项贷款基金 Of Which：Earmarked Loan Funds Designated by the Central Bank			1. 存放同业 Due from Banks and Other Financial Institutions	1.30	-0.05

续表
Continued

项　　目 Items	余　额 Balance	比年初增减额 Changes within the Year	项　　目 Items	余　额 Balance	比年初增减额 Changes within the Year
九、各项准备 Total Provisions	0.39	-0.03	2. 拆放同业 Placements with Banks and Other Financial Institutions	5.47	-1.21
十、所有者权益 Owner's Equity	7.84	-2.07	九、代理金融机构贷款 Lending on Behalf of Financial Institutions	4.00	0.22
其中：实收资本 Of Which: Paid-in Capital	10.88				
当年结益 Net Earnings	-1.38	-1.38	其中：代理人行专项贷款 Of Which: Agency Earmarked Loans of the Central Bank		
十一、其他 Others	-1.16	4.43	十、库存现金 Cash in Vault	0.03	
			十一、外币占款 Position for Foreign Exchange Purchase	3.00	-1.36
资金来源总计 Total Sources	**119.91**	**-8.26**	**资金运用总计 Total Uses**	**119.91**	**-8.26**

金融租赁公司人民币信贷收支表
Sources and Uses of Credit Funds of Financial Leasing Companies（RMB）

（2000 年末）

（Year - end of 2000）

单位：亿元
Unit：100 Million Yuan

项　目 Items	余　额 Balance	比年初增减额 Changes within the Year	项　目 Items	余　额 Balance	比年初增减额 Changes within the Year
一、各项存款 Total Deposits	68.51	1.66	一、各项贷款 Total Loans	88.13	3.69
1. 信托存款 Trust Deposits	33.26	1.50	1. 信托贷款 Trust Loans	7.89	- 2.09
2. 委托存款 Designated Deposits	33.59	- 0.17	其中：中长期信托贷款 Of Which：Medium and Long - term Trust Loans	1.09	
（1）委托存款 Designated Deposits	29.36	- 2.57	2. 委托贷款 Designated Loans	22.42	- 2.14
（2）委托投资基金 Designated Investment Funds	4.23	2.40	3. 抵押贷款 Mortagage Loans	0.92	- 0.01
3. 保证金存款 Guarantee Deposits	1.63	0.35	4. 贴现贷款 Discount		
4. 其他存款 Other Deposits	0.03	- 0.02	5. 融资租赁 Financing Leases	45.56	5.23
二、金融债券 Financial Bonds	4.10	- 1.30	6. 其他贷款 Other Loans	11.34	2.70
三、长期借款 Long - term Borrowing	9.52	2.46	二、委托投资 Designated Investments	4.60	1.79
四、证券业务款项 Securities Business Funds	0.47		三、投资 Investments	16.63	0.48
五、卖出回购证券 Repo	2.04	- 0.04	1. 短期投资 Short - term Investments	10.77	0.77
六、向中央银行借款 Borrowings from the Central Bank	2.08		2. 长期投资 Long - term Investments	5.86	- 0.29
七、同业往来 Inter - bank Transactions	33.53	9.57	四、证券业务款项 Securities Business Funds	0.01	0.01
1. 同业存放 Due to Banks and Other Financial Institutions	10.97	6.12	五、经营租赁 Operating Leases	1.81	0.03
2. 同业拆借 Placements from Banks and Other Financial Institutions	22.56	3.45	六、缴存准备金存款 Reserve Deposits with the Central Bank	1.23	0.20
			七、缴存人行特种存款 Special Deposits with the Central Bank		
八、代理金融机构贷款基金 Loan Funds on Behalf of Financial Institutions	5.35	- 0.09	八、同业往来 Inter - bank Transactions	11.39	4.66
其中：人行委托专项贷款基金 Of Which：Earmarked Loan Funds Designated by the Central Bank			1. 存放同业 Due from Banks and Other Financial Institutions	2.38	1.12

续表
Continued

项 目 Items	余 额 Balance	比年初增减额 Changes within the Year	项 目 Items	余 额 Balance	比年初增减额 Changes within the Year
九、各项准备 Total Provisions	0.39	0.02	2. 拆放同业 Placements with Banks and Other Financial Institutions	9.01	3.54
十、所有者权益 Owner's Equity	8.42	0.55	九、代理金融机构贷款 Lending on Behalf of Financial Institutions	4.00	
其中：实收资本 Of Which: Paid - in Capital	10.88				
当年结益 Net Earnings	0.09	0.09	其中：代理人行专项贷款 Of Which: Agency Earmarked Loans of the Central Bank		
十一、其他 Others	- 2.72	- 1.10			
			十、库存现金 Cash in Vault	0.02	- 0.01
			十一、外币占款 Position for Foreign Exchange Purchase	3.87	0.88
资金来源总计 Total Sources	**131.69**	**11.73**	**资金运用总计 Total Uses**	**131.69**	**11.73**

金融租赁公司人民币信贷收支表

Sources and Uses of Credit Funds of Financial Leasing Companies（RMB）

（2001 年末）

（Year - end of 2001）

单位：亿元

Unit：100 Million Yuan

项目 Items	余额 Balance	比年初增减额 Changes within the Year	项目 Items	余额 Balance	比年初增减额 Changes within the Year
一、各项存款 Total Deposits	66.26	11.72	一、各项贷款 Total Loans	106.08	27.34
1. 信托存款 Trust Deposits	6.82	-9.94	1. 信托贷款 Trust Loans	5.79	-1.20
2. 委托存款 Designated Deposits	42.90	10.61	其中：中长期信托贷款 Of Which：Medium and Long - term Trust Loans	2.16	
（1）委托存款 Designated Deposits	33.23	5.17	2. 委托贷款 Designated Loans	26.05	3.76
（2）委托投资基金 Designated Investment Funds	9.67	5.44	3. 抵押贷款 Mortagage Loans	0.37	-0.70
3. 保证金存款 Guarantee Deposits	7.02	5.33	4. 票据融资 Paper Financing		
4. 其他存款 Other Deposits	9.52	5.72	其中：贴现 Of Which：Discount		
二、金融债券 Financial Bonds	4.30	0.20	5. 融资租赁 Financing Leases	63.82	21.30
三、应付及暂收款 Accounts Payable and Receipts on Account	18.05	-3.29	6. 各项垫款 Total Advances		
其中：应付及预提利息 Of Which：Accounts Payable and Accrued	0.84	-0.64	7. 其他贷款 Other Loans	10.05	4.18
			二、委托投资 Designated Investments	4.20	-5.04
四、长期借款 Long - term Borrowing	27.18	17.78	三、投资 Investments	19.11	2.54
五、证券业务款项 Securities Business Funds	0.01		1. 短期投资 Short - term Investments	11.93	1.43
六、卖出回购证券 Repo	2.37	-0.03	2. 长期投资 Long - term Investments	7.18	1.11
七、向中央银行借款 Borrowings from the Central Bank	1.78	-0.30	四、应收及预付款 Accounts Receivable and Advance Payments	22.74	8.10
八、同业往来 Inter - bank Transactions	22.88	-11.95	其中：应收利息 Of Which：Interest Receivable	5.69	0.31
1. 同业存放 Due to Banks and Other Financial Institutions	8.31	-2.68	五、证券业务款项 Securities Business Funds	0.01	
2. 同业拆借 Placements from Banks and Other Financial Institutions	14.57	-9.27	六、经营租赁 Operating Leases	1.60	-0.21
九、代理金融机构贷款基金 Loan Funds on Behalf of Financial Institutions	5.35		七、买入返售证券 Reverse Repo	0.18	-0.27

续表
Continued

项　目 Items	余　额 Balance	比年初增减额 Changes within the Year	项　目 Items	余　额 Balance	比年初增减额 Changes within the Year
其中：中央银行委托专项贷款基金 Of Which: Earmarked Loan Funds Designated by the Central Bank			八、存放中央银行准备金存款 Reserve Deposits with the Central Bank	1.10	-0.08
			九、存放中央银行特种存款 Special Deposits with the Central Bank		
			十、同业往来 Inter-bank Transactions	10.20	1.34
十、各项准备 Total Provisions	0.61	0.22	1. 存放同业 Due from Banks and Other Financial Institutions	6.14	3.65
其中：贷款呆账准备金 Of Which: Provisions for Bad Loans	0.50	0.20	2. 拆放同业 Placements with Banks and Other Financial Institutions	4.06	-2.31
十一、所有者权益 Owner's Equity	27.39	17.27	十一、代理金融机构贷款 Lending on Behalf of Financial Institutions	4.00	
其中：实收资本 Of Which: Paid-in Capital	28.41	15.99	其中：代理人行专项贷款 Of Which: Agency Earmarked Loans of the Central Bank		
当年结益 Net Earnings	0.51	0.51	十二、库存现金 Cash in Vault	0.04	0.01
十二、其他 Others	-4.88	2.26	十三、外币占款 Position for Foreign Exchange Purchase	2.04	0.15
资金来源总计 Total Sources	**171.30**	**33.88**	**资金运用总计 Total Uses**	**171.30**	**33.88**

金融租赁公司人民币信贷收支表
Sources and Uses of Credit Funds of Financial Leasing Companies (RMB)

（2002年末）

(Year-end of 2002)

单位：亿元

Unit: 100 Million Yuan

项目 Items	余额 Balance	比年初增减额 Changes within the Year	项目 Items	余额 Balance	比年初增减额 Changes within the Year
一、各项存款 Total Deposits	59.96	-3.05	一、各项贷款 Total Loans	122.10	24.42
1.信托存款 Trust Deposits	3.16	-1.94	1.信托贷款 Trust Loans	4.44	-0.28
2.委托存款 Designated Deposits	36.28	-5.10	其中：中长期信托贷款 Of Which: Medium and Long-term Trust Loans	1.09	
（1）委托存款 Designated Deposits	25.26	-6.48			
（2）委托投资基金 Designated Investment Funds	11.02	1.38	2.委托贷款 Designated Loans	23.61	0.38
3.保证金存款 Guarantee Deposits	13.96	6.94	3.抵押贷款 Mortagage Loans	0.37	
4.其他存款 Other Deposits	6.56	-2.95	4.票据融资 Paper Financing		
二、金融债券 Financial Bonds	0.19	-0.01	其中：贴现 Of Which: Discount		
三、应付及暂收款 Accounts Payable and Receipts on Account	11.13	-3.73	5.融资租赁 Financing Leases	89.44	28.61
			6.各项垫款 Total Advances		
其中：应付及预提利息 Of Which: Interest Payable and Accrued	1.19	0.29	7.其他贷款 Other Loans	4.24	-4.29
四、长期借款 Long-term Borrowing	37.10	9.90	二、委托投资 Designated Investments	0.14	-4.04
五、证券业务款项 Securities Business Funds		-0.01	三、投资 Investments	19.74	8.71
六、卖出回购证券 Repo	0.20	-0.10	1.短期投资 Short-term Investments	11.87	6.82
七、向中央银行借款 Borrowings from the Central Bank	0.36		2.长期投资 Long-term Investments	7.87	1.89
八、同业往来 Inter-bank Transactions	21.63	6.20	四、应收及预付款 Accounts Receivable and Advance Payments	18.33	4.94
1.同业存放 Due to Banks and Other Financial Institutions	9.56	3.09	其中：应收利息 Of Which: Interest Receivable	1.39	-0.17
			五、证券业务款项 Securities Business Funds		-0.01
2.同业拆借 Placements from Banks and Other Financial Institutions	12.07	3.11	六、经营租赁 Operating Leases	5.26	3.90
九、代理金融机构贷款基金 Loan Funds on Behalf of Financial Institutions	1.12		七、买入返售证券 Reverse Repo	0.08	

续表
Continued

项　目 Items	余　额 Balance	比年初增减额 Changes within the Year	项　目 Items	余　额 Balance	比年初增减额 Changes within the Year
其中：中央银行委托专项贷款基金 Of Which: Earmarked Loan Funds Designated by the Central Bank			八、存放中央银行准备金存款 Reserve Deposits with the Central Bank	0.56	-0.50
			九、存放中央银行特种存款 Special Deposits with the Central Bank		
			十、同业往来 Inter-bank Transactions	7.84	-2.04
十、各项准备 Total Provisions	1.28	0.75	1. 存放同业 Due from Banks and Other Financial Institutions	6.08	-0.06
其中：贷款呆账准备金 Of Which: Provisions for Bad Loans	1.14	0.69			
十一、所有者权益 Owner's Equity	40.42	11.67	2. 拆放同业 Placements with Banks and Other Financial Institutions	1.76	-1.98
其中：实收资本 Of Which: Paid-in Capital	42.54	12.15	十一、代理金融机构贷款 Lending on Behalf of Financial Institutions		
当年结益 Net Earnings	1.07	1.07			
十二、其他 Others	2.53	13.35	其中：代理人行专项贷款 Of Which: Agency Earmarked Loans of the Central Bank		
			十二、库存现金 Cash in Vault	0.04	
			十三、外币占款 Position for Foreign Exchange Purchase	1.83	-0.41
资金来源总计 Total Sources	**175.92**	**34.97**	**资金运用总计 Total Uses**	**175.92**	**34.97**

金融租赁公司人民币信贷收支表
Sources and Uses of Credit Funds of Financial Leasing Companies（RMB）

（2003 年末）

（Year - end of 2003）

单位：亿元
Unit：100 Million Yuan

项目 Items	余额 Balance	比年初增减额 Changes within the Year	项目 Items	余额 Balance	比年初增减额 Changes within the Year
一、各项存款 Total Deposits	64.26	4.29	一、各项贷款 Total Loans	161.87	39.74
1. 信托存款 Trust Deposits	2.97	-0.19	1. 信托贷款 Trust Loans	3.80	-0.64
2. 委托存款 Designated Deposits	39.17	2.88	其中：中长期信托贷款 Of Which：Medium and Long - term Trust Loans	1.09	
（1）委托存款 Designated Deposits	28.38	3.11	2. 委托贷款 Designated Loans	26.08	2.47
（2）委托投资基金 Designated Investment Funds	10.79	-0.23	3. 抵押贷款 Mortagage Loans	0.37	
3. 保证金存款 Guarantee Deposits	19.13	5.17	4. 票据融资 Paper Financing		
4. 其他存款 Other Deposits	2.99	-3.57	其中：贴现 Of Which：Discount		
二、金融债券 Financial Bonds	0.15	-0.04	5. 融资租赁 Financing Leases	125.84	36.37
三、应付及暂收款 Accounts Payable and Receipts on Account	17.95	7.54	6. 各项垫款 Total Advances		
其中：应付及预提利息 Of Which：Interest Payable and Accrued	5.10	3.91	7. 其他贷款 Other Loans	5.78	1.54
			二、委托投资 Designated Investments	0.08	-0.06
四、长期借款 Long - term Borrowing	68.64	31.39	三、投资 Investments	18.63	-1.11
五、证券业务款项 Securities Business Funds			1. 短期投资 Short - term Investments	10.47	-1.40
六、卖出回购证券 Repo	0.10	-0.10	2. 长期投资 Long - term Investments	8.16	0.29
七、向中央银行借款 Borrowings from the Central Bank	0.36		四、应收及预付款 Accounts Receivable and Advance Payments	19.13	2.22
八、同业往来 Inter - bank Transactions	24.44	2.96			
1. 同业存放 Due to Banks and Other Financial Institutions	9.38	-0.61	其中：应收利息 Of Which：Interest Receivable	1.21	-0.17
			五、证券业务款项 Securities Business Funds		
2. 同业拆借 Placements from Banks and Other Financial Institutions	15.06	3.57	六、经营租赁 Operating Leases	8.84	3.58
九、代理金融机构贷款基金 Loan Funds on Behalf of Financial Institutions	1.12		七、买入返售证券 Reverse Repo	0.08	

续表
Continued

项　　目 Items	余　额 Balance	比年初增减额 Changes within the Year	项　　目 Items	余　额 Balance	比年初增减额 Changes within the Year
其中：中央银行委托专项贷款基金 Of Which: Earmarked Loan Funds Designated by the Central Bank			八、存放中央银行准备金存款 Reserve Deposits with the Central Bank	1.31	0.74
			九、存放中央银行特种存款 Special Deposits with the Central Bank		
十、各项准备 Total Provisions	1.78	0.52	十、同业往来 Inter－bank Transactions	8.65	0.81
其中：贷款损失准备 Of Which: Provisions for Loan Losses	0.66	0.22	1. 存放同业 Due from Banks and Other Financial Institutions	7.28	1.20
十一、所有者权益 Owner's Equity	42.76	2.85	2. 拆放同业 Placements with Banks and Other Financial Institutions	1.37	－0.39
其中：实收资本 Of Which: Paid－in Capital	46.28	4.14	十一、代理金融机构贷款 Lending on Behalf of Financial Institutions		
当年结益 Net Earnings	1.30	1.30	其中：代理人行专项贷款 Of Which: Agency Earmarked Loans of the Central Bank		
十二、其他 Others	－0.66	－3.05	十二、库存现金 Cash in Vault	0.03	－0.01
			十三、外币占款 Position for Foreign Exchange Purchase	2.28	0.45
资金来源总计 Total Sources	**220.90**	**46.36**	**资金运用总计 Total Uses**	**220.90**	**46.36**

金融租赁公司人民币信贷收支表

Sources and Uses of Credit Funds of Financial Leasing Companies（RMB）

（2004 年末）

（Year－end of 2004）

单位：亿元

Unit：100 Million Yuan

项　目 Items	余　额 Balance	比年初增减额 Changes within the Year	项　目 Items	余　额 Balance	比年初增减额 Changes within the Year
一、各项存款 Total Deposits	67.87	6.61	一、各项贷款 Total Loans	149.69	－12.30
1. 信托存款 Trust Deposits	4.64	1.67	1. 信托贷款 Trust Loans	1.73	－2.06
2. 委托存款 Designated Deposits	42.77	3.60	其中：中长期信托贷款 Of Which：Medium and Long－term Trust Loans		－1.09
（1）委托存款 Designated Deposits	33.54	5.16	2. 委托贷款 Designated Loans	34.51	1.18
（2）委托投资基金 Designated Investment Funds	9.23	－1.56	3. 抵押贷款 Mortagage Loans		－0.37
3. 保证金存款 Guarantee Deposits	17.20	1.07	4. 票据融资 Paper Financing		
4. 其他存款 Other Deposits	3.26	0.27	其中：贴现 Of Which：Discount		
二、金融债券 Financial Bonds	0.05	－0.10	5. 融资租赁 Financing Leases	107.10	－11.62
三、应付及暂收款 Accounts Payable and Receipts on Account	17.48	－0.80	6. 各项垫款 Total Advances		
其中：应付及预提利息 Of Which：Interest Payable and Accrued	4.86	4.46	7. 其他贷款 Other Loans	6.35	0.57
			二、委托投资 Designated Investments	0.08	
四、长期借款 Long－term Borrowing	50.47	－16.46	三、投资 Investments	14.33	－4.30
五、证券业务款项 Securities Business Funds			1. 短期投资 Short－term Investments	5.99	－4.48
六、卖出回购资产 Assets Repo（Including Securities）	0.10		2. 长期投资 Long－term Investments	8.34	0.18
七、向中央银行借款 Borrowings from the Central Bank	0.36		四、应收及预付款 Accounts Receivable and Advance Payments	24.07	5.00
八、同业往来 Inter－bank Transactions	18.01	－6.43	其中：应收利息 Of Which：Interest Receivable	1.15	0.03
1. 同业存放 Due to Banks and Other Financial Institutions	8.74	－0.64	五、证券业务款项 Securities Business Funds		
2. 同业拆借 Placements from Banks and Other Financial Institutions	9.27	－5.79	六、经营租赁 Operating Leases	4.38	－4.46

续表
Continued

项　目 Items	余　额 Balance	比年初增减额 Changes within the Year	项　目 Items	余　额 Balance	比年初增减额 Changes within the Year
九、代理金融机构贷款基金 Loan Funds on Behalf of Financial Institutions	1.12		七、买入返售资产 Assets Reverse Repo（Including Securities）	0.08	
其中：中央银行委托专项贷款基金 Of Which：Earmarked Loan Funds Designated by the Central Bank			八、存放中央银行准备金存款 Reserve Deposits with the Central Bank	1.57	0.26
			九、存放中央银行特种存款 Special Deposits with the Central Bank		
			十、同业往来 Inter－bank Transactions	6.64	－2.00
十、各项准备 Total Provisions	4.77	3.00	1. 存放同业 Due from Banks and Other Financial Institutions	5.49	－1.79
其中：贷款损失准备 Of Which：Provisions for Loan Losses	2.08	1.37	2. 拆放同业 Placements with Banks and Other Financial Institutions	1.15	－0.21
十一、所有者权益 Owner's Equity	38.25	－4.06	十一、代理金融机构贷款 Lending on Behalf of Financial Institutions		
其中：实收资本 Of Which：Paid－in Capital	50.80	4.52	其中：代理人行专项贷款 Of Which：Agency Earmarked Loans of the Central Bank		
当年结益 Net Earnings	－0.03	－0.03	十二、库存现金 Cash in Vault	0.01	－0.02
十二、其他 Others	0.82	－3.41	十三、外币占款 Position for Foreign Exchange Purchase	－1.55	－3.83
资金来源总计 Total Sources	**199.30**	**－21.65**	**资金运用总计 Total Uses**	**199.30**	**－21.65**

金融租赁公司人民币信贷收支表

Sources and Uses of Credit Funds of Financial Leasing Companies（RMB）

（2005 年末）

（Year - end of 2005）

单位：亿元

Unit：100 Million Yuan

项目 Items	余额 Balance	比年初增减额 Changes within the Year	项目 Items	余额 Balance	比年初增减额 Changes within the Year
一、各项存款 Total Deposits	51.62	-16.90	一、各项贷款 Total Loans	125.94	-23.73
1. 信托存款 Trust Deposits	4.34	-0.30	1. 信托贷款 Trust Loans	1.63	-0.08
2. 委托存款 Designated Deposits	33.25	-9.58	其中：中长期信托贷款 Of Which：Medium and Long - term Trust Loans		
（1）委托存款 Designated Deposits	24.66	-8.94	2. 委托贷款 Designated Loans	22.65	-11.86
（2）委托投资基金 Designated Investment Funds	8.59	-0.64	3. 抵押贷款 Mortagage Loans		
3. 保证金存款 Guarantee Deposits	10.77	-7.02	4. 票据融资 Paper Financing		
4. 其他存款 Other Deposits	3.26		其中：贴现 Of Which：Discount		
二、金融债券 Financial Bonds		-0.05	5. 融资租赁 Financing Leases	96.28	-10.82
三、应付及暂收款 Accounts Payable and Receipts on Account	14.95	-1.90	6. 各项垫款 Total Advances		
其中：应付及预提利息 Of Which：Interest Payable and Accrued	1.57	-3.29	7. 其他贷款 Other Loans	5.38	-0.97
			二、委托投资 Designated Investments		-0.08
四、长期借款 Long - term Borrowing	55.76	5.29	三、投资 Investments	11.06	-3.25
五、证券业务款项 Securities Business Funds			1. 短期投资 Short - term Investments	5.76	-0.23
六、卖出回购资产 Assets Repo（Including Securities）	0.10		2. 长期投资 Long - term Investments	5.30	-3.02
七、向中央银行借款 Borrowings from the Central Bank	0.35	-0.01	四、应收及预付款 Accounts Receivable and Advance Payments	30.41	6.87
八、同业往来 Inter - bank Transactions	15.04	-2.97	其中：应收利息 Of Which：Interest Receivable	0.71	-0.44
1. 同业存放 Due to Banks and Other Financial Institutions	7.32	-1.42	五、证券业务款项 Securities Business Funds		
2. 同业拆借 Placements from Banks and Other Financial Institutions	7.72	-1.55	六、经营租赁 Operating Leases	8.27	3.89

续表
Continued

项目 Items	余额 Balance	比年初增减额 Changes within the Year	项目 Items	余额 Balance	比年初增减额 Changes within the Year
九、代理金融机构贷款基金 Loan Funds on Behalf of Financial Institutions	4.10	2.98	七、买入返售资产 Assets Reverse Repo（Including Securities）	0.08	
其中：中央银行委托专项贷款基金 Of Which：Earmarked Loan Funds Designated by the Central Bank			八、存放中央银行准备金存款 Reserve Deposits with the Central Bank	1.89	0.32
			九、存放中央银行特种存款 Special Deposits with the Central Bank		
			十、同业往来 Inter－bank Transactions	10.00	3.36
十、各项准备 Total Provisions	20.22	15.24	1. 存放同业 Due from Banks and Other Financial Institutions	8.86	3.37
其中：贷款损失准备 Of Which：Provisions for Loan Losses	10.01	7.90			
十一、所有者权益 Owner's Equity	19.76	－18.36	2. 拆放同业 Placements with Banks and Other Financial Institutions	1.14	－0.01
其中：实收资本 Of Which：Paid－in Capital	50.78				
当年结益 Net Earnings	0.22	0.22	十一、代理金融机构贷款 Lending on Behalf of Financial Institutions		
十二、其他 Others	4.74	4.52	其中：代理人行专项贷款 Of Which：Agency Earmarked Loans of the Central Bank		
			十二、库存现金 Cash in Vault	0.01	
			十三、外币占款 Position for Foreign Exchange Purchase	－1.02	0.46
资金来源总计 Total Sources	**186.64**	**－12.16**	**资金运用总计 Total Uses**	**186.64**	**－12.16**

14. 外资银行人民币信贷收支表（2002—2005 年）
Sources and Uses of Credit Funds of Foreign - funded Banks（RMB）（2002—2005）

外资银行人民币信贷收支表
Sources and Uses of Credit Funds of Foreign - funded Banks（RMB）

（2002 年末）

（Year - end of 2002）

单位：亿元

Unit：100 Million Yuan

项　目 Items	余　额 Balance	比年初增减额 Changes within the Year	项　目 Items	余　额 Balance	比年初增减额 Changes within the Year
一、各项存款 Total Deposits	214.41	72.06	一、各项贷款 Total Loans	393.63	-12.63
1. 企业存款 Deposits by Enterprises	210.06	69.77	1. 短期贷款 Short - term Loans	331.92	-6.53
(1) 活期存款 Demand Deposits	117.63	43.16	(1) 工业贷款 Loans to Industrial Sector		
(2) 定期存款 Time Deposits	92.43	26.61	(2) 商业贷款 Loans to Commercial Sector		
2. 机关团体存款 Deposits by Government Agencies and Social Organizations			其中：收购贷款 Of Which：Loans for the Purchase of Farm Products		
3. 储蓄存款 Savings Deposits	0.08	-0.11	(3) 建筑业贷款 Loans to Construction Sector		
(1) 活期储蓄 Demand Deposits	0.05	-0.08	(4) 农业贷款 Loans to Agricultural Sector		
(2) 定期储蓄 Time Deposits	0.03	-0.03	(5) 乡镇企业贷款 Loans to Village and Township Enterprises		
4. 农业存款 Deposits by Agricultural Sector			(6) 三资企业贷款		
5. 其他存款 Other Deposits	4.27	2.40	Loans to Foreign Investment Enterprises and Ventures		
二、代理财政性存款 Agency Fiscal Deposits			(7) 私营企业及个体贷款 Loans to Privately - run Enterprises and Self - employed Entities		
三、金融债券 Financial Bonds			(8) 其他短期贷款 Other Short - term Loans	331.92	-6.53
其中：政策性金融债券 Of Which：Policy Financial Bonds			其中：个人短期消费贷款 Of Which：Short - term Consumer Credit	0.52	0.40
四、应付及暂收款 Accounts Payable and Receipts on Account	5.50	-3.71	2. 中期流动资金贷款 Medium - term Working Capital Loans		
其中：应付及预提利息 Of Which：Interest Payable and Accrued	0.58	-0.22	3. 中长期贷款 Medium and Long - term Loans	52.53	1.10
五、卖出回购证券 Repo	1.00	1.00	(1) 基本建设贷款 Capital Construction Loans		
六、向中央银行借款 Borrowings from the Central Bank		-0.11	(2) 技术改造贷款 Technical Improvement Loans		

续表
Continued

项目 Items	余额 Balance	比年初增减额 Changes within the Year	项目 Items	余额 Balance	比年初增减额 Changes within the Year
七、同业往来 Inter - bank Transactions	231.94	-73.89	(3) 其他中长期贷款 Other Medium and Long - term Loans	52.53	1.10
1. 同业存放 Due to Banks and Other Financial Institutions	0.84	、0.31			
			其中：个人中长期消费贷款 Of Which: Medium and Long - term Consumer Credit		-2.00
2. 同业拆借 Placements from Banks and Other Financial Institutions	231.10	-74.20			
			4. 票据融资 Paper Financing	9.18	-7.20
八、委托存款及委托投资基金（净） Designated Deposits and Designated Investment Funds (Net)			其中：贴现 Of Which: Discount	9.18	-7.20
			5. 各项垫款 Total Advances		
1. 委托存款及委托投资基金 Designated Deposits and Designated Investment Funds					
			二、有价证券及投资 Securities and Investments	4.91	4.47
2. 减：委托贷款及委托投资 Minus: Designated Loans and Designated Investments			三、应收及预付款 Accounts Receivable and Advance Payments	1.51	0.46
九、代理金融机构委托贷款基金 Designated Loan Funds on Behalf of Financial Institutions			其中：应收利息 Of Which: Interest Receivable	0.98	0.14
			四、买入返售证券 Reverse Repo		
其中：中央银行委托贷款基金 Of Which: Loan Funds Designated by the Central Bank					
			五、存放中央银行准备金存款 Reserve Deposits with the Central Bank	69.42	7.96
十、各项准备 Total Provisions	3.97	1.23	六、存放中央银行特种存款 Special Deposits with the Central Bank		
其中：贷款损失准备 Of Which: Provisions for Loan Losses	3.96	3.96	七、缴存中央银行财政性存款 Fiscal Deposits with the Central Bank		
			八、同业往来 Inter - bank Transactions	58.56	49.95
十一、所有者权益 Owner's Equity	70.70	55.98			
			1. 存放同业 Due from Banks and Other Financial Institutions	54.98	46.62
其中：实收资本 Of Which: Paid - in Capital	66.11	52.29			
当年结益 Net Earnings	2.39	2.39	2. 拆放同业 Placements with Banks and Other Financial Institutions	3.58	3.33
十二、其他 Others	0.77	-2.19			
			九、代理金融机构贷款 Lending on Behalf of Financial Institutions		
			其中：代理人行专项贷款 Of Which: Agency Earmarked Loans of the Central Bank		
			十、库存现金 Cash in Vault	0.26	0.16
			十一、外汇占款 Position for Foreign Exchange Purchase		
资金来源总计 Total Sources	**528.29**	**50.37**	**资金运用总计 Total Uses**	**528.29**	**50.37**

外资银行人民币信贷收支表

Sources and Uses of Credit Funds of Foreign – funded Banks（RMB）

（2003年末）

（Year – end of 2003）

单位：亿元

Unit：100 Million Yuan

项目 Items	余额 Balance	比年初增减额 Changes within the Year	项目 Items	余额 Balance	比年初增减额 Changes within the Year
一、各项存款 Total Deposits	405.90	191.47	一、各项贷款 Total Loans	448.74	55.11
1. 企业存款 Deposits by Enterprises	386.28	176.20	1. 短期贷款 Short – term Loans	320.51	–11.41
（1）活期存款 Demand Deposits	188.60	70.95	（1）工业贷款 Loans to Industrial Sector		
（2）定期存款 Time Deposits	197.68	105.25	（2）商业贷款 Loans to Commercial Sector		
2. 机关团体存款 Deposits by Government Agencies and Social Organizations			其中：收购贷款 Of Which：Loans for the Purchase of Farm Products		
3. 储蓄存款 Savings Deposits	0.34	0.26	（3）建筑业贷款 Loans to Construction Sector		
（1）活期储蓄 Demand Deposits	0.25	0.20	（4）农业贷款 Loans to Agricultural Sector		
（2）定期储蓄 Time Deposits	0.09	0.06	（5）乡镇企业贷款 Loans to Village and Township Enterprises		
4. 农业存款 Deposits by Agricultural Sector			（6）三资企业贷款 Loans to Foreign Investment Enterprises and Ventures		
5. 其他存款 Other Deposits	19.28	15.01	（7）私营企业及个体贷款 Loans to Privately – run Enterprises and Self – employed Entities		
二、代理财政性存款 Agency Fiscal Deposits			（8）其他短期贷款 Other Short – term Loans	320.51	–11.41
三、金融债券 Financial Bonds			其中：个人短期消费贷款 Of Which：Short – term Consumer Credit	0.41	–0.11
其中：政策性金融债券 Of Which：Policy Financial Bonds			2. 中期流动资金贷款 Medium – term Working Capital Loans		
四、应付及暂收款 Accounts Payable and Receipts on Account	8.53	3.00	3. 中长期贷款 Medium and Long – term Loans	69.27	16.74
其中：应付及预提利息 Of Which：Interest Payable and Accrued	1.11	0.53	（1）基本建设贷款 Capital Construction Loans		
五、卖出回购证券 Repo	0.98	–0.02	（2）技术改造贷款 Technical Improvement Loans		
六、向中央银行借款 Borrowings from the Central Bank					
七、同业往来 Inter – bank Transactions	151.36	–80.58	（3）其他中长期贷款 Other Medium and Long – term Loans	69.27	16.74

续表
Continued

项　　目 Items	余　额 Balance	比年初增减额 Changes within the Year	项　　目 Items	余　额 Balance	比年初增减额 Changes within the Year
1. 同业存放 Due to Banks and Other Financial Institutions	52.02	51.18	其中：个人中长期消费贷款 Of Which: Medium and Long-term Consumer Credit	0.34	0.34
2. 同业拆借 Placements from Banks and Other Financial Institutions	99.34	-131.76	4. 票据融资 Paper Financing	58.96	49.78
八、委托存款及委托投资基金（净） Designated Deposits and Designated Investment Funds (Net)			其中：贴现 Of Which: Discount	58.96	49.78
1. 委托存款及委托投资基金 Designated Deposits and Designated Investment Funds			5. 各项垫款 Total Advances		
2. 减：委托贷款及委托投资 Minus: Designated Loans and Designated Investments			二、有价证券及投资 Securities and Investments	47.89	42.98
九、代理金融机构委托贷款基金 Designated Loan Funds on Behalf of Financial Institutions			三、应收及预付款 Accounts Receivable and Advance Payments	1.51	
其中：中央银行委托贷款基金 Of Which: Loan Funds Designated by the Central Bank			其中：应收利息 Of Which: Interest Receivable	1.03	0.05
十、各项准备 Total Provisions	3.28	-0.69	四、买入返售证券 Reverse Repo		
其中：贷款损失准备 Of Which: Provisions for Loan Losses	3.26	-0.70	五、存放中央银行准备金存款 Reserve Deposits with the Central Bank	115.67	46.25
十一、所有者权益 Owner's Equity	99.57	28.91	六、存放中央银行特种存款 Special Deposits with the Central Bank		
其中：实收资本 Of Which: Paid-in Capital	89.72	23.61	七、缴存中央银行财政性存款 Fiscal Deposits with the Central Bank		
当年结益 Net Earnings	5.14	5.14	八、同业往来 Inter-bank Transactions	75.18	16.60
十二、其他 Others	19.75	18.97	1. 存放同业 Due from Banks and Other Financial Institutions	64.20	9.20
			2. 拆放同业 Placements with Banks and Other Financial Institutions	10.98	7.40
			九、代理金融机构贷款 Lending on Behalf of Financial Institutions		
			其中：代理人行专项贷款 Of Which: Agency Earmarked Loans of the Central Bank		
			十、库存现金 Cash in Vault	0.38	0.12
			十一、外汇占款 Position for Foreign Exchange Purchase		
资金来源总计 Total Sources	**689.37**	**161.06**	**资金运用总计 Total Uses**	**689.37**	**161.06**

外资银行人民币信贷收支表

Sources and Uses of Credit Funds of Foreign - funded Banks（RMB）

（2004 年末）

（Year - end of 2004）

单位：亿元

Unit：100 Million Yuan

项 目 Items	余 额 Balance	比年初增减额 Changes within the Year	项 目 Items	余 额 Balance	比年初增减额 Changes within the Year
一、各项存款 Total Deposits	601.33	195.50	一、各项贷款 Total Loans	668.59	216.60
1. 企业存款 Deposits by Enterprises	549.49	163.26	1. 短期贷款 Short - term Loans	496.26	177.16
（1）活期存款 Demand Deposits	303.08	114.56	（1）工业贷款 Loans to Industrial Sector		
（2）定期存款 Time Deposits	246.41	48.70	（2）商业贷款 Loans to Commercial Sector		
2. 机关团体存款 Deposits by Government Agencies and Social Organizations			其中：收购贷款 Of Which：Loans for the Purchase of Farm Products		
3. 储蓄存款 Savings Deposits	0.29	- 0.05	（3）建筑业贷款 Loans to Construction Sector		
（1）活期储蓄 Demand Deposits	0.21	- 0.04	（4）农业贷款 Loans to Agricultural Sector		
（2）定期储蓄 Time Deposits	0.08	- 0.01	（5）乡镇企业贷款 Loans to Village and Township Enterprises		
4. 农业存款 Deposits by Agricultural Sector			（6）三资企业贷款 Loans to Foreign Investment Enterprises and Ventures		
5. 其他存款 Other Deposits	51.55	32.29	（7）私营企业及个体贷款 Loans to Privately - run Enterprises and Self - employed Entities		
二、代理财政性存款 Agency Fiscal Deposits			（8）其他短期贷款 Other Short - term Loans	496.26	177.16
三、金融债券 Financial Bonds			其中：个人短期消费贷款 Of Which：Short - term Consumer Credit	0.93	0.52
其中：政策性金融债券 Of Which：Policy Financial Bonds			2. 中期流动资金贷款 Medium - term Working Capital Loans		
四、应付及暂收款 Accounts Payable and Receipts on Account	18.10	9.57	3. 中长期贷款 Medium and Long - term Loans	96.24	26.97
其中：应付及预提利息 Of Which：Interest Payable and Accrued	1.93	0.82	（1）基本建设贷款 Capital Construction Loans		
五、卖出回购资产 Assets Repo（Including Securities）	21.18	15.60	（2）技术改造贷款 Technical Improvement Loans		
六、向中央银行借款 Borrowings from the Central Bank		- 0.06	（3）其他中长期贷款 Other Medium and Long - term Loans	96.24	26.97
七、同业往来 Inter - bank Transactions	235.10	85.12			

续表
Continued

项　目 Items	余　额 Balance	比年初增减额 Changes within the Year	项　目 Items	余　额 Balance	比年初增减额 Changes within the Year
1. 同业存放 Due to Banks and Other Financial Institutions	67.49	15.47	其中：个人中长期消费贷款 Of Which: Medium and Long - term Consumer Credit	3.27	0.56
2. 同业拆借 Placements from Banks and Other Financial Institutions	167.61	69.65	4. 票据融资 Paper Financing	76.09	12.47
八、委托存款及委托投资基金(净) Designated Deposits and Designated Investment Funds (Net)			其中：贴现 Of Which: Discount	76.09	12.47
1. 委托存款及委托投资基金 Designated Deposits and Designated Investment Funds			5. 各项垫款 Total Advances		
2. 减：委托贷款及委托投资 Minus: Designated Loans and Designated Investments			二、有价证券及投资 Securities and Investments	122.74	74.85
九、代理金融机构委托贷款基金 Designated Loan Funds on Behalf of Financial Institutions			三、应收及预付款 Accounts Receivable and Advance Payments	3.64	2.14
其中：中央银行委托贷款基金 Of Which: Loan Funds Designated by the Central Bank			其中：应收利息 Of Which: Interest Receivable	2.25	1.22
十、各项准备 Total Provisions	4.91	1.63	四、买入返售资产 Assets Reverse Repo (Including Securities)		
其中：贷款损失准备 Of Which: Provisions for Loan Losses	4.88	1.62	五、存放中央银行准备金贷款 Reserve Deposits with the Central Bank	156.60	41.52
十一、所有者权益 Owner's Equity	139.72	40.17	六、存放中央银行特种存款 Special Deposits with the Central Bank		
其中：实收资本 Of Which: Paid - in Capital	125.05	35.33	七、缴存中央银行财政性存款 Fiscal Deposits with the Central Bank		
当年结益 Net Earnings	6.38	6.38	八、同业往来 Inter - bank Transactions	89.84	14.22
十二、其他 Others	21.68	2.03	1. 存放同业 Due from Banks and Other Financial Institutions	86.72	22.08
			2. 拆放同业 Placements with Banks and Other Financial Institutions	3.12	-7.86
			九、代理金融机构贷款 Lending on Behalf of Financial Institutions		
			其中：代理人行专项贷款 Of Which: Agency Earmarked Loans of the Central Bank		
			十、库存现金 Cash in Vault	0.61	0.23
			十一、外汇占款 Position for Foreign Exchange Purchase		
资金来源总计 Total Sources	**1042.02**	**349.56**	**资金运用总计 Total Uses**	**1042.02**	**349.56**

外资银行人民币信贷收支表

Sources and Uses of Credit Funds of Foreign－funded Banks（RMB）

（2005年末）

（Year－end of 2005）

单位：亿元

Unit：100 Million Yuan

项目 Items	余额 Balance	比年初增减额 Changes within the Year	项目 Items	余额 Balance	比年初增减额 Changes within the Year
一、各项存款 Total Deposits	980.22	378.89	一、各项贷款 Total Loans	1089.42	420.82
1. 企业存款 Deposits by Enterprises	851.98	302.06	1. 短期贷款 Short－term Loans	745.79	249.53
（1）活期存款 Demand Deposits	463.00	159.92	（1）工业贷款 Loans to Industrial Sector		
（2）定期存款 Time Deposits	388.98	142.14	（2）商业贷款 Loans to Commercial Sector		
2. 机关团体存款 Deposits by Government Agencies and Social Organizations			其中：收购贷款 Of Which：Loans for the Purchase of Farm Products		
3. 储蓄存款 Savings Deposits	0.40	0.11	（3）建筑业贷款 Loans to Construction Sector		
（1）活期储蓄 Demand Deposits	0.23	0.02	（4）农业贷款 Loans to Agricultural Sector		
（2）定期储蓄 Time Deposits	0.17	0.09	（5）乡镇企业贷款 Loans to Village and Township Enterprises		
4. 农业存款 Deposits by Agricultural Sector			（6）三资企业贷款 Loans to Foreign Investment Enterprises and Ventures		
5. 其他存款 Other Deposits	127.84	76.72	（7）私营企业及个体贷款 Loans to Privately－run Enterprises and Self－employed Entities		
二、代理财政性存款 Agency Fiscal Deposits			（8）其他短期贷款 Other Short－term Loans	745.79	249.53
三、金融债券 Financial Bonds			其中：个人短期消费贷款 Of Which：Short－term Consumer Credit	7.10	6.17
其中：政策性金融债券 Of Which：Policy Financial Bonds			2. 中期流动资金贷款 Medium－term Working Capital Loans		
四、应付及暂收款 Accounts Payable and Receipts on Account	28.88	11.54	3. 中长期贷款 Medium and Long－term Loans	261.49	165.25
其中：应付及预提利息 Of Which：Interest Payable and Accrued	3.36	1.43	（1）基本建设贷款 Capital Construction Loans		
五、卖出回购资产 Assets Repo（Including Securities）	53.69	32.51	（2）技术改造贷款 Technical Improvement Loans		
六、向中央银行借款 Borrowings from the Central Bank					
七、同业往来 Inter－bank Transactions	371.38	136.28	（3）其他中长期贷款 Other Medium and Long－term Loans	261.49	165.25

续表
Continued

项　目 Items	余　额 Balance	比年初增减额 Changes within the Year	项　目 Items	余　额 Balance	比年初增减额 Changes within the Year
1. 同业存放 Due to Banks and Other Financial Institutions	91.95	24.46	其中：个人中长期消费贷款 Of Which：Medium and Long－term Consumer Credit	10.08	6.81
2. 同业拆借 Placements from Banks and Other Financial Institutions	279.43	111.82	4. 票据融资 Paper Financing	82.14	6.04
			其中：贴现 Of Which：Discount	82.14	6.04
八、委托存款及委托投资基金(净) Designated Deposits and Designated Investment Funds（Net）			5. 各项垫款 Total Advances		
1. 委托存款及委托投资基金 Designated Deposits and Designated Investment Funds			二、有价证券及投资 Securities and Investments	133.63	10.89
			三、应收及预付款 Accounts Receivable and Advance Payments	8.83	5.19
2. 减：委托贷款及委托投资 Minus：Designated Loans and Designated Investments			其中：应收利息 Of Which：Interest Receivable	4.36	2.11
九、代理金融机构委托贷款基金 Designated Loan Funds on Behalf of Financial Institutions			四、买入返售资产 Assets Reverse Repo（Including Securities）	2.40	2.40
其中：中央银行委托贷款基金 Of Which：Loan Funds Designated by the Central Bank			五、存放中央银行准备金贷款 Reserve Deposits with the Central Bank	298.10	141.50
十、各项准备 Total Provisions	11.56	6.65	六、存放中央银行特种存款 Special Deposits with the Central Bank		
其中：贷款损失准备 Of Which：Provisions for Loan Losses	11.45	6.57	七、缴存中央银行财政性存款 Fiscal Deposits with the Central Bank		
十一、所有者权益 Owner's Equity	205.46	64.75	八、同业往来 Inter－bank Transactions	136.89	47.05
其中：实收资本 Of Which：Paid－in Capital	179.46	53.40	1. 存放同业 Due from Banks and Other Financial Institutions	124.82	38.10
当年结益 Net Earnings	9.85	9.85	2. 拆放同业 Placements with Banks and Other Financial Institutions	12.07	8.95
十二、其他 Others	19.36	－2.10			
			九、代理金融机构贷款 Lending on Behalf of Financial Institutions		
			其中：代理人行专项贷款 Of Which：Agency Earmarked Loans of the Central Bank		
			十、库存现金 Cash in Vault	1.28	0.67
			十一、外汇占款 Position for Foreign Exchange Purchase		
资金来源总计 Total Sources	**1670.55**	**628.52**	**资金运用总计 Total Uses**	**1670.55**	**628.52**

（二）外汇信贷收支统计
Sources and Uses of Credit Funds（Foreign Currency）

1. 金融机构外汇信贷收支表*（1993—2005年）
Sources and Uses of Credit Funds of Financial Institutions（Foreign Currency）（1993—2005年）

金融机构外汇信贷收支表
Sources and Uses of Credit Funds of Financial Institutions（Foreign Currency）

（1993年末）

（Year - end of 1993）

单位：亿美元

Unit：100 Million US Dollars

项　目 Items	余　额 Balance	比年初增减额 Changes within the Year	项　目 Items	余　额 Balance	比年初增减额 Changes within the Year
一、外汇存款 Total Deposits	675.28	114.21	一、外汇贷款 Total Loans	673.39	144.52
1. 居民外汇存款 Deposits by Resident Sector	534.10	112.40	1. 短期外汇贷款 Short - term Loans	299.11	79.58
（1）企业存款 Deposits by Enterprises	316.82	50.43	2. 中长期外汇贷款 Medium and Long - term Loans	337.98	62.37
（2）储蓄存款 Savings Deposits	139.70	45.45	3. 其他贷款 Other Loans	36.30	2.57
（3）其他存款 Other Deposits	77.58	16.52	二、投资 Investments	152.74	- 10.40
2. 非居民外汇存款 Deposits by Non - resident Sector	141.19	1.81	三、存放境外同业资金 Due from Overseas Banks and Other Financial Institutions	370.61	- 10.21
二、境外筹资 Overseas Financing	254.04	55.40	四、委托贷款 Designated Loans	160.07	36.56
三、委托借款 Designated Borrowing	153.47	26.65	五、人民银行往来 Transactions with the Central Bank	4.25	2.53
四、人民银行往来 Transactions with the Central Bank	47.10	18.06	六、国内同业往来 Domestic Inter - bank Transactions	95.97	18.67
五、国内同业往来 Domestic Inter - bank Transactions	117.32	11.26	其中：同业拆出 Of Which：Placements with Banks and Other Financial Institutions	26.71	7.60

续表
Continued

项 目 Items	余 额 Balance	比年初增减额 Changes within the Year	项 目 Items	余 额 Balance	比年初增减额 Changes within the Year
其中：同业拆入 Of Which: Placements from Banks and Other Financial Institutions	39.52	12.74	七、库存现金 Cash in Vault	13.91	4.86
六、自有资金 Own Capital	83.91	6.66			
七、当年结益 Net Earnings	16.58	16.58			
八、外汇买卖 Foreign Exchange Dealings	71.05	-59.80			
九、其他 Others	52.18	-2.48			
资金来源总计 Total Sources	**1470.93**	**186.54**	**资金运用总计 Total Uses**	**1470.93**	**186.54**

* 本表机构包括中国工商银行（1993—2005年）、中国农业银行（1993—2005年）、中国银行（1993—2005年）、中国建设银行（1993—2005年）、交通银行（1993—2005年）、中信实业银行（1993年并入，2005年更名为中信银行）、中国光大银行（1993—2005年）、华夏银行（1993—2005年）、广东发展银行（1993—2005年）、深圳发展银行（1993—2005年）、招商银行（1993—2005年）、福建兴业银行（1993年并入，2003年更名为兴业银行）、中国投资银行（1993—1998年）、信托投资公司（1993—2005年）、上海浦东发展银行（1994—2005年）、财务公司（1994—2005年）、国家开发银行（1995—2005年）、中国进出口银行（1995—2005年）、海南发展银行（1996—1997年）、中国民生银行（1997—2005年）、金融租赁公司（1998—2005年）、城市合作银行（1998年）、城市商业银行（1999—2005年）、中国农业发展银行（2001—2005年）、农村信用合作社（2001—2005年）、外资银行（2002—2005年）、农村商业银行（2002—2005年）、恒丰银行（2004—2005年）、浙商银行（2004—2005年）、农村合作银行（2005年）。

* Financial institutions of this statement include Industrial and Commercial Bank of China (1993—2005), Agricultural Bank of China (1993—2005), Bank of China (1993—2005), China Construction Bank (1993—2005), Bank of Communications (1993—2005), CITIC Industrial Bank (Included in this statement Since 1993 and renamed as China CITIC Bank in 2005), China Everbright Bank (1993—2005), Huaxia Bank (1993—2005), Guang Dong Development Bank (1993—2005), Shenzhen Development Bank (1993—2005), China Merchants Bank (1993—2005), Fujian Industrial Bank (Included in this statement from 1993 to 2005 and renamed as Industrial Bank in 2003), China Investment Bank (1993—1998), Trust and Investment Companies (1993—2005), Shanghai Pudong Development Bank (1994—2005), Finance Companies (1994—2005), China Development Bank (1995—2005), the Export - Import Bank of China (1995—2005), Hainan Development Bank (1996—1997), China Minsheng Banking Corporation (1997—2005), Financial Leasing Companies (1998—2005), Urban Cooperative Banks (1998), City Commercial Banks (1999—2005), Agricultural Development Bank of China (2001—2005), Rural Credit Cooperatives (2001—2005), Foreign - funded Banks (2002—2005), Rural Commercial Banks (2002—2005), Evergrowing Bank (2004—2005), China Zheshang Bank (2004—2005), Rural Cooperative Banks (2005).

金融机构外汇信贷收支表

Sources and Uses of Credit Funds of Financial Institutions（Foreign Currency）

（1994年末）

（Year - end of 1994）

单位：亿美元

Unit：100 Million US Dollars

项目 Items	余额 Balance	比年初增减额 Changes within the Year	项目 Items	余额 Balance	比年初增减额 Changes within the Year
一、外汇存款 Total Deposits	741.97	59.93	一、外汇贷款 Total Loans	650.26	- 89.89
1. 居民外汇存款 Deposits by Resident Sector	574.90	33.28	1. 短期外汇贷款 Short - term Loans	307.97	35.01
（1）企业存款 Deposits by Enterprises	297.46	- 20.51	2. 中长期外汇贷款 Medium and Long - term Loans	299.24	- 43.72
（2）储蓄存款 Savings Deposits	185.05	44.74	3. 其他贷款 Other Loans	43.05	11.16
（3）其他存款 Other Deposits	92.39	9.05	二、投资 Investments	162.01	6.07
2. 非居民外汇存款 Deposits by Non - resident Sector	167.07	26.65	三、存放境外同业资金 Due from Overseas Banks and Other Financial Institutions	366.97	12.70
二、境外筹资 Overseas Financing	159.47	13.49	四、委托贷款 Designated Loans	341.06	72.46
三、委托借款 Designated Borrowing	314.40	57.72	五、人民银行往来 Transactions with the Central Bank	4.01	0.33
四、人民银行往来 Transactions with the Central Bank	55.61	- 0.49	六、国内同业往来 Domestic Inter - bank Transactions	108.87	3.88
五、国内同业往来 Domestic Inter - bank Transactions	174.35	70.77	其中：同业拆出 Of Which：Placements with Baoks and Other Financial Institutions	31.64	8.51
其中：同业拆入 Of Which：Placements from Banks and Other Financial Institutions	30.39	3.36	七、库存现金 Cash in Vault	14.16	0.06
六、自有资金 Own Capital	96.74	9.87			
七、当年结益 Net Earnings	16.60	16.60			
八、外汇买卖 Foreign Exchange Dealings	39.79	- 31.97			
九、其他 Others	48.41	- 10.53			
资金来源总计 Total Sources	**1647.34**	**185.39**	**资金运用总计 Total Uses**	**1647.34**	**185.39**

金融机构外汇信贷收支表

Sources and Uses of Credit Funds of Financial Institutions (Foreign Currency)

(1995年末)

(Year - end of 1995)

单位：亿美元

Unit: 100 Million US Dollars

项目 Items	余额 Balance	比年初增减额 Changes within the Year	项目 Items	余额 Balance	比年初增减额 Changes within the Year
一、外汇存款 Total Deposits	760.76	61.88	一、外汇贷款 Total Loans	713.22	93.55
1. 居民外汇存款 Deposits by Resident Sector	634.80	47.75	1. 短期外汇贷款 Short - term Loans	427.90	51.22
(1) 企业存款 Deposits by Enterprises	282.27	4.30	2. 中长期外汇贷款 Medium and Long - term Loans	216.22	20.20
(2) 储蓄存款 Savings Deposits	222.38	37.22	3. 其他贷款 Other Loans	69.10	22.13
(3) 其他存款 Other Deposits	130.15	5.93	二、投资 Investments	120.53	-45.20
2. 非居民外汇存款 Deposits by Non - resident Sector	125.96	14.43	三、境外筹资贷款 On - lending of Overseas Financing	57.29	-8.14
二、境外筹资 Overseas Financing	128.26	-22.95	四、委托贷款 Designated Loans	271.92	-66.47
三、委托借款 Designated Borrowing	259.20	-74.05	五、人民银行往来 Transactions with the Central Bank	28.16	11.46
四、人民银行往来 Transactions with the Central Bank	67.74	12.13	六、国内同业往来 Domestic Inter - bank Transactions	100.06	6.76
五、国内同业往来 Domestic Inter - bank Transactions	174.51	-2.06	其中：同业拆出 Of Which: Placements with Banks and Other Financial Institutions	33.73	-0.83
其中：同业拆入 Of Which: Placements from Banks and Other Financial Institutions	38.29	7.58	七、国外同业往来 Overseas Inter - bank Transactions	360.66	-12.16
六、国外同业往来 Overseas Inter - bank Transactions	61.62	-14.09	其中：同业拆出 Of Which: Placements with Banks and Other Financial Institutions	46.55	6.92
其中：同业拆入 Of Which: Placements from Banks and Other Financial Institutions	41.94	-10.75	八、库存现金 Cash in Vault	14.35	0.19
七、所有者权益 Owner's Equity	137.50	7.42	九、外汇买卖 Foreign Exchange Dealings	38.22	6.89
八、当年结益 Net Earnings	25.35	25.35	十、其他 Others	1226.70	163.82
九、外汇买卖 Foreign Exchange Dealings	101.56	13.46			
十、其他 Others	1214.60	143.60			
资金来源总计 Total Sources	**2931.10**	**150.70**	**资金运用总计 Total Uses**	**2931.10**	**150.70**

金融机构外汇信贷收支表

Sources and Uses of Credit Funds of Financial Institutions（Foreign Currency）

（1996年末）

（Year - end of 1996）

单位：亿美元

Unit：100 Million US Dollars

项目 Items	余额 Balance	比年初增减额 Changes within the Year	项目 Items	余额 Balance	比年初增减额 Changes within the Year
一、外汇存款 Total Deposits	700.28	50.75	一、外汇贷款 Total Loans	766.44	54.79
1. 居民外汇存款 Deposits by Resident Sector	685.55	46.67	1. 短期外汇贷款 Short - term Loans	318.97	30.71
（1）企业存款 Deposits by Enterprises	302.20	20.11	2. 中长期外汇贷款 Medium and Long - term Loans	351.15	7.61
（2）储蓄存款 Savings Deposits	250.79	28.56	3. 其他贷款 Other Loans	96.32	16.92
（3）其他存款 Other Deposits	132.56	-2.00	二、投资 Investments	142.19	21.63
2. 非居民外汇存款 Deposits by Non - resident Sector	14.73	4.08	三、境外筹资贷款 On - lending of Overseas Financing	57.89	-1.42
二、境外筹资 Overseas Financing	126.05	-2.21	四、委托境外借款转贷款 On - lending of Overseas Designated Borrowing	288.08	15.45
三、委托境外借款 Overseas Designated Borrowing	268.90	11.53	五、人民银行往来 Transactions with the Central Bank	29.56	1.24
四、人民银行往来 Transactions with the Central Bank	201.76	111.86	六、国内同业往来 Domestic Inter - bank Transactions	87.97	-11.50
五、国内同业往来 Domestic Inter - bank Transactions	100.19	-71.75	其中：同业拆出 Of Which：Placements with Banks and Other Financial Institutions	38.28	1.43
其中：同业拆入 Of Which：Placements from Banks and Other Financial Institutions	31.99	-6.94	七、国外同业往来 Overseas Inter - bank Transactions	382.81	21.03
六、国外同业往来 Overseas Inter - bank Transactions	180.21	3.15	其中：同业拆出 Of Which：Placements with Banks and Other Financial Institutions	54.84	1.93
其中：同业拆入 Of Which：Placements from Banks and Other Financial Institutions	25.11	-17.80	八、库存现金 Cash in Vault	13.67	-0.68
七、所有者权益 Owner's Equity	186.21	24.51	九、外汇买卖 Foreign Exchange Dealings		
八、当年结益 Net Earnings	18.28	18.28	十、其他 Others	41.25	0.39
九、外汇买卖 Foreign Exchange Dealings	112.46	49.22			
十、其他 Others	-84.48	-94.41			
资金来源总计 Total Sources	**1809.86**	**100.93**	**资金运用总计 Total Uses**	**1809.86**	**100.93**

金融机构外汇信贷收支表

Sources and Uses of Credit Funds of Financial Institutions (Foreign Currency)

(1997年末)

(Year－end of 1997)

单位：亿美元

Unit：100 Million US Dollars

项目 Items	余额 Balance	比年初增减额 Changes within the Year	项目 Items	余额 Balance	比年初增减额 Changes within the Year
一、外汇存款 Total Deposits	768.71	71.29	一、外汇贷款 Total Loans	843.31	41.69
1. 居民外汇存款 Deposits by Resident Sector	752.20	69.52	1. 短期外汇贷款 Short－term Loans	370.72	47.53
(1) 企业存款 Deposits by Enterprises	337.27	34.29	2. 中长期外汇贷款 Medium and Long－term Loans	320.99	－30.23
(2) 储蓄存款 Savings Deposits	292.29	41.37	3. 其他贷款 Other Loans	151.60	24.39
(3) 其他存款 Other Deposits	122.64	－6.14	二、投资 Investments	155.28	11.88
2. 非居民外汇存款 Deposits by Non－resident Sector	16.51	1.77	三、境外筹资贷款 On－lending of Overseas Financing	50.24	－7.44
二、境外筹资 Overseas Financing	118.68	－6.46	四、委托境外借款转贷款 On－lending of Overseas Designated Borrowing	287.31	2.74
三、委托境外借款 Overseas Designated Borrowing	265.79	－3.00	五、人民银行往来 Transactions with the Central Bank	18.35	－11.31
四、人民银行往来 Transactions with the Central Bank	192.89	－8.85	六、国内同业往来 Domestic Inter－bank Transactions	67.49	－20.09
五、国内同业往来 Domestic Inter－bank Transactions	82.16	－24.14	其中：同业拆出 Of Which: Placements with Banks and Other Financial Institutions	37.71	－1.34
其中：同业拆入 Of Which: Placements from Banks and Other Financial Institutions	38.74	6.41	七、国外同业往来 Overseas Inter－bank Transactions	487.01	103.52
六、国外同业往来 Overseas Inter－bank Transactions	188.69	7.31	其中：同业拆出 Of Which: Placements with Banks and Other Financial Institutions	67.26	12.58
其中：同业拆入 Of Which: Placements from Banks and Other Financial Institutions	30.71	5.88	八、库存现金 Cash in Vault	14.79	1.11
七、所有者权益 Owner's Equity	210.78	11.36	九、外汇买卖 Foreign Exchange Dealings		
八、当年结益 Net Earnings	18.74	18.74	十、其他 Others	43.92	8.40
九、外汇买卖 Foreign Exchange Dealings	103.76	－9.36			
十、其他 Others	17.50	73.61			
资金来源总计 Total Sources	**1967.70**	**130.50**	**资金运用总计 Total Uses**	**1967.70**	**130.50**

金融机构外汇信贷收支表

Sources and Uses of Credit Funds of Financial Institutions（Foreign Currency）

（1998 年末）

（Year – end of 1998）

单位：亿美元

Unit：100 Million US Dollars

项　目 Items	余　额 Balance	比年初增减额 Changes within the Year	项　目 Items	余　额 Balance	比年初增减额 Changes within the Year
一、各项存款 Total Deposits	884.72	117.57	一、各项贷款 Total Loans	886.14	3.56
1. 单位活期存款 Demand Deposits by Enterprises	121.22	–30.81	1. 短期贷款 Short – term Loans	339.97	–23.48
其中：中资企业存款 Of Which：Deposits by Chinese – funded Enterprises	54.64	–22.13	（1）境内短期贷款 Domestic Short – term Loans	333.79	–21.32
			其中：中资企业贷款 Of Which：Loans to Chinese – funded Enterprises	161.44	–12.58
外商投资企业存款 Deposits by Foreign – funded Enterprises	53.18	–10.15	外商投资企业贷款 Loans to Foreign – funded Enterprises	99.07	–8.83
2. 单位定期存款 Time Deposits by Enterprises	263.36	35.07			
其中：中资企业存款 Of Which：Deposits by Chinese – funded Enterprises	203.39	29.16	（2）境外短期贷款 Overseas Short – term Loans	6.18	–2.16
			2. 中长期贷款 Medium and Long – term Loans	313.19	21.85
外商投资企业存款 Deposits by Foreign – funded Enterprises	31.16	8.58	（1）境内中长期贷款 Domestic Medium and Long – term Loans	303.95	19.93
3. 储蓄存款 Savings Deposits	412.46	121.07			
其中：定期存款 Of Which：Time Deposits	384.96	117.03	其中：中资企业贷款 Of Which：Loans to Chinese – funded Enterprises	154.89	1.88
4. 信托存款 Trust Deposits	10.30	–0.32	外商投资企业贷款 Loans to Foreign – funded Enterprises	31.00	–5.43
5. 委托存款 Designated Deposits	12.16	1.26			
6. 其他类存款 Other Deposits	48.30	–8.53	（2）境外中长期贷款 Overseas Medium and Long – term Loans	9.24	1.92
7. 境外存款 Foreign Deposits	16.92	–0.17	3. 进出口贸易融资 Financing for Import and Export Trades	37.65	–14.53
二、境外筹资 Overseas Financing	348.39	–18.06	4. 票据融资 Paper Financing	0.76	–0.91
三、向中央银行借款 Borrowings from the Central Bank	20.73	–0.20	5. 融资租赁 Financing Leases	7.33	–0.30
四、中央银行存款 Deposits by the Central Bank	187.17	15.73	6. 信托贷款 Trust Loans	64.73	–19.35
五、同业存放 Due to Banks and Other Financial Institutions	12.50	–16.03	7. 委托贷款 Designated Loans	12.28	–3.36

续表
Continued

项　目 Items	余　额 Balance	比年初增减额 Changes within the Year	项　目 Items	余　额 Balance	比年初增减额 Changes within the Year
其中：境外同业存放 Of Which: Due to Overseas Banks and Other Financial Institutions	9.12	-17.08	8. 逾期类贷款 Overdue Loans	110.23	43.64
			二、有价证券及投资 Securities and Investments	192.82	38.37
六、同业拆入 Placements from Banks and Other Financial Institutions	19.19	-6.30	三、境外筹资转贷款 On-lending of Overseas Financing	310.57	0.07
			四、存放中央银行 Deposits with the Central Bank	18.39	-0.29
其中：境外同业拆入 Of Which: Placements from Overseas Banks and Other Financial Institutions	16.42	-4.39	其中：缴存准备金 Of Which: Reserves with the Central Bank	11.22	-0.72
七、外汇买卖 Foreign Exchange Dealings	83.15	-18.20	五、存放同业 Due from Banks and Other Financial Institutions	404.38	-16.26
其中：结售汇 Of Which: Purchase and Sale of Foreign Exchange	63.12	-31.80	其中：存放境外同业 Of Which: Due from Overseas Banks and Other Financial Institutions	401.99	-15.14
八、境外联行存放 Due to Overseas Branches	157.83	-22.19			
九、证券业务款项 Securities Business Funds	0.20	-0.22	六、拆放同业 Placements with Banks and Other Financial Institutions	81.95	11.18
十、所有者权益 Owner's Equity	268.47	34.79			
其中：实收资本 Of Which: Paid-in Capital	137.46	14.83	其中：拆放境外同业 Of Which: Placements with Overseas Banks and Other Financial Institutions	80.93	11.13
当年结益 Net Earnings	25.55	25.55	七、存放境外联行 Due from Overseas Branches	48.03	-23.92
十一、其他 Others	-24.74	-74.39	八、证券业务占款 Funding of Securities Purchase	0.06	0.03
			九、库存现金 Cash in Vault	15.27	-0.24
资金来源总计 Total Sources	**1957.61**	**12.50**	**资金运用总计 Total Uses**	**1957.61**	**12.50**

金融机构外汇信贷收支表

Sources and Uses of Credit Funds of Financial Institutions（Foreign Currency）

（1999 年末）

（Year - end of 1999）

单位：亿美元

Unit：100 Million US Dollars

项目 Items	余额 Balance	比年初增减额 Changes within the Year	项目 Items	余额 Balance	比年初增减额 Changes within the Year
一、各项存款 Total Deposits	1031.71	148.86	一、各项贷款 Total Loans	803.05	-15.07
1. 单位活期存款 Demand Deposits by Enterprises	134.00	12.82	1. 短期贷款 Short - term Loans	304.61	-6.39
其中：中资企业存款 Of Which：Deposits by Chinese - funded Enterprises	63.05	8.44	（1）境内短期贷款 Domestic Short - term Loans	301.93	-2.89
			其中：中资企业贷款 Of Which：Loans to Chinese - funded Enterprises	144.46	10.39
外商投资企业存款 Deposits by Foreign - funded Enterprises	57.66	4.43			
			外商投资企业贷款 Loans to Foreign - funded Enterprises	83.04	-15.92
2. 单位定期存款 Time Deposits by Enterprises	264.01	0.28			
其中：中资企业存款 Of Which：Deposits by Chinese - funded Enterprises	196.19	-7.25	（2）境外短期贷款 Overseas Short - term Loans	2.68	-3.50
			2. 中长期贷款 Medium and Long - term Loans	293.51	0.27
外商投资企业存款 Deposits by Foreign - funded Enterprises	33.04	1.90	（1）境内中长期贷款 Domestic Medium and Long - term Loans	285.36	1.35
3. 储蓄存款 Savings Deposits	553.46	141.07			
			其中：中资企业贷款 Of Which：Loans to Chinese - funded Enterprises	156.02	16.76
其中：定期存款 Of Which：Time Deposits	516.18	131.25			
4. 信托存款 Trust Deposits	9.07	-0.41	外商投资企业贷款 Loans to Foreign - funded Enterprises	27.01	-3.99
5. 委托存款 Designated Deposits	13.05	1.22			
			（2）境外中长期贷款 Overseas Medium and Long - term Loans	8.15	-1.08
6. 其他类存款 Other Deposits	47.97	-0.70			
7. 境外存款 Foreign Deposits	10.15	-5.42	3. 进出口贸易融资 Financing for Import and Export Trades	27.96	-7.56
二、境外筹资 Overseas Financing	324.17	-12.77			
			4. 票据融资 Paper Financing	0.72	-0.04
三、向中央银行借款 Borrowings from the Central Bank	20.10	-0.63	5. 融资租赁 Financing Leases	5.24	-1.15
四、中央银行存款 Deposits by the Central Bank	154.83	-31.77	6. 信托贷款 Trust Loans	38.17	-11.72
五、同业存放 Due to Banks and Other Financial Institutions	11.24	-5.33	7. 委托贷款 Designated Loans	13.17	1.11

续表
Continued

项目 Items	余额 Balance	比年初增减额 Changes within the Year	项目 Items	余额 Balance	比年初增减额 Changes within the Year
其中：境外同业存放 Of Which: Due to Overseas Banks and Other Financial Institutions	7.45	-5.59	8. 逾期类贷款 Overdue Loans	119.67	10.41
			二、有价证券及投资 Securities and Investments	297.67	106.31
六、同业拆入 Placements from Banks and Other Financial Institutions	9.55	-6.24	三、境外筹资转贷款 On-lending of Overseas Financing	299.96	-10.44
			四、存放中央银行 Deposits with the Central Bank	18.89	0.41
其中：境外同业拆入 Of Which: Placements from Overseas Banks and Other Financial Institutions	7.88	-5.37	其中：缴存准备金 Of Which: Reserves with the Central Bank	12.34	1.11
七、外汇买卖 Foreign Exchange Dealings	96.35	13.27	五、存放同业 Due from Banks and Other Financial Institutions	270.25	-133.29
其中：结售汇 Of Which: Purchase and Sale of Foreign Exchange	69.90	0.77	其中：存放境外同业 Of Which: Due from Overseas Banks and Other Financial Institutions	268.06	-133.13
八、境外联行存放 Due to Overseas Branches	120.92	-51.68			
九、证券业务款项 Securities Business Funds	0.22	0.04	六、拆放同业 Placements with Banks and Other Financial Institutions	118.39	36.62
十、所有者权益 Owner's Equity	251.05	-1.93	其中：拆放境外同业 Of Which: Placements with Overseas Banks and Other Financial Institutions	117.65	36.72
其中：实收资本 Of Which: Paid-in Capital	127.57	5.63			
当年结益 Net Earnings	16.42	16.42	七、存放境外联行 Due from Overseas Branches	86.96	24.40
十一、其他 Others	-93.69	-27.01	八、证券业务占款 Funding of Securities Purchase	0.09	0.03
			九、库存现金 Cash in Vault	31.19	15.84
资金来源总计 Total Sources	**1926.45**	**24.81**	**资金运用总计 Total Uses**	**1926.45**	**24.81**

金融机构外汇信贷收支表

Sources and Uses of Credit Funds of Financial Institutions（Foreign Currency）

（2000 年末）

（Year - end of 2000）

单位：亿美元

Unit：100 Million US Dollars

项目 Items	余额 Balance	比年初增减额 Changes within the Year	项目 Items	余额 Balance	比年初增减额 Changes within the Year
一、各项存款 Total Deposits	1282.60	250.62	一、各项贷款 Total Loans	611.49	-55.58
1. 单位活期存款 Demand Deposits by Enterprises	137.29	2.96	1. 短期贷款 Short - term Loans	213.41	-29.90
其中：中资企业存款 Of Which：Deposits by Chinese - funded Enterprises	63.33	0.28	（1）境内短期贷款 Domestic Short - term Loans	211.22	-29.41
			其中：中资企业贷款 Of Which：Loans to Chinese - funded Enterprises	97.47	-25.20
外商投资企业存款 Deposits by Foreign - funded Enterprises	60.65	2.50			
			外商投资企业贷款 Loans to Foreign - funded Enterprises	61.13	-6.95
2. 单位定期存款 Time Deposits by Enterprises	322.50	58.19			
其中：中资企业存款 Of Which：Deposits by Chinese - funded Enterprises	237.64	41.12	（2）境外短期贷款 Overseas Short - term Loans	2.19	-0.49
			2. 中长期贷款 Medium and Long - term Loans	223.11	-24.08
外商投资企业存款 Deposits by Foreign - funded Enterprises	43.82	10.78	（1）境内中长期贷款 Domestic Medium and Long - term Loans	215.00	-24.04
3. 储蓄存款 Savings Deposits	729.50	176.04			
			其中：中资企业贷款 Of Which：Loans to Chinese - funded Enterprises	123.27	-9.74
其中：定期存款 Of Which：Time Deposits	683.55	167.37			
4. 信托存款 Trust Deposits	8.07	-0.97	外商投资企业贷款 Loans to Foreign - funded Enterprises	18.73	2.41
5. 委托存款 Designated Deposits	14.63	1.57			
			（2）境外中长期贷款 Overseas Medium and Long - term Loans	8.11	-0.04
6. 其他类存款 Other Deposits	62.41	14.51			
7. 境外存款 Foreign Deposits	8.20	-1.68	3. 进出口贸易融资 Financing for Import and Export Trades	20.82	-1.34
二、境外筹资 Overseas Financing	258.32	-65.83			
			4. 票据融资 Paper Financing	0.56	-0.16
三、向中央银行借款 Borrowings from the Central Bank	18.18	-1.92			
			5. 融资租赁 Financing Leases	4.37	-0.86
四、中央银行存款 Deposits by the Central Bank	98.86	-55.93			
			6. 信托贷款 Trust Loans	29.48	-4.95
五、同业存放 Due to Banks and Other Financial Institutions	10.59	0.46			
			7. 委托贷款 Designated Loans	12.97	-0.20

续表
Continued

项目 Items	余额 Balance	比年初增减额 Changes within the Year	项目 Items	余额 Balance	比年初增减额 Changes within the Year
其中：境外同业存放 Of Which: Due to Overseas Banks and Other Financial Institutions	7.55	0.10	8. 逾期类贷款 Overdue Loans	106.77	5.91
			二、有价证券及投资 Securities and Investments	410.89	113.60
六、同业拆入 Placements from Banks and Other Financial Institutions	10.94	1.39	三、境外筹资转贷款 On－lending of Overseas Financing	242.06	－46.76
			四、存放中央银行 Deposits with the Central Bank	26.06	7.17
其中：境外同业拆入 Of Which: Placements from Overseas Banks and Other Financial Institutions	9.83	1.95	其中：缴存准备金 Of Which: Reserves with the Central Bank	16.39	4.05
七、外汇买卖 Foreign Exchange Dealings	－52.50	－149.37	五、存放同业 Due from Banks and Other Financial Institutions	335.28	65.41
其中：结售汇 Of Which: Purchase and Sale of Foreign Exchange	51.47	－18.09	其中：存放境外同业 Of Which: Due from Overseas Banks and Other Financial Institutions	334.19	66.51
八、境外联行存放 Due to Overseas Branches	156.09	35.38			
九、证券业务款项 Securities Business Funds	0.69	0.47	六、拆放同业 Placements with Banks and Other Financial Institutions	302.28	183.95
十、所有者权益 Owner's Equity	269.59	18.64			
其中：实收资本 Of Which: Paid－in Capital	131.75	4.22	其中：拆放境外同业 Of Which: Placements with Overseas Banks and Other Financial Institutions	301.01	183.42
当年结益 Net Earnings	16.88	16.88			
			七、存放境外联行 Due from Overseas Branches	59.42	－27.33
十一、其他 Others	－42.30	198.84			
			八、证券业务占款 Funding of Securities Purchase	0.19	0.10
			九、库存现金 Cash in Vault	23.39	－7.81
资金来源总计 Total Sources	**2011.06**	**232.75**	**资金运用总计 Total Uses**	**2011.06**	**232.75**

金融机构外汇信贷收支表

Sources and Uses of Credit Funds of Financial Institutions（Foreign Currency）

（2001 年末）

（Year - end of 2001）

单位：亿美元

Unit：100 Million US Dollars

项　目 Items	余　额 Balance	比年初增减额 Changes within the Year	项　目 Items	余　额 Balance	比年初增减额 Changes within the Year
一、各项存款 Total Deposits	1348.78	61.15	一、各项贷款 Total Loans	806.47	-42.83
1. 单位活期存款 Demand Deposits by Enterprises	157.91	18.33	1. 短期贷款 Short - term Loans	213.47	-2.03
其中：中资企业存款 Of Which：Deposits by Chinese - funded Enterprises	94.47	20.98	（1）境内短期贷款 Domestic Short - term Loans	211.04	-0.67
外商投资企业存款 Deposits by Foreign - funded Enterprises	47.91	-4.90	其中：中资企业贷款 Of Which：Loans to Chinese - funded Enterprises	113.49	3.20
2. 单位定期存款 Time Deposits by Enterprises	295.01	-27.36	外商投资企业贷款 Loans to Foreign - funded Enterprises	69.81	0.75
其中：中资企业存款 Of Which：Deposits by Chinese - funded Enterprises	217.49	-19.99	（2）境外短期贷款 Overseas Short - term Loans	2.43	-1.36
外商投资企业存款 Deposits by Foreign - funded Enterprises	36.52	-7.28	2. 中长期贷款 Medium and Long - term Loans	239.37	-14.55
3. 储蓄存款 Savings Deposits	815.62	82.35	（1）境内中长期贷款 Domestic Medium and Long - term Loans	225.69	-16.32
其中：定期存款 Of Which：Time Deposits	739.06	52.57	其中：中资企业贷款 Of Which：Loans to Chinese - funded Enterprises	119.71	-15.02
4. 信托存款 Trust Deposits	5.42	-1.79	外商投资企业贷款 Loans to Foreign - funded Enterprises	20.77	-4.74
5. 委托存款 Designated Deposits	15.11	0.76	（2）境外中长期贷款 Overseas Medium and Long - term Loans	13.68	1.77
6. 其他类存款 Other Deposits	50.85	-11.80	3. 进出口贸易融资 Financing for Import and Export Trades	25.68	
7. 境外存款 Foreign Deposits	8.86	0.66	4. 票据融资 Paper Financing	0.79	0.22
二、境外筹资 Overseas Financing	260.44	-23.71	其中：贴现 Of Which：Discount	0.46	0.17
三、向中央银行借款 Borrowings from the Central Bank	7.58	-10.60	5. 融资租赁 Financing Leases	3.66	-0.38
四、中央银行存款 Deposits by the Central Bank	91.23	-43.94	6. 信托贷款 Trust Loans	36.24	-5.34
五、同业存放 Due to Banks and Other Financial Institutions	11.92	7.77			

续表
Continued

项目 Items	余额 Balance	比年初增减额 Changes within the Year	项目 Items	余额 Balance	比年初增减额 Changes within the Year
其中：境外同业存放 Of Which: Due to Overseas Banks and Other Financial Institutions	3.16	2.05	7. 委托贷款 Designated Loans	14.03	1.54
六、应付及暂收款 Accounts Payable and Receipts on Account	123.77	-8.98	8. 各项垫款 Total Advances	56.34	5.96
其中：应付及预提利息 Of Which: Interest Payable and Accrued	33.62	-9.34	9. 境外筹资转贷款 On-lending of Overseas Financing	216.89	-28.25
七、同业拆入 Placements from Banks and Other Financial Institutions	14.09	6.28	二、有价证券及投资 Securities and Investments	754.58	304.16
其中：境外同业拆入 Of Which: Placements from Overseas Banks and Other Financial Institutions	13.48	6.28	三、应收及预付款 Accounts Receivable and Advance Payments	136.20	-38.66
八、外汇买卖 Foreign Exchange Dealings	12.23	-5.74	其中：应收及预付利息 Of Which: Interest Receivable and Paid in Advance	26.30	-12.52
其中：结售汇 Of Which: Purchase and Sale of Foreign Exchange	81.38	-15.81	四、存放中央银行 Deposits with the Central Bank	28.83	3.07
九、境外联行存放 Due to Overseas Branches	89.18	-79.24	其中：缴存准备金 Of Which: Reserves with the Central Bank	17.69	1.94
十、证券业务款项 Securities Business Funds	1.65	0.96	五、存放同业 Due from Banks and Other Financial Institutions	59.52	24.20
十一、各项准备 Total Provisions	44.64	32.40	其中：存放境外同业 Of Which: Due from Overseas Banks and Other Financial Institutions	58.45	24.22
其中：贷款呆账准备金 Of Which: Provisions for Bad Loans	14.55	8.42	六、拆放同业 Placements with Banks and Other Financial Institutions	526.52	-153.43
十二、所有者权益 Owner's Equity	383.44	88.16	其中：拆放境外同业 Of Which: Placements with Overseas Banks and Other Financial Institutions	522.92	-155.76
其中：实收资本 Of Which: Paid-in Capital	206.73	48.64	七、存放境外联行 Due from Overseas Branches	36.03	-36.60
当年结益 Net Earnings	11.41	11.41	八、证券业务占款 Funding of Securities Purchase	0.10	-0.09
十三、其他 Others	-17.45	35.04	九、库存现金 Cash in Vault	23.25	-0.27
资金来源总计 Total Sources	**2371.50**	**59.55**	**资金运用总计 Total Uses**	**2371.50**	**59.55**

金融机构外汇信贷收支表

Sources and Uses of Credit Funds of Financial Institutions（Foreign Currency）

（2002 年末）

（Year－end of 2002）

单位：亿美元

Unit：100 Million US Dollars

项目 Items	余额 Balance	比年初增减额 Changes within the Year	项目 Items	余额 Balance	比年初增减额 Changes within the Year
一、各项存款 Total Deposits	1506.67	107.20	一、各项贷款 Total Loans	1027.98	90.92
1. 单位活期存款 Demand Deposits by Enterprises	212.43	34.82	1. 短期贷款 Short－term Loans	311.02	42.10
其中：中资企业存款 Of Which：Deposits by Chinese－funded Enterprises	106.04	15.61	（1）境内短期贷款 Domestic Short－term Loans	303.97	43.12
			其中：中资企业贷款 Of Which：Loans to Chinese－funded Enterprises	146.17	25.70
外商投资企业存款 Deposits by Foreign－funded Enterprises	86.49	20.71	外商投资企业贷款 Loans to Foreign－funded Enterprises	129.06	14.97
2. 单位定期存款 Time Deposits by Enterprises	303.43	－13.15			
其中：中资企业存款 Of Which：Deposits by Chinese－funded Enterprises	212.24	－5.10	（2）境外短期贷款 Overseas Short－term Loans	7.05	－1.02
			2. 中长期贷款 Medium and Long－term Loans	373.26	45.04
外商投资企业存款 Deposits by Foreign－funded Enterprises	46.53	－14.12	（1）境内中长期贷款 Domestic Medium and Long－term Loans	341.18	44.75
3. 储蓄存款 Savings Deposits	893.59	77.79			
			其中：中资企业贷款 Of Which：Loans to Chinese－funded Enterprises	193.97	49.12
其中：定期存款 Of Which：Time Deposits	784.27	45.15			
4. 信托存款 Trust Deposits	4.88	0.17	外商投资企业贷款 Loans to Foreign－funded Enterprises	62.41	－10.18
5. 委托存款 Designated Deposits	10.59	－4.03			
			（2）境外中长期贷款 Overseas Medium and Long－term Loans	32.08	0.29
6. 其他类存款 Other Deposits	61.38	7.44			
7. 境外存款 Foreign Deposits	20.37	4.16	3. 进出口贸易融资 Financing for Import and Export Trades	48.94	18.99
二、境外筹资 Overseas Financing	235.87	－23.07			
			4. 票据融资 Paper Financing	6.44	2.91
三、境外同业存放 Due to Overseas Banks and Other Financial Institutions	6.43	3.08			
			其中：贴现 Of Which：Discount	5.80	2.68
四、应付及暂收款 Accounts Payable and Receipts on Account	136.21	22.99	5. 融资租赁 Financing Leases	1.98	－0.28
			6. 信托贷款 Trust Loans	15.50	－1.81

续表
Continued

项 目 Items	余 额 Balance	比年初增减额 Changes within the Year	项 目 Items	余 额 Balance	比年初增减额 Changes within the Year
其中：应付及预提利息 Of Which: Interest Payable and Accrued	22.28	-10.90	7.委托贷款 Designated Loans	11.93	-1.52
			8.各项垫款 Total Advances	51.99	-4.61
五、境外同业拆入 Placements from Overseas Banks and Other Financial Institutions	77.38	54.87	9.境外筹资转贷款 On-lending of Overseas Financing	206.92	-9.90
六、外汇买卖 Foreign Exchange Dealings	153.42	140.30	二、有价证券及投资 Securities and Investments	903.36	145.04
其中：结售汇 Of Which: Purchase and Sale of Foreign Exchange	109.19	15.51	三、应收及预付款 Accounts Receivable and Advance Payments	115.29	-11.36
七、境外联行存放 Due to Overseas Branches	175.32	-71.49	其中：应收及预付利息 Of Which: Interest Receivable and Paid in Advance	19.02	-9.47
八、证券业务款项 Securities Business Funds		-1.52			
			四、存放境外同业 Due from Overseas Banks and Other Financial Institutions	85.01	24.62
九、各项准备 Total Provisions	57.28	5.64			
其中：贷款呆账准备金 Of Which: Provisions for Bad Loans	26.45	7.86	五、拆放境外同业 Placements with Overseas Banks and Other Financial Institutions	585.77	55.97
十、所有者权益 Owner's Equity	500.81	89.66			
			六、存放境外联行 Due from Overseas Branches	139.75	21.54
其中：实收资本 Of Which: Paid-in Capital	352.93	123.14			
			七、证券业务占款 Funding of Securities Purchase		-0.10
当年结益 Net Earnings	27.86	27.86			
			八、库存现金 Cash in Vault	24.60	1.18
十一、其他 Others	32.37	0.15			
资金来源总计 Total Sources	**2881.76**	**327.81**	**资金运用总计 Total Uses**	**2881.76**	**327.81**

金融机构外汇信贷收支表

Sources and Uses of Credit Funds of Financial Institutions（Foreign Currency）

（2003 年末）

（Year - end of 2003）

单位：亿美元

Unit：100 Million US Dollars

项　目 Items	余　额 Balance	比年初增减额 Changes within the Year	项　目 Items	余　额 Balance	比年初增减额 Changes within the Year
一、各项存款 Total Deposits	1487.06	-19.21	一、各项贷款 Total Loans	1301.77	276.04
1. 单位活期存款 Demand Deposits by Enterprises	246.43	34.62	1. 短期贷款 Short - term Loans	451.44	141.83
其中：中资企业存款 Of Which：Deposits by Chinese - funded Enterprises	130.33	24.55	（1）境内短期贷款 Domestic Short - term Loans	443.55	140.84
外商投资企业存款 Deposits by Foreign - funded Enterprises	96.81	10.09	其中：中资企业贷款 Of Which：Loans to Chinese - funded Enterprises	228.91	83.75
2. 单位定期存款 Time Deposits by Enterprises	272.83	-31.22	外商投资企业贷款 Loans to Foreign - funded Enterprises	182.51	53.43
其中：中资企业存款 Of Which：Deposits by Chinese - funded Enterprises	190.59	-21.49	（2）境外短期贷款 Overseas Short - term Loans	7.89	0.99
外商投资企业存款 Deposits by Foreign - funded Enterprises	40.38	-6.25	2. 中长期贷款 Medium and Long - term Loans	465.20	90.90
3. 储蓄存款 Savings Deposits	855.14	-38.44	（1）境内中长期贷款 Domestic Medium and Long - term Loans	426.15	83.97
其中：定期存款 Of Which：Time Deposits	722.33	-61.95	其中：中资企业贷款 Of Which：Loans to Chinese - funded Enterprises	241.03	47.26
4. 信托存款 Trust Deposits	2.69	-1.78	外商投资企业贷款 Loans to Foreign - funded Enterprises	67.82	5.23
5. 委托存款 Designated Deposits	11.11	0.53	（2）境外中长期贷款 Overseas Medium and Long - term Loans	39.05	6.93
6. 其他类存款 Other Deposits	72.72	11.33	3. 进出口贸易融资 Financing for Import and Export Trades	110.24	61.39
7. 境外存款 Foreign Deposits	26.14	5.75	4. 票据融资 Paper Financing	7.59	1.36
二、境外筹资 Overseas Financing	214.33	-19.19	其中：贴现 Of Which：Discount	6.08	0.49
三、同业存放 Due to Banks and Other Financial Institutions	42.78	-15.34	5. 融资租赁 Financing Leases	1.51	-0.47
其中：境外同业存放 Of Which：Due to Overseas Banks and Other Financial Institutions	23.33	-14.50	6. 信托贷款 Trust Loans	11.03	-3.07

续表
Continued

项 目 Items	余 额 Balance	比年初增减额 Changes within the Year	项 目 Items	余 额 Balance	比年初增减额 Changes within the Year
四、应付及暂收款 Accounts Payable and Receipts on Account	128.56	-6.85	7. 委托贷款 Designated Loans	12.13	0.22
其中：应付及预提利息 Of Which: Interest Payable and Accrued	18.34	-3.91	8. 各项垫款 Total Advances	47.16	-4.74
			9. 境外筹资转贷款 On-lending of Overseas Financing	195.47	-11.38
五、境外同业拆入 Placements from Overseas Banks and Other Financial Institutions	102.96	25.58	二、有价证券及投资 Securities and Investments	873.68	-29.73
			三、应收及预付款 Accounts Receivable and Advance Payments	144.79	30.52
六、外汇买卖 Foreign Exchange Dealings	178.88	22.13	其中：应收及预付利息 Of Which: Interest Receivable and Paid in Advance	12.11	-6.64
其中：结售汇 Of Which: Purchase and Sale of Foreign Exchange	92.59	-16.54	四、存放同业 Due from Banks and Other Financial Institutions	144.10	57.08
七、境外联行存放 Due to Overseas Branches	238.94	95.15	其中：存放境外同业 Of Which: Due from Overseas Banks and Other Financial Institutions	144.10	57.08
八、证券业务款项 Securities Business Funds					
九、各项准备 Total Provisions	276.92	219.81			
其中：贷款损失准备 Of Which: Provisions for Loan Losses	275.96	275.96	五、拆放境外同业 Placements with Overseas Banks and Other Financial Institutions	369.64	-216.14
十、所有者权益 Owner's Equity	708.61	209.77	六、存放境外联行 Due from Overseas Branches	124.48	-13.18
其中：实收资本 Of Which: Paid-in Capital	675.62	323.45	七、证券业务占款 Funding of Securities Purchase		
当年结益 Net Earnings	27.53	27.53	八、库存现金 Cash in Vault	28.78	4.17
十一、其他 Others	-391.80	-403.09			
资金来源总计 Total Sources	**2987.24**	**108.76**	**资金运用总计 Total Uses**	**2987.24**	**108.76**

金融机构外汇信贷收支表
Sources and Uses of Credit Funds of Financial Institutions（Foreign Currency）

（2004 年末）

（Year - end of 2004）

单位：亿美元

Unit：100 Million US Dollars

项目 Items	余额 Balance	比年初增减额 Changes within the Year	项目 Items	余额 Balance	比年初增减额 Changes within the Year
一、各项存款 Total Deposits	1530.25	38.82	一、各项贷款 Total Loans	1354.84	166.87
1. 单位活期存款 Demand Deposits by Enterprises	307.70	58.65	1. 短期贷款 Short - term Loans	480.59	78.62
其中：中资企业存款 Of Which：Deposits by Chinese - funded Enterprises	164.52	34.26	（1）境内短期贷款 Domestic Short - term Loans	469.79	76.05
外商投资企业存款 Deposits by Foreign - funded Enterprises	116.62	17.69	其中：中资企业贷款 Of Which：Loans to Chinese - funded Enterprises	204.58	14.06
2. 单位定期存款 Time Deposits by Enterprises	268.49	- 5.71	外商投资企业贷款 Loans to Foreign - funded Enterprises	228.15	51.59
其中：中资企业存款 Of Which：Deposits by Chinese - funded Enterprises	186.12	- 3.07	（2）境外短期贷款 Overseas Short - term Loans	10.80	2.57
外商投资企业存款 Deposits by Foreign - funded Enterprises	41.48	- 1.79	2. 中长期贷款 Medium and Long - term Loans	520.04	72.81
3. 储蓄存款 Savings Deposits	802.37	- 53.01	（1）境内中长期贷款 Domestic Medium and Long - term Loans	470.32	62.24
其中：定期存款 Of Which：Time Deposits	635.18	- 87.30	其中：中资企业贷款 Of Which：Loans to Chinese - funded Enterprises	232.29	- 2.76
4. 信托存款 Trust Deposits	3.00	0.50	外商投资企业贷款 Loans to Foreign - funded Enterprises	102.74	39.34
5. 委托存款 Designated Deposits	- 6.13	- 17.23	（2）境外中长期贷款 Overseas Medium and Long - term Loans	49.72	10.57
6. 其他类存款 Other Deposits	116.97	43.77	3. 进出口贸易融资 Financing for Import and Export Trades	138.23	29.89
7. 境外存款 Foreign Deposits	37.85	11.85	4. 票据融资 Paper Financing	12.17	2.53
二、境外筹资 Overseas Financing	230.85	20.33	其中：贴现 Of Which：Discount	11.16	3.04
三、同业存放 Due to Banks and Other Financial Institutions	18.74	- 24.12	5. 融资租赁 Financing Leases	0.82	- 0.69
其中：境外同业存放 Of Which：Due to Overseas Banks and Other Financial Institutions	4.23	- 19.15	6. 信托贷款 Trust Loans	2.74	- 0.07

续表
Continued

项　目 Items	余　额 Balance	比年初增减额 Changes within the Year	项　目 Items	余　额 Balance	比年初增减额 Changes within the Year
四、应付及暂收款 Accounts Payable and Receipts on Account	104.01	-22.66	7. 委托贷款 Designated Loans	2.08	-10.04
			8. 各项垫款 Total Advances	12.33	-8.42
其中：应付及预提利息 Of Which: Interest Payable and Accrued	16.19	-1.73	9. 境外筹资转贷款 On-lending of Overseas Financing	185.84	2.24
五、同业拆入 Placements from Banks and Other Financial Institutions	42.07	-61.43	二、有价证券及投资 Securities and Investments	1149.92	314.64
			三、应收及预付款 Accounts Receivable and Advance Payments	125.70	-12.83
其中：境外同业拆入 Of Which: Placements from Overseas Banks and Other Financial Institutions	42.07	-61.43	其中：应收及预付利息 Of Which: Interest Receivable and Paid in Advance	20.36	-0.74
六、外汇买卖 Foreign Exchange Dealings	375.40	207.96	四、存放同业 Due from Banks and Other Financial Institutions	50.08	-94.42
其中：结售汇 Of Which: Purchase and Sale of Foreign Exchange	74.51	-18.69	其中：存放境外同业 Of Which: Due from Overseas Banks and Other Financial Institutions	50.03	-94.47
七、境外联行存放 Due to Overseas Branches	318.40	68.14			
八、证券业务款项 Securities Business Funds			五、拆放同业 Placements with Banks and Other Financial Institutions	446.98	77.46
九、各项准备 Total Provisions	43.34	-233.41			
其中：贷款损失准备 Of Which: Provisions for Loan Losses	35.62	-224.24	其中：拆放境外同业 Of Which: Placements with Overseas Banks and Other Financial Institutions	446.98	77.56
十、所有者权益 Owner's Equity	647.13	-30.27	六、存放境外联行 Due from Overseas Branches	208.94	81.53
其中：实收资本 Of Which: Paid-in Capital	231.16	-413.86	七、证券业务占款 Funding of Securities Purchase		
当年结益 Net Earnings	66.87	66.87	八、库存现金 Cash in Vault	32.07	3.24
十一、其他 Others	58.34	573.13			
资金来源总计 Total Sources	**3368.53**	**536.49**	**资金运用总计 Total Uses**	**3368.53**	**536.49**

金融机构外汇信贷收支表

Sources and Uses of Credit Funds of Financial Institutions（Foreign Currency）

（2005 年末）

（Year - end of 2005）

单位：亿美元

Unit：100 Million US Dollars

项 目 Items	余 额 Balance	比年初增减额 Changes within the Year	项 目 Items	余 额 Balance	比年初增减额 Changes within the Year
一、各项存款 Total Deposits	1615.70	67.97	一、各项贷款 Total Loans	1505.30	170.82
1. 单位活期存款 Demand Deposits by Enterprises	394.07	86.25	1. 短期贷款 Short - term Loans	459.77	5.03
其中：中资企业存款 Of Which：Deposits by Chinese - funded Enterprises	215.90	50.94	（1）境内短期贷款 Domestic Short - term Loans	448.10	4.09
			其中：中资企业贷款 Of Which：Loans to Chinese - funded Enterprises	187.12	5.82
外商投资企业存款 Deposits by Foreign - funded Enterprises	128.59	10.28	外商投资企业贷款 Loans to Foreign - funded Enterprises	223.06	- 8.90
2. 单位定期存款 Time Deposits by Enterprises	300.70	32.15			
其中：中资企业存款 Of Which：Deposits by Chinese - funded Enterprises	162.80	- 23.47	（2）境外短期贷款 Overseas Short - term Loans	11.67	0.94
			2. 中长期贷款 Medium and Long - term Loans	679.05	155.48
外商投资企业存款 Deposits by Foreign - funded Enterprises	39.91	- 2.04	（1）境内中长期贷款 Domestic Medium and Long - term Loans	614.34	140.42
3. 储蓄存款 Savings Deposits	743.81	- 58.61			
			其中：中资企业贷款 Of Which：Loans to Chinese - funded Enterprises	281.00	51.08
其中：定期存款 Of Which：Time Deposits	576.58	- 58.64			
4. 信托存款 Trust Deposits	0.52	- 2.48	外商投资企业贷款 Loans to Foreign - funded Enterprises	131.56	27.38
5. 委托存款 Designated Deposits	7.27	- 3.89			
			（2）境外中长期贷款 Overseas Medium and Long - term Loans	64.71	15.06
6. 其他类存款 Other Deposits	121.64	4.64			
7. 境外存款 Foreign Deposits	47.69	9.91	3. 进出口贸易融资 Financing for Import and Export Trades	177.52	40.44
二、境外筹资 Overseas Financing	210.64	- 20.38			
			4. 票据融资 Paper Financing	10.90	- 1.17
三、同业存放 Due to Banks and Other Financial Institutions	15.79	- 2.29			
			其中：贴现 Of Which：Discount	9.78	- 1.28
其中：境外同业存放 Of Which：Due to Overseas Banks and Other Financial Institutions	3.00	- 0.59	5. 融资租赁 Financing Leases	0.64	- 0.19
			6. 信托贷款 Trust Loans	2.14	- 0.61

续表
Continued

项　目 Items	余　额 Balance	比年初增减额 Changes within the Year	项　目 Items	余　额 Balance	比年初增减额 Changes within the Year
四、应付及暂收款 Accounts Payable and Receipts on Account	313.90	210.74	7.委托贷款 Designated Loans	8.02	0.05
其中：应付及预提利息 Of Which: Interest Payable and Accrued	28.83	12.56	8.各项垫款 Total Advances	10.94	0.92
			9.境外筹资转贷款 On-lending of Overseas Financing	156.32	-29.13
五、同业拆入 Placements from Banks and Other Financial Institutions	36.33	-5.65	二、有价证券及投资 Securities and Investments	1230.30	80.31
			三、应收及预付款 Accounts Receivable and Advance Payments	165.04	41.23
其中：境外同业拆入 Of Which: Placements from Overseas Banks and Other Financial Institutions	36.33	-5.65	其中：应收及预付利息 Of Which: Interest Receivable and Paid in Advance	35.52	11.58
六、外汇买卖 Foreign Exchange Dealings	500.26	155.36	四、存放同业 Due from Banks and Other Financial Institutions	78.71	28.34
其中：结售汇 Of Which: Purchase and Sale of Foreign Exchange	68.45	-6.16	其中：存放境外同业 Of Which: Due from Overseas Banks and Other Financial Institutions	78.71	28.39
七、境外联行存放 Due to Overseas Branches	318.31	-29.87			
八、证券业务款项 Securities Business Funds			五、拆放同业 Placements with Banks and Other Financial Institutions	565.23	118.72
九、各项准备 Total Provisions	47.04	3.80	其中：拆放境外同业 Of Which: Placements with Overseas Banks and Other Financial Institutions	565.16	118.65
其中：贷款损失准备 Of Which: Provisions for Loan Losses	40.56	4.63			
十、所有者权益 Owner's Equity	315.68	-181.77	六、存放境外联行 Due from Overseas Branches	288.56	79.03
其中：实收资本 Of Which: Paid-in Capital	240.96	157.15	七、证券业务占款 Funding of Securities Purchase		
当年结益 Net Earnings	70.91	70.91	八、库存现金 Cash in Vault	28.11	-5.94
十一、其他 Others	487.60	314.60			
资金来源总计 Total Sources	**3861.25**	**512.51**	**资金运用总计 Total Uses**	**3861.25**	**512.51**

2. 国家银行外汇信贷收支表*（1993—2005 年）
Sources and Uses of Credit Funds of State Banks（Foreign Currency）（1993—2005）

国家银行外汇信贷收支表
Sources and Uses of Credit Funds of State Banks（Foreign Currency）

（1993 年末）

（Year - end of 1993）

单位：亿美元

Unit：100 Million US Dollars

项　目 Items	余　额 Balance	比年初增减额 Changes within the Year	项　目 Items	余　额 Balance	比年初增减额 Changes within the Year
一、外汇存款合计 Total Deposits	627.12	96.67	一、各项外汇贷款 Total Loans	456.85	96.64
1. 居民外汇存款 Deposits by Resident Sector	485.93	94.85	1. 短期外汇贷款 Short - term Loans	255.44	69.52
（1）企业存款 Deposits by Enterprises	297.08	42.16	其中：外商投资企业贷款 Of Which：Loans to Foreign - funded Enterprises	52.05	15.84
其中：外商投资企业存款 Of Which：Deposits by Foreign - funded Enterprises	73.94	28.84	2. 中长期外汇贷款 Medium and Long - term Loans	180.05	29.15
单位定期存款 Time Deposits by Enterprises	36.92	6.23	其中：基本建设贷款 Of Which：Capital Construction Loans	6.40	- 121.07
（2）储蓄存款 Savings Deposits	138.28	45.48	技术改造贷款 Technical Improvement Loans	149.95	147.47
其中：定期储蓄存款 Of Which：Time Deposits	40.87	12.78	3. 其他贷款 Other Loans	21.36	- 2.03
（3）其他存款 Other Deposits	50.57	7.22	二、投资 Investments	135.47	- 13.55
2. 非居民外汇存款 Deposits by Non - resident Sector	141.18	1.81	1. 投资 Investments	3.09	- 3.34
其中：使领馆及驻华机构存款 Of Which：Deposits by Foreign Embassies and Consulates and Institutions in China	1.80	0.61	其中：境内投资 Of Which：Domestic	0.03	
			2. 购买有价证券 Purchase of Securities	132.38	- 10.20
二、境外筹资 Overseas Financing	82.19	9.21	三、委托贷款 Designated Loans	155.61	35.66
1. 境外短期借款 Overseas Short - term Borrowing	40.16	- 2.17	四、存放境外同业资金 Due from Overseas Banks and Other Financial Institutions	355.14	- 13.00
2. 境外中长期商业借款 Overseas Medium and Long - term Commercial Borrowing	42.03	11.38	五、人民银行往来 Transactions with the Central Bank	3.99	2.41
其中：境外发行债券 Of Which：Overseas Bonds Issue	30.74	5.85	其中：缴存人行准备金 Of Which：Reserves with the Central Bank	0.58	0.58

续表
Continued

项 目 Items	余 额 Balance	比年初增减额 Changes within the Year	项 目 Items	余 额 Balance	比年初增减额 Changes within the Year
三、委托借款 Designated Borrowing	152.49	31.98	六、国内同业往来 Domestic Inter - bank Transactions	78.87	18.47
四、人民银行往来 Transactions with the Central Bank	46.86	18.19	其中：同业拆出 Of Which: Placements with Banks and Other Financial Institutions	18.38	8.53
五、国内同业往来 Domestic Inter - bank Transactions	79.47	16.07			
其中：同业拆入 Of Which: Placements from Banks and Other Financial Institutions	17.62	11.13	七、库存现金 Cash in Vault	13.63	4.69
			其中：外汇券 Of Which: Foreign Currency Certificate		
六、自有资金 Own Capital	60.12	3.03			
七、当年结益 Net Earnings	15.34	15.34			
八、外汇买卖 Foreign Exchange Dealings	70.51	-60.11			
九、其他 Others	65.46	0.94			
资金来源总计 Total Sources	**1199.56**	**131.32**	**资金运用总计 Total Uses**	**1199.56**	**131.32**

* 本表机构包括中国工商银行（1993—2005年）、中国农业银行（1993—2005年）、中国银行（1993—2005年）、中国建设银行（1993—2005年）、交通银行（1993—1997年）、中信实业银行（1993—1997年）、国家开发银行（1995—2005年）、中国进出口银行（1995—2005年）、中国农业发展银行（2001—2005年）。

* State Banks of this statement include Industrial and Commercial Bank of China (1993—2005), Agricultural Bank of China (1993—2005), Bank of China (1993—2005), China Construction Bank (1993—2005), Bank of Communications (1993—1997), CITIC Industrial Bank (1993—1997), China Development Bank (1995—2005), the Export - Import Bank of China (1995—2005), and Agricultural Development Bank of China (2001—2005).

国家银行外汇信贷收支表

Sources and Uses of Credit Funds of State Banks（Foreign Currency）

（1994年末）

（Year - end of 1994）

单位：亿美元

Unit：100 Million US Dollars

项目 Items	余额 Balance	比年初增减额 Changes within the Year	项目 Items	余额 Balance	比年初增减额 Changes within the Year
一、外汇存款合计 Total Deposits	673.13	42.02	一、各项外汇贷款 Total Loans	510.49	60.67
1. 居民外汇存款 Deposits by Resident Sector	506.53	15.83	1. 短期外汇贷款 Short - term Loans	247.09	22.02
（1）企业存款 Deposits by Enterprises	266.59	-28.58	其中：外商投资企业贷款 Of Which：Loans to Foreign - funded Enterprises	68.41	9.93
其中：外商投资企业存款 Of Which：Deposits by Foreign - funded Enterprises	73.24	-8.13	2. 中长期外汇贷款 Medium and Long - term Loans	232.53	34.10
单位定期存款 Time Deposits by Enterprises	54.69	17.50	其中：基本建设贷款 Of Which：Capital Construction Loans	7.87	-0.57
（2）储蓄存款 Savings Deposits	182.76	43.91	技术改造贷款 Technical Improvement Loans	5.90	0.46
其中：定期储蓄存款 Of Which：Time Deposits	55.48	14.58	3. 其他贷款 Other Loans	30.87	4.55
（3）其他存款 Other Deposits	57.18	0.50	二、投资 Investments	145.45	7.34
2. 非居民外汇存款 Deposits by Non - resident Sector	166.60	26.19	1. 投资 Investments	4.91	0.80
其中：使领馆及驻华机构存款 Of Which：Deposits by Foreign Embassies and Consulates and Institutions in China	2.12	0.31	其中：境内投资 Of Which：Domestic	0.26	0.23
			2. 购买有价证券 Purchase of Securities	140.54	6.54
二、境外筹资 Overseas Financing	86.31	0.71	三、委托贷款 Designated Loans	213.49	52.68
1. 境外短期借款 Overseas Short - term Borrowing	39.35	-3.15	四、存放境外同业资金 Due from Overseas Banks and Other Financial Institutions	357.96	11.02
2. 境外中长期商业借款 Overseas Medium and Long - term Commercial Borrowing	46.96	3.86	五、人民银行往来 Transactions with the Central Bank	3.75	0.26
其中：境外发行债券 Of Which：Overseas Bonds Issue	34.62	2.31	六、缴存人行准备金 Reserves with the Central Bank	11.89	10.03
三、委托借款 Designated Borrowing	190.79	40.30	七、国内同业往来 Domestic Inter - bank Transactions	75.65	-1.81

续表
Continued

项目 Items	余额 Balance	比年初增减额 Changes within the Year	项目 Items	余额 Balance	比年初增减额 Changes within the Year
四、人民银行往来 Transactions with the Central Bank	55.56	-0.30	其中：同业拆出 Of Which: Placements with Banks and Other Financial Institutions		4.02
五、国内同业往来 Domestic Inter-bank Transactions	127.29	65.82			
其中：同业拆入 Of Which: Placements from Banks and Other Financial Institutions	13.99	-2.99	八、库存现金 Cash in Vault	13.85	0.02
			九、联行往来 Transactions with Branches	113.98	11.06
六、所有者权益 Owner's Equity	68.69	6.34	其中：国内联行往来 Of Which: Transactions with Domestic Branches	83.09	24.81
七、当年结益 Net Earnings	14.50	14.50	十、其他 Others	902.56	179.73
八、外汇买卖 Foreign Exchange Dealings	39.34	-31.88			
九、联行往来 Transactions with Branches	79.19	9.79			
其中：国内联行往来 Of Which: Transactions with Domestic Branches	70.32	24.53			
十、其他 Others	1014.30	183.70			
资金来源总计 Total Sources	**2349.10**	**331.00**	**资金运用总计 Total Uses**	**2349.10**	**331.00**

国家银行外汇信贷收支表

Sources and Uses of Credit Funds of State Banks（Foreign Currency）

（1995 年末）

（Year - end of 1995）

单位：亿美元

Unit：100 Million US Dollars

项目 Items	余额 Balance	比年初增减额 Changes within the Year	项目 Items	余额 Balance	比年初增减额 Changes within the Year
一、外汇存款合计 Total Deposits	666.56	42.21	一、各项外汇贷款 Total Loans	541.56	66.99
1. 居民外汇存款 Deposits by Resident Sector	548.94	32.04	1. 短期外汇贷款 Short - term Loans	358.16	44.15
（1）企业存款 Deposits by Enterprises	252.02	-1.06	其中：外商投资企业贷款 Of Which：Loans to Foreign - funded Enterprises	64.24	9.00
其中：外商投资企业存款 Of Which：Deposits by Foreign - funded Enterprises	68.86	1.95	2. 中长期外汇贷款 Medium and Long - term Loans	136.57	12.48
单位定期存款 Time Deposits by Enterprises	90.07	17.59	其中：外汇储备贷款 Of Which：Foreign Exchange Reserve Loans	0.75	—
（2）储蓄存款 Savings Deposits	218.79	35.97	3. 其他贷款 Other Loans	46.83	13.36
其中：定期储蓄存款 Of Which：Time Deposits	196.73	44.53	二、投资 Investments	101.96	-46.95
（3）其他存款 Other Deposits	74.48	-3.17	1. 投资 Investments	5.47	0.56
（4）外债专户存款 Earmarked Deposits for Foreign Debt	3.65	0.30	其中：境内投资 Of Which：Domestic	0.39	0.13
			2. 购买有价证券 Purchase of Securities	96.49	-47.51
2. 非居民外汇存款 Deposits by Non - resident Sector	117.62	10.17	三、委托贷款 Designated Loans	249.69	50.12
其中：使领馆及驻华机构存款 Of Which：Deposits by Foreign Embassies and Consulates and Institutions in China	2.29	0.16	四、境外筹资贷款 On - lending of Overseas Financing	55.49	-9.34
			五、人民银行往来 Transactions with the Central Bank	26.83	10.59
二、境外筹资 Overseas Financing	60.60	-15.03	其中：缴存人行准备金 Of Which：Reserves with the Central Bank	22.38	9.87
1. 境外短期借款 Overseas Short - term Borrowing	27.97	-7.47			
2. 境外中长期商业借款 Overseas Medium and Long - term Commercial Borrowing	2.03	-1.43	六、国内同业往来 Domestic Inter - bank Transactions	68.44	-7.22
			其中：同业拆出 Of Which：Placements with Banks and Other Financial Institutions	14.62	-5.28
3. 境外发行债券 Overseas Bonds Issue	30.60	-6.13			
三、委托借款 Designated Borrowing	243.85	46.42			

续表
Continued

项 目 Items	余 额 Balance	比年初增减额 Changes within the Year	项 目 Items	余 额 Balance	比年初增减额 Changes within the Year
四、人民银行往来 Transactions with the Central Bank	60.41	4.85	七、国外同业往来 Overseas Inter - bank Transactions	341.24	-16.52
其中：外汇储备存款 Of Which: Foreign Exchange Reserve Deposits			其中：拆放同业 Of Which: Placements with Banks and Other Financial Institutions	37.44	5.75
五、国内同业往来 Domestic Inter - bank Transactions	119.65	-6.83	八、库存现金 Cash in Vault	13.94	0.11
其中：同业拆入 Of Which: Placements from Banks and Other Financial Institutions	10.19	-1.83	九、外汇买卖 Foreign Exchange Dealings	35.30	7.05
			其中：结售汇 Of Which: Purchase and Sale of Foreign Exchange	10.24	2.67
六、国外同业往来 Overseas Inter - bank Transactions	56.26	-15.93			
其中：同业拆入 Of Which: Placements from Banks and Other Financial Institutions	37.90	-12.19	十、联行往来 Transactions with Branches	151.33	35.19
			其中：国内联行往来 Of Which: Transactions with Domestic Branches		
七、所有者权益 Owner's Equity	106.20	8.64	十一、系统内往来 Internal Funds Allocation	328.01	76.18
其中：实收资本 Of Which: Paid - in Capital	45.39	2.23	十二、其他 Others	667.81	56.29
八、当年结益 Net Earnings	21.43	21.43			
九、外汇买卖 Foreign Exchange Dealings	92.64	10.80			
其中：结售汇 Of Which: Purchase and Sale of Foreign Exchange	60.14	38.65			
十、联行往来 Transactions with Branches	93.33	11.80			
其中：国内联行往来 Of Which: Transactions with Domestic Branches		—			
十一、系统内往来 Internal Funds Allocation	335.25	87.35			
十二、其他 Others	725.42	29.79			
资金来源总计 Total Sources	**2581.60**	**225.50**	**资金运用总计 Total Uses**	**2581.60**	**225.50**

国家银行外汇信贷收支表

Sources and Uses of Credit Funds of State Banks（Foreign Currency）

（1996年末）

（Year－end of 1996）

单位：亿美元

Unit：100 Million US Dollars

项目 Items	余额 Balance	比年初增减额 Changes within the Year	项目 Items	余额 Balance	比年初增减额 Changes within the Year
一、外汇存款合计 Total Deposits	593.71	38.54	一、各项外汇贷款 Total Loans	581.62	40.12
1. 居民外汇存款 Deposits by Resident Sector	590.87	38.01	1. 短期外汇贷款 Short－term Loans	239.24	23.31
（1）企业存款 Deposits by Enterprises	265.28	13.54	其中：外商投资企业贷款 Of Which：Loans to Foreign－funded Enterprises	77.29	13.59
其中：外商投资企业存款 Of Which：Deposits by Foreign－funded Enterprises	68.80	－0.07	2. 中长期外汇贷款 Medium and Long－term Loans	276.30	6.73
单位定期存款 Time Deposits by Enterprises	139.66	49.03	其中：外汇储备贷款 Of Which：Foreign Exchange Reserve Loans	10.68	7.42
（2）储蓄存款 Savings Deposits	245.71	27.08	3. 其他贷款 Other Loans	66.08	10.08
其中：定期存款 Of Which：Time Deposits	224.49	26.30	二、投资 Investments	123.65	21.65
（3）其他存款 Other Deposits	74.57	4.75	1. 投资 Investments	6.07	0.60
（4）外债专户存款 Earmarked Deposits for Foreign Debt	5.31	2.14	其中：境内投资 Of Which：Domestic	0.09	0.30
			2. 购买有价证券 Purchase of Securities	117.58	21.05
2. 非居民外汇存款 Deposits by Non－resident Sector	2.84	0.53	三、委托境外借款转贷款 On－lending of Overseas Designated Borrowing	264.22	14.19
其中：使领馆及驻华机构存款 Of Which：Deposits by Foreign Embassies and Consulates and Institutions in China	2.19	0.10	四、境外筹资贷款 On－lending of Overseas Financing	51.52	4.49
二、境外筹资 Overseas Financing	50.01	－10.59	五、人民银行往来 Transactions with the Central Bank	27.98	0.98
1. 境外短期借款 Overseas Short－term Borrowing	1.95	0.85	其中：缴存人行准备金 Of Which：Reserves with the Central Bank	23.59	1.21
2. 境外中长期商业借款 Overseas Medium and Long－term Commercial Borrowing	23.45	－5.45	六、国内同业往来 Domestic Inter－bank Transactions	47.72	－20.15
3. 境外发行债券 Overseas Bonds Issue	24.61	－5.99	其中：同业拆出 Of Which：Placements with Banks and Other Financial Institutions	15.34	1.53
三、委托境外借款 Overseas Designated Borrowing	254.70	10.92			

续表
Continued

项目 Items	余额 Balance	比年初增减额 Changes within the Year	项目 Items	余额 Balance	比年初增减额 Changes within the Year
四、人民银行往来 Transactions with the Central Bank	191.50	108.83	七、国外同业往来 Overseas Inter - bank Transactions	359.90	17.54
其中：外汇储备存款 Of Which: Foreign Exchange Reserve Deposits	16.36	12.15	其中：拆放同业 Of Which: Placements with Banks and Other Financial Institutions	43.24	0.57
五、国内同业往来 Domestic Inter - bank Transactions	42.20	- 74.83	八、库存现金 Cash in Vault	13.02	- 0.92
其中：同业拆入 Of Which: Placements from Banks and Other Financial Institutions	6.59	- 3.58	九、联行往来 Transactions with Branches	188.32	31.68
六、国外同业往来 Overseas Inter - bank Transactions	173.74	117.48			
其中：同业拆入 Of Which: Placements from Banks and Other Financial Institutions	19.70	- 19.16			
七、所有者权益 Owner's Equity	147.63	21.73			
其中：实收资本 Of Which: Paid - in Capital	84.04	11.64			
八、当年结益 Net Earnings	14.55	14.55			
九、外汇买卖 Foreign Exchange Dealings	107.56	50.32			
其中：结售汇 Of Which: Purchase and Sale of Foreign Exchange	98.73	47.74			
十、联行往来 Transactions with Branches	112.40	14.01			
十一、系统内往来 Internal Funds Allocation	0.57	- 9.38			
十二、其他 Others	- 30.62	- 65.29			
资金来源总计 Total Sources	**1658.00**	**100.70**	**资金运用总计 Total Uses**	**1658.00**	**100.70**

国家银行外汇信贷收支表

Sources and Uses of Credit Funds of State Banks（Foreign Currency）

（1997年末）

（Year – end of 1997）

单位：亿美元

Unit：100 Million US Dollars

项目 Items	余额 Balance	比年初增减额 Changes within the Year	项目 Items	余额 Balance	比年初增减额 Changes within the Year
一、外汇存款合计 Total Deposits	648.86	54.05	一、各项外汇贷款 Total Loans	665.14	41.15
1. 居民外汇存款 Deposits by Resident Sector	646.72	54.77	1. 短期外汇贷款 Short – term Loans	299.99	52.27
（1）企业存款 Deposits by Enterprises	291.82	25.80	其中：外商投资企业贷款 Of Which：Loans to Foreign – funded Enterprises	84.32	7.18
其中：外商投资企业存款 Of Which：Deposits by Foreign – funded Enterprises	64.80	-4.44	2. 中长期外汇贷款 Medium and Long – term Loans	250.55	-28.65
单位定期存款 Time Deposits by Enterprises	177.12	36.25	其中：外汇储备贷款 Of Which：Foreign Exchange Reserve Loans	14.87	5.63
（2）储蓄存款 Savings Deposits	284.65	38.81	3. 其他贷款 Other Loans	114.60	17.53
其中：定期储蓄存款 Of Which：Time Deposits	262.73	37.26	二、投资 Investments	139.64	10.22
（3）其他存款 Other Deposits	65.65	-9.13	1. 投资 Investments	13.31	1.55
（4）外债专户存款 Earmarked Deposits for Foreign Debt	4.60	-0.71	其中：境内投资 Of Which：Domestic	0.13	0.04
			2. 购买有价证券 Purchase of Securities	126.33	8.67
2. 非居民外汇存款 Deposits by Non – resident Sector	2.14	-0.72	三、委托境外借款转贷款 On – lending of Overseas Designated Borrowing	260.00	-4.57
其中：使领馆及驻华机构存款 Of Which：Deposits by Foreign Embassies and Consulates and Institutions in China	1.92	-0.29	四、境外筹资贷款 On – lending of Overseas Financing	40.80	-10.51
二、境外筹资 Overseas Financing	41.77	-8.30	五、人民银行往来 Transactions with the Central Bank	16.91	-11.20
1. 境外短期借款 Overseas Short – term Borrowing	0.12	-1.83	其中：缴存人行准备金 Of Which：Reserves with the Central Bank	11.19	-12.40
2. 境外中长期商业借款 Overseas Medium and Long – term Commercial Borrowing	18.80	-4.71	六、国内同业往来 Domestic Inter – bank Transactions	29.63	-18.56
3. 境外发行债券 Overseas Bonds Issue	22.85	-1.76	其中：同业拆出 Of Which：Placements with Banks and Other Financial Institutions	14.50	-1.11
三、委托借款 Designated Borrowing	250.30	-6.20			

续表
Continued

项 目 Items	余 额 Balance	比年初增减额 Changes within the Year	项 目 Items	余 额 Balance	比年初增减额 Changes within the Year
四、人民银行往来 Transactions with the Central Bank	182.42	-9.06	七、国外同业往来 Overseas Inter-bank Transactions	458.45	98.11
其中：外汇储备存款 Of Which: Foreign Exchange Reserve Deposits	16.95	0.58	其中：拆放同业 Of Which: Placements with Banks and Other Financial Institutions	53.51	10.27
五、国内同业往来 Domestic Inter-bank Transactions	40.66	-15.34	八、库存现金 Cash in Vault	13.90	0.87
其中：同业拆入 Of Which: Placements from Banks and Other Financial Institutions	9.49	2.05	九、联行往来 Transactions with Branches	172.41	-18.18
六、国外同业往来 Overseas Inter-bank Transactions	181.06	6.10			
其中：同业拆入 Of Which: Placements from Banks and Other Financial Institutions	23.76	4.04			
七、所有者权益 Owner's Equity	169.55	6.07			
其中：实收资本 Of Which: Paid-in Capital	80.26	-4.23			
八、当年结益 Net Earnings	15.00	15.00			
九、外汇买卖 Foreign Exchange Dealings	100.80	-7.09			
其中：结售汇 Of Which: Purchase and Sale of Foreign Exchange	96.86	-2.58			
十、联行往来 Transactions with Branches	134.18	19.17			
十一、系统内往来 Internal Funds Allocation	2.52	1.24			
十二、其他 Others	29.76	31.69			
资金来源总计 Total Sources	**1796.88**	**87.33**	**资金运用总计 Total Uses**	**1796.88**	**87.33**

国家银行外汇信贷收支表

Sources and Uses of Credit Funds of State Banks（Foreign Currency）

（1998 年末）

（Year - end of 1998）

单位：亿美元

Unit：100 Million US Dollars

项目 Items	余额 Balance	比年初增减额 Changes within the Year	项目 Items	余额 Balance	比年初增减额 Changes within the Year
一、各项存款 Total Deposits	702.32	115.46	一、各项贷款 Total Loans	659.40	24.43
1. 单位活期存款 Demand Deposits by Enterprises	97.14	- 18.45	1. 短期贷款 Short - term Loans	288.32	- 6.99
其中：中资企业存款 Of Which：Deposits by Chinese - funded Enterprises	46.95	- 12.07	（1）境内短期贷款 Domestic Short - term Loans	288.32	- 6.63
			其中：中资企业贷款 Of Which：Loans to Chinese - funded Enterprises	136.82	- 5.12
外商投资企业存款 Deposits by Foreign - funded Enterprises	43.90	- 7.63	外商投资企业贷款 Loans to Foreign - funded Enterprises	85.66	- 4.72
2. 单位定期存款 Time Deposits by Enterprises	193.08	31.58			
其中：中资企业存款 Of Which：Deposits by Chinese - funded Enterprises	158.13	28.82	（2）境外短期贷款 Overseas Short - term Loans		- 0.36
			2. 中长期贷款 Medium and Long - term Loans	288.26	20.16
外商投资企业存款 Deposits by Foreign - funded Enterprises	13.75	3.98	（1）境内中长期贷款 Domestic Medium and Long - term Loans	285.21	19.29
3. 储蓄存款 Savings Deposits	376.56	108.29			
其中：定期存款 Of Which：Time Deposits	351.90	104.56	其中：中资企业贷款 Of Which：Loans to Chinese - funded Enterprises	147.98	2.41
4. 其他类存款 Other Deposits	33.94	- 5.02	外商投资企业贷款 Loans to Foreign - funded Enterprises	29.97	- 4.11
5. 境外存款 Foreign Deposits	1.60	- 0.94	（2）境外中长期贷款 Overseas Medium and Long - term Loans	3.05	0.87
二、境内中长期借款 Domestic Medium and Long - term Borrowing	0.24	- 0.15			
			3. 进出口贸易融资 Financing for Import and Export Trades	27.24	- 12.98
三、卖出回购证券 Repo	0.34	0.34			
四、境外筹资 Overseas Financing	296.71	- 6.95	4. 票据融资 Paper Financing	0.66	- 0.76
五、向中央银行借款 Borrowings from the Central Bank	20.62	- 0.19	5. 逾期类贷款 Overdue Loans	54.92	25.00
六、中央银行存款 Deposits by the Central Bank	144.61	12.59	二、投资 Investments	158.09	43.65
七、同业存放 Due to Banks and Other Financial Institutions	20.39	- 14.47	1. 购买有价证券 Purchase of Securities	140.37	38.28

续表
Continued

项 目 Items	余 额 Balance	比年初增减额 Changes within the Year	项 目 Items	余 额 Balance	比年初增减额 Changes within the Year
1. 境内同业存放 Due to Domestic Banks and Other Financial Institutions	11.63	-1.48	其中：购买境外有价证券 Of Which: Purchase of Foreign Securities	140.37	38.28
2. 境外同业存放 Due to Overseas Banks and Other Financial Institutions	8.76	-12.99	2. 其他投资 Other Investments	17.72	5.37
			其中：投资境外 Of Which: Overseas	0.56	0.09
八、同业拆入 Placements from Banks and Other Financial Institutions	7.98	0.13	三、境外筹资转贷款 On-lending of Overseas Financing	305.71	2.53
1. 境内同业拆入 Placements from Domestic Banks and Other Financial Institutions	2.49	0.88	四、存放中央银行 Deposits with the Central Bank	14.79	-0.17
			其中：缴存准备金 Of Which: Reserves with the Central Bank	8.85	-1.10
2. 境外同业拆入 Placements from Overseas Banks and Other Financial Institutions	5.49	-0.75			
			五、存放同业 Due from Banks and Other Financial Institutions	392.83	-16.33
九、委托基金存款 Designated Fund Deposits	0.11	0.03			
十、外汇买卖 Foreign Exchange Dealings	74.26	-23.22	1. 存放境内同业 Due from Domestic Banks and Other Financial Institutions	7.96	-0.56
其中：结售汇 Of Which: Purchase and Sale of Foreign Exchange	63.66	-30.08	2. 存放境外同业 Due from Overseas Banks and Other Financial Institutions	384.87	-15.77
十一、境内联行存放 Due to Domestic Branches	-17.33	-19.15			
			六、拆放同业 Placements with Banks and Other Financial Institutions	37.86	10.51
十二、境外联行存放 Due to Overseas Branches	157.57	-21.66			
十三、所有者权益 Owner's Equity	204.28	30.17	1. 拆放境内同业 Placements with Domestic Banks and Other Financial Institutions	5.53	1.12
其中：实收资本 Of Which: Paid-in Capital	85.32	9.47			
当年结益 Net Earnings	21.56	21.56	2. 拆放境外同业 Placements with Overseas Banks and Other Financial Institutions	32.33	9.39
十四、其他 Others	2.77	-32.57	七、存放境外联行 Due from Overseas Branches	33.11	-24.48
			八、库存现金 Cash in Vault	13.08	0.22
资金来源总计 Total Sources	**1614.87**	**40.36**	**资金运用总计 Total Uses**	**1614.87**	**40.36**

国家银行外汇信贷收支表

Sources and Uses of Credit Funds of State Banks（Foreign Currency）

（1999 年末）

（Year - end of 1999）

单位：亿美元

Unit：100 Million US Dollars

项　目 Items	余　额 Balance	比年初增减额 Changes within the Year	项　目 Items	余　额 Balance	比年初增减额 Changes within the Year
一、各项存款 Total Deposits	829.10	126.94	一、各项贷款 Total Loans	611.68	1.16
1. 单位活期存款 Demand Deposits by Enterprises	106.60	9.56	1. 短期贷款 Short - term Loans	267.39	6.37
其中：中资企业存款 Of Which：Deposits by Chinese - funded Enterprises	52.24	5.31	（1）境内短期贷款 Domestic Short - term Loans	267.39	6.37
外商投资企业存款 Deposits by Foreign - funded Enterprises	47.96	4.09	其中：中资企业贷款 Of Which：Loans to Chinese - funded Enterprises	123.78	14.31
2. 单位定期存款 Time Deposits by Enterprises	189.10	- 4.02	外商投资企业贷款 Loans to Foreign - funded Enterprises	73.28	- 12.29
其中：中资企业存款 Of Which：Deposits by Chinese - funded Enterprises	151.57	- 6.60	（2）境外短期贷款 Overseas Short - term Loans		
外商投资企业存款 Deposits by Foreign - funded Enterprises	14.78	1.03	2. 中长期贷款 Medium and Long - term Loans	272.17	3.13
3. 储蓄存款 Savings Deposits	501.05	124.59	（1）境内中长期贷款 Domestic Medium and Long - term Loans	268.16	2.17
其中：定期存款 Of Which：Time Deposits	467.76	115.93	其中：中资企业贷款 Of Which：Loans to Chinese - funded Enterprises	151.67	19.23
4. 其他类存款 Other Deposits	31.68	- 2.26	外商投资企业贷款 Loans to Foreign - funded Enterprises	25.37	- 4.60
5. 境外存款 Foreign Deposits	0.67	- 0.93	（2）境外中长期贷款 Overseas Medium and Long - term Loans	4.01	0.96
二、境内中长期借款 Domestic Medium and Long - term Borrowing	2.50	2.26	3. 进出口贸易融资 Financing for Import and Export Trades	19.06	- 6.01
三、卖出回购证券 Repo		- 0.35	4. 票据融资 Paper Financing	0.60	- 0.06
四、境外筹资 Overseas Financing	292.91	- 3.96	5. 逾期类贷款 Overdue Loans	52.46	- 2.27
五、向中央银行借款 Borrowings from the Central Bank	20.04	- 0.58	二、投资 Investments	259.06	100.98
六、中央银行存款 Deposits by the Central Bank	112.39	- 31.66	1. 购买有价证券 Purchase of Securities	240.62	100.25
七、同业存放 Due to Banks and Other Financial Institutions	24.32	- 0.57			

续表
Continued

项目 Items	余额 Balance	比年初增减额 Changes within the Year	项目 Items	余额 Balance	比年初增减额 Changes within the Year
1. 境内同业存放 Due to Domestic Banks and Other Financial Institutions	16.91	4.71	其中：购买境外有价证券 Of Which: Purchase of Foreign Securities	239.45	99.08
2. 境外同业存放 Due to Overseas Banks and Other Financial Institutions	7.41	-5.28	2. 其他投资 Other Investments	18.44	0.73
			其中：投资境外 Of Which: Overseas	0.57	0.01
八、同业拆入 Placements from Banks and Other Financial Institutions	3.20	-5.14	三、境外筹资转贷款 On-lending of Overseas Financing	297.42	-8.11
1. 境内同业拆入 Placements from Domestic Banks and Other Financial Institutions	1.03	-1.82	四、存放中央银行 Deposits with the Central Bank	14.79	-0.04
			其中：缴存准备金 Of Which: Reserves with the Central Bank	10.40	1.55
2. 境外同业拆入 Placements from Overseas Banks and Other Financial Institutions	2.17	-3.32			
			五、存放同业 Due from Banks and Other Financial Institutions	279.56	-113.71
九、委托基金存款 Designated Fund Deposits	0.03	0.03			
十、外汇买卖 Foreign Exchange Dealings	81.81	7.86	1. 存放境内同业 Due from Domestic Banks and Other Financial Institutions	33.82	25.28
其中：结售汇 Of Which: Purchase and Sale of Foreign Exchange	68.83	-0.22	2. 存放境外同业 Due from Overseas Banks and Other Financial Institutions	245.74	-138.99
十一、境内联行存放 Due to Domestic Branches	-37.18	-19.07			
			六、拆放同业 Placements with Banks and Other Financial Institutions	64.46	25.68
十二、境外联行存放 Due to Overseas Branches	120.66	-51.68			
十三、所有者权益 Owner's Equity	195.31	4.68	1. 拆放境内同业 Placements with Domestic Banks and Other Financial Institutions	5.10	-1.35
其中：实收资本 Of Which: Paid-in Capital	76.26	4.68	2. 拆放境外同业 Placements with Overseas Banks and Other Financial Institutions	59.36	27.03
当年结益 Net Earnings	13.75	13.75			
十四、其他 Others	-21.88	12.73	七、存放境外联行 Due from Overseas Branches	69.64	22.01
			八、库存现金 Cash in Vault	26.60	13.52
资金来源总计 Total Sources	**1623.21**	**41.49**	**资金运用总计 Total Uses**	**1623.21**	**41.49**

国家银行外汇信贷收支表

Sources and Uses of Credit Funds of State Banks（Foreign Currency）

（2000 年末）

（Year - end of 2000）

单位：亿美元

Unit：100 Million US Dollars

项目 Items	余额 Balance	比年初增减额 Changes within the Year	项目 Items	余额 Balance	比年初增减额 Changes within the Year
一、各项存款 Total Deposits	1028.76	199.39	一、各项贷款 Total Loans	454.41	-21.63
1. 单位活期存款 Demand Deposits by Enterprises	109.08	2.16	1. 短期贷款 Short - term Loans	185.93	-19.14
其中：中资企业存款 Of Which：Deposits by Chinese - funded Enterprises	54.04	1.80	（1）境内短期贷款 Domestic Short - term Loans	185.93	-19.14
			其中：中资企业贷款 Of Which：Loans to Chinese - funded Enterprises	82.64	-19.35
外商投资企业存款 Deposits by Foreign - funded Enterprises	50.01	1.56	外商投资企业贷款 Loans to Foreign - funded Enterprises	53.61	-4.77
2. 单位定期存款 Time Deposits by Enterprises	227.72	38.32			
其中：中资企业存款 Of Which：Deposits by Chinese - funded Enterprises	183.36	31.47	（2）境外短期贷款 Overseas Short - term Loans		
			2. 中长期贷款 Medium and Long - term Loans	211.19	-12.62
外商投资企业存款 Deposits by Foreign - funded Enterprises	18.24	3.46	（1）境内中长期贷款 Domestic Medium and Long - term Loans	205.00	-14.80
3. 储蓄存款 Savings Deposits	649.04	147.99	其中：中资企业贷款 Of Which：Loans to Chinese - funded Enterprises	120.46	-8.27
其中：定期存款 Of Which：Time Deposits	608.83	141.07			
4. 其他类存款 Other Deposits	42.83	11.22	外商投资企业贷款 Loans to Foreign - funded Enterprises	17.62	2.94
5. 境外存款 Foreign Deposits	0.09	-0.30	（2）境外中长期贷款 Overseas Medium and Long - term Loans	6.19	2.18
二、境内中长期借款 Domestic Medium and Long - term Borrowing	1.43	-1.07			
			3. 进出口贸易融资 Financing for Import and Export Trades	12.46	-0.80
三、卖出回购证券 Repo	0.10	0.10			
四、境外筹资 Overseas Financing	235.91	-56.98	4. 票据融资 Paper Financing	0.34	-0.26
五、向中央银行借款 Borrowings from the Central Bank	18.18	-1.86	5. 逾期类贷款 Overdue Loans	44.49	11.19
六、中央银行存款 Deposits by the Central Bank	86.02	-26.32	二、投资 Investments	352.42	93.75
七、同业存放 Due to Banks and Other Financial Institutions	18.32	-4.66	1. 购买有价证券 Purchase of Securities	329.80	89.50

续表
Continued

项目 Items	余额 Balance	比年初增减额 Changes within the Year	项目 Items	余额 Balance	比年初增减额 Changes within the Year
1. 境内同业存放 Due to Domestic Banks and Other Financial Institutions	10.79	-4.78	其中：购买境外有价证券 Of Which: Purchase of Foreign Securities	318.51	79.37
2. 境外同业存放 Due to Overseas Banks and Other Financial Institutions	7.53	0.12	2. 其他投资 Other Investments	22.62	4.25
			其中：投资境外 Of Which: Overseas	0.90	0.33
八、同业拆入 Placements from Banks and Other Financial Institutions	6.14	2.94	三、境外筹资转贷款 On-lending of Overseas Financing	239.72	-46.56
1. 境内同业拆入 Placements from Domestic Banks and Other Financial Institutions	3.30	2.27	四、存放中央银行 Deposits with the Central Bank	20.64	5.85
			其中：缴存准备金 Of Which: Reserves with the Central Bank	13.99	3.59
2. 境外同业拆入 Placements from Overseas Banks and Other Financial Institutions	2.84	0.67	五、存放同业 Due from Banks and Other Financial Institutions	322.27	43.19
九、委托基金存款 Designated Fund Deposits	-0.01	-0.05			
十、外汇买卖 Foreign Exchange Dealings	-62.84	-145.26	1. 存放境内同业 Due from Domestic Banks and Other Financial Institutions	10.74	-22.98
其中：结售汇 Of Which: Purchase and Sale of Foreign Exchange	58.51	-9.98	2. 存放境外同业 Due from Overseas Banks and Other Financial Institutions	311.53	66.17
十一、境内联行存放 Due to Domestic Branches	-12.23	22.22	六、拆放同业 Placements with Banks and Other Financial Institutions	196.79	132.40
十二、境外联行存放 Due to Overseas Branches	156.07	35.62			
十三、所有者权益 Owner's Equity	211.17	15.99	1. 拆放境内同业 Placements with Domestic Banks and Other Financial Institutions	4.47	-0.63
其中：实收资本 Of Which: Paid-in Capital	75.94	-0.32	2. 拆放境外同业 Placements with Overseas Banks and Other Financial Institutions	192.32	133.03
当年结益 Net Earnings	11.89	11.89			
十四、其他 Others	-24.87	146.79	七、存放境外联行 Due from Overseas Branches	56.77	-12.66
			八、库存现金 Cash in Vault	19.13	-7.49
资金来源总计 Total Sources	**1662.15**	**186.85**	**资金运用总计 Total Uses**	**1662.15**	**186.85**

国家银行外汇信贷收支表

Sources and Uses of Credit Funds of State Banks（Foreign Currency）

（2001 年末）

（Year - end of 2001）

单位：亿美元

Unit：100 Million US Dollars

项 目 Items	余 额 Balance	比年初增减额 Changes within the Year	项 目 Items	余 额 Balance	比年初增减额 Changes within the Year
一、各项存款 Total Deposits	1076.28	44.46	一、各项贷款 Total Loans	653.77	-41.14
1. 单位活期存款 Demand Deposits by Enterprises	123.51	12.16	1. 短期贷款 Short - term Loans	159.32	-2.55
其中：中资企业存款 Of Which：Deposits by Chinese - funded Enterprises	83.08	18.88	(1) 境内短期贷款 Domestic Short - term Loans	159.32	-2.55
外商投资企业存款 Deposits by Foreign - funded Enterprises	35.05	-7.11	其中：中资企业贷款 Of Which：Loans to Chinese - funded Enterprises	85.35	2.57
2. 单位定期存款 Time Deposits by Enterprises	201.99	-25.49	外商投资企业贷款 Loans to Foreign - funded Enterprises	53.97	0.05
其中：中资企业存款 Of Which：Deposits by Chinese - funded Enterprises	164.18	-19.00	(2) 境外短期贷款 Overseas Short - term Loans		
外商投资企业存款 Deposits by Foreign - funded Enterprises	13.37	-4.86	2. 中长期贷款 Medium and Long - term Loans	214.17	-14.91
3. 储蓄存款 Savings Deposits	715.35	65.95	(1) 境内中长期贷款 Domestic Medium and Long - term Loans	207.14	-15.64
其中：定期存款 Of Which：Time Deposits	650.50	41.13	其中：中资企业贷款 Of Which：Loans to Chinese - funded Enterprises	113.43	-15.44
4. 其他类存款 Other Deposits	35.25	-8.25	外商投资企业贷款 Loans to Foreign - funded Enterprises	18.51	-4.35
5. 境外存款 Foreign Deposits	0.18	0.09	(2) 境外中长期贷款 Overseas Medium and Long - term Loans	7.03	0.73
二、境内中长期借款 Domestic Medium and Long - term Borrowing	1.40	-0.03	3. 进出口贸易融资 Financing for Import and Export Trades	13.87	-1.60
三、卖出回购证券 Repo	0.40	0.29	4. 票据融资 Paper Financing	0.65	0.31
四、境外筹资 Overseas Financing	228.98	-14.54	其中：贴现 Of Which：Discount	0.37	0.27
五、向中央银行借款 Borrowings from the Central Bank	7.58	-10.60	5. 各项垫款 Total Advances	51.71	5.90
六、中央银行存款 Deposits by the Central Bank	90.22	-32.10	6. 境外筹资转贷款 On - lending of Overseas Financing	214.05	-28.29
七、应付及暂收款 Accounts Payable and Receipts on Account	73.16	-17.97			

续表
Continued

项目 Items	余额 Balance	比年初增减额 Changes within the Year	项目 Items	余额 Balance	比年初增减额 Changes within the Year
其中：应付及预提利息 Of Which: Interest Payable and Accrued	25.41	-9.12	二、投资 Investments	610.66	256.88
八、同业存放 Due to Banks and Other Financial Institutions	47.29	37.61	1. 购买有价证券 Purchase of Securities	486.27	156.18
1. 境内同业存放 Due to Domestic Banks and Other Financial Institutions	44.17	35.58	其中：购买境外有价证券 Of Which: Purchase of Foreign Securities	455.98	137.14
2. 境外同业存放 Due to Overseas Banks and Other Financial Institutions	3.12	2.03	2. 其他投资 Other Investments	124.39	100.70
九、同业拆入 Placements from Banks and Other Financial Institutions	12.37	7.34	其中：投资境外 Of Which: Overseas	0.61	-0.29
1. 境内同业拆入 Placements from Domestic Banks and Other Financial Institutions	3.41	-0.03	三、应收及预付款 Accounts Receivable and Advance Payments	80.94	-41.76
2. 境外同业拆入 Placements from Overseas Banks and Other Financial Institutions	8.96	7.37	其中：应收及预付利息 Of Which: Interest Receivable and Paid in Advance	12.80	-10.67
十、委托基金存款（净） Designated Fund Deposits (Net)	0.01	0.01	四、买入返售证券 Reverse Repo		
十一、外汇买卖 Foreign Exchange Dealings	-3.66	-10.71	五、存放中央银行 Deposits with the Central Bank	22.11	1.79
其中：结售汇 Of Which: Purchase and Sale of Foreign Exchange	83.30	-20.73	其中：缴存准备金 Of Which: Reserves with the Central Bank	14.44	1.10
十二、境内联行存放 Due to Domestic Branches	-35.59	-27.98	六、存放同业 Due from Banks and Other Financial Institutions	44.51	30.14
十三、境外联行存放 Due to Overseas Branches	79.90	-88.50	1. 存放境内同业 Due from Domestic Banks and Other Financial Institutions	8.07	3.59
十四、各项准备 Total Provisions	41.48	31.85	2. 存放境外同业 Due from Overseas Banks and Other Financial Institutions	36.44	26.55
其中：贷款呆账准备金 Of Which: Provisions for Bad Loans	12.21	8.18	七、拆放同业 Placements with Banks and Other Financial Institutions	437.48	-137.00
十五、所有者权益 Owner's Equity	295.77	83.98	（1）拆放境内同业 Placements with Domestic Banks and Other Financial Institutions	9.42	4.93
其中：实收资本 Of Which: Paid-in Capital	120.99	44.55	（2）拆放境外同业 Placements with Overseas Banks and Other Financial Institutions	428.06	-141.93
当年结益 Net Earnings	9.37	9.35	八、存放境外联行 Due from Overseas Branches	34.46	-35.51
十六、其他 Others	-13.40	29.49	九、库存现金 Cash in Vault	18.26	-0.80
资金来源总计 Total Sources	**1902.19**	**32.60**	**资金运用总计 Total Uses**	**1902.19**	**32.60**

国家银行外汇信贷收支表

Sources and Uses of Credit Funds of State Banks（Foreign Currency）

（2002 年末）

（Year - end of 2002）

单位：亿美元

Unit：100 Million US Dollars

项　目 Items	余　额 Balance	比年初增减额 Changes within the Year	项　目 Items	余　额 Balance	比年初增减额 Changes within the Year
一、各项存款 Total Deposits	1140.05	64.08	一、各项贷款 Total Loans	729.58	70.09
1. 单位活期存款 Demand Deposits by Enterprises	135.01	12.24	1. 短期贷款 Short - term Loans	187.10	28.32
其中：中资企业存款 Of Which：Deposits by Chinese - funded Enterprises	88.89	10.05	（1）境内短期贷款 Domestic Short - term Loans	187.10	28.32
			其中：中资企业贷款 Of Which：Loans to Chinese - funded Enterprises	108.09	21.11
外商投资企业存款 Deposits by Foreign - funded Enterprises	37.36	4.41	外商投资企业贷款 Loans to Foreign - funded Enterprises	57.92	6.12
2. 单位定期存款 Time Deposits by Enterprises	190.08	- 11.22			
其中：中资企业存款 Of Which：Deposits by Chinese - funded Enterprises	155.72	- 7.97	（2）境外短期贷款 Overseas Short - term Loans		
			2. 中长期贷款 Medium and Long - term Loans	268.07	47.90
外商投资企业存款 Deposits by Foreign - funded Enterprises	9.77	- 3.60	（1）境内中长期贷款 Domestic Medium and Long - term Loans	260.04	46.78
3. 储蓄存款 Savings Deposits	774.07	59.50	其中：中资企业贷款 Of Which：Loans to Chinese - funded Enterprises	175.00	49.44
其中：定期存款 Of Which：Time Deposits	685.51	35.38			
4. 其他类存款 Other Deposits	40.73	3.58	外商投资企业贷款 Loans to Foreign - funded Enterprises	16.81	- 1.68
5. 境外存款 Foreign Deposits	0.16	- 0.02			
二、境内中长期借款 Domestic Medium and Long - term Borrowing		- 1.40	（2）境外中长期贷款 Overseas Medium and Long - term Loans	8.03	1.12
三、卖出回购证券 Repo	1.16	0.76	3. 进出口贸易融资 Financing for Import and Export Trades	21.97	8.13
四、境外筹资 Overseas Financing	219.79	- 9.18	4. 票据融资 Paper Financing	0.69	0.04
五、向中央银行借款 Borrowings from the Central Bank	3.39	- 4.27	其中：贴现 Of Which：Discount	0.28	- 0.09
六、中央银行存款 Deposits by the Central Bank	91.00	0.80	5. 各项垫款 Total Advances	47.77	- 4.23
七、应付及暂收款 Accounts Payable and Receipts on Account	87.11	13.70	6. 境外筹资转贷款 On - lending of Overseas Financing	203.98	- 10.07

续表
Continued

项　目 Items	余　额 Balance	比年初增减额 Changes within the Year	项　目 Items	余　额 Balance	比年初增减额 Changes within the Year
其中：应付及预提利息 Of Which: Interest Payable and Accrued	16.97	-8.43	二、投资 Investments	747.48	135.92
八、同业存放 Due to Banks and Other Financial Institutions	51.22	-3.00	1. 购买有价证券 Purchase of Securities	606.35	120.04
1. 境内同业存放 Due to Domestic Banks and Other Financial Institutions	45.12	-5.98	其中：购买境外有价证券 Of Which: Purchase of Foreign Securities	602.63	119.49
2. 境外同业存放 Due to Overseas Banks and Other Financial Institutions	6.10	2.98	2. 其他投资 Other Investments	141.13	15.88
九、同业拆入 Placements from Banks and Other Financial Institutions	71.09	58.74	其中：投资境外 Of Which: Overseas	5.66	-8.25
1. 境内同业拆入 Placements from Domestic Banks and Other Financial Institutions	8.08	4.67	三、应收及预付款 Accounts Receivable and Advance Payments	68.75	-14.09
2. 境外同业拆入 Placements from Overseas Banks and Other Financial Institutions	63.01	54.07	其中：应收及预付利息 Of Which: Interest Receivable and Paid in Advance	8.71	-4.11
十、委托基金存款（净） Designated Fund Deposits (Net)	0.02	0.01	四、买入返售证券 Reverse Repo		
十一、外汇买卖 Foreign Exchange Dealings	131.65	134.05	五、存放中央银行 Deposits with the Central Bank	23.07	0.96
其中：结售汇 Of Which: Purchase and Sale of Foreign Exchange	94.24	-1.37	其中：缴存准备金 Of Which: Reserves with the Central Bank	15.38	0.94
十二、境内联行存放 Due to Domestic Branches	-33.67	3.57	六、存放同业 Due from Banks and Other Financial Institutions	46.89	2.90
十三、境外联行存放 Due to Overseas Branches	32.82	-47.08	1. 存放境内同业 Due from Domestic Banks and Other Financial Institutions	2.58	-5.75
十四、各项准备 Total Provisions	43.97	2.44	2. 存放境外同业 Due from Overseas Banks and Other Financial Institutions	44.31	8.65
其中：贷款呆账准备金 Of Which: Provisions for Bad Loans	14.59	2.32	七、拆放同业 Placements with Banks and Other Financial Institutions	505.23	67.85
十五、所有者权益 Owner's Equity	381.09	83.24	1. 拆放境内同业 Placements with Domestic Banks and Other Financial Institutions	7.48	-2.03
其中：实收资本 Of Which: Paid-in Capital	240.98	117.98	2. 拆放境外同业 Placements with Overseas Banks and Other Financial Institutions	497.75	69.88
当年结益 Net Earnings	22.10	22.10			
十六、其他 Others	-16.33	-2.08	八、存放境外联行 Due from Overseas Branches	65.03	30.57
			九、库存现金 Cash in Vault	18.33	0.18
资金来源总计 Total Sources	**2204.36**	**294.38**	**资金运用总计 Total Uses**	**2204.36**	**294.38**

国家银行外汇信贷收支表

Sources and Uses of Credit Funds of State Banks（Foreign Currency）

（2003 年末）

（Year - end of 2003）

单位：亿美元

Unit：100 Million US Dollars

项目 Items	余额 Balance	比年初增减额 Changes within the Year	项目 Items	余额 Balance	比年初增减额 Changes within the Year
一、各项存款 Total Deposits	1093.30	-46.82	一、各项贷款 Total Loans	936.55	206.96
1. 单位活期存款 Demand Deposits by Enterprises	154.96	20.57	1. 短期贷款 Short - term Loans	297.76	111.35
其中：中资企业存款 Of Which：Deposits by Chinese - funded Enterprises	110.12	21.49	（1）境内短期贷款 Domestic Short - term Loans	297.69	111.28
			其中：中资企业贷款 Of Which：Loans to Chinese - funded Enterprises	182.23	74.85
外商投资企业存款 Deposits by Foreign - funded Enterprises	37.00	-0.59	外商投资企业贷款 Loans to Foreign - funded Enterprises	90.66	32.72
2. 单位定期存款 Time Deposits by Enterprises	153.07	-37.65			
其中：中资企业存款 Of Which：Deposits by Chinese - funded Enterprises	128.56	-26.96	（2）境外短期贷款 Overseas Short - term Loans	0.07	0.07
			2. 中长期贷款 Medium and Long - term Loans	335.02	66.09
外商投资企业存款 Deposits by Foreign - funded Enterprises	4.80	-5.14	（1）境内中长期贷款 Domestic Medium and Long - term Loans	322.34	61.44
3. 储蓄存款 Savings Deposits	733.73	-40.37			
			其中：中资企业贷款 Of Which：Loans to Chinese - funded Enterprises	212.43	37.85
其中：定期存款 Of Which：Time Deposits	629.38	-56.16			
4. 其他类存款 Other Deposits	51.38	10.64	外商投资企业贷款 Loans to Foreign - funded Enterprises	18.20	1.39
5. 境外存款 Foreign Deposits	0.16	-0.01			
			（2）境外中长期贷款 Overseas Medium and Long - term Loans	12.68	4.65
二、境内中长期借款 Domestic Medium and Long - term Borrowing	5.00	5.00			
			3. 进出口贸易融资 Financing for Import and Export Trades	65.95	43.97
三、卖出回购证券 Repo	13.08	11.92			
四、境外筹资 Overseas Financing	206.26	-13.60	4. 票据融资 Paper Financing	1.08	0.39
五、向中央银行借款 Borrowings from the Central Bank	3.28	-0.11	其中：贴现 Of Which：Discount	0.72	0.44
六、中央银行存款 Deposits by the Central Bank	64.89	-26.11	5. 各项垫款 Total Advances	44.17	-3.51
七、应付及暂收款 Accounts Payable and Receipts on Account	87.35	0.05	6. 境外筹资转贷款 On - lending of Overseas Financing	192.57	-11.33

续表
Continued

项　目 Items	余　额 Balance	比年初增减额 Changes within the Year	项　目 Items	余　额 Balance	比年初增减额 Changes within the Year
其中：应付及预提利息 Of Which: Interest Payable and Accrued	14.16	-2.81	二、投资 Investments	722.39	-25.29
八、同业存放 Due to Banks and Other Financial Institutions	61.19	-21.47	1. 购买有价证券 Purchase of Securities	593.70	-12.83
1. 境内同业存放 Due to Domestic Banks and Other Financial Institutions	38.37	-6.77	其中：购买境外有价证券 Of Which: Purchase of Foreign Securities	592.06	-10.75
2. 境外同业存放 Due to Overseas Banks and Other Financial Institutions	22.82	-14.70	2. 其他投资 Other Investments	128.69	-12.46
九、同业拆入 Placements from Banks and Other Financial Institutions	83.34	12.25	其中：投资境外 Of Which: Overseas	4.55	-1.13
1. 境内同业拆入 Placements from Domestic Banks and Other Financial Institutions	3.90	-4.18	三、应收及预付款 Accounts Receivable and Advance Payments	104.96	36.13
2. 境外同业拆入 Placements from Overseas Banks and Other Financial Institutions	79.44	16.43	其中：应收及预付利息 Of Which: Interest Receivable and Paid in Advance	4.34	-4.38
十、委托基金存款（净） Designated Fund Deposits (Net)	0.01	-0.01	四、买入返售证券 Reverse Repo	0.10	0.10
十一、外汇买卖 Foreign Exchange Dealings	147.24	15.57	五、存放中央银行 Deposits with the Central Bank	25.23	2.16
其中：结售汇 Of Which: Purchase and Sale of Foreign Exchange	104.98	10.89	其中：缴存准备金 Of Which: Reserves with the Central Bank	15.93	0.55
十二、境内联行存放 Due to Domestic Branches	-37.90	-4.46	六、存放同业 Due from Banks and Other Financial Institutions	112.17	63.29
十三、境外联行存放 Due to Overseas Branches	58.42	57.02	1. 存放境内同业 Due from Domestic Banks and Other Financial Institutions	19.95	17.37
十四、各项准备 Total Provisions	265.34	221.36	2. 存放境外同业 Due from Overseas Banks and Other Financial Institutions	92.22	45.92
其中：贷款呆账准备金 Of Which: Provisions for Bad Loans	265.34	221.36	七、拆放同业 Placements with Banks and Other Financial Institutions	740.32	235.07
十五、所有者权益 Owner's Equity	584.53	203.42	（1）拆放境内同业 Placements with Domestic Banks and Other Financial Institutions	427.24	419.75
其中：实收资本 Of Which: Paid - in Capital	562.09	321.11	（2）拆放境外同业 Placements with Overseas Banks and Other Financial Institutions	313.08	-184.68
当年结益 Net Earnings	22.43	22.43			
十六、其他 Others	51.18	67.77	八、存放境外联行 Due from Overseas Branches	22.74	-40.34
			九、库存现金 Cash in Vault	22.05	3.70
资金来源总计 Total Sources	**2686.51**	**481.78**	**资金运用总计 Total Uses**	**2686.51**	**481.78**

国家银行外汇信贷收支表

Sources and Uses of Credit Funds of State Banks（Foreign Currency）

（2004 年末）

（Year - end of 2004）

单位：亿美元

Unit：100 Million US Dollars

项　　目 Items	余　额 Balance	比年初增减额 Changes within the Year	项　　目 Items	余　额 Balance	比年初增减额 Changes within the Year
一、各项存款 Total Deposits	1081.86	- 11.65	一、各项贷款 Total Loans	903.15	77.64
1. 单位活期存款 Demand Deposits by Enterprises	186.17	31.18	1. 短期贷款 Short - term Loans	269.00	24.58
其中：中资企业存款 Of Which：Deposits by Chinese - funded Enterprises	132.92	23.08	（1）境内短期贷款 Domestic Short - term Loans	268.95	24.59
外商投资企业存款 Deposits by Foreign - funded Enterprises	42.15	5.16	其中：中资企业贷款 Of Which：Loans to Chinese - funded Enterprises	156.12	10.22
			外商投资企业贷款 Loans to Foreign - funded Enterprises	88.19	10.65
2. 单位定期存款 Time Deposits by Enterprises	152.52	- 0.57			
其中：中资企业存款 Of Which：Deposits by Chinese - funded Enterprises	125.84	- 2.72	（2）境外短期贷款 Overseas Short - term Loans	0.05	- 0.01
			2. 中长期贷款 Medium and Long - term Loans	351.99	36.91
外商投资企业存款 Deposits by Foreign - funded Enterprises	4.36	- 0.44	（1）境内中长期贷款 Domestic Medium and Long - term Loans	338.26	35.83
3. 储蓄存款 Savings Deposits	663.26	- 70.59	其中：中资企业贷款 Of Which：Loans to Chinese - funded Enterprises	201.96	- 3.98
其中：定期存款 Of Which：Time Deposits	540.04	- 89.41			
4. 其他类存款 Other Deposits	79.31	27.89	外商投资企业贷款 Loans to Foreign - funded Enterprises	29.22	17.90
5. 境外存款 Foreign Deposits	0.60	0.44	（2）境外中长期贷款 Overseas Medium and Long - term Loans	13.73	1.08
二、境内中长期借款 Domestic Medium and Long - term Borrowing	6.00	1.00			
			3. 进出口贸易融资 Financing for Import and Export Trades	87.17	21.81
三、卖出回购资产 Assets Repo（Including Securities）	17.90	4.82			
四、境外筹资 Overseas Financing	226.58	19.89	4. 票据融资 Paper Financing	1.31	0.23
五、向中央银行借款 Borrowings from the Central Bank	3.00	- 0.28	其中：贴现 Of Which：Discount	1.03	0.31
六、中央银行存款 Deposits by the Central Bank	62.82	- 2.07	5. 各项垫款 Total Advances	11.00	- 7.88
七、应付及暂收款 Accounts Payable and Receipts on Account	63.97	- 24.81	6. 境外筹资转贷款 On - lending of Overseas Financing	182.68	1.99

续表
Continued

项 目 Items	余 额 Balance	比年初增减额 Changes within the Year	项 目 Items	余 额 Balance	比年初增减额 Changes within the Year
其中：应付及预提利息 Of Which: Interest Payable and Accrued	11.87	-2.29	二、投资 Investments	1015.10	292.36
八、同业存放 Due to Banks and Other Financial Institutions	60.07	-1.14	1. 购买有价证券 Purchase of Securities	816.53	241.38
1. 境内同业存放 Due to Domestic Banks and Other Financial Institutions	56.46	18.07	其中：购买境外有价证券 Of Which: Purchase of Foreign Securities	809.91	236.40
2. 境外同业存放 Due to Overseas Banks and Other Financial Institutions	3.61	-19.21	2. 其他投资 Other Investments	198.57	50.98
九、同业拆入 Placements from Banks and Other Financial Institutions	26.64	-56.73	其中：投资境外 Of Which: Overseas	0.66	-3.90
(1) 境内同业拆入 Placements from Domestic Banks and Other Financial Institutions	12.42	8.49	三、应收及预付款 Accounts Receivable and Advance Payments	96.98	-9.13
(2) 境外同业拆入 Placements from Overseas Banks and Other Financial Institutions	14.22	-65.22	其中：应收及预付利息 Of Which: Interest Receivable and Paid in Advance	12.27	-0.95
十、委托基金存款（净） Designated Fund Deposits (Net)	-0.01	-0.02	四、买入返售资产 Assets Reverse Repo (Including Securities)	0.15	0.05
十一、外汇买卖 Foreign Exchange Dealings	360.36	213.05	五、存放中央银行 Deposits with the Central Bank	25.58	0.35
其中：结售汇 Of Which: Purchase and Sale of Foreign Exchange	95.62	-9.70	其中：缴存准备金 Of Which: Reserves with the Central Bank	15.46	-0.47
十二、境内联行存放 Due to Domestic Branches	-14.21	23.95	六、存放同业 Due from Banks and Other Financial Institutions	26.04	-86.19
十三、境外联行存放 Due to Overseas Branches	50.81	-7.61	1. 存放境内同业 Due from Domestic Banks and Other Financial Institutions	10.88	-9.07
十四、各项准备 Total Provisions	31.03	-234.33	2. 存放境外同业 Due from Overseas Banks and Other Financial Institutions	15.16	-77.12
其中：贷款损失准备 Of Which: Provisions for Loan Losses	24.56	-224.91	七、拆放同业 Placements with Banks and Other Financial Institutions	379.55	-360.79
十五、所有者权益 Owner's Equity	538.27	-46.23	(1) 拆放境内同业 Placements with Domestic Banks and Other Financial Institutions	3.78	-423.46
其中：实收资本 Of Which: Paid-in Capital	135.39	-426.70	(2) 拆放境外同业 Placements with Overseas Banks and Other Financial Institutions	375.77	62.67
当年结益 Net Earnings	65.35	65.35			
十六、其他 Others	42.51	102.67	八、存放境外联行 Due from Overseas Branches	86.32	63.58
			九、库存现金 Cash in Vault	24.73	2.64
资金来源总计 Total Sources	**2557.60**	**-19.49**	**资金运用总计 Total Uses**	**2557.60**	**-19.49**

国家银行外汇信贷收支表

Sources and Uses of Credit Funds of State Banks（Foreign Currency）

（2005 年末）

（Year – end of 2005）

单位：亿美元

Unit：100 Million US Dollars

项目 Items	余额 Balance	比年初增减额 Changes within the Year	项目 Items	余额 Balance	比年初增减额 Changes within the Year
一、各项存款 Total Deposits	1106.37	24.45	一、各项贷款 Total Loans	985.11	108.12
1. 单位活期存款 Demand Deposits by Enterprises	250.57	64.38	1. 短期贷款 Short – term Loans	234.32	– 8.77
其中：中资企业存款 Of Which：Deposits by Chinese – funded Enterprises	179.59	46.27	（1）境内短期贷款 Domestic Short – term Loans	234.32	– 8.72
			其中：中资企业贷款 Of Which：Loans to Chinese – funded Enterprises	128.50	– 3.93
外商投资企业存款 Deposits by Foreign – funded Enterprises	47.57	3.80	外商投资企贷款 Loans to Fureign Funded Enterprises	77.55	– 8.16
2. 单位定期存款 Time Deposits by Enterprises	173.78	21.24	（2）境外短期贷款 Overseas Short – term Loans		– 0.05
其中：中资企业存款 Of Which：Deposits by Chinese – funded Enterprises	93.15	– 32.82	2. 中长期贷款 Medium and Long – term Loans	474.50	118.81
外商投资企业存款 Deposits by Foreign – funded Enterprises	4.17	– 0.64	（1）境内中长期贷款 Domestic Medium and Long – term Loans	452.88	110.92
3. 储蓄存款 Savings Deposits	596.72	– 66.56	其中：中资企业贷款 Of Which：Loans to Chinese – funded Enterprises	242.96	43.36
其中：定期存款 Of Which：Time Deposits	479.00	– 61.05	外商投资企业贷款 Loans to Foreign – funded Enterprises	34.67	4.01
4. 其他类存款 Other Deposits	83.62	4.30	（2）境外中长期贷款 Overseas Medium and Long – term Loans	21.62	7.89
5. 境外存款 Foreign Deposits	1.68	1.09	3. 进出口贸易融资 Financing for Import and Export Trades	113.17	27.15
二、境内中长期筹资 Domestic Medium and Long – term Borrowing	30.03	24.03	4. 票据融资 Paper Financing	0.73	– 0.58
三、卖出回购资产 Assets Repo（Including Securities）	65.15	47.25	其中：贴现 Of Which：Discount	0.68	– 0.34
四、境外筹资 Overseas Financing	206.32	– 20.43	5. 各项垫款 Total Advances	9.20	0.60
五、向中央银行借款 Borrowings from the Central Bank		– 3.00	6. 境外筹资转贷款 On – lending of Overseas Financing	153.19	– 29.09
六、中央银行存款 Deposits by the Central Bank	35.43	– 25.53			
七、应付及暂收款 Accounts Payable and Receipts on Account	246.32	183.44			

续表
Continued

项　　目 Items	余　额 Balance	比年初增减额 Changes within the Year	项　　目 Items	余　额 Balance	比年初增减额 Changes within the Year
其中：应付及预提利息 Of Which：Interest Payable and Accrued	22.20	10.25	二、投资 Investments	1090.13	74.96
八、同业存放 Due to Banks and Other Financial Institutions	65.42	5.80	1. 购买有价证券 Purchase of Securities	1074.57	257.92
1. 境内同业存放 Due to Domestic Banks and Other Financial Institutions	63.18	6.53	其中：购买境外有价证券 Of Which：Purchase of Foreign Securities	1064.79	254.86
2. 境外同业存放 Due to Overseas Banks and Other Financial Institutions	2.24	-0.73	2. 其他投资 Other Investments	15.56	-182.96
九、同业拆入 Placements from Banks and Other Financial Institutions	24.72	-1.87	其中：投资境外 Of Which：Overseas	0.67	0.01
1. 境内同业拆入 Placements from Domestic Banks and Other Financial Institutions	23.40	11.03	三、应收及预付款 Accounts Receivable and Advance Payments	122.80	27.76
2. 境外同业拆入 Placements from Overseas Banks and Other Financial Institutions	1.32	-12.90	其中：应收及预付利息 Of Which：Interest Receivable and Paid in Advance	26.59	10.72
十、委托基金存款（净） Designated Fund Deposits（Net）	-0.01		四、买入返售资产 Assets Reverse Repo（Including Securities）	3.25	2.60
十一、外汇买卖 Foreign Exchange Dealings	491.14	149.97	五、存放中央银行 Deposits with the Central Bank	33.91	10.27
其中：结售汇 Of Which：Purchase and Sale of Foreign Exchange	58.06	-37.49	其中：缴存准备金 Of Which：Reserves with the Central Bank	21.04	5.58
十二、境内联行存放 Due to Domestic Branches	-25.39	-11.66	六、存放同业 Due from Banks and Other Financial Institutions	37.79	11.52
十三、境外联行存放 Due to Overseas Branches	15.25	-65.10	1. 存放境内同业 Due from Domestic Banks and Other Financial Institutions	5.77	-5.07
十四、各项准备 Total Provisions	27.92	-2.70	2. 存放境外同业 Due from Overseas Banks and Other Financial Institutions	32.02	16.59
其中：贷款损失准备 Of Which：Provisions for Loan Losses	23.46	-1.12	七、拆放同业 Placements with Banks and Other Financial Institutions	475.72	96.68
十五、所有者权益 Owner's Equity	213.83	-189.42	1. 拆放境内同业 Placements with Domestic Banks and Other Financial Institutions	4.89	1.11
其中：实收资本 Of Which：Paid-in Capital	153.10	151.00	2. 拆放境外同业 Placements with Overseas Banks and Other Financial Institutions	470.83	95.57
当年结益 Net Earnings	64.42	64.42			
十六、其他 Others	439.88	297.33	八、存放境外联行 Due from Overseas Branches	172.62	86.29
			九、库存现金 Cash in Vault	21.05	-5.64
资金来源总计 Total Sources	**2942.38**	**412.56**	**资金运用总计 Total Uses**	**2942.38**	**412.56**

3. 政策性银行外汇信贷收支表*（1998—2005 年）
Sources and Uses of Credit Funds of Policy Banks（Foreign Currency）（1998—2005）

政策性银行外汇信贷收支表
Sources and Uses of Credit Funds of Policy Banks（Foreign Currency）

（1998 年末）

（Year - end of 1998）

单位：亿美元
Unit：100 Million US Dollars

项目 Items	余额 Balance	比年初增减额 Changes within the Year	项目 Items	余额 Balance	比年初增减额 Changes within the Year
一、各项存款 Total Deposits	0.45	-0.49	一、各项贷款 Total Loans	5.79	2.55
1. 单位活期存款 Demand Deposits by Enterprises	0.45	-0.48	1. 短期贷款 Short - term Loans	3.31	2.77
其中：中资企业存款 Of Which：Deposits by Chinese - funded Enterprises	0.45	-0.48	（1）境内短期贷款 Domestic Short - term Loans	3.31	2.77
外商投资企业存款 Deposits by Foreign - funded Enterprises			其中：中资企业贷款 Of Which：Loans to Chinese - funded Enterprises	3.31	2.77
2. 单位定期存款 Time Deposits by Enterprises			外商投资企业贷款 Loans to Foreign - funded Enterprises		
其中：中资企业存款 Of Which：Deposits by Chinese - funded Enterprises			（2）境外短期贷款 Overseas Short - term Loans		
外商投资企业存款 Deposits by Foreign - funded Enterprises			2. 中长期贷款 Medium and Long - term Loans	1.63	-0.57
3. 储蓄存款 Savings Deposits			（1）境内中长期贷款 Domestic Medium and Long - term Loans	1.20	-1.00
其中：定期存款 Of Which：Time Deposits			其中：中资企业贷款 Of Which：Loans to Chinese - funded Enterprises		
4. 其他类存款 Other Deposits		-0.01	外商投资企业贷款 Loans to Foreign - funded Enterprises		
5. 境外存款 Foreign Deposits			（2）境外中长期贷款 Overseas Medium and Long - term Loans	0.43	0.43
二、境内中长期借款 Domestic Medium and Long - term Borrowing			3. 进出口贸易融资 Financing for Import and Export Trades	0.82	0.34
三、卖出回购证券 Repo					
四、境外筹资 Overseas Financing	19.63	6.04	4. 票据融资 Paper Financing		
五、向中央银行借款 Borrowings from the Central Bank	0.32	0.17	5. 逾期类贷款 Overdue Loans	0.03	0.01

续表
Continued

项　目 Items	余　额 Balance	比年初增减额 Changes within the Year	项　目 Items	余　额 Balance	比年初增减额 Changes within the Year
六、中央银行存款 Deposits by the Central Bank	1.10		二、投资 Investments	0.06	-0.56
七、同业存放 Due to Banks and Other Financial Institutions			1. 购买有价证券 Purchase of Securities	0.05	-0.56
			其中：购买境外有价证券 Of Which: Purchase of Foreign Securities	0.05	-0.56
1. 境内同业存放 Due to Domestic Banks and Other Financial Institutions			2. 其他投资 Other Investments	0.01	
2. 境外同业存放 Due to Overseas Banks and Other Financial Institutions			其中：投资境外 Of Which: Overseas	0.01	
八、同业拆入 Placements from Banks and Other Financial Institutions	3.18	3.18	三、境外筹资转贷款 On-lending of Overseas Financing	17.63	6.59
			四、存放中央银行 Deposits with the Central Bank		
1. 境内同业拆入 Placements from Domestic Banks and Other Financial Institutions	1.88	1.88	其中：缴存准备金 Of Which: Reserves with the Central Bank		
2. 境外同业拆入 Placements from Overseas Banks and Other Financial Institutions	1.30	1.30	五、存放同业 Due from Banks and Other Financial Institutions	0.32	-0.02
九、委托基金存款 Designated Fund Deposits			1. 存放境内同业 Due from Domestic Banks and Other Financial Institutions	0.04	0.02
十、外汇买卖 Foreign Exchange Dealings	0.12	-0.15	2. 存放境外同业 Due from Overseas Banks and Other Financial Institutions	0.28	-0.04
其中：结售汇 Of Which: Purchase and Sale of Foreign Exchange					
十一、境内联行存放 Due to Domestic Branches			六、拆放同业 Placements with Banks and Other Financial Institutions		-0.37
十二、境外联行存放 Due to Overseas Branches			1. 拆放境内同业 Placements with Domestic Banks and Other Financial Institutions		-0.01
十三、所有者权益 Owner's Equity	1.83	0.34			
其中：实收资本 Of Which: Paid-in Capital	1.42	0.17	2. 拆放境外同业 Placements with Overseas Banks and Other Financial Institutions		-0.36
当年结益 Net Earnings	0.16	0.16	七、存放境外联行 Due from Overseas Branches		
十四、其他 Others	-2.83	-0.90	八、库存现金 Cash in Vault		
资金来源总计 Total Sources	**23.80**	**8.19**	**资金运用总计 Total Uses**	**23.80**	**8.19**

* 本表机构包括国家开发银行（1995—2005年）、中国进出口银行（1995—2005年）、中国农业发展银行（2001—2005年）。

* Policy Banks of this statement include the China Development Bank (1995—2005), the Export-Import Bank of China (1995—2005), and Agricultural Development Bank of China (2001—2005).

政策性银行外汇信贷收支表

Sources and Uses of Credit Funds of Policy Banks（Foreign Currency）

（1999 年末）

（Year - end of 1999）

单位：亿美元

Unit：100 Million US Dollars

项　目 Items	余　额 Balance	比年初增减额 Changes within the Year
一、各项存款 Total Deposits	0.16	-0.29
1. 单位活期存款 Demand Deposits by Enterprises	0.15	-0.30
其中：中资企业存款 Of Which：Deposits by Chinese - funded Enterprises	0.15	-0.30
外商投资企业存款 Deposits by Foreign - funded Enterprises		
2. 单位定期存款 Time Deposits by Enterprises		
其中：中资企业存款 Of Which：Deposits by Chinese - funded Enterprises		
外商投资企业存款 Deposits by Foreign - funded Enterprises		
3. 储蓄存款 Savings Deposits		
其中：定期存款 Of Which：Time Deposits		
4. 其他类存款 Other Deposits	0.01	0.01
5. 境外存款 Foreign Deposits		
二、境内中长期借款 Domestic Medium and Long - term Borrowing	1.00	1.00
三、卖出回购证券 Repo		
四、境外筹资 Overseas Financing	35.32	15.69
五、向中央银行借款 Borrowings from the Central Bank	0.10	-0.22
六、中央银行存款 Deposits by the Central Bank	1.10	
七、同业存放 Due to Banks and Other Financial Institutions		

项　目 Items	余　额 Balance	比年初增减额 Changes within the Year
一、各项贷款 Total Loans	3.18	-2.61
1. 短期贷款 Short - term Loans	0.71	-2.60
（1）境内短期贷款 Domestic Short - term Loans	0.71	-2.60
其中：中资企业贷款 Of Which：Loans to Chinese - funded Enterprises	0.71	-2.60
外商投资企业贷款 Loans to Foreign - funded Enterprises		
（2）境外短期贷款 Overseas Short - term Loans		
2. 中长期贷款 Medium and Long - term Loans	1.76	0.13
（1）境内中长期贷款 Domestic Medium and Long - term Loans	1.20	
其中：中资企业贷款 Of Which：Loans to Chinese - funded Enterprises		
外商投资企业贷款 Loans to Foreign - funded Enterprises		
（2）境外中长期贷款 Overseas Medium and Long - term Loans	0.56	0.13
3. 进出口贸易融资 Financing for Import and Export Trades	0.62	-0.20
4. 票据融资 Paper Financing		
5. 逾期类贷款 Overdue Loans	0.09	0.06
二、投资 Investments	0.42	0.36
1. 购买有价证券 Purchase of Securities	0.40	0.35

续表
Continued

项　目 Items	余　额 Balance	比年初增减额 Changes within the Year	项　目 Items	余　额 Balance	比年初增减额 Changes within the Year
1. 境内同业存放 Due to Domestic Banks and Other Financial Institutions			其中：购买境外有价证券 Of Which: Purchase of Foreign Securities	0.40	0.35
2. 境外同业存放 Due to Overseas Banks and Other Financial Institutions			2. 其他投资 Other Investments	0.02	0.01
			其中：投资境外 Of Which: Overseas	0.02	0.01
八、同业拆入 Placements from Banks and Other Financial Institutions	1.07	-2.11	三、境外筹资转贷款 On-lending of Overseas Financing	31.08	13.45
1. 境内同业拆入 Placements from Domestic Banks and Other Financial Institutions	0.92	-0.96	四、存放中央银行 Deposits with the Central Bank		
			其中：缴存准备金 Of Which: Reserves with the Central Bank		
2. 境外同业拆入 Placements from Overseas Banks and Other Financial Institutions	0.15	-1.15	五、存放同业 Due from Banks and Other Financial Institutions	0.31	-0.01
九、委托基金存款 Designated Fund Deposits					
十、外汇买卖 Foreign Exchange Dealings	-0.07	-0.19	1. 存放境内同业 Due from Domestic Banks and Other Financial Institutions		-0.04
其中：结售汇 Of Which: Purchase and Sale of Foreign Exchange			2. 存放境外同业 Due from Overseas Banks and Other Financial Institutions	0.31	0.03
十一、境内联行存放 Due to Domestic Branches			六、拆放同业 Placements with Banks and Other Financial Institutions	3.00	3.00
十二、境外联行存放 Due to Overseas Branches					
十三、所有者权益 Owner's Equity	2.18	0.35	1. 拆放境内同业 Placements with Domestic Banks and Other Financial Institutions	0.30	0.30
其中：实收资本 Of Which: Paid-in Capital	1.72	0.30	2. 拆放境外同业 Placements with Overseas Banks and Other Financial Institutions	2.70	2.70
当年结益 Net Earnings	0.06	0.06			
十四、其他 Others	-2.87	-0.04	七、存放境外联行 Due from Overseas Branches		
			八、库存现金 Cash in Vault		
资金来源总计 Total Sources	**37.99**	**14.19**	**资金运用总计 Total Uses**	**37.99**	**14.19**

政策性银行外汇信贷收支表
Sources and Uses of Credit Funds of Policy Banks（Foreign Currency）

（2000 年末）

（Year - end of 2000）

单位：亿美元

Unit：100 Million US Dollars

项　　目 Items	余　额 Balance	比年初增减额 Changes within the Year	项　　目 Items	余　额 Balance	比年初增减额 Changes within the Year
一、各项存款 Total Deposits	0.08	-0.08	一、各项贷款 Total Loans	4.90	1.72
1. 单位活期存款 Demand Deposits by Enterprises	0.07	-0.08	1. 短期贷款 Short - term Loans	2.07	1.36
其中：中资企业存款 Of Which：Deposits by Chinese - funded Enterprises	0.07	-0.08	（1）境内短期贷款 Domestic Short - term Loans	2.07	1.36
			其中：中资企业贷款 Of Which：Loans to Chinese - funded Enterprises	2.07	1.36
外商投资企业存款 Deposits by Foreign - funded Enterprises			外商投资企业贷款 Loans to Foreign - funded Enterprises		
2. 单位定期存款 Time Deposits by Enterprises					
其中：中资企业存款 Of Which：Deposits by Chinese - funded Enterprises			（2）境外短期贷款 Overseas Short - term Loans		
			2. 中长期贷款 Medium and Long - term Loans	2.18	0.42
外商投资企业存款 Deposits by Foreign - funded Enterprises			（1）境内中长期贷款 Domestic Medium and Long - term Loans	0.10	-1.10
3. 储蓄存款 Savings Deposits			其中：中资企业贷款 Of Which：Loans to Chinese - funded Enterprises		
其中：定期存款 Of Which：Time Deposits					
4. 其他类存款 Other Deposits	0.01		外商投资企业贷款 Loans to Foreign - funded Enterprises		
5. 境外存款 Foreign Deposits			（2）境外中长期贷款 Overseas Medium and Long - term Loans	2.08	1.52
二、境内中长期借款 Domestic Medium and Long - term Borrowing		-1.00	3. 进出口贸易融资 Financing for Import and Export Trades	0.54	-0.08
三、卖出回购证券 Repo	0.10	0.10			
四、境外筹资 Overseas Financing	32.36	-2.96	4. 票据融资 Paper Financing		
五、向中央银行借款 Borrowings from the Central Bank		-0.10	其中：贴现 Of Which：Discount		
六、中央银行存款 Deposits by the Central Bank	0.42	-0.68	5. 逾期类贷款 Overdue Loans	0.12	0.03
七、同业存放 Due to Banks and Other Financial Institutions			二、投资 Investments	0.72	0.30

续表
Continued

项　目 Items	余　额 Balance	比年初增减额 Changes within the Year	项　目 Items	余　额 Balance	比年初增减额 Changes within the Year
1. 境内同业存放 Due to Domestic Banks and Other Financial Institutions			1. 购买有价证券 Purchase of Securities	0.71	0.31
2. 境外同业存放 Due to Overseas Banks and Other Financial Institutions			其中：购买境外有价证券 Of Which: Purchase of Foreign Securities	0.71	0.31
八、同业拆入 Placements from Banks and Other Financial Institutions	1.23	0.16	2. 其他投资 Other Investments	0.01	-0.01
1. 境内同业拆入 Placements from Domestic Banks and Other Financial Institutions	0.30	-0.62	其中：投资境外 Of Which: Overseas	0.01	-0.01
2. 境外同业拆入 Placements from Overseas Banks and Other Financial Institutions	0.93	0.78	三、境外筹资转贷款 On-lending of Overseas Financing	41.93	10.85
九、委托基金存款 Designated Fund Deposits			四、存放中央银行 Deposits with the Central Bank		
十、外汇买卖 Foreign Exchange Dealings	4.83	4.83	其中：缴存准备金 Of Which: Reserves with the Central Bank		
其中：结售汇 Of Which: Purchase and Sale of Foreign Exchange			五、存放同业 Due from Banks and Other Financial Institutions	0.09	-0.22
十一、境内联行存放 Due to Domestic Branches	10.29	10.29	1. 存放境内同业 Due from Domestic Banks and Other Financial Institutions		
十二、境外联行存放 Due to Overseas Branches			2. 存放境外同业 Due from Overseas Banks and Other Financial Institutions	0.09	-0.22
十三、所有者权益 Owner's Equity	3.52	1.34	六、拆放同业 Placements with Banks and Other Financial Institutions	2.01	-0.99
其中：实收资本 Of Which: Paid-in Capital	2.72	1.00	1. 拆放境内同业 Placements with Domestic Banks and Other Financial Institutions		-0.30
当年结益 Net Earnings	0.34	0.34	2. 拆放境外同业 Placements with Overseas Banks and Other Financial Institutions	2.01	-0.69
十四、其他 Others	-3.18	-0.24	七、存放境外联行 Due from Overseas Branches		
			八、库存现金 Cash in Vault		
资金来源总计 **Total Sources**	**49.65**	**11.66**	**资金运用总计** **Total Uses**	**49.65**	**11.66**

政策性银行外汇信贷收支表

Sources and Uses of Credit Funds of Policy Banks（Foreign Currency）

（2001 年末）

（Year - end of 2001）

单位：亿美元

Unit：100 Million US Dollars

项　目 Items	余　额 Balance	比年初增减额 Changes within the Year	项　目 Items	余　额 Balance	比年初增减额 Changes within the Year
一、各项存款 Total Deposits	0.07	-0.01	一、各项贷款 Total Loans	57.65	10.83
1. 单位活期存款 Demand Deposits by Enterprises	0.07		1. 短期贷款 Short - term Loans	2.89	0.82
其中：中资企业存款 Of Which：Deposits by Chinese - funded Enterprises	0.07		（1）境内短期贷款 Domestic Short - term Loans	2.89	0.82
外商投资企业存款 Deposits by Foreign - funded Enterprises			其中：中资企业贷款 Of Which：Loans to Chinese - funded Enterprises	2.89	0.82
			外商投资企业贷款 Loans to Foreign - funded Enterprises		
2. 单位定期存款 Time Deposits by Enterprises			（2）境外短期贷款 Overseas Short - term Loans		
其中：中资企业存款 Of Which：Deposits by Chinese - funded Enterprises			2. 中长期贷款 Medium and Long - term Loans	3.68	1.50
外商投资企业存款 Deposits by Foreign - funded Enterprises			（1）境内中长期贷款 Domestic Medium and Long - term Loans	0.10	
3. 储蓄存款 Savings Deposits			其中：中资企业贷款 Of Which：Loans to Chinese - funded Enterprises		
其中：定期存款 Of Which：Time Deposits					
4. 其他类存款 Other Deposits		-0.01	外商投资企业贷款 Loans to Foreign - funded Enterprises		
5. 境外存款 Foreign Deposits			（2）境外中长期贷款 Overseas Medium and Long - term Loans	3.58	1.50
二、境内中长期借款 Domestic Medium and Long - term Borrowing			3. 进出口贸易融资 Financing for Import and Export Trades	0.47	-0.15
三、卖出回购证券 Repo	0.40	0.30			
四、境外筹资 Overseas Financing	52.14	19.78	4. 票据融资 Paper Financing		
五、向中央银行借款 Borrowings from the Central Bank			其中：贴现 Of Which：Discount		
六、中央银行存款 Deposits by the Central Bank	0.42		5. 各项垫款 Total Advances		
七、应付及暂收款 Accounts Payable and Receipts on Account	16.50	5.81	6. 境外筹资转贷款 On - lending of Overseas Financing	50.61	8.66
			二、投资 Investments	3.87	3.15

续表
Continued

项　目 Items	余　额 Balance	比年初增减额 Changes within the Year	项　目 Items	余　额 Balance	比年初增减额 Changes within the Year
其中：应付及预提利息 Of Which: Interest Payable and Accrued	0.02	-0.04	1.购买有价证券 Purchase of Securities	3.86	3.15
八、同业存放 Due to Banks and Other Financial Institutions			其中：购买境外有价证券 Of Which: Purchase of Foreign Securities	3.86	3.15
1.境内同业存放 Due to Domestic Banks and Other Financial Institutions			2.其他投资 Other Investments	0.01	
2.境外同业存放 Due to Overseas Banks and Other Financial Institutions			其中：投资境外 Of Which: Overseas	0.01	
九、同业拆入 Placements from Banks and Other Financial Institutions	1.33	0.10	三、应收及预付款 Accounts Receivable and Advance Payments	19.66	5.33
1.境内同业拆入 Placements from Domestic Banks and Other Financial Institutions		-0.30	其中：应收及预付利息 Of Which: Interest Receivable and Paid in Advance	0.15	0.03
2.境外同业拆入 Placements from Overseas Banks and Other Financial Institutions	1.33	0.40	四、买入返售证券 Reverse Repo		
十、委托基金存款（净） Designated Fund Deposits (Net)			五、存放中央银行 Deposits with the Central Bank		
十一、外汇买卖 Foreign Exchange Dealings	10.52	5.69	其中：缴存准备金 Of Which: Reserves with the Central Bank		
其中：结售汇 Of Which: Purchase and Sale of Foreign Exchange			六、存放同业 Due from Banks and Other Financial Institutions	0.66	0.57
十二、境内联行存放 Due to Domestic Branches	-0.01	-10.30	1.存放境内同业 Due from Domestic Banks and Other Financial Institutions	0.56	0.56
十三、境外联行存放 Due to Overseas Branches			2.存放境外同业 Due from Overseas Banks and Other Financial Institutions	0.10	0.01
十四、各项准备 Total Provisions	0.53	0.53	七、拆放同业 Placements with Banks and Other Financial Institutions	5.13	3.12
其中：贷款呆账准备金 Of Which: Provisions for Bad Loans			1.拆放境内同业 Placements with Domestic Banks and Other Financial Institutions		
十五、所有者权益 Owner's Equity	2.34	-1.18	2.拆放境外同业 Placements with Overseas Banks and Other Financial Institutions	5.13	3.12
其中：实收资本 Of Which: Paid-in Capital	2.60	-0.12	八、存放境外联行 Due from Overseas Branches		
当年结益 Net Earnings	-0.01	-0.01	九、库存现金 Cash in Vault		
十六、其他 Others	2.75	2.28			
资金来源总计 Total Sources	**86.99**	**23.00**	**资金运用总计 Total Uses**	**86.99**	**23.00**

政策性银行外汇信贷收支表

Sources and Uses of Credit Funds of Policy Banks（Foreign Currency）

（2002 年末）

（Year - end of 2002）

单位：亿美元

Unit：100 Million US Dollars

项目 Items	余额 Balance	比年初增减额 Changes within the Year	项目 Items	余额 Balance	比年初增减额 Changes within the Year
一、各项存款 Total Deposits	0.13	0.06	一、各项贷款 Total Loans	73.33	15.68
1. 单位活期存款 Demand Deposits by Enterprises	0.10	0.03	1. 短期贷款 Short - term Loans	1.81	-1.08
其中：中资企业存款 Of Which：Deposits by Chinese - funded Enterprises	0.08	0.01	（1）境内短期贷款 Domestic Short - term Loans	1.81	-1.08
外商投资企业存款 Deposits by Foreign - funded Enterprises			其中：中资企业贷款 Of Which：Loans to Chinese - funded Enterprises	1.81	-1.08
2. 单位定期存款 Time Deposits by Enterprises	0.03	0.03	外商投资企业贷款 Loans to Foreign - funded Enterprises		
其中：中资企业存款 Of Which：Deposits by Chinese - funded Enterprises			（2）境外短期贷款 Overseas Short - term Loans		
外商投资企业存款 Deposits by Foreign - funded Enterprises			2. 中长期贷款 Medium and Long - term Loans	12.18	8.50
			（1）境内中长期贷款 Domestic Medium and Long - term Loans	6.29	6.19
3. 储蓄存款 Savings Deposits			其中：中资企业贷款 Of Which：Loans to Chinese - funded Enterprises	0.20	0.20
其中：定期存款 Of Which：Time Deposits					
4. 其他类存款 Other Deposits			外商投资企业贷款 Loans to Foreign - funded Enterprises		
5. 境外存款 Foreign Deposits			（2）境外中长期贷款 Overseas Medium and Long - term Loans	5.89	2.31
二、境内中长期借款 Domestic Medium and Long - term Borrowing					
			3. 进出口贸易融资 Financing for Import and Export Trades	0.32	-0.15
三、卖出回购证券 Repo	0.20	-0.20			
四、境外筹资 Overseas Financing	61.11	8.97	4. 票据融资 Paper Financing		
五、向中央银行借款 Borrowings from the Central Bank			其中：贴现 Of Which：Discount		
六、中央银行存款 Deposits by the Central Bank	0.42		5. 各项垫款 Total Advances	0.03	0.03
七、应付及暂收款 Accounts Payable and Receipts on Account	16.92	0.11	6. 境外筹资转贷款 On - lending of Overseas Financing	58.99	8.38
			二、投资 Investments	3.97	0.10

续表
Continued

项　目 Items	余　额 Balance	比年初增减额 Changes within the Year	项　目 Items	余　额 Balance	比年初增减额 Changes within the Year
其中：应付及预提利息 Of Which: Interest Payable and Accrued	0.03	0.01	1. 购买有价证券 Purchase of Securities	3.96	0.10
八、同业存放 Due to Banks and Other Financial Institutions			其中：购买境外有价证券 Of Which: Purchase of Foreign Securities	3.66	-0.20
1. 境内同业存放 Due to Domestic Banks and Other Financial Institutions			2. 其他投资 Other Investments	0.01	
2. 境外同业存放 Due to Overseas Banks and Other Financial Institutions			其中：投资境外 Of Which: Overseas	0.01	
九、同业拆入 Placements from Banks and Other Financial Institutions	0.37	-0.94	三、应收及预付款 Accounts Receivable and Advance Payments	16.53	-3.72
1. 境内同业拆入 Placements from Domestic Banks and Other Financial Institutions	0.12	0.12	其中：应收及预付利息 Of Which: Interest Receivable and Paid in Advance	0.11	-0.04
2. 境外同业拆入 Placements from Overseas Banks and Other Financial Institutions	0.25	-1.06	四、买入返售证券 Reverse Repo		
十、委托基金存款（净） Designated Fund Deposits (Net)			五、存放中央银行 Deposits with the Central Bank		
			其中：缴存准备金 Of Which: Reserves with the Central Bank		
十一、外汇买卖 Foreign Exchange Dealings	20.80	10.02	六、存放同业 Due from Banks and Other Financial Institutions	0.87	0.20
其中：结售汇 Of Which: Purchase and Sale of Foreign Exchange	4.91	4.91	1. 存放境内同业 Due from Domestic Banks and Other Financial Institutions	0.60	0.04
十二、境内联行存放 Due to Domestic Branches	0.04	0.04	2. 存放境外同业 Due from Overseas Banks and Other Financial Institutions	0.27	0.16
十三、境外联行存放 Due to Overseas Branches			七、拆放同业 Placements with Banks and Other Financial Institutions	8.13	3.00
十四、各项准备 Total Provisions	0.62	0.09			
其中：贷款呆账准备金 Of Which: Provisions for Bad Loans	0.62	0.09	1. 拆放境内同业 Placements with Domestic Banks and Other Financial Institutions	0.43	0.43
十五、所有者权益 Owner's Equity	4.62	0.21	2. 拆放境外同业 Placements with Overseas Banks and Other Financial Institutions	7.70	2.57
其中：实收资本 Of Which: Paid-in Capital	4.62				
当年结益 Net Earnings	0.27	0.27	八、存放境外联行 Due from Overseas Branches		
十六、其他 Others	-2.40	-3.10	九、库存现金 Cash in Vault		
资金来源总计 Total Sources	**102.83**	**15.26**	**资金运用总计 Total Uses**	**102.83**	**15.26**

政策性银行外汇信贷收支表

Sources and Uses of Credit Funds of Policy Banks（Foreign Currency）

（2003年末）

（Year - end of 2003）

单位：亿美元

Unit：100 Million US Dollars

项　目 Items	余　额 Balance	比年初增减额 Changes within the Year	项　目 Items	余　额 Balance	比年初增减额 Changes within the Year
一、各项存款 Total Deposits	2.72	2.59	一、各项贷款 Total Loans	101.31	27.98
1. 单位活期存款 Demand Deposits by Enterprises	2.20	2.10	1. 短期贷款 Short - term Loans	1.96	0.15
其中：中资企业存款 Of Which：Deposits by Chinese - funded Enterprises	1.48	1.40	（1）境内短期贷款 Domestic Short - term Loans	1.96	0.15
			其中：中资企业贷款 Of Which：Loans to Chinese - funded Enterprises	1.96	0.15
外商投资企业存款 Deposits by Foreign - funded Enterprises	0.02	0.02			
			外商投资企业贷款 Loans to Foreign - funded Enterprises		
2. 单位定期存款 Time Deposits by Enterprises	0.04	0.01			
其中：中资企业贷款 Of Which：Loans to Chinese - funded Enterprises	0.01	0.01	（2）境外短期贷款 Overseas Short - term Loans		
			2. 中长期贷款 Medium and Long - term Loans	29.29	17.11
外商投资企业贷款 Loans to Foreign - funded Enterprises					
			（1）境内中长期贷款 Domestic Medium and Long - term Loans	21.33	15.04
3. 储蓄存款 Savings Deposits					
			其中：中资企业贷款 Of Which：Loans to Chinese - funded Enterprises	10.88	10.68
其中：定期存款 Of Which：Time Deposits					
4. 其他类存款 Other Deposits	0.48	0.48	外商投资企业贷款 Loans to Foreign - funded Enterprises	0.26	0.26
5. 境外存款 Foreign Deposits					
			（2）境外中长期贷款 Overseas Medium and Long - term Loans	7.96	2.07
二、境内中长期借款 Domestic Medium and Long - term Borrowing	5.00	5.00			
			3. 进出口贸易融资 Financing for Import and Export Trades	6.32	6.00
三、卖出回购证券 Repo		- 0.20			
四、境外筹资 Overseas Financing	66.77	5.62	4. 票据融资 Paper Financing		
五、向中央银行借款 Borrowings from the Central Bank			其中：贴现 Of Which：Discount		
六、中央银行存款 Deposits by the Central Bank	5.00	4.58	5. 各项垫款 Total Advances	0.06	0.03
七、应付及暂收款 Accounts Payable and Receipts on Account	14.15	- 2.80	6. 境外筹资转贷款 On - lending of Overseas Financing	63.68	4.69
			二、投资 Investments	7.57	3.58

续表
Continued

项目 Items	余额 Balance	比年初增减额 Changes within the Year	项目 Items	余额 Balance	比年初增减额 Changes within the Year
其中：应付及预提利息 Of Which: Interest Payable and Accrued	0.02	-0.01	1. 购买有价证券 Purchase of Securities	7.56	3.58
八、同业存放 Due to Banks and Other Financial Institutions			其中：购买境外有价证券 Of Which: Purchase of Foreign Securities	7.26	3.58
1. 境内同业存放 Due to Domestic Banks and Other Financial Institutions			2. 其他投资 Other Investments	0.01	
2. 境外同业存放 Due to Overseas Banks and Other Financial Institutions			其中：投资境外 Of Which: Overseas	0.01	
九、同业拆入 Placements from Banks and Other Financial Institutions	2.29	1.92	三、应收及预付款 Accounts Receivable and Advance Payments	13.80	-2.75
1. 境内同业拆入 Placements from Domestic Banks and Other Financial Institutions	0.28	0.16	其中：应收及预付利息 Of Which: Interest Receivable and Paid in Advance	0.12	0.01
2. 境外同业拆入 Placements from Overseas Banks and Other Financial Institutions	2.01	1.76	四、买入返售证券 Reverse Repo		
十、委托基金存款（净） Designated Fund Deposits (Net)			五、存放中央银行 Deposits with the Central Bank		
			其中：缴存准备金 Of Which: Reserves with the Central Bank		
十一、外汇买卖 Foreign Exchange Dealings	25.38	4.55	六、存放同业 Due from Banks and Other Financial Institutions	6.99	6.12
其中：结售汇 Of Which: Purchase and Sale of Foreign Exchange	9.47	4.56	1. 存放境内同业 Due from Domestic Banks and Other Financial Institutions	1.35	0.75
十二、境内联行存放 Due to Domestic Branches			2. 存放境外同业 Due from Overseas Banks and Other Financial Institutions	5.64	5.37
十三、境外联行存放 Due to Overseas Branches			七、拆放同业 Placements with Banks and Other Financial Institutions	3.07	-5.07
十四、各项准备 Total Provisions	1.28	0.66			
其中：贷款呆账准备金 Of Which: Provisions for Bad Loans	1.28	0.66	1. 拆放境内同业 Placements with Domestic Banks and Other Financial Institutions	0.48	0.04
十五、所有者权益 Owner's Equity	4.86	0.24	2. 拆放境外同业 Placements with Overseas Banks and Other Financial Institutions	2.59	-5.11
其中：实收资本 Of Which: Paid-in Capital	4.62				
当年结益 Net Earnings	0.41	0.41	八、存放境外联行 Due from Overseas Branches		
十六、其他 Others	5.29	7.70	九、库存现金 Cash in Vault		
资金来源总计 Total Sources	**132.74**	**29.86**	**资金运用总计 Total Uses**	**132.74**	**29.86**

政策性银行外汇信贷收支表

Sources and Uses of Credit Funds of Policy Banks（Foreign Currency）

（2004 年末）

（Year – end of 2004）

单位：亿美元

Unit：100 Million US Dollars

项　目 Items	余　额 Balance	比年初增减额 Changes within the Year	项　目 Items	余　额 Balance	比年初增减额 Changes within the Year
一、各项存款 Total Deposits	2.95	0.23	一、各项贷款 Total Loans	124.06	22.75
1. 单位活期存款 Demand Deposits by Enterprises	1.27	– 0.93	1. 短期贷款 Short – term Loans	3.60	1.64
其中：中资企业存款 Of Which：Deposits by Chinese – funded Enterprises	0.54	– 0.94	（1）境内短期贷款 Domestic Short – term Loans	3.60	1.64
外商投资企业存款 Deposits by Foreign – funded Enterprises	0.05	0.03	其中：中资企业贷款 Of Which：Loans to Chinese – funded Enterprises	3.10	1.14
2. 单位定期存款 Time Deposits by Enterprises	0.33	0.29	外商投资企业贷款 Loans to Foreign – funded Enterprises	0.50	0.50
其中：中资企业存款 Of Which：Deposits by Chinese – funded Enterprises	0.30	0.29	（2）境外短期贷款 Overseas Short – term Loans		
外商投资企业存款 Deposits by Foreign – funded Enterprises			2. 中长期贷款 Medium and Long – term Loans	42.08	12.79
3. 储蓄存款 Savings Deposits			（1）境内中长期贷款 Domestic Medium and Long – term Loans	28.74	7.41
其中：定期存款 Of Which：Time Deposits			其中：中资企业贷款 Of Which：Loans to Chinese – funded Enterprises	13.26	2.38
4. 其他类存款 Other Deposits	0.93	0.45	外商投资企业贷款 Loans to Foreign – funded Enterprises	4.20	3.94
5. 境外存款 Foreign Deposits	0.42	0.42	（2）境外中长期贷款 Overseas Medium and Long – term Loans	13.34	5.38
二、境内中长期借款 Domestic Medium and Long – term Borrowing	6.00	1.00	3. 进出口贸易融资 Financing for Import and Export Trades	15.26	8.94
三、卖出回购资产 Assets Repo（Including Securities）	0.19	0.19			
四、境外筹资 Overseas Financing	84.76	17.99	4. 票据融资 Paper Financing		
五、向中央银行借款 Borrowings from the Central Bank			其中：贴现 Of Which：Discount		
六、中央银行存款 Deposits by the Central Bank	5.00		5. 各项垫款 Total Advances	0.10	0.04
七、应付及暂收款 Accounts Payable and Receipts on Account	4.96	– 9.19	6. 境外筹资转贷款 On – lending of Overseas Financing	63.02	– 0.66
			二、投资 Investments	9.81	2.24

续表
Continued

项 目 Items	余 额 Balance	比年初增减额 Changes within the Year	项 目 Items	余 额 Balance	比年初增减额 Changes within the Year
其中：应付及预提利息 Of Which: Interest Payable and Accrued	0.24	0.22	1. 购买有价证券 Purchase of Securities	9.80	2.24
八、同业存放 Due to Banks and Other Financial Institutions	0.01	0.01	其中：购买境外有价证券 Of Which: Purchase of Foreign Securities	9.50	2.24
1. 境内同业存放 Due to Domestic Banks and Other Financial Institutions			2. 其他投资 Other Investments	0.01	
2. 境外同业存放 Due to Overseas Banks and Other Financial Institutions	0.01	0.01	其中：投资境外 Of Which: Overseas	0.01	
九、同业拆入 Placements from Banks and Other Financial Institutions	3.78	1.49	三、应收及预付款 Accounts Receivable and Advance Payments	4.95	-8.85
1. 境内同业拆入 Placements from Domestic Banks and Other Financial Institutions	0.79	0.51	其中：应收及预付利息 Of Which: Interest Receivable and Paid in Advance	0.16	0.04
2. 境外同业拆入 Placements from Overseas Banks and Other Financial Institutions	2.99	0.98	四、买入返售资产 Assets Reverse Repo (Including Securities)		
十、委托基金存款（净）Designated Fund Deposits (Net)			五、存放中央银行 Deposits with the Central Bank		
十一、外汇买卖 Foreign Exchange Dealings	25.52	0.14	其中：缴存准备金 Of Which: Reserves with the Central Bank		
其中：结售汇 Of Which: Purchase and Sale of Foreign Exchange	7.71	-1.76	六、存放同业 Due from Banks and Other Financial Institutions	6.58	-0.41
十二、境内联行存放 Due to Domestic Branches			1. 存放境内同业 Due from Domestic Banks and Other Financial Institutions	2.61	1.26
十三、境外联行存放 Due to Overseas Branches			2. 存放境外同业 Due from Overseas Banks and Other Financial Institutions	3.97	-1.67
十四、各项准备 Total Provisions	1.51	0.23	七、拆放同业 Placements with Banks and Other Financial Institutions	3.21	0.14
其中：贷款损失准备 Of Which: Provisions for Loan Losses	1.51	0.23	1. 拆放境内同业 Placements with Domestic Banks and Other Financial Institutions	0.70	0.22
十五、所有者权益 Owner's Equity	8.25	3.39	2. 拆放境外同业 Placements with Overseas Banks and Other Financial Institutions	2.51	-0.08
其中：实收资本 Of Which: Paid - in Capital	8.22	3.60			
当年结益 Net Earnings	0.15	0.15	八、存放境外联行 Due from Overseas Branches		
十六、其他 Others	5.68	0.39	九、库存现金 Cash in Vault		
资金来源总计 Total Sources	**148.61**	**15.87**	**资金运用总计 Total Uses**	**148.61**	**15.87**

政策性银行外汇信贷收支表

Sources and Uses of Credit Funds of Policy Banks（Foreign Currency）

（2005 年末）

（Year - end of 2005）

单位：亿美元

Unit：100 Million US Dollars

项目 Items	余额 Balance	比年初增减额 Changes within the Year	项目 Items	余额 Balance	比年初增减额 Changes within the Year
一、各项存款 Total Deposits	65.38	62.43	一、各项贷款 Total Loans	237.55	113.49
1. 单位活期存款 Demand Deposits by Enterprises	48.15	46.88	1. 短期贷款 Short - term Loans	4.81	1.21
其中：中资企业存款 Of Which：Deposits by Chinese - funded Enterprises	32.56	32.02	（1）境内短期贷款 Domestic Short - term Loans	4.81	1.21
外商投资企业存款 Deposits by Foreign - funded Enterprises	1.17	1.12	其中：中资企业贷款 Of Which：Loans to Chinese - funded Enterprises	3.86	0.76
			外商投资企业贷款 Loans to Foreign - funded Enterprises	0.40	- 0.10
2. 单位定期存款 Time Deposits by Enterprises	15.10	14.77			
其中：中资企业存款 Of Which：Deposits by Chinese - funded Enterprises	0.08	- 0.22	（2）境外短期贷款 Overseas Short - term Loans		
外商投资企业存款 Deposits by Foreign - funded Enterprises			2. 中长期贷款 Medium and Long - term Loans	151.66	109.58
			（1）境内中长期贷款 Domestic Medium and Long - term Loans	130.04	101.30
3. 储蓄存款 Savings Deposits			其中：中资企业贷款 Of Which：Loans to Chinese - funded Enterprises	43.86	30.60
其中：定期存款 Of Which：Time Deposits					
4. 其他类存款 Other Deposits	0.54	- 0.39	外商投资企业贷款 Loans to Foreign - funded Enterprises	8.74	4.54
5. 境外存款 Foreign Deposits	1.59	1.17	（2）境外中长期贷款 Overseas Medium and Long - term Loans	21.62	8.28
二、境内中长期筹资 Domestic Medium and Long - term Borrowing	30.02	24.02			
三、卖出回购资产 Assets Repo（Including Securities）		- 0.19	3. 进出口贸易融资 Financing for Import and Export Trades	23.25	7.99
四、境外筹资 Overseas Financing	104.57	19.81	4. 票据融资 Paper Financing		
五、向中央银行借款 Borrowings from the Central Bank			其中：贴现 Of Which：Discount		
六、中央银行存款 Deposits by the Central Bank		- 5.00	5. 各项垫款 Total Advances	0.14	0.04
七、应付及暂收款 Accounts Payable and Receipts on Account	7.61	3.92	6. 境外筹资转贷款 On - lending of Overseas Financing	57.69	- 5.33
			二、投资 Investments	32.36	22.55

续表
Continued

项　目 Items	余　额 Balance	比年初增减额 Changes within the Year	项　目 Items	余　额 Balance	比年初增减额 Changes within the Year
其中：应付及预提利息 Of Which：Interest Payable and Accrued	2.72	2.48	1. 购买有价证券 Purchase of Securities	32.29	22.49
八、同业存放 Due to Banks and Other Financial Institutions	0.01		其中：购买境外有价证券 Of Which：Purchase of Foreign Securities	31.99	22.49
1. 境内同业存放 Due to Domestic Banks and Other Financial Institutions			2. 其他投资 Other Investments	0.07	0.06
			其中：投资境外 Of Which：Overseas	0.01	
2. 境外同业存放 Due to Overseas Banks and Other Financial Institutions	0.01		三、应收及预付款 Accounts Receivable and Advance Payments	1.93	－1.75
九、同业拆入 Placements from Banks and Other Financial Institutions	4.13	0.35	其中：应收及预付利息 Of Which：Interest Receivable and Paid in Advance	1.91	1.75
1. 境内同业拆入 Placements from Domestic Banks and Other Financial Institutions	2.89	2.10	四、买入返售资产 Assets Reverse Repo（Including Securities）		
2. 境外同业拆入 Placements from Overseas Banks and Other Financial Institutions	1.24	－1.75	五、存放中央银行 Deposits with the Central Bank	0.22	0.22
十、委托基金存款（净） Designated Fund Deposits（Net）			其中：缴存准备金 Of Which：Reserves with the Central Bank		
十一、外汇买卖 Foreign Exchange Dealings	64.87	39.35	六、存放同业 Due from Banks and Other Financial Institutions	4.17	－2.41
其中：结售汇 Of Which：Purchase and Sale of Foreign Exchange	－0.04	－7.75	1. 存放境内同业 Due from Domestic Banks and Other Financial Institutions	2.62	0.01
十二、境内联行存放 Due to Domestic Branches			2. 存放境外同业 Due from Overseas Banks and Other Financial Institutions	1.55	－2.42
十三、境外联行存放 Due to Overseas Branches					
十四、各项准备 Total Provisions	2.26	0.75	七、拆放同业 Placements with Banks and Other Financial Institutions	14.97	11.76
其中：贷款损失准备 Of Which：Provisions for Loan Losses	2.11	0.60	1. 拆放境内同业 Placements with Domestic Banks and Other Financial Institutions	2.44	1.747
十五、所有者权益 Owner's Equity	5.53	3.40	2. 拆放境外同业 Placements with Overseas Banks and Other Financial Institutions	12.53	10.02
其中：实收资本 Of Which：Paid－in Capital	3.10	1.00			
当年结益 Net Earnings	2.25	2.25	八、存放境外联行 Due from Overseas Branches		
十六、其他 Others	6.82	－4.98	九、库存现金 Cash in Vault		
资金来源总计 Total Sources	**291.20**	**143.86**	**资金运用总计 Total Uses**	**291.20**	**143.86**

4. 国有商业银行外汇信贷收支表*（1998—2005 年）

Sources and Uses of Credit Funds of State - owned Commercial Banks（Foreign Currency）（1998—2005）

国有商业银行外汇信贷收支表

Sources and Uses of Credit Funds of State - owned Commercial Banks（Foreign Currency）

（1998 年末）

（Year - end of 1998）

单位：亿美元

Unit：100 Million US Dollars

项　目 Items	余　额 Balance	比年初增减额 Changes within the Year	项　目 Items	余　额 Balance	比年初增减额 Changes within the Year
一、各项存款 Total Deposits	701.87	115.94	一、各项贷款 Total Loans	653.61	21.88
1. 单位活期存款 Demand Deposits by Enterprises	96.69	- 17.97	1. 短期贷款 Short - term Loans	285.01	- 9.76
其中：中资企业存款 Of Which：Deposits by Chinese - funded Enterprises	46.51	- 11.59	（1）境内短期贷款 Domestic Short - term Loans	285.01	- 9.40
外商投资企业存款 Deposits by Foreign - funded Enterprises	43.90	- 7.63	其中：中资企业贷款 Of Which：Loans to Chinese - funded Enterprises	133.51	- 7.89
			外商投资企业贷款 Loans to Foreign - funded Enterprises	85.66	- 4.72
2. 单位定期存款 Time Deposits by Enterprises	193.08	31.58	（2）境外短期贷款 Overseas Short - term Loans		- 0.36
其中：中资企业存款 Of Which：Deposits by Chinese - funded Enterprises	158.13	28.82	2. 中长期贷款 Medium and Long - term Loans	286.64	20.72
外商投资企业存款 Deposits by Foreign - funded Enterprises	13.75	3.98	（1）境内中长期贷款 Domestic Medium and Long - term Loans	284.02	20.29
3. 储蓄存款 Savings Deposits	376.56	108.29	其中：中资企业贷款 Of Which：Loans to Chinese - funded Enterprises	147.98	2.41
其中：定期存款 Of Which：Time Deposits	351.90	104.56	外商投资企业贷款 Loans to Foreign - funded Enterprises	29.97	- 4.11
4. 其他类存款 Other Deposits	33.94	- 5.02	（2）境外中长期贷款 Overseas Medium and Long - term Loans	2.62	0.43
5. 境外存款 Foreign Deposits	1.60	- 0.94	3. 进出口贸易融资 Financing for Import and Export Trades	26.42	- 13.32
二、境内中长期借款 Domestic Medium and Long - term Borrowing	0.24	- 0.15	4. 票据融资 Paper Financing	0.66	- 0.76
三、卖出回购证券 Repo	0.34	0.34	5. 逾期类贷款 Overdue Loans	54.88	25.00
四、境外筹资 Overseas Financing	277.07	- 13.00			
五、向中央银行借款 Borrowings from the Central Bank	20.30	- 0.37			

续表
Continued

项 目 Items	余 额 Balance	比年初增减额 Changes within the Year	项 目 Items	余 额 Balance	比年初增减额 Changes within the Year
六、中央银行存款 Deposits by the Central Bank	143.52	12.59	二、投资 Investments	158.02	44.21
七、同业存放 Due to Banks and Other Financial Institutions	27.83	-12.09	1. 购买有价证券 Purchase of Securities	140.32	38.84
			其中：购买境外有价证券 Of Which: Purchase of Foreign Securities	140.32	38.84
1. 境内同业存放 Due to Domestic Banks and Other Financial Institutions	19.07	0.90	2. 其他投资 Other Investments	17.70	5.37
2. 境外同业存放 Due to Overseas Banks and Other Financial Institutions	8.76	-12.99	其中：投资境外 Of Which: Overseas	0.55	0.09
八、同业拆入 Placements from Banks and Other Financial Institutions	6.11	-1.74	三、境外筹资转贷款 On-lending of Overseas Financing	288.07	-4.06
			四、存放中央银行 Deposits with the Central Bank	14.79	-0.17
1. 境内同业拆入 Placements from Domestic Banks and Other Financial Institutions	1.91	0.30	其中：缴存准备金 Of Which: Reserves with the Central Bank	8.85	-1.10
2. 境外同业拆入 Placements from Overseas Banks and Other Financial Institutions	4.20	-2.04	五、存放同业 Due from Banks and Other Financial Institutions	392.62	-16.22
九、委托基金存款 Designated Fund Deposits	0.11	0.03	1. 存放境内同业 Due from Domestic Banks and Other Financial Institutions	8.02	-0.50
十、外汇买卖 Foreign Exchange Dealings	74.14	-23.07			
其中：结售汇 Of Which: Purchase and Sale of Foreign Exchange	63.66	-30.08	2. 存放境外同业 Due from Overseas Banks and Other Financial Institutions	384.60	-15.72
十一、境内联行存放 Due to Domestic Branches	-17.33	-19.15	六、拆放同业 Placements with Banks and Other Financial Institutions	38.30	11.25
十二、境外联行存放 Due to Overseas Branches	157.57	-21.66			
十三、所有者权益 Owner's Equity	202.45	29.84	1. 拆放境内同业 Placements with Domestic Banks and Other Financial Institutions	5.97	1.51
其中：实收资本 Of Which: Paid-in Capital	83.90	9.29	2. 拆放境外同业 Placements with Overseas Banks and Other Financial Institutions	32.33	9.75
当年结益 Net Earnings	21.40	21.40	七、存放境外联行 Due from Overseas Branches	33.11	-24.48
十四、其他 Others	-2.62	-34.88	八、库存现金 Cash in Vault	13.08	0.22
资金来源总计 Total Sources	**1591.60**	**32.63**	**资金运用总计 Total Uses**	**1591.60**	**32.63**

* 本表机构包括中国工商银行、中国农业银行、中国银行、中国建设银行。

* State-owned Commercial Banks of this statement include the Industrial and Commercial Bank of China, Agricultural Bank of China, Bank of China and China Construction Bank.

国有商业银行外汇信贷收支表

Sources and Uses of Credit Funds of State - owned Commercial Banks（Foreign Currency）

（1999 年末）

（Year - end of 1999）

单位：亿美元

Unit：100 Million US Dollars

项目 Items	余额 Balance	比年初增减额 Changes within the Year	项目 Items	余额 Balance	比年初增减额 Changes within the Year
一、各项存款 Total Deposits	828.94	127.23	一、各项贷款 Total Loans	608.52	3.78
1. 单位活期存款 Demand Deposits by Enterprises	106.45	9.86	1. 短期贷款 Short - term Loans	266.68	8.97
其中：中资企业存款 Of Which：Deposits by Chinese - funded Enterprises	52.09	5.61	（1）境内短期贷款 Domestic Short - term Loans	266.68	8.97
外商投资企业存款 Deposits by Foreign - funded Enterprises	47.96	4.09	其中：中资企业贷款 Of Which：Loans to Chinese - funded Enterprises	123.07	16.91
2. 单位定期存款 Time Deposits by Enterprises	189.10	- 4.02	外商投资企业贷款 Loans to Foreign - funded Enterprises	73.28	- 12.29
其中：中资企业存款 Of Which：Deposits by Chinese - funded Enterprises	151.57	- 6.60	（2）境外短期贷款 Overseas Short - term Loans		
外商投资企业存款 Deposits by Foreign - funded Enterprises	14.78	1.03	2. 中长期贷款 Medium and Long - term Loans	270.43	3.01
3. 储蓄存款 Savings Deposits	501.05	124.59	（1）境内中长期贷款 Domestic Medium and Long - term Loans	266.97	2.17
其中：定期存款 Of Which：Time Deposits	467.76	115.93	其中：中资企业贷款 Of Which：Loans to Chinese - funded Enterprises	151.67	19.23
4. 其他类存款 Other Deposits	31.67	- 2.27	外商投资企业贷款 Loans to Foreign - funded Enterprises	25.37	- 4.60
5. 境外存款 Foreign Deposits	0.67	- 0.93	（2）境外中长期贷款 Overseas Medium and Long - term Loans	3.46	0.84
二、境内中长期借款 Domestic Medium and Long - term Borrowing	1.50	1.26	3. 进出口贸易融资 Financing for Import and Export Trades	18.44	- 5.81
三、卖出回购证券 Repo		- 0.35	4. 票据融资 Paper Financing	0.60	- 0.06
四、境外筹资 Overseas Financing	257.59	- 19.65	5. 逾期类贷款 Overdue Loans	52.37	- 2.33
五、向中央银行借款 Borrowings from the Central Bank	19.94	- 0.36	二、投资 Investments	258.64	100.62
六、中央银行存款 Deposits by the Central Bank	111.29	- 31.66	1. 购买有价证券 Purchase of Securities	240.22	99.90
七、同业存放 Due to Banks and Other Financial Institutions	24.72	- 7.61			

续表
Continued

项目 Items	余额 Balance	比年初增减额 Changes within the Year	项目 Items	余额 Balance	比年初增减额 Changes within the Year
1. 境内同业存放 Due to Domestic Banks and Other Financial Institutions	17.31	-2.33	其中：购买境外有价证券 Of Which: Purchase of Foreign Securities	239.05	98.73
2. 境外同业存放 Due to Overseas Banks and Other Financial Institutions	7.41	-5.28	2. 其他投资 Other Investments	18.42	0.72
			其中：投资境外 Of Which: Overseas	0.55	
八、同业拆入 Placements from Banks and Other Financial Institutions	3.15	-3.32	三、境外筹资转贷款 On-lending of Overseas Financing	266.34	-21.56
1. 境内同业拆入 Placements from Domestic Banks and Other Financial Institutions	1.13	-1.14	四、存放中央银行 Deposits with the Central Bank	14.79	-0.04
2. 境外同业拆入 Placements from Overseas Banks and Other Financial Institutions	2.02	-2.18	其中：缴存准备金 Of Which: Reserves with the Central Bank	10.40	1.55
九、委托基金存款 Designated Fund Deposits	0.03	0.03	五、存放同业 Due from Banks and Other Financial Institutions	279.25	-113.74
十、外汇买卖 Foreign Exchange Dealings	81.88	8.05	1. 存放境内同业 Due from Domestic Banks and Other Financial Institutions	33.82	25.28
其中：结售汇 Of Which: Purchase and Sale of Foreign Exchange	68.83	-0.22	2. 存放境外同业 Due from Overseas Banks and Other Financial Institutions	245.43	-139.02
十一、境内联行存放 Due to Domestic Branches	-37.18	-19.07			
十二、境外联行存放 Due to Overseas Branches	120.66	-51.68	六、拆放同业 Placements with Banks and Other Financial Institutions	61.79	22.57
十三、所有者权益 Owner's Equity	193.12	4.32	1. 拆放境内同业 Placements with Domestic Banks and Other Financial Institutions	5.13	-1.76
其中：实收资本 Of Which: Paid-in Capital	74.54	4.38	2. 拆放境外同业 Placements with Overseas Banks and Other Financial Institutions	56.66	24.33
当年结益 Net Earnings	13.69	13.69			
十四、其他 Others	-20.07	19.97	七、存放境外联行 Due from Overseas Branches	69.64	22.01
			八、库存现金 Cash in Vault	26.60	13.52
资金来源总计 Total Sources	**1585.57**	**27.16**	**资金运用总计 Total Uses**	**1585.57**	**27.16**

国有商业银行外汇信贷收支表

Sources and Uses of Credit Funds of State - owned Commercial Banks（Foreign Currency）

（2000年末）

（Year - end of 2000）

单位：亿美元

Unit：100 Million US Dollars

项目 Items	余额 Balance	比年初增减额 Changes within the Year	项目 Items	余额 Balance	比年初增减额 Changes within the Year
一、各项存款 Total Deposits	1028.68	199.47	一、各项贷款 Total Loans	449.50	-23.36
1. 单位活期存款 Demand Deposits by Enterprises	109.01	2.24	1. 短期贷款 Short - term Loans	183.86	-20.50
其中：中资企业存款 Of Which：Deposits by Chinese - funded Enterprises	53.97	1.88	（1）境内短期贷款 Domestic Short - term Loans	183.86	-20.50
外商投资企业存款 Deposits by Foreign - funded Enterprises	50.01	1.56	其中：中资企业贷款 Of Which：Loans to Chinese - funded Enterprises	80.57	-20.71
2. 单位定期存款 Time Deposits by Enterprises	227.72	38.32	外商投资企业贷款 Loans to Foreign - funded Enterprises	53.61	-4.77
其中：中资企业存款 Of Which：Deposits by Chinese - funded Enterprises	183.36	31.47	（2）境外短期贷款 Overseas Short - term Loans		
外商投资企业存款 Deposits by Foreign - funded Enterprises	18.24	3.46	2. 中长期贷款 Medium and Long - term Loans	209.00	-13.06
3. 储蓄存款 Savings Deposits	649.04	147.99	（1）境内中长期贷款 Domestic Medium and Long - term Loans	204.89	-13.71
其中：定期存款 Of Which：Time Deposits	608.83	141.07	其中：中资企业贷款 Of Which：Loans to Chinese - funded Enterprises	120.46	-8.27
4. 其他类存款 Other Deposits	42.82	11.22	外商投资企业贷款 Loans to Foreign - funded Enterprises	17.62	2.94
5. 境外存款 Foreign Deposits	0.09	-0.30	（2）境外中长期贷款 Overseas Medium and Long - term Loans	4.11	0.65
二、境内中长期借款 Domestic Medium and Long - term Borrowing	1.43	-0.07	3. 进出口贸易融资 Financing for Import and Export Trades	11.92	-0.72
三、卖出回购证券 Repo					
四、境外筹资 Overseas Financing	203.55	-54.01	4. 票据融资 Paper Financing	0.34	-0.26
五、向中央银行借款 Borrowings from the Central Bank	18.18	-1.76	5. 逾期类贷款 Overdue Loans	44.38	11.18
六、中央银行存款 Deposits by the Central Bank	85.60	-25.65	二、投资 Investments	351.70	93.45
七、同业存放 Due to Banks and Other Financial Institutions	18.73	-4.65	1. 购买有价证券 Purchase of Securities	329.09	89.19

续表
Continued

项目 Items	余额 Balance	比年初增减额 Changes within the Year	项目 Items	余额 Balance	比年初增减额 Changes within the Year
1. 境内同业存放 Due to Domestic Banks and Other Financial Institutions	11.20	-4.77	其中：购买境外有价证券 Of Which: Purchase of Foreign Securities	317.80	79.06
2. 境外同业存放 Due to Overseas Banks and Other Financial Institutions	7.53	0.12	2. 其他投资 Other Investments	22.61	4.26
			其中：投资境外 Of Which: Overseas	0.89	0.34
八、同业拆入 Placements from Banks and Other Financial Institutions	5.22	2.07	三、境外筹资转贷款 On-lending of Overseas Financing	197.80	-57.40
1. 境内同业拆入 Placements from Domestic Banks and Other Financial Institutions	3.30	2.17	四、存放中央银行 Deposits with the Central Bank	20.64	5.85
			其中：缴存准备金 Of Which: Reserves with the Central Bank	13.99	3.59
2. 境外同业拆入 Placements from Overseas Banks and Other Financial Institutions	1.92	-0.10	五、存放同业 Due from Banks and Other Financial Institutions	322.18	43.41
九、委托基金存款 Designated Fund Deposits	-0.01	-0.05			
十、外汇买卖 Foreign Exchange Dealings	-67.67	-150.09	1. 存放境内同业 Due from Domestic Banks and Other Financial Institutions	10.74	-22.98
其中：结售汇 Of Which: Purchase and Sale of Foreign Exchange	58.51	-9.98	2. 存放境外同业 Due from Overseas Banks and Other Financial Institutions	311.44	66.39
十一、境内联行存放 Due to Domestic Branches	-22.52	11.93	六、拆放同业 Placements with Banks and Other Financial Institutions	194.78	133.06
十二、境外联行存放 Due to Overseas Branches	156.07	35.62			
十三、所有者权益 Owner's Equity	207.65	14.66	1. 拆放境内同业 Placements with Domestic Banks and Other Financial Institutions	4.47	-0.66
其中：实收资本 Of Which: Paid-in Capital	73.22	-1.32	2. 拆放境外同业 Placements with Overseas Banks and Other Financial Institutions	190.31	133.72
当年结益 Net Earnings	11.55	11.55			
十四、其他 Others	-22.41	147.39	七、存放境外联行 Due from Overseas Branches	56.77	-12.66
			八、库存现金 Cash in Vault	19.13	-7.49
资金来源总计 Total Sources	**1612.50**	**174.86**	**资金运用总计 Total Uses**	**1612.50**	**174.86**

国有商业银行外汇信贷收支表

Sources and Uses of Credit Funds of State - owned Commercial Banks（Foreign Currency）

（2001 年末）

（Year - end of 2001）

单位：亿美元

Unit：100 Million US Dollars

项 目 Items	余 额 Balance	比年初增减额 Changes within the Year	项 目 Items	余 额 Balance	比年初增减额 Changes within the Year
一、各项存款 Total Deposits	1076.21	44.47	一、各项贷款 Total Loans	596.12	- 51.95
1. 单位活期存款 Demand Deposits by Enterprises	123.44	12.16	1. 短期贷款 Short - term Loans	156.43	- 3.37
其中：中资企业存款 Of Which：Deposits by Chinese - funded Enterprises	83.01	18.88	（1）境内短期贷款 Domestic Short - term Loans	156.43	- 3.37
外商投资企业存款 Deposits by Foreign - funded Enterprises	35.05	- 7.11	其中：中资企业贷款 Of Which：Loans to Chinese - funded Enterprises	82.46	1.75
2. 单位定期存款 Time Deposits by Enterprises	201.99	- 25.49	外商投资企业贷款 Loans to Foreign - funded Enterprises	53.97	0.05
其中：中资企业存款 Of Which：Deposits by Chinese - funded Enterprises	164.18	- 19.00	（2）境外短期贷款 Overseas Short - term Loans		
外商投资企业存款 Deposits by Foreign - funded Enterprises	13.37	- 4.86	2. 中长期贷款 Medium and Long - term Loans	210.49	- 16.41
3. 储蓄存款 Savings Deposits	715.35	65.95	（1）境内中长期贷款 Domestic Medium and Long - term Loans	207.04	- 15.64
其中：定期存款 Of Which：Time Deposits	650.50	41.13	其中：中资企业贷款 Of Which：Loans to Chinese - funded Enterprises	113.43	- 15.44
4. 其他类存款 Other Deposits	35.25	- 8.24	外商投资企业贷款 Loans to Foreign - funded Enterprises	18.51	- 4.35
5. 境外存款 Foreign Deposits	0.18	0.09	（2）境外中长期贷款 Overseas Medium and Long - term Loans	3.45	- 0.77
二、境内中长期借款 Domestic Medium and Long - term Borrowing	1.40	- 0.03	3. 进出口贸易融资 Financing for Import and Export Trades	13.40	- 1.44
三、卖出回购证券 Repo			4. 票据融资 Paper Financing	0.65	0.31
四、境外筹资 Overseas Financing	176.83	- 34.33	其中：贴现 Of Which：Discount	0.37	0.27
五、向中央银行借款 Borrowings from the Central Bank	7.58	- 10.60	5. 各项垫款 Total Advances	51.71	5.90
六、中央银行存款 Deposits by the Central Bank	89.80	- 32.10	6. 境外筹资转贷款 On - lending of Overseas Financing	163.44	- 36.94
七、应付及暂收款 Accounts Payable and Receipts on Account	56.66	- 23.78	二、投资 Investments	606.79	253.73

续表
Continued

项目 Items	余额 Balance	比年初增减额 Changes within the Year	项目 Items	余额 Balance	比年初增减额 Changes within the Year
其中：应付及预提利息 Of Which: Interest Payable and Accrued	25.39	-9.07	1. 购买有价证券 Purchase of Securities	482.41	153.03
八、同业存放 Due to Banks and Other Financial Institutions	47.98	36.99	其中：购买境外有价证券 Of Which: Purchase of Foreign Securities	452.12	133.99
1. 境内同业存放 Due to Domestic Banks and Other Financial Institutions	44.86	34.96	2. 其他投资 Other Investments	124.38	100.70
2. 境外同业存放 Due to Overseas Banks and Other Financial Institutions	3.12	2.03	其中：投资境外 Of Which: Overseas	0.60	-0.29
九、同业拆入 Placements from Banks and Other Financial Institutions	11.04	6.94	三、应收及预付款 Accounts Receivable and Advance Payments	61.28	-47.08
1. 境内同业拆入 Placements from Domestic Banks and Other Financial Institutions	3.41	-0.03	其中：应收及预付利息 Of Which: Interest Receivable and Paid in Advance	12.66	-10.70
2. 境外同业拆入 Placements from Overseas Banks and Other Financial Institutions	7.63	6.97	四、买入返售证券 Reverse Repo		
十、委托基金存款（净） Designated Fund Deposits (Net)	0.01	0.01	五、存放中央银行 Deposits with the Central Bank	22.11	1.79
十一、外汇买卖 Foreign Exchange Dealings	-14.18	-16.39	其中：缴存准备金 Of Which: Reserves with the Central Bank	14.44	1.10
其中：结售汇 Of Which: Purchase and Sale of Foreign Exchange	83.30	-20.73	六、存放同业 Due from Banks and Other Financial Institutions	44.42	30.14
十二、境内联行存放 Due to Domestic Branches	-35.59	-17.69	1. 存放境内同业 Due from Domestic Banks and Other Financial Institutions	8.08	3.60
十三、境外联行存放 Due to Overseas Branches	79.90	-88.50	2. 存放境外同业 Due from Overseas Banks and Other Financial Institutions	36.34	26.54
十四、各项准备 Total Provisions	40.95	31.32	七、拆放同业 Placements with Banks and Other Financial Institutions	432.35	-140.12
其中：贷款呆账准备金 Of Which: Provisions for Bad Loans	11.69	7.66	1. 拆放境内同业 Placements with Domestic Banks and Other Financial Institutions	9.42	4.93
十五、所有者权益 Owner's Equity	293.43	85.69	2. 拆放境外同业 Placements with Overseas Banks and Other Financial Institutions	422.93	-145.05
其中：实收资本 Of Which: Paid-in Capital	118.38	45.16	八、存放境外联行 Due from Overseas Branches	34.46	-35.51
当年结益 Net Earnings	9.38	9.38	九、库存现金 Cash in Vault	18.26	-0.80
十六、其他 Others	-16.23	28.20			
资金来源总计 Total Sources	**1815.79**	**10.20**	**资金运用总计 Total Uses**	**1815.79**	**10.20**

国有商业银行外汇信贷收支表

Sources and Uses of Credit Funds of State - owned Commercial Banks（Foreign Currency）

（2002年末）

（Year - end of 2002）

单位：亿美元

Unit：100 Million US Dollars

项　　目 Items	余　额 Balance	比年初增减额 Changes within the Year	项　　目 Items	余　额 Balance	比年初增减额 Changes within the Year
一、各项存款 Total Deposits	1139.92	64.02	一、各项贷款 Total Loans	656.26	54.42
1. 单位活期存款 Demand Deposits by Enterprises	134.91	12.21	1. 短期贷款 Short - term Loans	185.29	29.39
其中：中资企业存款 Of Which：Deposits by Chinese - funded Enterprises	88.81	10.04	（1）境内短期贷款 Domestic Short - term Loans	185.29	29.39
外商投资企业存款 Deposits by Foreign - funded Enterprises	37.36	4.41	其中：中资企业贷款 Of Which：Loans to Chinese - funded Enterprises	106.28	22.18
2. 单位定期存款 Time Deposits by Enterprises	190.05	- 11.25	外商投资企业贷款 Loans to Foreign - funded Enterprises	57.92	6.12
其中：中资企业存款 Of Which：Deposits by Chinese - funded Enterprises	155.72	- 7.97	（2）境外短期贷款 Overseas Short - term Loans		
外商投资企业存款 Deposits by Foreign - funded Enterprises	9.77	- 3.60	2. 中长期贷款 Medium and Long - term Loans	255.91	39.42
3. 储蓄存款 Savings Deposits	774.07	59.50	（1）境内中长期贷款 Domestic Medium and Long - term Loans	253.76	40.60
其中：定期存款 Of Which：Time Deposits	685.51	35.38	其中：中资企业贷款 Of Which：Loans to Chinese - funded Enterprises	174.80	49.24
4. 其他类存款 Other Deposits	40.73	3.58	外商投资企业贷款 Loans to Foreign - funded Enterprises	16.81	- 1.68
5. 境外存款 Foreign Deposits	0.16	- 0.02	（2）境外中长期贷款 Overseas Medium and Long - term Loans	2.15	- 1.18
二、境内中长期借款 Domestic Medium and Long - term Borrowing		- 1.40	3. 进出口贸易融资 Financing for Import and Export Trades	21.65	8.28
三、卖出回购证券 Repo	0.96	0.96	4. 票据融资 Paper Financing	0.69	0.04
四、境外筹资 Overseas Financing	158.68	- 18.14	其中：贴现 Of Which：Discount	0.28	- 0.09
五、向中央银行借款 Borrowings from the Central Bank	3.39	- 4.27	5. 各项垫款 Total Advances	47.74	- 4.26
六、中央银行存款 Deposits by the Central Bank	90.58	0.80	6. 境外筹资转贷款 On - lending of Overseas Financing	144.98	- 18.45
七、应付及暂收款 Accounts Payable and Receipts on Account	70.19	13.58	二、投资 Investments	743.50	135.81

续表
Continued

项 目 Items	余 额 Balance	比年初增减额 Changes within the Year	项 目 Items	余 额 Balance	比年初增减额 Changes within the Year
其中：应付及预提利息 Of Which: Interest Payable and Accrued	16.94	-8.44	1. 购买有价证券 Purchase of Securities	602.38	119.93
			其中：购买境外有价证券 Of Which: Purchase of Foreign Securities	598.96	119.68
八、同业存放 Due to Banks and Other Financial Institutions	51.83	-3.05	2. 其他投资 Other Investments	141.12	15.88
1. 境内同业存放 Due to Domestic Banks and Other Financial Institutions	45.73	-6.03	其中：投资境外 Of Which: Overseas	5.65	-8.25
2. 境外同业存放 Due to Overseas Banks and Other Financial Institutions	6.10	2.98	三、应收及预付款 Accounts Receivable and Advance Payments	52.21	-10.38
九、同业拆入 Placements from Banks and Other Financial Institutions	70.84	59.80	其中：应收及预付利息 Of Which: Interest Receivable and Paid in Advance	8.61	-4.06
1. 境内同业拆入 Placements from Domestic Banks and Other Financial Institutions	8.08	4.67	四、买入返售证券 Reverse Repo		
			五、存放中央银行 Deposits with the Central Bank	23.07	0.96
2. 境外同业拆入 Placements from Overseas Banks and Other Financial Institutions	62.76	55.13	其中：缴存准备金 Of Which: Reserves with the Central Bank	15.38	0.94
十、委托基金存款（净） Designated Fund Deposits (Net)	0.02	0.01			
			六、存放同业 Due from Banks and Other Financial Institutions	46.66	2.69
十一、外汇买卖 Foreign Exchange Dealings	110.85	124.04			
其中：结售汇 Of Which: Purchase and Sale of Foreign Exchange	89.33	-6.28	1. 存放境内同业 Due from Domestic Banks and Other Financial Institutions	2.62	-5.80
十二、境内联行存放 Due to Domestic Branches	-33.71	3.53	2. 存放境外同业 Due from Overseas Banks and Other Financial Institutions	44.04	8.49
十三、境外联行存放 Due to Overseas Branches	32.82	-47.08	七、拆放同业 Placements with Banks and Other Financial Institutions	497.10	64.85
十四、各项准备 Total Provisions	43.35	2.34			
其中：贷款呆账准备金 Of Which: Provisions for Bad Loans	13.97	2.23	1. 拆放境内同业 Placements with Domestic Banks and Other Financial Institutions	7.05	-2.46
十五、所有者权益 Owner's Equity	376.47	83.03	2. 拆放境外同业 Placements with Overseas Banks and Other Financial Institutions	490.05	67.31
其中：实收资本 Of Which: Paid-in Capital	236.36	117.98	八、存放境外联行 Due from Overseas Branches	65.03	30.57
当年结益 Net Earnings	21.83	21.83	九、库存现金 Cash in Vault	18.33	0.18
十六、其他 Others	-14.03	0.93			
资金来源总计 Total Sources	**2102.16**	**279.10**	**资金运用总计 Total Uses**	**2102.16**	**279.10**

国有商业银行外汇信贷收支表

Sources and Uses of Credit Funds of State - owned Commercial Banks（Foreign Currency）

（2003年末）

（Year - end of 2003）

单位：亿美元

Unit：100 Million US Dollars

项　目 Items	余　额 Balance	比年初增减额 Changes within the Year	项　目 Items	余　额 Balance	比年初增减额 Changes within the Year
一、各项存款 Total Deposits	1090.57	-49.42	一、各项贷款 Total Loans	835.26	178.98
1. 单位活期存款 Demand Deposits by Enterprises	152.75	18.46	1. 短期贷款 Short - term Loans	295.80	111.20
其中：中资企业存款 Of Which：Deposits by Chinese - funded Enterprises	108.63	20.08	（1）境内短期贷款 Domestic Short - term Loans	295.73	111.13
			其中：中资企业贷款 Of Which：Loans to Chinese - funded Enterprises	180.27	74.70
外商投资企业存款 Deposits by Foreign - funded Enterprises	36.98	-0.61	外商投资企业贷款 Loans to Foreign - funded Enterprises	90.66	32.72
2. 单位定期存款 Time Deposits by Enterprises	153.03	-37.66			
其中：中资企业存款 Of Which：Deposits by Chinese - funded Enterprises	128.55	-26.97	（2）境外短期贷款 Overseas Short - term Loans	0.07	0.07
			2. 中长期贷款 Medium and Long - term Loans	305.74	48.97
外商投资企业存款 Deposits by Foreign - funded Enterprises	4.80	-5.14	（1）境内中长期贷款 Domestic Medium and Long - term Loans	301.02	46.40
3. 储蓄存款 Savings Deposits	733.73	-40.37			
			其中：中资企业贷款 Of Which：Loans to Chinese - funded Enterprises	201.55	27.17
其中：定期存款 Of Which：Time Deposits	629.38	-56.16			
4. 其他类存款 Other Deposits	50.90	10.16	外商投资企业贷款 Loans to Foreign - funded Enterprises	17.95	1.14
5. 境外存款 Foreign Deposits	0.16	-0.01			
			（2）境外中长期贷款 Overseas Medium and Long - term Loans	4.72	2.57
二、境内中长期借款 Domestic Medium and Long - term Borrowing			3. 进出口贸易融资 Financing for Import and Export Trades	59.64	37.98
三、卖出回购证券 Repo	13.08	12.12			
四、境外筹资 Overseas Financing	139.49	-19.22	4. 票据融资 Paper Financing	1.08	0.39
五、向中央银行借款 Borrowings from the Central Bank	3.28	-0.11	其中：贴现 Of Which：Discount	0.72	0.44
六、中央银行存款 Deposits by the Central Bank	59.89	-30.69	5. 各项垫款 Total Advances	44.11	-3.54
七、应付及暂收款 Accounts Payable and Receipts on Account	73.20	2.85	6. 境外筹资转贷款 On - lending of Overseas Financing	128.89	-16.02
			二、投资 Investments	714.82	-28.86

续表
Continued

项　目 Items	余　额 Balance	比年初增减额 Changes within the Year	项　目 Items	余　额 Balance	比年初增减额 Changes within the Year
其中：应付及预提利息 Of Which: Interest Payable and Accrued	14.14	-2.80	1. 购买有价证券 Purchase of Securities	586.14	-16.41
八、同业存放 Due to Banks and Other Financial Institutions	61.72	-21.56	其中：购买境外有价证券 Of Which: Purchase of Foreign Securities	584.80	-14.33
1. 境内同业存放 Due to Domestic Banks and Other Financial Institutions	38.91	-6.85	2. 其他投资 Other Investments	128.68	-12.45
2. 境外同业存放 Due to Overseas Banks and Other Financial Institutions	22.81	-14.71	其中：投资境外 Of Which: Overseas	4.54	-1.12
九、同业拆入 Placements from Banks and Other Financial Institutions	81.34	10.50	三、应收及预付款 Accounts Receivable and Advance Payments	91.16	38.88
1. 境内同业拆入 Placements from Domestic Banks and Other Financial Institutions	3.90	-4.18	其中：应收及预付利息 Of Which: Interest Receivable and Paid in Advance	4.22	-4.39
2. 境外同业拆入 Placements from Overseas Banks and Other Financial Institutions	77.44	14.68	四、买入返售证券 Reverse Repo	0.10	0.10
十、委托基金存款（净） Designated Fund Deposits (Net)	0.01	-0.01	五、存放中央银行 Deposits with the Central Bank	25.23	2.16
十一、外汇买卖 Foreign Exchange Dealings	121.88	11.03	其中：缴存准备金 Of Which: Reserves with the Central Bank	15.93	0.55
其中：结售汇 Of Which: Purchase and Sale of Foreign Exchange	95.50	6.32	六、存放同业 Due from Banks and Other Financial Institutions	106.07	57.43
十二、境内联行存放 Due to Domestic Branches	-37.90	-4.46	1. 存放境内同业 Due from Domestic Banks and Other Financial Institutions	19.50	16.88
十三、境外联行存放 Due to Overseas Branches	58.42	57.02	2. 存放境外同业 Due from Overseas Banks and Other Financial Institutions	86.57	40.55
十四、各项准备 Total Provisions	264.07	220.71	七、拆放同业 Placements with Banks and Other Financial Institutions	737.73	240.62
其中：贷款呆账准备金 Of Which: Provisions for Bad Loans	264.07	220.71	1. 拆放境内同业 Placements with Domestic Banks and Other Financial Institutions	427.24	420.19
十五、所有者权益 Owner's Equity	579.67	203.19	2. 拆放境外同业 Placements with Overseas Banks and Other Financial Institutions	310.49	-179.57
其中：实收资本 Of Which: Paid-in Capital	557.47	321.11	八、存放境外联行 Due from Overseas Branches	22.74	-40.34
当年结益 Net Earnings	22.02	22.02	九、库存现金 Cash in Vault	22.05	3.70
十六、其他 Others	46.44	60.72			
资金来源总计 Total Sources	**2555.16**	**452.67**	**资金运用总计 Total Uses**	**2555.16**	**452.67**

国有商业银行外汇信贷收支表

Sources and Uses of Credit Funds of State - owned Commercial Banks（Foreign Currency）

（2004 年末）

（Year - end of 2004）

单位：亿美元

Unit：100 Million US Dollars

项　目 Items	余　额 Balance	比年初增减额 Changes within the Year	项　目 Items	余　额 Balance	比年初增减额 Changes within the Year
一、各项存款 Total Deposits	1078.90	-11.89	一、各项贷款 Total Loans	779.09	54.87
1. 单位活期存款 Demand Deposits by Enterprises	184.88	32.09	1. 短期贷款 Short - term Loans	265.40	22.94
其中：中资企业存款 Of Which：Deposits by Chinese - funded Enterprises	132.37	24.01	（1）境内短期贷款 Domestic Short - term Loans	265.35	22.95
外商投资企业存款 Deposits by Foreign - funded Enterprises	42.10	5.13	其中：中资企业贷款 Of Which：Loans to Chinese - funded Enterprises	153.02	9.08
2. 单位定期存款 Time Deposits by Enterprises	152.20	-0.85	外商投资企业贷款 Loans to Foreign - funded Enterprises	87.69	10.15
其中：中资企业存款 Of Which：Deposits by Chinese - funded Enterprises	125.54	-3.01	（2）境外短期贷款 Overseas Short - term Loans	0.05	-0.01
外商投资企业存款 Deposits by Foreign - funded Enterprises	4.36	-0.44	2. 中长期贷款 Medium and Long - term Loans	309.92	24.12
3. 储蓄存款 Savings Deposits	663.26	-70.59	（1）境内中长期贷款 Domestic Medium and Long - term Loans	309.53	28.43
其中：定期存款 Of Which：Time Deposits	540.04	-89.41	其中：中资企业贷款 Of Which：Loans to Chinese - funded Enterprises	188.70	-6.36
4. 其他类存款 Other Deposits	78.38	27.44	外商投资企业贷款 Loans to Foreign - funded Enterprises	25.03	13.97
5. 境外存款 Foreign Deposits	0.18	0.02	（2）境外中长期贷款 Overseas Medium and Long - term Loans	0.39	-4.31
二、境内中长期借款 Domestic Medium and Long - term Borrowing			3. 进出口贸易融资 Financing for Import and Export Trades	71.91	12.86
三、卖出回购资产 Assets Repo（Including Securities）	17.70	4.62	4. 票据融资 Paper Financing	1.31	0.23
四、境外筹资 Overseas Financing	141.83	1.91	其中：贴现 Of Which：Discount	1.03	0.31
五、向中央银行借款 Borrowings from the Central Bank	3.00	-0.28	5. 各项垫款 Total Advances	10.89	-7.92
六、中央银行存款 Deposits by the Central Bank	57.82	-2.07	6. 境外筹资转贷款 On - lending of Overseas Financing	119.66	2.64
七、应付及暂收款 Accounts Payable and Receipts on Account	59.01	-15.63	二、投资 Investments	1005.30	290.13

续表
Continued

项　目 Items	余　额 Balance	比年初增减额 Changes within the Year	项　目 Items	余　额 Balance	比年初增减额 Changes within the Year
其中：应付及预提利息 Of Which: Interest Payable and Accrued	11.62	-2.52	1. 购买有价证券 Purchase of Securities	806.74	239.15
八、同业存放 Due to Banks and Other Financial Institutions	60.60	-1.14	其中：购买境外有价证券 Of Which: Purchase of Foreign Securities	800.42	234.17
1. 境内同业存放 Due to Domestic Banks and Other Financial Institutions	57.00	18.07	2. 其他投资 Other Investments	198.56	50.98
2. 境外同业存放 Due to Overseas Banks and Other Financial Institutions	3.60	-19.21	其中：投资境外 Of Which: Overseas	0.65	-3.90
九、同业拆入 Placements from Banks and Other Financial Institutions	23.15	-58.22	三、应收及预付款 Accounts Receivable and Advance Payments	92.03	-0.27
1. 境内同业拆入 Placements from Domestic Banks and Other Financial Institutions	11.92	7.99	其中：应收及预付利息 Of Which: Interest Receivable and Paid in Advance	12.10	-0.99
2. 境外同业拆入 Placements from Overseas Banks and Other Financial Institutions	11.23	-66.21	四、买入返售资产 Assets Reverse Repo (Including Securities)	0.15	0.05
十、委托基金存款（净） Designated Fund Deposits (Net)	-0.01	-0.02	五、存放中央银行 Deposits with the Central Bank	25.58	0.35
十一、外汇买卖 Foreign Exchange Dealings	334.84	212.91	其中：缴存准备金 Of Which: Reserves with the Central Bank	15.46	-0.47
其中：结售汇 Of Which: Purchase and Sale of Foreign Exchange	87.91	-7.93	六、存放同业 Due from Banks and Other Financial Institutions	20.34	-85.80
十二、境内联行存放 Due to Domestic Branches	-14.20	23.96	1. 存放境内同业 Due from Domestic Banks and Other Financial Institutions	9.15	-10.35
十三、境外联行存放 Due to Overseas Branches	50.81	-7.61	2. 存放境外同业 Due from Overseas Banks and Other Financial Institutions	11.19	-75.45
十四、各项准备 Total Provisions	29.52	-234.57	七、拆放同业 Placements with Banks and Other Financial Institutions	377.04	-360.71
其中：贷款呆账准备金 Of Which: Provisions for Bad Loans	23.05	-225.14	1. 拆放境内同业 Placements with Domestic Banks and Other Financial Institutions	3.78	-423.46
十五、所有者权益 Owner's Equity	530.02	-49.62	2. 拆放境外同业 Placements with Overseas Banks and Other Financial Institutions	373.26	62.75
其中：实收资本 Of Which: Paid-in Capital	127.17	-430.30			
当年结益 Net Earnings	65.20	65.20	八、存放境外联行 Due from Overseas Branches	86.32	63.58
十六、其他 Others	37.59	102.49	九、库存现金 Cash in Vault	24.73	2.64
资金来源总计 Total Sources	**2410.58**	**-35.16**	**资金运用总计 Total Uses**	**2140.58**	**-35.16**

国有商业银行外汇信贷收支表

Sources and Uses of Credit Funds of State – owned Commercial Banks（Foreign Currency）

（2005 年末）

（Year – end of 2005）

单位：亿美元

Unit：100 Million US Dollars

项目 Items	余额 Balance	比年初增减额 Changes within the Year	项目 Items	余额 Balance	比年初增减额 Changes within the Year
一、各项存款 Total Deposits	1041.00	–37.97	一、各项贷款 Total Loans	747.58	–5.33
1. 单位活期存款 Demand Deposits by Enterprises	202.43	17.52	1. 短期贷款 Short – term Loans	229.51	–9.98
其中：中资企业存款 Of Which：Deposits by Chinese – funded Enterprises	147.03	14.25	（1）境内短期贷款 Domestic Short – term Loans	229.51	–9.93
外商投资企业存款 Deposits by Foreign – funded Enterprises	46.40	2.68	其中：中资企业贷款 Of Which：Loans to Chinese – funded Enterprises	124.64	–4.69
2. 单位定期存款 Time Deposits by Enterprises	158.68	6.46	外商投资企业贷款 Loans to Foreign – funded Enterprises	77.15	–8.06
其中：中资企业存款 Of Which：Deposits by Chinese – funded Enterprises	93.07	–32.61	（2）境外短期贷款 Overseas Short – term Loans		–0.05
外商投资企业存款 Deposits by Foreign – funded Enterprises	4.17	–0.64	2. 中长期贷款 Medium and Long – term Loans	322.85	9.25
3. 储蓄存款 Savings Deposits	596.72	–66.56	（1）境内中长期贷款 Domestic Medium and Long – term Loans	322.84	9.63
其中：定期存款 Of Which：Time Deposits	479.00	–61.05	其中：中资企业贷款 Of Which：Loans to Chinese – funded Enterprises	199.09	12.76
4. 其他类存款 Other Deposits	83.08	4.69	外商投资企业贷款 Loans to Foreign – funded Enterprises	25.93	–0.54
5. 境外存款 Foreign Deposits	0.09	–0.08	（2）境外中长期贷款 Overseas Medium and Long – term Loans	0.01	–0.38
二、境内中长期借款 Domestic Medium and Long – term Borrowing	0.01	0.01	3. 进出口贸易融资 Financing for Import and Export Trades	89.92	19.17
三、卖出回购资产 Assets Repo（Including Securities）	65.15	47.45	4. 票据融资 Paper Financing	0.73	–0.58
四、境外筹资 Overseas Financing	101.75	–40.24	其中：贴现 Of Which：Discount	0.68	–0.34
五、向中央银行借款 Borrowings from the Central Bank		–3.00	5. 各项垫款 Total Advances	9.07	0.57
六、中央银行存款 Deposits by the Central Bank	35.43	–20.53	6. 境外筹资转贷款 On – lending of Overseas Financing	95.50	–23.76
七、应付及暂收款 Accounts Payable and Receipts on Account	238.71	179.52	二、投资 Investments	1057.77	52.41

续表
Continued

项　目 Items	余　额 Balance	比年初增减额 Changes within the Year	项　目 Items	余　额 Balance	比年初增减额 Changes within the Year
其中：应付及预提利息 Of Which: Interest Payable and Accrued	19.49	7.78	1. 购买有价证券 Purchase of Securities	1042.28	235.43
八、同业存放 Due to Banks and Other Financial Institutions	65.97	5.81	其中：购买境外有价证券 Of Which: Purchase of Foreign Securities	1032.80	232.37
1. 境内同业存放 Due to Domestic Banks and Other Financial Institutions	63.74	6.55	2. 其他投资 Other Investments	15.49	-183.02
2. 境外同业存放 Due to Overseas Banks and Other Financial Institutions	2.23	-0.74	其中：投资境外 Of Which: Overseas	0.66	0.01
九、同业拆入 Placements from Banks and Other Financial Institutions	22.37	-0.73	三、应收及预付款 Accounts Receivable and Advance Payments	120.88	29.52
1. 境内同业拆入 Placements from Domestic Banks and Other Financial Institutions	22.30	10.43	其中：应收及预付利息 Of Which: Interest Receivable and Paid in Advance	24.69	8.99
2. 境外同业拆入 Placements from Overseas Banks and Other Financial Institutions	0.07	-11.16	四、买入返售资产 Assets Reverse Repo (Including Securities)	3.25	2.60
十、委托基金存款（净） Designated Fund Deposits (Net)	-0.01		五、存放中央银行 Deposits with the Central Bank	33.69	10.06
十一、外汇买卖 Foreign Exchange Dealings	426.27	110.62	其中：缴存准备金 Of Which: Reserves with the Central Bank	21.04	5.58
其中：结售汇 Of Which: Purchase and Sale of Foreign Exchange	58.10	-29.74	六、存放同业 Due from Banks and Other Financial Institutions	34.97	14.41
十二、境内联行存放 Due to Domestic Branches	-25.39	-11.65	1. 存放境内同业 Due from Domestic Banks and Other Financial Institutions	4.49	-4.61
十三、境外联行存放 Due to Overseas Branches	15.25	-65.10	2. 存放境外同业 Due from Overseas Banks and Other Financial Institutions	30.48	19.02
十四、各项准备 Total Provisions	25.67	-3.44	七、拆放同业 Placements with Banks and Other Financial Institutions	462.56	86.03
其中：贷款损失准备 Of Which: Provisions for Loan Losses	21.35	-1.72	1. 拆放境内同业 Placements with Domestic Banks and Other Financial Institutions	4.26	0.48
十五、所有者权益 Owner's Equity	208.30	-192.82	2. 拆放境外同业 Placements with Overseas Banks and Other Financial Institutions	458.30	85.55
其中：实收资本 Of Which: Paid-in Capital	150.00	150.00			
当年结益 Net Earnings	62.17	62.17	八、存放境外联行 Due from Overseas Branches	172.62	86.29
十六、其他 Others	433.89	302.42	九、库存现金 Cash in Vault	21.05	-5.64
资金来源总计 Total Sources	**2654.37**	**270.35**	**资金运用总计 Total Uses**	**2654.37**	**270.35**

5. 其他商业银行外汇信贷收支表*（1993—2005 年）

Sources and Uses of Credit Funds of Other Commercial Banks（Foreign Currency）（1993—2005）

其他商业银行外汇信贷收支表

Sources and Uses of Credit Funds of Other Commercial Banks（Foreing Currency）

（1993 年末）

（Year－end of 1993）

单位：亿美元

Unit：100 Million US Dollars

项　目 Items	余　额 Balance	比年初增减额 Changes within the Year	项　目 Items	余　额 Balance	比年初增减额 Changes within the Year
一、各项外汇存款 Total Deposits	24.91	9.18	一、各项外汇贷款 Total Loans	38.02	7.53
1. 居民外汇存款 Deposits by Resident Sector	24.91	9.18	1. 流动资金贷款 Working Capital Loans	17.07	2.74
（1）企业存款 Deposits by Enterprises	19.73	8.27	2. 固定资产贷款 Fixed Assets Loans	6.01	0.20
（2）储蓄存款 Savings Deposits	1.41	－0.03	3. 信托贷款 Trust Loans	0.03	－0.01
定期存款 Time Deposits	0.72	－0.34	4. 委托贷款 Designated Loans	10.90	1.68
活期存款 Demand Deposits	0.69	0.31	5. 贴现 Discount	0.02	0.01
（3）信托存款 Trust Deposits	0.02	0.02	6. 其他贷款 Other Loans	4.00	2.92
（4）委托存款 Designated Deposits	0.81	0.55	二、投资 Investments	0.52	0.34
（5）其他存款 Other Deposits	2.94	0.37	三、有价证券 Securities	0.55	0.31
2. 非居民外汇存款 Deposits by Non－resident Sector			四、境外外汇存款 Foreign Exchange Deposits with Overseas Financial Institutions	3.72	1.20
二、境外筹资 Overseas Financing	16.42	3.08	五、境外拆放 Placements with Overseas Banks and Other Financial Institutions	2.72	1.77
三、人民银行往来 Transactions with the Central Bank	0.24	－0.13	六、人民银行往来 Transactions with the Central Bank	0.25	0.11
四、国内同业往来 Domestic Inter－bank Transactions	5.95	0.53	其中：缴存人行准备金 Of Which：Reserves with the Central Bank	0.06	0.06
其中：同业拆入 Of Which：Placements from Banks and Other Financial Institutions	4.30	0.80	七、国内同业往来 Domestic Inter－bank Transactions	7.71	－0.05
五、外汇买卖 Foreign Exchange Dealings	0.53	0.31	其中：拆放同业 Of Which：Placements with Banks and Other Financial Institutions	2.86	－1.66
六、兑换 Exchange	1.12	0.52			

续表
Continued

项　目 Items	余　额 Balance	比年初增减额 Changes within the Year	项　目 Items	余　额 Balance	比年初增减额 Changes within the Year
七、应付及暂收款 Accounts Payable and Receipts on Account	2.35	-1.28	八、兑换 Exchange	1.07	0.60
			九、应收及暂付款 Accounts Receivalole and Paid in Advance	3.75	0.14
八、呆账准备金 Provisions for Bad Loans	0.06	-0.04			
九、自有资金 Own Capital	4.75	0.68	十、现金 Cash in Vault	0.28	0.18
十、结益 Net Earnings	0.26	0.26	十一、系统内往来 Internal Funds Allocation	8.06	4.25
十一、系统内往来 Internal Funds Allocation	9.73	3.98			
十二、其他 Others	0.28	-0.18			
资金来源总计 Total Sources	**66.65**	**16.38**	**资金运用总计 Total Uses**	**66.65**	**16.38**

* 本表机构包括中国光大银行（1993—2005年）、华夏银行（1993—2005年）、广东发展银行（1993—2005年）、深圳发展银行（1993—2005年）、招商银行（1993—2005年）、福建兴业银行（1993年并入，2003年更名为兴业银行）、中国投资银行（1993—1998年）、上海浦东发展银行（1994—2005年）、海南发展银行（1996—1997年）、中国民生银行（1997—2005年）、交通银行（1998—2005年）、中信实业银行（1998年并入，2005年更名为中信银行）、恒丰银行（2004—2005年）、浙商银行（2004—2005年）。

* Other Commercial Banks of this statement include China Everbright Bank (1993—2005), Huaxia Bank (1993—2005), Guangdong Development Bank (1993—2005), Shenzhen Development Bank (1993—2005), China Merchants Bank (1993—2005), Fujian Industrial Bank (Included in this statement from 1993 to 2005 and renamed as Industrial Bank in 2003), China Investment Bank (1993—1998), Shanghai Pudong Development Bank (1994—2005), Hainan Development Bank (1996—1997), China Minsheng Banking Corporation (1997—2005), Bank of Communications (1998—2005), CITIC Industrial Bank (Included in this statement from 1998 to 2005 and renamed as China CITIC Bank in 2005), Evergrowing Bank (2004—2005), and China Zheshang Bank (2004—2005).

其他商业银行外汇信贷收支表

Sources and Uses of Credit Funds of Other Commercial Banks（Foreign Currency）

（1994年末）

（Year-end of 1994）

单位：亿美元

Unit：100 Million US Dollars

项　目 Items	余　额 Balance	比年初增减额 Changes within the Year	项　目 Items	余　额 Balance	比年初增减额 Changes within the Year
一、各项外汇存款 Total Deposits	33.16	24.66	一、各项外汇贷款 Total Loans	34.20	29.28
1. 居民外汇存款 Deposits by Resident Sector	32.69	24.19	1. 流动资金贷款 Working Capital Loans	20.14	17.23
（1）企业存款 Deposits by Enterprises	25.70	18.47	2. 固定资产贷款 Fixed Assets Loans	1.88	1.78
（2）储蓄存款 Savings Deposits	2.29	2.08	3. 信托贷款 Trust Loans	0.02	0.02
定期存款 Time Deposits	1.39	1.31	4. 委托贷款 Designated Loans	0.61	0.37
活期存款 Demand Deposits	0.90	0.77	5. 贴现 Discount	0.11	0.10
（3）信托存款 Trust Deposits	0.03	0.03	6. 其他贷款 Other Loans	11.44	9.78
（4）委托存款 Designated Deposits	0.75	0.51	二、投资 Investments	0.47	0.32
（5）其他存款 Other Deposits	3.92	3.10	三、有价证券 Securities	0.32	-0.23
2. 非居民外汇存款 Deposits by Non-resident Sector	0.47	0.47	四、境外外汇存款 Foreign Exchange Deposits with Overseas Financial Institutions	2.65	0.22
二、境外筹资 Overseas Financing	3.73	3.65	五、境外拆放 Placements with Overseas Banks and Other Financial Institutions	3.88	3.16
三、人民银行往来 Transactions with the Central Bank	0.06	0.06	六、人民银行往来 Transactions with the Central Bank	0.26	0.21
四、国内同业往来 Domestic Inter-bank Transactions	2.69	2.68	七、缴存人行准备金 Reserves with the Central Bank	0.07	0.07
其中：同业拆入 Of Which：Placements from Banks and Other Financial Institutions	2.22	2.22	八、国内同业往来 Domestic Inter-bank Transactions	6.85	6.12
五、外汇买卖 Foreign Exchange Dealings	0.42	0.43	其中：拆放同业 Of Which：Placements with Banks and Other Financial Institutions	4.52	4.10
六、兑换 Exchange	1.86	1.85	九、兑换 Exchange	1.81	1.81
七、应付及暂收款 Accounts Payable and Receipts on Account	7.28	6.22	十、应收及预付款 Accounts Receivable and Advance Payments	6.42	5.57
八、呆账准备金 Provisions for Bad Loans	0.14	0.14			

续表
Continued

项目 Items	余额 Balance	比年初增减额 Changes within the Year	项目 Items	余额 Balance	比年初增减额 Changes within the Year
九、自有资金 Own Capital	4.97	4.21	十一、现金 Cash in Vault	0.30	0.20
十、结益 Net Earnings	0.93	0.93	十二、系统内往来 Internal Funds Allocation	13.91	10.32
十一、系统内往来 Internal Funds Allocation	14.23	10.64	十三、其他 Others	3.92	3.21
十二、其他 Others	5.59	4.79			
资金来源总计 Total Sources	**75.06**	**60.26**	**资金运用总计 Total Uses**	**75.06**	**60.26**

其他商业银行外汇信贷收支表

Sources and Uses of Credit Funds of Other Commercial Banks（Foreign Currency）

（1995年末）

（Year－end of 1995）

单位：亿美元

Unit：100 Million US Dollars

项目 Items	余额 Balance	比年初增减额 Changes within the Year	项目 Items	余额 Balance	比年初增减额 Changes within the Year
一、各项外汇存款 Total Deposits	53.87	15.12	一、各项外汇贷款 Total Loans	58.57	16.99
1.居民外汇存款 Deposits by Resident Sector	45.53	10.86	1.短期贷款 Short－term Loans	23.48	2.59
（1）企业存款 Deposits by Enterprises	29.49	4.60	其中：三资企业贷款 Of Which：Loans to Foreign Investment Enterprises and Ventures		
其中：三资企业存款 Of Which：Deposits by Foreign Investment Enterprises and Ventures			2.中长期贷款 Medium and Long－term Loans	12.84	5.66
企业定期存款 Time Deposits by Enterprises			其中：外汇储备贷款 Of Which：Foreign Exchange Reserve Loans		
（2）储蓄存款 Savings Deposits	3.59	1.25	3.境外贷款 Foreign Loans	8.41	2.90
其中：定期存款 Of Which：Time Deposits	2.57	1.14	4.其他贷款 Other Loans	13.84	5.84
（3）外债专户存款 Earmarked Deposits for Foreign Debt	1.15	－0.66	二、投资 Investments	0.95	0.36
（4）其他存款 Other Deposits	11.30	5.67	三、购买有价证券 Purchase of Securities	0.47	0.15
2.非居民外汇存款 Deposits by Non－resident Sector	8.34	4.26	四、境外筹资贷款 On－lending of Overseas Financing	1.80	1.20
二、境外筹资 Overseas Financing	4.53	－0.54	五、境外委托借款转贷款 On－lending of Overseas Designated Borrowing	10.33	－1.37
三、境外委托借款 Overseas Designated Borrowing	12.48	0.08	六、人民银行往来 Transactions with the Central Bank	1.33	0.87
四、人民银行往来 Transactions with the Central Bank	6.24	6.18	其中：缴存人行准备金 Of Which：Reserves with the Central Bank	0.67	0.58
其中：外汇储备存款 Of Which：Foreign Exchange Reserve Deposits			七、国内同业往来 Domestic Inter－bank Transactions	12.95	4.20
五、国内同业往来 Domestic Inter－bank Transactions	8.57	2.18	其中：拆放同业 Of Which：Placements with Banks and Other Financial Institutions	6.00	3.05
其中：同业拆入 Of Which：Placements from Banks and Other Financial Institutions		－0.35	八、国外同业往来 Overseas Inter－bank Transactions	10.20	1.96

续表
Continued

项目 Items	余额 Balance	比年初增减额 Changes within the Year	项目 Items	余额 Balance	比年初增减额 Changes within the Year
六、国外同业往来 Overseas Inter - bank Transactions	2.17	0.06	其中：拆放同业 Of Which: Placements with Banks and Other Financial Institutions	5.78	-0.34
其中：同业拆入 Of Which: Placements from Banks and Other Financial Institutions	2.12	0.74	九、外汇买卖 Foreign Exchange Dealings	2.92	-0.17
七、外汇买卖 Foreign Exchange Dealings	5.56	2.16	其中：结售汇 Of Which: Purchase and Sale of Foreign Exchange	7.68	7.43
其中：结售汇 Of Which: Purchase and Sale of Foreign Exchange	5.62	4.92	十、现金 Cash in Vault	0.41	0.09
八、所有者权益 Owner's Equity	5.70	-0.85	十一、系统内往来 Internal Funds Allocation	17.95	2.73
其中：实收资本 Of Which: Paid - in Capital	2.38	—	十二、其他 Others	20.53	7.12
九、结益 Net Earnings	2.23	2.23			
十、系统内往来 Internal Funds Allocation	18.07	3.10			
十一、其他 Others	18.99	4.41			
资金来源总计 Total Sources	**138.41**	**34.13**	**资金运用总计 Total Uses**	**138.41**	**34.13**

其他商业银行外汇信贷收支表

Sources and Uses of Credit Funds of Other Commercial Banks（Foreign Currency）

（1996 年末）

（Year – end of 1996）

单位：亿美元

Unit：100 Million US Dollars

项目 Items	余额 Balance	比年初增减额 Changes within the Year	项目 Items	余额 Balance	比年初增减额 Changes within the Year
一、各项外汇存款 Total Deposits	63.14	11.75	一、各项外汇贷款 Total Loans	67.22	13.28
1. 居民外汇存款 Deposits by Resident Sector	51.25	8.20	1. 短期贷款 Short – term Loans	27.32	1.25
（1）企业存款 Deposits by Enterprises	36.71	7.12	其中：三资企业贷款 Of Which：Loans to Foreign Investment Enterprises and Ventures	7.11	– 0.20
其中：三资企业存款 Of Which：Deposits by Foreign Investment Enterprises and Ventures	6.03	0.74	2. 中长期贷款 Medium and Long – term Loans	11.89	4.27
企业定期存款 Time Deposits by Enterprises	24.26	6.16	其中：外汇储备贷款 Of Which：Foreign Exchange Reserve Loans	6.19	6.19
（2）储蓄存款 Savings Deposits	5.08	1.49	3. 境外贷款 Foreign Loans	11.94	8.21
其中：定期存款 Of Which：Time Deposits	3.57	1.00	4. 其他贷款 Other Loans	16.07	4.23
（3）外债专户存款 Earmarked Deposits for Foreign Debts	0.94	– 0.21	二、投资 Investments	1.49	0.08
			1. 投资 Investments	0.65	– 0.29
（4）其他存款 Other Deposits	8.52	– 0.20	其中：境内投资 Of Which：Domestic	0.52	0.29
2. 非居民外汇存款 Deposits by Non – resident Sector	11.89	3.55	2. 购买有价证券 Purchase of Securities	0.84	0.37
二、境外筹资 Overseas Financing	4.91	0.38	三、融资租赁 Financing Leases	0.34	– 0.11
三、境外委托借款 Overseas Designated Borrowing	9.72	– 0.99	四、境外筹资贷款 On – lending of Overseas Financing	2.83	– 0.47
四、人民银行往来 Transactions with the Central Bank	9.16	3.02	五、境外委托借款转贷款 On – lending of Overseas Designated Borrowing	9.72	– 0.99
其中：外汇储备存款 Of Which：Foreign Exchange Reserve Deposits	8.48	2.36	六、人民银行往来 Transactions with the Central Bank	1.58	0.25
五、国内同业往来 Domestic Inter – bank Transactions	9.41	0.80	其中：缴存人行准备金 Of Which：Reserves with the Central Bank	0.92	0.25
其中：同业拆入 Of Which：Placements from Banks and Other Financial Institutions	4.98	0.68	七、国内同业往来 Domestic Inter – bank Transactions	16.87	3.79

续表
Continued

项　目 Items	余　额 Balance	比年初增减额 Changes within the Year	项　目 Items	余　额 Balance	比年初增减额 Changes within the Year
六、国外同业往来 Overseas Inter - bank Transactions	3.16	0.99	其中：拆放同业 Of Which: Placements with Banks and Other Financial Institutions	9.87	2.97
其中：同业拆入 Of Which: Placements from Banks and Other Financial Institutions	3.06	0.94	八、国外同业往来 Overseas Inter - bank Transactions	14.16	3.96
七、外汇买卖 Foreign Exchange Dealings	2.15	-0.48	其中：拆放同业 Of Which: Placements with Banks and Other Financial Institutions	9.30	3.52
其中：结售汇 Of Which: Purchase and Sale of Foreign Exchange	-16.32	-5.72	九、现金 Cash in Vault	0.65	0.24
八、所有者权益 Owner's Equity	8.94	0.33			
其中：实收资本 Of Which: Paid - in Capital	5.27	1.24			
九、结益 Net Earnings	1.64	1.64			
十、系统内往来 Intemal Funds Allocation	1.36	1.28			
十一、其他 Others	1.27	1.31			
资金来源总计 Total Sources	**114.86**	**20.03**	**资金运用总计 Total Uses**	**114.86**	**20.03**

其他商业银行外汇信贷收支表

Sources and Uses of Credit Funds of Other Commercial Banks（Foreign Currency）

（1997 年末）

（Year – end of 1997）

单位：亿美元

Unit：100 Million US Dollars

项　目 Items	余　额 Balance	比年初增减额 Changes within the Year	项　目 Items	余　额 Balance	比年初增减额 Changes within the Year
一、各项外汇存款 Total Deposits	76.70	13.25	一、各项外汇贷款 Total Loans	75.68	8.45
1. 居民外汇存款 Deposits by Resident Sector	62.33	10.77	1. 短期贷款 Short – term Loans	28.12	0.69
（1）企业存款 Deposits by Enterprises	44.53	7.79	其中：三资企业贷款 Of Which：Loans to Foreign Investment Enterprises and Ventures	7.09	– 0.04
其中：三资企业存款 Of Which：Deposits by Foreign Investment Enterprises and Ventures	5.58	– 0.46	2. 中长期贷款 Medium and Long – term Loans	12.45	0.56
企业定期存款 Time Deposits by Enterprises	31.45	7.16	其中：外汇储备贷款 Of Which：Foreign Exchange Reserve Loans	5.70	– 0.49
（2）储蓄存款 Savings Deposits	7.65	2.57	3. 境外贷款 Foreign Loans	14.58	2.64
其中：定期存款 Of Which：Time Deposits	5.80	2.23	4. 其他贷款 Other Loans	20.53	4.56
（3）外债专户存款 Earmarked Deposits for Foreign Debts	1.34	0.40	二、投资 Investments	2.54	1.05
（4）其他存款 Other Deposits	8.81	0.01	1. 投资 Investments	0.79	0.14
2. 非居民外汇存款 Deposits by Non – resident Sector	14.37	2.48	其中：境内投资 Of Which：Domestic	0.27	– 0.18
二、境外筹资 Overseas Financing	7.06	2.15	2. 购买有价证券 Purchase of Securities	1.75	0.91
三、境外委托借款 Overseas Designated Borrowing	8.13	– 1.52	三、融资租赁 Financing Leases	0.21	– 0.13
四、人民银行往来 Transactions with the Central Bank	9.37	0.21	四、境外筹资贷款 On – lending of Overseas Financing	3.31	0.48
其中：外汇储备存款 Of Which：Foreign Exchange Reserve Deposits	7.52	– 0.96	五、境外委托借款转贷款 On – lending of Overseas Designated Borrowing	8.73	– 0.92
五、国内同业往来 Domestic Inter – bank Transactions	8.42	– 1.26	六、人民银行往来 Transactions with the Central Bank	1.44	– 0.12
其中：同业拆入 Of Which：Placements from Banks and Other Financial Institutions	4.25	– 0.12	其中：缴存人行准备金 Of Which：Reserves with the Central Bank	0.82	– 0.07
			七、国内同业往来 Domestic Inter – bank Transactions	15.51	– 1.36

续表
Continued

项目 Items	余额 Balance	比年初增减额 Changes within the Year	项目 Items	余额 Balance	比年初增减额 Changes within the Year
六、国外同业往来 Overseas Inter - bank Transactions	3.06	-0.04	其中：拆放同业 Of Which: Placements with Banks and Other Financial Institutions	9.28	-0.59
其中：同业拆入 Of Which: Placements from Banks and Other Financial Institutions	2.46	-0.54	八、国外同业往来 Overseas Inter - bank Transactions	18.41	4.10
七、外汇买卖 Foreign Exchange Dealings	-0.20	-2.29	其中：拆放同业 Of Which: Placements with Banks and Other Financial Institutions	11.93	2.79
其中：结售汇 Of Which: Purchase and Sale of Foreign Exchange	-23.92	-7.96	九、现金 Cash in Vault	0.89	0.24
八、所有者权益 Owner's Equity	10.66	0.26			
其中：实收资本 Of Which: Paid - in Capital	6.18	0.91			
九、结益 Net Earnings	2.93	2.93			
十、系统内往来 Internal Funds Allocation	-0.40	-2.09			
十一、其他 Others	0.99	0.19			
资金来源总计 Total Sources	**126.72**	**11.79**	**资金运用总计 Total Uses**	**126.72**	**11.79**

其他商业银行外汇信贷收支表

Sources and Uses of Credit Funds of Other Commercial Banks（Foreign Currency）

（1998 年末）

（Year - end of 1998）

单位：亿美元

Unit：100 Million US Dollars

项目 Items	余额 Balance	比年初增减额 Changes within the Year	项目 Items	余额 Balance	比年初增减额 Changes within the Year
一、各项存款 Total Deposits	149.16	10.66	一、各项贷款 Total Loans	120.86	-5.83
1. 单位活期存款 Demand Deposits by Enterprises	20.55	-5.17	1. 短期贷款 Short - term Loans	48.31	-13.90
其中：中资企业存款 Of Which：Deposits by Chinese - funded Enterprises	4.88	-2.59	（1）境内短期贷款 Domestic Short - term Loans	42.13	-11.58
			其中：中资企业贷款 Of Which：Loans to Chinese - funded Enterprises	19.83	-4.68
外商投资企业存款 Deposits by Foreign - funded Enterprises	8.82	-2.67	外商投资企业贷款 Loans to Foreign - funded Enterprises	12.95	-4.07
2. 单位定期存款 Time Deposits by Enterprises	68.40	4.60	（2）境外短期贷款 Overseas Short - term Loans	6.18	-2.32
其中：中资企业存款 Of Which：Deposits by Chinese - funded Enterprises	44.26	1.62	2. 中长期贷款 Medium and Long - term Loans	28.39	0.72
外商投资企业存款 Deposits by Foreign - funded Enterprises	16.77	4.65	（1）境内中长期贷款 Domestic Medium and Long - term Loans	22.03	-0.51
3. 储蓄存款 Savings Deposits	35.33	12.43	其中：中资企业贷款 Of Which：Loans to Chinese - funded Enterprises	6.24	-0.63
其中：定期存款 Of Which：Time Deposits	32.59	12.15			
4. 其他类存款 Other Deposits	11.01	-0.63	外商投资企业贷款 Loans to Foreign - funded Enterprises	0.95	-1.33
5. 境外存款 Foreign Deposits	13.87	-0.57	（2）境外中长期贷款 Overseas Medium and Long - term Loans	6.36	1.23
二、境内中长期借款 Domestic Medium and Long - term Borrowing	0.08				
三、卖出回购证券 Repo			3. 进出口贸易融资 Financing for Import and Export Trades	10.29	-1.58
四、境外筹资 Overseas Financing	12.92	-3.77	4. 票据融资 Paper Financing	0.10	-0.16
五、向中央银行借款 Borrowings from the Central Bank	0.11	0.04	5. 逾期类贷款 Overdue Loans	33.77	9.09
六、中央银行存款 Deposits by the Central Bank	40.46	3.14	二、投资 Investments	21.78	-5.47
七、同业存放 Due to Banks and Other Financial Institutions	4.26	-1.56	1. 购买有价证券 Purchase of Securities	20.29	-5.67

续表
Continued

项目 Items	余额 Balance	比年初增减额 Changes within the Year	项目 Items	余额 Balance	比年初增减额 Changes within the Year
1. 境内同业存放 Due to Domestic Banks and Other Financial Institutions	3.90	-1.09	其中：购买境外有价证券 Of Which: Purchase of Foreign Securities	20.19	-5.77
2. 境外同业存放 Due to Overseas Banks and Other Financial Institutions	0.36	-0.47	2. 其他投资 Other Investments	1.49	0.20
			其中：投资境外 Of Which: Overseas	0.06	-0.02
八、同业拆入 Placements from Banks and Other Financial Institutions	4.75	-8.47	三、境外筹资转贷款 On-lending of Overseas Financing	4.69	-2.17
1. 境内同业拆入 Placements from Domestic Banks and Other Financial Institutions	3.08	-6.75	四、存放中央银行 Deposits with the Central Bank	3.14	-0.13
			其中：缴存准备金 Of Which: Reserves with the Central Bank	2.37	0.37
2. 境外同业拆入 Placements from Overseas Banks and Other Financial Institutions	1.67	-1.72	五、存放同业 Due from Banks and Other Financial Institutions	19.64	-1.31
九、委托基金存款 Designated Fund Deposits	0.06	-0.14			
十、外汇买卖 Foreign Exchange Dealings	4.16	1.18	1. 存放境内同业 Due from Domestic Banks and Other Financial Institutions	4.71	-1.08
其中：结售汇 Of Which: Purchase and Sale of Foreign Exchange	0.41	-0.90	2. 存放境外同业 Due from Overseas Banks and Other Financial Institutions	14.93	-0.23
十一、境内联行存放 Due to Domestic Branches	-1.84	-10.35	六、拆放同业 Placements with Banks and Other Financial Institutions	54.67	2.70
十二、境外联行存放 Due to Overseas Branches	0.26	-0.54			
十三、所有者权益 Owner's Equity	32.10	3.57	1. 拆放境内同业 Placements with Domestic Banks and Other Financial Institutions	6.24	-2.37
其中：实收资本 Of Which: Paid-in Capital	21.45	3.22	2. 拆放境外同业 Placements with Overseas Banks and Other Financial Institutions	48.43	5.07
当年结益 Net Earnings	4.54	4.54			
十四、其他 Others	-4.81	-5.31	七、存放境外联行 Due from Overseas Branches	14.92	0.56
			八、库存现金 Cash in Vault	1.97	0.10
资金来源总计 Total Sources	**241.67**	**-11.55**	**资金运用总计 Total Uses**	**241.67**	**-11.55**

其他商业银行外汇信贷收支表

Sources and Uses of Credit Funds of Other Commercial Banks（Foreign Currency）

（1999 年末）

（Year - end of 1999）

单位：亿美元

Unit：100 Million US Dollars

项　目 Items	余　额 Balance	比年初增减额 Changes within the Year	项　目 Items	余　额 Balance	比年初增减额 Changes within the Year
一、各项存款 Total Deposits	168.61	19.43	一、各项贷款 Total Loans	110.26	-8.37
1. 单位活期存款 Demand Deposits by Enterprises	21.09	0.57	1. 短期贷款 Short - term Loans	34.91	-11.74
其中：中资企业存款 Of Which：Deposits by Chinese - funded Enterprises	5.54	0.66	（1）境内短期贷款 Domestic Short - term Loans	32.23	-8.24
外商投资企业存款 Deposits by Foreign - funded Enterprises	8.99	0.17	其中：中资企业贷款 Of Which：Loans to Chinese - funded Enterprises	17.20	-2.63
			外商投资企业贷款 Loans to Foreign - funded Enterprises	9.32	-3.59
2. 单位定期存款 Time Deposits by Enterprises	72.58	4.14			
其中：中资企业存款 Of Which：Deposits by Chinese - funded Enterprises	43.67	-0.59	（2）境外短期贷款 Overseas Short - term Loans	2.68	-3.50
			2. 中长期贷款 Medium and Long - term Loans	24.09	-3.66
外商投资企业存款 Deposits by Foreign - funded Enterprises	17.65	0.93	（1）境内中长期贷款 Domestic Medium and Long - term Loans	19.83	-1.56
3. 储蓄存款 Savings Deposits	51.28	15.93			
			其中：中资企业贷款 Of Which：Loans to Chinese - funded Enterprises	4.00	-2.24
其中：定期存款 Of Which：Time Deposits	47.45	14.84			
4. 其他类存款 Other Deposits	14.17	3.17	外商投资企业贷款 Loans to Foreign - funded Enterprises	1.58	0.63
5. 境外存款 Foreign Deposits	9.49	-4.38			
			（2）境外中长期贷款 Overseas Medium and Long - term Loans	4.26	-2.10
二、境内中长期借款 Domestic Medium and Long - term Borrowing		-0.08			
			3. 进出口贸易融资 Financing for Import and Export Trades	8.60	-1.72
三、卖出回购证券 Repo	-0.28	-0.28			
四、境外筹资 Overseas Financing	10.17	-2.75	4. 票据融资 Paper Financing	0.12	0.02
五、向中央银行借款 Borrowings from the Central Bank	0.05	-0.06	5. 逾期类贷款 Overdue Loans	42.54	8.73
六、中央银行存款 Deposits by the Central Bank	40.35	-0.11	二、投资 Investments	27.74	6.00
七、同业存放 Due to Banks and Other Financial Institutions	3.13	-1.09	1. 购买有价证券 Purchase of Securities	26.29	6.02

续表
Continued

项　目 Items	余　额 Balance	比年初增减额 Changes within the Year	项　目 Items	余　额 Balance	比年初增减额 Changes within the Year
1. 境内同业存放 Due to Domestic Banks and Other Financial Institutions	3.10	-0.76	其中：购买境外有价证券 Of Which: Purchase of Foreign Securities	24.93	4.76
2. 境外同业存放 Due to Overseas Banks and Other Financial Institutions	0.03	-0.33	2. 其他投资 Other Investments	1.45	-0.02
			其中：投资境外 Of Which: Overseas	0.09	0.03
八、同业拆入 Placements from Banks and Other Financial Institutions	5.26	0.76	三、境外筹资转贷款 On-lending of Overseas Financing	2.32	-2.37
1. 境内同业拆入 Placements from Domestic Banks and Other Financial Institutions	4.72	1.77	四、存放中央银行 Deposits with the Central Bank	3.49	0.35
			其中：缴存准备金 Of Which: Reserves with the Central Bank	1.93	-0.44
2. 境外同业拆入 Placements from Overseas Banks and Other Financial Institutions	0.54	-1.01	五、存放同业 Due from Banks and Other Financial Institutions	27.41	8.12
九、委托基金存款 Designated Fund Deposits	-0.15	-0.21			
十、外汇买卖 Foreign Exchange Dealings	8.48	4.35	1. 存放境内同业 Due from Domestic Banks and Other Financial Institutions	6.66	1.98
其中：结售汇 Of Which: Purchase and Sale of Foreign Exchange	1.72	1.21	2. 存放境外同业 Due from Overseas Banks and Other Financial Institutions	20.75	6.14
十一、境内联行存放 Due to Domestic Branches	3.39	6.06	六、拆放同业 Placements with Banks and Other Financial Institutions	62.13	7.50
十二、境外联行存放 Due to Overseas Branches	0.26				
十三、所有者权益 Owner's Equity	31.32	-0.47	1. 拆放境内同业 Placements with Domestic Banks and Other Financial Institutions	4.22	-1.98
其中：实收资本 Of Which: Paid-in Capital	21.83	0.63	2. 拆放境外同业 Placements with Overseas Banks and Other Financial Institutions	57.91	9.48
当年结益 Net Earnings	3.20	3.20			
十四、其他 Others	-15.51	-9.48	七、存放境外联行 Due from Overseas Branches	17.32	2.40
			八、库存现金 Cash in Vault	4.41	2.44
资金来源总计 Total Sources	**255.08**	**16.07**	**资金运用总计 Total Uses**	**255.08**	**16.07**

其他商业银行外汇信贷收支表

Sources and Uses of Credit Funds of Other Commercial Banks（Foreign Currency）

（2000年末）

（Year – end of 2000）

单位：亿美元

Unit：100 Million US Dollars

项 目 Items	余 额 Balance	比年初增减额 Changes within the Year	项 目 Items	余 额 Balance	比年初增减额 Changes within the Year
一、各项存款 Total Deposits	218.42	49.80	一、各项贷款 Total Loans	89.40	– 20.87
1. 单位活期存款 Demand Deposits by Enterprises	22.98	1.88	1. 短期贷款 Short – term Loans	26.71	– 7.97
其中：中资企业存款 Of Which：Deposits by Chinese – funded Enterprises	5.34	– 0.20	（1）境内短期贷款 Domestic Short – term Loans	24.57	– 7.43
外商投资企业存款 Deposits by Foreign – funded Enterprises	9.89	0.90	其中：中资企业贷款 Of Which：Loans to Chinese – funded Enterprises	12.90	– 4.30
			外商投资企业贷款 Loans to Foreign – funded Enterprises	7.20	– 2.06
2. 单位定期存款 Time Deposits by Enterprises	91.32	18.74	（2）境外短期贷款 Overseas Short – term Loans	2.14	– 0.54
其中：中资企业存款 Of Which：Deposits by Chinese – funded Enterprises	53.03	9.36	2. 中长期贷款 Medium and Long – term Loans	14.22	– 9.88
外商投资企业存款 Deposits by Foreign – funded Enterprises	23.58	5.93	（1）境内中长期贷款 Domestic Medium and Long – term Loans	12.18	– 7.66
3. 储蓄存款 Savings Deposits	78.37	27.09	其中：中资企业贷款 Of Which：Loans to Chinese – funded Enterprises	2.62	– 1.38
其中：定期存款 Of Which：Time Deposits	72.85	25.40	外商投资企业贷款 Loans to Foreign – funded Enterprises	1.11	– 0.47
4. 其他类存款 Other Deposits	17.77	3.60	（2）境外中长期贷款 Overseas Medium and Long – term Loans	2.04	– 2.22
5. 境外存款 Foreign Deposits	7.98	– 1.51	3. 进出口贸易融资 Financing for Import and Export Trades	7.96	– 0.64
二、境内中长期借款 Domestic Medium and Long – term Borrowing					
三、卖出回购证券 Repo	– 0.13	0.15			
四、境外筹资 Overseas Financing	4.84	– 5.33	4. 票据融资 Paper Financing	0.22	0.10
五、向中央银行借款 Borrowings from the Central Bank		– 0.05	5. 逾期类贷款 Overdue Loans	40.29	– 2.48
六、中央银行存款 Deposits by the Central Bank	12.83	– 27.52	二、投资 Investments	45.91	18.17
七、同业存放 Due to Banks and Other Financial Institutions	5.12	1.99	1. 购买有价证券 Purchase of Securities	43.80	17.51

续表
Continued

项目 Items	余额 Balance	比年初增减额 Changes within the Year	项目 Items	余额 Balance	比年初增减额 Changes within the Year
1. 境内同业存放 Due to Domestic Banks and Other Financial Institutions	5.09	1.99	其中：购买境外有价证券 Of Which: Purchase of Foreign Securities	41.52	16.59
2. 境外同业存放 Due to Overseas Banks and Other Financial Institutions	0.03		2. 其他投资 Other Investments	2.11	0.66
			其中：投资境外 Of Which: Overseas	0.25	0.16
八、同业拆入 Placements from Banks and Other Financial Institutions	5.29	0.03	三、境外筹资转贷款 On – lending of Overseas Financing	2.15	– 0.17
1. 境内同业拆入 Placements from Domestic Banks and Other Financial Institutions	3.29	– 1.43	四、存放中央银行 Deposits with the Central Bank	4.83	1.34
2. 境外同业拆入 Placements from Overseas Banks and Other Financial Institutions	2.00	1.46	其中：缴存准备金 Of Which: Reserves with the Central Bank	2.39	0.46
			五、存放同业 Due from Banks and Other Financial Institutions	24.40	– 3.01
九、委托基金存款 Designated Fund Deposits	– 0.08	0.07			
十、外汇买卖 Foreign Exchange Dealings	7.70	– 0.77	1. 存放境内同业 Due from Domestic Banks and Other Financial Institutions	4.33	– 2.33
其中：结售汇 Of Which: Purchase and Sale of Foreign Exchange	– 4.93	– 6.64	2. 存放境外同业 Due from Overseas Banks and Other Financial Institutions	20.07	– 0.68
十一、境内联行存放 Due to Domestic Branches	0.30	3.96			
			六、拆放同业 Placements with Banks and Other Financial Institutions	111.86	49.73
十二、境外联行存放 Due to Overseas Branches	0.03	– 0.23			
十三、所有者权益 Owner's Equity	34.43	3.17	1. 拆放境内同业 Placements with Domestic Banks and Other Financial Institutions	4.15	– 0.07
其中：实收资本 Of Which: Paid – in Capital	26.41	4.58	2. 拆放境外同业 Placements with Overseas Banks and Other Financial Institutions	107.71	49.80
当年结益 Net Earnings	4.16	4.16			
十四、其他 Others	– 3.49	4.90	七、存放境外联行 Due from Overseas Branches	2.65	– 14.67
			八、库存现金 Cash in Vault	4.06	– 0.35
资金来源总计 Total Sources	**285.26**	**30.17**	**资金运用总计 Total Uses**	**285.26**	**30.17**

其他商业银行外汇信贷收支表

Sources and Uses of Credit Funds of Other Commercial Banks（Foreign Currency）

（2001 年末）

（Year - end of 2001）

单位：亿美元

Unit：100 Million US Dollars

项　目 Items	余　额 Balance	比年初增减额 Changes within the Year	项　目 Items	余　额 Balance	比年初增减额 Changes within the Year
一、各项存款 Total Deposits	232.41	13.89	一、各项贷款 Total Loans	94.45	0.72
1. 单位活期存款 Demand Deposits by Enterprises	27.75	4.76	1. 短期贷款 Short - term Loans	51.00	1.02
其中：中资企业存款 Of Which：Deposits by Chinese - funded Enterprises	6.25	0.91	（1）境内短期贷款 Domestic Short - term Loans	48.79	2.55
			其中：中资企业贷款 Of Which：Loans to Chinese - funded Enterprises	24.75	1.71
外商投资企业存款 Deposits by Foreign - funded Enterprises	11.66	1.76	外商投资企业贷款 Loans to Foreign - funded Enterprises	15.25	0.52
2. 单位定期存款 Time Deposits by Enterprises	88.13	- 3.29			
其中：中资企业存款 Of Which：Deposits by Chinese - funded Enterprises	51.05	- 2.00	（2）境外短期贷款 Overseas Short - term Loans	2.21	- 1.53
			2. 中长期贷款 Medium and Long - term Loans	25.19	- 1.64
外商投资企业存款 Deposits by Foreign - funded Enterprises	21.47	- 2.10	（1）境内中长期贷款 Domestic Medium and Long - term Loans	18.77	- 2.33
3. 储蓄存款 Savings Deposits	93.45	15.02			
其中：定期存款 Of Which：Time Deposits	83.52	10.61	其中：中资企业贷款 Of Which：Loans to Chinese - funded Enterprises	4.83	- 0.69
4. 其他类存款 Other Deposits	14.43	- 3.27	外商投资企业贷款 Loans to Foreign - funded Enterprises	1.99	- 0.58
5. 境外存款 Foreign Deposits	8.65	0.67			
			（2）境外中长期贷款 Overseas Medium and Long - term Loans	6.42	0.69
二、境内中长期借款 Domestic Medium and Long - term Borrowing		- 2.70			
			3. 进出口贸易融资 Financing for Import and Export Trades	11.36	1.56
三、卖出回购证券 Repo	1.02	0.92			
四、境外筹资 Overseas Financing	4.54	- 0.30	4. 票据融资 Paper Financing	0.14	- 0.09
五、向中央银行借款 Borrowings from the Central Bank			其中：贴现 Of Which：Discount	0.08	- 0.11
六、中央银行存款 Deposits by the Central Bank	1.01	- 11.84	5. 各项垫款 Total Advances	4.35	- 0.18
七、应付及暂收款 Accounts Payable and Receipts on Account	28.99	4.71	6. 境外筹资转贷款 On - lending of Overseas Financing	2.41	0.05
			二、投资 Investments	89.09	43.18

续表
Continued

项　目 Items	余　额 Balance	比年初增减额 Changes within the Year	项　目 Items	余　额 Balance	比年初增减额 Changes within the Year
其中：应付及预提利息 Of Which：Interest Payable and Accrued	5.11	0.11	1. 购买有价证券 Purchase of Securities	84.88	40.72
			其中：购买境外有价证券 Of Which：Purchase of Foreign Securities	77.46	35.58
八、同业存放 Due to Banks and Other Financial Institutions	12.16	7.04	2. 其他投资 Other Investments	4.21	2.46
1. 境内同业存放 Due to Domestic Banks and Other Financial Institutions	12.13	7.03	其中：投资境外 Of Which：Overseas	2.71	2.46
2. 境外同业存放 Due to Overseas Banks and Other Financial Institutions	0.03	0.01	三、应收及预付款 Accounts Receivable and Advance Payments	32.49	3.60
九、同业拆入 Placements from Banks and Other Financial Institutions	6.27	0.98	其中：应收及预付利息 Of Which：Interest Receivable and Paid in Advance	8.37	－0.66
1. 境内同业拆入 Placements from Domestic Banks and Other Financial Institutions	4.84	1.55	四、买入返售证券 Reverse Repo	0.10	－0.13
			五、存放中央银行 Deposits with the Central Bank	6.11	1.28
2. 境外同业拆入 Placements from Overseas Banks and Other Financial Institutions	1.43	－0.57	其中：缴存准备金 Of Which：Reserves with the Central Bank	3.24	0.85
十、委托基金存款（净） Designated Fund Deposits（Net）	0.02	0.10	六、存放同业 Due from Banks and Other Financial Institutions	21.88	－2.57
十一、外汇买卖 Foreign Exchange Dealings	13.99	6.30			
其中：结售汇 Of Which：Purchase and Sale of Foreign Exchange	－2.00	2.93	1. 存放境内同业 Due from Domestic Banks and Other Financial Institutions	5.97	1.75
十二、境内联行存放 Due to Domestic Branches	3.19	3.42	2. 存放境外同业 Due from Overseas Banks and Other Financial Institutions	15.91	－4.32
十三、境外联行存放 Due to Overseas Branches	9.28	9.25			
十四、各项准备 Total Provisions	1.69	0.08	七、拆放同业 Placements with Banks and Other Financial Institutions	97.96	－13.90
其中：贷款呆账准备金 Of Which：Provisions for Bad Loans	1.61	0.10	1. 拆放境内同业 Placements with Domestic Banks and Other Financial Institutions	4.13	－0.02
十五、所有者权益 Owner's Equity	34.18	－0.26	2. 拆放境外同业 Placements with Overseas Banks and Other Financial Institutions	93.83	－13.88
其中：实收资本 Of Which：Paid－in Capital	28.25	1.80			
当年结益 Net Earnings	1.81	1.81	八、存放境外联行 Due from Overseas Branches	1.57	－1.08
十六、其他 Others	－0.54		九、库存现金 Cash in Vault	4.56	0.49
资金来源总计 Total Sources	**348.21**	**31.59**	**资金运用总计 Total Uses**	**348.21**	**31.59**

其他商业银行外汇信贷收支表

Sources and Uses of Credit Funds of Other Commercial Banks（Foreign Currency）

（2002 年末）

（Year - end of 2002）

单位：亿美元

Unit：100 Million US Dollars

项　目 Items	余　额 Balance	比年初增减额 Changes within the Year	项　目 Items	余　额 Balance	比年初增减额 Changes within the Year
一、各项存款 Total Deposits	257.61	25.18	一、各项贷款 Total Loans	115.80	21.33
1. 单位活期存款 Demand Deposits by Enterprises	35.23	7.62	1. 短期贷款 Short - term Loans	55.88	7.69
其中：中资企业存款 Of Which：Deposits by Chinese - funded Enterprises	8.95	2.70	(1) 境内短期贷款 Domestic Short - term Loans	53.13	7.15
外商投资企业存款 Deposits by Foreign - funded Enterprises	16.02	4.36	其中：中资企业贷款 Of Which：Loans to Chinese - funded Enterprises	29.73	2.67
2. 单位定期存款 Time Deposits by Enterprises	85.55	-0.81	外商投资企业贷款 Loans to Foreign - funded Enterprises	16.22	3.24
其中：中资企业存款 Of Which：Deposits by Chinese - funded Enterprises	53.96	2.85	(2) 境外短期贷款 Overseas Short - term Loans	2.75	0.54
外商投资企业存款 Deposits by Foreign - funded Enterprises	15.12	-6.68	2. 中长期贷款 Medium and Long - term Loans	33.00	5.08
3. 储蓄存款 Savings Deposits	106.99	13.54	(1) 境内中长期贷款 Domestic Medium and Long - term Loans	27.15	5.65
其中：定期存款 Of Which：Time Deposits	89.33	5.81	其中：中资企业贷款 Of Which：Loans to Chinese - funded Enterprises	12.52	3.32
4. 其他类存款 Other Deposits	20.08	3.72	外商投资企业贷款 Loans to Foreign - funded Enterprises	2.05	0.96
5. 境外存款 Foreign Deposits	9.76	1.11	(2) 境外中长期贷款 Overseas Medium and Long - term Loans	5.85	-0.57
二、境内中长期借款 Domestic Medium and Long - term Borrowing			3. 进出口贸易融资 Financing for Import and Export Trades	19.02	7.64
三、卖出回购证券 Repo	0.44	-0.58			
四、境外筹资 Overseas Financing	2.36	-2.18	4. 票据融资 Paper Financing	1.05	0.83
五、向中央银行借款 Borrowings from the Central Bank			其中：贴现 Of Which：Discount	0.85	0.77
六、中央银行存款 Deposits by the Central Bank		-0.40	5. 各项垫款 Total Advances	4.16	-0.19
七、应付及暂收款 Accounts Payable and Receipts on Account	29.97	13.05	6. 境外筹资转贷款 On - lending of Overseas Financing	2.69	0.28
			二、投资 Investments	94.66	6.03

续表
Continued

项目 Items	余额 Balance	比年初增减额 Changes within the Year	项目 Items	余额 Balance	比年初增减额 Changes within the Year
其中：应付及预提利息 Of Which: Interest Payable and Accrued	3.48	-1.63	1. 购买有价证券 Purchase of Securities	91.89	8.07
八、同业存放 Due to Banks and Other Financial Institutions	12.98	1.25	其中：购买境外有价证券 Of Which: Purchase of Foreign Securities	83.20	6.80
1. 境内同业存放 Due to Domestic Banks and Other Financial Institutions	12.86	1.16	2. 其他投资 Other Investments	2.77	-2.04
2. 境外同业存放 Due to Overseas Banks and Other Financial Institutions	0.12	0.09	其中：投资境外 Of Which: Overseas	0.12	-2.21
九、同业拆入 Placements from Banks and Other Financial Institutions	11.35	5.08	三、应收及预付款 Accounts Receivable and Advance Payments	24.96	4.68
1. 境内同业拆入 Placements from Domestic Banks and Other Financial Institutions	4.36	-0.48	其中：应收及预付利息 Of Which: Interest Receivable and Paid in Advance	4.35	-4.13
2. 境外同业拆入 Placements from Overseas Banks and Other Financial Institutions	6.99	5.56	四、买入返售证券 Reverse Repo	0.52	0.42
十、委托基金存款（净） Designated Fund Deposits (Net)	0.03	-0.03	五、存放中央银行 Deposits with the Central Bank	7.65	1.54
十一、外汇买卖 Foreign Exchange Dealings	16.74	2.64	其中：缴存准备金 Of Which: Reserves with the Central Bank	4.49	1.25
其中：结售汇 Of Which: Purchase and Sale of Foreign Exchange	14.78	16.79	六、存放同业 Due from Banks and Other Financial Institutions	37.23	16.22
十二、境内联行存放 Due to Domestic Branches	-2.69	-5.00	1. 存放境内同业 Due from Domestic Banks and Other Financial Institutions	8.47	2.69
十三、境外联行存放 Due to Overseas Branches	9.28		2. 存放境外同业 Due from Overseas Banks and Other Financial Institutions	28.76	13.53
十四、各项准备 Total Provisions	5.65	3.95	七、拆放同业 Placements with Banks and Other Financial Institutions	87.08	-10.82
其中：贷款呆账准备金 Of Which: Provisions for Bad Loans	4.79	3.18	1. 拆放境内同业 Placements with Domestic Banks and Other Financial Institutions	5.35	1.22
十五、所有者权益 Owner's Equity	30.01	-4.13	2. 拆放境外同业 Placements with Overseas Banks and Other Financial Institutions	81.73	-12.04
其中：实收资本 Of Which: Paid-in Capital	27.26	-0.99			
当年结益 Net Earnings	2.77	2.77	八、存放境外联行 Due from Overseas Branches	0.46	-1.11
十六、其他 Others		0.30	九、库存现金 Cash in Vault	5.37	0.84
资金来源总计 Total Sources	**373.73**	**39.13**	**资金运用总计 Total Uses**	**373.73**	**39.13**

其他商业银行外汇信贷收支表

Sources and Uses of Credit Funds of Other Commercial Banks（Foreign Currency）

（2003 年末）

（Year－end of 2003）

单位：亿美元

Unit：100 Million US Dollars

项目 Items	余额 Balance	比年初增减额 Changes within the Year	项目 Items	余额 Balance	比年初增减额 Changes within the Year
一、各项存款 Total Deposits	271.14	13.51	一、各项贷款 Total Loans	158.87	43.46
1. 单位活期存款 Demand Deposits by Enterprises	44.34	9.11	1. 短期贷款 Short－term Loans	67.82	12.20
其中：中资企业存款 Of Which：Deposits by Chinese－funded Enterprises	12.02	3.07	（1）境内短期贷款 Domestic Short－term Loans	65.48	12.61
			其中：中资企业贷款 Of Which：Loans to Chinese－funded Enterprises	38.05	8.32
外商投资企业存款 Deposits by Foreign－funded Enterprises	21.60	5.58	外商投资企业贷款 Loans to Foreign－funded Enterprises	20.10	3.88
2. 单位定期存款 Time Deposits by Enterprises	91.46	5.90	（2）境外短期贷款 Overseas Short－term Loans	2.34	－0.41
其中：中资企业存款 Of Which：Deposits by Chinese－funded Enterprises	57.66	3.63	2. 中长期贷款 Medium and Long－term Loans	52.31	19.44
外商投资企业存款 Deposits by Foreign－funded Enterprises	14.35	－0.71	（1）境内中长期贷款 Domestic Medium and Long－term Loans	45.03	18.01
3. 储蓄存款 Savings Deposits	104.88	－2.12	其中：中资企业贷款 Of Which：Loans to Chinese－funded Enterprises	19.00	6.48
其中：定期存款 Of Which：Time Deposits	80.51	－8.82	外商投资企业贷款 Loans to Foreign－funded Enterprises	3.39	1.34
4. 其他类存款 Other Deposits	20.35	0.27	（2）境外中长期贷款 Overseas Medium and Long－term Loans	7.28	1.43
5. 境外存款 Foreign Deposits	10.11	0.35	3. 进出口贸易融资 Financing for Import and Export Trades	31.77	12.75
二、境内中长期借款 Domestic Medium and Long－term Borrowing			4. 票据融资 Paper Financing	1.34	0.29
三、卖出回购证券 Repo	1.17	0.73	其中：贴现 Of Which：Discount	1.12	0.27
四、境外筹资 Overseas Financing	2.75	0.39	5. 各项垫款 Total Advances	2.94	－1.22
五、向中央银行借款 Borrowings from the Central Bank			6. 境外筹资转贷款 On－lending of Overseas Financing	2.69	
六、中央银行存款 Deposits by the Central Bank			二、投资 Investments	95.14	0.49
七、应付及暂收款 Accounts Payable and Receipts on Account	21.70	－8.27			

续表
Continued

项　　目 Items	余　额 Balance	比年初增减额 Changes within the Year	项　　目 Items	余　额 Balance	比年初增减额 Changes within the Year
其中：应付及预提利息 Of Which: Interest Payable and Accrued	2.30	-1.18	1. 购买有价证券 Purchase of Securities	91.30	-0.58
			其中：购买境外有价证券 Of Which: Purchase of Foreign Securities	81.80	-7.23
八、同业存放 Due to Banks and Other Financial Institutions	23.40	10.31	2. 其他投资 Other Investments	3.84	1.07
1. 境内同业存放 Due to Domestic Banks and Other Financial Institutions	23.21	10.22	其中：投资境外 Of Which: Overseas	0.12	
2. 境外同业存放 Due to Overseas Banks and Other Financial Institutions	0.19	0.09	三、应收及预付款 Accounts Receivable and Advance Payments	19.66	-5.30
九、同业拆入 Placements from Banks and Other Financial Institutions	13.04	1.69	其中：应收及预付利息 Of Which: Interest Receivable and Paid in Advance	2.66	-1.69
1. 境内同业拆入 Placements from Domestic Banks and Other Financial Institutions	4.32	-0.04	四、买入返售证券 Reverse Repo	1.88	1.10
			五、存放中央银行 Deposits with the Central Bank	8.99	1.34
2. 境外同业拆入 Placements from Overseas Banks and Other Financial Institutions	8.72	1.73	其中：缴存准备金 Of Which: Reserves with the Central Bank	5.55	1.06
十、委托基金存款（净） Designated Fund Deposits (Net)	-0.16	-0.19	六、存放同业 Due from Banks and Other Financial Institutions	37.34	0.11
十一、外汇买卖 Foreign Exchange Dealings	12.18	-4.56			
其中：结售汇 Of Which: Purchase and Sale of Foreign Exchange	-13.28	-28.06	1. 存放境内同业 Due from Domestic Banks and Other Financial Institutions	7.60	-0.87
十二、境内联行存放 Due to Domestic Branches	-1.74	0.94	2. 存放境外同业 Due from Overseas Banks and Other Financial Institutions	29.74	0.98
十三、境外联行存放 Due to Overseas Branches	0.14	-9.14	七、拆放同业 Placements with Banks and Other Financial Institutions	56.02	-31.06
十四、各项准备 Total Provisions	6.27	0.62			
其中：贷款呆账准备金 Of Which: Provisions for Bad Loans	5.57	0.74	1. 拆放境内同业 Placements with Domestic Banks and Other Financial Institutions	7.76	2.41
十五、所有者权益 Owner's Equity	35.07	5.09	2. 拆放境外同业 Placements with Overseas Banks and Other Financial Institutions	48.26	-33.47
其中：实收资本 Of Which: Paid-in Capital	27.83	0.57			
当年结益 Net Earnings	3.01	3.01	八、存放境外联行 Due from Overseas Branches	1.79	1.33
十六、其他 Others	0.28	0.52	九、库存现金 Cash in Vault	5.55	0.17
资金来源总计 Total Sources	**385.24**	**11.64**	**资金运用总计 Total Uses**	**385.24**	**11.64**

其他商业银行外汇信贷收支表

Sources and Uses of Credit Funds of Other Commercial Banks（Foreign Currency）

（2004 年末）

（Year - end of 2004）

单位：亿美元

Unit：100 Million US Dollars

项　目 Items	余　额 Balance	比年初增减额 Changes within the Year	项　目 Items	余　额 Balance	比年初增减额 Changes within the Year
一、各项存款 Total Deposits	306.15	34.92	一、各项贷款 Total Loans	164.60	13.07
1. 单位活期存款 Demand Deposits by Enterprises	58.66	14.38	1. 短期贷款 Short - term Loans	68.36	4.86
其中：中资企业存款 Of Which：Deposits by Chinese - funded Enterprises	18.28	6.09	（1）境内短期贷款 Domestic Short - term Loans	65.33	4.17
外商投资企业存款 Deposits by Foreign - funded Enterprises	25.73	4.56	其中：中资企业贷款 Of Which：Loans to Chinese - funded Enterprises	37.67	1.23
2. 单位定期存款 Time Deposits by Enterprises	82.69	- 8.48	外商投资企业贷款 Loans to Foreign - funded Enterprises	22.41	2.74
其中：中资企业存款 Of Which：Deposits by Chinese - funded Enterprises	59.07	2.80	（2）境外短期贷款 Overseas Short - term Loans	3.03	0.69
			2. 中长期贷款 Medium and Long - term Loans	55.70	3.76
外商投资企业存款 Deposits by Foreign - funded Enterprises	9.00	- 6.60	（1）境内中长期贷款 Domestic Medium and Long - term Loans	47.71	3.05
3. 储蓄存款 Savings Deposits	116.14	11.26	其中：中资企业贷款 Of Which：Loans to Chinese - funded Enterprises	17.66	- 1.57
其中：定期存款 Of Which：Time Deposits	78.64	- 1.89			
4. 其他类存款 Other Deposits	36.01	15.23	外商投资企业贷款 Loans to Foreign - funded Enterprises	3.58	- 0.02
5. 境外存款 Foreign Deposits	12.65	2.53	（2）境外中长期贷款 Overseas Medium and Long - term Loans	7.99	0.71
二、境内中长期借款 Domestic Medium and Long - term Borrowing			3. 进出口贸易融资 Financing for Import and Export Trades	35.28	5.28
三、卖出回购资产 Assets Repo（Including Securities）	0.21	- 0.62			
四、境外筹资 Overseas Financing	3.49	0.74	4. 票据融资 Paper Financing	1.05	- 0.52
五、向中央银行借款 Borrowings from the Central Bank			其中：贴现 Of Which：Discount	0.88	- 0.47
六、中央银行存款 Deposits by the Central Bank			5. 各项垫款 Total Advances	1.22	- 0.61
七、应付及暂收款 Accounts Payable and Receipts on Account	26.29	4.60	6. 境外筹资转贷款 On - lending of Overseas Financing	2.99	0.30
			二、投资 Investments	116.66	21.52

续表
Continued

项目 Items	余额 Balance	比年初增减额 Changes within the Year	项目 Items	余额 Balance	比年初增减额 Changes within the Year
其中：应付及预提利息 Of Which: Interest Payable and Accrued	2.33	0.03	1. 购买有价证券 Purchase of Securities	111.51	20.21
八、同业存放 Due to Banks and Other Financial Institutions	19.79	-3.63	其中：购买境外有价证券 Of Which: Purchase of Foreign Securities	103.50	19.17
1. 境内同业存放 Due to Domestic Banks and Other Financial Institutions	19.57	-3.66	2. 其他投资 Other Investments	5.15	1.31
			其中：投资境外 Of Which: Overseas	0.12	
2. 境外同业存放 Due to Overseas Banks and Other Financial Institutions	0.22	0.03	三、应收及预付款 Accounts Receivable and Advance Payments	17.82	-2.41
九、同业拆入 Placements from Banks and Other Financial Institutions	7.52	-5.52	其中：应收及预付利息 Of Which: Interest Receivable and Paid in Advance	3.60	-0.04
1. 境内同业拆入 Placements from Domestic Banks and Other Financial Institutions	5.11	0.79	四、买入返售资产 Assets Reverse Repo (Including Securities)	1.24	0.24
2. 境外同业拆入 Placements from Overseas Banks and Other Financial Institutions	2.41	-6.31	五、存放中央银行 Deposits with the Central Bank	9.47	0.48
			其中：缴存准备金 Of Which: Reserves with the Central Bank	4.32	-1.23
十、委托基金存款（净） Designated Fund Deposits (Net)	-6.93	-6.77			
十一、外汇买卖 Foreign Exchange Dealings	8.52	-3.62	六、存放同业 Due from Banks and Other Financial Institutions	30.78	-6.56
其中：结售汇 Of Which: Purchase and Sale of Foreign Exchange	-22.15	-8.88	1. 存放境内同业 Due from Domestic Banks and Other Financial Institutions	10.51	2.91
十二、境内联行存放 Due to Domestic Branches	-7.55	-5.92	2. 存放境外同业 Due from Overseas Banks and Other Financial Institutions	20.27	-9.47
十三、境外联行存放 Due to Overseas Branches	0.05	-0.09			
十四、各项准备 Total Provisions	6.73	0.46	七、拆放同业 Placements with Banks and Other Financial Institutions	68.87	12.85
其中：贷款损失准备 Of Which: Provisions for Loan Losses	5.80	0.23	1. 拆放境内同业 Placements with Domestic Banks and Other Financial Institutions	8.59	0.83
十五、所有者权益 Owner's Equity	46.95	11.94			
其中：实收资本 Of Which: Paid - in Capital	35.35	7.52	2. 拆放境外同业 Placements with Overseas Banks and Other Financial Institutions	60.28	12.02
当年结益 Net Earnings	-1.92	-1.92	八、存放境外联行 Due from Overseas Branches	0.78	-1.01
十六、其他 Others	5.04	12.17	九、库存现金 Cash in Vault	6.04	0.48
资金来源总计 Total Sources	**416.26**	**38.66**	**资金运用总计 Total Uses**	**416.26**	**38.66**

其他商业银行外汇信贷收支表

Sources and Uses of Credit Funds of Other Commercial Banks（Foreign Currency）

（2005年末）

（Year - end of 2005）

单位：亿美元

Unit：100 Million US Dollars

项目 Items	余额 Balance	比年初增减额 Changes within the Year	项目 Items	余额 Balance	比年初增减额 Changes within the Year
一、各项存款 Total Deposits	330.53	24.29	一、各项贷款 Total Loans	171.41	6.71
1. 单位活期存款 Demand Deposits by Enterprises	69.04	10.33	1. 短期贷款 Short - term Loans	70.60	2.18
其中：中资企业存款 Of Which：Deposits by Chinese - funded Enterprises	20.82	2.50	（1）境内短期贷款 Domestic Short - term Loans	66.84	1.45
			其中：中资企业贷款 Of Which：Loans to Chinese - funded Enterprises	42.14	4.32
外商投资企业存款 Deposits by Foreign - funded Enterprises	22.82	-2.93	外商投资企业贷款 Loans to Foreign - funded Enterprises	15.85	-6.45
2. 单位定期存款 Time Deposits by Enterprises	91.60	8.91			
其中：中资企业存款 Of Which：Deposits by Chinese - funded Enterprises	66.06	7.01	（2）境外短期贷款 Overseas Short - term Loans	3.76	0.73
			2. 中长期贷款 Medium and Long - term Loans	51.45	-4.19
外商投资企业存款 Deposits by Foreign - funded Enterprises	5.72	-3.30	（1）境内中长期贷款 Domestic Medium and Long - term Loans	45.35	-2.30
3. 储蓄存款 Savings Deposits	119.70	3.54			
其中：定期存款 Of Which：Time Deposits	77.65	-1.00	其中：中资企业贷款 Of Which：Loans to Chinese - funded Enterprises	16.74	-0.92
4. 其他类存款 Other Deposits	35.62	-0.41	外商投资企业贷款 Loans to Foreign - funded Enterprises	3.59	0.01
5. 境外存款 Foreign Deposits	14.57	1.92			
二、境内中长期借款 Domestic Medium and Long - term Borrowing			（2）境外中长期贷款 Overseas Medium and Long - term Loans	6.10	-1.89
			3. 进出口贸易融资 Financing for Import and Export Trades	43.21	7.92
三、卖出回购资产 Assets Repo（Including Securities）	0.79	0.58			
四、境外筹资 Overseas Financing	3.68	0.19	4. 票据融资 Paper Financing	1.66	0.60
五、向中央银行借款 Borrowings from the Central Bank			其中：贴现 Of Which：Discount	1.12	0.24
六、中央银行存款 Deposits by the Central Bank			5. 各项垫款 Total Advances	1.51	0.21
七、应付及暂收款 Accounts Payable and Receipts on Account	51.86	25.43	6. 境外筹资转贷款 On - lending of Overseas Financing	2.98	-0.01
			二、投资 Investments	124.82	8.14

续表
Continued

项 目 Items	余 额 Balance	比年初增减额 Changes within the Year	项 目 Items	余 额 Balance	比年初增减额 Changes within the Year
其中：应付及预提利息 Of Which: Interest Payable and Accrued	2.81	0.48	1. 购买有价证券 Purchase of Securities	107.46	-4.07
八、同业存放 Due to Banks and Other Financial Institutions	19.91	0.13	其中：购买境外有价证券 Of Which: Purchase of Foreign Securities	95.79	-7.73
1. 境内同业存放 Due to Domestic Banks and Other Financial Institutions	19.57	0.01	2. 其他投资 Other Investments	17.36	12.21
			其中：投资境外 Of Which: Overseas	10.12	10.00
2. 境外同业存放 Due to Overseas Banks and Other Financial Institutions	0.34	0.12	三、应收及预付款 Accounts Receivable and Advance Payments	30.25	12.35
九、同业拆入 Placements from Banks and Other Financial Institutions	17.60	10.18	其中：应收及预付利息 Of Which: Interest Receivable and Paid in Advance	2.69	-0.91
1. 境内同业拆入 Placements from Domestic Banks and Other Financial Institutions	14.59	9.48	四、买入返售资产 Assets Reverse Repo (Including Securities)	0.54	-0.70
2. 境外同业拆入 Placements from Overseas Banks and Other Financial Institutions	3.01	0.70	五、存放中央银行 Deposits with the Central Bank	12.38	2.91
十、委托基金存款（净） Designated Fund Deposits (Net)		-4.47	其中：缴存准备金 Of Which: Reserves with the Central Bank	6.20	1.88
十一、外汇买卖 Foreign Exchange Dealings	2.42	5.31	六、存放同业 Due from Banks and Other Financial Institutions	56.08	25.29
其中：结售汇 Of Which: Purchase and Sale of Foreign Exchange	7.73	29.87	1. 存放境内同业 Due from Domestic Banks and Other Financial Institutions	26.75	16.24
十二、境内联行存放 Due to Domestic Branches	-5.71	1.73	2. 存放境外同业 Due from Overseas Banks and Other Financial Institutions	29.33	9.05
十三、境外联行存放 Due to Overseas Branches		-0.05			
十四、各项准备 Total Provisions	12.44	5.71	七、拆放同业 Placements with Banks and Other Financial Institutions	92.91	24.00
其中：贷款损失准备 Of Which: Provisions for Loan Losses	10.96	5.16	1. 拆放境内同业 Placements with Domestic Banks and Other Financial Institutions	5.14	-3.45
十五、所有者权益 Owner's Equity	35.91	0.03			
其中：实收资本 Of Which: Paid-in Capital	24.29		2. 拆放境外同业 Placements with Overseas Banks and Other Financial Institutions	87.77	27.45
当年结益 Net Earnings	1.77	1.77	八、存放境外联行 Due from Overseas Branches	1.85	1.07
十六、其他 Others	26.24	10.09	九、库存现金 Cash in Vault	5.43	-0.62
资金来源总计 Total Sources	**495.67**	**79.15**	**资金运用总计 Total Uses**	**495.67**	**79.15**

6. 城市商业银行外汇信贷收支表（1999—2005 年）

Sources and Uses of Credit Funds of City Commercial Banks（Foreign Currency）（1999—2005）

城市商业银行外汇信贷收支表

Sources and Uses of Credit Funds of City Commercial Banks（Foreign Currency）

（1999 年末）

（Year - end of 1999）

单位：亿美元

Unit：100 Million US Dollars

项目 Items	余额 Balance	比年初增减额 Changes within the Year	项目 Items	余额 Balance	比年初增减额 Changes within the Year
一、各项存款 Total Deposits	3.10	1.27	一、各项贷款 Total Loans	0.88	0.26
1. 单位活期存款 Demand Deposits by Enterprises	0.55	0.09	1. 短期贷款 Short - term Loans	0.43	- 0.01
其中：中资企业存款 Of Which：Deposits by Chinese - funded Enterprises	0.06	0.04	（1）境内短期贷款 Domestic Short - term Loans	0.43	- 0.01
外商投资企业存款 Deposits by Foreign - funded Enterprises	0.29	- 0.08	其中：中资企业贷款 Of Which：Loans to Chinese - funded Enterprises	0.12	- 0.06
2. 单位定期存款 Time Deposits by Enterprises	1.16	0.55	外商投资企业贷款 Loans to Foreign - funded Enterprises	0.14	0.01
其中：中资企业存款 Of Which：Deposits by Chinese - funded Enterprises	0.34	0.19	（2）境外短期贷款 Overseas Short - term Loans		
外商投资企业存款 Deposits by Foreign - funded Enterprises	0.53	0.29	2. 中长期贷款 Medium and Long - term Loans	0.13	0.06
3. 储蓄存款 Savings Deposits	1.13	0.55	（1）境内中长期贷款 Domestic Medium and Long - term Loans	0.08	0.01
其中：定期存款 Of Which：Time Deposits	0.96	0.47	其中：中资企业贷款 Of Which：Loans to Chinese - funded Enterprises	0.06	0.06
4. 其他类存款 Other Deposits	0.26	0.08	外商投资企业贷款 Loans to Foreign - funded Enterprises		
5. 境外存款 Foreign Deposits			（2）境外中长期贷款 Overseas Medium and Long - term Loans	0.05	0.05
二、境内中长期借款 Domestic Medium and Long - term Borrowing			3. 进出口贸易融资 Financing for Import and Export Trades	0.25	0.17
三、卖出回购证券 Repo			4. 票据融资 Paper Financing		- 0.01
四、境外筹资 Overseas Financing					
五、向中央银行借款 Borrowings from the Central Bank			5. 逾期类贷款 Overdue Loans	0.07	0.05

续表
Continued

项　目 Items	余　额 Balance	比年初增减额 Changes within the Year	项　目 Items	余　额 Balance	比年初增减额 Changes within the Year
六、中央银行存款 Deposits by the Central Bank			二、投资 Investments	0.10	0.10
七、同业存放 Due to Banks and Other Financial Institutions	0.73	0.21	1. 购买有价证券 Purchase of Securities	0.10	0.10
			其中：购买境外有价证券 Of Which: Purchase of Foreign Securities		
1. 境内同业存放 Due to Domestic Banks and Other Financial Institutions	0.73	0.21	2. 其他投资 Other Investments		
2. 境外同业存放 Due to Overseas Banks and Other Financial Institutions			其中：投资境外 Of Which: Overseas		
八、同业拆入 Placements from Banks and Other Financial Institutions	0.04	0.04	三、境外筹资转贷款 On-lending of Overseas Financing		
			四、存放中央银行 Deposits with the Central Bank	0.21	
1. 境内同业拆入 Placements from Domestic Banks and Other Financial Institutions	0.04	0.04	其中：缴存准备金 Of Which: Reserves with the Central Bank		
2. 境外同业拆入 Placements from Overseas Banks and Other Financial Institutions			五、存放同业 Due from Banks and Other Financial Institutions	3.48	1.33
九、委托基金存款 Designated Fund Deposits					
十、外汇买卖 Foreign Exchange Dealings	0.91	0.67	1. 存放境内同业 Due from Domestic Banks and Other Financial Institutions	2.47	0.88
其中：结售汇 Of Which: Purchase and Sale of Foreign Exchange	0.90	0.68	2. 存放境外同业 Due from Overseas Banks and Other Financial Institutions	1.01	0.45
十一、境内联行存放 Due to Domestic Branches	0.22	0.06	六、拆放同业 Placements with Banks and Other Financial Institutions	1.89	0.65
十二、境外联行存放 Due to Overseas Branches			1. 拆放境内同业 Placements with Domestic Banks and Other Financial Institutions	1.54	0.36
十三、所有者权益 Owner's Equity	1.03	0.29			
其中：实收资本 Of Which: Paid-in Capital	0.80	0.20	2. 拆放境外同业 Placements with Overseas Banks and Other Financial Institutions	0.35	0.29
当年结益 Net Earnings	0.16	0.16	七、存放境外联行 Due from Overseas Branches		
十四、其他 Others	0.68	-0.10	八、库存现金 Cash in Vault	0.15	0.10
资金来源总计 Total Sources	**6.71**	**2.44**	**资金运用总计 Total Uses**	**6.71**	**2.44**

城市商业银行外汇信贷收支表

Sources and Uses of Credit Funds of City Commercial Banks（Foreign Currency）

（2000年末）

（Year - end of 2000）

单位：亿美元

Unit：100 Million US Dollars

项　目 Items	余　额 Balance	比年初增减额 Changes within the Year	项　目 Items	余　额 Balance	比年初增减额 Changes within the Year
一、各项存款 Total Deposits	5.67	2.57	一、各项贷款 Total Loans	1.32	0.44
1. 单位活期存款 Demand Deposits by Enterprises	0.69	0.14	1. 短期贷款 Short - term Loans	0.62	0.19
其中：中资企业存款 Of Which：Deposits by Chinese - funded Enterprises	0.11	0.05	（1）境内短期贷款 Domestic Short - term Loans	0.62	0.19
外商投资企业存款 Deposits by Foreign - funded Enterprises	0.29		其中：中资企业贷款 Of Which：Loans to Chinese - funded Enterprises	0.33	0.21
2. 单位定期存款 Time Deposits by Enterprises	2.59	1.43	外商投资企业贷款 Loans to Foreign - funded Enterprises	0.16	0.02
其中：中资企业存款 Of Which：Deposits by Chinese - funded Enterprises	0.68	0.33	（2）境外短期贷款 Overseas Short - term Loans		
外商投资企业存款 Deposits by Foreign - funded Enterprises	1.81	1.28	2. 中长期贷款 Medium and Long - term Loans	0.20	0.07
3. 储蓄存款 Savings Deposits	2.10	0.97	（1）境内中长期贷款 Domestic Medium and Long - term Loans	0.20	0.12
其中：定期存款 Of Which：Time Deposits	1.87	0.91	其中：中资企业贷款 Of Which：Loans to Chinese - funded Enterprises	0.06	
4. 其他类存款 Other Deposits	0.29	0.03	外商投资企业贷款 Loans to Foreign - funded Enterprises		
5. 境外存款 Foreign Deposits			（2）境外中长期贷款 Overseas Medium and Long - term Loans		-0.05
二、境内中长期借款 Domestic Medium and Long - term Borrowing			3. 进出口贸易融资 Financing for Import and Export Trades	0.38	0.13
三、卖出回购证券 Repo			4. 票据融资 Paper Financing		
四、境外筹资 Overseas Financing			5. 逾期类贷款 Overdue Loans	0.12	0.05
五、向中央银行借款 Borrowings from the Central Bank			二、投资 Investments	0.84	0.74
六、中央银行存款 Deposits by the Central Bank			1. 购买有价证券 Purchase of Securities	0.84	0.74
七、同业存放 Due to Banks and Other Financial Institutions	1.30	0.57			

续表
Continued

项目 Items	余额 Balance	比年初增减额 Changes within the Year	项目 Items	余额 Balance	比年初增减额 Changes within the Year
1. 境内同业存放 Due to Domestic Banks and Other Financial Institutions	1.30	0.57	其中：购买境外有价证券 Of Which: Purchase of Foreign Securities	0.84	0.84
2. 境外同业存放 Due to Overseas Banks and Other Financial Institutions			2. 其他投资 Other Investments		
八、同业拆入 Placements from Banks and Other Financial Institutions	0.09	0.05	其中：投资境外 Of Which: Overseas		
			三、境外筹资转贷款 On-lending of Overseas Financing		
1. 境内同业拆入 Placements from Domestic Banks and Other Financial Institutions	0.09	0.05	四、存放中央银行 Deposits with the Central Bank	0.04	-0.17
2. 境外同业拆入 Placements from Overseas Banks and Other Financial Institutions			其中：缴存准备金 Of Which: Reserves with the Central Bank		
			五、存放同业 Due from Banks and Other Financial Institutions	3.43	-0.05
九、委托基金存款 Designated Fund Deposits					
十、外汇买卖 Foreign Exchange Dealings	1.32	0.41	1. 存放境内同业 Due from Domestic Banks and Other Financial Institutions	2.14	-0.33
其中：结售汇 Of Which: Purchase and Sale of Foreign Exchange	1.20	0.30	2. 存放境外同业 Due from Overseas Banks and Other Financial Institutions	1.29	0.28
十一、境内联行存放 Due to Domestic Branches		-0.22			
十二、境外联行存放 Due to Overseas Branches			六、拆放同业 Placements with Banks and Other Financial Institutions	4.70	2.81
十三、所有者权益 Owner's Equity	1.43	0.42	1. 拆放境内同业 Placements with Domestic Banks and Other Financial Institutions	3.71	2.17
其中：实收资本 Of Which: Paid-in Capital	0.92	0.12	2. 拆放境外同业 Placements with Overseas Banks and Other Financial Institutions	0.99	0.64
当年结益 Net Earnings	0.28	0.28			
十四、其他 Others	0.67	-0.03	七、存放境外联行 Due from Overseas Branches		
			八、库存现金 Cash in Vault	0.15	
资金来源总计 Total Sources	**10.48**	**3.77**	**资金运用总计 Total Uses**	**10.48**	**3.77**

城市商业银行外汇信贷收支表

Sources and Uses of Credit Funds of City Commercial Banks（Foreign Currency）

（2001 年末）

（Year - end of 2001）

单位：亿美元

Unit：100 Million US Dollars

项　目 Items	余　额 Balance	比年初增减额 Changes within the Year	项　目 Items	余　额 Balance	比年初增减额 Changes within the Year
一、各项存款 Total Deposits	7.43	1.76	一、各项贷款 Total Loans	2.60	1.29
1. 单位活期存款 Demand Deposits by Enterprises	1.23	0.54	1. 短期贷款 Short - term Loans	1.22	0.56
其中：中资企业存款 Of Which：Deposits by Chinese - funded Enterprises	0.23	0.12	（1）境内短期贷款 Domestic Short - term Loans	1.20	0.54
外商投资企业存款 Deposits by Foreign - funded Enterprises	0.72	0.43	其中：中资企业贷款 Of Which：Loans to Chinese - funded Enterprises	0.74	0.39
2. 单位定期存款 Time Deposits by Enterprises	3.29	0.70	外商投资企业贷款 Loans to Foreign - funded Enterprises	0.31	0.13
其中：中资企业存款 Of Which：Deposits by Chinese - funded Enterprises	1.00	0.32	（2）境外短期贷款 Overseas Short - term Loans	0.02	0.02
外商投资企业存款 Deposits by Foreign - funded Enterprises	1.48	-0.33	2. 中长期贷款 Medium and Long - term Loans	0.86	0.65
3. 储蓄存款 Savings Deposits	2.72	0.62	（1）境内中长期贷款 Domestic Medium and Long - term Loans	0.51	0.30
其中：定期存款 Of Which：Time Deposits	2.30	0.43	其中：中资企业贷款 Of Which：Loans to Chinese - funded Enterprises	0.07	
4. 其他类存款 Other Deposits	0.16	-0.13	外商投资企业贷款 Loans to Foreign - funded Enterprises	0.13	0.13
5. 境外存款 Foreign Deposits	0.03	0.03	（2）境外中长期贷款 Overseas Medium and Long - term Loans	0.35	0.35
二、境内中长期借款 Domestic Medium and Long - term Borrowing			3. 进出口贸易融资 Financing for Import and Export Trades	0.43	0.03
三、卖出回购证券 Repo			4. 票据融资 Paper Financing	0.01	0.01
四、境外筹资 Overseas Financing			其中：贴现 Of Which：Discount	0.01	0.01
五、向中央银行借款 Borrowings from the Central Bank			5. 各项垫款 Total Advances	0.08	0.04
六、中央银行存款 Deposits by the Central Bank			6. 境外筹资转贷款 On - lending of Overseas Financing		
七、应付及暂收款 Accounts Payable and Receipts on Account	0.16		二、投资 Investments	2.65	1.81

续表
Continued

项　目 Items	余　额 Balance	比年初增减额 Changes within the Year	项　目 Items	余　额 Balance	比年初增减额 Changes within the Year
其中：应付及预提利息 Of Which: Interest Payable and Accrued	0.07	-0.03	1. 购买有价证券 Purchase of Securities	0.82	-0.02
			其中：购买境外有价证券 Of Which: Purchase of Foreign Securities	0.23	-0.61
八、同业存放 Due to Banks and Other Financial Institutions	1.82	0.52	2. 其他投资 Other Investments	1.83	1.83
1. 境内同业存放 Due to Domestic Banks and Other Financial Institutions	1.82	0.52	其中：投资境外 Of Which: Overseas		
2. 境外同业存放 Due to Overseas Banks and Other Financial Institutions			三、应收及预付款 Accounts Receivable and Advance Payments	0.08	-0.07
九、同业拆入 Placements from Banks and Other Financial Institutions	0.03	-0.06	其中：应收及预付利息 Of Which: Interest Receivable and Paid in Advance	0.08	-0.01
1. 境内同业拆入 Placements from Domestic Banks and Other Financial Institutions	0.03	-0.06	四、买入返售证券 Reverse Repo		
2. 境外同业拆入 Placements from Overseas Banks and Other Financial Institutions			五、存放中央银行 Deposits with the Central Bank	0.11	0.07
			其中：缴存准备金 Of Which: Reserves with the Central Bank		
十、委托基金存款（净） Designated Fund Deposits (Net)			六、存放同业 Due from Banks and Other Financial Institutions	4.35	0.92
十一、外汇买卖 Foreign Exchange Dealings	0.80	-0.52			
其中：结售汇 Of Which: Purchase and Sale of Foreign Exchange	0.57	-0.63	1. 存放境内同业 Due from Domestic Banks and Other Financial Institutions	2.95	0.81
十二、境内联行存放 Due to Domestic Branches	-0.09	-0.12	2. 存放境外同业 Due from Overseas Banks and Other Financial Institutions	1.40	0.11
十三、境外联行存放 Due to Overseas Branches			七、拆放同业 Placements with Banks and Other Financial Institutions	4.25	-0.45
十四、各项准备 Total Provisions	0.03	0.02			
其中：贷款呆账准备金 Of Which: Provisions for Bad Loans	0.03	0.02	1. 拆放境内同业 Placements with Domestic Banks and Other Financial Institutions	3.22	-0.49
十五、所有者权益 Owner's Equity	2.60	1.20			
其中：实收资本 Of Which: Paid-in Capital	1.47	0.55	2. 拆放境外同业 Placements with Overseas Banks and Other Financial Institutions	1.03	0.04
当年结益 Net Earnings	0.32	0.32	八、存放境外联行 Due from Overseas Branches		
十六、其他 Others	1.47	0.82	九、库存现金 Cash in Vault	0.21	0.05
资金来源总计 Total Sources	**14.25**	**3.62**	**资金运用总计 Total Uses**	**14.25**	**3.62**

城市商业银行外汇信贷收支表

Sources and Uses of Credit Funds of City Commercial Banks（Foreign Currency）

（2002 年末）

（Year - end of 2002）

单位：亿美元

Unit：100 Million US Dollars

项 目 Items	余 额 Balance	比年初增减额 Changes within the Year	项 目 Items	余 额 Balance	比年初增减额 Changes within the Year
一、各项存款 Total Deposits	11.22	3.77	一、各项贷款 Total Loans	3.81	1.24
1. 单位活期存款 Demand Deposits by Enterprises	2.17	0.93	1. 短期贷款 Short - term Loans	1.91	0.69
其中：中资企业存款 Of Which：Deposits by Chinese - funded Enterprises	0.66	0.42	（1）境内短期贷款 Domestic Short - term Loans	1.88	0.68
			其中：中资企业贷款 Of Which：Loans to Chinese - funded Enterprises	0.99	0.25
外商投资企业存款 Deposits by Foreign - funded Enterprises	1.13	0.42	外商投资企业贷款 Loans to Foreign - funded Enterprises	0.75	0.44
2. 单位定期存款 Time Deposits by Enterprises	5.05	1.76			
其中：中资企业存款 Of Which：Deposits by Chinese - funded Enterprises	1.56	0.49	（2）境外短期贷款 Overseas Short - term Loans	0.03	0.01
			2. 中长期贷款 Medium and Long - term Loans	1.10	0.24
外商投资企业存款 Deposits by Foreign - funded Enterprises	1.59	0.11	（1）境内中长期贷款 Domestic Medium and Long - term Loans	0.87	0.36
3. 储蓄存款 Savings Deposits	3.50	0.77	其中：中资企业贷款 Of Which：Loans to Chinese - funded Enterprises	0.15	0.08
其中：定期存款 Of Which：Time Deposits	2.99	0.67			
4. 其他类存款 Other Deposits	0.44	0.28	外商投资企业贷款 Loans to Foreign - funded Enterprises	0.05	-0.08
5. 境外存款 Foreign Deposits	0.06	0.03	（2）境外中长期贷款 Overseas Medium and Long - term Loans	0.23	-0.12
二、境内中长期借款 Domestic Medium and Long - term Borrowing			3. 进出口贸易融资 Financing for Import and Export Trades	0.73	0.30
三、卖出回购证券 Repo					
四、境外筹资 Overseas Financing			4. 票据融资 Paper Financing	0.02	0.01
五、向中央银行借款 Borrowings from the Central Bank			其中：贴现 Of Which：Discount		-0.01
六、中央银行存款 Deposits by the Central Bank			5. 各项垫款 Total Advances	0.05	
七、应付及暂收款 Accounts Payable and Receipts on Account	0.16		6. 境外筹资转贷款 On - lending of Overseas Financing		
			二、投资 Investments	9.56	6.85

续表
Continued

项　　目 Items	余　额 Balance	比年初增减额 Changes within the Year	项　　目 Items	余　额 Balance	比年初增减额 Changes within the Year
其中：应付及预提利息 Of Which: Interest Payable and Accrued	0.06	-0.01	1. 购买有价证券 Purchase of Securities	9.03	8.15
八、同业存放 Due to Banks and Other Financial Institutions	7.09	5.26	其中：购买境外有价证券 Of Which: Purchase of Foreign Securities	7.84	7.55
1. 境内同业存放 Due to Domestic Banks and Other Financial Institutions	7.09	5.26	2. 其他投资 Other Investments	0.53	-1.30
2. 境外同业存放 Due to Overseas Banks and Other Financial Institutions			其中：投资境外 Of Which: Overseas	0.53	0.53
九、同业拆入 Placements from Banks and Other Financial Institutions	0.27	0.24	三、应收及预付款 Accounts Receivable and Advance Payments	0.09	0.01
1. 境内同业拆入 Placements from Domestic Banks and Other Financial Institutions	0.27	0.24	其中：应收及预付利息 Of Which: Interest Receivable and Paid in Advance	0.06	-0.02
2. 境外同业拆入 Placements from Overseas Banks and Other Financial Institutions			四、买入返售证券 Reverse Repo		
十、委托基金存款（净） Designated Fund Deposits (Net)			五、存放中央银行 Deposits with the Central Bank	0.14	0.03
十一、外汇买卖 Foreign Exchange Dealings	1.45	0.61	其中：缴存准备金 Of Which: Reserves with the Central Bank		
其中：结售汇 Of Which: Purchase and Sale of Foreign Exchange	1.01	0.41	六、存放同业 Due from Banks and Other Financial Institutions	7.88	2.95
十二、境内联行存放 Due to Domestic Branches	-0.01	0.07	1. 存放境内同业 Due from Domestic Banks and Other Financial Institutions	6.07	2.57
十三、境外联行存放 Due to Overseas Branches			2. 存放境外同业 Due from Overseas Banks and Other Financial Institutions	1.81	0.38
十四、各项准备 Total Provisions	0.17	0.14	七、拆放同业 Placements with Banks and Other Financial Institutions	5.83	1.48
其中：贷款呆账准备金 Of Which: Provisions for Bad Loans	0.17	0.14	1. 拆放境内同业 Placements with Domestic Banks and Other Financial Institutions	3.30	-0.02
十五、所有者权益 Owner's Equity	3.41	0.56	2. 拆放境外同业 Placements with Overseas Banks and Other Financial Institutions	2.53	1.50
其中：实收资本 Of Which: Paid-in Capital	2.07	0.40	八、存放境外联行 Due from Overseas Branches		
当年结益 Net Earnings	0.25	0.25	九、库存现金 Cash in Vault	0.28	0.07
十六、其他 Others	3.83	1.98			
资金来源总计 Total Sources	**27.59**	**12.63**	**资金运用总计 Total Uses**	**27.59**	**12.63**

城市商业银行外汇信贷收支表
Sources and Uses of Credit Funds of City Commercial Banks（Foreign Currency）

（2003年末）

（Year - end of 2003）

单位：亿美元

Unit：100 Million US Dollars

项目 Items	余额 Balance	比年初增减额 Changes within the Year	项目 Items	余额 Balance	比年初增减额 Changes within the Year
一、各项存款 Total Deposits	14.25	3.02	一、各项贷款 Total Loans	7.85	4.04
1. 单位活期存款 Demand Deposits by Enterprises	3.90	1.73	1. 短期贷款 Short - term Loans	2.69	0.78
其中：中资企业存款 Of Which：Deposits by Chinese - funded Enterprises	1.68	1.02	（1）境内短期贷款 Domestic Short - term Loans	2.69	0.81
外商投资企业存款 Deposits by Foreign - funded Enterprises	1.67	0.54	其中：中资企业贷款 Of Which：Loans to Chinese - funded Enterprises	1.56	0.57
			外商投资企业贷款 Loans to Foreign - funded Enterprises	1.00	0.25
2. 单位定期存款 Time Deposits by Enterprises	5.28	0.23	（2）境外短期贷款 Overseas Short - term Loans		- 0.03
其中：中资企业存款 Of Which：Deposits by Chinese - funded Enterprises	2.28	0.72	2. 中长期贷款 Medium and Long - term Loans	2.09	0.99
外商投资企业存款 Deposits by Foreign - funded Enterprises	1.70	0.11	（1）境内中长期贷款 Domestic Medium and Long - term Loans	1.93	1.06
3. 储蓄存款 Savings Deposits	4.05	0.54	其中：中资企业贷款 Of Which：Loans to Chinese - funded Enterprises	0.78	0.63
其中：定期存款 Of Which：Time Deposits	3.42	0.42	外商投资企业贷款 Loans to Foreign - funded Enterprises	0.29	0.24
4. 其他类存款 Other Deposits	0.94	0.50	（2）境外中长期贷款 Overseas Medium and Long - term Loans	0.16	- 0.07
5. 境外存款 Foreign Deposits	0.08	0.02	3. 进出口贸易融资 Financing for Import and Export Trades	2.09	1.36
二、境内中长期借款 Domestic Medium and Long - term Borrowing			4. 票据融资 Paper Financing	0.93	0.91
三、卖出回购证券 Repo			其中：贴现 Of Which：Discount		
四、境外筹资 Overseas Financing			5. 各项垫款 Total Advances	0.05	
五、向中央银行借款 Borrowings from the Central Bank			6. 境外筹资转贷款 On - lending of Overseas Financing		
六、中央银行存款 Deposits by the Central Bank			二、投资 Investments	5.10	- 4.46
七、应付及暂收款 Accounts Payable and Receipts on Account	3.68	3.52			

续表
Continued

项 目 Items	余 额 Balance	比年初增减额 Changes within the Year	项 目 Items	余 额 Balance	比年初增减额 Changes within the Year
其中：应付及预提利息 Of Which: Interest Payable and Accrued	0.07	0.01	1. 购买有价证券 Purchase of Securities	4.60	-4.43
			其中：购买境外有价证券 Of Which: Purchase of Foreign Securities	3.27	-4.57
八、同业存放 Due to Banks and Other Financial Institutions	9.26	2.17	2. 其他投资 Other Investments	0.50	-0.03
1. 境内同业存放 Due to Domestic Banks and Other Financial Institutions	9.26	2.17	其中：投资境外 Of Which: Overseas	0.50	-0.03
2. 境外同业存放 Due to Overseas Banks and Other Financial Institutions			三、应收及预付款 Accounts Receivable and Advance Payments	0.36	0.27
九、同业拆入 Placements from Banks and Other Financial Institutions	0.49	0.22	其中：应收及预付利息 Of Which: Interest Receivable and Paid in Advance	0.07	0.01
1. 境内同业拆入 Placements from Domestic Banks and Other Financial Institutions	0.49	0.22	四、买入返售证券 Reverse Repo		
2. 境外同业拆入 Placements from Overseas Banks and Other Financial Institutions			五、存放中央银行 Deposits with the Central Bank	0.16	0.02
			其中：缴存准备金 Of Which: Reserves with the Central Bank		
十、委托基金存款（净） Designated Fund Deposits (Net)			六、存放同业 Due from Banks and Other Financial Institutions	21.20	12.66
十一、外汇买卖 Foreign Exchange Dealings	2.38	0.93			
其中：结售汇 Of Which: Purchase and Sale of Foreign Exchange	1.52	0.51	1. 存放境内同业 Due from Domestic Banks and Other Financial Institutions	9.81	3.11
十二、境内联行存放 Due to Domestic Branches	0.26	0.19	2. 存放境外同业 Due from Foreign Banks and Other Financial Institutions	11.39	9.55
十三、境外联行存放 Due to Overseas Branches			七、拆放同业 Placements with Banks and Other Financial Institutions	4.70	-1.13
十四、各项准备 Total Provisions	0.12	-0.05			
其中：贷款呆账准备金 Of Which: Provisions for Bad Loans	0.05	-0.12	1. 拆放境内同业 Placements with Domestic Banks and Other Financial Institutions	2.41	-0.89
十五、所有者权益 Owner's Equity	4.49	0.71	2. 拆放境外同业 Placements with Overseas Banks and Other Financial Institutions	2.29	-0.24
其中：实收资本 Of Which: Paid-in Capital	2.47				
当年结益 Net Earnings	0.84	0.84	八、存放境外联行 Due from Overseas Branches		
十六、其他 Others	4.82	0.79	九、库存现金 Cash in Vault	0.38	0.10
资金来源总计 Total Sources	**39.75**	**11.50**	**资金运用总计 Total Uses**	**39.75**	**11.50**

城市商业银行外汇信贷收支表

Sources and Uses of Credit Funds of City Commercial Banks（Foreign Currency）

（2004年末）

（Year - end of 2004）

单位：亿美元

Unit：100 Million US Dollars

项目 Items	余额 Balance	比年初增减额 Changes within the Year	项目 Items	余额 Balance	比年初增减额 Changes within the Year
一、各项存款 Total Deposits	18.78	4.52	一、各项贷款 Total Loans	9.19	1.34
1.单位活期存款 Demand Deposits by Enterprises	5.83	1.92	1.短期贷款 Short - term Loans	3.51	0.82
其中：中资企业存款 Of Which：Deposits by Chinese - funded Enterprises	2.70	1.02	（1）境内短期贷款 Domestic Short - term Loans	3.51	0.82
外商投资企业存款 Deposits by Foreign - funded Enterprises	2.53	0.85	其中：中资企业贷款 Of Which：Loans to Chinese - funded Enterprises	1.74	0.18
2.单位定期存款 Time Deposits by Enterprises	5.14	-0.14	外商投资企业贷款 Loans to Foreign - funded Enterprises	1.60	0.60
其中：中资企业存款 Of Which：Deposits by Chinese - funded Enterprises	0.62	-1.66	（2）境外短期贷款 Overseas Short - term Loans		
外商投资企业存款 Deposits by Foreign - funded Enterprises	1.88	0.18	2.中长期贷款 Medium and Long - term Loans	2.28	0.19
3.储蓄存款 Savings Deposits	5.76	1.71	（1）境内中长期贷款 Domestic Medium and Long - term Loans	2.17	0.24
其中：定期存款 Of Which：Time Deposits	4.68	1.26	其中：中资企业贷款 Of Which：Loans to Chinese - funded Enterprises	0.92	0.14
4.其他类存款 Other Deposits	1.95	1.01	外商投资企业贷款 Loans to Foreign - funded Enterprises	0.26	-0.03
5.境外存款 Foreign Deposits	0.10	0.02	（2）境外中长期贷款 Overseas Medium and Long - term Loans	0.11	-0.05
二、境内中长期借款 Domestic Medium and Long - term Borrowing			3.进出口贸易融资 Financing for Import and Export Trades	2.72	0.63
三、卖出回购资产 Assets Repo（Including Securities）	0.02	0.02	4.票据融资 Paper Financing	0.56	-0.37
四、境外筹资 Overseas Financing			其中：贴现 Of Which：Discount		
五、向中央银行借款 Borrowings from the Central Bank			5.各项垫款 Total Advances	0.12	0.07
六、中央银行存款 Deposits by the Central Bank			6.境外筹资转贷款 On - lending of Overseas Financing		
七、应付及暂收款 Accounts Payable and Receipts on Account	0.97	-2.71	二、投资 Investments	7.31	2.17

续表
Continued

项　目 Items	余　额 Balance	比年初增减额 Changes within the Year	项　目 Items	余　额 Balance	比年初增减额 Changes within the Year
其中：应付及预提利息 Of Which: Interest Payable and Accrued	0.07		1. 购买有价证券 Purchase of Securities	6.79	2.15
八、同业存放 Due to Banks and Other Financial Institutions	9.23	-0.03	其中：购买境外有价证券 Of Which: Purchase of Foreign Securities	4.99	0.68
1. 境内同业存放 Due to Domestic Banks and Other Financial Institutions	9.23	-0.03	2. 其他投资 Other Investments	0.52	0.02
2. 境外同业存放 Due to Overseas Banks and Other Financial Institutions			其中：投资境外 Of Which: Overseas	0.50	
九、同业拆入 Placements from Banks and Other Financial Institutions	1.03	0.54	三、应收及预付款 Accounts Receivable and Advance Payments	0.28	-0.08
1. 境内同业拆入 Placements from Domestic Banks and Other Financial Institutions	0.98	0.49	其中：应收及预付利息 Of Which: Interest Receivable and Paid in Advance	0.06	-0.01
2. 境外同业拆入 Placements from Overseas Banks and Other Financial Institutions	0.05	0.05	四、买入返售资产 Assets Reverse Repo (Including Securities)	0.08	0.08
十、委托基金存款（净） Designated Fund Deposits (Net)	0.01	0.01	五、存放中央银行 Deposits with the Central Bank	0.28	0.12
十一、外汇买卖 Foreign Exchange Dealings	2.03	-0.43	其中：缴存准备金 Of Which: Reserves with the Central Bank	0.01	0.01
其中：结售汇 Of Which: Purchase and Sale of Foreign Exchange	1.66	0.06	六、存放同业 Due from Banks and Other Financial Institutions	17.95	-3.50
十二、境内联行存放 Due to Domestic Branches	0.07	-0.20	1. 存放境内同业 Due from Domestic Banks and Other Financial Institutions	12.58	2.52
十三、境外联行存放 Due to Overseas Branches			2. 存放境外同业 Due from Overseas Banks and Other Financial Institutions	5.37	-6.02
十四、各项准备 Total Provisions	0.21	0.09	七、拆放同业 Placements with Banks and Other Financial Institutions	6.32	1.61
其中：贷款呆账准备金 Of Which: Provisions for Bad Loans	0.21	0.16	1. 拆放境内同业 Placements with Domestic Banks and Other Financial Institutions	3.20	0.79
十五、所有者权益 Owner's Equity	2.36	-2.07	2. 拆放境外同业 Placements with Overseas Banks and Other Financial Institutions	3.12	0.82
其中：实收资本 Of Which: Paid-in Capital	1.65	-0.82			
当年结益 Net Earnings	0.69	0.69	八、存放境外联行 Due from Overseas Branches		
十六、其他 Others	7.23	2.15	九、库存现金 Cash in Vault	0.53	0.15
资金来源总计 Total Sources	**41.94**	**1.89**	**资金运用总计 Total Uses**	**41.94**	**1.89**

城市商业银行外汇信贷收支表

Sources and Uses of Credit Funds of City Commercial Banks（Foreign Currency）

（2005年末）

（Year - end of 2005）

单位：亿美元

Unit：100 Million US Dollars

项目 Items	余额 Balance	比年初增减额 Changes within the Year	项目 Items	余额 Balance	比年初增减额 Changes within the Year
一、各项存款 Total Deposits	20.95	2.17	一、各项贷款 Total Loans	9.30	0.11
1. 单位活期存款 Demand Deposits by Enterprises	6.62	0.79	1. 短期贷款 Short - term Loans	4.16	0.65
其中：中资企业存款 Of Which：Deposits by Chinese - funded Enterprises	2.34	-0.36	（1）境内短期贷款 Domestic Short - term Loans	4.16	0.65
外商投资企业存款 Deposits by Foreign - funded Enterprises	3.72	1.19	其中：中资企业贷款 Of Which：Loans to Chinese - funded Enterprises	2.34	0.60
2. 单位定期存款 Time Deposits by Enterprises	5.50	0.36	外商投资企业贷款 Loans to Foreign - funded Enterprises	1.70	0.10
其中：中资企业存款 Of Which：Deposits by Chinese - funded Enterprises	2.62	2.00	（2）境外短期贷款 Overseas Short - term Loans		
外商投资企业存款 Deposits by Foreign - funded Enterprises	1.97	0.09	2. 中长期贷款 Medium and Long - term Loans	1.92	-0.36
3. 储蓄存款 Savings Deposits	6.66	0.90	（1）境内中长期贷款 Domestic Medium and Long - term Loans	1.78	-0.39
其中：定期存款 Of Which：Time Deposits	5.58	0.90	其中：中资企业贷款 Of Which：Loans to Chinese - funded Enterprises	0.73	-0.19
4. 其他类存款 Other Deposits	2.12	0.17	外商投资企业贷款 Loans to Foreign - funded Enterprises	0.23	-0.03
5. 境外存款 Foreign Deposits	0.05	-0.05	（2）境外中长期贷款 Overseas Medium and Long - term Loans	0.14	0.03
二、境内中长期筹资 Domestic Medium and Long - term Borrowing			3. 进出口贸易融资 Financing for Import and Export Trades	2.45	-0.27
三、卖出回购资产 Assets Repo（Including Securities）	0.04	0.02			
四、境外筹资 Overseas Financing			4. 票据融资 Paper Financing	0.54	-0.02
五、向中央银行借款 Borrowings from the Central Bank			其中：贴现 Of Which：Discount	0.01	0.01
六、中央银行存款 Deposits by the Central Bank			5. 各项垫款 Total Advances	0.23	0.11
七、应付及暂收款 Accounts Payable and Receipts on Account	1.03	0.06	6. 境外筹资转贷款 On - lending of Overseas Financing		
			二、投资 Investments	9.25	1.94

续表
Continued

项目 Items	余额 Balance	比年初增减额 Changes within the Year	项目 Items	余额 Balance	比年初增减额 Changes within the Year
其中：应付及预提利息 Of Which: Interest Payable and Accrued	0.12	0.05	1. 购买有价证券 Purchase of Securities	8.88	2.09
八、同业存放 Due to Banks and Other Financial Institutions	10.04	0.81	其中：购买境外有价证券 Of Which: Purchase of Foreign Securities	5.08	0.09
1. 境内同业存放 Due to Domestic Banks and Other Financial Institutions	10.04	0.81	2. 其他投资 Other Investments	0.37	-0.15
2. 境外同业存放 Due to Overseas Banks and Other Financial Institutions			其中：投资境外 Of Which: Overseas	0.35	-0.15
九、同业拆入 Placements from Banks and Other Financial Institutions	0.93	-0.10	三、应收及预付款 Accounts Receivable and Advance Payments	0.32	0.04
1. 境内同业拆入 Placements from Domestic Banks and Other Financial Institutions	0.93	-0.05	其中：应收及预付利息 Of Which: Interest Receivable and Paid in Advance	0.07	0.01
2. 境外同业拆入 Placements from Overseas Banks and Other Financial Institutions		-0.05	四、买入返售资产 Assets Reverse Repo (Including Securities)		-0.08
十、委托基金存款（净） Designated Fund Deposits (Net)	0.01		五、存放中央银行 Deposits with the Central Bank	0.89	0.61
十一、外汇买卖 Foreign Exchange Dealings	1.90	-0.18	其中：缴存准备金 Of Which: Reserves with the Central Bank	0.30	0.30
其中：结售汇 Of Which: Purchase and Sale of Foreign Exchange	1.46	-0.25	六、存放同业 Due from Banks and Other Financial Institutions	20.34	2.33
十二、境内联行存放 Due to Domestic Branches	1.44	1.35	1. 存放境内同业 Due from Domestic Banks and Other Financial Institutions	15.84	3.20
十三、境外联行存放 Due to Overseas Branches			2. 存放境外同业 Due from Overseas Banks and Other Financial Institutions	4.50	-0.87
十四、各项准备 Total Provisions	0.17	-0.04	七、拆放同业 Placements with Banks and Other Financial Institutions	5.65	-0.67
其中：贷款损失准备 Of Which: Provisions for Loan Losses	0.16	-0.05	1. 拆放境内同业 Placements with Domestic Banks and Other Financial Institutions	4.14	0.94
十五、所有者权益 Owner's Equity	1.87	0.47	2. 拆放境外同业 Placements with Overseas Banks and Other Financial Institutions	1.51	-1.61
其中：实收资本 Of Which: Paid-in Capital	0.85	0.10	八、存放境外联行 Due from Overseas Branches		
当年结益 Net Earnings	0.98	0.98	九、库存现金 Cash in Vault	0.63	0.10
十六、其他 Others	8.00	-0.18			
资金来源总计 Total Sources	**46.38**	**4.38**	**资金运用总计 Total Uses**	**46.38**	**4.38**

7. 农村商业银行外汇信贷收支表（2002—2005 年）

Sources and Uses of Credit Funds of Rural Commercial Banks（Foreign Currency）（2002—2005）

农村商业银行外汇信贷收支表

Sources and Uses of Credit Funds of Rural Commercial Banks（Foreign Currency）

（2002 年末）

（Year - end of 2002）

单位：亿美元

Unit：100 Million US Dollars

项　目 Items	余　额 Balance	比年初增减额 Changes within the Year	项　目 Items	余　额 Balance	比年初增减额 Changes within the Year
一、各项存款 Total Deposits	0.26	0.26	一、各项贷款 Total Loans	0.05	0.05
1. 单位活期存款 Demand Deposits by Enterprises	0.04	0.04	1. 短期贷款 Short - term Loans		
其中：中资企业存款 Of Which：Deposits by Chinese - funded Enterprises	0.01	0.01	（1）境内短期贷款 Domestic Short - term Loans		
外商投资企业存款 Deposits by Foreign - funded Enterprises	0.03	0.03	其中：中资企业贷款 Of Which：Loans to Chinese - funded Enterprises		
			外商投资企业贷款 Loans to Foreign - funded Enterprises		
2. 单位定期存款 Time Deposits by Enterprises	0.01	0.01	（2）境外短期贷款 Overseas Short - term Loans		
其中：中资企业存款 Of Which：Deposits by Chinese - funded Enterprises			2. 中长期贷款 Medium and Long - term Loans		
外商投资企业存款 Deposits by Foreign - funded Enterprises	0.01	0.01	（1）境内中长期贷款 Domestic Medium and Long - term Loans		
3. 储蓄存款 Savings Deposits	0.21	0.21	其中：中资企业贷款 Of Which：Loans to Chinese - funded Enterprises		
其中：定期存款 Of Which：Time Deposits	0.21	0.21	外商投资企业贷款 Loans to Foreign - funded Enterprises		
4. 其他类存款 Other Deposits			（2）境外中长期贷款 Overseas Medium and Long - term Loans		
5. 境外存款 Foreign Deposits					
二、境内中长期借款 Domestic Medium and Long - term Borrowing			3. 进出口贸易融资 Financing for Import and Export Trades	0.05	0.05
三、卖出回购证券 Repo					
四、境外筹资 Overseas Financing			4. 票据融资 Paper Financing		
五、向中央银行借款 Borrowings from the Central Bank			其中：贴现 Of Which：Discount		
六、中央银行存款 Deposits by the Central Bank			5. 各项垫款 Total Advances		

续表
Continued

项　目 Items	余　额 Balance	比年初增减额 Changes within the Year	项　目 Items	余　额 Balance	比年初增减额 Changes within the Year
七、应付及暂收款 Accounts Payable and Receipts on Account			6. 境外筹资转贷款 On – lending of Overseas Financing		
其中：应付及预提利息 Of Which: Interest Payable and Accrued			二、投资 Investments		
八、同业存放 Due to Banks and Other Financial Institutions			1. 购买有价证券 Purchase of Securities		
1. 境内同业存放 Due to Domestic Banks and Other Financial Institutions			其中：购买境外有价证券 Of Which: Purchase of Foreign Securities		
2. 境外同业存放 Due to Overseas Banks and Other Financial Institutions			2. 其他投资 Other Investments		
九、同业拆入 Placements from Banks and Other Financial Institutions			其中：投资境外 Of Which: Overseas		
1. 境内同业拆入 Placements from Domestic Banks and Other Financial Institutions			三、应收及预付款 Accounts Receivable and Advance Payments	0.01	0.01
2. 境外同业拆入 Placements from Overseas Banks and Other Financial Institutions			其中：应收及预付利息 Of Which: Interest Receivable and Paid in Advance		
十、委托基金存款（净） Designated Fund Deposits (Net)			四、买入返售证券 Reverse Repo		
十一、外汇买卖 Foreign Exchange Dealings	0.04	0.04	五、存放中央银行 Deposits with the Central Bank	0.01	0.01
其中：结售汇 Of Which: Purchase and Sale of Foreign Exchange	0.04	0.04	其中：缴存准备金 Of Which: Reserves with the Central Bank		
十二、境内联行存放 Due to Domestic Branches			六、存放同业 Due from Banks and Other Financial Institutions	0.39	0.24
十三、境外联行存放 Due to Overseas Branches			1. 存放境内同业 Due from Domestic Banks and Other Financial Institutions	0.34	0.19
十四、各项准备 Total Provisions			2. 存放境外同业 Due from Overseas Banks and Other Financial Institutions	0.05	0.05
其中：贷款呆账准备金 Of Which: Provisions for Bad Loans			七、拆放同业 Placements with Banks and Other Financial Institutions		
十五、所有者权益 Owner's Equity	0.17	0.02	1. 拆放境内同业 Placements with Domestic Banks and Other Financial Institutions		
其中：实收资本 Of Which: Paid – in Capital	0.16	0.01	2. 拆放境外同业 Placements with Overseas Banks and Other Financial Institutions		
当年结益 Net Earnings	0.01	0.01	八、存放境外联行 Due from Overseas Branches		
十六、其他 Others			九、库存现金 Cash in Vault	0.01	0.01
资金来源总计 Total Sources	**0.47**	**0.32**	**资金运用总计 Total Uses**	**0.47**	**0.32**

农村商业银行外汇信贷收支表
Sources and Uses of Credit Funds of Rural Commercial Banks（Foreign Currency）

（2003 年末）

（Year - end of 2003）

单位：亿美元

Unit：100 Million US Dollars

项目 Items	余额 Balance	比年初增减额 Changes within the Year	项目 Items	余额 Balance	比年初增减额 Changes within the Year
一、各项存款 Total Deposits	0.50	0.24	一、各项贷款 Total Loans	0.20	0.15
1. 单位活期存款 Demand Deposits by Enterprises	0.14	0.10	1. 短期贷款 Short - term Loans	0.08	0.08
其中：中资企业存款 Of Which：Deposits by Chinese - funded Enterprises	0.05	0.04	（1）境内短期贷款 Domestic Short - term Loans	0.08	0.08
外商投资企业存款 Deposits by Foreign - funded Enterprises	0.09	0.06	其中：中资企业贷款 Of Which：Loans to Chinese - funded Enterprises	0.05	0.05
2. 单位定期存款 Time Deposits by Enterprises	0.03	0.02	外商投资企业贷款 Loans to Foreign - funded Enterprises	0.03	0.03
其中：中资企业存款 Of Which：Deposits by Chinese - funded Enterprises	0.01	0.01	（2）境外短期贷款 Overseas Short - term Loans		
外商投资企业存款 Deposits by Foreign - funded Enterprises	0.02	0.01	2. 中长期贷款 Medium and Long - term Loans		
3. 储蓄存款 Savings Deposits	0.30	0.09	（1）境内中长期贷款 Domestic Medium and Long - term Loans		
其中：定期存款 Of Which：Time Deposits	0.28	0.07	其中：中资企业贷款 Of Which：Loans to Chinese - funded Enterprises		
4. 其他类存款 Other Deposits	0.03	0.03	外商投资企业贷款 Loans to Foreign - funded Enterprises		
5. 境外存款 Foreign Deposits			（2）境外中长期贷款 Overseas Medium and Long - term Loans		
二、境内中长期借款 Domestic Medium and Long - term Borrowing			3. 进出口贸易融资 Financing for Import and Export Trades	0.12	0.07
三、卖出回购证券 Repo			4. 票据融资 Paper Financing		
四、境外筹资 Overseas Financing			其中：贴现 Of Which：Discount		
五、向中央银行借款 Borrowings from the Central Bank			5. 各项垫款 Total Advances		
六、中央银行存款 Deposits by the Central Bank					
七、应付及暂收款 Accounts Payable and Receipts on Account	0.05	0.05	6. 境外筹资转贷款 On - lending of Overseas Financing		

续表
Continued

项　目 Items	余　额 Balance	比年初增减额 Changes within the Year	项　目 Items	余　额 Balance	比年初增减额 Changes within the Year
其中：应付及预提利息 Of Which: Interest Payable and Accrued			二、投资 Investments	0.03	0.03
八、同业存放 Due to Banks and Other Financial Institutions	0.26	0.26	1. 购买有价证券 Purchase of Securities	0.03	0.03
1. 境内同业存放 Due to Domestic Banks and Other Financial Institutions	0.26	0.26	其中：购买境外有价证券 Of Which: Purchase of Foreign Securities		
2. 境外同业存放 Due to Overseas Banks and Other Financial Institutions			2. 其他投资 Other Investments		
九、同业拆入 Placements from Banks and Other Financial Institutions	0.03	0.03	其中：投资境外 Of Which: Overseas		
1. 境内同业拆入 Placements from Domestic Banks and Other Financial Institutions	0.03	0.03	三、应收及预付款 Accounts Receivable and Advance Payments	0.04	0.03
2. 境外同业拆入 Placements from Overseas Banks and Other Financial Institutions			其中：应收及预付利息 Of Which: Interest Receivable and Paid in Advance		
十、委托基金存款（净） Designated Fund Deposits (Net)			四、买入返售证券 Reverse Repo		
十一、外汇买卖 Foreign Exchange Dealings	0.12	0.08	五、存放中央银行 Deposits with the Central Bank		-0.01
其中：结售汇 Of Which: Purchase and Sale of Foreign Exchange	0.12	0.08	其中：缴存准备金 Of Which: Reserves with the Central Bank		
十二、境内联行存放 Due to Domestic Branches			六、存放同业 Due from Banks and Other Financial Institutions	0.83	0.44
十三、境外联行存放 Due to Overseas Branches			1. 存放境内同业 Due from Domestic Banks and Other Financial Institutions	0.80	0.46
十四、各项准备 Total Provisions			2. 存放境外同业 Due from Overseas Banks and Other Financial Institutions	0.03	-0.02
其中：贷款呆账准备金 Of Which: Provisions for Bad Loans			七、拆放同业 Placements with Banks and Other Financial Institutions		
十五、所有者权益 Owner's Equity	0.18	0.02	1. 拆放境内同业 Placements with Domestic Banks and Other Financial Institutions		
其中：实收资本 Of Which: Paid-in Capital	0.16		2. 拆放境外同业 Placements with Overseas Banks and Other Financial Institutions		
当年结益 Net Earnings	0.02	0.02	八、存放境外联行 Due from Overseas Branches		
十六、其他 Others	-0.02	-0.03	九、库存现金 Cash in Vault	0.02	0.01
资金来源总计 Total Sources	**1.12**	**0.65**	**资金运用总计 Total Uses**	**1.12**	**0.65**

农村商业银行外汇信贷收支表

Sources and Uses of Credit Funds of Rural Commercial Banks（Foreign Currency）

（2004年末）

（Year－end of 2004）

单位：亿美元

Unit：100 Million US Dollars

项 目 Items	余 额 Balance	比年初增减额 Changes within the Year	项 目 Items	余 额 Balance	比年初增减额 Changes within the Year
一、各项存款 Total Deposits	0.62	0.12	一、各项贷款 Total Loans	0.35	0.15
1.单位活期存款 Demand Deposits by Enterprises	0.19	0.05	1.短期贷款 Short－term Loans	0.24	0.16
其中：中资企业存款 Of Which：Deposits by Chinese－funded Enterprises	0.06	0.01	（1）境内短期贷款 Domestic Short－term Loans	0.24	0.16
外商投资企业存款 Deposits by Foreign－funded Enterprises	0.12	0.03	其中：中资企业贷款 Of Which：Loans to Chinese－funded Enterprises	0.22	0.17
2.单位定期存款 Time Deposits by Enterprises	0.02	－0.01	外商投资企业贷款 Loans to Foreign－funded Enterprises	0.02	－0.01
其中：中资企业存款 Of Which：Deposits by Chinese－funded Enterprises		－0.01	（2）境外短期贷款 Overseas Short－term Loans		
外商投资企业存款 Deposits by Foreign－funded Enterprises	0.02		2.中长期贷款 Medium and Long－term Loans		
3.储蓄存款 Savings Deposits	0.31	0.01	（1）境内中长期贷款 Domestic Medium and Long－term Loans		
其中：定期存款 Of Which：Time Deposits	0.29	0.01	其中：中资企业贷款 Of Which：Loans to Chinese－funded Enterprises		
4.其他类存款 Other Deposits	0.10	0.07	外商投资企业贷款 Loans to Foreign－funded Enterprises		
5.境外存款 Foreign Deposits			（2）境外中长期贷款 Overseas Medium and Long－term Loans		
二、境内中长期借款 Domestic Medium and Long－term Borrowing			3.进出口贸易融资 Financing for Import and Export Trades	0.11	－0.01
三、卖出回购资产 Assets Repo（Including Securities）			4.票据融资 Paper Financing		
四、境外筹资 Overseas Financing			其中：贴现 Of Which：Discount		
五、向中央银行借款 Borrowings from the Central Bank			5.各项垫款 Total Advances		
六、中央银行存款 Deposits by the Central Bank			6.境外筹资转贷款 On－lending of Overseas Financing		
七、应付及暂收款 Accounts Payable and Receipts on Account		－0.05			

续表
Continued

项目 Items	余额 Balance	比年初增减额 Changes within the Year	项目 Items	余额 Balance	比年初增减额 Changes within the Year
其中：应付及预提利息 Of Which: Interest Payable and Accrued			二、投资 Investments	0.03	
八、同业存放 Due to Banks and Other Financial Institutions	0.46	0.20	1. 购买有价证券 Purchase of Securities	0.03	
1. 境内同业存放 Due to Domestic Banks and Other Financial Institutions	0.46	0.20	其中：购买境外有价证券 Of Which: Purchase of Foreign Securities		
2. 境外同业存放 Due to Overseas Banks and Other Financial Institutions			2. 其他投资 Other Investments		
			其中：投资境外 Of Which: Overseas		
九、同业拆入 Placements from Banks and Other Financial Institutions		-0.03	三、应收及预付款 Accounts Receivable and Advance Payments		-0.04
1. 境内同业拆入 Placements from Domestic Banks and Other Financial Institutions		-0.03	其中：应收及预付利息 Of Which: Interest Receivable and Paid in Advance		
2. 境外同业拆入 Placements from Overseas Banks and Other Financial Institutions			四、买入返售资产 Assets Reverse Repo (Including Securities)		
十、委托基金存款（净） Designated Fund Deposits (Net)			五、存放中央银行 Deposits with the Central Bank		
十一、外汇买卖 Foreign Exchange Dealings	0.07	-0.07	其中：缴存准备金 Of Which: Reserves with the Central Bank		
其中：结售汇 Of Which: Purchase and Sale of Foreign Exchange	0.07	-0.07	六、存放同业 Due from Banks and Other Financial Institutions	1.00	0.17
十二、境内联行存放 Due to Domestic Branches			1. 存放境内同业 Due from Domestic Banks and Other Financial Institutions	0.90	0.10
十三、境外联行存放 Due to Overseas Branches			2. 存放境外同业 Due from Overseas Banks and Other Financial Institutions	0.10	0.07
十四、各项准备 Total Provisions			七、拆放同业 Placements with Banks and Other Financial Institutions		
其中：贷款呆账准备金 Of Which: Provisions for Bad Loans					
十五、所有者权益 Owner's Equity	0.23	0.07	1. 拆放境内同业 Placements with Domestic Banks and Other Financial Institutions		
其中：实收资本 Of Which: Paid - in Capital	0.18	0.02	2. 拆放境外同业 Placements with Overseas Banks and Other Financial Institutions		
当年结益 Net Earnings	0.05	0.05			
十六、其他 Others	0.01	0.03	八、存放境外联行 Due from Overseas Branches		
			九、库存现金 Cash in Vault	0.01	-0.01
资金来源总计 Total Sources	**1.39**	**0.27**	**资金运用总计 Total Uses**	**1.39**	**0.27**

农村商业银行外汇信贷收支表

Sources and Uses of Credit Funds of Rural Commercial Banks（Foreign Currency）

（2005年末）

（Year - end of 2005）

单位：亿美元

Unit：100 Million US Dollars

项目 Items	余额 Balance	比年初增减额 Changes within the Year	项目 Items	余额 Balance	比年初增减额 Changes within the Year
一、各项存款 Total Deposits	2.68	1.65	一、各项贷款 Total Loans	0.44	-0.10
1. 单位活期存款 Demand Deposits by Enterprises	0.64	0.15	1. 短期贷款 Short - term Loans	0.20	-0.16
其中：中资企业存款 Of Which：Deposits by Chinese - funded Enterprises	0.16	0.09	（1）境内短期贷款 Domestic Short - term Loans	0.20	-0.16
外商投资企业存款 Deposits by Foreign - funded Enterprises	0.48	0.07	其中：中资企业贷款 Of Which：Loans to Chinese - funded Enterprises	0.07	-0.15
2. 单位定期存款 Time Deposits by Enterprises	0.03	-0.04	外商投资企业贷款 Loans to Foreign - funded Enterprises	0.13	-0.01
其中：中资企业存款 Of Which：Deposits by Chinese - funded Enterprises	0.02	-0.03	（2）境外短期贷款 Overseas Short - term Loans		
外商投资企业存款 Deposits by Foreign - funded Enterprises	0.01	-0.01	2. 中长期贷款 Medium and Long - term Loans		
3. 储蓄存款 Savings Deposits	1.89	1.53	（1）境内中长期贷款 Domestic Medium and Long - term Loans		
其中：定期存款 Of Which：Time Deposits	0.99	0.65	其中：中资企业贷款 Of Which：Loans to Chinese - funded Enterprises		
4. 其他类存款 Other Deposits	0.12	0.01	外商投资企业贷款 Loans to Foreign - funded Enterprises		
5. 境外存款 Foreign Deposits			（2）境外中长期贷款 Overseas Medium and Long - term Loans		
二、境内中长期筹资 Domestic Medium and Long - term Borrowing			3. 进出口贸易融资 Financing for Import and Export Trades	0.24	0.06
三、卖出回购资产 Assets Repo（Including Securities）			4. 票据融资 Paper Financing		
四、境外筹资 Overseas Financing			其中：贴现 Of Which：Discount		
五、向中央银行借款 Borrowings from the Central Bank			5. 各项垫款 Total Advances		
六、中央银行存款 Deposits by the Central Bank			6. 境外筹资转贷款 On - lending of Overseas Financing		
七、应付及暂收款 Accounts Payable and Receipts on Account	0.04	0.02	二、投资 Investments	0.03	

续表
Continued

项 目 Items	余 额 Balance	比年初增减额 Changes within the Year	项 目 Items	余 额 Balance	比年初增减额 Changes within the Year
其中：应付及预提利息 Of Which: Interest Payable and Accrued	0.02	0.02	1. 购买有价证券 Purchase of Securities	0.03	
			其中：购买境外有价证券 Of Which: Purchase of Foreign Securities		
八、同业存放 Due to Banks and Other Financial Institutions	0.31	-0.15	2. 其他投资 Other Investments		
1. 境内同业存放 Due to Domestic Banks and Other Financial Institutions	0.31	-0.15	其中：投资境外 Of Which: Overseas		
2. 境外同业存放 Due to Overseas Banks and Other Financial Institutions			三、应收及预付款 Accounts Receivable and Advance Payments	0.01	0.01
九、同业拆入 Placements from Banks and Other Financial Institutions			其中：应收及预付利息 Of Which: Interest Receivable and Paid in Advance	0.01	0.01
1. 境内同业拆入 Placements from Domestic Banks and Other Financial Institutions			四、买入返售资产 Assets Reverse Repo (Including Securities)		
2. 境外同业拆入 Placements from Overseas Banks and Other Financial Institutions			五、存放中央银行 Deposits with the Central Bank	0.14	0.14
十、委托基金存款（净） Designated Fund Deposits (Net)			其中：缴存准备金 Of Which: Reserves with the Central Bank	0.06	0.06
十一、外汇买卖 Foreign Exchange Dealings	0.15		六、存放同业 Due from Banks and Other Financial Institutions	3.18	1.81
其中：结售汇 Of Which: Purchase and Sale of Foreign Exchange	0.49	0.35	1. 存放境内同业 Due from Domestic Banks and Other Financial Institutions	2.73	1.46
十二、境内联行存放 Due to Domestic Branches	0.02	0.02	2. 存放境外同业 Due from Overseas Banks and Other Financial Institutions	0.45	0.35
十三、境外联行存放 Due to Overseas Branches					
十四、各项准备 Total Provisions	0.03	0.02	七、拆放同业 Placements with Banks and Other Financial Institutions		
其中：贷款损失准备 Of Which: Provisions for Loan Losses	0.01		1. 拆放境内同业 Placements with Domestic Banks and Other Financial Institutions		
十五、所有者权益 Owner's Equity	0.13	0.08	2. 拆放境外同业 Placements with Overseas Banks and Other Financial Institutions		
其中：实收资本 Of Which: Paid - in Capital					
当年结益 Net Earnings	0.08	0.08	八、存放境外联行 Due from Overseas Branches		
十六、其他 Others	0.57	0.33	九、库存现金 Cash in Vault	0.13	0.11
资金来源总计 Total Sources	**3.93**	**1.97**	**资金运用总计 Total Uses**	**3.93**	**1.97**

8. 农村信用合作社外汇信贷收支表（2001—2005 年）
Sources and Uses of Credit Funds of Rural Credit Cooperatives（Foreign Currency）（2001—2005）

农村信用合作社外汇信贷收支表
Sources and Uses of Credit Funds of Rural Credit Cooperatives（Foreign Currency）

（2001 年末）
（Year－end of 2001）

单位：亿美元
Unit：100 Million US Dollars

项目 Items	余额 Balance	比年初增减额 Changes within the Year	项目 Items	余额 Balance	比年初增减额 Changes within the Year
一、各项存款 Total Deposits	4.28	0.92	一、各项贷款 Total Loans		
1. 单位活期存款 Demand Deposits by Enterprises	0.11	0.10	1. 短期贷款 Short－term Loans		
其中：中资企业存款 Of Which：Deposits by Chinese－funded Enterprises	0.01	0.01	（1）境内短期贷款 Domestic Short－term Loans		
外商投资企业存款 Deposits by Foreign－funded Enterprises	0.07	0.07	其中：中资企业贷款 Of Which：Loans to Chinese－funded Enterprises		
2. 单位定期存款 Time Deposits by Enterprises	0.04	0.03	外商投资企业贷款 Loans to Foreign－funded Enterprises		
其中：中资企业存款 Of Which：Deposits by Chinese－funded Enterprises			（2）境外短期贷款 Overseas Short－term Loans		
外商投资企业存款 Deposits by Foreign－funded Enterprises	0.02	0.02	2. 中长期贷款 Medium and Long－term Loans		
3. 储蓄存款 Savings Deposits	4.11	0.77	（1）境内中长期贷款 Domestic Medium and Long－term Loans		
其中：定期存款 Of Which：Time Deposits	2.74	0.40	其中：中资企业贷款 Of Which：Loans to Chinese－funded Enterprises		
4. 其他类存款 Other Deposits	0.02	0.02	外商投资企业贷款 Loans to Foreign－funded Enterprises		
5. 境外存款 Foreign Deposits			（2）境外中长期贷款 Overseas Medium and Long－term Loans		
二、境内中长期借款 Domestic Medium and Long－term Borrowing			3. 进出口贸易融资 Financing for Import and Export Trades		
三、卖出回购证券 Repo			4. 票据融资 Paper Financing		
四、境外筹资 Overseas Financing			其中：贴现 Of Which：Discount		
五、向中央银行借款 Borrowings from the Central Bank			5. 各项垫款 Total Advances		
六、中央银行存款 Deposits by the Central Bank					

续表
Continued

项　目 Items	余　额 Balance	比年初增减额 Changes within the Year	项　目 Items	余　额 Balance	比年初增减额 Changes within the Year
七、应付及暂收款 Accounts Payable and Receipts on Account	0.11	0.05	6. 境外筹资转贷款 On – lending of Overseas Financing		
其中：应付及预提利息 Of Which: Interest Payable and Accrued	0.08	0.02	二、投资 Investments		
			1. 购买有价证券 Purchase of Securities		
八、同业存放 Due to Banks and Other Financial Institutions	0.01	0.01	其中：购买境外有价证券 Of Which: Purchase of Foreign Securities		
1. 境内同业存放 Due to Domestic Banks and Other Financial Institutions	0.01	0.01	2. 其他投资 Other Investments		
2. 境外同业存放 Due to Overseas Banks and Other Financial Institutions			其中：投资境外 Of Which: Overseas		
九、同业拆入 Placements from Banks and Other Financial Institutions			三、应收及预付款 Accounts Receivable and Advance Payments	0.02	0.01
1. 境内同业拆入 Placements from Domestic Banks and Other Financial Institutions			其中：应收及预付利息 Of Which: Interest Receivable and Paid in Advance		-0.01
2. 境外同业拆入 Placements from Overseas Banks and Other Financial Institutions			四、买入返售证券 Reverse Repo		
十、委托基金存款（净） Designated Fund Deposits (Net)			五、存放中央银行 Deposits with the Central Bank	0.34	0.32
			其中：缴存准备金 Of Which: Reserves with the Central Bank		
十一、外汇买卖 Foreign Exchange Dealings	0.82	0.66	六、存放同业 Due from Banks and Other Financial Institutions	5.53	1.98
其中：结售汇 Of Which: Purchase and Sale of Foreign Exchange	0.81	0.66	1. 存放境内同业 Due from Domestic Banks and Other Financial Institutions	3.37	0.04
十二、境内联行存放 Due to Domestic Branches					
十三、境外联行存放 Due to Overseas Branches			2. 存放境外同业 Due from Overseas Banks and Other Financial Institutions	2.16	1.94
十四、各项准备 Total Provisions			七、拆放同业 Placements with Banks and Other Financial Institutions		
其中：贷款呆账准备金 Of Which: Provisions for Bad Loans					
十五、所有者权益 Owner's Equity	0.89	0.69	1. 拆放境内同业 Placements with Domestic Banks and Other Financial Institutions		
其中：实收资本 Of Which: Paid – in Capital	0.84	0.64	2. 拆放境外同业 Placements with Overseas Banks and Other Financial Institutions		
当年结益 Net Earnings	0.05	0.05			
十六、其他 Others	-0.02	-0.02	八、存放境外联行 Due from Overseas Branches		
			九、库存现金 Cash in Vault	0.20	
资金来源总计 Total Sources	**6.09**	**2.31**	**资金运用总计 Total Uses**	**6.09**	**2.31**

农村信用合作社外汇信贷收支表

Sources and Uses of Credit Funds of Rural Credit Cooperatives（Foreign Currency）

（2002年末）

（Year - end of 2002）

单位：亿美元

Unit：100 Million US Dollars

项目 Items	余额 Balance	比年初增减额 Changes within the Year	项目 Items	余额 Balance	比年初增减额 Changes within the Year
一、各项存款 Total Deposits	5.86	1.58	一、各项贷款 Total Loans	0.20	0.20
1. 单位活期存款 Demand Deposits by Enterprises	0.29	0.17	1. 短期贷款 Short - term Loans	0.18	0.18
其中：中资企业存款 Of Which：Deposits by Chinese - funded Enterprises	0.02	0.01	（1）境内短期贷款 Domestic Short - term Loans	0.18	0.18
外商投资企业存款 Deposits by Foreign - funded Enterprises	0.23	0.15	其中：中资企业贷款 Of Which：Loans to Chinese - funded Enterprises	0.13	0.13
2. 单位定期存款 Time Deposits by Enterprises	0.16	0.13	外商投资企业贷款 Loans to Foreign - funded Enterprises	0.05	0.05
其中：中资企业存款 Of Which：Deposits by Chinese - funded Enterprises			（2）境外短期贷款 Overseas Short - term Loans		
外商投资企业存款 Deposits by Foreign - funded Enterprises	0.15	0.13	2. 中长期贷款 Medium and Long - term Loans		
3. 储蓄存款 Savings Deposits	5.38	1.27	（1）境内中长期贷款 Domestic Medium and Long - term Loans		
其中：定期存款 Of Which：Time Deposits	3.63	0.89	其中：中资企业贷款 Of Which：Loans to Chinese - funded Enterprises		
4. 其他类存款 Other Deposits	0.03	0.01	外商投资企业贷款 Loans to Foreign - funded Enterprises		
5. 境外存款 Foreign Deposits			（2）境外中长期贷款 Overseas Medium and Long - term Loans		
二、境内中长期借款 Domestic Medium and Long - term Borrowing			3. 进出口贸易融资 Financing for Import and Export Trades	0.02	0.02
三、卖出回购证券 Repo			4. 票据融资 Paper Financing		
四、境外筹资 Overseas Financing			其中：贴现 Of Which：Discount		
五、向中央银行借款 Borrowings from the Central Bank			5. 各项垫款 Total Advances		
六、中央银行存款 Deposits by the Central Bank			6. 境外筹资转贷款 On - lending of Overseas Financing		
七、应付及暂收款 Accounts Payable and Receipts on Account	0.20	0.09	二、投资 Investments		

续表
Continued

项目 Items	余额 Balance	比年初增减额 Changes within the Year	项目 Items	余额 Balance	比年初增减额 Changes within the Year
其中：应付及预提利息 Of Which: Interest Payable and Accrued	0.06	-0.02	1. 购买有价证券 Purchase of Securities		
八、同业存放 Due to Banks and Other Financial Institutions	0.03	0.02	其中：购买境外有价证券 Of Which: Purchase of Foreign Securities		
1. 境内同业存放 Due to Domestic Banks and Other Financial Institutions	0.03	0.02	2. 其他投资 Other Investments		
			其中：投资境外 Of Which: Overseas		
2. 境外同业存放 Due to Overseas Banks and Other Financial Institutions			三、应收及预付款 Accounts Receivable and Advance Payments	0.14	0.12
九、同业拆入 Placements from Banks and Other Financial Institutions			其中：应收及预付利息 Of Which: Interest Receivable and Paid in Advance		
1. 境内同业拆入 Placements from Domestic Banks and Other Financial Institutions			四、买入返售证券 Reverse Repo		
			五、存放中央银行 Deposits with the Central Bank	0.07	-0.27
2. 境外同业拆入 Placements from Overseas Banks and Other Financial Institutions			其中：缴存准备金 Of Which: Reserves with the Central Bank		
十、委托基金存款（净） Designated Fund Deposits (Net)			六、存放同业 Due from Banks and Other Financial Institutions	6.87	1.47
十一、外汇买卖 Foreign Exchange Dealings	0.41	-0.48			
其中：结售汇 Of Which: Purchase and Sale of Foreign Exchange	0.41	-0.47	1. 存放境内同业 Due from Domestic Banks and Other Financial Institutions	4.63	1.39
十二、境内联行存放 Due to Domestic Branches	-0.01	-0.01	2. 存放境外同业 Due from Overseas Banks and Other Financial Institutions	2.24	0.08
十三、境外联行存放 Due to Overseas Branches			七、拆放同业 Placements with Banks and Other Financial Institutions	0.18	0.18
十四、各项准备 Total Provisions					
其中：贷款呆账准备金 Of Which: Provisions for Bad Loans			1. 拆放境内同业 Placements with Domestic Banks and Other Financial Institutions	0.05	0.05
十五、所有者权益 Owner's Equity	1.25	0.56	2. 拆放境外同业 Placements with Overseas Banks and Other Financial Institutions	0.13	0.13
其中：实收资本 Of Which: Paid-in Capital	1.13	0.44			
当年结益 Net Earnings	0.13	0.13	八、存放境外联行 Due from Overseas Branches		
十六、其他 Others		0.03	九、库存现金 Cash in Vault	0.28	0.09
资金来源总计 Total Sources	**7.74**	**1.79**	**资金运用总计 Total Uses**	**7.74**	**1.79**

农村信用合作社外汇信贷收支表

Sources and Uses of Credit Funds of Rural Credit Cooperatives（Foreign Currency）

（2003 年末）

（Year－end of 2003）

单位：亿美元

Unit：100 Million US Dollars

项目 Items	余额 Balance	比年初增减额 Changes within the Year	项目 Items	余额 Balance	比年初增减额 Changes within the Year
一、各项存款 Total Deposits	6.03	0.18	一、各项贷款 Total Loans	1.05	0.85
1. 单位活期存款 Demand Deposits by Enterprises	0.32	0.03	1. 短期贷款 Short－term Loans	0.75	0.57
其中：中资企业存款 Of Which：Deposits by Chinese－funded Enterprises	0.04	0.02	（1）境内短期贷款 Domestic Short－term Loans	0.75	0.57
外商投资企业存款 Deposits by Foreign－funded Enterprises	0.24	0.01	其中：中资企业贷款 Of Which：Loans to Chinese－funded Enterprises	0.56	0.43
2. 单位定期存款 Time Deposits by Enterprises	0.08	－0.08	外商投资企业贷款 Loans to Foreign－funded Enterprises	0.19	0.14
其中：中资企业存款 Of Which：Deposits by Chinese－funded Enterprises	0.01	0.01	（2）境外短期贷款 Overseas Short－term Loans		
外商投资企业存款 Deposits by Foreign－funded Enterprises	0.07	－0.08	2. 中长期贷款 Medium and Long－term Loans		
3. 储蓄存款 Savings Deposits	5.55	0.18	（1）境内中长期贷款 Domestic Medium and Long－term Loans		
其中：定期存款 Of Which：Time Deposits	3.64	0.02	其中：中资企业贷款 Of Which：Loans to Chinese－funded Enterprises		
4. 其他类存款 Other Deposits	0.08	0.05	外商投资企业贷款 Loans to Foreign－funded Enterprises		
5. 境外存款 Foreign Deposits			（2）境外中长期贷款 Overseas Medium and Long－term Loans		
二、境内中长期借款 Domestic Medium and Long－term Borrowing			3. 进出口贸易融资 Financing for Import and Export Trades	0.30	0.28
三、卖出回购证券 Repo			4. 票据融资 Paper Financing		
四、境外筹资 Overseas Financing			其中：贴现 Of Which：Discount		
五、向中央银行借款 Borrowings from the Central Bank			5. 各项垫款 Total Advances		
六、中央银行存款 Deposits by the Central Bank			6. 境外筹资转贷款 On－lending of Overseas Financing		
七、应付及暂收款 Accounts Payable and Receipts on Account	0.50	0.30	二、投资 Investments		

续表
Continued

项　　目 Items	余　额 Balance	比年初增减额 Changes within the Year	项　　目 Items	余　额 Balance	比年初增减额 Changes within the Year
其中：应付及预提利息 Of Which：Interest Payable and Accrued	0.06		1. 购买有价证券 Purchase of Securities		
八、同业存放 Due to Banks and Other Financial Institutions	0.83	0.80	其中：购买境外有价证券 Of Which：Purchase of Foreign Securities		
1. 境内同业存放 Due to Domestic Banks and Other Financial Institutions	0.83	0.80	2. 其他投资 Other Investments		
			其中：投资境外 Of Which：Overseas		
2. 境外同业存放 Due to Overseas Banks and Other Financial Institutions			三、应收及预付款 Accounts Receivable and Advance Payments	0.44	0.30
九、同业拆入 Placements from Banks and Other Financial Institutions			其中：应收及预付利息 Of Which：Interest Receivable and Paid in Advance		
1. 境内同业拆入 Placements from Domestic Banks and Other Financial Institutions			四、买入返售证券 Reverse Repo		
			五、存放中央银行 Deposits with the Central Bank	0.38	0.31
2. 境外同业拆入 Placements from Overseas Banks and Other Financial Institutions			其中：缴存准备金 Of Which：Reserves with the Central Bank		
十、委托基金存款（净） Designated Fund Deposits（Net）			六、存放同业 Due from Banks and Other Financial Institutions	6.95	0.10
十一、外汇买卖 Foreign Exchange Dealings	0.61	0.08			
其中：结售汇 Of Which：Purchase and Sale of Foreign Exchange	0.59	0.11	1. 存放境内同业 Due from Domestic Banks and Other Financial Institutions	5.32	0.70
十二、境内联行存放 Due to Domestic Branches	-0.01		2. 存放境外同业 Due from Overseas Banks and Other Financial Institutions	1.63	-0.60
十三、境外联行存放 Due to Overseas Branches			七、拆放同业 Placements with Banks and Other Financial Institutions	0.12	-0.06
十四、各项准备 Total Provisions	0.01	0.01			
其中：贷款呆账准备金 Of Which：Provisions for Bad Loans			1. 拆放境内同业 Placements with Domestic Banks and Other Financial Institutions		-0.05
十五、所有者权益 Owner's Equity	1.25	0.12	2. 拆放境外同业 Placements with Overseas Banks and Other Financial Institutions	0.12	-0.01
其中：实收资本 Of Which：Paid - in Capital	1.09	-0.04			
当年结益 Net Earnings	0.16	0.16	八、存放境外联行 Due from Overseas Branches		
十六、其他 Others	0.04	0.06	九、库存现金 Cash in Vault	0.32	0.05
资金来源总计 Total Sources	**9.26**	**1.55**	**资金运用总计 Total Uses**	**9.26**	**1.55**

农村信用合作社外汇信贷收支表
Sources and Uses of Credit Funds of Rural Credit Cooperatives（Foreign Currency）

（2004 年末）

（Year - end of 2004）

单位：亿美元

Unit：100 Million US Dollars

项　目 Items	余　额 Balance	比年初增减额 Changes within the Year	项　目 Items	余　额 Balance	比年初增减额 Changes within the Year
一、各项存款 Total Deposits	6.18	0.05	一、各项贷款 Total Loans	0.45	-0.71
1. 单位活期存款 Demand Deposits by Enterprises	0.60	0.20	1. 短期贷款 Short - term Loans	0.32	-0.49
其中：中资企业存款 Of Which：Deposits by Chinese - funded Enterprises	0.05		（1）境内短期贷款 Domestic Short - term Loans	0.32	-0.49
			其中：中资企业贷款 Of Which：Loans to Chinese - funded Enterprises	0.02	-0.56
外商投资企业存款 Deposits by Foreign - funded Enterprises	0.54	0.24	外商投资企业贷款 Loans to Foreign - funded Enterprises	0.30	0.08
2. 单位定期存款 Time Deposits by Enterprises	0.06	-0.03			
其中：中资企业存款 Of Which：Deposits by Chinese - funded Enterprises		-0.01	（2）境外短期贷款 Overseas Short - term Loans		
			2. 中长期贷款 Medium and Long - term Loans	0.02	
外商投资企业存款 Deposits by Foreign - funded Enterprises	0.05	-0.02	（1）境内中长期贷款 Domestic Medium and Long - term Loans	0.02	
3. 储蓄存款 Savings Deposits	5.42	-0.14			
其中：定期存款 Of Which：Time Deposits	3.16	-0.49	其中：中资企业贷款 Of Which：Loans to Chinese - funded Enterprises	0.02	
4. 其他类存款 Other Deposits	0.10	0.02	外商投资企业贷款 Loans to Foreign - funded Enterprises		
5. 境外存款 Foreign Deposits			（2）境外中长期贷款 Overseas Medium and Long - term Loans		
二、境内中长期借款 Domestic Medium and Long - term Borrowing					
			3. 进出口贸易融资 Financing for Import and Export Trades	0.11	-0.22
三、卖出回购资产 Assets Repo（Including Securities）					
四、境外筹资 Overseas Financing			4. 票据融资 Paper Financing		
五、向中央银行借款 Borrowings from the Central Bank			其中：贴现 Of Which：Discount		
六、中央银行存款 Deposits by the Central Bank			5. 各项垫款 Total Advances		
七、应付及暂收款 Accounts Payable and Receipts on Account	0.23	-0.28	6. 境外筹资转贷款 On - lending of Overseas Financing		
			二、投资 Investments		

续表
Continued

项　目 Items	余　额 Balance	比年初增减额 Changes within the Year	项　目 Items	余　额 Balance	比年初增减额 Changes within the Year
其中：应付及预提利息 Of Which: Interest Payable and Accrued	0.05	-0.01	1. 购买有价证券 Purchase of Securities		
			其中：购买境外有价证券 Of Which: Purchase of Foreign Securities		
八、同业存放 Due to Banks and Other Financial Institutions	0.39	-0.44	2. 其他投资 Other Investments		
1. 境内同业存放 Due to Domestic Banks and Other Financial Institutions	0.39	-0.44	其中：投资境外 Of Which: Overseas		
2. 境外同业存放 Due to Overseas Banks and Other Financial Institutions			三、应收及预付款 Accounts Receivable and Advance Payments	0.01	-0.43
九、同业拆入 Placements from Banks and Other Financial Institutions			其中：应收及预付利息 Of Which: Interest Receivable and Paid in Advance	0.01	0.01
1. 境内同业拆入 Placements from Domestic Banks and Other Financial Institutions			四、买入返售资产 Assets Reverse Repo (Including Securities)		
2. 境外同业拆入 Placements from Overseas Banks and Other Financial Institutions			五、存放中央银行 Deposits with the Central Bank	0.04	-0.34
			其中：缴存准备金 Of Which: Reserves with the Central Bank		
十、委托基金存款（净） Designated Fund Deposits (Net)			六、存放同业 Due from Banks and Other Financial Institutions	7.96	0.87
十一、外汇买卖 Foreign Exchange Dealings	0.46	-0.31			
其中：结售汇 Of Which: Purchase and Sale of Foreign Exchange	0.46	-0.29	1. 存放境内同业 Due from Domestic Banks and Other Financial Institutions	5.85	0.42
十二、境内联行存放 Due to Domestic Branches	0.04	0.05	2. 存放境外同业 Due from Overseas Banks and Other Financial Institutions	2.11	0.45
十三、境外联行存放 Due to Overseas Branches			七、拆放同业 Placements with Banks and Other Financial Institutions	0.10	-0.02
十四、各项准备 Total Provisions	0.01				
其中：贷款呆账准备金 Of Which: Provisions for Bad Loans			1. 拆放境内同业 Placements with Domestic Banks and Other Financial Institutions		
十五、所有者权益 Owner's Equity	1.58	0.34	2. 拆放境外同业 Placements with Overseas Banks and Other Financial Institutions	0.10	-0.02
其中：实收资本 Of Which: Paid - in Capital	1.34	0.13			
当年结益 Net Earnings	0.16	0.16	八、存放境外联行 Due from Overseas Branches		
十六、其他 Others	0.02	-0.01	九、库存现金 Cash in Vault	0.35	0.03
资金来源总计 Total Sources	**8.91**	**-0.60**	**资金运用总计 Total Uses**	**8.91**	**-0.60**

农村信用合作社外汇信贷收支表

Sources and Uses of Credit Funds of Rural Credit Cooperatives（Foreign Currency）

（2005 年末）

（Year – end of 2005）

单位：亿美元

Unit：100 Million US Dollars

项 目 Items	余 额 Balance	比年初增减额 Changes within the Year	项 目 Items	余 额 Balance	比年初增减额 Changes within the Year
一、各项存款 Total Deposits	3.64	– 2.03	一、各项贷款 Total Loans	0.41	0.16
1. 单位活期存款 Demand Deposits by Enterprises	0.25	0.02	1. 短期贷款 Short – term Loans	0.18	– 0.02
其中：中资企业存款 Of Which：Deposits by Chinese – funded Enterprises	0.06	0.03	（1）境内短期贷款 Domestic Short – term Loans	0.18	– 0.02
外商投资企业存款 Deposits by Foreign – funded Enterprises	0.19	– 0.01	其中：中资企业贷款 Of Which：Loans to Chinese – funded Enterprises	0.01	
2. 单位定期存款 Time Deposits by Enterprises	0.01	0.01	外商投资企业贷款 Loans to Foreign – funded Enterprises	0.17	– 0.02
其中：中资企业存款 Of Which：Deposits by Chinese – funded Enterprises			（2）境外短期贷款 Overseas Short – term Loans		
外商投资企业存款 Deposits by Foreign – funded Enterprises	0.01	0.01	2. 中长期贷款 Medium and Long – term Loans	0.01	– 0.01
3. 储蓄存款 Savings Deposits	3.29	– 2.07	（1）境内中长期贷款 Domestic Medium and Long – term Loans	0.01	– 0.01
其中：定期存款 Of Which：Time Deposits	2.09	– 1.02	其中：中资企业贷款 Of Which：Loans to Chinese – funded Enterprises	0.01	– 0.01
4. 其他类存款 Other Deposits	0.09	0.01	外商投资企业贷款 Loans to Foreign – funded Enterprises		
5. 境外存款 Foreign Deposits			（2）境外中长期贷款 Overseas Medium and Long – term Loans		
二、境内中长期筹资 Domestic Medium and Long – term Borrowing			3. 进出口贸易融资 Financing for Import and Export Trades	0.22	0.19
三、卖出回购资产 Assets Repo（Including Securities）			4. 票据融资 Paper Financing		
四、境外筹资 Overseas Financing			其中：贴现 Of Which：Discount		
五、向中央银行借款 Borrowings from the Central Bank			5. 各项垫款 Total Advances		
六、中央银行存款 Deposits by the Central Bank			6. 境外筹资转贷款 On – lending of Overseas Financing		
七、应付及暂收款 Accounts Payable and Receipts on Account	0.06	– 0.15	二、投资 Investments		

续表
Continued

项　目 Items	余　额 Balance	比年初增减额 Changes within the Year	项　目 Items	余　额 Balance	比年初增减额 Changes within the Year
其中：应付及预提利息 Of Which: Interest Payable and Accrued	0.05		1. 购买有价证券 Purchase of Securities		
			其中：购买境外有价证券 Of Which: Purchase of Foreign Securities		
八、同业存放 Due to Banks and Other Financial Institutions	0.39				
			2. 其他投资 Other Investments		
1. 境内同业存放 Due to Domestic Banks and Other Financial Institutions	0.39				
			其中：投资境外 Of Which: Overseas		
2. 境外同业存放 Due to Overseas Banks and Other Financial Institutions			三、应收及预付款 Accounts Receivable and Advance Payments		-0.01
九、同业拆入 Placements from Banks and Other Financial Institutions			其中：应收及预付利息 Of Which: Interest Receivable and Paid in Advance		-0.01
1. 境内同业拆入 Placements from Domestic Banks and Other Financial Institutions			四、买入返售资产 Assets Reverse Repo (Including Securities)		
2. 境外同业拆入 Placements from Overseas Banks and Other Financial Institutions			五、存放中央银行 Deposits with the Central Bank	0.12	0.08
			其中：缴存准备金 Of Which: Reserves with the Central Bank	0.11	0.11
十、委托基金存款（净） Designated Fund Deposits (Net)					
十一、外汇买卖 Foreign Exchange Dealings	0.47	-0.05	六、存放同业 Due from Banks and Other Financial Institutions	4.74	-2.60
其中：结售汇 Of Which: Purchase and Sale of Foreign Exchange	0.59	0.13			
			1. 存放境内同业 Due from Domestic Banks and Other Financial Institutions	3.25	-2.06
十二、境内联行存放 Due to Domestic Branches	-0.01	0.01			
			2. 存放境外同业 Due from Overseas Banks and Other Financial Institutions	1.49	-0.54
十三、境外联行存放 Due to Overseas Branches					
十四、各项准备 Total Provisions	0.03	0.03	七、拆放同业 Placements with Banks and Other Financial Institutions	0.12	0.02
其中：贷款损失准备 Of Which: Provisions for Loan Losses	0.02	0.02			
			1. 拆放境内同业 Placements with Domestic Banks and Other Financial Institutions		
十五、所有者权益 Owner's Equity	0.18	0.05			
其中：实收资本 Of Which: Paid-in Capital	0.07	-0.01	2. 拆放境外同业 Placements with Overseas Banks and Other Financial Institutions	0.12	0.02
当年结益 Net Earnings	0.08	0.08			
			八、存放境外联行 Due from Overseas Branches		
十六、其他 Others	0.85	-0.33			
			九、库存现金 Cash in Vault	0.22	-0.12
资金来源总计 Total Sources	**5.61**	**-2.47**	**资金运用总计 Total Uses**	**5.61**	**-2.47**

9. 财务公司外汇信贷收支表（1994—2005年）
Sources and Uses of Credit Funds of Finance Companies（Foreign Currency）（1994—2005）

财务公司外汇信贷收支表
Sources and Uses of Credit Funds of Finance Companies（Foreign Currency）

（1994年末）

（Year - end of 1994）

单位：亿美元

Unit：100 Million US Dollars

项　目 Items	余　额 Balance	比年初增减额 Changes within the Year	项　目 Items	余　额 Balance	比年初增减额 Changes within the Year
一、外汇存款 Total Deposits	5.17	1.08	一、外汇贷款 Total Loans	5.52	0.80
二、境外筹资 Overseas Financing	0.95	0.22	1. 短期外汇贷款 Short - term Loans	4.93	0.81
1. 境外短期借款 Overseas Short - term Borrowing	0.95	0.30	2. 中长期外汇贷款 Medium and Long - term Loans	0.59	- 0.01
2. 境外中长期借款 Overseas Medium and Long - term Borrowing		- 0.08	二、各项投资 Investments	0.29	- 0.02
其中：境外发行债券 Of Which：Overseas Bonds Issue			1. 投资 Investments	0.25	- 0.03
			其中：境外投资 Of Which：Overseas	0.04	0.04
三、委托借款 Designated Borrowing	0.01	- 0.02	2. 购买有价证券 Purchase of Securities	0.04	0.01
四、外汇自有资金 Banks' Own Working Capital	2.67	0.76	其中：购买海外债券 Of Which：Purchase of Foreign Securities		
五、同业往来 Inter - bank Transactions	1.71	- 0.21			
其中：境内借款 Of Which：Domestic Borrowing	1.45	0.30	三、租赁 Leases	0.16	0.03
六、结益 Net Earnings	0.17	0.17	四、委托贷款 Designated Loans	0.47	0.10
七、其他 Others	0.69	- 0.26	五、存放同业资金 Due from Banks and Other Financial Institutions	2.50	0.01
			其中：境外 Of Which：Overseas	0.20	0.05
			六、缴存准备金 Reserves with the Central Bank		
			七、同业往来 Inter - bank Transactions	1.55	0.47
			其中：同业拆出 Of Which：Placements with Banks and Other Financial Institutions	1.16	0.41
			八、其他 Others	0.88	0.35
资金来源总计 Total Sources	**11.37**	**1.74**	**资金运用总计 Total Uses**	**11.37**	**1.74**

财务公司外汇信贷收支表

Sources and Uses of Credit Funds of Finance Companies（Foreign Currency）

（1995 年末）

（Year - end of 1995）

单位：亿美元

Unit：100 Million US Dollars

项　目 Items	余　额 Balance	比年初增减额 Changes within the Year	项　目 Items	余　额 Balance	比年初增减额 Changes within the Year
一、外汇存款 Total Deposits	6.57	0.99	一、外汇贷款 Total Loans	4.78	-0.99
二、境外筹资 Overseas Financing	0.46	-0.60	1. 短期外汇贷款 Short - term Loans	4.21	-0.92
1. 境外短期借款 Overseas Short - term Borrowing	0.40	-0.60	2. 中长期外汇贷款 Medium and Long - term Loans	0.57	-0.07
2. 境外中长期借款 Overseas Medium and Long - term Borrowing	0.06		二、各项投资 Investments	0.36	0.07
			1. 投资 Investments	0.32	0.07
三、境外发行债券 Overseas Bonds Issue			其中：境内投资 Of Which：Domestic	0.04	-0.07
其中：短期债券 Of Which：Short - term Bonds			2. 购买有价证券 Purchase of Securities	0.04	
四、委托借款 Designated Borrowing	0.01		其中：购买海外债券 Of Which：Purchase of Foreign Securities		
五、境外同业往来 Overseas Inter - bank Transactions	0.34	0.17			
其中：拆入资金 Of Which：Placements from Banks and Other Financial Institutions	0.28	0.11	三、租赁 Leases	0.17	0.03
			四、委托贷款 Designated Loans	0.56	0.09
六、国内同业往来 Domestic Inter - bank Transactions	1.98	0.41	五、境外同业往来 Overseas Inter - bank Transactions		-0.23
其中：拆入资金 Of Which：Placements from Banks and Other Financial Institutions	1.96	0.63	其中：拆出资金 Of Which：Placements with Banks and Other Financial Institutions		-0.03
七、外汇买卖 Foreign Exchange Dealings			六、国内同业往来 Domestic Inter - bank Transactions	6.37	2.10
八、所有者权益 Owner's Equity	3.29	0.26	其中：拆出资金 Of Which：Placements with Banks and Other Financial Institutions	2.17	0.70
其中：实收资本 Of Which：Paid - in Capital	3.05	0.40			
九、结益 Net Earnings	0.26	0.26	七、缴存准备金 Reserves with the Central Bank		
十、贷款呆账准备金 Provisions for Bad Loans	0.02		八、其他资产 Other Assets	0.98	0.10
十一、投资风险准备 Provisions for Investment Risk					
十二、其他负债 Other Liabilities	0.29	-0.32			
资金来源总计 Total Sources	**13.22**	**1.17**	**资金运用总计 Total Uses**	**13.22**	**1.17**

财务公司外汇信贷收支表

Sources and Uses of Credit Funds of Finance Companies（Foreign Currency）

（1996年末）

（Year - end of 1996）

单位：亿美元

Unit：100 Million US Dollars

项　目 Items	余额 Balance	比年初增减额 Changes within the Year	项　目 Items	余额 Balance	比年初增减额 Changes within the Year
一、外汇存款 Total Deposits	10.04	3.47	一、外汇贷款 Total Loans	6.35	1.57
二、境外筹资 Overseas Financing	0.56	0.10	1. 短期外汇贷款 Short - term Loans	5.65	1.44
1. 境外短期借款 Overseas Short - term Borrowing	0.53	0.13	2. 中长期外汇贷款 Medium and Long - term Loans	0.7	0.13
2. 境外中长期借款 Overseas Medium and Long - term Borrowing	0.03	- 0.03	二、各项投资 Investments	0.35	- 0.01
三、境外发行债券 Overseas Bonds Issue			1. 投资 Investments	0.31	- 0.01
其中：短期债券 Of Which：Short - term Bonds			其中：境内投资 Of Which：Domestic	0.04	
四、委托境外借款 Overseas Designated Borrowing	1.13	1.12	2. 购买有价证券 Purchase of Securities	0.04	
五、境外同业往来 Overseas Inter - bank Transactions	0.36	0.02	其中：购买海外债券 Of Which：Purchase of Foreign Securities		
其中：拆入资金 Of Which：Placements from Banks and Other Financial Institutions	0.36	0.08	三、租赁 Leases	0.13	- 0.04
			四、委托贷款 Designated Loans	4.29	3.73
六、国内同业往来 Domestic Inter - bank Transactions	2.94	0.96	五、境外同业往来 Overseas Inter - bank Transactions		
其中：拆入资金 Of Which：Placements from Banks and Other Financial Institutions	2.91	0.95	其中：拆出资金 Of Which：Placements with Banks and Other Financial Institutions		
七、外汇买卖 Foreign Exchange Dealings	- 0.03	0.03	六、国内同业往来 Domestic Inter - bank Transactions	6.71	0.34
八、所有者权益 Owner's Equity	3.64	0.01	其中：拆出资金 Of Which：Placements with Banks and Other Financial Institutions	1.64	- 0.53
其中：实收资本 Of Which：Paid - in Capital	3.21	0.16			
九、结益 Net Earnings	0.37	0.37	七、缴存准备金 Reserves with the Central Bank		
十、贷款呆账准备金 Provisions for Bad Loans	0.03	0.01	八、其他资产 Other Assets	1.59	0.61
十一、投资风险准备 Provisions for Investment Risk					
十二、其他负债 Other Liabilities	0.38	0.11			
资金来源总计 Total Sources	**19.42**	**6.20**	**资金运用总计 Total Uses**	**19.42**	**6.20**

财务公司外汇信贷收支表

Sources and Uses of Credit Funds of Finance Companies（Foreign Currency）

（1997 年末）

（Year – end of 1997）

单位：亿美元

Unit：100 Million US Dollars

项　目 Items	余　额 Balance	比年初增减额 Changes within the Year	项　目 Items	余　额 Balance	比年初增减额 Changes within the Year
一、外汇存款 Total Deposits	15.81	5.77	一、外汇贷款 Total Loans	9.24	2.89
二、境外筹资 Overseas Financing	1.38	0.82	1. 短期外汇贷款 Short – term Loans	8.36	2.71
1. 境外短期借款 Overseas Short – term Borrowing	1.22	0.69	2. 中长期外汇贷款 Medium and Long – term Loans	0.88	0.18
2. 境外中长期借款 Overseas Medium and Long – term Borrowing	0.16	0.13	二、各项投资 Investments	0.25	– 0.10
三、境外发行债券 Overseas Bonds Issue			1. 投资 Investments	0.21	– 0.10
其中：短期债券 Of Which：Short – term Bonds			其中：境内投资 Of Which：Domestic	0.16	0.12
四、委托境外借款 Overseas Designated Borrowing	3.02	1.89	2. 购买有价证券 Purchase of Securities	0.04	
五、境外同业往来 Overseas Inter – bank Transactions	1.35	0.99	其中：购买海外债券 Of Which：Purchase of Foreign Securities		
其中：拆入资金 Of Which：Placements from Banks and Other Financial Institutions	1.35	0.99	三、租赁 Leases	0.02	– 0.11
			四、委托贷款 Designated Loans	11.00	6.71
六、国内同业往来 Domestic Inter – bank Transactions	2.70	– 0.24	五、境外同业往来 Overseas Inter – bank Transactions	0.03	0.03
其中：拆入资金 Of Which：Placements from Banks and Other Financial Institutions	2.36	– 0.55	其中：拆出资金 Of Which：Placements with Banks and Other Financial Institutions		
七、外汇买卖 Foreign Exchange Dealings		0.03	六、国内同业往来 Domestic Inter – bank Transactions	7.98	1.27
八、所有者权益 Owner's Equity	5.49	1.48	其中：拆出资金 Of Which：Placements with Banks and Other Financial Institutions	1.29	– 0.35
其中：实收资本 Of Which：Paid – in Capital	4.77	1.56			
九、结益 Net Earnings	0.29	0.29	七、缴存准备金 Reserves with the Central Bank		
十、贷款呆账准备金 Provisions for Bad Loans	0.05	0.02	八、其他资产 Other Assets	2.12	0.53
十一、投资风险准备 Provisions for Investment Risk					
十二、其他负债 Other Liabilities	0.55	0.17			
资金来源总计 Total Sources	**30.64**	**11.22**	**资金运用总计 Total Uses**	**30.64**	**11.22**

财务公司外汇信贷收支表

Sources and Uses of Credit Funds of Finance Companies（Foreign Currency）

（1998 年末）

（Year - end of 1998）

单位：亿美元

Unit：100 Million US Dollars

项目 Items	余额 Balance	比年初增减额 Changes within the Year	项目 Items	余额 Balance	比年初增减额 Changes within the Year
一、各项存款 Total Deposits	12.21	-7.1	一、各项贷款 Total Loans	16.35	-4.71
1. 企业存款 Deposits by Enterprises	4.56	-3.42	1. 短期贷款 Short - term Loans	5.30	-2.77
其中：定期存款 Of Which：Time Deposits	1.30	-1.54	2. 中长期贷款 Medium and Long - term Loans	0.90	0.13
2. 信托存款 Trust Deposits	0.27	0.20	3. 信托贷款 Trust Loans		
3. 委托存款 Designated Deposits	7.38	-3.89	其中：中长期信托贷款 Of Which：Medium and Long - term Trust Loans		
4. 其他存款 Other Deposits			4. 委托贷款 Designated Loans	7.57	-3.88
二、境内中长期借款 Domestic Medium and Long - term Borrowing			5. 融资租赁 Financing Leases	0.03	0.01
三、境外筹资 Overseas Financing	0.88	-0.14	6. 票据融资 Paper Financing		
四、证券业务款项 Securities Business Funds			7. 逾期类贷款 Overdue Loans	2.55	1.81
五、卖出回购证券 Repo			二、信托投资 Trust Investments		
六、同业存放 Due to Banks and Other Financial Institutions	0.38	-0.23	1. 短期信托投资 Short - term Trust Investments		
其中：境外同业存放 Of Which：Due to Overseas Banks and Other Financial Institutions		-0.25	其中：境外 Of Which：Overseas		
			2. 中长期信托投资 Medium and Long - term Trust Investments		
七、同业拆入 Placements from Banks and Other Financial Institutions	2.04	-1.53	其中：境外 Of Which：Overseas		
			三、投资 Investments	0.20	-0.06
其中：境外同业拆入 Of Which：Placements from Overseas Banks and Other Financial Institutions	0.03	-0.10	1. 购买有价证券 Purchase of Securities	0.02	-0.04
			其中：购买境外有价证券 Of Which：Purchase of Foreign Securities		
八、外汇买卖 Foreign Exchange Dealings	0.07	0.03			
九、各项准备 Total Provisions	0.07	0.01	2. 其他投资 Other Investments	0.18	-0.02

续表
Continued

项 目 Items	余 额 Balance	比年初增减额 Changes within the Year	项 目 Items	余 额 Balance	比年初增减额 Changes within the Year
十、所有者权益 Owner's Equity	7.08	1.04	其中：投资境外 Of Which: Overseas	0.02	0.02
其中：实收资本 Of Which: Paid - in Capital	6.11	0.84	四、证券业务占款 Funding of Securities Purchase		
当年结益 Net Earnings	0.34	0.34	五、经营租赁 Operating Leases		
十一、其他 Others	- 0.32	0.47	六、境外筹资转贷款 On - lending of Overseas Financing		
			七、存放中央银行 Deposits with the Central Bank	0.21	0.20
			其中：缴存准备金 Of Which: Reserves with the Central Bank		
			八、存放同业 Due from Banks and Other Financial Institutions	4.52	- 3.12
			其中：存放境外同业 Of Which: Due from Overseas Banks and Other Financial Institutions		
			九、拆放同业 Placements with Banks and Other Financial Institutions	1.13	0.23
			其中：拆放境外同业 Of Which: Placements with Overseas Banks and Other Financial Institutions		
			十、库存现金 Cash in Vault		
资金来源总计 Total Sources	**22.41**	**- 7.46**	**资金运用总计 Total Uses**	**22.41**	**- 7.46**

财务公司外汇信贷收支表

Sources and Uses of Credit Funds of Finance Companies（Foreign Currency）

（1999 年末）

（Year - end of 1999）

单位：亿美元

Unit：100 Million US Dollars

项目 Items	余额 Balance	比年初增减额 Changes within the Year	项目 Items	余额 Balance	比年初增减额 Changes within the Year
一、各项存款 Total Deposits	15.51	3.30	一、各项贷款 Total Loans	16.39	0.09
1. 企业存款 Deposits by Enterprises	6.46	1.90	1. 短期贷款 Short - term Loans	3.82	- 1.46
其中：定期存款 Of Which：Time Deposits	0.69	- 0.61	2. 中长期贷款 Medium and Long - term Loans	0.50	- 0.31
2. 信托存款 Trust Deposits	0.48	0.21	3. 信托贷款 Trust Loans		
3. 委托存款 Designated Deposits	8.57	1.19	其中：中长期信托贷款 Of Which：Medium and Long - term Trust Loans		
4. 其他存款 Other Deposits			4. 委托贷款 Designated Loans	8.76	1.19
二、境内中长期借款 Domestic Medium and Long - term Borrowing	0.18	0.18	5. 融资租赁 Financing Leases	0.06	0.03
三、境外筹资 Overseas Financing	0.85	- 0.03	6. 票据融资 Paper Financing		
四、证券业务款项 Securities Business Funds			7. 逾期类贷款 Overdue Loans	3.25	0.64
五、卖出回购证券 Repo			二、信托投资 Trust Investments		
六、同业存放 Due to Banks and Other Financial Institutions	0.33	- 0.03	1. 短期信托投资 Short - term Trust Investments		
其中：境外同业存放 Of Which：Due to Overseas Banks and Other Financial Institutions			其中：境外 Of Which：Overseas		
			2. 中长期信托投资 Medium and Long - term Trust Investments		
七、同业拆入 Placements from Banks and Other Financial Institutions	1.51	- 0.53	其中：境外 Of Which：Overseas		
			三、投资 Investments	0.28	0.08
其中：境外同业拆入 Of Which：Placements from Overseas Banks and Other Financial Institutions	0.03		1. 购买有价证券 Purchase of Securities	0.11	0.09
			其中：购买境外有价证券 Of Which：Purchase of Foreign Securities	0.09	0.09
八、外汇买卖 Foreign Exchange Dealings	- 0.04	- 0.12			
九、各项准备 Total Provisions	0.07		2. 其他投资 Other Investments	0.17	- 0.01

续表
Continued

项　目 Items	余　额 Balance	比年初增减额 Changes within the Year	项　目 Items	余　额 Balance	比年初增减额 Changes within the Year
十、所有者权益 Owner's Equity	7.27	0.31	其中：投资境外 Of Which: Overseas	0.02	
其中：实收资本 Of Which: Paid - in Capital	6.28	0.20	四、证券业务占款 Funding of Securities Purchase		
当年结益 Net Earnings	0.34	0.34	五、经营租赁 Operating Leases		
十一、其他 Others	0.21	0.48	六、境外筹资转贷款 On - lending of Overseas Financing		
			七、存放中央银行 Deposits with the Central Bank	0.31	0.10
			其中：缴存准备金 Of Which: Reserves with the Central Bank	0.01	0.01
			八、存放同业 Due from Banks and Other Financial Institutions	7.64	3.24
			其中：存放境外同业 Of Which: Due from Overseas Banks and Other Financial Institutions		
			九、拆放同业 Placements with Banks and Other Financial Institutions	1.27	0.15
			其中：拆放境外同业 Of Which: Placements with Overseas Banks and Other Financial Institutions		
			十、库存现金 Cash in Vault		-0.10
资金来源总计 Total Sources	**25.89**	**3.56**	**资金运用总计 Total Uses**	**25.89**	**3.56**

财务公司外汇信贷收支表

Sources and Uses of Credit Funds of Finance Companies（Foreign Currency）

（2000 年末）

（Year－end of 2000）

单位：亿美元

Unit：100 Million US Dollars

项目 Items	余额 Balance	比年初增减额 Changes within the Year	项目 Items	余额 Balance	比年初增减额 Changes within the Year
一、各项存款 Total Deposits	15.99	0.48	一、各项贷款 Total Loans	14.11	－2.20
1. 企业存款 Deposits by Enterprises	5.31	－1.15	1. 短期贷款 Short－term Loans	1.83	－1.99
其中：定期存款 Of Which：Time Deposits	0.77	0.08	2. 中长期贷款 Medium and Long－term Loans	0.15	－0.28
2. 信托存款 Trust Deposits	0.11	－0.37	3. 信托贷款 Trust Loans		
3. 委托存款 Designated Deposits	10.57	2.00	其中：中长期信托贷款 Of Which：Medium and Long－term Trust Loans		
4. 其他存款 Other Deposits			4. 委托贷款 Designated Loans	8.88	0.12
二、境内中长期借款 Domestic Medium and Long－term Borrowing	0.06	－0.12	5. 融资租赁 Financing Leases	0.06	
三、境外筹资 Overseas Financing	0.63	－0.22	6. 票据融资 Paper Financing		
四、证券业务款项 Securities Business Funds			7. 逾期类贷款 Overdue Loans	3.19	－0.05
五、卖出回购证券 Repo			二、信托投资 Trust Investments	0.05	0.05
六、同业存放 Due to Banks and Other Financial Institutions	0.18	－0.15	1. 短期信托投资 Short－term Trust Investments	0.05	0.05
其中：境外同业存放 Of Which：Due to Overseas Banks and Other Financial Institutions			其中：境外 Of Which：Overseas		
			2. 中长期信托投资 Medium and Long－term Trust Investments		
七、同业拆入 Placements from Banks and Other Financial Institutions	1.81	0.31	其中：境外 Of Which：Overseas		
其中：境外同业拆入 Of Which：Placements from Overseas Banks and Other Financial Institutions	0.03		三、投资 Investments	1.41	1.12
			1. 购买有价证券 Purchase of Securities	1.26	1.15
			其中：购买境外有价证券 Of Which：Purchase of Foreign Securities	0.28	0.19
八、外汇买卖 Foreign Exchange Dealings	0.05	－0.06			
九、各项准备 Total Provisions	0.05	－0.02	2. 其他投资 Other Investments	0.15	－0.03

续表
Continued

项目 Items	余额 Balance	比年初增减额 Changes within the Year	项目 Items	余额 Balance	比年初增减额 Changes within the Year
十、所有者权益 Owner's Equity	7.24	0.19	其中：投资境外 Of Which: Overseas		-0.02
其中：实收资本 Of Which: Paid-in Capital	6.40	0.17	四、证券业务占款 Funding of Securities Purchase		
当年结益 Net Earnings	0.33	0.33	五、经营租赁 Operating Leases		
十一、其他 Others	0.28	0.07	六、境外筹资转贷款 On-lending of Overseas Financing		
			七、存放中央银行 Deposits with the Central Bank	0.47	0.16
			其中：缴存准备金 Of Which: Reserves with the Central Bank	0.01	
			八、存放同业 Due from Banks and Other Financial Institutions	8.00	0.36
			其中：存放境外同业 Of Which: Due from Overseas Banks and Other Financial Institutions		
			九、拆放同业 Placements with Banks and Other Financial Institutions	2.25	0.99
			其中：拆放境外同业 Of Which: Placements with Overseas Banks and Other Financial Institutions		
			十、库存现金 Cash in Vault		
资金来源总计 Total Sources	**26.29**	**0.48**	**资金运用总计 Total Uses**	**26.29**	**0.48**

财务公司外汇信贷收支表

Sources and Uses of Credit Funds of Finance Companies（Foreign Currency）

（2001 年末）

（Year－end of 2001）

单位：亿美元

Unit：100 Million US Dollars

项　　目 Items	余　额 Balance	比年初增减额 Changes within the Year	项　　目 Items	余　额 Balance	比年初增减额 Changes within the Year
一、各项存款 Total Deposits	18.61	2.62	一、各项贷款 Total Loans	16.43	2.07
1. 企业存款 Deposits by Enterprises	6.77	1.46	1. 短期贷款 Short－term Loans	3.13	－1.58
其中：定期存款 Of Which：Time Deposits	1.45	0.68	2. 中长期贷款 Medium and Long－term Loans	1.62	1.16
2. 信托存款 Trust Deposits	0.12	0.01	3. 信托贷款 Trust Loans	0.09	0.09
3. 委托存款 Designated Deposits	11.72	1.15	其中：中长期信托贷款 Of Which：Medium and Long－term Trust Loans		
4. 其他存款 Other Deposits			4. 委托贷款 Designated Loans	11.34	2.46
二、境内中长期借款 Domestic Medium and Long－term Borrowing	0.03	－0.03	5. 融资租赁 Financing Leases	0.07	0.01
三、境外筹资 Overseas Financing	0.80	－0.11	6. 票据融资 Paper Financing		
四、证券业务款项 Securities Business Funds			其中：贴现 Of Which：Discount		
五、卖出回购证券 Repo			7. 各项垫款 Total Advances		
六、同业存放 Due to Banks and Other Financial Institutions	0.10	－0.04	8. 境外筹资转贷款 On－lending of Overseas Financing	0.18	－0.07
			二、信托投资 Trust Investments		－0.05
其中：境外同业存放 Of Which：Due to Overseas Banks and Other Financial Institutions			1. 短期信托投资 Short－term Trust Investments		－0.05
			其中：境外 Of Which：Overseas		
七、同业拆入 Placements from Banks and Other Financial Institutions	1.19	－0.62	2. 中长期信托投资 Medium and Long－term Trust Investments		
其中：境外同业拆入 Of Which：Placements from Overseas Banks and Other Financial Institutions	0.03		其中：境外 Of Which：Overseas		
			三、投资 Investments	1.68	0.27
八、外汇买卖 Foreign Exchange Dealings	－0.30	－0.36	1. 购买有价证券 Purchase of Securities	1.30	0.04
九、应付及暂收款 Accounts Payable and Receipts on Account	1.34	－0.05			

续表
Continued

项目 Items	余额 Balance	比年初增减额 Changes within the Year	项目 Items	余额 Balance	比年初增减额 Changes within the Year
其中：应付及预提利息 Of Which: Interest Payable and Accrued	0.38	0.09	其中：购买境外有价证券 Of Which: Purchase of Foreign Securities	0.72	0.44
十、各项准备 Total Provisions	0.08	0.02	2. 其他投资 Other Investments	0.38	0.23
其中：贷款呆账准备金 Of Which: Provisions for Bad Loans	0.08	0.03	其中：投资境外 Of Which: Overseas		
			四、证券业务占款 Funding of Securities Purchaseess		
十一、所有者权益 Owner's Equity	7.94	0.62	五、经营租赁 Operating Leases		
其中：实收资本 Of Which: Paid - in Capital	7.21	0.71	六、买入返售证券 Reverse Repo		
当年结益 Net Earnings	0.36	0.36	七、应收及预付款项 Accounts Receivable and Advance Payments	2.63	1.78
十二、其他 Others	0.06	0.39	其中：应收及预付利息 Of Which: Interest Receivable and Paid in Advance	0.41	-0.11
			八、存放中央银行 Deposits with the Central Bank	0.01	-0.46
			其中：缴存准备金 Of Which: Reserves with the Central Bank	0.01	
			九、存放同业 Due from Banks and Other Financial Institutions	8.36	0.34
			其中：存放境外同业 Of Which: Due from Overseas Banks and Other Financial Institutions		
			十、拆放同业 Placements with Banks and Other Financial Institutions	0.74	-1.51
			其中：拆放境外同业 Of Which: Placements with Overseas Banks and Other Financial Institutions		
			十一、库存现金 Cash in Vault		
资金来源总计 Total Sources	**29.85**	**2.44**	**资金运用总计 Total Uses**	**29.85**	**2.44**

财务公司外汇信贷收支表

Sources and Uses of Credit Funds of Finance Companies（Foreign Currency）

（2002 年末）

（Year - end of 2002）

单位：亿美元

Unit：100 Million US Dollars

项　目 Items	余　额 Balance	比年初增减额 Changes within the Year	项　目 Items	余　额 Balance	比年初增减额 Changes within the Year
一、各项存款 Total Deposits	17.96	-0.40	一、各项贷款 Total Loans	15.13	-0.97
1. 企业存款 Deposits by Enterprises	8.12	1.57	1. 短期贷款 Short - term Loans	4.02	1.07
其中：定期存款 Of Which：Time Deposits	0.93	-0.46	2. 中长期贷款 Medium and Long - term Loans	2.30	0.79
2. 信托存款 Trust Deposits	1.14	1.01	3. 信托贷款 Trust Loans	0.09	
3. 委托存款 Designated Deposits	8.70	-2.98	其中：中长期信托贷款 Of Which：Medium and Long - term Trust Loans		
4. 其他存款 Other Deposits			4. 委托贷款 Designated Loans	8.52	-2.79
二、境内中长期借款 Domestic Medium and Long - term Borrowing	0.02	-0.01	5. 融资租赁 Financing Leases	0.03	-0.03
三、境外筹资 Overseas Financing	0.48	-0.11	6. 票据融资 Paper Financing		
四、证券业务款项 Securities Business Funds			其中：贴现 Of Which：Discount		
五、卖出回购证券 Repo	0.78	0.78	7. 各项垫款 Total Advances		
六、同业存放 Due to Banks and Other Financial Institutions	0.43	0.40	8. 境外筹资转贷款 On - lending of Overseas Financing	0.17	-0.01
其中：境外同业存放 Of Which：Due to Overseas Banks and Other Financial Institutions			二、信托投资 Trust Investments		
			1. 短期信托投资 Short - term Trust Investments		
			其中：境外 Of Which：Overseas		
七、同业拆入 Placements from Banks and Other Financial Institutions	0.95	-0.10	2. 中长期信托投资 Medium and Long - term Trust Investments		
其中：境外同业拆入 Of Which：Placements from Overseas Banks and Other Financial Institutions	0.03		其中：境外 Of Which：Overseas		
			三、投资 Investments	2.41	0.80
八、外汇买卖 Foreign Exchange Dealings	-0.10	0.16	1. 购买有价证券 Purchase of Securities	1.73	0.44
九、应付及暂收款 Accounts Payable and Receipts on Account	1.30				

续表
Continued

项　目 Items	余　额 Balance	比年初增减额 Changes within the Year	项　目 Items	余　额 Balance	比年初增减额 Changes within the Year
其中：应付及预提利息 Of Which：Interest Payable and Accrued	0.33	-0.03	其中：购买境外有价证券 Of Which：Purchase of Foreign Securities	1.73	1.01
十、各项准备 Total Provisions	0.11	0.03	2. 其他投资 Other Investments	0.68	0.36
其中：贷款呆账准备金 Of Which：Provisions for Bad Loans	0.11	0.03	其中：投资境外 Of Which：Overseas		
			四、证券业务占款 Funding of Securities Purchase		
十一、所有者权益 Owner's Equity	8.05	0.49	五、经营租赁 Operating Leases		
其中：实收资本 Of Which：Paid-in Capital	7.31	0.61	六、买入返售证券 Reverse Repo	0.33	0.33
当年结益 Net Earnings	0.12	0.12	七、应收及预付款项 Accounts Receivable and Advance Payments	2.49	
十二、其他 Others	0.10	0.05	其中：应收及预付利息 Of Which：Interest Receivable and Paid in Advance	0.22	-0.10
			八、存放中央银行 Deposits with the Central Bank		-0.01
			其中：缴存准备金 Of Which：Reserves with the Central Bank		-0.01
			九、存放同业 Due from Banks and Other Financial Institutions	9.26	1.24
			其中：存放境外同业 Of Which：Due from Overseas Banks and Other Financial Institutions		
			十、拆放同业 Placements with Banks and Other Financial Institutions	0.43	-0.13
			其中：拆放境外同业 Of Which：Placements with Overseas Banks and Other Financial Institutions		
			十一、库存现金 Cash in Vault	0.03	0.03
资金来源总计 Total Sources	**30.08**	**1.29**	**资金运用总计 Total Uses**	**30.08**	**1.29**

财务公司外汇信贷收支表

Sources and Uses of Credit Funds of Finance Companies（Foreign Currency）

（2003 年末）

（Year－end of 2003）

单位：亿美元

Unit：100 Million US Dollars

项 目 Items	余 额 Balance	比年初增减额 Changes within the Year	项 目 Items	余 额 Balance	比年初增减额 Changes within the Year
一、各项存款 Total Deposits	18.13	0.20	一、各项贷款 Total Loans	17.95	3.12
1. 企业存款 Deposits by Enterprises	8.09		1. 短期贷款 Short－term Loans	2.64	－1.08
其中：定期存款 Of Which：Time Deposits	1.93	1.03	2. 中长期贷款 Medium and Long－term Loans	5.34	3.04
2. 信托存款 Trust Deposits	0.05	－1.09	3. 信托贷款 Trust Loans	0.15	0.06
3. 委托存款 Designated Deposits	9.99	1.29	其中：中长期信托贷款 Of Which：Medium and Long－term Trust Loans		
4. 其他存款 Other Deposits			4. 委托贷款 Designated Loans	9.53	1.01
二、境内中长期借款 Domestic Medium and Long－term Borrowing	0.01	－0.01	5. 融资租赁 Financing Leases	0.03	
三、境外筹资 Overseas Financing	0.15	－0.33	6. 票据融资 Paper Financing	0.12	0.12
四、证券业务款项 Securities Business Funds			其中：贴现 Of Which：Discount	0.12	0.12
五、卖出回购证券 Repo	0.09	－0.69	7. 各项垫款 Total Advances		
六、同业存放 Due to Banks and Other Financial Institutions		－0.43	8. 境外筹资转贷款 On－lending of Overseas Financing	0.14	－0.03
其中：境外同业存放 Of Which：Due to Overseas Banks and Other Financial Institutions			二、信托投资 Trust Investments		
			1. 短期信托投资 Short－term Trust Investments		
			其中：境外 Of Which：Overseas		
七、同业拆入 Placements from Banks and Other Financial Institutions	1.09	0.45	2. 中长期信托投资 Medium and Long－term Trust Investments		
其中：境外同业拆入 Of Which：Placements from Overseas Banks and Other Financial Institutions	0.03		其中：境外 Of Which：Overseas		
			三、投资 Investments	2.89	0.48
八、外汇买卖 Foreign Exchange Dealings	－0.05	－0.07	1. 购买有价证券 Purchase of Securities	2.59	0.86
九、应付及暂收款 Accounts Payable and Receipts on Account	1.66	0.39			

续表
Continued

项　目 Items	余　额 Balance	比年初增减额 Changes within the Year	项　目 Items	余　额 Balance	比年初增减额 Changes within the Year
其中：应付及预提利息 Of Which: Interest Payable and Accrued	0.18	-0.15	其中：购买境外有价证券 Of Which: Purchase of Foreign Securities	1.65	-0.08
十、各项准备 Total Provisions	0.16	0.05	2. 其他投资 Other Investments	0.30	-0.38
其中：贷款呆账准备金 Of Which: Provisions for Bad Loans	0.15	0.05	其中：投资境外 Of Which: Overseas		
			四、证券业务占款 Funding of Securities Purchase		
十一、所有者权益 Owner's Equity	8.39	0.51	五、经营租赁 Operating Leases		
其中：实收资本 Of Which: Paid-in Capital	7.51	0.40	六、买入返售证券 Reverse Repo		-0.33
当年结益 Net Earnings	0.18	0.18	七、应收及预付款项 Accounts Receivable and Advance Payments	2.03	-0.37
十二、其他 Others	0.98	0.93	其中：应收及预付利息 Of Which: Interest Receivable and Paid in Advance	0.15	-0.03
			八、存放中央银行 Deposits with the Central Bank		
			其中：缴存准备金 Of Which: Reserves with the Central Bank		
			九、存放同业 Due from Banks and Other Financial Institutions	7.40	-1.84
			其中：存放境外同业 Of Which: Due from Overseas Banks and Other Financial Institutions		
			十、拆放同业 Placements with Banks and Other Financial Institutions	0.34	-0.03
			其中：拆放境外同业 Of Which: Placements with Overseas Banks and Other Financial Institutions		
			十一、库存现金 Cash in Vault		-0.03
资金来源总计 Total Sources	**30.61**	**1.00**	**资金运用总计 Total Uses**	**30.61**	**1.00**

财务公司外汇信贷收支表

Sources and Uses of Credit Funds of Finance Companies（Foreign Currency）

（2004 年末）

（Year - end of 2004）

单位：亿美元

Unit：100 Million US Dollars

项　目 Items	余　额 Balance	比年初增减额 Changes within the Year	项　目 Items	余　额 Balance	比年初增减额 Changes within the Year
一、各项存款 Total Deposits	10.95	-7.18	一、各项贷款 Total Loans	7.95	-9.66
1. 企业存款 Deposits by Enterprises	10.22	2.13	1. 短期贷款 Short - term Loans	2.64	0.34
其中：定期存款 Of Which：Time Deposits	0.52	-1.41	2. 中长期贷款 Medium and Long - term Loans	4.69	-0.65
2. 信托存款 Trust Deposits	0.33	0.28	3. 信托贷款 Trust Loans	0.06	-0.09
3. 委托存款 Designated Deposits	0.40	-9.59	其中：中长期信托贷款 Of Which：Medium and Long - term Trust Loans		
4. 其他存款 Other Deposits			4. 委托贷款 Designated Loans	0.40	-9.13
二、境内中长期借款 Domestic Medium and Long - term Borrowing		-0.01	5. 融资租赁 Financing Leases	0.06	0.03
三、境外筹资 Overseas Financing	0.11	-0.04	6. 票据融资 Paper Financing		-0.12
四、证券业务款项 Securities Business Funds			其中：贴现 Of Which：Discount		-0.12
五、卖出回购资产 Assets Repo（Including Securities）		-0.09	7. 各项垫款 Total Advances		
六、同业存放 Due to Banks and Other Financial Institutions			8. 境外筹资转贷款 On - lending of Overseas Financing	0.10	-0.04
其中：境外同业存放 Of Which：Due to Overseas Banks and Other Financial Institutions			二、信托投资 Trust Investments		
			1. 短期信托投资 Short - term Trust Investments		
七、同业拆入 Placements from Banks and Other Financial Institutions	0.49	-0.41	其中：境外 Of Which：Overseas		
其中：境外同业拆入 Of Which：Placements from Overseas Banks and Other Financial Institutions			2. 中长期信托投资 Medium and Long - term Trust Investments		
			其中：境外 Of Which：Overseas		
			三、投资 Investments	2.48	-0.41
八、外汇买卖 Foreign Exchange Dealings	0.03	0.04	1. 购买有价证券 Purchase of Securities	2.08	-0.51
九、应付及暂收款 Accounts Payable and Receipts on Account	1.04	-0.54			

续表
Continued

项　目 Items	余　额 Balance	比年初增减额 Changes within the Year	项　目 Items	余　额 Balance	比年初增减额 Changes within the Year
其中：应付及预提利息 Of Which: Interest Payable and Accrued	0.05	-0.07	其中：购买境外有价证券 Of Which: Purchase of Foreign Securities	1.80	0.15
十、各项准备 Total Provisions	0.21	0.05	2. 其他投资 Other Investments	0.40	0.10
其中：贷款呆账准备金 Of Which: Provisions for Bad Loans	0.18	0.05	其中：投资境外 Of Which: Overseas		
十一、所有者权益 Owner's Equity	8.58	0.30	四、证券业务占款 Funding of Securities Purchase		
			五、经营租赁 Operating Leases		
其中：实收资本 Of Which: Paid - in Capital	7.59	0.23	六、买入返售资产 Assets Reverse Repo (Including Securities)		
当年结益 Net Earnings	0.34	0.34	七、应收及预付款项 Accounts Receivable and Advance Payments	0.53	-1.46
十二、其他 Others	-0.30	-1.28	其中：应收及预付利息 Of Which: Interest Receivable and Paid in Advance	0.13	0.02
			八、存放中央银行 Deposits with the Central Bank		
			其中：缴存准备金 Of Which: Reserves with the Central Bank		
			九、存放同业 Due from Banks and Other Financial Institutions	9.94	2.50
			其中：存放境外同业 Of Which: Due from Overseas Banks and Other Financial Institutions		
			十、拆放同业 Placements with Banks and Other Financial Institutions	0.21	-0.13
			其中：拆放境外同业 Of Which: Placements with Overseas Banks and Other Financial Institutions		
			十一、库存现金 Cash in Vault		
资金来源总计 Total Sources	**21.11**	**-9.16**	**资金运用总计 Total Uses**	**21.11**	**-9.16**

财务公司外汇信贷收支表

Sources and Uses of Credit Funds of Finance Companies（Foreign Currency）

（2005年末）

（Year - end of 2005）

单位：亿美元

Unit：100 Million US Dollars

项目 Items	余额 Balance	比年初增减额 Changes within the Year	项目 Items	余额 Balance	比年初增减额 Changes within the Year
一、各项存款 Total Deposits	19.43	2.59	一、各项贷款 Total Loans	17.06	3.23
1. 企业存款 Deposits by Enterprises	12.51	2.29	1. 短期贷款 Short - term Loans	3.59	0.96
其中：定期存款 Of Which：Time Deposits	0.76	0.24	2. 中长期贷款 Medium and Long - term Loans	6.41	1.72
2. 信托存款 Trust Deposits	0.05	-0.28	3. 信托贷款 Trust Loans	0.06	
3. 委托存款 Designated Deposits	6.87	0.58	其中：中长期信托贷款 Of Which：Medium and Long - term Trust Loans		
4. 其他存款 Other Deposits			4. 委托贷款 Designated Loans	6.87	0.58
二、境内中长期筹资 Domestic Medium and Long - term Borrowing			5. 融资租赁 Financing Leases	0.05	-0.01
三、境外筹资 Overseas Financing	0.06	-0.05	6. 票据融资 Paper Financing		
四、证券业务款项 Securities Business Funds			其中：贴现 Of Which：Discount		
五、卖出回购资产 Assets Repo（Including Securities）			7. 各项垫款 Total Advances		
六、同业存放 Due to Banks and Other Financial Institutions			8. 境外筹资转贷款 On - lending of Overseas Financing	0.08	-0.02
其中：境外同业存放 Of Which：Due to Overseas Banks and Other Financial Institutions			二、信托投资 Trust Investments		
			1. 短期信托投资 Short - term Trust Investments		
			其中：境外 Of Which：Overseas		
七、同业拆入 Placements from Banks and Other Financial Institutions	0.32	-0.17	2. 中长期信托投资 Medium and Long - term Trust Investments		
其中：境外同业拆入 Of Which：Placements from Overseas Banks and Other Financial Institutions			其中：境外 Of Which：Overseas		
			三、投资 Investments	2.28	-0.20
八、外汇买卖 Foreign Exchange Dealings	-0.14	-0.17	1. 购买有价证券 Purchase of Securities	1.91	-0.17
九、应付及暂收款 Accounts Payable and Receipts on Account	1.43	0.40			

续表
Continued

项目 Items	余额 Balance	比年初增减额 Changes within the Year	项目 Items	余额 Balance	比年初增减额 Changes within the Year
其中：应付及预提利息 Of Which: Interest Payable and Accrued	0.08	0.03	其中：购买境外有价证券 Of Which: Purchase of Foreign Securities	1.70	-0.10
十、各项准备 Total Provisions	0.58	0.13	2. 其他投资 Other Investments	0.37	-0.03
其中：贷款损失准备 Of Which: Provisions for Loan Losses	0.44	0.04	其中：投资境外 Of Which: Overseas		
			四、证券业务占款 Funding of Securities Purchase		
十一、所有者权益 Owner's Equity	6.74	-1.57	五、经营租赁 Operating Leases		
其中：实收资本 Of Which: Paid-in Capital	6.68	-0.91	六、买入返售资产 Assets Reverse Repo (Including Securities)		
当年结益 Net Earnings	0.20	0.20			
十二、其他 Others	0.02	0.31	七、应收及预付款项 Accounts Receivable and Advance Payments	0.50	-0.02
			其中：应收及预付利息 Of Which: Interest Receivable and Paid in Advance	0.11	
			八、存放中央银行 Deposits with the Central Bank	0.38	0.38
			其中：缴存准备金 Of Which: Reserves with the Central Bank	0.37	0.37
			九、存放同业 Due from Banks and Other Financial Institutions	8.11	-1.83
			其中：存放境外同业 Of Which: Due from Overseas Banks and Other Financial Institutions		
			十、拆放同业 Placements with Banks and Other Financial Institutions	0.10	-0.10
			其中：拆放境外同业 Of Which: Placements with Overseas Banks and Other Financial Institutions		
			十一、库存现金 Cash in Vault	0.01	0.01
资金来源总计 Total Sources	**28.44**	**1.47**	**资金运用总计 Total Uses**	**28.44**	**1.47**

10. 信托投资公司外汇信贷收支表（1993—2005）

Sources and Uses of Credit Funds of Financial Trust and Investment Companies（Foreign Currency）（1993—2005）

信托投资公司外汇信贷收支表

Sources and Uses of Credit Funds of Financial Trust and Investment Companies（Foreign Currency）

（1993 年末）

（Year - end of 1993）

单位：亿美元

Unit：100 Million US Dollars

项　目 Items	余　额 Balance	比年初增减额 Changes within the Year	项　目 Items	余　额 Balance	比年初增减额 Changes within the Year
一、外汇存款 Total Deposits	23.25	8.36	一、外汇贷款 Total Loans	178.52	40.35
1. 信托存款 Trust Deposits	15.50	5.55	1. 短期外汇贷款 Short - term Loans	26.60	7.33
其中：企业单位存款 Of Which：Deposits by Enterprises	6.15	1.04	2. 中长期外汇贷款 Medium and Long - term Loans	154.92	33.02
2. 委托存款 Designated Deposits	4.46	2.01	二、各项投资 Investments	16.21	2.50
3. 其他存款 Other Deposits	3.29	0.80	1. 投资 Investments	15.20	3.42
二、境外筹资 Overseas Financing	155.43	43.11	其中：境外投资 Of Which：Overseas	2.08	1.27
1. 境外短期借款 Overseas Short - term Borrowing	10.10	1.49	2. 购买有价证券 Purchase of Securities	1.01	- 0.92
2. 境外中长期借款 Overseas Medium and Long - term Borrowing	145.33	41.62	其中：购买海外证券 Of Which：Purchase of Foreign Securities	0.91	- 0.97
其中：境外发行债券 Of Which：Overseas Bonds Issue	18.97	9.87	三、租赁 Leases	9.50	1.02
三、委托借款 Designated Borrowing	0.98	- 5.33	四、委托贷款 Designated Loans	4.46	0.90
四、外汇自有资金 Banks' Own Working Capital	19.04	2.95	五、存放同业资金 Due from Banks and Other Financial Institutions	9.04	- 0.18
五、同业往来 Inter - bank Transactions	31.90	- 5.34	其中：境外 Of Which：Overseas	2.88	- 1.39
其中：同业拆入 Of Which：Placements from Banks and Other Financial Institutions	17.61	7.75	六、缴存准备金 Reserves with the Central Bank		
			七、同业往来 Inter - bank Transactions	9.39	0.25
六、结益 Net Earnings	0.99	0.99	其中：同业拆出 Of Which：Placements with Banks and Other Financial Institutions	5.47	0.73
七、其他 Others	- 4.47	0.10			
资金来源总计 Total Sources	**227.12**	**44.84**	**资金运用总计 Total Uses**	**227.12**	**44.84**

信托投资公司外汇信贷收支表

Sources and Uses of Credit Funds of Financial Trust and Investment Companies (Foreign Currency)

(1994年末)

(Year－end of 1994)

单位：亿美元

Unit: 100 Million US Dollars

项　目 Items	余　额 Balance	比年初增减额 Changes within the Year	项　目 Items	余　额 Balance	比年初增减额 Changes within the Year
一、外汇存款 Total Deposits	30.52	6.26	一、外汇贷款 Total Loans	100.03	16.72
1. 信托存款 Trust Deposits	18.32	2.63	1. 短期外汇贷款 Short－term Loans	35.80	8.66
其中：企业单位存款 Of Which: Deposits by Enterprises	5.74	－0.45	2. 中长期外汇贷款 Medium and Long－term Loans	61.23	8.06
			二、各项投资 Investments	15.80	－0.44
2. 委托存款 Designated Deposits	8.56	3.73	1. 投资 Investments	14.63	－0.60
3. 其他存款 Other Deposits	3.64	－0.10	其中：境外投资 Of Which: Overseas	0.42	－1.63
二、境外筹资 Overseas Financing	68.49	10.73	2. 购买有价证券 Purchase of Securities	1.17	0.16
1. 境外短期借款 Overseas Short－term Borrowing	12.35	2.29	其中：购买海外证券 Of Which: Purchase of Foreign Securities	0.17	－0.74
2. 境外中长期借款 Overseas Medium and Long－term Borrowing	56.14	8.44	三、租赁 Leases	11.20	1.73
其中：境外发行债券 Of Which: Overseas Bonds Issue	21.06	2.09	四、委托贷款 Designated Loans	127.10	26.22
三、委托借款 Designated Borrowing	123.59	24.86	五、存放同业资金 Due from Banks and Other Financial Institutions	10.36	1.15
四、外汇自有资金 Banks' Own Working Capital	20.42	1.11			
五、同业往来 Inter－bank Transactions	42.65	10.52	其中：境外 Of Which: Overseas	2.29	－0.59
其中：同业拆入 Of Which: Placements from Banks and Other Financial Institutions	12.73	－5.26	六、缴存准备金 Reserves with the Central Bank	0.05	0.05
			七、同业往来 Inter－bank Transactions	14.44	4.78
六、结益 Net Earnings	1.00	1.00	其中：同业拆出 Of Which: Placements with Banks and Other Financial Institutions	5.72	0.05
七、其他 Others	16.49	6.50			
			八、其他 Others	24.18	0.77
资金来源总计 Total Sources	**303.16**	**50.98**	**资金运用总计 Total Uses**	**303.16**	**50.98**

信托投资公司外汇信贷收支表

Sources and Uses of Credit Funds of Financial Trust and Investment Companies（Foreign Currency）

（1995 年末）

（Year－end of 1995）

单位：亿美元

Unit：100 Million US Dollars

项目 Items	余额 Balance	比年初增减额 Changes within the Year	项目 Items	余额 Balance	比年初增减额 Changes within the Year
一、外汇存款 Total Deposits	32.97	2.77	一、外汇贷款 Total Loans	106.54	5.77
1. 信托存款 Trust Deposits	20.32	1.27	1. 短期外汇贷款 Short－term Loans	41.53	4.88
其中：企业单位存款 Of Which：Deposits by Enterprises	7.49	－0.37	2. 中长期外汇贷款 Medium and Long－term Loans	65.01	0.89
2. 委托存款 Designated Deposits	9.73	1.90	二、各项投资 Investments	16.57	0.96
3. 其他存款 Other Deposits	2.92	－0.40	1. 投资 Investments	14.77	0.34
二、境外筹资 Overseas Financing	39.69	－4.35	其中：境内投资 Of Which：Domestic	6.71	2.58
1. 境外短期借款 Overseas Short－term Borrowing	13.53	1.71	2. 购买有价证券 Purchase of Securities	1.80	0.62
2. 境外中长期借款 Overseas Medium and Long－term Borrowing	26.16	－6.06	其中：购买海外证券 Of Which：Purchase of Foreign Securities	0.18	
三、境外发行债券 Overseas Bonds Issue	22.98	－2.43	三、租赁 Leases	10.8	－1.17
其中：短期债券 Of Which：Short－term Bonds			四、委托贷款 Designated Loans	10.84	－115.81
四、委托借款 Designated Borrowing	2.37	－121.03	五、境外同业往来 Overseas Inter－bank Transactions	2.15	－0.36
五、境外同业往来 Overseas Inter－bank Transactions	2.54	1.29	其中：拆出资金 Of Which：Placements with Banks and Other Financial Institutions	0.55	0.19
其中：同业拆入 Of Which：Placements from Banks and Other Financial Institutions	1.64	0.58	六、国内同业往来 Domestic Inter－bank Transactions	18.05	－3.35
六、国内同业往来 Domestic Inter－bank Transactions	44.04	1.91	其中：拆出资金 Of Which：Placements with Banks and Other Financial Institutions	12.76	1.14
其中：同业拆入 Of Which：Placements from Banks and Other Financial Institutions	21.14	9.12	七、缴存准备金 Reserves with the Central Bank	0.07	－0.24
七、外汇买卖 Foreign Exchange Dealings	3.37	0.51	八、其他 Others	28.83	0.93

续表
Continued

项目 Items	余额 Balance	比年初增减额 Changes within the Year	项目 Items	余额 Balance	比年初增减额 Changes within the Year
八、所有者权益 Owner's Equity	21.27	-0.82			
其中：实收资本 Of Which: Paid-in Capital	19.11	1.67			
九、结益 Net Earnings	1.37	1.37			
十、呆账准备金 Provisions for Bad Loans	0.44	0.14			
十一、投资风险准备 Provisions for Investment Risk	0.02	0.01			
十二、其他 Others	22.79	7.36			
资金来源总计 Total Sources	**193.85**	**-113.27**	**资金运用总计 Total Uses**	**193.85**	**-113.27**

信托投资公司外汇信贷收支表

Sources and Uses of Credit Funds of Financial Trust and Investment Companies（Foreign Currency）

（1996年末）

（Year - end of 1996）

单位：亿美元

Unit：100 Million US Dollars

项目 Items	余额 Balance	比年初增减额 Changes within the Year	项目 Items	余额 Balance	比年初增减额 Changes within the Year
一、外汇存款 Total Deposits	31.32	-1.65	一、外汇贷款 Total Loans	106.77	0.23
1. 信托存款 Trust Deposits	20.02	0.30	1. 短期外汇贷款 Short - term Loans	45.95	4.42
其中：企业单位存款 Of Which：Deposits by Enterprises	6.33	-1.16	2. 中长期外汇贷款 Medium and Long - term Loans	60.82	-4.19
			二、各项投资 Investments	16.71	0.14
2. 委托存款 Designated Deposits	8.50	-1.23	1. 投资 Investments	15.01	0.24
3. 其他存款 Other Deposits	2.80	-0.12	其中：境内投资 Of Which：Domestic	7.11	0.40
二、境外筹资 Overseas Financing	42.76	3.07	2. 购买有价证券 Purchase of Securities	1.7	-0.10
1. 境外短期借款 Overseas Short - term Borrowing	19.30	5.77	其中：购买海外证券 Of Which：Purchase of Foreign Securities	0.32	0.14
2. 境外中长期借款 Overseas Medium and Long - term Borrowing	23.46	-2.70	三、融资租赁 Financing Leases	9.91	-0.89
三、境外发行债券 Overseas Bonds Issue	22.50	-0.48	四、委托境外借款转贷款 On - lending of Overseas Designated Borrowing	9.57	-1.27
其中：短期债券 Of Which：Short - term Bonds					
四、委托境外借款 Overseas Designated Borrowing	3.07	0.70	五、境外同业往来 Overseas Inter - bank Transactions	1.92	-0.23
五、境外同业往来 Overseas Inter - bank Transactions	2.85	0.31	其中：拆出资金 Of Which：Placements with Banks and Other Financial Institutions	0.67	0.12
其中：同业拆入 Of Which：Placements from Banks and Other Financial Institutions	1.90	0.26	六、国内同业往来 Domestic Inter - bank Transactions	22.7	4.65
六、国内同业往来 Domestic Inter - bank Transactions	45.24	1.20	其中：拆出资金 Of Which：Placements with Banks and Other Financial Institutions	12.73	-0.03
其中：同业拆入 Of Which：Placements from Banks and Other Financial Institutions	17.50	-3.64	七、缴存准备金 Reserves with the Central Bank	0.03	-0.04
七、外汇买卖 Foreign Exchange Dealings	2.75	-0.62	八、其他 Others	29.59	0.76

续表
Continued

项　　目 Items	余　额 Balance	比年初增减额 Changes within the Year	项　　目 Items	余　额 Balance	比年初增减额 Changes within the Year
八、所有者权益 Owner's Equity	25.08	2.44			
其中：实收资本 Of Which：Paid - in Capital	14.12	-4.99			
九、结益 Net Earnings	1.50	1.50			
十、呆账准备金 Provisions for Bad Loans	0.52	0.08			
十一、投资风险准备 Provisions for Investment Risk	0.02				
十二、其他 Others	19.59	-3.20			
资金来源总计 Total Sources	**197.20**	**3.35**	**资金运用总计 Total Uses**	**197.20**	**3.35**

信托投资公司外汇信贷收支表

Sources and Uses of Credit Funds of Financial Trust and Investment Companies（Foreign Currency）

（1997年末）

（Year - end of 1997）

单位：亿美元

Unit：100 Million US Dollars

项目 Items	余额 Balance	比年初增减额 Changes within the Year	项目 Items	余额 Balance	比年初增减额 Changes within the Year
一、外汇存款 Total Deposits	24.79	-2.27	一、外汇贷款 Total Loans	87.41	-12.16
1.信托存款 Trust Deposits	16.58	-1.27	1.短期外汇贷款 Short - term Loans	33.7	-7.88
其中：企业单位存款 Of Which：Deposits by Enterprises	9.58	3.35	2.中长期外汇贷款 Medium and Long - term Loans	53.71	-4.28
			二、各项投资 Investments	12.24	0.10
2.委托存款 Designated Deposits	5.33	-1.19	1.投资 Investments	11.42	0.97
3.其他存款 Other Deposits	2.88	0.19	其中：境内投资 Of Which：Domestic	6.51	0.31
二、境外筹资 Overseas Financing	36.75	-5.29	2.购买有价证券 Purchase of Securities	0.82	-0.87
1.境外短期借款 Overseas Short - term Borrowing	17.10	-1.90	其中：购买海外证券 Of Which：Purchase of Foreign Securities		-0.35
2.境外中长期借款 Overseas Medium and Long - term Borrowing	19.65	-3.39	三、租赁 Leases	6.33	-2.01
三、境外发行债券 Overseas Bonds Issue	21.22	-1.03	四、委托贷款 Designated Loans	4.5	-1.27
其中：短期债券 Of Which：Short - term Bonds	0.46	0.46	五、境外同业往来 Overseas Inter - bank Transactions	1.48	-0.53
四、委托借款 Designated Borrowing	1.25	0.03	其中：拆出资金 Of Which：Placements with Banks and Other Financial Institutions	0.17	-0.50
五、境外同业往来 Overseas Inter - bank Transactions	3.21	0.35			
其中：同业拆入 Of Which：Placements from Banks and Other Financial Institutions	3.14	1.49	六、国内同业往来 Domestic Inter - bank Transactions	22.3	0.47
			其中：拆出资金 Of Which：Placements with Banks and Other Financial Institutions	13.92	1.19
六、国内同业往来 Domestic Inter - bank Transactions	30.37	-6.90			
其中：同业拆入 Of Which：Placements from Banks and Other Financial Institutions	22.64	5.92	七、缴存准备金 Reserves with the Central Bank	-0.03	
			八、其他 Others	35.45	10.02
七、外汇买卖 Foreign Exchange Dealings	3.10	-0.04			

续表
Continued

项　目 Items	余　额 Balance	比年初增减额 Changes within the Year	项　目 Items	余　额 Balance	比年初增减额 Changes within the Year
八、所有者权益 Owner's Equity	23.83	3.44			
其中：实收资本 Of Which：Paid - in Capital	21.11	7.65			
九、结益 Net Earnings	0.29	0.29			
十、呆账准备金 Provisions for Bad Loans	1.01	0.45			
十一、投资风险准备 Provisions for Investment Risk	0.17	0.14			
十二、其他 Others	23.72	5.42			
资金来源总计 Total Sources	**169.71**	**-5.41**	**资金运用总计 Total Uses**	**169.71**	**-5.41**

信托投资公司外汇信贷收支表

Sources and Uses of Credit Funds of Financial Trust and Investment Companies（Foreign Currency）

（1998 年末）

（Year - end of 1998）

单位：亿美元

Unit：100 Million US Dollars

项　目 Items	余　额 Balance	比年初增减额 Changes within the Year	项　目 Items	余　额 Balance	比年初增减额 Changes within the Year
一、各项存款 Total Deposits	18.84	-2.30	一、各项贷款 Total Loans	84.83	-12.05
1. 信托存款 Trust Deposits	9.85	-0.41	1. 短期信托贷款 Short - term Trust Loans	17.20	-11.92
2. 委托存款 Designated Deposits	4.61	-0.23	其中：境外短期 Of Which：Overseas Short - term Loans	0.26	-0.95
3. 其他存款 Other Deposits	4.38	-1.66			
			2. 中长期信托贷款 Medium and Long - term Trust Loans	40.24	-7.38
二、境内中长期借款 Domestic Medium and Long - term Borrowing	8.59	-0.92			
			其中：境外中长期 Of Which：Overseas Medium and Long - term Loans	0.79	-1.05
三、境外筹资 Overseas Financing	37.42	-7.01			
四、证券业务款项 Securities Business Funds	0.20	-0.22	3. 委托贷款 Designated Loans	4.71	0.52
五、卖出回购证券 Repo			4. 融资租赁 Financing Leases	3.94	-1.13
六、同业存放 Due to Banks and Other Financial Institutions	0.73	-3.35	5. 票据融资 Paper Financing		
			6. 逾期类贷款 Overdue Loans	18.74	7.86
其中：境外同业存放 Of Which：Due to Overseas Banks and Other Financial Institutions		-3.37			
			二、信托投资 Trust Investments	4.21	1.28
			1. 短期信托投资 Short - term Trust Investments	0.37	0.10
七、同业拆入 Placements from Banks and Other Financial Institutions	23.48	-3.27			
			其中：境外 Of Which：Overseas		
其中：境外同业拆入 Of Which：Placements from Overseas Banks and Other Financial Institutions	9.23	-1.81	2. 中长期信托投资 Medium and Long - term Trust Investments	3.84	1.18
			其中：境外 Of Which：Overseas	0.12	0.01
八、外汇买卖 Foreign Exchange Dealings	3.98	3.46			
			三、投资 Investments	8.47	-0.85
九、各项准备 Total Provisions	0.76	-0.10			
			1. 购买有价证券 Purchase of Securities	0.87	-0.22
十、所有者权益 Owner's Equity	23.27	-0.50			
			其中：购买境外有价证券 Of Which：Purchase of Foreign Securities	0.15	-0.57
其中：实收资本 Of Which：Paid - in Capital	22.96	0.86			
当年结益 Net Earnings	-0.99	-0.99	2. 其他投资 Other Investments	7.60	-0.63

续表
Continued

项 目 Items	余 额 Balance	比年初增减额 Changes within the Year	项 目 Items	余 额 Balance	比年初增减额 Changes within the Year
十一、其他 Others	-3.13	-0.68	其中：投资境外 Of Which: Overseas	0.58	0.11
			四、证券业务占款 Funding of Securities Purchase	0.06	0.03
			五、经营租赁 Operating Leases	0.02	
			六、境外筹资转贷款 On - lending of Overseas Financing	0.18	-0.29
			七、存放中央银行 Deposits with the Central Bank	0.09	-0.33
			其中：缴存准备金 Of Which: Reserves with the Central Bank	0.01	
			八、存放同业 Due from Banks and Other Financial Institutions	7.20	-1.31
			其中：存放境外同业 Of Which: Due from Overseas Banks and Other Financial Institutions	1.69	0.45
			九、拆放同业 Placements with Banks and Other Financial Institutions	8.90	-0.79
			其中：拆放境外同业 Of Which: Placements with Overseas Banks and Other Financial Institutions	0.11	-3.29
			十、库存现金 Cash in Vault	0.18	-0.58
资金来源总计 Total Sources	**114.14**	**-14.89**	**资金运用总计 Total Uses**	**114.14**	**-14.89**

信托投资公司外汇信贷收支表

Sources and Uses of Credit Funds of Financial Trust and Investment Companies（Foreign Currency）

（1999年末）

（Year－end of 1999）

单位：亿美元

Unit：100 Million US Dollars

项目 Items	余额 Balance	比年初增减额 Changes within the Year	项目 Items	余额 Balance	比年初增减额 Changes within the Year
一、各项存款 Total Deposits	15.29	－1.83	一、各项贷款 Total Loans	60.30	－7.68
1. 信托存款 Trust Deposits	8.95	－0.35	1. 短期信托贷款 Short－term Trust Loans	10.31	－4.12
2. 委托存款 Designated Deposits	4.60	0.21	其中：境外短期 Of Which：Overseas Short－term Loans	0.03	－0.01
3. 其他存款 Other Deposits	1.74	－1.69	2. 中长期信托贷款 Medium and Long－term Trust Loans	22.13	－6.03
二、境内中长期借款 Domestic Medium and Long－term Borrowing	5.88	－1.32	其中：境外中长期 Of Which：Overseas Medium and Long－term Loans	0.11	－0.03
三、境外筹资 Overseas Financing	19.78	－6.04	3. 委托贷款 Designated Loans	4.41	－0.08
四、证券业务款项 Securities Business Funds	0.22	0.04	4. 融资租赁 Financing Leases	2.29	－0.76
五、卖出回购证券 Repo			5. 票据融资 Paper Financing		
六、同业存放 Due to Banks and Other Financial Institutions	0.73	0.01	6. 逾期类贷款 Overdue Loans	21.16	3.31
其中：境外同业存放 Of Which：Due to Overseas Banks and Other Financial Institutions			二、信托投资 Trust Investments	3.09	0.07
七、同业拆入 Placements from Banks and Other Financial Institutions	17.60	－2.25	1. 短期信托投资 Short－term Trust Investments	0.39	0.02
			其中：境外 Of Which：Overseas		
其中：境外同业拆入 Of Which：Placements from Overseas Banks and Other Financial Institutions	5.13	－1.05	2. 中长期信托投资 Medium and Long－term Trust Investments	2.70	0.05
			其中：境外 Of Which：Overseas	0.08	
八、外汇买卖 Foreign Exchange Dealings	4.73	0.54	三、投资 Investments	7.36	－0.89
九、各项准备 Total Provisions	0.98	0.35	1. 购买有价证券 Purchase of Securities	0.53	－0.36
十、所有者权益 Owner's Equity	15.12	－6.73	其中：购买境外有价证券 Of Which：Purchase of Foreign Securities	0.15	－0.01
其中：实收资本 Of Which：Paid－in Capital	21.38	－0.07			

续表
Continued

项　目 Items	余　额 Balance	比年初增减额 Changes within the Year	项　目 Items	余　额 Balance	比年初增减额 Changes within the Year
当年结益 Net Earnings	-1.03	-1.03	2. 其他投资 Other Investments	6.83	-0.53
十一、其他 Others	2.06	5.34	其中：投资境外 Of Which: Overseas	0.62	0.19
			四、证券业务占款 Funding of Securities Purchase	0.09	0.03
			五、经营租赁 Operating Leases		
			六、境外筹资转贷款 On-lending of Overseas Financing	0.22	0.04
			七、存放中央银行 Deposits with the Central Bank	0.09	
			其中：缴存准备金 Of Which: Reserves with the Central Bank		-0.01
			八、存放同业 Due from Banks and Other Financial Institutions	4.84	-1.93
			其中：存放境外同业 Of Which: Due from Overseas Banks and Other Financial Institutions	0.55	-0.74
			九、拆放同业 Placements with Banks and Other Financial Institutions	6.37	-1.41
			其中：拆放境外同业 Of Which: Placements with Overseas Banks and Other Financial Institutions	0.04	-0.07
			十、库存现金 Cash in Vault	0.03	-0.12
资金来源总计 Total Sources	**82.39**	**-11.89**	**资金运用总计 Total Uses**	**82.39**	**-11.89**

信托投资公司外汇信贷收支表

Sources and Uses of Credit Funds of Financial Trust and Investment Companies（Foreign Currency）

（2000 年末）

（Year－end of 2000）

单位：亿美元

Unit：100 Million US Dollars

项　目 Items	余　额 Balance	比年初增减额 Changes within the Year	项　目 Items	余　额 Balance	比年初增减额 Changes within the Year
一、各项存款 Total Deposits	13.63	－1.63	一、各项贷款 Total Loans	49.28	－10.77
1. 信托存款 Trust Deposits	7.96	－0.96	1. 短期信托贷款 Short－term Trust Loans	8.25	－1.66
2. 委托存款 Designated Deposits	4.14	－0.46	其中：境外短期 Of Which：Overseas Short－term Loans	0.01	－0.02
3. 其他存款 Other Deposits	1.53	－0.21	2. 中长期信托贷款 Medium and Long－term Trust Loans	16.53	－5.61
二、境内中长期借款 Domestic Medium and Long－term Borrowing	5.68	－0.20	其中：境外中长期 Of Which：Overseas Medium and Long－term Loans	0.12	0.01
三、境外筹资 Overseas Financing	16.49	－3.29	3. 委托贷款 Designated Loans	4.09	－0.32
四、证券业务款项 Securities Business Funds	0.69	0.47	4. 融资租赁 Financing Leases	1.93	－0.35
五、卖出回购证券 Repo			5. 票据融资 Paper Financing		
六、同业存放 Due to Banks and Other Financial Institutions	0.15	－0.57	6. 逾期类贷款 Overdue Loans	18.48	－2.83
其中：境外同业存放 Of Which：Due to Overseas Banks and Other Financial Institutions			二、信托投资 Trust Investments	2.44	－0.65
七、同业拆入 Placements from Banks and Other Financial Institutions	16.50	－1.10	1. 短期信托投资 Short－term Trust Investments	0.14	－0.25
			其中：境外 Of Which：Overseas		
其中：境外同业拆入 Of Which：Placements from Overseas Banks and Other Financial Institutions	4.94	－0.19	2. 中长期信托投资 Medium and Long－term Trust Investments	2.30	－0.40
			其中：境外 Of Which：Overseas	0.04	－0.04
八、外汇买卖 Foreign Exchange Dealings	0.86	－3.64	三、投资 Investments	7.75	0.40
九、各项准备 Total Provisions	0.85	－0.12	1. 购买有价证券 Purchase of Securities	0.53	
十、所有者权益 Owner's Equity	14.31	－1.14	其中：购买境外有价证券 Of Which：Purchase of Foreign Securities	0.21	0.06
其中：实收资本 Of Which：Paid－in Capital	21.05	－0.33			

续表
Continued

项　目 Items	余　额 Balance	比年初增减额 Changes within the Year	项　目 Items	余　额 Balance	比年初增减额 Changes within the Year
当年结益 Net Earnings	0.24	0.24	2. 其他投资 Other Investments	7.22	0.40
十一、其他 Others	2.87	1.11	其中：投资境外 Of Which: Overseas	0.51	-0.11
			四、证券业务占款 Funding of Securities Purchase	0.19	0.10
			五、经营租赁 Operating Leases		
			六、境外筹资转贷款 On-lending of Overseas Financing	0.19	-0.03
			七、存放中央银行 Deposits with the Central Bank	0.09	
			其中：缴存准备金 Of Which: Reserves with the Central Bank		
			八、存放同业 Due from Banks and Other Financial Institutions	6.31	1.51
			其中：存放境外同业 Of Which: Due from Overseas Banks and Other Financial Institutions	1.30	0.75
			九、拆放同业 Placements with Banks and Other Financial Institutions	5.74	-0.68
			其中：拆放境外同业 Of Which: Placements with Overseas Banks and Other Financial Institutions		-0.04
			十、库存现金 Cash in Vault	0.04	0.01
资金来源总计 Total Sources	**72.03**	**-10.11**	**资金运用总计 Total Uses**	**72.03**	**-10.11**

信托投资公司外汇信贷收支表
Sources and Uses of Credit Funds of Financial Trust and Investment Companies（Foreign Currency）

（2001 年末）

（Year－end of 2001）

单位：亿美元

Unit：100 Million US Dollars

项　目 Items	余　额 Balance	比年初增减额 Changes within the Year	项　目 Items	余　额 Balance	比年初增减额 Changes within the Year
一、各项存款 Total Deposits	9.56	－2.59	一、各项贷款 Total Loans	36.47	－5.57
1. 信托存款 Trust Deposits	5.33	－1.79	1. 短期信托贷款 Short－term Trust Loans	10.64	－0.70
2. 委托存款 Designated Deposits	3.35	－0.50	其中：境外短期 Of Which：Overseas Short－term Loans	0.04	0.03
3. 其他存款 Other Deposits	0.88	－0.30	2. 中长期信托贷款 Medium and Long－term Trust Loans	21.38	－3.99
二、境内中长期借款 Domestic Medium and Long－term Borrowing	7.66	－4.37	其中：境外中长期 Of Which：Overseas Medium and Long－term Loans	0.46	－0.28
三、境外筹资 Overseas Financing	25.67	－8.76			
四、证券业务款项 Securities Business Funds	1.65	0.96	3. 委托贷款 Designated Loans	2.69	－0.92
五、卖出回购证券 Repo			4. 融资租赁 Financing Leases	1.30	－0.23
六、同业存放 Due to Banks and Other Financial Institutions	0.27	0.27	5. 票据融资 Paper Financing		
其中：境外同业存放 Of Which：Due to Overseas Banks and Other Financial Institutions			其中：贴现 Of Which：Discount		
			6. 各项垫款 Total Advances	0.21	0.21
			7. 境外筹资转贷款 On－lending of Overseas Financing	0.25	0.06
七、同业拆入 Placements from Banks and Other Financial Institutions	12.46	－0.63	二、信托投资 Trust Investments	2.03	－0.13
其中：境外同业拆入 Of Which：Placements from Overseas Banks and Other Financial Institutions	3.05	－0.49	1. 短期信托投资 Short－term Trust Investments	0.05	－0.09
			其中：境外 Of Which：Overseas		
八、外汇买卖 Foreign Exchange Dealings	0.46	－1.07	2. 中长期信托投资 Medium and Long－term Trust Investments	1.98	－0.04
九、应付及暂收款 Accounts Payable and Receipts on Account	19.95	4.29	其中：境外 Of Which：Overseas	0.06	0.02
其中：应付及预提利息 Of Which：Interest Payable and Accrued	2.57	－0.42	三、投资 Investments	48.31	2.13
			1. 购买有价证券 Purchase of Securities	5.99	1.04
十、各项准备 Total Provisions	1.35	0.44			

续表
Continued

项　目 Items	余　额 Balance	比年初增减额 Changes within the Year	项　目 Items	余　额 Balance	比年初增减额 Changes within the Year
其中：贷款呆账准备金 Of Which: Provisions for Bad Loans	0.61	0.09	其中：购买境外有价证券 Of Which: Purchase of Foreign Securities	4.64	0.68
十一、所有者权益 Owner's Equity	41.19	1.42	2. 其他投资 Other Investments	42.32	1.09
其中：实收资本 Of Which: Paid - in Capital	47.09	-0.09	其中：投资境外 Of Which: Overseas	28.89	0.73
当年结益 Net Earnings	-0.48	-0.46	四、证券业务占款 Funding of Securities Purchase	0.10	-0.09
十二、其他 Others	3.83	3.62	五、经营租赁 Operating Leases		-0.07
			六、买入返售证券 Reverse Repo		
			七、应收及预付款项 Accounts Receivable and Advance Payments	19.54	-2.13
			其中：应收及预付利息 Of Which: Interest Receivable and Paid in Advance	4.61	-1.04
			八、存放中央银行 Deposits with the Central Bank	0.14	0.05
			其中：缴存准备金 Of Which: Reserves with the Central Bank		
			九、存放同业 Due from Banks and Other Financial Institutions	9.20	0.49
			其中：存放境外同业 Of Which: Due from Overseas Banks and Other Financial Institutions	2.54	-0.06
			十、拆放同业 Placements with Banks and Other Financial Institutions	8.24	-1.09
			其中：拆放境外同业 Of Which: Placements with Overseas Banks and Other Financial Institutions		
			十一、库存现金 Cash in Vault	0.02	-0.01
资金来源总计 Total Sources	**124.05**	**-6.42**	**资金运用总计 Total Uses**	**124.05**	**-6.42**

信托投资公司外汇信贷收支表

Sources and Uses of Credit Funds of Financial Trust and Investment Companies（Foreign Currency）

（2002年末）

（Year - end of 2002）

单位：亿美元

Unit：100 Million US Dollars

项　目 Items	余　额 Balance	比年初增减额 Changes within the Year	项　目 Items	余　额 Balance	比年初增减额 Changes within the Year
一、各项存款 Total Deposits	7.54	-0.24	一、各项贷款 Total Loans	23.20	-0.29
1.信托存款 Trust Deposits	3.72	-0.80	1.短期信托贷款 Short - term Trust Loans	2.82	-1.01
2.委托存款 Designated Deposits	1.84	-0.94	其中：境外短期 Of Which：Overseas Short - term Loans	0.03	
3.其他存款 Other Deposits	1.98	1.50	2.中长期信托贷款 Medium and Long - term Trust Loans	12.58	4.73
二、境内中长期借款 Domestic Medium and Long - term Borrowing	5.56	-0.28	其中：境外中长期 Of Which：Overseas Medium and Long - term Loans	4.56	4.10
三、境外筹资 Overseas Financing	12.79	-10.85	3.委托贷款 Designated Loans	3.41	1.27
四、证券业务款项 Securities Business Funds		-1.52	4.融资租赁 Financing Leases	0.38	-0.24
五、卖出回购证券 Repo			5.票据融资 Paper Financing		
六、同业存放 Due to Banks and Other Financial Institutions	0.05	-0.22	其中：贴现 Of Which：Discount		
其中：境外同业存放 Of Which：Due to Overseas Banks and Other Financial Institutions			6.各项垫款 Total Advances	0.01	-0.20
七、同业拆入 Placements from Banks and Other Financial Institutions	2.06	-2.61	7.境外筹资转贷款 On - lending of Overseas Financing	0.08	-0.10
其中：境外同业拆入 Of Which：Placements from Overseas Banks and Other Financial Institutions	0.40	-2.38	8.其他贷款 Other Loans	3.92	-4.74
八、外汇买卖 Foreign Exchange Dealings	3.03	3.21	二、信托投资 Trust Investments	1.69	-0.57
九、应付及暂收款 Accounts Payable and Receipts on Account	12.15	-2.08	1.短期信托投资 Short - term Trust Investments	0.08	-0.34
其中：应付及预提利息 Of Which：Interest Payable and Accrued	0.59	-0.38	其中：境外 Of Which：Overseas		
			2.中长期信托投资 Medium and Long - term Trust Investments	1.61	-0.23
			其中：境外 Of Which：Overseas		
			三、投资 Investments	41.84	-3.19
十、各项准备 Total Provisions	1.33	0.06	1.购买有价证券 Purchase of Securities	8.09	2.58

续表
Continued

项 目 Items	余 额 Balance	比年初增减额 Changes within the Year	项 目 Items	余 额 Balance	比年初增减额 Changes within the Year
其中：贷款呆账准备金 Of Which: Provisions for Bad Loans	0.93	0.38	其中：购买境外有价证券 Of Which: Purchase of Foreign Securities	7.68	3.52
十一、所有者权益 Owner's Equity	42.63	1.89	2. 其他投资 Other Investments	33.75	-5.77
其中：实收资本 Of Which: Paid-in Capital	39.68	0.18	其中：投资境外 Of Which: Overseas	23.11	-5.53
当年结益 Net Earnings	0.91	0.91	四、证券业务占款 Funding of Securities Purchase		-0.10
十二、其他 Others	8.67	4.22	五、经营租赁 Operating Leases		
			六、买入返售证券 Reverse Repo		
			七、应收及预付款项 Accounts Receivable and Advance Payments	15.30	-1.59
			其中：应收及预付利息 Of Which: Interest Receivable and Paid in Advance	3.77	-0.28
			八、存放中央银行 Deposits with the Central Bank	0.06	-0.08
			其中：缴存准备金 Of Which: Reserves with the Central Bank		
			九、存放同业 Due from Banks and Other Financial Institutions	7.00	-1.37
			其中：存放境外同业 Of Which: Due from Overseas Banks and Other Financial Institutions	2.42	-0.11
			十、拆放同业 Placements with Banks and Other Financial Institutions	6.71	-1.22
			其中：拆放境外同业 Of Which: Placements with Overseas Banks and Other Financial Institutions		
			十一、库存现金 Cash in Vault	0.01	-0.01
资金来源总计 Total Sources	**95.81**	**-8.42**	**资金运用总计 Total Uses**	**95.81**	**-8.42**

信托投资公司外汇信贷收支表

Sources and Uses of Credit Funds of Financial Trust and Investment Companies（Foreign Currency）

（2003 年末）

（Year - end of 2003）

单位：亿美元

Unit：100 Million US Dollars

项　目 Items	余　额 Balance	比年初增减额 Changes within the Year
一、各项存款 Total Deposits	5.40	-1.68
1. 信托存款 Trust Deposits	2.55	-0.76
2. 委托存款 Designated Deposits	1.27	-0.52
3. 其他存款 Other Deposits	1.58	-0.40
二、境内中长期借款 Domestic! Medium and Long - term Borrowing	6.18	0.66
三、境外筹资 Overseas Financing	4.75	-5.62
四、证券业务款项 Securities Business Funds		
五、卖出回购证券 Repo		
六、同业存放 Due to Banks and Other Financial Institutions	0.03	-0.02
其中：境外同业存放 Of Which：Due to Overseas Banks and Other Financial Institutions		
七、同业拆入 Placements from Banks and Other Financial Institutions	1.52	-0.17
其中：境外同业拆入 Of Which：Placements from Overseas Banks and Other Financial Institutions	0.32	-0.08
八、外汇买卖 Foreign Exchange Dealings	16.27	10.15
九、应付及暂收款 Accounts Payable and Receipts on Account	7.53	-3.65
其中：应付及预提利息 Of Which：Interest Payable and Accrued	0.56	
十、各项准备 Total Provisions	1.20	-0.04

项　目 Items	余　额 Balance	比年初增减额 Changes within the Year
一、各项贷款 Total Loans	14.99	-6.90
1. 短期信托贷款 Short - term Trust Loans	2.33	-0.43
其中：境外短期 Of Which：Overseas Short - term Loans	0.02	-0.01
2. 中长期信托贷款 Medium and Long - term Trust Loans	7.40	-3.83
其中：境外中长期 Of Which：Overseas Medium and Long - term Loans	3.30	-1.14
3. 委托贷款 Designated Loans	2.60	-0.79
4. 融资租赁 Financing Leases	0.26	-0.12
5. 票据融资 Paper Financing		
其中：贴现 Of Which：Discount		
6. 各项垫款 Total Advances	0.01	
7. 境外筹资转贷款 On - lending of Overseas Financing	0.07	-0.01
8. 其他贷款 Other Loans	2.32	-1.72
二、信托投资 Trust Investments	1.66	-0.02
1. 短期信托投资 Short - term Trust Investments	0.09	0.01
其中：境外 Of Which：Overseas		
2. 中长期信托投资 Medium and Long - term Trust Investments	1.57	-0.03
其中：境外 Of Which：Overseas		
三、投资 Investments	40.61	-1.12

续表
Continued

项　目 Items	余　额 Balance	比年初增减额 Changes within the Year	项　目 Items	余　额 Balance	比年初增减额 Changes within the Year
其中：贷款呆账准备金 Of Which: Provisions for Bad Loans	1.09	-0.04	1. 购买有价证券 Purchase of Securities	0.66	-7.83
十一、所有者权益 Owner's Equity	39.54	-1.39	其中：购买境外有价证券 Of Which: Purchase of Foreign Securities	0.25	-7.83
其中：实收资本 Of Which: Paid-in Capital	39.94	0.84			
当年结益 Net Earnings	-0.46	-0.46	2. 其他投资 Other Investments	39.95	6.71
十二、其他 Others	1.32	-7.69	其中：投资境外 Of Which: Overseas	14.72	-8.39
			四、证券业务占款 Funding of Securities Purchase		
			五、经营租赁 Operating Leases		
			六、买入返售证券 Reverse Repo		
			七、应收及预付款项 Accounts Receivable and Advance Payments	13.50	-0.79
			其中：应收及预付利息 Of Which: Interest Receivable and Paid in Advance	3.07	-0.46
			八、存放中央银行 Deposits with the Central Bank	0.01	
			其中：缴存准备金 Of Which: Reserves with the Central Bank		
			九、存放同业 Due from Banks and Other Financial Institutions	5.52	-1.45
			其中：存放境外同业 Of Which: Due from Overseas Banks and Other Financial Institutions	1.19	-1.23
			十、拆放同业 Placements with Banks and Other Financial Institutions	7.39	0.79
			其中：拆放境外同业 Of Which: Placements with Overseas Banks and Other Financial Institutions		
			十一、库存现金 Cash in Vault	0.05	0.04
资金来源总计 Total Sources	**83.73**	**-9.45**	**资金运用总计 Total Uses**	**83.73**	**-9.45**

信托投资公司外汇信贷收支表

Sources and Uses of Credit Funds of Financial Trust and Investment Companies（Foreign Currency）

（2004 年末）

（Year - end of 2004）

单位：亿美元

Unit：100 Million US Dollars

项　目 Items	余　额 Balance	比年初增减额 Changes within the Year	项　目 Items	余　额 Balance	比年初增减额 Changes within the Year
一、各项存款 Total Deposits	4.02	-1.17	一、各项贷款 Total Loans	5.37	-1.47
1. 信托存款 Trust Deposits	2.12	-0.24	1. 短期信托贷款 Short - term Trust Loans	1.93	-0.18
2. 委托存款 Designated Deposits	0.40	-0.86	其中：境外短期 Of Which：Overseas Short - term Loans		
3. 其他存款 Other Deposits	1.50	-0.07	2. 中长期信托贷款 Medium and Long - term Trust Loans	0.66	-0.10
二、境内中长期借款 Domestic Medium and Long - term Borrowing	0.83	0.03	其中：境外中长期 Of Which：Overseas Medium and Long - term Loans	0.12	
三、境外筹资 Overseas Financing	0.39	-0.11	3. 委托贷款 Designated Loans	1.68	-0.91
四、证券业务款项 Securities Business Funds			4. 融资租赁 Financing Leases	0.22	-0.04
五、卖出回购资产 Assets Repo（Including Securities）			5. 票据融资 Paper Financing		
六、同业存放 Due to Banks and Other Financial Institutions			其中：贴现 Of Which：Discount		
其中：境外同业存放 Of Which：Due to Overseas Banks and Other Financial Institutions			6. 各项垫款 Total Advances		-0.01
			7. 境外筹资转贷款 On - lending of Overseas Financing	0.07	
七、同业拆入 Placements from Banks and Other Financial Institutions	1.19	-0.10	8. 其他贷款 Other Loans	0.81	-0.23
			二、信托投资 Trust Investments	1.50	-0.16
其中：境外同业拆入 Of Which：Placements from Overseas Banks and Other Financial Institutions	0.25		1. 短期信托投资 Short - term Trust Investments	0.08	-0.01
			其中：境外 Of Which：Overseas		
八、外汇买卖 Foreign Exchange Dealings	4.11	-0.38	2. 中长期信托投资 Medium and Long - term Trust Investments	1.42	-0.15
九、应付及暂收款 Accounts Payable and Receipts on Account	3.36	-0.68	其中：境外 Of Which：Overseas		
其中：应付及预提利息 Of Which：Interest Payable and Accrued	0.43	0.24	三、投资 Investments	1.95	0.18

续表
Continued

项目 Items	余额 Balance	比年初增减额 Changes within the Year	项目 Items	余额 Balance	比年初增减额 Changes within the Year
十、各项准备 Total Provisions	0.43	-0.31	1. 购买有价证券 Purchase of Securities	0.11	-0.04
其中：贷款呆账准备金 Of Which: Provisions for Bad Loans	0.32	-0.30	其中：购买境外有价证券 Of Which: Purchase of Foreign Securities	0.06	-0.02
十一、所有者权益 Owner's Equity	7.76	-0.34	2. 其他投资 Other Investments	1.84	0.22
其中：实收资本 Of Which: Paid-in Capital	8.68	0.19	其中：投资境外 Of Which: Overseas	0.15	0.04
当年结益 Net Earnings	0.14	0.14	四、证券业务占款 Funding of Securities Purchase		
十二、其他 Others	-0.40	-0.10	五、经营租赁 Operating Leases		
			六、买入返售资产 Assets Reverse Repo (Including Securities)		
			七、应收及预付款项 Accounts Receivable and Advance Payments	5.15	-0.32
			其中：应收及预付利息 Of Which: Interest Receivable and Paid in Advance	2.11	-0.10
			八、存放中央银行 Deposits with the Central Bank		
			其中：缴存准备金 Of Which: Reserves with the Central Bank		
			九、存放同业 Due from Banks and Other Financial Institutions	3.69	-1.21
			其中：存放境外同业 Of Which: Due from Overseas Banks and Other Financial Institutions	0.81	-0.14
			十、拆放同业 Placements with Banks and Other Financial Institutions	4.02	-0.14
			其中：拆放境外同业 Of Which: Placements with Overseas Banks and Other Financial Institutions		
			十一、库存现金 Cash in Vault	0.01	-0.04
资金来源总计 Total Sources	**21.69**	**-3.16**	**资金运用总计 Total Uses**	**21.69**	**-3.16**

信托投资公司外汇信贷收支表

Sources and Uses of Credit Funds of Financial Trust and Investment Companies（Foreign Currency）

（2005 年末）

（Year－end of 2005）

单位：亿美元

Unit：100 Million US Dollars

项　目 Items	余　额 Balance	比年初增减额 Changes within the Year	项　目 Items	余　额 Balance	比年初增减额 Changes within the Year
一、各项存款 Total Deposits	1.77	－2.25	一、各项贷款 Total Loans	3.76	－1.60
1. 信托存款 Trust Deposits	0.42	－1.70	1. 短期信托贷款 Short－term Trust Loans	0.49	－0.24
2. 委托存款 Designated Deposits	0.39	－0.01	其中：境外短期 Of Which：Overseas Short－term Loans		
3. 其他存款 Other Deposits	0.96	－0.54	2. 中长期信托贷款 Medium and Long－term Trust Loans	1.49	－0.36
二、境内中长期筹资 Domestic Medium and Long－term Borrowing	0.24	－0.59	其中：境外中长期 Of Which：Overseas Medium and Long－term Loans	0.12	
三、境外筹资 Overseas Financing	0.34	－0.05	3. 委托贷款 Designated Loans	1.14	－0.54
四、证券业务款项 Securities Business Funds			4. 融资租赁 Financing Leases	0.08	－0.14
五、卖出回购资产 Assets Repo（Including Securities）			5. 票据融资 Paper Financing		
六、同业存放 Due to Banks and Other Financial Institutions			其中：贴现 Of Which：Discount		
其中：境外同业存放 Of Which：Due to Overseas Banks and Other Financial Institutions			6. 各项垫款 Total Advances		
			7. 境外筹资转贷款 On－lending of Overseas Financing	0.07	
七、同业拆入 Placements from Banks and Other Financial Institutions	1.15	－0.02	8. 其他贷款 Other Loans	0.49	－0.32
			二、信托投资 Trust Investments	1.40	－0.10
其中：境外同业拆入 Of Which：Placements from Overseas Banks and Other Financial Institutions	0.25		1. 短期信托投资 Short－term Trust Investments		－0.08
			其中：境外 Of Which：Overseas		
八、外汇买卖 Foreign Exchange Dealings	4.29	0.32	2. 中长期信托投资 Medium and Long－term Trust Investments	1.40	－0.02
九、应付及暂收款 Accounts Payable and Receipts on Account	3.32	－0.23	其中：境外 Of Which：Overseas		
其中：应付及预提利息 Of Which：Interest Payable and Accrued	0.32	－0.11	三、投资 Investments	1.83	－0.12
十、各项准备 Total Provisions	0.30	－0.13	1. 购买有价证券 Purchase of Securities	0.07	－0.04

续表
Continued

项 目 Items	余 额 Balance	比年初增减额 Changes within the Year	项 目 Items	余 额 Balance	比年初增减额 Changes within the Year
其中：贷款损失准备 Of Which: Provisions for Loan Losses	0.22	－0.10	其中：购买境外有价证券 Of Which: Purchase of Foreign Securities	0.04	－0.02
十一、所有者权益 Owner's Equity	5.70	－1.31	2. 其他投资 Other Investments	1.76	－0.08
其中：实收资本 Of Which: Paid－in Capital	6.51	－1.44	其中：投资境外 Of Which: Overseas	0.11	－0.05
当年结益 Net Earnings	0.06	0.06	四、证券业务占款 Funding of Securities Purchase		
十二、其他 Others	0.32	0.01	五、经营租赁 Operating Leases		
			六、买入返售资产 Assets Reverse Repo (Including Securities)		
			七、应收及预付款项 Accounts Receivable and Advance Payments	4.72	－0.43
			其中：应收及预付利息 Of Which: Interest Receivable and Paid in Advance	2.07	－0.04
			八、存放中央银行 Deposits with the Central Bank		
			其中：缴存准备金 Of Which: Reserves with the Central Bank		
			九、存放同业 Due from Banks and Other Financial Institutions	1.90	－1.79
			其中：存放境外同业 Of Which: Due from Overseas Banks and Other Financial Institutions	0.10	－0.71
			十、拆放同业 Placements with Banks and Other Financial Institutions	3.81	－0.21
			其中：拆放境外同业 Of Which: Placements with Overseas Banks and Other Financial Institutions		
			十一、库存现金 Cash in Vault	0.01	
资金来源总计 Total Sources	**17.43**	**－4.25**	**资金运用总计 Total Uses**	**17.43**	**－4.25**

11. 金融租赁公司外汇信贷收支表（1998—2005年）
Sources and Uses of Credit Funds of Financial Leasing Companies（Foreign Currency）（1998—2005）

金融租赁公司外汇信贷收支表
Sources and Uses of Credit Funds of Financial Leasing Companies（Foreign Currency）

（1998年末）

（Year－end of 1998）

单位：亿美元

Unit：100 Million US Dollars

项目 Items	余额 Balance	比年初增减额 Changes within the Year	项目 Items	余额 Balance	比年初增减额 Changes within the Year
一、各项存款 Total Deposits	0.31	－0.44	一、各项贷款 Total Loans	3.30	－0.04
1. 信托存款 Trust Deposits	0.18	－0.45	1. 短期信托贷款 Short－term Trust Loans	0.41	－0.86
2. 委托存款 Designated Deposits			其中：境外短期 Of Which：Overseas Short－term Loans		
3. 其他存款 Other Deposits	0.13	0.01	2. 中长期信托贷款 Medium and Long－term Trust Loans	0.11	0.09
二、境内中长期借款 Domestic Medium and Long－term Borrowing	0.41		其中：境外中长期 Of Which：Overseas Medium and Long－term Loans	0.02	0.02
三、境外筹资 Overseas Financing	0.46	－0.19	3. 委托贷款 Designated Loans		
四、证券业务款项 Securities Business Funds			4. 融资租赁 Financing Leases	2.54	0.87
五、卖出回购证券 Repo			5. 票据融资 Paper Financing		
六、同业存放 Due to Banks and Other Financial Institutions	0.06	0.06	6. 逾期类贷款 Overdue Loans	0.24	－0.14
其中：境外同业存放 Of Which：Due to Overseas Banks and Other Financial Institutions			二、信托投资 Trust Investments		
			1. 短期信托投资 Short－term Trust Investments		
七、同业拆入 Placements from Banks and Other Financial Institutions	0.26	－0.08	其中：境外 Of Which：Overseas		
			2. 中长期信托投资 Medium and Long－term Trust Investments		
其中：境外同业拆入 Of Which：Placements from Overseas Banks and Other Financial Institutions			其中：境外 Of Which：Overseas		
八、外汇买卖 Foreign Exchange Dealings	0.50	0.29	三、投资 Investments	0.08	0.01
九、各项准备 Total Provisions	0.02		1. 购买有价证券 Purchase of Securities		

续表
Continued

项　目 Items	余　额 Balance	比年初增减额 Changes within the Year	项　目 Items	余　额 Balance	比年初增减额 Changes within the Year
十、所有者权益 Owner's Equity	1.01	0.23	其中：购买境外有价证券 Of Which: Purchase of Foreign Securities		
其中：实收资本 Of Which: Paid - in Capital	1.02	0.24	2. 其他投资 Other Investments	0.08	0.01
当年结益 Net Earnings	-0.01	-0.01	其中：投资境外 Of Which: Overseas	0.04	0.03
十一、其他 Others	0.70	-0.15	四、证券业务占款 Funding of Securities Purchase		
			五、经营租赁 Operating Leases		
			六、境外筹资转贷款 On - lending of Overseas Financing		
			七、存放中央银行 Deposits with the Central Bank		
			其中：缴存准备金 Of Which: Reserves with the Central Bank		
			八、存放同业 Due from Banks and Other Financial Institutions	0.23	0.04
			其中：存放境外同业 Of Which: Due from Overseas Banks and Other Financial Institutions		
			九、拆放同业 Placements with Banks and Other Financial Institutions	0.12	0.01
			其中：拆放境外同业 Of Which: Placements with Overseas Banks and Other Financial Institutions		
			十、库存现金 Cash in Vault		
资金来源总计 Total Sources	**3.73**	**0.02**	**资金运用总计 Total Uses**	**3.73**	**0.02**

金融租赁公司外汇信贷收支表

Sources and Uses of Credit Funds of Financial Leasing Companies（Foreign Currency）

（1999 年末）

（Year－end of 1999）

单位：亿美元

Unit：100 Million US Dollars

项目 Items	余额 Balance	比年初增减额 Changes within the Year	项目 Items	余额 Balance	比年初增减额 Changes within the Year
一、各项存款 Total Deposits	0.24	－0.06	一、各项贷款 Total Loans	2.82	－0.47
1. 信托存款 Trust Deposits	0.12	－0.06	1. 短期信托贷款 Short－term Trust Loans	0.34	－0.06
2. 委托存款 Designated Deposits			其中：境外短期 Of Which：Overseas Short－term Loans		
3. 其他存款 Other Deposits	0.12		2. 中长期信托贷款 Medium and Long－term Trust Loans	0.11	
二、境内中长期借款 Domestic Medium and Long－term Borrowing	0.42	0.01	其中：境外中长期 Of Which：Overseas Medium and Long－term Loans		－0.02
三、境外筹资 Overseas Financing	0.46		3. 委托贷款 Designated Loans		
四、证券业务款项 Securities Business Funds			4. 融资租赁 Financing Leases	2.20	－0.34
五、卖出回购证券 Repo			5. 票据融资 Paper Financing		
六、同业存放 Due to Banks and Other Financial Institutions		－0.06	6. 逾期类贷款 Overdue Loans	0.17	－0.07
其中：境外同业存放 Of Which：Due to Overseas Banks and Other Financial Institutions			二、信托投资 Trust Investments		
			1. 短期信托投资 Short－term Trust Investments		
七、同业拆入 Placements from Banks and Other Financial Institutions	0.22	－0.04	其中：境外 Of Which：Overseas		
			2. 中长期信托投资 Medium and Long－term Trust Investments		
其中：境外同业拆入 Of Which：Placements from Overseas Banks and Other Financial Institutions	0.02	0.02	其中：境外 Of Which：Overseas		
八、外汇买卖 Foreign Exchange Dealings	0.45	－0.05	三、投资 Investments	0.07	－0.01
九、各项准备 Total Provisions	0.01	－0.01	1. 购买有价证券 Purchase of Securities		
十、所有者权益 Owner's Equity	1.01		其中：购买境外有价证券 Of Which：Purchase of Foreign Securities		
其中：实收资本 Of Which：Paid－in Capital	1.02		2. 其他投资 Other Investments	0.07	－0.01

续表
Continued

项 目 Items	余 额 Balance	比年初增减额 Changes within the Year	项 目 Items	余 额 Balance	比年初增减额 Changes within the Year
当年结益 Net Earnings	-0.01	-0.01	其中：投资境外 Of Which: Overseas	0.03	-0.01
十一、其他 Others	0.44	-0.26	四、证券业务占款 Funding of Securities Purchase		
			五、经营租赁 Operating Leases		
			六、境外筹资转贷款 On-lending of Overseas Financing		
			七、存放中央银行 Deposits with the Central Bank		
			其中：缴存准备金 Of Which: Reserves with the Central Bank		
			八、存放同业 Due from Banks and Other Financial Institutions	0.22	-0.01
			其中：存放境外同业 Of Which: Due from Overseas Banks and Other Financial Institutions		
			九、拆放同业 Placements with Banks and Other Financial Institutions	0.14	0.02
			其中：拆放境外同业 Of Which: Placements with Overseas Banks and Other Financial Institutions		
			十、库存现金 Cash in Vault		
资金来源总计 Total Sources	**3.25**	**-0.47**	**资金运用总计 Total Uses**	**3.25**	**-0.47**

金融租赁公司外汇信贷收支表

Sources and Uses of Credit Funds of Financial Leasing Companies（Foreign Currency）

（2000 年末）

（Year－end of 2000）

单位：亿美元

Unit：100 Million US Dollars

项目 Items	余额 Balance	比年初增减额 Changes within the Year	项目 Items	余额 Balance	比年初增减额 Changes within the Year
一、各项存款 Total Deposits	0.25	0.01	一、各项贷款 Total Loans	2.44	－0.38
1. 信托存款 Trust Deposits	0.11	－0.01	1. 短期信托贷款 Short－term Trust Loans	0.36	0.02
2. 委托存款 Designated Deposits	0.01	0.01	其中：境外短期 Of Which：Overseas Short－term Loans		
3. 其他存款 Other Deposits	0.13	0.01	2. 中长期信托贷款 Medium and Long－term Trust Loans	0.07	－0.04
二、境内中长期借款 Domestic Medium and Long－term Borrowing	0.42		其中：境外中长期 Of Which：Overseas Medium and Long－term Loans		
三、境外筹资 Overseas Financing	0.45	－0.01	3. 委托贷款 Designated Loans		
四、证券业务款项 Securities Business Funds			4. 融资租赁 Financing Leases	1.80	－0.40
五、卖出回购证券 Repo			5. 票据融资 Paper Financing		
六、同业存放 Due to Banks and Other Financial Institutions	0.04	0.01	6. 逾期类贷款 Overdue Loans	0.21	0.04
其中：境外同业存放 Of Which：Due to Overseas Banks and Other Financial Institutions			二、信托投资 Trust Investments		
			1. 短期信托投资 Short－term Trust Investments		
七、同业拆入 Placements from Banks and Other Financial Institutions	0.20	0.01	其中：境外 Of Which：Overseas		
其中：境外同业拆入 Of Which：Placements from Overseas Banks and Other Financial Institutions	0.02		2. 中长期信托投资 Medium and Long－term Trust Investments		
			其中：境外 Of Which：Overseas		
八、外汇买卖 Foreign Exchange Dealings	0.41	－0.04	三、投资 Investments	0.07	
九、各项准备 Total Provisions	0.01		1. 购买有价证券 Purchase of Securities		
十、所有者权益 Owner's Equity	1.01		其中：购买境外有价证券 Of Which：Purchase of Foreign Securities		
其中：实收资本 Of Which：Paid－in Capital	1.02				

续表
Continued

项目 Items	余额 Balance	比年初增减额 Changes within the Year	项目 Items	余额 Balance	比年初增减额 Changes within the Year
当年结益 Net Earnings	-0.01	-0.01	2. 其他投资 Other Investments	0.07	
十一、其他 Others	0.06	-0.38	其中：投资境外 Of Which: Overseas	0.03	
			四、证券业务占款 Funding of Securities Purchase		
			五、经营租赁 Operating Leases		
			六、境外筹资转贷款 On-lending of Overseas Financing		
			七、存放中央银行 Deposits with the Central Bank		
			其中：缴存准备金 Of Which: Reserves with the Central Bank		
			八、存放同业 Due from Banks and Other Financial Institutions	0.21	-0.01
			其中：存放境外同业 Of Which: Due from Overseas Banks and Other Financial Institutions		
			九、拆放同业 Placements with Banks and Other Financial Institutions	0.13	-0.01
			其中：拆放境外同业 Of Which: Placements with Overseas Banks and Other Financial Institutions		
			十、库存现金 Cash in Vault		
资金来源总计 Total Sources	**2.85**	**-0.40**	**资金运用总计 Total Uses**	**2.85**	**-0.40**

金融租赁公司外汇信贷收支表

Sources and Uses of Credit Funds of Financial Leasing Companies（Foreign Currency）

（2001 年末）

（Year－end of 2001）

单位：亿美元

Unit：100 Million US Dollars

项目 Items	余额 Balance	比年初增减额 Changes within the Year	项目 Items	余额 Balance	比年初增减额 Changes within the Year
一、各项存款 Total Deposits	0.22		一、各项贷款 Total Loans	2.26	－0.12
1.信托存款 Trust Deposits	0.09		1.短期信托贷款 Short－term Trust Loans	0.41	－0.06
2.委托存款 Designated Deposits	0.01		其中：境外短期 Of Which：Overseas Short－term Loans		
3.其他存款 Other Deposits	0.12		2.中长期信托贷款 Medium and Long－term Trust Loans	0.07	0.03
二、境内中长期借款 Domestic Medium and Long－term Borrowing	0.42		其中：境外中长期 Of Which：Overseas Medium and Long－term Loans		
三、境外筹资 Overseas Financing	0.45		3.委托贷款 Designated Loans		
四、证券业务款项 Securities Business Funds			4.融资租赁 Financing Leases	1.78	－0.09
五、卖出回购证券 Repo			5.票据融资 Paper Financing		
六、同业存放 Due to Banks and Other Financial Institutions	0.05	0.01	其中：贴现 Of Which：Discount		
其中：境外同业存放 Of Which：Due to Overseas Banks and Other Financial Institutions			6.各项垫款 Total Advances		
			7.境外筹资转贷款 On－lending of Overseas Financing		
七、同业拆入 Placements from Banks and Other Financial Institutions	0.35	－0.03	二、信托投资 Trust Investments		
其中：境外同业拆入 Of Which：Placements from Overseas Banks and Other Financial Institutions	0.01	－0.03	1.短期信托投资 Short－term Trust Investments		
			其中：境外 Of Which：Overseas		
			2.中长期信托投资 Medium and Long－term Trust Investments		
八、外汇买卖 Foreign Exchange Dealings	0.11	－0.05			
九、应付及暂收款 Accounts Payable and Receipts on Account	0.06	－0.01	其中：境外 Of Which：Overseas		
其中：应付及预提利息 Of Which：Interest Payable and Accrued			三、投资 Investments	0.09	
十、各项准备 Total Provisions	0.01		1.购买有价证券 Purchase of Securities		

续表
Continued

项　目 Items	余　额 Balance	比年初增减额 Changes within the Year	项　目 Items	余　额 Balance	比年初增减额 Changes within the Year
其中：贷款呆账准备金 Of Which: Provisions for Bad Loans	0.01		其中：购买境外有价证券 Of Which: Purchase of Foreign Securities		
十一、所有者权益 Owner's Equity	0.88		2. 其他投资 Other Investments	0.09	
其中：实收资本 Of Which: Paid－in Capital	0.89		其中：投资境外 Of Which: Overseas	0.03	
当年结益 Net Earnings	－0.01	－0.01	四、证券业务占款 Funding of Securities Purchase		
十二、其他 Others	0.63	－0.11	五、经营租赁 Operating Leases		
			六、买入返售证券 Reverse Repo		
			七、应收及预付款项 Accounts Receivable and Advance Payments	0.51	－0.09
			其中：应收及预付利息 Of Which: Interest Receivable and Paid in Advance	0.04	
			八、存放中央银行 Deposits with the Central Bank		
			其中：缴存准备金 Of Which: Reserves with the Central Bank		
			九、存放同业 Due from Banks and Other Financial Institutions	0.23	0.02
			其中：存放境外同业 Of Which: Due from Overseas Banks and Other Financial Institutions		
			十、拆放同业 Placements with Banks and Other Financial Institutions	0.09	
			其中：拆放境外同业 Of Which: Placements with Overseas Banks and Other Financial Institutions		
			十一、库存现金 Cash in Vault		
资金来源总计 Total Sources	**3.18**	**－0.19**	**资金运用总计 Total Uses**	**3.18**	**－0.19**

金融租赁公司外汇信贷收支表

Sources and Uses of Credit Funds of Financial Leasing Companies（Foreign Currency）

（2002 年末）

（Year - end of 2002）

单位：亿美元

Unit：100 Million US Dollars

项　目 Items	余　额 Balance	比年初增减额 Changes within the Year	项　目 Items	余　额 Balance	比年初增减额 Changes within the Year
一、各项存款 Total Deposits	0.15	-0.01	一、各项贷款 Total Loans	2.02	-0.01
1. 信托存款 Trust Deposits	0.02		1. 短期信托贷款 Short - term Trust Loans		-0.02
2. 委托存款 Designated Deposits		-0.01	其中：境外短期 Of Which：Overseas Short - term Loans		
3. 其他存款 Other Deposits	0.13		2. 中长期信托贷款 Medium and Long - term Trust Loans		
二、境内中长期借款 Domestic Medium and Long - term Borrowing	0.42		其中：境外中长期 Of Which：Overseas Medium and Long - term Loans		
三、境外筹资 Overseas Financing	0.45		3. 委托贷款 Designated Loans		
四、证券业务款项 Securities Business Funds			4. 融资租赁 Financing Leases	1.57	
五、卖出回购证券 Repo			5. 票据融资 Paper Financing		
六、同业存放 Due to Banks and Other Financial Institutions		-0.05	其中：贴现 Of Which：Discount		
其中：境外同业存放 Of Which：Due to Overseas Banks and Other Financial Institutions			6. 各项垫款 Total Advances		
			7. 境外筹资转贷款 On - lending of Overseas Financing		
七、同业拆入 Placements from Banks and Other Financial Institutions	0.19	-0.04	8. 其他贷款 Other Loans	0.45	0.01
			二、信托投资 Trust Investments		
其中：境外同业拆入 Of Which：Placements from Overseas Banks and Other Financial Institutions	0.01		1. 短期信托投资 Short - term Trust Investments		
八、外汇买卖 Foreign Exchange Dealings	0.18	0.04	其中：境外 Of Which：Overseas		
九、应付及暂收款 Accounts Payable and Receipts on Account	0.04	-0.02	2. 中长期信托投资 Medium and Long - term Trust Investments		
其中：应付及预提利息 Of Which：Interest Payable and Accrued			其中：境外 Of Which：Overseas		
			三、投资 Investments	0.08	

续表
Continued

项目 Items	余额 Balance	比年初增减额 Changes within the Year	项目 Items	余额 Balance	比年初增减额 Changes within the Year
十、各项准备 Total Provisions	0.01		1. 购买有价证券 Purchase of Securities		
其中：贷款呆账准备金 Of Which: Provisions for Bad Loans	0.01		其中：购买境外有价证券 Of Which: Purchase of Foreign Securities		
十一、所有者权益 Owner's Equity	0.71		2. 其他投资 Other Investments	0.08	
其中：实收资本 Of Which: Paid - in Capital	0.74		其中：投资境外 Of Which: Overseas	0.02	
当年结益 Net Earnings	-0.01	-0.01	四、证券业务占款 Funding of Securities Purchase		
十二、其他 Others	0.61	-0.08	五、经营租赁 Operating Leases		
			六、买入返售证券 Reverse Repo		
			七、应收及预付款项 Accounts Receivable and Advance Payments	0.49	
			其中：应收及预付利息 Of Which: Interest Receivable and Paid in Advance	0.03	
			八、存放中央银行 Deposits with the Central Bank		
			其中：缴存准备金 Of Which: Reserves with the Central Bank		
			九、存放同业 Due from Banks and Other Financial Institutions	0.10	-0.13
			其中：存放境外同业 Of Which: Due from Overseas Banks and Other Financial Institutions		
			十、拆放同业 Placements with Banks and Other Financial Institutions	0.07	-0.02
			其中：拆放境外同业 Of Which: Placements with Overseas Banks and Other Financial Institutions		
			十一、库存现金 Cash in Vault		
资金来源总计 Total Sources	**2.76**	**-0.16**	**资金运用总计 Total Uses**	**2.76**	**-0.16**

金融租赁公司外汇信贷收支表

Sources and Uses of Credit Funds of Financial Leasing Companies（Foreign Currency）

（2003 年末）

（Year - end of 2003）

单位：亿美元

Unit：100 Million US Dollars

项　目 Items	余　额 Balance	比年初增减额 Changes within the Year	项　目 Items	余　额 Balance	比年初增减额 Changes within the Year
一、各项存款 Total Deposits	0.15		一、各项贷款 Total Loans	1.67	-0.35
1. 信托存款 Trust Deposits	0.02		1. 短期信托贷款 Short - term Trust Loans		
2. 委托存款 Designated Deposits			其中：境外短期 Of Which：Overseas Short - term Loans		
3. 其他存款 Other Deposits	0.13		2. 中长期信托贷款 Medium and Long - term Trust Loans		
二、境内中长期借款 Domestic Medium and Long - term Borrowing	0.42		其中：境外中长期 Of Which：Overseas Medium and Long - term Loans		
三、境外筹资 Overseas Financing	0.42	-0.03	3. 委托贷款 Designated Loans		
四、证券业务款项 Securities Business Funds			4. 融资租赁 Financing Leases	1.22	-0.35
五、卖出回购证券 Repo			5. 票据融资 Paper Financing		
六、同业存放 Due to Banks and Other Financial Institutions			其中：贴现 Of Which：Discount		
其中：境外同业存放 Of Which：Due to Overseas Banks and Other Financial Institutions			6. 各项垫款 Total Advances		
			7. 境外筹资转贷款 On - lending of Overseas Financing		
七、同业拆入 Placements from Banks and Other Financial Institutions	0.25	0.06	8. 其他贷款 Other Loans	0.45	
			二、信托投资 Trust Investments		
其中：境外同业拆入 Of Which：Placements from Overseas Banks and Other Financial Institutions	0.01		1. 短期信托投资 Short - term Trust Investments		
			其中：境外 Of Which：Overseas		
八、外汇买卖 Foreign Exchange Dealings	0.14	-0.04			
九、应付及暂收款 Accounts Payable and Receipts on Account	0.02	-0.02	2. 中长期信托投资 Medium and Long - term Trust Investments		
其中：应付及预提利息 Of Which：Interest Payable and Accrued			其中：境外 Of Which：Overseas		
			三、投资 Investments	0.04	-0.04

续表
Continued

项　目 Items	余　额 Balance	比年初增减额 Changes within the Year	项　目 Items	余　额 Balance	比年初增减额 Changes within the Year
十、各项准备 Total Provisions	0.01		1. 购买有价证券 Purchase of Securities		
其中：贷款呆账准备金 Of Which: Provisions for Bad Loans	0.01		其中：购买境外有价证券 Of Which: Purchase of Foreign Securities		
十一、所有者权益 Owner's Equity	0.59	-0.12	2. 其他投资 Other Investments	0.04	-0.04
其中：实收资本 Of Which: Paid-in Capital	0.74		其中：投资境外 Of Which: Overseas		-0.02
当年结益 Net Earnings	-0.04	-0.04	四、证券业务占款 Funding of Securities Purchase		
十二、其他 Others	0.50	-0.11	五、经营租赁 Operating Leases		
			六、买入返售证券 Reverse Repo		
			七、应收及预付款项 Accounts Receivable and Advance Payments	0.60	0.11
			其中：应收及预付利息 Of Which: Interest Receivable and Paid in Advance	0.03	
			八、存放中央银行 Deposits with the Central Bank		
			其中：缴存准备金 Of Which: Reserves with the Central Bank		
			九、存放同业 Due from Banks and Other Financial Institutions	0.09	-0.01
			其中：存放境外同业 Of Which: Due from Overseas Banks and Other Financial Institutions		
			十、拆放同业 Placements with Banks and Other Financial Institutions	0.04	-0.03
			其中：拆放境外同业 Of Which: Placements with Overseas Banks and Other Financial Institutions		
			十一、库存现金 Cash in Vault	0.06	0.06
资金来源总计 Total Sources	**2.50**	**-0.26**	**资金运用总计 Total Uses**	**2.50**	**-0.26**

金融租赁公司外汇信贷收支表

Sources and Uses of Credit Funds of Financial Leasing Companies（Foreign Currency）

（2004 年末）

（Year－end of 2004）

单位：亿美元

Unit：100 Million US Dollars

项目 Items	余额 Balance	比年初增减额 Changes within the Year	项目 Items	余额 Balance	比年初增减额 Changes within the Year
一、各项存款 Total Deposits	0.18	0.03	一、各项贷款 Total Loans	0.91	－0.76
1. 信托存款 Trust Deposits	0.05	0.03	1. 短期信托贷款 Short－term Trust Loans		
2. 委托存款 Designated Deposits			其中：境外短期 Of Which：Overseas Short－term Loans		
3. 其他存款 Other Deposits	0.13		2. 中长期信托贷款 Medium and Long－term Trust Loans		
二、境内中长期借款 Domestic Medium and Long－term Borrowing	0.71	0.29	其中：境外中长期 Of Which：Overseas Medium and Long－term Loans		
三、境外筹资 Overseas Financing	0.28	－0.14	3. 委托贷款 Designated Loans		
四、证券业务款项 Securities Business Funds			4. 融资租赁 Financing Leases	0.54	－0.68
五、卖出回购资产 Assets Repo（Including Securities）			5. 票据融资 Paper Financing		
六、同业存放 Due to Banks and Other Financial Institutions			其中：贴现 Of Which：Discount		
其中：境外同业存放 Of Which：Due to Overseas Banks and Other Financial Institutions			6. 各项垫款 Total Advances		
			7. 境外筹资转贷款 On－lending of Overseas Financing		
七、同业拆入 Placements from Banks and Other Financial Institutions	0.23	－0.02	8. 其他贷款 Other Loans	0.37	－0.08
			二、信托投资 Trust Investments		
其中：境外同业拆入 Of Which：Placements from Overseas Banks and Other Financial Institutions		－0.01	1. 短期信托投资 Short－term Trust Investments		
八、外汇买卖 Foreign Exchange Dealings	－0.18	－0.32	其中：境外 Of Which：Overseas		
九、应付及暂收款 Accounts Payable and Receipts on Account	0.03	0.01	2. 中长期信托投资 Medium and Long－term Trust Investments		
其中：应付及预提利息 Of Which：Interest Payable and Accrued	0.01	0.01	其中：境外 Of Which：Overseas		
			三、投资 Investments	0.03	－0.01

续表
Continued

项　目 Items	余　额 Balance	比年初增减额 Changes within the Year	项　目 Items	余　额 Balance	比年初增减额 Changes within the Year
十、各项准备 Total Provisions	0.54	0.53	1. 购买有价证券 Purchase of Securities		
其中：贷款呆账准备金 Of Which: Provisions for Bad Loans	0.41	0.40	其中：购买境外有价证券 Of Which: Purchase of Foreign Securities		
十一、所有者权益 Owner's Equity	-0.40	-1.03	2. 其他投资 Other Investments	0.03	-0.01
其中：实收资本 Of Which: Paid-in Capital	0.74		其中：投资境外 Of Which: Overseas		
当年结益 Net Earnings	-0.01	-0.01	四、证券业务占款 Funding of Securities Purchase		
十二、其他 Others	0.20	-0.30	五、经营租赁 Operating Leases		
			六、买入返售资产 Assets Reverse Repo (Including Securities)		
			七、应收及预付款项 Accounts Receivable and Advance Payments	0.63	-0.01
			其中：应收及预付利息 Of Which: Interest Receivable and Paid in Advance	0.03	
			八、存放中央银行 Deposits with the Central Bank		
			其中：缴存准备金 Of Which: Reserves with the Central Bank		
			九、存放同业 Due from Banks and Other Financial Institutions		-0.09
			其中：存放境外同业 Of Which: Due from Overseas Banks and Other Financial Institutions		
			十、拆放同业 Placements with Banks and Other Financial Institutions	0.02	-0.02
			其中：拆放境外同业 Of Which: Placements with Overseas Banks and Other Financial Institutions		
			十一、库存现金 Cash in Vault		-0.06
资金来源总计 Total Sources	**1.59**	**-0.95**	**资金运用总计 Total Uses**	**1.59**	**-0.95**

金融租赁公司外汇信贷收支表

Sources and Uses of Credit Funds of Financial Leasing Companies（Foreign Currency）

（2005 年末）

（Year - end of 2005）

单位：亿美元

Unit：100 Million US Dollars

项目 Items	余额 Balance	比年初增减额 Changes within the Year	项目 Items	余额 Balance	比年初增减额 Changes within the Year
一、各项存款 Total Deposits	0.12	-0.06	一、各项贷款 Total Loans	0.82	-0.08
1. 信托存款 Trust Deposits	0.05		1. 短期信托贷款 Short - term Trust Loans		
2. 委托存款 Designated Deposits	0.01	0.01	其中：境外短期 Of Which：Overseas Short - term Loans		
3. 其他存款 Other Deposits	0.06	-0.07	2. 中长期信托贷款 Medium and Long - term Trust Loans		
二、境内中长期筹资 Domestic Medium and Long - term Borrowing	0.68		其中：境外中长期 Of Which：Overseas Medium and Long - term Loans		
三、境外筹资 Overseas Financing	0.24	-0.04	3. 委托贷款 Designated Loans	0.01	0.01
四、证券业务款项 Securities Business Funds			4. 融资租赁 Financing Leases	0.51	-0.04
五、卖出回购资产 Assets Repo（Including Securities）			5. 票据融资 Paper Financing		
六、同业存放 Due to Banks and Other Financial Institutions			其中：贴现 Of Which：Discount		
其中：境外同业存放 Of Which：Due to Overseas Banks and Other Financial Institutions			6. 各项垫款 Total Advances		
			7. 境外筹资转贷款 On - lending of Overseas Financing		
七、同业拆入 Placements from Banks and Other Financial Institutions	0.17	-0.06	8. 其他贷款 Other Loans	0.30	-0.05
			二、信托投资 Trust Investments		
其中：境外同业拆入 Of Which：Placements from Overseas Banks and Other Financial Institutions			1. 短期信托投资 Short - term Trust Investments		
			其中：境外 Of Which：Overseas		
八、外汇买卖 Foreign Exchange Dealings	-0.12	0.05	2. 中长期信托投资 Medium and Long - term Trust Investments		
九、应付及暂收款 Accounts Payable and Receipts on Account	0.09	0.06	其中：境外 Of Which：Overseas		
其中：应付及预提利息 Of Which：Interest Payable and Accrued	0.03	0.02	三、投资 Investments	0.04	0.01

续表
Continued

项　目 Items	余　额 Balance	比年初增减额 Changes within the Year	项　目 Items	余　额 Balance	比年初增减额 Changes within the Year
十、各项准备 Total Provisions	0.89	0.34	1. 购买有价证券 Purchase of Securities		
其中：贷款损失准备 Of Which: Provisions for Loan Losses	0.66	0.23	其中：购买境外有价证券 Of Which: Purchase of Foreign Securities		
十一、所有者权益 Owner's Equity	-0.78	-0.38	2. 其他投资 Other Investments	0.04	0.01
其中：实收资本 Of Which: Paid-in Capital	0.74		其中：投资境外 Of Which: Overseas		
当年结益 Net Earnings	-0.02	-0.02	四、证券业务占款 Funding of Securities Purchase		
十二、其他 Others	0.18	-0.02	五、经营租赁 Operating Leases		
			六、买入返售资产 Assets Reverse Repo (Including Securities)		
			七、应收及预付款项 Accounts Receivable and Advance Payments	0.59	-0.04
			其中：应收及预付利息 Of Which: Interest Receivable and Paid in Advance	0.03	
			八、存放中央银行 Deposits with the Central Bank		
			其中：缴存准备金 Of Which: Reserves with the Central Bank		
			九、存放同业 Due from Banks and Other Financial Institutions		
			其中：存放境外同业 Of Which: Due from Overseas Banks and Other Financial Institutions		
			十、拆放同业 Placements with Banks and Other Financial Institutions	0.02	
			其中：拆放境外同业 Of Which: Placements with Overseas Banks and Other Financial Institutions		
			十一、库存现金 Cash in Vault		
资金来源总计 Total Sources	**1.47**	**-0.11**	**资金运用总计 Total Uses**	**1.47**	**-0.11**

12. 外资银行外汇信贷收支表（2002—2005 年）
Sources and Uses of Credit Funds of Foreign－funded Banks（Foreign Currency）（2002—2005）

外资银行外汇信贷收支表
Sources and Uses of Credit Funds of Foreign－funded Banks（Foreign Currency）
（2002 年末）
（Year－end of 2002）

单位：亿美元
Unit：100 Million US Dollars

项目 Items	余额 Balance	比年初增减额 Changes within the Year	项目 Items	余额 Balance	比年初增减额 Changes within the Year
一、各项存款 Total Deposits	66.01	13.09	一、各项贷款 Total Loans	138.33	－0.54
1. 单位活期存款 Demand Deposits by Enterprises	32.24	11.68	1. 短期贷款 Short－term Loans	60.69	6.25
其中：中资企业存款 Of Which：Deposits by Chinese－funded Enterprises	0.50	0.33	（1）境内短期贷款 Domestic Short－term Loans	56.50	6.06
			其中：中资企业贷款 Of Which：Loans to Chinese－funded Enterprises	2.49	0.47
外商投资企业存款 Deposits by Foreign－funded Enterprises	31.40	11.30	其中：外商投资企业贷款 Of Which：Loans to Foreign－funded Enterprises	53.81	5.48
2. 单位定期存款 Time Deposits by Enterprises	19.94	－4.14			
其中：中资企业存款 Of Which：Deposits by Chinese－funded Enterprises	0.11	－0.02	（2）境外短期贷款 Overseas Short－term Loans	4.02	0.02
			2. 中长期贷款 Medium and Long－term Loans	65.83	－11.66
外商投资企业存款 Deposits by Foreign－funded Enterprises	19.73	－4.08	（1）境内中长期贷款 Domestic Medium and Long－term Loans	48.00	－11.51
3. 储蓄存款 Savings Deposits	3.43	2.50	其中：中资企业贷款 Of Which：Loans to Chinese－funded Enterprises	3.29	－2.68
其中：定期存款 Of Which：Time Deposits	2.60	2.20			
4. 其他类存款 Other Deposits	0.23	－0.03	外商投资企业贷款 Loans to Foreign－funded Enterprises	42.69	－8.43
5. 境外存款 Foreign Deposits	10.17	3.08			
二、境内中长期借款 Domestic Medium and Long－term Borrowing	0.02	0.02	（2）境外中长期贷款 Overseas Medium and Long－term Loans	17.83	－0.15
三、卖出回购证券 Repo			3. 进出口贸易融资 Financing for Import and Export Trades	7.14	2.86
四、境外筹资 Overseas Financing		－0.75	4. 票据融资 Paper Financing	4.67	2.01
五、向中央银行借款 Borrowings from the Central Bank			其中：贴现 Of Which：Discount	4.67	2.01
六、中央银行存款 Deposits by the Central Bank			5. 各项垫款 Total Advances		
七、应付及暂收款 Accounts Payable and Receipts on Account	5.28	－1.75	6. 境外筹资转贷款 On－lending of Overseas Financing		

续表
Continued

项　目 Items	余　额 Balance	比年初增减额 Changes within the Year	项　目 Items	余　额 Balance	比年初增减额 Changes within the Year
其中：应付及预提利息 Of Which: Interest Payable and Accrued	0.79	-0.41	二、投资 Investments	7.03	-0.11
八、同业存放 Due to Banks and Other Financial Institutions	5.79	-4.68	1. 购买有价证券 Purchase of Securities	3.75	1.97
1. 境内同业存放 Due to Domestic Banks and Other Financial Institutions	5.58	-4.69	其中：购买境外有价证券 Of Which: Purchase of Foreign Securities	0.08	-0.09
2. 境外同业存放 Due to Overseas Banks and Other Financial Institutions	0.21	0.01	2. 其他投资 Other Investments	3.28	-2.09
九、同业拆入 Placements from Banks and Other Financial Institutions	29.58	-7.74	其中：投资境外 Of Which: Overseas	3.26	-1.96
1. 境内同业拆入 Placements from Domestic Banks and Other Financial Institutions	22.65	-5.36	三、应收及预付款 Accounts Receivable and Advance Payments	3.06	-0.49
2. 境外同业拆入 Placements from Overseas Banks and Other Financial Institutions	6.93	-2.38	其中：应收及预付利息 Of Which: Interest Receivable and Paid in Advance	1.88	-0.84
十、委托基金存款（净） Designated Fund Deposits (Net)			四、买入返售证券 Reverse Repo		
十一、外汇买卖 Foreign Exchange Dealings			五、存放中央银行 Deposits with the Central Bank	4.76	-3.43
其中：结售汇 Of Which: Purchase and Sale of Foreign Exchange			其中：缴存准备金 Of Which: Reserves with the Central Bank	2.92	0.48
十二、境内联行存放 Due to Domestic Branches	-0.44	2.29	六、存放同业 Due from Banks and Other Financial Institutions	23.87	12.03
十三、境外联行存放 Due to Overseas Branches	133.22	-24.41	1. 存放境内同业 Due from Domestic Banks and Other Financial Institutions	18.45	9.98
十四、各项准备 Total Provisions	6.03	-1.00	2. 存放境外同业 Due from Overseas Banks and Other Financial Institutions	5.42	2.05
其中：贷款呆账准备金 Of Which: Provisions for Bad Loans	5.84	1.79	七、拆放同业 Placements with Banks and Other Financial Institutions	24.58	-18.82
十五、所有者权益 Owner's Equity	33.49	7.05	1. 拆放境内同业 Placements with Domestic Banks and Other Financial Institutions	21.11	-15.15
其中：实收资本 Of Which: Paid-in Capital	33.61	4.51	2. 拆放境外同业 Placements with Overseas Banks and Other Financial Institutions	3.84	-3.30
当年结益 Net Earnings	1.57	1.57			
十六、其他 Others	-2.79	-1.42	八、存放境外联行 Due from Overseas Branches	74.27	-7.91
			九、库存现金 Cash in Vault	0.29	-0.03
资金来源总计 Total Sources	**276.19**	**-19.30**	**资金运用总计 Total Uses**	**276.19**	**-19.30**

外资银行外汇信贷收支表

Sources and Uses of Credit Funds of Foreign - funded Banks（Foreign Currency）

（2003年末）

（Year - end of 2003）

单位：亿美元

Unit：100 Million US Dollars

项目 Items	余额 Balance	比年初增减额 Changes within the Year	项目 Items	余额 Balance	比年初增减额 Changes within the Year
一、各项存款 Total Deposits	78.31	12.30	一、各项贷款 Total Loans	163.15	25.08
1. 单位活期存款 Demand Deposits by Enterprises	36.43	4.19	1. 短期贷款 Short - term Loans	79.27	18.92
其中：中资企业存款 Of Which：Deposits by Chinese - funded Enterprises	0.40	- 0.10	（1）境内短期贷款 Domestic Short - term Loans	73.98	17.51
外商投资企业存款 Deposits by Foreign - funded Enterprises	36.00	4.60	其中：中资企业贷款 Of Which：Loans to Chinese - funded Enterprises	3.49	1.02
2. 单位定期存款 Time Deposits by Enterprises	19.50	- 0.45	其中：外商投资企业贷款 Of Which：Loans to Foreign - funded Enterprises	70.42	16.62
其中：中资企业存款 Of Which：Deposits by Chinese - funded Enterprises	0.14	0.03	（2）境外短期贷款 Overseas Short - term Loans	5.26	1.39
外商投资企业存款 Deposits by Foreign - funded Enterprises	19.32	- 0.41	2. 中长期贷款 Medium and Long - term Loans	69.32	3.36
3. 储蓄存款 Savings Deposits	6.60	3.20	（1）境内中长期贷款 Domestic Medium and Long - term Loans	50.43	2.29
其中：定期存款 Of Which：Time Deposits	5.11	2.52	其中：中资企业贷款 Of Which：Loans to Chinese - funded Enterprises	2.78	- 0.62
4. 其他类存款 Other Deposits	0.18	- 0.05	外商投资企业贷款 Loans to Foreign - funded Enterprises	45.73	2.96
5. 境外存款 Foreign Deposits	15.61	5.43	（2）境外中长期贷款 Overseas Medium and Long - term Loans	18.88	1.05
二、境内中长期借款 Domestic Medium and Long - term Borrowing		- 0.02			
三、卖出回购证券 Repo			3. 进出口贸易融资 Financing for Import and Export Trades	10.01	2.92
四、境外筹资 Overseas Financing			4. 票据融资 Paper Financing	4.55	- 0.12
五、向中央银行借款 Borrowings from the Central Bank			其中：贴现 Of Which：Discount	4.55	- 0.12
六、中央银行存款 Deposits by the Central Bank			5. 各项垫款 Total Advances		
七、应付及暂收款 Accounts Payable and Receipts on Account	6.08	0.80	6. 境外筹资转贷款 On - lending of Overseas Financing		
其中：应付及预提利息 Of Which：Interest Payable and Accrued	1.01	0.22	二、投资 Investments	7.27	0.24

续表
Continued

项 目 Items	余 额 Balance	比年初增减额 Changes within the Year	项 目 Items	余 额 Balance	比年初增减额 Changes within the Year
八、同业存放 Due to Banks and Other Financial Institutions	10.39	4.60	1. 购买有价证券 Purchase of Securities	3.80	0.05
			其中：购买境外有价证券 Of Which: Purchase of Foreign Securities	0.10	0.02
1. 境内同业存放 Due to Domestic Banks and Other Financial Institutions	10.07	4.49	2. 其他投资 Other Investments	3.48	0.20
2. 境外同业存放 Due to Overseas Banks and Other Financial Institutions	0.32	0.11	其中：投资境外 Of Which: Overseas	3.47	0.21
九、同业拆入 Placements from Banks and Other Financial Institutions	34.80	5.22	三、应收及预付款 Accounts Receivable and Advance Payments	3.19	0.13
1. 境内同业拆入 Placements from Domestic Banks and Other Financial Institutions	20.37	-2.28	其中：应收及预付利息 Of Which: Interest Receivable and Paid in Advance	1.79	-0.09
2. 境外同业拆入 Placements from Overseas Banks and Other Financial Institutions	14.43	7.50	四、买入返售证券 Reverse Repo		
			五、存放中央银行 Deposits with the Central Bank	6.93	2.17
十、委托基金存款（净） Designated Fund Deposits (Net)			其中：缴存准备金 Of Which: Reserves with the Central Bank	3.64	0.72
十一、外汇买卖 Foreign Exchange Dealings					
其中：结售汇 Of Which: Purchase and Sale of Foreign Exchange			六、存放同业 Due from Banks and Other Financial Institutions	36.48	12.65
十二、境内联行存放 Due to Domestic Branches	-1.10	-0.66	1. 存放境内同业 Due from Domestic Banks and Other Financial Institutions	28.57	10.16
十三、境外联行存放 Due to Overseas Branches	180.38	47.27			
			2. 存放境外同业 Due from Overseas Banks and Other Financial Institutions	7.91	2.49
十四、各项准备 Total Provisions	3.80	-2.15			
其中：贷款呆账准备金 Of Which: Provisions for Bad Loans	3.75	-2.03	七、拆放同业 Placements with Banks and Other Financial Institutions	27.28	2.72
十五、所有者权益 Owner's Equity	34.57	1.41	1. 拆放境内同业 Placements with Domestic Banks and Other Financial Institutions	21.89	0.80
其中：实收资本 Of Which: Paid - in Capital	33.79	0.55	2. 拆放境外同业 Placements with Overseas Banks and Other Financial Institutions	5.89	2.26
当年结益 Net Earnings	1.39	1.39			
十六、其他 Others	-2.64	0.08	八、存放境外联行 Due from Overseas Branches	99.95	25.83
			九、库存现金 Cash in Vault	0.34	0.05
资金来源总计 Total Sources	**344.59**	**68.87**	**资金运用总计 Total Uses**	**344.59**	**68.87**

外资银行外汇信贷收支表

Sources and Uses of Credit Funds of Foreign - funded Banks（Foreign Currency）

（2004 年末）

（Year - end of 2004）

单位：亿美元

Unit：100 Million US Dollars

项目 Items	余额 Balance	比年初增减额 Changes within the Year	项目 Items	余额 Balance	比年初增减额 Changes within the Year
一、各项存款 Total Deposits	108.46	25.95	一、各项贷款 Total Loans	262.86	87.23
1. 单位活期存款 Demand Deposits by Enterprises	46.37	7.37	1. 短期贷款 Short - term Loans	135.86	48.73
其中：中资企业存款 Of Which：Deposits by Chinese - funded Enterprises	0.88	0.45	（1）境内短期贷款 Domestic Short - term Loans	128.16	46.63
外商投资企业存款 Deposits by Foreign - funded Enterprises	45.40	6.91	其中：中资企业贷款 Of Which：Loans to Chinese - funded Enterprises	5.73	2.28
2. 单位定期存款 Time Deposits by Enterprises	26.11	4.97	其中：外商投资企业贷款 Of Which：Loans to Foreign - funded Enterprises	115.50	37.49
其中：中资企业存款 Of Which：Deposits by Chinese - funded Enterprises	0.07	-0.07	（2）境外短期贷款 Overseas Short - term Loans	7.71	2.10
外商投资企业存款 Deposits by Foreign - funded Enterprises	26.04	5.09	2. 中长期贷款 Medium and Long - term Loans	104.91	32.80
3. 储蓄存款 Savings Deposits	11.49	4.77	（1）境内中长期贷款 Domestic Medium and Long - term Loans	77.06	23.95
其中：定期存款 Of Which：Time Deposits	8.38	3.22	其中：中资企业贷款 Of Which：Loans to Chinese - funded Enterprises	6.86	3.83
4. 其他类存款 Other Deposits	0.19	-0.01	外商投资企业贷款 Loans to Foreign - funded Enterprises	69.37	21.22
5. 境外存款 Foreign Deposits	24.31	8.87	（2）境外中长期贷款 Overseas Medium and Long - term Loans	27.85	8.85
二、境内中长期借款 Domestic Medium and Long - term Borrowing			3. 进出口贸易融资 Financing for Import and Export Trades	12.84	2.39
三、卖出回购资产 Assets Repo（Including Securities）					
四、境外筹资 Overseas Financing			4. 票据融资 Paper Financing	9.25	3.31
五、向中央银行借款 Borrowings from the Central Bank			其中：贴现 Of Which：Discount	9.25	3.31
六、中央银行存款 Deposits by the Central Bank			5. 各项垫款 Total Advances		
七、应付及暂收款 Accounts Payable and Receipts on Account	8.13	1.81	6. 境外筹资转贷款 On - lending of Overseas Financing		
			二、投资 Investments	6.83	-0.49

续表
Continued

项目 Items	余额 Balance	比年初增减额 Changes within the Year	项目 Items	余额 Balance	比年初增减额 Changes within the Year
其中：应付及预提利息 Of Which: Interest Payable and Accrued	1.38	0.36	1. 购买有价证券 Purchase of Securities	3.75	-0.05
			其中：购买境外有价证券 Of Which: Purchase of Foreign Securities	0.35	0.25
八、同业存放 Due to Banks and Other Financial Institutions	9.20	-1.19	2. 其他投资 Other Investments	3.09	-0.44
1. 境内同业存放 Due to Domestic Banks and Other Financial Institutions	8.80	-1.22	其中：投资境外 Of Which: Overseas	3.08	-0.44
2. 境外同业存放 Due to Overseas Banks and Other Financial Institutions	0.40	0.03	三、应收及预付款 Accounts Receivable and Advance Payments	4.30	1.04
九、同业拆入 Placements from Banks and Other Financial Institutions	51.42	15.42	其中：应收及预付利息 Of Which: Interest Receivable and Paid in Advance	2.17	0.34
1. 境内同业拆入 Placements from Domestic Banks and Other Financial Institutions	26.28	5.34	四、买入返售资产 Assets Reverse Repo (Including Securities)	0.27	0.27
2. 境外同业拆入 Placements from Overseas Banks and Other Financial Institutions	25.14	10.08	五、存放中央银行 Deposits with the Central Bank	10.55	3.05
十、委托基金存款（净） Designated Fund Deposits (Net)			其中：缴存准备金 Of Which: Reserves with the Central Bank	5.11	1.25
十一、外汇买卖 Foreign Exchange Dealings			六、存放同业 Due from Banks and Other Financial Institutions	52.97	15.88
其中：结售汇 Of Which: Purchase and Sale of Foreign Exchange			1. 存放境内同业 Due from Domestic Banks and Other Financial Institutions	46.76	18.12
十二、境内联行存放 Due to Domestic Branches	1.06	2.46	2. 存放境外同业 Due from Overseas Banks and Other Financial Institutions	6.21	-2.24
十三、境外联行存放 Due to Overseas Branches	267.55	75.85	七、拆放同业 Placements with Banks and Other Financial Institutions	29.52	1.05
十四、各项准备 Total Provisions	4.19	0.12	1. 拆放境内同业 Placements with Domestic Banks and Other Financial Institutions	21.81	-1.02
其中：贷款呆账准备金 Of Which: Provisions for Bad Loans	4.13	0.12	2. 拆放境外同业 Placements with Overseas Banks and Other Financial Institutions	7.71	2.07
十五、所有者权益 Owner's Equity	41.80	6.75	八、存放境外联行 Due from Overseas Branches	121.83	18.95
其中：实收资本 Of Which: Paid-in Capital	40.24	5.58	九、库存现金 Cash in Vault	0.40	0.06
当年结益 Net Earnings	2.06	2.06			
十六、其他 Others	-2.28	-0.13			
资金来源总计 Total Sources	**489.53**	**127.04**	**资金运用总计 Total Uses**	**489.53**	**127.04**

外资银行外汇信贷收支表

Sources and Uses of Credit Funds of Foreign－funded Banks（Foreign Currency）

（2005 年末）

（Year－end of 2005）

单位：亿美元

Unit：100 Million US Dollars

项目 Items	余额 Balance	比年初增减额 Changes within the Year	项目 Items	余额 Balance	比年初增减额 Changes within the Year
一、各项存款 Total Deposits	129.94	21.43	一、各项贷款 Total Loans	316.93	54.27
1. 单位活期存款 Demand Deposits by Enterprises	54.93	8.51	1. 短期贷款 Short－term Loans	146.20	10.37
其中：中资企业存款 Of Which：Deposits by Chinese－funded Enterprises	1.20	0.32	（1）境内短期贷款 Domestic Short－term Loans	138.30	10.08
外商投资企业存款 Deposits by Foreign－funded Enterprises	53.64	8.19	其中：中资企业贷款 Of Which：Loans to Chinese－funded Enterprises	10.09	4.10
2. 单位定期存款 Time Deposits by Enterprises	28.14	1.97	其中：外商投资企业贷款 Of Which：Loans to Foreign－funded Enterprises	127.59	5.71
其中：中资企业存款 Of Which：Deposits by Chinese－funded Enterprises	0.15	0.08	（2）境外短期贷款 Overseas Short－term Loans	7.90	0.26
外商投资企业存款 Deposits by Foreign－funded Enterprises	27.99	1.90	2. 中长期贷款 Medium and Long－term Loans	144.58	39.74
3. 储蓄存款 Savings Deposits	15.48	4.00	（1）境内中长期贷款 Domestic Medium and Long－term Loans	107.76	30.70
其中：定期存款 Of Which：Time Deposits	11.24	2.86	其中：中资企业贷款 Of Which：Loans to Chinese－funded Enterprises	14.09	7.23
4. 其他类存款 Other Deposits	0.21	0.03	外商投资企业贷款 Loans to Foreign－funded Enterprises	92.89	23.52
5. 境外存款 Foreign Deposits	31.19	6.92	（2）境外中长期贷款 Overseas Medium and Long－term Loans	36.82	9.04
二、境内中长期借款 Domestic Medium and Long－term Borrowing			3. 进出口贸易融资 Financing for Import and Export Trades	18.18	5.34
三、卖出回购资产 Assets Repo（Including Securities）			4. 票据融资 Paper Financing	7.97	－1.18
四、境外筹资 Overseas Financing			其中：贴现 Of Which：Discount	7.97	－1.18
五、向中央银行借款 Borrowings from the Central Bank			5. 各项垫款 Total Advances		
六、中央银行存款 Deposits by the Central Bank			6. 境外筹资转贷款 On－lending of Overseas Financing		
七、应付及暂收款 Accounts Payable and Receipts on Account	9.75	1.71	二、投资 Investments	10.66	3.83
其中：应付及预提利息 Of Which：Interest Payable and Accrued	3.20	1.83	1. 购买有价证券 Purchase of Securities	6.02	2.27

续表
Continued

项 目 Items	余 额 Balance	比年初增减额 Changes within the Year	项 目 Items	余 额 Balance	比年初增减额 Changes within the Year
八、同业存放 Due to Banks and Other Financial Institutions	8.97	-0.23	其中：购买境外有价证券 Of Which: Purchase of Foreign Securities	0.27	-0.08
1. 境内同业存放 Due to Domestic Banks and Other Financial Institutions	8.56	-0.24	2. 其他投资 Other Investments	4.65	1.56
			其中：投资境外 Of Which: Overseas	4.59	1.51
2. 境外同业存放 Due to Overseas Banks and Other Financial Institutions	0.41	0.01	三、应收及预付款 Accounts Receivable and Advance Payments	5.84	1.55
九、同业拆入 Placements from Banks and Other Financial Institutions	60.16	8.77	其中：应收及预付利息 Of Which: Interest Receivable and Paid in Advance	3.95	1.79
1. 境内同业拆入 Placements from Domestic Banks and Other Financial Institutions	28.41	2.16	四、买入返售资产 Assets Reverse Repo (Including Securities)		-0.27
2. 境外同业拆入 Placements from Overseas Banks and Other Financial Institutions	31.75	6.61	五、存放中央银行 Deposits with the Central Bank	8.12	-2.46
			其中：缴存准备金 Of Which: Reserves with the Central Bank	4.00	-1.13
十、委托基金存款（净） Designated Fund Deposits (Net)					
十一、外汇买卖 Foreign Exchange Dealings			六、存放同业 Due from Banks and Other Financial Institutions	69.58	16.60
其中：结售汇 Of Which: Purchase and Sale of Foreign Exchange			1. 存放境内同业 Due from Domestic Banks and Other Financial Institutions	58.95	12.18
十二、境内联行存放 Due to Domestic Branches	0.48	-0.83	2. 存放境外同业 Due from Overseas Banks and Other Financial Institutions	10.63	4.42
十三、境外联行存放 Due to Overseas Branches	303.06	35.27			
十四、各项准备 Total Provisions	4.67	0.43	七、拆放同业 Placements with Banks and Other Financial Institutions	41.28	11.79
其中：贷款损失准备 Of Which: Provisions for Loan Losses	4.63	0.46	1. 拆放境内同业 Placements with Domestic Banks and Other Financial Institutions	36.35	14.57
十五、所有者权益 Owner's Equity	51.92	10.18			
其中：实收资本 Of Which: Paid-in Capital	48.56	8.32	2. 拆放境外同业 Placements with Overseas Banks and Other Financial Institutions	4.93	-2.78
当年结益 Net Earnings	3.32	3.32	八、存放境外联行 Due from Overseas Branches	114.08	-8.33
十六、其他 Others	-1.83	0.48	九、库存现金 Cash in Vault	0.63	0.23
资金来源总计 Total Sources	**567.12**	**77.21**	**资金运用总计 Total Uses**	**567.12**	**77.21**

（三）本外币信贷收支统计

Sources and Uses of Credit Funds（Domestic and Foreign Currency Combined）

1. 金融机构本外币信贷收支表*（2002—2005 年）

Sources and Uses of Credit Funds of Financial Institutions（Domestic and Foreign Currency Combined）（2002—2005）

金融机构本外币信贷收支表

Sources and Uses of Credit Funds of Financial Institutions

（Domestic and Foreign Currency Combined）

（2002 年末）

（Year - end of 2002）

汇率：8.2773　　　　单位：亿元

Exchange Rate：8.2773　　　　Unit：100 Million Yuan

项　目 Items	余　额 Balance	比年初增减额 Changes within the Year	项　目 Items	余　额 Balance	比年初增减额 Changes within the Year
一、各项存款 Total Deposits	183388.48	28675.45	一、各项贷款 Total Loans	139802.90	19228.12
1. 企事业单位存款 Deposits by Enterprises and Public Institutions	64298.47	9714.53	1. 短期贷款 Short - term Loans	76822.41	8104.24
			2. 中长期贷款 Medium and Long - term Loans	51731.61	8810.88
（1）活期存款 Demand Deposits	45352.99	6670.69	3. 信托贷款 Trust Loans	353.20	- 71.31
（2）定期存款 Time Deposits	18945.48	3043.84	4. 委托贷款 Designated Loans	2044.21	53.58
2. 储蓄存款 Savings Deposits	94307.13	13877.54	5. 其他贷款 Other Loans	2232.64	99.93
（1）活期储蓄 Demand Deposits	29026.58	6071.33	6. 票据融资 Paper Financing	5805.31	2256.01
（2）定期储蓄 Time Deposits	65280.55	7806.21	7. 各项垫款 Total Advances	813.52	- 25.21
3. 信托存款 Trust Deposits	261.15	- 25.97	二、有价证券及投资 Securities and Investments	34267.11	4506.75
4. 委托存款 Designated Deposits	2281.24	30.26			
5. 其他存款 Other Deposits	22240.49	5079.09			
二、所有者权益 Owner's Equity	10400.00	1057.25			
其中：实收资本 Of Which：Paid - in Capital	9033.20	155.64			

续表
Continued

项 目 Items	余 额 Balance	比年初增减额 Changes within the Year	项 目 Items	余 额 Balance	比年初增减额 Changes within the Year
当年结益 Net Earnings	979.61	979.61			
三、其他 Others	-19718.47	-5997.83			
资金来源总计 Total Sources	**174070.01**	**23734.87**	**资金运用总计 Total Uses**	**174070.01**	**23734.87**

* 本表机构包括中国人民银行、政策性银行、国有商业银行、其他商业银行、城市商业银行、农村商业银行、农村合作银行、城市信用合作社、农村信用合作社、信托投资公司、财务公司、金融租赁公司、邮政储汇局、外资银行。

* The following institutions are included in the statement: the People's Bank of China, State-owned Commercial Banks, Other Commercial Banks, City Commercial Banks, Rural Commercial Banks, Rural Cooperative Banks, Urban Credit Cooperatives, Rural Credit Cooperatives, Finance Companies, Financial Leasing Companies, Postal Savings Bureau and Foreign-funded Banks.

金融机构本外币信贷收支表

Sources and Uses of Credit Funds of Financial Institutions

（Domestic and Foreign Currency Combined）

（2003年末）

（Year - end of 2003）

汇率：8.2767　　　　　　　　　　　　　　　　　　单位：亿元

Exchange Rate：8.2767　　　　　　　　　　　　　Unit：100 Million Yuan

项目 Items	余额 Balance	比年初增减额 Changes within the Year	项目 Items	余额 Balance	比年初增减额 Changes within the Year
一、各项存款 Total Deposits	220363.53	37028.45	一、各项贷款 Total Loans	169771.00	29936.31
1.企事业单位存款 Deposits by Enterprises and Public Institutions	76784.87	12575.92	1.短期贷款 Short - term Loans	87397.88	10670.31
（1）活期存款 Demand Deposits	53585.88	8413.98	2.中长期贷款 Medium and Long - term Loans	67251.74	15359.57
（2）定期存款 Time Deposits	23198.99	4161.94	3.信托贷款 Trust Loans	344.25	16.97
2.储蓄存款 Savings Deposits	110695.26	16313.03	4.委托贷款 Designated Loans	2128.75	103.48
（1）活期储蓄 Demand Deposits	36218.17	7151.88	5.其他贷款 Other Loans	2682.82	451.61
（2）定期储蓄 Time Deposits	74477.09	9161.15	6.票据融资 Paper Financing	9233.59	3414.37
3.信托存款 Trust Deposits	261.63	-2.19	7.各项垫款 Total Advances	731.97	-80.00
4.委托存款 Designated Deposits	2310.67	60.05	二、有价证券及投资 Securities and Investments	37490.62	3585.98
5.其他存款 Other Deposits	30311.10	8081.64			
二、所有者权益 Owner's Equity	10835.81	968.98			
其中：实收资本 Of Which：Paid - in Capital	10889.72	1907.64			
当年结益 Net Earnings	744.09	744.09			
三、其他 Others	-23937.72	-4475.14			
资金来源总计 Total Sources	**207261.62**	**33522.29**	**资金运用总计 Total Uses**	**207261.62**	**33522.29**

金融机构本外币信贷收支表
Sources and Uses of Credit Funds of Financial Institutions
(Domestic and Foreign Currency Combined)

(2004年末)

(Year - end of 2004)

汇率：8.2765 单位：亿元

Exchange Rate：8.2765 Unit：100 Million Yuan

项目 Items	余额 Balance	比年初增减额 Changes within the Year	项目 Items	余额 Balance	比年初增减额 Changes within the Year
一、各项存款 Total Deposits	254089.45	33726.51	一、各项贷款 Total Loans	189411.08	24054.15
1. 企事业单位存款 Deposits by Enterprises and Public Institutions	89438.25	12084.03	1. 短期贷款 Short - term Loans	90818.17	7151.14
			2. 中长期贷款 Medium and Long - term Loans	81006.85	14190.29
(1) 活期存款 Demand Deposits	61833.60	7477.25	3. 信托贷款 Trust Loans	238.24	25.06
(2) 定期存款 Time Deposits	27604.65	4606.78	4. 委托贷款 Designated Loans	2522.82	418.20
2. 储蓄存款 Savings Deposits	126196.22	15490.52	5. 其他贷款 Other Loans	2816.95	256.16
(1) 活期储蓄 Demand Deposits	42800.27	6572.63	6. 票据融资 Paper Financing	11622.24	2046.94
(2) 定期储蓄 Time Deposits	83395.95	8917.89	7. 各项垫款 Total Advances	385.81	- 33.64
3. 信托存款 Trust Deposits	281.39	20.25	二、有价证券及投资 Securities and Investments	40448.38	3567.04
4. 委托存款 Designated Deposits	2701.42	404.52			
5. 其他存款 Other Deposits	35472.17	5727.19			
二、所有者权益 Owner's Equity	12949.03	2528.46			
其中：实收资本 Of Which: Paid - in Capital	11930.57	1378.64			
当年结益 Net Earnings	1034.97	1034.97			
三、其他 Others	- 37179.02	- 8633.78			
资金来源总计 Total Sources	**229859.46**	**27621.19**	**资金运用总计 Total Uses**	**229859.46**	**27621.19**

金融机构本外币信贷收支表

Sources and Uses of Credit Funds of Financial Institutions

（Domestic and Foreign Currency Combined）

（2005 年末）

（Year - end of 2005）

汇率：8.0702　　　　单位：亿元

Exchange Rate：8.0702　　　　Unit：100 Million Yuan

项　目 Items	余　额 Balance	比年初增减额 Changes within the Year	项　目 Items	余　额 Balance	比年初增减额 Changes within the Year
一、各项存款 Total Deposits	300208.55	44147.06	一、各项贷款 Total Loans	206838.48	24617.14
1. 企事业单位存款 Deposits by Enterprises and Public Institutions	101750.55	12195.28	1. 短期贷款 Short - term Loans	91157.45	6441.56
			2. 中长期贷款 Medium and Long - term Loans	92940.53	13026.34
（1）活期存款 Demand Deposits	66222.96	4285.40	3. 信托贷款 Trust Loans	418.49	111.37
（2）定期存款 Time Deposits	35527.59	7909.88	4. 委托贷款 Designated Loans	2789.59	210.05
2. 储蓄存款 Savings Deposits	147053.74	20858.35	5. 其他贷款 Other Loans	2899.17	91.79
（1）活期储蓄 Demand Deposits	50137.03	7335.35	6. 票据融资 Paper Financing	16319.16	4699.52
（2）定期储蓄 Time Deposits	96916.71	13523.00	7. 各项垫款 Total Advances	314.09	36.51
3. 信托存款 Trust Deposits	445.57	107.51	二、有价证券及投资 Securities and Investments	44870.95	4494.00
4. 委托存款 Designated Deposits	3079.15	234.78			
5. 其他存款 Other Deposits	47879.54	10751.14			
二、所有者权益 Owner's Equity	18753.35	5188.94			
其中：实收资本 Of Which：Paid - in Capital	14248.15	2179.63			
当年结益 Net Earnings	4439.65	4439.65			
三、其他 Others	- 67252.47	- 20224.86			
资金来源总计 Total Sources	**251709.43**	**29111.14**	**资金运用总计 Total Uses**	**251709.43**	**29111.14**

2. 政策性银行本外币信贷收支表* (2002—2005 年)

Sources and Uses of Credit Funds of Policy Banks (Domestic and Foreign Currency Combined) (2002—2005)

政策性银行本外币信贷收支表

Sources and Uses of Credit Funds of Policy Banks (Domestic and Foreign Currency Combined)

(2002 年末)

(Year - end of 2002)

汇率: 8.2773　　　　单位: 亿元

Exchange Rate: 8.2773　　　　Unit: 100 Million Yuan

项　目 Items	余　额 Balance	比年初增减额 Changes within the Year	项　目 Items	余　额 Balance	比年初增减额 Changes within the Year
一、各项存款 Total Deposits	712.31	159.27	一、各项贷款 Total Loans	17212.90	1503.89
1. 企事业单位存款 Deposits by Enterprises and Public Institutions	707.13	157.24	1. 短期贷款 Short - term Loans	7511.40	55.67
(1) 活期存款 Demand Deposits	689.73	151.31	2. 中长期贷款 Medium and Long - term Loans	9210.29	1379.82
(2) 定期存款 Time Deposits	17.40	5.93	3. 其他贷款 Other Loans	490.94	68.13
2. 储蓄存款 Savings Deposits			4. 票据融资 Paper Financing		
(1) 活期储蓄 Demand Deposits			5. 各项垫款 Total Advances	0.27	0.27
(2) 定期储蓄 Time Deposits			二、有价证券及投资 Securities and Investments	1445.81	44.45
3. 其他存款 Other Deposits	5.18	2.03	三、应收及预付款 Accounts Receivable and Advance Payments	346.46	- 232.10
二、债券发行及境外筹资 Bonds Issue & Overseas Financing	10190.86	1375.87	其中: 应收利息 Of Which: Interest Receivable	198.59	- 64.70
三、应付及暂收款 Accounts Receivable and Receipts on Account	441.66	- 259.33	四、买入返售证券 Reverse Repo	98.13	54.23
其中: 应付及预收利息 Of Which: Interest Payable and Received in Advance	244.07	- 140.52	五、存放中央银行存款 Deposits with the Central Bank	275.22	90.00
四、卖出回购证券 Repo	1.66	- 1.64	六、同业往来 Inter - bank Transactions	144.07	1.40
五、向中央银行借款 Borrowings from the Central Bank	6501.65	- 248.00	七、库存现金 Cash in Vault	1.99	0.34
六、同业往来 Inter - bank Transactions	60.95	7.94			
七、代理境内贷款资金 Agency Domestic Lending Funds					
八、各项准备 Total Provisions	352.84	142.28			

续表
Continued

项　　目 Items	余　额 Balance	比年初增减额 Changes within the Year	项　　目 Items	余　额 Balance	比年初增减额 Changes within the Year
其中：贷款呆账准备金 Of Which：Provisions for Bad Loans	352.84	142.28			
九、所有者权益 Owner's Equity	992.75	186.35			
其中：实收资本 Of Which：Paid - in Capital	705.67	24.47			
当年结益 Net Earnings	225.89	225.89			
十、其他 Others	269.90	99.47			
资金来源总计 Total Sources	**19524.58**	**1462.21**	**资金运用总计 Total Uses**	**19524.58**	**1462.21**

*　本表机构包括国家开发银行、中国进出口银行、中国农业发展银行。

*　Policy Banks of this statement include the China Development Bank，the Export - Import Bank of China，and Agricultural Development Bank of China.

政策性银行本外币信贷收支表

Sources and Uses of Credit Funds of Policy Banks（Domestic and Foreign Currency Combined）

（2003 年末）

（Year - end of 2003）

汇率：8.2767　　　　单位：亿元

Exchange Rate：8.2767　　　　Unit：100 Million Yuan

项目 Items	余额 Balance	比年初增减额 Changes within the Year	项目 Items	余额 Balance	比年初增减额 Changes within the Year
一、各项存款 Total Deposits	971.40	259.08	一、各项贷款 Total Loans	19328.34	2115.43
1. 企事业单位存款 Deposits by Enterprises and Public Institutions	958.02	250.93	1. 短期贷款 Short - term Loans	7259.58	- 251.83
（1）活期存款 Demand Deposits	905.36	215.67	2. 中长期贷款 Medium and Long - term Loans	11488.76	2278.47
（2）定期存款 Time Deposits	52.66	35.26	3. 其他贷款 Other Loans	579.36	88.42
2. 储蓄存款 Savings Deposits			4. 票据融资 Paper Financing	0.11	0.11
（1）活期储蓄 Demand Deposits			5. 各项垫款 Total Advances	0.53	0.26
（2）定期储蓄 Time Deposits			二、有价证券及投资 Securities and Investments	1413.16	- 32.76
3. 其他存款 Other Deposits	13.38	8.15	三、应收及预付款 Accounts Receivable and Advance Payments	162.67	- 183.81
二、债券发行及境外筹资 Bonds Issue & Overseas Financing	12004.34	1813.15	其中：应收利息 Of Which：Interest Receivable	41.85	- 156.74
三、应付及暂收款 Accounts Receivable and Receipts on Account	275.55	- 166.27	四、买入返售证券 Reverse Repo		- 98.13
其中：应付及预收利息 Of Which：Interest Payable and Received in Advance	122.60	- 121.47	五、存放中央银行存款 Deposits with the Central Bank	521.23	246.00
四、卖出回购证券 Repo		- 1.66	六、同业往来 Inter - bank Transactions	136.41	- 7.73
五、向中央银行借款 Borrowings from the Central Bank	6507.00	5.35	七、库存现金 Cash in Vault	1.57	- 0.42
六、同业往来 Inter - bank Transactions	67.69	6.74			
七、代理境内贷款资金 Agency Domestic Lending Funds					
八、各项准备 Total Provisions	519.51	166.66			
其中：贷款呆账准备金 Of Which：Provisions for Bad Loans	429.51	76.66			
九、所有者权益 Owner's Equity	973.17	- 19.60			
其中：实收资本 Of Which：Paid - in Capital	715.37	9.82			
当年结益 Net Earnings	104.54	104.54			
十、其他 Others	244.72	- 24.87			
资金来源总计 Total Sources	**21563.38**	**2038.58**	**资金运用总计 Total Uses**	**21563.38**	**2038.58**

政策性银行本外币信贷收支表

Sources and Uses of Credit Funds of Policy Banks（Domestic and Foreign Currency Combined）

（2004 年末）

（Year - end of 2004）

汇率：8.2765　　　　单位：亿元

Exchange Rate：8.2765　　　　Unit：100 Million Yuan

项 目 Items	余 额 Balance	比年初增减额 Changes within the Year	项 目 Items	余 额 Balance	比年初增减额 Changes within the Year
一、各项存款 Total Deposits	1274.87	303.24	一、各项贷款 Total Loans	22228.24	2899.90
1. 企事业单位存款 Deposits by Enterprises and Public Institutions	1261.57	303.55	1. 短期贷款 Short - term Loans	7784.40	524.82
（1）活期存款 Demand Deposits	1138.90	233.54	2. 中长期贷款 Medium and Long - term Loans	13794.43	2305.67
（2）定期存款 Time Deposits	122.67	70.01	3. 其他贷款 Other Loans	647.89	68.53
2. 储蓄存款 Savings Deposits			4. 票据融资 Paper Financing	0.66	0.55
（1）活期储蓄 Demand Deposits			5. 各项垫款 Total Advances	0.86	0.33
（2）定期储蓄 Time Deposits			二、有价证券及投资 Securities and Investments	1526.00	112.84
3. 其他存款 Other Deposits	13.30	- 0.31	三、应收及预付款 Accounts Receivable and Advance Payments	84.02	- 78.47
二、债券发行及境外筹资 Bonds Issue & Overseas Financing	14690.98	2686.64	其中：应收利息 Of Which：Interest Receivable	27.77	- 14.07
三、应付及暂收款 Accounts Receivable and Receipts on Account	227.01	- 48.14	四、买入返售资产 Assets Reverse Repo（Including Securities）		
其中：应付及预收利息 Of Which：Interest Payable and Received in Advance	157.04	34.44	五、存放中央银行存款 Deposits with the Central Bank	526.17	4.94
四、卖出回购资产 Assets Repo（Including Securities）	31.65	31.65	六、同业往来 Inter - bank Transactions	120.17	- 16.28
五、向中央银行借款 Borrowings from the Central Bank	6099.00	- 408.00	七、库存现金 Cash in Vault	1.72	0.15
六、同业往来 Inter - bank Transactions	59.09	- 8.60			
七、代理境内贷款资金 Agency Domestic Lending Funds	1.23	1.23			
八、各项准备 Total Provisions	559.73	40.22			
其中：贷款呆账准备金 Of Which：Provisions for Bad Loans	559.73	130.22			
九、所有者权益 Owner's Equity	1117.98	161.52			
其中：实收资本 Of Which：Paid - in Capital	715.66	0.29			
当年结益 Net Earnings	130.91	130.91			
十、其他 Others	424.78	163.32			
资金来源总计 Total Sources	**24486.32**	**2923.08**	**资金运用总计 Total Uses**	**24486.32**	**2923.08**

政策性银行本外币信贷收支表

Sources and Uses of Credit Funds of Policy Banks（Domestic and Foreign Currency Combined）

（2005 年末）

（Year - end of 2005）

汇率：8.0702　　　　单位：亿元

Exchange Rate：8.0702　　　　Unit：100 Million Yuan

项　目 Items	余　额 Balance	比年初增减额 Changes within the Year	项　目 Items	余　额 Balance	比年初增减额 Changes within the Year
一、各项存款 Total Deposits	2132.99	858.12	一、各项贷款 Total Loans	26497.06	4268.82
1. 企事业单位存款 Deposits by Enterprises and Public Institutions	2113.83	852.26	1. 短期贷款 Short - term Loans	8907.97	1123.57
			2. 中长期贷款 Medium and Long - term Loans	16934.23	3139.80
（1）活期存款 Demand Deposits	1857.30	718.40			
（2）定期存款 Time Deposits	256.53	133.86	3. 其他贷款 Other Loans	653.19	5.30
2. 储蓄存款 Savings Deposits			4. 票据融资 Paper Financing	0.58	- 0.08
（1）活期储蓄 Demand Deposits			5. 各项垫款 Total Advances	1.09	0.23
（2）定期储蓄 Time Deposits			二、有价证券及投资 Securities and Investments	1576.53	50.53
3. 其他存款 Other Deposits	19.16	5.86	三、应收及预付款 Accounts Receivable and Advance Payments	125.64	52.11
二、债券发行及境外筹资 Bonds Issue & Overseas Financing	18996.42	4305.44			
			其中：应收利息 Of Which：Interest Receivable	59.73	31.96
三、应付及暂收款 Accounts Receivable and Receipts on Account	321.55	105.03	四、买入返售资产 Assets Reverse Repo（Including Securities）	36.00	36.00
其中：应付及预收利息 Of Which：Interest Payable and Received in Advance	235.16	78.12	五、存放中央银行存款 Deposits with the Central Bank	796.27	270.05
四、卖出回购资产 Assets Repo（Including Securities）		- 31.65	六、同业往来 Inter - bank Transactions	491.02	370.86
五、向中央银行借款 Borrowings from the Central Bank	5230.00	- 869.00	七、库存现金 Cash in Vault	1.90	0.18
六、同业往来 Inter - bank Transactions	406.57	347.48			
七、代理境内贷款资金 Agency Domestic Lending Funds	2.41	1.18			
八、各项准备 Total Provisions	490.22	- 69.51			
其中：贷款呆账准备金 Of Which：Provisions for Bad Loans	478.18	- 81.55			
九、所有者权益 Owner's Equity	1523.16	405.18			
其中：实收资本 Of Which：Paid - in Capital	715.80	0.23			
当年结益 Net Earnings	274.06	274.06			
十、其他 Others	421.10	- 3.72			
资金来源总计 Total Sources	**29524.42**	**5048.55**	**资金运用总计 Total Uses**	**29524.42**	**5048.55**

3. 国有商业银行本外币信贷收支表*（2002—2005 年）

Sources and Uses of Credit Funds of State – owned Commercial Banks（Domestic and Foreign Currency Combined）（2002 – 2005）

国有商业银行本外币信贷收支表

Sources and Uses of Credit Funds of State – owned Commercial Banks（Domestic and Foreign Currency Combined）

（2002 年末）

（Year – end of 2002）

汇率：8.2773 单位：亿元

Exchange Rate：8.2773 Unit：100 Million Yuan

项目 Items	余额 Balance	比年初增减额 Changes within the Year	项目 Items	余额 Balance	比年初增减额 Changes within the Year
一、各项存款 Total Deposits	111317.76	14908.88	一、各项贷款 Total Loans	79510.22	9848.43
1. 企事业单位存款 Deposits by Enterprises and Public Institutions	37963.66	3732.00	1. 短期贷款 Short – term Loans	39837.99	3353.71
			2. 中长期贷款 Medium and Long – term Loans	35141.11	5296.94
（1）活期存款 Demand Deposits	27974.64	2491.51			
（2）定期存款 Time Deposits	9989.02	1240.49	3. 其他贷款 Other Loans	1379.31	– 84.01
2. 储蓄存款 Savings Deposits	63062.59	8751.89	4. 票据融资 Paper Financing	2440.69	1320.16
（1）活期储蓄 Demand Deposits	19623.32	3971.15	5. 各项垫款 Total Advances	711.12	– 38.37
（2）定期储蓄 Time Deposits	43439.27	4780.74	二、有价证券及投资 Securities and Investments	27669.96	3204.91
3. 其他存款 Other Deposits	10291.51	2424.99	三、应收及预付款 Accounts Receivable and Advance Payments	2485.56	– 421.79
二、债券发行及境外筹资 Bonds Issue & Overseas Financing	1313.90	– 162.03	其中：应收利息 Of Which：Interest Receivable	1193.04	– 275.34
三、应付及暂收款 Accounts Receivable and Receipts on Account	2136.96	31.97	四、买入返售证券 Reverse Repo	1509.99	1199.34
其中：应付及预收利息 Of Which：Interest Payable and Received in Advance	793.78	– 17.66	五、存放中央银行存款 Deposits with the Central Bank	11463.45	1036.52
			六、同业往来 Inter – bank Transactions	5578.55	471.91
四、卖出回购证券 Repo	607.80	157.79	七、库存现金 Cash in Vault	905.65	60.95
五、向中央银行借款 Borrowings from the Central Bank	1786.15	– 43.38			
六、同业往来 Inter – bank Transactions	6135.69	– 42.76			
七、代理境内贷款资金 Agency Domestic Lending Funds	13.44	1.20			
八、各项准备 Total Provisions	1398.72	481.67			

续表
Continued

项 目 Items	余 额 Balance	比年初增减额 Changes within the Year	项 目 Items	余 额 Balance	比年初增减额 Changes within the Year
其中：贷款呆账准备金 Of Which: Provisions for Bad Loans	797.02	151.34			
九、所有者权益 Owner's Equity	6812.45	428.83			
其中：实收资本 Of Which: Paid - in Capital	5171.98	-67.02			
当年结益 Net Earnings	230.27	230.27			
十、其他 Others	-2399.49	-361.90			
资金来源总计 Total Sources	**129123.38**	**15400.27**	**资金运用总计 Total Uses**	**129123.38**	**15400.27**

* 本表机构包括中国工商银行、中国农业银行、中国银行、中国建设银行。

* The following institutions are included in the statement: Industrial and Commercial Bank of China, Agricultural Bank of China, Bank of China and China Construction Bank.

国有商业银行本外币信贷收支表

Sources and Uses of Credit Funds of State - owned Commercial Banks（Domestic and Foreign Currency Combined）

（2003 年末）

（Year - end of 2003）

汇率：8.2767
Exchange Rate：8.2767

单位：亿元
Unit：100 Million Yuan

项目 Items	余额 Balance	比年初增减额 Changes within the Year	项目 Items	余额 Balance	比年初增减额 Changes within the Year
一、各项存款 Total Deposits	128601.41	17283.40	一、各项贷款 Total Loans	94123.01	14457.20
1. 企事业单位存款 Deposits by Enterprises and Public Institutions	43186.38	5306.50	1. 短期贷款 Short - term Loans	43192.23	3356.20
			2. 中长期贷款 Medium and Long - term Loans	44240.82	8940.09
（1）活期存款 Demand Deposits	31881.56	4088.29			
（2）定期存款 Time Deposits	11304.82	1218.21	3. 其他贷款 Other Loans	1560.36	181.63
2. 储蓄存款 Savings Deposits	72923.26	9777.36	4. 票据融资 Paper Financing	4488.96	2048.21
（1）活期储蓄 Demand Deposits	24336.90	4671.23	5. 各项垫款 Total Advances	640.64	- 68.93
（2）定期储蓄 Time Deposits	48586.36	5106.13	二、有价证券及投资 Securities and Investments	31268.88	3597.41
3. 其他存款 Other Deposits	12491.77	2199.54	三、应收及预付款 Accounts Receivable and Advance Payments	2501.07	20.74
二、债券发行及境外筹资 Bonds Issue & Overseas Financing	1154.88	- 159.29	其中：应收利息 Of Which：Interest Receivable	851.56	- 342.43
三、应付及暂收款 Accounts Receivable and Receipts on Account	2748.16	613.74	四、买入返售证券 Reverse Repo	1143.10	- 81.80
其中：应付及预收利息 Of Which：Interest Payable and Received in Advance	872.29	78.49	五、存放中央银行存款 Deposits with the Central Bank	13081.99	1618.20
四、卖出回购证券 Repo	136.90	117.39	六、同业往来 Inter - bank Transactions	7689.86	2067.46
五、向中央银行借款 Borrowings from the Central Bank	1933.83	147.68	七、库存现金 Cash in Vault	1016.58	110.78
六、同业往来 Inter - bank Transactions	5930.97	- 600.61			
七、代理境内贷款资金 Agency Domestic Lending Funds	11.52	- 1.80			
八、各项准备 Total Provisions	4169.00	2631.64			
其中：贷款呆账准备金 Of Which：Provisions for Bad Loans	3626.06	2463.26			
九、所有者权益 Owner's Equity	8928.89	2255.15			
其中：实收资本 Of Which：Paid - in Capital	6625.20	1453.22			
当年结益 Net Earnings	- 31.58	- 31.58			
十、其他 Others	- 2791.07	- 497.31			
资金来源总计 Total Sources	**150824.49**	**21789.99**	**资金运用总计 Total Uses**	**150824.49**	**21789.99**

国有商业银行本外币信贷收支表

Sources and Uses of Credit Funds of State – owned Commercial Banks（Domestic and Foreign Currency Combined）

（2004 年末）

（Year – end of 2004）

汇率：8.2765　　　　单位：亿元

Exchange Rate：8.2765　　　　Unit：100 Million Yuan

项目 Items	余额 Balance	比年初增减额 Changes within the Year	项目 Items	余额 Balance	比年初增减额 Changes within the Year
一、各项存款 Total Deposits	144417.48	16114.25	一、各项贷款 Total Loans	101182.99	10675.82
1. 企事业单位存款 Deposits by Enterprises and Public Institutions	50033.47	6073.73	1. 短期贷款 Short – term Loans	40605.94	351.01
			2. 中长期贷款 Medium and Long – term Loans	51294.55	7535.81
（1）活期存款 Demand Deposits	36366.70	3711.95			
（2）定期存款 Time Deposits	13666.77	2361.78	3. 其他贷款 Other Loans	1585.55	128.32
2. 储蓄存款 Savings Deposits	81171.76	8246.93	4. 票据融资 Paper Financing	7401.36	2714.42
（1）活期储蓄 Demand Deposits	28039.10	3701.26	5. 各项垫款 Total Advances	295.59	– 53.74
（2）定期储蓄 Time Deposits	53132.66	4545.67	二、有价证券及投资 Securities and Investments	40312.18	9040.30
3. 其他存款 Other Deposits	13212.25	1793.59	三、应收及预付款 Accounts Receivable and Advance Payments	3247.08	738.74
二、债券发行及境外筹资 Bonds Issue & Overseas Financing	1834.89	676.48			
			其中：应收利息 Of Which：Interest Receivable	953.14	– 188.20
三、应付及暂收款 Accounts Receivable and Receipts on Account	2832.47	66.24			
			四、买入返售资产 Assets Reverse Repo（Including Securities）	1220.77	– 47.30
其中：应付及预收利息 Of Which：Interest Payable and Received in Advance	911.34	39.05			
			五、存放中央银行存款 Deposits with the Central Bank	14853.05	1771.03
四、卖出回购资产 Assets Repo（Including Securities）	227.03	11.99	六、同业往来 Inter – bank Transactions	3834.63	– 3856.03
五、向中央银行借款 Borrowings from the Central Bank	1910.81	– 266.51	七、库存现金 Cash in Vault	1094.09	77.17
六、同业往来 Inter – bank Transactions	5024.93	– 847.70			
七、代理境内贷款资金 Agency Domestic Lending Funds	20.01	8.48			
八、各项准备 Total Provisions	2507.31	– 1661.87			
其中：贷款呆账准备金 Of Which：Provisions for Bad Loans	1737.61	– 1727.93			
九、所有者权益 Owner's Equity	7174.32	996.88			
其中：实收资本 Of Which：Paid – in Capital	6682.49	57.29			
当年结益 Net Earnings	731.57	731.57			
十、其他 Others	– 204.46	3301.49			
资金来源总计 Total Sources	**165744.79**	**18399.73**	**资金运用总计 Total Uses**	**165744.79**	**18399.73**

国有商业银行本外币信贷收支表

Sources and Uses of Credit Funds of State - owned Commercial Banks（Domestic and Foreign Currency Combined）

（2005 年末）

（Year - end of 2005）

汇率：8.0702　　　　单位：亿元

Exchange Rate：8.0702　　　　Unit：100 Million Yuan

项目 Items	余额 Balance	比年初增减额 Changes within the Year	项目 Items	余额 Balance	比年初增减额 Changes within the Year
一、各项存款 Total Deposits	166579.26	20390.78	一、各项贷款 Total Loans	102257.06	7393.78
1. 企事业单位存款 Deposits by Enterprises and Public Institutions	54801.24	4608.26	1. 短期贷款 Short - term Loans	35028.65	- 439.75
(1) 活期存款 Demand Deposits	36873.33	387.32	2. 中长期贷款 Medium and Long - term Loans	55954.56	5718.43
(2) 定期存款 Time Deposits	17927.91	4220.94	3. 其他贷款 Other Loans	1496.39	- 79.10
2. 储蓄存款 Savings Deposits	91849.89	10677.92	4. 票据融资 Paper Financing	9580.01	2179.77
(1) 活期储蓄 Demand Deposits	32024.58	3985.38	5. 各项垫款 Total Advances	197.45	14.43
(2) 定期储蓄 Time Deposits	59825.31	6692.54	二、有价证券及投资 Securities and Investments	58891.42	18659.76
3. 其他存款 Other Deposits	19928.13	5104.60	三、应收及预付款 Accounts Receivable and Advance Payments	6049.22	3550.44
二、债券发行及境外筹资 Bonds Issue & Overseas Financing	2016.12	210.94	其中：应收利息 Of Which：Interest Receivable	813.24	- 193.71
三、应付及暂收款 Accounts Receivable and Receipts on Account	5235.11	2403.39	四、买入返售资产 Assets Reverse Repo（Including Securities）	3645.98	2420.96
其中：应付及预收利息 Of Which：Interest Payable and Received in Advance	1295.97	389.39	五、存放中央银行存款 Deposits with the Central Bank	16146.01	1309.06
四、卖出回购资产 Assets Repo（Including Securities）	2020.02	1792.99	六、同业往来 Inter - bank Transactions	4553.46	730.85
五、向中央银行借款 Borrowings from the Central Bank	1516.07	- 394.32	七、库存现金 Cash in Vault	1134.53	24.22
六、同业往来 Inter - bank Transactions	6212.18	1407.21			
七、代理境内贷款资金 Agency Domestic Lending Funds	0.21	- 2.47			
八、各项准备 Total Provisions	2876.04	454.81			
其中：贷款呆账准备金 Of Which：Provisions for Bad Loans	2475.53	737.73			
九、所有者权益 Owner's Equity	8851.12	2459.72			
其中：实收资本 Of Which：Paid - in Capital	8043.94	1361.36			
当年结益 Net Earnings	1404.10	1404.10			
十、其他 Others	- 2628.45	5366.02			
资金来源总计 Total Sources	**192677.68**	**34089.07**	**资金运用总计 Total Uses**	**192677.68**	**34089.07**

4. 其他商业银行本外币信贷收支表*（2002—2005 年）

Sources and Uses of Credit Funds of Other Commercial Banks (Domestic and Foreign Currency Combined) (2002 - 2005)

其他商业银行本外币信贷收支表

Sources and Uses of Credit Funds of Other Commercial Banks (Domestic and Foreign Currency Combined)

（2002 年末）

(Year - end of 2002)

汇率：8.2773　　　　单位：亿元

Exchange Rate: 8.2773　　　　Unit: 100 Million Yuan

项目 Items	余额 Balance	比年初增减额 Changes within the Year	项目 Items	余额 Balance	比年初增减额 Changes within the Year
一、各项存款 Total Deposits	24868.04	6389.00	一、各项贷款 Total Loans	17024.78	4762.54
1. 企事业单位存款 Deposits by Enterprises and Public Institutions	15479.38	3475.33	1. 短期贷款 Short - term Loans	10791.58	2292.70
			2. 中长期贷款 Medium and Long - term Loans	3788.86	1444.27
（1）活期存款 Demand Deposits	10021.17	2365.20			
（2）定期存款 Time Deposits	5458.21	1110.13	3. 其他贷款 Other Loans	179.74	65.62
2. 储蓄存款 Savings Deposits	5232.74	1335.84	4. 票据融资 Paper Financing	2176.12	953.65
（1）活期储蓄 Demand Deposits	2119.15	637.08	5. 各项垫款 Total Advances	88.48	6.30
（2）定期储蓄 Time Deposits	3113.59	698.76	二、有价证券及投资 Securities and Investments	4759.86	1143.67
3. 其他存款 Other Deposits	4155.92	1577.83	三、应收及预付款 Accounts Receivable and Advance Payments	619.55	47.93
二、债券发行及境外筹资 Bonds Issue & Overseas Financing	19.55	-18.05			
			其中：应收利息 Of Which: Interest Receivable	108.23	-107.16
三、应付及暂收款 Accounts Receivable and Receipts on Account	643.09	203.87			
			四、买入返售证券 Reverse Repo	727.28	117.28
其中：应付及预收利息 Of Which: Interest Payable and Received in Advance	158.68	15.93	五、存放中央银行存款 Deposits with the Central Bank	3711.62	309.56
四、卖出回购证券 Repo	262.32	-0.67	六、同业往来 Inter - bank Transactions	1757.14	224.34
五、向中央银行借款 Borrowings from the Central Bank	34.58	-38.68	七、库存现金 Cash in Vault	167.84	26.58
六、同业往来 Inter - bank Transactions	1889.07	16.74			
七、代理境内贷款资金 Agency Domestic Lending Funds	19.66	4.27			
八、各项准备 Total Provisions	442.64	135.91			

续表
Continued

项　目 Items	余　额 Balance	比年初增减额 Changes within the Year	项　目 Items	余　额 Balance	比年初增减额 Changes within the Year
其中：贷款呆账准备金 Of Which：Provisions for Bad Loans	414.29	121.39			
九、所有者权益 Owner's Equity	1188.69	47.16			
其中：实收资本 Of Which：Paid - in Capital	548.31	37.59			
当年结益 Net Earnings	133.57	133.57			
十、其他 Others	- 599.57	- 107.65			
资金来源总计 Total Sources	**28768.07**	**6631.90**	**资金运用总计 Total Uses**	**28768.07**	**6631.90**

* 本表机构包括中国光大银行、华夏银行、广东发展银行、深圳发展银行、招商银行、上海浦东发展银行、福建兴业银行（2003 年更名为兴业银行）、恒丰银行（2004 年）、中国民生银行、交通银行、中信实业银行（2005 年更名为中信银行）、浙商银行（2004 年）。

* The following institutions are included in the statement：China Everbright Bank，Huaxia Bank，Guangdong Development Bank，Shenzhen Development Bank，China Merchants Bank，Shanghai Pudong Development Bank，Fujian Industrial Bank（Renamed as Industrial Bank in 2003），Evergrowing Bank（2004），China Minshang Bank，Bank of Communications，CITIC Industrial Bank（Renamed as China CITIC Bank in 2005），and China Zheshang Bank（2004）.

其他商业银行本外币信贷收支表

Sources and Uses of Credit Funds of Other Commercial Banks（Domestic and Foreign Currency Combined）

（2003 年末）

（Year – end of 2003）

汇率：8.2767　　　　单位：亿元

Exchange Rate：8.2767　　　　Unit：100 Million Yuan

项　目 Items	余　额 Balance	比年初增减额 Changes within the Year	项　目 Items	余　额 Balance	比年初增减额 Changes within the Year
一、各项存款 Total Deposits	32865.46	7994.41	一、各项贷款 Total Loans	23682.53	6719.70
1. 企事业单位存款 Deposits by Enterprises and Public Institutions	19646.88	4164.76	1. 短期贷款 Short – term Loans	14535.95	3805.64
			2. 中长期贷款 Medium and Long – term Loans	6330.39	2542.21
（1）活期存款 Demand Deposits	12421.61	2397.41			
（2）定期存款 Time Deposits	7225.27	1767.35	3. 其他贷款 Other Loans	285.23	105.49
2. 储蓄存款 Savings Deposits	6719.55	1486.86	4. 票据融资 Paper Financing	2453.62	277.50
（1）活期储蓄 Demand Deposits	2818.58	699.55	5. 各项垫款 Total Advances	77.34	– 11.14
（2）定期储蓄 Time Deposits	3900.97	787.31	二、有价证券及投资 Securities and Investments	5827.14	1073.87
3. 其他存款 Other Deposits	6499.03	2342.79	三、应收及预付款 Accounts Receivable and Advance Payments	550.78	– 68.76
二、债券发行及境外筹资 Bonds Issue & Overseas Financing	62.11	49.16			
			其中：应收利息 Of Which：Interest Receivable	70.20	– 38.09
三、应付及暂收款 Accounts Receivable and Receipts on Account	607.52	– 32.21			
			四、买入返售证券 Reverse Repo	447.49	– 301.47
其中：应付及预收利息 Of Which：Interest Payable and Received in Advance	176.08	17.31			
			五、存放中央银行存款 Deposits with the Central Bank	4628.42	916.80
四、卖出回购证券 Repo	299.75	73.37	六、同业往来 Inter – bank Transactions	1523.92	– 238.57
五、向中央银行借款 Borrowings from the Central Bank	26.02	– 8.56	七、库存现金 Cash in Vault	190.91	23.05
六、同业往来 Inter – bank Transactions	1946.11	59.16			
七、代理境内贷款资金 Agency Domestic Lending Funds	17.52	– 2.14			
八、各项准备 Total Provisions	561.33	118.71			
其中：贷款呆账准备金 Of Which：Provisions for Bad Loans	526.59	111.73			
九、所有者权益 Owner's Equity	1417.36	225.39			
其中：实收资本 Of Which：Paid – in Capital	656.77	108.46			
当年结益 Net Earnings	146.17	146.17			
十、其他 Others	– 951.99	– 352.67			
资金来源总计 Total Sources	**36851.19**	**8124.62**	**资金运用总计 Total Uses**	**36851.19**	**8124.62**

其他商业银行本外币信贷收支表

Sources and Uses of Credit Funds of Other Commercial Banks（Domestic and Foreign Currency Combined）

（2004 年末）

（Year - end of 2004）

汇率：8.2765　　单位：亿元

Exchange Rate：8.2765　　Unit：100 Million Yuan

项目 Items	余额 Balance	比年初增减额 Changes within the Year	项目 Items	余额 Balance	比年初增减额 Changes within the Year
一、各项存款 Total Deposits	40598.84	7791.63	一、各项贷款 Total Loans	28859.41	4798.40
1. 企事业单位存款 Deposits by Enterprises and Public Institutions	23017.62	3603.11	1. 短期贷款 Short - term Loans	16748.51	2675.00
			2. 中长期贷款 Medium and Long - term Loans	9054.37	2728.35
（1）活期存款 Demand Deposits	14561.79	2159.10			
（2）定期存款 Time Deposits	8455.83	1444.01	3. 其他贷款 Other Loans	316.73	46.20
2. 储蓄存款 Savings Deposits	8419.52	1696.58	4. 票据融资 Paper Financing	2667.78	- 668.52
（1）活期储蓄 Demand Deposits	3568.39	746.57	5. 各项垫款 Total Advances	72.02	17.37
（2）定期储蓄 Time Deposits	4851.13	950.01	二、有价证券及投资 Securities and Investments	8093.79	2266.65
3. 其他存款 Other Deposits	9161.70	2491.94	三、应收及预付款 Accounts Receivable and Advance Payments	565.83	0.70
二、债券发行及境外筹资 Bonds Issue & Overseas Financing	456.65	394.54			
			其中：应收利息 Of Which：Interest Receivable	116.48	19.68
三、应付及暂收款 Accounts Receivable and Receipts on Account	776.79	159.64			
			四、买入返售资产 Assets Reverse Repo（Including Securities）	740.53	- 12.84
其中：应付及预收利息 Of Which：Interest Payable and Received in Advace	236.11	60.03			
			五、存放中央银行存款 Deposits with the Central Bank	5614.21	985.79
四、卖出回购资产 Assets Repo（Including Securities）	312.38	- 493.51	六、同业往来 Inter - bank Transactions	1292.99	- 185.60
五、向中央银行借款 Borrowings from the Central Bank	15.18	- 319.55	七、库存现金 Cash in Vault	223.02	32.06
六、同业往来 Inter - bank Transactions	1661.27	- 273.24			
七、代理境内贷款资金 Agency Domestic Lending Funds	13.54	- 3.98			
八、各项准备 Total Provisions	735.84	175.18			
其中：贷款呆账准备金 Of Which：Provisions for Bad Loans	693.05	167.16			
九、所有者权益 Owner's Equity	1606.00	232.78			
其中：实收资本 Of Which：Paid - in Capital	972.97	316.21			
当年结益 Net Earnings	- 96.69	- 96.69			
十、其他 Others	- 786.71	221.67			
资金来源总计 Total Sources	**45389.78**	**7885.16**	**资金运用总计 Total Uses**	**45389.78**	**7885.16**

其他商业银行本外币信贷收支表

Sources and Uses of Credit Funds of Other Commercial Banks (Domestic and Foreign Currency Combined)

(2005年末)

(Year-end of 2005)

汇率：8.0702 单位：亿元

Exchange Rate: 8.0702 Unit: 100 Million Yuan

项目 Items	余额 Balance	比年初增减额 Changes within the Year	项目 Items	余额 Balance	比年初增减额 Changes within the Year
一、各项存款 Total Deposits	49201.16	8594.72	一、各项贷款 Total Loans	34845.29	5983.51
1. 企事业单位存款 Deposits by Enterprises and Public Institutions	26787.63	3786.28	1. 短期贷款 Short-term Loans	18527.85	1763.91
(1) 活期存款 Demand Deposits	16066.76	1513.26	2. 中长期贷款 Medium and Long-term Loans	11303.51	2265.66
(2) 定期存款 Time Deposits	10720.87	2273.02	3. 其他贷款 Other Loans	372.79	55.64
2. 储蓄存款 Savings Deposits	10948.80	2528.44	4. 票据融资 Paper Financing	4550.80	1883.69
(1) 活期储蓄 Demand Deposits	4300.27	731.74	5. 各项垫款 Total Advances	90.34	14.61
(2) 定期储蓄 Time Deposits	6648.53	1796.70	二、有价证券及投资 Securities and Investments	10369.38	2234.44
3. 其他存款 Other Deposits	11464.73	2280.00	三、应收及预付款 Accounts Receivable and Advance Payments	803.84	237.12
二、债券发行及境外筹资 Bonds Issue & Overseas Financing	761.92	221.78	其中：应收利息 Of Which: Interest Receivable	118.07	1.61
三、应付及暂收款 Accounts Receivable and Receipts on Account	1230.48	452.34	四、买入返售资产 Assets Reverse Repo (Including Securities)	2488.66	1748.13
其中：应付及预收利息 Of Which: Interest Payable and Received in Advance	307.04	70.93	五、存放中央银行存款 Deposits with the Central Bank	5642.41	28.20
四、卖出回购资产 Assets Repo (Including Securities)	299.89	-12.49	六、同业往来 Inter-bank Transactions	2124.40	830.12
五、向中央银行借款 Borrowings from the Central Bank	12.40	-2.78	七、库存现金 Cash in Vault	243.41	20.31
六、同业往来 Inter-bank Transactions	2603.00	943.64			
七、代理境内贷款资金 Agency Domestic Lending Funds	12.75	-0.79			
八、各项准备 Total Provisions	944.11	208.27			
其中：贷款呆账准备金 Of Which: Provisions for Bad Loans	874.38	182.40			
九、所有者权益 Owner's Equity	2080.91	479.86			
其中：实收资本 Of Which: Paid-in Capital	1177.29	209.75			
当年结益 Net Earnings	445.55	445.55			
十、其他 Others	-629.23	197.28			
资金来源总计 Total Sources	**56517.39**	**11081.83**	**资金运用总计 Total Uses**	**56517.39**	**11081.83**

5. 城市商业银行本外币信贷收支表（2002—2005年）

Sources and Uses of Credit Funds of City Commercial Banks（Domestic and Foreign Currency Combined）（2002-2005）

城市商业银行本外币信贷收支表

Sources and Uses of Credit Funds of City Commercial Banks（Domestic and Foreign Currency Combined）

（2002年末）

（Year-end of 2002）

汇率：8.2773　　　　单位：亿元

Exchange Rate：8.2773　　　　Unit：100 Million Yuan

项目 Items	余额 Balance	比年初增减额 Changes within the Year	项目 Items	余额 Balance	比年初增减额 Changes within the Year
一、各项存款 Total Deposits	8983.03	2159.79	一、各项贷款 Total Loans	5924.93	1481.00
1. 企事业单位存款 Deposits by Enterprises and Public Institutions	5918.18	1328.97	1. 短期贷款 Short-term Loans	3554.32	555.47
（1）活期存款 Demand Deposits	4602.81	957.13	2. 中长期贷款 Medium and Long-term Loans	1567.28	470.83
（2）定期存款 Time Deposits	1315.37	371.84	3. 其他贷款 Other Loans	6.03	2.49
2. 储蓄存款 Savings Deposits	2471.22	572.20	4. 票据融资 Paper Financing	783.99	443.38
（1）活期储蓄 Demand Deposits	980.65	234.85	5. 各项垫款 Total Advances	13.31	8.83
（2）定期储蓄 Time Deposits	1490.57	337.35	二、有价证券及投资 Securities and Investments	2382.76	874.82
3. 其他存款 Other Deposits	593.63	258.62	三、应收及预付款 Accounts Receivable and Advance Payments	237.43	21.05
二、债券发行及境外筹资 Bonds Issue & Overseas Financing			其中：应收利息 Of Which：Interest Receivable	75.87	-16.11
三、应付及暂收款 Accounts Receivable and Receipts on Account	141.16	13.46	四、买入返售证券 Reverse Repo	520.05	251.99
其中：应付及预收利息 Of Which：Interest Payable and Received in Advance	41.84	2.35	五、存放中央银行存款 Deposits with the Central Bank	995.47	162.35
四、卖出回购证券 Repo	1111.11	659.25	六、同业往来 Inter-bank Transactions	637.40	85.67
五、向中央银行借款 Borrowings from the Central Bank	165.73	-20.34	七、库存现金 Cash in Vault	73.71	15.97
六、同业往来 Inter-bank Transactions	517.18	72.86			
七、代理境内贷款资金 Agency Domestic Lending Funds	4.39	-0.29			
八、各项准备 Total Provisions	66.47	30.75			

续表
Continued

项　目 Items	余　额 Balance	比年初增减额 Changes within the Year	项　目 Items	余　额 Balance	比年初增减额 Changes within the Year
其中：贷款呆账准备金 Of Which：Provisions for Bad Loans	66.21	30.88			
九、所有者权益 Owner's Equity	429.67	88.09			
其中：实收资本 Of Which：Paid - in Capital	367.58	39.63			
当年结益 Net Earnings	37.96	37.96			
十、其他 Others	-646.99	-110.72			
资金来源总计 Total Sources	**10771.75**	**2892.85**	**资金运用总计 Total Uses**	**10771.75**	**2892.85**

城市商业银行本外币信贷收支表

Sources and Uses of Credit Funds of City Commercial Banks（Domestic and Foreign Currency Combined）

（2003年末）

（Year - end of 2003）

汇率：8.2767　　　　单位：亿元

Exchange Rate：8.2767　　　　Unit：100 Million Yuan

项目 Items	余额 Balance	比年初增减额 Changes within the Year	项目 Items	余额 Balance	比年初增减额 Changes within the Year
一、各项存款 Total Deposits	11725.13	2742.01	一、各项贷款 Total Loans	7726.55	1800.12
1.企事业单位存款 Deposits by Enterprises and Public Institutions	7516.84	1600.18	1.短期贷款 Short - term Loans	4341.96	801.43
(1) 活期存款 Demand Deposits	5740.03	1138.74	2.中长期贷款 Medium and Long - term Loans	2533.05	966.09
(2) 定期存款 Time Deposits	1776.81	461.44	3.其他贷款 Other Loans	17.26	11.23
2.储蓄存款 Savings Deposits	3139.28	667.99	4.票据融资 Paper Financing	824.72	25.12
(1) 活期储蓄 Demand Deposits	1257.16	276.51	5.各项垫款 Total Advances	9.56	- 3.75
(2) 定期储蓄 Time Deposits	1882.12	391.48	二、有价证券及投资 Securities and Investments	2998.00	615.02
3.其他存款 Other Deposits	1069.01	473.84	三、应收及预付款 Accounts Receivable and Advance Payments	214.00	- 23.28
二、债券发行及境外筹资 Bonds Issue & Overseas Financing			其中：应收利息 Of Which：Interest Receivable	51.84	- 23.99
三、应付及暂收款 Accounts Receivable and Receipts on Account	180.20	38.86			
其中：应付及预收利息 Of Which：Interest Payable and Received in Advance	41.97	0.13	四、买入返售证券 Reverse Repo	345.42	- 172.93
			五、存放中央银行存款 Deposits with the Central Bank	1429.65	434.19
四、卖出回购证券 Repo	968.46	- 142.06	六、同业往来 Inter - bank Transactions	840.58	197.75
五、向中央银行借款 Borrowings from the Central Bank	177.75	12.02	七、库存现金 Cash in Vault	89.43	15.71
六、同业往来 Inter - bank Transactions	684.50	167.38			
七、代理境内贷款资金 Agency Domestic Lending Funds	5.04	0.65			
八、各项准备 Total Provisions	99.60	33.18			
其中：贷款呆账准备金 Of Which：Provisions for Bad Loans	97.19	32.36			
九、所有者权益 Owner's Equity	508.21	77.24			
其中：实收资本 Of Which：Paid - in Capital	418.63	51.05			
当年结益 Net Earnings	54.22	54.22			
十、其他 Others	- 705.26	- 62.70			
资金来源总计 Total Sources	**13643.63**	**2866.58**	**资金运用总计 Total Uses**	**13643.63**	**2866.58**

城市商业银行本外币信贷收支表

Sources and Uses of Credit Funds of City Commercial Banks (Domestic and Foreign Currency Combined)

(2004年末)

(Year - end of 2004)

汇率：8.2765

Exchange Rate: 8.2765

单位：亿元

Unit: 100 Million Yuan

项目 Items	余额 Balance	比年初增减额 Changes Within the Year	项目 Items	余额 Balance	比年初增减额 Changes within the Year
一、各项存款 Total Deposits	14145.58	2503.51	一、各项贷款 Total Loans	9030.98	1405.29
1. 企事业单位存款 Deposits by Enterprises and Public Institutions	8693.80	1179.68	1. 短期贷款 Short - term Loans	4702.01	386.92
(1) 活期存款 Demand Deposits	6481.70	744.39	2. 中长期贷款 Medium and Long - term Loans	3423.53	878.72
(2) 定期存款 Time Deposits	2212.10	435.29	3. 其他贷款 Other Loans	22.52	5.26
2. 储蓄存款 Savings Deposits	3864.30	723.52	4. 票据融资 Paper Financing	868.25	129.28
(1) 活期储蓄 Demand Deposits	1484.11	225.46	5. 各项垫款 Total Advances	14.67	5.11
(2) 定期储蓄 Time Deposits	2380.19	498.06	二、有价证券及投资 Securities and Investments	3579.63	581.63
3. 其他存款 Other Deposits	1587.48	600.31	三、应收及预付款 Accounts Receivable and Advance Payments	181.06	- 19.33
二、债券发行及境外筹资 Bonds Issue & Overseas Financing	30.00	30.00	其中：应收利息 Of Which: Interest Receivable	39.81	- 13.88
三、应付及暂收款 Accounts Receivable and Receipts on Account	178.54	- 2.46	四、买入返售资产 Assets Reverse Repo (Including Securities)	436.01	- 150.58
其中：应付及预收利息 Of Which: Interest Payable and Received in Advance	53.05	11.01	五、存放中央银行存款 Deposits with the Central Bank	1990.21	560.56
四、卖出回购资产 Assets Repo (Including Securities)	1075.60	12.83	六、同业往来 Inter - bank Transactions	701.20	- 139.32
五、向中央银行借款 Borrowings from the Central Bank	119.30	- 88.78	七、库存现金 Cash in Vault	98.54	9.12
六、同业往来 Inter - bank Transactions	442.41	- 220.14			
七、代理境内贷款资金 Agency Domestic Lending Funds	7.38	2.34			
八、各项准备 Total Provisions	167.02	67.42			
其中：贷款呆账准备金 Of Which: Provisions for Bad Loans	164.68	67.50			
九、所有者权益 Owner's Equity	583.61	85.50			
其中：实收资本 Of Which: Paid - in Capital	471.87	53.24			
当年结益 Net Earnings	87.41	87.41			
十、其他 Others	- 731.81	- 142.85			
资金来源总计 Total Sources	**16017.63**	**2247.37**	**资金运用总计 Total Uses**	**16017.63**	**2247.37**

城市商业银行本外币信贷收支表

Sources and Uses of Credit Funds of City Commercial Banks（Domestic and Foreign Currency Combined）

（2005年末）

（Year - end of 2005）

汇率：8.0702 单位：亿元

Exchange Rate：8.0702 Unit：100 Million Yuan

项目 Items	余额 Balance	比年初增减额 Changes within the Year	项目 Items	余额 Balance	比年初增减额 Changes within the Year
一、各项存款 Total Deposits	17198.23	3012.06	一、各项贷款 Total Loans	10887.63	1830.50
1. 企事业单位存款 Deposits by Enterprises and Public Institutions	10011.63	1319.18	1. 短期贷款 Short - term Loans	5360.47	640.34
			2. 中长期贷款 Medium and Long - term Loans	4111.22	679.96
（1）活期存款 Demand Deposits	7291.38	817.77			
（2）定期存款 Time Deposits	2720.25	501.41	3. 其他贷款 Other Loans	19.75	- 2.77
2. 储蓄存款 Savings Deposits	4955.58	1082.97	4. 票据融资 Paper Financing	1375.52	506.97
（1）活期储蓄 Demand Deposits	1799.34	313.05	5. 各项垫款 Total Advances	20.67	6.00
（2）定期储蓄 Time Deposits	3156.24	769.92	二、有价证券及投资 Securities and Investments	4178.27	595.70
3. 其他存款 Other Deposits	2231.02	609.91	三、应收及预付款 Accounts Receivable and Advance Payments	169.01	- 12.14
二、债券发行及境外筹资 Bonds Issue & Overseas Financing	73.00	43.00			
			其中：应收利息 Of Which：Interest Receivable	29.32	- 10.42
三、应付及暂收款 Accounts Receivable and Receipts on Account	275.94	95.68			
			四、买入返售资产 Assets Reverse Repo（Including Securities）	704.26	266.49
其中：应付及预收利息 Of Which：Interest Payable and Received in Advance	74.12	20.86			
			五、存放中央银行存款 Deposits with the Central Bank	2098.06	96.52
四、卖出回购资产 Assets Repo（Including Securities）	807.14	- 268.46	六、同业往来 Inter - bank Transactions	1063.65	352.83
五、向中央银行借款 Borrowings from the Central Bank	65.36	- 54.54	七、库存现金 Cash in Vault	112.10	13.23
六、同业往来 Inter - bank Transactions	581.86	138.91			
七、代理境内贷款资金 Agency Domestic Lending Funds	7.97	0.59			
八、各项准备 Total Provisions	209.11	41.56			
其中：贷款呆账准备金 Of Which：Provisions for Bad Loans	199.45	34.40			
九、所有者权益 Owner's Equity	826.70	250.94			
其中：实收资本 Of Which：Paid - in Capital	596.89	125.38			
当年结益 Net Earnings	120.73	120.73			
十、其他 Others	- 832.33	- 116.61			
资金来源总计 Total Sources	**19212.98**	**3143.13**	**资金运用总计 Total Uses**	**19212.98**	**3143.13**

6. 农村商业银行本外币信贷收支表（2002—2005 年）

Sources and Uses of Credit Funds of Rural Commercial Banks（Domestic and Foreign Currency Combined）（2002 – 2005）

农村商业银行本外币信贷收支表

Sources and Uses of Credit Funds of Rural Commercial Banks（Domestic and Foreign Currency Combined）

（2002 年末）

（Year – end of 2002）

汇率：8.2773
Exchange Rate：8.2773

单位：亿元
Unit：100 Million Yuan

项 目 Items	余 额 Balance	比年初增减额 Changes within the Year	项 目 Items	余 额 Balance	比年初增减额 Changes within the Year
一、各项存款 Total Deposits	257.44	60.48	一、各项贷款 Total Loans	145.45	45.30
1. 企事业单位存款 Deposits by Enterprises and Public Institutions	31.06	11.84	1. 短期贷款 Short – term Loans	118.93	31.12
（1）活期存款 Demand Deposits	0.36	0.34	2. 中长期贷款 Medium and Long – term Loans	6.08	5.01
（2）定期存款 Time Deposits	30.70	11.50	3. 其他贷款 Other Loans	0.42	0.40
2. 储蓄存款 Savings Deposits	143.11	23.45	4. 票据融资 Paper Financing	20.02	8.77
（1）活期储蓄 Demand Deposits	34.38	11.14	5. 各项垫款 Total Advances		
（2）定期储蓄 Time Deposits	108.73	12.31	二、有价证券及投资 Securities and Investments	87.38	20.44
3. 其他存款 Other Deposits	83.27	25.19	三、应收及预付款 Accounts Receivable and Advance Payments	1.25	0.46
二、债券发行及境外筹资 Bonds Issue & Overseas Financing			其中：应收利息 Of Which：Interest Receivable	0.01	
三、应付及暂收款 Accounts Receivable and Receipts on Account	5.37	– 1.65	四、买入返售证券 Reverse Repo		
其中：应付及预收利息 Of Which：Interest Payable and Received in Advance	3.80	0.01	五、存放中央银行存款 Deposits with the Central Bank	26.38	1.85
四、卖出回购证券 Repo			六、同业往来 Inter – bank Transactions	35.99	13.49
五、向中央银行借款 Borrowings from the Central Bank			七、库存现金 Cash in Vault	1.97	0.11
六、同业往来 Inter – bank Transactions	30.99	13.76			
七、代理境内贷款资金 Agency Domestic Lending Funds	0.01	– 0.13			
八、各项准备 Total Provisions	3.92	– 0.02			

续表
Continued

项　目 Items	余　额 Balance	比年初增减额 Changes within the Year	项　目 Items	余　额 Balance	比年初增减额 Changes within the Year
其中：贷款呆账准备金 Of Which：Provisions for Bad Loans	3.92	－0.02			
九、所有者权益 Owner's Equity	6.58	1.54			
其中：实收资本 Of Which：Paid－in Capital	3.58	0.85			
当年结益 Net Earnings	0.60	0.60			
十、其他 Others	－5.89	7.67			
资金来源总计 Total Sources	**298.42**	**81.65**	**资金运用总计 Total Uses**	**298.42**	**81.65**

农村商业银行本外币信贷收支表

Sources and Uses of Credit Funds of Rural Commercial Banks (Domestic and Foreign Currency Combined)

(2003年末)

(Year - end of 2003)

汇率：8.2767　　　　单位：亿元

Exchange Rate：8.2767　　　　Unit：100 Million Yuan

项目 Items	余额 Balance	比年初增减额 Changes within the Year	项目 Items	余额 Balance	比年初增减额 Changes within the Year
一、各项存款 Total Deposits	346.90	89.46	一、各项贷款 Total Loans	206.72	61.27
1. 企事业单位存款 Deposits by Enterprises and Public Institutions	52.19	21.13	1. 短期贷款 Short - term Loans	180.58	61.65
			2. 中长期贷款 Medium and Long - term Loans	15.82	9.74
(1) 活期存款 Demand Deposits	1.17	0.81			
(2) 定期存款 Time Deposits	51.02	20.32	3. 其他贷款 Other Loans	1.02	0.60
2. 储蓄存款 Savings Deposits	175.15	32.04	4. 票据融资 Paper Financing	9.30	- 10.72
(1) 活期储蓄 Demand Deposits	48.11	13.73	5. 各项垫款 Total Advances		
(2) 定期储蓄 Time Deposits	127.04	18.31	二、有价证券及投资 Securities and Investments	97.53	10.15
3. 其他存款 Other Deposits	119.56	36.29	三、应收及预付款 Accounts Receivable and Advance Payments	2.43	1.18
二、债券发行及境外筹资 Bonds Issue & Overseas Financing			其中：应收利息 Of Which: Interest Receivable	0.01	
三、应付及暂收款 Accounts Receivable and Receipts on Account	8.44	2.66	四、买入返售证券 Reverse Repo		
其中：应付及预收利息 Of Which: Interest Payable and Received in Advance	4.66	0.86	五、存放中央银行存款 Deposits with the Central Bank	39.30	12.92
			六、同业往来 Inter - bank Transactions	34.00	- 1.99
四、卖出回购证券 Repo			七、库存现金 Cash in Vault	2.85	0.88
五、向中央银行借款 Borrowings from the Central Bank					
六、同业往来 Inter - bank Transactions	13.51	- 17.48			
七、代理境内贷款资金 Agency Domestic Lending Funds	0.01				
八、各项准备 Total Provisions	8.33	4.41			
其中：贷款呆账准备金 Of Which: Provisions for Bad Loans	8.33	4.42			
九、所有者权益 Owner's Equity	4.65	- 1.48			
其中：实收资本 Of Which: Paid - in Capital	3.54				
当年结益 Net Earnings	0.86	0.86			
十、其他 Others	0.99	6.84			
资金来源总计 Total Sources	**382.83**	**84.41**	**资金运用总计 Total Uses**	**382.83**	**84.41**

农村商业银行本外币信贷收支表
Sources and Uses of Credit Funds of Rural Commercial Banks（Domestic and Foreign Currency Combined）

（2004 年末）

（Year – end of 2004）

汇率：8.2765　　单位：亿元

Exchange Rate：8.2765　　Unit：100 Million Yuan

项目 Items	余额 Balance	比年初增减额 Changes within the Year	项目 Items	余额 Balance	比年初增减额 Changes within the Year
一、各项存款 Total Deposits	500.80	153.90	一、各项贷款 Total Loans	309.70	103.67
1. 企事业单位存款 Deposits by Enterprises and Public Institutions	72.46	20.27	1. 短期贷款 Short – term Loans	265.98	88.58
			2. 中长期贷款 Medium and Long – term Loans	28.70	13.12
（1）活期存款 Demand Deposits	1.64	0.47			
（2）定期存款 Time Deposits	70.82	19.80	3. 其他贷款 Other Loans	0.92	– 0.10
2. 储蓄存款 Savings Deposits	256.03	80.88	4. 票据融资 Paper Financing	14.10	2.07
（1）活期储蓄 Demand Deposits	78.79	30.68	5. 各项垫款 Total Advances		
（2）定期储蓄 Time Deposits	177.24	50.20	二、有价证券及投资 Securities and Investments	110.76	13.23
3. 其他存款 Other Deposits	172.31	52.75	三、应收及预付款 Accounts Receivable and Advance Payments	1.37	– 1.06
二、债券发行及境外筹资 Bonds Issue & Overseas Financing					
三、应付及暂收款 Accounts Receivable and Receipts on Account	15.26	6.59	其中：应收利息 Of Which：Interest Receivable		– 0.01
			四、买入返售资产 Assets Reverse Repo（Including Securities）	14.23	13.23
其中：应付及预收利息 Of Which：Interest Payable and Received in Advance	6.97	2.31	五、存放中央银行存款 Deposits with the Central Bank	75.43	36.13
四、卖出回购资产 Assets Repo（Including Securities）	7.98	4.97	六、同业往来 Inter – bank Transactions	39.05	6.04
五、向中央银行借款 Borrowings from the Central Bank		– 2.73	七、库存现金 Cash in Vault	4.94	2.09
六、同业往来 Inter – bank Transactions	7.22	– 3.28			
七、代理境内贷款资金 Agency Domestic Lending Funds	0.02	0.01			
八、各项准备 Total Provisions	6.72	– 1.61			
其中：贷款呆账准备金 Of Which：Provisions for Bad Loans	6.72	– 1.61			
九、所有者权益 Owner's Equity	27.04	22.59			
其中：实收资本 Of Which：Paid – in Capital	11.80	8.26			
当年结益 Net Earnings	8.10	8.10			
十、其他 Others	– 9.56	– 7.11			
资金来源总计 Total Sources	**555.48**	**173.33**	**资金运用总计 Total Uses**	**555.48**	**173.33**

农村商业银行本外币信贷收支表

Sources and Uses of Credit Funds of Rural Commercial Banks (Domestic and Foreign Currency Combined)

(2005年末)

(Year - end of 2005)

汇率：8.0702　　　　单位：亿元

Exchange Rate: 8.0702　　　　Unit: 100 Million Yuan

项目 Items	余额 Balance	比年初增减额 Changes within the Year	项目 Items	余额 Balance	比年初增减额 Changes within the Year
一、各项存款 Total Deposits	2585.29	1722.20	一、各项贷款 Total Loans	1579.85	1035.72
1. 企事业单位存款 Deposits by Enterprises and Public Institutions	198.82	85.16	1. 短期贷款 Short - term Loans	1023.83	569.69
			2. 中长期贷款 Medium and Long - term Loans	413.71	350.84
(1) 活期存款 Demand Deposits	5.18	1.07			
(2) 定期存款 Time Deposits	193.64	84.09	3. 其他贷款 Other Loans	1.93	0.43
2. 储蓄存款 Savings Deposits	1327.88	881.11	4. 票据融资 Paper Financing	140.36	114.74
(1) 活期储蓄 Demand Deposits	416.48	284.90	5. 各项垫款 Total Advances	0.02	0.02
(2) 定期储蓄 Time Deposits	911.40	596.21	二、有价证券及投资 Securities and Investments	523.04	352.68
3. 其他存款 Other Deposits	1058.59	755.93	三、应收及预付款 Accounts Receivable and Advance Payments	27.70	25.36
二、债券发行及境外筹资 Bonds Issue & Overseas Financing			其中：应收利息 Of Which: Interest Receivable	1.20	1.18
三、应付及暂收款 Accounts Receivable and Receipts on Account	74.80	46.26	四、买入返售资产 Assets Reverse Repo (Including Securities)	116.10	101.87
其中：应付及预收利息 Of Which: Interest Payable and Received in Advance	50.90	38.86	五、存放中央银行存款 Deposits with the Central Bank	266.36	140.06
四、卖出回购资产 Assets Repo (Including Securities)	102.31	89.33	六、同业往来 Inter - bank Transactions	389.33	321.75
五、向中央银行借款 Borrowings from the Central Bank			七、库存现金 Cash in Vault	27.38	18.44
六、同业往来 Inter - bank Transactions	16.94	-1.63			
七、代理境内贷款资金 Agency Domestic Lending Funds	0.20	0.18			
八、各项准备 Total Provisions	41.06	29.85			
其中：贷款呆账准备金 Of Which: Provisions for Bad Loans	40.95	29.74			
九、所有者权益 Owner's Equity	155.61	107.98			
其中：实收资本 Of Which: Paid - in Capital	72.48	46.65			
当年结益 Net Earnings	29.40	29.40			
十、其他 Others	-46.45	1.71			
资金来源总计 Total Sources	**2929.76**	**1995.88**	**资金运用总计 Total Uses**	**2929.76**	**1995.88**

7. 农村信用合作社本外币信贷收支表（2002—2005年）

Sources and Uses of Credit Funds of Rural Credit Cooperatives（Domestic and Foreign Currency Combined）（2002 - 2005）

农村信用合作社本外币信贷收支表

Sources and Uses of Credit Funds of Rural Credit Cooperatives（Domestic and Foreign Currency Combined）

（2002年末）

（Year - end of 2002）

汇率：8.2773　　单位：亿元

Exchange Rate：8.2773　　Unit：100 Million Yuan

项　目 Items	余　额 Balance	比年初增减额 Changes within the Year	项　目 Items	余　额 Balance	比年初增减额 Changes within the Year
一、各项存款 Total Deposits	19668.76	2543.96	一、各项贷款 Total Loans	13794.47	1907.98
1. 企事业单位存款 Deposits by Enterprises and Public Institutions	779.57	206.74	1. 短期贷款 Short - term Loans	12895.82	1613.91
（1）活期存款 Demand Deposits	5.12	2.57	2. 中长期贷款 Medium and Long - term Loans	717.10	213.84
（2）定期存款 Time Deposits	774.45	204.17	3. 其他贷款 Other Loans	0.19	0.19
2. 储蓄存款 Savings Deposits	15450.40	1699.63	4. 票据融资 Paper Financing	181.36	80.04
（1）活期储蓄 Demand Deposits	4117.22	719.96	5. 各项垫款 Total Advances		
（2）定期储蓄 Time Deposits	11333.18	979.67	二、有价证券及投资 Securities and Investments	1801.65	350.03
3. 其他存款 Other Deposits	3438.79	637.59	三、应收及预付款 Accounts Receivable and Advance Payments	261.46	- 22.26
二、债券发行及境外筹资 Bonds Issue & Overseas Financing	0.06	- 0.02	其中：应收利息 Of Which：Interest Receivable	145.75	- 27.34
三、应付及暂收款 Accounts Receivable and Receipts on Account	495.88	43.72	四、买入返售证券 Reverse Repo	2.00	2.00
其中：应付及预收利息 Of Which：Interest Payable and Received in Advance	246.59	25.28	五、存放中央银行存款 Deposits with the Central Bank	2568.65	319.36
四、卖出回购证券 Repo	37.80	22.10	六、同业往来 Inter - bank Transactions	2076.87	551.20
五、向中央银行借款 Borrowings from the Central Bank	946.75	259.48	七、库存现金 Cash in Vault	347.57	31.83
六、同业往来 Inter - bank Transactions	892.58	254.36			
七、代理境内贷款资金 Agency Domestic Lending Funds	30.41	- 4.24			
八、各项准备 Total Provisions	166.12	11.17			

续表
Continued

项　　目 Items	余　额 Balance	比年初增减额 Changes within the Year	项　　目 Items	余　额 Balance	比年初增减额 Changes within the Year
其中：贷款呆账准备金 Of Which：Provisions for Bad Loans	166.13	11.18			
九、所有者权益 Owner's Equity	－269.03	25.37			
其中：实收资本 Of Which：Paid－in Capital	485.56	66.53			
当年结益 Net Earnings	－58.42	－58.42			
十、其他 Others	－1116.66	－15.76			
资金来源总计 Total Sources	**20852.67**	**3140.14**	**资金运用总计 Total Uses**	**20852.67**	**3140.14**

农村信用合作社本外币信贷收支表

Sources and Uses of Credit Funds of Rural Credit Cooperatives（Domestic and Foreign Currency Combined）

（2003 年末）

（Year – end of 2003）

汇率：8.2767
Exchange Rate：8.2767

单位：亿元
Unit：100 Million Yuan

项目 Items	余额 Balance	比年初增减额 Changes within the Year	项目 Items	余额 Balance	比年初增减额 Changes within the Year
一、各项存款 Total Deposits	23760.15	4091.67	一、各项贷款 Total Loans	16987.38	3192.94
1. 企事业单位存款 Deposits by Enterprises and Public Institutions	1027.83	248.75	1. 短期贷款 Short – term Loans	15446.63	2550.96
（1）活期存款 Demand Deposits	7.39	2.81	2. 中长期贷款 Medium and Long – term Loans	1097.71	380.45
（2）定期存款 Time Deposits	1020.44	245.94	3. 其他贷款 Other Loans	2.50	2.31
2. 储蓄存款 Savings Deposits	18050.90	2600.55	4. 票据融资 Paper Financing	440.54	259.22
（1）活期储蓄 Demand Deposits	5111.30	993.51	5. 各项垫款 Total Advances		
（2）定期储蓄 Time Deposits	12939.60	1607.04	二、有价证券及投资 Securities and Investments	2067.55	264.51
3. 其他存款 Other Deposits	4681.42	1242.37	三、应收及预付款 Accounts Receivable and Advance Payments	238.20	– 22.37
二、债券发行及境外筹资 Bonds Issue & Overseas Financing	0.05	– 0.01	其中：应收利息 Of Which：Interest Receivable	117.07	– 28.65
三、应付及暂收款 Accounts Receivable and Receipts on Account	586.46	79.14	四、买入返售证券 Reverse Repo	1.50	– 0.50
其中：应付及预收利息 Of Which：Interest Payable and Received in Advance	290.64	44.42	五、存放中央银行存款 Deposits with the Central Bank	2941.82	372.98
四、卖出回购证券 Repo	14.74	– 23.06	六、同业往来 Inter – bank Transactions	2712.85	633.07
五、向中央银行借款 Borrowings from the Central Bank	1013.67	67.30	七、库存现金 Cash in Vault	412.36	64.85
六、同业往来 Inter – bank Transactions	1168.35	274.50			
七、代理境内贷款资金 Agency Domestic Lending Funds	42.70	10.63			
八、各项准备 Total Provisions	202.34	36.13			
其中：贷款呆账准备金 Of Which：Provisions for Bad Loans	201.94	39.64			
九、所有者权益 Owner's Equity	– 133.16	147.59			
其中：实收资本 Of Which：Paid – in Capital	621.64	161.49			
当年结益 Net Earnings	– 5.47	– 5.47			
十、其他 Others	– 1293.64	– 178.41			
资金来源总计 Total Sources	**25361.66**	**4505.48**	**资金运用总计 Total Uses**	**25361.66**	**4505.48**

农村信用合作社本外币信贷收支表
Sources and Uses of Credit Funds of Rural Credit Cooperatives (Domestic and Foreign Currency Combined)

(2004 年末)

(Year - end of 2004)

汇率：8.2765 单位：亿元

Exchange Rate: 8.2765 Unit: 100 Million Yuan

项 目 Items	余 额 Balance	比年初增减额 Changes within the Year	项 目 Items	余 额 Balance	比年初增减额 Changes within the Year
一、各项存款 Total Deposits	27340.16	3623.18	一、各项贷款 Total Loans	19241.56	2525.64
1. 企事业单位存款 Deposits by Enterprises and Public Institutions	1149.52	122.03	1. 短期贷款 Short - term Loans	17394.36	2295.91
(1) 活期存款 Demand Deposits	7.20	0.19	2. 中长期贷款 Medium and Long - term Loans	1509.23	366.87
(2) 定期存款 Time Deposits	1142.32	121.84	3. 其他贷款 Other Loans	0.94	- 1.83
2. 储蓄存款 Savings Deposits	20811.01	2758.66	4. 票据融资 Paper Financing	336.82	- 135.52
(1) 活期储蓄 Demand Deposits	6223.84	1112.27	5. 各项垫款 Total Advances	0.21	0.21
(2) 定期储蓄 Time Deposits	14587.17	1646.39	二、有价证券及投资 Securities and Investments	2380.75	313.03
3. 其他存款 Other Deposits	5379.63	742.49	三、应收及预付款 Accounts Receivable and Advance Payments	224.81	- 12.98
二、债券发行及境外筹资 Bonds Issue & Overseas Financing	0.04	- 0.01	其中：应收利息 Of Which: Interest Receivable	96.83	- 20.14
三、应付及暂收款 Accounts Receivable and Receipts on Account	676.20	75.90	四、买入返售资产 Assets Reverse Repo (Including Securities)	122.72	75.67
其中：应付及预收利息 Of Which: Interest Payable and Received in Advance	342.93	52.62	五、存放中央银行存款 Deposits with the Central Bank	4024.78	1082.07
四、卖出回购资产 Assets Repo (Including Securities)	38.00	- 22.19	六、同业往来 Inter - bank Transactions	2813.22	137.49
五、向中央银行借款 Borrowings from the Central Bank	991.11	- 63.97	七、库存现金 Cash in Vault	458.53	46.13
六、同业往来 Inter - bank Transactions	835.52	- 80.87			
七、代理境内贷款资金 Agency Domestic Lending Funds	109.25	48.35			
八、各项准备 Total Provisions	242.51	40.13			
其中：贷款呆账准备金 Of Which: Provisions for Bad Loans	236.11	34.24			
九、所有者权益 Owner's Equity	732.30	886.30			
其中：实收资本 Of Which: Paid - in Capital	1437.40	801.55			
当年结益 Net Earnings	96.55	96.55			
十、其他 Others	- 1698.72	- 339.77			
资金来源总计 Total Sources	**29266.37**	**4167.05**	**资金运用总计 Total Uses**	**29266.37**	**4167.05**

农村信用合作社本外币信贷收支表

Sources and Uses of Credit Funds of Rural Credit Cooperatives（Domestic and Foreign Currency Combined）

（2005 年末）

（Year - end of 2005）

汇率：8.0702
Exchange Rate：8.0702

单位：亿元
Unit：100 Million Yuan

项 目 Items	余 额 Balance	比年初增减额 Changes within the Year	项 目 Items	余 额 Balance	比年初增减额 Changes within the Year
一、各项存款 Total Deposits	27634.86	1507.46	一、各项贷款 Total Loans	18684.13	1272.97
1. 企事业单位存款 Deposits by Enterprises and Public Institutions	1052.91	18.13	1. 短期贷款 Short - term Loans	16807.07	1115.14
			2. 中长期贷款 Medium and Long - term Loans	1556.76	133.68
（1）活期存款 Demand Deposits	5.26	1.40			
（2）定期存款 Time Deposits	1047.65	16.73	3. 其他贷款 Other Loans	1.76	1.52
2. 储蓄存款 Savings Deposits	21765.85	1665.08	4. 票据融资 Paper Financing	317.30	22.26
（1）活期储蓄 Demand Deposits	6691.59	681.88	5. 各项垫款 Total Advances	1.24	0.37
（2）定期储蓄 Time Deposits	15074.26	983.20	二、有价证券及投资 Securities and Investments	2099.87	- 167.16
3. 其他存款 Other Deposits	4816.10	- 175.75	三、应收及预付款 Accounts Receivable and Advance Payments	302.65	42.52
二、债券发行及境外筹资 Bonds Issue & Overseas Financing	0.04		其中：应收利息 Of Which：Interest Receivable	81.92	- 13.67
三、应付及暂收款 Accounts Receivable and Receipts on Account	756.29	88.28	四、买入返售资产 Assets Reverse Repo（Including Securities）	157.69	44.25
其中：应付及预收利息 Of Which：Interest Payable and Received in Advance	352.05	27.74	五、存放中央银行存款 Deposits with the Central Bank	4319.89	463.24
四、卖出回购资产 Assets Repo（Including Securities）	229.58	211.15	六、同业往来 Inter - bank Transactions	2620.28	- 74.16
五、向中央银行借款 Borrowings from the Central Bank	637.33	- 346.69	七、库存现金 Cash in Vault	467.41	23.79
六、同业往来 Inter - bank Transactions	711.74	- 82.32			
七、代理境内贷款资金 Agency Domestic Lending Funds	128.30	7.89			
八、各项准备 Total Provisions	321.72	91.88			
其中：贷款呆账准备金 Of Which：Provisions for Bad Loans	291.18	77.67			
九、所有者权益 Owner's Equity	1320.35	697.18			
其中：实收资本 Of Which：Paid - in Capital	1717.79	207.68			
当年结益 Net Earnings	120.33	120.33			
十、其他 Others	- 3088.29	- 569.38			
资金来源总计 Total Sources	**28651.92**	**1605.45**	**资金运用总计 Total Uses**	**28651.92**	**1605.45**

8. 财务公司本外币信贷收支表（2002—2005 年）

Sources and Uses of Credit Funds of Finance Companies (Domestic and Foreign Currency Combined) (2002 - 2005)

财务公司本外币信贷收支表

Sources and Uses of Credit Funds of Finance Companies

(Domestic and Foreign Currency Combined)

（2002 年末）

(Year - end of 2002)

汇率：8.2773 单位：亿元

Exchange Rate: 8.2773 Unit: 100 Million Yuan

项目 Items	余额 Balance	比年初增减额 Changes within the Year	项目 Items	余额 Balance	比年初增减额 Changes within the Year
一、各项存款 Total Deposits	3467.65	648.38	一、各项贷款 Total Loans	2194.11	247.08
1. 企业存款 Deposits by Enterprises	2282.60	613.82	1. 短期贷款 Short - term Loans	667.55	137.40
(1) 活期存款 Demand Deposits	1321.30	548.25	2. 中长期贷款 Medium and Long - term Loans	356.38	66.45
(2) 定期存款 Time Deposits	961.30	65.57	3. 委托贷款 Designated Loans	1089.12	34.90
2. 委托存款 Designated Deposits	1161.71	23.23	4. 信托贷款 Trust Loans	17.43	-0.08
3. 信托存款 Trust Deposits	19.74	9.92	5. 票据融资 Paper Financing	60.24	8.96
4. 其他存款 Other Deposits	3.60	1.41	其中：贴现 Of Which: Discount	60.24	8.96
二、借款及筹资 Borrowing and Financing	6.69	-1.65	6. 融资租赁 Financing Leases	1.98	-0.47
三、应付及暂收款 Accounts Receivable and Receipts on Account	127.89	-10.59	7. 各项垫款 Total Advances		
			8. 境外筹资转贷款 On - lending of Overseas Financing	1.41	-0.08
其中：应付及预提利息 Of Which: Interest Payable and Accrued	26.45	1.42	二、委托投资 Designated Investments	64.30	-0.30
四、证券业务款项 Securities Business Funds	22.68	17.90	三、投资 Investments	543.14	255.86
五、卖出回购证券 Repo	78.84	56.22	四、应收及预付款 Accounts Receivable and Advance Payments	112.82	27.37
六、向中央银行借款 Borrowings from the Central Bank	7.06	-0.03	其中：应收利息 Of Which: Interest Receivable	12.72	-2.72
七、同业往来 Inter - bank Transactions	90.37	6.11	五、证券业务占款 Funding of Securities Purchase	3.59	-4.17
八、代理金融机构贷款基金 Designated Loan Funds on Behalf of Financial Institutions	1.21	1.16	六、买入返售证券 Reverse Repo	157.48	137.56

续表
Continued

项　目 Items	余　额 Balance	比年初增减额 Changes within the Year	项　目 Items	余　额 Balance	比年初增减额 Changes within the Year
其中：中央银行委托贷款基金 Of Which：Loan Funds Designated by the Central Bank			七、存放中央银行存款 Deposits with the Central Bank	136.89	16.98
			八、同业往来 Inter－bank Transactions	874.73	237.10
九、各项准备 Total Provisions	21.45	4.80	九、现金 Cash	0.28	0.21
其中：贷款呆账准备金 Of Which：Provisions for Bad Loans	19.19	4.11			
十、所有者权益 Owner's Equity	357.05	59.23			
其中：实收资本 Of Which：Paid－in Capital	307.77	51.31			
当年结益 Net Earnings	29.35	29.35			
十一、其他 Others	－93.55	136.16			
资金来源总计 Total Sources	**4087.34**	**917.69**	**资金运用总计 Total Uses**	**4087.34**	**917.69**

财务公司本外币信贷收支表
Sources and Uses of Credit Funds of Finance Companies
(Domestic and Foreign Currency Combined)

（2003 年末）

(Year - end of 2003)

汇率：8.2767　　单位：亿元

Exchange Rate：8.2767　　Unit：100 Million Yuan

项目 Items	余额 Balance	比年初增减额 Changes within the Year	项目 Items	余额 Balance	比年初增减额 Changes within the Year
一、各项存款 Total Deposits	4358.01	895.13	一、各项贷款 Total Loans	2649.58	468.58
1. 企业存款 Deposits by Enterprises	2927.22	643.15	1. 短期贷款 Short - term Loans	749.57	88.91
（1）活期存款 Demand Deposits	1683.82	360.74	2. 中长期贷款 Medium and Long - term Loans	538.60	182.24
（2）定期存款 Time Deposits	1243.40	282.41	3. 委托贷款 Designated Loans	1176.33	93.38
2. 委托存款 Designated Deposits	1409.25	253.72	4. 信托贷款 Trust Loans	28.50	11.10
3. 信托存款 Trust Deposits	15.84	- 3.90	5. 票据融资 Paper Financing	143.57	83.33
4. 其他存款 Other Deposits	5.70	2.16	其中：贴现 Of Which：Discount	143.57	83.33
二、借款及筹资 Borrowing and Financing	8.36	1.67	6. 融资租赁 Financing Leases	8.25	6.27
三、应付及暂收款 Accounts Receivable and Receipts on Account	121.92	- 0.70	7. 各项垫款 Total Advances	3.60	3.60
			8. 境外筹资转贷款 On - lending of Overseas Financing	1.16	- 0.25
其中：应付及预提利息 Of Which：Interest Payable and Accrued	26.00	- 0.18	二、委托投资 Designated Investments	191.52	127.37
四、证券业务款项 Securities Business Funds	0.17	- 22.51	三、投资 Investments	762.47	225.12
五、卖出回购证券 Repo	119.60	41.53	四、应收及预付款 Accounts Receivable and Advance Payments	78.08	- 23.33
六、向中央银行借款 Borrowings from the Central Bank	5.62	0.09	其中：应收利息 Of Which：Interest Receivable	10.77	1.34
七、同业往来 Inter - bank Transactions	86.08	3.64	五、证券业务占款 Funding of Securities Purchase	3.42	- 0.17
八、代理金融机构贷款基金 Designated Loan Funds on Behalf of Financial Institutions		- 1.21	六、买入返售证券 Reverse Repo	189.01	30.81
其中：中央银行委托贷款基金 Of Which：Loan Funds Designated by the Central Bank			七、存放中央银行存款 Deposits with the Central Bank	206.97	70.13
			八、同业往来 Inter - bank Transactions	972.21	99.12
九、各项准备 Total Provisions	31.49	10.32			

续表
Continued

项　目 Items	余　额 Balance	比年初增减额 Changes within the Year	项　目 Items	余　额 Balance	比年初增减额 Changes within the Year
其中：贷款呆账准备金 Of Which：Provisions for Bad Loans	25.23	8.31	九、现金 Cash in Vault	0.08	-0.20
十、所有者权益 Owner's Equity	396.27	45.78			
其中：实收资本 Of Which：Paid-in Capital	329.34	27.15			
当年结益 Net Earnings	36.63	36.63			
十一、其他 Others	-74.18	23.69			
资金来源总计 Total Sources	**5053.34**	**997.43**	**资金运用总计 Total Uses**	**5053.34**	**997.43**

财务公司本外币信贷收支表

Sources and Uses of Credit Funds of Finance Companies

（Domestic and Foreign Currency Combined）

（2004 年末）

（Year – end of 2004）

汇率：8.2765
Exchange Rate：8.2765

单位：亿元
Unit：100 Million Yuan

项　目 Items	余　额 Balance	比年初增减额 Changes within the Year	项　目 Items	余　额 Balance	比年初增减额 Changes within the Year
一、各项存款 Total Deposits	4954.14	595.95	一、各项贷款 Total Loans	3097.11	435.05
1. 企业存款 Deposits by Enterprises	3315.84	385.80	1. 短期贷款 Short – term Loans	863.12	122.65
（1）活期存款 Demand Deposits	2058.83	373.72	2. 中长期贷款 Medium and Long – term Loans	627.88	89.06
（2）定期存款 Time Deposits	1257.01	12.08	3. 委托贷款 Designated Loans	1453.71	277.56
2. 委托存款 Designated Deposits	1603.87	197.26	4. 信托贷款 Trust Loans	19.49	– 9.01
3. 信托存款 Trust Deposits	26.59	10.75	5. 票据融资 Paper Financing	113.71	– 49.92
4. 其他存款 Other Deposits	7.84	2.14	其中：贴现 Of Which：Discount	110.91	– 49.91
二、借款及筹资 Borrowing and Financing	7.98	– 0.37	6. 融资租赁 Financing Leases	15.99	7.75
三、应付及暂收款 Accounts Receivable and Receipts on Account	93.72	– 26.33	7. 各项垫款 Total Advances	2.38	– 2.71
			8. 境外筹资转贷款 On – lending of Overseas Financing	0.83	– 0.33
其中：应付及预提利息 Of Which：Interest Payable and Accrued	25.00	0.77	二、委托投资 Designated Investments	157.60	– 33.84
四、证券业务款项 Securities Business Funds	1.24	1.07	三、投资 Investments	946.69	184.55
五、卖出回购资产 Assets Repo（Including Securities）	227.34	29.69	四、应收及预付款 Accounts Receivable and Advance Payments	55.09	– 22.24
六、向中央银行借款 Borrowings from the Central Bank	5.51	– 7.91	其中：应收利息 Of Which：Interest Receivable	10.42	0.36
七、同业往来 Inter – bank Transactions	67.25	– 12.98	五、证券业务占款 Funding of Securities Purchase	1.14	– 2.28
八、代理金融机构贷款基金 Designated Loan Funds on Behalf of Financial Institutions			六、买入返售资产 Assets Reverse Repo（Including Securities）	72.85	– 115.88
其中：中央银行委托贷款基金 Of Which：Loan Funds Designated by the Central Bank			七、存放中央银行存款 Deposits with the Central Bank	260.91	53.95
九、各项准备 Total Provisions	47.38	15.77	八、同业往来 Inter – bank Transactions	1112.65	138.52

续表
Continued

项　目 Items	余　额 Balance	比年初增减额 Changes within the Year	项　目 Items	余　额 Balance	比年初增减额 Changes within the Year
其中：贷款呆账准备金 Of Which：Provisions for Bad Loans	28.24	3.47	九、现金 Cash in Vault	0.09	0.01
十、所有者权益 Owner's Equity	451.72	56.60			
其中：实收资本 Of Which：Paid－in Capital	363.28	36.30			
当年结益 Net Earnings	44.13	44.13			
十一、其他 Others	－152.15	－13.65			
资金来源总计 Total Sources	**5704.13**	**637.84**	**资金运用总计 Total Uses**	**5704.13**	**637.84**

财务公司本外币信贷收支表
Sources and Uses of Credit Funds of Finance Companies
(Domestic and Foreign Currency Combined)

(2005 年末)

(Year - end of 2005)

汇率：8.0702　　　　单位：亿元

Exchange Rate：8.0702　　　　Unit：100 Million Yuan

项　目 Items	余　额 Balance	比年初增减额 Changes within the Year	项　目 Items	余　额 Balance	比年初增减额 Changes within the Year
一、各项存款 Total Deposits	6199.78	1196.91	一、各项贷款 Total Loans	3855.01	711.07
1. 企业存款 Deposits by Enterprises	4254.15	939.19	1. 短期贷款 Short - term Loans	1070.92	208.47
(1) 活期存款 Demand Deposits	2648.06	576.88	2. 中长期贷款 Medium and Long - term Loans	857.35	229.10
(2) 定期存款 Time Deposits	1606.09	362.31	3. 委托贷款 Designated Loans	1720.12	219.21
2. 委托存款 Designated Deposits	1903.20	249.43	4. 信托贷款 Trust Loans	23.02	3.46
3. 信托存款 Trust Deposits	38.59	12.29	5. 票据融资 Paper Financing	82.93	- 30.81
4. 其他存款 Other Deposits	3.84	- 4.00	其中：贴现 Of Which：Discount	82.93	- 28.01
二、借款及筹资 Borrowing and Financing	7.16	- 0.82	6. 融资租赁 Financing Leases	97.26	81.39
三、应付及暂收款 Accounts Receivable and Receipts on Account	82.94	- 12.39	7. 各项垫款 Total Advances	2.80	0.47
			8. 境外筹资转贷款 On - lending of Overseas Financing	0.61	- 0.22
其中：应付及预提利息 Of Which：Interest Payable and Accrued	29.70	4.67	二、委托投资 Designated Investments	134.83	- 22.75
四、证券业务款项 Securities Business Funds	0.02	- 1.22	三、投资 Investments	852.20	- 94.21
五、卖出回购资产 Assets Repo (Including Securities)	244.41	17.67	四、应收及预付款 Accounts Receivable and Advance Payments	56.01	5.56
六、向中央银行借款 Borrowings from the Central Bank	2.91	- 2.60	其中：应收利息 Of Which：Interest Receivable	9.52	0.69
七、同业往来 Inter - bank Transactions	60.53	- 6.72	五、证券业务占款 Funding of Securities Purchase	0.01	- 1.13
八、代理金融机构贷款基金 Designated Loan Funds on Behalf of Financial Institutions			六、买入返售资产 Assets Reverse Repo (Including Securities)	103.28	30.43
其中：中央银行委托贷款基金 Of Which：Loan Funds Designated by the Central Bank			七、存放中央银行存款 Deposits with the Central Bank	326.36	66.37
九、各项准备 Total Provisions	66.51	12.21	八、同业往来 Inter - bank Transactions	1641.49	528.14

续表
Continued

项目 Items	余额 Balance	比年初增减额 Changes within the Year	项目 Items	余额 Balance	比年初增减额 Changes within the Year
其中：贷款呆账准备金 Of Which: Provisions for Bad Loans	30.54	-1.40	九、现金 Cash in Vault	0.10	0.01
十、所有者权益 Owner's Equity	496.32	54.08			
其中：实收资本 Of Which: Paid-in Capital	403.21	39.29			
当年结益 Net Earnings	61.28	61.28			
十一、其他 Others	-191.29	-33.63			
资金来源总计 **Total Sources**	**6969.29**	**1223.49**	**资金运用总计** **Total Uses**	**6969.29**	**1223.49**

9. 信托投资公司本外币信贷收支表（2002—2005 年）

Sources and Uses of Credit Funds of Financial Trust and Investment Companies (Domestic and Foreign Currency Combined) (2002 - 2005)

信托投资公司本外币信贷收支表

Sources and Uses of Credit Funds of Financial Trust and Investment Companies (Domestic and Foreign Currency Combined)

（2002 年末）

(Year - end of 2002)

汇率：8.2773 单位：亿元

Exchange Rate: 8.2773 Unit: 100 Million Yuan

项目 Items	余额 Balance	比年初增减额 Changes within the Year	项目 Items	余额 Balance	比年初增减额 Changes within the Year
一、各项存款 Total Deposits	1512.64	-62.77	一、各项贷款 Total Loans	1403.14	-56.97
1. 信托存款 Trust Deposits	237.83	-34.51	1. 信托贷款 Trust Loans	330.90	-24.31
2. 委托存款及投资基金 Designated Deposits and Investment Funds	1207.00	-16.98	其中：中长期信托贷款 Of Which: Medium and Long-term Trust Loans	173.37	8.46
3. 其他存款 Other Deposits	67.81	-11.28	2. 委托贷款 Designated Loans	931.48	10.23
二、借款及筹资 Borrowing and Financing	408.65	-13.82	3. 票据融资 Paper Financing		
三、应付及暂收款 Accounts Receivable and Receipts on Account	375.54	-87.97	其中：贴现 Of Which: Discount		
			4. 融资租赁 Financing Leases	10.40	-3.46
其中：应付及预提利息 Of Which: Interest Payable and Accrued	40.93	-5.25	5. 各项垫款 Total Advances	0.32	-2.24
四、证券业务款项 Securities Business Funds	43.75	-293.41	6. 境外筹资转贷款 On-lending of Overseas Financing	0.67	-0.85
五、卖出回购证券 Repo	21.70	10.35	7. 其他贷款 Other Loans	129.37	-36.34
六、向中央银行借款 Borrowings from the Central Bank	30.09	-0.42	二、委托投资 Designated Investments	283.36	-0.03
七、同业往来 Inter-bank Transactions	130.39	-28.76	三、投资 Investments	940.34	70.98
八、代理金融机构贷款基金 Designated Loan Funds on Behalf of Financial Institutions	2.39	1.86	四、应收及预付款 Accounts Receivable and Advance Payments	384.56	-77.53
九、各项准备 Total Provisions	31.36	2.58	其中：应收利息及预付利息 Of Which: Interest Receivable and Paid in Advance	64.61	-8.15
其中：贷款呆账准备金 Of Which: Provisions for Bad Loans	16.82	4.42	五、证券业务占款 Funding of Securities Purchase	15.11	-38.63

续表
Continued

项　目 Items	余　额 Balance	比年初增减额 Changes within the Year	项　目 Items	余　额 Balance	比年初增减额 Changes within the Year
十、所有者权益 Owner's Equity	944.11	－6.38	六、买入返售证券 Reverse Repo	11.48	3.83
其中：实收资本 Of Which：Paid－in Capital	799.83	29.18	七、存放中央银行存款 Deposits with the Central Bank	16.24	－9.89
当年结益 Net Earnings	2.02	2.02	八、同业往来 Inter－bank Transactions	190.20	－221.74
十一、其他 Others	－255.77	148.20	九、库存现金 Cash in Vault	0.42	－0.56
资金来源总计 Total Sources	**3244.85**	**－330.54**	**资金运用总计 Total Uses**	**3244.85**	**－330.54**

信托投资公司本外币信贷收支表

Sources and Uses of Credit Funds of Financial Trust and Investment Companies

（Domestic and Foreign Currency Combined）

（2003 年末）

（Year－end of 2003）

汇率：8.2767　　　　单位：亿元

Exchange Rate：8.2767　　　　Unit：100 Million Yuan

项　目 Items	余　额 Balance	比年初增减额 Changes within the Year	项　目 Items	余　额 Balance	比年初增减额 Changes within the Year
一、各项存款 Total Deposits	1624.42	128.80	一、各项贷款 Total Loans	1333.50	－33.15
1. 信托存款 Trust Deposits	241.90	－0.32	1. 信托贷款 Trust Loans	292.69	－12.49
2. 委托存款及投资基金 Designated Deposits and Investment Funds	1311.20	121.11	其中：中长期信托贷款 Of Which：Medium and Long－term Trust Loans	133.69	－24.25
3. 其他存款 Other Deposits	71.32	8.01	2. 委托贷款 Designated Loans	926.34	7.63
二、借款及筹资 Borrowing and Financing	428.54	41.52	3. 票据融资 Paper Financing	0.10	
三、应付及暂收款 Accounts Receivable and Receipts on Account	298.86	－48.92	其中：贴现 Of Which：Discount		
			4. 融资租赁 Financing Leases	8.28	－2.03
其中：应付及预提利息 Of Which：Interest Payable and Accrued	33.17	－5.45	5. 各项垫款 Total Advances	0.25	－0.07
四、证券业务款项 Securities Business Funds	25.34	－12.06	6. 境外筹资转贷款 On－lending of Overseas Financing	0.58	－0.09
五、卖出回购证券 Repo	32.10	11.40	7. 其他贷款 Other Loans	105.26	－26.10
六、向中央银行借款 Borrowings from the Central Bank	15.12	－13.65	二、委托投资 Designated Investments	470.35	170.97
七、同业往来 Inter－bank Transactions	134.42	12.11	三、投资 Investments	1009.42	80.12
八、代理金融机构贷款基金 Designated Loan Funds on Behalf of Financial Institutions		－2.39	四、应收及预付款 Accounts Receivable and Advance Payments	342.89	－4.21
九、各项准备 Total Provisions	33.45	4.50	其中：应收利息及预付利息 Of Which：Interest Receivable and Paid in Advance	55.44	－6.98
其中：贷款呆账准备金 Of Which：Provisions for Bad Loans	23.05	4.08	五、证券业务占款 Funding of Securities Purchase	9.19	－4.69
十、所有者权益 Owner's Equity	982.52	50.53	六、买入返售证券 Reverse Repo	24.87	13.74
其中：实收资本 Of Which：Paid－in Capital	847.83	62.89	七、存放中央银行存款 Deposits with the Central Bank	11.11	－4.08
当年结益 Net Earnings	－0.24	－0.24	八、同业往来 Inter－bank Transactions	202.11	12.45
十一、其他 Others	－170.69	59.63	九、库存现金 Cash in Vault	0.64	0.32
资金来源总计 Total Sources	**3404.08**	**231.47**	**资金运用总计 Total Uses**	**3404.08**	**231.47**

信托投资公司本外币信贷收支表

Sources and Uses of Credit Funds of Financial Trust and Investment Companies

(Domestic and Foreign Currency Combined)

（2004 年末）

（Year – end of 2004）

汇率：8.2765 单位：亿元

Exchange Rate：8.2765 Unit：100 Million Yuan

项目 Items	余额 Balance	比年初增减额 Changes within the Year	项目 Items	余额 Balance	比年初增减额 Changes within the Year
一、各项存款 Total Deposits	1748.61	165.61	一、各项贷款 Total Loans	1330.51	174.56
1. 信托存款 Trust Deposits	245.52	4.09	1. 信托贷款 Trust Loans	215.83	34.43
2. 委托存款及投资基金 Designated Deposits and Investment Funds	1451.82	179.47	其中：中长期信托贷款 Of Which：Medium and Long – term Trust Loans	59.28	14.21
3. 其他存款 Other Deposits	51.27	– 17.95	2. 委托贷款 Designated Loans	1034.60	139.46
二、借款及筹资 Borrowing and Financing	66.24	– 9.09	3. 票据融资 Paper Financing		
三、应付及暂收款 Accounts Receivable and Receipts on Account	162.41	– 17.19	其中：贴现 Of Which：Discount		
			4. 融资租赁 Financing Leases	7.14	– 0.15
其中：应付及预提利息 Of Which：Interest Payable and Accrued	30.41	3.20	5. 各项垫款 Total Advances	0.04	– 0.21
四、证券业务款项 Securities Business Funds	6.20	– 6.87	6. 境外筹资转贷款 On – lending of Overseas Financing	0.58	
五、卖出回购资产 Assets Repo（Including Securities）	40.07	– 2.87	7. 其他贷款 Other Loans	72.32	1.03
六、向中央银行借款 Borrowings from the Central Bank	0.90	– 0.05	二、委托投资 Designated Investments	517.75	47.45
七、同业往来 Inter – bank Transactions	89.08	– 31.45	三、投资 Investments	327.10	– 42.73
八、代理金融机构贷款基金 Designated Loan Funds on Behalf of Financial Institutions			四、应收及预付款 Accounts Receivable and Advance Payments	185.62	– 2.17
九、各项准备 Total Provisions	38.67	12.24	其中：应收利息及预付利息 Of Which：Interest Receivable and Paid in Advance	38.11	– 5.88
其中：贷款呆账准备金 Of Which：Provisions for Bad Loans	18.33	3.45	五、证券业务占款 Funding of Securities Purchase	1.07	– 4.65
十、所有者权益 Owner's Equity	505.17	– 8.44	六、买入返售资产 Assets Reverse Repo（Including Securities）	3.31	– 21.06
其中：实收资本 Of Which：Paid – in Capital	501.73	9.45			
当年结益 Net Earnings	6.26	6.26	七、存放中央银行存款 Deposits with the Central Bank	5.53	– 4.67
十一、其他 Others	– 143.06	22.92	八、同业往来 Inter – bank Transactions	143.18	– 21.55
			九、库存现金 Cash in Vault	0.22	– 0.37
资金来源总计 Total Sources	**2514.29**	**124.81**	**资金运用总计 Total Uses**	**2514.29**	**124.81**

信托投资公司本外币信贷收支表
Sources and Uses of Credit Funds of Financial Trust and Investment Companies
(Domestic and Foreign Currency Combined)

(2005年末)

(Year - end of 2005)

汇率：8.0702
Exchange Rate: 8.0702

单位：亿元
Unit: 100 Million Yuan

项目 Items	余额 Balance	比年初增减额 Changes within the Year	项目 Items	余额 Balance	比年初增减额 Changes within the Year
一、各项存款 Total Deposits	1842.75	33.00	一、各项贷款 Total Loans	1530.48	120.04
1. 信托存款 Trust Deposits	401.57	99.09	1. 信托贷款 Trust Loans	392.97	108.59
2. 委托存款及投资基金 Designated Deposits and Investment Funds	1384.85	-72.30	其中：中长期信托贷款 Of Which: Medium and Long-term Trust Loans	161.91	53.50
3. 其他存款 Other Deposits	56.33	6.21	2. 委托贷款 Designated Loans	1046.74	2.62
二、借款及筹资 Borrowing and Financing	54.43	-10.87	3. 票据融资 Paper Financing	0.05	0.05
三、应付及暂收款 Accounts Receivable and Receipts on Account	137.16	-33.74	其中：贴现 Of Which: Discount		
			4. 融资租赁 Financing Leases	5.15	-2.06
其中：应付及预提利息 Of Which: Interest Payable and Accrued	7.66	-22.33	5. 各项垫款 Total Advances	0.04	
四、证券业务款项 Securities Business Funds	3.31	-2.27	6. 境外筹资转贷款 On-lending of Overseas Financing	0.55	-0.03
五、卖出回购资产 Assets Repo (Including Securities)	35.77	-2.30	7. 其他贷款 Other Loans	84.98	10.87
六、向中央银行借款 Borrowings from the Central Bank	0.84	-0.01	二、委托投资 Designated Investments	527.26	9.19
七、同业往来 Inter-bank Transactions	71.31	-21.07	三、投资 Investments	311.35	-24.74
八、代理金融机构贷款基金 Designated Loan Funds on Behalf of Financial Institutions			四、应收及预付款 Accounts Receivable and Advance Payments	140.89	-49.41
九、各项准备 Total Provisions	39.78	0.27	其中：应收利息及预付利息 Of Which: Interest Receivable and Paid in Advance	20.57	-17.79
其中：贷款呆账准备金 Of Which: Provisions for Bad Loans	15.32	-2.53	五、证券业务占款 Funding of Securities Purchase	0.44	-0.01
十、所有者权益 Owner's Equity	526.12	0.71	六、买入返售资产 Assets Reverse Repo (Including Securities)	0.85	-2.65
其中：实收资本 Of Which: Paid-in Capital	540.22	15.96			
当年结益 Net Earnings	1.23	1.23	七、存放中央银行存款 Deposits with the Central Bank	3.45	-2.24
十一、其他 Others	-55.23	82.21	八、同业往来 Inter-bank Transactions	140.34	-4.52
			九、库存现金 Cash in Vault	1.18	0.27
资金来源总计 Total Sources	**2656.24**	**45.93**	**资金运用总计 Total Uses**	**2656.24**	**45.93**

10. 金融租赁公司本外币信贷收支表（2002—2005 年）

Sources and Uses of Credit Funds of Financial Leasing Companies（Domestic and Foreign Currency Combined）（2002 – 2005）

金融租赁公司本外币信贷收支表（2002—2005 年）

Sources and Uses of Credit Funds of Financial Leasing Companies

（Domestic and Foreign Currency Combined）

（2002 年末）

（Year – end of 2002）

汇率：8.2773
Exchange Rate：8.2773

单位：亿元
Unit：100 Million Yuan

项　目 Items	余　额 Balance	比年初增减额 Changes within the Year	项　目 Items	余　额 Balance	比年初增减额 Changes within the Year
一、各项存款 Total Deposits	61.21	– 3.09	一、各项贷款 Total Loans	138.82	24.28
1. 信托存款 Trust Deposits	3.36	– 1.94	1. 信托贷款 Trust Loans	4.47	– 0.45
2. 委托存款及投资基金 Designated Deposits and Investment Funds	36.28	– 5.14	其中：中长期信托贷款 Of Which：Medium and Long – term Trust Loans	1.09	
3. 其他存款 Other Deposits	21.57	3.99	2. 委托贷款 Designated Loans	23.61	0.38
二、借款及筹资 Borrowing and Financing	44.48	9.89	3. 票据融资 Paper Financing		
三、应付及暂收款 Accounts Receivable and Receipts on Account	11.50	– 3.87	其中：贴现 Of Which：Discount		
其中：应付及预提利息 Of Which：Interest Payable and Accrued	1.19	0.29	4. 融资租赁 Financing Leases	102.43	28.63
			5. 各项垫款 Total Advances		
四、证券业务款项 Securities Business Funds		– 0.01	6. 境外筹资转贷款 On – lending of Overseas Financing		
五、卖出回购证券 Repo	0.20	– 0.10	7. 其他贷款 Other Loans	8.31	– 4.28
六、向中央银行借款 Borrowings from the Central Bank	0.36		二、委托投资 Designated Investments	0.14	– 4.04
七、同业往来 Inter – bank Transactions	23.23	5.48	三、投资 Investments	20.40	8.69
八、代理金融机构贷款基金 Designated Loan Funds on Behalf of Financial Institutions	1.12		四、应收及预付款 Accounts Receivable and Advance Payments	22.38	4.92
九、各项准备 Total Provisions	1.37	0.75	其中：应收利息及预付利息 Of Which：Interest Receivable and Paid in Advance	1.60	– 0.17
其中：贷款呆账准备金 Of Which：Provisions for Bad Loans	1.22	0.69	五、证券业务占款 Funding of Securities Purchase		– 0.01

续表
Continued

项目 Items	余额 Balance	比年初增减额 Changes within the Year	项目 Items	余额 Balance	比年初增减额 Changes within the Year
十、所有者权益 Owner's Equity	46.27	11.62	六、买入返售证券 Reverse Repo	0.08	
其中：实收资本 Of Which: Paid - in Capital	48.66	12.15	七、存放中央银行存款 Deposits with the Central Bank	0.56	-0.50
当年结益 Net Earnings	1.02	1.02	八、同业往来 Inter - bank Transactions	9.19	-3.33
十一、其他 Others	1.88	9.34	九、库存现金 Cash in Vault	0.05	
资金来源总计 Total Sources	**191.62**	**30.01**	**资金运用总计 Total Uses**	**191.62**	**30.01**

金融租赁公司本外币信贷收支表
Sources and Uses of Credit Funds of Financial Leasing Companies
（Domestic and Foreign Currency Combined）

（2003 年末）

（Year－end of 2003）

汇率：8.2767　　　　单位：亿元

Exchange Rate：8.2767　　　　Unit：100 Million Yuan

项　目 Items	余　额 Balance	比年初增减额 Changes within the Year	项　目 Items	余　额 Balance	比年初增减额 Changes within the Year
一、各项存款 Total Deposits	65.51	4.29	一、各项贷款 Total Loans	175.64	36.79
1. 信托存款 Trust Deposits	3.17	－0.19	1. 信托贷款 Trust Loans	3.82	－0.65
2. 委托存款及投资基金 Designated Deposits and Investment Funds	39.17	2.88	其中：中长期信托贷款 Of Which：Medium and Long－term Trust Loans	1.09	
3. 其他存款 Other Deposits	23.17	1.60	2. 委托贷款 Designated Loans	26.08	2.47
二、借款及筹资 Borrowing and Financing	75.72	31.09	3. 票据融资 Paper Financing		
三、应付及暂收款 Accounts Receivable and Receipts on Account	18.10	7.35	其中：贴现 Of Which：Discount		
			4. 融资租赁 Financing Leases	135.91	33.45
其中：应付及预提利息 Of Which：Interest Payable and Accrued	5.10	3.91	5. 各项垫款 Total Advances		
四、证券业务款项 Securities Business Funds			6. 境外筹资转贷款 On－lending of Overseas Financing		
五、卖出回购证券 Repo	0.10	－0.10	7. 其他贷款 Other Loans	9.83	1.52
六、向中央银行借款 Borrowings from the Central Bank	0.36		二、委托投资 Designated Investments	0.08	－0.06
七、同业往来 Inter－bank Transactions	26.54	3.46	三、投资 Investments	18.92	－1.48
八、代理金融机构贷款基金 Designated Loan Funds on Behalf of Financial Institutions	1.12		四、应收及预付款 Accounts Receivable and Advance Payments	24.13	3.17
九、各项准备 Total Provisions	1.87	0.52	其中：应收利息及预付利息 Of Which：Interest Receivable and Paid in Advance	1.42	－0.17
其中：贷款呆账准备金 Of Which：Provisions for Bad Loans	0.74	0.22	五、证券业务占款 Funding of Securities Purchase		
十、所有者权益 Owner's Equity	47.63	1.83	六、买入返售证券 Reverse Repo	0.08	
其中：实收资本 Of Which：Paid－in Capital	52.40	4.14	七、存放中央银行存款 Deposits with the Central Bank	1.31	0.74
当年结益 Net Earnings	0.96	0.96	八、同业往来 Inter－bank Transactions	9.71	0.52
十一、其他 Others	－6.55	－8.28	九、库存现金 Cash in Vault	0.53	0.48
资金来源总计 Total Sources	**230.40**	**40.16**	**资金运用总计 Total Uses**	**230.40**	**40.16**

金融租赁公司本外币信贷收支表

Sources and Uses of Credit Funds of Financial Leasing Companies

(Domestic and Foreign Currency Combined)

(2004 年末)

(Year - end of 2004)

汇率: 8.2765
Exchange Rate: 8.2765

单位: 亿元
Unit: 100 Million Yuan

项目 Items	余额 Balance	比年初增减额 Changes within the Year	项目 Items	余额 Balance	比年初增减额 Changes within the Year
一、各项存款 Total Deposits	69.32	6.81	一、各项贷款 Total Loans	157.20	-18.56
1. 信托存款 Trust Deposits	5.04	1.87	1. 信托贷款 Trust Loans	1.75	-2.06
2. 委托存款及投资基金 Designated Deposits and Investment Funds	42.77	3.60	其中: 中长期信托贷款 Of Which: Medium and Long-term Trust Loans		-1.09
3. 其他存款 Other Deposits	21.51	1.34	2. 委托贷款 Designated Loans	34.51	1.18
二、借款及筹资 Borrowing and Financing	58.71	-15.30	3. 票据融资 Paper Financing		
三、应付及暂收款 Accounts Receivable and Receipts on Account	17.72	-0.71	其中: 贴现 Of Which: Discount		
			4. 融资租赁 Financing Leases	111.55	-17.24
其中: 应付及预提利息 Of Which: Interest Payable and Accrued	4.97	4.57	5. 各项垫款 Total Advances		
四、证券业务款项 Securities Business Funds			6. 境外筹资转贷款 On-lending of Overseas Financing		
五、卖出回购资产 Assets Repo (Including Securities)	0.10		7. 其他贷款 Other Loans	9.39	-0.44
六、向中央银行借款 Borrowings from the Central Bank	0.36		二、委托投资 Designated Investments	0.08	
七、同业往来 Inter-bank Transactions	19.94	-6.60	三、投资 Investments	14.54	-4.38
八、代理金融机构贷款基金 Designated Loan Funds on Behalf of Financial Institutions	1.12		四、应收及预付款 Accounts Receivable and Advance Payments	29.26	4.89
九、各项准备 Total Provisions	9.20	7.34	其中: 应收利息及预付利息 Of Which: Interest Receivable and Paid in Advance	1.36	0.03
其中: 贷款呆账准备金 Of Which: Provisions for Bad Loans	5.47	4.68	五、证券业务占款 Funding of Securities Purchase		
十、所有者权益 Owner's Equity	34.95	-12.53	六、买入返售资产 Assets Reverse Repo (Including Securities)	0.08	
其中: 实收资本 Of Which: Paid-in Capital	56.92	4.52			
当年结益 Net Earnings	-0.15	-0.15	七、存放中央银行存款 Deposits with the Central Bank	1.57	0.26
十一、其他 Others	-1.89	-0.23	八、同业往来 Inter-bank Transactions	6.79	-2.91
			九、库存现金 Cash in Vault	0.01	-0.52
资金来源总计 Total Sources	**209.53**	**-21.22**	**资金运用总计 Total Uses**	**209.53**	**-21.22**

金融租赁公司本外币信贷收支表

Sources and Uses of Credit Funds of Financial Leasing Companies
（Domestic and Foreign Currency Combined）

（2005 年末）

（Year – end of 2005）

汇率：8.0702　　单位：亿元

Exchange Rate：8.0702　　Unit：100 Million Yuan

项　目 Items	余　额 Balance	比年初增减额 Changes within the Year	项　目 Items	余　额 Balance	比年初增减额 Changes within the Year
一、各项存款 Total Deposits	52.60	–17.37	一、各项贷款 Total Loans	132.64	–24.50
1. 信托存款 Trust Deposits	4.73	–0.31	1. 信托贷款 Trust Loans	1.65	–0.08
2. 委托存款及投资基金 Designated Deposits and Investment Funds	33.33	–9.50	其中：中长期信托贷款 Of Which：Medium and Long – term Trust Loans		
3. 其他存款 Other Deposits	14.54	–7.56	2. 委托贷款 Designated Loans	22.73	–11.78
二、借款及筹资 Borrowing and Financing	63.19	4.73	3. 票据融资 Paper Financing		
三、应付及暂收款 Accounts Receivable and Receipts on Account	15.64	–1.45	其中：贴现 Of Which：Discount		
其中：应付及预提利息 Of Which：Interest Payable and Accrued	1.80	–3.17	4. 融资租赁 Financing Leases	100.40	–11.26
			5. 各项垫款 Total Advances		
四、证券业务款项 Securities Business Funds			6. 境外筹资转贷款 On – lending of Overseas Financing		
五、卖出回购资产 Assets Repo（Including Securities）	0.10		7. 其他贷款 Other Loans	7.86	–1.38
六、向中央银行借款 Borrowings from the Central Bank	0.35	–0.01	二、委托投资 Designated Investments		–0.08
七、同业往来 Inter – bank Transactions	16.42	–3.52	三、投资 Investments	11.34	–3.18
八、代理金融机构贷款基金 Designated Loan Funds on Behalf of Financial Institutions	4.10	2.98	四、应收及预付款 Accounts Receivable and Advance Payments	35.14	6.41
九、各项准备 Total Provisions	27.44	17.89	其中：应收利息及预付利息 Of Which：Interest Receivable and Paid in Advance	0.92	–0.44
其中：贷款呆账准备金 Of Which：Provisions for Bad Loans	15.30	9.61	五、证券业务占款 Funding of Securities Purchase		
十、所有者权益 Owner's Equity	13.48	–21.33	六、买入返售资产 Assets Reverse Repo（Including Securities）	0.08	
其中：实收资本 Of Which：Paid – in Capital	56.77	–0.13			
当年结益 Net Earnings	0.09	0.09	七、存放中央银行存款 Deposits with the Central Bank	1.89	0.32
十一、其他 Others	–2.08	0.40	八、同业往来 Inter – bank Transactions	10.14	3.35
			九、库存现金 Cash in Vault	0.01	
资金来源总计 Total Sources	**191.24**	**–17.68**	**资金运用总计 Total Uses**	**191.24**	**–17.68**

11. 外资银行本外币信贷收支表（2002—2005 年）

Sources and Uses of Credit Funds of Foreign - funded Banks（Domestic and Foreign Currency Combined）（2002 - 2005）

外资银行本外币信贷收支表

Sources and Uses of Credit Funds of Foreign - funded Banks

（Domestic and Foreign Currency Combined）

（2002 年末）

（Year - end of 2002）

汇率：8.2773　　　　单位：亿元

Exchange Rate：8.2773　　　　Unit：100 Million Yuan

项　目 Items	余　额 Balance	比年初增减额 Changes within the Year	项　目 Items	余　额 Balance	比年初增减额 Changes within the Year
一、各项存款 Total Deposits	760.76	180.43	一、各项贷款 Total Loans	1538.65	- 17.10
1. 企事业单位存款 Deposits by Enterprises and Public Institutions	641.94	132.27	1. 短期贷款 Short - term Loans	834.23	45.32
(1) 活期存款 Demand Deposits	384.47	139.91	2. 中长期贷款 Medium and Long - term Loans	597.42	- 95.40
(2) 定期存款 Time Deposits	257.47	- 7.64	3. 其他贷款 Other Loans	59.14	23.53
2. 储蓄存款 Savings Deposits	28.45	20.55	4. 票据融资 Paper Financing	47.86	9.45
(1) 活期储蓄 Demand Deposits	6.90	2.35	5. 各项垫款 Total Advances		
(2) 定期储蓄 Time Deposits	21.55	18.20	二、有价证券及投资 Securities and Investments	63.11	3.56
3. 其他存款 Other Deposits	90.37	27.61	三、应收及预付款 Accounts Receivable and Advance Payments	26.79	- 3.63
二、债券发行及境外筹资 Bonds Issue & Overseas Financing	0.18	- 6.03	其中：应收利息 Of Which：Interest Receivable	16.53	- 6.81
三、应付及暂收款 Accounts Receivable and Receipts on Account	49.22	- 18.21	四、买入返售证券 Reverse Repo		
其中：应付及预收利息 Of Which：Interest Payable and Received in Advance	7.14	- 3.63	五、存放中央银行存款 Deposits with the Central Bank	108.80	- 20.41
四、卖出回购证券 Repo	1.00	1.00	六、同业往来 Inter - bank Transactions	459.57	- 6.26
五、向中央银行借款 Borrowings from the Central Bank		- 0.11	七、库存现金 Cash in Vault	2.68	- 0.07
六、同业往来 Inter - bank Transactions	524.72	- 176.70			
七、代理境内贷款资金 Agency Domestic Lending Funds					

续表
Continued

项　　目 Items	余　额 Balance	比年初增减额 Changes within the Year	项　　目 Items	余　额 Balance	比年初增减额 Changes within the Year
八、各项准备 Total Provisions	53.85	-7.10			
其中：贷款呆账准备金 Of Which: Provisions for Bad Loans	52.33	18.79			
九、所有者权益 Owner's Equity	347.88	114.35			
其中：实收资本 Of Which: Paid-in Capital	344.31	89.63			
当年结益 Net Earnings	15.38	15.38			
十、其他 Others	461.99	-131.54			
资金来源总计 Total Sources	**2199.60**	**-43.91**	**资金运用总计 Total Uses**	**2199.60**	**-43.91**

外资银行本外币信贷收支表

Sources and Uses of Credit Funds of Foreign - funded Banks

(Domestic and Foreign Currency Combined)

(2003年末)

(Year - end of 2003)

汇率：8.2767 单位：亿元

Exchange Rate: 8.2767 Unit: 100 Million Yuan

项目 Items	余额 Balance	比年初增减额 Changes within the Year	项目 Items	余额 Balance	比年初增减额 Changes within the Year
一、各项存款 Total Deposits	1054.09	293.30	一、各项贷款 Total Loans	1799.10	262.58
1.企事业单位存款 Deposits by Enterprises and Public Institutions	849.19	207.16	1.短期贷款 Short - term Loans	976.56	145.12
（1）活期存款 Demand Deposits	490.10	105.59	2.中长期贷款 Medium and Long - term Loans	642.98	44.46
（2）定期存款 Time Deposits	359.09	101.57	3.其他贷款 Other Loans	82.92	24.22
2.储蓄存款 Savings Deposits	54.90	26.64	4.票据融资 Paper Financing	96.64	48.78
（1）活期储蓄 Demand Deposits	12.57	5.84	5.各项垫款 Total Advances		
（2）定期储蓄 Time Deposits	42.33	20.80	二、有价证券及投资 Securities and Investments	108.05	44.94
3.其他存款 Other Deposits	150.00	59.50	三、应收及预付款 Accounts Receivable and Advance Payments	27.94	1.11
二、债券发行及境外筹资 Bonds Issue & Overseas Financing		-0.18	其中：应收利息 Of Which: Interest Receivable	15.84	-0.69
三、应付及暂收款 Accounts Receivable and Receipts on Account	58.85	9.63	四、买入返售证券 Reverse Repo		
其中：应付及预收利息 Of Which: Interest Payable and Received in Advance	9.45	2.32	五、存放中央银行存款 Deposits with the Central Bank	172.99	64.21
四、卖出回购证券 Repo	0.98	-0.02	六、同业往来 Inter - bank Transactions	607.06	146.57
五、向中央银行借款 Borrowings from the Central Bank			七、库存现金 Cash in Vault	3.18	0.50
六、同业往来 Inter - bank Transactions	525.36	0.64			
七、代理境内贷款资金 Agency Domestic Lending Funds					
八、各项准备 Total Provisions	34.76	-18.43			
其中：贷款呆账准备金 Of Which: Provisions for Bad Loans	34.28	-17.48			
九、所有者权益 Owner's Equity	385.65	40.48			
其中：实收资本 Of Which: Paid - in Capital	369.42	28.16			
当年结益 Net Earnings	16.63	16.63			
十、其他 Others	658.63	194.49			
资金来源总计 Total Sources	**2718.32**	**519.91**	**资金运用总计 Total Uses**	**2718.32**	**519.91**

外资银行本外币信贷收支表

Sources and Uses of Credit Funds of Foreign - funded Banks

（Domestic and Foreign Currency Combined）

（2004 年末）

（Year - end of 2004）

汇率：8.2765 单位：亿元

Exchange Rate：8.2765 Unit：100 Million Yuan

项　目 Items	余　额 Balance	比年初增减额 Changes within the Year	项　目 Items	余　额 Balance	比年初增减额 Changes within the Year
一、各项存款 Total Deposits	1498.98	410.24	一、各项贷款 Total Loans	2844.24	938.64
1. 企事业单位存款 Deposits by Enterprises and Public Institutions	1149.37	265.32	1. 短期贷款 Short - term Loans	1620.74	580.54
（1）活期存款 Demand Deposits	686.91	175.53	2. 中长期贷款 Medium and Long - term Loans	964.52	298.44
（2）定期存款 Time Deposits	462.46	89.79	3. 其他贷款 Other Loans	106.30	19.74
2. 储蓄存款 Savings Deposits	95.35	39.40	4. 票据融资 Paper Financing	152.68	39.92
（1）活期储蓄 Demand Deposits	25.91	12.77	5. 各项垫款 Total Advances		
（2）定期储蓄 Time Deposits	69.44	26.63	二、有价证券及投资 Securities and Investments	179.30	70.85
3. 其他存款 Other Deposits	254.26	105.52	三、应收及预付款 Accounts Receivable and Advance Payments	39.24	10.81
二、债券发行及境外筹资 Bonds Issue & Overseas Financing			其中：应收利息 Of Which：Interest Receivable	20.24	4.08
三、应付及暂收款 Accounts Receivable and Receipts on Account	85.39	24.53	四、买入返售资产 Assets Reverse Repo（Including Securities）	2.21	2.21
其中：应付及预收利息 Of Which：Interest Payable and Received in Advance	13.37	3.78	五、存放中央银行存款 Deposits with the Central Bank	243.95	66.76
			六、同业往来 Inter - bank Transactions	772.59	154.42
四、卖出回购资产 Assets Repo（Including Securities）	21.18	15.60	七、库存现金 Cash in Vault	3.89	0.66
五、向中央银行借款 Borrowings from the Central Bank		-0.06			
六、同业往来 Inter - bank Transactions	736.74	202.81			
七、代理境内贷款资金 Agency Domestic Lending Funds					
八、各项准备 Total Provisions	39.62	2.66			
其中：贷款呆账准备金 Of Which：Provisions for Bad Loans	39.04	2.56			
九、所有者权益 Owner's Equity	485.73	96.10			
其中：实收资本 Of Which：Paid - in Capital	458.07	81.53			
当年结益 Net Earnings	23.47	23.47			
十、其他 Others	1217.78	492.47			
资金来源总计 Total Sources	**4085.42**	**1244.35**	**资金运用总计 Total Uses**	**4085.42**	**1244.35**

外资银行本外币信贷收支表
Sources and Uses of Credit Funds of Foreign - funded Banks
(Domestic and Foreign Currency Combined)

(2005 年末)

(Year - end of 2005)

汇率：8.0702　　　　单位：亿元

Exchange Rate：8.0702　　　　Unit：100 Million Yuan

项　目 Items	余 额 Balance	比年初增减额 Changes within the Year	项　目 Items	余 额 Balance	比年初增减额 Changes within the Year
一、各项存款 Total Deposits	2028.89	529.46	一、各项贷款 Total Loans	3647.07	804.51
1. 企事业单位存款 Deposits by Enterprises and Public Institutions	1522.36	371.61	1. 短期贷款 Short - term Loans	1923.40	302.91
(1) 活期存款 Demand Deposits	906.31	219.03	2. 中长期贷款 Medium and Long - term Loans	1428.28	464.34
(2) 定期存款 Time Deposits	616.05	152.58	3. 其他贷款 Other Loans	148.93	42.63
2. 储蓄存款 Savings Deposits	125.34	30.11	4. 票据融资 Paper Financing	146.46	-5.37
(1) 活期储蓄 Demand Deposits	34.43	8.58	5. 各项垫款 Total Advances		
(2) 定期储蓄 Time Deposits	90.91	21.53	二、有价证券及投资 Securities and Investments	219.66	40.36
3. 其他存款 Other Deposits	381.19	127.74	三、应收及预付款 Accounts Receivable and Advance Payments	55.96	16.82
二、债券发行及境外筹资 Bonds Issue & Overseas Financing			其中：应收利息 Of Which：Interest Receivable	36.23	16.09
三、应付及暂收款 Accounts Receivable and Receipts on Account	107.62	23.77	四、买入返售资产 Assets Reverse Repo (Including Securities)	2.40	0.19
其中：应付及预收利息 Of Which：Interest Payable and Received in Advance	29.22	15.94	五、存放中央银行存款 Deposits with the Central Bank	363.61	119.45
			六、同业往来 Inter - bank Transactions	1031.62	259.17
四、卖出回购资产 Assets Repo (Including Securities)	53.69	32.51	七、库存现金 Cash in Vault	6.36	2.47
五、向中央银行借款 Borrowings from the Central Bank					
六、同业往来 Inter - bank Transactions	929.26	192.77			
七、代理境内贷款资金 Agency Domestic Lending Funds					
八、各项准备 Total Provisions	49.27	9.26			
其中：贷款呆账准备金 Of Which：Provisions for Bad Loans	48.80	9.37			
九、所有者权益 Owner's Equity	624.46	138.37			
其中：实收资本 Of Which：Paid - in Capital	571.41	112.33			
当年结益 Net Earnings	36.61	36.61			
十、其他 Others	1533.49	316.83			
资金来源总计 Total Sources	**5326.68**	**1242.97**	**资金运用总计 Total Uses**	**5326.68**	**1242.97**

（四）城乡储蓄存款统计
Savings Deposits in Urban and Rural Areas

1. 全国城乡储蓄存款情况表
Savings Deposits in Urban and Rural Areas

全国城乡储蓄存款情况表
Savings Deposits in Urban and Rural Areas

（年末余额）

（Year - end Balance）

单位：亿元

Unit：100 Million Yuan

年份 Year	总计 Total	其中：定期 Of Which：Time	城镇储蓄 Urban Savings	其中：定期 Of Which：Time	农户储蓄 Rural Savings	其中：定期 Of Which：Time
1952	8.6	4.8	8.6	4.8	—	
1953	12.3	6.8	12.2	6.8	0.1	
1954	15.9	9.8	14.3	9.8	1.6	
1955	19.9	13.3	16.9	13.3	3.0	
1956	26.7	15.6	22.4	15.6	4.3	
1957	35.2	19.6	27.9	19.6	7.3	
1958	55.2	23.9	35.1	23.9	20.1	
1959	68.3	31.6	47.3	31.6	21.0	
1960	66.3	37.3	51.1	37.3	15.2	
1961	55.4	29.7	39.2	29.7	16.2	
1962	41.2	25.6	31.4	25.6	9.8	
1963	45.7	29.4	35.6	29.4	10.1	
1964	55.5	37.0	44.8	37.0	10.7	
1965	65.2	43.4	52.3	43.4	12.9	
1966	72.3	46.9	57.7	46.9	14.6	
1967	73.8	48.9	59.8	48.9	14.0	
1968	78.3	50.3	62.3	50.3	16.0	
1969	75.9	49.4	61.0	49.4	14.9	
1970	79.5	53.8	64.5	53.8	15.0	
1971	90.3	61.4	73.3	61.4	17.0	
1972	105.2	69.6	85.1	69.6	20.1	
1973	121.2	77.7	94.1	77.7	27.1	
1974	136.4	86.7	105.8	86.7	30.6	
1975	149.7	94.5	114.6	94.5	35.1	
1976	159.1	100.6	122.2	100.6	36.9	
1977	181.6	111.7	135.1	111.7	46.5	
1978	210.6	128.9	154.9	128.9	55.7	
1979	281.0	166.4	202.6	166.4	78.4	
1980	395.8	304.9	278.8	228.6	117.0	76.3

注：1979 年以前定期储蓄存款中不含农户定期储蓄存款。

Notes：Time savings deposits prior to 1979 did not include those by rural households.

全国城乡储蓄存款情况表（续）

Savings Deposits in Urban and Rural Areas（Continued）

（年末余额）

（Year－end Balance）

单位：亿元

Unit：100 Million Yuan

年份 Year	总计 Total	其中：定期 Of Which：Time	城镇储蓄 Urban Savings	其中：定期 Of Which：Time	农户储蓄 Rural Savings	其中：定期 Of Which：Time
1981	523.4	396.4	353.8	289.4	169.6	107.0
1982	675.4	519.3	447.3	365.2	228.1	154.1
1983	892.9	682.4	572.6	463.9	320.3	218.5
1984	1214.7	900.9	776.6	615.4	438.1	285.5
1985	1622.6	1225.2	1057.8	841.2	564.8	384.0
1986	2237.8	1729.2	1471.7	1189.3	766.1	539.9
1987	3083.4	2357.8	2075.5	1647.9	1007.9	709.9
1988	3819.1	2845.3	2679.9	2057.0	1139.2	788.3
1989	5184.5	4208.5	3780.4	3131.8	1404.1	1076.7
1990	7119.6	5909.4	5278.6	4455.6	1841.0	1453.8
1991	9244.9	7634.9	6925.5	5808.6	2319.4	1826.3
1992	11757.3	9445.0	8889.9	7171.1	2867.4	2273.9
1993	15203.54	12108.34	11627.30	9263.10	3576.24	2845.24
1994	21518.80	16838.70	16702.80	13028.10	4816.00	3810.60
1995	29662.26	23778.25	23466.70	18765.05	6195.56	5013.20
1996	38520.84	30873.21	30850.23	24578.83	7670.61	6294.38
1997	46279.80	36226.74	37147.63	28731.10	9132.17	7495.64
1998	53407.47	41791.57	42966.44	33299.05	10441.03	8492.52
1999	59621.83	44955.11	48404.58	36051.89	11217.25	8903.22
2000	64332.38	46141.66	51977.13	36650.47	12355.25	9491.19
2001	73762.43	51434.86	59941.07	41017.81	13821.36	10417.05
2002	86910.65	58788.94	71504.85	47485.84	15405.80	11303.10
2003	103617.65	68498.67	85612.66	55589.17	18004.99	12909.50
2004	119555.39	78138.86	98789.22	63577.81	20766.17	14561.05
2005	141050.99	92263.54	119311.66	77206.15	21739.33	15057.39

2. 全国城乡储蓄存款增减额情况表

Ups and Downs of Savings Deposits in Urban and Rural Areas

全国城乡储蓄存款增减额情况表

Ups and Downs of Savings Deposits in Urban and Rural Areas

（比上年末）

（Compared with the End of Previous Year）

单位：亿元

Unit：100 Million Yuan

年份 Year	总计 Total	其中：定期 Of Which：Time	城镇储蓄 Urban Savings	其中：定期 Of Which：Time	农户储蓄 Rural Savings	其中：定期 Of Which：Time
1953	3.7	2.0	3.6	2.0	0.1	
1954	3.6	3.0	2.1	3.0	1.5	
1955	4.0	3.5	2.6	3.5	1.4	
1956	6.8	2.3	5.5	2.3	1.3	
1957	8.5	4.0	5.5	4.0	3.0	
1958	20.0	4.3	7.2	4.3	12.8	
1959	13.1	7.7	12.2	7.7	0.9	
1960	-2.0	5.7	3.8	5.7	-5.8	
1961	-10.9	-7.6	11.9	7.6	1.0	
1962	-14.2	-4.1	-7.8	-4.1	-6.4	
1963	4.5	3.8	4.2	3.8	0.3	
1964	9.8	7.6	9.2	7.6	0.6	
1965	9.7	6.4	7.5	6.4	2.2	
1966	7.1	3.5	5.4	3.5	1.7	
1967	1.5	2.0	2.1	2.0	-0.6	
1968	4.5	1.4	2.5	1.4	2.0	
1969	-2.4	-0.9	-1.3	-0.9	-1.1	
1970	3.6	4.4	3.5	4.4	0.1	
1971	10.8	7.7	8.8	7.6	2.0	
1972	14.9	8.2	11.8	8.2	3.1	
1973	16.0	8.1	9.0	8.1	7.0	
1974	15.2	9.0	11.7	9.0	3.5	
1975	13.3	7.8	8.8	7.8	4.5	
1976	9.4	6.1	7.6	6.1	1.8	
1977	22.5	11.1	12.9	11.1	9.6	
1978	29.0	17.2	19.8	17.2	9.2	
1979	70.4	37.5	47.7	37.5	22.7	
1980	114.8	138.5	76.2	62.2	38.6	76.3

全国城乡储蓄存款增减额情况表（续）

Ups and Downs of Savings Deposits in Urban and Rural Areas（Continued）

（比上年末）

（Compared with the End of Previous Year）

单位：亿元

Unit: 100 Million Yuan

年份 Year	总计 Total	其中：定期 Of Which: Time	城镇储蓄 Urban Savings	其中：定期 Of Which: Time	农户储蓄 Rural Savings	其中：定期 Of Which: Time
1981	127.6	91.5	75.0	60.8	52.6	30.7
1982	152.0	122.9	93.5	75.8	58.6	47.1
1983	217.5	163.1	125.3	98.7	92.2	64.4
1984	321.8	218.5	204.0	151.5	117.8	67.0
1985	407.9	324.3	281.2	225.8	126.7	98.5
1986	615.2	504.0	413.9	348.1	201.3	155.9
1987	845.6	628.6	603.8	458.6	241.8	170.0
1988	735.7	487.5	604.4	409.1	131.3	78.4
1989	1365.4	1363.2	1100.5	1074.8	264.9	288.4
1990	1935.1	1700.9	1498.2	1323.8	436.9	377.1
1991	2125.3	1725.5	1646.9	1353.0	478.4	372.5
1992	2512.4	1810.1	1964.4	1362.5	548.0	447.6
1993	3446.24	2663.34	2737.40	2092.00	708.84	571.34
1994	6315.26	4730.36	5075.50	3765.00	1239.76	965.36
1995	8143.46	6939.55	6763.90	5736.95	1379.56	1202.60
1996	8858.58	7094.96	7383.53	5813.78	1475.05	1281.18
1997	7758.96	5353.53	6297.40	4152.27	1461.56	1201.26
1998	7127.67	5564.83	5818.81	4567.95	1308.86	996.88
1999	6214.36	3163.54	5438.14	2752.84	776.22	410.70
2000	4710.55	1186.55	3572.55	598.58	1138.00	587.97
2001	9430.05	5293.20	7963.94	4367.34	1466.11	925.86
2002	13148.22	7354.08	11563.78	6468.03	1584.44	886.05
2003	16707.00	9709.73	14107.81	8103.33	2599.19	1606.40
2004	15937.74	9640.19	13176.56	7988.64	2761.18	1651.55
2005	21495.60	14124.68	20522.44	13628.34	973.16	496.34

3. 全国人均储蓄存款情况表
National Per Capita Savings Deposits

全国人均储蓄存款情况表
National Per Capita Savings Deposits

年份 Year	总人口（亿人）Total Population（100 Millions）	其中 Of Which		城乡储蓄存款余额（亿元）Balance of Urban and Rural Savings Deposits（100 Million Yuan）	其中 Of Which		全国人均储蓄存款（元）National Per Capita Savings Deposits（Yuan）	城镇人均储蓄存款（元）Urban Per Capita Savings Deposits（Yuan）	农户人均储蓄存款（元）Rural Per Capita Savings Deposits（Yuan）
		城镇人口 Urban Population	乡村人口 Rural Population		城镇储蓄 Urban Savings	农户储蓄 Rural Savings			
1952	5.75	0.72	5.03	8.6	8.6	—	1.50	11.94	—
1953	5.88	0.78	5.10	12.3	12.2	0.1	2.09	15.64	0.02
1954	6.02	0.82	5.20	15.9	14.3	1.6	2.64	17.44	0.31
1955	6.15	0.83	5.32	19.9	16.9	3.0	3.24	20.36	0.56
1956	6.28	0.92	5.36	26.7	22.4	4.3	4.25	24.35	0.80
1957	6.46	0.99	5.47	35.2	27.9	7.3	5.45	28.18	1.33
1958	6.60	1.07	5.53	55.2	35.1	20.1	8.36	32.80	3.63
1959	6.72	1.24	5.48	68.3	47.3	21.0	10.16	38.15	3.83
1960	6.62	1.31	5.31	66.3	51.1	15.2	10.02	39.01	2.86
1961	6.59	1.27	5.32	55.4	39.2	16.2	8.41	30.87	3.05
1962	6.73	1.17	5.56	41.1	31.4	9.7	6.11	26.84	1.74
1963	6.91	1.16	5.75	45.7	35.6	10.1	6.61	30.69	1.76
1964	7.04	1.29	5.75	55.5	44.8	10.7	7.88	34.73	1.86
1965	7.25	1.30	5.95	65.2	52.3	12.9	8.99	40.23	2.17
1966	7.45	1.33	6.12	72.3	57.7	14.6	9.70	43.38	2.39
1967	7.63	1.35	6.28	73.9	59.8	14.1	9.69	44.30	2.25
1968	7.85	1.38	6.47	78.3	62.3	16.0	9.97	45.14	2.47
1969	8.07	1.41	6.66	75.9	61.0	14.9	9.41	43.26	2.24
1970	8.30	1.44	6.86	79.5	64.5	15.0	9.58	44.79	2.19
1971	8.25	1.47	7.05	90.3	73.3	17.0	10.95	49.86	2.41
1972	8.71	1.49	7.22	105.2	85.1	20.1	12.08	57.11	2.78
1973	8.92	1.53	7.39	121.2	94.1	27.1	13.59	61.50	3.67
1974	9.09	1.56	7.53	136.4	105.8	30.6	15.01	67.82	4.06
1975	9.24	1.60	7.64	149.7	114.6	35.1	16.20	71.63	4.59
1976	9.37	1.63	7.74	159.1	122.2	36.9	16.98	74.97	4.77
1977	9.50	1.67	7.83	181.6	135.1	46.5	19.12	80.90	5.94
1978	9.62	1.72	7.90	210.6	154.9	55.7	21.89	90.06	7.05
1979	9.75	1.85	7.90	281.0	202.6	78.4	28.82	109.51	9.92
1980	9.87	1.91	7.96	395.8	278.8	117.0	40.10	145.97	14.70

全国人均储蓄存款情况表（续）
National Per Capita Savings Deposits (Continued)

年 份 Year	总人口（亿人）Total Population (100 Millions)	其中 Of Which		城乡储蓄存款余额（亿元）Balance of Urban and Rural Savings Deposits (100 Million Yuan)	其中 Of Which		全国人均储蓄存款（元）National Per Capita Savings Deposits (Yuan)	城镇人均储蓄存款（元）Urban Per Capita Savings Deposits (Yuan)	农户人均储蓄存款（元）Rural Per Capita Savings Deposits (Yuan)
		城镇人口 Urban Population	乡村人口 Rural Population		城镇储蓄 Urban Savings	农户储蓄 Rural Savings			
1981	10.01	2.02	7.99	523.4	353.8	169.6	52.29	175.15	21.23
1982	10.16	2.11	8.05	675.4	447.3	228.1	66.48	211.99	28.34
1983	10.27	2.41	7.86	892.9	572.6	320.3	86.94	237.59	40.75
1984	10.38	3.31	7.07	1214.7	776.6	438.1	117.02	234.62	61.97
1985	10.50	3.84	6.66	1622.6	1057.8	564.8	154.53	275.47	84.80
1986	10.65	4.41	6.24	2237.8	1471.7	766.1	210.12	333.72	122.77
1987	10.81	5.04	5.77	3083.4	2075.5	1007.9	285.24	411.81	174.68
1988	10.96	5.44	5.52	3819.1	2679.9	1139.2	348.46	492.63	206.38
1989	11.12	5.55	5.57	5184.5	3780.4	1404.1	466.23	681.15	252.08
1990	11.43	5.72	5.71	7119.6	5278.6	1841.0	622.89	922.83	322.42
1991	11.58	3.05	8.53	9244.9	6925.5	2319.4	798.35	2270.66	271.91
1992	11.72	3.24	8.48	11757.3	8889.9	2867.4	1003.18	2743.80	338.14
1993	11.86	3.34	8.52	15203.54	11627.30	3576.24	1281.92	3481.23	419.75
1994	11.99	3.43	8.56	21518.80	16702.80	4816.00	1794.73	4869.62	562.62
1995	12.12	3.52	8.60	29662.30	23466.70	6195.60	2447.38	6666.68	720.42
1996	12.24	3.60	8.64	38520.84	30850.23	7670.61	3147.13	8569.51	887.80
1997	12.36	3.94	8.42	46279.80	37147.63	9132.17	3744.32	9428.33	1084.58
1998	12.48	4.16	8.32	53407.47	42966.44	10441.03	4279.44	10328.47	1254.93
1999	12.58	4.38	8.20	59621.83	48404.58	11217.25	4739.41	11051.27	1367.96
2000	12.67	4.59	8.08	64332.38	51977.13	12355.25	5077.54	11323.99	1529.12
2001	12.76	4.80	7.96	73762.43	59941.07	13821.36	5780.75	12487.72	1736.35
2002	12.84	5.02	7.82	86910.65	71504.85	15405.80	6768.74	14243.99	1970.05
2003	12.92	5.24	7.68	103617.65	85612.66	18004.99	8019.94	16338.29	2344.40
2004	13.00	5.43	7.57	119555.39	98789.22	20766.17	9196.57	18193.23	2743.22
2005	13.07	5.62	7.45	141050.99	119311.66	21739.33	10791.97	21229.83	2918.03

4. 储蓄存款分地区数据
Balance of Savings Deposits by Regions

全国各地区城乡储蓄存款余额表
Balance of Savings Deposits by Regions

（1997 年末）

（Year - end of 1997）

单位：亿元

Unit：100 Million Yuan

项目 Items / 地区 Regions	城乡储蓄合计 Total of Savings Deposits in Urban and Rural Areas	其中：定期 Of Which：Time	城镇储蓄合计 Total of Savings Deposits in Urban Areas	其中：定期 Of Which：Time	农村储蓄合计 Total of Savings Deposits in Rural Areas	其中：定期 Of Which：Time
全　国 National Total	**46279.80**	**36226.74**	**37147.63**	**28731.10**	**9132.17**	**7495.64**
总　行 Headquarters	27.46	21.11	27.46	21.11		
北　京 Beijing	1966.49	1675.65	1762.13	1492.79	204.36	182.86
天　津 Tianjin	863.36	735.98	741.43	631.82	121.93	104.16
河　北 Hebei	2685.10	2260.43	1917.00	1590.76	768.10	669.67
山　西 Shanxi	1236.83	1070.20	955.51	818.25	281.32	251.95
内蒙古 Inner Mongolia	605.01	446.24	523.67	390.91	81.34	55.33
辽　宁 Liaoning	2726.39	2293.90	2350.09	1967.76	376.30	326.14
吉　林 Jilin	1140.38	909.15	1003.68	798.05	136.70	111.10
黑龙江 Heilongjiang	1689.72	1338.40	1528.08	1210.50	161.64	127.90
上　海 Shanghai	2729.57	1843.25	2556.83	1673.62	172.74	169.63
江　苏 Jiangsu	3102.62	2657.49	2463.37	2087.81	639.25	569.68
浙　江 Zhejiang	2292.90	1869.52	1635.43	1304.18	657.47	565.34
安　徽 Anhui	1036.47	832.90	788.75	638.89	247.72	194.01
福　建 Fujian	1324.37	999.32	1153.48	862.38	170.89	136.94
江　西 Jiangxi	928.24	740.12	750.39	599.22	177.85	140.90
山　东 Shandong	3246.54	2695.03	2457.72	2021.76	788.82	673.27
河　南 Henan	2230.15	1725.36	1673.44	1277.15	556.71	448.21
湖　北 Hubei	1410.57	1066.54	1145.54	845.79	265.03	220.75
湖　南 Hunan	1303.80	1027.40	919.15	708.41	384.65	318.99
广　东 Guangdong	6312.78	4314.19	4786.93	3202.05	1525.85	1112.14
广　西 Guangxi	1013.14	675.10	815.15	534.04	197.99	141.06
海　南 Hainan	360.83	256.70	317.58	225.01	43.25	31.69
四　川 Sichuan	1646.85	1341.36	1210.39	974.86	436.46	366.50
贵　州 Guizhou	362.87	275.26	317.69	244.13	45.18	31.13
云　南 Yunnan	806.07	619.38	656.85	507.85	149.22	111.53
西　藏 Tibet	30.45	22.28	30.45	22.28		
陕　西 Shanxi	1090.43	839.73	846.79	641.18	243.64	198.55
甘　肃 Gansu	570.70	452.21	493.69	395.53	77.01	56.68
青　海 Qinghai	113.15	87.41	105.60	82.12	7.55	5.29
宁　夏 Ningxia	168.85	136.26	147.56	119.46	21.29	16.80
新　疆 Xinjiang	676.13	543.77	621.32	505.38	54.81	38.39
重　庆 Chongqing	581.55	455.07	444.49	336.03	137.06	119.04

全国各地区城乡储蓄存款余额表（续一）
Balance of Savings Deposits by Regions（Continued）

（1998年末）

（Year-end of 1998）

单位：亿元

Unit：100 Million Yuan

项目 Items / 地区 Regions	城乡储蓄合计 Total of Savings Deposits in Urban and Rural Areas	其中：定期 Of Which: Time	城镇储蓄合计 Total of Savings Deposits in Urban Areas	其中：定期 Of Which: Time	农村储蓄合计 Total of Savings Deposits in Rural Areas	其中：定期 Of Which: Time
全　国 National Total	**53407.47**	**41791.57**	**42966.44**	**33299.05**	**10441.03**	**8492.52**
总　行 Headquarters	29.43	23.03	29.43	23.03		
北　京 Beijing	2277.73	1844.34	2053.73	1647.34	224.00	197.00
天　津 Tianjin	1020.15	855.74	880.83	738.53	139.32	117.21
河　北 Hebei	3208.08	2693.19	2272.10	1882.01	935.98	811.18
山　西 Shanxi	1436.64	1246.41	1092.91	939.33	343.73	307.08
内蒙古 Inner Mongolia	705.72	504.58	610.35	442.79	95.37	61.79
辽　宁 Liaoning	3190.46	2654.09	2757.26	2281.78	433.20	372.31
吉　林 Jilin	1287.72	1008.91	1125.75	880.39	161.97	128.52
黑龙江 Heilongjiang	1906.69	1506.01	1730.17	1369.24	176.52	136.77
上　海 Shanghai	2372.94	2017.16	2180.69	1829.37	192.25	187.79
江　苏 Jiangsu	3657.78	3114.45	2948.03	2484.89	709.75	629.56
浙　江 Zhejiang	2846.81	2300.30	2075.59	1643.99	771.22	656.31
安　徽 Anhui	1175.11	940.36	895.99	723.47	279.12	216.89
福　建 Fujian	1565.18	1141.86	1367.81	986.44	197.37	155.42
江　西 Jiangxi	1068.60	831.46	873.80	677.59	194.80	153.87
山　东 Shandong	3728.78	3080.42	2850.01	2331.74	878.77	748.68
河　南 Henan	2657.22	2079.70	1997.48	1548.79	659.74	530.91
湖　北 Hubei	1577.98	1160.27	1297.45	931.90	280.53	228.37
湖　南 Hunan	1506.29	1170.50	1075.37	815.97	430.92	354.53
广　东 Guangdong	7541.11	5120.15	5823.64	3885.00	1717.47	1235.15
广　西 Guangxi	1150.09	754.97	943.99	612.48	206.10	142.49
海　南 Hainan	414.25	295.88	366.50	261.66	47.75	34.22
四　川 Sichuan	2002.08	1613.04	1476.54	1172.11	525.54	440.93
贵　州 Guizhou	423.08	307.70	366.04	269.96	57.04	37.74
云　南 Yunnan	912.89	680.20	751.45	558.15	161.44	122.05
西　藏 Tibet	33.45	23.35	33.45	23.35		
陕　西 Shanxi	1241.63	921.17	973.03	710.34	268.60	210.83
甘　肃 Gansu	663.11	506.52	574.65	443.87	88.46	62.65
青　海 Qinghai	130.42	97.04	121.01	90.99	9.41	6.05
宁　夏 Ningxia	192.36	148.89	168.67	130.84	23.69	18.05
新　疆 Xinjiang	759.14	597.17	696.30	554.35	62.84	42.82
重　庆 Chongqing	724.54	552.72	556.42	407.40	168.12	145.32

全国各地区城乡储蓄存款余额表（续二）

Balance of Savings Deposits by Regions（Continued）

（1999 年末）

（Year - end of 1999）

单位：亿元

Unit：100 Million Yuan

项目 Items / 地区 Regions	城乡储蓄合计 Total of Savings Deposits in Urban and Rural Areas	其中：定期 Of Which: Time	城镇储蓄合计 Total of Savings Deposits in Urban Areas	其中：定期 Of Which: Time	农村储蓄合计 Total of Savings Deposits in Rural Areas	其中：定期 Of Which: Time
全　国 National Total	**59621.83**	**44955.11**	**48404.58**	**36051.89**	**11217.25**	**8903.22**
总　行 Headquarters	8.08	5.23	8.08	5.23		
北　京 Beijing	2681.25	2060.99	2429.61	1844.12	251.64	216.87
天　津 Tianjin	1130.18	918.46	975.04	789.44	155.14	129.02
河　北 Hebei	3681.24	3021.88	2590.25	2089.01	1090.99	932.87
山　西 Shanxi	1613.72	1377.79	1259.53	1059.15	354.19	318.64
内蒙古 Inner Mongolia	796.63	535.92	691.56	472.99	105.07	62.93
辽　宁 Liaoning	3555.76	2871.86	3077.83	2464.76	477.93	407.10
吉　林 Jilin	1422.58	1071.20	1249.35	938.88	173.23	132.32
黑龙江 Heilongjiang	2122.24	1627.60	1931.52	1485.09	190.72	142.51
上　海 Shanghai	2597.12	2119.82	2392.83	1921.49	204.29	198.33
江　苏 Jiangsu	4132.38	3437.39	3363.04	2771.99	769.34	665.40
浙　江 Zhejiang	3262.69	2508.60	2421.43	1810.61	841.26	697.99
安　徽 Anhui	1302.46	1018.41	1004.65	790.28	297.81	228.13
福　建 Fujian	1739.01	1167.50	1525.53	1009.04	213.48	158.46
江　西 Jiangxi	1161.14	870.09	958.79	715.83	202.35	154.26
山　东 Shandong	4109.02	3301.95	3168.64	2514.58	940.38	787.37
河　南 Henan	2939.96	2282.02	2239.50	1718.90	700.46	563.12
湖　北 Hubei	1705.93	1224.67	1435.43	1009.06	270.50	215.61
湖　南 Hunan	1688.40	1240.65	1245.36	887.38	443.04	353.27
广　东 Guangdong	8183.78	5154.17	6417.08	3973.55	1766.70	1180.62
广　西 Guangxi	1257.26	783.69	1054.10	653.11	203.16	130.58
海　南 Hainan	397.85	263.27	348.05	229.73	49.80	33.54
四　川 Sichuan	2385.19	1865.40	1775.57	1356.03	609.62	509.37
贵　州 Guizhou	484.51	328.48	420.99	288.70	63.52	39.78
云　南 Yunnan	1028.92	728.03	851.75	598.22	177.17	129.81
西　藏 Tibet	36.82	23.61	36.82	23.61		
陕　西 Shanxi	1371.95	1027.18	1097.15	814.91	274.80	212.27
甘　肃 Gansu	737.50	556.68	641.91	490.10	95.59	66.58
青　海 Qinghai	142.86	101.13	132.92	95.08	9.94	6.05
宁　夏 Ningxia	211.59	157.27	187.08	139.15	24.51	18.12
新　疆 Xinjiang	824.68	631.18	765.43	591.17	59.25	40.01
重　庆 Chongqing	909.10	672.97	707.78	500.69	201.32	172.28

全国各地区城乡储蓄存款余额表（续三）
Balance of Savings Deposits by Regions (Continued)

（2000年末）

(Year - end of 2000)

单位：亿元

Unit: 100 Million Yuan

项目 Items / 地区 Regions	城乡储蓄合计 Total of Savings Deposits in Urban and Rural Areas	其中：定期 Of Which: Time	城镇储蓄合计 Total of Savings Deposits in Urban Areas	其中：定期 Of Which: Time	农村储蓄合计 Total of Savings Deposits in Rural Areas	其中：定期 Of Which: Time
全　国 National Total	**64332.38**	**46141.66**	**51977.13**	**36650.47**	**12355.25**	**9491.19**
总　行 Headquarters	22.40	1.01	22.40	1.01		
北　京 Beijing	2923.13	2095.99	2663.22	1878.75	259.91	217.24
天　津 Tianjin	1172.40	910.34	1011.47	780.95	160.93	129.39
河　北 Hebei	3957.07	3152.36	2672.85	2081.45	1284.22	1070.91
山　西 Shanxi	1748.42	1450.32	1364.02	1109.94	384.40	340.38
内蒙古 Inner Mongolia	875.74	556.42	760.79	491.67	114.95	64.75
辽　宁 Liaoning	3790.60	2914.06	3278.45	2487.58	512.15	426.48
吉　林 Jilin	1512.52	1076.59	1319.94	934.98	192.58	141.61
黑龙江 Heilongjiang	2285.48	1672.85	2071.57	1520.56	213.91	152.29
上　海 Shanghai	2524.05	1987.09	2321.14	1792.30	202.91	194.79
江　苏 Jiangsu	4457.55	3563.93	3601.33	2842.00	856.22	721.93
浙　江 Zhejiang	3594.65	2585.23	2661.19	1844.49	933.46	740.74
安　徽 Anhui	1446.45	1089.64	1119.23	845.06	327.22	244.58
福　建 Fujian	1767.59	1074.90	1541.74	917.30	225.85	157.60
江　西 Jiangxi	1243.15	885.30	1003.02	705.26	240.13	180.04
山　东 Shandong	4466.72	3465.41	3343.59	2545.02	1123.13	920.39
河　南 Henan	3182.07	2393.64	2373.86	1758.18	808.21	635.46
湖　北 Hubei	1908.81	1317.75	1615.93	1091.93	292.88	225.82
湖　南 Hunan	1874.22	1315.23	1375.06	926.85	499.16	388.38
广　东 Guangdong	8665.79	5076.18	6868.42	3965.15	1797.37	1111.03
广　西 Guangxi	1374.47	800.82	1153.44	668.29	221.03	132.53
海　南 Hainan	404.19	245.37	354.47	214.39	49.72	30.98
四　川 Sichuan	2693.17	2012.50	2055.95	1488.56	637.22	523.94
贵　州 Guizhou	539.48	336.31	466.91	293.77	72.57	42.54
云　南 Yunnan	1138.22	750.67	937.49	610.62	200.73	140.05
西　藏 Tibet	40.48	23.41	40.48	23.41		
陕　西 Shanxi	1522.70	1101.64	1228.23	880.61	294.47	221.03
甘　肃 Gansu	818.76	593.99	709.35	521.27	109.41	72.72
青　海 Qinghai	159.07	104.44	146.95	97.59	12.12	6.85
宁　夏 Ningxia	229.35	160.59	204.01	142.91	25.34	17.68
新　疆 Xinjiang	908.55	653.58	835.95	607.91	72.60	45.67
重　庆 Chongqing	1085.12	774.10	854.66	580.71	230.46	193.39

全国各地区城乡储蓄存款余额表（续四）

Balance of Savings Deposits by Regions（Continued）

（2001 年末）

（Year - end of 2001）

单位：亿元

Unit：100 Million Yuan

项目 Items / 地区 Regions	城乡储蓄合计 Total of Savings Deposits in Urban and Rural Areas	其中：定期 Of Which: Time	城镇储蓄合计 Total of Savings Deposits in Urban Areas	其中：定期 Of Which: Time	农村储蓄合计 Total of Savings Deposits in Rural Areas	其中：定期 Of Which: Time
全　国 National Total	**73762.43**	**51434.86**	**59941.07**	**41017.81**	**13821.36**	**10417.05**
总　行 Headquarters	0.08		0.08			
北　京 Beijing	3536.32	2404.32	3253.87	2178.94	282.45	225.38
天　津 Tianjin	1284.95	976.74	1117.34	845.55	167.61	131.19
河　北 Hebei	4364.51	3419.72	2973.31	2270.12	1391.20	1149.60
山　西 Shanxi	1979.72	1597.85	1522.54	1201.41	457.18	396.44
内蒙古 Inner Mongolia	986.74	609.52	834.76	526.51	151.98	83.01
辽　宁 Liaoning	4131.55	3139.04	3584.44	2682.91	547.11	456.13
吉　林 Jilin	1676.06	1170.98	1465.18	1014.34	210.88	156.64
黑龙江 Heilongjiang	2578.45	1846.03	2341.28	1676.03	237.17	170.00
上　海 Shanghai	3001.89	2204.59	2781.82	1996.80	220.07	207.79
江　苏 Jiangsu	5172.83	4027.73	4217.93	3237.02	954.90	790.71
浙　江 Zhejiang	4262.38	2937.67	3178.03	2107.11	1084.35	830.56
安　徽 Anhui	1700.47	1255.06	1322.01	975.62	378.46	279.44
福　建 Fujian	2030.93	1142.34	1792.83	983.90	238.10	158.44
江　西 Jiangxi	1429.52	986.60	1157.33	786.76	272.19	199.84
山　东 Shandong	5063.42	3856.51	3764.68	2802.84	1298.74	1053.67
河　南 Henan	3634.51	2696.14	2746.66	2007.88	887.85	688.26
湖　北 Hubei	2287.40	1575.90	1947.70	1315.47	339.70	260.43
湖　南 Hunan	2183.73	1501.16	1620.79	1067.87	562.94	433.29
广　东 Guangdong	9930.12	5624.23	7986.58	4478.37	1943.54	1145.86
广　西 Guangxi	1538.61	868.25	1289.90	724.84	248.71	143.41
海　南 Hainan	427.32	250.52	378.07	220.79	49.25	29.73
四　川 Sichuan	3123.38	2282.84	2403.51	1694.38	719.87	588.46
贵　州 Guizhou	641.67	380.87	551.36	329.80	90.31	51.07
云　南 Yunnan	1298.52	834.57	1074.82	681.85	223.70	152.72
西　藏 Tibet	50.18	26.62	50.18	26.62		
陕　西 Shanxi	1768.47	1254.87	1436.50	1010.29	331.97	244.58
甘　肃 Gansu	920.71	652.50	799.53	574.21	121.18	78.29
青　海 Qinghai	188.53	116.23	174.23	108.69	14.30	7.54
宁　夏 Ningxia	257.97	173.95	227.87	153.79	30.10	20.16
新　疆 Xinjiang	994.30	692.15	905.41	637.06	88.89	55.09
重　庆 Chongqing	1317.17	929.37	1040.50	700.04	276.67	229.33

全国各地区城乡储蓄存款余额表（续五）
Balance of Savings Deposits by Regions (Continued)

（2002年末）

（Year - end of 2002）

单位：亿元

Unit: 100 Million Yuan

项目 Items / 地区 Regions	城乡储蓄合计 Total of Savings Deposits in Urban and Rural Areas	其中：定期 Of Which: Time	城镇储蓄合计 Total of Savings Deposits in Urban Areas	其中：定期 Of Which: Time	农村储蓄合计 Total of Savings Deposits in Rural Areas	其中：定期 Of Which: Time
全　国 National Total	**86910.65**	**58788.94**	**71504.85**	**47485.84**	**15405.80**	**11303.10**
总　行 Headquarters	2.50		2.50			
北　京 Beijing	4389.69	2875.81	4073.07	2634.71	316.62	241.10
天　津 Tianjin	1486.41	1096.34	1308.28	962.97	178.13	133.37
河　北 Hebei	4808.29	3680.17	3317.47	2462.47	1490.82	1217.70
山　西 Shanxi	2307.32	1797.63	1768.74	1339.42	538.58	458.21
内蒙古 Inner Mongolia	1137.93	685.06	959.04	588.54	178.89	96.52
辽　宁 Liaoning	4665.05	3454.50	4070.54	2959.68	594.51	494.82
吉　林 Jilin	1878.45	1295.92	1643.34	1119.51	235.11	176.41
黑龙江 Heilongjiang	2915.65	2033.47	2654.52	1847.44	261.13	186.03
上　海 Shanghai	3891.45	2730.13	3638.86	2498.19	252.59	231.94
江　苏 Jiangsu	6276.20	4720.09	5333.79	3959.18	942.41	760.91
浙　江 Zhejiang	5212.69	3445.31	3935.39	2500.22	1277.30	945.09
安　徽 Anhui	2047.51	1473.85	1609.13	1155.50	438.38	318.35
福　建 Fujian	2430.46	1385.45	2157.05	1206.87	273.41	178.58
江　西 Jiangxi	1706.63	1125.02	1397.16	904.44	309.47	220.58
山　东 Shandong	5803.52	4276.17	4355.18	3129.17	1448.34	1147.00
河　南 Henan	4196.01	3050.43	3211.67	2293.25	984.34	757.18
湖　北 Hubei	2754.54	1854.89	2364.69	1564.83	389.85	290.06
湖　南 Hunan	2576.40	1715.02	1947.53	1243.82	628.87	471.20
广　东 Guangdong	11813.35	6538.36	9633.48	5320.84	2179.87	1217.52
广　西 Guangxi	1733.53	943.28	1453.04	786.65	280.49	156.63
海　南 Hainan	483.51	272.90	427.35	240.69	56.16	32.21
四　川 Sichuan	3665.20	2599.54	2886.23	1971.89	778.97	627.65
贵　州 Guizhou	758.65	430.14	646.58	370.62	112.07	59.52
云　南 Yunnan	1499.75	931.28	1243.47	762.29	256.28	168.99
西　藏 Tibet	70.38	32.47	70.38	32.47		
陕　西 Shanxi	2108.09	1460.44	1737.91	1192.15	370.18	268.29
甘　肃 Gansu	1042.39	711.22	898.08	621.62	144.31	89.60
青　海 Qinghai	222.37	130.48	206.32	122.68	16.05	7.80
宁　夏 Ningxia	306.75	200.36	269.30	177.35	37.45	23.01
新　疆 Xinjiang	1137.64	760.32	1024.17	691.67	113.47	68.65
重　庆 Chongqing	1582.33	1082.90	1260.57	824.72	321.76	258.18

全国各地区城乡储蓄存款余额表（续六）
Balance of Savings Deposits by Regions（Continued）

（2003 年末）

（Year – end of 2003）

单位：亿元

Unit：100 Million Yuan

地区 Regions \ 项目 Items	城乡储蓄合计 Total of Savings Deposits in Urban and Rural Areas	其中：定期 Of Which：Time	城镇储蓄合计 Total of Savings Deposits in Urban Areas	其中：定期 Of Which：Time	农村储蓄合计 Total of Savings Deposits in Rural Areas	其中：定期 Of Which：Time
全　国 National Total	**103617.65**	**68498.67**	**85612.66**	**55589.17**	**18004.99**	**12909.50**
总　行 Headquarters	6.70		6.70			
北　京 Beijing	5293.54	3413.04	4926.48	3146.02	367.06	267.02
天　津 Tianjin	1825.53	1294.09	1593.95	1132.15	231.58	161.94
河　北 Hebei	5457.00	4064.09	3804.12	2734.27	1652.88	1329.82
山　西 Shanxi	2781.54	2072.57	2102.75	1519.27	678.79	553.30
内蒙古 Inner Mongolia	1355.51	796.70	1133.12	674.45	222.39	122.25
辽　宁 Liaoning	5434.88	3972.15	4741.97	3390.66	692.91	581.49
吉　林 Jilin	2161.39	1462.84	1904.88	1272.50	256.51	190.34
黑龙江 Heilongjiang	3342.43	2293.98	3033.12	2066.60	309.31	227.38
上　海 Shanghai	5103.15	3462.29	4789.12	3180.64	314.03	281.65
江　苏 Jiangsu	7638.17	5588.07	6507.76	4702.95	1130.41	885.12
浙　江 Zhejiang	6452.21	4118.52	4878.58	3004.59	1573.63	1113.93
安　徽 Anhui	2475.83	1750.63	1961.39	1378.13	514.44	372.50
福　建 Fujian	2924.65	1687.86	2578.13	1460.26	346.52	227.60
江　西 Jiangxi	2015.45	1278.73	1647.19	1021.61	368.26	257.12
山　东 Shandong	6768.35	4854.18	5121.90	3584.39	1646.45	1269.79
河　南 Henan	4919.09	3525.62	3796.31	2663.30	1122.78	862.32
湖　北 Hubei	3296.52	2175.87	2847.58	1853.57	448.94	322.30
湖　南 Hunan	3036.45	1970.84	2322.18	1441.55	714.27	529.29
广　东 Guangdong	14061.77	7634.02	11555.76	6296.59	2506.01	1337.43
广　西 Guangxi	1971.67	1032.78	1641.09	857.65	330.58	175.13
海　南 Hainan	546.87	296.36	482.93	260.69	63.94	35.67
四　川 Sichuan	4333.82	3041.88	3453.81	2330.90	880.01	710.98
贵　州 Guizhou	912.83	498.69	773.65	427.40	139.18	71.29
云　南 Yunnan	1766.50	1065.00	1465.09	872.44	301.41	192.56
西　藏 Tibet	91.90	40.26	91.90	40.26		
陕　西 Shanxi	2519.94	1749.77	2101.03	1446.41	418.91	303.36
甘　肃 Gansu	1217.38	819.42	1051.75	718.43	165.63	100.99
青　海 Qinghai	260.50	149.40	242.17	141.03	18.33	8.37
宁　夏 Ningxia	377.70	243.50	321.96	209.11	55.74	34.39
新　疆 Xinjiang	1371.83	880.02	1219.36	793.89	152.47	86.13
重　庆 Chongqing	1896.56	1265.52	1514.95	967.49	381.61	298.03

全国各地区城乡储蓄存款余额表（续七）

Balance of Savings Deposits by Regions（Continued）

（2004 年末）

（Year - end of 2004）

单位：亿元

Unit: 100 Million Yuan

项 目 Items / 地 区 Regions	城乡储蓄合计 Total of Savings Deposits in Urban and Rural Areas	其中：定期 Of Which: Time	城镇储蓄合计 Total of Savings Deposits in Urban Areas	其中：定期 Of Which: Time	农村储蓄合计 Total of Savings Deposits in Rural Areas	其中：定期 Of Which: Time
全 国 National Total	**119555.39**	**78138.86**	**98789.22**	**63577.81**	**20766.17**	**14561.05**
总 行 Headquarters	354.35		354.35			
北 京 Beijing	6122.35	3966.16	5692.80	3657.36	429.55	308.80
天 津 Tianjin	2116.67	1475.18	1815.19	1267.33	301.48	207.85
河 北 Hebei	6207.48	4517.25	4358.33	3054.59	1849.15	1462.66
山 西 Shanxi	3342.31	2421.93	2532.86	1769.05	809.45	652.88
内蒙古 Inner Mongolia	1603.87	915.36	1334.49	772.03	269.38	143.33
辽 宁 Liaoning	6048.52	4389.43	5338.96	3796.71	709.56	592.72
吉 林 Jilin	2405.59	1635.36	2114.58	1421.69	291.01	213.67
黑龙江 Heilongjiang	3585.45	2453.49	3268.87	2221.65	316.58	231.84
上 海 Shanghai	6116.13	4229.98	5739.75	3896.36	376.38	333.62
江 苏 Jiangsu	8863.10	6461.75	7621.99	5495.12	1241.11	966.63
浙 江 Zhejiang	7364.06	4626.69	5558.02	3398.04	1806.04	1228.65
安 徽 Anhui	2972.36	2075.99	2355.65	1633.25	616.71	442.74
福 建 Fujian	3322.26	1898.15	2905.74	1629.88	416.52	268.27
江 西 Jiangxi	2347.72	1465.77	1906.34	1162.72	441.38	303.05
山 东 Shandong	7721.46	5465.11	5791.36	4028.21	1930.10	1436.90
河 南 Henan	5607.30	3946.41	4338.80	2986.27	1268.50	960.14
湖 北 Hubei	3865.70	2551.28	3340.70	2173.51	525.00	377.77
湖 南 Hunan	3483.23	2214.84	2697.96	1639.29	785.27	575.55
广 东 Guangdong	16193.41	8683.77	13272.82	7188.16	2920.59	1495.61
广 西 Guangxi	2240.10	1128.72	1838.44	930.41	401.66	198.31
海 南 Hainan	615.92	323.52	546.17	286.04	69.75	37.48
四 川 Sichuan	5019.44	3559.19	3999.81	2735.18	1019.63	824.01
贵 州 Guizhou	1094.55	582.01	911.03	495.46	183.52	86.55
云 南 Yunnan	2052.12	1197.15	1679.23	967.64	372.89	229.51
西 藏 Tibet	107.49	44.11	107.49	44.11		
陕 西 Shanxi	2948.35	2070.48	2459.18	1717.72	489.17	352.76
甘 肃 Gansu	1384.88	928.07	1193.20	811.67	191.68	116.40
青 海 Qinghai	299.28	172.45	278.08	162.74	21.20	9.71
宁 夏 Ningxia	425.52	277.63	348.78	227.96	76.74	49.67
新 疆 Xinjiang	1534.67	991.62	1359.12	890.71	175.55	100.91
重 庆 Chongqing	2189.73	1469.99	1729.11	1116.92	460.62	353.07

全国各地区城乡储蓄存款余额表（续八）

Balance of Savings Deposits by Regions（Continued）

（2005 年末）

（Year－end of 2005）

单位：亿元

Unit：100 Million Yuan

项目 Items / 地区 Regions	城乡储蓄合计 Total of Savings Deposits in Urban and Rural Areas	其中：定期 Of Which：Time	城镇储蓄合计 Total of Savings Deposits in Urban Areas	其中：定期 Of Which：Time	农村储蓄合计 Total of Savings Deposits in Rural Areas	其中：定期 Of Which：Time
全　国 National Total	**141050.99**	**92263.54**	**119311.66**	**77206.15**	**21739.33**	**15057.39**
总　行 Headquarters	410.00		410.00			
北　京 Beijing	7477.74	4957.15	6969.06	4596.02	508.68	361.13
天　津 Tianjin	2461.45	1696.27	2116.60	1462.03	344.85	234.24
河　北 Hebei	7084.03	5096.75	5060.62	3505.03	2023.41	1591.72
山　西 Shanxi	4119.68	2945.48	3142.92	2155.69	976.76	789.79
内蒙古 Inner Mongolia	1973.60	1099.55	1638.04	927.90	335.56	171.65
辽　宁 Liaoning	6950.24	5053.06	6143.94	4391.19	806.30	661.87
吉　林 Jilin	2798.07	1880.62	2457.56	1635.67	340.51	244.95
黑龙江 Heilongjiang	4078.59	2778.47	3709.64	2513.13	368.95	265.34
上　海 Shanghai	7665.60	5486.58	7665.60	5486.58		
江　苏 Jiangsu	10581.27	7717.14	9474.66	6866.59	1106.61	850.55
浙　江 Zhejiang	8746.02	5473.28	7795.81	4854.03	950.21	619.25
安　徽 Anhui	3508.67	2445.54	2786.39	1924.52	722.28	521.02
福　建 Fujian	3903.05	2241.55	3416.30	1940.29	486.75	301.26
江　西 Jiangxi	2752.88	1712.27	2233.65	1357.38	519.23	354.89
山　东 Shandong	9035.14	6385.73	7006.65	4856.10	2028.49	1529.63
河　南 Henan	6488.55	4541.25	5000.44	3410.04	1488.11	1131.21
湖　北 Hubei	4465.80	2921.22	3911.17	2537.71	554.63	383.51
湖　南 Hunan	4092.12	2596.32	3189.47	1931.13	902.65	665.19
广　东 Guangdong	19051.35	10280.82	15929.15	8681.67	3122.20	1599.15
广　西 Guangxi	2561.34	1285.29	2098.24	1073.09	463.10	212.20
海　南 Hainan	697.57	370.58	621.91	331.07	75.66	39.51
四　川 Sichuan	5902.68	4212.24	4730.13	3263.40	1172.55	948.84
贵　州 Guizhou	1350.90	712.13	1125.36	613.09	225.54	99.04
云　南 Yunnan	2430.29	1399.14	1916.75	1090.60	513.54	308.54
西　藏 Tibet	123.09	48.08	123.09	48.08		
陕　西 Shanxi	3533.97	2434.18	2959.37	2017.66	574.60	416.52
甘　肃 Gansu	1586.65	1047.32	1352.01	905.60	234.64	141.72
青　海 Qinghai	348.94	202.91	324.41	191.63	24.53	11.28
宁　夏 Ningxia	509.50	331.60	402.91	259.13	106.59	72.47
新　疆 Xinjiang	1816.38	1170.89	1601.89	1056.31	214.49	114.58
重　庆 Chongqing	2545.85	1740.13	1997.96	1323.80	547.89	416.33

外汇储蓄存款分地区表
Savings Deposits in Foreign Currency by Regions
(年末余额)
(Year - end Balance)

单位：亿美元
Unit: 100 Million US Dollars

地区名称 Region	1997	1998	1999	2000	2001	2002	2003	2004	2005
全 国 National Total	**292.29**	**412.46**	**553.46**	**729.50**	**815.62**	**893.59**	**855.14**	**802.37**	**743.81**
总 行 Headquarters	2.56	2.15	1.25	1.11	1.16	1.22	1.53	49.96	79.77
北 京 Beijing	50.90	68.71	89.03	112.45	128.28	141.32	138.69	124.67	103.85
天 津 Tianjin	6.70	9.49	12.44	16.44	18.84	20.91	20.06	17.45	15.09
河 北 Hebei	3.04	4.53	6.30	8.93	10.96	12.09	11.78	10.01	8.53
山 西 Shanxi	1.53	2.34	3.20	4.63	5.55	6.27	6.52	6.33	6.04
内蒙古 Inner Mongolia	0.98	1.48	2.01	2.83	3.34	3.76	3.84	3.46	3.05
辽 宁 Liaoning	15.54	24.13	34.18	46.68	52.52	58.00	53.32	45.05	39.69
吉 林 Jilin	4.36	6.64	9.33	12.85	14.59	16.34	14.93	12.42	11.21
黑龙江 Heilongjiang	6.03	8.80	12.04	16.07	17.94	19.89	18.34	15.16	12.71
上 海 Shanghai	48.34	64.23	83.85	103.02	107.61	121.51	114.96	102.07	95.03
江 苏 Jiangsu	14.20	21.11	29.04	39.86	45.48	51.34	49.28	40.41	34.60
浙 江 Zhejiang	12.70	19.43	30.60	45.90	54.19	56.43	52.80	45.62	46.73
安 徽 Anhui	2.25	3.02	3.80	5.10	5.92	6.82	6.78	6.11	5.34
福 建 Fujian	14.18	21.02	29.76	40.27	44.98	48.10	42.00	34.97	30.37
江 西 Jiangxi	2.34	3.33	4.45	5.98	6.85	7.59	7.34	5.66	4.79
山 东 Shandong	8.99	12.83	17.58	24.40	28.52	31.74	30.23	25.29	22.86
河 南 Henan	3.58	5.21	7.24	10.36	12.34	13.77	13.65	11.96	10.05
湖 北 Hubei	4.64	6.47	8.35	11.11	12.52	14.10	14.13	12.23	11.76
湖 南 Hunan	3.46	5.01	6.44	8.44	9.45	10.55	10.18	8.87	7.63
广 东 Guangdong	66.19	94.43	124.64	161.03	175.70	187.72	184.72	173.70	150.74
广 西 Guangxi	2.65	3.44	4.41	6.07	6.94	7.59	7.12	6.30	5.40
海 南 Hainan	2.16	3.10	3.77	4.57	4.60	4.64	4.24	3.57	3.02
四 川 Sichuan	4.50	6.58	9.15	12.46	14.11	15.34	14.17	11.33	9.88
贵 州 Guizhou	0.67	0.86	1.08	1.43	1.66	1.78	1.69	1.51	1.37
云 南 Yunnan	2.10	3.13	4.46	6.24	6.92	7.50	6.99	5.90	5.28
西 藏 Tibet	0.03	0.04	0.06	0.08	0.11	0.12	0.12	0.11	0.10
陕 西 Shanxi	3.55	4.77	6.40	8.83	10.34	11.65	11.09	9.17	8.03
甘 肃 Gansu	1.00	1.68	2.22	3.14	3.69	4.02	3.81	3.36	2.87
青 海 Qinghai	0.14	0.18	0.26	0.38	0.47	0.55	0.56	0.54	0.47
宁 夏 Ningxia	0.24	0.32	0.43	0.59	0.69	0.77	0.77	0.65	0.57
新 疆 Xinjiang	1.14	1.78	2.62	3.82	4.12	4.39	4.09	3.79	2.87
重 庆 Chongqing	1.60	2.22	3.07	4.43	5.23	5.77	5.41	4.74	4.11

5. 全国各地区分机构储蓄存款余额表
Balance of Savings Deposits by Regions and Institutions

全国各地区分机构储蓄存款余额表
Balance of Savings Deposits by Regions and Institutions

（1997 年末）

（Year – end of 1997）

单位：亿元

Unit：100 Million Yuan

地 区 Regions	城乡储蓄 Savings Deposits in Urban and Rural Areas	其中：国有商业银行 Of Which：State – owned Commercial Banks	其他商业银行 Other Commercial Banks	农村信用社 Rural Credit Cooperatives	邮政储汇局 Postal Savings Bureau
全 国 National Total	**46279.80**	**30724.21**	**536.20**	**9132.17**	**2644.56**
总 行 Headquarters	27.46	0.23	26.28		
北 京 Beijing	1966.49	1563.66	15.26	204.36	115.70
天 津 Tianjin	863.36	640.79	0.87	121.93	58.07
河 北 Hebei	2685.10	1569.33	0.30	768.10	161.47
山 西 Shanxi	1236.83	820.99		281.32	84.31
内蒙古 Inner Mongolia	605.01	447.76		81.34	50.06
辽 宁 Liaoning	2726.39	1883.56	32.12	376.30	142.80
吉 林 Jilin	1140.38	803.30	1.98	136.70	66.50
黑龙江 Heilongjiang	1689.72	1222.95	13.69	161.64	184.18
上 海 Shanghai	2729.57	2262.17	35.91	172.74	132.48
江 苏 Jiangsu	3102.62	2022.80	9.49	639.25	244.79
浙 江 Zhejiang	2292.90	1327.83	10.59	657.47	99.49
安 徽 Anhui	1036.47	650.60	0.98	247.72	86.53
福 建 Fujian	1324.37	933.42	45.85	170.89	119.79
江 西 Jiangxi	928.24	633.13		177.85	58.37
山 东 Shandong	3246.54	1952.15	31.89	788.82	205.94
河 南 Henan	2230.15	1296.80	5.49	556.71	124.29
湖 北 Hubei	1410.57	1002.32	6.95	265.03	48.35
湖 南 Hunan	1303.80	739.35	0.90	384.65	101.17
广 东 Guangdong	6312.78	3837.25	271.21	1525.85	141.80
广 西 Guangxi	1013.14	706.05	0.49	197.99	43.94
海 南 Hainan	360.83	242.21	15.35	43.25	22.82
四 川 Sichuan	1646.85	990.28	4.88	436.46	96.42
贵 州 Guizhou	362.87	261.86		45.18	28.49
云 南 Yunnan	806.07	575.04	0.86	149.22	40.08
西 藏 Tibet	30.45	27.92			1.85
陕 西 Shanxi	1090.43	734.43	2.26	243.64	52.59
甘 肃 Gansu	570.70	441.36	1.46	77.01	28.38
青 海 Qinghai	113.15	95.76		7.55	5.93
宁 夏 Ningxia	168.85	134.23		21.29	8.66
新 疆 Xinjiang	676.13	541.77		54.81	48.32
重 庆 Chongqing	581.55	362.92	1.12	137.06	40.98

全国各地区分机构储蓄存款余额表（续一）

Balance of Savings Deposits by Regions and Institutions (Continued)

（1998 年末）

(Year - end of 1998)

单位：亿元

Unit: 100 Million Yuan

地 区 Regions	城乡储蓄 Savings Deposits in Urban and Rural Areas	其中：国有商业银行 Of Which: State - owned Commercial Banks	其他商业银行 Other Commercial Banks	农村信用社 Rural Credit Cooperatives	邮政储汇局 Postal Savings Bureau
全 国 National Total	**53407.47**	**35376.75**	**684.73**	**10441.03**	**3201.76**
总 行 Headquarters	29.43	0.42	27.66		
北 京 Beijing	2277.73	1800.32	29.06	224.00	140.10
天 津 Tianjin	1020.15	774.43	0.92	139.32	61.41
河 北 Hebei	3208.08	1854.39	0.77	935.98	196.15
山 西 Shanxi	1436.64	949.41	0.38	343.73	101.45
内蒙古 Inner Mongolia	705.72	522.79		95.37	56.28
辽 宁 Liaoning	3190.46	2204.75	53.23	433.20	159.97
吉 林 Jilin	1287.72	915.72	2.55	161.97	79.88
黑龙江 Heilongjiang	1906.69	1382.71	14.21	176.52	213.01
上 海 Shanghai	2372.94	1843.79	47.81	192.25	140.86
江 苏 Jiangsu	3657.78	2401.94	17.07	709.75	287.25
浙 江 Zhejiang	2846.81	1714.71	20.01	771.22	111.87
安 徽 Anhui	1175.11	729.49	1.13	279.12	104.05
福 建 Fujian	1565.18	1108.50	51.97	197.37	146.99
江 西 Jiangxi	1068.60	730.71		194.80	77.28
山 东 Shandong	3728.78	2249.49	36.94	878.77	253.09
河 南 Henan	2657.22	1509.06	6.26	659.74	165.02
湖 北 Hubei	1577.98	1097.52	11.17	280.53	80.84
湖 南 Hunan	1506.29	858.63	0.91	430.92	132.37
广 东 Guangdong	7541.11	4763.06	309.72	1717.47	172.87
广 西 Guangxi	1150.09	813.00	0.71	206.10	63.37
海 南 Hainan	414.25	297.27	31.40	47.75	31.53
四 川 Sichuan	2002.08	1195.98	6.35	525.54	116.23
贵 州 Guizhou	423.08	300.48		57.04	34.04
云 南 Yunnan	912.89	661.31	1.87	161.44	43.34
西 藏 Tibet	33.45	30.14			2.44
陕 西 Shanxi	1241.63	834.01	5.19	268.60	67.25
甘 肃 Gansu	663.11	505.65	4.16	88.46	37.35
青 海 Qinghai	130.42	108.60		9.41	8.20
宁 夏 Ningxia	192.36	150.71		23.69	12.23
新 疆 Xinjiang	759.14	608.38		62.84	53.35
重 庆 Chongqing	724.54	459.35	3.27	168.12	51.68

全国各地区分机构储蓄存款余额表（续二）

Balance of Savings Deposits by Regions and Institutions（Continued）

（1999年末）

（Year - end of 1999）

单位：亿元

Unit：100 Million Yuan

地区 Regions	城乡储蓄 Savings Deposits in Urban and Rural Areas	其中：国有商业银行 Of Which：State - owned Commercial Banks	其他商业银行 Other Commercial Banks	农村信用社 Rural Credit Cooperatives	邮政储汇局 Postal Savings Bureau
全　国 National Total	**59621.83**	**39885.84**	**755.41**	**11217.25**	**3816.74**
总　行 Headquarters	8.08	0.12	7.97		
北　京 Beijing	2681.25	2110.52	56.67	251.64	159.90
天　津 Tianjin	1130.18	857.31	0.70	155.14	70.34
河　北 Hebei	3681.24	2109.93	1.16	1090.99	231.27
山　西 Shanxi	1613.72	1066.47	0.96	354.19	123.96
内蒙古 Inner Mongolia	796.63	586.19		105.07	70.82
辽　宁 Liaoning	3555.76	2452.32	65.73	477.93	180.15
吉　林 Jilin	1422.58	1003.91	2.34	173.23	97.39
黑龙江 Heilongjiang	2122.24	1535.73	13.99	190.72	249.20
上　海 Shanghai	2597.12	2014.35	63.05	204.29	142.39
江　苏 Jiangsu	4132.38	2719.88	25.90	769.34	333.09
浙　江 Zhejiang	3262.69	2012.02	27.32	841.26	136.91
安　徽 Anhui	1302.46	809.02	1.99	297.81	123.65
福　建 Fujian	1739.01	1257.33	55.96	213.48	158.87
江　西 Jiangxi	1161.14	783.66		202.35	100.42
山　东 Shandong	4109.02	2452.76	45.86	940.38	322.90
河　南 Henan	2939.96	1668.43	6.35	700.46	225.22
湖　北 Hubei	1705.93	1206.58	17.92	270.50	108.58
湖　南 Hunan	1688.40	998.34	1.48	443.04	156.77
广　东 Guangdong	8183.78	5407.67	320.70	1766.70	198.39
广　西 Guangxi	1257.26	918.30	0.77	203.16	79.43
海　南 Hainan	397.85	301.79	1.44	49.80	39.34
四　川 Sichuan	2385.19	1472.28	8.28	609.62	137.05
贵　州 Guizhou	484.51	342.64		63.52	40.24
云　南 Yunnan	1028.92	754.01	3.22	177.17	45.36
西　藏 Tibet	36.82	32.49			3.46
陕　西 Shanxi	1371.95	921.22	9.82	274.80	92.12
甘　肃 Gansu	737.50	556.01	8.22	95.59	45.45
青　海 Qinghai	142.86	118.09		9.94	10.58
宁　夏 Ningxia	211.59	162.79		24.51	17.23
新　疆 Xinjiang	824.68	665.23		59.25	59.60
重　庆 Chongqing	909.10	588.41	7.56	201.32	56.65

全国各地区分机构储蓄存款余额表（续三）

Balance of Savings Deposits by Regions and Institutions（Continued）

（2000 年末）

（Year - end of 2000）

单位：亿元

Unit：100 Million Yuan

地　区 Regions	城乡储蓄 Savings Deposits in Urban and Rural Areas	其中：国有商业银行 Of Which：State - owned Commercial Banks	其他商业银行 Other Commercial Banks	农村信用社 Rural Credit Cooperatives	邮政储汇局 Postal Savings Bureau
全　国 National Total	**64332.38**	**42734.90**	**947.04**	**12355.25**	**4578.00**
总　行 Headquarters	22.40	20.47	1.93		
北　京 Beijing	2923.13	2291.07	78.37	259.91	170.31
天　津 Tianjin	1172.40	882.25	1.24	160.93	69.91
河　北 Hebei	3957.07	2257.86	3.12	1284.22	260.86
山　西 Shanxi	1748.42	1137.54	2.94	384.40	150.41
内蒙古 Inner Mongolia	875.74	635.23		114.95	88.19
辽　宁 Liaoning	3790.60	2551.51	89.88	512.15	224.89
吉　林 Jilin	1512.52	1050.33	2.54	192.58	118.91
黑龙江 Heilongjiang	2285.48	1612.12	18.04	213.91	285.30
上　海 Shanghai	2524.05	1882.54	80.13	202.91	153.54
江　苏 Jiangsu	4457.55	2872.82	38.78	856.22	402.76
浙　江 Zhejiang	3594.65	2221.85	36.91	933.46	167.95
安　徽 Anhui	1446.45	900.13	2.24	327.22	151.29
福　建 Fujian	1767.59	1275.14	59.55	225.85	170.84
江　西 Jiangxi	1243.15	807.79	2.73	240.13	132.64
山　东 Shandong	4466.72	2562.87	54.53	1123.13	426.83
河　南 Henan	3182.07	1777.94	8.50	808.21	282.17
湖　北 Hubei	1908.81	1330.15	25.73	292.88	152.97
湖　南 Hunan	1874.22	1113.42	2.91	499.16	183.27
广　东 Guangdong	8665.79	5949.91	369.65	1797.37	222.52
广　西 Guangxi	1374.47	1002.68	1.00	221.03	96.89
海　南 Hainan	404.19	305.96	1.67	49.72	41.78
四　川 Sichuan	2693.17	1721.27	11.83	637.22	167.86
贵　州 Guizhou	539.48	378.67		72.57	45.23
云　南 Yunnan	1138.22	829.21	5.77	200.73	51.43
西　藏 Tibet	40.48	35.59			4.75
陕　西 Shanxi	1522.70	1004.97	17.98	294.47	125.05
甘　肃 Gansu	818.76	601.23	13.70	109.41	56.16
青　海 Qinghai	159.07	129.70		12.12	12.71
宁　夏 Ningxia	229.35	173.64		25.34	21.87
新　疆 Xinjiang	908.55	722.12		72.60	68.65
重　庆 Chongqing	1085.12	696.96	15.37	230.46	70.08

全国各地区分机构储蓄存款余额表（续四）

Balance of Savings Deposits by Regions and Institutions（Continued）

（2001 年末）

（Year - end of 2001）

单位：亿元

Unit：100 Million Yuan

地　区 Regions	城乡储蓄 Savings Deposits in Urban and Rural Areas	其中：国有商业银行 Of Which：State - owned Commercial Banks	其他商业银行 Other Commercial Banks	农村信用社 Rural Credit Cooperatives	邮政储汇局 Postal Savings Bureau
全　国 National Total	**73762.43**	**48395.21**	**3121.56**	**13821.36**	**5911.65**
总　行 Headquarters	0.08	0.08			
北　京 Beijing	3536.32	2731.99	210.13	282.45	204.52
天　津 Tianjin	1284.95	941.02	30.42	167.61	90.42
河　北 Hebei	4364.51	2486.10	44.63	1391.20	327.26
山　西 Shanxi	1979.72	1257.60	20.82	457.18	203.40
内蒙古 Inner Mongolia	986.74	700.74	2.02	151.98	112.02
辽　宁 Liaoning	4131.55	2710.93	286.58	547.11	265.38
吉　林 Jilin	1676.06	1139.64	46.72	210.88	142.68
黑龙江 Heilongjiang	2578.45	1773.46	116.38	237.17	359.44
上　海 Shanghai	3001.89	2194.95	233.28	220.07	183.76
江　苏 Jiangsu	5172.83	3285.95	287.91	954.90	516.51
浙　江 Zhejiang	4262.38	2628.54	158.34	1084.35	224.61
安　徽 Anhui	1700.47	1042.51	45.28	378.46	201.01
福　建 Fujian	2030.93	1460.59	87.66	238.10	206.02
江　西 Jiangxi	1429.52	890.75	23.41	272.19	197.52
山　东 Shandong	5063.42	2814.77	193.86	1298.74	575.35
河　南 Henan	3634.51	2055.06	131.26	887.85	379.74
湖　北 Hubei	2287.40	1562.54	98.75	339.70	223.49
湖　南 Hunan	2183.73	1295.22	27.16	562.94	233.65
广　东 Guangdong	9930.12	6799.90	675.42	1943.54	281.87
广　西 Guangxi	1538.61	1104.74	38.58	248.71	118.31
海　南 Hainan	427.32	320.51	10.29	49.25	47.02
四　川 Sichuan	3123.38	2032.80	74.32	719.87	212.56
贵　州 Guizhou	641.67	440.96	14.93	90.31	59.41
云　南 Yunnan	1298.52	932.70	45.50	223.70	75.21
西　藏 Tibet	50.18	43.24			6.81
陕　西 Shanxi	1768.47	1144.69	67.50	331.97	169.29
甘　肃 Gansu	920.71	660.80	37.27	121.18	74.12
青　海 Qinghai	188.53	153.29		14.30	16.40
宁　夏 Ningxia	257.97	190.22		30.10	28.35
新　疆 Xinjiang	994.30	773.47	14.25	88.89	86.03
重　庆 Chongqing	1317.17	825.50	98.86	276.67	89.49

全国各地区分机构储蓄存款余额表（续五）
Balance of Savings Deposits by Regions and Institutions (Continued)

（2002 年末）

(Year - end of 2002)

单位：亿元

Unit: 100 Million Yuan

地 区 Regions	城乡储蓄 Savings Deposits in Urban and Rural Areas	其中：国有商业银行 Of Which: State - owned Commercial Banks	其他商业银行 Other Commercial Banks	农村信用社 Rural Credit Cooperatives	邮政储汇局 Postal Savings Bureau
全 国 National Total	**86910.65**	**56655.38**	**4347.15**	**15405.80**	**7369.09**
总 行 Headquarters	2.50	2.49	0.01		
北 京 Beijing	4389.69	3332.68	334.29	316.62	250.66
天 津 Tianjin	1486.41	1082.41	48.82	178.13	100.62
河 北 Hebei	4808.29	2770.01	56.38	1490.82	385.89
山 西 Shanxi	2307.32	1434.09	36.98	538.58	250.53
内蒙古 Inner Mongolia	1137.93	799.47	3.06	178.89	134.04
辽 宁 Liaoning	4665.05	2965.53	382.62	594.51	325.31
吉 林 Jilin	1878.45	1256.95	60.56	235.11	163.67
黑龙江 Heilongjiang	2915.65	1970.52	143.08	261.13	437.09
上 海 Shanghai	3891.45	2784.46	362.58	252.59	246.97
江 苏 Jiangsu	6276.20	3949.55	395.57	942.41	675.53
浙 江 Zhejiang	5212.69	3214.79	234.03	1277.30	286.88
安 徽 Anhui	2047.51	1250.70	61.87	438.38	251.56
福 建 Fujian	2430.46	1755.73	110.81	273.41	263.77
江 西 Jiangxi	1706.63	1036.94	35.53	309.47	268.30
山 东 Shandong	5803.52	3216.56	251.31	1448.34	675.52
河 南 Henan	4196.01	2398.73	173.17	984.34	454.02
湖 北 Hubei	2754.54	1848.67	150.65	389.85	297.39
湖 南 Hunan	2576.40	1528.54	40.58	628.87	303.42
广 东 Guangdong	11813.35	8088.46	903.62	2179.87	376.28
广 西 Guangxi	1733.53	1237.67	48.10	280.49	138.70
海 南 Hainan	483.51	359.18	13.82	56.16	54.27
四 川 Sichuan	3665.20	2420.89	105.64	778.97	259.53
贵 州 Guizhou	758.65	511.96	18.92	112.07	71.62
云 南 Yunnan	1499.75	1061.41	61.19	256.28	95.36
西 藏 Tibet	70.38	60.59			9.79
陕 西 Shanxi	2108.09	1347.12	106.80	370.18	222.17
甘 肃 Gansu	1042.39	741.37	47.35	144.31	87.59
青 海 Qinghai	222.37	180.75		16.05	19.44
宁 夏 Ningxia	306.75	219.66		37.45	33.72
新 疆 Xinjiang	1137.64	866.70	21.70	113.47	104.10
重 庆 Chongqing	1582.33	960.78	138.13	321.76	125.33

全国各地区分机构储蓄存款余额表（续六）

Balance of Savings Deposits by Regions and Institutions（Continued）

（2003 年末）

（Year - end of 2003）

单位：亿元

Unit：100 Million Yuan

地 区 Regions	城乡储蓄 Savings Deposits in Urban and Rural Areas	其中：国有商业银行 Of Which：State - owned Commercial Banks	其他商业银行 Other Commercial Banks	农村信用社 Rural Credit Cooperatives	邮政储汇局 Postal Savings Bureau
全 国 National Total	**103617.65**	**66850.39**	**5851.47**	**18004.99**	**8984.43**
总 行 Headquarters	6.70	6.68	0.02		
北 京 Beijing	5293.54	3962.33	488.84	367.06	282.84
天 津 Tianjin	1825.53	1292.53	74.26	231.58	117.48
河 北 Hebei	5457.00	3144.14	72.42	1652.88	455.81
山 西 Shanxi	2781.54	1667.53	66.55	678.79	310.58
内蒙古 Inner Mongolia	1355.51	934.89	4.60	222.39	161.31
辽 宁 Liaoning	5434.88	3327.50	508.82	692.91	398.34
吉 林 Jilin	2161.39	1423.05	79.98	256.51	205.22
黑龙江 Heilongjiang	3342.43	2231.36	170.87	309.31	507.15
上 海 Shanghai	5103.15	3602.14	542.47	314.03	318.08
江 苏 Jiangsu	7638.17	4784.79	518.59	1130.41	802.57
浙 江 Zhejiang	6452.21	3949.92	325.08	1573.63	348.28
安 徽 Anhui	2475.83	1512.93	81.87	514.44	304.23
福 建 Fujian	2924.65	2083.69	144.34	346.52	315.82
江 西 Jiangxi	2015.45	1210.68	47.03	368.26	316.94
山 东 Shandong	6768.35	3741.10	313.42	1646.45	824.03
河 南 Henan	4919.09	2799.63	229.59	1122.78	542.55
湖 北 Hubei	3296.52	2186.91	207.76	448.94	371.11
湖 南 Hunan	3036.45	1788.53	57.05	714.27	386.49
广 东 Guangdong	14061.77	9527.92	1192.23	2506.01	506.94
广 西 Guangxi	1971.67	1383.54	57.66	330.58	168.41
海 南 Hainan	546.87	400.55	17.61	63.94	64.77
四 川 Sichuan	4333.82	2890.34	141.66	880.01	315.12
贵 州 Guizhou	912.83	607.86	22.73	139.18	88.71
云 南 Yunnan	1766.50	1241.31	79.01	301.41	112.21
西 藏 Tibet	91.90	78.55			13.35
陕 西 Shanxi	2519.94	1584.30	144.40	418.91	287.45
甘 肃 Gansu	1217.38	856.18	59.05	165.63	110.49
青 海 Qinghai	260.50	210.79		18.33	24.27
宁 夏 Ningxia	377.70	248.43		55.74	44.55
新 疆 Xinjiang	1371.83	1025.80	29.14	152.47	126.86
重 庆 Chongqing	1896.56	1144.49	174.44	381.61	152.46

全国各地区分机构储蓄存款余额表（续七）

Balance of Savings Deposits by Regions and Institutions (Continued)

（2004 年末）

(Year - end of 2004)

单位：亿元

Unit: 100 Million Yuan

地区 Regions	城乡储蓄 Savings Deposits in Urban and Rural Areas	其中：国有商业银行 Of Which: State - owned Commercial Banks	其他商业银行 Other Commercial Banks	农村信用社 Rural Credit Cooperatives	邮政储汇局 Postal Savings Bureau
全 国 National Total	**119555.39**	**75682.31**	**7458.26**	**20766.17**	**10787.25**
总 行 Headquarters	354.35	353.96	0.39		
北 京 Beijing	6122.35	4450.93	673.05	429.55	318.57
天 津 Tianjin	2116.67	1416.87	104.74	301.48	161.05
河 北 Hebei	6207.48	3557.01	92.39	1849.15	539.59
山 西 Shanxi	3342.31	1944.86	110.85	809.45	395.20
内蒙古 Inner Mongolia	1603.87	1081.78	5.90	269.38	181.71
辽 宁 Liaoning	6048.52	3632.05	630.77	709.56	460.66
吉 林 Jilin	2405.59	1540.75	94.63	291.01	242.12
黑龙江 Heilongjiang	3585.45	2392.02	196.05	316.58	543.93
上 海 Shanghai	6116.13	4227.86	717.21	376.38	391.90
江 苏 Jiangsu	8863.10	5489.57	640.97	1241.11	947.12
浙 江 Zhejiang	7364.06	4394.37	450.49	1806.04	413.82
安 徽 Anhui	2972.36	1803.99	100.53	616.71	369.12
福 建 Fujian	3322.26	2309.56	176.25	416.52	376.08
江 西 Jiangxi	2347.72	1365.85	60.13	441.38	390.18
山 东 Shandong	7721.46	4115.31	417.07	1930.10	948.53
河 南 Henan	5607.30	3131.88	275.90	1268.50	647.39
湖 北 Hubei	3865.70	2483.70	270.37	525.00	491.87
湖 南 Hunan	3483.23	2033.88	79.29	785.27	482.25
广 东 Guangdong	16193.41	10788.39	1481.16	2920.59	642.93
广 西 Guangxi	2240.10	1531.78	68.04	401.66	206.20
海 南 Hainan	615.92	445.10	23.09	69.75	77.97
四 川 Sichuan	5019.44	3310.36	173.83	1019.63	381.26
贵 州 Guizhou	1094.55	713.04	26.67	183.52	109.29
云 南 Yunnan	2052.12	1404.75	95.66	372.89	133.93
西 藏 Tibet	107.49	93.86			13.63
陕 西 Shanxi	2948.35	1832.53	178.02	489.17	345.18
甘 肃 Gansu	1384.88	955.14	68.20	191.68	141.29
青 海 Qinghai	299.28	237.50		21.20	31.28
宁 夏 Ningxia	425.52	251.11		76.74	56.80
新 疆 Xinjiang	1534.67	1121.01	39.61	175.55	149.66
重 庆 Chongqing	2189.73	1271.54	206.97	460.62	196.82

全国各地区分机构储蓄存款余额表（续八）

Balance of Savings Deposits by Regions and Institutions（Continued）

（2005年末）

（Year - end of 2005）

单位：亿元

Unit：100 Million Yuan

地　区 Regions	城乡储蓄 Savings Deposits in Urban and Rural Areas	其中：国有商业银行 Of Which：State - owned Commercial Banks	其他商业银行 Other Commercial Banks	农村信用社 Rural Credit Cooperatives	邮政储汇局 Postal Savings Bureau
全　国 National Total	**141050.99**	**87034.23**	**9982.74**	**21739.33**	**13599.02**
总　行 Headquarters	410.00	408.35	1.65		
北　京 Beijing	7477.74	5315.64	969.86	508.68	380.29
天　津 Tianjin	2461.45	1559.93	154.08	344.85	235.14
河　北 Hebei	7084.03	4066.73	122.98	2023.41	667.39
山　西 Shanxi	4119.68	2300.43	173.33	976.76	552.20
内蒙古 Inner Mongolia	1973.60	1286.03	8.60	335.56	213.62
辽　宁 Liaoning	6950.24	4024.97	784.15	806.30	583.16
吉　林 Jilin	2798.07	1716.13	116.58	340.51	320.34
黑龙江 Heilongjiang	4078.59	2654.60	247.98	368.95	625.68
上　海 Shanghai	7665.60	5173.68	1000.31		510.80
江　苏 Jiangsu	10581.27	6422.95	849.65	1106.61	1203.74
浙　江 Zhejiang	8746.02	5086.55	636.56	950.21	534.93
安　徽 Anhui	3508.67	2087.15	126.92	722.28	468.41
福　建 Fujian	3903.05	2688.44	238.54	486.75	443.53
江　西 Jiangxi	2752.88	1531.12	78.98	519.23	496.56
山　东 Shandong	9035.14	4623.47	547.04	2028.49	1150.49
河　南 Henan	6488.55	3470.44	352.13	1488.11	804.73
湖　北 Hubei	4465.80	2800.32	365.64	554.63	636.21
湖　南 Hunan	4092.12	2367.26	116.44	902.65	585.30
广　东 Guangdong	19051.35	12473.65	1945.18	3122.20	820.81
广　西 Guangxi	2561.34	1727.40	81.15	463.10	249.93
海　南 Hainan	697.57	499.20	28.13	75.66	94.58
四　川 Sichuan	5902.68	3812.90	231.03	1172.55	508.21
贵　州 Guizhou	1350.90	843.37	32.01	225.54	148.44
云　南 Yunnan	2430.29	1582.05	130.30	513.54	149.70
西　藏 Tibet	123.09	107.16			15.93
陕　西 Shanxi	3533.97	2080.15	250.01	574.60	475.44
甘　肃 Gansu	1586.65	1052.09	85.15	234.64	186.18
青　海 Qinghai	348.94	273.24		24.53	40.15
宁　夏 Ningxia	509.50	267.03		106.59	67.97
新　疆 Xinjiang	1816.38	1303.86	54.29	214.49	181.43
重　庆 Chongqing	2545.85	1427.94	254.07	547.89	247.70

(五) 金融机构分地区存贷款统计
Regional Deposits and Loans

金融机构各项存、贷款分地区情况表
Regional Deposits and Loans at Financial Institutions

(1997年末余额)

(Year - end Balance of 1997)

单位: 亿元

Unit: 100 Million Yuan

地区 Regions	各项存款 Total Deposits	企业存款 Deposits by Enterprises	财政存款 Fiscal Deposits	储蓄存款 Savings Deposits
全国 National Total	**82392.79**	**28656.25**	**1574.90**	**46279.80**
总行 Headquarters	3156.82	812.08	706.75	27.46
北京 Beijing	5224.09	2861.62	- 64.67	1966.49
天津 Tianjin	1620.46	638.88	7.88	863.36
河北 Hebei	3726.73	946.86	17.89	2685.10
山西 Shanxi	1775.94	447.85	16.50	1236.83
内蒙古 Inner Mongolia	799.41	194.61	15.54	605.01
辽宁 Liaoning	4025.13	1137.00	16.40	2726.39
吉林 Jilin	1617.11	385.16	29.75	1140.38
黑龙江 Heilongjiang	2401.15	661.11	28.39	1689.72
上海 Shanghai	6233.31	2971.55	115.09	2729.57
江苏 Jiangsu	5658.05	2204.40	22.84	3102.62
浙江 Zhejiang	4294.03	1583.48	54.52	2292.90
安徽 Anhui	1630.04	507.67	34.06	1036.47
福建 Fujian	2193.75	707.44	15.40	1324.37
江西 Jiangxi	1348.26	335.89	28.16	928.24
山东 Shandong	4913.78	1362.86	24.58	3246.54
河南 Henan	3223.61	888.23	17.14	2230.15
湖北 Hubei	2446.50	883.82	20.26	1410.57
湖南 Hunan	1926.26	504.84	21.67	1303.80
广东 Guangdong	11100.29	3984.94	220.55	6312.78
广西 Guangxi	1578.04	455.40	42.60	1013.14
海南 Hainan	740.30	265.62	5.29	360.83
四川 Sichuan	2754.34	889.76	31.67	1646.85
贵州 Guizhou	676.30	256.95	31.80	362.87
云南 Yunnan	1836.34	827.84	55.46	806.07
西藏 Tibet	84.96	49.91	5.17	30.45
陕西 Shanxi	1737.33	556.48	12.18	1090.43
甘肃 Gansu	929.68	316.88	8.47	570.70
青海 Qinghai	198.97	74.35	2.85	113.15
宁夏 Ningxia	262.96	76.31	10.53	168.85
新疆 Xinjiang	1207.13	443.53	13.17	676.13
重庆 Chongqing	1070.40	422.97	7.06	581.55

金融机构各项存、贷款分地区情况表（续一）

Regional Deposits and Loans at Financial Institutions（Continued）

（1997年末余额）

（Year－end Balance of 1997）

单位：亿元

Unit：100 Million Yuan

地　区 Regions	各项贷款 Total Loans	短期贷款 Short－term Loans	其中：票据融资 Of Which：Paper Financing	中长期贷款 Medium and Long－term Loans
全　国 National Total	**74914.07**	**55418.27**	**552.34**	**15468.65**
总　行 Headquarters	6335.68	1290.77	5.91	4302.31
北　京 Beijing	2561.77	1933.97	13.78	573.98
天　津 Tianjin	1453.97	1136.48	7.82	249.88
河　北 Hebei	3055.39	2502.61	14.51	446.62
山　西 Shanxi	1527.04	1179.27	9.62	296.55
内蒙古 Inner Mongolia	1018.07	796.92	3.08	210.22
辽　宁 Liaoning	3993.43	3138.42	34.77	589.18
吉　林 Jilin	2177.10	1777.67	8.20	279.36
黑龙江 Heilongjiang	2524.34	2119.16	6.16	361.96
上　海 Shanghai	4168.54	3315.44	73.71	578.79
江　苏 Jiangsu	4462.45	3631.60	89.32	594.87
浙　江 Zhejiang	3272.57	2641.09	23.32	414.98
安　徽 Anhui	1818.40	1448.71	16.84	321.66
福　建 Fujian	1694.45	1292.85	9.37	316.12
江　西 Jiangxi	1450.06	1145.56	3.57	272.99
山　东 Shandong	4424.49	3498.09	59.30	668.83
河　南 Henan	3168.88	2581.01	24.85	502.87
湖　北 Hubei	2969.94	2245.82	18.50	627.34
湖　南 Hunan	2081.07	1651.78	5.48	344.45
广　东 Guangdong	8200.87	6749.60	64.11	882.25
广　西 Guangxi	1429.85	1062.99	0.97	300.54
海　南 Hainan	744.22	425.55	1.64	150.91
四　川 Sichuan	2713.06	2086.49	13.50	493.91
贵　州 Guizhou	728.56	544.28	1.92	170.33
云　南 Yunnan	1497.85	1187.31	6.21	272.37
西　藏 Tibet	64.40	44.71		19.10
陕　西 Shanxi	1621.35	1199.60	8.32	361.49
甘　肃 Gansu	866.12	635.97	4.12	213.92
青　海 Qinghai	261.60	171.58	0.33	89.20
宁　夏 Ningxia	273.63	190.66	0.95	75.32
新　疆 Xinjiang	1215.39	931.70	2.89	242.36
重　庆 Chongqing	1139.10	860.31	19.23	243.66

金融机构各项存、贷款分地区情况表（续二）
Regional Deposits and Loans at Financial Institutions (Continued)

（1998年末余额）

(Year - end Balance of 1998)

单位：亿元

Unit: 100 Million Yuan

地　区 Regions	各项存款 Total Deposits	企业存款 Deposits by Enterprises	财政存款 Fiscal Deposits	储蓄存款 Savings Deposits
全　国 National Total	**95697.94**	**32486.63**	**2187.89**	**53407.47**
总　行 Headquarters	3411.52	977.23	807.59	29.43
北　京 Beijing	6661.91	3573.82	95.16	2277.73
天　津 Tianjin	1840.21	656.94	12.53	1020.15
河　北 Hebei	4389.40	1018.09	31.11	3208.08
山　西 Shanxi	2071.89	490.35	24.08	1436.64
内蒙古 Inner Mongolia	945.49	223.77	19.79	705.72
辽　宁 Liaoning	4685.10	1272.28	33.90	3190.46
吉　林 Jilin	1770.94	361.66	38.96	1287.72
黑龙江 Heilongjiang	2705.11	680.68	54.12	1906.69
上　海 Shanghai	6339.07	3298.60	138.19	2372.94
江　苏 Jiangsu	6601.08	2496.32	43.21	3657.78
浙　江 Zhejiang	5263.99	1948.37	63.96	2846.81
安　徽 Anhui	1912.32	594.65	32.27	1175.11
福　建 Fujian	2557.61	768.21	23.30	1565.18
江　西 Jiangxi	1566.65	374.96	53.33	1068.60
山　东 Shandong	5740.59	1479.89	50.85	3728.78
河　南 Henan	3744.98	907.24	49.22	2657.22
湖　北 Hubei	2805.03	980.80	38.72	1577.98
湖　南 Hunan	2229.65	563.11	28.22	1506.29
广　东 Guangdong	13268.91	4641.86	251.20	7541.11
广　西 Guangxi	1792.21	495.63	52.73	1150.09
海　南 Hainan	800.70	287.24	5.91	414.25
四　川 Sichuan	3326.45	1026.12	35.68	2002.08
贵　州 Guizhou	804.01	301.02	38.04	423.08
云　南 Yunnan	2071.31	910.69	71.97	912.89
西　藏 Tibet	95.67	53.91	6.54	33.45
陕　西 Shanxi	2032.74	632.22	22.57	1241.63
甘　肃 Gansu	1079.90	355.54	13.64	663.11
青　海 Qinghai	229.39	87.16	2.60	130.42
宁　夏 Ningxia	295.83	82.99	10.29	192.36
新　疆 Xinjiang	1350.90	461.55	13.94	759.14
重　庆 Chongqing	1307.38	483.81	21.28	724.54

金融机构各项存、贷款分地区情况表（续三）

Regional Deposits and Loans at Financial Institutions（Continued）

（1998 年末余额）

（Year - end Balance of 1998）

单位：亿元

Unit：100 Million Yuan

地　区 Regions	各项贷款 Total Loans	短期贷款 Short - term Loans	其中：票据融资 Of Which：Paper Financing	中长期贷款 Medium and Long - term Loans
全　国 National Total	**86524.13**	**60613.22**	**542.38**	**20717.78**
总　行 Headquarters	8029.34	1436.63	21.79	5690.87
北　京 Beijing	3084.93	2215.05	12.36	793.55
天　津 Tianjin	1629.14	1226.29	7.61	308.24
河　北 Hebei	3565.92	2738.87	20.26	695.41
山　西 Shanxi	1741.81	1301.19	13.25	369.41
内蒙古 Inner Mongolia	1139.26	863.74	3.42	261.36
辽　宁 Liaoning	4451.30	3332.51	33.37	774.19
吉　林 Jilin	2368.30	1865.45	5.86	387.21
黑龙江 Heilongjiang	2856.88	2317.48	5.84	464.64
上　海 Shanghai	4817.90	3674.46	57.78	759.35
江　苏 Jiangsu	5080.52	4099.07	84.11	713.95
浙　江 Zhejiang	3898.08	3068.64	21.26	598.38
安　徽 Anhui	2063.37	1593.73	12.67	407.36
福　建 Fujian	1943.22	1423.55	6.23	418.70
江　西 Jiangxi	1601.45	1213.46	4.75	342.92
山　东 Shandong	5098.84	3719.38	49.35	956.12
河　南 Henan	3688.69	2905.23	27.31	644.62
湖　北 Hubei	3501.85	2365.98	20.37	992.01
湖　南 Hunan	2245.25	1689.15	6.05	453.78
广　东 Guangdong	9505.41	7528.56	69.25	1207.76
广　西 Guangxi	1519.41	1057.60	1.67	382.79
海　南 Hainan	805.46	438.50	0.31	178.80
四　川 Sichuan	3157.29	2292.78	16.08	695.10
贵　州 Guizhou	840.89	592.12	3.18	231.60
云　南 Yunnan	1715.36	1294.45	4.76	374.99
西　藏 Tibet	66.96	45.75		20.16
陕　西 Shanxi	1859.56	1296.19	11.71	484.48
甘　肃 Gansu	985.42	692.85	4.35	270.37
青　海 Qinghai	291.66	189.59	0.49	100.74
宁　夏 Ningxia	310.95	202.81	0.69	100.28
新　疆 Xinjiang	1318.43	961.14	3.31	310.21
重　庆 Chongqing	1341.38	971.03	12.92	328.51

注：本表“中长期贷款”项目中包含“中期流动资金贷款”数据。

Notes：The coverage of medium and long - term loans of this statement include the data of medium - term working capital loans.

金融机构各项存、贷款分地区情况表（续四）
Regional Deposits and Loans at Financial Institutions (Continued)

（1999 年末余额）

(Year - end Balance of 1999)

单位：亿元

Unit: 100 Million Yuan

地　区 Regions	各项存款 Total Deposits	企业存款 Deposits by Enterprises	财政存款 Fiscal Deposits	储蓄存款 Savings Deposits
全　国 National Total	**108778.94**	**37182.36**	**2128.06**	**59621.83**
总　行 Headquarters	3061.58	807.30	650.04	8.08
北　京 Beijing	8351.77	4477.46	84.54	2681.25
天　津 Tianjin	2058.73	736.00	8.11	1130.18
河　北 Hebei	5013.50	1111.13	24.12	3681.24
山　西 Shanxi	2350.57	558.43	30.23	1613.72
内蒙古 Inner Mongolia	1089.39	249.25	23.89	796.63
辽　宁 Liaoning	5297.61	1423.12	26.03	3555.76
吉　林 Jilin	2016.25	424.76	45.24	1422.58
黑龙江 Heilongjiang	3038.00	771.88	43.40	2122.24
上　海 Shanghai	7093.33	3748.69	138.55	2597.12
江　苏 Jiangsu	7490.78	2784.53	48.34	4132.38
浙　江 Zhejiang	6283.90	2418.33	80.53	3262.69
安　徽 Anhui	2197.77	666.64	42.77	1302.46
福　建 Fujian	2925.09	890.61	41.24	1739.01
江　西 Jiangxi	1779.51	456.02	64.99	1161.14
山　东 Shandong	6563.94	1725.26	58.49	4109.02
河　南 Henan	4180.98	995.71	39.00	2939.96
湖　北 Hubei	3141.50	1165.17	40.93	1705.93
湖　南 Hunan	2534.42	657.28	27.09	1688.40
广　东 Guangdong	14984.94	5342.00	302.61	8183.78
广　西 Guangxi	2008.97	564.81	56.99	1257.26
海　南 Hainan	824.95	289.38	5.55	397.85
四　川 Sichuan	3925.06	1168.14	51.68	2385.19
贵　州 Guizhou	945.82	358.34	31.87	484.51
云　南 Yunnan	2245.12	940.79	57.14	1028.92
西　藏 Tibet	128.54	62.63	8.16	36.82
陕　西 Shanxi	2286.00	704.16	27.60	1371.95
甘　肃 Gansu	1222.23	399.29	17.81	737.50
青　海 Qinghai	263.82	97.28	4.23	142.86
宁　夏 Ningxia	343.90	98.63	14.76	211.59
新　疆 Xinjiang	1548.70	544.57	13.10	824.68
重　庆 Chongqing	1582.23	544.77	19.04	909.10

金融机构各项存、贷款分地区情况表（续五）

Regional Deposits and Loans at Financial Institutions（Continued）

（1999年末余额）

（Year - end Balance of 1999）

单位：亿元

Unit：100 Million Yuan

地区 Regions	各项贷款 Total Loans	短期贷款 Short - term Loans	其中：票据融资 Of Which：Paper Financing	中长期贷款 Medium and Long - term Loans
全国 National Total	**93734.28**	**63887.55**	**511.46**	**23968.32**
总行 Headquarters	5647.89	1250.77	4.60	3413.53
北京 Beijing	3827.01	2763.65	13.29	959.83
天津 Tianjin	1825.27	1303.07	6.14	408.41
河北 Hebei	4011.46	2887.23	15.52	971.85
山西 Shanxi	1851.10	1351.17	12.33	406.19
内蒙古 Inner Mongolia	1183.73	867.01	7.24	297.04
辽宁 Liaoning	4945.95	3441.78	27.26	1124.53
吉林 Jilin	2711.15	1985.67	5.59	591.68
黑龙江 Heilongjiang	3263.68	2441.20	2.82	712.99
上海 Shanghai	5424.42	3996.70	65.45	1068.77
江苏 Jiangsu	5552.92	4313.10	96.72	955.61
浙江 Zhejiang	4655.30	3472.49	20.83	941.91
安徽 Anhui	2341.03	1671.32	11.26	566.71
福建 Fujian	2255.46	1610.31	15.36	540.39
江西 Jiangxi	1692.33	1263.89	3.36	379.41
山东 Shandong	5683.53	3903.34	34.21	1270.03
河南 Henan	4229.17	3088.92	32.76	946.17
湖北 Hubei	3532.72	2345.57	24.81	1028.72
湖南 Hunan	2405.34	1697.48	6.26	610.17
广东 Guangdong	10879.51	7961.11	57.10	1983.79
广西 Guangxi	1646.56	1054.12	1.17	512.73
海南 Hainan	748.45	359.27	0.49	235.68
四川 Sichuan	3927.16	2391.21	13.31	1329.52
贵州 Guizhou	899.83	608.89	3.13	274.92
云南 Yunnan	1825.11	1330.23	1.44	440.29
西藏 Tibet	73.11	48.00		22.87
陕西 Shanxi	2105.82	1344.59	8.74	666.77
甘肃 Gansu	1051.35	743.71	6.14	280.36
青海 Qinghai	304.03	196.46	0.30	105.14
宁夏 Ningxia	338.37	212.12	0.59	115.99
新疆 Xinjiang	1333.82	925.02	2.09	356.58
重庆 Chongqing	1561.66	1058.09	11.11	449.71

金融机构各项存、贷款分地区情况表（续六）
Regional Deposits and Loans at Financial Institutions (Continued)

（2000 年末余额）

(Year – end Balance of 2000)

单位：亿元

Unit: 100 Million Yuan

地 区 Regions	各项存款 Total Deposits	企业存款 Deposits by Enterprises	财政存款 Fiscal Deposits	储蓄存款 Savings Deposits
全 国 National Total	**123804.35**	**44093.73**	**3508.09**	**64332.38**
总 行 Headquarters	4276.52	1040.43	1726.68	22.40
北 京 Beijing	9778.84	5449.26	71.20	2923.13
天 津 Tianjin	2281.89	871.31	12.20	1172.40
河 北 Hebei	5526.96	1263.96	34.85	3957.07
山 西 Shanxi	2628.39	677.29	33.75	1748.42
内蒙古 Inner Mongolia	1270.14	304.11	31.66	875.74
辽 宁 Liaoning	5936.34	1743.55	26.44	3790.60
吉 林 Jilin	2229.40	531.55	41.33	1512.52
黑龙江 Heilongjiang	3333.35	880.26	47.09	2285.48
上 海 Shanghai	7793.19	4436.55	179.68	2524.05
江 苏 Jiangsu	8416.84	3219.34	61.06	4457.55
浙 江 Zhejiang	7300.09	2889.09	111.92	3594.65
安 徽 Anhui	2474.43	753.54	55.08	1446.45
福 建 Fujian	3114.34	1002.18	39.58	1767.59
江 西 Jiangxi	1966.76	526.91	77.32	1243.15
山 东 Shandong	7471.39	2077.19	76.44	4466.72
河 南 Henan	4753.36	1207.41	46.58	3182.07
湖 北 Hubei	3572.78	1343.01	53.72	1908.81
湖 南 Hunan	2874.31	763.10	38.67	1874.22
广 东 Guangdong	16874.78	6316.71	389.30	8665.79
广 西 Guangxi	2269.07	665.77	64.92	1374.47
海 南 Hainan	889.08	307.89	7.10	404.19
四 川 Sichuan	4515.84	1373.08	61.77	2693.17
贵 州 Guizhou	1106.62	429.58	39.61	539.48
云 南 Yunnan	2465.79	1038.40	53.90	1138.22
西 藏 Tibet	145.00	73.42	7.49	40.48
陕 西 Shanxi	2663.03	853.48	39.72	1522.70
甘 肃 Gansu	1402.95	463.38	23.18	818.76
青 海 Qinghai	308.37	118.66	3.87	159.07
宁 夏 Ningxia	396.48	125.57	18.64	229.35
新 疆 Xinjiang	1863.51	702.20	12.48	908.55
重 庆 Chongqing	1904.51	645.55	20.82	1085.12

金融机构各项存、贷款分地区情况表（续七）

Regional Deposits and Loans at Financial Institutions（Continued）

（2000 年末余额）

（Year - end Balance of 2000）

单位：亿元

Unit：100 Million Yuan

地　区 Regions	各项贷款 Total Loans	短期贷款 Short - term Loans	其中：票据融资 Of Which：Paper Financing	中长期贷款 Medium and Long - term Loans
全　国 National Total	**99371.07**	**65748.07**	**1263.93**	**27931.19**
总　行 Headquarters	4279.92	1374.04	40.54	1973.05
北　京 Beijing	5946.61	3446.88	107.18	2365.80
天　津 Tianjin	1863.61	1316.42	14.69	433.29
河　北 Hebei	4134.12	2834.60	27.53	1170.86
山　西 Shanxi	2132.90	1323.53	32.15	698.50
内蒙古 Inner Mongolia	1340.85	851.27	4.57	461.98
辽　宁 Liaoning	5217.87	3562.04	60.60	1238.75
吉　林 Jilin	2646.16	1876.26	5.35	636.86
黑龙江 Heilongjiang	3146.95	2330.24	15.93	716.23
上　海 Shanghai	5968.49	4347.56	118.41	1292.85
江　苏 Jiangsu	5977.29	4560.81	163.41	1169.23
浙　江 Zhejiang	5424.53	3958.19	60.64	1212.27
安　徽 Anhui	2379.20	1649.38	14.74	633.18
福　建 Fujian	2438.77	1727.97	15.76	605.02
江　西 Jiangxi	1739.85	1204.90	4.59	474.44
山　东 Shandong	6212.43	4093.66	92.58	1586.46
河　南 Henan	4356.95	3115.99	53.02	1056.09
湖　北 Hubei	3495.04	2198.73	40.96	1159.41
湖　南 Hunan	2403.38	1634.97	14.24	681.21
广　东 Guangdong	11691.54	8396.65	229.03	2485.54
广　西 Guangxi	1613.25	942.60	2.72	583.06
海　南 Hainan	635.46	268.70	2.73	253.46
四　川 Sichuan	4056.43	2385.30	37.01	1472.67
贵　州 Guizhou	1065.40	614.28	2.04	433.07
云　南 Yunnan	1988.79	1298.63	14.37	630.74
西　藏 Tibet	80.61	50.64		27.90
陕　西 Shanxi	2194.04	1340.17	22.54	751.35
甘　肃 Gansu	1171.24	706.27	13.04	431.19
青　海 Qinghai	365.94	170.24	0.41	188.44
宁　夏 Ningxia	383.22	206.92	1.17	164.52
新　疆 Xinjiang	1403.13	904.45	4.82	447.26
重　庆 Chongqing	1617.02	1055.77	47.18	496.42

金融机构各项存、贷款分地区情况表（续八）

Regional Deposits and Loans at Financial Institutions (Continued)

(2001 年末余额)

(Year - end Balance of 2001)

单位：亿元

Unit: 100 Million Yuan

地 区 Regions	各项存款 Total Deposits	企业存款 Deposits by Enterprises	财政存款 Fiscal Deposits	储蓄存款 Savings Deposits
全 国 National Total	**143617.17**	**51546.63**	**3369.75**	**73762.43**
总 行 Headquarters	4321.42	1751.82	1049.15	0.08
北 京 Beijing	12233.62	6765.88	105.55	3536.32
天 津 Tianjin	2562.74	946.88	12.93	1284.95
河 北 Hebei	6136.90	1370.83	41.32	4364.51
山 西 Shanxi	3090.73	821.93	45.74	1979.72
内蒙古 Inner Mongolia	1498.83	375.07	61.50	986.74
辽 宁 Liaoning	6613.58	1974.43	41.73	4131.55
吉 林 Jilin	2484.11	589.19	46.64	1676.06
黑龙江 Heilongjiang	3742.07	955.71	52.41	2578.45
上 海 Shanghai	9607.56	5437.29	199.29	3001.89
江 苏 Jiangsu	9699.78	3610.59	79.94	5172.83
浙 江 Zhejiang	8830.12	3475.65	136.33	4262.38
安 徽 Anhui	2907.31	857.44	75.97	1700.47
福 建 Fujian	3614.24	1163.27	45.93	2030.93
江 西 Jiangxi	2286.63	605.17	100.88	1429.52
山 东 Shandong	8495.11	2302.68	114.04	5063.42
河 南 Henan	5530.20	1398.27	81.19	3634.51
湖 北 Hubei	4238.57	1556.77	80.27	2287.40
湖 南 Hunan	3342.90	873.88	52.80	2183.73
广 东 Guangdong	19447.77	7110.56	422.44	9930.12
广 西 Guangxi	2518.58	703.01	76.27	1538.61
海 南 Hainan	873.89	289.04	11.39	427.32
四 川 Sichuan	5256.80	1553.25	93.35	3123.38
贵 州 Guizhou	1341.12	520.80	48.44	641.67
云 南 Yunnan	2779.75	1082.52	76.33	1298.52
西 藏 Tibet	212.90	125.69	9.67	50.18
陕 西 Shanxi	3204.89	1049.17	66.16	1768.47
甘 肃 Gansu	1615.76	539.78	35.16	920.71
青 海 Qinghai	391.04	142.23	17.17	188.53
宁 夏 Ningxia	468.89	152.73	30.18	257.97
新 疆 Xinjiang	1975.43	694.27	29.89	994.30
重 庆 Chongqing	2294.08	750.82	29.73	1317.17

金融机构各项存、贷款分地区情况表（续九）

Regional Deposits and Loans at Financial Institutions（Continued）

（2001 年末余额）

（Year - end Balance of 2001）

单位：亿元

Unit：100 Million Yuan

地　区 Regions	各项存款 Total Deposits	短期贷款 Short - term Loans	中长期贷款 Medium and Long - term Loans	票据融资 Paper Financing
全　国 National Total	**112314.70**	**67327.23**	**39238.08**	**2814.04**
总　行 Headquarters	4540.47	1394.38	1934.43	239.63
北　京 Beijing	7440.80	3321.75	3826.70	275.48
天　津 Tianjin	2159.87	1384.19	637.76	56.54
河　北 Hebei	4550.34	2933.38	1535.48	51.63
山　西 Shanxi	2408.42	1431.75	863.83	63.30
内蒙古 Inner Mongolia	1470.87	854.90	598.77	5.98
辽　宁 Liaoning	5615.96	3767.71	1670.43	76.05
吉　林 Jilin	2828.29	1999.26	778.53	17.75
黑龙江 Heilongjiang	3358.57	2428.31	911.57	13.21
上　海 Shanghai	7340.30	4156.08	2542.36	426.24
江　苏 Jiangsu	6671.70	4613.51	1678.20	258.57
浙　江 Zhejiang	6482.23	4184.40	2017.17	143.71
安　徽 Anhui	2605.38	1731.12	764.98	28.19
福　建 Fujian	2864.75	1656.70	980.87	182.49
江　西 Jiangxi	1880.94	1282.80	566.77	7.99
山　东 Shandong	7011.21	4538.47	2015.86	148.21
河　南 Henan	4885.73	3336.17	1447.99	74.73
湖　北 Hubei	3788.36	2263.82	1392.87	78.66
湖　南 Hunan	2787.91	1772.42	927.69	35.67
广　东 Guangdong	13100.46	8074.91	4457.81	388.97
广　西 Guangxi	1764.04	955.73	750.39	7.44
海　南 Hainan	644.79	278.25	314.72	1.88
四　川 Sichuan	4498.55	2544.78	1801.82	41.88
贵　州 Guizhou	1212.24	587.73	607.69	12.48
云　南 Yunnan	2173.45	1271.95	848.51	28.90
西　藏 Tibet	96.63	54.18	41.58	
陕　西 Shanxi	2537.53	1377.15	1005.78	56.54
甘　肃 Gansu	1268.38	711.57	524.42	19.80
青　海 Qinghai	422.03	176.24	244.55	0.59
宁　夏 Ningxia	441.39	202.12	229.56	3.57
新　疆 Xinjiang	1591.10	968.71	597.70	7.67
重　庆 Chongqing	1871.99	1072.74	721.28	60.29

注：自 2001 年起，本表“短期贷款”不再包含“票据融资”数据。

Note：As of 2001，the coverage of short - term loans of this statement didn’t include the data of paper financing.

金融机构各项存、贷款分地区情况表（续十）

Regional Deposits and Loans at Financial Institutions（Continued）

（2002 年末余额）

（Year - end Balance of 2002）

单位：亿元

Unit：100 Million Yuan

地　区 Regions	各项存款 Total Deposits	企业存款 Deposits by Enterprises	财政存款 Fiscal Deposits	储蓄存款 Savings Deposits
全　国 National Total	**170917.40**	**60028.57**	**3481.90**	**86910.65**
总　行 Headquarters	4627.72	2059.85	1076.89	2.50
北　京 Beijing	15414.18	8584.28	125.99	4389.69
天　津 Tianjin	3019.42	1116.56	23.28	1486.41
河　北 Hebei	6855.15	1477.96	60.50	4808.29
山　西 Shanxi	3708.75	960.28	71.01	2307.32
内蒙古 Inner Mongolia	1735.24	422.88	56.86	1137.93
辽　宁 Liaoning	7600.38	2150.91	56.20	4665.05
吉　林 Jilin	2878.33	699.90	56.88	1878.45
黑龙江 Heilongjiang	4236.71	1054.59	59.35	2915.65
上　海 Shanghai	12325.88	6951.74	148.41	3891.45
江　苏 Jiangsu	11882.42	4280.81	90.84	6276.20
浙　江 Zhejiang	11242.85	4335.52	165.00	5212.69
安　徽 Anhui	3449.26	978.23	57.34	2047.51
福　建 Fujian	4253.02	1262.10	55.20	2430.46
江　西 Jiangxi	2707.33	702.32	109.00	1706.63
山　东 Shandong	10247.79	2739.34	131.87	5803.52
河　南 Henan	6451.60	1572.82	64.44	4196.01
湖　北 Hubei	5023.00	1765.17	66.76	2754.54
湖　南 Hunan	3923.14	931.27	57.54	2576.40
广　东 Guangdong	22984.28	7775.34	477.66	11813.35
广　西 Guangxi	2784.15	682.86	64.37	1733.53
海　南 Hainan	834.00	236.13	12.55	483.51
四　川 Sichuan	6075.03	1665.14	83.43	3665.20
贵　州 Guizhou	1553.03	547.75	41.55	758.65
云　南 Yunnan	3121.29	1106.61	69.38	1499.75
西　藏 Tibet	282.96	170.58	6.28	70.38
陕　西 Shanxi	3802.59	1226.16	64.55	2108.09
甘　肃 Gansu	1806.33	582.27	33.58	1042.39
青　海 Qinghai	467.24	167.86	14.80	222.37
宁　夏 Ningxia	578.15	193.27	29.80	306.75
新　疆 Xinjiang	2225.31	706.05	18.58	1137.64
重　庆 Chongqing	2820.99	922.10	32.00	1582.33

金融机构各项存、贷款分地区情况表（续十一）

Regional Deposits and Loans at Financial Institutions（Continued）

（2002 年末余额）

（Year - end Balance of 2002）

单位：亿元

Unit：100 Million Yuan

地 区 Regions	各项存款 Total Deposits	短期贷款 Short - term Loans	中长期贷款 Medium and Long - term Loans	票据融资 Paper Financing
全 国 National Total	**131293.93**	**74247.90**	**48642.04**	**5752.02**
总 行 Headquarters	4391.80	1355.09	1775.71	365.45
北 京 Beijing	9235.09	3644.02	4835.70	741.62
天 津 Tianjin	2523.06	1496.64	846.93	93.88
河 北 Hebei	5038.21	3120.43	1674.66	214.88
山 西 Shanxi	2903.18	1633.19	1066.83	161.60
内蒙古 Inner Mongolia	1649.88	906.42	713.41	19.42
辽 宁 Liaoning	6249.33	3932.03	1994.55	258.24
吉 林 Jilin	3057.74	2035.46	948.96	34.32
黑龙江 Heilongjiang	3623.95	2502.62	1082.49	30.22
上 海 Shanghai	9366.54	4962.89	3510.50	685.15
江 苏 Jiangsu	8235.91	5389.29	2335.62	420.94
浙 江 Zhejiang	8612.80	5320.35	2748.32	416.70
安 徽 Anhui	2941.60	1929.14	868.02	64.50
福 建 Fujian	3110.05	1809.88	1174.80	116.33
江 西 Jiangxi	2130.76	1360.41	723.38	27.11
山 东 Shandong	8536.59	5325.24	2505.76	357.30
河 南 Henan	5553.58	3673.39	1702.63	153.58
湖 北 Hubei	4313.92	2331.65	1775.98	158.76
湖 南 Hunan	3227.48	1949.99	1181.34	61.27
广 东 Guangdong	15428.57	8577.99	5866.38	791.88
广 西 Guangxi	1941.07	1006.07	892.47	29.48
海 南 Hainan	647.45	260.38	359.06	9.38
四 川 Sichuan	5158.78	2794.94	2150.57	127.17
贵 州 Guizhou	1403.92	657.77	731.79	9.54
云 南 Yunnan	2418.49	1300.41	1051.75	48.83
西 藏 Tibet	121.11	64.84	55.40	0.01
陕 西 Shanxi	2952.79	1493.28	1228.29	140.83
甘 肃 Gansu	1469.82	807.07	623.37	26.18
青 海 Qinghai	480.01	185.68	289.71	3.99
宁 夏 Ningxia	524.56	230.68	281.22	10.03
新 疆 Xinjiang	1801.15	998.51	746.66	36.00
重 庆 Chongqing	2244.72	1192.13	899.84	137.42

金融机构各项存、贷款分地区情况表（续十二）

Regional Deposits and Loans at Financial Institutions (Continued)

（2003 年末余额）

(Year - end Balance of 2003)

单位：亿元

Unit: 100 Million Yuan

地　区 Regions	各项存款 Total Deposits	企业存款 Deposits by Enterprises	财政存款 Fiscal Deposits	储蓄存款 Savings Deposits
全　国 National Total	**208055.59**	**72487.05**	**5126.94**	**103617.65**
总　行 Headquarters	6121.04	2307.36	2237.53	6.70
北　京 Beijing	18342.98	10007.47	163.11	5293.54
天　津 Tianjin	4044.33	1551.93	22.05	1825.53
河　北 Hebei	7969.83	1732.42	96.61	5457.00
山　西 Shanxi	4683.60	1259.26	68.30	2781.54
内蒙古 Inner Mongolia	2090.82	544.23	41.90	1355.51
辽　宁 Liaoning	8949.07	2432.93	71.15	5434.88
吉　林 Jilin	3307.26	760.49	59.07	2161.39
黑龙江 Heilongjiang	4813.27	1172.47	39.41	3342.43
上　海 Shanghai	15576.86	8396.68	97.55	5103.15
江　苏 Jiangsu	15378.58	5718.32	159.17	7638.17
浙　江 Zhejiang	14758.14	5714.54	214.95	6452.21
安　徽 Anhui	4190.20	1234.15	66.04	2475.83
福　建 Fujian	5178.28	1561.00	51.74	2924.65
江　西 Jiangxi	3239.58	862.90	121.65	2015.45
山　东 Shandong	12438.21	3396.56	148.65	6768.35
河　南 Henan	7618.01	1827.47	85.42	4919.09
湖　北 Hubei	5986.35	2068.05	85.30	3296.52
湖　南 Hunan	4669.00	1169.34	53.67	3036.45
广　东 Guangdong	27213.65	9019.15	713.09	14061.77
广　西 Guangxi	3175.35	790.99	62.17	1971.67
海　南 Hainan	992.07	308.08	21.23	546.87
四　川 Sichuan	7235.79	2015.11	94.01	4333.82
贵　州 Guizhou	1898.58	655.50	45.98	912.83
云　南 Yunnan	3750.97	1344.71	88.82	1766.50
西　藏 Tibet	320.88	181.62	4.76	91.90
陕　西 Shanxi	4593.21	1455.35	84.48	2519.94
甘　肃 Gansu	2129.62	699.07	26.17	1217.38
青　海 Qinghai	538.54	187.81	15.00	260.50
宁　夏 Ningxia	746.93	247.65	24.66	377.70
新　疆 Xinjiang	2666.09	766.20	18.87	1371.83
重　庆 Chongqing	3438.63	1098.15	44.41	1896.56

金融机构各项存、贷款分地区情况表（续十三）

Regional Deposits and Loans at Financial Institutions（Continued）

（2003 年末余额）

（Year - end Balance of 2003）

单位：亿元

Unit：100 Million Yuan

地　区 Regions	各项存款 Total Deposits	短期贷款 Short - term Loans	中长期贷款 Medium and Long - term Loans	票据融资 Paper Financing
全　国 National Total	**158996.23**	**83661.15**	**63401.40**	**9170.73**
总　行 Headquarters	4941.46	1312.65	1823.77	853.49
北　京 Beijing	11347.15	4350.94	6059.36	920.36
天　津 Tianjin	3431.95	1679.94	1468.35	187.68
河　北 Hebei	5654.81	3335.49	1933.64	369.62
山　西 Shanxi	3552.29	1934.30	1311.71	258.08
内蒙古 Inner Mongolia	1924.11	982.99	876.15	56.28
辽　宁 Liaoning	7227.80	4345.41	2426.97	388.53
吉　林 Jilin	3288.87	2073.50	1115.53	62.62
黑龙江 Heilongjiang	3981.26	2534.42	1317.80	122.11
上　海 Shanghai	11496.11	5287.86	5069.01	874.09
江　苏 Jiangsu	11299.55	6873.28	3636.35	700.24
浙　江 Zhejiang	12014.29	7036.28	4310.99	493.31
安　徽 Anhui	3374.57	2078.21	1089.59	134.57
福　建 Fujian	3837.51	2039.24	1548.27	241.11
江　西 Jiangxi	2545.29	1504.72	974.33	51.08
山　东 Shandong	10467.13	6226.64	3279.50	636.17
河　南 Henan	6422.66	4025.09	2138.15	235.95
湖　北 Hubei	5000.75	2465.73	2137.14	296.99
湖　南 Hunan	3796.33	2156.68	1509.36	119.30
广　东 Guangdong	18215.17	9293.05	7489.09	1225.70
广　西 Guangxi	2320.65	1087.88	1168.06	54.29
海　南 Hainan	733.11	278.94	423.05	14.24
四　川 Sichuan	5910.61	3039.99	2610.63	191.60
贵　州 Guizhou	1714.04	649.90	1023.19	36.63
云　南 Yunnan	2955.56	1414.39	1438.71	86.48
西　藏 Tibet	144.44	73.73	70.66	0.02
陕　西 Shanxi	3548.23	1715.17	1518.15	213.78
甘　肃 Gansu	1727.73	917.13	753.20	44.88
青　海 Qinghai	564.84	204.53	348.43	11.33
宁　夏 Ningxia	681.59	288.02	365.07	25.14
新　疆 Xinjiang	2101.63	1076.24	923.49	77.26
重　庆 Chongqing	2774.83	1378.86	1193.73	187.81

金融机构各项存、贷款分地区情况表（续十四）

Regional Deposits and Loans at Financial Institutions (Continued)

（2004年末余额）

(Year - end Balance of 2004)

单位：亿元

Unit: 100 Million Yuan

地 区 Regions	各项存款 Total Deposits	企业存款 Deposits by Enterprises	财政存款 Fiscal Deposits	储蓄存款 Savings Deposits
全 国 National Total	**241424.32**	**84669.47**	**6236.17**	**119555.39**
总 行 Headquarters	6591.39	2675.20	1752.46	354.35
北 京 Beijing	21650.71	12334.98	240.86	6122.35
天 津 Tianjin	4758.72	1850.21	35.34	2116.67
河 北 Hebei	9249.94	2083.56	156.20	6207.48
山 西 Shanxi	5811.69	1538.00	138.92	3342.31
内蒙古 Inner Mongolia	2576.38	690.08	82.78	1603.87
辽 宁 Liaoning	10204.92	2816.81	100.26	6048.52
吉 林 Jilin	3683.49	804.95	124.41	2405.59
黑龙江 Heilongjiang	5313.28	1331.85	75.89	3585.45
上 海 Shanghai	18214.24	9823.62	157.30	6116.13
江 苏 Jiangsu	18222.21	6750.57	240.47	8863.10
浙 江 Zhejiang	17236.61	6558.02	316.75	7364.06
安 徽 Anhui	5045.33	1489.54	102.46	2972.36
福 建 Fujian	5992.82	1842.60	92.64	3322.26
江 西 Jiangxi	3758.30	991.67	161.30	2347.72
山 东 Shandong	14516.07	3874.64	225.83	7721.46
河 南 Henan	8634.60	1988.24	104.01	5607.30
湖 北 Hubei	7033.86	2354.43	155.08	3865.70
湖 南 Hunan	5500.48	1377.41	128.39	3483.23
广 东 Guangdong	30819.96	10030.30	1012.96	16193.41
广 西 Guangxi	3673.14	959.12	84.23	2240.10
海 南 Hainan	1110.82	361.20	20.28	615.92
四 川 Sichuan	8462.13	2378.93	139.42	5019.44
贵 州 Guizhou	2322.24	840.74	59.30	1094.55
云 南 Yunnan	4404.37	1688.80	108.46	2052.12
西 藏 Tibet	361.74	207.46	9.78	107.49
陕 西 Shanxi	5380.29	1665.93	155.64	2948.35
甘 肃 Gansu	2484.13	824.39	52.92	1384.88
青 海 Qinghai	601.73	212.55	27.33	299.28
宁 夏 Ningxia	841.17	260.31	41.75	425.52
新 疆 Xinjiang	2959.78	832.50	44.73	1534.67
重 庆 Chongqing	4007.79	1230.83	87.99	2189.73

金融机构各项存、贷款分地区情况表（续十五）

Regional Deposits and Loans at Financial Institutions（Continued）

（2004年末余额）

（Year－end Balance of 2004）

单位：亿元

Unit：100 Million Yuan

地 区 Regions	各项存款 Total Deposits	短期贷款 Short－term Loans	中长期贷款 Medium and Long－term Loans	票据融资 Paper Financing
全 国 National Total	**178197.78**	**86840.60**	**76702.88**	**11521.45**
总 行 Headquarters	6126.19	1434.44	1608.35	1829.98
北 京 Beijing	12625.24	4739.52	7098.14	763.60
天 津 Tianjin	3844.84	1771.53	1789.90	169.23
河 北 Hebei	6152.23	3423.37	2216.68	503.21
山 西 Shanxi	4016.13	2036.26	1584.43	341.46
内蒙古 Inner Mongolia	2239.78	1039.63	1124.08	68.14
辽 宁 Liaoning	7754.39	4289.43	2988.04	439.65
吉 林 Jilin	3435.02	1986.65	1303.67	109.31
黑龙江 Heilongjiang	4038.77	2391.23	1417.13	222.19
上 海 Shanghai	12929.30	5228.13	6635.59	769.37
江 苏 Jiangsu	13491.35	7337.82	4970.82	1082.58
浙 江 Zhejiang	14350.75	8114.96	5501.76	502.35
安 徽 Anhui	3900.59	2208.75	1433.07	201.60
福 建 Fujian	4367.04	2213.06	1914.64	232.48
江 西 Jiangxi	2854.01	1472.97	1272.83	99.42
山 东 Shandong	11783.67	6601.44	3977.36	824.67
河 南 Henan	7095.10	4200.53	2487.20	378.57
湖 北 Hubei	5377.66	2548.33	2472.25	301.30
湖 南 Hunan	4257.34	2348.31	1790.25	109.52
广 东 Guangdong	19549.10	8929.17	9040.95	1410.39
广 西 Guangxi	2759.67	1072.68	1585.45	95.44
海 南 Hainan	801.20	263.42	507.24	18.50
四 川 Sichuan	6475.92	3081.76	2988.33	348.78
贵 州 Guizhou	2020.02	708.23	1267.90	39.93
云 南 Yunnan	3398.30	1488.12	1804.89	96.60
西 藏 Tibet	167.89	84.65	82.53	0.71
陕 西 Shanxi	3829.57	1783.08	1734.77	201.11
甘 肃 Gansu	1907.36	998.53	836.98	61.09
青 海 Qinghai	619.85	218.41	386.85	14.15
宁 夏 Ningxia	762.14	308.39	425.37	25.24
新 疆 Xinjiang	2214.66	1155.10	989.75	46.26
重 庆 Chongqing	3052.66	1362.75	1465.64	214.61

金融机构各项存、贷款分地区情况表（续十六）

Regional Deposits and Loans at Financial Institutions (Continued)

（2005 年末余额）

(Year - end Balance of 2005)

单位：亿元

Unit: 100 Million Yuan

地 区 Regions	各项存款 Total Deposits	企业存款 Deposits by Enterprises	财政存款 Fiscal Deposits	储蓄存款 Savings Deposits
全 国 National Total	**287169.52**	**96143.74**	**7996.26**	**141050.99**
总 行 Headquarters	8906.15	4019.08	2767.14	410.00
北 京 Beijing	26809.87	15228.80	251.47	7477.74
天 津 Tianjin	5714.88	2216.28	43.55	2461.45
河 北 Hebei	10764.93	2360.31	154.94	7084.03
山 西 Shanxi	7088.71	1748.98	174.61	4119.68
内蒙古 Inner Mongolia	3298.15	844.80	123.06	1973.60
辽 宁 Liaoning	11982.54	3133.66	116.61	6950.24
吉 林 Jilin	4270.49	877.66	108.61	2798.07
黑龙江 Heilongjiang	6135.10	1387.79	95.81	4078.59
上 海 Shanghai	21395.85	10795.84	237.55	7665.60
江 苏 Jiangsu	22001.44	7531.73	203.39	10581.27
浙 江 Zhejiang	20494.15	7088.26	375.30	8746.02
安 徽 Anhui	5993.83	1661.44	138.69	3508.67
福 建 Fujian	7248.40	2164.84	128.32	3903.05
江 西 Jiangxi	4445.47	1050.22	176.91	2752.88
山 东 Shandong	17103.52	4123.87	259.66	9035.14
河 南 Henan	10004.01	2138.71	130.98	6488.55
湖 北 Hubei	8185.27	2503.80	208.12	4465.80
湖 南 Hunan	6498.25	1553.52	156.84	4092.12
广 东 Guangdong	35908.11	11399.01	1107.74	19051.35
广 西 Guangxi	4202.86	1012.47	100.46	2561.34
海 南 Hainan	1262.14	393.92	19.26	697.57
四 川 Sichuan	9905.97	2538.26	177.43	5902.68
贵 州 Guizhou	2777.54	895.81	61.64	1350.90
云 南 Yunnan	5140.52	1773.64	113.95	2430.29
西 藏 Tibet	455.11	219.64	15.87	123.09
陕 西 Shanxi	6447.66	1849.94	195.19	3533.97
甘 肃 Gansu	2895.84	872.28	80.50	1586.65
青 海 Qinghai	733.09	220.40	55.27	348.94
宁 夏 Ningxia	985.34	292.25	47.12	509.50
新 疆 Xinjiang	3427.50	909.45	64.38	1816.38
重 庆 Chongqing	4686.92	1337.06	105.90	2545.85

金融机构各项存、贷款分地区情况表（续十七）
Regional Deposits and Loans at Financial Institutions（Continued）

（2005 年末余额）

（Year - end Balance of 2005）

单位：亿元
Unit：100 Million Yuan

地　区 Regions	各项存款 Total Deposits	短期贷款 Short - term Loans	中长期贷款 Medium and Long - term Loans	票据融资 Paper Financing
全　国 National Total	**194690.39**	**87449.16**	**87460.42**	**16231.18**
总　行 Headquarters	7260.51	1379.30	1895.69	2474.94
北　京 Beijing	13856.26	4823.73	7884.46	1120.97
天　津 Tianjin	4452.63	1943.38	2204.27	211.72
河　北 Hebei	6415.23	3380.46	2474.74	549.27
山　西 Shanxi	4228.97	2108.19	1699.42	380.74
内蒙古 Inner Mongolia	2588.56	1126.84	1359.95	98.13
辽　宁 Liaoning	7982.40	3821.80	3451.61	655.10
吉　林 Jilin	3332.92	1828.72	1351.97	139.38
黑龙江 Heilongjiang	3658.50	2074.43	1372.26	196.34
上　海 Shanghai	14380.38	5186.98	7788.80	1070.83
江　苏 Jiangsu	15396.58	7809.96	5689.27	1738.47
浙　江 Zhejiang	16557.67	9283.91	6237.66	798.61
安　徽 Anhui	4313.56	2247.12	1745.73	256.80
福　建 Fujian	5068.68	2366.93	2350.80	324.57
江　西 Jiangxi	3018.99	1494.47	1352.14	155.87
山　东 Shandong	13381.75	7152.65	4590.24	1217.14
河　南 Henan	7434.52	4088.16	2736.62	585.00
湖　北 Hubei	5654.60	2386.64	2787.82	380.19
湖　南 Hunan	4509.06	2252.92	2101.89	146.39
广　东 Guangdong	20880.30	8106.10	10483.48	2115.09
广　西 Guangxi	3056.87	1146.89	1811.78	96.90
海　南 Hainan	874.32	253.70	583.85	34.61
四　川 Sichuan	6751.01	2959.39	3272.77	457.51
贵　州 Guizhou	2303.94	775.47	1466.07	59.00
云　南 Yunnan	3987.58	1607.50	2227.49	142.98
西　藏 Tibet	178.63	84.48	94.15	
陕　西 Shanxi	3989.06	1679.22	1919.89	294.42
甘　肃 Gansu	1923.45	936.24	894.96	86.39
青　海 Qinghai	638.57	188.67	434.88	14.77
宁　夏 Ningxia	833.90	344.40	458.63	26.87
新　疆 Xinjiang	2272.08	1138.67	994.62	116.55
重　庆 Chongqing	3508.85	1471.86	1742.49	285.62

二、现金收支统计
Cash Receipts and Expenditures

（一）金融机构现金收支表
Cash Receipts and Expenditures of Financial Institutions

金融机构现金收支表
Cash Receipts and Expenditures of Financial Institutions

（年累计额）

（Yearly Accumulated Amount）

单位：亿元

Unit：100 Million Yuan

项目 Items	1998	1999	2000	2001
一、商品销售收入 Commodity Sales Receipts	25851.26	27731.11	32593.12	35716.15
二、服务业收入 Service Receipts	9970.88	11387.59	13316.44	14956.78
三、税款收入 Tax Receipts	1194.60	1387.26	1585.84	1831.46
四、城乡个体经营收入 Receipts of Self－employed Entities	8455.97	9068.03	10651.94	11598.11
五、储蓄存款收入 Receipts of Savings Deposits	130888.14	154778.30	183022.79	217656.52
六、其他金融机构收入 Receipts of Other Financial Institutions	2753.77	2391.84	3059.47	2710.36
七、居民归还贷款收入 Receipts of Paying Back Loans by Households	3353.54	3597.28	4077.75	5059.78
八、汇兑收入 Remittance Receipts	3622.95	4577.35	5935.30	6203.53
九、有价证券收入 Receipts of Securities	1663.67	1421.50	1917.45	1644.64
十、其他收入 Other Receipts	16211.75	17058.78	20907.01	24002.85
其中：兑换外币收入 Of Which：Receipts of Foreign Currency Exchanges	128.83	178.77	206.95	160.02
收入合计 **Total**	**203966.53**	**233399.04**	**277067.11**	**321380.18**

续表
Continued

项　目 Items	1998	1999	2000	2001
一、工资支出 Wages Payments	18231.21	19001.89	20397.89	21537.38
1. 国家工资及奖金支出 Wages and Bonus Payments by Government	8733.28	9094.70	9797.61	10394.60
2. 国家对个人其他支出 Other Payments to Individuals by Government	4740.30	4797.54	4606.50	4464.24
3. 部队存款支出 Deposits Payments to Army	512.99	562.47	632.97	725.38
4. 其他单位工资性支出 Wages Payments to Other Enterprises	4244.64	4547.18	5360.81	5953.16
二、农副产品采购支出 Expenditures on Agricultural Products	3733.87	5863.36	7126.01	7639.64
三、工矿及其他产品采购支出 Expenditures on Industrial and Other Products	5289.97	3962.61	4653.23	5244.92
四、行政企事业管理费支出 Administrative Expenditures of Public Institutions and Enterprises	11074.90	12901.68	15298.21	17640.14
五、城乡个体经营支出 Expenditures of Self - employed Entities	10026.55	11438.10	13318.47	14814.90
六、储蓄存款支出 Expenditures of Savings Deposits	129307.84	154844.09	184906.95	218043.85
七、其他金融机构支出 Expenditures of Other Financial Institutions	2278.34	1977.35	2105.63	2477.49
八、居民提取贷款支出 Withdrawing of Loans by Households	3189.87	3396.08	3977.12	4955.41
九、汇兑支出 Remittance Expenditures	2744.41	3080.46	3789.83	3996.83
十、有价证券支出 Expenditures on Security Purchases	1361.23	1126.47	1303.74	1392.44
十一、其他支出 Other Expenditures	17754.89	18058.28	21387.19	24673.33
其中：兑换外币支出 Of Which：Expenditures on Foreign Currency Exchanges	175.00	106.11	117.27	242.65
支出合计 Total	**204993.08**	**235650.37**	**278264.27**	**322416.33**
投放（+）. 回笼（-） Cash Outflow，Cash Inflow	1026.55	2251.33	1197.16	1036.15
附：代发工资 Added：Acting as an Agent in Paying Wages	3662.79	4698.14	5962.76	7876.08

金融机构现金收支表
Cash Receipts and Expenditures of Financial Institutions

（年累计额）

（Yearly Accumulated Amount）

单位：亿元

Unit：100 Million Yuan

项目 Items	2002	2003	2004	2005
一、商品销售收入 Commodity Sales Receipts	40101.42	48545.93	57943.88	61763.35
二、服务业收入 Service Receipts	16848.92	19369.25	22864.95	24091.14
三、税款收入 Tax Receipts	2114.03	2513.66	2880.27	3157.10
四、城乡个体经营收入 Receipts of Self－employed Entities	12645.45	15458.07	19109.48	20229.56
五、储蓄存款收入 Receipts of Savings Deposits	252322.50	321577.79	404743.91	454954.30
六、其他金融机构收入 Receipts of Other Financial Institutions	2259.55	2272.24	2565.18	2347.20
七、居民归还贷款收入 Receipts of Paying Back Loans by Households	6260.65	8062.83	10290.10	11874.89
八、汇兑收入 Remittance Receipts	5900.60	5091.69	5444.28	5326.06
九、有价证券收入 Receipts of Securities	952.27	1124.33	1147.95	927.84
十、其他收入 Other Receipts	26187.62	31512.10	40889.15	42307.02
其中：兑换外币收入 Of Which：Receipts of Foreign Currency Exchanges	115.91	164.93	185.50	206.71
收入合计 Total	**365593.01**	**455527.89**	**567879.15**	**626978.46**

续表
Continued

项　目 Items	2002	2003	2004	2005
一、工资支出 Wages Payments	23743.93	28640.98	34307.01	36962.99
1. 国家工资及奖金支出 Wages and Bonus Payments by Government	11389.65	13286.50	15565.12	16049.48
2. 国家对个人其他支出 Other Payments to Individuals by Government	4517.56	5195.65	5845.07	6126.62
3. 部队存款支出 Deposits Payments to Army	762.65	851.99	943.32	901.92
4. 其他单位工资性支出 Wages Payments to Other Enterprises	7074.07	9306.84	11953.50	13884.97
二、农副产品采购支出 Expenditures on Agricultural Products	8340.32	10483.21	13058.57	14898.00
三、工矿及其他产品采购支出 Expenditures on Industrial and Other Products	6328.72	8741.46	11124.87	12697.34
四、行政企事业管理费支出 Administrative Expenditures of Public Institutions and Enterprises	19997.17	23767.93	27241.30	28585.02
五、城乡个体经营支出 Expenditures of Self - employed Entities	16779.47	20958.32	24773.93	26449.82
六、储蓄存款支出 Expenditures of Savings Deposits	251240.17	318132.01	401910.07	451555.72
七、其他金融机构支出 Expenditures of Other Financial Institutions	2339.60	2233.11	2353.45	2122.61
八、居民提取贷款支出 Withdrawing of Loans by Households	6362.38	8079.85	9466.62	10321.97
九、汇兑支出 Remittance Expenditures	3930.52	3280.16	3279.98	2981.03
十、有价证券支出 Expenditures on Security Purchases	941.21	1002.35	923.03	762.03
十一、其他支出 Other Expenditures	27178.75	32676.48	41162.63	42205.30
其中：兑换外币支出 Of Which：Expenditures on Foreign Currency Exchanges	503.55	824.98	1042.73	1377.83
支出合计 **Total**	**367182.24**	**457995.86**	**569601.46**	**629541.83**
投放（+）.回笼（-） Cash Outflow，Cash Inflow	1589.23	2467.97	1722.31	2563.37
附：代发工资 Added：Acting as an Agent in Paying Wages	8674.46	10602.00	14527.48	17367.10

(二) 国家银行现金收支表
Cash Receipts and Expenditures of State Banks

国家银行现金收支表
Cash Receipts and Expenditures of State Banks

(年累计额)

(Yearly Accumulated Amount)

单位：亿元

Unit：100 Million Yuan

项　目 Items	1953	1954	1955	1956	1957
一、商品销售收入 Commodity Sales Receipts	199.18	229.34	258.93	320.89	340.91
二、服务事业收入 Service Receipts	10.08	13.81	17.26	24.34	30.01
三、农村信用收入 Receipts of Rural Credit	12.21	4.02	5.10	15.00	30.56
四、税款收入 Tax Receipts	14.11	20.70	19.86	17.09	15.61
五、城镇储蓄存款收入 Receipts of Savings Deposits	18.53	33.82	46.32	59.19	67.58
六、汇兑收入 Remittance Receipts	12.39	9.76	8.30	10.85	13.87
七、其他收入 Other Receipts	29.79	28.56	25.34	23.22	18.19
收入合计 Total	**296.29**	**340.01**	**381.11**	**470.58**	**516.73**
投放 Cash Outflow	11.86	1.84		16.94	

续表
Continued

项目 Items	1953	1954	1955	1956	1957
一、工资和对个人其他支出 Wages and Other Payments to Individuals	77.86	91.00	108.92	157.42	176.83
1. 国家工资支出 Wages Payments by Government	65.23	76.87	90.92	134.40	148.88
2. 国家对个人其他支出 Other Payments to Individuals by Government				2.43	7.79
3. 部队存款支出 Deposits Payments to Army	12.63	14.13	18.00	20.59	20.16
4. 城镇集体单位工资支出 Wages Payments by Collective Enterprises					
二、农副产品采购支出 Expenditures on Agricultural Products	74.82	99.57	110.08	87.65	74.49
三、农村财政信用支出 Expenditures of Rural Fiscal Credit	15.69	4.56	6.79	30.09	57.48
四、行政管理费支出 Administrative Expenditures	16.02	21.32	27.71	40.56	38.30
五、工矿产品收购支出 Expenditures on Industrial Products	5.24	5.78	6.78	9.04	10.31
六、城镇储蓄存款支出 Expenditures of Savings Deposits	13.99	35.30	44.77	70.88	64.67
七、汇兑支出 Remittance Expenditures	13.90	13.76	11.45	15.34	19.05
八、其他支出 Other Expenditures	90.63	70.56	64.56	76.54	71.09
支出合计 **Total**	**308.15**	**341.85**	**381.06**	**487.52**	**512.22**
回笼 Cash Inflow			0.05		4.51

国家银行现金收支表
Cash Receipts and Expenditures of State Banks

（年累计额）

（Yearly Accumulated Amount）

单位：亿元

Unit：100 Million Yuan

项　目 Items	1958	1959	1960	1961	1962
一、商品销售收入 Commodity Sales Receipts	358.98	417.33	427.79	380.64	413.38
二、服务事业收入 Service Receipts	34.95	43.70	62.13	77.86	68.65
三、农村信用收入 Receipts of Rural Credit	30.92	66.32	48.25	43.18	29.85
四、税款收入 Tax Receipts	15.33	16.67	8.73	7.91	11.20
五、城镇储蓄存款收入 Receipts of Savings Deposits	111.75	123.39	156.97	99.27	55.50
六、汇兑收入 Remittance Receipts	15.43	18.99	19.92	18.10	16.70
七、其他收入 Other Receipts	28.68	60.96	36.16	40.23	37.91
收入合计 Total	**596.04**	**747.36**	**759.95**	**667.19**	**633.19**
投放 Cash Outflow	15.05	7.29	20.78	29.77	

续表
Continued

项　　目 Items	1958	1959	1960	1961	1962
一、工资和对个人其他支出 Wages and Other Payments to Individuals	196.53	277.63	312.88	310.29	286.87
1. 国家工资支出 Wayes Payments by Government	162.19	211.21	254.11	238.53	199.43
2. 国家对个人其他支出 Other Payments to Individuals by Government	15.71	15.33	16.36	21.91	33.62
3. 部队存款支出 Deposits Payments to Army	18.63	17.39	16.10	16.86	18.77
4. 城镇集体单位工资支出 Wages Payments by Collective Enterprises		33.70	26.31	32.99	35.05
二、农副产品采购支出 Expenditures on Agricultural Products	62.88	81.24	47.73	45.52	67.49
三、农村财政信用支出 Expenditures of Rural Fiscal Credit	86.28	89.54	111.12	109.26	93.35
四、行政管理费支出 Administrative Expenditures	52.82	59.42	64.41	44.81	35.45
五、工矿产品收购支出 Expenditures on Industrial Products	22.71	14.84	13.52	6.97	5.10
六、城镇储蓄存款支出 Expenditures of Savings Deposits	111.08	120.43	152.98	107.44	64.89
七、汇兑支出 Remittance Expenditures	22.21	23.80	24.37	21.75	19.98
八、其他支出 Other Expenditures	56.58	87.75	53.72	50.92	40.89
支出合计 Total	**611.09**	**754.65**	**780.73**	**696.96**	**614.02**
回笼 Cash Inflow					19.17

国家银行现金收支表
Cash Receipts and Expenditures of State Banks
（年累计额）
（Yearly Accumulated Amount）

单位：亿元
Unit: 100 Million Yuan

项　目 Items	1963	1964	1965	1966	1967
一、商品销售收入 Commodity Sales Receipts	412.75	441.92	468.78	509.01	545.12
二、服务事业收入 Service Receipts	53.26	53.84	54.94	56.07	54.88
三、农村信用收入 Receipts of Rural Credit	27.13	28.39	28.22	32.84	35.09
四、税款收入 Tax Receipts	10.91	9.78	8.25	5.52	4.39
五、城镇储蓄存款收入 Receipts of Savings Deposits			64.20	67.44	
六、汇兑收入 Remittance Receipts			18.59	18.86	
七、其他收入 Other Receipts	93.47	105.25	32.75	35.36	118.28
收入合计 Total	**597.52**	**639.18**	**675.73**	**725.10**	**757.76**
投放 Cash Outflow			10.86	17.66	13.43

续表
Continued

项　　目 Items	1963	1964	1965	1966	1967
一、工资和对个人其他支出 Wages and Other Payments to Individuals	269.89	289.11	305.28	320.32	329.88
1. 国家工资支出 Wayes Payments by Government	192.88	206.18	214.84	226.53	235.52
2. 国家对个人其他支出 Other Payments to Individuals by Government	26.19	25.65	26.41	26.20	23.28
3. 部队存款支出 Deposits Payments to Army	20.58	22.66	23.07	22.20	21.46
4. 城镇集体单位工资支出 Wages Payments by Collective Enterprises	30.24	34.62	40.96	45.39	49.62
二、农副产品采购支出 Expenditures on Agricultural Products	85.37	97.30	113.40	125.37	122.53
三、农村财政信用支出 Expenditures of Rural Fiscal Credit	82.54	86.31	104.66	116.91	133.19
四、行政管理费支出 Administrative Expenditures	34.80	39.39	40.68	46.37	46.49
五、工矿产品收购支出 Expenditures on Industrial Products			4.66	5.71	
六、城镇储蓄存款支出 Expenditures of Savings Deposits			59.61	64.63	
七、汇兑支出 Remittance Expenditures			24.29	24.01	
八、其他支出 Other Expenditures	108.30	117.16	34.01	39.44	139.10
支出合计 Total	**580.90**	**629.27**	**686.59**	**742.76**	**771.19**
回笼 Cash Inflow	16.62	9.91			

国家银行现金收支表
Cash Receipts and Expenditures of State Banks
（年累计额）
（Yearly Accumulated Amount）

单位：亿元
Unit：100 Million Yuan

项目 Items	1968	1969	1970	1971	1972
一、商品销售收入 Commodity Sales Receipts	518.41	559.10	576.11	609.31	675.03
二、服务事业收入 Service Receipts	55.65	56.80	59.34	69.14	79.62
三、农村信用收入 Receipts of Rural Credit	34.72	34.91	34.85	35.51	38.18
四、税款收入 Tax Receipts	4.67				
五、城镇储蓄存款收入 Receipts of Savings Deposits					
六、汇兑收入 Remittance Receipts					
七、其他收入 Other Receipts	111.70	142.46	142.46	158.10	173.51
收入合计 Total	**725.15**	**793.27**	**812.76**	**872.06**	**966.34**
投放 Cash Outflow	12.16	3.05		12.55	15.06

续表
Continued

项目 Items	1968	1969	1970	1971	1972
一、工资和对个人其他支出 Wages and Other Payments to Individuals	326.79	343.23	359.34	395.20	438.26
1. 国家工资支出 Wayes Payments by Government	234.94	244.26	258.68	283.69	317.35
2. 国家对个人其他支出 Other Payments to Individuals by Government	19.55	21.32	22.59	26.42	28.14
3. 部队存款支出 Deposits Payments to Army	25.00	29.25	28.24	30.33	30.76
4. 城镇集体单位工资支出 Wages Payments by Collective Enterprises	47.30	48.40	49.83	54.76	62.01
二、农副产品采购支出 Expenditures on Agricultural Products	113.75	103.42	99.71	113.16	123.43
三、农村财政信用支出 Expenditures of Rural Fiscal Credit	128.20	143.57	145.74	158.98	179.42
四、行政管理费支出 Administrative Expenditures	41.59	47.59	47.72	52.02	57.62
五、工矿产品收购支出 Expenditures on Industrial Products					
六、城镇储蓄存款支出 Expenditures of Savings Deposits					
七、汇兑支出 Remittance Expenditures					
八、其他支出 Other Expenditures	126.98	158.51	146.75	165.25	182.67
支出合计 **Total**	**737.31**	**796.32**	**799.26**	**884.61**	**981.40**
回笼 Cash Inflow			13.50		

国家银行现金收支表

Cash Receipts and Expenditures of State Banks

（年累计额）

（Yearly Accumulated Amount）

单位：亿元

Unit：100 Million Yuan

项目 Items	1973	1974	1975	1976	1977
一、商品销售收入 Commodity Sales Receipts	732.96	767.01	811.51	841.97	893.08
二、服务事业收入 Service Receipts	80.88	83.78	87.19	88.23	96.80
三、农村信用收入 Receipts of Rural Credit	41.94	42.90	44.21	44.93	52.59
四、税款收入 Tax Receipts	6.13	6.17	6.17	7.15	7.51
五、城镇储蓄存款收入 Receipts of Savings Deposits	92.75	100.49	104.53	107.15	117.48
六、汇兑收入 Remittance Receipts	24.38	25.44	25.64	24.76	25.34
七、其他收入 Other Receipts	53.36	48.35	48.89	47.82	49.39
收入合计 Total	**1032.40**	**1074.14**	**1128.14**	**1162.01**	**1242.19**
投放 Cash Outflow	14.82	10.56	6.03	21.32	

续表
Continued

项　目 Items	1973	1974	1975	1976	1977
一、工资和对个人其他支出 Wages and Other Payments to Individuals	457.34	476.54	494.73	517.76	540.72
1. 国家工资支出 Wayes Payments by Government	321.05	330.06	337.80	350.71	364.76
2. 国家对个人其他支出 Other Payments to Individuals by Government	33.87	37.90	41.53	46.38	51.83
3. 部队存款支出 Deposits Payments to Army	32.83	32.62	33.54	32.54	29.14
4. 城镇集体单位工资支出 Wages Payments by Collective Enterprises	69.59	75.96	81.86	88.13	94.99
二、农副产品采购支出 Expenditures on Agricultural Products	133.57	130.38	131.68	125.70	123.54
三、农村财政信用支出 Expenditures of Rural Fiscal Credit	201.05	212.60	234.76	252.87	271.78
四、行政管理费支出 Administrative Expenditures	65.65	73.17	77.47	84.61	89.14
五、工矿产品收购支出 Expenditures on Industrial Products	6.85	6.89	6.45	7.31	7.36
六、城镇储蓄存款支出 Expenditures of Savings Deposits	87.96	93.70	100.57	104.80	110.44
七、汇兑支出 Remittance Expenditures	30.40	32.83	33.03	33.53	35.16
八、其他支出 Other Expenditures	64.40	58.59	55.48	56.75	55.53
支出合计 Total	**1047.22**	**1084.70**	**1134.17**	**1183.33**	**1233.67**
回笼 Cash Inflow					8.52

国家银行现金收支表
Cash Receipts and Expenditures of State Banks

（年累计额）

（Yearly Accumulated Amount）

单位：亿元

Unit：100 Million Yuan

项　目 Items	1978	1979	1980	1981
一、商品销售收入 Commodity Sales Receipts	952.69	1115.20	1365.19	1587.99
其中：县以下商品销售收入 Of Which：Below the County			852.90	1000.38
二、服务事业收入 Service Receipts	104.91	122.02	142.71	156.88
三、农村信用收入 Receipts of Rural Credit	54.16	76.87	122.97	178.76
1. 农村信用社收入 Receipts of Rural Credit Cooperatives				
2. 社队现金收入 Cash Receipts of Communities				
3. 社队企事业收入 Receipts of Community Enterprises and Public Institutions				
四、税款收入 Tax Receipts	5.43	5.58	6.33	8.76
五、城镇储蓄存款收入 Receipts of Savings Deposits	142.85	221.31	291.60	350.32
六、汇兑收入 Remittance Receipts	26.44	30.10	37.28	41.91
七、其他收入 Other Receipts	49.50	55.33	67.04	77.54
收入合计 Total	**1335.98**	**1626.41**	**2033.12**	**2402.16**
投放 Cash Outflow	16.59	55.68	81.89	50.13

续表
Continued

项目 Items	1978	1979	1980	1981
一、工资和对个人其他支出 Wages and Other Payments to Individuals	617.40	729.63	896.63	969.52
1. 国家工资支出 Wages Payments by Government	409.98	462.81	565.76	539.82
2. 国家职工奖金支出 Bonus Payments by Government to Individuals				63.15
3. 国家对个人其他支出 Other Payments to Individuals by Government	61.18	93.60	109.84	122.01
4. 国家退休职工工资支出 Wages Payments by Government to Retired Employees				
5. 部队存款支出 Deposits Payments to Army	32.64	37.26	42.58	40.95
6. 城镇集体单位工资支出 Wages Payments by Collective Enterprises	113.60	135.96	155.70	165.16
7. 城镇集体单位奖金支出 Bonus Payments by Collective Enterprises				11.50
8. 城镇集体单位对个人其他支出 Other Payments by Collective Enterprises to Individuals			22.75	26.93
9. 城镇集体单位退休职工工资支出 Wages Payments by Collective Enterprises to Retired Employees				
二、农副产品采购支出 Expenditures on Agricultural Products	128.07	197.59	272.54	356.04
三、农村财政信用支出 Expenditures of Rural Fiscal Credit	296.67	359.57	457.88	546.78
1. 农村信用社支出 Expenditures by Rural Credit Cooperatives				
2. 社队现金支出 Cash Expenditures of Communities			88.99	96.11
其中：社员分配 Of Which: Allocation to Associators			88.99	96.11
3. 社队企事业支出 Expenditures of Community Enterprises				
其中：工资及对个人其他支出 Of Which: Wages and Other Payments to Individuals				
四、行政管理费支出 Administrative Expenditures	87.82	106.27	133.54	149.63
五、工矿产品收购支出 Expenditures on Industrial Products	7.08	8.83	15.03	16.96
六、城镇储蓄存款支出 Expenditures of Savings Deposits	129.77	182.88	224.98	291.34
七、汇兑支出 Remittance Expenditures	38.40	42.18	47.10	50.10
八、其他支出 Other Expenditures	47.36	55.14	67.31	71.92
支出合计 **Total**	**1352.57**	**1682.09**	**2115.01**	**2452.29**
回笼 Cash Inflow				

国家银行现金收支表
Cash Receipts and Expenditures of State Banks
（年累计额）
（Yearly Accumulated Amount）

单位：亿元
Unit: 100 Million Yuan

项 目 Items	1982	1983	1984
一、商品销售收入 Commodity Sales Receipts	1767.29	2027.94	2345.52
其中：县以下商品销售收入 Of Which: Below the County	1131.24	1276.93	1505.13
二、服务事业收入 Service Receipts	169.66	194.25	238.64
三、农村信用收入 Receipts of Rural Credit	285.57	429.42	537.24
1. 农村信用社收入 Receipts of Rural Credit Cooperatives	251.43	377.16	456.81
2. 社队现金收入 Cash Receipts of Communities	12.56	20.96	31.23
3. 社队企事业收入 Receipts of Community Enterprises and Public Institutions	21.58	31.30	49.20
四、税款收入 Tax Receipts	11.28	17.99	23.89
五、城镇储蓄存款收入 Receipts of Savings Deposits	451.22	597.70	845.87
六、汇兑收入 Remittance Receipts	43.36	50.47	61.84
七、其他收入 Other Receipts	91.19	110.92	154.64
收入合计 Total	**2819.57**	**3428.69**	**4207.64**
投放 Cash Outflow	42.79	90.65	262.33

续表
Continued

项 目 Items	1982	1983	1984
一、工资和对个人其他支出 Wages and Other Payments to Individuals	1046.22	1157.80	1415.74
1. 国家工资支出 Wages Payments by Government	566.83	606.40	699.13
2. 国家职工奖金支出 Bonus Payments by Government to Individuals	71.99	79.58	121.06
3. 国家对个人其他支出 Other Payments to Individuals by Government	144.24	133.47	188.40
4. 国家退休职工工资支出 Wages Payments by Government to Retired Employees		47.54	57.65
5. 部队存款支出 Deposits Payments to Army	41.83	44.32	47.62
6. 城镇集体单位工资支出 Wages Payments by Collective Enterprises	177.64	193.60	228.08
7. 城镇集体单位奖金支出 Bonus Payments by Collective Enterprises	13.30	15.70	24.34
8. 城镇集体单位对个人其他支出 Other Payments by Collective Enterprises to Individuals	30.39	24.41	34.50
9. 城镇集体单位退休职工工资支出 Wages Payments by Collective Enterprises to Retired Employees		12.78	14.96
二、农副产品采购支出 Expenditures on Agricultural Products	450.55	669.45	789.46
三、农村财政信用支出 Expenditures of Rural Fiscal Credit	681.23	836.00	1068.12
1. 农村信用社支出 Expenditures by Rural Credit Cooperatives	565.04	706.08	888.16
2. 社队现金支出 Cash Expenditures of Communities	62.25	55.59	64.22
其中：社员分配 Of Which：Allocation to Associators	30.65	20.41	10.94
3. 社队企事业支出 Expenditures of Community Enterprises	53.94	74.33	115.74
其中：工资及对个人其他支出 Of Which：Wages and Other Payments to Individuals	27.44	36.89	54.59
四、行政管理费支出 Administrative Expenditures	166.65	196.42	271.08
五、工矿产品收购支出 Expenditures on Industrial Products	16.93	21.41	32.55
六、城镇储蓄存款支出 Expenditures of Savings Deposits	370.19	481.41	664.36
七、汇兑支出 Remittance Expenditures	53.11	58.67	69.47
八、其他支出 Other Expenditures	77.48	98.18	159.19
支出合计 **Total**	**2862.36**	**3519.34**	**4469.97**
回笼 Cash Inflow			

国家银行现金收支表

Cash Receipts and Expenditures of State Banks

(年累计额)

(Yearly Accumulated Amount)

单位：亿元

Unit: 100 Million Yuan

项目 Items	1985	1986	1987	1988	1989
一、商品销售收入 Commodity Sales Receipts	2863.70	3279.39	3895.67	5216.25	5482.51
其中：县及县以下商品销售收入 Of Which: County & Below the County	1766.01	2032.35	2425.08	3177.43	3214.69
二、服务事业收入 Service Receipts	321.66	385.70	491.23	651.01	786.93
三、税款收入 Tax Receipts	36.10	44.38	59.03	80.21	110.18
四、农村信用社收入 Receipts of Rural Credit Cooperatives	580.36	697.28	896.40	1049.89	1113.24
五、乡镇企事业收入 Receipts of Village and Township Enterprises and Public Institutions	84.17	100.35	151.46	229.44	229.35
其中：商品销售收入 Of Which: Commodity Sales Receipts	36.53	43.91	71.12	108.44	109.31
服务事业收入 Service Receipts	6.73	6.85	11.56	16.39	18.11
六、城乡个体经营收入 Receipts of Self - employed Entities	36.09	42.36	70.79	110.66	115.31
七、储蓄存款收入 Receipts of Savings Deposits	1241.99	1658.18	2566.97	4336.08	5726.65
八、城市信用社收入 Receipts of Urban Credit Cooperatives			72.56	138.36	206.69
九、汇兑收入 Remittance Receipts	82.53	95.83	218.65	187.52	224.99
十、其他收入 Other Receipts	252.49	309.94	291.02	726.39	948.98
其中：金融债券收入 Of Which: Receipts of Financial Bonds		21.54			
十一、债券收入 Receipts of Bonds			65.79	84.65	105.02
收入合计 Total	**5499.09**	**6613.41**	**8779.57**	**12810.46**	**15049.85**
投放 Cash Outflow	195.72	230.53	236.11	676.67	209.99

续表
Continued

项　目 Items	1985	1986	1987	1988	1989
一、工资和对个人其他支出 Wages and Other Payments to Individuals	1786.43	2158.13	2512.43	3178.72	3680.12
1. 国家工资支出 Wages Payments by Government	868.20	1059.80	1172.90	1420.79	1672.34
2. 国家职工奖金支出 Bonus Payments by Government to Individuals	137.45	157.65	213.60	294.58	337.73
3. 国家对个人其他支出 Other Payments to Individuals by Government	338.44	423.74	519.69	703.85	818.55
4. 部队存款支出 Deposits Payments to Army	61.42	68.48	70.79	81.13	98.18
5. 城镇集体单位工资性支出 Wages Payments by Collective Enterprises	380.92	448.46	416.01	514.16	571.24
6. 城镇集体单位对个人其他支出 Other Payments by Collective Enterprises to Individuals			119.44	164.21	182.08
二、农副产品采购支出 Expenditures on Agricultural Products	834.77	1012.94	1189.02	1496.10	1534.95
三、工矿产品收购支出 Expenditures on Industrial Products	55.04	62.01	97.49	167.50	164.91
四、行政企业管理费支出 Administrative Expenditures of Enterprises	364.75	412.94	529.99	796.79	925.07
五、农村信用社支出 Expenditures of Rural Credit Cooperatives	1094.82	1222.14	1524.79	1934.88	1805.22
六、乡镇企事业支出 Expenditures of Village and Township Enterprises and Public Institutions	169.32	220.59	323.59	458.54	460.37
其中：工资性支出 Of Which：Wages Payments	62.24	80.19	115.37	146.89	160.66
七、城乡个体经营支出 Expenditures of Self – employed Entities	56.93	67.92	112.66	181.77	191.48
八、储蓄存款支出 Expenditures of Savings Deposits	1008.91	1311.72	2106.09	4057.28	5025.51
九、城市信用社支出 Expenditures of Urban Credit Cooperatives			67.82	188.04	226.59
十、汇兑支出 Remittance Expenditures	93.26	106.27	135.77	198.59	231.86
十一、其他支出 Other Expenditures	230.58	269.28	388.08	774.48	943.00
其中：金融债券支出 Of Which：Financial Bonds Expenditures		4.56			
十二、债券支出 Bonds Expenditures			27.95	54.44	70.76
支出合计 Total	**5694.81**	**6843.94**	**9015.68**	**13487.13**	**15259.84**
回笼 Cash Inflow					

国家银行现金收支表
Cash Receipts and Expenditures of State Banks
（年累计额）
（Yearly Accumulated Amount）

单位：亿元
Unit: 100 Million Yuan

项目 Items	1990	1991	1992	1993	1994
一、商品销售收入 Commodity Sales Receipts	5690.57	6602.10	8316.52	11287.65	14384.67
其中：县及县以下商品销售收入 Of Which: County & Below the County	3299.73	3740.97	4434.48	5389.72	6351.67
二、服务事业收入 Service Receipts	958.85	1200.57	1668.33	2443.64	3389.87
三、税款收入 Tax Receipts	126.84	156.31	192.84	269.70	388.70
四、农村信用社收入 Receipts of Rural Credit Cooperatives	1353.59	1662.69	2076.27	2861.19	3330.82
五、乡镇企事业收入 Receipts of Village and Township Enterprises and Public Institutions	270.60	359.62	531.29	860.63	1516.22
其中：商品销售收入 Of Which: Commodity Sales Receipts	124.03	163.31	229.24	377.63	494.64
服务事业收入 Service Receipts	21.80	30.64	47.44	120.60	130.15
六、城乡个体经营收入 Receipts of Self-employed Entities	138.64	191.90	263.29	430.68	881.76
七、储蓄存款收入 Receipts of Savings Deposits	6910.54	8996.17	14174.77	23778.03	36829.75
八、城市信用社收入 Receipts of Urban Credit Cooperatives	281.38	404.93	637.25	1251.51	2268.71
九、汇兑收入 Remittance Receipts	293.34	405.84	637.66	833.00	1285.37
十、其他收入 Other Receipts	1042.43	1321.15	2376.12	4482.02	6323.54
其中：金融债券收入 Of Which: Receipts of Financial Bonds					
十一、债券收入 Receipts of Bonds	104.29	163.81	373.67	489.84	647.70
收入合计 Total	**17171.07**	**21465.09**	**31248.01**	**48987.89**	**71247.08**
投放 Cash Outflow	300.35	533.43	1158.20	1478.01	1423.91

续表
Continued

项目 Items	1990	1991	1992	1993	1994
一、工资和对个人其他支出 Wages and Other Payments to Individuals	4177.47	4863.58	6104.09	7930.11	11174.54
1. 国家工资支出 Wages Payments by Government	1968.88	2256.26	2678.63	3413.26	5136.19
2. 国家职工奖金支出 Bonus Payments by Government to Individuals	365.14	436.05	565.41	757.85	1033.78
3. 国家对个人其他支出 Other Payments to Individuals by Government	914.42	1084.95	1473.55	1877.54	2530.75
4. 部队存款支出 Deposits Payments to Army	118.41	132.17	158.04	206.78	301.21
5. 城镇集体单位工资性支出 Wages Payments by Collective Enterprises	611.39	714.31	894.18	1185.23	1532.36
6. 城镇集体单位对个人其他支出 Other Payments by Collective Enterprises to Individuals	199.23	239.84	334.28	489.45	640.25
二、农副产品采购支出 Expenditures on Agricultural Products	1744.29	1874.15	1857.42	2264.60	3144.50
三、工矿产品收购支出 Expenditures on Industrial Products	190.69	267.21	442.14	710.79	958.52
四、行政企业管理费支出 Administrative Expenditures of Enterprises	1100.23	1392.76	2082.17	3438.39	4701.02
五、农村信用社支出 Expenditures of Rural Credit Cooperatives	1946.73	2438.08	3339.17	4216.47	4399.86
六、乡镇企事业支出 Expenditures of Village and Township Enterprises and Public Institutions	508.05	667.63	977.21	1370.67	2059.06
其中：工资性支出 Of Which：Wages Payments	167.72	215.48	282.87	366.25	515.39
七、城乡个体经营支出 Expenditures of Self - employed Entities	216.82	292.74	457.31	739.93	1239.08
八、储蓄存款支出 Expenditures of Savings Deposits	5817.93	7948.68	13315.41	22963.68	34435.44
九、城市信用社支出 Expenditures of Urban Credit Cooperatives	264.92	343.95	628.59	1320.41	2124.87
十、汇兑支出 Remittance Expenditures	272.85	360.97	570.22	844.47	1224.78
十一、其他支出 Other Expenditures	1118.95	1417.83	2370.65	4418.98	6789.88
其中：金融债券支出 Of Which：Financial Bonds Expenditures					
十二、债券支出 Bonds Expenditures	112.49	130.94	261.83	247.40	419.44
支出合计 **Total**	**17471.42**	**21998.52**	**32406.21**	**50465.90**	**72670.99**
回笼 Cash Inflow					

国家银行现金收支表

Cash Receipts and Expenditures of State Banks

（年累计额）

（Yearly Accumulated Amount）

单位：亿元

Unit：100 Million Yuan

项　　目 Items	1995	1996	1997
一、商品销售收入 Commodity Sales Receipts	17203.12	19108.89	19897.29
其中：县及县以下商品销售收入 Of Which：County & Below the County	7685.03	8415.07	8475.43
二、服务事业收入 Service Receipts	4202.97	5136.50	5986.29
三、税款收入 Tax Receipts	516.04	644.37	734.20
四、农村信用社收入 Receipts of Rural Credit Cooperatives	3646.25	2820.61	1628.50
五、乡镇企事业收入 Receipts of Village and Township Enterprises and Public Institutions	2096.39	2669.20	3106.84
其中：商品销售收入 Of Which：Commodity Sales Receipts	681.19	813.15	939.01
服务事业收入 Service Receipts	181.23	230.14	280.07
六、城乡个体经营收入 Receipts of Self－employed Entities	1446.21	2104.78	2660.78
七、储蓄存款收入 Receipts of Savings Deposits	52522.79	68525.70	85185.97
八、城市信用社收入 Receipts of Urban Credit Cooperatives	3553.80	4752.11	5462.66
九、汇兑收入 Remittance Receipts	1846.91	2133.52	2583.49
十、其他收入 Other Receipts	8880.36	11779.37	14287.21
其中：金融债券收入 Of Which：Receipts of Financial Bonds			
十一、债券收入 Receipts of Bonds	806.28	588.23	1110.61
收入合计 **Total**	**96721.12**	**120263.28**	**142643.84**
投放 Cash Outflow	596.79	916.63	1375.60

续表
Continued

项 目 Items	1995	1996	1997
一、工资和对个人其他支出 Wages and Other Payments to Individuals	12931.13	14013.01	14489.76
1. 国家工资支出 Wages Payments by Government	5938.00	6424.49	6597.07
2. 国家职工奖金支出 Bonus Payments by Government to Individuals	1156.67	1251.17	1280.98
3. 国家对个人其他支出 Other Payments to Individuals by Government	3029.58	3312.96	3406.39
4. 部队存款支出 Deposits Payments to Army	317.43	366.20	424.85
5. 城镇集体单位工资性支出 Wages Payments by Collective Enterprises	1713.35	1776.60	1816.89
6. 城镇集体单位对个人其他支出 Other Payments by Collective Enterprises to Individuals	776.10	881.59	963.58
二、农副产品采购支出 Expenditures on Agricultural Products	3589.58	3695.46	4361.17
三、工矿产品收购支出 Expenditures on Industrial Products	1152.04	1335.30	1365.92
四、行政企业管理费支出 Administrative Expenditures of Enterprises	5608.01	6599.89	7201.81
五、农村信用社支出 Expenditures of Rural Credit Cooperatives	4691.05	3876.01	2399.52
六、乡镇企事业支出 Expenditures of Village and Township Enterprises and Public Institutions	2655.10	3172.79	3531.47
其中：工资性支出 Of Which：Wages Payments	607.52	725.14	736.84
七、城乡个体经营支出 Expenditures of Self - employed Entities	1835.71	2488.79	3032.02
八、储蓄存款支出 Expenditures of Savings Deposits	49757.13	66787.46	85106.18
九、城市信用社支出 Expenditures of Urban Credit Cooperatives	2934.31	3601.22	4057.69
十、汇兑支出 Remittance Expenditures	1697.87	2057.63	2334.97
十一、其他支出 Other Expenditures	9908.60	12945.73	15388.52
其中：金融债券支出 Of Which：Financial Bonds Expenditures			
十二、债券支出 Bonds Expenditures	557.38	606.62	750.41
支出合计 **Total**	**97317.91**	**121179.91**	**144019.44**
回笼 Cash Inflow			

国家银行现金收支表

Cash Receipts and Expenditures of State Banks

（年累计额）

（Yearly Accumulated Amount）

单位：亿元

Unit：100 Million Yuan

项　目 Items	1998	1999	2000	2001
一、商品销售收入 Commodity Sales Receipts	19352.46	20396.15	23644.75	25297.33
二、服务业收入 Service Receipts	7426.96	8512.02	9986.03	11129.30
三、税款收入 Tax Receipts	901.54	1021.05	1173.18	1342.69
四、城乡个体经营收入 Receipts of Self-employed Entities	3336.44	3518.84	4246.96	4527.22
五、储蓄存款收入 Receipts of Savings Deposits	96222.36	115149.97	138447.02	163323.81
六、其他金融机构收入 Receipts of Other Financial Institutions	2186.87	1833.07	2345.68	2088.34
七、居民归还贷款收入 Receipts of Paying Back Loans by Households	665.71	850.40	1055.60	1369.30
八、汇兑收入 Remittance Receipts	3138.54	3970.23	5255.67	5481.24
九、有价证券收入 Receipts of Securities	1359.82	1137.19	1526.24	1242.63
十、其他收入 Other Receipts	11769.37	12403.01	15196.99	16566.62
其中：兑换外币收入 Of Which：Receipts of Foreign Currency Exchanges	122.27	174.69	201.06	156.96
收入合计 Total	**146360.07**	**168791.93**	**202878.12**	**232368.48**

续表
Continued

项　目 Items	1998	1999	2000	2001
一、工资支出 Wages Payments	14836.49	15353.26	16339.21	17129.13
1. 国家工资及奖金支出 Wages and Bonus Payments by Government	7667.31	7924.23	8446.03	8863.55
2. 国家对个人其他支出 Other Payments to Individuals by Government	3957.69	3944.07	3798.50	3655.49
3. 部队存款支出 Deposits Payments to Army	497.38	546.95	617.19	707.02
4. 其他单位工资性支出 Wages Payments by Other Enterprises	2714.11	2938.01	3477.49	3903.07
二、农副产品采购支出 Expenditures on Agricultural Products	3040.46	4381.42	5083.11	5272.18
三、工矿及其他产品采购支出 Expenditures on Industrial and Other Products	3135.34	2252.40	2850.96	3192.98
四、行政企事业管理费支出 Administrative Expenditures of Public Institutions and Enterprises	8259.76	9360.02	10939.83	12186.76
五、城乡个体经营支出 Expenditures of Self - employed Entities	4226.15	4791.91	5559.46	6042.71
六、储蓄存款支出 Expenditures of Savings Deposits	95119.25	115208.05	140445.51	164119.44
七、其他金融机构支出 Expenditures of Other Financial Institutions	1802.67	1498.42	1587.68	1859.83
八、居民提取贷款支出 Withdrawing of Loans by Households	581.37	780.90	1019.09	1125.07
九、汇兑支出 Remittance Expenditures	2506.57	2810.60	3480.02	3663.22
十、有价证券支出 Expenditures of Securities	1085.12	863.22	1053.95	1128.03
十一、其他支出 Other Expenditures	12544.45	12691.48	15201.50	16824.32
其中：兑换外币支出 Of Which：Expenditures on Foreign Currency Exchanges	159.92	97.18	100.87	224.72
支出合计 **Total**	**147137.63**	**169991.68**	**203560.32**	**232543.67**
投放（+）．回笼（-） Cash Outflow，Cash Inflow	777.56	1199.75	682.20	175.19
附：代发工资 Added：Acting as an Agent in Paying Wages	3386.87	4307.06	5419.06	6837.44

国家银行现金收支表
Cash Receipts and Expenditures of State Banks

（年累计额）

（Yearly Accumulated Amount）

单位：亿元

Unit：100 Million Yuan

项 目 Items	2002	2003	2004	2005
一、商品销售收入 Commodity Sales Receipts	27917.17	33762.11	39758.39	42128.14
二、服务业收入 Service Receipts	12642.37	14561.06	17039.64	17953.20
三、税款收入 Tax Receipts	1528.59	1835.82	2111.72	2305.93
四、城乡个体经营收入 Receipts of Self - employed Entities	4823.30	6351.84	8159.95	8896.21
五、储蓄存款收入 Receipts of Savings Deposits	185310.89	239463.21	295065.56	324754.32
六、其他金融机构收入 Receipts of Other Financial Institutions	1797.34	1842.25	2091.40	1896.13
七、居民归还贷款收入 Receipts of Paying Back Loans by Households	1474.86	1797.36	2101.89	2206.41
八、汇兑收入 Remittance Receipts	5027.96	3997.20	4084.59	3884.98
九、有价证券收入 Receipts of Securities	651.22	722.99	680.73	531.95
十、其他收入 Other Receipts	16963.42	19482.18	24845.37	23519.58
其中：兑换外币收入 Of Which：Receipts of Foreign Currency Exchanges	111.31	156.20	162.54	195.06
收入合计 Total	**258137.12**	**323816.02**	**395939.24**	**428076.85**

续表
Continued

项　目 Items	2002	2003	2004	2005
一、工资支出 Wages Payments	18679.74	22284.45	26254.45	27846.10
1. 国家工资及奖金支出 Wages and Bonus Payments by Government	9666.30	11180.63	12954.93	13361.66
2. 国家对个人其他支出 Other Payments to Individuals by Government	3639.23	4145.12	4667.42	4841.69
3. 部队存款支出 Deposits Payments to Army	740.60	830.73	898.62	874.21
4. 其他单位工资性支出 Wages Payments to Other Enterprises	4633.61	6127.97	7733.48	8768.54
二、农副产品采购支出 Expenditures on Agricultural Products	5741.00	7153.45	8760.39	10240.68
三、工矿及其他产品采购支出 Expenditures on Industrial and Other Products	3889.17	5368.39	6995.91	7940.79
四、行政企事业管理费支出 Administrative Expenditures of Public Institutions and Enterprises	13506.67	15576.44	17736.90	18460.62
五、城乡个体经营支出 Expenditures of Self - employed Entities	6517.31	8272.43	9935.25	10607.21
六、储蓄存款支出 Expenditures of Savings Deposits	184709.22	236392.91	291357.43	320228.90
七、其他金融机构支出 Expenditures of Other Financial Institutions	1793.47	1818.00	1925.42	1719.58
八、居民提取贷款支出 Withdrawing of Loans by Households	1156.21	1425.67	1422.33	1314.18
九、汇兑支出 Remittance Expenditures	3593.96	2885.40	2851.42	2496.58
十、有价证券支出 Expenditures of Securities	677.68	723.51	610.19	494.20
十一、其他支出 Other Expenditures	17185.49	19601.54	24460.06	23179.54
其中：兑换外币支出 Of Which：Expenditures on Foreign Currency Exchanges	473.34	772.30	964.78	1292.24
支出合计 Total	**257449.92**	**321502.19**	**392309.75**	**424528.38**
投放（+）．回笼（-） Cash Outflow，Cash Inflow	-687.20	-2313.83	-3629.49	-3548.47
附：代发工资 Added：Acting as an Agent in Paying Wages	7247.06	8651.16	10869.91	13366.00

(三) 其他商业银行现金收支表
Cash Receipts and Expenditures of Other Commercial Banks

其他商业银行现金收支表
Cash Receipts and Expenditures of Other Commercial Banks

(年累计额)

(Yearly Accumulated Amount)

单位: 亿元

Unit: 100 Million Yuan

项　目 Items	1993	1994	1995	1996	1997
一、商品销售收入 Commodity Sales Receipts	122.60	206.85	325.94	567.24	738.83
其中: 县以下商品销售收入 Of Which: Below the County	12.72	24.88	32.66	57.03	66.71
二、服务事业收入 Service Receipts	40.45	71.17	107.28	166.55	225.17
三、税款收入 Tax Receipts	1.52	3.60	5.73	7.49	8.79
四、农村信用收入 Receipts of Rural Credit		0.28	0.85	1.57	1.43
五、乡镇企事业收入 Receipts of Village and Township Enterprises and Public Institutions	17.04	28.83	49.67	84.50	104.61
其中: 商品销售收入 Of Which: Commodity Sales Receipts	10.24	14.15	22.77	36.05	38.67
服务事业收入 Service Receipts	2.47	5.63	7.88	15.20	12.84
六、城乡个体经营收入 Receipts of Self - employed Entities	9.39	13.70	32.40	75.75	95.84
七、储蓄存款收入 Receipts of Savings Deposits	249.53	408.02	745.86	1413.39	2099.12
八、其他金融机构收入 Receipts of Other Financial Institutions	3.43	8.80	19.47	81.65	139.47
九、汇兑收入 Remittance Receipts	4.16	10.45	17.57	19.59	38.31
十、其他收入 Other Receipts	67.32	83.79	160.42	304.87	387.35
十一、债券收入 Receipts of Bonds	8.31	11.79	10.72	36.18	62.11
收入合计 Total	**523.75**	**847.28**	**1475.91**	**2758.78**	**3901.03**

续表
Continued

项 目 Items	1993	1994	1995	1996	1997
一、工资和对个人其他支出 Wages and Other Payments to Individuals	42.72	76.74	112.51	180.29	232.19
1. 国家工资支出 Wages Payments by Government	16.42	32.15	47.30	72.81	100.18
2. 国家职工奖金支出 Bonus Payments by Government to Individuals	4.58	8.34	11.02	19.72	27.56
3. 国家对个人其他支出 Other Payments to Individuals by Government	5.47	9.67	14.88	30.04	41.92
4. 部队存款支出 Deposits Payments to Army	0.37	0.53	0.93	1.13	1.41
5. 城镇集体工资奖金支出 Wages and Bonus Payments by Collective Enterprises	9.31	15.44	21.90	32.03	33.72
6. 城镇集体单位对个人其他支出 Other Payments by Collective Enterprises to Individuals	6.57	10.61	16.48	24.56	27.40
二、农副产品采购支出 Expenditures on Agricultural Products	17.10	24.86	33.73	47.13	54.92
三、工矿产品收购支出 Expenditures on Industrial Products	24.20	34.64	45.48	59.17	65.41
四、行政企业管理费支出 Administrative Expenditures of Enterprises	34.98	64.58	103.82	187.55	271.73
五、农村信用社支出 Expenditures of Rural Credit Cooperatives	0.05	0.16	1.02	0.88	0.91
六、乡镇企事业支出 Expenditures of Village and Township Enterprises and Public Institutions	12.85	22.57	36.49	60.70	75.26
其中：工资性支出 Of Which：Wages Payments	1.60	3.13	3.62	6.73	6.47
七、城乡个体经营支出 Expenditures of Self - employed Entities	11.58	17.85	35.98	78.77	95.01
八、城镇储蓄存款支出 Expenditures of Savings Deposits	243.37	402.64	731.97	1437.28	2120.36
九、其他金融机构支出 Expenditures of Other Financial Institutions	3.96	8.50	21.90	57.72	94.24
十、汇兑支出 Remittance Expenditures	0.16	0.75	3.24	4.78	4.07
十一、其他支出 Other Expenditures	66.55	105.51	171.74	336.83	395.56
十二、债券支出 Bonds Expenditures	9.33	10.38	13.04	26.73	38.68
其中：金融债券支出 Of Which：Financial Bonds Expenditures					
支出合计 **Total**	**466.85**	**769.18**	**1310.92**	**2477.83**	**3448.34**
投放（+）.回笼（-） Cash Outflow，Cash Inflow	-56.90	-78.10	-164.99	-280.95	-452.69

其他商业银行现金收支表
Cash Receipts and Expenditures of Other Commercial Banks

（年累计额）

（Yearly Accumulated Amount）

单位：亿元

Unit：100 Million Yuan

项　　目 Items	1998	1999	2000	2001
一、商品销售收入 Commodity Sales Receipts	1780.86	2039.64	2605.31	3405.99
二、服务业收入 Service Receipts	632.10	725.82	880.95	1080.41
三、税款收入 Tax Receipts	36.82	43.38	58.52	74.57
四、城乡个体经营收入 Receipts of Self-employed Entities	167.50	189.44	262.61	372.84
五、储蓄存款收入 Receipts of Savings Deposits	4632.34	5800.85	8131.33	13378.85
六、其他金融机构收入 Receipts of Other Financial Institutions	233.46	255.88	347.38	294.66
七、居民归还贷款收入 Receipts of Paying Back Loans by Households	19.61	29.04	51.38	84.57
八、汇兑收入 Remittance Receipts	93.59	156.12	194.69	243.09
九、有价证券收入 Receipts of Securities	158.46	144.71	208.87	209.13
十、其他收入 Other Receipts	600.27	622.88	961.56	1812.23
其中：兑换外币收入 Of Which：Receipts of Foreign Currency Exchanges	2.71	2.44	3.95	1.52
收入合计 Total	**8355.01**	**10007.76**	**13702.60**	**20956.34**

续表
Continued

项目 Items	1998	1999	2000	2001
一、工资支出 Wages Payments	583.68	617.77	728.64	900.76
1. 国家工资及奖金支出 Wages and Bonus Payments by Government	309.68	323.54	369.83	494.82
2. 国家对个人其他支出 Other Payments to Individuals by Government	147.10	152.99	173.74	171.82
3. 部队存款支出 Deposits Payments to Army	5.59	5.21	5.90	8.03
4. 其他单位工资性支出 Wages Payments by Other Enterprises	121.31	136.03	179.17	226.09
二、农副产品采购支出 Expenditures on Agricultural Products	74.65	130.95	152.64	207.69
三、工矿及其他产品采购支出 Expenditures on Industrial and Other Products	164.89	132.69	167.31	207.93
四、行政企事业管理费支出 Administrative Expenditures of Public Institutions and Enterprises	905.45	1104.46	1449.29	2069.36
五、城乡个体经营支出 Expenditures of Self - employed Entities	201.30	252.08	331.17	514.45
六、储蓄存款支出 Expenditures of Savings Deposits	4575.22	5809.52	8214.02	13601.49
七、其他金融机构支出 Expenditures of Other Financial Institutions	183.80	202.51	200.60	249.13
八、居民提取贷款支出 Withdrawing of Loans by Households	16.72	23.72	44.90	72.57
九、汇兑支出 Remittance Expenditures	18.26	20.33	22.41	33.44
十、有价证券支出 Expenditures of Securities	119.42	118.19	129.52	143.68
十一、其他支出 Other Expenditures	566.87	576.59	816.57	1414.51
其中：兑换外币支出 Of Which：Expenditures on Foreign Currency Exchanges	8.57	7.52	15.34	14.70
支出合计 Total	**7410.26**	**8988.81**	**12257.07**	**19415.01**
投放（+）. 回笼（-） Cash Outflow，Cash Inflow	- 944.75	- 1018.95	- 1445.53	- 1541.33
附：代发工资 Added：Acting as an Agent in Paying Wages	135.63	212.20	303.27	435.75

其他商业银行现金收支表

Cash Receipts and Expenditures of Other Commercial Banks

（年累计额）

（Yearly Accumulated Amount）

单位：亿元

Unit：100 Million Yuan

项　目 Items	2002	2003	2004	2005
一、商品销售收入 Commodity Sales Receipts	4143.33	5188.56	6168.16	6321.69
二、服务业收入 Service Receipts	1193.34	1285.87	1525.74	1572.28
三、税款收入 Tax Receipts	96.01	108.44	126.04	130.61
四、城乡个体经营收入 Receipts of Self - employed Entities	438.49	495.28	538.62	569.45
五、储蓄存款收入 Receipts of Savings Deposits	18935.03	23555.92	32883.89	37858.97
六、其他金融机构收入 Receipts of Other Financial Institutions	228.67	187.11	207.45	169.66
七、居民归还贷款收入 Receipts of Paying Back Loans by Households	97.59	125.60	165.24	124.80
八、汇兑收入 Remittance Receipts	394.06	608.81	751.71	831.32
九、有价证券收入 Receipts of Securities	133.95	157.96	200.58	192.83
十、其他收入 Other Receipts	2670.51	3925.42	5450.97	6427.15
其中：兑换外币收入 Of Which：Receipts of Foreign Currency Exchanges	3.83	7.63	12.52	10.01
收入合计 **Total**	**28330.98**	**35638.97**	**48018.40**	**54198.76**

续表
Continued

项　目 Items	2002	2003	2004	2005
一、工资支出 Wages Payments	1090.78	1436.94	1774.03	1800.12
1. 国家工资及奖金支出 Wages and Bonus Payments by Government	563.04	719.25	839.47	763.50
2. 国家对个人其他支出 Other Payments to Individuals by Government	178.69	202.87	210.73	203.79
3. 部队存款支出 Deposits Payments to Army	8.44	9.86	18.37	14.52
4. 其他单位工资性支出 Wages Payments by Other Enterprises	340.61	504.96	705.46	818.31
二、农副产品采购支出 Expenditures on Agricultural Products	265.77	415.62	505.34	537.93
三、工矿及其他产品采购支出 Expenditures on Industrial and Other Products	247.47	342.48	454.41	627.10
四、行政企事业管理费支出 Administrative Expenditures of Public Institutions and Enterprises	2498.54	3321.18	3762.07	3640.77
五、城乡个体经营支出 Expenditures of Self-employed Entities	683.88	797.32	797.75	957.53
六、储蓄存款支出 Expenditures of Savings Deposits	19082.43	23672.00	33052.47	37528.43
七、其他金融机构支出 Expenditures of Other Financial Institutions	231.90	204.25	171.69	139.51
八、居民提取贷款支出 Withdrawing of Loans by Households	108.78	156.43	207.88	131.85
九、汇兑支出 Remittance Expenditures	37.26	79.33	130.06	152.13
十、有价证券支出 Expenditures of Securities	123.75	102.18	129.93	101.68
十一、其他支出 Other Expenditures	2241.63	3347.41	4528.74	5399.50
其中：兑换外币支出 Of Which：Expenditures on Foreign Currency Exchanges	29.46	51.20	64.28	75.39
支出合计 **Total**	**26612.19**	**33875.14**	**45514.37**	**51016.55**
投放（+）．回笼（-） Cash Outflow，Cash Inflow	-1718.79	-1763.83	-2504.03	-3182.21
附：代发工资 Added：Acting as an Agent in Paying Wages	664.97	896.69	2190.40	2059.46

(四) 城市商业银行现金收支表
Cash Receipts and Expenditures of City Commercial Banks

城市商业银行现金收支表
Cash Receipts and Expenditures of City Commercial Banks

(年累计额)

(Yearly Accumulated Amount)

单位：亿元

Unit：100 Million Yuan

项　目 Items	1997
一、商品销售收入 Commodity Sales Receipts	1281.50
其中：县以下商品销售收入 Of Which：Below the County	23.93
二、服务事业收入 Service Receipts	390.33
三、税款收入 Tax Receipts	18.76
四、农村信用收入 Receipts of Rural Credit	6.25
五、乡镇企事业收入 Receipts of Village and Township Enterprises and Public Institutions	92.38
其中：商品销售收入 Of Which：Commodity Sales Receipts	27.50
服务事业收入 Service Receipts	8.28
六、城乡个体经营收入 Receipts of Self－employed Entities	603.80
七、储蓄存款收入 Savings Deposits Receipts	2054.71
八、其他金融机构收入 Receipts of Other Financial Institutions	97.22
九、汇兑收入 Remittance Receipts	32.78
十、其他收入 Other Receipts	757.31
十一、债券收入 Receipts of Bonds	137.85
收入合计 **Total**	**5472.89**

续表
Continued

项　目 Items	1997
一、工资和对个人其他支出 Wages and Other Payments to Individuals	476.36
1. 国家工资支出 Wages Payments by Government	66.62
2. 国家职工奖金支出 Bonus Payments by Government to Individuals	13.46
3. 国家对个人其他支出 Other Payments to Individuals by Government	36.70
4. 部队存款支出 Deposits Payments to Army	6.07
5. 城镇集体工资奖金支出 Wages and Bonus Payments by Collective Enterprises	199.22
6. 城镇集体单位对个人其他支出 Other Payments by Collective Enterprises to Individuals	154.29
二、农副产品采购支出 Expenditures on Agricultural Products	137.10
三、工矿产品收购支出 Expenditures on Industrial Products	189.94
四、行政企业管理费支出 Administrative Expenditures of Enterprises	561.78
五、农村信用社支出 Expenditures of Rural Credit Cooperatives	5.76
六、乡镇企事业支出 Expenditures of Village and Township Enterprises and Public Institutions	70.57
其中：工资性支出 Of Which：Wages Payments	23.91
七、城乡个体经营支出 Expenditures of Self－employed Entities	433.49
八、城镇储蓄存款支出 Expenditures of Savings Deposits	2022.95
九、其他金融机构支出 Expenditures of Other Financial Institutions	101.58
十、汇兑支出 Remittance Expenditures	4.28
十一、其他支出 Other Expenditures	666.68
十二、债券支出 Expenditures of Bonds	135.42
其中：金融债券支出 Of Which：Expenditures of Financial Bonds	
支出合计 Total	**4805.91**
投放（＋）．回笼（－） Cash Outflow，Cash Inflow	－666.98

城市商业银行现金收支表

Cash Receipts and Expenditures of City Commercial Banks

（年累计额）

（Yearly Accumulated Amount）

单位：亿元

Unit：100 Million Yuan

项目 Items	1998	1999	2000	2001
一、商品销售收入 Commodity Sales Receipts	1623.10	1980.41	2446.31	2787.13
二、服务业收入 Service Receipts	531.58	695.97	842.33	992.69
三、税款收入 Tax Receipts	37.88	49.66	54.23	70.97
四、城乡个体经营收入 Receipts of Self - employed Entities	974.82	1211.52	1289.73	1331.02
五、储蓄存款收入 Receipts of Savings Deposits	3587.41	4564.31	5127.83	6395.69
六、其他金融机构收入 Receipts of Other Financial Institutions	146.68	168.99	249.95	199.34
七、居民归还贷款收入 Receipts of Paying Back Loans by Households	39.69	55.94	55.35	67.72
八、汇兑收入 Remittance Receipts	149.69	176.44	175.87	167.03
九、有价证券收入 Receipts of Securities	83.36	106.12	152.24	165.44
十、其他收入 Other Receipts	634.11	688.27	875.72	1119.29
其中：兑换外币收入 Of Which：Receipts of Foreign Currency Exchanges	0.99	1.19	1.10	1.32
收入合计 Total	**7808.32**	**9697.63**	**11269.56**	**13296.32**

续表
Continued

项目 Items	1998	1999	2000	2001
一、工资支出 Wages Payments	555.08	666.33	750.60	816.22
1. 国家工资及奖金支出 Wages and Bonus Payments by Government	180.83	229.77	278.73	291.91
2. 国家对个人其他支出 Other Payments to Individuals by Government	131.88	174.74	175.92	175.32
3. 部队存款支出 Deposits Payments to Army	2.04	2.79	1.97	2.25
4. 其他单位工资性支出 Wages Payments by Other Enterprises	240.33	259.03	293.98	346.74
二、农副产品采购支出 Expenditures on Agricultural Products	106.47	227.46	246.85	314.24
三、工矿及其他产品采购支出 Expenditures on Industrial and Other Products	393.19	347.12	443.79	498.98
四、行政企事业管理费支出 Administrative Expenditures of Public Institutions and Enterprises	819.80	1144.71	1420.56	1727.93
五、城乡个体经营支出 Expenditures of Self - employed Entities	826.09	1101.83	1243.33	1438.75
六、储蓄存款支出 Expenditures of Savings Deposits	3508.34	4425.18	5049.78	6154.52
七、其他金融机构支出 Expenditures of Other Financial Institutions	124.26	128.32	193.82	242.12
八、居民提取贷款支出 Withdrawing of Loans by Households	25.46	42.51	48.00	62.18
九、汇兑支出 Remittance Expenditures	12.48	17.51	18.98	21.87
十、有价证券支出 Expenditures of Securities	93.98	99.88	89.32	95.44
十一、其他支出 Other Expenditures	634.83	690.86	820.18	1125.99
其中：兑换外币支出 Of Which：Expenditures on Foreign Currency Exchanges	2.41	1.13	0.89	2.49
支出合计 Total	**7099.98**	**8891.71**	**10325.21**	**12498.24**
投放（+）. 回笼（-） Cash Outflow，Cash Inflow	-708.34	-805.92	-944.35	-798.08
附：代发工资 Added：Acting as an Agent in Paying Wages	30.82	50.44	93.86	370.47

城市商业银行现金收支表
Cash Receipts and Expenditures of City Commercial Banks

（年累计额）

（Yearly Accumulated Amount）

单位：亿元

Unit：100 Million Yuan

项目 Items	2002	2003	2004	2005
一、商品销售收入 Commodity Sales Receipts	3285.48	3851.77	4605.19	5150.73
二、服务业收入 Service Receipts	1073.81	1289.41	1525.59	1559.13
三、税款收入 Tax Receipts	91.59	112.17	131.94	160.92
四、城乡个体经营收入 Receipts of Self - employed Entities	1861.79	2202.59	2598.87	2638.39
五、储蓄存款收入 Receipts of Savings Deposits	8456.31	10564.55	14126.58	17061.03
六、其他金融机构收入 Receipts of Other Financial Institutions	138.70	124.95	153.63	108.68
七、居民归还贷款收入 Receipts of Paying Back Loans by Households	75.29	98.77	119.71	143.02
八、汇兑收入 Remittance Receipts	142.29	136.54	216.83	185.23
九、有价证券收入 Receipts of Securities	128.21	201.68	168.83	136.07
十、其他收入 Other Receipts	1341.74	1676.51	2178.56	2706.57
其中：兑换外币收入 Of Which：Receipts of Foreign Currency Exchanges	0.71	1.07	10.36	2.12
收入合计 Total	**16595.21**	**20258.94**	**25825.73**	**29849.77**

续表
Continued

项 目 Items	2002	2003	2004	2005
一、工资支出 Wages Payments	976.14	1225.07	1551.74	1893.31
1. 国家工资及奖金支出 Wages and Bonus Payments by Government	370.94	453.07	563.37	669.44
2. 国家对个人其他支出 Other Payments to Individuals by Government	195.40	224.99	235.10	257.88
3. 部队存款支出 Deposits Payments to Army	5.23	2.96	3.96	2.14
4. 其他单位工资性支出 Wages Payments by Other Enterprises	404.57	544.05	749.31	963.85
二、农副产品采购支出 Expenditures on Agricultural Products	399.39	538.01	646.24	626.31
三、工矿及其他产品采购支出 Expenditures on Industrial and Other Products	586.21	776.22	953.27	1073.69
四、行政企事业管理费支出 Administrative Expenditures of Public Institutions and Enterprises	2069.45	2467.43	2797.99	3036.86
五、城乡个体经营支出 Expenditures of Self - employed Entities	2203.46	2909.75	3289.87	3342.99
六、储蓄存款支出 Expenditures of Savings Deposits	8173.72	10345.80	14203.51	17519.72
七、其他金融机构支出 Expenditures of Other Financial Institutions	208.60	114.24	137.07	117.36
八、居民提取贷款支出 Withdrawing of Loans by Households	72.39	84.69	67.43	61.63
九、汇兑支出 Remittance Expenditures	22.73	26.39	29.23	40.60
十、有价证券支出 Expenditures of Securities	120.26	151.28	143.99	120.76
十一、其他支出 Other Expenditures	1365.32	1693.49	2098.36	2410.24
其中：兑换外币支出 Of Which：Expenditures on Foreign Currency Exchanges	0.31	1.05	9.94	8.05
支出合计 Total	**16197.67**	**20332.37**	**25918.70**	**30243.47**
投放（+）．回笼（-） Cash Outflow，Cash Inflow	-397.54	73.43	92.97	393.70
附：代发工资 Added：Acting as an Agent in Paying Wages	453.92	574.58	772.45	1039.34

(五) 城市信用合作社现金收支表
Cash Receipts and Expenditures of Urban Credit Cooperatives

城市信用合作社现金收支表
Cash Receipts and Expenditures of Urban Credit Cooperatives

(年累计额)

(Yearly Accumulated Amount)

单位：亿元

Unit：100 Million Yuan

项 目 Items	1990	1991	1992	1993
一、商品销售收入 Commodity Sales Receipts	312.91	393.23	545.61	1040.75
二、服务事业收入 Service Receipts	52.01	72.39	113.42	225.49
三、税款收入 Tax Receipts	4.03	5.61	7.84	13.84
四、乡镇企事业收入 Receipts of Village and Township Enterprises and Public Institutions		17.92	32.38	74.09
五、信用收入 Credit Receipts	25.35	72.24	50.78	82.55
六、城乡个体经营收入 Receipts of Self - employed Entities	152.32	255.70	321.62	514.26
七、储蓄存款收入 Receipts of Savings Deposits	248.14	336.86	717.85	1428.15
八、债券收入 Receipts of Bonds		43.49	60.65	109.00
九、其他收入 Other Receipts	117.02	122.92	250.36	511.80
收入合计 Total	**911.78**	**1320.36**	**2100.51**	**3999.93**

续表
Continued

项　目 Items	1990	1991	1992	1993
一、城镇集体单位工资支出 Wages Payments by Collective Enterprises	122.47	136.87	177.81	291.40
二、城镇集体单位奖金支出 Bonus Payments by Collective Enterprises	50.38	14.54	21.40	43.48
三、城镇集体单位对个人其他支出 Other Payments by Collective Enterprises to Individuals		58.46	96.18	191.09
四、农副产品采购支出 Expenditures on Agricultural Products	45.60	62.79	108.20	196.46
五、工矿产品收购支出 Expenditures on Industrial Products	50.47	68.14	122.64	262.91
六、行政管理费支出 Administrative Expenditures	68.96	94.11	168.47	355.77
七、乡镇企事业支出 Expenditures of Village and Township Enterprises and Public Institutions		23.75	44.48	97.39
八、农村信用支出 Expenditures of Rural Credit	23.95	73.53	49.57	75.05
九、城乡个体经营支出 Expenditures of Self - employed Entities	171.78	257.96	393.97	666.48
十、城镇储蓄存款支出 Expenditures of Savings Deposits	224.10	307.13	681.24	1374.41
十一、债券支出 Expenditures of Bonds		46.35	36.63	49.78
十二、其他支出 Other Expenditures	133.15	131.46	267.76	559.59
支出合计 **Total**	**890.86**	**1275.09**	**2168.35**	**4163.81**
投放（+）．回笼（-） Cash Outflows，Cash Inflow	-20.92	-45.27	67.84	163.88

城市信用合作社现金收支表

Cash Receipts and Expenditures of Urban Credit Cooperatives

（年累计额）

（Yearly Accumulated Amount）

单位：亿元

Unit: 100 Million Yuan

项 目 Items	1994	1995	1996	1997
一、商品销售收入 Commodity Sales Receipts	1744.63	2407.60	2585.70	1545.20
二、服务事业收入 Service Receipts	391.26	569.39	691.83	455.94
三、税款收入 Tax Receipts	25.83	41.99	52.54	46.26
四、乡镇企事业收入 Receipts of Village and Township Enterprises and Public Institutions	162.60	262.61	322.95	292.07
五、信用收入 Credit Receipts	166.71	251.66	325.68	314.09
六、城乡个体经营收入 Receipts of Self - employed Entities	914.10	1496.32	1947.18	1509.91
七、储蓄存款收入 Receipts of Savings Deposits	2802.34	4660.54	6540.58	5811.58
八、债券收入 Receipts of Bonds	159.66	188.27	212.62	105.85
九、其他收入 Other Receipts	859.83	1229.39	1572.46	1096.04
收入合计 Total	**7226.96**	**11107.77**	**14251.54**	**11176.94**

续表
Continued

项　目 Items	1994	1995	1996	1997
一、城镇集体单位工资支出 Wages Payments by Collective Enterprises	454.48	567.09	594.92	376.37
二、城镇集体单位奖金支出 Bonus Payments by Collective Enterprises	79.54	103.20	117.65	68.90
三、城镇集体单位对个人其他支出 Other Payments by Collective Enterprises to Individuals	301.03	401.75	450.65	312.97
四、农副产品采购支出 Expenditures on Agricultural Products	316.55	413.95	428.62	303.45
五、工矿产品收购支出 Expenditures on Industrial Products	401.02	514.28	523.57	339.48
六、行政管理费支出 Administrative Expenditures	538.75	699.39	741.84	343.45
七、乡镇企事业支出 Expenditures of Village and Township Enterprises and Public Institutions	177.64	266.14	325.78	295.63
八、农村信用支出 Expenditures of Rural Credit	168.70	231.50	305.45	278.79
九、城乡个体经营支出 Expenditures of Self - employed Entities	1003.80	1480.46	1801.17	1510.69
十、城镇储蓄存款支出 Expenditures of Savings Deposits	2635.56	4391.55	6327.54	5686.38
十一、债券支出 Expenditures of Bonds	112.53	165.20	211.80	66.26
十二、其他支出 Other Expenditures	932.64	1278.70	1584.59	1126.31
支出合计 Total	**7122.24**	**10513.21**	**13413.58**	**10708.68**
投放（+）. 回笼（-） Cash Outflows，Cash Inflow	-104.72	-594.56	-837.96	-468.26

城市信用合作社现金收支表
Cash Receipts and Expenditures of Urban Credit Cooperatives

（年累计额）

（Yearly Accumulated Amount）

单位：亿元

Unit：100 Million Yuan

项　目 Items	1998	1999	2000	2001
一、商品销售收入 Commodity Sales Receipts	971.97	865.04	817.32	485.21
二、服务事业收入 Service Receipts	340.04	285.28	224.77	135.49
三、税款收入 Tax Receipts	50.26	63.64	37.51	21.20
四、城乡个体经营收入 Receipts of Self－employed Entities	1210.22	1082.39	1164.12	906.51
五、储蓄存款收入 Receipts of Savings Deposits	4831.76	4696.12	3735.38	2033.29
六、其他金融机构收入 Receipts of Other Financial Institutions	51.79	36.58	27.14	11.49
七、居民归还贷款收入 Receipts of Paying Back Loans by Households	249.07	229.27	194.30	86.81
八、汇兑收入 Remittance Receipts	61.50	53.41	30.36	9.40
九、有价证券收入 Receipts of Securities	30.92	15.34	12.78	8.71
十、其他收入 Other Receipts	483.30	401.25	351.49	186.38
其中：兑换外币收入 Of Which：Receipts of Foreign Currency Exchanges	0.43	0.14	0.16	0.12
收入合计 Total	**8280.83**	**7728.32**	**6595.17**	**3884.49**

续表
Continued

项　目 Items	1998	1999	2000	2001
一、工资支出 Wages Payments	443.19	373.97	299.13	175.22
1. 国家工资及奖金支出 Wages and Bonus Payments by Government	141.33	128.11	100.10	62.51
2. 国家对个人其他支出 Other Payments to Individuals by Government	115.43	92.67	62.27	32.79
3. 部队存款支出 Deposits Payments to Army	1.43	0.94	0.96	0.58
4. 其他单位工资性支出 Wages Payments by Other Enterprises	185.00	152.25	135.80	79.34
二、农副产品采购支出 Expenditures on Agricultural Products	158.16	242.11	215.06	123.52
三、工矿及其他产品采购支出 Expenditures on Industrial and Other Products	371.02	248.70	259.57	133.13
四、行政企事业管理费支出 Administrative Expenditures of Public Institutions and Enterprises	299.57	288.17	249.95	175.73
五、城乡个体经营支出 Expenditures of Self - employed Entities	1348.69	1336.99	1381.40	1047.14
六、储蓄存款支出 Expenditures of Savings Deposits	4867.33	4822.11	3771.90	2044.32
七、其他金融机构支出 Expenditures of Other Financial Institutions	44.68	25.58	23.24	13.77
八、居民提取贷款支出 Withdrawing of Loans by Households	209.68	187.30	168.48	75.73
九、汇兑支出 Remittance Expenditures	29.40	22.94	12.93	5.52
十、有价证券支出 Expenditures of Securities	31.01	22.47	14.98	6.74
十一、其他支出 Other Expenditures	587.31	469.51	388.23	213.59
其中：兑换外币支出 Of Which：Expenditures on Foreign Currency Exchanges	0.40	0.15	0.11	0.08
支出合计 Total	**8390.04**	**8039.85**	**6784.87**	**4014.41**
投放（+）．回笼（-） Cash Outflows，Cash Inflow	109.21	311.53	189.70	129.92
附：代发工资 Added：Acting as an Agent in Paying Wages	18.61	13.40	10.43	4.40

城市信用合作社现金收支表
Cash Receipts and Expenditures of Urban Credit Cooperatives

（年累计额）

（Yearly Accumulated Amount）

单位：亿元

Unit：100 Million Yuan

项目 Items	2002	2003	2004	2005
一、商品销售收入 Commodity Sales Receipts	370.74	451.45	571.24	603.58
二、服务事业收入 Service Receipts	106.94	128.88	169.50	190.79
三、税款收入 Tax Receipts	18.66	21.31	27.45	33.19
四、城乡个体经营收入 Receipts of Self－employed Entities	541.82	525.15	625.09	731.42
五、储蓄存款收入 Receipts of Savings Deposits	1619.45	1920.13	2501.10	2993.86
六、其他金融机构收入 Receipts of Other Financial Institutions	1.90	3.67	5.66	3.02
七、居民归还贷款收入 Receipts of Paying Back Loans by Households	60.93	77.43	98.79	86.88
八、汇兑收入 Remittance Receipts	4.84	4.85	3.55	1.74
九、有价证券收入 Receipts of Securities	5.60	4.22	3.86	4.60
十、其他收入 Other Receipts	161.80	222.68	387.86	484.86
其中：兑换外币收入 Of Which：Receipts of Foreign Currency Exchanges				
收入合计 Total	**2892.68**	**3359.77**	**4394.10**	**5133.94**

续表
Continued

项　目 Items	2002	2003	2004	2005
一、工资支出 Wages Payments	158.15	183.56	239.88	264.38
1. 国家工资及奖金支出 Wages and Bonus Payments by Government	58.36	64.03	62.86	57.35
2. 国家对个人其他支出 Other Payments to Individuals by Government	24.77	26.51	34.94	46.96
3. 部队存款支出 Deposits Payments to Army	1.11	0.32	0.16	0.44
4. 其他单位工资性支出 Wages Payments by Other Enterprises	73.91	92.70	141.92	159.63
二、农副产品采购支出 Expenditures on Agricultural Products	86.11	116.35	138.35	172.73
三、工矿及其他产品采购支出 Expenditures on Industrial and Other Products	91.31	107.88	162.56	196.66
四、行政企事业管理费支出 Administrative Expenditures of Public Institutions and Enterprises	162.35	213.95	249.48	283.76
五、城乡个体经营支出 Expenditures of Self - employed Entities	635.27	667.24	830.04	949.69
六、储蓄存款支出 Expenditures of Savings Deposits	1632.96	1911.53	2496.29	2946.82
七、其他金融机构支出 Expenditures of Other Financial Institutions	5.34	6.89	6.92	5.25
八、居民提取贷款支出 Withdrawing of Loans by Households	61.10	80.76	73.88	66.97
九、汇兑支出 Remittance Expenditures	1.37	1.92	1.43	0.97
十、有价证券支出 Expenditures of Securities	2.98	2.30	1.59	1.35
十一、其他支出 Other Expenditures	178.56	244.18	400.28	490.49
其中：兑换外币支出 Of Which：Expenditures on Foreign Currency Exchanges	0.01			-0.04
支出合计 Total	**3015.50**	**3536.56**	**4600.70**	**5379.07**
投放（+）. 回笼（-） Cash Outflows，Cash Inflow	122.82	176.79	206.60	245.13
附：代发工资 Added：Acting as an Agent in Paying Wages	2.23	5.31	4.23	6.52

（六）农村信用合作社现金收支表
Cash Receipts and Expenditures of Rural Credit Cooperatives

农村信用合作社现金收支表
Cash Receipts and Expenditures of Rural Credit Cooperatives

（年累计额）

（Yearly Accumulated Amount）

单位：亿元

Unit：100 Million Yuan

项　目 Items	1983	1984
一、社队现金收入 Cash Receipts of Communities	13.37	12.39
二、社队企事业收入 Receipts of Community Enterprises and Public Institutions	11.35	20.34
三、社员存贷款收入 Deposits and Loan Receipts of Associators	70.06	122.17
四、代理业务收入 Receipts of Agency Business	8.01	8.41
五、其他收入 Other Receipts	7.95	11.21
收入合计 Total	**110.74**	**174.52**
一、社队现金支出 Cash Expenditures of Communities	28.55	28.33
其中：社员分配 Of Which：Allocation to Associators	9.28	5.54
二、社队企事业支出 Expenditures of Community Enterprises and Public Institutions	22.28	42.39
其中：工资及对个人其他 Of Which：Wages and Other Payments to Individuals	5.57	8.00
三、社员存贷款支出 Deposits and Loans Payments to Associators	51.88	107.68
四、代理业务支出 Expenditures of Agency Business	9.04	10.66
五、其他支出 Other Expenditures	11.15	14.37
支出合计 Total	**122.90**	**203.43**
投放（+）．回笼（-） Cash Outflows，Cash Inflow	12.16	28.91

农村信用合作社现金收支表

Cash Receipts and Expenditures of Rural Credit Cooperatives

（年累计额）

（Yearly Accumulated Amount）

单位：亿元

Unit：100 Million Yuan

项目 Items	1985	1986	1987	1988	1989
一、集体现金收入 Collective Cash Receipts	94.68	95.71	117.04	141.08	139.34
二、乡镇企事业收入 Receipts of Village and Township Enterprises and Public Institutions	220.09	259.83	360.71	473.35	465.89
三、个人存款收入 Receipts of Individual Deposits	950.35	1147.44	1616.28	2194.25	2393.52
四、代理业务收入 Receipts of Agency Business	7.79				
其中：商品销售收入 Of Which：Commodity Sales Receipts					
五、农户贷款收入 Receipts of Loans to Farmers	168.27	202.77	330.87	361.47	333.07
六、商品销售收入 Commodity Sales Receipts	31.90	37.42	39.17	43.83	40.76
七、其他收入 Other Receipts	135.16	160.86	214.74	294.66	337.58
收入合计 Total	**1608.24**	**1904.03**	**2678.81**	**3508.64**	**3710.16**
一、集体现金支出 Collective Cash Expenditures	231.60	224.26	258.35	292.62	276.77
其中：农户分配 Of Which：Allocation to Farmers	54.45	49.33	50.84	47.01	44.06
二、乡镇企事业支出 Expenditures of Village and Township Enterprises and Public Institutions	460.12	527.85	689.03	851.01	816.05
其中：工资性支出 Of Which：Wages Payments	106.96	119.56	148.33	173.63	173.51
三、个人存款支出 Expenditures of Individual Deposits	1003.58	1121.16	1604.28	2354.58	2440.01
四、代理业务支出 Expenditures of Agency Business	8.15				
其中：农产品采购支出 Of Which：Expenditures on Agricultural Products					
五、农户贷款支出 Expenditures of Loans to Farmers	139.13	238.59	374.05	361.06	319.46
六、农副产品收购支出 Expenditures on Agricultural Products	24.36	27.38	30.51	41.07	32.13
七、其他支出 Other Expenditures	188.78	224.29	288.90	388.04	447.83
支出合计 Total	**2055.72**	**2363.53**	**3245.12**	**4288.38**	**4332.25**
投放（+）．回笼（-） Cash Outflows，Cash Inflow	447.48	459.50	566.31	779.74	622.09

农村信用合作社现金收支表

Cash Receipts and Expenditures of Rural Credit Cooperatives

（年累计额）

（Yearly Accumulated Amount）

单位：亿元

Unit：100 Million Yuan

项目 Items	1990	1991	1992	1993	1994
一、集体现金收入 Collective Cash Receipts	160.63	203.05	293.05	405.06	679.52
二、乡镇企事业收入 Receipts of Village and Township Enterprises and Public Institutions	534.38	688.06	989.68	1473.95	2183.93
三、个人存款收入 Receipts of Individual Deposits	2837.40	3581.13	4992.84	7393.60	10274.85
四、代理业务收入 Receipts of Agency Business					212.10
其中：商品销售收入 Of Which：Commodity Sales Receipts					72.28
五、农户贷款收入 Receipts of Loans to Farmers	439.08	539.96	623.36	737.94	1214.75
六、商品销售收入 Commodity Sales Receipts	39.97	40.25	47.24	49.97	
七、其他收入 Other Receipts	391.80	480.89	668.19	1068.33	1252.87
收入合计 Total	**4403.26**	**5533.34**	**7614.36**	**11128.85**	**15818.02**
一、集体现金支出 Collective Cash Expenditures	307.68	364.71	496.49	659.78	943.35
其中：农户分配 Of Which：Allocation to Farmers	48.05	52.91	66.49	90.84	137.35
二、乡镇企事业支出 Expenditures of Village and Township Enterprises and Public Institutions	902.75	1120.03	1615.08	2239.56	3016.08
其中：工资性支出 Of Which：Wages Payments	182.80	209.36	294.29	393.58	785.12
三、个人存款支出 Expenditures of Individual Deposits	2707.34	3480.98	5006.07	7403.58	9815.67
四、代理业务支出 Expenditures of Agency Business					252.97
其中：农产品采购支出 Of Which：Expenditures on Agricultural Products					37.60
五、农户贷款支出 Expenditures of Loans to Farmers	481.07	589.37	675.66	743.08	1282.83
六、农副产品收购支出 Expenditures on Agricultural Products	33.78	34.81	33.89	35.58	
七、其他支出 Other Expenditures	535.39	661.77	913.31	1330.76	1524.85
支出合计 Total	**4968.01**	**6251.67**	**8740.50**	**12412.34**	**16835.75**
投放（+）.回笼（-） Cash Outflows，Cash Inflow	564.75	718.33	1126.14	1283.49	1017.73

农村信用合作社现金收支表
Cash Receipts and Expenditures of Rural Credit Cooperatives

（年累计额）

（Yearly Accumulated Amount）

单位：亿元

Unit：100 Million Yuan

项目 Items	1995	1996	1997
一、集体现金收入 Collective Cash Receipts	911.65	1054.96	1440.47
二、乡镇企事业收入 Receipts of Village and Township Enterprises and Public Institutions	2865.05	3503.89	4423.20
三、个人存款收入 Receipts of Individual Deposits	13617.19	15759.71	19579.08
四、代理业务收入 Receipts of Agency Business	275.07	331.47	376.58
其中：商品销售收入 Of Which：Commodity Sales Receipts	110.61	139.43	165.72
五、农户贷款收入 Receipts of Loans to Farmers	1696.45	2079.53	2366.59
六、商品销售收入 Commodity Sales Receipts			
七、其他收入 Other Receipts	1798.57	2457.85	3505.29
收入合计 Total	**21163.98**	**25187.41**	**31691.21**
一、集体现金支出 Collective Cash Expenditures	1145.85	1275.33	1651.11
其中：农户分配 Of Which：Allocation to Farmers	116.54	118.16	141.79
二、乡镇企事业支出 Expenditures of Village and Township Enterprises and Public Institutions	3752.78	4338.65	5318.74
其中：工资性支出 Of Which：Wages Payments	565.04	707.40	720.10
三、个人存款支出 Expenditures of Individual Deposits	13074.97	15192.80	19076.38
四、代理业务支出 Expenditures of Agency Business	346.54	412.04	505.52
其中：农产品采购支出 Of Which：Expenditures on Agricultural Products	46.61	47.24	78.34
五、农户贷款支出 Expenditures of Loans to Farmers	1764.31	2206.45	2476.57
六、农副产品收购支出 Expenditures on Agricultural Products			
七、其他支出 Other Expenditures	2144.22	2828.49	3993.50
支出合计 Total	**22228.67**	**26253.76**	**33021.82**
投放（+）. 回笼（-） Cash Outflows，Cash Inflow	1064.69	1066.35	1130.61

农村信用合作社现金收支表

Cash Receipts and Expenditures of Rural Credit Cooperatives

（年累计额）

（Yearly Accumulated Amount）

单位：亿元

Unit：100 Million Yuan

项 目 Items	1998	1999	2000	2001
一、商品销售收入 Commodity Sales Receipts	2122.86	2449.87	3079.43	3740.49
二、服务业事收入 Service Receipts	1040.21	1168.50	1382.36	1618.89
三、税款收入 Tax Receipts	168.10	209.54	262.39	322.03
四、城乡个体经营收入 Receipts of Self－employed Entities	2766.98	3065.84	3688.52	4460.51
五、储蓄存款收入 Receipts of Savings Deposits	21614.26	24567.06	27581.22	32524.88
六、其他金融机构收入 Receipts of Other Financial Institutions	134.97	97.31	89.32	116.53
七、居民归还贷款收入 Receipts of Paying Back Loans by Households	2379.46	2432.62	2721.12	3451.38
八、汇兑收入 Remittance Receipts	179.64	221.16	278.72	302.77
九、有价证券收入 Receipts of Securities	31.11	18.14	17.33	18.73
十、其他收入 Other Receipts	2724.71	2943.37	3521.24	4318.34
其中：兑换外币收入 Of Which：Receipts of Foreign Currency Exchanges	2.44	0.31	0.67	0.11
收入合计 Total	**33162.30**	**37173.41**	**42621.65**	**50874.55**

续表
Continued

项　目 Items	1998	1999	2000	2001
一、工资支出 Wages Payments	1812.77	1990.59	2280.29	2516.05
1. 国家工资及奖金支出 Wages and Bonus Payments by Government	434.12	489.05	602.91	681.81
2. 国家对个人其他支出 Other Payments to Individuals by Government	388.20	433.09	396.07	428.82
3. 部队存款支出 Deposits Payments to Army	6.55	6.58	6.95	7.49
4. 其他单位工资性支出 Wages Payments by Other Enterprises	983.90	1061.87	1274.36	1397.93
二、农副产品采购支出 Expenditures on Agricultural Products	354.13	881.41	1428.35	1722.02
三、工矿及其他产品采购支出 Expenditures on Industrial and Other Products	1225.53	981.70	931.61	1211.89
四、行政企事业管理费支出 Administrative Expenditures of Public Institutions and Enterprises	790.32	1004.32	1238.59	1480.35
五、城乡个体经营支出 Expenditures of Self - employed Entities	3424.32	3955.28	4803.11	5771.85
六、储蓄存款支出 Expenditures of Savings Deposits	21237.70	24579.24	27425.74	32124.09
七、其他金融机构支出 Expenditures of Other Financial Institutions	122.93	122.53	100.29	112.65
八、居民提取贷款支出 Withdrawing of Loans by Households	2356.64	2361.64	2696.65	3619.86
九、汇兑支出 Remittance Expenditures	177.71	209.07	255.49	272.78
十、有价证券支出 Expenditures of Securities	31.71	22.71	15.97	18.55
十一、其他支出 Other Expenditures	3130.06	3281.06	3816.56	4705.73
其中：兑换外币支出 Of Which：Expenditures on Foreign Currency Exchanges	3.70	0.12	0.05	0.67
支出合计 **Total**	**34663.82**	**39389.55**	**44992.65**	**53555.82**
投放（+）. 回笼（-） Cash Outflows，Cash Inflow	1501.52	2216.14	2371.00	2681.27
附：代发工资 Added：Acting as an Agent in Paying Wages	90.86	115.04	136.13	228.03

农村信用合作社现金收支表
Cash Receipts and Expenditures of Rural Credit Cooperatives

（年累计额）

(Yearly Accumulated Amount)

单位：亿元

Unit: 100 Million Yuan

项目 Items	2002	2003	2004	2005
一、商品销售收入 Commodity Sales Receipts	4384.69	5292.04	6571.52	5854.14
二、服务事业收入 Service Receipts	1832.45	2104.03	2570.45	2538.39
三、税款收入 Tax Receipts	379.18	435.94	476.82	479.76
四、城乡个体经营收入 Receipts of Self - employed Entities	4980.06	5883.20	7079.41	6370.23
五、储蓄存款收入 Receipts of Savings Deposits	38000.82	46073.98	59559.84	64855.13
六、其他金融机构收入 Receipts of Other Financial Institutions	92.95	114.25	106.56	161.85
七、居民归还贷款收入 Receipts of Paying Back Loans by Households	4551.98	5963.67	7794.04	8821.74
八、汇兑收入 Remittance Receipts	331.45	344.29	383.66	351.58
九、有价证券收入 Receipts of Securities	33.29	37.48	93.95	60.31
十、其他收入 Other Receipts	5050.15	6205.31	7839.30	8022.83
其中：兑换外币收入 Of Which: Receipts of Foreign Currency Exchanges	0.05	0.02	0.02	-0.50
收入合计 Total	**59637.02**	**72454.19**	**92475.55**	**97515.96**

续表
Continued

项目 Items	2002	2003	2004	2005
一、工资支出 Wages Payments	2839.10	3510.95	4305.25	4053.71
1. 国家工资及奖金支出 Wages and Bonus Payments by Government	731.00	869.51	1054.34	934.25
2. 国家对个人其他支出 Other Payments to Individuals by Government	479.47	596.16	671.73	691.80
3. 部队存款支出 Deposits Payments to Army	7.26	8.12	10.96	10.01
4. 其他单位工资性支出 Wages Payments by Other Enterprises	1621.37	2037.16	2568.22	2417.65
二、农副产品采购支出 Expenditures on Agricultural Products	1848.06	2259.79	2930.94	2860.78
三、工矿及其他产品采购支出 Expenditures on Industrial and Other Products	1514.56	2146.49	2497.45	2316.24
四、行政企事业管理费支出 Administrative Expenditures of Public Institutions and Enterprises	1760.17	2188.92	2623.90	2696.67
五、城乡个体经营支出 Expenditures of Self - employed Entities	6739.55	8311.59	9794.15	9126.55
六、储蓄存款支出 Expenditures of Savings Deposits	37641.85	45809.77	60132.52	65344.65
七、其他金融机构支出 Expenditures of Other Financial Institutions	100.28	89.72	111.85	131.01
八、居民提取贷款支出 Withdrawing of Loans by Households	4963.89	6332.30	7684.70	8541.29
九、汇兑支出 Remittance Expenditures	275.20	287.12	262.41	274.15
十、有价证券支出 Expenditures of Securities	16.54	23.08	37.15	41.89
十一、其他支出 Other Expenditures	5619.94	6853.95	8437.69	8985.97
其中：兑换外币支出 Of Which：Expenditures on Foreign Currency Exchanges	0.44	0.43	3.59	2.00
支出合计 **Total**	**63319.14**	**77813.68**	**98818.01**	**104372.91**
投放（+）．回笼（-） Cash Outflows，Cash Inflow	3682.12	5359.49	6342.46	6856.95
附：代发工资 Added：Acting as an Agent in Paying Wages	306.27	474.27	675.62	756.58

三、货币统计（1993—2005 年）

Monetary Statistics（1993—2005）

货币统计编制说明

货币统计包括货币供应量统计、概览及部门资产负债表统计两部分。中国人民银行于 1994 年发布《货币供应量统计和公布暂行办法》（银发［1994］267 号），按季度对外提供货币供应量、各资产负债表与概览。2002 年，按照国际货币基金组织《货币与金融统计手册》的概念、定义和分类，以中国人民银行和中国境内各金融机构的本、外币业务统计数据为基础开始编制新的中国货币统计数据。

1. 货币供应量：统计机构范围是除证券公司、保险公司以外的银行业金融机构，与银行概览的机构范围一致。

- M0：流通中现金
- M1：M0 + 活期存款
- M2：M1 + 准货币（定期存款 + 储蓄存款 + 其他存款）

2. 货币概览：由货币当局资产负债表与汇总的存款货币银行资产负债表合并编制而成。

其中：货币当局即中国人民银行（1949—2005 年）①；存款货币银行包括国有商业银行②（1993—2005 年）、其他商业银行③（1993—2005 年）、城市信用社（1993—2005 年）、农村信用社（1993—2005 年）、财务公司（1993—2005 年）、城市商业银行（2002—2005 年）、农村商业银行（2002—2005 年）、外资银行（2002—2005 年）、邮政储汇局（2004—2005 年）、农村合作银行（2005 年）。

3. 银行概览：由货币概览与特定存款机构资产负债表合并而成。

其中：特定存款机构包括信托投资公司（1993—2005 年）、金融租赁公司（1993—2005 年）、国家开发银行（1996—2005 年）、中国进出口银行（1996—2005 年）。

一、货币统计制度主要调整说明

- **1997 年** 中国人民银行对金融统计制度进行了调整：一是扩大了统计范围，将各商业银行所属的房地产信贷部、国际业务部和信用卡部等部门、机构数据并入表中；二是对统计数据的

---

① 括号中的年份为此机构数据并表的起止年份。

② 国有商业银行包括中国农业银行（1993—2005 年）、中国银行（1993—2005 年）、中国工商银行（1993—2005 年）、中国建设银行（1993—2005 年），2002 年之前还包括中国农业发展银行。

③ 其他商业银行包括中国光大银行（1993—2005 年）、华夏银行（1993—2005 年）、广东发展银行（1993—2005 年）、深圳发展银行（1993—2005 年）、招商银行（1993—2005 年）、上海浦东发展银行（1993—2005 年）、福建兴业银行（1993 年并入，2003 年更名为兴业银行）、烟台住房储蓄银行（1993 年并入，2003 年更名为恒丰银行）、蚌埠住房储蓄银行（1993 年并入，2001 年改制为城市商业银行）、中国投资银行（1995—1999 年）、中国民生银行（1996—2005 年）、海南发展银行（1995—1998 年）、交通银行（1995—2005 年）、中信实业银行（1995 年并入，2005 年更名为中信银行）、浙商银行（2004—2005 年）。

项目设置进行了细化，对原来不准确的归并关系予以调整，对有关误差与遗漏作了重新修订，自1997年第一季度起的数据与历史数据不完全可比。

- **2001年**　调整货币当局资产负债表中"对政府债权"项目归属，即涵盖人民银行所持有的国家债券；6月份调整货币与准货币（货币供应量 M_2）归属，将"证券公司客户保证金"计入"其他存款"项下。

- **2002年**　按照国际货币基金组织《货币与金融统计手册》的概念、定义和分类，对货币统计制度进行修订，2002年及以后各期数据与历史数据不完全可比。修订的主要内容包括：(1)一是调整报表机构，将在华外资银行纳入统计机构范围中；将政策性银行从国有商业银行范围剔除，将城市商业银行与城市信用社报表分开等；二是扩大统计范围，将境内金融机构的外汇业务数据纳入报表；三是对过去报表中存在的错误与遗漏进行修订，如在各资产负债表中将"再贴现"计入"向中央银行借款"项下，而不在"对非金融机构债权"中扣减。(2)对市场退出的金融机构，如城市信用社、信托投资公司等，相关数据自第二年年初一次性剔除。(3)将各表中的"对非货币金融机构债权"及"对非货币金融机构负债"更名为"对特定存款机构债权"及"对特定存款机构负债"。在各表中增设"对其他金融机构债权"、"对其他金融机构负债"。

- **2003年**　调整货币统计报表部分项目归属，如细分"债券投资"的对象和"回购"的对手方，调整相关债权、负债项目的归属；存款货币银行资产负债表中，"再贴现"不再从"对非金融机构债权"中扣减，而归属为"对中央银行负债"。

- **2004年**　(1)新增邮政储汇局资产负债表。(2)调整货币统计报表部分项目归属：一是对资产（证券、贷款、票据）转让业务开始按"回购式"与"买断式"两种方式进行统计，在货币统计报表中将资产转让业务按交易对手纳入"对特定存款机构债权"、"对其他金融机构债权"、"对特定存款机构负债"、"对其他金融机构负债"四个项目；二是为反映金融机构发行与持有境内外币债券的情况，增设了"境内有价证券投资"、"境内发行债券"等指标，在货币统计报表中将"境内有价证券投资"指标计入对"对特定存款机构债权"项目，将"境内发行债券"计入"债券"项目。

二、主要指标解释

（一）货币当局资产负债表主要项目

1. 国外资产（净）：国外资产与国外负债轧抵后的净额，主要是中国人民银行所掌握的以人民币计值的国家外汇储备、黄金及在国际金融机构往来的头寸净值。

2. 对政府债权：中国人民银行对政府的借款与透支以及买断的国家债券。

3. 对存款货币银行债权：中国人民银行对存款货币银行发放的信用贷款、再贴现和债券回购等性质的融资。

4. 对特定存款机构债权：中国人民银行对特定存款机构发放的信用贷款及购买特定存款机构发行的债券等。

5. 对其他金融机构债权：中国人民银行对其他金融机构发放的信用贷款等。

6. 对非金融部门债权：中国人民银行为支持老少边穷地区经济开发所发放的专项贷款。

7. 储备货币：中国人民银行所发行的货币、各金融机构在中国人民银行的准备金存款、邮政储蓄转存款和机关团体存款。

8. 国外负债：以人民币计值的中国人民银行对非居民的负债，主要包括国际金融机构在中国人民银行的存款等。

9. 政府存款：各级财政在中国人民银行账户上的预算收入与支出的余额。

（二）存款货币银行资产负债表主要项目

1. 国外资产：存款货币银行以人民币计值的对非居民的债权，主要包括购买的有价证券、国外同业往来和库存外币现金。

2. 储备资产：存款货币银行存放中国人民银行的准备金存款、库存现金及持有的中国人民银行债券。

3. 对政府债权：存款货币银行持有的国家债券。

4. 对非金融机构债权：存款货币银行对非金融机构的各种贷款和投资等。

5. 对特定存款机构的债权：存款货币银行存放和拆出给特定存款机构的款项以及持有这些机构发行的债券等。

6. 对其他金融机构的债权：存款货币银行存放和拆出给其他金融机构的款项以及持有这些机构发行的债券等。

7. 国外负债：存款货币银行以人民币计值的对非居民的负债，主要包括非居民外汇存款、境外筹资、委托借款和国外同业往来等。

8. 对非金融机构负债：存款货币银行吸收的非金融机构的各项本、外币存款等。

9. 对中央银行负债：存款货币银行向中国人民银行借入款项，包括再贷款、再贴现、回购等。

10. 对特定存款机构负债：存款货币银行从特定存款机构吸收的存款和拆入款项等。

（三）特定存款机构资产负债表主要项目

1. 储备资产：特定存款机构存放中国人民银行的准备金存款、库存现金及持有的中央银行债券。

2. 国内信贷：特定存款机构在国内发放的各种贷款等。

3. 对政府债权：特定存款机构持有的国家债券。

4. 对存款货币银行的债权：特定存款机构存放和拆出给存款货币银行的款项等。

5. 对其他金融机构的债权：特定存款机构存放和拆出给其他金融机构的款项以及持有这些机构发行的债券等。

6. 对非金融机构负债：特定存款机构吸收的非金融机构的各项本、外币存款等。

7. 对中央银行负债：特定存款机构向中国人民银行借入款项等。

8. 对存款货币银行负债：特定存款机构从存款货币银行吸收的存款和拆入款项等。

9. 对其他金融机构负债：特定存款机构从其他金融机构吸收的存款和拆入款项等。

Compilation Instructions for Monetary Statistics

Monetary statistics consists of two parts, statistics on Money Supply and Survey and Sectoral Balance Sheets. Since the implementation of the *Provisional Rules on the Compilation and Dissemination of Money Supply Statistics* (PBC Document No. 267 [1994]) in 1994, the People's Bank of China (henceforth PBC) has been releasing the quarterly data on money supply and survey and sectoral balance sheets. Beginning from 2002, a new monetary statistics system was adopted. This new system complies with the concepts, definitions and classifications as defined in the IMF's *Monetary and Financial Statistics Manual*. Data in this new system is based on the domestic and foreign currency businesses of the People's Bank of China and financial institutions operating in China.

A. Money Supply: Institutional coverage of money supply is the same as that of banking survey and includes all financial institutions other than the securities firms and insurance corporations.

- M0: currency in circulation
- M1: M0 + demand deposits
- M2: M1 + quasi – money (time deposits + savings deposits + other deposits)

B. Money Survey: The money survey is the consolidation of the balance sheet of monetary authority and the aggregated balance sheet of deposit money banks.

In which: monetary authority is the People's Bank of China (1949—2005)①; deposit money banks include the state – owned commercial banks② (1993—2005), other commercial banks③(1993—2005), urban credit cooperatives (1993—2005), rural credit cooperatives (1993—2005), finance companies (1993—2005), city commercial banks (2002—2005), rural commercial banks (2002—2005), foreign – funded banks (2002—2005), Postal Savings Bureau! (2004—2005) and rural cooperative banks (2005).

C. Banking Survey: The banking survey is the consolidation of money survey and the balance sheet of specific depository institutions.

---

① The figures in the bracket refer to the period during which the data of the institution was covered in this statement (the same applies hereinafter).

② The State – owned Commercial Banks include Agricultural Bank of China (1993—2005), Bank of China (1993—2005), Industrial and Commercial Bank of China (1993—2005) and China Construction Bank (1993—2005). Prior to 2002, the Agricultural Development Bank of China was also included.

③ The Other Commercial Banks include the China Everbright Bank (1993—2005), Huaxia Bank (1993—2005), Guangdong Development Bank (1993—2005), Shenzhen Development Bank (1993—2005), China Merchants Bank (1993—2005), Shanghai Pudong Development Bank (1993—2005), Fujian Industrial Bank (Included in 1993 and renamed as Industrial Bank in 2003), Yantai Housing and Savings Bank (included in 1993 and renamed as Evergrowing Bank in 2003), Bengbu Housing and Savings Bank (Re – organized to be a city commercial bank in 2001), Hainan Develoment Bank (1995—1998), China Minsheng Banking Corporation (1996—2005), China Investment Bank (1995—1999), Bank of Communications (1995—2005), CITIC Industrial Bank (Included Since 1995 and renamed as China CITIC Bank in 2005) and China Zheshang Bank (2004—2005).

In which: specific depository institutions include China Development Bank (1996—2005), the Export – Import Bank of China (1996—2005), trust and investment companies (1993—2005) and financial leasing companies (1993—2005).

1. Major Adjustments in Monetary Statistics

● 1997 A comprehensive adjustment to the financial statistical framework was made by the People's Bank of China, including (i) the coverage of data collection was extended to include data of real estate credit businesses, international businesses, credit card businesses and other businesses of commercial banks; (ii) the items were refined, the previous inaccurate relationships between items and indicators were corrected, and the errors and omissions item was modified. As a result, the data before and after the first quarter of 1997 were not entirely comparable.

● 2001 The claims on government in the balance sheet of monetary authority were adjusted to include government bonds held by the People's Bank of China. The coverage of money and quasi – money (M_2) was adjusted in June, so that other deposits included margins account of securities companies maintained with financial institutions.

● 2002 The concepts, definitions and classifications presented in the *Money and Financial Statistics Manual*, which was compiled by the IMF, were adopted in 2002, and adjustments to the financial statistical framework were made accordingly. Therefore, data in and after 2002 were not entirely comparable with those of the previous years. Major adjustments included: (i) The institutional coverage was expanded to include foreign – funded banks; policy banks as a group were excluded from the group of state – owned commercial banks; and the reporting forms of city commercial banks were separated from those of the urban credit cooperatives. Secondly, the statistical coverage was expanded to cover the data on foreign exchange businesses of domestic financial institutions. Thirdly, errors and omissions in previous reporting forms were revised. For instance, rediscount in the balance sheet of financial institutions was included in liabilities to the central bank, instead of being deducted from claims on non – financial institutions. (ii) All relevant statistics of liquidated financial institutions, such as urban credit cooperatives, trust and investment companies, were removed from the opening balances of the reporting forms in the following year after their market exit. (iii) In all relevant statistical statements, claims on non – monetary financial institutions and liabilities to non – monetary financial institutions were renamed as claims on specific depository institutions and liabilities to specific depository institutions, and claims on other financial institutions and liabilities to other financial institutions were added.

● 2003 The classifications of some items were adjusted in the monetary statistics reporting forms. For instance, securities investments and repos were classified according to investors and counterparts and their classification under claims and liabilities was adjusted. In the balance sheet of deposit money banks, data of rediscount was no longer deducted from claims on non – financial institutions, but became a component of liabilities to the central bank.

● 2004 (i) The balance sheet of postal savings bureau was presented. (ii) The classifications of some items were adjusted in the monetary statistics reporting forms: firstly, in respect of securities, loans and commercial papers, transfer businesses were reported separately into repurchases and outright purchases, and these transactions were classified into four categories according to the counterparts of the transactions, i.e. claims on specific depository institutions, claims on other financial institutions, liabilities to specific depository institutions and liabilities to other financial institutions. Secondly, in order to reflect the issuance and holding of domestic foreign – currency – dominated bonds by financial institutions, items like investments in domestic securities and domestic issuance of bonds were added. In the monetary statistics reporting forms, investments in domestic securities were included in the claims on specific depository institutions, while domestic issuance of bonds was included in bonds.

2. Notes on Major Indicators

A. Major Items of the Balance Sheet of the Monetary Authority

a) Foreign Assets (Net): The value of foreign assets netted against foreign liabilities, mainly including RMB equivalent of the official foreign exchange reserves, gold reserve and position with international financial institutions.

b) Claims on Government: Lending by the People's Bank of China to government, overdraft of the central government on the accounts with the People's Bank of China and outright purchases of government bonds.

c) Claims on Deposit Money Banks: Financing by the People's Bank of China in forms of lending, rediscount and repos, etc. to other deposit money banks.

d) Claims on Specific Depository Institutions: Financing by the People's Bank of China in forms of lending to specific depository institutions and purchasing of bonds issued by specific depository institutions.

e) Claims on Other Financial Institutions: Financing by the People's Bank of China in forms of lending, etc. to other financial institutions.

f) Claims on Non – financial Sectors: Earmarked loans of the People's Bank of China to old revolutionary bases, poor, remote, and minority – inhabited areas for economic development.

g) Reserve Money: Currency issued by the People's Bank of China, required reserve deposits of financial institutions with the PBC, postal savings deposited with the PBC and government agencies and organizations deposits.

h) Foreign Liabilities: RMB equivalent of claims on the People's Bank of China held by non – residents, such as deposits of international financial institutions in the People's Bank of China.

i) Deposits by Government: The net balance of budgetary revenue against expenditures of fiscal authorities at various levels with the People's Bank of China.

B. Major Items of the Balance Sheet of Deposit Money Banks

a) Foreign Assets: RMB equivalent of claims on non – residents by deposit money banks, including securities purchased, inter – bank transactions with foreign banks and foreign currency in vault.

b) Reserve Assets: Required reserve deposits by deposit money banks with the People's Bank of China, bonds issued by the People's Bank of China and cash in vault held by deposit money banks.

c) Claims on Government: Government securities held by deposit money banks.

d) Claims on Non – financial Institutions: Loans to and investments in non – financial institutions by deposit money banks.

e) Claims on Specific Depository Institutions: Deposits with and loans to specific depository institutions and holdings of bonds issued by specific depository institutions.

f) Claims on Other Financial Institutions: Deposits with and loans to other financial institutions and holdings of bonds issued by these institutions.

g) Foreign Liabilities: Liabilities to non – residents by deposit money banks in RMB equivalent value, including foreign exchange deposits of non – residents, external borrowing, trust borrowing and inter – bank transactions with foreign banks.

h) Liabilities to Non – financial Institutions: RMB & foreign – currency – denominated deposits of non – financial institutions with deposit money banks.

i) Liabilities to Central Bank: Borrowing from the People's Bank of China in forms of central bank lending, rediscount and repos, etc. by deposit money banks.

j) Liabilities to Specific Depository Institutions: Deposits of and borrowing from specific depository institutions by deposit money banks.

C. Major Items of the Balance Sheet of Specific Depository Institutions

a) Reserve Assets: Required reserve deposits with the People's Bank of China, holdings of bonds issued by the People's Bank of China and cash in vault.

b) Domestic Credit: Loans issued domestically by specific depository institutions.

c) Claims on Government: Government securities held by specific depository institutions.

d) Claims on Deposit Money Banks: Deposits with and loans to deposit money banks by specific depository institutions.

e) Claims on Other Financial Institutions: Deposits with and loans to other financial institutions and holdings of bonds issued by other financial institutions by specific depository institutions.

f) Claims on Non – financial Institutions: RMB & foreign – currency – denominated deposits of non – financial institutions with specific depository institutions.

g) Liabilities to Central Bank: Borrowing from the People's Bank of China by specific depository institutions.

h) Liabilities to Deposit Money Banks: Deposits of and borrowing from deposit money banks by specific depository institutions.

i) Liabilities to Other Financial Institutions: Deposits of and borrowing from other financial institutions by specific depository institutions.

（一）货币供应量统计
Money Supply Statistics

各层次货币供应量
Composition of Money Supply
（期末余额）
（Period - end Balance）

单位：亿元
Unit：100 Million Yuan

项目 Items / 时间 Time	货币和准货币 Money and Quasi - money（M2）	货币 Money（M1）			准货币 Quasi - money			
			流通中现金 Currency in Circulation（M0）	活期存款 Demand Deposits		定期存款 Time Deposits	储蓄存款 Savings Deposits	其他存款 Other Deposits
1993.03	29460.2	14032.5	4557.9	9474.6	15427.7	1105.1	12526.3	1796.3
1993.06	30860.2	14701.1	4863.6	9837.5	16159.1	1104.8	13100.9	1953.4
1993.09	31795.6	14422.9	5074.8	9348.1	17372.7	1129.0	14323.5	1920.2
1993.12	34879.8	16280.4	5864.7	10415.7	18599.4	1247.9	15203.5	2148.0
1994.03	37010.3	16437.0	5834.6	10602.4	20573.3	1278.6	17157.3	2137.4
1994.06	40039.5	17676.4	5781.5	11894.9	22363.1	1604.7	18349.9	2408.5
1994.09	43513.5	19009.5	6412.9	12596.6	24504.0	1787.6	19970.2	2746.2
1994.12	46923.5	20540.7	7288.6	13252.1	26382.8	1943.1	21518.8	2920.9
1995.03	50297.1	21026.2	7271.0	13755.2	29270.9	2202.6	23762.7	3305.6
1995.06	53150.3	21420.4	7003.9	14416.5	31729.9	2645.9	25572.1	3511.9
1995.09	56813.2	22493.0	7368.9	15124.1	34320.2	3095.8	27569.7	3654.7
1995.12	60750.5	23987.1	7885.3	16101.8	36763.4	3324.2	29662.2	3777.0
1996.03	64512.1	23909.3	8169.1	15740.2	40602.8	3724.8	33296.5	3581.5
1996.06	68132.8	24620.1	7665.7	16954.4	43512.7	4300.8	35457.9	3754.0
1996.09	72042.6	26336.0	8409.0	17927.0	45706.6	4674.5	37084.9	3947.2
1996.12	76094.9	28514.8	8802.0	19712.8	47580.1	5041.9	38520.8	4017.4

注：1994 年中国人民银行下发《货币供应量统计和公布暂行办法》，开始按季度对外公布货币供应量数据，本书将该数据溯至 1993 年。

Notes："Provisional Rules on the Statistics and Dissemination of Money Supply" is published by the People's Bank of China in 1994 and data on Money Supply is disseminated quarterly since then. Data of 1993 is processed when compling this book.

各层次货币供应量
Composition of Money Supply
(期末余额)
(Period - end Balance)

单位：亿元
Unit：100 Million Yuan

项 目 Items / 时 间 Time	货币和准货币 Money and Quasi - money（M2）							
		货币 Money（M1）			准货币 Quasi - money			
			流通中现金 Currency in Circulation（M0）	活期存款 Demand Deposits		定期存款 Time Deposits	储蓄存款 Savings Deposits	其他存款 Other Deposits
1997.01	78331.45	31056.28	11493.22	19563.06	47275.17	5419.31	39141.26	2714.60
1997.02	78680.67	29702.32	10075.22	19627.10	48978.35	5436.12	40896.15	2646.08
1997.03	79581.25	29629.00	9280.12	20348.88	49952.25	5692.20	41556.77	2703.28
1997.04	80679.02	29990.85	9277.12	20713.73	50688.17	5735.34	42122.16	2830.67
1997.05	81168.58	30275.09	9065.65	21209.44	50893.49	5802.87	42295.16	2795.46
1997.06	82811.51	31074.73	9121.58	21953.15	51736.78	6056.31	42771.16	2909.31
1997.07	83458.48	31100.33	9126.58	21973.75	52358.15	6076.27	43312.08	2969.80
1997.08	84745.98	31594.99	9327.35	22267.64	53150.99	6250.98	43914.92	2985.09
1997.09	85892.36	32244.60	9426.13	22818.47	53647.76	6498.12	44139.45	3010.19
1997.10	86644.34	32421.56	9488.81	22932.75	54222.78	6544.41	44720.33	2958.04
1997.11	87590.32	32909.15	9784.58	23124.57	54681.17	6571.02	45068.43	3041.72
1997.12	90995.32	34826.27	10177.61	24648.66	56169.05	6738.54	46279.80	3150.71
1998.01	92211.42	35585.57	13108.38	22477.19	56625.85	6662.84	46514.18	3448.83
1998.02	92023.72	33395.02	10886.06	22508.96	58628.70	6640.80	48537.54	3450.36
1998.03	92037.75	33110.71	10201.04	22909.67	58927.04	6764.24	48686.48	3476.32
1998.04	92661.53	33360.30	10172.50	23187.80	59301.23	6856.11	48984.56	3460.56
1998.05	93936.14	33552.90	9984.37	23568.53	60383.24	7053.43	49699.45	3630.36
1998.06	94657.61	33775.71	9720.44	24055.27	60881.90	7348.05	49949.89	3583.96
1998.07	96313.99	34355.51	10037.84	24317.67	61958.48	7541.36	50749.82	3667.30
1998.08	97298.68	35049.57	10129.07	24920.50	62249.11	7679.28	50900.91	3668.92
1998.09	99794.54	36501.39	10528.03	25973.36	63293.15	7974.82	51580.74	3737.59
1998.10	100779.30	36734.44	10501.33	26233.11	64044.86	8032.25	52257.11	3755.50
1998.11	102229.21	37414.47	10671.30	26743.17	64814.74	8090.79	52952.32	3771.63
1998.12	104498.54	38953.68	11204.15	27749.53	65544.86	8301.92	53407.47	3835.47

各层次货币供应量
Composition of Money Supply
（期末余额）
（Period－end Balance）

单位：亿元
Unit：100 Million Yuan

项目 Items / 时间 Time	货币和准货币 Money and Quasi－money（M2）	货币 Money（M1）	流通中现金 Currency in Circulation（M0）	活期存款 Demand Deposits	准货币 Quasi－money	定期存款 Time Deposits	储蓄存款 Savings Deposits	其他存款 Other Deposits
1999.01	105500.32	39010.82	11996.72	27014.10	66489.50	8382.69	54293.67	3813.14
1999.02	107778.35	38749.18	12784.24	25964.94	69029.17	8444.14	56767.47	3817.56
1999.03	108438.22	38053.61	11341.63	26711.98	70384.61	8641.86	57814.65	3928.10
1999.04	109218.31	38052.71	11225.41	26827.30	71165.60	8819.82	58369.07	3976.71
1999.05	110060.88	38003.93	10888.93	27115.00	72056.95	9017.25	58967.84	4071.86
1999.06	111363.48	38821.78	10880.52	27941.26	72541.70	9175.51	59173.48	4192.71
1999.07	111414.14	38990.67	11199.00	27791.67	72423.47	9042.49	59147.55	4233.43
1999.08	112827.01	40095.09	11395.16	28699.93	72731.92	9162.70	59187.26	4381.96
1999.09	115079.29	41913.95	12255.24	29658.71	73165.34	9281.87	59364.31	4519.16
1999.10	115389.63	42265.08	12153.88	30111.20	73124.55	9222.45	59269.90	4632.20
1999.11	116559.25	43370.16	12482.62	30887.54	73189.09	9238.65	59185.38	4765.06
1999.12	119897.87	45837.24	13455.49	32381.75	74060.63	9476.84	59621.83	4961.96
2000.01	121220.38	46570.05	16093.97	30476.08	74650.33	9481.63	60241.84	4926.86
2000.02	121583.35	44679.20	13983.01	30696.19	76904.15	9597.74	62270.25	5036.16
2000.03	122606.82	45158.45	13235.40	31923.05	77448.37	9877.86	62492.29	5078.22
2000.04	124121.87	46319.03	13675.50	32643.53	77802.84	10202.35	62536.12	5064.37
2000.05	124053.25	46490.23	13075.45	33414.78	77563.02	10271.92	62195.39	5095.71
2000.06	126605.33	48024.40	13006.04	35018.36	78580.93	10547.00	62842.38	5191.55
2000.07	126323.92	47803.09	13156.47	34646.62	78520.83	10492.17	62841.50	5187.16
2000.08	127790.30	48885.38	13378.68	35506.70	78904.92	10674.16	62861.11	5369.65
2000.09	130473.84	50616.89	13894.69	36722.20	79856.95	11149.15	63243.27	5464.53
2000.10	129522.44	49952.84	13589.45	36363.39	79569.60	10994.72	63122.34	5452.54
2000.11	130994.07	50787.49	13877.70	36909.79	80206.58	11028.47	63492.06	5686.05
2000.12	134610.26	53147.15	14652.65	38494.50	81463.11	11261.08	64332.38	5869.65

各层次货币供应量
Composition of Money Supply
（期末余额）
（Period - end Balance）

单位：亿元
Unit：100 Million Yuan

项目 Items / 时间 Time	货币和准货币 Money and Quasi - money（M2）	货币 Money（M1）	流通中现金 Currency in Circulation（M0）	活期存款 Demand Deposits	准货币 Quasi - money	定期存款 Time Deposits	储蓄存款 Savings Deposits	其他存款 Other Deposits
2001.01	137543.63	54406.23	17018.98	37387.25	83137.40	11272.77	66547.31	5317.32
2001.02	136210.17	51997.68	14910.39	37087.29	84212.49	11613.19	67343.36	5255.94
2001.03	138744.46	53033.36	14362.12	38671.24	85711.10	11962.25	68365.13	5383.72
2001.04	139949.85	53261.32	14622.99	38638.33	86688.53	12621.84	68618.46	5448.23
2001.05	139015.84	52542.99	13942.28	38600.71	86472.85	12110.41	68393.54	5968.90
2001.06	147809.67	55187.36	13943.44	41243.92	92622.31	12614.22	69628.58	10379.51
2001.07	149228.73	53502.80	14071.62	39431.18	95725.93	12338.53	69677.77	13709.63
2001.08	149941.76	55808.92	14370.13	41438.79	94132.84	12735.24	70558.48	10839.12
2001.09	151642.64	56643.96	15064.58	41579.38	94998.68	13567.26	71252.65	10178.77
2001.10	151497.25	56114.90	14484.61	41630.29	95382.35	13521.06	71818.81	10042.48
2001.11	154088.33	56579.56	14780.03	41799.53	97508.77	13538.87	72323.82	11646.08
2001.12	158301.92	59871.59	15688.80	44182.79	98430.33	14180.14	73762.43	10487.76
2002.01	159639.27	60576.06	16725.89	43850.17	99063.21	12846.37	74953.71	11263.13
2002.02	160935.59	58702.87	16641.55	42061.32	102232.72	12932.33	78114.33	11186.06
2002.03	164064.57	59474.83	15544.63	43930.20	104589.74	13081.62	78728.30	12779.82
2002.04	164570.56	60461.31	15864.18	44597.13	104109.25	13905.60	79728.20	10475.45
2002.05	166023.00	61246.86	15243.07	46003.79	104776.14	13585.04	80394.30	10796.80
2002.06	169601.24	63144.00	15097.35	48046.65	106457.24	14099.29	81711.79	10646.16
2002.07	170851.14	63487.78	15357.66	48130.12	107363.36	14291.23	82527.90	10544.23
2002.08	173250.92	64868.83	15712.61	49156.22	108382.09	14764.37	83275.97	10341.75
2002.09	176985.21	66799.76	16233.58	50566.18	110185.45	15783.93	84139.05	10262.47
2002.10	177294.15	67100.25	16014.66	51085.59	110193.90	15239.79	84725.13	10228.98
2002.11	179736.26	67992.78	16346.39	51646.39	111743.48	15722.45	85693.49	10327.54
2002.12	185006.97	70881.79	17278.03	53603.76	114125.18	16433.82	86910.65	10780.71

注：2001 年 6 月起，将证券公司客户保证金计入货币供应量（M2），含在其他存款内。

Notes：Margin account of security companies maintained with financial institutions is included in the other deposits，and then in the item of money supply from June 2001.

各层次货币供应量
Composition of Money Supply
（期末余额）
（Period – end Balance）

单位：亿元
Unit：100 Million Yuan

项目 Items / 时间 Time	货币和准货币 Money and Quasi – money（M2）							
		货币 Money（M1）			准货币 Quasi – money			
			流通中现金 Currency in Circulation（M0）	活期存款 Demand Deposits		定期存款 Time Deposits	储蓄存款 Savings Deposits	其他存款 Other Deposits
2003.01	190545.05	72405.66	21244.73	51160.93	118139.39	16906.53	90677.63	10555.23
2003.02	190108.41	69756.64	17937.17	51819.47	120351.77	16776.52	92824.21	10751.04
2003.03	194487.30	71438.82	17106.50	54332.32	123048.48	17377.09	94567.84	11103.55
2003.04	196130.13	71321.24	17441.14	53880.10	124808.89	18203.26	95194.12	11411.51
2003.05	199505.19	72777.84	17115.03	55662.81	126727.35	18544.84	96351.67	11830.84
2003.06	204907.42	75923.23	16956.89	58966.34	128984.19	18869.84	97674.57	12439.78
2003.07	206193.07	76152.77	17362.13	58790.64	130040.30	19118.75	98590.90	12330.65
2003.08	210591.90	77032.98	17606.76	59426.22	133558.92	19592.84	99255.58	14710.50
2003.09	213567.13	79163.88	18306.36	60857.52	134403.25	21261.13	100888.60	12253.52
2003.10	214469.36	80267.10	18250.67	62016.43	134202.26	20388.73	101381.89	12431.64
2003.11	216351.73	80814.93	18439.56	62375.37	135536.80	20658.55	102235.44	12642.81
2003.12	221222.82	84118.57	19745.99	64372.58	137104.25	20940.39	103617.65	12546.21
2004.01	225101.93	83805.90	22287.43	61518.47	141296.03	20920.59	109232.65	11142.79
2004.02	227050.72	83556.43	19893.44	63662.99	143494.29	20924.84	110646.38	11923.07
2004.03	231654.60	85815.57	19297.43	66518.14	145839.03	21645.35	111872.18	12321.50
2004.04	233627.86	85603.64	19878.40	65725.24	148024.22	23298.88	112175.44	12549.90
2004.05	234842.40	86780.37	19048.43	67731.94	148062.03	22836.18	112610.18	12615.67
2004.06	238427.49	88627.14	19017.58	69609.56	149800.35	23542.04	113792.47	12465.84
2004.07	238126.97	87982.23	19409.10	68573.13	150144.74	23447.20	114253.24	12444.30
2004.08	239729.19	89125.33	19517.94	69607.39	150603.86	23586.02	114489.63	12528.21
2004.09	243756.88	90439.05	20524.17	69914.88	153317.83	25071.91	115458.74	12787.18
2004.10	243740.32	90782.48	20078.25	70704.23	152957.84	24315.23	116000.99	12641.62
2004.11	247135.58	92387.13	20209.25	72177.88	154748.45	24215.96	117617.90	12914.59
2004.12	254106.95	95969.72	21468.30	74501.42	158137.23	25382.15	119555.39	13199.69

各层次货币供应量
Composition of Money Supply
（期末余额）
(Period - end Balance)

单位：亿元
Unit：100 Million Yuan

项目 Items / 时间 Time	货币和准货币 Money and Quasi - money（M2）	货币 Money（M1）	流通中现金 Currency in Circulation（M0）	活期存款 Demand Deposits	准货币 Quasi - money	定期存款 Time Deposits	储蓄存款 Savings Deposits	其他存款 Other Deposits
2005.01	257708.47	97079.03	24015.41	73063.62	160629.44	24939.47	122237.34	13452.63
2005.02	259357.29	92814.95	22667.97	70146.98	166542.34	25296.42	127823.44	13422.48
2005.03	264588.94	94743.19	21238.95	73504.24	169845.75	26543.24	129259.35	14043.16
2005.04	266992.66	94593.72	21666.56	72927.16	172398.94	28178.12	129816.83	14403.99
2005.05	269240.49	95802.01	20811.59	74990.42	173438.48	28201.05	130577.44	14659.99
2005.06	275785.53	98601.25	20848.76	77752.49	177184.28	29395.97	132339.14	15449.17
2005.07	276966.28	97674.10	21171.20	76502.90	179292.18	29673.70	133656.44	15962.04
2005.08	281288.22	99377.70	21351.56	78026.14	181910.52	30852.96	134505.01	16552.55
2005.09	287438.27	100964.00	22272.92	78691.08	186474.27	33320.65	136316.32	16837.30
2005.10	287591.61	101751.98	21892.98	79859.00	185839.63	32145.97	136827.11	16866.55
2005.11	292350.39	104125.78	22409.39	81716.39	188224.61	32229.65	138504.28	17490.68
2005.12	298755.67	107278.76	24031.67	83247.09	191476.91	33099.99	141050.99	17325.93

各层次货币供应量
Composition of Money Supply
（同比增长率）
（Comparable Growth Rate）

单位：%
Unit：%

项　目 Items / 时　间 Time	货币和准货币 Money and Quasi－money（M2）							
		货币 Money（M1）			准货币 Quasi－money			
			流通中现金 Currency in Circulation（M0）	活期存款 Demand Deposits		定期存款 Time Deposits	储蓄存款 Savings Deposits	其他存款 Other Deposits
1994.03	25.63	17.14	28.01	11.90	33.35	15.70	36.97	18.99
1994.06	29.74	20.24	18.87	20.91	38.39	45.25	40.07	23.30
1994.09	36.85	31.80	26.37	34.75	41.05	58.33	39.42	43.02
1994.12	34.53	26.17	24.28	27.23	41.85	55.71	41.54	35.98
1995.03	35.90	27.92	24.62	29.74	42.28	72.27	38.50	54.66
1995.06	32.74	21.18	21.14	21.20	41.89	64.88	39.36	45.81
1995.09	30.56	18.33	14.91	20.06	40.06	73.18	38.05	33.08
1995.12	29.47	16.78	8.19	21.50	39.35	71.08	37.85	29.31
1996.03	28.26	13.71	12.35	14.43	38.71	69.11	40.12	8.35
1996.06	28.19	14.94	9.45	17.60	37.13	62.55	38.66	6.89
1996.09	26.81	17.09	14.11	18.53	33.18	50.99	34.51	8.00
1996.12	25.26	18.88	11.63	22.43	29.42	51.67	29.86	6.36

注：同比增长速度按可比口径计算，1993年数据与上年度数据不可比，未列示该年份同比增速。

Notes：The comparable growth rate is calculated on comparable basis．Data of 1993 is not comparable with that of previous years，so the comparable growth rate of 1993 is not presented．

各层次货币供应量

Composition of Money Supply

（同比增长率）

(Comparable Growth Rate)

单位：%

Unit: %

项目 Items / 时间 Time	货币和准货币 Money and Quasi - money (M2)	货币 Money (M1)			准货币 Quasi - money			
			流通中现金 Currency in Circulation (M0)	活期存款 Demand Deposits		定期存款 Time Deposits	储蓄存款 Savings Deposits	其他存款 Other Deposits
1997.01	24.01	21.54	33.64	15.41	25.68	38.59	27.73	-11.32
1997.02	20.97	15.90	8.33	20.21	24.27	36.58	26.56	-15.17
1997.03	21.10	18.41	13.60	20.74	22.80	39.07	23.74	-8.50
1997.04	20.36	18.70	17.51	19.24	21.37	33.37	22.78	-10.29
1997.05	19.10	18.32	17.65	18.60	19.57	29.97	21.15	-12.31
1997.06	19.13	20.61	18.99	21.30	18.25	29.67	19.65	-12.78
1997.07	18.13	18.43	16.87	19.10	17.96	27.47	19.20	-9.56
1997.08	17.23	17.21	15.25	18.05	17.24	26.03	18.70	-11.64
1997.09	17.14	17.31	12.10	19.60	17.04	28.95	18.09	-11.97
1997.10	16.40	15.84	12.90	17.10	16.74	28.75	17.80	-12.98
1997.11	16.13	14.90	12.41	15.99	16.88	26.78	17.95	-10.30
1997.12	17.32	16.54	15.63	16.92	17.81	24.51	19.25	-8.89
1998.01	17.46	14.58	14.05	14.90	19.35	22.95	18.84	19.50
1998.02	16.71	12.43	8.05	14.68	19.29	22.16	18.68	22.52
1998.03	15.60	11.75	9.92	12.58	17.90	18.83	17.16	28.60
1998.04	14.59	11.23	9.65	11.94	16.56	19.54	16.29	14.65
1998.05	15.45	10.83	10.13	11.12	18.19	21.55	17.51	21.27
1998.06	14.30	8.69	6.57	9.58	17.70	21.33	16.80	23.20
1998.07	15.50	10.47	9.98	10.67	18.49	24.11	17.93	15.34
1998.08	15.01	10.93	8.60	11.91	17.44	22.85	16.84	14.95
1998.09	16.20	13.20	11.69	13.83	18.00	22.73	16.90	24.30
1998.10	16.29	13.30	10.67	14.39	18.07	23.73	17.13	18.38
1998.11	16.67	13.69	9.06	15.65	18.47	23.13	18.01	15.39
1998.12	14.80	11.85	10.09	12.58	16.70	23.20	15.40	21.70

注：1997 年，中国人民银行对金融统计制度进行了调整，该年度的同比增速不完全可比。

Notes: Financial statistic system was adjusted in 1997. Therefore, the comparable growth rate is not completely comparable that year.

各层次货币供应量
Composition of Money Supply
（同比增长率）
（Comparable Growth Rate）

单位：%
Unit：%

项 目 Items / 时 间 Time	货币和准货币 Money and Quasi - money（M2）							
		货币 Money（M1）			准货币 Quasi - money			
			流通中现金 Currency in Circulation （M0）	活期存款 Demand Deposits		定期存款 Time Deposits	储蓄存款 Savings Deposits	其他存款 Other Deposits
1999.01	14.38	9.63	-8.48	20.18	17.37	25.81	16.72	9.86
1999.02	17.95	16.03	17.44	15.35	19.06	27.16	18.60	9.90
1999.03	17.82	14.93	11.18	16.60	19.44	27.76	18.75	13.00
1999.04	17.87	14.07	10.35	15.70	20.01	28.64	19.16	14.92
1999.05	17.17	13.27	9.06	15.05	19.33	27.84	18.65	12.16
1999.06	17.65	14.94	11.93	16.65	19.15	24.87	18.47	16.99
1999.07	15.68	13.49	11.57	14.29	16.89	19.91	16.55	15.44
1999.08	15.96	14.40	12.50	15.17	16.84	19.32	16.28	19.43
1999.09	15.32	14.83	16.41	14.19	15.60	16.39	15.09	20.91
1999.10	14.50	15.06	15.74	14.78	14.18	14.82	13.42	23.34
1999.11	14.02	15.92	16.97	15.50	12.92	14.19	11.77	26.34
1999.12	14.74	17.67	20.09	16.69	12.99	14.15	11.64	29.34
2000.01	14.89	19.38	34.15	12.82	12.25	13.11	10.96	28.76
2000.02	12.79	15.30	9.38	18.22	11.39	13.66	9.69	31.45
2000.03	13.07	18.67	16.70	19.51	10.04	14.30	8.09	29.26
2000.04	13.65	21.72	21.83	21.68	9.33	15.68	7.14	27.33
2000.05	12.71	22.33	20.08	23.23	7.64	13.91	5.47	25.15
2000.06	13.69	23.70	19.54	25.33	8.32	14.95	6.20	23.79
2000.07	13.38	22.60	17.48	24.67	8.42	16.03	6.25	22.50
2000.08	13.26	21.92	17.41	23.72	8.49	16.50	6.21	22.52
2000.09	13.38	20.76	13.38	23.82	9.14	20.12	6.53	20.90
2000.10	12.25	18.19	11.81	20.76	8.81	19.22	6.50	17.69
2000.11	12.38	17.10	11.18	19.50	9.59	19.37	7.28	19.30
2000.12	12.27	15.95	8.90	18.88	10.00	18.83	7.90	18.29

各层次货币供应量
Composition of Money Supply
（同比增长率）
（Comparable Growth Rate）

单位:%
Unit:%

项目 Items / 时间 Time	货币和准货币 Money and Quasi - money（M2）	货币 Money（M1）	流通中现金 Currency in Circulation（M0）	活期存款 Demand Deposits	准货币 Quasi - money	定期存款 Time Deposits	储蓄存款 Savings Deposits	其他存款 Other Deposits
2001.01	13.47	16.83	5.75	22.68	11.37	18.89	10.47	7.93
2001.02	12.03	16.38	6.63	20.82	9.50	21.00	8.15	4.36
2001.03	13.16	17.44	8.51	21.14	10.67	21.10	9.40	6.02
2001.04	12.75	14.99	6.93	18.36	11.42	23.72	9.73	7.58
2001.05	12.06	13.02	6.63	15.52	11.49	17.90	9.97	17.14
2001.06	14.27	14.92	7.21	17.78	13.89	19.60	10.80	30.73
2001.07	13.52	11.92	6.96	13.81	14.43	17.60	10.88	32.81
2001.08	13.61	14.16	7.41	16.71	13.28	19.31	12.25	13.34
2001.09	13.55	12.26	8.42	13.72	14.34	21.69	12.66	17.10
2001.10	12.86	12.34	6.59	14.48	13.18	22.98	13.78	- 1.17
2001.11	13.19	11.40	6.50	13.25	14.25	22.76	13.91	7.55
2001.12	14.42	12.65	7.07	14.78	15.52	25.92	14.66	9.07
2002.01	12.97	9.44	- 1.72	14.40	15.24	23.51	12.63	24.93
2002.02	13.04	10.85	11.61	10.56	14.34	20.56	15.99	- 1.35
2002.03	14.39	10.12	8.23	10.81	16.96	18.20	15.16	27.96
2002.04	14.10	11.53	8.49	12.65	15.64	18.30	16.19	8.53
2002.05	13.98	14.53	9.33	16.36	13.66	20.67	17.55	- 13.85
2002.06	14.68	12.76	8.28	14.25	15.85	18.59	17.35	2.55
2002.07	14.42	16.95	9.14	19.68	12.98	22.78	18.44	- 23.10
2002.08	15.48	14.58	9.34	16.36	16.02	22.86	18.02	- 4.61
2002.09	16.50	15.95	7.76	18.85	16.84	22.61	18.08	0.80
2002.10	16.96	17.88	10.56	20.38	16.40	19.00	17.97	1.83
2002.11	16.57	18.54	10.60	21.30	15.40	22.30	18.49	- 11.34
2002.12	16.78	16.82	10.13	19.15	16.76	21.81	17.82	2.77

注：2001 年 6 月起，将证券公司客户保证金计入货币供应量（M2），含在其他存款内，同比增长速度按可比口径计算。

Notes: The comparable grouth rate is calculated on comparable basis. Margin account of security companies maitained with financial institutions is included in the money supply and the other deposits from 2001.

各层次货币供应量

Composition of Money Supply

（同比增长率）

（Comparable Growth Rate）

单位：%

Unit：%

项目 Items / 时间 Time	货币和准货币 Money and Quasi－money（M2）	货币 Money（M1）	流通中现金 Currency in Circulation（M0）	活期存款 Demand Deposits	准货币 Quasi－money	定期存款 Time Deposits	储蓄存款 Savings Deposits	其他存款 Other Deposits
2003.01	19.36	19.53	27.02	16.67	19.26	31.61	20.98	－6.29
2003.02	18.13	18.83	7.79	23.20	17.72	29.73	18.83	－3.89
2003.03	18.54	20.12	10.05	23.68	17.65	32.84	20.12	－13.12
2003.04	19.18	17.96	9.94	20.82	19.88	30.91	19.40	8.94
2003.05	20.17	18.83	12.28	21.00	20.95	36.51	19.85	9.58
2003.06	20.82	20.24	12.32	22.73	21.16	33.84	19.54	16.85
2003.07	20.69	19.95	13.05	22.15	21.12	33.78	19.46	16.94
2003.08	21.55	18.75	12.05	20.89	23.23	32.70	19.19	42.24
2003.09	20.67	18.51	12.77	20.35	21.98	34.70	19.91	19.40
2003.10	20.97	19.62	13.96	21.40	21.79	33.79	19.66	21.53
2003.11	20.37	18.86	12.81	20.77	21.29	31.40	19.30	22.42
2003.12	19.58	18.67	14.28	20.09	20.13	27.42	19.22	16.38
2004.01	18.14	15.74	4.91	20.25	19.60	23.74	20.46	5.57
2004.02	19.43	19.78	10.91	22.86	19.23	24.73	19.20	10.90
2004.03	19.11	20.12	12.81	22.43	18.52	24.56	18.30	10.97
2004.04	19.12	20.03	13.97	21.98	18.60	27.99	17.84	9.98
2004.05	17.49	18.63	11.30	20.87	16.84	23.14	16.87	6.63
2004.06	16.15	16.16	12.15	17.30	16.14	24.76	16.50	0.21
2004.07	15.28	14.97	11.79	15.91	15.46	22.64	15.89	0.92
2004.08	13.63	15.14	10.85	16.40	12.76	20.38	15.35	－14.83
2004.09	13.94	13.70	12.11	14.18	14.07	17.92	14.44	4.36
2004.10	13.45	12.57	10.01	13.32	13.98	19.26	14.42	1.69
2004.11	14.03	13.79	9.60	15.02	14.17	17.22	15.05	2.15
2004.12	14.67	13.58	8.72	15.06	15.34	21.21	15.38	5.21

各层次货币供应量
Composition of Money Supply
（同比增长率）
（Comparable Growth Rate）

单位：%
Unit：%

项　目 Items / 时　间 Time	货币和准货币 Money and Quasi－money（M2）							
		货币 Money（M1）			准货币 Quasi－money			
			流通中现金 Currency in Circulation（M0）	活期存款 Demand Deposits		定期存款 Time Deposits	储蓄存款 Savings Deposits	其他存款 Other Deposits
2005.01	14.29	15.32	7.75	18.05	13.68	19.21	11.91	20.73
2005.02	14.04	10.58	13.95	9.54	16.06	20.89	15.52	12.58
2005.03	14.03	9.92	10.06	9.88	16.46	22.63	15.54	13.97
2005.04	14.10	10.02	9.00	10.33	16.47	20.94	15.73	14.77
2005.05	14.65	10.40	9.26	10.72	17.14	23.49	15.96	16.20
2005.06	15.67	11.25	9.63	11.70	18.28	24.87	16.30	23.93
2005.07	16.31	11.02	9.08	11.56	19.41	26.56	16.98	28.27
2005.08	17.34	11.50	9.39	12.09	20.79	30.81	17.48	32.12
2005.09	17.92	11.64	8.52	12.55	21.63	32.90	18.06	31.67
2005.10	17.99	12.08	9.04	12.95	21.50	32.21	17.95	33.42
2005.11	18.30	12.71	10.89	13.22	21.63	33.09	17.76	35.43
2005.12	17.57	11.78	11.94	11.74	21.08	30.41	17.98	31.26

（二）货币概览
Monetary Survey

货币概览
Monetary Survey
（季末余额）
（Quarter－end Balance）

单位：亿元
Unit：100 Million Yuan

项目 Items	1993.03	1993.06	1993.09	1993.12
国外净资产 Net Foreign Assets	2154.2	1914.7	2061.0	2223.2
国内信贷 Domestic Credit	27351.7	28500.7	29560.3	33010.6
对政府债权（净） Claims on Government（Net）	1045.0	1093.1	1050.5	1183.8
对非金融部门债权 Claims on Non－financial Sectors	26093.2	27208.3	28365.1	31575.1
对非货币金融机构债权 Claims on Non－monetary Financial Institutions	213.5	199.3	144.7	251.7
货币和准货币 Money & Quasi－money	28113.6	29419.4	30353.2	33295.8
货币 Money	14032.5	14701.1	14422.9	16280.4
流通中现金 Currency in Circulation	4557.9	4863.6	5074.8	5864.7
活期存款 Demand Deposits	9474.6	9837.5	9348.1	10415.7
准货币 Quasi－money	14081.1	14718.3	15930.3	17015.4
定期存款 Time Deposits	1105.1	1104.8	1129.0	1247.9
储蓄存款 Savings Deposits	12526.3	13100.9	14323.5	15203.5
其他存款 Other Deposits	449.7	512.6	477.8	564.0
债券 Bonds	286.2	243.4	235.9	228.6
中央银行债券 Central Bank Bonds				
所有者权益 Owner's Equity	2338.7	2386.6	2625.8	2687.6
其中：实收资本 Of Which：Paid－in Capital	2338.7	2386.6	2625.8	2687.6
其他（净） Other Items（Net）	－1232.6	－1634.0	－1593.6	－978.2

货币概览
Monetary Survey
（季末余额）
(Quarter - end Balance)

单位：亿元
Unit: 100 Million Yuan

项　目 Items	1994.03	1994.06	1994.09	1994.12
国外净资产 Net Foreign Assets	3566.2	3604.3	4257.0	5064.0
国内信贷 Domestic Credit	34672.5	36546.2	38478.3	41243.8
对政府债权（净） Claims on Government (Net)	1256.4	1128.9	1136.9	1314.5
对非金融部门债权 Claims on Non - financial Sectors	32847.8	34830.6	36759.1	39368.3
对非货币金融机构债权 Claims on Non - monetary Financial Institutions	568.3	586.7	582.3	561.0
货币和准货币 Money & Quasi - money	35439.2	38292.6	41524.1	44827.2
货币 Money	16437.0	17676.4	19009.5	20540.7
流通中现金 Currency in Circulation	5834.6	5781.5	6412.9	7288.6
活期存款 Demand Deposits	10602.4	11894.9	12596.6	13252.1
准货币 Quasi - money	19002.2	20616.2	22514.6	24286.5
定期存款 Time Deposits	1278.6	1604.7	1787.6	1943.1
储蓄存款 Savings Deposits	17157.3	18349.9	19970.2	21518.4
其他存款 Other Deposits	566.3	661.6	756.8	825.0
债券 Bonds	231.3	216.0	217.2	195.7
中央银行债券 Central Bank Bonds	30.1	1.0	1.0	0.0
所有者权益 Owner's Equity	2948.3	3016.3	3061.2	3184.7
其中：实收资本 Of Which: Paid - in Capital	2897.3	2900.7	900.8	3101.1
其他（净） Other Items (Net)	- 410.2	- 1357.4	- 2068.2	- 1899.8

货币概览

Monetary Survey

（季末余额）

（Quarter－end Balance）

单位：亿元

Unit：100 Million Yuan

项目 Items	1995.03	1995.06	1995.09	1995.12
国外净资产 Net Foreign Assets	5075.6	5032.9	5415.9	6369.8
国内信贷 Domestic Credit	42816.8	43796.6	46089.8	50937.6
对政府债权（净） Claims on Government（Net）	1287.4	768.5	1003.2	1650.8
对非金融部门债权 Claims on Non－financial Sectors	40807.2	42393.5	44486.8	48766.1
对非货币金融机构债权 Claims on Non－monetary Financial Institutions	722.2	634.6	599.8	520.7
货币和准货币 Money & Quasi－money	47973.3	50687.7	54242.8	58252.0
货币 Money	21026.2	21420.4	22493.0	23987.1
流通中现金 Currency in Circulation	7271.0	7003.9	7368.9	7885.3
活期存款 Demand Deposits	13755.2	14416.5	15124.1	16101.8
准货币 Quasi－money	26947.1	29267.3	31749.8	34264.9
定期存款 Time Deposits	2202.6	2654.9	3095.8	3324.2
储蓄存款 Savings Deposits	23762.7	25572.1	27569.7	29662.2
其他存款 Other Deposits	981.8	1040.3	1084.3	1278.5
债券 Bonds	215.0	192.8	216.0	170.1
中央银行债券 Central Bank Bonds	0.4	0.1		
所有者权益 Owner's Equity	2930.9	3006.8	3165.2	3341.5
其中：实收资本 Of Which：Paid－in Capital	2739.1	2760.2	2912.5	2982.3
其他（净） Other Items（Net）	－3227.2	－5057.9	－6118.3	－4456.2

货币概览
Monetary Survey
（季末余额）
（Quarter－end Balance）

单位：亿元
Unit：100 Million Yuan

项目 Items	1996.03	1996.06	1996.09	1996.12
国外净资产 Net Foreign Assets	7290.3	7485.0	8707.6	9522.4
国内信贷 Domestic Credit	52651.9	56094.1	57568.1	61366.0
对政府债权（净） Claims on Government（Net）	2099.3	2115.0	2011.2	2161.7
对非金融部门债权 Claims on Non－financial Sectors	50112.6	53566.9	55103.7	58890.3
对非货币金融机构债权 Claims on Non－monetary Financial Institutions	440.0	412.2	453.2	314.0
货币和准货币 Money & Quasi－money	62242.0	65774.2	69548.2	73613.0
货币 Money	23909.3	24620.1	26336.0	28514.8
流通中现金 Currency in Circulation	8169.1	7665.7	8409.0	8802.0
活期存款 Demand Deposits	15740.2	16954.4	17927.0	19712.8
准货币 Quasi－money	38332.7	41154.1	43212.2	45098.2
定期存款 Time Deposits	3724.8	4300.8	4674.5	5041.9
储蓄存款 Savings Deposits	33296.5	35457.9	37084.9	38520.8
其他存款 Other Deposits	1311.4	1395.4	1452.8	1535.5
债券 Bonds	174.5	173.0	152.4	288.1
中央银行债券 Central Bank Bonds				
所有者权益 Owner's Equity	3242.8	3382.3	3619.8	3664.6
其中：实收资本 Of Which：Paid－in Capital	3031.4	3065.3	3083.4	3222.8
其他（净） Other Items（Net）	－5717.1	－5750.4	－7044.7	－6677.3

货币概览

Monetary Survey

（季末余额）

（Quarter - end Balance）

单位：亿元

Unit：100 Million Yuan

项目 Items	1997.03	1997.06	1997.09	1997.12
国外净资产 Net Foreign Assets	11200.1	11821.4	13245.3	14220.2
国内信贷 Domestic Credit	67372.4	68401.9	70650.5	75249.9
对政府债权（净） Claims on Government（Net）	1711.7	1393.3	1262.7	1592.6
对非金融部门债权 Claims on Non - financial Sectors	63019.0	64966.2	67058.5	70862.0
对非货币金融机构债权 Claims on Non - monetary Financial Institutions	2641.7	2042.4	2329.3	2795.3
货币和准货币 Money & Quasi - money	77896.3	80929.4	83916.8	88970.5
货币 Money	29629.0	31074.7	32244.6	34826.3
流通中现金 Currency in Circulation	9280.1	9121.6	9426.1	10177.6
活期存款 Demand Deposits	20348.9	21953.1	22818.5	24648.7
准货币 Quasi - money	48267.3	49854.7	51672.2	54144.2
定期存款 Time Deposits	5692.2	6056.3	6498.1	6738.5
储蓄存款 Savings Deposits	41556.8	42771.2	44139.5	46279.8
其他存款 Other Deposits	1018.3	1027.2	1034.6	1125.9
债券 Bonds	168.3	181.8	276.9	286.5
中央银行债券 Central Bank Bonds	58.7	34.3	36.0	21.3
所有者权益 Owner's Equity	3425.8	3538.1	3577.5	3677.6
其中：实收资本 Of Which：Paid - in Capital	3163.9	3371.8	3371.8	3406.1
其他（净） Other Items（Net）	- 2976.6	- 4460.3	- 3911.4	- 3485.8

货币概览
Monetary Survey
（季末余额）
(Quarter – end Balance)

单位：亿元
Unit: 100 Million Yuan

项　　目 Items	1998.03	1998.06	1998.09	1998.12
国外净资产 Net Foreign Assets	14681.8	14865.0	15387.1	15570.5
国内信贷 Domestic Credit	77150.4	80807.9	87703.4	92260.5
对政府债权（净） Claims on Government (Net)	1158.1	1869.5	4280.8	4826.6
对非金融部门债权 Claims on Non – financial Sectors	71599.4	74024.9	78187.4	81597.0
对非货币金融机构债权 Claims on Non – monetary Financial Institutions	4392.9	4913.5	5235.2	5836.9
货币和准货币 Money & Quasi – money	90048.7	92435.7	97547.2	102297.6
货币 Money	33110.7	33775.7	36501.4	38953.7
流通中现金 Currency in Circulation	10201.0	9720.4	10528.0	11204.2
活期存款 Demand Deposits	22909.7	24055.3	25973.4	27749.5
准货币 Quasi – money	56938.0	58660.0	61045.8	63343.9
定期存款 Time Deposits	6764.2	7348.1	7974.8	8301.9
储蓄存款 Savings Deposits	48686.5	49949.9	51580.7	53407.5
其他存款 Other Deposits	1487.3	1362.0	1490.3	1634.5
债券 Bonds	294.2	388.3	491.2	500.5
中央银行债券 Central Bank Bonds	22.3	4.5	9.2	60.2
所有者权益 Owner's Equity	3350.6	3307.8	5714.2	5837.9
其中：实收资本 Of Which: Paid – in Capital	3426.6	3391.6	6156.8	6205.7
其他（净） Other Items (Net)	– 1883.6	– 463.4	– 671.3	– 865.2

货币概览
Monetary Survey
（季末余额）
（Quarter - end Balance）

单位：亿元
Unit：100 Million Yuan

项目 Items	1999.03	1999.06	1999.09	1999.12
国外净资产 Net Foreign Assets	15148.7	14840.3	16109.8	17486.1
国内信贷 Domestic Credit	93562.5	96538.0	99465.4	104610.6
对政府债权（净） Claims on Government（Net）	4848.7	5084.5	5023.4	5859.0
对非金融部门债权 Claims on Non - financial Sectors	82725.8	85414.6	88181.2	91261.7
对非货币金融机构债权 Claims on Non - monetary Financial Institutions	5988.0	6038.9	6260.8	7489.9
货币和准货币 Money & Quasi - money	106261.6	109171.9	112891.4	117638.1
货币 Money	38053.6	38821.8	41913.9	45837.3
流通中现金 Currency in Circulation	11341.6	10880.5	12255.2	13455.5
活期存款 Demand Deposits	26712.0	27941.3	29658.7	32381.8
准货币 Quasi - money	68208.0	70350.1	70977.5	71800.9
定期存款 Time Deposits	8641.9	9175.5	9281.9	9476.8
储蓄存款 Savings Deposits	57814.6	59173.5	59364.3	59621.8
其他存款 Other Deposits	1751.5	2001.1	2331.3	2702.3
债券 Bonds	490.6	484.9	470.8	482.4
中央银行债券 Central Bank Bonds	65.5	68.0	67.0	72.4
实收资本 Paid - in Capital	6189.8	6188.7	6211.3	6225.8
其他（净） Other Items（Net）	- 4296.3	- 4535.2	- 4065.3	- 2321.9

货币概览
Monetary Survey
（季末余额）
（Quarter – end Balance）

单位：亿元
Unit: 100 Million Yuan

项目 Items	2000.03	2000.06	2000.09	2000.12
国外净资产 Net Foreign Assets	18439.5	19127.8	20044.0	20523.4
国内信贷 Domestic Credit	106846.6	110619.7	115383.8	121202.7
对政府债权（净） Claims on Government (Net)	5377.7	5018.8	5425.0	5862.6
对非金融部门债权 Claims on Non – financial Sectors	93507.1	92910.6	96726.1	101925.8
对非货币金融机构债权 Claims on Non – monetary Financial Institutions	7961.8	12690.3	13232.7	13414.3
货币和准货币 Money & Quasi – money	120399.6	124486.8	128352.6	132487.6
货币 Money	45158.5	48024.4	50616.9	53147.2
流通中现金 Currency in Circulation	13235.4	13006.0	13894.7	14652.7
活期存款 Demand Deposits	31923.1	35018.4	36722.2	38494.5
准货币 Quasi – money	75241.1	76462.4	77735.7	79340.4
定期存款 Time Deposits	9877.9	10547.0	11149.1	11261.1
储蓄存款 Savings Deposits	62492.3	62842.4	63243.3	64332.4
其他存款 Other Deposits	2870.9	3073.0	3343.3	3746.9
债券 Bonds	486.7	477.2	472.4	478.4
中央银行债券 Central Bank Bonds				
实收资本 Paid – in Capital	6241.0	6227.3	6250.5	6325.5
其他（净） Other Items (Net)	– 1841.2	– 1443.8	352.3	2434.6

货币概览
Monetary Survey
（季末余额）
（Quarter - end Balance）

单位：亿元
Unit：100 Million Yuan

项目 Items	2001.03	2001.06	2001.09	2001.12
国外净资产 Net Foreign Assets	22284.6	23582.9	24625.4	26685.4
国内信贷 Domestic Credit	115993.6	121639.1	124006.0	129589.8
对政府债权（净） Claims on Government（Net）	8811.3	8943.4	9054.1	10977.8
对非金融部门债权 Claims on Non - financial Sectors	94824.2	99125.6	101152.2	104152.6
对非货币金融机构债权 Claims on Non - monetary Financial Institutions	12358.1	13570.1	13799.7	14459.4
货币和准货币 Money & Quasi - money	136915.1	141885.6	146248.5	152888.5
货币 Money	53033.3	55187.4	56644.0	59871.6
流通中现金 Currency in Circulation	14362.1	13943.5	15064.6	15688.8
活期存款 Demand Deposits	38671.2	41243.9	41579.4	44182.8
准货币 Quasi - money	83881.8	86698.2	89604.5	93016.0
定期存款 Time Deposits	11962.3	12614.2	13567.3	14180.1
储蓄存款 Savings Deposits	68365.1	69628.6	71252.6	73762.4
其他存款 Other Deposits	3554.4	4455.4	4784.6	5074.3
债券 Bonds	478.2	371.4	362.0	371.0
中央银行债券 Central Bank Bonds				
实收资本 Paid - in Capital	6360.4	6422.6	6450.6	6551.9
其他（净） Other Items（Net）	-5475.5	-3457.6	-4429.7	-3536.2

货币概览
Monetary Survey
（月末余额）
（Month - end Balance）

单位：亿元
Unit：100 Million Yuan

项目 Items	2002.01	2002.02	2002.03	2002.04
国外净资产 Net Foreign Assets	25879.37	26325.15	26772.63	27154.89
国内信贷 Domestic Credit	147228.88	148320.65	151401.96	151589.05
对政府债权（净） Claims on Government（Net）	10269.21	10761.53	10897.07	10547.23
对非金融部门债权 Claims on Non - financial Sectors	113362.11	113983.17	116723.91	117701.54
对特定存款机构债权 Claims on Specific Depository Institutions	8045.64	7850.00	8055.89	8041.62
对其他金融机构债权 Claims on Other Financial Institutions	15551.92	15725.95	15725.09	15298.66
货币和准货币 Money & Quasi - money	157853.45	159182.97	162300.93	162825.22
货币 Money	60577.23	58703.97	59475.67	60462.04
流通中现金 Currency in Circulation	16727.06	16642.65	15545.47	15864.91
活期存款 Demand Deposits	43850.17	42061.32	43930.20	44597.13
准货币 Quasi - money	97276.22	100479.00	102825.26	102363.18
定期存款 Time Deposits	12846.37	12932.33	13081.62	13905.60
储蓄存款 Savings Deposits	74953.71	78114.33	78728.30	79728.20
其他存款 Other Deposits	9476.14	9432.34	11015.34	8729.38
外币存款 Deposits in Foreign Currency	11169.18	11283.32	11374.66	11362.37
债券 Bonds	516.83	626.13	548.18	855.41
中央银行债券 Central Bank Bonds				
实收资本 Paid - in Capital	7486.75	7538.25	7505.13	7582.06
其他（净） Other Items（Net）	-3917.96	-3984.87	-3554.31	-3881.12

货币概览
Monetary Survey
（月末余额）
（Month - end Balance）

单位：亿元
Unit：100 Million Yuan

项　目 Items	2002.05	2002.06	2002.07	2002.08
国外净资产 Net Foreign Assets	27644.72	27968.60	28512.61	29190.48
国内信贷 Domestic Credit	152363.48	155992.70	156749.93	158267.75
对政府债权（净） Claims on Government（Net）	10194.25	10942.30	11173.35	10908.49
对非金融部门债权 Claims on Non - financial Sectors	118894.13	121498.10	122136.73	123806.35
对特定存款机构债权 Claims on Specific Depository Institutions	7933.40	8179.40	8102.52	8141.30
对其他金融机构债权 Claims on Other Financial Institutions	15341.70	15372.90	15337.33	15411.61
货币和准货币 Money & Quasi - money	164268.36	167869.41	169122.95	171524.20
货币 Money	61247.53	63144.69	63488.41	64869.50
流通中现金 Currency in Circulation	15243.74	15098.04	15358.29	15713.28
活期存款 Demand Deposits	46003.79	48046.65	48130.12	49156.22
准货币 Quasi - money	103020.83	104724.72	105634.54	106654.70
定期存款 Time Deposits	13585.04	14099.29	14291.23	14764.37
储蓄存款 Savings Deposits	80394.30	81711.79	82527.90	83275.97
其他存款 Other Deposits	9041.49	8913.64	8815.41	8614.36
外币存款 Deposits in Foreign Currency	11554.50	11654.05	11643.39	11728.03
债券 Bonds	470.52	602.06	390.49	354.38
中央银行债券 Central Bank Bonds				
实收资本 Paid - in Capital	7466.38	7501.76	7550.03	7581.20
其他（净） Other Items（Net）	-3751.56	-3665.98	-3444.32	-3729.58

货币概览
Monetary Survey
（月末余额）
（Month－end Balance）

单位：亿元
Unit：100 Million Yuan

项目 Items	2002.09	2002.10	2002.11	2002.12
国外净资产 Net Foreign Assets	29335.46	30203.07	30806.01	31907.45
国内信贷 Domestic Credit	161256.24	161786.67	163889.99	168904.74
对政府债权（净） Claims on Government（Net）	10861.57	10757.10	10962.44	13297.59
对非金融部门债权 Claims on Non－financial Sectors	126592.23	127277.88	129049.06	131670.77
对特定存款机构债权 Claims on Specific Depository Institutions	8601.01	8510.97	8633.62	8674.26
对其他金融机构债权 Claims on Other Financial Institutions	15201.43	15240.72	15244.87	15262.12
货币和准货币 Money & Quasi－money	175254.87	175534.74	178018.43	183246.94
货币 Money	66800.29	67100.77	67993.28	70882.19
流通中现金 Currency in Circulation	16234.11	16015.18	16346.89	17278.43
活期存款 Demand Deposits	50566.18	51085.59	51646.39	53603.76
准货币 Quasi－money	108454.58	108433.97	110025.15	112364.75
定期存款 Time Deposits	15783.93	15239.79	15722.45	16433.82
储蓄存款 Savings Deposits	84139.05	84725.13	85693.49	86910.65
其他存款 Other Deposits	8531.60	8469.05	8609.21	9020.28
外币存款 Deposits in Foreign Currency	11708.69	11880.41	11941.43	12123.32
债券 Bonds	334.65	339.42	363.69	527.28
中央银行债券 Central Bank Bonds				
实收资本 Paid－in Capital	7574.73	7653.70	7530.90	7606.19
其他（净） Other Items（Net）	－4281.24	－3418.53	－3158.45	－2691.54

货币概览

Monetary Survey

（月末余额）

（Month - end Balance）

单位：亿元

Unit：100 Million Yuan

项目 Items	2003.01	2003.02	2003.03	2003.04
国外净资产 Net Foreign Assets	32897.66	33497.52	33906.07	34231.34
国内信贷 Domestic Credit	172042.54	173146.28	176577.01	177928.64
对政府债权（净） Claims on Government（Net）	12587.40	12520.34	11929.77	11475.42
对非金融部门债权 Claims on Non - financial Sectors	134701.18	135787.17	139446.28	141540.63
对特定存款机构债权 Claims on Specific Depository Institutions	8964.55	8951.42	9086.07	8905.37
对其他金融机构债权 Claims on Other Financial Institutions	15789.41	15887.35	16114.89	16007.22
货币和准货币 Money & Quasi - money	188918.38	188444.37	192832.44	194476.98
货币 Money	72406.05	69757.05	71439.21	71321.54
流通中现金 Currency in Circulation	21245.12	17937.58	17106.89	17441.44
活期存款 Demand Deposits	51160.93	51819.47	54332.32	53880.10
准货币 Quasi - money	116512.33	118687.32	121393.23	123155.44
定期存款 Time Deposits	16906.53	16776.52	17377.09	18203.26
储蓄存款 Savings Deposits	90677.63	92824.21	94567.84	95194.12
其他存款 Other Deposits	8928.17	9086.59	9448.30	9758.06
外币存款 Deposits in Foreign Currency	12040.99	12026.12	11958.89	11939.14
债券 Bonds	205.31	205.82	246.04	193.05
中央银行债券 Central Bank Bonds				
实收资本 Paid - in Capital	7624.98	7584.56	7438.03	7826.16
其他（净） Other Items（Net）	- 3849.46	- 1617.07	- 1992.32	- 2275.35

货 币 概 览

Monetary Survey

（月末余额）

（Month – end Balance）

单位：亿元

Unit：100 Million Yuan

项　　目 Items	2003.05	2003.06	2003.07	2003.08
国外净资产 Net Foreign Assets	34656.17	35056.26	35409.63	36337.94
国内信贷 Domestic Credit	180582.24	186322.61	187529.90	191352.87
对政府债权（净） Claims on Government（Net）	11018.27	11670.20	11573.99	11385.62
对非金融部门债权 Claims on Non – financial Sectors	144319.77	149493.49	150617.11	153591.75
对特定存款机构债权 Claims on Specific Depository Institutions	8947.24	9193.68	9354.14	9828.64
对其他金融机构债权 Claims on Other Financial Institutions	16296.96	15965.24	15984.66	16546.86
货币和准货币 Money & Quasi – money	197811.96	203071.74	204381.10	208692.40
货币 Money	72778.15	75923.52	76153.04	77033.30
流通中现金 Currency in Circulation	17115.34	16957.18	17362.40	17607.08
活期存款 Demand Deposits	55662.81	58966.34	58790.64	59426.22
准货币 Quasi – money	125033.81	127148.22	128228.06	131659.10
定期存款 Time Deposits	18544.84	18869.84	19118.75	19592.84
储蓄存款 Savings Deposits	96351.67	97674.57	98590.90	99255.58
其他存款 Other Deposits	10137.30	10603.81	10518.41	12810.68
外币存款 Deposits in Foreign Currency	11993.71	12097.14	12028.18	11984.19
债券 Bonds	144.87	145.37	95.29	44.78
中央银行债券 Central Bank Bonds				
实收资本 Paid – in Capital	7843.28	7832.74	7915.34	7929.31
其他（净） Other Items（Net）	– 2555.41	– 1768.12	– 1480.38	– 959.87

货币概览

Monetary Survey

（月末余额）

（Month - end Balance）

单位：亿元

Unit：100 Million Yuan

项　　目 Items	2003.09	2003.10	2003.11	2003.12
国外净资产 Net Foreign Assets	37099.03	38399.04	39487.21	37990.94
国内信贷 Domestic Credit	193805.35	194284.74	195248.09	201274.75
对政府债权（净） Claims on Government（Net）	11637.88	11185.15	11147.67	13131.47
对非金融部门债权 Claims on Non - financial Sectors	156287.88	156897.66	157999.01	158741.37
对特定存款机构债权 Claims on Specific Depository Institutions	9845.12	10092.71	10164.07	10039.02
对其他金融机构债权 Claims on Other Financial Institutions	16034.47	16109.22	15937.34	19362.89
货币和准货币 Money & Quasi - money	211611.50	212505.40	214358.84	219226.81
货币 Money	79164.14	80267.37	80815.22	84118.81
流通中现金 Currency in Circulation	18306.62	18250.94	18439.85	19746.23
活期存款 Demand Deposits	60857.52	62016.43	62375.37	64372.58
准货币 Quasi - money	132447.36	132238.03	133543.62	135108.00
定期存款 Time Deposits	21261.13	20388.73	20658.55	20940.39
储蓄存款 Savings Deposits	100888.60	101381.89	102235.44	103617.65
其他存款 Other Deposits	10297.63	10467.41	10649.63	10549.96
外币存款 Deposits in Foreign Currency	11852.73	11997.98	12019.47	11838.01
债券 Bonds	44.15	45.74	41.23	55.16
中央银行债券 Central Bank Bonds				
实收资本 Paid - in Capital	7890.73	7970.25	8020.65	9502.06
其他（净） Other Items（Net）	- 494.73	164.41	295.11	- 1356.35

货币概览

Monetary Survey

（月末余额）

（Month－end Balance）

单位：亿元

Unit：100 Million Yuan

项　目 Items	2004.01	2004.02	2004.03	2004.04
国外净资产 Net Foreign Assets	40225.97	40922.94	41739.51	42394.58
国内信贷 Domestic Credit	202800.38	204506.80	207930.72	209843.72
对政府债权（净） Claims on Government（Net）	12834.80	12589.91	12270.43	12068.85
对非金融部门债权 Claims on Non－financial Sectors	163218.29	165528.53	168947.50	171007.35
对特定存款机构债权 Claims on Specific Depository Institutions	10428.38	10811.18	10802.70	10986.00
对其他金融机构债权 Claims on Other Financial Institutions	16318.91	15577.18	15910.09	15781.52
货币和准货币 Money & Quasi－money	223229.16	225149.20	229726.91	231684.46
货币 Money	83806.09	83556.62	85815.79	85603.94
流通中现金 Currency in Circulation	22287.62	19893.63	19297.65	19878.70
活期存款 Demand Deposits	61518.47	63662.99	66518.14	65725.24
准货币 Quasi－money	139423.07	141592.58	143911.12	146080.52
定期存款 Time Deposits	20920.59	20924.84	21645.35	23298.88
储蓄存款 Savings Deposits	109232.65	110646.38	111872.18	112175.44
其他存款 Other Deposits	9269.83	10021.36	10393.59	10606.20
外币存款 Deposits in Foreign Currency	12037.18	11604.54	11662.03	11694.39
债券 Bonds	47.70	40.86	39.06	62.85
中央银行债券 Central Bank Bonds				
实收资本 Paid－in Capital	9558.50	9584.48	9662.13	9719.38
其他（净） Other Items（Net）	－1846.19	－949.34	－1419.90	－922.78

货币概览

Monetary Survey

（月末余额）

（Month - end Balance）

单位：亿元

Unit：100 Million Yuan

项目 Items	2004.05	2004.06	2004.07	2004.08
国外净资产 Net Foreign Assets	43227.26	45284.24	46468.63	47855.22
国内信贷 Domestic Credit	210276.42	209251.13	208284.12	209328.78
对政府债权（净） Claims on Government（Net）	11188.16	11195.43	10106.90	9775.99
对非金融部门债权 Claims on Non - financial Sectors	172104.76	169121.95	169063.74	170350.16
对特定存款机构债权 Claims on Specific Depository Institutions	11136.61	11313.88	11638.39	11730.21
对其他金融机构债权 Claims on Other Financial Institutions	15846.89	17619.87	17475.09	17472.42
货币和准货币 Money & Quasi - money	232897.23	236242.28	236199.28	237662.88
货币 Money	86780.65	88627.45	87982.45	89125.50
流通中现金 Currency in Circulation	19048.71	19017.89	19409.32	19518.11
活期存款 Demand Deposits	67731.94	69609.56	68573.13	69607.39
准货币 Quasi - money	146116.58	147614.83	148216.83	148537.38
定期存款 Time Deposits	22836.18	23542.04	23447.20	23586.02
储蓄存款 Savings Deposits	112610.18	113792.47	114253.24	114489.63
其他存款 Other Deposits	10670.22	10280.32	10516.39	10461.73
外币存款 Deposits in Foreign Currency	11882.83	11949.07	12163.69	12214.42
债券 Bonds	62.85	326.45	575.29	726.54
中央银行债券 Central Bank Bonds				
实收资本 Paid - in Capital	9759.79	10009.48	10040.51	10148.19
其他（净） Other Items（Net）	- 1099.02	- 3991.91	- 4226.02	- 3568.03

货币概览

Monetary Survey

（月末余额）

（Month – end Balance）

单位：亿元

Unit：100 Million Yuan

项目 Items	2004.09	2004.10	2004.11	2004.12
国外净资产 Net Foreign Assets	48752.21	50564.22	53938.63	55835.63
国内信贷 Domestic Credit	213262.22	212484.14	214547.67	220864.71
对政府债权（净） Claims on Government（Net）	10725.03	9704.57	10098.16	15465.44
对非金融部门债权 Claims on Non – financial Sectors	173104.48	173088.35	174372.34	176439.56
对特定存款机构债权 Claims on Specific Depository Institutions	11936.29	12175.17	12516.96	13198.89
对其他金融机构债权 Claims on Other Financial Institutions	17496.42	17516.05	17560.21	15760.82
货币和准货币 Money & Quasi – money	241696.40	241642.15	244848.03	251703.55
货币 Money	90439.21	90782.72	92387.36	95969.91
流通中现金 Currency in Circulation	20524.33	20078.49	20209.48	21468.49
活期存款 Demand Deposits	69914.88	70704.23	72177.88	74501.42
准货币 Quasi – money	151257.19	150859.43	152460.67	155733.64
定期存款 Time Deposits	25071.91	24315.23	24215.96	25382.15
储蓄存款 Savings Deposits	115458.74	116000.99	117617.90	119555.39
其他存款 Other Deposits	10726.54	10543.21	10626.81	10796.10
外币存款 Deposits in Foreign Currency	12285.67	12466.07	12197.05	12088.85
债券 Bonds	818.46	817.91	1281.59	1630.21
中央银行债券 Central Bank Bonds				
实收资本 Paid – in Capital	10268.48	10308.31	10496.04	10862.71
其他（净） Other Items（Net）	– 3054.58	– 2186.08	– 336.41	415.02

货币概览

Monetary Survey

（月末余额）

（Month - end Balance）

单位：亿元

Unit：100 Million Yuan

项目 Items	2005.01	2005.02	2005.03	2005.04
国外净资产 Net Foreign Assets	57287.93	58678.56	60017.39	61699.91
国内信贷 Domestic Credit	221994.31	222563.77	226463.77	227389.32
对政府债权（净） Claims on Government（Net）	12779.14	12357.20	12164.65	11270.18
对非金融部门债权 Claims on Non - financial Sectors	178503.10	179383.90	182592.72	183780.31
对特定存款机构债权 Claims on Specific Depository Institutions	13321.42	13506.92	14161.10	14911.42
对其他金融机构债权 Claims on Other Financial Institutions	17390.65	17315.75	17545.30	17427.41
货币和准货币 Money & Quasi - money	255345.86	257020.45	262197.68	264577.85
货币 Money	97079.93	92815.93	94744.19	94594.73
流通中现金 Currency in Circulation	24016.31	22668.95	21239.95	21667.57
活期存款 Demand Deposits	73063.62	70146.98	73504.24	72927.16
准货币 Quasi - money	158265.93	164204.52	167453.49	169983.12
定期存款 Time Deposits	24939.47	25296.42	26543.24	28178.12
储蓄存款 Savings Deposits	122237.34	127823.44	129259.35	129816.83
其他存款 Other Deposits	11089.12	11084.66	11650.90	11988.17
外币存款 Deposits in Foreign Currency	12066.34	12240.09	12460.57	12367.98
债券 Bonds	1671.37	1674.30	2216.03	2544.20
中央银行债券 Central Bank Bonds				
实收资本 Paid - in Capital	10890.30	10951.33	11057.43	12345.16
其他（净） Other Items（Net）	- 691.63	- 643.84	- 1450.55	- 2745.96

货币概览
Monetary Survey
（月末余额）
（Month - end Balance）

单位：亿元
Unit：100 Million Yuan

项目 Items	2005.05	2005.06	2005.07	2005.08
国外净资产 Net Foreign Assets	63272.74	65709.29	66547.40	68303.85
国内信贷 Domestic Credit	227246.57	231541.95	232541.40	236284.52
对政府债权（净） Claims on Government（Net）	10398.30	10475.59	9911.60	10421.13
对非金融部门债权 Claims on Non - financial Sectors	184079.65	183090.08	182843.50	184479.72
对特定存款机构债权 Claims on Specific Depository Institutions	15140.78	15787.24	16488.85	17927.19
对其他金融机构债权 Claims on Other Financial Institutions	17627.84	22189.04	23297.45	23456.48
货币和准货币 Money & Quasi - money	266724.84	272990.41	274301.53	278701.61
货币 Money	95803.02	98602.14	97674.98	99378.67
流通中现金 Currency in Circulation	20812.60	20849.65	21172.08	21352.53
活期存款 Demand Deposits	74990.42	77752.49	76502.90	78026.14
准货币 Quasi - money	170921.82	174388.27	176626.55	179322.94
定期存款 Time Deposits	28201.05	29395.97	29673.70	30852.96
储蓄存款 Savings Deposits	130577.44	132339.14	133656.44	134505.01
其他存款 Other Deposits	12143.33	12653.16	13296.41	13964.97
外币存款 Deposits in Foreign Currency	12220.95	12587.36	11959.69	11950.03
债券 Bonds	2445.26	2414.34	2624.39	3094.34
中央银行债券 Central Bank Bonds				
实收资本 Paid - in Capital	12062.42	12272.05	12325.20	12364.50
其他（净） Other Items（Net）	- 2934.16	- 3012.92	- 2122.01	- 1522.11

货币概览
Monetary Survey
（月末余额）
（Month - end Balance）

单位：亿元
Unit：100 Million Yuan

项目 Items	2005.09	2005.10	2005.11	2005.12
国外净资产 Net Foreign Assets	69628.64	72646.30	73925.89	75923.47
国内信贷 Domestic Credit	241657.42	241166.39	245392.64	250425.92
对政府债权（净） Claims on Government（Net）	11533.22	10698.21	11123.49	15160.11
对非金融部门债权 Claims on Non - financial Sectors	187272.48	186505.30	188698.71	189207.87
对特定存款机构债权 Claims on Specific Depository Institutions	20138.93	21058.49	22442.15	23416.87
对其他金融机构债权 Claims on Other Financial Institutions	22712.79	22904.39	23128.29	22641.07
货币和准货币 Money & Quasi - money	284832.32	284945.20	289634.81	296040.13
货币 Money	100964.95	101752.93	104127.26	107279.91
流通中现金 Currency in Circulation	22273.87	21893.93	22410.87	24032.82
活期存款 Demand Deposits	78691.08	79859.00	81716.39	83247.09
准货币 Quasi - money	183867.37	183192.27	185507.55	188760.22
定期存款 Time Deposits	33320.65	32145.97	32229.65	33099.99
储蓄存款 Savings Deposits	136316.32	136827.11	138504.28	141050.99
其他存款 Other Deposits	14230.40	14219.19	14773.62	14609.24
外币存款 Deposits in Foreign Currency	11658.96	11825.33	11864.42	11838.57
债券 Bonds	3416.47	3468.43	3788.42	4059.42
中央银行债券 Central Bank Bonds				
实收资本 Paid - in Capital	12419.40	12678.77	12784.09	13108.27
其他（净） Other Items（Net）	- 1041.09	894.96	1246.79	1303.00

(三) 银行概览
Banking Survey

银 行 概 览

Banking Survey

(季末余额)

(Quarter - end Balance)

单位: 亿元

Unit: 100 Million Yuan

项 目 Items	1993.03	1993.06	1993.09	1993.12
国外净资产 Net Foreign Assets	2154.2	1914.7	2061.0	2223.2
国内信贷 Domestic Credit	28938.1	30215.1	31316.2	34810.9
对政府债权(净) Claims on Government (Net)	1045.0	1093.1	1050.5	1183.8
对非金融部门债权 Claims on Non - financial Sectors	27893.1	29122.0	30265.7	33627.1
货币和准货币 Money & Quasi - money	29460.2	30860.2	31795.6	34879.8
货币 Money	14032.5	14701.1	14422.9	16280.4
流通中现金 Currency in Circulation	4557.9	4863.6	5074.8	5864.7
活期存款 Demand Deposits	9474.6	9837.5	9348.1	10415.7
准货币 Quasi - money	15427.7	16159.1	17372.7	18599.4
定期存款 Time Deposits	1105.1	1104.8	1129.0	1247.9
储蓄存款 Savings Deposits	12526.3	13100.9	14323.5	15203.5
其他存款 Other Deposits	1796.3	1953.4	1920.2	2148.0
债券 Bonds	306.9	264.6	258.1	247.9
所有者权益 Owner's Equity	2765.8	2843.9	3085.2	3147.5
其中: 实收资本 Of Which: Paid - in Capital	2765.8	2843.9	3085.2	3147.5
其他(净) Other Items (Net)	- 1440.6	- 1838.9	- 1761.7	- 1241.1

银行概览
Banking Survey
（季末余额）
（Quarter – end Balance）

单位：亿元
Unit：100 Million Yuan

项目 Items	1994.03	1994.06	1994.09	1994.12
国外净资产 Net Foreign Assets	3566.2	3604.3	4257.0	5064.0
国内信贷 Domestic Credit	36612.8	38678.5	40786.1	43103.7
对政府债权（净） Claims on Government（Net）	1270.0	1142.2	1152.2	1332.5
对非金融部门债权 Claims on Non – financial Sectors	35342.8	37536.3	39633.9	41771.2
货币和准货币 Money & Quasi – money	37010.3	40039.5	43513.5	46923.5
货币 Money	16437.0	17676.4	19009.5	20540.7
流通中现金 Currency in Circulation	5834.6	5781.5	6412.9	7288.6
活期存款 Demand Deposits	10602.4	11894.9	12596.6	13252.1
准货币 Quasi – money	20573.3	22363.1	24504.0	26382.8
定期存款 Time Deposits	1278.6	1604.7	1787.6	1943.1
储蓄存款 Savings Deposits	17157.3	18349.9	19970.2	21518.8
其他存款 Other Deposits	2137.4	2408.5	2746.2	2920.9
债券 Bonds	283.5	236.2	236.2	213.0
所有者权益 Owner's Equity	3449.4	3530.9	3590.3	3698.2
其中：实收资本 Of Which：Paid – in Capital	3327.6	3350.8	3349.1	3526.5
其他（净） Other Items（Net）	– 564.2	– 1523.8	– 2296.9	– 2667.0

银行概览

Banking Survey

（季末余额）

（Quarter - end Balance）

单位：亿元

Unit：100 Million Yuan

项　目 Items	1995.03	1995.06	1995.09	1995.12
国外净资产 Net Foreign Assets	5075.6	5032.9	5415.9	6369.8
国内信贷 Domestic Credit	44824.4	46040.8	48444.1	53333.8
对政府债权（净） Claims on Government（Net）	1307.7	791.9	1020.2	1666.7
对非金融部门债权 Claims on Non - financial Sectors	43534.7	45248.9	47423.9	51667.1
货币和准货币 Money & Quasi - money	50297.1	53150.3	56813.2	60750.5
货币 Money	21026.2	21420.4	22493.0	23987.1
流通中现金 Currency in Circulation	7271.0	7003.9	7368.9	7885.3
活期存款 Demand Deposits	13755.2	14416.5	15124.1	16101.8
准货币 Quasi - money	29270.9	31729.9	34320.2	36763.4
定期存款 Time Deposits	2202.6	2645.9	3095.8	3324.2
储蓄存款 Savings Deposits	23762.7	25572.1	27569.7	29662.2
其他存款 Other Deposits	3305.6	3511.9	3654.7	3777.0
债券 Bonds	232.2	213.0	234.0	189.1
所有者权益 Owner's Equity	3482.9	3569.9	3735.1	3886.9
其中：实收资本 Of Which：Paid - in Capital	3211.3	3243.2	3404.4	3431.7
其他（净） Other Items（Net）	- 4094.2	- 5859.5	- 6922.3	- 5122.9

银 行 概 览
Banking Survey

（季末余额）

（Quarter－end Balance）

单位：亿元

Unit：100 Million Yuan

项 目 Items	1996.03	1996.06	1996.09	1996.12
国外净资产 Net Foreign Assets	6822.1	7004.9	8368.7	9213.7
国内信贷 Domestic Credit	56484.0	60487.3	62051.7	66410.9
对政府债权（净） Claims on Government（Net）	2118.5	2135.9	2025.7	2180.4
对非金融部门债权 Claims on Non－financial Sectors	54365.5	58351.4	60026.0	64230.5
货币和准货币 Money & Quasi－money	64512.1	68132.8	72042.6	76094.9
货币 Money	23909.3	24620.1	26336.0	28514.8
流通中现金 Currency in Circulation	8169.1	7665.7	8409.0	8802.0
活期存款 Demand Deposits	15740.2	16954.4	17927.0	19712.8
准货币 Quasi－money	40602.8	43512.7	45706.6	47580.1
定期存款 Time Deposits	3724.8	4300.8	4674.5	5041.9
储蓄存款 Savings Deposits	33296.5	35457.9	37084.9	38520.8
其他存款 Other Deposits	3581.5	3754.0	3947.2	4017.4
债券 Bonds	185.2	182.6	162.0	299.8
所有者权益 Owner's Equity	3962.6	4153.8	4425.6	4480.5
其中：实收资本 Of Which：Paid－in Capital	3683.3	3745.7	3773.5	3918.0
其他（净） Other Items（Net）	－5353.8	－4977.0	－6209.8	－5250.6

银 行 概 览
Banking Survey
（季末余额）
（Quarter – end Balance）

单位：亿元
Unit：100 Million Yuan

项　　目 Items	1997.03	1997.06	1997.09	1997.12
国外净资产 Net Foreign Assets	10683.5	11283.9	12775.0	13660.7
国内信贷 Domestic Credit	69914.2	71849.9	74098.8	78681.1
对政府债权（净） Claims on Government（Net）	1737.8	1414.4	1281.3	1616.7
对非金融部门债权 Claims on Non – financial Sectors	68176.4	70435.5	72817.5	77064.4
货币和准货币 Money & Quasi – money	79581.3	82811.5	85892.4	90995.3
货币 Money	29629.0	31074.7	32244.6	34826.3
流通中现金 Currency in Circulation	9280.1	9121.6	9426.1	10177.6
活期存款 Demand Deposits	20348.9	21953.1	22818.5	24648.7
准货币 Quasi – money	49952.3	51736.8	53647.8	56169.0
定期存款 Time Deposits	5692.2	6056.3	6498.1	6738.5
储蓄存款 Savings Deposits	41556.8	42771.2	44139.5	46279.8
其他存款 Other Deposits	2703.3	2909.3	3010.2	3150.7
债券 Bonds	2667.3	2968.2	3307.7	3532.1
所有者权益 Owner's Equity	4250.3	4363.0	4473.8	4625.1
其中：实收资本 Of Which：Paid – in Capital	3904.8	4136.9	4224.7	4294.9
其他（净） Other Items（Net）	– 5901.2	– 7008.9	– 6800.1	– 6810.7

银 行 概 览

Banking Survey

（季末余额）

（Quarter－end Balance）

单位：亿元

Unit：100 Million Yuan

项　目 Items	1998.03	1998.06	1998.09	1998.12
国外净资产 Net Foreign Assets	14055.1	14299.8	14842.3	15042.0
国内信贷 Domestic Credit	79142.0	82725.1	89746.1	94420.3
对政府债权（净） Claims on Government（Net）	1174.8	1885.8	4297.7	4844.7
对非金融部门债权 Claims on Non－financial Sectors	77967.2	80839.3	85448.4	89575.6
货币和准货币 Money & Quasi－money	92037.7	94657.6	99794.5	104498.5
货币 Money	33110.7	33775.7	36501.4	38953.7
流通中现金 Currency in Circulation	10201.0	9720.4	10528.0	11204.2
活期存款 Demand Deposits	22909.7	24055.3	25973.4	27749.5
准货币 Quasi－money	58927.0	60881.9	63293.1	65544.8
定期存款 Time Deposits	6764.2	7348.0	7974.8	8301.9
储蓄存款 Savings Deposits	48686.5	49949.9	51580.7	53407.5
其他存款 Other Deposits	3476.3	3584.0	3737.6	3835.4
债券 Bonds	3637.7	4076.1	4555.4	5203.8
所有者权益 Owner's Equity	4358.6	4333.9	6751.7	6949.5
其中：实收资本 Of Which：Paid－in Capital	4334.9	4329.3	7130.9	7192.7
其他（净） Other Items（Net）	－6836.9	－6042.7	－6513.2	－7189.5

银行概览
Banking Survey
（季末余额）
（Quarter - end Balance）

单位：亿元
Unit：100 Million Yuan

项目 Items	1999.03	1999.06	1999.09	1999.12
国外净资产 Net Foreign Assets	14734.2	14417.6	15662.7	17028.2
国内信贷 Domestic Credit	95694.2	98885.1	101861.2	105806.7
对政府债权（净） Claims on Government（Net）	4865.9	5104.1	5040.3	5876.8
对非金融部门债权 Claims on Non - financial Sectors	90828.3	93781.0	96820.9	99929.9
货币和准货币 Money & Quasi - money	108438.2	111363.5	115079.3	119897.9
货币 Money	38053.6	38821.8	41913.9	45837.3
流通中现金 Currency in Circulation	11341.6	10880.5	12255.2	13455.5
活期存款 Demand Deposits	26712.0	27941.3	29658.7	32381.8
准货币 Quasi - money	70384.6	72541.7	73165.4	74060.6
定期存款 Time Deposits	8641.9	9175.5	9281.9	9476.8
储蓄存款 Savings Deposits	57814.6	59173.5	59364.3	59621.8
其他存款 Other Deposits	3928.1	4192.7	4519.2	4962.0
债券 Bonds	5388.0	5581.4	5708.2	6354.6
实收资本 Paid - in Capital	7193.8	7207.8	7244.5	7276.4
其他（净） Other Items（Net）	- 10591.6	- 10850.0	- 10508.1	- 10694.0

银 行 概 览

Banking Survey

（季末余额）

（Quarter - end Balance）

单位：亿元

Unit：100 Million Yuan

项 目 Items	2000.03	2000.06	2000.09	2000.12
国外净资产 Net Foreign Assets	17963.4	18630.8	19543.5	20124.3
国内信贷 Domestic Credit	107452.3	106751.2	111298.6	117241.3
对政府债权（净） Claims on Government（Net）	5396.3	5035.7	5542.5	5875.5
对非金融部门债权 Claims on Non - financial Sectors	102056.0	101715.5	105756.1	111365.8
货币和准货币 Money & Quasi - money	122606.8	126605.3	130473.8	134610.4
货币 Money	45158.5	48024.4	50616.9	53147.2
流通中现金 Currency in Circulation	13235.4	13006.0	13894.7	14652.7
活期存款 Demand Deposits	31923.1	35018.4	36722.2	38494.5
准货币 Quasi - money	77448.3	78580.9	79856.9	81463.2
定期存款 Time Deposits	9877.8	10547.0	11149.1	11261.1
储蓄存款 Savings Deposits	62492.3	62842.4	63243.3	64332.4
其他存款 Other Deposits	5078.2	5191.5	5464.5	5869.7
债券 Bonds	6447.3	6777.2	7039.9	7428.9
实收资本 Paid - in Capital	7285.8	7283.3	7309.2	7396.7
其他（净） Other Items（Net）	- 10924.2	- 15283.8	- 13980.8	- 12070.4

银行概览

Banking Survey

（季末余额）

（Quarter – end Balance）

单位：亿元

Unit: 100 Million Yuan

项　目 Items	2001.03	2001.06	2001.09	2001.12
国外净资产 Net Foreign Assets	21976.6	23264.4	24308.4	26424.7
国内信贷 Domestic Credit	113082.3	117789.2	120345.8	125555.0
对政府债权（净） Claims on Government (Net)	8827.4	8962.2	9071.9	11015.9
对非金融部门债权 Claims on Non – financial Sectors	104254.9	108827.0	111273.9	114539.1
货币和准货币 Money & Quasi – money	138744.5	147809.7	151642.7	158301.9
货币 Money	53033.4	55187.4	56644.0	59871.6
流通中现金 Currency in Circulation	14362.1	13943.4	15064.6	15688.8
活期存款 Demand Deposits	38671.3	41243.9	41579.4	44182.8
准货币 Quasi – money	85711.1	92622.3	94998.7	98430.3
定期存款 Time Deposits	11962.3	12614.2	13567.3	14180.1
储蓄存款 Savings Deposits	68365.1	69628.6	71252.6	73762.4
其他存款 Other Deposits	5383.7	10379.5	10178.8	10487.8
债券 Bonds	7555.1	7733.1	7995.2	8448.0
实收资本 Paid – in Capital	7445.8	7510.5	7560.2	7659.8
其他（净） Other Items (Net)	– 18686.5	– 21999.7	– 22543.9	– 22430.0

银行概览

Banking Survey

（月末余额）

（Month - end Balance）

单位：亿元

Unit：100 Million Yuan

项目 Items	2002.01	2002.02	2002.03	2002.04
国外净资产 Net Foreign Assets	25682.90	26109.53	26558.17	26955.63
国内信贷 Domestic Credit	150235.63	151570.59	154543.93	154775.61
对政府债权（净） Claims on Government（Net）	10285.23	10774.17	10914.27	10572.19
对非金融部门债权 Claims on Non - financial Sectors	123375.45	124046.78	126882.58	127887.33
对其他金融部门债权 Claims on Other Financial Sectors	16574.95	16749.64	16747.08	16316.09
货币和准货币 Money & Quasi - money	159639.27	160935.59	164064.57	164570.56
货币 Money	60576.06	58702.87	59474.83	60461.31
流通中现金 Currency in Circulation	16725.89	16641.55	15544.63	15864.18
活期存款 Demand Deposits	43850.17	42061.32	43930.20	44597.13
准货币 Quasi - money	99063.21	102232.72	104589.74	104109.25
定期存款 Time Deposits	12846.37	12932.33	13081.62	13905.60
储蓄存款 Savings Deposits	74953.71	78114.33	78728.30	79728.20
其他存款 Other Deposits	11263.13	11186.06	12779.82	10475.45
外币存款 Deposits in Foreign Currency	11218.40	11331.21	11419.77	11406.35
债券 Bonds	8595.18	8666.46	8740.99	9279.27
实收资本 Paid - in Capital	8885.56	8910.87	8866.35	8944.55
其他（净） Other Items（Net）	- 12419.88	- 12164.01	- 11989.58	- 12469.49

银行概览
Banking Survey
(月末余额)
(Month - end Balance)

单位：亿元
Unit: 100 Million Yuan

项目 Items	2002.05	2002.06	2002.07	2002.08
国外净资产 Net Foreign Assets	27460.47	27793.84	28344.02	29014.93
国内信贷 Domestic Credit	155707.11	159328.19	160256.53	161841.77
对政府债权（净） Claims on Government (Net)	10217.10	10965.46	11200.45	10938.47
对非金融部门债权 Claims on Non - financial Sectors	129127.65	131969.63	132702.87	134477.03
对其他金融部门债权 Claims on Other Financial Sectors	16362.36	16393.10	16353.21	16426.27
货币和准货币 Money & Quasi - money	166023.00	169601.24	170851.14	173250.92
货币 Money	61246.86	63144.00	63487.78	64868.83
流通中现金 Currency in Circulation	15243.07	15097.35	15357.66	15712.61
活期存款 Demand Deposits	46003.79	48046.65	48130.12	49156.22
准货币 Quasi - money	104776.14	106457.24	107363.36	108382.09
定期存款 Time Deposits	13585.04	14099.29	14291.23	14764.37
储蓄存款 Savings Deposits	80394.30	81711.79	82527.90	83275.97
其他存款 Other Deposits	10796.80	10646.16	10544.23	10341.75
外币存款 Deposits in Foreign Currency	11601.65	11693.68	11681.14	11766.59
债券 Bonds	8861.47	9065.77	9073.89	9122.51
实收资本 Paid - in Capital	8835.05	8878.29	8929.72	8957.43
其他（净） Other Items (Net)	- 12153.59	- 12116.95	- 11935.34	- 12240.75

银行概览

Banking Survey

（月末余额）

（Month－end Balance）

单位：亿元

Unit：100 Million Yuan

项目 Items	2002.09	2002.10	2002.11	2002.12
国外净资产 Net Foreign Assets	29166.07	30058.27	30667.43	31746.34
国内信贷 Domestic Credit	164611.86	165314.01	167226.47	172624.73
对政府债权（净） Claims on Government（Net）	10886.07	10784.75	10996.92	13331.91
对非金融部门债权 Claims on Non－financial Sectors	137502.53	138273.24	139969.48	143016.39
对其他金融部门债权 Claims on Other Financial Sectors	16223.26	16256.02	16260.07	16276.43
货币和准货币 Money & Quasi－money	176985.21	177294.15	179736.26	185006.97
货币 Money	66799.76	67100.25	67992.78	70881.79
流通中现金 Currency in Circulation	16233.58	16014.66	16346.39	17278.03
活期存款 Demand Deposits	50566.18	51085.59	51646.39	53603.76
准货币 Quasi－money	110185.45	110193.90	111743.48	114125.18
定期存款 Time Deposits	15783.93	15239.79	15722.45	16433.82
储蓄存款 Savings Deposits	84139.05	84725.13	85693.49	86910.65
其他存款 Other Deposits	10262.47	10228.98	10327.54	10780.71
外币存款 Deposits in Foreign Currency	11745.57	11916.79	11977.80	12159.08
债券 Bonds	9227.33	9475.84	9665.24	10102.35
实收资本 Paid－in Capital	8958.95	9038.93	8918.61	8991.97
其他（净） Other Items（Net）	－13139.13	－12353.43	－12404.01	－11889.30

银行概览
Banking Survey
（月末余额）
（Month – end Balance）

单位：亿元
Unit：100 Million Yuan

项　目 Items	2003.01	2003.02	2003.03	2003.04
国外净资产 Net Foreign Assets	32730.15	33312.38	33764.13	34139.11
国内信贷 Domestic Credit	175431.28	176628.97	180260.36	181886.01
对政府债权（净） Claims on Government（Net）	12623.54	12566.16	11978.61	11530.63
对非金融部门债权 Claims on Non – financial Sectors	145970.68	147136.91	151125.87	153312.03
对其他金融部门债权 Claims on Other Financial Sectors	16837.06	16925.90	17155.88	17043.35
货币和准货币 Money & Quasi – money	190545.05	190108.41	194487.30	196130.13
货币 Money	72405.66	69756.64	71438.82	71321.24
流通中现金 Currency in Circulation	21244.73	17937.17	17106.50	17441.14
活期存款 Demand Deposits	51160.93	51819.47	54332.32	53880.10
准货币 Quasi – money	118139.39	120351.77	123048.48	124808.89
定期存款 Time Deposits	16906.53	16776.52	17377.09	18203.26
储蓄存款 Savings Deposits	90677.63	92824.21	94567.84	95194.12
其他存款 Other Deposits	10555.23	10751.04	11103.55	11411.51
外币存款 Deposits in Foreign Currency	12075.50	12061.99	11996.03	11975.48
债券 Bonds	9778.06	9978.61	10051.97	9922.17
实收资本 Paid – in Capital	9005.57	9021.31	8875.25	9265.47
其他（净） Other Items（Net）	– 13242.75	– 11228.97	– 11386.06	– 11268.13

银行概览

Banking Survey

（月末余额）

（Month - end Balance）

单位：亿元

Unit：100 Million Yuan

项目 Items	2003.05	2003.06	2003.07	2003.08
国外净资产 Net Foreign Assets	34623.07	35014.31	35241.13	36132.11
国内信贷 Domestic Credit	184609.91	190670.26	191859.25	195550.23
对政府债权（净） Claims on Government（Net）	11071.00	11719.67	11615.53	11430.34
对非金融部门债权 Claims on Non - financial Sectors	156206.27	161952.89	163221.16	166492.44
对其他金融部门债权 Claims on Other Financial Sectors	17332.64	16997.70	17022.56	17627.45
货币和准货币 Money & Quasi - money	199505.19	204907.42	206193.07	210591.90
货币 Money	72777.84	75923.23	76152.77	77032.98
流通中现金 Currency in Circulation	17115.03	16956.89	17362.13	17606.76
活期存款 Demand Deposits	55662.81	58966.34	58790.64	59426.22
准货币 Quasi - money	126727.35	128984.19	130040.30	133558.92
定期存款 Time Deposits	18544.84	18869.84	19118.75	19592.84
储蓄存款 Savings Deposits	96351.67	97674.57	98590.90	99255.58
其他存款 Other Deposits	11830.84	12439.78	12330.65	14710.50
外币存款 Deposits in Foreign Currency	12059.73	12165.33	12063.75	12021.20
债券 Bonds	10130.67	10319.09	10574.35	10563.28
实收资本 Paid - in Capital	9282.39	9272.07	9305.88	9340.80
其他（净） Other Items（Net）	- 11745.00	- 10979.34	- 11036.67	- 10834.84

银 行 概 览

Banking Survey

（月末余额）

（Month－end Balance）

单位：亿元

Unit：100 Million Yuan

项　目 Items	2003.09	2003.10	2003.11	2003.12
国外净资产 Net Foreign Assets	36896.72	38202.33	39280.82	37732.92
国内信贷 Domestic Credit	198449.05	198847.68	199755.54	206283.64
对政府债权（净） Claims on Government（Net）	11688.67	11239.51	11198.02	13178.51
对非金融部门债权 Claims on Non－financial Sectors	169659.95	170448.70	171585.99	172700.24
对其他金融部门债权 Claims on Other Financial Sectors	17100.43	17159.47	16971.53	20404.89
货币和准货币 Money & Quasi－money	213567.13	214469.36	216351.73	221222.82
货币 Money	79163.88	80267.10	80814.93	84118.57
流通中现金 Currency in Circulation	18306.36	18250.67	18439.56	19745.99
活期存款 Demand Deposits	60857.52	62016.43	62375.37	64372.58
准货币 Quasi－money	134403.25	134202.26	135536.80	137104.25
定期存款 Time Deposits	21261.13	20388.73	20658.55	20940.39
储蓄存款 Savings Deposits	100888.60	101381.89	102235.44	103617.65
其他存款 Other Deposits	12253.52	12431.64	12642.81	12546.21
外币存款 Deposits in Foreign Currency	11894.88	12042.07	12066.86	11884.29
债券 Bonds	10986.54	11329.96	11544.46	11653.96
实收资本 Paid－in Capital	9305.73	9396.01	9458.13	10949.09
其他（净） Other Items（Net）	－10408.51	－10187.39	－10384.82	－11693.60

银 行 概 览

Banking Survey

（月末余额）

（Month - end Balance）

单位：亿元

Unit：100 Million Yuan

项　目 Items	2004.01	2004.02	2004.03	2004.04
国外净资产 Net Foreign Assets	39873.08	40566.76	41388.95	42031.85
国内信贷 Domestic Credit	207355.79	208726.85	212393.88	214218.83
对政府债权（净） Claims on Government（Net）	12880.24	12633.26	12313.71	12115.45
对非金融部门债权 Claims on Non - financial Sectors	177125.86	179492.43	183133.56	185292.50
对其他金融部门债权 Claims on Other Financial Sectors	17349.69	16601.16	16946.61	16810.88
货币和准货币 Money & Quasi - money	225101.93	227050.72	231654.60	233627.86
货币 Money	83805.90	83556.43	85815.57	85603.64
流通中现金 Currency in Circulation	22287.43	19893.44	19297.43	19878.40
活期存款 Demand Deposits	61518.47	63662.99	66518.14	65725.24
准货币 Quasi - money	141296.03	143494.29	145839.03	148024.22
定期存款 Time Deposits	20920.59	20924.84	21645.35	23298.88
储蓄存款 Savings Deposits	109232.65	110646.38	111872.18	112175.44
其他存款 Other Deposits	11142.79	11923.07	12321.50	12549.90
外币存款 Deposits in Foreign Currency	12078.49	11643.52	11700.99	11736.38
债券 Bonds	11597.26	11850.57	11804.23	11975.31
实收资本 Paid - in Capital	10649.75	10674.88	10761.83	10819.02
其他（净） Other Items（Net）	- 12198.56	- 11926.08	- 12138.82	- 11907.89

银行概览

Banking Survey

（月末余额）

（Month – end Balance）

单位：亿元

Unit：100 Million Yuan

项　　目 Items	2004.05	2004.06	2004.07	2004.08
国外净资产 Net Foreign Assets	42859.25	44919.38	46118.07	47464.98
国内信贷 Domestic Credit	214575.85	213923.99	211911.59	213768.63
对政府债权（净） Claims on Government (Net)	11233.03	11239.12	10150.18	9813.57
对非金融部门债权 Claims on Non – financial Sectors	186462.82	184029.85	183249.80	185446.97
对其他金融部门债权 Claims on Other Financial Sectors	16880.00	18655.02	18511.61	18508.09
货币和准货币 Money & Quasi – money	234842.40	238427.49	238126.97	239729.19
货币 Money	86780.37	88627.14	87982.23	89125.33
流通中现金 Currency in Circulation	19048.43	19017.58	19409.10	19517.94
活期存款 Demand Deposits	67731.94	69609.56	68573.13	69607.39
准货币 Quasi – money	148062.03	149800.35	150144.74	150603.86
定期存款 Time Deposits	22836.18	23542.04	23447.20	23586.02
储蓄存款 Savings Deposits	112610.18	113792.47	114253.24	114489.63
其他存款 Other Deposits	12615.67	12465.84	12444.30	12528.21
外币存款 Deposits in Foreign Currency	11928.36	12009.02	12202.65	12262.60
债券 Bonds	12123.38	12542.40	12340.46	13266.05
实收资本 Paid – in Capital	10859.42	11109.57	11140.21	11254.29
其他（净） Other Items (Net)	– 12318.46	– 15245.11	– 15780.63	– 15278.52

银行概览

Banking Survey

（月末余额）

（Month－end Balance）

单位：亿元

Unit：100 Million Yuan

项目 Items	2004.09	2004.10	2004.11	2004.12
国外净资产 Net Foreign Assets	48362.64	50154.89	53493.68	55348.92
国内信贷 Domestic Credit	217476.87	216754.66	218834.51	225261.84
对政府债权（净） Claims on Government（Net）	10761.85	9744.39	10137.77	15495.74
对非金融部门债权 Claims on Non－financial Sectors	188187.98	188467.22	190110.75	192983.35
对其他金融部门债权 Claims on Other Financial Sectors	18527.04	18543.05	18585.99	16782.75
货币和准货币 Money & Quasi－money	243756.88	243740.32	247135.58	254106.95
货币 Money	90439.05	90782.48	92387.13	95969.72
流通中现金 Currency in Circulation	20524.17	20078.25	20209.25	21468.30
活期存款 Demand Deposits	69914.88	70704.23	72177.88	74501.42
准货币 Quasi－money	153317.83	152957.84	154748.45	158137.23
定期存款 Time Deposits	25071.91	24315.23	24215.96	25382.15
储蓄存款 Savings Deposits	115458.74	116000.99	117617.90	119555.39
其他存款 Other Deposits	12787.18	12641.62	12914.59	13199.69
外币存款 Deposits in Foreign Currency	12338.40	12512.23	12235.59	12129.83
债券 Bonds	13541.43	13741.06	14295.15	15203.49
实收资本 Paid－in Capital	11375.53	11413.19	11600.92	11969.42
其他（净） Other Items（Net）	－15172.73	－14497.25	－12939.05	－12798.93

银行概览
Banking Survey
（月末余额）
(Month – end Balance)

单位：亿元
Unit: 100 Million Yuan

项目 Items	2005.01	2005.02	2005.03	2005.04
国外净资产 Net Foreign Assets	56902.35	58287.47	59610.80	61280.55
国内信贷 Domestic Credit	226979.44	227504.61	231100.62	231483.39
对政府债权（净） Claims on Government (Net)	12806.88	12383.80	12193.20	11298.99
对非金融部门债权 Claims on Non – financial Sectors	195734.46	196757.80	200339.19	201733.70
对其他金融部门债权 Claims on Other Financial Sectors	18438.10	18363.01	18568.23	18450.70
货币和准货币 Money & Quasi – money	257708.47	259357.29	264588.94	266992.66
货币 Money	97079.03	92814.95	94743.19	94593.72
流通中现金 Currency in Circulation	24015.41	22667.97	21238.95	21666.56
活期存款 Demand Deposits	73063.62	70146.98	73504.24	72927.16
准货币 Quasi – money	160629.44	166542.34	169845.75	172398.94
定期存款 Time Deposits	24939.47	25296.42	26543.24	28178.12
储蓄存款 Savings Deposits	122237.34	127823.44	129259.35	129816.83
其他存款 Other Deposits	13452.63	13422.48	14043.16	14403.99
外币存款 Deposits in Foreign Currency	12463.24	12632.50	12854.74	12881.41
债券 Bonds	15433.81	15436.73	16275.30	16759.12
实收资本 Paid – in Capital	11972.51	12032.69	12139.67	13478.01
其他（净） Other Items (Net)	– 13696.24	– 13667.13	– 15147.23	– 17347.26

银行概览

Banking Survey

（月末余额）

（Month - end Balance）

单位：亿元

Unit：100 Million Yuan

项目 Items	2005.05	2005.06	2005.07	2005.08
国外净资产 Net Foreign Assets	62873.28	65303.92	66147.98	67883.46
国内信贷 Domestic Credit	231307.40	235755.62	236149.92	238634.01
对政府债权（净） Claims on Government（Net）	10425.16	10502.67	9938.97	10452.67
对非金融部门债权 Claims on Non - financial Sectors	202209.40	202040.08	201888.15	203691.55
对其他金融部门债权 Claims on Other Financial Sectors	18672.84	23212.87	24322.80	24489.79
货币和准货币 Money & Quasi - money	269240.49	275785.53	276966.28	281288.22
货币 Money	95802.01	98601.25	97674.10	99377.70
流通中现金 Currency in Circulation	20811.59	20848.76	21171.20	21351.56
活期存款 Demand Deposits	74990.42	77752.49	76502.90	78026.14
准货币 Quasi - money	173438.48	177184.28	179292.18	181910.52
定期存款 Time Deposits	28201.05	29395.97	29673.70	30852.96
储蓄存款 Savings Deposits	130577.44	132339.14	133656.44	134505.01
其他存款 Other Deposits	14659.99	15449.17	15962.04	16552.55
外币存款 Deposits in Foreign Currency	12737.66	13108.20	12471.49	12462.49
债券 Bonds	16804.50	17114.39	17426.50	18344.49
实收资本 Paid - in Capital	13183.31	13393.29	13447.11	13487.43
其他（净） Other Items（Net）	- 17785.28	- 18341.87	- 18013.48	- 19065.16

银行概览
Banking Survey
（月末余额）
（Month – end Balance）

单位：亿元
Unit：100 Million Yuan

项目 Items	2005.09	2005.10	2005.11	2005.12
国外净资产 Net Foreign Assets	69170.50	72118.49	73622.51	75595.86
国内信贷 Domestic Credit	242219.66	241090.15	243946.28	248367.10
对政府债权（净） Claims on Government（Net）	11546.91	10712.86	11140.91	15197.27
对非金融部门债权 Claims on Non – financial Sectors	206928.18	206443.77	208648.59	209502.94
对其他金融部门债权 Claims on Other Financial Sectors	23744.57	23933.52	24156.78	23666.89
货币和准货币 Money & Quasi – money	287438.27	287591.61	292350.39	298755.67
货币 Money	100964.00	101751.98	104125.78	107278.76
流通中现金 Currency in Circulation	22272.92	21892.98	22409.39	24031.67
活期存款 Demand Deposits	78691.08	79859.00	81716.39	83247.09
准货币 Quasi – money	186474.27	185839.63	188224.61	191476.91
定期存款 Time Deposits	33320.65	32145.97	32229.65	33099.99
储蓄存款 Savings Deposits	136316.32	136827.11	138504.28	141050.99
其他存款 Other Deposits	16837.30	16866.55	17490.68	17325.93
外币存款 Deposits in Foreign Currency	12157.94	12327.23	12369.47	12358.60
债券 Bonds	18867.32	18940.14	19680.69	20378.79
实收资本 Paid – in Capital	13556.84	13813.48	13922.83	14252.11
其他（净） Other Items（Net）	–20630.21	–19463.82	–20754.59	–21782.21

（四）各部门资产负债表

Sectoral Balance Sheet

1. 货币当局资产负债表

Balance Sheet of Monetary Authority

货币当局资产负债表

Balance Sheet of Monetary Authority

（季末余额）

（Quarter – end Balance）

单位：亿元

Unit：100 Million Yuan

项　　目 Items	1993.03	1993.06	1993.09	1993.12
国外资产（净） Foreign Assets（Net）	1324.0	1286.5	1451.0	1549.5
外汇 Foreign Exchange	1222.0	1183.0	1332.2	1431.8
货币黄金 Monetary Gold	12.0	12.0	12.0	12.0
其他国外资产 Other Foreign Assets	90.0	91.5	106.8	105.7
对政府债权 Claims on Government	1339.6	1373.7	1399.8	1582.7
对存款货币银行债权 Claims on Deposit Money Banks	6671.7	6868.1	7879.6	9609.5
对非货币金融机构债权 Claims on Non – monetary Financial Institutions	213.5	199.3	144.7	251.7
对非金融部门债权 Claims on Non – financial Sectors	561.1	600.6	639.1	682.3
储备货币 Reserve Money	9846.1	10089.1	11075.9	13147.0
发行货币 Currency Issue	4867.3	5228.6	5438.3	6314.2
对金融机构负债 Liabilities to Financial Institutions	3844.6	3751.6	4439.6	5541.1
准备金 Reserves	2497.7	2582.8	2615.5	2884.6
存款货币银行 Reserves by Deposit Money Banks	2393.2	2463.5	2498.1	2754.1
存款 Deposits	1346.9	1168.8	1824.1	2656.5
存款货币银行 Deposits by Deposit Money Banks	1096.3	943.8	1581.0	2286.7
非金融机构存款 Deposits by Non – financial Institutions	1134.2	1108.9	1198.0	1291.7
债券 Bonds	0.0	0.0	0.0	0.0
政府存款 Deposits by Government	337.6	340.4	414.5	473.4
自有资金 Own Capital	310.3	310.3	310.3	310.3
其他负债 Other Liabilities	– 384.1	– 411.6	– 286.5	– 255.0

货币当局资产负债表
Balance Sheet of Monetary Authority

(季末余额)

(Quarter - end Balance)

单位：亿元

Unit：100 Million Yuan

项目 Items	1994.03	1994.06	1994.09	1994.12
国外资产（净） Foreign Assets（Net）	2437.6	3081.7	3816.8	4451.3
外汇 Foreign Exchange	2253.8	2888.0	3619.0	4263.9
货币黄金 Monetary Gold	12.0	12.0	12.0	12.0
其他国外资产 Other Foreign Assets	171.8	181.7	185.8	175.4
对政府债权 Claims on Government	1582.8	1582.8	1582.8	1687.7
对存款货币银行债权 Claims on Deposit Money Banks	9297.7	9383.1	9581.0	10451.0
对非货币金融机构债权 Claims on Non - monetary Financial Institutions	258.7	275.7	231.3	269.9
对非金融部门债权 Claims on Non - financial Sectors	682.9	696.1	708.3	728.3
储备货币 Reserve Money	13612.3	14138.3	15193.8	17217.8
发行货币 Currency Issue	6308.7	6258.6	6923.5	7883.9
对金融机构负债 Liabilities to Financial Institutions	5934.2	6399.3	6634.2	7468.3
准备金 Reserves	3072.5	3391.9	3683.3	3961.2
存款货币银行 Reserves by Deposit Money Banks	3002.4	3312.2	3571.9	3827.5
存款 Deposits	2861.7	3007.4	2950.9	3507.1
存款货币银行 Deposits by Deposit Money Banks	2527.7	2708.6	2590.9	3031.3
非金融机构存款 Deposits by Non - financial Institutions	1369.4	1480.4	1636.1	1865.6
债券 Bonds	30.1	1.0	1.0	0.0
政府存款 Deposits by Government	635.4	874.0	912.1	833.3
自有资金 Own Capital	280.5	280.5	280.5	265.7
其他负债 Other Liabilities	- 298.6	- 274.4	- 467.2	- 728.6

货币当局资产负债表
Balance Sheet of Monetary Authority

（季末余额）
（Quarter - end Balance）

单位：亿元
Unit：100 Million Yuan

项目 Items	1995.03	1995.06	1995.09	1995.12
国外资产（净） Foreign Assets（Net）	4992.7	5322.6	6020.1	6669.5
外汇 Foreign Exchange	4839.1	5192.6	5846.0	6511.4
货币黄金 Monetary Gold	12.0	12.0	12.0	12.0
其他国外资产 Other Foreign Assets	141.6	118.0	162.1	146.1
对政府债权 Claims on Government	1582.8	1582.8	1582.8	1582.8
对存款货币银行债权 Claims on Deposit Money Banks	10294.8	9990.1	10372.0	11510.3
对非货币金融机构债权 Claims on Non - monetary Financial Institutions	312.3	200.6	183.7	181.6
对非金融部门债权 Claims on Non - financial Sectors	739.8	744.0	697.7	680.1
储备货币 Reserve Money	17588.4	17297.0	18705.8	20759.8
发行货币 Currency Issue	7826.1	7595.5	7960.7	8574.0
对金融机构负债 Liabilities to Financial Institutions	7835.5	7664.4	8497.9	9672.5
准备金 Reserves	4252.1	4548.3	4933.5	5246.5
存款货币银行 Reserves by Deposit Money Banks	4129.0	4411.5	4776.6	5108.6
存款 Deposits	3583.4	3116.1	3564.4	4426.0
存款货币银行 Deposits by Deposit Money Banks	3204.7	2662.7	2982.6	3946.8
非金融机构存款 Deposits by Non - financial Institutions	1926.8	2037.1	2247.2	2513.3
债券 Bonds	0.4	0.1	0.0	197.1
政府存款 Deposits by Government	910.7	1498.1	1236.5	973.4
自有资金 Own Capital	265.7	263.8	371.2	371.1
其他负债 Other Liabilities	- 842.8	- 1218.9	- 1457.2	- 1677.1

货币当局资产负债表
Balance Sheet of Monetary Authority

（季末余额）
（Quarter－end Balance）

单位：亿元
Unit：100 Million Yuan

项　目 Items	1996.03	1996.06	1996.09	1996.12
国外资产（净） Foreign Assets（Net）	7329.4	7887.8	8729.1	9562.2
外汇 Foreign Exchange	7176.8	7712.6	8536.8	9330.0
货币黄金 Monetary Gold	12.0	12.0	12.0	12.0
其他国外资产 Other Foreign Assets	140.6	163.2	180.3	220.2
对政府债权 Claims on Government	1582.8	1582.8	1582.8	1582.8
对存款货币银行债权 Claims on Deposit Money Banks	11451.1	10936.5	11174.7	14518.4
对非货币金融机构债权 Claims on Non－monetary Financial Institutions	174.2	120.9	119.0	117.7
对非金融部门债权 Claims on Non－financial Sectors	680.1	674.9	668.4	685.7
储备货币 Reserve Money	21513.6	21349.6	22509.2	26888.5
发行货币 Currency Issue	8844.7	8343.4	9135.3	9434.8
对金融机构负债 Liabilities to Financial Institutions	10052.9	10261.6	10434.9	14354.9
准备金 Reserves	5628.7	6063.8	6501.1	7612.4
存款货币银行 Reserves by Deposit Money Banks	5487.6	5917.7	6327.2	6544.7
存款 Deposits	4424.2	4197.8	3933.8	6742.5
存款货币银行 Deposits by Deposit Money Banks	3964.5	3694.8	3443.9	6657.7
非金融机构存款 Deposits by Non－financial Institutions	2616.0	2744.6	2939.0	3098.8
债券 Bonds	0.0	0.0	0.0	0.0
政府存款 Deposits by Government	963.2	1132.6	1400.4	1225.4
自有资金 Own Capital	369.7	369.7	368.8	366.8
其他负债 Other Liabilities	－1628.9	－1649.0	－2004.4	－2013.9

货币当局资产负债表
Balance Sheet of Monetary Authority

（季末余额）

（Quarter - end Balance）

单位：亿元

Unit：100 Million Yuan

项 目 Items	1997.03	1997.06	1997.09	1997.12
国外资产（净） Foreign Assets（Net）	10664.2	11436.5	12515.6	13229.2
外汇 Foreign Exchange	10138.6	10916.1	12018.1	12649.3
货币黄金 Monetary Gold	12.0	12.0	12.0	12.0
其他国外资产 Other Foreign Assets	513.6	508.4	485.5	567.9
对政府债权 Claims on Government	1582.8	1582.8	1582.8	1582.8
对存款货币银行债权 Claims on Deposit Money Banks	13628.9	13235.9	13531.4	14357.9
对非货币金融机构债权 Claims on Non - monetary Financial Institutions	1658.7	1835.4	1898.0	2072.3
对非金融部门债权 Claims on Non - financial Sectors	661.7	643.7	169.4	171.0
储备货币 Reserve Money	26811.4	27485.2	28379.9	30632.8
发行货币 Currency Issue	10138.9	9959.1	10271.5	10981.1
对金融机构负债 Liabilities to Financial Institutions	13738.3	14463.4	14903.4	16114.9
准备金 Reserves	8073.6	8495.5	8913.4	9248.7
存款货币银行 Reserves by Deposit Money Banks	7703.0	8148.0	8578.7	8904.9
存款 Deposits	5664.7	5967.9	5990.0	6866.2
存款货币银行 Deposits by Deposit Money Banks	4508.2	4852.5	5187.9	6284.4
非金融机构存款 Deposits by Non - financial Institutions	2934.2	3062.7	3205.0	3536.8
债券 Bonds	118.9	118.9	118.9	118.9
政府存款 Deposits by Government	1434.3	1572.9	1722.3	1485.9
自有资金 Own Capital	366.2	366.3	366.2	366.2
其他（净） Other Items（Net）	- 534.5	- 809.0	- 890.1	- 1190.6

货币当局资产负债表
Balance Sheet of Monetary Authority
（季末余额）
(Quarter - end Balance)

单位：亿元
Unit: 100 Million Yuan

项目 Items	1998.03	1998.06	1998.09	1998.12
国外资产（净）Foreign Assets (Net)	13179.7	13169.7	13284.7	13560.3
外汇 Foreign Exchange	12651.4	12621.5	12729.3	13087.9
货币黄金 Monetary Gold	12.0	12.0	12.0	12.0
其他国外资产 Other Foreign Assets	516.3	536.2	543.4	460.4
对政府债权 Claims on Government	1582.8	1582.8	1582.8	1582.8
对存款货币银行债权 Claims on Deposit Money Banks	14014.5	13496.1	11370.2	13058.0
对非货币金融机构债权 Claims on Non - monetary Financial Institutions	2138.4	2404.0	2607.0	2962.8
对非金融部门债权 Claims on Non - financial Sectors	171.0	109.3	105.0	103.8
储备货币 Reserve Money	29213.4	30589.8	28177.4	31335.3
发行货币 Currency Issue	11058.0	10551.9	11343.9	12064.1
对金融机构负债 Liabilities to Financial Institutions	14479.5	16109.3	12657.5	14744.7
准备金 Reserves	7755.2	16109.3	12657.5	14744.7
存款货币银行 Reserves by Deposit Money Banks	7483.2	15388.2	12093.3	14033.6
存款 Deposits	6724.3			
存款货币银行 Deposits by Deposit Money Banks	4791.9			
非金融机构存款 Deposits by Non - financial Institutions	3675.9	3928.6	4176.0	4526.5
债券 Bonds	118.9	118.9	118.9	118.9
政府存款 Deposits by Government	1843.6	1381.1	1877.7	1726.1
自有资金 Own Capital	366.6	366.6	366.6	366.8
其他负债 Other Liabilities	- 456.1	- 1694.5	- 1590.9	- 2279.4

货币当局资产负债表
Balance Sheet of Monetary Authority

（季末余额）

（Quarter - end Balance）

单位：亿元

Unit：100 Million Yuan

项　目 Items	1999.03	1999.06	1999.09	1999.12
国外资产（净） Foreign Assets（Net）	13522.1	13549.9	14661.6	14458.5
外汇 Foreign Exchange	13107.1	13134.8	14252.3	14061.4
货币黄金 Monetary Gold	12.0	12.0	12.0	12.0
其他国外资产 Other Foreign Assets	403.0	403.1	397.3	385.1
对政府债权 Claims on Government	1582.8	1582.8	1582.8	1582.8
对存款货币银行债权 Claims on Deposit Money Banks	12195.3	11860.1	12535.4	15373.9
对非货币金融机构债权 Claims on Non - monetary Financial Institutions	3012.5	3047.8	3048.7	3833.1
对非金融部门债权 Claims on Non - financial Sectors	102.9	102.5	101.9	101.5
储备货币 Reserve Money	29185.8	28799.8	29393.2	33620.1
发行货币 Currency Issue	12251.0	11787.0	13401.8	15069.8
对金融机构负债 Liabilities to Financial Institutions	13430.0	13405.2	12315.4	14728.5
准备金 Reserves	13430.0	13405.2	12315.4	14728.5
存款货币银行 Reserves by Deposit Money Banks	12743.0	12574.5	11890.3	14200.7
存款 Deposits				
存款货币银行 Deposits by Deposit Money Banks				
非金融机构存款 Deposits by Non - financial Institutions	3504.8	3607.6	3676.0	3821.8
债券 Bonds	118.9	118.9	118.9	118.9
政府存款 Deposits by Government	1770.6	1709.2	2160.5	1785.5
自有资金 Own Capital	366.8	366.8	366.8	366.8
其他负债 Other Liabilities	- 1026.5	- 851.6	- 109.0	- 541.5

货币当局资产负债表
Balance Sheet of Monetary Authority

（季末余额）

（Quarter – end Balance）

单位：亿元

Unit: 100 Million Yuan

项　目 Items	2000.03	2000.06	2000.09	2000.12
国外资产（净） Foreign Assets (Net)	14648.8	14749.9	14775.0	15188.9
外汇 Foreign Exchange	14261.3	14374.8	14417.9	14814.5
黄金 Gold	12.0	12.0	12.0	12.0
其他国外资产 Other Foreign Assets	375.5	363.1	345.1	362.4
对政府债权 Claims on Government	1582.8	1582.8	1582.8	1582.8
对存款货币银行债权 Claims on Deposit Money Banks	13623.3	11433.7	11362.5	13519.2
对非货币金融机构债权 Claims on Non – monetary Financial Institutions	4346.3	7320.8	8366.0	8600.4
对非金融部门债权 Claims on Non – financial Sectors	101.3	117.9	115.9	110.2
储备货币 Reserve Money	32290.3	32469.9	33845.9	36491.4
发行货币 Currency Issue	14289.1	14070.5	15127.0	15938.3
对金融机构负债 Liabilities to Financial Institutions	13876.2	14163.9	14388.0	16019.0
准备金 Reserves	13876.2	14163.9	14388.0	16019.0
存款货币银行 Reserves by Deposit Money Banks	13486.8	13717.1	13983.3	15391.7
存款 Deposits				
存款货币银行 Deposits by Deposit Money Banks				
非金融机构存款 Deposits by Non – financial Institutions	4125.0	4235.5	4330.9	4534.1
债券 Bonds				
政府存款 Deposits by Government	2314.9	3047.7	2749.0	3100.4
自有资金 Own Capital	366.8	366.8	366.8	366.8
其他（净） Other Items (Net)	– 669.5	– 679.3	– 759.5	– 957.1

货币当局资产负债表
Balance Sheet of Monetary Authority

（季末余额）

（Quarter－end Balance）

单位：亿元

Unit：100 Million Yuan

项　目 Items	2001.03	2001.06	2001.09	2001.12
国外资产（净） Foreign Assets（Net）	15312.6	16505.3	17768.7	19351.3
外汇 Foreign Exchange	15089.0	16282.1	17505.3	18850.2
黄金 Gold	12.0	12.0	12.0	256.0
其他国外资产 Other Foreign Assets	211.6	211.2	251.4	245.1
对政府债权 Claims on Government	2731.1	2841.2	2811.5	2821.3
对存款货币银行债权 Claims on Deposit Money Banks	10067.9	11257.0	11205.3	11311.6
对非货币金融机构债权 Claims on Non－monetary Financial Institutions	8440.8	8322.4	8276.1	8547.3
对非金融部门债权 Claims on Non－financial Sectors	229.3	234.0	233.7	195.5
储备货币 Reserve Money	34697.7	34396.8	35727.5	39851.7
发行货币 Currency Issue	15577.1	15172.1	16423.5	16868.7
对金融机构负债 Liabilities to Financial Institutions	14127.9	13998.8	13847.4	17089.1
准备金 Reserves	14127.9	13998.8	13847.4	17089.1
存款货币银行 Reserves by Deposit Money Banks	13931.2	13758.2	13661.3	16853.4
存款 Deposits				
存款货币银行 Deposits by Deposit Money Banks				
非金融机构存款 Deposits by Non－financial Institutions	4992.7	5225.9	5456.6	5893.9
债券 Bonds				
政府存款 Deposits by Government	3450.3	3983.0	4283.8	2850.5
自有资金 Own Capital	355.2	355.2	355.2	355.2
其他（净） Other Items（Net）	－1721.5	424.9	－71.2	－830.4

货币当局资产负债表
Balance Sheet of Monetary Authority

(月末余额)

(Month – end Balance)

单位：亿元

Unit：100 Million Yuan

项 目 Items	2002.01	2002.02	2002.03	2002.04
国外资产 Foreign Assets	19005.61	19423.43	19655.71	19979.97
外汇 Foreign Exchange	18004.00	18425.00	18659.92	18977.74
货币黄金 Monetary Gold	256.00	256.00	256.00	256.00
其他国外资产 Other Foreign Assets	745.61	742.43	739.79	746.23
对政府债权 Claims on Government	2725.62	2725.62	2727.70	2657.70
其中：中央政府 Of Which：Central Government	2725.62	2725.62	2727.70	2657.70
对存款货币银行债权 Claims on Deposit Money Banks	9995.57	9923.15	9999.24	9970.30
对特定存款机构债权 Claims on Specific Depository Institutions	2620.79	2512.09	2483.84	2505.15
对其他金融机构债权 Claims on Other Financial Institutions	7064.61	7202.93	7208.54	7210.53
对非金融机构债权 Claims on Non – financial Institutions	217.19	217.08	217.07	216.98
其他资产 Other Assets	3681.64	3948.65	4756.07	4908.48
总资产 Total Assets	**45311.03**	**45952.95**	**47048.17**	**47449.11**
储备货币 Reserve Money	40054.21	40890.63	41221.08	40519.38
发行货币 Currency Issue	18053.95	18089.94	16941.05	17133.22
金融机构存款 Deposits by Financial Institutions	15946.35	16445.95	17760.44	16831.40
存款货币银行 Deposit Money Banks	15796.83	16308.09	17598.82	16536.71
特定存款机构 Specific Depository Institutions	141.48	132.20	157.72	289.16
其他金融机构 Other Financial Institutions	8.04	5.66	3.90	5.53
非金融机构存款 Deposits by Non – financial Institutions	6053.91	6354.74	6519.59	6554.76
活期存款 Demand Deposits	40.50	42.60	50.77	51.62
储蓄存款 Savings Deposits	6013.41	6312.14	6468.82	6503.14
发行债券 Bonds Issue				
国外负债 Foreign Liabilities	483.01	494.90	484.61	484.23
政府存款 Deposits by Government	3549.59	3045.34	3115.47	3841.95
自有资金 Own Capital	355.21	355.21	355.21	355.21
其他负债 Other Liabilities	869.01	1166.87	1871.80	2248.34
总负债 Total Liabilities	**45311.03**	**45952.95**	**47048.17**	**47449.11**

货币当局资产负债表
Balance Sheet of Monetary Authority

（月末余额）

（Month－end Balance）

单位：亿元

Unit：100 Million Yuan

项 目 Items	2002.05	2002.06	2002.07	2002.08
国外资产 Foreign Assets	20157.77	20277.50	20555.93	20999.66
外汇 Foreign Exchange	19143.27	19252.50	19515.88	19956.49
货币黄金 Monetary Gold	256.00	256.00	256.00	256.00
其他国外资产 Other Foreign Assets	758.50	769.00	784.05	787.17
对政府债权 Claims on Government	2577.12	2537.50	2521.58	2521.58
其中：中央政府 Of Which：Central Government	2577.12	2537.50	2521.58	2521.58
对存款货币银行债权 Claims on Deposit Money Banks	9942.97	9802.61	9816.05	9713.37
对特定存款机构债权 Claims on Specific Depository Institutions	2479.93	2479.07	2477.99	2486.99
对其他金融机构债权 Claims on Other Financial Institutions	7215.17	7218.98	7175.12	7208.64
对非金融机构债权 Claims on Non－financial Institutions	216.98	212.80	206.73	206.69
其他资产 Other Assets	4178.16	4084.36	4373.68	4610.43
总资产 Total Assets	**46768.10**	**46612.82**	**47127.08**	**47747.36**
储备货币 Reserve Money	40319.88	40554.45	41187.19	41469.80
发行货币 Currency Issue	16447.98	16473.99	16568.95	16995.19
金融机构存款 Deposits by Financial Institutions	17273.39	17365.64	17821.23	17624.88
存款货币银行 Deposit Money Banks	17101.61	17209.82	17615.32	17438.42
特定存款机构 Specific Depository Institutions	167.11	151.49	202.34	121.41
其他金融机构 Other Financial Institutions	4.67	4.33	3.57	65.05
非金融机构存款 Deposits by Non－financial Institutions	6598.51	6714.82	6797.01	6849.73
活期存款 Demand Deposits	54.98	87.33	113.55	105.42
储蓄存款 Savings Deposits	6543.53	6627.49	6683.46	6744.31
发行债券 Bonds Issue				
国外负债 Foreign Liabilities	491.37	454.39	470.18	460.60
政府存款 Deposits by Government	4433.67	4369.49	4408.75	4799.54
自有资金 Own Capital	219.75	219.75	219.75	219.75
其他负债 Other Liabilities	1303.43	1014.74	841.21	797.67
总负债 Total Liabilities	**46768.10**	**46612.82**	**47127.08**	**47747.36**

货币当局资产负债表
Balance Sheet of Monetary Authority

（月末余额）

（Month－end Balance）

单位：亿元

Unit：100 Million Yuan

项　　目 Items	2002.09	2002.10	2002.11	2002.12
国外资产 Foreign Assets	21424.68	21903.11	22545.61	23242.85
外汇 Foreign Exchange	20381.73	20859.69	21501.03	22107.39
货币黄金 Monetary Gold	256.00	256.00	256.00	337.24
其他国外资产 Other Foreign Assets	786.95	787.42	788.58	798.22
对政府债权 Claims on Government	2569.64	2541.85	2541.85	2863.79
其中：中央政府 Of Which：Central Government	2569.64	2541.85	2541.85	2863.79
对存款货币银行债权 Claims on Deposit Money Banks	9763.24	9737.03	9609.25	9982.56
对特定存款机构债权 Claims on Specific Depository Institutions	2447.05	2448.22	2419.30	2305.08
对其他金融机构债权 Claims on Other Financial Institutions	7214.52	7231.65	7238.94	7240.27
对非金融机构债权 Claims on Non－financial Institutions	206.47	206.40	206.90	206.74
其他资产 Other Assets	4638.30	4556.06	4534.32	5266.29
总资产 Total Assets	**48263.90**	**48624.32**	**49096.17**	**51107.58**
储备货币 Reserve Money	39863.97	40106.24	40901.79	45138.18
发行货币 Currency Issue	17713.56	17313.69	17704.40	18589.10
金融机构存款 Deposits by Financial Institutions	15271.63	15819.27	16065.02	19138.35
存款货币银行 Deposit Money Banks	15120.53	15667.51	15874.54	18939.54
特定存款机构 Specific Depository Institutions	143.92	130.10	183.72	193.01
其他金融机构 Other Financial Institutions	7.18	21.66	6.76	5.80
非金融机构存款 Deposits by Non－financial Institutions	6878.78	6973.28	7132.37	7410.73
活期存款 Demand Deposits	84.27	84.19	87.68	41.64
储蓄存款 Savings Deposits	6794.51	6889.09	7044.69	7369.09
发行债券 Bonds Issue	1937.50	1937.50	1837.50	1487.50
国外负债 Foreign Liabilities	442.18	443.09	443.09	423.06
政府存款 Deposits by Government	5121.48	5245.99	5038.96	3085.43
自有资金 Own Capital	219.75	219.75	219.75	219.75
其他负债 Other Liabilities	679.02	671.75	655.08	753.66
总负债 Total Liabilities	**48263.90**	**48624.32**	**49096.17**	**51107.58**

货币当局资产负债表

Balance Sheet of Monetary Authority

（月末余额）

（Month－end Balance）

单位：亿元

Unit：100 Million Yuan

项目 Items	2003.01	2003.02	2003.03	2003.04
国外资产 Foreign Assets	24474.47	24714.34	25222.19	25786.06
外汇 Foreign Exchange	23323.69	23553.02	24062.32	24630.64
货币黄金 Monetary Gold	337.24	337.24	337.24	337.24
其他国外资产 Other Foreign Assets	813.54	824.08	822.63	818.18
对政府债权 Claims on Government	2863.79	2863.79	2863.79	3007.23
其中：中央政府 Of Which：Central Government	2863.79	2863.79	2863.79	3007.23
对存款货币银行债权 Claims on Deposit Money Banks	9882.95	9505.26	9548.71	9562.81
对特定存款机构债权 Claims on Specific Depository Institutions	2305.31	2330.66	2270.66	2041.44
对其他金融机构债权 Claims on Other Financial Institutions	7244.73	7250.91	7268.43	7280.47
对非金融机构债权 Claims on Non－financial Institutions	206.70	206.65	206.57	206.56
其他资产 Other Assets	5358.60	5307.23	5426.82	6810.05
总资产 Total Assets	**52336.55**	**52178.84**	**52807.17**	**54694.62**
储备货币 Reserve Money	46091.51	45032.69	44111.31	42952.48
发行货币 Currency Issue	23277.91	19400.72	18675.97	18837.43
金融机构存款 Deposits by Financial Institutions	15324.07	17829.89	17426.67	16042.04
存款货币银行 Deposit Money Banks	15196.46	17543.00	17171.32	15915.03
特定存款机构 Specific Depository Institutions	122.38	277.64	246.24	121.52
其他金融机构 Other Financial Institutions	5.23	9.25	9.11	5.49
非金融机构存款 Deposits by Non－financial Institutions	7489.53	7802.08	8008.67	8073.01
活期存款 Demand Deposits	54.62	54.48	46.60	64.38
储蓄存款 Savings Deposits	7434.91	7747.60	7962.07	8008.63
发行债券 Bonds Issue	950.00	950.00	450.00	598.92
国外负债 Foreign Liabilities	433.83	451.54	433.47	436.82
政府存款 Deposits by Government	3736.57	4005.79	4494.01	5581.38
自有资金 Own Capital	219.75	219.75	219.75	219.75
其他负债 Other Liabilities	904.89	1519.07	3098.63	4905.27
总负债 Total Liabilities	**52336.55**	**52178.84**	**52807.17**	**54694.62**

货币当局资产负债表

Balance Sheet of Monetary Authority

（月末余额）

（Month – end Balance）

单位：亿元

Unit: 100 Million Yuan

项 目 Items	2003.05	2003.06	2003.07	2003.08
国外资产 Foreign Assets	26484.27	27151.36	27946.72	28904.92
外汇 Foreign Exchange	25310.95	25983.47	26781.67	27647.50
货币黄金 Monetary Gold	337.24	337.24	337.24	337.24
其他国外资产 Other Foreign Assets	836.08	830.65	827.81	920.18
对政府债权 Claims on Government	3007.23	3007.23	3007.24	3007.24
其中：中央政府 Of Which: Central Government	3007.23	3007.23	3007.24	3007.24
对存款货币银行债权 Claims on Deposit Money Banks	9605.26	9626.68	9621.16	10430.09
对特定存款机构债权 Claims on Specific Depository Institutions	1939.29	1773.03	1769.72	1791.31
对其他金融机构债权 Claims on Other Financial Institutions	7280.29	7283.76	7282.91	7283.85
对非金融机构债权 Claims on Non – financial Institutions	206.51	206.49	206.38	206.38
其他资产 Other Assets	5220.98	5242.11	5250.28	5119.66
总资产 Total Assets	**53743.83**	**54290.66**	**55084.41**	**56743.45**
储备货币 Reserve Money	42408.50	43205.96	43800.89	44682.09
发行货币 Currency Issue	18474.69	18485.14	18695.96	19108.53
金融机构存款 Deposits by Financial Institutions	15728.14	16323.71	16519.48	16801.48
存款货币银行 Deposit Money Banks	15573.11	16143.93	16314.93	16531.57
特定存款机构 Specific Depository Institutions	149 86	176.75	201.78	248.46
其他金融机构 Other Financial Institutions	5.17	3.03	2.77	21.45
非金融机构存款 Deposits by Non – financial Institutions	8205.67	8397.11	8585.45	8772.08
活期存款 Demand Deposits	78.84	104.94	121.41	141.37
储蓄存款 Savings Deposits	8126.83	8292.17	8464.04	8630.71
发行债券 Bonds Issue	1389.95	2379.70	3019.09	4103.56
国外负债 Foreign Liabilities	443.13	440.21	440.21	451.99
政府存款 Deposits by Government	6261.34	5802.93	5882.45	6048.14
自有资金 Own Capital	219.75	219.75	219.75	219.75
其他负债 Other Liabilities	3021.16	2242.11	1722.02	1237.92
总负债 Total Liabilities	**53743.83**	**54290.66**	**55084.41**	**56743.45**

货币当局资产负债表
Balance Sheet of Monetary Authority

（月末余额）

（Month－end Balance）

单位：亿元

Unit：100 Million Yuan

项　目 Items	2003.09	2003.10	2003.11	2003.12
国外资产 Foreign Assets	29944.86	31249.25	32576.25	31141.85
外汇 Foreign Exchange	28670.20	29982.19	31292.14	29841.80
货币黄金 Monetary Gold	337.24	337.24	337.24	337.24
其他国外资产 Other Foreign Assets	937.42	929.82	946.87	962.81
对政府债权 Claims on Government	3058.59	2926.11	2926.11	2901.02
其中：中央政府 Of Which：Central Government	3058.59	2926.11	2926.11	2901.02
对存款货币银行债权 Claims on Deposit Money Banks	10685.69	10737.08	10163.67	10619.47
对特定存款机构债权 Claims on Specific Depository Institutions	1664.29	1774.20	1664.39	1363.34
对其他金融机构债权 Claims on Other Financial Institutions	7284.11	7284.02	7283.73	7255.95
对非金融机构债权 Claims on Non－financial Institutions	206.38	206.29	206.29	206.25
其他资产 Other Assets	5104.64	5228.19	5148.80	8516.18
总资产 Total Assets	**57948.56**	**59405.14**	**59969.24**	**62004.06**
储备货币 Reserve Money	46730.40	48099.13	48670.68	52841.36
发行货币 Currency Issue	19987.97	19722.90	20006.63	21240.48
金融机构存款 Deposits by Financial Institutions	17944.84	19552.77	19694.99	22558.04
存款货币银行 Deposit Money Banks	17767.23	19113.22	19356.22	22274.41
特定存款机构 Specific Depository Institutions	173.93	230.88	337.26	280.31
其他金融机构 Other Financial Institutions	3.68	208.67	1.51	3.32
非金融机构存款 Deposits by Non－financial Institutions	8797.59	8823.46	8969.06	9042.84
活期存款 Demand Deposits	105.42	99.88	145.82	58.41
储蓄存款 Savings Deposits	8692.17	8723.58	8823.24	8984.43
发行债券 Bonds Issue	4398.16	3950.08	3758.06	3031.55
国外负债 Foreign Liabilities	450.25	471.10	457.58	482.58
政府存款 Deposits by Government	5996.02	6371.37	6601.61	4954.71
自有资金 Own Capital	219.75	219.75	219.75	219.75
其他负债 Other Liabilities	153.98	293.71	261.56	474.11
总负债 Total Liabilities	**57948.56**	**59405.14**	**59969.24**	**62004.06**

货币当局资产负债表
Balance Sheet of Monetary Authority

（月末余额）

（Month－end Balance）

单位：亿元

Unit：100 Million Yuan

项　目 Items	2004.01	2004.02	2004.03	2004.04
国外资产 Foreign Assets	32188.60	32973.48	33981.27	34894.69
外汇 Foreign Exchange	30977.22	31750.47	32758.19	33677.72
货币黄金 Monetary Gold	337.24	337.24	337.24	337.24
其他国外资产 Other Foreign Assets	874.14	885.77	885.84	879.73
对政府债权 Claims on Government	3023.11	3007.02	3007.02	3007.02
其中：中央政府 Of Which：Central Government	3023.11	3007.02	3007.02	3007.02
对存款货币银行债权 Claims on Deposit Money Banks	11088.67	10217.69	10071.60	9924.24
对特定存款机构债权 Claims on Specific Depository Institutions	1372.34	1342.30	1298.48	1306.93
对其他金融机构债权 Claims on Other Financial Institutions	7272.19	7276.60	7266.65	7265.38
对非金融机构债权 Claims on Non－financial Institutions	186.93	206.23	206.22	205.81
其他资产 Other Assets	9001.05	8620.06	8739.87	10037.20
总资产 Total Assets	**64132.89**	**63643.38**	**64571.11**	**66641.27**
储备货币 Reserve Money	53304.76	51691.66	50461.59	50921.75
发行货币 Currency Issue	24890.39	21622.30	20981.83	21538.14
金融机构存款 Deposits by Financial Institutions	28348.97	30003.45	29417.73	29309.70
存款货币银行 Deposit Money Banks	28195.63	29832.32	29234.66	28836.62
特定存款机构 Specific Depository Institutions	150.15	169.03	181.09	204.13
其他金融机构 Other Financial Institutions	3.19	2.10	1.98	268.95
非金融机构存款 Deposits by Non－financial Institutions	65.40	65.91	62.03	73.91
活期存款 Demand Deposits	65.40	65.91	62.03	73.91
储蓄存款 Savings Deposits				
发行债券 Bonds Issue	3250.07	4175.01	5957.08	6098.74
国外负债 Foreign Liabilities	482.58	493.16	517.67	518.65
政府存款 Deposits by Government	5332.91	5808.15	6423.33	6780.09
自有资金 Own Capital	219.75	219.75	219.75	219.75
其他负债 Other Liabilities	1542.82	1255.65	991.69	2102.29
总负债 Total Liabilities	**64132.89**	**63643.38**	**64571.11**	**66641.27**

货币当局资产负债表
Balance Sheet of Monetary Authority

（月末余额）

（Month - end Balance）

单位：亿元

Unit：100 Million Yuan

项目 Items	2004.05	2004.06	2004.07	2004.08
国外资产 Foreign Assets	35375.84	36419.14	37325.20	38254.98
外汇 Foreign Exchange	34160.36	35198.36	36107.17	37038.25
货币黄金 Monetary Gold	337.24	337.24	337.24	337.24
其他国外资产 Other Foreign Assets	878.24	883.54	880.79	879.49
对政府债权 Claims on Government	3007.02	3007.02	3007.02	3023.11
其中：中央政府 Of Which：Central Government	3007.02	3007.02	3007.02	3023.11
对存款货币银行债权 Claims on Deposit Money Banks	9743.53	9814.24	9803.02	9644.14
对特定存款机构债权 Claims on Specific Depository Institutions	1311.31	1319.36	1338.78	1263.64
对其他金融机构债权 Claims on Other Financial Institutions	7286.20	8891.03	8890.46	8890.14
对非金融机构债权 Claims on Non - financial Institutions	205.79	149.07	148.90	148.87
其他资产 Other Assets	8676.33	9265.16	9189.03	9172.78
总资产 Total Assets	**65606.02**	**68865.02**	**69702.41**	**70397.66**
储备货币 Reserve Money	49894.06	51305.77	50502.95	51583.20
发行货币 Currency Issue	20665.96	20695.17	20978.85	21216.64
金融机构存款 Deposits by Financial Institutions	29153.01	30531.87	29394.44	30209.19
存款货币银行 Deposit Money Banks	28888.56	30270.01	29091.42	29926.00
特定存款机构 Specific Depository Institutions	259.40	257.32	297.77	266.14
其他金融机构 Other Financial Institutions	5.05	4.54	5.25	17.05
非金融机构存款 Deposits by Non - financial Institutions	75.09	78.73	129.66	157.37
活期存款 Demand Deposits	75.09	78.73	129.66	157.37
储蓄存款 Savings Deposits				
发行债券 Bonds Issue	6159.70	7476.11	7636.76	7210.94
国外负债 Foreign Liabilities	518.65	524.91	525.13	520.88
政府存款 Deposits by Government	7345.59	7755.59	9050.32	9496.03
自有资金 Own Capital	219.75	219.75	219.75	219.75
其他负债 Other Liabilities	1468.27	1582.89	1767.50	1366.86
总负债 Total Liabilities	**65606.02**	**68865.02**	**69702.41**	**70397.66**

货币当局资产负债表
Balance Sheet of Monetary Authority

（月末余额）

（Month – end Balance）

单位：亿元

Unit: 100 Million Yuan

项目 Items	2004.09	2004.10	2004.11	2004.12
国外资产 Foreign Assets	39453.51	41239.99	44740.75	46960.13
外汇 Foreign Exchange	38237.41	40010.86	43490.01	45939.99
货币黄金 Monetary Gold	337.24	337.24	337.24	337.24
其他国外资产 Other Foreign Assets	878.86	891.89	913.50	682.90
对政府债权 Claims on Government	3007.02	2975.74	2969.62	2969.62
其中：中央政府 Of Which: Central Government	3007.02	2975.74	2969.62	2969.62
对存款货币银行债权 Claims on Deposit Money Banks	9639.99	9691.60	9621.40	9376.35
对特定存款机构债权 Claims on Specific Depository Institutions	1216.02	1217.16	1157.74	1047.85
对其他金融机构债权 Claims on Other Financial Institutions	8889.51	8889.71	8870.56	8865.09
对非金融机构债权 Claims on Non – financial Institutions	138.28	136.27	136.27	136.25
其他资产 Other Assets	9290.77	9268.41	9089.92	9300.04
总资产 Total Assets	**71635.10**	**73418.88**	**76586.26**	**78655.33**
储备货币 Reserve Money	53150.02	52667.34	53981.71	58856.11
发行货币 Currency Issue	22548.08	21841.88	21946.69	23104.00
金融机构存款 Deposits by Financial Institutions	30445.19	30692.66	31849.79	35672.79
存款货币银行 Deposit Money Banks	30025.87	30194.17	31533.85	35216.51
特定存款机构 Specific Depository Institutions	415.84	482.63	308.77	416.67
其他金融机构 Other Financial Institutions	3.48	15.86	7.17	39.61
非金融机构存款 Deposits by Non – financial Institutions	156.75	132.80	185.23	79.32
活期存款 Demand Deposits	156.75	132.80	185.23	79.32
储蓄存款 Savings Deposits				
发行债券 Bonds Issue	7662.62	9010.16	9551.03	11079.01
国外负债 Foreign Liabilities	525.70	525.53	546.52	562.28
政府存款 Deposits by Government	8973.23	9902.89	9862.24	5832.22
自有资金 Own Capital	219.75	219.75	219.75	219.75
其他负债 Other Liabilities	1103.78	1093.21	2425.01	2105.96
总负债 Total Liabilities	**71635.10**	**73418.88**	**76586.26**	**78655.33**

货币当局资产负债表
Balance Sheet of Monetary Authority

（月末余额）

（Month – end Balance）

单位：亿元

Unit：100 Million Yuan

项 目 Items	2005.01	2005.02	2005.03	2005.04
国外资产 Foreign Assets	48760.67	49932.23	51432.24	52113.42
外汇 Foreign Exchange	47486.88	48653.85	50163.35	50836.94
货币黄金 Monetary Gold	337.24	337.24	337.24	337.24
其他国外资产 Other Foreign Assets	936.55	941.14	931.65	939.24
对政府债权 Claims on Government	2969.62	2969.62	2969.62	2969.62
其中：中央政府 Of Which：Central Government	2969.62	2969.62	2969.62	2969.62
对存款货币银行债权 Claims on Deposit Money Banks	9351.18	9413.09	9092.62	8901.96
对特定存款机构债权 Claims on Specific Depository Institutions	1052.85	1053.40	994.75	934.40
对其他金融机构债权 Claims on Other Financial Institutions	8829.27	8841.66	8846.70	8850.09
对非金融机构债权 Claims on Non – financial Institutions	136.25	136.25	136.24	136.24
其他资产 Other Assets	9351.10	9321.64	9576.94	10800.35
总资产 Total Assets	**80450.94**	**81667.89**	**83049.11**	**84706.08**
储备货币 Reserve Money	58846.68	58845.59	57588.32	56219.53
发行货币 Currency Issue	26056.84	24914.68	23135.22	23502.86
金融机构存款 Deposits by Financial Institutions	32692.17	33821.61	34315.55	32593.34
存款货币银行 Deposit Money Banks	32374.53	33584.34	33975.62	32384.30
特定存款机构 Specific Depository Institutions	314.12	233.64	335.57	204.96
其他金融机构 Other Financial Institutions	3.52	3.63	4.36	4.08
非金融机构存款 Deposits by Non – financial Institutions	97.67	109.30	137.55	123.33
活期存款 Demand Deposits	97.67	109.30	137.55	123.33
储蓄存款 Savings Deposits				
发行债券 Bonds Issue	11541.63	12552.19	14733.37	16680.33
国外负债 Foreign Liabilities	598.01	598.01	617.37	623.06
政府存款 Deposits by Government	6955.21	7234.95	7728.56	8897.41
自有资金 Own Capital	219.75	219.75	219.75	219.75
其他负债 Other Liabilities	2289.66	2217.40	2161.74	2066.00
总负债 Total Liabilities	**80450.94**	**81667.89**	**83049.11**	**84706.08**

货币当局资产负债表
Balance Sheet of Monetary Authority
（月末余额）
（Month－end Balance）

单位：亿元
Unit：100 Million Yuan

项目 Items	2005.05	2005.06	2005.07	2005.08
国外资产 Foreign Assets	54240.69	55963.65	57604.51	58855.96
外汇 Foreign Exchange	52980.22	54698.13	56346.60	57636.78
货币黄金 Monetary Gold	337.24	337.24	337.24	337.24
其他国外资产 Other Foreign Assets	923.23	928.28	920.67	881.94
对政府债权 Claims on Government	2931.82	2929.71	2929.71	2929.71
其中：中央政府 Of Which：Central Government	2931.82	2929.71	2929.71	2929.71
对存款货币银行债权 Claims on Deposit Money Banks	8958.47	8630.45	8522.70	8105.11
对特定存款机构债权 Claims on Specific Depository Institutions	874.40	850.95	952.12	1751.17
对其他金融机构债权 Claims on Other Financial Institutions	8786.06	13370.94	14184.70	14101.62
对非金融机构债权 Claims on Non－financial Institutions	136.09	95.18	95.10	94.80
其他资产 Other Assets	10761.56	10725.96	10766.01	10805.11
总资产 Total Assets	**86689.09**	**92566.84**	**95054.85**	**96643.48**
储备货币 Reserve Money	56589.97	57360.22	58271.07	58782.17
发行货币 Currency Issue	22551.14	22641.25	22943.44	23219.90
金融机构存款 Deposits by Financial Institutions	33905.08	34575.43	35163.59	35379.12
存款货币银行 Deposit Money Banks	33658.28	34248.17	34903.67	35105.24
特定存款机构 Specific Depository Institutions	242.90	324.53	249.88	256.00
其他金融机构 Other Financial Institutions	3.90	2.73	10.04	17.88
非金融机构存款 Deposits by Non－financial Institutions	133.75	143.54	164.04	183.15
活期存款 Demand Deposits	133.75	143.54	164.04	183.15
储蓄存款 Savings Deposits				
发行债券 Bonds Issue	17267.91	16341.59	16187.10	16519.27
国外负债 Foreign Liabilities	611.17	622.30	624.30	641.66
政府存款 Deposits by Government	9885.39	9673.81	10509.90	10665.78
自有资金 Own Capital	219.75	219.75	219.75	219.75
其他负债 Other Liabilities	2114.90	8349.17	9242.73	9814.85
总负债 Total Liabilities	**86689.09**	**92566.84**	**95054.85**	**96643.48**

货币当局资产负债表

Balance Sheet of Monetary Authority

（月末余额）

（Month – end Balance）

单位：亿元

Unit：100 Million Yuan

项　　目 Items	2005.09	2005.10	2005.11	2005.12
国外资产 Foreign Assets	60121.43	61195.73	62137.35	63339.16
外汇 Foreign Exchange	58904.42	59979.12	60923.43	62139.96
货币黄金 Monetary Gold	337.24	337.24	337.24	337.24
其他国外资产 Other Foreign Assets	879.77	879.37	876.68	861.96
对政府债权 Claims on Government	2929.71	2892.43	2892.43	2892.43
其中：中央政府 Of Which：Central Government	2929.71	2892.43	2892.43	2892.43
对存款货币银行债权 Claims on Deposit Money Banks	8031.89	7969.97	7877.03	7817.72
对特定存款机构债权 Claims on Specific Depository Institutions	3131.43	3703.85	4212.28	4874.29
对其他金融机构债权 Claims on Other Financial Institutions	13331.94	13332.46	13332.37	13226.11
对非金融机构债权 Claims on Non – financial Institutions	94.80	94.80	94.75	66.73
其他资产 Other Assets	11203.32	11241.32	11249.29	11459.57
总资产 Total Assets	**98844.52**	**100430.56**	**101795.50**	**103676.01**
储备货币 Reserve Money	60771.21	59840.99	59136.68	64343.13
发行货币 Currency Issue	24368.87	23803.15	24245.95	25853.97
金融机构存款 Deposits by Financial Institutions	36209.05	35841.13	34638.49	38391.25
存款货币银行 Deposit Money Banks	35877.99	35602.13	34256.25	37929.33
特定存款机构 Specific Depository Institutions	328.36	234.61	373.13	453.18
其他金融机构 Other Financial Institutions	2.70	4.39	9.11	8.74
非金融机构存款 Deposits by Non – financial Institutions	193.29	196.71	252.24	97.91
活期存款 Demand Deposits	193.29	196.71	252.24	97.91
储蓄存款 Savings Deposits				
发行债券 Bonds Issue	16414.40	18094.50	20326.14	20296.00
国外负债 Foreign Liabilities	641.63	641.61	641.60	641.57
政府存款 Deposits by Government	9875.09	10938.02	10778.22	7527.23
自有资金 Own Capital	219.75	219.75	219.75	219.75
其他负债 Other Liabilities	10922.44	10695.69	10693.11	10648.33
总负债 Total Liabilities	**98844.52**	**100430.56**	**101795.50**	**103676.01**

2. 存款货币银行资产负债表
Balance Sheet of Deposit Money Banks

存款货币银行资产负债表
Balance Sheet of Deposit Money Banks

（季末余额）

（Quarter – end Balance）

单位：亿元

Unit：100 Million Yuan

项　目 Items	1993.03	1993.06	1993.09	1993.12
国外资产 Foreign Assets	2654.4	2537.6	2624.0	2948.9
储备资产 Reserve Assets	3876.1	3811.3	4397.7	5832.1
准备金 Reserves	2499.9	2583.9	2619.6	2887.7
在人行存款 Deposits with the Central Bank	1066.8	862.4	1414.6	2406.7
库存现金 Cash in Vault	309.4	365.0	363.5	537.7
中央银行债券 Central Bank Bonds				
对政府债权 Claims on Government	43.0	59.8	65.2	74.5
对其他部门债权 Claims on Other Sectors	25532.1	26607.7	27726.0	30892.8
对非货币金融机构债权 Claims on Non – monetary Financial Institutions				
对非金融部门负债 Liabilities to Non – financial Sectors	22416.8	23451.3	23984.9	26087.7
活期存款 Demand Deposits	8841.3	9246.0	8704.9	9692.9
定期存款 Time Deposits	1105.1	1104.8	1129.0	1247.9
储蓄存款 Savings Deposits	12020.7	12587.9	13673.2	14582.9
其他存款 Other Deposits	449.7	512.6	477.8	564.0
对中央银行负债 Liabilities to the Central Bank	6692.7	6856.3	7798.4	9680.3
对非货币金融机构负债 Liabilities to Non – monetary Financial Institutions				
国外负债 Foreign Liabilities	1824.2	1909.4	2014.0	2275.2
债券 Bonds	286.2	243.4	235.9	228.6
所有者权益 Owner's Equity	2028.4	2076.3	2315.5	2377.3
其中：实收资本 Of Which：Paid – in Capital	2028.4	2076.3	2315.5	2377.3
其他（净） Other Items（Net）	– 1142.7	– 1520.3	– 1535.8	– 900.8

存款货币银行资产负债表
Balance Sheet of Deposit Money Banks

（季末余额）

（Quarter - end Balance）

单位：亿元

Unit：100 Million Yuan

项 目 Items	1994.03	1994.06	1994.09	1994.12
国外资产 Foreign Assets	4306.9	3998.8	4018.5	4401.5
储备资产 Reserve Assets	5723.2	6311.7	6455.2	7518.4
准备金 Reserves	3069.4	3389.5	3667.0	3941.0
在人行存款 Deposits with the Central Bank	2179.7	2445.1	2277.6	2981.8
库存现金 Cash in Vault	474.1	477.1	510.6	595.6
中央银行债券 Central Bank Bonds	45.1	35.6	60.7	82.7
对政府债权 Claims on Government	309.0	420.1	466.2	460.1
对其他部门债权 Claims on Other Sectors	32164.9	34134.5	36050.8	38640.0
对非货币金融机构债权 Claims on Non - monetary Financial Institutions	540.3	555.3	597.3	645.0
对非金融部门负债 Liabilities to Non - financial Sectors	28235.2	31030.7	33475.1	35674.0
活期存款 Demand Deposits	9940.4	11203.0	11833.7	12389.9
定期存款 Time Deposits	1278.6	1604.7	1787.6	1943.1
储蓄存款 Savings Deposits	16449.9	17561.4	19097.0	20516.0
其他存款 Other Deposits	566.3	661.6	756.8	825.0
对中央银行负债 Liabilities to the Central Bank	9132.7	9407.5	9597.8	10316.5
对非货币金融机构负债 Liabilities to Non - monetary Financial Institutions	230.7	244.3	246.3	353.9
国外负债 Foreign Liabilities	3178.3	3476.2	3578.3	3788.8
债券 Bonds	231.3	216.0	217.2	195.7
所有者权益 Owner's Equity	2667.8	2735.8	2780.7	2919.0
其中：实收资本 Of Which：Paid - in Capital	2616.8	2620.2	2620.3	2835.4
其他（净） Other Items（Net）	- 586.6	- 1654.5	- 2246.7	- 1500.2

存款货币银行资产负债表
Balance Sheet of Deposit Money Banks

（季末余额）

（Quarter－end Balance）

单位：亿元

Unit：100 Million Yuan

项　目 Items	1995.03	1995.06	1995.09	1995.12
国外资产 Foreign Assets	3992.7	3731.7	3559.3	3899.6
储备资产 Reserve Assets	7807.5	7625.8	8547.8	9898.5
准备金 Reserves	4226.8	4524.1	4896.7	5249.8
在人行存款 Deposits with the Central Bank	3025.6	2510.1	3059.3	3959.5
库存现金 Cash in Vault	555.1	591.6	591.8	689.2
中央银行债券 Central Bank Bonds	23.3	22.6	24.0	197.1
对政府债权 Claims on Government	615.3	683.8	656.9	1041.4
对其他部门债权 Claims on Other Sectors	40067.4	41649.5	43789.1	48086.0
对非货币金融机构债权 Claims on Non－monetary Financial Institutions	691.2	737.9	750.8	776.1
对非金融部门负债 Liabilities to Non－financial Sectors	38766.5	41611.8	44626.2	47849.8
活期存款 Demand Deposits	12967.80	13630.20	14291.70	15201.60
定期存款 Time Deposits	2202.6	2645.9	3095.8	3324.2
储蓄存款 Savings Deposits	22614.3	24286.4	26154.4	28045.5
其他存款 Other Deposits	981.8	1049.3	1084.3	1278.5
对中央银行负债 Liabilities to the Central Bank	10145.7	9893.9	10203.1	11173.9
对非货币金融机构负债 Liabilities to Non－monetary Financial Institutions	281.3	303.9	334.7	437.0
国外负债 Foreign Liabilities	3909.8	4021.4	4163.5	4199.3
债券 Bonds	215.0	192.8	216.0	170.1
所有者权益 Owner's Equity	2665.2	2743.0	2794.0	2970.4
其中：实收资本 Of Which：Paid－in Capital	2473.4	2496.4	2541.3	2611.2
其他（净） Other Items（Net）	－2786.1	－4315.5	－5009.6	－2901.8

存款货币银行资产负债表
Balance Sheet of Deposit Money Banks

（季末余额）

（Quarter – end Balance）

单位：亿元

Unit：100 Million Yuan

项目 Items	1996.03	1996.06	1996.09	1996.12
国外资产 Foreign Assets	4055.9	3778.0	4214.8	4199.9
储备资产 Reserve Assets	10017.1	10377.9	10528.4	13694.9
准备金 Reserves	5619.7	6078.9	6485.8	6545.6
在人行存款 Deposits with the Central Bank	3721.8	3621.3	3316.3	6516.5
库存现金 Cash in Vault	675.6	677.7	726.3	632.8
中央银行债券 Central Bank Bonds				
对政府债权 Claims on Government	1479.7	1665.2	1828.8	1804.3
对其他部门债权 Claims on Other Sectors	49432.5	52892.0	54435.3	58231.6
对非货币金融机构债权 Claims on Non – monetary Financial Institutions	633.1	701.3	737.2	775.7
对非金融部门负债 Liabilities to Non – financial Sectors	51472.2	55388.6	58233.6	61715.7
活期存款 Demand Deposits	14949.5	16164.2	17030.9	18764.9
定期存款 Time Deposits	3724.8	4300.8	4674.5	5041.9
储蓄存款 Savings Deposits	31486.5	33528.2	35074.4	36373.4
其他存款 Other Deposits	1311.4	1395.4	1453.8	1535.5
对中央银行负债 Liabilities to the Central Bank	11160.6	10706.0	10918.5	14210.1
对非货币金融机构负债 Liabilities to Non – monetary Financial Institutions	367.3	410.0	403.0	579.4
国外负债 Foreign Liabilities	4095.0	4180.8	4236.3	4239.7
债券 Bonds	174.5	173.4	152.4	288.1
所有者权益 Owner's Equity	2873.1	3012.6	3251.0	3297.8
其中：实收资本 Of Which：Paid – in Capital	2661.7	2695.6	2714.6	2856.0
其他（净） Other Items（Net）	–4524.4	–4457.0	–5450.3	–5624.4

存款货币银行资产负债表
Balance Sheet of Deposit Money Banks

（季末余额）

（Quarter－end Balance）

单位：亿元

Unit：100 Million Yuan

项 目 Items	1997.03	1997.06	1997.09	1997.12
国外资产 Foreign Assets	4641.9	4531.3	4902.4	5249.0
储备资产 Reserve Assets	13613.9	14494.3	15039.7	16274.8
准备金 Reserves	7984.6	8393.0	8822.4	9143.3
在人行存款 Deposits with the Central Bank	4770.5	5263.8	5371.9	6328.0
库存现金 Cash in Vault	858.8	837.5	845.4	803.5
中央银行债券 Central Bank Bonds	60.3	84.7	92.9	97.7
对政府债权 Claims on Government	1563.3	1383.4	1402.3	1495.7
对其他部门债权 Claims on Other Sectors	62357.3	64322.5	66889.1	70691.0
对非货币金融机构债权 Claims on Non－monetary Financial Institutions	1882.1	1858.0	1995.5	2224.0
对非金融部门负债 Liabilities to Non－financial Sectors	65698.4	68756.5	71350.5	75309.9
活期存款 Demand Deposits	19682.7	21216.2	22119.0	23810.3
定期存款 Time Deposits	5692.2	6056.3	6498.1	6438.5
储蓄存款 Savings Deposits	39305.1	40456.8	41698.8	43635.2
其他存款 Other Deposits	1018.4	1027.2	1034.6	1425.9
对中央银行负债 Liabilities to the Central Bank	13338.9	12955.3	13246.9	14002.9
对非货币金融机构负债 Liabilities to Non－monetary Financial Institutions	899.0	1365.2	1564.2	1501.0
国外负债 Foreign Liabilities	4106.0	4146.2	4172.7	4258.1
债券 Bonds	168.3	181.8	276.9	286.5
所有者权益 Owner's Equity	3059.6	3171.8	3211.2	3311.4
其中：实收资本 Of Which：Paid－in Capital	3163.9	3371.8	3397.2	3406.1
其他（净） Other Items（Net）	－3151.4	－3902.6	－3500.5	－2637.6

存款货币银行资产负债表
Balance Sheet of Deposit Money Banks

（季末余额）

（Quarter – end Balance）

单位：亿元

Unit：100 Million Yuan

项目 Items	1998.03	1998.06	1998.09	1998.12
国外资产 Foreign Assets	5660.9	5742.2	5958.8	5962.9
储备资产 Reserve Assets	13639.2	16176.6	12988.0	15005.8
准备金 Reserves	7900.6	15345.2	12172.1	14145.8
在人行存款 Deposits with the Central Bank	4881.7			
库存现金 Cash in Vault	856.9	831.4	815.9	860.0
中央银行债券 Central Bank Bonds	96.6	114.5	109.7	58.7
对政府债权 Claims on Government	1418.9	1667.7	4575.7	4969.9
对其他部门债权 Claims on Other Sectors	71428.4	73915.6	78082.4	81493.2
对非货币金融机构债权 Claims on Non – monetary Financial Institutions	2254.5	2509.4	2628.2	2874.1
对非金融部门负债 Liabilities to Non – financial Sectors	76235.3	78877.0	82909.6	86627.8
活期存款 Demand Deposits	22210.9	23219.9	24931.5	26485.7
定期存款 Time Deposits	6764.2	7348.1	7975.5	8301.9
储蓄存款 Savings Deposits	45772.9	46947.0	48512.3	50205.7
其他存款 Other Deposits	1487.3	1362.0	1490.3	1634.5
对中央银行负债 Liabilities to the Central Bank	13695.5	13227.0	10800.6	12032.5
对非货币金融机构负债 Liabilities to Non – monetary Financial Institutions	762.1	1279.9	1207.7	1133.9
国外负债 Foreign Liabilities	4158.8	4046.9	3856.4	3952.7
债券 Bonds	294.2	388.3	491.2	500.5
所有者权益 Owner's Equity	2984.1	2941.3	5347.7	5471.1
其中：实收资本 Of Which：Paid – in Capital	3426.6	3391.6	6156.8	6205.7
其他（净） Other Items（Net）	– 3631.5	– 634.4	– 270.4	646.1

存款货币银行资产负债表
Balance Sheet of Deposit Money Banks

（季末余额）

（Quarter – end Balance）

单位：亿元

Unit：100 Million Yuan

项目 Items	1999.03	1999.06	1999.09	1999.12
国外资产 Foreign Assets	5516.2	5140.0	5997.9	6419.9
储备资产 Reserve Assets	13544.5	13508.8	13193.2	15919.1
准备金 Reserves	12635.1	12602.3	12046.7	14304.8
库存现金 Cash in Vault	909.4	906.5	1146.5	1614.3
中央银行债券 Central Bank Bonds	53.5	50.9	51.9	46.5
对政府债权 Claims on Government	5036.5	5210.9	5601.0	6061.7
对其他部门债权 Claims on Other Sectors	82622.9	85312.1	88079.3	91160.2
对非货币金融机构债权 Claims on Non – monetary Financial Institutions	2975.6	2991.1	3212.1	3656.8
对非金融部门负债 Liabilities to Non – financial Sectors	90217.9	93351.1	95423.4	100340.3
活期存款 Demand Deposits	25510.2	26623.0	28131.2	32356.2
定期存款 Time Deposits	8641.9	9175.5	9281.9	9476.8
储蓄存款 Savings Deposits	54314.4	55551.5	55679.0	55805.1
其他存款 Other Deposits	1751.4	2001.1	2331.3	2702.2
对中央银行负债 Liabilities to the Central Bank	11553.9	11637.0	11577.0	12013.7
对非货币金融机构负债 Liabilities to Non – monetary Financial Institutions	784.4	914.2	1465.0	1640.9
国外负债 Foreign Liabilities	3889.6	3849.5	3760.7	3392.2
债券 Bonds	490.6	484.9	470.8	482.4
实收资本 Paid – in Capital	6189.8	6188.7	6211.3	6225.8
其他（净） Other Items（Net）	– 3377.0	– 4211.6	– 2772.8	– 831.1

存款货币银行资产负债表
Balance Sheet of Deposit Money Banks

（季末余额）

（Quarter - end Balance）

单位：亿元

Unit：100 Million Yuan

项目 Items	2000.03	2000.06	2000.09	2000.12
国外资产 Foreign Assets	7022.4	7560.8	8336.9	8976.8
储备资产 Reserve Assets	13887.2	13469.6	14034.7	16082.2
准备金 Reserves	12833.5	12405.1	12802.4	14796.5
库存现金 Cash in Vault	1053.7	1064.5	1232.3	1285.7
中央银行债券 Central Bank Bonds	9.1	6.2	7.7	7.7
对政府债权 Claims on Government	6109.7	6483.7	6691.2	7380.1
对其他部门债权 Claims on Other Sectors	93405.8	92792.7	96610.2	101815.6
对非货币金融机构债权 Claims on Non - monetary Financial Institutions	3615.5	5369.1	4866.7	4813.9
对非金融部门负债 Liabilities to Non - financial Sectors	102972.5	107179.1	110056.3	113231.2
活期存款 Demand Deposits	31903.7	34999.2	36705.2	38468.8
定期存款 Time Deposits	9877.9	10547.0	11149.2	11261.1
储蓄存款 Savings Deposits	58320.0	58559.9	58858.6	59754.4
其他存款 Other Deposits	2870.9	3073.0	3343.3	3746.9
对中央银行负债 Liabilities to the Central Bank	11502.0	9266.3	8752.7	8938.6
对非货币金融机构负债 Liabilities to Non - monetary Financial Institutions	1424.9	1538.4	1547.9	1375.4
国外负债 Foreign Liabilities	3231.7	3182.9	3068.0	3642.3
债券 Bonds	486.7	477.2	472.4	478.4
实收资本 Paid - in Capital	6241.0	6227.3	6250.5	6325.5
其他（净） Other Items（Net）	- 1809.1	- 2189.1	399.6	5084.9

存款货币银行资产负债表
Balance Sheet of Deposit Money Banks
（季末余额）
（Quarter - end Balance）

单位：亿元
Unit: 100 Million Yuan

项目 Items	2001.03	2001.06	2001.09	2001.12
国外资产 Foreign Assets	10105.2	9760.4	9354.1	9752.6
储备资产 Reserve Assets	14548.0	14372.2	14656.1	18065.2
准备金 Reserves	13333.0	13143.5	13297.2	16885.3
库存现金 Cash in Vault	1215.0	1228.7	1358.9	1179.9
中央银行债券 Central Bank Bonds	5.3	6.8	6.8	5.7
对政府债权 Claims on Government	9530.5	10085.2	10526.4	11007.0
对其他部门债权 Claims on Other Sectors	94824.3	98891.6	100918.6	103957.1
对非货币金融机构债权 Claims on Non - monetary Financial Institutions	7413.8	7400.1	5523.6	5912.1
对非金融部门负债 Liabilities to Non - financial Sectors	117459.9	122612.1	125800.4	131245.3
活期存款 Demand Deposits	38656.5	41231.0	41723.0	44140.1
定期存款 Time Deposits	11962.2	12614.2	13567.3	14180.1
储蓄存款 Savings Deposits	63286.8	64311.5	65725.5	67850.8
其他存款 Other Deposits	3554.4	4455.4	4784.6	5074.3
对中央银行负债 Liabilities to the Central Bank	8909.1	9076.9	9073.1	9440.5
对非货币金融机构负债 Liabilities to Non - monetary Financial Institutions	1406.8	2225.1	2165.4	2499.8
国外负债 Foreign Liabilities	3133.1	2682.7	2497.4	2418.4
债券 Bonds	478.2	371.4	362.0	371.0
实收资本 Paid - in Capital	6360.4	6422.6	6450.6	6551.9
其他（净） Other Items（Net）	- 1320.4	- 2874.5	- 5363.3	- 3827.2

存款货币银行资产负债表

Balance Sheet of Deposit Money Banks

（月末余额）

（Month - end Balance）

单位：亿元

Unit：100 Million Yuan

项目 Items	2002.01	2002.02	2002.03	2002.04
国外资产 Foreign Assets	10443.20	10345.38	10537.53	10523.73
储备资产 Reserve Assets	16715.81	17270.94	18646.07	17125.24
准备金存款 Reserve Deposits	15388.92	15823.66	17250.49	15856.94
库存现金 Cash in Vault	1326.89	1447.28	1395.58	1268.30
中央银行债券 Central Bank Bonds				
对政府债权 Claims on Government	11093.18	11081.25	11284.84	11731.48
其中：中央政府 Of Which：Central Government	11093.18	11081.25	11284.84	11731.48
对非金融机构债权 Claims on Non - financial Institutions	113144.92	113766.09	116506.84	117484.56
对特定存款机构债权 Claims on Specific Depository Institutions	5424.85	5337.91	5572.05	5536.47
对其他金融机构债权 Claims on Other Financial Institutions	8487.31	8523.02	8516.55	8088.13
其他资产 Other Assets	19964.27	20381.40	21581.59	22458.23
总资产 Total Assets	**185273.54**	**186705.99**	**192645.47**	**192947.84**
对非金融机构负债 Liabilities to Non - financial Institutions	141372.60	142590.50	145296.41	147885.68
活期存款 Demand Deposits	43809.67	42018.72	43879.43	44545.51
定期存款 Time Deposits	12846.37	12932.33	13081.62	13905.60
储蓄存款 Savings Deposits	68940.30	71802.19	72259.48	73225.06
其他存款 Other Deposits	4607.08	4553.94	4701.22	4847.14
外币存款 Deposits in Foreign Currency	11169.18	11283.32	11374.66	11362.37
对中央银行负债 Liabilities to the Central Bank	11471.57	11320.83	11852.20	11773.16
对特定存款机构负债 Liabilities to Specific Depository Institutions	389.10	414.15	356.40	333.08
对其他金融机构负债 Liabilities to Other Financial Institutions	9785.47	9955.42	11984.03	8902.65
其中：计入广义货币的存款 Of Which：Deposits Included in Broad Money	4869.06	4878.40	6314.12	3882.24
国外负债 Foreign Liabilities	3086.43	2948.76	2936.00	2864.58
债券 Bonds	516.83	626.13	548.18	855.41
实收资本 Paid - in Capital	7131.54	7183.04	7149.92	7226.85
其他负债 Other Liabilities	11520.00	11667.16	12522.33	13106.43
总负债 Total Liabilities	**185273.54**	**186705.99**	**192645.47**	**192947.84**

存款货币银行资产负债表
Balance Sheet of Deposit Money Banks

（月末余额）

（Month – end Balance）

单位：亿元

Unit: 100 Million Yuan

项目 Items	2002.05	2002.06	2002.07	2002.08
国外资产 Foreign Assets	10791.97	11155.01	11470.25	11694.17
储备资产 Reserve Assets	17981.12	18125.67	17515.62	17221.43
准备金存款 Reserve Deposits	16776.88	16749.71	16304.96	15939.52
库存现金 Cash in Vault	1204.24	1375.96	1210.66	1281.91
中央银行债券 Central Bank Bonds				
对政府债权 Claims on Government	12050.80	12774.24	13060.52	13186.45
其中：中央政府 Of Which: Central Government	12050.80	12774.24	13060.52	13186.45
对非金融机构债权 Claims on Non – financial Institutions	118677.15	121285.31	121930.00	123599.66
对特定存款机构债权 Claims on Specific Depository Institutions	5453.47	5700.36	5624.53	5654.31
对其他金融机构债权 Claims on Other Financial Institutions	8126.53	8153.93	8162.21	8202.97
其他资产 Other Assets	21273.81	22513.84	22946.98	23148.13
总资产 Total Assets	**194354.85**	**199708.36**	**200710.11**	**202707.12**
对非金融机构负债 Liabilities to Non – financial Institutions	149904.99	154031.20	155098.35	157559.24
活期存款 Demand Deposits	45948.81	47959.32	48016.57	49050.80
定期存款 Time Deposits	13585.04	14099.29	14291.23	14764.37
储蓄存款 Savings Deposits	73850.77	75084.30	75844.44	76531.66
其他存款 Other Deposits	4965.87	5234.24	5302.72	5484.38
外币存款 Deposits in Foreign Currency	11554.50	11654.05	11643.39	11728.03
对中央银行负债 Liabilities to the Central Bank	12025.67	11995.55	12187.72	12008.46
对特定存款机构负债 Liabilities to Specific Depository Institutions	322.65	338.75	326.72	410.90
对其他金融机构负债 Liabilities to Other Financial Institutions	9371.11	9194.36	8948.95	8575.79
其中：计入广义货币的存款 Of Which: Deposits Included in Broad Money	4075.62	3679.40	3512.69	3129.98
国外负债 Foreign Liabilities	2813.65	3009.52	3043.39	3042.75
债券 Bonds	470.52	602.06	390.49	354.38
实收资本 Paid – in Capital	7246.63	7282.01	7330.28	7361.45
其他负债 Other Liabilities	12199.63	13254.91	13384.21	13394.15
总负债 Total Liabilities	**194354.85**	**199708.36**	**200710.11**	**202707.12**

存款货币银行资产负债表
Balance Sheet of Deposit Money Banks
（月末余额）
（Month - end Balance）

单位：亿元
Unit：100 Million Yuan

项目 Items	2002.09	2002.10	2002.11	2002.12
国外资产 Foreign Assets	11368.14	11691.73	11622.78	12382.89
储备资产 Reserve Assets	16711.75	17220.73	17556.02	20281.48
准备金存款 Reserve Deposits	15232.30	15922.43	16198.51	18970.80
库存现金 Cash in Vault	1479.45	1298.30	1357.51	1310.68
中央银行债券 Central Bank Bonds	200.28	994.25	940.25	793.29
对政府债权 Claims on Government	13413.41	13461.24	13459.55	13519.23
其中：中央政府 Of Which：Central Government	13413.41	13461.24	13459.55	13519.23
对非金融机构债权 Claims on Non - financial Institutions	126385.76	127071.48	128842.16	131464.03
对特定存款机构债权 Claims on Specific Depository Institutions	6153.96	6062.75	6214.32	6369.18
对其他金融机构债权 Claims on Other Financial Institutions	7986.91	8009.07	8005.93	8021.85
其他资产 Other Assets	24691.11	22862.65	23008.21	22497.42
总资产 Total Assets	**206911.32**	**207373.90**	**209649.22**	**215329.37**
对非金融机构负债 Liabilities to Non - financial Institutions	161137.45	161690.27	163830.14	167943.88
活期存款 Demand Deposits	50481.91	51001.40	51558.71	53562.12
定期存款 Time Deposits	15783.93	15239.79	15722.45	16433.82
储蓄存款 Savings Deposits	77344.54	77836.04	78648.80	79541.56
其他存款 Other Deposits	5818.38	5732.63	5958.75	6283.06
外币存款 Deposits in Foreign Currency	11708.69	11880.41	11941.43	12123.32
对中央银行负债 Liabilities to the Central Bank	11954.53	11973.59	11830.65	12359.78
对特定存款机构负债 Liabilities to Specific Depository Institutions	396.32	379.99	341.46	348.19
对其他金融机构负债 Liabilities to Other Financial Institutions	8508.16	8347.32	8363.16	8546.84
其中：计入广义货币的存款 Of Which：Deposits Included in Broad Money	2713.22	2736.42	2650.46	2737.22
国外负债 Foreign Liabilities	3015.18	2948.68	2919.29	3295.23
债券 Bonds	334.65	339.42	363.69	527.28
实收资本 Paid - in Capital	7354.98	7433.95	7311.15	7386.44
其他负债 Other Liabilities	14210.05	14260.68	14689.68	14921.73
总负债 Total Liabilities	**206911.32**	**207373.90**	**209649.22**	**215329.37**

存款货币银行资产负债表
Balance Sheet of Deposit Money Banks

（月末余额）

（Month – end Balance）

单位：亿元

Unit：100 Million Yuan

项 目 Items	2003.01	2003.02	2003.03	2003.04
国外资产 Foreign Assets	12587.27	12634.87	12495.92	12410.99
储备资产 Reserve Assets	17418.51	19033.22	18800.86	17423.35
准备金存款 Reserve Deposits	15385.72	17569.84	17231.48	16027.35
库存现金 Cash in Vault	2032.79	1463.38	1569.38	1396.00
中央银行债券 Central Bank Bonds	874.66	874.89	382.10	488.71
对政府债权 Claims on Government	13460.18	13662.34	13559.99	14049.57
其中：中央政府 Of Which：Central Government	13460.18	13662.34	13559.99	14049.57
对非金融机构债权 Claims on Non – financial Institutions	134494.48	135580.52	139239.71	141334.07
对特定存款机构债权 Claims on Specific Depository Institutions	6659.24	6620.76	6815.41	6863.93
对其他金融机构债权 Claims on Other Financial Institutions	8544.68	8636.44	8846.46	8726.75
其他资产 Other Assets	21239.00	21727.29	24450.84	25675.15
总资产 Total Assets	**215278.02**	**218770.33**	**224591.29**	**226972.52**
对非金融机构负债 Liabilities to Non – financial Institutions	169716.40	172107.10	177050.33	178270.01
活期存款 Demand Deposits	51106.31	51764.99	54285.72	53815.72
定期存款 Time Deposits	16906.53	16776.52	17377.09	18203.26
储蓄存款 Savings Deposits	83242.72	85076.61	86605.77	87185.49
其他存款 Other Deposits	6419.85	6462.86	6822.86	7126.40
外币存款 Deposits in Foreign Currency	12040.99	12026.12	11958.89	11939.14
对中央银行负债 Liabilities to the Central Bank	10320.62	10135.22	10152.75	10155.81
对特定存款机构负债 Liabilities to Specific Depository Institutions	452.72	387.46	401.52	408.76
对其他金融机构负债 Liabilities to Other Financial Institutions	8503.01	8733.11	8908.63	8979.30
其中：计入广义货币的存款 Of Which：Deposits Included in Broad Money	2508.32	2623.73	2625.44	2631.66
国外负债 Foreign Liabilities	3730.25	3400.15	3378.57	3528.89
债券 Bonds	205.31	205.82	246.04	193.05
实收资本 Paid – in Capital	7405.23	7364.81	7218.28	7606.41
其他负债 Other Liabilities	14944.48	16436.66	17235.17	17830.29
总负债 Total Liabilities	**215278.02**	**218770.33**	**224591.29**	**226972.52**

存款货币银行资产负债表
Balance Sheet of Deposit Money Banks

（月末余额）

（Month - end Balance）

单位：亿元

Unit：100 Million Yuan

项目 Items	2003.05	2003.06	2003.07	2003.08
国外资产 Foreign Assets	12094.37	12014.74	11315.16	11268.65
储备资产 Reserve Assets	16857.29	17958.23	17866.10	18276.98
准备金存款 Reserve Deposits	15497.95	16430.26	16532.53	16775.51
库存现金 Cash in Vault	1359.34	1527.97	1333.57	1501.47
中央银行债券 Central Bank Bonds	1086.73	1953.96	2443.60	3217.82
对政府债权 Claims on Government	14272.38	14465.90	14449.20	14426.52
其中：中央政府 Of Which：Central Government	14272.38	14465.90	14449.20	14426.52
对非金融机构债权 Claims on Non - financial Institutions	144113.26	149287.00	150410.73	153385.37
对特定存款机构债权 Claims on Specific Depository Institutions	7007.95	7420.65	7584.42	8037.33
对其他金融机构债权 Claims on Other Financial Institutions	9016.67	8681.48	8701.75	9263.01
其他资产 Other Assets	25670.45	25332.02	24498.43	24880.46
总资产 Total Assets	**230119.10**	**237113.98**	**237269.39**	**242756.14**
对非金融机构负债 Liabilities to Non - financial Institutions	181699.55	186970.48	187843.59	189462.73
活期存款 Demand Deposits	55583.97	58861.40	58669.23	59284.85
定期存款 Time Deposits	18544.84	18869.84	19118.75	19592.84
储蓄存款 Savings Deposits	88224.84	89382.40	90126.86	90624.87
其他存款 Other Deposits	7352.19	7759.70	7900.57	7975.98
外币存款 Deposits in Foreign Currency	11993.71	12097.14	12028.18	11984.19
对中央银行负债 Liabilities to the Central Bank	10209.37	10241.53	10246.22	10968.67
对特定存款机构负债 Liabilities to Specific Depository Institutions	419.70	381.62	351.34	306.27
对其他金融机构负债 Liabilities to Other Financial Institutions	9374.32	9698.97	9571.89	11677.66
其中：计入广义货币的存款 Of Which：Deposits Included in Broad Money	2785.11	2844.11	2617.84	4834.70
国外负债 Foreign Liabilities	3479.34	3669.63	3412.04	3383.64
债券 Bonds	144.87	145.37	95.29	44.78
实收资本 Paid - in Capital	7623.53	7612.99	7695.59	7709.56
其他负债 Other Liabilities	17168.42	18393.39	18053.43	19202.83
总负债 Total Liabilities	**230119.10**	**237113.98**	**237269.39**	**242756.14**

存款货币银行资产负债表
Balance Sheet of Deposit Money Banks

（月末余额）

（Month－end Balance）

单位：亿元

Unit：100 Million Yuan

项　目 Items	2003.09	2003.10	2003.11	2003.12
国外资产 Foreign Assets	11151.32	11694.45	11434.13	11121.47
储备资产 Reserve Assets	19779.88	20854.41	21209.56	24094.55
准备金存款 Reserve Deposits	18098.52	19382.44	19642.78	22600.31
库存现金 Cash in Vault	1681.36	1471.97	1566.78	1494.24
中央银行债券 Central Bank Bonds	3496.99	3413.25	3455.65	2890.07
对政府债权 Claims on Government	14575.31	14630.41	14823.17	15185.16
其中：中央政府 Of Which：Central Government	14575.31	14630.41	14823.17	15185.16
对非金融机构债权 Claims on Non－financial Institutions	156081.50	156691.37	157792.72	158535.12
对特定存款机构债权 Claims on Specific Depository Institutions	8180.83	8318.51	8499.68	8675.68
对其他金融机构债权 Claims on Other Financial Institutions	8750.36	8825.20	8653.61	12106.94
其他资产 Other Assets	23673.43	23570.68	23391.42	21804.14
总资产 Total Assets	**245689.62**	**247998.28**	**249259.94**	**254413.13**
对非金融机构负债 Liabilities to Non－financial Institutions	194213.57	195020.60	196527.38	199941.22
活期存款 Demand Deposits	60752.10	61337.38	62229.55	64314.17
定期存款 Time Deposits	21261.13	20335.19	20658.55	20940.39
储蓄存款 Savings Deposits	92196.43	92658.31	93412.20	94633.22
其他存款 Other Deposits	8151.18	8691.74	8207.61	8215.43
外币存款 Deposits in Foreign Currency	11852.73	11997.98	12019.47	11838.01
对中央银行负债 Liabilities to the Central Bank	10969.31	11188.85	10585.27	10772.38
对特定存款机构负债 Liabilities to Specific Depository Institutions	372.35	404.32	403.67	381.22
对其他金融机构负债 Liabilities to Other Financial Institutions	9622.91	9978.11	10022.39	9914.44
其中：计入广义货币的存款 Of Which：Deposits Included in Broad Money	2146.45	2395.18	2442.02	2334.53
国外负债 Foreign Liabilities	3546.90	4073.56	4065.59	3789.80
债券 Bonds	44.15	45.74	41.23	55.16
实收资本 Paid－in Capital	7670.98	7750.50	7800.90	9282.31
其他负债 Other Liabilities	19249.45	19536.60	19813.51	20276.60
总负债 Total Liabilities	**245689.62**	**247998.28**	**249259.94**	**254413.13**

存款货币银行资产负债表

Balance Sheet of Deposit Money Banks

（月末余额）

（Month – end Balance）

单位：亿元

Unit：100 Million Yuan

项 目 Items	2004.01	2004.02	2004.03	2004.04
国外资产 Foreign Assets	13034.99	12911.63	12350.58	11900.87
储备资产 Reserve Assets	30958.08	31858.11	31197.29	30846.81
准备金存款 Reserve Deposits	28206.51	30029.33	29398.38	29072.97
库存现金 Cash in Vault	2751.57	1828.78	1798.91	1773.84
中央银行债券 Central Bank Bonds	2881.50	3606.51	5166.51	5150.66
对政府债权 Claims on Government	15144.60	15391.04	15686.74	15841.92
其中：中央政府 Of Which：Central Government	15144.60	15391.04	15686.74	15841.92
对非金融机构债权 Claims on Non – financial Institutions	163031.36	165322.30	168741.28	170801.54
对特定存款机构债权 Claims on Specific Depository Institutions	9056.04	9468.88	9504.22	9679.07
对其他金融机构债权 Claims on Other Financial Institutions	9046.72	8300.58	8643.44	8516.14
其他资产 Other Assets	23252.35	23723.55	25696.02	25186.32
总资产 Total Assets	**266405.64**	**270582.60**	**276986.08**	**277923.33**
对非金融机构负债 Liabilities to Non – financial Institutions	210578.71	213950.25	219203.86	220743.50
活期存款 Demand Deposits	61453.07	63597.08	66456.11	65142.80
定期存款 Time Deposits	20920.59	20924.84	21645.35	23227.71
储蓄存款 Savings Deposits	109232.65	110646.38	111872.18	112175.45
其他存款 Other Deposits	6935.22	7177.41	7568.19	8503.15
外币存款 Deposits in Foreign Currency	12037.18	11604.54	11662.03	11694.39
对中央银行负债 Liabilities to the Central Bank	10903.51	10532.58	10358.13	10257.65
对特定存款机构负债 Liabilities to Specific Depository Institutions	357.48	363.89	301.78	301.63
对其他金融机构负债 Liabilities to Other Financial Institutions	10268.45	10552.72	10954.44	10726.82
其中：计入广义货币的存款 Of Which：Deposits Included in Broad Money	2334.61	2843.95	2825.40	2660.39
国外负债 Foreign Liabilities	4515.04	4469.01	4074.67	3882.33
债券 Bonds	47.70	40.86	39.06	62.85
实收资本 Paid – in Capital	9338.75	9364.73	9442.38	9499.63
其他负债 Other Liabilities	20396.00	21308.56	22611.76	22448.92
总负债 Total Liabilities	**266405.64**	**270582.60**	**276986.08**	**277923.33**

存款货币银行资产负债表
Balance Sheet of Deposit Money Banks

（月末余额）

（Month - end Balance）

单位：亿元

Unit: 100 Million Yuan

项 目 Items	2004.05	2004.06	2004.07	2004.08
国外资产 Foreign Assets	12344.57	14481.83	14066.99	14573.19
储备资产 Reserve Assets	30711.32	32212.15	30744.14	31819.22
准备金存款 Reserve Deposits	29001.32	30434.16	29068.14	30025.13
库存现金 Cash in Vault	1710.00	1777.99	1676.00	1794.09
中央银行债券 Central Bank Bonds	4964.41	6638.09	6794.82	6256.26
对政府债权 Claims on Government	15526.73	15944.00	16150.20	16248.91
其中：中央政府 Of Which: Central Government	15526.73	15944.00	16150.20	16248.91
对非金融机构债权 Claims on Non - financial Institutions	171898.97	168972.88	168914.84	170201.29
对特定存款机构债权 Claims on Specific Depository Institutions	9825.30	9994.52	10299.61	10466.57
对其他金融机构债权 Claims on Other Financial Institutions	8560.69	8728.84	8584.63	8582.28
其他资产 Other Assets	25972.85	26475.42	25426.63	24747.16
总资产 Total Assets	**279804.84**	**283447.73**	**280981.86**	**282894.88**
对非金融机构负债 Liabilities to Non - financial Institutions	222975.78	226868.83	226695.00	228202.56
活期存款 Demand Deposits	67141.95	68765.50	68443.47	69450.02
定期存款 Time Deposits	22761.12	23465.58	23447.20	23586.02
储蓄存款 Savings Deposits	112610.19	113792.46	114253.24	114489.63
其他存款 Other Deposits	8579.69	8896.22	8387.40	8462.47
外币存款 Deposits in Foreign Currency	11882.83	11949.07	12163.69	12214.42
对中央银行负债 Liabilities to the Central Bank	10090.29	10153.60	10155.32	9982.21
对特定存款机构负债 Liabilities to Specific Depository Institutions	312.27	339.96	332.53	326.40
对其他金融机构负债 Liabilities to Other Financial Institutions	10412.23	10116.39	9738.70	9776.02
其中：计入广义货币的存款 Of Which: Deposits Included in Broad Money	2650.65	2192.35	2128.99	1999.26
国外负债 Foreign Liabilities	3974.50	5091.82	4398.43	4452.07
债券 Bonds	62.85	326.45	575.29	726.54
实收资本 Paid - in Capital	9540.04	9789.73	9820.76	9928.44
其他负债 Other Liabilities	22436.88	20760.95	19265.83	19500.64
总负债 Total Liabilities	**279804.84**	**283447.73**	**280981.86**	**282894.88**

存款货币银行资产负债表
Balance Sheet of Deposit Money Banks

（月末余额）

（Month - end Balance）

单位：亿元

Unit：100 Million Yuan

项 目 Items	2004.09	2004.10	2004.11	2004.12
国外资产 Foreign Assets	14648.00	14445.70	14454.05	14052.82
储备资产 Reserve Assets	32387.90	32228.77	33492.22	37084.20
准备金存款 Reserve Deposits	30219.43	30341.98	31639.66	35293.31
库存现金 Cash in Vault	2168.47	1886.79	1852.56	1790.89
中央银行债券 Central Bank Bonds	6439.16	7537.40	7830.87	9217.17
对政府债权 Claims on Government	16691.24	16631.72	16990.78	18328.04
其中：中央政府 Of Which：Central Government	16691.24	16631.72	16990.78	18328.04
对非金融机构债权 Claims on Non - financial Institutions	172966.20	172952.08	174236.07	176303.31
对特定存款机构债权 Claims on Specific Depository Institutions	10720.27	10958.01	11359.22	12151.04
对其他金融机构债权 Claims on Other Financial Institutions	8606.91	8626.34	8689.65	6895.73
其他资产 Other Assets	24822.36	25787.65	25925.86	26456.67
总资产 Total Assets	**287282.04**	**289167.67**	**292978.72**	**300488.98**
对非金融机构负债 Liabilities to Non - financial Institutions	231363.63	232027.69	234779.48	240573.11
活期存款 Demand Deposits	69758.13	70571.43	71992.65	74422.10
定期存款 Time Deposits	25071.91	24315.23	24215.96	25382.15
储蓄存款 Savings Deposits	115458.74	116000.99	117617.90	119555.39
其他存款 Other Deposits	8789.18	8673.97	8755.92	9124.62
外币存款 Deposits in Foreign Currency	12285.67	12466.07	12197.05	12088.85
对中央银行负债 Liabilities to the Central Bank	9980.44	10012.56	9868.09	9690.06
对特定存款机构负债 Liabilities to Specific Depository Institutions	318.60	321.26	305.35	338.45
对其他金融机构负债 Liabilities to Other Financial Institutions	9620.21	9627.29	9605.19	9489.88
其中：计入广义货币的存款 Of Which：Deposits Included in Broad Money	1937.36	1869.24	1870.89	1671.48
国外负债 Foreign Liabilities	4823.60	4595.94	4709.65	4615.04
债券 Bonds	818.46	817.91	1281.59	1630.21
实收资本 Paid - in Capital	10048.73	10088.56	10276.29	10642.96
其他负债 Other Liabilities	20308.37	21676.46	22153.08	23509.27
总负债 Total Liabilities	**287282.04**	**289167.67**	**292978.72**	**300488.98**

存款货币银行资产负债表
Balance Sheet of Deposit Money Banks

（月末余额）

（Month – end Balance）

单位：亿元

Unit: 100 Million Yuan

项　目 Items	2005.01	2005.02	2005.03	2005.04
国外资产 Foreign Assets	13915.76	14064.29	13761.16	14902.49
储备资产 Reserve Assets	34530.21	36056.43	36209.62	34559.80
准备金存款 Reserve Deposits	32370.41	33693.48	34161.58	32564.41
库存现金 Cash in Vault	2159.80	2362.95	2048.04	1995.39
中央银行债券 Central Bank Bonds	9212.69	9600.91	11503.85	13361.46
对政府债权 Claims on Government	16764.73	16622.53	16923.59	17197.97
其中：中央政府 Of Which: Central Government	16764.73	16622.53	16923.59	17197.97
对非金融机构债权 Claims on Non – financial Institutions	178366.85	179247.65	182456.48	183644.07
对特定存款机构债权 Claims on Specific Depository Institutions	12268.57	12453.52	13166.35	13977.02
对其他金融机构债权 Claims on Other Financial Institutions	8561.38	8474.09	8698.60	8577.32
其他资产 Other Assets	27107.64	27399.28	27997.99	29128.51
总资产 Total Assets	**300727.83**	**303918.70**	**310717.64**	**315348.64**
对非金融机构负债 Liabilities to Non – financial Institutions	241717.63	244846.41	251540.64	253605.37
活期存款 Demand Deposits	72965.95	70037.68	73366.69	72803.83
定期存款 Time Deposits	24939.47	25296.42	26543.24	28178.12
储蓄存款 Savings Deposits	122237.34	127823.44	129259.35	129816.83
其他存款 Other Deposits	9508.53	9448.78	9910.79	10438.61
外币存款 Deposits in Foreign Currency	12066.34	12240.09	12460.57	12367.98
对中央银行负债 Liabilities to the Central Bank	9639.64	9664.18	9283.30	9075.45
对特定存款机构负债 Liabilities to Specific Depository Institutions	389.07	325.95	298.16	325.93
对其他金融机构负债 Liabilities to Other Financial Institutions	7952.51	8159.37	8332.69	8239.24
其中：计入广义货币的存款 Of Which: Deposits Included in Broad Money	1580.59	1635.88	1740.11	1549.56
国外负债 Foreign Liabilities	4790.49	4719.95	4558.64	4692.94
债券 Bonds	1671.37	1674.30	2216.03	2544.20
实收资本 Paid – in Capital	10670.55	10731.58	10837.68	12125.41
其他负债 Other Liabilities	23896.57	23796.96	23650.50	24740.10
总负债 Total Liabilities	**300727.83**	**303918.70**	**310717.64**	**315348.64**

存款货币银行资产负债表

Balance Sheet of Deposit Money Banks

（月末余额）

（Month - end Balance）

单位：亿元

Unit：100 Million Yuan

项目 Items	2005.05	2005.06	2005.07	2005.08
国外资产 Foreign Assets	14538.10	14928.13	14069.58	14355.41
储备资产 Reserve Assets	35717.78	36423.60	36970.53	37201.10
准备金存款 Reserve Deposits	33854.70	34509.83	35078.22	35221.44
库存现金 Cash in Vault	1863.08	1913.77	1892.31	1979.66
中央银行债券 Central Bank Bonds	13833.78	12351.83	12499.57	12881.02
对政府债权 Claims on Government	17351.87	17219.69	17491.79	18157.20
其中：中央政府 Of Which：Central Government	17351.87	17219.69	17491.79	18157.20
对非金融机构债权 Claims on Non - financial Institutions	183943.56	182994.90	182748.40	184384.92
对特定存款机构债权 Claims on Specific Depository Institutions	14266.38	14936.29	15536.73	16176.02
对其他金融机构债权 Claims on Other Financial Institutions	8841.78	8818.10	9112.75	9354.86
其他资产 Other Assets	31717.89	40276.57	39821.36	41472.65
总资产 Total Assets	**320211.14**	**327949.11**	**328250.71**	**333983.18**
对非金融机构负债 Liabilities to Non - financial Institutions	256350.58	262766.30	262824.82	266844.21
活期存款 Demand Deposits	74856.67	77608.95	76338.86	77842.99
定期存款 Time Deposits	28201.05	29395.97	29673.70	30852.96
储蓄存款 Savings Deposits	130577.44	132339.14	133656.44	134505.01
其他存款 Other Deposits	10494.47	10834.88	11196.13	11693.22
外币存款 Deposits in Foreign Currency	12220.95	12587.36	11959.69	11950.03
对中央银行负债 Liabilities to the Central Bank	9006.70	8668.42	8540.30	8070.46
对特定存款机构负债 Liabilities to Specific Depository Institutions	352.80	445.97	474.27	512.47
对其他金融机构负债 Liabilities to Other Financial Institutions	8372.28	8708.87	9265.76	9881.71
其中：计入广义货币的存款 Of Which：Deposits Included in Broad Money	1648.86	1818.28	2100.28	2271.75
国外负债 Foreign Liabilities	4894.88	4560.19	4502.39	4265.86
债券 Bonds	2445.26	2414.34	2624.39	3094.34
实收资本 Paid - in Capital	11842.67	12052.30	12105.45	12144.75
其他负债 Other Liabilities	26945.97	28332.72	27913.33	29169.38
总负债 Total Liabilities	**320211.14**	**327949.11**	**328250.71**	**333983.18**

存款货币银行资产负债表
Balance Sheet of Deposit Money Banks
（月末余额）
(Month – end Balance)

单位：亿元
Unit: 100 Million Yuan

项目 Items	2005.09	2005.10	2005.11	2005.12
国外资产 Foreign Assets	14386.92	16333.09	16636.19	17422.12
储备资产 Reserve Assets	37897.30	37751.15	36238.78	39969.54
准备金存款 Reserve Deposits	35643.37	35728.54	34280.47	37772.82
库存现金 Cash in Vault	2253.93	2022.61	1958.31	2196.72
中央银行债券 Central Bank Bonds	13511.35	14679.64	16508.15	16582.97
对政府债权 Claims on Government	18478.60	18743.80	19009.28	19794.91
其中：中央政府 Of Which: Central Government	18478.60	18743.80	19009.28	19794.91
对非金融机构债权 Claims on Non – financial Institutions	187177.68	186410.50	188603.96	189141.14
对特定存款机构债权 Claims on Specific Depository Institutions	17007.50	17354.64	18229.87	18542.58
对其他金融机构债权 Claims on Other Financial Institutions	9380.85	9571.93	9795.92	9414.96
其他资产 Other Assets	43593.88	42609.31	43448.58	44414.16
总资产 Total Assets	**341434.08**	**343454.06**	**348470.73**	**355282.38**
对非金融机构负债 Liabilities to Non – financial Institutions	271976.81	272543.93	276698.60	281791.54
活期存款 Demand Deposits	78497.79	79662.29	81464.15	83149.18
定期存款 Time Deposits	33320.65	32145.97	32229.65	33099.99
储蓄存款 Savings Deposits	136316.32	136827.11	138504.28	141050.99
其他存款 Other Deposits	12183.09	12083.23	12636.10	12652.81
外币存款 Deposits in Foreign Currency	11658.96	11825.33	11864.42	11838.57
对中央银行负债 Liabilities to the Central Bank	8034.91	8008.50	8038.18	7807.45
对特定存款机构负债 Liabilities to Specific Depository Institutions	472.00	466.13	443.07	637.20
对其他金融机构负债 Liabilities to Other Financial Institutions	9907.57	10223.87	10459.47	10110.83
其中：计入广义货币的存款 Of Which: Deposits Included in Broad Money	2047.31	2135.96	2137.52	1956.43
国外负债 Foreign Liabilities	4238.08	4240.91	4206.05	4196.24
债券 Bonds	3416.47	3468.43	3788.42	4059.42
实收资本 Paid – in Capital	12199.65	12459.02	12564.34	12888.52
其他负债 Other Liabilities	31188.59	32043.27	32272.60	33791.18
总负债 Total Liabilities	**341434.08**	**343454.06**	**348470.73**	**355282.38**

3. 国有商业银行资产负债表
Balance Sheet of State - owned Commercial Banks

国有商业银行资产负债表
Balance Sheet of State - owned Commercial Banks

（季末余额）

（Quarter - end Balance）

单位：亿元

Unit：100 Million Yuan

项目 Items	1993.03	1993.06	1993.09	1993.12
国外资产 Foreign Assets	2445.5	2319.8	2413.4	2720.7
储备资产 Reserve Assets	3346.5	3230.3	3793.7	4892.4
准备金 Reserves	2263.1	2314.3	2355.7	2578.1
在人行存款 Deposits with the Central Bank	843.1	632.7	1153.4	1901.9
库存现金 Cash in Vault	240.3	283.3	284.6	412.4
中央银行债券 Central Bank Bonds				
对政府债权 Claims on Government				
对其他部门债权 Claims on Other Sectors	21147.4	21916.1	22823.3	25581.4
对非货币金融机构债权 Claims on Non - monetary Financial Institutions				
对非金融部门负债 Liabilities to Non - financial Sectors	16491.8	17111.5	17508.4	18780.3
活期存款 Demand Deposits	7037.5	7239.4	6803.3	7416.9
定期存款 Time Deposits	855.7	842.9	849.6	909.7
储蓄存款 Savings Deposits	8561.2	8989.5	9819.9	10420.5
其他存款 Other Deposits	37.4	39.7	35.6	33.2
对中央银行负债 Liabilities to the Central Bank	6580.4	6750.6	7694.7	9555.7
对非货币金融机构负债 Liabilities to Non - monetary Financial Institutions				
国外负债 Foreign Liabilities	1712.2	1784.4	1886.4	2141.2
债券 Bonds	274.8	232.8	224.9	219.3
所有者权益 Owner's Equity	1445.6	1484.3	1701.3	1708.4
其中：实收资本 Of Which：Paid - in Capital	1445.6	1484.3	1701.3	1708.4
其他（净） Other Items（Net）	434.6	102.6	14.7	789.6

国有商业银行资产负债表
Balance Sheet of State - owned Commercial Banks

（季末余额）

（Quarter - end Balance）

单位：亿元

Unit：100 Million Yuan

项 目 Items	1994.03	1994.06	1994.09	1994.12
国外资产 Foreign Assets	3972.4	3703.9	3669.6	3950.8
储备资产 Reserve Assets	4958.5	5324.5	5387.2	6046.2
准备金 Reserves	2730.3	2982.4	3208.0	3418.2
在人行存款 Deposits with the Central Bank	1864.8	1989.9	1807.2	2209.4
库存现金 Cash in Vault	363.4	352.2	372.0	418.6
中央银行债券 Central Bank Bonds	11.1	7.0	15.2	9.8
对政府债权 Claims on Government	278.5	378.1	415.0	379.9
对其他部门债权 Claims on Other Sectors	26114.5	27516.0	28937.7	30995.0
对非货币金融机构债权 Claims on Non - monetary Financial Institutions	414.2	387.2	410.6	429.9
对非金融部门负债 Liabilities to Non - financial Sectors	20303.8	22147.9	23772.1	25029.0
活期存款 Demand Deposits	7596.3	8490.6	8944.6	9116.3
定期存款 Time Deposits	953.9	1172.3	1255.1	1311.3
储蓄存款 Savings Deposits	11713.3	12436.1	13509.3	14553.3
其他存款 Other Deposits	40.3	48.9	63.1	48.1
对中央银行负债 Liabilities to the Central Bank	9022.1	9294.4	9490.7	10182.2
对非货币金融机构负债 Liabilities to Non - monetary Financial Institutions	143.2	143.6	150.7	181.1
国外负债 Foreign Liabilities	3038.9	3335.4	3420.5	3614.9
债券 Bonds	223.0	208.0	210.1	188.9
所有者权益 Owner's Equity	1755.8	1786.2	1803.0	1848.2
其中：实收资本 Of Which：Paid - in Capital	1809.2	1801.8	1810.7	1811.6
其他（净） Other Items（Net）	1262.4	401.2	- 11.8	767.3

国有商业银行资产负债表

Balance Sheet of State - owned Commercial Banks

（季末余额）

（Quarter - end Balance）

单位：亿元

Unit：100 Million Yuan

项目 Items	1995.03	1995.06	1995.09	1995.12
国外资产 Foreign Assets	3454.3	3242.8	3031.2	3297.0
储备资产 Reserve Assets	6395.9	6090.1	6944.6	7795.1
准备金 Reserves	3643.9	3874.2	4178.0	4468.5
在人行存款 Deposits with the Central Bank	2360.0	1807.9	2359.9	2869.9
库存现金 Cash in Vault	392.0	408.0	406.7	456.7
中央银行债券 Central Bank Bonds	0.7	0.1	2.1	173.6
对政府债权 Claims on Government	423.0	492.4	465.9	486.3
对其他部门债权 Claims on Other Sectors	31384.3	32491.0	34168.3	37563.8
对非货币金融机构债权 Claims on Non - monetary Financial Institutions	420.3	428.5	432.8	456.3
对非金融部门负债 Liabilities to Non - financial Sectors	26977.9	28880.5	31067.5	33088.5
活期存款 Demand Deposits	9580.6	10005.0	10511.7	11049.0
定期存款 Time Deposits	1429.4	1700.1	1968.2	2100.1
储蓄存款 Savings Deposits	15913.3	17115.4	18520.9	19831.3
其他存款 Other Deposits	54.6	60.0	66.7	108.1
对中央银行负债 Liabilities to the Central Bank	10022.6	9823.4	10131.3	11095.2
对非货币金融机构负债 Liabilities to Non - monetary Financial Institutions	122.3	122.6	129.0	176.9
国外负债 Foreign Liabilities	3563.8	3662.0	3807.4	3833.8
债券 Bonds	207.5	188.2	213.6	169.6
所有者权益 Owner's Equity	1536.0	1590.0	1607.1	1788.5
其中：实收资本 Of Which：Paid - in Capital	1731.6	1746.6	1775.8	1819.7
其他（净） Other Items（Net）	- 351.6	- 1521.8	- 1911.0	- 380.4

国有商业银行资产负债表

Balance Sheet of State - owned Commercial Banks

（季末余额）

(Quarter - end Balance)

单位：亿元

Unit: 100 Million Yuan

项目 Items	1996.03	1996.06	1996.09	1996.12
国外资产 Foreign Assets	3397.8	3149.3	3532.5	3498.0
储备资产 Reserve Assets	8130.3	8371.9	8473.7	10195.9
准备金 Reserves	4778.5	5127.9	5464.5	5446.4
在人行存款 Deposits with the Central Bank	2893.6	2794.1	2520.6	4343.4
库存现金 Cash in Vault	458.2	449.9	488.6	406.1
中央银行债券 Central Bank Bonds	0.0	0.0	0.0	0.0
对政府债权 Claims on Government	799.3	932.9	984.5	967.1
对其他部门债权 Claims on Other Sectors	38232.1	40754.3	41484.3	44477.4
对非货币金融机构债权 Claims on Non - monetary Financial Institutions	342.4	338.6	346.8	332.1
对非金融部门负债 Liabilities to Non - financial Sectors	35799.7	38448.4	40300.5	42402.1
活期存款 Demand Deposits	11017.7	11852.4	12423.0	13512.3
定期存款 Time Deposits	2403.8	2777.2	2979.4	3168.0
储蓄存款 Savings Deposits	22310.7	23754.6	24840.7	25684.2
其他存款 Other Deposits	67.5	64.2	57.4	37.6
对中央银行负债 Liabilities to the Central Bank	11080.6	10615.9	10831.6	14088.5
对非货币金融机构负债 Liabilities to Non - monetary Financial Institutions	141.7	125.2	130.7	144.8
国外负债 Foreign Liabilities	3739.3	3820.4	3862.8	3839.0
债券 Bonds	172.2	172.6	151.5	280.5
所有者权益 Owner's Equity	1691.2	1871.6	2001.7	2010.4
其中：实收资本 Of Which: Paid - in Capital	1821.2	1820.0	1826.8	1926.5
其他（净） Other Items (Net)	- 1722.8	- 1507.1	- 2457.0	- 3294.8

国有商业银行资产负债表

Balance Sheet of State - owned Commercial Banks

（季末余额）

（Quarter - end Balance）

单位：亿元

Unit：100 Million Yuan

项目 Items	1997.03	1997.06	1997.09	1997.12
国外资产 Foreign Assets	3925.9	3806.9	4186.2	4525.9
储备资产 Reserve Assets	9822.6	10158.5	10595.9	10915.8
准备金 Reserves	5793.6	6077.6	6377.0	6583.9
在人行存款 Deposits with the Central Bank	3476.9	3551.2	3682.1	3828.8
库存现金 Cash in Vault	552.1	529.7	536.8	503.1
中央银行债券 Central Bank Bonds	38.3	52.7	57.4	62.0
对政府债权 Claims on Government	878.0	781.4	746.7	762.0
对其他部门债权 Claims on Other Sectors	47995.1	49306.8	51354.9	54374.6
对非货币金融机构债权 Claims on Non - monetary Financial Institutions	1193.4	1148.0	1301.5	1494.2
对非金融部门负债 Liabilities to Non - financial Sectors	45837.1	47768.9	49497.5	51905.5
活期存款 Demand Deposits	14168.9	15186.3	15746.6	16520.6
定期存款 Time Deposits	3661.6	3963.8	4283.7	4363.2
储蓄存款 Savings Deposits	27764.7	28401.5	29247.9	30725.6
其他存款 Other Deposits	241.9	217.3	219.3	296.1
对中央银行负债 Liabilities to the Central Bank	13233.4	12847.0	13149.1	13885.1
对非货币金融机构负债 Liabilities to Non - monetary Financial Institutions	606.3	1022.7	1270.3	1011.0
国外负债 Foreign Liabilities	3700.6	3750.7	3772.6	3906.2
债券 Bonds	165.3	178.8	270.2	277.6
所有者权益 Owner's Equity	1895.5	2008.2	2071.4	2028.3
其中：实收资本 Of Which：Paid - in Capital	1915.6	2098.9	2105.5	2105.8
其他（净） Other Items（Net）	- 1584.9	- 2322.0	- 1788.5	- 879.2

国有商业银行资产负债表
Balance Sheet of State - owned Commercial Banks

（季末余额）

(Quarter - end Balance)

单位：亿元

Unit: 100 Million Yuan

项目 Items	1998.03	1998.06	1998.09	1998.12
国外资产 Foreign Assets	4721.7	4808.4	4992.5	5021.9
储备资产 Reserve Assets	9026.9	11892.3	8694.6	9722.7
准备金 Reserves	5315.3	11368.5	8193.6	9196.9
在人行存款 Deposits with the Central Bank	3169.4			
库存现金 Cash in Vault	542.2	523.8	501.0	525.8
中央银行债券 Central Bank Bonds	60.8	67.7	71.8	22.8
对政府债权 Claims on Government	623.8	618.7	3444.3	3691.1
对其他部门债权 Claims on Other Sectors	54565.0	56317.4	59716.7	62314.0
对非货币金融机构债权 Claims on Non - monetary Financial Institutions	1519.4	1692.4	1687.7	1819.7
对非金融部门负债 Liabilities to Non - financial Sectors	52605.6	54467.9	57556.9	59477.8
活期存款 Demand Deposits	15548.7	16301.0	17566.2	18185.2
定期存款 Time Deposits	4470.2	4804.8	5279.2	5372.8
储蓄存款 Savings Deposits	32003.8	32902.3	34238.5	35378.0
其他存款 Other Deposits	582.9	459.8	473.0	541.8
对中央银行负债 Liabilities to the Central Bank	13559.6	13081.8	10658.5	11867.2
对非货币金融机构负债 Liabilities to Non - monetary Financial Institutions	434.3	925.5	811.0	644.4
国外负债 Foreign Liabilities	3861.7	3771.6	3604.4	3705.6
债券 Bonds	277.8	372.0	473.0	482.9
所有者权益 Owner's Equity	1813.3	1846.2	4331.5	4368.7
其中：实收资本 Of Which: Paid - in Capital	2088.1	2079.2	4836.9	4845.5
其他（净） Other Items (Net)	-2034.7	931.9	1172.3	2045.6

国有商业银行资产负债表
Balance Sheet of State - owned Commercial Banks
（季末余额）
（Quarter - end Balance）

单位：亿元
Unit：100 Million Yuan

项目 Items	1999.03	1999.06	1999.09	1999.12
国外资产 Foreign Assets	4759.3	4410.6	5151.8	5310.3
储备资产 Reserve Assets	9432.5	9457.0	8568.7	10158.6
准备金 Reserves	8866.4	8897.1	7853.8	9052.6
库存现金 Cash in Vault	566.1	559.9	714.9	1106.0
中央银行债券 Central Bank Bonds	22.1	21.7	23.7	20.8
对政府债权 Claims on Government	3688.2	3743.1	4081.0	4357.0
对其他部门债权 Claims on Other Sectors	63144.6	65103.3	67120.0	69573.1
对非货币金融机构债权 Claims on Non - monetary Financial Institutions	1883.2	1859.3	1915.8	2343.2
对非金融部门负债 Liabilities to Non - financial Sectors	63023.7	65349.6	66715.0	69769.8
活期存款 Demand Deposits	17917.4	18611.0	19533.8	22428.7
定期存款 Time Deposits	5716.9	6091.9	6132.9	6141.5
储蓄存款 Savings Deposits	38698.7	39727.9	39912.7	39887.1
其他存款 Other Deposits	690.7	918.8	1135.6	1312.5
对中央银行负债 Liabilities to the Central Bank	7811.2	7690.2	7591.5	7559.8
对非货币金融机构负债 Liabilities to Non - monetary Financial Institutions	551.3	676.0	1095.7	1243.8
国外负债 Foreign Liabilities	3676.6	3654.8	3570.5	3215.3
债券 Bonds	482.9	476.7	463.3	476.1
实收资本 Paid - in Capital	4844.9	4845.7	4850.0	4783.7
其他（净） Other Items（Net）	2539.3	1902.0	2575.0	4714.5

国有商业银行资产负债表
Balance Sheet of State - owned Commercial Banks
（季末余额）
(Quarter - end Balance)

单位：亿元
Unit: 100 Million Yuan

项目 Items	2000.03	2000.06	2000.09	2000.12
国外资产 Foreign Assets	5918.1	6315.4	6976.1	7453.4
储备资产 Reserve Assets	9171.2	8855.4	9096.8	9548.4
准备金 Reserves	8517.2	8203.1	8338.5	8773.2
库存现金 Cash in Vault	654.0	652.3	758.3	775.2
中央银行债券 Central Bank Bonds	2.4	2.0	2.1	2.1
对政府债权 Claims on Government	4358.5	4555.6	4671.7	5411.7
对其他部门债权 Claims on Other Sectors	71210.6	69312.2	72059.9	76061.8
对非货币金融机构债权 Claims on Non - monetary Financial Institutions	2373.0	3724.7	3121.4	2967.2
对非金融部门负债 Liabilities to Non - financial Sectors	72376.1	74850.5	76413.3	77505.0
活期存款 Demand Deposits	22480.4	24348.3	25382.7	26137.3
定期存款 Time Deposits	6506.8	6774.2	6997.9	6803.2
储蓄存款 Savings Deposits	42023.9	42169.9	42361.6	42734.9
其他存款 Other Deposits	1365.0	1558.1	1671.1	1829.6
对中央银行负债 Liabilities to the Central Bank	10844.6	8443.6	7861.2	8120.5
对非货币金融机构负债 Liabilities to Non - monetary Financial Institutions	1105.2	1209.8	1095.0	934.7
国外负债 Foreign Liabilities	3054.8	3009.2	2941.9	3055.7
债券 Bonds	480.9	471.8	467.4	473.7
实收资本 Paid - in Capital	4788.8	4787.3	4787.5	4793.0
其他（净） Other Items (Net)	383.4	-6.9	2361.7	6562.0

国有商业银行资产负债表

Balance Sheet of State – owned Commercial Banks

（季末余额）

（Quarter – end Balance）

单位：亿元

Unit：100 Million Yuan

项 目 Items	2001.03	2001.06	2001.09	2001.12
国外资产 Foreign Assets	8395.8	8016.4	7534.7	8006.2
储备资产 Reserve Assets	9247.8	8907.6	9232.5	10847.5
准备金 Reserves	8496.7	8157.4	8411.0	10158.4
库存现金 Cash in Vault	751.1	750.2	821.5	689.1
中央银行债券 Central Bank Bonds	2.2	0.7	0.7	0.6
对政府债权 Claims on Government	7203.2	7409.6	7622.9	7660.8
对其他部门债权 Claims on Other Sectors	67664.2	69626.1	70406.7	72307.3
对非货币金融机构债权 Claims on Non – monetary Financial Institutions	2878.7	3900.0	4110.4	4426.3
对非金融部门负债 Liabilities to Non – financial Sectors	80908.6	83270.3	85130.3	87670.3
活期存款 Demand Deposits	26232.4	27592.8	27800.7	28957.0
定期存款 Time Deposits	7400.9	7565.7	7946.8	7960.2
储蓄存款 Savings Deposits	45456.6	46084.3	47146.3	48395.2
其他存款 Other Deposits	1818.7	2027.5	2236.5	2357.9
对中央银行负债 Liabilities to the Central Bank	7927.0	7871.1	7827.3	8358.2
对非货币金融机构负债 Liabilities to Non – monetary Financial Institutions	936.2	1666.1	1768.7	2052.5
国外负债 Foreign Liabilities	2909.9	2475.1	2282.7	2213.4
债券 Bonds	473.5	370.8	361.7	370.7
实收资本 Paid – in Capital	4971.0	4787.0	4787.1	4814.5
其他（净） Other Items（Net）	– 2734.3	– 2580.0	– 3249.9	– 2230.9

国有商业银行资产负债表

Balance Sheet of State – owned Commercial Banks

（月末余额）

（Month – end Balance）

单位：亿元

Unit：100 Million Yuan

项目 Items	2002.01	2002.02	2002.03	2002.04
国外资产 Foreign Assets	7653.06	7648.71	7825.98	7825.09
储备资产 Reserve Assets	10747.78	11614.42	12710.14	11618.91
准备金存款 Reserve Deposits	9940.81	10721.89	11849.23	10882.01
库存现金 Cash in Vault	806.97	892.53	860.91	736.90
中央银行债券 Central Bank Bonds				
对政府债权 Claims on Government	7667.34	7665.81	7710.38	7878.60
其中：中央政府 Of Which：Central Government	7667.34	7665.81	7710.38	7878.60
对非金融机构债权 Claims on Non – financial Institutions	71293.07	71557.38	72998.10	73380.33
对特定存款机构债权 Claims on Specific Depository Institutions	3941.91	3862.72	4053.85	3931.15
对其他金融机构债权 Claims on Other Financial Institutions	7862.13	7826.33	7981.27	7757.28
其他资产 Other Assets	11269.97	11553.53	11999.32	12437.90
总资产 Total Assets	**120435.26**	**121728.90**	**125279.04**	**124829.26**
对非金融机构负债 Liabilities to Non – financial Institutions	96391.88	97334.86	99284.29	100218.91
活期存款 Demand Deposits	28802.82	27667.79	29048.75	28837.90
定期存款 Time Deposits	7075.01	7117.43	7198.27	7607.30
储蓄存款 Savings Deposits	49411.27	51418.62	51778.47	52447.07
其他存款 Other Deposits	2328.52	2270.33	2345.75	2391.81
外币存款 Deposits in Foreign Currency	8774.26	8860.69	8913.05	8934.83
对中央银行负债 Liabilities to the Central Bank	2733.67	2734.72	2730.88	2829.98
对特定存款机构负债 Liabilities to Specific Depository Institutions	266.68	273.88	227.70	200.21
对其他金融机构负债 Liabilities to Other Financial Institutions	7161.69	7189.04	8204.07	6034.43
其中：计入广义货币的存款. Of Which：Deposits Included in Broad Money	3542.94	3473.70	4491.38	2521.91
国外负债 Foreign Liabilities	1510.84	1488.53	1491.66	1475.72
债券 Bonds	88.82	103.47	101.41	329.86
实收资本 Paid – in Capital	5142.04	5188.63	5135.17	5179.15
其他负债 Other Liabilities	7139.64	7415.77	8103.86	8561.00
总负债 Total Liabilities	**120435.26**	**121728.90**	**125279.04**	**124829.26**

国有商业银行资产负债表

Balance Sheet of State - owned Commercial Banks

（月末余额）

（Month - end Balance）

单位：亿元

Unit：100 Million Yuan

项　　目 Items	2002.05	2002.06	2002.07	2002.08
国外资产 Foreign Assets	8099.52	8426.14	8732.42	8948.18
储备资产 Reserve Assets	12108.13	12240.47	12165.67	11982.19
准备金存款 Reserve Deposits	11398.67	11414.23	11454.39	11219.60
库存现金 Cash in Vault	709.46	826.24	711.28	762.59
中央银行债券 Central Bank Bonds				
对政府债权 Claims on Government	7936.52	8435.78	8447.79	8522.27
其中：中央政府 Of Which：Central Government	7936.52	8435.78	8447.79	8522.27
对非金融机构债权 Claims on Non - financial Institutions	74158.02	75712.00	75957.36	76825.82
对特定存款机构债权 Claims on Specific Depository Institutions	3843.42	3962.39	3931.06	3956.63
对其他金融机构债权 Claims on Other Financial Institutions	7722.28	7775.22	7767.33	7761.79
其他资产 Other Assets	11799.37	11925.39	12435.74	12462.05
总资产 Total Assets	**125667.26**	**128477.39**	**129437.37**	**130458.93**
对非金融机构负债 Liabilities to Non - financial Institutions	101681.76	103934.14	104716.62	106146.59
活期存款 Demand Deposits	29851.14	31007.57	31094.16	31635.09
定期存款 Time Deposits	7451.80	7524.64	7631.36	7863.63
储蓄存款 Savings Deposits	52869.39	53713.78	54304.30	54838.02
其他存款 Other Deposits	2443.98	2587.11	2598.84	2653.90
外币存款 Deposits in Foreign Currency	9065.45	9101.04	9087.96	9155.95
对中央银行负债 Liabilities to the Central Bank	2910.20	2975.98	3044.17	2902.48
对特定存款机构负债 Liabilities to Specific Depository Institutions	192.90	198.01	205.45	201.37
对其他金融机构负债 Liabilities to Other Financial Institutions	6391.60	6129.28	5971.29	5710.23
其中：计入广义货币的存款 Of Which：Deposits Included in Broad Money	2715.22	2323.67	2235.21	1970.92
国外负债 Foreign Liabilities	1456.33	1641.62	1627.45	1620.20
债券 Bonds	93.10	170.90	81.66	84.74
实收资本 Paid - in Capital	5178.79	5181.40	5185.17	5188.78
其他负债 Other Liabilities	7762.58	8246.06	8605.56	8604.54
总负债 Total Liabilities	**125667.26**	**128477.39**	**129437.37**	**130458.93**

国有商业银行资产负债表

Balance Sheet of State – owned Commercial Banks

(月末余额)

(Month – end Balance)

单位：亿元

Unit: 100 Million Yuan

项 目 Items	2002.09	2002.10	2002.11	2002.12
国外资产 Foreign Assets	8701.45	8993.57	8919.92	9594.90
储备资产 Reserve Assets	10798.41	11483.24	11470.68	11943.14
准备金存款 Reserve Deposits	9930.72	10726.97	10676.83	11189.24
库存现金 Cash in Vault	867.69	756.27	793.85	753.90
中央银行债券 Central Bank Bonds	0.35	785.85	747.45	586.43
对政府债权 Claims on Government	8519.71	8486.01	8485.64	8379.15
其中：中央政府 Of Which: Central Government	8519.71	8486.01	8485.64	8379.15
对非金融机构债权 Claims on Non – financial Institutions	78836.51	79147.60	80130.13	81548.56
对特定存款机构债权 Claims on Specific Depository Institutions	4228.17	4156.69	4247.81	4385.77
对其他金融机构债权 Claims on Other Financial Institutions	7652.67	7647.25	7627.19	7623.70
其他资产 Other Assets	13694.71	12378.05	12505.91	11434.37
总资产 Total Assets	**132431.98**	**133078.26**	**134134.73**	**135496.02**
对非金融机构负债 Liabilities to Non – financial Institutions	107886.90	108440.62	109475.90	110251.87
活期存款 Demand Deposits	32375.92	32819.44	32978.76	32934.32
定期存款 Time Deposits	8280.56	7993.15	8203.49	8415.94
储蓄存款 Savings Deposits	55373.19	55716.30	56241.79	56655.38
其他存款 Other Deposits	2750.29	2670.34	2733.93	2851.48
外币存款 Deposits in Foreign Currency	9106.94	9241.39	9317.93	9394.75
对中央银行负债 Liabilities to the Central Bank	2784.14	2756.31	2682.03	3165.26
对特定存款机构负债 Liabilities to Specific Depository Institutions	243.49	232.07	214.35	202.80
对其他金融机构负债 Liabilities to Other Financial Institutions	5593.78	5490.80	5572.16	5420.41
其中：计入广义货币的存款 Of Which: Deposits Included in Broad Money	1579.39	1635.50	1592.69	1519.30
国外负债 Foreign Liabilities	1590.97	1586.66	1514.45	1884.71
债券 Bonds	72.91	84.57	99.59	208.54
实收资本 Paid – in Capital	5143.15	5189.47	5045.95	5082.31
其他负债 Other Liabilities	9116.64	9297.76	9530.30	9280.12
总负债 Total Liabilities	**132431.98**	**133078.26**	**134134.73**	**135496.02**

国有商业银行资产负债表
Balance Sheet of State - owned Commercial Banks

（月末余额）
（Month - end Balance）

单位：亿元
Unit：100 Million Yuan

项目 Items	2003.01	2003.02	2003.03	2003.04
国外资产 Foreign Assets	9864.62	9848.79	9802.14	9716.33
储备资产 Reserve Assets	11359.59	12621.56	12494.79	11304.28
准备金存款 Reserve Deposits	10048.20	11752.01	11528.95	10493.27
库存现金 Cash in Vault	1311.39	869.55	965.84	811.01
中央银行债券 Central Bank Bonds	778.43	778.43	298.33	367.13
对政府债权 Claims on Government	8399.10	8463.13	8381.75	8496.33
其中：中央政府 Of Which：Central Government	8399.10	8463.13	8381.75	8496.33
对非金融机构债权 Claims on Non - financial Institutions	83750.18	84583.74	86828.51	87788.00
对特定存款机构债权 Claims on Specific Depository Institutions	4277.01	4263.67	4314.43	4305.54
对其他金融机构债权 Claims on Other Financial Institutions	7730.33	7867.37	8022.13	7947.04
其他资产 Other Assets	10551.28	10970.47	12478.89	13868.25
总资产 Total Assets	**136710.54**	**139397.16**	**142620.97**	**143792.90**
对非金融机构负债 Liabilities to Non - financial Institutions	112739.18	114515.70	117685.79	117985.80
活期存款 Demand Deposits	32047.29	32717.93	34318.83	33760.61
定期存款 Time Deposits	8845.01	8829.32	9137.39	9621.19
储蓄存款 Savings Deposits	59641.29	60778.03	61930.99	62271.35
其他存款 Other Deposits	2870.09	2882.38	3049.81	3083.30
外币存款 Deposits in Foreign Currency	9335.50	9308.04	9248.77	9249.35
对中央银行负债 Liabilities to the Central Bank	2545.37	2516.49	2504.18	2479.13
对特定存款机构负债 Liabilities to Specific Depository Institutions	225.37	226.87	210.73	203.75
对其他金融机构负债 Liabilities to Other Financial Institutions	5488.95	5666.83	5783.09	5590.41
其中：计入广义货币的存款 Of Which：Deposits Included in Broad Money	1414.05	1529.99	1522.89	1500.74
国外负债 Foreign Liabilities	2270.18	1962.03	1938.52	2021.73
债券 Bonds	0.47	0.47	0.47	0.46
实收资本 Paid - in Capital	5126.67	5076.75	4916.89	5282.37
其他负债 Other Liabilities	8314.35	9432.02	9581.30	10229.25
总负债 Total Liabilities	**136710.54**	**139397.16**	**142620.97**	**143792.90**

国有商业银行资产负债表

Balance Sheet of State - owned Commercial Banks

（月末余额）

（Month - end Balance）

单位：亿元

Unit：100 Million Yuan

项　目 Items	2003.05	2003.06	2003.07	2003.08
国外资产 Foreign Assets	9425.82	9290.47	8689.52	8629.38
储备资产 Reserve Assets	10697.33	11236.56	11466.69	11165.70
准备金存款 Reserve Deposits	9895.16	10329.71	10694.72	10280.59
库存现金 Cash in Vault	802.17	906.85	771.97	885.11
中央银行债券 Central Bank Bonds	883.71	1628.73	2042.43	2796.85
对政府债权 Claims on Government	8599.14	8701.12	8606.38	8614.81
其中：中央政府 Of Which：Central Government	8599.14	8701.12	8606.38	8614.81
对非金融机构债权 Claims on Non - financial Institutions	89340.66	92604.67	92909.69	94032.34
对特定存款机构债权 Claims on Specific Depository Institutions	4312.50	4545.92	4496.42	4709.03
对其他金融机构债权 Claims on Other Financial Institutions	8160.17	7935.78	7964.61	8369.55
其他资产 Other Assets	13649.07	12836.44	12751.37	13278.69
总资产 Total Assets	**145068.40**	**148779.69**	**148927.11**	**151596.35**
对非金融机构负债 Liabilities to Non - financial Institutions	119831.89	122449.28	123146.32	123939.35
活期存款 Demand Deposits	34784.80	36424.19	36336.27	36644.36
定期存款 Time Deposits	9684.97	9675.08	10001.74	10126.03
储蓄存款 Savings Deposits	62943.01	63659.48	64188.47	64547.93
其他存款 Other Deposits	3133.92	3329.71	3339.29	3451.36
外币存款 Deposits in Foreign Currency	9285.19	9360.82	9280.55	9169.67
对中央银行负债 Liabilities to the Central Bank	2490.86	2495.55	2501.95	2763.97
对特定存款机构负债 Liabilities to Specific Depository Institutions	210.01	202.47	184.86	155.05
对其他金融机构负债 Liabilities to Other Financial Institutions	5884.54	6036.79	5817.16	7395.76
其中：计入广义货币的存款 Of Which：Deposits Included in Broad Money	1651.82	1649.63	1481.18	3078.44
国外负债 Foreign Liabilities	1940.79	2089.15	1822.09	1757.67
债券 Bonds	0.46	0.46	0.42	0.42
实收资本 Paid - in Capital	5282.47	5239.65	5280.39	5280.39
其他负债 Other Liabilities	9427.38	10266.34	10173.92	10303.74
总负债 Total Liabilities	**145068.40**	**148779.69**	**148927.11**	**151596.35**

国有商业银行资产负债表

Balance Sheet of State - owned Commercial Banks

（月末余额）

（Month - end Balance）

单位：亿元

Unit：100 Million Yuan

项目 Items	2003.09	2003.10	2003.11	2003.12
国外资产 Foreign Assets	8453.22	8895.75	8652.14	8386.23
储备资产 Reserve Assets	12448.71	13204.70	13486.33	13507.45
准备金存款 Reserve Deposits	11483.17	12364.46	12584.70	12673.36
库存现金 Cash in Vault	965.54	840.24	901.63	834.09
中央银行债券 Central Bank Bonds	3124.84	3124.84	3099.73	2548.80
对政府债权 Claims on Government	8615.89	8646.14	8800.08	9013.08
其中：中央政府 Of Which：Central Government	8615.89	8646.14	8800.08	9013.08
对非金融机构债权 Claims on Non - financial Institutions	95568.63	95733.82	96036.78	96400.82
对特定存款机构债权 Claims on Specific Depository Institutions	4855.54	5012.53	5124.61	5358.90
对其他金融机构债权 Claims on Other Financial Institutions	7953.30	8004.39	7928.24	11377.39
其他资产 Other Assets	12071.96	12252.19	12066.42	9807.38
总资产 Total Assets	**153092.09**	**154874.36**	**155194.33**	**156400.05**
对非金融机构负债 Liabilities to Non - financial Institutions	126133.58	126631.42	127124.22	127119.80
活期存款 Demand Deposits	37101.58	37856.63	37856.78	37797.01
定期存款 Time Deposits	10838.90	10365.19	10392.86	10038.25
储蓄存款 Savings Deposits	65635.39	65921.02	66326.99	66850.39
其他存款 Other Deposits	3506.09	3430.83	3488.10	3475.38
外币存款 Deposits in Foreign Currency	9051.62	9057.75	9059.49	8958.77
对中央银行负债 Liabilities to the Central Bank	2964.14	3179.59	2634.29	2610.69
对特定存款机构负债 Liabilities to Specific Depository Institutions	177.17	210.69	189.15	197.57
对其他金融机构负债 Liabilities to Other Financial Institutions	5697.47	5880.92	5936.62	5769.14
其中：计入广义货币的存款 Of Which：Deposits Included in Broad Money	1135.51	1332.59	1359.00	1244.11
国外负债 Foreign Liabilities	1806.26	2214.67	2129.14	1985.53
债券 Bonds	0.41	0.41	0.41	0.37
实收资本 Paid - in Capital	5210.60	5262.05	5262.62	6672.40
其他负债 Other Liabilities	11102.46	11494.61	11917.88	12044.55
总负债 Total Liabilities	**153092.09**	**154874.36**	**155194.33**	**156400.05**

国有商业银行资产负债表

Balance Sheet of State – owned Commercial Banks

(月末余额)

(Month – end Balance)

单位：亿元

Unit：100 Million Yuan

项 目 Items	2004.01	2004.02	2004.03	2004.04
国外资产 Foreign Assets	10244.53	10256.68	9704.57	9194.00
储备资产 Reserve Assets	14244.48	14796.56	13882.91	13452.76
准备金存款 Reserve Deposits	12595.57	13781.80	12904.84	12537.59
库存现金 Cash in Vault	1648.91	1014.76	978.07	915.17
中央银行债券 Central Bank Bonds	2510.84	3320.69	4597.97	4562.94
对政府债权 Claims on Government	8991.42	9017.30	9167.59	9164.03
其中：中央政府 Of Which：Central Government	8991.42	9017.30	9167.59	9164.03
对非金融机构债权 Claims on Non – financial Institutions	98715.07	100079.35	101804.33	102709.48
对特定存款机构债权 Claims on Specific Depository Institutions	5416.43	5547.26	5745.89	5813.73
对其他金融机构债权 Claims on Other Financial Institutions	8415.52	7705.86	7931.84	8002.05
其他资产 Other Assets	10680.06	10745.79	11406.33	10906.69
总资产 Total Assets	**159218.35**	**161469.49**	**164241.43**	**163805.68**
对非金融机构负债 Liabilities to Non – financial Institutions	129658.70	131653.61	134349.11	134587.02
活期存款 Demand Deposits	37166.58	38699.68	40277.31	39569.96
定期存款 Time Deposits	10493.65	10506.47	10817.23	11767.88
储蓄存款 Savings Deposits	70706.96	71418.74	72084.67	72017.48
其他存款 Other Deposits	2233.74	2274.54	2388.37	2449.53
外币存款 Deposits in Foreign Currency	9057.77	8754.18	8781.53	8782.17
对中央银行负债 Liabilities to the Central Bank	2705.33	2581.48	2515.53	2467.67
对特定存款机构负债 Liabilities to Specific Depository Institutions	189.11	185.66	148.97	155.65
对其他金融机构负债 Liabilities to Other Financial Institutions	6159.66	6109.28	6212.68	5886.93
其中：计入广义货币的存款 Of Which：Deposits Included in Broad Money	1278.50	1608.56	1572.65	1402.75
国外负债 Foreign Liabilities	2403.88	2264.69	1744.62	1482.51
债券 Bonds	0.36	0.36	0.35	0.35
实收资本 Paid – in Capital	6664.32	6661.23	6671.96	6671.62
其他负债 Other Liabilities	11436.99	12013.18	12598.21	12553.93
总负债 Total Liabilities	**159218.35**	**161469.49**	**164241.43**	**163805.68**

国有商业银行资产负债表

Balance Sheet of State - owned Commercial Banks

（月末余额）

（Month - end Balance）

单位：亿元

Unit：100 Million Yuan

项目 Items	2004.05	2004.06	2004.07	2004.08
国外资产 Foreign Assets	9574.93	10863.05	10939.25	11203.54
储备资产 Reserve Assets	13627.55	14188.25	13590.16	14518.71
准备金存款 Reserve Deposits	12715.40	13243.89	12706.60	13556.00
库存现金 Cash in Vault	912.15	944.36	883.56	962.71
中央银行债券 Central Bank Bonds	4117.69	5367.39	5256.93	4648.17
对政府债权 Claims on Government	9040.21	9267.06	9448.38	9556.94
其中：中央政府 Of Which：Central Government	9040.21	9267.06	9448.38	9556.94
对非金融机构债权 Claims on Non - financial Institutions	103284.79	99800.23	99541.70	100167.07
对特定存款机构债权 Claims on Specific Depository Institutions	5907.93	5966.14	6100.98	6164.23
对其他金融机构债权 Claims on Other Financial Institutions	8032.23	8059.92	7959.57	7958.38
其他资产 Other Assets	11419.71	11025.03	10651.39	10430.31
总资产 Total Assets	**165005.04**	**164537.07**	**163488.36**	**164647.35**
对非金融机构负债 Liabilities to Non - financial Institutions	135766.69	137108.95	137099.88	138092.77
活期存款 Demand Deposits	40912.47	41493.29	41124.84	41827.07
定期存款 Time Deposits	11416.64	11564.62	11577.73	11665.74
储蓄存款 Savings Deposits	72087.18	72618.52	72904.30	73037.66
其他存款 Other Deposits	2458.28	2523.92	2470.22	2480.51
外币存款 Deposits in Foreign Currency	8892.12	8908.60	9022.79	9081.79
对中央银行负债 Liabilities to the Central Bank	2444.36	2436.88	2439.70	2419.14
对特定存款机构负债 Liabilities to Specific Depository Institutions	160.59	168.37	171.20	168.59
对其他金融机构负债 Liabilities to Other Financial Institutions	5768.79	5524.09	5337.72	5460.54
其中：计入广义货币的存款 Of Which：Deposits Included in Broad Money	1460.15	1186.61	1150.60	1083.88
国外负债 Foreign Liabilities	1465.72	1505.04	1504.23	1532.51
债券 Bonds	0.35	0.35	141.03	291.02
实收资本 Paid - in Capital	6671.39	6671.14	6671.33	6671.27
其他负债 Other Liabilities	12727.15	11122.25	10123.27	10011.51
总负债 Total Liabilities	**165005.04**	**164537.07**	**163488.36**	**164647.35**

国有商业银行资产负债表
Balance Sheet of State - owned Commercial Banks

（月末余额）

（Month - end Balance）

单位：亿元

Unit：100 Million Yuan

项　目 Items	2004.09	2004.10	2004.11	2004.12
国外资产 Foreign Assets	11325.00	11075.15	11036.21	10736.38
储备资产 Reserve Assets	14595.96	14514.82	15091.81	15171.02
准备金存款 Reserve Deposits	13448.29	13536.78	14139.68	14281.64
库存现金 Cash in Vault	1147.67	978.04	952.13	889.38
中央银行债券 Central Bank Bonds	4814.15	5739.31	5877.58	6759.71
对政府债权 Claims on Government	9739.61	9709.35	9833.00	11320.93
其中：中央政府 Of Which：Central Government	9739.61	9709.35	9833.00	11320.93
对非金融机构债权 Claims on Non - financial Institutions	101886.37	101730.77	102460.50	103706.95
对特定存款机构债权 Claims on Specific Depository Institutions	6292.97	6558.00	6944.66	7333.41
对其他金融机构债权 Claims on Other Financial Institutions	7954.71	7895.13	7990.57	6362.04
其他资产 Other Assets	10134.15	11185.53	11081.36	11529.42
总资产 Total Assets	**166742.92**	**168408.06**	**170315.69**	**172919.86**
对非金融机构负债 Liabilities to Non - financial Institutions	139491.18	139710.18	141124.58	142744.09
活期存款 Demand Deposits	41828.28	42292.60	42925.74	43288.80
定期存款 Time Deposits	12433.55	12019.56	12061.96	12407.07
储蓄存款 Savings Deposits	73589.56	73771.07	74682.89	75682.31
其他存款 Other Deposits	2550.32	2488.42	2534.35	2571.80
外币存款 Deposits in Foreign Currency	9089.47	9138.53	8919.64	8794.11
对中央银行负债 Liabilities to the Central Bank	2411.65	2395.94	2410.90	2402.27
对特定存款机构负债 Liabilities to Specific Depository Institutions	155.21	165.13	156.47	170.00
对其他金融机构负债 Liabilities to Other Financial Institutions	5387.48	5394.69	5409.16	5247.39
其中：计入广义货币的存款 Of Which：Deposits Included in Broad Money	1074.64	1008.45	1044.53	913.68
国外负债 Foreign Liabilities	1856.46	1744.95	1809.96	1718.66
债券 Bonds	374.02	374.02	494.12	661.07
实收资本 Paid - in Capital	6751.19	6751.08	6753.12	6730.88
其他负债 Other Liabilities	10315.73	11872.07	12157.38	13245.50
总负债 Total Liabilities	**166742.92**	**168408.06**	**170315.69**	**172919.86**

国有商业银行资产负债表

Balance Sheet of State - owned Commercial Banks

（月末余额）

（Month - end Balance）

单位：亿元

Unit：100 Million Yuan

项　目 Items	2005.01	2005.02	2005.03	2005.04
国外资产 Foreign Assets	10697.53	10720.96	10415.49	11536.00
储备资产 Reserve Assets	16090.87	17001.88	16951.25	15877.43
准备金存款 Reserve Deposits	14936.62	15697.67	15886.11	14895.65
库存现金 Cash in Vault	1154.25	1304.21	1065.14	981.78
中央银行债券 Central Bank Bonds	6463.05	6928.93	8538.06	9929.51
对政府债权 Claims on Government	9799.83	9741.89	10024.68	10059.80
其中：中央政府 Of Which：Central Government	9799.83	9741.89	10024.68	10059.80
对非金融机构债权 Claims on Non - financial Institutions	104927.41	105326.64	107133.09	107011.70
对特定存款机构债权 Claims on Specific Depository Institutions	7350.99	7490.30	8049.66	8441.34
对其他金融机构债权 Claims on Other Financial Institutions	7933.13	7929.56	8119.55	8021.55
其他资产 Other Assets	11641.42	11779.63	11397.10	12257.72
总资产 Total Assets	**174904.23**	**176919.79**	**180628.88**	**183135.05**
对非金融机构负债 Liabilities to Non - financial Institutions	144868.64	146975.51	150928.86	151576.52
活期存款 Demand Deposits	43445.06	41800.98	43865.24	43411.03
定期存款 Time Deposits	12339.47	12675.42	13478.75	14426.15
储蓄存款 Savings Deposits	77655.77	80960.44	81823.49	82012.73
其他存款 Other Deposits	2664.34	2656.15	2835.33	2930.18
外币存款 Deposits in Foreign Currency	8764.00	8882.52	8926.05	8796.43
对中央银行负债 Liabilities to the Central Bank	2373.62	2329.38	2267.00	2241.32
对特定存款机构负债 Liabilities to Specific Depository Institutions	191.47	162.30	158.51	161.88
对其他金融机构负债 Liabilities to Other Financial Institutions	3790.83	3916.71	3946.11	3780.99
其中：计入广义货币的存款 Of Which：Deposits Included in Broad Money	876.04	924.72	890.00	781.96
国外负债 Foreign Liabilities	1910.53	1809.36	1584.16	1590.69
债券 Bonds	661.06	661.06	1000.35	1000.35
实收资本 Paid - in Capital	6634.20	6634.20	6634.20	7875.73
其他负债 Other Liabilities	14473.88	14431.27	14109.69	14907.57
总负债 Total Liabilities	**174904.23**	**176919.79**	**180628.88**	**183135.05**

国有商业银行资产负债表

Balance Sheet of State－owned Commercial Banks

（月末余额）

（Month－end Balance）

单位：亿元

Unit：100 Million Yuan

项　目 Items	2005.05	2005.06	2005.07	2005.08
国外资产 Foreign Assets	11212.60	11294.62	10628.39	10966.36
储备资产 Reserve Assets	16806.33	16392.46	17788.98	17526.10
准备金存款 Reserve Deposits	15856.95	15428.44	16809.17	16493.32
库存现金 Cash in Vault	949.38	964.02	979.81	1032.78
中央银行债券 Central Bank Bonds	10441.08	9647.93	10019.65	10501.15
对政府债权 Claims on Government	10187.88	10299.18	10550.36	10833.03
其中：中央政府 Of Which：Central Government	10187.88	10299.18	10550.36	10833.03
对非金融机构债权 Claims on Non－financial Institutions	105414.72	102716.11	101914.30	102192.38
对特定存款机构债权 Claims on Specific Depository Institutions	8757.52	9179.29	9628.15	10327.43
对其他金融机构债权 Claims on Other Financial Institutions	8129.98	8134.52	8347.50	8603.91
其他资产 Other Assets	13985.43	19615.49	19640.26	20756.15
总资产 Total Assets	**184935.54**	**187279.60**	**188517.59**	**191706.51**
对非金融机构负债 Liabilities to Non－financial Institutions	153072.22	155253.58	156005.20	158223.64
活期存款 Demand Deposits	44558.50	45477.70	45247.91	46213.92
定期存款 Time Deposits	14569.00	14910.90	15276.32	15923.73
储蓄存款 Savings Deposits	82306.93	83028.96	83926.05	84382.93
其他存款 Other Deposits	2974.71	3134.76	3194.35	3264.78
外币存款 Deposits in Foreign Currency	8663.08	8701.26	8360.57	8438.28
对中央银行负债 Liabilities to the Central Bank	2178.29	1900.22	1890.88	1841.44
对特定存款机构负债 Liabilities to Specific Depository Institutions	160.20	198.19	177.84	230.18
对其他金融机构负债 Liabilities to Other Financial Institutions	3976.08	4301.87	4779.72	5314.23
其中：计入广义货币的存款 Of Which：Deposits Included in Broad Money	877.62	984.44	1186.43	1279.74
国外负债 Foreign Liabilities	1726.72	1409.47	1448.36	1224.65
债券 Bonds	1000.35	1000.36	1000.36	1130.39
实收资本 Paid－in Capital	7509.03	7509.03	7521.66	7507.04
其他负债 Other Liabilities	15312.65	15706.88	15693.57	16234.94
总负债 Total Liabilities	**184935.54**	**187279.60**	**188517.59**	**191706.51**

国有商业银行资产负债表

Balance Sheet of State - owned Commercial Banks

（月末余额）

（Month - end Balance）

单位：亿元

Unit：100 Million Yuan

项目 Items	2005.09	2005.10	2005.11	2005.12
国外资产 Foreign Assets	11194.21	13050.58	13230.19	13849.95
储备资产 Reserve Assets	17830.93	17185.03	15622.24	16400.93
准备金存款 Reserve Deposits	16707.46	16153.10	14645.39	15436.24
库存现金 Cash in Vault	1123.47	1031.93	976.85	964.69
中央银行债券 Central Bank Bonds	10737.30	11975.39	13454.37	12921.17
对政府债权 Claims on Government	11075.27	11137.57	11070.70	11418.27
其中：中央政府 Of Which：Central Government	11075.27	11137.57	11070.70	11418.27
对非金融机构债权 Claims on Non - financial Institutions	103333.11	102001.97	103300.75	103509.21
对特定存款机构债权 Claims on Specific Depository Institutions	10881.20	11047.60	11425.17	11501.25
对其他金融机构债权 Claims on Other Financial Institutions	8678.90	8802.77	8832.79	8324.20
其他资产 Other Assets	21599.49	21463.11	21778.81	22358.70
总资产 Total Assets	**195330.41**	**196664.02**	**198715.02**	**200283.68**
对非金融机构负债 Liabilities to Non - financial Institutions	160267.73	160537.47	162003.75	162835.05
活期存款 Demand Deposits	46270.52	47178.09	48036.95	47508.88
定期存款 Time Deposits	17148.02	16426.65	16257.52	16647.40
储蓄存款 Savings Deposits	85382.54	85372.38	86021.25	87034.23
其他存款 Other Deposits	3327.17	3285.11	3367.51	3357.01
外币存款 Deposits in Foreign Currency	8139.48	8275.24	8320.52	8287.53
对中央银行负债 Liabilities to the Central Bank	1854.50	1885.30	1998.74	1802.00
对特定存款机构负债 Liabilities to Specific Depository Institutions	201.78	168.90	137.89	370.82
对其他金融机构负债 Liabilities to Other Financial Institutions	5382.64	5577.98	5770.51	5411.78
其中：计入广义货币的存款 Of Which：Deposits Included in Broad Money	1112.56	1156.56	1155.93	986.17
国外负债 Foreign Liabilities	1205.83	1168.10	1108.61	970.94
债券 Bonds	1351.15	1352.08	1352.97	1353.84
实收资本 Paid - in Capital	7507.27	7772.16	7812.02	8043.94
其他负债 Other Liabilities	17559.51	18202.03	18530.53	19495.31
总负债 Total Liabilities	**195330.41**	**196664.02**	**198715.02**	**200283.68**

4. 其他商业银行资产负债表
Balance Sheet of Other Commercial Banks

其他商业银行资产负债表
Balance Sheet of Other Commercial Banks

(季末余额)

(Quarter – end Balance)

单位：亿元

Unit：100 Million Yuan

项 目 Items	1993.03	1993.06	1993.09	1993.12
国外资产 Foreign Assets	208.9	217.8	210.6	228.2
储备资产 Reserve Assets	256.6	271.6	296.1	502.1
准备金 Reserves	137.3	151.2	144.4	172.2
在中央银行存款 Deposits with the Central Bank	111.4	111.0	142.5	313.4
库存现金 Cash in Vault	7.9	9.4	9.2	16.5
中央银行债券 Central Bank Bonds				
对政府债权 Claims on Government	1.0	0.4	1.4	0.4
对其他部门债权 Claims on Other Sectors	921.4	1027.7	1080.3	1235.0
对非货币金融机构债权 Claims on Non – monetary Financial Institutions				
对非金融部门负债 Liabilities to Non – financial Sectors	1136.0	1297.9	1274.1	1549.8
活期存款 Demand Deposits	717.7	803.7	770.6	945.8
定期存款 Time Deposits	158.2	168.9	169.1	208.2
储蓄存款 Savings Deposits	133.7	150.6	179.3	210.4
其他存款 Other Deposits	126.4	174.7	155.1	185.4
对中央银行负债 Liabilities to the Central Bank	62.7	58.6	63.1	80.4
对非货币金融机构负债 Liabilities to Non – monetary Financial Institutions				
国外负债 Foreign Liabilities	112.0	125.0	127.6	134.0
债券 Bonds	11.1	10.2	10.6	8.8
所有者权益 Owner's Equity	117.8	124.6	132.6	144.7
其中：实收资本 Of Which：Paid – in Capital	117.8	124.6	132.6	144.7
其他（净） Other Items（Net）	– 51.7	– 98.8	– 19.6	48.0

其他商业银行资产负债表
Balance Sheet of Other Commercial Banks

（季末余额）
（Quarter – end Balance）

单位：亿元
Unit：100 Million Yuan

项目 Items	1994.03	1994.06	1994.09	1994.12
国外资产 Foreign Assets	334.5	294.9	348.9	450.7
储备资产 Reserve Assets	467.5	537.6	563.4	767.3
准备金 Reserves	186.7	222.7	252.1	281.1
在中央银行存款 Deposits with the Central Bank	266.6	299.9	293.8	466.4
库存现金 Cash in Vault	14.2	15.0	17.5	19.8
中央银行债券 Central Bank Bonds	15.6	14.4	34.9	52.7
对政府债权 Claims on Government	0.0	0.0	10.0	11.6
对其他部门债权 Claims on Other Sectors	1296.2	1466.1	1618.7	1788.6
对非货币金融机构债权 Claims on Non – monetary Financial Institutions	38.5	40.6	39.0	58.5
对非金融部门负债 Liabilities to Non – financial Sectors	1630.8	1945.3	2172.3	2427.7
活期存款 Demand Deposits	1037.6	1224.7	1308.0	1427.9
定期存款 Time Deposits	170.9	238.3	293.2	341.7
储蓄存款 Savings Deposits	255.4	294.3	347.7	413.0
其他存款 Other Deposits	166.9	188.0	223.4	245.1
对中央银行负债 Liabilities to the Central Bank	79.0	74.4	71.1	92.6
对非货币金融机构负债 Liabilities to Non – monetary Financial Institutions	29.7	33.8	36.1	91.0
国外负债 Foreign Liabilities	139.4	140.8	157.8	173.9
债券 Bonds	7.8	7.5	7.1	6.8
所有者权益 Owner's Equity	194.7	218.0	220.8	242.4
其中：实收资本 Of Which：Paid – in Capital	132.3	148.2	152.1	175.1
其他（净） Other Items（Net）	70.9	– 66.2	– 50.3	95.0

其他商业银行资产负债表
Balance Sheet of Other Commercial Banks

（季末余额）

（Quarter – end Balance）

单位：亿元

Unit：100 Million Yuan

项　目 Items	1995.03	1995.06	1995.09	1995.12
国外资产 Foreign Assets	538.4	488.9	528.1	602.6
储备资产 Reserve Assets	725.0	756.9	818.8	1052.4
准备金 Reserves	307.4	346.6	383.8	422.6
在人行存款 Deposits with the Central Bank	396.8	386.0	410.8	600.5
库存现金 Cash in Vault	20.8	24.3	24.2	29.3
中央银行债券 Central Bank Bonds	0.7	1.0	2.0	3.0
对政府债权 Claims on Government	95.2	75.6	87.9	114.7
对其他部门债权 Claims on Other Sectors	2114.5	2290.2	2384.1	2813.5
对非货币金融机构债权 Claims on Non – monetary Financial Institutions	75.7	98.6	85.3	96.0
对非金融部门负债 Liabilities to Non – financial Sectors	2758.5	3114.4	3423.5	3779.8
活期存款 Demand Deposits	1589.5	1736.7	1837.3	1994.8
定期存款 Time Deposits	413.8	529.4	630.1	680.3
储蓄存款 Savings Deposits	486.6	559.7	653.2	759.1
其他存款 Other Deposits	268.6	288.6	302.9	345.6
对中央银行负债 Liabilities to the Central Bank	80.0	36.6	37.9	43.7
对非货币金融机构负债 Liabilities to Non – monetary Financial Institutions	71.5	93.5	109.2	149.0
国外负债 Foreign Liabilities	346.0	359.4	356.1	365.5
债券 Bonds	6.7	3.8	1.0	0.2
所有者权益 Owner's Equity	268.9	275.1	299.3	281.8
其中：实收资本 Of Which：Paid – in Capital	197.5	205.0	219.6	223.5
其他（净） Other Items（Net）	17.9	– 171.6	– 320.8	62.2

其他商业银行资产负债表
Balance Sheet of Other Commercial Banks

（季末余额）
（Quarter - end Balance）

单位：亿元
Unit：100 Million Yuan

项　目 Items	1996.03	1996.06	1996.09	1996.12
国外资产 Foreign Assets	658.1	628.7	682.3	701.9
储备资产 Reserve Assets	938.3	1050.1	1094.3	1427.2
准备金 Reserves	447.0	522.2	602.6	647.5
在人行存款 Deposits with the Central Bank	461.8	496.4	457.4	752.7
库存现金 Cash in Vault	29.5	31.5	34.3	27.0
中央银行债券 Central Bank Bonds	0.0	0.0	0.0	0.0
对政府债权 Claims on Government	181.4	219.4	321.8	301.4
对其他部门债权 Claims on Other Sectors	2881.8	3406.3	3659.0	4089.5
对非货币金融机构债权 Claims on Non - monetary Financial Institutions	54.9	117.9	122.9	153.3
对非金融部门负债 Liabilities to Non - financial Sectors	3955.8	4713.2	5125.5	5703.6
活期存款 Demand Deposits	1966.2	2345.0	2538.1	2888.7
定期存款 Time Deposits	755.3	934.8	1078.6	1222.7
储蓄存款 Savings Deposits	886.7	1007.0	1122.4	1185.6
其他存款 Other Deposits	347.6	426.4	386.4	406.6
对中央银行负债 Liabilities to the Central Bank	44.3	51.4	48.1	81.2
对非货币金融机构负债 Liabilities to Non - monetary Financial Institutions	107.4	139.5	106.1	166.7
国外负债 Foreign Liabilities	355.7	360.4	373.5	400.7
债券 Bonds	0.1	0.1	0.1	6.9
所有者权益 Owner's Equity	320.6	356.5	393.5	429.4
其中：实收资本 Of Which：Paid - in Capital	236.6	275.3	274.9	292.9
其他（净） Other Items（Net）	- 69.4	- 198.7	- 166.5	- 115.2

其他商业银行资产负债表
Balance Sheet of Other Commercial Banks

（季末余额）
(Quarter – end Balance)

单位：亿元
Unit: 100 Million Yuan

项　目 Items	1997.03	1997.06	1997.09	1997.12
国外资产 Foreign Assets	713.6	722.1	715.4	722.1
储备资产 Reserve Assets	1151.9	1672.4	1528.1	2009.2
准备金 Reserves	604.6	664.2	695.6	736.9
在人行存款 Deposits with the Central Bank	504.2	967.8	793.2	1233.2
库存现金 Cash in Vault	43.1	40.4	39.3	39.1
中央银行债券 Central Bank Bonds	20.0	29.3	32.2	32.3
对政府债权 Claims on Government	291.7	241.3	253.3	252.1
对其他部门债权 Claims on Other Sectors	3489.4	3682.6	3858.0	4304.3
对非货币金融机构债权 Claims on Non – monetary Financial Institutions	358.5	380.0	400.1	461.1
对非金融部门负债 Liabilities to Non – financial Sectors	4982.6	5527.4	5732.8	6375.7
活期存款 Demand Deposits	2494.0	2845.5	2974.4	3466.7
定期存款 Time Deposits	1185.2	1261.9	1346.9	1453.3
储蓄存款 Savings Deposits	1168.8	1284.9	1288.1	1357.8
其他存款 Other Deposits	134.6	135.1	123.4	97.9
对中央银行负债 Liabilities to the Central Bank	58.2	51.1	38.6	59.7
对非货币金融机构负债 Liabilities to Non – monetary Financial Institutions	137.7	168.4	131.4	312.7
国外负债 Foreign Liabilities	386.5	373.6	375.7	304.2
债券 Bonds	0.1	0.1	1.3	4.9
所有者权益 Owner's Equity	459.6	479.7	488.9	530.7
其中：实收资本 Of Which: Paid – in Capital	273.8	277.3	278.3	298.0
其他（净） Other Items (Net)	0.4	127.4	18.4	193.2

其他商业银行资产负债表

Balance Sheet of Other Commercial Banks

（季末余额）

（Quarter - end Balance）

单位：亿元

Unit：100 Million Yuan

项　目 Items	1998.03	1998.06	1998.09	1998.12
国外资产 Foreign Assets	938.7	933.5	960.6	940.8
储备资产 Reserve Assets	1462.3	1448.8	1575.1	1995.3
准备金 Reserves	736.9	1405.8	1532.3	1948.9
在人行存款 Deposits with the Central Bank	681.1			
库存现金 Cash in Vault	44.3	43.0	42.8	46.4
中央银行债券 Central Bank Bonds	33.3	41.9	35.3	33.7
对政府债权 Claims on Government	266.4	385.6	413.1	460.2
对其他部门债权 Claims on Other Sectors	4337.3	4576.7	4918.0	5314.4
对非货币金融机构债权 Claims on Non - monetary Financial Institutions	455.2	555.8	682.4	780.9
对非金融部门负债 Liabilities to Non - financial Sectors	6074.0	6458.9	6889.1	7583.4
活期存款 Demand Deposits	3090.8	3289.4	3500.7	3890.2
定期存款 Time Deposits	1370.4	1498.9	1593.6	1761.5
储蓄存款 Savings Deposits	1449.8	1478.8	1555.8	1667.2
其他存款 Other Deposits	163.0	191.8	239.0	264.5
对中央银行负债 Liabilities to the Central Bank	79.8	77.6	72.7	77.8
对非货币金融机构负债 Liabilities to Non - monetary Financial Institutions	190.1	230.6	260.4	356.4
国外负债 Foreign Liabilities	287.1	265.5	242.7	238.8
债券 Bonds	12.2	13.5	16.4	16.4
所有者权益 Owner's Equity	525.5	537.2	530.0	538.2
其中：实收资本 Of Which：Paid - in Capital	298.5	298.5	298.6	306.2
其他（净） Other Items（Net）	324.5	359.0	573.2	714.30

其他商业银行资产负债表
Balance Sheet of Other Commercial Banks

（季末余额）
（Quarter – end Balance）

单位：亿元
Unit：100 Million Yuan

项　目 Items	1999.03	1999.06	1999.09	1999.12
国外资产 Foreign Assets	756.7	728.6	844.6	1108.7
储备资产 Reserve Assets	1317.4	1404.9	2028.0	2509.2
准备金 Reserves	1268.9	1355.5	1960.4	2405.5
库存现金 Cash in Vault	48.5	49.4	67.6	103.7
中央银行债券 Central Bank Bonds	27.2	27.1	25.3	24.3
对政府债权 Claims on Government	470.3	491.0	503.3	622.6
对其他部门债权 Claims on Other Sectors	5315.7	5524.4	5800.4	6190.2
对非货币金融机构债权 Claims on Non – monetary Financial Institutions	811.3	833.3	997.0	974.3
对非金融部门负债 Liabilities to Non – financial Sectors	7318.6	7735.8	8145.9	8968.4
活期存款 Demand Deposits	3572.1	3782.3	4075.5	4699.5
定期存款 Time Deposits	1741.2	1875.2	1913.3	2035.9
储蓄存款 Savings Deposits	1772.1	1807.8	1828.4	1880.8
其他存款 Other Deposits	233.2	270.5	328.7	352.2
对中央银行负债 Liabilities to the Central Bank	64.6	76.7	76.7	129.3
对非货币金融机构负债 Liabilities to Non – monetary Financial Institutions	114.1	109.4	196.7	226.2
国外负债 Foreign Liabilities	205.7	187.5	181.3	169.6
债券 Bonds	4.4	4.4	4.4	4.4
实收资本 Paid – in Capital	304.7	299.7	309.2	344.1
其他（净） Other Items（Net）	686.5	595.8	1284.4	1587.3

其他商业银行资产负债表
Balance Sheet of Other Commercial Banks

（季末余额）
（Quarter - end Balance）

单位：亿元
Unit：100 Million Yuan

项　目 Items	2000.03	2000.06	2000.09	2000.12
国外资产 Foreign Assets	1102.9	1242.0	1357.7	1520.6
储备资产 Reserve Assets	2136.4	2144.6	2326.0	3115.0
准备金 Reserves	2073.9	2080.3	2244.5	3020.6
库存现金 Cash in Vault	62.5	64.3	81.5	94.4
中央银行债券 Central Bank Bonds	5.2	2.6	4.5	4.5
对政府债权 Claims on Government	626.9	705.6	751.2	773.8
对其他部门债权 Claims on Other Sectors	6460.1	9195.4	7739.9	8464.0
对非货币金融机构债权 Claims on Non - monetary Financial Institutions	930.8	1267.2	1351.0	1412.9
对非金融部门负债 Liabilities to Non - financial Sectors	9050.5	10268.4	11158.6	11867.3
活期存款 Demand Deposits	4645.8	5422.7	5794.8	6088.3
定期存款 Time Deposits	2057.6	2301.9	2564.6	2715.8
储蓄存款 Savings Deposits	1961.0	2016.8	2123.9	2261.0
其他存款 Other Deposits	386.1	527.0	675.3	802.2
对中央银行负债 Liabilities to the Central Bank	139.4	117.2	115.1	96.8
对非货币金融机构负债 Liabilities to Non - monetary Financial Institutions	211.3	152.3	223.7	249.6
国外负债 Foreign Liabilities	169.6	166.0	118.7	123.2
债券 Bonds	4.4	4.4	4.3	4.3
实收资本 Paid - in Capital	339.3	309.4	314.5	348.8
其他（净） Other Items（Net）	1347.8	3539.7	1595.4	2600.8

其他商业银行资产负债表

Balance Sheet of Other Commercial Banks

（季末余额）

（Quarter - end Balance）

单位：亿元

Unit：100 Million Yuan

项 目 Items	2001.03	2001.06	2001.09	2001.12
国外资产 Foreign Assets	1706.4	1739.9	1833.8	1738.8
储备资产 Reserve Assets	2630.9	2882.4	2741.6	3454.1
准备金 Reserves	2543.7	2792.3	2627.3	3350.3
库存现金 Cash in Vault	87.2	90.1	114.3	103.8
中央银行债券 Central Bank Bonds	5.0	4.9	4.9	5.1
对政府债权 Claims on Government	1141.9	1290.1	1402.2	1526.8
对其他部门债权 Claims on Other Sectors	9125.8	10045.8	10768.7	11514.9
对非货币金融机构债权 Claims on Non - monetary Financial Institutions	700.4	995.6	1036.6	1066.4
对非金融部门负债 Liabilities to Non - financial Sectors	12478.3	14023.7	14621.9	15865.4
活期存款 Demand Deposits	6276.5	7060.9	7140.9	7699.8
定期存款 Time Deposits	2864.1	3227.9	3403.6	3695.7
储蓄存款 Savings Deposits	2451.9	2607.2	2833.6	3121.6
其他存款 Other Deposits	885.8	1127.7	1243.8	1348.3
对中央银行负债 Liabilities to the Central Bank	93.7	93.4	83.5	73.3
对非货币金融机构负债 Liabilities to Non - monetary Financial Institutions	296.4	338.0	334.6	363.4
国外负债 Foreign Liabilities	215.4	200.3	207.3	198.1
债券 Bonds	4.3	0.3		
实收资本 Paid - in Capital	359.3	373.6	376.2	390.0
其他（净） Other Items（Net）	1863.0	1929.4	2164.3	2415.9

其他商业银行资产负债表

Balance Sheet of Other Commercial Banks

（月末余额）

（Month－end Balance）

单位：亿元

Unit：100 Million Yuan

项目 Items	2002.01	2002.02	2002.03	2002.04
国外资产 Foreign Assets	1674.44	1687.56	1691.45	1692.59
储备资产 Reserve Assets	2792.41	2414.43	2911.38	2522.12
准备金存款 Reserve Deposits	2687.32	2305.95	2800.31	2405.53
库存现金 Cash in Vault	105.09	108.48	111.07	116.59
中央银行债券 Central Bank Bonds				
对政府债权 Claims on Government	1576.75	1588.70	1743.52	1800.05
其中：中央政府 Of Which：Central Government	1576.75	1588.70	1743.52	1800.05
对非金融机构债权 Claims on Non－financial Institutions	12714.78	12861.56	13508.92	13821.32
对特定存款机构债权 Claims on Specific Depository Institutions	1045.55	1052.51	1104.72	1162.69
对其他金融机构债权 Claims on Other Financial Institutions	413.55	445.61	301.54	139.01
其他资产 Other Assets	2279.69	2364.97	2796.00	3116.21
总资产 Total Assets	**22497.17**	**22415.34**	**24057.53**	**24253.99**
对非金融机构负债 Liabilities to Non－financial Institutions	17004.56	16933.31	17368.20	18423.62
活期存款 Demand Deposits	7328.51	7132.33	7362.97	7821.13
定期存款 Time Deposits	3369.41	3352.63	3437.60	3783.26
储蓄存款 Savings Deposits	3173.00	3309.33	3336.74	3511.37
其他存款 Other Deposits	1307.59	1297.86	1373.03	1461.23
外币存款 Deposits in Foreign Currency	1826.05	1841.16	1857.86	1846.63
对中央银行负债 Liabilities to the Central Bank	568.30	412.28	551.77	462.68
对特定存款机构负债 Liabilities to Specific Depository Institutions	81.40	100.92	94.41	92.45
对其他金融机构负债 Liabilities to Other Financial Institutions	2341.44	2419.41	3482.04	2484.24
其中：计入广义货币的存款 Of Which：Deposits Included in Broad Money	1196.32	1215.86	1671.63	1137.75
国外负债 Foreign Liabilities	118.66	141.81	121.26	111.69
债券 Bonds	55.48	127.12	69.38	170.06
实收资本 Paid－in Capital	546.76	547.21	546.20	562.22
其他负债 Other Liabilities	1780.57	1733.28	1824.27	1947.03
总负债 Total Liabilities	**22497.17**	**22415.34**	**24057.53**	**24253.99**

其他商业银行资产负债表
Balance Sheet of Other Commercial Banks
（月末余额）
(Month – end Balance)

单位：亿元
Unit: 100 Million Yuan

项目 Items	2002.05	2002.06	2002.07	2002.08
国外资产 Foreign Assets	1732.19	1719.56	1666.67	1658.57
储备资产 Reserve Assets	2792.78	2850.72	2284.64	2201.04
准备金存款 Reserve Deposits	2690.37	2741.22	2181.65	2089.70
库存现金 Cash in Vault	102.41	109.50	102.99	111.34
中央银行债券 Central Bank Bonds				
对政府债权 Claims on Government	1868.69	1893.48	2051.31	2094.87
其中：中央政府 Of Which: Central Government	1868.69	1893.48	2051.31	2094.87
对非金融机构债权 Claims on Non – financial Institutions	14027.78	14761.56	14892.24	15350.18
对特定存款机构债权 Claims on Specific Depository Institutions	1157.76	1259.72	1248.79	1247.46
对其他金融机构债权 Claims on Other Financial Institutions	183.77	205.93	192.59	205.24
其他资产 Other Assets	2677.08	3132.97	3116.22	3284.70
总资产 Total Assets	**24440.05**	**25823.94**	**25452.46**	**26042.06**
对非金融机构负债 Liabilities to Non – financial Institutions	18636.30	19820.64	19654.48	20252.63
活期存款 Demand Deposits	8037.52	8638.49	8445.06	8667.21
定期存款 Time Deposits	3608.31	3893.49	3875.04	3995.36
储蓄存款 Savings Deposits	3576.04	3711.85	3784.54	3892.43
其他存款 Other Deposits	1512.97	1649.26	1647.11	1773.47
外币存款 Deposits in Foreign Currency	1901.46	1927.55	1902.73	1924.16
对中央银行负债 Liabilities to the Central Bank	475.77	353.29	369.07	353.16
对特定存款机构负债 Liabilities to Specific Depository Institutions	89.99	101.45	80.60	67.61
对其他金融机构负债 Liabilities to Other Financial Institutions	2601.01	2668.10	2640.42	2636.00
其中：计入广义货币的存款 Of Which: Deposits Included in Broad Money	1162.29	1130.18	1077.04	1058.02
国外负债 Foreign Liabilities	115.20	103.36	103.95	101.88
债券 Bonds	61.46	99.50	42.91	48.42
实收资本 Paid – in Capital	569.68	568.21	568.21	571.60
其他负债 Other Liabilities	1890.64	2109.39	1992.82	2010.76
总负债 Total Liabilities	**24440.05**	**25823.94**	**25452.46**	**26042.06**

其他商业银行资产负债表

Balance Sheet of Other Commercial Banks

（月末余额）

（Month - end Balance）

单位：亿元

Unit：100 Million Yuan

项　目 Items	2002.09	2002.10	2002.11	2002.12
国外资产 Foreign Assets	1600.85	1644.17	1657.95	1720.47
储备资产 Reserve Assets	2798.33	2437.49	2658.47	3830.37
准备金存款 Reserve Deposits	2664.57	2326.84	2540.75	3707.00
库存现金 Cash in Vault	133.76	110.65	117.72	123.37
中央银行债券 Central Bank Bonds	198.93	198.94	183.34	202.79
对政府债权 Claims on Government	2177.55	2249.31	2279.78	2306.54
其中：中央政府 Of Which：Central Government	2177.55	2249.31	2279.78	2306.54
对非金融机构债权 Claims on Non - financial Institutions	15869.73	16040.99	16430.36	17136.09
对特定存款机构债权 Claims on Specific Depository Institutions	1437.18	1410.26	1456.42	1444.42
对其他金融机构债权 Claims on Other Financial Institutions	139.52	141.34	163.86	175.38
其他资产 Other Assets	3300.87	3003.45	2901.70	3161.10
总资产 Total Assets	**27522.96**	**27125.95**	**27731.88**	**29977.16**
对非金融机构负债 Liabilities to Non - financial Institutions	21375.57	21132.04	21659.28	23484.73
活期存款 Demand Deposits	9038.88	8924.44	9109.35	10141.16
定期存款 Time Deposits	4409.60	4179.05	4329.08	4750.03
储蓄存款 Savings Deposits	4026.63	4066.50	4163.78	4347.15
其他存款 Other Deposits	1954.31	1975.27	2087.07	2215.41
外币存款 Deposits in Foreign Currency	1946.15	1986.78	1970.00	2030.98
对中央银行负债 Liabilities to the Central Bank	439.49	489.56	514.44	326.13
对特定存款机构负债 Liabilities to Specific Depository Institutions	112.61	101.87	91.40	81.64
对其他金融机构负债 Liabilities to Other Financial Institutions	2588.48	2549.00	2478.63	2754.65
其中：计入广义货币的存款 Of Which：Deposits Included in Broad Money	940.65	920.10	870.94	994.55
国外负债 Foreign Liabilities	108.72	118.16	140.39	159.74
债券 Bonds	41.01	43.94	47.69	94.85
实收资本 Paid - in Capital	583.65	583.65	581.58	579.48
其他负债 Other Liabilities	2273.43	2107.73	2218.47	2495.94
总负债 Total Liabilities	**27522.96**	**27125.95**	**27731.88**	**29977.16**

其他商业银行资产负债表
Balance Sheet of Other Commercial Banks

（月末余额）
（Month – end Balance）

单位：亿元
Unit：100 Million Yuan

项目 Items	2003.01	2003.02	2003.03	2003.04
国外资产 Foreign Assets	1631.99	1660.49	1604.82	1577.07
储备资产 Reserve Assets	2316.46	2655.46	2713.68	2481.51
准备金存款 Reserve Deposits	2151.51	2531.68	2584.60	2354.64
库存现金 Cash in Vault	164.95	123.78	129.08	126.87
中央银行债券 Central Bank Bonds	96.17	96.40	83.21	104.13
对政府债权 Claims on Government	2249.41	2314.41	2325.01	2500.17
其中：中央政府 Of Which：Central Government	2249.41	2314.41	2325.01	2500.17
对非金融机构债权 Claims on Non – financial Institutions	17753.46	17799.41	18523.90	19217.78
对特定存款机构债权 Claims on Specific Depository Institutions	1482.98	1437.09	1514.25	1554.67
对其他金融机构债权 Claims on Other Financial Institutions	398.20	342.20	364.96	367.94
其他资产 Other Assets	3257.54	3036.45	3655.40	3737.63
总资产 Total Assets	**29186.21**	**29341.91**	**30785.23**	**31540.90**
对非金融机构负债 Liabilities to Non – financial Institutions	22961.40	22897.63	23914.82	24321.88
活期存款 Demand Deposits	9350.47	9357.15	9941.45	9897.26
定期存款 Time Deposits	4790.10	4629.11	4764.84	4953.40
储蓄存款 Savings Deposits	4553.24	4604.72	4729.50	4791.70
其他存款 Other Deposits	2273.08	2297.41	2469.67	2669.42
外币存款 Deposits in Foreign Currency	1994.51	2009.24	2009.36	2010.10
对中央银行负债 Liabilities to the Central Bank	41.38	24.65	18.42	30.10
对特定存款机构负债 Liabilities to Specific Depository Institutions	121.60	69.82	86.37	92.54
对其他金融机构负债 Liabilities to Other Financial Institutions	2622.73	2653.81	2708.61	2943.11
其中：计入广义货币的存款 Of Which：Deposits Included in Broad Money	903.11	913.46	901.83	930.75
国外负债 Foreign Liabilities	160.39	134.82	132.39	142.54
债券 Bonds	0.03	0.03	40.03	40.12
实收资本 Paid – in Capital	582.20	582.23	582.13	582.20
其他负债 Other Liabilities	2696.48	2978.92	3302.46	3388.41
总负债 Total Liabilities	**29186.21**	**29341.91**	**30785.23**	**31540.90**

其他商业银行资产负债表
Balance Sheet of Other Commercial Banks

（月末余额）
（Month－end Balance）

单位：亿元
Unit：100 Million Yuan

项 目 Items	2003.05	2003.06	2003.07	2003.08
国外资产 Foreign Assets	1538.53	1552.00	1448.29	1429.74
储备资产 Reserve Assets	2501.91	2991.96	2655.70	3254.37
准备金存款 Reserve Deposits	2384.42	2856.04	2537.93	3116.82
库存现金 Cash in Vault	117.49	135.92	117.77	137.55
中央银行债券 Central Bank Bonds	142.72	223.77	263.04	280.21
对政府债权 Claims on Government	2588.81	2676.84	2704.37	2669.67
其中：中央政府 Of Which：Central Government	2588.81	2676.84	2704.37	2669.67
对非金融机构债权 Claims on Non－financial Institutions	19942.52	21148.25	21635.83	22738.95
对特定存款机构债权 Claims on Specific Depository Institutions	1673.99	1748.53	1865.92	1992.62
对其他金融机构债权 Claims on Other Financial Institutions	426.58	360.52	304.72	444.92
其他资产 Other Assets	3740.57	3791.39	3280.50	3273.56
总资产 Total Assets	**32555.63**	**34493.26**	**34158.37**	**36084.04**
对非金融机构负债 Liabilities to Non－financial Institutions	25073.24	26935.46	26563.75	26903.19
活期存款 Demand Deposits	10270.82	11369.36	10980.79	10990.80
定期存款 Time Deposits	5057.31	5350.63	5257.09	5533.78
储蓄存款 Savings Deposits	4874.26	5039.38	5101.79	5171.85
其他存款 Other Deposits	2849.34	3120.14	3193.81	3124.41
外币存款 Deposits in Foreign Currency	2021.51	2055.95	2030.27	2082.35
对中央银行负债 Liabilities to the Central Bank	16.40	16.12	17.24	363.04
对特定存款机构负债 Liabilities to Specific Depository Institutions	85.97	84.66	90.61	69.79
对其他金融机构负债 Liabilities to Other Financial Institutions	3037.49	3177.45	3233.91	3857.18
其中：计入广义货币的存款 Of Which：Deposits Included in Broad Money	932.43	979.19	937.54	1584.25
国外负债 Foreign Liabilities	160.98	159.62	169.13	156.43
债券 Bonds	40.17	40.22	40.27	40.32
实收资本 Paid－in Capital	591.21	591.24	604.26	604.25
其他负债 Other Liabilities	3550.17	3488.49	3439.20	4089.84
总负债 Total Liabilities	**32555.63**	**34493.26**	**34158.37**	**36084.04**

其他商业银行资产负债表

Balance Sheet of Other Commercial Banks

（月末余额）

(Month – end Balance)

单位：亿元

Unit: 100 Million Yuan

项目 Items	2003.09	2003.10	2003.11	2003.12
国外资产 Foreign Assets	1421.72	1509.38	1421.09	1449.62
储备资产 Reserve Assets	3366.22	3537.72	3416.34	4768.81
准备金存款 Reserve Deposits	3206.73	3405.67	3276.27	4623.87
库存现金 Cash in Vault	159.49	132.05	140.07	144.94
中央银行债券 Central Bank Bonds	265.25	203.61	286.21	291.30
对政府债权 Claims on Government	2746.04	2747.56	2741.24	2799.58
其中：中央政府 Of Which: Central Government	2746.04	2747.56	2741.24	2799.58
对非金融机构债权 Claims on Non – financial Institutions	23228.86	23434.33	23711.00	23995.53
对特定存款机构债权 Claims on Specific Depository Institutions	2057.20	2074.64	2104.42	2042.51
对其他金融机构债权 Claims on Other Financial Institutions	371.55	302.78	307.89	264.21
其他资产 Other Assets	3292.96	2988.32	3005.50	3293.89
总资产 Total Assets	**36749.80**	**36798.34**	**36993.69**	**38905.45**
对非金融机构负债 Liabilities to Non – financial Institutions	28542.10	28335.01	28726.21	30513.53
活期存款 Demand Deposits	11604.27	11615.34	11841.29	12923.33
定期存款 Time Deposits	6264.27	5874.21	5997.40	6467.84
储蓄存款 Savings Deposits	5409.29	5458.27	5555.99	5851.47
其他存款 Other Deposits	3209.05	3186.45	3197.72	3151.58
外币存款 Deposits in Foreign Currency	2055.22	2200.74	2133.81	2119.31
对中央银行负债 Liabilities to the Central Bank	196.86	199.71	229.46	293.39
对特定存款机构负债 Liabilities to Specific Depository Institutions	108.24	122.66	140.66	112.26
对其他金融机构负债 Liabilities to Other Financial Institutions	3434.00	3612.89	3639.79	3637.48
其中：计入广义货币的存款 Of Which: Deposits Included in Broad Money	826.88	904.64	917.52	880.29
国外负债 Foreign Liabilities	179.15	173.87	155.67	181.17
债券 Bonds	38.20	40.42	36.48	50.08
实收资本 Paid – in Capital	604.53	604.24	605.52	667.73
其他负债 Other Liabilities	3646.72	3709.54	3459.90	3449.81
总负债 Total Liabilities	**36749.80**	**36798.34**	**36993.69**	**38905.45**

其他商业银行资产负债表

Balance Sheet of Other Commercial Banks

（月末余额）

（Month - end Balance）

单位：亿元

Unit：100 Million Yuan

项 目 Items	2004.01	2004.02	2004.03	2004.04
国外资产 Foreign Assets	1379.32	1240.46	1253.72	1272.58
储备资产 Reserve Assets	3470.38	3951.58	4329.40	4215.96
准备金存款 Reserve Deposits	3279.41	3792.91	4185.54	4041.80
库存现金 Cash in Vault	190.97	158.67	143.86	174.16
中央银行债券 Central Bank Bonds	265.22	126.57	264.90	300.10
对政府债权 Claims on Government	2778.23	2806.45	2840.89	2917.65
其中：中央政府 Of Which：Central Government	2778.23	2806.45	2840.89	2917.65
对非金融机构债权 Claims on Non - financial Institutions	25145.64	25519.63	26414.44	26888.15
对特定存款机构债权 Claims on Specific Depository Institutions	2047.50	2065.06	2071.52	2102.72
对其他金融机构债权 Claims on Other Financial Institutions	199.75	150.48	276.75	193.44
其他资产 Other Assets	3331.96	3568.37	3933.85	4102.79
总资产 Total Assets	**38618.00**	**39428.60**	**41385.47**	**41993.39**
对非金融机构负债 Liabilities to Non - financial Institutions	29289.24	29683.80	31175.80	31716.48
活期存款 Demand Deposits	11918.74	12312.01	13133.85	12840.32
定期存款 Time Deposits	6027.15	5946.03	6260.03	6822.10
储蓄存款 Savings Deposits	6046.10	6133.24	6258.57	6341.80
其他存款 Other Deposits	3166.49	3278.94	3468.17	3674.44
外币存款 Deposits in Foreign Currency	2130.76	2013.58	2055.18	2037.82
对中央银行负债 Liabilities to the Central Bank	289.65	184.28	107.14	65.84
对特定存款机构负债 Liabilities to Specific Depository Institutions	118.40	129.58	105.65	111.62
对其他金融机构负债 Liabilities to Other Financial Institutions	3613.88	3960.98	4187.43	4162.99
其中：计入广义货币的存款 Of Which：Deposits Included in Broad Money	898.91	1064.63	1069.55	1078.65
国外负债 Foreign Liabilities	176.52	181.06	159.39	146.50
债券 Bonds	43.59	37.16	34.25	58.56
实收资本 Paid - in Capital	668.56	669.39	669.74	693.17
其他负债 Other Liabilities	4418.16	4582.35	4946.07	5038.23
总负债 Total Liabilities	**38618.00**	**39428.60**	**41385.47**	**41993.39**

其他商业银行资产负债表
Balance Sheet of Other Commercial Banks

（月末余额）

(Month – end Balance)

单位：亿元

Unit: 100 Million Yuan

项目 Items	2004.05	2004.06	2004.07	2004.08
国外资产 Foreign Assets	1257.86	1310.04	1429.71	1566.30
储备资产 Reserve Assets	3977.19	4908.02	3974.48	4070.24
准备金存款 Reserve Deposits	3822.17	4756.07	3828.05	3912.83
库存现金 Cash in Vault	155.02	151.95	146.43	157.41
中央银行债券 Central Bank Bonds	538.82	783.62	812.15	894.79
对政府债权 Claims on Government	2781.54	2862.36	2987.74	2990.34
其中：中央政府 Of Which: Central Government	2781.54	2862.36	2987.74	2990.34
对非金融机构债权 Claims on Non – financial Institutions	27157.91	27186.33	27105.47	27338.34
对特定存款机构债权 Claims on Specific Depository Institutions	2137.76	2164.02	2145.57	2263.79
对其他金融机构债权 Claims on Other Financial Institutions	169.58	276.86	186.92	168.46
其他资产 Other Assets	4163.72	4390.54	4364.08	4057.30
总资产 Total Assets	**42184.38**	**43881.79**	**43006.12**	**43349.56**
对非金融机构负债 Liabilities to Non – financial Institutions	32130.89	33649.33	33004.31	33305.71
活期存款 Demand Deposits	13292.04	14047.97	13416.41	13551.36
定期存款 Time Deposits	6667.70	7047.85	6907.86	6945.00
储蓄存款 Savings Deposits	6398.07	6588.32	6593.26	6666.44
其他存款 Other Deposits	3702.30	3857.31	3903.01	3969.41
外币存款 Deposits in Foreign Currency	2070.78	2107.88	2183.77	2173.50
对中央银行负债 Liabilities to the Central Bank	40.33	30.30	31.25	26.13
对特定存款机构负债 Liabilities to Specific Depository Institutions	114.09	122.78	123.79	114.76
对其他金融机构负债 Liabilities to Other Financial Institutions	4093.76	4009.51	3924.35	3852.26
其中：计入广义货币的存款 Of Which: Deposits Included in Broad Money	1028.33	853.22	846.40	798.04
国外负债 Foreign Liabilities	152.85	174.81	171.41	162.20
债券 Bonds	58.43	322.92	350.95	350.95
实收资本 Paid – in Capital	693.18	847.20	853.51	946.25
其他负债 Other Liabilities	4900.85	4724.94	4546.55	4591.30
总负债 Total Liabilities	**42184.38**	**43881.79**	**43006.12**	**43349.56**

其他商业银行资产负债表

Balance Sheet of Other Commercial Banks

（月末余额）

（Month - end Balance）

单位：亿元

Unit：100 Million Yuan

项　目 Items	2004.09	2004.10	2004.11	2004.12
国外资产 Foreign Assets	1568.64	1677.60	1698.27	1672.05
储备资产 Reserve Assets	4442.20	4252.32	4489.55	5778.29
准备金存款 Reserve Deposits	4244.19	4080.63	4316.94	5605.25
库存现金 Cash in Vault	198.01	171.69	172.61	173.04
中央银行债券 Central Bank Bonds	1002.80	1141.07	1293.42	1596.78
对政府债权 Claims on Government	3015.37	3010.50	3076.09	3029.93
其中：中央政府 Of Which：Central Government	3015.37	3010.50	3076.09	3029.93
对非金融机构债权 Claims on Non - financial Institutions	27928.20	27980.95	28137.06	28941.41
对特定存款机构债权 Claims on Specific Depository Institutions	2327.57	2264.28	2246.69	2454.89
对其他金融机构债权 Claims on Other Financial Institutions	212.69	184.07	191.82	177.02
其他资产 Other Assets	4218.03	4170.08	4133.21	3974.14
总资产 Total Assets	**44715.50**	**44680.87**	**45266.11**	**47624.51**
对非金融机构负债 Liabilities to Non - financial Institutions	34631.03	34505.76	34942.01	37133.10
活期存款 Demand Deposits	13839.95	13944.27	14127.43	15242.55
定期存款 Time Deposits	7573.91	7206.16	7168.80	7771.04
储蓄存款 Savings Deposits	6858.17	6919.55	7143.35	7458.26
其他存款 Other Deposits	4139.58	4111.87	4220.13	4371.10
外币存款 Deposits in Foreign Currency	2219.42	2323.91	2282.30	2290.15
对中央银行负债 Liabilities to the Central Bank	29.89	18.96	16.89	15.48
对特定存款机构负债 Liabilities to Specific Depository Institutions	123.12	109.80	111.89	118.91
对其他金融机构负债 Liabilities to Other Financial Institutions	3793.51	3780.18	3830.33	3875.16
其中：计入广义货币的存款 Of Which：Deposits Included in Broad Money	747.03	766.73	741.47	671.72
国外负债 Foreign Liabilities	152.83	149.83	167.93	156.99
债券 Bonds	356.24	356.14	479.14	519.46
实收资本 Paid - in Capital	946.25	946.26	946.31	983.95
其他负债 Other Liabilities	4682.63	4813.94	4771.61	4821.46
总负债 Total Liabilities	**44715.50**	**44680.87**	**45266.11**	**47624.51**

其他商业银行资产负债表
Balance Sheet of Other Commercial Banks

(月末余额)

(Month – end Balance)

单位：亿元

Unit: 100 Million Yuan

项 目 Items	2005.01	2005.02	2005.03	2005.04
国外资产 Foreign Assets	1575.27	1721.66	1697.56	1727.28
储备资产 Reserve Assets	4349.69	4358.48	4982.69	4497.64
准备金存款 Reserve Deposits	4154.25	4154.57	4810.37	4300.36
库存现金 Cash in Vault	195.44	203.91	172.32	197.28
中央银行债券 Central Bank Bonds	1670.91	1379.34	1391.49	1523.81
对政府债权 Claims on Government	3024.11	2982.82	3064.64	3230.18
其中：中央政府 Of Which: Central Government	3024.11	2982.82	3064.64	3230.18
对非金融机构债权 Claims on Non – financial Institutions	29385.84	29533.11	30151.42	30668.05
对特定存款机构债权 Claims on Specific Depository Institutions	2460.98	2493.46	2680.45	2870.68
对其他金融机构债权 Claims on Other Financial Institutions	218.01	144.05	271.97	261.50
其他资产 Other Assets	4225.78	4018.30	4330.55	4554.12
总资产 Total Assets	**46910.59**	**46631.22**	**48570.77**	**49333.26**
对非金融机构负债 Liabilities to Non – financial Institutions	36337.65	35967.33	37620.17	38112.87
活期存款 Demand Deposits	14418.51	13836.99	14728.48	14332.50
定期存款 Time Deposits	7548.78	7583.28	7856.56	8316.31
储蓄存款 Savings Deposits	7564.00	7819.45	7963.31	8092.31
其他存款 Other Deposits	4513.86	4425.95	4611.33	4852.02
外币存款 Deposits in Foreign Currency	2292.50	2301.66	2460.49	2519.73
对中央银行负债 Liabilities to the Central Bank	16.33	14.20	14.20	14.17
对特定存款机构负债 Liabilities to Specific Depository Institutions	130.52	98.96	87.61	98.46
对其他金融机构负债 Liabilities to Other Financial Institutions	3779.52	3845.13	3981.28	3929.28
其中：计入广义货币的存款 Of Which: Deposits Included in Broad Money	637.65	643.13	785.82	697.81
国外负债 Foreign Liabilities	124.96	147.77	148.88	164.10
债券 Bonds	561.96	561.95	564.24	564.92
实收资本 Paid – in Capital	968.40	968.40	968.40	978.77
其他负债 Other Liabilities	4991.25	5027.48	5185.99	5470.69
总负债 Total Liabilities	**46910.59**	**46631.22**	**48570.77**	**49333.26**

其他商业银行资产负债表

Balance Sheet of Other Commercial Banks

（月末余额）

（Month - end Balance）

单位：亿元

Unit：100 Million Yuan

项 目 Items	2005.05	2005.06	2005.07	2005.08
国外资产 Foreign Assets	1661.36	1971.76	1875.10	1808.31
储备资产 Reserve Assets	4725.23	5585.55	4826.24	5164.12
准备金存款 Reserve Deposits	4559.03	5415.86	4650.18	4986.55
库存现金 Cash in Vault	166.20	169.69	176.06	177.57
中央银行债券 Central Bank Bonds	1348.69	1187.90	1090.06	1107.14
对政府债权 Claims on Government	3126.02	3064.96	3122.83	3258.92
其中：中央政府 Of Which：Central Government	3126.02	3064.96	3122.83	3258.92
对非金融机构债权 Claims on Non - financial Institutions	31254.66	32435.46	32578.48	33200.02
对特定存款机构债权 Claims on Specific Depository Institutions	2927.92	3077.44	3118.20	3138.79
对其他金融机构债权 Claims on Other Financial Institutions	323.95	325.51	354.62	419.37
其他资产 Other Assets	4678.85	5566.80	5350.91	5461.62
总资产 Total Assets	**50046.68**	**53215.38**	**52316.44**	**53558.29**
对非金融机构负债 Liabilities to Non - financial Institutions	38451.99	41126.18	40192.45	41078.00
活期存款 Demand Deposits	14708.54	15873.92	15080.86	15262.51
定期存款 Time Deposits	8139.82	8695.54	8566.85	8873.91
储蓄存款 Savings Deposits	8216.90	8563.78	8688.57	8872.65
其他存款 Other Deposits	4899.55	5196.57	5278.18	5587.26
外币存款 Deposits in Foreign Currency	2487.18	2796.37	2577.99	2481.67
对中央银行负债 Liabilities to the Central Bank	13.85	13.87	13.11	12.42
对特定存款机构负债 Liabilities to Specific Depository Institutions	113.10	145.07	140.77	97.34
对其他金融机构负债 Liabilities to Other Financial Institutions	3939.66	3925.34	3988.40	4066.16
其中：计入广义货币的存款 Of Which：Deposits Included in Broad Money	720.44	739.13	825.12	892.85
国外负债 Foreign Liabilities	170.84	153.24	139.63	147.91
债券 Bonds	565.04	561.68	561.10	631.22
实收资本 Paid - in Capital	978.76	1071.41	1075.96	1076.19
其他负债 Other Liabilities	5813.44	6218.59	6205.02	6449.05
总负债 Total Liabilities	**50046.68**	**53215.38**	**52316.44**	**53558.29**

其他商业银行资产负债表
Balance Sheet of Other Commercial Banks

（月末余额）

(Month - end Balance)

单位：亿元

Unit: 100 Million Yuan

项目 Items	2005.09	2005.10	2005.11	2005.12
国外资产 Foreign Assets	1739.98	1735.97	1840.05	1937.97
储备资产 Reserve Assets	5525.07	5540.87	5263.21	5826.09
准备金存款 Reserve Deposits	5310.40	5347.52	5084.81	5626.46
库存现金 Cash in Vault	214.67	193.35	178.40	199.63
中央银行债券 Central Bank Bonds	1161.11	1122.91	1529.66	1642.33
对政府债权 Claims on Government	3315.49	3323.24	3396.24	3494.62
其中：中央政府 Of Which: Central Government	3315.49	3323.24	3396.24	3494.62
对非金融机构债权 Claims on Non - financial Institutions	34311.98	34590.07	34921.98	35305.55
对特定存款机构债权 Claims on Specific Depository Institutions	3262.00	3374.51	3653.12	3643.89
对其他金融机构债权 Claims on Other Financial Institutions	325.18	355.49	556.73	502.76
其他资产 Other Assets	6049.55	5603.44	5776.95	6621.55
总资产 Total Assets	**55690.36**	**55646.50**	**56937.94**	**58974.76**
对非金融机构负债 Liabilities to Non - financial Institutions	43000.29	42564.27	43851.43	45699.58
活期存款 Demand Deposits	15717.20	15660.68	16115.69	16977.24
定期存款 Time Deposits	9780.57	9313.81	9507.29	9980.65
储蓄存款 Savings Deposits	9182.78	9283.12	9495.95	9982.74
其他存款 Other Deposits	5846.73	5837.10	6270.77	6333.35
外币存款 Deposits in Foreign Currency	2473.01	2469.56	2461.73	2425.60
对中央银行负债 Liabilities to the Central Bank	12.41	12.41	12.47	29.83
对特定存款机构负债 Liabilities to Specific Depository Institutions	113.88	123.13	107.21	122.53
对其他金融机构负债 Liabilities to Other Financial Institutions	4040.43	4234.71	4271.27	4259.05
其中：计入广义货币的存款 Of Which: Deposits Included in Broad Money	849.71	896.78	899.80	892.17
国外负债 Foreign Liabilities	157.26	167.82	164.18	175.35
债券 Bonds	628.85	728.62	828.04	859.13
实收资本 Paid - in Capital	1082.94	1077.93	1077.95	1177.29
其他负债 Other Liabilities	6654.30	6737.61	6625.39	6652.00
总负债 Total Liabilities	**55690.36**	**55646.50**	**56937.94**	**58974.76**

5. 城市商业银行资产负债表
Balance Sheet of City Commercial Banks

城市商业银行资产负债表
Balance Sheet of City Commercial Banks

（月末余额）

（Month - end Balance）

单位：亿元

Unit：100 Million Yuan

项目 Items	2002.01	2002.02	2002.03	2002.04
国外资产 Foreign Assets	36.05	39.74	36.80	55.95
储备资产 Reserve Assets	604.29	556.29	545.81	638.95
准备金存款 Reserve Deposits	541.54	495.05	482.48	582.07
库存现金 Cash in Vault	62.75	61.24	63.33	56.88
中央银行债券 Central Bank Bonds				
对政府债权 Claims on Government	899.12	916.07	973.75	1052.37
其中：中央政府 Of Which：Central Government	899.12	916.07	973.75	1052.37
对非金融机构债权 Claims on Non - financial Institutions	4645.70	4703.50	4882.04	4924.50
对特定存款机构债权 Claims on Specific Depository Institutions	321.00	325.76	321.77	348.38
对其他金融机构债权 Claims on Other Financial Institutions	171.54	173.87	158.67	156.87
其他资产 Other Assets	1511.49	1525.74	1626.85	1663.88
总资产 Total Assets	**8189.19**	**8240.97**	**8545.69**	**8840.90**
对非金融机构负债 Liabilities to Non - financial Institutions	6407.21	6417.14	6488.07	6828.68
活期存款 Demand Deposits	3362.12	3283.71	3309.12	3523.44
定期存款 Time Deposits	882.83	885.23	892.54	937.00
储蓄存款 Savings Deposits	1880.01	1969.00	1993.14	2051.29
其他存款 Other Deposits	223.42	217.99	231.96	253.57
外币存款 Deposits in Foreign Currency	58.83	61.21	61.31	63.38
对中央银行负债 Liabilities to the Central Bank	751.28	731.43	961.31	807.13
对特定存款机构负债 Liabilities to Specific Depository Institutions	16.66	15.76	10.84	18.41
对其他金融机构负债 Liabilities to Other Financial Institutions	206.78	271.18	229.65	320.92
其中：计入广义货币的存款 Of Which：Deposits Included in Broad Money	129.61	188.59	150.86	222.35
国外负债 Foreign Liabilities	0.22	0.24	0.25	0.38
债券 Bonds	9.87	33.69	15.80	23.13
实收资本 Paid - in Capital	329.28	330.69	335.94	336.53
其他负债 Other Liabilities	467.89	440.84	503.83	505.72
总负债 Total Liabilities	**8189.19**	**8240.97**	**8545.69**	**8840.90**

城市商业银行资产负债表

Balance Sheet of City Commercial Banks

（月末余额）

（Month – end Balance）

单位：亿元

Unit：100 Million Yuan

项目 Items	2002.05	2002.06	2002.07	2002.08
国外资产 Foreign Assets	54.89	64.09	66.43	73.37
储备资产 Reserve Assets	668.08	671.28	666.17	663.56
准备金存款 Reserve Deposits	611.36	608.80	603.39	596.41
库存现金 Cash in Vault	56.72	62.48	62.78	67.15
中央银行债券 Central Bank Bonds				
对政府债权 Claims on Government	1185.36	1320.33	1408.70	1378.10
其中：中央政府 Of Which: Central Government	1185.36	1320.33	1408.70	1378.10
对非金融机构债权 Claims on Non – financial Institutions	5007.02	5141.07	5224.08	5365.57
对特定存款机构债权 Claims on Specific Depository Institutions	354.36	378.54	349.36	358.02
对其他金融机构债权 Claims on Other Financial Institutions	174.22	149.19	178.73	219.45
其他资产 Other Assets	1586.00	1722.19	1699.08	1692.79
总资产 Total Assets	**9029.93**	**9446.69**	**9592.55**	**9750.86**
对非金融机构负债 Liabilities to Non – financial Institutions	6925.95	7176.31	7327.09	7525.40
活期存款 Demand Deposits	3565.34	3699.13	3759.82	3844.83
定期存款 Time Deposits	941.50	986.61	1027.89	1078.71
储蓄存款 Savings Deposits	2089.78	2147.27	2180.53	2224.79
其他存款 Other Deposits	266.03	275.68	289.36	301.52
外币存款 Deposits in Foreign Currency	63.30	67.62	69.49	75.55
对中央银行负债 Liabilities to the Central Bank	902.80	1001.44	1059.16	1084.42
对特定存款机构负债 Liabilities to Specific Depository Institutions	19.61	17.12	19.94	120.48
对其他金融机构负债 Liabilities to Other Financial Institutions	312.17	338.18	288.22	177.86
其中：计入广义货币的存款 Of Which: Deposits Included in Broad Money	197.87	225.23	200.21	100.53
国外负债 Foreign Liabilities	0.44	0.43	0.42	0.44
债券 Bonds	13.74	29.77	10.66	12.26
实收资本 Paid – in Capital	340.78	344.79	350.06	350.50
其他负债 Other Liabilities	514.44	538.65	537.00	479.50
总负债 Total Liabilities	**9029.93**	**9446.69**	**9592.55**	**9750.86**

城市商业银行资产负债表
Balance Sheet of City Commercial Banks

（月末余额）

（Month－end Balance）

单位：亿元

Unit：100 Million Yuan

项目 Items	2002.09	2002.10	2002.11	2002.12
国外资产 Foreign Assets	77.84	84.52	93.39	109.62
储备资产 Reserve Assets	680.30	713.65	706.13	1062.53
准备金存款 Reserve Deposits	618.40	646.91	637.53	991.13
库存现金 Cash in Vault	61.90	66.74	68.60	71.40
中央银行债券 Central Bank Bonds	0.94	9.40	9.40	4.00
对政府债权 Claims on Government	1441.97	1453.85	1417.40	1491.45
其中：中央政府 Of Which：Central Government	1441.97	1453.85	1417.40	1491.45
对非金融机构债权 Claims on Non－financial Institutions	5393.24	5488.63	5700.51	6181.10
对特定存款机构债权 Claims on Specific Depository Institutions	392.79	403.68	418.49	445.76
对其他金融机构债权 Claims on Other Financial Institutions	175.68	186.71	182.58	198.66
其他资产 Other Assets	1806.61	1729.99	1833.80	2030.35
总资产 Total Assets	**9969.37**	**10070.43**	**10361.70**	**11523.47**
对非金融机构负债 Liabilities to Non－financial Institutions	7806.80	7903.31	8139.27	8914.32
活期存款 Demand Deposits	3979.90	4031.96	4162.64	4712.46
定期存款 Time Deposits	1143.41	1136.61	1177.58	1273.61
储蓄存款 Savings Deposits	2274.83	2315.94	2358.42	2442.23
其他存款 Other Deposits	333.71	337.62	356.49	394.57
外币存款 Deposits in Foreign Currency	74.95	81.18	84.14	91.45
对中央银行负债 Liabilities to the Central Bank	1004.11	1012.80	1042.94	1276.47
对特定存款机构负债 Liabilities to Specific Depository Institutions	16.54	23.59	16.57	41.74
对其他金融机构负债 Liabilities to Other Financial Institutions	273.88	263.54	272.37	330.65
其中：计入广义货币的存款 Of Which：Deposits Included in Broad Money	183.94	180.43	186.66	222.91
国外负债 Foreign Liabilities	0.51	0.50	0.50	0.48
债券 Bonds	15.02	10.68	16.19	20.79
实收资本 Paid－in Capital	350.59	351.18	352.63	373.32
其他负债 Other Liabilities	501.92	504.83	521.23	565.70
总负债 Total Liabilities	**9969.37**	**10070.43**	**10361.70**	**11523.47**

城市商业银行资产负债表
Balance Sheet of City Commercial Banks

(月末余额)

(Month - end Balance)

单位：亿元

Unit: 100 Million Yuan

项目 Items	2003.01	2003.02	2003.03	2003.04
国外资产 Foreign Assets	95.14	99.68	103.75	112.81
储备资产 Reserve Assets	780.90	781.02	737.35	791.38
准备金存款 Reserve Deposits	696.92	706.02	662.91	727.70
库存现金 Cash in Vault	83.98	75.00	74.44	63.68
中央银行债券 Central Bank Bonds			0.50	17.39
对政府债权 Claims on Government	1545.76	1572.29	1524.31	1642.44
其中：中央政府 Of Which: Central Government	1545.76	1572.29	1524.31	1642.44
对非金融机构债权 Claims on Non - financial Institutions	6097.74	6096.78	6379.11	6515.50
对特定存款机构债权 Claims on Specific Depository Institutions	581.56	577.27	590.86	603.39
对其他金融机构债权 Claims on Other Financial Institutions	173.01	173.95	230.50	180.56
其他资产 Other Assets	1861.44	1843.09	2166.23	2117.07
总资产 Total Assets	**11135.55**	**11144.08**	**11732.61**	**11980.54**
对非金融机构负债 Liabilities to Non - financial Institutions	8649.37	8632.12	8860.81	9108.28
活期存款 Demand Deposits	4335.66	4267.24	4365.09	4471.96
定期存款 Time Deposits	1297.45	1293.63	1345.90	1407.79
储蓄存款 Savings Deposits	2509.72	2548.56	2612.05	2652.73
其他存款 Other Deposits	411.90	422.37	439.42	481.43
外币存款 Deposits in Foreign Currency	94.64	100.32	98.35	94.37
对中央银行负债 Liabilities to the Central Bank	202.97	196.85	185.49	182.36
对特定存款机构负债 Liabilities to Specific Depository Institutions	88.99	70.50	85.37	98.06
对其他金融机构负债 Liabilities to Other Financial Institutions	328.32	353.86	360.67	401.10
其中：计入广义货币的存款 Of Which: Deposits Included in Broad Money	190.84	180.05	200.52	199.97
国外负债 Foreign Liabilities	0.60	0.64	0.63	0.65
债券 Bonds			0.02	
实收资本 Paid - in Capital	378.07	377.97	379.08	387.76
其他负债 Other Liabilities	1487.23	1512.14	1860.54	1802.33
总负债 Total Liabilities	**11135.55**	**11144.08**	**11732.61**	**11980.54**

城市商业银行资产负债表
Balance Sheet of City Commercial Banks

（月末余额）

（Month - end Balance）

单位：亿元

Unit：100 Million Yuan

项目 Items	2003.05	2003.06	2003.07	2003.08
国外资产 Foreign Assets	120.57	138.68	134.52	141.63
储备资产 Reserve Assets	817.13	882.85	865.76	984.39
准备金存款 Reserve Deposits	748.99	806.43	795.05	899.35
库存现金 Cash in Vault	68.14	76.42	70.71	85.04
中央银行债券 Central Bank Bonds	60.24	101.30	137.47	109.64
对政府债权 Claims on Government	1665.36	1702.05	1757.25	1756.83
其中：中央政府 Of Which：Central Government	1665.36	1702.05	1757.25	1756.83
对非金融机构债权 Claims on Non - financial Institutions	6708.56	6993.28	7044.11	7299.00
对特定存款机构债权 Claims on Specific Depository Institutions	662.03	709.53	789.60	897.49
对其他金融机构债权 Claims on Other Financial Institutions	160.75	143.25	153.32	149.38
其他资产 Other Assets	2148.51	2360.37	2203.65	2154.49
总资产 Total Assets	**12343.15**	**13031.31**	**13085.68**	**13492.85**
对非金融机构负债 Liabilities to Non - financial Institutions	9374.75	9745.49	9916.47	10061.99
活期存款 Demand Deposits	4605.95	4798.38	4897.53	4955.05
定期存款 Time Deposits	1457.14	1529.92	1530.57	1537.84
储蓄存款 Savings Deposits	2706.94	2757.88	2800.60	2836.96
其他存款 Other Deposits	507.25	561.15	587.96	634.80
外币存款 Deposits in Foreign Currency	97.47	98.16	99.81	97.34
对中央银行负债 Liabilities to the Central Bank	185.29	208.56	199.04	309.76
对特定存款机构负债 Liabilities to Specific Depository Institutions	109.90	81.02	63.63	68.61
对其他金融机构负债 Liabilities to Other Financial Institutions	399.21	415.89	452.92	333.64
其中：计入广义货币的存款 Of Which：Deposits Included in Broad Money	200.39	214.82	199.11	172.00
国外负债 Foreign Liabilities	0.69	0.67	0.65	0.63
债券 Bonds				
实收资本 Paid - in Capital	388.27	389.80	392.65	392.76
其他负债 Other Liabilities	1885.04	2189.88	2060.32	2325.46
总负债 Total Liabilities	**12343.15**	**13031.31**	**13085.68**	**13492.85**

城市商业银行资产负债表

Balance Sheet of City Commercial Banks

（月末余额）

（Month - end Balance）

单位：亿元

Unit: 100 Million Yuan

项目 Items	2003.09	2003.10	2003.11	2003.12
国外资产 Foreign Assets	155.11	130.20	122.32	148.91
储备资产 Reserve Assets	1011.91	1009.55	1043.37	1506.46
准备金存款 Reserve Deposits	936.13	935.13	961.22	1420.18
库存现金 Cash in Vault	75.78	74.42	82.15	86.28
中央银行债券 Central Bank Bonds	57.41	50.54	47.91	33.79
对政府债权 Claims on Government	1757.88	1780.31	1823.71	1859.37
其中：中央政府 Of Which: Central Government	1757.88	1780.31	1823.71	1859.37
对非金融机构债权 Claims on Non - financial Institutions	7534.32	7518.21	7789.88	8074.13
对特定存款机构债权 Claims on Specific Depository Institutions	810.19	762.95	783.82	810.58
对其他金融机构债权 Claims on Other Financial Institutions	141.42	149.65	125.22	185.18
其他资产 Other Assets	2089.63	2047.34	1972.49	2159.45
总资产 Total Assets	**13557.87**	**13448.75**	**13708.72**	**14777.87**
对非金融机构负债 Liabilities to Non - financial Institutions	10456.70	10513.17	10710.85	11605.77
活期存款 Demand Deposits	5141.90	5228.47	5310.39	5919.58
定期存款 Time Deposits	1625.29	1570.77	1591.91	1733.17
储蓄存款 Savings Deposits	2913.96	2939.14	2979.55	3105.75
其他存款 Other Deposits	672.20	674.92	729.25	730.49
外币存款 Deposits in Foreign Currency	103.35	99.87	99.75	116.78
对中央银行负债 Liabilities to the Central Bank	263.84	270.15	230.56	262.54
对特定存款机构负债 Liabilities to Specific Depository Institutions	74.50	59.94	59.72	59.35
对其他金融机构负债 Liabilities to Other Financial Institutions	380.86	371.24	383.52	423.97
其中：计入广义货币的存款 Of Which: Deposits Included in Broad Money	184.05	157.94	165.50	210.13
国外负债 Foreign Liabilities	0.61	0.88	0.76	0.75
债券 Bonds		0.02		
实收资本 Paid - in Capital	406.78	405.94	412.32	425.76
其他负债 Other Liabilities	1974.58	1827.41	1910.99	1999.73
总负债 Total Liabilities	**13557.87**	**13448.75**	**13708.72**	**14777.87**

城市商业银行资产负债表
Balance Sheet of City Commercial Banks

（月末余额）

（Month - end Balance）

单位：亿元

Unit：100 Million Yuan

项目 Items	2004.01	2004.02	2004.03	2004.04
国外资产 Foreign Assets	120.49	119.37	105.82	108.50
储备资产 Reserve Assets	1049.27	1059.97	1044.97	1204.99
准备金存款 Reserve Deposits	940.46	971.95	962.45	1129.22
库存现金 Cash in Vault	108.81	88.02	82.52	75.77
中央银行债券 Central Bank Bonds	55.63	46.19	55.49	39.08
对政府债权 Claims on Government	1804.80	1808.49	1912.57	1961.94
其中：中央政府 Of Which：Central Government	1804.80	1808.49	1912.57	1961.94
对非金融机构债权 Claims on Non - financial Institutions	8077.14	8184.62	8303.03	8509.84
对特定存款机构债权 Claims on Specific Depository Institutions	914.88	922.61	910.24	904.17
对其他金融机构债权 Claims on Other Financial Institutions	88.95	96.64	106.55	97.56
其他资产 Other Assets	2141.18	2128.00	2303.44	2270.39
总资产 Total Assets	**14252.34**	**14365.89**	**14742.11**	**15096.47**
对非金融机构负债 Liabilities to Non - financial Institutions	11035.77	11060.18	11344.05	11624.97
活期存款 Demand Deposits	5377.30	5363.85	5526.81	5671.38
定期存款 Time Deposits	1679.74	1664.43	1692.45	1746.48
储蓄存款 Savings Deposits	3198.08	3228.79	3263.35	3307.92
其他存款 Other Deposits	670.24	692.74	751.76	785.19
外币存款 Deposits in Foreign Currency	110.41	110.37	109.68	114.00
对中央银行负债 Liabilities to the Central Bank	229.39	200.49	157.43	167.33
对特定存款机构负债 Liabilities to Specific Depository Institutions	40.48	36.75	33.78	22.45
对其他金融机构负债 Liabilities to Other Financial Institutions	427.94	398.54	437.39	531.76
其中：计入广义货币的存款 Of Which：Deposits Included in Broad Money	157.20	170.75	182.36	177.86
国外负债 Foreign Liabilities	0.80	0.94	2.14	1.25
债券 Bonds				
实收资本 Paid - in Capital	425.76	425.76	428.82	428.94
其他负债 Other Liabilities	2092.20	2243.23	2338.50	2319.77
总负债 Total Liabilities	**14252.34**	**14365.89**	**14742.11**	**15096.47**

城市商业银行资产负债表
Balance Sheet of City Commercial Banks

（月末余额）

（Month – end Balance）

单位：亿元

Unit：100 Million Yuan

项　目 Items	2004.05	2004.06	2004.07	2004.08
国外资产 Foreign Assets	111.51	98.27	98.13	109.91
储备资产 Reserve Assets	1207.36	1243.34	1254.42	1278.71
准备金存款 Reserve Deposits	1119.97	1156.99	1172.23	1184.78
库存现金 Cash in Vault	87.39	86.35	82.19	93.93
中央银行债券 Central Bank Bonds	40.68	43.82	252.43	261.37
对政府债权 Claims on Government	1894.84	1945.34	1776.96	1783.51
其中：中央政府 Of Which：Central Government	1894.84	1945.34	1776.96	1783.51
对非金融机构债权 Claims on Non – financial Institutions	8489.17	8682.82	8687.57	8777.90
对特定存款机构债权 Claims on Specific Depository Institutions	912.86	929.75	980.68	963.84
对其他金融机构债权 Claims on Other Financial Institutions	101.60	91.85	106.42	96.58
其他资产 Other Assets	2281.52	2404.20	2219.13	2175.66
总资产 Total Assets	**15039.54**	**15439.39**	**15375.74**	**15447.48**
对非金融机构负债 Liabilities to Non – financial Institutions	11744.85	12099.04	12132.73	12309.26
活期存款 Demand Deposits	5730.17	5887.97	5859.41	5939.90
定期存款 Time Deposits	1761.61	1847.65	1857.91	1887.27
储蓄存款 Savings Deposits	3324.93	3397.05	3425.40	3449.85
其他存款 Other Deposits	802.53	836.25	861.23	900.17
外币存款 Deposits in Foreign Currency	125.61	130.12	128.78	132.07
对中央银行负债 Liabilities to the Central Bank	156.01	153.03	153.45	155.08
对特定存款机构负债 Liabilities to Specific Depository Institutions	27.04	35.44	28.40	32.21
对其他金融机构负债 Liabilities to Other Financial Institutions	448.48	469.24	391.04	367.43
其中：计入广义货币的存款 Of Which：Deposits Included in Broad Money	161.40	151.28	131.13	116.48
国外负债 Foreign Liabilities	1.32	1.09	1.80	1.48
债券 Bonds				
实收资本 Paid – in Capital	430.99	431.14	431.22	431.31
其他负债 Other Liabilities	2230.85	2250.41	2237.10	2150.71
总负债 Total Liabilities	**15039.54**	**15439.39**	**15375.74**	**15447.48**

城市商业银行资产负债表

Balance Sheet of City Commercial Banks

（月末余额）

（Month – end Balance）

单位：亿元

Unit：100 Million Yuan

项目 Items	2004.09	2004.10	2004.11	2004.12
国外资产 Foreign Assets	109.05	111.53	116.51	121.07
储备资产 Reserve Assets	1305.46	1296.61	1405.52	2059.18
准备金存款 Reserve Deposits	1217.77	1205.22	1310.70	1965.01
库存现金 Cash in Vault	87.69	91.39	94.82	94.17
中央银行债券 Central Bank Bonds	78.80	104.47	77.90	175.08
对政府债权 Claims on Government	2010.85	2042.01	2155.95	2111.57
其中：中央政府 Of Which：Central Government	2010.85	2042.01	2155.95	2111.57
对非金融机构债权 Claims on Non – financial Institutions	8931.23	8943.48	9091.74	9242.06
对特定存款机构债权 Claims on Specific Depository Institutions	972.18	987.29	977.48	1031.22
对其他金融机构债权 Claims on Other Financial Institutions	111.61	123.86	123.91	151.58
其他资产 Other Assets	2379.73	2194.42	2241.20	2353.54
总资产 Total Assets	**15898.91**	**15803.67**	**16190.21**	**17245.30**
对非金融机构负债 Liabilities to Non – financial Institutions	12538.36	12543.81	12900.23	13962.29
活期存款 Demand Deposits	6000.51	5995.69	6183.21	6792.25
定期存款 Time Deposits	1947.69	1916.38	1935.37	2169.59
储蓄存款 Savings Deposits	3520.90	3557.78	3642.40	3816.61
其他存款 Other Deposits	935.59	936.25	996.42	1029.38
外币存款 Deposits in Foreign Currency	133.67	137.71	142.83	154.46
对中央银行负债 Liabilities to the Central Bank	152.74	146.28	143.06	120.22
对特定存款机构负债 Liabilities to Specific Depository Institutions	31.00	38.38	27.20	39.85
对其他金融机构负债 Liabilities to Other Financial Institutions	359.53	352.60	290.16	286.10
其中：计入广义货币的存款 Of Which：Deposits Included in Broad Money	114.83	93.65	84.48	85.65
国外负债 Foreign Liabilities	1.88	1.73	2.11	1.33
债券 Bonds			20.00	30.00
实收资本 Paid – in Capital	431.15	430.41	434.45	472.39
其他负债 Other Liabilities	2384.25	2290.46	2373.00	2333.12
总负债 Total Liabilities	**15898.91**	**15803.67**	**16190.21**	**17245.30**

城市商业银行资产负债表
Balance Sheet of City Commercial Banks

（月末余额）

（Month – end Balance）

单位：亿元

Unit：100 Million Yuan

项 目 Items	2005.01	2005.02	2005.03	2005.04
国外资产 Foreign Assets	118.08	117.00	97.49	94.29
储备资产 Reserve Assets	1415.73	1397.80	1380.08	1457.17
准备金存款 Reserve Deposits	1304.95	1282.60	1288.54	1371.27
库存现金 Cash in Vault	110.78	115.20	91.54	85.90
中央银行债券 Central Bank Bonds	192.72	125.42	182.64	201.26
对政府债权 Claims on Government	2109.82	2070.43	2022.78	2081.78
其中：中央政府 Of Which: Central Government	2109.82	2070.43	2022.78	2081.78
对非金融机构债权 Claims on Non – financial Institutions	9440.88	9498.34	9595.23	9766.66
对特定存款机构债权 Claims on Specific Depository Institutions	1033.45	1026.76	1023.83	1082.05
对其他金融机构债权 Claims on Other Financial Institutions	153.13	151.63	159.64	136.59
其他资产 Other Assets	2330.77	2280.37	2415.38	2569.63
总资产 Total Assets	**16794.58**	**16667.75**	**16877.07**	**17389.43**
对非金融机构负债 Liabilities to Non – financial Institutions	13420.90	13298.64	13527.34	13917.91
活期存款 Demand Deposits	6248.29	5991.61	6070.26	6210.03
定期存款 Time Deposits	2111.31	2110.75	2184.24	2277.08
储蓄存款 Savings Deposits	3842.55	3982.97	4021.77	4097.75
其他存款 Other Deposits	1076.54	1070.96	1114.88	1203.15
外币存款 Deposits in Foreign Currency	142.21	142.35	136.19	129.90
对中央银行负债 Liabilities to the Central Bank	107.67	103.05	97.82	84.39
对特定存款机构负债 Liabilities to Specific Depository Institutions	28.27	26.81	21.02	19.93
对其他金融机构负债 Liabilities to Other Financial Institutions	276.26	289.15	320.14	366.02
其中：计入广义货币的存款 Of Which: Deposits Included in Broad Money	66.47	67.60	64.27	69.77
国外负债 Foreign Liabilities	1.76	1.80	3.55	2.51
债券 Bonds	30.00	30.00	30.58	30.00
实收资本 Paid – in Capital	470.69	472.82	473.25	474.53
其他负债 Other Liabilities	2459.03	2445.48	2403.37	2494.14
总负债 Total Liabilities	**16794.58**	**16667.75**	**16877.07**	**17389.43**

城市商业银行资产负债表
Balance Sheet of City Commercial Banks
（月末余额）
（Month – end Balance）

单位：亿元
Unit：100 Million Yuan

项　目 Items	2005.05	2005.06	2005.07	2005.08
国外资产 Foreign Assets	95.69	105.82	102.96	106.23
储备资产 Reserve Assets	1384.30	1588.67	1459.51	1519.18
准备金存款 Reserve Deposits	1290.44	1494.51	1367.42	1413.51
库存现金 Cash in Vault	93.86	94.16	92.09	105.67
中央银行债券 Central Bank Bonds	223.81	239.95	187.44	188.46
对政府债权 Claims on Government	2066.67	2005.05	2094.75	2221.23
其中：中央政府 Of Which：Central Government	2066.67	2005.05	2094.75	2221.23
对非金融机构债权 Claims on Non – financial Institutions	9890.17	10187.30	10335.00	10515.93
对特定存款机构债权 Claims on Specific Depository Institutions	1010.76	1066.34	1044.83	998.53
对其他金融机构债权 Claims on Other Financial Institutions	195.55	164.34	168.61	162.08
其他资产 Other Assets	2700.87	2850.10	2787.01	2846.89
总资产 Total Assets	**17567.82**	**18207.57**	**18180.11**	**18558.53**
对非金融机构负债 Liabilities to Non – financial Institutions	14097.44	14523.57	14641.73	14996.92
活期存款 Demand Deposits	6342.19	6529.20	6507.41	6669.40
定期存款 Time Deposits	2270.07	2351.84	2344.91	2426.57
储蓄存款 Savings Deposits	4128.06	4218.98	4316.24	4372.07
其他存款 Other Deposits	1226.21	1278.25	1332.82	1390.39
外币存款 Deposits in Foreign Currency	130.91	145.30	140.35	138.49
对中央银行负债 Liabilities to the Central Bank	87.02	78.65	73.23	68.94
对特定存款机构负债 Liabilities to Specific Depository Institutions	32.74	51.24	46.17	65.27
对其他金融机构负债 Liabilities to Other Financial Institutions	314.12	318.71	291.62	315.69
其中：计入广义货币的存款 Of Which：Deposits Included in Broad Money	50.78	94.69	88.71	98.78
国外负债 Foreign Liabilities	1.74	2.05	1.16	1.13
债券 Bonds	30.47	30.42	30.40	30.00
实收资本 Paid – in Capital	478.06	484.90	488.06	483.38
其他负债 Other Liabilities	2526.23	2718.03	2607.74	2597.20
总负债 Total Liabilities	**17567.82**	**18207.57**	**18180.11**	**18558.53**

城市商业银行资产负债表
Balance Sheet of City Commercial Banks

（月末余额）
（Month – end Balance）

单位：亿元
Unit：100 Million Yuan

项目 Items	2005.09	2005.10	2005.11	2005.12
国外资产 Foreign Assets	109.39	131.02	103.86	98.58
储备资产 Reserve Assets	1593.39	1591.60	1646.98	2186.64
准备金存款 Reserve Deposits	1494.73	1484.73	1544.65	2079.59
库存现金 Cash in Vault	98.66	106.87	102.33	107.05
中央银行债券 Central Bank Bonds	184.19	191.79	197.81	247.73
对政府债权 Claims on Government	2184.25	2266.83	2370.88	2460.15
其中：中央政府 Of Which：Central Government	2184.25	2266.83	2370.88	2460.15
对非金融机构债权 Claims on Non – financial Institutions	10767.48	10783.72	10936.12	11125.46
对特定存款机构债权 Claims on Specific Depository Institutions	1025.57	1022.24	1109.26	1163.47
对其他金融机构债权 Claims on Other Financial Institutions	163.46	181.89	164.15	241.02
其他资产 Other Assets	3047.63	2982.22	2923.82	3068.10
总资产 Total Assets	**19075.36**	**19151.31**	**19452.88**	**20591.15**
对非金融机构负债 Liabilities to Non – financial Institutions	15365.66	15481.40	15868.52	16911.19
活期存款 Demand Deposits	6709.38	6848.09	6986.35	7652.20
定期存款 Time Deposits	2538.97	2496.27	2564.57	2675.88
储蓄存款 Savings Deposits	4522.17	4558.95	4675.34	4901.86
其他存款 Other Deposits	1435.12	1417.25	1483.75	1514.35
外币存款 Deposits in Foreign Currency	160.02	160.84	158.51	166.90
对中央银行负债 Liabilities to the Central Bank	62.21	60.34	67.21	64.77
对特定存款机构负债 Liabilities to Specific Depository Institutions	48.08	41.36	48.10	40.36
对其他金融机构负债 Liabilities to Other Financial Institutions	292.74	267.04	275.05	303.18
其中：计入广义货币的存款 Of Which：Deposits Included in Broad Money	84.66	82.24	81.08	75.88
国外负债 Foreign Liabilities	0.62	0.48	1.18	0.52
债券 Bonds	30.00	30.00	38.00	73.00
实收资本 Paid – in Capital	491.39	491.67	512.90	596.89
其他负债 Other Liabilities	2784.66	2779.02	2641.92	2601.24
总负债 Total Liabilities	**19075.36**	**19151.31**	**19452.88**	**20591.15**

6. 外资银行资产负债表
Balance Sheet of Foreign – funded Banks

外资银行资产负债表
Balance Sheet of Foreign – funded Banks
（月末余额）
（Month – end Balance）

单位：亿元
Unit：100 Million Yuan

项目 Items	2002.01	2002.02	2002.03	2002.04
国外资产 Foreign Assets	1044.34	934.00	943.95	908.52
储备资产 Reserve Assets	105.54	88.84	100.92	104.58
准备金存款 Reserve Deposits	105.42	88.75	100.76	104.49
库存现金 Cash in Vault	0.12	0.09	0.16	0.09
中央银行债券 Central Bank Bonds				
对政府债权 Claims on Government	3.99	5.96	5.99	6.10
其中：中央政府 Of Which：Central Government	3.99	5.96	5.99	6.10
对非金融机构债权 Claims on Non – financial Institutions	1397.49	1392.66	1388.39	1388.64
对特定存款机构债权 Claims on Specific Depository Institutions	41.77	38.39	37.90	43.21
对其他金融机构债权 Claims on Other Financial Institutions	3.14	7.83	8.16	2.87
其他资产 Other Assets	381.64	346.03	311.54	301.82
总资产 Total Assets	**2977.91**	**2813.71**	**2796.85**	**2755.74**
对非金融机构负债 Liabilities to Non – financial Institutions	545.41	552.94	593.74	560.50
活期存款 Demand Deposits	64.24	68.94	77.91	77.49
定期存款 Time Deposits	61.70	58.66	64.22	60.75
储蓄存款 Savings Deposits	1.01	1.06	1.15	1.29
其他存款 Other Deposits	0.03	0.01	0.15	0.31
外币存款 Deposits in Foreign Currency	418.43	424.27	450.31	420.66
对中央银行负债 Liabilities to the Central Bank	0.08	0.04	0.04	0.01
对特定存款机构负债 Liabilities to Specific Depository Institutions	11.64	11.70	10.08	10.99
对其他金融机构负债 Liabilities to Other Financial Institutions	62.44	64.52	56.93	52.58
其中：计入广义货币的存款 Of Which：Deposits Included in Broad Money				
国外负债 Foreign Liabilities	1451.57	1313.06	1317.64	1271.63
债券 Bonds	2.38	1.44	1.33	2.07
实收资本 Paid – in Capital	251.02	258.15	258.42	265.11
其他负债 Other Liabilities	653.37	611.86	558.67	592.85
总负债 Total Liabilities	**2977.91**	**2813.71**	**2796.85**	**2755.74**

外资银行资产负债表
Balance Sheet of Foreign - funded Banks

（月末余额）

（Month - end Balance）

单位：亿元

Unit：100 Million Yuan

项 目 Items	2002.05	2002.06	2002.07	2002.08
国外资产 Foreign Assets	870.35	907.34	971.26	981.00
储备资产 Reserve Assets	101.17	91.21	93.91	94.69
准备金存款 Reserve Deposits	101.05	91.06	93.74	94.55
库存现金 Cash in Vault	0.12	0.15	0.17	0.14
中央银行债券 Central Bank Bonds				
对政府债权 Claims on Government	6.40	6.50	7.41	8.02
其中：中央政府 Of Which：Central Government	6.40	6.50	7.41	8.02
对非金融机构债权 Claims on Non - financial Institutions	1376.20	1371.40	1375.01	1388.27
对特定存款机构债权 Claims on Specific Depository Institutions	41.91	40.90	41.98	39.77
对其他金融机构债权 Claims on Other Financial Institutions	1.06	1.01	0.66	0.60
其他资产 Other Assets	308.98	318.60	341.03	360.53
总资产 Total Assets	**2706.07**	**2736.96**	**2831.26**	**2872.88**
对非金融机构负债 Liabilities to Non - financial Institutions	577.31	597.15	615.62	631.20
活期存款 Demand Deposits	100.18	82.67	89.89	91.30
定期存款 Time Deposits	47.19	66.89	69.17	75.38
储蓄存款 Savings Deposits	1.34	1.43	1.78	2.09
其他存款 Other Deposits	0.02	0.18	0.79	0.34
外币存款 Deposits in Foreign Currency	428.58	445.98	453.99	462.09
对中央银行负债 Liabilities to the Central Bank	0.01	0.01	0.00	0.00
对特定存款机构负债 Liabilities to Specific Depository Institutions	9.55	9.57	8.08	7.50
对其他金融机构负债 Liabilities to Other Financial Institutions	54.40	43.47	39.60	37.89
其中：计入广义货币的存款 Of Which：Deposits Included in Broad Money				
国外负债 Foreign Liabilities	1236.99	1259.41	1306.86	1315.51
债券 Bonds	1.97	1.48	5.04	8.70
实收资本 Paid - in Capital	266.54	287.52	310.76	327.13
其他负债 Other Liabilities	559.30	538.35	545.30	544.95
总负债 Total Liabilities	**2706.07**	**2736.96**	**2831.26**	**2872.88**

外资银行资产负债表
Balance Sheet of Foreign - funded Banks

（月末余额）

（Month - end Balance）

单位：亿元

Unit：100 Million Yuan

项目 Items	2002.09	2002.10	2002.11	2002.12
国外资产 Foreign Assets	953.97	930.89	909.85	919.27
储备资产 Reserve Assets	112.01	102.06	90.73	109.06
准备金存款 Reserve Deposits	111.81	101.80	90.53	108.80
库存现金 Cash in Vault	0.20	0.26	0.20	0.26
中央银行债券 Central Bank Bonds				
对政府债权 Claims on Government	8.37	8.19	19.18	18.57
其中：中央政府 Of Which：Central Government	8.37	8.19	19.18	18.57
对非金融机构债权 Claims on Non - financial Institutions	1392.99	1393.27	1399.51	1374.25
对特定存款机构债权 Claims on Specific Depository Institutions	39.53	35.71	41.30	41.12
对其他金融机构债权 Claims on Other Financial Institutions	0.44	0.44	0.60	0.23
其他资产 Other Assets	370.93	391.83	365.11	418.47
总资产 Total Assets	**2878.24**	**2862.39**	**2826.28**	**2880.97**
对非金融机构负债 Liabilities to Non - financial Institutions	631.33	644.38	648.42	692.34
活期存款 Demand Deposits	97.35	101.20	102.74	118.90
定期存款 Time Deposits	87.66	88.02	96.10	93.05
储蓄存款 Savings Deposits	2.24	2.51	2.64	3.08
其他存款 Other Deposits	0.37			
外币存款 Deposits in Foreign Currency	443.71	452.65	446.94	477.31
对中央银行负债 Liabilities to the Central Bank				0.02
对特定存款机构负债 Liabilities to Specific Depository Institutions	9.79	9.61	6.69	10.28
对其他金融机构负债 Liabilities to Other Financial Institutions	32.36	31.01	28.20	23.63
其中：计入广义货币的存款 Of Which：Deposits Included in Broad Money				
国外负债 Foreign Liabilities	1310.26	1238.65	1259.73	1246.02
债券 Bonds	5.57	5.32	4.58	5.00
实收资本 Paid - in Capital	334.58	344.27	347.86	347.50
其他负债 Other Liabilities	554.35	589.15	530.80	556.18
总负债 Total Liabilities	**2878.24**	**2862.39**	**2826.28**	**2880.97**

外资银行资产负债表
Balance Sheet of Foreign - funded Banks

(月末余额)

(Month - end Balance)

单位：亿元

Unit：100 Million Yuan

项目 Items	2003.01	2003.02	2003.03	2003.04
国外资产 Foreign Assets	955.97	990.04	949.87	968.81
储备资产 Reserve Assets	94.81	90.66	100.04	98.50
准备金存款 Reserve Deposits	94.48	90.42	99.75	98.22
库存现金 Cash in Vault	0.33	0.24	0.29	0.28
中央银行债券 Central Bank Bonds				
对政府债权 Claims on Government	18.28	18.46	18.29	22.34
其中：中央政府 Of Which：Central Government	18.28	18.46	18.29	22.34
对非金融机构债权 Claims on Non - financial Institutions	1386.51	1392.12	1412.83	1417.57
对特定存款机构债权 Claims on Specific Depository Institutions	39.25	40.44	40.22	37.55
对其他金融机构债权 Claims on Other Financial Institutions	0.39	0.39	0.51	0.51
其他资产 Other Assets	406.70	382.49	375.26	395.32
总资产 Total Assets	**2901.91**	**2914.60**	**2897.02**	**2940.60**
对非金融机构负债 Liabilities to Non - financial Institutions	694.35	699.08	702.39	708.23
活期存款 Demand Deposits	111.21	108.06	116.96	125.38
定期存款 Time Deposits	99.17	108.98	113.82	121.36
储蓄存款 Savings Deposits	0.09	0.08	0.08	0.08
其他存款 Other Deposits				
外币存款 Deposits in Foreign Currency	483.88	481.96	471.53	461.41
对中央银行负债 Liabilities to the Central Bank	0.02			
对特定存款机构负债 Liabilities to Specific Depository Institutions	5.91	10.41	10.55	6.11
对其他金融机构负债 Liabilities to Other Financial Institutions	24.28	26.58	25.08	24.61
其中：计入广义货币的存款 Of Which：Deposits Included in Broad Money				
国外负债 Foreign Liabilities	1294.82	1298.40	1305.17	1362.11
债券 Bonds	4.73	5.24	5.46	2.42
实收资本 Paid - in Capital	354.19	356.26	360.24	361.28
其他负债 Other Liabilities	523.61	518.63	488.13	475.84
总负债 Total Liabilities	**2901.91**	**2914.60**	**2897.02**	**2940.60**

外资银行资产负债表

Balance Sheet of Foreign - funded Banks

（月末余额）

（Month - end Balance）

单位：亿元

Unit：100 Million Yuan

项　　目 Items	2003.05	2003.06	2003.07	2003.08
国外资产 Foreign Assets	977.84	1003.25	1013.70	1030.89
储备资产 Reserve Assets	99.30	105.70	122.52	124.94
准备金存款 Reserve Deposits	99.05	105.40	122.17	124.65
库存现金 Cash in Vault	0.25	0.30	0.35	0.29
中央银行债券 Central Bank Bonds				
对政府债权 Claims on Government	23.15	27.16	27.93	35.31
其中：中央政府 Of Which：Central Government	23.15	27.16	27.93	35.31
对非金融机构债权 Claims on Non - financial Institutions	1449.08	1466.09	1484.66	1501.68
对特定存款机构债权 Claims on Specific Depository Institutions	37.01	36.43	36.97	36.92
对其他金融机构债权 Claims on Other Financial Institutions	0.51	0.51	0.48	0.48
其他资产 Other Assets	407.67	398.63	401.45	403.99
总资产 Total Assets	**2994.56**	**3037.77**	**3087.71**	**3134.21**
对非金融机构负债 Liabilities to Non - financial Institutions	723.92	715.06	766.08	808.17
活期存款 Demand Deposits	121.28	122.64	126.49	139.53
定期存款 Time Deposits	137.53	133.68	144.88	156.59
储蓄存款 Savings Deposits	0.12	0.10	0.21	0.33
其他存款 Other Deposits				
外币存款 Deposits in Foreign Currency	464.99	458.64	494.50	511.72
对中央银行负债 Liabilities to the Central Bank		0.12	0.11	0.10
对特定存款机构负债 Liabilities to Specific Depository Institutions	5.79	6.14	4.99	5.31
对其他金融机构负债 Liabilities to Other Financial Institutions	25.33	26.49	33.02	32.85
其中：计入广义货币的存款 Of Which：Deposits Included in Broad Money				
国外负债 Foreign Liabilities	1375.22	1418.52	1418.50	1467.24
债券 Bonds	4.19	4.64	4.55	3.99
实收资本 Paid - in Capital	360.50	365.71	370.49	375.43
其他负债 Other Liabilities	499.61	501.09	489.97	441.12
总负债 Total Liabilities	**2994.56**	**3037.77**	**3087.71**	**3134.21**

外资银行资产负债表
Balance Sheet of Foreign – funded Banks

（月末余额）
（Month – end Balance）

单位：亿元
Unit: 100 Million Yuan

项　目 Items	2003.09	2003.10	2003.11	2003.12
国外资产 Foreign Assets	1085.46	1123.16	1205.68	1103.54
储备资产 Reserve Assets	129.30	148.85	151.22	171.02
准备金存款 Reserve Deposits	128.98	148.47	150.86	170.64
库存现金 Cash in Vault	0.32	0.38	0.36	0.38
中央银行债券 Central Bank Bonds				
对政府债权 Claims on Government	42.50	48.26	48.68	51.93
其中：中央政府 Of Which: Central Government	42.50	48.26	48.68	51.93
对非金融机构债权 Claims on Non – financial Institutions	1553.22	1606.26	1648.09	1476.16
对特定存款机构债权 Claims on Specific Depository Institutions	39.66	41.93	53.39	30.87
对其他金融机构债权 Claims on Other Financial Institutions	0.48	0.43	0.43	0.02
其他资产 Other Assets	446.98	472.50	512.72	496.92
总资产 Total Assets	**3297.60**	**3441.39**	**3620.21**	**3330.46**
对非金融机构负债 Liabilities to Non – financial Institutions	855.26	869.21	963.34	906.70
活期存款 Demand Deposits	157.17	163.40	160.13	189.34
定期存款 Time Deposits	179.62	184.07	197.39	199.06
储蓄存款 Savings Deposits	0.50	0.29	0.30	0.34
其他存款 Other Deposits				
外币存款 Deposits in Foreign Currency	517.97	521.45	605.52	517.96
对中央银行负债 Liabilities to the Central Bank	0.08	0.06	0.16	0.06
对特定存款机构负债 Liabilities to Specific Depository Institutions	3.37	3.94	3.70	2.57
对其他金融机构负债 Liabilities to Other Financial Institutions	33.48	35.12	37.01	30.10
其中：计入广义货币的存款 Of Which: Deposits Included in Broad Money				
国外负债 Foreign Liabilities	1559.20	1682.46	1778.54	1620.83
债券 Bonds	5.49	4.84	4.29	4.66
实收资本 Paid – in Capital	379.05	387.70	394.06	354.57
其他负债 Other Liabilities	461.67	458.06	439.11	410.97
总负债 Total Liabilities	**3297.60**	**3441.39**	**3620.21**	**3330.46**

外资银行资产负债表
Balance Sheet of Foreign – funded Banks

（月末余额）

（Month – end Balance）

单位：亿元

Unit：100 Million Yuan

项　目 Items	2004.01	2004.02	2004.03	2004.04
国外资产 Foreign Assets	1258.20	1260.40	1253.06	1288.09
储备资产 Reserve Assets	173.23	196.70	209.48	225.14
准备金存款 Reserve Deposits	172.86	196.27	208.94	224.65
库存现金 Cash in Vault	0.37	0.43	0.54	0.49
中央银行债券 Central Bank Bonds				
对政府债权 Claims on Government	57.67	63.85	81.66	85.54
其中：中央政府 Of Which：Central Government	57.67	63.85	81.66	85.54
对非金融机构债权 Claims on Non – financial Institutions	1747.26	1800.26	1919.37	2000.74
对特定存款机构债权 Claims on Specific Depository Institutions	46.01	51.06	50.00	43.98
对其他金融机构债权 Claims on Other Financial Institutions	0.15	0.27	0.27	0.27
其他资产 Other Assets	546.72	541.80	585.48	629.64
总资产 Total Assets	**3829.24**	**3914.34**	**4099.32**	**4273.40**
对非金融机构负债 Liabilities to Non – financial Institutions	1010.94	1007.51	1028.12	1086.79
活期存款 Demand Deposits	181.96	191.56	214.05	227.54
定期存款 Time Deposits	212.98	219.30	231.20	232.25
储蓄存款 Savings Deposits	0.29	0.38	0.39	0.18
其他存款 Other Deposits				
外币存款 Deposits in Foreign Currency	615.71	596.27	582.48	626.82
对中央银行负债 Liabilities to the Central Bank	0.05	0.36		
对特定存款机构负债 Liabilities to Specific Depository Institutions	2.90	3.41	3.43	3.19
对其他金融机构负债 Liabilities to Other Financial Institutions	30.94	33.40	29.31	26.59
其中：计入广义货币的存款 Of Which：Deposits Included in Broad Money				
国外负债 Foreign Liabilities	1932.57	2021.05	2167.24	2250.77
债券 Bonds	3.70	3.29	4.41	3.90
实收资本 Paid – in Capital	389.20	390.13	403.90	421.52
其他负债 Other Liabilities	458.94	455.19	462.91	480.64
总负债 Total Liabilities	**3829.24**	**3914.34**	**4099.32**	**4273.40**

外资银行资产负债表
Balance Sheet of Foreign – funded Banks

（月末余额）
(Month – end Balance)

单位：亿元
Unit: 100 Million Yuan

项目 Items	2004.05	2004.06	2004.07	2004.08
国外资产 Foreign Assets	1365.18	2175.14	1565.13	1656.36
储备资产 Reserve Assets	218.31	211.16	188.99	178.23
准备金存款 Reserve Deposits	217.81	210.66	188.31	177.58
库存现金 Cash in Vault	0.50	0.50	0.68	0.65
中央银行债券 Central Bank Bonds				
对政府债权 Claims on Government	83.47	84.19	89.41	84.02
其中：中央政府 Of Which: Central Government	83.47	84.19	89.41	84.02
对非金融机构债权 Claims on Non – financial Institutions	2084.90	2207.40	2245.17	2294.11
对特定存款机构债权 Claims on Specific Depository Institutions	48.17	45.36	42.76	35.93
对其他金融机构债权 Claims on Other Financial Institutions	0.37	0.27	0.27	0.14
其他资产 Other Assets	623.79	797.73	711.63	685.69
总资产 Total Assets	**4424.19**	**5521.25**	**4843.36**	**4934.48**
对非金融机构负债 Liabilities to Non – financial Institutions	1120.77	1145.14	1135.83	1128.23
活期存款 Demand Deposits	236.51	245.66	242.66	243.96
定期存款 Time Deposits	225.09	231.84	229.72	217.88
储蓄存款 Savings Deposits	0.15	0.32	0.14	0.16
其他存款 Other Deposits				
外币存款 Deposits in Foreign Currency	659.02	667.32	663.31	666.23
对中央银行负债 Liabilities to the Central Bank				
对特定存款机构负债 Liabilities to Specific Depository Institutions	2.88	5.83	2.75	3.47
对其他金融机构负债 Liabilities to Other Financial Institutions	20.18	21.80	20.63	43.88
其中：计入广义货币的存款 Of Which: Deposits Included in Broad Money				
国外负债 Foreign Liabilities	2353.52	3409.78	2719.89	2754.78
债券 Bonds	4.03	3.14	3.27	4.53
实收资本 Paid – in Capital	429.45	436.77	443.33	442.14
其他负债 Other Liabilities	493.36	498.79	517.66	557.45
总负债 Total Liabilities	**4424.19**	**5521.25**	**4843.36**	**4934.48**

外资银行资产负债表
Balance Sheet of Foreign - funded Banks

（月末余额）

（Month - end Balance）

单位：亿元

Unit：100 Million Yuan

项目 Items	2004.09	2004.10	2004.11	2004.12
国外资产 Foreign Assets	1609.55	1541.93	1565.35	1486.25
储备资产 Reserve Assets	190.20	179.53	192.06	244.56
准备金存款 Reserve Deposits	189.55	179.03	191.51	243.95
库存现金 Cash in Vault	0.65	0.50	0.55	0.61
中央银行债券 Central Bank Bonds				
对政府债权 Claims on Government	85.38	93.87	90.33	98.03
其中：中央政府 Of Which：Central Government	85.38	93.87	90.33	98.03
对非金融机构债权 Claims on Non - financial Institutions	2363.48	2399.30	2485.37	2558.58
对特定存款机构债权 Claims on Specific Depository Institutions	42.51	43.00	47.23	72.33
对其他金融机构债权 Claims on Other Financial Institutions	0.12	0.11	0.14	0.14
其他资产 Other Assets	713.25	657.80	665.82	700.06
总资产 Total Assets	**5004.49**	**4915.54**	**5046.30**	**5159.95**
对非金融机构负债 Liabilities to Non - financial Institutions	1148.21	1192.86	1217.70	1264.14
活期存款 Demand Deposits	243.69	246.21	272.99	305.30
定期存款 Time Deposits	218.14	237.22	240.84	251.88
储蓄存款 Savings Deposits	0.17	0.18	0.20	0.29
其他存款 Other Deposits				
外币存款 Deposits in Foreign Currency	686.21	709.25	703.67	706.67
对中央银行负债 Liabilities to the Central Bank				
对特定存款机构负债 Liabilities to Specific Depository Institutions	2.92	2.50	4.03	3.70
对其他金融机构负债 Liabilities to Other Financial Institutions	25.40	21.65	28.44	27.21
其中：计入广义货币的存款 Of Which：Deposits Included in Broad Money				
国外负债 Foreign Liabilities	2811.32	2698.32	2728.73	2737.14
债券 Bonds	8.16	7.71	8.29	11.64
实收资本 Paid - in Capital	447.37	452.87	454.06	471.97
其他负债 Other Liabilities	561.11	539.63	605.05	644.15
总负债 Total Liabilities	**5004.49**	**4915.54**	**5046.30**	**5159.95**

外资银行资产负债表
Balance Sheet of Foreign - funded Banks

(月末余额)

(Month - end Balance)

单位：亿元

Unit: 100 Million Yuan

项 目 Items	2005.01	2005.02	2005.03	2005.04
国外资产 Foreign Assets	1489.52	1466.60	1515.60	1510.18
储备资产 Reserve Assets	189.69	175.65	189.47	199.35
准备金存款 Reserve Deposits	189.04	175.05	188.74	198.60
库存现金 Cash in Vault	0.65	0.60	0.73	0.75
中央银行债券 Central Bank Bonds				
对政府债权 Claims on Government	101.37	104.07	120.83	114.56
其中：中央政府 Of Which: Central Government	101.37	104.07	120.83	114.56
对非金融机构债权 Claims on Non - financial Institutions	2618.16	2663.68	2785.12	2851.58
对特定存款机构债权 Claims on Specific Depository Institutions	101.62	100.44	93.45	114.60
对其他金融机构债权 Claims on Other Financial Institutions	0.10	0.10	0.10	0.10
其他资产 Other Assets	738.19	750.34	781.59	825.41
总资产 Total Assets	**5238.65**	**5260.88**	**5486.16**	**5615.78**
对非金融机构负债 Liabilities to Non - financial Institutions	1274.24	1313.38	1392.52	1414.20
活期存款 Demand Deposits	300.66	292.45	331.49	339.18
定期存款 Time Deposits	253.88	258.37	270.08	302.43
储蓄存款 Savings Deposits	0.26	0.22	0.21	0.25
其他存款 Other Deposits				
外币存款 Deposits in Foreign Currency	719.44	762.34	790.74	772.34
对中央银行负债 Liabilities to the Central Bank				
对特定存款机构负债 Liabilities to Specific Depository Institutions	3.22	2.96	2.92	2.18
对其他金融机构负债 Liabilities to Other Financial Institutions	27.77	28.74	30.62	28.10
其中：计入广义货币的存款 Of Which: Deposits Included in Broad Money				
国外负债 Foreign Liabilities	2752.32	2760.10	2821.12	2934.71
债券 Bonds	10.31	13.25	12.82	10.59
实收资本 Paid - in Capital	478.46	483.53	498.88	510.91
其他负债 Other Liabilities	692.33	658.92	727.28	715.09
总负债 Total Liabilities	**5238.65**	**5260.88**	**5486.16**	**5615.78**

外资银行资产负债表

Balance Sheet of Foreign – funded Banks

（月末余额）

（Month – end Balance）

单位：亿元

Unit：100 Million Yuan

项 目 Items	2005.05	2005.06	2005.07	2005.08
国外资产 Foreign Assets	1535.87	1521.29	1429.79	1441.91
储备资产 Reserve Assets	226.43	199.34	254.82	268.36
准备金存款 Reserve Deposits	225.51	198.54	253.88	267.38
库存现金 Cash in Vault	0.92	0.80	0.94	0.98
中央银行债券 Central Bank Bonds				
对政府债权 Claims on Government	128.49	126.36	61.12	65.81
其中：中央政府 Of Which：Central Government	128.49	126.36	61.12	65.81
对非金融机构债权 Claims on Non – financial Institutions	2945.87	3027.72	3041.43	3118.35
对特定存款机构债权 Claims on Specific Depository Institutions	107.89	107.96	111.03	104.47
对其他金融机构债权 Claims on Other Financial Institutions	0.04	0.03	0.16	0.20
其他资产 Other Assets	843.10	851.02	866.43	876.54
总资产 Total Assets	**5787.69**	**5833.72**	**5764.78**	**5875.64**
对非金融机构负债 Liabilities to Non – financial Institutions	1459.58	1461.06	1424.73	1455.05
活期存款 Demand Deposits	359.94	355.74	370.28	368.13
定期存款 Time Deposits	312.01	320.91	320.71	352.02
储蓄存款 Savings Deposits	0.33	0.34	0.35	1.01
其他存款 Other Deposits				
外币存款 Deposits in Foreign Currency	787.30	784.07	733.39	733.89
对中央银行负债 Liabilities to the Central Bank				
对特定存款机构负债 Liabilities to Specific Depository Institutions	6.87	4.03	5.37	7.47
对其他金融机构负债 Liabilities to Other Financial Institutions	32.74	35.52	44.02	53.90
其中：计入广义货币的存款 Of Which：Deposits Included in Broad Money				
国外负债 Foreign Liabilities	2994.84	2994.69	2912.52	2891.45
债券 Bonds	11.36	11.84	8.79	8.28
实收资本 Paid – in Capital	521.92	525.75	536.79	547.68
其他负债 Other Liabilities	760.38	800.83	832.56	911.81
总负债 Total Liabilities	**5787.69**	**5833.72**	**5764.78**	**5875.64**

外资银行资产负债表
Balance Sheet of Foreign - funded Banks

（月末余额）
(Month - end Balance)

单位：亿元
Unit: 100 Million Yuan

项目 Items	2005.09	2005.10	2005.11	2005.12
国外资产 Foreign Assets	1311.20	1381.69	1425.13	1500.79
储备资产 Reserve Assets	320.30	300.33	316.72	364.89
准备金存款 Reserve Deposits	319.32	299.28	315.70	363.61
库存现金 Cash in Vault	0.98	1.05	1.02	1.28
中央银行债券 Central Bank Bonds				
对政府债权 Claims on Government	82.43	88.40	76.96	101.82
其中：中央政府 Of Which: Central Government	82.43	88.40	76.96	101.82
对非金融机构债权 Claims on Non - financial Institutions	3151.16	3193.30	3229.61	3301.36
对特定存款机构债权 Claims on Specific Depository Institutions	105.20	114.76	121.27	118.39
对其他金融机构债权 Claims on Other Financial Institutions	0.37	0.25	0.26	3.00
其他资产 Other Assets	894.37	922.14	928.37	962.65
总资产 Total Assets	**5865.03**	**6000.87**	**6098.32**	**6352.90**
对非金融机构负债 Liabilities to Non - financial Institutions	1523.39	1561.95	1582.80	1695.52
活期存款 Demand Deposits	396.27	394.72	417.68	469.86
定期存款 Time Deposits	394.02	399.89	387.94	421.03
储蓄存款 Savings Deposits	1.04	0.36	0.38	0.40
其他存款 Other Deposits				
外币存款 Deposits in Foreign Currency	732.06	766.98	776.80	804.23
对中央银行负债 Liabilities to the Central Bank				
对特定存款机构负债 Liabilities to Specific Depository Institutions	2.14	1.63	19.42	1.60
对其他金融机构负债 Liabilities to Other Financial Institutions	46.23	47.67	40.43	42.50
其中：计入广义货币的存款 Of Which: Deposits Included in Broad Money				
国外负债 Foreign Liabilities	2873.64	2903.78	2931.54	3048.91
债券 Bonds	12.02	13.28	16.96	21.12
实收资本 Paid - in Capital	552.88	558.64	564.93	579.43
其他负债 Other Liabilities	854.73	913.92	942.24	963.82
总负债 Total Liabilities	**5865.03**	**6000.87**	**6098.32**	**6352.90**

7. 城市信用合作社资产负债表
Balance Sheet of Urban Credit Cooperatives

城市信用合作社资产负债表
Balance Sheet of Urban Credit Cooperatives

（季末余额）

（Quarter - end Balance）

单位：亿元

Unit：100 Million Yuan

项　目 Items	1993.03	1993.06	1993.09	1993.12
国外资产 Foreign Assets				
储备资产 Reserve Assets	198.7	228.2	232.8	331.2
准备金 Reserves	96.1	114.4	116.0	134.3
在人行存款 Deposits with the Central Bank	90.2	99.1	102.1	176.3
库存现金 Cash in Vault	12.4	14.7	14.7	20.6
中央银行债券 Central Bank Bonds				
对政府债权 Claims on Government	41.7	59.1	63.1	73.8
对其他部门债权 Claims on Other Sectors	573.5	610.0	646.9	777.4
对非货币金融机构债权 Claims on Non - monetary Financial Institutions				
对非金融部门负债 Liabilities to Non - financial Sectors	961.3	1081.1	1099.2	1339.7
活期存款 Demand Deposits	468.1	536.2	514.7	622.0
定期存款 Time Deposits	43.2	48.6	54.3	68.7
储蓄存款 Savings Deposits	244.0	273.4	312.3	375.8
其他存款 Other Deposits	206.0	222.9	217.9	273.2
对中央银行负债 Liabilities to the Central Bank	28.9	25.9	19.8	23.1
对非货币金融机构负债 Liabilities to Non - monetary Financial Institutions				
国外负债 Foreign Liabilities				
债券 Bonds				
所有者权益 Owner's Equity	59.2	63.4	69.0	84.1
其中：实收资本 Of Which：Paid - in Capital	59.2	63.4	69.0	84.1
其他（净） Other Items（Net）	- 235.5	- 273.1	- 245.2	- 264.5

城市信用合作社资产负债表
Balance Sheet of Urban Credit Cooperatives

（季末余额）

（Quarter－end Balance）

单位：亿元

Unit：100 Million Yuan

项　目 Items	1994.03	1994.06	1994.09	1994.12
国外资产 Foreign Assets				
储备资产 Reserve Assets	199.6	337.1	347.9	478.0
准备金 Reserves	145.7	175.6	197.6	230.5
在人行存款 Deposits with the Central Bank	31.0	135.9	120.6	214.5
库存现金 Cash in Vault	22.9	25.6	29.7	33.0
中央银行债券 Central Bank Bonds	18.4	14.2	10.6	20.2
对政府债权 Claims on Government	29.7	41.3	50.5	67.9
对其他部门债权 Claims on Other Sectors	979.7	1113.8	1258.3	1442.8
对非货币金融机构债权 Claims on Non－monetary Financial Institutions	82.7	116.4	133.1	139.6
对非金融部门负债 Liabilities to Non－financial Sectors	1481.0	1762.2	1987.8	2353.5
活期存款 Demand Deposits	654.4	777.5	845.6	999.2
定期存款 Time Deposits	89.0	125.0	161.9	204.4
储蓄存款 Savings Deposits	456.2	534.2	620.8	733.7
其他存款 Other Deposits	281.4	325.5	359.5	416.2
对中央银行负债 Liabilities to the Central Bank	24.0	32.2	29.4	34.7
对非货币金融机构负债 Liabilities to Non－monetary Financial Institutions	43.4	44.3	32.5	44.0
国外负债 Foreign Liabilities				
债券 Bonds				
所有者权益 Owner's Equity	123.5	131.0	135.6	161.5
其中：实收资本 Of Which：Paid－in Capital	87.2	94.0	100.7	111.1
其他（净） Other Items（Net）	－361.8	－346.9	－384.9	－445.2

城市信用合作社资产负债表
Balance Sheet of Urban Credit Cooperatives

（季末余额）

（Quarter - end Balance）

单位：亿元

Unit：100 Million Yuan

项目 Items	1995.03	1995.06	1995.09	1995.12
国外资产 Foreign Assets				
储备资产 Reserve Assets	484.1	508.7	522.2	662.7
准备金 Reserves	253.1	279.8	309.6	332.1
在人行存款 Deposits with the Central Bank	195.5	187.3	168.5	282.6
库存现金 Cash in Vault	35.5	41.6	44.1	48.0
中央银行债券 Central Bank Bonds	21.5	21.5	19.9	20.5
对政府债权 Claims on Government	93.7	112.7	101.8	98.2
对其他部门债权 Claims on Other Sectors	1621.5	1741.3	1868.4	2068.2
对非货币金融机构债权 Claims on Non - monetary Financial Institutions	150.9	165.4	184.3	189.6
对非金融部门负债 Liabilities to Non - financial Sectors	2531.1	2745.3	2953.7	3357.4
活期存款 Demand Deposits	992.1	1032.6	1053.6	1172.4
定期存款 Time Deposits	253.6	303.4	359.9	407.2
储蓄存款 Savings Deposits	862.5	970.8	1091.8	1259.5
其他存款 Other Deposits	422.9	438.5	448.4	518.3
对中央银行负债 Liabilities to the Central Bank	35.8	29.1	28.6	29.7
对非货币金融机构负债 Liabilities to Non - monetary Financial Institutions	51.8	47.2	51.0	57.6
国外负债 Foreign Liabilities				
债券 Bonds	0.2	0.2	0.8	0.2
所有者权益 Owner's Equity	176.7	180.3	187.4	200.8
其中：实收资本 Of Which：Paid - in Capital	127.0	130.6	129.2	136.0
其他（净） Other Items（Net）	-423.9	-452.5	-524.9	-606.5

城市信用合作社资产负债表
Balance Sheet of Urban Credit Cooperatives

（季末余额）

(Quarter - end Balance)

单位：亿元

Unit: 100 Million Yuan

项　目 Items	1996.03	1996.06	1996.09	1996.12
国外资产 Foreign Assets				
储备资产 Reserve Assets	617.6	603.7	616.8	779.0
准备金 Reserves	360.6	351.7	366.2	394.7
在人行存款 Deposits with the Central Bank	205.0	200.5	194.5	341.6
库存现金 Cash in Vault	52.0	51.5	56.1	42.7
中央银行债券 Central Bank Bonds				
对政府债权 Claims on Government	119.8	94.5	93.4	99.4
对其他部门债权 Claims on Other Sectors	2182.4	2239.6	2407.6	2631.1
对非货币金融机构债权 Claims on Non - monetary Financial Institutions	185.5	197.2	211.5	238.3
对非金融部门负债 Liabilities to Non - financial Sectors	3399.2	3405.0	3615.1	3998.3
活期存款 Demand Deposits	1072.2	986.1	1028.6	1171.9
定期存款 Time Deposits	411.6	417.8	443.1	474.6
储蓄存款 Savings Deposits	1442.7	1565.2	1677.0	1833.0
其他存款 Other Deposits	472.7	435.9	466.4	518.8
对中央银行负债 Liabilities to the Central Bank	30.9	33.5	34.3	33.7
对非货币金融机构负债 Liabilities to Non - monetary Financial Institutions	64.1	76.8	98.7	177.8
国外负债 Foreign Liabilities				
债券 Bonds	0.3	0.3	0.2	0.4
所有者权益 Owner's Equity	216.1	199.7	200.3	211.9
其中：实收资本 Of Which: Paid - in Capital	156.2	146.9	150.6	158.4
其他（净） Other Items (Net)	- 605.3	- 580.3	- 619.3	- 674.3

城市信用合作社资产负债表

Balance Sheet of Urban Credit Cooperatives

（季末余额）

（Quarter – end Balance）

单位：亿元

Unit：100 Million Yuan

项　目 Items	1997.03	1997.06	1997.09	1997.12
国外资产 Foreign Assets				
储备资产 Reserve Assets	735.2	807.7	941.3	1002.8
准备金 Reserves	437.9	460.2	496.2	525.5
在人行存款 Deposits with the Central Bank	230.8	284.4	380.9	411.3
库存现金 Cash in Vault	66.5	63.1	64.2	66.0
中央银行债券 Central Bank Bonds	1.9	2.7	3.3	3.3
对政府债权 Claims on Government	221.6	184.2	209.7	245.8
对其他部门债权 Claims on Other Sectors	3001.9	3174.5	3305.1	3516.8
对非货币金融机构债权 Claims on Non – monetary Financial Institutions	260.0	247.6	235.7	220.7
对非金融部门负债 Liabilities to Non – financial Sectors	4523.2	4768.2	4988.7	5382.5
活期存款 Demand Deposits	1753.8	1836.8	1957.9	2232.5
定期存款 Time Deposits	625.4	611.0	613.4	631.1
储蓄存款 Savings Deposits	2053.4	2224.1	2321.3	2419.7
其他存款 Other Deposits	90.6	96.3	96.1	99.2
对中央银行负债 Liabilities to the Central Bank	38.5	39.7	39.4	37.8
对非货币金融机构负债 Liabilities to Non – monetary Financial Institutions	119.4	135.7	130.3	139.6
国外负债 Foreign Liabilities				
债券 Bonds	2.1	1.9	3.0	2.7
所有者权益 Owner's Equity	251.2	265.5	258.2	280.8
其中：实收资本 Of Which：Paid – in Capital	209.0	227.5	234.9	252.6
其他（净） Other Items（Net）	– 713.8	– 794.3	– 724.5	– 854.0

城市信用合作社资产负债表
Balance Sheet of Urban Credit Cooperatives

（季末余额）

（Quarter – end Balance）

单位：亿元

Unit：100 Million Yuan

项　目 Items	1998.03	1998.06	1998.09	1998.12
国外资产 Foreign Assets				
储备资产 Reserve Assets	880.7	709.4	756.8	982.5
准备金 Reserves	523.5	645.1	690.2	908.4
在人行存款 Deposits with the Central Bank	290.8			
库存现金 Cash in Vault	66.4	64.3	66.6	74.1
中央银行债券 Central Bank Bonds	2.6	4.9	2.5	2.1
对政府债权 Claims on Government	243.8	360.2	367.9	388.2
对其他部门债权 Claims on Other Sectors	3586.1	3739.7	3816.1	4007.6
对非货币金融机构债权 Claims on Non – monetary Financial Institutions	202.0	213.7	207.3	225.9
对非金融部门负债 Liabilities to Non – financial Sectors	5311.4	5403.1	5560.2	6084.9
活期存款 Demand Deposits	2055.0	2125.8	2245.3	2583.8
定期存款 Time Deposits	627.1	643.8	659.8	683.5
储蓄存款 Savings Deposits	2541.3	2548.2	2572.6	2719.5
其他存款 Other Deposits	88.0	85.3	82.5	98.1
对中央银行负债 Liabilities to the Central Bank	34.8	39.3	37.0	39.1
对非货币金融机构负债 Liabilities to Non – monetary Financial Institutions	110.2	99.3	113.7	116.2
国外负债 Foreign Liabilities				
债券 Bonds	2.1	1.7	0.9	0.7
所有者权益 Owner's Equity	258.1	251.7	229.2	240.0
其中：实收资本 Of Which: Paid – in Capital	265.4	265.9	267.5	273.9
其他（净） Other Items（Net）	– 801.4	– 767.2	– 790.4	– 874.6

城市信用合作社资产负债表

Balance Sheet of Urban Credit Cooperatives

（季末余额）

（Quarter - end Balance）

单位：亿元

Unit：100 Million Yuan

项目 Items	1999.03	1999.06	1999.09	1999.12
国外资产 Foreign Assets				
储备资产 Reserve Assets	700.5	701.7	792.3	1042.9
准备金 Reserves	629.6	633.2	705.9	939.6
库存现金 Cash in Vault	70.9	68.5	86.4	103.3
中央银行债券 Central Bank Bonds	3.9	2.0	2.9	1.2
对政府债权 Claims on Government	390.1	445.4	473.1	502.7
对其他部门债权 Claims on Other Sectors	4075.2	4185.0	4312.5	4460.0
对非货币金融机构债权 Claims on Non - monetary Financial Institutions	231.6	250.0	248.8	294.7
对非金融部门负债 Liabilities to Non - financial Sectors	5919.5	6081.7	6177.9	6638.8
活期存款 Demand Deposits	2316.9	2440.1	2590.1	2972.3
定期存款 Time Deposits	681.5	702.9	705.1	728.0
储蓄存款 Savings Deposits	2842.4	2859.1	2800.8	2819.9
其他存款 Other Deposits	78.7	79.6	81.9	118.6
对中央银行负债 Liabilities to the Central Bank	45.6	52.0	87.4	143.1
对非货币金融机构负债 Liabilities to Non - monetary Financial Institutions	102.8	113.2	157.3	154.6
国外负债 Foreign Liabilities				
债券 Bonds	0.5	0.4	0.5	0.4
实收资本 Paid - in Capital	279.6	292.4	298.0	314.7
其他（净） Other Items（Net）	-946.7	-955.6	-891.5	-950.1

城市信用合作社资产负债表
Balance Sheet of Urban Credit Cooperatives

（季末余额）

（Quarter - end Balance）

单位：亿元

Unit: 100 Million Yuan

项 目 Items	2000.03	2000.06	2000.09	2000.12
国外资产 Foreign Assets				
储备资产 Reserve Assets	723.4	723.5	874.7	1078.3
准备金 Reserves	648.1	649.7	794.7	989.4
库存现金 Cash in Vault	75.3	73.8	80.0	88.9
中央银行债券 Central Bank Bonds	1.4	1.3	1.2	1.2
对政府债权 Claims on Government	538.6	583.0	606.5	623.9
对其他部门债权 Claims on Other Sectors	4314.8	4489.9	4653.5	4695.1
对非货币金融机构债权 Claims on Non - monetary Financial Institutions	266.4	327.1	346.6	386.4
对非金融部门负债 Liabilities to Non - financial Sectors	6153.7	6452.0	6609.5	6786.6
活期存款 Demand Deposits	2712.5	2998.7	3151.0	3475.7
定期存款 Time Deposits	711.2	743.2	786.0	792.3
储蓄存款 Savings Deposits	2632.2	2605.0	2579.7	2403.3
其他存款 Other Deposits	97.8	105.1	92.8	115.3
对中央银行负债 Liabilities to the Central Bank	208.9	290.9	300.1	314.3
对非货币金融机构负债 Liabilities to Non - monetary Financial Institutions	93.4	162.4	214.7	177.2
国外负债 Foreign Liabilities				
债券 Bonds	0.2	0.3	0.1	
实收资本 Paid - in Capital	309.0	309.2	317.0	324.1
其他（净） Other Items (Net)	-920.6	-1090.0	-958.9	-817.3

城市信用合作社资产负债表

Balance Sheet of Urban Credit Cooperatives

（季末余额）

（Quarter - end Balance）

单位：亿元

Unit：100 Million Yuan

项目 Items	2001.03	2001.06	2001.09	2001.12
国外资产 Foreign Assets				
储备资产 Reserve Assets	685.9	669.6	784.0	1047.5
准备金 Reserves	612.8	599.9	709.5	976.2
库存现金 Cash in Vault	73.1	69.7	74.5	71.3
中央银行债券 Central Bank Bonds	1.1	1.2	1.2	0.1
对政府债权 Claims on Government	616.2	738.3	792.9	890.9
对其他部门债权 Claims on Other Sectors	4644.4	4856.8	5001.1	5495.5
对非货币金融机构债权 Claims on Non - monetary Financial Institutions	289.5	298.5	322.8	366.3
对非金融部门负债 Liabilities to Non - financial Sectors	6403.9	6727.1	7058.1	7812.4
活期存款 Demand Deposits	3193.1	3383.3	3533.7	4051.1
定期存款 Time Deposits	813.0	871.0	960.0	1020.1
储蓄存款 Savings Deposits	2277.9	2304.6	2347.2	2512.6
其他存款 Other Deposits	119.9	168.2	217.2	228.7
对中央银行负债 Liabilities to the Central Bank	350.2	369.1	382.1	316.3
对非货币金融机构负债 Liabilities to Non - monetary Financial Institutions	156.9	207.2	49.0	70.1
国外负债 Foreign Liabilities				
债券 Bonds	0.1		0.1	0.1
实收资本 Paid - in Capital	323.7	330.6	331.0	363.7
其他（净） Other Items（Net）	-997.7	-1069.6	-918.3	-762.3

城市信用合作社资产负债表
Balance Sheet of Urban Credit Cooperatives

（月末余额）

（Month – end Balance）

单位：亿元

Unit：100 Million Yuan

项目 Items	2002.01	2002.02	2002.03	2002.04
国外资产 Foreign Assets				
储备资产 Reserve Assets	106.02	97.86	88.30	92.06
准备金存款 Reserve Deposits	93.66	85.38	75.91	80.27
库存现金 Cash in Vault	12.36	12.48	12.39	11.79
中央银行债券 Central Bank Bonds				
对政府债权 Claims on Government	22.52	21.80	21.35	24.65
其中：中央政府 Of Which: Central Government	22.52	21.80	21.35	24.65
对非金融机构债权 Claims on Non – financial Institutions	621.24	606.29	592.99	606.69
对特定存款机构债权 Claims on Specific Depository Institutions	5.67	4.77	4.02	4.92
对其他金融机构债权 Claims on Other Financial Institutions	6.24	6.91	5.97	5.93
其他资产 Other Assets	301.22	293.44	282.27	291.55
总资产 Total Assets	**1062.91**	**1031.07**	**994.90**	**1025.80**
对非金融机构负债 Liabilities to Non – financial Institutions	905.23	865.25	834.76	852.87
活期存款 Demand Deposits	287.20	263.60	244.93	253.50
定期存款 Time Deposits	79.94	79.99	75.57	81.49
储蓄存款 Savings Deposits	527.86	511.40	499.36	504.01
其他存款 Other Deposits	10.23	10.26	14.90	13.87
外币存款 Deposits in Foreign Currency				
对中央银行负债 Liabilities to the Central Bank	29.49	32.84	35.26	40.12
对特定存款机构负债 Liabilities to Specific Depository Institutions	0.51	0.51	0.49	0.51
对其他金融机构负债 Liabilities to Other Financial Institutions	3.31	3.40	3.46	3.31
其中：计入广义货币的存款 Of Which: Deposits Included in Broad Money	0.01	0.03	0.05	0.05
国外负债 Foreign Liabilities				
债券 Bonds	0.16	0.31	0.18	0.21
实收资本 Paid – in Capital	34.15	31.53	31.31	33.17
其他负债 Other Liabilities	90.06	97.23	89.44	95.61
总负债 Total Liabilities	**1062.91**	**1031.07**	**994.90**	**1025.80**

城市信用合作社资产负债表
Balance Sheet of Urban Credit Cooperatives

（月末余额）
（Month - end Balance）

单位：亿元
Unit：100 Million Yuan

项目 Items	2002.05	2002.06	2002.07	2002.08
国外资产 Foreign Assets				
储备资产 Reserve Assets	92.76	86.73	95.75	104.89
准备金存款 Reserve Deposits	82.13	74.78	84.89	93.49
库存现金 Cash in Vault	10.63	11.95	10.86	11.40
中央银行债券 Central Bank Bonds				
对政府债权 Claims on Government	24.80	24.52	24.39	25.24
其中：中央政府 Of Which：Central Government	24.80	24.52	24.39	25.24
对非金融机构债权 Claims on Non - financial Institutions	615.65	620.98	624.29	638.29
对特定存款机构债权 Claims on Specific Depository Institutions	4.83	4.83	6.37	6.68
对其他金融机构债权 Claims on Other Financial Institutions	5.62	5.62	5.53	5.66
其他资产 Other Assets	285.58	297.15	287.39	287.60
总资产 Total Assets	**1029.24**	**1039.83**	**1043.72**	**1068.36**
对非金融机构负债 Liabilities to Non - financial Institutions	861.95	871.83	883.96	899.74
活期存款 Demand Deposits	257.21	260.02	270.27	279.73
定期存款 Time Deposits	81.83	85.91	86.67	89.92
储蓄存款 Savings Deposits	506.58	508.22	510.25	512.45
其他存款 Other Deposits	16.33	17.68	16.77	17.64
外币存款 Deposits in Foreign Currency				
对中央银行负债 Liabilities to the Central Bank	39.90	39.26	38.00	39.17
对特定存款机构负债 Liabilities to Specific Depository Institutions	0.50	0.49	0.49	0.49
对其他金融机构负债 Liabilities to Other Financial Institutions	3.30	3.21	3.00	3.11
其中：计入广义货币的存款 Of Which：Deposits Included in Broad Money	0.05	0.12	0.02	0.03
国外负债 Foreign Liabilities				
债券 Bonds	0.17	0.34	0.17	0.19
实收资本 Paid - in Capital	33.30	33.86	34.64	34.90
其他负债 Other Liabilities	90.12	90.84	83.46	90.76
总负债 Total Liabilities	**1029.24**	**1039.83**	**1043.72**	**1068.36**

城市信用合作社资产负债表
Balance Sheet of Urban Credit Cooperatives

（月末余额）

（Month - end Balance）

单位：亿元

Unit：100 Million Yuan

项目 Items	2002.09	2002.10	2002.11	2002.12
国外资产 Foreign Assets				
储备资产 Reserve Assets	93.59	98.84	106.58	159.96
准备金存款 Reserve Deposits	79.74	86.86	94.07	147.39
库存现金 Cash in Vault	13.85	11.98	12.51	12.57
中央银行债券 Central Bank Bonds	0.06	0.06	0.06	0.06
对政府债权 Claims on Government	27.51	28.90	30.61	35.84
其中：中央政府 Of Which：Central Government	27.51	28.90	30.61	35.84
对非金融机构债权 Claims on Non - financial Institutions	645.05	649.79	654.18	674.46
对特定存款机构债权 Claims on Specific Depository Institutions	6.86	6.86	7.73	7.42
对其他金融机构债权 Claims on Other Financial Institutions	6.11	6.16	5.81	4.21
其他资产 Other Assets	288.74	290.94	293.23	310.34
总资产 Total Assets	**1067.92**	**1081.55**	**1098.20**	**1192.29**
对非金融机构负债 Liabilities to Non - financial Institutions	903.93	915.91	941.48	1010.55
活期存款 Demand Deposits	277.05	280.14	292.84	333.92
定期存款 Time Deposits	92.70	95.38	99.04	103.40
储蓄存款 Savings Deposits	514.48	518.35	527.74	549.53
其他存款 Other Deposits	19.70	22.04	21.86	23.70
外币存款 Deposits in Foreign Currency				
对中央银行负债 Liabilities to the Central Bank	39.86	40.28	37.54	35.66
对特定存款机构负债 Liabilities to Specific Depository Institutions	0.49	0.49	0.49	0.49
对其他金融机构负债 Liabilities to Other Financial Institutions	3.02	2.98	2.97	3.61
其中：计入广义货币的存款 Of Which：Deposits Included in Broad Money	0.03	0.05	0.02	0.29
国外负债 Foreign Liabilities				
债券 Bonds	0.07	0.16	0.15	1.32
实收资本 Paid - in Capital	36.00	35.99	36.11	37.88
其他负债 Other Liabilities	84.55	85.74	79.46	102.78
总负债 Total Liabilities	**1067.92**	**1081.55**	**1098.20**	**1192.29**

城市信用合作社资产负债表
Balance Sheet of Urban Credit Cooperatives

（月末余额）

（Month - end Balance）

单位：亿元

Unit：100 Million Yuan

项　目 Items	2003.01	2003.02	2003.03	2003.04
国外资产 Foreign Assets				
储备资产 Reserve Assets	110.80	104.78	100.41	110.82
准备金存款 Reserve Deposits	96.78	92.41	87.46	98.35
库存现金 Cash in Vault	14.02	12.37	12.95	12.47
中央银行债券 Central Bank Bonds	0.06	0.06	0.06	0.06
对政府债权 Claims on Government	35.63	37.87	32.27	39.56
其中：中央政府 Of Which：Central Government	35.63	37.87	32.27	39.56
对非金融机构债权 Claims on Non - financial Institutions	673.18	680.13	680.70	698.83
对特定存款机构债权 Claims on Specific Depository Institutions	9.32	10.43	11.43	11.25
对其他金融机构债权 Claims on Other Financial Institutions	4.60	3.87	4.79	3.99
其他资产 Other Assets	290.15	303.32	312.57	311.29
总资产 Total Assets	**1123.74**	**1140.46**	**1142.23**	**1175.80**
对非金融机构负债 Liabilities to Non - financial Institutions	968.46	986.10	989.05	1021.67
活期存款 Demand Deposits	291.58	295.26	295.35	311.08
定期存款 Time Deposits	107.63	111.59	116.89	121.88
储蓄存款 Savings Deposits	546.46	555.83	552.62	558.14
其他存款 Other Deposits	22.79	23.42	24.19	30.57
外币存款 Deposits in Foreign Currency				
对中央银行负债 Liabilities to the Central Bank	24.44	24.39	27.82	31.12
对特定存款机构负债 Liabilities to Specific Depository Institutions	0.39	0.39	0.39	0.38
对其他金融机构负债 Liabilities to Other Financial Institutions	4.30	4.29	3.27	3.27
其中：计入广义货币的存款 Of Which：Deposits Included in Broad Money	0.13	0.04	0.01	0.01
国外负债 Foreign Liabilities				
债券 Bonds	0.02	0.02		
实收资本 Paid - in Capital	37.22	37.23	36.23	36.71
其他负债 Other Liabilities	88.91	88.04	85.47	82.65
总负债 Total Liabilities	**1123.74**	**1140.46**	**1142.23**	**1175.80**

城市信用合作社资产负债表
Balance Sheet of Urban Credit Cooperatives

(月末余额)

(Month - end Balance)

单位：亿元

Unit: 100 Million Yuan

项目 Items	2003.05	2003.06	2003.07	2003.08
国外资产 Foreign Assets				
储备资产 Reserve Assets	113.20	107.54	116.84	117.40
准备金存款 Reserve Deposits	102.10	94.75	105.58	104.80
库存现金 Cash in Vault	11.10	12.79	11.26	12.60
中央银行债券 Central Bank Bonds	0.06	0.06	0.06	0.65
对政府债权 Claims on Government	38.72	40.53	40.17	40.40
其中：中央政府 Of Which: Central Government	38.72	40.53	40.17	40.40
对非金融机构债权 Claims on Non - financial Institutions	713.91	745.35	754.39	781.65
对特定存款机构债权 Claims on Specific Depository Institutions	12.97	10.47	11.24	9.32
对其他金融机构债权 Claims on Other Financial Institutions	3.99	3.67	3.79	4.10
其他资产 Other Assets	324.19	342.73	330.22	338.06
总资产 Total Assets	**1207.04**	**1250.35**	**1256.71**	**1291.58**
对非金融机构负债 Liabilities to Non - financial Institutions	1043.95	1078.27	1091.41	1124.50
活期存款 Demand Deposits	317.77	334.37	338.96	359.53
定期存款 Time Deposits	123.59	126.15	127.31	129.91
储蓄存款 Savings Deposits	568.91	580.80	586.50	591.65
其他存款 Other Deposits	33.68	36.95	38.64	43.41
外币存款 Deposits in Foreign Currency				
对中央银行负债 Liabilities to the Central Bank	30.47	28.99	28.60	28.80
对特定存款机构负债 Liabilities to Specific Depository Institutions	0.38	0.38	0.38	0.39
对其他金融机构负债 Liabilities to Other Financial Institutions	3.55	3.24	3.24	3.23
其中：计入广义货币的存款 Of Which: Deposits Included in Broad Money	0.01	0.01	0.01	0.01
国外负债 Foreign Liabilities				
债券 Bonds				
实收资本 Paid - in Capital	36.70	36.88	37.55	37.69
其他负债 Other Liabilities	91.99	102.59	95.53	96.97
总负债 Total Liabilities	**1207.04**	**1250.35**	**1256.71**	**1291.58**

城市信用合作社资产负债表
Balance Sheet of Urban Credit Cooperatives

（月末余额）

（Month - end Balance）

单位：亿元

Unit：100 Million Yuan

项目 Items	2003.09	2003.10	2003.11	2003.12
国外资产 Foreign Assets				
储备资产 Reserve Assets	112.90	119.63	130.58	201.21
准备金存款 Reserve Deposits	98.15	106.93	116.34	186.65
库存现金 Cash in Vault	14.75	12.70	14.24	14.56
中央银行债券 Central Bank Bonds	0.65	0.45	0.26	2.64
对政府债权 Claims on Government	44.63	45.58	46.47	51.40
其中：中央政府 Of Which：Central Government	44.63	45.58	46.47	51.40
对非金融机构债权 Claims on Non - financial Institutions	816.00	829.34	835.57	856.46
对特定存款机构债权 Claims on Specific Depository Institutions	14.43	16.39	12.96	12.56
对其他金融机构债权 Claims on Other Financial Institutions	5.01	5.09	4.62	4.38
其他资产 Other Assets	337.56	338.99	344.26	358.59
总资产 Total Assets	**1331.18**	**1355.47**	**1374.72**	**1487.24**
对非金融机构负债 Liabilities to Non - financial Institutions	1152.28	1172.87	1174.89	1270.64
活期存款 Demand Deposits	369.09	378.54	377.20	440.29
定期存款 Time Deposits	129.41	129.68	126.50	126.52
储蓄存款 Savings Deposits	600.83	611.78	617.28	647.58
其他存款 Other Deposits	52.95	52.87	53.91	56.25
外币存款 Deposits in Foreign Currency				
对中央银行负债 Liabilities to the Central Bank	33.65	35.23	39.86	37.81
对特定存款机构负债 Liabilities to Specific Depository Institutions	0.39	0.39	0.39	0.39
对其他金融机构负债 Liabilities to Other Financial Institutions	3.48	3.56	4.92	6.10
其中：计入广义货币的存款 Of Which：Deposits Included in Broad Money	0.01	0.01		
国外负债 Foreign Liabilities				
债券 Bonds				
实收资本 Paid - in Capital	37.75	37.79	37.68	38.81
其他负债 Other Liabilities	103.63	105.63	116.98	133.49
总负债 Total Liabilities	**1331.18**	**1355.47**	**1374.72**	**1487.24**

城市信用合作社资产负债表
Balance Sheet of Urban Credit Cooperatives

(月末余额)

(Month – end Balance)

单位：亿元

Unit: 100 Million Yuan

项目 Items	2004.01	2004.02	2004.03	2004.04
国外资产 Foreign Assets				
储备资产 Reserve Assets	132.36	130.55	126.47	133.86
准备金存款 Reserve Deposits	114.74	115.85	112.38	119.37
库存现金 Cash in Vault	17.62	14.70	14.09	14.49
中央银行债券 Central Bank Bonds	2.64	0.06	0.06	0.06
对政府债权 Claims on Government	56.56	56.36	56.15	55.95
其中：中央政府 Of Which: Central Government	56.56	56.36	56.15	55.95
对非金融机构债权 Claims on Non – financial Institutions	856.18	869.65	887.74	910.40
对特定存款机构债权 Claims on Specific Depository Institutions	14.25	14.24	14.34	16.27
对其他金融机构债权 Claims on Other Financial Institutions	4.11	4.71	4.72	4.30
其他资产 Other Assets	332.64	346.27	351.90	356.72
总资产 Total Assets	**1398.74**	**1421.84**	**1441.38**	**1477.56**
对非金融机构负债 Liabilities to Non – financial Institutions	1214.34	1232.12	1256.57	1292.09
活期存款 Demand Deposits	377.50	380.69	389.81	410.08
定期存款 Time Deposits	125.57	129.24	133.90	136.30
储蓄存款 Savings Deposits	658.04	666.39	675.15	687.85
其他存款 Other Deposits	53.23	55.80	57.71	57.86
外币存款 Deposits in Foreign Currency				
对中央银行负债 Liabilities to the Central Bank	37.13	34.49	30.99	31.92
对特定存款机构负债 Liabilities to Specific Depository Institutions	0.11	0.11	0.11	0.12
对其他金融机构负债 Liabilities to Other Financial Institutions	2.97	1.11	2.61	1.60
其中：计入广义货币的存款 Of Which: Deposits Included in Broad Money				
国外负债 Foreign Liabilities				
债券 Bonds				
实收资本 Paid – in Capital	37.01	37.05	37.09	37.46
其他负债 Other Liabilities	107.18	116.96	114.01	114.37
总负债 Total Liabilities	**1398.74**	**1421.84**	**1441.38**	**1477.56**

城市信用合作社资产负债表
Balance Sheet of Urban Credit Cooperatives

（月末余额）

（Month - end Balance）

单位：亿元

Unit：100 Million Yuan

项　目 Items	2004.05	2004.06	2004.07	2004.08
国外资产 Foreign Assets				
储备资产 Reserve Assets	146.52	134.33	151.30	147.21
准备金存款 Reserve Deposits	132.44	119.92	137.06	132.17
库存现金 Cash in Vault	14.08	14.41	14.24	15.04
中央银行债券 Central Bank Bonds	0.55	0.25	0.54	0.54
对政府债权 Claims on Government	50.00	52.85	51.38	52.21
其中：中央政府 Of Which：Central Government	50.00	52.85	51.38	52.21
对非金融机构债权 Claims on Non - financial Institutions	920.93	929.92	945.91	957.74
对特定存款机构债权 Claims on Specific Depository Institutions	16.47	17.06	16.49	16.82
对其他金融机构债权 Claims on Other Financial Institutions	5.63	5.45	6.45	6.66
其他资产 Other Assets	365.69	394.61	381.48	386.97
总资产 Total Assets	**1505.79**	**1534.47**	**1553.55**	**1568.15**
对非金融机构负债 Liabilities to Non - financial Institutions	1314.96	1334.35	1357.88	1373.79
活期存款 Demand Deposits	419.49	427.73	431.76	438.18
定期存款 Time Deposits	137.34	137.97	144.48	145.42
储蓄存款 Savings Deposits	701.28	712.47	724.48	731.21
其他存款 Other Deposits	56.85	56.18	57.16	58.98
外币存款 Deposits in Foreign Currency				
对中央银行负债 Liabilities to the Central Bank	32.25	32.56	33.38	33.15
对特定存款机构负债 Liabilities to Specific Depository Institutions	0.13	0.13	0.14	0.11
对其他金融机构负债 Liabilities to Other Financial Institutions	2.51	2.32	2.69	1.65
其中：计入广义货币的存款 Of Which：Deposits Included in Broad Money				
国外负债 Foreign Liabilities				
债券 Bonds				
实收资本 Paid - in Capital	37.52	37.52	39.13	39.13
其他负债 Other Liabilities	118.42	127.59	120.33	120.32
总负债 Total Liabilities	**1505.79**	**1534.47**	**1553.55**	**1568.15**

城市信用合作社资产负债表
Balance Sheet of Urban Credit Cooperatives

（月末余额）

（Month – end Balance）

单位：亿元

Unit：100 Million Yuan

项目 Items	2004.09	2004.10	2004.11	2004.12
国外资产 Foreign Assets				
储备资产 Reserve Assets	138.09	160.02	182.31	280.89
准备金存款 Reserve Deposits	120.06	144.38	166.66	263.96
库存现金 Cash in Vault	18.03	15.64	15.65	16.93
中央银行债券 Central Bank Bonds	0.93	1.08	1.07	2.14
对政府债权 Claims on Government	50.85	50.53	49.33	46.38
其中：中央政府 Of Which：Central Government	50.85	50.53	49.33	46.38
对非金融机构债权 Claims on Non – financial Institutions	974.22	986.65	1004.01	1024.21
对特定存款机构债权 Claims on Specific Depository Institutions	18.03	18.05	17.51	20.51
对其他金融机构债权 Claims on Other Financial Institutions	6.96	5.09	5.57	6.34
其他资产 Other Assets	401.99	392.08	408.86	419.33
总资产 Total Assets	**1591.07**	**1613.50**	**1668.66**	**1799.80**
对非金融机构负债 Liabilities to Non – financial Institutions	1390.48	1424.00	1478.48	1588.85
活期存款 Demand Deposits	448.85	463.25	486.62	555.39
定期存款 Time Deposits	147.55	153.82	161.01	170.79
储蓄存款 Savings Deposits	737.79	744.27	764.27	791.01
其他存款 Other Deposits	56.29	62.66	66.58	71.66
外币存款 Deposits in Foreign Currency				
对中央银行负债 Liabilities to the Central Bank	33.32	32.09	30.79	31.17
对特定存款机构负债 Liabilities to Specific Depository Institutions	0.31	0.11	0.11	0.51
对其他金融机构负债 Liabilities to Other Financial Institutions	1.69	1.05	0.88	1.97
其中：计入广义货币的存款 Of Which：Deposits Included in Broad Money				
国外负债 Foreign Liabilities				
债券 Bonds				
实收资本 Paid – in Capital	40.22	39.61	41.62	48.53
其他负债 Other Liabilities	125.05	116.64	116.78	128.77
总负债 Total Liabilities	**1591.07**	**1613.50**	**1668.66**	**1799.80**

城市信用合作社资产负债表

Balance Sheet of Urban Credit Cooperatives

（月末余额）

（Month－end Balance）

单位：亿元

Unit：100 Million Yuan

项目 Items	2005.01	2005.02	2005.03	2005.04
国外资产 Foreign Assets				
储备资产 Reserve Assets	186.39	186.85	165.45	182.30
准备金存款 Reserve Deposits	169.34	169.67	150.70	166.12
库存现金 Cash in Vault	17.05	17.18	14.75	16.18
中央银行债券 Central Bank Bonds	2.75	3.26	3.36	3.45
对政府债权 Claims on Government	48.17	46.42	44.63	46.49
其中：中央政府 Of Which：Central Government	48.17	46.42	44.63	46.49
对非金融机构债权 Claims on Non－financial Institutions	1011.72	1018.49	1046.97	1070.50
对特定存款机构债权 Claims on Specific Depository Institutions	17.56	17.72	17.41	13.98
对其他金融机构债权 Claims on Other Financial Institutions	5.81	4.63	3.90	3.80
其他资产 Other Assets	423.68	424.89	448.36	465.52
总资产 Total Assets	**1696.08**	**1702.26**	**1730.08**	**1786.04**
对非金融机构负债 Liabilities to Non－financial Institutions	1501.40	1518.09	1539.16	1599.01
活期存款 Demand Deposits	487.33	468.19	476.54	500.28
定期存款 Time Deposits	161.52	166.93	173.05	184.61
储蓄存款 Savings Deposits	790.18	826.63	826.74	845.50
其他存款 Other Deposits	62.37	56.34	62.83	68.62
外币存款 Deposits in Foreign Currency				
对中央银行负债 Liabilities to the Central Bank	27.06	24.60	21.81	21.15
对特定存款机构负债 Liabilities to Specific Depository Institutions	0.28	0.28	0.28	0.08
对其他金融机构负债 Liabilities to Other Financial Institutions	1.57	1.42	2.71	1.28
其中：计入广义货币的存款 Of Which：Deposits Included in Broad Money				
国外负债 Foreign Liabilities				
债券 Bonds				
实收资本 Paid－in Capital	45.66	46.14	45.16	45.31
其他负债 Other Liabilities	120.11	111.73	120.96	119.21
总负债 Total Liabilities	**1696.08**	**1702.26**	**1730.08**	**1786.04**

城市信用合作社资产负债表
Balance Sheet of Urban Credit Cooperatives

（月末余额）

（Month – end Balance）

单位：亿元

Unit：100 Million Yuan

项目 Items	2005.05	2005.06	2005.07	2005.08
国外资产 Foreign Assets				
储备资产 Reserve Assets	184.48	186.14	179.25	183.89
准备金存款 Reserve Deposits	168.43	170.63	163.19	168.68
库存现金 Cash in Vault	16.05	15.51	16.06	15.21
中央银行债券 Central Bank Bonds	4.24	3.63	2.55	2.78
对政府债权 Claims on Government	47.32	47.08	45.97	50.41
其中：中央政府 Of Which：Central Government	47.32	47.08	45.97	50.41
对非金融机构债权 Claims on Non – financial Institutions	1089.22	1116.77	1077.23	1102.44
对特定存款机构债权 Claims on Specific Depository Institutions	13.50	14.49	18.73	19.47
对其他金融机构债权 Claims on Other Financial Institutions	4.06	3.96	3.96	4.75
其他资产 Other Assets	471.16	476.79	455.67	468.64
总资产 Total Assets	**1813.98**	**1848.86**	**1783.36**	**1832.38**
对非金融机构负债 Liabilities to Non – financial Institutions	1618.95	1639.06	1590.27	1623.28
活期存款 Demand Deposits	498.55	521.65	491.93	502.50
定期存款 Time Deposits	185.61	186.09	180.19	182.63
储蓄存款 Savings Deposits	863.73	859.90	862.49	875.04
其他存款 Other Deposits	71.06	71.42	55.66	63.11
外币存款 Deposits in Foreign Currency				
对中央银行负债 Liabilities to the Central Bank	20.59	20.59	19.21	19.43
对特定存款机构负债 Liabilities to Specific Depository Institutions	0.08	0.08	0.08	0.08
对其他金融机构负债 Liabilities to Other Financial Institutions	0.81	0.72	0.73	1.23
其中：计入广义货币的存款 Of Which：Deposits Included in Broad Money				
国外负债 Foreign Liabilities				
债券 Bonds				
实收资本 Paid – in Capital	45.34	47.54	46.79	47.91
其他负债 Other Liabilities	128.21	140.87	126.28	140.45
总负债 Total Liabilities	**1813.98**	**1848.86**	**1783.36**	**1832.38**

城市信用合作社资产负债表
Balance Sheet of Urban Credit Cooperatives

（月末余额）

（Month - end Balance）

单位：亿元

Unit：100 Million Yuan

项　　目 Items	2005.09	2005.10	2005.11	2005.12
国外资产 Foreign Assets				
储备资产 Reserve Assets	178.46	201.66	211.54	330.43
准备金存款 Reserve Deposits	161.17	185.12	193.93	311.34
库存现金 Cash in Vault	17.29	16.54	17.61	19.09
中央银行债券 Central Bank Bonds	3.16	2.98	2.98	2.48
对政府债权 Claims on Government	51.55	51.95	62.00	64.37
其中：中央政府 Of Which：Central Government	51.55	51.95	62.00	64.37
对非金融机构债权 Claims on Non - financial Institutions	1079.14	1086.51	1111.15	1148.38
对特定存款机构债权 Claims on Specific Depository Institutions	15.85	16.40	15.80	17.64
对其他金融机构债权 Claims on Other Financial Institutions	5.38	5.99	4.20	5.51
其他资产 Other Assets	485.11	478.35	499.63	481.66
总资产 Total Assets	**1818.65**	**1843.84**	**1907.30**	**2050.47**
对非金融机构负债 Liabilities to Non - financial Institutions	1603.07	1627.27	1686.32	1813.11
活期存款 Demand Deposits	508.13	520.36	540.08	613.42
定期存款 Time Deposits	184.40	185.20	196.73	202.34
储蓄存款 Savings Deposits	849.79	861.13	884.23	926.35
其他存款 Other Deposits	60.75	60.58	65.28	71.00
外币存款 Deposits in Foreign Currency				
对中央银行负债 Liabilities to the Central Bank	18.93	17.80	18.28	16.88
对特定存款机构负债 Liabilities to Specific Depository Institutions	0.09	0.08	0.08	0.06
对其他金融机构负债 Liabilities to Other Financial Institutions	1.21	1.15	1.45	2.98
其中：计入广义货币的存款 Of Which：Deposits Included in Broad Money				1.44
国外负债 Foreign Liabilities				
债券 Bonds				
实收资本 Paid - in Capital	45.19	45.42	47.18	52.73
其他负债 Other Liabilities	150.16	152.12	153.99	164.71
总负债 Total Liabilities	**1818.65**	**1843.84**	**1907.30**	**2050.47**

8. 农村信用合作社资产负债表
Balance Sheet of Rural Credit Cooperatives

农村信用合作社资产负债表
Balance Sheet of Rural Credit Cooperatives

（季末余额）

(Quarter - end Balance)

单位：亿元

Unit: 100 Million Yuan

项目 Items	1993.03	1993.06	1993.09	1993.12
国外资产 Foreign Assets				
储备资产 Reserve Assets	509.7	525.5	546.8	605.8
准备金 Reserves	443.5	454.2	479.6	506.8
在人行存款 Deposits with the Central Bank	17.4	13.7	12.2	10.8
库存现金 Cash in Vault	48.8	57.6	55.0	88.2
中央银行债券 Central Bank Bonds				
对政府债权 Claims on Government				
对其他部门债权 Claims on Other Sectors	2750.2	2911.2	3035.3	3143.8
对非货币金融机构债权 Claims on Non - monetary Financial Institutions				
对非金融部门负债 Liabilities to Non - financial Sectors	3716.5	3852.6	4000.8	4297.2
活期存款 Demand Deposits	599.3	642.7	600.9	682.2
定期存款 Time Deposits	35.4	35.5	38.2	38.8
储蓄存款 Savings Deposits	3081.8	3174.4	3361.7	3576.2
其他存款 Other Deposits				
对中央银行负债 Liabilities to the Central Bank				
对非货币金融机构负债 Liabilities to Non - monetary Financial Institutions				
国外负债 Foreign Liabilities				
债券 Bonds				
所有者权益 Owner's Equity	377.0	373.6	383.2	407.8
其中：实收资本 Of Which: Paid - in Capital	377.0	373.6	383.2	407.8
其他（净） Other Items (Net)	- 833.6	- 789.5	- 801.9	- 955.4

农村信用合作社资产负债表

Balance Sheet of Rural Credit Cooperatives

（季末余额）

（Quarter – end Balance）

单位：亿元

Unit：100 Million Yuan

项 目 Items	1994.03	1994.06	1994.09	1994.12
国外资产 Foreign Assets				
储备资产 Reserve Assets	628.9	682.7	767.2	884.7
准备金 Reserves	540.2	582.7	622.8	672.1
在人行存款 Deposits with the Central Bank	15.1	15.8	53.0	88.4
库存现金 Cash in Vault	73.6	84.2	91.4	124.2
中央银行债券 Central Bank Bonds				
对政府债权 Claims on Government				
对其他部门债权 Claims on Other Sectors	3576.8	3836.7	4023.7	4168.6
对非货币金融机构债权 Claims on Non – monetary Financial Institutions				
对非金融部门负债 Liabilities to Non – financial Sectors	4693.5	5020.7	5301.0	5681.1
活期存款 Demand Deposits	626.0	676.3	708.2	805.4
定期存款 Time Deposits	42.5	47.6	54.6	59.7
储蓄存款 Savings Deposits	4025.0	4296.8	4538.2	4816.0
其他存款 Other Deposits				
对中央银行负债 Liabilities to the Central Bank				
对非货币金融机构负债 Liabilities to Non – monetary Financial Institutions				
国外负债 Foreign Liabilities				
债券 Bonds				
所有者权益 Owner's Equity	554.9	545.2	571.2	616.9
其中：实收资本 Of Which：Paid – in Capital	554.5	536.4	515.9	694.4
其他（净） Other Items（Net）	– 1042.7	– 1046.5	– 1081.3	– 1244.7

农村信用合作社资产负债表
Balance Sheet of Rural Credit Cooperatives

（季末余额）

（Quarter – end Balance）

单位：亿元

Unit：100 Million Yuan

项目 Items	1995.03	1995.06	1995.09	1995.12
国外资产 Foreign Assets				
储备资产 Reserve Assets	910.7	1025.8	1060.3	1218.3
准备金 Reserves	735.4	787.3	831.0	875.4
在人行存款 Deposits with the Central Bank	68.5	120.9	112.6	187.8
库存现金 Cash in Vault	106.8	117.6	116.7	155.1
中央银行债券 Central Bank Bonds				
对政府债权 Claims on Government				338.5
对其他部门债权 Claims on Other Sectors	4641.4	4771.1	5019.7	5234.2
对非货币金融机构债权 Claims on Non – monetary Financial Institutions				
对非金融部门负债 Liabilities to Non – financial Sectors	6162.5	6486.7	6782.7	7172.9
活期存款 Demand Deposits	748.6	772.5	808.5	892.0
定期存款 Time Deposits	62.0	73.7	85.7	85.3
储蓄存款 Savings Deposits	5351.9	5640.5	5888.5	6195.6
其他存款 Other Deposits				
对中央银行负债 Liabilities to the Central Bank				
对非货币金融机构负债 Liabilities to Non – monetary Financial Institutions				
国外负债 Foreign Liabilities				
债券 Bonds				
所有者权益 Owner's Equity	622.8	637.2	635.1	631.9
其中：实收资本 Of Which：Paid – in Capital	366.3	362.7	363.8	377.7
其他（净） Other Items（Net）	– 1233.2	– 1327.0	– 1337.8	– 1013.8

农村信用合作社资产负债表
Balance Sheet of Rural Credit Cooperatives

（季末余额）

（Quarter－end Balance）

单位：亿元

Unit：100 Million Yuan

项目 Items	1996.03	1996.06	1996.09	1996.12
国外资产 Foreign Assets				
储备资产 Reserve Assets	1201.5	1242.1	1294.7	1935.6
准备金 Reserves	917.1	980.5	1018.2	712.0
在人行存款 Deposits with the Central Bank	148.6	116.9	129.3	1066.7
库存现金 Cash in Vault	135.8	144.7	147.2	156.9
中央银行债券 Central Bank Bonds				
对政府债权 Claims on Government	367.6	390.4	404.6	406.3
对其他部门债权 Claims on Other Sectors	5643.5	5954.0	6282.9	6364.7
对非货币金融机构债权 Claims on Non－monetary Financial Institutions				
对非金融部门负债 Liabilities to Non－financial Sectors	7731.8	8156.9	8434.8	8793.5
活期存款 Demand Deposits	793.2	850.2	887.0	1007.4
定期存款 Time Deposits	92.2	105.7	113.5	115.5
储蓄存款 Savings Deposits	6846.4	7201.0	7434.3	7670.6
其他存款 Other Deposits				
对中央银行负债 Liabilities to the Central Bank				
对非货币金融机构负债 Liabilities to Non－monetary Financial Institutions				
国外负债 Foreign Liabilities				
债券 Bonds				
所有者权益 Owner's Equity	559.8	548.2	558.4	547.7
其中：实收资本 Of Which：Paid－in Capital	376.7	378.8	384.2	401.1
其他（净） Other Items（Net）	－1079.0	－1118.6	－1011.0	－634.6

农村信用合作社资产负债表
Balance Sheet of Rural Credit Cooperatives

（季末余额）

（Quarter – end Balance）

单位：亿元

Unit：100 Million Yuan

项　目 Items	1997.03	1997.06	1997.09	1997.12
国外资产 Foreign Assets				
储备资产 Reserve Assets	1830.1	1777.1	1883.5	2242.7
准备金 Reserves	1109.3	1147.2	1203.7	1246.7
在人行存款 Deposits with the Central Bank	523.8	425.6	474.7	800.8
库存现金 Cash in Vault	197.0	204.3	205.1	195.2
中央银行债券 Central Bank Bonds				
对政府债权 Claims on Government	132.8	140.2	153.3	186.4
对其他部门债权 Claims on Other Sectors	7165.7	7401.0	7612.2	7661.5
对非货币金融机构债权 Claims on Non – monetary Financial Institutions	35.9	39.3	33.5	31.4
对非金融部门负债 Liabilities to Non – financial Sectors	9453.3	9744.9	10128.4	10609.2
活期存款 Demand Deposits	971.8	1034.6	1113.6	1264.8
定期存款 Time Deposits	121.7	135.2	150.1	158.8
储蓄存款 Savings Deposits	8318.2	8546.3	8841.4	9132.2
其他存款 Other Deposits	41.6	28.8	23.3	53.4
对中央银行负债 Liabilities to the Central Bank	4.7	13.3	15.8	16.4
对非货币金融机构负债 Liabilities to Non – monetary Financial Institutions	5.1	6.4	4.5	2.9
国外负债 Foreign Liabilities				
债券 Bonds	0.4	0.3	1.7	0.4
所有者权益 Owner's Equity	343.7	293.2	250.3	310.0
其中：实收资本 Of Which：Paid – in Capital	678.9	670.7	669.9	630.5
其他（净） Other Items（Net）	– 642.7	– 700.5	– 718.2	– 816.9

农村信用合作社资产负债表

Balance Sheet of Rural Credit Cooperatives

（季末余额）

（Quarter - end Balance）

单位：亿元

Unit：100 Million Yuan

项　目 Items	1998.03	1998.06	1998.09	1998.12
国外资产 Foreign Assets				
储备资产 Reserve Assets	2171.0	2044.4	1877.7	2207.5
准备金 Reserves	1271.6	1844.1	1672.8	1993.8
在人行存款 Deposits with the Central Bank	695.4			
库存现金 Cash in Vault	204.0	200.3	204.9	213.7
中央银行债券 Central Bank Bonds				
对政府债权 Claims on Government	238.8	250.3	293.2	375.4
对其他部门债权 Claims on Other Sectors	8097.6	8414.0	8678.2	8813.7
对非货币金融机构债权 Claims on Non - monetary Financial Institutions	37.1	30.2	36.1	34.5
对非金融部门负债 Liabilities to Non - financial Sectors	11145.0	11436.0	11665.3	12164.4
活期存款 Demand Deposits	1158.2	1195.1	1283.7	1447.7
定期存款 Time Deposits	163.2	186.0	200.0	205.1
储蓄存款 Savings Deposits	9778.0	10017.7	10145.5	10441.0
其他存款 Other Deposits	45.6	37.2	36.1	70.6
对中央银行负债 Liabilities to the Central Bank	17.5	24.8	28.7	41.8
对非货币金融机构负债 Liabilities to Non - monetary Financial Institutions	3.5	3.1	2.9	1.9
国外负债 Foreign Liabilities				
债券 Bonds	1.5	0.5	0.3	0.1
所有者权益 Owner's Equity	237.3	147.5	94.4	151.4
其中：实收资本 Of Which：Paid - in Capital	660.5	629.9	636.8	658.1
其他（净） Other Items（Net）	-860.3	-873.0	-906.4	-928.5

农村信用合作社资产负债表

Balance Sheet of Rural Credit Cooperatives

（季末余额）

（Quarter – end Balance）

单位：亿元

Unit：100 Million Yuan

项　目 Items	1999.03	1999.06	1999.09	1999.12
国外资产 Foreign Assets				
储备资产 Reserve Assets	2006.9	1867.9	1720.7	2128.6
准备金 Reserves	1783.2	1639.3	1443.1	1827.4
库存现金 Cash in Vault	223.7	228.6	277.6	301.2
中央银行债券 Central Bank Bonds				
对政府债权 Claims on Government	437.9	468.8	488.1	461.8
对其他部门债权 Claims on Other Sectors	9033.0	9429.3	9719.3	9769.2
对非货币金融机构债权 Claims on Non – monetary Financial Institutions	36.7	35.3	37.8	32.8
对非金融部门负债 Liabilities to Non – financial Sectors	12614.8	12863.6	12957.2	13361.4
活期存款 Demand Deposits	1365.4	1445.7	1558.2	1803.1
定期存款 Time Deposits	212.4	230.5	235.2	264.8
储蓄存款 Savings Deposits	11001.2	11156.6	11137.1	11217.3
其他存款 Other Deposits	35.8	30.8	26.7	76.2
对中央银行负债 Liabilities to the Central Bank	67.6	173.9	213.1	214.4
对非货币金融机构负债 Liabilities to Non – monetary Financial Institutions	2.2	2.6	2.7	3.1
国外负债 Foreign Liabilities				
债券 Bonds	0.1	0.1		
实收资本 Paid – in Capital	638.9	627.4	630.7	653.8
其他（净） Other Items（Net）	– 1809.1	– 1866.3	– 1837.8	– 1840.3

农村信用合作社资产负债表

Balance Sheet of Rural Credit Cooperatives

（季末余额）

（Quarter - end Balance）

单位：亿元

Unit：100 Million Yuan

项目 Items	2000.03	2000.06	2000.09	2000.12
国外资产 Foreign Assets				
储备资产 Reserve Assets	1783.8	1675.0	1659.8	2232.5
准备金 Reserves	1521.9	1401.1	1347.4	1905.4
库存现金 Cash in Vault	261.9	273.9	312.4	327.1
中央银行债券 Central Bank Bonds				
对政府债权 Claims on Government	454.3	501.5	525.7	500.7
对其他部门债权 Claims on Other Sectors	10288.6	10624.9	10909.4	11161.9
对非货币金融机构债权 Claims on Non - monetary Financial Institutions	32.0	37.7	35.5	35.5
对非金融部门负债 Liabilities to Non - financial Sectors	13765.8	13992.1	14195.7	15128.9
活期存款 Demand Deposits	1730.5	1869.8	2021.4	2288.3
定期存款 Time Deposits	286.6	316.7	341.2	388.1
储蓄存款 Savings Deposits	11702.8	11768.1	11793.4	12355.3
其他存款 Other Deposits	45.9	37.5	39.7	97.2
对中央银行负债 Liabilities to the Central Bank	302.4	408.0	469.7	399.7
对非货币金融机构负债 Liabilities to Non - monetary Financial Institutions	2.4	2.3	2.9	2.9
国外负债 Foreign Liabilities				
债券 Bonds	0.1	0.1	0.1	
实收资本 Paid - in Capital	669.5	687.3	691.1	716.0
其他（净） Other Items（Net）	-2181.5	-2250.7	-2229.1	-2316.9

农村信用合作社资产负债表

Balance Sheet of Rural Credit Cooperatives

（季末余额）

(Quarter - end Balance)

单位：亿元

Unit: 100 Million Yuan

项　目 Items	2001.03	2001.06	2001.09	2001.12
国外资产 Foreign Assets				
储备资产 Reserve Assets	1899.2	1826.0	1796.7	2583.5
准备金 Reserves	1595.7	1507.3	1448.1	2267.9
库存现金 Cash in Vault	303.5	318.7	348.6	315.6
中央银行债券 Central Bank Bonds				
对政府债权 Claims on Government	506.7	572.0	614.9	744.2
对其他部门债权 Claims on Other Sectors	11916.3	12456.7	12891.5	12744.3
对非货币金融机构债权 Claims on Non - monetary Financial Institutions	36.2	37.1	37.2	36.0
对非金融部门负债 Liabilities to Non - financial Sectors	15793.6	16246.0	16540.5	17272.7
活期存款 Demand Deposits	2215.3	2400.9	2547.7	2710.6
定期存款 Time Deposits	430.5	478.7	535.1	588.4
储蓄存款 Savings Deposits	13100.4	13315.3	13398.4	13821.4
其他存款 Other Deposits	47.4	51.1	59.3	152.3
对中央银行负债 Liabilities to the Central Bank	530.9	736.2	773.1	685.7
对非货币金融机构负债 Liabilities to Non - monetary Financial Institutions	6.3	2.9	3.1	1.6
国外负债 Foreign Liabilities				
债券 Bonds	0.1	0.1	0.1	0.1
实收资本 Paid - in Capital	737.2	761.2	780.7	787.6
其他（净） Other Items (Net)	- 2709.7	- 2854.6	- 2757.2	- 2639.7

农村信用合作社资产负债表

Balance Sheet of Rural Credit Cooperatives

（月末余额）

（Month - end Balance）

单位：亿元

Unit：100 Million Yuan

项目 Items	2002.01	2002.02	2002.03	2002.04
国外资产 Foreign Assets	27.56	28.52	30.51	29.38
储备资产 Reserve Assets	2167.70	2261.03	2077.75	1928.72
准备金存款 Reserve Deposits	1832.97	1892.42	1734.42	1586.86
库存现金 Cash in Vault	334.73	368.61	343.33	341.86
中央银行债券 Central Bank Bonds				
对政府债权 Claims on Government	764.87	715.78	682.94	816.73
其中：中央政府 Of Which：Central Government	764.87	715.78	682.94	816.73
对非金融机构债权 Claims on Non - financial Institutions	12888.00	13042.19	13509.83	13810.60
对特定存款机构债权 Claims on Specific Depository Institutions	52.07	40.37	35.43	35.62
对其他金融机构债权 Claims on Other Financial Institutions	0.24	0.24	0.24	0.64
其他资产 Other Assets	2913.29	3121.51	3300.31	3342.70
总资产 Total Assets	**18813.73**	**19209.64**	**19637.01**	**19964.39**
对非金融机构负债 Liabilities to Non - financial Institutions	17179.59	17600.10	17801.25	17957.80
活期存款 Demand Deposits	2651.24	2426.34	2544.26	2620.12
定期存款 Time Deposits	586.76	603.40	624.96	654.34
储蓄存款 Savings Deposits	13826.26	14459.77	14520.88	14578.69
其他存款 Other Deposits	79.20	72.64	72.20	64.89
外币存款 Deposits in Foreign Currency	36.13	37.95	38.95	39.76
对中央银行负债 Liabilities to the Central Bank	716.52	726.27	878.17	1020.99
对特定存款机构负债 Liabilities to Specific Depository Institutions	3.33	2.53	4.19	2.01
对其他金融机构负债 Liabilities to Other Financial Institutions	0.47	0.83	0.85	0.89
其中：计入广义货币的存款 Of Which：Deposits Included in Broad Money	0.01	0.02	0.02	
国外负债 Foreign Liabilities				
债券 Bonds	0.07	0.07	0.06	0.06
实收资本 Paid - in Capital	411.38	410.85	418.49	425.92
其他负债 Other Liabilities	502.37	468.99	534.00	556.72
总负债 Total Liabilities	**18813.73**	**19209.64**	**19637.01**	**19964.39**

农村信用合作社资产负债表
Balance Sheet of Rural Credit Cooperatives

（月末余额）

(Month - end Balance)

单位：亿元

Unit: 100 Million Yuan

项　目 Items	2002.05	2002.06	2002.07	2002.08
国外资产 Foreign Assets	22.45	23.86	22.70	20.27
储备资产 Reserve Assets	1935.08	1934.25	1940.28	1911.46
准备金存款 Reserve Deposits	1614.07	1572.42	1621.36	1586.28
库存现金 Cash in Vault	321.01	361.83	318.92	325.18
中央银行债券 Central Bank Bonds				
对政府债权 Claims on Government	870.92	930.45	924.25	907.50
其中：中央政府 Of Which: Central Government	870.92	930.45	924.25	907.50
对非金融机构债权 Claims on Non - financial Institutions	14001.11	14180.08	14331.94	14547.50
对特定存款机构债权 Claims on Specific Depository Institutions	37.38	35.94	36.11	35.52
对其他金融机构债权 Claims on Other Financial Institutions	0.84	0.72	0.12	0.91
其他资产 Other Assets	3384.83	3736.17	3612.80	3598.05
总资产 Total Assets	**20252.61**	**20841.47**	**20868.20**	**21021.21**
对非金融机构负债 Liabilities to Non - financial Institutions	18155.12	18496.26	18590.75	18710.38
活期存款 Demand Deposits	2690.77	2809.87	2816.80	2909.07
定期存款 Time Deposits	678.52	699.66	721.25	747.82
储蓄存款 Savings Deposits	14677.39	14871.51	14931.34	14929.86
其他存款 Other Deposits	68.24	70.02	75.94	77.36
外币存款 Deposits in Foreign Currency	40.20	45.20	45.42	46.27
对中央银行负债 Liabilities to the Central Bank	1078.63	1107.90	1120.06	1144.27
对特定存款机构负债 Liabilities to Specific Depository Institutions	1.60	3.68	3.74	5.12
对其他金融机构负债 Liabilities to Other Financial Institutions	1.42	3.29		2.47
其中：计入广义货币的存款 Of Which: Deposits Included in Broad Money				
国外负债 Foreign Liabilities				
债券 Bonds	0.06	0.06	0.05	0.06
实收资本 Paid - in Capital	431.62	422.40	427.39	431.69
其他负债 Other Liabilities	584.16	807.88	726.21	727.22
总负债 Total Liabilities	**20252.61**	**20841.47**	**20868.20**	**21021.21**

农村信用合作社资产负债表
Balance Sheet of Rural Credit Cooperatives

（月末余额）

（Month - end Balance）

单位：亿元

Unit：100 Million Yuan

项　目 Items	2002.09	2002.10	2002.11	2002.12
国外资产 Foreign Assets	22.47	23.61	22.33	21.94
储备资产 Reserve Assets	1965.93	2104.22	2220.36	2848.46
准备金存款 Reserve Deposits	1567.80	1755.72	1859.80	2503.21
库存现金 Cash in Vault	398.13	348.50	360.56	345.25
中央银行债券 Central Bank Bonds				
对政府债权 Claims on Government	964.35	950.23	902.59	921.93
其中：中央政府 Of Which：Central Government	964.35	950.23	902.59	921.93
对非金融机构债权 Claims on Non - financial Institutions	14682.44	14725.94	14807.94	14674.17
对特定存款机构债权 Claims on Specific Depository Institutions	34.38	32.56	32.09	33.08
对其他金融机构债权 Claims on Other Financial Institutions	0.91	0.91	0.91	1.21
其他资产 Other Assets	3708.65	3617.93	3667.91	3551.32
总资产 Total Assets	**21379.13**	**21455.40**	**21654.13**	**22052.11**
对非金融机构负债 Liabilities to Non - financial Institutions	18972.83	19046.74	19271.59	19674.12
活期存款 Demand Deposits	3052.40	3065.44	3138.36	3266.28
定期存款 Time Deposits	766.83	767.77	774.31	773.14
储蓄存款 Savings Deposits	15019.83	15082.81	15217.59	15405.80
其他存款 Other Deposits	87.04	83.06	93.38	180.37
外币存款 Deposits in Foreign Currency	46.73	47.66	47.95	48.53
对中央银行负债 Liabilities to the Central Bank	1153.48	1132.27	1084.65	985.32
对特定存款机构负债 Liabilities to Specific Depository Institutions	5.02	4.06	3.66	3.05
对其他金融机构负债 Liabilities to Other Financial Institutions	0.00	2.55	1.37	2.92
其中：计入广义货币的存款 Of Which：Deposits Included in Broad Money		0.16		
国外负债 Foreign Liabilities				
债券 Bonds	0.07	0.06	0.06	0.06
实收资本 Paid - in Capital	440.56	455.20	470.80	489.91
其他负债 Other Liabilities	807.17	814.52	822.00	896.73
总负债 Total Liabilities	**21379.13**	**21455.40**	**21654.13**	**22052.11**

农村信用合作社资产负债表

Balance Sheet of Rural Credit Cooperatives

（月末余额）

（Month – end Balance）

单位：亿元

Unit：100 Million Yuan

项 目 Items	2003.01	2003.02	2003.03	2003.04
国外资产 Foreign Assets	20.55	22.14	22.53	23.65
储备资产 Reserve Assets	2492.10	2549.24	2420.56	2390.63
准备金存款 Reserve Deposits	2038.45	2171.10	2038.36	2013.43
库存现金 Cash in Vault	453.65	378.14	382.20	377.20
中央银行债券 Central Bank Bonds				
对政府债权 Claims on Government	822.73	855.32	835.92	868.82
其中：中央政府 Of Which：Central Government	822.73	855.32	835.92	868.82
对非金融机构债权 Claims on Non – financial Institutions	14969.52	15178.11	15658.13	16038.18
对特定存款机构债权 Claims on Specific Depository Institutions	251.52	275.02	303.32	311.76
对其他金融机构债权 Claims on Other Financial Institutions	65.65	58.52	63.97	63.66
其他资产 Other Assets	3555.22	3856.76	4103.18	3961.74
总资产 Total Assets	**22177.29**	**22795.11**	**23407.61**	**23658.44**
对非金融机构负债 Liabilities to Non – financial Institutions	19892.77	20558.42	20977.31	21216.81
活期存款 Demand Deposits	3120.78	3149.81	3334.17	3405.87
定期存款 Time Deposits	796.64	826.51	869.51	906.25
储蓄存款 Savings Deposits	15834.41	16430.25	16621.95	16754.07
其他存款 Other Deposits	92.84	103.02	102.20	101.13
外币存款 Deposits in Foreign Currency	48.10	48.83	49.48	49.49
对中央银行负债 Liabilities to the Central Bank	1015.86	1022.26	1096.27	1142.32
对特定存款机构负债 Liabilities to Specific Depository Institutions	4.90	3.93	2.57	2.38
对其他金融机构负债 Liabilities to Other Financial Institutions	8.76	5.87	5.60	3.20
其中：计入广义货币的存款 Of Which：Deposits Included in Broad Money				
国外负债 Foreign Liabilities				
债券 Bonds	0.06	0.06	0.06	0.05
实收资本 Paid – in Capital	456.59	464.08	473.66	486.04
其他负债 Other Liabilities	798.35	740.49	852.14	807.64
总负债 Total Liabilities	**22177.29**	**22795.11**	**23407.61**	**23658.44**

农村信用合作社资产负债表
Balance Sheet of Rural Credit Cooperatives

（月末余额）

（Month - end Balance）

单位：亿元

Unit：100 Million Yuan

项目 Items	2003.05	2003.06	2003.07	2003.08
国外资产 Foreign Assets	20.54	19.10	17.81	20.12
储备资产 Reserve Assets	2353.95	2315.21	2365.99	2344.49
准备金存款 Reserve Deposits	1997.94	1923.89	2008.33	1968.03
库存现金 Cash in Vault	356.01	391.32	357.66	376.46
中央银行债券 Central Bank Bonds			0.50	0.50
对政府债权 Claims on Government	883.05	901.89	910.84	909.66
其中：中央政府 Of Which：Central Government	883.05	901.89	910.84	909.66
对非金融机构债权 Claims on Non - financial Institutions	16326.79	16663.19	16971.76	17323.65
对特定存款机构债权 Claims on Specific Depository Institutions	292.50	322.13	331.17	338.62
对其他金融机构债权 Claims on Other Financial Institutions	66.85	64.10	63.80	65.74
其他资产 Other Assets	4178.34	4425.77	4248.69	4151.74
总资产 Total Assets	**24122.02**	**24711.39**	**24910.56**	**25154.52**
对非金融机构负债 Liabilities to Non - financial Institutions	21624.56	22084.69	22289.38	22478.95
活期存款 Demand Deposits	3547.62	3759.36	3830.74	3950.27
定期存款 Time Deposits	941.42	952.33	970.93	991.89
储蓄存款 Savings Deposits	16973.70	17185.77	17290.06	17316.29
其他存款 Other Deposits	111.96	137.11	146.85	169.99
外币存款 Deposits in Foreign Currency	49.86	50.12	50.80	50.51
对中央银行负债 Liabilities to the Central Bank	1165.57	1171.42	1178.51	1182.23
对特定存款机构负债 Liabilities to Specific Depository Institutions	2.55	1.88	1.90	2.71
对其他金融机构负债 Liabilities to Other Financial Institutions	6.88	16.50	11.01	9.32
其中：计入广义货币的存款 Of Which：Deposits Included in Broad Money				
国外负债 Foreign Liabilities				
债券 Bonds	0.05	0.05	0.05	0.05
实收资本 Paid - in Capital	494.33	520.26	525.47	531.85
其他负债 Other Liabilities	828.08	916.59	904.24	949.41
总负债 Total Liabilities	**24122.02**	**24711.39**	**24910.56**	**25154.52**

农村信用合作社资产负债表
Balance Sheet of Rural Credit Cooperatives

（月末余额）

(Month - end Balance)

单位：亿元

Unit: 100 Million Yuan

项目 Items	2003.09	2003.10	2003.11	2003.12
国外资产 Foreign Assets	18.72	17.56	17.35	17.13
储备资产 Reserve Assets	2366.96	2429.92	2531.77	3349.87
准备金存款 Reserve Deposits	1905.98	2022.27	2108.25	2940.19
库存现金 Cash in Vault	460.98	407.65	423.52	409.68
中央银行债券 Central Bank Bonds	0.50	0.88	3.05	6.02
对政府债权 Claims on Government	920.06	914.28	915.47	919.29
其中：中央政府 Of Which: Central Government	920.06	914.28	915.47	919.29
对非金融机构债权 Claims on Non - financial Institutions	17678.95	17842.11	18011.43	17759.69
对特定存款机构债权 Claims on Specific Depository Institutions	350.91	352.83	365.63	363.80
对其他金融机构债权 Claims on Other Financial Institutions	74.09	66.83	66.09	61.43
其他资产 Other Assets	4249.80	4161.89	4201.94	4269.00
总资产 Total Assets	**25659.99**	**25786.30**	**26112.73**	**26746.23**
对非金融机构负债 Liabilities to Non - financial Institutions	22864.27	23016.50	23308.03	23765.25
活期存款 Demand Deposits	4126.75	4167.60	4227.04	4387.79
定期存款 Time Deposits	1019.48	1027.48	1034.16	1019.75
储蓄存款 Savings Deposits	17473.97	17563.96	17765.22	18004.99
其他存款 Other Deposits	194.19	208.35	232.58	302.77
外币存款 Deposits in Foreign Currency	49.88	49.11	49.03	49.95
对中央银行负债 Liabilities to the Central Bank	1190.04	1180.17	1133.76	1046.44
对特定存款机构负债 Liabilities to Specific Depository Institutions	4.34	2.36	2.88	1.75
对其他金融机构负债 Liabilities to Other Financial Institutions	4.59	23.48	4.73	7.35
其中：计入广义货币的存款 Of Which: Deposits Included in Broad Money				
国外负债 Foreign Liabilities				
债券 Bonds	0.05	0.05	0.05	0.05
实收资本 Paid - in Capital	544.72	560.32	596.24	625.53
其他负债 Other Liabilities	1051.98	1003.42	1067.04	1299.86
总负债 Total Liabilities	**25659.99**	**25786.30**	**26112.73**	**26746.23**

农村信用合作社资产负债表
Balance Sheet of Rural Credit Cooperatives

（月末余额）

（Month - end Balance）

单位：亿元

Unit：100 Million Yuan

项　目 Items	2004.01	2004.02	2004.03	2004.04
国外资产 Foreign Assets	18.28	20.55	19.29	23.49
储备资产 Reserve Assets	2995.84	2842.96	2736.87	2738.57
准备金存款 Reserve Deposits	2364.05	2395.04	2276.09	2263.64
库存现金 Cash in Vault	631.79	447.92	460.78	474.93
中央银行债券 Central Bank Bonds	7.00	10.78	129.39	129.47
对政府债权 Claims on Government	945.66	1141.09	1126.23	1144.78
其中：中央政府 Of Which：Central Government	945.66	1141.09	1126.23	1144.78
对非金融机构债权 Claims on Non - financial Institutions	18334.54	18700.25	19168.18	19613.88
对特定存款机构债权 Claims on Specific Depository Institutions	400.76	414.56	430.85	449.95
对其他金融机构债权 Claims on Other Financial Institutions	88.24	59.22	57.54	57.71
其他资产 Other Assets	4280.69	4465.48	4724.43	4512.79
总资产 Total Assets	**27071.01**	**27654.89**	**28392.78**	**28670.64**
对非金融机构负债 Liabilities to Non - financial Institutions	24473.28	24982.27	25474.63	25760.09
活期存款 Demand Deposits	4075.76	4212.42	4455.66	4514.76
定期存款 Time Deposits	1024.07	1060.60	1092.98	1126.23
储蓄存款 Savings Deposits	19116.59	19435.98	19627.04	19804.67
其他存款 Other Deposits	206.07	222.50	248.48	263.72
外币存款 Deposits in Foreign Currency	50.79	50.77	50.47	50.71
对中央银行负债 Liabilities to the Central Bank	1073.52	1083.94	1110.51	1175.49
对特定存款机构负债 Liabilities to Specific Depository Institutions	3.16	5.07	6.53	5.32
对其他金融机构负债 Liabilities to Other Financial Institutions	10.10	28.44	49.42	67.41
其中：计入广义货币的存款 Of Which：Deposits Included in Broad Money		0.01	0.84	1.13
国外负债 Foreign Liabilities				
债券 Bonds	0.05	0.05	0.05	0.04
实收资本 Paid - in Capital	654.27	680.08	726.95	740.69
其他负债 Other Liabilities	856.63	875.04	1024.69	921.60
总负债 Total Liabilities	**27071.01**	**27654.89**	**28392.78**	**28670.64**

农村信用合作社资产负债表

Balance Sheet of Rural Credit Cooperatives

（月末余额）

（Month – end Balance）

单位：亿元

Unit: 100 Million Yuan

项　目 Items	2004.05	2004.06	2004.07	2004.08
国外资产 Foreign Assets	20.92	21.55	19.98	21.33
储备资产 Reserve Assets	2756.87	2724.89	2765.34	2746.36
准备金存款 Reserve Deposits	2312.75	2249.56	2326.68	2283.85
库存现金 Cash in Vault	444.12	475.33	438.66	462.51
中央银行债券 Central Bank Bonds	131.40	280.81	287.35	284.21
对政府债权 Claims on Government	1159.37	1202.01	1189.80	1181.09
其中：中央政府 Of Which: Central Government	1159.37	1202.01	1189.80	1181.09
对非金融机构债权 Claims on Non – financial Institutions	19792.67	19885.57	20030.31	20141.07
对特定存款机构债权 Claims on Specific Depository Institutions	447.60	462.81	570.92	579.44
对其他金融机构债权 Claims on Other Financial Institutions	63.27	61.33	62.58	63.63
其他资产 Other Assets	4592.24	4806.49	4455.25	4257.72
总资产 Total Assets	**28964.34**	**29445.46**	**29381.53**	**29274.85**
对非金融机构负债 Liabilities to Non – financial Institutions	26043.14	26426.81	26404.47	26314.31
活期存款 Demand Deposits	4591.66	4708.38	4606.27	4623.69
定期存款 Time Deposits	1149.33	1166.03	1174.73	1159.11
储蓄存款 Savings Deposits	19979.15	20208.86	20274.19	20179.42
其他存款 Other Deposits	271.49	292.34	297.56	301.41
外币存款 Deposits in Foreign Currency	51.51	51.20	51.72	50.68
对中央银行负债 Liabilities to the Central Bank	1165.94	1154.19	1152.62	1153.10
对特定存款机构负债 Liabilities to Specific Depository Institutions	4.43	4.32	3.16	4.17
对其他金融机构负债 Liabilities to Other Financial Institutions	42.37	33.78	23.34	10.98
其中：计入广义货币的存款 Of Which: Deposits Included in Broad Money	0.77	0.38		
国外负债 Foreign Liabilities				
债券 Bonds	0.04	0.04	0.04	0.04
实收资本 Paid – in Capital	770.07	834.03	845.92	858.66
其他负债 Other Liabilities	938.35	992.29	951.98	933.59
总负债 Total Liabilities	**28964.34**	**29445.46**	**29381.53**	**29274.85**

农村信用合作社资产负债表
Balance Sheet of Rural Credit Cooperatives

（月末余额）
（Month – end Balance）

单位：亿元
Unit：100 Million Yuan

项 目 Items	2004.09	2004.10	2004.11	2004.12
国外资产 Foreign Assets	20.73	23.90	22.25	21.23
储备资产 Reserve Assets	2797.29	2946.83	3203.51	4476.81
准备金存款 Reserve Deposits	2232.83	2447.29	2708.05	4021.17
库存现金 Cash in Vault	564.46	499.54	495.46	455.64
中央银行债券 Central Bank Bonds	366.54	373.43	376.01	386.77
对政府债权 Claims on Government	1197.58	1206.72	1228.97	1157.81
其中：中央政府 Of Which：Central Government	1197.58	1206.72	1228.97	1157.81
对非金融机构债权 Claims on Non – financial Institutions	20213.78	20176.92	20139.79	19748.26
对特定存款机构债权 Claims on Specific Depository Institutions	593.29	596.16	590.59	621.52
对其他金融机构债权 Claims on Other Financial Institutions	68.07	71.87	83.21	84.18
其他资产 Other Assets	4386.91	4387.09	4562.79	4516.80
总资产 Total Assets	**29644.19**	**29782.92**	**30207.12**	**31013.38**
对非金融机构负债 Liabilities to Non – financial Institutions	26517.53	26674.66	26957.23	27348.35
活期存款 Demand Deposits	4710.97	4757.17	4834.14	4986.21
定期存款 Time Deposits	1154.78	1142.63	1153.34	1141.83
储蓄存款 Savings Deposits	20285.15	20420.94	20594.61	20766.17
其他存款 Other Deposits	316.04	302.53	323.85	403.08
外币存款 Deposits in Foreign Currency	50.59	51.39	51.29	51.06
对中央银行负债 Liabilities to the Central Bank	1155.74	1119.02	1067.67	990.17
对特定存款机构负债 Liabilities to Specific Depository Institutions	2.95	3.30	3.61	2.95
对其他金融机构负债 Liabilities to Other Financial Institutions	8.11	5.77	0.86	27.28
其中：计入广义货币的存款 Of Which：Deposits Included in Broad Money				0.02
国外负债 Foreign Liabilities				
债券 Bonds	0.04	0.04	0.04	0.04
实收资本 Paid – in Capital	890.81	926.54	1102.91	1443.77
其他负债 Other Liabilities	1069.01	1053.59	1074.80	1200.82
总负债 Total Liabilities	**29644.19**	**29782.92**	**30207.12**	**31013.38**

农村信用合作社资产负债表
Balance Sheet of Rural Credit Cooperatives

(月末余额)

(Month – end Balance)

单位：亿元

Unit: 100 Million Yuan

项目 Items	2005.01	2005.02	2005.03	2005.04
国外资产 Foreign Assets	19.44	20.40	16.89	18.55
储备资产 Reserve Assets	3361.56	3549.73	3211.60	3034.52
准备金存款 Reserve Deposits	2824.26	2968.07	2685.57	2509.08
库存现金 Cash in Vault	537.30	581.66	526.03	525.44
央行债券 Central Bank Bonds	389.76	387.90	626.73	634.32
对政府债权 Claims on Government	1095.05	1078.87	1075.82	1092.60
其中：中央政府 Of Which: Central Government	1095.05	1078.87	1075.82	1092.60
对非金融机构债权 Claims on Non – financial Institutions	19664.58	19900.09	20287.57	20682.50
对特定存款机构债权 Claims on Specific Depository Institutions	650.45	679.81	671.16	667.78
对其他金融机构债权 Claims on Other Financial Institutions	89.83	88.55	80.43	78.89
其他资产 Other Assets	4696.98	5038.57	5383.65	5274.86
总资产 Total Assets	**29967.65**	**30743.92**	**31353.85**	**31484.02**
对非金融机构负债 Liabilities to Non – financial Institutions	26478.65	27321.05	27719.35	27752.73
活期存款 Demand Deposits	4645.96	4344.80	4571.34	4571.94
定期存款 Time Deposits	1051.43	1061.57	1095.16	1117.18
储蓄存款 Savings Deposits	20402.56	21545.84	21638.29	21624.65
其他存款 Other Deposits	332.46	322.05	367.66	392.34
外币存款 Deposits in Foreign Currency	46.24	46.79	46.90	46.62
对中央银行负债 Liabilities to the Central Bank	983.31	955.26	969.72	976.68
对特定存款机构负债 Liabilities to Specific Depository Institutions	30.98	32.11	25.25	40.84
对其他金融机构负债 Liabilities to Other Financial Institutions	29.10	32.61	17.37	58.66
其中：计入广义货币的存款 Of Which: Deposits Included in Broad Money	0.02	0.02	0.01	0.01
国外负债 Foreign Liabilities				
债券 Bonds	0.04	0.04	0.04	0.34
实收资本 Paid – in Capital	1563.40	1617.15	1662.16	1682.65
其他负债 Other Liabilities	882.17	785.70	959.96	972.12
总负债 Total Liabilities	**29967.65**	**30743.92**	**31353.85**	**31484.02**

农村信用合作社资产负债表
Balance Sheet of Rural Credit Cooperatives
（月末余额）
（Month－end Balance）

单位：亿元
Unit：100 Million Yuan

项目 Items	2005.05	2005.06	2005.07	2005.08
国外资产 Foreign Assets	16.22	17.02	16.73	16.40
储备资产 Reserve Assets	3017.70	2998.50	2981.68	2872.26
准备金存款 Reserve Deposits	2529.34	2487.43	2508.52	2383.31
库存现金 Cash in Vault	488.36	511.07	473.16	488.95
央行债券 Central Bank Bonds	706.34	122.13	60.00	41.50
对政府债权 Claims on Government	1087.26	1039.98	1015.62	904.96
其中：中央政府 Of Which：Central Government	1087.26	1039.98	1015.62	904.96
对非金融机构债权 Claims on Non－financial Institutions	20872.62	20372.93	20557.13	20013.04
对特定存款机构债权 Claims on Specific Depository Institutions	660.07	636.66	685.91	598.30
对其他金融机构债权 Claims on Other Financial Institutions	76.22	76.16	96.48	76.21
其他资产 Other Assets	5344.18	6643.81	6414.21	6204.26
总资产 Total Assets	**31780.61**	**31907.19**	**31827.76**	**30726.93**
对非金融机构负债 Liabilities to Non－financial Institutions	27974.46	27848.99	27890.52	26966.51
活期存款 Demand Deposits	4649.48	4633.47	4546.53	4187.87
定期存款 Time Deposits	1131.59	1075.03	1085.98	1025.79
储蓄存款 Savings Deposits	21754.57	21693.39	21805.32	21305.13
其他存款 Other Deposits	392.97	402.10	409.24	404.88
外币存款 Deposits in Foreign Currency	45.85	45.00	43.45	42.84
对中央银行负债 Liabilities to the Central Bank	967.15	937.41	907.92	886.85
对特定存款机构负债 Liabilities to Specific Depository Institutions	37.41	44.96	101.64	44.60
对其他金融机构负债 Liabilities to Other Financial Institutions	37.52	65.19	40.33	36.02
其中：计入广义货币的存款 Of Which：Deposits Included in Broad Money	0.01	0.01	0.01	0.01
国外负债 Foreign Liabilities				
债券 Bonds	0.04	0.04	0.04	0.04
实收资本 Paid－in Capital	1722.94	1806.15	1821.86	1828.03
其他负债 Other Liabilities	1041.09	1204.45	1065.45	964.88
总负债 Total Liabilities	**31780.61**	**31907.19**	**31827.76**	**30726.93**

农村信用合作社资产负债表
Balance Sheet of Rural Credit Cooperatives

（月末余额）
（Month－end Balance）

单位：亿元
Unit：100 Million Yuan

项　目 Items	2005.09	2005.10	2005.11	2005.12
国外资产 Foreign Assets	16.89	17.49	20.48	14.74
储备资产 Reserve Assets	3092.41	3107.29	3299.37	4779.68
准备金存款 Reserve Deposits	2512.01	2605.00	2799.34	4314.05
库存现金 Cash in Vault	580.40	502.29	500.03	465.63
央行债券 Central Bank Bonds	420.01	411.72	410.71	609.23
对政府债权 Claims on Government	883.63	903.45	969.08	1019.94
其中：中央政府 Of Which：Central Government	883.63	903.45	969.08	1019.94
对非金融机构债权 Claims on Non－financial Institutions	19869.98	19775.83	19703.80	19008.74
对特定存款机构债权 Claims on Specific Depository Institutions	604.37	613.05	642.26	653.00
对其他金融机构债权 Claims on Other Financial Institutions	78.00	81.78	85.70	80.14
其他资产 Other Assets	6313.13	6345.81	6462.71	5588.82
总资产 Total Assets	**31278.42**	**31256.42**	**31594.11**	**31754.29**
对非金融机构负债 Liabilities to Non－financial Institutions	27337.03	27381.28	27721.29	27674.26
活期存款 Demand Deposits	4361.00	4349.45	4417.38	4436.07
定期存款 Time Deposits	1039.60	1038.02	1049.89	1047.60
储蓄存款 Savings Deposits	21472.55	21550.54	21791.34	21739.33
其他存款 Other Deposits	421.98	401.10	420.87	422.01
外币存款 Deposits in Foreign Currency	41.90	42.17	41.81	29.25
对中央银行负债 Liabilities to the Central Bank	845.77	786.71	697.77	639.55
对特定存款机构负债 Liabilities to Specific Depository Institutions	32.60	35.75	42.47	19.97
对其他金融机构负债 Liabilities to Other Financial Institutions	27.48	－15.87	11.98	64.92
其中：计入广义货币的存款 Of Which：Deposits Included in Broad Money	0.01	0.01	0.01	
国外负债 Foreign Liabilities				
债券 Bonds	0.04	0.04	0.04	0.04
实收资本 Paid－in Capital	1830.62	1822.75	1857.44	1717.79
其他负债 Other Liabilities	1204.88	1245.76	1263.12	1637.76
总负债 Total Liabilities	**31278.42**	**31256.42**	**31594.11**	**31754.29**

9. 邮政储汇局资产负债表
Balance Sheet of Postal Saving Bureau

邮政储汇局资产负债表
Balance Sheet of Postal Saving Bureau

（月末余额）

（Month - end Balance）

单位：亿元

Unit：100 Million Yuan

项目 Items	2004.01	2004.02	2004.03	2004.04
国外资产 Foreign Assets				
储备资产 Reserve Assets	8386.69	8408.82	8321.90	8372.35
准备金存款 Reserve Deposits	8238.55	8309.41	8208.02	8258.82
库存现金 Cash in Vault	148.14	99.41	113.88	113.53
中央银行债券 Central Bank Bonds	19.75	79.72	89.54	83.09
对政府债权 Claims on Government	17.38	18.66	27.82	42.46
其中：中央政府 Of Which：Central Government	17.38	18.66	27.82	42.46
对非金融机构债权 Claims on Non - financial Institutions	45.00	45.00	45.00	45.00
对特定存款机构债权 Claims on Specific Depository Institutions	158.12	397.20	227.17	286.77
对其他金融机构债权 Claims on Other Financial Institutions	18.96	20.28	13.33	15.92
其他资产 Other Assets	766.96	659.74	1130.21	1033.34
总资产 Total Assets	**9412.86**	**9629.42**	**9854.97**	**9878.93**
对非金融机构负债 Liabilities to Non - financial Institutions	9315.09	9576.03	9778.91	9831.35
活期存款 Demand Deposits				
定期存款 Time Deposits				
储蓄存款 Savings Deposits	9315.09	9576.03	9778.91	9831.35
其他存款 Other Deposits				
外币存款 Deposits in Foreign Currency				
对中央银行负债 Liabilities to the Central Bank	44.12	29.75	21.61	35.50
对特定存款机构负债 Liabilities to Specific Depository Institutions				
对其他金融机构负债 Liabilities to Other Financial Institutions				
其中：计入广义货币的存款 Of Which：Deposits Included in Broad Money				
国外负债 Foreign Liabilities				
债券 Bonds				
实收资本 Paid - in Capital				
其他负债 Other Liabilities	53.65	23.64	54.45	12.08
总负债 Total Liabilities	**9412.86**	**9629.42**	**9854.97**	**9878.93**

邮政储汇局资产负债表
Balance Sheet of Postal Saving Bureau

（月末余额）

（Month – end Balance）

单位：亿元

Unit：100 Million Yuan

项　目 Items	2004.05	2004.06	2004.07	2004.08
国外资产 Foreign Assets				
储备资产 Reserve Assets	8358.91	8380.27	8353.51	8344.89
准备金存款 Reserve Deposits	8267.03	8280.46	8248.03	8250.23
库存现金 Cash in Vault	91.88	99.81	105.48	94.66
中央银行债券 Central Bank Bonds	71.83	68.85	60.85	39.81
对政府债权 Claims on Government	48.12	51.18	88.87	106.37
其中：中央政府 Of Which: Central Government	48.12	51.18	88.87	106.37
对非金融机构债权 Claims on Non – financial Institutions	45.00	45.00	45.00	45.00
对特定存款机构债权 Claims on Specific Depository Institutions	289.36	344.77	376.30	374.76
对其他金融机构债权 Claims on Other Financial Institutions	12.39	8.01	6.70	7.93
其他资产 Other Assets	1168.39	1258.46	1285.98	1349.86
总资产 Total Assets	**9994.00**	**10156.54**	**10217.21**	**10268.62**
对非金融机构负债 Liabilities to Non – financial Institutions	9936.83	10083.91	10148.82	10190.14
活期存款 Demand Deposits				
定期存款 Time Deposits				
储蓄存款 Savings Deposits	9936.83	10083.91	10148.82	10190.14
其他存款 Other Deposits				
外币存款 Deposits in Foreign Currency				
对中央银行负债 Liabilities to the Central Bank	38.38	33.89	32.76	33.41
对特定存款机构负债 Liabilities to Specific Depository Institutions				
对其他金融机构负债 Liabilities to Other Financial Institutions				
其中：计入广义货币的存款 Of Which: Deposits Included in Broad Money				
国外负债 Foreign Liabilities				
债券 Bonds				
实收资本 Paid – in Capital				
其他负债 Other Liabilities	18.79	38.74	35.63	45.07
总负债 Total Liabilities	**9994.00**	**10156.54**	**10217.21**	**10268.62**

邮政储汇局资产负债表
Balance Sheet of Postal Saving Bureau

（月末余额）

（Month - end Balance）

单位：亿元

Unit：100 Million Yuan

项目 Items	2004.09	2004.10	2004.11	2004.12
国外资产 Foreign Assets				
储备资产 Reserve Assets	8486.80	8439.43	8488.05	8510.86
准备金存款 Reserve Deposits	8342.97	8316.86	8373.56	8356.34
库存现金 Cash in Vault	143.83	122.57	114.49	154.52
中央银行债券 Central Bank Bonds	41.80	41.80	46.77	123.03
对政府债权 Claims on Government	102.78	122.28	156.60	192.21
其中：中央政府 Of Which：Central Government	102.78	122.28	156.60	192.21
对非金融机构债权 Claims on Non - financial Institutions	45.00	45.00	45.00	110.24
对特定存款机构债权 Claims on Specific Depository Institutions	409.96	425.56	465.78	546.14
对其他金融机构债权 Claims on Other Financial Institutions	6.70	6.70	15.70	7.13
其他资产 Other Assets	1226.78	1342.24	1407.21	1359.98
总资产 Total Assets	**10319.82**	**10423.01**	**10625.11**	**10849.59**
对非金融机构负债 Liabilities to Non - financial Institutions	10231.79	10348.00	10544.03	10787.25
活期存款 Demand Deposits				
定期存款 Time Deposits				
储蓄存款 Savings Deposits	10231.79	10348.00	10544.03	10787.25
其他存款 Other Deposits				
外币存款 Deposits in Foreign Currency				
对中央银行负债 Liabilities to the Central Bank	35.38	38.68	36.82	26.24
对特定存款机构负债 Liabilities to Specific Depository Institutions				
对其他金融机构负债 Liabilities to Other Financial Institutions				
其中：计入广义货币的存款 Of Which：Deposits Included in Broad Money				
国外负债 Foreign Liabilities				
债券 Bonds				
实收资本 Paid - in Capital				
其他负债 Other Liabilities	52.65	36.33	44.26	36.10
总负债 Total Liabilities	**10319.82**	**10423.01**	**10625.11**	**10849.59**

邮政储汇局资产负债表
Balance Sheet of Postal Saving Bureau
（月末余额）
（Month – end Balance）

单位：亿元
Unit: 100 Million Yuan

项　目 Items	2005.01	2005.02	2005.03	2005.04
国外资产 Foreign Assets				
储备资产 Reserve Assets	8469.48	8724.13	8822.40	8700.21
准备金存款 Reserve Deposits	8339.28	8595.34	8654.56	8523.68
库存现金 Cash in Vault	130.20	128.79	167.84	176.53
央行债券 Central Bank Bonds	318.60	607.18	606.18	926.43
对政府债权 Claims on Government	164.08	184.78	169.97	165.15
其中：中央政府 Of Which: Central Government	164.08	184.78	169.97	165.15
对非金融机构债权 Claims on Non – financial Institutions		6.70	6.70	6.70
对特定存款机构债权 Claims on Specific Depository Institutions	581.50	572.50	557.15	709.58
对其他金融机构债权 Claims on Other Financial Institutions	6.70		0.99	0.13
其他资产 Other Assets	1557.62	1574.90	1757.03	1553.69
总资产 Total Assets	**11097.98**	**11670.19**	**11920.42**	**12061.89**
对非金融机构负债 Liabilities to Non – financial Institutions	11006.00	11606.08	11852.61	11924.87
活期存款 Demand Deposits				
定期存款 Time Deposits				
储蓄存款 Savings Deposits	11006.00	11606.08	11852.61	11924.87
其他存款 Other Deposits				
外币存款 Deposits in Foreign Currency				
对中央银行负债 Liabilities to the Central Bank	25.37	27.91	28.46	28.06
对特定存款机构负债 Liabilities to Specific Depository Institutions				
对其他金融机构负债 Liabilities to Other Financial Institutions			12.57	21.17
其中：计入广义货币的存款 Of Which: Deposits Included in Broad Money				
国外负债 Foreign Liabilities				
债券 Bonds				
实收资本 Paid – in Capital				
其他负债 Other Liabilities	66.61	36.20	26.78	87.79
总负债 Total Liabilities	**11097.98**	**11670.19**	**11920.42**	**12061.89**

邮政储汇局资产负债表
Balance Sheet of Postal Saving Bureau

（月末余额）

（Month - end Balance）

单位：亿元

Unit：100 Million Yuan

项　目 Items	2005.05	2005.06	2005.07	2005.08
国外资产 Foreign Assets				
储备资产 Reserve Assets	8702.21	8770.80	8762.28	8728.91
准备金存款 Reserve Deposits	8579.69	8650.40	8643.22	8618.65
库存现金 Cash in Vault	122.52	120.40	119.06	110.26
央行债券 Central Bank Bonds	976.63	998.03	968.76	886.38
对政府债权 Claims on Government	248.15	141.09	115.07	141.38
其中：中央政府 Of Which：Central Government	248.15	141.09	115.07	141.38
对非金融机构债权 Claims on Non - financial Institutions	6.70	6.70	9.68	14.56
对特定存款机构债权 Claims on Specific Depository Institutions	667.28	718.75	805.49	805.31
对其他金融机构债权 Claims on Other Financial Institutions	13.75	4.80	25.20	12.71
其他资产 Other Assets	1584.48	1748.30	1722.57	1933.05
总资产 Total Assets	**12199.20**	**12388.47**	**12409.05**	**12522.30**
对非金融机构负债 Liabilities to Non - financial Institutions	12075.46	12284.56	12367.41	12452.64
活期存款 Demand Deposits				
定期存款 Time Deposits				
储蓄存款 Savings Deposits	12075.46	12284.56	12367.41	12452.64
其他存款 Other Deposits				
外币存款 Deposits in Foreign Currency				
对中央银行负债 Liabilities to the Central Bank	23.10	11.23	0.14	0.08
对特定存款机构负债 Liabilities to Specific Depository Institutions				
对其他金融机构负债 Liabilities to Other Financial Institutions	14.10	14.10	14.10	14.10
其中：计入广义货币的存款 Of Which：Deposits Included in Broad Money				
国外负债 Foreign Liabilities				
债券 Bonds				
实收资本 Paid - in Capital				
其他负债 Other Liabilities	86.54	78.58	27.40	55.48
总负债 Total Liabilities	**12199.20**	**12388.47**	**12409.05**	**12522.30**

邮政储汇局资产负债表

Balance Sheet of Postal Saving Bureau

(月末余额)

(Month – end Balance)

单位：亿元

Unit: 100 Million Yuan

项　目 Items	2005.09	2005.10	2005.11	2005.12
国外资产 Foreign Assets				
储备资产 Reserve Assets	8390.96	8989.83	8945.63	8635.27
准备金存款 Reserve Deposits	8230.09	8874.34	8819.85	8259.18
库存现金 Cash in Vault	160.87	115.49	125.78	376.09
央行债券 Central Bank Bonds	851.78	838.25	809.91	1054.76
对政府债权 Claims on Government	211.48	280.32	412.28	541.25
其中：中央政府 Of Which: Central Government	211.48	280.32	412.28	541.25
对非金融机构债权 Claims on Non – financial Institutions	15.42	17.63	48.70	90.70
对特定存款机构债权 Claims on Specific Depository Institutions	926.39	980.10	1070.57	1265.82
对其他金融机构债权 Claims on Other Financial Institutions	27.16	24.27	52.50	49.74
其他资产 Other Assets	2266.86	1794.39	2017.82	2149.26
总资产 Total Assets	**12690.05**	**12924.79**	**13357.41**	**13786.80**
对非金融机构负债 Liabilities to Non – financial Institutions	12595.08	12804.58	13189.87	13599.02
活期存款 Demand Deposits				
定期存款 Time Deposits				
储蓄存款 Savings Deposits	12594.88	12804.58	13189.87	13599.02
其他存款 Other Deposits				
外币存款 Deposits in Foreign Currency	0.20			
对中央银行负债 Liabilities to the Central Bank	0.07	0.06		0.16
对特定存款机构负债 Liabilities to Specific Depository Institutions	14.10	14.10	14.10	6.00
对其他金融机构负债 Liabilities to Other Financial Institutions				
其中：计入广义货币的存款 Of Which: Deposits Included in Broad Money				
国外负债 Foreign Liabilities				
债券 Bonds				
实收资本 Paid – in Capital				
其他负债 Other Liabilities	80.80	106.05	153.44	181.62
总负债 Total Liabilities	**12690.05**	**12924.79**	**13357.41**	**13786.80**

10. 特定存款机构资产负债表
Balance Sheet of Specific Depository Institutions

特定存款机构资产负债表

Balance Sheet of Specific Depository Institutions

（季末余额）

（Quarter - end Balance）

单位：亿元

Unit：100 Million Yuan

项　目 Items	1993.03	1993.06	1993.09	1993.12
国外资产 Foreign Assets				
储备资产 Reserve Assets	95.9	95.8	92.3	111.1
准备金存款 Reserve Deposits	37.3	38.4	36.5	40.3
在人行存款 Deposits with the Central Bank	58.6	57.4	55.8	70.8
库存现金 Cash in Vault				
中央银行债券 Central Bank Bonds				
国内信贷 Domestic Credit	1799.9	1913.7	1900.6	2052.0
委托信贷 Designated Credit	816.5	869.5	900.6	989.0
信托信贷 Trust Credit	339.3	340.7	359.9	379.1
其他信贷 Other Credit	644.1	703.5	640.1	683.9
对政府债权 Claims on Government	0.0	0.0	0.0	0.0
对存款货币银行债权 Claims on Deposit Money Banks	165.3	175.9	144.0	165.0
对非金融机构负债 Liabilities to Non - financial Institutions	1346.6	1440.8	1442.4	1584.0
信托存款 Trust Deposits	220.7	232.0	218.9	248.3
委托存款 Designated Deposits	903.0	976.2	998.1	1096.5
其他存款 Other Deposits	222.9	232.6	225.4	239.2
国外负债 Foreign Liabilities				
债券 Bonds	20.7	21.2	22.2	19.3
对中央银行负债 Liabilities to the Central Bank	41.4	39.7	32.7	35.3
对存款货币银行负债 Liabilities to Deposit Money Banks	274.5	266.8	192.6	199.5
所有者权益 Owner's Equity	427.1	457.3	459.4	459.9
其中：实收资本 Of Which：Paid - in Capital	427.1	457.3	459.4	459.9
其他（净） Other Items（Net）	- 49.2	- 40.4	- 12.4	30.1

特定存款机构资产负债表
Balance Sheet of Specific Depository Institutions

（季末余额）
（Quarter - end Balance）

单位：亿元
Unit: 100 Million Yuan

项目 ItemsItems	1994.03	1994.06	1994.09	1994.12
国外资产 Foreign Assets				
储备资产 Reserve Assets	123.2	135.8	154.5	167.5
准备金存款 Reserve Deposits	44.3	50.2	62.4	64.0
在人行存款 Deposits with the Central Bank	75.7	81.8	87.2	99.6
库存现金 Cash in Vault	3.2	3.8	4.9	3.9
中央银行债券 Central Bank Bonds	1.6	1.1	1.3	1.0
国内信贷 Domestic Credit	2495.0	2705.7	2874.8	2402.8
委托信贷 Designated Credit	1017.6	1100.1	1208.5	1278.3
信托信贷 Trust Credit	397.3	435.0	482.9	487.0
其他信贷 Other Credit	1080.1	1170.6	1183.4	637.5
对政府债权 Claims on Government	13.6	13.3	15.3	18.1
对存款货币银行债权 Claims on Deposit Money Banks	183.8	182.1	204.8	211.6
对非金融机构负债 Liabilities to Non - financial Institutions	1571.1	1746.9	1989.4	2096.3
信托存款 Trust Deposits	261.8	297.8	377.8	453.6
委托存款 Designated Deposits	1170.0	1291.9	1419.9	1479.6
其他存款 Other Deposits	139.3	157.2	191.7	163.1
国外负债 Foreign Liabilities				
债券 Bonds	22.1	19.2	18.0	17.3
对中央银行负债 Liabilities to the Central Bank	52.3	36.3	28.9	27.9
对存款货币银行负债 Liabilities to Deposit Money Banks	370.5	371.9	360.4	316.7
所有者权益 Owner's Equity	501.1	514.6	529.1	513.5
其中：实收资本 Of Which: Paid - in Capital	430.3	450.1	448.3	425.4
其他（净） Other Items (Net)	300.1	349.1	324.9	-170.7

特定存款机构资产负债表
Balance Sheet of Specific Depository Institutions

（季末余额）

（Quarter－end Balance）

单位：亿元

Unit：100 Million Yuan

项　目 Items	1995.03	1995.06	1995.09	1995.12
国外资产 Foreign Assets				
储备资产 Reserve Assets	159.0	154.4	154.8	165.6
准备金存款 Reserve Deposits	78.7	83.9	90.0	79.3
在人行存款 Deposits with the Central Bank	75.5	66.1	60.9	83.4
库存现金 Cash in Vault	4.8	4.4	3.9	2.9
中央银行债券 Central Bank Bonds	0.5	0.8	0.2	0.0
国内信贷 Domestic Credit	2727.5	2855.4	2937.1	2901.0
委托信贷 Designated Credit	1431.6	1508.3	1553.0	1461.8
信托信贷 Trust Credit	551.4	594.3	617.2	694.4
其他信贷 Other Credit	744.5	752.8	766.9	744.8
对政府债权 Claims on Government	20.3	23.4	17.0	15.9
对存款货币银行债权 Claims on Deposit Money Banks	188.5	171.3	180.1	179.1
对非金融机构负债 Liabilities to Non－financial Institutions	2323.8	2462.6	2570.4	2498.5
信托存款 Trust Deposits	510.3	566.1	592.7	625.3
委托存款 Designated Deposits	1641.9	1726.5	1799.4	1676.6
其他存款 Other Deposits	171.6	170.0	178.3	196.6
国外负债 Foreign Liabilities				
债券 Bonds	16.8	20.1	18.0	19.0
对中央银行负债 Liabilities to the Central Bank	27.2	26.2	24.6	23.9
对存款货币银行负债 Liabilities to Deposit Money Banks	329.7	322.3	313.6	344.2
所有者权益 Owner's Equity	552.0	563.1	569.9	545.4
其中：实收资本 Of Which：Paid－in Capital	472.2	483.0	491.9	449.4
其他（净） Other Items（Net）	－153.7	－189.0	－207.3	－169.4

特定存款机构资产负债表
Balance Sheet of Specific Depository Institutions
（季末余额）
（Quarter – end Balance）

单位：亿元
Unit：100 Million Yuan

项目 Items	1996.03	1996.06	1996.09	1996.12
国外资产 Foreign Assets	119.1	105.2	101.3	95.4
储备资产 Reserve Assets	276.4	215.4	176.6	175.1
准备金存款 Reserve Deposits	76.4	80.7	88.5	87.7
在人行存款 Deposits with the Central Bank	196.8	131.2	84.8	84.3
库存现金 Cash in Vault	3.2	3.5	3.3	3.1
中央银行债券 Central Bank Bonds				
国内信贷 Domestic Credit	4252.9	4784.5	4922.3	5340.2
委托信贷 Designated Credit	1321.8	1389.7	1452.2	1441.0
信托信贷 Trust Credit	550.1	568.8	604.6	682.5
其他信贷 Other Credit	2381.0	2826.0	2865.5	3216.7
对政府债权 Claims on Government	19.2	20.5	14.5	18.7
对存款货币银行债权 Claims on Deposit Money Banks	233.1	275.6	306.1	236.7
对非金融机构负债 Liabilities to Non – financial Institutions	2270.1	2358.6	2494.4	2481.9
信托存款 Trust Deposits	531.9	569.7	599.8	604.4
委托存款 Designated Deposits	1531.3	1601.6	1691.2	1655.1
其他存款 Other Deposits	206.9	187.3	203.4	222.4
国外负债 Foreign Liabilities	587.3	585.3	440.2	404.1
债券 Bonds	10.7	9.2	9.6	11.7
对中央银行负债 Liabilities to the Central Bank	23.0	23.4	23.1	22.8
对存款货币银行负债 Liabilities to Deposit Money Banks	213.9	221.4	235.2	306.4
所有者权益 Owner's Equity	719.8	771.5	805.8	815.9
其中：实收资本 Of Which：Paid – in Capital	651.9	680.4	690.1	695.2
其他（净） Other Items（Net）	1075.9	1431.8	1512.5	1823.3

特定存款机构资产负债表
Balance Sheet of Specific Depository Institutions

（季末余额）

（Quarter – end Balance）

单位：亿元

Unit：100 Million Yuan

项目 Items	1997.03	1997.06	1997.09	1997.12
国外资产 Foreign Assets	92.7	70.6	58.8	70.4
储备资产 Reserve Assets	151.1	192.3	206.5	182.0
准备金存款 Reserve Deposits	66.2	67.5	78.0	76.9
在人行存款 Deposits with the Central Bank	81.0	121.4	124.8	102.1
库存现金 Cash in Vault	3.9	3.4	3.7	3.0
中央银行债券 Central Bank Bonds				
国内信贷 Domestic Credit	5157.4	5469.2	5759.0	6202.4
委托信贷 Designated Credit	1173.5	1215.8	1246.7	1256.6
信托信贷 Trust Credit	437.9	469.8	463.6	478.5
其他信贷 Other Credit	3546.0	3783.6	4048.7	4467.3
对政府债权 Claims on Government	26.0	21.1	18.6	24.1
对存款货币银行债权 Claims on Deposit Money Banks	275.8	310.0	312.7	333.8
对非金融机构负债 Liabilities to Non – financial Institutions	1684.9	1882.1	1975.6	2024.8
信托存款 Trust Deposits	424.2	416.9	455.2	493.8
委托存款 Designated Deposits	1229.7	1360.1	1401.4	1411.5
其他存款 Other Deposits	31.0	105.1	119.0	119.5
国外负债 Foreign Liabilities	609.3	608.1	529.2	629.9
债券 Bonds	2499.0	2786.4	3030.8	3255.3
对中央银行负债 Liabilities to the Central Bank	41.2	36.0	35.8	35.6
对存款货币银行负债 Liabilities to Deposit Money Banks	166.2	167.9	186.5	203.3
所有者权益 Owner's Equity	825.5	824.9	896.3	974.5
其中：实收资本 Of Which：Paid – in Capital	722.0	765.1	827.5	888.8
其他（净） Other Items（Net）	– 123.1	– 242.2	– 298.6	– 310.7

特定存款机构资产负债表
Balance Sheet of Specific Depository Institutions

（季末余额）
（Quarter－end Balance）

单位：亿元
Unit: 100 Million Yuan

项　　目 Items	1998.03	1998.06	1998.09	1998.12
国外资产 Foreign Assets	38.2	43.3	43.9	46.1
储备资产 Reserve Assets	156.5	124.2	107.9	105.7
准备金存款 Reserve Deposits	73.6	120.4	104.4	102.3
在人行存款 Deposits with the Central Bank	78.5			
库存现金 Cash in Vault	4.4	3.8	3.5	3.4
中央银行债券 Central Bank Bonds				
国内信贷 Domestic Credit	6367.8	6814.4	7261.0	7978.6
委托信贷 Designated Credit	1274.0	1316.9	1333.4	1313.7
信托信贷 Trust Credit	491.9	469.9	475.4	501.4
其他信贷 Other Credit	4601.9	5027.6	5452.2	6163.5
对政府债权 Claims on Government	16.6	16.3	17.0	18.1
对存款货币银行债权 Claims on Deposit Money Banks	322.7	317.9	385.5	345.7
对非金融机构负债 Liabilities to Non－financial Institutions	2159.8	2221.9	2247.3	2200.9
信托存款 Trust Deposits	605.8	589.1	589.7	597.2
委托存款 Designated Deposits	1443.7	1499.3	1514.3	1491.6
其他存款 Other Deposits	110.3	133.5	143.3	112.1
国外负债 Foreign Liabilities	664.9	608.5	588.7	574.5
债券 Bonds	3343.5	3687.8	4064.2	4703.3
对中央银行负债 Liabilities to the Central Bank	36.3	34.2	34.0	37.3
对存款货币银行负债 Liabilities to Deposit Money Banks	188.2	193.5	197.0	173.1
所有者权益 Owner's Equity	1008.0	1026.0	1037.5	1111.6
其中：实收资本 Of Which: Paid－in Capital	908.3	937.7	974.1	987.0
其他（净） Other Items (Net)	－498.9	－455.8	－353.4	－306.5

特定存款机构资产负债表
Balance Sheet of Specific Depository Institutions

（季末余额）

（Quarter - end Balance）

单位：亿元

Unit：100 Million Yuan

项　目 Items	1999.03	1999.06	1999.09	1999.12
国外资产 Foreign Assets	28.3	57.9	45.4	46.0
储备资产 Reserve Assets	173.0	229.9	129.3	188.7
准备金存款 Reserve Deposits	168.6	225.3	124.9	185.3
库存现金 Cash in Vault	4.4	4.6	4.4	3.4
中央银行债券 Central Bank Bonds				
国内信贷 Domestic Credit	8102.5	8366.4	8639.7	8668.2
委托信贷 Designated Credit	1296.5	1304.2	1294.6	1277.3
信托信贷 Trust Credit	464.0	460.8	456.2	426.5
其他信贷 Other Credit	6342.0	6601.4	6888.9	6964.4
对政府债权 Claims on Government	17.2	19.6	16.9	17.8
对存款货币银行债权 Claims on Deposit Money Banks	319.1	454.8	450.2	469.7
对非金融机构负债 Liabilities to Non - financial Institutions	2176.7	2191.6	2187.9	2259.8
信托存款 Trust Deposits	592.3	582.1	574.6	652.9
委托存款 Designated Deposits	1464.1	1483.1	1457.9	1461.5
其他存款 Other Deposits	120.3	126.4	155.4	145.4
国外负债 Foreign Liabilities	442.8	480.6	492.5	503.9
债券 Bonds	4897.4	5096.5	5237.4	5872.2
对中央银行负债 Liabilities to the Central Bank	38.0	68.5	68.7	236.1
对存款货币银行负债 Liabilities to Deposit Money Banks	171.1	171.9	168.3	166.8
实收资本 Paid - in Capital	1003.9	1019.3	1033.2	1050.6
其他（净） Other Items（Net）	- 89.8	100.2	93.5	- 699.0

特定存款机构资产负债表
Balance Sheet of Specific Depository Institutions

（季末余额）

（Quarter – end Balance）

单位：亿元

Unit：100 Million Yuan

项目 Items	2000.03	2000.06	2000.09	2000.12
国外资产 Foreign Assets	44.5	49.9	50.2	58.9
储备资产 Reserve Assets	102.2	182.1	147.9	111.0
准备金 Reserves	97.8	178.6	144.6	108.2
库存现金 Cash in Vault	4.4	3.5	3.3	2.8
中央银行债券 Central Bank Bonds	0.1			
国内信贷 Domestic Credit	8548.9	8804.9	9030.0	9440.1
委托信贷 Designated Credit	1254.3	1249.1	1221.3	1199.2
信托信贷 Trust Credit	398.7	371.9	348.0	350.5
其他信贷 Other Credit	6895.9	7183.9	7460.7	7890.4
对政府债权 Claims on Government	18.6	16.9	17.5	13.0
对存款货币银行债权 Claims on Deposit Money Banks	536.6	403.5	481.2	483.6
对非金融部门负债 Liabilities to Non – financial Sectors	2208.7	2118.5	2122.2	2122.8
信托存款 Trust Deposits	593.1	521.0	502.2	505.6
委托存款 Designated Deposits	1448.6	1447.6	1428.2	1414.3
其他存款 Other Deposits	167.0	149.9	191.8	202.9
国外负债 Foreign Liabilities	520.6	546.9	550.7	458.0
债券 Bonds	5960.7	6300.0	6567.5	6950.5
对中央银行负债 Liabilities to the Central Bank	195.7	195.7	195.7	195.8
对存款货币银行负债 Liabilities to Deposit Money Banks	194.8	177.1	183.3	192.4
实收资本 Paid – in Capital	1044.9	1056.0	1058.7	1071.2
其他（净） Other Items（Net）	– 874.5	– 936.9	– 951.3	– 884.1

特定存款机构资产负债表
Balance Sheet of Specific Depository Institutions

（季末余额）
（Quarter - end Balance）

单位：亿元
Unit：100 Million Yuan

项 目 Items	2001.03	2001.06	2001.09	2001.12
国外资产 Foreign Assets	399.8	395.7	370.7	422.8
储备资产 Reserve Assets	90.0	139.6	83.4	106.1
准备金 Reserves	87.7	137.6	81.5	104.6
库存现金 Cash in Vault	2.3	2.0	1.9	1.5
中央银行债券 Central Bank Bonds				
国内信贷 Domestic Credit	9430.6	9701.4	10121.7	10386.5
委托信贷 Designated Credit	1147.7	1145.3	1149.1	1138.0
信托信贷 Trust Credit	486.6	468.6	465.4	426.2
其他信贷 Other Credit	7796.3	8087.5	8507.2	8822.3
对政府债权 Claims on Government	16.1	18.8	17.8	38.1
对存款货币银行债权 Claims on Deposit Money Banks	517.4	493.0	517.5	507.1
对非金融部门负债 Liabilities to Non - financial Sectors	1829.4	1812.1	1784.7	1724.2
信托存款 Trust Deposits	356.3	344.6	323.6	308.7
委托存款 Designated Deposits	1339.4	1339.4	1344.8	1327.8
其他存款 Other Deposits	133.7	128.1	116.3	87.7
国外负债 Foreign Liabilities	707.8	714.3	687.7	683.5
债券 Bonds	7076.9	7361.7	7633.3	8077.0
对中央银行负债 Liabilities to the Central Bank	205.7	205.6	213.2	206.2
对存款货币银行负债 Liabilities to Deposit Money Banks	153.1	143.2	165.7	161.6
实收资本 Paid - in Capital	1085.4	1087.9	1109.7	1107.9
其他（净） Other Items（Net）	- 604.4	- 576.3	- 483.2	- 499.8

特定存款机构资产负债表
Balance Sheet of Specific Depository Institutions
（月末余额）
（Month – end Balance）

单位：亿元
Unit：100 Million Yuan

项　目 Items	2002.01	2002.02	2002.03	2002.04
国外资产 Foreign Assets	431.69	363.45	364.82	386.19
储备资产 Reserve Assets	91.40	85.97	99.92	241.37
准备金存款 Reserve Deposits	90.23	84.87	99.08	240.64
库存现金 Cash in Vault	1.17	1.10	0.84	0.73
中央银行债券 Central Bank Bonds				
对政府债权 Claims on Government	16.02	12.64	17.20	24.96
其中：中央政府 Of Which：Central Government	16.02	12.64	17.20	24.96
国内信贷 Domestic Credit	10013.34	10063.61	10158.67	10185.79
委托贷款 Designated Credit	1018.67	1012.75	1007.34	995.86
信托贷款 Trust Credit	393.23	411.21	397.58	411.80
其他贷款 Other Credit	8601.44	8639.65	8753.75	8778.13
对存款货币银行债权 Claims on Deposit Money Banks	718.56	711.71	607.77	712.56
对其他金融机构债权 Claims on Other Financial Institutions	1023.03	1023.69	1021.99	1017.43
其他资产 Other Assets	2133.43	1951.68	1977.56	1909.17
总资产 Total Assets	**14427.47**	**14212.75**	**14247.93**	**14477.47**
对非金融机构负债 Liabilities to Non – financial Institutions	1833.49	1800.12	1807.92	1788.38
信托存款 Trust Deposits	254.57	248.47	244.17	244.08
委托存款 Designated Deposits	1178.91	1171.70	1166.33	1151.68
其他存款 Other Deposits	350.79	332.06	352.31	348.64
外币存款 Deposits in Foreign Currency	49.22	47.89	45.11	43.98
债券 Bonds	8078.35	8040.33	8192.81	8423.86
国外负债 Foreign Liabilities	628.16	579.07	579.28	585.45
对中央银行负债 Liabilities to the Central Bank	226.13	104.56	80.38	78.52
对存款货币银行负债 Liabilities to Deposit Money Banks	369.58	421.18	345.52	319.09
对其他金融机构负债 Liabilities to Other Financial Institutions	33.43	32.62	33.36	29.29
其中：计入广义货币的存款 Of Which：Deposits Included in Broad Money	2.72	1.49	1.67	1.67
实收资本 Paid – in Capital	1398.81	1372.62	1361.22	1362.49
其他负债 Other Liabilities	1859.52	1862.25	1847.44	1890.39
总负债 Total Liabilities	**14427.47**	**14212.75**	**14247.93**	**14477.47**

特定存款机构资产负债表

Balance Sheet of Specific Depository Institutions

（月末余额）

（Month - end Balance）

单位：亿元

Unit：100 Million Yuan

项 目 Items	2002.05	2002.06	2002.07	2002.08
国外资产 Foreign Assets	393.87	414.16	433.51	424.26
储备资产 Reserve Assets	117.14	90.50	116.73	69.84
准备金存款 Reserve Deposits	116.47	89.81	116.10	69.17
库存现金 Cash in Vault	0.67	0.69	0.63	0.67
中央银行债券 Central Bank Bonds				
对政府债权 Claims on Government	22.85	23.21	27.10	29.98
其中：中央政府 Of Which：Central Government	22.85	23.21	27.10	29.98
国内信贷 Domestic Credit	10233.52	10471.52	10566.14	10670.68
委托贷款 Designated Credit	994.45	947.78	972.32	979.66
信托贷款 Trust Credit	387.39	388.74	363.26	341.50
其他贷款 Other Credit	8851.68	9135.00	9230.56	9349.52
对存款货币银行债权 Claims on Deposit Money Banks	669.08	636.00	595.04	523.77
对其他金融机构债权 Claims on Other Financial Institutions	1020.66	1020.19	1015.88	1014.66
其他资产 Other Assets	1889.66	1884.11	1830.63	1826.61
总资产 Total Assets	**14346.78**	**14539.69**	**14585.03**	**14559.80**
对非金融机构负债 Liabilities to Non - financial Institutions	1799.86	1770.46	1764.89	1764.26
信托存款 Trust Deposits	242.21	227.78	223.59	211.95
委托存款 Designated Deposits	1148.25	1098.18	1121.39	1136.30
其他存款 Other Deposits	362.25	404.87	382.16	377.45
外币存款 Deposits in Foreign Currency	47.15	39.63	37.75	38.56
债券 Bonds	8390.95	8463.71	8683.40	8768.13
国外负债 Foreign Liabilities	578.12	588.92	602.10	599.81
对中央银行负债 Liabilities to the Central Bank	72.37	62.71	61.22	61.39
对存款货币银行负债 Liabilities to Deposit Money Banks	336.60	427.73	353.22	354.65
对其他金融机构负债 Liabilities to Other Financial Institutions	30.17	25.17	24.55	27.18
其中：计入广义货币的存款 Of Which：Deposits Included in Broad Money	2.60	1.69	1.68	1.69
实收资本 Paid - in Capital	1368.67	1376.53	1379.69	1376.23
其他负债 Other Liabilities	1770.04	1824.46	1715.96	1608.15
总负债 Total Liabilities	**14346.78**	**14539.69**	**14585.03**	**14559.80**

特定存款机构资产负债表
Balance Sheet of Specific Depository Institutions

（月末余额）

（Month – end Balance）

单位：亿元

Unit：100 Million Yuan

项　目 Items	2002.09	2002.10	2002.11	2002.12
国外资产 Foreign Assets	438.45	464.29	472.56	460.24
储备资产 Reserve Assets	71.43	73.50	138.59	131.68
准备金存款 Reserve Deposits	70.90	72.98	138.09	131.28
库存现金 Cash in Vault	0.53	0.52	0.50	0.40
中央银行债券 Central Bank Bonds				
对政府债权 Claims on Government	24.50	27.65	34.48	34.32
其中：中央政府 Of Which：Central Government	24.50	27.65	34.48	34.32
国内信贷 Domestic Credit	10910.30	10995.36	10920.42	11345.62
委托贷款 Designated Credit	982.53	987.87	959.12	926.83
信托贷款 Trust Credit	342.58	294.64	297.77	297.39
其他贷款 Other Credit	9585.19	9712.85	9663.53	10121.40
对存款货币银行债权 Claims on Deposit Money Banks	533.44	509.25	495.91	465.16
对其他金融机构债权 Claims on Other Financial Institutions	1021.83	1015.30	1015.20	1014.31
其他资产 Other Assets	1886.29	1923.36	2006.08	1990.13
总资产 Total Assets	**14886.24**	**15008.71**	**15083.24**	**15441.46**
对非金融机构负债 Liabilities to Non – financial Institutions	1766.08	1794.64	1753.03	1794.52
信托存款 Trust Deposits	219.43	217.76	214.74	210.22
委托存款 Designated Deposits	1132.66	1141.08	1100.79	1071.38
其他存款 Other Deposits	377.11	399.42	401.13	477.16
外币存款 Deposits in Foreign Currency	36.88	36.38	36.37	35.76
债券 Bonds	8892.68	9136.42	9301.55	9575.07
国外负债 Foreign Liabilities	607.84	609.09	611.14	621.35
对中央银行负债 Liabilities to the Central Bank	66.82	62.40	65.68	74.09
对存款货币银行负债 Liabilities to Deposit Money Banks	431.33	343.36	334.93	385.06
对其他金融机构负债 Liabilities to Other Financial Institutions	29.49	27.97	32.64	20.49
其中：计入广义货币的存款 Of Which：Deposits Included in Broad Money	1.67	1.67	1.67	1.67
实收资本 Paid – in Capital	1384.22	1385.23	1387.71	1385.78
其他负债 Other Liabilities	1707.78	1649.60	1596.56	1585.10
总负债 Total Liabilities	**14886.24**	**15008.71**	**15083.24**	**15441.46**

特定存款机构资产负债表
Balance Sheet of Specific Depository Institutions
（月末余额）
（Month - end Balance）

单位：亿元
Unit：100 Million Yuan

项　目 Items	2003.01	2003.02	2003.03	2003.04
国外资产 Foreign Assets	460.67	495.68	544.96	540.63
储备资产 Reserve Assets	75.93	229.17	201.78	74.35
准备金存款 Reserve Deposits	75.54	228.76	201.39	74.05
库存现金 Cash in Vault	0.39	0.41	0.39	0.30
中央银行债券 Central Bank Bonds			3.32	2.50
对政府债权 Claims on Government	36.14	45.82	48.84	55.21
其中：中央政府 Of Which：Central Government	36.14	45.82	48.84	55.21
国内信贷 Domestic Credit	11269.50	11349.74	11679.59	11771.40
委托贷款 Designated Credit	914.95	921.59	913.38	917.55
信托贷款 Trust Credit	270.43	268.53	280.70	289.74
其他贷款 Other Credit	10084.12	10159.62	10485.51	10564.11
对存款货币银行债权 Claims on Deposit Money Banks	498.35	454.28	450.52	469.49
对其他金融机构债权 Claims on Other Financial Institutions	1047.65	1038.55	1040.99	1036.13
其他资产 Other Assets	1958.92	1970.64	1712.51	1564.69
总资产 Total Assets	**15347.16**	**15583.88**	**15682.51**	**15514.40**
对非金融机构负债 Liabilities to Non - financial Institutions	1659.90	1698.65	1690.72	1688.12
信托存款 Trust Deposits	216.54	224.87	230.34	233.16
委托存款 Designated Deposits	1042.60	1057.66	1048.76	1049.38
其他存款 Other Deposits	366.25	380.25	374.48	369.24
外币存款 Deposits in Foreign Currency	34.51	35.87	37.14	36.34
债券 Bonds	9572.75	9772.79	9805.93	9729.12
国外负债 Foreign Liabilities	628.18	680.82	686.90	632.86
对中央银行负债 Liabilities to the Central Bank	70.78	72.07	73.78	62.50
对存款货币银行负债 Liabilities to Deposit Money Banks	374.95	322.62	320.45	442.09
对其他金融机构负债 Liabilities to Other Financial Institutions	40.24	44.41	50.23	45.23
其中：计入广义货币的存款 Of Which：Deposits Included in Broad Money	1.67	1.67	1.67	1.67
实收资本 Paid - in Capital	1380.59	1436.75	1437.22	1439.31
其他负债 Other Liabilities	1619.77	1555.77	1617.28	1475.17
总负债 Total Liabilities	**15347.16**	**15583.88**	**15682.51**	**15514.40**

特定存款机构资产负债表
Balance Sheet of Specific Depository Institutions

(月末余额)
(Month - end Balance)

单位：亿元
Unit: 100 Million Yuan

项目 Items	2003.05	2003.06	2003.07	2003.08
国外资产 Foreign Assets	596.13	584.82	428.19	385.77
储备资产 Reserve Assets	106.37	86.21	92.99	136.60
准备金存款 Reserve Deposits	106.06	85.92	92.72	136.28
库存现金 Cash in Vault	0.31	0.29	0.27	0.32
中央银行债券 Central Bank Bonds	2.50		65.30	36.59
对政府债权 Claims on Government	52.73	49.47	41.54	44.72
其中：中央政府 Of Which: Central Government	52.73	49.47	41.54	44.72
国内信贷 Domestic Credit	11886.50	12459.40	12604.05	12900.69
委托贷款 Designated Credit	914.01	919.51	925.84	947.78
信托贷款 Trust Credit	285.59	291.50	268.39	266.17
其他贷款 Other Credit	10686.90	11248.39	11409.82	11686.74
对存款货币银行债权 Claims on Deposit Money Banks	513.30	475.87	493.55	438.82
对其他金融机构债权 Claims on Other Financial Institutions	1035.68	1032.46	1037.90	1080.59
其他资产 Other Assets	1609.90	1538.79	1592.93	1714.50
总资产 Total Assets	**15803.11**	**16227.02**	**16356.45**	**16738.28**
对非金融机构负债 Liabilities to Non - financial Institutions	1757.89	1902.49	1846.14	1935.16
信托存款 Trust Deposits	229.62	231.30	233.06	230.06
委托存款 Designated Deposits	1053.37	1050.46	1049.87	1078.51
其他存款 Other Deposits	408.88	552.54	527.64	589.58
外币存款 Deposits in Foreign Currency	66.02	68.19	35.57	37.01
债券 Bonds	9985.80	10173.72	10479.06	10518.50
国外负债 Foreign Liabilities	629.23	626.77	596.69	591.60
对中央银行负债 Liabilities to the Central Bank	72.08	78.85	86.93	215.88
对存款货币银行负债 Liabilities to Deposit Money Banks	343.78	406.73	361.40	500.60
对其他金融机构负债 Liabilities to Other Financial Institutions	48.97	48.39	58.54	46.89
其中：计入广义货币的存款 Of Which: Deposits Included in Broad Money	1.67	1.67	1.67	1.67
实收资本 Paid - in Capital	1439.11	1439.33	1390.54	1411.49
其他负债 Other Liabilities	1526.25	1550.74	1537.15	1518.16
总负债 Total Liabilities	**15803.11**	**16227.02**	**16356.45**	**16738.28**

特定存款机构资产负债表

Balance Sheet of Specific Depository Institutions

（月末余额）

（Month - end Balance）

单位：亿元

Unit：100 Million Yuan

项　目 Items	2003.09	2003.10	2003.11	2003.12
国外资产 Foreign Assets	404.33	407.87	404.42	357.15
储备资产 Reserve Assets	81.48	134.44	243.51	194.74
准备金存款 Reserve Deposits	81.22	134.17	243.22	194.50
库存现金 Cash in Vault	0.26	0.27	0.29	0.24
中央银行债券 Central Bank Bonds	3.47	54.42	94.59	56.16
对政府债权 Claims on Government	50.79	54.36	50.35	47.04
其中：中央政府 Of Which：Central Government	50.79	54.36	50.35	47.04
国内信贷 Domestic Credit	13372.07	13551.04	13586.98	13958.87
委托贷款 Designated Credit	922.92	941.41	953.19	930.92
信托贷款 Trust Credit	270.15	271.43	263.74	269.01
其他贷款 Other Credit	12179.00	12338.20	12370.05	12758.94
对存款货币银行债权 Claims on Deposit Money Banks	473.80	494.39	527.35	481.73
对其他金融机构债权 Claims on Other Financial Institutions	1065.96	1050.25	1034.19	1042.00
其他资产 Other Assets	1705.44	1710.73	1804.19	1826.41
总资产 Total Assets	**17157.34**	**17457.50**	**17745.58**	**17964.10**
对非金融机构负债 Liabilities to Non - financial Institutions	1996.37	2006.65	2038.90	2040.86
信托存款 Trust Deposits	232.15	228.91	226.47	223.80
委托存款 Designated Deposits	1053.56	1070.85	1075.71	1041.44
其他存款 Other Deposits	668.51	662.80	689.33	729.34
外币存款 Deposits in Foreign Currency	42.15	44.09	47.39	46.28
债券 Bonds	10942.39	11284.22	11503.23	11598.80
国外负债 Foreign Liabilities	606.64	604.58	610.81	615.17
对中央银行负债 Liabilities to the Central Bank	90.36	89.79	91.55	89.06
对存款货币银行负债 Liabilities to Deposit Money Banks	388.35	379.08	392.09	451.55
对其他金融机构负债 Liabilities to Other Financial Institutions	47.77	47.21	46.80	41.07
其中：计入广义货币的存款 Of Which：Deposits Included in Broad Money	1.67	1.67	1.67	1.67
实收资本 Paid - in Capital	1415.00	1425.76	1437.48	1447.03
其他负债 Other Liabilities	1670.46	1620.21	1624.72	1680.56
总负债 Total Liabilities	**17157.34**	**17457.50**	**17745.58**	**17964.10**

特定存款机构资产负债表

Balance Sheet of Specific Depository Institutions

（月末余额）

（Month – end Balance）

单位：亿元

Unit：100 Million Yuan

项 目 Items	2004.01	2004.02	2004.03	2004.04
国外资产 Foreign Assets	221.22	217.27	218.28	202.33
储备资产 Reserve Assets	90.87	230.27	97.71	107.36
准备金存款 Reserve Deposits	90.68	230.08	97.49	107.06
库存现金 Cash in Vault	0.19	0.19	0.22	0.30
中央银行债券 Central Bank Bonds	84.31	113.75	150.87	147.96
对政府债权 Claims on Government	45.44	43.35	43.28	46.60
其中：中央政府 Of Which：Central Government	45.44	43.35	43.28	46.60
国内信贷 Domestic Credit	13907.57	13963.90	14186.06	14285.15
委托贷款 Designated Credit	939.33	975.82	965.81	989.84
信托贷款 Trust Credit	180.36	186.33	193.80	198.67
其他贷款 Other Credit	12787.88	12801.75	13026.45	13096.64
对存款货币银行债权 Claims on Deposit Money Banks	333.26	343.92	323.18	328.38
对其他金融机构债权 Claims on Other Financial Institutions	1030.78	1023.98	1036.52	1029.36
其他资产 Other Assets	1120.01	1110.41	1103.50	1117.46
总资产 Total Assets	**16833.46**	**17046.85**	**17159.40**	**17264.60**
对非金融机构负债 Liabilities to Non – financial Institutions	1912.60	1939.02	1965.20	1984.02
信托存款 Trust Deposits	216.14	207.63	217.49	222.10
委托存款 Designated Deposits	1028.50	1082.62	1080.25	1105.70
其他存款 Other Deposits	626.65	609.79	628.50	614.23
外币存款 Deposits in Foreign Currency	41.31	38.98	38.96	41.99
债券 Bonds	11549.56	11809.71	11765.17	11912.46
国外负债 Foreign Liabilities	574.11	573.45	568.84	565.06
对中央银行负债 Liabilities to the Central Bank	85.86	75.59	77.97	72.17
对存款货币银行负债 Liabilities to Deposit Money Banks	256.22	215.49	253.31	216.79
对其他金融机构负债 Liabilities to Other Financial Institutions	35.31	33.25	30.03	29.88
其中：计入广义货币的存款 Of Which：Deposits Included in Broad Money	1.67	1.67	1.67	1.67
实收资本 Paid – in Capital	1091.25	1090.40	1099.70	1099.64
其他负债 Other Liabilities	1328.55	1309.94	1399.18	1384.58
总负债 Total Liabilities	**16833.46**	**17046.85**	**17159.40**	**17264.60**

特定存款机构资产负债表
Balance Sheet of Specific Depository Institutions

（月末余额）

（Month - end Balance）

单位：亿元

Unit：100 Million Yuan

项目 Items	2004.05	2004.06	2004.07	2004.08
国外资产 Foreign Assets	196.28	204.62	248.91	237.96
储备资产 Reserve Assets	155.58	168.21	193.47	156.30
准备金存款 Reserve Deposits	155.30	167.90	193.13	156.13
库存现金 Cash in Vault	0.28	0.31	0.34	0.17
中央银行债券 Central Bank Bonds	149.16	111.79	129.93	97.03
对政府债权 Claims on Government	44.87	43.69	41.03	37.58
其中：中央政府 Of Which：Central Government	44.87	43.69	41.03	37.58
国内信贷 Domestic Credit	14358.06	14907.90	14940.02	15096.81
委托贷款 Designated Credit	981.88	976.55	954.61	1005.89
信托贷款 Trust Credit	204.17	203.33	199.66	198.84
其他贷款 Other Credit	13172.01	13728.02	13785.75	13892.08
对存款货币银行债权 Claims on Deposit Money Banks	343.95	330.66	370.04	308.96
对其他金融机构债权 Claims on Other Financial Institutions	1033.11	1035.15	1034.68	1035.67
其他资产 Other Assets	1112.72	1192.32	1082.29	1096.43
总资产 Total Assets	**17393.73**	**17994.34**	**18040.37**	**18066.74**
对非金融机构负债 Liabilities to Non - financial Institutions	1989.31	2243.80	2085.66	2112.99
信托存款 Trust Deposits	223.51	224.31	227.74	226.20
委托存款 Designated Deposits	1101.28	1091.99	1070.14	1130.99
其他存款 Other Deposits	618.99	867.55	728.63	707.62
外币存款 Deposits in Foreign Currency	45.53	59.95	59.15	48.18
债券 Bonds	12060.53	12215.95	12516.08	12539.51
国外负债 Foreign Liabilities	564.29	569.48	621.69	628.20
对中央银行负债 Liabilities to the Central Bank	70.95	67.60	65.58	69.86
对存款货币银行负债 Liabilities to Deposit Money Banks	230.09	282.30	199.98	203.96
对其他金融机构负债 Liabilities to Other Financial Institutions	30.21	30.24	27.33	26.30
其中：计入广义货币的存款 Of Which：Deposits Included in Broad Money	1.67	1.67	1.67	1.67
实收资本 Paid - in Capital	1099.63	1100.09	1102.61	1106.10
其他负债 Other Liabilities	1348.72	1484.88	1421.44	1379.82
总负债 Total Liabilities	**17393.73**	**17994.34**	**18040.37**	**18066.74**

特定存款机构资产负债表
Balance Sheet of Specific Depository Institutions
（月末余额）
（Month - end Balance）

单位：亿元
Unit: 100 Million Yuan

项目 Items	2004.09	2004.10	2004.11	2004.12
国外资产 Foreign Assets	268.36	302.88	271.07	252.69
储备资产 Reserve Assets	308.00	345.42	186.03	313.78
准备金存款 Reserve Deposits	307.84	345.18	185.80	313.59
库存现金 Cash in Vault	0.16	0.24	0.23	0.19
中央银行债券 Central Bank Bonds	216.76	235.03	329.29	278.25
对政府债权 Claims on Government	36.82	39.82	39.61	30.30
其中：中央政府 Of Which: Central Government	36.82	39.82	39.61	30.30
国内信贷 Domestic Credit	15083.50	15378.87	15738.41	16543.79
委托贷款 Designated Credit	1002.84	994.05	1019.51	1055.25
信托贷款 Trust Credit	199.51	211.04	213.47	216.56
其他贷款 Other Credit	13881.15	14173.78	14505.43	15271.98
对存款货币银行债权 Claims on Deposit Money Banks	334.65	311.64	320.61	319.93
对其他金融机构债权 Claims on Other Financial Institutions	1030.62	1027.00	1025.78	1021.93
其他资产 Other Assets	1094.18	991.42	982.73	894.22
总资产 Total Assets	**18372.89**	**18632.08**	**18893.53**	**19654.89**
对非金融机构负债 Liabilities to Non - financial Institutions	2111.70	2142.90	2324.65	2442.90
信托存款 Trust Deposits	231.69	236.66	243.84	232.58
委托存款 Designated Deposits	1125.72	1115.57	1150.15	1183.70
其他存款 Other Deposits	701.56	744.51	892.12	985.64
外币存款 Deposits in Foreign Currency	52.73	46.16	38.54	40.98
债券 Bonds	12722.97	12923.15	13013.56	13573.28
国外负债 Foreign Liabilities	657.93	712.21	716.02	739.40
对中央银行负债 Liabilities to the Central Bank	68.03	79.69	80.68	112.85
对存款货币银行负债 Liabilities to Deposit Money Banks	206.11	196.11	198.08	263.03
对其他金融机构负债 Liabilities to Other Financial Institutions	22.51	22.00	24.09	25.56
其中：计入广义货币的存款 Of Which: Deposits Included in Broad Money	1.67	1.67	1.67	1.67
实收资本 Paid - in Capital	1107.05	1104.88	1104.88	1106.71
其他负债 Other Liabilities	1476.59	1451.14	1431.57	1391.16
总负债 Total Liabilities	**18372.89**	**18632.08**	**18893.53**	**19654.89**

特定存款机构资产负债表

Balance Sheet of Specific Depository Institutions

（月末余额）

（Month - end Balance）

单位：亿元

Unit：100 Million Yuan

项 目 Items	2005.01	2005.02	2005.03	2005.04
国外资产 Foreign Assets	320.68	322.96	301.07	295.09
储备资产 Reserve Assets	181.44	110.04	257.91	124.14
准备金存款 Reserve Deposits	180.54	109.06	256.91	123.13
库存现金 Cash in Vault	0.90	0.98	1.00	1.01
中央银行债券 Central Bank Bonds	284.72	213.63	221.37	235.80
对政府债权 Claims on Government	27.74	26.60	28.55	28.81
其中：中央政府 Of Which：Central Government	27.74	26.60	28.55	28.81
国内信贷 Domestic Credit	17231.36	17373.90	17746.47	17953.39
委托贷款 Designated Credit	1089.73	1120.50	1114.30	1137.53
信托贷款 Trust Credit	284.79	290.40	296.66	326.15
其他贷款 Other Credit	15856.84	15963.00	16335.51	16489.71
对存款货币银行债权 Claims on Deposit Money Banks	351.30	330.42	330.41	331.01
对其他金融机构债权 Claims on Other Financial Institutions	1047.45	1047.26	1022.93	1023.29
其他资产 Other Assets	898.14	863.71	866.45	994.23
总资产 Total Assets	**20342.83**	**20288.52**	**20775.16**	**20985.76**
对非金融机构负债 Liabilities to Non - financial Institutions	2758.74	2728.56	2784.76	2927.58
信托存款 Trust Deposits	287.94	292.30	297.12	318.75
委托存款 Designated Deposits	1206.11	1224.14	1207.76	1244.83
其他存款 Other Deposits	867.79	819.71	885.71	850.57
外币存款 Deposits in Foreign Currency	396.90	392.41	394.17	513.43
债券 Bonds	13762.44	13762.43	14059.27	14214.92
国外负债 Foreign Liabilities	706.26	714.05	707.66	714.45
对中央银行负债 Liabilities to the Central Bank	36.45	36.20	42.52	45.96
对存款货币银行负债 Liabilities to Deposit Money Banks	360.17	359.01	386.68	307.77
对其他金融机构负债 Liabilities to Other Financial Institutions	23.57	20.56	23.07	25.24
其中：计入广义货币的存款 Of Which：Deposits Included in Broad Money	1.67	1.67	1.67	1.67
实收资本 Paid - in Capital	1082.21	1081.36	1082.24	1132.85
其他负债 Other Liabilities	1612.99	1586.35	1688.96	1616.99
总负债 Total Liabilities	**20342.83**	**20288.52**	**20775.16**	**20985.76**

特定存款机构资产负债表

Balance Sheet of Specific Depository Institutions

（月末余额）

（Month – end Balance）

单位：亿元

Unit：100 Million Yuan

项目 Items	2005.05	2005.06	2005.07	2005.08
国外资产 Foreign Assets	302.08	299.22	361.11	380.25
储备资产 Reserve Assets	152.88	211.19	152.86	146.66
准备金存款 Reserve Deposits	151.87	210.30	151.98	145.69
库存现金 Cash in Vault	1.01	0.89	0.88	0.97
中央银行债券 Central Bank Bonds	228.99	235.99	188.43	153.29
对政府债权 Claims on Government	26.86	27.08	27.37	31.54
其中：中央政府 Of Which：Central Government	26.86	27.08	27.37	31.54
国内信贷 Domestic Credit	18129.75	18950.00	19044.65	19211.83
委托贷款 Designated Credit	1130.90	1168.56	1187.55	1161.06
信托贷款 Trust Credit	329.75	338.23	340.58	350.51
其他贷款 Other Credit	16669.10	17443.21	17516.52	17700.26
对存款货币银行债权 Claims on Deposit Money Banks	335.71	396.54	370.54	393.65
对其他金融机构债权 Claims on Other Financial Institutions	1045.00	1023.83	1025.35	1033.31
其他资产 Other Assets	1016.21	986.11	1050.37	1110.40
总资产 Total Assets	**21237.48**	**22129.96**	**22220.68**	**22460.93**
对非金融机构负债 Liabilities to Non – financial Institutions	3031.70	3315.18	3175.76	3098.37
信托存款 Trust Deposits	334.75	356.66	352.42	360.70
委托存款 Designated Deposits	1235.54	1278.63	1303.78	1240.29
其他存款 Other Deposits	944.70	1159.05	1007.76	984.92
外币存款 Deposits in Foreign Currency	516.71	520.84	511.80	512.46
债券 Bonds	14359.24	14700.05	14802.11	15250.15
国外负债 Foreign Liabilities	701.54	704.59	760.53	800.64
对中央银行负债 Liabilities to the Central Bank	47.51	46.27	123.71	40.15
对存款货币银行负债 Liabilities to Deposit Money Banks	302.83	447.88	463.50	277.52
对其他金融机构负债 Liabilities to Other Financial Institutions	24.47	24.19	22.82	18.85
其中：计入广义货币的存款 Of Which：Deposits Included in Broad Money	1.67	1.67	1.67	1.67
实收资本 Paid – in Capital	1120.89	1121.24	1121.91	1122.93
其他负债 Other Liabilities	1649.30	1770.56	1750.34	1852.32
总负债 Total Liabilities	**21237.48**	**22129.96**	**22220.68**	**22460.93**

特定存款机构资产负债表
Balance Sheet of Specific Depository Institutions
（月末余额）
（Month – end Balance）

单位：亿元
Unit：100 Million Yuan

项 目 Items	2005.09	2005.10	2005.11	2005.12
国外资产 Foreign Assets	339.39	309.87	578.55	549.73
储备资产 Reserve Assets	229.49	132.98	273.43	314.00
准备金存款 Reserve Deposits	228.54	132.03	271.95	312.85
库存现金 Cash in Vault	0.95	0.95	1.48	1.15
中央银行债券 Central Bank Bonds	107.45	166.31	263.11	209.53
对政府债权 Claims on Government	13.69	14.65	17.42	37.16
其中：中央政府 Of Which：Central Government	13.69	14.65	17.42	37.16
国内信贷 Domestic Credit	19655.70	19938.47	19949.88	20295.07
委托贷款 Designated Credit	1154.32	1139.77	1149.63	1060.21
信托贷款 Trust Credit	371.99	372.58	370.64	393.63
其他贷款 Other Credit	18129.39	18426.12	18429.61	18841.23
对存款货币银行债权 Claims on Deposit Money Banks	381.76	391.23	394.93	615.38
对其他金融机构债权 Claims on Other Financial Institutions	1031.78	1029.13	1028.49	1025.82
其他资产 Other Assets	937.00	1006.84	1083.29	913.26
总资产 Total Assets	**22696.26**	**22989.48**	**23589.10**	**23959.95**
对非金融机构负债 Liabilities to Non – financial Institutions	3104.21	3147.59	3220.44	3235.05
信托存款 Trust Deposits	380.32	382.02	389.43	402.48
委托存款 Designated Deposits	1232.95	1238.18	1234.25	1114.97
其他存款 Other Deposits	991.96	1025.49	1091.71	1197.57
外币存款 Deposits in Foreign Currency	498.98	501.90	505.05	520.03
债券 Bonds	15450.85	15471.71	15892.27	16319.37
国外负债 Foreign Liabilities	797.53	837.68	881.93	877.34
对中央银行负债 Liabilities to the Central Bank	41.61	42.69	43.80	37.36
对存款货币银行负债 Liabilities to Deposit Money Banks	280.35	408.67	381.37	337.22
对其他金融机构负债 Liabilities to Other Financial Institutions	19.37	21.14	18.87	16.20
其中：计入广义货币的存款 Of Which：Deposits Included in Broad Money	1.67	1.67	1.67	1.67
实收资本 Paid – in Capital	1137.44	1134.71	1138.74	1143.84
其他负债 Other Liabilities	1864.90	1925.29	2011.68	1993.57
总负债 Total Liabilities	**22696.26**	**22989.48**	**23589.10**	**23959.95**

11. 财务公司资产负债表
Balance Sheet of Finance Companies

财务公司资产负债表
Balance Sheet of Finance Companies
（季末余额）
（Quarter – end Balance）

单位：亿元
Unit：100 Million Yuan

项　目 Items	1993.03	1993.06	1993.09	1993.12
国外资产 Foreign Assets				
储备资产 Reserve Assets	8.1	9.9	7.9	7.4
准备金 Reserves	3.4	4.0	3.5	3.1
在人行存款 Deposits with the Central Bank	4.7	5.9	4.4	4.3
库存现金 Cash in Vault				
中央银行债券 Central Bank Bonds				
对政府债权 Claims on Government	0.3	0.3	0.7	0.3
对其他部门债权 Claims on Other Sectors	139.6	142.7	140.2	155.2
对非货币金融机构债权 Claims on Non – monetary Financial Institutions				
对非金融部门负债 Liabilities to Non – financial Sectors	111.2	108.2	102.4	120.7
活期存款 Demand Deposits	18.7	24.0	15.4	26.0
定期存款 Time Deposits	12.6	8.9	17.8	22.5
储蓄存款 Savings Deposits				
其他存款 Other Deposits	79.9	75.3	69.2	72.2
对中央银行负债 Liabilities to the Central Bank	20.7	21.2	20.8	21.1
对非货币金融机构负债 Liabilities to Non – monetary Financial Institutions				
国外负债 Foreign Liabilities				
债券 Bonds	0.3	0.4	0.4	0.5
所有者权益 Owner's Equity	28.8	30.4	29.4	32.3
其中：实收资本 Of Which：Paid – in Capital	28.8	30.4	29.4	32.3
其他（净） Other Items（Net）	– 13.0	– 7.3	– 4.2	– 11.7

财务公司资产负债表
Balance Sheet of Finance Companies

（季末余额）

（Quarter - end Balance）

单位：亿元

Unit：100 Million Yuan

项　目 Items	1994.03	1994.06	1994.09	1994.12
国外资产 Foreign Assets				
储备资产 Reserve Assets	8.9	12.5	12.3	14.3
准备金 Reserves	6.7	8.8	9.3	11.2
在人行存款 Deposits with the Central Bank	2.2	3.6	3.0	3.1
库存现金 Cash in Vault	0.0	0.1	0.0	0.0
中央银行债券 Central Bank Bonds				
对政府债权 Claims on Government	0.8	0.7	0.7	0.7
对其他部门债权 Claims on Other Sectors	167.7	201.9	212.4	245.0
对非货币金融机构债权 Claims on Non - monetary Financial Institutions	4.9	11.1	14.6	17.0
对非金融部门负债 Liabilities to Non - financial Sectors	126.1	154.6	160.9	182.7
活期存款 Demand Deposits	26.1	33.9	27.3	41.1
定期存款 Time Deposits	22.3	21.5	22.8	26.0
储蓄存款 Savings Deposits				
其他存款 Other Deposits	77.7	99.2	110.8	115.6
对中央银行负债 Liabilities to the Central Bank	7.6	6.5	6.6	7.0
对非货币金融机构负债 Liabilities to Non - monetary Financial Institutions	14.4	22.6	27.0	37.8
国外负债 Foreign Liabilities				
债券 Bonds	0.5	0.5	0.0	0.0
所有者权益 Owner's Equity	38.9	55.4	50.1	50.0
其中：实收资本 Of Which：Paid - in Capital	33.6	39.8	40.9	43.2
其他（净） Other Items（Net）	-5.2	-13.4	-4.6	-0.5

财务公司资产负债表
Balance Sheet of Finance Companies
（季末余额）
（Quarter - end Balance）

单位：亿元
Unit：100 Million Yuan

项目 Items	1995.03	1995.06	1995.09	1995.12
国外资产 Foreign Assets				
储备资产 Reserve Assets	27.2	31.6	32.9	45.4
准备金 Reserves	22.4	23.5	25.3	26.6
在人行存款 Deposits with the Central Bank	4.8	8.0	7.5	18.7
库存现金 Cash in Vault	0.0	0.1	0.1	0.1
中央银行债券 Central Bank Bonds	0.4	0.0	0.0	0.0
对政府债权 Claims on Government	3.4	3.1	1.3	3.7
对其他部门债权 Claims on Other Sectors	305.7	355.9	348.6	406.3
对非货币金融机构债权 Claims on Non - monetary Financial Institutions	44.3	45.4	48.4	34.2
对非金融部门负债 Liabilities to Non - financial Sectors	336.5	384.9	398.8	451.2
活期存款 Demand Deposits	57.0	83.4	80.6	93.4
定期存款 Time Deposits	43.8	39.3	51.9	51.3
储蓄存款 Savings Deposits				
其他存款 Other Deposits	235.7	262.2	266.3	306.5
对中央银行负债 Liabilities to the Central Bank	7.3	5.1	5.3	5.3
对非货币金融机构负债 Liabilities to Non - monetary Financial Institutions	35.7	40.6	45.5	53.5
国外负债 Foreign Liabilities				
债券 Bonds	0.6	0.6	0.6	0.1
所有者权益 Owner's Equity	60.8	60.4	65.1	67.4
其中：实收资本 Of Which：Paid - in Capital	51.0	51.5	52.9	54.3
其他（净） Other Items（Net）	- 59.9	- 55.6	- 84.1	- 87.9

财务公司资产负债表
Balance Sheet of Finance Companies

（季末余额）
（Quarter－end Balance）

单位：亿元
Unit：100 Million Yuan

项目 Items	1996.03	1996.06	1996.09	1996.12
国外资产 Foreign Assets				
储备资产 Reserve Assets	46.5	60.6	67.1	69.2
准备金 Reserves	33.6	47.1	52.5	57.0
在人行存款 Deposits with the Central Bank	12.8	13.4	14.5	12.1
库存现金 Cash in Vault	0.1	0.1	0.1	0.1
中央银行债券 Central Bank Bonds				
对政府债权 Claims on Government	11.6	28.0	24.5	30.1
对其他部门债权 Claims on Other Sectors	492.7	537.8	601.5	668.9
对非货币金融机构债权 Claims on Non－monetary Financial Institutions	50.3	47.6	56.0	52.0
对非金融部门负债 Liabilities to Non－financial Sectors	585.7	655.7	757.7	818.2
活期存款 Demand Deposits	100.2	130.5	155.2	184.6
定期存款 Time Deposits	61.9	56.3	59.9	61.1
储蓄存款 Savings Deposits				
其他存款 Other Deposits	423.6	468.9	542.6	572.5
对中央银行负债 Liabilities to the Central Bank	4.8	5.2	4.5	6.7
对非货币金融机构负债 Liabilities to Non－monetary Financial Institutions	54.1	68.5	67.5	90.1
国外负债 Foreign Liabilities				
债券 Bonds	1.9	0.4	0.6	0.3
所有者权益 Owner's Equity	85.4	90.6	97.1	98.4
其中：实收资本 Of Which：Paid－in Capital	71.0	74.6	78.1	77.1
其他（净） Other Items（Net）	－130.8	－146.4	－178.3	－193.5

财务公司资产负债表
Balance Sheet of Finance Companies

（季末余额）
（Quarter – end Balance）

单位：亿元
Unit：100 Million Yuan

项　目 Items	1997.03	1997.06	1997.09	1997.12
国外资产 Foreign Assets	2.4	2.1	1.0	1.0
储备资产 Reserve Assets	74.1	78.7	91.0	104.3
准备金 Reserves	39.3	43.8	49.9	50.4
在人行存款 Deposits with the Central Bank	34.7	34.8	41.0	53.8
库存现金 Cash in Vault	0.1	0.1	0.1	0.1
中央银行债券 Central Bank Bonds				
对政府债权 Claims on Government	39.1	36.4	39.3	49.5
对其他部门债权 Claims on Other Sectors	705.4	757.8	759.0	833.8
对非货币金融机构债权 Claims on Non – monetary Financial Institutions	34.4	43.1	24.7	16.6
对非金融部门负债 Liabilities to Non – financial Sectors	902.2	947.1	1003.1	1037.1
活期存款 Demand Deposits	294.1	313.1	326.6	325.7
定期存款 Time Deposits	98.3	84.4	104.1	132.2
储蓄存款 Savings Deposits				
其他存款 Other Deposits	509.8	549.6	572.4	579.2
对中央银行负债 Liabilities to the Central Bank	4.1	4.2	4.0	4.0
对非货币金融机构负债 Liabilities to Non – monetary Financial Institutions	30.6	32.0	27.9	34.8
国外负债 Foreign Liabilities	18.9	22.0	24.4	47.6
债券 Bonds	0.4	0.8	0.8	1.0
所有者权益 Owner's Equity	109.6	125.1	142.5	161.5
其中：实收资本 Of Which：Paid – in Capital	86.6	97.5	108.7	119.2
其他（净） Other Items（Net）	– 210.4	– 213.1	– 287.7	– 280.8

财务公司资产负债表
Balance Sheet of Finance Companies
（季末余额）
（Quarter - end Balance）

单位：亿元
Unit：100 Million Yuan

项 目 Items	1998.03	1998.06	1998.09	1998.12
国外资产 Foreign Assets	1.0	0.4	0.1	0.1
储备资产 Reserve Assets	98.5	81.7	83.8	97.9
准备金 Reserves	53.3	81.5	83.3	97.8
在人行存款 Deposits with the Central Bank	45.1			
库存现金 Cash in Vault	0.1	0.2	0.5	0.1
中央银行债券 Central Bank Bonds	0.0	0.0	0.0	0.2
对政府债权 Claims on Government	46.2	53.0	57.1	54.9
对其他部门债权 Claims on Other Sectors	842.4	867.7	953.5	1043.5
对非货币金融机构债权 Claims on Non - monetary Financial Institutions	40.9	17.4	14.7	13.2
对非金融部门负债 Liabilities to Non - financial Sectors	1099.5	1111.1	1238.0	1317.3
活期存款 Demand Deposits	358.2	308.5	335.5	378.7
定期存款 Time Deposits	133.4	214.7	242.9	279.1
储蓄存款 Savings Deposits				
其他存款 Other Deposits	607.9	587.9	659.6	659.5
对中央银行负债 Liabilities to the Central Bank	3.9	3.6	3.6	6.7
对非货币金融机构负债 Liabilities to Non - monetary Financial Institutions	24.0	21.4	19.7	15.2
国外负债 Foreign Liabilities	10.0	9.9	9.4	8.3
债券 Bonds	1.0	0.6	0.6	0.4
所有者权益 Owner's Equity	150.0	158.7	162.6	172.7
其中：实收资本 Of Which：Paid - in Capital	114.2	118.1	116.9	122.0
其他（净） Other Items（Net）	- 259.4	- 285.1	- 324.7	- 310.8

财务公司资产负债表

Balance Sheet of Finance Companies

（季末余额）

（Quarter – end Balance）

单位：亿元

Unit：100 Million Yuan

项目 Items	1999.03	1999.06	1999.09	1999.12
国外资产 Foreign Assets	0.2	0.8	1.6	0.9
储备资产 Reserve Assets	87.2	77.3	83.6	79.9
准备金 Reserves	87.0	77.2	83.5	79.8
库存现金 Cash in Vault	0.2	0.1	0.1	0.1
中央银行债券 Central Bank Bonds	0.2	0.2	0.2	0.2
对政府债权 Claims on Government	50.0	62.8	55.5	50.2
对其他部门债权 Claims on Other Sectors	1054.5	1070.0	1127.1	1235.0
对非货币金融机构债权 Claims on Non – monetary Financial Institutions	12.8	13.3	13.3	11.9
对非金融部门负债 Liabilities to Non – financial Sectors	1341.2	1320.5	1427.4	1602.1
活期存款 Demand Deposits	338.3	344.0	373.6	452.7
定期存款 Time Deposits	289.8	275.1	295.3	306.8
储蓄存款 Savings Deposits				
其他存款 Other Deposits	713.1	701.4	758.5	842.6
对中央银行负债 Liabilities to the Central Bank	6.7	6.7	6.7	6.6
对非货币金融机构负债 Liabilities to Non – monetary Financial Institutions	14.2	13.0	12.7	13.3
国外负债 Foreign Liabilities	7.3	7.3	8.9	7.3
债券 Bonds	2.8	3.4	2.6	1.5
实收资本 Paid – in Capital	121.8	123.5	123.5	129.6
其他（净） Other Items（Net）	– 289.1	– 250.0	– 300.5	– 382.3

财务公司资产负债表
Balance Sheet of Finance Companies
（季末余额）
（Quarter - end Balance）

单位：亿元
Unit：100 Million Yuan

项　　目 Items	2000.03	2000.06	2000.09	2000.12
国外资产 Foreign Assets	1.4	3.5	3.2	2.7
储备资产 Reserve Assets	72.4	71.1	77.3	98.1
准备金 Reserves	72.3	70.9	77.2	98.0
库存现金 Cash in Vault	0.1	0.2	0.1	0.1
中央银行债券 Central Bank Bonds	0.2	0.2	0.0	0.0
对政府债权 Claims on Government	60.9	65.3	62.6	69.9
对其他部门债权 Claims on Other Sectors	1202.1	1243.2	1321.0	1432.8
对非货币金融机构债权 Claims on Non - monetary Financial Institutions	13.4	13.0	12.3	12.0
对非金融部门负债 Liabilities to Non - financial Sectors	1626.3	1616.0	1679.2	1943.1
活期存款 Demand Deposits	334.5	359.7	355.4	479.1
定期存款 Time Deposits	315.7	411.0	459.4	561.4
储蓄存款 Savings Deposits				
其他存款 Other Deposits	976.1	845.3	864.4	902.6
对中央银行负债 Liabilities to the Central Bank	6.6	6.6	6.6	7.3
对非货币金融机构负债 Liabilities to Non - monetary Financial Institutions	12.7	11.6	11.8	11.1
国外负债 Foreign Liabilities	7.3	7.3	7.3	7.3
债券 Bonds	1.1	0.8	0.5	0.3
实收资本 Paid - in Capital	134.4	134.2	140.4	143.6
其他（净） Other Items（Net）	-438.0	-380.2	-369.4	-497.2

财务公司资产负债表
Balance Sheet of Finance Companies

（季末余额）

(Quarter - end Balance)

单位：亿元

Unit: 100 Million Yuan

项目 Items	2001.03	2001.06	2001.09	2001.12
国外资产 Foreign Assets	3.0	4.1	6.7	7.6
储备资产 Reserve Assets	84.3	86.7	101.3	132.7
准备金 Reserves	84.2	86.6	101.2	132.6
库存现金 Cash in Vault	0.1	0.1	0.1	0.1
中央银行债券 Central Bank Bonds				
对政府债权 Claims on Government	62.6	75.2	93.6	184.3
对其他部门债权 Claims on Other Sectors	1473.5	1906.3	1850.5	1895.0
对非货币金融机构债权 Claims on Non - monetary Financial Institutions	12.5	16.5	16.6	17.1
对非金融部门负债 Liabilities to Non - financial Sectors	1875.5	2345.1	2449.7	2624.5
活期存款 Demand Deposits	739.3	793.2	700.1	721.6
定期存款 Time Deposits	453.7	471.0	721.7	915.7
储蓄存款 Savings Deposits				
其他存款 Other Deposits	682.5	1080.9	1027.9	987.2
对中央银行负债 Liabilities to the Central Bank	7.3	7.1	7.1	7.1
对非货币金融机构负债 Liabilities to Non - monetary Financial Institutions	11.1	10.9	10.0	12.3
国外负债 Foreign Liabilities	7.8	7.4	7.4	6.9
债券 Bonds	0.2	0.1	0.1	0.1
实收资本 Paid - in Capital	149.2	170.2	175.7	196.1
其他（净） Other Items (Net)	- 415.2	- 452.0	- 581.3	- 610.3

财务公司资产负债表
Balance Sheet of Finance Companies
（月末余额）

（Month - end Balance）

单位：亿元

Unit：100 Million Yuan

项目 Items	2002.01	2002.02	2002.03	2002.04
国外资产 Foreign Assets	7.64	6.81	8.52	11.89
储备资产 Reserve Assets	101.61	98.17	103.16	102.94
准备金存款 Reserve Deposits	101.48	98.06	103.05	102.86
库存现金 Cash in Vault	0.13	0.11	0.11	0.08
中央银行债券 Central Bank Bonds				
对政府债权 Claims on Government	158.60	167.14	146.92	152.99
其中：中央政府 Of Which：Central Government	158.60	167.14	146.92	152.99
对非金融机构债权 Claims on Non - financial Institutions	1916.61	1940.13	1967.19	1973.44
对特定存款机构债权 Claims on Specific Depository Institutions	16.88	13.39	14.37	10.49
对其他金融机构债权 Claims on Other Financial Institutions	30.46	62.21	60.73	25.55
其他资产 Other Assets	916.53	777.84	848.92	893.54
总资产 Total Assets	**3148.33**	**3065.69**	**3149.81**	**3170.84**
对非金融机构负债 Liabilities to Non - financial Institutions	2536.73	2486.63	2517.88	2628.82
活期存款 Demand Deposits	774.80	671.81	751.34	870.05
定期存款 Time Deposits	736.77	782.32	734.67	727.75
储蓄存款 Savings Deposits				
其他存款 Other Deposits	969.99	974.89	979.41	974.94
外币存款 Deposits in Foreign Currency	55.17	57.61	52.46	56.08
对中央银行负债 Liabilities to the Central Bank	28.48	19.88	31.59	19.19
对特定存款机构负债 Liabilities to Specific Depository Institutions	8.88	8.83	8.66	8.51
对其他金融机构负债 Liabilities to Other Financial Institutions	9.24	6.88	7.57	6.15
其中：计入广义货币的存款 Of Which：Deposits Included in Broad Money	0.19	0.19	0.19	0.19
国外负债 Foreign Liabilities	5.14	5.14	5.16	5.16
债券 Bonds	0.04	0.04	0.01	0.01
实收资本 Paid - in Capital	256.91	255.94	264.14	264.14
其他负债 Other Liabilities	302.91	282.35	314.80	238.86
总负债 Total Liabilities	**3148.33**	**3065.69**	**3149.81**	**3170.84**

财务公司资产负债表
Balance Sheet of Finance Companies

(月末余额)

(Month - end Balance)

单位：亿元

Unit：100 Million Yuan

项目 Items	2002.05	2002.06	2002.07	2002.08
国外资产 Foreign Assets	12.25	13.71	10.23	12.12
储备资产 Reserve Assets	105.99	114.51	116.69	118.32
准备金存款 Reserve Deposits	105.90	114.43	116.60	118.25
库存现金 Cash in Vault	0.09	0.08	0.09	0.07
中央银行债券 Central Bank Bonds				
对政府债权 Claims on Government	158.10	163.19	196.66	250.45
其中：中央政府 Of Which：Central Government	158.10	163.19	196.66	250.45
对非金融机构债权 Claims on Non - financial Institutions	1998.32	2020.80	2026.67	2019.71
对特定存款机构债权 Claims on Specific Depository Institutions	13.82	18.04	10.90	10.22
对其他金融机构债权 Claims on Other Financial Institutions	38.72	16.27	17.28	9.35
其他资产 Other Assets	873.16	970.69	1054.15	1084.52
总资产 Total Assets	**3200.36**	**3317.21**	**3432.58**	**3504.69**
对非金融机构负债 Liabilities to Non - financial Institutions	2641.52	2702.76	2855.65	2934.30
活期存款 Demand Deposits	882.27	854.53	932.84	1013.90
定期存款 Time Deposits	720.39	782.70	820.13	856.18
储蓄存款 Savings Deposits				
其他存款 Other Deposits	984.58	1000.25	1020.39	1001.65
外币存款 Deposits in Foreign Currency	54.28	65.28	82.29	62.57
对中央银行负债 Liabilities to the Central Bank	25.32	24.63	34.22	31.91
对特定存款机构负债 Liabilities to Specific Depository Institutions	8.48	8.42	8.40	8.33
对其他金融机构负债 Liabilities to Other Financial Institutions	7.15	8.75	8.20	8.21
其中：计入广义货币的存款 Of Which：Deposits Included in Broad Money	0.21	0.21	0.21	0.48
国外负债 Foreign Liabilities	4.68	4.70	4.70	4.70
债券 Bonds	0.01			
实收资本 Paid - in Capital	264.91	280.95	288.44	289.46
其他负债 Other Liabilities	248.29	287.00	232.97	227.78
总负债 Total Liabilities	**3200.36**	**3317.21**	**3432.58**	**3504.69**

财务公司资产负债表
Balance Sheet of Finance Companies

（月末余额）

（Month - end Balance）

单位：亿元

Unit：100 Million Yuan

项　目 Items	2002.09	2002.10	2002.11	2002.12
国外资产 Foreign Assets	11.15	14.49	18.84	16.18
储备资产 Reserve Assets	123.91	131.76	133.75	136.95
准备金存款 Reserve Deposits	123.84	131.67	133.67	136.89
库存现金 Cash in Vault	0.07	0.09	0.08	0.06
中央银行债券 Central Bank Bonds				
对政府债权 Claims on Government	273.97	284.75	324.36	365.77
其中：中央政府 Of Which：Central Government	273.97	284.75	324.36	365.77
对非金融机构债权 Claims on Non - financial Institutions	2089.73	2117.48	2205.93	2276.31
对特定存款机构债权 Claims on Specific Depository Institutions	15.06	16.97	10.51	11.59
对其他金融机构债权 Claims on Other Financial Institutions	11.59	26.26	24.98	18.47
其他资产 Other Assets	1162.69	1110.46	1087.61	1255.75
总资产 Total Assets	**3688.10**	**3702.17**	**3805.98**	**4081.02**
对非金融机构负债 Liabilities to Non - financial Institutions	3074.81	3098.32	3181.53	3353.65
活期存款 Demand Deposits	1029.41	1101.82	1102.46	1261.82
定期存款 Time Deposits	943.24	916.98	973.56	953.57
储蓄存款 Savings Deposits				
其他存款 Other Deposits	1013.60	1010.70	1033.06	1060.14
外币存款 Deposits in Foreign Currency	88.56	68.82	72.45	78.12
对中央银行负债 Liabilities to the Central Bank	30.39	39.30	44.00	85.90
对特定存款机构负债 Liabilities to Specific Depository Institutions	8.33	8.29	8.29	8.16
对其他金融机构负债 Liabilities to Other Financial Institutions	17.62	7.40	7.51	11.02
其中：计入广义货币的存款 Of Which：Deposits Included in Broad Money	9.21	0.19	0.19	0.19
国外负债 Foreign Liabilities	4.72	4.72	4.24	4.26
债券 Bonds				
实收资本 Paid - in Capital	297.54	305.24	307.24	306.94
其他负债 Other Liabilities	254.69	238.90	253.17	311.09
总负债 Total Liabilities	**3688.10**	**3702.17**	**3805.98**	**4081.02**

财务公司资产负债表
Balance Sheet of Finance Companies

（月末余额）

（Month – end Balance）

单位：亿元

Unit: 100 Million Yuan

项　目 Items	2003.01	2003.02	2003.03	2003.04
国外资产 Foreign Assets	18.43	13.46	11.99	11.98
储备资产 Reserve Assets	147.87	141.31	142.99	147.34
准备金存款 Reserve Deposits	147.79	141.17	142.91	147.27
库存现金 Cash in Vault	0.08	0.14	0.08	0.07
中央银行债券 Central Bank Bonds				
对政府债权 Claims on Government	379.27	390.86	395.77	432.90
其中：中央政府 Of Which: Central Government	379.27	390.86	395.77	432.90
对非金融机构债权 Claims on Non – financial Institutions	2256.79	2277.56	2324.43	2343.72
对特定存款机构债权 Claims on Specific Depository Institutions	12.92	12.16	9.42	10.09
对其他金融机构债权 Claims on Other Financial Institutions	172.50	190.14	158.96	162.51
其他资产 Other Assets	947.33	948.38	978.65	996.41
总资产 Total Assets	**3935.11**	**3973.87**	**4022.21**	**4104.95**
对非金融机构负债 Liabilities to Non – financial Institutions	3267.21	3274.33	3355.72	3354.73
活期存款 Demand Deposits	1217.96	1223.35	1249.87	1203.98
定期存款 Time Deposits	894.44	899.49	956.41	997.45
储蓄存款 Savings Deposits				
其他存款 Other Deposits	1072.83	1076.53	1071.20	1082.16
外币存款 Deposits in Foreign Currency	81.98	74.96	78.24	71.14
对中央银行负债 Liabilities to the Central Bank	5.53	5.53	5.52	5.73
对特定存款机构负债 Liabilities to Specific Depository Institutions	5.56	5.54	5.54	5.54
对其他金融机构负债 Liabilities to Other Financial Institutions	25.66	21.87	22.34	13.63
其中：计入广义货币的存款 Of Which: Deposits Included in Broad Money	0.19	0.19	0.19	0.19
国外负债 Foreign Liabilities	4.26	4.26	1.86	1.86
债券 Bonds				
实收资本 Paid – in Capital	301.36	301.36	301.36	301.36
其他负债 Other Liabilities	325.53	360.98	329.87	422.10
总负债 Total Liabilities	**3935.11**	**3973.87**	**4022.21**	**4104.95**

财务公司资产负债表
Balance Sheet of Finance Companies

（月末余额）

（Month – end Balance）

单位：亿元

Unit：100 Million Yuan

项目 Items	2003.05	2003.06	2003.07	2003.08
国外资产 Foreign Assets	10.80	11.04	11.04	16.67
储备资产 Reserve Assets	147.75	155.75	150.35	154.12
准备金存款 Reserve Deposits	147.67	155.67	150.26	154.04
库存现金 Cash in Vault	0.08	0.08	0.09	0.08
中央银行债券 Central Bank Bonds		0.10	0.10	29.97
对政府债权 Claims on Government	448.55	366.70	357.30	353.92
其中：中央政府 Of Which：Central Government	448.55	366.70	357.30	353.92
对非金融机构债权 Claims on Non – financial Institutions	2369.85	2470.83	2445.01	2571.95
对特定存款机构债权 Claims on Specific Depository Institutions	8.87	8.96	17.14	20.45
对其他金融机构债权 Claims on Other Financial Institutions	197.25	173.08	210.46	228.30
其他资产 Other Assets	969.92	914.27	1038.21	1027.61
总资产 Total Assets	**4152.99**	**4100.73**	**4229.61**	**4402.99**
对非金融机构负债 Liabilities to Non – financial Institutions	3475.16	3391.18	3504.53	3584.72
活期存款 Demand Deposits	1260.22	1218.02	1356.38	1386.56
定期存款 Time Deposits	1068.03	1021.18	1004.23	1033.25
储蓄存款 Savings Deposits				
其他存款 Other Deposits	1075.78	1081.98	1075.07	1096.07
外币存款 Deposits in Foreign Currency	71.13	70.00	68.85	68.84
对中央银行负债 Liabilities to the Central Bank	5.73	5.72	5.72	5.72
对特定存款机构负债 Liabilities to Specific Depository Institutions	5.10	5.07	4.97	4.41
对其他金融机构负债 Liabilities to Other Financial Institutions	17.37	22.65	20.63	45.68
其中：计入广义货币的存款 Of Which：Deposits Included in Broad Money	0.46	0.46		
国外负债 Foreign Liabilities	1.66	1.67	1.67	1.67
债券 Bonds				
实收资本 Paid – in Capital	301.36	300.74	316.07	318.36
其他负债 Other Liabilities	346.61	373.70	376.02	442.43
总负债 Total Liabilities	**4152.99**	**4100.73**	**4229.61**	**4402.99**

财务公司资产负债表
Balance Sheet of Finance Companies

（月末余额）
（Month－end Balance）

单位：亿元
Unit：100 Million Yuan

项　目 Items	2003.09	2003.10	2003.11	2003.12
国外资产 Foreign Assets	16.88	18.09	15.26	15.62
储备资产 Reserve Assets	181.65	201.45	199.36	207.04
准备金存款 Reserve Deposits	181.58	201.36	199.28	206.98
库存现金 Cash in Vault	0.07	0.09	0.08	0.06
中央银行债券 Central Bank Bonds	48.34	32.93	18.49	7.52
对政府债权 Claims on Government	398.75	402.15	398.89	440.22
其中：中央政府 Of Which：Central Government	398.75	402.15	398.89	440.22
对非金融机构债权 Claims on Non－financial Institutions	2573.60	2611.79	2669.56	2850.43
对特定存款机构债权 Claims on Specific Depository Institutions	18.12	21.80	18.76	20.36
对其他金融机构债权 Claims on Other Financial Institutions	203.97	295.49	220.58	213.75
其他资产 Other Assets	941.39	1062.82	1045.56	1200.89
总资产 Total Assets	**4382.70**	**4646.52**	**4586.46**	**4955.83**
对非金融机构负债 Liabilities to Non－financial Institutions	3610.94	3860.07	3872.58	4096.13
活期存款 Demand Deposits	1313.11	1537.58	1467.21	1632.86
定期存款 Time Deposits	1096.59	1135.02	1206.45	1227.33
储蓄存款 Savings Deposits				
其他存款 Other Deposits	1130.08	1121.95	1130.74	1164.77
外币存款 Deposits in Foreign Currency	71.16	65.52	68.18	71.17
对中央银行负债 Liabilities to the Central Bank	5.51	7.56	8.51	11.72
对特定存款机构负债 Liabilities to Specific Depository Institutions	4.34	4.34	7.17	7.33
对其他金融机构负债 Liabilities to Other Financial Institutions	69.03	50.90	15.80	40.30
其中：计入广义货币的存款 Of Which：Deposits Included in Broad Money				
国外负债 Foreign Liabilities	1.68	1.68	1.48	1.52
债券 Bonds				
实收资本 Paid－in Capital	318.61	323.52	323.52	328.51
其他负债 Other Liabilities	372.59	398.45	357.40	470.32
总负债 Total Liabilities	**4382.70**	**4646.52**	**4586.46**	**4955.83**

财务公司资产负债表
Balance Sheet of Finance Companies

（月末余额）
（Month - end Balance）

单位：亿元
Unit：100 Million Yuan

项　目 Items	2004.01	2004.02	2004.03	2004.04
国外资产 Foreign Assets	13.72	13.72	13.81	13.76
储备资产 Reserve Assets	225.50	220.39	227.97	247.56
准备金存款 Reserve Deposits	225.38	220.31	227.87	247.48
库存现金 Cash in Vault	0.12	0.08	0.10	0.08
中央银行债券 Central Bank Bonds	20.42	22.50	28.39	35.15
对政府债权 Claims on Government	442.44	448.06	423.08	418.34
其中：中央政府 Of Which：Central Government	442.44	448.06	423.08	418.34
对非金融机构债权 Claims on Non - financial Institutions	2935.38	2941.14	3048.55	3028.91
对特定存款机构债权 Claims on Specific Depository Institutions	19.29	18.25	16.66	23.63
对其他金融机构债权 Claims on Other Financial Institutions	230.46	262.58	249.90	142.35
其他资产 Other Assets	945.58	1032.11	1016.30	1136.61
总资产 Total Assets	**4832.79**	**4958.75**	**5024.66**	**5046.31**
对非金融机构负债 Liabilities to Non - financial Institutions	3990.79	4145.03	4159.31	4243.08
活期存款 Demand Deposits	1522.55	1604.87	1580.88	1565.31
定期存款 Time Deposits	1234.90	1274.12	1291.68	1345.74
储蓄存款 Savings Deposits				
其他存款 Other Deposits	1165.58	1190.31	1207.68	1253.19
外币存款 Deposits in Foreign Currency	67.76	75.73	79.07	78.84
对中央银行负债 Liabilities to the Central Bank	15.09	9.47	7.17	6.62
对特定存款机构负债 Liabilities to Specific Depository Institutions	3.32	3.31	3.31	3.28
对其他金融机构负债 Liabilities to Other Financial Institutions	22.96	20.97	29.60	37.12
其中：计入广义货币的存款 Of Which：Deposits Included in Broad Money				
国外负债 Foreign Liabilities	1.27	1.27	1.28	1.30
债券 Bonds				
实收资本 Paid - in Capital	330.63	332.62	333.68	335.95
其他负债 Other Liabilities	468.73	446.08	490.31	418.96
总负债 Total Liabilities	**4832.79**	**4958.75**	**5024.66**	**5046.31**

财务公司资产负债表
Balance Sheet of Finance Companies

（月末余额）

（Month – end Balance）

单位：亿元

Unit：100 Million Yuan

项目 Items	2004.05	2004.06	2004.07	2004.08
国外资产 Foreign Assets	13.52	13.48	13.59	14.42
储备资产 Reserve Assets	235.17	246.56	249.66	253.17
准备金存款 Reserve Deposits	235.07	246.46	249.57	253.08
库存现金 Cash in Vault	0.10	0.10	0.09	0.09
中央银行债券 Central Bank Bonds	62.67	90.65	121.87	124.67
对政府债权 Claims on Government	417.95	427.92	467.31	437.22
其中：中央政府 Of Which：Central Government	417.95	427.92	467.31	437.22
对非金融机构债权 Claims on Non – financial Institutions	3067.47	3135.72	3176.77	3250.66
对特定存款机构债权 Claims on Specific Depository Institutions	27.30	29.46	30.76	30.21
对其他金融机构债权 Claims on Other Financial Institutions	173.08	222.61	255.18	279.51
其他资产 Other Assets	1116.93	1153.90	1122.30	1138.91
总资产 Total Assets	**5114.09**	**5320.30**	**5437.44**	**5528.77**
对非金融机构负债 Liabilities to Non – financial Institutions	4334.11	4427.14	4681.08	4749.29
活期存款 Demand Deposits	1631.90	1615.68	1815.37	1864.32
定期存款 Time Deposits	1353.89	1420.53	1408.53	1408.63
储蓄存款 Savings Deposits				
其他存款 Other Deposits	1268.46	1311.16	1347.81	1371.56
外币存款 Deposits in Foreign Currency	79.86	79.77	109.37	104.78
对中央银行负债 Liabilities to the Central Bank	5.88	5.75	5.16	5.20
对特定存款机构负债 Liabilities to Specific Depository Institutions	3.11	3.09	3.09	3.09
对其他金融机构负债 Liabilities to Other Financial Institutions	31.14	50.64	35.90	36.23
其中：计入广义货币的存款 Of Which：Deposits Included in Broad Money		0.86	0.86	0.86
国外负债 Foreign Liabilities	1.09	1.10	1.10	1.10
债券 Bonds				
实收资本 Paid – in Capital	337.16	356.30	362.40	362.40
其他负债 Other Liabilities	401.60	476.28	348.71	371.46
总负债 Total Liabilities	**5114.09**	**5320.30**	**5437.44**	**5528.77**

财务公司资产负债表

Balance Sheet of Finance Companies

（月末余额）

（Month－end Balance）

单位：亿元

Unit：100 Million Yuan

项 目 Items	2004.09	2004.10	2004.11	2004.12
国外资产 Foreign Assets	14.29	14.29	14.39	14.90
储备资产 Reserve Assets	253.51	259.49	164.08	260.97
准备金存款 Reserve Deposits	253.42	259.40	264.01	260.91
库存现金 Cash in Vault	0.09	0.09	0.07	0.06
中央银行债券 Central Bank Bonds	130.68	132.78	154.66	170.20
对政府债权 Claims on Government	430.93	339.89	343.96	313.63
其中：中央政府 Of Which：Central Government	430.93	339.89	343.96	313.63
对非金融机构债权 Claims on Non－financial Institutions	3335.37	3300.10	3348.54	3464.67
对特定存款机构债权 Claims on Specific Depository Institutions	24.25	26.16	26.07	25.75
对其他金融机构债权 Claims on Other Financial Institutions	243.86	337.80	278.19	106.17
其他资产 Other Assets	1095.56	1205.74	1169.29	1379.79
总资产 Total Assets	**5528.45**	**5616.25**	**5599.18**	**5736.08**
对非金融机构负债 Liabilities to Non－financial Institutions	4663.13	4837.74	4786.03	4877.64
活期存款 Demand Deposits	1710.98	1824.70	1943.56	1978.60
定期存款 Time Deposits	1447.87	1494.34	1344.71	1252.70
储蓄存款 Savings Deposits				
其他存款 Other Deposits	1403.27	1419.11	1405.74	1559.10
外币存款 Deposits in Foreign Currency	101.01	99.59	92.02	87.24
对中央银行负债 Liabilities to the Central Bank	4.72	4.59	4.96	5.51
对特定存款机构负债 Liabilities to Specific Depository Institutions	3.09	2.04	2.04	2.53
对其他金融机构负债 Liabilities to Other Financial Institutions	41.48	67.02	42.35	21.76
其中：计入广义货币的存款 Of Which：Deposits Included in Broad Money	0.86	0.41	0.41	0.41
国外负债 Foreign Liabilities	1.11	1.11	0.92	0.92
债券 Bonds				
实收资本 Paid－in Capital	364.40	364.45	366.45	362.45
其他负债 Other Liabilities	450.52	339.30	396.43	465.27
总负债 Total Liabilities	**5528.45**	**5616.25**	**5599.18**	**5736.08**

财务公司资产负债表
Balance Sheet of Finance Companies

（月末余额）

（Month – end Balance）

单位：亿元

Unit：100 Million Yuan

项目 Items	2005.01	2005.02	2005.03	2005.04
国外资产 Foreign Assets	14.90	16.55	16.55	15.06
储备资产 Reserve Assets	247.41	240.96	231.86	234.57
准备金存款 Reserve Deposits	247.31	240.87	231.77	234.49
库存现金 Cash in Vault	0.10	0.09	0.09	0.08
中央银行债券 Central Bank Bonds	165.04	158.02	144.53	130.84
对政府债权 Claims on Government	321.39	306.64	297.51	303.16
其中：中央政府 Of Which：Central Government	321.39	306.64	297.51	303.16
对非金融机构债权 Claims on Non – financial Institutions	3513.17	3506.17	3641.59	3761.12
对特定存款机构债权 Claims on Specific Depository Institutions	21.57	22.08	23.09	21.05
对其他金融机构债权 Claims on Other Financial Institutions	142.08	143.93	55.38	74.22
其他资产 Other Assets	1204.27	1223.20	1169.59	1312.98
总资产 Total Assets	**5629.83**	**5617.55**	**5580.10**	**5853.00**
对非金融机构负债 Liabilities to Non – financial Institutions	4742.00	4732.53	4670.75	4870.35
活期存款 Demand Deposits	1915.88	1920.52	1780.75	1889.64
定期存款 Time Deposits	1161.97	1140.38	1180.65	1248.22
储蓄存款 Savings Deposits				
其他存款 Other Deposits	1569.69	1574.96	1617.33	1637.33
外币存款 Deposits in Foreign Currency	94.46	96.67	92.02	95.16
对中央银行负债 Liabilities to the Central Bank	7.28	10.78	5.29	10.68
对特定存款机构负债 Liabilities to Specific Depository Institutions	4.33	2.53	2.57	2.56
对其他金融机构负债 Liabilities to Other Financial Institutions	39.39	37.58	21.89	53.74
其中：计入广义货币的存款 Of Which：Deposits Included in Broad Money	0.41	0.41	0.01	0.01
国外负债 Foreign Liabilities	0.92	0.92	0.93	0.93
债券 Bonds				
实收资本 Paid – in Capital	363.23	363.31	363.31	365.14
其他负债 Other Liabilities	472.68	469.90	515.36	549.60
总负债 Total Liabilities	**5629.83**	**5617.55**	**5580.10**	**5853.00**

财务公司资产负债表

Balance Sheet of Finance Companies

（月末余额）

（Month - end Balance）

单位：亿元

Unit：100 Million Yuan

项　目 Items	2005.05	2005.06	2005.07	2005.08
国外资产 Foreign Assets	15.06	15.47	14.72	13.90
储备资产 Reserve Assets	247.03	298.41	283.43	289.79
准备金存款 Reserve Deposits	246.93	298.33	283.34	289.70
库存现金 Cash in Vault	0.10	0.08	0.09	0.09
中央银行债券 Central Bank Bonds	111.02	125.69	145.54	126.99
对政府债权 Claims on Government	312.86	309.84	294.79	299.15
其中：中央政府 Of Which：Central Government	312.86	309.84	294.79	299.15
对非金融机构债权 Claims on Non - financial Institutions	3797.46	3777.53	3855.56	3993.40
对特定存款机构债权 Claims on Specific Depository Institutions	20.14	17.19	11.65	15.24
对其他金融机构债权 Claims on Other Financial Institutions	97.59	106.72	114.16	73.35
其他资产 Other Assets	1507.99	1724.41	1758.13	1800.74
总资产 Total Assets	**6109.15**	**6375.26**	**6477.98**	**6612.56**
对非金融机构负债 Liabilities to Non - financial Institutions	5109.40	5306.97	5418.05	5541.99
活期存款 Demand Deposits	2076.12	2105.66	2147.37	2199.95
定期存款 Time Deposits	1279.83	1446.59	1509.03	1575.19
储蓄存款 Savings Deposits				
其他存款 Other Deposits	1655.61	1649.06	1667.19	1661.23
外币存款 Deposits in Foreign Currency	97.84	105.66	94.46	105.62
对中央银行负债 Liabilities to the Central Bank	11.57	7.35	7.31	3.50
对特定存款机构负债 Liabilities to Specific Depository Institutions	2.40	2.40	2.40	2.43
对其他金融机构负债 Liabilities to Other Financial Institutions	57.21	47.35	106.77	80.27
其中：计入广义货币的存款 Of Which：Deposits Included in Broad Money	0.01	0.01	0.01	0.37
国外负债 Foreign Liabilities	0.74	0.74	0.72	0.72
债券 Bonds				
实收资本 Paid - in Capital	359.31	354.86	361.54	364.67
其他负债 Other Liabilities	568.52	655.59	581.19	618.98
总负债 Total Liabilities	**6109.15**	**6375.26**	**6477.98**	**6612.56**

财务公司资产负债表
Balance Sheet of Finance Companies
（月末余额）
(Month – end Balance)

单位：亿元
Unit: 100 Million Yuan

项目 Items	2005.09	2005.10	2005.11	2005.12
国外资产 Foreign Assets	13.09	13.48	13.47	13.75
储备资产 Reserve Assets	290.81	292.01	294.89	326.41
准备金存款 Reserve Deposits	290.75	291.93	294.81	326.36
库存现金 Cash in Vault	0.06	0.08	0.08	0.05
中央银行债券 Central Bank Bonds	126.97	108.34	74.22	51.64
对政府债权 Claims on Government	285.24	278.92	265.86	266.04
其中：中央政府 Of Which: Central Government	285.24	278.92	265.86	266.04
对非金融机构债权 Claims on Non – financial Institutions	4192.16	4256.05	4299.25	4303.12
对特定存款机构债权 Claims on Specific Depository Institutions	13.21	6.71	14.57	8.32
对其他金融机构债权 Claims on Other Financial Institutions	98.83	114.93	94.45	174.42
其他资产 Other Assets	1764.20	1841.53	1835.88	1899.32
总资产 Total Assets	**6784.51**	**6911.97**	**6892.59**	**7043.02**
对非金融机构负债 Liabilities to Non – financial Institutions	5599.79	5716.67	5765.42	6013.95
活期存款 Demand Deposits	2009.06	2112.81	2158.01	2553.25
定期存款 Time Deposits	1729.93	1736.08	1750.02	1599.98
储蓄存款 Savings Deposits				
其他存款 Other Deposits	1758.29	1767.30	1762.22	1759.42
外币存款 Deposits in Foreign Currency	102.51	100.48	95.17	101.30
对中央银行负债 Liabilities to the Central Bank	3.27	3.18	3.18	11.91
对特定存款机构负债 Liabilities to Specific Depository Institutions	2.43	2.40	2.40	2.39
对其他金融机构负债 Liabilities to Other Financial Institutions	102.63	96.27	73.91	16.41
其中：计入广义货币的存款 Of Which: Deposits Included in Broad Money	0.37	0.37	0.70	0.77
国外负债 Foreign Liabilities	0.73	0.73	0.54	0.52
债券 Bonds				
实收资本 Paid – in Capital	393.05	392.03	392.55	402.32
其他负债 Other Liabilities	682.61	700.69	654.59	595.52
总负债 Total Liabilities	**6784.51**	**6911.97**	**6892.59**	**7043.02**

四、国际金融统计

International Financing Statistics

（一）黄金、外汇储备

Gold and Foreign Exchange Reserves

黄金、外汇储备
Gold and Foreign Exchange Reserves

年份 Year	黄金储备 Gold Reserves （万盎司）（10 000 OZ.）	外汇储备 Foreign Exchange Reserves （亿美元）（100 Million US Dollars）	年份 Year	黄金储备 Gold Reserves （万盎司）（10 000 OZ.）	外汇储备 Foreign Exchange Reserves （亿美元）（100 Million US Dollars）
1952	500	1.39	1975	1280	8.99
1953	500	1.14	1976	1280	12.55
1954	500	1.06	1977	1280	23.45
1955	500	1.93	1978	1280	15.57
1956	500	1.23	1979	1280	21.54
1957	500	1.28	1980	1280	22.62
1958	500	0.86	1981	1267	47.73
1959	400	1.30	1982	1267	111.25
1960	400	1.02	1983	1267	143.42
1961	400	1.27	1984	1267	144.20
1962	300	1.38	1985	1267	119.13
1963	300	1.73	1986	1267	105.14
1964	300	2.36	1987	1267	152.36
1965	500	2.81	1988	1267	175.48
1966	500	4.20	1989	1267	170.22
1967	500	3.50	1990	1267	285.94
1968	700	3.32	1991	1267	426.64
1969	700	4.98	1992	1267	194.40
1970	700	1.91	1993	1267	212.00
1971	900	2.02	1994	1267	516.20
1972	900	5.43	1995	1267	735.97
1973	900	0.83	1996	1267	1050.29
1974	1280	3.69			

注：“外汇储备”统计口径从 1992 年起不含“中国银行外汇结存”。

Note: The item Bank of China balance was not covered in the statistic of foreign exchange reserves since 1992.

黄金、外汇储备
Gold and Foreign Exchange Reserves

年　份 Year	黄金储备（万盎司） Gold Reserves（10 000 OZ.）	外汇储备（亿美元） Foreign Exchange Reserves （100 Million US Dollars）
1997.01	1267	1086.79
1997.02	1267	1103.15
1997.03	1267	1120.55
1997.04	1267	1144.08
1997.05	1267	1175.75
1997.06	1267	1209.41
1997.07	1267	1259.46
1997.08	1267	1303.40
1997.09	1267	1340.74
1997.10	1267	1378.97
1997.11	1267	1388.73
1997.12	1267	1398.90
1998.01	1267	1404.86
1998.02	1267	1403.33
1998.03	1267	1406.17
1998.04	1267	1405.16
1998.05	1267	1409.05
1998.06	1267	1405.10
1998.07	1267	1405.99
1998.08	1267	1407.38
1998.09	1267	1411.07
1998.10	1267	1437.00
1998.11	1267	1445.88
1998.12	1267	1449.59
1999.01	1267	1450.90
1999.02	1267	1465.15
1999.03	1267	1466.25
1999.04	1267	1466.65
1999.05	1267	1467.45
1999.06	1267	1470.51
1999.07	1267	1487.37
1999.08	1267	1507.30
1999.09	1267	1515.11
1999.10	1267	1528.47
1999.11	1267	1537.70
1999.12	1267	1546.75

黄金、外汇储备
Gold and Foreign Exchange Reserves

年　份 Year	黄金储备（万盎司） Gold Reserves（10 000 OZ.）	外汇储备（亿美元） Foreign Exchange Reserves （100 Million US Dollars）
2000.01	1267	1561.00
2000.02	1267	1565.59
2000.03	1267	1568.20
2000.04	1267	1568.46
2000.05	1267	1580.19
2000.06	1267	1585.68
2000.07	1267	1585.96
2000.08	1267	1592.17
2000.09	1267	1600.92
2000.10	1267	1613.44
2000.11	1267	1639.11
2000.12	1267	1655.74
2001.01	1267	1686.23
2001.02	1267	1747.73
2001.03	1267	1758.47
2001.04	1267	1771.78
2001.05	1267	1790.00
2001.06	1267	1808.38
2001.07	1267	1844.92
2001.08	1267	1900.53
2001.09	1267	1957.64
2001.10	1267	2030.29
2001.11	1267	2083.15
2001.12	1608	2121.65
2002.01	1608	2174.00
2002.02	1608	2235.31
2002.03	1608	2276.05
2002.04	1608	2338.24
2002.05	1608	2384.73
2002.06	1608	2427.63
2002.07	1608	2465.34
2002.08	1608	2530.90
2002.09	1608	2586.30
2002.10	1608	2655.39
2002.11	1608	2746.25
2002.12	1929	2864.07

黄金、外汇储备
Gold and Foreign Exchange Reserves

年　份 Year	黄金储备（万盎司） Gold Reserves（10 000 OZ.）	外汇储备（亿美元） Foreign Exchange Reserves （100 Million US Dollars）
2003.01	1929	3044.57
2003.02	1929	3082.52
2003.03	1929	3160.09
2003.04	1929	3262.91
2003.05	1929	3400.61
2003.06	1929	3464.76
2003.07	1929	3564.86
2003.08	1929	3647.34
2003.09	1929	3838.63
2003.10	1929	4009.92
2003.11	1929	4203.61
2003.12	1929	4032.51
2004.01	1929	4157.20
2004.02	1929	4266.39
2004.03	1929	4398.22
2004.04	1929	4490.17
2004.05	1929	4585.60
2004.06	1929	4706.39
2004.07	1929	4829.82
2004.08	1929	4961.69
2004.09	1929	5145.38
2004.10	1929	5424.43
2004.11	1929	5738.82
2004.12	1929	6099.32
2005.01	1929	6236.46
2005.02	1929	6426.10
2005.03	1929	6591.44
2005.04	1929	6707.74
2005.05	1929	6910.12
2005.06	1929	7109.73
2005.07	1929	7327.33
2005.08	1929	7532.09
2005.09	1929	7690.04
2005.10	1929	7849.02
2005.11	1929	7942.23
2005.12	1929	8188.72

（二）人民币对美元汇率
Exchange Rate of RMB to US Dollar

人民币对美元汇率

Exchange Rate of RMB to US Dollar

单位：100美元折人民币元

Unit：RMB to Every 100 US Dollars

年份 Year	期末数 Year - end Figure	年平均数 Year - average Figure	年份 Year	期末数 Year - end Figure	年平均数 Year - average Figure
1952	261.70	226.45	1975	196.63	185.98
1953	261.70	261.70	1976	188.03	194.14
1954	261.70	261.70	1977	173.00	185.78
1955	246.76	246.76	1978	157.71	168.36
1956	246.18	246.18	1979	149.62	155.49
1957	246.18	246.18	1980	153.03	149.84
1958	246.18	246.18	1981	174.55	170.50
1959	246.18	246.18	1982	192.27	189.25
1960	246.18	246.18	1983	198.09	197.57
1961	246.18	246.18	1984	279.57	232.70
1962	246.18	246.18	1985	320.12	293.67
1963	246.18	246.18	1986	372.21	345.28
1964	246.18	246.18	1987	372.21	372.21
1965	246.18	246.18	1988	372.21	372.21
1966	246.18	246.18	1989	472.21	376.51
1967	246.18	246.18	1990	522.21	478.32
1968	246.18	246.18	1991	543.42	532.22
1969	246.18	246.18	1992	575.18	551.46
1970	246.18	246.18	1993	580.00	576.20
1971	226.73	246.11	1994	844.62	861.87
1972	224.01	224.51	1995	831.74	835.09
1973	202.02	198.94	1996	829.82	829.90
1974	183.97	196.12			

人民币对美元汇率
Exchange Rate of RMB to US Dollar

单位：1美元折人民币元
Unit：RMB to Every 1 US Dollar

年份 Year	期末数 Month - end Figure	月平均数 Month - average Figure
1997.01	8.2938	8.2963
1997.02	8.2948	8.2929
1997.03	8.2964	8.2957
1997.04	8.2949	8.2957
1997.05	8.2921	8.2929
1997.06	8.2908	8.2921
1997.07	8.2901	8.2911
1997.08	8.2884	8.2894
1997.09	8.2852	8.2872
1997.10	8.2836	8.2838
1997.11	8.2796	8.2811
1997.12	8.2798	8.2796
1998.01	8.2785	8.2796
1998.02	8.2790	8.2791
1998.03	8.2791	8.2792
1998.04	8.2781	8.2792
1998.05	8.2795	8.2790
1998.06	8.2798	8.2797
1998.07	8.2799	8.2798
1998.08	8.2800	8.2799
1998.09	8.2782	8.2790
1998.10	8.2776	8.2778
1998.11	8.2782	8.2778
1998.12	8.2787	8.2779
1999.01	8.2778	8.2790
1999.02	8.2789	8.2780
1999.03	8.2800	8.2787
1999.04	8.2794	8.2792
1999.05	8.2786	8.2785
1999.06	8.2786	8.2780
1999.07	8.2773	8.2777
1999.08	8.2771	8.2773
1999.09	8.2775	8.2774
1999.10	8.2774	8.2782
1999.11	8.2782	8.2782
1999.12	8.2793	8.2793

人民币对美元汇率
Exchange Rate of RMB to US Dollar

单位：1美元折人民币元

Unit：RMB to Every 1 US Dollar

年份 Year	期末数 Month - end Figure	月平均数 Month - average Figure
2000.01	8.2781	8.2793
2000.02	8.2786	8.2779
2000.03	8.2788	8.2786
2000.04	8.2795	8.2793
2000.05	8.2772	8.2777
2000.06	8.2780	8.2772
2000.07	8.2794	8.2793
2000.08	8.2786	8.2796
2000.09	8.2798	8.2786
2000.10	8.2780	8.2786
2000.11	8.2774	8.2774
2000.12	8.2781	8.2772
2001.01	8.2786	8.2771
2001.02	8.2781	8.2770
2001.03	8.2779	8.2776
2001.04	8.2773	8.2771
2001.05	8.2777	8.2772
2001.06	8.2770	8.2771
2001.07	8.2767	8.2771
2001.08	8.2767	8.2770
2001.09	8.2769	8.2768
2001.10	8.2768	8.2768
2001.11	8.2774	8.2769
2001.12	8.2766	8.2770
2002.01	8.2765	8.2767
2002.02	8.2766	8.2766
2002.03	8.2774	8.2770
2002.04	8.2770	8.2772
2002.05	8.2766	8.2769
2002.06	8.2771	8.2770
2002.07	8.2766	8.2768
2002.08	8.2767	8.2767
2002.09	8.2771	8.2770
2002.10	8.2771	8.2769
2002.11	8.2771	8.2769
2002.12	8.2773	8.2772

人民币对美元汇率

Exchange Rate of RMB to US Dollar

单位：1美元折人民币元

Unit: RMB to Every 1 US Dollar

年份 Year	期末数 Month - end Figure	月平均数 Month - average Figure
2003.01	8.2766	8.2768
2003.02	8.2774	8.2773
2003.03	8.2771	8.2772
2003.04	8.2770	8.2771
2003.05	8.2770	8.2769
2003.06	8.2774	8.2770
2003.07	8.2773	8.2773
2003.08	8.2771	8.2770
2003.09	8.2770	8.2771
2003.10	8.2767	8.2767
2003.11	8.2772	8.2769
2003.12	8.2767	8.2770
2004.01	8.2770	8.2769
2004.02	8.2770	8.2771
2004.03	8.2771	8.2771
2004.04	8.2769	8.2769
2004.05	8.2769	8.2771
2004.06	8.2766	8.2767
2004.07	8.2769	8.2767
2004.08	8.2767	8.2768
2004.09	8.2766	8.2767
2004.10	8.2765	8.2765
2004.11	8.2765	8.2765
2004.12	8.2765	8.2765
2005.01	8.2765	8.2765
2005.02	8.2765	8.2765
2005.03	8.2765	8.2765
2005.04	8.2765	8.2765
2005.05	8.2765	8.2765
2005.06	8.2765	8.2765
2005.07	8.1080	8.2369
2005.08	8.0973	8.1019
2005.09	8.0930	8.0922
2005.10	8.0840	8.0889
2005.11	8.0796	8.0840
2005.12	8.0702	8.0759

中国金融统计（1949—2005年）

China Financial Statistics（1949—2005）

（下册）

主　编　苏　宁

Editor－in－chief　Su Ning

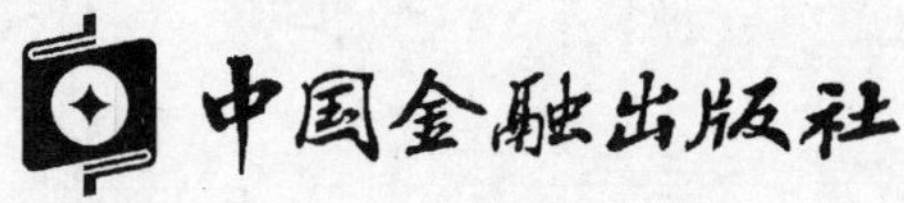

第二部分
Part Ⅱ

金融统计主要指标时间序列表
Time Series of Major Financial Indicators

第二部分编制说明

一、资料编制的基本原则

编者在统一、规范、准确的基础上，科学组织金融机构主要统计指标，合理设置统计数据属性，按照先后顺序形成时间序列表，对特别指标、特定事件给出专栏注释，充分突出科学、实用、连续的特点。

金融机构信贷收支主要指标时间序列表分为“金融机构、国家银行、政策性银行、国有商业银行、其他商业银行、农村信用社”六类主要机构，选取“各项存款、企业存款、储蓄存款、流通中货币、各项贷款、农业贷款、中长期贷款、有价证券及投资”等主要指标加工而成，设置“期末余额”、“比上期增减额”和“比去年同期增长（%）”三种属性，其项目含义和涵盖的机构范围与本书第一部分的信贷收支统计一致。

- 期末余额：为存量概念，反映该统计指标期末的数据存量。本表中，1990 年以前为年末存量，1990 年起为月末存量。
- 比上期增减额：为流量概念，反映统计指标当期的变化情况。本表中，1990 年以前为年度数据增减额，1990 年起为月度数据增减额。由于自 1993 年之后引入了年初结转的制度做法，1993 年之后各年度的 1 月份比上期增减额即为比年初增减额。
- 比去年同期增长（%）：为同比增幅，反映该统计指标自去年同期以来的变化幅度。

在同比增长幅度的计算方法上，本书以计算期当年的统计口径对基期的数据进行可比调整之后进行同比增长幅度的计算，即以“计算期期末余额”为分子，以“按照计算期统计口径调整后的基期期末余额”作为分母计算。在基期到计算期之间发生不良贷款剥离或者票据置换时，在计算增速时以“基期期末的余额数”作为分母，“计算期期末余额数 + 基期到计算期之间发生的剥离数”作为分子计算。

二、金融统计制度各年度主要调整说明

- **1978—1989 年**　汇兑在途资金不在“各项存款”中反映。
- **1985 年**　停用“基本建设存款”指标，将其数据并入“企业存款”中。
- **1988 年**　增设“金融债券”项目，将其数据从“其他类存款”中调出，将“乡镇企业贷款”数据从“农业贷款”项下调至“流动资金贷款”项下。
- **1990 年**　将邮政储蓄存款纳入“城镇储蓄存款”项下。
- **1994 年**　“农业存款”项目不包括农村信用社转存款及缴存准备金存款；“其他存款”中的某些项目调入“企业存款”等项目内。
- **1997 年**　（1）扩大了统计范围，将各商业银行所属房地产信贷部、国际业务部和信用卡部等部门数据并入表中。（2）将“部队存款”从“机关团体存款”中调出。（3）拆分“信托类存款”项目为“信托存款”和“委托存款”两项。（4）“金融债券”仅反映金融机构所发行的被金融系统以外各部门所持有的金融债券数值。（5）调整“有价证券及投资”归属：一是将金融机构之间交叉持有的有价证券投资数据轧差反映，二是将非银行金融机构的信托投资、自营证券部分并入。

● **1998 年**　(1) 自 3 月起，财政预算外存款被列为一般性存款，因此，在金融机构、国家银行信贷收支表中，将“财政预算外存款”从“财政存款”项下调出。银行类信贷收支表中，将“财政预算外存款”、“机关团体存款”从“财政存款”项下调至“其他存款”项内。(2) 自 4 月起，金融机构、国家银行、国有商业银行信贷收支表中，“保函垫款”从“其他”项中调至“其他短期贷款”内。(3) 中国工商银行“申购新股冻结款”自本年起从“活期储蓄”中调入“同业存放”项内。

● **1999 年**　(1) 金融机构信贷收支表中的“各项存款”中增加财务、信托、租赁公司的“租赁保证金”数据。(2) 年末，中国工商银行、中国银行、中国建设银行、国家开发银行进行不良资产剥离和划转，相关报表的“余额”为剥离后的实际数据，“比年初增减额”为“本年余额增减数”与“本年剥离数”之和。

● **2000 年**　(1) 河南、湖北、江苏等省的部分城市信用社更名为农村信用社，从 2 月起，各省的部分农村基金会并入农村信用社，致使农村信用社数据发生较大变化。(2) 中国工商银行将在“储蓄存款”项内的“证券清算资金”自 2000 年 1 月 1 日起改为归入“同业存放”项下的“证券公司存放”。(3) 中国工商银行、中国农业银行、中国银行、中国建设银行、国家开发银行的不良资产剥离和划转工作在不断进行，相关报表的“余额”为剥离后的实际数据，“比年初增减额”为“本年余额增减数”与“本年剥离数”之和。

● **2001 年**　(1) 将交通银行和中信实业银行数据从国家银行数据调入其他商业银行数据中。(2) 将“贴现”从“短期贷款”中调出，调入到新增设项目“票据融资”中。(3) 将“各项垫款”从“短期贷款”中调出，调入新增设项目“各项垫款”项下。(4) 将“逾期类贷款”数据按其来源分别返还到“各项贷款”的分类项目中。

● **2002 年**　(1) 从本年开始，将外资银行纳入金融统计体系中。(2) 由于信托投资公司关闭机构较多，相关报表数据变化较大。(3) 在金融机构和国家银行信贷收支表中，各金融机构的“贴现及转贴现”与人民银行的“再贴现”数据加总后反映在“票据融资”项目中，计入“各项贷款”。(4) 中国建设银行和中国工商银行进行了会计制度改革，这两家机构报送的 2001 年年末数据于 2002 年年初结转数据差异较大。(5) 考虑到信托投资公司的市场退出因素，相关信贷收支表中余额数据为剔除市场退出机构后的实际数据，增减额数据为包含退出机构的可比数据。

● **2003 年**　(1) 将“证券公司股票质押贷款”从“其他类短期贷款”中调至“拆放同业”项下，这一调整引起各金融机构“各项贷款”和“同业往来”数据变动。(2) 调整各汇总类信贷收支表中“金融债券”项目的归属关系，将并表机构之间相互持有的金融债券予以轧差。(3) 中国工商银行和中国建设银行政策性住房委托贷款并账，引起“各项贷款”和“同业往来”数据变动。(4) 农村信用社自本年起细化投资类会计科目，在金融机构信贷收支表中，将投资其他金融机构的金融性债券数据轧差。

● **2004 年**　(1)“票据融资”、“其中：贴现”项目仅反映各金融机构直贴的票据和从其他金融机构买入的买断式转贴现票据，不再扣减“再贴现”。(2) 在国有商业银行、政策性银行和农村信用社信贷收支表中，“邮政储汇局定期存款”计入“各项存款”内。(3) 在金融机构和国家银行信贷收支表中，将“财政预算外存款”计入“各项存款”下的财政存款项目，在其余各信贷收支表中“财政预算外存款”不再计入“各项存款”，而计入“代理财政性存款”项目。(4) 中国建设银行将财政预算内基本建设资金地质勘探费存款从“财政预算外存款”调至“企业活期存款”中，将土地储备贷款自“房地产开发企业流动资金贷款”调入“其他地产开发贷款”，致使“建筑业贷款”和“基本建设贷款”发生变化。(5) 6 月，中国银行、中国建设银行和交通银行进行了不良贷款剥离和划转。

● **2005 年**　(1) 终止“其他长期负债”项下的“住房公积金存款”，将其纳入“其他存款”项下。(2) 5 月、6 月，中国工商银行进行了不良贷款剥离和划转。(3) 本年有 53 家农村信用社改制为农村商业银行或者农村合作银行，导致相关数据有较大变动。

三、主要指标解释

● 各项存款：金融机构资金来源的主要项目，包括企业存款、财政存款、储蓄存款、农业存款、其他存款等。

● 企业存款：金融机构吸收的各种所有制形式、各行业企业单位的存款，有活期存款与定期存款之分。

● 财政存款：1998—2003 年期间，指中国人民银行和金融机构代理的各项财政预算内存款，1998 年之前和 2004—2005 年还包含了财政预算外存款。

● 储蓄存款：金融机构吸收的城镇居民和农户的个人储蓄存款，有活期储蓄存款与定期储蓄存款之分。

● 农村（业）存款：农村集体单位、乡镇企业、各种专业户和承包户的生产周转金、积累基金等，主要是中国农业银行和农村信用社吸收的农业企业存款。1994 年之前指标名称为“农村存款”。从 1994 年开始，该指标内涵未变，改称为“农业存款”。

● 流通中货币：由中国人民银行发行的、扣除金融机构库存现金之外的全部流通中纸币、硬币之和。

● 各项贷款：金融机构资金运用的主要项目，包括短期贷款、中长期贷款、信托贷款、票据融资和各项垫款等。

● 短期贷款：金融机构发放的期限在 1 年以下（含 1 年）的用于流动资金的贷款，包括工业贷款、商业贷款、建筑业贷款、农业贷款、乡镇企业贷款、私营企业及个体贷款、其他短期贷款等。

在主要指标时间序列表中，将 1978 年之前国家银行发放的所有贷款均作为短期贷款。1978 年之后，将流动资金贷款作为短期贷款，将固定资产（金）贷款作为中长期贷款。

● 中长期贷款：金融机构发放的期限在 1 年以上的用于基本建设、技术改造等的贷款，包括基本建设贷款、住房开发贷款，以及技术改造贷款和其他中长期贷款。

1998—2005 年，将中期流动资金贷款并入中长期贷款项下的其他中长期贷款项目中。

● 票据融资：商业票据的贴现和转贴现形成的资金运用。

2001 年之前，票据融资包含在其他短期贷款指标中。从 2001 年起，票据融资在各项贷款下单列。

● 有价证券及投资：金融机构购买的以生息为目的的各类有价证券，如自营投资、信托投资、长期投资等。

1994 年之前，有价证券及投资指标数据由有价证券和投资两项归并而成。

四、汇总类机构涵盖范围

● 金融机构：包括国家银行、其他商业银行、城市商业银行、农村商业银行、城市信用社、农村信用合作社、农村合作银行、外资银行、财务公司、信托投资公司、金融租赁公司。

● 国家银行：包括中国人民银行、政策性银行、国有商业银行、邮政储汇局。

● 政策性银行：包括国家开发银行、中国进出口银行、中国农业发展银行。

● 国有商业银行：包括中国工商银行、中国农业银行、中国银行、中国建设银行。

● 其他商业银行：交通银行、中信实业银行、光大银行、华夏银行、广东发展银行、深圳发展银行、招商银行、上海浦东发展银行、福建兴业银行、民生银行、恒丰银行、浙商银行。

具体各表所涵盖机构范围及各家机构并入的时间详见第一部分相关报表的附加注释。

五、其他说明

对于年度间金融统计制度变化引起的统计项目内涵发生较大变化的，如果确实无法进行可比口径调整，在同比增长栏的相应位置以“—”代替，表示不可比。

Compilation Instructions for Part Ⅱ

1. Basic Principles

Throughout the compilation process, all data are processed consistently and accurately; indicators are chosen scientifically and the attributes of each indicator are designed on a reasonable basis. Tables are compiled over time and notes are written for specific indicators and events. These characters make the material sound, practical and continuous.

Time series of major indicators extracted from the statements of sources and uses of credit funds include six categories of institutions, financial institutions, state banks, policy banks, state - owned commercial banks, other commercial banks and rural credit cooperatives, which include total deposits, deposits by enterprises, savings deposits, currency in circulation, total loans, loans to agricultural sector, medium and long - term loans and securities and investments. Three attributes are designed, which are balance, changes compared with previous period and increase rate year - on - year. The definitions , conceptual coverage and institutions covered are consistent with those noted in other parts of this book.

- Balance at the End of the Period: Stock concept, measuring the amount of the indicator at the end of each period. End - of - year data are provided prior to 1990, and end - of - month data are provided from 1990 on.

- Changes Compared with Previous Period: Flow concept, measuring the changes during the reporting period. Before 1990, the change were measured on an annual basis for each year. From 1990 onward, monthly flow data were presented. With the implementation of the opening balance adjustment from 1993, monthly flow data for each January since then reflected the changes over the opening balances of each year.

- Increase Rate Year - on - year (%): Relative growth data, reflecting percentage changes compared with the same period of previous year. Before 1990, annual change was presented yearly, and subsequent to 1990, annual change was presented monthly.

The method used to calculate the increase rate year - on - year (%) in this part is based on a comparable basis. The data at base period are adjusted on a consistent basis with the method applicable during the current period. The numerator is the balance at the end of the current period, and the denominator is the balance at the end of base period adjusted to be consistent with the method applicable during the current period. When non - performing loans were transferred to asset management companies or replaced by special bills between the base period and the current period, the balance at the end of base period is taken as the denominator. The balance at the end of current period was adjusted to include the balance of loans transferred or replaced between the base period and the current period, and this amount was taken as numerator for the calculation.

2. Major Changes in Financial Statistical Framework

- 1978 - 1989 Funds in the process of remittance were not included in total deposits.

- 1985　Capital construction deposits were removed, which became part of deposits by enterprises.

- 1988　Financial bonds became a separate item, which were previously part of other deposits; loans to village and township enterprises were removed from loans to agricultural sector to working capital loans.

- 1990　Post savings deposits began to be included in urban savings deposits.

- 1994　Re-deposits and required reserves by rural credit cooperatives were excluded from deposits by agricultural sectors; some components of other deposits were reclassified into deposits by enterprises and others.

- 1997　(i) The coverage of data collection was extended to include data of real estate credit businesses, international businesses, credit card businesses and other businesses of commercial banks; (ii) deposits by the army became separated from deposits by government agencies and organizations; (iii) trust deposits were split into trust deposits and designated deposits; (iv) financial bonds only reflected bonds issued by financial institutions and held by non-financial sectors; (v) securities and investments were adjusted to reflect the net position of securities cross – held among financial institutions and trust investments and proprietary securities held by non – bank financial institutions.

- 1998　(i) As of March, extra – budgetary fiscal deposits were treated as ordinary deposits. Therefore, in the statement of sources and uses of credit funds of state banks and the statement of sources and uses of credit funds of financial institutions, extra – budgetary fiscal deposits were separated from fiscal deposits since March, 1998. In the statement of sources and uses of credit funds of banking institutions, extra – budgetary deposit and deposits by government agencies and organizations were transferred from fiscal deposits to other deposits; (ii) in the statements of sources and uses of credit funds of financial institutions, sources and uses of credit funds of state banks and sources and uses of credit funds of state – owned commercial banks, advance under letter of guarantee were transferred from other loans to other short – term loans since April, 1998; (iii) in the reporting form of Industrial and Commercial Bank of China, deposits frozen for new shares application were transferred from demand deposits to due to banks and other financial institutions since 1998.

- 1999　(i) In the statement of sources and uses of credit funds of financial institutions, security deposits for leases of finance corporations, trust and investment companies and financial leasing companies were included in total deposits; (ii) the non-performing assets of the Industrial and Commercial Bank of China, Bank of China, Construction Bank of China and State Development Bank were transferred to asset management companies at the end of 1999. The balances in the reporting forms of these institutions reflected the balances remaining after the NPLs transfer, while the amount in the changes within the year reflected the sum of actual movement in the balances and the NPLs transferred.

- 2000　(i) Some Urban credit cooperatives in Henan Province, Hubei Province and Jiangsu Province were renamed as rural credit cooperatives. For all the provinces, some of local cooperative foundations were merged into rural credit cooperatives since February, 2000. Such changes led to large changes of data on rural credit cooperatives; (ii) as of January 1, 2000, the Industrial and Commercial Bank of China reclassified security clearing fund, which was formerly under savings deposits, into deposits by security companies, a sub-item of due to banks and other financial institutions; (iii) the transfer of non – performing assets in the Industrial and Commercial Bank of China, Agricultural Bank of China, Bank of China, China Construction Bank and State Development Bank continued. The balances in the reporting forms of these institutions were the balances after the NPLs transfer, while the amount in the changes within the year reflected the sum of actual movement in the balances and NPLs transferred.

● 2001 (i) Bank of Communications and CITIC Industrial Bank were reclassified from state banks to other commercial banks, with their data being adjusted and classified accordingly; (ii) discount was transferred out of short – term loans into the newly established paper financing; (iii) total advances were transferred out of short – term loans into total advances, which were newly established; (iv) over – due loans were abolished as a separate item, and reclassified into the sub – item under total loans.

● 2002 (i) Since this year, data of foreign – funded banks were included in the financial statistical framework; (ii) with many trust and investment companies closed, data in related forms changed a lot; (iii) in the statement of sources and uses of credit funds of financial institutions and the statement of sources and uses of credit funds of state banks, the sum of discount and rediscount of financial institutions and rediscount of the People's Bank of China, were included in paper financing, a sub – item under total loans; (iv) China Construction Bank and Industrial and Commercial Bank of China reformed their accounting systems, leading to large variances between the data on December 31, 2001 and on January 1, 2002; (v) given the market exit of some trust and investment companies, balances in the related statements of sources and uses of credit funds did not include the liquidated trust and investment companies, while the changes within the year included the liquidated institutions and were, therefore, comparable with previous years.

● 2003 (i) Stock collateralized loans to securities firms were transferred from other short – term loans to placements with banks and other financial institutions, which resulted in variances in total loans and inter – bank transactions in the statement of sources and uses of credit funds of various financial institutions; (ii) financial bonds in various aggregate statements of sources and uses of credit funds were adjusted, and the balances reflected netted value of financial bonds cross – held by consolidated institutions; (iii) the consolidation of policy designated loans on housing held by the Industrial and Commercial Bank of China and China Construction Bank led to changes in total loans and inter – bank transactions; (iv) since this year, detailed accounting items of investments were adopted by rural credit cooperatives, and the balance of investments on financial bonds issued by other financial institutions was netted in the statement of sources and uses of credit funds of financial institutions.

● 2004 (i) Discount and paper financing only included commercial paper discounted by financial institutions and outright purchase of discounted commercial paper from other financial institutions, and rediscount was no longer deducted; (ii) in the statements of sources and uses of credit funds of state – owned commercial banks, policy banks and rural credit cooperatives, time deposits of postal savings bureau was included in total deposits; (iii) in the statement of sources and uses of credit funds of state banks and the statement of sources and uses of credit funds of financial institutions , extra – budgetary fiscal deposits were included in fiscal deposits under total deposits, while for other institutions, they were no longer included in total deposits, but in agency fiscal deposits; (iv) China Construction Bank transferred budgetary appropriation of capital construction funds for funding geological explorations from extra – budgetary deposits to demand deposits by enterprises, and transferred loans for land reserve from working capital loans of real estate development firms to other real estate development loans, leading to changes in loans to construction sector and in capital construction loans; (v) the non-performing loans in Bank of China, China Construction Bank and Bank of Communication were transferred in June.

● 2005　(i) Deposits by housing provident funds, which were previously included in other long - term liabilities, were removed, and related data were included in other deposits; (ii) the non - performing loans in the Industrial and Commercial Bank of China were transferred in May and June; (iii) Fifty - three rural credit cooperatives were restructured into rural commercial banks or rural cooperative banks. Such changes have led to the changes of relative data.

3. Notes on Major Statistical Indicators

● Total Deposits: Important sources of credit funds for financial institutions, including deposits by enterprises, fiscal deposits, savings deposits, deposits by agricultural sector, other deposits etc.

● Deposits by Enterprises: Deposits with financial institutions by enterprises regardless of their ownership and industries, further divided into demand deposits and time deposits.

● Fiscal Deposits: Deposits held by government sector with the People's Bank of China and other financial institutions acting as agents. From 1998 to 2003, fiscal deposits only refer to all kinds of budgetary fiscal deposits; but before 1998 and in 2004 and 2005, fiscal deposits also include extra - budgetary fiscal deposits.

● Savings Deposits: Deposits in financial institutions by urban and rural individuals, further divided into demand deposits and time deposits.

● Rural Deposits/Deposits by Agricultural Sector: Deposits by rural collectives, township & village enterprises and rural households. Such deposits are used for providing working capital or are part of accumulated funds from operations. The majority of such deposits are deposits by agricultural enterprises with Agricultural Bank of China and rural credit cooperatives. These deposits were referred as rural deposits before 1994 and renamed as deposits by agricultural sector since then, without any change in its definition.

● Currency in Circulation: The sum of notes and coins issued by the People's Bank of China, excluding the amount of cash in vault held by financial institutions.

● Total Loans: Important uses of credit funds by financial institutions, including short - term loans, medium and long - term loans, trust loans, paper financing and total advances.

● Short - term Loans: Working capital loans issued by financial institutions with maturity equal to or less than one year, including loans industrial sector, loans to commercial sector, loans to construction sector, loans to agricultural sector, loans to township & village enterprises, loans to privately - run enterprises and self - employed business, other short - term loans, etc.

In time series of major indicators, all loans extended by state banks before 1978 were classified as short - term loans. After 1978, working capital loans were classified as short - term loans and fix - asset loans were categorised as medium and long - term loans.

● Medium and Long - term Loans: Loans issued by financial institutions with maturity longer than one year, for capital construction, and technology upgrading, etc, including capital construction loans, housing development loans, technical improvement loans and other medium and long – term loans.

From 1998 to 2005, medium – term working capital loans were included in other medium and long – term loans, which was the sub – item of medium and long – term loans.

- Paper Financing: Funds used for discounting and re-discounting of commercial papers.

Prior to 2001, paper financing was included in other short – term loans; as of 2001, paper financing became a separate item in total loans.

- Securities and Investments: Securities held by financial institutions for interest earning, including proprietary investments, trust investments and long – term investments, etc.

Prior to 1994, the data of securities and investments was the aggregate of the items securities and investments.

4. Institutional Coverage for Aggregated Data

- Financial Institutions: Including state banks, other commercial banks, city commercial banks, rural commercial banks, urban credit cooperatives, rural credit cooperatives, rural cooperative banks, foreign – funded banks, finance companies, trust and investment companies and financial leasing companies.

- State Banks: Including the People's Bank of China, policy banks, state – owned commercial banks and Postal Savings Bureau.

- Policy Banks: Including China Development Bank, The Export – Import Bank of China and the Agricultural Development Bank of China.

- State – owned Commercial Banks: Including the Industrial and Commercial Bank of China, Agricultural Bank of China, Bank of China and China Construction Bank.

- Other Commercial Banks: Including Bank of Communications, China CITIC Bank, China Everbright Bank, Huaxia Bank, Guangdong Development Bank, Shenzhen Development Bank, China Merchants Bank, Shanghai Pudong Development Bank, Industrial Bank, China Minsheng Banking Corporation, Evergrowing Bank, China Zheshang Bank.

Please refer to compilation notes on financial statistics for detailed information on institutions covered and when data of each institution were included.

5. Other Matters

Where the changes were due to implementation of new accounting concepts, and if the data could not be presented on adjusted regulations on a comparable basis, the rate of change over the year was substituted by a symbol "—", indicating that the data were incomparable.

一、人民币信贷收支主要指标时间序列表

Time Series of Major Indicators in Sources and Uses of Credit Funds (RMB)

（一）金融机构人民币信贷收支主要指标时间序列表（1949—1989 年年度时序、1990—2005 年月度时序）

Time Series of Major Indicators in Sources and Uses of Credit Funds of Financial Institutions（RMB）（Annual Series from 1949 to 1989，Monthly Series from 1990 to 2005）

金融机构人民币信贷收支主要指标时间序列表

Time Series of Major Indicators in Sources and Uses of Credit Funds of Financial Institutions（RMB）

年份 Year	各项存款 Total Deposits	企业存款 Deposits by Enterprises	财政存款 Fiscal Deposits	城镇储蓄存款 Urban Savings Deposits	农户储蓄存款 Savings Deposits by Rural Households	农村存款 Rural Deposits	流通中货币 Currency in Circulation
期末余额（亿元） Balance（100 Million Yuan）							
1949	1.49						
1950	26.45						
1951	65.98						
1952	93.30	33.00	19.50	8.60			27.50
1953	107.70	31.80	33.30	12.20	0.10	1.10	39.40
1954	154.10	34.40	61.30	14.30	1.60	4.30	41.20
1955	141.90	32.40	36.10	16.90	3.00	3.30	40.30
1956	136.80	45.00	16.40	22.40	4.30	6.40	57.30
1957	168.30	39.70	20.60	27.90	7.30	13.40	52.80
1958	304.00	77.60	49.90	35.10	20.10	16.40	67.80
1959	407.50	70.00	82.10	47.30	21.00	36.00	75.10
1960	468.50	86.00	146.60	51.10	15.20	43.40	95.90
1961	491.10	116.10	174.60	39.20	16.20	42.40	125.70
1962	411.80	152.30	79.90	31.40	9.80	24.00	106.50

续表
Continued

年 份 Year	各项存款 Total Deposits	企业存款 Deposits by Enterprises	财政存款 Fiscal Deposits	城镇储蓄存款 Urban Savings Deposits	农户储蓄存款 Savings Deposits by Rural Households	农村存款 Rural Deposits	流通中货币 Currency in Circulation
比上期增减额（亿元） Changes Compared with Previous Period (100 Million Yuan)							
1949							
1950	24.96						
1951	39.53						
1952	27.32						
1953	14.40	-1.20	13.80	3.60	0.10	1.10	11.90
1954	46.40	2.60	28.00	2.10	1.50	3.20	1.80
1955	-12.20	-2.00	-25.20	2.60	1.40	-1.00	-0.90
1956	-5.10	12.60	-19.70	5.50	1.30	3.10	17.00
1957	31.50	-5.30	4.20	5.50	3.00	7.00	-4.50
1958	135.70	37.90	29.30	7.20	12.80	3.00	15.00
1959	103.50	-7.60	32.20	12.20	0.90	19.60	7.30
1960	61.00	16.00	64.50	3.80	-5.80	7.40	20.80
1961	22.60	30.10	28.00	-11.90	1.00	-1.00	29.80
1962	-79.30	36.20	-94.70	-7.80	-6.40	-18.40	-19.20
比去年同期增长（%） Increase Rate Year-on-year (%)							
1949							
1950	1675.17						
1951	149.45						
1952	41.41						
1953	15.43	-3.64	70.77	41.86			43.27
1954	43.08	8.18	84.08	17.21	1500.00	290.91	4.57
1955	-7.92	-5.81	-41.11	18.18	87.50	-23.26	-2.18
1956	-3.59	38.89	-54.57	32.54	43.33	93.94	42.18
1957	23.03	-11.78	25.61	24.55	69.77	109.38	-7.85
1958	80.63	95.47	142.23	25.81	175.34	22.39	28.41
1959	34.05	-9.79	64.53	34.76	4.48	119.51	10.77
1960	14.97	22.86	78.56	8.03	-27.62	20.56	27.70
1961	4.82	35.00	19.10	-23.29	6.58	-2.30	31.07
1962	-16.15	31.18	-54.24	-19.90	-39.51	-43.40	-15.27

金融机构人民币信贷收支主要指标时间序列表
Time Series of Major Indicators in Sources and Uses of Credit Funds of Financial Institutions（RMB）

年份 Year	各项贷款 Total Loans	工业生产企业贷款 Loans to Industrial Production Enterprises	物资供销企业贷款 Loans to Material Supply and Sale Enterprises	商业企业贷款 Loans to Commercial Enterprises	建筑企业贷款 Loans to Construction Enterprises	农业贷款 Loans to Agricultural Sector	固定资产贷款 Fixed Asset Loans
	期末余额（亿元） Balance（100 Million Yuan）						
1949	1.04						
1950	18.64						
1951	65.77						
1952	108.00	9.50		93.80		4.20	
1953	134.80	13.00		114.30		6.80	
1954	185.80	14.60		161.80		8.80	
1955	206.60	18.10		175.30		12.40	
1956	239.20	27.90		172.60		35.50	
1957	283.00	30.30		216.40		33.20	
1958	498.15	89.20		342.40		63.85	
1959	814.70	254.80		495.30		61.10	
1960	983.90	362.80	30.80	506.30		77.50	
1961	814.80	167.10	25.30	537.50		75.00	
1962	691.70	119.80	27.00	459.00		76.30	
	比上期增减额（亿元） Changes Compared with Previous Period（100 Million Yuan）						
1949							
1950	17.60						
1951	47.13						
1952	42.23						
1953	26.80	3.50		20.50		2.60	
1954	51.00	1.60		47.50		2.00	
1955	20.80	3.50		13.50		3.60	
1956	32.60	9.80		-2.70		23.10	
1957	43.80	2.40		43.80		-2.30	
1958	215.15	58.90		126.00		30.65	
1959	316.55	165.60		152.90		-2.75	
1960	169.20	108.00	30.80	11.00		16.40	
1961	-169.10	-195.70	-5.50	31.20		-2.50	
1962	-123.10	-47.30	1.70	-78.50		1.30	
	比去年同期增长（%） Increase Rate Year-on-year（%）						
1949							
1950	1692.31						
1951	252.84						
1952	64.21						
1953	24.81	36.84		21.86		61.90	
1954	37.83	12.31		41.56		29.41	
1955	11.19	23.97		8.34		40.91	
1956	15.78	54.14		-1.54		186.29	
1957	18.31	8.60		25.38		-6.48	
1958	76.02	194.39		58.23		92.32	
1959	63.55	185.65		44.66		-4.31	
1960	20.77	42.39		2.22		26.84	
1961	-17.19	-53.94	-17.86	6.16		-3.23	
1962	-15.11	-28.31	6.72	-14.60		1.73	

金融机构人民币信贷收支主要指标时间序列表

Time Series of Major Indicators in Sources and Uses of Credit Funds of Financial Institutions (RMB)

年份 Year	各项存款 Total Deposits	企业存款 Deposits by Enterprises	财政存款 Fiscal Deposits	城镇储蓄存款 Urban Savings Deposits	农户储蓄存款 Savings Deposits by Rural Households	农村存款 Rural Deposits	流通中货币 Currency in Circulation
	期末余额（亿元） Balance (100 Million Yuan)						
1963	414.90	176.80	67.30	35.60	10.10	25.40	89.90
1964	439.34	156.10	84.80	44.80	10.70	34.74	80.00
1965	481.65	181.90	74.20	52.30	12.90	37.85	90.80
1966	554.75	185.00	95.80	57.70	14.60	49.45	108.50
1967	582.46	199.40	67.30	59.80	14.00	62.66	121.90
1968	621.62	211.80	92.30	62.30	16.00	63.82	134.10
1969	641.19	215.50	119.60	61.00	14.90	62.99	137.10
1970	702.40	226.10	176.80	64.50	15.00	66.40	123.60
1971	770.24	226.80	188.90	73.30	17.00	79.14	136.20
1972	781.60	239.00	172.60	85.10	20.10	76.60	151.20
1973	869.05	279.00	160.80	94.10	27.10	84.25	166.10
1974	903.09	324.80	137.30	105.80	30.60	98.39	176.60
1975	982.50	362.70	140.20	114.60	35.10	109.20	182.60
1976	993.16	389.80	97.90	122.20	36.90	114.46	204.00
1977	1080.44	384.70	151.90	135.10	46.50	113.34	195.40
	比上期增减额（亿元） Changes Compared with Previous Period (100 Million Yuan)						
1963	3.10	24.50	-12.60	4.20	0.30	1.40	-16.60
1964	24.44	-20.70	17.50	9.20	0.60	9.34	-9.90
1965	42.31	25.80	-10.60	7.50	2.20	3.11	10.80
1966	73.10	3.10	21.60	5.40	1.70	11.60	17.70
1967	27.71	14.40	-28.50	2.10	-0.60	13.21	13.40
1968	39.16	12.40	25.00	2.50	2.00	1.16	12.20
1969	19.57	3.70	27.30	-1.30	-1.10	-0.83	3.00
1970	61.21	10.60	57.20	3.50	0.10	3.41	-13.50
1971	67.84	0.70	12.10	8.80	2.00	12.74	12.60
1972	11.36	12.20	-16.30	11.80	3.10	-2.54	15.00
1973	87.45	40.00	-11.80	9.00	7.00	7.65	14.90
1974	34.04	45.80	-23.50	11.70	3.50	14.14	10.50
1975	79.41	37.90	2.90	8.80	4.50	10.81	6.00
1976	10.66	27.10	-42.30	7.60	1.80	5.26	21.40
1977	87.28	-5.10	54.00	12.90	9.60	-1.12	-8.60
	比去年同期增长（%） Increase Rate Year-on-year (%)						
1963	0.75	16.09	-15.77	13.38	3.06	5.83	-15.59
1964	5.89	-11.71	26.00	25.84	5.94	36.77	-11.01
1965	9.63	16.53	-12.50	16.74	20.56	8.95	13.50
1966	15.18	1.70	29.11	10.33	13.18	30.65	19.49
1967	5.00	7.78	-29.75	3.64	-4.11	26.71	12.35
1968	6.72	6.22	37.15	4.18	14.29	1.85	10.01
1969	3.15	1.75	29.58	-2.09	-6.88	-1.30	2.24
1970	9.55	4.92	47.83	5.74	0.67	5.41	-9.85
1971	9.66	0.31	6.84	13.64	13.33	19.19	10.19
1972	1.47	5.38	-8.63	16.10	18.24	-3.21	11.01
1973	11.19	16.74	-6.84	10.58	34.83	9.99	9.85
1974	3.92	16.42	-14.61	12.43	12.92	16.78	6.32
1975	8.79	11.67	2.11	8.32	14.71	10.99	3.40
1976	1.08	7.47	-30.17	6.63	5.13	4.82	11.72
1977	8.79	-1.31	55.16	10.56	26.02	-0.98	-4.22

金融机构人民币信贷收支主要指标时间序列表

Time Series of Major Indicators in Sources and Uses of Credit Funds of Financial Institutions（RMB）

年 份 Year	各项贷款 Total Loans	工业生产企业贷款 Loans to Industrial Production Enterprises	物资供销企业贷款 Loans to Material Supply and Sale Enterprises	商业企业贷款 Loans to Commercial Enterprises	建筑企业贷款 Loans to Construction Enterprises	农业贷款 Loans to Agricultural Sector	固定资产贷款 Fixed Asset Loans
	期末余额（亿元） Balance（100 Million Yuan）						
1963	576.50	76.90	31.50	384.40		79.30	
1964	588.75	76.00	31.60	396.60		81.35	
1965	656.65	93.20	41.30	431.30		87.45	
1966	766.85	122.30	52.20	498.60		88.65	
1967	806.95	173.60	51.80	483.00		91.75	
1968	902.55	213.10	62.50	525.00		93.45	
1969	959.05	234.00	69.10	547.50		97.55	
1970	1047.95	241.40	67.40	626.60		99.65	
1971	1130.76	251.90	126.00	667.20		68.46	
1972	1163.76	224.30	151.30	693.80		74.76	
1973	1287.06	231.10	179.60	776.90		76.86	
1974	1373.26	266.70	179.60	815.00		83.76	
1975	1486.98	293.50	179.10	884.70		96.68	
1976	1574.14	329.40	173.30	908.00		122.74	
1977	1699.54	334.20	187.90	996.90		134.54	
	比上期增减额（亿元） Changes Compared with Previous Period（100 Million Yuan）						
1963	-115.20	-42.90	4.50	-74.60		3.00	
1964	12.25	-0.90	0.10	12.20		2.05	
1965	67.90	17.20	9.70	34.70		6.10	
1966	110.20	29.10	10.90	67.30		1.20	
1967	40.10	51.30	-0.40	-15.60		3.10	
1968	95.60	39.50	10.70	42.00		1.70	
1969	56.50	20.90	6.60	22.50		4.10	
1970	88.90	7.40	-1.70	79.10		2.10	
1971	82.81	10.50	58.60	40.60		-31.19	
1972	33.00	-27.60	25.30	26.60		6.30	
1973	123.30	6.80	28.30	83.10		2.10	
1974	86.20	35.60	0.00	38.10		6.90	
1975	113.72	26.80	-0.50	69.70		12.92	
1976	87.16	35.90	-5.80	23.30		26.06	
1977	125.40	4.80	14.60	88.90		11.80	
	比去年同期增长（%） Increase Rate Year-on-year（%）						
1963	-16.65	-35.81	16.67	-16.25		3.93	
1964	2.12	-1.17	0.32	3.17		2.59	
1965	11.53	22.63	30.70	8.75		7.50	
1966	16.78	31.22	26.39	15.60		1.37	
1967	5.23	41.95	-0.77	-3.13		3.50	
1968	11.85	22.75	20.66	8.70		1.85	
1969	6.26	9.81	10.56	4.29		4.39	
1970	9.27	3.16	-2.46	14.45		2.15	
1971	7.90	4.35	86.94	6.48		-31.30	
1972	2.92	-10.96	20.08	3.99		9.20	
1973	10.59	3.03	18.70	11.98		2.81	
1974	6.70	15.40	0.00	4.90		8.98	
1975	8.28	10.05	-0.28	8.55		15.43	
1976	5.86	12.23	-3.24	2.63		26.95	
1977	7.97	1.46	8.42	9.79		9.61	

金融机构人民币信贷收支主要指标时间序列表
Time Series of Major Indicators in Sources and Uses of Credit Funds of Financial Institutions (RMB)

年 份 Year	各项存款 Total Deposits	企业存款 Deposits by Enterprises	财政存款 Fiscal Deposits	储蓄存款 Savings Deposits	农村存款 Rural Deposits	流通中货币 Currency in Circulation
	期末余额（亿元） Balance (100 Million Yuan)					
1978	1155.01	368.43	187.35	210.61	119.16	212.00
1979	1362.56	468.91	148.68	280.96	147.83	267.70
1980	1689.66	561.01	160.68	395.80	169.91	346.20
1981	2097.19	676.96	194.29	523.35	174.44	396.34
1982	2449.05	761.64	175.76	675.44	188.84	439.12
1983	2883.32	864.99	229.89	892.93	190.06	529.78
1984	3735.33	1251.79	210.93	1214.70	228.76	792.11
1985	4559.95	1735.89	404.10	1622.57	199.51	987.83
1986	5933.88	2265.94	348.61	2237.81	252.75	1218.36
1987	7392.40	2701.12	331.98	3083.41	289.60	1454.48
1988	8810.36	3010.26	294.10	3819.09	349.56	2134.03
1989	10709.57	3174.11	460.79	5184.46	331.37	2344.02
	比上期增减额（亿元） Changes Compared with Previous Period (100 Million Yuan)					
1978	74.57	-16.27	35.45	29.01	5.82	16.60
1979	207.55	100.48	-38.67	70.35	28.67	55.70
1980	327.10	92.10	12.00	114.84	22.08	78.50
1981	407.53	115.95	33.61	127.55	4.53	50.14
1982	351.86	84.68	-18.53	152.09	14.40	42.78
1983	434.27	103.35	54.13	217.49	1.22	90.66
1984	852.01	386.80	-18.96	321.77	38.70	262.33
1985	824.62	484.10	193.17	407.87	-29.25	195.72
1986	1373.93	530.05	-55.49	615.24	53.24	230.53
1987	1458.52	435.18	-16.63	845.60	36.85	236.12
1988	1417.96	309.14	-37.88	735.68	59.96	679.55
1989	1899.21	163.85	166.69	1365.37	-18.19	209.99
	比去年同期增长（%） Increase Rate Year-on-year (%)					
1978	6.90	-4.23	23.34	15.97	5.13	8.50
1979	17.97	27.27	-20.64	33.40	24.06	26.27
1980	24.01	19.64	8.07	40.87	14.94	29.32
1981	24.12	20.67	20.92	32.23	2.67	14.48
1982	16.78	12.51	-9.54	29.06	8.25	10.79
1983	17.73	13.57	30.80	32.20	0.65	20.65
1984	29.55	44.72	-8.25	36.04	20.36	49.52
1985	22.08	38.67	91.58	33.58	-12.79	24.71
1986	30.13	30.53	-13.73	37.92	26.69	23.34
1987	24.58	19.21	-4.77	37.79	14.58	19.38
1988	19.18	11.44	-11.41	23.86	20.70	46.72
1989	21.56	5.44	56.68	35.75	-5.20	9.84

金融机构人民币信贷收支主要指标时间序列表

Time Series of Major Indicators in Sources and Uses of Credit Funds of Financial Institutions（RMB）

年份 Year	各项贷款 Total Loans	流动资金贷款 Working Capital Loans				农业贷款 Loans to Agricultural Sector	固定资产贷款 Fixed Asset Loans			
			工业贷款 Loans to Industrial Sector	商业贷款 Loans to Commercial Sector	建筑业贷款 Loans to Construction Sector			基本建设贷款 Capital Construction Loans	技术改造贷款 Technical Improvement Loans	其他固定资产贷款 Other Fixed Asset Loans
期末余额（亿元） Balance（100 Million Yuan）										
1978	1890.42	1734.48	616.83	1117.65		155.94				
1979	2082.47	1902.89	670.64	1232.25		179.58				
1980	2478.08	2180.90	743.76	1437.14		249.67	47.51		47.51	
1981	2853.29	2488.56	839.13	1639.21		280.99	83.74		83.74	
1982	3162.70	2687.84	866.58	1806.60		322.88	151.98	13.36	138.62	
1983	3566.56	2995.56	973.53	2003.11		378.91	192.09	28.26	163.83	
1984	4746.80	3763.04	1316.88	2346.53		689.73	294.03	52.98	229.37	11.68
1985	6198.38	4554.19	1609.96	2723.49	93.56	775.57	686.25	213.14	417.55	55.56
1986	8142.72	5650.99	2232.34	3188.14	132.06	1095.60	975.97	297.89	585.87	92.21
1987	9814.09	6669.55	2639.84	3632.30	170.56	1427.70	1221.61	418.84	696.22	106.55
1988	11964.25	8026.14	3163.42	4264.98	252.64	1277.59	1558.20	501.17	892.93	164.10
1989	14248.81	10178.55	3888.14	5010.55	283.69	984.19	1780.18	581.42	1003.11	195.65
比上期增减额（亿元） Changes Compared with Previous Period（100 Million Yuan）										
1978	190.88	—	—	—		—				
1979	192.05	168.41	53.81	114.60		23.64				
1980	395.61	278.01	73.12	204.89		70.09	47.51		47.51	
1981	375.21	307.66	95.37	202.07		31.32	36.23		36.23	
1982	309.41	199.28	27.45	167.39		41.89	68.24	13.36	54.88	
1983	403.86	307.72	106.95	196.51		56.03	40.11	14.90	25.21	
1984	1180.24	767.48	343.35	343.42		310.82	101.94	24.72	65.54	11.68
1985	1451.58	791.15	293.08	376.96	93.56	85.84	392.22	160.16	188.18	43.88
1986	1944.34	1194.63	622.38	464.65	38.50	320.03	289.72	84.75	168.32	36.65
1987	1671.37	1018.56	407.50	444.16	38.50	332.10	245.64	120.95	110.35	14.34
1988	2150.16	1356.59	523.58	632.68	82.08	-150.11	336.59	82.33	196.71	57.55
1989	2284.56	2152.41	724.72	745.57	31.05	-293.40	221.98	80.25	110.18	31.55
比去年同期增长（%） Increase Rate Year-on-year（%）										
1978	11.23	—	—	—		—				
1979	10.16	9.71	8.72	10.25		15.16				
1980	19.00	14.61	10.90	16.63		39.03				
1981	15.14	14.11	12.82	14.06		12.54	76.26		76.26	
1982	10.84	8.01	3.27	10.21		14.91	81.49		65.54	
1983	12.77	11.45	12.34	10.88		17.35	26.39	111.53	18.19	
1984	33.09	25.62	35.27	17.14		82.03	53.07	87.47	40.00	
1985	30.58	21.02	22.26	16.06		12.45	133.95	302.30	82.04	375.68
1986	31.37	26.23	38.66	17.06	41.15	41.26	42.22	39.76	40.31	65.96
1987	20.53	18.02	18.25	13.93	29.15	30.31	25.17	40.60	18.84	15.55
1988	21.91	20.34	19.83	17.42	48.12	-10.51	27.55	19.66	28.25	54.01
1989	19.09	26.82	22.91	17.48	12.29	-22.97	14.25	16.01	12.34	19.23

金融机构人民币信贷收支主要指标时间序列表

Time Series of Major Indicators in Sources and Uses of Credit Funds of Financial Institutions (RMB)

年 月 Year Month		各项存款 Total Deposits	企业存款 Deposits by Enterprises	财政存款 Fiscal Deposits	储蓄存款 Savings Deposits	活期储蓄 Demand Deposits	定期储蓄 Time Deposits	农村存款 Rural Deposits	流通中货币 Currency in Circulation
		期末余额（亿元） Balance (100 Million Yuan)							
1990	1	10744.06	3166.99	428.03	5350.83			277.32	2624.60
	2	11060.62	3188.73	424.03	5659.38			272.20	2287.20
	3	11435.60	3346.71	431.00	5823.97			284.23	2154.64
	4	11763.33	3460.42	476.98	5937.67			288.83	2129.69
	5	12027.52	3542.41	447.24	6090.24			297.80	2090.05
	6	12262.48	3565.05	430.46	6285.29			306.73	2096.20
	7	12616.35	3650.10	458.50	6484.95			307.31	2132.06
	8	12889.15	3753.92	448.94	6621.77			317.85	2178.77
	9	13130.83	3887.84	424.40	6721.30			327.73	2300.44
	10	13418.11	3884.17	505.46	6880.33			338.19	2383.23
	11	13693.57	4006.19	475.54	7012.76			359.81	2490.03
	12	13942.94	4063.90	427.11	7119.56			393.58	2644.87
		比上期增减额（亿元） Changes Compared with Previous Period (100 Million Yuan)							
1990	1	34.49	-7.12	-32.76	166.37			-54.05	280.58
	2	316.56	21.74	-4.00	308.55			-5.12	-337.40
	3	374.98	157.98	6.97	164.59			12.03	-132.56
	4	327.73	113.71	45.98	113.70			4.60	-24.95
	5	264.19	81.99	-29.74	152.57			8.97	-39.64
	6	234.96	22.64	-16.78	195.05			8.93	6.15
	7	353.87	85.05	28.04	199.66			0.58	35.86
	8	272.80	103.82	-9.56	136.82			10.54	46.71
	9	241.68	133.92	-24.54	99.53			9.88	121.67
	10	287.28	-3.67	81.06	159.03			10.46	82.79
	11	275.46	122.02	-29.92	132.43			21.62	106.80
	12	249.37	57.71	-48.43	106.80			33.77	154.84
		比去年同期增长（%） Increase Rate Year-on-year (%)							
1990	1	23.27	11.30	17.92	39.45			-8.76	6.91
	2	24.98	13.38	20.56	39.83			-1.32	1.42
	3	25.88	15.53	20.85	40.37			2.43	2.65
	4	26.44	15.65	25.03	39.93			1.81	2.95
	5	26.76	16.71	16.84	39.57			3.44	2.62
	6	29.31	20.68	27.36	40.21			7.91	0.73
	7	30.48	23.94	24.62	39.86			10.25	2.05
	8	31.01	26.14	23.84	39.26			13.70	4.73
	9	31.01	30.33	-4.37	38.75			18.01	10.47
	10	31.23	28.10	7.83	39.00			20.70	12.52
	11	30.38	26.75	2.84	38.39			22.17	13.13
	12	30.19	28.03	-7.31	37.33			18.77	12.83

金融机构人民币信贷收支主要指标时间序列表
Time Series of Major Indicators in Sources and Uses of Credit Funds of Financial Institutions（RMB）

年 月 Year Month	各项贷款 Total Loans	短期贷款 Short - term Loans				农业贷款 Loans to Agricultural Sector	中长期贷款 Medium and Long - term Loans				有价证券及投资 Securities and Investments
			工业贷款 Loans to Industrial Sector	商业贷款 Loans to Commercial Sector	建筑业贷款 Loans to Construction Sector			基本建设贷款 Capital Construction Loans	技术改造贷款 Technical Improvement Loans	其他中长期贷款 Other Medium and Long - term Loans	
期末余额（亿元） Balance（100 Million Yuan）											
1990 1	14247.48	10158.48	3967.40	4899.71	282.57	1009.76	1766.67	581.06	992.40	193.21	179.40
2	14275.06	10155.22	4005.93	4844.69	281.26	1040.39	1770.32	581.84	996.26	192.22	179.20
3	14600.62	10362.18	4153.30	4878.39	284.48	1125.18	1782.58	589.61	996.56	196.41	181.06
4	14806.56	10463.70	4221.51	4885.60	288.26	1186.33	1796.91	602.88	997.88	196.15	182.54
5	14956.50	10530.95	4268.55	4886.84	289.78	1229.78	1817.66	612.30	1005.55	199.81	183.44
6	15229.59	10715.43	4345.25	4969.12	293.90	1260.84	1850.72	630.19	1017.16	203.37	185.34
7	15390.95	10813.40	4396.61	5001.45	297.03	1285.06	1879.19	646.62	1028.07	204.50	192.91
8	15659.54	11007.92	4468.11	5100.46	298.61	1309.44	1909.78	664.64	1036.77	208.37	214.46
9	16177.19	11439.85	4686.90	5290.64	300.76	1329.45	1953.36	690.42	1051.22	211.72	225.64
10	16544.15	11757.02	4744.97	5529.96	302.70	1321.34	1999.19	714.43	1069.60	215.16	243.76
11	16909.86	12073.37	4838.61	5737.37	306.86	1291.87	2056.17	740.23	1096.77	219.17	253.42
12	17511.02	12480.42	4990.17	5966.59	316.77	1244.09	2214.89	818.29	1163.80	232.80	259.06
比上期增减额（亿元） Changes Compared with Previous Period（100 Million Yuan）											
1990 1	-1.33	-20.07	79.26	-110.84	-1.12	25.57	-13.51	-0.36	-10.71	-2.44	1.83
2	27.58	-3.26	38.53	-55.02	-1.31	30.63	3.65	0.78	3.86	-0.99	-0.20
3	325.56	206.96	147.37	33.70	3.22	84.79	12.26	7.77	0.30	4.19	1.86
4	205.94	101.52	68.21	7.21	3.78	61.15	14.33	13.27	1.32	-0.26	1.48
5	149.94	67.25	47.04	1.24	1.52	43.45	20.75	9.42	7.67	3.66	0.90
6	273.09	184.48	76.70	82.28	4.12	31.06	33.06	17.89	11.61	3.56	1.90
7	161.36	97.97	51.36	32.33	3.13	24.22	28.47	16.43	10.91	1.13	7.57
8	268.59	194.52	71.50	99.01	1.58	24.38	30.59	18.02	8.70	3.87	21.55
9	517.65	431.93	218.79	190.18	2.15	20.01	43.58	25.78	14.45	3.35	11.18
10	366.96	317.17	58.07	239.32	1.94	-8.11	45.83	24.01	18.38	3.44	18.12
11	365.71	316.35	93.64	207.41	4.16	-29.47	56.98	25.80	27.17	4.01	9.66
12	601.16	407.05	151.56	229.22	9.91	-47.78	158.72	78.06	67.03	13.63	5.64
比去年同期增长（%） Increase Rate Year - on - year（%）											
1990 1	17.37	18.59	25.44	15.10	11.94	17.65	14.03	16.46	12.24	16.22	6.12
2	17.78	18.83	26.26	14.89	11.25	19.27	14.62	16.43	13.04	17.61	6.00
3	18.93	20.15	28.85	15.32	12.07	20.83	15.30	18.30	13.15	17.70	4.23
4	19.42	20.43	28.57	15.65	12.19	21.92	15.57	19.86	13.28	14.77	4.52
5	20.00	20.99	28.95	16.20	11.50	23.56	15.98	20.96	13.16	15.89	5.36
6	20.91	21.81	29.65	16.96	12.01	25.13	17.41	23.50	14.26	15.71	6.49
7	21.17	22.03	29.95	17.13	13.00	25.80	18.04	24.81	14.97	13.83	10.86
8	22.33	23.42	30.93	18.93	12.28	26.60	18.76	26.53	14.93	15.33	23.22
9	24.07	25.57	33.79	20.66	12.77	28.22	19.84	29.51	15.25	14.62	29.19
10	24.50	25.59	32.36	21.61	12.56	28.92	21.49	32.33	16.17	16.34	38.93
11	23.65	24.34	29.90	20.87	13.21	28.87	21.40	33.86	15.14	16.46	44.75
12	22.89	22.61	28.34	19.08	11.66	26.41	24.42	40.74	16.02	18.99	45.89

金融机构人民币信贷收支主要指标时间序列表

Time Series of Major Indicators in Sources and Uses of Credit Funds of Financial Institutions（RMB）

年 月 Year Month		各项存款 Total Deposits	企业存款 Deposits by Enterprises	财政存款 Fiscal Deposits	储蓄存款 Savings Deposits	活期储蓄 Demand Deposits	定期储蓄 Time Deposits	农村存款 Rural Deposits	流通中货币 Currency in Circulation
		期末余额（亿元） Balance（100 Million Yuan）							
1991	1	14232.37	4184.36	427.47	7305.40			391.14	2836.70
	2	14662.74	4234.28	446.51	7670.86			347.83	2815.36
	3	15049.47	4393.28	446.43	7916.27			359.63	2585.61
	4	15446.87	4576.03	452.47	8063.81			370.28	2526.81
	5	15803.77	4740.41	463.77	8190.37			383.38	2486.85
	6	16003.45	4747.33	440.83	8368.32			392.00	2517.25
	7	16366.62	4849.17	450.39	8550.34			401.31	2581.10
	8	16732.16	5001.87	450.14	8672.80			419.14	2632.08
	9	17097.44	5182.97	475.87	8775.18			429.52	2730.03
	10	17497.00	5269.56	558.37	8939.28			447.85	2879.34
	11	17959.91	5438.99	592.20	9115.25			476.21	3002.58
	12	17972.84	5215.29	504.29	9244.84			506.82	3177.80
		比上期增减额（亿元） Changes Compared with Previous Period（100 Million Yuan）							
1991	1	289.43	120.46	0.36	185.84			-2.44	191.83
	2	430.37	49.92	19.04	365.46			-43.31	-21.34
	3	386.73	159.00	-0.08	245.41			11.80	-229.75
	4	397.40	182.75	6.04	147.54			10.65	-58.80
	5	356.90	164.38	11.30	126.56			13.10	-39.96
	6	199.68	6.92	-22.94	177.95			8.62	30.40
	7	363.17	101.84	9.56	182.02			9.31	63.85
	8	365.54	152.70	-0.25	122.46			17.83	50.98
	9	365.28	181.10	25.73	102.38			10.38	97.95
	10	399.56	86.59	82.50	164.10			18.33	149.31
	11	462.91	169.43	33.83	175.97			28.36	123.24
	12	12.93	-223.70	-87.91	129.59			30.61	175.22
		比去年同期增长（%） Increase Rate Year-on-year（%）							
1991	1	32.47	32.12	-0.13	36.53			41.04	8.08
	2	32.57	32.79	5.30	35.54			27.78	23.09
	3	31.60	31.27	3.58	35.93			26.53	20.00
	4	31.31	32.24	-5.14	35.81			28.20	18.65
	5	31.40	33.82	3.70	34.48			28.74	18.99
	6	30.51	33.16	2.41	33.14			27.80	20.09
	7	29.73	32.85	-1.77	31.85			30.59	21.06
	8	29.82	33.24	0.27	30.97			31.87	20.81
	9	30.21	33.31	12.13	30.56			31.06	18.67
	10	30.40	35.67	10.47	29.93			32.43	20.82
	11	31.16	35.76	24.53	29.98			32.35	20.58
	12	28.90	28.33	18.07	29.85			28.77	20.15

金融机构人民币信贷收支主要指标时间序列表
Time Series of Major Indicators in Sources and Uses of Credit Funds of Financial Institutions（RMB）

年 月 Year Month		各项贷款 Total Loans	短期贷款 Short-term Loans				农业贷款 Loans to Agricultural Sector	中长期贷款 Medium and Long-term Loans				有价证券及投资 Securities and Investments
				工业贷款 Loans to Industrial Sector	商业贷款 Loans to Commercial Sector	建筑业贷款 Loans to Construction Sector			基本建设贷款 Capital Construction Loans	技术改造贷款 Technical Improvement Loans	其他中长期贷款 Other Medium and Long-term Loans	
期末余额（亿元） Balance（100 Million Yuan）												
1991	1	17594.65	12486.49	5008.29	5930.19	317.37	1302.75	2219.81	822.43	1162.78	234.60	266.91
	2	17639.62	12465.04	5043.69	5855.01	320.02	1334.21	2238.30	830.34	1176.59	231.37	271.81
	3	17937.88	12609.50	5128.65	5864.20	329.51	1432.13	2267.91	850.54	1183.58	233.79	273.56
	4	18148.92	12673.47	5188.09	5825.40	338.48	1513.04	2305.64	876.38	1191.91	237.36	278.60
	5	18341.71	12757.86	5261.13	5806.72	341.68	1558.70	2342.18	895.95	1206.49	239.74	285.30
	6	18622.56	12940.80	5332.93	5889.30	341.23	1591.93	2382.11	914.98	1225.55	241.58	290.73
	7	18832.58	13066.75	5402.81	5920.83	48.27	1612.49	2420.99	936.69	1240.10	244.20	292.12
	8	19120.78	13234.38	5485.80	5978.84	349.48	1640.99	2481.32	970.95	1263.12	247.25	303.37
	9	19643.10	13527.87	5579.05	6155.40	349.15	1657.79	2715.72	1113.18	1351.87	250.68	323.35
	10	20063.35	13869.85	5647.67	6410.31	350.08	1643.63	2784.35	1151.30	1380.45	252.60	369.54
	11	20486.00	14246.76	5763.06	6657.04	351.57	1606.39	2858.46	1195.60	1407.28	255.59	415.76
	12	21116.40	14624.69	5916.78	6845.38	363.62	1562.37	3046.15	1259.11	1519.95	267.08	430.41
比上期增减额（亿元） Changes Compared with Previous Period（100 Million Yuan）												
1991	1	83.63	6.07	18.12	-36.40	0.60	58.66	4.92	4.14	-1.02	1.80	7.85
	2	44.97	-21.45	35.40	-75.18	2.65	31.46	18.49	7.91	13.81	-3.23	4.90
	3	298.26	144.46	84.96	9.19	9.49	97.92	29.61	20.20	6.99	2.42	1.75
	4	211.04	63.97	59.44	-38.80	8.97	80.91	37.73	25.84	8.33	3.57	5.04
	5	192.79	84.39	73.04	-18.68	3.20	45.66	36.54	19.57	14.58	2.38	6.70
	6	280.85	182.94	71.80	82.58	-0.45	33.23	39.93	19.03	19.06	1.84	5.43
	7	210.02	125.95	69.88	31.53	7.04	20.56	38.88	21.71	14.55	2.62	1.39
	8	288.20	167.63	82.99	58.01	1.21	28.50	60.33	34.26	23.02	3.05	11.25
	9	522.32	293.49	93.25	176.56	-0.33	16.80	234.40	142.23	88.75	3.43	19.98
	10	420.25	341.98	68.62	254.91	0.93	-14.16	68.63	38.12	28.58	1.92	46.19
	11	422.65	376.91	115.39	246.73	1.49	-37.24	74.11	44.30	26.83	2.99	46.22
	12	630.40	377.93	153.72	188.34	12.05	-44.02	187.69	63.51	112.67	11.49	14.65
比去年同期增长（%） Increase Rate Year-on-year（%）												
1991	1	23.49	22.92	26.24	21.03	12.32	29.02	25.65	41.54	17.17	21.42	48.78
	2	23.57	22.75	25.91	20.85	13.78	28.24	26.43	42.71	18.10	20.37	51.68
	3	22.86	21.69	23.48	20.21	15.83	27.28	27.23	44.25	18.77	19.03	51.09
	4	22.57	21.12	22.90	19.24	17.42	27.54	28.31	45.37	19.44	21.01	52.62
	5	22.63	21.15	23.25	18.82	17.91	26.75	28.86	46.33	19.98	19.98	55.53
	6	22.28	20.77	22.73	18.52	16.10	26.26	28.71	45.19	20.49	18.79	56.86
	7	22.36	20.84	22.89	18.38	17.25	25.48	28.83	44.86	20.62	19.41	51.43
	8	22.10	20.23	22.78	17.22	17.04	25.32	29.93	46.09	21.83	18.66	41.46
	9	21.42	18.25	19.03	16.35	16.09	24.70	39.03	61.23	28.60	18.40	43.30
	10	21.27	17.97	19.02	15.92	15.65	24.39	39.27	61.15	29.06	17.40	51.60
	11	21.15	18.00	19.11	16.03	14.57	24.35	39.02	61.52	28.31	16.62	64.06
	12	20.59	17.18	18.57	14.73	14.79	25.58	37.53	53.87	30.60	14.73	66.14

金融机构人民币信贷收支主要指标时间序列表

Time Series of Major Indicators in Sources and Uses of Credit Funds of Financial Institutions（RMB）

年　月 Year Month		各项存款 Total Deposits	企业存款 Deposits by Enterprises	财政存款 Fiscal Deposits	储蓄存款 Savings Deposits	活期储蓄 Demand Deposits	定期储蓄 Time Deposits	农村存款 Rural Deposits	流通中货币 Currency in Circulation
		期末余额（亿元）Balance（100 Million Yuan）							
1992	1	18139.14	5180.95	594.65	9418.61			609.58	3824.24
	2	18818.67	5359.20	584.60	9928.62			590.49	3274.89
	3	19343.39	5602.05	627.19	10109.80			622.80	3117.18
	4	19993.72	5933.27	688.45	10241.26			650.54	3121.20
	5	20552.78	6211.00	690.38	10409.28			687.47	3111.18
	6	20954.12	6397.68	584.32	10611.09			725.84	3155.92
	7	21576.39	6714.10	540.27	10753.17			767.25	3278.63
	8	22168.30	6968.35	635.54	10865.21			815.83	3387.53
	9	22097.78	6848.48	487.41	11039.17			835.79	3559.38
	10	22555.59	7084.73	425.39	11211.73			873.34	3732.59
	11	22839.59	7202.88	363.30	11357.62			908.19	3989.10
	12	23143.81	7074.94	250.16	11757.28			948.84	4336.00
		比上期增减额（亿元）Changes Compared with Previous Period（100 Million Yuan）							
1992	1	166.30	-34.34	90.36	173.77			102.76	646.44
	2	679.53	178.25	-10.05	510.01			-19.09	-549.35
	3	524.72	242.85	42.59	181.18			32.31	-157.71
	4	650.33	331.22	61.26	131.46			27.74	4.02
	5	559.06	277.73	1.93	168.02			36.93	-10.02
	6	401.34	186.68	-106.06	201.81			38.37	44.74
	7	622.27	316.42	-44.05	142.08			41.41	122.71
	8	591.91	254.25	95.27	112.04			48.58	108.90
	9	-70.52	-119.87	-148.13	173.96			19.96	171.85
	10	457.81	236.25	-62.02	172.56			37.55	173.21
	11	284.00	118.15	-62.09	145.89			34.85	256.51
	12	304.22	-127.94	-113.14	399.66			40.65	346.90
		比去年同期增长（%）Increase Rate Year-on-year（%）							
1992	1	27.45	23.82	39.11	28.93			55.85	34.81
	2	28.34	26.57	30.93	29.43			69.76	16.32
	3	28.53	27.51	40.49	27.71			73.18	20.56
	4	29.44	29.66	52.15	27.00			75.69	23.52
	5	30.05	31.02	48.86	27.09			79.32	25.11
	6	30.94	34.76	32.55	26.80			85.16	25.37
	7	31.83	38.46	19.96	25.76			91.19	27.02
	8	32.49	39.31	41.19	25.28			94.64	28.70
	9	29.25	32.13	2.43	25.80			94.59	30.38
	10	28.91	34.45	-23.82	25.42			95.01	29.63
	11	27.17	32.43	-38.65	24.60			90.71	32.86
	12	28.77	35.66	-50.39	27.18			87.21	36.45

金融机构人民币信贷收支主要指标时间序列表

Time Series of Major Indicators in Sources and Uses of Credit Funds of Financial Institutions（RMB）

年 月 Year Month		各项贷款 Total Loans	短期贷款 Short－term Loans	工业贷款 Loans to Industrial Sector	商业贷款 Loans to Commercial Sector	建筑业贷款 Loans to Construction Sector	农业贷款 Loans to Agricultural Sector	中长期贷款 Medium and Long－term Loans	基本建设贷款 Capital Construction Loans	技术改造贷款 Technical Improvement Loans	其他中长期贷款 Other Medium and Long－term Loans	有价证券及投资 Securities and Investments
期末余额（亿元） Balance（100 Million Yuan）												
1992	1	21187.65	14646.50	5889.32	6893.48	366.86	1602.01	3032.22	1262.36	1505.49	264.37	440.57
	2	21278.93	14688.27	5947.53	6844.91	365.33	1647.07	3040.87	1270.82	1506.15	263.90	444.15
	3	21691.18	14908.68	6036.75	6896.32	376.62	1768.52	3076.66	1291.11	1519.52	266.03	443.45
	4	22158.47	15072.33	6122.34	6908.34	392.13	1862.02	3221.39	1373.97	1575.26	272.16	471.06
	5	22494.21	15223.33	6206.81	6915.76	404.98	1920.05	3294.47	1412.04	1607.03	275.40	501.80
	6	22989.77	15484.96	6276.00	7048.33	414.40	1957.86	3371.03	1442.88	1647.97	280.17	534.17
	7	23404.12	15798.95	6413.10	7159.69	433.72	2000.20	3438.86	1478.23	1677.95	282.67	583.12
	8	23814.00	16029.19	6487.94	7269.88	439.72	2041.22	3494.36	1504.30	1703.62	286.43	616.59
	9	23999.21	16093.29	6485.07	7327.39	425.75	2055.54	3572.54	1544.14	1736.88	291.53	664.12
	10	24481.74	16442.26	6585.53	7534.28	434.83	2048.72	3635.68	1565.73	1774.22	295.72	723.94
	11	24989.56	16855.01	6747.47	7752.51	437.46	2025.50	3684.65	1582.94	1801.89	299.83	777.56
	12	25742.81	17258.08	6862.60	8007.63	436.22	1984.15	3924.02	1685.73	1927.82	310.47	845.97
比上期增减额（亿元） Changes Compared with Previous Period（100 Million Yuan）												
1992	1	71.25	21.81	－27.46	48.10	3.24	39.64	－13.93	3.25	－14.46	－2.71	10.16
	2	91.28	41.77	58.21	－48.57	－1.53	45.06	8.65	8.46	0.66	－0.47	3.58
	3	412.25	220.41	89.22	51.41	11.29	121.45	35.79	20.29	13.37	2.13	－0.70
	4	467.29	163.65	85.59	12.02	15.51	93.50	144.73	82.86	55.74	6.13	27.61
	5	335.74	151.00	84.47	7.42	12.85	58.03	73.08	38.07	31.77	3.24	30.74
	6	495.56	261.63	69.19	132.57	9.42	37.81	76.56	30.84	40.94	4.77	32.37
	7	414.35	313.99	137.10	111.36	19.32	42.34	67.83	35.35	29.98	2.50	48.95
	8	409.88	230.24	74.84	110.19	6.00	41.02	55.50	26.07	25.67	3.76	33.47
	9	185.21	64.10	－2.87	57.51	－13.97	14.32	78.18	39.84	33.26	5.10	47.53
	10	482.53	348.97	100.46	206.89	9.08	－6.82	63.14	21.59	37.34	4.19	59.82
	11	507.82	412.75	161.94	218.23	2.63	－23.22	48.97	17.21	27.67	4.11	53.62
	12	753.25	403.07	115.13	255.12	－1.24	－41.35	239.37	102.79	125.93	10.64	68.41
比去年同期增长（%） Increase Rate Year－on－year（%）												
1992	1	20.42	17.30	17.59	16.24	15.59	22.97	36.60	53.49	29.47	12.69	65.06
	2	20.63	17.84	17.92	16.91	14.16	23.45	35.86	53.05	28.01	14.06	63.40
	3	20.92	18.23	17.71	17.60	14.30	23.49	35.66	51.80	28.38	13.79	62.10
	4	22.09	18.93	18.01	18.59	15.85	23.06	39.72	56.78	32.16	14.66	69.08
	5	22.64	19.33	17.97	19.10	18.53	23.18	40.66	57.60	33.20	14.87	75.89
	6	23.45	19.66	17.68	19.68	21.44	22.99	41.51	57.70	34.47	15.97	83.73
	7	24.27	20.91	18.70	20.92	24.54	24.04	42.04	57.81	35.31	15.75	99.62
	8	24.55	21.12	18.27	21.59	25.82	24.39	40.83	54.93	34.87	15.85	103.25
	9	22.18	18.96	16.24	19.04	21.94	23.99	31.55	38.71	28.48	16.30	105.39
	10	22.02	18.55	16.61	17.53	24.21	24.65	30.58	36.00	28.52	17.07	95.90
	11	21.98	18.31	17.08	16.46	24.43	26.09	28.90	32.40	28.04	17.31	87.02
	12	21.91	18.01	15.99	16.98	19.97	27.00	28.82	33.88	26.83	16.25	96.55

金融机构人民币信贷收支主要指标时间序列表
Time Series of Major Indicators in Sources and Uses of Credit Funds of Financial Institutions (RMB)

年 月 Year Month		各项存款 Total Deposits	企业存款 Deposits by Enterprises	财政存款 Fiscal Deposits	储蓄存款 Savings Deposits	活期储蓄 Demand Deposits	定期储蓄 Time Deposits	农村存款 Rural Deposits	流通中货币 Currency in Circulation
		期末余额（亿元） Balance (100 Million Yuan)							
1993	1	24238.08	7477.27	307.92	12246.37	2493.99	9752.38	911.07	5021.19
	2	24978.70	7769.56	342.74	12564.74	2595.28	9969.46	947.78	4639.35
	3	25380.05	8054.91	366.47	12526.31	2690.07	9836.24	964.90	4557.93
	4	25875.64	8381.70	367.83	12546.01	2795.80	9750.21	998.43	4704.50
	5	26300.55	8579.54	335.31	12764.93	2881.50	9883.43	1016.13	4745.84
	6	26469.62	8311.90	369.25	13109.84	3002.80	10107.04	1004.59	4863.56
	7	26564.05	7939.01	435.94	13532.55	3019.14	10513.41	964.90	4908.30
	8	26831.71	7835.73	464.38	13910.63	3014.58	10896.05	952.78	4907.59
	9	27195.03	7863.19	443.39	14233.19	3017.10	11216.09	947.02	5074.82
	10	28020.83	8123.06	568.32	14615.19	3050.42	11564.77	953.53	5159.56
	11	29128.18	8697.03	577.99	14968.81	3112.77	11856.04	996.99	5398.60
	12	29645.99	8673.77	502.34	15203.54	3232.51	11971.03	1073.56	5864.70
		比上期增减额（亿元） Changes Compared with Previous Period (100 Million Yuan)							
1993	1	469.88	58.47	62.20	452.55	140.97	311.58	-40.76	685.19
	2	740.62	292.29	34.82	318.37	101.29	217.08	36.71	-381.84
	3	401.35	285.35	23.73	-38.43	94.79	-133.22	17.12	-81.42
	4	495.59	326.79	1.36	19.70	105.73	-86.03	33.53	146.57
	5	424.91	197.84	-32.52	218.92	85.70	133.22	17.70	41.34
	6	169.07	-267.64	33.94	344.91	121.30	223.61	-11.54	117.72
	7	94.43	-372.89	66.69	422.71	16.34	406.37	-39.69	44.74
	8	267.66	-103.28	28.44	378.08	-4.56	382.64	-12.12	-0.71
	9	363.32	27.46	-20.99	322.56	2.52	320.04	-5.76	167.23
	10	825.80	259.87	124.93	382.00	33.32	348.68	6.51	84.74
	11	1107.35	573.97	9.67	353.62	62.35	291.27	43.46	239.04
	12	517.81	-23.25	-75.65	234.73	119.74	114.99	76.57	466.10
		比去年同期增长（%） Increase Rate Year-on-year (%)							
1993	1	33.62	44.32	-48.22	30.02			49.46	31.30
	2	32.73	44.98	-41.37	26.55			60.51	41.66
	3	31.21	43.79	-41.57	23.90			54.93	46.22
	4	29.42	41.27	-46.57	22.50			53.48	50.73
	5	27.97	38.13	-51.43	22.63	—	—	47.81	52.54
	6	26.32	29.92	-36.81	23.55	—	—	38.40	54.11
	7	23.12	18.24	-19.31	25.85	—	—	25.76	49.71
	8	21.04	12.45	-26.93	28.03	—	—	16.79	44.87
	9	23.07	14.82	-9.03	28.93	—	—	13.31	42.58
	10	24.23	14.66	33.60	30.36	—	—	9.18	38.23
	11	27.53	20.74	59.09	31.80	—	—	9.78	35.33
	12	28.09	22.60	100.81	29.31	—	—	13.14	35.26

金融机构人民币信贷收支主要指标时间序列表

Time Series of Major Indicators in Sources and Uses of Credit Funds of Financial Institutions（RMB）

年 月 Year Month	各项贷款 Total Loans	短期贷款 Short－term Loans				农业贷款 Loans to Agricultural Sector	中长期贷款 Medium and Long－term Loans				有价证券及投资 Securities and Investments
			工业贷款 Loans to Industrial Sector	商业贷款 Loans to Commercial Sector	建筑业贷款 Loans to Construction Sector			基本建设贷款 Capital Construction Loans	技术改造贷款 Technical Improvement Loans	其他中长期贷款 Other Medium and Long－term Loans	
期末余额（亿元） Balance（100 Million Yuan）											
1993 1	26813.07	17703.22	7045.77	8079.18	445.76	2033.18	3933.28				703.17
2	27258.50	17925.78	7095.00	8127.76	451.30	2153.88	3963.11				718.25
3	27339.44	17876.96	7067.38	8116.83	446.79	2200.49	3993.91				728.10
4	27894.27	18206.78	7184.55	8246.48	463.68	2268.63	4053.27				725.49
5	28201.57	18337.99	7235.39	8274.98	467.84	2304.05	4113.74				722.80
6	28465.28	18477.81	7298.84	8345.14	468.74	2315.91	4171.59				842.17
7	28663.60	18533.63	7311.19	8336.85	473.36	2339.02	4206.35				833.81
8	29022.52	18768.51	7418.95	8429.85	465.37	2359.25	4252.45				812.75
9	29636.25	19239.46	7631.31	8638.01	467.85	2382.39	4406.31				798.72
10	30398.30	19778.30	7838.39	8897.88	480.36	2393.00	4620.41				803.63
11	31603.58	20543.71	8156.63	9243.49	502.66	2405.98	4940.88				834.24
12	32955.83	21370.61	8451.93	9625.24	527.19	2401.28	5197.21				863.09
比上期增减额（亿元） Changes Compared with Previous Period（100 Million Yuan）											
1993 1	193.33	147.79	104.91	8.51	8.88	42.88	－18.08				36.50
2	445.43	222.56	49.23	48.58	5.54	120.70	29.83				15.08
3	80.94	－48.82	－27.62	－10.93	－4.51	46.61	30.80				9.85
4	554.83	329.82	117.17	129.65	16.89	68.14	59.36				－2.61
5	307.30	131.21	50.84	28.50	4.16	35.42	60.47				－2.69
6	263.71	139.82	63.45	70.16	0.90	11.86	57.85				119.37
7	198.32	55.82	12.35	－8.29	4.62	23.11	34.76				－8.36
8	358.92	234.88	107.76	93.00	－7.99	20.23	46.10				－21.06
9	613.73	470.95	212.36	208.16	2.48	23.14	153.86				－14.03
10	762.05	538.84	207.08	259.87	12.51	10.61	214.10				4.91
11	1205.28	765.41	318.24	345.61	22.30	12.98	320.47				30.61
12	1352.25	826.90	295.30	381.76	24.53	－4.70	256.33				28.85
比去年同期增长（%） Increase Rate Year－on－year（%）											
1993 1	26.55	20.87	19.64	17.20	21.51	26.91	29.72				59.60
2	28.10	22.04	19.29	18.74	23.53	30.77	30.33				61.71
3	26.04	19.91	17.07	17.70	18.63	24.43	29.81				64.19
4	25.89	20.80	17.35	19.37	18.25	21.84	25.82				54.01
5	25.37	20.46	16.57	19.65	15.52	20.00	24.87				44.04
6	23.82	19.33	16.30	18.40	13.11	18.29	23.75				57.66
7	22.47	17.31	14.00	16.44	9.14	16.94	22.32				42.99
8	21.87	17.09	14.35	15.96	5.83	15.58	21.69				31.81
9	23.49	19.55	17.68	17.89	9.89	15.90	23.34				20.27
10	24.17	20.29	19.02	18.10	10.47	16.80	27.09				11.01
11	26.47	21.88	20.88	19.23	14.90	18.78	34.09				7.29
12	28.02	23.83	23.16	20.20	20.85	21.02	32.45				2.02

金融机构人民币信贷收支主要指标时间序列表

Time Series of Major Indicators in Sources and Uses of Credit Funds of Financial Institutions (RMB)

年　月 Year Month		各项存款 Total Deposits							流通中货币 Currency in Circulation
			企业存款 Deposits by Enterprises	财政存款 Fiscal Deposits	储蓄存款 Savings Deposits	活期储蓄 Demand Deposits	定期储蓄 Time Deposits	农业存款 Deposits by Agricultural Sector	
期末余额（亿元） Balance (100 Million Yuan)									
1994	1	29475.77	9687.92	577.29	15599.07	3353.77	12245.30	839.44	6659.03
	2	30646.66	9772.67	642.49	16676.40	3561.35	13115.05	782.49	6305.19
	3	31842.90	10397.68	664.25	17157.16	3563.46	13593.70	829.03	5834.60
	4	32689.08	10947.76	628.78	17338.65	3586.53	13752.12	843.48	5813.99
	5	34022.32	11521.74	837.56	17783.45	3712.22	14071.23	859.59	5729.03
	6	35164.04	11924.32	902.94	18349.09	3904.94	14444.15	890.14	5781.47
	7	36295.89	12211.50	1005.17	18955.47	4059.15	14896.32	892.99	5970.24
	8	37411.70	12651.45	971.14	19437.40	4158.92	15278.48	921.62	6084.49
	9	38044.79	12692.80	941.11	19970.00	4294.99	15675.01	936.21	6412.85
	10	39015.66	12929.25	1048.02	20470.49	4346.99	16123.50	956.61	6554.72
	11	39837.13	13194.53	963.17	20996.86	4474.89	16521.97	999.82	6866.57
	12	40502.54	13278.98	862.26	21518.79	4680.15	16838.64	1063.19	7288.60
比上期增减额（亿元） Changes Compared with Previous Period (100 Million Yuan)									
1994	1	242.52	-92.42	83.77	395.53	49.57	345.96	-61.53	794.33
	2	1170.89	84.75	65.20	1077.33	207.58	869.75	-56.95	-353.84
	3	1196.24	625.01	21.76	480.77	2.11	478.65	46.54	-470.59
	4	846.18	550.08	-35.47	181.49	23.07	158.41	14.45	-20.61
	5	1333.24	573.98	208.78	444.80	125.69	319.11	16.11	-84.96
	6	1141.72	402.58	65.38	565.64	192.72	372.92	30.55	52.44
	7	1131.85	287.18	102.23	606.38	154.21	452.17	2.85	188.77
	8	1115.81	439.95	-34.03	481.93	99.77	382.16	28.63	114.25
	9	633.09	41.35	-30.03	532.60	136.07	396.53	14.59	328.36
	10	970.87	236.45	106.91	500.49	52.00	448.49	20.40	141.87
	11	821.47	265.28	-84.85	526.37	127.90	398.47	43.21	311.85
	12	665.41	84.45	-100.91	521.93	205.26	316.67	63.37	422.03
比去年同期增长（%） Increase Rate Year-on-year (%)									
1994	1	21.61	29.56	87.48	27.38	34.47	25.56	-7.86	32.62
	2	22.69	25.78	87.46	32.72	37.22	31.55	-17.44	35.91
	3	25.46	29.08	81.26	36.97	32.47	38.20	-14.08	28.01
	4	26.33	30.62	70.94	38.20	28.28	41.04	-15.52	23.58
	5	29.36	34.29	149.79	39.31	28.83	42.37	-15.41	20.72
	6	32.85	43.46	144.53	39.96	30.04	42.91	-11.39	18.87
	7	36.64	53.82	130.58	40.07	34.45	41.69	-7.45	21.64
	8	39.43	61.46	109.13	39.73	37.96	40.22	-3.27	23.98
	9	39.90	61.42	112.25	40.31	42.35	39.75	-1.14	26.37
	10	39.24	59.17	84.41	40.06	42.50	39.42	0.32	27.04
	11	36.76	51.71	66.64	40.27	43.76	39.35	0.28	27.19
	12	36.62	53.09	71.65	41.54	44.78	40.66	-0.97	24.28

金融机构人民币信贷收支主要指标时间序列表

Time Series of Major Indicators in Sources and Uses of Credit Funds of Financial Institutions（RMB）

年 月 Year Month	各项贷款 Total Loans	短期贷款 Short-term Loans					中长期贷款 Medium and Long-term Loans				有价证券及投资 Securities and Investments
			工业贷款 Loans to Industrial Sector	商业贷款 Loans to Commercial Sector	建筑业贷款 Loans to Construction Sector	农业贷款 Loans to Agricultural Sector		基本建设贷款 Capital Construction Loans	技术改造贷款 Technical Improvement Loans	其他中长期贷款 Other Medium and Long-term Loans	
期末余额（亿元） Balance（100 Million Yuan）											
1994 1	32871.56	22064.38	8495.78	8442.17	532.43	874.96	6579.22				1342.61
2	33046.87	22176.25	8524.98	8410.31	536.03	897.32	6596.75				1410.72
3	33542.34	22507.42	8595.73	8410.62	536.05	1007.65	6711.34				1427.34
4	34243.54	22990.55	8785.00	8541.33	546.09	1091.87	6840.09				1651.59
5	34883.73	23416.77	9007.55	8599.61	558.54	1127.93	6972.47				1838.01
6	35608.07	23903.51	9163.09	8810.62	572.58	1144.52	7102.79				1909.24
7	36224.16	24263.01	9292.75	8934.06	586.18	1142.91	7245.81				1935.16
8	36855.98	24686.89	9412.41	9108.31	593.88	1158.91	7322.06				2000.74
9	37476.11	25085.73	9498.30	9371.50	591.87	1154.35	7424.79				2158.73
10	38288.57	25717.17	9638.50	9715.91	598.43	1163.36	7487.54				2228.62
11	38788.31	26317.28	9767.29	10089.87	604.12	1159.46	7322.06				2371.35
12	39975.99	26948.70	9948.26	10509.84	617.21	1143.85	7774.92				2462.42
比上期增减额（亿元） Changes Compared with Previous Period（100 Million Yuan）											
1994 1	112.17	58.61	10.72	-76.15	3.14	30.59	3.32				54.54
2	175.32	111.87	29.20	-31.87	3.60	22.36	17.53				68.11
3	495.47	331.18	70.75	0.32	0.02	110.33	114.58				16.62
4	701.20	483.12	189.27	130.71	10.04	84.22	128.75				224.25
5	640.20	426.22	222.55	58.28	12.45	36.05	132.38				186.42
6	724.34	486.74	155.54	211.01	14.04	16.59	130.32				71.23
7	616.09	359.50	129.66	123.44	13.60	-1.61	143.02				25.92
8	631.82	423.88	119.66	174.25	7.70	16.00	76.25				65.58
9	620.13	398.84	85.89	263.19	-2.01	-4.56	102.73				157.99
10	812.46	631.44	140.20	344.41	6.56	9.01	62.75				69.89
11	499.74	600.11	128.79	373.96	5.69	-3.90	-165.48				142.73
12	1187.68	631.42	180.97	419.97	13.09	-15.61	452.86				91.07
比去年同期增长（%） Increase Rate Year-on-year（%）											
1994 1	22.60	—	20.58	4.49	19.44	—	67.27				90.94
2	21.24	—	20.15	3.48	18.77	—	66.45				96.41
3	22.69	—	21.63	3.62	19.98	—	68.04				96.04
4	22.76	—	22.28	3.58	17.77	—	68.75				127.65
5	23.69	—	24.49	3.92	19.39	—	69.49				154.29
6	25.09	—	25.54	5.58	22.15	—	70.27				126.70
7	26.38	—	27.10	7.16	23.83	—	72.26				132.09
8	26.99	—	26.87	8.05	27.61	—	72.18				146.17
9	26.45	—	24.46	8.49	26.51	—	68.50				170.27
10	25.96	—	22.97	9.19	24.58	—	62.05				177.32
11	22.73	—	19.75	9.16	20.18	—	48.19				184.25
12	21.30	—	17.70	9.19	17.08	—	49.60				185.30

金融机构人民币信贷收支主要指标时间序列表

Time Series of Major Indicators in Sources and Uses of Credit Funds of Financial Institutions（RMB）

年 月 Year Month		各项存款 Total Deposits	企业存款 Deposits by Enterprises	财政存款 Fiscal Deposits	储蓄存款 Savings Deposits	活期储蓄 Demand Deposits	定期储蓄 Time Deposits	农业存款 Deposits by Agricultural Sector	流通中货币 Currency in Circulation
		期末余额（亿元） Balance（100 Million Yuan）							
1995	1	41309.96	13148.43	982.41	22331.81	4664.10	17667.71	936.15	9213.05
	2	43188.10	13566.35	807.34	23740.97	4889.58	18851.39	962.66	7764.94
	3	44191.79	14200.52	1154.50	23764.30	4892.91	18871.39	991.95	7271.03
	4	45463.14	14517.71	1563.74	24219.06	4911.41	19307.65	989.00	7268.05
	5	46759.18	14965.15	1726.85	24819.86	4979.02	19840.84	998.31	7045.89
	6	47806.03	15273.45	1652.45	25573.11	5159.17	20413.94	1023.18	7003.94
	7	48836.76	15610.94	1414.88	26353.38	5228.75	21124.63	1024.75	7092.88
	8	49669.11	16125.58	1206.45	26833.89	5238.82	21595.07	1053.56	7241.90
	9	50753.18	16301.93	1303.78	27569.72	5376.38	22193.34	1081.88	7368.94
	10	51794.44	16633.12	1330.09	28183.69	5408.89	22774.80	1095.69	7420.06
	11	52826.43	16957.38	1279.84	28844.45	5627.69	23216.76	1115.47	7731.83
	12	53882.10	17323.82	1005.40	29662.25	5884.01	23778.24	1196.22	7885.34
		比上期增减额（亿元） Changes Compared with Previous Period（100 Million Yuan）							
1995	1	384.55	-290.30	116.33	795.68	-6.49	802.17	-122.15	1924.45
	2	1878.14	417.92	-175.07	1409.16	225.48	1183.68	26.51	-1448.11
	3	1003.69	634.17	347.16	23.33	3.33	20.00	29.29	-493.91
	4	1271.35	317.19	409.24	454.76	18.50	436.26	-2.95	-2.98
	5	1296.04	447.44	163.11	600.80	67.61	533.19	9.31	-222.16
	6	1046.85	308.30	-74.40	753.25	180.15	573.10	24.87	-41.95
	7	1030.73	337.49	-237.57	780.27	69.57	710.70	1.57	88.94
	8	832.35	514.64	-208.43	480.51	10.07	470.44	28.81	149.02
	9	1084.07	176.35	97.33	735.83	137.56	598.27	28.32	127.04
	10	1041.26	331.19	26.31	613.97	32.51	581.46	13.81	51.12
	11	1031.99	324.26	-50.25	660.76	218.79	441.97	19.78	311.77
	12	1055.67	366.44	-274.44	817.80	256.32	561.48	80.75	153.51
		比去年同期增长（%） Increase Rate Year-on-year（%）							
1995	1	40.15	35.72	70.18	43.16	39.07	44.28	11.52	38.35
	2	40.92	38.82	25.66	42.36	37.30	43.74	23.03	23.15
	3	38.78	36.57	73.81	38.51	37.31	38.82	19.65	24.62
	4	39.08	32.61	148.69	39.68	36.94	40.40	17.25	25.01
	5	37.44	29.89	106.18	39.57	34.13	41.00	16.14	22.99
	6	35.95	28.09	83.01	39.37	32.12	41.33	14.95	21.14
	7	34.55	27.84	40.76	39.03	28.81	41.81	14.75	18.80
	8	32.76	27.46	24.23	38.05	25.97	41.34	14.32	19.02
	9	33.40	28.43	38.54	38.06	25.18	41.58	15.56	14.91
	10	32.75	28.65	26.91	37.68	24.43	41.25	14.54	13.20
	11	32.61	28.52	32.88	37.38	25.76	40.52	11.57	12.60
	12	33.03	30.46	16.60	37.84	25.72	41.21	12.51	8.19

金融机构人民币信贷收支主要指标时间序列表

Time Series of Major Indicators in Sources and Uses of Credit Funds of Financial Institutions（RMB）

年 月 Year Month		各项贷款 Total Loans	短期贷款 Short－term Loans	工业贷款 Loans to Industrial Sector	商业贷款 Loans to Commercial Sector	建筑业贷款 Loans to Construction Sector	农业贷款 Loans to Agricultural Sector	中长期贷款 Medium and Long－term Loans	基本建设贷款 Capital Construction Loans	技术改造贷款 Technical Improvement Loans	其他中长期贷款 Other Medium and Long－term Loans	有价证券及投资 Securities and Investments
		期末余额（亿元） Balance（100 Million Yuan）										
1995	1	41546.10	27694.40	10060.81	10668.28	636.22	1199.53	8681.57				2862.88
	2	41968.29	27986.98	10115.81	10683.22	637.70	1270.41	8698.31				2898.33
	3	42453.45	28256.94	10199.08	10687.68	645.41	1346.29	8793.10				3098.43
	4	43179.95	28752.12	10381.93	10732.72	665.13	1429.82	8884.03				3264.47
	5	43619.18	29033.10	10482.85	10772.52	672.48	1467.50	8949.11				3416.25
	6	44073.06	29221.95	10545.52	10887.88	672.43	1477.45	9117.34				3552.78
	7	44824.48	29699.58	10679.18	11023.11	687.02	1516.81	9212.70				3607.48
	8	45643.68	30191.72	10855.76	11193.82	701.97	1549.55	9467.74				3655.77
	9	46513.49	30712.86	10998.35	11452.15	714.26	1562.82	9708.01				3806.13
	10	47515.17	31453.97	11196.73	11817.43	730.16	1574.30	9828.18				3852.80
	11	48629.70	32206.46	11395.10	12230.95	742.74	1572.90	9984.51				4018.80
	12	50544.09	33371.97	11774.70	12837.13	799.34	1544.79	10699.32				4215.72
		比上期增减额（亿元） Changes Compared with Previous Period（100 Million Yuan）										
1995	1	341.83	256.25	47.59	53.40	2.21	53.28	2.31				11.77
	2	422.19	292.58	55.00	14.94	1.48	70.88	16.74				35.45
	3	485.16	269.96	83.27	4.46	7.71	75.88	94.79				200.10
	4	726.50	495.18	182.85	45.04	19.72	83.53	90.93				166.04
	5	439.23	280.98	100.92	39.80	7.35	37.68	65.08				151.78
	6	453.88	188.85	62.67	115.36	－0.05	9.95	168.23				136.53
	7	751.42	477.63	133.66	135.23	14.59	39.36	95.36				54.70
	8	819.20	492.14	176.58	170.71	14.95	32.74	255.04				48.29
	9	869.81	521.14	142.59	258.33	12.29	13.27	240.27				150.36
	10	1001.68	741.11	198.38	365.28	15.90	11.48	120.17				46.67
	11	1114.53	752.49	198.37	413.52	12.58	－1.4	156.33				166.00
	12	1914.39	1165.51	379.60	606.18	56.60	－28.11	714.81				196.92
		比去年同期增长（%） Increase Rate Year－on－year（%）										
1995	1	26.39	25.52	18.42	26.37	19.49	37.10	31.95				113.23
	2	27.00	26.20	18.66	27.03	18.97	41.58	31.86				105.45
	3	26.57	25.54	18.65	27.07	20.40	33.61	31.02				117.08
	4	26.10	25.06	18.18	25.66	21.80	30.95	29.88				97.66
	5	25.04	23.98	16.38	25.27	20.40	30.11	28.35				85.87
	6	23.77	22.25	15.09	23.58	17.44	29.09	28.36				86.08
	7	23.74	22.41	14.92	23.38	17.20	32.71	27.15				86.42
	8	23.84	22.30	15.33	22.90	18.20	33.71	29.30				82.72
	9	24.12	22.43	15.79	22.20	20.68	35.39	30.75				76.31
	10	24.10	22.31	16.17	21.63	22.01	35.32	31.26				72.88
	11	25.37	22.38	16.67	21.22	22.95	35.66	36.36				69.47
	12	26.44	23.84	18.36	22.14	29.51	35.05	37.61				71.20

金融机构人民币信贷收支主要指标时间序列表
Time Series of Major Indicators in Sources and Uses of Credit Funds of Financial Institutions（RMB）

年 月 Year Month		各项存款 Total Deposits	企业存款 Deposits by Enterprises	财政存款 Fiscal Deposits	储蓄存款 Savings Deposits	活期储蓄 Demand Deposits	定期储蓄 Time Deposits	农业存款 Deposits by Agricultural Sector	流通中货币 Currency in Circulation
		期末余额（亿元） Balance（100 Million Yuan）							
1996	1	54373.49	17449.96	1117.76	30356.54	5900.80	24455.74	1144.42	8600.45
	2	55668.77	17094.21	1191.63	32026.25	6171.38	25854.87	1018.02	9300.83
	3	57498.77	17620.88	1126.19	33296.48	6116.11	27180.37	1068.79	8169.05
	4	59316.48	18330.02	1456.95	34018.53	6005.57	28012.96	1075.06	7894.94
	5	60508.23	18912.75	1315.94	34622.10	6141.34	28480.76	1099.25	7705.52
	6	61768.70	19318.30	1281.35	35457.91	6523.45	28934.46	1151.84	7665.69
	7	63117.01	19678.60	1559.08	36048.67	6589.68	29458.99	1149.71	7809.31
	8	64470.87	20127.21	1545.74	36705.80	6717.21	29988.59	1177.13	8093.35
	9	65180.51	20504.12	1522.28	37085.17	6850.56	30234.61	1208.04	8409.00
	10	66449.17	20959.29	1676.86	37671.42	7119.98	30551.44	1247.41	8404.75
	11	67253.38	21371.27	1788.75	37917.26	7218.46	30698.80	1265.95	8704.56
	12	68595.59	22450.17	1274.16	38520.84	7647.64	30873.20	1364.09	8802.01
		比上期增减额（亿元） Changes Compared with Previous Period（100 Million Yuan）							
1996	1	570.26	26.08	117.53	641.17	-25.93	667.10	-46.32	715.11
	2	1295.28	-355.75	73.87	1669.71	270.58	1399.13	-126.4	700.38
	3	1830.00	526.67	-65.44	1270.23	-55.27	1325.50	50.77	-1131.78
	4	1817.71	709.14	330.76	722.05	-110.54	832.59	6.27	-274.11
	5	1191.75	582.73	-141.01	603.57	135.77	467.80	24.19	-189.42
	6	1260.47	405.55	-34.59	835.81	382.11	453.70	52.59	-39.83
	7	1348.31	360.30	277.73	590.76	66.23	524.53	-2.13	143.62
	8	1353.86	448.61	-13.34	657.13	127.53	529.60	27.42	284.04
	9	709.64	376.91	-23.46	379.37	133.35	246.02	30.91	315.65
	10	1268.66	455.17	154.58	586.25	269.42	316.83	39.37	-4.25
	11	804.21	411.98	111.89	245.84	98.48	147.36	18.54	299.81
	12	1342.21	1078.90	-514.59	603.58	429.18	174.40	98.14	97.45
		比去年同期增长（%） Increase Rate Year-on-year（%）							
1996	1	31.62	32.72	13.78	35.93	26.52	38.42	22.25	-6.65
	2	28.90	26.00	47.60	34.90	26.21	37.15	5.75	19.78
	3	30.11	24.09	-2.45	40.11	25.00	44.03	7.75	12.35
	4	30.47	26.26	-6.83	40.46	22.28	45.09	8.70	8.63
	5	29.40	26.38	-23.80	39.49	23.34	43.55	10.11	9.36
	6	29.21	26.48	-22.46	38.65	26.44	41.74	12.57	9.45
	7	29.24	26.06	10.19	36.79	26.03	39.45	12.19	10.10
	8	29.80	24.82	28.12	36.79	28.22	38.87	11.73	11.76
	9	28.43	25.78	16.76	34.51	27.42	36.23	11.66	14.11
	10	28.29	26.01	26.07	33.66	31.63	34.15	13.85	13.27
	11	27.31	26.03	39.76	31.45	28.27	32.23	13.49	12.58
	12	27.31	29.59	26.73	29.86	29.97	29.84	14.03	11.62

金融机构人民币信贷收支主要指标时间序列表

Time Series of Major Indicators in Sources and Uses of Credit Funds of Financial Institutions（RMB）

年 月 Year Month		各项贷款 Total Loans	短期贷款 Short - term Loans	工业贷款 Loans to Industrial Sector	商业贷款 Loans to Commercial Sector	建筑业贷款 Loans to Construction Sector	农业贷款 Loans to Agricultural Sector	中长期贷款 Medium and Long - term Loans	基本建设贷款 Capital Construction Loans	技术改造贷款 Technical Improvement Loans	其他中长期贷款 Other Medium and Long - term Loans	有价证券及投资 Securities and Investments
		期末余额（亿元） Balance（100 Million Yuan）										
1996	1	50552.45	33710.30	11848.97	12765.02	798.05	1583.89	10569.65				4169.96
	2	51079.56	34039.24	11962.03	12821.42	807.41	1631.95	10620.07				4255.03
	3	51901.67	34584.57	12142.75	12958.18	824.63	1722.80	10749.62				4453.07
	4	52817.41	35250.47	12419.76	13078.23	844.09	1832.87	10868.22				4617.10
	5	53379.66	35569.60	12560.64	13083.83	858.82	1886.78	10978.07				4810.10
	6	54381.34	36221.69	12857.56	13352.06	867.16	1900.98	11166.59				4899.70
	7	55192.53	36749.67	13076.85	13505.24	887.97	1939.80	11270.45				5108.05
	8	56075.73	37322.07	13237.06	13729.99	901.19	1958.76	11386.53				5183.29
	9	56932.63	37842.80	13394.30	13991.47	910.02	1970.94	11532.98				5345.40
	10	57959.73	38603.01	13659.26	14313.87	925.13	1990.52	11647.78				5272.22
	11	58765.45	39124.57	13864.35	14528.13	952.81	1974.19	11856.77				5344.36
	12	61156.55	40210.01	14213.27	15332.64	973.79	1919.12	12672.59				5644.85
		比上期增减额（亿元） Changes Compared with Previous Period（100 Million Yuan）										
1996	1	79.23	156.63	58.56	－27.13	－4.22	42.85	－61.69				35.72
	2	527.11	328.94	113.06	56.40	9.36	48.06	50.42				85.07
	3	822.11	545.33	180.72	136.76	17.22	90.85	129.55				198.04
	4	915.74	665.90	277.01	120.05	19.46	110.07	118.60				164.03
	5	562.25	319.13	140.88	5.60	14.73	53.91	109.85				193.00
	6	1001.68	652.09	296.92	268.23	8.34	14.20	188.52				89.60
	7	811.19	527.98	219.29	153.18	20.81	38.82	103.86				208.35
	8	883.17	572.40	160.21	224.75	13.22	18.96	116.08				75.24
	9	856.93	520.73	157.24	261.48	8.83	12.18	146.45				162.11
	10	1027.10	760.21	264.96	322.40	15.11	19.58	114.80				－73.18
	11	805.72	521.56	205.09	214.26	27.68	－16.33	208.99				72.14
	12	2391.10	1085.44	348.92	804.51	20.98	－55.07	815.82				300.49
		比去年同期增长（%） Increase Rate Year－on－year（%）										
1996	1	21.68	21.72	17.77	19.65	25.44	32.04	21.75				45.66
	2	21.71	21.63	18.25	20.01	26.61	28.46	22.09				46.81
	3	22.26	22.39	19.06	21.24	27.77	27.97	22.25				43.72
	4	22.32	22.60	19.63	21.85	26.91	28.19	22.33				41.43
	5	22.38	22.51	19.82	21.46	27.71	28.57	22.67				40.80
	6	23.39	23.95	21.92	22.63	28.96	28.67	22.48				37.91
	7	23.13	23.74	22.45	22.52	29.25	27.89	22.34				41.60
	8	22.86	23.62	21.94	22.66	28.38	26.41	20.27				41.78
	9	22.40	23.21	21.78	22.17	27.41	26.11	18.80				40.44
	10	21.98	22.73	21.99	21.13	26.70	26.44	18.51				36.84
	11	20.84	21.48	21.67	18.78	28.28	25.51	18.75				32.98
	12	21.00	20.49	20.71	19.44	21.82	24.23	18.44				33.90

金融机构人民币信贷收支主要指标时间序列表

Time Series of Major Indicators in Sources and Uses of Credit Funds of Financial Institutions（RMB）

年 月 Year Month		各项存款 Total Deposits	企业存款 Deposits by Enterprises	财政存款 Fiscal Deposits	储蓄存款 Savings Deposits	活期储蓄 Demand Deposits	定期储蓄 Time Deposits	农业存款 Deposits by Agricultural Sector	流通中货币 Currency in Circulation
期末余额（亿元） Balance（100 Million Yuan）									
1997	1	68202.22	22873.80	1363.37	39141.26	7632.75	31508.51	1162.02	11493.22
	2	70193.32	22976.34	1587.66	40896.15	8020.03	32876.12	1123.01	10075.22
	3	72020.23	23883.13	1718.94	41556.77	8474.06	33082.71	1191.95	9280.12
	4	73096.37	24265.75	1735.97	42122.16	8750.23	33371.93	1203.28	9277.12
	5	73871.06	24804.83	1767.44	42295.16	8706.34	33588.82	1220.44	9065.65
	6	75448.64	25674.11	1758.27	42771.16	8708.22	34062.94	1258.70	9121.58
	7	76132.10	25732.70	1799.71	43312.08	8635.81	34676.27	1272.78	9126.58
	8	77136.05	26142.74	1716.92	43914.92	8820.94	35093.98	1306.98	9327.35
	9	78315.48	26879.36	1848.70	44139.45	8762.38	35377.07	1351.72	9426.13
	10	79134.21	26992.38	1978.27	44720.33	8840.97	35879.36	1377.20	9488.81
	11	79907.31	27168.82	2101.21	45068.43	9036.56	36031.87	1415.43	9784.58
	12	82392.80	28656.25	1574.90	46279.80	10053.06	36226.74	1532.99	10177.61
比上期增减额（亿元） Changes Compared with Previous Period（100 Million Yuan）									
1997	1	-1249.75	-1332.98	-27.07	360.36	-44.19	404.55	-87.21	2691.21
	2	1991.11	102.55	224.29	1754.90	387.29	1367.61	-39.01	-1418.00
	3	1826.94	906.79	131.28	660.62	454.03	206.59	68.94	-795.10
	4	1076.13	382.62	17.03	565.39	276.17	289.22	11.33	-3.00
	5	774.68	539.08	31.47	172.99	-43.89	216.88	17.16	-211.48
	6	1577.58	869.28	-9.17	475.99	1.87	474.12	38.26	55.93
	7	683.47	58.59	41.44	540.92	-72.41	613.33	14.09	5.00
	8	1003.93	410.04	-82.79	602.84	185.13	417.71	34.19	200.77
	9	1179.43	736.60	131.79	224.53	-58.56	283.09	44.74	98.78
	10	818.73	113.02	129.57	580.89	78.60	502.29	25.47	62.68
	11	773.10	176.44	122.94	348.10	195.59	152.51	38.24	295.77
	12	2485.47	1487.43	-526.31	1211.37	1016.50	194.87	117.55	393.04
比去年同期增长（%） Increase Rate Year-on-year（%）									
1997	1	25.43	31.08	21.97	28.94	29.35	28.84	1.54	33.64
	2	26.09	34.41	33.23	27.70	29.96	27.16	10.31	8.33
	3	25.26	35.54	52.63	24.81	38.55	21.72	11.52	13.60
	4	23.23	32.38	19.15	23.82	45.70	19.13	11.93	17.51
	5	22.08	31.15	34.31	22.16	41.77	17.94	11.02	17.65
	6	22.15	32.90	37.22	20.63	33.49	17.72	9.28	18.99
	7	20.62	30.76	15.43	20.15	31.05	17.71	10.70	16.87
	8	19.64	29.89	11.07	19.64	31.22	17.02	11.03	15.25
	9	20.15	31.09	21.44	19.02	27.91	17.01	11.89	12.10
	10	19.09	28.78	17.97	18.71	24.17	17.44	10.40	12.90
	11	18.82	27.13	17.47	18.86	25.19	17.37	11.81	12.41
	12	20.11	27.64	23.60	20.14	31.45	17.34	12.38	15.63

金融机构人民币信贷收支主要指标时间序列表
Time Series of Major Indicators in Sources and Uses of Credit Funds of Financial Institutions（RMB）

年 月 Year Month	各项贷款 Total Loans	短期贷款 Short－term Loans					中长期贷款 Medium and Long－term Loans				有价证券及投资 Securities and Investments
			工业贷款 Loans to Industrial Sector	商业贷款 Loans to Commercial Sector	建筑业贷款 Loans to Construction Sector	农业贷款 Loans to Agricultural Sector		基本建设贷款 Capital Construction Loans	技术改造贷款 Technical Improvement Loans	其他中长期贷款 Other Medium and Long－term Loans	
期末余额（亿元） Balance（100 Million Yuan）											
1997 1	64527.37	47995.36	14473.64	15906.60	1413.32	2718.05	13501.44	6549.74	4401.69	2550.01	3803.37
2	64840.53	48336.40	14547.67	15929.45	1415.85	2772.94	13475.72	6573.23	4398.72	2503.77	3811.85
3	65796.10	48914.18	14741.41	15953.92	1430.21	2912.52	13628.61	6674.92	4412.96	2540.73	3967.45
4	66471.13	49372.80	14836.72	16026.78	1439.99	3016.37	13703.54	6703.34	4422.15	2578.05	3738.78
5	67102.69	49837.82	14980.73	16096.93	1452.45	3078.06	13761.64	6803.93	4435.54	2522.17	3742.68
6	68169.66	50512.33	15204.73	16275.06	1479.58	3102.74	14052.77	6996.46	4485.51	2570.80	3629.72
7	68699.94	50831.65	15257.87	16432.46	1478.55	3137.04	14075.15	7000.85	4492.59	2581.71	3575.53
8	69518.02	51481.61	15395.96	16739.10	1495.10	3189.16	14185.84	7061.86	4536.54	2587.44	3636.85
9	70564.45	52245.37	15630.12	17066.14	1515.33	3232.56	14385.54	7158.40	4629.65	2597.49	3703.83
10	71353.52	52825.80	15795.18	17346.45	1521.93	3249.17	14522.07	7234.57	4657.21	2630.29	3665.86
11	72221.80	53495.48	15957.16	17645.58	1540.64	3252.51	14692.82	7339.86	4668.25	2684.71	3676.39
12	74914.07	55418.27	16526.63	18356.61	1591.06	3314.64	15468.65	7693.07	4886.00	2889.58	3671.74
比上期增减额（亿元） Changes Compared with Previous Period（100 Million Yuan）											
1997 1	316.20	331.14	67.20	2.00	－5.78	62.42	－117.81	－5.82	－74.51	－37.49	－312.99
2	313.15	341.04	74.03	22.85	2.54	54.89	－25.73	23.48	－2.97	－46.24	8.48
3	955.58	577.79	193.74	24.46	14.36	139.58	152.89	101.70	14.24	36.95	155.60
4	675.64	458.62	95.32	72.86	9.78	103.85	74.93	28.42	9.19	37.32	－228.67
5	631.60	465.04	144.01	70.15	12.47	61.69	58.11	100.59	13.39	－55.87	3.90
6	1066.97	674.50	224.00	178.13	27.13	24.68	291.13	192.54	49.97	48.62	－112.96
7	503.27	319.33	53.14	157.41	－1.03	34.30	22.37	4.38	7.08	10.91	－54.20
8	818.09	649.96	138.09	306.64	16.54	52.12	110.70	61.02	43.95	5.73	61.32
9	1046.45	763.78	234.16	327.04	20.24	43.40	199.70	96.54	93.11	10.05	66.98
10	789.07	580.43	165.06	280.30	6.60	16.61	136.53	76.17	27.55	32.81	－37.97
11	868.28	669.67	161.98	299.14	18.71	3.34	170.74	105.29	11.04	54.41	10.53
12	2692.27	1922.78	569.47	711.03	50.41	62.13	775.84	353.21	217.75	204.88	－4.65
比去年同期增长（%） Increase Rate Year－on－year（%）											
1997 1	27.64	—	—	—	—	—	—	—	—	—	—
2	26.94	—	—	—	—	—	—	—	—	—	—
3	26.77	—	—	—	—	—	—	—	—	—	—
4	25.85	—	—	—	—	—	—	—	—	—	—
5	25.71	—	—	—	—	—	—	—	—	—	—
6	25.35	—	—	—	—	—	—	—	—	—	—
7	24.47	—	—	—	—	—	—	—	—	—	—
8	23.97	—	—	—	—	—	—	—	—	—	—
9	23.94	—	—	—	—	—	—	—	—	—	—
10	23.11	—	—	—	—	—	—	—	—	—	—
11	22.90	—	—	—	—	—	—	—	—	—	—
12	22.50	—	—	—	—	—	—	—	—	—	—

金融机构人民币信贷收支主要指标时间序列表

Time Series of Major Indicators in Sources and Uses of Credit Funds of Financial Institutions (RMB)

年 月 Year Month		各项存款 Total Deposits	企业存款 Deposits by Enterprises	财政存款 Fiscal Deposits	储蓄存款 Savings Deposits	活期储蓄 Demand Deposits	定期储蓄 Time Deposits	农业存款 Deposits by Agricultural Sector	流通中货币 Currency in Circulation
		期末余额(亿元) Balance (100 Million Yuan)							
1998	1	80862.83	26728.38	1652.99	46514.18	9509.77	37004.41	1307.46	13108.38
	2	82414.81	26668.30	1765.21	47865.30	9729.12	38136.18	1342.15	10886.06
	3	84175.36	27154.03	2143.64	48686.48	9777.27	38909.21	1401.88	10201.04
	4	84445.84	27453.11	1768.23	48984.56	9763.58	39220.98	1400.25	10172.49
	5	86166.93	27979.57	2032.69	49699.45	10059.12	39640.33	1412.41	9984.37
	6	86895.11	28629.48	1776.30	49949.89	10125.17	39824.72	1439.09	9720.44
	7	88581.30	29008.47	2096.07	50749.82	10629.90	40119.92	1459.35	10037.84
	8	89230.85	29617.93	1867.51	50900.91	10551.79	40349.12	1497.08	10129.07
	9	91881.37	30858.42	2380.85	51580.74	10931.15	40649.59	1549.44	10528.03
	10	92969.82	31056.33	2440.51	52257.11	11205.62	41051.49	1573.52	10501.33
	11	94419.46	31538.63	2636.83	52952.32	11471.96	41480.36	1625.72	10671.30
	12	95697.94	32486.63	2187.89	53407.47	11615.90	41791.57	1748.01	11204.15
		比上期增减额(亿元) Changes Compared with Previous Period (100 Million Yuan)							
1998	1	-1434.34	-1857.77	73.47	722.17	35.61	686.56	-203.36	2930.77
	2	1551.98	-60.08	112.22	1351.12	219.35	1131.77	34.69	-2222.32
	3	1760.55	485.73	401.39	821.18	48.15	773.03	59.73	-685.02
	4	270.48	299.09	-375.40	298.08	-13.69	311.77	-1.62	-28.55
	5	1721.07	526.46	264.46	714.89	295.54	419.35	12.16	-188.13
	6	728.20	649.91	-256.38	250.44	66.05	184.39	26.68	-263.93
	7	1686.20	378.99	319.76	799.93	504.73	295.20	20.26	317.40
	8	649.55	609.46	-228.56	151.08	-78.12	229.20	37.74	91.23
	9	2650.50	1240.49	513.34	679.83	379.36	300.47	52.36	398.96
	10	1088.44	197.90	59.66	676.37	274.47	401.90	24.08	-26.71
	11	1449.65	482.30	196.32	695.21	266.34	428.87	52.20	169.98
	12	1278.50	948.01	-448.93	455.15	143.94	311.21	122.29	532.85
		比去年同期增长(%) Increase Rate Year-on-year (%)							
1998	1	18.19	16.85	21.24	18.84	24.59	17.44	12.52	14.05
	2	18.01	16.07	11.18	17.04	21.31	16.00	19.51	8.05
	3	16.52	13.70	26.43	17.16	15.38	17.61	17.61	9.92
	4	15.11	13.14	3.22	16.29	11.58	17.53	16.37	9.65
	5	16.28	12.80	16.51	17.51	15.54	18.02	15.73	10.13
	6	14.81	11.51	2.39	16.78	16.27	16.92	14.33	6.57
	7	15.98	12.73	18.23	17.17	23.09	15.70	14.66	9.98
	8	15.31	13.29	10.53	15.91	19.62	14.97	14.54	8.60
	9	16.94	14.80	30.81	16.86	24.75	14.90	14.63	11.69
	10	17.09	15.06	25.23	16.85	26.75	14.42	14.26	10.67
	11	17.74	16.08	27.37	17.49	26.95	15.12	14.86	9.06
	12	15.68	13.37	41.50	15.40	15.55	15.36	14.03	10.09

金融机构人民币信贷收支主要指标时间序列表

Time Series of Major Indicators in Sources and Uses of Credit Funds of Financial Institutions（RMB）

年 月 Year Month		各项贷款 Total Loans	短期贷款 Short－term Loans	工业贷款 Loans to Industrial Sector	商业贷款 Loans to Commercial Sector	建筑业贷款 Loans to Construction Sector	农业贷款 Loans to Agricultural Sector	中长期贷款 Medium and Long－term Loans	基本建设贷款 Capital Construction Loans	技术改造贷款 Technical Improvement Loans	其他中长期贷款 Other Medium and Long－term Loans	有价证券及投资 Securities and Investments
		期末余额（亿元） Balance（100 Million Yuan）										
1998	1	74837.52	54418.72	16217.78	18138.08	1482.44	3921.20	16195.78	8035.09	4820.58	3340.11	3656.05
	2	75030.94	54390.33	16209.24	18074.32	1482.94	3944.87	16304.39	8138.32	4787.16	3378.91	3660.82
	3	75928.91	55056.96	16372.03	18112.22	1501.81	4062.40	16429.45	8142.80	4797.69	3488.96	3541.07
	4	76570.65	55429.27	16472.11	18054.23	1507.55	4154.89	16583.05	8207.23	4805.35	3570.47	3630.15
	5	77313.97	55814.76	16604.60	18059.86	1523.84	4192.26	16828.63	8351.59	4827.33	3649.71	3829.41
	6	78805.94	56660.00	16905.06	18181.62	1537.84	4283.78	17438.08	8690.83	4884.60	3862.65	3885.64
	7	79562.39	57088.81	16997.89	17165.39	1548.17	4323.67	17618.95	8805.68	4885.80	3927.47	4009.20
	8	80885.00	57808.27	17194.73	17007.16	1572.88	4381.10	18153.81	9000.48	4926.78	4226.55	6735.93
	9	82644.94	58680.87	17448.98	18875.47	1595.76	4448.42	18915.11	9466.54	4995.23	4453.34	7510.28
	10	83421.25	58987.15	17446.02	19077.61	1596.56	4442.03	19240.46	9542.89	5051.18	4646.39	7674.29
	11	84596.88	59543.24	17546.39	19481.06	1601.05	4422.85	19798.57	9868.90	5064.68	4864.99	7782.84
	12	86524.13	60613.22	17821.47	19752.43	1628.73	4444.24	20717.78	10442.75	5118.22	5156.81	8112.24
		比上期增减额（亿元） Changes Compared with Previous Period（100 Million Yuan）										
1998	1	－179.10	－224.84	－124.46	－144.35	12.45	112.86	－80.94	－43.10	－62.18	24.34	－29.82
	2	193.43	－28.40	－8.55	－63.76	0.50	23.67	108.62	103.23	－33.42	38.81	4.77
	3	897.99	666.66	162.80	37.90	18.88	117.53	125.05	4.48	10.52	110.05	－119.75
	4	623.70	354.26	100.08	－57.99	5.74	92.49	153.60	64.43	7.66	81.51	89.08
	5	743.31	385.49	132.49	5.63	16.28	37.37	245.57	144.36	21.98	79.23	199.26
	6	1491.95	845.22	300.46	121.76	14.00	91.52	609.44	339.24	57.26	212.94	56.23
	7	756.42	428.79	92.82	－1016.24	10.33	39.89	180.87	114.85	1.20	64.82	123.56
	8	1322.65	719.49	196.84	－158.22	24.71	57.43	534.86	194.80	40.98	299.08	2726.73
	9	1759.89	872.57	254.25	1868.31	22.87	67.32	761.30	466.06	68.44	226.80	774.34
	10	776.34	306.30	－2.96	202.13	0.81	－6.39	325.35	76.35	55.95	193.05	164.01
	11	1175.63	556.09	100.37	403.45	4.49	－19.18	558.12	326.02	13.50	218.60	108.55
	12	1927.25	1069.98	275.08	271.37	27.68	21.39	919.21	573.85	53.54	291.82	329.40
		比去年同期增长（%） Increase Rate Year－on－year（%）										
1998	1	16.00	13.38	12.05	14.03	4.89	44.27	19.96	22.68	9.52	30.98	－3.87
	2	15.74	12.52	11.42	13.46	4.74	42.26	20.99	23.81	8.83	34.95	－3.96
	3	15.43	12.56	11.06	13.53	5.01	39.48	20.55	21.99	8.72	37.32	－10.75
	4	15.21	12.25	11.02	12.65	4.69	37.74	21.01	22.44	8.67	38.50	－2.91
	5	15.23	11.98	10.84	12.19	4.92	36.20	22.29	22.75	8.83	44.70	2.32
	6	15.61	12.15	11.18	11.71	3.94	38.06	24.09	24.22	8.90	50.25	7.05
	7	15.82	12.29	11.40	4.46	4.71	37.83	25.18	25.78	8.75	52.13	12.13
	8	16.36	12.27	11.68	1.60	5.20	37.37	27.97	27.45	8.60	63.35	85.21
	9	17.13	12.30	11.64	10.60	5.31	37.61	31.49	32.24	7.90	71.45	102.77
	10	16.92	11.64	10.45	9.98	4.90	36.71	32.49	31.91	8.46	76.65	109.35
	11	17.13	11.28	9.96	10.40	3.92	35.98	34.75	34.46	8.49	81.21	111.70
	12	15.49	9.34	7.83	7.60	2.37	34.08	33.93	35.74	4.75	78.46	120.94

金融机构人民币信贷收支主要指标时间序列表

Time Series of Major Indicators in Sources and Uses of Credit Funds of Financial Institutions (RMB)

年 月 Year Month		各项存款 Total Deposits	企业存款 Deposits by Enterprises	财政存款 Fiscal Deposits	储蓄存款 Savings Deposits	活期储蓄 Demand Deposits	定期储蓄 Time Deposits	农业存款 Deposits by Agricultural Sector	流通中货币 Currency in Circulation
期末余额（亿元） Balance (100 Million Yuan)									
1999	1	95970.20	31842.29	2263.03	54293.67	11964.47	42329.20	1744.23	11996.72
	2	97229.16	31122.71	2045.58	56767.47	12802.48	43964.99	1566.86	12784.24
	3	99438.13	31869.25	2132.05	57814.65	12645.53	45169.12	1651.56	11341.63
	4	100214.80	32102.61	2016.49	58369.07	12502.71	45866.36	1684.46	11225.41
	5	101473.55	32541.52	2107.39	58967.84	12521.87	46445.97	1702.97	10888.93
	6	102761.64	33410.79	2065.99	59173.48	12591.96	46581.52	1745.46	10880.52
	7	102898.38	33084.38	2488.19	59147.55	12817.38	46330.17	1765.75	11199.00
	8	103773.43	33959.44	2150.27	59187.26	13104.84	46082.42	1821.69	11395.16
	9	105523.94	34881.42	2505.89	59364.31	13590.31	45774.00	1870.74	12255.24
	10	105898.87	35158.30	2466.69	59269.90	13807.55	45462.35	1894.79	12153.88
	11	107311.52	35818.65	3014.11	59185.38	14088.50	45096.88	1986.97	12482.62
	12	108778.94	37182.36	2128.06	59621.83	14666.72	44955.11	2126.33	13455.49
比上期增减额（亿元） Changes Compared with Previous Period (100 Million Yuan)									
1999	1	353.70	-615.21	77.68	924.87	352.23	572.64	-3.04	792.56
	2	1258.95	-719.58	-217.45	2473.79	838.00	1635.79	-177.38	787.52
	3	2208.97	746.54	86.47	1047.18	-156.95	1204.13	84.70	-1442.61
	4	776.67	233.36	-115.56	554.42	-142.82	697.24	32.90	-116.22
	5	1258.75	438.92	90.90	598.77	19.17	579.60	18.50	-336.48
	6	1288.10	869.27	-41.39	205.64	70.09	135.55	42.49	-8.41
	7	136.72	-326.41	422.19	-25.93	225.42	-251.35	20.29	318.48
	8	875.07	875.07	-337.91	39.71	287.46	-247.75	55.94	196.16
	9	1750.52	921.97	355.62	177.07	485.48	-308.41	49.05	860.08
	10	374.92	276.88	-39.21	-94.41	217.24	-311.65	24.04	-101.36
	11	1412.64	660.34	547.43	-84.52	280.95	-365.47	92.18	328.74
	12	1467.41	1363.70	-886.06	436.45	578.22	-141.77	139.36	972.87
比去年同期增长（%） Increase Rate Year-on-year (%)									
1999	1	18.67	19.13	38.76	16.72	25.81	14.39	33.41	-8.48
	2	17.15	16.70	17.41	18.60	31.59	15.28	16.74	17.44
	3	18.12	17.36	-0.54	18.75	29.33	16.09	17.81	11.18
	4	18.66	16.94	14.04	19.16	28.05	16.94	20.30	10.35
	5	17.75	16.30	3.67	18.65	24.48	17.17	20.57	9.06
	6	18.25	16.70	16.31	18.47	24.36	16.97	21.29	11.93
	7	16.15	14.05	18.71	16.55	20.58	15.48	21.00	11.57
	8	16.29	14.66	15.14	16.28	24.20	14.21	21.68	12.50
	9	14.84	13.04	5.25	15.09	24.33	12.61	20.74	16.41
	10	13.89	13.21	1.07	13.42	23.22	10.74	20.42	15.74
	11	13.64	13.57	14.31	11.77	22.81	8.72	22.22	16.97
	12	13.53	14.34	-2.74	11.48	26.04	7.43	21.64	20.09

金融机构人民币信贷收支主要指标时间序列表

Time Series of Major Indicators in Sources and Uses of Credit Funds of Financial Institutions（RMB）

年　月 Year Month		各项贷款 Total Loans	短期贷款 Short－term Loans	工业贷款 Loans to Industrial Sector	商业贷款 Loans to Commercial Sector	建筑业贷款 Loans to Construction Sector	农业贷款 Loans to Agricultural Sector	中长期贷款 Medium and Long－term Loans	基本建设贷款 Capital Construction Loans	技术改造贷款 Technical Improvement Loans	其他中长期贷款 Other Medium and Long－term Loans	有价证券及投资 Securities and Investments
期末余额（亿元） Balance（100 Million Yuan）												
1999	1	86532.97	60621.59	17706.28	19771.81	1689.19	4499.98	20633.60	10367.47	5071.26	5194.87	8035.82
	2	87057.21	61003.37	17781.42	19750.86	1695.09	4553.59	20706.27	10465.89	5061.81	5178.57	8015.29
	3	87825.58	61369.41	17878.73	19674.53	1703.56	4645.04	21024.24	10645.98	5071.90	5306.36	8188.66
	4	88399.85	61563.96	17925.23	19575.89	1715.53	4755.30	21308.31	10784.48	5073.13	5450.70	8138.51
	5	89021.35	61781.05	17989.66	19497.86	1733.59	4813.59	21606.37	10959.63	5067.86	5578.88	8364.66
	6	90620.29	62710.54	18293.63	19660.05	1775.00	4865.81	22270.10	11378.76	5097.39	5793.95	8537.43
	7	91157.63	62928.61	18253.71	19650.29	1776.29	4904.96	22509.52	11474.39	5119.32	5915.81	8795.16
	8	92101.23	63374.37	18297.24	19700.79	1783.38	4900.50	22892.29	11630.24	5131.58	6130.47	8623.35
	9	93390.41	64088.32	18451.75	19798.91	1808.91	4926.72	23439.75	11891.23	5157.80	6390.72	9177.91
	10	93866.35	64134.72	18435.22	19794.22	1807.72	4908.67	23720.85	12029.69	5166.96	6524.20	9261.50
	11	94929.68	64628.10	18516.05	19941.05	1797.39	4878.50	24180.68	12237.31	5223.71	6719.66	9202.76
	12	93734.28	63887.55	17948.87	19890.86	1476.86	4792.39	23968.32	11840.11	5025.87	7102.34	12505.79
比上期增减额（亿元） Changes Compared with Previous Period（100 Million Yuan）												
1999	1	144.67	67.73	－114.52	29.88	45.90	55.91	－29.54	－61.19	－43.05	74.70	－62.80
	2	524.24	381.79	75.14	－20.95	5.91	53.61	72.67	98.43	－9.46	－16.30	－20.54
	3	768.37	366.04	97.31	－76.33	8.47	91.45	317.96	180.10	10.09	127.77	173.39
	4	574.24	194.54	46.50	－98.65	11.97	110.26	284.08	138.50	1.22	144.36	－50.16
	5	621.52	217.11	64.44	－78.02	18.06	58.29	298.06	175.14	－5.26	128.18	226.15
	6	1598.95	929.47	303.97	162.18	41.41	52.22	663.73	419.13	29.54	215.06	172.76
	7	537.34	218.07	－39.92	－9.76	1.29	39.15	239.44	95.64	21.92	121.88	257.74
	8	943.61	445.76	43.53	50.50	7.09	－4.46	382.78	155.85	12.26	214.67	－171.81
	9	1289.18	713.95	154.50	98.12	25.53	26.23	547.46	260.99	26.22	260.25	554.56
	10	475.95	46.41	－16.53	－4.68	－1.18	－18.06	281.08	138.47	9.15	133.46	83.59
	11	1063.32	493.37	80.83	146.83	－10.33	－30.17	459.83	207.62	56.75	195.46	－58.74
	12	2305.02	1171.35	433.36	205.91	86.61	－86.11	1293.37	625.72	105.61	562.04	3303.03
比去年同期增长（%） Increase Rate Year－on－year（%）												
1999	1	15.60	11.36	9.18	9.01	13.95	14.76	27.40	29.03	5.20	55.53	119.79
	2	16.00	12.12	9.70	9.28	14.31	15.43	27.00	28.60	5.74	53.26	118.95
	3	15.64	11.43	9.20	8.63	13.43	14.33	27.97	30.74	5.72	52.09	131.25
	4	15.45	11.07	8.82	8.43	13.80	14.45	28.49	31.40	5.57	52.66	124.19
	5	15.14	10.69	8.34	7.96	13.76	14.82	28.39	31.23	4.98	52.86	118.43
	6	14.99	10.68	8.21	8.13	15.42	13.59	27.71	30.93	4.36	50.00	119.72
	7	14.57	10.23	7.39	14.48	14.73	13.44	27.76	30.31	4.78	50.63	119.37
	8	13.87	9.63	6.41	15.84	13.38	11.86	26.10	29.22	4.16	45.05	28.02
	9	13.00	9.22	5.75	4.89	13.36	10.75	23.92	25.61	3.25	43.50	22.20
	10	12.52	8.73	5.67	3.76	13.23	10.51	23.29	26.06	2.29	40.41	20.68
	11	12.21	8.54	5.53	2.36	12.26	10.30	22.13	24.00	3.14	38.12	18.24
	12	12.25	8.52	6.32	1.95	15.60	7.83	22.92	23.17	4.12	41.08	54.16

金融机构人民币信贷收支主要指标时间序列表
Time Series of Major Indicators in Sources and Uses of Credit Funds of Financial Institutions (RMB)

年 Year	月 Month	各项存款 Total Deposits	企业存款 Deposits by Enterprises	财政存款 Fiscal Deposits	储蓄存款 Savings Deposits	活期储蓄 Demand Deposits	定期储蓄 Time Deposits	农业存款 Deposits by Agricultural Sector	流通中货币 Currency in Circulation
					期末余额(亿元) Balance (100 Million Yuan)				
2000	1	107778.82	35659.16	2412.93	60241.84	14975.00	45266.84	1989.98	16093.97
	2	109962.65	36010.98	2146.24	62270.25	15726.83	46543.42	1939.59	13983.01
	3	112346.37	37387.11	2702.67	62492.29	16001.83	46490.46	2043.04	13235.40
	4	113386.35	38357.08	2634.15	62536.12	16115.39	46420.73	2047.80	13675.50
	5	114679.66	39056.12	3378.95	62195.39	16066.60	46128.79	2101.13	13075.45
	6	117443.25	40739.83	3489.45	62842.38	16640.16	46202.22	2194.38	13006.04
	7	117155.09	40239.49	3662.40	62841.50	16642.47	46199.03	2190.16	13156.47
	8	118127.02	41146.52	3383.41	62861.11	16764.26	46096.85	2268.50	13378.68
	9	120048.33	42685.74	3143.65	63243.27	17308.88	45934.39	2349.83	13894.69
	10	119955.19	42147.46	3685.56	63122.34	17135.05	45987.29	2341.86	13589.45
	11	121868.23	42541.59	4427.74	63492.06	17404.70	46087.36	2443.12	13877.70
	12	123804.35	44093.73	3508.09	64332.38	18190.72	46141.66	2642.86	14652.65
					比上期增减额(亿元) Changes Compared with Previous Period (100 Million Yuan)				
2000	1	-613.59	-1436.05	289.21	886.15	450.63	435.52	-145.09	2638.48
	2	2183.83	351.82	-266.69	2028.41	751.83	1276.58	-50.39	-2110.96
	3	2383.72	1376.13	556.43	222.04	275.00	-52.96	103.45	-747.61
	4	1039.98	969.97	-68.52	43.83	113.56	-69.73	4.76	440.10
	5	1293.31	699.04	744.80	-340.73	-48.79	-291.94	53.33	-600.05
	6	2763.59	1683.71	110.50	646.99	573.56	73.43	93.25	-69.41
	7	-288.16	-500.34	172.95	-0.88	2.31	-3.19	-4.22	150.43
	8	971.92	907.03	-278.99	19.61	121.79	-102.18	78.34	222.21
	9	1921.31	1539.22	-239.76	382.16	544.62	-162.46	81.33	516.01
	10	-93.16	-538.28	541.91	-120.93	-173.83	52.90	-7.97	-305.24
	11	1913.05	394.13	742.18	369.72	269.65	100.07	101.26	288.25
	12	1936.14	1552.14	-919.65	840.32	786.02	54.30	199.74	774.95
					比去年同期增长(%) Increase Rate Year-on-year (%)				
2000	1	12.30	11.99	6.62	10.96	25.16	6.94	14.09	34.15
	2	13.10	15.71	4.92	9.69	22.84	5.86	23.79	9.38
	3	12.98	17.31	26.76	8.09	26.54	2.93	23.71	16.70
	4	13.14	19.48	30.63	7.14	28.90	1.21	21.57	21.83
	5	13.01	20.02	60.34	5.47	28.31	-0.68	23.38	20.08
	6	14.29	21.94	68.90	6.20	32.15	-0.81	25.72	19.54
	7	13.86	21.63	47.19	6.25	29.84	-0.28	24.04	17.48
	8	13.83	21.16	57.35	6.21	27.92	0.03	24.53	17.41
	9	13.76	22.37	25.45	6.53	27.36	0.35	25.61	13.38
	10	13.27	19.88	49.41	6.50	24.10	1.15	23.59	11.81
	11	13.56	18.77	46.90	7.28	23.54	2.20	22.96	11.18
	12	13.81	18.59	64.85	7.90	24.03	2.64	24.29	8.90

金融机构人民币信贷收支主要指标时间序列表

Time Series of Major Indicators in Sources and Uses of Credit Funds of Financial Institutions（RMB）

年 月 Year Month	各项贷款 Total Loans	短期贷款 Short-term Loans					中长期贷款 Medium and Long-term Loans				有价证券及投资 Securities and Investments
			工业贷款 Loans to Industrial Sector	商业贷款 Loans to Commercial Sector	建筑业贷款 Loans to Construction Sector	农业贷款 Loans to Agricultural Sector		基本建设贷款 Capital Construction Loans	技术改造贷款 Technical Improvement Loans	其他中长期贷款 Other Medium and Long-term Loans	
期末余额（亿元） Balance（100 Million Yuan）											
2000 1	93838.17	64225.34	17924.79	19898.84	1486.49	4852.32	23851.23	11710.47	5015.77	7124.99	12569.43
2	94352.89	64472.00	18038.65	19820.58	1491.00	4895.89	24040.69	11804.66	5027.18	7208.85	12694.87
3	95776.52	65456.07	18340.26	19846.54	1510.53	5024.41	24605.00	12122.84	5047.67	7434.49	12657.30
4	96604.25	65910.96	18415.43	19730.54	1521.45	5136.15	24936.27	12298.13	5048.40	7589.74	13077.85
5	96174.88	65263.96	18214.56	19312.79	1522.86	5072.58	25093.43	12444.98	4998.80	7649.65	13611.30
6	94847.87	63711.09	17830.38	18209.27	1537.16	4930.23	25302.95	12492.10	4918.25	7892.60	13579.39
7	94362.51	62958.05	17358.34	17836.90	1552.57	4941.73	25509.84	12679.32	4830.72	7999.80	14742.06
8	94874.36	63174.12	17231.24	17669.83	1575.14	4985.16	25806.66	12819.85	4803.91	8182.90	15159.62
9	95995.51	63798.70	17088.89	17705.33	1610.41	5025.78	26323.62	13129.17	4802.27	8392.18	16696.80
10	96709.81	64133.09	17054.58	17703.41	1618.21	5025.60	26679.51	13325.13	4822.60	8531.78	16827.23
11	98180.28	65043.07	17084.39	17819.91	1630.43	4978.27	27180.85	13515.86	4841.39	8823.60	17647.15
12	99371.07	65748.07	17019.33	17868.50	1617.05	4888.99	27931.19	13742.22	4861.07	9327.90	19651.07
比上期增减额（亿元） Changes Compared with Previous Period（100 Million Yuan）											
2000 1	681.51	389.26	-5.36	7.08	11.23	77.93	156.34	52.93	10.97	92.44	66.44
2	519.47	269.15	17.97	-7.97	4.51	43.57	169.06	71.21	13.66	84.19	125.51
3	1449.96	1004.44	305.14	30.28	19.53	131.90	569.99	318.26	25.01	226.72	-37.58
4	1001.07	608.49	110.22	-77.31	10.92	118.71	350.61	175.82	12.08	162.71	420.49
5	795.02	420.82	49.51	-25.92	2.18	76.27	314.15	182.87	30.87	100.41	533.78
6	1757.11	1104.37	222.73	73.96	41.81	49.41	631.92	162.51	92.97	376.44	-32.03
7	902.36	397.32	-29.63	72.58	15.58	68.25	444.09	225.93	21.83	196.33	1162.95
8	999.52	521.20	-38.12	-11.56	-20.39	56.73	479.44	198.45	11.29	269.70	417.55
9	1573.86	990.90	81.17	114.75	35.27	47.29	602.89	366.07	66.96	169.86	1539.7
10	840.65	429.50	-2.27	44.21	8.19	2.45	387.14	199.74	46.31	141.09	130.53
11	1534.69	955.09	43.63	136.82	12.22	-44.48	521.01	194.85	28.07	298.09	820.22
12	1291.67	784.04	-16.81	60.18	-13.39	-89.67	771.29	231.49	35.83	503.97	2005.24
比去年同期增长（%） Increase Rate Year-on-year（%）											
2000 1	12.80	9.11	6.87	1.98	12.10	7.83	23.88	24.62	5.40	40.47	56.42
2	12.71	8.87	6.52	2.05	11.98	7.52	24.26	24.12	5.86	42.54	58.38
3	13.38	9.86	7.65	2.60	12.57	8.25	25.10	25.01	6.15	43.38	54.57
4	13.77	10.50	7.99	2.72	12.42	8.23	25.07	25.04	6.36	42.56	60.69
5	13.87	10.79	7.87	3.00	11.37	8.50	24.80	24.71	7.08	41.09	62.72
6	13.80	10.91	7.30	2.52	11.13	8.35	23.92	21.54	8.28	42.35	59.06
7	14.12	11.16	7.37	2.94	11.93	8.88	24.58	22.50	8.24	42.73	67.62
8	14.04	11.20	6.91	2.62	10.34	10.13	24.59	22.56	8.20	42.14	75.80
9	14.15	11.50	6.45	2.69	10.73	10.51	24.25	22.95	8.95	39.01	81.92
10	14.47	12.09	6.54	2.94	11.26	10.96	24.41	23.20	9.66	38.32	81.69
11	14.80	12.72	6.31	2.87	12.58	10.74	24.20	22.70	9.00	38.74	91.76
12	17.64	15.25	9.57	3.43	36.10	10.86	28.52	28.77	14.01	38.36	57.14

金融机构人民币信贷收支主要指标时间序列表

Time Series of Major Indicators in Sources and Uses of Credit Funds of Financial Institutions（RMB）

年 月 Year Month		各项存款 Total Deposits							流通中货币 Currency in Circulation
			企业存款 Deposits by Enterprises	财政存款 Fiscal Deposits	储蓄存款 Savings Deposits			农业存款 Deposits by Agricultural Sector	
						活期储蓄 Demand Deposits	定期储蓄 Time Deposits		
期末余额（亿元） Balance（100 Million Yuan）									
2001	1	124987.67	43488.62	4131.87	66547.31	19259.28	47288.03	2360.11	17018.98
	2	125502.38	43410.73	3749.11	67343.36	19029.15	48314.21	2392.07	14910.39
	3	128899.71	45147.08	3960.67	68365.13	19711.22	48653.91	2534.37	14362.12
	4	130930.13	45739.54	5012.39	68618.46	19803.80	48814.66	2544.24	14622.99
	5	130420.46	45093.41	4538.71	68393.54	19494.20	48899.34	2608.04	13942.28
	6	135189.54	47956.80	4502.18	69628.58	20376.97	49251.61	2753.32	13943.44
	7	133699.41	45869.33	4970.05	69677.77	20180.14	49497.63	2698.00	14071.62
	8	137138.40	47973.92	4873.39	70558.48	20775.55	49782.93	2812.28	14370.13
	9	139116.33	49028.77	4817.91	71252.65	21235.89	50016.76	2905.67	15064.58
	10	140065.90	48831.58	5393.22	71818.81	21337.06	50481.75	2916.07	14484.61
	11	140286.55	48855.92	4787.14	72323.82	21436.78	50887.04	2945.16	14780.03
	12	143617.17	51546.63	3369.75	73762.43	22327.57	51434.86	3083.26	15688.80
比上期增减额（亿元） Changes Compared with Previous Period（100 Million Yuan）									
2001	1	1488.22	-858.54	626.18	2242.52	1076.19	1166.33	-297.48	2366.33
	2	514.71	-77.89	-382.76	796.05	-230.13	1026.18	31.96	-2108.59
	3	3397.33	1736.35	211.56	1021.77	682.07	339.70	142.30	-548.27
	4	2030.42	592.46	1051.72	253.33	92.58	160.75	9.87	260.87
	5	-509.67	-646.13	-473.68	-224.92	-309.60	84.68	63.80	-680.71
	6	4769.08	2863.39	-36.53	1235.04	882.77	352.27	145.28	1.16
	7	-1490.13	-2087.47	467.87	49.19	-196.83	246.02	-55.32	128.18
	8	3438.99	2104.59	-96.66	880.71	595.41	285.30	114.28	298.51
	9	1977.93	1054.85	-55.48	694.17	460.34	233.83	93.39	694.45
	10	949.57	-197.19	575.31	566.16	101.17	464.99	10.40	-579.97
	11	220.65	24.34	-606.08	505.01	99.72	405.29	29.09	295.42
	12	3330.62	2690.71	-1417.39	1438.61	890.79	547.82	138.10	908.77
比去年同期增长（%） Increase Rate Year-on-year（%）									
2001	1	15.97	21.96	71.24	10.47	28.61	4.47	18.60	5.75
	2	14.13	20.55	74.68	8.15	21.00	3.80	23.33	6.63
	3	14.73	20.76	46.55	9.40	23.18	4.65	24.05	8.51
	4	15.47	19.25	90.28	9.73	22.89	5.16	24.24	6.93
	5	13.73	15.46	34.32	9.97	21.33	6.01	24.13	6.63
	6	15.11	17.72	29.02	10.80	22.46	6.60	25.47	7.21
	7	14.12	13.99	35.70	10.88	21.26	7.14	23.19	6.96
	8	16.09	16.59	44.04	12.25	23.93	8.00	23.97	7.41
	9	15.88	14.86	53.26	12.66	22.69	8.89	23.65	8.42
	10	16.77	15.86	46.33	13.78	24.52	9.77	24.52	6.59
	11	15.11	14.84	8.12	13.91	23.17	10.41	20.55	6.50
	12	16.00	16.90	-3.94	14.66	22.74	11.47	16.66	7.07

金融机构人民币信贷收支主要指标时间序列表

Time Series of Major Indicators in Sources and Uses of Credit Funds of Financial Institutions（RMB）

年 月 Year Month	各项贷款 Total Loans	短期贷款 Short - term Loans	工业贷款 Loans to Industrial Sector	商业贷款 Loans to Commercial Sector	建筑业贷款 Loans to Construction Sector	农业贷款 Loans to Agricultural Sector	中长期贷款 Medium and Long - term Loans	基本建设贷款 Capital Construction Loans	技术改造贷款 Technical Improvement Loans	其他中长期贷款 Other Medium and Long - term Loans	票据融资 Paper Financing	有价证券及投资 Securities and Investments
期末余额（亿元） Balance（100 Million Yuan）												
2001 1	100687.23	63386.93	17790.60	18515.15	1780.35	5009.99	33166.28	14072.86	4833.97	14259.45	1510.91	20217.88
2	101425.74	63566.03	17815.98	18411.51	1787.05	5108.26	33630.89	14294.32	4879.43	14457.14	1555.99	20202.62
3	102470.64	63816.97	17744.67	18275.65	1812.11	5296.79	34313.56	14492.42	4883.41	14937.73	1657.39	20417.70
4	103491.81	64030.13	17730.42	18183.61	1823.71	5475.82	34961.81	14689.00	4895.59	15377.22	1832.00	20663.39
5	104714.59	64394.18	17752.17	18105.94	1943.90	5594.72	35374.03	14824.61	4885.81	15663.61	1904.41	20851.50
6	106553.42	65320.03	18063.71	18201.89	1955.66	5674.18	36023.19	15051.39	4877.88	16093.92	2142.85	21231.51
7	107094.17	65316.34	17954.32	18162.34	1927.11	5734.02	36394.56	15233.95	4854.38	16306.23	2258.58	21506.72
8	107614.13	65267.07	17909.97	18071.32	1920.36	5800.75	36881.02	15446.01	4864.73	16570.28	2369.76	21685.08
9	108973.37	65764.83	18027.78	18075.65	1940.60	5865.05	37599.53	15715.38	4900.14	16984.01	2579.25	21695.61
10	108989.38	65637.98	18028.37	18005.59	1935.10	5857.12	37732.44	15677.45	4908.82	17146.17	2591.33	21986.35
11	110090.33	66126.99	18196.17	18218.37	1960.03	5817.94	38245.77	15880.82	4922.13	17442.82	2694.04	21900.69
12	112314.70	67327.23	18636.68	18563.41	2099.58	5711.48	39238.08	16270.78	5000.68	17966.62	2814.04	23112.65
比上期增减额（亿元） Changes Compared with Previous Period（100 Million Yuan）												
2001 1	1285.38	548.51	150.00	- 19.36	39.98	87.63	476.67	81.40	10.40	384.87	248.01	114.23
2	738.51	179.10	25.38	- 103.64	6.70	98.27	464.61	221.46	45.46	197.69	45.08	- 15.26
3	1044.90	250.94	- 71.31	- 135.86	25.06	188.53	682.67	198.10	3.98	480.59	101.40	215.08
4	1021.17	213.16	- 14.25	- 92.04	11.60	179.03	648.25	196.58	12.18	439.49	174.61	245.69
5	1222.78	364.05	21.75	- 77.67	120.19	118.90	412.22	135.61	- 9.78	286.39	72.41	188.11
6	1838.83	925.85	311.54	95.95	11.76	79.46	649.16	226.78	- 7.93	430.31	238.44	380.01
7	540.75	- 3.69	- 109.39	- 39.55	- 28.55	59.84	371.37	182.56	- 23.50	212.31	115.73	275.21
8	519.96	- 49.27	- 44.35	- 91.02	- 6.75	66.73	486.46	212.06	10.35	264.05	111.18	178.36
9	1359.24	497.76	117.81	4.33	20.24	64.30	718.51	269.37	35.41	413.73	209.49	10.53
10	16.01	- 126.85	0.59	- 70.06	- 5.50	- 7.93	132.91	- 37.93	8.68	162.16	12.08	290.74
11	1100.95	489.01	167.80	212.78	24.93	- 39.18	513.33	203.37	13.31	296.65	102.71	- 85.66
12	2224.37	1200.24	440.51	345.04	139.55	- 106.46	992.31	389.96	78.55	523.80	120.00	1211.96
比去年同期增长（%） Increase Rate Year - on - year（%）												
2001 1	14.69	12.50	8.95	6.18	23.21	11.98	32.64	27.45	13.41	50.11	159.43	52.69
2	14.85	12.40	8.94	5.72	23.28	12.99	33.25	28.51	14.02	49.98	171.99	59.25
3	14.20	11.16	6.56	4.79	23.35	13.79	32.63	25.87	10.63	53.04	177.36	61.42
4	14.10	10.85	6.04	4.83	23.23	14.66	32.47	25.77	12.95	51.06	187.15	58.08
5	14.61	11.16	5.95	4.67	30.95	15.69	32.07	25.08	12.25	50.83	180.22	51.17
6	14.90	10.80	5.63	4.18	24.44	16.75	32.85	21.61	2.36	60.94	182.91	55.01
7	14.60	11.13	5.90	4.43	21.35	16.54	30.35	21.25	6.26	52.19	200.88	42.35
8	14.00	10.88	6.31	4.14	26.08	16.60	28.48	24.62	9.65	41.17	195.25	39.27
9	13.64	10.32	6.45	2.76	24.57	16.80	27.95	23.18	8.37	41.60	185.29	29.80
10	12.69	10.03	6.60	2.87	23.61	16.59	25.50	21.18	8.15	37.51	170.34	30.52
11	12.06	9.75	7.32	3.27	24.22	16.86	24.03	20.94	7.81	33.79	153.98	23.95
12	12.86	10.38	9.50	3.89	29.84	16.82	24.67	18.40	4.21	38.94	122.64	17.39

金融机构人民币信贷收支主要指标时间序列表

Time Series of Major Indicators in Sources and Uses of Credit Funds of Financial Institutions (RMB)

年 月 Year Month		各项存款 Total Deposits	企业存款 Deposits by Enterprises	财政存款 Fiscal Deposits	储蓄存款 Savings Deposits	活期储蓄 Demand Deposits	定期储蓄 Time Deposits	农业存款 Deposits by Agricultural Sector	流通中货币 Currency in Circulation
		期末余额（亿元） Balance (100 Million Yuan)							
2002	1	143388.45	49088.51	3867.46	74953.71	22743.20	52210.51	3088.20	16725.89
	2	144349.17	47690.18	3404.23	78114.33	23801.77	54312.56	2822.60	16641.55
	3	147209.94	49330.57	3433.46	78728.30	24021.63	54706.67	2956.88	15544.63
	4	150603.98	50707.16	4174.77	79728.20	24636.13	55092.07	3033.31	15864.18
	5	153258.08	51473.28	4756.96	80394.30	24894.65	55499.65	3111.44	15243.07
	6	157645.11	53510.35	4798.14	81711.79	25552.62	56159.17	3237.09	15097.35
	7	158780.22	53481.43	4777.87	82527.90	25858.66	56669.24	3263.03	15357.66
	8	161671.05	54800.76	5198.57	83275.97	26248.80	57027.17	3358.42	15712.61
	9	165674.85	56898.03	5458.57	84139.05	26771.92	57367.13	3510.38	16233.58
	10	166454.92	56693.61	5664.99	84725.13	26866.46	57858.67	3532.50	16014.66
	11	168595.90	57608.26	5526.52	85693.49	27349.33	58344.16	3613.28	16346.39
	12	170917.40	60028.57	3481.90	86910.65	28121.71	58788.94	3764.24	17278.03
		比上期增减额（亿元） Changes Compared with Previous Period (100 Million Yuan)							
2002	1	138.93	-1407.35	514.24	1276.14	422.63	853.51	-1.92	1037.09
	2	965.71	-1397.70	-463.15	3160.62	1058.57	2102.05	-265.60	-84.34
	3	2869.21	1640.39	29.23	613.97	219.86	394.11	134.28	-1096.92
	4	3406.46	1377.91	741.31	999.90	614.50	385.40	76.43	319.55
	5	2656.95	766.14	582.19	666.10	258.52	407.58	78.13	-621.11
	6	4462.15	2037.05	41.18	1317.49	657.97	659.52	125.65	-145.72
	7	1138.35	-28.92	-20.27	816.11	306.04	510.07	25.94	260.31
	8	2895.72	1319.50	420.69	748.07	390.14	357.93	95.39	354.95
	9	4004.68	2097.32	260.01	863.08	523.12	339.96	151.96	520.97
	10	780.05	-204.44	206.42	586.08	94.54	491.54	22.12	-218.92
	11	2141.53	914.67	-138.47	968.36	482.87	485.49	80.78	331.73
	12	2329.96	2420.29	-2044.62	1217.16	772.38	444.78	150.96	931.64
		比去年同期增长（%） Increase Rate Year-on-year (%)							
2002	1	14.65	12.69	-6.40	12.63	18.09	10.41	30.85	-1.72
	2	14.95	9.68	-9.20	15.99	25.08	12.42	18.00	11.61
	3	14.13	9.07	-13.31	15.16	21.87	12.44	16.67	8.23
	4	14.95	10.66	-16.71	16.19	24.40	12.86	19.22	8.49
	5	17.44	13.94	4.81	17.55	27.70	13.50	19.30	9.33
	6	16.54	11.40	6.57	17.35	25.40	14.03	17.57	8.28
	7	18.68	16.38	-3.87	18.44	28.14	14.49	20.94	9.14
	8	17.81	14.02	6.67	18.02	26.34	14.55	19.42	9.34
	9	19.01	15.83	13.30	18.08	26.06	14.70	20.81	7.76
	10	18.76	15.89	5.04	17.97	25.91	14.61	21.14	10.56
	11	20.10	17.68	15.45	18.49	27.58	14.65	22.69	10.60
	12	18.91	16.19	3.33	17.82	25.95	14.30	22.09	10.13

金融机构人民币信贷收支主要指标时间序列表

Time Series of Major Indicators in Sources and Uses of Credit Funds of Financial Institutions（RMB）

年 月 Year Month		各项贷款 Total Loans	短期贷款 Short－term Loans	工业贷款 Loans to Industrial Sector	商业贷款 Loans to Commercial Sector	建筑业贷款 Loans to Construction Sector	农业贷款 Loans to Agricultural Sector	中长期贷款 Medium and Long－term Loans	基本建设贷款 Capital Construction Loans	技术改造贷款 Technical Improvement Loans	其他中长期贷款 Other Medium and Long－term Loans	票据融资 Paper Financing	有价证券及投资 Securities and Investments
		期末余额（亿元） Balance（100 Million Yuan）											
2002	1	113194.69	66508.50	17425.12	18477.27	1892.24	5913.24	40450.93	19299.41	1973.79	19177.73	3509.83	23576.60
	2	113709.88	66715.19	17579.20	18465.42	1876.54	6009.87	40770.93	19443.97	1960.61	19366.35	3505.49	23566.93
	3	116255.00	68501.44	18279.72	18492.50	1962.80	6326.19	41424.57	19731.64	1951.94	19740.99	3628.38	24136.63
	4	117179.02	68919.43	18238.91	18195.38	2008.96	6594.38	41707.64	19805.50	1948.83	19953.31	3866.65	24465.97
	5	118286.23	69346.08	18545.82	18032.59	2228.78	6725.76	42357.01	20009.41	1959.99	20387.61	3900.53	24753.81
	6	121137.64	70707.42	19053.47	17997.04	2344.94	6852.59	43448.49	20543.79	1987.28	20917.42	4333.57	25349.85
	7	121754.40	70745.47	19151.15	17864.54	2385.56	6943.41	43881.20	20708.34	1989.66	21183.20	4466.28	25618.01
	8	123483.62	71333.65	19287.71	17762.37	2442.37	7044.47	44722.23	21002.83	1990.62	21728.78	4774.21	25822.14
	9	126366.74	72585.31	19649.97	17831.22	2573.64	7123.00	45931.11	21457.42	2000.50	22473.19	5182.71	26155.39
	10	127089.14	72659.95	19603.37	17849.17	2615.75	7112.63	46547.71	21638.03	2020.07	22889.61	5209.42	26265.90
	11	128627.75	73223.83	19787.22	17874.52	2679.13	7061.87	47274.29	21771.65	1993.43	23509.21	5467.45	26318.92
	12	131293.93	74247.90	20190.47	17973.12	2747.99	6884.58	48642.04	22434.61	2029.78	24177.65	5752.02	26789.73
		比上期增减额（亿元） Changes Compared with Previous Period（100 Million Yuan）											
2002	1	239.94	12.27	－54.16	－134.97	28.34	206.10	243.94	39.04	8.89	196.01	－10.22	53.22
	2	529.51	207.43	154.68	－11.79	－15.7	96.63	320.00	144.56	－13.18	188.62	－4.34	2.94
	3	2554.12	1786.24	700.52	27.07	86.26	316.32	653.64	287.67	－8.67	374.64	122.89	570.61
	4	936.61	418.63	－40.48	－296.86	46.17	268.19	283.31	74.10	－3.11	212.32	238.27	331.76
	5	1110.19	426.67	306.91	－162.79	219.82	131.38	649.37	203.91	11.16	434.30	33.88	288.77
	6	2929.20	1361.48	507.66	－35.55	116.16	126.83	1091.48	534.38	27.29	529.81	433.04	608.64
	7	619.57	38.04	97.67	－132.5	40.62	90.82	432.71	164.55	2.38	265.78	132.71	268.94
	8	1736.20	588.62	136.84	－102.00	56.81	101.06	843.31	294.49	0.96	547.86	307.93	207.93
	9	2885.13	1251.66	362.26	68.84	131.27	78.53	1208.9	454.59	9.88	744.43	408.50	334.84
	10	722.39	74.64	－46.60	17.95	42.11	－10.37	616.60	180.61	19.57	416.42	26.71	110.17
	11	1538.81	563.87	183.84	25.35	63.38	－50.76	726.60	133.62	－26.64	619.62	258.03	53.44
	12	2673.34	1025.76	403.44	98.71	68.92	－177.29	1368.10	663.19	36.38	668.53	284.57	474.45
		比去年同期增长（%） Increase Rate Year－on－year（%）											
2002	1	10.83	4.53	－2.05	－0.20	6.28	18.03	21.87	37.14	－59.17	34.25	30.46	16.60
	2	10.55	4.54	－1.33	0.29	5.01	17.65	21.13	36.03	－59.82	33.71	29.49	16.64
	3	11.86	6.88	3.02	1.19	8.32	19.43	20.64	36.15	－60.03	31.94	28.93	18.20
	4	11.64	7.15	2.87	0.06	10.16	20.43	19.19	34.83	－60.19	29.51	29.78	18.39
	5	11.43	7.19	4.47	－0.41	14.66	20.22	19.63	34.97	－59.88	29.90	29.60	18.71
	6	12.18	7.74	5.48	－1.13	19.91	20.77	20.50	36.49	－59.26	29.70	34.04	19.39
	7	12.20	7.80	6.67	－1.64	23.79	21.09	20.45	35.94	－59.01	29.61	34.02	19.11
	8	13.26	8.77	7.69	－1.71	27.18	21.44	21.13	35.98	－59.08	30.81	39.27	19.07
	9	14.56	9.83	9.00	－1.35	32.62	21.45	22.02	36.54	－59.17	31.99	46.35	20.55
	10	15.35	10.14	8.74	－0.87	35.17	21.44	23.22	38.02	－58.85	33.15	53.24	19.46
	11	15.73	10.19	8.74	－1.89	36.69	21.38	23.45	37.09	－59.50	34.40	62.02	20.17
	12	15.82	9.74	8.34	－3.18	30.88	20.54	23.80	37.88	－59.41	34.19	65.46	15.90

金融机构人民币信贷收支主要指标时间序列表
Time Series of Major Indicators in Sources and Uses of Credit Funds of Financial Institutions（RMB）

年　月 Year Month		各项存款 Total Deposits	企业存款 Deposits by Enterprises	财政存款 Fiscal Deposits	储蓄存款 Savings Deposits	活期储蓄 Demand Deposits	定期储蓄 Time Deposits	农业存款 Deposits by Agricultural Sector	流通中货币 Currency in Circulation
		期末余额（亿元） Balance（100 Million Yuan）							
2003	1	173465.88	58629.42	4158.88	90677.63	29790.64	60886.99	3595.08	21244.73
	2	176585.78	58962.52	4489.22	92824.21	30146.88	62677.33	3627.14	17937.17
	3	182295.33	61657.84	4867.22	94567.84	30676.16	63891.68	3834.97	17106.50
	4	184627.83	61866.31	5888.25	95194.12	30848.03	64346.09	3887.81	17441.14
	5	188954.27	63603.23	6529.61	96351.67	31286.20	65065.47	4040.35	17115.03
	6	194306.47	66657.97	6128.64	97674.57	31995.42	65679.15	4237.80	16956.89
	7	195520.53	66354.00	6189.74	98590.90	32416.12	66174.78	4309.23	17362.13
	8	197725.62	67214.38	6401.44	99255.58	32758.13	66497.45	4433.71	17606.76
	9	202869.28	70086.22	6290.83	100888.60	33584.97	67303.63	4622.35	18306.36
	10	204076.95	70176.94	6669.33	101381.89	33599.63	67782.26	4682.26	18250.67
	11	206119.57	70509.62	6937.03	102235.44	34166.64	68068.80	4740.47	18439.56
	12	208055.59	72487.05	5126.94	103617.65	35118.98	68498.67	4898.33	19745.99
		比上期增减额（亿元） Changes Compared with Previous Period（100 Million Yuan）							
2003	1	2583.03	-1310.84	688.67	3691.88	1629.04	2062.84	-170.49	3966.70
	2	3119.90	333.10	330.34	2146.58	356.24	1790.34	32.06	-3307.56
	3	5713.53	2696.06	378.00	1743.63	529.28	1214.35	207.83	-830.67
	4	2337.13	208.47	1021.03	626.28	171.87	454.41	52.84	334.64
	5	4330.50	1737.48	641.36	1157.55	438.17	719.38	152.54	-326.11
	6	5353.99	3054.76	-400.97	1322.90	709.22	613.68	197.45	-158.14
	7	1215.30	-303.98	61.10	916.33	420.70	495.63	71.43	405.24
	8	2205.10	860.39	211.70	664.68	342.01	322.67	124.48	244.63
	9	5143.62	2871.82	-110.61	1633.02	826.84	806.18	188.64	699.60
	10	1207.70	90.73	378.50	493.29	14.66	478.63	59.91	-55.69
	11	2042.62	332.68	267.70	853.55	567.01	286.54	58.21	188.89
	12	1936.02	1977.43	-1810.09	1382.21	952.34	429.87	157.86	1306.43
		比去年同期增长（%） Increase Rate Year-on-year（%）							
2003	1	20.98	19.44	7.54	20.98	30.99	16.62	16.41	27.02
	2	22.33	23.64	31.87	18.83	26.66	15.40	28.50	7.79
	3	23.83	24.99	41.76	20.12	27.70	16.79	29.70	10.05
	4	22.59	22.01	41.04	19.40	25.21	16.80	28.17	9.94
	5	23.29	23.57	37.26	19.85	25.67	17.24	29.85	12.28
	6	23.26	24.57	27.73	19.54	25.21	16.95	30.91	12.32
	7	23.14	24.07	29.55	19.46	25.36	16.77	32.06	13.05
	8	22.30	22.65	23.14	19.19	24.80	16.61	32.02	12.05
	9	22.45	23.18	15.25	19.91	25.45	17.32	31.68	12.77
	10	22.60	23.78	17.73	19.66	25.06	17.15	32.55	13.96
	11	22.26	22.39	25.52	19.30	24.93	16.67	31.20	12.81
	12	21.73	20.75	47.25	19.22	24.88	16.52	30.13	14.28

金融机构人民币信贷收支主要指标时间序列表

Time Series of Major Indicators in Sources and Uses of Credit Funds of Financial Institutions（RMB）

年 月 Year Month	各项贷款 Total Loans	短期贷款 Short－term Loans					中长期贷款 Medium and Long－term Loans				票据融资 Paper Financing	有价证券及投资 Securities and Investments
			工业贷款 Loans to Industrial Sector	商业贷款 Loans to Commercial Sector	建筑业贷款 Loans to Construction Sector	农业贷款 Loans to Agricultural Sector		基本建设贷款 Capital Construction Loans	技术改造贷款 Technical Improvement Loans	其他中长期贷款 Other Medium and Long－term Loans		
期末余额（亿元） Balance（100 Million Yuan）												
2003 1	134622.95	75590.55	20534.91	18046.94	2905.72	7228.86	49991.72	22848.58	2049.88	25093.26	6401.55	26387.87
2	135714.13	76041.09	20502.72	18060.08	2936.48	7378.13	50448.38	23081.02	2067.21	25300.15	6569.62	26656.09
3	139436.53	77717.60	20876.46	18088.80	3040.76	7731.19	52032.26	23846.72	2097.82	26087.72	7046.78	26439.82
4	141377.15	78195.47	20830.31	17921.40	3088.20	7990.90	52909.69	24083.15	2090.09	26736.45	7593.56	27077.93
5	143908.41	79201.99	21083.35	17817.60	3149.04	8145.53	53907.98	24397.56	2112.76	27397.66	8127.62	27406.01
6	149156.56	81290.08	21620.58	17923.65	3276.14	8311.09	56013.38	25388.73	2111.78	28512.87	9163.20	27756.97
7	150216.81	80850.87	21365.76	17738.04	3165.22	8455.26	57279.61	25797.50	2135.13	29346.98	9385.85	27731.19
8	153025.17	81888.69	21920.35	17830.69	3375.99	8630.82	58378.92	26317.56	2163.21	29898.15	10007.53	27963.28
9	156059.89	82731.62	22263.70	17900.29	3150.38	8741.30	60215.29	27281.50	2165.86	30767.93	10346.65	28070.98
10	156676.17	83153.19	22413.33	17934.30	3139.45	8752.34	60896.33	27616.38	2172.89	31107.06	9843.00	28107.02
11	157701.12	83402.44	22512.48	17957.98	3067.03	8704.51	61801.48	27950.38	2202.55	31648.55	9702.53	28204.53
12	158996.23	83661.15	22756.00	17994.41	3002.14	8411.35	63401.40	28857.12	2208.75	32335.53	9170.73	30259.47
比上期增减额（亿元） Changes Compared with Previous Period（100 Million Yuan）												
2003 1	3266.13	1425.64	353.00	92.28	152.11	348.64	1194.64	364.89	19.52	810.23	633.90	－45.69
2	1091.18	450.54	－32.19	13.14	30.76	149.27	456.66	232.44	17.33	206.89	168.07	268.22
3	3724.83	1676.60	373.74	28.72	104.28	353.06	1583.88	765.70	30.61	787.57	477.16	－215.74
4	1944.69	477.87	－46.15	－167.40	47.44	259.71	877.43	236.43	－7.73	648.73	546.78	639.71
5	2533.77	1006.51	253.04	－103.80	60.84	154.63	1000.81	314.41	22.67	663.73	534.06	331.81
6	5249.85	2088.10	537.23	106.05	127.10	165.56	2105.39	991.17	－0.98	1115.20	1035.58	351.42
7	1061.81	－439.21	－254.82	－185.61	－110.92	144.17	1266.67	408.77	23.35	834.55	222.65	－25.19
8	2808.36	1037.82	554.59	92.65	210.77	175.56	1099.31	520.06	28.08	551.17	621.68	232.10
9	3034.73	842.93	343.35	69.60	－225.61	110.48	1836.38	963.94	2.65	869.79	339.12	107.69
10	616.27	421.57	149.63	34.01	－10.93	11.04	681.03	334.88	7.03	339.12	－503.65	36.04
11	1024.96	249.25	99.15	23.68	－72.42	－47.83	905.16	334.00	29.66	541.50	－140.47	97.51
12	1295.09	258.71	243.52	36.43	－64.89	－293.16	1599.91	906.74	6.20	686.97	－531.80	2054.94
比去年同期增长（%） Increase Rate Year－on－year（%）												
2003 1	18.93	13.66	17.85	－2.33	53.56	22.25	23.59	18.39	3.86	30.85	82.40	11.92
2	19.35	13.98	16.63	－2.20	56.48	22.77	23.74	18.71	5.44	30.64	87.42	13.11
3	19.94	13.45	14.21	－2.18	54.92	22.21	25.61	20.86	7.47	32.15	94.22	9.54
4	20.65	13.46	14.21	－1.51	53.72	21.18	26.86	21.60	7.25	34.00	96.39	10.68
5	21.66	14.21	13.68	－1.19	41.29	21.11	27.27	21.93	7.79	34.38	108.38	10.71
6	23.13	14.97	13.47	－0.41	39.71	21.28	28.92	23.58	6.26	36.31	111.45	9.50
7	23.28	14.28	11.56	－0.71	32.68	21.77	30.53	24.58	7.31	38.54	110.15	8.25
8	23.92	14.80	13.65	0.38	38.23	22.52	30.54	25.30	8.67	37.60	109.62	8.29
9	23.50	13.98	13.30	0.39	22.41	22.72	31.10	27.14	8.27	36.91	99.64	7.32
10	23.28	14.44	14.33	0.48	20.02	23.05	30.83	27.63	7.57	35.90	88.95	7.00
11	22.60	13.90	13.77	0.47	14.48	23.26	30.73	28.38	10.49	34.62	77.46	7.16
12	21.10	12.68	12.71	0.12	9.25	22.18	30.34	28.63	8.82	33.74	59.44	12.95

金融机构人民币信贷收支主要指标时间序列表

Time Series of Major Indicators in Sources and Uses of Credit Funds of Financial Institutions（RMB）

年 月 Year Month		各项存款 Total Deposits	企业存款 Deposits by Enterprises	财政存款 Fiscal Deposits	储蓄存款 Savings Deposits	活期储蓄 Demand Deposits	定期储蓄 Time Deposits	农业存款 Deposits by Agricultural Sector	流通中货币 Currency in Circulation
期末余额（亿元） Balance（100 Million Yuan）									
2004	1	210248.48	70153.31	5988.93	109232.65	37586.78	71645.87	4564.95	22287.43
	2	214639.78	71876.44	6370.40	110646.38	37557.98	73088.40	4701.35	19893.44
	3	220563.25	75025.89	6844.31	111872.18	38301.33	73570.85	4959.13	19297.43
	4	222360.32	75873.31	7223.49	112175.44	38681.67	73493.77	5000.81	19878.40
	5	225048.71	77118.07	7808.85	112610.18	38817.15	73793.03	5070.71	19048.43
	6	229670.82	79357.97	8192.30	113792.47	39617.79	74174.68	5174.66	19017.58
	7	230192.75	78202.74	9453.14	114253.24	39890.95	74362.29	5073.97	19409.10
	8	232473.01	78973.93	10132.97	114489.63	40001.40	74488.23	5124.54	19517.94
	9	235029.68	80546.23	9551.21	115458.74	40680.18	74778.56	5212.93	20524.17
	10	236483.03	80239.29	10506.65	116000.99	40774.04	75226.95	5269.27	20078.25
	11	239788.54	81449.91	10452.74	117617.90	40471.30	77146.60	5364.51	20209.25
	12	241424.32	84669.47	6236.17	119555.39	41416.53	78138.86	5526.32	21468.30
比上期增减额（亿元） Changes Compared with Previous Period（100 Million Yuan）									
2004	1	2229.76	-2870.07	316.40	5606.68	2459.11	3147.57	-333.57	2541.44
	2	4391.30	1723.13	381.47	1413.73	-28.80	1442.53	136.40	-2393.99
	3	5923.47	3149.45	473.91	1225.80	743.35	482.45	257.78	-596.01
	4	1797.07	847.42	379.18	303.26	380.34	-77.08	41.68	580.97
	5	2688.39	1244.76	585.36	434.74	135.48	299.26	69.90	-829.97
	6	4622.11	2239.90	383.45	1182.29	800.64	381.65	103.95	-30.85
	7	521.93	-1155.23	1260.84	460.77	273.16	187.61	-100.69	391.52
	8	2280.26	771.19	679.83	236.39	110.45	125.94	50.57	108.84
	9	2556.67	1572.30	-581.76	969.11	678.78	290.33	88.39	1006.23
	10	1453.35	-306.94	955.44	542.25	93.86	448.39	56.34	-445.92
	11	3305.51	1210.62	-53.91	1616.91	-302.74	1919.65	95.24	131.00
	12	1635.78	3219.56	-4216.57	1937.49	945.23	992.26	161.81	1259.05
比去年同期增长（%） Increase Rate Year-on-year（%）									
2004	1	21.20	19.66	10.99	20.46	26.17	17.67	26.98	4.91
	2	21.54	21.90	10.83	19.20	24.58	16.61	29.62	10.91
	3	20.99	21.68	10.66	18.30	24.86	15.15	29.31	12.81
	4	20.44	22.64	0.67	17.84	25.39	14.22	28.63	13.97
	5	19.10	21.25	-0.14	16.87	24.07	13.41	25.50	11.30
	6	18.20	19.05	9.73	16.50	23.82	12.93	22.11	12.15
	7	17.73	17.86	24.88	15.89	23.06	12.37	17.75	11.79
	8	17.57	17.50	30.39	15.35	22.11	12.02	15.58	10.85
	9	15.85	14.92	24.27	14.44	21.13	11.11	12.78	12.11
	10	15.88	14.34	29.41	14.42	21.35	10.98	12.54	10.01
	11	16.33	15.52	25.19	15.05	18.45	13.34	13.16	9.60
	12	16.04	16.81	-4.24	15.38	17.93	14.07	12.82	8.72

金融机构人民币信贷收支主要指标时间序列表

Time Series of Major Indicators in Sources and Uses of Credit Funds of Financial Institutions（RMB）

年 月 Year Month	各项贷款 Total Loans	短期贷款 Short－term Loans					中长期贷款 Medium and Long－term Loans				票据融资 Paper Financing	有价证券及投资 Securities and Investments
			工业贷款 Loans to Industrial Sector	商业贷款 Loans to Commercial Sector	建筑业贷款 Loans to Construction Sector	农业贷款 Loans to Agricultural Sector		基本建设贷款 Capital Construction Loans	技术改造贷款 Technical Improvement Loans	其他中长期贷款 Other Medium and Long－term Loans		
期末余额（亿元） Balance（100 Million Yuan）												
2004 1	161730.64	84590.83	23128.10	18033.76	2935.54	8759.61	64943.47	29574.54	2260.45	33108.48	9471.41	29804.24
2	163810.61	85690.35	23257.77	18069.31	2927.14	9192.50	65663.96	29947.43	2290.91	33425.62	9661.33	29876.23
3	167442.53	87245.06	23587.22	18240.75	2898.77	9550.73	67375.12	30745.44	2345.60	34284.08	10006.87	30191.91
4	169435.02	87470.78	23686.80	17970.18	2883.21	9827.14	68619.89	31275.73	2373.50	34970.66	10488.55	30198.05
5	170566.13	87771.51	23732.99	17921.32	2850.60	9944.02	69447.41	31624.04	2411.30	35412.07	10477.30	29897.26
6	169905.94	86150.29	23271.68	17152.36	2574.03	10002.22	70239.76	32165.97	2318.78	35755.01	10723.18	30389.94
7	169884.39	85680.18	22973.30	17060.20	2666.81	10090.62	70683.23	32191.48	2326.64	36165.11	10708.89	30576.06
8	171040.15	85924.76	23044.95	17082.64	2677.84	10188.93	71414.53	32519.23	2326.69	36568.61	10804.11	30722.74
9	173473.07	87007.64	23470.77	17176.90	2689.56	10254.01	72608.60	32929.50	2314.62	37364.48	10927.06	31314.35
10	173728.97	86775.23	23275.90	17238.08	2679.73	10230.00	73384.04	33423.04	2337.57	37623.43	10617.91	31089.05
11	175224.01	86613.94	23537.23	17219.38	2788.74	10145.99	74694.15	33986.64	2242.65	38464.86	10917.95	31412.84
12	178197.78	86840.60	23896.61	17074.11	2780.13	9843.11	76702.88	35050.64	2312.67	39339.57	11521.45	30931.01
比上期增减额（亿元） Changes Compared with Previous Period（100 Million Yuan）												
2004 1	2539.63	1228.69	205.62	－9.92	1.41	368.70	1287.95	528.93	46.74	712.28	－26.73	－163.78
2	2079.97	1100.03	129.67	35.55	－8.40	432.89	720.65	372.89	30.46	317.30	189.92	80.51
3	3731.34	1646.66	329.45	171.44	－28.37	400.98	1717.96	798.01	54.69	865.26	345.54	307.16
4	1995.29	228.32	99.58	－270.57	－15.56	277.61	1244.97	530.29	27.90	686.78	481.68	6.14
5	1132.13	301.68	46.19	－48.86	－32.61	117.32	827.59	348.31	37.80	441.48	－11.25	－300.79
6	2821.11	942.66	241.35	104.26	－79.16	115.30	1605.57	804.77	38.30	762.50	248.57	492.68
7	－19.41	－468.13	－298.38	－92.15	92.78	89.31	443.62	25.51	7.86	410.25	－14.29	186.12
8	1156.69	245.45	71.66	22.43	11.03	98.71	731.36	327.75	0.05	403.56	95.22	146.68
9	2502.47	1147.55	425.81	94.27	11.72	94.98	1198.95	410.26	－12.07	800.76	122.95	591.61
10	256.27	－232.05	－194.87	61.17	－9.83	－23.83	775.45	493.54	22.94	258.97	－309.15	－225.30
11	1495.04	124.56	261.33	－18.70	109.01	－84.02	1024.27	563.60	－94.91	555.58	300.04	323.79
12	2982.75	235.01	359.38	－145.27	－8.61	－299.02	2009.36	1064.01	70.02	875.33	603.50	－481.83
比去年同期增长（%） Increase Rate Year－on－year（%）												
2004 1	20.14	11.91	12.63	－0.07	1.03	21.18	29.91	29.44	10.27	31.94	47.96	12.95
2	20.71	12.69	13.44	0.05	－0.32	24.59	30.16	29.75	10.82	32.12	47.06	12.08
3	20.16	12.38	12.98	0.84	－4.67	24.09	29.50	28.93	11.81	31.45	42.01	14.19
4	19.92	11.98	13.71	0.27	－6.64	23.53	29.71	29.87	13.56	30.82	38.13	11.52
5	18.60	10.94	12.57	0.58	－9.48	22.62	28.84	29.62	14.13	29.28	28.91	9.09
6	16.32	9.25	10.89	0.57	－15.41	21.57	26.86	27.73	16.00	26.90	17.05	9.49
7	15.48	9.27	10.81	1.10	－9.51	20.55	24.83	25.80	15.10	24.69	14.13	10.26
8	14.12	8.18	8.34	0.70	－14.83	19.24	23.74	24.56	13.60	23.74	7.99	9.87
9	13.50	8.47	8.58	0.84	－8.36	18.82	21.95	21.67	12.91	22.84	5.64	11.55
10	13.22	7.64	6.98	0.99	－8.36	18.40	21.86	21.98	13.60	22.34	7.90	10.61
11	13.43	7.12	7.67	0.75	－2.64	18.09	22.20	22.54	7.76	22.90	12.56	11.38
12	14.39	7.07	8.10	－0.26	－0.82	18.65	22.28	22.37	10.63	23.00	25.66	2.22

金融机构人民币信贷收支主要指标时间序列表

Time Series of Major Indicators in Sources and Uses of Credit Funds of Financial Institutions (RMB)

年　月 Year Month		各项存款 Total Deposits	企业存款 Deposits by Enterprises	财政存款 Fiscal Deposits	储蓄存款 Savings Deposits	活期储蓄 Demand Deposits	定期储蓄 Time Deposits	农业存款 Deposits by Agricultural Sector	流通中货币 Currency in Circulation
		期末余额（亿元） Balance (100 Million Yuan)							
2005	1	245368.63	82971.54	7447.00	122237.34	42272.74	79964.60	5549.58	24015.41
	2	248752.10	81094.53	7841.06	127823.44	43961.19	83862.25	5155.43	22667.97
	3	255573.32	85044.34	8175.58	129259.35	44088.47	85170.88	5442.86	21238.95
	4	258882.32	85888.86	9416.43	129816.83	44087.19	85729.64	5462.38	21666.56
	5	262848.38	87514.29	10278.34	130577.44	44106.42	86471.02	5543.12	20811.59
	6	269140.58	90273.49	10054.89	132339.14	44871.83	87467.31	5711.35	20848.76
	7	270736.45	88747.26	11015.56	133656.44	45239.00	88417.44	5619.63	21171.20
	8	275100.41	90773.63	11303.73	134505.01	45393.80	89111.21	5759.80	21351.56
	9	279882.41	93166.96	10618.62	136316.32	46164.46	90151.86	5970.65	22272.92
	10	281465.66	92567.09	11620.22	136827.11	45994.48	90832.63	5981.65	21892.98
	11	285504.74	93943.85	11427.10	138504.28	47161.10	91343.18	6081.12	22409.39
	12	287169.52	96143.74	7996.26	141050.99	48787.45	92263.54	6203.78	24031.67
		比上期增减额（亿元） Changes Compared with Previous Period (100 Million Yuan)							
2005	1	2117.17	-1813.24	1209.15	2683.12	854.89	1828.23	22.43	2547.11
	2	3383.48	-1877.01	394.06	5586.10	1688.45	3897.65	-394.15	-1347.44
	3	6821.22	3949.81	334.52	1435.91	127.28	1308.63	287.43	-1429.02
	4	3309.00	844.52	1240.85	557.48	-1.28	558.76	19.52	427.61
	5	3966.06	1625.43	861.91	760.61	19.23	741.38	80.74	-854.97
	6	6292.20	2759.20	-223.45	1761.70	765.41	996.29	168.23	37.17
	7	1595.86	-1526.23	960.67	1317.30	367.17	950.13	-91.72	322.44
	8	4363.96	2026.37	288.17	848.57	154.80	693.77	140.17	180.36
	9	4782.01	2393.33	-685.11	1811.31	770.66	1040.65	210.85	921.36
	10	1583.24	-599.87	1001.60	510.79	-169.98	680.77	11.00	-379.94
	11	4039.08	1376.76	-193.12	1677.17	1166.62	510.55	99.47	516.41
	12	1664.79	2199.89	-3430.84	2546.71	1626.35	920.36	122.66	1622.28
		比去年同期增长（%） Increase Rate Year-on-year (%)							
2005	1	16.70	18.27	24.35	11.91	12.47	11.61	21.57	7.75
	2	15.90	12.82	23.09	15.52	17.05	14.74	9.66	13.95
	3	15.87	13.35	19.45	15.54	15.11	15.77	9.75	10.06
	4	16.43	13.20	30.36	15.73	13.97	16.65	9.23	9.00
	5	16.78	13.48	31.62	15.96	13.63	17.18	9.32	9.26
	6	17.19	13.75	22.74	16.30	13.26	17.92	10.37	9.63
	7	17.61	13.48	16.53	16.98	13.41	18.90	10.75	9.08
	8	18.34	14.94	11.55	17.48	13.48	19.63	12.40	9.39
	9	19.08	15.67	11.18	18.06	13.48	20.56	14.54	8.52
	10	19.02	15.36	10.60	17.95	12.80	20.74	13.52	9.04
	11	19.07	15.34	9.32	17.76	16.53	18.40	13.36	10.89
	12	18.95	13.55	28.22	17.98	17.80	18.08	12.26	11.94

金融机构人民币信贷收支主要指标时间序列表

Time Series of Major Indicators in Sources and Uses of Credit Funds of Financial Institutions（RMB）

年 月 Year Month	各项贷款 Total Loans	短期贷款 Short－term Loans	工业贷款 Loans to Industrial Sector	商业贷款 Loans to Commercial Sector	建筑业贷款 Loans to Construction Sector	农业贷款 Loans to Agricultural Sector	中长期贷款 Medium and Long－term Loans	基本建设贷款 Capital Construction Loans	技术改造贷款 Technical Improvement Loans	其他中长期贷款 Other Medium and Long－term Loans	票据融资 Paper Financing	有价证券及投资 Securities and Investments
	期末余额（亿元） Balance（100 Million Yuan）											
2005 1	181082.96	87601.34	24451.15	16786.47	2839.07	10694.32	78194.81	35678.98	2347.16	40168.67	12020.60	30722.41
2	182042.30	88025.35	24607.82	16758.09	2861.58	10826.28	78726.19	35906.56	2358.51	40461.12	12030.89	30629.10
3	185461.32	89437.51	24911.99	16799.46	2880.86	11218.37	80084.75	36791.14	2398.07	40895.54	12586.55	30989.85
4	186889.10	89549.76	24926.30	16752.68	2855.21	11578.89	80752.84	37069.42	2408.01	41275.41	13167.85	31273.36
5	186274.10	88551.46	24017.67	16438.08	2850.43	11767.65	81059.58	37203.25	2406.52	41449.81	13272.38	31319.25
6	186178.70	86853.05	22463.89	15896.35	2966.86	11785.48	81931.27	37643.03	2432.97	41855.27	14027.42	31208.56
7	185859.75	86281.06	22275.46	15779.11	2933.30	11880.94	82085.30	37776.61	2427.87	41880.82	14066.51	31560.81
8	187756.60	86660.46	22345.64	15793.95	2944.63	12018.46	82782.57	38271.52	2436.77	42074.28	14875.45	32369.04
9	190941.90	87523.88	22668.99	16040.12	2970.77	12006.99	84284.89	39100.65	2432.79	42751.45	15491.90	32703.73
10	191168.27	87379.35	22532.98	16125.39	2959.50	11954.57	84801.72	39393.07	2424.07	42984.58	15332.28	33123.44
11	193416.93	87890.53	22571.45	16485.33	3002.38	11891.22	85642.97	39608.38	2385.73	43648.86	16223.79	33457.84
12	194690.39	87449.16	22516.66	16447.55	2983.72	11529.93	87460.42	40336.50	2361.05	44762.87	16231.18	34942.14
	比上期增减额（亿元） Changes Compared with Previous Period（100 Million Yuan）											
2005 1	2810.28	1003.41	307.65	－26.32	8.97	514.04	1253.25	626.15	45.24	581.86	500.19	－133.79
2	959.43	424.08	156.67	－28.37	22.51	131.99	531.39	227.58	11.35	292.46	10.29	－93.31
3	3606.66	1586.66	304.18	41.37	19.28	472.77	1371.70	884.59	39.56	447.55	555.66	360.75
4	1420.43	105.42	14.30	－46.79	－25.65	357.37	667.58	278.27	9.94	379.37	581.30	283.51
5	1089.20	336.74	－30.24	2.29	6.62	194.79	632.76	347.77	－1.49	286.48	104.67	45.89
6	4653.00	1998.20	774.55	271.88	155.53	159.29	1867.46	1116.80	26.44	724.22	755.61	－110.69
7	－313.91	－567.31	－188.44	－117.24	－33.56	97.63	154.40	133.58	－5.09	25.91	39.08	352.25
8	1896.86	379.42	70.19	14.84	11.34	137.51	697.26	494.91	8.90	193.45	808.94	808.23
9	3453.01	1112.37	323.35	246.17	26.14	103.64	1521.07	829.14	－3.98	695.91	616.46	334.69
10	264.42	－109.14	－136.02	85.27	－11.27	－36.05	519.49	292.41	－8.72	235.80	－159.62	419.17
11	2250.73	513.11	38.47	359.94	42.87	－62.45	841.39	215.30	－38.34	664.43	891.51	334.40
12	1453.71	－273.72	－54.78	－37.77	－18.66	－283.79	1830.06	728.12	－24.68	1126.62	7.39	1484.30
	比去年同期增长（%） Increase Rate Year－on－year（%）											
2005 1	14.23	6.79	8.76	－2.07	3.44	23.65	21.68	21.53	9.62	22.63	26.94	3.08
2	13.37	5.92	8.83	－2.42	4.50	19.26	21.15	20.78	8.66	22.34	24.55	2.52
3	13.00	5.74	8.60	－3.11	6.19	19.29	20.10	20.52	7.81	20.56	25.80	2.64
4	12.51	5.59	8.20	－1.92	5.88	19.56	18.89	19.36	6.97	19.28	25.57	3.56
5	12.40	5.61	7.86	－1.64	7.32	20.11	18.39	19.15	5.23	18.61	26.70	4.76
6	13.53	6.94	10.31	－0.73	17.22	20.43	18.55	19.80	4.92	18.32	30.82	2.69
7	13.36	6.86	10.92	－0.88	11.89	20.34	18.03	20.12	4.35	17.05	31.36	3.22
8	13.70	7.00	10.88	－0.93	11.85	20.52	17.80	20.43	4.73	16.29	37.69	5.36
9	14.05	6.87	10.25	－0.04	12.33	20.48	17.95	21.45	5.11	15.66	41.78	4.44
10	14.04	7.03	10.59	0.10	12.33	20.40	17.41	20.53	3.70	15.49	44.41	6.54
11	14.35	7.82	9.52	2.30	9.47	20.79	16.48	19.16	6.38	14.69	48.60	6.51
12	13.25	7.22	7.64	2.95	9.14	21.58	15.81	17.62	2.09	15.00	40.88	12.97

（二）国家银行人民币信贷收支主要指标时间序列表（1949—1989 年年度时序、1990—2005 年月度时序）

Time Series of Major Indicators in Sources and Uses of Credit Funds of State Banks（RMB）（Annual Series from 1949 to 1989, Monthly Series from 1990 to 2005）

国家银行人民币信贷收支主要指标时间序列表
Time Series of Major Indicators in Sources and Uses of Credit Funds of State Banks（RMB）

年 份 Year	各项存款 Total Deposits	企业存款 Deposits by Enterprises	财政存款 Fiscal Deposits	储蓄存款 Savings Deposits	农村存款 Rural Deposits
期末余额（亿元） Balance（100 Million Yuan）					
1949	1.1				
1950	24.3	10.6	2.9	1.3	
1951	58.8	20.5	10.2	5.5	
1952	93.3	33.0	19.5	8.6	
1953	107.6	31.8	33.3	12.2	1.1
1954	152.5	34.4	61.3	14.3	4.3
1955	141.7	32.4	36.1	16.9	6.1
1956	134.1	45.0	16.4	22.4	8.0
1957	165.5	39.7	20.6	27.9	17.9
1958	295.3	77.6	49.9	35.1	27.8
1959	398.7	70.0	82.1	47.3	48.2
1960	459.8	86.0	146.6	51.1	49.9
1961	488.7	116.1	174.6	39.2	56.2
1962	409.6	152.3	79.9	31.4	31.6
比上期增减额（亿元） Changes Compared with Previous Period（100 Million Yuan）					
1949					
1950	23.2	10.6	2.9	1.3	
1951	34.5	9.9	7.3	4.2	
1952	34.5	12.5	9.3	3.1	
1953	14.3	-1.2	13.8	3.6	1.1
1954	44.9	2.6	28.0	2.1	3.2
1955	-10.8	-2.0	-25.2	2.6	1.8
1956	-7.6	12.6	-19.7	5.5	1.9
1957	31.4	-5.3	4.2	5.5	9.9
1958	129.8	37.9	29.3	7.2	9.9
1959	103.4	-7.6	32.2	12.2	20.4
1960	61.1	16.0	64.5	3.8	1.7
1961	28.9	30.1	28.0	-11.9	6.3
1962	-79.1	36.2	-94.7	-7.8	-24.6
比去年同期增长（%） Increase Rate Year-on-year（%）					
1949					
1950	2109.09				
1951	141.98	93.40	251.72	323.08	
1952	58.67	60.98	91.18	56.36	
1953	15.33	-3.64	70.77	41.86	
1954	41.73	8.18	84.08	17.21	290.91
1955	-7.08	-5.81	-41.11	18.18	41.86
1956	-5.36	38.89	-54.57	32.54	31.15
1957	23.42	-11.78	25.61	24.55	123.75
1958	78.43	95.47	142.23	25.81	55.31
1959	35.02	-9.79	64.53	34.76	73.38
1960	15.32	22.86	78.56	8.03	3.53
1961	6.29	35.00	19.10	-23.29	12.63
1962	-16.19	31.18	-54.24	-19.90	-43.77

国家银行人民币信贷收支主要指标时间序列表
Time Series of Major Indicators in Sources and Uses of Credit Funds of State Banks（RMB）

年份 Year	各项贷款 Total Loans	工业生产企业贷款 Loans to Industrial Production Enterprises	物资供销企业贷款 Loans to Material Supply and Sale Enterprises	商业企业贷款 Loans to Commercial Enterprises	农业贷款 Loans to Agricultural Sector
	期末余额（亿元） Balance（100 Million Yuan）				
1949	0.7				
1950	18.2	1.7		14.7	0.8
1951	63.9	2.1		48.9	2.1
1952	108.0	9.5		93.8	4.2
1953	134.6	13.0		114.3	6.6
1954	184.6	14.6		161.8	7.6
1955	204.2	18.1		175.3	10.0
1956	233.9	27.9		172.6	30.2
1957	277.5	30.3		216.4	27.7
1958	477.7	89.2		342.4	43.4
1959	798.1	254.8		495.3	44.5
1960	969.2	362.8	30.8	506.3	62.8
1961	803.5	167.1	25.3	537.5	63.7
1962	682.1	119.8	27.0	459.0	66.7
	比上期增减额（亿元） Changes Compared with Previous Period（100 Million Yuan）				
1949					
1950	17.5	1.7		14.7	0.8
1951	45.7	0.4		34.2	1.3
1952	44.1	7.4		44.9	2.1
1953	26.6	3.5		20.5	2.4
1954	50.0	1.6		47.5	1.0
1955	19.6	3.5		13.5	2.4
1956	29.7	9.8		-2.7	20.2
1957	43.6	2.4		43.8	-2.5
1958	200.2	58.9		126.0	15.7
1959	320.4	165.6		152.9	1.1
1960	171.1	108.0	30.8	11.0	18.3
1961	-165.7	-195.7	-5.5	31.2	0.9
1962	-121.4	-47.3	1.7	-78.5	3.0
	比去年同期增长（%） Increase Rate Year-on-year（%）				
1949					
1950	2500.00				
1951	251.10	23.53		232.65	162.50
1952	69.01	352.38		91.82	100.00
1953	24.63	36.84		21.86	57.14
1954	37.15	12.31		41.56	15.15
1955	10.62	23.97		8.34	31.58
1956	14.54	54.14		-1.54	202.00
1957	18.64	8.60		25.38	-8.28
1958	72.14	194.39		58.23	56.68
1959	67.07	185.65		44.66	2.53
1960	21.44	42.39		2.22	41.12
1961	-17.10	-53.94	-17.86	6.16	1.43
1962	-15.11	-28.31	6.72	-14.60	4.71

国家银行人民币信贷收支主要指标时间序列表
Time Series of Major Indicators in Sources and Uses of Credit Funds of State Banks（RMB）

年　份 Year	各项存款 Total Deposits	企业存款 Deposits by Enterprises	财政存款 Fiscal Deposits	储蓄存款 Savings Deposits	农村存款 Rural Deposits
期末余额（亿元） Balance（100 Million Yuan）					
1963	414.0	176.8	67.3	35.6	34.6
1964	439.5	156.1	84.8	44.8	45.6
1965	481.0	181.9	74.2	52.3	50.1
1966	553.6	185.0	95.8	57.7	62.9
1967	575.1	199.4	67.3	59.8	69.3
1968	625.1	211.8	92.3	62.3	83.3
1969	641.7	215.5	119.6	61.0	78.4
1970	704.3	226.1	176.8	64.5	83.3
1971	767.6	226.8	188.9	73.3	93.5
1972	776.3	239.0	172.6	85.1	91.4
1973	865.0	279.0	160.8	94.1	107.3
1974	897.5	324.8	137.3	105.8	123.4
1975	975.1	362.7	140.2	114.6	136.9
1976	978.5	389.8	97.9	122.2	136.7
1977	1063.8	384.7	151.9	135.1	143.2
比上期增减额（亿元） Changes Compared with Previous Period（100 Million Yuan）					
1963	4.4	24.5	-12.6	4.2	3.0
1964	25.5	-20.7	17.5	9.2	11.0
1965	41.5	25.8	-10.6	7.5	4.5
1966	72.6	3.1	21.6	5.4	12.8
1967	21.5	14.4	-28.5	2.1	6.4
1968	50.0	12.4	25.0	2.5	14.0
1969	16.6	3.7	27.3	-1.3	-4.9
1970	62.6	10.6	57.2	3.5	4.9
1971	63.3	0.7	12.1	8.8	10.2
1972	8.7	12.2	-16.3	11.8	-2.1
1973	88.7	40.0	-11.8	9.0	15.9
1974	32.5	45.8	-23.5	11.7	16.1
1975	77.6	37.9	2.9	8.8	13.5
1976	3.4	27.1	-42.3	7.6	-0.2
1977	85.3	-5.1	54.0	12.9	6.5
比去年同期增长（%） Increase Rate Year-on-year（%）					
1963	1.07	16.09	-15.77	13.38	9.49
1964	6.16	-11.71	26.00	25.84	31.79
1965	9.44	16.53	-12.50	16.74	9.87
1966	15.09	1.70	29.11	10.33	25.55
1967	3.88	7.78	-29.75	3.64	10.17
1968	8.69	6.22	37.15	4.18	20.20
1969	2.66	1.75	29.58	-2.09	-5.88
1970	9.76	4.92	47.83	5.74	6.25
1971	8.99	0.31	6.84	13.64	12.24
1972	1.13	5.38	-8.63	16.10	-2.25
1973	11.43	16.74	-6.84	10.58	17.40
1974	3.76	16.42	-14.61	12.43	15.00
1975	8.65	11.67	2.11	8.32	10.94
1976	0.35	7.47	-30.17	6.63	-0.15
1977	8.72	-1.31	55.16	10.56	4.75

国家银行人民币信贷收支主要指标时间序列表
Time Series of Major Indicators in Sources and Uses of Credit Funds of State Banks（RMB）

年 份 Year	各项贷款 Total Loans	工业生产企业贷款 Loans to Industrial Production Enterprises	物资供销企业贷款 Loans to Material Supply and Sale Enterprises	商业企业贷款 Loans to Commercial Enterprises	农业贷款 Loans to Agricultural Sector
	期末余额（亿元）Balance（100 Million Yuan）				
1963	568.0	76.9	31.5	384.4	70.8
1964	578.9	76.0	31.6	396.6	71.5
1965	647.4	93.2	41.3	431.3	78.2
1966	755.9	122.3	52.2	498.6	77.7
1967	796.6	173.6	51.8	483.0	81.4
1968	890.3	213.1	62.5	525.0	81.2
1969	945.5	234.0	69.1	547.5	84.0
1970	1033.4	241.4	67.4	626.6	85.1
1971	1113.9	251.9	126.0	667.2	51.6
1972	1145.6	224.3	151.3	693.8	56.6
1973	1269.0	231.1	179.6	776.9	58.8
1974	1353.5	266.7	179.6	815.0	64.0
1975	1462.7	293.5	179.1	884.7	72.4
1976	1541.8	329.4	173.3	908.0	90.4
1977	1663.3	334.2	187.9	996.9	98.3
	比上期增减额（亿元）Changes Compared with Previous Period（100 Million Yuan）				
1963	-114.1	-42.9	4.5	-74.6	4.1
1964	10.9	-0.9	0.1	12.2	0.7
1965	68.5	17.2	9.7	34.7	6.7
1966	108.5	29.1	10.9	67.3	-0.5
1967	40.7	51.3	-0.4	-15.6	3.7
1968	93.7	39.5	10.7	42.0	-0.2
1969	55.2	20.9	6.6	22.5	2.8
1970	87.9	7.4	-1.7	79.1	1.1
1971	80.5	10.5	58.6	40.6	-33.5
1972	31.7	-27.6	25.3	26.6	5.0
1973	123.4	6.8	28.3	83.1	2.2
1974	84.5	35.6	0.0	38.1	5.2
1975	109.2	26.8	-0.5	69.7	8.4
1976	79.1	35.9	-5.8	23.3	18.0
1977	121.5	4.8	14.6	88.9	7.9
	比去年同期增长（%）Increase Rate Year-on-year（%）				
1963	-16.73	-35.81	16.67	-16.25	6.15
1964	1.92	-1.17	0.32	3.17	0.99
1965	11.83	22.63	30.70	8.75	9.37
1966	16.76	31.22	26.39	15.60	-0.64
1967	5.38	41.95	-0.77	-3.13	4.76
1968	11.76	22.75	20.66	8.70	-0.25
1969	6.20	9.81	10.56	4.29	3.45
1970	9.30	3.16	-2.46	14.45	1.31
1971	7.79	4.35	86.94	6.48	-39.37
1972	2.85	-10.96	20.08	3.99	9.69
1973	10.77	3.03	18.70	11.98	3.89
1974	6.66	15.40	0.00	4.90	8.84
1975	8.07	10.05	-0.28	8.55	13.13
1976	5.41	12.23	-3.24	2.63	24.86
1977	7.88	1.46	8.42	9.79	8.74

国家银行人民币信贷收支主要指标时间序列表
Time Series of Major Indicators in Sources and Uses of Credit Funds of State Banks（RMB）

年　份 Year	各项存款 Total Deposits	企业存款 Deposits by Enterprises	财政存款 Fiscal Deposits	储蓄存款 Savings Deposits	农村存款 Rural Deposits
			期末余额（亿元） Balance（100 Million Yuan）		
1978	1134.56	368.43	187.35	154.91	154.41
1979	1340.04	468.91	148.68	202.56	203.71
1980	1644.54	561.01	160.68	278.77	241.82
1981	2031.67	676.96	194.29	353.80	278.47
1982	2362.04	761.64	175.76	447.33	329.94
1983	2764.24	864.99	229.89	572.60	391.31
1984	3438.66	1251.79	210.93	776.58	370.21
1985	4244.73	1735.89	404.10	1057.76	449.10
1986	5446.29	2244.94	348.61	1470.77	560.80
1987	6651.25	2660.52	331.98	2067.41	631.95
1988	7448.82	2936.58	294.10	2659.16	669.53
1989	9027.03	3085.36	460.79	3730.88	715.87
			比上期增减额（亿元） Changes Compared with Previous Period（100 Million Yuan）		
1978	70.76	-16.27	35.45	19.81	11.21
1979	205.48	100.48	-38.67	47.65	49.30
1980	304.50	92.10	12.00	76.21	38.11
1981	387.13	115.95	33.61	75.03	36.65
1982	330.37	84.68	-18.53	93.53	51.47
1983	402.20	103.35	54.13	125.27	61.37
1984	674.42	386.80	-18.96	203.98	-21.10
1985	806.07	484.10	193.17	281.18	78.89
1986	1201.56	509.05	-55.49	413.01	111.70
1987	1204.96	415.58	-16.63	596.64	71.15
1988	797.57	276.06	-37.88	591.75	37.58
1989	1578.21	148.78	166.69	1071.72	46.34
			比去年同期增长（%） Increase Rate Year-on-year（%）		
1978	6.65	-4.23	23.34	14.66	7.83
1979	18.11	27.27	-20.64	30.76	31.93
1980	22.72	19.64	8.07	37.62	18.71
1981	23.54	20.67	20.92	26.91	15.16
1982	16.26	12.51	-9.54	26.44	18.48
1983	17.03	13.57	30.80	28.00	18.60
1984	24.40	44.72	-8.25	35.62	-5.39
1985	23.44	38.67	91.58	36.21	21.31
1986	28.31	29.33	-13.73	39.05	24.87
1987	22.12	18.51	-4.77	40.57	12.69
1988	11.99	10.38	-11.41	28.62	5.95
1989	21.19	5.07	56.68	40.30	6.92

国家银行人民币信贷收支主要指标时间序列表

Time Series of Major Indicators in Sources and Uses of Credit Funds of State Banks（RMB）

年份 Year	各项贷款 Total Loans	流动资金贷款 Working Capital Loans	工业贷款 Loans to Industrial Sector	商业贷款 Loans to Commercial Sector	建筑业贷款 Loans to Construction Sector	农业贷款 Loans to Agricultural Sector	固定资产贷款 Fixed Asset Loans	基本建设贷款 Capital Construction Loans	技术改造贷款 Technical Improvement Loans	其他固定资产贷款 Other Fixed Asset Loans
				期末余额（亿元） Balance（100 Million Yuan）						
1978	1849.96	1734.48	616.83	1117.65		115.48				
1979	2039.63	1902.89	670.64	1232.25		136.74				
1980	2400.49	2180.90	743.76	1437.14		172.08	47.51		47.51	
1981	2764.85	2478.81	839.13	1639.21		192.55	83.74		83.74	
1982	3052.27	2673.73	866.58	1806.60		212.45	151.98	13.36	138.62	
1983	3419.17	2978.14	973.53	2003.11		231.52	192.09	28.26	163.83	
1984	4423.61	3763.04	1316.88	2346.53		366.54	294.03	52.98	229.37	11.68
1985	5832.04	4554.19	1609.96	2723.49	93.56	409.23	686.25	213.14	417.55	55.56
1986	7597.75	5631.49	2225.14	3182.04	132.06	570.13	975.97	297.89	585.87	92.21
1987	9014.10	6606.15	2615.94	3614.60	170.56	691.11	1221.61	418.84	696.22	106.55
1988	10551.35	8026.14	3118.75	4224.82	252.64	403.61	1558.20	501.17	892.93	164.10
1989	12402.85	9493.41	3817.92	4952.86	283.69	470.55	1780.18	581.42	1003.11	195.65
				比上期增减额（亿元） Changes Compared with Previous Period（100 Million Yuan）						
1978	186.66	—	—	—		—				
1979	189.67	168.41	53.81	114.60		21.26				
1980	360.86	278.01	73.12	204.89		35.34	47.51		47.51	
1981	364.36	297.91	95.37	202.07		20.47	36.23		36.23	
1982	287.42	194.92	27.45	167.39		19.90	68.24	13.36	54.88	
1983	366.90	304.41	106.95	196.51		19.07	40.11	14.90	25.21	
1984	1004.44	784.90	343.35	343.42		135.02	101.94	24.72	65.54	11.68
1985	1408.43	791.15	293.08	376.96	93.56	42.69	392.22	160.16	188.18	43.88
1986	1765.71	1077.30	615.18	458.55	38.50	160.90	289.72	84.75	168.32	36.65
1987	1416.35	974.66	390.80	432.56	38.50	120.98	245.64	120.95	110.35	14.34
1988	1537.25	1419.99	502.81	610.22	82.08	-287.50	336.59	82.33	196.71	57.55
1989	1851.50	1467.27	699.17	728.04	31.05	66.94	221.98	80.25	110.18	31.55
				比去年同期增长（%） Increase Rate Year-on-year（%）						
1978	11.22	—	—	—		—				
1979	10.25	9.71	8.72	10.25		18.41				
1980	17.69	14.61	10.90	16.63		25.84				
1981	15.18	13.66	12.82	14.06		11.90	76.26		76.26	
1982	10.40	7.86	3.27	10.21		10.33	81.49		65.54	
1983	12.02	11.39	12.34	10.88		8.98	26.39	111.53	18.19	
1984	29.39	26.36	35.27	17.14		58.32	53.07	87.47	40.00	
1985	31.84	21.02	22.26	16.06		11.65	133.39	302.30	82.04	375.68
1986	30.28	23.66	38.21	16.84	41.15	39.32	42.22	39.76	40.31	65.96
1987	18.64	17.31	17.56	13.59	29.15	21.22	25.17	40.60	18.84	15.55
1988	17.05	21.49	19.22	16.88	48.12	-41.60	27.55	19.66	28.25	54.01
1989	17.55	18.28	22.42	17.23	12.29	16.59	14.25	16.01	12.34	19.23

国家银行人民币信贷收支主要指标时间序列表

Time Series of Major Indicators in Sources and Uses of Credit Funds of State Banks (RMB)

年　月 Year Month		各项存款 Total Deposits	企业存款 Deposits by Enterprises	财政存款 Fiscal Deposits	储蓄存款 Savings Deposits	农村存款 Rural Deposits
		期末余额（亿元）Balance (100 Million Yuan)				
1990	1	9082.25	3083.95	428.03	3835.88	732.10
	2	9345.84	3108.00	424.03	4060.39	760.09
	3	9654.39	3262.72	431.00	4198.15	749.74
	4	9911.67	3373.62	476.98	4284.77	733.47
	5	10108.08	3451.32	447.24	4405.02	731.50
	6	10312.52	3472.38	430.46	4548.40	767.66
	7	10629.84	3557.15	458.50	4703.09	778.62
	8	10848.01	3658.53	448.94	4812.86	777.21
	9	11053.10	3791.42	424.40	4891.72	784.08
	10	11303.35	3785.39	505.46	5000.19	825.49
	11	11541.61	3903.06	475.54	5094.66	873.70
	12	11653.99	3946.66	427.11	5192.93	844.09
		比上期增减额（亿元）Changes Compared with Previous Period (100 Million Yuan)				
1990	1	55.22	-1.41	-32.76	105.00	16.23
	2	263.59	24.05	-4.00	224.51	27.99
	3	308.55	154.72	6.97	137.76	-10.35
	4	257.28	110.90	45.98	86.62	-16.27
	5	196.41	77.70	-29.74	120.25	-1.97
	6	204.44	21.06	-16.78	143.38	36.16
	7	317.32	84.77	28.04	154.69	10.96
	8	218.17	101.38	-9.56	109.77	-1.41
	9	205.09	132.89	-24.54	78.86	6.87
	10	250.25	-6.03	81.06	108.47	41.41
	11	238.26	117.67	-29.92	94.47	48.21
	12	112.38	43.60	-48.43	98.27	-29.61
		比去年同期增长（%）Increase Rate Year-on-year (%)				
1990	1	24.73	11.23	17.92	44.14	18.38
	2	26.67	13.22	20.56	44.33	23.36
	3	27.98	15.87	20.85	44.05	30.29
	4	28.18	16.00	25.03	42.59	29.82
	5	28.17	17.10	16.84	41.80	28.75
	6	31.04	21.13	27.36	42.21	32.14
	7	32.42	24.43	24.62	41.85	32.09
	8	32.66	26.59	23.84	41.09	31.30
	9	32.04	30.73	-4.37	40.43	29.49
	10	31.66	28.25	7.83	40.40	29.70
	11	30.08	26.73	2.84	39.81	26.78
	12	29.10	27.92	-7.31	39.19	17.91

国家银行人民币信贷收支主要指标时间序列表

Time Series of Major Indicators in Sources and Uses of Credit Funds of State Banks（RMB）

年 月 Year Month	各项贷款 Total Loans	流动资金贷款 Working Capital Loans				农业贷款 Loans to Agricultural Sector	固定资产贷款 Fixed Asset Loans			
			工业贷款 Loans to Industrial Sector	商业贷款 Loans to Commercial Sector	建筑业贷款 Loans to Construction Sector			基本建设贷款 Capital Construction Loans	技术改造贷款 Technical Improvement Loans	其他固定资产贷款 Other Fixed Asset Loans
期末余额（亿元） Balance（100 Million Yuan）										
1990 1	12354.40	9457.51	3896.87	4842.62	282.57	468.60	1766.67	581.06	992.40	193.21
2	12339.78	9438.00	3933.80	4786.67	281.26	473.91	1770.32	581.84	996.26	192.22
3	12570.60	9623.68	4080.13	4820.02	284.48	498.42	1782.58	589.61	996.56	196.41
4	12697.14	9704.82	4146.06	4826.56	288.26	519.71	1796.91	602.88	997.88	196.15
5	12791.07	9757.40	4192.47	4827.04	289.78	536.59	1817.66	612.30	1005.55	199.81
6	13021.92	9923.74	4267.54	4908.34	293.90	553.32	1850.72	630.19	1017.16	203.37
7	13151.21	10009.96	4317.45	4940.78	297.03	559.87	1879.19	646.62	1028.07	204.50
8	13367.56	10184.53	4387.56	5039.16	298.61	566.52	1909.78	664.64	1036.77	208.37
9	13838.91	10597.89	4605.01	5228.36	300.76	573.61	1953.36	690.42	1051.22	211.72
10	14176.72	10894.92	4660.92	5465.76	302.70	572.21	1999.19	714.43	1069.60	215.16
11	14534.30	11202.13	4752.69	5672.28	306.86	566.03	2056.17	740.23	1096.77	219.17
12	15140.43	11593.98	4899.73	5895.57	316.77	571.93	2214.89	818.29	1163.80	232.80
比上期增减额（亿元） Changes Compared with Previous Period（100 Million Yuan）										
1990 1	-48.45	-35.90	78.95	-110.24	-1.12	-1.95	-13.51	-0.36	-10.71	-2.44
2	-14.62	-19.51	36.93	-55.95	-1.31	5.31	3.65	0.78	3.86	-0.99
3	230.82	185.68	146.33	33.35	3.22	24.51	12.26	7.77	0.30	4.19
4	126.54	81.14	65.93	6.54	3.78	21.29	14.33	13.27	1.32	-0.26
5	93.93	52.58	46.41	0.48	1.52	16.88	20.75	9.42	7.67	3.66
6	230.85	166.34	75.07	81.30	4.12	16.73	33.06	17.89	11.61	3.56
7	129.29	86.22	49.91	32.44	3.13	6.55	28.47	16.43	10.91	1.13
8	216.35	174.57	70.11	98.38	1.58	6.65	30.59	18.02	8.70	3.87
9	471.35	413.36	217.45	189.20	2.15	7.09	43.58	25.78	14.45	3.35
10	337.81	297.03	55.91	237.40	1.94	-1.40	45.83	24.01	18.38	3.44
11	357.58	307.21	91.77	206.52	4.16	-6.18	56.98	25.80	27.17	4.01
12	606.13	391.85	147.04	223.29	9.91	5.90	158.72	78.06	67.03	13.63
比去年同期增长（%） Increase Rate Year-on-year（%）										
1990 1	17.70	18.17	25.12	15.04	11.94	16.57	14.03	16.46	12.24	16.22
2	18.03	18.43	26.08	14.79	11.25	16.97	14.62	16.43	13.04	17.61
3	19.38	19.95	28.82	15.40	12.07	17.98	15.30	18.30	13.15	17.70
4	19.61	20.15	28.54	15.75	12.19	17.94	15.57	19.86	13.28	14.77
5	20.11	20.73	29.03	16.33	11.50	18.52	15.98	20.96	13.16	15.89
6	20.98	21.52	29.78	17.11	12.01	19.86	17.41	23.50	14.26	15.71
7	21.34	21.83	30.16	17.32	13.00	19.95	18.04	24.81	14.97	13.83
8	22.44	23.19	31.11	19.10	12.28	20.47	18.76	26.53	14.93	15.33
9	24.09	25.32	33.98	20.77	12.77	21.67	19.84	29.51	15.25	14.62
10	24.23	25.20	32.49	21.67	12.56	22.21	21.49	32.33	16.17	16.34
11	22.92	23.82	29.90	20.87	13.21	21.67	21.40	33.86	15.14	16.46
12	22.07	22.13	28.34	19.03	11.66	21.55	24.42	40.74	16.02	18.99

国家银行人民币信贷收支主要指标时间序列表

Time Series of Major Indicators in Sources and Uses of Credit Funds of State Banks (RMB)

年　月 Year Month		各项存款 Total Deposits	企业存款 Deposits by Enterprises	财政存款 Fiscal Deposits	储蓄存款 Savings Deposits	农村存款 Rural Deposits
		期末余额（亿元） Balance (100 Million Yuan)				
1991	1	11909.96	4074.43	427.47	5314.30	868.23
	2	12216.08	4123.32	446.51	5563.55	888.66
	3	12562.60	4280.77	446.43	5763.44	861.09
	4	12867.31	4460.13	452.47	5892.60	831.57
	5	13150.85	4619.68	463.77	5991.61	827.39
	6	13300.84	4625.07	440.83	6122.88	852.25
	7	13619.44	4725.06	450.39	6265.26	877.74
	8	13925.14	4876.36	450.14	6365.17	885.32
	9	14260.90	5052.89	475.87	6447.88	905.11
	10	14628.70	5136.85	558.37	6563.88	964.75
	11	15053.39	5299.87	592.20	6689.48	1045.79
	12	14881.59	5058.06	504.29	6790.90	1031.57
		比上期增减额（亿元） Changes Compared with Previous Period (100 Million Yuan)				
1991	1	255.97	127.77	0.36	121.37	24.14
	2	306.12	48.89	19.04	249.25	20.43
	3	346.52	157.45	-0.08	199.89	-27.57
	4	304.71	179.36	6.04	129.16	-29.52
	5	283.54	159.55	11.30	99.01	-4.18
	6	149.99	5.39	-22.94	131.27	24.86
	7	318.60	99.99	9.56	142.38	25.49
	8	305.70	151.30	-0.25	99.91	7.58
	9	335.76	176.53	25.73	82.71	19.79
	10	367.80	83.96	82.50	116.00	59.64
	11	424.69	163.02	33.83	125.60	81.04
	12	-171.80	-241.81	-87.91	101.42	-14.22
		比去年同期增长（%） Increase Rate Year-on-year (%)				
1991	1	31.13	32.12	-0.13	38.54	18.59
	2	30.71	32.67	5.30	37.02	16.92
	3	30.12	31.20	3.58	37.29	14.85
	4	29.82	32.21	-5.14	37.52	13.37
	5	30.10	33.85	3.70	36.02	13.11
	6	28.98	33.20	2.41	34.62	11.02
	7	28.12	32.83	-1.77	33.22	12.73
	8	28.37	33.29	0.27	32.25	13.91
	9	29.02	33.27	12.13	31.81	15.44
	10	29.42	35.70	10.47	31.27	16.87
	11	30.43	35.79	24.53	31.30	19.70
	12	27.70	28.16	18.07	30.77	22.21

国家银行人民币信贷收支主要指标时间序列表

Time Series of Major Indicators in Sources and Uses of Credit Funds of State Banks（RMB）

年 月 Year Month	各项贷款 Total Loans	流动资金贷款 Working Capital Loans				农业贷款 Loans to Agricultural Sector	固定资产贷款 Fixed Asset Loans			
			工业贷款 Loans to Industrial Sector	商业贷款 Loans to Commercial Sector	建筑业贷款 Loans to Construction Sector			基本建设贷款 Capital Construction Loans	技术改造贷款 Technical Improvement Loans	其他固定资产贷款 Other Fixed Asset Loans
期末余额（亿元） Balance（100 Million Yuan）										
1991 1	15136.12	11569.77	4914.89	5857.28	317.37	571.22	2219.81	822.43	1162.78	234.60
2	15119.45	11532.30	4946.79	5783.18	320.02	577.81	2238.30	830.34	1176.59	231.37
3	15295.31	11636.97	5028.71	5789.64	329.51	605.06	2267.91	850.54	1183.58	233.79
4	15405.12	11674.76	5087.67	5752.51	338.48	631.05	2305.64	876.38	1191.91	237.36
5	15525.77	11735.71	5158.68	5733.05	341.68	652.39	2342.18	895.95	1206.49	239.74
6	15747.51	11891.56	5228.51	5813.41	341.23	674.62	2382.11	914.98	1225.55	241.58
7	15909.64	12002.24	5297.21	5844.05	348.27	682.49	2420.99	936.69	1240.10	244.20
8	16140.90	12149.66	5378.63	5901.40	349.48	696.24	2481.32	970.95	1263.12	247.25
9	16635.06	12425.46	5470.73	6077.09	349.15	706.81	2715.72	1113.18	1351.87	250.68
10	17031.57	12752.47	5538.00	6330.00	350.08	706.65	2784.35	1151.30	1380.45	252.60
11	17465.54	13118.12	5651.34	6574.47	351.57	703.92	2858.46	1195.60	1407.28	255.59
12	18061.42	13476.71	5801.99	6757.52	363.62	708.72	3046.15	1259.11	1519.95	267.08
比上期增减额（亿元） Changes Compared with Previous Period（100 Million Yuan）										
1991 1	-4.31	-24.21	15.16	-38.29	0.60	-0.71	4.92	4.14	-1.02	1.80
2	-16.67	-37.47	31.90	-74.10	2.65	6.59	18.49	7.91	13.81	-3.23
3	175.86	104.67	81.92	6.46	9.49	27.25	29.61	20.20	6.99	2.42
4	109.81	37.79	58.96	-37.13	8.97	25.99	37.73	25.84	8.33	3.57
5	120.65	60.95	71.01	-19.46	3.20	21.34	36.54	19.57	14.58	2.38
6	221.74	155.85	69.83	80.36	-0.45	22.23	39.93	19.03	19.06	1.84
7	162.13	110.68	68.70	30.64	7.04	7.87	38.88	21.71	14.55	2.62
8	231.26	147.42	81.42	57.35	1.21	13.75	60.33	34.26	23.02	3.05
9	494.16	275.80	92.10	175.69	-0.33	10.57	234.40	142.23	88.75	3.43
10	396.51	327.01	67.27	252.91	0.93	-0.16	68.63	38.12	28.58	1.92
11	433.97	365.65	113.34	244.47	1.49	-2.73	74.11	44.30	26.83	2.99
12	595.88	358.59	150.65	183.05	12.05	4.80	187.69	63.51	112.67	11.49
比去年同期增长（%） Increase Rate Year-on-year（%）										
1991 1	22.52	22.33	26.12	20.95	12.32	21.90	25.65	41.54	17.17	21.42
2	22.53	22.19	25.75	20.82	13.78	21.92	26.43	42.71	18.10	20.37
3	21.68	20.92	23.25	20.12	15.83	21.40	27.23	44.25	18.77	19.03
4	21.33	20.30	22.71	19.18	17.42	21.42	28.31	45.37	19.44	21.01
5	21.38	20.27	23.05	18.77	17.91	21.58	28.86	46.33	19.98	19.98
6	20.93	19.83	22.52	18.44	16.10	21.92	28.71	45.19	20.49	18.79
7	20.97	19.90	22.69	18.28	17.25	21.90	28.83	44.86	20.62	19.41
8	20.75	19.30	22.59	17.11	17.04	22.90	29.93	46.09	21.83	18.66
9	20.20	17.24	18.80	16.23	16.09	23.22	39.03	61.23	28.60	18.40
10	20.14	17.05	18.82	15.81	15.65	23.49	39.27	61.15	29.06	17.40
11	20.17	17.10	18.91	15.91	14.57	24.36	39.02	61.52	28.31	16.62
12	19.29	16.24	18.41	14.62	14.79	23.92	37.53	53.87	30.60	14.73

国家银行人民币信贷收支主要指标时间序列表
Time Series of Major Indicators in Sources and Uses of Credit Funds of State Banks (RMB)

年 月 Year Month	各项存款 Total Deposits	企业存款 Deposits by Enterprises	财政存款 Fiscal Deposits	储蓄存款 Savings Deposits	农村存款 Rural Deposits
		期末余额（亿元） Balance (100 Million Yuan)			
1992 1	15114.82	5052.28	594.65	6904.87	1165.68
2	15714.16	5227.13	584.60	7254.26	1222.27
3	16128.99	5464.51	627.19	7404.87	1189.60
4	16645.19	5787.93	688.45	7509.78	1163.07
5	17098.55	6053.34	690.38	7642.32	1177.16
6	17382.71	6230.28	584.32	7784.03	1218.77
7	17870.72	6535.36	540.27	7892.10	1234.47
8	18313.66	6779.10	635.54	7981.68	1228.50
9	18159.50	6654.41	487.41	8119.16	1236.42
10	18528.60	6877.46	425.39	8246.04	1285.42
11	18757.74	6980.75	363.30	8349.38	1343.77
12	18907.80	6822.62	250.16	8677.29	1409.46
		比上期增减额（亿元） Changes Compared with Previous Period (100 Million Yuan)			
1992 1	233.23	-5.78	90.36	113.97	134.11
2	599.34	174.85	-10.05	349.39	56.59
3	414.83	237.38	42.59	150.61	-32.67
4	516.20	323.42	61.26	104.91	-26.53
5	453.36	265.41	1.93	132.54	14.09
6	284.16	176.94	-106.06	141.71	41.61
7	488.01	305.08	-44.05	108.07	15.70
8	442.94	243.74	95.27	89.58	-5.97
9	-154.16	-124.69	-148.13	137.48	7.92
10	369.10	223.05	-62.02	126.88	49.00
11	229.14	103.29	-62.09	103.34	58.35
12	150.06	-158.13	-113.14	327.91	65.69
		比去年同期增长（%） Increase Rate Year-on-year (%)			
1992 1	26.91	24.00	39.11	29.93	34.26
2	28.63	26.77	30.93	30.39	37.54
3	28.39	27.65	40.49	28.48	38.15
4	29.36	29.77	52.15	27.44	39.86
5	30.02	31.03	48.86	27.55	42.27
6	30.69	34.71	32.55	27.13	43.01
7	31.21	38.31	19.96	25.97	40.64
8	31.52	39.02	41.19	25.40	38.76
9	27.34	31.70	2.43	25.92	36.60
10	26.66	33.88	-23.82	25.63	33.24
11	24.61	31.72	-38.65	24.81	28.49
12	27.05	34.89	-50.39	27.78	36.63

国家银行人民币信贷收支主要指标时间序列表
Time Series of Major Indicators in Sources and Uses of Credit Funds of State Banks（RMB）

年 月 Year Month	各项贷款 Total Loans	流动资金贷款 Working Capital Loans	工业贷款 Loans to Industrial Sector	商业贷款 Loans to Commercial Sector	建筑业贷款 Loans to Construction Sector	农业贷款 Loans to Agricultural Sector	固定资产贷款 Fixed Asset Loans	基本建设贷款 Capital Construction Loans	技术改造贷款 Technical Improvement Loans	其他固定资产贷款 Other Fixed Asset Loans
期末余额（亿元） Balance（100 Million Yuan）										
1992 1	18065.60	13474.32	5774.72	6812.20	366.86	705.10	3032.22	1262.36	1505.49	264.37
2	18100.59	13485.57	5831.11	6763.08	365.33	717.56	3040.87	1270.82	1506.15	263.90
3	18339.46	13644.62	5917.99	6810.29	376.62	751.80	3076.66	1291.11	1519.52	266.03
4	18665.39	13764.43	6000.69	6818.59	392.13	783.32	3221.39	1373.97	1575.26	272.16
5	18905.91	13875.70	6081.16	6821.72	404.98	807.24	3294.47	1412.04	1607.03	275.40
6	19298.82	14093.40	6146.54	6950.70	414.40	821.21	3371.03	1442.88	1647.97	280.17
7	19610.90	14365.48	6279.79	7056.52	433.72	838.44	3438.85	1478.23	1677.95	282.67
8	19901.65	14552.04	6350.16	7161.45	439.72	854.23	3494.36	1504.30	1703.62	286.43
9	20000.97	14578.53	6348.24	7217.45	425.75	852.49	3572.54	1544.17	1736.88	291.53
10	20423.84	14890.35	6445.23	7418.46	434.83	856.66	3635.68	1565.73	1774.22	295.72
11	20882.24	15264.86	6602.58	7629.25	437.46	859.11	3684.65	1582.94	1801.89	299.83
12	21570.02	15634.84	6709.89	7876.51	436.22	859.55	3924.02	1685.73	1927.82	310.47
比上期增减额（亿元） Changes Compared with Previous Period（100 Million Yuan）										
1992 1	4.18	-2.39	-27.27	54.68	3.24	-3.62	-13.93	3.25	-14.46	-2.71
2	34.99	11.25	56.39	-49.12	-1.53	12.46	8.65	8.46	0.66	-0.47
3	238.87	159.05	86.88	47.21	11.29	34.24	35.79	20.29	13.37	2.13
4	325.93	119.81	82.70	8.30	15.51	31.52	144.73	82.86	55.74	6.13
5	240.52	111.27	80.47	3.13	12.85	23.92	73.08	38.07	31.77	3.24
6	392.91	217.70	65.38	128.98	9.42	13.97	76.56	30.84	40.94	4.77
7	312.08	272.08	133.25	105.82	19.32	17.23	67.82	35.35	29.98	2.50
8	290.75	186.56	70.37	104.93	6.00	15.79	55.51	26.07	25.67	3.76
9	99.32	26.49	-1.92	56.00	-13.97	-1.74	78.18	39.87	33.26	5.10
10	422.87	311.82	96.99	201.01	9.08	4.17	63.14	21.56	37.34	4.19
11	458.40	374.51	157.35	210.79	2.63	2.45	48.97	17.21	27.67	4.11
12	687.78	369.98	107.31	247.26	-1.24	0.44	239.37	102.79	125.93	10.64
比去年同期增长（%） Increase Rate Year-on-year（%）										
1992 1	19.35	16.46	17.49	16.30	15.59	23.44	36.60	53.49	29.47	12.69
2	19.72	16.94	17.88	16.94	14.16	24.19	35.86	53.05	28.01	14.06
3	19.90	17.25	17.68	17.63	14.30	24.25	35.66	51.80	28.38	13.79
4	21.16	17.90	17.95	18.53	15.85	24.13	39.72	56.78	32.16	14.66
5	21.77	18.23	17.88	18.99	18.53	23.74	40.66	57.60	33.20	14.87
6	22.55	18.52	17.56	19.56	21.44	21.73	41.51	57.70	34.47	15.97
7	23.26	19.69	18.55	20.75	24.54	22.85	42.04	57.81	35.31	15.75
8	23.30	19.77	18.06	21.35	25.82	22.69	40.83	54.93	34.87	15.85
9	20.23	17.33	16.04	18.76	21.94	20.61	31.55	38.72	28.48	16.30
10	19.92	16.76	16.38	17.20	24.21	21.23	30.58	36.00	28.52	17.07
11	19.56	16.36	16.83	16.04	24.43	22.05	28.90	32.40	28.04	17.31
12	19.43	16.01	15.65	16.56	19.97	21.28	28.82	33.88	26.83	16.25

国家银行人民币信贷收支主要指标时间序列表

Time Series of Major Indicators in Sources and Uses of Credit Funds of State Banks (RMB)

年　月 Year Month		各项存款 Total Deposits				
			企业存款 Deposits by Enterprises	财政存款 Fiscal Deposits	储蓄存款 Savings Deposits	农村存款 Rural Deposits
			期末余额（亿元） Balance (100 Million Yuan)			
1993	1	19294.01	6878.64	307.92	8964.11	1485.78
	2	19740.54	7124.68	342.74	9170.50	1404.88
	3	19963.87	7347.72	366.47	9157.35	1347.03
	4	20282.14	7624.12	367.83	9177.32	1320.22
	5	20583.18	7789.07	335.31	9352.71	1325.18
	6	20661.37	7501.90	369.25	9614.98	1340.81
	7	20751.64	7161.45	435.94	9945.22	1351.58
	8	20977.95	7055.51	464.38	10247.41	1372.99
	9	21284.77	7049.08	443.39	10505.03	1416.92
	10	22069.10	7293.40	568.32	10786.85	1482.97
	11	23021.74	7824.72	577.99	11044.26	1569.68
	12	23245.36	7671.62	502.34	11187.58	1752.85
			比上期增减额（亿元） Changes Compared with Previous Period (100 Million Yuan)			
1993	1	387.91	62.86	62.20	286.03	76.36
	2	446.53	246.04	34.82	206.39	-80.90
	3	223.33	223.04	23.73	-13.16	-57.86
	4	318.27	276.40	1.36	19.97	-26.81
	5	301.04	164.95	-32.52	175.40	4.96
	6	78.19	-287.17	33.94	262.26	15.64
	7	90.27	-340.45	66.69	330.24	10.77
	8	226.31	-105.93	28.44	302.20	21.40
	9	306.82	-6.44	-20.99	257.62	43.93
	10	784.33	244.32	124.93	281.82	66.05
	11	952.64	531.32	9.67	257.41	86.71
	12	223.62	-153.10	-75.65	143.32	183.17
			比去年同期增长（%） Increase Rate Year-on-year (%)			
1993	1	27.65	36.15	-48.22	29.82	27.46
	2	25.62	36.30	-41.37	26.42	14.94
	3	23.78	34.46	-41.57	23.67	13.23
	4	21.85	31.72	-46.57	22.20	13.51
	5	20.38	28.67	-51.43	22.38	12.57
	6	18.86	20.41	-36.81	23.52	10.01
	7	16.12	9.58	-19.31	26.01	9.49
	8	14.55	4.08	-26.93	28.39	11.76
	9	17.21	5.93	-9.03	29.39	14.60
	10	19.11	6.05	33.60	30.81	15.37
	11	22.73	12.09	59.09	32.28	16.81
	12	22.94	12.44	100.81	28.93	24.36

国家银行人民币信贷收支主要指标时间序列表

Time Series of Major Indicators in Sources and Uses of Credit Funds of State Banks（RMB）

年 月 Year Month		各项贷款 Total Loans	流动资金贷款 Working Capital Loans				农业贷款 Loans to Agricultural Sector	固定资产贷款 Fixed Asset Loans			
				工业贷款 Loans to Industrial Sector	商业贷款 Loans to Commercial Sector	建筑业贷款 Loans to Construction Sector			基本建设贷款 Capital Construction Loans	技术改造贷款 Technical Improvement Loans	其他固定资产贷款 Other Fixed Asset Loans
期末余额（亿元） Balance（100 Million Yuan）											
1993	1	21667.50	15710.93	6774.01	7881.59	443.51	867.34	3904.85	1680.25	1912.69	311.91
	2	21812.39	15790.97	6814.87	7904.53	448.91	886.94	3932.78	1695.42	1920.50	316.86
	3	21818.63	15746.67	6788.63	7889.64	444.16	897.31	3962.08	1712.24	1928.33	321.51
	4	22173.12	15991.87	6891.58	8005.05	461.03	917.74	4020.94	1748.89	1946.12	325.94
	5	22363.05	16085.20	6952.00	8025.70	464.93	931.88	4080.56	1782.31	1966.69	331.56
	6	22608.16	16224.46	7008.69	8103.00	465.81	938.69	4140.41	1814.01	1990.29	336.12
	7	22765.42	16239.94	7024.07	8091.85	470.48	944.98	4176.78	1845.66	1991.42	339.71
	8	23077.67	16442.40	7134.28	8181.55	462.64	959.15	4223.61	1870.66	2008.78	344.17
	9	23610.52	16857.55	7336.12	8380.45	465.00	970.81	4376.60	1955.26	2074.60	346.74
	10	24287.84	17322.87	7529.83	8622.53	477.34	979.41	4595.24	2097.60	2149.51	348.13
	11	25369.30	18007.00	7832.23	8957.05	499.57	998.57	4914.15	2291.96	2270.39	351.80
	12	26461.14	18688.69	8110.02	9314.15	523.66	1013.38	5170.52	2419.83	2391.39	359.31
比上期增减额（亿元） Changes Compared with Previous Period（100 Million Yuan）											
1993	1	51.97	67.72	61.57	-2.13	8.78	8.06	-19.70	-4.75	-17.03	2.07
	2	144.89	80.04	40.85	22.94	5.40	19.60	27.94	15.17	7.81	4.95
	3	6.23	-44.30	-26.23	-14.89	-4.75	10.37	29.29	16.82	7.83	4.64
	4	354.49	245.19	102.95	115.41	16.87	20.43	58.86	36.65	17.78	4.43
	5	189.93	93.33	60.42	20.65	3.90	14.14	59.63	33.43	20.58	5.63
	6	245.11	139.26	56.68	77.30	0.87	6.81	59.85	31.69	23.60	4.56
	7	157.26	15.48	15.38	-11.15	4.67	6.29	36.36	31.65	1.13	3.59
	8	312.25	202.46	110.21	89.70	-7.83	14.16	46.83	25.01	17.36	4.47
	9	532.85	415.15	201.84	198.89	2.36	11.66	153.00	84.60	65.83	2.57
	10	677.32	465.33	193.71	242.08	12.34	8.61	218.63	142.34	74.90	1.39
	11	1081.46	684.14	302.40	334.52	22.22	19.16	318.91	194.36	120.88	3.67
	12	1091.84	681.69	277.80	357.10	24.09	14.80	256.38	127.87	121.00	7.51
比去年同期增长（%） Increase Rate Year-on-year（%）											
1993	1	19.94	16.60	17.30	15.70	20.89	23.01	28.78	33.10	27.05	17.98
	2	20.51	17.10	16.87	16.88	22.88	23.60	29.33	33.41	27.51	20.07
	3	18.97	15.41	14.71	15.85	17.93	19.35	28.78	32.62	26.90	20.85
	4	18.79	16.18	14.85	17.40	17.57	17.16	24.82	27.29	23.54	19.76
	5	18.29	15.92	14.32	17.65	14.80	15.44	23.86	26.22	22.38	20.39
	6	17.15	15.12	14.03	16.58	12.41	14.31	22.82	25.72	20.77	19.97
	7	16.09	13.05	11.85	14.67	8.48	12.71	21.46	24.86	18.68	20.18
	8	15.96	12.99	12.35	14.24	5.21	12.28	20.87	24.35	17.91	20.16
	9	18.05	15.63	15.56	16.11	9.22	13.88	22.51	26.62	19.44	18.94
	10	18.92	16.34	16.83	16.23	9.78	14.33	26.39	33.97	21.15	17.72
	11	21.49	17.96	18.62	17.40	14.20	16.23	33.37	44.79	26.00	17.33
	12	22.68	19.53	20.87	18.25	20.04	17.90	31.77	43.55	24.05	15.73

国家银行人民币信贷收支主要指标时间序列表

Time Series of Major Indicators in Sources and Uses of Credit Funds of State Banks (RMB)

年 月 Year Month		各项存款 Total Deposits	企业存款 Deposits by Enterprises	财政存款 Fiscal Deposits	储蓄存款 Savings Deposits	活期储蓄 Demand Deposits	定期储蓄 Time Deposits	农业存款 Deposits by Agricultural Sector
		期末余额（亿元） Balance (100 Million Yuan)						
1994	1	21651.75	8691.65	577.29	11442.35	2381.12	9061.23	163.53
	2	22515.53	8747.62	642.49	12212.24	2515.09	9697.15	154.14
	3	23476.76	9298.98	664.25	12599.89	2539.33	10060.56	157.39
	4	24037.70	9767.74	628.78	12706.90	2566.27	10140.63	162.23
	5	25066.38	10252.54	837.56	13025.26	2663.71	10361.55	162.93
	6	25876.27	10572.65	902.94	13429.24	2801.29	10627.95	162.57
	7	26704.92	10796.43	1005.17	13899.42	2923.22	10976.20	167.16
	8	27511.16	11196.40	971.14	14278.94	3008.26	11270.68	172.74
	9	27897.76	11178.89	941.10	14706.94	3115.53	11591.41	169.37
	10	28577.75	11347.37	1048.01	15065.29	3140.66	11924.63	185.35
	11	29128.38	11576.93	963.18	15453.50	3230.68	12222.82	200.21
	12	29356.75	11466.58	862.24	15844.46	3374.74	12469.72	195.11
		比上期增减额（亿元） Changes Compared with Previous Period (100 Million Yuan)						
1994	1	246.90	-41.63	83.77	255.98	34.74	221.24	-13.02
	2	863.78	55.98	65.20	769.89	133.98	635.91	-9.39
	3	961.23	551.36	21.76	387.65	24.24	363.41	3.25
	4	560.94	468.76	-35.47	107.02	26.94	80.07	4.84
	5	1028.68	484.80	208.78	318.36	97.45	220.92	0.70
	6	809.89	320.11	65.38	403.98	137.58	266.40	-0.36
	7	828.65	223.78	102.23	470.18	121.93	348.25	4.59
	8	806.24	399.97	-34.03	379.52	85.04	294.48	5.58
	9	386.60	-17.51	-30.04	428.00	107.27	320.73	-3.37
	10	679.99	168.48	106.91	358.35	25.13	333.22	15.98
	11	550.63	229.56	-84.83	388.21	90.02	298.19	14.86
	12	228.37	-110.35	-100.94	390.96	144.06	246.90	-5.10
		比去年同期增长（%） Increase Rate Year-on-year (%)						
1994	1	12.22	26.36	87.48	27.65	—	—	—
	2	14.06	22.78	87.46	33.17	—	—	—
	3	17.60	26.56	81.26	37.59	—	—	—
	4	18.52	28.12	70.94	38.46	—	—	—
	5	21.78	31.63	149.79	39.27	—	—	—
	6	25.24	40.93	144.53	39.67	—	—	—
	7	28.69	50.76	130.58	39.76	—	—	—
	8	31.14	58.69	109.13	39.34	—	—	—
	9	31.07	58.59	112.25	40.00	—	—	—
	10	29.49	55.58	84.40	39.66	—	—	—
	11	26.53	47.95	66.64	39.92	—	—	—
	12	26.29	49.47	71.64	41.63	—	—	—

国家银行人民币信贷收支主要指标时间序列表

Time Series of Major Indicators in Sources and Uses of Credit Funds of State Banks（RMB）

期末余额（亿元）

Balance（100 Million Yuan）

年 月 Year Month		各项贷款 Total Loans	短期贷款 Short - term Loans	工业贷款 Loans to Industrial Sector	商业贷款 Loans to Commercial Sector	建筑业贷款 Loans to Construction Sector	农业贷款 Loans to Agricultural Sector	中长期贷款 Medium and Long - term Loans	基本建设贷款 Capital Construction Loans	技术改造贷款 Technical Improvement Loans	其他中长期贷款 Other Medium and Long - term Loans	有价证券及投资 Securities and Investments
1994	1	26430.31	19630.94	8076.09	8141.86	528.87	596.38	5974.89	2435.22	2302.85	1236.82	851.87
	2	26494.66	19661.05	8109.33	8090.64	532.50	608.09	5989.17	2443.60	2311.85	1233.72	909.88
	3	26792.47	19827.32	8161.71	8087.22	532.45	660.31	6110.70	2533.12	2359.72	1217.86	908.20
	4	27198.80	20137.97	8328.95	8196.46	542.40	704.33	6232.38	2601.10	2395.99	1235.29	1092.66
	5	27692.13	20471.63	8535.55	8245.49	554.76	722.84	6371.32	2700.67	2422.78	1247.87	1260.51
	6	28249.58	20875.79	8677.62	8435.58	568.61	734.02	6503.04	2764.72	2482.59	1255.73	1324.86
	7	28668.20	21134.52	8801.69	8531.85	582.12	721.10	6645.95	2829.12	2509.61	1307.22	1347.10
	8	29099.34	21459.67	8900.26	8687.88	589.73	734.02	6728.22	2858.33	2551.53	1318.36	1400.83
	9	29558.66	21816.16	8971.77	8948.92	587.58	734.63	6825.43	2897.20	2598.13	1330.10	1542.54
	10	30186.79	22365.89	9094.73	9279.87	594.08	745.23	6887.16	2901.52	2629.72	1355.92	1609.16
	11	30573.28	22909.09	9215.64	9650.30	599.63	751.91	6721.26	2670.23	2685.54	1365.49	1712.17
	12	31602.90	23427.77	9368.01	10052.72	612.53	755.80	7172.93	2766.21	2985.18	1421.54	1802.91

比上期增减额（亿元）

Changes Compared with Previous Period（100 Million Yuan）

年 月 Year Month		各项贷款 Total Loans	短期贷款 Short - term Loans	工业贷款 Loans to Industrial Sector	商业贷款 Loans to Commercial Sector	建筑业贷款 Loans to Construction Sector	农业贷款 Loans to Agricultural Sector	中长期贷款 Medium and Long - term Loans	基本建设贷款 Capital Construction Loans	技术改造贷款 Technical Improvement Loans	其他中长期贷款 Other Medium and Long - term Loans	有价证券及投资 Securities and Investments
1994	1	- 11.59	- 10.25	9.43	- 82.71	2.84	4.33	- 2.79	14.04	- 17.14	0.30	11.38
	2	64.35	30.10	33.25	- 51.22	3.63	11.71	14.28	8.38	8.99	- 3.10	58.01
	3	297.81	166.27	52.38	- 3.42	- 0.05	52.23	121.52	89.51	47.87	- 15.86	- 1.68
	4	406.33	310.65	167.24	109.24	9.95	44.01	121.68	67.99	36.27	17.43	184.46
	5	493.33	333.66	206.60	49.04	12.36	18.51	138.94	99.56	26.79	12.58	167.85
	6	557.45	404.16	142.07	190.09	13.85	11.18	131.72	64.05	59.81	7.86	64.35
	7	418.62	258.73	124.07	96.27	13.51	- 12.92	142.91	64.40	27.02	51.49	22.24
	8	431.14	325.15	98.57	156.03	7.61	12.92	82.27	29.21	41.92	11.14	53.73
	9	459.32	356.49	71.51	261.04	- 2.15	0.61	97.21	38.87	46.60	11.74	141.71
	10	628.13	549.73	122.96	330.95	6.50	10.60	61.73	4.32	31.59	25.82	66.62
	11	386.49	543.20	120.91	370.43	5.55	6.68	- 165.90	- 231.29	55.82	9.57	103.01
	12	1029.62	518.68	152.37	402.42	12.90	3.89	451.67	95.98	299.64	56.05	90.74

比去年同期增长（%）

Increase Rate Year - on - year（%）

年 月 Year Month		各项贷款 Total Loans	短期贷款 Short - term Loans	工业贷款 Loans to Industrial Sector	商业贷款 Loans to Commercial Sector	建筑业贷款 Loans to Construction Sector	农业贷款 Loans to Agricultural Sector	中长期贷款 Medium and Long - term Loans	基本建设贷款 Capital Construction Loans	技术改造贷款 Technical Improvement Loans	其他中长期贷款 Other Medium and Long - term Loans	有价证券及投资 Securities and Investments
1994	1	21.98	—	19.22	3.30	19.25	—	—	44.93	20.40	—	85.04
	2	21.47	—	18.99	2.35	18.62	—	—	44.13	20.38	—	94.94
	3	22.80	—	20.23	2.50	19.88	—	—	47.94	22.37	—	92.93
	4	22.67	—	20.86	2.39	17.65	—	—	48.73	23.12	—	133.62
	5	23.83	—	22.78	2.74	19.32	—	—	51.53	23.19	—	169.65
	6	24.95	—	23.81	4.10	22.07	—	—	52.41	24.74	—	133.09
	7	25.93	—	25.31	5.44	23.73	—	—	53.29	26.02	—	137.86
	8	26.09	—	24.75	6.19	27.47	—	—	52.80	27.02	—	151.93
	9	25.19	—	22.30	6.78	26.36	—	—	48.17	25.23	—	182.69
	10	24.29	—	20.78	7.62	24.46	—	—	38.33	22.34	—	185.68
	11	20.51	—	17.66	7.74	20.03	—	—	16.50	18.29	—	199.63
	12	19.43	—	15.51	7.93	16.97	—	—	14.31	24.83	—	198.43

国家银行人民币信贷收支主要指标时间序列表

Time Series of Major Indicators in Sources and Uses of Credit Funds of State Banks (RMB)

年 月 Year Month		各项存款 Total Deposits	企业存款 Deposits by Enterprises	财政存款 Fiscal Deposits	储蓄存款 Savings Deposits	活期储蓄 Demand Deposits	定期储蓄 Time Deposits	农业存款 Deposits by Agricultural Sector
期末余额（亿元） Balance (100 Million Yuan)								
1995	1	29765.23	11261.62	982.42	16448.03	3356.64	13091.39	176.15
	2	31035.51	11625.89	807.34	17374.54	3494.68	13879.86	179.29
	3	31806.27	12161.77	1154.50	17389.61	3530.26	13859.35	179.00
	4	32832.49	12410.80	1563.74	17742.89	3557.27	14185.62	180.35
	5	33837.57	12767.77	1726.85	18214.74	3608.15	14606.59	179.17
	6	34528.47	13002.82	1652.45	18778.07	3728.83	15049.24	174.51
	7	35174.43	13214.10	1414.88	19388.83	3781.43	15607.40	181.82
	8	35852.50	13699.82	1206.45	19775.77	3800.31	15975.46	184.64
	9	36632.16	13785.79	1303.78	20366.75	3918.39	16448.36	185.43
	10	37440.42	14066.64	1330.09	20830.31	3930.30	16900.01	202.19
	11	38171.85	14353.17	1279.84	21342.57	4123.19	17219.38	209.56
	12	38784.83	14519.63	1005.40	21941.03	4265.37	17675.66	216.83
比上期增减额（亿元） Changes Compared with Previous Period (100 Million Yuan)								
1995	1	357.41	-252.35	116.33	594.70	-6.49	601.19	-18.62
	2	1270.28	364.27	-175.08	926.51	138.04	788.47	3.14
	3	769.23	534.35	347.16	15.07	35.58	-20.51	-0.29
	4	1026.22	249.03	409.24	353.28	27.02	326.26	1.35
	5	1005.08	356.97	163.11	471.85	50.87	420.98	-1.18
	6	690.90	235.05	-74.40	563.33	120.68	442.65	-4.66
	7	645.96	211.28	-237.57	610.76	52.60	558.16	7.31
	8	678.07	485.72	-208.43	386.94	18.88	368.06	2.82
	9	779.66	85.97	97.33	590.98	118.08	472.90	0.79
	10	808.26	280.85	26.31	463.56	11.91	451.65	16.76
	11	731.43	286.53	-50.25	512.26	192.89	319.37	7.37
	12	612.98	166.46	-274.44	598.46	142.18	456.28	7.27
比去年同期增长（%） Increase Rate Year-on-year (%)								
1995	1	37.47	29.57	70.18	43.75	40.97	44.48	7.72
	2	37.84	32.90	25.66	42.27	38.95	43.13	16.32
	3	35.48	30.79	73.81	38.01	39.02	37.76	13.73
	4	36.59	27.06	148.69	39.63	38.62	39.89	11.17
	5	34.99	24.53	106.18	39.84	35.46	40.97	9.97
	6	33.44	22.99	83.01	39.83	33.11	41.60	7.34
	7	31.72	22.39	40.76	39.49	29.36	42.19	8.77
	8	30.32	22.36	24.23	38.50	26.33	41.74	6.89
	9	31.31	23.32	38.54	38.48	25.77	41.90	9.48
	10	31.01	23.96	26.92	38.27	25.14	41.72	9.09
	11	31.05	23.98	32.88	38.11	27.63	40.88	4.67
	12	32.12	26.63	16.60	38.48	26.39	41.75	11.13

国家银行人民币信贷收支主要指标时间序列表

Time Series of Major Indicators in Sources and Uses of Credit Funds of State Banks（RMB）

年 月 Year Month		各项贷款 Total Loans	短期贷款 Short - term Loans					中长期贷款 Medium and Long - term Loans				有价证券及投资 Securities and Investments
				工业贷款 Loans to Industrial Sector	商业贷款 Loans to Commercial Sector	建筑业贷款 Loans to Construction Sector	农业贷款 Loans to Agricultural Sector		基本建设贷款 Capital Construction Loans	技术改造贷款 Technical Improvement Loans	其他中长期贷款 Other Medium and Long - term Loans	
期末余额（亿元） Balance（100 Million Yuan）												
1995	1	31747.13	23968.56	9439.82	10184.89	620.32	783.78	7111.74				1859.39
	2	31865.80	24074.97	9480.01	10191.08	622.68	799.92	7120.21				1867.57
	3	32934.39	24157.13	9548.80	10164.61	629.66	813.72	8097.72				2010.67
	4	33389.91	24497.56	9699.07	10198.55	648.63	849.82	8184.25				2153.14
	5	33691.05	24715.31	9806.10	10219.59	655.79	871.16	8256.40				2280.22
	6	34087.08	24929.04	9856.67	10330.14	656.65	889.99	8429.34				2389.22
	7	34530.92	25266.44	9961.59	10444.34	671.35	901.02	8518.13				2451.69
	8	35203.90	25668.46	10114.79	10606.76	687.29	919.26	8771.83				2518.95
	9	35897.24	26108.86	10225.48	10847.86	699.59	937.22	9012.78				2633.28
	10	36697.97	26778.08	10411.46	11211.37	715.54	942.62	9128.15				2667.50
	11	37564.99	27449.65	10593.60	11599.49	728.68	951.07	9291.28				2803.85
	12	39393.40	28477.49	10918.99	12163.33	785.45	962.42	10025.58				3064.19
比上期增减额（亿元） Changes Compared with Previous Period（100 Million Yuan）												
1995	1	151.15	139.60	46.52	46.59	1.93	18.75	-7.62				-6.47
	2	118.67	106.41	40.19	6.19	2.36	16.14	8.47				8.18
	3	186.62	82.16	68.79	-26.47	6.98	13.80	95.54				143.10
	4	455.52	340.43	150.27	33.94	18.97	36.10	86.53				142.47
	5	301.14	217.75	107.03	21.04	7.16	21.34	72.15				127.08
	6	396.03	213.73	50.57	110.55	0.86	18.83	172.94				109.00
	7	443.84	337.40	104.92	114.20	14.70	11.03	88.79				62.47
	8	672.98	402.02	153.20	162.42	15.94	18.24	253.70				67.26
	9	693.34	440.40	110.69	241.10	12.30	17.96	240.95				114.33
	10	800.73	669.22	185.98	363.51	15.95	5.40	115.37				34.22
	11	867.02	671.57	182.14	388.12	13.14	8.45	163.13				136.35
	12	1828.41	1027.84	325.39	563.84	56.77	11.35	734.30				260.34
比去年同期增长（%） Increase Rate Year - on - year（%）												
1995	1	20.12	22.10	16.89	25.09	17.29	31.42	19.03				118.27
	2	20.27	22.45	16.90	25.96	16.94	31.55	18.88				105.25
	3	22.92	21.84	17.00	25.69	18.26	23.23	32.52				121.39
	4	22.76	21.65	16.45	24.43	19.59	20.66	31.32				97.05
	5	21.66	20.73	14.89	23.94	18.21	20.52	29.59				80.90
	6	20.66	19.42	13.59	22.46	15.48	21.25	29.62				80.34
	7	20.45	19.55	13.18	22.42	15.33	24.95	28.17				82.00
	8	20.98	19.61	13.65	22.09	16.54	25.24	30.37				79.82
	9	21.44	19.68	13.97	21.22	19.06	27.58	32.05				70.71
	10	21.57	19.73	14.48	20.81	20.45	26.49	32.54				65.77
	11	22.87	19.82	14.95	20.20	21.52	26.49	38.24				63.76
	12	24.65	21.55	16.56	21.00	28.23	27.34	39.77				69.96

国家银行人民币信贷收支主要指标时间序列表
Time Series of Major Indicators in Sources and Uses of Credit Funds of State Banks (RMB)

年 月 Year Month		各项存款 Total Deposits	企业存款 Deposits by Enterprises	财政存款 Fiscal Deposits	储蓄存款 Savings Deposits	活期储蓄 Demand Deposits	定期储蓄 Time Deposits	农业存款 Deposits by Agricultural Sector
		期末余额（亿元） Balance (100 Million Yuan)						
1996	1	39551.51	14719.51	1117.76	22519.37	4329.89	18189.48	203.19
	2	40433.65	14404.28	1191.63	23727.14	4516.66	19210.48	183.46
	3	41796.72	14848.20	1126.18	24684.89	4486.77	20198.12	181.34
	4	43244.77	15396.78	1456.95	25242.54	4418.46	20824.08	187.21
	5	44084.66	15868.22	1315.94	25698.14	4531.09	21167.05	187.62
	6	44937.58	16202.09	1281.35	26298.34	4819.82	21478.52	193.32
	7	45945.59	16438.53	1559.08	26727.71	4865.54	21862.17	199.90
	8	46869.47	16788.87	1545.74	27242.60	4977.61	22264.99	204.74
	9	47351.47	17038.11	1522.28	27523.92	5073.08	22450.84	205.29
	10	48332.47	17397.35	1676.86	27968.13	5300.99	22667.14	215.25
	11	48956.85	17756.63	1788.75	28130.61	5368.02	22762.59	225.39
	12	49596.52	18496.82	1274.16	28524.16	5647.04	22877.12	238.74
		比上期增减额（亿元） Changes Compared with Previous Period (100 Million Yuan)						
1996	1	664.54	99.32	117.53	533.59	20.98	512.61	-13.60
	2	882.14	-315.23	73.87	1207.77	186.77	1021.00	-19.73
	3	1363.07	443.92	-65.45	957.75	-29.89	987.64	-2.12
	4	1448.05	548.58	330.77	557.65	-68.31	625.96	5.87
	5	839.89	471.44	-141.01	455.60	112.63	342.97	0.41
	6	852.92	333.87	-34.59	600.20	288.73	311.47	5.70
	7	1008.01	236.44	277.73	429.37	45.72	383.65	6.58
	8	923.88	350.34	-13.34	514.89	112.07	402.82	4.84
	9	482.00	249.24	-23.46	281.32	95.47	185.85	0.55
	10	981.00	359.24	154.58	444.21	227.91	216.30	9.96
	11	624.38	359.28	111.89	162.48	67.03	95.45	10.14
	12	639.67	740.19	-514.59	393.55	279.02	114.53	13.35
		比去年同期增长（%） Increase Rate Year-on-year (%)						
1996	1	32.88	30.71	13.78	36.91	28.99	38.94	15.35
	2	30.28	23.90	47.60	36.56	29.24	38.41	2.33
	3	31.41	22.09	-2.45	41.95	27.09	45.74	1.31
	4	31.71	24.06	-6.83	42.27	24.21	46.80	3.80
	5	30.28	24.28	-23.80	41.08	25.58	44.91	4.72
	6	30.15	24.60	-22.46	40.05	29.26	42.72	10.78
	7	30.62	24.40	10.19	37.85	28.67	40.08	9.94
	8	30.73	22.55	28.12	37.76	30.98	39.37	10.89
	9	29.26	23.59	16.76	35.14	29.47	36.49	10.71
	10	29.09	23.68	26.07	34.27	34.87	34.13	6.46
	11	28.25	23.71	39.76	31.81	30.19	32.19	7.55
	12	27.88	27.39	26.73	30.00	32.39	29.43	10.10

国家银行人民币信贷收支主要指标时间序列表

Time Series of Major Indicators in Sources and Uses of Credit Funds of State Banks（RMB）

年 月 Year Month	各项贷款 Total Loans	短期贷款 Short - term Loans					中长期贷款 Medium and Long - term Loans				有价证券及投资 Securities and Investments
			工业贷款 Loans to Industrial Sector	商业贷款 Loans to Commercial Sector	建筑业贷款 Loans to Construction Sector	农业贷款 Loans to Agricultural Sector		基本建设贷款 Capital Construction Loans	技术改造贷款 Technical Improvement Loans	其他中长期贷款 Other Medium and Long - term Loans	
期末余额（亿元） Balance（100 Million Yuan）											
1996 1	39529.75	28765.03	11005.72	12093.34	786.39	975.75	9908.25				3066.89
2	39814.39	28998.96	11111.73	12145.16	795.94	992.84	9964.33				3106.51
3	40373.94	29386.22	11270.38	12263.07	813.05	1020.55	10092.51				3226.17
4	40962.49	29850.63	11515.78	12308.52	832.36	1061.82	10201.30				3355.10
5	41319.92	30087.91	11650.93	12300.26	846.54	1088.07	10314.80				3503.13
6	42113.22	30696.95	11899.59	12545.80	860.21	1115.81	10509.39				3575.11
7	42690.97	31146.17	12094.69	12694.72	874.96	1135.93	10608.83				3719.21
8	43274.56	31619.39	12243.44	12901.39	888.53	1144.11	10714.53				3750.72
9	43902.91	32109.92	12411.39	13153.79	897.20	1152.14	10864.52				3894.85
10	44726.14	32781.32	12637.68	13458.24	910.92	1173.31	10968.12				3794.16
11	45374.18	33254.21	12808.23	13653.19	934.37	1176.92	11175.79				3821.91
12	47434.52	34432.84	13099.96	14417.12	949.42	1209.61	12034.17				4097.80
比上期增减额（亿元） Changes Compared with Previous Period（100 Million Yuan）											
1996 1	32.98	92.16	60.29	- 18.14	- 1.87	13.35	- 80.02				36.04
2	284.64	233.93	106.01	51.82	9.55	17.09	56.08				39.62
3	559.55	387.26	158.65	117.91	17.11	27.71	128.18				119.66
4	588.55	464.41	245.40	45.45	19.31	41.27	108.79				128.93
5	357.43	237.28	135.15	- 8.26	14.18	26.25	113.50				148.03
6	793.30	609.04	248.66	245.54	13.67	27.74	194.59				71.98
7	577.75	449.22	195.10	148.92	14.75	20.12	99.44				144.10
8	583.59	473.22	148.75	206.67	13.57	8.18	105.70				31.51
9	628.35	490.53	167.95	252.40	8.67	8.03	149.99				144.13
10	823.23	671.40	226.29	304.45	13.72	21.17	103.60				- 100.69
11	648.04	472.89	170.55	194.95	23.45	3.61	207.67				27.75
12	2060.34	1178.63	291.73	763.93	15.05	32.69	858.38				275.89
比去年同期增长（%） Increase Rate Year - on - year（%）											
1996 1	24.51	20.01	16.59	18.74	26.77	24.49	39.32				64.94
2	24.94	20.45	17.21	19.17	27.82	24.12	39.94				66.34
3	22.59	21.65	18.03	20.64	29.13	25.42	24.63				60.45
4	22.68	21.85	18.73	20.69	28.33	24.95	24.65				55.82
5	22.64	21.74	18.81	20.36	29.09	24.90	24.93				53.63
6	23.55	23.14	20.73	21.45	31.00	25.37	24.68				49.64
7	23.63	23.27	21.41	21.55	30.33	26.07	24.54				51.70
8	22.93	23.18	21.04	21.63	29.28	24.46	22.15				48.90
9	22.30	22.98	21.38	21.26	28.25	22.93	20.55				47.91
10	21.88	22.42	21.38	20.04	27.31	24.47	20.16				42.24
11	20.79	21.15	20.91	17.71	28.23	23.75	20.28				36.31
12	20.41	20.91	19.97	18.53	20.88	25.68	20.03				33.73

国家银行人民币信贷收支主要指标时间序列表
Time Series of Major Indicators in Sources and Uses of Credit Funds of State Banks (RMB)

年　月 Year Month		各项存款 Total Deposits	企业存款 Deposits by Enterprises	财政存款 Fiscal Deposits	储蓄存款 Savings Deposits	活期储蓄 Demand Deposits	定期储蓄 Time Deposits	农业存款 Deposits by Agricultural Sector
		期末余额（亿元） Balance (100 Million Yuan)						
1997	1	49904.55	18193.53	1260.90	29058.21	5685.63	23372.58	213.16
	2	51427.92	18327.78	1489.72	30224.55	5959.28	24265.27	207.27
	3	52772.48	19040.07	1609.50	30730.31	6397.35	24332.96	218.11
	4	53667.80	19352.61	1701.30	31190.14	6683.70	24506.44	220.76
	5	54218.10	19846.20	1735.29	31231.28	6634.39	24596.89	221.17
	6	55340.74	20598.34	1725.16	31528.64	6577.59	24951.05	221.50
	7	55683.82	20576.20	1765.69	31901.60	6491.98	25409.62	233.27
	8	56402.94	20886.68	1681.03	32373.24	6665.71	25707.53	232.56
	9	57222.65	21450.74	1812.27	32469.56	6561.89	25907.67	235.03
	10	57855.33	21491.51	1942.54	32911.63	6643.48	26268.15	248.74
	11	58352.33	21558.16	2063.61	33179.21	6786.29	26392.92	253.71
	12	60005.43	22590.89	1534.78	34190.33	7647.79	26542.54	263.99
		比上期增减额（亿元） Changes Compared with Previous Period (100 Million Yuan)						
1997	1	-1043.99	-1142.03	-37.22	261.06	4.20	256.86	-25.79
	2	1523.36	134.23	228.82	1166.34	273.65	892.69	-5.89
	3	1344.57	712.29	119.77	505.76	438.07	67.69	10.84
	4	895.32	312.54	91.81	459.83	286.35	173.48	2.64
	5	550.30	493.58	33.99	41.14	-49.31	90.45	0.41
	6	1122.64	752.14	-10.13	297.36	-56.80	354.16	0.34
	7	343.07	-22.14	40.53	372.96	-85.61	458.57	11.76
	8	719.13	310.48	-84.66	471.64	173.73	297.91	-0.71
	9	819.71	564.06	131.24	96.32	-103.82	200.14	2.47
	10	632.64	40.76	130.27	442.07	81.59	360.48	13.71
	11	497.04	66.66	121.07	267.58	142.81	124.77	4.98
	12	1653.10	1032.73	-528.84	1011.12	861.50	149.62	10.28
		比去年同期增长（%） Increase Rate Year-on-year (%)						
1997	1	26.18	23.60	12.81	29.04	31.31	28.50	4.91
	2	27.19	27.24	25.02	27.38	31.94	26.31	12.98
	3	26.26	28.23	42.92	24.49	42.58	20.47	20.28
	4	24.10	25.69	16.77	23.56	51.27	17.68	17.92
	5	22.99	25.07	31.87	21.53	46.42	16.20	17.88
	6	23.15	27.13	34.64	19.89	36.47	16.17	14.58
	7	21.20	25.17	13.25	19.36	33.43	16.23	16.69
	8	20.34	24.41	8.75	18.83	33.91	15.46	13.59
	9	20.85	25.90	19.05	17.97	29.35	15.40	14.49
	10	19.70	23.53	15.84	17.68	25.33	15.89	15.56
	11	19.19	21.41	15.37	17.95	26.42	15.95	12.56
	12	20.99	22.13	20.45	19.86	35.43	16.02	10.58

国家银行人民币信贷收支主要指标时间序列表

Time Series of Major Indicators in Sources and Uses of Credit Funds of State Banks（RMB）

年 月 Year Month		各项贷款 Total Loans	短期贷款 Short - term Loans					中长期贷款 Medium and Long - term Loans				有价证券及投资 Securities and Investments
				工业贷款 Loans to Industrial Sector	商业贷款 Loans to Commercial Sector	建筑业贷款 Loans to Construction Sector	农业贷款 Loans to Agricultural Sector		基本建设贷款 Capital Construction Loans	技术改造贷款 Technical Improvement Loans	其他中长期贷款 Other Medium and Long - term Loans	
期末余额（亿元） Balance（100 Million Yuan）												
1997	1	51193.64	38130.95	13460.91	14952.01	1342.62	1253.24	12770.46	6475.99	4381.07	1913.40	2636.10
	2	51377.31	38292.62	13545.14	14971.85	1345.12	1262.13	12772.86	6496.35	4377.65	1898.86	2606.4
	3	51925.48	38681.40	13742.22	14989.67	1355.80	1297.64	12924.74	6594.99	4395.60	1934.16	2629.39
	4	52369.07	39034.97	13847.83	15070.92	1365.02	1330.86	12994.85	6624.22	4400.10	1970.53	2392.33
	5	52802.20	39371.63	13980.83	15148.93	1377.73	1347.99	13077.33	6734.05	4414.00	1929.28	2396.34
	6	53697.64	40003.66	14201.51	15383.67	1400.08	1368.88	13359.51	6924.55	4461.59	1973.37	2337.31
	7	54039.49	40285.95	14262.24	15549.49	1399.33	1375.96	13396.47	6928.22	4469.03	1999.22	2318.51
	8	54689.32	40819.09	14393.70	15854.48	1410.68	1385.71	13504.46	6983.49	4513.55	2007.42	2356.63
	9	55578.27	41508.26	14621.77	16183.72	1437.92	1418.56	13706.64	7078.70	4606.88	2021.06	2342.32
	10	56227.43	42007.20	14783.22	16468.62	1443.37	1425.17	13837.87	7154.88	4630.45	2052.54	2256.83
	11	57007.79	42610.26	14938.67	16763.71	1458.68	1437.52	14010.42	7257.85	4642.74	2109.83	2218.13
	12	59317.50	44259.19	15434.02	17410.52	1507.59	1536.29	14724.63	7574.47	4851.98	2298.18	2180.12
比上期增减额（亿元） Changes Compared with Previous Period（100 Million Yuan）												
1997	1	18.76	122.40	37.66	31.89	-14.16	11.57	-140.59	-7.91	-73.33	-59.35	-204.27
	2	183.65	161.66	84.23	19.84	2.50	8.88	2.39	20.36	-3.43	-14.54	-29.70
	3	548.20	388.79	197.09	17.81	10.68	35.51	151.90	98.64	17.96	35.30	22.99
	4	443.58	353.58	105.61	81.25	9.22	33.22	70.09	29.22	4.49	36.38	-237.06
	5	433.14	336.66	133.00	78.01	12.71	17.13	82.49	109.84	13.90	-41.25	4.01
	6	895.46	632.04	220.68	234.74	22.35	20.89	282.18	190.50	47.59	44.09	-59.02
	7	341.84	282.30	60.73	165.82	-0.75	7.09	36.95	3.66	7.44	25.85	-18.8
	8	649.83	533.14	131.47	304.99	11.35	9.74	107.99	55.27	44.52	8.20	38.11
	9	888.96	689.19	228.07	329.24	27.24	32.86	202.17	95.21	93.33	13.63	-14.30
	10	649.14	498.92	161.45	284.89	5.45	6.61	131.23	76.18	23.57	31.48	-85.49
	11	780.37	603.07	155.45	295.10	15.31	12.35	172.55	102.98	12.28	57.29	-38.70
	12	2309.69	1648.92	495.36	646.80	48.91	98.77	714.21	316.62	209.24	188.35	-38.01
比去年同期增长（%） Increase Rate Year - on - year（%）												
1997	1	29.51	—	—	—	—	—	—	—	—	—	—
	2	29.04	—	—	—	—	—	—	—	—	—	—
	3	28.61	—	—	—	—	—	—	—	—	—	—
	4	27.85	—	—	—	—	—	—	—	—	—	—
	5	27.79	—	—	—	—	—	—	—	—	—	—
	6	27.51	—	—	—	—	—	—	—	—	—	—
	7	26.58	—	—	—	—	—	—	—	—	—	—
	8	26.38	—	—	—	—	—	—	—	—	—	—
	9	26.59	—	—	—	—	—	—	—	—	—	—
	10	25.71	—	—	—	—	—	—	—	—	—	—
	11	25.64	—	—	—	—	—	—	—	—	—	—
	12	25.05	—	—	—	—	—	—	—	—	—	—

国家银行人民币信贷收支主要指标时间序列表
Time Series of Major Indicators in Sources and Uses of Credit Funds of State Banks (RMB)

年　月 Year Month		各项存款 Total Deposits	企业存款 Deposits by Enterprises	财政存款 Fiscal Deposits	储蓄存款 Savings Deposits	活期储蓄 Demand Deposits	定期储蓄 Time Deposits	农业存款 Deposits by Agricultural Sector
期末余额（亿元） Balance (100 Million Yuan)								
1998	1	58627.02	21016.13	1612.04	34260.41	7167.26	27093.15	239.19
	2	60431.06	21058.17	1706.88	35757.73	7974.14	27783.59	239.08
	3	61336.30	21505.93	2109.43	35775.15	7347.33	28427.82	244.96
	4	61455.12	21682.36	1737.34	36039.17	7344.64	28694.53	241.25
	5	62727.52	22024.46	2017.87	36629.09	7618.27	29010.82	240.14
	6	63361.68	22626.18	1760.31	36783.18	7639.48	29143.70	245.70
	7	64602.92	22809.23	2080.37	37463.26	8090.66	29372.60	248.24
	8	65227.90	23436.58	1851.88	37584.85	7990.61	29594.24	256.63
	9	67490.54	24423.38	2368.20	38226.49	8334.97	29891.52	266.76
	10	68266.84	24471.30	2422.93	38777.48	8557.20	30220.28	277.30
	11	69459.63	24860.32	2618.70	39349.92	8766.32	30583.60	287.58
	12	69782.21	25249.11	2169.60	39560.98	8722.20	30838.78	300.62
比上期增减额（亿元） Changes Compared with Previous Period (100 Million Yuan)								
1998	1	-1648.50	-1563.12	74.37	69.50	-478.26	547.76	-24.80
	2	1804.04	42.04	115.73	1497.32	806.88	690.44	-0.10
	3	1577.49	447.76	402.55	689.67	45.44	644.23	5.88
	4	118.82	176.43	-372.09	264.02	-2.69	266.71	-3.71
	5	1272.39	342.10	280.53	589.92	273.63	316.29	-1.12
	6	634.16	601.72	-257.56	154.09	21.21	132.88	5.57
	7	1241.22	183.05	320.06	680.08	451.18	228.90	2.53
	8	624.97	627.34	-228.49	121.59	-100.05	221.64	8.39
	9	2262.62	986.79	516.32	641.63	344.35	297.28	10.13
	10	776.31	47.93	54.73	550.99	222.23	328.76	10.54
	11	1192.77	389.02	195.76	572.43	209.12	363.31	10.28
	12	322.58	388.79	-449.09	211.06	-44.12	255.18	13.04
比去年同期增长（%） Increase Rate Year-on-year (%)								
1998	1	17.09	15.51	27.85	17.90	26.06	15.92	12.21
	2	15.84	14.90	15.98	16.08	22.53	14.50	15.35
	3	15.86	12.95	32.68	16.42	14.85	16.83	12.31
	4	14.15	12.04	3.31	15.55	9.89	17.09	9.28
	5	15.32	10.98	17.61	17.28	14.83	17.95	8.58
	6	14.12	9.84	3.22	16.67	16.14	16.80	10.93
	7	15.63	10.85	19.35	17.43	24.63	15.60	6.42
	8	15.25	12.21	11.70	16.10	19.88	15.12	10.35
	9	17.53	13.86	32.46	17.73	27.02	15.38	13.50
	10	17.56	13.86	26.41	17.82	28.81	15.05	11.48
	11	18.56	15.32	28.55	18.60	29.18	15.88	13.35
	12	15.76	11.77	43.66	15.71	14.05	16.19	13.88

国家银行人民币信贷收支主要指标时间序列表

Time Series of Major Indicators in Sources and Uses of Credit Funds of State Banks（RMB）

年 月 Year Month		各项贷款 Total Loans	短期贷款 Short - term Loans	工业贷款 Loans to Industrial Sector	商业贷款 Loans to Commercial Sector	建筑业贷款 Loans to Construction Sector	农业贷款 Loans to Agricultural Sector	中长期贷款 Medium and Long - term Loans	基本建设贷款 Capital Construction Loans	技术改造贷款 Technical Improvement Loans	其他中长期贷款 Other Medium and Long - term Loans	有价证券及投资 Securities and Investments
期末余额（亿元） Balance（100 Million Yuan）												
1998	1	59019.03	43243.93	15176.76	17230.66	1388.90	1512.81	15405.44	7909.97	4790.45	2705.02	2157.98
	2	59093.20	43190.99	15173.48	17180.41	1387.63	1517.49	15505.81	8010.99	4757.80	2737.02	2110.69
	3	59675.69	43638.62	15327.17	17212.92	1404.49	1537.73	15620.74	8013.07	4769.27	2838.40	2034.48
	4	60080.71	43864.76	15458.17	17160.79	1408.12	1557.89	15774.60	8066.80	4775.22	2932.58	2091.66
	5	60601.88	44168.58	15585.07	17163.27	1425.81	1573.30	15975.27	8212.35	4796.37	2966.55	2139.09
	6	61917.32	44869.40	15861.90	17298.55	1439.14	1639.80	16582.53	8547.92	4855.99	3178.62	2088.38
	7	62472.71	45231.14	15943.92	16198.78	1448.70	1657.84	16733.50	8652.59	4855.72	3225.19	2167.22
	8	63652.80	45866.98	16162.38	16049.30	1472.02	1681.90	17259.81	8846.06	4899.19	3514.56	4887.13
	9	65139.43	46607.28	16428.14	17923.10	1492.85	1726.62	17996.47	9306.46	4969.25	3720.76	5594.96
	10	65801.39	46914.57	16427.64	18145.12	1493.30	1730.31	18300.58	9379.58	5024.67	3896.33	5632.88
	11	66847.13	47384.23	16478.66	18542.18	1497.60	1730.70	18835.60	9702.96	5037.24	4095.40	5635.13
	12	68442.11	48105.68	16664.06	18746.74	1512.36	1781.63	19744.30	10267.76	5088.64	4387.89	6037.62
比上期增减额（亿元） Changes Compared with Previous Period（100 Million Yuan）												
1998	1	- 308.17	- 246.89	- 86.57	- 126.65	2.50	- 24.23	- 97.60	- 49.89	- 62.68	14.97	- 15.30
	2	74.18	- 52.92	- 3.28	- 50.25	- 1.27	4.69	100.37	101.02	- 32.65	32.00	- 47.30
	3	582.47	447.61	153.69	32.51	16.85	20.24	114.92	2.08	11.47	101.37	- 76.20
	4	389.10	210.21	131.00	- 52.13	3.63	20.16	153.87	53.74	5.95	94.18	57.18
	5	521.18	303.82	126.89	2.48	17.70	15.41	200.68	145.55	21.15	33.98	47.43
	6	1315.45	700.83	276.83	135.28	13.33	66.50	607.25	335.56	59.62	212.07	- 50.71
	7	555.39	361.73	82.02	- 1099.77	9.55	18.04	150.98	104.67	- 0.27	46.58	78.84
	8	1180.09	635.85	218.46	- 149.48	23.33	24.06	526.30	193.47	43.47	289.36	2719.91
	9	1486.64	740.29	265.76	1873.79	20.82	44.73	736.68	460.40	70.06	206.22	707.83
	10	661.93	307.28	- 0.49	222.02	0.45	3.68	304.10	73.13	55.42	175.55	37.91
	11	1045.78	469.67	51.01	397.06	4.30	0.39	535.04	323.38	12.57	199.09	2.26
	12	1594.97	721.44	185.40	204.55	14.76	50.93	908.69	564.80	51.40	292.49	402.49
比去年同期增长（%） Increase Rate Year - on - year（%）												
1998	1	15.29	13.41	12.75	15.24	3.45	20.71	20.63	22.14	9.34	41.37	- 18.14
	2	15.02	12.79	12.02	14.75	3.16	20.23	21.40	23.31	8.68	44.14	- 19.02
	3	14.93	12.82	11.53	14.83	3.59	18.50	20.86	21.50	8.50	46.75	- 22.63
	4	14.71	12.35	11.63	13.87	3.16	17.06	21.39	21.78	8.53	48.82	- 12.57
	5	14.76	12.16	11.47	13.30	3.49	16.71	22.16	21.95	8.66	53.76	- 10.74
	6	15.29	12.14	11.69	12.45	2.79	19.79	24.13	23.44	8.84	61.08	- 10.65
	7	15.59	12.25	11.79	4.18	3.53	20.49	24.91	24.89	8.65	61.32	- 6.53
	8	16.37	12.34	12.29	1.23	4.35	21.37	27.81	26.67	8.54	75.08	107.38
	9	17.18	12.26	12.35	10.75	3.82	21.72	31.30	31.47	7.87	84.10	138.86
	10	17.00	11.65	11.12	10.18	3.46	21.41	32.25	31.09	8.51	89.83	149.59
	11	17.24	11.17	10.31	10.61	2.67	20.39	34.44	33.69	8.50	94.11	154.05
	12	15.35	8.66	7.97	7.67	0.32	15.97	34.09	35.56	4.88	90.93	176.94

国家银行人民币信贷收支主要指标时间序列表

Time Series of Major Indicators in Sources and Uses of Credit Funds of State Banks (RMB)

年 月 Year Month		各项存款 Total Deposits	企业存款 Deposits by Enterprises	财政存款 Fiscal Deposits	储蓄存款 Savings Deposits	活期储蓄 Demand Deposits	定期储蓄 Time Deposits	农业存款 Deposits by Agricultural Sector
期末余额（亿元） Balance (100 Million Yuan)								
1999	1	70571.11	25118.23	2241.61	40420.44	9088.81	31331.63	304.56
	2	71459.24	24398.05	2025.63	42382.08	9770.19	32611.89	267.06
	3	73562.99	25185.93	2111.21	43275.20	9648.58	33626.62	278.35
	4	74108.01	25279.37	1995.49	43794.77	9551.50	34243.27	295.02
	5	75211.79	25670.99	2084.99	44323.78	9572.97	34750.81	292.91
	6	76178.26	26335.53	2043.02	44449.72	9613.13	34836.59	291.84
	7	76317.63	25987.62	2465.65	44455.64	9814.64	34641.00	293.04
	8	76925.40	26719.10	2127.26	44522.07	10071.61	34450.46	303.43
	9	78353.54	27400.01	2483.32	44702.63	10478.90	34223.73	305.66
	10	78548.86	27551.38	2443.12	44670.70	10667.42	34003.28	320.66
	11	79719.19	28110.80	2990.23	44598.35	10869.80	33728.55	338.76
	12	79973.51	28733.07	2106.33	44827.99	11225.32	33602.67	342.09
比上期增减额（亿元） Changes Compared with Previous Period (100 Million Yuan)								
1999	1	809.90	-133.63	76.58	857.40	364.50	492.90	3.93
	2	888.12	-720.19	-215.99	1961.64	681.38	1280.26	-37.49
	3	2103.76	787.89	85.58	893.12	-121.61	1014.73	11.29
	4	545.01	93.44	-115.71	519.57	-97.08	616.65	16.67
	5	1103.80	391.62	89.50	529.01	21.47	507.54	-2.11
	6	966.47	664.54	-41.97	125.95	40.16	85.79	-1.07
	7	139.36	-347.91	422.62	5.92	201.51	-195.59	1.20
	8	607.78	731.48	-338.39	66.44	256.97	-190.53	10.39
	9	1428.13	680.91	356.06	180.56	407.29	-226.73	2.23
	10	195.34	151.37	-40.20	-31.93	188.52	-220.45	15.00
	11	1170.32	559.42	547.11	-72.35	202.38	-274.73	18.10
	12	254.33	622.28	-883.91	229.64	355.52	-125.88	3.33
比去年同期增长（%） Increase Rate Year-on-year (%)								
1999	1	20.37	19.52	40.84	17.98	26.81	15.64	27.33
	2	19.58	15.86	18.67	20.80	33.80	17.38	11.70
	3	19.93	17.11	0.08	20.96	31.32	18.29	13.62
	4	20.59	16.59	14.86	21.52	30.05	19.34	22.29
	5	19.90	16.56	3.33	21.01	25.66	19.79	21.97
	6	20.23	16.39	16.06	20.84	25.83	19.53	18.78
	7	18.13	13.93	18.52	18.66	21.31	17.94	18.05
	8	17.93	14.01	14.87	18.46	26.04	16.41	18.24
	9	16.10	12.19	4.86	16.94	25.72	14.49	14.58
	10	15.06	12.59	0.83	15.20	24.66	12.52	15.64
	11	14.77	13.07	14.19	13.34	24.00	10.28	17.80
	12	14.60	13.80	-2.92	13.31	28.70	8.96	13.79

国家银行人民币信贷收支主要指标时间序列表

Time Series of Major Indicators in Sources and Uses of Credit Funds of State Banks（RMB）

年 月 Year Month		各项贷款 Total Loans	短期贷款 Short - term Loans					中长期贷款 Medium and Long - term Loans				有价证券及投资 Securities and Investments
				工业贷款 Loans to Industrial Sector	商业贷款 Loans to Commercial Sector	建筑业贷款 Loans to Construction Sector	农业贷款 Loans to Agricultural Sector		基本建设贷款 Capital Construction Loans	技术改造贷款 Technical Improvement Loans	其他中长期贷款 Other Medium and Long - term Loans	
期末余额（亿元） Balance（100 Million Yuan）												
1999	1	68470.51	48160.20	16585.25	18812.06	1564.11	1766.92	19692.17	10210.17	5036.08	4445.92	5710.81
	2	68807.13	48426.95	16669.59	18796.41	1570.48	1781.06	19751.00	10302.29	5029.82	4418.89	5707.17
	3	69409.14	48694.09	16772.46	18735.25	1578.35	1801.87	20052.25	10475.89	5041.93	4534.43	5809.26
	4	69807.03	48787.10	16824.66	18648.30	1587.95	1822.63	20319.86	10603.96	5040.37	4675.53	5768.64
	5	70264.78	48941.58	16909.61	18603.00	1603.39	1830.70	20602.35	10782.11	5035.82	4784.42	5900.02
	6	71589.48	49633.42	17191.23	18744.19	1642.32	1835.88	21232.59	11182.58	5065.16	4984.85	5956.35
	7	72021.62	49810.15	17182.75	18759.54	1641.79	1840.53	21459.01	11273.93	5086.23	5098.85	6127.53
	8	72684.20	50110.79	17214.01	18810.24	1647.07	1792.60	21798.31	11429.12	5097.35	5271.84	6061.71
	9	73757.27	50642.52	17350.52	18910.02	1669.38	1791.62	22328.07	11688.95	5123.65	5515.47	6528.97
	10	74190.39	50730.24	17345.45	18915.73	1665.76	1783.54	22610.48	11833.75	5132.07	5644.65	6551.60
	11	75153.72	51155.73	17428.53	19076.62	1652.55	1771.93	23071.71	12038.16	5180.13	5853.42	6455.13
	12	73695.85	50113.23	16786.51	18989.51	1322.84	1744.63	22791.76	11635.79	4981.52	6174.45	9675.01
比上期增减额（亿元） Changes Compared with Previous Period（100 Million Yuan）												
1999	1	16.65	48.65	-79.44	74.49	50.91	-10.53	-58.00	-63.78	-50.07	55.85	-17.65
	2	336.61	266.75	84.34	-15.66	6.37	14.14	58.83	92.13	-6.26	-27.04	-3.64
	3	602.02	267.14	102.88	-61.15	7.87	20.80	301.25	173.59	12.11	115.55	102.09
	4	397.89	93.01	52.19	-86.95	9.61	20.76	267.61	128.08	-1.57	141.10	-40.62
	5	457.74	154.47	84.95	-45.30	15.44	8.07	282.49	178.15	-4.55	108.89	131.38
	6	1324.72	691.86	281.62	141.19	38.94	5.19	630.24	400.47	29.34	200.43	56.33
	7	432.10	176.69	-8.48	15.35	-0.54	4.64	226.42	91.35	21.08	113.99	171.18
	8	662.57	300.65	31.26	50.70	5.28	-47.93	339.30	155.19	11.12	172.98	-65.81
	9	1073.11	531.73	136.51	99.78	22.31	-0.98	529.75	259.84	26.29	243.62	467.26
	10	433.11	87.73	-5.07	5.71	-3.61	-8.08	282.43	144.79	8.42	129.20	22.63
	11	963.32	425.48	83.09	160.88	-13.22	-11.61	461.24	204.41	48.06	208.77	-96.47
	12	2042.55	869.40	358.52	168.99	77.43	-27.30	1225.78	620.55	104.84	500.39	3219.87
比去年同期增长（%） Increase Rate Year - on - year（%）												
1999	1	15.98	11.33	9.28	9.18	12.62	16.80	27.83	29.08	5.13	64.36	164.64
	2	16.41	12.08	9.86	9.41	13.18	17.37	27.38	28.60	5.72	61.45	170.39
	3	16.28	11.54	9.43	8.84	12.38	17.18	28.37	30.73	5.72	59.75	185.54
	4	16.19	11.22	8.84	8.67	12.77	16.99	28.81	31.45	5.55	59.43	175.79
	5	15.94	10.81	8.50	8.39	12.45	16.36	28.96	31.29	4.99	61.28	175.82
	6	15.62	10.62	8.38	8.36	14.12	11.96	28.04	30.82	4.31	56.82	185.21
	7	15.28	10.12	7.77	15.81	13.33	11.02	28.24	30.30	4.75	58.09	182.74
	8	14.19	9.25	6.51	17.20	11.89	6.58	26.30	29.20	4.04	50.00	24.03
	9	13.23	8.66	5.61	5.51	11.83	3.76	24.07	25.60	3.11	48.23	16.69
	10	12.75	8.13	5.59	4.25	11.55	3.08	23.55	26.16	2.14	44.87	16.31
	11	12.43	7.96	5.76	2.88	10.35	2.38	22.49	24.07	2.84	42.93	14.55
	12	12.79	8.15	6.74	2.66	14.39	-2.08	23.06	23.29	3.86	44.80	60.25

国家银行人民币信贷收支主要指标时间序列表
Time Series of Major Indicators in Sources and Uses of Credit Funds of State Banks (RMB)

年 月 Year Month		各项存款 Total Deposits	企业存款 Deposits by Enterprises	财政存款 Fiscal Deposits	储蓄存款 Savings Deposits	活期储蓄 Demand Deposits	定期储蓄 Time Deposits	农业存款 Deposits by Agricultural Sector
		期末余额（亿元）Balance (100 Million Yuan)						
2000	1	79844.32	27848.09	2388.86	45597.42	11644.82	33952.60	314.93
	2	81512.22	28235.71	2124.13	47119.87	12215.18	34904.69	314.08
	3	83669.04	29391.19	2679.12	47372.74	12463.71	34909.03	330.07
	4	84335.62	29882.04	2611.57	47445.78	12571.34	34874.44	327.85
	5	85582.39	30508.52	3355.80	47149.96	12511.08	34638.88	332.45
	6	87541.21	31626.33	3463.06	47649.72	12956.48	34693.24	338.98
	7	87352.65	31293.20	3636.73	47643.63	12954.60	34689.03	334.62
	8	87937.18	31963.26	3357.09	47674.58	13058.81	34615.77	344.58
	9	89065.84	32887.38	3116.69	47988.92	13515.17	34473.75	347.28
	10	89142.71	32540.50	3657.71	47828.71	13334.49	34494.22	353.05
	11	90644.48	32827.28	4395.39	48094.77	13538.56	34556.21	375.45
	12	90892.70	33337.57	3477.25	48626.81	14043.86	34582.95	372.03
		比上期增减额（亿元）Changes Compared with Previous Period (100 Million Yuan)						
2000	1	-37.49	-883.09	286.40	827.44	480.45	346.99	-27.18
	2	1667.90	387.62	-264.73	1522.45	570.36	952.09	-0.85
	3	2156.82	1155.48	554.99	252.87	248.53	4.34	15.99
	4	666.58	490.85	-67.55	73.04	107.63	-34.59	-2.22
	5	1246.77	626.48	744.23	-295.82	-60.26	-235.56	4.60
	6	1958.82	1117.81	107.26	499.76	445.40	54.36	6.53
	7	-188.56	-333.13	173.67	-6.09	-1.88	-4.21	-4.36
	8	584.53	670.06	-279.64	30.95	104.21	-73.26	9.96
	9	1128.66	924.12	-240.40	314.34	456.36	-142.02	2.70
	10	76.87	-346.88	541.02	-160.21	-180.68	20.47	5.77
	11	1501.77	286.78	737.68	266.06	204.07	61.99	22.40
	12	248.22	510.29	-918.14	532.04	505.30	26.74	-3.42
		比去年同期增长（%）Increase Rate Year-on-year (%)						
2000	1	13.14	10.87	6.57	12.81	28.12	8.37	3.40
	2	14.07	15.73	4.86	11.18	25.02	7.03	17.61
	3	13.74	16.70	26.90	9.47	29.18	3.81	18.59
	4	13.80	18.21	30.87	8.34	31.62	1.84	11.13
	5	13.79	18.84	60.95	6.38	30.69	-0.32	13.50
	6	14.92	20.09	69.51	7.20	34.78	-0.41	16.15
	7	14.46	20.42	47.49	7.17	31.99	0.14	14.19
	8	14.31	19.63	57.81	7.08	29.66	0.48	13.56
	9	13.67	20.03	25.50	7.35	28.98	0.73	13.62
	10	13.49	18.11	49.71	7.07	25.00	1.44	10.10
	11	13.70	16.78	46.99	7.84	24.55	2.45	10.83
	12	13.65	16.03	65.09	8.47	25.11	2.92	8.75

国家银行人民币信贷收支主要指标时间序列表
Time Series of Major Indicators in Sources and Uses of Credit Funds of State Banks（RMB）

年　月 Year Month		各项贷款 Total Loans	短期贷款 Short－term Loans					中长期贷款 Medium and Long－term Loans				有价证券及投资 Securities and Investments
				工业贷款 Loans to Industrial Sector	商业贷款 Loans to Commercial Sector	建筑业贷款 Loans to Construction Sector	农业贷款 Loans to Agricultural Sector		基本建设贷款 Capital Construction Loans	技术改造贷款 Technical Improvement Loans	其他中长期贷款 Other Medium and Long－term Loans	
期末余额（亿元） Balance（100 Million Yuan）												
2000	1	73867.69	50415.75	16804.90	19049.01	1331.02	1736.93	22695.33	11510.23	4970.54	6214.56	9726.11
	2	74218.82	50584.28	16917.81	19010.51	1335.20	1747.65	22871.44	11603.50	4984.61	6283.33	9775.22
	3	75353.03	51163.83	17132.72	19030.36	1355.96	1761.58	23417.81	11920.49	5001.97	6495.35	9722.42
	4	75885.78	51377.18	17222.48	18922.90	1365.65	1752.54	23732.35	12093.23	5004.50	6634.62	10073.64
	5	75243.32	50566.21	16989.35	18494.38	1369.10	1626.19	23881.73	12237.89	4948.88	6694.96	10782.23
	6	73411.89	48587.61	16574.53	17338.53	1375.42	1431.70	24039.55	12288.22	4866.53	6884.80	10616.92
	7	72771.83	47761.06	16098.64	16970.66	1386.28	1395.15	24206.47	12458.87	4769.16	6978.44	11971.48
	8	73003.70	47713.93	15947.16	16807.93	1406.36	1379.02	24486.51	12587.40	4742.67	7156.44	12414.70
	9	73761.12	47997.73	15778.31	16829.72	1429.64	1376.63	24961.90	12884.93	4735.43	7341.54	13491.84
	10	74298.46	48198.40	15740.26	16825.20	1436.31	1362.80	25283.14	13072.54	4753.49	7457.11	13615.61
	11	75401.81	48843.12	15751.60	16920.21	1442.97	1326.99	25724.19	13257.89	4774.43	7691.87	14397.29
	12	76393.75	49242.11	15657.66	16958.48	1425.61	1289.42	26406.09	13454.76	4811.09	8140.24	16419.43
比上期增减额（亿元） Changes Compared with Previous Period（100 Million Yuan）												
2000	1	415.77	246.17	22.55	21.77	8.37	－2.53	143.77	58.21	8.76	76.80	0.53
	2	355.93	191.06	17.02	31.81	4.19	10.72	155.71	70.30	16.32	69.09	49.17
	3	1160.22	599.89	218.43	24.17	20.75	17.31	552.05	317.06	21.88	213.11	－52.81
	4	705.67	366.95	124.83	－68.78	9.70	－2.07	333.86	173.25	13.88	146.73	351.16
	5	582.35	256.85	17.24	－36.70	4.22	13.49	306.38	180.71	24.85	100.82	708.92
	6	1252.69	678.65	192.09	21.64	33.83	－2.73	580.21	165.70	91.17	323.34	－165.42
	7	747.66	323.80	－33.49	77.07	11.03	20.20	404.13	209.36	11.99	182.78	1354.84
	8	719.53	258.03	－62.48	－7.20	－22.88	－2.83	462.64	186.45	11.61	264.58	443.21
	9	1210.11	650.08	54.66	101.03	23.28	4.28	561.34	354.29	61.37	145.68	1079.65
	10	663.73	295.79	－6.01	41.61	7.05	－11.21	352.50	191.39	44.03	117.08	123.86
	11	1167.55	689.82	25.16	115.33	6.66	－32.94	460.72	189.47	30.22	241.03	781.99
	12	1092.81	478.01	－45.70	49.85	－17.35	－37.98	702.86	202.00	52.81	448.05	2023.47
比去年同期增长（%） Increase Rate Year－on－year（%）												
2000	1	13.39	8.67	7.35	2.66	11.13	－1.70	23.94	24.57	5.23	43.65	70.31
	2	13.35	8.47	6.91	2.92	10.94	－1.88	24.35	24.14	5.69	46.09	71.28
	3	14.04	9.10	7.55	3.38	11.70	－2.03	25.24	25.11	5.87	47.07	67.36
	4	14.40	9.65	7.96	3.50	11.64	－3.28	25.23	25.23	6.18	45.77	74.63
	5	14.48	9.82	7.52	3.55	10.83	－2.97	25.00	24.84	6.77	44.56	82.75
	6	14.11	9.66	6.88	2.89	10.26	－3.39	24.03	21.85	7.95	45.23	78.25
	7	14.47	9.92	6.73	3.21	10.97	－2.54	24.60	22.72	7.74	45.57	95.38
	8	14.41	9.78	6.18	2.90	9.22	－0.09	24.78	22.69	7.73	45.82	104.81
	9	14.39	9.91	5.66	2.89	9.16	0.21	24.34	22.99	8.37	42.02	106.69
	10	14.62	10.30	5.65	3.08	9.82	0.03	24.34	23.10	9.05	40.84	107.87
	11	14.70	10.73	5.29	2.81	11.10	－1.17	23.85	22.59	8.63	39.93	123.09
	12	13.70	10.18	3.09	2.20	6.70	－1.80	21.85	19.77	7.93	37.01	69.76

国家银行人民币信贷收支主要指标时间序列表
Time Series of Major Indicators in Sources and Uses of Credit Funds of State Banks (RMB)

年 月 Year Month		各项存款 Total Deposits	企业存款 Deposits by Enterprises	财政存款 Fiscal Deposits	储蓄存款 Savings Deposits	活期储蓄 Demand Deposits	定期储蓄 Time Deposits	农业存款 Deposits by Agricultural Sector
期末余额(亿元) Balance (100 Million Yuan)								
2001	1	86994.27	29011.92	4100.59	49113.42	14589.52	34523.90	332.75
	2	87828.67	29455.93	3717.52	49705.59	14404.05	35301.54	338.56
	3	90063.40	30469.14	3927.08	50534.95	14953.48	35581.47	347.55
	4	91306.11	30489.32	4980.73	50677.99	15007.37	35670.62	344.38
	5	90683.55	30345.27	4509.91	50458.55	14708.73	35749.82	366.64
	6	93360.26	31800.72	4466.32	51401.39	15381.72	36019.67	382.04
	7	92693.76	30581.47	4936.09	51432.47	15214.22	36218.25	376.55
	8	94684.26	31665.50	4838.75	52150.46	15698.65	36451.81	394.52
	9	95836.29	32214.63	4782.96	52673.42	16037.44	36635.98	395.31
	10	96702.04	32134.76	5356.71	53072.39	16079.37	36993.02	403.96
	11	96664.51	32192.40	4749.88	53378.09	16085.26	37292.83	405.19
	12	97346.93	33081.29	3330.60	54306.87	16626.64	37680.23	409.74
比上期增减额(亿元) Changes Compared with Previous Period (100 Million Yuan)								
2001	1	1445.63	-698.76	626.06	1801.04	967.63	833.41	-39.21
	2	834.40	444.01	-383.07	592.17	-185.47	777.64	5.81
	3	2234.73	1013.21	209.56	829.36	549.43	279.93	8.99
	4	1242.71	20.18	1053.65	143.04	53.89	89.15	-3.17
	5	-622.56	-144.05	-470.82	-219.44	-298.64	79.20	22.26
	6	2676.71	1455.45	-43.59	942.84	672.99	269.85	15.40
	7	-666.50	-1219.25	469.77	31.08	-167.50	198.58	-5.49
	8	1990.50	1084.03	-97.34	717.99	484.43	233.56	17.97
	9	1152.03	549.13	-55.79	522.96	338.79	184.17	0.79
	10	865.75	-79.87	573.75	398.97	41.93	357.04	8.65
	11	-37.53	57.64	-606.83	305.70	5.89	299.81	1.23
	12	682.42	888.89	-1419.28	928.78	541.38	387.40	4.55
比去年同期增长(%) Increase Rate Year-on-year (%)								
2001	1	15.04	16.25	71.72	10.48	28.52	4.29	5.66
	2	13.70	16.31	75.10	8.18	20.90	3.72	7.79
	3	13.72	15.69	46.62	9.39	23.03	4.52	5.30
	4	14.55	14.15	90.78	9.54	22.46	4.89	5.04
	5	12.02	11.01	34.44	9.75	20.61	5.82	10.28
	6	13.01	12.67	29.04	10.65	21.88	6.47	12.70
	7	12.30	9.24	35.78	10.73	20.57	7.06	12.53
	8	14.01	10.69	44.17	12.24	23.50	7.99	14.49
	9	14.22	9.89	53.50	12.68	22.04	9.02	13.83
	10	14.94	10.39	46.49	13.93	24.06	10.02	14.42
	11	13.00	9.66	8.09	13.99	22.31	10.74	7.92
	12	13.78	11.44	-4.20	14.78	22.06	11.84	10.14

国家银行人民币信贷收支主要指标时间序列表

Time Series of Major Indicators in Sources and Uses of Credit Funds of State Banks（RMB）

年 月 Year Month	各项贷款 Total Loans	短期贷款 Short－term Loans					中长期贷款 Medium and Long－term Loans				票据融资 Paper Financing	有价证券及投资 Securities and Investments
			工业贷款 Loans to Industrial Sector	商业贷款 Loans to Commercial Sector	建筑业贷款 Loans to Construction Sector	农业贷款 Loans to Agricultural Sector		基本建设贷款 Capital Construction Loans	技术改造贷款 Technical Improvement Loans	其他中长期贷款 Other Medium and Long－term Loans		
期末余额（亿元） Balance（100 Million Yuan）												
2001 1	73412.29	42303.56	15136.72	16506.38	1472.90	1283.26	30262.67	13527.30	4677.35	12058.02	561.24	17374.58
2	73801.89	42269.02	15153.36	16420.47	1479.29	1280.59	30635.30	13646.68	4707.21	12281.41	588.83	17382.16
3	74468.29	42259.14	15145.03	16293.41	1490.39	1299.47	31238.33	13828.66	4712.90	12696.77	665.71	17442.76
4	74987.66	42158.59	15138.10	16185.24	1487.70	1313.02	31742.75	14010.84	4723.37	13008.54	771.87	17561.87
5	75417.04	42167.98	15113.27	16079.86	1606.58	1332.41	32090.74	14147.88	4718.43	13224.43	842.56	16684.81
6	76497.38	42552.26	15337.38	16124.03	1609.70	1322.82	32553.54	14348.72	4715.78	13489.04	1077.51	16292.80
7	76707.22	42433.82	15267.73	16070.59	1578.19	1319.31	32826.91	14508.51	4701.88	13616.52	1126.45	17041.14
8	76924.01	42306.61	15206.26	16002.24	1574.22	1300.80	33175.86	14698.28	4717.87	13759.71	1120.15	17123.78
9	77691.43	42438.58	15269.22	15998.40	1573.32	1298.64	33787.77	14956.92	4753.18	14077.67	1144.68	17059.13
10	77524.26	42363.76	15296.48	15946.35	1557.42	1288.31	33794.16	14912.11	4742.53	14139.52	1044.07	17145.01
11	78139.89	42669.90	15413.33	16138.20	1565.97	1263.74	34167.45	15113.68	4754.55	14299.22	979.17	17107.91
12	80077.59	43679.83	15763.21	16463.49	1684.81	1272.27	34995.68	15495.17	4816.66	14683.85	1087.99	17913.39
比上期增减额（亿元） Changes Compared with Previous Period（100 Million Yuan）												
2001 1	624.90	103.65	12.36	－63.84	22.57	－4.57	371.85	75.56	9.94	286.35	121.06	95.90
2	389.60	－34.54	16.64	－85.91	6.39	－2.67	372.63	119.38	29.86	223.39	27.59	7.58
3	666.40	－9.88	－8.33	－127.06	11.10	18.88	603.03	181.98	5.69	415.36	76.88	60.60
4	519.37	－100.55	－6.93	－108.17	－2.69	13.55	504.42	182.18	10.47	311.77	106.16	119.11
5	429.38	9.39	－24.83	－105.38	118.88	19.39	347.99	137.04	－4.94	215.89	70.69	－877.06
6	1080.34	384.28	224.11	44.17	3.12	－9.59	462.80	200.84	－2.65	264.61	234.95	－392.01
7	209.84	－118.44	－69.65	－53.44	－31.51	－3.51	273.37	159.79	－13.9	127.48	48.94	748.34
8	216.79	－127.21	－61.47	－68.35	－3.97	－18.51	348.95	189.77	15.99	143.19	－6.30	82.64
9	767.42	131.97	62.96	－3.84	－0.90	－2.16	611.91	258.64	35.31	317.96	24.53	－64.65
10	－167.17	－74.82	27.26	－52.05	－15.90	－10.33	6.39	－44.81	－10.65	61.85	－100.61	85.88
11	615.63	306.14	116.85	191.85	8.55	－24.57	373.29	201.57	12.02	159.7	－64.90	－37.10
12	1937.70	1009.93	349.88	325.29	118.84	8.53	828.23	381.49	62.11	384.63	108.82	805.48
比去年同期增长（%） Increase Rate Year－on－year（%）												
2001 1	10.88	13.61	11.52	15.42	7.42	32.58	6.30	7.82	17.20	－0.03	27.09	0.46
2	11.41	13.52	12.27	14.48	7.87	32.37	7.57	8.88	17.80	1.76	33.34	6.90
3	12.29	13.32	11.96	13.58	8.65	33.57	9.81	9.43	14.72	8.22	50.75	7.27
4	12.77	12.86	11.91	12.80	8.46	34.08	11.27	10.88	17.17	9.27	74.79	8.00
5	11.67	10.39	10.09	9.80	16.79	24.73	11.92	11.64	15.34	10.83	90.79	2.61
6	8.90	5.15	7.56	2.96	15.07	9.09	11.99	13.01	12.19	10.70	144.00	0.12
7	7.28	1.79	3.72	－0.18	8.21	4.41	12.70	9.83	5.47	19.12	155.09	4.72
8	6.91	1.17	3.18	－1.40	15.58	1.94	12.70	14.18	8.44	12.71	153.66	5.22
9	7.31	0.18	1.98	－2.71	15.51	1.25	15.14	15.57	7.09	17.96	159.21	4.83
10	6.91	0.24	2.09	－2.50	14.37	0.25	14.39	15.33	6.93	16.37	136.43	5.36
11	7.64	0.85	2.77	－1.46	14.98	－1.88	15.60	16.81	6.99	17.74	121.73	5.13
12	10.21	2.03	4.17	－0.61	18.75	－1.19	19.81	16.18	3.39	30.96	146.37	10.08

国家银行人民币信贷收支主要指标时间序列表

Time Series of Major Indicators in Sources and Uses of Credit Funds of State Banks (RMB)

年　月 Year Month		各项存款 Total Deposits	企业存款 Deposits by Enterprises	财政存款 Fiscal Deposits	储蓄存款 Savings Deposits	活期储蓄 Demand Deposits	定期储蓄 Time Deposits	农业存款 Deposits by Agricultural Sector
期末余额（亿元） Balance (100 Million Yuan)								
2002	1	98589.95	31811.80	3835.97	55424.68	17070.44	38354.24	421.94
	2	99286.44	30757.56	3374.38	57730.75	17876.11	39854.64	384.94
	3	101442.88	32009.86	3404.47	58247.27	18074.28	40172.99	401.58
	4	103077.80	32203.81	4146.48	58950.21	18504.98	40445.23	395.93
	5	105142.17	32854.20	4729.08	59412.92	18679.11	40733.81	395.52
	6	107633.12	33794.83	4763.96	60341.27	19123.12	41218.15	402.78
	7	108473.51	33755.76	4746.87	60987.77	19384.14	41603.63	422.89
	8	110328.13	34455.42	5164.80	61582.33	19702.40	41879.93	425.55
	9	112502.61	35447.56	5421.89	62167.71	20057.06	42110.65	436.18
	10	113298.66	35481.04	5625.06	62605.39	20121.00	42484.39	442.24
	11	114380.55	35809.18	5486.86	63286.49	20455.47	42831.02	448.70
	12	113452.28	35980.06	3447.90	64024.46	20893.90	43130.56	465.72
比上期增减额（亿元） Changes Compared with Previous Period (100 Million Yuan)								
2002	1	1258.39	-287.57	514.92	1116.58	433.27	683.31	11.56
	2	696.49	-1054.24	-461.59	2306.07	805.67	1500.40	-37.00
	3	2156.44	1252.30	30.09	516.52	198.17	318.35	16.64
	4	1634.92	193.95	742.01	702.94	430.70	272.24	-5.65
	5	2064.37	650.39	582.60	462.71	174.13	288.58	-0.41
	6	2490.95	940.63	34.88	928.35	444.01	484.34	7.26
	7	840.39	-39.07	-17.09	646.50	261.02	385.48	20.11
	8	1854.62	699.66	417.93	594.56	318.26	276.30	2.66
	9	2174.48	992.14	257.09	585.38	354.66	230.72	10.63
	10	796.05	33.48	203.17	437.68	63.94	373.74	6.06
	11	1081.89	328.14	-138.20	681.10	334.47	346.63	6.46
	12	-928.27	170.88	-2038.96	737.97	438.43	299.54	17.02
比去年同期增长（%） Increase Rate Year-on-year (%)								
2002	1	13.33	9.65	-6.45	12.85	17.00	11.09	26.80
	2	13.05	4.42	-9.23	16.15	24.10	12.90	13.70
	3	12.63	5.06	-13.31	15.26	20.87	12.90	15.55
	4	12.89	5.62	-16.75	16.32	23.31	13.39	14.97
	5	15.94	8.27	4.86	17.75	26.99	13.94	7.88
	6	15.29	6.27	6.66	17.39	24.32	14.43	5.43
	7	17.02	10.38	-3.83	18.58	27.41	14.87	12.31
	8	16.52	8.81	6.74	18.09	25.50	14.89	7.87
	9	17.39	10.04	13.36	18.02	25.06	14.94	10.34
	10	17.16	10.41	5.01	17.96	25.14	14.84	9.48
	11	18.33	11.23	15.52	18.56	27.17	14.85	10.74
	12	16.54	8.76	3.52	17.89	25.67	14.46	13.66

国家银行人民币信贷收支主要指标时间序列表
Time Series of Major Indicators in Sources and Uses of Credit Funds of State Banks（RMB）

年 月 Year Month	各项贷款 Total Loans	短期贷款 Short-term Loans					中长期贷款 Medium and Long-term Loans				票据融资 Paper Financing	有价证券及投资 Securities and Investments
			工业贷款 Loans to Industrial Sector	商业贷款 Loans to Commercial Sector	建筑业贷款 Loans to Construction Sector	农业贷款 Loans to Agricultural Sector		基本建设贷款 Capital Construction Loans	技术改造贷款 Technical Improvement Loans	其他中长期贷款 Other Medium and Long-term Loans		
期末余额（亿元） Balance（100 Million Yuan）												
2002 1	80228.56	42386.27	14604.35	16423.12	1458.26	1279.59	36210.25	18517.06	1792.09	15901.10	1308.47	18405.49
2	80434.32	42353.77	14772.45	16425.19	1444.79	1286.62	36438.91	18645.50	1791.24	16002.17	1316.04	18408.61
3	81868.66	43165.05	15295.76	16403.98	1514.22	1316.89	36962.85	18917.84	1779.53	16265.48	1417.16	18637.07
4	82121.43	43307.48	15291.21	16158.63	1549.29	1314.91	37032.96	18948.29	1776.56	16308.11	1454.98	18713.54
5	82775.69	43433.94	15578.71	16000.88	1767.82	1314.64	37511.22	19148.09	1776.09	16587.04	1505.42	18738.68
6	84531.69	44045.18	15970.18	15938.63	1848.21	1320.75	38405.53	19648.97	1794.21	16962.35	1761.68	19185.92
7	84805.24	44077.71	16073.91	15838.12	1890.28	1322.07	38669.92	19775.26	1794.71	17099.95	1738.17	19188.21
8	85765.27	44260.39	16184.48	15706.44	1928.53	1321.07	39315.38	20035.69	1789.76	17489.93	1866.64	19294.81
9	87913.94	44906.97	16424.87	15733.02	2031.43	1320.41	40238.37	20451.18	1794.72	17992.47	2448.34	19357.12
10	88341.87	44928.29	16383.50	15733.42	2069.55	1312.34	40665.33	20609.50	1814.84	18240.99	2427.20	19297.450
11	89242.90	45216.39	16496.55	15720.80	2118.07	1297.09	41131.56	20701.54	1782.94	18647.08	2574.51	19274.35
12	90892.63	45800.67	16745.38	15760.12	2168.03	1286.04	42317.21	21370.27	1811.42	19135.52	2458.77	19488.39
比上期增减额（亿元） Changes Compared with Previous Period（100 Million Yuan）												
2002 1	-187.47	-239.56	-52.57	-122.24	8.32	0.17	162.41	30.54	11.72	120.15	-114.75	11.74
2	205.76	-32.50	168.10	2.07	-13.47	7.03	228.66	128.44	-0.85	101.07	7.57	3.12
3	1434.34	811.28	523.31	-21.21	69.43	30.27	523.94	272.34	-11.71	263.31	101.12	228.46
4	252.77	142.43	-4.55	-245.35	35.07	-1.98	70.11	30.45	-2.97	42.63	37.82	76.47
5	654.26	126.46	287.50	-157.75	218.53	-0.27	478.26	199.80	-0.47	278.93	50.44	25.14
6	1756.00	611.24	391.47	-62.25	80.39	6.11	894.31	500.88	18.12	375.31	256.26	447.24
7	273.55	32.53	103.73	-100.51	42.07	1.32	264.39	126.29	0.50	137.60	-23.51	2.29
8	960.03	182.68	110.57	-131.68	38.25	-1.00	645.46	260.43	-4.95	389.98	128.47	106.60
9	2148.67	646.58	240.39	26.58	102.90	-0.66	922.99	415.49	4.96	502.54	581.70	62.31
10	427.93	21.32	-41.37	0.40	38.12	-8.07	426.96	158.32	20.12	248.52	-21.14	-59.67
11	901.03	288.10	113.05	-12.62	48.52	-15.25	466.23	92.04	-31.9	406.09	147.31	-23.10
12	1649.73	584.28	248.83	39.32	49.96	-11.05	1185.65	668.73	28.48	488.44	-115.74	214.04
比去年同期增长（%） Increase Rate Year-on-year（%）												
2002 1	8.63	0.20	-3.52	-0.50	-0.99	-0.29	19.65	36.89	-61.69	31.87	30.13	12.69
2	8.34	0.20	-2.51	0.03	-2.33	0.47	18.94	36.63	-61.95	30.30	27.73	5.91
3	9.26	2.14	1.00	0.68	1.60	1.34	18.33	36.80	-62.24	28.11	25.98	6.85
4	8.84	2.73	1.01	-0.16	4.14	0.14	16.67	35.24	-62.39	25.36	17.95	6.56
5	9.10	3.00	3.08	-0.49	10.04	-1.33	16.89	35.34	-62.36	25.43	15.77	12.31
6	9.85	3.51	4.13	-1.15	14.82	-0.16	17.98	36.94	-61.95	25.75	15.20	17.76
7	9.92	3.87	5.28	-1.45	19.78	0.21	17.80	36.30	-61.83	25.58	10.67	12.60
8	10.86	4.62	6.43	-1.85	22.51	1.56	18.51	36.31	-62.06	27.11	19.70	12.68
9	12.55	5.82	7.57	-1.66	29.12	1.68	19.09	36.73	-62.24	27.81	56.50	13.47
10	13.42	6.05	7.11	-1.34	32.88	1.87	20.33	38.21	-61.73	29.01	72.61	12.55
11	10.74	5.97	7.03	-2.59	35.26	2.64	20.38	36.97	-62.50	30.41	97.24	12.66
12	13.07	4.86	6.23	-4.27	28.68	1.08	20.92	37.92	-62.39	30.32	76.14	8.79

国家银行人民币信贷收支主要指标时间序列表
Time Series of Major Indicators in Sources and Uses of Credit Funds of State Banks (RMB)

年 月 Year Month		各项存款 Total Deposits	企业存款 Deposits by Enterprises	财政存款 Fiscal Deposits	储蓄存款 Savings Deposits	活期储蓄 Demand Deposits	定期储蓄 Time Deposits	农业存款 Deposits by Agricultural Sector
		期末余额（亿元） Balance (100 Million Yuan)						
2003	1	116611.72	35789.44	4126.01	67076.21	22361.00	44715.21	435.76
	2	119147.73	36299.50	4458.10	68525.62	22585.01	45940.61	442.62
	3	123036.53	37991.23	4832.97	69893.05	23017.19	46875.86	453.08
	4	124305.40	37839.98	5854.79	70279.99	23103.60	47176.39	445.53
	5	127030.07	38779.55	6494.44	71069.83	23392.56	47677.27	454.02
	6	129614.64	40315.71	6087.79	71951.65	23874.78	48076.87	436.55
	7	130576.15	40286.29	6151.91	72652.50	24230.67	48421.83	440.16
	8	131917.13	40696.62	6363.01	73178.63	24516.40	48662.23	441.40
	9	134357.21	41916.32	6250.64	74327.57	25083.60	49243.97	458.81
	10	135266.09	42069.09	6624.42	74644.60	25078.05	49566.55	474.55
	11	136309.16	42131.95	6891.00	75150.23	25461.97	49688.26	473.54
	12	134650.27	41594.94	5083.45	75834.83	25944.22	49890.61	463.28
		比上期增减额（亿元） Changes Compared with Previous Period (100 Million Yuan)						
2003	1	3173.45	-106.51	689.81	2968.70	1424.78	1543.92	-30.59
	2	2536.01	510.06	332.09	1449.41	224.01	1225.40	6.86
	3	3888.80	1691.73	374.87	1367.43	432.18	935.25	10.46
	4	1268.87	-151.25	1021.82	386.94	86.41	300.53	-7.55
	5	2724.67	939.57	639.65	789.84	288.96	500.88	8.49
	6	2584.57	1536.16	-406.65	881.82	482.22	399.60	-17.47
	7	961.51	-29.42	64.12	700.85	355.89	344.96	3.61
	8	1340.98	410.33	211.10	526.13	285.73	240.40	1.24
	9	2440.08	1219.70	-112.37	1148.94	567.20	581.74	17.41
	10	908.88	152.77	373.78	317.03	-5.55	322.58	15.74
	11	1043.07	62.86	266.58	505.63	383.92	121.71	-1.01
	12	-1658.89	-537.01	-1807.55	684.60	482.25	202.35	-10.26
		比去年同期增长（%） Increase Rate Year-on-year (%)						
2003	1	18.28	12.50	7.56	21.02	30.99	16.58	3.28
	2	20.00	18.02	32.12	18.70	26.34	15.27	14.98
	3	21.29	18.69	41.96	19.99	27.35	16.69	12.82
	4	20.59	17.50	41.20	19.22	24.85	16.64	12.53
	5	20.82	18.04	37.33	19.62	25.23	17.05	14.79
	6	20.42	19.30	27.79	19.24	24.85	16.64	8.38
	7	20.38	19.35	29.60	19.13	25.00	16.39	4.08
	8	19.57	18.11	23.20	18.83	24.43	16.19	3.72
	9	19.43	18.25	15.29	19.56	25.06	16.94	5.19
	10	19.39	18.57	17.77	19.23	24.64	16.67	7.31
	11	19.17	17.66	25.59	18.75	24.48	16.01	5.54
	12	18.68	15.61	47.44	18.45	24.17	15.67	-0.52

国家银行人民币信贷收支主要指标时间序列表

Time Series of Major Indicators in Sources and Uses of Credit Funds of State Banks（RMB）

年 月 Year Month	各项贷款 Total Loans	短期贷款 Short－term Loans	工业贷款 Loans to Industrial Sector	商业贷款 Loans to Commercial Sector	建筑业贷款 Loans to Construction Sector	农业贷款 Loans to Agricultural Sector	中长期贷款 Medium and Long－term Loans	基本建设贷款 Capital Construction Loans	技术改造贷款 Technical Improvement Loans	其他中长期贷款 Other Medium and Long－term Loans	票据融资 Paper Financing	有价证券及投资 Securities and Investments
期末余额（亿元） Balance（100 Million Yuan）												
2003 1	93141.51	46476.09	16995.63	15787.99	2308.66	1292.97	43284.11	21721.41	1834.59	19728.11	3066.16	19466.98
2	93962.67	46539.16	16905.33	15783.37	2339.56	1297.44	43606.76	21932.33	1849.29	19825.14	3499.39	19546.90
3	96215.79	47149.49	17159.93	15740.17	2415.51	1305.85	44816.48	22619.14	1870.15	20327.19	3935.54	19430.53
4	96972.18	47102.22	17079.88	15577.59	2440.35	1327.14	45372.30	22807.28	1857.64	20707.38	4186.76	19697.67
5	98335.34	47420.74	17243.44	15457.75	2479.53	1329.06	46016.59	23064.70	1860.53	21091.36	4588.05	19846.23
6	101758.95	48371.50	17586.37	15494.62	2577.08	1322.63	47753.67	23991.11	1849.33	21913.23	5314.17	20070.91
7	102099.05	47847.92	17394.04	15317.04	2452.14	1320.76	48619.88	24331.77	1862.97	22425.14	5312.75	19919.59
8	103350.06	48058.01	17429.87	15332.65	2460.89	1322.96	49351.50	24849.27	1883.45	22618.78	5622.24	19872.08
9	105114.72	48094.52	17558.12	15337.37	2202.30	1314.59	50841.20	25743.41	1880.68	23217.11	5860.61	19896.46
10	105321.19	48205.99	17626.05	15297.94	2169.87	1308.65	51200.08	26029.66	1888.20	23282.22	5594.85	19913.04
11	105514.97	48077.83	17601.65	15259.40	2063.61	1293.71	51813.70	26304.39	1908.64	23600.67	5306.58	20009.71
12	106155.93	47987.46	17639.07	15168.83	1938.17	1271.81	53141.15	27184.87	1904.42	24051.86	4751.74	21860.55
比上期增减额（亿元） Changes Compared with Previous Period（100 Million Yuan）												
2003 1	2093.44	671.69	248.45	44.68	136.73	10.96	814.40	305.55	23.22	485.63	607.34	－22.09
2	821.16	63.07	－90.30	－4.62	30.90	4.47	322.65	210.92	14.70	97.03	433.23	79.92
3	2253.12	610.33	254.60	－43.20	75.95	8.41	1209.72	686.81	20.86	502.05	436.15	－116.37
4	756.39	－47.27	－80.05	－162.58	24.84	21.29	555.82	188.14	－12.51	380.19	251.22	267.14
5	1363.16	318.52	163.56	－119.84	39.18	1.92	644.29	257.42	2.89	383.98	401.29	148.56
6	3423.61	950.76	342.93	36.87	97.55	－6.43	1737.08	926.41	－11.20	821.87	726.12	224.68
7	340.10	－523.58	－192.33	－177.58	－124.94	－1.87	866.21	340.66	13.64	511.91	－1.42	－151.32
8	1251.01	210.09	35.83	15.61	8.75	2.20	731.62	517.50	20.48	193.64	309.49	－47.51
9	1764.66	36.51	128.25	4.72	－258.59	－8.37	1489.70	894.14	－2.77	598.33	238.37	24.38
10	206.47	111.47	67.93	－39.43	－32.43	－5.94	358.88	286.25	7.52	65.11	－265.76	16.58
11	193.78	－128.16	－24.40	－38.54	－106.26	－14.94	613.62	274.73	20.44	318.45	－288.27	96.67
12	640.96	－90.37	37.42	－90.57	－125.44	－21.90	1327.45	880.48	－4.22	451.19	－554.84	1850.84
比去年同期增长（%） Increase Rate Year－on－year（%）												
2003 1	16.10	9.65	16.37	－3.87	58.32	1.05	19.54	17.30	2.37	24.07	134.33	5.77
2	16.82	9.88	14.44	－3.91	61.93	0.84	19.67	17.63	3.24	23.89	165.90	6.18
3	17.52	9.23	12.19	－4.05	59.52	－0.84	21.25	19.57	5.09	24.97	177.71	4.26
4	18.08	8.76	11.70	－3.60	57.51	0.93	22.52	20.37	4.56	26.98	187.75	5.26
5	18.80	9.18	10.69	－3.39	40.26	1.10	22.67	20.45	4.75	27.16	204.77	5.91
6	20.38	9.82	10.12	－2.79	39.44	0.14	24.34	22.10	3.07	29.19	201.65	4.61
7	20.39	8.55	8.21	－3.29	29.72	－0.10	25.73	23.04	3.80	31.14	205.65	3.81
8	20.50	8.58	7.69	－2.38	27.60	0.14	25.53	24.03	5.23	29.32	201.20	2.99
9	19.57	7.10	6.90	－2.51	8.41	－0.44	26.35	25.88	4.79	29.04	139.37	2.79
10	19.22	7.30	7.58	－2.77	4.85	－0.28	25.91	26.30	4.04	27.64	130.51	3.19
11	18.23	6.33	6.70	－2.93	－2.57	－0.26	25.97	27.06	7.05	26.56	106.12	3.82
12	16.79	4.77	5.34	－3.75	－10.60	－1.11	25.58	27.21	5.13	25.69	93.26	12.17

国家银行人民币信贷收支主要指标时间序列表

Time Series of Major Indicators in Sources and Uses of Credit Funds of State Banks (RMB)

年　月 Year Month		各项存款 Total Deposits	企业存款 Deposits by Enterprises	财政存款 Fiscal Deposits	储蓄存款 Savings Deposits	活期储蓄 Demand Deposits	定期储蓄 Time Deposits	农业存款 Deposits by Agricultural Sector
		期末余额（亿元） Balance (100 Million Yuan)						
2004	1	137977.70	41530.07	5806.04	80022.05	27935.27	52086.78	442.27
	2	140966.52	42812.72	6218.18	80994.77	27909.20	53085.57	446.93
	3	144455.89	44626.77	6734.82	81863.58	28471.58	53392.00	456.12
	4	145032.67	44916.02	7108.56	81848.83	28647.95	53200.88	445.94
	5	146814.19	45735.31	7701.42	82024.00	28686.43	53337.57	445.32
	6	149030.09	46582.21	8095.91	82702.43	29197.31	53505.12	441.64
	7	150013.54	45978.03	9357.31	83053.12	29466.39	53586.73	438.07
	8	151673.01	46465.47	10032.35	83227.80	29576.02	53651.78	446.18
	9	152576.66	47193.18	9440.21	83821.35	30029.57	53791.78	448.38
	10	153852.84	47042.05	10384.87	84119.08	30047.64	54071.44	457.51
	11	155857.05	47830.13	10339.14	85226.93	29704.90	55522.03	466.75
	12	153556.60	48491.87	6105.73	86469.56	30205.96	56263.60	484.99
		比上期增减额（亿元） Changes Compared with Previous Period (100 Million Yuan)						
2004	1	3323.81	-837.87	368.17	4179.75	1986.04	2193.71	-21.04
	2	2988.82	1282.65	412.14	972.72	-26.07	998.79	4.66
	3	3489.37	1814.05	516.64	868.81	562.38	306.43	9.19
	4	576.78	289.25	373.74	-14.75	176.37	-191.12	-10.18
	5	1781.52	819.29	592.86	175.17	38.48	136.69	-0.62
	6	2215.90	846.90	394.49	678.43	510.88	167.55	-3.68
	7	983.45	-604.18	1261.40	350.69	269.08	81.61	-3.57
	8	1659.47	487.44	675.04	174.68	109.63	65.05	8.11
	9	903.65	727.71	-592.14	593.55	453.55	140.00	2.20
	10	1276.18	-151.13	944.66	297.73	18.07	279.66	9.13
	11	2004.21	788.08	-45.73	1107.85	-342.74	1450.59	9.24
	12	-2300.45	661.74	-4233.41	1242.63	501.06	741.57	18.24
		比去年同期增长（%） Increase Rate Year-on-year (%)						
2004	1	18.32	16.04	12.83	19.30	24.93	16.49	1.49
	2	18.31	17.94	13.29	18.20	23.57	15.55	0.97
	3	17.41	17.47	13.89	17.13	23.70	13.90	0.67
	4	16.67	18.70	3.01	16.46	24.00	12.77	0.09
	5	15.57	17.94	2.15	15.41	22.63	11.87	-1.92
	6	14.98	15.54	12.94	14.94	22.29	11.29	1.17
	7	14.89	14.13	28.74	14.32	21.61	10.67	-0.47
	8	14.98	14.18	33.61	13.73	20.64	10.25	1.08
	9	13.56	12.59	27.49	12.77	19.72	9.24	-2.27
	10	13.74	11.82	33.80	12.69	19.82	9.09	-3.59
	11	14.34	13.52	28.30	13.41	16.66	11.74	-1.43
	12	14.04	16.58	-1.75	14.02	16.43	12.77	4.69

国家银行人民币信贷收支主要指标时间序列表

Time Series of Major Indicators in Sources and Uses of Credit Funds of State Banks（RMB）

年 Year	月 Month	各项贷款 Total Loans	短期贷款 Short－term Loans	工业贷款 Loans to Industrial Sector	商业贷款 Loans to Commercial Sector	建筑业贷款 Loans to Construction Sector	农业贷款 Loans to Agricultural Sector	中长期贷款 Medium and Long－term Loans	基本建设贷款 Capital Construction Loans	技术改造贷款 Technical Improvement Loans	其他中长期贷款 Other Medium and Long－term Loans	票据融资 Paper Financing	有价证券及投资 Securities and Investments
期末余额（亿元） Balance（100 Million Yuan）													
2004	1	107258.27	47916.66	17616.29	15092.06	1742.54	1286.30	54180.56	27792.83	1945.58	24442.15	4882.17	21793.02
	2	108296.34	48116.74	17608.63	15091.55	1710.00	1294.34	54655.42	28104.59	1962.20	24588.63	5243.91	21845.23
	3	110380.32	48456.48	17678.93	15132.42	1637.80	1312.58	55837.04	28796.20	2001.78	25039.06	5804.91	22030.43
	4	111150.59	48211.80	17678.66	14910.10	1588.14	1328.88	56577.81	29146.97	2027.25	25403.59	6076.87	21939.69
	5	111804.85	48108.17	17655.01	14845.18	1542.70	1327.24	57106.54	29463.40	2051.92	25591.22	6302.37	21835.56
	6	110704.13	46446.36	17235.31	14100.98	1278.58	1331.47	57514.75	29949.00	1961.70	25604.05	6541.22	22139.23
	7	110540.00	46049.73	16989.41	14049.13	1221.94	1327.68	57716.48	29942.69	1959.83	25813.96	6570.15	22355.76
	8	111042.46	45927.77	16946.26	14070.49	1205.06	1328.87	58179.49	30231.23	1948.97	25999.29	6728.64	22505.18
	9	112536.34	46419.10	17178.17	14138.62	1168.81	1324.10	59059.91	30575.90	1926.53	26557.48	6848.11	22797.96
	10	112771.95	46190.83	17006.75	14180.14	1136.64	1316.15	59646.45	31010.35	1948.72	26687.38	6721.81	22600.09
	11	113902.22	45971.75	17200.79	14210.28	1227.20	1296.72	60687.06	31575.73	1848.79	27262.54	7027.11	22734.68
	12	116050.92	46164.00	17400.71	14079.90	1210.80	1296.59	62290.29	32586.45	1906.26	27797.58	7391.21	22494.86
比上期增减额（亿元） Changes Compared with Previous Period（100 Million Yuan）													
2004	1	1173.74	111.14	－12.14	－59.54	－46.73	13.75	857.46	459.38	36.54	361.54	201.82	－138.73
	2	1038.07	200.08	－7.66	－0.51	－32.54	8.04	474.86	311.76	16.62	146.48	361.74	52.21
	3	2083.98	339.74	70.30	40.87	－72.20	18.24	1181.62	691.61	39.58	450.43	561.00	185.20
	4	770.27	－244.68	－0.27	－222.32	－49.66	16.30	740.77	350.77	25.47	364.53	271.96	－90.74
	5	654.26	－103.63	－23.65	－64.92	－45.44	－1.64	528.73	316.43	24.67	187.63	225.50	－104.13
	6	1796.32	366.26	146.58	42.91	－95.79	7.98	1193.05	744.20	33.61	415.24	241.04	303.67
	7	－164.16	－396.65	－245.90	－51.85	－56.65	－3.79	201.73	－6.30	－1.87	209.90	28.93	216.53
	8	502.47	－121.96	－43.16	21.36	－16.88	1.19	463.00	288.53	－10.86	185.33	158.50	149.42
	9	1493.92	491.37	231.91	68.13	－36.24	－4.76	880.43	344.68	－22.44	558.19	119.46	292.78
	10	235.58	－228.31	－171.41	41.52	－32.18	－7.96	586.55	434.45	22.19	129.91	－126.29	－197.87
	11	1130.29	66.78	194.03	30.14	90.57	－19.42	754.76	565.38	－99.93	289.31	305.30	134.59
	12	2148.65	192.23	199.92	－130.38	－16.41	－0.14	1603.21	1010.70	57.47	535.04	364.10	－239.82
比去年同期增长（%） Increase Rate Year－on－year（%）													
2004	1	15.16	3.10	3.65	－4.41	－24.52	－0.52	25.17	27.95	6.05	23.90	59.23	11.95
	2	15.25	3.39	4.16	－4.38	－26.91	－0.24	25.34	28.14	6.11	24.03	49.85	11.76
	3	14.72	2.77	3.02	－3.86	－32.20	0.52	24.59	27.31	7.04	23.18	47.50	13.38
	4	14.62	2.36	3.51	－4.28	－34.92	0.13	24.70	27.80	9.13	22.68	45.14	11.38
	5	13.70	1.45	2.39	－3.96	－37.78	－0.14	24.10	27.74	10.29	21.34	37.36	10.02
	6	11.64	0.21	1.22	－3.91	－43.85	0.95	22.08	25.91	12.77	18.68	23.13	10.31
	7	11.10	0.48	0.93	－3.14	－43.30	0.81	20.32	24.12	11.85	16.91	23.71	12.23
	8	10.25	－0.21	0.47	－3.10	－44.19	0.73	19.48	22.70	10.05	16.72	19.72	13.25
	9	9.82	0.73	1.06	－2.68	－39.28	1.01	17.71	19.78	9.02	16.12	16.89	14.58
	10	9.82	0.03	－0.30	－2.16	－39.86	0.86	18.03	20.13	9.76	16.35	20.18	13.49
	11	10.69	－0.16	0.94	－1.72	－32.37	0.52	18.64	21.02	3.35	17.22	32.46	13.62
	12	12.05	0.43	1.86	－1.99	－28.84	2.24	18.69	20.82	6.60	17.25	55.59	2.90

国家银行人民币信贷收支主要指标时间序列表

Time Series of Major Indicators in Sources and Uses of Credit Funds of State Banks (RMB)

年 月 Year Month		各项存款 Total Deposits	企业存款 Deposits by Enterprises	财政存款 Fiscal Deposits	储蓄存款 Savings Deposits	活期储蓄 Demand Deposits	定期储蓄 Time Deposits	农业存款 Deposits by Agricultural Sector
		期末余额（亿元） Balance (100 Million Yuan)						
2005	1	158558.71	48634.28	7323.64	88661.77	30993.53	57668.24	466.21
	2	161590.90	47563.15	7727.79	92566.52	32181.99	60384.53	434.62
	3	166111.11	50228.59	8068.91	93676.12	32324.22	61351.90	450.72
	4	168052.93	50517.82	9298.47	93937.60	32266.71	61670.89	447.64
	5	170920.66	51587.75	10164.61	94382.39	32233.67	62148.72	442.61
	6	173498.41	52228.80	9941.14	95313.53	32625.60	62687.93	441.11
	7	175546.75	51522.92	10894.49	96293.47	32973.34	63320.13	455.85
	8	178172.66	52671.85	11179.38	96835.57	33069.15	63766.42	460.63
	9	180036.25	53577.45	10480.44	97977.42	33576.92	64400.50	474.12
	10	181590.50	53284.89	11477.02	98176.97	33377.78	64799.19	465.87
	11	183337.93	53738.30	11271.36	99211.11	34236.36	64974.75	435.78
	12	181120.65	53490.49	7822.19	100633.26	35158.26	65475.00	424.19
		比上期增减额（亿元） Changes Compared with Previous Period (100 Million Yuan)						
2005	1	3232.22	-16.78	1217.72	2192.40	787.93	1404.47	-18.80
	2	3032.19	-1071.13	404.15	3904.75	1188.46	2716.29	-31.59
	3	4520.21	2665.44	341.12	1109.60	142.23	967.37	16.10
	4	1941.82	289.23	1229.56	261.48	-57.51	318.99	-3.08
	5	2867.73	1069.93	866.14	444.79	-33.04	477.83	-5.03
	6	2577.75	641.05	-223.47	931.14	391.93	539.21	-1.50
	7	2048.34	-705.88	953.35	979.94	347.74	632.20	14.74
	8	2625.91	1148.93	284.89	542.10	95.81	446.29	4.78
	9	1863.59	905.60	-698.94	1141.85	507.77	634.08	13.49
	10	1554.25	-292.56	996.58	199.55	-199.14	398.69	-8.25
	11	1747.43	453.41	-205.66	1034.14	858.58	175.56	-30.09
	12	-2217.28	-247.81	-3449.17	1422.15	921.90	500.25	-11.59
		比去年同期增长（%） Increase Rate Year-on-year (%)						
2005	1	14.92	17.11	26.14	10.80	10.95	10.72	5.41
	2	14.63	11.10	24.28	14.29	15.31	13.75	-2.75
	3	14.99	12.55	19.81	14.43	13.53	14.91	-1.18
	4	15.87	12.47	30.81	14.77	12.63	15.92	0.38
	5	16.42	12.80	31.98	15.07	12.37	16.52	-0.61
	6	16.42	12.12	22.79	15.25	11.74	17.16	-0.12
	7	17.02	12.06	16.43	15.94	11.90	18.16	4.06
	8	17.47	13.36	11.43	16.35	11.81	18.85	3.24
	9	18.00	13.53	11.02	16.89	11.81	19.72	5.74
	10	18.03	13.27	10.52	16.71	11.08	19.84	1.83
	11	17.63	12.35	9.02	16.41	15.25	17.03	-6.64
	12	17.95	10.31	28.11	16.38	16.40	16.37	-12.54

国家银行人民币信贷收支主要指标时间序列表

Time Series of Major Indicators in Sources and Uses of Credit Funds of State Banks（RMB）

年 月 Year Month		各项贷款 Total Loans	短期贷款 Short - term Loans	工业贷款 Loans to Industrial Sector	商业贷款 Loans to Commercial Sector	建筑业贷款 Loans to Construction Sector	农业贷款 Loans to Agricultural Sector	中长期贷款 Medium and Long - term Loans	基本建设贷款 Capital Construction Loans	技术改造贷款 Technical Improvement Loans	其他中长期贷款 Other Medium and Long - term Loans	票据融资 Paper Financing	有价证券及投资 Securities and Investments
		期末余额（亿元） Balance（100 Million Yuan）											
2005	1	117370.96	46082.96	17867.64	13794.69	1249.61	1318.20	63419.00	33129.20	1928.13	28361.67	7655.31	22183.07
	2	117800.24	46125.12	17894.06	13750.02	1251.87	1325.76	63783.23	33330.18	1940.35	28512.70	7673.32	22232.83
	3	119870.03	46529.73	18041.27	13732.06	1245.58	1356.41	64814.00	34149.68	1965.23	28699.09	8319.29	22530.02
	4	119948.55	46164.72	17921.74	13693.61	1212.83	1395.52	65196.72	34395.11	1966.27	28835.34	8381.78	22550.09
	5	118355.71	44770.07	16879.84	13359.90	1183.72	1423.89	65265.97	34463.96	1964.01	28838.00	8153.56	22706.97
	6	116698.89	42166.43	14899.36	12691.33	1148.13	1419.37	65638.68	34761.63	1985.15	28891.90	8780.68	22716.57
	7	115864.63	41762.49	14783.54	12629.45	1121.28	1410.17	65687.28	34848.16	1970.73	28868.39	8298.26	22925.05
	8	116574.60	41725.66	14800.02	12656.25	1087.85	1411.82	66127.96	35241.50	1972.10	28914.36	8602.18	23289.33
	9	118233.00	42164.38	14908.60	12854.70	1056.72	1417.67	67181.42	35990.65	1965.64	29225.13	8763.25	23625.81
	10	118258.05	42020.00	14790.59	12910.72	1043.99	1398.21	67473.60	36207.04	1957.35	29309.21	8633.96	23754.72
	11	119954.54	42327.57	14775.53	13242.57	1027.93	1391.02	67909.00	36340.53	1936.68	29631.79	9588.98	23811.65
	12	120851.06	42045.65	14693.21	13198.71	1012.47	1384.22	69106.44	37016.03	1911.66	30178.75	9574.68	25067.51
		比上期增减额（亿元） Changes Compared with Previous Period（100 Million Yuan）											
2005	1	1320.49	121.95	218.52	-20.95	-11.63	21.63	925.72	542.75	39.66	343.31	264.52	-216.30
	2	429.28	42.14	26.41	-44.67	2.26	7.56	364.25	200.99	12.22	151.04	18.01	49.76
	3	2069.78	404.60	147.21	-17.96	-6.30	30.65	1030.77	819.51	24.87	186.39	645.97	297.19
	4	78.54	-364.98	-119.52	-38.45	-32.74	39.11	382.72	245.42	1.05	136.25	62.49	20.07
	5	102.80	-68.40	-163.52	-16.83	-17.71	30.14	395.50	282.78	-2.26	114.98	-228.08	156.88
	6	2778.71	802.01	347.85	145.05	3.51	2.40	1346.58	974.70	21.13	350.75	627.68	9.60
	7	-834.27	-403.96	-115.82	-61.88	-26.85	-9.20	48.61	86.52	-14.41	-23.50	-482.42	208.48
	8	709.98	-36.81	16.48	26.80	-33.43	1.66	440.67	393.34	1.36	45.97	303.92	364.28
	9	1658.36	438.70	108.58	198.45	-31.14	5.84	1053.44	749.14	-6.45	310.75	161.07	336.48
	10	25.05	-144.38	-118.01	56.02	-12.72	-19.46	292.19	216.40	-8.30	84.09	-129.29	128.91
	11	1696.50	307.58	-15.06	331.84	-16.06	-7.18	435.40	133.49	-20.67	322.58	955.02	56.93
	12	896.53	-281.94	-82.32	-43.86	-15.47	-6.81	1197.46	675.51	-25.01	546.96	-14.30	1255.86
		比去年同期增长（%） Increase Rate Year - on - year（%）											
2005	1	12.13	0.41	4.64	-3.38	-18.63	2.77	18.50	20.13	5.47	17.68	56.85	1.79
	2	11.45	0.08	4.84	-3.67	-16.95	2.72	18.14	19.51	5.20	17.60	46.37	1.77
	3	11.22	0.21	5.25	-4.05	-13.67	3.62	17.48	19.49	4.36	16.22	43.35	2.27
	4	10.52	-0.04	4.58	-2.88	-13.03	5.30	16.62	18.89	3.10	15.09	37.97	2.78
	5	9.97	0.03	3.79	-2.57	-11.62	7.70	16.23	18.58	1.75	14.70	29.41	3.99
	6	10.95	0.97	5.05	-1.98	-6.25	7.25	16.39	19.04	1.19	14.44	34.25	2.61
	7	10.36	0.97	5.89	-2.06	-4.10	6.87	16.06	19.36	0.56	13.42	26.31	2.55
	8	10.50	1.15	6.26	-2.02	-5.53	6.90	15.90	19.52	1.19	12.79	27.85	3.48
	9	10.51	1.03	5.46	-1.09	-5.27	7.72	15.95	20.62	2.03	11.59	27.98	3.63
	10	10.30	1.21	5.82	-0.98	-3.71	6.90	15.30	19.63	0.44	11.36	28.46	5.11
	11	10.70	2.37	4.54	1.15	-12.12	7.94	14.04	17.91	4.75	10.19	36.47	4.74
	12	9.42	1.33	2.87	1.77	-12.21	7.43	13.03	16.33	0.28	10.04	29.55	11.44

（三）政策性银行人民币信贷收支主要指标时间序列表（1997—2005 年月度时序）

Time Series of Major Indicators in Sources and Uses of Credit Funds of Policy Banks（RMB）（Monthly Series from 1997 to 2005）

政策性银行人民币信贷收支主要指标时间序列表

Time Series of Major Indicators in Sources and Uses of Credit Funds of Policy Banks（RMB）

年　月 Year Month	各项存款 Total Deposits	企业存款 Deposits by Enterprises	储蓄存款 Savings Deposits	活期储蓄 Demand Deposits	定期储蓄 Time Deposits	农业存款 Deposits by Agricultural Sector
期末余额（亿元）Balance（100 Million Yuan）						
1997　1	210.38	202.54				
2	195.71	187.98				
3	191.35	181.34				
4	185.98	176.12				
5	195.11	186.17				
6	217.30	204.52				
7	240.20	226.82				
8	283.94	268.88				
9	227.31	218.30				
10	223.61	215.84				
11	255.49	246.75				
12	366.21	347.15				
比上期增减额（亿元）Changes Compared with Previous Period（100 Million Yuan）						
1997　1	-82.54	-81.01				
2	-14.67	-14.56				
3	-4.35	-6.63				
4	-5.38	-5.23				
5	9.14	10.06				
6	22.18	18.34				
7	22.90	22.31				
8	43.74	42.06				
9	-56.64	-50.58				
10	-3.71	-2.47				
11	31.88	30.91				
12	110.72	100.40				
比去年同期增长（%）Increase Rate Year-on-year（%）						
1997　1						
2						
3						
4						
5						
6						
7						
8						
9						
10						
11						
12						

政策性银行人民币信贷收支主要指标时间序列表

Time Series of Major Indicators in Sources and Uses of Credit Funds of Policy Banks（RMB）

年 月 Year Month		各项贷款 Total Loans	短期贷款 Short－term Loans						中长期贷款 Medium and Long－term Loans				有价证券及投资 Securities and Investments
				工业贷款 Loans to Industrial Sector	商业贷款 Loans to Commercial Sector	建筑业贷款 Loans to Construction Sector	农业贷款 Loans to Agricultural Sector	贴现 Discount		基本建设贷款 Capital Construction Loans	技术改造贷款 Technical Improvement Loans	其他中长期贷款 Other Medium and Long－term Loans	
期末余额（亿元）Balance（100 Million Yuan）													
1997	1	8829.39	5727.67		5657.82			0.14	3100.78	2315.68	120.10	665.00	4.74
	2	8865.85	5729.04		5660.04			0.23	3134.19	2346.65	120.15	667.39	6.66
	3	8995.20	5756.59		5686.72			0.14	3236.72	2411.41	119.69	705.62	6.66
	4	9056.32	5766.31		5696.68			0.19	3288.35	2438.61	118.97	730.77	3.86
	5	9198.99	5786.52		5716.45			0.13	3410.05	2542.67	118.60	748.78	3.86
	6	9537.28	5960.16		5889.98			0.18	3573.81	2655.69	116.52	801.60	3.86
	7	10169.69	6075.24		6006.04			0.13	4091.12	3003.40	116.46	971.26	3.86
	8	10499.96	6311.43		6240.74			0.09	4184.16	3077.16	116.05	990.95	83.86
	9	10837.94	6540.25		6468.67			0.08	4293.76	3160.76	116.80	1016.20	83.86
	10	11129.96	6741.15		6667.30			0.19	4386.12	3223.89	116.28	1045.95	83.86
	11	11432.58	6937.86		6863.91			0.25	4492.16	3285.97	116.01	1090.18	2.05
	12	12124.08	7328.86		7246.12				4792.62	3454.28	118.69	1219.65	1.02
比上期增减额（亿元）Changes Compared with Previous Period（100 Million Yuan）													
1997	1	36.60	15.03		18.55			0.14	21.57	37.18	－0.19	－15.42	－1.77
	2	36.47	1.37		2.22			0.09	33.42	30.97	0.06	2.39	1.93
	3	129.36	27.54		26.68			－0.10	102.54	64.76	－0.46	38.24	
	4	61.12	9.72		9.96			0.05	51.63	27.20	－0.72	25.15	－2.81
	5	142.69	20.23		19.78			－0.05	121.71	104.06	－0.37	18.01	
	6	338.28	173.62		173.52			0.05	163.77	113.02	－2.08	52.83	
	7	632.40	115.08		116.06			－0.05	517.30	347.71	－0.06	169.65	
	8	330.27	236.19		234.70			－0.04	93.04	73.76	－0.41	19.69	80.00
	9	338.00	228.83		227.94			－0.01	109.61	83.61	0.75	25.25	
	10	292.03	200.91		198.63			0.11	92.36	63.13	－0.52	29.75	
	11	302.62	196.71		196.61			0.06	106.04	62.08	－0.27	44.23	－81.81
	12	691.50	391.00		382.21			－0.25	300.46	168.31	2.68	129.47	－1.03
比去年同期增长（%）Increase Rate Year－on－year（%）													
1997	1												
	2												
	3												
	4												
	5												
	6												
	7												
	8												
	9												
	10												
	11												
	12												

政策性银行人民币信贷收支主要指标时间序列表

Time Series of Major Indicators in Sources and Uses of Credit Funds of Policy Banks（RMB）

年　月 Year Month		各项存款 Total Deposits	企业存款 Deposits by Enterprises	储蓄存款 Savings Deposits	活期储蓄 Demand Deposits	定期储蓄 Time Deposits	农业存款 Deposits by Agricultural Sector
		期末余额（亿元） Balance（100 Million Yuan）					
1998	1	252.65	241.19				
	2	243.72	232.39				
	3	230.79	215.13				
	4	179.09	167.91				
	5	162.45	152.05				
	6	184.13	172.77				
	7	173.45	162.60				
	8	177.36	166.09				
	9	173.29	161.21				
	10	167.39	159.60				
	11	194.55	185.15				
	12	205.34	190.66				
		比上期增减额（亿元） Changes Compared with Previous Period（100 Million Yuan）					
1998	1	-117.34	-106.47				
	2	-8.92	-8.79				
	3	-12.92	-17.25				
	4	-51.72	-47.23				
	5	-16.63	-15.86				
	6	21.67	20.72				
	7	-10.67	-10.17				
	8	3.90	3.49				
	9	-4.07	-4.88				
	10	-5.90	-1.61				
	11	27.15	25.55				
	12	10.79	5.51				
		比去年同期增长（%） Increase Rate Year-on-year（%）					
1998	1	20.09	19.08				
	2	24.52	23.62				
	3	20.61	18.63				
	4	-3.72	-4.66				
	5	-16.74	-18.33				
	6	-15.27	-15.52				
	7	-27.79	-28.31				
	8	-37.54	-38.23				
	9	-23.76	-26.15				
	10	-25.14	-26.06				
	11	-23.86	-24.96				
	12	-43.93	-45.08				

政策性银行人民币信贷收支主要指标时间序列表

Time Series of Major Indicators in Sources and Uses of Credit Funds of Policy Banks（RMB）

年 月 Year Month	各项贷款 Total Loans	短期贷款 Short - term Loans	工业贷款 Loans to Industrial Sector	商业贷款 Loans to Commercial Sector	建筑业贷款 Loans to Construction Sector	农业贷款 Loans to Agricultural Sector	贴现 Discount	中长期贷款 Medium and Long - term Loans	基本建设贷款 Capital Construction Loans	技术改造贷款 Technical Improvement Loans	其他中长期贷款 Other Medium and Long - term Loans	有价证券及投资 Securities and Investments
	期末余额（亿元） Balance（100 Million Yuan）											
1998 1	12078.05	7263.43		7171.73			0.01	4807.34	3468.58	122.22	1216.54	1.02
2	12132.83	7219.35		7130.96			0.01	4899.14	3580.16	104.07	1214.91	0.01
3	12199.73	7211.08		7122.02				4972.21	3641.52	103.34	1227.35	0.01
4	12190.97	7132.31		7040.32			0.03	5036.82	3681.14	108.34	1247.34	0.01
5	10990.78	7079.91		6991.01			0.03	3889.33	3459.00	107.94	322.39	0.36
6	11260.33	7143.12		7026.26			0.02	4096.21	3656.29	108.78	331.14	0.36
7	11376.46	7271.03		5886.09				4074.25	3666.09	108.92	299.24	0.36
8	11469.69	7297.37		5605.89				4135.64	3717.69	107.92	310.03	0.36
9	11809.22	7352.78		7339.13				4416.08	3973.56	109.57	332.95	0.36
10	12067.67	7549.03		7533.02				4452.47	3972.01	136.72	343.74	0.36
11	12527.34	7802.05		7783.92				4632.50	4137.39	133.65	361.46	0.36
12	12119.04	7053.64		6971.71				4954.90	4410.61	143.78	400.51	0.36
	比上期增减额（亿元） Changes Compared with Previous Period（100 Million Yuan）											
1998 1	-49.84	-46.48		-45.98			0.01	-8.03	10.66	3.54	-22.23	
2	54.76	-44.10		-40.78				91.80	111.58	-18.15	-1.63	-1.01
3	66.89	-8.27		-8.94			-0.01	73.06	61.36	-0.74	12.44	
4	-8.77	-78.77		-81.70			0.03	64.61	39.61	5.00	19.99	
5	-1200.18	-52.40		-49.31				-1147.48	-222.13	-0.40	-924.95	0.35
6	269.53	63.21		35.25			-0.01	206.88	197.29	0.83	8.75	
7	116.13	127.91		-1140.17			-0.02	-21.97	9.80	0.14	-31.90	
8	93.23	26.34		-280.20				61.39	51.60	-1.00	10.79	
9	339.53	55.41		1733.24				280.44	255.87	1.65	22.92	
10	258.45	196.25		193.89				36.39	-1.55	27.15	10.79	
11	459.67	253.02		250.90				180.03	165.38	-3.07	17.72	
12	-408.30	-748.41		-812.21				322.40	273.22	10.13	39.05	
	比去年同期增长（%） Increase Rate Year - on - year（%）											
1998 1	36.79	26.81		26.76			-92.86	55.04	49.79	1.77	82.94	-78.48
2	36.85	26.01		25.99			-95.65	56.31	52.56	-13.38	82.04	-99.85
3	35.62	25.27		25.24			-100.00	53.62	51.01	-13.66	73.94	-99.85
4	34.61	23.69		23.59			-84.21	53.17	50.95	-8.94	70.69	-99.74
5	19.48	22.35		22.30			-76.92	14.05	36.04	-8.99	-56.94	-90.67
6	18.07	19.85		19.29			-88.89	14.62	37.68	-6.64	-58.69	-90.67
7	11.87	19.68		-2.00			-100.00	-0.41	22.06	-6.47	-69.19	-90.67
8	9.24	15.62		-10.17			-100.00	-1.16	20.82	-7.01	-68.71	-99.57
9	8.96	12.42		13.46			-100.00	2.85	25.72	-6.19	-67.24	-99.57
10	8.43	11.98		12.98			-100.00	1.51	23.21	17.58	-67.14	-99.57
11	9.58	12.46		13.40			-100.00	3.12	25.91	15.21	-66.84	-82.44
12	-0.04	-3.76		-3.79				3.39	27.69	21.14	-67.16	-64.71

政策性银行人民币信贷收支主要指标时间序列表

Time Series of Major Indicators in Sources and Uses of Credit Funds of Policy Banks (RMB)

年 月 Year Month		各项存款 Total Deposits	企业存款 Deposits by Enterprises	储蓄存款 Savings Deposits	活期储蓄 Demand Deposits	定期储蓄 Time Deposits	农业存款 Deposits by Agricultural Sector
		期末余额（亿元） Balance (100 Million Yuan)					
1999	1	182.66	171.82				
	2	151.63	140.74				
	3	142.73	127.04				
	4	136.01	132.49				
	5	185.98	182.57				
	6	274.23	270.22				
	7	266.72	261.02				
	8	245.98	238.88				
	9	259.79	253.30				
	10	298.61	290.67				
	11	355.81	349.41				
	12	376.36	368.06				
		比上期增减额（亿元） Changes Compared with Previous Period (100 Million Yuan)					
1999	1	-17.08	-13.55				
	2	-31.02	-31.08				
	3	-8.90	-13.70				
	4	-6.72	5.45				
	5	49.97	50.08				
	6	88.25	87.65				
	7	-7.50	-9.19				
	8	-20.75	-22.16				
	9	13.81	14.42				
	10	38.84	37.38				
	11	57.20	58.74				
	12	20.55	18.65				
		比去年同期增长（%） Increase Rate Year-on-year (%)					
1999	1	-27.71	-28.76				
	2	-37.78	-39.44				
	3	-38.16	-40.95				
	4	-24.05	-21.09				
	5	14.48	20.07				
	6	48.94	56.40				
	7	53.78	60.54				
	8	38.69	43.82				
	9	49.90	57.12				
	10	78.39	82.12				
	11	82.90	88.72				
	12	83.30	93.05				

政策性银行人民币信贷收支主要指标时间序列表

Time Series of Major Indicators in Sources and Uses of Credit Funds of Policy Banks（RMB）

年 月 Year Month		各项贷款 Total Loans	短期贷款 Short－term Loans						中长期贷款 Medium and Long－term Loans				有价证券及投资 Securities and Investments
				工业贷款 Loans to Industrial Sector	商业贷款 Loans to Commercial Sector	建筑业贷款 Loans to Construction Sector	农业贷款 Loans to Agricultural Sector	贴现 Discount		基本建设贷款 Capital Construction Loans	技术改造贷款 Technical Improvement Loans	其他中长期贷款 Other Medium and Long－term Loans	
期末余额（亿元） Balance（100 Million Yuan）													
1999	1	12109.45	7048.32		6986.62				4953.34	4406.82	152.13	394.39	0.36
	2	12106.97	7016.08		6954.16				4982.41	4432.16	152.48	397.77	0.36
	3	12133.69	6954.25		6891.74				5068.55	4506.38	151.06	411.11	0.36
	4	12047.04	6815.19		6755.01				5114.15	4548.97	145.53	419.65	0.36
	5	11997.60	6754.74		6696.06				5118.07	4580.02	130.46	407.59	0.36
	6	12214.93	6807.03		6745.60				5278.20	4742.37	132.78	403.05	0.36
	7	12289.70	6830.75		6767.30				5320.25	4794.60	134.27	391.38	0.36
	8	12367.50	6836.44		6770.55				5387.72	4863.39	134.61	389.72	0.36
	9	12550.88	6887.52		6803.55				5513.04	4976.17	132.83	404.04	0.36
	10	12720.66	6929.80		6842.69				5605.54	5066.99	132.39	406.16	0.36
	11	13017.08	7071.99		6991.01				5702.30	5162.22	126.97	413.11	0.36
	12	13094.82	7295.98		7188.09				5646.51	5052.53	113.92	480.06	0.36
比上期增减额（亿元） Changes Compared with Previous Period（100 Million Yuan）													
1999	1	－9.58	1.93		4.21				－8.80	－3.79	8.35	－13.36	
	2	－2.50	－32.24		－32.46				29.05	25.34	0.35	3.36	
	3	26.73	－61.83		－62.42				86.14	74.22	－1.42	13.34	
	4	－86.65	－139.06		－136.73				45.60	42.59	－5.53	8.54	
	5	－49.42	－60.45		－58.95				3.92	31.05	－15.07	－12.06	
	6	217.33	52.29		49.54				160.13	162.35	2.32	－4.54	
	7	74.76	23.72		21.70				42.04	52.23	1.49	－11.68	
	8	77.81	5.69		3.25				67.48	68.79	0.34	－1.65	
	9	183.39	51.08		33.00				125.33	112.78	－1.77	14.32	
	10	169.79	42.28		39.14				92.52	90.82	－0.44	2.13	
	11	296.42	142.20		148.32				96.76	95.23	－5.42	6.95	
	12	562.02	223.99		197.08				345.70	272.59	6.17	66.94	
比去年同期增长（%） Increase Rate Year－on－year（%）													
1999	1	0.26	－2.96		－2.58			－100.00	3.04	27.05	24.47	－67.58	－64.71
	2	－0.21	－2.82		－2.48			－100.00	1.70	23.80	46.52	－67.26	3500.00
	3	－0.54	－3.56		－3.23				1.94	23.75	46.18	－66.50	3500.00
	4	－1.18	－4.45		－4.05			－100.00	1.54	23.58	34.33	－66.36	3500.00
	5	9.16	－4.59		－4.22			－100.00	31.59	32.41	20.86	26.43	
	6	8.48	－4.71		－3.99			－100.00	28.86	29.70	22.06	21.72	
	7	8.03	－6.06		14.97				30.58	30.78	23.27	30.78	
	8	7.83	－6.32		20.78				30.28	30.82	24.73	25.70	
	9	6.28	－6.33		－7.30				24.84	25.23	21.23	21.35	
	10	5.41	－8.20		－9.16				25.90	27.57	－3.17	18.16	
	11	3.91	－9.36		－10.19				23.09	24.77	－5.00	14.29	
	12	12.05	3.44		3.10				22.06	23.22	－7.40	19.86	

政策性银行人民币信贷收支主要指标时间序列表

Time Series of Major Indicators in Sources and Uses of Credit Funds of Policy Banks (RMB)

年　月 Year Month		各项存款 Total Deposits	企业存款 Deposits by Enterprises	储蓄存款 Savings Deposits	活期储蓄 Demand Deposits	定期储蓄 Time Deposits	农业存款 Deposits by Agricultural Sector
期末余额（亿元）Balance (100 Million Yuan)							
2000	1	325.44	317.44				
	2	325.89	317.76				
	3	335.55	327.56				
	4	349.45	339.80				
	5	397.82	387.30				
	6	365.24	353.46				
	7	411.34	395.75				
	8	423.52	408.69				
	9	432.63	426.27				
	10	456.17	450.63				
	11	484.73	480.10				
	12	531.56	526.59				
比上期增减额（亿元）Changes Compared with Previous Period (100 Million Yuan)							
2000	1	-50.90	-50.60				
	2	0.45	0.32				
	3	9.66	9.80				
	4	13.90	12.24				
	5	48.37	47.50				
	6	-32.58	-33.84				
	7	46.10	42.29				
	8	12.18	12.94				
	9	9.11	17.58				
	10	23.54	24.36				
	11	28.56	29.47				
	12	46.83	46.49				
比去年同期增长（%）Increase Rate Year-on-year (%)							
2000	1	78.18	84.75				
	2	114.92	125.78				
	3	135.09	157.84				
	4	156.93	156.47				
	5	113.90	112.14				
	6	33.19	30.80				
	7	54.22	51.61				
	8	72.19	71.09				
	9	66.54	68.29				
	10	52.76	55.03				
	11	36.23	37.40				
	12	41.24	43.07				

政策性银行人民币信贷收支主要指标时间序列表

Time Series of Major Indicators in Sources and Uses of Credit Funds of Policy Banks（RMB）

年 Year	月 Month	各项贷款 Total Loans	短期贷款 Short-term Loans	工业贷款 Loans to Industrial Sector	商业贷款 Loans to Commercial Sector	建筑业贷款 Loans to Construction Sector	农业贷款 Loans to Agricultural Sector	贴现 Discount	中长期贷款 Medium and Long-term Loans	基本建设贷款 Capital Construction Loans	技术改造贷款 Technical Improvement Loans	其他中长期贷款 Other Medium and Long-term Loans	有价证券及投资 Securities and Investments
期末余额（亿元） Balance（100 Million Yuan）													
2000	1	12868.78	7328.17		7219.17				5449.26	4867.12	105.64	476.50	47.96
	2	12856.61	7292.45		7186.35				5475.56	4899.64	106.48	469.44	47.96
	3	12987.60	7262.61		7167.12				5631.96	5051.51	106.23	474.22	47.96
	4	13035.77	7234.43		7134.08				5714.23	5136.09	105.12	473.02	47.96
	5	13064.51	7174.33		7075.53				5799.19	5222.53	104.79	471.87	47.96
	6	13127.29	7134.64		7042.76				5895.48	5299.23	108.25	488.00	47.96
	7	13227.27	7145.16		7056.01				5982.81	5394.78	108.28	479.75	47.96
	8	13287.84	7139.44		7055.66				6051.02	5450.95	110.19	489.88	47.96
	9	13477.53	7151.75		7076.98				6208.79	5612.51	108.61	487.67	48.16
	10	13595.40	7153.88		7077.01				6325.38	5717.60	110.21	497.57	48.16
	11	13786.04	7251.28		7166.91				6398.26	5775.42	111.45	511.39	48.16
	12	14149.87	7374.57		7303.69				6668.95	5956.25	117.08	595.62	52.43
比上期增减额（亿元） Changes Compared with Previous Period（100 Million Yuan）													
2000	1	32.60	32.20		30.99				6.01	8.55	1.02	-3.56	
	2	-10.45	-35.72		-32.82				27.60	33.51	1.15	-7.06	
	3	130.99	-29.84		-19.23				156.40	151.86	-0.25	4.79	
	4	48.14	-28.18		-33.04				82.25	84.58	-1.12	-1.21	
	5	28.74	-60.10		-58.55				84.96	86.44	-0.32	-1.16	
	6	63.22	-39.69		-32.77				96.60	77.00	3.46	16.14	
	7	99.98	10.52		13.25				87.32	95.55	0.02	-8.25	
	8	60.59	-5.72		-0.35				68.23	56.17	1.92	10.14	
	9	189.67	12.31		21.32				157.76	161.56	-1.58	-2.22	0.2
	10	117.88	2.13		0.03				116.59	105.09	1.60	9.90	
	11	190.65	97.40		89.90				72.89	57.82	1.24	13.83	
	12	363.82	123.29		136.78				270.68	180.83	5.63	84.22	4.27
比去年同期增长（%） Increase Rate Year-on-year（%）													
2000	1	12.41	3.97		3.33				22.22	23.52	-11.81	20.82	13222.22
	2	12.34	3.94		3.34				22.06	23.57	-11.26	18.02	13222.22
	3	13.17	4.43		4.00				23.07	24.91	-10.59	15.35	13222.22
	4	14.39	6.15		5.61				23.58	25.60	-7.96	12.72	13222.22
	5	15.10	6.21		5.67				25.15	26.63	2.42	15.77	13222.22
	6	13.57	4.81		4.41				23.18	23.92	3.24	21.08	13222.22
	7	13.69	4.60		4.27				23.85	24.56	2.11	22.58	13222.22
	8	13.47	4.43		4.21				23.57	23.96	3.28	25.70	13222.22
	9	13.32	3.84		4.02				23.62	24.39	3.47	20.70	13277.78
	10	12.73	3.23		3.42				23.66	24.24	5.02	22.51	13277.78
	11	11.63	2.54		2.52				22.84	23.07	10.48	23.79	13277.78
	12	10.05	1.08		1.61				21.74	21.75	11.21	24.07	14463.89

政策性银行人民币信贷收支主要指标时间序列表

Time Series of Major Indicators in Sources and Uses of Credit Funds of Policy Banks (RMB)

年 月 Year Month		各项存款 Total Deposits	企业存款 Deposits by Enterprises	储蓄存款 Savings Deposits	活期储蓄 Demand Deposits	定期储蓄 Time Deposits	农业存款 Deposits by Agricultural Sector
		期末余额（亿元）Balance (100 Million Yuan)					
2001	1	459.61	456.60				
	2	455.62	451.80				
	3	394.39	391.35				
	4	400.99	398.37				
	5	399.27	396.23				
	6	395.44	392.20				
	7	403.80	401.17				
	8	435.54	433.28				
	9	436.49	434.05				
	10	449.24	446.99				
	11	485.63	482.60				
	12	552.38	549.27				
		比上期增减额（亿元）Changes Compared with Previous Period (100 Million Yuan)					
2001	1	-71.94	-69.97				
	2	-3.99	-4.80				
	3	-61.23	-60.45				
	4	6.60	7.02				
	5	-1.72	-2.14				
	6	-3.83	-4.03				
	7	8.36	8.97				
	8	31.74	32.11				
	9	0.95	0.77				
	10	12.75	12.94				
	11	36.39	35.61				
	12	66.75	66.67				
		比去年同期增长（%）Increase Rate Year-on-year (%)					
2001	1	41.23	43.84				
	2	39.81	42.18				
	3	17.54	19.47				
	4	14.75	17.24				
	5	0.36	2.31				
	6	8.27	10.96				
	7	-1.83	1.37				
	8	2.84	6.02				
	9	0.89	1.83				
	10	-1.52	-0.81				
	11	0.19	0.52				
	12	3.92	4.31				

政策性银行人民币信贷收支主要指标时间序列表

Time Series of Major Indicators in Sources and Uses of Credit Funds of Policy Banks（RMB）

年　月 Year Month	各项贷款 Total Loans	短期贷款 Short－term Loans	工业贷款 Loans to Industrial Sector	商业贷款 Loans to Commercial Sector	建筑业贷款 Loans to Construction Sector	农业贷款 Loans to Agricultural Sector	中长期贷款 Medium and Long－term Loans	基本建设贷款 Capital Construction Loans	技术改造贷款 Technical Improvement Loans	其他中长期贷款 Other Medium and Long－term Loans	票据融资 Paper Financing	有价证券及投资 Securities and Investments
期末余额（亿元） Balance（100 Million Yuan）												
2001　1	14270.22	7351.18		7285.62			6919.04	6009.65	125.58	783.81		83.93
2	14253.46	7289.66		7222.62			6963.80	6051.66	122.42	789.72		93.34
3	14243.19	7178.07		7098.73			7065.12	6135.65	123.01	806.46		93.34
4	14256.30	7098.53		7002.88			7157.77	6219.28	126.59	811.90		105.57
5	14250.66	7051.06		6946.91			7199.6	6263.96	127.35	808.29		105.57
6	14340.91	7048.38		6936.63			7292.53	6338.80	128.61	825.12		105.57
7	14455.07	7050.27		6951.39			7404.79	6448.54	123.84	832.41	0.01	104.42
8	14575.19	7018.46		6911.94			7556.72	6577.41	124.69	854.62	0.01	110.89
9	14738.25	7050.37		6920.70			7687.88	6704.64	124.16	859.08		110.89
10	14668.81	7091.17		6962.97			7577.64	6603.89	119.05	854.70		122.17
11	14912.55	7250.26		7123.33			7662.29	6697.42	120.20	844.67		76.07
12	15218.91	7431.85		7301.40			7787.06	6766.48	119.21	901.37		1369.31
比上期增减额（亿元） Changes Compared with Previous Period（100 Million Yuan）												
2001　1	－38.03	－25.07		－18.34			－1.49	－5.50	0.49	3.52		31.5
2	－16.76	－61.52		－63.00			44.76	42.01	－3.16	5.91		9.41
3	－10.27	－111.59		－123.89			101.32	83.99	0.59	16.74		
4	13.11	－79.54		－95.85			92.65	83.63	3.58	5.44		12.23
5	－5.64	－47.47		－55.97			41.83	44.68	0.76	－3.61		
6	90.25	－2.68		－10.28			92.93	74.84	1.26	16.83		
7	114.16	1.89		14.76			112.26	109.74	－4.77	7.29	0.01	－1.15
8	120.12	－31.81		－39.45			151.93	128.87	0.85	22.21		6.47
9	163.05	31.91		8.76			131.16	127.23	－0.53	4.46	－0.01	
10	－69.44	40.80		42.27			－110.24	－100.75	－5.11	－4.38		11.28
11	243.74	159.09		160.36			84.65	93.53	1.15	－10.03		－46.1
12	306.36	181.59		178.07			124.77	69.06	－0.99	56.70		1293.24
比去年同期增长（%） Increase Rate Year－on－year（%）												
2001　1	9.46	0.31		0.92			23.17	23.47	18.88	21.59		75.00
2	9.44	－0.04		0.50			23.40	23.51	14.97	23.92		94.62
3	8.27	－1.16		－0.95			21.82	21.47	15.80	25.64		94.62
4	7.97	－1.88		－1.84			21.69	21.10	20.42	26.74		120.12
5	7.70	－1.72		－1.82			20.67	19.95	21.53	26.49		120.12
6	7.88	－1.21		－1.51			20.31	19.62	18.81	26.18		120.12
7	7.93	－1.33		－1.48			20.43	19.53	14.38	28.96		117.72
8	8.23	－1.69		－2.04			21.29	20.67	13.16	27.71		131.21
9	8.09	－1.42		－2.21			20.77	19.46	14.32	33.25		130.25
10	6.68	－0.88		－1.61			16.94	15.50	8.02	31.10		153.68
11	6.69	－0.01		－0.61			16.98	15.96	7.85	27.38		57.95
12	6.54	0.78		－0.03			14.26	13.60	1.82	21.49		2511.69

政策性银行人民币信贷收支主要指标时间序列表

Time Series of Major Indicators in Sources and Uses of Credit Funds of Policy Banks (RMB)

年 月 Year Month		各项存款 Total Deposits	企业存款 Deposits by Enterprises	储蓄存款 Savings Deposits	活期储蓄 Demand Deposits	定期储蓄 Time Deposits	农业存款 Deposits by Agricultural Sector
期末余额（亿元）Balance (100 Million Yuan)							
2002	1	469.90	466.94				
	2	440.58	438.53				
	3	471.18	468.19				
	4	473.27	469.30				
	5	492.76	487.64				
	6	539.52	534.01				
	7	540.36	533.41				
	8	543.06	536.54				
	9	563.33	557.09				
	10	602.02	597.90				
	11	596.87	592.63				
	12	711.26	706.08				
比上期增减额（亿元）Changes Compared with Previous Period (100 Million Yuan)							
2002	1	-82.56	-82.37				
	2	-29.32	-28.41				
	3	30.60	29.66				
	4	2.09	1.11				
	5	19.49	18.34				
	6	46.76	46.37				
	7	0.84	-0.60				
	8	2.70	3.13				
	9	20.27	20.55				
	10	38.69	40.81				
	11	-5.15	-5.27				
	12	114.39	113.45				
比去年同期增长（%）Increase Rate Year-on-year (%)							
2002	1	2.24	2.26				
	2	-3.30	-2.94				
	3	19.47	19.63				
	4	18.03	17.81				
	5	23.42	23.07				
	6	36.44	36.16				
	7	33.82	32.96				
	8	24.69	23.83				
	9	29.06	28.35				
	10	34.01	33.76				
	11	22.91	22.80				
	12	28.76	28.55				

政策性银行人民币信贷收支主要指标时间序列表

Time Series of Major Indicators in Sources and Uses of Credit Funds of Policy Banks（RMB）

年 月 Year Month		各项贷款 Total Loans	短期贷款 Short－term Loans					中长期贷款 Medium and Long－term Loans				票据融资 Paper Financing	有价证券及投资 Securities and Investments
				工业贷款 Loans to Industrial Sector	商业贷款 Loans to Commercial Sector	建筑业贷款 Loans to Construction Sector	农业贷款 Loans to Agricultural Sector		基本建设贷款 Capital Construction Loans	技术改造贷款 Technical Improvement Loans	其他中长期贷款 Other Medium and Long－term Loans		
期末余额（亿元） Balance（100 Million Yuan）													
2002	1	15296.78	7487.84		7349.28			7808.94	6781.32	120.35	907.27		1371.41
	2	15323.57	7476.93		7340.76			7846.64	6818.81	124.49	903.34		1371.41
	3	15416.88	7448.73		7326.67			7968.15	6933.74	127.69	906.72		1377.04
	4	15379.10	7374.40		7241.89			8004.70	6984.73	132.18	887.79		1383.95
	5	15349.21	7292.66		7155.49			8056.55	7023.61	134.43	898.51		1383.95
	6	15612.99	7276.89		7130.32			8336.10	7257.30	140.04	938.76		1389.57
	7	15707.45	7299.09		7145.16			8408.33	7342.72	142.75	922.86	0.03	1384.23
	8	15783.16	7269.03		7107.07			8514.09	7442.19	146.68	925.22	0.04	1407.03
	9	15981.61	7297.15		7116.89			8684.43	7595.39	154.63	934.41	0.03	1413.33
	10	16122.08	7332.70		7145.10			8789.36	7692.52	156.27	940.57	0.02	1410.13
	11	16085.02	7344.69		7147.88			8740.31	7648.63	151.31	940.37	0.02	1410.13
	12	16605.94	7496.42		7212.18			9109.52	7979.69	156.17	973.66		1412.90
比上期增减额（亿元） Changes Compared with Previous Period（100 Million Yuan）													
2002	1	64.92	55.99		61.67			8.93	14.84	1.14	－7.05		2.10
	2	26.79	－10.91		－8.52			37.70	37.49	4.14	－3.93		
	3	93.31	－28.20		－14.09			121.51	114.93	3.20	3.38		5.63
	4	－37.78	－74.33		－84.78			36.55	50.99	4.49	－18.93		6.91
	5	－29.89	－81.74		－86.40			51.85	38.88	2.25	10.72		
	6	263.78	－15.77		－25.17			279.55	233.69	5.61	40.25		5.62
	7	94.46	22.20		14.84			72.23	85.42	2.71	－15.90	0.03	－5.34
	8	75.71	－30.06		－38.09			105.76	99.47	3.93	2.36	0.01	22.80
	9	198.45	28.12		9.82			170.34	153.20	7.95	9.19	－0.01	6.30
	10	140.47	35.55		28.21			104.93	97.13	1.64	6.16	－0.01	－3.20
	11	－37.06	11.99		2.78			－49.05	－43.89	－4.96	－0.20		
	12	520.92	151.73		64.30			369.21	331.06	4.86	33.29	－0.02	2.77
比去年同期增长（%） Increase Rate Year－on－year（%）													
2002	1	7.19	1.86		0.87			12.86	12.84	－4.16	15.75		1533.99
	2	7.51	2.57		1.64			12.68	12.68	1.69	14.39		1369.26
	3	8.24	3.77		3.21			12.78	13.01	3.80	12.43		1375.29
	4	7.88	3.89		3.41			11.83	12.31	4.42	9.35		1210.93
	5	7.71	3.43		3.00			11.90	12.13	5.56	11.16		1210.93
	6	8.87	3.24		2.79			14.31	14.49	8.89	13.77		1216.25
	7	8.66	3.53		2.79			13.55	13.87	15.27	10.86	200.00	1225.64
	8	8.29	3.57		2.82			12.67	13.15	17.64	8.26	300.00	1168.85
	9	8.44	3.50		2.83			12.96	13.29	24.54	8.77		1174.53
	10	9.91	3.41		2.62			15.99	16.48	31.26	10.05		1054.24
	11	7.86	1.30		0.34			14.07	14.20	25.88	11.33		1753.73
	12	9.11	0.87		－1.22			16.98	17.93	31.00	8.02		3.18

政策性银行人民币信贷收支主要指标时间序列表

Time Series of Major Indicators in Sources and Uses of Credit Funds of Policy Banks（RMB）

年　月 Year Month		各项存款 Total Deposits	企业存款 Deposits by Enterprises	储蓄存款 Savings Deposits	活期储蓄 Demand Deposits	定期储蓄 Time Deposits	农业存款 Deposits by Agricultural Sector
期末余额（亿元） Balance（100 Million Yuan）							
2003	1	561.38	557.07				
	2	583.03	578.74				
	3	585.37	580.46				
	4	566.47	560.26				
	5	594.90	588.36				
	6	756.34	750.42				
	7	722.81	716.66				
	8	775.13	770.81				
	9	876.13	866.77				
	10	887.48	878.07				
	11	912.87	903.82				
	12	948.83	939.45				
比上期增减额（亿元） Changes Compared with Previous Period（100 Million Yuan）							
2003	1	-149.89	-148.97				
	2	21.65	21.67				
	3	2.34	1.72				
	4	-18.90	-20.20				
	5	28.43	28.10				
	6	161.44	162.06				
	7	-33.53	-33.76				
	8	52.32	54.15				
	9	101.00	95.96				
	10	11.35	11.30				
	11	25.39	25.75				
	12	35.96	35.63				
比去年同期增长（%） Increase Rate Year-on-year（%）							
2003	1	19.47	19.30				
	2	32.33	31.97				
	3	24.23	23.98				
	4	19.69	19.38				
	5	20.73	20.65				
	6	40.19	40.53				
	7	33.76	34.35				
	8	42.73	43.66				
	9	55.53	55.59				
	10	47.42	46.86				
	11	52.94	52.51				
	12	33.40	33.05				

政策性银行人民币信贷收支主要指标时间序列表

Time Series of Major Indicators in Sources and Uses of Credit Funds of Policy Banks（RMB）

年　月 Year Month		各项贷款 Total Loans	短期贷款 Short - term Loans	工业贷款 Loans to Industrial Sector	商业贷款 Loans to Commercial Sector	建筑业贷款 Loans to Construction Sector	农业贷款 Loans to Agricultural Sector	中长期贷款 Medium and Long - term Loans	基本建设贷款 Capital Construction Loans	技术改造贷款 Technical Improvement Loans	其他中长期贷款 Other Medium and Long - term Loans	票据融资 Paper Financing	有价证券及投资 Securities and Investments
期末余额（亿元） Balance（100 Million Yuan）													
2003	1	16546.37	7509.86		7227.58			9036.51	7931.63	157.92	946.96		1428.34
	2	16576.89	7460.26		7187.96			9116.63	8003.42	161.10	952.11		1439.25
	3	16794.78	7374.97		7099.51			9419.81	8286.01	165.70	968.10		1310.20
	4	16748.26	7300.36		6986.13			9447.90	8339.37	170.35	938.18		1306.61
	5	16721.59	7252.00		6884.14			9469.59	8355.96	169.65	943.98		1306.62
	6	17263.79	7269.43		6860.61			9994.36	8754.69	175.73	1063.94		1308.01
	7	17361.12	7256.15		6823.12			10104.97	8856.69	178.57	1069.71		1362.89
	8	17590.60	7259.47		6789.83			10331.13	9064.11	180.12	1086.90		1334.28
	9	18000.13	7278.80		6762.27			10721.33	9271.30	183.86	1266.17		1305.36
	10	18144.45	7293.05		6736.63			10851.34	9364.27	185.42	1301.65	0.06	1354.72
	11	18101.73	7213.14		6706.51			10888.53	9347.94	182.68	1357.91	0.06	1390.90
	12	18489.81	7243.38		6747.48			11246.32	9584.14	182.20	1479.98	0.11	1350.50
比上期增减额（亿元） Changes Compared with Previous Period（100 Million Yuan）													
2003	1	- 59.58	13.43		15.39			- 73.01	- 48.06	1.75	- 26.7		15.44
	2	30.52	- 49.60		- 39.62			80.12	71.79	3.18	5.15		10.91
	3	217.89	- 85.29		- 88.45			303.18	282.59	4.60	15.99		- 129.05
	4	- 46.52	- 74.61		- 113.38			28.09	53.36	4.65	- 29.92		- 3.59
	5	- 26.67	- 48.36		- 101.99			21.69	16.59	- 0.70	5.80		0.01
	6	542.20	17.43		- 23.53			524.77	398.73	6.08	119.96		1.39
	7	97.33	- 13.28		- 37.49			110.61	102.00	2.84	5.77		54.88
	8	229.48	3.32		- 33.29			226.16	207.42	1.55	17.19		- 28.61
	9	409.53	19.33		- 27.56			390.20	207.19	3.74	179.27		- 28.92
	10	144.32	14.25		- 25.64			130.01	92.97	1.56	35.48	0.06	49.36
	11	- 42.72	- 79.91		- 30.12			37.19	- 16.33	- 2.74	56.26		36.18
	12	388.08	30.24		40.97			357.79	236.20	- 0.48	122.07	0.05	- 40.40
比去年同期增长（%） Increase Rate Year - on - year（%）													
2003	1	8.17	0.29		- 1.66			15.72	16.96	31.22	4.37		4.15
	2	8.18	- 0.22		- 2.08			16.19	17.37	29.41	5.40		4.95
	3	8.94	- 0.99		- 3.10			18.22	19.50	29.77	6.77		- 4.85
	4	8.90	- 1.00		- 3.53			18.03	19.39	28.88	5.68		- 5.59
	5	8.94	- 0.56		- 3.79			17.54	18.97	26.20	5.06		- 5.59
	6	10.57	- 0.10		- 3.78			19.89	20.63	25.49	13.33		- 5.87
	7	10.53	- 0.59		- 4.51			20.18	20.62	25.09	15.91	- 100.00	- 1.54
	8	11.45	- 0.13		- 4.46			21.34	21.79	22.80	17.47	- 100.00	- 5.17
	9	12.63	- 0.25		- 4.98			23.45	22.06	18.90	35.50	- 100.00	- 7.64
	10	12.54	- 0.54		- 5.72			23.46	21.73	18.65	38.39	200.00	- 3.93
	11	12.54	- 1.79		- 6.17			24.58	22.22	20.73	44.40	200.00	- 1.36
	12	11.34	- 3.38		- 6.44			23.46	20.11	16.67	52.00		- 4.42

政策性银行人民币信贷收支主要指标时间序列表

Time Series of Major Indicators in Sources and Uses of Credit Funds of Policy Banks（RMB）

年　月 Year Month	各项存款 Total Deposits	企业存款 Deposits by Enterprises	储蓄存款 Savings Deposits	活期储蓄 Demand Deposits	定期储蓄 Time Deposits	农业存款 Deposits by Agricultural Sector
期末余额（亿元） Balance（100 Million Yuan）						
2004　1	791.28	782.08				
2	788.78	780.02				
3	824.82	816.65				
4	795.27	788.23				
5	790.38	784.64				
6	1051.60	1046.12				
7	908.21	903.57				
8	889.91	886.70				
9	889.80	888.09				
10	966.52	963.41				
11	1128.66	1126.06				
12	1250.48	1248.30				
比上期增减额（亿元） Changes Compared with Previous Period（100 Million Yuan）						
2004　1	-157.78	-157.37				
2	-2.50	-2.06				
3	36.04	36.63				
4	-29.55	-28.42				
5	-4.89	-3.59				
6	261.22	261.48				
7	-143.39	-142.55				
8	-18.30	-16.87				
9	-0.11	1.39				
10	76.72	75.32				
11	162.14	162.65				
12	121.82	122.24				
比去年同期增长（%） Increase Rate Year-on-year（%）						
2004　1	40.95	40.39				
2	35.29	34.78				
3	40.91	40.69				
4	40.39	40.69				
5	32.86	33.36				
6	39.04	39.40				
7	25.65	26.08				
8	14.81	15.03				
9	1.56	2.46				
10	8.91	9.72				
11	23.64	24.59				
12	31.79	32.88				

政策性银行人民币信贷收支主要指标时间序列表

Time Series of Major Indicators in Sources and Uses of Credit Funds of Policy Banks（RMB）

年 月 Year Month	各项贷款 Total Loans	短期贷款 Short－term Loans	工业贷款 Loans to Industrial Sector	商业贷款 Loans to Commercial Sector	建筑业贷款 Loans to Construction Sector	农业贷款 Loans to Agricultural Sector	中长期贷款 Medium and Long－term Loans	基本建设贷款 Capital Construction Loans	技术改造贷款 Technical Improvement Loans	其他中长期贷款 Other Medium and Long－term Loans	票据融资 Paper Financing	有价证券及投资 Securities and Investments
期末余额（亿元） Balance（100 Million Yuan）												
2004 1	18560.54	7263.25		6779.88			11297.23	9665.80	175.61	1455.82	0.06	1372.08
2	18578.51	7233.52		6759.90			11344.91	9713.83	179.28	1451.80	0.08	1403.92
3	18786.35	7222.91		6754.70			11563.32	9889.75	182.74	1490.83	0.12	1445.48
4	18775.56	7178.04		6695.93			11597.29	9912.70	179.10	1505.49	0.23	1450.65
5	18798.76	7136.63		6657.28			11661.88	9961.48	176.25	1524.15	0.25	1451.65
6	19377.19	7242.02		6715.25			12134.97	10326.24	179.28	1629.45	0.20	1410.93
7	19463.93	7278.33		6752.89			12185.25	10340.77	179.58	1664.90	0.35	1427.64
8	19579.24	7307.82		6768.38			12271.04	10408.36	181.51	1681.17	0.38	1390.97
9	19612.01	7396.58		6825.13			12214.97	10282.37	183.26	1749.34	0.46	1532.72
10	20001.69	7502.88		6923.30			12498.33	10513.97	184.20	1800.16	0.48	1446.40
11	20458.10	7663.20		7056.96			12794.42	10735.40	179.61	1879.41	0.48	1517.48
12	21201.42	7754.59		7019.02			13446.17	11186.87	183.65	2075.65	0.66	1444.85
比上期增减额（亿元） Changes Compared with Previous Period（100 Million Yuan）												
2004 1	70.73	19.87		32.40			50.91	81.66	－6.59	－24.16	－0.05	21.58
2	17.97	－29.73		－19.98			47.68	48.03	3.67	－4.02	0.02	31.84
3	207.84	－10.61		－5.20			218.41	175.92	3.46	39.03	0.04	41.56
4	－10.79	－44.87		－58.77			33.97	22.95	－3.64	14.66	0.11	5.17
5	23.20	－41.41		－38.65			64.59	48.78	－2.85	18.66	0.02	1.00
6	578.43	105.39		57.97			473.09	364.76	3.03	105.30	－0.05	－40.72
7	86.74	36.31		37.64			50.28	14.53	0.30	35.45	0.15	16.71
8	115.31	29.49		15.49			85.79	67.59	1.93	16.27	0.03	－36.67
9	32.77	88.76		56.75			－56.07	－125.99	1.75	68.17	0.08	141.75
10	389.68	106.30		98.17			283.36	231.60	0.94	50.82	0.02	－86.32
11	456.41	160.32		133.66			296.09	221.43	－4.59	79.25		71.08
12	743.32	91.39		－37.94			651.75	451.47	4.04	196.24	0.18	－72.63
比去年同期增长（%） Increase Rate Year－on－year（%）												
2004 1	12.17	－3.28		－6.19			25.02	21.86	11.20	53.74	—	－3.94
2	12.07	－3.04		－5.96			24.44	21.37	11.28	52.48	—	－2.45
3	11.86	－2.06		－4.86			22.76	19.35	10.28	54.00	—	10.33
4	12.10	－1.68		－4.15			22.75	18.87	5.14	60.47	—	11.02
5	12.42	－1.59		－3.30			23.15	19.21	3.89	61.46	—	11.10
6	12.24	－0.38		－2.12			21.42	17.95	2.02	53.15	—	7.87
7	12.11	0.31		－1.03			20.59	16.76	0.57	55.64	—	4.75
8	11.31	0.67		－0.32			18.78	14.83	0.77	54.68	—	4.25
9	8.95	1.62		0.93			13.93	10.91	－0.33	38.16	—	17.42
10	10.24	2.88		2.77			15.18	12.28	－0.66	38.30	700.00	6.77
11	13.02	6.24		5.23			17.50	14.84	－1.68	38.40	700.00	9.10
12	14.67	7.06		4.02			19.56	16.72	0.80	40.25	500.00	6.99

政策性银行人民币信贷收支主要指标时间序列表

Time Series of Major Indicators in Sources and Uses of Credit Funds of Policy Banks (RMB)

年　月 Year Month		各项存款 Total Deposits	企业存款 Deposits by Enterprises	储蓄存款 Savings Deposits	活期储蓄 Demand Deposits	定期储蓄 Time Deposits	农业存款 Deposits by Agricultural Sector
期末余额（亿元） Balance (100 Million Yuan)							
2005	1	1087.35	1086.16				
	2	1033.15	1031.18				
	3	1135.23	1133.05				
	4	1111.20	1109.01				
	5	1225.55	1222.98				
	6	1495.91	1492.56				
	7	1326.86	1323.73				
	8	1332.87	1329.67				
	9	1392.06	1388.66				
	10	1478.40	1475.22				
	11	1563.00	1560.03				
	12	1605.40	1603.40				
比上期增减额（亿元） Changes Compared with Previous Period (100 Million Yuan)							
2005	1	-163.13	-162.14				
	2	-54.20	-54.98				
	3	102.08	101.87				
	4	-24.03	-24.04				
	5	114.35	113.97				
	6	270.36	269.58				
	7	-169.05	-168.83				
	8	6.01	5.94				
	9	59.19	58.99				
	10	86.34	86.56				
	11	84.60	84.81				
	12	42.40	43.37				
比去年同期增长（%） Increase Rate Year-on-year (%)							
2005	1	37.42	38.88				
	2	30.98	32.20				
	3	37.63	38.74				
	4	39.73	40.70				
	5	55.06	55.87				
	6	42.25	42.68				
	7	46.10	46.50				
	8	49.78	49.96				
	9	56.45	56.36				
	10	52.96	53.12				
	11	38.48	38.54				
	12	28.38	28.45				

政策性银行人民币信贷收支主要指标时间序列表

Time Series of Major Indicators in Sources and Uses of Credit Funds of Policy Banks（RMB）

年 月 Year Month	各项贷款 Total Loans	短期贷款 Short－term Loans					中长期贷款 Medium and Long－term Loans				票据融资 Paper Financing	有价证券及投资 Securities and Investments
			工业贷款 Loans to Industrial Sector	商业贷款 Loans to Commercial Sector	建筑业贷款 Loans to Construction Sector	农业贷款 Loans to Agricultural Sector		基本建设贷款 Capital Construction Loans	技术改造贷款 Technical Improvement Loans	其他中长期贷款 Other Medium and Long－term Loans		
期末余额（亿元） Balance（100 Million Yuan）												
2005 1	21298.48	7751.25		7032.33			13546.66	11260.34	183.38	2102.94	0.57	1431.79
2	21384.84	7776.43		7010.72			13608.01	11287.85	185.81	2134.35	0.40	1356.02
3	21767.83	7867.73		7018.20			13899.79	11491.67	188.48	2219.64	0.31	1345.84
4	21915.09	7919.67		7020.20			13995.13	11526.89	192.17	2276.07	0.29	1368.81
5	22072.29	7949.50		6981.79			14122.51	11585.72	187.53	2349.26	0.28	1358.77
6	22919.33	8222.11		7084.89			14696.92	11994.29	198.86	2503.77	0.30	1359.87
7	23002.92	8234.46		7106.17			14768.06	12054.52	199.35	2514.19	0.40	1317.34
8	23227.24	8299.81		7130.89			14926.93	12135.29	200.63	2591.01	0.50	1320.66
9	23756.71	8535.81		7262.92			15220.43	12301.96	204.11	2714.36	0.47	1254.47
10	24008.37	8651.34		7379.85			15356.53	12380.03	200.91	2775.59	0.50	1274.74
11	24275.24	8979.30		7640.81			15295.36	12240.39	192.66	2862.31	0.58	1348.43
12	24580.05	8869.19		7595.17			15710.28	12359.00	198.76	3152.52	0.58	1315.29
比上期增减额（亿元） Changes Compared with Previous Period（100 Million Yuan）												
2005 1	97.06	－3.34		13.31			100.49	73.47	－0.27	27.29	－0.09	－13.06
2	86.36	25.18		－21.61			61.35	27.51	2.43	31.41	－0.17	－75.77
3	382.99	91.30		7.48			291.78	203.82	2.67	85.29	－0.09	－10.18
4	147.26	51.94		2.00			95.34	35.22	3.69	56.43	－0.02	22.97
5	157.20	29.83		－38.41			127.38	58.83	－4.64	73.19	－0.01	－10.04
6	847.04	272.61		103.10			574.41	408.57	11.33	154.51	0.02	1.10
7	83.59	12.35		21.28			71.14	60.23	0.49	10.42	0.1	－42.53
8	224.32	65.35		24.72			158.87	80.77	1.28	76.82	0.1	3.32
9	529.47	236.00		132.03			293.50	166.67	3.48	123.35	－0.03	－66.19
10	251.66	115.53		116.93			136.10	78.07	－3.20	61.23	0.03	20.27
11	266.87	327.96		260.96			－61.17	－139.64	－8.25	86.72	0.08	73.69
12	304.81	－110.11		－45.64			414.92	118.61	6.10	290.21		－33.14
比去年同期增长（%） Increase Rate Year－on－year（%）												
2005 1	14.75	6.72		3.72			19.91	16.50	4.42	44.45	850.00	4.35
2	15.11	7.51		3.71			19.95	16.20	3.64	47.01	400.00	－3.41
3	15.87	8.93		3.90			20.21	16.20	3.14	48.89	158.33	－6.89
4	16.72	10.33		4.84			20.68	16.28	7.30	51.18	26.09	－5.64
5	17.41	11.39		4.87			21.10	16.31	6.40	54.14	12.00	－6.40
6	18.28	13.53		5.50			21.11	16.15	10.92	53.66	50.00	－3.62
7	18.18	13.14		5.23			21.20	16.57	11.01	51.01	14.29	－7.73
8	18.63	13.57		5.36			21.64	16.59	10.53	54.12	31.58	－5.05
9	21.13	15.40		6.41			24.60	19.64	11.38	55.16	2.17	－18.15
10	20.03	15.31		6.59			22.87	17.75	9.07	54.19	4.17	－11.87
11	18.66	17.17		8.27			19.55	14.02	7.27	52.30	20.83	－11.14
12	15.94	14.37		8.21			16.84	10.48	8.23	51.88	－12.12	－8.97

（四）国有商业银行人民币信贷收支主要指标时间序列表（1997—2005年月度时序）

Time Series of Major Indicators in Sources and Uses of Credit Funds of Stateowned Banks（RMB）（Monthly Series from 1997 to 2005）

国有商业银行人民币信贷收支主要指标时间序列表

Time Series of Major Indicators in Sources and Uses of Credit Funds of State - owned Banks（RMB）

年 月 Year Month		各项存款 Total Deposits	企业存款 Deposits by Enterprises	储蓄存款 Savings Deposits	活期储蓄 Demand Deposits	定期储蓄 Time Deposits	农业存款 Deposits by Agricultural Sector
		期末余额（亿元） Balance（100 Million Yuan）					
1997	1	42995.95	16110.67	26248.41	5153.92	21094.49	213.16
	2	44220.16	16254.93	27295.37	5404.62	21890.75	207.27
	3	45332.10	16879.65	27764.74	5835.12	21929.62	218.11
	4	46113.18	17184.10	28208.39	6122.66	22085.73	220.76
	5	46548.56	17615.15	28228.94	6068.43	22160.51	221.17
	6	47244.13	18132.56	28400.45	5995.71	22404.74	221.50
	7	47611.41	18164.73	28721.64	5908.78	22812.86	233.27
	8	48296.53	18427.20	29141.41	6071.44	23069.97	232.56
	9	48931.24	18935.96	29243.68	5951.15	23292.53	235.03
	10	49402.43	19030.14	29618.35	6023.00	23595.35	248.74
	11	49657.78	19055.31	29822.91	6135.49	23687.42	253.71
	12	51220.53	19701.47	30724.21	6930.99	23793.22	263.99
		比上期增减额（亿元） Changes Compared with Previous Period（100 Million Yuan）					
1997	1	-613.86	-858.69	292.41	42.18	250.23	-25.79
	2	1224.21	144.26	1046.96	250.70	796.26	-5.89
	3	1111.94	624.72	469.37	430.50	38.87	10.84
	4	781.08	304.45	443.65	287.54	156.11	2.65
	5	435.36	431.04	20.55	-54.23	74.78	0.41
	6	695.57	517.41	171.51	-72.72	244.23	0.33
	7	367.27	32.17	321.19	-86.93	408.12	11.77
	8	685.12	262.47	419.77	162.66	257.11	-0.71
	9	634.72	508.76	102.27	-120.29	222.56	2.47
	10	471.19	94.18	374.67	71.85	302.82	13.71
	11	255.36	25.18	204.56	112.49	92.07	4.97
	12	1562.73	646.16	901.29	795.49	105.80	10.28

国有商业银行人民币信贷收支主要指标时间序列表

Time Series of Major Indicators in Sources and Uses of Credit Funds of State - owned Banks（RMB）

年 月 Year Month		各项贷款 Total Loans	短期贷款 Short - term Loans	工业贷款 Loans to Industrial Sector	商业贷款 Loans to Commercial Sector	建筑业贷款 Loans to Construction Sector	农业贷款 Loans to Agricultural Sector	贴现 Discount	中长期贷款 Medium and Long - term Loans	基本建设贷款 Capital Construction Loans	技术改造贷款 Technical Improvement Loans	其他中长期贷款 Other Medium and Long - term Loans	有价证券及投资 Securities and Investments
		期末余额（亿元） Balance（100 Million Yuan）											
1997	1	39890.38	30974.98	12996.62	9020.07	1339.17	1246.91	336.19	8873.98	3734.72	4145.62	993.64	2886.55
	2	40041.32	31143.71	13084.58	9040.27	1341.32	1256.45	348.69	8846.46	3723.71	4141.35	981.40	2864.22
	3	40424.33	31478.12	13279.98	9028.63	1351.57	1292.32	371.02	8900.69	3758.56	4160.46	981.67	2883.78
	4	40763.37	31798.72	13383.88	9095.88	1360.28	1326.67	378.56	8918.29	3760.72	4166.05	991.52	2703.70
	5	41041.57	32108.28	13516.26	9154.39	1372.12	1343.57	378.15	8885.81	3767.86	4181.13	936.82	2717.28
	6	41578.20	32518.53	13728.80	9206.06	1390.10	1364.65	375.07	9016.89	3856.87	4227.91	932.11	2679.95
	7	41766.03	32711.84	13801.93	9265.13	1393.35	1371.67	357.77	9011.96	3849.01	4237.40	925.55	2712.12
	8	42062.30	32992.87	13928.98	9338.59	1404.02	1381.23	363.52	9029.38	3832.84	4280.14	916.40	2794.18
	9	42581.93	33422.91	14147.54	9430.82	1430.82	1414.23	352.54	9118.96	3844.25	4369.90	904.81	2768.99
	10	42928.18	33729.36	14309.40	9517.20	1438.03	1421.64	341.35	9159.05	3859.88	4393.32	905.85	2791.86
	11	43356.83	34095.13	14458.58	9606.68	1453.72	1433.56	352.07	9222.73	3904.30	4403.18	915.25	2744.72
	12	44823.69	35168.24	14904.16	9841.45	1501.86	1533.61	363.48	9619.53	4048.86	4608.54	962.13	2746.63
		比上期增减额（亿元） Changes Compared with Previous Period（100 Million Yuan）											
1997	1	7.29	153.69	60.17	30.31	- 14.51	13.74	50.67	- 150.32	- 32.05	- 68.92	- 49.35	- 85.78
	2	150.95	168.75	87.96	20.20	2.15	9.54	12.50	- 27.52	- 11.01	- 4.27	- 12.24	- 22.33
	3	382.99	334.39	195.40	- 11.64	10.25	35.87	22.33	54.23	34.85	19.11	0.27	19.56
	4	339.04	320.60	103.90	67.25	8.71	34.35	7.54	17.60	2.16	5.59	9.85	- 180.08
	5	278.16	309.56	132.38	58.51	11.84	16.90	- 0.41	- 32.48	7.14	15.08	- 54.70	13.58
	6	536.67	410.29	212.54	51.67	17.98	21.08	- 3.08	131.08	89.01	46.78	- 4.71	- 37.32
	7	187.83	193.30	73.13	59.07	3.25	7.02	- 17.30	- 4.93	- 7.86	9.49	- 6.56	32.16
	8	296.27	281.04	127.05	73.46	10.67	9.56	5.75	17.42	- 16.17	42.74	- 9.15	82.06
	9	519.62	430.04	218.56	92.23	26.80	33.00	- 10.98	89.58	11.41	89.76	- 11.59	- 25.19
	10	346.24	306.45	161.86	86.38	7.21	7.41	- 11.19	40.09	15.63	23.41	1.04	22.87
	11	428.67	365.77	149.18	89.48	15.69	11.92	10.72	63.68	44.42	9.86	9.40	- 47.14
	12	1466.86	1073.11	445.58	234.76	48.14	100.05	11.41	396.80	144.56	205.36	46.88	1.91

国有商业银行人民币信贷收支主要指标时间序列表
Time Series of Major Indicators in Sources and Uses of Credit Funds of State - owned Banks (RMB)

年 月 Year Month		各项存款 Total Deposits	企业存款 Deposits by Enterprises	储蓄存款 Savings Deposits	活期储蓄 Demand Deposits	定期储蓄 Time Deposits	农业存款 Deposits by Agricultural Sector
		期末余额(亿元) Balance (100 Million Yuan)					
1998	1	51041.88	18508.36	30762.22	6477.67	24284.55	239.19
	2	51868.51	18627.98	31436.68	6582.06	24854.62	239.08
	3	52856.67	19020.77	32003.39	6599.22	25404.17	244.93
	4	53391.09	19257.01	32249.89	6618.40	25631.49	241.25
	5	54319.62	19581.00	32793.96	6877.96	25916.00	240.14
	6	55037.39	20068.81	32901.00	6874.33	26026.67	245.70
	7	55997.51	20325.43	33554.76	7313.63	26241.13	248.24
	8	56777.23	20919.12	33635.04	7194.43	26440.61	256.63
	9	58360.21	21798.13	34237.34	7524.20	26713.14	266.76
	10	59014.26	21828.26	34744.29	7724.29	27020.00	277.30
	11	59924.02	22185.01	35256.83	7911.33	27345.50	287.58
	12	60378.85	22384.32	35376.75	7812.49	27564.26	300.62
		比上期增减额(亿元) Changes Compared with Previous Period (100 Million Yuan)					
1998	1	-1234.91	-1191.46	37.42	-451.06	488.48	-24.79
	2	826.64	119.61	674.46	104.39	570.07	-0.10
	3	988.16	392.78	566.70	17.15	549.55	5.85
	4	534.42	236.25	246.50	19.18	227.32	-3.68
	5	928.53	324.00	544.07	259.56	284.51	-1.12
	6	717.78	487.81	107.04	-3.63	110.67	5.57
	7	960.11	256.62	653.76	439.30	214.46	2.53
	8	779.73	593.69	80.28	-119.20	199.48	8.39
	9	1582.98	879.01	602.29	329.76	272.53	10.13
	10	654.04	30.13	506.96	200.10	306.86	10.54
	11	909.79	356.75	512.54	187.04	325.50	10.28
	12	454.83	199.31	119.93	-98.83	218.76	13.04
		比去年同期增长(%) Increase Rate Year-on-year (%)					
1998	1	16.36	14.88	17.20	25.68	15.12	12.21
	2	15.29	14.60	15.17	21.79	13.54	15.35
	3	14.59	12.68	15.27	13.09	15.84	12.30
	4	13.82	12.06	14.33	8.10	16.05	9.28
	5	14.72	11.16	16.17	13.34	16.95	8.58
	6	14.54	10.68	15.85	14.65	16.17	10.93
	7	15.57	11.89	16.83	23.78	15.03	6.42
	8	15.49	13.52	15.42	18.50	14.61	10.35
	9	17.15	15.12	17.08	26.43	14.69	13.50
	10	17.27	14.70	17.31	28.25	14.51	11.48
	11	18.41	16.42	18.22	28.94	15.44	13.35
	12	15.47	13.62	15.14	12.72	15.85	13.88

国有商业银行人民币信贷收支主要指标时间序列表

Time Series of Major Indicators in Sources and Uses of Credit Funds of State - owned Banks（RMB）

年 月 Year Month		各项贷款 Total Loans	短期贷款 Short - term Loans	工业贷款 Loans to Industrial Sector	商业贷款 Loans to Commercial Sector	建筑业贷款 Loans to Construction Sector	农业贷款 Loans to Agricultural Sector	贴现 Discount	中长期贷款 Medium and Long - term Loans	基本建设贷款 Capital Construction Loans	技术改造贷款 Technical Improvement Loans	其他中长期贷款 Other Medium and Long - term Loans	有价证券及投资 Securities and Investments
期末余额（亿元） Balance（100 Million Yuan）													
1998	1	44619.86	34299.14	14681.20	9750.45	1383.23	1510.52	373.24	10285.81	4379.27	4543.14	1363.40	2737.37
	2	44649.01	34319.57	14687.37	9747.92	1382.36	1515.84	366.86	10295.30	4369.39	4531.14	1394.77	2691.12
	3	45132.67	34761.34	14840.59	9785.34	1399.05	1535.61	372.33	10337.35	4312.05	4544.64	1480.66	2638.80
	4	45533.29	35077.06	14975.92	9815.96	1403.52	1556.16	379.00	10423.06	4325.05	4546.84	1551.17	2718.40
	5	47314.48	35448.05	15112.73	9870.73	1420.93	1571.69	385.82	11833.64	4706.94	4570.22	2556.48	2784.42
	6	48289.60	36030.79	15382.68	9962.75	1434.49	1638.34	401.08	12227.30	4845.74	4624.83	2756.73	2732.02
	7	48723.29	36297.75	15477.58	10006.88	1443.10	1656.57	401.97	12394.17	4940.97	4619.63	2833.56	2874.94
	8	49734.69	36861.27	15700.97	10126.40	1466.42	1680.63	399.83	12841.75	5081.18	4663.55	3097.02	5615.36
	9	50798.37	37482.71	15953.54	10260.25	1487.18	1725.22	396.73	13284.58	5284.11	4725.30	3275.17	6299.79
	10	51187.90	37604.56	15965.43	10290.73	1487.90	1728.86	368.90	13552.61	5358.48	4756.45	3437.68	6430.96
	11	51734.80	37805.34	16019.11	10437.49	1491.35	1729.27	346.77	13898.59	5510.56	4774.20	3613.83	6428.20
	12	53611.02	39128.48	16168.66	11427.53	1505.85	1780.05	338.45	14454.28	5789.37	4810.96	3853.95	6726.52
比上期增减额（亿元） Changes Compared with Previous Period（100 Million Yuan）													
1998	1	- 202.08	- 121.15	- 50.57	- 66.57	2.56	- 22.01	9.94	- 80.25	- 53.66	- 65.58	38.99	- 9.33
	2	29.15	20.43	6.17	- 2.53	- 0.87	5.32	- 6.38	9.49	- 9.88	- 12.00	31.37	- 46.25
	3	438.66	441.76	153.22	37.42	16.69	19.77	5.46	42.06	- 57.35	13.50	85.91	- 52.33
	4	384.71	299.82	135.33	30.62	4.47	20.55	6.67	85.70	13.00	2.20	70.50	79.60
	5	1781.21	371.01	136.81	54.77	17.41	15.54	6.83	1410.58	381.89	23.38	1005.31	66.02
	6	975.12	582.73	269.95	92.02	13.56	66.65	15.25	393.67	138.80	54.61	200.26	- 52.40
	7	433.69	266.97	94.90	44.13	8.62	18.22	0.89	166.86	95.23	- 5.20	76.83	142.92
	8	1011.39	563.51	223.39	119.52	23.31	24.06	- 2.14	447.58	140.20	43.92	263.46	2740.41
	9	1063.68	621.44	252.57	133.85	20.77	44.60	- 3.11	442.83	202.94	61.75	178.14	684.43
	10	389.50	121.83	11.89	30.48	0.71	3.64	- 27.83	268.02	74.36	31.14	162.52	131.17
	11	546.91	200.78	53.68	146.76	3.45	0.41	- 22.13	345.98	152.08	17.75	176.15	- 2.76
	12	1876.23	1323.15	149.55	990.04	14.5	50.78	- 8.32	555.69	278.81	36.76	240.12	298.32
比去年同期增长（%） Increase Rate Year - on - year（%）													
1998	1	11.86	10.73	12.96	8.10	3.29	21.14	11.02	15.91	17.26	9.59	37.21	- 5.17
	2	11.51	10.20	12.25	7.83	3.06	20.64	5.21	16.38	17.34	9.41	42.12	- 6.04
	3	11.65	10.43	11.75	8.38	3.51	18.83	0.35	16.14	14.73	9.23	50.83	- 8.50
	4	11.68	10.29	11.90	7.92	3.18	17.30	0.12	16.87	15.01	9.14	56.44	0.54
	5	15.26	10.38	11.81	7.83	3.56	16.98	2.03	33.17	24.92	9.31	172.89	2.47
	6	16.12	10.77	12.05	8.22	3.19	20.06	6.93	35.60	25.64	9.39	195.75	1.94
	7	16.63	10.93	12.14	8.01	3.57	20.77	12.35	37.53	28.37	9.02	206.15	6.00
	8	18.22	11.70	12.72	8.44	4.44	21.68	9.99	42.22	32.57	8.96	237.96	100.97
	9	19.27	12.12	12.77	8.79	3.94	21.99	12.53	45.68	37.45	8.13	261.97	127.51
	10	19.21	11.45	11.57	8.13	3.47	21.61	8.07	47.97	38.82	8.27	279.50	130.35
	11	19.29	10.84	10.79	8.65	2.59	20.63	- 1.51	50.70	41.14	8.43	294.85	134.20
	12	19.57	11.21	8.48	16.12	0.27	16.07	- 6.89	50.26	42.99	4.39	300.56	144.90

国有商业银行人民币信贷收支主要指标时间序列表
Time Series of Major Indicators in Sources and Uses of Credit Funds of State-owned Banks (RMB)

年 月 Year Month		各项存款 Total Deposits	企业存款 Deposits by Enterprises	储蓄存款 Savings Deposits	活期储蓄 Demand Deposits	定期储蓄 Time Deposits	农业存款 Deposits by Agricultural Sector
		期末余额（亿元） Balance (100 Million Yuan)					
1999	1	61213.25	22411.86	36180.13	8153.91	28026.22	304.56
	2	62180.62	21731.42	37959.45	8791.62	29167.83	267.06
	3	63984.69	22472.79	38698.23	8637.99	30060.24	278.32
	4	64651.46	22598.66	39180.65	8562.74	30617.91	295.02
	5	65510.50	22897.16	39651.88	8584.65	31067.23	292.91
	6	66266.31	23371.94	39726.52	8610.69	31115.83	291.84
	7	66067.19	23087.21	39744.83	8809.46	30935.38	293.04
	8	66952.74	23791.24	39781.35	9041.12	30740.23	303.43
	9	67807.71	24322.62	39912.74	9407.27	30505.47	305.66
	10	68076.21	24523.84	39864.96	9582.34	30282.62	320.66
	11	68537.31	24966.36	39748.44	9739.94	30008.50	338.76
	12	69324.91	25363.69	39885.84	10023.01	29862.83	342.09
		比上期增减额（亿元） Changes Compared with Previous Period (100 Million Yuan)					
1999	1	845.16	19.43	801.32	339.31	462.01	3.93
	2	967.41	-680.43	1779.32	637.71	1141.61	-37.49
	3	1804.06	741.37	738.78	-153.63	892.41	11.26
	4	666.76	125.87	482.42	-75.25	557.67	16.70
	5	859.05	298.50	471.23	21.91	449.32	-2.11
	6	755.80	474.78	74.63	26.03	48.60	-1.07
	7	-199.12	-284.73	18.32	198.77	-180.45	1.20
	8	885.56	704.04	36.51	231.67	-195.16	10.39
	9	854.96	531.37	131.39	366.15	-234.76	2.23
	10	268.50	201.22	-47.78	175.07	-222.85	15.00
	11	461.11	442.52	-116.51	157.60	-274.11	18.10
	12	787.59	397.32	137.40	283.07	-145.67	3.33
		比去年同期增长（%） Increase Rate Year-on-year (%)					
1999	1	20.22	21.09	17.61	25.88	15.41	27.33
	2	19.88	16.66	20.75	33.57	17.35	11.70
	3	21.05	18.15	20.92	30.89	18.33	13.63
	4	21.09	17.35	21.49	29.38	19.45	22.29
	5	20.60	16.94	20.91	24.81	19.88	21.97
	6	20.40	16.46	20.75	25.26	19.55	18.78
	7	17.98	13.59	18.45	20.45	17.89	18.05
	8	17.92	13.73	18.27	25.67	16.26	18.24
	9	16.19	11.58	16.58	25.03	14.20	14.58
	10	15.36	12.35	14.74	24.05	12.07	15.64
	11	14.37	12.54	12.74	23.11	9.74	17.80
	12	14.82	13.31	12.75	28.29	8.34	13.79

国有商业银行人民币信贷收支主要指标时间序列表
Time Series of Major Indicators in Sources and Uses of Credit Funds of State - owned Banks（RMB）

年 月 Year Month	各项贷款 Total Loans	短期贷款 Short - term Loans						中长期贷款 Medium and Long - term Loans				有价证券及投资 Securities and Investments
			工业贷款 Loans to Industrial Sector	商业贷款 Loans to Commercial Sector	建筑业贷款 Loans to Construction Sector	农业贷款 Loans to Agricultural Sector	贴现 Discount		基本建设贷款 Capital Construction Loans	技术改造贷款 Technical Improvement Loans	其他中长期贷款 Other Medium and Long - term Loans	
期末余额（亿元） Balance（100 Million Yuan）												
1999 1	53678.95	39250.25	16106.34	11493.10	1557.73	1765.57	350.98	14400.63	5735.76	4750.46	3914.41	6728.04
2	53994.71	39537.14	16194.03	11512.54	1563.48	1779.78	360.88	14429.96	5801.63	4744.18	3884.15	6724.68
3	54534.94	39858.77	16297.62	11515.94	1571.68	1800.15	363.33	14648.55	5905.58	4755.03	3987.94	6840.85
4	55022.04	40123.66	16357.97	11577.99	1581.27	1821.36	350.90	14870.93	5990.77	4760.22	4119.94	6793.32
5	55504.94	40331.63	16442.96	11593.81	1596.88	1829.30	342.98	15146.24	6137.67	4770.91	4237.66	6894.49
6	56532.12	40899.36	16707.32	11670.99	1635.53	1834.42	339.08	15605.77	6369.61	4799.71	4436.45	6980.78
7	56872.03	41060.83	16709.60	11671.22	1634.77	1839.07	321.12	15784.20	6410.16	4820.77	4553.27	7160.72
8	57416.35	41341.68	16741.11	11714.54	1639.04	1791.07	321.54	16047.72	6493.24	4832.60	4721.88	7110.61
9	58240.36	41772.46	16871.56	11783.15	1661.33	1790.13	333.40	16441.06	6636.47	4856.68	4947.91	7642.14
10	58493.77	41835.79	16870.65	11756.11	1658.27	1782.18	316.50	16631.19	6692.42	4866.80	5071.97	7708.93
11	59105.14	42090.36	16952.90	11774.25	1644.98	1770.68	308.12	16988.15	6801.28	4914.62	5272.26	7775.43
12	57456.22	40686.99	16287.35	11466.08	1315.79	1742.61	291.15	16745.15	6510.84	4729.30	5505.01	11039.44
比上期增减额（亿元） Changes Compared with Previous Period（100 Million Yuan）												
1999 1	56.17	108.63	-62.80	85.42	51.04	-10.01	12.03	-52.27	-59.78	-57.85	65.36	1.72
2	315.76	286.89	87.69	19.43	5.75	14.21	9.90	29.34	65.87	-6.28	-30.25	-3.37
3	540.23	321.65	103.59	3.41	8.20	20.38	2.44	218.57	103.95	10.84	103.78	116.17
4	487.07	264.87	60.35	62.05	9.59	21.21	-12.43	222.37	85.18	5.19	132.00	-47.53
5	482.92	207.99	84.99	15.82	15.61	7.94	-7.91	275.31	146.90	10.69	117.72	101.17
6	1027.17	567.72	264.36	77.18	38.65	5.11	-3.90	459.53	231.94	28.80	198.79	86.29
7	339.90	161.47	2.29	0.23	-0.76	4.65	-17.96	178.42	40.55	21.06	116.81	179.94
8	544.33	280.86	31.50	43.32	4.27	-47.99	0.43	263.53	83.08	11.84	168.61	-50.11
9	824.05	430.80	130.46	68.62	22.29	-0.95	11.86	393.35	143.23	24.07	226.05	531.53
10	253.39	63.31	-0.91	-27.05	-3.06	-7.95	-16.91	190.13	55.95	10.12	124.06	66.79
11	611.37	254.58	82.25	18.14	-13.29	-11.50	-8.37	356.96	108.86	47.82	200.28	66.50
12	1367.17	508.51	334.98	-52.07	77.94	-28.07	-16.97	861.21	350.18	98.91	412.12	3264.07
比去年同期增长（%） Increase Rate Year - on - year（%）												
1999 1	20.26	14.38	9.71	17.87	12.62	16.88	-5.97	40.00	30.98	4.56	187.11	145.79
2	20.89	15.15	10.26	18.10	13.10	17.41	-1.63	40.16	32.78	4.70	178.48	149.88
3	20.79	14.61	9.82	17.69	12.34	17.23	-2.41	41.70	36.95	4.63	169.33	159.24
4	20.84	14.39	9.23	17.95	12.66	17.04	-7.41	42.67	38.51	4.69	165.60	149.90
5	17.31	13.78	8.80	17.46	12.38	16.39	-11.11	27.99	30.40	4.39	65.76	147.61
6	17.07	13.51	8.61	17.15	14.01	11.97	-15.46	27.63	31.45	3.78	60.93	155.52
7	16.72	13.12	7.96	16.63	13.28	11.02	-20.11	27.35	29.73	4.35	60.69	149.07
8	15.45	12.15	6.62	15.68	11.77	6.57	-19.58	24.97	27.79	3.62	52.47	26.63
9	14.65	11.44	5.75	14.84	11.71	3.76	-15.96	23.76	25.59	2.78	51.07	21.31
10	14.27	11.25	5.67	14.24	11.45	3.08	-14.20	22.72	24.89	2.32	47.54	19.87
11	14.25	11.33	5.83	12.81	10.30	2.39	-11.15	22.23	23.42	2.94	45.89	20.96
12	12.80	8.87	6.92	2.58	14.42	-2.10	-13.98	23.49	23.53	4.21	47.49	64.12

国有商业银行人民币信贷收支主要指标时间序列表

Time Series of Major Indicators in Sources and Uses of Credit Funds of State - owned Banks（RMB）

年　月 Year Month		各项存款 Total Deposits	企业存款 Deposits by Enterprises	储蓄存款 Savings Deposits	活期储蓄 Demand Deposits	定期储蓄 Time Deposits	农业存款 Deposits by Agricultural Sector
		期末余额（亿元） Balance（100 Million Yuan）					
2000	1	69021.42	24638.50	40590.82	10431.31	30159.51	314.93
	2	70724.83	25007.84	41899.45	10940.70	30958.75	314.08
	3	71991.38	26009.19	42023.95	11131.47	30892.48	330.07
	4	72553.59	26370.16	42088.65	11253.25	30835.40	327.85
	5	72982.53	26949.28	41780.37	11181.44	30598.93	332.45
	6	74486.18	27871.21	42169.90	11565.71	30604.19	338.98
	7	74162.74	27599.58	42136.47	11564.07	30572.40	334.62
	8	74903.20	28199.93	42115.52	11641.11	30474.41	344.58
	9	75954.72	28888.26	42361.63	12054.31	30307.32	347.28
	10	75588.12	28660.54	42170.65	11870.37	30300.28	353.05
	11	76157.19	28876.39	42344.77	12033.14	30311.63	375.45
	12	76945.23	29158.29	42734.90	12447.96	30286.94	372.03
		比上期增减额（亿元） Changes Compared with Previous Period（100 Million Yuan）					
2000	1	- 215.68	- 723.33	762.99	469.25	293.74	- 27.18
	2	1703.41	369.34	1308.63	509.39	799.24	- 0.85
	3	1266.55	1001.35	124.50	190.77	- 66.27	15.99
	4	562.21	360.97	64.70	121.78	- 57.08	- 2.22
	5	428.94	579.12	- 308.28	- 71.81	- 236.47	4.60
	6	1503.65	921.93	389.53	384.27	5.26	6.53
	7	- 323.44	- 271.63	- 33.43	- 1.64	- 31.79	- 4.36
	8	740.46	600.35	- 20.95	77.04	- 97.99	9.96
	9	1051.52	688.33	246.11	413.20	- 167.09	2.70
	10	- 366.60	- 227.72	- 190.98	- 183.94	- 7.04	5.77
	11	569.07	215.85	174.12	162.77	11.35	22.40
	12	788.04	281.90	390.13	414.82	- 24.69	- 3.42
		比去年同期增长（%） Increase Rate Year - on - year（%）					
2000	1	12.76	9.94	12.19	27.93	7.61	3.40
	2	13.74	15.08	10.38	24.44	6.14	17.61
	3	12.51	15.74	8.59	28.87	2.77	18.59
	4	12.22	16.69	7.42	31.42	0.71	11.13
	5	11.41	17.70	5.37	30.25	- 1.51	13.50
	6	12.40	19.25	6.15	34.32	- 1.64	16.15
	7	12.25	19.54	6.02	31.27	- 1.17	14.19
	8	11.87	18.53	5.87	28.76	- 0.86	13.56
	9	12.01	18.77	6.14	28.14	- 0.65	13.62
	10	11.03	16.87	5.78	23.88	0.06	10.10
	11	11.12	15.66	6.53	23.54	1.01	10.83
	12	10.99	14.96	7.14	24.19	1.42	8.75

国有商业银行人民币信贷收支主要指标时间序列表
Time Series of Major Indicators in Sources and Uses of Credit Funds of State - owned Banks（RMB）

年 月 Year Month		各项贷款 Total Loans	短期贷款 Short - term Loans						中长期贷款 Medium and Long - term Loans				有价证券及投资 Securities and Investments
				工业贷款 Loans to Industrial Sector	商业贷款 Loans to Commercial Sector	建筑业贷款 Loans to Construction Sector	农业贷款 Loans to Agricultural Sector	贴现 Discount		基本建设贷款 Capital Construction Loans	技术改造贷款 Technical Improvement Loans	其他中长期贷款 Other Medium and Long - term Loans	
期末余额（亿元） Balance（100 Million Yuan）													
2000	1	57856.42	40999.53	16322.90	11506.32	1323.55	1735.19	332.95	16837.04	6565.77	4726.31	5544.96	11110.36
	2	58194.85	41192.63	16431.49	11502.60	1327.95	1745.96	329.20	16982.38	6626.52	4736.14	5619.72	11160.48
	3	59105.53	41732.38	16635.65	11534.57	1349.11	1759.88	335.52	17352.73	6778.71	4752.35	5821.67	11096.00
	4	59558.74	41962.44	16725.81	11474.03	1358.92	1751.22	356.48	17576.17	6861.45	4753.62	5961.10	11440.88
	5	58778.45	41121.66	16484.67	11088.80	1362.46	1624.26	369.37	17636.53	6919.18	4697.21	6020.14	12226.45
	6	56740.63	39067.48	16048.95	9950.23	1368.81	1429.83	372.92	17655.97	6884.94	4608.58	6162.45	12133.16
	7	56003.62	38260.73	15591.12	9572.04	1379.51	1392.75	377.51	17725.77	6956.92	4507.80	6261.05	13478.85
	8	56133.81	38190.44	15437.83	9410.42	1400.98	1376.94	371.65	17926.25	7023.97	4479.33	6422.95	13958.41
	9	56603.15	38354.43	15260.25	9401.74	1423.84	1374.65	380.71	18231.90	7160.16	4473.05	6598.69	15131.64
	10	56990.19	38543.48	15225.80	9404.81	1430.63	1360.82	378.86	18428.97	7242.77	4490.71	6695.49	15335.04
	11	57749.40	38961.44	15232.54	9392.53	1437.55	1325.15	389.75	18770.51	7368.52	4510.05	6891.94	16158.46
	12	58250.69	39100.38	15132.53	9261.65	1418.73	1287.58	441.60	19134.41	7380.81	4541.64	7211.96	18309.70
比上期增减额（亿元） Changes Compared with Previous Period（100 Million Yuan）													
2000	1	385.67	256.21	39.71	2.62	7.97	-2.25	41.76	128.98	44.73	7.46	76.79	71.15
	2	341.50	215.61	12.71	66.57	4.40	10.77	-3.75	123.64	36.80	11.76	75.08	49.73
	3	936.73	560.14	207.68	36.30	21.16	17.30	6.32	376.02	152.26	20.74	203.02	-64.49
	4	626.14	383.65	125.23	-21.86	9.81	-1.69	20.96	242.78	83.26	12.61	146.91	344.82
	5	444.50	227.01	9.23	6.60	4.31	12.88	12.91	217.37	93.78	24.06	99.53	787.75
	6	1045.89	603.08	171.20	38.91	33.87	-2.68	3.53	441.55	80.84	84.90	275.81	-90.60
	7	650.67	343.6	-15.44	66.75	10.86	19.68	4.59	306.97	110.67	8.58	187.72	1345.15
	8	617.86	234.87	-64.30	-6.09	-21.49	-2.51	-5.85	383.08	124.97	9.62	248.49	478.38
	9	922.07	530.30	45.94	70.56	22.86	4.38	9.06	391.61	192.96	62.33	136.32	1173.03
	10	513.42	284.17	-2.41	49.20	7.18	-11.20	-1.85	228.33	86.40	43.63	98.30	203.48
	11	823.38	463.05	20.56	8.05	6.92	-32.82	10.89	361.19	129.86	28.62	202.71	823.72
	12	602.20	217.99	-51.76	-119.30	-18.82	-37.96	51.85	384.86	17.42	47.74	319.70	2152.57
比去年同期增长（%） Increase Rate Year - on - year（%）													
2000	1	13.42	9.35	7.55	2.41	11.10	-1.72	-5.13	24.60	25.50	5.82	46.05	65.14
	2	13.39	9.10	7.04	2.82	10.98	-1.90	-8.78	25.20	24.71	6.21	49.12	65.97
	3	13.98	9.62	7.64	3.10	11.74	-2.05	-7.65	25.90	25.10	6.40	50.33	62.20
	4	14.11	9.86	8.00	2.36	11.69	-3.28	1.59	25.65	24.71	6.55	49.08	68.41
	5	13.92	9.85	7.50	2.28	10.86	-3.00	7.70	24.80	23.25	6.82	47.29	77.37
	6	13.70	9.80	6.83	1.94	10.32	-3.42	9.98	23.95	20.03	7.94	46.91	73.88
	7	14.16	10.21	6.72	2.51	11.03	-2.59	17.56	24.50	21.00	7.65	47.26	88.29
	8	14.16	10.03	6.13	2.08	9.43	-0.12	15.59	24.84	21.37	7.59	47.26	96.35
	9	14.13	10.16	5.59	2.08	9.34	0.18	14.19	24.24	21.66	8.34	43.29	98.04
	10	14.51	10.67	5.58	2.73	9.97	0.00	19.71	24.19	21.94	9.01	41.73	98.97
	11	14.72	11.11	5.19	2.64	11.28	-1.21	26.50	23.70	21.89	8.53	40.19	107.86
	12	13.81	10.77	3.02	2.13	6.75	-1.79	51.68	21.20	17.76	7.78	36.81	65.90

国有商业银行人民币信贷收支主要指标时间序列表

Time Series of Major Indicators in Sources and Uses of Credit Funds of State－owned Banks（RMB）

年 月 Year Month		各项存款 Total Deposits	企业存款 Deposits by Enterprises	储蓄存款 Savings Deposits	活期储蓄 Demand Deposits	定期储蓄 Time Deposits	农业存款 Deposits by Agricultural Sector
		期末余额（亿元） Balance（100 Million Yuan）					
2001	1	77703.93	28555.32	44400.67	13407.37	30993.30	332.75
	2	78729.74	29004.14	44796.94	13197.63	31599.31	338.56
	3	80648.85	30077.78	45456.60	13699.02	31757.58	347.55
	4	80774.87	30090.95	45542.36	13755.92	31786.44	344.38
	5	80550.28	29949.04	45247.08	13442.39	31804.69	366.64
	6	83168.44	31408.52	46084.27	14072.22	32012.05	382.04
	7	81946.50	30180.29	46044.97	13888.36	32156.61	376.55
	8	83921.85	31232.23	46688.68	14352.02	32336.66	394.52
	9	85053.31	31780.58	47146.29	14671.44	32474.85	395.31
	10	85237.08	31687.77	47458.77	14689.86	32768.91	403.96
	11	85670.62	31709.80	47657.08	14662.43	32994.65	405.19
	12	87509.57	32532.03	48395.21	15108.26	33286.95	409.74
		比上期增减额（亿元） Changes Compared with Previous Period（100 Million Yuan）					
2001	1	763.80	－628.80	1666.28	959.35	706.93	－39.21
	2	1025.81	448.82	396.27	－209.74	606.01	5.81
	3	1919.11	1073.64	659.66	501.39	158.27	8.99
	4	126.02	13.17	85.76	56.90	28.86	－3.17
	5	－224.59	－141.91	－295.28	－313.53	18.25	22.26
	6	2618.16	1459.48	837.19	629.83	207.36	15.40
	7	－1221.94	－1228.23	－39.30	－183.86	144.56	－5.49
	8	1975.35	1051.94	643.71	463.66	180.05	17.97
	9	1131.46	548.35	457.61	319.42	138.19	0.79
	10	183.77	－92.81	312.48	18.42	294.06	8.65
	11	433.54	22.03	198.31	－27.43	225.74	1.23
	12	1838.95	822.23	738.13	445.83	292.30	4.55
		比去年同期增长（%） Increase Rate Year－on－year（%）					
2001	1	12.58	15.90	9.39	28.53	2.76	5.66
	2	11.32	15.98	6.92	20.63	2.07	7.79
	3	12.03	15.64	8.17	23.07	2.80	5.30
	4	11.33	14.11	8.21	22.24	3.08	5.04
	5	10.37	11.13	8.30	20.22	3.94	10.28
	6	11.66	12.69	9.28	21.67	4.60	12.70
	7	10.50	9.35	9.28	20.10	5.18	12.53
	8	12.04	10.75	10.86	23.29	6.11	14.49
	9	11.98	10.01	11.29	21.71	7.15	13.83
	10	12.77	10.56	12.54	23.75	8.15	14.42
	11	12.49	9.81	12.55	21.85	8.85	7.92
	12	13.73	11.57	13.25	21.37	9.91	10.14

国有商业银行人民币信贷收支主要指标时间序列表

Time Series of Major Indicators in Sources and Uses of Credit Funds of State－owned Banks（RMB）

年 月 Year Month	各项贷款 Total Loans	短期贷款 Short－term Loans	工业贷款 Loans to Industrial Sector	商业贷款 Loans to Commercial Sector	建筑业贷款 Loans to Construction Sector	农业贷款 Loans to Agricultural Sector	中长期贷款 Medium and Long－term Loans	基本建设贷款 Capital Construction Loans	技术改造贷款 Technical Improvement Loans	其他中长期贷款 Other Medium and Long－term Loans	票据融资 Paper Financing	有价证券及投资 Securities and Investments
期末余额（亿元） Balance（100 Million Yuan）												
2001 1	58913.24	34952.38	15136.72	9220.76	1472.90	1283.26	23114.80	7517.66	4551.78	11045.36	561.24	18306.67
2	59319.43	34979.36	15153.36	9197.85	1479.29	1280.59	23442.50	7595.02	4584.79	11262.69	588.83	18285.16
3	59995.83	35081.06	15145.03	9194.68	1490.39	1299.47	23943.96	7693.01	4589.89	11661.06	665.71	18381.51
4	60502.43	35060.06	15138.10	9182.35	1487.70	1313.02	24356.05	7791.56	4596.79	11967.70	771.87	18487.87
5	60932.50	35116.91	15113.27	9132.94	1606.58	1332.41	24657.27	7883.92	4591.08	12182.27	842.56	18604.13
6	61922.46	35503.88	15337.38	9187.40	1609.70	1322.82	25027.00	8009.91	4587.17	12429.92	1077.51	18799.38
7	62018.31	35383.55	15267.73	9119.20	1578.19	1319.31	25188.27	8059.97	4578.03	12550.27	1126.45	18996.77
8	62114.72	35288.15	15206.26	9090.30	1574.22	1300.80	25385.04	8120.88	4593.18	12670.98	1120.14	19137.39
9	62719.52	35388.21	15269.22	9077.70	1573.32	1298.64	25866.23	8252.28	4629.02	12984.93	1144.68	19200.00
10	62621.81	35272.60	15296.48	8983.38	1557.42	1288.31	25982.87	8308.21	4623.48	13051.18	1044.07	19333.60
11	63029.88	35419.65	15413.33	9014.88	1565.97	1263.74	26307.69	8416.27	4634.36	13257.06	979.17	19085.49
12	64663.14	36247.97	15763.21	9162.09	1684.81	1272.27	27013.09	8728.70	4697.45	13586.94	1087.99	18955.48
比上期增减额（亿元） Changes Compared with Previous Period（100 Million Yuan）												
2001 1	663.01	128.72	12.36	－45.50	22.57	－4.57	373.42	81.07	9.46	282.89	121.06	－9.94
2	406.19	26.98	16.64	－22.91	6.39	－2.67	327.70	77.36	33.01	217.33	27.59	－21.51
3	676.41	101.70	－8.33	－3.17	11.10	18.88	501.46	97.99	5.10	398.37	76.88	96.35
4	506.59	－21.00	－6.93	－12.33	－2.69	13.55	412.09	98.55	6.90	306.64	106.16	106.36
5	430.07	56.85	－24.83	－49.41	118.88	19.39	301.22	92.36	－5.71	214.57	70.69	116.26
6	989.96	386.97	224.11	54.46	3.12	－9.59	369.73	125.99	－3.91	247.65	234.95	195.25
7	95.85	－120.33	－69.65	－68.20	－31.51	－3.51	161.27	50.06	－9.14	120.35	48.94	197.39
8	96.41	－95.40	－61.47	－28.90	－3.97	－18.51	196.77	60.91	15.15	120.71	－6.31	140.62
9	604.8	100.06	62.96	－12.60	－0.90	－2.16	481.19	131.40	35.84	313.95	24.54	62.61
10	－97.71	－115.61	27.26	－94.32	－15.90	－10.33	116.64	55.93	－5.54	66.25	－100.61	133.60
11	408.07	147.05	116.85	31.50	8.55	－24.57	324.82	108.06	10.88	205.88	－64.90	－248.11
12	1633.26	828.32	349.88	147.21	118.84	8.53	705.40	312.43	63.09	329.88	108.82	－130.01
比去年同期增长（%） Increase Rate Year－on－year（%）												
2001 1	14.12	4.38	2.84	1.35	10.22	－1.62	33.05	18.98	7.72	63.41	68.57	64.81
2	14.15	4.03	2.84	0.57	10.33	－2.38	33.50	19.42	8.15	63.55	78.87	63.88
3	13.49	3.11	1.51	0.22	9.43	－2.27	32.77	18.18	7.79	62.15	98.41	65.70
4	13.19	2.45	0.71	0.31	8.44	－1.42	32.43	18.18	7.67	60.53	116.53	61.64
5	13.34	2.39	0.51	－0.19	16.82	－1.13	32.00	18.01	7.13	59.25	128.11	52.18
6	13.72	2.45	0.86	－0.05	14.50	－1.76	30.42	18.76	5.34	54.49	188.94	54.94
7	12.91	1.67	0.53	－1.46	11.32	－3.47	28.55	17.69	5.07	50.14	198.39	40.94
8	11.95	1.27	0.56	－1.73	12.39	－4.68	26.14	16.61	5.22	44.50	201.40	37.11
9	11.29	0.76	0.68	－2.62	10.53	－5.16	24.74	15.43	4.64	41.83	200.67	26.90
10	10.14	0.06	0.87	－4.14	8.86	－5.15	23.08	14.84	3.52	38.76	175.58	26.09
11	9.29	－0.13	1.50	－3.90	8.93	－4.66	21.21	14.29	3.11	34.67	151.23	18.12
12	10.98	2.29	4.17	－1.07	18.75	－1.19	21.23	18.26	3.43	31.14	146.37	3.53

国有商业银行人民币信贷收支主要指标时间序列表
Time Series of Major Indicators in Sources and Uses of Credit Funds of State - owned Banks (RMB)

年　月 Year Month		各项存款 Total Deposits	企业存款 Deposits by Enterprises	储蓄存款 Savings Deposits	活期储蓄 Demand Deposits	定期储蓄 Time Deposits	农业存款 Deposits by Agricultural Sector
期末余额（亿元） Balance (100 Million Yuan)							
2002	1	88230.18	31344.87	49411.27	15561.38	33849.89	421.94
	2	89116.77	30319.04	51418.62	16302.75	35115.87	384.94
	3	91047.66	31541.68	51778.47	16457.21	35321.26	401.58
	4	91903.31	31734.53	52447.07	16891.44	35555.63	395.93
	5	93321.83	32366.57	52869.39	17058.15	35811.24	395.52
	6	95614.84	33260.85	53713.78	17456.51	36257.27	402.78
	7	96389.28	33222.38	54304.30	17695.31	36608.99	422.89
	8	97770.54	33918.88	54838.02	17982.27	36855.75	425.55
	9	99638.61	34890.48	55373.19	18318.99	37054.20	436.18
	10	100098.28	34883.13	55716.30	18354.41	37361.89	442.24
	11	101164.45	35216.55	56241.79	18627.43	37614.36	448.70
	12	101882.40	35273.98	56655.38	18890.27	37765.11	465.72
比上期增减额（亿元） Changes Compared with Previous Period (100 Million Yuan)							
2002	1	726.14	-205.18	1014.82	442.59	572.23	11.56
	2	886.59	-1025.83	2007.35	741.37	1265.98	-37.00
	3	1930.89	1222.64	359.85	154.46	205.39	16.64
	4	855.65	192.85	668.60	434.23	234.37	-5.65
	5	1418.52	632.04	422.32	166.71	255.61	-0.41
	6	2293.01	894.28	844.39	398.36	446.03	7.26
	7	774.44	-38.47	590.52	238.80	351.72	20.11
	8	1381.26	696.50	533.72	286.96	246.76	2.66
	9	1868.07	971.60	535.17	336.72	198.45	10.63
	10	459.67	-7.35	343.11	35.42	307.69	6.06
	11	1066.17	333.42	525.49	273.02	252.47	6.46
	12	717.95	57.43	413.59	262.84	150.75	17.02
比去年同期增长（%） Increase Rate Year - on - year (%)							
2002	1	13.55	9.77	11.28	16.07	9.22	26.80
	2	13.19	4.53	14.78	23.53	11.13	13.70
	3	12.89	4.87	13.91	20.13	11.22	15.55
	4	13.78	5.46	15.16	22.79	11.86	14.97
	5	15.86	8.07	16.85	26.90	12.60	7.88
	6	14.97	5.90	16.56	24.05	13.26	5.43
	7	17.62	10.08	17.94	27.41	13.85	12.31
	8	16.50	8.60	17.45	25.29	13.98	7.87
	9	17.15	9.79	17.45	24.86	14.10	10.34
	10	17.44	10.08	17.40	24.95	14.02	9.48
	11	18.09	11.06	18.01	27.04	14.00	10.74
	12	16.42	8.43	17.07	25.03	13.45	13.66

国有商业银行人民币信贷收支主要指标时间序列表

Time Series of Major Indicators in Sources and Uses of Credit Funds of State-owned Banks（RMB）

年 月 Year Month	各项贷款 Total Loans	短期贷款 Short-term Loans	工业贷款 Loans to Industrial Sector	商业贷款 Loans to Commercial Sector	建筑业贷款 Loans to Construction Sector	农业贷款 Loans to Agricultural Sector	中长期贷款 Medium and Long-term Loans	基本建设贷款 Capital Construction Loans	技术改造贷款 Technical Improvement Loans	其他中长期贷款 Other Medium and Long-term Loans	票据融资 Paper Financing	有价证券及投资 Securities and Investments
期末余额（亿元） Balance（100 Million Yuan）												
2002 1	64487.16	34898.43	14604.35	9073.84	1458.26	1279.59	28205.80	11735.74	1671.74	14798.32	1059.36	19451.21
2	64715.34	34876.84	14772.45	9084.43	1444.79	1286.62	28396.87	11826.69	1666.75	14903.43	1116.03	19431.42
3	66114.84	35716.32	15295.76	9077.31	1514.22	1316.89	28799.30	11984.10	1651.83	15163.37	1275.62	19787.30
4	66443.12	35933.08	15291.21	8916.74	1549.29	1314.91	28832.96	11963.56	1644.38	15225.02	1351.07	20032.28
5	67169.11	36141.29	15578.71	8845.40	1767.82	1314.64	29259.38	12124.49	1641.66	15493.23	1443.33	20052.45
6	68695.41	36768.28	15970.18	8808.30	1848.21	1320.75	29878.31	12391.67	1654.17	15832.47	1729.52	20574.70
7	68896.41	36778.62	16073.91	8692.96	1890.28	1322.07	30076.44	12432.54	1651.96	15991.94	1721.91	20634.49
8	69787.34	36991.36	16184.48	8599.37	1928.53	1321.07	30616.18	12593.50	1643.08	16379.60	1856.94	20747.20
9	71741.01	37609.82	16424.87	8616.13	2031.43	1320.41	31369.04	12855.78	1640.09	16873.17	2441.89	20783.94
10	72030.77	37595.59	16383.50	8588.32	2069.55	1312.34	31691.15	12916.98	1658.57	17115.60	2422.98	21650.98
11	72969.73	37871.70	16496.55	8572.92	2118.07	1297.09	32206.38	13052.91	1631.63	17521.84	2571.21	21712.43
12	74078.14	38304.25	16745.38	8547.94	2168.03	1286.04	33022.94	13390.58	1655.25	17977.11	2434.97	21515.74
比上期增减额（亿元） Changes Compared with Previous Period（100 Million Yuan）												
2002 1	-193.39	-295.54	-52.57	-183.90	8.32	0.17	153.52	15.70	10.59	127.23	-55.80	15.79
2	228.18	-21.59	168.10	10.59	-13.47	7.03	191.07	90.95	-4.99	105.11	56.67	-19.79
3	1399.50	839.48	523.31	-7.12	69.43	30.27	402.43	157.41	-14.92	259.94	159.59	355.88
4	328.28	216.76	-4.55	-160.57	35.07	-1.98	33.66	-20.54	-7.45	61.65	75.45	244.98
5	725.99	208.21	287.50	-71.34	218.53	-0.27	426.42	160.93	-2.72	268.21	92.26	20.17
6	1526.30	626.99	391.47	-37.10	80.39	6.11	618.93	267.18	12.51	339.24	286.19	522.25
7	201.00	10.34	103.73	-115.34	42.07	1.32	198.13	40.87	-2.21	159.47	-7.61	59.79
8	890.93	212.74	110.57	-93.59	38.25	-1.00	539.74	160.96	-8.88	387.66	135.03	112.71
9	1953.67	618.46	240.39	16.76	102.90	-0.66	752.86	262.28	-2.99	493.57	584.95	36.74
10	289.76	-14.23	-41.37	-27.81	38.12	-8.07	322.11	61.20	18.48	242.43	-18.91	867.04
11	938.96	276.11	113.05	-15.40	48.52	-15.25	515.23	135.93	-26.94	406.24	148.23	61.45
12	1108.41	432.55	248.83	-24.98	49.96	-11.05	816.56	337.67	23.62	455.27	-136.24	-196.69
比去年同期增长（%） Increase Rate Year-on-year（%）												
2002 1	9.46	-0.15	-3.52	-1.59	-0.99	-0.29	22.02	56.11	-63.27	33.98	88.75	6.25
2	9.10	-0.29	-2.51	-1.23	-2.33	0.47	21.13	55.72	-63.65	32.33	89.53	6.27
3	10.20	1.81	1.00	-1.28	1.60	1.34	20.28	55.78	-64.01	30.03	91.62	7.65
4	9.82	2.49	1.01	-2.89	4.14	0.14	18.38	53.55	-64.23	27.22	75.04	8.35
5	10.24	2.92	3.08	-3.15	10.04	-1.33	18.66	53.79	-64.24	27.18	71.30	7.78
6	10.94	3.56	4.13	-4.13	14.82	-0.16	19.38	54.70	-63.94	27.37	60.51	9.44
7	11.09	3.94	5.28	-4.67	19.78	0.21	19.41	54.25	-63.92	27.42	52.86	8.62
8	12.35	4.83	6.43	-5.40	22.51	1.56	20.61	55.08	-64.23	29.27	65.78	8.41
9	14.38	6.28	7.57	-5.08	29.12	1.68	21.27	55.78	-64.57	29.94	113.33	8.25
10	15.03	6.59	7.11	-4.40	32.88	1.87	21.97	55.47	-64.13	31.14	132.07	11.99
11	15.77	6.92	7.03	-4.90	35.26	2.64	22.42	55.09	-64.79	32.17	162.59	13.76
12	14.56	5.67	6.23	-6.70	28.68	1.08	22.25	53.41	-64.76	32.31	123.80	13.51

国有商业银行人民币信贷收支主要指标时间序列表

Time Series of Major Indicators in Sources and Uses of Credit Funds of State - owned Banks (RMB)

年 月 Year Month		各项存款 Total Deposits	企业存款 Deposits by Enterprises	储蓄存款 Savings Deposits	活期储蓄 Demand Deposits	定期储蓄 Time Deposits	农业存款 Deposits by Agricultural Sector
		期末余额(亿元) Balance (100 Million Yuan)					
2003	1	104434.80	35232.38	59641.29	20411.83	39229.46	435.76
	2	106304.54	35720.75	60778.03	20572.78	40205.25	442.62
	3	109609.51	37410.76	61930.99	20944.11	40986.88	453.08
	4	109811.12	37279.73	62271.35	21044.75	41226.60	445.53
	5	111735.07	38191.19	62943.01	21302.45	41640.56	454.02
	6	114373.37	39565.28	63659.48	21710.01	41949.47	436.55
	7	115115.99	39569.63	64188.47	21990.93	42197.54	440.16
	8	116006.92	39925.81	64547.93	22193.44	42354.49	441.40
	9	118432.82	41049.55	65635.39	22775.64	42859.75	458.81
	10	118930.73	41191.02	65921.02	22767.76	43153.26	474.55
	11	119536.23	41228.13	66326.99	23090.31	43236.68	473.54
	12	119575.12	40655.49	66850.39	23473.19	43377.20	463.28
		比上期增减额(亿元) Changes Compared with Previous Period (100 Million Yuan)					
2003	1	2552.81	42.46	2902.86	1479.24	1423.62	-30.59
	2	1869.74	488.37	1136.74	160.95	975.79	6.86
	3	3304.97	1690.01	1152.96	371.33	781.63	10.46
	4	201.61	-131.03	340.36	100.64	239.72	-7.55
	5	1923.95	911.46	671.66	257.70	413.96	8.49
	6	2638.30	1374.09	716.47	407.56	308.91	-17.47
	7	742.62	4.35	528.99	280.92	248.07	3.61
	8	890.93	356.18	359.46	202.51	156.95	1.24
	9	2425.90	1123.74	1087.46	582.20	505.26	17.41
	10	497.91	141.47	285.63	-7.88	293.51	15.74
	11	605.50	37.11	405.97	322.55	83.42	-1.01
	12	38.89	-572.64	523.40	382.88	140.52	-10.26
		比去年同期增长(%) Increase Rate Year-on-year (%)					
2003	1	18.37	12.40	20.70	31.17	15.89	3.28
	2	19.29	17.82	18.20	26.19	14.49	14.98
	3	20.39	18.61	19.61	27.26	16.04	12.82
	4	19.49	17.47	18.73	24.59	15.95	12.53
	5	19.73	18.00	19.05	24.88	16.28	14.79
	6	19.62	18.95	18.52	24.37	15.70	8.38
	7	19.43	19.11	18.20	24.28	15.27	4.08
	8	18.65	17.71	17.71	23.42	14.92	3.72
	9	18.86	17.65	18.53	24.33	15.67	5.19
	10	18.81	18.08	18.32	24.05	15.50	7.31
	11	18.16	17.07	17.93	23.96	14.95	5.54
	12	17.37	15.26	17.99	24.26	14.86	-0.52

国有商业银行人民币信贷收支主要指标时间序列表
Time Series of Major Indicators in Sources and Uses of Credit Funds of State-owned Banks（RMB）

年 月 Year Month		各项贷款 Total Loans	短期贷款 Short-term Loans					中长期贷款 Medium and Long-term Loans				票据融资 Paper Financing	有价证券及投资 Securities and Investments
				工业贷款 Loans to Industrial Sector	商业贷款 Loans to Commercial Sector	建筑业贷款 Loans to Construction Sector	农业贷款 Loans to Agricultural Sector		基本建设贷款 Capital Construction Loans	技术改造贷款 Technical Improvement Loans	其他中长期贷款 Other Medium and Long-term Loans		
期末余额（亿元） Balance（100 Million Yuan）													
2003	1	76399.07	38966.24	16995.63	8560.42	2308.66	1292.97	34062.89	13789.78	1676.67	18596.44	3054.79	21676.85
	2	77191.84	39078.90	16905.33	8595.41	2339.56	1297.44	34305.49	13928.92	1688.19	18688.38	3490.09	21774.64
	3	79229.88	39774.52	17159.93	8640.66	2415.51	1305.85	35212.09	14333.13	1704.46	19174.50	3928.99	21329.91
	4	80034.84	39801.86	17079.88	8591.46	2440.35	1327.14	35739.82	14467.90	1687.29	19584.63	4182.26	21419.17
	5	81427.47	40168.74	17243.44	8573.61	2479.53	1329.06	36362.48	14708.74	1690.88	19962.86	4586.29	22180.45
	6	84307.95	41102.07	17586.37	8634.01	2577.08	1322.63	37574.81	15236.42	1673.60	20664.79	5311.46	23350.82
	7	84552.92	40591.78	17394.04	8493.93	2452.14	1320.76	38330.42	15475.08	1684.40	21170.94	5312.22	23625.54
	8	85567.05	40798.53	17429.87	8542.82	2460.89	1322.96	38835.88	15785.16	1703.33	21347.39	5614.33	24399.43
	9	86872.27	40815.73	17558.12	8575.10	2202.30	1314.59	39935.38	16472.11	1696.82	21766.45	5802.77	24973.01
	10	86893.33	40912.94	17626.05	8561.31	2169.87	1308.65	40164.26	16665.39	1702.77	21796.10	5495.86	25169.48
	11	87051.98	40864.69	17601.65	8552.89	2063.61	1293.71	40740.69	16956.45	1725.96	22058.28	5129.74	25418.34
	12	87210.09	40744.08	17639.07	8421.35	1938.17	1271.81	41710.40	17600.73	1722.23	22387.44	4480.03	25352.53
比上期增减额（亿元） Changes Compared with Previous Period（100 Million Yuan）													
2003	1	2165.50	658.27	248.45	29.30	136.73	10.96	887.45	353.61	21.47	512.37	619.77	161.13
	2	792.77	112.66	-90.30	34.99	30.90	4.47	242.60	139.14	11.52	91.94	435.30	97.79
	3	2038.04	695.62	254.60	45.25	75.95	8.41	906.60	404.21	16.27	486.12	438.90	-444.73
	4	804.96	27.34	-80.05	-49.20	24.84	21.29	527.73	134.77	-17.17	410.13	253.27	89.26
	5	1392.63	366.88	163.56	-17.85	39.18	1.92	622.66	240.84	3.59	378.23	404.03	761.28
	6	2880.48	933.33	342.93	60.40	97.55	-6.43	1212.33	527.68	-17.28	701.93	725.17	1170.37
	7	244.97	-510.29	-192.33	-140.08	-124.94	-1.87	755.61	238.66	10.80	506.15	0.76	274.72
	8	1014.13	206.75	35.83	48.89	8.75	2.20	505.46	310.08	18.93	176.45	302.11	773.89
	9	1305.22	17.20	128.25	32.28	-258.59	-8.37	1099.50	686.95	-6.51	419.06	188.44	573.58
	10	21.06	97.21	67.93	-13.79	-32.43	-5.94	228.88	193.28	5.95	29.65	-306.91	196.47
	11	158.65	-48.25	-24.40	-8.42	-106.26	-14.94	576.43	291.06	23.19	262.18	-366.12	248.86
	12	158.11	-120.61	37.42	-131.54	-125.44	-21.90	969.71	644.28	-3.73	329.16	-649.71	-65.81
比去年同期增长（%） Increase Rate Year-on-year（%）													
2003	1	18.47	11.66	16.37	-5.66	58.32	1.05	20.77	17.50	0.29	25.67	188.36	11.44
	2	19.28	12.05	14.44	-5.38	61.93	0.84	20.81	17.78	1.29	25.40	212.72	12.06
	3	19.84	11.36	12.19	-4.81	59.52	-0.84	22.27	19.60	3.19	26.45	208.01	7.80
	4	20.46	10.77	11.70	-3.65	57.51	0.93	23.95	20.93	2.61	28.63	209.55	6.92
	5	21.23	11.14	10.69	-3.07	40.26	1.10	24.28	21.31	3.00	28.85	217.76	10.61
	6	22.73	11.79	10.12	-1.98	39.44	0.14	25.76	22.96	1.17	30.52	207.11	13.49
	7	22.72	10.37	8.21	-2.29	29.72	-0.10	27.44	24.47	1.96	32.39	208.51	14.50
	8	22.61	10.29	7.69	-0.66	27.60	0.14	26.85	25.34	3.67	30.33	202.34	17.60
	9	21.09	8.52	6.90	-0.48	8.41	-0.44	27.31	28.13	3.46	29.00	137.63	20.16
	10	20.63	8.82	7.58	-0.31	4.85	-0.28	26.74	29.02	2.66	27.35	126.82	16.25
	11	19.30	7.90	6.70	-0.23	-2.57	-0.26	26.50	29.91	5.78	25.89	99.51	17.07
	12	17.73	6.37	5.34	-1.48	-10.60	-1.11	26.31	31.44	4.05	24.53	83.99	17.83

国有商业银行人民币信贷收支主要指标时间序列表

Time Series of Major Indicators in Sources and Uses of Credit Funds of State – owned Banks（RMB）

年　月 Year Month	各项存款 Total Deposits	企业存款 Deposits by Enterprises	储蓄存款 Savings Deposits			农业存款 Deposits by Agricultural Sector
				活期储蓄 Demand Deposits	定期储蓄 Time Deposits	
			期末余额（亿元） Balance（100 Million Yuan）			
2004　1	122068.01	40747.97	70706.96	25377.29	45329.67	442.27
2	124471.69	42032.70	71418.74	25303.30	46115.44	446.93
3	127209.36	43810.10	72084.67	25765.16	46319.51	456.12
4	127377.65	44127.79	72017.48	25894.89	46122.59	445.94
5	128464.59	44950.69	72087.18	25874.31	46212.87	445.32
6	129874.30	45536.09	72618.52	26292.25	46326.27	441.64
7	129623.57	45074.45	72904.30	26509.10	46395.20	438.07
8	130557.28	45578.77	73037.66	26587.14	46450.52	446.18
9	132012.14	46305.09	73589.56	27020.20	46569.36	448.38
10	132174.71	46078.65	73771.07	26981.78	46789.29	457.51
11	133814.03	46704.08	74682.89	26627.21	48055.68	466.75
12	135487.87	47243.57	75682.31	27019.26	48663.05	484.99
			比上期增减额（亿元） Changes Compared with Previous Period（100 Million Yuan）			
2004　1	2792.85	-680.51	3856.02	1903.56	1952.46	-21.04
2	2403.68	1284.73	711.78	-73.99	785.77	4.66
3	2737.67	1777.40	665.93	461.86	204.07	9.19
4	168.29	317.69	-67.19	129.73	-196.92	-10.18
5	1086.94	822.90	69.70	-20.58	90.28	-0.62
6	1409.71	585.40	531.34	417.94	113.40	-3.68
7	-250.73	-461.64	285.78	216.85	68.93	-3.57
8	933.71	504.32	133.36	78.04	55.32	8.11
9	1454.86	726.32	551.90	433.06	118.84	2.20
10	162.57	-226.44	181.51	-38.42	219.93	9.13
11	1639.32	625.43	911.82	-354.57	1266.39	9.24
12	1673.84	539.49	999.42	392.05	607.37	18.24
			比去年同期增长（%） Increase Rate Year-on-year（%）			
2004　1	18.04	15.65	18.55	24.33	15.55	1.49
2	18.24	17.67	17.51	22.99	14.70	0.97
3	17.21	17.11	16.40	23.02	13.01	0.67
4	17.11	18.37	15.65	23.05	11.88	0.09
5	16.06	17.70	14.53	21.46	10.98	-1.92
6	14.64	15.09	14.07	21.11	10.43	1.17
7	13.71	13.91	13.58	20.55	9.95	-0.47
8	13.67	14.16	13.15	19.80	9.67	1.08
9	12.56	12.80	12.12	18.64	8.66	-2.27
10	12.21	11.87	11.91	18.51	8.43	-3.59
11	13.05	13.28	12.60	15.32	11.15	-1.43
12	14.39	16.20	13.21	15.11	12.19	4.69

国有商业银行人民币信贷收支主要指标时间序列表

Time Series of Major Indicators in Sources and Uses of Credit Funds of State - owned Banks（RMB）

年 月 Year Month	各项贷款 Total Loans	短期贷款 Short - term Loans	工业贷款 Loans to Industrial Sector	商业贷款 Loans to Commercial Sector	建筑业贷款 Loans to Construction Sector	农业贷款 Loans to Agricultural Sector	中长期贷款 Medium and Long - term Loans	基本建设贷款 Capital Construction Loans	技术改造贷款 Technical Improvement Loans	其他中长期贷款 Other Medium and Long - term Loans	票据融资 Paper Financing	有价证券及投资 Securities and Investments
期末余额（亿元） Balance（100 Million Yuan）												
2004 1	88513.29	40653.41	17616.29	8312.18	1742.54	1286.30	42698.89	18127.03	1769.97	22801.89	4882.11	25221.20
2	89533.43	40883.22	17608.63	8331.65	1710.00	1294.34	43126.11	18390.77	1782.92	22952.42	5243.83	26210.15
3	91409.56	41233.58	17678.93	8377.72	1637.80	1312.58	44089.31	18906.45	1819.04	23363.82	5804.78	27854.21
4	92191.02	41033.75	17678.66	8214.16	1588.14	1328.88	44796.51	19234.27	1848.14	23714.10	6076.65	27780.35
5	92822.10	40971.54	17655.01	8187.90	1542.70	1327.24	45260.67	19501.92	1875.67	23883.08	6302.12	27338.67
6	91199.68	39204.35	17235.31	7385.74	1278.58	1331.47	45252.52	19622.76	1782.42	23847.34	6541.01	28880.42
7	90948.84	38771.39	16989.41	7296.23	1221.94	1327.68	45404.01	19601.93	1780.25	24021.83	6569.80	29144.47
8	91336.00	38619.94	16946.26	7302.10	1205.06	1328.87	45781.24	19822.86	1767.46	24190.92	6728.26	28739.56
9	92807.72	39022.52	17178.17	7313.49	1168.81	1324.10	46728.34	20293.54	1743.27	24691.53	6847.64	29301.77
10	92655.66	38687.94	17006.75	7256.83	1136.64	1316.15	47033.53	20496.39	1764.52	24772.62	6721.33	30414.98
11	93329.50	38308.54	17200.79	7153.32	1227.20	1296.72	47778.03	20840.32	1669.18	25268.53	7026.63	31077.89
12	94734.92	38409.40	17400.71	7060.87	1210.80	1296.59	48729.55	21399.58	1722.62	25607.35	7390.55	31991.80
比上期增减额（亿元） Changes Compared with Previous Period（100 Million Yuan）												
2004 1	1103.02	91.27	- 12.14	- 91.94	- 46.73	13.75	806.55	377.72	43.13	385.70	201.88	- 131.44
2	1020.14	229.81	- 7.66	19.47	- 32.54	8.04	427.22	263.74	12.95	150.53	361.72	988.95
3	1876.13	350.36	70.30	46.07	- 72.20	18.24	963.20	515.68	36.12	411.40	560.95	1644.06
4	781.46	- 199.83	- 0.27	- 163.56	- 49.66	16.30	707.20	327.82	29.10	350.28	271.87	- 73.86
5	631.08	- 62.21	- 23.65	- 26.26	- 45.44	- 1.64	464.16	267.65	27.53	168.98	225.47	- 441.68
6	1274.64	260.89	146.58	- 15.05	- 95.79	7.98	776.69	379.45	30.58	366.66	241.09	1541.75
7	- 250.90	- 432.99	- 245.90	- 89.51	- 56.65	- 3.79	151.48	- 20.84	- 2.17	174.49	28.78	264.05
8	387.19	- 151.45	- 43.16	5.87	- 16.88	1.19	377.24	220.94	- 12.79	169.09	158.47	- 404.91
9	1471.76	402.62	231.91	11.39	- 36.24	- 4.76	947.10	470.67	- 24.19	500.62	119.38	562.21
10	- 152.12	- 334.62	- 171.41	- 56.66	- 32.18	- 7.96	305.18	202.85	21.25	81.08	- 126.31	1113.21
11	673.89	- 93.53	194.03	- 103.51	90.57	- 19.42	458.67	343.94	- 95.34	210.07	305.30	662.91
12	1405.35	100.83	199.92	- 92.45	- 16.41	- 0.14	951.49	559.24	53.43	338.82	363.92	913.91
比去年同期增长（%） Increase Rate Year - on - year（%）												
2004 1	15.86	4.33	3.65	- 2.90	- 24.52	- 0.52	25.35	31.45	5.56	22.61	59.82	16.35
2	15.99	4.62	4.16	- 3.07	- 26.91	- 0.24	25.71	32.03	5.61	22.82	50.25	20.37
3	15.37	3.67	3.02	- 3.04	- 32.20	0.52	25.21	31.91	6.72	21.85	47.74	30.59
4	15.19	3.10	3.51	- 4.39	- 34.92	0.13	25.34	32.94	9.53	21.09	45.30	29.70
5	13.99	2.00	2.39	- 4.50	- 37.78	- 0.14	24.47	32.59	10.93	19.64	37.41	23.26
6	11.61	0.32	1.22	- 5.34	- 43.85	0.95	22.52	30.49	13.90	17.35	23.19	23.68
7	10.99	0.51	0.93	- 4.83	- 43.30	0.81	20.50	28.34	13.04	15.37	23.71	23.36
8	10.13	- 0.37	0.47	- 5.31	- 44.19	0.73	19.90	27.22	11.03	15.21	19.88	17.79
9	10.17	0.58	1.06	- 5.53	- 39.28	1.01	18.98	24.77	10.04	15.29	18.04	17.33
10	9.97	- 0.48	- 0.30	- 6.04	- 39.86	0.86	19.06	24.54	10.90	15.50	22.34	20.84
11	10.54	- 1.29	0.94	- 7.16	- 32.37	0.52	19.20	24.43	3.88	16.38	37.02	22.27
12	11.95	- 0.75	1.86	- 6.81	- 28.84	2.24	18.71	23.05	7.21	16.18	65.02	26.19

国有商业银行人民币信贷收支主要指标时间序列表

Time Series of Major Indicators in Sources and Uses of Credit Funds of State - owned Banks (RMB)

年　月 Year Month		各项存款 Total Deposits	企业存款 Deposits by Enterprises	储蓄存款 Savings Deposits			农业存款 Deposits by Agricultural Sector
					活期储蓄 Demand Deposits	定期储蓄 Time Deposits	
期末余额（亿元） Balance (100 Million Yuan)							
2005	1	139203.09	47548.13	77655.77	27790.39	49865.38	466.21
	2	141273.67	46531.97	80960.44	28823.79	52136.65	434.62
	3	145092.89	49095.55	81823.49	28905.93	52917.56	450.72
	4	145778.93	49408.81	82012.73	28843.61	53169.12	447.64
	5	147503.88	50364.77	82306.93	28743.97	53562.96	442.61
	6	149817.05	50736.24	83028.96	29020.99	54007.97	441.11
	7	150977.18	50199.18	83926.05	29365.71	54560.34	455.85
	8	153207.98	51342.18	84382.93	29427.58	54955.35	460.63
	9	155557.92	52188.78	85382.54	29886.46	55496.08	474.12
	10	155816.05	51809.69	85372.38	29641.00	55731.38	465.87
	11	157243.58	52178.26	86021.25	30360.27	55660.98	435.78
	12	158178.25	51887.10	87034.23	31074.52	55959.71	424.19
比上期增减额（亿元） Changes Compared with Previous Period (100 Million Yuan)							
2005	1	1944.65	145.38	1973.43	771.10	1202.33	- 18.80
	2	2070.58	- 1016.16	3304.67	1033.40	2271.27	- 31.59
	3	3819.22	2563.58	863.05	82.14	780.91	16.10
	4	686.04	313.26	189.24	- 62.32	251.56	- 3.08
	5	1724.95	955.96	294.20	- 99.64	393.84	- 5.03
	6	2313.17	371.47	722.03	277.02	445.01	- 1.50
	7	1160.13	- 537.06	897.09	344.72	552.37	14.74
	8	2230.80	1143.00	456.88	61.87	395.01	4.78
	9	2349.94	846.60	999.61	458.88	540.73	13.49
	10	258.13	- 379.09	- 10.16	- 245.46	235.30	- 8.25
	11	1427.53	368.57	648.87	719.27	- 70.40	- 30.09
	12	934.67	- 291.16	1012.98	714.25	298.73	- 11.59
比去年同期增长（%） Increase Rate Year - on - year (%)							
2005	1	14.04	16.69	9.83	9.51	10.01	5.41
	2	13.50	10.70	13.36	13.91	13.06	- 2.75
	3	14.06	12.06	13.51	12.19	14.24	- 1.18
	4	14.45	11.97	13.88	11.39	15.28	0.38
	5	14.82	12.04	14.18	11.09	15.90	- 0.61
	6	15.36	11.42	14.34	10.38	16.58	- 0.12
	7	16.47	11.37	15.12	10.78	17.60	4.06
	8	17.35	12.64	15.53	10.68	18.31	3.24
	9	17.84	12.71	16.03	10.61	19.17	5.74
	10	17.89	12.44	15.73	9.86	19.11	1.83
	11	17.51	11.72	15.18	14.02	15.83	- 6.64
	12	16.75	9.83	15.00	15.01	14.99	- 12.54

国有商业银行人民币信贷收支主要指标时间序列表

Time Series of Major Indicators in Sources and Uses of Credit Funds of State - owned Banks（RMB）

年 月 Year Month		各项贷款 Total Loans	短期贷款 Short - term Loans	工业贷款 Loans to Industrial Sector	商业贷款 Loans to Commercial Sector	建筑业贷款 Loans to Construction Sector	农业贷款 Loans to Agricultural Sector	中长期贷款 Medium and Long - term Loans	基本建设贷款 Capital Construction Loans	技术改造贷款 Technical Improvement Loans	其他中长期贷款 Other Medium and Long - term Loans	票据融资 Paper Financing	有价证券及投资 Securities and Investments
		期末余额（亿元） Balance（100 Million Yuan）											
2005	1	95957.91	38331.71	17867.64	6762.36	1249.61	1318.20	49757.77	21868.87	1744.75	26144.15	7654.74	31587.61
	2	96300.84	38348.69	17894.06	6739.30	1251.87	1325.76	50060.65	22042.33	1754.55	26263.77	7672.93	32234.77
	3	97987.63	38661.99	18041.27	6713.86	1245.58	1356.41	50799.64	22658.01	1776.75	26364.88	8318.99	34707.33
	4	97918.88	38245.05	17921.74	6673.41	1212.83	1395.52	51087.01	22868.21	1774.10	26444.70	8381.49	36524.13
	5	96168.97	36820.56	16879.84	6378.10	1183.72	1423.89	51029.03	22878.23	1776.48	26374.32	8153.27	37467.44
	6	93706.06	33944.34	14899.36	5606.45	1148.13	1419.37	50868.25	22767.34	1786.29	26314.62	8780.37	42853.83
	7	92788.29	33528.03	14783.54	5523.28	1121.28	1410.17	50845.80	22793.64	1771.38	26280.78	8297.86	43925.13
	8	93274.23	33425.86	14800.02	5525.37	1087.85	1411.82	51127.89	23106.21	1771.46	26250.22	8601.68	45416.42
	9	94403.16	33628.57	14908.60	5591.78	1056.72	1417.67	51887.86	23688.69	1761.53	26437.64	8762.78	46479.01
	10	94176.53	33368.66	14790.59	5530.87	1043.99	1398.21	52043.93	23827.01	1756.43	26460.49	8633.45	47894.92
	11	95606.14	33348.26	14775.53	5601.75	1027.93	1391.02	52540.50	24100.15	1744.01	26696.34	9588.40	49733.68
	12	96223.99	33176.44	14693.21	5603.53	1012.47	1384.22	53349.16	24657.03	1712.91	26979.22	9574.10	50355.01
		比上期增减额（亿元） Changes Compared with Previous Period（100 Million Yuan）											
2005	1	1223.46	125.29	218.52	- 34.26	- 11.63	21.63	825.25	469.29	39.93	316.03	264.62	- 323.12
	2	324.93	16.96	26.41	- 23.06	2.26	7.56	302.91	173.48	9.79	119.64	18.18	647.16
	3	1686.78	313.30	147.21	- 25.44	- 6.30	30.65	738.98	615.68	22.20	101.10	646.06	2472.56
	4	- 68.75	- 416.92	- 119.52	- 40.45	- 32.74	39.11	287.36	210.19	- 2.65	79.82	62.50	1816.80
	5	- 54.23	- 98.23	- 163.52	21.58	- 17.71	30.14	268.29	223.96	2.39	41.94	- 228.07	943.31
	6	1972.59	529.41	347.85	41.95	3.51	2.40	813.08	566.13	9.80	237.15	627.66	5386.39
	7	- 917.78	- 416.32	- 115.82	- 83.16	- 26.85	- 9.20	- 22.45	26.29	- 14.9	- 33.84	- 482.51	1071.30
	8	485.96	- 102.15	16.48	2.08	- 33.43	1.66	282.09	312.56	0.08	- 30.55	303.82	1491.29
	9	1128.90	202.69	108.58	66.42	- 31.14	5.84	759.96	582.48	- 9.93	187.41	161.10	1062.59
	10	- 226.63	- 259.91	- 118.01	- 60.92	- 12.72	- 19.46	156.08	138.33	- 5.10	22.85	- 129.33	1415.91
	11	1429.64	- 20.38	- 15.06	70.89	- 16.06	- 7.18	496.57	273.14	- 12.42	235.85	954.95	1838.76
	12	617.84	- 171.83	- 82.32	1.78	- 15.47	- 6.81	808.66	556.89	- 31.11	282.88	- 14.30	621.33
		比去年同期增长（%） Increase Rate Year - on - year（%）											
2005	1	11.68	- 0.72	4.64	- 9.18	- 18.63	2.77	18.37	22.07	5.57	16.42	56.84	25.24
	2	10.79	- 1.24	4.84	- 9.66	- 16.95	2.72	17.90	21.26	5.35	16.18	46.36	22.99
	3	10.37	- 1.32	5.25	- 10.47	- 13.67	3.62	17.00	21.21	4.48	14.57	43.35	24.60
	4	9.36	- 1.85	4.58	- 9.17	- 13.03	5.30	15.79	20.24	2.69	13.21	37.97	31.47
	5	8.55	- 1.94	3.79	- 8.62	- 11.62	7.70	15.20	19.74	1.31	12.59	29.41	37.05
	6	9.47	- 1.35	5.05	- 8.78	- 6.25	7.25	15.28	20.57	0.22	12.06	34.25	48.38
	7	8.76	- 1.32	5.89	- 8.81	- 4.10	6.87	14.85	20.83	- 0.50	11.11	26.31	50.72
	8	8.83	- 1.20	6.26	- 8.85	- 5.53	6.90	14.52	21.06	0.23	10.20	27.85	58.03
	9	8.33	- 1.70	5.46	- 8.08	- 5.27	7.72	13.82	21.12	1.05	8.73	27.98	58.62
	10	8.26	- 1.52	5.82	- 8.21	- 3.71	6.90	13.42	20.60	- 0.46	8.47	28.46	57.47
	11	9.01	- 0.60	4.54	- 5.89	- 12.12	7.94	12.69	19.92	4.48	7.27	36.47	60.03
	12	8.04	- 1.30	2.87	- 4.63	- 12.21	7.43	12.15	19.39	- 0.56	6.96	29.55	57.40

（五）其他商业银行人民币信贷收支主要指标时间序列表（1993—2005年月度时序）

Time Series of Major Indicators in Sources and Uses of Credit Funds of Other Commercial Banks（RMB）（Monthly Series from 1997 to 2005）

其他商业银行人民币信贷收支主要指标时间序列表

Time Series of Major Indicators in Sources and Uses of Credit Funds of Other Commercial Banks（RMB）

年 月 Year Month	各项存款 Total Deposits	企业存款 Deposits by Enterprises	储蓄存款 Savings Deposits	活期储蓄 Demand Deposits	定期储蓄 Time Deposits	农村存款 Deposits by Agricultural Sector
	期末余额（亿元）Balance（100 Million Yuan）					
1993 1	256.14	138.58	38.11	20.38	17.74	4.00
2	279.08	153.24	41.11	22.29	18.82	3.65
3	297.76	164.67	43.20	23.99	19.21	3.63
4	320.31	179.00	44.61	25.45	19.17	4.45
5	327.16	184.54	45.98	26.10	19.87	4.50
6	340.94	192.23	47.16	26.48	20.68	4.19
7	337.92	181.36	49.62	27.44	22.18	4.09
8	343.30	186.11	51.95	28.02	23.93	4.12
9	375.14	211.98	54.15	28.69	25.46	3.82
10	393.74	224.26	58.62	29.54	29.08	3.40
11	422.01	238.45	61.72	30.94	30.78	3.08
12	458.61	262.98	63.94	31.74	32.20	3.26
	比上期增减额（亿元）Changes Compared with Previous Period（100 Million Yuan）					
1993 1	0.83	-0.46	3.62	2.26	1.36	0.11
2	22.94	14.66	3.00	1.91	1.08	-0.35
3	18.68	11.43	2.09	1.70	0.39	-0.01
4	22.55	14.33	1.42	1.45	-0.04	0.82
5	6.86	5.55	1.36	0.66	0.70	0.04
6	13.78	7.68	1.18	0.37	0.81	-0.31
7	-3.02	-10.87	2.46	0.96	1.50	-0.10
8	5.39	4.75	2.34	0.59	1.75	0.03
9	31.84	25.87	2.19	0.67	1.52	-0.30
10	18.59	12.27	4.47	0.85	3.62	-0.42
11	28.27	14.19	3.10	1.40	1.70	-0.32
12	36.60	24.53	2.22	0.80	1.42	0.18

其他商业银行人民币信贷收支主要指标时间序列表

Time Series of Major Indicators in Sources and Uses of Credit Funds of Other Commercial Banks（RMB）

年 月 Year Month		各项贷款 Total Loans	短期贷款 Short－term Loans				农业贷款 Loans to Agricultural Sector	中长期贷款 Medium and Long－term Loans	贴现 Discount	有价证券及投资 Securities and Investments
				工业贷款 Loans to Industrial Sector	商业贷款 Loans to Commercial Sector	建筑业及基建企业贷款 Loans to Construction and Infrastructure				
期末余额（亿元） Balance（100 Million Yuan）										
1993	1	239.00	128.06	52.90	50.15	2.26	2.77	23.21	0.12	19.93
	2	257.75	141.28	54.86	56.95	2.39	3.42	23.30	0.12	22.83
	3	266.03	145.04	59.31	56.40	2.63	3.34	25.48	0.12	24.91
	4	284.46	158.11	63.82	61.91	2.65	3.61	25.96	0.22	26.14
	5	290.52	159.31	63.92	63.04	2.91	3.72	26.21	0.34	25.82
	6	290.75	158.55	61.95	64.00	2.94	3.62	23.93	0.22	29.38
	7	291.68	157.29	57.67	66.27	2.88	3.59	22.17	0.12	31.11
	8	298.34	161.20	59.82	67.21	2.72	3.73	21.40	0.08	30.78
	9	310.94	173.23	64.15	72.86	2.85	3.45	22.19	0.05	31.06
	10	329.77	195.01	73.88	82.24	3.02	3.51	17.18	0.33	32.64
	11	345.31	204.77	79.69	84.44	3.09	3.43	18.10	0.02	32.61
	12	364.28	217.07	84.71	87.18	3.54	3.94	18.23	0.26	35.82
比上期增减额（亿元） Changes Compared with Previous Period（100 Million Yuan）										
1993	1	10.79	7.05	2.54	3.14	0.11	0.06	1.49		－1.91
	2	18.75	13.22	1.96	6.80	0.13	0.65	0.10		2.90
	3	8.28	3.76	4.45	－0.55	0.24	－0.07	2.18		2.09
	4	18.43	13.07	4.51	5.51	0.02	0.26	0.48	0.10	1.23
	5	6.06	1.20	0.11	1.13	0.26	0.12	0.25	0.12	－0.33
	6	0.23	－0.75	－1.97	0.97	0.03	－0.10	－2.28	－0.12	3.56
	7	0.93	－1.26	－4.28	2.26	－0.05	－0.03	－1.76	－0.09	1.73
	8	6.67	3.91	2.15	0.94	－0.16	0.14	－0.77	－0.04	－0.35
	9	12.60	12.03	4.33	5.65	0.13	－0.28	0.80	－0.03	0.29
	10	18.83	21.78	9.73	9.38	0.17	0.06	－5.01	0.28	1.58
	11	15.54	9.76	5.81	2.19	0.07	－0.08	0.91	－0.31	－0.02
	12	18.97	12.31	5.02	2.74	0.44	0.51	0.14	0.24	3.21

其他商业银行人民币信贷收支主要指标时间序列表

Time Series of Major Indicators in Sources and Uses of Credit Funds of Other Commercial Banks (RMB)

年 月 Year Month		各项存款 Total Deposits	企业存款 Deposits by Enterprises	储蓄存款 Savings Deposits			农业存款 Deposits by Agricultural Sector
					活期储蓄 Demand Deposits	定期储蓄 Time Deposits	
期末余额（亿元）Balance (100 Million Yuan)							
1994	1	447.74	272.71	68.16	33.20	34.96	2.85
	2	462.34	284.06	72.15	33.73	38.43	2.67
	3	491.41	306.91	76.03	34.22	41.81	3.17
	4	531.96	340.15	79.33	35.87	43.46	3.72
	5	565.41	365.16	83.60	37.45	46.15	3.90
	6	600.22	393.90	88.84	39.19	49.65	3.76
	7	647.10	430.59	94.81	41.20	53.61	3.74
	8	685.53	445.18	100.43	42.78	57.65	3.47
	9	704.46	456.24	104.00	43.14	60.86	4.01
	10	729.23	471.62	108.39	44.35	64.05	3.05
	11	750.29	477.64	114.44	46.48	67.96	2.90
	12	827.51	541.56	124.56	51.96	72.60	2.95
比上期增减额（亿元）Changes Compared with Previous Period (100 Million Yuan)							
1994	1	-7.59	-13.47	4.19	1.85	2.34	-0.44
	2	14.60	11.35	3.99	0.53	3.47	-0.18
	3	29.07	22.85	3.87	0.49	3.38	0.49
	4	40.55	33.24	3.30	1.65	1.65	0.56
	5	33.45	25.01	4.27	1.58	2.69	0.18
	6	34.81	28.73	5.24	1.74	3.50	-0.14
	7	46.88	36.69	5.97	2.01	3.96	-0.02
	8	38.43	14.59	5.62	1.58	4.04	-0.27
	9	18.93	11.06	3.57	0.36	3.21	0.54
	10	24.77	15.38	4.39	1.21	3.19	-0.96
	11	21.06	6.02	6.05	2.13	3.91	-0.15
	12	77.22	63.92	10.12	5.48	4.64	0.05
比去年同期增长（%）Increase Rate Year-on-year (%)							
1994	1	74.80	96.79	78.85	62.90	97.07	-28.75
	2	65.67	85.37	75.50	51.32	104.20	-26.85
	3	65.04	86.38	76.00	42.64	117.65	-12.67
	4	66.08	90.03	77.83	40.94	126.71	-16.40
	5	72.82	97.88	81.82	43.49	132.26	-13.33
	6	76.05	104.91	88.38	48.00	140.09	-10.26
	7	91.50	137.42	91.07	50.15	141.70	-8.56
	8	99.69	139.20	93.32	52.68	140.91	-15.78
	9	87.79	115.23	92.06	50.37	139.04	4.97
	10	85.21	110.30	84.90	50.14	120.25	-10.29
	11	77.79	100.31	85.42	50.23	120.79	-5.84
	12	80.44	105.93	94.81	63.71	125.47	-9.51

其他商业银行人民币信贷收支主要指标时间序列表
Time Series of Major Indicators in Sources and Uses of Credit Funds of Other Commercial Banks（RMB）

年 月 Year Month		各项贷款 Total Loans	短期贷款 Short - term Loans	工业贷款 Loans to Industrial Sector	商业贷款 Loans to Commercial Sector	建筑业及基建企业贷款 Loans to Construction and Infrastructure	农业贷款 Loans to Agricultural Sector	中长期贷款 Medium and Long - term Loans	贴现 Discount	有价证券及投资 Securities and Investments
		期末余额（亿元） Balance（100 Million Yuan）								
1994	1	376.45	207.73	86.15	83.42	3.56	9.69	12.25	0.29	27.12
	2	382.50	216.23	94.35	83.79	3.53	4.17	13.76	0.27	31.36
	3	396.21	222.89	89.43	93.90	3.60	9.93	14.72	0.28	32.15
	4	417.24	243.25	97.00	104.30	3.69	3.96	13.53	0.34	36.57
	5	436.61	253.63	105.56	102.12	3.78	3.86	13.41	0.38	41.35
	6	451.44	264.65	105.25	110.71	3.97	3.19	14.01	0.45	41.70
	7	480.68	281.86	105.06	125.49	4.06	3.13	13.90	0.64	48.02
	8	507.41	296.85	108.90	133.51	4.15	3.15	14.95	0.62	46.15
	9	532.92	301.77	112.73	133.10	4.29	2.90	21.00	0.57	45.46
	10	558.13	312.12	118.07	136.36	4.36	2.65	20.70	0.40	43.68
	11	575.62	317.38	122.50	136.95	4.49	2.55	21.26	0.98	53.57
	12	613.63	324.52	128.34	134.31	4.69	2.59	22.88	1.45	60.28
		比上期增减额（亿元） Changes Compared with Previous Period（100 Million Yuan）								
1994	1	11.06	3.81	-7.03	10.03	0.30	5.76	-1.83	0.03	4.67
	2	6.06	8.51	8.20	0.37	-0.03	-5.51	1.51	-0.02	4.24
	3	13.71	6.65	-4.93	10.11	0.07	5.76	0.96	0.01	0.79
	4	21.03	20.36	7.57	10.40	0.09	-5.97	-1.19	0.06	4.42
	5	19.37	10.38	8.56	-2.18	0.09	-0.10	-0.12	0.04	4.77
	6	14.83	11.02	-0.31	8.59	0.19	-0.67	0.60	0.07	0.35
	7	29.24	17.21	-0.19	14.78	0.09	-0.06	-0.11	0.19	6.32
	8	26.73	14.99	3.84	8.02	0.09	0.02	1.05	-0.02	-1.87
	9	25.51	4.92	3.83	-0.41	0.14	-0.25	6.05	-0.05	-0.69
	10	25.21	10.35	5.34	3.26	0.07	-0.25	-0.30	-0.17	-1.78
	11	17.49	5.26	4.43	0.59	0.13	-0.10	0.56	0.58	9.89
	12	38.01	7.14	5.84	-2.64	0.20	0.04	1.62	0.47	6.71
		比去年同期增长（%） Increase Rate Year - on - year（%）								
1994	1	57.51	62.21	62.85	66.34	57.52	249.82	-47.22	141.67	36.08
	2	48.40	53.05	71.98	47.13	47.70	21.93	-40.94	125.00	37.36
	3	48.93	53.67	50.78	66.49	36.88	197.31	-42.23	133.33	29.06
	4	46.68	53.85	51.99	68.47	39.25	9.70	-47.88	54.55	39.90
	5	50.29	59.21	65.14	61.99	29.90	3.76	-48.84	11.76	60.15
	6	55.27	66.92	69.90	72.98	35.03	-11.88	-41.45	104.55	41.93
	7	64.80	79.20	82.17	89.36	40.97	-12.81	-37.30	433.33	54.36
	8	70.08	84.15	82.05	98.65	52.57	-15.55	-30.14	675.00	49.94
	9	71.39	74.20	75.73	82.68	50.53	-15.94	-5.36	1040.00	46.36
	10	69.25	60.05	59.81	65.81	44.37	-24.50	20.49	21.21	33.82
	11	66.70	54.99	53.72	62.19	45.31	-25.66	17.46	4800.00	64.27
	12	68.45	49.50	51.51	54.06	32.49	-34.26	25.51	457.69	68.29

其他商业银行人民币信贷收支主要指标时间序列表

Time Series of Major Indicators in Sources and Uses of Credit Funds of Other Commercial Banks (RMB)

年 月 Year Month		各项存款 Total Deposits	企业存款 Deposits by Enterprises	储蓄存款 Savings Deposits			农业存款 Deposits by Agricultural Sector
					活期储蓄 Demand Deposits	定期储蓄 Time Deposits	
期末余额（亿元） Balance (100 Million Yuan)							
1995	1	920.24	616.65	141.39	54.50	86.89	3.34
	2	959.78	643.25	150.88	58.25	92.63	2.16
	3	1022.57	692.25	160.33	59.45	100.88	2.32
	4	1069.75	727.94	168.11	60.79	107.32	2.50
	5	1119.67	772.01	175.24	61.42	113.82	2.45
	6	1187.78	812.13	183.69	63.11	120.58	2.48
	7	1247.58	859.49	195.74	64.31	131.43	2.48
	8	1304.33	890.33	205.03	64.26	140.77	2.42
	9	1338.89	914.18	214.15	66.11	148.04	2.30
	10	1373.00	930.06	224.50	68.99	155.51	2.20
	11	1416.07	955.67	235.89	70.35	165.54	2.26
	12	1530.34	1023.85	254.87	78.06	176.81	2.11
比上期增减额（亿元） Changes Compared with Previous Period (100 Million Yuan)							
1995	1	-2.26	-4.75	8.19	-0.03	8.22	0.39
	2	39.54	26.60	9.49	3.75	5.74	-1.18
	3	62.79	49.00	9.45	1.20	8.25	0.16
	4	47.18	35.69	7.78	1.34	6.44	0.18
	5	49.92	44.07	7.13	0.63	6.50	-0.05
	6	68.11	40.12	8.45	1.69	6.76	0.03
	7	59.80	47.36	12.05	1.20	10.85	
	8	56.75	30.84	9.29	-0.05	9.34	-0.06
	9	34.56	23.85	9.12	1.85	7.27	-0.12
	10	34.11	15.88	10.35	2.88	7.47	-0.10
	11	43.07	25.61	11.39	1.36	10.03	0.06
	12	114.27	68.18	18.98	7.71	11.27	-0.15
比去年同期增长（%） Increase Rate Year-on-year (%)							
1995	1	105.53	126.12	107.44	64.16	148.54	17.19
	2	107.59	126.45	109.12	72.69	141.04	-19.10
	3	108.09	125.55	110.88	73.73	141.28	-26.81
	4	101.10	114.01	111.91	69.47	146.94	-32.80
	5	98.03	111.42	109.62	64.01	146.63	-37.18
	6	97.89	106.18	106.76	61.04	142.86	-34.04
	7	92.80	99.61	106.46	56.09	145.16	-33.69
	8	90.27	99.99	104.15	50.21	144.18	-30.26
	9	90.06	100.37	105.91	53.25	143.25	-42.64
	10	88.28	97.21	107.12	55.56	142.79	-27.87
	11	88.74	100.08	106.13	51.36	143.58	-22.07
	12	84.93	89.06	104.62	50.23	143.54	-28.47

其他商业银行人民币信贷收支主要指标时间序列表

Time Series of Major Indicators in Sources and Uses of Credit Funds of Other Commercial Banks（RMB）

年 月 Year Month	各项贷款 Total Loans	短期贷款 Short - term Loans				农业贷款 Loans to Agricultural Sector	中长期贷款 Medium and Long - term Loans	贴现 Discount	有价证券及投资 Securities and Investments
			工业贷款 Loans to Industrial Sector	商业贷款 Loans to Commercial Sector	建筑业及基建企业贷款 Loans to Construction and Infrastructure				
期末余额（亿元） Balance（100 Million Yuan）									
1995 1	789.08	421.58	176.69	160.74	15.91	2.53	76.01	1.81	64.78
2	793.40	418.89	174.21	161.89	15.03	2.54	77.17	2.25	67.02
3	854.45	451.98	185.29	177.56	15.74	2.85	77.93	2.89	73.14
4	881.22	469.89	189.94	185.73	16.50	2.76	78.52	2.98	77.93
5	905.86	487.54	192.98	195.13	16.69	2.48	79.59	3.10	84.83
6	920.89	491.16	196.06	194.77	15.78	2.52	83.10	3.74	90.08
7	968.03	501.97	200.62	198.41	15.52	2.59	83.85	4.36	98.48
8	1026.79	528.80	224.77	199.56	14.64	2.55	84.43	5.37	108.96
9	1065.90	544.40	234.85	203.85	14.63	2.52	90.26	7.39	113.10
10	1073.81	540.53	234.84	198.29	14.62	2.51	89.34	7.52	121.52
11	1106.73	555.26	241.56	205.31	14.07	2.89	87.31	8.25	120.99
12	1153.62	595.64	253.64	227.31	13.89	2.74	98.92	10.02	133.11
比上期增减额（亿元） Changes Compared with Previous Period（100 Million Yuan）									
1995 1	25.02	6.89	8.09	8.73	0.29	-0.06	-0.60	0.26	-0.70
2	4.32	-2.69	-2.48	1.15	-0.88	0.01	1.16	0.44	2.24
3	61.05	33.09	11.08	15.67	0.71	0.31	0.76	0.64	6.12
4	26.77	17.91	4.65	8.17	0.76	-0.09	0.59	0.09	4.79
5	24.64	17.65	3.04	9.40	0.19	-0.28	1.07	0.12	6.90
6	15.03	3.62	3.08	-0.36	-0.91	0.04	3.51	0.64	5.25
7	47.14	10.81	4.56	3.64	-0.26	0.07	0.75	0.62	8.40
8	58.76	26.83	24.15	1.15	-0.88	-0.04	0.58	1.01	10.48
9	39.11	15.60	10.08	4.29	-0.01	-0.03	5.83	2.02	4.14
10	7.91	-3.87	-0.01	-5.56	-0.01	-0.01	-0.92	0.13	8.42
11	32.92	14.73	6.72	7.02	-0.55	0.38	-2.03	0.73	-0.53
12	46.89	40.38	12.08	22.00	-0.18	-0.15	11.61	1.77	12.12
比去年同期增长（%） Increase Rate Year - on - year（%）									
1995 1	109.61	102.95	105.10	92.69	346.91	-73.89	520.49	524.14	138.86
2	107.42	93.72	84.64	93.21	325.78	-39.09	460.83	733.33	113.71
3	115.66	102.78	107.19	89.09	337.22	-71.30	429.42	932.14	127.50
4	111.20	93.17	95.81	78.07	347.15	-30.30	480.34	776.47	113.10
5	107.48	92.22	82.82	91.08	341.53	-35.75	493.51	715.79	105.15
6	103.99	85.59	86.28	75.93	297.48	-21.00	493.15	731.11	116.02
7	101.39	78.09	90.96	58.11	282.27	-17.25	503.24	581.25	105.08
8	102.36	78.14	106.40	49.47	252.77	-19.05	464.75	766.13	136.10
9	100.01	80.40	108.33	53.16	241.03	-13.10	329.81	1196.49	148.79
10	92.39	73.18	98.90	45.42	235.32	-5.28	331.59	1780.00	178.21
11	92.27	74.95	97.19	49.92	213.36	13.33	310.68	741.84	125.85
12	88.00	83.54	97.63	69.24	196.16	5.79	332.34	591.03	120.82

其他商业银行人民币信贷收支主要指标时间序列表

Time Series of Major Indicators in Sources and Uses of Credit Funds of Other Commercial Banks (RMB)

年 月 Year Month		各项存款 Total Deposits	企业存款 Deposits by Enterprises	储蓄存款 Savings Deposits	活期储蓄 Demand Deposits	定期储蓄 Time Deposits	农业存款 Deposits by Agricultural Sector
期末余额（亿元）Balance (100 Million Yuan)							
1996	1	1518.96	1017.41	266.23	80.61	185.62	2.32
	2	1515.45	993.98	283.08	80.89	202.19	1.80
	3	1582.67	1045.67	299.62	80.98	218.64	2.09
	4	1684.15	1132.42	315.40	82.06	233.34	2.24
	5	1768.61	1201.79	324.08	84.44	239.64	2.33
	6	1838.45	1246.62	336.30	90.80	245.50	2.55
	7	1900.47	1294.65	347.87	94.17	253.70	2.37
	8	1974.62	1337.01	362.64	98.16	264.48	2.29
	9	2033.00	1381.86	376.06	104.11	271.95	2.24
	10	2094.01	1418.45	385.46	110.19	275.27	2.34
	11	2144.85	1453.68	391.09	116.10	274.99	2.25
	12	2348.82	1612.14	411.40	130.80	280.60	2.38
比上期增减额（亿元）Changes Compared with Previous Period (100 Million Yuan)							
1996	1	-11.37	-6.44	11.36	2.55	8.81	0.21
	2	-3.52	-23.43	16.85	0.28	16.57	-0.52
	3	67.20	51.69	16.54	0.09	16.45	0.29
	4	101.48	86.75	15.78	1.08	14.70	0.15
	5	84.46	69.37	8.68	2.38	6.30	0.09
	6	69.84	44.83	12.22	6.36	5.86	0.22
	7	62.02	48.03	11.57	3.37	8.20	-0.18
	8	74.15	42.36	14.77	3.99	10.78	-0.08
	9	58.37	44.85	13.42	5.95	7.47	-0.05
	10	61.01	36.59	9.40	6.08	3.32	0.10
	11	50.84	35.23	5.63	5.91	-0.28	-0.09
	12	203.97	158.46	20.31	14.70	5.61	0.13
比去年同期增长（%）Increase Rate Year-on-year (%)							
1996	1	65.06	64.99	88.29	47.91	113.63	-30.54
	2	57.90	54.52	87.62	38.87	118.28	-16.67
	3	54.77	51.05	86.88	36.22	116.73	-9.91
	4	57.43	55.57	87.62	34.99	117.42	-10.40
	5	57.96	55.67	84.93	37.48	110.54	-4.90
	6	54.78	53.50	83.08	43.88	103.60	2.82
	7	52.33	50.63	77.72	46.43	93.03	-4.44
	8	51.39	50.17	76.87	52.75	87.88	-5.37
	9	51.84	51.16	75.61	57.48	83.70	-2.61
	10	52.51	52.51	71.70	59.72	77.01	6.36
	11	51.46	52.11	65.79	65.03	66.12	-0.44
	12	53.48	57.46	61.42	67.56	58.70	12.80

其他商业银行人民币信贷收支主要指标时间序列表

Time Series of Major Indicators in Sources and Uses of Credit Funds of Other Commercial Banks（RMB）

年 月 Year Month		各项贷款 Total Loans	短期贷款 Short－term Loans				农业贷款 Loans to Agricultural Sector	中长期贷款 Medium and Long－term Loans	贴现 Discount	有价证券及投资 Securities and Investments
				工业贷款 Loans to Industrial Sector	商业贷款 Loans to Commercial Sector	建筑业及基建企业贷款 Loans to Construction and Infrastructure				
		期末余额（亿元） Balance（100 Million Yuan）								
1996	1	1164.67	598.38	251.29	234.30	11.66	2.81	74.14	10.35	125.71
	2	1179.61	604.76	252.98	239.03	11.46	2.93	64.69	10.83	156.94
	3	1199.76	605.46	253.53	238.45	11.59	2.89	64.51	13.37	173.72
	4	1239.04	623.91	261.41	246.86	11.70	2.41	64.14	15.11	181.56
	5	1267.03	636.25	266.97	248.76	12.29	2.68	64.00	17.25	204.06
	6	1307.84	661.41	281.10	254.40	6.82	2.83	65.38	20.93	202.38
	7	1328.42	664.65	284.77	251.70	12.87	2.73	67.56	22.93	231.04
	8	1369.79	673.07	286.56	257.48	12.53	2.69	70.78	25.23	272.23
	9	1412.72	682.57	292.62	265.06	12.46	2.65	71.78	28.73	263.43
	10	1440.30	697.80	304.38	268.03	13.63	2.65	75.80	30.18	286.91
	11	1504.27	740.70	334.58	274.27	17.25	2.68	79.25	34.00	289.90
	12	1638.55	812.59	364.23	300.49	22.61	3.86	87.08	37.64	307.60
		比上期增减额（亿元） Changes Compared with Previous Period（100 Million Yuan）								
1996	1	11.05	6.27	7.05	1.57	－2.23	0.07	17.97	0.33	14.06
	2	14.94	6.38	1.69	4.73	－0.20	0.12	－9.45	0.48	8.61
	3	20.15	0.70	0.55	－0.58	0.13	－0.04	－0.18	2.54	16.78
	4	39.28	18.45	7.88	8.41	0.11	－0.48	－0.37	1.74	7.84
	5	27.99	12.34	5.56	1.90	0.59	0.27	－0.14	2.14	22.50
	6	40.81	25.16	14.13	5.64	－5.47	0.15	1.38	3.68	－1.68
	7	20.58	3.24	3.67	－2.70	6.05	－0.10	2.18	2.00	28.66
	8	41.37	8.42	1.79	5.78	－0.34	－0.04	3.22	2.30	41.19
	9	42.92	9.50	6.06	7.58	－0.07	－0.04	1.00	3.50	－8.80
	10	27.59	15.23	11.76	2.97	1.17		4.02	1.45	23.48
	11	63.97	42.90	30.20	6.24	3.62	0.03	3.45	3.82	2.99
	12	134.28	71.89	29.65	26.22	5.36	1.18	7.83	3.64	17.70
		比去年同期增长（%） Increase Rate Year－on－year（%）								
1996	1	47.60	41.94	42.22	45.76	－26.71	11.07	－2.46	471.82	94.06
	2	48.68	44.37	45.22	47.65	－23.75	15.35	－16.17	381.33	134.17
	3	40.41	33.96	36.83	34.29	－26.37	1.40	－17.22	362.63	137.52
	4	40.61	32.78	37.63	32.91	－29.09	－12.68	－18.31	407.05	132.98
	5	39.87	30.50	38.34	27.48	－26.36	8.06	－19.59	456.45	140.55
	6	42.02	34.66	43.37	30.62	－56.78	12.30	－21.32	459.63	124.67
	7	37.23	32.41	41.94	26.86	－17.07	5.41	－19.43	425.92	134.61
	8	33.41	27.28	27.49	29.02	－14.41	5.49	－16.17	369.83	149.84
	9	32.54	25.38	24.60	30.03	－14.83	5.16	－20.47	288.77	132.92
	10	34.13	29.10	29.61	35.17	－6.77	5.58	－15.16	301.33	136.10
	11	35.92	33.40	38.51	33.59	22.60	－7.27	－9.23	312.12	139.61
	12	42.04	36.42	43.60	32.19	62.78	40.88	－11.97	275.65	131.09

其他商业银行人民币信贷收支主要指标时间序列表

Time Series of Major Indicators in Sources and Uses of Credit Funds of Other Commercial Banks (RMB)

年 月 Year Month		各项存款 Total Deposits	企业存款 Deposits by Enterprises	储蓄存款 Savings Deposits	活期储蓄 Demand Deposits	定期储蓄 Time Deposits	农业存款 Deposits by Agricultural Sector
		期末余额(亿元) Balance (100 Million Yuan)					
1997	1	2132.00	1601.80	439.48	133.35	306.13	1.58
	2	2142.21	1623.42	455.19	136.85	318.34	1.63
	3	2213.84	1696.61	453.88	136.33	317.55	1.74
	4	2250.66	1727.31	457.71	141.70	316.01	2.35
	5	2282.39	1754.91	454.71	139.30	315.41	2.23
	6	2388.23	1840.01	470.99	141.37	329.62	2.45
	7	2438.98	1871.92	487.86	150.23	337.63	2.42
	8	2507.52	1927.58	499.25	152.22	347.03	2.63
	9	2604.30	2019.16	505.54	156.11	349.43	2.56
	10	2600.33	2029.58	512.45	158.62	353.83	2.70
	11	2676.75	2102.16	518.45	164.18	354.27	2.88
	12	2957.91	2363.12	536.20	179.42	356.78	3.23
		比上期增减额(亿元) Changes Compared with Previous Period (100 Million Yuan)					
1997	1	3.99	-53.88	26.06	4.30	21.76	-0.55
	2	10.18	21.62	15.71	3.50	12.21	0.04
	3	71.65	73.19	-1.30	-0.52	-0.78	0.11
	4	36.80	30.70	3.81	5.36	-1.55	0.61
	5	31.73	27.60	-2.99	-2.40	-0.59	-0.12
	6	105.87	85.11	16.28	2.07	14.21	0.23
	7	50.71	31.89	16.86	8.85	8.01	-0.04
	8	68.53	55.66	11.39	1.99	9.40	0.21
	9	96.78	91.59	6.28	3.89	2.39	-0.07
	10	-3.96	10.42	6.92	2.51	4.41	0.14
	11	76.41	72.59	5.99	5.55	0.44	0.18
	12	281.16	260.95	17.75	15.24	2.51	0.35
		比去年同期增长(%) Increase Rate Year-on-year (%)					
1997	1	40.36	57.44	65.08	65.43	64.92	-31.90
	2	41.36	63.33	60.80	69.18	57.45	-9.44
	3	39.88	62.25	51.49	68.35	45.24	-16.75
	4	33.64	52.53	45.12	72.68	35.43	4.91
	5	29.05	46.02	40.31	64.97	31.62	-4.29
	6	29.90	47.60	40.05	55.69	34.26	-3.92
	7	28.34	44.59	40.24	59.53	33.08	2.11
	8	26.99	44.17	37.67	55.07	31.21	14.85
	9	28.10	46.12	34.43	49.95	28.49	14.29
	10	24.18	43.08	32.95	43.95	28.54	15.38
	11	24.80	44.61	32.57	41.41	28.83	28.00
	12	25.93	46.58	30.34	37.17	27.15	35.71

其他商业银行人民币信贷收支主要指标时间序列表

Time Series of Major Indicators in Sources and Uses of Credit Funds of Other Commercial Banks（RMB）

年 月 Year Month		各项贷款 Total Loans	短期贷款 Short－term Loans						中长期贷款 Medium and Long－term Loans				有价证券及投资 Securities and Investments
				工业贷款 Loans to Industrial Sector	商业贷款 Loans to Commercial Sector	建筑业及基建企业贷款 Loans to Construction and Infrastructure	农业贷款 Loans to Agricultural Sector	贴现 Discount		基本建设贷款 Capital Construction Loans	技术改造贷款 Technical Improvement Loans	其他中长期贷款 Other Medium and Long－term Loans	
期末余额（亿元） Balance（100 Million Yuan）													
1997	1	1540.08	1210.36	280.35	275.63	37.26	2.08	36.93	113.20	39.28	4.87	69.05	307.41
	2	1542.31	1213.72	279.09	267.54	37.01	1.22	35.93	110.14	36.21	4.95	68.98	308.27
	3	1571.99	1230.36	288.18	273.69	39.14	1.20	36.03	111.46	37.94	5.09	68.43	329.83
	4	1566.74	1198.67	277.97	262.34	39.23	1.01	32.48	110.43	37.37	5.10	67.96	334.83
	5	1592.50	1198.89	282.51	254.39	38.69	1.02	33.91	110.53	36.88	4.87	68.78	316.57
	6	1644.94	1251.03	297.63	262.81	39.95	0.99	33.54	113.65	37.68	4.97	71.00	322.51
	7	1674.71	1256.30	298.16	265.72	39.52	0.97	37.83	114.02	37.74	4.88	71.40	325.32
	8	1709.00	1278.80	306.75	265.80	39.74	0.94	41.69	115.82	35.74	4.78	75.30	331.30
	9	1752.68	1307.37	313.21	278.86	34.80	0.85	43.36	125.17	40.99	4.91	79.27	365.53
	10	1790.72	1338.39	318.28	280.66	34.67	1.15	41.12	131.77	42.67	5.88	83.22	375.68
	11	1827.01	1373.94	328.30	286.70	34.51	1.17	42.57	133.86	42.35	5.20	86.31	392.71
	12	1976.71	1552.11	377.66	327.32	38.91	1.52	50.73	163.60	50.95	5.54	107.11	406.74
比上期增减额（亿元） Changes Compared with Previous Period（100 Million Yuan）													
1997	1	65.00	15.55	9.49	－15.74	7.99	－0.03	4.13	7.54	1.66	0.32	5.56	－10.54
	2	2.21	3.35	－1.26	－8.09	－0.25	－0.86	－0.99	－3.07	－3.07	0.08	－0.08	0.85
	3	29.70	16.65	9.09	6.15	2.13	－0.02	0.10	1.32	1.73	0.14	－0.55	21.57
	4	－5.26	－31.70	－10.21	－11.35	0.08	－0.19	－3.55	－1.03	－0.57	0.01	－0.47	4.99
	5	25.76	0.21	4.54	－7.95	－0.54	0.01	1.43	0.10	－0.49	－0.23	0.82	－18.25
	6	52.44	52.14	15.12	8.42	1.26	－0.02	－0.37	3.12	0.81	0.10	2.21	5.94
	7	29.78	5.27	0.54	2.90	－0.43	－0.03	4.29	0.37	0.06	－0.09	0.40	2.80
	8	34.28	22.50	8.59	0.08	0.22	－0.03	3.86	1.80	－2.00	－0.10	3.90	5.99
	9	43.69	28.57	6.45	13.06	－4.94	－0.09	1.68	9.35	5.25	0.13	3.97	34.23
	10	38.04	31.01	5.08	1.80	－0.13	0.30	－2.25	6.62	1.69	0.97	3.96	10.15
	11	36.27	35.55	10.02	6.05	－0.17	0.02	1.45	2.06	－0.33	－0.69	3.08	17.02
	12	149.70	178.17	49.36	40.62	4.41	0.34	8.16	29.75	8.60	0.35	20.80	14.03
比去年同期增长（%） Increase Rate Year－on－year（%）													
1997	1	32.23	—	—	—	—	—	—	—	—	—	—	—
	2	30.75	—	—	—	—	—	—	—	—	—	—	—
	3	31.03	—	—	—	—	—	—	—	—	—	—	—
	4	26.45	—	—	—	—	—	—	—	—	—	—	—
	5	25.69	—	—	—	—	—	—	—	—	—	—	—
	6	25.78	—	—	—	—	—	—	—	—	—	—	—
	7	26.07	—	—	—	—	—	—	—	—	—	—	—
	8	24.76	—	—	—	—	—	—	—	—	—	—	—
	9	24.06	—	—	—	—	—	—	—	—	—	—	—
	10	24.33	—	—	—	—	—	—	—	—	—	—	—
	11	21.45	—	—	—	—	—	—	—	—	—	—	—
	12	20.64	—	—	—	—	—	—	—	—	—	—	—

其他商业银行人民币信贷收支主要指标时间序列表

Time Series of Major Indicators in Sources and Uses of Credit Funds of Other Commercial Banks (RMB)

年 月 Year Month		各项存款 Total Deposits	企业存款 Deposits by Enterprises	储蓄存款 Savings Deposits			农业存款 Deposits by Agricultural Sector
					活期储蓄 Demand Deposits	定期储蓄 Time Deposits	
期末余额（亿元） Balance (100 Million Yuan)							
1998	1	2897.13	2210.05	580.55	190.77	389.78	2.03
	2	2833.08	2142.03	589.66	189.17	400.49	2.44
	3	2869.23	2179.35	592.00	187.52	404.48	2.46
	4	2950.39	2242.17	595.92	191.53	404.39	2.65
	5	3056.89	2342.03	600.28	194.32	405.96	2.78
	6	3123.19	2390.81	599.52	193.76	405.76	2.91
	7	3189.56	2441.53	612.98	205.46	407.52	2.89
	8	3205.12	2445.70	620.37	209.73	410.64	3.80
	9	3430.02	2618.77	635.07	218.78	416.29	3.21
	10	3484.91	2663.46	646.11	224.08	422.03	3.05
	11	3539.25	2699.45	658.37	229.28	429.09	3.11
	12	3839.99	2958.36	684.73	247.22	437.51	3.05
比上期增减额（亿元） Changes Compared with Previous Period (100 Million Yuan)							
1998	1	-145.06	-154.20	16.66	7.33	9.33	-1.22
	2	-64.04	-68.02	9.11	-1.60	10.71	0.41
	3	31.61	37.32	2.34	-1.65	3.99	0.02
	4	81.15	62.81	3.92	4.00	-0.08	0.19
	5	106.53	99.87	4.37	2.80	1.57	0.13
	6	66.29	48.78	-0.76	-0.56	-0.20	0.13
	7	66.38	50.72	13.46	11.70	1.76	-0.01
	8	15.58	4.19	7.39	4.27	3.12	0.91
	9	224.89	173.06	14.70	9.05	5.65	-0.59
	10	54.90	44.69	11.04	5.30	5.74	-0.16
	11	54.35	36.00	12.26	5.20	7.06	0.07
	12	300.74	258.91	26.36	17.94	8.42	-0.07
比去年同期增长（%） Increase Rate Year-on-year (%)							
1998	1	33.49	37.97	32.10	43.06	27.32	28.48
	2	29.96	31.95	29.54	38.23	25.81	49.69
	3	26.92	28.45	30.43	37.55	27.38	41.38
	4	28.42	29.81	30.20	35.17	27.97	12.77
	5	31.37	33.46	32.01	39.50	28.71	24.66
	6	28.26	29.94	27.29	37.06	23.10	18.78
	7	28.20	30.43	25.65	36.76	20.70	19.42
	8	25.79	26.88	24.26	37.78	18.33	44.49
	9	29.99	29.70	25.62	40.14	19.13	25.39
	10	32.18	31.23	26.08	41.27	19.27	12.96
	11	30.45	28.41	26.99	39.65	21.12	7.99
	12	27.80	25.19	27.70	37.79	22.63	-5.57

其他商业银行人民币信贷收支主要指标时间序列表

Time Series of Major Indicators in Sources and Uses of Credit Funds of Other Commercial Banks（RMB）

年 月 Year Month		各项贷款 Total Loans	短期贷款 Short－term Loans						中长期贷款 Medium and Long－term Loans				有价证券及投资 Securities and Investments
				工业贷款 Loans to Industrial Sector	商业贷款 Loans to Commercial Sector	建筑业及基建企业贷款 Loans to Construction and Infrastructure	农业贷款 Loans to Agricultural Sector	贴现 Discount		基本建设贷款 Capital Construction Loans	技术改造贷款 Technical Improvement Loans	其他中长期贷款 Other Medium and Long－term Loans	
期末余额（亿元） Balance（100 Million Yuan）													
1998	1	1985.34	1523.99	363.15	316.94	38.49	1.60	54.40	178.14	56.76	5.74	115.64	407.07
	2	1999.19	1519.96	363.44	310.05	41.90	1.46	54.81	178.77	57.41	5.63	115.73	414.86
	3	2082.63	1547.51	366.03	312.70	44.73	1.50	52.12	186.97	59.78	5.53	121.66	394.81
	4	2113.87	1562.03	363.06	316.78	44.60	1.73	51.77	190.43	61.25	6.39	122.79	405.02
	5	2149.89	1574.00	368.85	317.97	43.32	1.94	47.42	206.26	62.50	6.86	136.90	475.81
	6	2233.36	1640.15	383.53	312.85	44.40	1.94	41.89	221.07	64.90	6.50	149.67	557.98
	7	2272.25	1644.03	375.88	315.72	44.55	1.18	39.13	236.23	66.53	9.45	160.25	566.50
	8	2316.35	1662.23	375.85	313.20	44.67	1.70	42.80	243.68	73.87	5.43	164.38	578.24
	9	2401.44	1728.26	379.80	313.03	45.78	1.49	48.58	254.91	76.65	5.94	172.32	600.89
	10	2415.41	1699.40	371.77	297.56	43.27	1.46	49.53	266.07	78.70	7.82	179.55	664.27
	11	2416.45	1729.55	379.38	299.84	44.36	1.22	54.07	273.93	79.26	8.95	185.72	712.42
	12	2608.44	1886.61	411.56	319.52	48.80	1.08	62.38	290.33	85.25	9.74	195.34	738.12
比上期增减额（亿元） Changes Compared with Previous Period（100 Million Yuan）													
1998	1	－16.78	－38.21	－18.35	－11.34	－2.38	0.09	3.68	7.96	2.03	0.55	5.38	－2.27
	2	13.86	－4.02	0.29	－6.89	3.41	－0.14	0.41	0.63	0.65	－0.11	0.09	7.79
	3	62.76	27.56	2.59	2.65	2.83	0.04	－2.69	8.20	2.37	－0.11	5.94	－20.05
	4	29.36	12.65	－2.97	4.08	－0.12	0.23	－0.35	3.46	1.47	0.86	1.13	10.20
	5	36.03	11.99	5.79	1.19	－1.28	0.21	－4.34	15.82	1.25	0.47	14.10	70.79
	6	83.46	66.14	14.68	－5.12	1.08		－5.54	14.81	2.40	－0.36	12.77	82.17
	7	38.88	3.87	－7.65	2.87	0.15	－0.77	－2.76	15.16	1.63	2.95	10.58	8.52
	8	44.09	18.20	－0.03	－2.52	0.11	0.52	3.67	7.43	7.34	－4.03	4.12	11.73
	9	85.13	66.05	3.95	－0.16	1.11	－0.21	5.79	11.25	2.78	0.52	7.95	22.66
	10	13.95	－28.88	－8.03	－15.47	－2.51	－0.03	0.94	11.16	2.05	1.88	7.23	63.37
	11	46.03	30.15	7.61	2.27	1.08	－0.24	4.54	7.86	0.56	1.13	6.17	48.15
	12	146.98	157.05	32.18	19.68	4.45	－0.14	8.30	16.41	5.99	0.79	9.63	25.70
比去年同期增长（%） Increase Rate Year－on－year（%）													
1998	1	28.91	25.91	29.53	14.99	3.30	－23.08	47.31	57.37	44.50	17.86	67.47	32.42
	2	29.62	25.23	30.22	15.89	13.21	19.67	52.55	62.31	58.55	13.74	67.77	34.58
	3	32.48	25.78	27.01	14.25	14.28	25.00	44.66	67.75	57.56	8.64	77.79	19.70
	4	34.92	30.31	30.61	20.75	13.69	71.29	59.39	72.44	63.90	25.29	80.68	20.96
	5	35.00	31.29	30.56	24.99	11.97	90.20	39.84	86.61	69.47	40.86	99.04	50.30
	6	35.77	31.10	28.86	19.04	11.14	95.96	24.90	94.52	72.24	30.78	110.80	73.01
	7	35.68	30.86	26.07	18.82	12.73	21.65	3.44	107.18	76.29	93.65	124.44	74.14
	8	35.54	29.98	22.53	17.83	12.41	80.85	2.66	110.40	106.69	13.60	118.30	74.54
	9	37.02	32.19	21.26	12.25	31.55	75.29	12.04	103.65	87.00	20.98	117.38	64.39
	10	34.88	26.97	16.81	6.02	24.81	26.96	20.45	101.92	84.44	32.99	115.75	76.82
	11	34.73	25.88	15.56	4.58	28.54	4.27	27.01	104.64	87.15	72.12	115.18	81.41
	12	31.96	21.55	8.98	－2.38	25.42	－28.95	22.96	77.46	67.32	75.81	82.37	81.47

其他商业银行人民币信贷收支主要指标时间序列表

Time Series of Major Indicators in Sources and Uses of Credit Funds of Other Commercial Banks (RMB)

年 月 Year Month		各项存款 Total Deposits	企业存款 Deposits by Enterprises	储蓄存款 Savings Deposits	活期储蓄 Demand Deposits	定期储蓄 Time Deposits	农业存款 Deposits by Agricultural Sector
		期末余额（亿元） Balance (100 Million Yuan)					
1999	1	3531.38	2684.53	666.75	246.07	420.68	2.65
	2	3585.57	2705.30	703.41	263.30	440.11	2.03
	3	3582.02	2712.35	695.88	247.76	448.12	2.36
	4	3668.29	2771.31	708.52	251.26	457.26	2.35
	5	3673.11	2764.81	717.21	252.47	464.74	2.25
	6	3864.23	2949.00	706.59	248.43	458.16	2.73
	7	3825.87	2894.56	703.58	254.04	449.54	2.46
	8	3923.24	2970.23	706.61	262.83	443.78	2.39
	9	4148.33	3149.75	723.83	285.17	438.66	2.36
	10	4134.94	3136.17	716.75	286.91	429.84	2.37
	11	4246.59	3237.28	723.52	298.81	424.71	3.01
	12	4669.74	3607.18	755.41	328.43	426.98	3.99
		比上期增减额（亿元） Changes Compared with Previous Period (100 Million Yuan)					
1999	1	-250.25	-242.68	11.95	3.61	8.34	-0.38
	2	54.19	20.77	36.66	17.23	19.43	-0.62
	3	-3.54	7.06	-7.53	-15.54	8.01	0.33
	4	86.27	58.95	12.65	3.51	9.14	-0.01
	5	4.80	-6.50	8.68	1.20	7.48	-0.11
	6	191.11	184.19	-10.63	-4.04	-6.59	0.48
	7	-38.36	-54.44	-3.01	5.61	-8.62	-0.27
	8	97.37	75.67	3.03	8.79	-5.76	-0.06
	9	225.10	179.52	17.23	22.34	-5.11	-0.03
	10	-13.39	-13.57	-7.09	1.74	-8.83	0.01
	11	111.66	101.11	6.79	11.91	-5.12	0.64
	12	423.14	369.89	31.89	29.62	2.27	0.98
		比去年同期增长（%） Increase Rate Year-on-year (%)					
1999	1	21.89	21.47	14.85	28.99	7.93	30.54
	2	26.56	26.30	19.29	39.19	9.89	-16.80
	3	24.84	24.46	17.55	32.12	10.79	-4.07
	4	24.33	23.60	18.90	31.19	13.07	-11.32
	5	20.16	18.05	19.48	29.92	14.48	-19.06
	6	23.73	23.35	17.86	28.22	12.91	-6.19
	7	19.95	18.56	14.78	23.64	10.31	-14.88
	8	22.41	21.45	13.90	25.32	8.07	-37.11
	9	20.94	20.28	13.98	30.35	5.37	-26.48
	10	18.65	17.75	10.93	28.04	1.85	-22.30
	11	19.99	19.92	9.90	30.33	-1.02	-3.22
	12	21.61	21.93	10.32	32.85	-2.41	30.82

其他商业银行人民币信贷收支主要指标时间序列表

Time Series of Major Indicators in Sources and Uses of Credit Funds of Other Commercial Banks（RMB）

年 月 Year Month		各项贷款 Total Loans	短期贷款 Short－term Loans	工业贷款 Loans to Industrial Sector	商业贷款 Loans to Commercial Sector	建筑业及基建企业贷款 Loans to Construction and Infrastructure	农业贷款 Loans to Agricultural Sector	贴现 Discount	中长期贷款 Medium and Long－term Loans	基本建设贷款 Capital Construction Loans	技术改造贷款 Technical Improvement Loans	其他中长期贷款 Other Medium and Long－term Loans	有价证券及投资 Securities and Investments
		期末余额（亿元） Balance（100 Million Yuan）											
1999	1	2541.05	1873.38	403.64	294.95	58.95	1.06	62.83	259.39	68.80	9.72	180.87	709.21
	2	2573.85	1883.96	396.06	291.81	59.33	1.03	63.99	262.11	69.05	10.02	183.04	707.80
	3	2588.04	1871.63	393.24	287.80	59.22	1.02	57.82	266.70	71.47	10.27	184.96	754.10
	4	2587.12	1851.68	391.91	287.89	57.34	1.19	52.33	263.72	72.40	11.28	180.04	745.73
	5	2609.84	1845.60	385.08	282.33	56.04	1.15	50.17	269.25	73.09	12.34	183.82	765.06
	6	2691.46	1925.09	391.71	299.74	54.41	1.19	48.01	286.74	82.16	10.53	194.05	787.68
	7	2710.30	1922.36	392.67	292.04	53.79	1.20	46.96	284.18	82.03	10.44	191.71	827.71
	8	2761.03	1955.22	397.59	294.29	53.94	1.24	50.86	284.33	81.04	10.33	192.96	808.79
	9	2840.66	2025.40	405.69	296.94	55.56	1.21	48.82	291.47	80.75	10.78	199.94	831.09
	10	2861.44	2027.86	394.49	296.06	59.54	1.13	53.57	282.66	72.93	10.76	198.97	894.93
	11	2926.77	2082.15	394.82	292.79	61.97	0.80	66.71	275.88	74.26	10.53	191.09	933.81
	12	3090.21	2289.96	419.61	316.19	66.83	0.93	69.64	289.40	77.36	11.41	200.63	947.96
		比上期增减额（亿元） Changes Compared with Previous Period（100 Million Yuan）											
1999	1	10.12	－37.33	－4.86	－17.74	－4.02	－0.02	0.46	23.88	2.86	－0.01	21.03	－15.63
	2	32.75	10.55	－7.58	－3.15	0.38	－0.03	1.16	2.72	0.25	0.30	2.17	－1.40
	3	14.22	－12.32	－2.82	－4.01	－0.11	－0.01	－6.17	4.60	2.43	0.25	1.92	46.30
	4	－0.91	－19.95	－1.33	0.09	－1.88	0.17	－5.49	－2.97	0.93	1.02	－4.92	－8.37
	5	22.70	－6.10	－6.83	－5.57	－1.30	－0.05	－2.16	5.53	0.69	1.06	3.78	19.33
	6	81.65	79.50	6.63	17.41	－1.63	0.04	－2.16	17.49	9.06	－1.81	10.24	22.62
	7	18.82	－2.73	0.96	－7.70	－0.62	0.01	－1.05	－2.56	－0.13	－0.09	－2.34	40.04
	8	50.73	32.86	4.92	2.25	0.15	0.04	3.90	0.15	－0.99	－0.11	1.25	－18.92
	9	79.63	70.17	8.10	2.65	1.62	－0.03	－2.05	7.14	－0.29	0.45	6.98	22.30
	10	20.79	2.46	－11.20	－0.88	3.98	－0.08	4.75	－8.81	－7.82	－0.02	－0.97	63.84
	11	65.33	54.29	0.33	－3.27	2.43	－0.34	13.14	－6.78	1.34	－0.23	－7.89	38.88
	12	163.44	207.82	24.79	23.40	4.86	0.13	2.94	13.51	3.09	0.88	9.54	14.14
		比去年同期增长（%） Increase Rate Year－on－year（%）											
1999	1	27.99	22.93	11.15	－6.94	53.16	－33.75	15.50	45.61	21.21	69.34	56.41	74.22
	2	28.74	23.95	8.98	－5.88	41.60	－29.45	16.75	46.62	20.28	77.98	58.16	70.61
	3	24.27	20.94	7.43	－7.96	32.39	－32.00	10.94	42.64	19.56	85.71	52.03	91.00
	4	22.39	18.54	7.95	－9.12	28.57	－31.21	1.08	38.49	18.20	76.53	46.62	84.12
	5	21.39	17.26	4.40	－11.21	29.36	－40.72	5.80	30.54	16.94	79.88	34.27	60.79
	6	20.51	17.37	2.13	－4.19	22.55	－38.66	14.61	29.71	26.59	62.00	29.65	41.17
	7	19.28	16.93	4.47	－7.50	20.74	1.69	20.01	20.30	23.30	10.48	19.63	46.11
	8	19.20	17.63	5.78	－6.04	20.75	－27.06	18.83	16.68	9.71	90.24	17.39	39.87
	9	18.29	17.19	6.82	－5.14	21.36	－18.79	0.49	14.34	5.35	81.48	16.03	38.31
	10	18.47	19.33	6.11	－0.50	37.60	－22.60	8.16	6.24	－7.33	37.60	10.82	34.72
	11	18.90	20.39	4.07	－2.35	39.70	－34.43	23.38	0.71	－6.31	17.65	2.89	31.08
	12	18.47	21.38	1.96	－1.04	36.95	－13.89	11.64	－0.32	－9.26	17.15	2.71	28.43

其他商业银行人民币信贷收支主要指标时间序列表

Time Series of Major Indicators in Sources and Uses of Credit Funds of Other Commercial Banks（RMB）

年 月 Year Month		各项存款 Total Deposits	企业存款 Deposits by Enterprises	储蓄存款 Savings Deposits			农业存款 Deposits by Agricultural Sector
					活期储蓄 Demand Deposits	定期储蓄 Time Deposits	
期末余额（亿元） Balance（100 Million Yuan）							
2000	1	4469.94	3353.14	774.78	343.75	431.03	3.21
	2	4520.33	3389.14	784.80	344.38	440.42	3.18
	3	4687.91	3515.13	784.48	347.17	437.31	2.56
	4	4939.65	3732.23	804.92	367.23	437.69	2.48
	5	4936.49	3710.00	795.07	362.88	432.19	3.09
	6	5498.03	4170.00	819.54	385.95	433.59	3.05
	7	5331.90	3987.15	820.01	384.28	435.73	3.50
	8	5560.37	4123.46	835.40	398.31	437.09	3.19
	9	6152.09	4612.39	881.23	434.37	446.86	3.14
	10	5924.39	4370.34	866.48	419.76	446.72	3.25
	11	6060.60	4417.70	885.20	431.26	453.94	3.28
	12	6685.53	4968.01	947.04	482.55	464.49	3.42
比上期增减额（亿元） Changes Compared with Previous Period（100 Million Yuan）							
2000	1	-248.43	-300.94	19.25	15.26	3.99	-0.78
	2	50.39	36.00	10.02	0.63	9.39	-0.03
	3	167.58	125.99	-0.32	2.79	-3.11	-0.62
	4	251.74	217.10	20.44	20.06	0.38	-0.08
	5	-3.16	-22.23	-9.85	-4.35	-5.50	0.61
	6	561.54	460.00	24.47	23.07	1.40	-0.04
	7	-166.13	-182.85	0.47	-1.67	2.14	0.45
	8	228.47	136.31	15.39	14.03	1.36	-0.31
	9	591.72	488.93	45.83	36.06	9.77	-0.05
	10	-227.70	-242.05	-14.75	-14.61	-0.14	0.11
	11	136.21	47.36	18.72	11.50	7.22	0.03
	12	624.93	550.31	61.84	51.29	10.55	0.14
比去年同期增长（%） Increase Rate Year-on-year（%）							
2000	1	26.58	24.91	16.20	39.70	2.46	21.13
	2	26.07	25.28	11.57	30.79	0.07	56.65
	3	30.87	29.60	12.73	40.12	-2.41	8.47
	4	34.66	34.67	13.61	46.16	-4.28	5.53
	5	34.40	34.19	10.86	43.73	-7.00	37.33
	6	42.28	41.40	15.99	55.36	-5.36	11.72
	7	39.36	37.75	16.55	51.27	-3.07	42.28
	8	41.73	38.83	18.23	51.55	-1.51	33.47
	9	48.30	46.44	21.75	52.32	1.87	33.05
	10	43.28	39.35	20.89	46.30	3.93	37.13
	11	42.72	36.46	22.35	44.33	6.88	8.97
	12	43.17	37.73	25.37	46.93	8.78	-14.29

其他商业银行人民币信贷收支主要指标时间序列表

Time Series of Major Indicators in Sources and Uses of Credit Funds of Other Commercial Banks（RMB）

年 月 Year Month	各项贷款 Total Loans	短期贷款 Short－term Loans	工业贷款 Loans to Industrial Sector	商业贷款 Loans to Commercial Sector	建筑业及基建企业贷款 Loans to Construction and Infrastructure	农业贷款 Loans to Agricultural Sector	贴现 Discount	中长期贷款 Medium and Long－term Loans	基本建设贷款 Capital Construction Loans	技术改造贷款 Technical Improvement Loans	其他中长期贷款 Other Medium and Long－term Loans	有价证券及投资 Securities and Investments
期末余额（亿元） Balance（100 Million Yuan）												
2000 1	3114.27	2266.52	407.02	309.08	67.97	0.93	86.99	298.53	79.62	11.37	207.54	967.92
2	3149.77	2286.94	408.44	317.33	65.25	0.89	80.14	300.11	80.43	9.20	210.48	980.52
3	3240.63	2378.06	431.10	323.65	65.75	1.10	93.40	297.40	82.32	9.29	205.79	958.64
4	3350.49	2462.34	438.44	322.57	63.95	1.09	114.64	301.21	83.87	10.52	206.82	985.40
5	3432.30	2525.44	450.54	330.83	63.49	1.59	130.03	299.16	84.26	10.72	204.18	1132.25
6	3716.08	2809.73	471.63	370.73	66.46	1.15	180.01	320.76	75.61	10.87	234.28	1219.37
7	3759.61	2813.47	472.26	373.89	63.58	0.74	193.64	327.23	76.48	10.87	239.88	1243.19
8	3905.91	2938.11	481.88	378.25	65.36	0.74	236.38	349.84	83.90	11.39	254.55	1248.14
9	4122.73	3143.43	503.91	387.77	73.48	0.72	285.13	368.95	86.91	11.49	270.55	1321.12
10	4256.03	3240.12	517.21	400.67	75.97	0.84	337.88	388.04	88.36	11.49	288.19	1333.46
11	4447.97	3415.77	535.92	415.55	78.88	0.72	356.24	401.53	90.29	11.52	299.72	1330.18
12	4534.63	3540.59	556.32	418.63	77.84	0.70	371.60	445.14	94.41	7.84	342.89	1344.01
比上期增减额（亿元） Changes Compared with Previous Period（100 Million Yuan）												
2000 1	12.26	－34.05	－13.44	－0.15	0.98		7.89	9.31	0.52	－0.04	8.83	19.92
2	35.50	20.42	1.42	8.25	－2.72	－0.04	－6.85	1.58	0.81	－2.17	2.94	12.60
3	90.86	91.12	22.66	6.32	0.50	0.21	13.26	－2.71	1.89	0.09	－4.69	－21.88
4	109.86	84.28	7.34	－1.08	－1.80	－0.01	21.24	3.81	1.55	1.23	1.03	26.76
5	81.81	63.10	12.10	8.26	－0.46	0.50	15.39	－2.05	0.39	0.20	－2.64	146.85
6	283.78	284.29	21.09	39.90	2.97	－0.44	49.98	21.60	－8.65	0.15	30.10	87.12
7	43.53	3.74	0.63	3.16	－2.88	－0.41	13.63	6.47	0.87		5.60	23.82
8	146.30	124.64	9.62	4.36	1.78		42.74	22.61	7.42	0.52	14.67	4.95
9	216.82	205.32	22.03	9.52	8.12	－0.02	48.75	19.11	3.01	0.10	16.00	72.98
10	133.30	96.69	13.30	12.90	2.49	0.12	52.75	19.09	1.45		17.64	12.34
11	191.94	175.65	18.71	14.88	2.91	－0.12	18.36	13.49	1.93	0.03	11.53	－3.28
12	86.66	124.82	20.40	3.08	－1.04	－0.02	15.36	43.61	4.12	－3.68	43.17	13.83
比去年同期增长（%） Increase Rate Year－on－year（%）												
2000 1	22.56	20.99	0.84	4.79	15.30	－12.26	38.45	15.09	15.73	16.98	14.75	36.48
2	22.38	21.39	3.13	8.75	9.98	－13.59	25.24	14.50	16.48	－8.18	14.99	38.53
3	25.22	27.06	9.63	12.46	11.03	7.84	61.54	11.51	15.18	－9.54	11.26	27.12
4	29.51	32.98	11.87	12.05	11.53	－8.40	119.07	14.22	15.84	－6.74	14.87	32.14
5	31.51	36.84	17.00	17.18	13.29	38.26	159.18	11.11	15.28	－13.13	11.08	47.99
6	38.07	45.95	20.40	23.68	22.15	－3.36	274.94	11.86	－7.97	3.23	20.73	54.81
7	38.72	46.36	20.27	28.03	18.20	－38.33	312.35	15.15	－6.77	4.12	25.13	50.20
8	41.47	50.27	21.20	28.53	21.17	－40.32	364.77	23.04	3.53	10.26	31.92	54.32
9	45.13	55.20	24.21	30.59	32.25	－40.50	484.04	26.58	7.63	6.59	35.32	58.96
10	48.74	59.78	31.11	35.33	27.59	－25.66	530.73	37.28	21.16	6.78	44.84	49.00
11	51.98	64.05	35.74	41.93	27.29	－10.00	434.01	45.55	21.59	9.40	56.85	42.45
12	46.74	54.61	32.58	32.40	16.47	－24.73	433.60	53.81	22.04	－31.29	70.91	41.78

其他商业银行人民币信贷收支主要指标时间序列表

Time Series of Major Indicators in Sources and Uses of Credit Funds of Other Commercial Banks (RMB)

年 月 Year Month		各项存款 Total Deposits	企业存款 Deposits by Enterprises	储蓄存款 Savings Deposits	活期储蓄 Demand Deposits	定期储蓄 Time Deposits	农业存款 Deposits by Agricultural Sector
		期末余额(亿元) Balance (100 Million Yuan)					
2001	1	12284.80	8709.78	2381.06	978.08	1402.98	3.23
	2	11904.38	8324.27	2366.35	951.91	1414.44	3.67
	3	12697.08	8949.33	2451.91	1015.31	1436.60	3.25
	4	13299.80	9388.96	2514.01	1047.50	1466.51	3.06
	5	12991.05	8905.56	2486.21	1031.39	1454.82	3.49
	6	14468.78	10065.14	2607.25	1116.84	1490.41	3.84
	7	13601.80	9186.70	2592.83	1091.00	1501.83	3.48
	8	14600.30	9911.46	2719.42	1179.09	1540.33	3.84
	9	15200.09	10292.20	2833.61	1251.02	1582.59	3.91
	10	15101.64	10086.64	2889.19	1265.31	1623.88	3.82
	11	15199.23	10071.43	2933.53	1280.27	1653.26	4.14
	12	16560.89	11117.07	3121.56	1397.97	1723.59	4.77
		比上期增减额(亿元) Changes Compared with Previous Period (100 Million Yuan)					
2001	1	264.20	86.03	119.56	72.96	46.60	-0.19
	2	-380.42	-385.51	-14.71	-26.17	11.46	0.44
	3	792.70	625.06	85.56	63.40	22.16	-0.42
	4	602.72	439.63	62.10	32.19	29.91	-0.19
	5	-308.75	-483.40	-27.80	-16.11	-11.69	0.43
	6	1477.73	1159.58	121.04	85.45	35.59	0.35
	7	-866.98	-878.44	-14.42	-25.84	11.42	-0.36
	8	998.50	724.76	126.59	88.09	38.50	0.36
	9	599.79	380.74	114.19	71.93	42.26	0.07
	10	-98.45	-205.56	55.58	14.29	41.29	-0.09
	11	97.59	-15.21	44.34	14.96	29.38	0.32
	12	1361.66	1045.64	188.03	117.70	70.33	0.63
		比去年同期增长(%) Increase Rate Year-on-year (%)					
2001	1	41.37	39.47	24.25	53.72	9.61	0.62
	2	35.48	32.15	21.00	47.38	7.99	15.41
	3	38.63	36.23	25.03	54.62	10.14	26.95
	4	39.02	35.99	26.45	53.19	12.43	23.39
	5	35.80	29.42	26.38	52.03	12.88	12.94
	6	38.82	32.94	29.27	54.61	15.13	25.90
	7	34.09	26.11	28.61	51.45	15.91	-0.57
	8	39.76	32.54	32.99	58.17	18.54	20.38
	9	34.37	25.74	33.42	54.80	20.28	24.52
	10	38.13	29.32	36.89	59.51	23.27	17.54
	11	36.21	27.67	36.20	56.39	23.82	26.22
	12	37.77	28.96	38.06	54.55	27.07	39.47

其他商业银行人民币信贷收支主要指标时间序列表

Time Series of Major Indicators in Sources and Uses of Credit Funds of Other Commercial Banks（RMB）

年 Year	月 Month	各项贷款 Total Loans	短期贷款 Short - term Loans	工业贷款 Loans to Industrial Sector	商业贷款 Loans to Commercial Sector	建筑业及基建企业贷款 Loans to Construction and Infrastructure	农业贷款 Loans to Agricultural Sector	中长期贷款 Medium and Long - term Loans	基本建设贷款 Capital Construction Loans	技术改造贷款 Technical Improvement Loans	其他中长期贷款 Other Medium and Long - term Loans	票据融资 Paper Financing	有价证券及投资 Securities and Investments
期末余额（亿元） Balance（100 Million Yuan）													
2001	1	8766.74	6627.95	1340.55	1072.29	107.83	6.66	1373.76	304.6	107.54	961.62	733.49	2047.06
	2	8937.31	6757.98	1376.07	1078.77	106.78	6.61	1413.06	306.21	111.69	995.16	735.16	2012.65
	3	9071.12	6835.18	1390.40	1078.13	111.33	6.10	1465.84	310.65	111.78	1043.41	743.02	2146.85
	4	9331.41	6932.17	1405.76	1089.66	117.50	6.07	1542.80	319.47	113.80	1109.53	829.26	2216.12
	5	9558.99	7127.47	1454.59	1121.19	115.42	6.07	1585.51	320.50	112.37	1152.64	817.98	2307.99
	6	9995.90	7470.79	1529.97	1163.50	119.38	5.88	1697.12	336.76	106.83	1253.53	799.14	2433.33
	7	10184.91	7552.59	1525.95	1191.33	123.44	6.30	1753.49	350.01	108.67	1294.81	845.28	2504.18
	8	10298.52	7525.38	1546.56	1169.47	127.94	6.85	1819.33	365.84	100.74	1352.75	918.78	2589.06
	9	10727.43	7698.21	1596.04	1168.16	141.85	6.81	1906.83	374.32	100.30	1432.21	1085.91	2647.44
	10	10874.03	7683.78	1600.27	1151.73	151.56	6.80	1948.67	374.83	101.27	1472.57	1203.38	2722.77
	11	11262.24	7848.48	1656.91	1167.93	168.11	8.36	2032.67	365.57	101.64	1565.46	1342.07	2712.63
	12	11462.17	8084.26	1690.65	1180.56	169.37	7.09	2136.25	369.95	108.96	1657.34	1202.76	2864.61
比上期增减额（亿元） Changes Compared with Previous Period（100 Million Yuan）													
2001	1	339.86	111.04	97.39	-7.23	4.30	1.46	79.29	14.59	1.01	63.69	147.70	-22.64
	2	170.57	130.03	35.52	6.48	-1.05	-0.05	39.30	1.61	4.15	33.54	1.67	-34.41
	3	133.81	77.20	14.33	-0.64	4.55	-0.51	52.78	4.44	0.09	48.25	7.86	134.20
	4	260.29	96.99	15.36	11.53	6.17	-0.03	76.96	8.82	2.02	66.12	86.24	69.27
	5	227.58	195.30	48.83	31.53	-2.08		42.71	1.03	-1.43	43.11	-11.28	91.87
	6	436.91	343.32	75.38	42.31	3.96	-0.19	111.61	16.26	-5.54	100.89	-18.84	125.34
	7	189.01	81.80	-4.02	27.83	4.06	0.42	56.37	13.25	1.84	41.28	46.14	70.85
	8	113.61	-27.21	20.61	-21.86	4.50	0.55	65.84	15.83	-7.93	57.94	73.50	84.88
	9	428.91	172.83	49.48	-1.31	13.91	-0.04	87.50	8.48	-0.44	79.46	167.13	58.38
	10	146.60	-14.43	4.23	-16.43	9.71	-0.01	41.84	0.51	0.97	40.36	117.47	75.33
	11	388.21	164.70	56.64	16.20	16.55	1.56	84.00	-9.26	0.37	92.89	138.69	-10.14
	12	199.93	235.78	33.74	12.63	1.26	-1.27	103.58	4.38	7.32	91.88	-139.31	151.98
比去年同期增长（%） Increase Rate Year - on - year（%）													
2001	1	42.43	62.10	50.79	69.51	42.93	149.44	91.17	94.24	23.92	102.44	380.06	28.24
	2	43.83	63.74	53.79	68.85	47.26	156.20	94.99	94.26	26.82	107.77	409.68	26.09
	3	41.75	60.30	49.80	65.27	53.35	117.86	96.20	80.14	24.42	115.22	350.51	41.13
	4	42.61	59.85	50.33	70.97	66.27	151.87	100.86	78.07	22.00	123.97	354.51	42.53
	5	41.95	59.89	52.28	69.65	64.58	72.44	104.76	77.77	18.76	130.80	289.46	30.04
	6	39.96	56.39	53.43	62.44	63.38	94.70	104.85	87.61	9.51	127.33	184.91	29.66
	7	41.75	59.22	55.74	66.27	75.47	100.64	105.69	90.75	7.64	127.94	199.60	31.56
	8	39.69	55.66	56.03	62.40	80.86	142.05	103.59	86.44	-0.80	127.03	172.21	34.71
	9	39.55	52.70	56.17	58.12	78.92	152.22	100.99	88.09	-2.02	121.25	160.02	31.61
	10	38.46	50.47	55.11	54.79	85.62	141.99	101.46	87.08	-0.13	121.27	156.93	34.32
	11	37.39	46.92	57.05	50.45	99.44	226.56	100.29	79.12	-0.14	120.80	153.88	33.90
	12	36.17	46.21	56.33	45.43	99.92	179.13	88.89	74.55	11.38	101.83	105.63	39.87

其他商业银行人民币信贷收支主要指标时间序列表
Time Series of Major Indicators in Sources and Uses of Credit Funds of Other Commercial Banks（RMB）

年 月 Year Month		各项存款 Total Deposits	企业存款 Deposits by Enterprises	储蓄存款 Savings Deposits	活期储蓄 Demand Deposits	定期储蓄 Time Deposits	农业存款 Deposits by Agricultural Sector
		期末余额（亿元） Balance（100 Million Yuan）					
2002	1	15956.00	10433.53	3173.00	1414.57	1758.43	4.19
	2	15882.15	10228.26	3309.33	1454.85	1854.48	4.31
	3	16321.85	10533.93	3336.74	1465.71	1871.03	3.57
	4	17479.14	11335.46	3511.37	1584.88	1926.49	3.87
	5	17727.11	11365.62	3576.04	1603.26	1972.78	4.19
	6	19031.77	12227.20	3711.85	1657.38	2054.47	4.85
	7	18916.30	11976.60	3784.54	1676.31	2108.23	4.26
	8	19506.68	12310.93	3892.43	1725.25	2167.18	4.30
	9	20649.39	13077.47	4026.63	1805.10	2221.53	4.49
	10	20387.33	12730.35	4066.50	1804.50	2262.00	4.57
	11	20908.02	13060.14	4163.78	1856.56	2307.22	4.80
	12	22735.91	14479.70	4347.15	1972.94	2374.21	5.34
		比上期增减额（亿元） Changes Compared with Previous Period（100 Million Yuan）					
2002	1	-599.41	-627.25	49.50	14.66	34.84	-0.58
	2	-73.85	-205.27	136.33	40.28	96.05	0.12
	3	439.70	305.67	27.41	10.86	16.55	-0.74
	4	1157.29	801.53	174.63	119.17	55.46	0.30
	5	247.97	30.16	64.67	18.38	46.29	0.32
	6	1304.66	861.58	135.81	54.12	81.69	0.66
	7	-115.47	-250.60	72.69	18.93	53.76	-0.59
	8	590.38	334.33	107.89	48.94	58.95	0.04
	9	1142.71	766.54	134.20	79.85	54.35	0.19
	10	-262.06	-347.12	39.87	-0.60	40.47	0.08
	11	520.69	329.79	97.28	52.06	45.22	0.23
	12	1827.89	1419.56	183.37	116.38	66.99	0.54
		比去年同期增长（%） Increase Rate Year-on-year（%）					
2002	1	29.88	19.79	33.26	44.63	25.34	29.72
	2	33.41	22.87	39.85	52.83	31.11	17.44
	3	28.55	17.71	36.09	44.36	30.24	9.85
	4	31.42	20.73	39.67	51.30	31.37	26.47
	5	36.46	27.62	43.83	55.45	35.60	20.06
	6	31.54	21.48	42.37	48.40	37.85	26.30
	7	39.07	30.37	45.96	53.65	40.38	22.41
	8	33.60	24.21	43.13	46.32	40.70	11.98
	9	35.85	27.06	42.10	44.29	40.37	14.83
	10	35.00	26.21	40.75	42.61	39.30	19.63
	11	37.56	29.68	41.94	45.01	39.56	15.94
	12	37.29	30.25	39.26	41.13	37.75	11.95

其他商业银行人民币信贷收支主要指标时间序列表

Time Series of Major Indicators in Sources and Uses of Credit Funds of Other Commercial Banks（RMB）

年 月 Year Month		各项贷款 Total Loans	短期贷款 Short - term Loans	工业贷款 Loans to Industrial Sector	商业贷款 Loans to Commercial Sector	建筑业及基建企业贷款 Loans to Construction and Infrastructure	农业贷款 Loans to Agricultural Sector	中长期贷款 Medium and Long - term Loans	基本建设贷款 Capital Construction Loans	技术改造贷款 Technical Improvement Loans	其他中长期贷款 Other Medium and Long - term Loans	票据融资 Paper Financing	有价证券及投资 Securities and Investments
		期末余额（亿元） Balance（100 Million Yuan）											
2002	1	11786.55	8117.90	1725.26	1173.98	186.42	9.18	2174.50	388.62	107.40	1678.48	1445.38	2901.90
	2	11939.26	8159.96	1688.46	1153.49	181.66	6.94	2237.38	401.28	100.93	1735.17	1490.90	2917.27
	3	12585.69	8668.71	1820.92	1193.54	183.96	7.07	2323.72	418.09	98.67	1806.96	1539.66	2962.74
	4	12909.69	8630.21	1803.91	1140.85	197.30	7.43	2434.49	433.54	101.73	1899.22	1791.78	3047.70
	5	13107.33	8732.40	1808.85	1133.69	195.73	9.54	2544.10	434.60	102.34	2007.16	1777.64	3104.05
	6	13855.04	9206.58	1894.58	1144.98	217.27	8.52	2691.05	451.86	106.43	2132.76	1905.48	3216.52
	7	13969.45	9099.96	1892.35	1111.67	218.89	8.73	2803.61	481.43	108.41	2213.77	2012.45	3372.09
	8	14407.90	9320.63	1927.82	1134.46	234.10	9.02	2913.00	499.72	107.44	2305.84	2120.28	3444.74
	9	14895.96	9698.97	1999.85	1172.46	252.91	8.30	3092.96	522.91	109.44	2460.61	2048.77	3822.40
	10	15035.62	9706.12	1994.34	1184.21	251.43	5.66	3235.38	527.51	110.10	2597.77	2038.79	3903.32
	11	15407.71	9869.02	2046.56	1209.00	258.94	4.75	3419.97	551.81	110.94	2757.22	2061.85	3968.73
	12	16066.25	10329.04	2125.50	1241.96	268.76	4.94	3515.74	534.73	112.14	2868.87	2167.42	3976.40
		比上期增减额（亿元） Changes Compared with Previous Period（100 Million Yuan）											
2002	1	306.27	17.92	29.36	-8.18	17.20	2.09	61.02	17.16	-1.91	45.77	224.71	19.35
	2	152.71	42.06	-36.80	-20.49	-4.76	-2.24	62.88	12.66	-6.47	56.69	45.52	15.37
	3	646.43	508.75	132.46	40.05	2.30	0.13	86.34	16.81	-2.26	71.79	48.76	45.47
	4	324.00	-38.50	-17.01	-52.69	13.34	0.36	110.77	15.45	3.06	92.26	252.12	84.96
	5	197.64	102.19	4.94	-7.16	-1.57	2.11	109.61	1.06	0.61	107.94	-14.14	56.35
	6	747.71	474.18	85.73	11.29	21.54	-1.02	146.95	17.26	4.09	125.60	127.84	112.47
	7	114.41	-106.62	-2.23	-33.31	1.62	0.21	112.56	29.57	1.98	81.01	106.97	155.57
	8	438.45	220.67	35.47	22.79	15.21	0.29	109.39	18.29	-0.97	92.07	107.83	72.65
	9	488.06	378.34	72.03	38.00	18.81	-0.72	179.96	23.19	2.00	154.77	-71.51	377.66
	10	139.66	7.15	-5.51	11.75	-1.48	-2.64	142.42	4.60	0.66	137.16	-9.98	80.92
	11	372.09	162.90	52.22	24.79	7.51	-0.91	184.59	24.30	0.84	159.45	23.06	65.41
	12	658.54	460.02	78.94	32.96	9.82	0.19	95.77	-17.08	1.20	111.65	105.57	7.67
		比去年同期增长（%） Increase Rate Year - on - year（%）											
2002	1	34.45	22.48	28.70	9.48	72.88	37.84	58.29	27.58	-0.13	74.55	97.06	41.76
	2	33.59	20.75	22.70	6.93	70.13	4.99	58.34	31.05	-9.63	74.36	102.80	44.95
	3	38.74	26.82	30.96	10.70	65.24	15.90	58.52	34.59	-11.73	73.18	107.22	38.00
	4	38.35	24.50	28.32	4.70	67.91	22.41	57.80	35.71	-10.61	71.17	116.07	37.52
	5	37.12	22.52	24.35	1.11	69.58	57.17	60.46	35.60	-8.93	74.14	117.32	34.49
	6	38.61	23.23	23.83	-1.59	82.00	44.90	58.57	34.18	-0.37	70.14	138.44	32.19
	7	37.16	20.49	24.01	-6.69	77.33	38.57	59.89	37.55	-0.24	70.97	138.08	34.66
	8	39.90	23.86	24.65	-2.99	82.98	31.68	60.11	36.60	6.65	70.46	130.77	33.05
	9	38.86	25.99	25.30	0.37	78.29	21.88	62.20	39.70	9.11	71.81	88.67	44.38
	10	38.27	26.32	24.63	2.82	65.89	-16.76	66.03	40.73	8.72	76.41	69.42	43.36
	11	36.81	25.74	23.52	3.52	54.03	-43.18	68.25	50.95	9.15	76.13	53.63	46.31
	12	40.17	27.77	25.72	5.20	58.68	-30.32	64.58	44.54	2.92	73.10	80.20	38.81

其他商业银行人民币信贷收支主要指标时间序列表

Time Series of Major Indicators in Sources and Uses of Credit Funds of Other Commercial Banks (RMB)

年 月 Year Month		各项存款 Total Deposits	企业存款 Deposits by Enterprises	储蓄存款 Savings Deposits	活期储蓄 Demand Deposits	定期储蓄 Time Deposits	农业存款 Deposits by Agricultural Sector
期末余额（亿元） Balance (100 Million Yuan)							
2003	1	22291.25	13750.76	4553.21	2058.09	2495.15	4.83
	2	22214.69	13596.61	4604.72	2038.11	2566.61	4.81
	3	23264.79	14306.89	4729.50	2076.57	2652.93	5.07
	4	23774.41	14429.36	4791.70	2104.28	2687.42	5.04
	5	24539.86	14857.35	4874.26	2132.38	2741.88	5.15
	6	26536.38	16182.43	5039.38	2217.23	2822.15	5.08
	7	26269.47	15650.68	5101.79	2228.51	2873.28	5.91
	8	26630.79	15920.70	5171.85	2255.36	2916.49	12.76
	9	28484.74	17225.26	5409.29	2380.09	3029.20	14.13
	10	28231.44	16843.66	5458.27	2377.75	3080.52	11.70
	11	28717.17	17019.03	5555.99	2426.57	3129.42	12.32
	12	30621.18	18522.86	5851.47	2616.84	3234.63	15.93
比上期增减额（亿元） Changes Compared with Previous Period (100 Million Yuan)							
2003	1	-447.54	-731.63	206.20	85.29	120.91	-0.51
	2	-76.56	-154.15	51.48	-19.98	71.46	-0.02
	3	1050.10	710.28	124.78	38.46	86.32	0.26
	4	509.62	122.47	62.20	27.71	34.49	-0.03
	5	765.45	427.99	82.56	28.10	54.46	0.11
	6	1996.52	1325.08	165.12	84.85	80.27	-0.07
	7	-266.91	-531.75	62.41	11.28	51.13	0.83
	8	361.32	270.02	70.06	26.85	43.21	6.85
	9	1853.95	1304.56	237.44	124.73	112.71	1.37
	10	-253.30	-381.60	48.98	-2.34	51.32	-2.43
	11	485.73	175.37	97.72	48.82	48.90	0.62
	12	1904.01	1503.83	295.48	190.27	105.21	3.61
比去年同期增长（%） Increase Rate Year-on-year (%)							
2003	1	39.70	31.79	43.50	45.49	41.90	15.27
	2	39.87	32.93	39.14	40.09	38.40	11.60
	3	42.54	35.82	41.74	41.68	41.79	42.02
	4	36.02	27.29	36.46	32.77	39.50	30.23
	5	38.43	30.72	36.30	33.00	38.99	22.91
	6	39.43	32.35	35.76	33.78	37.37	4.74
	7	38.87	30.68	34.81	32.94	36.29	38.73
	8	36.52	29.32	32.87	30.73	34.58	196.74
	9	37.94	31.72	34.34	31.85	36.36	214.70
	10	38.48	32.31	34.23	31.77	36.19	156.02
	11	37.35	30.31	33.44	30.70	35.64	156.67
	12	34.68	27.92	34.60	32.64	36.24	198.31

其他商业银行人民币信贷收支主要指标时间序列表
Time Series of Major Indicators in Sources and Uses of Credit Funds of Other Commercial Banks（RMB）

年　月 Year Month	各项贷款 Total Loans	短期贷款 Short－term Loans	工业贷款 Loans to Industrial Sector	商业贷款 Loans to Commercial Sector	建筑业及基建企业贷款 Loans to Construction and Infrastructure	农业贷款 Loans to Agricultural Sector	中长期贷款 Medium and Long－term Loans	基本建设贷款 Capital Construction Loans	技术改造贷款 Technical Improvement Loans	其他中长期贷款 Other Medium and Long－term Loans	票据融资 Paper Financing	有价证券及投资 Securities and Investments
期末余额（亿元） Balance（100 Million Yuan）												
2003 1	16683.49	10474.12	2228.94	1283.79	281.78	5.02	3805.65	592.25	109.28	3104.12	2348.09	3845.10
2	16707.20	10635.68	2276.45	1286.70	280.75	5.22	3887.25	605.69	109.05	3172.51	2126.47	3889.42
3	17359.02	11166.56	2390.47	1339.66	295.59	6.60	4117.24	634.97	114.81	3367.46	2020.92	3945.92
4	18003.89	11331.37	2432.59	1327.10	317.72	6.73	4302.33	660.22	118.79	3523.32	2315.63	4187.01
5	18667.41	11699.14	2497.15	1342.55	331.98	7.48	4508.49	695.06	122.25	3691.18	2406.45	4441.00
6	19819.85	12364.80	2647.35	1391.98	351.45	7.73	4710.29	739.26	128.05	3842.98	2691.00	4671.47
7	20232.42	12248.80	2630.51	1383.64	362.82	6.95	5015.76	787.00	135.30	4093.46	2911.41	4808.45
8	21182.69	12738.17	3107.23	1451.39	558.66	23.90	5225.31	777.60	137.14	4310.57	3162.63	4905.31
9	21609.53	13140.12	3289.22	1501.43	581.53	24.77	5419.95	824.92	136.23	4458.80	2990.36	4991.03
10	21751.09	13308.90	3336.25	1547.47	601.37	25.49	5614.18	851.35	131.95	4630.88	2767.65	4946.98
11	22009.67	13526.70	3448.62	1591.45	621.81	25.45	5792.85	886.97	134.77	4771.11	2625.49	5001.62
12	22367.56	13974.59	3575.32	1675.66	662.17	31.73	5897.44	882.65	138.80	4875.99	2442.53	5039.76
比上期增减额（亿元） Changes Compared with Previous Period（100 Million Yuan）												
2003 1	675.97	204.19	103.51	41.96	12.84	0.08	289.53	57.52	－2.86	234.87	180.67	－124.70
2	23.71	161.56	47.51	2.91	－1.03	0.20	81.60	13.44	－0.23	68.39	－221.62	44.32
3	651.82	530.88	114.02	52.96	14.84	1.38	229.99	29.28	5.76	194.95	－105.55	56.50
4	644.87	164.81	42.12	－12.56	22.13	0.13	185.09	25.25	3.98	155.86	294.71	241.09
5	663.52	367.77	64.56	15.45	14.26	0.75	206.16	34.84	3.46	167.86	90.82	253.99
6	1152.44	665.66	150.20	49.43	19.47	0.25	201.80	44.20	5.80	151.80	284.55	230.47
7	412.57	－116.00	－16.84	－8.34	11.37	－0.78	305.47	47.74	7.25	250.48	220.41	136.98
8	950.27	489.37	476.72	67.75	195.84	16.95	209.55	－9.40	1.84	217.11	251.22	96.86
9	426.84	401.95	181.99	50.04	22.87	0.87	194.64	47.32	－0.91	148.23	－172.27	85.72
10	141.56	168.78	47.03	46.04	19.84	0.72	194.23	26.43	－4.28	172.08	－222.71	－44.05
11	258.58	217.80	112.37	43.98	20.44	－0.04	178.67	35.62	2.82	140.23	－142.16	54.64
12	357.89	447.89	126.70	84.21	40.36	6.28	104.59	－4.32	4.03	104.88	－182.96	38.14
比去年同期增长（%） Increase Rate Year－on－year（%）												
2003 1	41.55	29.02	29.19	9.35	51.15	－45.32	75.01	52.40	1.75	84.94	62.45	32.50
2	39.93	30.34	34.82	11.55	54.55	－24.78	73.74	50.94	8.05	82.84	42.63	33.32
3	37.93	28.81	31.28	12.24	60.68	－6.65	77.18	51.87	16.36	86.36	31.26	33.18
4	39.46	31.30	34.85	16.33	61.03	－9.42	76.72	52.29	16.77	85.51	29.24	37.38
5	42.42	33.97	38.05	18.42	69.61	－21.59	77.21	59.93	19.45	83.90	35.37	43.07
6	43.05	34.30	39.73	21.57	61.76	－9.27	75.04	63.60	20.31	80.19	41.22	45.23
7	44.83	34.60	39.01	24.46	65.75	－20.39	78.90	63.47	24.80	84.91	44.67	42.60
8	47.02	36.67	61.18	27.94	138.64	164.97	79.38	55.61	27.64	86.94	49.16	42.40
9	45.07	35.48	64.47	28.06	129.94	198.43	75.24	57.76	24.48	81.21	45.96	30.57
10	44.66	37.12	67.29	30.68	139.18	350.35	73.52	61.39	19.85	78.26	35.75	26.74
11	42.85	37.06	68.51	31.63	140.14	435.79	69.38	60.74	21.48	73.04	27.34	26.03
12	39.22	35.29	68.21	34.92	146.38	542.31	67.74	65.06	23.77	69.96	12.69	26.74

其他商业银行人民币信贷收支主要指标时间序列表

Time Series of Major Indicators in Sources and Uses of Credit Funds of Other Commercial Banks (RMB)

年 月 Year Month		各项存款 Total Deposits	企业存款 Deposits by Enterprises	储蓄存款 Savings Deposits	活期储蓄 Demand Deposits	定期储蓄 Time Deposits	农业存款 Deposits by Agricultural Sector
		期末余额(亿元) Balance (100 Million Yuan)					
2004	1	29460.20	17033.55	6046.10	2661.81	3381.29	13.60
	2	30123.66	17321.20	6133.24	2687.47	3445.77	13.17
	3	31931.33	18412.74	6258.57	2758.59	3499.98	12.74
	4	32478.13	18668.27	6341.80	2818.25	3523.55	11.63
	5	32940.11	18927.59	6398.07	2835.55	3562.52	11.71
	6	34528.91	19990.96	6588.32	2938.09	3650.23	14.17
	7	33822.84	19256.26	6593.26	2919.77	3673.49	14.09
	8	34134.24	19392.51	6666.44	2941.60	3724.84	15.84
	9	35429.33	20229.38	6858.17	3046.32	3811.85	16.29
	10	35215.96	19968.30	6919.55	3060.89	3858.66	16.74
	11	35838.74	20134.43	7143.35	3108.63	4034.72	16.03
	12	38064.97	21847.75	7458.26	3258.01	4200.25	19.98
		比上期增减额(亿元) Changes Compared with Previous Period (100 Million Yuan)					
2004	1	-1102.04	-1259.85	191.19	41.53	149.66	-2.33
	2	663.46	287.65	87.14	25.66	61.48	-0.43
	3	1807.67	1091.54	125.33	71.12	54.21	-0.43
	4	546.80	255.53	83.23	59.66	23.57	-1.11
	5	461.98	259.32	56.27	17.30	38.97	0.08
	6	1588.80	1063.37	190.25	102.54	87.71	2.46
	7	-706.07	-734.70	4.94	-18.32	23.26	-0.08
	8	311.40	136.25	73.18	21.83	51.35	1.75
	9	1295.09	836.87	191.73	104.72	87.01	0.45
	10	-213.37	-261.08	61.38	14.57	46.81	0.45
	11	622.78	166.13	223.80	47.74	176.06	-0.71
	12	2226.23	1713.32	314.91	149.38	165.53	3.95
		比去年同期增长(%) Increase Rate Year-on-year (%)					
2004	1	32.98	23.87	32.79	29.33	35.63	181.57
	2	36.48	27.39	33.19	31.86	34.25	173.80
	3	38.11	28.70	32.33	32.84	31.93	151.28
	4	37.44	29.38	32.35	33.93	31.11	130.75
	5	35.04	27.40	31.26	32.98	29.93	127.38
	6	30.86	23.53	30.74	32.51	29.34	178.94
	7	29.50	23.04	29.23	31.02	27.85	138.41
	8	28.70	21.81	28.90	30.43	27.72	24.14
	9	24.89	17.44	26.79	27.99	25.84	15.29
	10	25.60	18.55	26.77	28.73	25.26	43.08
	11	25.34	18.31	28.57	28.11	28.93	30.11
	12	24.82	17.95	27.46	24.50	29.85	25.42

其他商业银行人民币信贷收支主要指标时间序列表

Time Series of Major Indicators in Sources and Uses of Credit Funds of Other Commercial Banks（RMB）

年　月 Year Month	各项贷款 Total Loans	短期贷款 Short－term Loans					中长期贷款 Medium and Long－term Loans				票据融资 Paper Financing	有价证券及投资 Securities and Investments
			工业贷款 Loans to Industrial Sector	商业贷款 Loans to Commercial Sector	建筑业及基建企业贷款 Loans to Construction and Infrastructure	农业贷款 Loans to Agricultural Sector		基本建设贷款 Capital Construction Loans	技术改造贷款 Technical Improvement Loans	其他中长期贷款 Other Medium and Long－term Loans		
期末余额（亿元） Balance（100 Million Yuan）												
2004　1	23711.93	14280.53	3911.61	1786.98	778.63	23.02	6179.92	912.65	145.23	5122.04	3194.67	4974.66
2	24034.13	14588.10	4043.22	1818.63	799.55	25.23	6374.53	970.95	156.62	5246.96	3013.41	4878.33
3	24870.49	15235.14	4273.56	1935.14	835.74	25.91	6721.94	1045.12	173.02	5503.80	2852.91	5052.75
4	25341.06	15228.84	4334.35	1879.04	856.03	26.95	7039.95	1146.36	176.68	5716.91	3010.81	5236.13
5	25624.98	15492.28	4410.74	1918.18	871.19	26.77	7231.97	1185.15	181.43	5865.39	2838.21	5369.87
6	25707.67	15433.65	4361.43	1876.50	867.50	27.83	7439.39	1216.80	178.45	6044.14	2784.31	5714.69
7	25662.14	15264.80	4333.70	1843.91	1019.02	30.78	7615.89	1255.36	183.56	6176.97	2726.15	5856.50
8	25889.47	15398.50	4415.07	1842.52	1047.08	29.68	7760.26	1276.62	185.31	6298.33	2671.36	6053.33
9	26490.73	15788.67	4564.80	1874.04	1085.01	31.12	7984.16	1326.26	191.90	6466.00	2652.43	6269.83
10	26531.43	15805.70	4574.31	1906.03	1106.70	32.04	8148.02	1364.13	194.56	6589.33	2509.70	6435.20
11	26681.25	15841.75	4600.28	1871.95	1119.73	28.56	8317.11	1372.07	193.50	6751.54	2449.20	6688.23
12	27496.99	16182.72	4728.56	1895.36	1147.08	31.87	8593.28	1421.68	202.01	6969.59	2659.06	7128.25
比上期增减额（亿元） Changes Compared with Previous Period（100 Million Yuan）												
2004　1	443.48	303.71	150.14	30.58	35.19	0.22	262.53	32.94	6.43	223.16	－129.04	－65.10
2	322.20	307.57	131.61	31.65	20.92	2.21	194.61	58.30	11.39	124.92	－181.26	－96.33
3	836.36	647.04	230.34	116.51	36.19	0.68	347.41	74.17	16.40	256.84	－160.50	174.42
4	470.57	－6.30	60.79	－56.10	20.29	1.04	318.01	101.24	3.66	213.11	157.90	183.38
5	283.92	263.44	76.39	39.14	15.16	－0.18	192.02	38.79	4.75	148.48	－172.60	133.74
6	544.30	370.23	87.07	44.43	25.39	1.66	228.63	35.88	4.02	188.73	－53.40	344.82
7	－45.53	－168.84	－27.72	－32.59	151.52	2.96	176.50	38.56	5.10	132.84	－58.17	141.81
8	227.35	133.72	81.37	－1.38	28.07	－1.11	144.36	21.25	1.76	121.35	－54.78	196.83
9	601.24	390.15	149.72	31.52	37.92	1.44	223.91	49.65	6.58	167.68	－18.94	216.50
10	40.72	17.04	9.52	31.99	21.69	0.93	163.87	37.89	2.66	123.32	－142.73	165.37
11	149.83	36.06	25.97	－34.09	13.04	－3.48	169.08	7.92	－1.05	162.21	－60.49	253.03
12	815.75	340.97	128.28	23.42	27.34	3.30	276.18	49.62	8.50	218.06	209.86	440.02
比去年同期增长（%） Increase Rate Year－on－year（%）												
2004　1	42.08	36.34	75.49	39.20	176.33	358.57	62.39	54.10	32.90	65.01	35.72	29.38
2	43.80	37.16	77.61	41.31	184.79	383.33	63.99	60.30	43.62	65.39	41.31	25.43
3	43.25	36.44	78.77	44.45	182.74	292.58	63.26	64.59	50.70	63.44	40.96	28.05
4	40.73	34.40	78.18	41.59	169.43	300.45	63.63	73.63	48.73	62.26	29.86	25.06
5	37.26	32.42	76.63	42.88	162.42	257.89	60.41	70.51	48.41	58.90	17.86	20.92
6	32.03	28.29	69.90	40.99	155.11	267.79	58.39	65.17	44.83	57.54	3.34	22.33
7	29.11	28.12	69.93	39.49	188.88	351.65	52.26	60.05	40.84	51.14	－6.40	21.80
8	24.39	24.25	46.48	32.88	92.63	26.69	48.92	64.72	40.23	46.35	－15.55	23.40
9	24.16	23.42	42.93	30.55	91.58	28.06	47.70	61.29	46.00	45.24	－14.10	25.62
10	23.25	21.98	41.20	28.74	88.87	28.09	45.51	60.73	52.75	42.51	－13.99	30.08
11	22.23	20.29	37.35	23.04	84.75	14.62	43.94	55.17	48.77	41.72	－13.19	33.72
12	23.52	18.87	36.07	18.25	77.62	2.33	46.07	61.55	50.58	43.14	－1.86	41.44

其他商业银行人民币信贷收支主要指标时间序列表

Time Series of Major Indicators in Sources and Uses of Credit Funds of Other Commercial Banks（RMB）

年　月 Year Month		各项存款 Total Deposits	企业存款 Deposits by Enterprises	储蓄存款 Savings Deposits	活期储蓄 Demand Deposits	定期储蓄 Time Deposits	农业存款 Deposits by Agricultural Sector
		期末余额（亿元） Balance（100 Million Yuan）					
2005	1	37261.37	20809.00	7564.00	3278.68	4285.32	17.21
	2	36845.84	20272.14	7819.45	3328.07	4491.38	16.24
	3	38450.83	21390.68	7963.31	3363.08	4600.23	17.06
	4	38887.28	21434.65	8092.31	3385.84	4706.47	16.60
	5	39266.33	21609.92	8216.90	3392.03	4824.87	16.54
	6	41650.90	23218.69	8563.78	3498.27	5065.51	18.23
	7	40905.70	22360.08	8688.57	3486.97	5201.60	17.68
	8	41924.69	22825.29	8872.65	3528.05	5344.60	18.09
	9	43859.65	24091.74	9182.78	3620.85	5561.93	18.47
	10	43432.34	23587.07	9283.12	3625.19	5657.93	17.90
	11	44694.01	24199.31	9495.95	3700.10	5795.85	18.72
	12	46533.61	25491.21	9982.74	3960.89	6021.85	20.84
		比上期增减额（亿元） Changes Compared with Previous Period（100 Million Yuan）					
2005	1	-810.36	-1021.99	105.05	20.62	84.43	-2.77
	2	-415.53	-536.86	255.45	49.39	206.06	-0.97
	3	1604.99	1118.54	143.86	35.01	108.85	0.82
	4	436.45	43.97	129.00	22.76	106.24	-0.46
	5	379.05	175.27	124.59	6.19	118.40	-0.06
	6	2384.57	1608.77	346.88	106.24	240.64	1.69
	7	-745.20	-858.61	124.79	-11.30	136.09	-0.55
	8	1018.99	465.21	184.08	41.08	143.00	0.41
	9	1934.96	1266.45	310.13	92.80	217.33	0.38
	10	-427.31	-504.67	100.34	4.34	96.00	-0.57
	11	1261.67	612.24	212.83	74.91	137.92	0.82
	12	1839.60	1291.90	486.79	260.79	226.00	2.12
		比去年同期增长（%） Increase Rate Year-on-year（%）					
2005	1	26.48	22.16	25.11	23.17	26.62	26.54
	2	22.32	17.04	27.49	23.84	30.34	23.31
	3	20.42	16.17	27.24	21.91	31.44	33.91
	4	19.73	14.82	27.60	20.14	33.57	42.73
	5	19.21	14.17	28.43	19.63	35.43	41.25
	6	20.63	16.15	29.98	19.07	38.77	28.65
	7	20.94	16.12	31.78	19.43	41.60	25.48
	8	22.82	17.70	33.09	19.94	43.49	14.20
	9	23.79	19.09	33.90	18.86	45.91	13.38
	10	23.33	18.12	34.16	18.44	46.63	6.93
	11	24.71	20.19	32.93	19.03	43.65	16.78
	12	22.25	16.68	33.85	21.57	43.37	4.30

其他商业银行人民币信贷收支主要指标时间序列表

Time Series of Major Indicators in Sources and Uses of Credit Funds of Other Commercial Banks（RMB）

年　月 Year Month	各项贷款 Total Loans	短期贷款 Short－term Loans	工业贷款 Loans to Industrial Sector	商业贷款 Loans to Commercial Sector	建筑业及基建企业贷款 Loans to Construction and Infrastructure	农业贷款 Loans to Agricultural Sector	中长期贷款 Medium and Long－term Loans	基本建设贷款 Capital Construction Loans	技术改造贷款 Technical Improvement Loans	其他中长期贷款 Other Medium and Long－term Loans	票据融资 Paper Financing	有价证券及投资 Securities and Investments
	期末余额（亿元） Balance（100 Million Yuan）											
2005　1	27922.15	16305.06	4804.15	1884.04	1157.30	32.58	8763.67	1480.28	207.24	7076.15	2782.77	7249.18
2	28070.27	16359.85	4884.74	1904.50	1166.84	34.10	8870.91	1499.99	208.66	7162.26	2762.34	6948.36
3	28622.59	16799.24	5035.43	1956.51	1191.95	35.82	9071.67	1535.89	215.77	7320.01	2674.37	7234.03
4	29094.41	16713.96	5112.67	1954.47	1194.17	37.37	9240.14	1560.00	225.25	7454.89	3056.03	7746.39
5	29617.63	16787.68	5194.18	1976.07	1191.43	40.09	9422.73	1603.39	226.40	7592.94	3321.37	7524.72
6	30691.02	17474.52	5518.61	2076.12	1325.75	43.42	9726.05	1690.45	229.24	7806.36	3405.66	7623.62
7	30838.35	17188.97	5470.46	2015.18	1322.19	43.35	9751.53	1688.04	229.44	7834.05	3811.71	7685.71
8	31459.27	17269.13	5507.50	2006.98	1355.43	49.38	9869.31	1733.41	234.19	7901.71	4230.59	8008.45
9	32501.51	17638.77	5651.12	2046.79	1406.65	52.78	10109.54	1769.93	235.21	8104.40	4665.34	8278.98
10	32683.45	17593.14	5641.77	2045.95	1406.12	51.97	10245.84	1800.91	235.37	8209.56	4749.53	8432.73
11	33023.29	17767.92	5706.12	2074.13	1436.53	51.93	10499.74	1823.39	233.63	8442.72	4662.07	9139.23
12	33461.99	17958.06	5733.65	2099.90	1430.83	54.28	10888.36	1877.52	236.95	8773.89	4537.41	9362.14
	比上期增减额（亿元） Changes Compared with Previous Period（100 Million Yuan）											
2005　1	425.15	108.42	76.26	－13.96	8.90	0.71	186.43	57.59	6.23	122.61	124.39	79.93
2	148.13	54.79	80.59	20.47	9.54	1.53	107.26	19.72	1.43	86.11	－20.44	－300.82
3	552.28	439.37	150.69	52.00	25.11	1.71	200.74	35.89	7.10	157.75	－87.97	285.67
4	471.83	－85.27	77.24	－2.03	2.22	1.55	168.46	24.11	9.48	134.87	381.67	512.36
5	523.29	73.74	81.51	21.59	－2.74	2.73	182.64	43.42	1.16	138.06	265.33	－221.67
6	1073.34	686.81	324.43	100.05	134.32	3.32	303.31	87.05	2.84	213.42	84.29	98.90
7	147.35	－285.53	－48.15	－60.93	－3.56	－0.07	25.46	－2.42	0.19	27.69	406.06	62.09
8	620.92	80.16	37.04	－8.20	33.24	6.04	117.79	45.37	4.75	67.67	418.87	322.74
9	1042.21	369.63	143.62	39.80	51.22	3.39	240.22	36.52	1.02	202.68	434.75	270.53
10	181.98	－45.62	－9.35	－0.83	－0.54	－0.80	136.31	30.99	0.16	105.16	84.20	153.75
11	339.80	174.77	64.35	28.17	30.42	－0.05	253.89	22.47	－1.74	233.16	－87.47	706.50
12	438.70	190.13	27.52	25.78	－5.70	2.35	388.63	54.13	3.32	331.18	－124.66	222.91
	比去年同期增长（％） Increase Rate Year－on－year（％）											
2005　1	19.70	17.18	26.30	10.25	52.37	44.14	42.15	62.66	47.51	38.35	－12.88	45.72
2	18.71	15.09	24.19	9.46	49.58	37.57	39.49	54.92	37.70	36.69	－8.32	42.43
3	16.94	13.08	21.02	5.55	46.10	40.56	35.27	47.36	28.75	33.18	－6.24	43.17
4	16.63	12.57	21.10	8.60	42.90	40.89	31.55	36.45	31.45	30.58	1.52	47.94
5	17.38	11.13	20.85	7.51	40.10	52.04	30.59	35.65	28.64	29.62	17.04	40.13
6	19.38	13.22	26.53	10.64	52.83	56.02	30.74	38.93	28.46	29.16	22.32	33.40
7	20.17	12.61	26.23	9.29	29.75	40.84	28.04	34.47	24.99	26.83	39.82	31.23
8	21.51	12.15	24.74	8.93	29.45	66.37	27.18	35.78	26.38	25.46	58.37	32.30
9	22.69	11.72	23.80	9.22	29.64	69.60	26.62	33.45	22.57	25.34	75.89	32.04
10	23.19	11.31	23.34	7.34	27.06	62.20	25.75	32.02	20.98	24.59	89.25	31.04
11	23.77	12.16	24.04	10.80	28.29	81.83	26.24	32.89	20.74	25.05	90.35	36.65
12	21.69	10.97	21.26	10.79	24.74	70.32	26.71	32.06	17.30	25.89	70.64	31.34

（六）农村信用合作社人民币信贷收支主要指标时间序列表（1953—1989 年度时序、1990—2005 年月度时序）

Time Series of Major Indicators in Sources and Uses of Credit Funds of Rural Credit Cooperatives（RMB）（Annual Series from 1953 to 1989, Monthly Series from 1990 to 2005）

农村信用合作社人民币信贷收支主要指标时间序列表

Time Series of Major Indicators in Sources and Uses of Credit Funds of Rural Credit Cooperatives（RMB）

年份 Year	存款合计 Total Deposits	集体农业存款 Deposits by Agricultural Collectives	乡镇企业存款 Deposits by Village and Township Enterprises	农户储蓄存款 Savings Deposits by Rural Households	贷款合计 Total Loans	集体农业贷款 Loans to Agricultural Collectives	乡镇企业贷款 Loans to Village and Township Enterprises	农户贷款 Loans to Rural Households
				期末余额（亿元） Balance（100 Million Yuan）				
1953	0.1			0.1	0.2	0.2		
1954	1.6			1.6	1.2	1.2		
1955	6.1	3.1		3.0	3.0	3.0		
1956	10.8	6.5		4.3	10.2	4.1		6.1
1957	20.7	13.4		7.3	9.5	4.2		5.3
1958	40.3	20.2		20.1	24.7	13.6		11.1
1959	45.0	24.0		21.0	22.9	16.0		6.9
1960	43.1	27.9		15.2	22.3	12.7		9.6
1961	47.1	30.9		16.2	17.6	9.5		8.1
1962	28.2	18.4		9.8	15.6	7.9		7.7
1963	31.4	21.3		10.1	13.8	5.6		8.2
1964	42.8	32.1		10.7	14.1	4.2		9.9
				比上期增减额（亿元） Changes Compared with Previous Period（100 Million Yuan）				
1953								
1954	1.5			1.5	1.0	1.0		
1955	4.5	3.1		1.4	1.8	1.8		
1956	4.7	3.4		1.3	7.2	1.1		6.1
1957	9.9	6.9		3.0	-0.7	0.1		-0.8
1958	19.6	6.8		12.8	15.2	9.4		5.8
1959	4.7	3.8		0.9	-1.8	2.4		-4.2
1960	-1.9	3.9		-5.8	-0.6	-3.3		2.7
1961	4.0	3.0		1.0	-4.7	-3.2		-1.5
1962	-18.9	-12.5		-6.4	-2.0	-1.6		-0.4
1963	3.2	2.9		0.3	-1.8	-2.3		0.5
1964	11.4	10.8		0.6	0.3	-1.4		1.7
				比去年同期增长（%） Increase Rate Year-on-year（%）				
1953								
1954	1500.00			1500.00	500.00	500.00		
1955	281.25			87.50	150.00	150.00		
1956	77.05	109.68		43.33	240.00	36.67		
1957	91.67	106.15		69.77	-6.86	2.44		-13.11
1958	94.69	50.75		175.34	160.00	223.81		109.43
1959	11.66	18.81		4.48	-7.29	17.65		-37.84
1960	-4.22	16.25		-27.62	-2.62	-20.63		39.13
1961	9.28	10.75		6.58	-21.08	-25.20		-15.63
1962	-40.13	-40.45		-39.51	-11.36	-16.84		-4.94
1963	11.35	15.76		3.06	-11.54	-29.11		6.49
1964	36.31	50.70		5.94	2.17	-25.00		20.73

农村信用合作社人民币信贷收支主要指标时间序列表
Time Series of Major Indicators in Sources and Uses of Credit Funds of Rural Credit Cooperatives（RMB）

年 份 Year	存款合计 Total Deposits	集体农业存款 Deposits by Agricultural Collectives	乡镇企业存款 Deposits by Village and Township Enterpries	农户储蓄存款 Savings Deposits by Rural Households	贷款合计 Total Loans	集体农业贷款 Loans to Agricultural Collectives	乡镇企业贷款 Loans to Village and Township Enterprises	农户贷款 Loans to Rural Households
期末余额（亿元） Balance（100 Million Yuan）								
1965	48.0	35.1		12.9	13.5	3.1		10.4
1966	60.9	46.3		14.6	15.2	3.8		11.4
1967	73.2	59.2		14.0	14.6	3.6		11.0
1968	75.7	59.7		16.0	16.5	4.0		12.5
1969	73.3	58.4		14.9	17.8	4.5		13.3
1970	76.4	61.4		15.0	18.8	5.6		13.2
1971	90.3	64.2		17.0	19.4	6.0	0.8	12.6
1972	90.9	61.5		20.1	21.1	7.9	1.2	12.0
1973	104.8	67.3		27.1	20.8	7.8	1.5	11.5
1974	121.2	78.1		30.6	22.0	10.7		11.3
1975	135.1	85.1		35.1	26.7	15.4		11.3
1976	141.2	89.4		36.9	35.8	17.1	7.0	11.7
比上期增减额（亿元） Changes Compared with Previous Period（100 Million Yuan）								
1965	5.2	3.0		2.2	-0.6	-1.1		0.5
1966	12.9	11.2		1.7	1.7	0.7		1.0
1967	12.3	12.9		-0.6	-0.6	-0.2		-0.4
1968	2.5	0.5		2.0	1.9	0.4		1.5
1969	-2.4	-1.3		-1.1	1.3	0.5		0.8
1970	3.1	3.0		0.1	1.0	1.1		-0.1
1971	13.9	2.8		2.0	0.6	0.4	0.8	-0.6
1972	0.6	-2.7		3.1	1.7	1.9	0.4	-0.6
1973	13.9	5.8		7.0	-0.3	-0.1	0.3	-0.5
1974	16.4	10.8		3.5	1.2	2.9	-1.5	-0.2
1975	13.9	7.0		4.5	4.7	4.7		
1976	6.1	4.3		1.8	9.1	1.7	7.0	0.4
比去年同期增长（%） Increase Rate Year-on-year（%）								
1965	12.15	9.35		20.56	-4.26	-26.19		5.05
1966	26.88	31.91		13.18	12.59	22.58		9.62
1967	20.20	27.86		-4.11	-3.95	-5.26		-3.51
1968	3.42	0.84		14.29	13.01	11.11		13.64
1969	-3.17	-2.18		-6.88	7.88	12.50		6.40
1970	4.23	5.14		0.67	5.62	24.44		-0.75
1971	18.19	4.56		13.33	3.19	7.14		-4.55
1972	0.66	-4.21		18.24	8.76	31.67	50.00	-4.76
1973	15.29	9.43		34.83	-1.42	-1.27	25.00	-4.17
1974	15.65	16.05		12.92	5.77	37.18	-100.00	-1.74
1975	11.47	8.96		14.71	21.36	43.93		
1976	4.52	5.05		5.13	34.08	11.04		3.54

农村信用合作社人民币信贷收支主要指标时间序列表
Time Series of Major Indicators in Sources and Uses of Credit Funds of Rural Credit Cooperatives (RMB)

年　份 Year	存款合计 Total Deposits	集体农业存款 Deposits by Agricultural Collectives	乡镇企业存款 Deposits by Village and Township Enterprises	农户储蓄存款 Savings Deposits by Rural Households	贷款合计 Total Loans	集体农业贷款 Loans to Agricultural Collectives	乡镇企业贷款 Loans to Village and Township Enterprises	农户贷款 Loans to Rural Households
				期末余额（亿元） Balance (100 Million Yuan)				
1977	151.3	89.3		46.5	39.7	18.4	9.9	11.4
1978	166.0	93.8		55.7	45.1	21.8	12.1	11.2
1979	215.9	98.3	21.9	78.4	47.5	22.4	14.2	10.9
1980	272.3	105.5	29.5	117.0	81.6	34.5	31.1	16.0
1981	319.6	113.2	29.7	169.6	96.4	35.7	35.5	25.2
1982	389.9	121.1	33.7	228.1	121.2	34.8	42.3	44.1
1983	487.4	91.8	62.3	319.9	163.7	28.2	60.1	75.4
1984	624.9	89.9	81.1	438.1	354.5	38.4	135.0	181.1
1985	724.9	71.9	72.1	564.8	400.0	41.4	164.4	194.2
1986	962.3	83.9	91.7	766.1	568.5	44.6	265.9	258.0
1987	1225.2	89.9	104.7	1005.7	771.4	64.5	359.3	347.6
1988	1399.8	98.4	128.3	1142.3	908.6	80.1	456.1	372.4
1989	1669.5	92.3	126.2	1412.1	1094.9	107.3	571.0	415.7
				比上期增减额（亿元） Changes Compared with Previous Period (100 Million Yuan)				
1977	10.1	-0.1		9.6	3.9	1.3	2.9	-0.3
1978	14.7	4.5		9.2	5.4	3.4	2.2	-0.2
1979	49.9	4.5	21.9	22.7	2.4	0.6	2.1	-0.3
1980	56.4	7.2	7.6	38.6	34.1	12.1	16.9	5.1
1981	47.3	7.7	0.2	52.6	14.8	1.2	4.4	9.2
1982	70.3	7.9	4.0	58.5	24.8	-0.9	6.8	18.9
1983	97.5	-29.3	28.6	91.8	42.5	-6.6	17.8	31.3
1984	137.5	-1.9	18.8	118.2	190.8	10.2	74.9	105.7
1985	100.0	-18.0	-9.0	126.7	45.5	3.0	29.4	13.1
1986	237.4	12.0	19.6	201.3	168.5	3.2	101.5	63.8
1987	262.9	6.0	13.0	239.6	202.9	19.9	93.4	89.6
1988	174.6	8.5	23.6	136.6	137.2	15.6	96.8	24.8
1989	269.7	-6.1	-2.1	269.8	186.3	27.2	114.9	43.3
				比去年同期增长（%） Increase Rate Year-on-year (%)				
1977	7.15	-0.11		26.02	10.89	7.60	41.43	-2.56
1978	9.72	5.04		19.78	13.60	18.48	22.22	-1.75
1979	30.06	4.80		40.75	5.32	2.75	17.36	-2.68
1980	26.12	7.32	34.70	49.23	71.79	54.02	119.01	46.79
1981	17.37	7.30	0.68	44.96	18.14	3.48	14.15	57.50
1982	22.00	6.98	13.47	34.49	25.73	-2.52	19.15	75.00
1983	25.01	-24.19	84.87	40.25	35.07	-18.97	42.08	70.98
1984	28.21	-2.07	30.18	36.95	116.55	36.17	124.63	140.19
1985	16.00	-20.02	-11.10	28.92	12.83	7.81	21.78	7.23
1986	32.75	16.69	27.18	35.64	42.13	7.73	61.74	32.85
1987	27.32	7.15	14.18	31.28	35.69	44.62	35.13	34.73
1988	14.25	9.45	22.54	13.58	17.79	24.19	26.94	7.13
1989	19.27	-6.20	-1.64	23.62	20.50	33.96	25.19	11.63

农村信用合作社人民币信贷收支主要指标时间序列表
Time Series of Major Indicators in Sources and Uses of Credit Funds of Rural Credit Cooperatives（RMB）

年 月 Year Month		存款合计 Total Deposits	集体存款 Deposits by Collectives	农户储蓄存款 Savings Deposits by Rural Households	活期储蓄 Demand Deposits	定期储蓄 Time Deposits
期末余额（亿元） Balance（100 Million Yuan）						
1990	1	1675.95	213.93	1462.02	331.19	1130.83
	2	1753.08	210.12	1542.96	337.11	1205.85
	3	1785.58	217.83	1567.75	326.32	1241.43
	4	1812.20	219.62	1592.58	322.51	1270.07
	5	1847.53	225.63	1621.90	325.69	1296.21
	6	1903.01	233.01	1670.00	341.71	1328.29
	7	1945.89	234.28	1711.61	352.78	1358.83
	8	1977.65	241.49	1736.16	355.60	1380.56
	9	2005.53	250.35	1755.18	361.33	1393.85
	10	2061.59	259.49	1802.10	378.53	1423.57
	11	2113.86	276.96	1836.90	389.15	1447.75
	12	2144.40	303.40	1841.00	387.18	1453.82
比上期增减额（亿元） Changes Compared with Previous Period（100 Million Yuan）						
1990	1	16.96	-40.96	57.92	3.82	54.10
	2	77.13	-3.81	80.94	5.92	75.02
	3	32.50	7.71	24.79	-10.79	35.58
	4	26.62	1.79	24.83	-3.81	28.64
	5	35.33	6.01	29.32	3.18	26.14
	6	55.48	7.38	48.10	16.02	32.08
	7	42.88	1.27	41.61	11.07	30.54
	8	31.76	7.21	24.55	2.82	21.73
	9	27.88	8.86	19.02	5.73	13.29
	10	56.06	9.14	46.92	17.20	29.72
	11	52.27	17.47	34.80	10.62	24.18
	12	30.54	26.44	4.10	-1.97	6.07
比去年同期增长（%） Increase Rate Year-on-year（%）						
1990	1	21.11	-8.03	27.00	-2.25	39.19
	2	23.75	-0.27	27.95	-3.09	40.53
	3	26.25	3.92	30.14	-0.13	41.41
	4	27.80	3.56	32.06	2.29	42.60
	5	28.55	5.03	32.68	3.74	42.68
	6	30.08	7.97	33.90	6.96	43.18
	7	30.38	10.69	33.63	8.89	42.01
	8	30.65	13.96	33.36	10.91	40.70
	9	31.07	17.88	33.20	13.72	39.39
	10	32.17	20.35	34.07	18.37	38.97
	11	31.76	22.00	33.37	19.88	37.54
	12	29.26	19.03	31.12	18.27	35.02

农村信用合作社人民币信贷收支主要指标时间序列表

Time Series of Major Indicators in Sources and Uses of Credit Funds of Rural Credit Cooperatives (RMB)

年 月 Year Month	贷款合计 Total Loans	集体农业贷款 Loans to Agricultural Collectives	乡镇企业贷款 Loans to Village and Township Enterprises	农户贷款 Loans to Rural Households
		期末余额（亿元）Balance (100 Million Yuan)		
1990 1	1131.22	107.23	555.80	435.23
2	1170.00	108.96	568.28	459.77
3	1255.74	114.92	588.14	517.16
4	1316.31	118.88	604.55	555.92
5	1358.47	123.18	617.59	578.95
6	1388.41	125.84	632.14	589.08
7	1415.96	127.60	642.06	601.60
8	1449.87	130.06	658.91	612.87
9	1476.41	132.85	673.74	619.08
10	1482.33	132.70	689.13	607.07
11	1460.67	132.97	694.64	578.21
12	1410.78	134.05	700.35	517.69
		比上期增减额（亿元）Changes Compared with Previous Period (100 Million Yuan)		
1990 1	42.95	0.86	15.93	22.72
2	38.78	1.73	12.48	24.54
3	85.74	5.96	19.86	57.39
4	60.57	3.96	16.41	38.76
5	42.16	4.30	13.04	23.03
6	29.94	2.66	14.55	10.13
7	27.55	1.76	9.92	12.52
8	33.91	2.46	16.85	11.27
9	26.54	2.79	14.83	6.21
10	5.92	-0.15	15.39	-12.01
11	-21.66	0.27	5.51	-28.86
12	-49.89	1.08	5.71	-60.52
		比去年同期增长（%）Increase Rate Year-on-year (%)		
1990 1	19.88	31.64	22.59	11.07
2	21.38	32.10	22.88	14.52
3	22.98	33.29	23.80	17.19
4	24.76	33.39	25.58	19.44
5	26.69	35.48	27.00	21.84
6	28.32	36.52	28.56	23.35
7	28.64	35.61	27.87	24.62
8	29.97	34.47	29.53	25.83
9	31.84	35.42	31.22	27.74
10	32.96	34.53	32.72	28.36
11	32.96	33.32	32.23	28.85
12	29.64	26.02	29.73	25.50

农村信用合作社人民币信贷收支主要指标时间序列表

Time Series of Major Indicators in Sources and Uses of Credit Funds of Rural Credit Cooperatives（RMB）

年 月 Year Month		存款合计 Total Deposits				
			集体存款 Deposits by Collectives	农户储蓄存款 Savings Deposits by Rural Households		
					活期储蓄 Demand Deposits	定期储蓄 Time Deposits
		期末余额（亿元） Balance（100 Million Yuan）				
1991	1	2201.03	300.32	1900.71	400.37	1500.34
	2	2274.33	267.18	2007.15	425.85	1581.30
	3	2324.39	275.01	2049.38	416.95	1632.43
	4	2347.67	280.93	2066.74	408.22	1658.52
	5	2379.79	289.23	2090.56	411.62	1678.94
	6	2431.17	296.97	2134.20	428.71	1705.49
	7	2473.19	303.98	2169.21	440.24	1728.97
	8	2506.51	317.44	2189.07	443.68	1745.39
	9	2531.72	325.46	2206.26	449.39	1756.87
	10	2592.13	340.45	2251.68	467.17	1784.51
	11	2660.14	362.06	2298.08	484.79	1813.29
	12	2709.33	389.97	2319.36	493.03	1826.33
		比上期增减额（亿元） Changes Compared with Previous Period（100 Million Yuan）				
1991	1	56.63	-3.08	59.71	13.19	46.52
	2	73.30	-33.14	106.44	25.48	80.96
	3	50.06	7.83	42.23	-8.90	51.13
	4	23.28	5.92	17.36	-8.73	26.09
	5	32.12	8.30	23.82	3.40	20.42
	6	51.38	7.74	43.64	17.09	26.55
	7	42.02	7.01	35.01	11.53	23.48
	8	33.32	13.46	19.86	3.44	16.42
	9	25.21	8.02	17.19	5.71	11.48
	10	60.41	14.99	45.42	17.78	27.64
	11	68.01	21.61	46.40	17.62	28.78
	12	49.19	27.91	21.28	8.24	13.04
		比去年同期增长（%） Increase Rate Year-on-year（%）				
1991	1	31.33	40.38	30.01	20.89	32.68
	2	29.73	27.16	30.08	26.32	31.14
	3	30.18	26.25	30.72	27.77	31.50
	4	29.55	27.92	29.77	26.58	30.58
	5	28.81	28.19	28.90	26.38	29.53
	6	27.75	27.45	27.80	25.46	28.40
	7	27.10	29.75	26.74	24.79	27.24
	8	26.74	31.45	26.09	24.77	26.43
	9	26.24	30.00	25.70	24.37	26.04
	10	25.73	31.20	24.95	23.42	25.35
	11	25.84	30.73	25.11	24.58	25.25
	12	26.34	28.53	25.98	27.34	25.62

农村信用合作社人民币信贷收支主要指标时间序列表

Time Series of Major Indicators in Sources and Uses of Credit Funds of Rural Credit Cooperatives (RMB)

年 月 Year Month	贷款合计 Total Loans	集体农业贷款 Loans to Agricultural Collectives	乡镇企业贷款 Loans to Village and Township Enterprises	农户贷款 Loans to Rural Households
	期末余额（亿元） Balance (100 Million Yuan)			
1991 1	1494.27	137.65	724.22	571.90
2	1534.09	140.04	737.77	595.21
3	1643.68	146.47	770.13	661.13
4	1731.79	152.71	796.32	714.39
5	1779.83	156.19	816.56	737.48
6	1816.17	160.14	839.19	743.66
7	1842.08	162.47	851.94	751.71
8	1873.63	166.26	868.67	759.52
9	1892.32	168.72	883.21	758.80
10	1885.62	167.68	893.95	739.60
11	1852.62	166.44	900.15	700.09
12	1808.69	168.07	912.71	632.36
	比上期增减额（亿元） Changes Compared with Previous Period (100 Million Yuan)			
1991 1	83.49	3.60	23.87	54.21
2	39.82	2.39	13.55	23.31
3	109.59	6.43	32.36	65.92
4	88.11	6.24	26.19	53.26
5	48.04	3.48	20.24	23.09
6	36.34	3.95	22.63	6.18
7	25.91	2.33	12.75	8.05
8	31.55	3.79	16.73	7.81
9	18.69	2.46	14.54	-0.72
10	-6.70	-1.04	10.74	-19.20
11	-33.00	-1.24	6.20	-39.51
12	-43.93	1.63	12.56	-67.73
	比去年同期增长（%） Increase Rate Year-on-year (%)			
1991 1	32.09	28.37	30.30	31.40
2	31.12	28.52	29.83	29.46
3	30.89	27.45	30.94	27.84
4	31.56	28.46	31.72	28.51
5	31.02	26.80	32.22	27.38
6	30.81	27.26	32.75	26.24
7	30.09	27.33	32.69	24.95
8	29.23	27.83	31.83	23.93
9	28.17	27.00	31.09	22.57
10	27.21	26.36	29.72	21.83
11	26.83	25.17	29.59	21.08
12	28.20	25.38	30.32	22.15

农村信用合作社人民币信贷收支主要指标时间序列表

Time Series of Major Indicators in Sources and Uses of Credit Funds of Rural Credit Cooperatives（RMB）

年 月 Year Month	存款合计 Total Deposits				
		集体存款 Deposits by Collectives	农户储蓄存款 Savings Deposits by Rural Households		
				活期储蓄 Demand Deposits	定期储蓄 Time Deposits
			期末余额（亿元）Balance（100 Million Yuan）		
1992 1	2742.56	370.06	2372.50	433.83	1938.67
2	2876.75	352.83	2523.92	463.57	2060.35
3	2925.23	374.09	2551.14	459.24	2091.90
4	2963.50	390.82	2572.68	459.17	2113.51
5	3016.96	414.20	2602.76	466.85	2135.91
6	3100.83	443.89	2656.94	492.38	2164.56
7	3151.00	466.71	2684.29	504.99	2179.30
8	3204.54	502.90	2701.64	515.25	2186.39
9	3261.58	528.48	2733.10	534.45	2198.65
10	3320.21	549.01	2771.2	552.25	2218.95
11	3382.44	576.02	2806.42	568.82	2237.60
12	3478.46	611.05	2867.41	593.52	2273.89
			比上期增减额（亿元）Changes Compared with Previous Period（100 Million Yuan）		
1992 1	33.23	-19.91	53.14	-59.2	112.34
2	134.19	-17.23	151.42	29.74	121.68
3	48.48	21.26	27.22	-4.33	31.55
4	38.27	16.73	21.54	-0.07	21.61
5	53.46	23.38	30.08	7.68	22.40
6	83.87	29.69	54.18	25.53	28.65
7	50.17	22.82	27.35	12.61	14.74
8	53.54	36.19	17.35	10.26	7.09
9	57.04	25.58	31.46	19.20	12.26
10	58.63	20.53	38.10	17.80	20.30
11	62.23	27.01	35.22	16.57	18.65
12	96.02	35.03	60.99	24.70	36.29
			比去年同期增长（%）Increase Rate Year-on-year（%）		
1992 1	24.60	23.22	24.82	8.36	29.22
2	26.49	32.06	25.75	8.86	30.29
3	25.85	36.03	24.48	10.14	28.15
4	26.23	39.12	24.48	12.48	27.43
5	26.77	43.21	24.50	13.42	27.22
6	27.54	49.47	24.49	14.85	26.92
7	27.41	53.53	23.75	14.71	26.05
8	27.85	58.42	23.41	16.13	25.27
9	28.83	62.38	23.88	18.93	25.15
10	28.09	61.26	23.07	18.21	24.35
11	27.15	59.10	22.12	17.33	23.40
12	28.39	56.69	23.63	20.38	24.51

农村信用合作社人民币信贷收支主要指标时间序列表

Time Series of Major Indicators in Sources and Uses of Credit Funds of Rural Credit Cooperatives (RMB)

年 月 Year Month		贷款合计 Total Loans	集体农业贷款 Loans to Agricultural Collectives	乡镇企业贷款 Loans to Village and Township Enterprises	农户贷款 Loans to Rural Households
期末余额（亿元）Balance (100 Million Yuan)					
1992	1	1882.31	173.73	942.51	665.79
	2	1944.59	176.08	970.28	696.23
	3	2092.33	187.76	1024.18	770.07
	4	2195.62	196.53	1059.74	822.53
	5	2261.62	202.35	1089.61	847.79
	6	2319.59	207.99	1125.17	857.47
	7	2375.13	213.45	1155.62	869.11
	8	2431.11	218.48	1187.59	881.58
	9	2474.69	223.14	1223.54	878.08
	10	2487.58	221.86	1250.08	861.87
	11	2483.66	222.12	1275.07	826.81
	12	2452.80	222.34	1294.69	757.58
比上期增减额（亿元）Changes Compared with Previous Period (100 Million Yuan)					
1992	1	73.62	5.66	29.80	33.43
	2	62.28	2.35	27.77	30.44
	3	147.74	11.68	53.90	73.84
	4	103.29	8.77	35.56	52.46
	5	66.00	5.82	29.87	25.26
	6	57.97	5.64	35.56	9.68
	7	55.54	5.46	30.45	11.64
	8	55.98	5.03	31.97	12.47
	9	43.58	4.66	35.95	-3.50
	10	12.89	-1.28	26.54	-16.21
	11	-3.92	0.26	24.99	-35.06
	12	-30.86	0.22	19.62	-69.23
比去年同期增长（%）Increase Rate Year-on-year (%)					
1992	1	25.97	26.21	30.14	16.42
	2	26.76	25.74	31.52	16.97
	3	27.30	28.19	32.99	16.48
	4	26.78	28.69	33.08	15.14
	5	27.07	29.55	33.44	14.96
	6	27.72	29.88	34.08	15.30
	7	28.94	31.38	35.65	15.62
	8	29.75	31.41	36.71	16.07
	9	30.78	32.25	38.53	15.72
	10	31.92	32.31	39.84	16.53
	11	34.06	33.45	41.65	18.10
	12	35.61	32.29	41.85	19.80

农村信用合作社人民币信贷收支主要指标时间序列表

Time Series of Major Indicators in Sources and Uses of Credit Funds of Rural Credit Cooperatives（RMB）

年 月 Year Month		存款合计 Total Deposits				
			集体存款 Deposits by Collectives	农户储蓄存款 Savings Deposits by Rural Households	活期储蓄 Demand Deposits	定期储蓄 Time Deposits
		期末余额（亿元）Balance（100 Million Yuan）				
1993	1	3594.67	582.47	3012.20	624.77	2387.43
	2	3728.37	614.91	3113.46	645.01	2468.45
	3	3716.48	634.73	3081.75	646.02	2435.73
	4	3729.86	658.31	3071.55	655.75	2415.80
	5	3777.03	672.63	3104.40	670.45	2433.95
	6	3852.55	678.19	3174.36	699.20	2475.16
	7	3898.48	649.58	3248.90	700.11	2548.79
	8	3949.90	641.35	3308.55	692.59	2615.96
	9	4000.63	638.96	3361.67	693.90	2667.77
	10	4076.95	633.21	3443.74	700.72	2743.02
	11	4176.36	654.18	3522.18	712.37	2809.81
	12	4297.26	721.02	3576.24	731.00	2845.24
		比上期增减额（亿元）Changes Compared with Previous Period（100 Million Yuan）				
1993	1	117.01	-27.91	144.92	32.48	112.44
	2	133.70	32.44	101.26	20.24	81.02
	3	-11.89	19.82	-31.71	1.01	-32.72
	4	13.38	23.58	-10.20	9.73	-19.93
	5	47.17	14.32	32.85	14.70	18.15
	6	75.52	5.56	69.96	28.75	41.21
	7	45.93	-28.61	74.54	0.91	73.63
	8	51.42	-8.23	59.65	-7.52	67.17
	9	50.73	-2.39	53.12	1.31	51.81
	10	76.32	-5.75	82.07	6.82	75.25
	11	99.41	20.97	78.44	11.65	66.79
	12	120.90	66.84	54.06	18.63	35.43
		比去年同期增长（%）Increase Rate Year-on-year（%）				
1993	1	31.07	57.40	26.96	44.01	23.15
	2	29.60	74.28	23.36	39.14	19.81
	3	27.05	69.67	20.80	40.67	16.44
	4	25.86	68.44	19.39	42.81	14.30
	5	25.19	62.39	19.27	43.61	13.95
	6	24.24	52.78	19.47	42.00	14.35
	7	23.72	39.18	21.03	38.64	16.95
	8	23.26	27.53	22.46	34.42	19.65
	9	22.66	20.91	23.00	29.83	21.34
	10	22.79	15.34	24.27	26.88	23.62
	11	23.47	13.57	25.50	25.24	25.57
	12	23.54	18.00	24.72	23.16	25.13

农村信用合作社人民币信贷收支主要指标时间序列表
Time Series of Major Indicators in Sources and Uses of Credit Funds of Rural Credit Cooperatives (RMB)

年　月 Year Month		贷款合计 Total Loans	集体农业贷款 Loans to Agricultural Collectives	乡镇企业贷款 Loans to Village and Township Enterprises	农户贷款 Loans to Rural Households
期末余额（亿元） Balance (100 Million Yuan)					
1993	1	2540.87	227.16	1344.66	787.76
	2	2728.87	238.49	1431.70	860.69
	3	2750.17	243.31	1416.44	888.84
	4	2839.68	248.64	1456.17	927.70
	5	2884.96	254.29	1479.46	939.43
	6	2911.22	254.51	1498.53	938.20
	7	2963.96	256.99	1535.83	943.05
	8	2995.58	258.50	1560.47	943.48
	9	3035.32	260.15	1588.49	944.56
	10	3068.43	260.31	1621.82	939.27
	11	3101.33	261.23	1661.95	922.44
	12	3143.86	262.12	1730.89	880.57
比上期增减额（亿元） Changes Compared with Previous Period (100 Million Yuan)					
1993	1	86.95	4.50	50.41	28.28
	2	188.00	11.33	87.04	72.93
	3	21.30	4.82	-15.26	28.15
	4	89.51	5.33	39.73	38.86
	5	45.28	5.65	23.29	11.73
	6	26.26	0.22	19.07	-1.23
	7	52.74	2.48	37.30	4.85
	8	31.62	1.51	24.64	0.43
	9	39.74	1.65	28.02	1.08
	10	33.11	0.16	33.33	-5.29
	11	32.90	0.92	40.13	-16.83
	12	42.53	0.89	68.94	-41.87
比去年同期增长（%） Increase Rate Year-on-year (%)					
1993	1	34.99	30.75	42.67	18.32
	2	40.33	35.44	47.56	23.62
	3	31.44	29.59	38.30	15.42
	4	29.33	26.52	37.41	12.79
	5	27.56	25.67	35.78	10.81
	6	25.51	22.37	33.18	9.41
	7	24.79	20.40	32.90	8.51
	8	23.22	18.32	31.40	7.02
	9	22.65	16.59	29.83	7.57
	10	23.35	17.33	29.74	8.98
	11	24.87	17.61	30.34	11.57
	12	28.17	17.89	33.69	16.23

农村信用合作社人民币信贷收支主要指标时间序列表

Time Series of Major Indicators in Sources and Uses of Credit Funds of Rural Credit Cooperatives（RMB）

年 月 Year Month		存款合计 Total Deposits				
			集体存款 Deposits by Collectives	农户储蓄存款 Savings Deposits by Rural Households		
					活期储蓄 Demand Deposits	定期储蓄 Time Deposits
期末余额（亿元） Balance（100 Million Yuan）						
1994	1	4362.15	673.07	3689.08	795.57	2893.51
	2	4578.51	625.68	3952.83	855.77	3097.06
	3	4693.49	668.48	4025.01	833.34	3191.67
	4	4754.82	677.53	4077.29	821.94	3255.35
	5	4859.85	692.75	4167.10	835.99	3331.11
	6	5020.64	723.82	4296.82	880.96	3415.86
	7	5114.76	722.09	4392.67	899.92	3492.75
	8	5205.29	745.42	4459.87	905.38	3554.49
	9	5301.06	762.83	4538.23	928.31	3609.92
	10	5406.66	768.22	4638.44	946.30	3692.14
	11	5546.15	796.72	4749.43	976.99	3772.44
	12	5681.14	865.12	4816.02	1005.47	3810.55
比上期增减额（亿元） Changes Compared with Previous Period（100 Million Yuan）						
1994	1	64.99	-48.06	113.05	7.45	105.60
	2	216.36	-47.39	263.75	60.20	203.55
	3	114.98	42.80	72.18	-22.43	94.61
	4	61.33	9.05	52.28	-11.40	63.68
	5	105.03	15.22	89.81	14.05	75.76
	6	160.79	31.07	129.72	44.97	84.75
	7	94.12	-1.73	95.85	18.96	76.89
	8	90.53	23.33	67.20	5.46	61.74
	9	95.77	17.41	78.36	22.93	55.43
	10	105.60	5.39	100.21	17.99	82.22
	11	139.49	28.50	110.99	30.69	80.30
	12	134.99	68.40	66.59	28.48	38.11
比去年同期增长（%） Increase Rate Year-on-year（%）						
1994	1	21.35	15.55	22.47	27.34	21.20
	2	22.80	1.75	26.96	32.68	25.47
	3	26.29	5.32	30.61	29.00	31.04
	4	27.48	2.92	32.74	25.34	34.75
	5	28.67	2.99	34.23	24.69	36.86
	6	30.32	6.73	35.36	26.00	38.01
	7	31.20	11.16	35.20	28.54	37.04
	8	31.78	16.23	34.80	30.72	35.88
	9	32.51	19.39	35.00	33.78	35.32
	10	32.62	21.32	34.69	35.05	34.60
	11	32.80	21.79	34.84	37.15	34.26
	12	32.20	19.99	34.67	37.55	33.93

农村信用合作社人民币信贷收支主要指标时间序列表

Time Series of Major Indicators in Sources and Uses of Credit Funds of Rural Credit Cooperatives（RMB）

年　月 Year Month	贷款合计 Total Loans	农业贷款 Loans to Agricultural Sector	短期农业贷款 Short－term Loans to Agricultural Sector	农业中长期贷款 Medium and Long－term Loans to Agricultural Sector	乡镇企业贷款 Loans to Village and Township Enterprises	其他贷款 Other Loans	贴现 Discount
				期末余额（亿元） Balance（100 Million Yuan）			
1994　1	3362.53	690.29	268.89	75.19	1824.05	848.19	
2	3430.12	703.10	285.06	76.08	1853.28	873.74	
3	3576.77	759.84	337.41	75.71	1911.62	905.31	
4	3726.75	809.98	383.59	76.88	1968.21	948.56	
5	3789.49	829.58	401.23	77.01	1994.48	965.43	
6	3836.74	835.52	407.31	77.02	2022.29	978.93	
7	3910.54	848.76	418.68	76.85	2056.71	1005.07	
8	3982.37	857.76	421.74	75.86	2090.11	1034.50	
9	4023.67	855.59	416.83	75.44	2114.29	1053.79	
10	4079.75	849.64	415.48	74.94	2154.76	1075.35	
11	4110.45	830.70	405.00	75.98	2191.17	1088.58	
12	4168.55	808.38	385.45	74.39	2279.42	1080.75	
				比上期增减额（亿元） Changes Compared with Previous Period（100 Million Yuan）			
1994　1	107.52	33.24	20.49	3.95	45.00	29.28	
2	67.59	12.81	16.17	0.89	29.23	25.55	
3	146.65	56.74	52.35	－0.37	58.34	31.57	
4	149.98	50.14	46.18	1.17	56.59	43.25	
5	62.74	19.60	17.64	0.13	26.27	16.87	
6	47.25	5.94	6.08	0.01	27.81	13.50	
7	73.80	13.24	11.37	－0.17	34.42	26.14	
8	71.83	9.00	3.06	－0.99	33.40	29.43	
9	41.30	－2.17	－4.91	－0.42	24.18	19.29	
10	56.08	－5.95	－1.35	－0.50	40.47	21.56	
11	30.70	－18.94	－10.48	1.04	36.41	13.23	
12	58.10	－22.32	－19.55	－1.59	88.25	－7.83	
				比去年同期增长（%） Increase Rate Year－on－year（%）			
1994　1	32.34	—	—	—	—	—	
2	25.70	—	—	—	—	—	
3	30.06	—	—	—	—	—	
4	31.24	—	—	—	—	—	
5	31.35	—	—	—	—	—	
6	31.79	—	—	—	—	—	
7	31.94	—	—	—	—	—	
8	32.94	—	—	—	—	—	
9	32.56	—	—	—	—	—	
10	32.96	—	—	—	—	—	
11	32.54	—	—	—	—	—	
12	32.59	—	—	—	—	—	

农村信用合作社人民币信贷收支主要指标时间序列表

Time Series of Major Indicators in Sources and Uses of Credit Funds of Rural Credit Cooperatives（RMB）

年 月 Year Month		存款合计 Total Deposits				
			集体存款 Deposits by Collectives	农户储蓄存款 Savings Deposits by Rural Households		
					活期储蓄 Demand Deposits	定期储蓄 Time Deposits
		期末余额（亿元）Balance（100 Million Yuan）				
1995	1	5713.87	756.67	4957.20	994.37	3962.83
	2	6161.19	781.21	5379.98	1073.61	4306.37
	3	6162.52	810.63	5351.89	1038.82	4313.07
	4	6221.16	806.16	5415.00	1020.26	4394.74
	5	6318.61	816.70	5501.91	1029.36	4472.55
	6	6486.71	846.19	5640.52	1077.95	4562.57
	7	6582.03	840.45	5741.58	1083.52	4658.06
	8	6667.53	866.50	5801.03	1073.29	4727.74
	9	6782.63	894.14	5888.49	1090.86	4797.63
	10	6868.32	891.30	5977.02	1094.16	4882.86
	11	6980.20	903.65	6076.55	1113.59	4962.96
	12	7172.84	977.28	6195.56	1182.37	5013.19
		比上期增减额（亿元）Changes Compared with Previous Period（100 Million Yuan）				
1995	1	45.01	-103.90	148.91	-7.88	156.79
	2	447.32	24.54	422.78	79.24	343.54
	3	1.33	29.42	-28.09	-34.79	6.70
	4	58.64	-4.47	63.11	-18.56	81.67
	5	97.45	10.54	86.91	9.10	77.81
	6	168.10	29.49	138.61	48.59	90.02
	7	95.32	-5.74	101.06	5.57	95.49
	8	85.50	26.05	59.45	-10.23	69.68
	9	115.10	27.64	87.46	17.57	69.89
	10	85.69	-2.84	88.53	3.30	85.23
	11	111.88	12.35	99.53	19.43	80.10
	12	192.64	73.63	119.01	68.78	50.23
		比去年同期增长（%）Increase Rate Year-on-year（%）				
1995	1	30.99	12.42	34.37	24.99	36.96
	2	34.57	24.86	36.10	25.46	39.05
	3	31.30	21.26	32.97	24.66	35.14
	4	30.84	18.99	32.81	24.13	35.00
	5	30.02	17.89	32.03	23.13	34.27
	6	29.20	16.91	31.27	22.36	33.57
	7	28.69	16.39	30.71	20.40	33.36
	8	28.09	16.24	30.07	18.55	33.01
	9	27.95	17.21	29.75	17.51	32.90
	10	27.03	16.02	28.86	15.63	32.25
	11	25.86	13.42	27.94	13.98	31.56
	12	26.26	12.96	28.64	17.59	31.56

农村信用合作社人民币信贷收支主要指标时间序列表

Time Series of Major Indicators in Sources and Uses of Credit Funds of Rural Credit Cooperatives (RMB)

年 月 Year Month		贷款合计 Total Loans	农业贷款 Loans to Agricultural Sector	短期农业贷款 Short - term Loans to Agricultural Sector	农业中长期贷款 Medium and Long - term Loans to Agricultural Sector	乡镇企业贷款 Loans to Village and Township Enterprises	其他贷款 Other Loans	贴现 Discount
		期末余额（亿元） Balance (100 Million Yuan)						
1995	1	4311.01	847.55	413.21	74.93	2311.21	1125.74	26.51
	2	4528.11	917.50	467.95	77.01	2391.44	1190.47	28.70
	3	4641.42	979.56	529.72	79.60	2420.93	1207.65	33.28
	4	4781.77	1035.44	577.24	81.92	2462.21	1249.35	34.77
	5	4837.84	1055.35	593.85	81.91	2486.03	1262.17	34.29
	6	4771.06	1047.54	584.93	80.56	2463.67	1223.22	36.63
	7	4905.80	1087.77	613.21	81.04	2523.40	1255.37	39.26
	8	4987.54	1108.67	627.74	81.53	2564.46	1275.65	38.76
	9	5019.69	1107.58	623.08	80.87	2595.86	1274.01	42.24
	10	5102.21	1121.16	629.17	81.81	2634.97	1302.59	43.49
	11	5145.55	1111.58	618.94	81.99	2673.81	1311.07	49.09
	12	5234.24	1094.85	579.62	76.59	2779.10	1301.87	58.42
		比上期增减额（亿元） Changes Compared with Previous Period (100 Million Yuan)						
1995	1	132.43	43.04	34.58	1.29	32.94	49.37	7.08
	2	217.10	69.95	54.74	2.08	80.23	64.73	2.19
	3	113.31	62.06	61.77	2.59	29.49	17.18	4.58
	4	140.35	55.88	47.52	2.32	41.28	41.70	1.49
	5	56.07	19.91	16.61	-0.01	23.82	12.82	-0.48
	6	-66.78	-7.81	-8.92	-1.35	-22.36	-38.95	2.34
	7	134.74	40.23	28.28	0.48	59.73	32.15	2.63
	8	81.74	20.90	14.53	0.49	41.06	20.28	-0.50
	9	32.15	-1.09	-4.66	-0.66	31.40	-1.64	3.48
	10	82.52	13.58	6.09	0.94	39.11	28.58	1.25
	11	43.34	-9.58	-10.23	0.18	38.84	8.48	5.60
	12	88.69	-16.73	-39.32	-5.40	105.29	-9.20	9.33
		比去年同期增长（%） Increase Rate Year - on - year (%)						
1995	1	28.21	22.78	53.67	-0.35	26.71	32.72	—
	2	32.01	30.49	64.16	1.22	29.04	36.25	—
	3	29.77	28.92	57.00	5.14	26.64	33.40	—
	4	28.31	27.84	50.48	6.56	25.10	31.71	—
	5	27.66	27.21	48.01	6.36	24.65	30.74	—
	6	24.35	25.38	43.61	4.60	21.83	24.95	—
	7	25.45	28.16	46.46	5.45	22.69	24.90	—
	8	25.24	29.25	48.85	7.47	22.69	23.31	—
	9	24.75	29.45	49.48	7.20	22.78	20.90	—
	10	25.06	31.96	51.43	9.17	22.29	21.13	—
	11	25.18	33.81	52.82	7.91	22.03	20.44	—
	12	25.57	35.44	50.37	2.96	21.92	20.46	—

农村信用合作社人民币信贷收支主要指标时间序列表

Time Series of Major Indicators in Sources and Uses of Credit Funds of Rural Credit Cooperatives（RMB）

年 月 Year Month		存款合计 Total Deposits				
			集体存款 Deposits by Collectives	农户储蓄存款 Savings Deposits by Rural Households		
					活期储蓄 Demand Deposits	定期储蓄 Time Deposits
		期末余额（亿元）Balance（100 Million Yuan）				
1996	1	7205.88	938.91	6266.97	1130.92	5136.05
	2	7459.70	832.75	6626.95	1193.68	5433.27
	3	7731.73	885.37	6846.36	1178.12	5668.24
	4	7830.62	885.61	6945.01	1138.05	5806.96
	5	7945.75	909.30	7036.45	1146.69	5889.76
	6	8156.99	955.97	7201.02	1218.50	5982.52
	7	8244.27	947.43	7296.84	1222.14	6074.70
	8	8346.46	970.10	7376.36	1229.35	6147.01
	9	8434.82	1000.50	7434.32	1254.91	6179.41
	10	8546.10	1029.81	7516.29	1277.79	6238.50
	11	8605.86	1038.31	7567.55	1295.13	6272.42
	12	8793.58	1122.97	7670.61	1376.23	6294.38
		比上期增减额（亿元）Changes Compared with Previous Period（100 Million Yuan）				
1996	1	33.01	-37.66	70.67	-50.61	121.28
	2	253.82	-106.16	359.98	62.76	297.22
	3	272.03	52.62	219.41	-15.56	234.97
	4	98.89	0.24	98.65	-40.07	138.72
	5	115.13	23.69	91.44	8.64	82.80
	6	211.24	46.67	164.57	71.81	92.76
	7	87.28	-8.54	95.82	3.64	92.18
	8	102.19	22.67	79.52	7.21	72.31
	9	88.36	30.40	57.96	25.56	32.40
	10	111.28	29.31	81.97	22.88	59.09
	11	59.76	8.50	51.26	17.34	33.92
	12	187.72	84.66	103.06	81.10	21.96
		比去年同期增长（%）Increase Rate Year-on-year（%）				
1996	1	26.11	24.08	26.42	13.73	29.61
	2	21.08	6.60	23.18	11.18	26.17
	3	25.46	9.22	27.92	13.41	31.42
	4	25.87	9.86	28.26	11.55	32.13
	5	25.75	11.34	27.89	11.40	31.69
	6	25.75	12.97	27.67	13.04	31.12
	7	25.25	12.73	27.09	12.79	30.41
	8	25.18	11.96	27.16	14.54	30.02
	9	24.36	11.90	26.25	15.04	28.80
	10	24.43	15.54	25.75	16.78	27.76
	11	23.29	14.90	24.54	16.30	26.38
	12	22.60	14.91	23.81	16.40	25.56

农村信用合作社人民币信贷收支主要指标时间序列表

Time Series of Major Indicators in Sources and Uses of Credit Funds of Rural Credit Cooperatives (RMB)

年 月 Year Month		贷款合计 Total Loans	农业贷款 Loans to Agricultural Sector	短期农业贷款 Short-term Loans to Agricultural Sector	农业中长期贷款 Medium and Long-term Loans to Agricultural Sector	乡镇企业贷款 Loans to Village and Township Enterprises	其他贷款 Other Loans	贴现 Discount
		期末余额（亿元） Balance (100 Million Yuan)						
1996	1	5367.29	1138.80	605.33	76.93	2813.54	1352.29	62.66
	2	5481.75	1172.00	636.18	76.82	2863.17	1377.03	69.55
	3	5643.53	1250.16	699.37	78.28	2903.92	1411.97	72.48
	4	5826.97	1337.30	768.64	79.55	2968.39	1449.84	71.44
	5	5915.11	1384.65	796.03	80.93	2994.09	1465.59	70.78
	6	5954.00	1400.27	782.33	78.95	3020.15	1462.96	70.62
	7	6096.51	1439.78	801.14	79.22	3076.11	1507.93	72.69
	8	6194.57	1467.50	811.96	80.85	3121.66	1532.85	72.56
	9	6282.86	1481.74	816.15	80.76	3169.03	1558.75	73.34
	10	6369.94	1493.75	814.56	80.96	3216.70	1589.31	70.18
	11	6381.55	1481.27	794.59	80.69	3232.84	1597.95	69.49
	12	6364.68	1486.61	705.65	73.23	3264.66	1538.58	74.83
		比上期增减额（亿元） Changes Compared with Previous Period (100 Million Yuan)						
1996	1	133.03	48.94	29.43	0.49	33.92	45.94	4.23
	2	114.46	33.20	30.85	-0.11	49.63	24.74	6.89
	3	161.78	78.16	63.19	1.46	40.75	34.94	2.93
	4	183.44	87.14	69.27	1.27	64.47	37.87	-1.04
	5	88.14	47.35	27.39	1.38	25.70	15.75	-0.66
	6	38.89	15.62	-13.70	-1.98	26.06	-2.63	-0.16
	7	142.51	39.51	18.81	0.27	55.96	44.97	2.07
	8	98.06	27.72	10.82	1.63	45.55	24.92	-0.13
	9	88.29	14.24	4.19	-0.09	47.37	25.90	0.78
	10	87.08	12.01	-1.59	0.20	47.67	30.56	-3.16
	11	11.61	-12.48	-19.97	-0.27	16.14	8.64	-0.69
	12	-16.87	5.34	-88.94	-7.46	31.82	-59.37	5.34
		比去年同期增长（%） Increase Rate Year-on-year (%)						
1996	1	24.50	34.36	46.49	2.67	21.73	20.12	136.36
	2	21.06	27.74	35.95	-0.25	19.73	15.67	142.33
	3	21.59	27.62	32.03	-1.66	19.95	16.92	117.79
	4	21.86	29.15	33.16	-2.89	20.56	16.05	105.46
	5	22.27	31.20	34.05	-1.20	20.44	16.12	106.42
	6	24.79	33.67	33.75	-2.00	22.59	19.60	92.79
	7	24.27	32.36	30.65	-2.25	21.90	20.12	85.15
	8	24.20	32.37	29.35	-0.83	21.73	20.16	87.20
	9	25.16	33.78	30.99	-0.14	22.08	22.35	73.63
	10	24.85	33.23	29.47	-1.04	22.08	22.01	61.37
	11	24.02	33.26	28.38	-1.59	20.91	21.88	41.56
	12	21.60	35.78	21.74	-4.39	17.47	18.18	28.09

农村信用合作社人民币信贷收支主要指标时间序列表

Time Series of Major Indicators in Sources and Uses of Credit Funds of Rural Credit Cooperatives（RMB）

年 月 Year Month	各项存款 Total Deposits					
		企业存款 Deposits by Enterprises	储蓄存款 Savings Deposits			农业存款 Deposits by Agricultural Sector
				活期储蓄 Demand Deposits	定期储蓄 Time Deposits	
期末余额（亿元） Balance（100 Million Yuan）						
1997 1	8822.14	122.25	7711.77	1324.59	6387.18	947.15
2	9264.32	120.18	8188.05	1431.62	6756.43	913.83
3	9457.38	121.66	8318.22	1449.67	6868.55	971.84
4	9513.70	126.08	8365.84	1426.75	6939.09	980.01
5	9612.64	129.21	8445.70	1431.84	7013.86	996.75
6	9755.48	135.25	8546.27	1480.70	7065.57	1034.58
7	9846.71	138.36	8634.23	1470.53	7163.70	1036.83
8	9986.15	142.32	8734.46	1477.88	7256.58	1071.20
9	10142.35	150.07	8841.39	1510.24	7331.15	1113.60
10	10260.49	155.70	8942.55	1504.98	7437.57	1125.24
11	10363.69	156.58	9012.43	1547.17	7465.26	1157.83
12	10624.22	158.81	9132.17	1636.53	7495.64	1264.77
比上期增减额（亿元） Changes Compared with Previous Period（100 Million Yuan）						
1997 1	-38.02	5.94	52.78	-46.21	98.99	-60.81
2	442.17	-2.07	476.28	107.03	369.25	-33.33
3	193.07	1.48	130.17	18.05	112.12	58.01
4	56.33	4.42	47.63	-22.91	70.54	8.17
5	98.94	3.13	79.85	5.08	74.77	16.74
6	142.82	6.03	100.57	48.86	51.71	37.83
7	91.26	3.12	87.97	-10.16	98.13	2.25
8	139.42	3.95	100.23	7.35	92.88	34.37
9	156.21	7.75	106.93	32.36	74.57	42.40
10	118.13	5.63	101.16	-5.26	106.42	11.64
11	103.20	0.88	69.88	42.18	27.70	32.59
12	260.54	2.24	119.74	89.36	30.38	106.94
比去年同期增长（%） Increase Rate Year-on-year（%）						
1997 1	22.43	—	23.05	17.12	24.36	—
2	24.19	—	23.56	19.93	24.35	—
3	22.32	—	21.50	23.05	21.18	—
4	21.49	—	20.46	25.37	19.50	—
5	20.98	—	20.03	24.87	19.09	—
6	19.60	—	18.68	21.52	18.10	—
7	19.44	—	18.33	20.32	17.93	—
8	19.65	—	18.41	20.22	18.05	—
9	20.24	—	18.93	20.35	18.64	—
10	20.06	—	18.98	17.78	19.22	—
11	20.43	—	19.09	19.46	19.02	—
12	20.82	—	19.05	18.91	19.08	—

农村信用合作社人民币信贷收支主要指标时间序列表

Time Series of Major Indicators in Sources and Uses of Credit Funds of Rural Credit Cooperatives (RMB)

年 月 Year Month		各项贷款 Total Loans											有价证券及投资 Securities and Investments
			短期贷款 Short - term Loans						中长期贷款 Medium and Long - term Loans				
				工业贷款 Loans to Industrial Sector	商业贷款 Loans to Commercial Sector	建筑业及基建企业贷款 Loans to Construction and Infrastructure	农业贷款 Loans to Agricultural Sector	贴现 Discount		基本建设贷款 Capital Construction Loans	技术改造贷款 Technical Improvement Loans	其他中长期贷款 Other Medium and Long - term Loans	
期末余额(亿元) Balance (100 Million Yuan)													
1997	1	6521.10	6099.51				1461.10	84.32	421.59			421.59	414.46
	2	6675.12	6249.23				1507.97	84.17	425.89			425.89	417.00
	3	6855.93	6434.87				1611.69	84.08	421.06			421.06	442.56
	4	6992.06	6573.24				1682.26	83.18	418.82			418.82	437.58
	5	7092.42	6678.69				1726.81	80.57	413.73			413.73	466.01
	6	7072.80	6663.09				1730.88	76.22	409.71			409.71	468.32
	7	7144.79	6740.50				1757.98	67.26	404.29			404.29	465.46
	8	7230.65	6832.81				1800.51	64.53	397.84			397.84	468.41
	9	7279.10	6886.16				1810.85	59.69	392.94			392.94	486.37
	10	7323.20	6933.40				1820.16	53.68	389.80			389.80	504.66
	11	7332.16	6951.46				1811.27	51.33	380.70			380.70	516.14
	12	7326.14	6956.39				1774.31	52.92	369.75			369.75	521.74
比上期增减额(亿元) Changes Compared with Previous Period (100 Million Yuan)													
1997	1	167.77	169.70				50.20	9.81	- 1.93			- 1.93	10.29
	2	154.02	149.71				46.87	- 0.15	4.31			4.31	2.54
	3	180.80	185.64				103.72	- 0.09	- 4.84			- 4.84	25.56
	4	136.13	138.37				70.57	- 0.90	- 2.24			- 2.24	- 4.98
	5	100.35	105.44				44.55	- 2.61	- 5.09			- 5.09	28.43
	6	- 19.62	- 15.60				4.07	- 4.35	- 4.02			- 4.02	2.32
	7	71.99	77.41				27.10	- 8.96	- 5.42			- 5.42	- 2.86
	8	85.85	92.30				42.53	- 2.74	- 6.45			- 6.45	2.95
	9	48.47	53.37				10.35	- 4.83	- 4.90			- 4.90	17.96
	10	44.10	47.24				9.31	- 6.01	- 3.14			- 3.14	18.29
	11	8.98	18.07				- 8.89	- 2.35	- 9.09			- 9.09	11.49
	12	- 6.05	4.91				- 36.97	1.59	- 10.96			- 10.96	5.60
比去年同期增长(%) Increase Rate Year - on - year (%)													
1997	1	21.49	—				—	—	—			—	—
	2	21.76	—				—	—	—			—	—
	3	21.48	—				—	—	—			—	—
	4	19.99	—				—	—	—			—	—
	5	19.90	—				—	—	—			—	—
	6	18.79	—				—	—	—			—	—
	7	17.19	—				—	—	—			—	—
	8	16.72	—				—	—	—			—	—
	9	15.85	—				—	—	—			—	—
	10	14.96	—				—	—	—			—	—
	11	14.89	—				—	—	—			—	—
	12	15.10	—				—	—	—			—	—

农村信用合作社人民币信贷收支主要指标时间序列表

Time Series of Major Indicators in Sources and Uses of Credit Funds of Rural Credit Cooperatives（RMB）

年 月 Year Month		各项存款 Total Deposits	企业存款 Deposits by Enterprises	储蓄存款 Savings Deposits	活期储蓄 Demand Deposits	定期储蓄 Time Deposits	农业存款 Deposits by Agricultural Sector
		期末余额（亿元） Balance（100 Million Yuan）					
1998	1	10493.62	163.05	9222.89	1581.79	7641.10	1064.04
	2	10975.51	166.18	9663.24	1664.44	7998.80	1098.86
	3	11163.25	168.77	9778.00	1678.14	8099.86	1152.69
	4	11206.07	179.06	9812.28	1661.35	8150.93	1154.74
	5	11322.44	184.60	9910.74	1670.49	8240.25	1167.99
	6	11459.61	192.10	10017.67	1718.49	8299.18	1188.99
	7	11572.19	194.94	10112.18	1743.23	8368.95	1206.58
	8	11623.58	199.54	10129.90	1750.29	8379.61	1234.04
	9	11691.07	206.47	10145.47	1773.48	8371.99	1277.27
	10	11793.44	210.61	10232.95	1807.69	8425.26	1289.99
	11	11916.38	210.44	10311.18	1844.61	8466.57	1331.43
	12	12191.47	211.87	10441.03	1948.51	8492.52	1441.00
		比上期增减额（亿元） Changes Compared with Previous Period（100 Million Yuan）					
1998	1	-232.28	-13.38	16.52	-71.45	87.97	-178.09
	2	481.89	3.13	440.35	82.65	357.70	34.82
	3	187.74	2.59	114.76	13.70	101.06	53.83
	4	42.83	10.29	34.28	-16.79	51.07	2.05
	5	116.36	5.54	98.46	9.14	89.32	13.25
	6	137.18	7.50	106.94	48.01	58.93	21.00
	7	112.58	2.85	94.50	24.73	69.77	17.59
	8	51.40	4.60	17.73	7.07	10.66	27.46
	9	67.50	6.93	15.58	23.19	-7.61	43.23
	10	102.35	4.14	87.46	34.20	53.26	12.72
	11	122.94	-0.17	78.23	36.92	41.31	41.44
	12	275.12	1.44	129.87	103.91	25.96	109.57
		比去年同期增长（%） Increase Rate Year-on-year（%）					
1998	1	18.95	33.37	19.59	19.42	19.63	12.34
	2	18.47	38.28	18.02	16.26	18.39	20.25
	3	18.04	38.72	17.55	15.76	17.93	18.61
	4	17.79	42.02	17.29	16.44	17.46	17.83
	5	17.79	42.87	17.35	16.67	17.49	17.18
	6	17.47	42.03	17.22	16.06	17.46	14.92
	7	17.52	40.89	17.12	18.54	16.82	16.37
	8	16.40	40.21	15.98	18.43	15.48	15.20
	9	15.27	37.58	14.75	17.43	14.20	14.70
	10	14.94	35.27	14.43	20.11	13.28	14.64
	11	14.98	34.40	14.41	19.22	13.41	14.99
	12	14.75	33.41	14.33	19.06	13.30	13.93

农村信用合作社人民币信贷收支主要指标时间序列表

Time Series of Major Indicators in Sources and Uses of Credit Funds of Rural Credit Cooperatives (RMB)

年 月 Year Month		各项贷款 Total Loans	短期贷款 Short－term Loans	工业贷款 Loans to Industrial Sector	商业贷款 Loans to Commercial Sector	建筑业及基建企业贷款 Loans to Construction and Infrastructure	农业贷款 Loans to Agricultural Sector	贴现 Discount	中长期贷款 Medium and Long－term Loans	基本建设贷款 Capital Construction Loans	技术改造贷款 Technical Improvement Loans	其他中长期贷款 Other Medium and Long－term Loans	有价证券及投资 Securities and Investments
期末余额（亿元） Balance (100 Million Yuan)													
1998	1	7514.93	7110.21				2404.48	57.84	399.43			399.43	506.31
	2	7593.80	7186.37				2423.62	55.51	402.42			402.42	540.22
	3	7784.54	7378.73				2521.19	55.31	405.78			405.78	551.96
	4	7918.32	7530.77				2593.28	56.25	387.52			387.52	563.30
	5	8000.99	7593.91				2615.10	52.88	407.05			407.05	569.09
	6	8055.05	7669.24				2640.04	49.04	385.78			385.78	609.74
	7	8139.23	7753.80		0.11		2662.64	46.66	385.40			385.40	633.61
	8	8223.66	7848.13				2695.47	46.80	375.52			375.52	648.61
	9	8292.92	7911.07				2713.49	46.44	381.56			381.56	678.54
	10	8328.93	7942.57				2708.11	43.58	386.36			386.36	752.64
	11	8342.75	7950.82				2688.84	45.67	391.92			391.92	818.51
	12	8340.18	7973.42				2659.29	48.86	366.76			366.76	848.91
比上期增减额（亿元） Changes Compared with Previous Period (100 Million Yuan)													
1998	1	96.91	101.21	－0.19	－0.01		138.27	4.20	－2.92			－2.92	－17.98
	2	78.86	76.15				19.14	－2.34	2.99			2.99	33.91
	3	190.76	192.38				97.57	－0.19	3.36			3.36	11.74
	4	133.78	152.04				72.09	0.94	－18.26			－18.26	11.34
	5	82.66	63.13				21.81	－3.38	19.53			19.53	5.79
	6	54.05	75.33				24.94	－3.84	－21.28			－21.28	40.64
	7	84.20	84.58		0.11		22.60	－2.38	－0.38			－0.38	23.87
	8	84.42	94.32		－0.11		32.83	0.15	－9.88			－9.88	15.01
	9	69.27	62.95				18.02	－0.36	6.04			6.04	29.93
	10	36.01	31.50				－5.37	－2.86	4.79			4.79	74.10
	11	13.80	8.24				－19.27	2.09	5.56			5.56	65.87
	12	－2.56	22.60				－29.55	3.19	－25.16			－25.16	30.40
比去年同期增长（%） Increase Rate Year－on－year (%)													
1998	1	15.24	16.57				64.57	－31.40	－5.26			－5.26	22.16
	2	13.76	15.00				60.72	－34.05	－5.51			－5.51	29.55
	3	13.54	14.67				56.43	－34.22	－3.63			－3.63	24.72
	4	13.25	14.57				54.15	－32.38	－7.47			－7.47	28.73
	5	12.81	13.70				51.44	－34.37	－1.61			－1.61	22.12
	6	13.89	15.10				52.53	－35.66	－5.84			－5.84	30.20
	7	13.92	15.03				51.46	－30.63	－4.67			－4.67	36.13
	8	13.73	14.86				49.71	－27.48	－5.61			－5.61	38.47
	9	13.93	14.88				49.85	－22.20	－2.90			－2.90	39.51
	10	13.73	14.56				48.78	－18.82	－0.88			－0.88	49.14
	11	13.78	14.38				48.45	－11.03	2.95			2.95	58.58
	12	13.84	14.62				49.88	－7.67	－0.81			－0.81	62.71

农村信用合作社人民币信贷收支主要指标时间序列表

Time Series of Major Indicators in Sources and Uses of Credit Funds of Rural Credit Cooperatives（RMB）

年 月 Year Month		各项存款 Total Deposits	企业存款 Deposits by Enterprises	储蓄存款 Savings Deposits	活期储蓄 Demand Deposits	定期储蓄 Time Deposits	农业存款 Deposits by Agricultural Sector
		期末余额（亿元） Balance（100 Million Yuan）					
1999	1	12155.80	212.86	10453.70	1934.91	8518.79	1423.76
	2	12410.23	215.13	10850.15	2049.95	8800.20	1286.15
	3	12642.31	218.36	11001.21	2051.48	8949.73	1359.43
	4	12665.73	222.93	11007.32	2005.61	9001.71	1376.03
	5	12722.65	229.94	11040.02	1997.84	9042.18	1396.40
	6	12891.34	238.38	11156.61	2047.38	9109.23	1437.79
	7	12912.45	240.09	11155.17	2062.71	9092.46	1458.56
	8	12953.94	243.88	11143.81	2076.17	9067.64	1504.09
	9	12992.72	242.68	11137.05	2116.38	9020.67	1550.77
	10	12969.63	247.58	11099.18	2132.42	8966.76	1560.18
	11	13047.39	263.69	11085.27	2179.19	8906.08	1632.51
	12	13358.09	265.16	11217.25	2314.03	8903.22	1767.65
		比上期增减额（亿元） Changes Compared with Previous Period（100 Million Yuan）					
1999	1	16.65	2.00	54.13	-4.88	59.01	-8.81
	2	254.44	2.28	396.45	115.04	281.41	-137.61
	3	232.07	3.22	151.06	1.53	149.53	73.28
	4	23.43	4.57	6.12	-45.86	51.98	16.60
	5	56.92	7.01	32.70	-7.77	40.47	20.37
	6	168.67	8.43	116.59	49.53	67.06	41.38
	7	21.12	1.72	-1.45	15.33	-16.78	20.78
	8	41.48	3.79	-11.36	13.46	-24.82	45.53
	9	38.78	-1.20	-6.76	40.21	-46.97	46.68
	10	-23.09	4.90	-37.87	16.04	-53.91	9.41
	11	77.75	16.10	-13.91	46.77	-60.68	72.33
	12	310.70	1.47	131.98	134.84	-2.86	135.14
		比去年同期增长（%） Increase Rate Year-on-year（%）					
1999	1	15.84	30.55	13.35	22.32	11.49	33.81
	2	13.07	29.46	12.28	23.16	10.02	17.04
	3	13.25	29.38	12.51	22.25	10.49	17.94
	4	13.03	24.50	12.18	20.72	10.44	19.16
	5	12.37	24.56	11.39	19.60	9.73	19.56
	6	12.49	24.09	11.37	19.14	9.76	20.93
	7	11.58	23.16	10.31	18.33	8.65	20.88
	8	11.45	22.22	10.01	18.62	8.21	21.88
	9	11.13	17.54	9.77	19.33	7.75	21.41
	10	9.97	17.55	8.47	17.96	6.43	20.95
	11	9.49	25.30	7.51	18.14	5.19	22.61
	12	9.57	25.15	7.43	18.76	4.84	22.67

农村信用合作社人民币信贷收支主要指标时间序列表

Time Series of Major Indicators in Sources and Uses of Credit Funds of Rural Credit Cooperatives (RMB)

年 月 Year Month		各项贷款 Total Loans	短期贷款 Short - term Loans						中长期贷款 Medium and Long - term Loans				有价证券及投资 Securities and Investments
				工业贷款 Loans to Industrial Sector	商业贷款 Loans to Commercial Sector	建筑业及基建企业贷款 Loans to Construction and Infrastructure	农业贷款 Loans to Agricultural Sector	贴现 Discount		基本建设贷款 Capital Construction Loans	技术改造贷款 Technical Improvement Loans	其他中长期贷款 Other Medium and Long - term Loans	
		期末余额（亿元） Balance (100 Million Yuan)											
1999	1	8369.04	8003.63				2726.30	50.87	365.41			365.41	848.30
	2	8472.77	8106.47				2765.60	53.83	366.30			366.30	824.12
	3	8608.65	8240.56				2836.32	53.13	368.09			368.09	862.15
	4	8755.59	8385.58				2925.54	51.58	370.01			370.01	854.19
	5	8851.63	8478.53	0.05	0.20		2975.61	49.04	373.10			373.10	898.31
	6	8970.76	8597.68				3022.90	47.63	373.08			373.08	927.34
	7	9053.94	8678.97				3056.60	44.67	374.97			374.97	951.49
	8	9164.65	8783.91				3100.20	43.10	380.74			380.74	939.19
	9	9246.82	8860.92				3127.18	42.82	385.90			385.90	960.54
	10	9252.60	8863.26				3117.54	42.01	389.34			389.34	984.14
	11	9272.70	8880.95				3099.08	41.34	391.75			391.75	977.33
	12	9225.59	8836.42				3039.64	43.31	389.17			389.17	1005.39
		比上期增减额（亿元） Changes Compared with Previous Period (100 Million Yuan)											
1999	1	138.44	138.76				65.40	2.02	-0.32			-0.32	0.23
	2	103.73	102.84				39.30	2.96	0.89			0.89	-24.18
	3	135.90	134.11				70.72	-0.70	1.79			1.79	38.02
	4	146.95	145.03				89.22	-1.54	1.92			1.92	-7.96
	5	96.02	92.93	0.05	0.20		50.07	-2.55	3.09			3.09	44.13
	6	119.15	119.17	-0.05	-0.20		47.29	-1.40	-0.02			-0.02	29.03
	7	83.18	81.29				33.70	-2.91	1.89			1.89	24.14
	8	110.71	104.94				43.59	-1.56	5.77			5.77	-12.30
	9	82.16	77.00				26.99	-0.29	5.16			5.16	21.35
	10	5.79	2.35				-9.64	-0.81	3.44			3.44	23.60
	11	20.08	17.67				-18.47	-0.67	2.41			2.41	-6.81
	12	-47.11	-44.53				-59.44	1.97	-2.58			-2.58	28.06
		比去年同期增长（%） Increase Rate Year - on - year (%)											
1999	1	11.37	12.57				13.38	-12.05	-8.52			-8.52	67.55
	2	11.57	12.80				14.11	-3.03	-8.98			-8.98	52.55
	3	10.59	11.68				12.50	-3.94	-9.29			-9.29	56.20
	4	10.57	11.35				12.81	-8.30	-4.52			-4.52	51.64
	5	10.63	11.65				13.79	-7.26	-8.34			-8.34	57.85
	6	11.37	12.11				14.50	-2.88	-3.29			-3.29	52.09
	7	11.24	11.93				14.80	-4.26	-2.71			-2.71	50.17
	8	11.44	11.92				15.02	-7.91	1.39			1.39	44.80
	9	11.50	12.01				15.25	-7.80	1.14			1.14	41.56
	10	11.09	11.59				15.12	-3.60	0.77			0.77	30.76
	11	11.15	11.70				15.26	-9.48	-0.04			-0.04	19.40
	12	10.62	10.82				14.30	-11.36	6.11			6.11	18.43

农村信用合作社人民币信贷收支主要指标时间序列表

Time Series of Major Indicators in Sources and Uses of Credit Funds of Rural Credit Cooperatives（RMB）

年　月 Year Month		各项存款 Total Deposits	企业存款 Deposits by Enterprises	储蓄存款 Savings Deposits	活期储蓄 Demand Deposits	定期储蓄 Time Deposits	农业存款 Deposits by Agricultural Sector
期末余额（亿元） Balance（100 Million Yuan）							
2000	1	13259.63	267.99	11251.60	2275.65	8975.95	1659.19
	2	13659.18	274.76	11700.38	2441.89	9258.49	1607.37
	3	13764.78	286.98	11702.85	2470.64	9232.21	1697.00
	4	13734.86	298.00	11662.67	2447.72	9214.95	1701.73
	5	13776.62	304.77	11649.45	2462.09	9187.36	1750.87
	6	13995.21	317.15	11768.14	2549.29	9218.85	1835.49
	7	14016.47	323.15	11783.50	2553.04	9230.46	1836.55
	8	14079.98	331.86	11764.46	2555.68	9208.78	1904.72
	9	14198.71	341.74	11793.44	2593.20	9200.24	1980.20
	10	14244.14	347.65	11842.24	2613.57	9228.67	1969.23
	11	14422.09	359.55	11927.51	2657.37	9270.14	2045.80
	12	15129.43	388.64	12355.25	2864.06	9491.19	2244.11
比上期增减额（亿元） Changes Compared with Previous Period（100 Million Yuan）							
2000	1	-96.89	1.46	46.13	-33.05	79.18	-116.93
	2	399.55	6.77	448.78	166.24	282.54	-51.82
	3	105.60	12.22	2.47	28.75	-26.28	89.63
	4	-29.92	11.02	-40.18	-22.92	-17.26	4.73
	5	41.76	6.77	-13.22	14.37	-27.59	49.14
	6	218.59	12.38	118.69	87.20	31.49	84.62
	7	21.26	6.00	15.36	3.75	11.61	1.06
	8	63.51	8.71	-19.04	2.64	-21.68	68.17
	9	118.73	9.88	28.98	37.52	-8.54	75.48
	10	45.43	5.91	48.80	20.37	28.43	-10.97
	11	177.95	11.90	85.27	43.80	41.47	76.57
	12	707.34	29.09	427.74	206.69	221.05	198.31
比去年同期增长（%） Increase Rate Year-on-year（%）							
2000	1	9.08	25.90	7.63	17.61	5.37	16.54
	2	10.06	27.72	7.84	19.12	5.21	24.98
	3	8.88	31.43	6.38	20.43	3.16	24.83
	4	8.44	33.67	5.95	22.04	2.37	23.67
	5	8.28	32.54	5.52	23.24	1.61	25.38
	6	8.56	33.04	5.48	24.51	1.20	27.66
	7	8.55	34.60	5.63	23.77	1.52	25.92
	8	8.69	36.08	5.57	23.10	1.56	26.64
	9	9.28	40.82	5.89	22.53	1.99	27.69
	10	9.83	40.42	6.69	22.56	2.92	26.22
	11	10.54	36.35	7.60	21.94	4.09	25.32
	12	13.26	46.57	10.15	23.77	6.60	26.95

农村信用合作社人民币信贷收支主要指标时间序列表

Time Series of Major Indicators in Sources and Uses of Credit Funds of Rural Credit Cooperatives (RMB)

年 月 Year Month	各项贷款 Total Loans	短期贷款 Short－term Loans	工业贷款 Loans to Industrial Sector	商业贷款 Loans to Commercial Sector	建筑业及基建企业贷款 Loans to Construction and Infrastructure	农业贷款 Loans to Agricultural Sector	贴现 Discount	中长期贷款 Medium and Long－term Loans	基本建设贷款 Capital Construction Loans	技术改造贷款 Technical Improvement Loans	其他中长期贷款 Other Medium and Long－term Loans	有价证券及投资 Securities and Investments
期末余额（亿元） Balance（100 Million Yuan）												
2000 1	9392.38	9016.60				3106.77	49.09	375.78			375.78	1018.32
2	9465.48	9086.50				3137.29	49.36	378.98			378.98	1052.59
3	9669.78	9285.69				3251.14	46.63	384.09			384.09	1073.10
4	9855.60	9466.13				3371.23	46.55	389.47			389.47	1099.61
5	9923.18	9531.06				3433.59	44.63	392.12			392.12	1081.52
6	10020.66	9623.52				3485.61	45.29	397.14			397.14	1105.72
7	10111.06	9711.22				3535.01	43.06	399.84			399.84	1112.46
8	10206.24	9825.74				3594.42	43.62	380.50			380.50	1127.31
9	10284.76	9905.67				3637.77	47.90	379.09			379.09	1150.36
10	10337.89	9960.20				3651.55	48.18	377.69			377.69	1151.21
11	10374.34	9993.30				3640.41	54.43	381.04			381.04	1165.02
12	10489.29	10109.36				3587.98	78.28	379.93			379.93	1173.30
比上期增减额（亿元） Changes Compared with Previous Period（100 Million Yuan）												
2000 1	207.73	204.14				79.82	5.73	3.59			3.59	11.97
2	73.10	69.90				30.52	0.27	3.20			3.20	34.27
3	204.30	199.19				113.85	－2.73	5.11			5.11	20.51
4	185.82	180.44				120.09	－0.08	5.38			5.38	26.51
5	67.58	64.93				62.36	－1.92	2.65			2.65	－18.09
6	97.48	92.46				52.02	0.66	5.02			5.02	24.20
7	90.40	87.70				49.40	－2.23	2.70			2.70	6.74
8	95.18	114.52				59.41	0.56	－19.34			－19.34	14.85
9	78.52	79.93				43.35	4.28	－1.41			－1.41	23.05
10	53.13	54.53				13.78	0.28	－1.40			－1.40	0.85
11	36.45	33.10				－11.14	6.25	3.35			3.35	13.81
12	114.95	116.06				－52.43	23.85	－1.11			－1.11	8.28
比去年同期增长（%） Increase Rate Year－on－year（%）												
2000 1	12.23	12.66				13.96	－3.50	2.84			2.84	20.04
2	11.72	12.09				13.44	－8.30	3.46			3.46	27.72
3	12.33	12.68				14.63	－12.23	4.35			4.35	24.47
4	12.56	12.89				15.23	－9.75	5.26			5.26	28.73
5	12.11	12.41	－100.00	－100.00		15.39	－8.99	5.10			5.10	20.39
6	11.70	11.93				15.31	－4.91	6.45			6.45	19.24
7	11.68	11.89				15.65	－3.60	6.63			6.63	16.92
8	11.37	11.86				15.94	1.21	－0.06			－0.06	20.03
9	11.22	11.79				16.33	11.86	－1.76			－1.76	19.76
10	11.73	12.38				17.13	14.69	－2.99			－2.99	16.98
11	11.88	12.53				17.47	31.66	－2.73			－2.73	19.20
12	13.70	14.41				18.04	80.74	－2.37			－2.37	16.70

农村信用合作社人民币信贷收支主要指标时间序列表

Time Series of Major Indicators in Sources and Uses of Credit Funds of Rural Credit Cooperatives（RMB）

年 月 Year	Month	各项存款 Total Deposits	企业存款 Deposits by Enterprises	储蓄存款 Savings Deposits	活期储蓄 Demand Deposits	定期储蓄 Time Deposits	农业存款 Deposits by Agricultural Sector
期末余额（亿元）Balance（100 Million Yuan）							
2001	1	15264.13	398.40	12765.84	2938.85	9826.99	2013.17
	2	15564.49	411.60	13016.02	2948.95	10067.07	2042.85
	3	15797.70	430.97	13100.39	3006.55	10093.84	2172.99
	4	15841.55	446.57	13119.02	3006.14	10112.88	2187.30
	5	15939.11	460.11	13160.62	3018.59	10142.03	2229.34
	6	16247.32	479.14	13315.30	3119.09	10196.21	2359.07
	7	16265.79	493.41	13364.03	3119.85	10244.18	2309.13
	8	16379.81	515.54	13358.18	3119.36	10238.82	2404.98
	9	16542.44	535.67	13398.45	3155.51	10242.94	2496.41
	10	16645.29	553.81	13483.76	3190.03	10293.73	2497.84
	11	16800.03	566.54	13591.47	3245.47	10346.00	2526.45
	12	17263.45	588.96	13821.36	3404.31	10417.05	2657.77
比上期增减额（亿元）Changes Compared with Previous Period（100 Million Yuan）							
2001	1	9.35	3.21	317.22	48.20	269.02	-255.33
	2	300.36	13.20	250.18	10.10	240.08	29.68
	3	233.21	19.37	84.37	57.60	26.77	130.14
	4	43.85	15.60	18.63	-0.41	19.04	14.31
	5	97.56	13.54	41.60	12.45	29.15	42.04
	6	308.21	19.03	154.68	100.50	54.18	129.73
	7	18.47	14.27	48.73	0.76	47.97	-49.94
	8	114.02	22.13	-5.85	-0.49	-5.36	95.85
	9	162.63	20.13	40.27	36.15	4.12	91.43
	10	102.85	18.14	85.31	34.52	50.79	1.43
	11	154.74	12.73	107.71	55.44	52.27	28.61
	12	463.42	22.42	229.89	158.84	71.05	131.32
比去年同期增长（%）Increase Rate Year-on-year（%）							
2001	1	15.12	48.66	13.46	29.14	9.48	21.33
	2	13.95	49.80	11.24	20.77	8.73	27.09
	3	14.77	50.17	11.94	21.69	9.33	28.05
	4	15.34	49.86	12.49	22.81	9.74	28.53
	5	15.70	50.97	12.97	22.60	10.39	27.33
	6	16.09	51.08	13.15	22.35	10.60	28.53
	7	16.05	52.69	13.41	22.20	10.98	25.73
	8	16.33	55.35	13.55	22.06	11.19	26.26
	9	16.51	56.75	13.61	21.68	11.33	26.07
	10	16.86	59.30	13.86	22.06	11.54	26.84
	11	16.49	57.57	13.95	22.13	11.61	23.49
	12	14.11	51.54	11.87	18.86	9.75	18.43

农村信用合作社人民币信贷收支主要指标时间序列表

Time Series of Major Indicators in Sources and Uses of Credit Funds of Rural Credit Cooperatives (RMB)

期末余额（亿元）

Balance (100 Million Yuan)

年 月 Year Month	各项贷款 Total Loans	短期贷款 Short-term Loans	工业贷款 Loans to Industrial Sector	商业贷款 Loans to Commercial Sector	建筑业及基建企业贷款 Loans to Construction and Infrastructure	农业贷款 Loans to Agricultural Sector	中长期贷款 Medium and Long-term Loans	基本建设贷款 Capital Construction Loans	技术改造贷款 Technical Improvement Loans	其他中长期贷款 Other Medium and Long-term Loans	票据融资 Paper Financing	有价证券及投资 Securities and Investments
2001 1	10786.59	10322.47				3706.35	386.69			386.69	77.43	1156.96
2	10954.88	10461.50				3806.85	402.91			402.91	90.47	1168.55
3	11212.45	10705.65				3976.89	414.29			414.29	92.51	1210.55
4	11428.83	10905.81				4141.53	432.84			432.84	90.18	1261.01
5	11586.45	11048.76				4241.78	442.11			442.11	95.58	1291.25
6	11736.00	11173.90				4330.68	465.93			465.93	96.17	1292.68
7	11883.51	11295.45				4393.80	471.14			471.14	116.92	1327.30
8	12037.17	11416.82				4478.55	483.78			483.78	136.57	1350.45
9	12160.31	11553.40				4544.67	466.67			466.67	140.24	1346.13
10	12162.51	11551.28				4547.23	481.96			481.96	129.27	1370.20
11	12156.93	11536.78				4529.90	498.03			498.03	122.12	1410.72
12	11971.16	11355.21				4417.57	503.38			503.38	112.57	1517.35

比上期增减额（亿元）

Changes Compared with Previous Period (100 Million Yuan)

年 月 Year Month	各项贷款 Total Loans	短期贷款 Short-term Loans	工业贷款 Loans to Industrial Sector	商业贷款 Loans to Commercial Sector	建筑业及基建企业贷款 Loans to Construction and Infrastructure	农业贷款 Loans to Agricultural Sector	中长期贷款 Medium and Long-term Loans	基本建设贷款 Capital Construction Loans	技术改造贷款 Technical Improvement Loans	其他中长期贷款 Other Medium and Long-term Loans	票据融资 Paper Financing	有价证券及投资 Securities and Investments
2001 1	210.54	205.17				91.71	5.68			5.68	-0.31	-19.91
2	168.29	139.03				100.50	16.22			16.22	13.04	11.59
3	257.57	244.15				170.04	11.38			11.38	2.04	42.00
4	216.38	200.16				164.64	18.55			18.55	-2.33	50.46
5	157.62	142.95				100.25	9.27			9.27	5.40	30.24
6	149.55	125.14				88.90	23.82			23.82	0.59	1.43
7	147.51	121.55				63.12	5.21			5.21	20.75	34.62
8	153.66	121.37				84.75	12.64			12.64	19.65	23.15
9	123.14	136.58				66.12	-17.11			-17.11	3.67	-4.32
10	2.20	-2.12				2.56	15.29			15.29	-10.97	24.07
11	-5.58	-14.50				-17.33	16.07			16.07	-7.15	40.52
12	-185.77	-181.57				-112.33	5.35			5.35	-9.55	106.63

比去年同期增长（%）

Increase Rate Year-on-year (%)

年 月 Year Month	各项贷款 Total Loans	短期贷款 Short-term Loans	工业贷款 Loans to Industrial Sector	商业贷款 Loans to Commercial Sector	建筑业及基建企业贷款 Loans to Construction and Infrastructure	农业贷款 Loans to Agricultural Sector	中长期贷款 Medium and Long-term Loans	基本建设贷款 Capital Construction Loans	技术改造贷款 Technical Improvement Loans	其他中长期贷款 Other Medium and Long-term Loans	票据融资 Paper Financing	有价证券及投资 Securities and Investments
2001 1	14.84	15.11				19.30	2.90			2.90	57.73	13.61
2	15.74	15.76				21.34	6.31			6.31	83.29	11.02
3	15.95	15.87				22.32	7.86			7.86	98.39	12.81
4	15.96	15.78				22.85	11.14			11.14	93.73	14.68
5	16.76	16.47				23.54	12.75			12.75	114.16	19.39
6	17.12	16.66				24.24	17.32			17.32	112.34	16.91
7	17.53	16.83				24.29	17.83			17.83	171.53	19.31
8	17.94	16.71				24.60	27.14			27.14	213.09	19.79
9	18.24	17.20				24.93	23.10			23.10	192.78	17.02
10	17.65	16.54				24.53	27.61			27.61	168.31	19.02
11	17.18	16.08				24.43	30.70			30.70	124.36	21.09
12	14.13	13.20				23.12	32.49			32.49	43.80	29.32

农村信用合作社人民币信贷收支主要指标时间序列表

Time Series of Major Indicators in Sources and Uses of Credit Funds of Rural Credit Cooperatives（RMB）

年 月 Year Month		各项存款 Total Deposits	企业存款 Deposits by Enterprises	储蓄存款 Savings Deposits	活期储蓄 Demand Deposits	定期储蓄 Time Deposits	农业存款 Deposits by Agricultural Sector
				期末余额（亿元） Balance（100 Million Yuan）			
2002	1	17140.92	590.19	13826.26	3385.30	10440.96	2595.04
	2	17562.11	606.31	14459.77	3579.90	10879.87	2376.63
	3	17762.73	628.10	14520.88	3589.33	10931.55	2493.22
	4	17920.51	657.47	14578.69	3621.56	10957.13	2569.46
	5	18117.98	681.31	14677.39	3673.11	11004.28	2642.10
	6	18455.05	702.51	14871.51	3800.78	11070.73	2757.92
	7	18544.69	723.70	14931.34	3818.24	11113.10	2764.04
	8	18667.60	750.22	14929.86	3820.75	11109.11	2853.64
	9	18924.36	770.09	15019.83	3880.66	11139.17	2992.06
	10	19000.83	770.35	15082.81	3896.86	11185.95	3005.59
	11	19222.61	776.94	15217.59	3964.87	11252.72	3075.61
	12	19620.23	775.84	15405.80	4102.70	11303.10	3199.50
				比上期增减额（亿元） Changes Compared with Previous Period（100 Million Yuan）			
2002	1	51.46	18.54	109.48	-0.66	110.14	-13.18
	2	421.19	16.12	633.51	194.60	438.91	-218.41
	3	200.62	21.79	61.11	9.43	51.68	116.59
	4	157.78	29.37	57.81	32.23	25.58	76.24
	5	197.47	23.84	98.70	51.55	47.15	72.64
	6	337.07	21.20	194.12	127.67	66.45	115.82
	7	89.64	21.19	59.83	17.46	42.37	6.12
	8	122.91	26.52	-1.48	2.51	-3.99	89.60
	9	256.76	19.87	89.97	59.91	30.06	138.42
	10	76.47	0.26	62.98	16.20	46.78	13.53
	11	221.78	6.59	134.78	68.01	66.77	70.02
	12	397.62	-1.10	188.21	137.83	50.38	123.89
				比去年同期增长（%） Increase Rate Year-on-year（%）			
2002	1	12.30	48.14	8.31	15.19	6.25	28.90
	2	12.83	47.31	11.09	21.40	8.07	16.34
	3	12.44	45.74	10.84	19.38	8.30	14.74
	4	13.12	47.23	11.13	20.47	8.35	17.47
	5	13.67	48.08	11.53	21.68	8.50	18.51
	6	13.59	46.62	11.69	21.86	8.58	16.91
	7	14.01	46.67	11.73	22.39	8.48	19.70
	8	13.97	45.52	11.77	22.49	8.50	18.66
	9	14.40	43.76	12.10	22.98	8.75	19.85
	10	14.15	39.10	11.86	22.16	8.67	20.33
	11	14.42	37.14	11.96	22.17	8.76	21.74
	12	13.65	31.73	11.46	20.51	8.51	20.38

农村信用合作社人民币信贷收支主要指标时间序列表

Time Series of Major Indicators in Sources and Uses of Credit Funds of Rural Credit Cooperatives (RMB)

年 月 Year Month		各项贷款 Total Loans	短期贷款 Short - term Loans	工业贷款 Loans to Industrial Sector	商业贷款 Loans to Commercial Sector	建筑业及基建企业贷款 Loans to Construction and Infrastructure	农业贷款 Loans to Agricultural Sector	中长期贷款 Medium and Long - term Loans	基本建设贷款 Capital Construction Loans	技术改造贷款 Technical Improvement Loans	其他中长期贷款 Other Medium and Long - term Loans	票据融资 Paper Financing	有价证券及投资 Securities and Investments
		期末余额（亿元） Balance (100 Million Yuan)											
2002	1	12187.14	11577.28		0.06		4603.26	513.26			513.26	96.60	1460.18
	2	12349.76	11728.53		0.07		4694.25	523.74			523.74	97.49	1403.62
	3	12721.45	12081.39		0.07		4977.88	542.65			542.65	97.41	1466.44
	4	13082.79	12405.37		0.08		5247.39	561.65			561.65	115.77	1540.42
	5	13277.42	12581.45		0.07		5377.28	580.67			580.67	115.30	1591.23
	6	13475.30	12745.73		0.08		5499.60	602.83			602.83	126.74	1632.78
	7	13610.50	12864.41				5587.91	621.30			621.30	124.79	1643.01
	8	13798.08	13014.18	0.01			5688.87	646.89			646.89	137.01	1654.85
	9	13928.60	13123.97	0.01			5768.11	673.41			673.41	131.22	1716.36
	10	13960.17	13146.65	0.01			5768.53	688.78			688.78	124.74	1714.06
	11	13984.90	13153.81				5733.90	696.23			696.23	134.86	1723.73
	12	13792.73	12894.27				5563.64	717.10			717.10	181.36	1801.65
		比上期增减额（亿元） Changes Compared with Previous Period (100 Million Yuan)											
2002	1	300.66	295.38	-0.05	0.06		204.83	10.00			10.00	-4.72	8.56
	2	162.62	151.25		0.01		90.99	10.48			10.48	0.89	-56.56
	3	371.69	352.86				283.63	18.91			18.91	-0.08	62.82
	4	361.34	323.98		0.01		269.51	19.00			19.00	18.36	73.98
	5	194.63	176.08		-0.01		129.89	19.02			19.02	-0.47	50.81
	6	197.88	164.28		0.01		122.32	22.16			22.16	11.44	41.55
	7	135.20	118.68		-0.08		88.31	18.47			18.47	-1.95	10.23
	8	187.58	149.77	0.01			100.96	25.59			25.59	12.22	11.84
	9	130.52	109.79				79.24	26.52			26.52	-5.79	61.51
	10	31.57	22.68				0.42	15.37			15.37	-6.48	-2.30
	11	24.73	7.16	-0.01			-34.63	7.45			7.45	10.12	9.67
	12	-192.17	-259.54				-170.26	20.87			20.87	46.50	77.92
		比去年同期增长（%） Increase Rate Year - on - year (%)											
2002	1	12.98	12.16				24.20	32.73			32.73	24.76	26.21
	2	12.73	12.11				23.31	29.99			29.99	7.76	20.12
	3	13.46	12.85				25.17	30.98			30.98	5.30	21.14
	4	14.47	13.75				26.70	29.76			29.76	28.38	22.16
	5	14.59	13.87				26.77	31.34			31.34	20.63	23.23
	6	14.82	14.07				26.99	29.38			29.38	31.79	26.31
	7	14.53	13.89				27.18	31.87			31.87	6.73	23.79
	8	14.63	13.99				27.02	33.72			33.72	0.32	22.54
	9	14.54	13.59				26.92	44.30			44.30	-6.43	27.50
	10	14.78	13.81				26.86	42.91			42.91	-3.50	25.10
	11	15.04	14.02				26.58	39.80			39.80	10.43	22.19
	12	15.22	13.55				25.94	42.46			42.46	61.11	18.74

农村信用合作社人民币信贷收支主要指标时间序列表

Time Series of Major Indicators in Sources and Uses of Credit Funds of Rural Credit Cooperatives（RMB）

年 月 Year Month		各项存款 Total Deposits					
			企业存款 Deposits by Enterprises	储蓄存款 Savings Deposits			农业存款 Deposits by Agricultural Sector
					活期储蓄 Demand Deposits	定期储蓄 Time Deposits	
期末余额（亿元） Balance（100 Million Yuan）							
2003	1	19841.98	798.74	15834.41	4211.53	11622.88	3061.76
	2	20506.75	828.44	16430.25	4364.75	12065.50	3088.01
	3	20928.39	871.40	16621.95	4422.99	12198.96	3273.49
	4	21168.14	908.39	16754.07	4457.83	12296.24	3343.75
	5	21574.23	943.51	16973.70	4552.10	12421.60	3483.97
	6	22031.58	954.37	17185.77	4662.94	12522.83	3694.20
	7	22241.31	973.11	17290.06	4699.83	12590.23	3763.61
	8	22427.25	994.10	17316.29	4709.86	12606.43	3877.76
	9	22819.45	1021.92	17473.97	4803.47	12670.50	4048.04
	10	22974.39	1029.91	17563.96	4823.53	12740.43	4088.45
	11	23263.64	1036.82	17765.22	4931.40	12833.82	4143.18
	12	23710.20	1024.50	18004.99	5095.49	12909.50	4298.54
比上期增减额（亿元） Changes Compared with Previous Period（100 Million Yuan）							
2003	1	222.64	23.40	429.08	108.60	320.48	-138.27
	2	664.77	29.70	595.84	153.22	442.62	26.25
	3	421.64	42.96	191.70	58.24	133.46	185.48
	4	239.75	36.99	132.12	34.84	97.28	70.26
	5	406.09	35.12	219.63	94.27	125.36	140.22
	6	457.35	10.86	212.07	110.84	101.23	210.23
	7	209.73	18.74	104.29	36.89	67.40	69.41
	8	185.94	20.99	26.23	10.03	16.20	114.15
	9	392.20	27.82	157.68	93.61	64.07	170.28
	10	154.94	7.99	89.99	20.06	69.93	40.41
	11	289.25	6.91	201.26	107.87	93.39	54.73
	12	446.56	-12.32	239.77	164.09	75.68	155.36
比去年同期增长（%） Increase Rate Year-on-year（%）							
2003	1	15.76	35.34	14.52	24.41	11.32	17.99
	2	16.77	36.64	13.63	21.92	10.90	29.93
	3	17.82	38.74	14.47	23.23	11.59	31.30
	4	18.12	38.16	14.92	23.09	12.22	30.13
	5	19.08	38.48	15.65	23.93	12.88	31.86
	6	19.38	35.85	15.56	22.68	13.12	33.95
	7	19.93	34.46	15.80	23.09	13.29	36.16
	8	20.14	32.51	15.98	23.27	13.48	35.89
	9	20.58	32.70	16.34	23.78	13.75	35.29
	10	20.91	33.69	16.45	23.78	13.90	36.03
	11	21.02	33.45	16.74	24.38	14.05	34.71
	12	20.85	32.05	16.87	24.20	14.21	34.35

农村信用合作社人民币信贷收支主要指标时间序列表

Time Series of Major Indicators in Sources and Uses of Credit Funds of Rural Credit Cooperatives (RMB)

年 月 Year Month	各项贷款 Total Loans	短期贷款 Short - term Loans					中长期贷款 Medium and Long - term Loans				票据融资 Paper Financing	有价证券及投资 Securities and Investments
			工业贷款 Loans to Industrial Sector	商业贷款 Loans to Commercial Sector	建筑业及基建企业贷款 Loans to Construction and Infrastructure	农业贷款 Loans to Agricultural Sector		基本建设贷款 Capital Construction Loans	技术改造贷款 Technical Improvement Loans	其他中长期贷款 Other Medium and Long-term Loans		
期末余额（亿元） Balance (100 Million Yuan)												
2003 1	14304.35	13410.75				5902.07	739.78			739.78	153.82	1777.71
2	14516.95	13616.21				6045.32	750.76			750.76	149.98	1823.14
3	15017.74	14066.22				6387.87	786.32			786.32	165.20	1815.58
4	15398.22	14397.05				6626.27	829.05			829.05	172.12	1858.71
5	15668.55	14635.71				6776.50	864.96			864.96	167.88	1870.59
6	16008.58	14928.10				6947.53	911.95			911.95	168.53	1915.13
7	16295.05	15182.52				7094.12	916.94			916.94	195.59	1958.03
8	16591.75	15399.44				7249.74	982.33			982.33	209.98	2015.40
9	16938.85	15649.89				7365.58	1021.12			1021.12	267.84	2051.72
10	17072.56	15769.37				7381.05	1042.48			1042.48	260.71	2062.68
11	17233.43	15810.23				7338.73	1064.66			1064.66	358.54	2071.04
12	16978.69	15440.44				7056.38	1097.71			1097.71	440.54	2067.55
比上期增减额（亿元） Changes Compared with Previous Period (100 Million Yuan)												
2003 1	512.27	517.17				339.30	22.60			22.60	-27.50	-25.33
2	212.60	205.46				143.25	10.98			10.98	-3.84	45.43
3	500.79	450.01				342.55	35.56			35.56	15.22	-7.56
4	380.48	330.83				238.40	42.73			42.73	6.92	43.13
5	270.33	238.66				150.23	35.91			35.91	-4.24	11.88
6	340.03	292.39				171.03	46.99			46.99	0.65	44.54
7	286.47	254.42				146.59	4.99			4.99	27.06	42.90
8	296.70	216.92				155.62	65.39			65.39	14.39	57.37
9	347.10	250.45				115.84	38.79			38.79	57.86	36.32
10	133.71	119.48				15.47	21.36			21.36	-7.13	10.96
11	160.87	40.86				-42.32	22.18			22.18	97.83	8.36
12	-254.74	-369.79				-282.35	33.05			33.05	82.00	-3.49
比去年同期增长（%） Increase Rate Year - on - year (%)												
2003 1	17.37	15.84		-100.00		28.22	44.13			44.13	59.23	21.75
2	17.55	16.09		-100.00		28.78	43.35			43.35	53.84	29.89
3	18.05	16.43		-100.00		28.33	44.90			44.90	69.59	23.81
4	17.70	16.05		-100.00		26.28	47.61			47.61	48.67	20.66
5	18.01	16.33		-100.00		26.02	48.96			48.96	45.60	17.56
6	18.80	17.12		-100.00		26.33	51.28			51.28	32.97	17.29
7	19.72	18.02				26.95	47.58			47.58	56.74	19.17
8	20.25	18.33	-100.00			27.44	51.85			51.85	53.26	21.79
9	21.61	19.25	-100.00			27.69	51.63			51.63	104.12	19.54
10	22.29	19.95	-100.00			27.95	51.35			51.35	109.00	20.34
11	23.23	20.20				27.99	52.92			52.92	165.86	20.15
12	23.10	19.75				26.83	53.08			53.08	142.91	14.76

农村信用合作社人民币信贷收支主要指标时间序列表

Time Series of Major Indicators in Sources and Uses of Credit Funds of Rural Credit Cooperatives（RMB）

年 月 Year Month	各项存款 Total Deposits	企业存款 Deposits by Enterprises	储蓄存款 Savings Deposits	活期储蓄 Demand Deposits	定期储蓄 Time Deposits	农业存款 Deposits by Agricultural Sector
期末余额（亿元） Balance（100 Million Yuan）						
2004 1	24426.04	1027.48	19116.59	5522.48	13594.11	4003.72
2	24939.67	1062.44	19435.98	5519.69	13916.29	4137.44
3	25432.45	1094.83	19627.04	5622.71	14004.33	4377.99
4	25717.19	1128.16	19804.67	5722.90	14081.77	4433.60
5	25999.92	1151.29	19979.15	5796.45	14182.70	4509.72
6	26379.82	1168.62	20208.86	5932.35	14276.51	4612.43
7	26359.95	1177.05	20274.19	5939.66	14334.53	4513.26
8	26267.51	1161.25	20179.42	5894.29	14285.13	4528.46
9	26471.91	1157.17	20285.15	5978.52	14306.63	4608.90
10	26632.13	1144.96	20420.94	6038.48	14382.46	4653.02
11	26912.85	1155.66	20594.61	6048.71	14545.90	4728.41
12	27289.10	1144.08	20766.17	6205.12	14561.05	4867.34
比上期增减额（亿元） Changes Compared with Previous Period（100 Million Yuan）						
2004 1	759.78	4.02	1110.22	426.72	683.50	-294.98
2	513.63	34.96	319.39	-2.79	322.18	133.72
3	492.78	32.39	191.06	103.02	88.04	240.55
4	284.74	33.33	177.63	100.19	77.44	55.61
5	282.73	23.13	174.48	73.55	100.93	76.12
6	379.90	17.33	229.71	135.90	93.81	102.71
7	-19.87	8.43	65.33	7.31	58.02	-99.17
8	-92.44	-15.80	-94.77	-45.37	-49.40	15.20
9	204.40	-4.08	105.73	84.23	21.50	80.44
10	160.22	-12.21	135.79	59.96	75.83	44.12
11	280.72	10.70	173.67	10.23	163.44	75.39
12	376.25	-11.58	171.56	156.41	15.15	138.93
比去年同期增长（%） Increase Rate Year-on-year（%）						
2004 1	23.27	28.64	20.73	31.13	16.96	30.77
2	21.80	28.25	18.29	26.46	15.34	33.98
3	21.71	25.64	18.08	27.12	14.80	33.74
4	21.67	24.19	18.21	28.38	14.52	32.59
5	20.70	22.02	17.71	27.34	14.18	29.44
6	19.94	22.45	17.59	27.22	14.00	24.86
7	18.71	20.96	17.26	26.38	13.85	19.92
8	17.31	16.81	16.53	25.15	13.32	16.78
9	16.21	13.23	16.09	24.46	12.91	13.86
10	16.12	11.17	16.27	25.19	12.89	13.81
11	15.88	11.46	15.93	22.66	13.34	14.13
12	15.29	11.67	15.34	21.78	12.79	13.23

农村信用合作社人民币信贷收支主要指标时间序列表

Time Series of Major Indicators in Sources and Uses of Credit Funds of Rural Credit Cooperatives (RMB)

年 月 Year Month	各项贷款 Total Loans	短期贷款 Short－term Loans	工业贷款 Loans to Industrial Sector	商业贷款 Loans to Commercial Sector	建筑业及基建企业贷款 Loans to Construction and Infrastructure	农业贷款 Loans to Agricultural Sector	中长期贷款 Medium and Long－term Loans	基本建设贷款 Capital Construction Loans	技术改造贷款 Technical Improvement Loans	其他中长期贷款 Other Medium and Long－term Loans	票据融资 Paper Financing	有价证券及投资 Securities and Investments
期末余额（亿元） Balance (100 Million Yuan)												
2004 1	17638.99	16018.21				7399.68	1215.47	5.23		1210.24	405.31	2101.12
2	18183.03	16519.18				7820.13	1237.06	5.95		1231.11	426.79	2113.67
3	18651.45	16948.34				8160.21	1288.39	5.78		1282.61	414.72	2114.32
4	19098.78	17332.30				8423.72	1333.92	8.23		1325.69	432.56	2139.92
5	19279.83	17496.91				8542.78	1377.81	7.71		1370.10	405.10	2154.97
6	19352.78	17522.76	0.15	0.27	0.25	8595.43	1413.85	5.78	0.02	1408.05	416.17	2233.77
7	19480.69	17637.01	0.15	0.28	0.27	8685.31	1443.64	4.90	0.02	1438.72	400.04	2353.56
8	19581.62	17724.59	0.15	0.29	0.28	8771.09	1455.03	4.24	0.02	1450.77	401.98	2372.05
9	19662.03	17809.98				8839.60	1467.95	3.68		1464.27	384.06	2399.26
10	19634.14	17804.63				8823.09	1475.89	4.59		1471.30	353.40	2414.71
11	19597.53	17752.69				8761.49	1485.01	4.64		1480.37	359.53	2452.47
12	19237.84	17391.74				8455.70	1509.09	4.57		1504.52	336.80	2380.75
比上期增减额（亿元） Changes Compared with Previous Period (100 Million Yuan)												
2004 1	628.25	643.35				355.26	51.93	0.24		51.69	－67.03	33.40
2	544.04	500.97				420.45	21.59	0.72		20.87	21.48	12.55
3	567.07	520.90				382.50	58.24	－0.17		58.41	－12.07	0.65
4	450.13	386.56				264.71	45.73	2.45		43.28	17.84	25.60
5	182.07	165.56				119.50	43.96	－0.52		44.48	－27.46	15.05
6	193.68	138.13	0.15	0.27	0.25	104.56	44.49	－1.93	0.02	46.40	11.07	78.80
7	130.01	116.20		0.01	0.02	90.78	29.94	－0.88		30.82	－16.13	119.79
8	101.88	88.46		0.01	0.01	86.19	11.46	－0.66		12.12	1.94	18.49
9	149.19	149.36	－0.15	－0.29	－0.28	98.09	17.73	－0.56	－0.02	18.31	－17.92	27.21
10	－27.47	－4.96				－16.33	7.97	0.91		7.06	－30.66	15.45
11	－36.61	－51.94				－61.60	9.12	0.05		9.07	6.13	37.76
12	－350.73	－352.62				－301.94	24.71	－0.07		24.78	－22.73	－71.72
比去年同期增长（%） Increase Rate Year－on－year (%)												
2004 1	23.31	19.44				25.37	64.30			63.59	162.78	18.19
2	25.25	21.32				29.36	64.77			63.98	183.88	15.94
3	24.85	21.14				28.41	64.73			63.99	150.81	16.45
4	24.69	21.04				27.78	61.75			60.76	151.18	15.13
5	23.70	20.20				26.71	60.12			59.23	141.30	15.20
6	22.28	18.77				25.10	56.75			56.11	146.94	16.64
7	20.93	17.55				23.80	59.16			58.62	104.53	20.20
8	19.38	16.47				22.33	49.73			49.30	91.44	17.70
9	17.80	15.56				21.73	45.78			45.42	42.13	16.94
10	16.66	14.65				21.26	43.56			43.12	30.15	17.07
11	15.28	14.02				21.12	41.42			40.99	－5.83	18.42
12	14.88	14.47				21.69	39.42			39.00	28.86	15.15

农村信用合作社人民币信贷收支主要指标时间序列表

Time Series of Major Indicators in Sources and Uses of Credit Funds of Rural Credit Cooperatives（RMB）

年 月 Year Month		各项存款 Total Deposits	企业存款 Deposits by Enterprises	储蓄存款 Savings Deposits			农业存款 Deposits by Agricultural Sector
					活期储蓄 Demand Deposits	定期储蓄 Time Deposits	
期末余额（亿元） Balance（100 Million Yuan）							
2005	1	26426.81	1053.42	20402.56	6075.83	14326.73	4533.13
	2	27271.30	1063.54	21545.84	6478.44	15067.40	4246.96
	3	27658.63	1097.26	21638.29	6435.19	15203.10	4467.28
	4	27692.00	1120.13	21624.65	6410.21	15214.44	4468.76
	5	27914.28	1134.54	21754.57	6448.26	15306.31	4548.22
	6	27790.27	1081.23	21693.39	6528.72	15164.67	4529.19
	7	27832.56	1089.31	21805.32	6532.22	15273.10	4443.54
	8	26906.95	1028.35	21305.13	6431.29	14873.84	4081.80
	9	27274.95	1042.60	21472.55	6520.42	14952.13	4248.41
	10	27319.14	1040.97	21550.54	6518.01	15032.53	4236.63
	11	27652.92	1053.13	21791.34	6659.73	15131.61	4298.21
	12	27605.61	1050.86	21739.33	6681.94	15057.39	4296.85
比上期增减额（亿元） Changes Compared with Previous Period（100 Million Yuan）							
2005	1	346.36	20.61	346.11	84.74	261.37	8.05
	2	844.49	10.12	1143.28	402.61	740.67	-286.17
	3	387.33	33.72	92.45	-43.25	135.70	220.32
	4	33.37	22.87	-13.64	-24.98	11.34	1.48
	5	222.28	14.41	129.92	38.05	91.87	79.46
	6	-124.01	-53.31	-61.18	80.46	-141.64	-19.03
	7	42.29	8.08	111.93	3.50	108.43	-85.65
	8	-925.61	-60.96	-500.19	-100.93	-399.26	-361.74
	9	368.00	14.25	167.42	89.13	78.29	166.61
	10	44.19	-1.63	77.99	-2.41	80.40	-11.78
	11	333.78	12.16	240.80	141.72	99.08	61.58
	12	-47.31	-2.27	-52.01	22.21	-74.22	-1.36
比去年同期增长（%） Increase Rate Year-on-year（%）							
2005	1	8.19	2.52	6.73	10.02	5.39	13.22
	2	9.35	0.10	10.86	17.37	8.27	2.65
	3	8.75	0.22	10.25	14.45	8.56	2.04
	4	7.68	-0.71	9.19	12.01	8.04	0.79
	5	7.36	-1.45	8.89	11.24	7.92	0.85
	6	5.35	-7.48	7.35	10.05	6.22	-1.80
	7	5.59	-7.45	7.55	9.98	6.55	-1.54
	8	2.43	-11.44	5.58	9.11	4.12	-9.86
	9	3.03	-9.90	5.85	9.06	4.51	-7.82
	10	2.58	-9.08	5.53	7.94	4.52	-8.95
	11	2.75	-8.87	5.81	10.10	4.03	-9.10
	12	1.16	-8.15	4.69	7.68	3.41	-11.72

农村信用合作社人民币信贷收支主要指标时间序列表

Time Series of Major Indicators in Sources and Uses of Credit Funds of Rural Credit Cooperatives (RMB)

年 月 Year Month		各项贷款 Total Loans	短期贷款 Short - term Loans					中长期贷款 Medium and Long - term Loans				票据融资 Paper Financing	有价证券及投资 Securities and Investments
				工业贷款 Loans to Industrial Sector	商业贷款 Loans to Commercial Sector	建筑业及基建企业贷款 Loans to Construction and Infrastructure	农业贷款 Loans to Agricultural Sector		基本建设贷款 Capital Construction Loans	技术改造贷款 Technical Improvement Loans	其他中长期贷款 Other Medium and Long - term Loans		
期末余额（亿元） Balance (100 Million Yuan)													
2005	1	19150.21	17287.62				9109.44	1534.06	4.56		1529.50	327.42	2368.35
	2	19388.94	17517.49				9230.86	1540.65	4.64		1536.01	326.87	2376.51
	3	19787.94	17872.40				9550.02	1579.15	4.67		1574.48	335.29	2352.03
	4	20194.23	18230.08				9834.43	1605.60	4.67		1600.93	357.25	2354.64
	5	20452.76	18451.53				9974.68	1635.86	4.68		1631.18	364.23	2352.93
	6	19946.85	17932.64	0.59	0.03		9797.00	1670.27	4.52		1665.75	342.53	2281.42
	7	20140.12	18082.8	0.56	0.04		9902.92	1692.39	4.58		1687.81	362.98	2189.57
	8	19705.90	17826.14	0.48	0.04		9968.81	1547.43	4.62		1542.81	330.26	1909.28
	9	19558.25	17645.42	0.47	0.05		9913.46	1605.37	4.56		1600.81	305.40	1896.12
	10	19471.87	17580.13	0.47	0.05		9822.97	1609.66	4.52		1605.14	280.24	1909.95
	11	19383.33	17477.32	0.47	0.05		9754.85	1636.54	4.57		1631.97	267.41	2020.43
	12	18680.86	16805.66	0.47	0.06		9331.01	1556.66	5.00		1551.66	317.30	2099.87
比上期增减额（亿元） Changes Compared with Previous Period (100 Million Yuan)													
2005	1	775.00	698.89				486.00	43.49	- 1.53		45.02	32.38	101.32
	2	238.78	229.92				121.44	6.59	0.08		6.51	- 0.55	8.16
	3	586.56	529.34				399.81	51.63	0.03		51.60	8.42	- 24.48
	4	398.53	350.46				281.07	25.91			25.91	21.96	2.61
	5	268.41	230.64				144.50	30.95	0.01		30.94	6.98	- 1.71
	6	- 196.52	- 231.16	0.59	0.03		- 44.64	56.07	- 0.16		56.23	- 21.70	- 71.51
	7	198.27	154.81	- 0.03	0.01		108.07	22.47	0.06		22.41	20.45	- 91.85
	8	- 435.22	- 257.59	- 0.08			65.46	- 145.03	0.04		- 145.07	- 32.72	- 280.29
	9	119.99	68.19	- 0.01	0.01		59.74	76.67	- 0.06		76.73	- 24.86	- 13.16
	10	- 50.29	- 31.73				- 74.97	6.82	- 0.04		6.86	- 25.16	13.83
	11	- 86.66	- 101.06				- 67.31	27.01	0.05		26.96	- 12.83	110.48
	12	- 545.08	- 525.29		0.01		- 356.16	- 68.86	0.43		- 69.29	49.89	79.44
比去年同期增长（%） Increase Rate Year - on - year (%)													
2005	1	10.22	9.62				24.80	27.89	- 12.81		28.06	- 19.22	12.72
	2	8.23	7.68				19.64	26.19	- 22.02		26.42	- 23.41	12.44
	3	8.13	7.54				19.03	24.63	- 19.20		24.83	- 19.15	11.24
	4	7.67	7.16				18.63	22.31	- 43.26		22.71	- 17.41	10.03
	5	8.05	7.47				18.67	20.65	- 39.30		20.99	- 10.09	9.19
	6	6.00	5.35	293.33	- 88.89	- 100.00	16.82	20.94	- 21.80	- 100.00	21.12	- 17.69	2.13
	7	6.31	5.53	273.33	- 85.71	- 100.00	16.84	19.99	- 6.53	- 100.00	20.09	- 9.26	- 6.97
	8	3.54	3.55	220.00	- 86.21	- 100.00	16.44	9.08	8.96	- 100.00	9.08	- 17.84	- 19.51
	9	3.37	3.08				15.88	13.02	23.91		12.99	- 20.48	- 20.97
	10	3.26	2.93				15.24	12.87	- 1.53		12.92	- 20.70	- 20.90
	11	3.01	2.66				15.29	14.00	- 1.51		14.04	- 25.62	- 17.62
	12	2.06	1.73				15.20	7.57	9.41		7.57	- 5.79	- 11.80

二、外汇信贷收支主要指标时间序列表

Time Series of Major Indicators in Sources and Uses of Credit Funds (Foreign Currency)

(一)金融机构外汇信贷收支主要指标时间序列表(1998—2005年月度时序)

Time Series of Major Indicators in Sources and Uses of Credit Funds of Financial Institutions (Foreign Currency) (Monthly Series from 1998 to 2005)

金融机构外汇信贷收支主要指标时间序列表

Time Series of Major Indicators in Sources and Uses of Credit Funds of Financial Institutions (Foreign Currency)

年 月 Year Month	各项存款 Total Deposits	单位活期存款 Demand Deposits by Enterprises	单位定期存款 Time Deposits by Enterprises	储蓄存款 Savings Deposits	定期储蓄 Time Deposits	境外存款 Foreign Deposits	境外筹资 Overseas Financing
	期末余额(亿美元) Balance (100 Million US Dollars)						
1998 1	754.76	130.52	224.85	301.60	278.82	16.18	361.84
2	770.21	133.31	228.93	311.95	289.07	16.33	362.14
3	779.57	131.02	235.27	322.49	299.85	16.26	361.08
4	782.18	122.95	238.98	331.42	308.10	16.83	349.00
5	793.37	126.31	242.89	339.60	315.55	16.94	354.22
6	805.39	121.12	243.99	350.41	326.20	16.81	345.83
7	820.25	120.54	253.04	364.29	339.99	15.70	341.15
8	849.51	125.26	261.28	379.46	354.61	14.75	340.02
9	862.40	125.90	263.42	387.50	363.26	16.96	338.18
10	861.43	128.63	253.33	396.53	371.54	16.74	346.10
11	874.81	126.44	256.83	406.30	380.07	16.08	356.09
12	884.72	121.22	263.36	412.46	384.96	16.92	348.39
	比上期增减额(亿美元) Changes Compared with Previous Period (100 Million US Dollars)						
1998 1	-12.67	-21.56	-3.56	10.21	10.89	-0.91	-4.61
2	15.49	2.79	4.10	10.35	10.25	0.15	0.30
3	9.34	-2.29	6.33	10.54	10.78	-0.07	-1.06
4	2.62	-8.07	3.71	8.93	8.25	0.57	-12.08
5	11.20	3.36	3.91	8.18	7.45	0.11	5.22
6	12.02	-5.19	1.10	10.81	10.65	-0.13	-8.39
7	14.87	-0.58	9.03	13.88	13.79	-1.11	-4.68
8	29.25	4.72	8.25	15.17	14.62	-0.95	-1.13
9	12.88	0.62	2.13	8.04	8.65	2.21	-1.84
10	-0.95	2.73	-10.07	9.03	8.28	-0.22	7.92
11	13.37	-2.19	3.50	9.77	8.53	-0.66	9.99
12	9.90	-5.23	6.52	6.15	4.89	0.84	-7.70

金融机构外汇信贷收支主要指标时间序列表

Time Series of Major Indicators in Sources and Uses of Credit Funds of Financial Institutions (Foreign Currency)

年 月 Year Month		各项贷款 Total Loans	短期贷款 Short - term Loans	境内短期贷款 Domestic Short - term Loans	中长期贷款 Medium and Long - term Loans	境内中长期贷款 Domestic Medium and Long - term Loans	进出口贸易融资 Financing for Import and Export Trades	票据融资 Paper Financing	境外筹资转贷款 On - lending of Overseas Financing	有价证券及投资 Securities and Investments
		期末余额（亿美元） Balance (100 Million US Dollars)								
1998	1	1179.01	349.27	341.63	285.59	277.79	51.53	1.56	308.90	155.74
	2	1181.41	337.73	330.51	295.58	287.73	48.11	1.37	307.90	152.15
	3	1183.93	341.07	333.42	294.10	286.21	48.93	1.36	310.38	156.94
	4	1180.87	339.71	332.60	295.28	287.10	48.39	1.27	307.93	156.69
	5	1179.63	341.64	334.74	296.92	288.72	46.69	1.41	306.45	163.35
	6	1180.63	342.37	335.69	298.81	290.68	46.88	1.38	302.16	168.30
	7	1175.28	338.98	332.39	298.16	289.69	45.46	1.37	300.90	164.38
	8	1170.99	333.03	326.57	301.53	292.94	44.45	1.50	300.66	175.02
	9	1172.88	329.23	322.90	305.06	296.41	44.93	1.30	297.89	170.24
	10	1181.12	327.54	321.01	305.97	297.11	44.68	1.12	305.87	170.36
	11	1199.24	328.44	321.74	311.81	302.83	42.71	1.07	315.89	184.87
	12	1196.71	339.97	333.79	313.19	303.95	37.65	0.76	310.57	192.81
		比上期增减额（亿美元） Changes Compared with Previous Period (100 Million US Dollars)								
1998	1	- 14.65	- 14.55	- 13.85	- 5.75	- 6.24	- 0.66	- 0.11	- 1.60	1.29
	2	2.40	- 11.56	- 11.13	9.99	9.94	- 3.42	- 0.19	- 1.00	- 3.60
	3	2.50	3.33	2.90	- 1.48	- 1.52	0.82	- 0.01	2.48	4.79
	4	- 3.04	- 1.36	- 0.82	1.18	0.87	- 0.54	- 0.09	- 2.45	- 0.25
	5	- 1.26	1.93	2.14	1.64	1.62	- 1.70	0.14	- 1.48	6.66
	6	0.99	0.73	0.95	1.89	1.96	0.19	- 0.03	- 4.29	4.95
	7	- 5.36	- 3.39	- 3.30	- 0.65	- 0.99	- 1.42	- 0.01	- 1.26	- 3.92
	8	- 4.28	- 5.95	- 5.82	3.39	3.27	- 1.01	0.13	- 0.24	10.64
	9	1.90	- 3.80	- 3.67	3.51	3.45	0.48	- 0.20	- 2.77	- 4.78
	10	8.22	- 1.69	- 1.89	0.91	0.70	- 0.25	- 0.18	7.98	0.12
	11	18.14	0.90	0.73	5.85	5.72	- 1.97	- 0.05	10.02	14.51
	12	- 2.52	11.54	12.06	1.37	1.12	- 5.05	- 0.31	- 5.32	7.94

注：从 2001 年起“境外筹资转贷款”纳入各项贷款统计，按此口径对 1998—2000 年各项贷款进行了可比口径调整。

Note: As of 2001, the data of on - lending of overseas financing were included in the date of total loans, adjustment on the data of total loans of related sheets was made on comparable basis from 1998 to 2000.

金融机构外汇信贷收支主要指标时间序列表

Time Series of Major Indicators in Sources and Uses of Credit Funds of Financial Institutions（Foreign Currency）

年 月 Year Month		各项存款 Total Deposits	单位活期存款 Demand Deposits by Enterprises	单位定期存款 Time Deposits by Enterprises	储蓄存款 Savings Deposits	定期储蓄 Time Deposits	境外存款 Foreign Deposits	境外筹资 Overseas Financing
期末余额（亿美元） Balance（100 Million US Dollars）								
1999	1	886.01	124.91	260.83	420.44	392.23	15.17	336.27
	2	896.10	127.06	258.47	431.58	401.86	14.40	332.86
	3	895.07	125.61	251.48	441.75	412.18	13.18	328.02
	4	900.37	125.91	248.51	449.90	419.94	12.37	326.31
	5	910.20	126.17	250.05	459.50	428.37	11.66	325.04
	6	921.74	129.77	247.82	470.13	437.68	11.59	326.78
	7	929.05	131.99	240.44	483.40	450.03	11.85	318.78
	8	953.84	131.98	249.56	498.11	464.28	11.86	319.00
	9	981.02	131.77	259.48	514.19	479.56	11.22	325.89
	10	998.98	130.72	263.54	527.53	491.60	11.13	327.05
	11	1017.53	131.22	266.47	542.68	505.76	10.74	323.82
	12	1031.71	134.00	264.01	553.46	516.18	10.15	324.17
比上期增减额（亿美元） Changes Compared with Previous Period（100 Million US Dollars）								
1999	1	3.28	3.80	-2.61	8.08	7.32	-0.42	-0.67
	2	10.08	2.15	-2.36	11.14	9.63	-0.77	-3.41
	3	-1.02	-1.45	-6.99	10.17	10.32	-1.22	-4.84
	4	5.27	0.30	-2.99	8.15	7.76	-0.81	-1.71
	5	9.83	0.26	1.56	9.60	8.43	-0.71	-1.27
	6	11.54	3.60	-2.25	10.63	9.31	-0.07	1.74
	7	7.31	2.22	-7.38	13.27	12.35	0.26	-8.00
	8	24.81	-0.01	9.13	14.71	14.25	0.01	0.22
	9	27.17	-0.21	9.92	16.08	15.28	-0.64	6.89
	10	17.94	-1.05	4.07	13.34	12.04	-0.09	1.16
	11	18.66	0.50	2.92	15.15	14.16	-0.39	-3.23
	12	14.09	2.78	-3.10	10.78	10.42	-0.59	0.35
比去年同期增长（%） Increase Rate Year-on-year（%）								
1999	1	17.39	-4.30	16.00	39.40	40.67	-6.24	-7.07
	2	16.34	-4.69	12.90	38.35	39.02	-11.82	-8.09
	3	14.82	-4.13	6.89	36.98	37.46	-18.94	-9.16
	4	15.11	2.41	3.99	35.75	36.30	-26.50	-6.50
	5	14.73	-0.11	2.95	35.31	35.75	-31.17	-8.24
	6	14.45	7.14	1.57	34.17	34.18	-31.05	-5.51
	7	13.26	9.50	-4.98	32.70	32.37	-24.52	-6.56
	8	12.28	5.36	-4.49	31.27	30.93	-19.59	-6.18
	9	13.75	4.66	-1.50	32.69	32.02	-33.84	-3.63
	10	15.97	1.62	4.03	33.04	32.31	-33.51	-5.50
	11	16.31	3.78	3.75	33.57	33.07	-33.21	-9.06
	12	16.62	10.54	0.25	34.19	34.09	-40.01	-6.95

金融机构外汇信贷收支主要指标时间序列表

Time Series of Major Indicators in Sources and Uses of Credit Funds of Financial Institutions（Foreign Currency）

年 月 Year Month	各项贷款 Total Loans	短期贷款 Short－term Loans	境内短期贷款 Domestic Short－term Loans	中长期贷款 Medium and Long－term Loans	境内中长期贷款 Domestic Medium and Long－term Loans	进出口贸易融资 Financing for Import and Export Trades	票据融资 Paper Financing	境外筹资转贷款 On－lending of Overseas Financing	有价证券及投资 Securities and Investments
	期末余额（亿美元） Balance（100 Million US Dollars）								
1999 1	1171.25	336.34	330.80	309.51	300.18	36.68	0.74	308.82	208.20
2	1168.39	333.99	329.09	310.87	301.96	35.68	0.66	308.09	195.25
3	1169.59	333.98	329.71	312.36	303.22	35.55	0.58	304.80	184.64
4	1167.90	334.42	330.37	311.68	302.77	34.72	0.55	302.66	179.87
5	1162.29	328.04	324.41	310.47	301.56	33.46	0.56	303.91	207.45
6	1155.68	328.33	324.99	305.82	297.04	33.69	0.55	300.16	226.48
7	1152.71	325.17	322.04	309.31	300.57	32.43	0.54	297.36	221.83
8	1149.41	324.28	321.39	309.17	300.58	31.35	0.60	296.46	219.15
9	1156.96	324.93	322.17	309.42	300.72	29.82	0.53	302.77	232.50
10	1159.21	325.06	322.42	307.90	299.23	28.20	0.75	306.67	238.99
11	1148.15	321.30	319.00	305.27	297.03	28.67	0.75	302.13	268.29
12	1103.01	304.61	301.93	293.51	285.36	27.96	0.72	299.96	297.67
	比上期增减额（亿美元） Changes Compared with Previous Period（100 Million US Dollars）								
1999 1	－6.73	－2.52	－1.88	－3.18	－3.27	－1.01	－0.02	－1.58	16.84
2	－2.84	－2.35	－1.71	1.37	1.78	－1.00	－0.08	－0.73	－12.95
3	1.18	－0.02	0.61	1.48	1.27	－0.13	－0.08	－3.29	－10.61
4	－1.70	0.42	0.66	－0.68	－0.44	－0.83	－0.03	－2.14	－4.77
5	－5.59	－6.38	－5.96	－1.21	－1.23	－1.26	0.01	1.25	27.58
6	－6.60	0.29	0.58	－4.64	－4.51	0.23	－0.01	－3.75	19.03
7	－2.98	－3.16	－2.95	3.49	3.53	－1.26	－0.01	－2.80	－4.65
8	－3.31	－0.89	－0.65	－0.14	0.01	－1.08	0.06	－0.90	－2.70
9	7.50	0.65	0.78	0.25	0.13	－1.53	－0.07	6.31	13.35
10	2.35	0.13	0.25	－1.54	－1.49	－1.62	0.22	3.92	6.49
11	－11.12	－3.76	－3.42	－2.63	－2.22	0.47		4.54	29.30
12	3.31	11.17	10.79	6.64	6.75	1.48	－0.03	－2.17	29.38
	比去年同期增长（%） Increase Rate Year－on－year（%）								
1999 1	－0.66	－3.70	－3.17	8.38	8.06	－28.82	－52.56	－0.03	33.68
2	－1.10	－1.11	－0.43	5.17	4.95	－25.84	－51.82	0.06	28.33
3	－1.21	－2.08	－1.11	6.21	5.94	－27.35	－57.35	－1.80	17.65
4	－1.10	－1.56	－0.67	5.55	5.46	－28.25	－56.69	－1.71	14.79
5	－1.47	－3.98	－3.09	4.56	4.45	－28.34	－60.28	－0.83	27.00
6	－2.11	－4.10	－3.19	2.35	2.19	－28.14	－60.14	－0.66	34.57
7	－1.92	－4.07	－3.11	3.74	3.76	－28.66	－60.58	－1.18	34.95
8	－1.84	－2.63	－1.59	2.53	2.61	－29.47	－60.00	－1.40	25.21
9	－1.36	－1.31	－0.23	1.43	1.45	－33.63	－59.23	1.64	36.57
10	－1.86	－0.76	0.44	0.63	0.71	－36.88	－33.04	0.26	40.29
11	－4.26	－2.17	－0.85	－2.10	－1.92	－32.87	－29.91	－4.36	45.12
12	－3.78	－2.21	－1.20	－0.42	－0.08	－19.92	－5.26	－3.42	54.39

金融机构外汇信贷收支主要指标时间序列表
Time Series of Major Indicators in Sources and Uses of Credit Funds of Financial Institutions（Foreign Currency）

年 月 Year Month		各项存款 Total Deposits	单位活期存款 Demand Deposits by Enterprises	单位定期存款 Time Deposits by Enterprises	储蓄存款 Savings Deposits	定期储蓄 Time Deposits	境外存款 Foreign Deposits	境外筹资 Overseas Financing
期末余额（亿美元） Balance（100 Million US Dollars）								
2000	1	1044.67	127.53	271.40	567.94	529.91	9.68	322.52
	2	1062.51	128.43	272.68	583.03	544.15	10.04	320.94
	3	1079.16	129.31	274.78	594.76	555.67	9.25	315.20
	4	1093.37	128.60	278.29	606.46	566.62	8.96	315.36
	5	1110.80	130.57	279.84	618.89	578.12	8.76	291.60
	6	1136.78	130.63	288.63	634.20	594.38	8.66	287.23
	7	1169.97	132.48	302.50	650.86	609.77	8.65	288.04
	8	1184.27	131.14	303.30	666.14	623.76	8.38	286.67
	9	1204.25	128.73	306.68	683.26	640.40	8.86	277.90
	10	1226.82	133.50	308.02	699.17	655.41	7.50	274.43
	11	1274.35	135.67	333.49	715.20	670.89	7.60	273.28
	12	1282.60	137.29	322.50	729.50	683.55	8.20	258.32
比上期增减额（亿美元） Changes Compared with Previous Period（100 Million US Dollars）								
2000	1	12.70	-6.80	7.09	14.48	13.73	-0.20	-1.63
	2	17.84	0.90	1.28	15.09	14.24	0.36	-1.58
	3	16.65	0.88	2.10	11.73	11.52	-0.79	-5.74
	4	14.21	-0.71	3.51	11.70	10.95	-0.29	0.16
	5	17.42	1.97	1.55	12.43	11.50	-0.20	-23.76
	6	25.98	0.06	8.79	15.31	16.26	-0.10	-4.37
	7	33.19	1.85	13.87	16.66	15.39	-0.01	0.81
	8	14.30	-1.34	0.80	15.28	13.99	-0.27	-1.37
	9	19.98	-2.41	3.38	17.12	16.64	0.48	-8.77
	10	22.58	4.77	1.34	15.91	15.01	-1.36	-3.47
	11	47.53	2.17	25.47	16.03	15.48	0.10	-1.15
	12	8.24	1.62	-10.99	14.30	12.66	0.60	-14.96
比去年同期增长（%） Increase Rate Year-on-year（%）								
2000	1	17.90	2.10	4.05	35.08	35.10	-36.19	-4.09
	2	18.57	1.08	5.50	35.09	35.41	-30.28	-3.58
	3	20.56	2.95	9.26	34.64	34.81	-29.82	-3.91
	4	21.44	2.14	11.99	34.80	34.93	-27.57	-3.36
	5	22.04	3.49	11.91	34.69	34.96	-24.87	-10.29
	6	23.32	0.66	16.47	34.90	35.80	-25.28	-12.10
	7	25.93	0.37	25.81	34.64	35.50	-27.00	-9.64
	8	24.16	-0.64	21.53	33.73	34.35	-29.34	-10.13
	9	22.75	-2.31	18.19	32.88	33.54	-21.03	-14.73
	10	22.81	2.13	16.88	32.54	33.32	-32.61	-16.09
	11	25.23	3.39	25.15	31.79	32.65	-29.24	-15.61
	12	24.32	2.46	22.15	31.81	32.42	-19.21	-20.31

金融机构外汇信贷收支主要指标时间序列表
Time Series of Major Indicators in Sources and Uses of Credit Funds of Financial Institutions (Foreign Currency)

年　月 Year Month		各项贷款 Total Loans	短期贷款 Short – term Loans	境内短期贷款 Domestic Short – term Loans	中长期贷款 Medium and Long – term Loans	境内中长期贷款 Domestic Medium and Long – term Loans	进出口贸易融资 Financing for Import and Export Trades	票据融资 Paper Financing	境外筹资转贷款 On – lending of Overseas Financing	有价证券及投资 Securities and Investments
		期末余额（亿美元） Balance (100 Million US Dollars)								
2000	1	1098.83	306.65	303.95	292.05	284.24	23.68	0.49	294.30	317.05
	2	1092.24	304.07	301.34	291.06	283.17	21.68	0.46	293.84	283.10
	3	1085.86	301.73	298.97	289.59	281.69	22.81	0.47	289.24	293.71
	4	1086.22	298.87	296.31	291.56	282.73	23.71	0.53	290.20	288.59
	5	1051.25	288.91	286.15	285.82	277.77	23.01	0.56	272.32	298.27
	6	960.78	246.34	243.59	257.35	248.94	22.74	0.52	262.41	294.81
	7	937.56	237.20	234.75	252.73	244.38	21.90	0.47	262.52	313.93
	8	922.61	229.23	226.85	246.84	238.35	21.82	0.50	259.97	330.01
	9	908.07	226.20	224.18	243.24	234.58	20.56	0.55	258.10	341.76
	10	899.74	224.01	222.08	242.25	234.06	19.87	0.57	255.78	369.68
	11	896.04	222.33	220.74	238.76	230.24	19.74	0.62	255.05	385.16
	12	853.55	213.41	211.22	223.11	215.00	20.82	0.56	242.06	410.89
		比上期增减额（亿美元） Changes Compared with Previous Period (100 Million US Dollars)								
2000	1	- 8.42	- 4.02	- 4.04	- 0.73	- 0.39	0.04	- 0.23	- 3.93	19.69
	2	- 6.37	- 2.43	- 2.46	- 3.09	- 3.17	- 1.99	- 0.03	0.31	- 33.90
	3	- 6.34	- 2.34	- 2.37	- 1.48	- 1.49	1.12	0.01	- 4.60	10.56
	4	0.80	- 2.82	- 2.62	1.98	1.05	0.90	0.06	0.96	- 5.12
	5	- 23.83	- 5.84	- 6.04	- 0.47	0.31	- 0.69	0.03	- 17.55	9.68
	6	- 6.21	0.02	0.03	- 2.74	- 3.10	0.29	- 0.04	- 4.78	- 3.39
	7	- 3.61	- 2.89	- 2.59	0.10	0.16	- 1.14	- 0.05	- 1.27	19.12
	8	- 8.64	- 4.57	- 4.50	- 5.23	- 5.37	- 0.08	0.03	- 2.34	16.10
	9	- 12.10	- 2.54	- 2.18	- 3.27	- 3.44	- 0.24	0.05	- 1.30	11.72
	10	- 6.80	- 1.18	- 1.09	- 0.89	- 0.42	- 0.70	0.02	- 2.32	27.93
	11	- 2.73	- 1.51	- 1.17	- 3.32	- 3.65	- 0.13	0.05	- 0.72	15.48
	12	- 18.09	0.22	- 0.38	- 4.94	- 4.53	1.28	- 0.06	- 9.22	25.73
		比去年同期增长（%） Increase Rate Year – on – year (%)								
2000	1	- 1.94	- 0.61	0.24	0.76	1.30	- 29.47	- 33.78	- 4.70	52.28
	2	- 2.17	- 0.63	0.02	- 0.39	- 0.06	- 33.07	- 30.30	- 4.38	45.02
	3	- 2.82	- 1.34	- 0.90	- 1.37	- 1.00	- 29.68	- 18.97	- 4.85	59.07
	4	- 2.66	- 2.31	- 1.88	- 0.72	- 0.71	- 25.40	- 3.64	- 3.86	60.44
	5	- 4.32	- 2.19	- 1.94	- 0.74	- 0.47	- 24.66		- 10.03	43.78
	6	- 4.31	- 2.27	- 2.11	- 0.13		- 24.31	- 5.45	- 10.50	30.20
	7	- 4.43	- 2.21	- 2.02	- 1.43	- 1.34	- 24.88	- 12.96	- 10.09	41.54
	8	- 4.92	- 3.35	- 3.22	- 3.11	- 3.17	- 22.55	- 16.67	- 10.60	50.63
	9	- 6.54	- 4.32	- 4.13	- 4.24	- 4.35	- 19.38	3.77	- 12.89	47.02
	10	- 7.35	- 4.72	- 4.54	- 4.03	- 3.98	- 17.23	- 24.00	- 14.76	54.71
	11	- 6.69	- 4.08	- 3.88	- 4.29	- 4.50	- 19.04	- 17.33	- 13.72	43.59
	12	- 8.89	- 7.90	- 7.80	- 8.37	- 8.60	- 20.24	- 22.22	- 16.17	38.06

金融机构外汇信贷收支主要指标时间序列表

Time Series of Major Indicators in Sources and Uses of Credit Funds of Financial Institutions（Foreign Currency）

年 月 Year Month		各项存款 Total Deposits	单位活期存款 Demand Deposits by Enterprises	单位定期存款 Time Deposits by Enterprises	储蓄存款 Savings Deposits	定期储蓄 Time Deposits	境外存款 Foreign Deposits	境外筹资 Overseas Financing
期末余额（亿美元） Balance（100 Million US Dollars）								
2001	1	1300.74	134.31	324.15	749.27	701.42	7.78	289.81
	2	1288.20	135.29	316.23	742.66	693.96	7.93	287.85
	3	1292.51	132.11	324.14	740.04	690.34	8.62	285.96
	4	1318.52	131.99	343.04	745.51	693.94	9.13	281.44
	5	1346.73	143.40	352.86	756.35	698.90	8.61	278.27
	6	1339.97	144.23	341.15	759.58	700.84	9.14	275.78
	7	1335.65	142.61	330.58	772.09	709.67	9.31	274.05
	8	1347.38	145.49	327.53	785.24	719.24	9.05	276.06
	9	1347.88	141.02	326.12	793.99	726.33	8.95	272.19
	10	1356.63	151.08	316.28	804.01	733.12	8.38	268.87
	11	1353.35	156.65	302.33	811.23	738.07	8.85	266.81
	12	1348.78	157.91	295.01	815.62	739.06	8.86	260.44
比上期增减额（亿美元） Changes Compared with Previous Period（100 Million US Dollars）								
2001	1	13.11	-5.27	1.78	16.00	14.93	-0.42	5.66
	2	-12.54	0.98	-7.92	-6.61	-7.46	0.15	-1.96
	3	4.31	-3.18	7.91	-2.62	-3.62	0.69	-1.89
	4	26.01	-0.12	18.90	5.47	3.60	0.51	-4.52
	5	28.21	11.41	9.82	10.84	4.96	-0.52	-3.17
	6	-6.76	0.83	-11.71	3.23	1.94	0.53	-2.49
	7	-4.32	-1.62	-10.57	12.51	8.83	0.17	-1.73
	8	11.73	2.88	-3.05	13.15	9.57	-0.26	2.01
	9	0.50	-4.47	-1.41	8.75	7.09	-0.10	-3.87
	10	8.75	10.06	-9.84	10.02	6.79	-0.57	-3.32
	11	-3.28	5.57	-13.95	7.22	4.95	0.47	-2.06
	12	-4.57	1.26	-7.32	4.39	0.99	0.01	-6.37
比去年同期增长（%） Increase Rate Year-on-year（%）								
2001	1	24.51	5.32	19.44	31.93	32.37	-19.63	-10.14
	2	21.24	5.34	15.97	27.38	27.53	-21.02	-10.31
	3	19.77	2.17	17.96	24.43	24.24	-6.81	-9.28
	4	20.59	2.64	23.27	22.93	22.47	1.90	-10.76
	5	21.24	9.83	26.09	22.21	20.89	-1.71	-4.57
	6	17.87	10.41	18.20	19.77	17.91	5.54	-3.99
	7	14.16	7.65	9.28	18.63	16.38	7.63	-4.86
	8	13.77	10.94	7.99	17.88	15.31	8.00	-3.70
	9	11.93	9.55	6.34	16.21	13.42	1.02	-2.05
	10	10.58	13.17	2.68	14.99	11.86	11.73	-2.03
	11	6.20	15.46	-9.34	13.43	10.01	16.45	-2.37
	12	5.16	15.02	-8.52	11.81	8.12	8.05	0.82

金融机构外汇信贷收支主要指标时间序列表
Time Series of Major Indicators in Sources and Uses of Credit Funds of Financial Institutions (Foreign Currency)

年　月 Year Month	各项贷款 Total Loans	短期贷款 Short－term Loans	境内短期贷款 Domestic Short－term Loans	中长期贷款 Medium and Long－term Loans	境内中长期贷款 Domestic Medium and Long－term Loans	进出口贸易融资 Financing for Import and Export Trades	票据融资 Paper Financing	境外筹资转贷款 On－lending of Overseas Financing	有价证券及投资 Securities and Investments
	期末余额（亿美元） Balance (100 Million US Dollars)								
2001　1	841.82	211.70	208.20	251.21	239.85	24.83	0.68	241.45	482.64
2	837.14	210.29	206.94	249.79	238.51	22.41	0.72	240.66	519.84
3	836.10	212.03	208.46	250.60	238.71	23.39	0.65	237.35	551.73
4	834.25	209.97	206.53	247.40	235.46	22.93	0.68	238.56	603.66
5	832.73	208.35	205.19	248.12	235.87	23.26	0.73	237.72	591.51
6	832.05	211.45	208.47	246.77	234.18	24.15	0.57	234.99	567.44
7	824.36	207.46	204.51	254.43	241.11	23.57	0.62	224.19	583.92
8	829.94	207.56	204.60	254.10	240.12	24.27	1.21	228.87	591.27
9	824.50	207.02	204.01	251.04	237.03	24.33	0.81	227.68	600.21
10	818.90	210.23	207.28	246.45	232.00	23.71	0.82	224.40	579.75
11	812.78	213.92	211.00	240.01	225.76	24.15	0.60	222.50	618.15
12	806.47	213.47	211.04	239.37	225.69	25.68	0.79	216.89	754.58
	比上期增减额（亿美元） Changes Compared with Previous Period (100 Million US Dollars)								
2001　1	－7.48	－3.81	－3.52	－2.70	－2.15	－0.86	0.11	－3.69	32.23
2	－4.68	－1.41	－1.26	－1.42	－1.34	－2.42	0.04	－0.79	37.20
3	－1.03	1.74	1.52	0.81	0.20	0.98	－0.07	－3.31	31.89
4	－1.85	－2.06	－1.93	－3.20	－3.25	－0.46	0.03	1.21	51.93
5	－1.55	－1.62	－1.34	0.72	0.41	0.33	0.05	－0.84	－12.15
6	－0.69	3.10	3.28	－1.35	－1.69	0.89	－0.16	－2.73	－24.07
7	－7.67	－3.99	－3.96	7.66	6.93	－0.58	0.05	－10.80	16.48
8	5.58	0.10	0.09	－0.33	－0.99	0.70	0.59	4.68	7.35
9	－5.44	－0.54	－0.59	－3.06	－3.09	0.06	－0.40	－1.19	8.94
10	－5.60	3.21	3.27	－4.59	－5.03	－0.62	0.01	－3.28	－20.46
11	－6.12	3.69	3.72	－6.44	－6.24	0.44	－0.22	－1.90	38.40
12	－6.31	－0.45	0.04	－0.64	－0.07	1.53	0.19	－5.61	136.43
	比去年同期增长（%） Increase Rate Year－on－year (%)								
2001　1	－9.64	4.82	4.55	9.88	8.90	11.11	38.78	－14.76	52.25
2	－9.54	6.27	6.09	10.49	9.58	10.15	56.52	－15.16	83.63
3	－9.10	7.78	7.53	11.33	10.23	8.99	38.30	－14.95	87.87
4	－9.35	8.27	7.99	9.34	8.53	2.91	28.30	－14.82	109.20
5	－7.53	10.36	10.31	9.46	8.22	7.48	30.36	－9.65	98.34
6	－7.66	12.82	12.88	7.85	6.43	10.20	9.62	－9.24	92.48
7	－8.29	14.31	14.23	6.91	5.11	13.15	31.91	－12.86	86.00
8	－6.88	17.20	17.11	8.24	6.23	16.77	142.00	－10.29	79.16
9	－6.26	18.54	18.20	8.42	6.45	19.26	47.27	－10.33	75.62
10	－6.18	20.90	20.56	6.75	4.32	20.33	43.86	－10.79	56.82
11	－6.59	24.36	23.82	5.42	3.13	23.35	－3.23	－11.28	60.49
12	－5.53	24.36	24.53	7.29	4.97	23.34	41.07	－10.40	83.64

金融机构外汇信贷收支主要指标时间序列表
Time Series of Major Indicators in Sources and Uses of Credit Funds of Financial Institutions（Foreign Currency）

年 月 Year Month		各项存款 Total Deposits	单位活期存款 Demand Deposits by Enterprises	单位定期存款 Time Deposits by Enterprises	储蓄存款 Savings Deposits	定期储蓄 Time Deposits	境外存款 Foreign Deposits	境外筹资 Overseas Financing
期末余额（亿美元） Balance（100 Million US Dollars）								
2002	1	1386.84	172.87	308.72	820.57	742.57	16.34	255.24
	2	1400.74	179.55	306.92	830.61	749.88	16.57	247.23
	3	1412.30	175.24	312.27	839.17	756.00	16.46	245.16
	4	1409.90	169.29	307.76	846.09	761.40	16.08	245.11
	5	1436.27	181.73	306.93	855.44	767.18	16.26	242.97
	6	1445.46	188.76	296.92	865.53	773.58	16.87	267.08
	7	1444.04	190.13	295.41	868.47	774.28	17.60	264.31
	8	1455.40	194.10	296.76	874.73	777.53	17.54	263.86
	9	1453.07	188.11	297.15	877.62	779.12	17.67	262.52
	10	1475.40	204.36	293.70	884.74	782.50	19.22	258.06
	11	1484.16	203.85	298.84	887.67	783.53	19.50	236.92
	12	1506.67	212.43	303.43	893.59	784.27	20.37	235.87
比上期增减额（亿美元） Changes Compared with Previous Period（100 Million US Dollars）								
2002	1	-12.86	-4.74	-7.86	4.77	3.45	0.13	-3.84
	2	13.90	6.68	-1.80	10.04	7.31	0.23	-8.01
	3	11.56	-4.31	5.35	8.56	6.12	-0.11	-2.07
	4	-2.40	-5.95	-4.51	6.92	5.40	-0.38	-0.05
	5	26.37	12.44	-0.83	9.35	5.78	0.18	-2.14
	6	9.43	7.03	-10.01	10.09	6.40	0.61	24.25
	7	-1.42	1.37	-1.51	2.94	0.70	0.73	-2.76
	8	11.36	3.97	1.35	6.26	3.25	-0.06	-0.46
	9	-2.33	-5.99	0.39	2.89	1.59	0.13	-1.34
	10	22.34	16.25	-3.45	7.12	3.38	1.55	-4.46
	11	8.79	-0.51	5.14	2.93	1.03	0.28	-21.13
	12	22.52	8.58	4.59	5.92	0.74	0.87	-1.06
比去年同期增长（%） Increase Rate Year-on-year（%）								
2002	1	2.51	11.07	-11.15	9.36	5.78	8.72	-12.16
	2	4.52	15.67	-10.09	11.68	7.97	13.65	-14.33
	3	5.21	16.13	-10.48	13.25	9.43	10.17	-14.46
	4	2.91	12.80	-16.79	13.32	9.62	3.01	-13.14
	5	2.53	10.25	-18.98	12.94	9.68	7.54	-12.92
	6	3.80	14.24	-18.91	13.82	10.32	6.91	-3.42
	7	3.99	16.92	-17.18	12.33	9.02	10.07	-3.85
	8	3.76	15.51	-15.95	11.26	8.03	8.47	-4.68
	9	3.69	16.42	-15.48	10.40	7.20	7.55	-3.82
	10	4.57	18.11	-13.84	9.91	6.67	20.20	-4.29
	11	5.47	14.50	-8.61	9.29	6.10	17.40	-11.45
	12	7.50	18.80	-4.91	9.43	6.06	25.66	-9.69

金融机构外汇信贷收支主要指标时间序列表

Time Series of Major Indicators in Sources and Uses of Credit Funds of Financial Institutions (Foreign Currency)

年 月 Year Month		各项贷款 Total Loans	短期贷款 Short-term Loans	境内短期贷款 Domestic Short-term Loans	中长期贷款 Medium and Long-term Loans	境内中长期贷款 Domestic Medium and Long-term Loans	进出口贸易融资 Financing for Import and Export Trades	票据融资 Paper Financing	境外筹资转贷款 On-lending of Overseas Financing	有价证券及投资 Securities and Investments
期末余额(亿美元) Balance (100 Million US Dollars)										
2002	1	939.45	272.58	264.62	336.49	304.85	29.56	3.54	213.70	734.85
	2	950.20	275.44	267.68	344.93	313.64	27.84	3.23	211.97	720.65
	3	958.06	288.29	280.15	339.37	307.64	29.89	3.66	211.26	782.33
	4	964.63	292.05	284.42	332.95	303.03	32.15	4.16	215.37	809.09
	5	973.50	297.91	289.89	332.39	300.56	34.84	4.39	215.73	831.12
	6	983.62	301.28	293.68	334.59	302.73	37.51	5.04	218.44	826.44
	7	987.60	299.21	292.87	341.35	309.50	40.14	5.41	215.53	827.22
	8	985.84	301.00	294.52	338.67	306.10	43.03	5.53	215.75	886.14
	9	996.45	301.65	295.49	348.19	315.79	46.83	5.87	212.58	867.47
	10	998.38	302.31	296.15	351.44	318.48	45.84	6.07	211.81	873.96
	11	1003.35	307.47	301.16	352.29	319.20	47.15	6.51	208.23	933.66
	12	1027.98	311.02	303.97	373.26	341.18	48.94	6.44	206.92	903.36
比上期增减额(亿美元) Changes Compared with Previous Period (100 Million US Dollars)										
2002	1	1.33	3.66	3.77	8.27	8.42	-0.39	0.01	-3.12	-24.33
	2	11.08	2.86	3.06	8.44	8.79	-1.72	-0.31	-1.73	-13.64
	3	7.86	12.85	12.47	-5.56	-6.00	2.05	0.43	-0.71	61.68
	4	6.58	3.76	4.27	-6.42	-4.61	2.26	0.50	4.11	26.77
	5	8.86	5.86	5.47	-0.56	-2.47	2.69	0.23	0.36	22.02
	6	10.61	3.37	3.79	2.20	2.17	2.67	0.65	2.71	-4.51
	7	3.99	-2.07	-0.81	6.76	6.77	2.63	0.37	-2.91	0.79
	8	-1.77	1.79	1.65	-2.68	-3.40	2.89	0.12	0.22	58.91
	9	10.62	0.65	0.97	9.52	9.69	3.80	0.34	-3.17	-18.67
	10	1.92	0.66	0.66	3.25	2.69	-0.99	0.20	-0.77	6.50
	11	5.12	5.16	5.01	0.85	0.72	1.31	0.44	-3.58	59.82
	12	24.72	3.55	2.81	20.97	21.98	1.79	-0.07	-1.31	-30.30
比去年同期增长(%) Increase Rate Year-on-year (%)										
2002	1	-5.41	1.02	0.64	-4.47	-4.32	4.56	6.63	-11.49	50.69
	2	-3.71	2.67	2.28	-1.86	-1.39	7.32	-15.89	-11.92	37.27
	3	-2.51	7.13	7.05	-2.96	-2.92	9.89	-6.63	-10.99	40.45
	4	-1.41	10.96	10.96	-4.04	-3.81	19.78	-5.45	-9.72	32.84
	5	-0.37	13.19	13.04	-3.97	-4.40	28.80	-4.57	-9.25	39.19
	6	0.81	12.64	13.23	-2.69	-2.74	34.44	10.53	-7.04	44.15
	7	1.93	13.10	14.39	-2.90	-2.94	47.14	24.08	-3.86	40.21
	8	1.43	13.30	14.71	-2.65	-2.94	51.94	25.97	-5.73	48.34
	9	3.14	13.92	15.23	0.95	1.22	64.89	56.12	-6.63	43.05
	10	3.96	12.89	14.15	3.15	3.69	65.13	80.65	-5.61	49.13
	11	5.31	12.87	14.25	6.18	6.66	67.26	107.99	-6.41	49.48
	12	8.81	14.35	15.18	13.78	15.17	63.35	86.67	-4.60	18.70

金融机构外汇信贷收支主要指标时间序列表
Time Series of Major Indicators in Sources and Uses of Credit Funds of Financial Institutions（Foreign Currency）

年 月 Year Month		各项存款 Total Deposits	单位活期存款 Demand Deposits by Enterprises	单位定期存款 Time Deposits by Enterprises	储蓄存款 Savings Deposits	定期储蓄 Time Deposits	境外存款 Foreign Deposits	境外筹资 Overseas Financing
		期末余额（亿美元） Balance（100 Million US Dollars）						
2003	1	1496.11	205.66	298.51	896.51	785.75	21.02	235.57
	2	1494.91	214.91	284.57	900.27	787.13	20.70	240.70
	3	1487.93	211.92	278.83	900.82	786.36	21.26	238.61
	4	1485.98	209.83	276.81	901.73	785.01	21.86	230.98
	5	1496.60	222.56	271.48	905.35	785.49	22.50	229.57
	6	1510.60	231.12	270.59	908.58	784.99	23.50	225.54
	7	1499.52	226.99	268.16	904.63	778.13	24.45	219.26
	8	1495.07	228.54	270.09	895.75	767.87	24.04	215.16
	9	1480.68	225.09	274.81	879.33	751.38	24.23	216.44
	10	1501.13	242.78	279.45	868.36	738.59	25.63	218.65
	11	1504.73	252.45	285.33	860.98	729.71	24.48	217.87
	12	1487.06	246.43	272.83	855.14	722.33	26.14	214.33
		比上期增减额（亿美元） Changes Compared with Previous Period（100 Million US Dollars）						
2003	1	-10.55	-6.15	-5.54	2.92	1.48	0.63	-0.35
	2	-1.20	9.25	-13.94	3.76	1.38	-0.32	5.13
	3	-7.00	-2.99	-5.74	0.55	-0.77	0.56	-2.09
	4	-1.95	-2.09	-2.02	0.91	-1.35	0.60	-7.63
	5	11.03	12.73	-5.33	3.62	0.48	0.64	0.99
	6	14.00	8.56	-0.89	3.23	-0.50	1.00	-4.03
	7	-11.07	-4.13	-2.43	-3.95	-6.86	0.95	-6.27
	8	-4.46	1.55	1.93	-8.88	-10.26	-0.41	-4.11
	9	-14.39	-3.45	4.72	-16.42	-16.49	0.19	1.28
	10	20.46	17.69	4.64	-10.97	-12.79	1.40	2.21
	11	3.59	9.67	5.88	-7.38	-8.88	-1.15	-0.78
	12	-17.67	-6.02	-12.50	-5.84	-7.38	1.66	-3.54
		比去年同期增长（%） Increase Rate Year-on-year（%）						
2003	1	7.88	18.97	-3.31	9.25	5.81	28.64	-7.71
	2	6.72	19.69	-7.28	8.39	4.97	24.92	-2.64
	3	5.36	20.93	-10.71	7.35	4.02	29.16	-2.67
	4	5.40	23.95	-10.06	6.58	3.10	35.95	-5.76
	5	4.20	22.47	-11.55	5.83	2.39	38.38	-5.52
	6	4.51	22.44	-8.87	4.97	1.47	39.30	-15.55
	7	3.84	19.39	-9.22	4.16	0.50	38.92	-17.04
	8	2.73	17.74	-8.99	2.40	-1.24	37.06	-18.46
	9	1.90	19.66	-7.52	0.19	-3.56	37.13	-17.55
	10	1.74	18.80	-4.85	-1.85	-5.61	33.35	-15.27
	11	1.39	23.84	-4.52	-3.01	-6.87	25.54	-8.04
	12	-1.30	16.01	-10.08	-4.30	-7.90	28.38	-9.13

金融机构外汇信贷收支主要指标时间序列表

Time Series of Major Indicators in Sources and Uses of Credit Funds of Financial Institutions (Foreign Currency)

年 月 Year Month		各项贷款 Total Loans	短期贷款 Short - term Loans	境内短期贷款 Domestic Short - term Loans	中长期贷款 Medium and Long - term Loans	境内中长期贷款 Domestic Medium and Long - term Loans	进出口贸易融资 Financing for Import and Export Trades	票据融资 Paper Financing	境外筹资转贷款 On - lending of Overseas Financing	有价证券及投资 Securities and Investments
		期末余额（亿美元） Balance (100 Million US Dollars)								
2003	1	1039.79	314.44	307.68	375.34	342.80	55.00	6.50	207.46	892.16
	2	1046.24	319.38	313.03	377.63	344.77	55.98	6.41	206.33	892.32
	3	1078.94	333.31	327.07	384.43	350.02	62.97	6.92	207.13	946.02
	4	1106.42	344.00	337.92	390.16	353.06	72.64	6.49	206.62	958.84
	5	1137.24	355.81	349.38	398.57	360.94	81.29	6.64	207.76	933.51
	6	1173.41	370.04	362.76	414.74	376.99	89.66	7.05	204.52	953.19
	7	1185.89	388.95	381.35	415.46	378.09	90.69	7.18	202.32	985.05
	8	1215.70	406.65	399.63	428.09	390.37	95.12	7.10	197.25	978.95
	9	1264.01	425.99	418.46	454.01	413.88	97.18	7.31	198.11	939.28
	10	1281.82	437.00	429.53	463.38	425.00	96.79	6.98	199.58	925.03
	11	1306.30	447.55	440.24	466.06	427.60	108.89	7.24	198.02	874.11
	12	1301.77	451.44	443.55	465.20	426.15	110.24	7.59	195.47	873.68
		比上期增减额（亿美元） Changes Compared with Previous Period (100 Million US Dollars)								
2003	1	12.82	4.82	4.96	1.01	0.59	6.11	0.27	0.61	- 11.36
	2	6.45	4.94	5.35	2.29	1.97	0.98	- 0.09	- 1.13	0.16
	3	32.76	13.94	14.05	6.83	5.28	6.99	0.51	0.80	53.73
	4	27.48	10.69	10.85	5.73	3.04	9.67	- 0.43	- 0.51	12.82
	5	32.01	11.81	11.46	8.42	7.89	8.69	0.15	1.14	- 25.25
	6	36.18	14.23	13.38	16.18	16.06	8.37	0.41	- 3.24	19.69
	7	12.49	18.91	18.59	0.72	1.10	1.04	0.13	- 2.20	31.86
	8	29.80	17.70	18.28	12.63	12.28	4.42	- 0.08	- 5.07	- 6.11
	9	48.31	19.34	18.83	25.92	23.51	2.06	0.21	0.86	- 39.67
	10	17.83	11.01	11.07	9.37	11.12	- 0.38	- 0.33	1.47	- 14.25
	11	24.46	10.55	10.71	2.68	2.60	12.09	0.26	- 1.56	- 50.92
	12	- 4.52	3.89	3.31	- 0.86	- 1.45	1.35	0.35	- 2.55	- 0.43
		比去年同期增长（%） Increase Rate Year - on - year (%)								
2003	1	10.70	15.36	16.27	11.55	12.45	86.06	90.62	- 2.92	21.41
	2	10.11	15.95	16.94	9.48	9.93	101.08	98.45	- 2.66	23.82
	3	12.63	15.62	16.75	13.28	13.78	110.67	95.48	- 1.95	20.92
	4	14.71	17.79	18.81	17.18	16.51	125.94	60.64	- 4.06	18.51
	5	16.83	19.44	20.52	19.90	20.08	133.32	54.78	- 3.69	12.32
	6	19.30	22.82	23.52	23.95	24.53	139.03	42.14	- 6.37	15.34
	7	20.09	29.99	30.21	21.71	22.16	125.93	34.46	- 6.13	19.08
	8	23.32	35.10	35.69	26.40	27.53	121.06	30.51	- 8.57	10.47
	9	26.86	41.22	41.62	30.39	31.06	107.52	26.25	- 6.81	8.28
	10	28.40	44.55	45.04	31.85	33.45	111.15	15.95	- 5.77	5.84
	11	30.21	45.56	46.18	32.29	33.96	130.94	14.02	- 4.90	- 6.38
	12	26.63	45.15	45.92	24.63	24.90	125.26	17.86	- 5.53	- 3.29

金融机构外汇信贷收支主要指标时间序列表

Time Series of Major Indicators in Sources and Uses of Credit Funds of Financial Institutions（Foreign Currency）

年 月 Year Month		各项存款 Total Deposits						境外筹资 Overseas Financing
			单位活期存款 Demand Deposits by Enterprises	单位定期存款 Time Deposits by Enterprises	储蓄存款 Savings Deposits	定期储蓄 Time Deposits	境外存款 Foreign Deposits	
期末余额（亿美元） Balance（100 Million US Dollars）								
2004	1	1509.64	269.88	274.23	852.53	717.09	26.66	207.98
	2	1457.99	263.20	249.06	832.42	695.72	26.92	208.08
	3	1467.56	271.58	248.30	825.71	685.44	29.35	204.61
	4	1474.04	261.05	262.45	819.04	676.02	31.13	196.77
	5	1497.72	283.44	256.70	821.65	672.28	33.16	197.37
	6	1510.69	295.24	273.92	803.55	647.67	35.12	193.74
	7	1536.89	299.37	269.50	826.39	666.03	35.11	198.83
	8	1549.15	309.25	254.47	833.09	668.81	35.85	207.20
	9	1559.03	290.92	273.39	837.56	668.85	36.33	226.96
	10	1583.82	309.10	282.62	835.51	662.14	36.28	232.46
	11	1552.59	316.08	272.57	809.98	642.36	36.74	236.23
	12	1530.25	307.70	268.49	802.37	635.18	37.85	230.85
比上期增减额（亿美元） Changes Compared with Previous Period（100 Million US Dollars）								
2004	1	18.21	20.83	0.03	-2.85	-5.39	0.66	-2.54
	2	-51.72	-6.68	-25.17	-20.11	-21.37	0.26	0.10
	3	9.64	8.38	-0.76	-6.71	-10.28	2.43	-3.47
	4	6.48	-10.53	14.15	-6.67	-9.42	1.78	-7.84
	5	23.68	22.39	-5.75	2.61	-3.74	2.03	0.60
	6	12.97	11.80	17.22	-18.10	-24.61	1.96	-3.63
	7	26.20	4.13	-4.42	22.84	18.36	-0.01	5.09
	8	12.26	9.88	-15.03	6.70	2.78	0.74	8.37
	9	9.88	-18.33	18.92	4.47	0.04	0.48	19.76
	10	24.79	18.18	9.23	-2.05	-6.71	-0.05	5.50
	11	-31.23	6.98	-10.05	-25.53	-19.78	0.46	3.77
	12	-22.34	-8.38	-4.08	-7.61	-7.18	1.11	-5.38
比去年同期增长（%） Increase Rate Year-on-year（%）								
2004	1	0.90	31.23	-8.13	-4.91	-8.74	26.83	-11.71
	2	-2.47	22.47	-12.48	-7.54	-11.61	30.05	-13.55
	3	-1.37	28.15	-10.95	-8.34	-12.83	38.05	-14.25
	4	-0.80	24.41	-5.19	-9.17	-13.88	42.41	-14.81
	5	0.07	27.35	-5.44	-9.25	-14.41	47.38	-14.03
	6	0.01	27.74	1.23	-11.56	-17.49	49.45	-14.10
	7	2.49	31.89	0.50	-8.65	-14.41	43.60	-9.32
	8	3.62	35.32	-5.78	-7.00	-12.90	49.13	-3.70
	9	5.29	29.25	-0.52	-4.75	-10.98	49.94	4.86
	10	5.51	27.32	1.13	-3.78	-10.35	41.55	6.32
	11	3.18	25.20	-4.47	-5.92	-11.97	50.08	8.43
	12	2.90	24.86	-1.59	-6.17	-12.07	44.74	7.71

金融机构外汇信贷收支主要指标时间序列表
Time Series of Major Indicators in Sources and Uses of Credit Funds of Financial Institutions (Foreign Currency)

年　月 Year Month	各项贷款 Total Loans	短期贷款 Short－term Loans	境内短期贷款 Domestic Short－term Loans	中长期贷款 Medium and Long－term Loans	境内中长期贷款 Domestic Medium and Long－term Loans	进出口贸易融资 Financing for Import and Export Trades	票据融资 Paper Financing	境外筹资转贷款 On－lending of Overseas Financing	有价证券及投资 Securities and Investments
期末余额（亿美元） Balance (100 Million US Dollars)									
2004 1	1329.27	470.87	462.58	471.76	432.49	118.01	10.40	193.40	1024.42
2	1363.78	483.79	475.51	480.49	441.19	130.59	10.86	193.78	1065.21
3	1401.69	504.91	496.55	488.13	447.95	142.76	12.28	190.20	999.20
4	1422.30	513.62	505.02	497.52	456.06	148.18	12.96	187.27	1008.18
5	1440.50	525.48	516.95	504.79	462.30	148.90	13.09	186.82	992.20
6	1346.20	493.31	484.43	482.13	437.10	153.48	13.43	176.97	943.61
7	1338.36	494.24	484.90	484.55	438.66	145.07	12.93	175.15	974.65
8	1344.34	526.10	516.26	457.81	412.27	144.74	12.74	176.52	1014.08
9	1346.31	490.99	480.58	502.00	451.28	139.53	13.51	173.94	1088.36
10	1333.59	492.14	481.61	491.65	440.08	135.28	12.95	176.08	1145.92
11	1354.77	487.66	477.25	507.31	456.51	139.24	12.50	183.99	1176.64
12	1354.84	480.59	469.79	520.04	470.32	138.23	12.17	185.84	1149.92
比上期增减额（亿美元） Changes Compared with Previous Period (100 Million US Dollars)									
2004 1	21.76	11.60	11.55	4.50	4.40	7.08	0.74	－2.10	189.14
2	34.62	12.92	12.93	8.77	8.74	12.58	0.46	0.38	40.79
3	37.80	21.12	21.04	7.60	6.72	12.17	1.42	－3.58	－66.01
4	20.61	8.71	8.47	9.39	8.11	5.42	0.68	－2.93	8.98
5	18.20	11.86	11.93	7.27	6.24	0.72	0.13	－0.45	－15.98
6	25.21	9.97	9.61	12.54	9.97	7.16	0.35	2.04	－48.59
7	－7.85	0.93	0.47	2.42	1.56	－8.41	－0.50	－1.81	31.04
8	6.01	31.86	31.36	－26.73	－26.38	－0.33	－0.19	1.37	39.43
9	1.96	－35.11	－35.68	44.18	39.00	－5.21	0.78	－2.58	74.28
10	－12.72	1.14	1.02	－10.33	－11.18	－4.25	－0.57	2.14	57.56
11	21.18	10.70	10.82	0.47	1.25	3.96	－0.45	7.91	30.72
12	0.09	－7.08	－7.47	12.73	13.81	－1.00	－0.32	1.85	－26.72
比去年同期增长（%） Increase Rate Year－on－year (%)									
2004 1	27.84	49.75	50.34	25.69	26.16	114.56	60.00	－6.78	14.82
2	30.35	51.48	51.91	27.25	27.98	133.28	69.42	－6.08	19.38
3	29.91	51.48	51.82	26.98	27.98	126.71	77.46	－8.17	5.62
4	28.55	49.31	49.45	27.52	29.17	103.99	99.69	－9.37	5.15
5	26.67	47.69	47.96	26.66	28.09	83.17	97.14	－10.08	6.28
6	24.91	44.70	45.15	24.74	25.27	74.06	90.64	－7.66	－1.01
7	22.93	37.90	38.20	25.10	25.32	62.81	80.22	－7.55	－1.06
8	20.41	39.74	39.73	15.17	14.62	54.88	79.58	－4.48	3.59
9	15.97	25.15	24.91	18.32	17.53	46.23	85.09	－6.19	15.87
10	13.36	22.26	21.93	13.70	11.83	42.43	85.67	－5.81	23.88
11	12.86	18.38	17.98	16.40	14.99	30.24	72.79	－1.08	34.61
12	13.26	15.79	15.41	19.35	18.62	27.74	60.61	1.16	31.62

金融机构外汇信贷收支主要指标时间序列表

Time Series of Major Indicators in Sources and Uses of Credit Funds of Financial Institutions（Foreign Currency）

年 月 Year Month		各项存款 Total Deposits						境外筹资 Overseas Financing
			单位活期存款 Demand Deposits by Enterprises	单位定期存款 Time Deposits by Enterprises	储蓄存款 Savings Deposits	定期储蓄 Time Deposits	境外存款 Foreign Deposits	
期末余额（亿美元） Balance（100 Million US Dollars）								
2005	1	1583.65	334.77	290.26	794.99	627.06	33.47	231.19
	2	1618.50	338.44	310.06	796.05	628.60	37.82	230.41
	3	1627.56	350.77	308.00	790.65	620.31	37.27	223.91
	4	1631.38	354.38	315.08	787.96	615.52	38.53	233.28
	5	1608.61	364.45	306.32	773.09	598.92	38.21	227.28
	6	1652.86	407.66	310.89	765.41	592.75	39.09	211.55
	7	1604.71	372.97	306.32	757.81	585.53	38.41	209.28
	8	1611.18	415.99	279.48	746.12	577.27	41.50	216.18
	9	1575.12	362.07	304.33	740.70	574.16	42.40	208.61
	10	1598.60	387.66	299.06	742.78	573.68	43.78	212.87
	11	1607.59	392.63	306.65	739.83	572.25	46.14	215.68
	12	1615.70	394.07	300.70	743.81	576.58	47.69	210.64
比上期增减额（亿美元） Changes Compared with Previous Period（100 Million US Dollars）								
2005	1	35.92	26.95	21.71	-7.43	-8.16	-4.31	0.17
	2	34.85	3.67	19.80	1.06	1.54	4.35	-0.78
	3	9.06	12.33	-2.06	-5.40	-8.29	-0.55	-6.50
	4	3.82	3.61	7.08	-2.69	-4.79	1.26	9.37
	5	-22.77	10.07	-8.76	-14.87	-16.60	-0.32	-6.00
	6	44.25	43.21	4.57	-7.68	-6.17	0.88	-15.73
	7	-48.15	-34.69	-4.57	-7.60	-7.22	-0.68	-2.27
	8	6.47	43.02	-26.84	-11.69	-8.26	3.09	6.90
	9	-36.06	-53.92	24.85	-5.42	-3.11	0.90	-7.57
	10	23.48	25.59	-5.27	2.08	-0.48	1.38	4.26
	11	8.99	4.97	7.59	-2.95	-1.43	2.36	2.81
	12	8.11	1.44	-5.95	3.98	4.33	1.55	-5.04
比去年同期增长（%） Increase Rate Year-on-year（%）								
2005	1	4.90	24.04	5.85	-6.75	-12.55	25.54	11.16
	2	11.01	28.59	24.49	-4.37	-9.65	40.49	10.73
	3	10.90	29.16	24.04	-4.25	-9.50	26.98	9.43
	4	10.67	35.75	20.05	-3.79	-8.95	23.77	18.55
	5	7.40	28.58	19.33	-5.91	-10.91	15.23	15.15
	6	9.41	38.08	13.50	-4.75	-8.48	11.30	9.19
	7	4.41	24.58	13.66	-8.30	-12.09	9.40	5.26
	8	4.00	34.52	9.83	-10.44	-13.69	15.76	4.33
	9	1.03	24.46	11.32	-11.56	-14.16	16.71	-8.09
	10	0.93	25.42	5.82	-11.10	-13.36	20.67	-8.43
	11	3.54	24.22	12.50	-8.66	-10.91	25.59	-8.70
	12	5.58	28.07	12.00	-7.30	-9.23	26.00	-8.75

金融机构外汇信贷收支主要指标时间序列表

Time Series of Major Indicators in Sources and Uses of Credit Funds of Financial Institutions (Foreign Currency)

年　月 Year Month		各项贷款 Total Loans	短期贷款 Short - term Loans	境内短期贷款 Domestic Short - term Loans	中长期贷款 Medium and Long - term Loans	境内中长期贷款 Domestic Medium and Long - term Loans	进出口贸易融资 Financing for Import and Export Trades	票据融资 Paper Financing	境外筹资转贷款 On - lending of Overseas Financing	有价证券及投资 Securities and Investments
		期末余额（亿美元） Balance (100 Million US Dollars)								
2005	1	1448.58	492.69	481.68	593.69	543.38	144.89	12.54	180.42	1185.85
	2	1447.87	491.58	480.30	593.41	542.81	144.80	12.50	181.10	1190.20
	3	1468.69	499.06	487.62	604.25	552.48	149.22	12.87	178.82	1197.18
	4	1479.69	493.75	482.02	615.74	563.11	154.52	12.67	178.25	1280.92
	5	1496.81	502.73	489.54	616.46	562.27	166.37	12.91	173.90	1259.45
	6	1496.63	494.92	482.22	621.13	566.54	176.21	13.33	168.67	1246.02
	7	1519.22	522.76	508.51	620.62	566.21	174.08	13.35	166.02	1219.29
	8	1500.15	499.99	485.51	628.73	572.93	169.60	12.89	165.85	1222.31
	9	1496.44	493.89	480.16	631.54	574.86	169.96	13.16	164.22	1233.84
	10	1532.01	485.65	471.36	672.95	613.81	175.49	10.86	163.83	1261.81
	11	1515.17	471.87	457.47	673.85	614.98	175.88	10.47	159.41	1278.35
	12	1505.30	459.77	448.10	679.05	614.34	177.52	10.90	156.32	1230.30
		比上期增减额（亿美元） Changes Compared with Previous Period (100 Million US Dollars)								
2005	1	87.79	19.85	19.57	65.67	65.01	6.99	0.47	-5.43	35.93
	2	-0.68	-1.10	-1.37	-0.28	-0.57	-0.08	-0.05	0.69	4.35
	3	20.81	7.48	7.32	10.86	9.68	4.41	0.37	-2.28	6.98
	4	10.99	-5.33	-5.62	11.48	10.62	5.31	-0.20	-0.57	83.74
	5	24.90	14.66	13.20	2.03	0.47	12.12	0.25	-4.33	-21.47
	6	18.35	4.60	5.09	7.81	7.41	10.38	0.41	-4.85	-13.43
	7	22.60	27.85	26.30	-0.50	-0.32	-2.13	0.03	-2.65	-26.73
	8	-19.09	-22.77	-23.00	8.08	6.70	-4.48	-0.46	-0.17	3.02
	9	-3.69	-6.10	-5.35	2.83	1.94	0.36	0.26	-1.63	11.53
	10	35.52	-8.26	-8.82	41.39	38.94	5.53	-2.30	-0.39	27.97
	11	-16.81	-13.76	-13.87	0.90	1.17	0.39	-0.39	-4.42	16.54
	12	-9.87	-12.09	-9.36	5.21	-0.63	1.64	0.44	-3.10	-48.05
		比去年同期增长（%） Increase Rate Year - on - year (%)								
2005	1	17.97	13.58	13.24	33.31	33.77	24.96	20.77	-0.56	15.76
	2	14.93	10.32	9.87	30.82	31.00	12.86	15.19	-0.40	11.73
	3	13.31	7.19	6.69	31.00	31.19	6.33	4.89	0.27	19.81
	4	12.44	4.33	3.79	30.84	31.18	6.03	-2.16	1.54	27.05
	5	12.75	4.77	3.94	29.35	29.52	13.65	-1.22	-0.54	26.94
	6	13.13	3.99	3.28	29.75	30.63	15.34	-0.74	-4.46	32.05
	7	15.48	9.43	8.60	29.00	30.09	20.56	3.33	-4.98	25.10
	8	13.55	-1.52	-2.45	38.30	40.04	17.74	1.26	-5.82	20.53
	9	13.11	4.28	3.68	26.69	28.37	22.40	-2.66	-5.36	13.37
	10	16.85	2.36	1.63	37.77	40.48	30.33	-16.14	-6.73	10.11
	11	13.78	0.47	-0.36	33.70	35.69	26.90	-16.24	-13.14	8.64
	12	13.05	-0.57	-0.76	31.43	31.57	29.01	-10.44	-15.67	6.99

（二）国家银行外汇信贷收支主要指标时间序列表（1998—2005 年月度时序）

Time Series of Major Indicators in Sources and Uses of Credit Funds of State Banks（Foreign Currency）（Monthly Series from 1998 to 2005）

国家银行外汇信贷收支主要指标时间序列表
Time Series of Major Indicators in Sources and Uses of Credit Funds of State Banks（Foreign Currency）

年 月 Year Month	各项存款 Total Deposits						境外筹资 Overseas Financing
		单位活期存款 Demand Deposits by Enterprises	单位定期存款 Time Deposits by Enterprises	储蓄存款 Savings Deposits	定期储蓄 Time Deposits	境外存款 Foreign Deposits	
期末余额（亿美元） Balance（100 Million US Dollars）							
1998 1	577.65	102.50	158.50	277.58	257.36	2.50	299.95
2	593.63	105.44	163.65	286.81	266.41	2.39	300.25
3	600.74	102.47	167.98	296.17	276.01	1.98	300.29
4	601.83	96.26	169.69	304.11	283.30	1.89	287.89
5	612.81	98.12	173.40	311.45	290.01	1.78	296.52
6	628.16	95.51	176.52	321.04	299.44	1.83	288.29
7	641.34	94.57	183.49	333.38	311.77	2.15	286.94
8	663.75	99.22	187.70	346.78	324.67	1.71	286.53
9	675.07	100.24	188.29	354.15	332.52	1.64	284.24
10	675.26	103.34	178.96	362.28	339.91	1.63	293.81
11	688.28	100.26	183.94	371.22	347.64	1.59	304.15
12	702.32	97.14	193.08	376.56	351.90	1.60	296.71
比上期增减额（亿美元） Changes Compared with Previous Period（100 Million US Dollars）							
1998 1	-9.21	-13.08	-3.01	9.31	10.02	-0.05	-3.71
2	15.93	2.94	5.15	9.23	9.05	-0.13	0.30
3	7.11	-2.97	4.33	9.36	9.60	-0.41	0.04
4	1.11	-6.21	1.71	7.94	7.29	-0.09	-12.39
5	10.98	1.86	3.71	7.34	6.71	-0.11	8.63
6	15.36	-2.61	3.12	9.59	9.43	0.05	-8.23
7	13.18	-0.94	6.97	12.34	12.33	0.32	-1.35
8	22.41	4.65	4.21	13.40	12.90	-0.44	-0.41
9	11.34	1.02	0.59	7.37	7.85	-0.07	-2.29
10	0.21	3.10	-9.33	8.13	7.39	-0.01	9.57
11	13.02	-3.08	4.98	8.94	7.73	-0.04	10.34
12	14.05	-3.13	9.14	5.34	4.26	0.01	-7.44

国家银行外汇信贷收支主要指标时间序列表

Time Series of Major Indicators in Sources and Uses of Credit Funds of State Banks (Foreign Currency)

年 月 Year Month		各项贷款 Total Loans	短期贷款 Short-term Loans	境内短期贷款 Domestic Short-term Loans	中长期贷款 Medium and Long-term Loans	境内中长期贷款 Domestic Medium and Long-term Loans	进出口贸易融资 Financing for Import and Export Trades	票据融资 Paper Financing	境外筹资转贷款 On-lending of Overseas Financing	有价证券及投资 Securities and Investments
期末余额（亿美元） Balance (100 Million US Dollars)										
1998	1	926.44	283.31	283.15	263.30	260.93	40.56	1.32	301.92	116.18
	2	926.58	273.84	273.84	272.85	270.59	36.86	1.14	301.16	112.91
	3	932.19	277.17	277.17	269.88	267.67	37.28	1.16	303.24	121.37
	4	929.16	277.44	277.44	270.76	268.39	36.27	1.05	300.90	121.91
	5	932.86	280.67	280.67	273.21	270.76	34.92	1.19	299.45	128.91
	6	934.14	282.79	282.79	275.06	272.52	35.25	1.15	295.62	135.12
	7	930.82	280.80	280.80	274.33	271.77	34.19	1.14	294.37	130.60
	8	930.86	277.53	277.53	277.82	275.11	33.39	1.29	294.38	140.98
	9	931.83	276.37	276.37	280.44	277.69	33.70	1.13	291.91	136.04
	10	941.25	276.05	276.05	281.11	278.16	33.69	0.97	300.36	135.33
	11	960.04	277.63	277.63	287.38	284.31	31.44	0.93	310.48	149.38
	12	965.11	288.32	288.32	288.26	285.21	27.24	0.66	305.71	158.09
比上期增减额（亿美元） Changes Compared with Previous Period (100 Million US Dollars)										
1998	1	-9.17	-11.99	-11.79	-4.81	-5.00	0.33	-0.09	-1.26	1.74
	2	0.12	-9.47	-9.31	9.55	9.66	-3.70	-0.18	-0.76	-3.27
	3	5.59	3.33	3.33	-2.97	-2.92	0.42	0.02	2.08	8.48
	4	-3.02	0.29	0.29	0.88	0.72	-1.01	-0.11	-2.34	0.53
	5	3.71	3.21	3.21	2.45	2.37	-1.35	0.14	-1.45	7.00
	6	1.28	2.12	2.12	1.85	1.76	0.33	-0.04	-3.83	6.21
	7	-3.32	-1.99	-1.99	-0.73	-0.75	-1.06	-0.01	-1.25	-4.52
	8	0.02	-3.27	-3.27	3.49	3.34	-0.80	0.15	0.01	10.40
	9	0.97	-1.16	-1.16	2.62	2.58	0.31	-0.16	-2.47	-4.94
	10	9.45	-0.32	-0.32	0.67	0.47	-0.01	-0.16	8.45	-0.71
	11	18.80	1.58	1.58	6.27	6.15	-2.25	-0.04	10.12	14.05
	12	5.04	10.70	10.70	0.87	0.89	-4.19	-0.27	-4.77	8.72

国家银行外汇信贷收支主要指标时间序列表

Time Series of Major Indicators in Sources and Uses of Credit Funds of State Banks（Foreign Currency）

年　月 Year Month	各项存款 Total Deposits	单位活期存款 Demand Deposits by Enterprises	单位定期存款 Time Deposits by Enterprises	储蓄存款 Savings Deposits	定期储蓄 Time Deposits	境外存款 Foreign Deposits	境外筹资 Overseas Financing
			期末余额（亿美元） Balance（100 Million US Dollars）				
1999　1	704.61	99.02	191.43	383.80	358.43	1.63	294.52
2	713.52	101.81	186.92	393.95	367.24	1.70	293.66
3	714.41	100.10	181.64	403.36	376.75	1.52	289.05
4	721.16	101.15	179.85	410.81	383.85	1.50	287.54
5	730.25	100.85	180.55	419.45	391.42	1.55	288.16
6	741.55	102.54	182.69	428.70	399.55	1.59	289.84
7	747.15	105.10	175.15	440.44	410.45	1.57	282.47
8	768.18	103.76	183.33	453.18	422.86	1.66	283.52
9	790.97	104.04	190.56	467.20	436.14	1.64	290.54
10	804.86	103.04	193.50	478.70	446.57	1.55	293.33
11	818.97	104.01	192.70	491.93	458.92	1.58	291.90
12	829.10	106.60	189.10	501.05	467.76	0.67	292.91
			比上期增减额（亿美元） Changes Compared with Previous Period（100 Million US Dollars）				
1999　1	2.43	1.98	-1.69	7.34	6.60	0.03	-2.35
2	8.91	2.79	-4.51	10.15	8.81	0.07	-0.86
3	0.89	-1.71	-5.28	9.41	9.51	-0.18	-4.61
4	6.75	1.05	-1.79	7.45	7.10	-0.02	-1.51
5	9.09	-0.30	0.70	8.64	7.57	0.05	0.62
6	11.30	1.69	2.14	9.25	8.13	0.04	1.68
7	5.60	2.56	-7.54	11.74	10.90	-0.02	-7.37
8	21.03	-1.34	8.18	12.74	12.41	0.09	1.05
9	22.79	0.28	7.23	14.02	13.28	-0.02	7.02
10	13.89	-1.00	2.94	11.50	10.43	-0.09	2.79
11	14.11	0.97	-0.80	13.23	12.35	0.03	-1.43
12	10.13	2.59	-3.60	9.12	8.84	-0.91	1.01
			比去年同期增长（%） Increase Rate Year-on-year（%）				
1999　1	21.98	-3.40	20.78	38.27	39.27	-34.80	-1.81
2	20.21	-3.44	14.22	37.36	37.85	-28.27	-2.19
3	18.93	-2.31	8.13	36.19	36.50	-23.23	-3.74
4	19.83	5.08	5.99	35.09	35.49	-20.63	-2.96
5	19.16	2.78	4.12	34.68	34.97	-12.92	-2.82
6	18.05	7.36	3.50	33.53	33.43	-13.11	0.54
7	16.50	11.13	-4.55	32.11	31.65	-26.98	-1.56
8	15.73	4.58	-2.33	30.68	30.24	-2.92	-1.05
9	17.17	3.79	1.21	31.92	31.16		2.22
10	19.19	-0.29	8.12	32.14	31.38	-4.91	-0.16
11	18.99	3.74	4.76	32.52	32.01	-0.63	-4.03
12	18.05	9.75	-2.06	33.06	32.92	-58.13	-1.28

国家银行外汇信贷收支主要指标时间序列表

Time Series of Major Indicators in Sources and Uses of Credit Funds of State Banks (Foreign Currency)

年　月 Year Month	各项贷款 Total Loans	短期贷款 Short－term Loans	境内短期贷款 Domestic Short－term Loans	中长期贷款 Medium and Long－term Loans	境内中长期贷款 Domestic Medium and Long－term Loans	进出口贸易融资 Financing for Import and Export Trades	票据融资 Paper Financing	境外筹资转贷款 On－lending of Overseas Financing	有价证券及投资 Securities and Investments
期末余额（亿美元） Balance (100 Million US Dollars)									
1999 1	954.29	285.59	285.59	281.86	278.76	26.69	0.63	304.42	174.69
2	954.34	284.99	284.99	282.69	279.45	25.97	0.58	304.21	162.74
3	954.94	285.92	285.92	284.30	280.95	26.44	0.48	301.06	152.87
4	955.28	287.78	287.78	284.49	281.12	25.72	0.47	299.36	148.18
5	951.51	283.72	283.72	284.46	281.04	24.41	0.49	300.44	174.99
6	947.15	283.84	283.84	281.12	277.70	24.49	0.48	296.75	193.63
7	945.65	282.63	282.63	284.13	280.59	23.52	0.47	293.93	189.13
8	945.07	282.37	282.37	284.68	280.98	22.34	0.51	293.35	185.52
9	953.51	284.42	284.42	285.59	281.75	20.42	0.44	300.06	197.63
10	958.51	285.89	285.89	284.60	280.73	19.36	0.67	304.02	203.04
11	949.16	283.97	283.97	282.38	278.37	19.86	0.66	299.47	230.87
12	909.10	267.39	267.39	272.17	268.16	19.06	0.60	297.42	259.06
比上期增减额（亿美元） Changes Compared with Previous Period (100 Million US Dollars)									
1999 1	－7.60	－3.29	－3.29	－2.97	－3.02	－0.57	－0.03	－1.11	16.61
2	0.03	－0.60	－0.60	0.83	0.69	－0.72	－0.05	－0.21	－11.95
3	0.59	0.93	0.93	1.61	1.50	0.47	－0.10	－3.15	－9.87
4	0.34	1.86	1.86	0.19	0.17	－0.72	－0.01	－1.70	－4.69
5	－3.77	－4.06	－4.06	－0.03	－0.08	－1.31	0.02	1.08	26.81
6	－4.36	0.12	0.12	－3.34	－3.34	0.08	－0.01	－3.69	18.64
7	－1.48	－1.21	－1.21	3.01	2.89	－0.97	－0.01	－2.82	－4.50
8	－0.60	－0.26	－0.26	0.55	0.39	－1.18	0.04	－0.58	－3.61
9	8.44	2.05	2.05	0.91	0.77	－1.92	－0.07	6.71	12.11
10	4.98	1.47	1.47	－0.99	－1.02	－1.06	0.23	3.96	5.41
11	－9.35	－1.92	－1.92	－2.20	－2.34	0.50	－0.01	－4.55	27.83
12	5.78	11.28	11.28	5.58	5.58	1.39	－0.06	－2.05	28.19
比去年同期增长（%） Increase Rate Year－on－year (%)									
1999 1	3.45	0.80	0.86	8.70	8.50	－34.20	－52.27	0.83	50.36
2	3.44	4.07	4.07	5.16	4.84	－29.54	－49.12	1.01	44.13
3	2.88	3.16	3.16	6.93	6.56	－29.08	－58.62	－0.72	25.95
4	3.23	3.72	3.72	6.64	6.32	－29.09	－55.24	－0.51	19.71
5	2.44	1.09	1.09	5.66	5.35	－30.10	－58.82	0.33	35.75
6	1.80	0.37	0.37	3.63	3.33	－30.52	－58.26	0.38	43.30
7	1.93	0.65	0.65	4.74	4.42	－31.21	－58.77	－0.15	44.84
8	1.87	1.75	1.75	3.64	3.31	－33.09	－60.47	－0.35	31.59
9	2.68	2.91	2.91	2.99	2.62	－39.41	－61.06	2.79	45.27
10	2.17	3.56	3.56	2.38	2.07	－42.53	－30.93	1.22	50.03
11	－0.80	2.28	2.28	－0.62	－0.96	－36.83	－29.03	－3.55	54.57
12	－0.72	2.40	2.40	1.03	0.70	－22.02	－9.09	2.71	63.88

国家银行外汇信贷收支主要指标时间序列表

Time Series of Major Indicators in Sources and Uses of Credit Funds of State Banks（Foreign Currency）

年 月 Year Month		各项存款 Total Deposits						境外筹资 Overseas Financing
			单位活期存款 Demand Deposits by Enterprises	单位定期存款 Time Deposits by Enterprises	储蓄存款 Savings Deposits	定期储蓄 Time Deposits	境外存款 Foreign Deposits	
期末余额（亿美元） Balance（100 Million US Dollars）								
2000	1	840.00	101.22	193.67	513.34	479.44	0.33	291.38
	2	855.78	102.38	194.78	526.90	492.17	0.31	289.89
	3	866.29	102.47	194.48	536.96	502.10	0.31	283.74
	4	878.80	102.40	196.43	547.01	511.56	0.25	284.10
	5	891.52	103.20	197.46	557.54	521.24	0.20	260.53
	6	910.84	101.25	203.63	570.43	535.11	0.23	256.29
	7	941.33	105.06	215.56	584.50	548.09	0.24	257.19
	8	952.57	103.56	215.39	597.13	559.73	0.21	255.90
	9	969.34	101.32	218.25	611.41	573.71	0.21	254.37
	10	983.14	103.69	217.34	624.20	585.83	0.11	250.94
	11	1027.41	108.58	242.11	637.35	598.53	0.15	250.40
	12	1028.76	109.08	227.72	649.04	608.83	0.09	235.91
比上期增减额（亿美元） Changes Compared with Previous Period（100 Million US Dollars）								
2000	1	10.63	-5.70	4.27	12.29	11.68	-0.06	-1.51
	2	15.78	1.16	1.11	13.56	12.73	-0.02	-1.49
	3	10.51	0.09	-0.30	10.06	9.93		-6.15
	4	12.51	-0.07	1.95	10.05	9.46	-0.06	0.36
	5	12.72	0.80	1.03	10.53	9.68	-0.05	-23.57
	6	19.32	-1.95	6.17	12.89	13.87	0.03	-4.24
	7	30.49	3.81	11.93	14.07	12.98	0.01	0.90
	8	11.24	-1.50	-0.17	12.63	11.64	-0.03	-1.29
	9	16.77	-2.24	2.86	14.28	13.98		-1.53
	10	13.80	2.37	-0.91	12.79	12.12	-0.10	-3.43
	11	44.27	4.89	24.77	13.15	12.70	0.04	-0.54
	12	1.35	0.50	-14.39	11.69	10.30	-0.06	-14.49
比去年同期增长（%） Increase Rate Year-on-year（%）								
2000	1	19.21	2.22	1.17	33.75	33.76	-79.75	-1.07
	2	19.94	0.56	4.21	33.75	34.02	-81.76	-1.28
	3	21.26	2.37	7.07	33.12	33.27	-79.61	-1.84
	4	21.86	1.24	9.22	33.15	33.27	-83.33	-1.20
	5	22.08	2.33	9.37	32.92	33.17	-87.10	-9.59
	6	22.83	-1.26	11.46	33.06	33.93	-85.53	-11.58
	7	25.99	-0.04	23.07	32.71	33.53	-84.71	-8.95
	8	24.01	-0.19	17.49	31.76	32.37	-87.35	-9.74
	9	22.55	-2.61	14.53	30.87	31.54	-87.20	-12.45
	10	22.15	0.63	12.32	30.39	31.18	-92.90	-14.45
	11	25.45	4.39	25.64	29.56	30.42	-90.51	-14.22
	12	24.08	2.33	20.42	29.54	30.16	-86.57	-19.46

国家银行外汇信贷收支主要指标时间序列表

Time Series of Major Indicators in Sources and Uses of Credit Funds of State Banks (Foreign Currency)

年　月 Year Month	各项贷款 Total Loans	短期贷款 Short－term Loans	境内短期贷款 Domestic Short－term Loans	中长期贷款 Medium and Long－term Loans	境内中长期贷款 Domestic Medium and Long－term Loans	进出口贸易融资 Financing for Import and Export Trades	票据融资 Paper Financing	境外筹资转贷款 On－lending of Overseas Financing	有价证券及投资 Securities and Investments
期末余额（亿美元） Balance (100 Million US Dollars)									
2000　1	908.41	270.34	270.34	272.45	268.44	14.79	0.39	291.81	277.15
2	904.99	269.32	269.32	271.84	267.72	13.18	0.36	291.27	241.46
3	898.64	267.24	267.24	270.70	266.56	14.18	0.37	286.64	248.31
4	900.98	264.65	264.65	272.88	267.74	15.12	0.43	287.67	239.92
5	868.18	255.79	255.79	268.69	263.37	14.13	0.47	269.77	248.03
6	776.77	212.27	212.27	239.78	234.03	13.76	0.43	259.84	244.63
7	756.35	205.46	205.46	235.86	230.19	13.26	0.40	259.92	264.79
8	745.62	199.92	199.92	230.13	224.37	13.06	0.42	257.31	280.71
9	738.20	197.15	197.15	226.93	220.94	12.55	0.45	255.71	288.94
10	731.91	195.48	195.48	227.20	221.55	11.96	0.46	253.43	314.72
11	730.90	195.15	195.15	225.20	219.04	11.62	0.40	252.58	327.39
12	694.13	185.93	185.93	211.19	205.00	12.46	0.34	239.72	352.42
比上期增减额（亿美元） Changes Compared with Previous Period (100 Million US Dollars)									
2000　1	－5.27	－3.34	－3.34	0.94	0.94	0.05	－0.21	－3.88	18.41
2	－3.20	－0.61	－0.61	－1.58	－1.69	－1.60	－0.03	0.23	－35.63
3	－6.31	－2.08	－2.08	－1.09	－1.11	1.00	0.01	－4.64	6.79
4	2.80	－2.55	－2.55	2.19	1.19	0.94	0.06	1.04	－8.39
5	－21.70	－4.74	－4.74	1.08	0.90	－1.00	0.04	－17.57	8.11
6	－7.12	0.26	0.26	－2.37	－2.80	0.20	－0.04	－4.80	－3.33
7	－0.83	－0.64	－0.64	0.92	1.00	－0.80	－0.03	－1.30	20.16
8	－4.40	－2.14	－2.14	－5.06	－5.15	－0.20	0.02	－2.39	15.94
9	－4.97	－2.26	－2.26	－2.89	－3.12	0.51	0.03	－1.03	8.21
10	－4.77	－0.66	－0.66	0.37	0.71	－0.60	0.01	－2.28	25.77
11	－0.07	－0.12	－0.12	－1.58	－2.09	－0.35	－0.06	－0.85	12.67
12	－12.35	－0.26	－0.26	－3.55	－3.58	1.05	－0.06	－9.09	25.04
比去年同期增长（%） Increase Rate Year－on－year (%)									
2000　1		4.34	4.34	2.35	2.05	－36.38	－38.10	－4.14	58.65
2	－0.34	4.35	4.35	1.49	1.19	－40.78	－37.93	－4.00	48.41
3	－1.06	3.28	3.28	0.53	0.26	－38.05	－22.92	－4.54	62.43
4	－0.81	1.73	1.73	1.23	0.62	－32.66	－8.51	－3.65	61.91
5	－2.69	1.51	1.51	1.62	0.97	－33.14	－4.08	－9.84	41.74
6	－3.00	1.56	1.56	1.99	1.17	－32.54	－10.42	－10.34	26.38
7	－2.93	1.77	1.77	1.23	0.49	－33.16	－14.89	－9.92	40.04
8	－3.34	1.10	1.10	－0.74	－1.48	－30.53	－17.65	－10.56	51.36
9	－4.72	－0.42	－0.42	－2.07	－2.86	－21.50	2.27	－12.90	46.24
10	－5.71	－1.16	－1.16	－1.59	－2.25	－20.30	－31.34	－14.79	55.03
11	－4.79	－0.54	－0.54	－1.38	－2.18	－24.07	－39.39	－13.77	41.83
12	－6.99	－4.88	－4.88	－4.79	－5.68	－26.86	－43.33	－16.24	36.07

国家银行外汇信贷收支主要指标时间序列表
Time Series of Major Indicators in Sources and Uses of Credit Funds of State Banks（Foreign Currency）

年 月 Year Month		各项存款 Total Deposits	单位活期存款 Demand Deposits by Enterprises	单位定期存款 Time Deposits by Enterprises	储蓄存款 Savings Deposits	定期储蓄 Time Deposits	境外存款 Foreign Deposits	境外筹资 Overseas Financing
期末余额（亿美元） Balance（100 Million US Dollars）								
2001	1	1039.03	106.34	226.48	662.68	621.82	0.09	249.64
	2	1028.54	107.32	219.12	657.50	615.63	0.17	247.44
	3	1027.61	103.03	223.62	654.47	611.82	0.16	245.78
	4	1053.51	103.11	245.51	658.82	614.65	0.11	242.21
	5	1073.08	113.19	248.55	667.86	618.82	0.15	239.56
	6	1064.13	112.99	237.72	670.18	620.10	0.13	237.24
	7	1059.67	111.26	228.67	680.40	627.30	0.06	236.48
	8	1066.54	112.34	223.97	691.26	635.10	0.08	238.75
	9	1066.52	109.13	223.06	697.31	639.99	0.06	237.91
	10	1076.21	118.43	216.29	705.46	645.48	0.10	235.15
	11	1074.49	122.09	205.10	711.43	649.52	0.23	234.65
	12	1076.28	123.51	201.99	715.35	650.50	0.18	228.98
比上期增减额（亿美元） Changes Compared with Previous Period（100 Million US Dollars）								
2001	1	7.21	-5.01	-1.00	13.28	12.45		6.12
	2	-10.49	0.98	-7.36	-5.18	-6.19	0.08	-2.20
	3	-0.93	-4.29	4.50	-3.03	-3.81	-0.01	-1.66
	4	25.90	0.08	21.89	4.35	2.83	-0.05	-3.57
	5	19.57	10.08	3.04	9.04	4.17	0.04	-2.65
	6	-8.95	-0.20	-10.83	2.32	1.28	-0.02	-2.32
	7	-4.46	-1.73	-9.05	10.22	7.20	-0.07	-0.76
	8	6.87	1.08	-4.70	10.86	7.80	0.02	2.27
	9	-0.02	-3.21	-0.91	6.05	4.89	-0.02	-0.84
	10	9.69	9.30	-6.77	8.15	5.49	0.04	-2.76
	11	-1.72	3.66	-11.19	5.97	4.04	0.13	-0.50
	12	1.79	1.42	-3.11	3.92	0.98	-0.05	-5.67
比去年同期增长（%） Increase Rate Year-on-year（%）								
2001	1	23.69	5.06	16.94	29.09	29.70	-72.73	-14.32
	2	20.19	4.83	12.50	24.79	25.08	-45.16	-14.64
	3	18.62	0.55	14.98	21.88	21.85	-48.39	-13.38
	4	19.88	0.69	24.99	20.44	20.15	-56.00	-14.74
	5	20.37	9.68	25.87	19.79	18.72	-25.00	-8.05
	6	16.83	11.60	16.74	17.49	15.88	-43.48	-7.43
	7	12.57	5.90	6.08	16.41	14.45	-75.00	-8.05
	8	11.96	8.48	3.98	15.76	13.47	-61.90	-6.70
	9	10.03	7.71	2.20	14.05	11.55	-71.43	-6.47
	10	9.47	14.22	-0.48	13.02	10.18	-9.09	-6.29
	11	4.58	12.44	-15.29	11.62	8.52	53.33	-6.29
	12	4.62	13.23	-11.30	10.22	6.84	100.00	-2.94

国家银行外汇信贷收支主要指标时间序列表
Time Series of Major Indicators in Sources and Uses of Credit Funds of State Banks（Foreign Currency）

年　月 Year Month	各项贷款 Total Loans	短期贷款 Short - term Loans	境内短期贷款 Domestic Short - term Loans	中长期贷款 Medium and Long - term Loans	境内中长期贷款 Domestic Medium and Long - term Loans	进出口贸易融资 Financing for Import and Export Trades	票据融资 Paper Financing	境外筹资转贷款 On - lending of Overseas Financing	有价证券及投资 Securities and Investments
期末余额（亿美元） Balance（100 Million US Dollars）									
2001　1	687.82	160.07	160.07	227.02	220.80	14.57	0.34	238.30	382.34
2	684.88	158.54	158.54	226.15	219.93	12.58	0.37	237.50	416.51
3	681.40	159.05	159.05	225.22	219.07	13.13	0.32	234.29	442.41
4	677.44	156.92	156.92	222.01	215.87	12.56	0.35	235.42	491.58
5	676.58	155.95	155.95	222.41	216.15	12.52	0.43	234.55	477.31
6	673.36	157.99	157.99	221.00	214.65	12.85	0.37	231.83	451.82
7	668.10	156.22	156.22	227.58	221.31	12.60	0.40	221.04	464.30
8	674.09	156.44	156.44	227.32	220.76	13.11	0.92	225.71	464.71
9	669.43	156.02	156.02	224.70	218.08	13.12	0.48	224.50	470.79
10	662.97	157.65	157.65	220.54	213.61	12.36	0.51	221.22	446.97
11	655.92	158.36	158.36	215.09	208.02	12.49	0.47	219.36	478.09
12	653.77	159.32	159.32	214.17	207.14	13.87	0.65	214.05	610.66
比上期增减额（亿美元） Changes Compared with Previous Period（100 Million US Dollars）									
2001　1	- 7.11	- 1.77	- 1.77	- 2.09	- 2.01	- 0.90		- 4.04	28.56
2	- 2.94	- 1.53	- 1.53	- 0.87	- 0.87	- 1.99	0.03	- 0.80	34.17
3	- 3.48	0.51	0.51	- 0.93	- 0.86	0.55	- 0.05	- 3.21	25.90
4	- 3.96	- 2.13	- 2.13	- 3.21	- 3.20	- 0.57	0.03	1.13	49.17
5	- 0.85	- 0.97	- 0.97	0.40	0.28	- 0.04	0.08	- 0.87	- 14.27
6	- 3.28	2.02	2.02	- 1.43	- 1.53	0.33	- 0.06	- 2.72	- 25.49
7	- 5.24	- 1.75	- 1.75	6.55	6.66	- 0.25	0.03	- 10.79	12.48
8	6.02	0.22	0.22	- 0.23	- 0.55	0.51	0.52	4.67	0.41
9	- 4.66	- 0.42	- 0.42	- 2.62	- 2.68	0.01	- 0.44	- 1.21	6.08
10	- 6.52	1.63	1.63	- 4.19	- 4.49	- 0.76	0.03	- 3.28	- 23.82
11	- 7.07	0.69	0.69	- 5.44	- 5.57	0.13	- 0.04	- 1.86	31.12
12	- 2.07	0.97	0.97	- 0.89	- 0.85	1.38	0.18	- 5.31	132.57
比去年同期增长（%） Increase Rate Year - on - year（%）									
2001　1	- 7.63	- 1.78	- 1.78	8.91	8.22	8.52	- 12.82	- 15.11	37.98
2	- 7.63	- 0.96	- 0.96	9.60	8.97	6.60	2.78	- 15.49	72.50
3	- 7.37	0.01	0.01	9.73	9.12	2.96	- 13.51	- 15.25	78.20
4	- 8.10	0.31	0.31	7.52	- 7.21	- 18.60	- 15.16	- 15.16	104.92
5	- 6.00	2.14	2.14	6.88	- 0.99	- 8.51	- 9.98	- 9.98	92.47
6	- 6.21	3.51	3.51	5.00	4.87	0.00	- 13.95	- 9.56	84.70
7	- 6.97	4.67	4.67	3.16	2.99	4.15	0.00	- 13.20	75.34
8	- 5.67	6.05	6.05	4.46	4.22	9.65	119.05	- 10.59	65.54
9	- 5.68	6.97	6.97	4.60	4.44	6.06	6.67	- 10.73	62.94
10	- 5.97	8.59	8.59	2.41	1.90	5.02	10.87	- 11.22	42.02
11	- 6.93	9.51	9.51	0.70	0.30	9.21	17.50	- 11.66	46.03
12	- 5.81	10.14	10.14	1.43	1.06	11.32	91.18	- 10.71	73.28

国家银行外汇信贷收支主要指标时间序列表

Time Series of Major Indicators in Sources and Uses of Credit Funds of State Banks（Foreign Currency）

年 月 Year Month		各项存款 Total Deposits	单位活期存款 Demand Deposits by Enterprises	单位定期存款 Time Deposits by Enterprises	储蓄存款 Savings Deposits	定期储蓄 Time Deposits	境外存款 Foreign Deposits	境外筹资 Overseas Financing
		期末余额（亿美元） Balance（100 Million US Dollars）						
2002	1	1063.89	115.69	195.63	718.48	653.04	0.34	227.03
	2	1074.27	120.49	193.20	727.32	659.62	0.24	224.93
	3	1080.56	115.07	196.33	734.42	664.84	0.25	222.88
	4	1083.16	114.08	193.20	739.59	668.76	0.21	222.90
	5	1098.65	119.85	193.05	747.76	673.89	0.18	224.03
	6	1103.39	126.29	182.68	755.18	678.87	0.17	247.88
	7	1101.89	123.63	181.78	756.87	679.09	0.23	246.55
	8	1111.46	126.61	183.80	761.25	681.29	0.15	246.84
	9	1105.63	121.89	180.59	762.68	682.18	0.14	245.17
	10	1122.02	131.49	180.97	768.46	684.93	0.31	242.10
	11	1131.57	132.90	187.55	770.59	685.71	0.17	221.07
	12	1140.05	135.01	190.08	774.07	685.51	0.16	219.79
		比上期增减额（亿美元） Changes Compared with Previous Period（100 Million US Dollars）						
2002	1	-12.08	-7.08	-5.67	3.91	2.91	0.16	-1.94
	2	10.38	4.80	-2.43	8.84	6.58	-0.10	-2.10
	3	6.29	-5.42	3.13	7.10	5.22	0.01	-2.05
	4	2.60	-0.99	-3.13	5.17	3.92	-0.04	0.02
	5	15.49	5.77	-0.15	8.17	5.13	-0.03	1.13
	6	4.74	6.44	-10.37	7.42	4.98	-0.01	23.85
	7	-1.50	-2.66	-0.90	1.69	0.22	0.06	-1.33
	8	9.57	2.98	2.02	4.38	2.20	-0.08	0.29
	9	-5.83	-4.72	-3.21	1.43	0.89	-0.01	-1.67
	10	16.39	9.60	0.38	5.78	2.75	0.17	-3.07
	11	9.55	1.41	6.58	2.13	0.78	-0.14	-21.03
	12	8.48	2.11	2.53	3.48	-0.20	-0.01	-1.28
		比去年同期增长（%） Increase Rate Year-on-year（%）						
2002	1	2.39	8.79	-13.60	8.42	5.02	277.78	-9.06
	2	4.45	12.27	-11.81	10.62	7.15	41.18	-9.10
	3	5.15	11.69	-12.18	12.22	8.67	56.25	-9.32
	4	2.81	10.64	-21.29	12.26	8.80	90.91	-7.97
	5	2.38	5.88	-22.31	11.96	8.90	20.00	-6.48
	6	3.69	11.77	-23.14	12.68	9.48	30.77	4.48
	7	3.98	11.12	-20.49	11.24	8.26	283.33	4.26
	8	4.21	12.70	-17.92	10.12	7.27	87.50	3.39
	9	3.67	11.69	-19.02	9.37	6.59	133.33	3.05
	10	4.26	11.03	-16.31	8.93	6.11	210.00	2.96
	11	5.31	8.85	-8.53	8.32	5.57	-26.09	-5.79
	12	5.93	9.31	-5.87	8.21	5.38	-11.11	-4.01

国家银行外汇信贷收支主要指标时间序列表
Time Series of Major Indicators in Sources and Uses of Credit Funds of State Banks (Foreign Currency)

年 月 Year Month	各项贷款 Total Loans	短期贷款 Short - term Loans	境内短期贷款 Domestic Short - term Loans	中长期贷款 Medium and Long - term Loans	境内中长期贷款 Domestic Medium and Long - term Loans	进出口贸易融资 Financing for Import and Export Trades	票据融资 Paper Financing	境外筹资转贷款 On - lending of Overseas Financing	有价证券及投资 Securities and Investments
期末余额(亿美元) Balance (100 Million US Dollars)									
2002 1	659.95	159.80	159.80	223.74	216.92	13.46	0.59	210.89	590.23
2	666.03	161.16	161.16	231.86	224.82	12.58	0.17	209.16	585.04
3	671.20	170.90	170.87	227.02	219.76	13.67	0.36	208.43	643.81
4	676.70	172.65	172.65	225.42	220.45	15.04	0.46	212.44	665.56
5	683.82	176.55	176.55	226.99	219.42	16.14	0.47	212.79	687.11
6	695.47	182.07	182.07	229.31	221.53	17.80	0.45	215.43	681.55
7	698.82	181.82	181.82	235.20	227.40	17.81	0.57	212.48	682.45
8	694.98	182.71	182.71	232.29	224.18	17.87	0.59	212.73	739.89
9	701.71	184.14	184.14	240.40	232.11	19.09	0.72	209.58	720.61
10	702.91	183.41	183.41	244.14	235.65	17.76	0.75	208.80	725.48
11	705.88	186.42	186.30	245.37	236.79	19.83	0.70	205.18	778.11
12	729.58	187.10	187.10	268.07	260.04	21.97	0.69	203.98	747.48
比上期增减额(亿美元) Changes Compared with Previous Period (100 Million US Dollars)									
2002 1	0.46	1.02	1.02	3.57	3.66	- 0.38	- 0.06	- 3.16	- 21.33
2	6.08	1.36	1.36	8.12	7.90	- 0.88	- 0.42	- 1.73	- 5.19
3	5.17	9.74	9.71	- 4.84	- 5.06	1.09	0.19	- 0.73	58.77
4	5.50	1.75	1.78	- 1.60	0.69	1.37	0.10	4.01	21.75
5	7.12	3.90	3.90	1.57	- 1.03	1.10	0.01	0.35	21.55
6	11.65	5.52	5.52	2.32	2.11	1.66	- 0.02	2.64	- 5.56
7	3.35	- 0.25	- 0.25	5.89	5.87	0.01	0.12	- 2.95	0.90
8	- 3.84	0.89	0.89	- 2.91	- 3.22	0.06	0.02	0.25	57.44
9	6.73	1.43	1.43	8.11	7.93	1.22	0.13	- 3.15	- 19.28
10	1.20	- 0.73	- 0.73	3.74	3.54	- 1.33	0.03	- 0.78	4.87
11	2.97	3.01	2.89	1.23	1.14	2.07	- 0.05	- 3.62	52.63
12	23.70	0.68	0.80	22.70	23.25	2.14	- 0.01	- 1.20	- 30.63
比去年同期增长(%) Increase Rate Year - on - year (%)									
2002 1	- 4.05	- 0.17	- 0.17	- 1.44	- 1.76	- 7.62	73.53	- 11.50	54.37
2	- 2.75	1.65	1.65	2.52	2.22		- 54.05	- 11.93	40.46
3	- 1.50	7.45	7.43	0.80	0.31	4.11	12.50	- 11.04	45.52
4	- 0.11	10.02	10.02	1.54	2.12	19.75	31.43	- 9.76	35.39
5	1.06	13.21	13.21	2.04	1.50	28.91	9.30	- 9.28	43.95
6	3.29	15.26	15.26	3.76	3.21	38.52	21.62	- 7.07	50.85
7	4.60	16.39	16.39	3.36	2.75	41.35	42.50	- 3.87	46.98
8	3.10	16.79	16.79	2.19	1.55	36.31	- 35.87	- 5.75	59.22
9	4.82	18.02	18.02	6.99	6.43	45.50	50.00	- 6.65	53.06
10	6.03	16.34	16.34	10.72	10.33	43.69	47.06	- 5.61	62.31
11	7.62	17.73	17.66	14.08	13.83	58.77	48.94	- 6.46	62.75
12	11.59	17.44	17.44	25.15	25.52	58.40	6.15	- 4.70	22.40

国家银行外汇信贷收支主要指标时间序列表

Time Series of Major Indicators in Sources and Uses of Credit Funds of State Banks（Foreign Currency）

年 月 Year Month	各项存款 Total Deposits						境外筹资 Overseas Financing
		单位活期存款 Demand Deposits by Enterprises	单位定期存款 Time Deposits by Enterprises	储蓄存款 Savings Deposits	定期储蓄 Time Deposits	境外存款 Foreign Deposits	
期末余额（亿美元） Balance（100 Million US Dollars）							
2003 1	1132.37	131.78	184.06	776.68	687.12	0.16	219.54
2	1129.32	139.55	169.46	779.35	687.96	0.20	218.83
3	1123.20	133.96	169.15	778.96	686.78	0.22	217.00
4	1123.06	133.92	168.20	779.22	685.52	0.20	217.19
5	1131.66	143.23	164.97	782.16	686.13	0.20	218.69
6	1140.70	149.51	164.42	783.56	685.01	0.23	214.48
7	1127.49	142.42	162.29	779.87	678.98	0.29	211.41
8	1114.16	141.87	157.79	771.90	669.83	0.24	207.28
9	1100.18	141.49	158.57	756.73	655.66	0.09	208.60
10	1102.25	154.27	156.33	747.00	644.56	0.04	210.60
11	1105.03	156.16	160.81	739.94	636.50	0.14	209.83
12	1093.30	154.96	153.07	733.73	629.38	0.16	206.26
比上期增减额（亿美元） Changes Compared with Previous Period（100 Million US Dollars）							
2003 1	-7.75	-2.61	-6.66	2.58	1.58	-0.01	-0.32
2	-3.05	7.77	-14.60	2.67	0.84	0.04	-0.71
3	-6.12	-5.59	-0.31	-0.39	-1.18	0.02	-1.83
4	-0.14	-0.04	-0.95	0.26	-1.26	-0.02	0.19
5	8.60	9.31	-3.23	2.94	0.61		1.50
6	9.04	6.28	-0.55	1.40	-1.12	0.03	-4.21
7	-13.21	-7.09	-2.13	-3.69	-6.03	0.06	-3.07
8	-13.33	-0.55	-4.50	-7.97	-9.15	-0.05	-4.13
9	-13.98	-0.38	0.78	-15.17	-14.17	-0.15	1.32
10	2.07	12.78	-2.24	-9.73	-11.10	-0.05	2.00
11	2.78	1.89	4.48	-7.06	-8.06	0.10	-0.77
12	-11.73	-1.20	-7.74	-6.21	-7.12	0.02	-3.57
比去年同期增长（%） Increase Rate Year-on-year（%）							
2003 1	6.44	13.91	-5.91	8.10	5.22	-52.94	-3.30
2	5.12	15.82	-12.29	7.15	4.30	-16.67	-2.71
3	3.95	16.42	-13.84	6.06	3.30	-12.00	-2.64
4	3.68	17.39	-12.94	5.36	2.51	-4.76	-2.56
5	3.00	19.51	-14.55	4.60	1.82	11.11	-2.38
6	3.38	18.39	-10.00	3.76	0.90	35.29	-13.47
7	2.32	15.20	-10.72	3.04	-0.02	26.09	-14.25
8	0.24	12.05	-14.15	1.40	-1.68	60.00	-16.03
9	-0.49	16.08	-12.19	-0.78	-3.89	-35.71	-14.92
10	-1.76	17.32	-13.62	-2.79	-5.89	-87.10	-13.01
11	-2.35	17.50	-14.26	-3.98	-7.18	-17.65	-5.08
12	-4.10	14.78	-19.47	-5.21	-8.19		-6.16

国家银行外汇信贷收支主要指标时间序列表
Time Series of Major Indicators in Sources and Uses of Credit Funds of State Banks (Foreign Currency)

年 月 Year Month		各项贷款 Total Loans	短期贷款 Short-term Loans	境内短期贷款 Domestic Short-term Loans	中长期贷款 Medium and Long-term Loans	境内中长期贷款 Domestic Medium and Long-term Loans	进出口贸易融资 Financing for Import and Export Trades	票据融资 Paper Financing	境外筹资转贷款 On-lending of Overseas Financing	有价证券及投资 Securities and Investments
		期末余额（亿美元） Balance (100 Million US Dollars)								
2003	1	739.19	190.97	190.97	270.52	261.97	24.87	0.65	204.49	738.58
	2	743.41	194.45	194.45	272.43	263.84	24.82	0.80	203.32	729.78
	3	760.33	204.01	204.01	274.73	265.73	29.20	0.86	204.14	772.68
	4	779.63	213.22	213.22	278.56	266.61	34.95	0.82	203.58	786.11
	5	799.20	221.27	221.27	283.49	271.43	40.11	0.83	204.67	758.89
	6	823.66	233.54	233.54	293.29	281.26	46.07	0.85	201.41	778.46
	7	830.54	242.52	242.52	292.39	280.57	46.70	1.14	199.26	825.56
	8	849.13	253.16	253.16	303.17	291.43	48.98	1.05	194.16	816.01
	9	890.33	269.66	269.66	323.64	311.62	51.56	1.14	195.10	779.86
	10	906.86	279.20	279.16	329.71	317.51	51.34	1.03	196.50	761.82
	11	923.06	287.16	287.12	331.91	319.69	58.94	0.96	194.94	713.80
	12	936.55	297.76	297.69	335.02	322.34	65.95	1.08	192.57	722.39
		比上期增减额（亿美元） Changes Compared with Previous Period (100 Million US Dollars)								
2003	1	9.60	4.56	4.56	1.59	1.07	2.89	-0.04	0.59	-9.10
	2	4.22	3.48	3.48	1.91	1.87	-0.05	0.15	-1.17	-8.80
	3	16.92	9.56	9.56	2.30	1.89	4.38	0.06	0.82	42.90
	4	19.30	9.21	9.21	3.83	0.88	5.75	-0.04	-0.56	13.43
	5	19.57	8.05	8.05	4.93	4.82	5.16	0.01	1.09	-27.22
	6	24.46	12.27	12.27	9.80	9.83	5.96	0.02	-3.26	19.57
	7	6.88	8.98	8.98	-0.90	-0.69	0.63	0.29	-2.15	47.10
	8	18.59	10.64	10.64	10.78	10.86	2.28	-0.09	-5.10	-9.55
	9	41.20	16.50	16.50	20.47	20.19	2.58	0.09	0.94	-36.15
	10	16.53	9.54	9.50	6.07	5.89	-0.22	-0.11	1.40	-18.04
	11	16.20	7.96	7.96	2.20	2.18	7.60	-0.07	-1.56	-48.02
	12	13.49	10.60	10.57	3.11	2.65	7.01	0.12	-2.37	8.59
		比去年同期增长（%） Increase Rate Year-on-year (%)								
2003	1	12.01	19.51	19.51	20.91	20.77	84.77	10.17	-3.03	25.13
	2	11.62	20.66	20.66	17.50	17.36	97.30	370.59	-2.79	24.74
	3	13.28	19.37	19.39	21.02	20.92	113.61	138.89	-2.06	20.02
	4	15.21	23.50	23.50	23.57	20.94	132.38	78.26	-4.17	18.11
	5	16.87	25.33	25.33	24.89	23.70	148.51	76.60	-3.82	10.45
	6	18.43	28.27	28.27	27.90	26.96	158.82	88.89	-6.51	14.22
	7	18.85	33.38	33.38	24.32	23.38	162.21	100.00	-6.22	20.97
	8	22.18	38.56	38.56	30.51	30.00	174.09	77.97	-8.73	10.29
	9	26.88	46.44	46.44	34.63	34.26	170.09	58.33	-6.91	8.22
	10	29.02	52.23	52.21	35.05	34.74	189.08	37.33	-5.89	5.01
	11	30.77	54.04	54.12	35.27	35.01	197.23	37.14	-4.99	-8.26
	12	28.37	59.14	59.11	24.97	23.96	200.18	56.52	-5.59	-3.36

国家银行外汇信贷收支主要指标时间序列表

Time Series of Major Indicators in Sources and Uses of Credit Funds of State Banks（Foreign Currency）

年 月 Year Month		各项存款 Total Deposits						境外筹资 Overseas Financing
			单位活期存款 Demand Deposits by Enterprises	单位定期存款 Time Deposits by Enterprises	储蓄存款 Savings Deposits	定期储蓄 Time Deposits	境外存款 Foreign Deposits	
期末余额（亿美元） Balance（100 Million US Dollars）								
2004	1	1105.07	167.88	154.70	731.56	625.36	0.20	204.10
	2	1068.51	162.89	141.84	712.06	605.44	0.14	204.23
	3	1072.56	167.64	144.15	705.99	596.14	0.16	200.80
	4	1073.26	161.32	152.68	699.12	587.06	0.18	192.96
	5	1086.89	174.47	149.72	700.02	583.65	0.17	193.60
	6	1091.39	180.20	170.42	676.85	558.53	0.26	189.98
	7	1107.07	187.60	152.12	696.96	575.49	0.16	194.98
	8	1119.29	192.96	146.46	698.75	574.69	0.15	203.32
	9	1119.06	176.53	156.69	699.84	573.30	0.24	223.02
	10	1123.41	185.05	158.49	696.27	566.82	0.28	228.51
	11	1096.99	193.03	150.89	671.15	548.57	0.44	232.18
	12	1081.86	186.17	152.52	663.26	540.04	0.60	226.58
比上期增减额（亿美元） Changes Compared with Previous Period（100 Million US Dollars）								
2004	1	11.56	12.89	1.61	-2.29	-4.09	0.04	-2.59
	2	-36.56	-4.99	-12.86	-19.50	-19.92	-0.06	0.13
	3	4.05	4.75	2.31	-6.07	-9.30	0.02	-3.43
	4	0.70	-6.32	8.53	-6.87	-9.08	0.02	-7.84
	5	13.63	13.15	-2.96	0.90	-3.41	-0.01	0.64
	6	4.50	5.73	20.70	-23.17	-25.12	0.09	-3.62
	7	15.68	7.40	-18.30	20.11	16.96	-0.10	5.00
	8	12.22	5.36	-5.66	1.79	-0.80	-0.01	8.34
	9	-0.23	-16.43	10.23	1.09	-1.39	0.09	19.70
	10	4.35	8.52	1.80	-3.57	-6.48	0.04	5.49
	11	-26.42	7.98	-7.60	-25.12	-18.25	0.16	3.67
	12	-15.13	-6.86	1.63	-7.89	-8.53	0.16	-5.60
比去年同期增长（%） Increase Rate Year-on-year（%）								
2004	1	-2.41	27.39	-15.95	-5.81	-8.99	25.00	-7.03
	2	-5.38	16.73	-16.30	-8.63	-11.99	-30.00	-6.67
	3	-4.51	25.14	-14.78	-9.37	-13.20	-27.27	-7.47
	4	-4.43	20.46	-9.23	-10.28	-14.36	-10.00	-11.16
	5	-3.96	21.81	-9.24	-10.50	-14.94	-15.00	-11.47
	6	-4.32	20.53	3.65	-13.62	-18.46	13.04	-11.42
	7	-1.81	31.72	-6.27	-10.63	-15.24	-44.83	-7.77
	8	0.46	36.01	-7.18	-9.48	-14.20	-37.50	-1.91
	9	1.72	24.77	-1.19	-7.52	-12.56	166.67	6.91
	10	1.92	19.95	1.38	-6.79	-12.06	600.00	8.50
	11	-0.73	23.61	-6.17	-9.30	-13.81	214.29	10.65
	12	-1.05	20.14	-0.36	-9.60	-14.19	275.00	9.85

国家银行外汇信贷收支主要指标时间序列表
Time Series of Major Indicators in Sources and Uses of Credit Funds of State Banks (Foreign Currency)

年 月 Year Month	各项贷款 Total Loans	短期贷款 Short－term Loans	境内短期贷款 Domestic Short－term Loans	中长期贷款 Medium and Long－term Loans	境内中长期贷款 Domestic Medium and Long－term Loans	进出口贸易融资 Financing for Import and Export Trades	票据融资 Paper Financing	境外筹资转贷款 On－lending of Overseas Financing	有价证券及投资 Securities and Investments
期末余额（亿美元） Balance (100 Million US Dollars)									
2004 1	944.93	302.67	302.63	337.93	325.43	68.67	1.12	190.45	914.08
2	965.65	310.54	310.50	344.03	331.60	75.11	1.03	190.84	966.97
3	981.90	321.27	321.23	345.17	332.41	83.46	1.16	187.19	900.77
4	993.85	325.29	325.24	351.58	338.34	88.12	1.30	184.37	907.94
5	1004.07	329.82	329.73	356.31	343.07	89.39	1.32	183.90	890.82
6	901.03	293.05	292.96	328.99	315.14	92.18	1.28	174.13	843.99
7	895.92	294.46	294.38	329.23	315.61	87.07	1.13	172.31	873.21
8	897.60	326.09	326.01	298.09	285.96	86.92	1.04	173.65	913.02
9	897.57	287.26	287.18	340.71	323.94	85.64	1.22	171.02	988.50
10	885.82	288.22	288.14	329.06	311.83	82.43	1.43	173.12	1021.86
11	896.35	277.49	277.41	341.82	326.35	84.02	1.17	180.96	1050.82
12	903.15	269.00	268.95	351.99	338.26	87.17	1.31	182.68	1015.10
比上期增减额（亿美元） Changes Compared with Previous Period (100 Million US Dollars)									
2004 1	8.13	4.83	4.86	2.76	2.94	2.68	0.04	－2.14	191.34
2	20.72	7.87	7.87	6.10	6.17	6.44	－0.09	0.39	52.89
3	16.25	10.73	10.73	1.14	0.81	8.35	0.13	－3.65	－66.20
4	11.95	4.02	4.01	6.41	5.93	4.66	0.14	－2.82	7.17
5	10.22	4.53	4.49	4.73	4.73	1.27	0.02	－0.47	－17.12
6	8.23	1.47	1.46	7.93	7.29	3.42	－0.04	2.13	－46.83
7	－5.08	1.43	1.44	0.24	0.47	－5.12	－0.14	－1.82	29.22
8	1.68	31.63	31.63	－31.14	－29.64	－0.14	－0.09	1.33	39.81
9	－0.02	－38.83	－38.83	42.62	37.98	－1.28	0.18	－2.62	75.48
10	－11.76	0.96	0.96	－11.63	－12.10	－3.21	0.20	2.09	33.36
11	10.51	4.43	4.43	－2.42	－0.65	1.59	－0.26	7.84	28.96
12	6.81	－8.49	－8.46	10.17	11.90	3.15	0.14	1.73	－35.72
比去年同期增长（%） Increase Rate Year－on－year (%)									
2004 1	27.83	58.49	58.47	24.92	24.22	176.12	72.31	－6.87	23.76
2	29.89	59.70	59.68	26.28	25.68	202.62	28.75	－6.14	32.50
3	29.14	57.48	57.46	25.64	25.09	185.82	34.88	－8.30	16.58
4	27.48	52.56	52.54	26.21	26.90	152.13	58.54	－9.44	15.50
5	25.63	49.06	49.02	25.69	26.39	122.86	59.04	－10.15	17.38
6	22.90	41.86	41.81	24.19	24.57	101.45	50.59	－7.64	8.42
7	21.27	37.19	37.16	24.66	25.04	87.77		－7.55	5.77
8	18.82	43.92	43.89	9.95	10.21	78.75		－4.44	11.89
9	13.32	20.71	20.68	16.17	15.26	67.32	7.89	－6.24	26.75
10	9.95	16.93	16.92	10.50	9.31	61.78	38.83	－5.85	34.13
11	9.16	9.96	9.94	13.61	13.10	43.62	21.88	－1.07	47.21
12	8.32	3.19	3.19	15.59	15.87	33.13	21.30	1.04	40.52

国家银行外汇信贷收支主要指标时间序列表

Time Series of Major Indicators in Sources and Uses of Credit Funds of State Banks（Foreign Currency）

年 月 Year Month	各项存款 Total Deposits	单位活期存款 Demand Deposits by Enterprises	单位定期存款 Time Deposits by Enterprises	储蓄存款 Savings Deposits	定期储蓄 Time Deposits	境外存款 Foreign Deposits	境外筹资 Overseas Financing
期末余额（亿美元） Balance（100 Million US Dollars）							
2005 1	1122.13	211.71	174.06	656.38	532.39	0.54	226.90
2	1134.36	207.11	192.15	657.29	534.78	0.87	226.14
3	1142.67	213.76	192.96	651.13	525.58	0.92	219.58
4	1141.08	228.83	184.44	641.84	519.86	0.93	228.88
5	1124.28	234.36	176.68	627.88	504.32	1.39	222.87
6	1127.42	250.49	169.73	620.28	498.98	0.99	207.19
7	1107.72	238.56	169.66	612.64	491.15	0.99	204.97
8	1120.50	279.73	150.47	602.00	482.80	1.34	211.91
9	1081.21	229.80	168.88	595.91	479.16	1.66	204.30
10	1098.78	245.63	170.64	596.70	477.73	1.74	208.49
11	1105.31	250.27	179.08	593.31	475.86	1.75	211.34
12	1106.37	250.57	173.78	596.72	479.00	1.68	206.32
比上期增减额（亿美元） Changes Compared with Previous Period（100 Million US Dollars）							
2005 1	40.21	25.52	21.52	-6.90	-7.66	-0.05	0.15
2	12.23	-4.60	18.09	0.91	2.39	0.33	-0.76
3	8.31	6.65	0.81	-6.16	-9.20	0.05	-6.56
4	-1.59	15.07	-8.52	-9.29	-5.72	0.01	9.30
5	-16.80	5.53	-7.76	-13.96	-15.54	0.46	-6.01
6	3.14	16.13	-6.95	-7.60	-5.34	-0.40	-15.68
7	-19.70	-11.93	-0.07	-7.64	-7.83		-2.22
8	12.78	41.17	-19.19	-10.64	-8.35	0.35	6.94
9	-39.26	-49.93	18.41	-6.06	-3.62	0.32	-7.61
10	17.54	15.83	1.76	0.76	-1.45	0.08	4.19
11	6.53	4.64	8.44	-3.39	-1.87	0.01	2.85
12	1.06	0.30	-5.30	3.41	3.14	-0.07	-5.02
比去年同期增长（%） Increase Rate Year-on-year（%）							
2005 1	1.54	26.11	12.51	-10.28	-14.87	170.00	11.17
2	6.16	27.15	35.47	-7.69	-11.67	521.43	10.73
3	6.54	27.51	33.86	-7.77	-11.84	475.00	9.35
4	6.32	41.85	20.80	-8.19	-11.45	416.67	18.62
5	3.44	34.33	18.01	-10.31	-13.59	717.65	15.12
6	3.30	39.01	-0.40	-8.36	-10.66	280.77	9.06
7	0.06	27.16	11.53	-12.10	-14.66	518.75	5.12
8	0.11	44.97	2.74	-13.85	-15.99	793.33	4.22
9	-3.38	30.18	7.78	-14.85	-16.42	591.67	-8.39
10	-2.19	32.74	7.67	-14.30	-15.72	521.43	-8.76
11	0.76	29.65	18.68	-11.60	-13.25	297.73	-8.98
12	2.27	34.59	13.94	-10.03	-11.30	180.00	-8.94

国家银行外汇信贷收支主要指标时间序列表

Time Series of Major Indicators in Sources and Uses of Credit Funds of State Banks (Foreign Currency)

年　月 Year Month	各项贷款 Total Loans	短期贷款 Short－term Loans	境内短期贷款 Domestic Short－term Loans	中长期贷款 Medium and Long－term Loans	境内中长期贷款 Domestic Medium and Long－term Loans	进出口贸易融资 Financing for Import and Export Trades	票据融资 Paper Financing	境外筹资转贷款 On－lending of Overseas Financing	有价证券及投资 Securities and Investments
期末余额（亿美元） Balance (100 Million US Dollars)									
2005　1	980.36	277.61	277.56	424.68	410.53	88.42	1.31	177.23	1059.33
2	979.35	277.38	277.33	423.33	409.10	88.24	1.29	177.97	1061.84
3	983.69	275.95	275.90	426.96	412.31	92.47	1.40	175.66	1066.25
4	985.58	270.53	270.48	433.04	418.27	94.41	1.30	175.02	1151.88
5	986.87	274.77	274.66	429.35	414.28	100.14	1.15	170.66	1130.63
6	973.18	263.30	263.24	430.38	414.73	103.86	1.19	165.52	1110.74
7	991.67	287.81	287.81	429.10	413.53	101.86	1.06	162.88	1086.02
8	971.62	262.35	262.35	433.29	416.97	103.09	0.97	162.75	1087.92
9	968.01	255.63	255.63	434.83	418.16	106.19	0.91	161.13	1101.78
10	999.84	248.48	248.48	472.43	454.51	107.87	0.84	160.66	1130.04
11	987.24	239.01	239.01	472.44	455.07	108.86	0.89	156.26	1146.19
12	985.11	234.32	234.32	474.50	452.88	113.17	0.73	153.19	1090.13
比上期增减额（亿美元） Changes Compared with Previous Period (100 Million US Dollars)									
2005　1	77.06	16.42	16.42	64.54	64.13	1.59	0.01	－5.46	44.16
2	－1.03	－0.24	－0.24	－1.35	－1.43	－0.18	－0.03	0.75	2.51
3	4.35	－1.42	－1.42	3.63	3.20	4.23	0.11	－2.32	4.41
4	1.89	－5.41	－5.41	6.08	5.97	1.93	－0.10	－0.63	85.63
5	9.07	9.90	9.84	－2.38	－2.69	6.02	－0.15	－4.33	－21.25
6	4.83	0.96	1.01	4.16	3.58	4.26	0.04	－4.78	－19.89
7	18.52	24.51	24.57	－1.27	－1.19	－2.00	－0.13	－2.63	－24.72
8	－20.07	－25.46	－25.46	4.19	3.44	1.22	－0.09	－0.14	1.90
9	－3.59	－6.71	－6.71	1.54	1.19	3.10	－0.06	－1.61	13.86
10	31.82	－7.16	－7.16	37.59	36.34	1.69	－0.07	－0.47	28.26
11	－12.61	－9.48	－9.48	0.01	0.57	0.99	0.05	－4.40	16.15
12	－2.12	－4.68	－4.68	2.07	－2.19	4.30	－0.16	－3.07	－56.06
比去年同期增长（%） Increase Rate Year－on－year (%)									
2005　1	15.53	4.36	4.35	36.10	36.98	29.68	17.86	－0.70	15.89
2	12.94	1.64	1.63	33.30	34.00	18.32	25.24	－0.51	9.81
3	11.52	－2.20	－2.21	33.91	34.63	11.55	20.69	0.19	18.37
4	10.36	－5.07	－5.08	33.20	34.04	7.84		1.38	26.87
5	10.14	－3.37	－3.38	30.76	31.40	13.04	－12.88	－0.71	26.98
6	10.93	－3.97	－3.96	32.17	33.01	13.56	－7.03	－4.72	31.67
7	13.62	3.89	3.91	31.69	32.44	17.94	－7.08	－5.24	24.43
8	11.18	－14.00	－13.98	46.85	47.37	19.54	－7.69	－6.05	19.21
9	10.78	－4.71	－4.68	28.93	30.46	24.94	－26.23	－5.55	11.51
10	15.84	－7.51	－7.49	44.91	47.17	31.86	－41.26	－6.96	10.64
11	13.08	－7.35	－7.32	39.51	40.80	30.54	－23.93	－13.42	9.13
12	11.99	－6.17	－6.15	36.07	35.20	30.76	－44.27	－15.92	7.44

（三）政策性银行外汇信贷收支主要指标时间序列表（1998—2005年月度时序）

Time Series of Major Indicators in Sources and Uses of Credit Funds of Policy Banks（Foreign Currency）（Monthly Series from 1998 to 2005）

政策性银行外汇信贷收支主要指标时间序列表
Time Series of Major Indicators in Sources and Uses of Credit Funds of Policy Banks（Foreign Currency）

年 月 Year Month	各项存款 Total Deposits						境外筹资 Overseas Financing
		单位活期存款 Demand Deposits by Enterprises	单位定期存款 Time Deposits by Enterprises	储蓄存款 Savings Deposits		境外存款 Foreign Deposits	
					定期储蓄 Time Deposits		
期末余额（亿美元） Balance（100 Million US Dollars）							
1998 1	0.54	0.53					13.85
2	0.67	0.66					14.58
3	0.79	0.78					14.87
4	0.71	0.71					14.65
5	0.73	0.72					15.49
6	0.64	0.64					16.80
7	0.73	0.71					17.63
8	0.55	0.55					18.49
9	0.57	0.57					18.99
10	0.54	0.54					19.98
11	0.58	0.58					19.90
12	0.45	0.45					19.63
比上期增减额（亿美元） Changes Compared with Previous Period（100 Million US Dollars）							
1998 1	-0.40	-0.40					0.26
2	0.13	0.13					0.73
3	0.12	0.12					0.29
4	-0.08	-0.07					-0.22
5	0.02	0.01					0.84
6	-0.09	-0.08					1.31
7	0.09	0.07					0.83
8	-0.18	-0.16					0.86
9	0.02	0.02					0.50
10	-0.03	-0.03					0.99
11	0.04	0.04					-0.08
12	-0.13	-0.13					-0.27

政策性银行外汇信贷收支主要指标时间序列表
Time Series of Major Indicators in Sources and Uses of Credit Funds of Policy Banks (Foreign Currency)

年 月 Year Month	各项贷款 Total Loans								有价证券及投资 Securities and Investments
		短期贷款 Short-term Loans		中长期贷款 Medium and Long-term Loans		进出口贸易融资 Financing for Import and Export Trades	票据融资 Paper Financing	境外筹资转贷款 On-lending of Overseas Financing	
			境内短期贷款 Domestic Short-term Loans		境内中长期贷款 Domestic Medium and Long-term Loans				
期末余额（亿美元） Balance (100 Million US Dollars)									
1998 1	14.88	0.85	0.85	1.95	1.95	0.51		11.55	0.42
2	15.71	1.08	1.08	1.95	1.95	0.51		12.15	0.18
3	16.46	1.56	1.56	1.95	1.95	0.43		12.45	0.18
4	16.74	1.85	1.85	1.34	1.20	0.53		12.96	0.13
5	17.88	2.18	2.18	1.38	1.20	0.58		13.69	0.13
6	19.37	2.35	2.35	2.48	2.20	0.59		13.90	0.13
7	20.50	2.61	2.61	2.48	2.20	0.64		14.73	0.13
8	21.62	2.52	2.52	2.61	2.20	0.72		15.73	0.13
9	22.55	2.99	2.99	2.61	2.20	0.77		16.13	0.13
10	23.31	3.04	3.04	2.63	2.20	0.79		16.81	0.06
11	23.58	3.17	3.17	2.13	1.70	0.84		17.41	0.06
12	23.42	3.31	3.31	1.63	1.20	0.82		17.63	0.06
比上期增减额（亿美元） Changes Compared with Previous Period (100 Million US Dollars)									
1998 1	0.60	0.31	0.31	-0.25	-0.25	0.03		0.51	-0.20
2	0.83	0.23	0.23					0.60	-0.24
3	0.75	0.48	0.48			-0.08		0.30	
4	0.28	0.29	0.29	-0.61	-0.75	0.10		0.51	-0.05
5	1.14	0.33	0.33	0.04		0.05		0.73	
6	1.49	0.17	0.17	1.10	1.00	0.01		0.21	
7	1.13	0.26	0.26			0.05		0.83	
8	1.12	-0.09	-0.09	0.13		0.08		1.00	
9	0.93	0.47	0.47			0.05		0.40	
10	0.76	0.05	0.05	0.02		0.02		0.68	-0.07
11	0.27	0.13	0.13	-0.50	-0.50	0.05		0.60	
12	-0.16	0.14	0.14	-0.50	-0.50	-0.02		0.22	

政策性银行外汇信贷收支主要指标时间序列表

Time Series of Major Indicators in Sources and Uses of Credit Funds of Policy Banks（Foreign Currency）

年 月 Year Month		各项存款 Total Deposits	单位活期存款 Demand Deposits by Enterprises	单位定期存款 Time Deposits by Enterprises	储蓄存款 Savings Deposits	定期储蓄 Time Deposits	境外存款 Foreign Deposits	境外筹资 Overseas Financing
		期末余额（亿美元）Balance（100 Million US Dollars）						
1999	1	0.53	0.53					20.86
	2	0.47	0.47					20.84
	3	0.42	0.42					21.24
	4	0.42	0.42					21.80
	5	0.56	0.56					27.80
	6	0.24	0.24					27.99
	7	0.34	0.33					29.05
	8	0.20	0.19					30.44
	9	0.16	0.15					31.01
	10	0.21	0.20					32.38
	11	0.19	0.18					34.50
	12	0.16	0.15					35.32
		比上期增减额（亿美元）Changes Compared with Previous Period（100 Million US Dollars）						
1999	1	0.08	0.08					1.23
	2	-0.06	-0.06					-0.02
	3	-0.05	-0.05					0.40
	4							0.56
	5	0.14	0.14					6.00
	6	-0.32	-0.32					0.19
	7	0.10	0.09					1.06
	8	-0.14	-0.14					1.39
	9	-0.04	-0.04					0.57
	10	0.05	0.05					1.37
	11	-0.02	-0.02					2.12
	12	-0.03	-0.03					0.82
		比去年同期增长（%）Increase Rate Year-on-year（%）						
1999	1	-1.85						50.61
	2	-29.85	-28.79					42.94
	3	-46.84	-46.15					42.84
	4	-40.85	-40.85					48.81
	5	-23.29	-22.22					79.47
	6	-62.50	-62.50					66.61
	7	-53.42	-53.52					64.78
	8	-63.64	-65.45					64.63
	9	-71.93	-73.68					63.30
	10	-61.11	-62.96					62.06
	11	-67.24	-68.97					73.37
	12	-64.44	-66.67					79.93

政策性银行外汇信贷收支主要指标时间序列表

Time Series of Major Indicators in Sources and Uses of Credit Funds of Policy Banks (Foreign Currency)

年 月 Year Month	各项贷款 Total Loans	短期贷款 Short - term Loans	境内短期贷款 Domestic Short - term Loans	中长期贷款 Medium and Long - term Loans	境内中长期贷款 Domestic Medium and Long - term Loans	进出口贸易融资 Financing for Import and Export Trades	票据融资 Paper Financing	境外筹资转贷款 On - lending of Overseas Financing	有价证券及投资 Securities and Investments
	期末余额（亿美元） Balance (100 Million US Dollars)								
1999 1	24.31	3.38	3.38	1.64	1.20	0.70		18.36	0.06
2	24.87	3.40	3.40	1.67	1.20	0.70		19.07	0.06
3	25.43	3.56	3.56	1.67	1.20	0.70		19.45	0.06
4	26.27	3.74	3.74	1.69	1.20	0.70		20.09	0.06
5	27.49	0.03	0.03	1.69	1.20	0.63		25.09	0.06
6	27.50	0.04	0.04	1.72	1.20	0.62		25.07	0.06
7	28.59	0.14	0.14	1.73	1.20	0.62		26.05	0.11
8	30.07	0.21	0.21	1.75	1.20	0.62		27.44	0.11
9	30.67	0.37	0.37	1.75	1.20	0.62		27.86	0.11
10	33.08	0.48	0.48	1.76	1.20	0.62		30.15	0.11
11	33.36	0.65	0.65	1.76	1.20	0.62		30.26	0.11
12	34.26	0.71	0.71	1.76	1.20	0.62		31.08	0.42
	比上期增减额（亿美元） Changes Compared with Previous Period (100 Million US Dollars)								
1999 1	0.89	0.07	0.07	0.01		- 0.12		0.73	
2	0.56	0.02	0.02	0.03				0.71	
3	0.56	0.16	0.16					0.38	
4	0.84	0.18	0.18	0.02				0.64	
5	1.22	- 3.71	- 3.71			- 0.07		5.00	
6	0.01	0.01	0.01	0.03		- 0.01		- 0.02	
7	1.09	0.10	0.10	0.01				0.98	0.05
8	1.48	0.07	0.07	0.02				1.39	
9	0.60	0.16	0.16					0.42	
10	2.41	0.11	0.11	0.01				2.29	
11	0.28	0.17	0.17					0.11	
12	0.90	0.06	0.06					0.82	0.31
	比去年同期增长（%） Increase Rate Year - on - year (%)								
1999 1	63.37	297.65	297.65	- 15.90	- 38.46	37.25		58.96	- 85.71
2	58.31	214.81	214.81	- 14.36	- 38.46	37.25		56.95	- 66.67
3	54.50	128.21	128.21	- 14.36	- 38.46	62.79		56.22	- 66.67
4	56.93	102.16	102.16	26.12		32.08		55.02	- 53.85
5	53.75	- 98.62	- 98.62	22.46		8.62		83.27	- 53.85
6	41.97	- 98.30	- 98.30	- 30.65	- 45.45	5.08		80.36	- 53.85
7	39.46	- 94.64	- 94.64	- 30.24	- 45.45	- 3.13		76.85	- 15.38
8	39.08	- 91.67	- 91.67	- 32.95	- 45.45	- 13.89		74.44	- 15.38
9	36.01	- 87.63	- 87.63	- 32.95	- 45.45	- 19.48		72.72	- 15.38
10	41.91	- 84.21	- 84.21	- 33.08	- 45.45	- 21.52		79.36	83.33
11	41.48	- 79.50	- 79.50	- 17.37	- 29.41	- 26.19		73.81	83.33
12	46.29	- 78.55	- 78.55	7.98		- 24.39		76.29	600.00

政策性银行外汇信贷收支主要指标时间序列表

Time Series of Major Indicators in Sources and Uses of Credit Funds of Policy Banks（Foreign Currency）

年 月 Year Month	各项存款 Total Deposits	单位活期存款 Demand Deposits by Enterprises	单位定期存款 Time Deposits by Enterprises	储蓄存款 Savings Deposits	定期储蓄 Time Deposits	境外存款 Foreign Deposits	境外筹资 Overseas Financing
	期末余额（亿美元） Balance（100 Million US Dollars）						
2000 1	0.25	0.24					36.31
2	0.25	0.24					37.15
3	0.09	0.08					37.70
4	0.10	0.09					38.31
5	0.12	0.11					39.43
6	0.12	0.11					40.82
7	0.12	0.11					41.40
8	0.14	0.13					41.54
9	0.10	0.09					42.35
10	0.10	0.09					42.91
11	0.23	0.22					43.51
12	0.08	0.07					32.36
	比上期增减额（亿美元） Changes Compared with Previous Period（100 Million US Dollars）						
2000 1	0.09	0.09					0.99
2							0.84
3	-0.16	-0.16					0.55
4	0.01	0.01					0.61
5	0.02	0.02					1.12
6							1.39
7							0.58
8	0.02	0.02					0.14
9	-0.04	-0.04					0.81
10							0.56
11	0.13	0.13					0.60
12	-0.15	-0.15					-11.15
	比去年同期增长（%） Increase Rate Year-on-year（%）						
2000 1	-52.83	-54.72					74.07
2	-46.81	-48.94					78.26
3	-78.57	-80.95					77.50
4	-76.19	-78.57					75.73
5	-78.57	-80.36					41.83
6	-50.00	-54.17					45.84
7	-64.71	-66.67					42.51
8	-30.00	-31.58					36.47
9	-37.50	-40.00					36.57
10	-52.38	-55.00					32.52
11	21.05	22.22					26.12
12	-50.00	-53.33					-8.38

政策性银行外汇信贷收支主要指标时间序列表

Time Series of Major Indicators in Sources and Uses of Credit Funds of Policy Banks (Foreign Currency)

年 月 Year Month	各项贷款 Total Loans	短期贷款 Short – term Loans	境内短期贷款 Domestic Short – term Loans	中长期贷款 Medium and Long – term Loans	境内中长期贷款 Domestic Medium and Long – term Loans	进出口贸易融资 Financing for Import and Export Trades	票据融资 Paper Financing	境外筹资转贷款 On – lending of Overseas Financing	有价证券及投资 Securities and Investments
期末余额（亿美元）Balance (100 Million US Dollars)									
2000 1	35.50	0.91	0.91	1.76	1.20	0.77		32.04	0.42
2	36.62	0.96	0.96	1.77	1.21	0.77		33.10	0.41
3	37.38	1.15	1.15	1.77	1.21	0.77		33.67	0.41
4	39.43	1.30	1.30	2.78	1.21	0.72		34.59	0.41
5	40.66	1.45	1.45	3.45	1.88	0.72		35.00	0.41
6	42.29	1.63	1.63	2.88	1.21	0.72		36.92	0.41
7	42.87	1.78	1.78	2.93	1.21	0.72		37.30	0.86
8	42.22	1.78	1.78	2.35	0.56	0.66		36.91	0.61
9	42.96	1.89	1.89	2.47	0.56	0.51		37.50	0.61
10	43.81	1.87	1.87	2.48	0.52	0.51		38.36	0.53
11	44.65	2.04	2.04	2.51	0.52	0.45		39.03	0.53
12	46.83	2.07	2.07	2.18	0.10	0.54		41.93	0.72
比上期增减额（亿美元）Changes Compared with Previous Period (100 Million US Dollars)									
2000 1	1.24	0.20	0.20			0.15		0.96	
2	1.12	0.05	0.05	0.01	0.01			1.06	-0.01
3	0.76	0.19	0.19					0.57	
4	2.05	0.15	0.15	1.01		-0.05		0.92	
5	1.23	0.15	0.15	0.67	0.67			0.41	
6	1.63	0.18	0.18	-0.57	-0.67			1.92	
7	0.58	0.15	0.15	0.05				0.38	0.45
8	-0.65			-0.58	-0.65	-0.06		-0.39	-0.25
9	0.74	0.11	0.11	0.12		-0.15		0.59	
10	0.85	-0.02	-0.02	0.01	-0.04			0.86	-0.08
11	0.84	0.17	0.17	0.03		-0.06		0.67	
12	2.18	0.03	0.03	-0.33	-0.42	0.09		2.90	0.19
比去年同期增长（%）Increase Rate Year – on – year (%)									
2000 1	46.03	-73.08	-73.08	7.32		10.00		74.51	600.00
2	47.25	-71.76	-71.76	5.99	0.83	10.00		73.57	583.33
3	46.99	-67.70	-67.70	5.99	0.83	10.00		73.11	583.33
4	50.10	-65.24	-65.24	64.50	0.83	2.86		72.18	583.33
5	47.91	4733.33	4733.33	104.14	56.67	14.29		39.50	583.33
6	53.78	3975.00	3975.00	67.44	0.83	16.13		47.27	583.33
7	49.95	1171.43	1171.43	69.36	0.83	16.13		43.19	681.82
8	40.41	747.62	747.62	34.29	-53.33	6.45		34.51	454.55
9	40.07	410.81	410.81	41.14	-53.33	-17.74		34.60	454.55
10	32.44	289.58	289.58	40.91	-56.67	-17.74		27.23	381.82
11	33.84	213.85	213.85	42.61	-56.67	-27.42		28.98	381.82
12	36.69	191.55	191.55	23.86	-91.67	-12.90		34.91	71.43

政策性银行外汇信贷收支主要指标时间序列表
Time Series of Major Indicators in Sources and Uses of Credit Funds of Policy Banks（Foreign Currency）

年 月 Year Month		各项存款 Total Deposits	单位活期存款 Demand Deposits by Enterprises	单位定期存款 Time Deposits by Enterprises	储蓄存款 Savings Deposits	定期储蓄 Time Deposits	境外存款 Foreign Deposits	境外筹资 Overseas Financing
期末余额（亿美元） Balance（100 Million US Dollars）								
2001	1	0.18	0.15					46.06
	2	0.18	0.15					46.86
	3	0.55	0.52					47.15
	4	0.15	0.12					47.93
	5	0.08	0.06					49.33
	6	0.10	0.09					49.36
	7	0.08	0.07					50.29
	8	0.08	0.07					50.23
	9	0.11	0.10					50.27
	10	0.10	0.09					51.35
	11	0.06	0.05					51.62
	12	0.07	0.07					52.14
比上期增减额（亿美元） Changes Compared with Previous Period（100 Million US Dollars）								
2001	1	0.10	0.08					13.70
	2							0.80
	3	0.37	0.37					0.29
	4	-0.40	-0.40					0.78
	5	-0.07	-0.06					1.40
	6	0.02	0.03					0.03
	7	-0.02	-0.02					0.93
	8							-0.06
	9	0.03	0.03					0.04
	10	-0.01	-0.01					1.08
	11	-0.04	-0.04					0.27
	12	0.01	0.02					0.52
比去年同期增长（%） Increase Rate Year-on-year（%）								
2001	1	-28.00	-37.50					26.85
	2	-28.00	-37.50					26.14
	3	511.11	550.00					25.07
	4	50.00	33.33					25.11
	5	-33.33	-45.45					25.11
	6	-16.67	-18.18					20.92
	7	-33.33	-36.36					21.47
	8	-42.86	-46.15					20.92
	9	10.00	11.11					18.70
	10							19.67
	11	-73.91	-77.27					18.64
	12	-12.50						61.12

政策性银行外汇信贷收支主要指标时间序列表
Time Series of Major Indicators in Sources and Uses of Credit Funds of Policy Banks (Foreign Currency)

年 月 Year Month		各项贷款 Total Loans	短期贷款 Short - term Loans	境内短期贷款 Domestic Short - term Loans	中长期贷款 Medium and Long - term Loans	境内中长期贷款 Domestic Medium and Long - term Loans	进出口贸易融资 Financing for Import and Export Trades	票据融资 Paper Financing	境外筹资转贷款 On - lending of Overseas Financing	有价证券及投资 Securities and Investments
期末余额（亿美元） Balance (100 Million US Dollars)										
2001	1	47.50	2.22	2.22	2.28	0.10	0.59		42.41	1.46
	2	48.34	2.22	2.22	2.28	0.10	0.59		43.25	1.88
	3	49.18	2.69	2.69	2.32	0.10	0.51		43.66	2.27
	4	49.86	2.39	2.39	2.45	0.10	0.51		44.51	4.61
	5	51.86	2.46	2.46	2.52	0.10	0.51		46.37	4.72
	6	51.73	2.48	2.48	2.63	0.10	0.54		46.08	4.40
	7	52.77	2.51	2.51	2.65	0.10	0.50		47.11	2.59
	8	54.58	2.57	2.57	2.98	0.10	0.50		48.53	3.28
	9	55.38	2.71	2.71	3.14	0.10	0.52		49.01	2.36
	10	56.40	2.74	2.74	3.41	0.10	0.54		49.71	2.27
	11	56.99	2.85	2.85	3.53	0.10	0.54		50.07	2.07
	12	57.65	2.89	2.89	3.68	0.10	0.47		50.61	3.87
比上期增减额（亿美元） Changes Compared with Previous Period (100 Million US Dollars)										
2001	1	0.68	0.15	0.15	0.10		-0.03		0.46	0.74
	2	0.84							0.84	0.42
	3	0.84	0.47	0.47	0.04		-0.08		0.41	0.39
	4	0.68	-0.30	-0.30	0.13				0.85	2.34
	5	2.00	0.07	0.07	0.07				1.86	0.11
	6	-0.13	0.02	0.02	0.11		0.03		-0.29	-0.32
	7	1.04	0.03	0.03	0.02		-0.04		1.03	-1.81
	8	1.81	0.06	0.06	0.33				1.42	0.69
	9	0.80	0.14	0.14	0.16		0.02		0.48	-0.92
	10	1.02	0.03	0.03	0.27		0.02		0.70	-0.09
	11	0.59	0.11	0.11	0.12				0.36	-0.20
	12	0.66	0.04	0.04	0.15		-0.07		0.54	1.80
比去年同期增长（%） Increase Rate Year - on - year (%)										
2001	1	33.80	143.96	143.96	29.55	-91.67	-23.38		32.37	247.62
	2	32.00	131.25	131.25	28.81	-91.74	-23.38		30.66	358.54
	3	31.57	133.91	133.91	31.07	-91.74	-33.77		29.67	453.66
	4	26.45	83.85	83.85	-11.87	-91.74	-29.17		28.68	1024.39
	5	27.55	69.66	69.66	-26.96	-94.68	-29.17		32.49	1051.22
	6	22.32	52.15	52.15	-8.68	-91.74	-25.00		24.81	973.17
	7	23.09	41.01	41.01	-9.56	-91.74	-30.56		26.30	201.16
	8	29.28	44.38	44.38	26.81	-82.14	-24.24		31.48	437.70
	9	28.91	43.39	43.39	27.13	-82.14	1.96		30.69	286.89
	10	28.74	46.52	46.52	37.50	-80.77	5.88		29.59	328.30
	11	27.64	39.71	39.71	40.64	-80.77	20.00		28.29	290.57
	12	23.10	39.61	39.61	68.81		-12.96		20.70	437.50

政策性银行外汇信贷收支主要指标时间序列表
Time Series of Major Indicators in Sources and Uses of Credit Funds of Policy Banks（Foreign Currency）

年 月 Year Month	各项存款 Total Deposits	单位活期存款 Demand Deposits by Enterprises	单位定期存款 Time Deposits by Enterprises	储蓄存款 Savings Deposits	定期储蓄 Time Deposits	境外存款 Foreign Deposits	境外筹资 Overseas Financing
期末余额（亿美元） Balance（100 Million US Dollars）							
2002 1	0.07	0.07					52.27
2	0.07	0.07					52.32
3	0.06	0.06					52.46
4	0.06	0.06					53.46
5	0.27	0.27					54.84
6	0.05	0.05					56.06
7	0.08	0.08					57.65
8	0.22	0.22					58.27
9	0.08	0.08					59.36
10	0.09	0.09					59.72
11	0.14	0.14					60.03
12	0.13	0.10	0.03				61.11
比上期增减额（亿美元） Changes Compared with Previous Period（100 Million US Dollars）							
2002 1							0.13
2							0.05
3	-0.01	-0.01					0.14
4							1.00
5	0.21	0.21					1.38
6	-0.22	-0.22					1.22
7	0.03	0.03					1.59
8	0.14	0.14					0.62
9	-0.14	-0.14					1.09
10	0.01	0.01					0.36
11	0.05	0.05					0.31
12	-0.01	-0.04	0.03				1.08
比去年同期增长（%） Increase Rate Year-on-year（%）							
2002 1	-61.11	-53.33					13.48
2	-61.11	-53.33					11.65
3	-89.09	-88.46					11.26
4	-60.00	-50.00					11.54
5	237.50	350.00					11.17
6	-50.00	-44.44					13.57
7		14.29					14.64
8	175.00	214.29					16.01
9	-27.27	-20.00					18.08
10	-10.00						16.30
11	133.33	180.00					16.29
12	85.71	42.86	—				17.20

政策性银行外汇信贷收支主要指标时间序列表
Time Series of Major Indicators in Sources and Uses of Credit Funds of Policy Banks (Foreign Currency)

年　月 Year Month		各项贷款 Total Loans	短期贷款 Short－term Loans	境内短期贷款 Domestic Short－term Loans	中长期贷款 Medium and Long－term Loans	境内中长期贷款 Domestic Medium and Long－term Loans	进出口贸易融资 Financing for Import and Export Trades	票据融资 Paper Financing	境外筹资转贷款 On－lending of Overseas Financing	有价证券及投资 Securities and Investments
		期末余额（亿美元） Balance (100 Million US Dollars)								
2002	1	58.15	2.96	2.96	3.92	0.30	0.46		50.81	5.38
	2	58.68	2.97	2.97	4.19	0.30	0.37		51.15	5.21
	3	60.01	3.07	3.07	4.44	0.30	0.37		52.13	5.69
	4	60.74	2.30	2.30	4.63	0.30	0.37		53.44	5.78
	5	61.94	2.45	2.45	4.84	0.30	0.37		54.28	5.54
	6	63.26	2.45	2.45	5.02	0.30	0.36		55.43	6.62
	7	63.90	2.55	2.55	5.23	0.36	0.36		55.76	6.46
	8	65.11	2.55	2.55	5.95	0.76	0.36		56.25	6.44
	9	70.03	1.58	1.58	10.66	5.21	0.32		57.45	4.01
	10	71.16	2.12	2.12	10.87	5.21	0.32		57.83	3.92
	11	71.37	1.87	1.87	11.18	5.41	0.32		57.98	3.54
	12	73.33	1.81	1.81	12.18	6.29	0.32		58.99	3.97
		比上期增减额（亿美元） Changes Compared with Previous Period (100 Million US Dollars)								
2002	1	0.50	0.07	0.07	0.24	0.20	－0.01		0.20	1.51
	2	0.53	0.01	0.01	0.27		－0.09		0.34	－0.17
	3	1.33	0.10	0.10	0.25				0.98	0.48
	4	0.73	－0.77	－0.77	0.19				1.31	0.09
	5	1.20	0.15	0.15	0.21				0.84	－0.24
	6	1.32			0.18		－0.01		1.15	1.08
	7	0.64	0.10	0.10	0.21	0.06			0.33	－0.16
	8	1.21			0.72	0.40			0.49	－0.02
	9	4.92	－0.97	－0.97	4.71	4.45	－0.04		1.20	－2.43
	10	1.13	0.54	0.54	0.21				0.38	－0.09
	11	0.21	－0.25	－0.25	0.31	0.20			0.15	－0.38
	12	1.96	－0.06	－0.06	1.00	0.88			1.01	0.43
		比去年同期增长（%） Increase Rate Year－on－year (%)								
2002	1	22.42	33.33	33.33	71.93	200.00	－22.03		19.81	268.49
	2	21.39	33.78	33.78	83.77	200.00	－37.29		18.27	177.13
	3	22.02	14.13	14.13	91.38	200.00	－27.45		19.40	150.66
	4	21.82	－3.77	－3.77	88.98	200.00	－27.45		20.06	25.38
	5	19.44	－0.41	－0.41	92.06	200.00	－27.45		17.06	17.37
	6	22.29	－1.21	－1.21	90.87	200.00	－33.33		20.29	50.45
	7	21.09	1.59	1.59	97.36	260.00	－28.00		18.36	149.42
	8	19.29	－0.78	－0.78	99.66	660.00	－28.00		15.91	96.34
	9	26.45	－41.70	－41.70	239.49	5110.00	－38.46		17.22	69.92
	10	26.17	－22.63	－22.63	218.77	5110.00	－40.74		16.33	72.69
	11	25.23	－34.39	－34.39	216.71	5310.00	－40.74		15.80	71.01
	12	27.20	－37.37	－37.37	230.98	6190.00	－31.91		16.56	2.58

政策性银行外汇信贷收支主要指标时间序列表
Time Series of Major Indicators in Sources and Uses of Credit Funds of Policy Banks（Foreign Currency）

年 月 Year Month		各项存款 Total Deposits	单位活期存款 Demand Deposits by Enterprises	单位定期存款 Time Deposits by Enterprises	储蓄存款 Savings Deposits	定期储蓄 Time Deposits	境外存款 Foreign Deposits	境外筹资 Overseas Financing
期末余额（亿美元）Balance（100 Million US Dollars）								
2003	1	0.21	0.18	0.03				62.04
	2	0.32	0.29	0.03				62.39
	3	0.53	0.13	0.35				63.07
	4	0.55	0.15	0.35				63.84
	5	4.53	4.31	0.03				64.66
	6	4.77	4.41	0.17				64.41
	7	0.93	0.50	0.03				64.24
	8	1.12	0.70	0.03				63.70
	9	1.73	1.18	0.03				65.16
	10	1.95	1.39	0.03				65.59
	11	2.47	1.95	0.03				65.87
	12	2.72	2.20	0.04				66.77
比上期增减额（亿美元）Changes Compared with Previous Period（100 Million US Dollars）								
2003	1	0.08	0.08					0.89
	2	0.11	0.11					0.35
	3	0.21	-0.16	0.32				0.68
	4	0.02	0.02					0.77
	5	3.98	4.16	-0.32				0.82
	6	0.24	0.10	0.14				-0.25
	7	-3.84	-3.91	-0.14				-0.17
	8	0.19	0.20					-0.54
	9	0.61	0.48					1.46
	10	0.22	0.21					0.43
	11	0.52	0.56					0.28
	12	0.25	0.25	0.01				0.90
比去年同期增长（%）Increase Rate Year-on-year（%）								
2003	1	200.00	157.14	—				18.69
	2	357.14	314.29	—				19.25
	3	783.33	116.67	—				20.22
	4	816.67	150.00	—				19.42
	5	1577.78	1496.30	—				17.91
	6	9440.00	8720.00	—				14.89
	7	1062.50	525.00	—				11.43
	8	409.09	218.18	—				9.32
	9	2062.50	1375.00	—				9.77
	10	2066.67	1444.44	—				9.83
	11	1664.29	1292.86	—				9.73
	12	1992.31	2100.00	33.33				9.26

政策性银行外汇信贷收支主要指标时间序列表

Time Series of Major Indicators in Sources and Uses of Credit Funds of Policy Banks (Foreign Currency)

年 月 Year Month		各项贷款 Total Loans	短期贷款 Short-term Loans	境内短期贷款 Domestic Short-term Loans	中长期贷款 Medium and Long-term Loans	境内中长期贷款 Domestic Medium and Long-term Loans	进出口贸易融资 Financing for Import and Export Trades	票据融资 Paper Financing	境外筹资转贷款 On-lending of Overseas Financing	有价证券及投资 Securities and Investments
		期末余额（亿美元）Balance (100 Million US Dollars)								
2003	1	74.30	1.83	1.83	12.26	6.29	0.32		59.86	3.59
	2	74.60	1.83	1.83	12.28	6.28	0.32		60.14	4.64
	3	76.29	1.87	1.87	13.46	7.12	0.32		60.61	6.58
	4	78.68	2.41	2.41	14.32	7.67	0.32		61.60	6.08
	5	83.72	2.46	2.46	18.55	11.78	0.32		62.36	5.75
	6	83.32	0.91	0.91	19.59	12.79	0.63		62.14	5.86
	7	83.97	1.33	1.33	19.77	13.01	0.85		61.97	6.90
	8	84.44	1.36	1.36	21.20	14.28	0.89		60.94	7.72
	9	90.31	1.36	1.36	25.74	18.55	0.97		62.19	8.91
	10	91.75	1.75	1.75	26.41	18.97	0.93		62.61	7.76
	11	96.31	1.81	1.81	26.79	19.33	4.82		62.84	7.69
	12	101.31	1.96	1.96	29.29	21.33	6.32		63.68	7.57
		比上期增减额（亿美元）Changes Compared with Previous Period (100 Million US Dollars)								
2003	1	0.97	0.02	0.02	0.08				0.87	-0.40
	2	0.30			0.02	-0.01			0.28	1.05
	3	1.69	0.04	0.04	1.18	0.84			0.47	1.94
	4	2.39	0.54	0.54	0.86	0.55			0.99	-0.50
	5	5.04	0.05	0.05	4.23	4.11			0.76	-0.33
	6	-0.40	-1.55	-1.55	1.04	1.01	0.31		-0.22	0.11
	7	0.65	0.42	0.42	0.18	0.22	0.22		-0.17	1.04
	8	0.47	0.03	0.03	1.43	1.27	0.04		-1.03	0.82
	9	5.87			4.54	4.27	0.08		1.25	1.19
	10	1.44	0.39	0.39	0.67	0.42	-0.04		0.42	-1.15
	11	4.56	0.06	0.06	0.38	0.36	3.89		0.23	-0.07
	12	5.00	0.15	0.15	2.50	2.00	1.50		0.84	-0.12
		比去年同期增长（%）Increase Rate Year-on-year (%)								
2003	1	27.77	-38.18	-38.18	212.76	1996.67	-30.43		17.81	-33.27
	2	27.13	-38.38	-38.38	193.08	1993.33	-13.51		17.58	-10.94
	3	27.13	-39.09	-39.09	203.15	2273.33	-13.51		16.27	15.64
	4	29.54	4.78	4.78	209.29	2456.67	-13.51		15.27	5.19
	5	35.16	0.41	0.41	283.26	3826.67	-13.51		14.89	3.79
	6	31.71	-62.86	-62.86	290.24	4163.33	75.00		12.11	-11.48
	7	31.41	-47.84	-47.84	278.01	3513.89	136.11		11.14	6.81
	8	29.69	-46.67	-46.67	256.30	1778.95	147.22		8.34	19.88
	9	28.96	-13.92	-13.92	141.46	256.05	203.13		8.25	122.19
	10	28.93	-17.45	-17.45	142.96	264.11	190.63		8.27	97.96
	11	34.94	-3.21	-3.21	139.62	257.30	1406.25		8.38	117.23
	12	38.16	8.29	8.29	140.48	239.11	1875.00		7.95	90.68

政策性银行外汇信贷收支主要指标时间序列表

Time Series of Major Indicators in Sources and Uses of Credit Funds of Policy Banks（Foreign Currency）

年 月 Year Month		各项存款 Total Deposits	单位活期存款 Demand Deposits by Enterprises	单位定期存款 Time Deposits by Enterprises	储蓄存款 Savings Deposits	定期储蓄 Time Deposits	境外存款 Foreign Deposits	境外筹资 Overseas Financing
		期末余额（亿美元） Balance（100 Million US Dollars）						
2004	1	2.36	1.67	0.03				66.14
	2	2.19	1.45	0.04				66.38
	3	2.18	1.52	0.04				65.03
	4	2.56	1.86	0.04				65.02
	5	2.99	2.09	0.11				65.24
	6	4.87	3.50	0.03			0.12	65.07
	7	4.68	3.35	0.03				71.86
	8	3.36	2.20	0.03				71.87
	9	4.06	2.70	0.03			0.11	74.55
	10	3.26	1.88	0.03			0.11	83.73
	11	2.36	1.08	0.03			0.11	83.93
	12	2.95	1.27	0.33			0.42	84.76
		比上期增减额（亿美元） Changes Compared with Previous Period（100 Million US Dollars）						
2004	1	-0.36	-0.53	-0.01				-0.63
	2	-0.17	-0.22	0.01				0.24
	3	-0.01	0.07					-1.35
	4	0.38	0.34					-0.01
	5	0.43	0.23	0.07				0.22
	6	1.88	1.41	-0.08			0.12	-0.17
	7	-0.19	-0.15				-0.12	6.79
	8	-1.32	-1.15					0.01
	9	0.70	0.50				0.11	2.68
	10	-0.80	-0.82					9.18
	11	-0.90	-0.80					0.20
	12	0.59	0.19	0.30			0.31	0.83
		比去年同期增长（%） Increase Rate Year-on-year（%）						
2004	1	1023.81	827.78					6.61
	2	584.38	400.00	33.33				6.40
	3	311.32	1069.23	-88.57				3.11
	4	365.45	1140.00	-88.57				1.85
	5	-34.00	-51.51	266.67				0.90
	6	2.10	-20.63	-82.35				1.02
	7	403.23	570.00				—	11.86
	8	200.00	214.29					12.83
	9	134.68	128.81				—	14.41
	10	67.18	35.25				—	27.66
	11	-4.45	-44.62				—	27.42
	12	8.46	-42.27	725.00			—	26.94

政策性银行外汇信贷收支主要指标时间序列表

Time Series of Major Indicators in Sources and Uses of Credit Funds of Policy Banks（Foreign Currency）

年 月 Year Month		各项贷款 Total Loans	短期贷款 Short-term Loans	境内短期贷款 Domestic Short-term Loans	中长期贷款 Medium and Long-term Loans	境内中长期贷款 Domestic Medium and Long-term Loans	进出口贸易融资 Financing for Import and Export Trades	票据融资 Paper Financing	境外筹资转贷款 On-lending of Overseas Financing	有价证券及投资 Securities and Investments
		期末余额（亿美元） Balance（100 Million US Dollars）								
2004	1	101.40	1.98	1.98	29.47	21.52	6.86		63.03	6.28
	2	102.49	2.01	2.01	29.58	21.65	7.48		63.36	5.97
	3	103.01	2.04	2.04	30.46	22.16	8.57		61.88	6.42
	4	105.48	2.04	2.04	31.64	22.88	9.70		62.04	6.96
	5	107.67	1.83	1.83	32.37	23.59	11.17		62.24	7.12
	6	112.02	1.63	1.63	33.57	24.17	14.69		62.05	7.00
	7	113.22	2.03	2.03	33.75	24.40	15.85		61.51	6.86
	8	113.91	2.58	2.58	33.42	23.86	16.39		61.43	9.76
	9	118.22	2.76	2.76	37.32	24.90	16.50		61.55	8.79
	10	119.48	2.96	2.96	37.90	24.99	16.06		62.47	6.92
	11	120.36	3.55	3.55	38.27	25.33	16.11		62.34	6.81
	12	124.06	3.60	3.60	42.08	28.74	15.26		63.02	9.81
		比上期增减额（亿美元） Changes Compared with Previous Period（100 Million US Dollars）								
2004	1	0.09	0.02	0.02	0.18	0.19	0.54		-0.65	-1.29
	2	1.09	0.03	0.03	0.11	0.13	0.62		0.33	-0.31
	3	0.52	0.03	0.03	0.88	0.51	1.09		-1.48	0.45
	4	2.47			1.18	0.72	1.13		0.16	0.54
	5	2.19	-0.21	-0.21	0.73	0.71	1.47		0.20	0.16
	6	4.35	-0.20	-0.20	1.20	0.58	3.52		-0.19	-0.12
	7	1.20	0.40	0.40	0.18	0.23	1.16		-0.54	-0.14
	8	0.69	0.55	0.55	-0.33	-0.54	0.54		-0.08	2.90
	9	4.31	0.18	0.18	3.90	1.04	0.11		0.12	-0.97
	10	1.26	0.20	0.20	0.58	0.09	-0.44		0.92	-1.87
	11	0.88	0.59	0.59	0.37	0.34	0.05		-0.13	-0.11
	12	3.70	0.05	0.05	3.81	3.41	-0.85		0.68	3.00
		比去年同期增长（%） Increase Rate Year-on-year（%）								
2004	1	36.47	8.20	8.20	140.38	242.13	2043.75		5.30	74.93
	2	37.39	9.84	9.84	140.88	244.75	2237.50		5.35	28.66
	3	35.02	9.09	9.09	126.30	211.24	2578.13		2.10	-2.43
	4	34.06	-15.35	-15.35	120.95	198.31	2931.25		0.71	14.47
	5	28.61	-25.61	-25.61	74.50	100.25	3390.63		-0.19	23.83
	6	34.45	79.12	79.12	71.36	88.98	2231.75		-0.14	19.45
	7	34.83	52.63	52.63	70.71	87.55	1764.71		-0.74	-0.58
	8	34.90	89.71	89.71	57.64	67.09	1741.57		0.80	26.42
	9	30.90	102.94	102.94	44.99	34.23	1601.03		-1.03	-1.35
	10	30.22	69.14	69.14	43.51	31.73	1626.88		-0.22	-10.82
	11	24.97	96.13	96.13	42.85	31.04	234.23		-0.80	-11.44
	12	22.46	83.67	83.67	43.67	34.74	141.46		-1.04	29.59

政策性银行外汇信贷收支主要指标时间序列表
Time Series of Major Indicators in Sources and Uses of Credit Funds of Policy Banks（Foreign Currency）

年 月 Year Month		各项存款 Total Deposits	单位活期存款 Demand Deposits by Enterprises	单位定期存款 Time Deposits by Enterprises	储蓄存款 Savings Deposits	定期储蓄 Time Deposits	境外存款 Foreign Deposits	境外筹资 Overseas Financing
期末余额（亿美元） Balance（100 Million US Dollars）								
2005	1	47.24	15.35	31.03			0.42	82.93
	2	47.15	14.82	31.09			0.77	83.47
	3	47.70	15.30	31.24			0.82	82.65
	4	62.12	45.77	15.24			0.82	82.80
	5	63.00	46.33	15.17			1.28	81.10
	6	63.12	46.65	15.17			0.90	80.67
	7	63.31	47.10	15.12			0.90	89.33
	8	63.73	46.97	15.37			1.19	94.76
	9	62.13	45.35	15.47			1.18	94.12
	10	62.56	45.71	15.53			1.18	99.20
	11	63.43	46.30	15.41			1.61	104.23
	12	65.38	48.15	15.10			1.59	104.57
比上期增减额（亿美元） Changes Compared with Previous Period（100 Million US Dollars）								
2005	1	44.29	14.08	30.70				-1.83
	2	-0.09	-0.53	0.06			0.35	0.54
	3	0.55	0.48	0.15			0.05	-0.82
	4	14.42	30.47	-16.00				0.15
	5	0.88	0.56	-0.07			0.46	-1.70
	6	0.12	0.32				-0.38	-0.43
	7	0.19	0.45	-0.05				8.66
	8	0.42	-0.13	0.25			0.29	5.43
	9	-1.60	-1.62	0.10			-0.01	-0.64
	10	0.43	0.36	0.06				5.08
	11	0.87	0.59	-0.12			0.43	5.03
	12	1.95	1.85	-0.31			-0.02	0.34
比去年同期增长（%） Increase Rate Year-on-year（%）								
2005	1	1901.69	819.16	103333.33			—	25.39
	2	2052.97	922.07	77625.00			—	25.75
	3	2088.07	906.58	78000.00			—	27.10
	4	2326.56	2360.75	38000.00			—	27.35
	5	2007.02	2116.75	13690.91			—	24.31
	6	1196.10	1232.86	50466.67			650.00	23.97
	7	1252.78	1305.97	50300.00			—	24.31
	8	1796.73	2035.00	51133.33			—	31.85
	9	1430.30	1579.63	51466.67			972.73	26.25
	10	1819.02	2331.38	51666.67			972.73	18.48
	11	2587.71	4187.04	51266.67			1363.64	24.19
	12	2116.27	3691.34	4475.76			278.57	23.37

政策性银行外汇信贷收支主要指标时间序列表
Time Series of Major Indicators in Sources and Uses of Credit Funds of Policy Banks (Foreign Currency)

年 月 Year Month		各项贷款 Total Loans	短期贷款 Short－term Loans	境内短期贷款 Domestic Short－term Loans	中长期贷款 Medium and Long－term Loans	境内中长期贷款 Domestic Medium and Long－term Loans	进出口贸易融资 Financing for Import and Export Trades	票据融资 Paper Financing	境外筹资转贷款 On－lending of Overseas Financing	有价证券及投资 Securities and Investments
		期末余额（亿美元） Balance (100 Million US Dollars)								
2005	1	183.06	3.58	3.58	102.69	88.93	15.29		61.40	13.28
	2	184.27	3.43	3.43	103.39	89.16	15.43		61.92	12.33
	3	185.10	3.86	3.86	103.78	89.13	16.11		61.25	11.07
	4	188.03	4.15	4.15	105.79	91.02	16.91		61.08	9.44
	5	187.19	4.36	4.36	106.10	91.03	16.92		59.71	8.78
	6	189.55	3.19	3.19	110.29	94.64	16.59		59.36	9.05
	7	191.07	4.03	4.03	110.25	94.77	18.12		58.55	18.64
	8	193.29	4.79	4.79	111.35	95.12	18.20		58.83	17.09
	9	199.29	6.21	6.21	114.55	97.97	20.13		58.28	14.64
	10	223.64	5.71	5.71	136.06	118.14	23.25		58.50	11.02
	11	224.15	5.12	5.12	138.57	121.21	22.92		57.42	33.07
	12	237.55	4.81	4.81	151.66	130.04	23.25		57.69	32.36
		比上期增减额（亿美元） Changes Compared with Previous Period (100 Million US Dollars)								
2005	1	59.00	－0.02	－0.02	60.61	60.19	0.03		－1.62	3.47
	2	1.21	－0.15	－0.15	0.70	0.23	0.14		0.52	－0.95
	3	0.83	0.43	0.43	0.39	－0.03	0.68		－0.67	－1.26
	4	2.93	0.29	0.29	2.01	1.89	0.80		－0.17	－1.63
	5	－0.84	0.21	0.21	0.31	0.01	0.01		－1.37	－0.66
	6	2.36	－1.17	－1.17	4.19	3.61	－0.33		－0.35	0.27
	7	1.52	0.84	0.84	－0.04	0.13	1.53		－0.81	9.59
	8	2.22	0.76	0.76	1.10	0.35	0.08		0.28	－1.55
	9	6.00	1.42	1.42	3.20	2.85	1.93		－0.55	－2.45
	10	24.35	－0.50	－0.50	21.51	20.17	3.12		0.22	－3.62
	11	0.51	－0.59	－0.59	2.51	3.07	－0.33		－1.08	22.05
	12	13.40	－0.31	－0.31	13.09	8.83	0.33		0.27	－0.71
		比去年同期增长（%） Increase Rate Year－on－year (%)								
2005	1	80.53	80.81	80.81	248.46	313.24	122.89		－2.59	111.46
	2	79.79	70.65	70.65	249.53	311.82	106.28		－2.27	106.53
	3	79.69	89.22	89.22	240.71	302.21	87.98		－1.02	72.43
	4	78.26	103.43	103.43	234.36	297.81	74.33		－1.55	35.63
	5	73.86	138.25	138.25	227.77	285.88	51.48		－4.06	23.31
	6	69.21	95.71	95.71	228.54	291.56	12.93		－4.34	29.29
	7	68.76	98.52	98.52	226.67	288.40	14.32		－4.81	171.72
	8	69.69	85.66	85.66	233.18	298.66	11.04		－4.23	75.10
	9	68.58	125.00	125.00	206.94	293.45	22.00		－5.31	66.55
	10	87.18	92.91	92.91	259.00	372.75	44.77		－6.36	59.25
	11	86.23	44.23	44.23	262.09	378.52	42.27		－7.89	385.61
	12	91.48	33.61	33.61	260.41	352.47	52.36		－8.46	229.87

（四）国有商业银行外汇信贷收支主要指标时间序列表（1998—2005 年月度时序）

Time Series of Major Indicators in Sources and Uses of Credit Funds of State－owned Commercial Banks（Foreign Currency）（Monthly Series from 1998 to 2005）

国有商业银行外汇信贷收支主要指标时间序列表

Time Series of Major Indicators in Sources and Uses of Credit Funds of State－owned Commercial Banks（Foreign Currency）

年 月 Year Month	各项存款 Total Deposits	单位活期存款 Demand Deposits by Enterprises	单位定期存款 Time Deposits by Enterprises	储蓄存款 Savings Deposits	定期储蓄 Time Deposits	境外存款 Foreign Deposits	境外筹资 Overseas Financing
期末余额（亿美元） Balance（100 Million US Dollars）							
1998 1	577.11	101.97	158.50	277.58	257.36	2.50	286.10
2	592.96	104.78	163.65	286.81	266.41	2.37	285.68
3	599.93	101.69	167.98	296.17	276.01	1.98	285.41
4	601.12	95.55	169.69	304.11	283.30	1.89	273.24
5	612.08	97.40	173.40	311.45	290.01	1.78	281.03
6	627.52	94.87	176.52	321.04	299.44	1.83	271.49
7	640.62	93.86	183.49	333.38	311.77	2.15	269.30
8	663.20	98.67	187.70	346.78	324.67	1.71	268.04
9	674.50	99.67	188.29	354.15	332.52	1.64	265.25
10	674.71	102.79	178.96	362.28	339.91	1.63	273.82
11	687.70	99.68	183.94	371.22	347.64	1.59	284.25
12	701.87	96.69	193.08	376.56	351.90	1.60	277.07
比上期增减额（亿美元） Changes Compared with Previous Period（100 Million US Dollars）							
1998 1	－8.84	－12.69	－3.01	9.31	10.02	－0.05	－3.97
2	15.85	2.81	5.15	9.23	9.05	－0.13	－0.42
3	6.97	－3.09	4.33	9.36	9.60	－0.39	－0.27
4	1.19	－6.14	1.71	7.94	7.29	－0.09	－12.17
5	10.96	1.85	3.71	7.34	6.71	－0.11	7.79
6	15.45	－2.53	3.12	9.59	9.43	0.05	－9.54
7	13.10	－1.01	6.97	12.34	12.33	0.32	－2.19
8	22.58	4.81	4.21	13.40	12.90	－0.44	－1.26
9	11.31	1.00	0.59	7.37	7.85	－0.07	－2.79
10	0.22	3.12	－9.33	8.13	7.39	－0.01	8.57
11	12.98	－3.11	4.98	8.94	7.73	－0.04	10.43
12	14.18	－2.99	9.14	5.34	4.26	0.01	－7.18

国有商业银行外汇信贷收支主要指标时间序列表
Time Series of Major Indicators in Sources and Uses of Credit Funds of State - owned Commercial Banks (Foreign Currency)

年 Year	月 Month	各项贷款 Total Loans	短期贷款 Short - term Loans	境内短期贷款 Domestic Short - term Loans	中长期贷款 Medium and Long - term Loans	境内中长期贷款 Domestic Medium and Long - term Loans	进出口贸易融资 Financing for Import and Export Trades	票据融资 Paper Financing	境外筹资转贷款 On - lending of Overseas Financing	有价证券及投资 Securities and Investments
		期末余额（亿美元） Balance (100 Million US Dollars)								
1998	1	911.60	282.46	282.30	261.35	258.98	40.06	1.32	290.37	115.76
	2	910.88	272.76	272.76	270.90	268.64	36.36	1.14	289.01	112.73
	3	915.72	275.61	275.61	267.94	265.73	36.85	1.16	290.79	121.19
	4	912.42	275.61	275.61	269.41	267.19	35.73	1.05	287.94	121.77
	5	914.99	278.49	278.49	271.84	269.57	34.33	1.19	285.76	128.78
	6	914.76	280.44	280.44	272.59	270.33	34.65	1.15	281.71	134.98
	7	910.33	278.19	278.19	271.86	269.58	33.55	1.14	279.64	130.45
	8	909.24	275.00	275.00	275.21	272.91	32.68	1.29	278.65	140.85
	9	909.29	273.39	273.39	277.83	275.49	32.94	1.13	275.78	135.90
	10	918.00	273.02	273.02	278.49	275.97	32.90	0.97	283.56	135.26
	11	936.50	274.47	274.47	285.27	282.63	30.60	0.93	293.07	149.33
	12	941.68	285.01	285.01	286.64	284.02	26.42	0.66	288.07	158.02
		比上期增减额（亿美元） Changes Compared with Previous Period (100 Million US Dollars)								
1998	1	-12.27	-12.32	-12.12	-4.57	-4.76	0.31	-0.09	-1.77	1.94
	2	-0.70	-9.70	-9.54	9.55	9.66	-3.70	-0.18	-1.36	-3.03
	3	4.83	2.85	2.85	-2.96	-2.91	0.49	0.02	1.78	8.46
	4	-3.29			1.47	1.46	-1.12	-0.11	-2.85	0.58
	5	2.58	2.88	2.88	2.43	2.38	-1.40	0.14	-2.18	7.00
	6	-0.23	1.95	1.95	0.75	0.76	0.32	-0.04	-4.05	6.20
	7	-4.43	-2.25	-2.25	-0.73	-0.75	-1.10	-0.01	-2.07	-4.53
	8	-1.09	-3.19	-3.19	3.35	3.33	-0.87	0.15	-0.99	10.40
	9	0.05	-1.61	-1.61	2.62	2.58	0.26	-0.16	-2.87	-4.95
	10	8.71	-0.37	-0.37	0.66	0.48	-0.04	-0.16	7.78	-0.64
	11	18.52	1.45	1.45	6.79	6.67	-2.30	-0.04	9.51	14.05
	12	5.20	10.55	10.55	1.37	1.39	-4.18	-0.27	-5.00	8.71

国有商业银行外汇信贷收支主要指标时间序列表

Time Series of Major Indicators in Sources and Uses of Credit Funds of State - owned Commercial Banks（Foreign Currency）

年 月 Year Month	各项存款 Total Deposits	单位活期存款 Demand Deposits by Enterprises	单位定期存款 Time Deposits by Enterprises	储蓄存款 Savings Deposits	定期储蓄 Time Deposits	境外存款 Foreign Deposits	境外筹资 Overseas Financing
期末余额（亿美元） Balance（100 Million US Dollars）							
1999 1	704.08	98.49	191.43	383.80	358.43	1.63	273.66
2	713.03	101.34	186.92	393.95	367.24	1.70	272.82
3	713.98	99.68	181.64	403.36	376.75	1.52	267.82
4	720.75	100.73	179.85	410.81	383.85	1.50	265.74
5	729.68	100.29	180.55	419.45	391.42	1.55	260.36
6	741.30	102.30	182.69	428.70	399.55	1.59	261.85
7	746.81	104.77	175.15	440.44	410.45	1.57	253.41
8	767.98	103.58	183.33	453.18	422.86	1.66	253.07
9	790.81	103.89	190.56	467.20	436.14	1.64	259.53
10	804.65	102.84	193.50	478.70	446.57	1.55	260.95
11	818.79	103.83	192.70	491.93	458.92	1.58	257.40
12	828.94	106.45	189.10	501.05	467.76	0.67	257.59
比上期增减额（亿美元） Changes Compared with Previous Period（100 Million US Dollars）							
1999 1	2.35	1.90	-1.69	7.34	6.60	0.03	-3.58
2	8.97	2.85	-4.51	10.15	8.81	0.07	-0.84
3	0.93	-1.66	-5.28	9.41	9.51	-0.18	-5.00
4	6.75	1.05	-1.79	7.45	7.10	-0.02	-2.08
5	8.95	-0.44	0.70	8.64	7.57	0.05	-5.38
6	11.60	2.01	2.14	9.25	8.13	0.04	1.49
7	5.53	2.47	-7.54	11.74	10.90	-0.02	-8.44
8	21.17	-1.19	8.18	12.74	12.41	0.09	-0.34
9	22.83	0.31	7.23	14.02	13.28	-0.02	6.46
10	13.84	-1.05	2.94	11.50	10.43	-0.09	1.42
11	14.14	0.99	-0.80	13.23	12.35	0.03	-3.55
12	10.15	2.62	-3.60	9.12	8.84	-0.91	0.19
比去年同期增长（%） Increase Rate Year - on - year（%）							
1999 1	22.00	-3.41	20.78	38.27	39.27	-34.80	-4.35
2	20.26	-3.28	14.22	37.36	37.85	-28.27	-4.50
3	19.01	-1.98	8.13	36.19	36.50	-23.23	-6.16
4	19.90	5.42	5.99	35.09	35.49	-20.63	-5.65
5	19.21	2.97	4.12	34.68	34.97	-12.92	-7.36
6	18.13	7.83	3.50	33.53	33.43	-13.11	-3.55
7	16.58	11.62	-4.55	32.11	31.65	-26.98	-5.90
8	15.80	4.98	-2.33	30.68	30.24	-2.92	-5.58
9	17.24	4.23	1.21	31.92	31.16		-2.16
10	19.26	0.05	8.12	32.14	31.38	-4.91	-4.70
11	19.07	4.16	4.76	32.52	32.01	-0.63	-9.45
12	18.10	10.09	-2.06	33.06	32.92	-58.13	-7.03

国有商业银行外汇信贷收支主要指标时间序列表
Time Series of Major Indicators in Sources and Uses of Credit Funds of State – owned Commercial Banks (Foreign Currency)

年 月 Year Month		各项贷款 Total Loans	短期贷款 Short – term Loans	境内短期贷款 Domestic Short – term Loans	中长期贷款 Medium and Long – term Loans	境内中长期贷款 Domestic Medium and Long – term Loans	进出口贸易融资 Financing for Import and Export Trades	票据融资 Paper Financing	境外筹资转贷款 On – lending of Overseas Financing	有价证券及投资 Securities and Investments
期末余额（亿美元） Balance (100 Million US Dollars)										
1999	1	929.99	282.21	282.21	280.23	277.57	25.99	0.63	286.06	174.62
	2	929.49	281.60	281.60	281.04	278.27	25.27	0.58	285.14	162.67
	3	929.52	282.37	282.37	282.63	279.75	25.74	0.48	281.61	152.81
	4	929.04	284.04	284.04	282.82	279.93	25.02	0.47	279.27	148.12
	5	924.01	283.70	283.70	282.76	279.84	23.77	0.49	275.35	174.93
	6	919.67	283.80	283.80	279.42	276.52	23.87	0.48	271.68	193.57
	7	917.08	282.49	282.49	282.40	279.39	22.90	0.47	267.88	189.03
	8	915.03	282.16	282.16	282.95	279.80	21.72	0.51	265.91	185.40
	9	922.85	284.05	284.05	283.85	280.56	19.80	0.44	272.20	197.52
	10	925.43	285.41	285.41	282.83	279.52	18.74	0.67	273.86	202.93
	11	915.81	283.32	283.32	280.63	277.19	19.24	0.66	269.20	230.76
	12	874.86	266.68	266.68	270.43	266.97	18.44	0.60	266.34	258.64
比上期增减额（亿美元） Changes Compared with Previous Period (100 Million US Dollars)										
1999	1	-8.49	-3.36	-3.36	-2.98	-3.02	-0.45	-0.03	-1.84	16.60
	2	-0.53	-0.61	-0.61	0.82	0.71	-0.72	-0.05	-0.92	-11.95
	3	0.02	0.77	0.77	1.59	1.48	0.47	-0.10	-3.53	-9.86
	4	-0.48	1.67	1.67	0.19	0.18	-0.72	-0.01	-2.34	-4.69
	5	-5.03	-0.34	-0.34	-0.06	-0.09	-1.25	0.02	-3.92	26.81
	6	-4.38	0.10	0.10	-3.36	-3.32	0.10	-0.01	-3.67	18.64
	7	-2.57	-1.31	-1.31	2.98	2.87	-0.97	-0.01	-3.80	-4.56
	8	-2.07	-0.33	-0.33	0.55	0.41	-1.18	0.04	-1.97	-3.63
	9	7.83	1.89	1.89	0.89	0.75	-1.92	-0.07	6.29	12.12
	10	2.58	1.36	1.36	-1.02	-1.02	-1.06	0.23	1.66	5.41
	11	-9.64	-2.09	-2.09	-2.20	-2.35	0.50	-0.01	-4.66	27.83
	12	4.89	11.22	11.22	5.59	5.59	1.39	-0.06	-2.86	27.88
比去年同期增长（%） Increase Rate Year – on – year (%)										
1999	1	2.47	-0.09	-0.03	8.89	8.86	-35.12	-52.27	-1.48	50.85
	2	2.49	3.24	3.24	5.31	5.16	-30.50	-49.12	-1.34	44.30
	3	1.95	2.45	2.45	7.09	6.89	-30.15	-58.62	-3.16	26.09
	4	2.25	3.06	3.06	6.55	6.35	-29.97	-61.79	-3.01	19.79
	5	1.43	1.87	1.87	5.57	5.37	-30.76	-58.82	-3.64	35.84
	6	0.95	1.20	1.20	3.94	3.73	-31.11	-58.26	-3.56	43.41
	7	1.08	1.55	1.55	5.06	4.83	-31.74	-58.77	-4.21	44.89
	8	0.98	2.60	2.60	3.99	3.71	-33.54	-60.47	-4.57	31.63
	9	1.84	3.90	3.90	3.33	3.01	-39.89	-61.06	-1.30	45.34
	10	1.16	4.54	4.54	2.72	2.45	-43.04	-30.93	-3.42	50.03
	11	-1.87	3.22	3.22	-0.49	-0.79	-37.12	-29.03	-8.14	54.55
	12	-1.89	3.34	3.34	1.00	0.71	-21.94	-9.09	-7.54	63.68

国有商业银行外汇信贷收支主要指标时间序列表

Time Series of Major Indicators in Sources and Uses of Credit Funds of State - owned Commercial Banks（Foreign Currency）

年 月 Year Month		各项存款 Total Deposits						境外筹资 Overseas Financing
			单位活期存款 Demand Deposits by Enterprises	单位定期存款 Time Deposits by Enterprises	储蓄存款 Savings Deposits	定期储蓄 Time Deposits	境外存款 Foreign Deposits	
期末余额（亿美元） Balance（100 Million US Dollars）								
2000	1	839.75	100.98	193.67	513.34	479.44	0.33	255.07
	2	855.53	102.14	194.78	526.90	492.17	0.31	252.74
	3	866.20	102.39	194.48	536.96	502.10	0.31	246.04
	4	878.70	102.31	196.43	547.01	511.56	0.25	245.78
	5	891.40	103.09	197.46	557.54	521.24	0.20	221.09
	6	910.71	101.13	203.63	570.43	535.11	0.23	215.47
	7	941.21	104.95	215.56	584.50	548.09	0.24	215.79
	8	952.43	103.43	215.39	597.13	559.73	0.21	214.37
	9	969.24	101.23	218.25	611.41	573.71	0.21	212.02
	10	983.03	103.60	217.34	624.20	585.83	0.11	208.03
	11	1027.18	108.36	242.11	637.35	598.53	0.15	206.89
	12	1028.68	109.01	227.72	649.04	608.83	0.09	203.55
比上期增减额（亿美元） Changes Compared with Previous Period（100 Million US Dollars）								
2000	1	10.54	-5.79	4.27	12.29	11.68	-0.06	-2.49
	2	15.78	1.16	1.11	13.56	12.73	-0.02	-2.33
	3	10.67	0.25	-0.30	10.06	9.93		-6.70
	4	12.50	-0.08	1.95	10.05	9.46	-0.06	-0.26
	5	12.70	0.78	1.03	10.53	9.68	-0.05	-24.69
	6	19.31	-1.96	6.17	12.89	13.87	0.03	-5.62
	7	30.50	3.82	11.93	14.07	12.98	0.01	0.32
	8	11.22	-1.52	-0.17	12.63	11.64	-0.03	-1.42
	9	16.81	-2.20	2.86	14.28	13.98		-2.35
	10	13.79	2.37	-0.91	12.79	12.12	-0.10	-3.99
	11	44.15	4.76	24.77	13.15	12.70	0.04	-1.14
	12	1.50	0.65	-14.39	11.69	10.30	-0.06	-3.34
比去年同期增长（%） Increase Rate Year - on - year（%）								
2000	1	19.27	2.53	1.17	33.75	33.76	-79.75	-6.79
	2	19.98	0.79	4.21	33.75	34.02	-81.76	-7.36
	3	21.32	2.72	7.07	33.12	33.27	-79.61	-8.13
	4	21.92	1.57	9.22	33.15	33.27	-83.33	-7.51
	5	22.16	2.79	9.37	32.92	33.17	-87.10	-15.08
	6	22.86	-1.14	11.46	33.06	33.93	-85.53	-17.71
	7	26.03	0.17	23.07	32.71	33.53	-84.71	-14.85
	8	24.02	-0.14	17.49	31.76	32.37	-87.35	-15.29
	9	22.56	-2.56	14.53	30.87	31.54	-87.20	-18.31
	10	22.17	0.74	12.32	30.39	31.18	-92.90	-20.28
	11	25.45	4.36	25.64	29.56	30.42	-90.51	-19.62
	12	24.10	2.40	20.42	29.54	30.16	-86.57	-20.98

国有商业银行外汇信贷收支主要指标时间序列表

Time Series of Major Indicators in Sources and Uses of Credit Funds of State - owned Commercial Banks (Foreign Currency)

年　月 Year Month	各项贷款 Total Loans	短期贷款 Short - term Loans	境内短期贷款 Domestic Short - term Loans	中长期贷款 Medium and Long - term Loans	境内中长期贷款 Domestic Medium and Long - term Loans	进出口贸易融资 Financing for Import and Export Trades	票据融资 Paper Financing	境外筹资转贷款 On - lending of Overseas Financing	有价证券及投资 Securities and Investments
期末余额（亿美元）Balance (100 Million US Dollars)									
2000 1	872.92	269.43	269.43	270.70	267.25	14.02	0.39	259.77	276.73
2	868.38	268.36	268.36	270.08	266.52	12.41	0.36	258.17	241.04
3	861.26	266.09	266.09	268.93	265.35	13.41	0.37	252.97	247.90
4	861.56	263.35	263.35	270.10	266.53	14.40	0.43	253.09	239.51
5	827.53	254.34	254.34	265.24	261.49	13.41	0.47	234.78	247.62
6	734.51	210.64	210.64	236.92	232.84	13.04	0.43	222.93	244.22
7	713.48	203.68	203.68	232.93	228.98	12.54	0.40	222.62	263.93
8	703.40	198.14	198.14	227.78	223.82	12.40	0.42	220.40	280.11
9	695.26	195.26	195.26	224.47	220.39	12.04	0.45	218.22	288.33
10	688.09	193.61	193.61	224.72	221.03	11.44	0.46	215.07	314.18
11	686.27	193.11	193.11	222.70	218.52	11.17	0.40	213.56	326.85
12	647.30	183.86	183.86	209.00	204.89	11.92	0.34	197.80	351.70
比上期增减额（亿美元）Changes Compared with Previous Period (100 Million US Dollars)									
2000 1	-6.50	-3.54	-3.54	0.94	0.95	-0.10	-0.21	-4.84	18.41
2	-4.32	-0.66	-0.66	-1.59	-1.70	-1.60	-0.03	-0.83	-35.63
3	-7.07	-2.27	-2.27	-1.10	-1.12	1.00	0.01	-5.20	6.80
4	0.74	-2.70	-2.70	1.18	1.19	0.99	0.06	0.11	-8.39
5	-22.92	-4.89	-4.89	0.41	0.23	-1.00	0.04	-17.98	8.11
6	-8.74	0.08	0.08	-1.79	-2.12	0.20	-0.04	-6.71	-3.33
7	-1.42	-0.79	-0.79	0.87	1.00	-0.80	-0.03	-1.69	19.71
8	-3.76	-2.14	-2.14	-4.49	-4.50	-0.14	0.02	-2.00	16.20
9	-5.71	-2.37	-2.37	-3.01	-3.13	0.66	0.03	-1.62	8.20
10	-5.65	-0.64	-0.64	0.36	0.75	-0.61	0.01	-3.15	25.85
11	-0.87	-0.29	-0.29	-1.60	-2.09	-0.28	-0.06	-1.51	12.66
12	-14.54	-0.29	-0.29	-3.24	-3.17	0.96	-0.06	-11.98	24.86
比去年同期增长（%）Increase Rate Year - on - year (%)									
2000 1	-1.20	5.27	5.27	2.32	2.06	-37.63	-38.10	-9.19	58.48
2	-1.61	5.26	5.26	1.47	1.20	-42.18	-37.93	-9.19	48.21
3	-2.38	4.17	4.17	0.50	0.25	-39.36	-22.92	-9.90	62.23
4	-2.25	2.61	2.61	0.85	0.61	-33.65	-8.51	-9.10	61.70
5	-4.20	1.01	1.01	1.01	0.73	-34.37	-4.08	-14.34	41.55
6	-4.69	1.00	1.00	1.59	1.18	-33.81	-10.42	-15.65	26.20
7	-4.58	1.19	1.19	0.82	0.49	-34.50	-14.89	-15.09	39.68
8	-4.78	0.55	0.55	-0.96	-1.26	-31.58	-17.65	-15.21	51.13
9	-6.21	-0.95	-0.95	-2.34	-2.65	-21.62	2.27	-17.76	46.01
10	-7.08	-1.65	-1.65	-1.86	-2.02	-20.44	-31.34	-19.41	54.86
11	-6.20	-1.03	-1.03	-1.66	-1.94	-23.96	-39.39	-18.58	41.67
12	-8.71	-5.41	-5.41	-4.99	-5.30	-27.33	-43.33	-22.20	36.01

国有商业银行外汇信贷收支主要指标时间序列表

Time Series of Major Indicators in Sources and Uses of Credit Funds of State - owned Commercial Banks（Foreign Currency）

年 月 Year Month		各项存款 Total Deposits	单位活期存款 Demand Deposits by Enterprises	单位定期存款 Time Deposits by Enterprises	储蓄存款 Savings Deposits	定期储蓄 Time Deposits	境外存款 Foreign Deposits	境外筹资 Overseas Financing
期末余额（亿美元） Balance（100 Million US Dollars）								
2001	1	1038.85	106.19	226.48	662.68	621.82	0.09	203.57
	2	1028.36	107.17	219.12	657.50	615.63	0.17	200.58
	3	1027.07	102.52	223.62	654.47	611.82	0.16	198.62
	4	1053.35	102.98	245.51	658.82	614.65	0.11	194.28
	5	1072.99	113.13	248.55	667.86	618.82	0.15	190.23
	6	1064.03	112.90	237.72	670.18	620.10	0.13	187.88
	7	1059.58	111.18	228.67	680.40	627.30	0.06	186.19
	8	1066.46	112.27	223.97	691.26	635.10	0.08	188.52
	9	1066.42	109.04	223.06	697.31	639.99	0.06	187.64
	10	1076.11	118.34	216.29	705.46	645.48	0.10	183.81
	11	1074.43	122.03	205.10	711.43	649.52	0.23	183.03
	12	1076.21	123.44	201.99	715.35	650.50	0.18	176.83
比上期增减额（亿美元） Changes Compared with Previous Period（100 Million US Dollars）								
2001	1	7.11	-5.09	-1.00	13.28	12.45		-7.59
	2	-10.49	0.98	-7.36	-5.18	-6.19	0.08	-2.99
	3	-1.29	-4.65	4.50	-3.03	-3.81	-0.01	-1.96
	4	26.28	0.46	21.89	4.35	2.83	-0.05	-4.34
	5	19.64	10.15	3.04	9.04	4.17	0.04	-4.05
	6	-8.96	-0.23	-10.83	2.32	1.28	-0.02	-2.35
	7	-4.45	-1.72	-9.05	10.22	7.20	-0.07	-1.69
	8	6.88	1.09	-4.70	10.86	7.80	0.02	2.33
	9	-0.04	-3.23	-0.91	6.05	4.89	-0.02	-0.88
	10	9.69	9.30	-6.77	8.15	5.49	0.04	-3.83
	11	-1.68	3.69	-11.19	5.97	4.04	0.13	-0.78
	12	1.78	1.41	-3.11	3.92	0.98	-0.05	-6.20
比去年同期增长（%） Increase Rate Year-on-year（%）								
2001	1	23.71	5.16	16.94	29.09	29.70	-72.73	-20.19
	2	20.20	4.92	12.50	24.79	25.08	-45.16	-20.64
	3	18.57	0.13	14.98	21.88	21.85	-48.39	-19.27
	4	19.88	0.65	24.99	20.44	20.15	-56.00	-20.95
	5	20.37	9.74	25.87	19.79	18.72	-25.00	-13.96
	6	16.84	11.64	16.74	17.49	15.88	-43.48	-12.80
	7	12.58	5.94	6.08	16.41	14.45	-75.00	-13.72
	8	11.97	8.55	3.98	15.76	13.47	-61.90	-12.06
	9	10.03	7.72	2.20	14.05	11.55	-71.43	-11.50
	10	9.47	14.23	-0.48	13.02	10.18	-9.09	-11.64
	11	4.60	12.62	-15.29	11.62	8.52	53.33	-11.53
	12	4.62	13.24	-11.30	10.22	6.84	100.00	-13.13

国有商业银行外汇信贷收支主要指标时间序列表

Time Series of Major Indicators in Sources and Uses of Credit Funds of State－owned Commercial Banks（Foreign Currency）

年　月 Year Month		各项贷款 Total Loans	短期贷款 Short－term Loans	境内短期贷款 Domestic Short－term Loans	中长期贷款 Medium and Long－term Loans	境内中长期贷款 Domestic Medium and Long－term Loans	进出口贸易融资 Financing for Import and Export Trades	票据融资 Paper Financing	境外筹资转贷款 On－lending of Overseas Financing	有价证券及投资 Securities and Investments
		期末余额（亿美元） Balance（100 Million US Dollars）								
2001	1	640.32	157.85	157.85	224.74	220.70	13.97	0.34	195.90	380.87
	2	636.54	156.32	156.32	223.87	219.83	11.98	0.37	194.26	414.63
	3	632.22	156.36	156.36	222.90	218.97	12.62	0.32	190.63	440.14
	4	627.58	154.54	154.54	219.55	215.76	12.05	0.35	190.91	486.97
	5	624.72	153.49	153.49	219.89	216.05	12.01	0.43	188.18	472.59
	6	621.62	155.50	155.50	218.36	214.54	12.30	0.37	185.75	447.41
	7	615.31	153.71	153.71	224.93	221.23	12.09	0.40	173.92	461.70
	8	619.52	153.88	153.88	224.34	220.66	12.61	0.92	177.18	461.44
	9	614.05	153.30	153.30	221.55	217.96	12.60	0.48	175.49	468.44
	10	606.57	154.92	154.92	217.13	213.51	11.82	0.51	171.51	444.70
	11	598.92	155.50	155.50	211.56	207.92	11.95	0.47	169.28	476.02
	12	596.12	156.43	156.43	210.49	207.04	13.40	0.65	163.44	606.79
		比上期增减额（亿美元） Changes Compared with Previous Period（100 Million US Dollars）								
2001	1	－7.76	－1.92	－1.92	－2.19	－2.01	－0.87		－4.49	27.81
	2	－3.78	－1.53	－1.53	－0.87	－0.87	－1.99	0.03	－1.64	33.76
	3	－4.32	0.04	0.04	－0.97	－0.86	0.64	－0.05	－3.63	25.51
	4	－4.64	－1.82	－1.82	－3.35	－3.21	－0.57	0.03	0.28	46.83
	5	－2.85	－1.05	－1.05	0.33	0.28	－0.04	0.08	－2.73	－14.38
	6	－3.17	2.01	2.01	－1.54	－1.52	0.29	－0.06	－2.43	－25.18
	7	－6.29	－1.79	－1.79	6.54	6.66	－0.21	0.03	－11.83	14.29
	8	4.25	0.17	0.17	－0.55	－0.54	0.52	0.52	3.26	－0.26
	9	－5.46	－0.56	－0.56	－2.79	－2.70	－0.01	－0.44	－1.69	7.00
	10	－7.54	1.60	1.60	－4.46	－4.49	－0.78	0.03	－3.98	－23.74
	11	－7.65	0.58	0.58	－5.55	－5.57	0.13	－0.04	－2.23	31.32
	12	－2.73	0.93	0.93	－1.04	－0.85	1.45	0.18	－5.84	130.77
		比去年同期增长（%） Increase Rate Year－on－year（%）								
2001	1	－9.31	－2.41	－2.41	8.77	8.66	10.20	－12.82	－20.96	37.66
	2	－9.30	－1.57	－1.57	9.47	9.42	8.38	2.78	－21.41	72.02
	3	－9.06	－0.72	－0.72	9.59	9.58	5.07	－13.51	－21.23	77.58
	4	－9.68	－0.21	－0.21	7.72	7.74	－6.11	－18.60	－21.15	103.35
	5	－7.65	1.64	1.64	7.32	7.38	0.52	－8.51	－16.31	90.88
	6	－7.85	3.03	3.03	5.15	5.36	1.30	－13.95	－15.25	83.20
	7	－8.78	4.26	4.26	3.32	3.49	6.06	0.00	－19.83	74.93
	8	－7.76	5.61	5.61	4.23	4.43	11.45	119.05	－17.64	64.72
	9	－7.82	6.52	6.52	4.36	4.66	6.23	6.67	－17.85	62.46
	10	－8.17	8.12	8.12	2.02	2.09	5.07	10.87	－18.50	41.54
	11	－9.18	9.11	9.11	0.24	0.49	8.77	17.50	－18.97	45.64
	12	－7.90	9.71	9.71	0.73	1.06	12.42	91.18	－17.37	72.53

国有商业银行外汇信贷收支主要指标时间序列表

Time Series of Major Indicators in Sources and Uses of Credit Funds of State - owned Commercial Banks（Foreign Currency）

年 月 Year Month		各项存款 Total Deposits	单位活期存款 Demand Deposits by Enterprises	单位定期存款 Time Deposits by Enterprises	储蓄存款 Savings Deposits	定期储蓄 Time Deposits	境外存款 Foreign Deposits	境外筹资 Overseas Financing
		期末余额（亿美元） Balance（100 Million US Dollars）						
2002	1	1063.82	115.62	195.63	718.48	653.04	0.34	174.76
	2	1074.20	120.42	193.20	727.32	659.62	0.24	172.61
	3	1080.50	115.01	196.33	734.42	664.84	0.25	170.42
	4	1083.10	114.02	193.20	739.59	668.76	0.21	169.44
	5	1098.38	119.58	193.05	747.76	673.89	0.18	169.19
	6	1103.33	126.23	182.68	755.18	678.87	0.17	191.82
	7	1101.81	123.55	181.78	756.87	679.09	0.23	188.90
	8	1111.25	126.40	183.80	761.25	681.29	0.15	188.57
	9	1105.54	121.80	180.59	762.68	682.18	0.14	185.81
	10	1121.93	131.40	180.97	768.46	684.93	0.31	182.38
	11	1131.43	132.76	187.55	770.59	685.71	0.17	161.04
	12	1139.92	134.91	190.05	774.07	685.51	0.16	158.68
		比上期增减额（亿美元） Changes Compared with Previous Period（100 Million US Dollars）						
2002	1	-12.08	-7.08	-5.67	3.91	2.91	0.16	-2.06
	2	10.38	4.80	-2.43	8.84	6.58	-0.10	-2.15
	3	6.30	-5.41	3.13	7.10	5.22	0.01	-2.19
	4	2.60	-0.99	-3.13	5.17	3.92	-0.04	-0.98
	5	15.28	5.56	-0.15	8.17	5.13	-0.03	-0.25
	6	4.95	6.65	-10.37	7.42	4.98	-0.01	22.63
	7	-1.52	-2.68	-0.90	1.69	0.22	0.06	-2.92
	8	9.44	2.85	2.02	4.38	2.20	-0.08	-0.33
	9	-5.71	-4.60	-3.21	1.43	0.89	-0.01	-2.76
	10	16.39	9.60	0.38	5.78	2.75	0.17	-3.43
	11	9.50	1.36	6.58	2.13	0.78	-0.14	-21.34
	12	8.49	2.15	2.50	3.48	-0.20	-0.01	-2.36
		比去年同期增长（%） Increase Rate Year - on - year（%）						
2002	1	2.40	8.88	-13.60	8.42	5.02	277.78	-14.15
	2	4.46	12.36	-11.81	10.62	7.15	41.18	-13.94
	3	5.20	12.18	-12.18	12.22	8.67	56.25	-14.20
	4	2.82	10.72	-21.29	12.26	8.80	90.91	-12.79
	5	2.37	5.70	-22.31	11.96	8.90	20.00	-11.06
	6	3.69	11.81	-23.14	12.68	9.48	30.77	2.10
	7	3.99	11.13	-20.49	11.24	8.26	283.33	1.46
	8	4.20	12.59	-17.92	10.12	7.27	87.50	0.03
	9	3.67	11.70	-19.02	9.37	6.59	133.33	-0.98
	10	4.26	11.04	-16.31	8.93	6.11	210.00	-0.78
	11	5.31	8.79	-8.53	8.32	5.57	-26.09	-12.01
	12	5.92	9.29	-5.89	8.21	5.38	-11.11	-10.26

国有商业银行外汇信贷收支主要指标时间序列表

Time Series of Major Indicators in Sources and Uses of Credit Funds of State - owned Commercial Banks (Foreign Currency)

年 月 Year Month		各项贷款 Total Loans	短期贷款 Short - term Loans	境内短期贷款 Domestic Short - term Loans	中长期贷款 Medium and Long - term Loans	境内中长期贷款 Domestic Medium and Long - term Loans	进出口贸易融资 Financing for Import and Export Trades	票据融资 Paper Financing	境外筹资转贷款 On - lending of Overseas Financing	有价证券及投资 Securities and Investments
		期末余额（亿美元） Balance (100 Million US Dollars)								
2002	1	601.80	156.84	156.84	219.82	216.62	13.00	0.59	160.08	584.84
	2	607.35	158.19	158.19	227.68	224.52	12.21	0.17	158.00	579.83
	3	611.19	167.84	167.81	222.58	219.46	13.30	0.36	156.29	638.13
	4	615.96	170.35	170.35	220.79	220.15	14.67	0.46	159.00	659.78
	5	621.89	174.11	174.11	222.15	219.12	15.77	0.47	158.51	681.57
	6	632.22	179.63	179.63	224.29	221.23	17.43	0.45	160.01	674.93
	7	634.92	179.27	179.27	229.97	227.04	17.45	0.57	156.72	676.00
	8	629.87	180.16	180.16	226.35	223.42	17.50	0.59	156.48	733.45
	9	631.70	182.56	182.56	229.76	226.92	18.77	0.72	152.13	716.60
	10	631.76	181.29	181.29	233.27	230.44	17.44	0.75	150.97	721.56
	11	634.51	184.55	184.43	234.19	231.38	19.51	0.70	147.19	774.57
	12	656.26	185.29	185.29	255.91	253.76	21.65	0.69	144.98	743.50
		比上期增减额（亿美元） Changes Compared with Previous Period (100 Million US Dollars)								
2002	1	-0.04	0.94	0.94	3.33	3.46	-0.37	-0.06	-3.35	-22.85
	2	5.55	1.35	1.35	7.86	7.90	-0.79	-0.42	-2.08	-5.01
	3	3.84	9.65	9.62	-5.10	-5.06	1.09	0.19	-1.71	58.30
	4	4.77	2.51	2.54	-1.79	0.69	1.37	0.10	2.71	21.65
	5	5.93	3.76	3.76	1.36	-1.03	1.10	0.01	-0.49	21.79
	6	10.33	5.52	5.52	2.14	2.11	1.66	-0.02	1.50	-6.64
	7	2.70	-0.36	-0.36	5.68	5.81	0.02	0.12	-3.29	1.07
	8	-5.05	0.89	0.89	-3.62	-3.62	0.05	0.02	-0.24	57.45
	9	1.83	2.40	2.40	3.41	3.50	1.27	0.13	-4.35	-16.85
	10	0.06	-1.27	-1.27	3.51	3.52	-1.33	0.03	-1.16	4.96
	11	2.75	3.26	3.14	0.92	0.94	2.07	-0.05	-3.78	53.01
	12	21.75	0.74	0.86	21.72	22.38	2.14	-0.01	-2.21	-31.07
		比去年同期增长（%） Increase Rate Year - on - year (%)								
2002	1	-6.02	-0.64	-0.64	-2.19	-1.85	-6.94	73.53	-18.28	53.55
	2	-4.59	1.20	1.20	1.70	2.13	1.92	-54.05	-18.67	39.84
	3	-3.33	7.34	7.32	-0.14	0.22	5.39	12.50	-18.01	44.98
	4	-1.85	10.23	10.23	0.56	2.03	21.74	31.43	-16.71	35.49
	5	-0.46	13.43	13.43	1.01	1.41	31.31	9.30	-15.77	44.22
	6	1.71	15.52	15.52	2.72	3.12	41.71	21.62	-13.86	50.85
	7	3.19	16.63	16.63	2.26	2.64	44.33	42.50	-9.89	46.42
	8	1.67	17.08	17.08	0.90	1.25	38.78	-35.87	-11.68	58.95
	9	2.87	19.07	19.07	3.70	4.10	48.97	50.00	-13.31	52.98
	10	4.16	17.02	17.02	7.44	7.94	47.55	47.06	-11.98	62.26
	11	5.95	18.68	18.60	10.70	11.28	63.26	48.94	-13.05	62.72
	12	10.08	18.46	18.46	21.56	22.55	61.57	6.15	-11.29	22.52

国有商业银行外汇信贷收支主要指标时间序列表

Time Series of Major Indicators in Sources and Uses of Credit Funds of State - owned Commercial Banks（Foreign Currency）

年　月 Year Month		各项存款 Total Deposits	单位活期存款 Demand Deposits by Enterprises	单位定期存款 Time Deposits by Enterprises	储蓄存款 Savings Deposits	定期储蓄 Time Deposits	境外存款 Foreign Deposits	境外筹资 Overseas Financing
		期末余额（亿美元）Balance（100 Million US Dollars）						
2003	1	1132.15	131.59	184.03	776.68	687.12	0.16	157.50
	2	1129.00	139.27	169.43	779.35	687.96	0.20	156.44
	3	1122.66	133.82	168.80	778.96	686.78	0.22	153.93
	4	1122.51	133.77	167.86	779.22	685.52	0.20	153.35
	5	1127.15	138.93	164.95	782.16	686.13	0.20	154.03
	6	1135.94	145.10	164.26	783.56	685.01	0.23	150.07
	7	1126.56	141.91	162.26	779.87	678.98	0.29	147.17
	8	1113.05	141.17	157.76	771.90	669.83	0.24	143.58
	9	1098.47	140.31	158.55	756.73	655.66	0.09	143.44
	10	1100.29	152.87	156.30	747.00	644.56	0.04	145.01
	11	1102.56	154.21	160.78	739.94	636.50	0.14	143.96
	12	1090.57	152.75	153.03	733.73	629.38	0.16	139.49
		比上期增减额（亿美元）Changes Compared with Previous Period（100 Million US Dollars）						
2003	1	-7.84	-2.70	-6.66	2.58	1.58	-0.01	-1.21
	2	-3.15	7.68	-14.60	2.67	0.84	0.04	-1.06
	3	-6.34	-5.45	-0.63	-0.39	-1.18	0.02	-2.51
	4	-0.15	-0.05	-0.94	0.26	-1.26	-0.02	-0.58
	5	4.64	5.16	-2.91	2.94	0.61		0.68
	6	8.79	6.17	-0.69	1.40	-1.12	0.03	-3.96
	7	-9.38	-3.19	-2.00	-3.69	-6.03	0.06	-2.90
	8	-13.51	-0.74	-4.50	-7.97	-9.15	-0.05	-3.59
	9	-14.58	-0.86	0.79	-15.17	-14.17	-0.15	-0.14
	10	1.82	12.56	-2.25	-9.73	-11.10	-0.05	1.57
	11	2.27	1.34	4.48	-7.06	-8.06	0.10	-1.05
	12	-11.99	-1.46	-7.75	-6.21	-7.12	0.02	-4.47
		比去年同期增长（%）Increase Rate Year - on - year（%）						
2003	1	6.42	13.81	-5.93	8.10	5.22	-52.94	-9.88
	2	5.10	15.65	-12.30	7.15	4.30	-16.67	-9.37
	3	3.90	16.36	-14.02	6.06	3.30	-12.00	-9.68
	4	3.64	17.32	-13.12	5.36	2.51	-4.76	-9.50
	5	2.62	16.18	-14.56	4.60	1.82	11.11	-8.96
	6	2.96	14.95	-10.08	3.76	0.90	35.29	-21.77
	7	2.25	14.86	-10.74	3.04	-0.02	26.09	-22.09
	8	0.16	11.69	-14.17	1.40	-1.68	60.00	-23.86
	9	-0.64	15.20	-12.20	-0.78	-3.89	-35.71	-22.80
	10	-1.93	16.34	-13.63	-2.79	-5.89	-87.10	-20.49
	11	-2.55	16.16	-14.27	-3.98	-7.18	-17.65	-10.61
	12	-4.33	13.22	-19.48	-5.21	-8.19		-12.09

国有商业银行外汇信贷收支主要指标时间序列表
Time Series of Major Indicators in Sources and Uses of Credit Funds of State - owned Commercial Banks (Foreign Currency)

年 月 Year Month		各项贷款 Total Loans	短期贷款 Short - term Loans	境内短期贷款 Domestic Short - term Loans	中长期贷款 Medium and Long - term Loans	境内中长期贷款 Domestic Medium and Long - term Loans	进出口贸易融资 Financing for Import and Export Trades	票据融资 Paper Financing	境外筹资转贷款 On - lending of Overseas Financing	有价证券及投资 Securities and Investments
期末余额（亿美元） Balance (100 Million US Dollars)										
2003	1	664.91	189.14	189.14	258.28	255.69	24.55	0.65	144.63	735.00
	2	668.80	192.62	192.62	260.14	257.56	24.50	0.80	143.18	725.14
	3	684.05	202.14	202.14	261.27	258.61	28.88	0.86	143.54	766.10
	4	700.96	210.81	210.81	264.25	258.94	34.63	0.82	141.98	780.05
	5	715.49	218.81	218.81	264.95	259.65	39.79	0.83	142.31	753.14
	6	740.35	232.63	232.63	273.72	268.48	45.43	0.85	139.27	772.60
	7	746.57	241.19	241.19	272.62	267.56	45.85	1.14	137.29	818.66
	8	764.69	251.81	251.81	281.97	277.15	48.09	1.05	133.21	808.30
	9	800.02	268.30	268.30	297.90	293.07	50.59	1.14	132.91	770.95
	10	815.11	277.45	277.41	303.32	298.55	50.40	1.03	133.88	754.07
	11	826.73	285.35	285.31	305.11	300.35	54.11	0.96	132.10	706.11
	12	835.26	295.80	295.73	305.74	301.02	59.64	1.08	128.89	714.82
比上期增减额（亿美元） Changes Compared with Previous Period (100 Million US Dollars)										
2003	1	8.63	4.54	4.54	1.51	1.07	2.89	- 0.04	- 0.28	- 8.68
	2	3.89	3.48	3.48	1.86	1.87	- 0.05	0.15	- 1.45	- 9.86
	3	15.25	9.52	9.52	1.13	1.05	4.38	0.06	0.36	40.96
	4	16.91	8.67	8.67	2.98	0.33	5.75	- 0.04	- 1.56	13.95
	5	14.53	8.00	8.00	0.70	0.71	5.16	0.01	0.33	- 26.91
	6	24.86	13.82	13.82	8.77	8.83	5.64	0.02	- 3.04	19.46
	7	6.22	8.56	8.56	- 1.10	- 0.92	0.42	0.29	- 1.98	46.06
	8	18.12	10.62	10.62	9.35	9.59	2.24	- 0.09	- 4.08	- 10.36
	9	35.33	16.49	16.49	15.93	15.92	2.50	0.09	- 0.30	- 37.35
	10	15.09	9.15	9.11	5.42	5.48	- 0.19	- 0.11	0.97	- 16.88
	11	11.62	7.90	7.90	1.79	1.80	3.71	- 0.07	- 1.78	- 47.96
	12	8.53	10.45	10.42	0.63	0.67	5.53	0.12	- 3.21	8.71
比去年同期增长（%） Increase Rate Year - on - year (%)										
2003	1	10.49	20.59	20.59	17.50	18.04	88.85	10.17	- 9.65	25.68
	2	10.12	21.76	21.76	14.26	14.72	100.66	370.59	- 9.38	25.06
	3	11.92	20.44	20.46	17.38	17.84	117.14	138.89	- 8.16	20.05
	4	13.80	23.75	23.75	19.68	17.62	136.06	78.26	- 10.70	18.23
	5	15.05	25.67	25.67	19.27	18.50	152.31	76.60	- 10.22	10.50
	6	17.10	29.51	29.51	22.04	21.36	160.64	88.89	- 12.96	14.47
	7	17.58	34.54	34.54	18.55	17.85	162.75	100.00	- 12.40	21.10
	8	21.40	39.77	39.77	24.57	24.05	174.80	77.97	- 14.87	10.21
	9	26.65	46.97	46.97	29.66	29.15	169.53	58.33	- 12.63	7.58
	10	29.02	53.04	53.02	30.03	29.56	188.99	37.33	- 11.32	4.51
	11	30.29	54.62	54.70	30.28	29.81	177.34	37.14	- 10.25	- 8.84
	12	27.28	59.64	59.60	19.47	18.62	175.47	56.52	- 11.10	- 3.86

国有商业银行外汇信贷收支主要指标时间序列表

Time Series of Major Indicators in Sources and Uses of Credit Funds of State - owned Commercial Banks（Foreign Currency）

年 月 Year Month	各项存款 Total Deposits	单位活期存款 Demand Deposits by Enterprises	单位定期存款 Time Deposits by Enterprises	储蓄存款 Savings Deposits	定期储蓄 Time Deposits	境外存款 Foreign Deposits	境外筹资 Overseas Financing
	期末余额（亿美元） Balance（100 Million US Dollars）						
2004 1	1102.71	166.21	154.68	731.56	625.36	0.20	137.96
2	1066.31	161.43	141.81	712.06	605.44	0.14	137.84
3	1070.39	166.12	144.12	705.99	596.14	0.16	135.77
4	1070.70	159.46	152.64	699.12	587.06	0.18	127.94
5	1083.89	172.37	149.62	700.02	583.65	0.17	128.36
6	1086.55	176.70	170.40	676.85	558.53	0.15	124.91
7	1102.39	184.26	152.08	696.96	575.49	0.16	123.12
8	1115.93	190.74	146.44	698.75	574.69	0.15	131.46
9	1115.02	173.85	156.67	699.84	573.30	0.12	148.47
10	1120.15	183.17	158.46	696.27	566.82	0.17	144.78
11	1094.63	191.95	150.86	671.15	548.57	0.33	148.25
12	1078.90	184.88	152.20	663.26	540.04	0.18	141.83
	比上期增减额（亿美元） Changes Compared with Previous Period（100 Million US Dollars）						
2004 1	11.92	13.42	1.63	-2.29	-4.09	0.04	-1.96
2	-36.40	-4.78	-12.87	-19.50	-19.92	-0.06	-0.12
3	4.08	4.69	2.31	-6.07	-9.30	0.02	-2.07
4	0.31	-6.66	8.52	-6.87	-9.08	0.02	-7.83
5	13.19	12.91	-3.02	0.90	-3.41	-0.01	0.42
6	2.66	4.33	20.78	-23.17	-25.12	-0.02	-3.45
7	15.84	7.56	-18.32	20.11	16.96	0.01	-1.79
8	13.54	6.48	-5.64	1.79	-0.80	-0.01	8.34
9	-0.91	-16.89	10.23	1.09	-1.39	-0.03	17.01
10	5.13	9.32	1.79	-3.57	-6.48	0.05	-3.69
11	-25.52	8.78	-7.60	-25.12	-18.25	0.16	3.47
12	-15.73	-7.07	1.34	-7.89	-8.53	-0.15	-6.42
	比去年同期增长（%） Increase Rate Year - on - year（%）						
2004 1	-2.60	26.31	-15.95	-5.81	-8.99	25.00	-12.41
2	-5.55	15.91	-16.30	-8.63	-11.99	-30.00	-11.89
3	-4.66	24.14	-14.62	-9.37	-13.20	-27.27	-11.80
4	-4.62	19.20	-9.07	-10.28	-14.36	-10.00	-16.57
5	-3.84	24.07	-9.29	-10.50	-14.94	-15.00	-16.67
6	-4.35	21.78	3.74	-13.62	-18.46	-34.78	-16.77
7	-2.15	29.84	-6.27	-10.63	-15.24	-44.83	-16.34
8	0.26	35.11	-7.18	-9.48	-14.20	-37.50	-8.44
9	1.51	23.90	-1.19	-7.52	-12.56	33.33	3.51
10	1.80	19.82	1.38	-6.79	-12.06	325.00	-0.16
11	-0.72	24.47	-6.17	-9.30	-13.81	135.71	2.98
12	-1.07	21.03	-0.54	-9.60	-14.19	12.50	1.68

国有商业银行外汇信贷收支主要指标时间序列表

Time Series of Major Indicators in Sources and Uses of Credit Funds of State - owned Commercial Banks (Foreign Currency)

年　月 Year Month		各项贷款 Total Loans	短期贷款 Short - term Loans	境内短期贷款 Domestic Short - term Loans	中长期贷款 Medium and Long - term Loans	境内中长期贷款 Domestic Medium and Long - term Loans	进出口贸易融资 Financing for Import and Export Trades	票据融资 Paper Financing	境外筹资转贷款 On - lending of Overseas Financing	有价证券及投资 Securities and Investments
		期末余额（亿美元） Balance (100 Million US Dollars)								
2004	1	843.51	300.69	300.65	308.45	303.91	61.80	1.12	127.42	907.80
	2	863.13	308.53	308.49	314.45	309.94	67.62	1.03	127.47	961.16
	3	878.88	319.23	319.19	314.70	310.24	74.90	1.16	125.31	894.51
	4	888.36	323.25	323.20	319.94	315.46	78.41	1.30	122.33	901.16
	5	896.41	328.00	327.91	323.93	319.47	78.22	1.32	121.67	883.71
	6	789.02	291.42	291.33	295.43	290.98	77.49	1.28	112.08	837.00
	7	782.69	292.42	292.34	295.48	291.20	71.22	1.13	110.80	866.36
	8	783.71	323.51	323.43	264.68	262.11	70.53	1.04	112.22	903.14
	9	779.35	284.50	284.42	303.38	299.03	69.14	1.22	109.47	979.70
	10	766.33	285.26	285.18	291.15	286.83	66.37	1.43	110.65	1014.94
	11	776.01	273.95	273.87	303.56	301.03	67.91	1.17	118.62	1044.01
	12	779.09	265.40	265.35	309.92	309.53	71.91	1.31	119.66	1005.30
		比上期增减额（亿美元） Changes Compared with Previous Period (100 Million US Dollars)								
2004	1	8.00	4.81	4.84	2.57	2.75	2.12	0.04	-1.50	192.63
	2	19.62	7.84	7.84	6.00	6.03	5.82	-0.09	0.05	53.36
	3	15.75	10.70	10.70	0.25	0.30	7.28	0.13	-2.16	-66.65
	4	9.48	4.02	4.01	5.24	5.22	3.51	0.14	-2.98	6.65
	5	8.05	4.75	4.71	3.99	4.01	-0.19	0.02	-0.66	-17.45
	6	3.89	1.67	1.66	6.75	6.74	-0.10	-0.04	2.31	-46.71
	7	-6.32	1.02	1.03	0.04	0.21	-6.28	-0.14	-1.28	29.36
	8	1.04	31.08	31.08	-30.78	-29.08	-0.68	-0.09	1.42	36.78
	9	-4.36	-39.01	-39.01	38.70	36.92	-1.39	0.18	-2.75	76.56
	10	-13.03	0.76	0.76	-12.23	-12.20	-2.77	0.20	1.18	35.24
	11	9.67	3.84	3.84	-2.76	-0.96	1.54	-0.26	7.97	29.07
	12	3.08	-8.54	-8.51	6.35	8.49	4.00	0.14	1.04	-38.71
		比去年同期增长（%） Increase Rate Year - on - year (%)								
2004	1	26.86	58.98	58.96	19.42	18.86	151.73	72.31	-11.90	23.51
	2	29.06	60.18	60.15	20.88	20.34	176.00	28.75	-10.97	32.55
	3	28.48	57.93	57.91	20.45	19.96	159.35	34.88	-12.70	16.76
	4	26.73	53.34	53.31	21.07	21.83	126.42	58.54	-13.84	15.53
	5	25.29	49.90	49.86	22.26	23.04	96.58	59.04	-14.50	17.34
	6	21.60	41.71	41.67	20.81	21.50	71.96	50.59	-10.98	8.34
	7	19.74	37.11	37.07	21.31	22.00	56.68		-10.63	5.83
	8	17.04	43.67	43.63	6.37	7.28	47.97		-6.82	11.73
	9	11.33	20.30	20.26	13.68	14.05	37.91	7.89	-8.68	27.08
	10	7.67	16.60	16.59	7.61	7.87	32.94	38.83	-8.46	34.59
	11	7.33	9.41	9.39	11.05	11.96	26.67	21.88	-1.20	47.85
	12	6.60	2.66	2.66	12.89	14.53	21.63	21.30	2.07	40.64

国有商业银行外汇信贷收支主要指标时间序列表

Time Series of Major Indicators in Sources and Uses of Credit Funds of State - owned Commercial Banks（Foreign Currency）

年 月 Year Month		各项存款 Total Deposits	单位活期存款 Demand Deposits by Enterprises	单位定期存款 Time Deposits by Enterprises	储蓄存款 Savings Deposits	定期储蓄 Time Deposits	境外存款 Foreign Deposits	境外筹资 Overseas Financing
期末余额（亿美元） Balance（100 Million US Dollars）								
2005	1	1074.88	196.36	143.03	656.38	532.39	0.12	143.97
	2	1087.21	192.29	161.06	657.29	534.78	0.10	142.67
	3	1094.98	198.47	161.72	651.13	525.58	0.10	136.93
	4	1078.95	183.05	169.20	641.84	519.86	0.11	146.09
	5	1061.29	188.04	161.51	627.88	504.32	0.10	141.77
	6	1064.30	203.85	154.56	620.28	498.98	0.09	126.53
	7	1044.41	191.46	154.54	612.64	491.15	0.09	115.64
	8	1056.77	232.75	135.10	602.00	482.80	0.15	117.15
	9	1019.09	184.45	153.42	595.91	479.16	0.48	110.18
	10	1036.22	199.92	155.12	596.70	477.73	0.56	109.29
	11	1041.87	203.96	163.68	593.31	475.86	0.13	107.11
	12	1041.00	202.43	158.68	596.72	479.00	0.09	101.75
比上期增减额（亿美元） Changes Compared with Previous Period（100 Million US Dollars）								
2005	1	-4.09	11.45	-9.19	-6.90	-7.66	-0.05	1.98
	2	12.33	-4.07	18.03	0.91	2.39	-0.02	-1.30
	3	7.77	6.18	0.66	-6.16	-9.20	0.00	-5.74
	4	-16.03	-15.42	7.48	-9.29	-5.72	0.01	9.16
	5	-17.66	4.99	-7.69	-13.96	-15.54	-0.01	-4.32
	6	3.01	15.81	-6.95	-7.60	-5.34	-0.01	-15.24
	7	-19.89	-12.39	-0.02	-7.64	-7.83		-10.89
	8	12.36	41.29	-19.44	-10.64	-8.35	0.06	1.51
	9	-37.68	-48.30	18.32	-6.09	-3.64	0.33	-6.97
	10	17.13	15.47	1.70	0.79	-1.43	0.08	-0.89
	11	5.65	4.04	8.56	-3.39	-1.87	-0.43	-2.18
	12	-0.87	-1.53	-5.00	3.41	3.14	-0.04	-5.36
比去年同期增长（%） Increase Rate Year - on - year（%）								
2005	1	-2.52	18.14	-7.53	-10.28	-14.87	-40.00	4.36
	2	1.96	19.12	13.57	-7.69	-11.67	-28.57	3.50
	3	2.30	19.47	12.21	-7.77	-11.84	-37.50	0.85
	4	0.77	14.79	10.85	-8.19	-11.45	-38.89	14.19
	5	-2.09	9.09	7.95	-10.31	-13.59	-41.18	10.45
	6	-2.05	15.37	-9.30	-8.36	-10.66	-40.00	1.30
	7	-5.26	3.91	1.62	-12.10	-14.66	-43.75	-6.08
	8	-5.30	22.02	-7.74	-13.85	-15.99		-10.89
	9	-8.60	6.10	-2.07	-14.85	-16.42	300.00	-25.79
	10	-7.49	9.14	-2.11	-14.30	-15.72	229.41	-24.51
	11	-4.82	6.26	8.50	-11.60	-13.25	-60.61	-27.75
	12	-3.51	9.49	4.26	-10.03	-11.30	-50.00	-28.26

国有商业银行外汇信贷收支主要指标时间序列表

Time Series of Major Indicators in Sources and Uses of Credit Funds of State - owned Commercial Banks（Foreign Currency）

年　月 Year Month	各项贷款 Total Loans	短期贷款 Short - term Loans	境内短期贷款 Domestic Short - term Loans	中长期贷款 Medium and Long - term Loans	境内中长期贷款 Domestic Medium and Long - term Loans	进出口贸易融资 Financing for Import and Export Trades	票据融资 Paper Financing	境外筹资转贷款 On - lending of Overseas Financing	有价证券及投资 Securities and Investments
期末余额（亿美元） Balance（100 Million US Dollars）									
2005 1	797.28	274.03	273.98	321.98	321.59	73.13	1.31	115.82	1046.05
2	795.06	273.95	273.90	319.93	319.93	72.81	1.29	116.05	1049.52
3	798.57	272.08	272.03	323.19	323.19	76.35	1.40	114.40	1055.18
4	797.52	266.38	266.33	327.25	327.25	77.48	1.30	113.94	1142.43
5	799.69	270.41	270.30	323.25	323.25	83.22	1.15	110.96	1121.85
6	783.65	260.11	260.05	320.10	320.10	87.28	1.19	106.16	1101.69
7	800.62	283.79	283.79	318.84	318.75	83.75	1.06	104.33	1067.37
8	778.32	257.56	257.56	321.94	321.85	84.88	0.97	103.92	1070.83
9	768.74	249.44	249.44	320.28	320.19	86.06	0.91	102.85	1087.15
10	776.22	242.77	242.77	336.38	336.37	84.63	0.84	102.16	1119.03
11	763.08	233.88	233.88	333.88	333.87	85.94	0.89	98.83	1113.12
12	747.58	229.51	229.51	322.85	322.84	89.92	0.73	95.50	1057.77
比上期增减额（亿美元） Changes Compared with Previous Period（100 Million US Dollars）									
2005 1	18.06	16.44	16.44	3.93	3.93	1.56	0.01	-3.84	40.69
2	-2.21	-0.08	-0.08	-2.04	-1.66	-0.32	-0.03	0.23	3.47
3	3.50	-1.86	-1.86	3.25	3.25	3.54	0.11	-1.65	5.66
4	-1.03	-5.71	-5.71	4.08	4.08	1.13	-0.10	-0.46	87.25
5	9.91	9.70	9.64	-2.71	-2.71	6.02	-0.15	-2.96	-20.58
6	2.50	2.13	2.18	-0.01	-0.01	4.59	0.04	-4.42	-20.16
7	16.95	23.67	23.73	-1.27	-1.36	-3.53	-0.13	-1.83	-34.32
8	-22.25	-26.21	-26.21	3.11	3.11	1.14	-0.09	-0.41	3.46
9	-9.61	-8.14	-8.14	-1.66	-1.66	1.17	-0.06	-1.07	16.32
10	7.48	-6.67	-6.67	16.09	16.18	-1.42	-0.07	-0.69	31.88
11	-13.14	-8.88	-8.88	-2.51	-2.51	1.31	0.05	-3.33	-5.91
12	-15.49	-4.37	-4.37	-11.01	-11.01	3.98	-0.16	-3.33	-55.35
比去年同期增长（%） Increase Rate Year - on - year（%）									
2005 1	7.71	3.85	3.85	15.81	17.41	19.35	17.86	0.24	15.23
2	5.01	1.19	1.18	12.96	14.59	8.61	25.24	0.38	9.19
3	3.52	-2.78	-2.79	13.90	15.53	2.78	20.69	0.79	17.96
4	2.30	-5.76	-5.76	13.31	14.91	-0.38		2.87	26.77
5	2.49	-4.17	-4.18	11.08	12.62	7.56	-12.88	0.99	27.01
6	2.65	-4.53	-4.52	9.86	11.53	13.68	-7.03	-4.93	31.69
7	5.65	3.23	3.26	9.41	10.99	18.74	-7.08	-5.48	23.26
8	2.67	-14.79	-14.77	23.31	24.49	21.51	-7.69	-7.04	18.63
9	2.01	-5.97	-5.94	7.03	8.56	25.64	-26.23	-5.68	11.02
10	4.72	-8.56	-8.53	17.06	18.82	28.75	-41.26	-7.31	10.31
11	1.72	-8.02	-7.99	11.45	12.38	27.76	-23.93	-16.35	6.67
12	-0.67	-6.71	-6.69	5.61	5.74	26.19	-44.27	-19.86	5.27

（五）其他商业银行外汇信贷收支主要指标时间序列表（1998—2005 年月度时序）

Time Series of Major Indicators in Sources and Uses of Credit Funds of Other Commercial Banks（Foreign Currency）（Monthly Series from 1998 to 2005）

其他商业银行外汇信贷收支主要指标时间序列表

Time Series of Major Indicators in Sources and Uses of Credit Funds of Other Commercial Banks（Foreign Currency）

年 月 Year Month		各项存款 Total Deposits	单位活期存款 Demand Deposits by Enterprises	单位定期存款 Time Deposits by Enterprises	储蓄存款 Savings Deposits	定期储蓄 Time Deposits	境外存款 Foreign Deposits	境外筹资 Overseas Financing
期末余额（亿美元） Balance（100 Million US Dollars）								
1998	1	136.64	23.66	64.58	23.83	21.35	13.58	16.26
	2	135.93	23.57	63.51	24.88	22.47	13.75	15.72
	3	140.30	24.32	65.53	26.02	23.62	14.09	16.15
	4	141.83	22.16	66.95	26.98	24.55	14.76	15.87
	5	143.77	23.23	67.09	27.80	25.27	15.01	14.66
	6	141.69	21.82	65.19	28.94	26.42	14.80	14.49
	7	143.07	22.11	67.22	30.45	27.84	13.34	14.09
	8	149.71	21.97	71.20	32.17	29.51	12.82	14.39
	9	151.24	21.77	73.19	32.80	30.29	13.77	12.92
	10	150.80	21.50	72.36	33.72	31.18	13.63	12.45
	11	150.84	21.46	70.91	34.53	31.96	13.02	12.61
	12	149.16	20.55	68.40	35.33	32.59	13.87	12.92
比上期增减额（亿美元） Changes Compared with Previous Period（100 Million US Dollars）								
1998	1	-1.87	-2.06	0.79	0.92	0.90	-0.86	-0.43
	2	-0.71	-0.09	-1.07	1.05	1.12	0.17	-0.54
	3	4.38	0.75	2.02	1.14	1.15	0.34	0.43
	4	1.53	-2.16	1.42	0.96	0.93	0.67	-0.28
	5	1.94	1.07	0.14	0.82	0.72	0.25	-1.21
	6	-2.08	-1.41	-1.90	1.14	1.15	-0.21	-0.17
	7	1.38	0.29	2.02	1.51	1.42	-1.46	-0.40
	8	6.63	-0.14	3.98	1.72	1.67	-0.52	0.30
	9	1.53	-0.20	1.99	0.63	0.78	0.95	-1.47
	10	-0.44	-0.27	-0.83	0.92	0.89	-0.14	-0.47
	11	0.04	-0.04	-1.45	0.81	0.78	-0.61	0.16
	12	-1.68	-0.92	-2.52	0.80	0.63	0.85	0.31

其他商业银行外汇信贷收支主要指标时间序列表
Time Series of Major Indicators in Sources and Uses of Credit Funds of Other Commercial Banks (Foreign Currency)

年 月 Year Month		各项贷款 Total Loans	短期贷款 Short－term Loans	境内短期贷款 Domestic Short－term Loans	中长期贷款 Medium and Long－term Loans	境内中长期贷款 Domestic Medium and Long－term Loans	进出口贸易融资 Financing for Import and Export Trades	票据融资 Paper Financing	境外筹资转贷款 On－lending of Overseas Financing	有价证券及投资 Securities and Investments
		期末余额（亿美元） Balance (100 Million US Dollars)								
1998	1	130.58	60.02	52.54	27.41	21.80	10.84	0.24	6.55	27.26
	2	131.05	58.33	51.12	27.95	22.18	11.12	0.23	6.32	26.87
	3	132.80	58.54	50.89	28.09	22.23	11.53	0.20	6.28	23.21
	4	132.86	56.92	49.81	28.38	22.38	11.99	0.22	6.25	22.41
	5	131.39	55.89	48.99	27.54	21.61	11.61	0.22	6.24	22.40
	6	130.67	54.36	47.68	27.11	21.34	11.33	0.23	5.99	21.40
	7	129.83	53.04	46.45	27.16	21.07	10.93	0.22	5.96	21.85
	8	127.83	50.68	44.22	26.96	20.90	10.66	0.21	6.01	21.99
	9	128.76	49.61	43.28	27.58	21.50	11.08	0.17	5.78	21.15
	10	128.24	48.23	41.70	27.73	21.65	10.85	0.14	5.31	22.11
	11	127.83	47.40	40.70	28.07	21.98	11.13	0.13	5.23	22.91
	12	125.55	48.31	42.13	28.39	22.03	10.29	0.10	4.69	21.78
		比上期增减额（亿美元） Changes Compared with Previous Period (100 Million US Dollars)								
1998	1	－2.95	－2.18	－1.50	－0.27	－0.75	－1.02	－0.02	－0.30	0.01
	2	0.47	－1.69	－1.42	0.54	0.38	0.28	－0.01	－0.23	－0.39
	3	1.75	0.21	－0.23	0.14	0.05	0.41	－0.03	－0.04	－3.66
	4	0.06	－1.62	－1.08	0.29	0.15	0.46	0.02	－0.03	－0.80
	5	－1.47	－1.03	－0.82	－0.84	－0.77	－0.38		－0.01	－0.01
	6	－0.72	－1.53	－1.31	－0.43	－0.27	－0.28	0.01	－0.25	－1.00
	7	－0.84	－1.32	－1.23	0.05	－0.27	－0.40	－0.01	－0.03	0.45
	8	－2.00	－2.36	－2.23	－0.20	－0.17	－0.27	－0.01	0.05	0.13
	9	0.93	－1.07	－0.94	0.62	0.60	0.42	－0.04	－0.23	－0.83
	10	－0.52	－1.38	－1.58	0.15	0.15	－0.23	－0.03	－0.47	0.96
	11	－0.41	－0.83	－1.00	0.34	0.33	0.28	－0.01	－0.08	0.80
	12	－2.29	0.90	1.42	0.32	0.05	－0.84	－0.03	－0.54	－1.13

其他商业银行外汇信贷收支主要指标时间序列表

Time Series of Major Indicators in Sources and Uses of Credit Funds of Other Commercial Banks（Foreign Currency）

年 月 Year Month		各项存款 Total Deposits	单位活期存款 Demand Deposits by Enterprises	单位定期存款 Time Deposits by Enterprises	储蓄存款 Savings Deposits	定期储蓄 Time Deposits	境外存款 Foreign Deposits	境外筹资 Overseas Financing
		期末余额（亿美元） Balance（100 Million US Dollars）						
1999	1	149.37	21.72	67.72	36.04	33.30	13.43	13.01
	2	150.98	21.24	69.70	36.99	34.08	12.60	12.09
	3	148.73	21.15	67.95	37.72	34.86	11.55	12.14
	4	148.02	21.18	66.74	38.38	35.48	10.77	11.68
	5	148.80	21.77	67.59	39.32	36.32	10.01	11.62
	6	148.37	22.96	63.14	40.65	37.47	9.99	11.83
	7	149.12	22.24	63.37	42.18	38.90	10.28	11.25
	8	152.30	22.07	64.60	44.09	40.70	10.20	11.61
	9	157.04	22.01	67.33	46.06	42.61	9.58	11.73
	10	160.26	21.87	68.42	47.84	44.17	9.58	11.84
	11	164.93	21.31	71.86	49.67	45.92	9.16	10.58
	12	168.61	21.09	72.58	51.28	47.45	9.49	10.17
		比上期增减额（亿美元） Changes Compared with Previous Period（100 Million US Dollars）						
1999	1	0.19	1.20	-0.72	0.69	0.69	-0.44	0.09
	2	1.61	-0.48	1.98	0.95	0.78	-0.83	-0.92
	3	-2.25	-0.09	-1.75	0.73	0.78	-1.05	0.05
	4	-0.71	0.03	-1.21	0.66	0.62	-0.78	-0.46
	5	0.78	0.59	0.85	0.94	0.84	-0.76	-0.06
	6	-0.42	1.19	-4.45	1.33	1.15	-0.02	0.21
	7	0.78	-0.72	0.25	1.53	1.43	0.29	-0.58
	8	3.17	-0.17	1.23	1.91	1.80	-0.08	0.36
	9	4.74	-0.06	2.72	1.97	1.91	-0.62	0.12
	10	3.20	-0.14	1.09	1.78	1.56		0.11
	11	4.67	-0.56	3.44	1.83	1.75	-0.42	-1.26
	12	3.68	-0.22	0.70	1.61	1.53	0.33	-0.41
		比去年同期增长（%） Increase Rate Year-on-year（%）						
1999	1	9.32	-8.20	4.86	51.24	55.97	-1.10	-19.99
	2	11.09	-9.89	9.75	48.67	51.67	-8.36	-23.09
	3	6.01	-13.03	3.69	44.97	47.59	-18.03	-24.83
	4	4.36	-4.42	-0.31	42.25	44.52	-27.03	-26.40
	5	3.50	-6.28	0.75	41.44	43.73	-33.31	-20.74
	6	4.70	5.22	-3.14	40.46	41.82	-32.50	-18.36
	7	4.24	0.59	-5.73	38.52	39.73	-22.94	-20.16
	8	1.73	0.46	-9.27	37.05	37.92	-20.44	-19.32
	9	3.85	1.10	-7.98	40.43	40.67	-30.43	-9.21
	10	6.27	1.72	-5.44	41.87	41.66	-29.71	-4.90
	11	9.34	-0.70	1.37	43.85	43.68	-29.65	-16.10
	12	13.04	2.68	6.10	45.15	45.60	-31.58	-21.28

其他商业银行外汇信贷收支主要指标时间序列表

Time Series of Major Indicators in Sources and Uses of Credit Funds of Other Commercial Banks (Foreign Currency)

年 Year	月 Month	各项贷款 Total Loans	短期贷款 Short－term Loans	境内短期贷款 Domestic Short－term Loans	中长期贷款 Medium and Long－term Loans	境内中长期贷款 Domestic Medium and Long－term Loans	进出口贸易融资 Financing for Import and Export Trades	票据融资 Paper Financing	境外筹资转贷款 On－lending of Overseas Financing	有价证券及投资 Securities and Investments
		期末余额（亿美元） Balance（100 Million US Dollars）								
1999	1	122.78	46.34	40.80	27.41	21.00	9.85	0.10	4.33	21.75
	2	121.60	44.94	40.04	27.20	21.34	9.56	0.09	3.71	21.24
	3	122.31	43.68	39.41	27.07	21.11	8.93	0.09	3.55	20.44
	4	121.19	42.24	38.19	26.84	21.13	8.81	0.08	3.14	20.60
	5	120.46	39.81	36.18	26.60	20.92	8.82	0.07	3.31	21.36
	6	120.06	40.22	36.88	25.24	19.70	8.98	0.07	3.23	21.92
	7	119.42	38.44	35.31	26.20	20.82	8.69	0.07	3.24	21.84
	8	118.09	37.73	34.84	25.61	20.54	8.76	0.08	2.93	22.83
	9	117.58	36.80	34.04	25.03	20.04	9.14	0.09	2.44	23.87
	10	115.61	35.83	33.19	24.44	19.51	8.58	0.09	2.42	24.92
	11	114.64	34.27	31.97	24.18	19.81	8.54	0.09	2.42	26.44
	12	112.58	34.91	32.23	24.09	19.83	8.60	0.12	2.32	27.74
		比上期增减额（亿美元） Changes Compared with Previous Period（100 Million US Dollars）								
1999	1	－0.57	－0.33	0.31	－0.36	－0.39	－0.47		－0.36	0.01
	2	－1.18	－1.40	－0.76	－0.21	0.34	－0.29	－0.01	－0.62	－0.51
	3	0.71	－1.26	－0.63	－0.13	－0.23	－0.63		－0.16	－0.80
	4	－1.12	－1.44	－1.22	－0.23	0.02	－0.12	－0.01	－0.41	0.16
	5	－0.73	－2.43	－2.01	－0.24	－0.21	0.01	－0.01	0.17	0.76
	6	－0.40	0.41	0.70	－1.36	－1.22	0.16		－0.08	0.56
	7	－0.64	－1.78	－1.57	0.96	1.12	－0.29		0.01	－0.08
	8	－1.33	－0.71	－0.47	－0.59	－0.28	0.07	0.01	－0.31	0.99
	9	－0.51	－0.93	－0.80	－0.58	－0.50	0.38	0.01	－0.49	1.04
	10	－1.97	－0.97	－0.85	－0.59	－0.53	－0.56		－0.02	1.04
	11	－0.97	－1.56	－1.22	－0.26	0.30	－0.04			1.52
	12	－2.06	0.64	0.26	－0.09	0.02	0.06	0.03	－0.10	1.30
		比去年同期增长（%） Increase Rate Year－on－year（%）								
1999	1	－5.44	－22.79	－22.34	2.74	－0.33	－9.13	－58.33	－33.89	－20.21
	2	－6.67	－22.96	－21.67	0.04	－0.37	－14.03	－60.87	－41.30	－20.95
	3	－7.37	－25.38	－22.56	－0.95	－1.68	－22.55	－55.00	－43.47	－11.93
	4	－8.26	－25.79	－23.33	－2.82	－2.27	－26.52	－63.64	－49.76	－8.08
	5	－7.79	－28.77	－26.15	－0.67	0.34	－24.03	－68.18	－46.96	－4.64
	6	－7.58	－26.01	－22.65	－4.21	－4.28	－20.74	－69.57	－46.08	2.43
	7	－7.48	－27.53	－23.98	－0.76	2.51	－20.49	－68.18	－45.64	－0.05
	8	－7.10	－25.55	－21.21	－2.44	1.73	－17.82	－61.90	－51.25	3.91
	9	－8.20	－25.82	－21.35	－6.95	－3.75	－17.51	－47.06	－57.79	12.86
	10	－9.37	－25.71	－20.41	－9.65	－6.96	－20.92	－35.71	－54.43	12.62
	11	－9.84	－27.70	－21.45	－11.72	－7.00	－23.27	－30.77	－53.73	15.41
	12	－9.84	－27.72	－23.48	－13.06	－7.12	－16.42	20.00	－50.53	27.36

其他商业银行外汇信贷收支主要指标时间序列表

Time Series of Major Indicators in Sources and Uses of Credit Funds of Other Commercial Banks（Foreign Currency）

年 月 Year Month		各项存款 Total Deposits						境外筹资 Overseas Financing
			单位活期存款 Demand Deposits by Enterprises	单位定期存款 Time Deposits by Enterprises	储蓄存款 Savings Deposits	定期储蓄 Time Deposits	境外存款 Foreign Deposits	
期末余额（亿美元） Balance（100 Million US Dollars）								
2000	1	171.53	20.90	75.32	53.39	49.44	9.35	10.03
	2	173.84	20.58	75.15	54.91	50.91	9.72	10.02
	3	178.72	21.20	77.50	56.55	52.46	8.92	10.70
	4	180.84	20.98	78.59	58.12	53.90	8.70	10.67
	5	185.41	21.79	79.49	59.97	55.66	8.55	10.68
	6	190.94	23.28	82.14	62.29	57.96	8.42	10.59
	7	192.77	21.94	82.88	64.80	60.29	8.40	10.58
	8	197.20	22.24	83.83	67.34	62.55	8.17	10.57
	9	202.38	22.62	84.33	70.10	65.14	8.63	4.76
	10	206.80	22.89	86.64	73.12	67.94	7.38	4.74
	11	211.45	22.23	87.26	75.92	70.62	7.43	4.77
	12	218.42	22.98	91.32	78.37	72.85	7.98	4.84
比上期增减额（亿美元） Changes Compared with Previous Period（100 Million US Dollars）								
2000	1	2.91	-0.20	2.74	2.11	1.99	-0.14	-0.14
	2	2.31	-0.32	-0.17	1.52	1.47	0.37	-0.01
	3	4.88	0.62	2.35	1.64	1.55	-0.80	0.68
	4	2.12	-0.22	1.09	1.57	1.44	-0.22	-0.03
	5	4.57	0.81	0.90	1.85	1.76	-0.15	0.01
	6	5.53	1.49	2.65	2.32	2.30	-0.13	-0.09
	7	1.83	-1.34	0.74	2.51	2.33	-0.02	-0.01
	8	4.43	0.30	0.95	2.54	2.26	-0.23	-0.01
	9	5.18	0.38	0.50	2.76	2.59	0.46	-5.81
	10	4.42	0.27	2.31	3.02	2.80	-1.25	-0.02
	11	4.65	-0.66	0.62	2.80	2.68	0.05	0.03
	12	6.97	0.75	4.06	2.45	2.23	0.55	0.07
比去年同期增长（%） Increase Rate Year-on-year（%）								
2000	1	14.84	-3.78	11.22	48.14	48.47	-30.38	-22.91
	2	15.14	-3.11	7.82	48.45	49.38	-22.86	-17.12
	3	20.16	0.24	14.05	49.92	50.49	-22.77	-11.86
	4	22.17	-0.94	17.76	51.43	51.92	-19.22	-8.65
	5	24.60	0.09	17.61	52.52	53.25	-14.59	-8.09
	6	28.71	1.39	30.09	53.23	54.68	-15.72	-10.48
	7	29.24	-1.35	30.75	53.63	54.99	-18.29	-5.96
	8	29.48	0.77	29.77	52.73	53.69	-19.90	-8.96
	9	28.86	2.77	25.21	52.19	52.87	-9.92	-59.42
	10	29.04	4.66	26.63	52.84	53.81	-22.96	-59.97
	11	28.21	4.32	21.40	52.85	53.79	-18.89	-54.91
	12	29.54	8.96	25.82	52.83	53.53	-15.91	-52.41

其他商业银行外汇信贷收支主要指标时间序列表

Time Series of Major Indicators in Sources and Uses of Credit Funds of Other Commercial Banks (Foreign Currency)

年 月 Year Month		各项贷款 Total Loans	短期贷款 Short-term Loans	境内短期贷款 Domestic Short-term Loans	中长期贷款 Medium and Long-term Loans	境内中长期贷款 Domestic Medium and Long-term Loans	进出口贸易融资 Financing for Import and Export Trades	票据融资 Paper Financing	境外筹资转贷款 On-lending of Overseas Financing	有价证券及投资 Securities and Investments
		期末余额（亿美元） Balance (100 Million US Dollars)								
2000	1	110.22	33.60	30.90	22.32	18.39	8.57	0.10	2.30	29.04
	2	108.42	32.10	29.37	21.95	18.05	8.21	0.10	2.37	30.95
	3	108.55	31.84	29.08	21.69	17.86	8.31	0.09	2.38	34.45
	4	107.50	31.66	29.10	21.22	17.46	8.24	0.10	2.31	37.61
	5	106.89	30.38	27.82	19.68	16.83	8.55	0.09	2.33	38.01
	6	107.81	31.11	28.56	19.30	16.63	8.62	0.08	2.34	39.17
	7	106.02	28.75	26.50	18.53	15.89	8.27	0.07	2.38	38.74
	8	104.77	27.68	25.50	18.36	15.65	8.37	0.08	2.43	40.09
	9	98.49	27.89	26.07	17.98	15.30	7.58	0.10	2.16	40.22
	10	97.08	27.47	25.74	16.72	14.17	7.47	0.11	2.13	42.51
	11	95.33	26.64	25.05	15.39	12.92	7.69	0.22	2.25	44.99
	12	91.55	26.71	24.57	14.22	12.18	7.96	0.22	2.15	45.91
		比上期增减额（亿美元） Changes Compared with Previous Period (100 Million US Dollars)								
2000	1	-2.35	-1.08	-1.10	-1.78	-1.45	-0.03	-0.02	-0.02	1.30
	2	-1.80	-1.50	-1.53	-0.37	-0.34	-0.36		0.07	1.91
	3	0.13	-0.26	-0.29	-0.26	-0.19	0.10	-0.01	0.01	3.50
	4	-1.05	-0.18	0.02	-0.47	-0.40	-0.07	0.01	-0.07	3.16
	5	-0.61	-1.28	-1.28	-1.54	-0.63	0.31	-0.01	0.02	0.40
	6	0.92	0.73	0.74	-0.38	-0.20	0.07	-0.01	0.01	1.16
	7	-1.79	-2.36	-2.06	-0.77	-0.74	-0.35	-0.01	0.04	-0.43
	8	-1.25	-1.07	-1.00	-0.17	-0.24	0.10	0.01	0.05	1.35
	9	-6.28	0.21	0.57	-0.38	-0.35	-0.79	0.02	-0.27	0.13
	10	-1.41	-0.42	-0.33	-1.26	-1.13	-0.11	0.01	-0.03	2.29
	11	-1.75	-0.83	-0.69	-1.33	-1.25	0.22	0.11	0.12	2.48
	12	-3.78	0.07	-0.48	-1.17	-0.74	0.27		-0.10	0.92
		比去年同期增长（%） Increase Rate Year-on-year (%)								
2000	1	-10.23	-27.49	-24.26	-18.57	-12.43	-12.99		-46.88	33.52
	2	-10.84	-28.57	-26.65	-19.30	-15.42	-14.12	11.11	-36.12	45.72
	3	-11.25	-27.11	-26.21	-19.87	-15.40	-6.94		-32.96	68.54
	4	-11.30	-25.05	-23.80	-20.94	-17.37	-6.47	25.00	-26.43	82.57
	5	-11.27	-23.69	-23.11	-26.02	-19.55	-3.06	28.57	-29.61	77.95
	6	-10.20	-22.65	-22.56	-23.53	-15.58	-4.01	14.29	-27.55	78.70
	7	-11.22	-25.21	-24.95	-29.27	-23.68	-4.83		-26.54	77.38
	8	-11.28	-26.64	-26.81	-28.31	-23.81	-4.45		-17.06	75.60
	9	-16.24	-24.21	-23.41	-28.17	-23.65	-17.07	11.11	-11.48	68.50
	10	-16.03	-23.33	-22.45	-31.59	-27.37	-12.94	22.22	-11.98	70.72
	11	-16.84	-22.26	-21.65	-36.35	-34.78	-9.95	144.44	-7.02	70.16
	12	-18.68	-23.49	-23.77	-40.97	-38.58	-7.44	83.33	-7.33	65.50

其他商业银行外汇信贷收支主要指标时间序列表

Time Series of Major Indicators in Sources and Uses of Credit Funds of Other Commercial Banks（Foreign Currency）

年 月 Year	Month	各项存款 Total Deposits	单位活期存款 Demand Deposits by Enterprises	单位定期存款 Time Deposits by Enterprises	储蓄存款 Savings Deposits	定期储蓄 Time Deposits	境外存款 Foreign Deposits	境外筹资 Overseas Financing
		期末余额（亿美元） Balance（100 Million US Dollars）						
2001	1	223.61	22.47	94.28	80.90	75.18	7.69	4.82
	2	222.66	23.16	93.79	79.44	73.89	7.75	4.90
	3	227.51	23.55	97.24	79.87	74.08	8.46	4.67
	4	226.24	23.76	94.04	80.88	74.78	9.03	4.73
	5	234.54	25.13	100.28	82.58	75.57	8.47	4.74
	6	235.66	25.89	99.39	83.39	76.15	9.01	4.73
	7	236.01	25.30	98.43	85.52	77.70	9.23	4.71
	8	240.40	27.06	99.62	87.66	79.37	8.96	4.52
	9	240.51	26.12	98.43	90.18	81.43	8.59	4.53
	10	239.67	26.98	95.47	91.97	82.71	8.27	4.54
	11	238.84	27.99	92.89	93.14	83.56	8.61	4.51
	12	232.41	27.75	88.13	93.45	83.52	8.65	4.54
		比上期增减额（亿美元） Changes Compared with Previous Period（100 Million US Dollars）						
2001	1	5.09	-0.52	2.86	2.47	2.27	-0.29	-0.02
	2	-0.95	0.69	-0.49	-1.46	-1.29	0.06	0.08
	3	4.85	0.39	3.45	0.43	0.19	0.71	-0.23
	4	-1.27	0.21	-3.20	1.01	0.70	0.57	0.06
	5	8.30	1.37	6.24	1.70	0.79	-0.56	0.01
	6	1.12	0.76	-0.89	0.81	0.58	0.54	-0.01
	7	0.35	-0.59	-0.96	2.13	1.55	0.22	-0.02
	8	4.39	1.76	1.19	2.14	1.67	-0.27	-0.19
	9	0.11	-0.94	-1.19	2.52	2.06	-0.37	0.01
	10	-0.84	0.86	-2.96	1.79	1.28	-0.32	0.01
	11	-0.83	1.01	-2.58	1.17	0.85	0.34	-0.03
	12	-6.43	-0.24	-4.76	0.31	-0.04	0.04	0.03
		比去年同期增长（%） Increase Rate Year-on-year（%）						
2001	1	30.36	7.51	25.17	51.53	52.06	-17.75	-51.94
	2	28.08	12.54	24.80	44.67	45.14	-20.27	-51.10
	3	27.30	11.08	25.47	41.24	41.21	-5.16	-56.36
	4	25.11	13.25	19.66	39.16	38.74	3.79	-55.67
	5	26.50	15.33	26.15	37.70	35.77	-0.94	-55.62
	6	23.42	11.21	21.00	33.87	31.38	7.01	-55.34
	7	22.43	15.31	18.76	31.98	28.88	9.88	-55.48
	8	21.91	21.67	18.84	30.18	26.89	9.67	-57.24
	9	18.84	15.47	16.72	28.64	25.01	-0.46	-4.83
	10	15.89	17.87	10.19	25.78	21.74	12.06	-4.22
	11	12.95	25.91	6.45	22.68	18.32	15.88	-5.45
	12	6.41	20.76	-3.49	19.24	14.65	8.40	-6.20

其他商业银行外汇信贷收支主要指标时间序列表

Time Series of Major Indicators in Sources and Uses of Credit Funds of Other Commercial Banks (Foreign Currency)

年　月 Year Month		各项贷款 Total Loans	短期贷款 Short－term Loans	境内短期贷款 Domestic Short－term Loans	中长期贷款 Medium and Long－term Loans	境内中长期贷款 Domestic Medium and Long－term Loans	进出口贸易融资 Financing for Import and Export Trades	票据融资 Paper Financing	境外筹资转贷款 On－lending of Overseas Financing	有价证券及投资 Securities and Investments
		期末余额（亿美元） Balance (100 Million US Dollars)								
2001	1	91.27	47.98	44.53	26.06	20.84	9.75	0.34	2.59	49.40
	2	90.77	48.18	44.88	25.49	20.35	9.45	0.35	2.61	52.37
	3	93.36	49.44	45.92	26.77	20.95	9.82	0.33	2.53	56.56
	4	94.05	49.76	46.37	26.79	20.91	9.97	0.33	2.61	58.63
	5	93.93	49.06	45.90	27.12	21.06	10.29	0.30	2.64	60.26
	6	95.18	49.97	46.99	27.02	20.81	10.90	0.20	2.63	61.57
	7	95.07	49.15	46.20	28.10	21.05	10.55	0.22	2.63	64.93
	8	94.73	48.99	46.23	27.70	20.52	10.75	0.29	2.64	70.96
	9	94.42	49.15	46.36	27.09	19.95	10.81	0.33	2.67	74.63
	10	95.03	50.21	47.46	26.51	19.23	10.96	0.29	2.67	77.23
	11	96.81	52.75	50.03	25.80	18.50	11.20	0.12	2.64	83.83
	12	94.45	51.00	48.79	25.19	18.77	11.36	0.14	2.41	89.09
		比上期增减额（亿美元） Changes Compared with Previous Period (100 Million US Dollars)								
2001	1	－2.46	－2.00	－1.71	－0.77	－0.26	－0.05	0.11	0.23	3.49
	2	－0.50	0.20	0.35	－0.57	－0.49	－0.30	0.01	0.02	2.97
	3	2.59	1.26	1.04	1.28	0.60	0.37	－0.02	－0.08	4.19
	4	0.69	0.32	0.45	0.02	－0.04	0.15		0.08	2.07
	5	－0.12	－0.70	－0.47	0.33	0.15	0.32	－0.03	0.03	1.63
	6	1.25	0.91	1.09	－0.10	－0.25	0.61	－0.10	－0.01	1.31
	7	－0.11	－0.82	－0.79	1.08	0.24	－0.35	0.02		3.36
	8	－0.34	－0.16	0.03	－0.40	－0.53	0.20	0.07	0.01	6.03
	9	－0.31	0.16	0.13	－0.61	－0.57	0.06	0.04	0.03	3.67
	10	0.61	1.06	1.10	－0.58	－0.72	0.15	－0.04		2.60
	11	1.78	2.54	2.57	－0.71	－0.73	0.24	－0.17	－0.03	6.60
	12	－2.36	－1.75	－1.24	－0.61	0.27	0.16	0.02	－0.23	5.26
		比去年同期增长（%） Increase Rate Year－on－year (%)								
2001	1	－17.19	44.78	46.29	16.76	13.32	13.77	240.00	12.61	70.11
	2	－16.28	52.28	55.24	16.13	12.74	15.10	250.00	10.13	69.21
	3	－13.99	57.55	60.45	23.42	17.30	18.17	266.67	6.30	64.18
	4	－12.51	59.49	61.91	26.25	19.76	21.00	230.00	12.99	55.89
	5	－12.12	63.97	67.76	37.80	25.13	20.35	233.33	13.30	58.54
	6	－11.72	63.03	67.22	40.00	25.14	26.45	150.00	12.39	57.19
	7	－10.33	73.74	77.42	51.65	32.47	27.57	214.29	10.50	67.60
	8	－9.58	79.98	84.62	50.87	31.12	28.43	262.50	8.64	77.00
	9	－4.13	82.58	84.70	50.67	30.39	42.61	230.00	23.61	85.55
	10	－2.11	85.83	87.66	58.55	35.71	46.72	163.64	25.35	81.67
	11	1.55	101.41	103.37	67.64	43.19	45.64	－45.45	17.33	86.33
	12	3.17	94.29	102.36	77.14	54.11	42.71	－36.36	12.09	94.05

其他商业银行外汇信贷收支主要指标时间序列表
Time Series of Major Indicators in Sources and Uses of Credit Funds of Other Commercial Banks（Foreign Currency）

年 月 Year Month		各项存款 Total Deposits						境外筹资 Overseas Financing
			单位活期存款 Demand Deposits by Enterprises	单位定期存款 Time Deposits by Enterprises	储蓄存款 Savings Deposits	定期储蓄 Time Deposits	境外存款 Foreign Deposits	
期末余额（亿美元） Balance（100 Million US Dollars）								
2002	1	231.00	27.68	84.81	94.23	83.95	8.63	4.54
	2	233.04	28.96	84.87	95.18	84.56	8.80	4.14
	3	235.94	28.80	85.91	96.47	85.35	8.62	4.11
	4	233.81	26.64	85.34	97.79	86.44	7.98	4.19
	5	241.78	30.70	84.12	99.10	87.05	8.26	3.19
	6	243.43	30.47	83.88	100.73	87.65	8.16	3.24
	7	240.47	31.08	83.66	101.55	87.75	8.32	2.28
	8	243.12	32.34	83.10	102.94	88.37	8.16	2.34
	9	245.52	31.00	85.16	103.95	88.67	8.21	2.62
	10	251.20	35.30	84.08	104.78	88.89	9.00	2.35
	11	249.58	34.08	81.97	105.14	88.81	9.13	2.34
	12	257.61	35.23	85.55	106.99	89.33	9.76	2.36
比上期增减额（亿美元） Changes Compared with Previous Period（100 Million US Dollars）								
2002	1	-1.43	0.07	-1.55	0.78	0.43	-0.02	
	2	2.04	1.28	0.06	0.95	0.61	0.17	-0.40
	3	2.90	-0.16	1.04	1.29	0.79	-0.18	-0.03
	4	-2.13	-2.16	-0.57	1.32	1.09	-0.64	0.08
	5	7.97	4.06	-1.22	1.31	0.61	0.28	-1.00
	6	1.65	-0.23	-0.24	1.63	0.60	-0.10	0.05
	7	-2.96	0.61	-0.22	0.82	0.10	0.16	-0.96
	8	2.65	1.26	-0.56	1.39	0.62	-0.16	0.06
	9	2.40	-1.34	2.06	1.01	0.30	0.05	0.28
	10	5.68	4.30	-1.08	0.83	0.22	0.79	-0.27
	11	-1.62	-1.22	-2.11	0.36	-0.08	0.13	-0.01
	12	8.03	1.15	3.58	1.85	0.52	0.63	0.02
比去年同期增长（%） Increase Rate Year-on-year（%）								
2002	1	3.30	23.19	-10.04	16.48	11.67	12.22	-5.81
	2	4.66	25.04	-9.51	19.81	14.44	13.55	-15.51
	3	3.71	22.29	-11.65	20.78	15.21	1.89	-11.99
	4	3.35	12.12	-9.24	20.91	15.59	-11.63	-11.42
	5	3.09	22.16	-16.11	20.00	15.19	-2.48	-32.70
	6	3.30	17.69	-15.60	20.79	15.10	-9.43	-31.50
	7	1.89	22.85	-15.00	18.74	12.93	-9.86	-51.59
	8	1.13	19.51	-16.57	17.43	11.34	-8.93	-48.23
	9	2.08	18.68	-13.47	15.27	8.89	-4.42	-42.16
	10	4.81	30.84	-11.92	13.93	7.47	8.83	-48.24
	11	4.50	21.76	-11.76	12.88	6.28	6.04	-48.12
	12	10.84	26.95	-2.93	14.49	6.96	12.83	-48.02

其他商业银行外汇信贷收支主要指标时间序列表

Time Series of Major Indicators in Sources and Uses of Credit Funds of Other Commercial Banks (Foreign Currency)

年 月 Year Month		各项贷款 Total Loans	短期贷款 Short - term Loans	境内短期贷款 Domestic Short - term Loans	中长期贷款 Medium and Long - term Loans	境内中长期贷款 Domestic Medium and Long - term Loans	进出口贸易融资 Financing for Import and Export Trades	票据融资 Paper Financing	境外筹资转贷款 On - lending of Overseas Financing	有价证券及投资 Securities and Investments
期末余额（亿美元） Balance (100 Million US Dollars)										
2002	1	95.83	49.71	47.56	28.01	21.51	11.21	0.18	2.43	85.86
	2	98.12	50.76	48.61	29.86	23.39	10.62	0.14	2.43	85.56
	3	100.11	52.92	50.79	29.45	23.09	10.84	0.14	2.44	86.88
	4	100.57	53.20	51.26	28.90	22.24	11.43	0.23	2.54	91.03
	5	104.23	54.79	52.74	29.41	22.68	12.98	0.26	2.55	91.82
	6	103.85	52.14	50.14	31.04	24.21	13.39	0.51	2.62	92.72
	7	106.13	52.06	50.06	31.24	24.46	15.42	0.60	2.66	89.90
	8	107.63	51.75	49.85	30.66	23.92	17.85	0.59	2.64	91.08
	9	112.00	52.41	50.49	32.55	25.82	19.57	0.77	2.62	90.88
	10	113.14	52.96	51.08	32.32	25.60	20.32	0.87	2.63	92.03
	11	115.17	54.56	52.65	33.18	26.48	19.70	1.00	2.69	96.58
	12	115.80	55.88	53.13	33.00	27.15	19.02	1.05	2.69	94.66
比上期增减额（亿美元） Changes Compared with Previous Period (100 Million US Dollars)										
2002	1	1.36	1.52	1.58	0.09	0.01	-0.17	-0.04	0.02	-2.77
	2	2.29	1.05	1.05	1.85	1.88	-0.59	-0.04		-0.30
	3	1.99	2.16	2.18	-0.41	-0.30	0.22		0.01	1.32
	4	0.46	0.28	0.47	-0.55	-0.85	0.59	0.09	0.10	4.15
	5	3.66	1.59	1.48	0.51	0.44	1.55	0.03	0.01	0.79
	6	-0.38	-2.65	-2.60	1.63	1.53	0.41	0.25	0.07	0.90
	7	2.28	-0.08	-0.08	0.20	0.25	2.03	0.09	0.04	-2.82
	8	1.50	-0.31	-0.21	-0.58	-0.54	2.43	-0.01	-0.02	1.18
	9	4.37	0.66	0.64	1.89	1.90	1.72	0.18	-0.02	-0.20
	10	1.14	0.55	0.59	-0.23	-0.22	0.75	0.10	0.01	1.15
	11	2.03	1.60	1.57	0.86	0.88	-0.62	0.13	0.06	4.55
	12	0.63	1.32	0.48	-0.18	0.67	-0.68	0.05		-1.92
比去年同期增长（%） Increase Rate Year - on - year (%)										
2002	1	5.00	3.61	6.80	7.48	3.21	14.97	-47.06	-6.18	73.81
	2	8.10	5.35	8.31	17.14	14.94	12.38	-60.00	-6.90	63.38
	3	7.23	7.04	10.61	10.01	10.21	10.39	-57.58	-3.56	53.61
	4	6.93	6.91	10.55	7.88	6.36	14.64	-30.30	-2.68	55.26
	5	10.97	11.68	14.90	8.44	7.69	26.14	-13.33	-3.41	52.37
	6	9.11	4.34	6.70	14.88	16.34	22.84	155.00	-0.38	50.59
	7	11.63	5.92	8.35	11.17	16.20	46.16	172.73	1.14	38.46
	8	13.62	5.63	7.83	10.69	16.57	66.05	103.45		28.35
	9	18.62	6.63	8.91	20.16	29.42	81.04	133.33	-1.87	21.77
	10	19.06	5.48	7.63	21.92	33.13	85.40	200.00	-1.50	19.16
	11	18.96	3.43	5.24	28.60	43.14	75.89	733.33	1.89	15.21
	12	22.60	9.57	8.90	31.00	44.65	67.43	650.00	11.62	6.25

其他商业银行外汇信贷收支主要指标时间序列表
Time Series of Major Indicators in Sources and Uses of Credit Funds of Other Commercial Banks（Foreign Currency）

年 月 Year Month	各项存款 Total Deposits	单位活期存款 Demand Deposits by Enterprises	单位定期存款 Time Deposits by Enterprises	储蓄存款 Savings Deposits	定期储蓄 Time Deposits	境外存款 Foreign Deposits	境外筹资 Overseas Financing
	期末余额（亿美元）Balance（100 Million US Dollars）						
2003 1	252.80	33.63	83.80	107.01	88.85	9.55	2.41
2	254.70	35.86	83.22	107.71	89.06	9.33	2.44
3	255.55	37.59	80.31	108.21	89.14	9.56	2.42
4	255.18	35.98	81.48	108.55	88.78	9.27	2.43
5	256.45	38.14	79.72	108.84	88.41	9.70	2.52
6	261.48	40.74	79.80	110.26	88.74	9.90	2.63
7	258.82	39.96	79.47	109.64	87.75	10.06	2.63
8	266.09	43.91	82.40	108.58	86.61	9.84	2.65
9	263.74	40.68	85.80	107.12	84.21	9.86	2.61
10	281.00	46.63	92.43	105.85	82.59	9.95	2.66
11	271.30	46.20	91.80	105.09	81.25	8.81	2.68
12	271.14	44.34	91.46	104.88	80.51	10.11	2.75
	比上期增减额（亿美元）Changes Compared with Previous Period（100 Million US Dollars）						
2003 1	-4.83	-1.60	-1.76	0.01	-0.48	-0.21	0.05
2	1.90	2.23	-0.58	0.70	0.21	-0.22	0.03
3	0.85	1.73	-2.91	0.50	0.08	0.23	-0.02
4	-0.37	-1.61	1.17	0.34	-0.36	-0.29	0.01
5	1.27	2.16	-1.76	0.29	-0.37	0.43	0.09
6	5.03	2.60	0.08	1.42	0.33	0.20	0.11
7	-2.66	-0.78	-0.33	-0.62	-0.99	0.16	
8	7.27	3.95	2.93	-1.06	-1.14	-0.22	0.02
9	-2.35	-3.23	3.40	-1.46	-2.40	0.02	-0.04
10	17.26	5.95	6.63	-1.27	-1.62	0.09	0.05
11	-9.70	-0.43	-0.63	-0.76	-1.34	-1.14	0.02
12	-0.16	-1.86	-0.34	-0.21	-0.74	1.30	0.07
	比去年同期增长（%）Increase Rate Year-on-year（%）						
2003 1	9.44	21.50	-1.19	13.56	5.84	10.66	-46.92
2	9.29	23.83	-1.94	13.16	5.32	6.02	-41.06
3	8.31	30.52	-6.52	12.17	4.44	10.90	-41.12
4	9.14	35.06	-4.52	11.00	2.71	16.17	-42.00
5	6.07	24.23	-5.23	9.83	1.56	17.43	-21.00
6	7.41	33.71	-4.86	9.46	1.24	21.32	-18.83
7	7.63	28.57	-5.01	7.97		20.91	15.35
8	9.45	35.78	-0.84	5.48	-1.99	20.59	13.25
9	7.42	31.23	0.75	3.05	-5.03	20.10	-0.38
10	11.86	32.10	9.93	1.02	-7.09	10.56	13.19
11	8.70	35.56	11.99	-0.05	-8.51	-3.50	14.53
12	5.25	25.86	6.91	-1.97	-9.87	3.59	16.53

其他商业银行外汇信贷收支主要指标时间序列表

Time Series of Major Indicators in Sources and Uses of Credit Funds of Other Commercial Banks (Foreign Currency)

年　月 Year Month	各项贷款 Total Loans	短期贷款 Short－term Loans	境内短期贷款 Domestic Short－term Loans	中长期贷款 Medium and Long－term Loans	境内中长期贷款 Domestic Medium and Long－term Loans	进出口贸易融资 Financing for Import and Export Trades	票据融资 Paper Financing	境外筹资转贷款 On－lending of Overseas Financing	有价证券及投资 Securities and Investments
	期末余额（亿美元）Balance (100 Million US Dollars)								
2003 1	118.99	55.56	52.82	33.57	27.63	21.84	1.10	2.72	95.52
2	121.46	55.48	53.13	34.58	28.56	23.28	1.19	2.75	94.93
3	130.21	59.22	56.88	37.57	31.19	25.19	1.36	2.74	101.07
4	136.30	60.41	58.06	39.22	32.99	28.61	1.23	2.78	99.37
5	144.64	61.23	58.83	43.50	37.23	31.77	1.42	2.84	100.59
6	151.01	62.56	59.72	46.54	40.01	33.59	1.68	2.86	104.88
7	156.19	66.22	63.48	47.63	40.81	34.24	1.58	2.81	103.57
8	163.76	68.68	66.33	50.62	43.60	35.74	1.83	2.84	105.10
9	166.02	71.32	68.88	51.63	44.54	34.73	1.75	2.80	100.11
10	169.87	72.73	70.40	54.01	46.81	34.65	1.82	2.86	103.37
11	172.76	72.76	70.45	53.71	46.76	38.03	1.61	2.86	100.80
12	158.87	67.82	65.48	52.31	45.03	31.77	1.34	2.69	95.14
	比上期增减额（亿美元）Changes Compared with Previous Period (100 Million US Dollars)								
2003 1	3.58	－0.06	－0.05	0.70	0.61	2.82	0.05	0.03	0.87
2	2.47	－0.08	0.31	1.01	0.93	1.44	0.09	0.03	－0.59
3	8.75	3.74	3.75	2.99	2.63	1.91	0.17	－0.01	6.14
4	6.09	1.19	1.18	1.65	1.80	3.42	－0.13	0.04	－1.70
5	8.34	0.82	0.77	4.28	4.24	3.16	0.19	0.06	1.22
6	6.37	1.33	0.89	3.04	2.78	1.82	0.26	0.02	4.29
7	5.18	3.66	3.76	1.09	0.80	0.65	－0.10	－0.05	－1.31
8	7.57	2.46	2.85	2.99	2.79	1.50	0.25	0.03	1.53
9	2.26	2.64	2.55	1.01	0.94	－1.01	－0.08	－0.04	－4.99
10	3.85	1.41	1.52	2.38	2.27	－0.08	0.07	0.06	3.26
11	2.89	0.03	0.05	－0.30	－0.05	3.38	－0.21		－2.57
12	－13.89	－4.94	－4.97	－1.40	－1.73	－6.26	－0.27	－0.17	－5.66
	比去年同期增长（%）Increase Rate Year－on－year (%)								
2003 1	24.17	11.77	11.06	19.85	28.45	94.83	511.11	11.93	11.25
2	23.79	9.30	9.30	15.81	22.10	119.21	750.00	13.17	10.95
3	30.07	11.90	11.99	27.57	35.08	132.38	871.43	12.30	16.33
4	35.53	13.55	13.27	35.71	48.34	150.31	434.78	9.45	9.16
5	38.77	11.75	11.55	47.91	64.15	144.76	446.15	11.37	9.55
6	45.41	19.98	19.11	49.94	65.26	150.86	229.41	9.16	13.11
7	47.17	27.20	26.81	52.46	66.84	122.05	163.33	5.64	15.21
8	52.15	32.71	33.06	65.10	82.27	100.22	210.17	7.58	15.39
9	48.23	36.08	36.42	58.62	72.50	77.47	127.27	6.87	10.16
10	50.14	37.33	37.82	67.11	82.85	70.52	109.20	8.75	12.32
11	50.00	33.36	33.81	61.87	76.59	93.05	61.00	6.32	4.37
12	37.19	21.37	23.24	58.52	65.86	67.03	27.62		0.51

其他商业银行外汇信贷收支主要指标时间序列表
Time Series of Major Indicators in Sources and Uses of Credit Funds of Other Commercial Banks（Foreign Currency）

年 月 Year Month	各项存款 Total Deposits						境外筹资 Overseas Financing
		单位活期存款 Demand Deposits by Enterprises	单位定期存款 Time Deposits by Enterprises	储蓄存款 Savings Deposits	定期储蓄 Time Deposits	境外存款 Foreign Deposits	
期末余额（亿美元） Balance（100 Million US Dollars）							
2004 1	272.15	48.24	88.72	104.00	79.15	9.87	2.80
2	258.45	47.54	77.61	102.55	77.23	9.96	2.91
3	264.05	50.61	76.45	102.03	76.33	10.42	2.95
4	262.61	46.24	76.86	101.77	75.86	10.55	2.95
5	267.41	50.76	74.24	103.09	75.78	11.03	2.94
6	276.53	53.03	74.01	107.44	75.43	13.12	2.93
7	286.69	52.40	82.69	109.54	76.57	12.72	3.03
8	287.11	54.46	76.33	113.63	79.13	13.03	3.06
9	297.40	54.65	81.66	116.17	80.00	12.96	3.13
10	313.30	60.32	90.39	117.04	79.85	12.24	3.14
11	312.69	60.05	88.79	116.38	78.14	12.86	3.27
12	306.15	58.66	82.69	116.14	78.64	12.65	3.49
比上期增减额（亿美元） Changes Compared with Previous Period（100 Million US Dollars）							
2004 1	0.92	3.96	-2.45	-0.88	-1.38	-0.25	0.05
2	-13.70	-0.70	-11.11	-1.45	-1.92	0.09	0.11
3	5.60	3.07	-1.16	-0.52	-0.90	0.46	0.04
4	-1.44	-4.37	0.41	-0.26	-0.47	0.13	
5	4.80	4.52	-2.62	1.32	-0.08	0.48	-0.01
6	9.12	2.27	-0.23	4.35	-0.35	2.09	-0.01
7	10.16	-0.63	8.68	2.10	1.14	-0.40	0.10
8	0.42	2.06	-6.36	4.09	2.56	0.31	0.03
9	10.29	0.19	5.33	2.54	0.87	-0.07	0.07
10	15.90	5.67	8.73	0.87	-0.15	-0.72	0.01
11	-0.61	-0.27	-1.60	-0.66	-1.71	0.62	0.13
12	-6.54	-1.39	-6.10	-0.24	0.50	-0.21	0.22
比去年同期增长（%） Increase Rate Year-on-year（%）							
2004 1	7.65	43.44	5.87	-2.81	-10.92	3.35	16.18
2	1.47	32.57	-6.74	-4.79	-13.28	6.75	19.26
3	3.33	34.64	-4.81	-5.71	-14.37	9.00	21.90
4	2.91	28.52	-5.67	-6.25	-14.55	13.81	21.40
5	4.27	33.09	-6.87	-5.28	-14.29	13.71	16.67
6	5.76	30.17	-7.26	-2.56	-15.00	32.53	11.41
7	10.77	31.13	4.05	-0.09	-12.74	26.44	15.21
8	7.90	24.03	-7.37	4.65	-8.64	32.42	15.47
9	12.76	34.34	-4.83	8.45	-5.00	31.44	19.92
10	11.49	29.36	-2.21	10.57	-3.32	23.02	18.05
11	15.26	29.98	-3.28	10.74	-3.83	45.97	22.01
12	12.91	32.30	-9.59	10.74	-2.32	25.12	26.91

其他商业银行外汇信贷收支主要指标时间序列表
Time Series of Major Indicators in Sources and Uses of Credit Funds of Other Commercial Banks（Foreign Currency）

年　月 Year Month		各项贷款 Total Loans	短期贷款 Short – term Loans	境内短期贷款 Domestic Short – term Loans	中长期贷款 Medium and Long – term Loans	境内中长期贷款 Domestic Medium and Long – term Loans	进出口贸易融资 Financing for Import and Export Trades	票据融资 Paper Financing	境外筹资转贷款 On – lending of Overseas Financing	有价证券及投资 Securities and Investments
		期末余额（亿美元） Balance（100 Million US Dollars）								
2004	1	168.17	71.27	68.88	53.33	46.06	36.20	1.73	2.74	93.35
	2	175.29	71.89	69.47	54.60	47.40	41.35	1.79	2.74	82.13
	3	181.35	73.95	71.46	54.93	47.60	44.84	1.84	2.84	80.65
	4	181.11	73.31	70.87	55.53	48.12	44.88	1.77	2.74	79.25
	5	180.81	74.49	72.08	55.61	48.19	43.38	1.72	2.75	80.55
	6	174.18	69.40	67.12	55.08	47.89	43.83	1.48	2.66	79.36
	7	171.55	67.74	65.39	56.18	48.39	41.89	1.28	2.67	81.89
	8	171.92	66.17	63.76	57.03	49.13	42.85	1.40	2.70	79.71
	9	167.92	66.95	64.53	56.43	48.59	38.84	1.22	2.75	80.03
	10	165.35	65.75	63.21	56.28	48.16	38.21	0.96	2.79	104.97
	11	169.77	68.51	65.86	56.28	48.01	39.78	1.01	2.86	107.99
	12	164.60	68.36	65.33	55.70	47.71	35.28	1.05	2.99	116.66
		比上期增减额（亿美元） Changes Compared with Previous Period（100 Million US Dollars）								
2004	1	8.39	3.16	3.11	0.80	0.81	4.25	0.14	0.05	– 1.79
	2	7.12	0.62	0.59	1.27	1.34	5.15	0.06		– 11.22
	3	6.06	2.06	1.99	0.33	0.20	3.49	0.05	0.10	– 1.48
	4	– 0.24	– 0.64	– 0.59	0.60	0.52	0.04	– 0.07	– 0.10	– 1.40
	5	– 0.30	1.18	1.21	0.08	0.07	– 1.50	– 0.05	0.01	1.30
	6	1.61	– 0.48	– 0.35	0.06	0.29	2.40	– 0.23	– 0.09	– 1.19
	7	– 2.64	– 1.67	– 1.74	1.09	0.49	– 1.93	– 0.20	0.01	2.53
	8	0.38	– 1.57	– 1.63	0.86	0.75	0.95	0.13	0.03	– 2.18
	9	– 4.01	0.78	0.77	– 0.60	– 0.54	– 4.01	– 0.19	0.05	0.32
	10	– 2.56	– 1.20	– 1.32	– 0.15	– 0.43	– 0.62	– 0.26	0.04	24.94
	11	4.43	2.77	2.66		– 0.15	1.56	0.06	0.07	3.02
	12	– 5.17	– 0.15	– 0.53	– 0.58	– 0.30	– 4.50	0.04	0.13	8.67
		比去年同期增长（%） Increase Rate Year – on – year（%）								
2004	1	41.33	28.28	30.41	58.86	66.70	65.75	57.27	0.74	– 2.27
	2	44.32	29.58	30.75	57.89	65.97	77.62	50.42	– 0.36	– 13.48
	3	39.28	24.87	25.63	46.21	52.61	78.01	35.29	3.65	– 20.20
	4	32.88	21.35	22.06	41.59	45.86	56.87	43.90	– 1.44	– 20.25
	5	25.01	21.66	22.52	27.84	29.44	36.54	21.13	– 3.17	– 19.92
	6	20.80	18.30	20.11	19.62	21.17	36.29	– 11.31	– 6.99	– 24.33
	7	15.10	9.24	10.26	19.17	20.00	28.07	– 18.35	– 4.98	– 20.93
	8	10.01	3.04	3.06	13.83	14.04	25.35	– 22.40	– 4.93	– 24.16
	9	6.10	0.32	0.36	10.44	10.42	17.45	– 29.71	– 1.79	– 20.06
	10	2.19	– 3.27	– 3.68	5.30	4.14	15.93	– 46.70	– 2.45	1.55
	11	3.04	0.49	0.03	5.88	3.93	9.73	– 36.02		7.13
	12	8.80	7.59	6.81	7.61	7.26	17.19	– 20.15	11.15	22.62

其他商业银行外汇信贷收支主要指标时间序列表

Time Series of Major Indicators in Sources and Uses of Credit Funds of Other Commercial Banks（Foreign Currency）

年 月 Year Month		各项存款 Total Deposits	单位活期存款 Demand Deposits by Enterprises	单位定期存款 Time Deposits by Enterprises	储蓄存款 Savings Deposits	定期储蓄 Time Deposits	境外存款 Foreign Deposits	境外筹资 Overseas Financing
		期末余额（亿美元） Balance（100 Million US Dollars）						
2005	1	304.06	56.74	85.37	115.27	77.79	9.74	3.51
	2	321.73	61.20	85.83	115.29	77.55	12.05	3.49
	3	319.69	61.49	86.21	115.93	77.95	11.55	3.57
	4	325.95	55.62	98.26	122.29	78.60	11.97	3.63
	5	321.16	58.63	97.12	121.38	77.99	11.71	3.66
	6	359.43	80.55	111.47	121.10	77.55	12.27	3.67
	7	336.43	61.93	108.90	120.77	77.40	11.40	3.63
	8	326.04	63.26	100.39	119.17	76.90	11.51	3.59
	9	326.83	60.23	104.40	119.23	76.74	12.23	3.63
	10	327.44	63.98	99.72	120.10	77.33	12.09	3.70
	11	328.64	65.07	98.16	119.99	77.20	13.50	3.68
	12	330.53	69.04	91.60	119.70	77.65	14.57	3.68
		比上期增减额（亿美元） Changes Compared with Previous Period（100 Million US Dollars）						
2005	1	-2.18	-1.97	2.68	-0.89	-0.86	-2.91	0.02
	2	17.67	4.46	0.46	0.02	-0.24	2.31	-0.02
	3	-2.04	0.29	0.38	0.64	0.40	-0.50	0.08
	4	6.26	-5.87	12.05	6.36	0.65	0.42	0.06
	5	-4.79	3.01	-1.14	-0.91	-0.61	-0.26	0.03
	6	38.27	21.92	14.35	-0.28	-0.44	0.56	0.01
	7	-23.00	-18.62	-2.57	-0.33	-0.15	-0.87	-0.04
	8	-10.39	1.33	-8.51	-1.60	-0.50	0.11	-0.04
	9	0.79	-3.03	4.01	0.06	-0.16	0.72	0.04
	10	0.61	3.75	-4.68	0.87	0.59	-0.14	0.07
	11	1.20	1.09	-1.56	-0.11	-0.13	1.41	-0.02
	12	1.89	3.97	-6.56	-0.29	0.45	1.07	
		比去年同期增长（%） Increase Rate Year-on-year（%）						
2005	1	11.73	17.62	-3.78	10.84	-1.72	-1.32	25.36
	2	24.48	28.73	10.59	12.42	0.41	20.98	19.93
	3	21.07	21.50	12.77	13.62	2.12	10.84	21.02
	4	24.12	20.29	27.84	20.16	3.61	13.46	23.05
	5	20.10	15.50	30.82	17.74	2.92	6.17	24.49
	6	29.98	51.90	50.61	12.71	2.81	-6.48	25.26
	7	17.35	18.19	31.70	10.25	1.08	-10.38	19.80
	8	13.56	16.16	31.52	4.88	-2.82	-11.67	17.32
	9	9.90	10.21	27.85	2.63	-4.08	-5.63	15.97
	10	4.51	6.07	10.32	2.61	-3.16	-1.23	17.83
	11	5.10	8.36	10.55	3.10	-1.20	4.98	12.54
	12	7.96	17.70	10.78	3.07	-1.26	15.18	5.44

其他商业银行外汇信贷收支主要指标时间序列表

Time Series of Major Indicators in Sources and Uses of Credit Funds of Other Commercial Banks（Foreign Currency）

年 月 Year Month		各项贷款 Total Loans	短期贷款 Short－term Loans	境内短期贷款 Domestic Short－term Loans	中长期贷款 Medium and Long－term Loans	境内中长期贷款 Domestic Medium and Long－term Loans	进出口贸易融资 Financing for Import and Export Trades	票据融资 Paper Financing	境外筹资转贷款 On－lending of Overseas Financing	有价证券及投资 Securities and Investments
期末余额（亿美元） Balance（100 Million US Dollars）										
2005	1	169.50	69.00	65.98	54.49	46.74	40.36	1.20	3.02	109.57
2005	2	168.56	67.23	64.45	54.76	47.06	40.75	1.20	2.96	111.92
2005	3	173.79	70.25	67.67	56.75	48.97	40.76	1.60	3.00	114.71
2005	4	178.56	71.54	69.00	56.45	48.95	44.38	1.70	3.06	112.77
2005	5	183.24	72.69	70.02	55.82	48.33	48.28	1.90	3.09	113.04
2005	6	191.02	74.00	71.21	56.19	49.06	54.86	1.53	3.01	119.81
2005	7	188.90	73.17	70.33	53.94	47.06	55.75	1.65	3.00	116.99
2005	8	185.19	73.81	70.85	54.49	47.74	50.79	1.74	2.96	118.15
2005	9	184.58	75.99	73.05	53.68	46.86	48.70	1.81	2.95	116.35
2005	10	186.56	75.27	72.26	54.37	47.61	50.90	1.50	3.03	115.60
2005	11	181.56	72.15	69.07	53.39	46.69	50.24	1.32	3.01	117.01
2005	12	171.41	70.60	66.84	51.45	45.35	43.21	1.66	2.98	124.82
比上期增减额（亿美元） Changes Compared with Previous Period（100 Million US Dollars）										
2005	1	4.80	0.58	0.59	－1.15	－0.91	5.07	0.14	0.03	－7.11
2005	2	－0.97	－1.79	－1.55	0.26	0.31	0.39		－0.06	2.35
2005	3	5.27	3.03	3.23	2.01	1.93	0.01	0.41	0.04	2.79
2005	4	4.75	1.30	1.34	－0.32	－0.04	3.63	0.09	0.06	－1.94
2005	5	4.67	1.14	1.01	－0.63	－0.62	3.89	0.20	0.03	0.27
2005	6	7.79	1.31	1.19	0.38	0.74	6.58	－0.37	－0.08	6.77
2005	7	－2.12	－0.83	－0.88	－2.25	－2.00	0.89	0.13	－0.01	－2.82
2005	8	－3.72	0.63	0.51	0.55	0.68	－4.96	0.08	－0.04	1.16
2005	9	－0.58	2.20	2.22	－0.82	－0.89	－2.08	0.08	－0.01	－1.80
2005	10	1.98	－0.71	－0.78	0.70	0.76	2.19	－0.32	0.08	－0.75
2005	11	－5.01	－3.13	－3.20	－0.98	－0.92	－0.66	－0.18	－0.02	1.41
2005	12	－10.15	－1.55	－2.23	－1.94	－1.34	－7.03	0.34	－0.03	7.81
比去年同期增长（%） Increase Rate Year－on－year（%）										
2005	1	5.69	3.28	2.48	3.28	2.76	16.88	－30.06	10.22	17.38
2005	2	0.84	－0.10	－0.62	1.36	0.51	3.26	－32.40	8.03	36.27
2005	3	0.38	1.22	1.13	4.41	4.14	－4.75	－11.96	5.63	42.23
2005	4	3.14	3.87	3.87	2.70	2.93	3.25	－3.39	11.68	42.30
2005	5	5.89	3.76	3.52	1.42	1.49	15.79	11.05	12.36	40.34
2005	6	9.67	6.63	6.09	2.02	2.44	25.17	3.38	13.16	50.97
2005	7	10.11	8.02	7.55	－3.99	－2.75	33.09	28.91	12.36	42.86
2005	8	7.72	11.55	11.12	－4.45	－2.83	18.53	24.29	9.63	48.22
2005	9	9.92	13.50	13.20	－4.87	－3.56	25.39	48.36	7.27	45.38
2005	10	12.83	14.48	14.32	－3.39	－1.14	33.21	56.25	8.60	10.13
2005	11	6.94	5.31	4.87	－5.14	－2.75	26.29	30.69	5.24	8.35
2005	12	4.14	3.28	2.31	－7.63	－4.95	22.48	58.10	－0.33	6.99

（六）农村信用合作社外汇信贷收支主要指标时间序列表（2001—2005 年月度时序）

Time Series of Major Indicators in Sources and Uses of Credit Funds of Rural Credit Cooperatives（Foreign Currency）（Monthly Series from 2001 to 2005）

农村信用合作社外汇信贷收支主要指标时间序列表

Time Series of Major Indicators in Sources and Uses of Credit Funds of Rural Credit Cooperatives（Foreign Currency）

年 月 Year Month		各项存款 Total Deposits						境外筹资 Overseas Financing
			单位活期存款 Demand Deposits by Enterprises	单位定期存款 Time Deposits by Enterprises	储蓄存款 Savings Deposits	定期储蓄 Time Deposits	境外存款 Foreign Deposits	
		期末余额（亿美元） Balance（100 Million US Dollars）						
2001	1	3.55	0.01	0.02	3.52	2.47		
	2	3.63	0.02	0.02	3.59	2.54		
	3	3.58	0.01	0.02	3.55	2.52		
	4	3.70	0.02	0.05	3.63	2.57		
	5	3.79	0.02	0.05	3.72	2.59		
	6	3.87	0.03	0.05	3.79	2.63		
	7	3.92	0.03	0.03	3.86	2.65		
	8	3.99	0.04	0.02	3.93	2.69		
	9	4.04	0.03	0.02	3.99	2.73		
	10	4.10	0.05	0.02	4.03	2.74		
	11	4.13	0.06	0.02	4.05	2.75		
	12	4.28	0.11	0.04	4.11	2.74		
		比上期增减额（亿美元） Changes Compared with Previous Period（100 Million US Dollars）						
2001	1	0.19		0.01	0.18	0.13		
	2	0.08	0.01		0.07	0.07		
	3	-0.05	-0.01		-0.04	-0.02		
	4	0.12	0.01	0.03	0.08	0.05		
	5	0.09			0.09	0.02		
	6	0.08	0.01		0.07	0.04		
	7	0.05		-0.02	0.07	0.02		
	8	0.07	0.01	-0.01	0.07	0.04		
	9	0.05	-0.01		0.06	0.04		
	10	0.06	0.02		0.04	0.01		
	11	0.03	0.01		0.02	0.01		
	12	0.15	0.05	0.02	0.06	-0.01		

注：2001 年，农村信用社未发放外汇贷款。

Note：The rural credit cooperatives didn 't have lending in foreign currency in 2001.

农村信用合作社外汇信贷收支主要指标时间序列表

Time Series of Major Indicators in Sources and Uses of Credit Funds of Rural Credit Cooperatives (Foreign Currency)

年 月 Year Month	各项存款 Total Deposits						境外筹资 Overseas Financing
		单位活期存款 Demand Deposits by Enterprises	单位定期存款 Time Deposits by Enterprises	储蓄存款 Savings Deposits		境外存款 Foreign Deposits	
					定期储蓄 Time Deposits		
期末余额（亿美元） Balance (100 Million US Dollars)							
2002 1	4.37	0.09	0.04	4.22	2.83		
2	4.58	0.14	0.04	4.38	2.91		
3	4.69	0.16	0.03	4.46	2.94		
4	4.81	0.15	0.08	4.56	3.05		
5	4.85	0.16	0.07	4.58	3.05		
6	5.46	0.21	0.07	5.16	3.49		
7	5.49	0.18	0.06	5.22	3.55		
8	5.57	0.16	0.12	5.27	3.59		
9	5.64	0.17	0.14	5.31	3.63		
10	5.75	0.23	0.14	5.34	3.63		
11	5.80	0.28	0.13	5.35	3.63		
12	5.86	0.29	0.16	5.38	3.63		
比上期增减额（亿美元） Changes Compared with Previous Period (100 Million US Dollars)							
2002 1	0.09	-0.03	0.01	0.11	0.09		
2	0.21	0.05		0.16	0.08		
3	0.11	0.02	-0.01	0.08	0.03		
4	0.12	-0.01	0.05	0.10	0.11		
5	0.04	0.01	-0.01	0.02			
6	0.61	0.05		0.58	0.44		
7	0.03	-0.03	-0.01	0.06	0.06		
8	0.08	-0.02	0.06	0.05	0.04		
9	0.07	0.01	0.02	0.04	0.04		
10	0.11	0.06		0.03			
11	0.05	0.05	-0.01	0.01			
12	0.06	0.01	0.03	0.03			
比去年同期增长（%） Increase Rate Year-on-year (%)							
2002 1	23.10	800.00	100.00	19.89	14.57		
2	26.17	600.00	100.00	22.01	14.57		
3	31.01	1500.00	50.00	25.63	16.67		
4	30.00	650.00	60.00	25.62	18.68		
5	27.97	700.00	40.00	23.12	17.76		
6	41.09	600.00	40.00	36.15	32.70		
7	40.05	500.00	100.00	35.23	33.96		
8	39.60	300.00	500.00	34.10	33.46		
9	39.60	466.67	600.00	33.08	32.97		
10	40.24	360.00	600.00	32.51	32.48		
11	40.44	366.67	550.00	32.10	32.00		
12	36.92	163.64	300.00	30.90	32.48		

农村信用合作社外汇信贷收支主要指标时间序列表

Time Series of Major Indicators in Sources and Uses of Credit Funds of Rural Credit Cooperatives（Foreign Currency）

年 月 Year Month	各项贷款 Total Loans								有价证券及投资 Securities and Investments
		短期贷款		中长期贷款		进出口贸易融资 Financing for Import and Export Trades	票据融资 Paper Financing	境外筹资转贷款 On-lending of Overseas Financing	
		Short-term Loans	境内短期贷款 Domestic Short-term Loans	Medium and Long-term Loans	境内中长期贷款 Domestic Medium and Long-term Loans				
期末余额（亿美元） Balance（100 Million US Dollars）									
2002 1	0.01					0.01			
2									
3									
4	0.01	0.01	0.01						
5	0.01	0.01	0.01						
6	0.04	0.04	0.04						
7	0.04	0.04	0.04						
8	0.05	0.04	0.04			0.01			
9	0.08	0.06	0.06			0.02			
10	0.12	0.11	0.11			0.01			
11	0.17	0.16	0.16			0.01			
12	0.20	0.18	0.18			0.02			
比上期增减额（亿美元） Changes Compared with Previous Period（100 Million US Dollars）									
2002 1	0.01					0.01			
2	-0.01					-0.01			
3									
4	0.01	0.01	0.01						
5									
6	0.03	0.03	0.03						
7									
8	0.01					0.01			
9	0.03	0.02	0.02			0.01			
10	0.04	0.05	0.05			-0.01			
11	0.05	0.05	0.05						
12	0.03	0.02	0.02			0.01			
比去年同期增长（%） Increase Rate Year-on-year（%）									
2002 1	—					—			
2									
3									
4	—	—	—						
5	—	—	—						
6	—	—	—						
7	—	—	—						
8	—	—	—			—			
9	—	—	—			—			
10	—	—	—			—			
11	—	—	—			—			
12	—	—	—			—			

农村信用合作社外汇信贷收支主要指标时间序列表

Time Series of Major Indicators in Sources and Uses of Credit Funds of Rural Credit Cooperatives（Foreign Currency）

年　月 Year Month		各项存款 Total Deposits						境外筹资 Overseas Financing
			单位活期存款 Demand Deposits by Enterprises	单位定期存款 Time Deposits by Enterprises	储蓄存款 Savings Deposits	定期储蓄 Time Deposits	境外存款 Foreign Deposits	
		期末余额（亿美元） Balance（100 Million US Dollars）						
2003	1	5.82	0.23	0.15	5.42	3.66		
	2	5.90	0.24	0.15	5.48	3.69		
	3	5.98	0.23	0.16	5.53	3.71		
	4	5.98	0.26	0.16	5.52	3.72		
	5	6.02	0.25	0.16	5.58	3.74		
	6	6.06	0.27	0.16	5.60	3.76		
	7	6.14	0.31	0.13	5.63	3.77		
	8	6.09	0.32	0.09	5.61	3.75		
	9	6.02	0.26	0.07	5.61	3.74		
	10	5.93	0.27	0.06	5.55	3.68		
	11	5.92	0.29	0.06	5.52	3.66		
	12	6.03	0.32	0.08	5.55	3.64		
		比上期增减额（亿美元） Changes Compared with Previous Period（100 Million US Dollars）						
2003	1	-0.03	-0.06	-0.01	0.05	0.04		
	2	0.08	0.01		0.06	0.03		
	3	0.08	-0.01	0.01	0.05	0.02		
	4		0.03		-0.01	0.01		
	5	0.04	-0.01		0.06	0.02		
	6	0.04	0.02		0.02	0.02		
	7	0.08	0.04	-0.03	0.03	0.01		
	8	-0.05	0.01	-0.04	-0.02	-0.02		
	9	-0.07	-0.06	-0.02		-0.01		
	10	-0.09	0.01	-0.01	-0.06	-0.06		
	11	-0.01	0.02		-0.03	-0.02		
	12	0.11	0.03	0.02	0.03	-0.02		
		比去年同期增长（%） Increase Rate Year-on-year（%）						
2003	1	33.18	155.56	275.00	28.44	29.33		
	2	28.82	71.43	275.00	25.11	26.80		
	3	27.51	43.75	433.33	23.99	26.19		
	4	24.32	73.33	100.00	21.05	21.97		
	5	24.12	56.25	128.57	21.83	22.62		
	6	10.99	28.57	128.57	8.53	7.74		
	7	11.84	72.22	116.67	7.85	6.20		
	8	9.34	100.00	-25.00	6.45	4.46		
	9	6.74	52.94	-50.00	5.65	3.03		
	10	3.13	17.39	-57.14	3.93	1.38		
	11	2.07	3.57	-53.85	3.18	0.83		
	12	2.90	10.34	-50.00	3.16	0.28		

农村信用合作社外汇信贷收支主要指标时间序列表

Time Series of Major Indicators in Sources and Uses of Credit Funds of Rural Credit Cooperatives（Foreign Currency）

年 月 Year Month		各项贷款 Total Loans	短期贷款 Short－term Loans	境内短期贷款 Domestic Short－term Loans	中长期贷款 Medium and Long－term Loans	境内中长期贷款 Domestic Medium and Long－term Loans	进出口贸易融资 Financing for Import and Export Trades	票据融资 Paper Financing	境外筹资转贷款 On－lending of Overseas Financing	有价证券及投资 Securities and Investments
		期末余额（亿美元） Balance（100 Million US Dollars）								
2003	1	0.30	0.26	0.26			0.04			
	2	0.32	0.29	0.29			0.03			
	3	0.44	0.37	0.37			0.07			
	4	0.52	0.45	0.45			0.07			
	5	0.56	0.49	0.49			0.07			
	6	0.63	0.55	0.55			0.08			
	7	0.68	0.59	0.59			0.09			
	8	0.81	0.67	0.67			0.14			
	9	0.90	0.73	0.73			0.17			
	10	0.89	0.73	0.73			0.16			
	11	0.92	0.76	0.76			0.16			
	12	1.05	0.75	0.75			0.30			
		比上期增减额（亿美元） Changes Compared with Previous Period（100 Million US Dollars）								
2003	1	0.10	0.08	0.08			0.02			
	2	0.02	0.03	0.03			－0.01			
	3	0.12	0.08	0.08			0.04			
	4	0.08	0.08	0.08						
	5	0.04	0.04	0.04						
	6	0.07	0.06	0.06			0.01			
	7	0.05	0.04	0.04			0.01			
	8	0.13	0.08	0.08			0.05			
	9	0.09	0.06	0.06			0.03			
	10	－0.01					－0.01			
	11	0.03	0.03	0.03						
	12	0.13	－0.01	－0.01			0.14			
		比去年同期增长（%） Increase Rate Year－on－year（%）								
2003	1	2900.00	—	—			300.00			
	2	—	—	—			—			
	3	—	—	—			—			
	4	5100.00	4400.00	4400.00			—			
	5	5500.00	4800.00	4800.00			—			
	6	1475.00	1275.00	1275.00			—			
	7	1600.00	1375.00	1375.00			—			
	8	1520.00	1575.00	1575.00			1300.00			
	9	1025.00	1116.67	1116.67			750.00			
	10	641.67	563.64	563.64			1500.00			
	11	441.18	375.00	375.00			1500.00			
	12	425.00	316.67	316.67			1400.00			

农村信用合作社外汇信贷收支主要指标时间序列表

Time Series of Major Indicators in Sources and Uses of Credit Funds of Rural Credit Cooperatives (Foreign Currency)

年 月 Year Month		各项存款 Total Deposits	单位活期存款 Demand Deposits by Enterprises	单位定期存款 Time Deposits by Enterprises	储蓄存款 Savings Deposits	定期储蓄 Time Deposits	境外存款 Foreign Deposits	境外筹资 Overseas Financing
期末余额（亿美元） Balance (100 Million US Dollars)								
2004	1	6.13	0.34	0.10	5.60	3.64		
	2	6.13	0.40	0.08	5.59	3.61		
	3	6.10	0.40	0.07	5.54	3.56		
	4	6.12	0.43	0.06	5.56	3.54		
	5	6.23	0.51	0.07	5.57	3.49		
	6	6.18	0.46	0.06	5.58	3.45		
	7	6.26	0.58	0.06	5.55	3.40		
	8	6.13	0.53	0.06	5.46	3.30		
	9	6.11	0.55	0.06	5.44	3.26		
	10	6.21	0.60	0.05	5.48	3.24		
	11	6.19	0.60	0.05	5.44	3.19		
	12	6.18	0.60	0.06	5.42	3.16		
比上期增减额（亿美元） Changes Compared with Previous Period (100 Million US Dollars)								
2004	1		-0.06	0.01	0.04	-0.01		
	2		0.06	-0.02	-0.01	-0.03		
	3	-0.03		-0.01	-0.05	-0.05		
	4	0.02	0.03	-0.01	0.02	-0.02		
	5	0.11	0.08	0.01	0.01	-0.05		
	6	-0.05	-0.05	-0.01	0.01	-0.04		
	7	0.08	0.12		-0.03	-0.05		
	8	-0.13	-0.05		-0.09	-0.10		
	9	-0.02	0.02		-0.02	-0.04		
	10	0.10	0.05	-0.01	0.04	-0.02		
	11	-0.02			-0.04	-0.05		
	12	-0.01		0.01	-0.02	-0.03		
比去年同期增长（%） Increase Rate Year-on-year (%)								
2004	1	5.33	47.83	-33.33	3.32	-0.55		
	2	3.90	66.67	-46.67	2.01	-2.17		
	3	2.01	73.91	-56.25	0.18	-4.04		
	4	2.34	65.38	-62.50	0.72	-4.84		
	5	3.49	104.00	-56.25	-0.18	-6.68		
	6	1.98	70.37	-62.50	-0.36	-8.24		
	7	1.95	87.10	-53.85	-1.42	-9.81		
	8	0.66	65.63	-33.33	-2.67	-12.00		
	9	1.50	111.54	-14.29	-3.03	-12.83		
	10	4.72	122.22	-16.67	-1.26	-11.96		
	11	4.56	106.90	-16.67	-1.45	-12.84		
	12	2.49	87.50	-25.00	-2.34	-13.19		

农村信用合作社外汇信贷收支主要指标时间序列表

Time Series of Major Indicators in Sources and Uses of Credit Funds of Rural Credit Cooperatives（Foreign Currency）

年 月 Year Month		各项贷款 Total Loans	短期贷款 Short－term Loans	境内短期贷款 Domestic Short－term Loans	中长期贷款 Medium and Long－term Loans	境内中长期贷款 Domestic Medium and Long－term Loans	进出口贸易融资 Financing for Import and Export Trades	票据融资 Paper Financing	境外筹资转贷款 On－lending of Overseas Financing	有价证券及投资 Securities and Investments
期末余额（亿美元） Balance（100 Million US Dollars）										
2004	1	1.22	0.95	0.95	0.02	0.02	0.25			
	2	1.17	0.95	0.95	0.02	0.02	0.20			
	3	1.25	1.03	1.03	0.02	0.02	0.20			
	4	1.25	0.97	0.97	0.02	0.02	0.26			
	5	1.07	0.76	0.76	0.02	0.02	0.29			
	6	1.12	0.77	0.77	0.02	0.02	0.33			
	7	1.04	0.76	0.76	0.02	0.02	0.26			
	8	0.55	0.32	0.32	0.02	0.02	0.21			
	9	0.52	0.34	0.34	0.02	0.02	0.16			
	10	0.52	0.37	0.37	0.02	0.02	0.13			
	11	0.51	0.38	0.38	0.02	0.02	0.11			
	12	0.45	0.32	0.32	0.02	0.02	0.11			
比上期增减额（亿美元） Changes Compared with Previous Period（100 Million US Dollars）										
2004	1	0.06	0.14	0.14			－0.08			
	2	－0.05					－0.05			
	3	0.08	0.08	0.08						
	4		－0.06	－0.06			0.06			
	5	－0.18	－0.21	－0.21			0.03			
	6	0.05	0.01	0.01			0.04			
	7	－0.08	－0.01	－0.01			－0.07			
	8	－0.49	－0.44	－0.44			－0.05			
	9	－0.03	0.02	0.02			－0.05			
	10		0.03	0.03			－0.03			
	11	－0.01	0.01	0.01			－0.02			
	12	－0.06	－0.06	－0.06						
比去年同期增长（%） Increase Rate Year－on－year（%）										
2004	1	306.67	265.38	265.38	—	—	525.00			
	2	265.63	227.59	227.59	—	—	566.67			
	3	184.09	178.38	178.38	—	—	185.71			
	4	140.38	115.56	115.56	—	—	271.43			
	5	91.07	55.10	55.10	—	—	314.29			
	6	77.78	40.00	40.00	—	—	312.50			
	7	52.94	28.81	28.81	—	—	188.89			
	8	－32.10	－52.24	－52.24	—	—	50.00			
	9	－42.22	－53.42	－53.42	—	—	－5.88			
	10	－41.57	－49.32	－49.32	—	—	－18.75			
	11	－44.57	－50.00	－50.00	—	—	－31.25			
	12	－57.14	－57.33	－57.33	—	—	－63.33			

农村信用合作社外汇信贷收支主要指标时间序列表

Time Series of Major Indicators in Sources and Uses of Credit Funds of Rural Credit Cooperatives（Foreign Currency）

年　月 Year Month		各项存款 Total Deposits						境外筹资 Overseas Financing
			单位活期存款 Demand Deposits by Enterprises	单位定期存款 Time Deposits by Enterprises	储蓄存款 Savings Deposits	定期储蓄 Time Deposits	境外存款 Foreign Deposits	
		期末余额（亿美元） Balance（100 Million US Dollars）						
2005	1	5.59	0.22		5.28	3.06		
	2	5.65	0.21		5.36	3.05		
	3	5.67	0.24		5.33	3.02		
	4	5.63	0.30		5.26	2.98		
	5	5.55	0.25		5.22	2.94		
	6	5.44	0.25		5.11	2.84		
	7	5.37	0.27		5.02	2.78		
	8	5.29	0.29		4.92	2.74		
	9	5.18	0.23		4.86	2.72		
	10	5.22	0.31		4.82	2.71		
	11	5.18	0.32		4.79	2.70		
	12	3.64	0.25	0.01	3.29	2.09		
		比上期增减额（亿美元） Changes Compared with Previous Period（100 Million US Dollars）						
2005	1	-0.08	-0.01		-0.08	-0.05		
	2	0.06	-0.01		0.08	-0.01		
	3	0.02	0.03		-0.03	-0.03		
	4	-0.04	0.06		-0.07	-0.04		
	5	-0.08	-0.05		-0.04	-0.04		
	6	-0.11			-0.11	0.10		
	7	-0.07	0.02		-0.09	-0.06		
	8	-0.08	0.02		-0.10	-0.04		
	9	-0.11	-0.06		-0.06	-0.02		
	10	0.04	0.08		-0.04	-0.01		
	11	-0.04	0.01		-0.03	-0.01		
	12	-1.54	-0.07	0.01	-1.50	-0.61		
		比去年同期增长（%） Increase Rate Year-on-year（%）						
2005	1	-8.81	-35.29	-100.00	-5.71	-15.93		
	2	-7.83	-47.50	-100.00	-4.11	-15.51		
	3	-7.05	-40.00	-100.00	-3.79	-15.17		
	4	-8.01	-30.23	-100.00	-5.40	-15.82		
	5	-10.91	-50.98	-100.00	-6.28	-15.76		
	6	-11.97	-45.65	-100.00	-8.42	-17.68		
	7	-14.22	-53.45	-100.00	-9.55	-18.24		
	8	-13.70	-45.28	-100.00	-9.89	-16.97		
	9	-15.22	-58.18	-100.00	-10.66	-16.56		
	10	-15.94	-48.33	-100.00	-12.04	-16.36		
	11	-16.32	-46.67	-100.00	-11.95	-15.36		
	12	-41.10	-58.33	-83.33	-39.30	-33.86		

农村信用合作社外汇信贷收支主要指标时间序列表

Time Series of Major Indicators in Sources and Uses of Credit Funds of Rural Credit Cooperatives（Foreign Currency）

年 月 Year Month	各项贷款 Total Loans	短期贷款 Short - term Loans	境内短期贷款 Domestic Short - term Loans	中长期贷款 Medium and Long - term Loans	境内中长期贷款 Domestic Medium and Long - term Loans	进出口贸易融资 Financing for Import and Export Trades	票据融资 Paper Financing	境外筹资转贷款 On - lending of Overseas Financing	有价证券及投资 Securities and Investments
期末余额（亿美元） Balance（100 Million US Dollars）									
2005 1	0.31	0.23	0.23	0.02	0.02	0.06			
2	0.30	0.22	0.22	0.02	0.02	0.06			
3	0.33	0.23	0.23	0.02	0.02	0.08			
4	0.35	0.23	0.23	0.02	0.02	0.10			
5	0.43	0.24	0.24	0.02	0.02	0.17			
6	0.30	0.15	0.15	0.02	0.02	0.13			
7	0.32	0.15	0.15	0.02	0.02	0.15			
8	0.36	0.21	0.21	0.02	0.02	0.13			
9	0.34	0.20	0.20	0.02	0.02	0.12			
10	0.33	0.20	0.20	0.01	0.01	0.12			
11	0.33	0.17	0.17	0.01	0.01	0.15			
12	0.41	0.18	0.18	0.01	0.01	0.22			
比上期增减额（亿美元） Changes Compared with Previous Period（100 Million US Dollars）									
2005 1	0.06	0.03	0.03			0.03			
2	-0.01	-0.01	-0.01						
3	0.03	0.01	0.01			0.02			
4	0.02					0.02			
5	0.08	0.01	0.01			0.07			
6	-0.13	-0.09	-0.09			-0.04			
7	0.02					0.02			
8	0.04	0.06	0.06			-0.02			
9	-0.02	-0.01	-0.01			-0.01			
10	-0.01			-0.01	-0.01				
11		-0.03	-0.03			0.03			
12	0.08	0.01	0.01			0.07			
比去年同期增长（%） Increase Rate Year - on - year（%）									
2005 1	-74.59	-75.79	-75.79			-76.00			
2	-74.36	-76.84	-76.84			-70.00			
3	-73.60	-77.67	-77.67			-60.00			
4	-72.00	-76.29	-76.29			-61.54			
5	-59.81	-68.42	-68.42			-41.38			
6	-73.21	-80.52	-80.52			-60.61			
7	-69.23	-80.26	-80.26			-42.31			
8	-34.55	-34.38	-34.38			-38.10			
9	-34.62	-41.18	-41.18			-25.00			
10	-36.54	-45.95	-45.95	-50.00	-50.00	-7.69			
11	-35.29	-55.26	-55.26	-50.00	-50.00	36.36			
12	-8.89	-43.75	-43.75	-50.00	-50.00	100.00			

三、本外币信贷收支主要指标时间序列表

Time Series of Major Indicators in Sources and Uses of Credit Funds (Domestic and Foreign Currency Combined)

（一）金融机构本外币信贷收支主要指标时间序列表（2002—2005 年月度时序）

Time Series of Major Indicators in Sources and Uses of Credit Funds of Financial Institutions (Domestic and Foreign Currency Combined) (Monthly Series from 2002 to 2005)

金融机构本外币信贷收支主要指标时间序列表

Time Series of Major Indicators in Sources and Uses of Credit Funds of Financial Institutions (Domestic and Foreign Currency Combined)

年 月 Year Month		各项存款 Total Deposits	企事业单位存款 Deposits by Enterprises and Establishments			储蓄存款 Savings Deposits		
				活期存款 Demand Deposits	定期存款 Time Deposits		活期储蓄 Demand Deposits	定期储蓄 Time Deposits
期末余额（亿元） Balance (100 Million Yuan)								
2002	1	154866.65	53074.35	37672.88	15401.47	81745.19	23388.83	58356.36
	2	155942.51	51716.61	36244.02	15472.59	84988.85	24469.91	60518.94
	3	158899.91	53365.71	37699.35	15666.36	85674.44	24710.04	60964.40
	4	162273.79	54655.65	38202.76	16452.89	86731.29	25337.13	61394.16
	5	165145.63	55517.83	39392.39	16125.44	87474.35	25625.08	61849.27
	6	169609.23	57530.50	40973.42	16557.08	88875.90	26313.69	62562.21
	7	170731.66	57499.98	40763.72	16736.26	89715.84	26638.22	63077.62
	8	173716.92	58863.51	41642.88	17220.63	90515.88	27053.36	63462.52
	9	177702.04	60914.63	42671.17	18243.46	91403.15	27587.21	63815.94
	10	178667.06	60816.04	43145.24	17670.80	92048.20	27712.69	64335.51
	11	180880.53	61769.14	43573.19	18195.95	93040.89	28211.29	64829.60
	12	183388.48	64298.47	45352.99	18945.48	94307.13	29026.58	65280.55

续表
Continued

年 月 Year Month		各项存款 Total Deposits	企事业单位存款 Deposits by Enterprises and Establishments	活期存款 Demand Deposits	定期存款 Time Deposits	储蓄存款 Savings Deposits	活期储蓄 Demand Deposits	定期储蓄 Time Deposits
		比上期增减额（亿元）Changes Compared with Previous Period（100 Million Yuan）						
2002	1	32.41	-1511.74	-1011.24	-500.50	1315.60	433.58	882.02
	2	1081.92	-1357.11	-1428.57	71.46	3243.66	1081.08	2162.58
	3	2965.84	1649.10	1455.33	193.77	685.59	240.13	445.46
	4	3386.30	1291.26	504.74	786.52	1056.85	627.09	429.76
	5	2874.68	862.20	1189.64	-327.44	743.06	287.95	455.11
	6	4540.74	2012.65	1581.01	431.64	1401.55	688.61	712.94
	7	1125.67	-30.52	-209.69	179.17	839.94	324.53	515.41
	8	2990.15	1363.70	879.33	484.37	800.04	415.14	384.90
	9	3986.01	2051.17	1028.33	1022.84	887.27	533.85	353.42
	10	966.32	-98.61	474.06	-572.67	645.05	125.48	519.57
	11	2213.95	953.12	427.96	525.16	992.69	498.60	494.09
	12	2515.55	2529.31	1779.79	749.52	1266.24	815.29	450.95
		比去年同期增长（%）Increase Rate Year-on-year（%）						
2002	1	13.65	11.20	12.27	8.68	12.35	18.97	9.90
	2	14.10	8.66	9.39	7.01	15.63	25.90	11.94
	3	13.42	8.11	9.31	5.33	15.00	22.77	12.12
	4	13.99	9.03	11.00	4.73	15.95	25.22	12.52
	5	16.22	11.76	14.51	5.57	17.16	28.29	13.09
	6	15.54	9.73	11.47	5.64	17.06	26.10	13.63
	7	17.52	14.42	16.69	9.24	17.93	28.68	13.91
	8	16.71	12.39	13.51	9.77	17.45	26.86	13.85
	9	17.83	14.14	15.77	10.50	17.43	26.54	13.89
	10	17.67	14.37	17.25	7.90	17.29	26.38	13.76
	11	18.98	16.26	18.25	11.75	17.70	27.96	13.74
	12	18.06	15.27	16.53	12.36	17.12	26.39	13.42

金融机构本外币信贷收支主要指标时间序列表

Time Series of Major Indicators in Sources and Uses of Credit Funds of Financial Institutions (Domestic and Foreign Currency Combined)

年 月 Year Month	各项贷款 Total Loans	短期贷款 Short - term Loans	中长期贷款 Medium and Long - term Loans	票据融资 Paper Financing	有价证券及投资 Securities and Investments
期末余额（亿元）Balance (100 Million Yuan)					
2002 1	120969.86	68764.55	43235.73	3539.13	29658.59
2	121574.39	68994.93	43625.83	3532.22	29531.41
3	124185.15	70887.78	44233.71	3658.70	30612.26
4	125163.52	71336.79	44463.57	3901.07	31162.82
5	126343.29	71811.73	45108.05	3936.80	31632.61
6	129279.22	73201.21	46217.93	4375.26	32190.28
7	129928.46	73221.95	46706.35	4511.08	32464.53
8	131643.13	73825.07	47525.28	4819.98	33156.35
9	134614.63	75082.17	48813.08	5231.31	33336.47
10	135352.73	75162.39	49456.74	5259.31	33499.74
11	136932.91	75770.43	50190.41	5519.88	34046.87
12	139802.90	76822.41	51731.61	5805.31	34267.11
比上期增减额（亿元）Changes Compared with Previous Period (100 Million Yuan)					
2002 1	250.51	42.59	312.09	-10.17	-147.74
2	621.56	231.12	390.10	-6.91	-109.85
3	2619.79	1892.86	607.88	126.48	1081.77
4	990.93	449.63	230.10	242.37	552.97
5	1182.75	474.96	644.48	35.73	470.72
6	3017.78	1389.61	1109.88	438.46	571.72
7	652.04	20.74	488.42	135.82	275.02
8	1721.66	603.56	821.21	308.90	695.61
9	2973.51	1257.10	1287.82	411.33	180.72
10	738.86	80.22	643.66	28.75	163.93
11	1581.63	608.04	733.69	260.57	548.59
12	2878.08	1055.38	1541.55	283.95	223.89
比去年同期增长（%）Increase Rate Year - on - year (%)					
2002 1	9.62	4.41	19.74	30.21	22.27
2	9.50	4.47	19.30	28.96	20.29
3	10.82	6.89	18.80	28.52	22.30
4	10.71	7.28	17.43	29.35	21.22
5	10.60	7.39	17.87	29.17	22.63
6	11.39	7.90	18.81	33.77	23.91
7	11.49	7.97	18.72	33.91	23.01
8	12.44	8.92	19.38	39.13	24.50
9	13.79	9.96	20.54	46.44	24.78
10	14.58	10.23	21.82	53.46	24.82
11	15.04	10.28	22.29	62.34	25.77
12	15.37	9.88	23.16	65.64	16.51

金融机构本外币信贷收支主要指标时间序列表

Time Series of Major Indicators in Sources and Uses of Credit Funds of Financial Institutions（Domestic and Foreign Currency Combined）

年 月 Year Month		各项存款 Total Deposits	企事业单位存款 Deposits by Enterprises and Establishments	活期存款 Demand Deposits	定期存款 Time Deposits	储蓄存款 Savings Deposits	活期储蓄 Demand Deposits	定期储蓄 Time Deposits
期末余额（亿元） Balance（100 Million Yuan）								
2003	1	185848.84	62802.38	43425.19	19377.19	98097.69	30707.33	67390.36
	2	188959.58	63096.84	43964.84	19132.00	100276.15	31083.44	69192.71
	3	194611.10	65719.99	46034.88	19685.11	102023.95	31623.58	70400.37
	4	196927.12	65894.07	45399.69	20494.38	102657.71	31814.12	70843.59
	5	201341.53	67692.43	46900.60	20791.83	103845.17	32278.22	71566.95
	6	206810.28	70810.81	49701.21	21109.60	105195.26	33018.48	72176.78
	7	207932.45	70452.56	49113.85	21338.71	106078.77	33463.13	72615.64
	8	210100.29	71341.64	49512.86	21828.78	106669.76	33816.55	72853.21
	9	215125.16	74224.05	50687.96	23536.09	108166.92	34644.03	73522.89
	10	216501.51	74499.38	51797.34	22702.04	108569.08	34673.76	73895.32
	11	218574.35	74960.90	51940.14	23020.76	109362.00	35253.22	74108.78
	12	220363.53	76784.87	53585.88	23198.99	110695.26	36218.17	74477.09
比上期增减额（亿元） Changes Compared with Previous Period（100 Million Yuan）								
2003	1	2494.80	-1407.88	-1746.71	338.83	3715.46	1641.04	2074.42
	2	3110.74	294.46	539.65	-245.19	2178.46	376.11	1802.35
	3	5655.34	2623.89	2070.04	553.85	1747.80	540.14	1207.66
	4	2320.65	174.08	-635.19	809.27	633.76	190.54	443.22
	5	4421.91	1798.92	1500.91	298.01	1187.46	464.10	723.36
	6	5470.52	3118.40	2800.61	317.79	1350.09	740.26	609.83
	7	1123.42	-358.26	-587.36	229.10	883.51	444.65	438.86
	8	2167.85	889.09	399.01	490.08	590.99	353.42	237.57
	9	5024.86	2882.39	1175.10	1707.29	1497.16	827.48	669.68
	10	1376.35	275.34	1109.38	-834.04	402.16	29.73	372.43
	11	2072.83	461.52	142.80	318.72	792.92	579.46	213.46
	12	1789.18	1824.97	1645.74	178.23	1333.26	964.95	368.31
比去年同期增长（%） Increase Rate Year-on-year（%）								
2003	1	20.01	18.33	15.27	25.81	20.00	31.29	15.48
	2	21.17	22.00	21.30	23.65	17.99	27.03	14.33
	3	22.47	23.15	22.11	25.65	19.08	27.98	15.48
	4	21.35	20.56	18.84	24.56	18.36	25.56	15.39
	5	21.92	21.93	19.06	28.94	18.71	25.96	15.71
	6	21.93	23.08	21.30	27.50	18.36	25.48	15.37
	7	21.79	22.53	20.48	27.50	18.24	25.62	15.12
	8	20.94	21.20	18.90	26.76	17.85	25.00	14.80
	9	21.06	21.85	18.79	29.01	18.34	25.58	15.21
	10	21.18	22.50	20.05	28.47	17.95	25.12	14.86
	11	20.84	21.36	19.20	26.52	17.54	24.96	14.31
	12	20.16	19.42	18.15	22.45	17.38	24.78	14.09

金融机构本外币信贷收支主要指标时间序列表

Time Series of Major Indicators in Sources and Uses of Credit Funds of Financial Institutions (Domestic and Foreign Currency Combined)

年 月 Year Month		各项贷款 Total Loans	短期贷款 Short-term Loans	中长期贷款 Medium and Long-term Loans	票据融资 Paper Financing	有价证券及投资 Securities and Investments
期末余额（亿元） Balance (100 Million Yuan)						
2003	1	143228.63	78192.91	53098.25	6455.28	33771.80
	2	144374.40	78684.81	53574.21	6622.79	34055.18
	3	148366.98	80476.40	55214.02	7104.00	34270.15
	4	150535.28	81042.75	56139.09	7647.23	35014.27
	5	153321.95	82147.01	57207.03	8182.62	35132.56
	6	158869.86	84353.11	59446.35	9221.52	35646.91
	7	160033.00	84070.36	60718.61	9445.25	35884.73
	8	163087.57	85254.55	61922.32	10066.30	36066.20
	9	166521.95	86257.39	63973.24	10407.06	35845.38
	10	167285.59	86770.20	64731.57	9900.83	35763.09
	11	168513.48	87106.85	65659.15	9762.45	35439.71
	12	169771.00	87397.88	67251.74	9233.59	37490.62
比上期增减额（亿元） Changes Compared with Previous Period (100 Million Yuan)						
2003	1	3371.40	1465.16	1202.86	636.06	-140.67
	2	1145.77	491.90	475.96	167.51	283.38
	3	3995.50	1791.77	1640.08	481.21	215.70
	4	2172.41	566.35	925.08	543.23	745.72
	5	2798.94	1104.26	1070.45	535.39	122.74
	6	5549.59	2206.09	2239.31	1038.90	514.81
	7	1165.23	-282.74	1272.70	223.73	238.41
	8	3054.57	1184.19	1203.71	621.05	181.48
	9	3434.38	1002.83	2050.93	340.76	-220.83
	10	763.64	512.81	758.33	-506.23	-82.29
	11	1227.90	336.66	927.58	-138.38	-323.38
	12	1257.50	291.03	1592.58	-528.86	2050.91
比去年同期增长（%） Increase Rate Year-on-year (%)						
2003	1	18.40	13.71	22.81	82.46	13.87
	2	18.75	14.04	22.80	87.50	15.32
	3	19.47	13.53	24.82	94.22	11.95
	4	20.27	13.61	26.26	96.08	12.36
	5	21.35	14.39	26.82	107.89	11.06
	6	22.89	15.23	28.62	110.80	10.74
	7	23.17	14.82	30.00	109.41	10.54
	8	23.89	15.48	30.29	108.88	8.78
	9	23.70	14.88	31.06	98.97	7.53
	10	23.59	15.44	30.89	88.25	6.75
	11	23.06	14.96	30.82	76.86	4.09
	12	21.44	13.77	30.00	59.04	9.40

金融机构本外币信贷收支主要指标时间序列表

Time Series of Major Indicators in Sources and Uses of Credit Funds of Financial Institutions（Domestic and Foreign Currency Combined）

年 月 Year Month		各项存款 Total Deposits	企事业单位存款 Deposits by Enterprises and Establishments			储蓄存款 Savings Deposits		
				活期存款 Demand Deposits	定期存款 Time Deposits		活期储蓄 Demand Deposits	定期储蓄 Time Deposits
期末余额（亿元） Balance（100 Million Yuan）								
2004	1	222743.94	74657.08	51466.18	23190.90	116289.11	38707.85	77581.26
	2	226696.21	76116.45	53129.74	22986.71	117536.26	38689.49	78846.77
	3	232710.43	79328.84	55627.84	23701.00	118706.74	39462.41	79244.33
	4	234560.84	80206.43	54734.88	25471.55	118954.49	39865.39	79089.10
	5	237445.06	81588.84	56627.62	24961.22	119410.77	40053.44	79357.33
	6	242174.10	84068.71	58259.30	25809.41	120443.17	40907.94	79535.23
	7	242913.32	82911.26	57233.15	25678.11	121093.08	41218.17	79874.91
	8	245294.83	83639.66	57947.15	25692.51	121684.84	41361.10	80023.74
	9	247933.14	85216.72	57881.89	27334.83	122390.93	42076.54	80314.39
	10	249591.36	85136.55	58482.14	26654.41	122916.11	42208.92	80707.19
	11	252638.69	86321.92	59849.87	26472.05	124321.66	41858.54	82463.12
	12	254089.45	89438.25	61833.60	27604.65	126196.22	42800.27	83395.95
比上期增减额（亿元） Changes Compared with Previous Period（100 Million Yuan）								
2004	1	2381.00	-2697.14	-2890.17	193.03	5583.41	2480.21	3103.20
	2	3962.94	1459.37	1663.56	-204.19	1247.15	-18.36	1265.51
	3	6003.55	3212.39	2498.10	714.29	1170.48	772.92	397.56
	4	1850.41	877.59	-892.96	1770.55	247.75	402.98	-155.23
	5	2884.22	1382.41	1892.74	-510.33	456.28	188.05	268.23
	6	4729.04	2479.87	1631.68	848.19	1032.40	854.50	177.90
	7	739.22	-1157.45	-1026.15	-131.30	649.91	310.23	339.68
	8	2381.51	728.40	714.00	14.40	291.76	142.93	148.83
	9	2638.31	1577.06	-65.26	1642.32	1006.09	715.44	290.65
	10	1658.22	-80.17	600.25	-680.42	525.18	132.38	392.80
	11	3047.33	1185.37	1367.73	-182.36	1405.55	-350.38	1755.93
	12	1450.76	3116.33	1983.73	1132.60	1874.56	941.73	932.83
比去年同期增长（%） Increase Rate Year-on-year（%）								
2004	1	19.85	18.88	18.52	19.68	18.54	26.05	15.12
	2	19.97	20.63	20.85	20.15	17.21	24.47	13.95
	3	19.58	20.71	20.84	20.40	16.35	24.79	12.56
	4	19.11	21.72	20.56	24.29	15.87	25.31	11.64
	5	17.93	20.53	20.74	20.05	14.99	24.09	10.89
	6	17.10	18.72	17.22	22.26	14.49	23.89	10.20
	7	16.82	17.68	16.53	20.34	14.15	23.17	10.00
	8	16.75	17.24	17.03	17.70	13.79	22.31	9.84
	9	15.25	14.81	14.19	16.14	13.15	21.45	9.24
	10	15.28	14.28	12.91	17.41	13.21	21.73	9.22
	11	15.58	15.16	15.23	14.99	13.68	18.74	11.27
	12	15.30	16.48	15.39	18.99	14.00	18.17	11.98

金融机构本外币信贷收支主要指标时间序列表

Time Series of Major Indicators in Sources and Uses of Credit Funds of Financial Institutions (Domestic and Foreign Currency Combined)

年 月 Year Month		各项贷款 Total Loans	短期贷款 Short - term Loans	中长期贷款 Medium and Long - term Loans	票据融资 Paper Financing	有价证券及投资 Securities and Investments
		期末余额（亿元） Balance (100 Million Yuan)				
2004	1	172732.96	88488.12	68848.33	9557.49	38283.25
	2	175098.44	89694.57	69640.91	9751.20	38692.98
	3	179044.51	91424.18	71415.55	10108.53	38462.27
	4	181207.36	91721.96	72737.92	10595.77	38542.59
	5	182489.12	92120.89	73625.48	10585.65	38109.64
	6	181047.56	90233.32	74230.25	10834.30	38199.69
	7	180961.93	89770.98	74693.91	10815.88	38643.06
	8	182166.92	90279.05	75203.84	10909.55	39116.02
	9	184616.02	91071.36	76763.57	11038.89	40322.24
	10	184766.42	90848.35	77453.39	10725.04	40573.29
	11	186436.84	90650.12	78892.93	11021.40	41151.37
	12	189411.08	90818.17	81006.85	11622.24	40448.38
		比上期增减额（亿元） Changes Compared with Previous Period (100 Million Yuan)				
2004	1	2720.22	1324.88	1325.49	-20.62	1401.91
	2	2371.86	1206.95	793.04	193.71	418.25
	3	4039.11	1821.57	1781.14	357.33	-239.23
	4	2165.64	300.37	1322.57	487.24	80.32
	5	1282.79	399.89	887.63	-10.12	-432.95
	6	3029.57	1025.09	1709.32	251.46	90.05
	7	-84.11	-460.38	463.82	-18.42	443.37
	8	1205.93	508.95	509.98	93.67	472.96
	9	2518.60	856.96	1564.62	129.33	1206.22
	10	150.79	-222.63	689.82	-313.84	251.05
	11	1670.43	213.10	1028.22	296.35	578.08
	12	2983.23	176.38	2114.56	600.85	-702.99
		比去年同期增长（%） Increase Rate Year - on - year (%)				
2004	1	20.60	13.17	29.66	48.06	13.36
	2	21.28	13.99	29.99	47.24	13.66
	3	20.75	13.72	29.36	42.29	12.23
	4	20.45	13.29	29.58	38.56	10.08
	5	19.09	12.26	28.71	29.37	8.47
	6	16.84	10.54	26.74	17.52	7.16
	7	15.94	10.36	24.85	14.54	7.69
	8	14.51	9.43	23.24	8.41	8.46
	9	13.66	9.15	21.74	6.10	12.49
	10	13.23	8.25	21.38	8.35	13.45
	11	13.40	7.60	21.86	12.93	16.12
	12	14.31	7.44	22.11	25.95	7.89

金融机构本外币信贷收支主要指标时间序列表

Time Series of Major Indicators in Sources and Uses of Credit Funds of Financial Institutions（Domestic and Foreign Currency Combined）

年 月 Year Month		各项存款 Total Deposits	企事业单位存款 Deposits by Enterprises and Establishments			储蓄存款 Savings Deposits		
				活期存款 Demand Deposits	定期存款 Time Deposits		活期储蓄 Demand Deposits	定期储蓄 Time Deposits
		期末余额（亿元） Balance（100 Million Yuan）						
2005	1	258475.91	88144.60	60802.49	27342.11	128817.12	43662.62	85154.50
	2	262147.76	86461.89	58598.86	27863.03	134412.03	45347.16	89064.87
	3	269043.29	90496.60	61403.87	29092.73	135803.23	45498.33	90304.90
	4	272384.55	91429.57	60643.30	30786.27	136338.45	45514.41	90824.04
	5	276162.32	93066.09	62328.97	30737.12	136975.93	45547.93	91428.00
	6	282820.27	96220.46	64251.09	31969.37	138673.97	46300.83	92373.14
	7	283747.54	94254.96	62097.05	32157.91	139800.70	46635.83	93164.87
	8	288146.95	96405.15	63288.31	33116.84	140546.56	46761.07	93785.49
	9	292629.82	98560.18	62775.71	35784.47	142310.74	47512.20	94798.54
	10	294388.89	98118.66	63554.29	34564.37	142831.75	47361.50	95470.25
	11	298493.40	99593.61	64885.55	34708.06	144481.79	48515.00	95966.79
	12	300208.55	101750.55	66222.96	35527.59	147053.74	50137.03	96916.71
		比上期增减额（亿元） Changes Compared with Previous Period（100 Million Yuan）						
2005	1	2414.41	-1410.67	-1135.07	-275.60	2621.73	860.94	1760.79
	2	3671.86	-1682.71	-2203.63	520.92	5594.91	1684.54	3910.37
	3	6895.53	4034.71	2805.01	1229.70	1391.20	151.17	1240.03
	4	3340.79	932.96	-760.57	1693.53	535.22	16.08	519.14
	5	3776.32	1635.26	1685.15	-49.89	637.48	33.52	603.96
	6	6657.95	3154.37	1922.12	1232.25	1698.04	752.90	945.14
	7	927.26	-1965.50	-2154.04	188.54	1126.73	335.00	791.73
	8	4399.41	2150.19	1191.26	958.93	745.86	125.24	620.62
	9	4482.88	2155.03	-512.60	2667.63	1764.18	751.13	1013.05
	10	1759.06	-441.52	778.58	-1220.10	521.01	-150.70	671.71
	11	4104.51	1474.95	1331.26	143.69	1650.04	1153.50	496.54
	12	1715.16	2156.94	1337.41	819.53	2571.95	1622.03	949.92
		比去年同期增长（%） Increase Rate Year-on-year（%）						
2005	1	16.04	18.07	18.14	17.90	10.77	12.80	9.76
	2	15.64	13.59	10.29	21.21	14.36	17.21	12.96
	3	15.61	14.08	10.38	22.75	14.40	15.30	13.96
	4	16.13	13.99	10.80	20.87	14.61	14.17	14.84
	5	16.29	14.07	10.07	23.14	14.71	13.72	15.21
	6	16.78	14.45	10.28	23.87	15.14	13.18	16.14
	7	16.81	13.68	8.50	25.23	15.45	13.14	16.64
	8	17.47	15.26	9.22	28.90	15.79	13.06	17.20
	9	18.03	15.66	8.45	30.91	16.28	12.92	18.03
	10	17.95	15.25	8.67	29.68	16.20	12.21	18.29
	11	18.15	15.37	8.41	31.11	16.22	15.90	16.38
	12	18.15	13.77	7.10	28.70	16.53	17.14	16.21

金融机构本外币信贷收支主要指标时间序列表

Time Series of Major Indicators in Sources and Uses of Credit Funds of Financial Institutions (Domestic and Foreign Currency Combined)

年 月 Year Month	各项贷款 Total Loans	短期贷款 Short - term Loans	中长期贷款 Medium and Long - term Loans	票据融资 Paper Financing	有价证券及投资 Securities and Investments
	期末余额（亿元） Balance (100 Million Yuan)				
2005 1	193072.01	91678.95	83108.54	12124.40	40537.09
2	194025.74	92094.10	83637.58	12134.28	40479.76
3	197616.44	93567.85	85085.71	12693.06	40897.97
4	199135.41	93636.11	85848.88	13272.71	41874.97
5	198662.24	92711.93	86161.71	13379.23	41743.18
6	198565.85	90949.16	87072.08	14137.76	41521.21
7	198177.74	90519.40	87117.24	14174.80	41446.80
8	199903.86	90708.86	87873.58	14979.83	42266.32
9	203052.76	91520.43	89396.09	15598.43	42689.23
10	203552.89	91304.90	90241.82	15420.04	43323.87
11	205658.82	91702.28	91087.19	16308.42	43786.54
12	206838.48	91157.45	92940.53	16319.16	44870.95
	比上期增减额（亿元） Changes Compared with Previous Period (100 Million Yuan)				
2005 1	3535.61	1167.33	1795.89	504.05	160.14
2	953.82	415.23	529.04	9.88	-57.33
3	3778.30	1648.22	1461.28	558.77	418.21
4	1511.48	61.48	762.65	579.66	976.73
5	1295.39	457.83	649.70	106.66	-131.79
6	4805.37	2036.63	1932.07	759.10	-221.97
7	-407.63	-435.22	38.86	37.03	-74.41
8	1724.56	188.84	755.89	805.03	819.52
9	3415.96	1060.25	1541.09	618.60	422.91
10	536.89	-180.67	848.05	-178.39	634.64
11	2107.35	399.05	845.32	888.38	462.67
12	1358.50	-377.79	1865.58	10.75	1084.41
	比去年同期增长（%） Increase Rate Year - on - year (%)				
2005 1	14.47	7.09	22.34	26.89	5.89
2	13.47	6.12	21.70	24.47	4.62
3	13.02	5.81	20.72	25.59	6.33
4	12.50	5.53	19.57	25.29	8.65
5	12.42	5.57	19.01	26.42	9.53
6	13.50	6.81	19.16	30.50	8.70
7	13.33	6.87	18.47	31.06	7.26
8	13.53	6.48	18.67	37.31	8.05
9	13.83	6.64	18.26	41.31	5.87
10	14.03	6.71	18.30	43.78	6.78
11	14.14	7.38	17.21	47.98	6.40
12	13.06	6.76	16.46	40.42	10.93

（二）政策性银行本外币信贷收支主要指标时间序列表（2002—2005 年月度时序）

Time Series of Major Indicators in Sources and Uses of Credit Funds of Policy Banks（Domestic and Foreign Currency Combined）（Monthly Series from 2002 to 2005）

政策性银行本外币信贷收支主要指标时间序列表

Time Series of Major Indicators in Sources and Uses of Credit Funds of Policy Banks（Domestic and Foreign Currency Combined）

年 Year	月 Month	各项存款 Total Deposits	企事业单位存款 Deposits by Enterprises and Establishments	活期存款 Demand Deposits	定期存款 Time Deposits	储蓄存款 Savings Deposits	活期储蓄 Demand Deposits	定期储蓄 Time Deposits	债券发行及境外筹资 Bonds Issue & Overseas Financing
		期末余额（亿元） Balance（100 Million Yuan）							
2002	1	470.47	467.51	457.24	10.27				8826.01
	2	441.12	439.07	430.14	8.93				8788.41
	3	471.64	468.65	462.51	6.14				8941.74
	4	473.77	469.80	464.21	5.59				9151.64
	5	494.96	489.84	484.25	5.59				9100.12
	6	539.95	534.44	525.44	9.00				9177.76
	7	541.05	534.10	525.11	8.99				9365.78
	8	544.90	538.38	528.61	9.77				9405.58
	9	563.98	557.74	546.74	11.00				9539.38
	10	602.76	598.64	588.20	10.44				9741.14
	11	598.01	593.77	580.44	13.33				9908.87
	12	712.31	707.13	689.73	17.40				10190.86
		比上期增减额（亿元） Changes Compared with Previous Period（100 Million Yuan）							
2002	1	-82.57	-82.38	-81.18	-1.20				11.02
	2	-29.35	-28.44	-27.10	-1.34				-37.60
	3	30.52	29.58	32.37	-2.79				153.33
	4	2.13	1.15	1.70	-0.55				209.90
	5	21.19	20.04	20.04					-51.52
	6	44.99	44.60	41.19	3.41				77.64
	7	1.10	-0.34	-0.33	-0.01				188.02
	8	3.85	4.28	3.50	0.78				39.80
	9	19.08	19.36	18.13	1.23				133.80
	10	38.78	40.90	41.46	-0.56				201.76
	11	-4.75	-4.87	-7.76	2.89				167.73
	12	114.30	113.36	109.29	4.07				281.99
		比去年同期增长（%） Increase Rate Year-on-year（%）							
2002	1	2.02	2.11	0.64	191.76				13.50
	2	-3.51	-3.09	-4.61	315.35				12.92
	3	18.23	18.46	18.08	56.23				12.99
	4	17.77	17.63	17.43	36.34				14.61
	5	23.76	23.48	23.12	65.38				12.28
	6	36.27	36.02	35.05	133.16				13.12
	7	33.76	32.93	32.02	122.52				14.13
	8	24.92	24.09	23.06	126.16				12.89
	9	28.95	28.26	27.38	95.04				13.79
	10	33.94	33.71	32.87	107.14				14.03
	11	23.02	22.93	21.42	168.21				13.51
	12	28.82	28.60	26.65	230.17				15.48

政策性银行本外币信贷收支主要指标时间序列表

Time Series of Major Indicators in Sources and Uses of Credit Funds of Policy Banks (Domestic and Foreign Currency Combined)

年　月 Year Month		各项贷款 Total Loans				有价证券及投资 Securities and Investments
			短期贷款 Short - term Loans	中长期贷款 Medium and Long - term Loans	票据融资 Paper Financing	
期末余额（亿元） Balance (100 Million Yuan)						
2002	1	15778.08	7512.30	7841.39		1415.94
	2	15809.24	7501.47	7881.30		1414.58
	3	15913.59	7474.10	8004.88		1424.11
	4	15881.81	7393.40	8043.02		1431.82
	5	15861.86	7312.90	8096.61		1429.82
	6	16136.56	7297.13	8377.63		1444.39
	7	16236.37	7320.20	8451.61	0.03	1437.65
	8	16322.00	7290.14	8563.26	0.04	1460.38
	9	16561.11	7310.23	8772.57	0.03	1446.51
	10	16710.96	7350.25	8879.28	0.02	1442.65
	11	16675.67	7360.17	8832.78	0.02	1439.44
	12	17212.90	7511.40	9210.29		1445.81
比上期增减额（亿元） Changes Compared with Previous Period (100 Million Yuan)						
2002	1	69.07	56.57	10.92		14.58
	2	31.16	- 10.83	39.91		- 1.36
	3	104.35	- 27.37	123.58		9.53
	4	- 31.78	- 80.70	38.14		7.71
	5	- 19.95	- 80.50	53.59		- 2.00
	6	274.70	- 15.77	281.02		14.57
	7	99.81	23.07	73.98	0.03	- 6.74
	8	85.63	- 30.06	111.65	0.01	22.73
	9	239.11	20.09	209.31	- 0.01	- 13.87
	10	149.85	40.02	106.71	- 0.01	- 3.86
	11	- 35.29	9.92	- 46.50		- 3.21
	12	537.23	151.23	377.51	- 0.02	6.37
比去年同期增长（%） Increase Rate Year - on - year (%)						
2002	1	7.60	1.94	13.02		1374.02
	2	7.89	2.65	12.87		1198.26
	3	8.62	3.80	12.99		1169.71
	4	8.27	3.87	12.05		896.19
	5	8.05	3.42	12.13		888.33
	6	9.26	3.23	14.54		916.89
	7	9.03	3.52	13.80	200.00	1041.81
	8	8.62	3.56	12.95	300.00	958.09
	9	8.98	3.36	13.73		1008.86
	10	10.41	3.32	16.74		923.23
	11	8.39	1.19	14.84		1443.80
	12	9.66	0.75	17.82		3.17

政策性银行本外币信贷收支主要指标时间序列表

Time Series of Major Indicators in Sources and Uses of Credit Funds of Policy Banks（Domestic and Foreign Currency Combined）

年 月 Year Month		各项存款 Total Deposits	企事业单位存款 Deposits by Enterprises and Establishments	活期存款 Demand Deposits	定期存款 Time Deposits	储蓄存款 Savings Deposits	活期储蓄 Demand Deposits	定期储蓄 Time Deposits	债券发行及境外筹资 Bonds Issue & Overseas Financing
		期末余额（亿元） Balance（100 Million Yuan）							
2003	1	563.14	558.83	533.42	25.41				10197.44
	2	585.62	581.29	552.26	29.03				10400.52
	3	589.74	584.42	557.66	26.76				10439.32
	4	571.02	564.37	540.69	23.68				10318.97
	5	632.35	624.23	605.59	18.64				10532.47
	6	795.82	788.32	762.15	26.17				10718.36
	7	730.52	721.09	697.76	23.33				10972.21
	8	784.30	776.78	752.49	24.29				10957.26
	9	890.33	876.69	835.13	41.56				11432.36
	10	903.68	889.85	857.02	32.83				11779.94
	11	933.25	920.13	881.12	39.01				12001.31
	12	971.40	958.02	905.36	52.66				12004.34
		比上期增减额（亿元） Changes Compared with Previous Period（100 Million Yuan）							
2003	1	-149.18	-148.26	-156.27	8.01				6.25
	2	22.48	22.46	18.84	3.62				203.08
	3	4.12	3.13	5.40	-2.27				38.80
	4	-18.72	-20.05	-16.97	-3.08				-120.35
	5	61.33	59.86	64.90	-5.04				213.50
	6	163.47	164.09	156.56	7.53				185.89
	7	-65.30	-67.23	-64.39	-2.84				253.85
	8	53.78	55.69	54.73	0.96				-14.95
	9	106.03	99.91	82.64	17.27				475.10
	10	13.35	13.16	21.89	-8.73				347.58
	11	29.57	30.28	24.10	6.18				221.37
	12	38.15	37.89	24.24	13.65				3.03
		比去年同期增长（%） Increase Rate Year-on-year（%）							
2003	1	19.70	19.53	16.66	147.42				15.54
	2	32.76	32.39	28.39	225.08				18.34
	3	25.04	24.70	20.57	335.83				16.75
	4	20.53	20.13	16.48	323.61				12.76
	5	27.76	27.44	25.06	233.45				15.74
	6	47.39	47.50	45.05	190.78				16.79
	7	35.02	35.01	32.88	159.51				17.15
	8	43.93	44.28	42.35	148.62				16.50
	9	57.87	57.19	52.75	277.82				19.84
	10	49.92	48.65	45.70	214.46				20.93
	11	56.06	54.96	51.80	192.65				21.12
	12	36.37	35.48	31.26	202.64				17.80

政策性银行本外币信贷收支主要指标时间序列表

Time Series of Major Indicators in Sources and Uses of Credit Funds of Policy Banks (Domestic and Foreign Currency Combined)

年 月 Year Month		各项贷款 Total Loans	短期贷款 Short - term Loans	中长期贷款 Medium and Long - term Loans	票据融资 Paper Financing	有价证券及投资 Securities and Investments
		期末余额（亿元） Balance (100 Million Yuan)				
2003	1	17161.30	7525.01	9137.95		1458.04
	2	17194.51	7475.41	9218.37		1477.63
	3	17426.22	7390.45	9531.21		1364.63
	4	17399.48	7320.31	9566.41		1356.90
	5	17414.49	7272.36	9623.10		1354.18
	6	17953.46	7276.96	10156.48		1356.49
	7	18056.09	7267.12	10268.61		1420.03
	8	18289.48	7270.69	10506.58		1398.19
	9	18747.60	7290.02	10934.42		1379.08
	10	18903.81	7307.53	11069.89	0.06	1418.91
	11	18899.08	7228.12	11110.39	0.06	1454.53
	12	19328.34	7259.58	11488.76	0.11	1413.16
		比上期增减额（亿元） Changes Compared with Previous Period (100 Million Yuan)				
2003	1	-51.61	13.60	-72.34		12.12
	2	33.21	-49.60	80.42		19.59
	3	231.71	-84.96	312.84		-113.00
	4	-26.74	-70.14	35.20		-7.73
	5	15.01	-47.95	56.69		-2.72
	6	538.97	4.60	533.38		2.31
	7	102.63	-9.84	112.13		63.54
	8	233.39	3.57	237.97		-21.84
	9	458.12	19.33	427.84		-19.11
	10	156.21	17.51	135.47	0.06	39.83
	11	-4.73	-79.41	40.50		35.62
	12	429.26	31.46	378.37	0.05	-41.37
		比去年同期增长（%） Increase Rate Year - on - year (%)				
2003	1	8.77	0.17	16.53		2.97
	2	8.76	-0.35	16.97		4.46
	3	9.51	-1.12	19.07		-4.18
	4	9.56	-0.99	18.94		-5.23
	5	9.79	-0.55	18.85		-5.29
	6	11.26	-0.28	21.23		-6.09
	7	11.21	-0.73	21.50	-100.00	-1.23
	8	12.05	-0.27	22.69	-100.00	-4.26
	9	13.20	-0.28	24.64	-100.00	-4.66
	10	13.12	-0.58	24.67	200.00	-1.65
	11	13.33	-1.79	25.79	200.00	1.05
	12	12.29	-3.35	24.74		-2.26

政策性银行本外币信贷收支主要指标时间序列表

Time Series of Major Indicators in Sources and Uses of Credit Funds of Policy Banks（Domestic and Foreign Currency Combined）

年 月 Year Month		各项存款 Total Deposits	企事业单位存款 Deposits by Enterprises and Establishments			储蓄存款 Savings Deposits			债券发行及境外筹资 Bonds Issue & Overseas Financing
				活期存款 Demand Deposits	定期存款 Time Deposits		活期储蓄 Demand Deposits	定期储蓄 Time Deposits	
期末余额（亿元） Balance（100 Million Yuan）									
2004	1	810.84	796.14	742.18	53.96				12096.86
	2	806.92	792.35	734.97	57.38				12359.02
	3	842.87	829.53	772.98	56.55				12303.25
	4	816.47	803.98	754.22	49.76				12450.45
	5	815.20	802.88	753.15	49.73				12600.33
	6	1091.86	1075.35	1023.75	51.60				12754.38
	7	946.98	931.54	862.62	68.92				13190.74
	8	917.78	905.22	841.77	63.45				13214.19
	9	923.36	910.62	854.22	56.40				13419.84
	10	993.50	979.22	924.73	54.49				13695.98
	11	1148.15	1135.21	1079.13	56.08				13988.13
	12	1274.87	1261.57	1138.90	122.67				14690.98
比上期增减额（亿元） Changes Compared with Previous Period（100 Million Yuan）									
2004	1	-160.79	-161.88	-163.18	1.30				92.52
	2	-3.92	-3.79	-7.21	3.42				262.16
	3	35.95	37.18	38.01	-0.83				-55.77
	4	-26.40	-25.55	-18.76	-6.79				147.20
	5	-1.27	-1.10	-1.07	-0.03				149.88
	6	276.66	272.47	270.60	1.87				154.05
	7	-144.88	-143.81	-161.13	17.32				436.36
	8	-29.20	-26.32	-20.85	-5.47				23.45
	9	5.58	5.40	12.45	-7.05				205.65
	10	70.14	68.60	70.51	-1.91				276.14
	11	154.65	155.99	154.40	1.59				292.15
	12	126.72	126.36	59.77	66.59				702.85
比去年同期增长（%） Increase Rate Year-on-year（%）									
2004	1	43.99	42.47	39.14	112.36				18.63
	2	37.79	36.31	33.08	97.66				18.83
	3	42.92	41.94	38.61	111.32				17.85
	4	42.98	42.46	39.49	110.14				20.66
	5	28.92	28.62	24.37	166.79				19.63
	6	37.20	36.41	34.32	97.17				19.00
	7	29.63	29.18	23.63	195.41				20.22
	8	17.02	16.53	11.86	161.22				20.60
	9	3.71	3.87	2.29	35.71				17.38
	10	9.94	10.04	7.90	65.98				16.27
	11	23.03	23.37	22.47	43.76				16.56
	12	31.24	31.69	25.80	132.95				22.38

政策性银行本外币信贷收支主要指标时间序列表

Time Series of Major Indicators in Sources and Uses of Credit Funds of Policy Banks（Domestic and Foreign Currency Combined）

年　月 Year Month		各项贷款 Total Loans				有价证券及投资 Securities and Investments
			短期贷款 Short－term Loans	中长期贷款 Medium and Long－term Loans	票据融资 Paper Financing	
		期末余额（亿元） Balance（100 Million Yuan）				
2004	1	19400.02	7279.67	11541.22	0.06	1424.02
	2	19426.93	7250.16	11589.76	0.08	1453.35
	3	19639.00	7239.78	11815.45	0.12	1498.65
	4	19648.61	7194.91	11859.15	0.23	1508.24
	5	19689.87	7151.74	11929.78	0.25	1510.54
	6	20304.34	7255.49	12412.81	0.20	1468.83
	7	20401.11	7295.17	12464.58	0.35	1484.39
	8	20521.92	7329.17	12547.57	0.38	1471.65
	9	20590.48	7419.40	12523.88	0.46	1605.50
	10	20990.52	7527.42	12812.02	0.48	1503.67
	11	21454.17	7692.56	13111.13	0.48	1573.83
	12	22228.24	7784.40	13794.43	0.66	1526.00
		比上期增减额（亿元） Changes Compared with Previous Period（100 Million Yuan）				
2004	1	71.68	20.09	52.46	－0.05	10.86
	2	26.91	－29.51	48.54	0.02	29.33
	3	212.07	－10.38	225.69	0.04	45.30
	4	9.61	－44.87	43.70	0.11	9.59
	5	41.26	－43.17	70.63	0.02	2.30
	6	614.47	103.75	483.03	－0.05	－41.71
	7	96.77	39.68	51.77	0.15	15.56
	8	120.81	34.00	82.99	0.03	－12.74
	9	68.56	90.23	－23.69	0.08	133.85
	10	400.04	108.02	288.14	0.02	－101.83
	11	463.65	165.14	299.11		70.16
	12	774.07	91.84	683.30	0.18	－47.83
		比去年同期增长（%） Increase Rate Year－on－year（%）				
2004	1	13.05	－3.26	26.30		－2.33
	2	12.98	－3.01	25.72		－1.64
	3	12.70	－2.04	23.97		9.82
	4	12.93	－1.71	23.97		11.15
	5	13.07	－1.66	23.97		11.55
	6	13.09	－0.30	22.22		8.28
	7	12.99	0.39	21.39		4.53
	8	12.21	0.80	19.43		5.25
	9	9.83	1.77	14.54		16.42
	10	11.04	3.01	15.74	700.00	5.97
	11	13.52	6.43	18.01	700.00	8.20
	12	15.00	7.23	20.07	500.00	7.98

政策性银行本外币信贷收支主要指标时间序列表

Time Series of Major Indicators in Sources and Uses of Credit Funds of Policy Banks（Domestic and Foreign Currency Combined）

年 月 Year Month		各项存款 Total Deposits	企事业单位存款 Deposits by Enterprises and Establishments	活期存款 Demand Deposits	定期存款 Time Deposits	储蓄存款 Savings Deposits	活期储蓄 Demand Deposits	定期储蓄 Time Deposits	债券发行及境外筹资 Bonds Issue & Overseas Financing
期末余额（亿元） Balance（100 Million Yuan）									
2005	1	1478.31	1469.95	1103.63	366.32				14939.54
	2	1423.37	1411.11	1052.83	358.28				14944.00
	3	1530.01	1518.30	1166.64	351.66				15434.05
	4	1625.33	1614.00	1399.86	214.14				15921.08
	5	1746.90	1731.92	1515.33	216.59				15951.34
	6	2018.38	2004.25	1772.72	231.53				16260.62
	7	1840.28	1828.26	1625.16	203.10				16631.32
	8	1848.99	1834.53	1608.34	226.19				17392.98
	9	1894.90	1880.90	1649.15	231.75				17688.05
	10	1984.16	1970.31	1691.19	279.12				17699.05
	11	2075.46	2058.62	1823.30	235.32				18367.81
	12	2132.99	2113.83	1857.30	256.53				18996.42
比上期增减额（亿元） Changes Compared with Previous Period（100 Million Yuan）									
2005	1	203.44	208.38	-35.27	243.65				248.56
	2	-54.94	-58.84	-50.80	-8.04				4.46
	3	106.64	107.19	113.81	-6.62				490.05
	4	95.32	95.70	233.22	-137.52				487.03
	5	121.57	117.92	115.47	2.45				30.26
	6	271.48	272.33	257.39	14.94				309.28
	7	-178.10	-175.99	-147.56	-28.43				370.70
	8	8.71	6.27	-16.82	23.09				761.66
	9	45.91	46.37	40.81	5.56				295.07
	10	89.26	89.41	42.04	47.37				11.00
	11	91.30	88.31	132.11	-43.80				668.76
	12	57.53	55.21	34.00	21.21				628.61
比去年同期增长（%） Increase Rate Year-on-year（%）									
2005	1	82.32	84.63	48.70	578.87				23.50
	2	76.40	78.09	43.25	524.40				20.92
	3	81.52	83.03	50.93	521.86				25.45
	4	99.07	100.75	85.60	330.35				27.88
	5	114.29	115.71	101.20	335.53				26.59
	6	84.86	86.38	73.16	348.70				27.49
	7	94.33	96.26	88.40	194.69				26.08
	8	101.46	102.66	91.07	256.49				31.62
	9	105.22	106.55	93.06	310.90				31.81
	10	99.71	101.21	82.88	412.24				29.23
	11	80.77	81.34	68.96	319.61				31.31
	12	67.31	67.56	63.08	109.12				29.31

政策性银行本外币信贷收支主要指标时间序列表
Time Series of Major Indicators in Sources and Uses of Credit Funds of Policy Banks (Domestic and Foreign Currency Combined)

年　月 Year Month		各项贷款 Total Loans	短期贷款 Short - term Loans	中长期贷款 Medium and Long - term Loans	票据融资 Paper Financing	有价证券及投资 Securities and Investments
		期末余额（亿元） Balance (100 Million Yuan)				
2005	1	22813.69	7780.84	14396.63	0.57	1541.69
	2	22909.90	7804.78	14463.72	0.40	1458.05
	3	23300.03	7899.71	14758.81	0.31	1437.40
	4	23471.39	7954.03	14870.69	0.29	1447.00
	5	23621.64	7985.58	15000.70	0.28	1431.45
	6	24487.96	8248.51	15609.58	0.30	1434.66
	7	24552.04	8267.12	15662.00	0.40	1468.52
	8	24792.26	8338.55	15828.51	0.50	1459.00
	9	25369.50	8586.03	16147.41	0.47	1372.95
	10	25816.20	8697.51	16456.42	0.50	1363.84
	11	26086.31	9020.69	16414.92	0.58	1615.65
	12	26497.06	8907.97	16934.23	0.58	1576.53
		比上期增减额（亿元） Changes Compared with Previous Period (100 Million Yuan)				
2005	1	585.45	-3.56	602.20	-0.09	15.69
	2	96.21	23.94	67.09	-0.17	-83.64
	3	390.13	94.93	295.09	-0.09	-20.65
	4	171.36	54.32	111.88	-0.02	9.60
	5	150.25	31.55	130.01	-0.01	-15.55
	6	866.32	262.93	608.88	0.02	3.21
	7	64.08	18.61	52.42	0.10	33.86
	8	240.22	71.43	166.51	0.10	-9.52
	9	577.24	247.48	318.90	-0.03	-86.05
	10	446.70	111.48	309.01	0.03	-9.11
	11	270.11	323.18	-41.50	0.08	251.81
	12	410.75	-112.72	519.31		-39.12
		比去年同期增长（%） Increase Rate Year - on - year (%)				
2005	1	17.60	6.88	24.74	850.00	8.26
	2	17.93	7.65	24.80	400.00	0.32
	3	18.64	9.12	24.91	158.33	-4.09
	4	19.46	10.55	25.39	26.09	-4.06
	5	19.97	11.66	25.74	12.00	-5.24
	6	20.60	13.69	25.75	50.00	-2.33
	7	20.35	13.32	25.65	14.29	-1.07
	8	20.81	13.77	26.15	31.58	-0.86
	9	23.21	15.72	28.93	2.17	-14.48
	10	22.99	15.54	28.45	4.17	-9.30
	11	21.59	17.27	25.20	20.83	2.66
	12	19.20	14.43	22.76	-12.12	3.31

（三）国有商业银行本外币信贷收支主要指标时间序列表（2002—2005 年月度时序）

Time Series of Major Indicators in Sources and Uses of Credit Funds of State - owned Commercial Banks（Domestic and Foreign Currency Combined）（Monthly Series from 2002 to 2005）

国有商业银行本外币信贷收支主要指标时间序列表

Time Series of Major Indicators in Sources and Uses of Credit Funds of State - owned Commercial Banks（Domestic and Foreign Currency Combined）

年 月 Year Month		各项存款 Total Deposits	企事业单位存款 Deposits by Enterprises and Establishments	活期存款 Demand Deposits	定期存款 Time Deposits	储蓄存款 Savings Deposits	活期储蓄 Demand Deposits	定期储蓄 Time Deposits	债券发行及境外筹资 Bonds Issue & Overseas Financing
					期末余额（亿元） Balance（100 Million Yuan）				
2002	1	97034.98	33921.09	25226.89	8694.20	55357.74	16102.98	39254.76	1458.81
	2	98007.58	32914.88	24198.37	8716.51	57438.39	16863.11	40575.28	1441.06
	3	99991.36	34118.79	25295.41	8823.38	57857.54	17033.12	40824.42	1423.10
	4	100868.06	34277.38	25070.95	9206.43	58568.64	17477.71	41090.93	1414.88
	5	102412.64	34954.10	25904.48	9049.62	59058.23	17669.51	41388.72	1412.70
	6	104747.16	35817.64	26780.97	9036.67	59964.47	18088.11	41876.36	1600.11
	7	105508.46	35749.38	26613.55	9135.83	60568.61	18339.09	42229.52	1575.84
	8	106967.90	36486.18	27101.35	9384.83	61138.62	18644.07	42494.55	1573.11
	9	108789.31	37393.42	27618.13	9775.29	61685.97	18985.27	42700.70	1550.32
	10	109384.59	37468.68	27977.60	9491.08	62076.93	19045.80	43031.13	1510.40
	11	110529.57	37867.88	28111.97	9755.91	62620.04	19329.98	43290.06	1333.72
	12	111317.76	37963.66	27974.64	9989.02	63062.59	19623.32	43439.27	1313.90
					比上期增减额（亿元） Changes Compared with Previous Period（100 Million Yuan）				
2002	1	626.10	-310.57	-256.24	-54.33	1047.04	450.81	596.23	-17.12
	2	972.60	-1006.21	-1028.52	22.31	2080.65	760.13	1320.52	-17.75
	3	1983.78	1203.91	1097.04	106.87	419.15	170.01	249.14	-17.96
	4	876.70	158.59	-224.46	383.05	711.10	444.59	266.51	-8.22
	5	1544.58	676.72	833.53	-156.81	489.59	191.80	297.79	-2.18
	6	2334.52	863.54	876.49	-12.95	906.24	418.60	487.64	187.41
	7	761.30	-68.26	-167.42	99.16	604.14	250.98	353.16	-24.27
	8	1459.44	736.80	487.80	249.00	570.01	304.98	265.03	-2.73
	9	1821.41	907.24	516.78	390.46	547.35	341.20	206.15	-22.79
	10	595.28	75.26	359.47	-284.21	390.96	60.53	330.43	-39.92
	11	1144.98	399.20	134.37	264.83	543.11	284.18	258.93	-176.68
	12	788.19	95.78	-137.33	233.11	442.55	293.34	149.21	-19.82
					比去年同期增长（%） Increase Rate Year - on - year（%）				
2002	1	12.43	8.34	10.80	1.80	10.97	17.15	8.62	-14.09
	2	12.34	3.82	5.86	-1.47	14.33	24.50	10.57	-13.88
	3	12.16	4.09	7.20	-3.88	13.73	21.21	10.87	-14.11
	4	12.71	3.95	7.59	-4.82	14.85	23.77	11.44	-12.69
	5	14.51	6.11	10.04	-3.75	16.31	27.59	12.08	-11.02
	6	13.89	4.39	7.74	-4.40	16.14	24.86	12.74	2.05
	7	16.31	8.36	12.15	-1.37	17.21	28.00	13.07	1.42
	8	15.33	7.27	10.26	-0.54	16.65	25.83	13.04	
	9	15.88	8.30	11.32	0.59	16.57	25.35	13.05	-0.99
	10	16.19	8.74	13.02	-2.19	16.47	25.41	12.91	-1.55
	11	16.88	10.03	12.82	2.69	16.95	27.38	12.82	-12.69
	12	15.45	7.77	8.98	4.55	16.10	25.43	12.33	-10.98

国有商业银行本外币信贷收支主要指标时间序列表

Time Series of Major Indicators in Sources and Uses of Credit Funds of State - owned Commercial Banks (Domestic and Foreign Currency Combined)

年　月 Year Month		各项贷款 Total Loans	短期贷款 Short - term Loans	中长期贷款 Medium and Long - term Loans	票据融资 Paper Financing	有价证券及投资 Securities and Investments
期末余额（亿元） Balance (100 Million Yuan)						
2002	1	69467.93	36196.48	30025.25	1064.21	24291.64
	2	69742.16	36186.15	30281.34	1117.40	24230.49
	3	71174.15	37105.60	30641.85	1278.63	25069.31
	4	71541.55	37343.14	30660.40	1354.89	25493.30
	5	72316.18	37582.32	31098.07	1447.19	25693.53
	6	73928.40	38255.09	31734.84	1733.25	26161.20
	7	74151.49	38262.41	31979.79	1726.65	26229.46
	8	75000.75	38482.55	32489.65	1861.83	26817.78
	9	76969.61	39120.85	33270.76	2447.82	26715.41
	10	77260.03	39096.26	33621.97	2429.19	27623.28
	11	78221.57	39399.26	34144.79	2576.98	28123.64
	12	79510.22	39837.99	35141.11	2440.69	27669.96
比上期增减额（亿元） Changes Compared with Previous Period (100 Million Yuan)						
2002	1	- 193.86	- 287.80	181.08	- 56.32	- 173.41
	2	274.23	- 10.33	256.09	53.19	- 61.15
	3	1431.99	919.45	360.51	161.23	838.82
	4	367.40	237.54	18.55	76.26	423.99
	5	774.63	239.18	437.67	92.30	200.23
	6	1612.22	672.77	636.77	286.06	467.67
	7	223.09	7.32	244.95	- 6.60	68.26
	8	849.26	220.14	509.86	135.18	588.32
	9	1968.86	638.30	781.11	585.99	- 102.37
	10	290.42	- 24.59	351.21	- 18.63	907.87
	11	961.54	303.00	522.82	147.79	500.36
	12	1288.65	438.73	996.32	- 136.29	- 453.68
比去年同期增长（%） Increase Rate Year - on - year (%)						
2002	1	8.18	- 0.17	20.22	88.68	13.20
	2	7.98	- 0.24	19.71	88.79	11.57
	3	9.11	2.01	18.82	91.31	13.82
	4	8.90	2.76	17.14	74.88	13.21
	5	9.40	3.28	17.45	71.04	14.11
	6	10.23	3.98	18.26	60.40	16.26
	7	10.49	4.38	18.23	52.84	14.95
	8	11.54	5.25	19.26	65.09	16.82
	9	13.52	6.72	20.11	113.10	15.77
	10	14.22	6.95	21.03	131.73	20.03
	11	15.05	7.34	21.69	162.13	22.14
	12	14.24	6.11	22.21	123.23	15.40

国有商业银行本外币信贷收支主要指标时间序列表

Time Series of Major Indicators in Sources and Uses of Credit Funds of State - owned Commercial Banks（Domestic and Foreign Currency Combined）

年 月 Year Month		各项存款 Total Deposits	企事业单位存款 Deposits by Enterprises and Establishments			储蓄存款 Savings Deposits			债券发行及境外筹资 Bonds Issue & Overseas Financing
				活期存款 Demand Deposits	定期存款 Time Deposits		活期储蓄 Demand Deposits	定期储蓄 Time Deposits	
期末余额（亿元） Balance（100 Million Yuan）									
2003	1	113805.20	37844.63	27476.51	10368.12	66069.56	21153.11	44916.45	1304.03
	2	115649.76	38275.90	28044.19	10231.71	67229.08	21329.27	45899.81	1295.39
	3	118901.84	39915.55	29380.98	10534.57	68378.45	21707.05	46671.40	1274.51
	4	119102.26	39776.34	28765.78	11010.56	68720.94	21820.29	46900.65	1269.75
	5	121064.52	40706.48	29656.13	11050.35	69416.92	22097.30	47319.62	1275.34
	6	123776.12	42126.01	31091.30	11034.71	70145.38	22525.78	47619.60	1242.64
	7	124440.95	42087.37	30742.48	11344.89	70643.69	22826.04	47817.65	1218.62
	8	125219.78	42400.13	30968.29	11431.84	70937.02	23038.32	47898.70	1188.87
	9	127524.73	43523.20	31372.02	12151.18	71898.81	23612.19	48286.62	1187.64
	10	128037.60	43749.90	32091.03	11658.87	72103.79	23615.66	48488.13	1200.64
	11	128662.46	43835.44	32111.70	11723.74	72451.64	23946.48	48505.16	1191.98
	12	128601.41	43186.38	31881.56	11304.82	72923.26	24336.90	48586.36	1154.88
比上期增减额（亿元） Changes Compared with Previous Period（100 Million Yuan）									
2003	1	2487.19	-35.25	-316.76	281.51	2923.66	1487.44	1436.22	-10.14
	2	1844.56	431.27	567.68	-136.41	1159.52	176.16	983.36	-8.64
	3	3252.08	1639.65	1336.79	302.86	1149.37	377.78	771.59	-20.88
	4	200.42	-139.21	-615.20	475.99	342.49	113.24	229.25	-4.76
	5	1962.26	930.14	890.35	39.79	695.98	277.01	418.97	5.59
	6	2711.60	1419.53	1435.17	-15.64	728.46	428.48	299.98	-32.70
	7	664.83	-38.64	-348.82	310.18	498.31	300.26	198.05	-24.02
	8	778.83	312.76	225.81	86.95	293.33	212.28	81.05	-29.75
	9	2304.95	1123.07	403.73	719.34	961.79	573.87	387.92	-1.23
	10	512.87	226.70	719.01	-492.31	204.98	3.47	201.51	13.00
	11	624.86	85.54	20.67	64.87	347.85	330.82	17.03	-8.66
	12	-61.05	-649.06	-230.14	-418.92	471.62	390.42	81.20	-37.10
比去年同期增长（%） Increase Rate Year - on - year（%）									
2003	1	17.28	11.57	8.92	19.25	19.35	31.36	14.42	-10.61
	2	18.00	16.29	15.89	17.38	17.05	26.48	13.12	-10.11
	3	18.91	16.99	16.15	19.39	18.18	27.44	14.32	-10.44
	4	18.08	16.04	14.74	19.60	17.33	24.85	14.14	-10.26
	5	18.21	16.46	14.48	22.11	17.54	25.06	14.33	-9.72
	6	18.17	17.61	16.09	22.11	16.98	24.53	13.71	-22.34
	7	17.94	17.73	15.51	24.18	16.63	24.47	13.23	-22.67
	8	17.06	16.21	14.27	21.81	16.03	23.57	12.72	-24.43
	9	17.22	16.39	13.59	24.31	16.56	24.37	13.08	-23.39
	10	17.05	16.76	14.70	22.84	16.15	23.99	12.68	-20.51
	11	16.41	15.76	14.23	20.17	15.70	23.88	12.05	-10.63
	12	15.53	13.76	13.97	13.17	15.64	24.02	11.85	-12.10

国有商业银行本外币信贷收支主要指标时间序列表

Time Series of Major Indicators in Sources and Uses of Credit Funds of State - owned Commercial Banks (Domestic and Foreign Currency Combined)

年 月 Year Month		各项贷款 Total Loans				有价证券及投资 Securities and Investments
			短期贷款 Short - term Loans	中长期贷款 Medium and Long - term Loans	票据融资 Paper Financing	
期末余额（亿元）Balance (100 Million Yuan)						
2003	1	81902.22	40531.59	36200.55	3060.21	27760.10
	2	82727.66	40673.26	36458.72	3496.68	27789.83
	3	84891.79	41447.65	37374.64	3936.14	27670.96
	4	85836.69	41546.72	37927.02	4189.06	27875.55
	5	87349.58	41979.86	38555.37	4593.15	28414.20
	6	90436.07	43027.69	39840.39	5318.49	29745.94
	7	90732.51	42588.23	40586.94	5321.66	30401.85
	8	91896.57	42882.76	41169.88	5623.01	31089.70
	9	93494.07	43036.44	42401.10	5812.23	31354.09
	10	93639.73	43209.26	42674.72	5504.36	31410.54
	11	93894.96	43226.58	43266.11	5137.68	31262.92
	12	94123.01	43192.23	44240.82	4488.96	31268.88
比上期增减额（亿元）Changes Compared with Previous Period (100 Million Yuan)						
2003	1	2236.41	695.56	899.82	619.46	88.63
	2	825.44	141.67	258.17	436.47	29.73
	3	2164.13	774.39	915.92	439.46	- 118.87
	4	944.90	99.07	552.38	252.92	204.59
	5	1512.89	433.14	628.35	404.09	538.65
	6	3086.49	1047.83	1285.02	725.34	1331.74
	7	296.44	- 439.46	746.55	3.17	655.91
	8	1164.06	294.53	582.94	301.35	687.85
	9	1597.50	153.68	1231.22	189.22	264.39
	10	145.66	172.82	273.62	- 307.87	56.45
	11	255.23	17.32	591.39	- 366.68	- 147.62
	12	228.05	- 34.35	974.71	- 648.72	5.96
比去年同期增长（%）Increase Rate Year - on - year (%)						
2003	1	17.90	11.98	20.57	187.56	14.28
	2	18.62	12.40	20.40	212.93	14.64
	3	19.27	11.70	21.97	207.84	10.38
	4	19.98	11.26	23.70	209.18	9.34
	5	20.79	11.70	23.98	217.38	10.59
	6	22.33	12.48	25.54	206.85	13.70
	7	22.36	11.31	26.91	208.21	15.91
	8	22.53	11.43	26.72	202.02	15.93
	9	21.47	10.01	27.44	137.45	17.36
	10	21.20	10.52	26.93	126.59	13.71
	11	20.04	9.71	26.71	99.37	11.16
	12	18.38	8.42	25.89	83.92	13.01

国有商业银行本外币信贷收支主要指标时间序列表

Time Series of Major Indicators in Sources and Uses of Credit Funds of State - owned Commercial Banks（Domestic and Foreign Currency Combined）

年 月 Year Month		各项存款 Total Deposits	企事业单位存款 Deposits by Enterprises and Establishments			储蓄存款 Savings Deposits			债券发行及境外筹资 Bonds Issue & Overseas Financing
				活期存款 Demand Deposits	定期存款 Time Deposits		活期储蓄 Demand Deposits	定期储蓄 Time Deposits	
期末余额（亿元） Balance（100 Million Yuan）									
2004	1	131194.91	43403.87	31629.96	11773.91	76762.04	26256.28	50505.76	1142.27
	2	133297.60	44542.64	32862.44	11680.20	77312.49	26185.83	51126.66	1141.30
	3	136069.05	46377.97	34367.96	12010.01	77928.23	26674.41	51253.82	1124.15
	4	136239.59	46710.93	33679.70	13031.23	77804.00	26822.39	50981.61	1059.28
	5	137435.82	47615.73	34960.76	12654.97	77881.21	26837.53	51043.68	1062.77
	6	138867.11	48408.86	35434.02	12974.84	78220.58	27271.57	50949.01	1034.19
	7	138747.92	47858.34	35021.78	12836.56	78672.95	27514.46	51158.49	1160.07
	8	139793.34	48369.43	35491.75	12877.68	78821.02	27613.98	51207.04	1379.04
	9	141240.74	49040.67	35310.40	13730.27	79381.85	28067.51	51314.34	1602.82
	10	141445.51	48906.07	35574.99	13331.08	79533.73	28053.16	51480.57	1572.28
	11	142873.84	49541.43	36230.84	13310.59	80237.71	27641.77	52595.94	1721.10
	12	144417.48	50033.47	36366.70	13666.77	81171.76	28039.10	53132.66	1834.89
比上期增减额（亿元） Changes Compared with Previous Period（100 Million Yuan）									
2004	1	2891.68	-555.87	-1024.79	468.92	3837.21	1918.44	1918.77	-16.14
	2	2102.69	1138.77	1232.48	-93.71	550.45	-70.45	620.90	-0.97
	3	2771.45	1835.33	1505.52	329.81	615.74	488.58	127.16	-17.15
	4	170.54	332.96	-688.26	1021.22	-124.23	147.98	-272.21	-64.87
	5	1196.23	904.80	1281.06	-376.26	77.21	15.14	62.07	3.49
	6	1431.29	793.13	473.26	319.87	339.37	434.04	-94.67	-28.58
	7	-119.19	-550.52	-412.24	-138.28	452.37	242.89	209.48	125.88
	8	1045.42	511.09	469.97	41.12	148.07	99.52	48.55	218.97
	9	1447.40	671.24	-181.35	852.59	560.83	453.53	107.30	223.78
	10	204.77	-134.60	264.59	-399.19	151.88	-14.35	166.23	-30.54
	11	1428.33	635.36	655.85	-20.49	703.98	-411.39	1115.37	148.82
	12	1543.64	492.04	135.86	356.18	934.05	397.33	536.72	113.79
比去年同期增长（%） Increase Rate Year - on - year（%）									
2004	1	16.32	14.69	15.12	13.56	16.18	24.12	12.44	-12.40
	2	16.30	16.37	17.18	14.16	15.00	22.77	11.39	-11.90
	3	15.49	16.19	16.97	14.01	13.97	22.88	9.82	-11.80
	4	15.40	17.43	17.08	18.35	13.22	22.92	8.70	-16.58
	5	14.51	16.97	17.89	14.52	12.19	21.45	7.87	-16.67
	6	13.18	14.91	13.97	17.58	11.51	21.07	6.99	-16.77
	7	12.51	13.71	13.92	13.15	11.37	20.54	6.99	-4.80
	8	12.67	14.08	14.61	12.65	11.11	19.86	6.91	16.00
	9	11.77	12.68	12.55	13.00	10.41	18.87	6.27	34.96
	10	11.46	11.79	10.86	14.34	10.30	18.79	6.17	30.95
	11	12.06	13.02	12.83	13.54	10.75	15.43	8.43	44.39
	12	13.30	15.85	14.07	20.89	11.31	15.21	9.36	58.88

国有商业银行本外币信贷收支主要指标时间序列表

Time Series of Major Indicators in Sources and Uses of Credit Funds of State－owned Commercial Banks（Domestic and Foreign Currency Combined）

年 月 Year Month		各项贷款 Total Loans	短期贷款 Short－term Loans	中长期贷款 Medium and Long－term Loans	票据融资 Paper Financing	有价证券及投资 Securities and Investments
		期末余额（亿元）Balance（100 Million Yuan）				
2004	1	95494.91	43142.26	45251.87	4891.35	32735.16
	2	96677.52	43436.88	45728.81	5252.33	34165.73
	3	98684.17	43875.87	46694.16	5814.37	35258.23
	4	99543.91	43709.20	47444.71	6087.39	35239.04
	5	100241.68	43686.34	47941.93	6313.07	34653.03
	6	97729.88	41616.23	47697.60	6551.59	35808.02
	7	97427.11	41191.81	47849.60	6579.18	36315.19
	8	97822.49	41297.50	47971.88	6736.90	36214.56
	9	99258.10	41377.23	49239.26	6857.78	37410.37
	10	98998.30	41048.93	49443.28	6733.18	38815.12
	11	99752.07	40575.83	50290.39	7036.33	39718.63
	12	101182.99	40605.94	51294.55	7401.36	40312.18
		比上期增减额（亿元）Changes Compared with Previous Period（100 Million Yuan）				
2004	1	1169.64	131.27	827.91	202.19	1463.28
	2	1182.61	294.62	476.94	360.98	1430.57
	3	2006.65	438.99	965.35	562.04	1092.50
	4	859.74	－166.67	750.55	273.02	－19.19
	5	697.77	－22.86	497.22	225.68	－586.01
	6	1306.35	274.58	832.30	240.73	1154.99
	7	－302.80	－424.44	151.99	27.59	507.17
	8	395.40	105.69	122.28	157.73	－100.63
	9	1435.60	79.75	1267.38	120.87	1195.81
	10	－259.84	－328.34	204.01	－124.59	1404.75
	11	753.79	－61.76	435.80	303.14	903.51
	12	1430.86	30.08	1004.13	365.04	593.55
		比去年同期增长（%）Increase Rate Year－on－year（%）				
2004	1	16.60	6.44	25.00	59.84	17.92
	2	16.86	6.79	25.43	50.21	23.00
	3	16.25	5.86	24.94	47.72	27.42
	4	15.97	5.20	25.09	45.32	26.42
	5	14.76	4.06	24.35	37.45	21.96
	6	12.29	2.17	22.42	23.23	20.38
	7	11.59	2.23	20.55	23.67	19.45
	8	10.60	1.77	19.14	19.85	16.48
	9	10.25	1.59	18.67	18.03	19.32
	10	9.80	0.43	18.38	22.36	23.57
	11	10.30	－0.71	18.72	37.00	27.05
	12	11.56	－0.56	18.38	64.93	28.92

国有商业银行本外币信贷收支主要指标时间序列表
Time Series of Major Indicators in Sources and Uses of Credit Funds of State－owned Commercial Banks（Domestic and Foreign Currency Combined）

年 Year	月 Month	各项存款 Total Deposits	企事业单位存款 Deposits by Enterprises and Establishments	活期存款 Demand Deposits	定期存款 Time Deposits	储蓄存款 Savings Deposits	活期储蓄 Demand Deposits	定期储蓄 Time Deposits	债券发行及境外筹资 Bonds Issue & Overseas Financing
		期末余额（亿元） Balance（100 Million Yuan）							
2005	1	148099.42	50357.20	36833.91	13523.29	83088.27	28816.56	54271.71	1821.51
	2	150271.88	49456.51	35448.06	14008.45	86400.48	29837.74	56562.74	1810.75
	3	154155.56	52076.63	37259.34	14817.29	87212.57	29945.07	57267.50	2067.66
	4	154709.00	52324.29	36497.76	15826.53	87324.92	29853.15	57471.77	2146.29
	5	156287.70	53257.85	37352.06	15905.79	87503.60	29766.60	57737.00	2110.46
	6	158625.74	53702.56	37512.39	16190.17	88162.71	30024.94	58137.77	1984.27
	7	159445.15	53004.49	36475.17	16529.32	88893.33	30350.77	58542.56	1874.68
	8	161764.92	54320.84	37303.13	17017.71	89257.49	30392.76	58864.73	1976.80
	9	163805.43	54923.12	36533.53	18389.59	90205.25	30831.32	59373.93	2083.90
	10	164192.92	54679.81	36999.19	17680.62	90196.08	30602.72	59593.36	2076.59
	11	165661.56	55148.66	37568.63	17580.03	90814.99	31309.23	59505.76	2059.38
	12	166579.26	54801.24	36873.33	17927.91	91849.89	32024.58	59825.31	2016.12
		比上期增减额（亿元） Changes Compared with Previous Period（100 Million Yuan）							
2005	1	1910.94	164.22	347.90	－183.68	1916.30	777.36	1138.94	16.33
	2	2172.46	－900.69	－1385.85	485.16	3312.21	1021.18	2291.03	－10.76
	3	3883.68	2620.12	1811.28	808.84	812.09	107.33	704.76	256.91
	4	553.44	247.66	－761.58	1009.24	112.35	－91.92	204.27	78.63
	5	1578.70	933.56	854.30	79.26	178.68	－86.55	265.23	－35.83
	6	2338.04	444.71	160.33	284.38	659.11	258.34	400.77	－126.19
	7	819.41	－698.07	－1037.22	339.15	730.62	325.83	404.79	－109.59
	8	2319.77	1316.35	827.96	488.39	364.16	41.99	322.17	102.12
	9	2040.51	602.28	－769.60	1371.88	947.76	438.56	509.20	107.10
	10	387.49	－243.31	465.66	－708.97	－9.17	－228.60	219.43	－7.31
	11	1468.64	468.85	569.44	－100.59	618.91	706.51	－87.60	－17.21
	12	917.70	－347.42	－695.30	347.88	1034.90	715.35	319.55	－43.26
		比去年同期增长（%） Increase Rate Year－on－year（%）							
2005	1	12.89	16.02	16.45	14.86	8.24	9.75	7.46	59.46
	2	12.73	11.03	7.87	19.93	11.75	13.95	10.63	58.66
	3	13.29	12.29	8.41	23.37	11.91	12.26	11.73	83.93
	4	13.56	12.02	8.37	21.45	12.24	11.30	12.73	102.62
	5	13.72	11.85	6.84	25.69	12.36	10.91	13.11	98.58
	6	14.23	10.94	5.87	24.78	12.71	10.10	14.11	91.87
	7	14.92	10.75	4.15	28.77	12.99	10.31	14.43	61.60
	8	15.72	12.30	5.10	32.15	13.24	10.06	14.95	43.35
	9	15.98	12.00	3.46	33.93	13.63	9.85	15.71	30.01
	10	16.08	11.81	4.00	32.63	13.41	9.09	15.76	32.08
	11	15.95	11.32	3.69	32.08	13.18	13.27	13.14	19.65
	12	15.35	9.53	1.39	31.18	13.15	14.21	12.60	9.88

国有商业银行本外币信贷收支主要指标时间序列表

Time Series of Major Indicators in Sources and Uses of Credit Funds of State - owned Commercial Banks (Domestic and Foreign Currency Combined)

年 月 Year Month	各项贷款 Total Loans	短期贷款 Short - term Loans	中长期贷款 Medium and Long - term Loans	票据融资 Paper Financing	有价证券及投资 Securities and Investments
			期末余额（亿元） Balance (100 Million Yuan)		
2005 1	102556.58	40599.71	52422.58	7665.61	40245.20
2	102881.21	40615.99	52708.58	7683.59	40921.03
3	104596.91	40913.88	53474.43	8330.55	43440.62
4	104519.69	40449.73	53795.52	8392.27	45979.49
5	102787.52	39058.61	53704.42	8162.80	46752.42
6	100191.81	36097.12	53517.56	8790.19	51972.05
7	99279.70	35828.93	53431.02	8306.47	52579.36
8	99576.60	35511.44	53734.78	8609.50	54087.28
9	100624.56	35647.23	54479.97	8770.15	55277.27
10	100451.50	35331.21	54763.18	8640.26	56941.07
11	101771.52	35237.93	55238.08	9595.57	58727.23
12	102257.06	35028.65	55954.56	9580.01	58891.42
			比上期增减额（亿元） Changes Compared with Previous Period (100 Million Yuan)		
2005 1	1372.78	261.32	857.73	264.66	13.54
2	324.63	16.26	286.03	17.97	675.83
3	1715.69	297.89	765.82	646.97	2519.59
4	- 77.20	- 464.12	321.10	61.71	2538.87
5	27.89	- 17.92	246.00	- 229.32	772.93
6	1993.12	546.91	812.95	627.95	5219.63
7	- 935.32	- 277.69	- 93.25	- 483.71	607.31
8	295.43	- 318.09	303.34	303.02	1507.92
9	1047.36	135.54	745.00	160.66	1189.99
10	- 174.31	- 316.53	282.87	- 129.90	1663.80
11	1319.46	- 93.49	474.72	955.31	1786.16
12	484.25	- 209.83	716.12	- 15.55	164.19
			比去年同期增长（%） Increase Rate Year - on - year (%)		
2005 1	11.39	- 0.46	18.23	56.76	22.94
2	10.37	- 1.10	17.62	46.33	19.77
3	9.86	- 1.41	16.83	43.31	23.21
4	8.83	- 2.09	15.65	37.90	30.48
5	8.10	- 2.08	14.97	29.34	34.92
6	9.02	- 1.53	15.00	34.18	45.14
7	8.39	- 1.19	14.44	26.26	44.79
8	8.26	- 2.21	14.79	27.81	49.35
9	7.75	- 2.08	13.34	27.90	47.76
10	7.85	- 2.06	13.45	28.33	46.70
11	8.36	- 1.15	12.48	36.38	47.86
12	7.31	- 1.74	11.68	29.45	46.09

（四）其他商业银行本外币信贷收支主要指标时间序列表（2002—2005 年月度时序）

Time Series of Major Indicators in Sources and Uses of Credit Funds of Other Commercial Banks（Domestic and Foreign Currency Combined）（Monthly Series from 2002 to 2005）

其他商业银行本外币信贷收支主要指标时间序列表

Time Series of Major Indicators in Sources and Uses of Credit Funds of Other Commercial Banks（Domestic and Foreign Currency Combined）

年 月 Year Month		各项存款 Total Deposits	企事业单位存款 Deposits by Enterprises and Establishments			储蓄存款 Savings Deposits			债券发行及境外筹资 Bonds Issue & Overseas Financing
				活期存款 Demand Deposits	定期存款 Time Deposits		活期储蓄 Demand Deposits	定期储蓄 Time Deposits	
期末余额（亿元） Balance（100 Million Yuan）									
2002	1	17868.02	11364.62	7293.24	4071.38	3952.93	1499.65	2453.28	37.64
	2	17810.94	11170.45	7115.34	4055.11	4097.07	1542.75	2554.32	34.26
	3	18274.81	11483.38	7334.69	4148.69	4135.26	1557.79	2577.47	34.01
	4	19414.38	12262.36	7772.73	4489.63	4320.76	1678.84	2641.92	34.73
	5	19728.22	12315.92	8011.34	4304.58	4396.25	1702.97	2693.28	26.41
	6	21046.77	13173.74	8585.94	4587.80	4545.65	1765.65	2780.00	26.86
	7	20906.50	12926.32	8358.76	4567.56	4625.03	1790.55	2834.48	18.88
	8	21519.02	13266.43	8583.18	4683.25	4744.47	1845.88	2898.59	19.41
	9	22681.60	14038.96	8924.48	5114.48	4887.03	1931.61	2955.42	21.71
	10	22466.45	13718.47	8843.48	4874.99	4933.73	1936.00	2997.73	19.50
	11	22973.84	14020.70	9013.17	5007.53	5034.01	1991.72	3042.29	19.41
	12	24868.04	15479.38	10021.17	5458.21	5232.74	2119.15	3113.59	19.55
比上期增减额（亿元） Changes Compared with Previous Period（100 Million Yuan）									
2002	1	-611.02	-639.43	-362.73	-276.70	56.03	17.58	38.45	0.04
	2	-57.08	-194.17	-177.90	-16.27	144.14	43.10	101.04	-3.38
	3	463.87	312.93	219.35	93.58	38.19	15.04	23.15	-0.25
	4	1139.57	778.98	438.04	340.94	185.50	121.05	64.45	0.72
	5	313.84	53.56	238.61	-185.05	75.49	24.13	51.36	-8.32
	6	1318.55	857.82	574.60	283.22	149.40	62.68	86.72	0.45
	7	-140.27	-247.42	-227.18	-20.24	79.38	24.90	54.48	-7.98
	8	612.52	340.11	224.42	115.69	119.44	55.33	64.11	0.53
	9	1162.58	772.53	341.30	431.23	142.56	85.73	56.83	2.30
	10	-215.15	-320.49	-81.00	-239.49	46.70	4.39	42.31	-2.21
	11	507.39	302.23	169.69	132.54	100.28	55.72	44.56	-0.09
	12	1894.20	1458.68	1008.00	450.68	198.73	127.43	71.30	0.14
比去年同期增长（%） Increase Rate Year-on-year（%）									
2002	1	26.40	17.45	20.38	12.54	29.57	46.25	21.13	-42.75
	2	29.56	20.21	22.61	16.22	35.48	54.60	26.07	-48.37
	3	25.34	15.42	16.79	13.07	32.83	46.51	25.74	-46.34
	4	27.96	18.32	20.68	14.43	35.72	52.90	26.68	-45.40
	5	32.12	23.86	28.74	15.69	38.69	56.32	29.46	-58.88
	6	28.18	18.66	21.76	13.27	37.85	50.04	31.09	-55.01
	7	34.40	26.60	31.68	18.24	40.12	54.92	32.15	-68.20
	8	29.71	21.05	23.30	17.12	37.72	47.94	31.92	-66.75
	9	31.94	23.99	25.61	21.25	36.51	45.96	30.97	-57.93
	10	31.50	23.59	25.38	20.47	35.15	44.26	29.86	-48.40
	11	33.75	26.63	28.77	22.95	35.89	46.50	29.74	-61.96
	12	34.54	28.18	30.98	23.35	34.35	43.17	28.94	-48.01

其他商业银行本外币信贷收支主要指标时间序列表
Time Series of Major Indicators in Sources and Uses of Credit Funds of Other Commercial Banks（Domestic and Foreign Currency Combined）

年 月 Year Month		各项贷款 Total Loans				有价证券及投资 Securities and Investments
			短期贷款 Short－term Loans	中长期贷款 Medium and Long－term Loans	票据融资 Paper Financing	
期末余额（亿元） Balance（100 Million Yuan）						
2002	1	12579.63	8529.37	2406.20	1446.91	3612.48
	2	12751.25	8580.10	2484.41	1492.09	3625.33
	3	13414.37	9106.83	2567.31	1540.84	3681.88
	4	13742.16	9070.49	2673.70	1793.67	3801.11
	5	13970.03	9185.84	2787.56	1779.77	3864.00
	6	14714.31	9638.04	2947.82	1909.68	3983.93
	7	14847.86	9530.92	3062.07	2017.41	4116.22
	8	15298.70	9748.95	3166.68	2125.20	4198.65
	9	15822.96	10132.77	3362.32	2055.16	4574.65
	10	15972.05	10144.51	3502.85	2045.98	4665.06
	11	16360.81	10320.53	3694.53	2070.10	4768.09
	12	17024.78	10791.58	3788.86	2176.12	4759.86
比上期增减额（亿元） Changes Compared with Previous Period（100 Million Yuan）						
2002	1	317.39	30.49	61.61	224.44	－3.71
	2	171.62	50.73	78.24	45.18	12.85
	3	663.12	526.73	82.87	48.75	56.55
	4	327.79	－36.34	106.39	252.83	119.23
	5	227.87	115.35	113.86	－13.90	62.89
	6	744.28	452.20	160.26	129.91	119.93
	7	133.55	－107.12	114.25	107.73	132.29
	8	450.84	218.03	104.61	107.79	82.43
	9	524.26	383.82	195.64	－70.04	376.00
	10	149.09	11.74	140.53	－9.18	90.41
	11	388.76	176.02	191.68	24.12	103.03
	12	663.97	471.05	94.33	106.02	－8.23
比去年同期增长（%） Increase Rate Year－on－year（%）						
2002	1	32.11	21.41	51.38	96.51	47.09
	2	31.61	19.89	52.99	102.17	48.21
	3	36.27	25.71	52.13	106.63	40.79
	4	35.93	23.51	51.53	115.59	40.70
	5	35.15	21.93	54.02	116.93	37.67
	6	36.45	22.24	53.47	138.47	35.37
	7	35.33	19.74	54.18	138.15	35.33
	8	38.04	22.92	54.58	130.70	32.19
	9	37.49	25.02	57.78	88.79	40.11
	10	36.98	25.25	61.57	69.68	38.76
	11	35.62	24.57	64.49	54.13	39.97
	12	39.05	26.86	61.60	80.76	32.14

其他商业银行本外币信贷收支主要指标时间序列表

Time Series of Major Indicators in Sources and Uses of Credit Funds of Other Commercial Banks（Domestic and Foreign Currency Combined）

年 月 Year Month		各项存款 Total Deposits	企事业单位存款 Deposits by Enterprises and Establishments	活期存款 Demand Deposits	定期存款 Time Deposits	储蓄存款 Savings Deposits	活期储蓄 Demand Deposits	定期储蓄 Time Deposits	债券发行及境外筹资 Bonds Issue & Overseas Financing
		期末余额（亿元） Balance（100 Million Yuan）							
2003	1	24383.51	14722.70	9238.99	5483.71	5438.92	2208.43	3230.49	13.35
	2	24322.96	14582.27	9264.35	5317.92	5496.32	2192.49	3303.83	13.49
	3	25379.95	15282.76	9853.17	5429.59	5625.12	2234.38	3390.74	53.31
	4	25886.52	15401.62	9773.74	5627.88	5690.16	2267.88	3422.28	49.67
	5	26662.64	15832.90	10115.72	5717.18	5775.12	2301.49	3473.63	50.25
	6	28700.71	17180.14	11169.05	6011.09	5952.04	2395.32	3556.72	51.18
	7	28411.88	16639.32	10724.13	5915.19	6009.31	2409.73	3599.58	51.22
	8	28833.24	16966.20	10750.02	6216.18	6070.61	2437.25	3633.36	51.47
	9	30667.66	18272.16	11297.44	6974.72	6295.91	2569.72	3726.19	49.22
	10	30557.35	17994.71	11355.08	6639.63	6334.33	2570.27	3764.06	51.81
	11	30962.96	18161.35	11403.57	6757.78	6425.86	2623.90	3801.96	58.10
	12	32865.46	19646.88	12421.61	7225.27	6719.55	2818.58	3900.97	62.11
		比上期增减额（亿元） Changes Compared with Previous Period（100 Million Yuan）							
2003	1	-487.54	-759.42	-785.21	25.79	206.23	89.40	116.83	0.40
	2	-60.55	-140.43	25.36	-165.79	57.40	-15.94	73.34	0.14
	3	1056.99	700.49	588.82	111.67	128.80	41.89	86.91	39.82
	4	506.57	118.86	-79.43	198.29	65.04	33.50	31.54	-3.64
	5	776.12	431.28	341.98	89.30	84.96	33.61	51.35	0.58
	6	2038.07	1347.24	1053.33	293.91	176.92	93.83	83.09	0.93
	7	-288.83	-540.82	-444.92	-95.90	57.27	14.41	42.86	0.04
	8	421.36	326.88	25.89	300.99	61.30	27.52	33.78	0.25
	9	1834.42	1305.96	547.42	758.54	225.30	132.47	92.83	-2.25
	10	-110.31	-277.45	57.64	-335.09	38.42	0.55	37.87	2.59
	11	405.61	166.64	48.49	118.15	91.53	53.63	37.90	6.29
	12	1902.50	1485.53	1018.04	467.49	293.69	194.68	99.01	4.01
		比去年同期增长（%） Increase Rate Year-on-year（%）							
2003	1	36.46	29.55	26.68	34.69	37.59	47.26	31.68	-64.53
	2	36.56	30.54	30.20	31.14	34.15	42.12	29.34	-60.62
	3	38.88	33.09	34.34	30.87	36.03	43.43	31.55	56.75
	4	33.34	25.60	25.74	25.35	31.69	35.09	29.54	43.02
	5	35.15	28.56	26.27	32.82	31.36	35.15	28.97	90.27
	6	36.37	30.41	30.09	31.02	30.94	35.66	27.94	90.54
	7	35.90	28.72	28.30	29.50	29.93	34.58	26.99	171.29
	8	33.99	27.89	25.25	32.73	27.95	32.04	25.35	165.17
	9	35.21	30.15	26.59	36.37	28.83	33.04	26.08	126.72
	10	36.01	31.17	28.40	36.20	28.39	32.76	25.56	165.69
	11	34.77	29.53	26.52	34.95	27.65	31.74	24.97	199.33
	12	32.16	26.92	23.95	32.37	28.41	33.01	25.29	217.70

其他商业银行本外币信贷收支主要指标时间序列表

Time Series of Major Indicators in Sources and Uses of Credit Funds of Other Commercial Banks (Domestic and Foreign Currency Combined)

年　月 Year Month		各项贷款 Total Loans				有价证券及投资 Securities and Investments
			短期贷款 Short - term Loans	中长期贷款 Medium and Long - term Loans	票据融资 Paper Financing	
期末余额（亿元）Balance (100 Million Yuan)						
2003	1	17668.29	10934.00	4083.40	2357.23	4635.62
	2	17712.58	11094.94	4173.43	2136.34	4675.15
	3	18436.72	11656.69	4428.20	2032.17	4782.49
	4	19132.10	11831.42	4626.97	2325.80	5009.47
	5	19864.50	12205.91	4868.52	2418.23	5273.46
	6	21069.80	12882.67	5095.48	2704.88	5539.56
	7	21525.25	12796.96	5410.02	2924.45	5665.75
	8	22538.17	13306.62	5644.32	3177.77	5775.24
	9	22983.77	13730.44	5847.32	3004.86	5819.57
	10	23157.02	13910.82	6061.22	2782.75	5802.42
	11	23439.57	14128.96	6237.40	2638.78	5836.04
	12	23682.53	14535.95	6330.39	2453.62	5827.14
比上期增减额（亿元）Changes Compared with Previous Period (100 Million Yuan)						
2003	1	705.46	203.69	295.22	181.11	-117.65
	2	44.29	160.94	90.03	-220.89	39.53
	3	724.14	561.75	254.77	-104.17	107.34
	4	695.38	174.73	198.77	293.63	226.98
	5	732.40	374.49	241.55	92.43	263.99
	6	1205.30	676.76	226.96	286.65	266.10
	7	455.45	-85.71	314.54	219.57	126.19
	8	1012.92	509.66	234.30	253.32	109.49
	9	445.60	423.82	203.00	-172.91	44.33
	10	173.25	180.38	213.90	-222.11	-17.15
	11	282.55	218.14	176.18	-143.97	33.62
	12	242.96	406.99	92.99	-185.16	-8.90
比去年同期增长（%）Increase Rate Year - on - year (%)						
2003	1	40.45	28.19	69.70	62.91	28.32
	2	38.91	29.31	67.98	43.18	28.96
	3	37.44	28.00	72.48	31.89	29.89
	4	39.22	30.44	73.05	29.67	31.79
	5	42.19	32.88	74.65	35.87	36.48
	6	43.19	33.66	72.86	41.64	39.05
	7	44.97	34.27	76.68	44.96	37.64
	8	47.32	36.49	78.24	49.53	37.55
	9	45.26	35.51	73.91	46.21	27.21
	10	44.98	37.13	73.04	36.01	24.38
	11	43.27	36.90	68.83	27.47	22.40
	12	39.11	34.70	67.08	12.75	22.42

其他商业银行本外币信贷收支主要指标时间序列表

Time Series of Major Indicators in Sources and Uses of Credit Funds of Other Commercial Banks（Domestic and Foreign Currency Combined）

年 月 Year Month	各项存款 Total Deposits	企事业单位存款 Deposits by Enterprises and Establishments			储蓄存款 Savings Deposits			债券发行及境外筹资 Bonds Issue & Overseas Financing
			活期存款 Demand Deposits	定期存款 Time Deposits		活期储蓄 Demand Deposits	定期储蓄 Time Deposits	
期末余额（亿元） Balance（100 Million Yuan）								
2004 1	31712.70	18167.08	11405.17	6761.91	6906.84	2867.46	4039.38	55.98
2	32262.82	18357.06	11768.32	6588.74	6982.02	2897.03	4084.99	49.72
3	34116.85	19464.40	12571.21	6893.19	7103.01	2971.27	4131.74	44.99
4	34651.71	19687.23	12228.54	7458.69	7184.11	3032.71	4151.40	69.85
5	35153.53	19962.28	12679.71	7282.57	7251.30	3061.56	4189.74	68.20
6	36817.68	21042.46	13381.81	7660.65	7477.53	3203.03	4274.50	332.65
7	36195.80	20374.43	12781.89	7592.54	7499.86	3192.62	4307.24	338.62
8	36510.67	20475.05	12898.05	7577.00	7606.98	3227.17	4379.81	318.46
9	37890.70	21357.51	13107.56	8249.95	7819.63	3345.65	4473.98	315.35
10	37809.18	21215.74	13261.33	7954.41	7888.27	3368.69	4519.58	316.52
11	38426.78	21366.35	13462.50	7903.85	8106.58	3425.16	4681.42	431.02
12	40598.84	23017.62	14561.79	8455.83	8419.52	3568.39	4851.13	456.65
比上期增减额（亿元） Changes Compared with Previous Period（100 Million Yuan）								
2004 1	-1094.51	-1247.43	-997.52	-249.91	183.90	45.64	138.26	-6.13
2	550.12	189.98	363.15	-173.17	75.18	29.57	45.61	-6.26
3	1854.03	1107.34	802.89	304.45	120.99	74.24	46.75	-4.73
4	534.86	222.83	-342.67	565.50	81.10	61.44	19.66	24.86
5	501.82	275.05	451.17	-176.12	67.19	28.85	38.34	-1.65
6	1664.15	1080.18	702.10	378.08	226.23	141.47	84.76	264.45
7	-621.88	-668.03	-599.92	-68.11	22.33	-10.41	32.74	5.97
8	314.87	100.62	116.16	-15.54	107.12	34.55	72.57	-20.16
9	1380.03	882.46	209.51	672.95	212.65	118.48	94.17	-3.11
10	-81.52	-141.77	153.77	-295.54	68.64	23.04	45.60	1.17
11	617.60	150.61	201.17	-50.56	218.31	56.47	161.84	114.50
12	2172.06	1651.27	1099.29	551.98	312.94	143.23	169.71	25.63
比去年同期增长（%） Increase Rate Year-on-year（%）								
2004 1	30.79	23.40	23.45	23.31	26.99	29.84	25.04	319.33
2	33.43	25.89	27.03	23.90	27.03	32.13	23.64	268.57
3	35.20	27.36	27.59	26.96	26.27	32.98	21.85	-15.61
4	34.61	27.83	25.12	32.53	26.25	33.72	21.31	40.63
5	32.57	26.08	25.35	27.38	25.56	33.03	20.62	35.72
6	28.95	22.48	19.81	27.44	25.63	33.72	20.18	549.96
7	28.08	22.45	19.19	28.36	24.80	32.49	19.66	561.11
8	27.11	20.68	19.98	21.89	25.31	32.41	20.54	518.73
9	24.02	16.89	16.02	18.28	24.20	30.20	20.07	540.69
10	24.52	17.90	16.79	19.80	24.53	31.06	20.07	510.92
11	24.60	17.65	18.06	16.96	26.16	30.54	23.13	641.86
12	24.00	17.16	17.23	17.03	25.30	26.60	24.36	635.23

其他商业银行本外币信贷收支主要指标时间序列表
Time Series of Major Indicators in Sources and Uses of Credit Funds of Other Commercial Banks (Domestic and Foreign Currency Combined)

年　月 Year Month		各项贷款 Total Loans				有价证券及投资 Securities and Investments
			短期贷款 Short－term Loans	中长期贷款 Medium and Long－term Loans	票据融资 Paper Financing	
期末余额（亿元） Balance (100 Million Yuan)						
2004	1	25103.90	14870.46	6621.32	3208.99	5747.29
	2	25484.93	15183.15	6826.48	3028.20	5558.10
	3	26371.53	15847.22	7176.62	2868.15	5720.33
	4	26840.07	15835.63	7499.58	3025.44	5891.94
	5	27121.63	16108.84	7692.31	2852.48	6036.51
	6	27149.48	16008.03	7895.40	2796.56	6371.50
	7	27082.14	15825.54	8080.88	2736.76	6534.27
	8	27312.47	15946.18	8232.26	2682.98	6713.14
	9	27880.34	16342.70	8451.20	2662.49	6932.23
	10	27900.00	16349.91	8613.83	2517.61	7303.91
	11	28086.51	16408.85	8782.94	2457.60	7582.08
	12	28859.41	16748.51	9054.37	2667.78	8093.79
比上期增减额（亿元） Changes Compared with Previous Period (100 Million Yuan)						
2004	1	513.07	329.94	269.22	－127.91	－79.85
	2	381.03	312.69	205.16	－180.79	－189.19
	3	886.60	664.07	350.14	－160.05	162.23
	4	468.54	－11.59	322.96	157.29	171.61
	5	281.56	273.21	192.73	－172.96	144.57
	6	557.62	366.16	229.15	－55.31	334.99
	7	－67.37	－182.48	185.47	－59.82	162.77
	8	230.35	120.66	151.38	－53.77	178.87
	9	567.86	396.48	218.96	－20.50	219.09
	10	19.68	7.23	162.63	－144.88	371.68
	11	186.52	58.95	169.10	－60.00	278.17
	12	772.94	339.68	271.45	210.18	511.71
比去年同期增长（%） Increase Rate Year－on－year (%)						
2004	1	42.08	36.00	62.15	36.13	23.98
	2	43.88	36.85	63.57	41.75	18.89
	3	43.04	35.95	62.07	41.14	19.61
	4	40.29	33.84	62.08	30.08	17.62
	5	36.53	31.98	58.00	17.96	14.47
	6	31.37	27.88	55.46	3.41	15.02
	7	28.28	27.32	49.85	－6.40	15.33
	8	23.53	23.35	46.31	－15.55	16.24
	9	23.61	22.43	44.98	－11.37	19.12
	10	22.77	20.89	42.54	－9.51	25.88
	11	22.09	19.44	41.23	－6.84	29.92
	12	24.10	18.43	43.44	8.75	38.90

其他商业银行本外币信贷收支主要指标时间序列表

Time Series of Major Indicators in Sources and Uses of Credit Funds of Other Commercial Banks（Domestic and Foreign Currency Combined）

年 月 Year Month		各项存款 Total Deposits	企事业单位存款 Deposits by Enterprises and Establishments	活期存款 Demand Deposits	定期存款 Time Deposits	储蓄存款 Savings Deposits	活期储蓄 Demand Deposits	定期储蓄 Time Deposits	债券发行及境外筹资 Bonds Issue & Overseas Financing
		期末余额（亿元） Balance（100 Million Yuan）							
2005	1	39777.98	21985.20	13729.58	8255.62	8518.01	3588.88	4929.13	539.05
	2	39508.58	21488.99	13195.06	8293.93	8773.64	3640.44	5133.20	540.41
	3	41096.75	22613.10	14042.75	8570.35	8922.81	3677.40	5245.41	545.43
	4	41585.05	22708.24	13578.25	9129.99	9104.44	3747.44	5357.00	536.79
	5	41924.51	22899.00	13954.78	8944.22	9221.52	3751.16	5470.36	537.17
	6	44625.44	24807.75	15189.35	9618.40	9566.01	3858.67	5707.34	543.79
	7	43633.61	23745.22	14294.84	9450.38	9667.74	3838.58	5829.16	521.95
	8	44564.94	24150.52	14462.85	9687.67	9837.59	3870.30	5967.29	597.74
	9	46504.60	25424.20	14797.84	10626.36	10147.64	3964.68	6182.96	594.82
	10	46079.28	24910.35	14789.71	10120.64	10253.96	3970.91	6283.05	678.97
	11	47349.34	25518.20	15216.87	10301.33	10465.37	4045.79	6419.58	772.76
	12	49201.16	26787.63	16066.76	10720.87	10948.80	4300.27	6648.53	761.92
		比上期增减额（亿元） Changes Compared with Previous Period（100 Million Yuan）							
2005	1	-828.46	-1016.15	-823.92	-192.23	97.65	20.35	77.30	-1.09
	2	-269.40	-496.21	-534.52	38.31	255.63	51.56	204.07	1.36
	3	1588.17	1124.11	847.69	276.42	149.17	36.96	112.21	5.02
	4	488.30	95.14	-464.50	559.64	181.63	70.04	111.59	-8.64
	5	339.46	190.76	376.53	-185.77	117.08	3.72	113.36	0.38
	6	2700.93	1908.75	1234.57	674.18	344.49	107.51	236.98	6.62
	7	-991.83	-1062.53	-894.51	-168.02	101.73	-20.09	121.82	-21.84
	8	931.33	405.30	168.01	237.29	169.85	31.72	138.13	75.79
	9	1939.66	1273.68	334.99	938.69	310.05	94.38	215.67	-2.92
	10	-425.32	-513.85	-8.13	-505.72	106.32	6.23	100.09	84.15
	11	1270.06	607.85	427.16	180.69	211.41	74.88	136.53	93.79
	12	1851.82	1269.43	849.89	419.54	483.43	254.48	228.95	-10.84
		比去年同期增长（%） Increase Rate Year-on-year（%）							
2005	1	25.43	21.02	20.38	22.09	23.33	25.16	22.03	862.93
	2	22.46	17.06	12.12	25.88	25.66	25.66	25.66	986.91
	3	20.46	16.18	11.71	24.33	25.62	23.77	26.95	1112.34
	4	20.01	15.35	11.04	22.41	26.73	23.57	29.04	668.49
	5	19.26	14.71	10.06	22.82	27.17	22.52	30.57	687.64
	6	21.21	17.89	13.51	25.56	27.93	20.47	33.52	63.47
	7	20.55	16.54	11.84	24.47	28.91	20.23	35.33	54.14
	8	22.06	17.95	12.13	27.86	29.32	19.93	36.25	87.70
	9	22.73	19.04	12.90	28.81	29.77	18.50	38.20	88.62
	10	21.87	17.41	11.53	27.23	29.99	17.88	39.02	114.51
	11	23.22	19.43	13.03	30.33	29.10	18.12	37.13	79.29
	12	21.19	16.38	10.34	26.79	30.04	20.51	37.05	66.85

其他商业银行本外币信贷收支主要指标时间序列表
Time Series of Major Indicators in Sources and Uses of Credit Funds of Other Commercial Banks（Domestic and Foreign Currency Combined）

年　月 Year Month		各项贷款 Total Loans	短期贷款 Short - term Loans	中长期贷款 Medium and Long - term Loans	票据融资 Paper Financing	有价证券及投资 Securities and Investments
期末余额（亿元） Balance（100 Million Yuan）						
2005	1	29325.07	16876.23	9214.64	2792.67	8156.04
	2	29465.30	16916.19	9324.18	2772.26	7874.68
	3	30061.06	17380.69	9541.43	2687.64	8183.47
	4	30572.17	17306.07	9707.28	3070.08	8679.76
	5	31134.12	17389.30	9884.67	3337.06	8460.35
	6	32271.96	18086.94	10191.11	3418.34	8615.16
	7	32369.85	17782.20	10188.84	3825.11	8634.32
	8	32958.58	17866.68	10310.45	4244.67	8965.28
	9	33995.39	18253.84	10543.89	4680.01	9220.71
	10	34191.66	18201.67	10685.39	4761.62	9367.21
	11	34490.14	18350.85	10931.09	4672.71	10084.56
	12	34845.29	18527.85	11303.51	4550.80	10369.38
比上期增减额（亿元） Changes Compared with Previous Period（100 Million Yuan）						
2005	1	464.97	113.26	176.88	125.57	21.10
	2	140.26	39.96	109.56	- 20.42	- 281.36
	3	595.71	464.48	217.23	- 84.62	308.79
	4	511.12	- 74.61	165.84	382.45	496.29
	5	562.01	83.24	177.44	266.97	- 219.41
	6	1137.79	697.62	306.42	81.28	154.81
	7	96.52	- 305.51	- 2.38	406.78	19.16
	8	588.66	84.44	121.61	419.55	330.96
	9	1036.74	387.13	233.43	435.34	255.43
	10	196.24	- 52.19	141.50	81.61	146.50
	11	298.41	149.14	245.69	- 88.91	717.35
	12	355.08	176.95	372.44	- 121.91	284.82
比去年同期增长（%） Increase Rate Year - on - year（%）						
2005	1	16.81	13.49	39.17	- 12.97	41.91
	2	15.62	11.41	36.59	- 8.45	41.68
	3	13.99	9.68	32.95	- 6.29	43.06
	4	13.90	9.29	29.44	1.48	47.32
	5	14.79	7.95	28.50	16.99	40.15
	6	18.87	12.99	29.08	22.23	35.21
	7	19.52	12.36	26.08	39.77	32.14
	8	20.67	12.04	25.24	58.21	33.55
	9	21.93	11.69	24.76	75.78	33.01
	10	22.55	11.32	24.05	89.13	28.25
	11	22.79	11.83	24.46	90.13	33.01
	12	20.74	10.62	24.84	70.58	28.12

（五）农村信用合作社本外币信贷收支主要指标时间序列表（2002—2005 年月度时序）

Time Series of Major Indicators in Sources and Uses of Credit Funds of Rural Credit Cooperatives（Domestic and Foreign Currency Combined）（Monthly Series from 2002 to 2005）

农村信用合作社本外币信贷收支主要指标时间序列表

Time Series of Major Indicators in Sources and Uses of Credit Funds of Rural Credit Cooperatives（Domestic and Foreign Currency Combined）

年　月 Year Month	各项存款 Total Deposits	企事业单位存款 Deposits by Enterprises and Establishments	活期存款 Demand Deposits	定期存款 Time Deposits	储蓄存款 Savings Deposits	活期储蓄 Demand Deposits	定期储蓄 Time Deposits	债券发行及境外筹资 Bonds Issue & Overseas Financing
				期末余额（亿元） Balance（100 Million Yuan）				
2002 1	17177.05	591.23	4.14	587.09	13861.18	3396.80	10464.38	0.07
2	17600.06	607.81	4.02	603.79	14496.06	3592.08	10903.98	0.07
3	17801.68	629.74	4.50	625.24	14557.84	3601.92	10955.92	0.06
4	17960.27	659.30	4.32	654.98	14616.46	3634.07	10982.39	0.06
5	18158.18	683.21	4.12	679.09	14715.33	3685.77	11029.56	0.06
6	18500.25	704.82	4.54	700.28	14914.20	3814.57	11099.63	0.06
7	18590.11	725.71	3.96	721.75	14974.50	3832.05	11142.45	0.05
8	18713.87	752.68	3.81	748.87	14973.44	3834.62	11138.82	0.06
9	18971.09	772.67	4.67	768.00	15063.81	3894.56	11169.25	0.07
10	19048.49	773.42	4.45	768.97	15127.04	3911.01	11216.03	0.06
11	19270.56	780.30	4.94	775.36	15261.89	3979.10	11282.79	0.06
12	19668.76	779.57	5.12	774.45	15450.40	4117.22	11333.18	0.06
				比上期增减额（亿元） Changes Compared with Previous Period（100 Million Yuan）				
2002 1	52.25	18.40	1.59	16.81	110.41	-0.46	110.87	-0.01
2	423.01	16.58	-0.12	16.70	634.88	195.28	439.60	
3	201.62	21.93	0.48	21.45	61.78	9.84	51.94	-0.01
4	158.59	29.56	-0.18	29.74	58.62	32.15	26.47	
5	197.91	23.91	-0.20	24.11	98.87	51.70	47.17	
6	342.07	21.61	0.42	21.19	198.87	128.80	70.07	
7	89.86	20.89	-0.58	21.47	60.30	17.48	42.82	-0.01
8	123.76	26.97	-0.15	27.12	-1.06	2.57	-3.63	0.01
9	257.22	19.99	0.86	19.13	90.37	59.94	30.43	0.01
10	77.40	0.75	-0.22	0.97	63.23	16.45	46.78	-0.01
11	222.07	6.88	0.49	6.39	134.85	68.09	66.76	
12	398.20	-0.73	0.18	-0.91	188.51	138.12	50.39	
				比去年同期增长（%） Increase Rate Year-on-year（%）				
2002 1	12.32	48.33	6800.00	47.31	8.33	15.24	6.26	-41.67
2	12.86	47.58	518.46	46.83	11.12	21.45	8.09	-41.67
3	12.47	46.03	625.81	45.20	10.88	19.46	8.32	-50.00
4	13.16	47.46	575.00	46.71	11.16	20.54	8.37	-50.00
5	13.70	48.30	543.75	47.61	11.55	21.73	8.52	-50.00
6	13.64	46.90	521.92	46.17	11.75	21.92	8.63	-50.00
7	14.06	46.95	442.47	46.36	11.78	22.44	8.54	-58.33
8	14.02	45.87	408.00	45.35	11.82	22.53	8.55	-50.00
9	14.45	44.12	469.51	43.47	12.15	23.01	8.80	-46.15
10	14.20	39.49	345.00	38.94	11.91	22.19	8.72	-50.00
11	14.47	37.56	182.29	37.12	12.01	22.20	8.82	-25.00
12	13.70	32.09	243.62	31.56	11.51	20.54	8.56	-25.00

农村信用合作社本外币信贷收支主要指标时间序列表

Time Series of Major Indicators in Sources and Uses of Credit Funds of Rural Credit Cooperatives (Domestic and Foreign Currency Combined)

年 月 Year Month	各项贷款 Total Loans	短期贷款 Short - term Loans	中长期贷款 Medium and Long - term Loans	票据融资 Paper Financing	有价证券及投资 Securities and Investments
	期末余额（亿元） Balance (100 Million Yuan)				
2002 1	12187.26	11577.31	513.26	96.60	1460.18
2	12349.77	11728.54	523.74	97.49	1403.62
3	12721.49	12081.42	542.65	97.41	1466.44
4	13082.88	12405.44	561.65	115.77	1540.42
5	13277.51	12581.53	580.67	115.30	1591.23
6	13475.61	12746.03	602.83	126.74	1632.78
7	13610.88	12864.78	621.30	124.79	1643.01
8	13798.53	13014.52	646.89	137.01	1654.85
9	13929.26	13124.50	673.41	131.22	1716.36
10	13961.24	13147.61	688.78	124.74	1714.06
11	13986.25	13155.06	696.23	134.86	1723.73
12	13794.47	12895.82	717.10	181.36	1801.65
	比上期增减额（亿元） Changes Compared with Previous Period (100 Million Yuan)				
2002 1	300.77	295.40	10.00	-4.72	8.56
2	162.51	151.23	10.48	0.89	-56.56
3	371.72	352.88	18.91	-0.08	62.82
4	361.39	324.02	19.00	18.36	73.98
5	194.63	176.09	19.02	-0.47	50.81
6	198.10	164.50	22.16	11.44	41.55
7	135.27	118.75	18.47	-1.95	10.23
8	187.65	149.74	25.59	12.22	11.84
9	130.73	109.98	26.52	-5.79	61.51
10	31.98	23.11	15.37	-6.48	-2.30
11	25.01	7.45	7.45	10.12	9.67
12	-191.78	-259.24	20.87	46.50	77.92
	比去年同期增长（%） Increase Rate Year - on - year (%)				
2002 1	12.99	12.16	32.73	24.76	26.21
2	12.73	12.11	29.99	7.76	20.12
3	13.46	12.85	30.98	5.30	21.14
4	14.47	13.75	29.76	28.38	22.16
5	14.60	13.87	31.34	20.62	23.23
6	14.82	14.07	29.38	31.79	26.31
7	14.54	13.89	31.87	6.73	23.79
8	14.63	13.99	33.72	0.32	22.54
9	14.55	13.60	44.30	-6.43	27.50
10	14.79	13.82	42.91	-3.50	25.10
11	15.05	14.03	39.80	10.43	22.19
12	15.23	13.57	42.46	61.11	18.74

农村信用合作社本外币信贷收支主要指标时间序列表
Time Series of Major Indicators in Sources and Uses of Credit Funds of Rural Credit Cooperatives（Domestic and Foreign Currency Combined）

年 月 Year Month		各项存款 Total Deposits	企事业单位存款 Deposits by Enterprises and Establishments			储蓄存款 Savings Deposits			债券发行及境外筹资 Bonds Issue & Overseas Financing
				活期存款 Demand Deposits	定期存款 Time Deposits		活期储蓄 Demand Deposits	定期储蓄 Time Deposits	
期末余额（亿元） Balance（100 Million Yuan）									
2003	1	19890.08	801.88	3.97	797.91	15879.22	4226.08	11653.14	0.06
	2	20555.58	831.67	3.91	827.76	16475.65	4379.60	12096.05	0.06
	3	20977.87	874.59	3.75	870.84	16667.73	4438.03	12229.70	0.06
	4	21217.63	911.81	4.26	907.55	16799.82	4472.75	12327.07	0.05
	5	21624.09	946.91	4.12	942.79	17019.87	4567.32	12452.55	0.05
	6	22081.70	957.79	4.21	953.58	17232.20	4678.21	12553.99	0.05
	7	22292.11	976.70	4.73	971.97	17336.71	4715.26	12621.45	0.05
	8	22477.76	997.52	4.88	992.64	17362.76	4725.29	12637.47	0.05
	9	22869.33	1024.65	4.56	1020.09	17520.41	4818.96	12701.45	0.05
	10	23023.50	1032.70	4.73	1027.97	17609.92	4839.02	12770.90	0.05
	11	23312.67	1039.78	5.12	1034.66	17810.91	4946.82	12864.09	0.05
	12	23760.15	1027.83	7.39	1020.44	18050.90	5111.30	12939.60	0.05
比上期增减额（亿元） Changes Compared with Previous Period（100 Million Yuan）									
2003	1	221.60	22.80	-0.61	23.41	428.87	108.29	320.58	
	2	665.50	29.79	-0.06	29.85	596.43	153.52	442.91	
	3	422.29	42.92	-0.16	43.08	192.08	58.43	133.65	
	4	239.76	37.22	0.51	36.71	132.09	34.72	97.37	-0.01
	5	406.46	35.10	-0.14	35.24	220.05	94.57	125.48	
	6	457.61	10.88	0.09	10.79	212.33	110.89	101.44	
	7	210.41	18.91	0.52	18.39	104.51	37.05	67.46	
	8	185.65	20.82	0.15	20.67	26.05	10.03	16.02	
	9	391.57	27.13	-0.32	27.45	157.65	93.67	63.98	
	10	154.17	8.05	0.17	7.88	89.51	20.06	69.45	
	11	289.17	7.08	0.39	6.69	200.99	107.80	93.19	
	12	447.48	-11.95	2.27	-14.22	239.99	164.48	75.51	
比去年同期增长（%） Increase Rate Year-on-year（%）									
2003	1	15.79	35.63	-4.11	35.91	14.56	24.41	11.36	-14.29
	2	16.79	36.83	-2.74	37.09	13.66	21.92	10.93	-14.29
	3	17.84	38.88	-16.67	39.28	14.49	23.21	11.63	
	4	18.14	38.30	-1.39	38.56	14.94	23.08	12.24	-16.67
	5	19.09	38.60		38.83	15.66	23.92	12.90	-16.67
	6	19.36	35.89	-7.27	36.17	15.54	22.64	13.10	-16.67
	7	19.91	34.59	19.44	34.67	15.77	23.05	13.27	
	8	20.11	32.53	28.08	32.55	15.96	23.23	13.45	-16.67
	9	20.55	32.61	-2.36	32.82	16.31	23.74	13.72	-28.57
	10	20.87	33.52	6.29	33.68	16.41	23.73	13.86	-16.67
	11	20.98	33.25	3.64	33.44	16.70	24.32	14.02	-16.67
	12	20.80	31.85	44.34	31.76	16.83	24.14	14.17	-16.67

农村信用合作社本外币信贷收支主要指标时间序列表

Time Series of Major Indicators in Sources and Uses of Credit Funds of Rural Credit Cooperatives (Domestic and Foreign Currency Combined)

年 月 Year Month		各项贷款 Total Loans				有价证券及投资 Securities and Investments
			短期贷款 Short - term Loans	中长期贷款 Medium and Long - term Loans	票据融资 Paper Financing	
期末余额（亿元） Balance (100 Million Yuan)						
2003	1	14306.81	13412.91	739.78	153.82	1777.71
	2	14519.61	13618.65	750.76	149.98	1823.14
	3	15021.44	14069.32	786.32	165.20	1815.58
	4	15402.43	14400.71	829.05	172.12	1858.71
	5	15673.16	14639.76	864.96	167.88	1870.59
	6	16013.81	14932.66	911.95	168.53	1915.13
	7	16300.61	15187.37	916.94	195.59	1958.03
	8	16598.42	15404.97	982.33	209.98	2015.40
	9	16946.26	15655.90	1021.12	267.84	2051.72
	10	17079.92	15775.44	1042.48	260.71	2062.68
	11	17241.07	15816.52	1064.66	358.54	2071.04
	12	16987.38	15446.63	1097.71	440.54	2067.55
比上期增减额（亿元） Changes Compared with Previous Period (100 Million Yuan)						
2003	1	512.37	517.24	22.52	-27.50	-25.33
	2	212.80	205.74	10.98	-3.84	45.43
	3	501.83	450.67	35.56	15.22	-7.56
	4	380.99	331.39	42.73	6.92	43.13
	5	270.73	239.05	35.91	-4.24	11.88
	6	340.65	292.90	46.99	0.65	44.54
	7	286.80	254.71	4.99	27.06	42.90
	8	297.81	217.60	65.39	14.39	57.37
	9	347.84	250.93	38.79	57.86	36.32
	10	133.66	119.54	21.36	-7.13	10.96
	11	161.15	41.08	22.18	97.83	8.36
	12	-253.69	-369.89	33.05	82.00	-3.49
比去年同期增长（%） Increase Rate Year - on - year (%)						
2003	1	17.39	15.86	44.13	59.23	21.75
	2	17.57	16.12	43.35	53.84	29.89
	3	18.08	16.45	44.90	69.59	23.81
	4	17.73	16.08	47.61	48.67	20.66
	5	18.04	16.36	48.96	45.60	17.56
	6	18.84	17.16	51.28	32.97	17.29
	7	19.76	18.05	47.58	56.74	19.17
	8	20.29	18.37	51.85	53.26	21.79
	9	21.66	19.29	51.63	104.12	19.54
	10	22.34	19.99	51.35	109.00	20.34
	11	23.27	20.23	52.92	165.86	20.15
	12	23.15	19.78	53.08	142.91	14.76

农村信用合作社本外币信贷收支主要指标时间序列表

Time Series of Major Indicators in Sources and Uses of Credit Funds of Rural Credit Cooperatives（Domestic and Foreign Currency Combined）

年 月 Year Month	各项存款 Total Deposits	企事业单位存款 Deposits by Enterprises and Establishments			储蓄存款 Savings Deposits			债券发行及境外筹资 Bonds Issue & Overseas Financing
			活期存款 Demand Deposits	定期存款 Time Deposits		活期储蓄 Demand Deposits	定期储蓄 Time Deposits	
期末余额（亿元） Balance（100 Million Yuan）								
2004 1	24476.83	1031.18	6.26	1024.92	19162.99	5538.74	13624.25	0.05
2	24990.44	1066.47	5.23	1061.24	19482.25	5536.08	13946.17	0.05
3	25482.92	1098.78	5.22	1093.56	19672.88	5639.09	14033.79	0.05
4	25767.90	1132.27	5.54	1126.73	19850.69	5739.65	14111.04	0.04
5	26051.43	1156.06	6.18	1149.88	20025.22	5813.65	14211.57	0.04
6	26431.02	1173.04	6.48	1166.56	20254.99	5949.94	14305.05	0.04
7	26411.67	1182.28	7.08	1175.20	20320.10	5957.46	14362.64	0.04
8	26318.19	1166.11	6.55	1159.56	20224.61	5912.20	14312.41	0.04
9	26522.50	1162.20	6.92	1155.28	20330.15	5996.58	14333.57	0.04
10	26683.52	1150.32	7.28	1143.04	20466.35	6057.04	14409.31	0.04
11	26964.14	1161.07	7.33	1153.74	20639.64	6067.32	14572.32	0.04
12	27340.16	1149.52	7.20	1142.32	20811.01	6223.84	14587.17	0.04
比上期增减额（亿元） Changes Compared with Previous Period（100 Million Yuan）								
2004 1	759.85	3.69	-0.75	4.44	1110.64	427.17	683.47	
2	513.61	35.29	-1.03	36.32	319.26	-2.66	321.92	
3	492.48	32.31	-0.01	32.32	190.63	103.01	87.62	
4	284.98	33.49	0.32	33.17	177.81	100.56	77.25	-0.01
5	283.53	23.79	0.64	23.15	174.53	74.00	100.53	
6	379.59	16.98	0.30	16.68	229.77	136.29	93.48	
7	-19.35	9.24	0.60	8.64	65.11	7.52	57.59	
8	-93.48	-16.17	-0.53	-15.64	-95.49	-45.26	-50.23	
9	204.31	-3.91	0.37	-4.28	105.54	84.38	21.16	
10	161.02	-11.88	0.36	-12.24	136.20	60.46	75.74	
11	280.62	10.75	0.05	10.70	173.29	10.28	163.01	
12	376.02	-11.55	-0.13	-11.42	171.37	156.52	14.85	
比去年同期增长（%） Increase Rate Year-on-year（%）								
2004 1	23.22	28.60	57.68	28.45	20.68	31.06	16.91	-16.67
2	21.76	28.23	33.76	28.21	18.25	26.41	15.30	-16.67
3	21.66	25.63	39.20	25.58	18.03	27.06	14.75	-16.67
4	21.63	24.18	30.05	24.15	18.16	28.32	14.47	-20.00
5	20.66	22.09	50.00	21.97	17.66	27.29	14.13	-20.00
6	19.90	22.47	53.92	22.33	17.54	27.18	13.95	-20.00
7	18.67	21.05	49.68	20.91	17.21	26.34	13.80	-20.00
8	17.27	16.90	34.22	16.82	16.48	25.12	13.25	-20.00
9	16.18	13.42	51.75	13.25	16.04	24.44	12.85	-20.00
10	16.09	11.39	53.91	11.19	16.22	25.17	12.83	-20.00
11	15.86	11.66	43.16	11.51	15.88	22.65	13.28	-20.00
12	15.26	11.84	-2.57	11.94	15.29	21.77	12.73	-20.00

农村信用合作社本外币信贷收支主要指标时间序列表
Time Series of Major Indicators in Sources and Uses of Credit Funds of Rural Credit Cooperatives (Domestic and Foreign Currency Combined)

年 月 Year Month		各项贷款 Total Loans	短期贷款 Short－term Loans	中长期贷款 Medium and Long－term Loans	票据融资 Paper Financing	有价证券及投资 Securities and Investments
		期末余额（亿元）Balance (100 Million Yuan)				
2004	1	17649.08	16026.11	1215.60	405.31	2101.12
	2	18192.71	16527.03	1237.20	426.79	2113.67
	3	18661.80	16956.88	1288.53	414.72	2114.32
	4	19109.10	17340.34	1334.06	432.56	2139.92
	5	19288.70	17503.21	1377.95	405.10	2154.97
	6	19362.10	17529.19	1413.99	416.17	2233.77
	7	19489.21	17643.26	1443.78	400.04	2353.56
	8	19586.14	17727.23	1455.17	401.98	2372.05
	9	19666.29	17812.79	1468.09	384.06	2399.26
	10	19638.41	17807.67	1476.03	353.40	2414.71
	11	19601.70	17755.76	1485.15	359.55	2452.47
	12	19241.56	17394.36	1509.23	336.82	2380.75
		比上期增减额（亿元）Changes Compared with Previous Period (100 Million Yuan)				
2004	1	628.75	644.56	51.93	－67.03	33.40
	2	543.63	500.92	21.60	21.48	12.55
	3	567.74	521.59	58.24	－12.07	0.65
	4	450.09	386.05	45.73	17.84	25.60
	5	180.63	163.83	43.96	－27.46	15.05
	6	194.13	138.26	44.49	11.07	78.80
	7	129.21	116.02	29.94	－16.13	119.79
	8	97.88	84.85	11.46	1.94	18.49
	9	148.93	149.53	17.73	－17.92	27.21
	10	－27.46	－4.73	7.97	－30.66	15.45
	11	－36.71	－51.91	9.12	6.15	37.76
	12	－351.18	－353.07	24.71	－22.73	－71.72
		比去年同期增长（%）Increase Rate Year－on－year (%)				
2004	1	23.36	19.48	64.32	163.50	18.19
	2	25.30	21.36	64.79	184.56	15.94
	3	24.89	21.18	64.75	151.04	16.45
	4	24.72	21.07	61.77	151.31	15.13
	5	23.72	20.21	60.14	141.30	15.20
	6	22.30	18.78	56.76	146.94	16.64
	7	20.94	17.55	59.18	104.53	20.20
	8	19.36	16.44	49.75	91.44	17.70
	9	17.79	15.53	45.79	43.39	16.94
	10	16.71	14.62	43.57	35.55	17.07
	11	15.41	14.00	41.44	0.28	18.42
	12	15.06	14.44	39.43	－23.54	15.15

农村信用合作社本外币信贷收支主要指标时间序列表

Time Series of Major Indicators in Sources and Uses of Credit Funds of Rural Credit Cooperatives（Domestic and Foreign Currency Combined）

年 月 Year Month		各项存款 Total Deposits	企事业单位存款 Deposits by Enterprises and Establishments			储蓄存款 Savings Deposits			债券发行及境外筹资 Bonds Issue & Overseas Financing
				活期存款 Demand Deposits	定期存款 Time Deposits		活期储蓄 Demand Deposits	定期储蓄 Time Deposits	
期末余额（亿元）Balance（100 Million Yuan）									
2005	1	26473.05	1055.23	3.78	1051.45	20446.24	6094.22	14352.02	0.04
	2	27318.09	1065.31	3.73	1061.58	21590.15	6497.52	15092.63	0.04
	3	27705.53	1099.26	4.09	1095.17	21682.37	6454.30	15228.07	0.04
	4	27738.62	1122.65	5.46	1117.19	21668.18	6429.08	15239.10	0.34
	5	27960.13	1136.61	5.01	1131.60	21797.73	6467.90	15330.64	0.04
	6	27835.27	1083.33	8.30	1075.03	21735.63	6547.49	15188.14	0.04
	7	27876.01	1091.48	5.50	1085.98	21845.96	6550.35	15295.61	0.04
	8	26949.79	1030.72	4.93	1025.79	21344.93	6448.92	14896.01	0.04
	9	27316.85	1044.44	4.84	1039.60	21511.89	6537.71	14974.18	0.04
	10	27361.31	1043.47	5.45	1038.02	21589.51	6535.09	15054.42	0.04
	11	27694.73	1055.70	5.81	1049.89	21830.04	6676.62	15153.42	0.04
	12	27634.86	1052.91	5.26	1047.65	21765.85	6691.59	15074.26	0.04
比上期增减额（亿元）Changes Compared with Previous Period（100 Million Yuan）									
2005	1	345.65	20.45	-0.08	20.53	345.47	84.51	260.96	
	2	845.04	10.08	-0.05	10.13	1143.91	403.30	740.61	
	3	387.44	33.95	0.36	33.59	92.22	-43.22	135.44	
	4	33.09	23.39	1.37	22.02	-14.19	-25.22	11.03	0.30
	5	221.51	13.96	-0.45	14.41	129.55	38.01	91.54	-0.30
	6	-124.86	-53.28	3.29	-56.57	-62.10	80.40	-142.50	
	7	40.74	8.15	-2.80	10.95	110.33	2.86	107.47	
	8	-926.22	-60.76	-0.57	-60.19	-501.03	-101.43	-399.60	
	9	367.06	13.72	-0.09	13.81	166.96	88.79	78.17	
	10	44.46	-0.97	0.61	-1.58	77.62	-2.62	80.24	
	11	333.42	12.23	0.36	11.87	240.53	141.53	99.00	
	12	-59.87	-2.79	-0.55	-2.24	-64.19	14.97	-79.16	
比去年同期增长（%）Increase Rate Year-on-year（%）									
2005	1	8.16	2.33	-39.62	2.59	6.70	10.03	5.34	-20.00
	2	9.31	-0.11	-28.68	0.03	10.82	17.37	8.22	-20.00
	3	8.72	0.04	-21.65	0.15	10.21	14.46	8.51	-20.00
	4	7.65	-0.85	-1.44	-0.85	9.16	12.01	7.99	750.00
	5	7.33	-1.68	-18.93	-1.59	8.85	11.24	7.87	
	6	5.31	-7.65	28.09	-7.85	7.31	10.04	6.17	
	7	5.54	-7.68	-22.32	-7.59	7.51	9.95	6.50	
	8	2.40	-11.61	-24.73	-11.54	5.54	9.08	4.08	
	9	3.00	-10.13	-30.06	-10.01	5.81	9.02	4.47	
	10	2.54	-9.29	-25.14	-9.19	5.49	7.89	4.48	
	11	2.71	-9.08	-20.74	-9.00	5.77	10.04	3.99	
	12	1.08	-8.40	-26.94	-8.29	4.59	7.52	3.34	

农村信用合作社本外币信贷收支主要指标时间序列表

Time Series of Major Indicators in Sources and Uses of Credit Funds of Rural Credit Cooperatives (Domestic and Foreign Currency Combined)

年　月 Year Month		各项贷款 Total Loans				有价证券及投资 Securities and Investments
			短期贷款 Short－term Loans	中长期贷款 Medium and Long－term Loans	票据融资 Paper Financing	
期末余额（亿元） Balance (100 Million Yuan)						
2005	1	19152.71	17289.48	1534.20	327.42	2368.35
	2	19391.30	17519.25	1540.79	326.87	2376.51
	3	19790.62	17874.30	1579.29	335.29	2352.03
	4	20197.06	18231.92	1605.74	357.25	2354.64
	5	20456.27	18453.50	1636.00	364.23	2352.93
	6	19949.27	17933.84	1670.41	342.53	2281.42
	7	20142.64	18084.00	1692.53	362.98	2189.57
	8	19708.77	17827.78	1547.57	330.26	1909.28
	9	19560.95	17647.04	1605.51	305.40	1896.12
	10	19474.57	17581.74	1609.77	280.24	1909.95
	11	19386.01	17478.69	1636.65	267.41	2020.43
	12	18684.13	16807.07	1556.76	317.30	2099.87
比上期增减额（亿元） Changes Compared with Previous Period (100 Million Yuan)						
2005	1	775.44	699.07	43.49	32.38	101.32
	2	238.64	229.82	6.59	－0.55	8.16
	3	586.88	529.48	51.63	8.42	－24.48
	4	398.67	350.39	25.91	21.96	2.61
	5	269.10	230.78	30.95	6.98	－1.71
	6	－197.61	－231.93	56.07	－21.70	－71.51
	7	198.37	154.81	22.47	20.45	－91.85
	8	－434.88	－257.16	－145.03	－32.72	－280.29
	9	119.82	68.17	76.67	－24.86	－13.16
	10	－50.29	－31.74	6.79	－25.16	13.83
	11	－86.68	－101.30	27.01	－12.83	110.48
	12	－544.49	－525.25	－68.87	49.89	79.44
比去年同期增长（%） Increase Rate Year－on－year (%)						
2005	1	10.17	9.57	27.89	－19.22	12.72
	2	8.19	7.64	26.19	－23.41	12.44
	3	8.09	7.50	24.63	－19.15	11.24
	4	7.63	7.12	22.30	－17.41	10.03
	5	8.02	7.44	20.65	－10.09	9.19
	6	5.96	5.32	20.94	－17.69	2.13
	7	6.28	5.50	19.99	－9.26	－6.97
	8	3.53	3.55	9.08	－17.84	－19.51
	9	3.36	3.07	13.02	－20.48	－20.97
	10	3.25	2.92	12.87	－20.70	－20.90
	11	3.00	2.65	13.99	－25.63	－17.62
	12	2.06	1.72	7.57	－5.80	－11.80

专栏［1］：农业贷款

农业贷款始终在金融机构的信贷业务中占有重要地位。1993 年之前，农业贷款反映金融机构向各农业公有制企业发放的贷款，这里的农业指物质产品平衡表体系（MPS）下与工业、商业、建筑业、交通运输业并列的五大物质生产部门之一。1993 年，取消 MPS 的国民收入核算之后，中国国民经济核算体系进入了国民账户体系（SNA）的发展阶段，农业贷款的内涵随之发生了变迁，主要包括农村信用社发放的农户贷款、农村工商业贷款、农业经济组织贷款等以及商业银行发放的农林牧渔业贷款，农副产品收购贷款不包含在内。本专栏将信贷收支表中列示的短期农业贷款和数据源中的中长期农业贷款数据汇总为农业贷款数据。

金融机构人民币农业贷款时间序列表

单位：亿元

年　份	期末余额	年　份	期末余额
1949		1978	155.94
1950		1979	179.58
1951		1980	249.67
1952	4.20	1981	280.99
1953	6.80	1982	322.88
1954	8.80	1983	378.91
1955	12.40	1984	689.73
1956	35.50	1985	775.57
1957	33.20	1986	1095.60
1958	63.85	1987	1427.70
1959	61.10	1988	1277.59
1960	77.50	1989	984.19
1961	75.00	1990	1244.09
1962	76.30	1991	1562.37
1963	79.30	1992	1984.15
1964	81.35	1993	2401.28
1965	87.45	1994	2886.50
1966	88.65	1995	3649.58
1967	91.75	1996	4415.86
1968	93.45	1997	4541.17
1969	97.55	1998	5987.13
1970	99.65	1999	6809.49
1971	68.46	2000	7446.49
1972	74.76	2001	8658.21
1973	76.86	2002	10163.35
1974	83.76	2003	11967.82
1975	96.68	2004	13531.79
1976	122.74	2005	15105.72
1977	134.54		

注：1994—1996 年间，中长期农业贷款数据为按照可比口径加工的数据，在此基础上汇总金融机构信贷收支表中的短期农业贷款数据得到金融机构农业贷款数据。该三年的农业短期贷款年末余额分别为 1143.85 亿元、1544.79 亿元、1919.12 亿元。

Box 1: Loans to Agricultural Sector

Loans to agricultural sector have all along been an important part in the credit businesses of financial institutions. Prior to 1993, it reflected loans lent to state – owned agricultural enterprises. The agricultural sector mentioned referred to the five material production sectors within the Material Production System ("MPS") and the other four sectors being industry, commerce, construction and transportation. With replacement of MPS by the System of National Accounts ("SNA") in 1993, the definition of loans to agricultural sector was changed and covered loans to rural households, loans to industrial and commercial enterprises in rural areas, loans to rural economic organizations by rural credit cooperatives and loans to agriculture, forestry, animal husbandry and fishery by commercial banks. However, loans for the purchase of agricultural products were not included. In the following table, the medium and long – term loans to agricultural sector and the short – term loans to agricultural sector listed in the statement of the sources and uses of credit funds of financial institutions are aggregated and presented as loans to agricultural sector.

Loans to Agricultural Sector from Financial Institutions

Unit: 100 Million Yuan

Year	Balance at Year – end	Year	Balance at Year – end
1949		1978	155.94
1950		1979	179.58
1951		1980	249.67
1952	4.20	1981	280.99
1953	6.80	1982	322.88
1954	8.80	1983	378.91
1955	12.40	1984	689.73
1956	35.50	1985	775.57
1957	33.20	1986	1095.60
1958	63.85	1987	1427.70
1959	61.10	1988	1277.59
1960	77.50	1989	984.19
1961	75.00	1990	1244.09
1962	76.30	1991	1562.37
1963	79.30	1992	1984.15
1964	81.35	1993	2401.28
1965	87.45	1994	2886.50
1966	88.65	1995	3649.58
1967	91.75	1996	4415.86
1968	93.45	1997	4541.17
1969	97.55	1998	5987.13
1970	99.65	1999	6809.49
1971	68.46	2000	7446.49
1972	74.76	2001	8658.21
1973	76.86	2002	10163.35
1974	83.76	2003	11967.82
1975	96.68	2004	13531.79
1976	122.74	2005	15105.72
1977	134.54		

Note: The medium and long – term loans to agricultural sector in 1994, 1995 and 1996 were complied on a comparable basis, and then added to short – term loans to agricultural sector extracted from the statement of the sources and uses of credit funds of financial institutions to get the balance of loans to agricultural sector. The short – term loans to agricultural sector at the end of these three years were 114.385 billion yuan, 154.479 million yuan and 191.912 billion yuan, respectively.

专栏［2］：个人消费贷款

1998年以来，中国经济全面告别“短缺”，扩大内需和刺激消费成为基本的经济战略方针。中国人民银行于1999年发布《关于开展个人消费信贷指导意见》，鼓励所有的商业银行发展所有的消费信贷业务。个人消费贷款逐步成为商业银行重要的资产业务，商业银行的贷款投向结构发生重要变化。从2001年起，金融统计指标体系中设置“个人消费贷款”及细项指标，反映金融机构发放个人消费贷款的数量、期限等情况，并在信贷收支表中设置个人短期和中长期消费贷款项目。

金融机构人民币个人消费贷款统计表

单位：亿元

年　份	期末余额
2001	6990.26
2002	10672.11
2003	15735.71
2004	19882.05
2005	21951.21

Box 2: Consumer Credit

In 1998, The lacking in supply became a thing in the past in the Chinese economy. China has adopted the strategic principle of boosting domestic demand and consumption since then. In 1999, the People's Bank of China issued *Opinions on Expanding Consumer Credit Services* to encourage all the commercial banks to develop consumer credit services. Consumer credit has gradually become an important asset business of commercial banks, and the structure of commercial banks' asset portfolio has taken on significant changes. Since 2001, consumer credit and various sub – items were added to the the financial statistical framework to collect and record the amount and the maturity of consumer credit. Correspondingly, short – term consumer credit and medium and long – term consumer credit became separate items in the statement of sources and uses of credit funds.

Consumer Credit of Financial Institutions (RMB)

Unit: 100 Million Yuan

Year	Balance at Year – end
2001	6990.26
2002	10672.11
2003	15735.71
2004	19882.05
2005	21951.21

专栏［3］：不良贷款剥离

1999 年，为防范和化解金融风险，推动国有银行的商业化改革，国务院决定设立四家金融资产管理公司收购、管理和处置国有银行剥离的不良贷款。2004 年 6 月以来，为加快国有商业银行股份制改造，在对国有商业银行注资的基础上实施不良资产剥离和划转。本专栏按照机构和业务类别列示历年金融机构期末不良贷款剥离累计额情况。现行金融统计中，对不良贷款的剥离与划转在各相关信贷收支表中按照“余额真实反映、比较数可比”的原则进行处理。

金融机构不良贷款剥离情况统计表

（期末累计额）

单位：亿元、亿美元

机构 \ 时间	金融机构		国家银行		政策性银行		国有商业银行		其他商业银行	
	人民币	外汇	人民币	外汇	人民币	外汇	人民币	外汇	人民币	外汇
1999.12	3500	45.8	3500	45.8	484		3016	45.8		
2000.01	3769	45.8	3769	45.8	743		3026	45.8		
2000.02	3772	46.2	3772	46.2	744		3028	46.2		
2000.03	3798	46.2	3798	46.2	744		3054	46.2		
2000.04	3972	46.2	3972	46.2	744		3228	46.2		
2000.05	5196	57.7	5196	57.7	744		4452	57.7		
2000.06	8281	135.7	8280	135.7	745		7536	135.7		
2000.07	9668	156.7	9668	156.7	745		8923	156.7		
2000.08	10156	162.8	10156	162.8	745		9411	162.8		
2000.09	10609	164.7	10609	164.7	745		9864	164.7		
2000.10	10734	166.2	10734	166.2	745		9989	166.2		
2000.11	10799	167.2	10799	167.2	745		10054	167.2		
2000.12	10900	187.7	10900	187.7	745		10155	187.7		
2004.06	14258	307.2	13797	299.0	745		13052	307.2	461	8.2
2005.05	15954	315.0	15493	306.8	745		14748	315.0	461	8.2
2005.06	20389	333.5	19928	325.3	745		19183	333.5	461	8.2

Box3: Transfer of Non – performing Loans

In order to prevent and dissolve financial risks, and to promote the commercial – orientation reforms in the state – owned commercial banks, the State Council decided to set up four asset management companies in 1999, to acquire, manage and dispose of non – performing loans transferred from state – owned commercial banks. As of June 2004, additional equity was injected into the state – owned commercial banks, accompanied by the transferring of non – performing loans in order to speed up the reform processes. In the following tables, we have listed the accumulative balances of non – performing loans transferred from financial institutions at the end of each period, by institution and currency denomination. In the current financial statistics, the transfer of non – performing loans is recorded and complied in the principle of "outstanding balance in its true volume, comparability of comparable figures".

Transfer of Non – performing Loans from Financial Institutions

(Accumulative Balances at Period – end)

Unit: 100 Million Yuan and 100 Million US Dollars

Institution / Time	Financial Institutions		State Banks		Policy Banks		State – owned Commercial Banks		Other Commercial Banks	
	RMB	USD	RMB	USD	RMB	USD	RMB	USD	RMB	USD
1999.12	3500	45.8	3500	45.8	484		3016	45.8		
2000.01	3769	45.8	3769	45.8	743		3026	45.8		
2000.02	3772	46.2	3772	46.2	744		3028	46.2		
2000.03	3798	46.2	3798	46.2	744		3054	46.2		
2000.04	3972	46.2	3972	46.2	744		3228	46.2		
2000.05	5196	57.7	5196	57.7	744		4452	57.7		
2000.06	8281	135.7	8280	135.7	745		7536	135.7		
2000.07	9668	156.7	9668	156.7	745		8923	156.7		
2000.08	10156	162.8	10156	162.8	745		9411	162.8		
2000.09	10609	164.7	10609	164.7	745		9864	164.7		
2000.10	10734	166.2	10734	166.2	745		9989	166.2		
2000.11	10799	167.2	10799	167.2	745		10054	167.2		
2000.12	10900	187.7	10900	187.7	745		10155	187.7		
2004.06	14258	307.2	13797	299.0	745		13052	307.2	461	8.2
2005.05	15954	315.0	15493	306.8	745		14748	315.0	461	8.2
2005.06	20389	333.5	19928	325.3	745		19183	333.5	461	8.2

前　言

原建设部(现住房和城乡建设部)和原人事部(现人力资源和社会保障部)从 2003 年起实施注册公用设备工程师(暖通空调、动力)执业资格考试制度。

本教程的编写老师都是本专业有较深造诣的教授和高级工程师,分别来自北京建筑大学、北京工业大学、北京交通大学、北京工商大学、郑州大学及北京市建筑设计研究院。为了帮助公用设备工程师们准备考试,教师们根据多年教学实践经验和考生的回馈意见,依据考试大纲和现行教材、规范,为学员们编写了这本教程。本教程的目的是为了指导复习,因此力求简明扼要,联系实际,着重对概念和规范的理解应用,并注意突出重点,是一套值得考生信赖的考前辅导和培训用书。

本教程严格按现行考试大纲编写,并在多年教学实践中不断加以改进。为方便考生复习,本教程分上、下册出版,上册第 1 至第 11 章为上午段公共基础考试内容,下册第 12 至第 18 章为下午段专业基础考试内容,所选例题及练习题大多来自真题,并注有年号,考生做题时,可对此部分题多加关注。

本教程可与《2019 注册公用设备工程师(暖通空调、动力)执业资格考试基础考试历年真题详解(2005～2018)》配套使用。

(1)在结构设置上,首先对大纲要求的知识点进行精炼阐述,然后辅以典型例题并进行解析,每一小节后附经典练习,并在每一章后提供提示及参考答案。

(2)例题、练习题、模拟题等试题多来自历年真题,考生可在复习、练习过程中熟悉本考试的深度和广度。

(3)全书是对考试大纲内容的精炼,考生通过本书的复习和练习,可在较短时间内完成对考试大纲的理解和掌握。

特别提醒,《中华人民共和国城乡规划法》(2015 年版)对原第二十四条第二款第二项作了修订,本书已更新。《中华人民共和国环境保护法》(自 2015 年 1 月 1 日起施行),本书也已更新。

本书中的部分知识点和试题配有视频讲解,考生可扫描书中"二维码"在线学习,或者扫描封面"二维码",登录"注考大师",获取更多学习资源。

本书由李洪欣、曹纬浚担任主编。参与或协助本书编写的老师有王连俊、王健、冯东、刘燕、刘世奎、乔春生、孙惠镐、许小重、许怡生、杨松林、李兆年、李魁元、吴昌泽、陈向东、陈璐、范元玮、侯云芬、赵知敬、钱民刚、谢亚勃、穆静波、魏京花、朱强、卢纪富、沈超、蒋全科、贾玲华、毛怀珍、刘宝生、张翠兰、毛元钰、李平、邓华、陈庆年、李广秋、郭虹、曹京、楼香林、杨守俊、王志刚、何承奎、曹铎、罗滨、吴莎莎、张文革、罗金标、徐华萍、栾彩虹、孙国樑、张炳珍。

由于考试涉及面广，书中难免存在疏漏和不足，真诚地希望读者批评指正，提出宝贵意见，以便本书再版时改进。

最后，祝愿各位考生取得好的成绩！

李洪欣
2019 年 1 月

主编致考生

一、注册公用设备工程师(暖通空调、动力)在专业考试之前进行基础考试是和国外接轨的做法。通过基础考试并达到职业实践年限后就可以申请参加专业考试。基础考试是考大学中的基础课程,按考试大纲的安排,上午考试段考 11 科,120 道题,4 个小时,每题 1 分,共 120 分;下午考试段考 7 科,60 道题,4 个小时,每题 2 分,共 120 分;上、下午共 240 分。试题均为 4 选 1 的单选题,平均每题时间上午 2 分钟,下午 4 分钟,因此不会有复杂的论证和计算,主要是检验考生的基本概念和基本知识。考生在复习时不要偏重难度大或过于复杂的知识,而应将复习的注意力主要放在弄清基本概念和基本知识方面。

二、考生在复习本教程之前,应认真阅读"考试大纲",清楚地了解考试的内容和范围,以便合理制订自己的复习计划。复习时一定要紧扣"考试大纲"的内容,将全面复习与突出重点相结合。着重对"考试大纲"要求掌握的基本概念、基本理论、基本计算方法、计算公式和步骤,以及基本知识的应用等内容有系统、有条理地重点掌握,明白其中的道理和关系,掌握分析问题的方法。同时还应会使用为减少计算工作量或简化、方便计算所制作的表格等。本教程中每章前均有一节"复习指导",具体说明本章的复习重点、难点和复习中要注意的问题,建议考生认真阅读每章的"复习指导",参考"复习指导"的意见进行复习。在对基本概念、基本原理和基本知识有一个整体把握的基础上,对每章节的重点、难点进行重点复习和重点掌握。

三、注册公用设备工程师(暖通空调、动力)基础考试上、下午试卷共计 240 分,上、下午不分段计算成绩,这几年及格线都是 55%,也就是说,上、下午试卷总分达到 132 分就可以通过。因此,考生在准备考试时应注意扬长避短。从道理上讲,自己较弱的科目更应该努力复习,但毕竟时间和精力有限,如 2009 年新增加的"信号与信息技术",据了解,非信息专业的考生大多未学过,短时间内要掌握好比较困难,而"信号与信息技术"总共只有 6 道题,6 分,只占总分的 2.5%,也就是说,即使"信号与信息技术"1 分未得,其他科目也还有 234 分,从 234 分中考 132 分是完全可以做到的。因此考生可以根据考试分科题量、分数分配和自己的具体情况,计划自己的复习重点和主要得分科目。当然一些主要得分科目是不能放松的,如"高等数学"24 题(上午段)24 分,"工程热力学"10 题(下午段)20 分,"传热学"10 题(下午段)20 分,都是不能放松的;其他科目则可根据自己过去对课程的掌握情况有所侧重,争取在自己过去学得好的课程中多得分。

四、在考试拿到试卷时,建议考生不要顺着题序顺次往下做。因为有的题会比较难,有的题不很熟悉,耽误的时间会比较多,以致到最后时间不够,题做不完,有些题会做但时间来不及,这就太得不偿失了。建议考生将做题过程分为四遍:

(1)首先用 15～20 分钟将题从头到尾看一遍,一是首先解答出自己很熟悉很有把握的题;

二是将那些需要稍加思考估计能在平均答题时间里做出的题做个记号。这里说的平均答题时间，是指上午段4个小时考120道题，平均每题2分钟；下午段4个小时考60道题，平均每题4分钟，这个2分钟（上午）、4分钟（下午）就是平均答题时间。将估计在这个时间里能做出来的题做上记号。

(2)第二遍做这些做了记号的题，这些题应该在考试时间里能做完，做完了这些题可以说就考出了考生的基本水平，不管考生基础如何，复习得怎么样，考得如何，至少不会因为题没做完而遗憾了。

(3)这些会做或基本会做的题做完以后，如果还有时间，就做那些需要稍多花费时间的题，能做几个算几个，并适当抽时间检查一下已答题的答案。

(4)考试时间将近结束时，比如还剩5分钟要收卷了，这时你就应看看还有多少道题没有答，这些题确实不会了，建议考生也不要放弃。既然是单选，那也不妨估个答案，答对了也是有分的。建议考生回头看看已答题目的答案，A、B、C、D各有多少，虽然整个卷子四种答案的数量并不一定是平均的，但还是可以这样考虑，看看已答的题A、B、C、D中哪个答案最少，然后将不会做没有答的题按这个前边最少的答案通填，这样其中会有1/4可能还会多于1/4的题能得分，如果考生前边答对的题离及格正好差几分，这样一补充就能及格了。

五、基础考试是不允许带书和资料的，2012年前，考试时会给每位考生发一本“考试手册”，载有公式和一些数据，考后收回。但从2012年起，取消了“考试手册”的配发。据说原因是考生使用不多，事实上也没有更多时间去翻手册。因此一些重要的公式、规定，考生一定要自己记住。

六、本教程每节后均附有习题，并在每章后附有提示及参考答案。建议考生在复习好本教程内容的基础上，多做习题。多做习题能帮助巩固已学的概念、理论、方法和公式等，并能发现自己的不足，哪些地方理解得不正确，哪些地方没有掌握好；同时熟能生巧，提高解题速度。本教程在最后提供了两套模拟试题，建议考生在复习完本教程以后，集中时间，排除干扰，模拟考试气氛，将模拟试题全部做一遍，以接近实战地检验一下自己的复习效果。

注册公用设备工程师考试已经进行了十多年，分析这些年的考题，特别是近两年的考题，可以总结出考题考查的一些新趋势。一个趋势就是考试题目考查点越来越细，越来越深入；另一个趋势就是有的题目考查得更加综合，一个题目可能涉及几个知识点，考题难度加大。这都对考生的备考提出了更高的要求。因此，考生需要对大纲涉及的考点做到真正理解，并在此基础上能够灵活应用。

复习中若遇到疑问，可写清楚问题发邮件至caowj0818@126.com（上册问题）、466362436@qq.com（下册问题），我们会尽快回复解答。相信这本教程能帮助大家准备好考试。

最后，祝愿各位考生取得好成绩！

曹纬浚

2019年1月

目　录

上　册

第一章 高等数学

复习指导

在注册工程师基础考试中，基础部分试卷试题总数为120道题，其中高等数学占24题。近几年，高等数学题微积分部分有18道题，线性代数、概率论与数理统计各3题。数学题的数量占上午试题总量的$\frac{1}{5}$，因而复习好数学是至关重要的。

一、考试大纲

1.1 空间解析几何

向量的线性运算；向量的数量积、向量积及混合积；两向量垂直、平行的条件；直线方程；平面方程；平面与平面、直线与直线、平面与直线之间的位置关系；点到平面、直线的距离；球面、母线平行于坐标轴的柱面、旋转轴为坐标轴的旋转曲面的方程；常用的二次曲面方程；空间曲线在坐标面上的投影曲线方程。

1.2 微分学

函数的有界性、单调性、周期性和奇偶性；数列极限与函数极限的定义及其性质；无穷小和无穷大的概念及其关系；无穷小的性质及无穷小的比较；极限的四则运算；函数连续的概念；函数间断点及其类型；导数与微分的概念；导数的几何意义和物理意义；平面曲线的切线和法线；导数和微分的四则运算；高阶导数；微分中值定理；洛必达法则；一元函数的切线与法线，空间曲线的切线与法平面、曲面的切平面及法线；函数单调性的判别；函数的极值；函数曲线的凹凸性、拐点；偏导数与全微分的概念；二阶偏导数；多元函数的极值和条件极值；多元函数的最大、最小值及其简单应用。

1.3 积分学

原函数与不定积分的概念；不定积分的基本性质；基本积分公式；定积分的基本概念和性质(包括定积分中值定理)；积分上限的函数及其导数；牛顿-莱布尼兹公式；不定积分和定积分的换元积分法与分部积分法；有理函数、三角函数的有理式和简单无理函数的积分；广义积分；二重积分与三重积分的概念、性质、计算和应用；两类曲线积分的概念、性质和计算；求平面图形的面积、平面曲线的弧长和旋转体的体积。

1.4 无穷级数

数项级数的敛散性概念；收敛级数的和；级数的基本性质与级数收敛的必要条件；几何级数与p级数及其收敛性；正项级数敛散性的判别法；任意项级数的绝对收敛与条件收敛；幂级数及其收敛半径、收敛区间和收敛域；幂级数的和函数；函数的泰勒级数展开；函数的傅里叶系数与傅里叶级数。

1.5 常微分方程

常微分方程的基本概念；变量可分离的微分方程；齐次微分方程；一阶线性微分方程；全微

分方程;可降阶的高阶微分方程;线性微分方程解的性质及解的结构定理;二阶常系数齐次线性微分方程。

1.6　线性代数

行列式的性质及计算;行列式按行按列展开定理的应用;矩阵的运算;逆矩阵的概念、性质及求法;矩阵的初等变换和初等矩阵;矩阵的秩;等价矩阵的概念和性质;向量的线性表示;向量组的线性相关和线性无关;线性方程组有解的判定;线性方程组求解;矩阵的特征值和特征向量的概念与性质;相似矩阵的概念和性质;矩阵的相似对角化;二次型及其矩阵表示;合同矩阵的概念和性质;二次型的秩;惯性定理;二次型及其矩阵的正定性。

1.7　概率论与数理统计

随机事件与样本空间;事件的关系与运算;概率的基本性质;古典型概率;条件概率;概率的基本公式;事件的独立性;独立重复试验;随机变量;随机变量的分布函数;离散型随机变量的概率分布;连续型随机变量的概率密度;常见随机变量的分布;随机变量的数学期望、方差、标准差及其性质;随机变量函数的数学期望;矩、协方差、相关系数及其性质;总体;个体;简单随机样本;统计量;样本均值;样本方差和样本矩;χ^2 分布;t 分布;F 分布;点估计的概念;估计量与估计值;矩估计法;最大似然估计法;估计量的评选标准;区间估计的概念;单个正态总体的均值和方差的区间估计;两个正态总体的均值差和方差比的区间估计;显著性检验;单个正态总体的均值和方差的假设检验。

二、复习指导

在复习中,首先要熟悉大纲,按大纲的要求分清哪些属于考试要求,哪些不属于考试要求,有的放矢地做好复习工作。建议考生除了复习本复习教程上的内容外,还可结合同济大学编的《高等数学》上、下册(第六版或第七版)课本一起复习。由于复习教程篇幅所限,有的内容显得简单了,结合书本复习,可进一步充实相关的内容。另外,在教科书中还附有大量的习题,可在复习时做练习题用。

关于考试的试题基础部分在上午考,时间为 4 个小时,考题有 120 道,也就是要在 240 分钟内做完 120 道题,平均 2 分钟做 1 道题,这一点也是我们在复习中应该注意的。这样,大的定理证明、复杂的计算题、计算量大大超过 2 分钟的题目就不可能在试题中出现。试题的形式都是单选题,从给出的四个选项中挑一个。如果题目是以计算题形式给出的,可通过正确的计算选择其中一个答案。

有的从形式上看也是计算题,但涉及的内容有奇偶函数,不妨先去判定一下。对常微分方程中的题目,如求二阶常系数线性非齐次方程的特解,可将给出的选项代入试题试算一下,求出方程的特解。对于线性代数中求可逆方阵的逆矩阵时,可将给出的选项代入试题,求出符合公式 $\boldsymbol{AB}=\boldsymbol{E}$ 的逆矩阵等。这对提高计算速度,减少复杂的计算有帮助。有的题目属于概念题,应认真回顾所学过的概念做出正确的选择,有的题目要求根据学过的定义、定理判定,要很好想一下这些定义、定理的具体内容,经分析后选出要求的答案。因而熟记书本的定义、定理性质是必要的。另外,熟悉一些题目的计算步骤,记住曾做过一些题目的结论也是必要的。并注意根据题目的要求,当能肯定选出某一选项后,其余三个选项,不论它所给出的内容是什么,也不再去验证它为什么错。除了有的题目给了四个选项,一时判定不了的,可以采取逐一排除的方法,得到最后的结论。这些做法在具体做题时需要灵活掌握。但可以肯定的是,选择题往往是从涉及概念性较强,计算比较灵活,而计算量又不很大的一类题目中选出。了解以上情况之后，从一开始复习就要加以注意。最后通过系统的复习达到对考试要求的内容有一个全面了解，应该记忆的定义、定理、性质和一些推导出来的结论要记住，应该记忆的公式要记牢，对各种类型的计算题解题的步骤要记住，只有这样，才能较好地应对这次考试。

下面按章、节讲一下每一部分的重点和难点，按复习教程所写的内容顺序进行。

(一)空间解析几何与向量代数

重点：(1)掌握利用向量的基本向量分解式或坐标表示式进行向量运算，如加法、减法、数乘，数量积、向量积、混合积的计算。

(2)熟练掌握利用两向量平行、两向量垂直坐标所具备的性质，设 $\vec{a}$，$\vec{b}$ 为非零向量，$\vec{a}=\{a_x,a_y,a_z\}$，$\vec{b}=\{b_x,b_y,b_z\}$，则①$\vec{a}\,/\!/\,\vec{b}\Leftrightarrow\vec{a}\times\vec{b}=0\Leftrightarrow\vec{a}=\lambda\vec{b}\Leftrightarrow\frac{a_x}{b_x}=\frac{a_y}{b_y}=\frac{a_z}{b_z}$；②$\vec{a}\perp\vec{b}\Leftrightarrow\vec{a}\cdot\vec{b}=0\Leftrightarrow a_xb_x+a_yb_y+a_zb_z=0$。会利用上述条件求直线方程、平面方程，或判定直线和平面间的某种位置关系，空间曲线在坐标面上的投影曲线。

(3)熟练掌握二次曲面类型的判别。

难点：利用两向量平行或垂直的条件求直线方程、平面方程，判定直线和平面的位置关系又是其中的难点。

(二)一元函数微分学

重点：(1)熟练掌握函数奇偶性、单调性、周期性、有界性的判定办法。

(2)熟练掌握求函数极限的方法，把两个重要极限、利用等价无穷小求极限等方法和用洛必达法则求极限方法灵活地结合在一起，解决求极限的问题。

(3)掌握利用函数在一点连续的定义，判定函数在一点的连续性或求某一个数值，会判定函数的间断点及间断点的类型。

(4)掌握用在一点导数的定义的两种形式求函数在一点的导数，并会利用在一点左、右导数的定义判定分段函数在交界点的可导性。掌握利用在一点导数的几何意义求切线方程、法线方程。

(5)熟练掌握复合函数、参数方程、隐函数、幂指函数的一阶导数以及高阶导数的计算。

(6)熟练掌握三个中值定理结论中的 ξ 值求法，会求函数的单调区间、函数的极值、函数的最值、函数的凹凸区间、拐点，会求函数的渐近线。其中，求各种给出函数的导数，确定函数曲线的单调性、凹凸区间等，又是这一节的**难点**。

(三)一元函数积分学

重点：(1)掌握原函数的概念，并要求把原函数的概念灵活地运用到求函数的不定积分中，计算出不定积分。

(2)熟练掌握利用不定积分公式、换元法、分部积分法，求不定积分。

其中，涉及利用原函数概念的不定积分计算，用换元积分法计算不定积分，是难点。

(3)掌握积分上限函数求导的方法，熟练掌握利用定积分的性质、奇偶函数在对称区间上积分的知识，利用定积分的换元积分和分部积分等求定积分。

(4)熟练掌握利用定积分求平面图形的面积和旋转体的体积、平面曲线的弧长、计算变力沿直线运动所做的功等。

(5)熟练掌握广义积分的计算，判定广义积分敛散性。

难点：计算不定积分、定积分及利用定积分求平面图形的面积和旋转体的体积。

（四）多元函数微分学

重点：(1)熟练掌握复合函数偏导数和全微分的计算，隐函数偏导数和全微分的计算。

(2)掌握二元函数在一点的连续性，偏导存在和全微分的概念及它们之间的联系。

(3)熟练掌握求空间曲线的切线和法平面、空间曲面的切平面和法线的方程的方法。

难点：二元函数连续性、偏导存在和可微概念之间的关系，求二元复合函数和隐函数的偏导、全微分是难点。

（五）多元函数积分学

重点：(1)熟练掌握二重积分的计算，并会在直角坐标系下把二重积分写成两种积分顺序下的二次积分，会把二重积分化为极坐标系下的二次积分。

(2)熟练掌握把三重积分化为在直角坐标系下、柱面坐标系下、球面坐标系下的三次积分（计算三重积分不是重点）。

(3)熟练掌握对弧长和坐标的曲线积分的计算。在对坐标的曲线积分中，一定要会利用与路径无关的条件，应用格林公式计算曲线积分。

难点：把三重积分化为直角、柱面、球面坐标系下三次积分，对弧长的曲线积分。

（六）级数

重点：(1)熟练掌握数项级数敛散性的判定。

(2)熟练掌握幂级数的收敛半经和收敛区间的求法。

(3)熟练掌握利用已知函数展开式，采用间接展开法，把函数展开成幂级数。

(4)掌握用狄利克雷收敛定理确定傅里叶级数的和函数，求在某点傅里叶级数的和。

难点：(1)数项级数敛散性的判定。

(2)用间接展开法把函数展开成幂级数。

（七）常微分方程

重点：(1)熟练掌握一阶微分方程中可分离变量方程、一阶线性方程通解的求法。

(2)熟练掌握二阶常系数线性齐次方程通解的计算方法。

(3)掌握列微分方程、解应用题方法。

难点：列微分方程、解应用题。

技巧：对于常微分方程的考题，使用“代入选项试算法”可会使题速度更快，不妨一试。

（八）线性代数

根据考试大纲的要求，线性代数需要掌握以下内容：行列式、矩阵、n 维向量、线性方程组、矩阵的特征值与特征向量、二次型。

行列式是线性代数的基本工具，而高阶行列式的计算一般都要用到行列式的相关性质。

矩阵是线性代数研究的主要对象，是求解线性方程组的有力工具。除了会矩阵的基本运算外，还应会求逆矩阵、矩阵的秩，进而会求解矩阵方程。

在求解线性方程组时会涉及解向量的最大线性无关组的问题，对于向量组要会求它的最大线性无关组。能熟练利用齐次及非齐次线性方程组解的性质，写出方程组的通解。

特征值与特征向量是矩阵理论中最基本的概念之一，对此，应熟练掌握。

关于二次型，首先要会写出它的矩阵形式，即找出它所对应的实对称阵。将一般二次型化为标准型时，也会遇到求二次型所对应矩阵的特征根的问题。

（九）概率论与数理统计

概率论与数理统计需要掌握的内容如下。

随机事件与概率、古典概型、一维随机变量的分布和数字特征、数理统计的基本概念、参数估计、假设检验。

对事件运算、古典概型、全概率公式、独立重复试验要会灵活运用这些工具解决具体问题。

对于随机变量可以有三种描述工具：分布函数、离散型随机变量的分布律、连续型随机变量的概率密度，需要熟悉它们的定义、性质，并且要会使用。比如，概率密度 $f(x)$ 中如果含未知数 A，则可用 $\int_{-\infty}^{+\infty} f(x)\mathrm{d}x = 1$ 定出 A。而对正态 $N(\mu,\sigma^2)$ 分布的随机变量要转化成标准正态 $N(0,1)$ 分布才可查表。

数字特征可从某个侧面反映随机变量分布的特点，数学期望和方差的性质及有关计算公式属于基本内容，用它们可以解决一些实际问题，应该予以关注。

统计量，比如样本均值 $\overline{X}$ 和方差 S^2，抽样分布是参数估计、假设检验的基础。

总之，大家应在基本概念清晰的基础上，熟练掌握有关的计算问题，特别是比较简捷的计算。

第一节　空间解析几何与向量代数

一、空间直角坐标

（一）空间直角坐标系

在空间取定一点 O，和以 O 为原点的两两垂直的三个数轴，依次记作 x 轴（横轴）、y 轴（纵轴）、z 轴（竖轴），构成一个空间直角坐标系（见图 1-1-1）。通常符合右手规则，即以右手握住 z 轴，当右手的四个手指从正向 x 轴以 $\frac{\pi}{2}$ 角度转向正向 y 轴时，大拇指的指向就是 z 轴的正向。并设 $\vec{i}$、$\vec{j}$、$\vec{k}$ 为 x 轴、y 轴、z 轴上的单位向量，又称为 $Oxyz$ 坐标系，或$[O, \vec{i}, \vec{j}, \vec{k}]$坐标系。

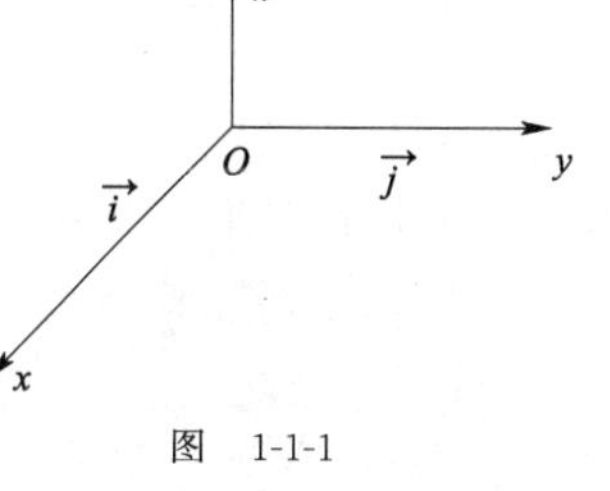

图 1-1-1

（二）两点间的距离

在空间直角坐标系中，$M_1(x_1, y_1, z_1)$与 $M_2(x_2, y_2, z_2)$之间的距离为

$$d=\sqrt{(x_2-x_1)^2+(y_2-y_1)^2+(z_2-z_1)^2} \tag{1-1-1}$$

（三）空间有向直线方向的确定

设有一条有向直线 L，它与三个坐标轴正向的夹角分别为 α、β、γ（$0\leqslant\alpha,\beta,\gamma\leqslant\pi$），称为直线 L 的方向角；$\{\cos\alpha, \cos\beta, \cos\gamma\}$称为直线 L 的方向余弦，三个方向余弦有以下关系

$$\cos^2\alpha+\cos^2\beta+\cos^2\gamma=1 \tag{1-1-2}$$

二、向量代数

（一）向量的概念

空间具有一定长度和方向的线段称为向量。以 A 为起点，B 为终点的向量，记作$\overrightarrow{AB}$，或简

记作$\vec{a}$。向量$\vec{a}$的长记作$|\vec{a}|$,又称为向量$\vec{a}$的模,两向量$\vec{a}$和$\vec{b}$若满足:①$|\vec{a}|=|\vec{b}|$,②$\vec{a}//\vec{b}$,③$\vec{a}$,$\vec{b}$指向同一侧,则称$\vec{a}=\vec{b}$。

与$\vec{a}$方向一致的单位向量记作$\vec{a}^0$,则$\vec{a}^0=\dfrac{\vec{a}}{|\vec{a}|}$。若$\vec{a}^0=\{\cos\alpha,\cos\beta,\cos\gamma\}$,也即为$\vec{a}$的方向余弦。

(二)向量的运算

1. 两向量的和

以$\vec{a}$、$\vec{b}$为边的平行四边形的对角线(见图1-1-2)所表示的向量$\vec{c}$,称向量$\vec{a}$与$\vec{b}$的和,记作

$$\vec{c}=\vec{a}+\vec{b} \tag{1-1-3}$$

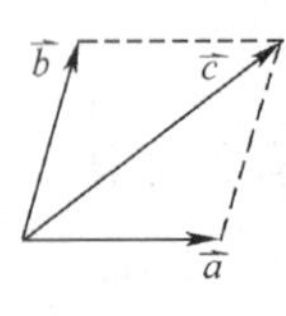

图 1-1-2

一般说,n个向量$\vec{a}_1,\vec{a}_2,\cdots,\vec{a}_n$的和可定义如下:先作向量$\vec{a}_1$,再以$\vec{a}_1$的终点为起点作向量$\vec{a}_2$,…,最后以向量$\vec{a}_{n-1}$的终点为起点作向量$\vec{a}_n$,则以向量$\vec{a}_1$的起点为起点、以向量$\vec{a}_n$的终点为终点的向量$\vec{b}$称为$\vec{a}_1,\vec{a}_2,\cdots,\vec{a}_n$的和,即

$$\vec{b}=\vec{a}_1+\vec{a}_2+\cdots+\vec{a}_n \tag{1-1-4}$$

2. 两向量的差

设$\vec{a}$为一向量,与$\vec{a}$的模相同,而方向相反的向量叫做$\vec{a}$的负向量,记作$-\vec{a}$,规定两个向量$\vec{a}$与$\vec{b}$的差为

$$\vec{a}-\vec{b}=\vec{a}+(-\vec{b}) \tag{1-1-5}$$

3. 向量与数的乘法

设λ是一个数,向量$\vec{a}$与λ的乘积$\lambda\vec{a}$规定为:

当$\lambda>0$时,$\lambda\vec{a}$表示一个向量,它的方向与$\vec{a}$的方向相同,它的模等于$|\vec{a}|$的λ倍,即$|\lambda\vec{a}|=\lambda|\vec{a}|$;

当$\lambda=0$时,$\lambda\vec{a}$是零向量,即$\lambda\vec{a}=\vec{0}$;

当$\lambda<0$时,$\lambda\vec{a}$表示一个向量,它的方向与$\vec{a}$的方向相反,模等于$|\vec{a}|$的$|\lambda|$倍,即$|\lambda\vec{a}|=|\lambda||\vec{a}|$。

4. 两向量的数量积

两向量的数量积为一数量,表示为

$$\vec{a}\cdot\vec{b}=|\vec{a}||\vec{b}|\cos(\widehat{\vec{a},\vec{b}}) \tag{1-1-6}$$

5. 两向量的向量积

两向量的向量积为一向量,记作$\vec{a}\times\vec{b}=\vec{c}$。

①$|\vec{c}|=|\vec{a}||\vec{b}|\sin(\widehat{\vec{a},\vec{b}})$,$|\vec{c}|$的几何意义为以$\vec{a}$、$\vec{b}$为边作出的平行四边形的面积;②$\vec{c}\perp\vec{a}$,$\vec{c}\perp\vec{b}$;③$\vec{c}$的正向按右手规则四个手指从$\vec{a}$以不超过$\pi$的角度转向$\vec{b}$,则大拇指的指向即为$\vec{c}$的方向。

6. 三个向量的混合积

$(\vec{a}\times\vec{b})\cdot\vec{c}$称为向量$\vec{a}$、$\vec{b}$、$\vec{c}$的混合积,记作$[\vec{a}\ \vec{b}\ \vec{c}]$,$|(\vec{a}\times\vec{b})\cdot\vec{c}|$的几何意义表示以$\vec{a}$、$\vec{b}$、$\vec{c}$为棱的平行六面体的体积。可推出,当向量$\vec{a}$、$\vec{b}$、$\vec{c}$共面时,混合积$[\vec{a}\ \vec{b}\ \vec{c}]=0$,即$(\vec{a}\times\vec{b})\cdot\vec{c}=0$。

(三)向量运算的性质($\vec{a}$、$\vec{b}$为向量,λ、μ为数量)

交换律

$\vec{a}+\vec{b}=\vec{b}+\vec{a}$,$\lambda\vec{a}=\vec{a}\lambda$,$\vec{a}\cdot\vec{b}=\vec{b}\cdot\vec{a}$

结合律

$(\vec{a}+\vec{b})+\vec{c}=\vec{a}+(\vec{b}+\vec{c}),(\lambda\mu)\vec{a}=\lambda(\mu\vec{a})$

$\lambda(\vec{a}\cdot\vec{b})=(\lambda\vec{a})\cdot\vec{b}=\vec{a}\cdot(\lambda\vec{b}),\lambda(\vec{a}\times\vec{b})=(\lambda\vec{a})\times\vec{b}=\vec{a}\times(\lambda\vec{b})$

分配律

$(\lambda+\mu)\vec{a}=\lambda\vec{a}+\mu\vec{a},\lambda(\vec{a}+\vec{b})=\lambda\vec{a}+\lambda\vec{b},(\vec{a}+\vec{b})\cdot\vec{c}=\vec{a}\cdot\vec{c}+\vec{b}\cdot\vec{c},(\vec{a}+\vec{b})\times\vec{c}=\vec{a}\times\vec{c}+\vec{b}\times\vec{c}$

向量的数量积满足交换律，即 $\vec{a}\cdot\vec{b}=\vec{b}\cdot\vec{a}$；

向量的向量积不满足交换律，即 $\vec{a}\times\vec{b}\neq\vec{b}\times\vec{a},\vec{a}\times\vec{b}=-\vec{b}\times\vec{a}$。

（四）向量在轴上的投影

给定向量$\overrightarrow{AB}$及 u 轴，过 A、B 点分别向 u 轴作垂直平面，与 u 轴交于 A_1、B_1，则有向线段$\overrightarrow{A_1B_1}$的值 A_1B_1 称为$\overrightarrow{AB}$在 u 轴上的投影，记作 $\mathrm{Prj_u}\,\overrightarrow{AB}$，向量的投影是一个数量。

设$\overrightarrow{AB}$与 u 轴的夹角为 α，则

$$\mathrm{Prj_u}\,\overrightarrow{AB}=|\overrightarrow{AB}|\cos\alpha$$

n 个向量的和在 u 轴上的投影为

$$\mathrm{Prj_u}(\vec{a}_1+\vec{a}_2+\cdots+\vec{a}_n)=\mathrm{Prj_u}\vec{a}_1+\mathrm{Prj_u}\vec{a}_2+\cdots+\mathrm{Prj_u}\vec{a}_n \qquad (1\text{-}1\text{-}7)$$

（五）向量的投影表示

设 $\vec{a}$ 的起点 A 坐标为 (x_1,y_1,z_1)，终点 B 坐标为 (x_2,y_2,z_2)，则 $\vec{a}=\overrightarrow{AB}=\{x_2-x_1,y_2-y_1,z_2-z_1\}$，记 $a_x=x_2-x_1,a_y=y_2-y_1,a_z=z_2-z_1$，$a_x$、$a_y$、$a_z$ 称为向量 $\vec{a}$ 在 x 轴、y 轴、z 轴上的投影。又设 $\vec{i}$、$\vec{j}$、$\vec{k}$ 依次为与 x、y、z 轴正向一致的单位向量，则

$$\vec{a}=a_x\vec{i}+a_y\vec{j}+a_z\vec{k}=(x_2-x_1)\vec{i}+(y_2-y_1)\vec{j}+(z_2-z_1)\vec{k} \qquad (1\text{-}1\text{-}8)$$

又可写成

$$\vec{a}=\{a_x,a_y,a_z\}=\{x_2-x_1,y_2-y_1,z_2-z_1\} \qquad (1\text{-}1\text{-}9)$$

式(1-1-8)又称为向量 $\vec{a}$ 按基本单位向量的分解式，式(1-1-9)又叫做向量 $\vec{a}$ 的坐标表示式。

（六）向量运算的坐标表示式

设 $\vec{a}=\{a_x,a_y,a_z\},\vec{b}=\{b_x,b_y,b_z\},\vec{c}=\{c_x,c_y,c_z\}$，则

$$\vec{a}\pm\vec{b}=\{a_x\pm b_x,a_y\pm b_y,a_z\pm b_z\}$$

$$\lambda\vec{a}=\{\lambda a_x,\lambda a_y,\lambda a_z\}$$

$$\vec{a}\cdot\vec{b}=a_xb_x+a_yb_y+a_zb_z$$

$$\vec{a}\times\vec{b}=\begin{vmatrix}\vec{i}&\vec{j}&\vec{k}\\a_x&a_y&a_z\\b_x&b_y&b_z\end{vmatrix}=\begin{vmatrix}a_y&a_z\\b_y&b_z\end{vmatrix}\vec{i}-\begin{vmatrix}a_x&a_z\\b_x&b_z\end{vmatrix}\vec{j}+\begin{vmatrix}a_x&a_y\\b_x&b_y\end{vmatrix}\vec{k} \qquad (1\text{-}1\text{-}10)$$

$$[\vec{a}\,\vec{b}\,\vec{c}]=(\vec{a}\times\vec{b})\cdot\vec{c}$$

$$=\begin{vmatrix}a_x&a_y&a_z\\b_x&b_y&b_z\\c_x&c_y&c_z\end{vmatrix}=\begin{vmatrix}b_y&b_z\\c_y&c_z\end{vmatrix}a_x-\begin{vmatrix}b_x&b_z\\c_x&c_z\end{vmatrix}a_y+\begin{vmatrix}b_x&b_y\\c_x&c_y\end{vmatrix}a_z$$

向量的模和方向余弦的坐标表示式：

设 $\vec{a}=\{a_x,a_y,a_z\}$，α、β、γ 为 $\vec{a}$ 的方向角，则 $|\vec{a}|=\sqrt{a_x^2+a_y^2+a_z^2}$，

$$\cos\alpha=\frac{a_x}{|\vec{a}|}=\frac{a_x}{\sqrt{a_x^2+a_y^2+a_z^2}}$$

$$\cos\beta=\frac{a_y}{|\vec{a}|}=\frac{a_y}{\sqrt{a_x^2+a_y^2+a_z^2}} \quad (1\text{-}1\text{-}11)$$

$$\cos\gamma=\frac{a_z}{|\vec{a}|}=\frac{a_z}{\sqrt{a_x^2+a_y^2+a_z^2}}$$

且满足 $\cos^2\alpha+\cos^2\beta+\cos^2\gamma=1$。

(七)两向量的夹角、平行与垂直坐标表示

设 $\vec{a}=\{a_x,a_y,a_z\}$，$\vec{b}=\{b_x,b_y,b_z\}$，则

$$\cos(\widehat{\vec{a},\vec{b}})=\frac{\vec{a}\cdot\vec{b}}{|\vec{a}||\vec{b}|}=\frac{a_xb_x+a_yb_y+a_zb_z}{\sqrt{a_x^2+a_y^2+a_z^2}\sqrt{b_x^2+b_y^2+b_z^2}}$$

$$0\leqslant(\widehat{\vec{a},\vec{b}})\leqslant\pi \quad (1\text{-}1\text{-}12)$$

$$\vec{a}/\!/\vec{b}\Leftrightarrow\vec{a}\times\vec{b}=\vec{0}\Leftrightarrow\vec{a}=\lambda\vec{b}\Leftrightarrow\frac{a_x}{b_x}=\frac{a_y}{b_y}=\frac{a_z}{b_z}$$

$$\vec{a}\perp\vec{b}\Leftrightarrow\vec{a}\cdot\vec{b}=0\Leftrightarrow a_xb_x+a_yb_y+a_zb_z=0$$

三、平面

(一)平面的一般方程

$$Ax+By+Cz+D=0$$

其中，平面法向量 $\vec{n}=\{A,B,C\}$。

(二)平面的点法式方程

过定点 (x_0,y_0,z_0)，以 $\vec{n}=\{A,B,C\}$ 为法线向量的平面方程为

$$A(x-x_0)+B(y-y_0)+C(z-z_0)=0$$

称为平面的点法式方程。

(三)平面的截距式方程

设 a,b,c 分别为平面在 x 轴、y 轴、z 轴上的截距，则平面方程为：

$$\frac{x}{a}+\frac{y}{b}+\frac{z}{c}=1 \quad (1\text{-}1\text{-}13)$$

该方程又称为平面的截距式方程。

(四)两平面的夹角(通常指锐角)

设两平面方程为

$$\pi_1 \qquad A_1x+B_1y+C_1z+D_1=0$$

$$\pi_2 \qquad A_2x+B_2y+C_2z+D_2=0$$

则两平面夹角 φ 的余弦为

$$\cos\varphi=\frac{|A_1A_2+B_1B_2+C_1C_2|}{\sqrt{A_1^2+B_1^2+C_1^2}\sqrt{A_2^2+B_2^2+C_2^2}} \quad (1\text{-}1\text{-}14)$$

两平面平行的充分必要条件为

$$\frac{A_1}{A_2}=\frac{B_1}{B_2}=\frac{C_1}{C_2}\neq\frac{D_1}{D_2} \quad (1\text{-}1\text{-}15)$$

两平面垂直的充分必要条件为

$$A_1A_2+B_1B_2+C_1C_2=0 \tag{1-1-16}$$

（五）三平面的交点

设三个平面方程为 $A_ix+B_iy+C_iz+D_i=0$（其中，$i=1,2,3$），若系数行列式 $D\neq 0$，则三平面有唯一交点，交点坐标即方程组的解。

（六）点到平面的距离

若平面方程为 $Ax+By+Cz+D=0$，平面外一点 $M(x_1,y_1,z_1)$，则点 M 到平面的距离为

$$d=\frac{|Ax_1+By_1+Cz_1+D|}{\sqrt{A^2+B^2+C^2}} \tag{1-1-17}$$

（七）点到直线的距离

设点 $M_0(x_0,y_0,z_0)$ 是直线 L 外的一点，$M_1(x_1,y_1,z_1)$ 是直线 L 上的任意取定的点，且直线 L 的方向向量为 $\vec{S}$，点 M_0 到直线 L 的距离为 d，设点 $M_0(x_0,y_0,z_0)$，L：$\frac{x-x_1}{m}=\frac{y-y_1}{n}=\frac{z-z_1}{p}$，则

$$d=\frac{|\overrightarrow{M_0M_1}\times\vec{S}|}{|\vec{S}|}=\left|\frac{\begin{vmatrix}\vec{i} & \vec{j} & \vec{k}\\ x_1-x_0 & y_1-y_0 & z_1-z_0\\ m & n & p\end{vmatrix}}{\sqrt{m^2+n^2+p^2}}\right| \tag{1-1-18}$$

四、空间直线

（一）空间直线的一般方程

设空间直线 L 由两个平面 π_1 和 π_2 的交线给出，设 π_1 和 π_2 的方程分别为 $A_1x+B_1y+C_1z+D_1=0$ 和 $A_2x+B_2y+C_2z+D_2=0$，则 L 的方程为

$$\begin{cases}A_1x+B_1y+C_1z+D_1=0\\ A_2x+B_2y+C_2z+D_2=0\end{cases} \tag{1-1-19}$$

（二）空间直线的点向式方程（或对称式方程）与参数方程

设直线 L 上一点 $M_0(x_0,y_0,z_0)$ 和它的一个方向向量 $\vec{S}=\{m,n,p\}$，则 L 的方程为

$$\frac{x-x_0}{m}=\frac{y-y_0}{n}=\frac{z-z_0}{p} \tag{1-1-20}$$

称为直线的点向式方程（或对称式方程）。

设 $\frac{x-x_0}{m}=\frac{y-y_0}{n}=\frac{z-z_0}{p}=t$，得到空间直线 L 的参数方程为

$$x=x_0+mt,y=y_0+nt,z=z_0+pt \tag{1-1-21}$$

在空间直线的点向式方程中，当 m、n、p 中有一个为 0，例如 $m=0$，而 n、$p\neq 0$ 时，则方程组应理解为 $x-x_0=0$，$\frac{y-y_0}{n}=\frac{z-z_0}{p}$。此时直线与 x 轴垂直。

当 m、n、p 中有两个为 0，例如 $m=n=0$，而 $p\neq 0$ 时，则方程组应理解为 $x-x_0=0$ 与 $y-y_0=0$ 联立。此时直线与 z 轴平行。

（三）两直线的夹角（通常指锐角）

设两直线的方程分别为 $\frac{x-x_1}{m_1}=\frac{y-y_1}{n_1}=\frac{z-z_1}{p_1}$，$\frac{x-x_2}{m_2}=\frac{y-y_2}{n_2}=\frac{z-z_2}{p_2}$，则两直线间夹角的余弦为

$$\cos\varphi=\frac{|m_1m_2+n_1n_2+p_1p_2|}{\sqrt{m_1^2+n_1^2+p_1^2}\sqrt{m_2^2+n_2^2+p_2^2}} \tag{1-1-22}$$

两条直线平行的充分必要条件为

$$\frac{m_1}{m_2}=\frac{n_1}{n_2}=\frac{p_1}{p_2} \tag{1-1-23}$$

两条直线垂直的充分必要条件为

$$m_1m_2+n_1n_2+p_1p_2=0$$

(四)两直线共面(平行或相交)的条件

设两直线的方程分别为

$$\frac{x-x_1}{m_1}=\frac{y-y_1}{n_1}=\frac{z-z_1}{p_1}$$

$$\frac{x-x_2}{m_2}=\frac{y-y_2}{n_2}=\frac{z-z_2}{p_2}$$

则它们共面的条件为

$$\begin{vmatrix} x_2-x_1 & y_2-y_1 & z_2-z_1 \\ m_1 & n_1 & p_1 \\ m_2 & n_2 & p_2 \end{vmatrix}=0 \tag{1-1-24}$$

(五)直线与平面的夹角

设平面 π 的方程为 $Ax+By+Cz+D=0$,直线 L 的方程为 $\frac{x-x_0}{m}=\frac{y-y_0}{n}=\frac{z-z_0}{p}$,则直线 L 和平面 π 间夹角 φ 的正弦为

$$\sin\varphi=\frac{|Am+Bn+Cp|}{\sqrt{A^2+B^2+C^2}\sqrt{m^2+n^2+p^2}} \tag{1-1-25}$$

直线与平面平行的条件为

$$Am+Bn+Cp=0 \tag{1-1-26}$$

直线与平面垂直的条件为

$$\frac{A}{m}=\frac{B}{n}=\frac{C}{p} \tag{1-1-27}$$

(六)空间曲线在坐标面的投影曲线方程

设空间曲线 C 的一般方程为

$$\begin{cases} F(x,y,z)=0 \\ G(x,y,z)=0 \end{cases}$$

空间曲线在坐标面上的投影得到的曲线,称为空间曲线在坐标面上的投影曲线。

空间曲线 C 在 xOy 平面上的投影曲线可表示为 $\begin{cases} H(x,y)=0 \\ z=0 \end{cases}$,其中方程 $H(x,y)=0$,由方程组 $\begin{cases} F(x,y,z)=0 \\ G(x,y,z)=0 \end{cases}$,消去字母 z 得到。$H(x,y)=0$ 又称为曲线 C 在 xOy 平面的投影柱面方程,$z=0$ 为 xOy 平面。

同理,消去方程组中变量 x 或变量 y,再分别和 $x=0$ 或 $y=0$ 联立,得到曲线 C 在 yOz 面或 xOz 面上的投影曲线方程。

$$\begin{cases}R(y,z)=0\\x=0\end{cases} \quad \text{或} \quad \begin{cases}T(x,z)=0\\y=0\end{cases}$$

五、柱面、锥面、旋转曲面、二次曲面

(一)柱面

动直线 L 平行于定直线并沿定曲线 C 移动形成的图形称为柱面,定曲线 C 叫做柱面的准线,动直线 L 叫做柱面的母线。只含 x、y 而缺 z 的方程 $F(x,y)=0$ 在空间直角坐标系中表示母线平行于 z 轴的柱面,其准线是 xOy 面上的曲线 $C:F(x,y)=0$。类似地,只含 x,z 而缺 y 的方程 $G(x,z)=0$ 和只含 y、z 而缺 x 的方程 $H(y,z)$ 分别表示母线平行于 y 轴和 x 轴的柱面。

(二)锥面

设直线 L 绕另一条与 L 相交的直线旋转一周,所得到的旋转曲面叫做圆锥面,两直线的交点叫做圆锥面的顶点,两直线的夹角 $\alpha(0<\alpha<\frac{\pi}{2})$ 叫做圆锥面的半顶角。

如圆锥面方程 $x^2+y^2=z^2$,锥面方程 $3x^2+4y^2=z^2$。

(三)旋转曲面

一条平面曲线绕其平面上的一条直线旋转一周所形成的曲面叫做旋转曲面,这条定直线叫做旋转曲面的轴。若 yOz 平面上曲线 L 的方程是 $f(y,z)=0$,将此曲线绕 Oy 轴旋转一周,得旋转曲面方程为 $f(y,\pm\sqrt{x^2+z^2})=0$,将此曲线绕 Oz 轴旋转一周,旋转曲面方程为 $f(\pm\sqrt{x^2+y^2},z)=0$(即绕某一个轴旋转,该变量坐标量不变,另一个变量改写为另两个变量平方和,再开方的形式)。如曲线 $L:\begin{cases}f(x,y)=0\\z=0\end{cases}$,绕 x 轴旋转一周产生的旋转面方程为 $f(x,\pm\sqrt{y^2+z^2})=0$,绕 y 轴旋转一周产生的旋转面方程为 $f(\pm\sqrt{x^2+z^2},y)=0$。

(四)二次曲面

三元二次方程所表示的曲面叫做二次曲面。常见的二次曲面有:

由方程 $\frac{x^2}{a^2}+\frac{y^2}{b^2}+\frac{z^2}{c^2}=1$ 所表示的曲面叫做椭球面(见图1-1-3a)。当 $a=b=c$ 时,方程 $x^2+y^2+z^2=a^2$ 表示的曲面叫做球面。

由方程 $\frac{x^2}{2p}+\frac{y^2}{2q}=z$($p$ 与 q 同号)所表示的曲面叫做椭圆抛物面(见图 1-1-3b)。

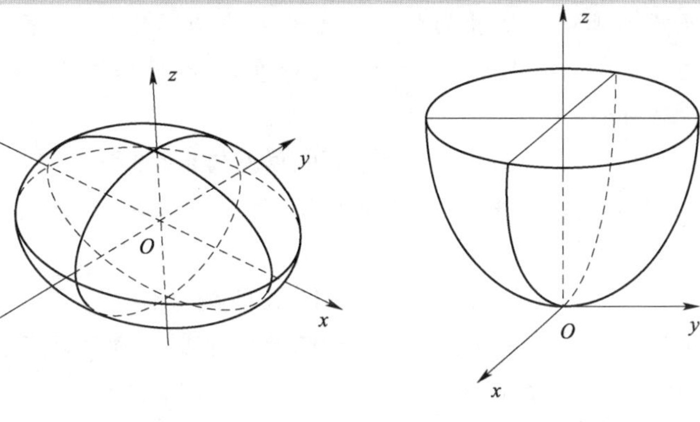

a)椭球面　　b)椭圆抛物面

图 1-1-3

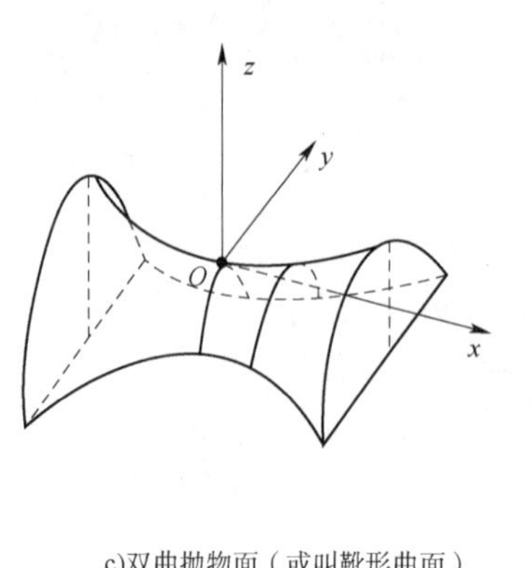

c)双曲抛物面（或叫靴形曲面）

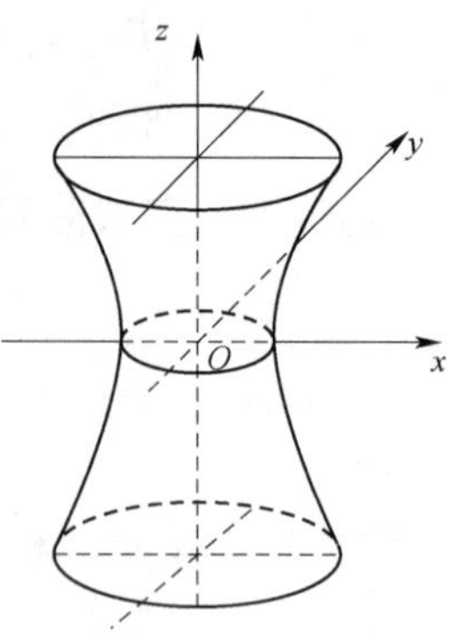

d)单叶双曲面

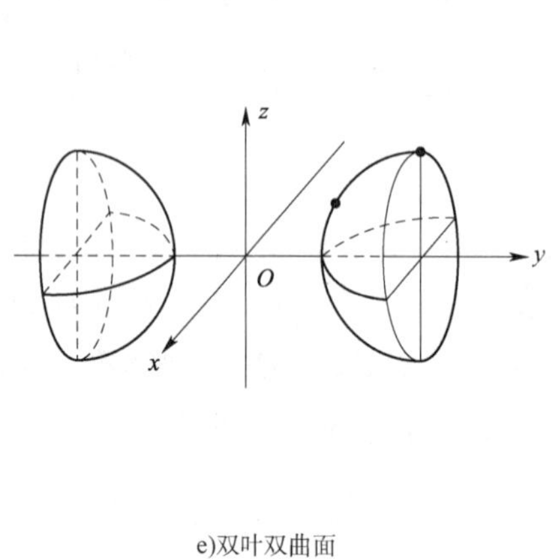

e)双叶双曲面

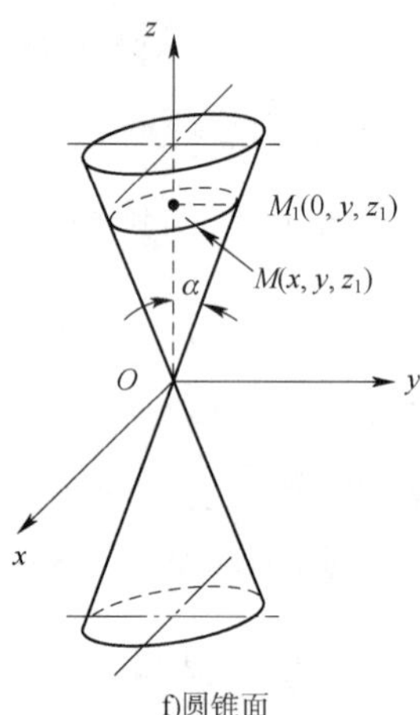

f)圆锥面

图 1-1-3

由方程$-\frac{x^2}{2p}+\frac{y^2}{2q}=z$($p$ 与 q 同号)所表示的曲面叫做双曲抛物面或鞍形曲面(见图 1-1-3c)。

由方程$\frac{x^2}{a^2}+\frac{y^2}{b^2}-\frac{z^2}{c^2}=1$($a,b,c$ 均不为 0)所表示的曲面叫做单叶双曲面(见图 1-1-3d)。

由方程$\frac{x^2}{a^2}-\frac{y^2}{b^2}+\frac{z^2}{c^2}=-1$($a,b,c$ 均不为 0)所表示的曲面叫做双叶双曲面(见图 1-1-3e)。

注:以上两式为双曲面标准式,等号左边两项正号、一项负号;等号右边+1 时是单叶双曲面,−1 时是双叶双曲面。曲面绕负项的轴。如等号左边两项负号、一项正号时,对等号两边均乘"−1",将等号左边变成两项正号、一项负号的标准式,再根据等号右边是"+1"或"−1"来判断是单叶还是双叶双曲面。

由方程 $z^2=a^2(x^2+y^2)(a\neq0)$所表示的曲面叫做圆锥面(见图 1-1-3f)。

【例 1-1-1】 设 $\vec{a},\vec{b}$ 向量互相平行,但方向相反,且$|\vec{a}|>|\vec{b}|>0$,则有:

A. $|\vec{a}+\vec{b}|=|\vec{a}|-|\vec{b}|$　　B. $|\vec{a}+\vec{b}|>|\vec{a}|-|\vec{b}|$

C. $|\vec{a}+\vec{b}|<|\vec{a}|-|\vec{b}|$　　D. $|\vec{a}+\vec{b}|=|\vec{a}|+|\vec{b}|$

解 由题设条件画出向量 $\vec{a}$、$\vec{b}$ 的示意图(见解图),根据向量的运算法则,两平行向量相加,取绝对值较大向量的方向。向量的模为绝对值较大向量的模减去绝对值较小向量的模。

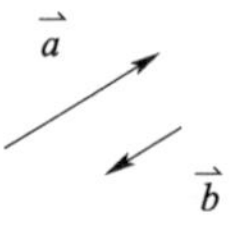

例 1-1-1 解图

答案:A

【例 1-1-2】 已知向量 $\vec{\alpha}=(-3,-2,1)$，$\vec{\beta}=(1,-4,-5)$，则 $|\vec{\alpha}\times\vec{\beta}|$ 等于：

A. 0　　B. 6　　C. $14\sqrt{3}$　　D. $14i+15j-10k$

解 $\vec{\alpha}\times\vec{\beta}=\begin{vmatrix}\vec{i} & \vec{j} & \vec{k}\\ -3 & -2 & 1\\ 1 & -4 & -5\end{vmatrix}=14\vec{i}-14\vec{j}+14\vec{k}$

$|\vec{\alpha}\times\vec{\beta}|=\sqrt{14^2+14^2+14^2}=\sqrt{3\times14^2}=14\sqrt{3}$

答案：C

【例 1-1-3】 求过已知点 $M_0(4,-1,3)$ 且平行于直线 $\frac{x-3}{2}=\frac{y}{1}=\frac{z-1}{5}$ 的直线方程。

解 已知 $M_0(4,-1,3)$，$\vec{S}=\{2,1,5\}$

则直线方程

$$\frac{x-4}{2}=\frac{y+1}{1}=\frac{z-3}{5}$$

【例 1-1-4】 过 z 轴和点 $(1,2,-1)$ 的平面方程是：

A. $x+2y-z-6=0$　　B. $2x-y=0$　　C. $y+2z=0$　　D. $x+z=0$

解 如解图所示。取 z 轴的方向向量 $\vec{S}=\{0,0,1\}$，连接原点 $O(0,0,0)$ 和点 $M(1,2,-1)$ 的向量 $\overrightarrow{OM}=\{1,2,-1\}$，过 z 轴和 $\overrightarrow{OM}$ 的平面的法向量为

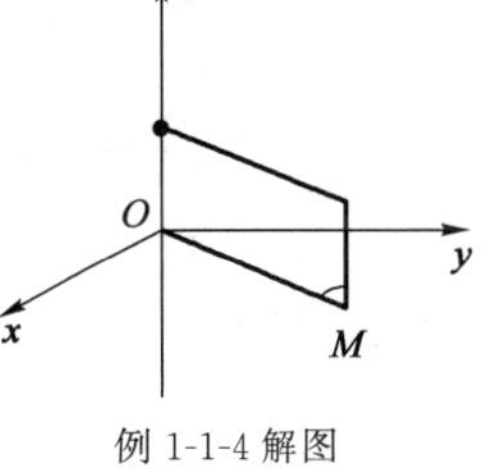

例 1-1-4 解图

$$\vec{n}=\begin{vmatrix}\vec{i} & \vec{j} & \vec{k}\\ 0 & 0 & 1\\ 1 & 2 & -1\end{vmatrix}=-2\vec{i}+\vec{j}$$

过 z 轴和点 $M(1,2,-1)$ 的平面方程为

$$-2(x-1)+(y-2)=0$$

化简得 $-2x+y=0$，即 $2x-y=0$。

答案：B

【例 1-1-5】 若向量 $\boldsymbol{\alpha}$，$\boldsymbol{\beta}$ 满足 $|\boldsymbol{\alpha}|=2$，$|\boldsymbol{\beta}|=\sqrt{2}$，且 $\boldsymbol{\alpha}\cdot\boldsymbol{\beta}=2$，则 $|\boldsymbol{\alpha}\times\boldsymbol{\beta}|$ 等于：

A. 2　　B. $2\sqrt{2}$　　C. $2+\sqrt{2}$　　D. 不能确定

解 $|\boldsymbol{\alpha}|=2$，$|\boldsymbol{\beta}|=\sqrt{2}$，$\boldsymbol{\alpha}\cdot\boldsymbol{\beta}=2$

由 $\boldsymbol{\alpha}\cdot\boldsymbol{\beta}=|\boldsymbol{\alpha}||\boldsymbol{\beta}|\cos(\widehat{\boldsymbol{\alpha\beta}})=2\cdot\sqrt{2}\cos(\widehat{\boldsymbol{\alpha\beta}})=2$

知 $\cos(\widehat{\boldsymbol{\alpha\beta}})=\frac{\sqrt{2}}{2}$，$(\widehat{\boldsymbol{\alpha\beta}})=\frac{\pi}{4}$

故 $|\boldsymbol{\alpha}\times\boldsymbol{\beta}|=|\boldsymbol{\alpha}||\boldsymbol{\beta}|\sin(\widehat{\boldsymbol{\alpha\beta}})=2\cdot\sqrt{2}\cdot\frac{\sqrt{2}}{2}=2$

答案：A

【例 1-1-6】 设空间直线的点向式方程为 $\frac{x}{0}=\frac{y}{1}=\frac{z}{2}$，则该直线过原点且：

A. 垂直于 Ox 轴　　B. 垂直于 Oy 轴，但不平行于 Ox 轴

C. 垂直于 Oz 轴但不平行于 Ox 轴　　D. 平行于 Ox 轴

解　由直线的点向式方程可知，直线过原点，方向向量 $\vec{S}=\{0,1,2\}$，方向向量在 x 轴的投影为 0，所以空间直线过原点且垂直于 Ox 轴。

答案：A

【例 1-1-7】　过直线 $L_1:\dfrac{x+1}{1}=\dfrac{y-2}{2}=\dfrac{z+3}{1}$ 和直线 $L_2:\begin{cases}x=-t+3\\y=-2t-1\\z=-t+1\end{cases}$ 的平面方程是：

A. $x+y-1=0$　　B. $-x+z+2=0$

C. $x+2y-z=0$　　C. $2x+2z-1=0$

解　解题时，对于直线方程应考虑它的方向向量，对于平面要考虑它的法向量，切记！

已知直线 L_1 的方向向量 $\vec{S_1}=\{1,2,1\}$，直线 $L_2:\begin{cases}x=-t+3\\y=-2t-1\\z=-t+1\end{cases}$ 可化为 $\dfrac{x-3}{-1}=\dfrac{y+1}{-2}=\dfrac{z-1}{-1}$，其方向向量 $\vec{S_2}=\{-1,-2,-1\}$，因 $\vec{S_1}$、$\vec{S_2}$ 坐标成比例，故 $L_1 /\!/ L_2$。分别在 L_1、L_2 上取点 $M_1(-1,2,-3)$，$M_2(3,-1,1)$，$\overrightarrow{M_1M_2}=\{4,-3,4\}$，所求平面的法向量 $\vec{n}\perp L_1$，$\vec{n}\perp\overrightarrow{M_1M_2}$，法向量

$\vec{n}=\begin{vmatrix}\vec{i} & \vec{j} & \vec{k}\\1 & 2 & 1\\4 & -3 & 4\end{vmatrix}=11\vec{i}-0\vec{j}-11\vec{k}$，可取 $\vec{n}=\{1,0,-1\}$。

已知 $M_1(-1,2,-3)$，$\vec{n}=\{1,0,-1\}$，则平面方程为

$$1(x+1)+0(y-2)-1(z+3)=0$$

即 $-x+z+2=0$

答案：B

【例 1-1-8】　已知直线 L_1 方程 $\dfrac{x-1}{1}=\dfrac{y}{-4}=\dfrac{z+3}{1}$，直线 L_2 方程，$\begin{cases}x=2t\\y=-2t-2\\z=-t\end{cases}$ 则这两条直线的夹角为：

A. $\dfrac{\pi}{3}$　　B. $\dfrac{\pi}{4}$　　C. 0　　D. $\dfrac{\pi}{2}$

解　L_1 的方向向量 $\vec{S_1}=\{1,-4.1\}$

L_2 写成点向式方程 $\dfrac{x}{2}=\dfrac{y+2}{-2}=\dfrac{z}{-1}=t$

$$\vec{S_2}=\{2,-2,-1\}$$

两直线的夹角通常指交成的锐角，设 L_1 和 L_2 的夹角为 φ，由计算公式

$$\cos\varphi=\frac{|1\times2+(-4)\times(-2)+1\times(-1)|}{\sqrt{1^2+(-4)^2+1^2}\sqrt{2^2+(-2)^2+(-1)^2}}=\frac{1}{\sqrt{2}}$$

得 $\varphi=\dfrac{\pi}{4}$

答案：B

【例 1-1-9】 设平面 π 的方程为 $3x-4y-5z-2=0$，以下选项中错误的是：

A. 平面 π 过点 $(-1,0,-1)$

B. 平面 π 的法向量为 $-3\vec{i}+4\vec{j}+5\vec{k}$

C. 平面 π 在 z 轴的截距是 $-\dfrac{2}{5}$

D. 平面 π 与平面 $-2x-y-2z+2=0$ 垂直

解 逐一验证选项 A、B、C 正确。

验证 D，两平面法向量为：$\vec{n_1}=\{3,-4,-5\}$，$\vec{n_2}=\{-2,-1,-2\}$。由条件知两平面垂直，那么两平面的法线向量也垂直，则 $\vec{n_1}\cdot\vec{n_2}=0$，但 $\vec{n_1}\cdot\vec{n_2}=-6+4+10=8\neq0$，选项 D 错误。

答案：D

【例 1-1-10】 已知直线 L：$\dfrac{x}{3}=\dfrac{y+1}{-1}=\dfrac{z-3}{2}$，平面 π：$-2x+2y+z-1=0$，则：

A. L 与 π 垂直相交　　B. L 平行于 π，但 L 不在 π 上

C. L 与 π 非垂直相交　　D. L 在 π 上

解 $\vec{S}=\{3,-1,2\}$，$\vec{n}=\{-2,2,1\}$，$\vec{S}\cdot\vec{n}\neq0$，$\vec{S}$ 与 $\vec{n}$ 不垂直。

故直线 L 不平行于平面 π，从而选项 B、D 不成立；又因为 $\vec{S}$ 不平行于 $\vec{n}$，所以 L 不垂直于平面 π，选项 A 不成立。即直线 L 与平面 π 非垂直相交。

答案：C

【例 1-1-11】 方程 $y^2+z^2-4x+8=0$ 表示：

A. 单叶双曲面　　B. 双叶双曲面

C. 锥面　　D. 旋转抛物面

解 将方程变形得 $y^2+z^2=4(x-2)$，而 $y^2+z^2=4x$ 表示顶点在 $(0,0,0)$，曲线 $y^2=4x$ 或 $z^2=4x$ 绕 x 轴旋转，得到的旋转抛物面，可知方程 $y^2+z^2=4(x-2)$ 为顶点在 $(2,0,0)$ 绕 x 轴旋转所得的旋转抛物面（见解图）。

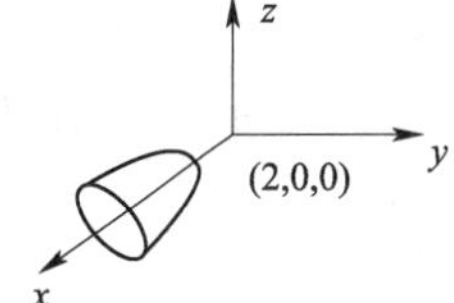

例 1-1-11 解图

答案：D

注：判断空间曲面的方法还可以使用截痕法（即可以令某一个坐标量 $z=0$，则可以观察图像在 xOy 平面上的投影，以此来判断整体图像的趋势），这不需要强行记忆上述公式，但需要较强的平面解析几何的功底，具体应用见后面的例题评注。

【例 1-1-12】 下列方程中代表锥面的是：

A. $\dfrac{x^2}{3}+\dfrac{y^2}{2}-z^2=0$　　B. $\dfrac{x^2}{3}-\dfrac{y^2}{2}-z^2=1$

C. $\dfrac{x^2}{3}+\dfrac{y^2}{2}-z^2=1$　　D. $\dfrac{x^2}{3}+\dfrac{y^2}{2}+z^2=1$

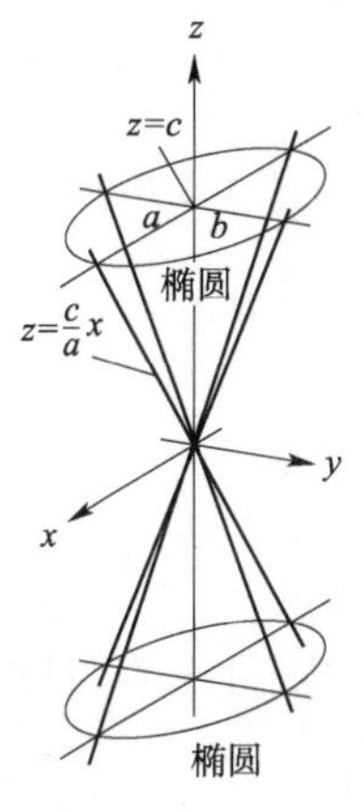

例 1-1-12 解图

解 选项 A 等号左边两项正项、一项负项，等号右边为 0，是锥面（见注）。

选项 D 等号左边三项均为正项，等号右边为 1 或其他正数，是椭球面。如等号右边为 0，就是一个点了。

将选项 B 等号两边均乘以"-1"，变成双曲面的标准式，等号右边变成"-1"，可以看出，选项 B 为双叶双曲面（绕 x 轴），选项 C 为单叶双曲面（绕 z 轴）。

答案:A

注:本题可以采用截痕法,在选项 A 中,令 $z=0$,可以看出,方程变为 $\frac{x^2}{3}+\frac{y^2}{2}=0$,这在 xOy 平面上是一个点,若令 $z=c$,c 为非零常数,则方程变为椭圆。再令 $x=0$,则方程变成 $\frac{y^2}{2}-z^2=0$,或者 $y=\pm\sqrt{2}z$,这是在 yOz 平面上从原点出发的两条对称直线,$y=0$ 亦是如此。由此看来,这就是一个椭圆锥曲面,故选 A,其他选项类似做法,如解图所示。

习　题

1-1-1　设 $\vec{\alpha}=\vec{i}+2\vec{j}+3\vec{k}$,$\vec{\beta}=\vec{i}-3\vec{j}-2\vec{k}$,与 $\vec{\alpha}$,$\vec{\beta}$ 都垂直的单位向量为(　　)。

A. $\pm(\vec{i}+\vec{j}-\vec{k})$　　B. $\pm\frac{1}{\sqrt{3}}(\vec{i}-\vec{j}+\vec{k})$

C. $\pm\frac{1}{\sqrt{3}}(-\vec{i}+\vec{j}+\vec{k})$　　D. $\pm\frac{1}{\sqrt{3}}(\vec{i}+\vec{j}-\vec{k})$

1-1-2　已知 $|\vec{a}|=1$,$|\vec{b}|=\sqrt{2}$,且 $(\widehat{\vec{a},\vec{b}})=\frac{\pi}{4}$,则 $|\vec{a}+\vec{b}|$ 等于(　　)。

A. 1　　B. $1+\sqrt{2}$　　C. 2　　D. $\sqrt{5}$

1-1-3　设 $\vec{a}$,$\vec{b}$,$\vec{c}$ 均为向量,下列等式中正确的是(　　)。

A. $(\vec{a}+\vec{b})\cdot(\vec{a}-\vec{b})=|\vec{a}|^2-|\vec{b}|^2$　　B. $\vec{a}(\vec{a}\cdot\vec{b})=|\vec{a}|^2\vec{b}$

C. $(\vec{a}\cdot\vec{b})^2=|\vec{a}|^2|\vec{b}|^2$　　D. $(\vec{a}+\vec{b})\times(\vec{a}-\vec{b})=\vec{a}\times\vec{a}-\vec{b}\times\vec{b}$

1-1-4　已知两条空间直线 L_1:$\begin{cases}3x+z=4\\y+2z=9\end{cases}$,$L_2$:$\begin{cases}6x-y=7\\3y+6z=1\end{cases}$,这两直线的关系为(　　)。

A. 平行但不重合　　B. 重合

C. 垂直　　D. 相交但不垂直

1-1-5　直线 L:$\frac{x+3}{2}=\frac{y+4}{1}=\frac{z}{3}$ 与平面 π:$4x-2y-2z=3$ 的位置关系为(　　)。

A. 相互平行　　B. L 在 π 上

C. 垂直相交　　D. 相交但不垂直

1-1-6　过点 $M_0(2,1,3)$ 且与直线 L:$\frac{x+1}{3}=\frac{y-1}{2}=\frac{z}{-1}$ 垂直相交的直线方程是(　　)。

A. $\frac{x-2}{-\frac{12}{7}}=\frac{y-1}{\frac{5}{7}}=\frac{z-3}{-\frac{24}{7}}$　　B. $\frac{x-2}{3}=\frac{y-1}{-2}=\frac{z-3}{4}$

C. $\frac{x-2}{2}=\frac{y-1}{-1}=\frac{z-3}{4}$　　D. $\frac{x-2}{3}=\frac{y-1}{-1}=\frac{z-3}{4}$

1-1-7　过点 $M(3,-2,1)$ 且与直线 L:$\begin{cases}x-y-z+1=0\\2x+y-3z+4=0\end{cases}$ 平行的直线方程是(　　)。

A. $\frac{x-3}{1}=\frac{y+2}{-1}=\frac{z-1}{-1}$　　B. $\frac{x-3}{2}=\frac{y+2}{1}=\frac{z-1}{-3}$

C. $\frac{x-3}{4}=\frac{y+2}{-1}=\frac{z-1}{3}$　　D. $\frac{x-3}{4}=\frac{y+2}{1}=\frac{z-1}{3}$

1-1-8　球面 $x^2+y^2+(z+3)^2=25$ 与平面 $z=1$ 的交线是(　　)。

A. $x^2+y^2=9$　　B. $x^2+y^2+(z-1)^2=9$

C. $\begin{cases} x=3\cos t \\ y=3\sin t \end{cases}$　　D. $\begin{cases} x^2+y^2=9 \\ z=1 \end{cases}$

1-1-9　已知平面 π 过点 $(1,1,0)$,$(0,0,1)$,$(0,1,1)$,则与平面 π 垂直且过点 $(1,1,1)$ 的直线的对称式方程为(　　)。

A. $\frac{x-1}{1}=\frac{y-1}{0}=\frac{z-1}{1}$　　B. $\frac{x-1}{-2}=\frac{y-1}{0}=\frac{z-1}{1}$

C. $\frac{x-1}{1}=\frac{z-1}{1}$　　D. $\frac{x-1}{1}=\frac{y-1}{0}=\frac{z-1}{-1}$

1-1-10　将椭圆 $\begin{cases} \frac{x^2}{9}+\frac{z^2}{4}=1 \\ y=0 \end{cases}$,绕 x 轴旋转一周所生成的旋转曲面的方程是(　　)。

A. $\frac{x^2}{9}+\frac{y^2}{9}+\frac{z^2}{4}=1$　　B. $\frac{x^2}{9}+\frac{z^2}{4}=1$

C. $\frac{x^2}{9}+\frac{y^2}{4}+\frac{z^2}{4}=1$　　D. $\frac{x^2}{9}+\frac{y^2}{4}+\frac{z^2}{9}=1$

1-1-11　母线平行 x 轴且通过曲线 $\begin{cases} 2x^2+y^2+z^2=16 \\ x^2-y^2+z^2=0 \end{cases}$ 的柱面方程是(　　)。

A. 椭圆柱面 $3x^2+2z^2=16$　　B. 椭圆柱面 $x^2+2y^2=16$

C. 双曲柱面 $3y^2-z^2=16$　　D. 抛物柱面 $3y^2-z=16$

1-1-12　直线 L_0:$\frac{x-1}{3}=\frac{y-2}{2}=\frac{z-3}{1}$ 在 xOy 平面上的投影直线方程为(　　)。

A. $\begin{cases} 2x+3y+4=0 \\ z=0 \end{cases}$　　B. $\begin{cases} 2x-3y+4=0 \\ z=0 \end{cases}$

C. $\begin{cases} y-2z+4=0 \\ z=0 \end{cases}$　　D. $\begin{cases} y+2z-4=0 \\ z=0 \end{cases}$

第二节　一元函数微分学

一、函数

(一)函数定义

设 X 与 Y 是实数的两个集合,若按照某规律(法则)对于每一个 $x\in X$,有唯一的数 $y\in Y$ 与之对应,则称在集合 X 上定义了一个单值函数,记为 $y=f(x)$。如果对于 x 的每一个值对应着多个 y 值,则称这种函数为多值函数。对应规律和定义域是函数的两大要素。函数定义域的确定:解析式表示的函数的定义域是使解析式中每一种运算都有意义的自变量 x 取值范围,实际问题可根据实际问题的性质来确定。

(二)基本初等函数,初等函数,分段函数

幂函数、指数函数、对数函数、三角函数、反三角函数及常数统称为基本初等函数。

由基本初等函数经过有限次的四则运算和有限次复合且用一个式子表示的函数称为初等函数。

分段函数也满足函数定义，它是由几个式子表示的，当自变量取一部分值时，函数由一个式子表示，当自变量取另一部分值时，函数由另一个式子表示。

（三）函数的几何特性

1. 函数的单调性

设函数 $f(x)$ 在区间 I 上有定义，若对于任意 x_1、$x_2\in I$，当 $x_1<x_2$ 时，都有 $f(x_1)<f(x_2)$ [或 $f(x_1)>f(x_2)$] 成立，则称函数 $f(x)$ 在区间 I 上单调增加（或单调减少）。

2. 函数的有界性

设函数 $f(x)$ 在区间 I 上有定义，若存在正数 M，使得对任何 $x\in I$，都有 $|f(x)|\leqslant M$ 成立，则称 $f(x)$ 在区间 I 上有界。若这样的 M 不存在，则称 $f(x)$ 在 I 上无界。

3. 函数的奇偶性

设函数 $f(x)$ 的定义域 D 是关于原点对称的，若 $x\in D$，$-x\in D$，对任何 $x\in D$，有 $f(-x)=f(x)$ 成立，则称 $f(x)$ 为偶函数；若对上述 x 有 $f(-x)=-f(x)$ 成立，则称 $f(x)$ 为奇函数。

4. 函数的周期性

设函数 $f(x)$ 的定义域为 D，若存在常数 $T\neq 0$，使得对于任何 $x\in D$，都有 $f(x+T)=f(x)$ 成立，则称 $f(x)$ 为周期函数，称满足上式的最小正数 T 为 $f(x)$ 的周期。

二、极限

极限是用来描述变量的变化趋势的，分为数列的极限、函数的极限。函数的极限又可根据 x 的变化趋势分为 $x\to x_0$ 和 $x\to\infty$ 两种。

（一）数列极限定义

数列 $\{x_n\}$，$\lim\limits_{n\to\infty}x_n=a$ 是指 $\forall\varepsilon>0$，$\exists N=N(\varepsilon)$，当 $n>N$ 时，有 $|x_n-a|<\varepsilon$ 成立。

（二）函数极限定义

函数极限 $\lim\limits_{x\to x_0}f(x)=A$ 是指 $\forall\varepsilon>0$，$\exists\delta=\delta(\varepsilon)>0$，当 $0<|x-x_0|<\delta$ 时，就有 $|f(x)-A|<\varepsilon$ 成立。

$\lim\limits_{x\to\infty}f(x)=A$ 是指 $\forall\varepsilon>0$，$\exists X>0$，当 $|x|>X$ 时，就有 $|f(x)-A|<\varepsilon$ 成立。

（三）函数 $f(x)$ 在 $x=x_0$ 的左右极限

若 $\lim\limits_{x\to x_0^+}f(x)=A$，称A为函数 $f(x)$ 在 $x\to x_0$ 时的右极限；若 $\lim\limits_{x\to x_0^-}f(x)=A$，称A为函数 $f(x)$ 在 $x\to x_0$ 时的左极限。

函数在一点的极限与其左右极限有以下关系

$$\lim_{x\to x_0}f(x)=A\Leftrightarrow\lim_{x\to x_0^+}f(x)=\lim_{x\to x_0^-}f(x)=A \tag{1-2-1}$$

（四）无穷大量、无穷小量

(1) 若 $\lim\limits_{x\to x_0(\text{或}\infty)}f(x)=0$，则称 $f(x)$ 是 $x\to x_0$（或 $x\to\infty$）时的无穷小量。

在同一极限过程中，函数的极限与无穷小量有如下关系

$$\lim f(x)=A\Leftrightarrow f(x)=A+\alpha(x) \tag{1-2-2}$$

其中 $\alpha(x)$ 为该极限过程中的无穷小量。

(2)无穷小量运算性质:有限个无穷小的和也是无穷小。有界函数与无穷小的乘积是无穷小。常数与无穷小的乘积是无穷小。有限个无穷小的乘积也是无穷小。

(3)若 $\lim\limits_{x\to x_0(\text{或}\infty)} f(x)=\infty$,则称 $f(x)$ 是 $x\to x_0$(或 $x\to\infty$)时的无穷大量。

(4)无穷大量与无穷小量的关系:在同一变化过程中,若 $\lim f(x)=0$,且 $f(x)\neq 0$,则 $\lim\dfrac{1}{f(x)}=\infty$;若 $\lim f(x)=\infty$,则 $\lim\dfrac{1}{f(x)}=0$。

(五)无穷小比较

(1)若在自变量的某一变化过程中 $\lim\alpha=0$,$\lim\beta=0$,如果 $\lim\dfrac{\beta}{\alpha}=0$,就称 β 是比 α 高阶的无穷小;如果 $\lim\dfrac{\beta}{\alpha}=\infty$,就称 β 是比 α 低阶的无穷小;如果 $\lim\dfrac{\beta}{\alpha}=c\neq 0$,就称 β 与 α 是同阶无穷小;如果 $\lim\dfrac{\beta}{\alpha}=1$,就称 β 与 α 是等价无穷小,记作 $\alpha\sim\beta$。

(2)等价无穷小量在求极限中的应用。设 $\alpha\sim\alpha'$,$\beta\sim\beta'$,且 $\lim\dfrac{\beta'}{\alpha'}$ 存在,则 $\lim\dfrac{\beta}{\alpha}=\lim\dfrac{\beta'}{\alpha'}$。求两个无穷小之比的极限时,分子及分母都可用等价无穷小来代替,如果用来代替的无穷小选得适当,可以使计算简化。

(3)在计算极限时常用的等价无穷小有,在 $x\to 0$ 时,$\sin x\sim x$,$\tan x\sim x$,$1-\cos x\sim\dfrac{1}{2}x^2$,$e^x-1\sim x$,$\ln(1+x)\sim x$,$\sqrt[n]{1+x}-1\sim\dfrac{1}{n}x$。

(六)在同一极限过程中有极限的函数具有的运算性质

设 $\lim f(x)=a$,$\lim g(x)=b$,则:

(1) $\lim[f(x)\pm g(x)]=\lim f(x)\pm\lim g(x)=a\pm b$。

(2) $\lim[f(x)g(x)]=\lim f(x)\cdot\lim g(x)=a\cdot b$。

$\lim kf(x)=k\lim f(x)=ka$(k 为常数)。

$\lim[f(x)]^n=[\lim f(x)]^n=a^n$($n$ 为正整数)。

(3) $\lim\dfrac{f(x)}{g(x)}=\dfrac{\lim f(x)}{\lim g(x)}=\dfrac{a}{b}(b\neq 0)$。

(4)若 $f(x)\geqslant 0$(或 $f(x)\leqslant 0$),且 $\lim f(x)=a$,则 $a\geqslant 0$(或 $a\leqslant 0$)。

(5)有极限的函数在该极限过程中有界。

(6)函数极限的唯一性。如果 $\lim f(x)$ 存在,那么这极限唯一。

(七)常用的求极限的方法

(1)利用极限与左右极限的关系,求分段函数在分界点处的极限。

(2)利用四则运算法则。

(3)利用极限存在准则:夹逼定理、单调有界数列必有极限。

(4)运用等价无穷小代替。

(5)利用无穷大量与无穷小量的关系。

(6)利用两个重要极限:$\lim\limits_{x\to 0}\dfrac{\sin x}{x}=1$,$\lim\limits_{x\to\infty}(1+\dfrac{1}{x})^x=e$ 或 $\lim\limits_{x\to 0}(1+x)^{\frac{1}{x}}=e$。

(7)利用公式

$$\lim_{x\to\infty}\frac{a_0x^n+a_1x^{n-1}+\cdots+a_n}{b_0x^m+b_1x^{m-1}+\cdots+b_m}=\begin{cases}\dfrac{a_0}{b_0} & n=m\\ \infty & n>m\\ 0 & n<m\end{cases}$$

其中，m，n 为正整数，a_0，b_0 不等于 0。

(8)利用变量替换。

(9)利用初等函数的连续性。

(10)利用若 $\lim f(x)=A>0$，$\lim g(x)=B$，则 $\lim f(x)^{g(x)}=A^B$。

(11)运用洛必达法则求未定型的极限。

三、函数的连续性

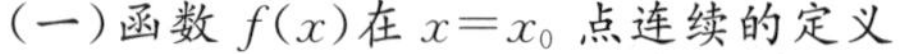

(一)函数 $f(x)$ 在 $x=x_0$ 点连续的定义

如果函数 $f(x)$ 在点 x_0 的某邻域有定义，若有 $\lim\limits_{x\to x_0}f(x)=f(x_0)$ 成立，则称 $f(x)$ 在 $x=x_0$ 处连续。还可以用增量来定义函数 $f(x)$ 在一点 x_0 的连续性，若有 $\lim\limits_{\Delta x\to 0}\Delta y=0$，其中 $\Delta x=x-x_0$，$\Delta y=f(x)-f(x_0)$，则称 $f(x)$ 在 x_0 处连续。

(二)函数 $f(x)$ 在 $x=x_0$ 点左、右连续性

若 $\lim\limits_{x\to x_0^+}f(x)=f(x_0)$ 或 $\lim\limits_{x\to x_0^-}f(x)=f(x_0)$，则称 $f(x)$ 在点 x_0 处右连续或左连续。函数 $f(x)$ 在 $x=x_0$ 点连续的充分必要条件为 $\lim\limits_{x\to x_0^+}f(x)=\lim\limits_{x\to x_0^-}f(x)=f(x_0)$。若 $f(x)$ 在区间 I 上每一点均连续(对区间端点应理解为左连续或右连续)，则称 $f(x)$ 在 I 上连续。

(三)连续函数的性质

(1)连续函数的和、差、积、商(分母不为零时)，仍为连续函数。

(2)连续函数的复合函数仍为连续函数。

(3)初等函数在其定义域内是连续的。

(四)函数的间断点及间断点的类型

若 $f(x)$ 在点 x_0 处不连续，则称 x_0 为 $f(x)$ 的一个间断点。当 $f(x)$ 在间断点 x_0 处左、右极限存在时，称 x_0 为第一类间断点。并称左右极限存在且相等的第一类间断点为可去间断点，称左右极限存在但不相等的第一类间断点为跳跃间断点；当 $f(x)$ 在间断点 x_0 处左右极限至少有一个不存在时，称 x_0 为第二类间断点。

第一类间断点又可细分为跳跃间断点和可去间断点，第二类间断点又可细分为无穷间断点和振荡间断点。

(五)闭区间 $[a,b]$ 上连续函数的性质

(1)根存在定理：若 $f(x)$ 在 $[a,b]$ 连续，且 $f(a)\cdot f(b)<0$，则至少存在一点 $x_0\in(a,b)$，使 $f(x_0)=0$。

(2)介值定理：若 $f(x)$ 在 $[a,b]$ 上连续且 $f(a)\neq f(b)$，对任意的数 c，$\min\{f(a),f(b)\}<c<\max\{f(a),f(b)\}$，则至少存在一点 $x_0\in(a,b)$，使得 $f(x_0)=c$。

(3)最值定理：若 $f(x)$ 在 $[a,b]$ 上连续，则 $f(x)$ 在 $[a,b]$ 上一定可取得最大值和最小值。

(4)有界性定理：闭区间上连续函数必有界。

【例 1-2-1】 判定函数 $f(x)=\ln(x+\sqrt{x^2+1})$ 的奇偶性。

解 利用函数奇偶性定义判定

$$\begin{aligned}f(-x)&=\ln[-x+\sqrt{(-x)^2+1}]=\ln(-x+\sqrt{x^2+1})\\&=\ln\frac{x^2+1-x^2}{\sqrt{x^2+1}+x}=\ln\frac{1}{\sqrt{x^2+1}+x}=\ln(x+\sqrt{x^2+1})^{-1}\\&=-\ln(x+\sqrt{x^2+1})=-f(x)\end{aligned}$$

$f(-x)=-f(x)$，由定义可知函数是奇函数。

【例 1-2-2】 假设当 $x\to+\infty$ 时，$f(x)$，$g(x)$ 都是无穷大量，则当 $x\to+\infty$ 时，下列结论正确的是：

A. $f(x)+g(x)$ 是无穷大量　　B. $\frac{f(x)+g(x)}{f(x)g(x)}\to0$

C. $\frac{g(x)}{f(x)}\to1$　　D. $f(x)-g(x)\to0$

解 $\lim\limits_{x\to+\infty}\frac{f(x)+g(x)}{f(x)g(x)}=\lim\limits_{x\to+\infty}\frac{1}{g(x)}+\lim\limits_{x\to+\infty}\frac{1}{f(x)}=0$。

答案：B

【例 1-2-3】 设 $f(x)$ 为偶函数，$g(x)$ 为奇函数，则下列函数中为奇函数的是：

A. $f[g(x)]$　　B. $f[f(x)]$　　C. $g[f(x)]$　　D. $g[g(x)]$

解 本题考查奇偶函数的性质。当 $f(-x)=-f(x)$ 时，$f(x)$ 为奇函数；当 $f(-x)=f(x)$ 时，$f(x)$ 为偶函数。

方法 1：

选项 D，设 $H(x)=g[g(x)]$，则

$$H(-x)=g[g(-x)]\xlongequal[\text{奇函数}]{g(x)\text{为}}g[-g(x)]=-g[g(x)]=-H(x)$$

故 $g[g(x)]$ 为奇函数。

方法 2：

采用特殊值法，题中 $f(x)$ 是偶函数，$g(x)$ 是奇函数，可设 $f(x)=x^2$，$g(x)=x$，则选项 A、B、C 均是偶函数，错误。

答案：D

【例 1-2-4】 求极限 $\lim\limits_{n\to\infty}\frac{\sqrt[3]{n^2}\sin n!}{n+1}$

解 $\lim\limits_{n\to\infty}\frac{\sqrt[3]{n^2}\sin n!}{n+1}=\lim\limits_{n\to\infty}\frac{n^{\frac{2}{3}}}{n+1}\cdot\sin n!$

当 $n\to\infty$ 时，$\frac{n^{\frac{2}{3}}}{n+1}\to0$，$|\sin n!|\leqslant1$

故原式 $=0$。

【例 1-2-5】 若 $\lim\limits_{x\to1}\frac{2x^2+ax+b}{x^2+x-2}=1$，则必有：

A. $a=-1$，$b=2$　　B. $a=-1$，$b=-2$

C. $a=-1$，$b=-1$　　D. $a=1$，$b=1$

解 因为$\lim\limits_{x\to1}(x^2+x-2)=0$，

故$\lim\limits_{x\to1}(2x^2+ax+b)=0$，即 $2+a+b=0$，得 $b=-2-a$，代入原式：

$$\lim_{x\to1}\frac{2x^2+ax-2-a}{x^2+x-2}=\lim_{x\to1}\frac{2(x+1)(x-1)+a(x-1)}{(x+2)(x-1)}=\lim_{x\to1}\frac{2\times2+a}{3}=1$$

故 $4+a=3$，得 $a=-1$，$b=-1$。

答案：C

注：本题体现了极限法则的逆用思想，因为题中 $x\to1$ 时，分母极限为 0，则分子极限也是 0，比值极限才有可能等于 1，如果分子极限为非 0 常数，则比值极限一定是无穷大。

【例 1-2-6】 若 $\lim\limits_{x\to0}(1-x)^{\frac{k}{x}}=2$，则常数 k 等于：

A. $-\ln2$　　B. $\ln2$　　C. 1　　D. 2

解 $\lim\limits_{x\to0}(1-x)^{\frac{k}{x}}=2$

利用基本极限公式$\lim\limits_{x\to0}(1+x)^{\frac{1}{x}}=e$ 变形

因 $\lim\limits_{x\to0}(1-x)^{\frac{k}{x}}=\lim\limits_{x\to0}[1+(-x)]^{-\frac{1}{x}(-k)}=\lim\limits_{x\to0}\{[1+(-x)]^{\frac{1}{-x}}\}^{-k}=e^{-k}$

所以 $e^{-k}=2$，$k=-\ln2$

答案：A

注：本题体现了基本极限公式的用法，$(1+无穷小)^{无穷大}=e$，这里的无穷小和无穷大互为倒数(乘积为 1)，因此要拼凑它。

【例 1-2-7】 设 $f(x)=\dfrac{1+e^{\frac{1}{x}}}{2+3e^{\frac{1}{x}}}$，问 $x=0$ 是否为间断点，若是间断点，是什么类型的间断点？

解 因 $x=0$ 函数没有定义，所以 $x=0$ 是间断点。

又因

$$\lim_{x\to0^+}f(x)=\lim_{x\to0^+}\frac{e^{\frac{1}{x}}\left(\dfrac{1}{e^{\frac{1}{x}}}+1\right)}{e^{\frac{1}{x}}\left(\dfrac{2}{e^{\frac{1}{x}}}+3\right)}=\frac{1}{3}$$

$$\lim_{x\to0^-}f(x)=\lim_{x\to0^-}\frac{1+e^{\frac{1}{x}}}{2+3e^{\frac{1}{x}}}=\frac{1}{2}$$

左右极限存在但不相等，所以 $x=0$ 是第一类间断点，属跳跃间断点。

【例 1-2-8】 下列极限计算中，错误的是：

A. $\lim\limits_{n\to\infty}\dfrac{2^n}{x}\sin\dfrac{x}{2^n}=1$　　B. $\lim\limits_{x\to\infty}\dfrac{\sin x}{x}=1$

C. $\lim\limits_{x\to0}(1-x)^{\frac{1}{x}}=e^{-1}$　　D. $\lim\limits_{x\to\infty}\left(1+\dfrac{1}{x}\right)^{2x}=e^2$

解 选项 A：$\lim\limits_{n\to\infty}\dfrac{2^n}{x}\sin\dfrac{x}{2^n}=\lim\limits_{n\to\infty}\dfrac{\sin\dfrac{x}{2^n}}{\dfrac{x}{2^n}}$，设$\dfrac{x}{2^n}=t$，当 $n\to\infty$，$t\to0$，原式$=\lim\limits_{t\to0}\dfrac{\sin t}{t}=1$

选项 B：$\lim\limits_{x\to\infty}\dfrac{\sin x}{x}=\lim\limits_{x\to\infty}\dfrac{1}{x}\sin x=0$(无穷小量与有界函数的乘积为无穷小量)

注意：$\lim\limits_{x\to 0}\frac{\sin x}{x}=1$

同理可验证选项 C：由$\lim\limits_{x\to 0}(1+kx)^{\frac{1}{x}}=\lim\limits_{x\to 0}(1+kx)^{\frac{1}{kx}\cdot k}=e^k$，知$\lim\limits_{x\to 0}(1-x)^{\frac{1}{x}}=\lim\limits_{x\to 0}[1+(-1)x]^{\frac{1}{-x}(-1)}=e^{-1}$

选项 D：$\lim\limits_{x\to 0}\left(1+\frac{1}{x}\right)^{2x}=\lim\limits_{x\to\infty}\left[\left(1+\frac{1}{x}\right)^{x}\right]^{2}=e^2$

答案：B

【例 1-2-9】 设 $f(x)$是定义在$[a,b]$上的单调增函数，$x_0\in(a,b)$，则有：

A. $f(x_0-0)$存在，但 $f(x_0+0)$不一定存在

B. $f(x_0+0)$存在，但 $f(x_0-0)$不一定存在

C. $f(x_0-0)$、$f(x_0+0)$都存在，但$\lim\limits_{x\to x_0}f(x)$不一定存在

D. $\lim\limits_{x\to x_0}f(x)$存在

解 画出函数在$[a,b]$上单调递增的 4 种图形（见解图）。

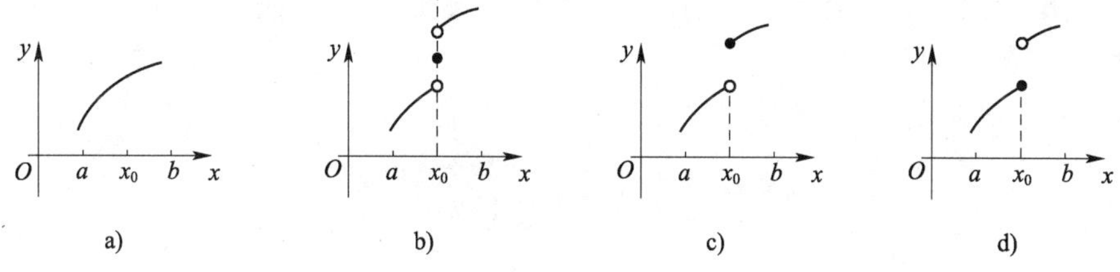

例 1-2-9 解图

通过对图形的分析，可知选项 C 正确。

答案：C

【例 1-2-10】 若$\lim\limits_{x\to\infty}\left(\frac{ax^2-3}{x^2+1}+bx+2\right)=\infty$，则 a 与 b 的值是：

A. $b\neq 0$，a 为任意实数　　B. $a\neq 0, b=0$

C. $a=1, b=0$　　D. $a=0, b=0$

解 通分，利用多项式的商在 $x\to\infty$时的结论得到

$$原式=\lim_{x\to\infty}\frac{ax^2-3+(bx+2)(x^2+1)}{x^2+1}=\lim_{x\to\infty}\frac{bx^3+(a+2)x^2+bx-1}{x^2+1}=\infty$$

仅需 x^3 项的系数不等于 0，即 $b\neq 0$，a 可以为任意实数。

答案：A

注：求有理多项式 $f(x)$极限时，若是讨论无穷大（$x\to\infty$），分子分母高次幂相等时，则观察高次幂的系数；若是讨论无穷小（$x\to 0$），低次幂相等时，看低次幂分子分母则观察低次幂的系数。例如：$\lim\limits_{x\to 0}\frac{ax+bx^2}{x}=2$，则 $a=2$ 且 b 为任意实数。

【例 1-2-11】 当 $x\to x_0$ 时，若 $f(x)$有极限，$g(x)$无极限，则下列结论正确的是：

A. $f(x)g(x)$当 $x\to x_0$ 时，必无极限

B. $f(x)g(x)$当 $x\to x_0$ 时，必有极限

C. $f(x)g(x)$当 $x\to x_0$ 时，可能有极限，也可能无极限

D. $f(x)g(x)$当 $x\to x_0$ 时，若有极限，则极限必为 0

解 举例说明：

(1)$\lim\limits_{x\to 0}x=0$，$\lim\limits_{x\to 0}\sin\dfrac{1}{x}$振荡无极限，而$\lim\limits_{x\to 0}x\sin\dfrac{1}{x}=0$(无穷小量乘有界函数的极限为0)。

(2)$\lim\limits_{x\to 0}x=0$，$\lim\limits_{x\to 0}\dfrac{1}{x^2}$无极限，$\lim\limits_{x\to 0}x\cdot\dfrac{1}{x^2}=\lim\limits_{x\to 0}\dfrac{1}{x}=\infty$无极限。

答案：C

四、导数与微分

(一)导数定义

设函数 $y=f(x)$在点 x_0 的某一邻域内有定义，当自变量 x 在点 x_0 给以增量 Δx(点 $x_0+\Delta x$ 仍在该邻域内)，设函数取得对应的增量 $\Delta y=f(x_0+\Delta x)-f(x_0)$。如果当 $\Delta x\to 0$ 时这两个增量的比的极限

$$\lim_{\Delta x\to 0}\frac{\Delta y}{\Delta x}=\lim_{\Delta x\to 0}\frac{f(x_0+\Delta x)-f(x_0)}{\Delta x} \tag{1-2-3}$$

存在，则称这个极限值为函数在点 x_0 的导数，并称函数在 x_0 可导或具有导数。若上述极限不存在，则称函数在 x_0 不可导。

函数 $y=f(x)$在点 x_0 的导数可记为

$$f'(x_0)=\lim_{\Delta x\to 0}\frac{f(x_0+\Delta x)-f(x_0)}{\Delta x} \tag{1-2-4}$$

也可记为 $y'\Big|_{x=x_0}$，$\dfrac{\mathrm{d}y}{\mathrm{d}x}\Big|_{x=x_0}$，$\dfrac{\mathrm{d}}{\mathrm{d}x}f(x)\Big|_{x=x_0}$。

用导数定义求函数 $f(x)$在 x_0 的导数还可用下式计算

$$f'(x_0)=\lim_{x\to x_0}\frac{f(x)-f(x_0)}{x-x_0} \tag{1-2-5}$$

(二)函数 $f(x)$在 $x=x_0$ 的单侧导数

$$f'_-(x_0)=\lim_{\Delta x\to 0^-}\frac{f(x_0+\Delta x)-f(x_0)}{\Delta x}\text{或}f'_-(x_0)=\lim_{x\to x_0^-}\frac{f(x)-f(x_0)}{x-x_0} \tag{1-2-6a}$$

$$f'_+(x_0)=\lim_{\Delta x\to 0^+}\frac{f(x_0+\Delta x)-f(x_0)}{\Delta x}\text{或}f'_+(x_0)=\lim_{x\to x_0^+}\frac{f(x)-f(x_0)}{x-x_0} \tag{1-2-6b}$$

分别称为函数 $f(x)$在 x_0 的左导数与右导数，统称为单侧导数。

函数 $f(x)$在 x_0 可导的充要条件是 $f'_+(x_0)=f'_-(x_0)$。

函数 $f(x)$在 x_0 可导，则函数在 x_0 点必连续；反之，不一定成立。

(三)$f(x)$在点 x_0 处的导数$f'(x_0)$的几何意义

导数 $f'(x_0)$几何意义表示曲线 $y=f(x)$在对应点(x_0,y_0)处的切线斜率。

已知函数 $y=f(x)$及其曲线上点(x_0,y_0)，则函数 $f(x)$在点(x_0,y_0)处的切线方程为

$$y-y_0=f'(x_0)(x-x_0)$$

法线方程为 $$y-y_0=-\frac{1}{f'(x_0)}(x-x_0)\qquad[f'(x_0)\neq 0]$$

函数在一点导数的物理意义为物体作变速直线运动，已知物体运动的距离 s 和时间 t 的函数：$s=s(t)$，导数 $s'(t_0)$表示物体在 t_0 时刻的瞬时速度。

（四）函数的导函数及求导函数公式

如果函数 $y=f(x)$ 在区间 (a,b) 内每一点都有导数，称这种对应关系所确定的函数为 $y=f(x)$ 的导函数，记为 $f'(x)$，y'，$\frac{dy}{dx}$，$\frac{d}{dx}f(x)$。即

$$f'(x)=\lim_{\Delta x\to 0}\frac{f(x+\Delta x)-f(x)}{\Delta x}\qquad x\in(a,b) \tag{1-2-7}$$

（五）常用的求导方法

1.利用导数的定义求导

特别是分段函数在交界点处的导数往往用在一点左、右导数定义计算。

2.利用基本导数公式表和导数的四则运算法则求导

基本导数公式：

$(c)'=0$ $\quad$ $(\ln x)'=\frac{1}{x}$

$(x^\mu)'=\mu x^{\mu-1}$ $\quad$ $(\arcsin x)'=\frac{1}{\sqrt{1-x^2}}$

$(\sin x)'=\cos x$ $\quad$ $(\arccos x)'=-\frac{1}{\sqrt{1-x^2}}$

$(\cos x)'=-\sin x$ $\quad$ $(\arctan x)'=\frac{1}{1+x^2}$

$(\tan x)'=\sec^2 x$ $\quad$ $(\text{arccot}\, x)'=-\frac{1}{1+x^2}$

$(\cot x)'=-\csc^2 x$ $\quad$ $(\text{sh}x)'=\text{ch}x$

$(\sec x)'=\sec x\tan x$ $\quad$ $(\text{ch}x)'=\text{sh}x$

$(\csc x)'=-\csc x\cot x$ $\quad$ $(\text{th}x)'=\frac{1}{\text{ch}^2 x}$

$(a^x)'=a^x\ln a$ $\quad$ $(\text{arsh}x)'=\frac{1}{\sqrt{1+x^2}}$

$(e^x)'=e^x$ $\quad$ $(\text{arch}x)'=\frac{1}{\sqrt{x^2-1}}$

$(\log_a x)'=\frac{1}{x\ln a}$ $\quad$ $(\text{arth}x)'=\frac{1}{1-x^2}$

函数和、差、积、商求导法则：

$$[f(x)\pm g(x)]'=f'(x)\pm g'(x)$$

$$[f(x)\cdot g(x)]'=f'(x)g(x)+f(x)g'(x)$$

$$\left[\frac{f(x)}{g(x)}\right]'=\frac{f'(x)g(x)-f(x)g'(x)}{[g(x)]^2}\qquad [g(x)\neq 0]$$

3.利用复合函数的求导法则求导

若 $u=\varphi(x)$ 在点 x 处可导，$y=f(u)$ 在相应点 u 处可导，则复合函数 $f[\varphi(x)]$ 在点 x 可导，且 $\frac{dy}{dx}=\frac{dy}{du}\cdot\frac{du}{dx}$ 或记为 $\{f[\varphi(x)]\}'=f'[\varphi(x)]\cdot\varphi'(x)$。

4. 反函数求导法

若 $y=f(x)$ 与 $x=\varphi(y)$ 互为反函数，$f(x)$ 在点 x 可导，$\varphi(y)$ 在相应点 y 处可导，且 $\frac{dx}{dy}=\varphi'(y)\neq 0$，则 $\frac{dy}{dx}=\frac{1}{\frac{dx}{dy}}$。

5. 参数方程求导法

设 $y=f(x)$ 的参数方程为 $x=\varphi(t)$，$y=\psi(t)$ 时，$\varphi(t)$ 与 $\psi(t)$ 均可导，$\varphi'(t)\neq 0$，则 $\frac{dy}{dx}=\frac{dy/dt}{dx/dt}=\frac{dy}{dt}\cdot\frac{dt}{dx}=\frac{\psi'(t)}{\varphi'(t)}$。

6. 隐函数求导法

若方程 $F(x,y)=0$ 确定了隐函数 $y=f(x)$，则由 $F[x,f(x)]=0$ 两边对 x 求导，并运用复合函数求导法则，就可求得 $f'(x)$。

对隐函数求导应熟练掌握。还可以应用多元函数隐函数的方法计算，可能更简单，见多元函数微分法。

7. 取对数求导法

求幂指函数或某些含有复杂的乘、除、乘方、开方运算函数的导数时，可以采用先取对数后求导的方法进行。[幂指函数：形如 $y=f(x)^{g(x)}$ 的函数]

8. 求函数的高阶导数

若 $f'(x)$ 在 (a,b) 内可导，则它的导数称为 $f(x)$ 的二阶导数。一般说来，$f(x)$ 的 $n-1$ 阶导数仍是 x 的函数，若它可导，则该导数称为函数 $f(x)$ 的 n 阶导数，记为 $y^{(n)}$，$f^{(n)}(x)$，$\frac{d^n y}{dx^n}$，$\frac{d^n f(x)}{dx^n}$。求 $y=f(x)$ 的 n 阶导数，可以利用求一阶导数的法则逐次地往下求导即可，但在计算过程中，要注意分析归纳，找出规律，写出 n 阶导数的表示式。

9. 参数方程的二阶导数

若方程 $x=\varphi(t)$，$y=\psi(t)$ 二阶可导，且 $\varphi'(t)\neq 0$。在求出一阶导数 $\frac{dy}{dx}=\frac{\psi'(t)}{\varphi'(t)}$ 后求二阶导数时，别忘乘 $\frac{dt}{dx}$，即 $\frac{d^2y}{dx^2}=\frac{d}{dx}\left(\frac{dy}{dx}\right)=\frac{d}{dt}\left[\frac{\psi'(t)}{\varphi'(t)}\right]\cdot\frac{dt}{dx}=\frac{\psi''\varphi'-\psi'\varphi''}{[\varphi'(t)]^3}$。

10. 隐函数的二阶导数

若 $F(x,y)=0$，求出一阶导数后，在求二阶导数时，把式中的 y 作为中间变量来求导，然后代入 y'，整理后得 y''。

（六）函数微分及微分公式

1. 微分定义

设函数 $y=f(x)$ 在某一区间 I 上有定义，x_0、$x_0+\Delta x$ 在 I 上，如果 $\Delta y=f(x_0+\Delta x)-f(x_0)$ 可表示为

$$\Delta y=A\Delta x+o(\Delta x) \tag{1-2-8}$$

其中 A 是不依赖于 Δx 的常数，$o(\Delta x)$ 为比 Δx 高阶的无穷小，则称 $f(x)$ 在点 x_0 可微。$dy=A\Delta x$ 称为 $f(x)$ 在点 x_0 处相应于自变量增量 Δx 的微分。$f(x)$ 在点 x_0 可微的充分必要条件是 $f(x)$ 在点 x_0 可导。记 $\Delta x=dx$，则 $dy=A\Delta x=f'(x_0)dx$。

函数 $y=f(x)$在任意点 x 的微分，称为函数的微分。记作 $dy=f'(x)dx$。

函数的微分就是求出函数$f'(x)$乘以 dx。函数的微分具有微分形式的不变性，即不论 u 是中间变量还是自变量，函数 $f(u)$的一阶微分都具有相同的形式，即 $df(u)=f'(u)du$。

2. 微分公式

$d(x^{\mu}) = \mu x^{\mu-1}dx$　　　　$d(e^{x}) = e^{x}dx$

$d(\sin x) = \cos x dx$　　　　$d(\log_a x) = \dfrac{1}{x\ln a}dx$

$d(\cos x) = -\sin x dx$　　　　$d(\ln x) = \dfrac{1}{x}dx$

$d(\tan x) = \sec^2 x dx$　　　　$d(\arcsin x) = \dfrac{1}{\sqrt{1-x^2}}dx$

$d(\cot x) = -\csc^2 x dx$　　　　$d(\arccos x) = -\dfrac{1}{\sqrt{1-x^2}}dx$

$d(\sec x) = \sec x\tan x dx$　　　　$d(\arctan x) = \dfrac{1}{1+x^2}dx$

$d(\csc x) = -\csc x\cot x dx$　　　　$d(\text{arccot}\, x) = -\dfrac{1}{1+x^2}dx$

$d(a^{x}) = a^{x}\ln a dx$

3. 函数和、差、积、商微分法则

$d(u\pm v) = du\pm dv$　　　　$d(cu) = cd(u)$　（c 为常数）

$d(uv) = vdu+udv$　　　　$d\left(\dfrac{u}{v}\right)=\dfrac{vdu-udv}{v^2}$

【例 1-2-12】　$y = 2^{\tan\frac{1}{x}}$，求 y'。

解　该题为复合函数求导，注意求导时要有从外到里层层剥开的思想。该题即为函数 $y=2^{\tan\frac{1}{x}}$，由 $y = 2^{u}, u = \tan V, V = \dfrac{1}{x}$ 复合而成，所以 $y' = (2^{u})'_{u}\cdot(\tan V)'_{V}\cdot\left(\dfrac{1}{x}\right)'$，即

$$y' = 2^{\tan\frac{1}{x}}\cdot\ln 2\cdot\sec^2\frac{1}{x}\cdot\left(-\frac{1}{x^2}\right)$$
$$=-\frac{\ln 2}{x^2}2^{\tan\frac{1}{x}}\cdot\sec^2\frac{1}{x}$$

【例 1-2-13】　$y=x^{\sin x}(x>0)$，求 y'。

解　本题属于幂指函数的求导问题，既不能使用幂函数的导数公式，也不能使用指数函数的导数公式。可利用对数求导法求解。即

$$\ln y = \sin x\ln x$$
$$\frac{1}{y}\cdot y' = \cos x\ln x+\frac{\sin x}{x}$$
$$y' = x^{\sin x}\left(\cos x\ln x+\frac{\sin x}{x}\right)$$

【例 1-2-14】　已知 $x^2+y^2-xy = 1$，求由方程确定的函数 y 的导数 y'。

解　**方法 1：**两边对 x 求导，求导时，把式中字母 y 看作 x 的函数。

$$2x+2y\frac{dy}{dx}-\left(y+x\frac{dy}{dx}\right)=0$$

$$2x + 2y\frac{dy}{dx} - y - x\frac{dy}{dx} = 0$$

$$(2y - x)\frac{dy}{dx} = y - 2x$$

$$\frac{dy}{dx} = \frac{y - 2x}{2y - x}$$

方法 2:利用二元方程确定的隐函数求导法则计算,这时先将原式写成 $F(x,y)=0$ 的形式。

$$x^2 + y^2 - xy - 1 = 0$$

设 $F(x,y) = x^2 + y^2 - xy - 1$,则

$$F_x = 2x - y, F_y = 2y - x$$

$$\frac{dy}{dx} = -\frac{F_x}{F_y} = -\frac{2x - y}{2y - x} = \frac{y - 2x}{2y - x}$$

注:用方法 2 求隐函数的导数显得简单,以后不妨用这种方法。

【例 1-2-15】 $y = \ln(x + \sqrt{x^2 - a^2})$,求$\frac{dy}{dx}$,$\frac{d^2y}{dx^2}$。

解 在计算一阶导数后,注意将其化为最简形式,再求二阶导数。

$$\frac{dy}{dx} = \frac{1}{x + \sqrt{x^2 - a^2}}\left(1 + \frac{x}{\sqrt{x^2 - a^2}}\right)$$

$$= \frac{1}{x + \sqrt{x^2 - a^2}} \cdot \frac{x + \sqrt{x^2 - a^2}}{\sqrt{x^2 - a^2}}$$

$$= \frac{1}{\sqrt{x^2 - a^2}}$$

$$\frac{d^2y}{dx^2} = -\frac{1}{2}(x^2 - a^2)^{-\frac{3}{2}} \cdot 2x$$

$$= -\frac{x}{(x^2 - a^2)^{\frac{3}{2}}}$$

【例 1-2-16】 设 $\begin{cases} x = e^{2t} \\ y = t - e^{-t} \end{cases}$,求$\frac{dy}{dx}$,$\frac{d^2y}{dx^2}$。

解 求参数方程的二阶导数$\frac{d^2y}{dx^2}$时,应在公式后面乘上 $\frac{dt}{dx}$ 一项。

$$\frac{dy}{dt} = 1 + e^{-t}, \frac{dx}{dt} = 2e^{2t}$$

$$\frac{dy}{dx} = \frac{\frac{dy}{dt}}{\frac{dx}{dt}} = \frac{1 + e^{-t}}{2e^{2t}} = \frac{1}{2}(e^{-2t} + e^{-3t})$$

$$\frac{d^2y}{dx^2} = \frac{d}{dt}\left(\frac{dy}{dx}\right) \cdot \frac{dt}{dx} = \frac{1}{2}(-2e^{-2t} - 3e^{-3t})\frac{1}{\frac{dx}{dt}}$$

$$= \frac{1}{2}(-2e^{-2t} - 3e^{-3t})\frac{1}{2e^{2t}} = -\frac{1}{2}e^{-4t} - \frac{3}{4}e^{-5t}$$

【例 1-2-17】 曲线 $y=x^3-6x$ 上切线平行于 x 轴的点是：

A. (0,0)　　B. $(\sqrt{2},1)$

C. $(-\sqrt{2},4\sqrt{2})$和$(\sqrt{2},-4\sqrt{2})$　　D. (1,2)和(-1,2)

解 切线平行 x 轴，即切线的斜率为0。

设曲线的切点坐标为(x_0,y_0)，则

$$y=x^3-6x,y'=3x^2-6,y'|_{x=x_0}=3x_0^2-6$$

令 $3x_0^2-6=0$，解得 $x_0=\pm\sqrt{2}$

所求切点坐标为$(\sqrt{2},-4\sqrt{2})$，$(-\sqrt{2},4\sqrt{2})$

答案：C

【例 1-2-18】 已知 $f(x)$是二阶可导函数，$y=e^{2f(x)}$，则$\frac{d^2y}{dx^2}$为：

A. $e^{2f(x)}$　　B. $e^{2f(x)}f''(x)$

C. $e^{2f(x)}[2f'(x)]$　　D. $2e^{2f(x)}[2(f'(x))^2+f''(x)]$

解 利用复合函数求导法则，题中 $f(x)$为 x 的二阶可导函数。

$$y'=(e^{2f(x)})'=2f'(x)e^{2f(x)}$$

$$y''=2[f''(x)e^{2f(x)}+f'(x)e^{2f(x)}\cdot 2f'(x)]=2e^{2f(x)}[2(f'(x))^2+f''(x)]$$

答案：D

【例 1-2-19】 设 $y=e^{\sin^2x}$，则 dy 为：

A. $e^x\mathrm{d}\sin^2x$　　B. $e^{\sin^2x}\mathrm{d}\sin^2x$

C. $e^{\sin^2x}\sin2x\mathrm{d}\sin x$　　D. $e^{\sin^2x}\mathrm{d}\sin x$

解 $\mathrm{d}y=y'\mathrm{d}x=e^{\sin^2x}\cdot2\sin x\cdot\cos x\mathrm{d}x=e^{\sin^2x}\cdot2\sin x\mathrm{d}\sin x=e^{\sin^2x}\mathrm{d}\sin^2x$

答案：B

五、微分中值定理

微分中值定理在研究函数中起着重要的作用，最重要的是拉格朗日中值定理，罗尔定理可看作它的特例，柯西定理是它的推广。

(一)罗尔定理

若 $f(x)$在$[a,b]$连续，在(a,b)内可导，且 $f(a)=f(b)$，则至少存在一点 $\xi\in(a,b)$，使$f'(\xi)=0$。

(二)拉格朗日中值定理

若 $f(x)$在$[a,b]$连续，在(a,b)内可导，则至少存在一点 $\xi\in(a,b)$，使得

$$f(b)-f(a)=f'(\xi)(b-a) \tag{1-2-9}$$

由拉格朗日中值定理可以证明：若 $f(x)$在区间 I 上的导数恒等于零，则 $f(x)$在 I 上为常数。

(三)柯西中值定理

若 $f(x)$，$F(x)$在$[a,b]$连续，在(a,b)内可导，且 $F'(x)\neq0$，则至少存在一点 $\xi\in(a,b)$，使得

$$\frac{f(b)-f(a)}{F(b)-F(a)}=\frac{f'(\xi)}{F'(\xi)} \tag{1-2-10}$$

(四)洛必达法则

若：(1) $\lim\limits_{x\to a(或\infty)}f(x)=\lim\limits_{x\to a(或\infty)}F(x)=0(或\infty)$；(2) $f'(x)$及 $F'(x)$在 $0<|x-x_0|<\delta$(或

$|x|>X$)处存在，且 $F'(x)\neq 0$，(3) $\lim\limits_{x\to a(\text{或}\infty)}\dfrac{f'(x)}{F'(x)}$存在(或$\infty$)，则

$$\lim_{x\to a(\text{或}\infty)}\frac{f(x)}{F(x)}=\lim_{x\to a(\text{或}\infty)}\frac{f'(x)}{F'(x)}=\text{存在(或}\infty\text{)} \tag{1-2-11}$$

满足以上条件的两个函数比的极限等于两个函数导数比的极限，在利用洛必达法则时，三个条件中有一条不满足就不能应用。对于未定型"$0\cdot\infty$"、"$\infty-\infty$"、"0^0"、"∞^0"、"1^∞"可化为"$\dfrac{0}{0}$"或"$\dfrac{\infty}{\infty}$"型的极限计算。在利用洛必达法则计算未定式的极限时，前面学过的计算极限的方法仍适用，例如等价无穷小替换，两个重要极限等。

(五)泰勒公式

若 $f(x)$在 x_0 的某一邻域(a,b)内具有 $n+1$ 阶导数，则$\forall x\in(a,b)$有下面式子成立

$$f(x)=f(x_0)+\frac{f'(x_0)}{1!}(x-x_0)+\cdots+\frac{f^{(n)}(x_0)}{n!}(x-x_0)^n+R_n(x) \tag{1-2-12}$$

该公式称为 $f(x)$的 n 阶泰勒公式，$R_n(x)$称为余项，其中 $R_n(x)$表达式为

$$R_n(x)=\frac{f^{(n+1)}(\zeta)}{(n+1)!}(x-x_0)^{n+1} \tag{1-2-13}$$

这里ζ是介于 x_0 与 x 之间的某个值。

在泰勒公式(1-2-12)中取 $x_0=0$，就得到工程中常用的麦克劳林公式

$$f(x)=f(0)+f'(0)x+\frac{f''(0)}{2!}x^2+\cdots+\frac{f^{(n)}(0)}{n!}x^n+R_n(x) \tag{1-2-14}$$

其中 $R_n(x)=\dfrac{f^{(n+1)}(\zeta)}{(n+1)!}x^{n+1}$，这里$\zeta$是介于 0 与 x 之间的某个值。

六、导数的应用

(一)判定函数的单调区间

设$y=f(x)$在区间(a,b)上可导，$\forall x\in(a,b)$，若$f'(x)>0$(或<0)[在个别点亦可$f'(x)=0$]，则 $f(x)$在区间(a,b)上严格单调增加(或减小)。

(二)求函数的极值

若函数 $f(x)$在点 x_0 的某一邻域内的任何点 x 恒有 $f(x)<f(x_0)$[或 $f(x)>f(x_0)$]，则函数 $f(x)$在点 x_0 有极大值(或极小值)，函数的极大值、极小值统称为函数的极值，点 x_0 为$f(x)$的极值点。函数的极值是局部的概念，在某一邻域内函数的极大(小)值不一定是函数在定义域内的最大(小)值。

极值存在的必要条件：若$f'(x_0)$存在，且 x_0 为 $f(x)$的极值点，则$f'(x_0)=0$。但逆命题不成立，即若$f'(x_0)=0$，但 x_0 不一定是函数 $f(x)$的极值点。导数为零的点称为函数的驻点。驻点以及连续但导数不存在的点称为函数可疑极值点。

极值存在的第一充分条件：设 $f(x)$在 x_0 的某一邻域内连续，且可导，若 $x<x_0$ 时，$f'(x)>0$[或$f'(x)<0$]；若 $x>x_0$ 时，$f'(x)<0$[或$f'(x)>0$]，则 $f(x)$在 x_0 取得极大值(或极小值)。对于连续但导数不存在的点的极值，同样要通过判定在该点两侧的导数符号来确定。

极值存在的第二充分条件：设$f(x)$具有二阶导数，且在x_0点$f'(x_0)=0$，若$f''(x_0)<0$

时，$f(x)$在 x_0 取得极大值，若 $f''(x_0)>0$ 时，$f(x)$在 x_0 取得极小值。

（三）函数的最大值、最小值

函数 $f(x)$在$[a,b]$上连续，则其在$[a,b]$上的最大值和最小值可通过比较端点、驻点、一阶导数不存在的点的函数值的大小来确定，即

$$f_{最大值}=\max\{f(a),f(b),f(x_1),f(x_2),\cdots,f(x_n)\}$$

$$f_{最小值}=\min\{f(a),f(b),f(x_1),f(x_2),\cdots,f(x_n)\}$$

其中，$x_1,x_2,\cdots,x_n$ 为 $f(x)$在$[a,b]$内的所有可能极值点。

在求解实际问题时，经常用到下面结论：若 $f(x)$在$[a,b]$上连续，且在(a,b)内只有唯一一个极值点 x_0，则当 $f(x_0)$为极大(小)值时，它就是 $f(x)$在$[a,b]$上的最大(小)值。

若 $f(x)$在$[a,b]$上单调增加(减少)，则 $f(a)$为其最小(大)值，$f(b)$为其最大(小)值。

（四）凹凸性，拐点

设 $f(x)$在$[a,b]$上连续，任给 $x_1,x_2\in(a,b)$恒有 $f(\frac{x_1+x_2}{2})>$(或$<$)$\frac{f(x_1)+f(x_2)}{2}$，则称$f(x)$在$[a,b]$上是凸(或凹)的。若曲线在 x_0 两旁凹凸性改变，则称点$(x_0,f(x_0))$为曲线的拐点。

函数凹凸性判别法则(充分条件)：设 $f''(x)$存在，若 $a<x<b$ 时，$f''(x)>0$ [或 $f''(x)<0$]在个别点 $f''(x)$可以为零，则曲线为凹(或凸)。

设 $f(x)$连续，若在点 x_0，$f''(x_0)=0$ 或 $f''(x_0)$不存在，且在 x_0 两侧 $f''(x)$改变符号时，则点$(x_0,f(x_0))$是拐点。

【例 1-2-20】 求 $\lim\limits_{x\to\infty}x(e^{\frac{1}{x}}-1)$。

解
$$原式\overset{\infty\cdot 0}{=}\lim_{x\to\infty}\frac{e^{\frac{1}{x}}-1}{\frac{1}{x}}\overset{\frac{0}{0}}{=}\lim_{x\to\infty}\frac{e^{\frac{1}{x}}(-\frac{1}{x^2})}{-\frac{1}{x^2}}=\lim_{x\to\infty}e^{\frac{1}{x}}=1$$

【例 1-2-21】 求 $\lim\limits_{x\to 0^+}x^{\sin x}$。

解
$$原式\overset{0^0}{=}\lim_{x\to 0^+}e^{\ln x^{\sin x}}=\lim_{x\to 0^+}e^{\sin x\ln x}=e^{\lim\limits_{x\to 0^+}\sin x\ln x}$$

因
$$\lim_{x\to 0^+}\sin x\ln x\overset{0\cdot\infty}{=}\lim_{x\to 0^+}\frac{\ln x}{\frac{1}{\sin x}}\overset{\frac{\infty}{\infty}}{=}\lim_{x\to 0^+}-\frac{\sin^2 x}{x\cos x}=-\lim_{x\to 0^+}\frac{x^2}{x\cos x}$$
$$=0\quad(x\to 0,\sin^2 x\sim x^2)$$

故
$$原式=e^0=1$$

【例 1-2-22】 求函数 $y=x^2e^{-x}$ 的单调区间、极值及此函数曲线的凹凸区间和拐点。

解 (1) $D:(-\infty,+\infty)$

(2) $y'=2xe^{-x}-x^2e^{-x}=xe^{-x}(2-x)$

$y''=2e^{-x}-2xe^{-x}-2xe^{-x}+x^2e^{-x}=e^{-x}(x^2-4x+2)$

(3) 令 $y'=0$，得 $x_1=0,x_2=2$

令 $y''=0$，得 $x_3=2-\sqrt{2},x_4=2+\sqrt{2}$

(4) 列表。

例 1-2-22 解表

x	$(-\infty,0)$	0	$(0,2-\sqrt{2})$	$2-\sqrt{2}$	$(2-\sqrt{2},2)$	2	$(2,2+\sqrt{2})$	$2+\sqrt{2}$	$(2+\sqrt{2},+\infty)$
y'	−	0	+	+	+	0	−	−	−
y''	+	+	+	0	−	−	−	0	+

函数在(0,2)单增,在$(-\infty,0)$与$(2,+\infty)$单减。

$$f_{极小}(0)=0,f_{极大}(2)=4e^{-2}$$

$(-\infty,2-\sqrt{2})$,$(2+\sqrt{2},+\infty)$为凹区间,$(2-\sqrt{2},2+\sqrt{2})$为凸区间,点$(2-\sqrt{2},(2-\sqrt{2})^2e^{\sqrt{2}-2})$,$(2+\sqrt{2},(2+\sqrt{2})^2e^{-(2+\sqrt{2})})$为拐点。

【例 1-2-23】 设$f(x)$在$(-\infty,+\infty)$上定义,且$x_0\neq0$是$f(x)$的极大值点,则有:

A. x_0是$f(x)$的拐点　　B. $-x_0$是$-f(-x)$的极小值点

C. $-x_0$是$-f(x)$的极小值点　　D. $f(x_0)>f(x)(-\infty<x<+\infty)$

解 设$x_0>0$,$f(x_0)>0$,画出下列几个示意图。

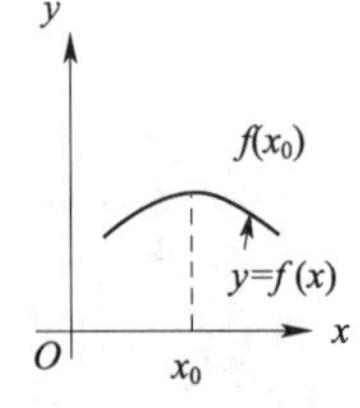

a)y=f(x),当x=x0时,y=f(x0)

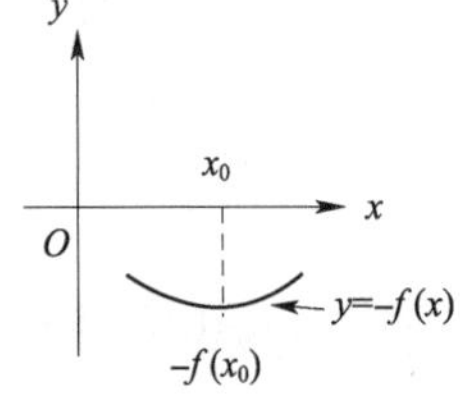

b)y=-f(x),当x=x0时,y=-f(x0)

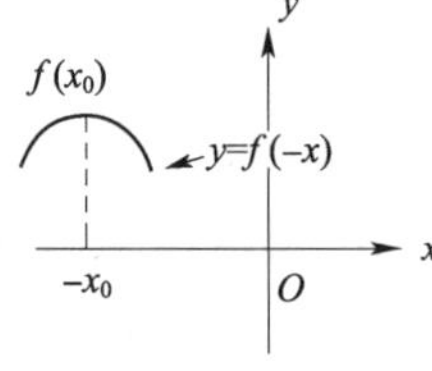

c)y=f(-x),当x=-x0时,y=f(x0)

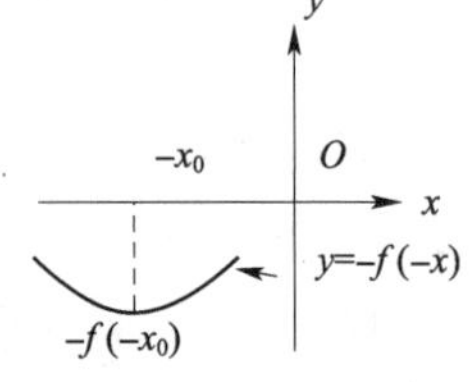

d)y=-f(-x),x=-x0时,y=-f(x0)

例 1-2-23 解图

通过对上述图形的分析,$-x_0$是$-f(-x)$的极小值点。

答案:B

【例 1-2-24】 下列极限式中,能够使用洛必达法则求极限的是:

A. $\lim\limits_{x\to0}\dfrac{1+\cos x}{e^x-1}$　　B. $\lim\limits_{x\to0}\dfrac{x-\sin x}{\sin x}$

C. $\lim\limits_{x\to0}\dfrac{x^2\sin\dfrac{1}{x}}{\sin x}$　　D. $\lim\limits_{x\to\infty}\dfrac{x+\sin x}{x-\sin x}$

解 $\lim\limits_{x\to0}\dfrac{x-\sin x}{\sin x}\overset{\frac{0}{0}}{=}\lim\limits_{x\to0}\dfrac{1-\cos x}{\cos x}=0$

答案:B

【例 1-2-25】 下列有关极限的命题中,正确的是:

A. 若$y=f(x)$在$x=x_0$处有$f'(x_0)=0$,则$f(x)$在$x=x_0$必取得极值

B. 极大值一定大于极小值

C. 若可导函数$y=f(x)$在$x=x_0$处取得极值,则必有$f'(x_0)=0$

D. 极大值就是最大值

解 选项 A,仅为$y=f(x)$在x_0取得极值的必要条件,错误;

选项 B,函数的极大值不一定大于极小值,错误;

选项 D,极大值也不一定就是函数的最大值,错误。

答案:C

【例 1-2-26】 下列说法中正确的是：

A. 若 $f'(x_0)=0$，则 $f(x_0)$必是 $f(x)$的极值

B. 若 $f(x_0)$是 $f(x)$的极值，则 $f(x)$在 x_0 处可导，且 $f'(x_0)=0$

C. 若 $f(x)$在 x_0 处可导，则 $f'(x_0)=0$ 是 $f(x)$在 x_0 取得极值的必要条件

D. 若 $f(x)$在 x_0 处可导，则 $f'(x_0)=0$ 是 $f(x)$在 x_0 取得极值的充分条件

解 函数 $f(x)$在点 x_0 处可导，则 $f'(x_0)=0$ 是 $f(x)$在 x_0 取得极值的必要条件。

答案：C

【例 1-2-27】 设函数 $f(x)$二阶可导，并且处处满足方程 $f''(x)+3(f'(x))^2+2e^x f(x)=0$，若 x_0 是该函数的一个驻点且 $f(x_0)<0$，则 $f(x)$在点 x_0：

A. 取得极大值　　B. 取得极小值

C. 不取得极值　　D. 不能确定

解 将 x_0 代入方程得 $f''(x_0)+3(f'(x_0))^2+2e^{x_0}f(x_0)=0$

因为 x_0 为该函数的一个驻点，所以 $f'(x_0)=0$。

化简 $f''(x_0)+2e^{x_0}f(x_0)=0$

$f''(x_0)=-2e^{x_0}f(x_0)>0$

利用函数取得极值的第二充分条件，$f(x)$在点 x_0 取得极小值。

答案：B

【例 1-2-28】 设 $f(x)=x(x-1)(x-2)$，则方程 $f'(x)=0$ 的实根个数是：

A. 3　　B. 2　　C. 1　　D. 0

解 $f(x)=x(x-1)(x-2)$

$f(x)$在$[0,1]$连续，在$(0,1)$可导，且 $f(0)=f(1)$

由罗尔定理可知，存在 $f'(\zeta_1)=0$，ζ_1 在$(0,1)$之间

$f(x)$在$[1,2]$连续，在$(1,2)$可导，且 $f(1)=f(2)$

由罗尔定理可知，存在 $f'(\zeta_2)=0$，ζ_2 在$(1,2)$之间

因为 $f'(x)=0$ 是二次方程，所以 $f'(x)=0$ 的实根个数为 2

答案：B

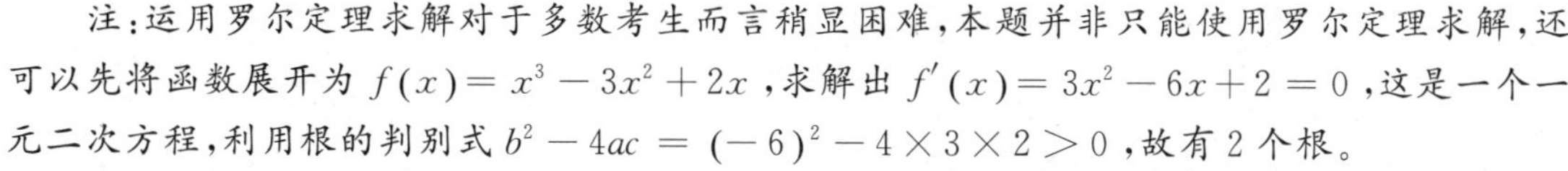

注：运用罗尔定理求解对于多数考生而言稍显困难，本题并非只能使用罗尔定理求解，还可以先将函数展开为 $f(x)=x^3-3x^2+2x$，求解出 $f'(x)=3x^2-6x+2=0$，这是一个一元二次方程，利用根的判别式 $b^2-4ac=(-6)^2-4\times3\times2>0$，故有 2 个根。

【例 1-2-29】 设函数 $f(x)$在$(-\infty,+\infty)$上是偶函数，且在$(0,+\infty)$内有 $f'(x)>0$，$f''(x)>0$，则在$(-\infty,0)$内必有：

A. $f'(x)>0$，$f''(x)>0$　　B. $f'(x)<0$，$f''(x)>0$

C. $f'(x)>0$，$f''(x)<0$　　D. $f'(x)<0$，$f''(x)<0$

解 已知 $f(x)$在$(-\infty,+\infty)$为偶函数，$f(x)$的图形关于 y 轴对称。又知 $f(x)$在$(0,+\infty)$上，$f'(x)>0$，$f''(x)>0$，因而函数 $f(x)$在$(0,+\infty)$上的图形单增且凹向。

由对称性可知，函数 $f(x)$在$(-\infty,0)$上图形单减且凹向，所以在$(-\infty,0)$上 $f'(x)<0$，$f''(x)>0$，选 B。

还可通过 $f(-x)=f(x)$，求出一阶、二阶导数，确定在$(-\infty,0)$上，y'、y''的符号。

答案：B

【例 1-2-30】 对于曲线 $y=\frac{1}{5}x^5-\frac{1}{3}x^3$，下列说法不正确的是：

A. 有 3 个极值点　　　　B. 有 3 个拐点

C. 有 2 个极值点　　　　D. 对称原点

解　求曲线的极值点：

$y=\frac{1}{5}x^5-\frac{1}{3}x^3$，$y'=x^4-x^2=x^2(x+1)(x-1)$

令 $y'=0$，驻点 $x=-1,0,1$，把定义域分成 $(-\infty,-1)$，$(-1,0)$，$(0,1)$，$(1,+\infty)$ 几个区间。列表。

例 1-2-30 解表

x	$(-\infty,-1)$	-1	$(-1,0)$	0	$(0,1)$	1	$(1,+\infty)$
$f'(x)$	$+$	0	$-$	0	$-$	0	$+$
$f(x)$	↗	极大点	↘	无极值	↘	极小点	↗

可知函数有 2 个极值点，选项 C 正确，选项 A 不正确。

本题选项 D 正确，因为 $f(x)$ 为奇函数，图形关于原点对称。

还可通过计算拐点的方法，确定选项 B 正确。

答案：A

习　题

1-2-1　$\lim\limits_{x\to\infty}\frac{3x^2+5}{5x+3}\sin\frac{2}{x}=(\quad)$。

A. 1　　B. $\frac{6}{5}$　　C. 2　　D. -1

1-2-2　极限 $\lim\limits_{x\to 0}\frac{\ln(1-tx^2)}{x\sin x}$ 的值等于（　　）。

A. t　　B. $-t$　　C. 1　　D. -1

1-2-3　当 $x\to 0$ 时，$x^2-\sin x$ 是 x 的（　　）。

A. 高价无穷小　　　　B. 同阶无穷小但不是等价无穷小

C. 低阶无穷小　　　　D. 等价无穷小

1-2-4　设 $f(x)=\begin{cases}\cos(x-1) & x>1\\ g(x) & x<1\end{cases}$，若 $\lim\limits_{x\to 1}f(x)=1$，则 $g(x)=(\quad)$。

A. $\arctan\frac{1}{x-1}$　　　　B. $\arcsin\frac{1}{x-1}$

C. $\tan(x-1)$　　　　D. $1+e^{\frac{1}{x-1}}$

1-2-5　$\lim\limits_{x\to 0}\frac{\sqrt{2-2\cos x}}{x}$ 的结果（　　）。

A. 不存在　　B. 1　　C. $\sqrt{2}$　　D. 2

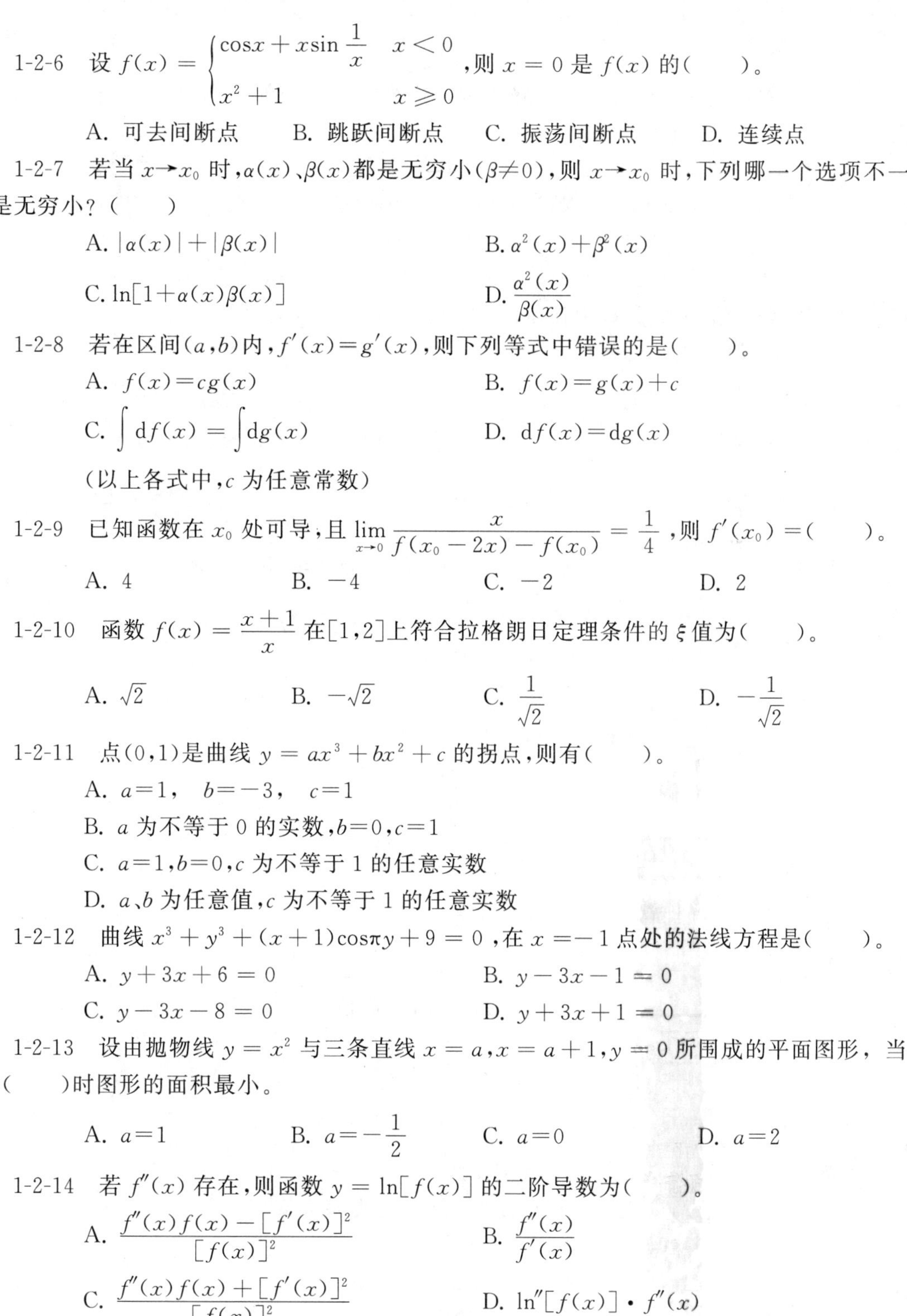

1-2-6　设 $f(x)=\begin{cases}\cos x+x\sin\dfrac{1}{x} & x<0\\ x^2+1 & x\geqslant 0\end{cases}$，则 $x=0$ 是 $f(x)$ 的（　　）。

A. 可去间断点　　B. 跳跃间断点　　C. 振荡间断点　　D. 连续点

1-2-7　若当 $x\to x_0$ 时，$\alpha(x)$、$\beta(x)$ 都是无穷小（$\beta\neq 0$），则 $x\to x_0$ 时，下列哪一个选项不一定是无穷小？（　　）

A. $|\alpha(x)|+|\beta(x)|$　　B. $\alpha^2(x)+\beta^2(x)$

C. $\ln[1+\alpha(x)\beta(x)]$　　D. $\dfrac{\alpha^2(x)}{\beta(x)}$

1-2-8　若在区间 (a,b) 内，$f'(x)=g'(x)$，则下列等式中错误的是（　　）。

A. $f(x)=cg(x)$　　B. $f(x)=g(x)+c$

C. $\int \mathrm{d}f(x)=\int \mathrm{d}g(x)$　　D. $\mathrm{d}f(x)=\mathrm{d}g(x)$

（以上各式中，c 为任意常数）

1-2-9　已知函数在 x_0 处可导，且 $\lim\limits_{x\to 0}\dfrac{x}{f(x_0-2x)-f(x_0)}=\dfrac{1}{4}$，则 $f'(x_0)=$（　　）。

A. 4　　B. -4　　C. -2　　D. 2

1-2-10　函数 $f(x)=\dfrac{x+1}{x}$ 在 $[1,2]$ 上符合拉格朗日定理条件的 ξ 值为（　　）。

A. $\sqrt{2}$　　B. $-\sqrt{2}$　　C. $\dfrac{1}{\sqrt{2}}$　　D. $-\dfrac{1}{\sqrt{2}}$

1-2-11　点 $(0,1)$ 是曲线 $y=ax^3+bx^2+c$ 的拐点，则有（　　）。

A. $a=1$，　$b=-3$，　$c=1$

B. a 为不等于 0 的实数，$b=0$，$c=1$

C. $a=1$，$b=0$，c 为不等于 1 的任意实数

D. a、b 为任意值，c 为不等于 1 的任意实数

1-2-12　曲线 $x^3+y^3+(x+1)\cos\pi y+9=0$，在 $x=-1$ 点处的法线方程是（　　）。

A. $y+3x+6=0$　　B. $y-3x-1=0$

C. $y-3x-8=0$　　D. $y+3x+1=0$

1-2-13　设由抛物线 $y=x^2$ 与三条直线 $x=a$，$x=a+1$，$y=0$ 所围成的平面图形，当 $a=$（　　）时图形的面积最小。

A. $a=1$　　B. $a=-\dfrac{1}{2}$　　C. $a=0$　　D. $a=2$

1-2-14　若 $f''(x)$ 存在，则函数 $y=\ln[f(x)]$ 的二阶导数为（　　）。

A. $\dfrac{f''(x)f(x)-[f'(x)]^2}{[f(x)]^2}$　　B. $\dfrac{f''(x)}{f'(x)}$

C. $\dfrac{f''(x)f(x)+[f'(x)]^2}{[f(x)]^2}$　　D. $\ln''[f(x)]\cdot f''(x)$

1-2-15　设参数方程 $\begin{cases}x=f(t)-\ln f(t)\\ y=tf(t)\end{cases}$ 确定了 y 是 x 的函数，且 $f'(t)$ 存在，$f(0)=2$，$f'(0)=2$，则当 $t=0$ 时，$\dfrac{\mathrm{d}y}{\mathrm{d}x}$ 的值等于（　　）。

A. $\frac{4}{3}$　　B. $-\frac{4}{3}$　　C. -2　　D. 2

1-2-16　设曲线 $y=\ln(1+x^2)$，M 是曲线上的点，若曲线在 M 点的切线平行于已知直线 $y-x+1=0$，则 M 点的坐标是（　　）。

A. $(-2,\ln5)$　　B. $(-1,\ln2)$　　C. $(1,\ln2)$　　D. $(2,\ln5)$

1-2-17　若 $f'(x)=g'(x)$，则下列等式（　　）成立。

A. $f(x)=g(x)$　　B. $f(x)>g(x)$

C. $f(x)<g(x)$　　D. $f(x)=g(x)+c$

1-2-18　设 $f(x)$ 的二阶导数存在，且 $f'(x)=f(1-x)$，则（　　）成立。

A. $f''(x)+f'(x)=0$　　B. $f''(x)-f'(x)=0$

C. $f''(x)+f(x)=0$　　D. $f''(x)-f(x)=0$

1-2-19　设函数 $f(x)=\begin{cases}e^{-x}+1 & x\leqslant0\\ ax+2 & x>0\end{cases}$，若 $f(x)$ 在 $x=0$ 处可导，则 a 的值是（　　）。

A. 1　　B. 2　　C. 0　　D. -1

1-2-20　设 $f(x)=\begin{cases}x^2\sin\frac{1}{x} & x>0\\ ax+b & x\leqslant0\end{cases}$ 在 $x=0$ 处可导，则 a,b 之值为（　　）。

A. $a=1,b=0$　　B. $a=0$，b 为任意常数

C. $a=0,b=0$　　D. $a=1$，b 任意常数

1-2-21　已知 $\begin{cases}x=\dfrac{1-t^2}{1+t^2}\\ y=\dfrac{2t}{1+t^2}\end{cases}$，则 $\frac{\mathrm{d}y}{\mathrm{d}x}$ 为（　　）。

A. $\frac{t^2-1}{2t}$　　B. $\frac{1-t^2}{2t}$　　C. $\frac{x^2-1}{2x}$　　D. $\frac{2t}{t^2-1}$

1-2-22　设 $y=(1+x)^{\frac{1}{x}}$，则 $y'(1)$ 等于（　　）。

A. 2　　B. e　　C. $\frac{1}{2}-\ln2$　　D. $1-\ln4$

1-2-23　函数 $f(x)=10\arctan x-3\ln x$ 的极大值是（　　）。

A. $10\arctan2-3\ln2$　　B. $\frac{5}{2}\pi-3$

C. $10\arctan3-3\ln3$　　D. $10\arctan\frac{1}{3}$

1-2-24　设 $f(x)$ 在 $(-a,a)$ 是连续偶函数，且当 $0<x<a$ 时，$f(x)<f(0)$，则（　　）。

A. $f(0)$ 是 $f(x)$ 在 $(-a,a)$ 的极大值，但不是最大值

B. $f(0)$ 是 $f(x)$ 在 $(-a,a)$ 的最小值

C. $f(0)$ 是 $f(x)$ 在 $(-a,a)$ 的极大值，也是最大值

D. $f(0)$ 是曲线 $y=f(x)$ 的拐点的纵坐标

1-2-25　曲线 $y=x^3(x-4)$ 既单增且向上凹的区间为（　　）。

A. $(-\infty,0)$　　B. $(0,+\infty)$　　C. $(2,+\infty)$　　D. $(3,+\infty)$

1-2-26　函数 $f(x)=\frac{x^2}{2}+2x+\ln|x|$ 在 $[-4,-1]$ 上的最大值为（　　）。

A. 2　　　　B. 1　　　　C. ln4　　　　D. $-\frac{3}{2}$

1-2-27　设函数 $f(x)$在$(-\infty,+\infty)$二阶可导,并且处处满足方程 $xf''(x)+3x(f'(x))^2=1-e^{-x}$,若 $x_0\neq 0$ 是该函数的一个驻点,则下列命题成立的是(　　)。

A. $(x_0 f(x_0))$是曲线 $y=f(x)$的拐点

B. $f(x_0)$是 $f(x)$的极小值

C. $f(x_0)$是 $f(x)$的极大值

D. $f(x_0)$不是极值,$(x_0,f(x_0))$也不是曲线 $y=f(x)$的拐点

第三节　一元函数积分学

一、不定积分

(一)不定积分的概念

1. 原函数定义

定义在某区间I上的函数$f(x)$,若存在函数$F(x)$,使得该区间上的一切x,均有$F'(x)=f(x)$或 $dF(x)=f(x)dx$,则称 $F(x)$为 $f(x)$在区间 I 上的原函数。

若函数 $f(x)$存在两个原函数,那么它们只相差一个常数。由于常数的导数为零,所以函数 $f(x)$如果有原函数,则 $f(x)$就有无穷多个原函数,可表示为 $F(x)+C$。

2. 不定积分定义

函数 $f(x)$的全体原函数称为 $f(x)$的不定积分,记作$\int f(x)dx$。

若 $F(x)$ 是 $f(x)$ 的一个原函数,则$\int f(x)dx=F(x)+C$(C为任意常数)

(1-3-1)

3. 不定积分的性质

利用原函数的定义和不定积分的概念可得到下面性质

$$\int kf(x)dx=k\int f(x)dx \quad (\text{常数 } k\neq 0)$$

$$\int [f(x)\pm g(x)]dx=\int f(x)dx\pm\int g(x)dx$$

$$d\int f(x)dx=f(x)dx,\ \frac{d}{dx}\int f(x)dx=f(x)$$

$$\int dF(x)=F(x)+C,\ \int F'(x)dx=F(x)+C$$

(二)不定积分的计算

1. 利用原函数的定义计算不定积分

2. 利用积分公式计算不定积分

常用的不定积分公式有:

$$\int kdx=kx+C \quad (k\text{ 是常数}) \qquad \int x^{\mu}dx=\frac{x^{\mu+1}}{\mu+1}+C \quad (\mu\neq -1)$$

$$\int \frac{dx}{x}=\ln|x|+C$$

$$\int \frac{dx}{1+x^2}=\arctan x+C \qquad \int \frac{dx}{\sqrt{1-x^2}}=\arcsin x+C$$

$\int \cos x\mathrm{d}x = \sin x + C$ $\int \sin x\mathrm{d}x = -\cos x + C$

$\int \frac{\mathrm{d}x}{\cos^2 x} = \int \sec^2 x\mathrm{d}x = \tan x + C$ $\int \frac{\mathrm{d}x}{\sin^2 x} = \int \csc^2 x\mathrm{d}x = -\cot x + C$

$\int \sec x\tan x\mathrm{d}x = \sec x + C$ $\int \csc x\cot x\mathrm{d}x = -\csc x + C$

$\int e^x\mathrm{d}x = e^x + C$ $\int a^x\mathrm{d}x = \frac{a^x}{\ln a} + C$

$\int \mathrm{sh}x\mathrm{d}x = \mathrm{ch}x + C$ $\int \mathrm{ch}x\mathrm{d}x = \mathrm{sh}x + C$

$\int \tan x\mathrm{d}x = -\ln|\cos x| + C$ $\int \cot x\mathrm{d}x = \ln|\sin x| + C$

$\int \sec x\mathrm{d}x = \ln|\sec x + \tan x| + C$ $\int \csc x\mathrm{d}x = \ln|\csc x - \cot x| + C$

$\int \frac{\mathrm{d}x}{a^2 + x^2} = \frac{1}{a}\arctan\frac{x}{a} + C$ $\int \frac{\mathrm{d}x}{x^2 - a^2} = \frac{1}{2a}\ln\left|\frac{x-a}{x+a}\right| + C$

$\int \frac{\mathrm{d}x}{\sqrt{a^2 - x^2}} = \arcsin\frac{x}{a} + C$ $\int \frac{\mathrm{d}x}{\sqrt{x^2 - a^2}} = \ln|x + \sqrt{x^2 - a^2}| + C$

$\int \frac{\mathrm{d}x}{\sqrt{x^2 + a^2}} = \ln(x + \sqrt{x^2 + a^2}) + C$

3. 换元积分法

第一类换元积分法：设 $f(u)$ 具有原函数 $F(u)$，而 $u=\varphi(x)$ 可导，则有

$$\int f[\varphi(x)]\varphi'(x)\mathrm{d}x = \int f(u)\mathrm{d}u = F[\varphi(x)] + C \tag{1-3-2}$$

第二类换元积分法：设 $x=\varphi(t)$ 在区间 $[\alpha,\beta]$ 上单调可导，且 $\varphi'(t)\neq 0$，又设 $f[\varphi(t)]\varphi'(t)$ 具有原函数 $F(t)$，则有

$$\int f(x)\mathrm{d}x = \int f[\varphi(t)]\varphi'(t)\mathrm{d}t = F(t) + c = F[\varphi^{-1}(x)] + C \tag{1-3-3}$$

式中，$\varphi^{-1}(x)$ 为 $x=\varphi(t)$ 的反函数。

用式(1-3-3)，在计算时可根据函数的特点适当选择代换函数。常用的代换有三角代换、根式代换、倒代换等。

三角代换，如被积函数 $f(x)$ 中含有

$$\sqrt{a^2 - x^2}，可设\ x = a\sin t\ \left(-\frac{\pi}{2} < t < \frac{\pi}{2}\right)$$

$$\sqrt{x^2 + a^2}，可设\ x = a\tan t\ \left(-\frac{\pi}{2} < t < \frac{\pi}{2}\right)$$

$$\sqrt{x^2 - a^2}，可设\ x = a\sec t\ \left(0 < t < \frac{\pi}{2}\right)$$

根式代换，如 $\int \frac{1}{\sqrt{2x-1}+1}\mathrm{d}x$，可设 $\sqrt{2x-1} = t$

倒代换，如 $\int \frac{1}{x\sqrt{x^2-1}}\mathrm{d}x$，可设 $x = \frac{1}{t}$ $(t > 0$ 或 $t < 0)$

4. 分部积分法

设 $u(x)$，$v(x)$ 可微，且 $\int v(x)\mathrm{d}u(x)$ 存在，由公式 $\mathrm{d}(uv)=u\mathrm{d}v+v\mathrm{d}u$ 得到分部积分公式

$$\int u\mathrm{d}v = uv - \int v\mathrm{d}u$$

或

$$\int uv'\mathrm{d}x = uv - \int vu'\mathrm{d}x \tag{1-3-4}$$

利用分部积分公式计算不定积分的方法称为分部积分法。

运用分部积分法时，需将被积函数转换为 u 与 v' 两个因式的乘积。正确把其中一部分看作 u，其余看作 v' 是利用好分部积分法公式的关键。应该记住 u 和 v' 设法的一般规律。如果被积函数是正整数次幂函数与正(余)弦函数的乘积或是正整数次幂函数与指数函数的乘积时，设幂函数为 u，其余的为 v'。如果被积函数是正整数次幂函数与对数函数的乘积或是幂函数与反三角函数的乘积时，设对数函数或反三角函数为 u，其余的为 v'。掌握了这些规律，对解决一部分不定积分是有利的，对后面求定积分也是有用的。在定积分分部积分法中，设 u 和 v' 的方法与不定积分方法完全一致。

5. 有理函数积分

有理函数是指两个多项式的商所表示的函数，即

$$R(x)=\frac{P_n(x)}{Q_m(x)}=\frac{a_0x^n+a_1x^{n-1}+\cdots+a_n}{b_0x^m+b_1x^{m-1}+\cdots+b_m}$$

式中 m,n 为非负整数，$a_0\neq0,b_0\neq0$，$P_n(x)$ 与 $Q_m(x)$ 无公因式。当次数 $m>n$ 时称为真分式，次数 $m\leqslant n$ 时称为假分式。计算时，先通过代数变形或多项式除法化假分式为真分式，再把真分式的分母在实数范围内因式分解，然后按规则转换为部分分式之和，用比较同次幂或代特殊值法确定待定系数，再积分。

运用上述方法可将真分式的不定积分化为下面四类积分：

Ⅰ. $\displaystyle\int\frac{A}{x-a}\mathrm{d}x$　　Ⅱ. $\displaystyle\int\frac{A}{(x-a)^n}\mathrm{d}x$

Ⅲ. $\displaystyle\int\frac{Mx+N}{x^2+Px+Q}\mathrm{d}x$　　Ⅳ. $\displaystyle\int\frac{Mx+N}{(x^2+Px+Q)^n}\mathrm{d}x$

以上是解有理函数不定积分的一般步骤，但在解此类题之前应先考虑是否有更简便的方法，这一点应注意。

6. 三角函数有理式的积分

三角函数有理式的不定积分可通过三角代换设 $\tan\frac{x}{2}=u$ 来解决，$\mathrm{d}x=\frac{2}{1+u^2}\mathrm{d}u$，$\sin x=\frac{2u}{1+u^2}$，$\cos x=\frac{1-u^2}{1+u^2}$ 化为有理函数的积分。对于三角函数的有理式积分，在解题前同样要考虑有没有更简便的方法来求解。

7. 简单无理函数的积分

$$\int R(x,\sqrt[n]{ax+b})\mathrm{d}x\quad,\quad\int R\left(x,\sqrt[n]{\frac{ax+b}{cx+d}}\right)\mathrm{d}x$$

可通过变量替换，设 $\sqrt[n]{ax+b}$，$\sqrt[n]{\frac{ax+b}{cx+d}}$ 为一新变量来解决。

【例 1-3-1】 已知 $\frac{\sin x}{1+x\sin x}$ 为 $f(x)$ 的一个原函数，求 $\int f(x)f'(x)\mathrm{d}x$。

解 $\displaystyle\int f(x)f'(x)\mathrm{d}x=\int f(x)\mathrm{d}f(x)=\frac{1}{2}f^2(x)+C$

由原函数定义可知

$$f(x)=\left(\frac{\sin x}{1+x\sin x}\right)'=\frac{\cos x(1+x\sin x)-\sin x(\sin x+x\cos x)}{(1+x\sin x)^2}$$

$$=\frac{\cos x-\sin^2 x}{(1+x\sin x)^2}$$

$$原式=\frac{1}{2}\left[\frac{\cos x-\sin^2 x}{(1+x\sin x)^2}\right]^2+C$$

【例 1-3-2】 已知 $f(x)$为连续的偶函数，则 $f(x)$的原函数中：

A. 有奇函数　　B. 都是奇函数

C. 都是偶函数　　D. 没有奇函数也没有偶函数

解 举例 $f(x)=x^2$，$\int x^2\mathrm{d}x=\frac{1}{3}x^3+C$

当 $C=0$ 时，为奇函数；

当 $C=1$ 时，$\int x^2\mathrm{d}x=\frac{1}{3}x^3+1$ 为非奇非偶函数。

答案：A

【例 1-3-3】 $f'(e^x)=1+x$，求 $f(x)$。

解 把式子转化为关于 $f(x)$形式的表达式，设 $e^x=t,x=\ln t$，则

$$f'(t)=1+\ln t$$

即

$$f'(x)=1+\ln x$$

$$f(x)=\int(1+\ln x)\mathrm{d}x=x+\int\ln x\mathrm{d}x$$

$$=x+x\ln x-\int 1\mathrm{d}x=x+x\ln x-x+C$$

$$=x\ln x+C$$

【例 1-3-4】 若 $\sec^2 x$ 是 $f(x)$的一个原函数，则 $\int xf(x)\mathrm{d}x$ 等于：

A. $\tan x+C$　　B. $x\tan x-\ln|\cos x|+C$

C. $x\sec^2 x+\tan x+C$　　D. $x\sec^2 x-\tan x+C$

解 $\int xf(x)\mathrm{d}x=\int x\mathrm{d}\sec^2 x=x\sec^2 x-\int\sec^2 x\mathrm{d}x=x\sec^2 x-\tan x+C$

答案：D

【例 1-3-5】 若 $\int f(x)\mathrm{d}x=x^3+C$，则$\int f(\cos x)\sin x\mathrm{d}x$ 等于：

A. $-\cos^3 x+C$　　B. $\sin^3 x+C$

C. $\cos^3 x+C$　　D. $\frac{1}{3}\cos^3 x+C$

解 已知 $\int f(x)\mathrm{d}x=x^3+C$，先将$\int f(\cos x)\sin x\mathrm{d}x$ 换成已给式子形式。

设 $\cos x=u$，$\mathrm{d}u=-\sin x\mathrm{d}x$，$\sin x\mathrm{d}x=-\mathrm{d}u$，则

$$\int f(\cos x)\sin x\mathrm{d}x=-\int f(u)\mathrm{d}u=-u^3+C=-(\cos x)^3+C=-\cos^3 x+C$$

答案：A

【例 1-3-6】 下列积分式中，正确的是：

A. $\int\cos(2x+3)\mathrm{d}x=\sin(2x+3)+C$　B. $\int e^{\sqrt{x}}\mathrm{d}x=e^{\sqrt{x}}+C$

C. $\int\ln x\mathrm{d}x=x\ln x-x+C$　D. $\int\frac{1}{\sqrt{4-x^2}}\mathrm{d}x=\frac{1}{2}\arcsin\frac{x}{2}+C$

解　计算如下

选项 A，$\int\cos(2x+3)\mathrm{d}x=\frac{1}{2}\int\cos(2x+3)\mathrm{d}(2x+3)=\frac{1}{2}\sin(2x+3)+C$，错误。

选项 B，设$\sqrt{x}=t, x=t^2, \mathrm{d}x=2t\mathrm{d}t$，$\int e^{\sqrt{x}}\mathrm{d}x=2\int e^t\cdot t\mathrm{d}t=2\left(te^t-\int e^t\mathrm{d}t\right)=2e^t(t-1)+C=2e^{\sqrt{x}}(\sqrt{x}-1)+C$ 错误。

选项 C，$\int\ln x\mathrm{d}x\xlongequal{\text{分部积分}}x\ln x-\int\mathrm{d}x=x\ln x-x+C$，正确。

选项 D，$\int\frac{1}{\sqrt{4-x^2}}\mathrm{d}x\xlongequal{\text{积分公式}}\arcsin\frac{x}{2}+C$，错误。

答案：C

二、定积分

（一）定积分概念

定积分的引入是应实际的需要而产生的，如数学中计算曲边梯形的面积，物理中计算变速直线运动的物体在时间$[t_1, t_2]$内所经过的路程等。

1. 定积分定义

设 $f(x)$是定义在$[a,b]$上的有界函数，在$[a,b]$中任意插入一些分点 $a=x_0<x_1<\cdots<x_n=b$，把$[a,b]$分成 n 个小区间，在每个小区间$[x_{i-1}, x_i]$上任意取一点 ξ_i，作函数值与小区间 Δx_i 的乘积 $f(\xi_i)\Delta x_i$（其中，$i=1,2,\cdots,n$），作和式$\sum_{i=1}^{n}f(\xi_i)\Delta x_i$，令 $\lambda=\max\{\Delta x_i(i=1,2,\cdots,n)\}\to 0$，如果上式极限（这个极限与区间的分法及各小区间上 ξ_i 的取法无关）存在，则称此极限为函数 $f(x)$在$[a,b]$上的定积分，记作 $\int_a^b f(x)\mathrm{d}x$，即

$$\int_a^b f(x)\mathrm{d}x=\lim_{\substack{n\to\infty\\ \lambda\to 0}}\sum_{i=1}^{n}f(\xi_i)\Delta x_i \tag{1-3-5}$$

2. 定积分的几何意义、物理意义

几何意义：

当在$[a,b]$上 $f(x)\geqslant 0$，$\int_a^b f(x)\mathrm{d}x$ 表示由曲线 $y=f(x)$，x 轴，直线 $x=a$、$x=b$ 所围成图形的面积；

当在$[a,b]$ 上 $f(x)\leqslant 0$，$\int_a^b f(x)\mathrm{d}x$ 表示由曲线 $y=f(x)$，x 轴，直线 $x=a$、$x=b$ 所围成图形的面积的负值；

当 $f(x)$ 可正可负，$\int_a^b f(x)\mathrm{d}x$ 表示由曲线 $y=f(x)$，x 轴，直线 $x=a$、$x=b$ 所围成图形的面积的代数和。

物理意义：$\int_a^b f(x)\mathrm{d}x$ 可以表示不同的物理量，如变速直线运动所经过的路程，变力所做的功。

为了以后计算和应用方便，对定积分作以下两点补充规定：

(1)当 $a=b$ 时，$\int_a^b f(x)\mathrm{d}x = 0$；

(2)当 $a>b$ 时，$\int_a^b f(x)\mathrm{d}x = -\int_b^a f(x)\mathrm{d}x$，即交换定积分的上下限时，绝对值不变而符号相反。

3. 定积分性质

(1)若 $f(x)$在$[a,b]$上可积，k 为常数，则

$$\int_a^b kf(x)\mathrm{d}x = k\int_a^b f(x)\mathrm{d}x \tag{1-3-6}$$

(2)若 $f(x)$，$g(x)$在$[a,b]$上可积，则

$$\int_a^b [f(x) \pm g(x)]\mathrm{d}x = \int_a^b f(x)\mathrm{d}x \pm \int_a^b g(x)\mathrm{d}x$$

(3)如果 $a<c<b$，$f(x)$有界，则 $f(x)$在$[a,b]$上可积的充要条件是 $f(x)$在$[a,c]$和$[c,b]$上都可积。且有

$$\int_a^b f(x)\mathrm{d}x = \int_a^c f(x)\mathrm{d}x + \int_c^b f(x)\mathrm{d}x \tag{1-3-7}$$

(4)如果在区间$[a,b]$上，$f(x)=1$ 则

$$\int_a^b 1\mathrm{d}x = \int_a^b \mathrm{d}x = b-a$$

(5)如果在区间$[a,b]$上，$f(x)\geqslant 0$，则 $\int_a^b f(x)\mathrm{d}x \geqslant 0\ (a<b)$。

(6)如果在区间$[a,b]$上，$f(x)\leqslant g(x)$，则有

$$\int_a^b f(x)\mathrm{d}x \leqslant \int_a^b g(x)\mathrm{d}x$$

(7)设 M 及 m 分别是 $f(x)$在区间$[a,b]$上的最大值及最小值，则

$$m(b-a) \leqslant \int_a^b f(x)\mathrm{d}x \leqslant M(b-a) \qquad (a<b)$$

(8)定积分中值定理

如果函数 $f(x)$在闭区间$[a,b]$上连续，则在积分区间$[a,b]$上至少存在一个点 ξ，使下式成立

$$\int_a^b f(x)\mathrm{d}x = f(\xi)(b-a) \qquad (a\leqslant \xi \leqslant b) \tag{1-3-8}$$

4. 积分上限函数

(1)设 $f(x)$ 在$[a,b]$上连续，$x\in[a,b]$，称$\int_a^x f(x)\mathrm{d}x$ 为积分上限函数，记作 $\phi(x) = \int_a^x f(x)\mathrm{d}x$，经常写成如下形式 $\phi(x) = \int_a^x f(t)\mathrm{d}t \quad (a\leqslant x\leqslant b)$。

(2)若 $f(x)$在$[a,b]$上连续，则积分上限函数的导数

$$\phi'(x) = \left[\int_a^x f(t)\mathrm{d}t\right]' = f(x) \qquad (a\leqslant x\leqslant b)$$

上式可说明积分上限函数 $\int_a^x f(t)\mathrm{d}t$ 是 $f(x)$ 的一个原函数。

(3)若 $f(x)$ 在$[a,b]$上连续，且 $g(x)$ 可导，则$[\int_a^{g(x)} f(t)\mathrm{d}t]' = f(u)\cdot g'(x) = f[g(x)]\cdot g'(x)$。

注：如果给出的函数为积分下限函数，求导时，可利用定积分的性质，化为积分上限函数，再利用积分上限求导的方法计算。

(二)定积分的计算

(1)利用定义计算：即分割、取近似、求和、取极限的方法。

(2)利用牛顿-莱布尼兹公式计算：设函数 $f(x)$在$[a,b]$上连续，$F(x)$为其原函数，则

$$\int_a^b f(x)\mathrm{d}x = F(x)\Big|_a^b = F(b) - F(a)$$

(3)利用换元法计算：若 $f(x)$在$[a,b]$上连续，$x=\varphi(t)$在$[\alpha,\beta]$上连续，且当 $t\in[\alpha,\beta]$时 $x=\varphi(t)\in[a,b]$，$a=\varphi(\alpha)$，$b=\varphi(\beta)$，$\varphi(t)$在$[\alpha,\beta]$上具有连续导数，则

$$\int_a^b f(x)\mathrm{d}x = \int_\alpha^\beta f[\varphi(t)]\varphi'(t)\mathrm{d}t \tag{1-3-9}$$

(4)利用分部积分法计算：设 $u=u(x)$、$v=v(x)$在$[a,b]$上可导，$u'(x)v(x)$在$[a,b]$上可积，则

$$\int_a^b u(x)v'(x)\mathrm{d}x = u(x)v(x)\Big|_a^b - \int_a^b u'(x)v(x)\mathrm{d}x \tag{1-3-10}$$

或

$$\int_a^b u(x)\mathrm{d}v(x) = u(x)v(x)\Big|_a^b - \int_a^b v(x)\mathrm{d}u(x)$$

定积分的换元法、分部积分法与不定积分采用的方法是一致的，只多了上下限。不定积分的换元法有第一、二类之分，并且有不同的公式，而定积分换元法只有一个计算式，从公式(1-3-10)左往右推，就是第二类换元法，从公式(1-3-10)右往左推就是第一类换元法。定积分分部积分中 u 与 $\mathrm{d}v$ 的取法与不定积分相同。

(5)利用定积分的性质计算。

(6)利用公式计算：

①$\int_0^{\frac{\pi}{2}} \sin^m x\,\mathrm{d}x = \int_0^{\frac{\pi}{2}} \cos^m x\,\mathrm{d}x$　　(m 为正整数)

$$= \begin{cases} \dfrac{m-1}{m}\times\dfrac{m-3}{m-2}\times\cdots\times\dfrac{5}{6}\times\dfrac{3}{4}\times\dfrac{1}{2}\times\dfrac{\pi}{2} & (m\text{ 为正偶数}) \\ \dfrac{m-1}{m}\times\dfrac{m-3}{m-2}\times\cdots\times\dfrac{6}{7}\times\dfrac{4}{5}\times\dfrac{2}{3}\times 1 & (m\text{ 为大于 1 的奇数}) \end{cases}$$

②$\int_0^{\pi} \sin^m x\,\mathrm{d}x = 2\int_0^{\frac{\pi}{2}} \sin^m x\,\mathrm{d}x$　　(m 为正整数)

③$\int_{-a}^{a} f(x)\mathrm{d}x = \begin{cases} 2\int_0^a f(x)\mathrm{d}x & f(x)\text{ 为偶函数} \\ 0 & f(x)\text{ 为奇函数} \end{cases}$

④$\int_a^{a+T} f(x)\mathrm{d}x = \int_0^T f(x)\mathrm{d}x$　　[a 为实数、T 为周期函数 $f(x)$ 的周期]

⑤$\int_0^{\pi} xf(\sin x)\mathrm{d}x = \dfrac{\pi}{2}\int_0^{\pi} f(\sin x)\mathrm{d}x$

【例 1-3-7】 $\frac{d}{dx}\int_{2x}^{0}e^{-t^2}dt$ 等于：

A. e^{4x^2} B. $2e^{-4x^2}$ C. $-2e^{-4x^2}$ D. e^{-x^2}

解 $\frac{d}{dx}\int_{2x}^{0}e^{-t^2}dt=-\frac{d}{dx}\int_{0}^{2x}e^{-t^2}dt=-e^{-4x^2}\cdot 2=-2e^{-4x^2}$

答案:C

注:该题是积分下限函数求导,可以利用定积分的性质将其转化为积分上限函数,故有 $\int_{2x}^{0}e^{-t^2}dt=-\int_{0}^{2x}e^{-t^2}dt$,然后利用公式即可求出。

【例 1-3-8】 设 $f(x)$在$(-\infty,+\infty)$连续,$x\neq 0$,求 $\varphi(x)=\int_{0}^{\frac{1}{x}}f(t)dt$ 的导数。

解 本题为积分上限函数,按前述公式计算。

$$\varphi'(x)=\frac{d}{dx}\int_{0}^{\frac{1}{x}}f(t)dt=f\left(\frac{1}{x}\right)\left(-\frac{1}{x^2}\right)=-\frac{1}{x^2}f\left(\frac{1}{x}\right)$$

【例 1-3-9】 设 f 连续,$f(0)=1$,那么$\lim\limits_{x\to 0}\frac{\int_{0}^{x}tf(t)dt}{x^2}$ 的值为:

A. 1 B. $\frac{1}{2}$ C. $\frac{3}{2}$ D. 2

解 $\lim\limits_{x\to 0}\frac{\int_{0}^{x}tf(t)dt}{x^2}\overset{\frac{0}{0}}{=}\lim\limits_{x\to 0}\frac{xf(x)}{2x}=\lim\limits_{x\to 0}\frac{f(x)}{2}=\frac{1}{2}$

答案:B

【例 1-3-10】 计算 $\int_{0}^{\pi}\sqrt{\sin^3 x-\sin^5 x}dx$ 。

解

$$\begin{aligned}原式&=\int_{0}^{\pi}\sqrt{\sin^3 x(1-\sin^2 x)}dx=\int_{0}^{\pi}(\sin x)^{\frac{3}{2}}\mid\cos x\mid dx\\&=\int_{0}^{\frac{\pi}{2}}(\sin x)^{\frac{3}{2}}\mid\cos x\mid dx+\int_{\frac{\pi}{2}}^{\pi}(\sin x)^{\frac{3}{2}}\mid\cos x\mid dx\\&=\frac{2}{5}(\sin x)^{\frac{5}{2}}\Big|_{0}^{\frac{\pi}{2}}-\frac{2}{5}(\sin x)^{\frac{5}{2}}\Big|_{\frac{\pi}{2}}^{\pi}=\frac{4}{5}\end{aligned}$$

【例 1-3-11】 计算 $\int_{-2}^{2}(\mid x\mid+x)e^{|x|}dx$。

解

$$原式=\int_{-2}^{2}\mid x\mid e^{|x|}dx+\int_{-2}^{2}xe^{|x|}dx$$

因 $f(x)=xe^{|x|}$ 为奇函数,故$\int_{-2}^{2}xe^{|x|}dx=0$,则

$$\begin{aligned}原式&=2\int_{0}^{2}\mid x\mid e^{|x|}dx\quad[因\ f(x)=\mid x\mid e^{|x|}\ 为偶函数]\\&=2\int_{0}^{2}xe^{x}dx=2\int_{0}^{2}xde^{x}\\&=2\left(xe^{x}\Big|_{0}^{2}-\int_{0}^{2}e^{x}dx\right)\end{aligned}$$

$$=2(2e^2-e^2+1)$$
$$=2(e^2+1)$$

【例 1-3-12】 设 $I_1=\int_0^{\frac{\pi}{2}}\sqrt[3]{1+x^2}\mathrm{d}x$，$I_2=\int_0^{\frac{\pi}{2}}\sqrt[3]{1+\sin^2 x}\,\mathrm{d}x$，那么：

A. $I_1\geqslant I_2$　　B. $I_1\leqslant I_2$　　C. $I_1=I_2$　　D. 无法确定

解 因在 $\left[0,\frac{\pi}{2}\right]$ 上，$x\geqslant\sin x$，$1+x^2\geqslant1+\sin^2 x$

由定积分性质可知 $\int_0^{\frac{\pi}{2}}\sqrt[3]{1+x^2}\mathrm{d}x\geqslant\int_0^{\frac{\pi}{2}}\sqrt[3]{1+\sin^2 x}\,\mathrm{d}x$，所以 $I_1\geqslant I_2$。

答案：A

【例 1-3-13】 设 $f(x)$ 为 $(-\infty,+\infty)$ 上的连续函数，且满足 $f(x)=3x^2-x\int_0^1 f(x)\mathrm{d}x$，求 $f(x)$ 的表达式。

解 因为 $f(x)$ 在 $[0,1]$ 上连续，所以 $\int_0^1 f(x)\mathrm{d}x$ 为一确定的值。

设 $\int_0^1 f(x)\mathrm{d}x=A$，则 $f(x)=3x^2-xA$

两边积分

$$\int_0^1 f(x)\mathrm{d}x=\int_0^1 3x^2\mathrm{d}x-\int_0^1 Ax\,\mathrm{d}x$$

$$A=1-\frac{A}{2}\cdot x^2\Big|_0^1,A=1-\frac{A}{2},A=\frac{2}{3}$$

$$f(x)=3x^2-Ax=3x^2-\frac{2}{3}x$$

注：该题的基本思想是将定积分（某个确定数字）设为未知量进行求解，最后再反代回原方程求出 $f(x)$ 的表达式。

【例 1-3-14】 设 $f''(u)$ 连续，已知 $n\int_0^1 xf''(2x)\mathrm{d}x=\int_0^2 tf''(t)\mathrm{d}t$，那么 n 为：

A. 2　　B. 1　　C. 3　　D. 4

解 设 $2x=t$，$x=\frac{t}{2}$，$\mathrm{d}x=\frac{1}{2}\mathrm{d}t$，当 $x=1$，$t=2$；当 $x=0$，$t=0$。

左 $=n\int_0^2\frac{t}{2}f''(t)\,\frac{1}{2}\mathrm{d}t=\frac{n}{4}\int_0^2 tf''(t)\mathrm{d}t=$ 右

所以 $\frac{n}{4}=1$，$n=4$

答案：D

三、广义积分

（一）无穷限积分

设 $f(x)$ 在 $[a,+\infty)$ 上有定义，且对任何 $b>a$，$f(x)$ 在 $[a,b]$ 上可积，若极限 $\lim\limits_{b\to+\infty}\int_a^b f(x)\mathrm{d}x$ 存在，则定义

$$\int_a^{+\infty}f(x)\mathrm{d}x=\lim_{b\to+\infty}\int_a^b f(x)\mathrm{d}x \tag{1-3-11}$$

并说 $f(x)$ 在 $[a,+\infty)$ 上广义积分存在或收敛；若上述极限不存在，就说广义积分不存在或发散。同理可定义

$$\int_{-\infty}^{b} f(x)\mathrm{d}x = \lim_{a\to-\infty}\int_{a}^{b} f(x)\mathrm{d}x \tag{1-3-12}$$

$$\int_{-\infty}^{+\infty} f(x)\mathrm{d}x = \int_{-\infty}^{c} f(x)\mathrm{d}x + \int_{c}^{+\infty} f(x)\mathrm{d}x \tag{1-3-13}$$

其中 c 为 $(-\infty,+\infty)$ 上任一点。只有当右边两个广义积分都存在时，广义积分才收敛。若有一个不存在，则广义积分发散。

（二）无界函数积分

设 $f(x)$ 在 $(a,b]$ 上有定义，在点 a 的右邻域内无界，对任何 $0<\varepsilon<b-a$，$f(x)$ 在 $[a+\varepsilon,b]$ 上可积，若极限 $\lim\limits_{\varepsilon\to0^+}\int_{a+\varepsilon}^{b} f(x)\mathrm{d}x$ 存在，则定义

$$\int_{a}^{b} f(x)\mathrm{d}x = \lim_{\varepsilon\to0^+}\int_{a+\varepsilon}^{b} f(x)\mathrm{d}x \tag{1-3-14}$$

并说 $f(x)$ 在 $(a,b]$ 上广义积分存在或收敛；若极限不存在，则说广义积分不存在或发散，同理，若 $f(x)$ 在 $[a,b)$ 上有定义，$f(x)$ 在点 b 左邻域无界的情况，若极限 $\lim\limits_{\varepsilon\to0^+}\int_{a}^{b-\varepsilon} f(x)\mathrm{d}x$ 存在，则定义

$$\int_{a}^{b} f(x)\mathrm{d}x = \lim_{\varepsilon\to0^+}\int_{a}^{b-\varepsilon} f(x)\mathrm{d}x \quad [f(x)\text{在点 } b \text{ 的左邻域无界}] \tag{1-3-15}$$

并说 $f(x)$ 在 $[a,b)$ 上广义积分存在或收敛；极限不存在，则称广义积分不存在或发散。

$$\int_{a}^{b} f(x)\mathrm{d}x = \lim_{\varepsilon_1\to0^+}\int_{a}^{c-\varepsilon_1} f(x)\mathrm{d}x + \lim_{\varepsilon_2\to0^+}\int_{c+\varepsilon_2}^{b} f(x)\mathrm{d}x \quad [a<c<b, f(x)\text{在点 } c \text{ 的邻域无界}] \tag{1-3-16}$$

只有当右边两个极限都存在时，广义积分 $\int_{a}^{b} f(x)\mathrm{d}x$ 才收敛；若其中一个发散，则广义积分发散。

上述广义积分，在计算中都是先通过计算定积分，再取极限求出最后的结果。在计算定积分时，常义积分所用的一切计算方法均能使用，在求极限时有时还要用到洛必达法则才能求出最后的极限。对于无界函数的积分，它很容易和常义积分混淆在一起，计算前要认真分析一下是常义积分还是广义积分，否则将会出现错误的结果。

【例 1-3-15】 求 $\int_{e}^{+\infty}\dfrac{1}{x(\ln x)^2}\mathrm{d}x$ 。

解　方法 1：

$$\text{原式} = \lim_{b\to+\infty}\int_{e}^{b}\frac{1}{(\ln x)^2}\mathrm{d}\ln x = \lim_{b\to+\infty}\left(-\frac{1}{\ln x}\right)\Bigg|_{e}^{b}$$

$$= -\lim_{b\to+\infty}\left(\frac{1}{\ln b} - \frac{1}{\ln e}\right) = 1$$

方法 2：

$$\text{原式} = \int_{e}^{+\infty}\frac{1}{(\ln x)^2}\mathrm{d}\ln x = -\frac{1}{\ln x}\Bigg|_{e}^{+\infty}$$

$$= -\left(\lim_{x\to+\infty}\frac{1}{\ln x} - 1\right) = 1$$

【例 1-3-16】 求$\int_{-1}^{1}\frac{1}{x^3}\mathrm{d}x$。

解 $\lim\limits_{x\to0}\frac{1}{x^3}=\infty$，$x=0$为无穷不连续点。

方法 1：

$$原式=\int_{-1}^{0}\frac{1}{x^3}\mathrm{d}x+\int_{0}^{1}\frac{1}{x^3}\mathrm{d}x$$

因

$$\begin{aligned}\int_{0}^{1}\frac{1}{x^3}\mathrm{d}x&=\lim_{\varepsilon\to0^+}\int_{\varepsilon}^{1}\frac{1}{x^3}\mathrm{d}x\\&=\lim_{\varepsilon\to0^+}-\frac{1}{2}\left(\frac{1}{x^2}\right)\Big|_{\varepsilon}^{1}\\&=-\frac{1}{2}\left(1-\lim_{\varepsilon\to0^+}\frac{1}{\varepsilon^2}\right)\\&=+\infty\end{aligned}$$

所以广义积分$\int_{-1}^{1}\frac{1}{x^3}\mathrm{d}x$发散。

方法 2：

因

$$\begin{aligned}\int_{0}^{1}\frac{1}{x^3}\mathrm{d}x&=-\frac{1}{2}\left(\frac{1}{x^2}\Big|_{0}^{1}\right)\\&=-\frac{1}{2}\left(1-\lim_{x\to0^+}\frac{1}{x^2}\right)\\&=+\infty\end{aligned}$$

所以广义积分$\int_{-1}^{1}\frac{1}{x^3}\mathrm{d}x$发散。

注：在广义积分中，只要有一项发散则发散，即便是左右对称的情况，例如本题，$\int_{0}^{1}\frac{1}{x^3}\mathrm{d}x=+\infty$，而$\int_{-1}^{0}\frac{1}{x^3}\mathrm{d}x=-\infty$，看似相加即可抵消，然而却不能用这种思维来处理本题，因为正无穷大与负无穷大之和未必是0，这种情况就是发散。

【例 1-3-17】 下列广义积分收敛的是：

A. $\int_{1}^{+\infty}\cos x\mathrm{d}x$　　B. $\int_{1}^{+\infty}\frac{1}{x^3}\mathrm{d}x$

C. $\int_{1}^{+\infty}\ln x\mathrm{d}x$　　D. $\int_{1}^{+\infty}e^x\mathrm{d}x$

解 对每一选项通过计算检验

A. $\int_{1}^{+\infty}\cos x\mathrm{d}x=\sin x\Big|_{1}^{+\infty}$，振荡无极限

B. $\int_{1}^{+\infty}\frac{1}{x^3}\mathrm{d}x=-\frac{1}{2}x^{-2}\Big|_{1}^{+\infty}=\frac{1}{2}$

C. $\int_{1}^{+\infty}\ln x\mathrm{d}x=(x\ln x-x)\Big|_{1}^{+\infty}=x(\ln x-1)\Big|_{1}^{+\infty}=\lim\limits_{x\to+\infty}x(\ln x-1)+1=+\infty$

D. $\int_{1}^{+\infty}e^x\mathrm{d}x=e^x\Big|_{1}^{+\infty}=+\infty$

答案：B

【例 1-3-18】 下列命题或等式中，错误的是：

A. 设 $f(x)$ 在 $[-a,a]$ 上连续且为偶函数，则 $\int_{-a}^{a} f(x)\mathrm{d}x = 2\int_{0}^{a} f(x)\mathrm{d}x$

B. 设 $f(x)$ 在 $[-a,a]$ 上连续且为奇函数，则 $\int_{-a}^{a} f(x)\mathrm{d}x = 0$

C. 设 $f(x)$ 是 $(-\infty,+\infty)$ 上连续的周期函数，周期为 T，则 $\int_{a}^{a+T} f(x)\mathrm{d}x = \int_{0}^{T} f(x)\mathrm{d}x$

D. $\int_{-1}^{1} \frac{1}{x^2}\mathrm{d}x = -\frac{1}{x}\Big|_{-1}^{1} = -2$

解 由定积分公式计算可知选项 A、B 正确。选项 C 计算如下：

$$\int_{a}^{a+T} f(x)\mathrm{d}x = \int_{a}^{0} f(x)\mathrm{d}x + \int_{0}^{T} f(x)\mathrm{d}x + \int_{T}^{a+T} f(x)\mathrm{d}x \qquad ①$$

将式子 $\int_{T}^{a+T} f(x)\mathrm{d}x$ 变形，设 $x = t+T, \mathrm{d}x = \mathrm{d}t$。当 $x = T$ 时，$t = 0$；当 $x = a+T$ 时，$t = a$。

$$\int_{T}^{a+T} f(x)\mathrm{d}x = \int_{0}^{a} f(t+T)\mathrm{d}t = \int_{0}^{a} f(t)\mathrm{d}t = \int_{0}^{a} f(x)\mathrm{d}x = -\int_{a}^{0} f(x)\mathrm{d}x$$

代入式 ①，得 $\int_{a}^{a+T} f(x)\mathrm{d}x = \int_{0}^{T} f(x)\mathrm{d}x$，正确。

选项 D 是广义积分，计算如下：

$\int_{-1}^{1} \frac{1}{x^2}\mathrm{d}x = \int_{-1}^{0} \frac{1}{x^2}\mathrm{d}x + \int_{0}^{1} \frac{1}{x^2}\mathrm{d}x$ （$x = 0$ 为无穷间断点）

而 $\int_{-1}^{0} \frac{1}{x^2}\mathrm{d}x = \lim\limits_{\varepsilon\to 0^+}\int_{-1}^{0-\varepsilon} \frac{1}{x^2}\mathrm{d}x = \lim\limits_{\varepsilon\to 0^+}\left(\frac{-1}{x}\right)\Big|_{-1}^{0-\varepsilon} = \lim\limits_{\varepsilon\to 0^+}\left(\frac{1}{\varepsilon}-1\right) = +\infty$，错误。

答案：D

四、定积分的应用

通过定积分定义导出的微分元素法，对解决几何方面和物理方面的实际问题行之有效。

（一）用元素法解题的主要步骤

（1）确定积分变量及变量的变化区间；

（2）找出所求量的微分元素；

（3）在积分区间上积分。而选对积分变量及变量的变化区间、正确写出所求量的微分元素是微分元素法的关键。

（二）定积分的应用

1. 定积分的几何应用

计算平面图形的面积，旋转体和平行截面面积为已知的立体的体积，平面曲线的弧长。

（1）平面图形的面积

直角坐标方程：设曲边梯形由曲边 $y = f(x)[f(x) \geqslant 0]$，直线 $x = a, x = b$ 以及 x 轴围成，如图 1-3-1 所示。

$$A = \int_{a}^{b} f(x)\mathrm{d}x$$

参数方程:设曲边由参数方程 $\begin{cases} x = \varphi(t) \\ y = \psi(t) \end{cases}$ 给出,直线 $x = a, x = b$ 以及 x 轴围成,如图 1-3-2 所示。

则
$$A = \int_a^b f(x)\mathrm{d}x = \int_{t_1}^{t_2} \psi(t)\varphi'(t)\mathrm{d}t$$
(当 $x = a$ 时,$t = t_1$,当 $x = b$ 时,$t = t_2$)

极坐标方程:设曲边方程为 $r = r(\theta)$ 以及射线 $\theta = \alpha, \theta = \beta$ 围成的图形,如图 1-3-3 所示。

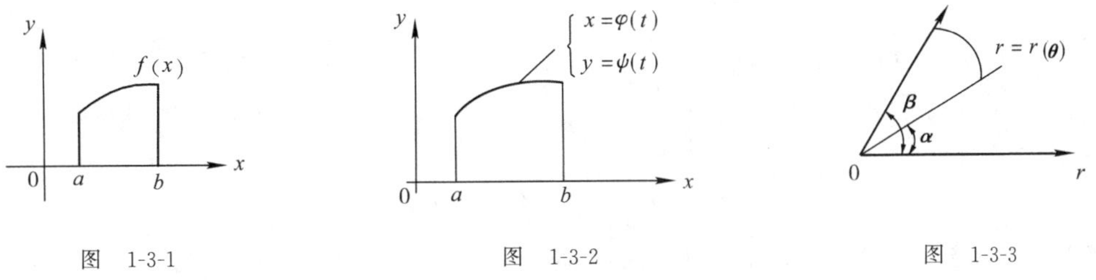

图 1-3-1　　图 1-3-2　　图 1-3-3

则
$$A = \int_\alpha^\beta \frac{1}{2} r^2(\theta)\mathrm{d}\theta$$

(2)体积

旋转体的体积:设由曲线 $y = f(x)$,直线 $x = a, x = b$ 以及 x 轴围成的平面图形,绕 x 轴旋转一周而生成的旋转体的体积,如图1-3-4所示。则
$$V_x = \int_a^b \pi[f(x)]^2 \mathrm{d}x$$

平行截面面积为已知的立体的体积:设立体由曲面 S,以及平面 $x = a$、$x = b$ 所围成,且对于 $[a,b]$ 上任一点 x 作垂直截面,截得的面积 $A = A(x)$ 为 x 的连续函数,如图 1-3-5 所示。则
$$V = \int_a^b A(x)\mathrm{d}x$$

图 1-3-4　　图 1-3-5

(3)平面曲线的弧长

直角坐标方程:曲线 C 的方程为 $y = f(x), a \leqslant x \leqslant b$,则 $s = \int_a^b \sqrt{1 + [f'(x)]^2}\mathrm{d}x$

参数方程:曲线 C 的方程为 $\begin{cases} x = \varphi(t) \\ y = \psi(t) \end{cases}, t_1 \leqslant t \leqslant t_2$,则 $s = \int_{t_1}^{t_2} \sqrt{[\varphi'(t)]^2 + [\psi'(t)]^2}\mathrm{d}t$

极坐标方程:曲线 C 的方程为 $r = r(\theta), \alpha \leqslant \theta \leqslant \beta$,则 $s = \int_\alpha^\beta \sqrt{[r(\theta)]^2 + [r'(\theta)]^2}\mathrm{d}\theta$

2. 定积分的物理应用

计算物体作变速直线运动所经历的路程及物体在变力作用下沿直线运动所做的功、水压力等。

【例 1-3-19】 计算抛物线 $y^2 = 2x$ 与直线 $y = x - 4$ 所围成平面图形的面积。

解 如解图所示，求交点$\begin{cases} y^2 = 2x \\ y = x - 4 \end{cases}$，得(8,4)和(2,−2)

选积分变量为 y，则

$$A = \int_{-2}^{4}\left(y + 4 - \frac{1}{2}y^2\right)dy$$

$$= \left(\frac{1}{2}y^2 + 4y - \frac{1}{6}y^3\right)\Bigg|_{-2}^{4} = 18$$

选积分变量为 x，则

$$A = \int_0^2 [\sqrt{2x} - (-\sqrt{2x})]dx + \int_2^8 [\sqrt{2x} - (x - 4)]dx$$

$$= \int_0^2 2\sqrt{2x}\,dx + \int_2^8 (\sqrt{2x} - x + 4)dx = 18$$

例 1-3-19 解图

【例 1-3-20】 曲线 $y=\ln x$，$y=\ln a$，$y=\ln b(0<a<b)$及 y 轴所围图形的面积为 A（见图），则 A 等于：

A. $\int_{\ln a}^{\ln b}\ln x dx$　　B. $\int_{e^a}^{e^b}e^x dx$

C. $\int_{\ln a}^{\ln b}e^y dy$　　D. $\int_{e^a}^{e^b}\ln x dx$

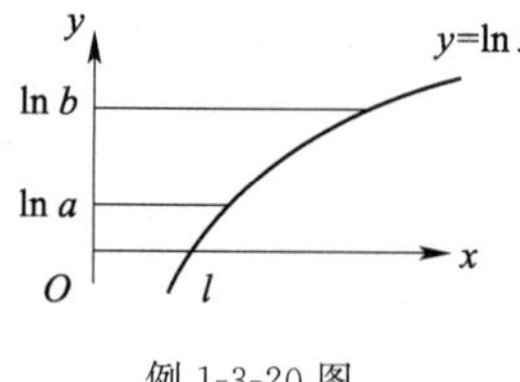

例 1-3-20 图

解 选积分变量为 y，$y\in[\ln a,\ln b]$，由 $y=\ln x$，得 $x=e^y$

则 $dA=e^y dy$，即 $A=\int_{\ln a}^{\ln b}e^y dy$

答案：C

【例 1-3-21】 计算：(1)求由直线 $x=0$，$x=2$，$y=0$ 与抛物线 $y=-x^2+1$ 所围成平面图形的面积 S；(2)求上述平面图形绕 x 轴旋转一周所得的旋转体的体积 V_x（见图）。

解 因为平面图形有一部分在 x 轴的上方，另有一部分在 x 轴下方，在计算面积 I_2 时需加一个负号。

例 1-3-21 图

(1) $S = \int_0^1 (-x^2 + 1)dx + \int_1^2 -(-x^2 + 1)dx$

$$= \left(-\frac{1}{3}x^3 + x\right)\Bigg|_0^1 + \left(\frac{1}{3}x^3 - x\right)\Bigg|_1^2$$

$$= 2$$

(2) $V_x = \int_0^1 \pi(-x^2 + 1)^2 dx + \int_1^2 \pi[-(-x^2 + 1)]^2 dx$

$$= \pi\int_0^2 (-x^2 + 1)^2 dx = \pi\int_0^2 (x^4 - 2x^2 + 1)dx$$

$$= \pi\left(\frac{1}{5}x^5 - \frac{2}{3}x^3 + x\right)\Bigg|_0^2 = \frac{46}{15}\pi$$

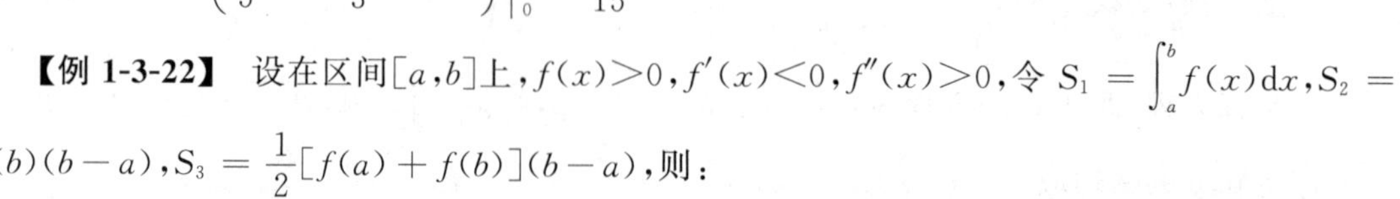
【例 1-3-22】 设在区间$[a,b]$上，$f(x)>0$，$f'(x)<0$，$f''(x)>0$，令 $S_1 = \int_a^b f(x)dx$，$S_2 = f(b)(b-a)$，$S_3 = \frac{1}{2}[f(a) + f(b)](b-a)$，则：

A. $S_1<S_2<S_3$　　B. $S_2<S_1<S_3$　　C. $S_3<S_1<S_2$　　D. $S_2<S_3<S_1$

解 在$[a,b]$上，$y=f(x)$如解图所示。

由已知　$f(x)>0$，图形在 x 轴上方

$f'(x)<0$，$f(x)$的图形单调减少

$f''(x)>0$，$f(x)$的图形为凹形

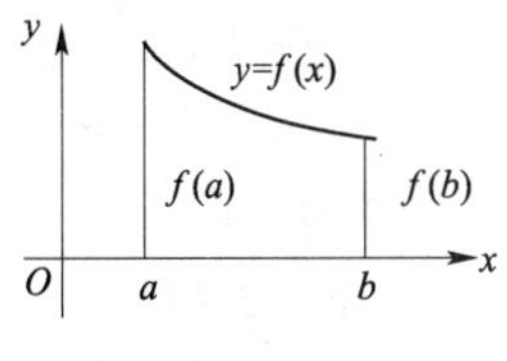

例 1-3-22 解图

$S_1=\int_a^b f(x)\mathrm{d}x$ 为由 $y=f(x)$，$x=a$，$x=b$ 及 x 轴所围成的图形面积。

$S_2=f(b)(b-a)$表示的是以最小值 $f(b)$为高，以$(b-a)$为底的长方形面积。

$S_3=\dfrac{1}{2}[f(a)+f(b)](b-a)$表示以 $f(a)$为下底，$f(b)$为上底，$(b-a)$为高的梯形面积。

由画出的图形可知，面积大小的顺序为 $S_2<S_1<S_3$。

答案：B

【例 1-3-23】 求由曲线 $y=2-x^2$ 与 $y=|x|$所围成图形的面积(见图)。下列表示式错误的是：

A. $\int_{-1}^{0}(2-x^2+x)\mathrm{d}x+\int_0^1(2-x^2-x)\mathrm{d}x$

B. $\int_0^1 2y\mathrm{d}y+\int_1^2 2\sqrt{2-y}\mathrm{d}y$

C. $2\int_0^1(2-x^2-x)\mathrm{d}x$

D. $\int_{-1}^{1}(2-x^2-x)\mathrm{d}x$

例 1-3-23 图

解　$\begin{cases}y=2-x^2\\y=x\end{cases}$ 与 $\begin{cases}y=2-x^2\\y=-x\end{cases}$ 的交点分别为$(1,1)$、$(-1,1)$，经分析 A、B、C 列式均正确。

A. 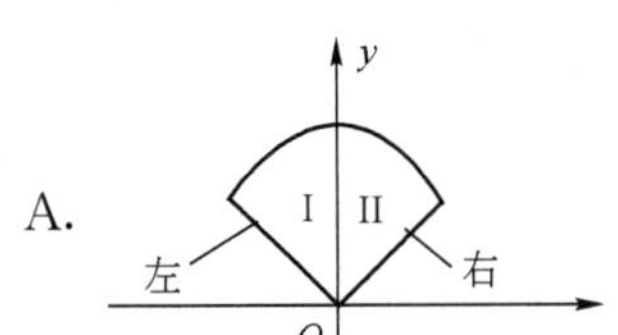

为按左右两部分分别列式计算面积。

B. 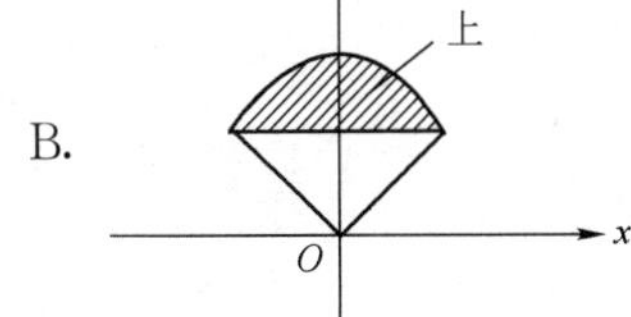

利用图形关于 y 轴的对称式，按上、下两部分分别列式计算面积。

C. 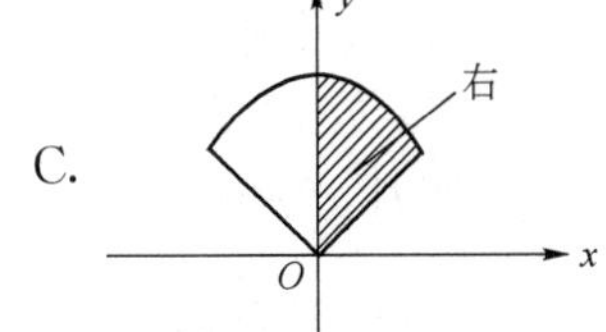

利用图形关于 y 轴对称，面积为右半部面积的 2 倍列式计算面积。

D. 列式错误在于对曲线 $y=2-x^2$ 与 $y=|x|$所围成图形的理解有误。

$$y=|x|=\begin{cases}x & x\geqslant 0\\-x & x<0\end{cases}$$

两交点坐标应为(−1,1)、(1,1)。选项 D 的被积函数 $f(x)=2-x^2-x$ 是由计算曲线 $y=2-x^2$、$y=x$ 与 y 轴所围成图形面积元素的表达式。

答案:D

【例 1-3-24】 由交点为(x_1,y_1)及(x_2,y_2)(其中 $x_1<x_2$)的两曲线 $y=f(x)>0$,$y=g(x)>0$[$f(x)\geqslant g(x)$]所围图形绕 x 轴旋转一周所得的旋转体体积 V 是:

A. $\int_{x_1}^{x_2}\pi[f(x)-g(x)]^2\mathrm{d}x$　　B. $\int_{x_1}^{x_2}\pi[f^2(x)-g^2(x)]\mathrm{d}x$

C. $\int_{x_1}^{x_2}[\pi f(x)]^2\mathrm{d}x-\int_{x_1}^{x_2}[\pi g(x)]^2\mathrm{d}x$　　D. $\int_{x_1}^{x_2}[\pi f(x)-\pi g(x)]\mathrm{d}x$

解 如解图所示,$x\in[x_1,x_2]$

$$\text{则 } \mathrm{d}V=\pi f^2(x)\mathrm{d}x-\pi g^2(x)\mathrm{d}x=\pi[f^2(x)-g^2(x)]\mathrm{d}x$$

$$V=\int_{x_1}^{x_2}\pi[f^2(x)-g^2(x)]\mathrm{d}x$$

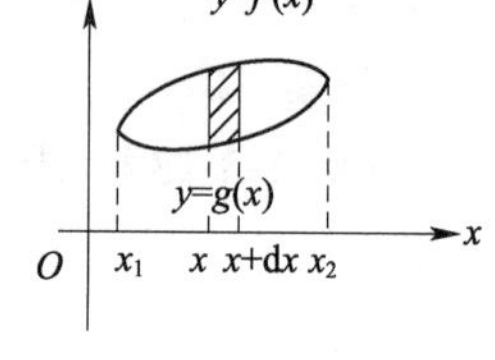

例 1-3-24 解图

答案:B

习　题

1-3-1 下列各式中正确的是(C 为任意常数)(　　)。

A. $\int f'(3-2x)\mathrm{d}x=-\frac{1}{2}f(3-2x)+C$

B. $\int f'(3-2x)\mathrm{d}x=-f(3-2x)+C$

C. $\int f'(3-2x)\mathrm{d}x=f(x)+C$

D. $\int f'(3-2x)\mathrm{d}x=\frac{1}{2}f(3-2x)+C$

1-3-2 设 $F(x)$ 是 $f(x)$ 的一个原函数,则 $\int e^{-x}f(e^{-x})\mathrm{d}x$ 等于(　　)。

A. $F(e^{-x})+C$　　B. $-F(e^{-x})+C$

C. $F(e^{x})+C$　　D. $-F(e^{x})+C$

1-3-3 计算积分 $\int\frac{f'(\ln x)}{x\sqrt{f(\ln x)}}\mathrm{d}x=$(　　)。

A. $\sqrt{f(\ln x)}+C$　　B. $-\sqrt{f(\ln x)}+C$

C. $2\sqrt{f(\ln x)}+C$　　D. $-2\sqrt{f(\ln x)}+C$

1-3-4 设 $f(x)$ 的一个原函数为 $\cos x$,$g(x)$ 的一个原函数为 x^2,则 $f[g(x)]=$(　　)。

A. $\cos x^2$　　B. $-\sin x^2$　　C. $\cos 2x$　　D. $-\sin 2x$

1-3-5 如果 $\int\frac{f'(\ln x)}{x}\mathrm{d}x=x^2+C$,则 $f(x)=$(　　)$+C$。

A. $\frac{1}{x^2}$　　B. e^x　　C. e^{2x}　　D. xe^x

1-3-6　设 $f(x)$连续，则$\lim\limits_{x \to a}\dfrac{x}{x-a}\displaystyle\int_a^x f(t)\mathrm{d}t$ 为(　　)。

A. 0　　B. a　　C. $af(a)$　　D. $f(a)$

1-3-7　设函数 $f(x)$ 在区间$[a,b]$上连续，则下列结论不正确的是(　　)。

A. $\displaystyle\int_a^b f(x)\mathrm{d}x$ 是 $f(x)$ 的一个原函数

B. $\displaystyle\int_a^x f(t)\mathrm{d}t$ 是 $f(x)$ 的一个原函数 $(a<x<b)$

C. $\displaystyle\int_x^b f(t)\mathrm{d}t$ 是 $-f(x)$ 的一个原函数$(a<x<b)$

D. $f(x)$ 在$[a,b]$上是可积的

1-3-8　若 $f(x)$为可导函数，且已知 $f(0)=0$，$f'(0)=2$，则$\lim\limits_{x \to 0}\dfrac{\int_0^x f(t)\mathrm{d}t}{x^2}=$(　　)。

A. 0　　B. 1　　C. 2　　D. 不存在

1-3-9　广义积分 $I=\displaystyle\int_e^{+\infty}\frac{\mathrm{d}x}{x(\ln x)^2}$，则(　　)。

A. $I-1$　　B. $I=-1$　　C. $I=\dfrac{1}{2}$　　D. 此广义积分发散

1-3-10　下列广义积分中发散的是(　　)。

A. $\displaystyle\int_2^{+\infty}\frac{1}{x\ln^3 x}\mathrm{d}x$　　B. $\displaystyle\int_0^{+\infty}e^{-x}\mathrm{d}x$

C. $\displaystyle\int_{-1}^0\frac{2}{\sqrt{1-x^2}}\mathrm{d}x$　　D. $\displaystyle\int_1^e\frac{1}{x\ln x}\mathrm{d}x$

1-3-11　设 $Q(x)=\displaystyle\int_0^{x^2}te^{-t}\mathrm{d}t$，则 $Q'(x)=$(　　)。

A. xe^{-x}　　B. $-xe^{-x}$　　C. $2x^3e^{-x^2}$　　D. $-2x^3e^{-x^2}$

1-3-12　$\displaystyle\int_0^a f(x)\mathrm{d}x=$(　　)。

A. $\displaystyle\int_0^{\frac{a}{2}}[f(x)+f(x-a)]\mathrm{d}x$　　B. $\displaystyle\int_0^{\frac{a}{2}}[f(x)+f(a-x)]\mathrm{d}x$

C. $\displaystyle\int_0^{\frac{a}{2}}[f(x)-f(a-x)]\mathrm{d}x$　　D. $\displaystyle\int_0^{\frac{a}{2}}[f(x)-f(x-a)]\mathrm{d}x$

1-3-13　设 $f(x)=\begin{cases}1, 0\leqslant x\leqslant \dfrac{1}{2}\\ 0, \dfrac{1}{2}<x\leqslant 1\end{cases}$，则 ξ 在等式 $f(\xi)=\displaystyle\int_0^1 f(x)\mathrm{d}x$ 中的情况是(　　)。

A. 在$[0,1]$内至少有一点 ξ，使该式成立

B. 在$[0,1]$内不存在 ξ，使该式成立

C. 在$[0,\frac{1}{2}]$，$(\frac{1}{2},1]$都存在 ξ，使该式成立

D. 仅在$[0,\frac{1}{2}]$中存在 ξ，使该式成立

1-3-14　下列结论中，错误的是(　　)。

A. $\int_{-a}^{a} f(x^2)\mathrm{d}x = 2\int_{0}^{a} f(x^2)\mathrm{d}x$　　B. $\int_{0}^{2\pi} \sin^{10} x\mathrm{d}x = \int_{0}^{2\pi} \cos^{10} x\mathrm{d}x$

C. $\int_{-\pi}^{\pi} \cos 5x \sin 7x \mathrm{d}x = 0$　　D. $\int_{0}^{1} 10^x \mathrm{d}x = 9$

1-3-15　设 $f(x)$ 在 $[-a,a]$ 上连续且为非零偶函数，则 $\varphi(x) = \int_{0}^{x} f(t)\mathrm{d}t$ 是(　　)。

A. 偶函数　　B. 奇函数　　C. 非奇非偶函数　　D. 不存在

1-3-16　设函数 $f(x)$ 在 $[0, +\infty]$ 上连续，且满足 $f(x) = xe^{-x} + e^x\int_{0}^{1} f(x)\mathrm{d}x$，则 $f(x)$ 是(　　)。

A. xe^{-x}　　B. $xe^{-x} - e^{x-1}$

C. e^{x-1}　　D. $(x-1)e^{-x}$

1-3-17　曲线 $y^2 = 4 - x$ 与 y 轴所围成部分的面积为(　　)。

A. $\int_{-2}^{2} (4 - y^2)\mathrm{d}y$　　B. $\int_{0}^{2} (4 - y^2)\mathrm{d}y$

C. $\int_{0}^{4} \sqrt{4 - x}\mathrm{d}x$　　D. $\int_{-4}^{4} \sqrt{4 - x}\mathrm{d}x$

1-3-18　在区间 $[0,2\pi]$ 上，曲线 $y = \sin x$ 与 $y = \cos x$ 之间所围图形的面积是(　　)。

A. $\int_{\frac{\pi}{4}}^{\pi} (\sin x - \cos x)\mathrm{d}x$　　B. $\int_{\frac{\pi}{4}}^{\frac{5}{4}\pi} (\sin x - \cos x)\mathrm{d}x$

C. $\int_{0}^{2\pi} (\sin x - \cos x)\mathrm{d}x$　　D. $\int_{0}^{\frac{5}{4}\pi} (\sin x - \cos x)\mathrm{d}x$

第四节　多元函数微分学

一、多元函数的概念

(一) n 元函数定义

设有集合 $E \subset R^n$(R^n 表示 n 维实数空间)，如果对于 E 中每一点 $P(x_1, x_2, \cdots, x_n)$，均有一个确定的 u 值与之对应，则称 u 为 $(x_1, x_2, \cdots, x_n)$ 的 n 元函数(当 $n \geqslant 2$ 时称为多元函数)。

在 R^n 中点 $P_1(x_1, x_2, \cdots, x_n)$ 和点 $P_2(y_1, y_2, \cdots, y_n)$ 间的距离公式为

$$|P_1P_2| = \sqrt{(y_1 - x_1)^2 + \cdots + (y_n - x_n)^2} \tag{1-4-1}$$

与点 P_0 的距离小于 $\delta(\delta > 0)$ 的点 M 的全体称为点 P_0 的 δ 邻域，记为 $U(P_0, \delta)$。用 $U(P_0)$ 表示点 P_0 的某一邻域；用 $\overline{U}(P_0, \delta)$ 表示某一去心的点 P_0 的 δ 邻域。

(当 $n=2$ 时，即二元函数的定义，二维空间两点间的距离公式及点 P_0 的 δ 邻域的概念同上。)

(二) 二元函数的极限

设二元函数 $z = f(x, y)$ 的定义域为 $D \subset R^2$，点 $P(x_0, y_0)$ 为 D 的聚点(即在 P_0 的任一邻域内，总含有 D 中无限多个点，则称 P_0 为 D 的聚点)。若 $\forall \varepsilon > 0$，$\exists \delta > 0$，使当 $0 < \sqrt{(x - x_0)^2 + (y - y_0)^2} < \delta$ 时，有 $|f(x, y) - A| < \varepsilon$ 成立，则称 A 为二元函数 $f(x, y)$，当 $(x, y) \to (x_0, y_0)$ 的极限，记为 $\lim\limits_{\substack{x \to x_0 \\ y \to y_0}} f(x, y) = A$，其中点 $(x, y) \to (x_0, y_0)$ 要求以任意方式进行，

极限均存在且相等，仅个别路径不行，这是二元函数极限与一元函数极限最大的不同之处。

二元函数比一元函数多了一个自变量，求极限时注意它们的区别与联系。关于一元函数的极限的运算法则和计算公式，可以推广到二元函数，但形式要比一元复杂得多。

（三）二元函数的连续性

设 $f(x,y)$ 的定义域为 D，$M_0(x_0,y_0)\in D$，且为 D 的聚点，若有 $\lim\limits_{\substack{x\to x_0\\ y\to y_0}} f(x,y)=f(x_0,y_0)$，则称 $f(x,y)$ 在点 M_0 连续。若 $f(x,y)$ 在区域 D 中的每一点均连续，则称 $f(x,y)$ 在 D 上连续。在有界闭区域上连续的二元函数，介值定理、最值定理仍成立。连续二元函数的和、差、积、商（分母不为零）仍为连续函数，二元连续函数的复合函数也具有相应的连续性。二元初等函数在定义域上连续。这些性质都可推广到三元以上的函数中。

二、二元函数的偏导数和全微分

（一）偏导数

1. 二元函数在一点的偏导数

设 $z=f(x,y)$ 在点 $P_0(x_0,y_0)$ 的某一邻域内有定义，$P_1(x_0+\Delta x,y_0)$ 为该邻域内的一点，若有

$$\lim_{\Delta x\to 0}\frac{f(x_0+\Delta x,y_0)-f(x_0,y_0)}{\Delta x} \tag{1-4-2}$$

存在，则称此极限为 $f(x,y)$ 在点 P_0 处对 x 的偏导数，记作 $z'_x\Big|_{(x_0,y_0)}$，$\dfrac{\partial z}{\partial x}\Big|_{(x_0,y_0)}$，$f'_x\Big|_{(x_0,y_0)}$，$\dfrac{\partial f}{\partial x}\Big|_{(x_0,y_0)}$。

类似地，函数 $z=f(x,y)$ 在点 $P_0(x_0,y_0)$ 处对 y 的偏导数定义为 $f'_y(x_0,y_0)=\lim\limits_{\Delta y\to 0}\dfrac{f(x_0,y_0+\Delta y)-f(x_0,y_0)}{\Delta y}$，记作 $z'_y|_{(x_0,y_0)}$，$\dfrac{\partial z}{\partial y}|_{(x_0,y_0)}$，$f'_y|_{(x_0,y_0)}$，$\dfrac{\partial f}{\partial y}|_{(x_0,y_0)}$。

2. 二元函数偏导函数

若 $z=f(x,y)$ 在定义域 D 内的每一点 (x,y) 处对 x（或 y）的偏导数都存在，称这种对应关系所确定的函数为函数 z 对 x（对 y）的偏导函数，记作 $\dfrac{\partial z}{\partial x}$，$z'_x$，$\dfrac{\partial f}{\partial x}$，$f'_x$（$\dfrac{\partial z}{\partial y}$，$z'_y$，$\dfrac{\partial f}{\partial y}$，$f'_y$）。

计算二元函数在一点的偏导数，可以用定义求，也可用先求出偏导函数再代值的方法计算。求二元函数的偏导函数时，只要把一个变量当作变量，另一个变量看作常数求导即可。对于二元分段函数，在分界点处的偏导数，必须用函数在一点偏导数定义计算。

对于一元函数，曾有函数在一点可导，在这一点必连续的结论；对于二元函数，函数在一点存在对 x、对 y 的偏导数，但不能保证函数在这一点连续。

3. 基本概念关系图（见图 1-4-1）

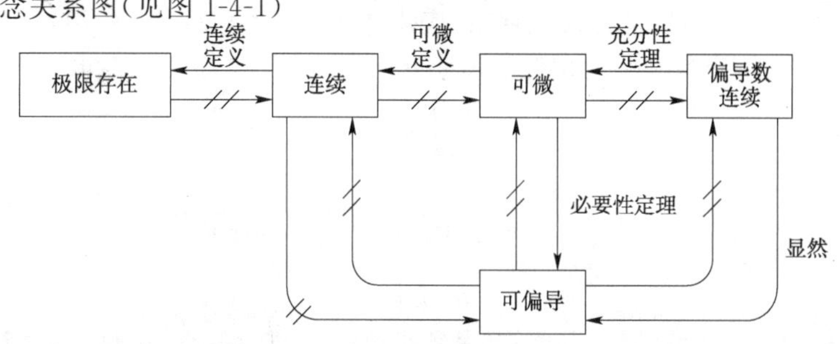

图 1-4-1

反例就不一一列举了，请大家记住结论即可。

4. 二元函数高阶偏导

函数 $z=f(x,y)$ 在 D 内的偏导数 $\frac{\partial z}{\partial x}$ 和 $\frac{\partial z}{\partial y}$ 仍是 x,y 的二元函数，如果 $\frac{\partial z}{\partial x}$ 和 $\frac{\partial z}{\partial y}$ 的偏导数也存在，则称它们的偏导数为 $z=f(x,y)$ 的二阶偏导数，按求导数次序不同有

$$\frac{\partial^2 z}{\partial x^2}=\frac{\partial}{\partial x}\left(\frac{\partial z}{\partial x}\right) \qquad \frac{\partial^2 z}{\partial x\partial y}=\frac{\partial}{\partial y}\left(\frac{\partial z}{\partial x}\right)$$

$$\frac{\partial^2 z}{\partial y^2}=\frac{\partial}{\partial y}\left(\frac{\partial z}{\partial y}\right) \qquad \frac{\partial^2 z}{\partial y\partial x}=\frac{\partial}{\partial x}\left(\frac{\partial z}{\partial y}\right)$$

其中，$\frac{\partial^2 z}{\partial x\partial y}$ 与 $\frac{\partial^2 z}{\partial y\partial x}$ 称为二阶混合偏导。类似可定义三阶、四阶以及 n 阶偏导。二阶及二阶以上的偏导数称为高阶偏导数。在 $\frac{\partial^2 z}{\partial x\partial y}$ 与 $\frac{\partial^2 z}{\partial y\partial x}$ 连续时，高阶混合偏导与求导的次序无关，即 $\frac{\partial^2 z}{\partial x\partial y}=\frac{\partial^2 z}{\partial y\partial x}$。即高阶混合偏导相等。

（二）全微分

（1）二元函数全微分定义：

设 $z=f(x,y)$ 在点 $P(x,y)$ 的某一邻域内有定义，点 $P_1(x+\Delta x,y+\Delta y)$ 在该邻域内，若全增量 $\Delta z=f(x+\Delta x,y+\Delta y)-f(x,y)$ 可表示为

$$\Delta z=A\Delta x+B\Delta y+o(\rho) \tag{1-4-3}$$

式中，A、B 与 Δx 及 Δy 无关；而仅与 x、y 有关，$\rho=\sqrt{(\Delta x)^2+(\Delta y)^2}$，$o(\rho)$ 表示关于 ρ 的高阶无穷小。则称 $f(x,y)$ 在 (x,y) 处可微。$A\Delta x+B\Delta y$ 为 $f(x,y)$ 在点 (x,y) 处的全微分，记作 $\mathrm{d}z=A\Delta x+B\Delta y$。

若 $z=f(x,y)$ 在区域 D 内每点均可微分，称 $f(x,y)$ 在区域 D 内可微。

函数 $z=f(x,y)$ 的全微分为

$$\mathrm{d}z=\frac{\partial z}{\partial x}\mathrm{d}x+\frac{\partial z}{\partial y}\mathrm{d}y \tag{1-4-4}$$

（2）如果函数 $z=f(x,y)$ 在点 (x,y) 处可微，则该函数在点 (x,y) 的偏导 $\frac{\partial z}{\partial x}$、$\frac{\partial z}{\partial y}$ 都存在，且 $\mathrm{d}z=\frac{\partial z}{\partial x}\mathrm{d}x+\frac{\partial z}{\partial y}\mathrm{d}y$。

（3）二元函数在 (x,y) 点可微、偏导存在、连续之间的关系（见图 1-4-2）：

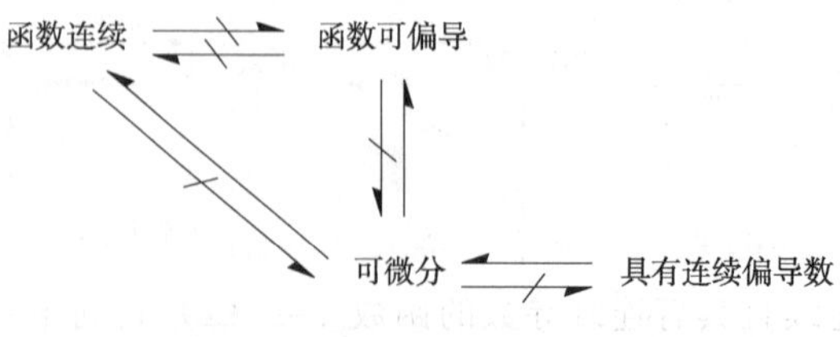

图 1-4-2

二元函数 $z=f(x,y)$ 在 (x,y) 点可微，函数在点 (x,y) 的偏导一定存在；但偏导存在，二元

函数在点(x,y)不一定可微。函数$z=f(x,y)$在点(x,y)可微,则函数在点(x,y)连续;但函数在点(x,y)连续,二元函数在这一点不一定可微。如果函数$z=f(x,y)$的偏导数$\frac{\partial z}{\partial x}$、$\frac{\partial z}{\partial y}$在点$(x,y)$连续,则二元函数在该点可微分。

这个结论一定要牢记,在考概念性题目中经常要用到。

(4)二元函数$f(x,y)$在一点(x_0,y_0)偏导的几何意义

二元函数$z=f(x,y)$在$P_0(x_0,y_0)$对x的偏导数$f'_x(x_0,y_0)$的几何意义为曲线C:$z=f(x,y)$,$y=y_0$在点$M_0(x_0,y_0,z_0)$的切线斜率。对y的偏导数$f'_y(x_0,y_0)$表示曲线C:$z=f(x,y)$,$x=x_0$在点$M_0(x_0,y_0,z_0)$的切线斜率。

(三)复合函数的微分法

1.复合函数全导数公式

设$u=\varphi(t)$,$v=\psi(t)$在点t可导,函数$z=f(u,v)$在对应点(u,v)具有连续偏导数,则复合函数$z=f[\varphi(t),\psi(t)]$在点t可导,且有

$$\frac{\mathrm{d}z}{\mathrm{d}t}=\frac{\partial z}{\partial u}\frac{\mathrm{d}u}{\mathrm{d}t}+\frac{\partial z}{\partial v}\frac{\mathrm{d}v}{\mathrm{d}t} \tag{1-4-5}$$

推广:设$u=f(x,y,z,t)$,$x=u(t)$,$y=v(t)$,$z=\omega(t)$,则

$$\frac{\mathrm{d}u}{\mathrm{d}t}=\frac{\partial u}{\partial x}\frac{\mathrm{d}x}{\mathrm{d}t}+\frac{\partial u}{\partial y}\frac{\mathrm{d}y}{\mathrm{d}t}+\frac{\partial u}{\partial z}\frac{\mathrm{d}z}{\mathrm{d}t}+\frac{\partial u}{\partial t} \tag{1-4-6}$$

式(1-4-5)、式(1-4-6)称函数z对t的全导数公式。

2.复合函数偏导数公式

推广到多个中间变量,多个自变量的情况有下面公式:

(1)设$z=f(u,v)$,$u=\varphi(x,y)$,$v=\psi(x,y)$,则

$$\frac{\partial z}{\partial x}=\frac{\partial z}{\partial u}\cdot\frac{\partial u}{\partial x}+\frac{\partial z}{\partial v}\cdot\frac{\partial v}{\partial x}\qquad\frac{\partial z}{\partial y}=\frac{\partial z}{\partial u}\cdot\frac{\partial u}{\partial y}+\frac{\partial z}{\partial v}\cdot\frac{\partial v}{\partial y} \tag{1-4-7}$$

(2)设$z=f(u,x,y)$,$u=\varphi(x,y)$,则复合函数$z=f[\varphi(x,y),x,y]$的偏导数

$$\frac{\partial z}{\partial x}=\frac{\partial f}{\partial u}\cdot\frac{\partial u}{\partial x}+\frac{\partial f}{\partial x}\qquad\frac{\partial z}{\partial y}=\frac{\partial f}{\partial u}\cdot\frac{\partial u}{\partial y}+\frac{\partial f}{\partial y} \tag{1-4-8}$$

(3)设$z=f(u,v,\omega)$,$u=\varphi(x,y)$,$v=\psi(x,y)$,$\omega=\omega(x,y)$,则

$$\frac{\partial z}{\partial x}=\frac{\partial z}{\partial u}\cdot\frac{\partial u}{\partial x}+\frac{\partial z}{\partial v}\cdot\frac{\partial v}{\partial x}+\frac{\partial z}{\partial \omega}\cdot\frac{\partial \omega}{\partial x} \tag{1-4-9a}$$

$$\frac{\partial z}{\partial y}=\frac{\partial z}{\partial u}\cdot\frac{\partial u}{\partial y}+\frac{\partial z}{\partial v}\cdot\frac{\partial v}{\partial y}+\frac{\partial z}{\partial \omega}\cdot\frac{\partial \omega}{\partial y} \tag{1-4-9b}$$

(四)隐函数的微分法

(1)设方程$F(x,y)=0$,满足$F(x_0,y_0)=0$,$F(x,y)$在点(x_0,y_0)的某一邻域内连续,且有连续的偏导数$F'_x(x,y)$、$F'_y(x,y)$,$F'_y(x_0,y_0)\neq 0$,则方程$F(x,y)=0$在点(x_0,y_0)的邻域内恒能唯一确定一个单值连续且具有连续导数的函数$y=f(x)$,它满足条件$y_0=f(x_0)$,并有

$$\frac{\mathrm{d}y}{\mathrm{d}x}=-\frac{F'_x(x,y)}{F'_y(x,y)} \tag{1-4-10}$$

(2)设方程 $F(x,y,z)=0$ 满足 $F(x_0,y_0,z_0)=0$，$F(x,y,z)$ 在点 (x_0,y_0,z_0) 的某一邻域内连续且有连续偏导数 $F'_x(x,y,z)$、$F'_y(x,y,z)$、$F'_z(x,y,z)$，$F'_z(x_0,y_0,z_0)\neq 0$，则在点 (x_0,y_0,z_0) 的邻域内，方程 $F(x,y,z)=0$ 恒能唯一确定一个单值且具有连续偏导数的函数 $z=f(x,y)$，它满足条件 $z_0=f(x_0,y_0)$，并有

$$\frac{\partial z}{\partial x}=-\frac{F'_x(x,y,z)}{F'_z(x,y,z)} \qquad \frac{\partial z}{\partial y}=-\frac{F'_y(x,y,z)}{F'_z(x,y,z)} \tag{1-4-11}$$

三、多元函数的应用

(一)空间曲线的切线与法平面

设空间曲线 γ 的参数方程为 $x=x(t)$，$y=y(t)$，$z=z(t)$，其中 $x(t)$，$y(t)$，$z(t)$ 均可微。曲线 γ 上的点 $M_0(x_0,y_0,z_0)$ 对应 $t=t_0$，且 $x'(t_0)$、$y'(t_0)$、$z'(t_0)$ 不同时为零，则曲线 γ 在点 M_0 处的切线方程为

$$\frac{x-x_0}{x'(t_0)}=\frac{y-y_0}{y'(t_0)}=\frac{z-z_0}{z'(t_0)} \tag{1-4-12}$$

过点 M_0 与切线垂直的平面称为曲线 γ 在点 M_0 处的法平面，它的方程为

$$x'(t_0)(x-x_0)+y'(t_0)(y-y_0)+z'(t_0)(z-z_0)=0$$

其中 $\{x'(t_0),y'(t_0),z'(t_0)\}$ 既是曲线 γ 在 M_0 处的切线的方向向量，又是 γ 在 M_0 处的法平面的法向量。

(二)曲面的切平面与法线

设曲面 Σ 的方程为 $F(x,y,z)=0$，$M_0(x_0,y_0,z_0)$ 为 Σ 上的一点，$F(x,y,z)$ 在点 M_0 可微，且 $F'_x(x_0,y_0,z_0)$，$F'_y(x_0,y_0,z_0)$，$F'_z(x_0,y_0,z_0)$ 不同时为零，则曲面 Σ 在点 M_0 处的切平面方程为

$$F'_x|_{M_0}(x-x_0)+F'_y|_{M_0}(y-y_0)+F'_z|_{M_0}(z-z_0)=0 \tag{1-4-13}$$

过点 M_0 与切平面垂直的直线称为曲面 Σ 在 M_0 的法线，法线方程为

$$\frac{x-x_0}{F'_x(x_0,y_0,z_0)}=\frac{y-y_0}{F'_y(x_0,y_0,z_0)}=\frac{z-z_0}{F'_z(x_0,y_0,z_0)} \tag{1-4-14}$$

其中，$\{F'_x,F'_y,F'_z\}_{M_0}$ 既是曲面 Σ 在点 M_0 处的切平面的法向量，又是曲面 Σ 在点 M_0 处的法线的方向向量。

(三)多元函数的极值

多元函数的极值问题分为无条件极值和条件极值两大类。对于自变量除了限定其在定义域内变化外，没有其他任何限制的极值问题，称为无条件极值；如果自变量还要受一定的其他条件限制，则称为条件极值。

1. 无条件极值

设函数 $z=f(x,y)$ 在点 (x_0,y_0) 的某个邻域内有定义，对于该邻域内异于点 (x_0,y_0) 的点 (x,y)，恒有 $f(x,y)<f(x_0,y_0)$ [或 $f(x,y)>f(x_0,y_0)$]，则称 $f(x_0,y_0)$ 为 $f(x,y)$ 的极大值(或极小值)，则称点 (x_0,y_0) 为极大值点(或极小值点)。

函数的极大值和极小值统称为函数的极值。使 $f(x,y)$ 的一阶偏导数均等于零的点称

为 $f(x,y)$ 的驻点。可偏导的函数在点 (x_0,y_0) 取得极值的必要条件是点 (x_0,y_0) 为它的驻点。

驻点和使 $f(x,y)$ 的一阶偏导数不存在的点统称为函数的极值可疑点，判断驻点是否为函数的极值点的方法如下：

设函数 $z=f(x,y)$ 在点 (x_0,y_0) 的某邻域内连续且有一阶及二阶连续偏导数，又 $f'_x(x_0,y_0)=0$，$f'_y(x_0,y_0)=0$，记 $A=f''_{xx}(x_0,y_0)$，$B=f''_{xy}(x_0,y_0)$，$C=f''_{yy}(x_0,y_0)$ 则

(1) $AC-B^2>0$ 时具有极值，且当 $A<0$ 时有极大值，当 $A>0$ 时有极小值；

(2) $AC-B^2<0$ 时没有极值；

(3) $AC-B^2=0$ 时可能有极值，也可能没有极值，需另找其他方法判断。

2. 条件极值

求解条件极值的基本方法是设法将它转化为无条件极值问题求解。常用的转化方法有两种：(1) 直接由约束条件找出变量之间的关系，代入目标函数将条件极值化为无条件极值；(2) 运用拉格朗日乘数法，构造辅助函数，将条件极值化为无条件极值。

拉格朗日乘数法：求 $z=f(x,y)$（目标函数）在约束条件 $\varphi(x,y)=0$ 下的极值，可构造函数

$$F(x,y,\lambda)=f(x,y)+\lambda\varphi(x,y) \tag{1-4-15}$$

将 $F(x,y,\lambda)$ 分别对 x、y、λ 求偏导，并令其为零，得到 $\begin{cases}F'_x=f'_x+\lambda\varphi'_x=0\\F'_y=f'_y+\lambda\varphi'_y=0\\F'_\lambda=\varphi(x,y)=0\end{cases}$ 方程组，解出 x、y、λ。得到 $F(x,y,\lambda)$ 的驻点 (x_0,y_0,λ_0)，则 (x_0,y_0) 就是原问题的极值可疑点。对于实际问题可根据问题本身的性质确定该极值可疑点是否为极值点。

这种方法可以推广到自变量多于两个，条件多于一个的情况。

在实际问题中，如果多元函数只有唯一可能极值点，而根据问题的性质可知，最大值（或最小值）一定存在，那么在这个可能极值点处，取得函数的最大值（或最小值）。

【例 1-4-1】 $f(x,y)=\ln\left(x+\dfrac{y}{2x}\right)$，求 $\left.\dfrac{\partial z}{\partial x}\right|_{(1,0)}$，$\left.\dfrac{\partial z}{\partial y}\right|_{(1,0)}$。

解

$$\frac{\partial z}{\partial x}=\frac{1}{x+\dfrac{y}{2x}}\left(1-\frac{y}{2x^2}\right)=\frac{2x^2-y}{x(2x^2+y)}，则\left.\frac{\partial z}{\partial x}\right|_{(1,0)}=1$$

$$\frac{\partial z}{\partial y}=\frac{1}{x+\dfrac{y}{2x}}\cdot\frac{1}{2x}=\frac{1}{2x^2+y}，则\left.\frac{\partial z}{\partial y}\right|_{(1,0)}=\frac{1}{2}$$

【例 1-4-2】 设 $z=z(x,y)$ 是由方程 $xz-xy+\ln(xyz)=0$ 所确定的可微函数，则 $\dfrac{\partial z}{\partial y}$ 等于：

A. $\dfrac{-xz}{xz+1}$　　B. $-x+\dfrac{1}{2}$

C. $\dfrac{z(-xz+y)}{x(xz+1)}$　　D. $\dfrac{z(xy-1)}{y(xz+1)}$

解 $F(x,y,z)=xz-xy+\ln(xyz)$

$$F_x=z-y+\frac{yz}{xyz}=z-y+\frac{1}{x}，F_y=-x+\frac{xz}{xyz}=-x+\frac{1}{y}，F_z=x+\frac{xy}{xyz}=x+\frac{1}{z}$$

$$\frac{\partial z}{\partial y}=-\frac{F_y}{F_z}=-\frac{\frac{-xy+1}{y}}{\frac{xz+1}{z}}=-\frac{(1-xy)z}{y(xz+1)}=\frac{z(xy-1)}{y(xz+1)}$$

答案:D

【例 1-4-3】 设方程 $x^2+y^2+z^2=4z$ 确定可微函数 $z=z(x,y)$,则全微分 $\mathrm{d}z$ 等于:

A. $\frac{1}{2-z}(y\mathrm{d}x+x\mathrm{d}y)$　　B. $\frac{1}{2-z}(x\mathrm{d}x+y\mathrm{d}y)$

C. $\frac{1}{2+z}(\mathrm{d}x+\mathrm{d}y)$　　D. $\frac{1}{2-z}(\mathrm{d}x-\mathrm{d}y)$

解 设函数 $F(x,y,z)=x^2+y^2+z^2-4z$,则

$F_x=2x,F_y=2y,F_z=2z-4$

$$\frac{\partial z}{\partial x}=-\frac{F_x}{F_z}=-\frac{2x}{2z-4}=-\frac{x}{z-2},\frac{\partial z}{\partial y}=-\frac{F_y}{F_z}=-\frac{2y}{2z-4}=-\frac{y}{z-2}$$

$$\mathrm{d}z=\frac{\partial z}{\partial x}\mathrm{d}x+\frac{\partial z}{\partial y}\mathrm{d}y=-\frac{x}{z-2}\mathrm{d}x-\frac{y}{z-2}\mathrm{d}y=\frac{1}{2-z}(x\mathrm{d}x+y\mathrm{d}y)$$

答案:B

【例 1-4-4】 设 $z=f\left(xy,\frac{x}{y}\right)$,函数 $z=f(u,v)$ 具有连续偏导数,求$\frac{\partial z}{\partial x},\frac{\partial z}{\partial y}$。

解

$$\frac{\partial z}{\partial x}=\frac{\partial z}{\partial u}\cdot y+\frac{\partial z}{\partial v}\cdot\frac{1}{y}=y\frac{\partial z}{\partial u}+\frac{1}{y}\frac{\partial z}{\partial v}$$

$$\frac{\partial z}{\partial y}=\frac{\partial z}{\partial u}\cdot x+\frac{\partial z}{\partial v}\left(-\frac{x}{y^2}\right)=x\frac{\partial z}{\partial u}-\frac{x}{y^2}\frac{\partial z}{\partial v}$$

【例 1-4-5】 求曲线 $x=t,y=t^2,z=t^3$ 在点(1,1,1)处的切线和法平面。

解 将点(1,1,1)代入曲线方程可得 $t=1$

$$\vec{s}=\{1,2t,3t^2\}\ ,\ \vec{s}\,|_{t=1}=\{1,2,3\}$$

切线方程　$$\frac{x-1}{1}=\frac{y-1}{2}=\frac{z-1}{3}$$

法平面方程　$$(x-1)+2(y-1)+3(z-1)=0$$

【例 1-4-6】 曲面 $x^2-4y^2+2z^2=6$ 上点(2,2.3)处的法线方程是:

A. $x-1=\frac{y-6}{-4}=\frac{z}{3}$　　B. $\frac{x-2}{-1}=\frac{y-2}{-4}=\frac{z-3}{3}$

C. $\frac{x-1}{1}=\frac{y-6}{4}=\frac{z-1}{2}$　　D. $\frac{x-2}{1}=\frac{y-2}{-4}=\frac{z-3}{3}$

解 曲面 $x^2-4y^2+2z^2-6=0$

$$F_x=2x,F_y=-8y,F_z=4z$$

$$\vec{n}_{切}=\{2x,-8y,4z\}|_{(2,2,3)}=\{4,-16,12\}$$

取切平面的法向量为法线的方向向量

$$\vec{S}=\{4,-16,12\}$$

即法线方程为　$$\frac{x-2}{4}=\frac{y-2}{-16}=\frac{z-3}{12}$$

化简 $$\frac{x-2}{1}=\frac{y-2}{-4}=\frac{z-3}{3}$$

答案:D

【例 1-4-7】 已知函数 $f\left(xy,\frac{x}{y}\right)=x^2$,则$\frac{\partial f(x,y)}{\partial x}+\frac{\partial f(x,y)}{\partial y}$等于:

A. $2x+2y$　　B. $x+y$　　C. $2x-2y$　　D. $x-y$

解 题目中需要求解$\frac{\partial f}{\partial x}$和$\frac{\partial f}{\partial y}$,故联想到采用换元的形式,将函数 $f\left(xy,\frac{x}{y}\right)$变形为 $f(u,v)$的形式。此时求解$\frac{\partial f}{\partial u}$和$\frac{\partial f}{\partial v}$,即可认为是求解$\frac{\partial f}{\partial x}$和$\frac{\partial f}{\partial y}$,再换写成 $f(x,y)$的形式。若不进行换元,将无法进行偏导数计算。

设 $u=xy,v=\frac{x}{y}$,那么 $x=\frac{u}{y},x=yv$

$x^2=\frac{u}{y}\cdot yv=u\cdot v$

原函数化为 $f(u,v)=uv$,即 $f(x,y)=xy$

$f'_x(x,y)=y,f'_y(x,y)=x$

$\frac{\partial f}{\partial x}+\frac{\partial f}{\partial y}=y+x$

答案:B

【例 1-4-8】 函数 $z=f(x,y)$在点(x_0,y_0)处具有偏导数是它在该点存在全微分的:

A. 必要不充分条件　　B. 充分不必要条件

C. 充分必要条件　　D. 既不充分也不必要条件

解 可通过图 1-4-1“基本概念关系图”得到结果。

答案:A

【例 1-4-9】 对于二元函数 $z=f(x,y)$在点(x_0,y_0)处连续是它在该点处偏导数存在的:

A. 必要不充分条件　　B. 充分不必要条件

C. 充分必要条件　　D. 既不充分也不必要条件

解 可通过图 1-4-1“基本概念关系图”得到结果。

答案:D

【例 1-4-10】 函数 $f(x,y)$在点 $P_0(x_0,y_0)$处有一阶偏导数是函数在该点连续的:

A. 必要条件　　B. 充分条件

C. 充分必要条件　　D. 既不充分也不必要条件

解 可通过图 1-4-1“基本概念关系图”得到结果。$f(x,y)$在点 $P_0(x_0,y_0)$处有一阶偏导数,不能说明 $f(x,y)$在点 $P_0(x_0,y_0)$处连续;同样,$f(x,y)$在点 $P_0(x_0,y_0)$处连续,也不能确定 $f(x,y)$在点 $P_0(x_0,y_0)$处有一阶偏导数。

答案:D

习　题

1-4-1 设 $z=u^2\ln v$,而 $u=\varphi(x,y)$,$v=\psi(y)$ 均为可导函数,则 $\frac{\partial z}{\partial y}$ 为(　　)。

A. $2u\ln v + u^2 \cdot \frac{1}{v}$　　B. $2\varphi'_y \ln v + u^2 \cdot \frac{1}{v}$

C. $2u\varphi'_y \ln v + u^2 \cdot \frac{1}{v} \cdot \psi'_y$　　D. $2u\psi'_y \cdot \frac{1}{v} \cdot \psi'_y$

1-4-2　已知 $y = y(x, z)$，由方程 $xyz = e^{x+y}$ 确定，则 $\frac{\partial y}{\partial x}$ 是(　　)。

A. $\frac{y(x-1)}{x(1-y)}$　B. $\frac{y}{x(1-y)}$　C. $\frac{yz}{1-y}$　D. $\frac{y(1-xz)}{x(1-y)}$

1-4-3　若函数 $z = \frac{\ln(xy)}{y}$，则当 $x = e, y = e^{-1}$ 时，全微分 $\mathrm{d}z$ 等于(　　)。

A. $e\mathrm{d}x + \mathrm{d}y$　　B. $e^2\mathrm{d}x - \mathrm{d}y$

C. $\mathrm{d}x + e^2\mathrm{d}y$　　D. $e\mathrm{d}x + e^2\mathrm{d}y$

1-4-4　在曲线 $x=t, y=t^2, z=t^3$ 上某点的切线平行于平面 $x+2y+z=4$，则该点的坐标为(　　)。

A. $\left(-\frac{1}{3}, \frac{1}{9}, -\frac{1}{27}\right), (-1, 1, -1)$　　B. $\left(-\frac{1}{3}, \frac{1}{9}, -\frac{1}{27}\right), (1, 1, 1)$

C. $\left(\frac{1}{3}, \frac{1}{9}, \frac{1}{27}\right), (1, 1, 1)$　　D. $\left(\frac{1}{3}, \frac{1}{9}, \frac{1}{27}\right), (-1, 1, -1)$

1-4-5　曲面 $z=x^2-y^2$ 与平面 $x-y-z-1=0$ 平行的切平面方程是(　　)。

A. $x-y-z-1=0$　　B. $x-y-z+1=0$

C. $x-y-z=0$　　D. $x-y-z-2=0$

1-4-6　二元函数 $z = x^3 - y^3 + 3x^2 + 3y^2 - 9x$ 的极大值点是(　　)。

A. $(1,0)$　　B. $(1,2)$

C. $(-3,0)$　　D. $(-3, 2)$

1-4-7　曲面 $xyz=1$ 上平行于 $x+y+z+3=0$ 的切平面方程是(　　)。

A. $x+y+z=0$　　B. $x+y+z=1$

C. $x+y+z=2$　　D. $x+y+z=3$

1-4-8　曲面 $z=x^2-y^2$ 在点$(\sqrt{2}, -1, 1)$处的法线方程是(　　)。

A. $\frac{x-\sqrt{2}}{2\sqrt{2}}=\frac{y+1}{-2}=\frac{z-1}{-1}$　　B. $\frac{x-\sqrt{2}}{2\sqrt{2}}=\frac{y+1}{-2}=\frac{z-1}{1}$

C. $\frac{x-\sqrt{2}}{2\sqrt{2}}=\frac{y+1}{2}=\frac{z-1}{-1}$　　D. $\frac{x-\sqrt{2}}{2\sqrt{2}}=\frac{y+1}{2}=\frac{z-1}{1}$

1-4-9　对于二元函数 $z=f(x,y)$，下列有关偏导数和全微分关系中正确的命题是(　　)。

A. 偏导数不连续，则全微分必不存在

B. 偏导数连续，则全微分必存在

C. 全微分存在，则偏导数必连续

D. 全微分存在，而偏导数不一定存在

1-4-10　若二元函数 $z=f(x,y)$在点 $P_0(x_0, y_0)$处的两个偏导数$\frac{\partial z}{\partial x}, \frac{\partial z}{\partial y}$存在，则(　　)。

A. $f(x,y)$在点 P_0 处连续　　B. $z=f(x,y_0)$在点 P_0 处连续

C. $dz=\left.\frac{\partial z}{\partial x}\right|_{P_0}dx+\left.\frac{\partial z}{\partial y}\right|_{P_0}dy$　　　　D. A、B、C 都不对

第五节　多元函数积分学

一、二重积分

(一)二重积分的概念与性质

1. 二重积分定义

设 $f(x,y)$为有界闭区域 D 上的有界函数，将 D 分割成 n 个小区域 $\Delta\sigma_1,\Delta\sigma_2,\cdots,\Delta\sigma_n$，$\Delta\sigma_i$ 也表示第 i 个小区域的面积，用 λ_i 表示 $\Delta\sigma_i(i=1,2,\cdots,n)$的直径($\Delta\sigma_i$ 上任意两点间距离的最大值)，在每一 $\Delta\sigma_i$ 上任取一点(x_i,y_i)，作积分和$\sum\limits_{i=1}^{n}f(x_i,y_i)\Delta\sigma_i$，如果当 $n\to\infty$时，$\|\lambda\|\to 0$($\|\lambda\|=\max\{\lambda_1,\cdots,\lambda_n\}$)积分和有极限 I，即

$$\lim_{\substack{n\to\infty\\ \|\lambda\|\to 0}}\sum_{i=1}^{n}f(x_i,y_i)\Delta\sigma_i=I \tag{1-5-1}$$

称 I 为二元函数 $f(x,y)$在闭区域 D 上的二重积分，记作$\iint\limits_D f(x,y)d\sigma$。

2. 二重积分存在的充分条件

若 $f(x,y)$在 D 上连续，则二重积分$\iint\limits_D f(x,y)d\sigma$一定存在。

3. 二重积分几何意义

若 $f(x,y)\geqslant 0$，则二重积分$\iint\limits_D f(x,y)d\sigma$表示以曲面$z=f(x,y)$为顶，以区域$D$为底，以$D$的边界为准线，母线平行于$Oz$轴的柱面围成的曲顶柱体的体积。当$f(x,y)=1$时，$\iint\limits_D 1dxdy$表示 D 的面积。

4. 二重积分的性质

(1) $\iint\limits_D kf(x,y)d\sigma=k\iint\limits_D f(x,y)d\sigma$　　(k 为常数)

(2) $\iint\limits_D[f(x,y)\pm g(x,y)]d\sigma=\iint\limits_D f(x,y)d\sigma\pm\iint\limits_D g(x,y)d\sigma$

(3) $\iint\limits_D f(x,y)d\sigma=\iint\limits_{D_1}f(x,y)d\sigma+\iint\limits_{D_2}f(x,y)d\sigma$　　(其中 $D=D_1+D_2$)

(4)在 D 上，$f(x,y)=1$，σ 为 D 的面积，则$\iint\limits_D 1d\sigma=\iint\limits_D d\sigma=\sigma$。

(5)在 D 上，$f(x,y)\leqslant\varphi(x,y)$，则$\iint\limits_D f(x,y)d\sigma\leqslant\iint\limits_D\varphi(x,y)d\sigma$。

(6)设 M,m 分别为 $f(x,y)$ 在闭区域 D 上的最大值、最小值，σ 是 D 的面积，则 $m\sigma\leqslant\iint\limits_D f(x,y)d\sigma\leqslant M\sigma$。

(7)设 $f(x,y)$ 在闭区域 D 上连续，σ 是 D 的面积，则在 D 上至少存在一点(ξ,η) 使

$$\iint_D f(x,y)\mathrm{d}\sigma = f(\xi,\eta)\sigma。$$

（二）二重积分的计算

1. 直角坐标系

计算二重积分时，可根据被积函数 $f(x,y)$ 和区域 D 的形状选择积分顺序，是先 y 后 x，还是先 x 后 y，把 D 用不等式组表示，再将二重积分化为累次积分计算。

若 $D=\{(x,y)\mid a\leqslant x\leqslant b, y_1(x)\leqslant y\leqslant y_2(x)\}$，则

$$\iint_D f(x,y)\mathrm{d}x\mathrm{d}y = \int_a^b \mathrm{d}x\int_{y_1(x)}^{y_2(x)} f(x,y)\mathrm{d}y \tag{1-5-2}$$

若 $D=\{(x,y)\mid c\leqslant y\leqslant d, x_1(y)\leqslant x\leqslant x_2(y)\}$，则

$$\iint_D f(x,y)\mathrm{d}x\mathrm{d}y = \int_c^d \mathrm{d}y\int_{x_1(y)}^{x_2(y)} f(x,y)\mathrm{d}x \tag{1-5-3}$$

2. 极坐标系

如果积分区域D的边界曲线用极坐标方程表示比较方便（如圆周等），且被积函数用极坐标表示也较方便（如含有x^2+y^2等），则可以利用直角坐标与极坐标的关系式$x=r\cos\theta, y=r\sin\theta$，面积元素 $\mathrm{d}x\mathrm{d}y=r\mathrm{d}r\mathrm{d}\theta$，将二重积分转化为极坐标计算

$$\iint_D f(x,y)\mathrm{d}x\mathrm{d}y = \iint_D f(r\cos\theta, r\sin\theta)r\mathrm{d}r\mathrm{d}\theta \tag{1-5-4}$$

在极坐标系下，若

(1)$D=\{(r,\theta)\mid \alpha\leqslant\theta\leqslant\beta, \varphi_1(\theta)\leqslant r\leqslant\varphi_2(\theta)\}$，则

$$\iint_D f(r\cos\theta, r\sin\theta)r\mathrm{d}r\mathrm{d}\theta = \int_\alpha^\beta \mathrm{d}\theta\int_{\varphi_1(\theta)}^{\varphi_2(\theta)} f(r\cos\theta, r\sin\theta)r\mathrm{d}r \tag{1-5-5}$$

(2)$D=\{(r,\theta)\mid \alpha\leqslant\theta\leqslant\beta, 0\leqslant r\leqslant\varphi(\theta)\}$，则

$$\iint_D f(r\cos\theta, r\sin\theta)r\mathrm{d}r\mathrm{d}\theta = \int_\alpha^\beta \mathrm{d}\theta\int_0^{\varphi(\theta)} f(r\cos\theta, r\sin\theta)r\mathrm{d}r \tag{1-5-6}$$

式中，α、$\beta\in[0,2\pi]$且 $\alpha<\beta$；$\varphi(\theta)$、$\varphi_1(\theta)$、$\varphi_2(\theta)$均为连续函数。式(1-5-5)对应于极点位于积分区域 D 外部的情况；式(1-5-6)对应于极点位于积分区域 D 内部或边界上的情形。

二、三重积分

（一）三重积分的一般概念

1. 三重积分定义

设 $f(x,y,z)$是空间有界闭区域 Ω 上的有界函数，用任意分法将 Ω 分成 n 份 $\Delta U_1, \Delta U_2, \cdots, \Delta U_n$（同时用它表示子区域的体积），在 ΔU_i 内任取一点(x_i, y_i, z_i)作积分和$\sum\limits_{i=1}^{n} f(x_i, y_i, z_i)\Delta U_i$，若当 $n\to\infty$，$\|\lambda\|\to 0$ 时[$\|\lambda\|$ 表示 $\Delta U_i(i=1,2,\cdots,n)$的最大直径]极限 $\lim\limits_{\substack{n\to\infty\\ \|\lambda\|\to 0}}\sum\limits_{i=1}^{n} f(x_i, y_i, z_i)\Delta U_i$ 存在，则称此极限值为 $f(x,y,z)$在 Ω 上的三重积分，记作 $\iiint\limits_{\Omega} f(x,y,z)\mathrm{d}U$。

2. 三重积分存在的充分条件

在有界闭区域 Ω 上连续函数 $f(x,y,z)$ 在 Ω 上必定可积。

3. 三重积分的性质

三重积分也有类似二重积分的 7 个性质(不再赘述)。

(二)三重积分的计算

三重积分的计算,也是根据被积函数和积分区域 Ω 的情况,选择一种合适的坐标系和积分顺序,将它化为累次积分进行计算。

1. 直角坐标

设 $\Omega=\{(x,y,z)\mid a\leqslant x\leqslant b,y_1(x)\leqslant y\leqslant y_2(x),z_1(x,y)\leqslant z\leqslant z_2(x,y)\}$,则

$$\iiint_{\Omega} f(x,y,z)\mathrm{d}x\mathrm{d}y\mathrm{d}z=\int_a^b \mathrm{d}x\int_{y_1(x)}^{y_2(x)}\mathrm{d}y\int_{z_1(x,y)}^{z_2(x,y)} f(x,y,z)\mathrm{d}z \tag{1-5-7}$$

同理可写出其他顺序,将三重积分化为三次积分。(在直角坐标系下,体积元素 $\mathrm{d}v=\mathrm{d}x\mathrm{d}y\mathrm{d}z$)

2. 柱坐标

设 $\Omega=\{(x,y,z)\mid \alpha\leqslant\theta\leqslant\beta,r_1(\theta)\leqslant r\leqslant r_2(\theta),z_1(r,\theta)\leqslant z\leqslant z_2(r,\theta)\}$,则

$$\iiint_{\Omega} f(x,y,z)\mathrm{d}x\mathrm{d}y\mathrm{d}z=\int_\alpha^\beta \mathrm{d}\theta\int_{r_1(\theta)}^{r_2(\theta)} r\mathrm{d}r\int_{z_1(r,\theta)}^{z_2(r,\theta)} f(r\cos\theta,r\sin\theta,z)\mathrm{d}z \tag{1-5-8}$$

同理也可写出其他顺序,将三重积分化为三次积分。

在柱坐标系下,体积元素 $\mathrm{d}v=r\mathrm{d}r\mathrm{d}\theta\mathrm{d}z$,直角坐标和柱坐标的关系 $x=r\cos\theta,y=r\sin\theta,z=z$。

3. 球面坐标

设 $\Omega=\{(x,y,z)\mid \alpha\leqslant\theta\leqslant\beta,\varphi_1(\theta)\leqslant\varphi\leqslant\varphi_2(\theta),r_1(\theta,\varphi)\leqslant r\leqslant r_2(\theta,\varphi)\}$,则

$$\iiint_{\Omega} f(x,y,z)\mathrm{d}x\mathrm{d}y\mathrm{d}z=\int_\alpha^\beta \mathrm{d}\theta\int_{\varphi_1(\theta)}^{\varphi_2(\theta)}\sin\varphi\mathrm{d}\varphi\int_{r_1(\theta,\varphi)}^{r_2(\theta,\varphi)} f(r\sin\varphi\cos\theta,r\sin\varphi\sin\theta,r\cos\varphi)r^2\mathrm{d}r \tag{1-5-9}$$

在球坐标系下,体积元素 $\mathrm{d}v=r^2\sin\varphi\mathrm{d}r\mathrm{d}\theta\mathrm{d}\varphi$,直角坐标和球面坐标的关系 $x=r\sin\varphi\cos\theta$,$y=r\sin\varphi\sin\theta,z=r\cos\varphi$。

在计算三重积分时,当积分区域 Ω 为圆柱形(或柱形)区域,或 Ω 的投影为圆域时,被积函数具有 $f(x^2+y^2)$ 的形式,一般可采用柱面坐标计算;当积分区域为球形区域或锥面与球面围成的区域,被积函数具有 $f(x^2+y^2+z^2)$ 的形式,用球面坐标计算较为方便。

【例 1-5-1】 设 D 域为 $0\leqslant x\leqslant y,0\leqslant y\leqslant 1$,则 $\iint\limits_D \mathrm{d}x\mathrm{d}y$ 为:

A. 1　　B. $\frac{1}{2}$　　C. 2　　D. 3

解　画出 D 域图形(见解图)

$\iint\limits_D \mathrm{d}x\mathrm{d}y$ 中被积函数 $f(x,y)=1$

二重积分在数值上等于 D 的面积,

所以 $\iint\limits_D \mathrm{d}x\mathrm{d}y=\frac{1}{2}\times1\times1=\frac{1}{2}$

例 1-5-1 解图

答案:B

【例 1-5-2】 若 D 域是以 $(0,0)$,$(1,0)$,$(0,1)$ 为顶点的三角形区域,由二重积分的几何意义知,$\iint\limits_D(1-x-y)\mathrm{d}\sigma$ 的值等于:

A. $\frac{1}{3}$　　　　B. $\frac{1}{2}$　　　　C. 1　　　　D. $\frac{1}{6}$

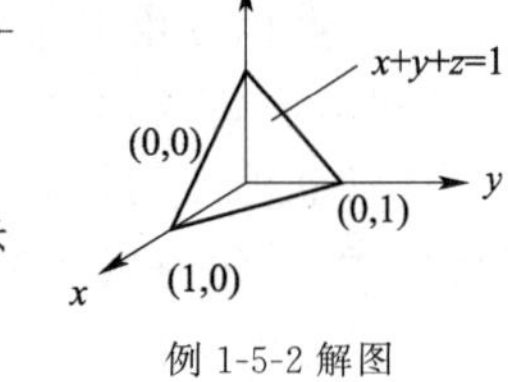

例 1-5-2 解图

解　由二重积分的几何意义知，$\iint\limits_D(1-x-y)\mathrm{d}\sigma$ 表示以 $z=1-x-y$ 为曲顶、D 为底的曲顶柱体的体积。

曲顶柱体见解图，曲顶为一平面，方程 $z=1-x-y$，该二重积分表示正三棱锥的体积，

所以 $$\iint\limits_D(1-x-y)\mathrm{d}\sigma=\frac{1}{3}\times\text{底面积}\times\text{高}=\frac{1}{3}\times\frac{1}{2}\times1\times1\times1=\frac{1}{6}$$

答案：D

【例 1-5-3】　将二重积分 $\iint\limits_D f(x,y)\mathrm{d}x\mathrm{d}y$ 化为直角坐标系下的二次积分，其中 D 由 $x+y=1$，$x-y=1$ 及 y 轴围成(见图)，要求用两种积分顺序表示。

解　(1)先 y 后 x

$$D:\begin{cases}0\leqslant x\leqslant 1\\ x-1\leqslant y\leqslant -x+1\end{cases}$$

$$\iint\limits_D f(x,y)\mathrm{d}x\mathrm{d}y=\int_0^1\mathrm{d}x\int_{x-1}^{1-x}f(x,y)\mathrm{d}y$$

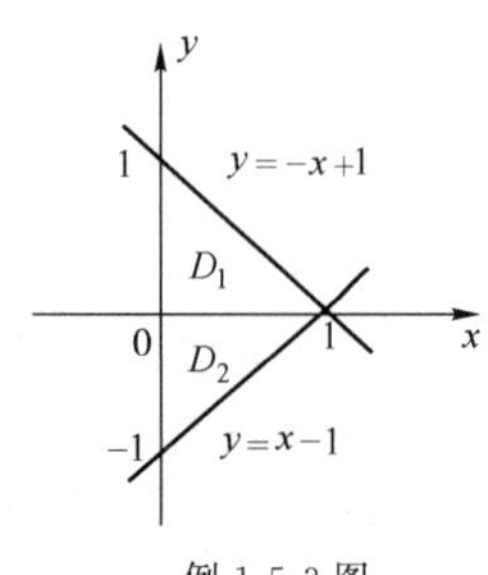

例 1-5-3 图

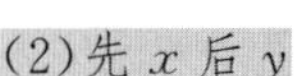
(2)先 x 后 y

由于右边界曲线由两个方程给出，把 D 分为 D_1、D_2 两部分，见图。

$$\iint\limits_D=\iint\limits_{D_1+D_2}=\iint\limits_{D_1}+\iint\limits_{D_2}$$

$$D_1:\begin{cases}0\leqslant y\leqslant 1\\ 0\leqslant x\leqslant 1-y\end{cases}\qquad D_2:\begin{cases}-1\leqslant y\leqslant 0\\ 0\leqslant x\leqslant 1+y\end{cases}$$

$$\iint\limits_D f(x,y)\mathrm{d}x\mathrm{d}y=\int_0^1\mathrm{d}y\int_0^{1-y}f(x,y)\mathrm{d}x+\int_{-1}^0\mathrm{d}y\int_0^{1+y}f(x,y)\mathrm{d}x$$

注：计算二重积分时，确定积分上下限：若 x 的范围简单(从 0 到 1)，则 y 的范围一定会变难(利用函数表示从 $x-1$ 到 $1-x$)，反之亦然。

【例 1-5-4】　设 $D:|x|\leqslant\pi,0\leqslant y\leqslant 1$，则 $\iint\limits_D(2+xy)\mathrm{d}\sigma$ 等于：

A. 0　　　　B. 2π　　　　C. 1　　　　D. 4π

解　画出积分区域 D 的图形(见解图)。

$$\iint\limits_D(2+xy)\mathrm{d}\sigma=\iint\limits_D 2\mathrm{d}\sigma+\iint\limits_D xy\,\mathrm{d}\sigma$$

首先，利用二重积分的对称性及二重积分的几何意义计算，积分区域 D 关于 y 轴对称，函数 $f(x,y)$ 满足 $f(-x,y)=-f(x,y)$，为关于变量 x 的奇函数，因而

$$\iint\limits_D xy\,\mathrm{d}\sigma=0$$

例 1-5-4 解图

其次，$\iint\limits_D 2\mathrm{d}\sigma = 2\iint\limits_D \mathrm{d}\sigma = 2\times D$ 的面积 $= 2\times 2\pi\times 1 = 4\pi$，故原式$=4\pi$。

答案：D

【例 1-5-5】 已知二重积分 $I=\int_0^1 \mathrm{d}x\int_x^{\sqrt{x}} \frac{\sin y}{y}\mathrm{d}y$。其值等于：

A. $2-\sin 1$　　B. $1-\sin 2$　　C. 0　　D. $1-\sin 1$

解 如解图所示，先对 y 积分时，被积函数无初等函数表示的原函数，需要改变积分顺序后再计算。

先作出曲线 $y=x$，$y=\sqrt{x}$，求交点 $(0,0)$、$(1,1)$，再作直线 $x=0$、$x=1$ 把积分区域还原。

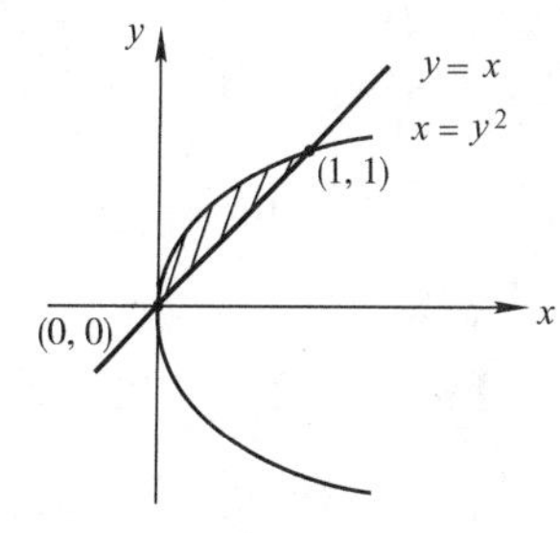

例 1-5-5 解图

按先 x 后 y 的顺序

$$D:\begin{cases}0\leqslant y\leqslant 1\\ y^2\leqslant x\leqslant y\end{cases}$$

$$I=\int_0^1 \mathrm{d}y\int_{y^2}^{y}\frac{\sin y}{y}\mathrm{d}x=\int_0^1 \frac{\sin y}{y}x\Big|_{y^2}^{y}\mathrm{d}y$$

$$=\int_0^1 (1-y)\sin y\mathrm{d}y = 1-\sin 1$$

答案：D

注：这是一个交换积分次序的题目，在交换积分次序时，最好画图。

【例 1-5-6】 若 D 域是 $x^2+y^2\leqslant 4, y\geqslant 0$，则 $\iint\limits_D \sin x^3y^2\mathrm{d}\sigma$ 的值等于：

A. 0　　B. 2　　C. 3　　D. 无法计算

解 画出积分区域 D 的图形，D 为上半圆和 x 轴围成的图形（见解图），图形关于 y 轴以称，方程 $f(x,y)=\sin x^3y^2$ 满足 $f(-x,y)=-f(x,y)$，为关于变量 x 的奇函数，由二重积分几何意义可知 $\iint\limits_D \sin x^3y^2\mathrm{d}\sigma=0$。

例 1-5-6 解图

答案：A

【例 1-5-7】 二次积分 $\int_0^1 \mathrm{d}x\int_{x^2}^{x} f(x,y)\mathrm{d}y$ 交换积分次序后的二次积分是：

A. $\int_{x^2}^{x}\mathrm{d}y\int_0^1 f(x,y)\mathrm{d}x$　　B. $\int_0^1\mathrm{d}y\int_{y^2}^{y} f(x,y)\mathrm{d}x$

C. $\int_y^{\sqrt{y}}\mathrm{d}y\int_0^1 f(x,y)\mathrm{d}x$　　D. $\int_0^1\mathrm{d}y\int_y^{\sqrt{y}} f(x,y)\mathrm{d}x$

解 根据给出的二重积分的上下限 $0\leqslant x\leqslant 1, x^2\leqslant y\leqslant x$ 画出积分区域 D，再写出先 x 后 y 的积分式。

D：$0\leqslant y\leqslant 1, y\leqslant x\leqslant \sqrt{y}$　（见解图）

$y=x$，即 $x=y$；$y=x^2$，得 $x=\sqrt{y}$

所以二次积分交换积分顺序后为 $\int_0^1\mathrm{d}y\int_y^{\sqrt{y}} f(x,y)\mathrm{d}x$。

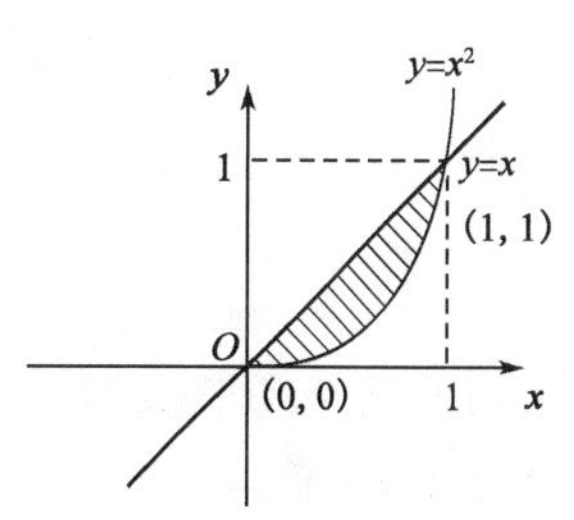

例 1-5-7 解图

答案：D

【例 1-5-8】 $I=\int_0^1 dy\int_0^{\sqrt{1-y}} 3x^2y^2dx$，则交换积分次序后得：

A. $I=\int_0^1 dx\int_0^{\sqrt{1-x}} 3x^2y^2dy$　　B. $I=\int_0^{\sqrt{1-y}} dx\int_0^1 3x^2y^2dy$

C. $I=\int_0^1 dx\int_0^{1-x^2} 3x^2y^2dy$　　D. $I=\int_0^1 dx\int_0^{1+x^2} 3x^2y^2dy$

解　画出积分区域 D(见解图)

由 $x=\sqrt{1-y}$，得 $x^2=1-y$，$y=1-x^2$

$D:\begin{cases}0\leqslant x\leqslant 1\\ 0\leqslant y\leqslant 1-x^2\end{cases}$

故 $I=\int_0^1 dx\int_0^{1-x^2} 3x^2y^2dy$ 。

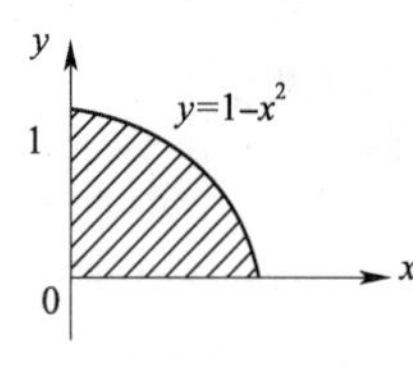

例 1-5-8 解图

答案：C

【例 1-5-9】 D 域由 x 轴，$x^2+y^2-2x=0(y\geqslant 0)$ 及 $x+y=2$ 所围成，$f(x,y)$ 是连续函数，化 $\iint\limits_D f(x,y)dxdy$ 为二次积分是：

A. $\int_0^{\frac{\pi}{4}} d\varphi\int_0^{2\cos\varphi} f(\rho\cos\varphi,\rho\sin\varphi)\rho d\rho$　　B. $\int_0^1 dy\int_{1-\sqrt{1-y^2}}^{2-y} f(x,y)dx$

C. $\int_0^{\frac{\pi}{2}} d\varphi\int_0^1 f(\rho\cos\varphi,\rho\sin\varphi)\rho d\rho$　　D. $\int_0^1 dx\int_0^{\sqrt{2x-x^2}} f(x,y)dy$

解　积分区域 D 为 $x^2+y^2-2x=0$，即 $(x-1)^2+y^2=1$。由解图可知，选项 A、C 积分变量 ρ、φ 的取值均有错误。

在化为直角坐标计算时，按先 x 后 y 的顺序积分

$D:\begin{cases}0\leqslant y\leqslant 1\\ 1-\sqrt{1-y^2}\leqslant x\leqslant 2-y\end{cases}$

$$\iint\limits_D f(x,y)dxdy=\int_0^1 dy\int_{1-\sqrt{1-y^2}}^{2-y} f(x,y)dx$$

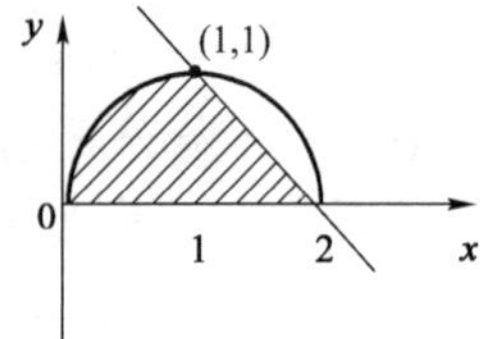

例 1-5-9 解图

答案：B

【例 1-5-10】 设 D 是由 $y=x^2-4$ 和 $y=0$ 围成的平面区域(见图)，则 $I=\iint\limits_D(ax+y)dxdy$：

A. $I>0$　　B. $I=0$

C. $I<0$　　D. I 的符号与参数 a 有关

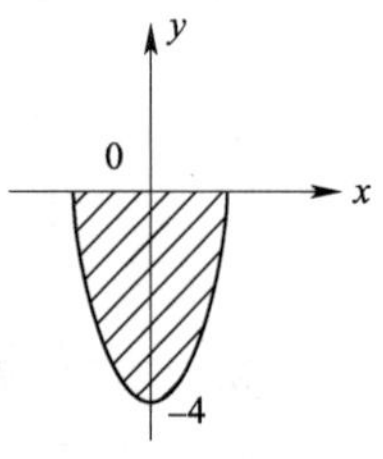

例 1-5-10 图

解

$$\iint\limits_D(ax+y)dxdy=\underset{(\mathrm{I})}{\iint\limits_D ax\,dxdy}+\underset{(\mathrm{II})}{\iint\limits_D y\,dxdy}$$

(I) 由于积分区域 D 关于 y 轴对称，被积函数满足 $f(-x,y)=-f(x,y)$，故 $\iint\limits_D ax\,dxdy=0$。

(II) 由于在积分区域 D 内，被积函数 $y\leqslant 0$，故 $\iint\limits_D y\,dxdy<0$。

答案:C

【例 1-5-11】 计算由曲面 $z=2-x^2-y^2$ 及 $z=\sqrt{x^2+y^2}$ 所围成立体的体积(见图)。

$z=2-x^2-y^2$

$z=\sqrt{x^2+y^2}$

例 1-5-11 图

解 利用三重积分计算(本题也可用二重积分计算)

投影区域 D_{xy}

$$\begin{cases} z=2-x^2-y^2 \\ z=\sqrt{x^2+y^2} \end{cases} \xrightarrow{\text{消字母}z} D_{xy}: x^2+y^2 \leqslant 1$$

利用柱面坐标计算

$$\Omega: \begin{cases} r \leqslant z \leqslant 2-r^2 \\ 0 \leqslant r \leqslant 1 \\ 0 \leqslant \theta \leqslant 2\pi \end{cases} \quad V=\iiint_{\Omega} \mathrm{d}V=\int_0^{2\pi} \mathrm{d}\theta \int_0^1 r \mathrm{d}r \int_r^{2-r^2} \mathrm{d}z=\frac{5}{6}\pi$$

【例 1-5-12】 计算由曲面 $z=\sqrt{x^2+y^2}$ 及 $z=x^2+y^2$ 所围成的立体体积的三次积分为:

A. $\int_0^{2\pi} \mathrm{d}\theta \int_0^1 r \mathrm{d}r \int_{r^2}^r \mathrm{d}z$　　B. $\int_0^{2\pi} \mathrm{d}\theta \int_0^1 r \mathrm{d}r \int_r^1 \mathrm{d}z$

C. $\int_0^{2\pi} \mathrm{d}\theta \int_0^{\frac{\pi}{4}} \sin\varphi \mathrm{d}\varphi \int_0^1 r^2 \mathrm{d}r$　　D. $\int_0^{2\pi} \mathrm{d}\theta \int_{\frac{\pi}{4}}^{\frac{\pi}{2}} \sin\varphi \mathrm{d}\varphi \int_0^1 r^2 \mathrm{d}r$

解 由已知条件画出积分区域,如解图所示。

$z=\sqrt{x^2+y^2}$ 为上半锥面,$z=x^2+y^2$ 为旋转抛物面。因 $z=x^2+y^2$,用球面坐标表示复杂,一般选用柱面坐标计算。选项 C、D 在化球面坐标时有错误。

化柱面坐标计算,求 D_{xy},消 z。由 $\begin{cases} z=\sqrt{x^2+y^2} \\ z=x^2+y^2 \end{cases}$ 得 $D_{xy}: x^2+y^2 \leqslant 1$

例 1-5-12 解图

$$\Omega \text{ 化为柱面坐标为 } \begin{cases} r^2 \leqslant z \leqslant r \\ 0 \leqslant r \leqslant 1 \\ 0 \leqslant \theta \leqslant 2\pi \end{cases}, \mathrm{d}V=r \mathrm{d}r \mathrm{d}\theta \mathrm{d}z$$

$$V=\iiint_{\Omega} 1 \mathrm{d}V=\int_0^{2\pi} \mathrm{d}\theta \int_0^1 r \mathrm{d}r \int_{r^2}^r 1 \mathrm{d}z$$

答案:A

【例 1-5-13】 设函数 $f(x,y)$ 在 $x^2+y^2 \leqslant 1$ 范围内连续,使 $\iint\limits_{x^2+y^2 \leqslant 1} f(x,y) \mathrm{d}x \mathrm{d}y=4\int_0^1 \mathrm{d}x \int_0^{\sqrt{1-x^2}} f(x,y) \mathrm{d}y$ 成立的充分条件是:

A. $f(-x,y)=f(x,y), f(x,-y)=-f(x,y)$

B. $f(-x,y)=f(x,y), f(x,-y)=f(x,y)$

C. $f(-x,y)=-f(x,y), f(x,-y)=-f(x,y)$

D. $f(-x,y)=-f(x,y), f(x,-y)=f(x,y)$

解 如解图所示,因为积分区域 D 关于 y 轴对称,函数 $f(x,y)$ 满足 $f(-x,y)=f(x,y)$,

所以 $\iint\limits_{D} f(x,y)\mathrm{d}x\mathrm{d}y = 2\iint\limits_{D_1} f(x,y)\mathrm{d}x\mathrm{d}y$

又因 D_1 关于 x 轴对称，函数 $f(x,y)$ 满足 $f(x,-y)=f(x,y)$

则 $\iint\limits_{D_1} f(x,y)\mathrm{d}x\mathrm{d}y = 2\iint\limits_{D_2} f(x,y)\mathrm{d}x\mathrm{d}y$

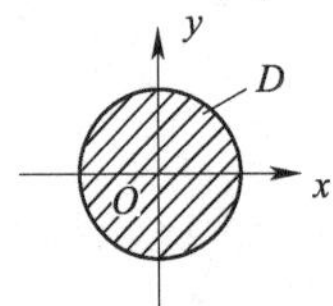

D：$x^2+y^2\leqslant 1$

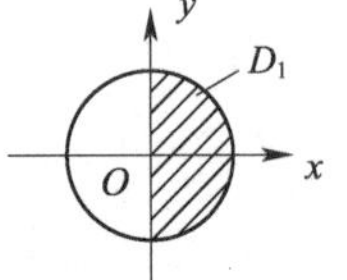

D_1：$x^2+y^2\leqslant 1(x\geqslant 0)$

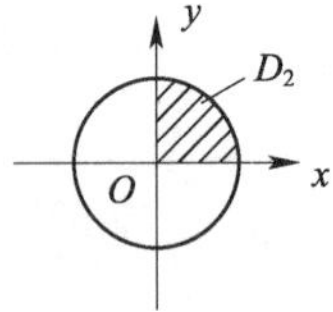

D_2：$x^2+y^2\leqslant 1(x\geqslant 0,y\geqslant 0)$

例 1-5-13 解图

故 $\iint\limits_{x^2+y^2\leqslant 1} f(x,y)\mathrm{d}x\mathrm{d}y = 4\iint\limits_{D_2} f(x,y)\mathrm{d}x\mathrm{d}y$，$D_2$：$\begin{cases}0\leqslant x\leqslant 1\\0\leqslant y\leqslant \sqrt{1-x^2}\end{cases}$

所以 $\iint\limits_{x^2+y^2\leqslant 1} f(x,y)\mathrm{d}x\mathrm{d}y = 4\int_0^1\mathrm{d}x\int_0^{\sqrt{1-x^2}} f(x,y)\mathrm{d}y$

答案：B

三、对弧长的曲线积分

(一)对弧长的曲线积分的概念

设 L 是平面上的可求长曲线，$f(x,y)$是定义在 L 上的有界函数，将 L 任意地分为 n 个小弧段$\overset{\frown}{M_{i-1}M_i}(i=1,2,\cdots,n)$，设$\overset{\frown}{M_{i-1}M_i}$的长为 Δs_i，在$\overset{\frown}{M_{i-1}M_i}$上任意取一点$(\xi_i,\eta_i)$作积分和$\sum\limits_{i=1}^{n}f(\xi_i,\eta_i)\Delta s_i$，若 $\lambda=\max\{\Delta s_i,(i=1,2,\cdots,n)\}\to 0$，上述和式极限存在，则称此极限为 $f(x,y)$在 L 上对弧长的曲线积分，记作 $\int_L f(x,y)\mathrm{d}s$。

(二)对弧长的曲线积分的性质

(1) $\int_L kf(x,y)\mathrm{d}s = k\int_L f(x,y)\mathrm{d}s$ (k 为常数)

(2)可加性：$\int_{\overset{\frown}{AB}} f(x,y)\mathrm{d}s = \int_{\overset{\frown}{AC}} f(x,y)\mathrm{d}s + \int_{\overset{\frown}{CB}} f(x,y)\mathrm{d}s$ (C 为$\overset{\frown}{AB}$上的任一点)

(3)与路径方向无关性：$\int_{\overset{\frown}{AB}} f(x,y)\mathrm{d}s = \int_{\overset{\frown}{BA}} f(x,y)\mathrm{d}s$

(三)对弧长的曲线积分的计算

(1)设曲线的参数方程为 $x=\varphi(t)$、$y=\psi(t)$，$\alpha\leqslant t\leqslant\beta$ 且 $\psi(t)$、$\varphi(t)$在$[\alpha,\beta]$上具有连续导数，则

$$\int_L f(x,y)\mathrm{d}s = \int_\alpha^\beta f[\varphi(t),\psi(t)]\sqrt{[\varphi'(t)]^2+[\psi'(t)]^2}\,\mathrm{d}t \quad (1\text{-}5\text{-}10)$$

(2)设曲线方程为 $y=y(x)$，$a\leqslant x\leqslant b$ 且 $y(x)$在$[a,b]$上具有连续导数，则

$$\int_L f(x,y)\mathrm{d}s = \int_a^b f[x,y(x)]\sqrt{1+[y'(x)]^2}\,\mathrm{d}x$$

在(2)式中，当 $f(x,y)=1$ 时，$\int_L \mathrm{d}s = \int_a^b \sqrt{1+(f'(x))^2}\,\mathrm{d}x$，可用它计算平面曲线的弧长，

与一元定积分应用求弧长公式一样。

(3)设曲线方程为 $x=x(y), c\leqslant y\leqslant d$，且 $x(y)$ 在 $[c,d]$ 上具有连续导数，则

$$\int_L f(x,y)\mathrm{d}s = \int_c^d f[x(y),y]\sqrt{1+[x'(y)]^2}\mathrm{d}y \tag{1-5-11}$$

在计算对弧长的曲线积分时，由于 $\mathrm{d}s>0$，化为定积分后，积分下限必须小于积分上限。

四、对坐标的曲线积分

(一)对坐标的曲线积分的概念和性质

设 L 为平面上的有向曲线，$P(x,y)$ 是定义在 L 上的有界函数，自 L 的起点至终点任意分 L 为 n 个弧段 $\widehat{M_{i-1}M_i}(i=1,2,\cdots,n)$，$\widehat{M_{i-1}M_i}$ 在 x 轴上的投影为 Δx_i，在 $\widehat{M_{i-1}M_i}$ 上任取一点 (ξ_i,η_i) 作积分和 $\sum\limits_{i=1}^{n}P(\xi_i,\eta_i)\Delta x_i$，如果 $\lambda=\max|\Delta x_i|,(i=1,2,\cdots,n)\}\to 0$，上述和式的极限存在，则称此极限为函数 $P(x,y)$ 沿曲线 L 对坐标 x 的曲线积分，记作 $\int_L P(x,y)\mathrm{d}x$，即

$$\int_L P(x,y)\,\mathrm{d}x=\lim_{\lambda\to 0}\sum_{i=1}^{n}P(\xi_i,\eta_i)\Delta x_i$$

同理，可以定义函数 $Q(x,y)$ 沿曲线 L 对坐标 y 的曲线积分

$$\int_L Q(x,y)\,\mathrm{d}y=\lim_{\lambda\to 0}\sum_{i=1}^{n}Q(\xi_i,\eta_i)\Delta y_i$$

一般平面曲线 L 对坐标的曲线积分表达式为

$$\int_L P(x,y)\mathrm{d}x+Q(x,y)\mathrm{d}y$$

对坐标的曲线积分具有以下性质：

1. 可加性

$$\int_L P\mathrm{d}x+Q\mathrm{d}y=\int_{L_1}P\mathrm{d}x+Q\mathrm{d}y+\int_{L_2}P\mathrm{d}x+Q\mathrm{d}y$$

其中，$L=L_1+L_2$。

2. 与积分曲线的方向有关

$$\int_L P(x,y)\mathrm{d}x+Q(x,y)\mathrm{d}y=-\int_{-L}P(x,y)\mathrm{d}x+Q(x,y)\mathrm{d}y \tag{1-5-12}$$

其中，L 和 $-L$ 方向相反。

(二)计算

(1)设曲线 L 的参数方程为 $x=\varphi(t)$、$y=\psi(t)$，L 的起点与终点所对应的参数依次为 α 与 β，且 $P(x,y)$、$Q(x,y)$ 连续，$\psi(t)$、$\varphi(t)$ 连续可微，则

$$\int_L P(x,y)\mathrm{d}x+Q(x,y)\mathrm{d}y=\int_\alpha^\beta\{P[\varphi(t),\psi(t)]\varphi'(t)+Q[\varphi(t),\psi(t)]\psi'(t)\}\mathrm{d}t \tag{1-5-13}$$

(2)设曲线 L 的方程 $y=y(x)$ 连续可微，起点与终点的横坐标依次为 a、b，则

$$\int_L P(x,y)\mathrm{d}x+Q(x,y)\mathrm{d}y=\int_a^b\{P[x,y(x)]+Q[x,y(x)]y'(x)\}\mathrm{d}x \tag{1-5-14}$$

(3)设曲线 L 的方程 $x=x(y)$ 连续可微，起点与终点的纵坐标依次为 c、d，则

$$\int_L P(x,y)\mathrm{d}x+Q(x,y)\mathrm{d}y=\int_c^d\{P[x(y),y]x'(y)+Q[x(y),y]\}\mathrm{d}y \tag{1-5-15}$$

(三)格林公式

设 D 为单连通域，$P(x,y)$、$Q(x,y)$ 在区域 D 上具有一阶连续偏导数，L 为 D 全部边界曲线的正向，即沿 L 前进时，D 始终在边界的左侧，则

$$\oint_L P\mathrm{d}x+Q\mathrm{d}y=\iint_D(\frac{\partial Q}{\partial x}-\frac{\partial P}{\partial y})\mathrm{d}x\mathrm{d}y \tag{1-5-16}$$

其中 L 为闭曲线的正向，D 为 L 所围成的区域。

式(1-5-16)称为格林公式。

(四)曲线积分与路径无关的条件

设 D 为一单连通域，函数 $P(x,y)$、$Q(x,y)$ 在 D 内具有一阶连续偏导数，则曲线积分 $\int_L P\mathrm{d}x+Q\mathrm{d}y$ 在 D 内与路径无关的充分必要条件为 $\frac{\partial P}{\partial y}=\frac{\partial Q}{\partial x}$ 在 D 上恒成立。

设 D 为单连通域，P、Q 具有一阶连续偏导数，则由格林公式可知下列 4 个条件相互等价。

(1)$\frac{\partial Q}{\partial x}=\frac{\partial P}{\partial y}$ 在 D 内恒成立。

(2)$\oint_L P(x,y)\mathrm{d}x+Q(x,y)\mathrm{d}y=0$，$L$ 是位于 D 内的任意一条光滑(或分段光滑)的闭曲线。

(3)设 L 是位于 D 内的任意一条光滑(或分段光滑)的曲线，曲线积分 $\int_L P(x,y)\mathrm{d}x+Q(x,y)\mathrm{d}y$ 与积分路径无关(即只依赖于曲线 L 的起点和终点位置)。

(4)存在可微函数 $u(x,y)$，在 D 内有 $\mathrm{d}u=P(x,y)\mathrm{d}x+Q(x,y)\mathrm{d}y$。

对于(4)中的函数 $u(x,y)$ 可按下面方法计算

$$\forall(x_0,y_0)\in D\quad u(x,y)=\int_{(x_0,y_0)}^{(x,y)}P(x,y)\mathrm{d}x+Q(x,y)\mathrm{d}y \tag{1-5-17}$$

在曲线积分与路径无关的条件下，$u(x,y)$ 可按下列两式之一求出

$$u(x,y)=\int_{x_0}^{x}P(x,y_0)\mathrm{d}x+\int_{y_0}^{y}Q(x,y)\mathrm{d}y \tag{1-5-18}$$

$$u(x,y)=\int_{x_0}^{x}P(x,y)\mathrm{d}x+\int_{y_0}^{y}Q(x_0,y)\mathrm{d}y \tag{1-5-19}$$

五、多元积分学的应用

(一)平面图形的面积

设 D 为 xOy 平面上的有界闭区域，则 D 的面积 A 为

$$A=\iint_D\mathrm{d}x\mathrm{d}y \tag{1-5-20}$$

(二)几何体的体积

设 Ω 为三维空间里的几何体，则 Ω 的体积 V 为

$$V=\iiint\limits_{\Omega}\mathrm{d}x\mathrm{d}y\mathrm{d}z \tag{1-5-21}$$

(三)曲顶柱体体积

设曲面 Σ 的方程为 $z=f(x,y)\geqslant 0,(x,y)\in D$，则 D 上以 Σ 为顶的曲顶柱体体积 V 为

$$V=\iint\limits_{D}f(x,y)\mathrm{d}x\mathrm{d}y \tag{1-5-22}$$

多元积分可用于计算曲面面积、平面薄片和空间物体的质量、重心、转动惯量、对质点的引力等。曲线积分可用于计算曲线形构件的质量、重心、转动惯量、引力、变力沿曲线运动所做的功等。

【例 1-5-14】 已知 $\int_L\sqrt{y}\,\mathrm{d}s$，其中 L 是抛物线 $y=x^2$ 上点 $A(0,0)$ 与点 $B(1,1)$ 之间的一段弧(见图)，其值为：

A. $\dfrac{1}{12}(5\sqrt{5}-1)$　　B. $5\sqrt{5}-1$　　C. $\dfrac{1}{12}$　　D. $\dfrac{5}{12}\sqrt{5}$

解 用对弧长的曲线积分的方法，计算如下：

抛物方程为 $y=x^2$，故 $y'=2x$，利用公式 $\int_L f(x)\sqrt{1+(y')^2}\,\mathrm{d}x$，

有：$\int_L\sqrt{y}\,\mathrm{d}s=\int_0^1\sqrt{x^2}\sqrt{1+4x^2}\,\mathrm{d}x$

$$=\int_0^1 x\sqrt{1+4x^2}\,\mathrm{d}x=\frac{1}{12}(5\sqrt{5}-1)$$

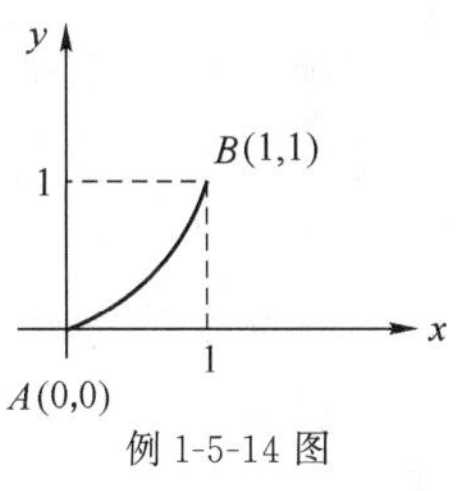

例 1-5-14 图

答案：A

【例 1-5-15】 设 L 是从 A(1,0)至 B(−1,2)的线段，则 $\int_L(x+y)\mathrm{d}s$ 等于：

A. $-2\sqrt{2}$　　B. $2\sqrt{2}$　　C. 2　　D. 0

解 如解图所示，线段 AB 的方程为

$$y-2=\frac{-2}{2}(x+1),y=-x+1$$

L 参数方程：$\begin{cases}y=-x+1\\x=x\end{cases}(-1\leqslant x\leqslant 1)$，$\mathrm{d}s=\sqrt{1+1}\,\mathrm{d}x=\sqrt{2}\,\mathrm{d}x$

例 1-5-15 解图

故 $\int_L(x+y)\mathrm{d}s=\int_{-1}^{1}[x+(-x+1)]\sqrt{2}\,\mathrm{d}x=\int_{-1}^{1}\sqrt{2}\,\mathrm{d}x=\sqrt{2}x\,|_{-1}^{1}=2\sqrt{2}$。

答案：B

【例 1-5-16】 已知 $\int_L(x+y)\mathrm{d}x+(x-y)\mathrm{d}y$，其中 L 为直线 $y=2x-1$ 上从(1,1)到(2,3)的有向线段(见图)。其值为：

A. 0　　B. $\dfrac{5}{2}$　　C. 1　　D. 2

解 本题为对坐标的曲线积分，计算方法如下：

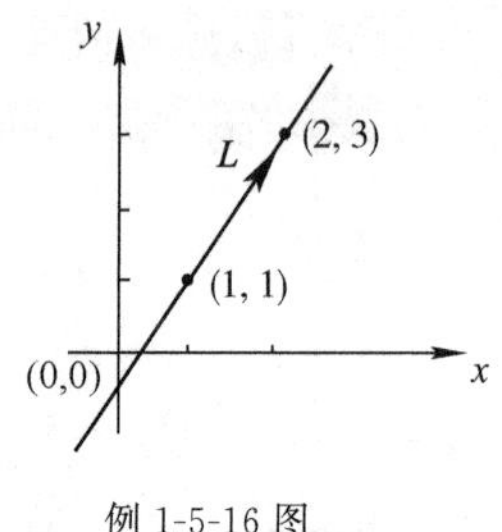

例 1-5-16 图

因为计算曲线 $y=2x-1$，故 $y'=2$，$\mathrm{d}y=2\mathrm{d}x$。将原式中所有的 y 替换为 x 的表达式，则：

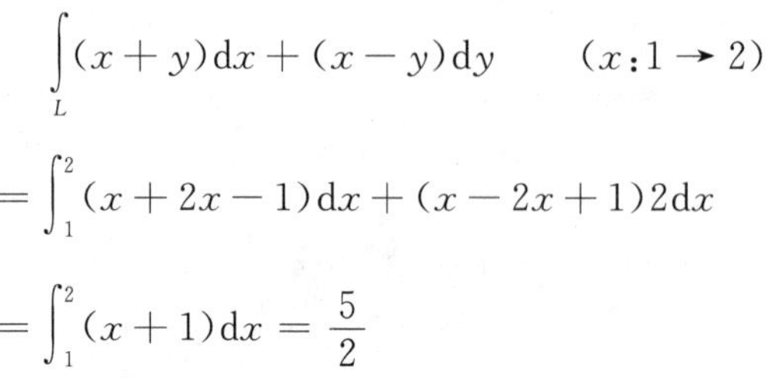

$$\int_L (x+y)\mathrm{d}x+(x-y)\mathrm{d}y \qquad (x:1\to 2)$$

$$=\int_1^2 (x+2x-1)\mathrm{d}x+(x-2x+1)2\mathrm{d}x$$

$$=\int_1^2 (x+1)\mathrm{d}x=\frac{5}{2}$$

答案：B

【例 1-5-17】 设 L 是椭圆 $\begin{cases}x=a\cos\theta\\ y=b\sin\theta\end{cases}$ $(a>0,b>0)$ 的上半椭圆周，沿顺时针方向，则曲线积分 $\int_L y^2\mathrm{d}x$ 等于：

A. $\frac{5}{3}ab^2$　　B. $\frac{4}{3}ab^2$　　C. $\frac{2}{3}ab^2$　　D. $\frac{1}{3}ab^2$

解 本题考查了参数方程形式的对坐标的曲线积分（也称第二类曲线积分），注意绕行方向为顺时针。

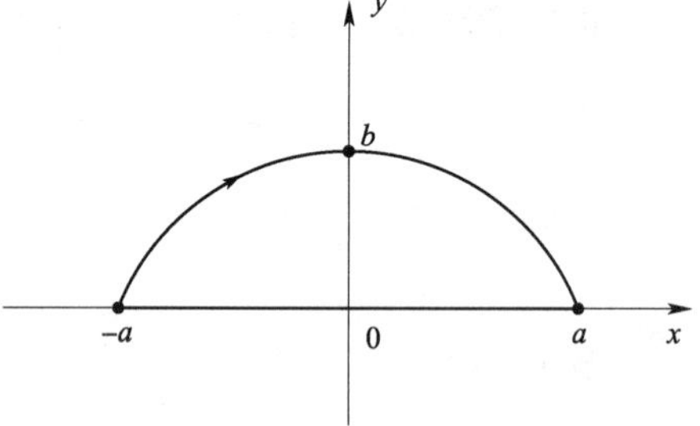

例 1-5-17 解图

积分路径 L 沿顺时针方向，取椭圆上半周，则角度 θ 的取值范围为 π 到 0。

根据 $x=a\cos\theta$，可知 $\mathrm{d}x=-a\sin\theta\mathrm{d}\theta$，因此原式有：

$$\int_L y^2\mathrm{d}x=\int_\pi^0 (b\sin\theta)^2(-a\sin\theta)\mathrm{d}\theta=\int_0^\pi ab^2\sin^3\theta\mathrm{d}\theta$$

$$=ab^2\int_0^\pi \sin^2\theta\mathrm{d}(-\cos\theta)$$

$$=-ab^2\int_0^\pi (1-\cos^2\theta)\mathrm{d}(\cos\theta)=\frac{4}{3}ab^2$$

答案：B

注：对坐标的曲线积分应注意积分路径的方向，然后写出积分变量的上下限，本题若取逆时针为绕行方向，则 θ 的范围应从 0 到 π。简单作图即可观察和验证。

【例 1-5-18】 设 L 是曲线 $y=\ln x$ 上从点 $(1,0)$ 至点 $(e,1)$ 的一段曲线，则曲线积分 $\int_L \frac{2y}{x}\mathrm{d}x+x\mathrm{d}y$ 等于：

A. e　　B. $e+2$　　C. 2　　D. $e-1$

解 见解图。

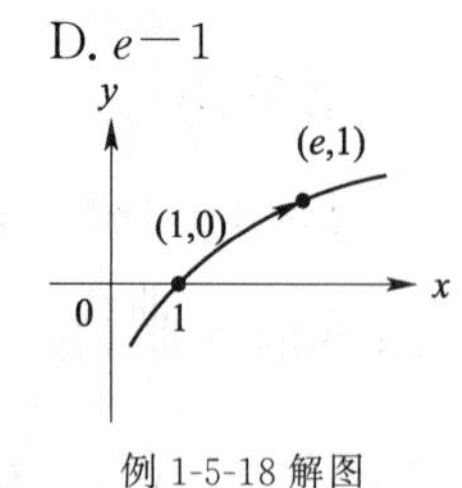

例 1-5-18 解图

$$L_1:\begin{cases}y=\ln x\\ x=x\end{cases} \qquad (x:1\to e)$$

$$\text{原式}=\int_1^e \frac{2\ln x}{x}\mathrm{d}x+x\cdot\frac{1}{x}\mathrm{d}x=\int_1^e\left(\frac{2\ln x}{x}+1\right)\mathrm{d}x$$

$=[(\ln x)^2+x]_1^e=(1+e)-(0+1)=e$

答案：A

习　　题

1-5-1　设 D 为由 $y=x, x=0, y=1$ 所围成的区域，则 $\iint\limits_D e^{-y}\mathrm{d}x\mathrm{d}y=$（　　）。

A. $\frac{1}{2}(e^{-1})$　　B. $-\frac{1}{2e}$　　C. $\frac{1}{2}(1+e)$　　D. $1-\frac{2}{e}$

1-5-2　化二次积分为极坐标系下的二次积分，$\int_0^1\mathrm{d}x\int_0^{x^2}f(x,y)\mathrm{d}y=$（　　）。

A. $\int_0^{\frac{\pi}{3}}\mathrm{d}\theta\int_0^{\sec\theta\tan\theta}f(r\cos\theta,r\sin\theta)r\mathrm{d}r$　　B. $\int_0^{\frac{\pi}{4}}\mathrm{d}\theta\int_0^{\sec\theta\tan\theta}f(r\cos\theta,r\sin\theta)r\mathrm{d}r$

C. $\int_0^{\frac{\pi}{3}}\mathrm{d}\theta\int_{\sec\theta\tan\theta}^{\sec\theta}f(r\cos\theta,r\sin\theta)r\mathrm{d}r$　　D. $\int_0^{\frac{\pi}{4}}\mathrm{d}\theta\int_{\sec\theta\tan\theta}^{\sec\theta}f(r\cos\theta,r\sin\theta)r\mathrm{d}r$

1-5-3　设 D 为圆域 $x^2+y^2\leqslant 4$，则下列式子中正确的是（　　）。

A. $\iint\limits_D\sin(x^2+y^2)\mathrm{d}x\mathrm{d}y=\iint\limits_D\sin 4\mathrm{d}x\mathrm{d}y$

B. $\iint\limits_D\sin(x^2+y^2)\mathrm{d}x\mathrm{d}y=\int_0^{2\pi}\mathrm{d}\theta\int_0^4\sin r^2\mathrm{d}r$

C. $\iint\limits_D\sin(x^2+y^2)\mathrm{d}x\mathrm{d}y=\int_0^{2\pi}\mathrm{d}\theta\int_0^2 r\sin r^2\mathrm{d}r$

D. $\iint\limits_D\sin(x^2+y^2)\mathrm{d}x\mathrm{d}y=\int_0^{2\pi}\mathrm{d}\theta\int_0^2\sin r^2\mathrm{d}r$

1-5-4　$I=\iint\limits_D xy\mathrm{d}\sigma$，$D$ 由 $y^2=x$ 及 $y=x-2$ 所围成，则化为二次积分后的结果为（　　）。

A. $I=\int_0^4\mathrm{d}x\int_{y+2}^{y^2}xy\mathrm{d}y$　　B. $I=\int_{-1}^2\mathrm{d}y\int_{y^2}^{y+2}xy\mathrm{d}x$

C. $I=\int_0^1\mathrm{d}x\int_{-\sqrt{x}}^{\sqrt{x}}xy\mathrm{d}y+\int_1^4\mathrm{d}x\int_{x-2}^{x}xy\mathrm{d}y$　　D. $I=\int_{-1}^2\mathrm{d}x\int_{y^2}^{y+2}xy\mathrm{d}y$

1-5-5　改变积分次序 $\int_0^3\mathrm{d}y\int_y^{6-y}f(x,y)\mathrm{d}x$，则有（　　）。

A. $\int_0^3\mathrm{d}x\int_x^{6-x}f(x,y)\mathrm{d}y$　　B. $\int_0^3\mathrm{d}x\int_0^x f(x,y)\mathrm{d}y+\int_3^6\mathrm{d}x\int_0^{6-x}f(x,y)\mathrm{d}y$

C. $\int_0^3\mathrm{d}x\int_0^x f(x,y)\mathrm{d}y$　　D. $\int_3^6\mathrm{d}x\int_0^{6-x}f(x,y)\mathrm{d}y$

1-5-6　曲线 $y=\frac{2}{3}x^{\frac{3}{2}}$ 上相应于 x 从 0 到 1 的一段弧的长度是（　　）。

A. $\frac{2}{3}(\sqrt[3]{4}-1)$　　B. $\frac{4}{3}\sqrt{2}$　　C. $\frac{2}{3}(2\sqrt{2}-1)$　　D. $\frac{4}{15}$

1-5-7 设 L 是连接 $A(1,0),B(0,1),C(-1,0)$ 的折线，则曲线积分 $\int_{ABC}\frac{\mathrm{d}x+\mathrm{d}y}{|x|+|y|}=$(　　)。

A. 0　　B. -2　　C. 2　　D. 4

1-5-8 两个圆柱体 $x^2+y^2\leqslant R^2, x^2+z^2\leqslant R^2$ 公共部分的体积 V 为(　　)。

A. $2\int_0^R \mathrm{d}x\int_0^{\sqrt{R^2-x^2}}\sqrt{R^2-x^2}\,\mathrm{d}y$　　B. $8\int_0^R \mathrm{d}x\int_0^{\sqrt{R^2-x^2}}\sqrt{R^2-x^2}\,\mathrm{d}y$

C. $\int_{-R}^R \mathrm{d}x\int_{-\sqrt{R^2-x^2}}^{\sqrt{R^2-x^2}}\sqrt{R^2-x^2}\,\mathrm{d}y$　　D. $4\int_{-R}^R \mathrm{d}x\int_{-\sqrt{R^2-x^2}}^{\sqrt{R^2-x^2}}\sqrt{R^2-x^2}\,\mathrm{d}y$

1-5-9 设平面闭区域 D 由 $x=0,y=0,x+y=\frac{1}{2},x+y=1$ 所围成，$I_1=\iint_D[\ln(x+y)]^3\mathrm{d}x\mathrm{d}y$，$I_2=\iint_D(x+y)^3\mathrm{d}x\mathrm{d}y$，$I_3=\iint_D[\sin(x+y)]^3\mathrm{d}x\mathrm{d}y$，则 I_1,I_2,I_3 之间的关系应是(　　)。

A. $I_1<I_2<I_3$　　B. $I_1<I_3<I_2$

C. $I_3<I_2<I_1$　　D. $I_3<I_1<I_2$

第六节　级　　数

一、常数项级数及其敛散性

(一)常数项级数的概念

1. 常数项级数定义

由无穷数列 $\{a_n\}$ 组成的表达式

$$\sum_{n=1}^{\infty}a_n=a_1+a_2+\cdots+a_n+\cdots \tag{1-6-1}$$

称为常数项无穷级数，简称常数项级数。a_n 称为级数的通项(或一般项)。

2. 常数项级数敛散性定义

$$S_n=\sum_{i=1}^{n}a_i=a_1+a_2+\cdots+a_n$$

称为级数式(1-6-1)的前 n 项和，简称部分和。若 $\lim\limits_{n\to\infty}S_n=S$ 存在，则称级数 $\sum\limits_{n=1}^{\infty}a_n$ 收敛，S 为该级数的和，即 $S=\sum\limits_{n=1}^{\infty}a_n$。若 $\lim\limits_{n\to\infty}S_n$ 不存在，则称级数 $\sum\limits_{n=1}^{\infty}a_n$ 发散。

由于 $a_n=S_n-S_{n-1}$，可以得到级数 $\sum\limits_{n=1}^{\infty}a_n$ 收敛的必要条件 $\lim\limits_{n\to\infty}a_n=0$。

(二)常数项级数的性质

(1)如果级数 $\sum\limits_{n=1}^{\infty}a_n$ 收敛于和 S，c 为常数，则 $\sum\limits_{n=1}^{\infty}ca_n$ 收敛，其和为 cS。

(2)如果级数 $\sum\limits_{n=1}^{\infty}a_n$、$\sum\limits_{n=1}^{\infty}b_n$ 都收敛，其和分别为 A、B，则 $\sum\limits_{n=1}^{\infty}(a_n\pm b_n)$ 收敛，其和为 $A\pm B$。

(3)一个级数收敛，另一个级数发散，则它们对应项的和或差所得的级数发散。

(4)两个发散级数对应项的和或差所得的级数敛散性不定。

(5)在级数中去掉、加上或改变有限项不会改变级数的收敛性。在收敛时和要改变。

(6)如果级数$\sum_{n=1}^{\infty}a_n$收敛,则对其任意加括号后所得的级数仍收敛且其和不变。若加括号后所成的级数发散,则原级数也发散。

二、正项级数敛散性判别法

各项为正数的级数$\sum_{n=1}^{\infty}a_n=a_1+a_2+\cdots+a_n+\cdots(a_n\geqslant 0)$称为正项级数,各项符号相同的级数都可以归入正项级数(负项级数各项乘以-1可化为正项级数来判定)。正项级数的部分和S_n构成一个单调增加(或不减少)的数列$\{S_n\}$。由极限存在准则可知,正项级数收敛的充要条件是其部分和数列$\{S_n\}$有上界。

(一)利用级数收敛的必要条件判别

设$\sum_{n=1}^{\infty}a_n$,其中$a_n\geqslant 0(n=1,2,\cdots)$。若$\lim\limits_{n\to\infty}a_n\neq 0$,则$\sum_{n=1}^{\infty}a_n$发散。

(二)正项级数收敛的基本定理

正项级数收敛的充要条件是其部分和数列有界。

(三)常用的正项级数敛散法

1.比较判别法

设$\sum_{n=1}^{\infty}a_n$、$\sum_{n=1}^{\infty}b_n$为两个正项级数,且$0\leqslant a_n\leqslant b_n(n=1,2,\cdots)$,那么若$\sum_{n=1}^{\infty}b_n$收敛,则$\sum_{n=1}^{\infty}a_n$收敛;若$\sum_{n=1}^{\infty}a_n$发散,则$\sum_{n=1}^{\infty}b_n$发散。

2.比较判别法的极限形式

设$\sum_{n=1}^{\infty}a_n$、$\sum_{n=1}^{\infty}b_n$为两个正项级数,若$\lim\limits_{n\to\infty}\frac{a_n}{b_n}=c$,则当:

(1)$0<c<+\infty$时,$\sum_{n=1}^{\infty}a_n$与$\sum_{n=1}^{\infty}b_n$具有相同的敛散性;

(2)$c=0$时,$\sum_{n=1}^{\infty}b_n$收敛,则$\sum_{n=1}^{\infty}a_n$也收敛;

(3)$c=+\infty$时,$\sum_{n=1}^{\infty}b_n$发散,则$\sum_{n=1}^{\infty}a_n$也发散。

在运用比较判别法时,常用下面三个级数作为比较的级数:①等比级数$\sum_{n=1}^{\infty}aq^{n-1}$,当$|q|<1$时级数收敛,当$|q|\geqslant 1$时发散。②调和级数$\sum_{n=1}^{\infty}\frac{1}{n}$,这是一个发散的级数。③$p$级数$\sum_{n=1}^{\infty}\frac{1}{n^p}(p>0$,实数),当$p>1$时,$p$级数收敛;当$p\leqslant 1$时,$p$级数发散。

3.比值判别法

设$\sum_{n=1}^{\infty}a_n$为正项级数,若$\lim\limits_{n\to\infty}\frac{a_{n+1}}{a_n}=\rho$,则当$\rho<1$时,级数收敛;当$\rho>1$(包括$+\infty$)时,级数发散,当$\rho=1$时,级数的敛散性不确定。

4.根值判别法

设$\sum_{n=1}^{\infty}a_n$为正项级数,若$\lim\limits_{n\to\infty}\sqrt[n]{a_n}=\rho$,则当$\rho<1$时,级数收敛;当$\rho>1$(包括$\rho=\infty$)时,级数

发散，当 $\rho=1$ 时，级数的敛散性不确定。

三、任意项级数敛散性的判定

（一）交错级数敛散性的判定（莱布尼茨定理）

设交错级数 $\sum_{n=1}^{\infty}(-1)^{n-1}a_n(a_n>0,n=1,2,\cdots)$，即 $a_1-a_2+a_3-a_4+a_5\cdots$ 组成的级数，满足条件：① $\lim_{n\to\infty}a_n=0$；② $a_n\geqslant a_{n+1}(n=1,2,\cdots)$。则交错级数收敛，且其和 $S\leqslant a_1$。

（二）一般异号级数敛散性的判定

若一个级数 $\sum_{n=1}^{\infty}a_n$ 各项为任意实数，$a_n(n=1,2,\cdots)$ 可正、可负和零，构成的级数，称为一般异号级数。一般异号级数敛散性的判定方法：

把级数各项取绝对值，化为正项级数判定。

设 $\sum_{n=1}^{\infty}a_n$，其中项 $a_n(n=1,2,\cdots)$ 为任意实数，若 $\sum_{n=1}^{\infty}|a_n|$ 收敛，则 $\sum_{n=1}^{\infty}a_n$ 也收敛；若各项取绝对值的级数 $\sum_{n=1}^{\infty}|a_n|$ 采用比值法或根值法判定得到级数发散，则原级数 $\sum_{n=1}^{\infty}a_n$ 一定发散。

设级数 $\sum_{n=1}^{\infty}a_n$ 为一般异号级数，若 $\lim_{n\to\infty}a_n\neq0$，则 $\sum_{n=1}^{\infty}a_n$ 发散。

（三）绝对收敛与条件收敛

设 $\sum_{n=1}^{\infty}a_n$，其中项 $a_n(n=1,2,\cdots)$ 为任意实数，若 $\sum_{n=1}^{\infty}|a_n|$ 收敛，则称 $\sum_{n=1}^{\infty}a_n$ 绝对收敛；若 $\sum_{n=1}^{\infty}|a_n|$ 发散，但 $\sum_{n=1}^{\infty}a_n$ 收敛，则称 $\sum_{n=1}^{\infty}a_n$ 条件收敛。

已知级数 $\sum_{n=1}^{\infty}a_n$，如果级数 $\sum_{n=1}^{\infty}a_n$ 绝对收敛，则级数 $\sum_{n=1}^{\infty}a_n$ 必定收敛。

四、幂级数及其敛散性

（一）幂级数

（1）形如 $a_0+a_1x+a_2x^2+\cdots+a_nx^n+\cdots$ 的级数称为幂级数，常数 $a_0,a_1,\cdots,a_n,\cdots$ 称为幂级数的系数。对于形如 $a_0+a_1(x-x_0)+a_2(x-x_0)^2+\cdots+a_n(x-x_0)^n+\cdots$ 的幂级数，令 $z=x-x_0$ 就可把它化为上面的形式。

（2）阿贝尔定理：如果级数 $\sum_{n=0}^{\infty}a_nx^n$ 在 $x=x_0(x_0\neq0)$ 时收敛，则适合不等式 $|x|<|x_0|$ 的一切 x 使该幂级数绝对收敛。反之，如果级数 $\sum_{n=0}^{\infty}a_nx^n$ 在 $x=x_0$ 时发散，则适合不等式 $|x|>|x_0|$ 的一切 x 使该幂级数发散。

（3）形如 $\sum_{n=0}^{\infty}a_nx^n$ 幂级数的收敛区间、收敛域：

①存在一个正数 $R(0<R<\infty)$，当 $|x|<R$ 时，幂级数收敛；当 $|x|>R$ 时，幂级数发散。称开区间 $(-R,R)$ 为幂级数的收敛区间。再通过判定端点 $x\pm R$ 的敛散性，得到级数的收敛域。有下列几种情况：$(-R,R)$ 或 $(-R,R]$ 或 $[-R,R)$ 或 $[-R,R]$。

②对任何实数 x 幂级数都收敛，幂级数的收敛区间、收敛域均为 $(-\infty,+\infty)$。

③除 $x=0$ 外幂级数均发散，收敛域只有一点 $x=0$。

对于情况①，常数 R 称为幂级数的收敛半径；情况②，幂级数的收敛半径 $R=+\infty$；情况③，收敛半径 $R=0$。

（二）幂级数收敛半径 R 的求法

1. 不缺项的幂级数

(1)设 $\sum_{n=0}^{\infty}a_nx^n$，若 $\lim_{n\to\infty}\left|\frac{a_{n+1}}{a_n}\right|=\rho$，则：①当 $0<\rho<\infty$ 时，$R=\frac{1}{\rho}$；②当 $\rho=0$ 时，$R=+\infty$；③当 $\rho=+\infty$ 时，$R=0$。其中，a_{n+1}、a_n 为幂级数连续两项的系数。

(2)对于形如 $\sum_{n=0}^{\infty}a_n(x-x_0)^n$ 的幂级数，令 $y=x-x_0$，将它化为 $\sum_{n=0}^{\infty}a_ny^n$ 的形式，再利用上面方法求出 R 值，回代 $y=x-x_0$，解不等式得到 x 的收敛范围。

2. 缺项的幂级数

对于 $\sum_{n=0}^{\infty}a_nx^n$ 级数中，缺少 x 的乘方次数为奇数次的项或缺少 x 的乘方次数为偶数次的项时，例如 $\sum_{n=0}^{\infty}a_nx^{2n}$、$\sum_{n=0}^{\infty}a_nx^{2n-1}$，可把级数看作为函数项级数，用比值法计算，即 $\lim_{n\to\infty}\left|\frac{U_{n+1}(x)}{U_n(x)}\right|=$

$\rho(x)\begin{cases}<1，解出|x|<R，级数绝对收敛。\\>1，解出|x|>R，级数发散。\end{cases}$

则 R 值为级数的收敛半径。

（其中 $U_{n+1}(x)$，$U_n(x)$ 为幂级数的相邻两项）

注：求幂级数的收敛半径 R，重点应放在"1. 不缺项的幂级数"这一部分。

（三）幂级数的运算

1. 幂级数的四则运算

设 $\sum_{n=0}^{\infty}a_nx^n$ 与 $\sum_{n=0}^{\infty}b_nx^n$ 的收敛半径分别为 R 与 R'，则：

(1) $\sum_{n=0}^{\infty}a_nx^n\pm\sum_{n=0}^{\infty}b_nx^n=\sum_{n=0}^{\infty}(a_n\pm b_n)x^n$，其收敛半径 $R=\min\{R,R'\}$；

(2) $\sum_{n=0}^{\infty}a_nx^n$ 与 $\sum_{n=0}^{\infty}b_nx^n$ 的积所得级数的收敛半径 $R=\min\{R,R'\}$；

(3) $\sum_{n=0}^{\infty}a_nx^n$ 与 $\sum_{n=0}^{\infty}b_nx^n(b_0\neq0)$ 的商所得到的级数，在比 R、R' 小得多的范围内收敛。

2. 幂级数的分析运算法

设幂级数 $\sum_{n=0}^{\infty}a_nx^n$ 的收敛半径为 R，和函数为 $S(x)$，则：

(1) $S(x)$ 在其收敛区间上连续。

(2) $S(x)$ 在 $(-R,R)$ 上可积，$\forall x\in(-R,R)$，有逐项积分公式

$$\int_0^x S(x)\mathrm{d}x=\int_0^x\sum_{n=0}^{\infty}a_nx^n\mathrm{d}x=\sum_{n=0}^{\infty}\int_0^x a_nx^n\mathrm{d}x \tag{1-6-2}$$

(3) $S(x)$ 在 $(-R,R)$ 上可导，且有逐项求导公式

$$S'(x)=(\sum_{n=0}^{\infty}a_nx^n)'=\sum_{n=0}^{\infty}(a_nx^n)'=\sum_{n=1}^{\infty}na_nx^{n-1} \tag{1-6-3}$$

逐项积分和逐项微分后的级数的收敛半径仍为 R，但端点 $x=\pm R$ 的敛散性可能会发生变化。

利用幂级数的四则运算和分析运算的性质以及一些函数幂级数的展开式可求出幂级数的

和函数，并由此可求出一些常数项级数的和。

（四）函数的幂级数展开式

1. 函数的泰勒级数与麦克劳林级数

设 $f(x)$ 在 $x=x_0$ 的各阶导数都存在，$a_n=\frac{1}{n!}f^{(n)}(x_0)$，$(n=1,2,\cdots)$，称为函数 $f(x)$ 的泰勒系数，以这些系数写成的幂级数称为 $f(x)$ 的泰勒级数，记为

$$f(x_0)+\frac{f'(x_0)}{1!}(x-x_0)+\cdots+\frac{1}{n!}f^{(n)}(x_0)(x-x_0)^n+\cdots \tag{1-6-4}$$

但此级数不一定收敛于 $f(x)$，只有当函数 $f(x)$ 在包含 $x=x_0$ 的某区间 I 内无限次可导，而且泰勒公式中的余项 $R_n(x)$，当 $x\in I$ 时，满足条件

$$\lim_{n\to\infty}R_n(x)=0 \tag{1-6-5}$$

其中 $R_n(x)=\frac{f^{(n+1)}(\xi)}{(n+1)!}(x-x_0)^{n+1}$，$\xi$ 是介于 x 与 x_0 之间的某个值。则 $f(x)$ 的泰勒级数，当 $x\in I$ 时，收敛于 $f(x)$，即

$$f(x)=f(x_0)+\frac{f'(x_0)}{1!}(x-x_0)+\cdots+\frac{1}{n!}f^{(n)}(x_0)(x-x_0)^n+\cdots \tag{1-6-6}$$

称为 $f(x)$ 在 $x=x_0$ 的泰勒级数展开式。当 $x_0=0$ 时，称为 $f(x)$ 的麦克劳林级数展开式

$$f(x)=f(0)+\frac{f'(0)}{1!}x+\frac{f''(0)}{2!}x^2+\cdots+\frac{1}{n!}f^{(n)}(0)x^n+\cdots \tag{1-6-7}$$

2. 函数的幂级数展开式

把函数展开为幂级数，实际上是一个对函数求高阶导数的问题。

通常用直接展开法和间接展开法将函数展开成幂级数。直接展开法是先求出 $f^{(n)}(x)$，$(n=1,2,\cdots)$，写出 $f(x)$ 的幂级数，求出收敛半径 R，然后再讨论在 $(-R,R)$ 内泰勒公式中的余项 $R_n(x)\to 0(n\to\infty)$，得到幂级数在该区间内收敛于 $f(x)$。间接展开法是利用一些已知函数的幂级数展开式如 e^x、$\sin x$、$\cos x$、$\ln(1+x)$、$(1+x)^m$ 等的展开式作为基础，再利用幂级数的四则运算和分析运算的性质，以及函数幂级数展开式的唯一性定理将函数展开成幂级数。

常用的函数展开式有

$$e^x=1+x+\frac{1}{2!}x^2+\cdots+\frac{1}{n!}x^n+\cdots=\sum_{n=0}^{\infty}\frac{x^n}{n!}\quad(-\infty,+\infty)$$

$$\sin x=x-\frac{1}{3!}x^3+\frac{1}{5!}x^5+\cdots+(-1)^n\frac{x^{2n+1}}{(2n+1)!}+\cdots=\sum_{n=0}^{\infty}(-1)^n\frac{x^{2n+1}}{(2n+1)!}\quad(-\infty,+\infty)$$

$$\cos x=1-\frac{1}{2!}x^2+\frac{1}{4!}x^4+\cdots+(-1)^n\frac{x^{2n}}{(2n)!}+\cdots=\sum_{n=0}^{\infty}(-1)^n\frac{x^{2n}}{(2n)!}\quad(-\infty,+\infty)$$

$$\ln(1+x)=x-\frac{x^2}{2}+\frac{x^3}{3}-\cdots+(-1)^n\frac{x^{n+1}}{n+1}+\cdots=\sum_{n=1}^{\infty}(-1)^{n-1}\frac{x^n}{n}\quad(-1,1]$$

$$(1+x)^m=1+mx+\frac{m(m-1)}{2!}x^2+\cdots+\frac{m(m-1)\cdots(m-n+1)}{n!}x^n+\cdots\quad(m\text{ 为任意常数})$$

当 $m>0$ 时，收敛于 $[-1,1]$；当 $-1<m<0$ 时，收敛于 $(-1,1]$；当 $m\leqslant -1$ 时，收敛于 $(-1,1)$。

$$\frac{1}{1+x}=1-x+x^2-\cdots+(-1)^n x^n+\cdots=\sum_{n=0}^{\infty}(-1)^n x^n\quad(-1,1)$$

$$\frac{1}{1-x}=1+x+x^2+\cdots+x^n+\cdots=\sum_{n=0}^{\infty}x^n \qquad (-1,1)$$

函数$\frac{1}{1+x}$、$\frac{1}{1-x}$的展开式应特别关注，在求函数展开式中经常用到。

五、傅里叶级数

(一)傅里叶系数、傅里叶级数

若周期为 2π 的函数 $f(x)$可积，则

$$\begin{aligned} a_n &= \frac{1}{\pi}\int_{-\pi}^{\pi} f(x)\cos nx\,dx \qquad (n=0,1,2,\cdots) \\ b_n &= \frac{1}{\pi}\int_{-\pi}^{\pi} f(x)\sin nx\,dx \qquad (n=1,2,\cdots) \end{aligned} \tag{1-6-8}$$

称为 $f(x)$的傅里叶系数。以傅里叶系数为系数写出的级数

$$\frac{a_0}{2}+\sum_{n=1}^{\infty}(a_n\cos nx+b_n\sin nx) \tag{1-6-9}$$

称为 $f(x)$的傅里叶级数。函数的傅里叶级数不一定收敛，即使收敛，它的和函数也不一定就是 $f(x)$，这一点值得注意。

(二)狄利克雷收敛定理

狄利克雷收敛定理：若$f(x)$是周期为2π的周期函数，且满足在一个周期内连续或只有有限个第一类间断点，并且至多只有有限个极值点，则$f(x)$的傅里叶级数收敛，并且当x是$f(x)$的连续点时，级数收敛于 $f(x)$，当 x 是 $f(x)$的间断点时，级数收敛于$\frac{f(x-0)+f(x+0)}{2}$。

只要函数满足狄利克雷收敛条件，那么傅里叶级数在连续点处收敛于函数在该点的函数值，在间断点处，收敛于函数在该点左极限与右极限的算术平均值。

(三)函数展开成傅里叶级数

(1)设函数 $f(x)$为以 2π 为周期函数，且满足狄利克雷收敛定理条件，则系数

$$a_0=\frac{1}{\pi}\int_{-\pi}^{\pi} f(x)\,dx$$

$$a_n=\frac{1}{\pi}\int_{-\pi}^{\pi} f(x)\cos nx\,dx \qquad (n=1,2,\cdots)$$

$$b_n=\frac{1}{\pi}\int_{-\pi}^{\pi} f(x)\sin nx\,dx \qquad (n=1,2,\cdots)$$

它的傅里叶级数为

$$f(x)=\frac{a_0}{2}+\sum_{n=1}^{\infty}(a_n\cos nx+b_n\sin nx) \qquad (\text{在 } f(x)\text{连续点处收敛})$$

(2)若周期为 2π 的连续函数 $f(x)$是奇函数，则

$$a_n=0 \qquad (n=0,1,2,\cdots)$$

$$b_n=\frac{2}{\pi}\int_{0}^{\pi} f(x)\sin nx\,dx \qquad (n=1,2,\cdots)$$

它的傅里叶级数只含有正弦项，即

$$f(x)=\sum_{n=1}^{\infty}b_n\sin nx\,dx \qquad (\text{在 } f(x)\text{连续点处收敛})$$

若周期为 2π 的连续函数 $f(x)$ 是偶函数，则

$$a_n=\frac{2}{\pi}\int_0^{\pi}f(x)\cos nx\,\mathrm{d}x \qquad (n=0,1,2,\cdots)$$

$$b_n=0 \qquad (n=1,2,\cdots)$$

它的傅里叶级数只含有常数项和余弦项，即

$$f(x)=\frac{a_0}{2}+\sum_{n=1}^{\infty}a_n\cos nx \qquad (\text{在 } f(x) \text{ 连续点处收敛})$$

分别称这样的级数为正弦级数和余弦级数。

(3)如果 $f(x)$ 在 $[-\pi,\pi]$ 上有定义，通过周期延拓，变成以 2π 为周期的周期函数，然后展开成傅里叶级数，在 $(-\pi,\pi)$ 上的展式即为 $f(x)$ 的展式，端点 $x=-\pi$、$x=\pi$ 由延拓后的函数来确定。若在该点连续，包括在内；若在该点间断，不包括在内。只定义在 $[0,\pi]$ 上的函数 $f(x)$，可先通过奇延拓（或偶延拓），再周期延拓得到以 2π 为周期的周期函数，展开成傅里叶级数，在 $(0,\pi)$ 上的展式即为 $f(x)$ 的展式，$x=0$、$x=\pi$ 点由延拓后的函数来确定，若在该点连续，包括在内；若在该点间断，不包括在内。

(4)周期为 $2l$ 的函数，也有相关的收敛定理，它的系数的计算公式为

$$a_n=\frac{1}{l}\int_{-l}^{l}f(x)\cos\frac{n\pi x}{l}\mathrm{d}x \qquad (n=0,1,2,\cdots)$$

$$b_n=\frac{1}{l}\int_{-l}^{l}f(x)\sin\frac{n\pi x}{l}\mathrm{d}x \qquad (n=1,2,\cdots) \qquad (1\text{-}6\text{-}10)$$

傅里叶级数为

$$f(x)=\frac{a_0}{2}+\sum_{n=1}^{\infty}\left(a_n\cos\frac{n\pi x}{l}+b_n\sin\frac{n\pi x}{l}\right) \qquad (\text{确定收敛域}) \qquad (1\text{-}6\text{-}11)$$

周期为 $2l$ 的奇（或偶）函数，定义在 $[-l,l]$ 上的函数及定义在 $[0,l]$ 上的函数可仿照周期为 2π 的函数，定义在 $[-\pi,\pi]$ 上函数及定义在 $[0,\pi]$ 上的函数来处理。

【例 1-6-1】 级数 $\sum\limits_{n=1}^{\infty}\frac{(-1)^n}{a_n}(a_n>0)$ 满足下列什么条件时收敛：

A. $\lim\limits_{n\to\infty}a_n=\infty$　　B. $\lim\limits_{n\to\infty}\frac{1}{a_n}=0$　　C. 发散　　D. 单调递增且 $\lim\limits_{n\to\infty}a_n=+\infty$

解　本题考查级数收敛的充分条件。

注意本题有 $(-1)^n$，显然 $\sum\limits_{n=1}^{\infty}\frac{(-1)^n}{a_n}(a_n>0)$ 是一个交错级数。

交错级数收敛，即 $\sum\limits_{n=1}^{\infty}(-1)^n a_n$，只要满足：① $a_n>a_{n+1}$，② $a_n\to0(n\to\infty)$。

在选项 D 中，已知 a_n 单调递增，即 $a_n<a_{n+1}$，所以 $\frac{1}{a_n}>\frac{1}{a_{n+1}}$

已知 $\lim\limits_{n\to\infty}a_n=+\infty$，所以 $\lim\limits_{n\to\infty}\frac{1}{a_n}=0$

故级数 $\sum\limits_{n=1}^{\infty}\frac{(-1)^n}{a_n}(a_n>0)$ 收敛

其他选项均不符合交错级数收敛的判别方法。

答案：D

【例 1-6-2】 级数 $\sum\limits_{n=1}^{\infty}(-1)^n\frac{1}{n^{p-1}}$：

A. 当 $1<p\leqslant 2$ 时条件收敛　　B. 当 $p>2$ 时条件收敛

C. 当 $p<1$ 时条件收敛　　D. 当 $p>1$ 时条件收敛

解 $\sum_{n=1}^{\infty}(-1)^n\frac{1}{n^{p-1}}$级数条件收敛应满足条件：①取绝对值后级数发散；②原级数收敛。

$\sum_{n=1}^{\infty}\left|(-1)^n\frac{1}{n^{p-1}}\right|=\sum_{n=1}^{\infty}\frac{1}{n^{p-1}}$，当 $0<p-1\leqslant 1$ 时，即 $1<p\leqslant 2$，取绝对值后级数发散，原级数 $\sum_{n=1}^{\infty}(-1)^n\frac{1}{n^{p-1}}$为交错级数。

在 $1<p\leqslant 2$ 时，取绝对值后的级数发散，而当 $p>1$ 时，满足莱布尼兹定理条件：①$\frac{1}{n^{p-1}}>\frac{1}{(n+1)^{p-1}}$；②$\lim\limits_{n\to\infty}\frac{1}{n^{p-1}}=0$，原级数收敛。

综合以上结论 $1<p\leqslant 2$ 和 $p>1$，应为 $1<p\leqslant 2$。

答案：A

【例 1-6-3】 幂级数 $x-\frac{x^2}{2}+\frac{x^3}{3}-\cdots+(-1)^{n-1}\frac{x^n}{n}+\cdots$的收敛半径和收敛域为：

A. 2；(−2 ,2)　　B. 2；(−2,2)　　C. 1；(−1,1)　　D. 1；(−1,1)

解

$$\rho=\lim_{n\to\infty}\left|\frac{a_{n+1}}{a_n}\right|=\lim_{n\to\infty}\frac{\frac{1}{n+1}}{\frac{1}{n}}=1$$

$R=\frac{1}{\rho}=1$，即 $|x|<1$ 收敛

当 $x=1$ 时，代入级数得

$1-\frac{1}{2}+\frac{1}{3}-\cdots+(-1)^{n-1}\frac{1}{n}+\cdots$ 为交错级数，满足莱布尼兹定理条件，收敛。

当 $x=-1$ 时，代入级数得

$-1-\frac{1}{2}-\frac{1}{3}-\cdots-\frac{1}{n}\cdots=-\left(1+\frac{1}{2}+\frac{1}{3}+\cdots+\frac{1}{n}+\cdots\right)$ 为调和级数，发散。

收敛域(−1,1]

答案：C

注：在求级数的收敛域时，要注意对两个端点的讨论。本题中，要对端点 $x=1$，$x=-1$ 加以讨论。

【例 1-6-4】 函数 $f(x)=\frac{1}{x}$，将其展开为 $x-3$ 的幂级数为：

A. $\frac{1}{3}\sum_{n=0}^{\infty}(-1)^n\left(\frac{x-3}{3}\right)^n$　(0,6)　　B. $\frac{1}{2}\sum_{n=0}^{\infty}(-1)^n\left(\frac{x-3}{4}\right)^n$　(0,6)

C. $\frac{1}{4}\sum_{n=0}^{\infty}(-1)^n\left(\frac{x-3}{4}\right)^n$　(0,6)　　D. $\sum_{n=0}^{\infty}(-1)^n\left(\frac{x-3}{3}\right)^n$　(0,6)

解

$$\frac{1}{x}=\frac{1}{3+x-3}=\frac{1}{3}\times\frac{1}{1+\frac{x-3}{3}}$$

利用已知$\frac{1}{1+x}=1-x+x^2-x^3+\cdots$，$x\subset(-1,1)$，展开式得到

$$\frac{1}{3}\times\frac{1}{1+\frac{x-3}{3}}=\frac{1}{3}\times\left[1-\frac{x-3}{3}+\left(\frac{x-3}{3}\right)^2-\left(\frac{x-3}{3}\right)^3+\cdots\right]$$

由 $-1<x<1$，代入 $-1<\frac{x-3}{3}<1$，得 $0<x<6$

$$\frac{1}{x}=\frac{1}{3}\times\left[1-\frac{x-3}{3}+\left(\frac{x-3}{3}\right)^2-\cdots\right]\quad(0,6)$$

答案:A

【例 1-6-5】 下列各级数发散的是:

A. $\sum\limits_{n=1}^{\infty}\sin\frac{1}{n}$　　B. $\sum\limits_{n=1}^{\infty}(-1)^{n-1}\frac{1}{\ln(n+1)}$

C. $\sum\limits_{n=1}^{\infty}\frac{n+1}{3^{\frac{n}{2}}}$　　D. $\sum\limits_{n=1}^{\infty}(-1)^{n-1}\left(\frac{2}{3}\right)^n$

解 选 A。分析如下:

$\sum\limits_{n=1}^{\infty}\sin\frac{1}{n}$ 为正项级数，对于 $\lim\limits_{n\to\infty}\frac{\sin\frac{1}{n}}{\frac{1}{n}}$，因 $\lim\limits_{x\to\infty}\frac{\sin\frac{1}{x}}{\frac{1}{x}}=\lim\limits_{t\to0}\frac{\sin t}{t}=1$，故 $\lim\limits_{n\to\infty}\frac{\sin\frac{1}{n}}{\frac{1}{n}}=1$

而 $\sum\limits_{n=1}^{\infty}\frac{1}{n}$ 发散，所以 $\sum\limits_{n=1}^{\infty}\sin\frac{1}{n}$ 发散

选项 B，$\sum\limits_{n=1}^{\infty}(-1)^{n-1}\frac{1}{\ln(n+1)}$ 为交错级数，可用莱布尼兹定理判定：① $u_n\geqslant u_{n+1}$；② $\lim\limits_{n\to\infty}u_n=0$。级数收敛。

选项 C，$\sum\limits_{n=1}^{\infty}\frac{n+1}{3^{\frac{n}{2}}}$ 为正项级数，用比值判别法 $\lim\limits_{n\to\infty}\frac{u_{n+1}}{u_n}=\frac{1}{\sqrt{3}}<1$，收敛。

选项 D，$\sum\limits_{n=1}^{\infty}(-1)^{n-1}\left(\frac{2}{3}\right)^n=\frac{2}{3}-\left(\frac{2}{3}\right)^2+\left(\frac{2}{3}\right)^3+\left(\frac{2}{3}\right)^4+\cdots$ 为等比级数，公比 $q=-\frac{2}{3}$，$|q|<1$，收敛。

答案:A

【例 1-6-6】 级数 $\sum\limits_{n=1}^{\infty}u_n$ 收敛的充要条件是:

A. $\lim\limits_{n\to\infty}u_n=0$　　B. $\lim\limits_{n\to\infty}\frac{u_{n+1}}{u_n}=r<1$

C. $u_n\leqslant\frac{1}{n^2}$　　D. $\lim\limits_{n\to\infty}S_n$ 存在，其中 $S_n=u_1+\cdots+u_n$

解 选项 A 错误：$\sum\limits_{n=1}^{\infty}u_n$ 收敛 $\Rightarrow\lim\limits_{n\to\infty}u_n=0$ 仅是级数收敛的必要条件，而非充分条件。例如调和级数 $\sum\limits_{n=1}^{\infty}\frac{1}{n}$，满足 $\lim\limits_{n\to\infty}u_n=\lim\limits_{n\to\infty}\frac{1}{n}=0$，但级数发散。

选项 B 错误：$\lim\limits_{n\to\infty}\frac{u_{n+1}}{u_n}=r<1$ 为正项级数收敛的充分条件，但所给级数并未说明是什么类型的级数。

选项 C 错误：此条件仅对正项级数收敛适用。

选项 D 正确：$\lim\limits_{n\to\infty}S_n$ 存在是级数 $\sum\limits_{n=1}^{\infty}u_n$ 收敛的充分必要条件，这是判定级数敛散性的基本定理。

答案:D

【例 1-6-7】 设部分和 $S_n=\sum_{k=1}^{n}a_k$,则数列$\{S_n\}$有界,是级数$\sum_{n=1}^{\infty}a_n$ 收敛的:

A. 充分不必要条件　　B. 必要不充分条件

C. 充分必要条件　　D. 既不充分条件也不必要条件

解 正项极数收敛的充要条件是其部分和数列$\{S_n\}$有上界,但在本题中数列$\{a_n\}$的 a_n 未给出$a_n\geqslant 0$ 的条件,所以选项 C 不成立。部分数列$\{S_n\}$有界仅是级数收敛的必要条件,但非充分条件。

例如:级数$\sum_{n=1}^{\infty}n$,$S_n=1+2+\cdots+n=\dfrac{n(n+1)}{2}$,部分数列$\{S_n\}$无界,级数一定发散;例如:极数$\sum_{n=1}^{\infty}(-1)^{n+1}$,$S_n=1-1+1\cdots+(-1)^{n+1}$,$|S_n|\leqslant 1$ 有界,但级数发散,选项 A、D 也不成立。所以选项 B 成立。

答案:B

【例 1-6-8】 级数$\sum_{n=1}^{\infty}\dfrac{\sin\dfrac{n\pi}{2}}{\sqrt{n^3}}$的收敛性是:

A. 绝对收敛　　B. 发散　　C. 条件收敛　　D. 无法判定

解 级数各项取绝对值,即$\sum_{n=1}^{\infty}\left|\dfrac{\sin\dfrac{n\pi}{2}}{\sqrt{n^3}}\right|$,因$\left|\dfrac{\sin\dfrac{n\pi}{2}}{\sqrt{n^3}}\right|\leqslant\dfrac{1}{n^{\frac{3}{2}}}$,而级数$\sum_{n=1}^{\infty}\dfrac{1}{n^{\frac{3}{2}}}$,$p=\dfrac{3}{2}>1$,收敛,由正项级数比较法知,级数$\sum_{n=1}^{\infty}\left|\dfrac{\sin\dfrac{n\pi}{2}}{\sqrt{n^3}}\right|$收敛,所以原级数$\sum_{n=1}^{\infty}\dfrac{\sin\dfrac{n\pi}{2}}{\sqrt{n^3}}$绝对收敛。

答案:A

【例 1-6-9】 已知数列$\{b_n\}$,有$\lim\limits_{n\to\infty}b_n=\infty$,且 $b_n\neq 0(n=1,2,3,\cdots)$,则级数$\sum_{n=1}^{\infty}\left(\dfrac{1}{b_n}-\dfrac{1}{b_{n+1}}\right)$的和为:

A. $\dfrac{1}{b_1}$　　B. $\dfrac{1}{2b_1}$　　C. $\dfrac{1}{b_1b_2}$　　D. ∞

解 $S_n=\left(\dfrac{1}{b_1}-\dfrac{1}{b_2}\right)+\left(\dfrac{1}{b_2}-\dfrac{1}{b_3}\right)+\cdots+\left(\dfrac{1}{b_n}-\dfrac{1}{b_{n+1}}\right)=\dfrac{1}{b_n}-\dfrac{1}{b_{n+1}}$

$$\lim_{n\to\infty}S_n=\lim_{n\to\infty}\left(\frac{1}{b_1}-\frac{1}{b_{n+1}}\right)=\frac{1}{b_1}(b_1\neq 0)$$

答案:A

【例 1-6-10】 级数$\sum_{n=1}^{\infty}(-1)^{n-1}x^n$ 的和函数是:

A. $\dfrac{1}{1+x}(-1<x<1)$　　B. $\dfrac{x}{1+x}(-1<x<1)$

C. $\dfrac{x}{1-x}(-1<x<1)$　　D. $\dfrac{1}{1-x}(-1<x<1)$

解 级数$\sum_{n=1}^{\infty}(-1)^{n-1}x^n=x-x^2+x^3-\cdots+(-1)^{n-1}x^n+\cdots$,公比 $q=-x$,$|q|=|-x|=|x|<1$,

等比级数收敛，级数的和函数 $S=\frac{a_1}{1-q}=\frac{x}{1-(-x)}=\frac{x}{1+x}\quad(-1<x<1)$。

答案：B

【例 1-6-11】 函数 e^x 展开成为 $x-1$ 的幂级数是：

A. $\sum_{n=0}^{\infty}\frac{(x-1)^n}{n!}$　　B. $e\sum_{n=0}^{\infty}\frac{(x-1)^n}{n!}$　　C. $\sum_{n=0}^{\infty}\frac{(n-1)^n}{n}$　　D. $\sum_{n=0}^{\infty}\frac{(x-1)^n}{ne}$

解 $e^x=e^{x-1+1}=ee^{x-1}$

已知 $e^x=1+\frac{1}{1!}x+\frac{1}{2!}x^2+\cdots+\frac{1}{n!}x^n+\cdots\quad(-\infty,+\infty)$

$$e^{x-1}=1+\frac{1}{1!}(x-1)+\frac{1}{2!}(x-1)^2+\cdots+\frac{1}{n!}(x-1)^n+\cdots$$

$$=\sum_{n=0}^{\infty}\frac{1}{n!}(x-1)^n\quad(-\infty,+\infty)$$

$$e^x=e\sum_{n=0}^{\infty}\frac{1}{n!}(x-1)^n\quad(-\infty,+\infty)$$

答案：B

注：求函数 $f(x)$ 的展开式时，一般都是用间接展开法，即利用已知函数的幂级数展开式计算。常用的 $\frac{1}{1+x}$、$\frac{1}{1-x}$ 及 e^x 函数的展开式应牢记，是近几年来的热门考点。

【例 1-6-12】 级数 $\sum_{n=1}^{\infty}\frac{(2x+1)^n}{n}$ 的收敛域是：

A. $(-1,1)$　　B. $[-1,1]$

C. $[-1,0)$　　D. $(-1,0)$

解 设 $2x+1=z$，级数为 $\sum_{n=1}^{\infty}\frac{z^n}{n}$。

$$\lim_{n\to\infty}\left|\frac{a_{n+1}}{a_n}\right|=\lim_{n\to\infty}\frac{\frac{1}{n+1}}{\frac{1}{n}}=1,\rho=1,R=\frac{1}{\rho}=1$$

当 $z=1$ 时，$\sum_{n=1}^{\infty}\frac{1}{n}$ 发散，当 $z=-1$ 时，$\sum_{n=1}^{\infty}\frac{(-1)^n}{n}$ 收敛，

所以 $-1\leqslant z<1$ 收敛，即 $-1\leqslant 2x+1<1$，$-1\leqslant x<0$。

答案：C

【例 1-6-13】 若级数 $\sum_{n=1}^{\infty}b_n$ 收敛，且 $\lim_{n\to\infty}\frac{a_n}{b_n}=1$，则级数 $\sum_{n=1}^{\infty}a_n$：

A. 收敛　　B. 发散

C. 收敛且其和与 $\sum_{n=1}^{\infty}b_n$ 的和相等　　D. 不一定收敛

解 如果 $\sum_{n=1}^{\infty}a_n$ 和 $\sum_{n=1}^{\infty}b_n$ 都是正项级数，且 $\lim_{n\to\infty}\frac{a_n}{b_n}=1$，由正项级数的比较判别法极限形式，可判定 $\sum_{n=1}^{\infty}a_n$ 一定收敛，但如果 $\sum_{n=1}^{\infty}a_n$ 和 $\sum_{n=1}^{\infty}b_n$ 不是正项级数，则结论不一定成立。

例如：$b_n=(-1)^n\frac{1}{\sqrt{n}}$，$a_n=(-1)^n\frac{1}{\sqrt{n}}+\frac{1}{n}$

可判定$\sum\limits_{n=1}^{\infty}b_n$收敛，而$\lim\limits_{n\to\infty}\dfrac{(-1)^n\dfrac{1}{\sqrt{n}}+\dfrac{1}{n}}{(-1)^n\dfrac{1}{\sqrt{n}}}=\lim\limits_{n\to\infty}(1+(-1)^n\dfrac{1}{\sqrt{n}})=1$

但$\sum\limits_{n=1}^{\infty}a_n$发散。因为$\sum\limits_{n=1}^{\infty}(-1)^n\sqrt{\dfrac{1}{n}}$收敛，$\sum\limits_{n=1}^{\infty}\dfrac{1}{n}$发散，对应项之和所得到的级数发散。

答案:D

【例 1-6-14】 下列命题中，正确的是：

A. 周期函数$f(x)$的傅里叶级数收敛于$f(x)$

B. 若$f(x)$有任意阶导数，则$f(x)$的泰勒级数收敛于$f(x)$

C. 正项级数收敛的充分必要条件是级数的部分和数列有界

D. 若正项级数收敛，则级数$\sum\limits_{n=1}^{\infty}\sqrt{a_n}$必收敛

解 选项A错误。由迪利克雷收敛定理知，周期函数在满足一定的条件下，展开成的傅里叶级数才收敛于$f(x)$。

选项B错误。若$f(x)$有任意阶导数，$f(x)$的泰勒级数在$\lim\limits_{n\to\infty}R_n(x)=0$的条件下才收敛于$f(x)$。

选项D错误。举例说明，$\sum\limits_{n=1}^{\infty}\dfrac{1}{n^2}$收敛（$p>1$），但$\sum\limits_{n=1}^{\infty}\dfrac{1}{n}$为调和级数发散。

选项C正确。正项级数收敛的充分必要条件是级数的部分和数列有界，这是正项级数收敛的基本定理。

答案:C

【例 1-6-15】 设级数$\sum\limits_{n=1}^{\infty}a_n(x-2)^n$在$x=0$处收敛，在$x=4$处发散，则级数的收敛域为：

A. $[0,4)$ B. $(0,4)$ C. $[0,4]$ D. $[-2,2]$

解 设$x-2=t$，级数$\sum\limits_{n=1}^{\infty}a_nt^n$，当$x=0$，$t=-2$，级数收敛

由阿贝尔定理可知，$\sum\limits_{n=1}^{\infty}a_nt^n$在$(-2,2)$收敛

因$t=-2$收敛，所在在$[-2,2)$收敛

又当$x=4$，$t=2$时，级数发散，由阿贝尔定理可知，$\sum\limits_{n=1}^{\infty}a_nt^n$在$(-\infty,-2)$和$(2,+\infty)$上发散

因$t=2$时发散，所以$\sum\limits_{n=1}^{\infty}a_nt^n$在$(-\infty,-2)$和$[2,+\infty)$上发散，在$(-2,2)$上收敛

所以级数$\sum\limits_{n=1}^{\infty}a_nt^n$的收敛域取公共部分$[-2,2)$

则原级数$\sum\limits_{n=1}^{\infty}a_n(x-2)^n$的收敛域为$[0,4)$

答案:A

【例 1-6-16】 周期为2的函数$f(x)$，它在一个周期内的表达式为$f(x)=x(-1\leqslant x<1)$，设它的傅里叶级数的和函数为$S(x)$，则$S\left(\dfrac{3}{2}\right)$等于：

A. 1 B. $-\dfrac{1}{2}$ C. -1 D. $\dfrac{1}{2}$

解 设函数 $f(x)$ 的傅里叶级数为

$$\frac{a_0}{2}+\sum_{n=1}^{\infty}a_n\cos\frac{n\pi x}{l}+b_n\sin\frac{n\pi x}{l}$$

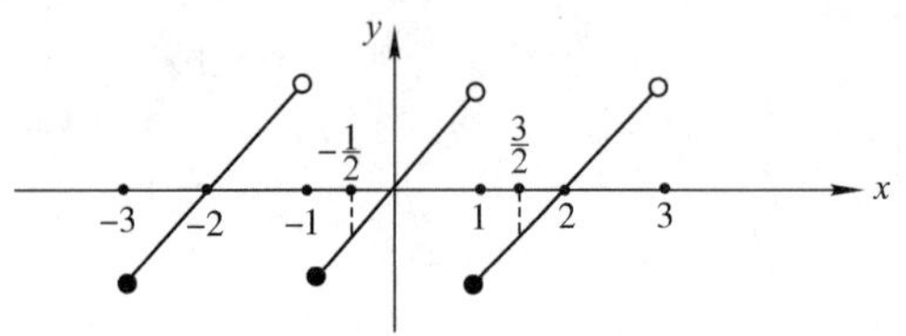

例 1-6-16 解图

由迪利克雷收敛可知，$x=\frac{3}{2}$ 是函数 $f(x)$ 的连续点(见解图)，级数的和函数 $S(x)$ 收敛于 $x=\frac{3}{2}$ 对应的函数值。

$$S\left(\frac{3}{2}\right)=S\left(-\frac{1}{2}\right)=f\left(-\frac{1}{2}\right)=x\Big|_{x=-\frac{1}{2}}=-\frac{1}{2}$$

答案:B

习 题

1-6-1 下列级数中，发散的级数是(　　)。

A. $\sum_{n=1}^{\infty}(-1)^n\frac{1}{\sqrt{n}}$　　B. $\sum_{n=1}^{\infty}\frac{n}{2^n}$　　C. $\sum_{n=1}^{\infty}\left(\frac{1}{n}-\frac{1}{n+1}\right)$　　D. $\sum_{n=1}^{\infty}\sin\frac{n\pi}{3}$

1-6-2 函数 $\sum_{n=1}^{\infty}\frac{(-1)^{n-1}}{n}$ 的收敛性是(　　)。

A. 绝对收敛　　B. 条件收敛

C. 等比级数收敛　　D. 发散

1-6-3 设级数 $\sum_{n=1}^{\infty}U_n$ 是条件收敛的，又设 $U_n{}^*=\frac{U_n+|U_n|}{2}$，$U_n{}^{**}=\frac{U_n-|U_n|}{2}$，则级数 $\sum_{n=1}^{\infty}U_n^*$ 和 $\sum_{n=1}^{\infty}U_n^{**}$ (　　)。

A. $\sum_{n=1}^{\infty}U_n^*$ 和 $\sum_{n=1}^{\infty}U_n^{**}$ 都是收敛的　　B. $\sum_{n=1}^{\infty}U_n^*$ 和 $\sum_{n=1}^{\infty}U_n^{**}$ 都是发散的

C. $\sum_{n=1}^{\infty}U_n^*$ 发散，但 $\sum_{n=1}^{\infty}U_n^{**}$ 收敛　　D. $\sum_{n=1}^{\infty}U_n^*$ 收敛，但 $\sum_{n=1}^{\infty}U_n^{**}$ 发散

1-6-4 已知幂级数 $\sum_{n=1}^{\infty}\frac{a^n-b^n}{a^n+b^n}x^n(0<a<b)$，则所给级数的收敛半径 R 等于(　　)。

A. b　　B. $\frac{1}{a}$

C. $\frac{1}{b}$　　D. R 的值与 a，b 无关

1-6-5 级数 $\sum_{n=1}^{\infty}\left(x^n+\frac{1}{2^nx^n}\right)$ 的收敛域为(　　)。

A. $|x|<1$　　B. $|x|>\frac{1}{2}$　　C. $\frac{1}{2}<|x|<1$　　D. 无法确定

1-6-6 设 $f(x)=\begin{cases}x & -\pi\leqslant x<0\\ 1 & 0\leqslant x\leqslant\pi\end{cases}$ 的傅里叶级数展开式为 $\frac{a_0}{2}+\sum_{n=1}^{\infty}(a_n\cos nx+b_n\sin nx)$，则其中的系数 $a_3=$(　　)。

A. $\frac{1}{\pi}$　　B. $\frac{2}{\pi}$　　C. $\frac{2}{9\pi}$　　D. 0

1-6-7　幂级数 $x^2-\frac{1}{2}x^3+\frac{1}{3}x^4-\cdots+\frac{(-1)^{n+1}}{n}x^{n+1}+\cdots(-1<x\leqslant 1)$ 的和是(　　)。

A. $x\sin x$　　B. $\frac{x^2}{1+x^2}$　　C. $x\ln(1-x)$　　D. $x\ln(1+x)$

1-6-8　若 $\lim\limits_{n\to\infty}\left|\frac{C_n}{C_{n+1}}\right|=3$，则幂级数 $\sum\limits_{n=0}^{\infty}C_n(x-1)^n$ 的敛散性为(　　)。

A. 必在 $|x|>3$ 时发散　　B. 必在 $|x|\leqslant 3$ 时发散

C. 在 $x=-3$ 处敛散性不定　　D. 其收敛半径为 3

1-6-9　函数 $f(x)=\frac{x}{x^2-5x+6}$ 展开成 $(x-5)$ 的级数的收敛区间是(　　)。

A. (10,1)　　B. (−1,1)　　C. (3,7)　　D. (4,5)

1-6-10　设 $f(x)=\begin{cases}x & 0\leqslant x\leqslant\frac{\pi}{2}\\ \pi & \frac{\pi}{2}<x<\pi\end{cases}$，$S(x)=\sum\limits_{n=1}^{\infty}b_n\sin nx$，其中 $b_n=\frac{2}{\pi}\int_0^{\pi}f(x)\sin nx\mathrm{d}x$，则 $S\left(-\frac{\pi}{2}\right)$ 的值是(　　)。

A. $\frac{\pi}{2}$　　B. $\frac{3\pi}{4}$　　C. $-\frac{3\pi}{4}$　　D. 0

第七节　常微分方程

一、微分方程的一般概念

含有未知函数的导数(或微分)的方程称为微分方程。未知函数为一元函数的微分方程称为常微分方程。方程中未知函数求导的最高阶数称为微分方程的阶。如果一个方程中未知函数对自变量的各阶导数的乘方次数都是一次，称为线性微分方程，否则称为非线性微分方程。在微分方程中，不含未知函数及其导数的项 $Q(x)$ 称为自由项。$Q(x)$ 为零的方程称为齐次方程，$Q(x)$ 不为零的方程称为非齐次方程。代入方程后能使方程成为恒等式的连续函数称为微分方程的解。若微分方程的解中，含有独立的任意常数的个数与方程的阶数相同，则称此解为微分方程的通解。方程中给出的特定条件称初始条件。通解中任意常数被初始条件确定后的解称为微分方程的特解。

二、一阶微分方程的解法

(一)可分离变量方程

若一阶方程 $F(x,y,y')=0$ 可化为 $f(x)\mathrm{d}x=g(y)\mathrm{d}y$ 或 $f(x)\mathrm{d}x-g(y)\mathrm{d}y=0$ 的形式，称为可分离变量方程。对变量已分离的方程，两边积分就可得到原方程的通解

$$\int g(y)\mathrm{d}y=\int f(x)\mathrm{d}x+C \tag{1-7-1}$$

其中，C 为任意常数。

(二)齐次方程

若一阶方程 $F(x,y,y')=0$，可化为 $y'=\varphi\left(\frac{y}{x}\right)$ 的形式，称为齐次方程。令 $u=\frac{y}{x}$，$y=xu$，

$y'=u+xu'$，代入方程则可将方程化为 $u+xu'=\varphi(u)$，分离变量后，两边积分得

$$\int \frac{\mathrm{d}u}{\varphi(u)-u}=\int \frac{\mathrm{d}x}{x}+C \tag{1-7-2}$$

其中 C 为任意常数。求出积分后，再把 $u=\dfrac{y}{x}$ 代入得原方程的通解。

若一阶方程 $F(x,y,y')=0$，可化为 $x'=\varphi\left(\dfrac{x}{y}\right)$ 的形式，也称为齐次方程，可设 $u=\dfrac{x}{y}$ 求通解。

（三）一阶线性方程

若一阶方程 $F(x,y,y')=0$ 可化为

$$y'+P(x)y=Q(x) \tag{1-7-3}$$

其中，$P(x)$、$Q(x)$ 是 x 的函数或常数，则该方程称为一阶线性微分方程，当 $Q(x)\neq 0$ 时，称为一阶线性非齐次方程。当 $Q(x)=0$ 时，$y'+P(x)y=0$ 称为一阶线性齐次微分方程。解一阶线性非齐次方程时，可先解对应的齐次方程，求出通解 $y=Ce^{-\int P(x)\mathrm{d}x}$，然后常数变易，将解中的 c 写成 $C(x)$，代入求出 $C(x)=\int Q(x)e^{\int P(x)\mathrm{d}x}\mathrm{d}x+C$，最后得到非齐次的通解

$$y=e^{-\int P(x)\mathrm{d}x}\left[\int Q(x)e^{\int P(x)\mathrm{d}x}\mathrm{d}x+C\right] \tag{1-7-4}$$

通常可以直接利用式(1-7-4)，求出一阶线性非齐次方程的通解。

将式(1-7-4)写成 $y=e^{-\int P(x)\mathrm{d}x}\int Q(x)e^{\int P(x)\mathrm{d}x}\mathrm{d}x+Ce^{-\int P(x)\mathrm{d}x}$ 形式，得到一阶非齐次方程的通解＝(第一项)非齐线性方程的一个特解＋(第二项)线性齐次方程的通解。

（四）全微分方程

若一阶微分方程 $P(x,y)\mathrm{d}x+Q(x,y)\mathrm{d}y=0$ 的左端恰好是某一函数 $u=u(x,y)$ 的全微分，称为全微分方程。即

$$\mathrm{d}u(x,y)=P(x,y)\mathrm{d}x+Q(x,y)\mathrm{d}y$$

这里，$\dfrac{\partial u}{\partial x}=P(x,y)$，$\dfrac{\partial u}{\partial y}=Q(x,y)$

那么 $u(x,y)=C$ 就是全微分方程的通解。

通解的求法：

当 $P(x,y)$、$Q(x,y)$ 在单连通域 G 内具有一阶连续偏导数，$\dfrac{\partial P}{\partial y}=\dfrac{\partial Q}{\partial x}$ 在区域 G 内恒成立，那么全微分方程的通解可通过计算下面积分求出

$$u(x,y)=\int_{x_0}^{x}P(x,y)\mathrm{d}x+\int_{y_0}^{y}Q(x_0,y)\mathrm{d}y=C \tag{1-7-5}$$

或

$$u(x,y)=\int_{x_0}^{x}P(x,y_0)\mathrm{d}x+\int_{y_0}^{y}Q(x,y)\mathrm{d}y=C \tag{1-7-6}$$

其中 x_0、y_0 是在区域 G 内适当选定的点 $M_0(x_0,y_0)$ 的坐标。

三、可降阶的高阶微分方程

（一）$y^{(n)}=f(x)$型

这种方程只需逐次积分，求出其通解。每次积分，方程的阶数降低一次，出现一个任意常数。

（二）$y''=f(x,y')$型

微分方程中不显含 y。

应牢记用下面方法变形，然后计算。

令 $y'=P(x)$，则 $y''=P'(x)$，方程化为$\frac{dP}{dx}=f(x,P)$，解微分方程求出 $P=\varphi(x,C_1)$，代入 $y'=P(x)$，从而把方程化为$\frac{dy}{dx}=\varphi(x,C_1)$，运用分离变量法，求得原方程的通解为

$$y=\int\varphi(x,C_1)dx+C_2 \tag{1-7-7}$$

（三）$y''=f(y,y')$型

微分方程中不显含 x。

令 $y'=P(y)$，则 $y''=\frac{dP}{dx}=\frac{dP}{dy}\cdot\frac{dy}{dx}=P\frac{dP}{dy}$，从而可将原方程化为 $P\frac{dP}{dy}=f(y,P)$，设其通解为 $P=\varphi(y,C_1)$，再运用分离变量法，求得原方程的通解为

$$\int\frac{dy}{\varphi(y,C_1)}=x+C_1 \tag{1-7-8}$$

【例 1-7-1】 函数 $y=3e^{2x}$是微分方程$\frac{d^2y}{dx^2}-4y=0$ 的：

A. 通解　　B. 特解

C. 是解，但既非通解也非特解　　D. 不是解

解 $y=3e^{2x}$，$y'=6e^{2x}$，$y''=12e^{2x}$，代入微分方程，得：

$$12e^{2x}-12e^{2x}=0$$

即验证是方程的解。

因为 $y=3e^{2x}$无任意常数 C，故非通解；又因题中未给出初始条件，故也非特解。

答案：C

【例 1-7-2】 判别一阶微分方程 $(e^{x+y}-e^x)dx+(e^{x+y}+e^y)dy=0$ 的类型，并求其通解。

解

$$e^x(e^y-1)dx+e^y(e^x+1)dy=0$$

$$\frac{e^x}{e^x+1}dx+\frac{e^y}{e^y-1}dy=0$$

微分方程为一阶可分离变量方程。

$$\int\frac{e^x}{e^x+1}dx+\int\frac{e^y}{e^y-1}dy=\ln c$$

$$\ln(e^x+1)+\ln(e^y-1)=\ln c$$

$$\ln(e^x+1)(e^y-1)=\ln c$$

$$(e^x+1)(e^y-1)=C$$

通解为$(e^x+1)(e^y-1)=C$

【例 1-7-3】 微分方程 $ydx+(y^2x-e^y)dy=0$ 是：

A. 可分离变量方程　　B. 可化为一阶线性的微分方程

C. 全微分方程　　D. 齐次方程

解　将方程变形：

$$y\mathrm{d}x+(y^2x-e^y)\mathrm{d}y=0, y\frac{\mathrm{d}x}{\mathrm{d}y}+y^2x-e^y=0$$

$$y\frac{\mathrm{d}x}{\mathrm{d}y}+y^2x=e^y, \frac{\mathrm{d}x}{\mathrm{d}y}+yx=\frac{1}{y}e^y$$

答案:B

【例 1-7-4】　微分方程 $xy'-y=x^2e^{2x}$ 通解 y 等于：

A. $x(\frac{1}{2}e^{2x}+C)$　　B. $x(e^{2x}+C)$

C. $x(\frac{1}{2}x^2e^{2x}+C)$　　D. $x^2e^{2x}+C$

解　$xy'-y=x^2e^{2x}, y'-\frac{1}{x}y=xe^{2x}$

$P(x)=-\frac{1}{x}, Q(x)=xe^{2x}$

$$y=e^{-\int(-\frac{1}{x})\mathrm{d}x}\left[\int xe^{2x}e^{\int(-\frac{1}{x})\mathrm{d}x}\mathrm{d}x+C\right]=e^{\ln x}(\int xe^{2x}e^{-\ln x}\mathrm{d}x+C)$$

$$=x(\int e^{2x}\mathrm{d}x+C)=x\left(\frac{1}{2}e^{2x}+C\right)$$

答案:A

【例 1-7-5】　微分方程 $y'+\frac{1}{x}y=2$ 满足初始条件 $y|_{x=1}=0$ 的特解是：

A. $x-\frac{1}{x}$　　B. $x+\frac{1}{x}$

C. $x+\frac{C}{x}$（C 为任意常数）　　D. $x+\frac{2}{x}$

解　$P(x)=\frac{1}{x}, Q(x)=2$

代入公式 $y=e^{-\int P(x)\mathrm{d}x}[\int Q(x)e^{\int P(x)\mathrm{d}x}\mathrm{d}x+C]$

通解为　$y=e^{-\int\frac{1}{x}\mathrm{d}x}[\int 2e^{\int\frac{1}{x}\mathrm{d}x}\mathrm{d}x+C]=e^{-\ln x}[\int 2x\mathrm{d}x+C]=\frac{1}{x}(x^2+C)$

当 $x=1, y=0$ 时，$C=-1$

特解为 $y=x-\frac{1}{x}$

答案:A

【例 1-7-6】　设 $\int_0^x f(t)\mathrm{d}t=2f(x)-4$，且 $f(0)=2$，则 $f(x)$ 是：

A. $e^{\frac{x}{2}}$　　B. $e^{\frac{x}{2}+1}$　　C. $2e^{\frac{x}{2}}$　　D. $\frac{1}{2}e^{2x}$

解　方程左边是积分上限函数，可利用积分上限函数求导的方法计算。方程两边求导，得 $f(x)=2f'(x)$

设 $f(x)=y, f'(x)=y'$，方程化为 $2y'=y$，解方程 $\frac{2}{y}\mathrm{d}y=\mathrm{d}x$，得 $2\ln y=x+C_1\Rightarrow\ln y=\frac{x}{2}+$

$\frac{C_1}{2}$，$y=e^{\frac{x}{2}+\frac{1}{2}}=Ce^{\frac{x}{2}}$，其中 $C=e^{\frac{1}{2}}$

代入初始条件 $x=0,y=2$，得 $C=2$

所以 $y=2e^{\frac{x}{2}}$，即 $f(x)=2e^{\frac{x}{2}}$

答案：C

【例 1-7-7】 已知微分方程 $y'+p(x)y=q(x)[q(x)\neq 0]$ 有两个不同的特解 $y_1(x)$，$y_2(x)$，C 为任意常数，则该微分方程的通解是：

A. $y=C(y_1-y_2)$　　B. $y=C(y_1+y_2)$

C. $y=y_1+C(y_1+y_2)$　　D. $y=y_1+C(y_1-y_2)$

解 $y'+p(x)y=q(x)$，$y_1(x)-y_2(x)$ 为对应齐次方程的解。

微分方程 $y'+p(x)y=q(x)$ 的通解为 $y=y_1+C(y_1-y_2)$

其中 y_1 为一阶非齐次方程的一个特解，$C(y_1-y_2)$ 为一阶齐次方程的通解。

答案：D

【例 1-7-8】 设 $p(x)$ 在 $(-\infty,+\infty)$ 连续且不恒等于 0，$y_1(x)$、$y_2(x)$ 是微分方程 $y'+p(x)y=0$ 的两个不同特解，则下列结论中不成立的是：

A. $\frac{y_2(x)}{y_1(x)}\equiv$ 常数（假设其中 $y_1(x)\neq 0$）

B. $C(y_1-y_2)$ 构成方程的通解

C. $(y_1-y_2)=$ 常数

D. $y_1(x)-y_2(x)$ 在任意一点不等于 0

解 因为 $p(x)$ 不恒等于 0，非零常数不可能是微分方程 $y'+p(x)y=0$ 的解。因为 $y_1(x)$，$y_2(x)$ 是方程两个不同的解，则 $y_1(x)-y_2(x)$ 也是这个方程的解，而 (y_1-y_2) 为非零常数，所以 $C(y_1-y_2)$ 构成方程的通解，选项 B 成立。

一阶线性齐次方程 $y'+p(x)y=0$ 任意两个解，只差一个常数因子，所以 $\frac{y_2(x)}{y_1(x)}\equiv$ 常数，选项 A 成立。

对于一阶微分方程 $y'+p(x)y=0$ 两个不同的解不能满足相同的初始条件使函数值相同，所以 $y_1(x)-y_2(x)$ 在任意一点不等于 0，选项 D 成立。

因为 $y_1(x)$，$y_2(x)$ 只差一个常数因子，$y_1-y_2\neq$ 常数，选项 C 不成立。

答案：C

四、高阶线性微分方程

（一）线性微分方程解的结构

二阶和二阶以上的微分方程称为高阶微分方程。形如

$$y''+P(x)y'+Q(x)y=f(x) \tag{1-7-9}$$

其中 $P(x)$、$Q(x)$ 为 x 的函数或常数。当 $f(x)\neq 0$ 时，方程称为二阶线性非齐次方程。

当 $f(x)=0$ 时，对应的方程

$$y''+P(x)y'+Q(x)y=0 \tag{1-7-10}$$

称为二阶线性齐次方程。

1. 二阶线性齐次微分方程（1-7-10）解的结构

(1)如果函数 $y_1(x)$ 与 $y_2(x)$ 是方程(1-7-10)的两个解，那么 $y=C_1y_1+C_2y_2$ 也是方程(1-7-10)的解，其中 C_1、C_2 是任意常数。

(2)如果 $y_1(x)$ 与 $y_2(x)$ 是方程(1-7-10)的两个线性无关的解，那么 $y=C_1y_1+C_2y_2$ 就是方程(1-7-10)的通解。

2. 二阶线性非齐次方程(1-7-9)解的结构

(1)若 y^* 是二阶非齐次线性方程(1-7-9)的一个特解，Y 是对应的线性齐次方程(1-7-10)的通解，那么 $y=Y+y^*$ 是二阶非齐次线性微分方程(1-7-9)的通解。

(2)若非齐次线性方程(1-7-9)的右端 $f(x)$ 是几个函数的和，如

$$y''+P(x)y'+Q(x)y=f_1(x)+f_2(x) \tag{1-7-11}$$

而 y_1^* 与 y_2^* 分别是方程 $y''+P(x)y'+Q(x)y=f_1(x)$ 与 $y''+P(x)y'+Q(x)y=f_2(x)$ 的特解，那么 $y_1^*+y_2^*$ 就是方程(1-7-11)的特解。

(二)二阶常系数线性齐次方程通解的计算

(1)定义：当二阶线性齐次方程 $y''+P(x)y'+Q(x)y=0$ 中 $P(x)$、$Q(x)$ 为常数时，即 $y''+py'+qy=0$(其中，p、q 为常数)，该方程称为二阶常系数线性齐次方程。

(2)二阶常系数线性齐次方程通解的计算：设二阶常系数线性齐次方程

$$y''+py'+qy=0 \tag{1-7-12}$$

(其中，p、q 均为常数)

求方程解(1-7-12)的步骤如下：

①写出对应的特征方程

$$r^2+pr+q=0 \tag{1-7-13}$$

②求出特征根(即特征方程的根)

$$r_{1,2}=\frac{-p\pm\sqrt{p^2-4q}}{2} \tag{1-7-14}$$

③按下面规则写出方程(1-7-12)的通解

若 $r_1\neq r_2$，为两个不同的实特征根，则方程的通解为

$$y=C_1e^{r_1x}+C_2e^{r_2x} \tag{1-7-15}$$

若 $r_1=r_2$，为重特征根，则方程的通解为

$$y=e^{r_1x}(C_1+C_2x) \tag{1-7-16}$$

若 $r_{1,2}=\alpha\pm i\beta$，为一对共轭复根，则方程的通解为

$$y=e^{\alpha x}(C_1\cos\beta x+C_2\sin\beta x) \tag{1-7-17}$$

(三)二阶常系数线性非齐次方程简介

$y''+py'+qy=f(x)$ 中，$f(x)=P_m(x)\cdot e^{\lambda x}$($P_m(x)$ 为某个多项式，乘指数函数 $e^{\lambda x}$)时方程通解的求法：

(1)二阶常系数线性非齐次方程的通解为

$y=\overline{y}$(二阶常系数线性齐次方程的通解)$+y^*$(二阶常系数线性非齐次方程的一个特解)

(2)二阶常系数线性齐次方程 $y''+py'+qy=0$ 的通解按“(二)二阶常系数线性齐次方程通解的计算”求出。

(3)当自由项 $f(x)=P_m(x)e^{\lambda x}$($P_m(x)$ 为某个多项式，乘指数函数 $e^{\lambda x}$)时，方程有形如 $y^*=x^kQ_m(x)e^{\lambda x}$ 的特解，其中 $Q_m(x)$ 与 $P_m(x)$ 为同次多项式，其系数待定，而 k 按 λ 不是特征方程

的根、是特征方程的单根或是特征方程的重根，依次取为 0，1 或 2。

注：考试大纲中没有“二阶常系数非齐次方程”，但 2013 年、2017 年试题中均出现过，应该是超纲了。为了帮助考生了解二阶常系数非齐次方程，我们特意加了一点简介。

【例 1-7-9】 求二阶线性齐次方程(1) $y''-y'-6y=0$；(2)$y''+9y=0$；(3)$y''+2y'+y=0$的通解。

解 (1) $r^2-r-6=0$

$r=3, r_2=-2$

$y=C_1e^{3x}+C_2e^{-2x}$

(2) $r^2+9=0$

$r_1=\pm 3i \qquad (\alpha=0, \beta=3)$

$y=C_1\cos 3x+C_2\sin 3x$

(3) $r^2+2r+1=0$

$r=-1$(重根)

$y=e^{-x}(C_1+C_2x)$

【例 1-7-10】 二阶微分方程 $xy''+y'=0$ 的通解是：

A. $C_1x^3+C_2$　　B. $C_1\ln x+C_2$

C. $C_1e^x+C_2$　　D. 不存在

解 本题为可降阶的高阶微分方程，不显含变量 y：

设 $$y'=P, y''=P'$$

方程转化为 $$xP'+P=0, x\frac{\mathrm{d}P}{\mathrm{d}x}=-P, \frac{1}{P}\mathrm{d}P=-\frac{1}{x}\mathrm{d}x$$

积分 $$\ln P=-\ln x+\ln C_1, P=\frac{C_1}{x}, 即\frac{\mathrm{d}y}{\mathrm{d}x}=\frac{C_1}{x}$$

故 $y=C_1\ln x+C_2$。

答案：B

【例 1-7-11】 微分方程 $y''-4y'+3y=0, y|_{x=0}=6, y'|_{x=0}=10$，满足初始条件的特解：

A. $y=4e^x+e^{3x}$　　B. $y=e^x+2e^{3x}$

C. $y=4e^x+2e^{3x}$　　D. $y=2e^x+4e^{3x}$

解 方程的特征方程为 $r^2-4r+3=0$，解得 $r_1=1, r_2=3$

则通解为 $y=C_1e^x+C_2e^{3x}$

求导 $y'=C_1e^x+3C_2e^{3x}$

代入初始条件 $\begin{cases}C_1+C_2=6\\C_1+3C_2=10\end{cases}\Rightarrow C_1=4, C_2=2$

方程的特解为 $y=4e^x+2e^{3x}$。

答案：C

【例 1-7-12】 由微分方程 $y''-y'=0$ 所确定的积分曲线方程，使其在点 $M(0,0)$和直线 $y=x$ 相切，则曲线方程为：

A. $y=C_1+C_2e^x$　　B. $y=-1+e^x$

C. $y=1+e^x$　　D. $y=2+e^{2x}$

解 $y''-y'=0$ 的特征方程为：$r^2-r=0$，解得 $r_1=0, r_2=1$

故通解为 $y=C_1e^{0x}+C_2e^x$，即 $y=C_1+C_2e^x$

初始条件为：$y|_{x=0}=0, y'|_{x=0}=1$

代入通解，得：

$$C_1+C_2=0; y'=C_2e^x, C_2=1$$

所以 $C_2=1, C_1=-1, y=-1+e^x$

答案：B

【例 1-7-13】 已知函数 $y_1(x), y_2(x), y_3(x)$ 都是方程 $y''(x)+P_1(x)y'(x)+P_2(x)y(x)=Q(x)$（以下称方程①）的特解，其中 P_1, P_2, Q 为已知非零连续函数，且 $\frac{y_1-y_2}{y_2-y_3}\neq$ 常数，方程①的通解是：

A. $y=C_1y_1+C_2y_2+y_3$　　B. $y=C_1y_1+C_2(y_1-y_3)+y_2$

C. $y=C_1(y_2-y_3)+C_2y_1+y_1$　　D. $y=(C_1+1)y_1+(C_2-C_1)y_2-C_2y_3$

（其中 C_1、C_2 为常数）

解 验证：y_1-y_2, y_2-y_3 是方程①对应的齐次方程的解，如将 y_1-y_2 代入方程，$(y''_1-y''_2)+P_1(y'_1-y'_2)+P_2(y_1-y_2)=y''_1+P_1y'_1+P_2y_1-(y''_2+P_1y'_2+P_2y_2)=Q(x)-Q(x)=0$。

所以 y_1-y_2 是方程①对应齐次方程的解。

同样验证 y_2-y_3 也是方程①对应齐次方程的解。

而已知$\frac{y_1-y_2}{y_2-y_3}\neq$常数，所以 y_1-y_2, y_2-y_3 是方程①对应齐次方程的两个线性无关的解。可知方程①对应齐次方程的通解为：$y=C_1(y_1-y_2)+C_2(y_2-y_3)$

所示方程①的通解是：$y=C_1(y_1-y_2)+C_2(y_2-y_3)+y_1$

解整理得：$y=(C_1+1)y_1+(C_2-C_1)y_2-C_2y_3$

答案：D

【例 1-7-14】 微分方程$\frac{d^2y}{dx^2}+2y=1$ 的通解为：

A. $\frac{1}{2}+C_1\cos\sqrt{2}x+C_2\sin\sqrt{2}x$　　B. $\frac{1}{2}+C_1e^{\sqrt{2}}x+C_2e^{-\sqrt{2}x}$

C. $C_1\cos\sqrt{2}x+C_2\sin\sqrt{2}x$　　D. $C_1e^{\sqrt{2}x}+C_2e^{-\sqrt{2}x}$

解 可直接看出 $y^*=\frac{1}{2}$是方程的一个特解，

$\frac{d^2y}{dx^2}+2y=0$ 的特征方程为：$r^2+2=0$，解得 $r_{1,2}=\pm\sqrt{2}i$

故齐次线性方程的通解为 $y=C_1\cos\sqrt{2}x+C_2\sin\sqrt{2}x$

原方程的通解为：$y=y^*+y$，即 $y=\frac{1}{2}+C_1\cos\sqrt{2}x+C_2\sin\sqrt{2}x$

答案：A

习　题

1-7-1　判断下列一阶微分方程中可化为一阶线性方程的是（　　）。

A. $(5-2xy-y^2)\mathrm{d}x-(x+y)^2\mathrm{d}y=0$　　B. $(x^2+y^2)\mathrm{d}x-xy\mathrm{d}y=0$

C. $(x\mathrm{e}^y-2y)\mathrm{d}y+e^{-y}\mathrm{d}x=0$　　D. $\mathrm{d}y-\mathrm{e}^x\mathrm{d}x=-2xy\mathrm{d}x$

1-7-2　微分方程 $y'=\dfrac{x}{y}+\dfrac{y}{x}, y|_{x=1}=2$ 的特解为(　　)。

A. $y^2=x^2(2+\ln x)$　　B. $y^2=4\ln x$

C. $y^2=2x^2(2+\ln x)$　　D. $y^2=x^2(4+\ln x)$

1-7-3　若方程 $y'+p(x)y=0$ 的一个特解为 $y=\cos 2x$,则该方程满足初始条件 $y|_{x=0}=2$ 的特解为(　　)。

A. $\cos 2x+2$　　B. $\cos 2x+1$

C. $2\cos x$　　D. $2\cos 2x$

1-7-4　设已知一阶线性方程 $\dfrac{\mathrm{d}y}{\mathrm{d}x}+p(x)y=q(x)$ 的两个解 $y_1(x), y_2(x)$,则该方程的通解为(　　)。

A. $C_1y_1(x)+C_2y_2(x)$　　B. $C_1y_1(x)+C_2[y_2(x)-y_1(x)]$

C. $y_1(x)+C[y_2(x)+y_1(x)]$　　D. $y_2(x)+C[y_2(x)-y_1(x)]$

1-7-5　微分方程 $(1+x^2)y''=2xy'$ 满足初始条件 $y|_{x=0}=1, y'|_{x=0}=3$ 的特解是(　　)。

A. x^3+3x+2　　B. $9x^3+3x+1$

C. x^3+3x+1　　D. $9x^3+3x+2$

1-7-6　下列函数中不是方程 $y''-2y'+y=0$ 的解的函数是(　　)。

A. x^2e^x　　B. e^x　　C. xe^x　　D. $(x+2)e^x$

1-7-7　已知 $r_1=3, r_2=-3$ 是方程 $y''+py'+qy=0$ (p 和 q 是常数)的特征方程的两个根,则该微分方程是(　　)。

A. $y''+9y'=0$　　B. $y''-9y'=0$　　C. $y''+9y=0$　　D. $y''-9y=0$

1-7-8　微分方程 $\dfrac{\mathrm{d}^2y}{\mathrm{d}x^2}+2y=1$ 的通解是(　　)。

A. $\dfrac{1}{2}+C_1\cos\sqrt{2}x+C_2\sin\sqrt{2}x$　　B. $\dfrac{1}{2}+C_1e^{\sqrt{2}x}+C_2e^{-\sqrt{2}x}$

C. $C_1\cos\sqrt{2}x+C_2\sin\sqrt{2}x$　　D. $C_1e^{\sqrt{2}x}+C_2e^{-\sqrt{2}x}$

第八节　线性代数

一、行列式及其计算

在 n 阶行列式

$$\boldsymbol{D}_n=\begin{vmatrix} a_{11} & a_{12} & \cdots & a_{1n} \\ \vdots & \vdots & & \vdots \\ a_{n1} & a_{n2} & \cdots & a_{nn} \end{vmatrix} \tag{1-8-1}$$

中,a_{ij} 称为第 i 行第 j 列的元素。对于二阶、三阶行列式在中学阶段大家就已知道

$$\boldsymbol{D}_2=\begin{vmatrix} a_{11} & a_{12} \\ a_{21} & a_{22} \end{vmatrix}=a_{11}a_{22}-a_{12}a_{21}$$

$$D_3=\begin{vmatrix} a_{11} & a_{12} & a_{13} \\ a_{21} & a_{22} & a_{23} \\ a_{31} & a_{32} & a_{33} \end{vmatrix}$$

$$=a_{11}a_{22}a_{33}+a_{12}a_{23}a_{31}+a_{13}a_{21}a_{32}-a_{13}a_{22}a_{31}-a_{11}a_{23}a_{32}-a_{12}a_{21}a_{33}$$

(一)n 阶行列式的计算

余子式:行列式中元素 a_{ij} 的余子式是将行列式中 a_{ij} 所在的行与列划去,剩下的元素按原顺序排成的低一阶行列式,叫做元素 a_{ij} 的余子式,记作 M_{ij}。

代数余子式:行列式中元素 a_{ij} 的代数余子式为 $(-1)^{i+j}M_{ij}$,可记作 A_{ij},即 $A_{ij}=(-1)^{i+j}M_{ij}$。

拉普拉斯展开定理[又称行列式按行(列)展开定理]及推论如下。

定理:n 阶行列式

$$D=\begin{vmatrix} a_{11} & a_{12} & \cdots & a_{1n} \\ a_{21} & a_{22} & \cdots & a_{2n} \\ \vdots & \vdots & & \vdots \\ a_{n1} & a_{n2} & \cdots & a_{nn} \end{vmatrix}$$

的值等于它的任意一行(列)的各元素与其对应代数余子式的乘积的和。

即
$$D=a_{i1}A_{i1}+a_{i2}A_{i2}+\cdots+a_{in}A_{in} \quad (i=1,2,\cdots,n)$$
$$D=a_{1j}A_{1j}+a_{2j}A_{2j}+\cdots+a_{nj}A_{nj} \quad (j=1,2,\cdots,n)$$

推论:n 阶行列式 D 的某一行(列)的各元素与另一行(列)对应的代数余子式的乘积之和等于零。

即
$$a_{i1}A_{j1}+a_{i2}A_{j2}+\cdots+a_{in}A_{jn}=0 \quad (i\neq j;i,j=1,2,\cdots,n)$$
$$a_{1i}A_{1j}+a_{2i}A_{2j}+\cdots+a_{ni}A_{nj}=0 \quad (i\neq j;i,j=1,2,\cdots,n)$$

(二)行列式的主要性质

(1)行列式与它的转置行列式相等。

(2)对换行列式的任意两行(列),行列式仅改变符号。

(3)行列式的任一行(列)的所有元素同乘以数 k,等于该行列式乘以数 k。

(4)行列式中如果有两行(列)元素成比例,则行列式为零。

(5)若行列式某一行(列)的各元素是两个数之和,则该行列式等于按此行(列)分成的两个相应行列式的和。

例如 $\begin{vmatrix} a_{11}+a'_{11} & a_{12}+a_{12}' \\ a_{21} & a_{22} \end{vmatrix}=\begin{vmatrix} a_{11} & a_{12} \\ a_{21} & a_{22} \end{vmatrix}+\begin{vmatrix} a'_{11} & a'_{12} \\ a_{21} & a_{22} \end{vmatrix}$

(6)将行列式的某一行(列)的各元素同乘以一个数后加到另一行(列)对应元素上,行列式值不变。

行列式的计算重点,放在会利用行列式的性质和拉普拉斯展开定理计算三、四阶行列式和简单的高阶行列式上。

【例 1-8-1】 解方程 $\begin{vmatrix} 1 & 1 & 1 & 1 \\ 1 & x & 2 & 2 \\ 2 & 2 & x & 3 \\ 3 & 3 & 3 & x \end{vmatrix}=0$。

解 由于 $\begin{vmatrix}1&1&1&1\\1&x&2&2\\2&2&x&3\\3&3&3&x\end{vmatrix}\xlongequal[\substack{-2r_1+r_3\\-3r_1+r_4}]{-r_1+r_2}\begin{vmatrix}1&1&1&1\\0&x-1&1&1\\0&0&x-2&1\\0&0&0&x-3\end{vmatrix}=(x-1)(x-2)(x-3)$

所以方程解为 $x=1,x=2,x=3$

【例 1-8-2】 计算行列式 $D=\begin{vmatrix}0&3&0&1\\a&d&e&f\\0&1&b&2\\0&0&0&c\end{vmatrix}$。

解 按第一行展开,得

$$D=(-1)^{1+2}3\begin{vmatrix}a&e&f\\0&b&2\\0&0&c\end{vmatrix}+(-1)^{1+4}\begin{vmatrix}a&d&e\\0&1&b\\0&0&0\end{vmatrix}=-3abc$$

或按第一列展开

$$D=(-1)^{2+1}a\begin{vmatrix}3&0&1\\1&b&2\\0&0&c\end{vmatrix}=-ac\begin{vmatrix}3&0\\1&b\end{vmatrix}=-3abc$$

【例 1-8-3】 设 $D=\begin{vmatrix}-1&5&7&-8\\1&1&1&1\\2&0&-9&6\\-3&4&3&7\end{vmatrix}$,则 $A_{41}+A_{42}+A_{43}+A_{44}=$:

A. 2　　B. 1　　C. -1　　D. 0

解 将行列式第 4 行换成(1　1　1　1)

则行列式为 $D_1=\begin{vmatrix}-1&5&7&-8\\1&1&1&1\\2&0&-9&6\\1&1&1&1\end{vmatrix}$

把 D_1 按第 4 行展开计算 $D_1=1\cdot A_{41}+1\cdot A_{42}+1\cdot A_{43}+1\cdot A_{44}$,而由行列式性质可知 $D_1=0$

所以 $A_{41}+A_{42}+A_{43}+A_{44}=0$,即 $D=0$。

答案:D

【例 1-8-4】 在函数 $f(x)=\begin{vmatrix}2x&1&-1\\-x&-x&x\\1&2&x\end{vmatrix}$ 中 x^3 的系数是:

A. 1　　B. -2　　C. -1　　D. 3

解 将行列式按第一行展开

$$f(x)=2x\begin{vmatrix}-x&x\\2&x\end{vmatrix}+1\times(-1)^{1+2}\begin{vmatrix}-x&x\\1&x\end{vmatrix}+(-1)\times(-1)^{1+3}\begin{vmatrix}-x&-x\\1&2\end{vmatrix}$$

可以看出,在展开式中含有 x^3 的项仅有 $2x\begin{vmatrix}-x&x\\2&x\end{vmatrix}=2x(-x^2-2x)=-2x^3-$

$4x^2$，其余均不含 x^3 的项。

所以 x^3 的系数为－2。

答案：B

【例 1-8-5】 行列式 $\boldsymbol{D}$ 非零的充分条件是：

A. $\boldsymbol{D}$ 的所有元素非零

B. $\boldsymbol{D}$ 至少有几个元素非零

C. $\boldsymbol{D}$ 的任意两行元素之间不成比例

D. 以 $\boldsymbol{D}$ 为系数行列式的齐次线性方程组有唯一解

解 逐个分析，选项 A、B、C 均不成立。

选项 D 成立。由线性齐次方程组克莱姆法则可知，线性齐次方程组的系数行列式 $\boldsymbol{D}=|\boldsymbol{A}|\neq 0$ 的充分条件是该方程组有唯一解。

答案：D

二、矩阵及其运算

(一)矩阵的概念

由 $m\times n$ 个数 $a_{ij}(i=1,2,\cdots,m;j=1,2,\cdots,n)$ 排成 m 行 n 列的数表

$$\boldsymbol{A}_{m\times n}=\begin{bmatrix} a_{11} & a_{12} & \cdots & a_{1n} \\ a_{21} & a_{22} & \cdots & a_{nn} \\ \vdots & \vdots & & \vdots \\ a_{m1} & a_{m2} & \cdots & a_{mn} \end{bmatrix} \tag{1-8-2}$$

叫做 m 行 n 列矩阵，这 $m\times n$ 个数叫做矩阵 $\boldsymbol{A}$ 的元素，a_{ij} 叫做矩阵 $\boldsymbol{A}$ 的第 i 行第 j 列元素。

若 $m=n$，则 $\boldsymbol{A}$ 为 n 阶方阵。

只有一行的矩阵称为行矩阵(或行向量)，只有一列的矩阵称为列矩阵(或列向量)。

元素都是零的矩阵称为零矩阵，记作 $\boldsymbol{0}$。

(二)矩阵的运算

1. 矩阵相等

如果两个 $m\times n$ 阶矩阵 $\boldsymbol{A}=(a_{ij})$，$\boldsymbol{B}=(b_{ij})$的对应元素相等，即

$$a_{ij}=b_{ij} \quad (i=1,2,\cdots,m;j=1,2,\cdots,n)$$

则称矩阵 $\boldsymbol{A}$ 与矩阵 $\boldsymbol{B}$ 相等，记作 $\boldsymbol{A}=\boldsymbol{B}$。

2. 矩阵的运算

$$\boldsymbol{A}\pm\boldsymbol{B}=\begin{bmatrix} a_{11}\pm b_{11} & \cdots & a_{1n}\pm b_{1n} \\ a_{21}\pm b_{21} & \cdots & a_{2n}\pm b_{2n} \\ \vdots & & \vdots \\ a_{m1}\pm b_{m1} & \cdots & a_{mn}\pm b_{mn} \end{bmatrix}$$

设 λ 为任意常数

$$\lambda\boldsymbol{A}=\begin{bmatrix} \lambda a_{11} & \cdots & \lambda a_{1n} \\ \lambda a_{21} & \cdots & \lambda a_{2n} \\ \vdots & & \vdots \\ \lambda a_{mn} & \cdots & \lambda a_{mn} \end{bmatrix}$$

$$
\boldsymbol{A}_{m\times n}\boldsymbol{B}_{n\times p}=\begin{bmatrix} a_{11} & \cdots & a_{1n} \\ a_{21} & \cdots & a_{2n} \\ \vdots & & \vdots \\ a_{m1} & \cdots & a_{mn} \end{bmatrix}\begin{bmatrix} b_{11} & \cdots & b_{1p} \\ b_{21} & \cdots & b_{2p} \\ \vdots & & \vdots \\ b_{n1} & \cdots & b_{np} \end{bmatrix}=\begin{bmatrix} c_{11} & \cdots & c_{1p} \\ c_{21} & \cdots & c_{2p} \\ \vdots & & \vdots \\ c_{m1} & \cdots & c_{mp} \end{bmatrix}=\boldsymbol{C}_{m\times p}
$$

其中 $C_{ij}=a_{i1}b_{1j}+a_{i2}b_{2j}+\cdots+a_{in}b_{nj}(i=1,2,\cdots,m;j=1,2,\cdots,p)$。

矩阵相乘时,必须满足左矩阵列数与右矩阵行数相同时才能相乘。

另外要注意,数乘矩阵的运算是用这个数乘矩阵的每一个元素,与数乘行列式运算不同,应特别注意它们的区别。

矩阵运算有下列性质:

(1)加法运算性质

设 $\boldsymbol{A}$、$\boldsymbol{B}$、$\boldsymbol{C}$ 均为 $m\times n$ 阶矩阵,则

$\boldsymbol{A}+\boldsymbol{B}=\boldsymbol{B}+\boldsymbol{A}$

$\boldsymbol{A}+\boldsymbol{B}+\boldsymbol{C}=(\boldsymbol{A}+\boldsymbol{B})+\boldsymbol{C}=\boldsymbol{A}+(\boldsymbol{B}+\boldsymbol{C})$

(2)数与矩阵相乘的运算性质(设 $\boldsymbol{A}$、$\boldsymbol{B}$ 均为 $m\times n$ 阶矩阵,λ、μ 为常数)

$\lambda(\boldsymbol{A}+\boldsymbol{B})=\lambda\boldsymbol{A}+\lambda\boldsymbol{B}$

$(\lambda+\mu)\boldsymbol{A}=\lambda\boldsymbol{A}+\mu\boldsymbol{A}$

$(\lambda\mu)\boldsymbol{A}=\lambda(\mu\boldsymbol{A})$

(3)矩阵乘法运算性质(假设运算均是可行的)

$(\boldsymbol{AB})\boldsymbol{C}=\boldsymbol{A}(\boldsymbol{BC})$

$\boldsymbol{A}(\boldsymbol{B}+\boldsymbol{C})=\boldsymbol{AB}+\boldsymbol{AC}$

$(\boldsymbol{B}+\boldsymbol{C})\boldsymbol{A}=\boldsymbol{BA}+\boldsymbol{CA}$

$\lambda(\boldsymbol{AB})=(\lambda\boldsymbol{A})\boldsymbol{B}=\boldsymbol{A}(\lambda\boldsymbol{B})$($\lambda$ 为常数)

对矩阵的运算还需要注意以下几点:

①矩阵的乘法不满足交换律即 $\boldsymbol{AB}\neq\boldsymbol{BA}$

②矩阵乘法运算不满足消去律即 $\boldsymbol{AB}=\boldsymbol{AC}$,且 $\boldsymbol{A}\neq\boldsymbol{0}$,不能推出 $\boldsymbol{B}=\boldsymbol{C}$,只有当方阵 $\boldsymbol{A}$ 可逆时,该结论才能成立。

③矩阵 $\boldsymbol{AB}=\boldsymbol{0}$ 不一定能推出 $\boldsymbol{A}=\boldsymbol{0}$ 或 $\boldsymbol{B}=\boldsymbol{0}$。例如$\begin{bmatrix} 1 & 1 \\ -1 & -1 \end{bmatrix}\begin{bmatrix} -1 & -1 \\ 1 & 1 \end{bmatrix}=\begin{bmatrix} 0 & 0 \\ 0 & 0 \end{bmatrix}$。

④由 $\boldsymbol{A}^2=\boldsymbol{A}$ 不一定能推出 $\boldsymbol{A}=\boldsymbol{0}$ 或 $\boldsymbol{A}=\boldsymbol{E}$,仅当方阵 $\boldsymbol{A}$ 可逆时 $\boldsymbol{A}=\boldsymbol{E}$;仅当 $\boldsymbol{A}-\boldsymbol{E}$ 可逆时,$\boldsymbol{A}=\boldsymbol{0}$。

⑤由 $\boldsymbol{A}^2=\boldsymbol{0}$,不一定能推出 $\boldsymbol{A}=\boldsymbol{0}$。例 $\boldsymbol{A}=\begin{bmatrix} 1 & -1 \\ 1 & -1 \end{bmatrix}$,$\boldsymbol{A}^2=\begin{bmatrix} 1 & -1 \\ 1 & -1 \end{bmatrix}\begin{bmatrix} 1 & -1 \\ 1 & -1 \end{bmatrix}=\begin{bmatrix} 0 & 0 \\ 0 & 0 \end{bmatrix}$。

(4)矩阵幂的性质

设矩阵 $\boldsymbol{A}$ 是 n 阶方阵,$\boldsymbol{A}$ 可以连乘,k 个 $\boldsymbol{A}$ 相乘记作 $\boldsymbol{A}^k$,叫 $\boldsymbol{A}$ 的 k 次幂。

矩阵的幂有性质:$\boldsymbol{A}^k\boldsymbol{A}^l=\boldsymbol{A}^{k+l}$,$(\boldsymbol{A}^k)^l=\boldsymbol{A}^{kl}$

设 $\boldsymbol{A}$ 是 n 阶方阵,$f(x)=a_nx^n+a_{n-1}x^{n-1}+\cdots+a_1x+a_0$,是一个一元 n 次多项式,用 $\boldsymbol{A}$ 代替多项式中的 x,得到矩阵多项式 $f(\boldsymbol{A})=a_n\boldsymbol{A}^n+a_{n-1}\boldsymbol{A}^{n-1}+\cdots+a_1\boldsymbol{A}+a_0\boldsymbol{E}$,其中 $\boldsymbol{E}$ 是 n 阶单位矩阵,矩阵多项式仍是一个 n 阶方阵。

(5)转置矩阵的定义和性质

转置矩阵的定义：把矩阵 $\boldsymbol{A}$ 的所有行换成相应的列所得的矩阵，称为矩阵 $\boldsymbol{A}$ 的转置矩阵，记作 $\boldsymbol{A}^{\mathrm{T}}$。

若
$$\boldsymbol{A}=\begin{bmatrix} a_{11} & a_{12} & \cdots & a_{1n} \\ a_{21} & a_{22} & \cdots & a_{2n} \\ \vdots & \vdots & & \vdots \\ a_{m1} & a_{m2} & \cdots & a_{mn} \end{bmatrix}$$

则
$$\boldsymbol{A}^{\mathrm{T}}=\begin{bmatrix} a_{11} & a_{21} & \cdots & a_{m1} \\ a_{12} & a_{22} & \cdots & a_{m2} \\ \vdots & \vdots & & \vdots \\ a_{1n} & a_{2n} & \cdots & a_{mn} \end{bmatrix}$$

矩阵转置的性质：

$$(\boldsymbol{A}^{\mathrm{T}})^{\mathrm{T}}=\boldsymbol{A}$$
$$(\lambda\boldsymbol{A})^{\mathrm{T}}=\lambda\boldsymbol{A}^{\mathrm{T}}(\lambda \text{ 为常数})$$
$$(\boldsymbol{A}+\boldsymbol{B})^{\mathrm{T}}=\boldsymbol{A}^{\mathrm{T}}+\boldsymbol{B}^{\mathrm{T}}$$
$$(\boldsymbol{AB})^{\mathrm{T}}=\boldsymbol{B}^{\mathrm{T}}\boldsymbol{A}^{\mathrm{T}}$$
$$(\boldsymbol{AB}\cdots\boldsymbol{C})^{\mathrm{T}}=\boldsymbol{C}^{\mathrm{T}}\cdots\boldsymbol{B}^{\mathrm{T}}\boldsymbol{A}^{\mathrm{T}}$$

(三)单位矩阵、对角矩阵、三角矩阵

主对角线上的元素为 1，主对角线外的其他元素全为 0 的 n 阶方阵，称为 n 阶单位矩阵，记作 $\boldsymbol{E}$，即 $E=\begin{bmatrix} 1 & & \\ & \ddots & \\ & & 1 \end{bmatrix}$。

除主对角线外，其他元素全部为零的方阵称为对角方阵，记作 Λ，即 $\boldsymbol{\Lambda}=\begin{bmatrix} a_{11} & & 0 \\ & \ddots & \\ 0 & & a_{nn} \end{bmatrix}$。

矩阵
$$\begin{bmatrix} a_{11} & \cdots & a_{1n} \\ & \ddots & \vdots \\ 0 & & a_{nn} \end{bmatrix} \qquad \begin{bmatrix} a_{11} & & 0 \\ \vdots & \ddots & \\ a_{n1} & \cdots & a_{nn} \end{bmatrix}$$
分别称为上三角矩阵和下三角矩阵。

(四)对称矩阵，反对称矩阵

若 n 阶方阵 $\boldsymbol{A}$ 满足 $\boldsymbol{A}=\boldsymbol{A}^{\mathrm{T}}$，则称 $\boldsymbol{A}$ 为对称矩阵；若 n 阶方阵满足 $\boldsymbol{A}=-\boldsymbol{A}^{\mathrm{T}}$，则称 $\boldsymbol{A}$ 为反对称矩阵。

(五)方阵的行列式

由 n 阶方阵 $\boldsymbol{A}$ 的元素按原次序组成的行列式叫做方阵 $\boldsymbol{A}$ 的行列式，记作 $|\boldsymbol{A}|$ 或 $\det A$。

方阵行列式性质：设 $\boldsymbol{A}$、$\boldsymbol{B}$ 是两个 n 阶方阵，则：① $|\boldsymbol{A}^{\mathrm{T}}|=|\boldsymbol{A}|$，$|k\boldsymbol{A}|=k^n|\boldsymbol{A}|$（$k$ 为常数），$|\boldsymbol{AB}|=|\boldsymbol{A}||\boldsymbol{B}|$，$|\boldsymbol{A}^k|=|\boldsymbol{A}|^k$（$k$ 为正整数），$|\boldsymbol{A}^{-1}|=\dfrac{1}{|\boldsymbol{A}|}=|\boldsymbol{A}|^{-1}$；②设 $\boldsymbol{A}$ 为 $\boldsymbol{m}$ 阶矩阵，$\boldsymbol{B}$ 为 $\boldsymbol{n}$ 阶矩阵，则行列式 $\begin{vmatrix} \boldsymbol{A} & \boldsymbol{0} \\ \boldsymbol{0} & \boldsymbol{B} \end{vmatrix}=|\boldsymbol{A}||\boldsymbol{B}|$。

（六）奇异矩阵，非奇异矩阵

若 n 阶方阵 $\mathbf{A}$，满足 $|\mathbf{A}|\neq 0$，则称 $\mathbf{A}$ 为非奇异矩阵；如果 $|\mathbf{A}|=0$，则称 $\mathbf{A}$ 为奇异矩阵。

（七）正交矩阵

若 $\mathbf{A}$ 为 n 阶方阵，如果 $\mathbf{A}^{\mathrm{T}}\mathbf{A}=\mathbf{A}\mathbf{A}^{\mathrm{T}}=\boldsymbol{E}$，则称 $\mathbf{A}$ 为正交矩阵。

三、矩阵的秩及逆矩阵

（一）矩阵的秩

在 $m\times n$ 矩阵 $\mathbf{A}$ 中任取 k 行、k 列（$k\leqslant\min\{m,n\}$），位于这些行列交叉处的元素构成一个 k 阶行列式，称为矩阵 $\mathbf{A}$ 的 k 阶子式。

矩阵 $\mathbf{A}$ 中不为零子式的最高阶数，称为矩阵 $\mathbf{A}$ 的秩，记为 $R(\mathbf{A})$。

如果矩阵 $\mathbf{A}$ 中至少有一个 k 阶子式不为零，而所有 $k+1$ 阶子式全为零，则 $R(\mathbf{A})=k$。

当 n 阶方阵 $\mathbf{A}$ 的秩 $R(\mathbf{A})=n$ 时，即 $\det\mathbf{A}\neq 0$，称方阵 $\mathbf{A}$ 为满秩的。

n 阶方阵 $\mathbf{A}$ 的秩 $R(\mathbf{A})=n$ 的充分必要条件是 $|\mathbf{A}|\neq 0$。

（二）矩阵的初等变换、初等矩阵

1. 矩阵的初等变换

（1）对调两行（对调 i、j 两行，记作 $r_i\leftrightarrow r_j$）；

（2）以数 $k\neq 0$ 乘以某一行中所有元素（第 i 行乘 k 记作 $r_i\times k$）；

（3）把某一行所有元素的 k 倍加到另一行对应元素上（第 j 行的 k 倍加到第 i 行上，记作 kr_j+r_i）。

以上是矩阵的初等行变换。

如果把其中的“行”换成“列”，即得矩阵的初等列变换（其中记号“r”换成“c”即可）。

矩阵的初等行（列）变换，统称矩阵的初等变换。

初等变换不改变矩阵的秩。任何一个满秩方阵经过有限次行（列）变换后，必可化为单位矩阵。

2. 初等矩阵

由单位矩阵 $\boldsymbol{E}=\begin{bmatrix}1&0&0&\cdots&0\\0&1&0&\cdots&0\\0&0&1&\cdots&0\\\vdots&\vdots&\vdots&&\vdots\\0&0&0&\cdots&1\end{bmatrix}$ 经过一次初等变换得到的矩阵称为初等矩阵。

三种初等变换对应着三种初等矩阵。

（1）对调两行或对调两列

交换 n 阶单位矩阵的第 i 行（列）和第 j 行（列）所得初等矩阵，可记作 $\boldsymbol{E}(i,j)$。

$$\boldsymbol{E}\xrightarrow[(c_i\leftrightarrow c_j)]{r_i\leftrightarrow r_j}\boldsymbol{E}(i,j)=\begin{bmatrix}1&0&0&\cdots&0\\0&0&1&\cdots&0\\\vdots&\vdots&\vdots&&\vdots\\0&1&0&\cdots&0\\\vdots&\vdots&\vdots&&\vdots\\0&0&0&\cdots&1\end{bmatrix}\begin{matrix}\\i\\\\j\\\\\\\end{matrix}$$

(2)以数 $k\neq0$ 乘某行或某列

把 n 阶单位矩阵第 i 行(列)乘以一个非零常数 k 所得的初等矩阵可记作 $\boldsymbol{E}[i(k)]$。

$$\boldsymbol{E}\xrightarrow[(kc_i)]{kr_i}\boldsymbol{E}[i(k)]=\begin{bmatrix}1&&&&\\&\ddots&&&\\&&1&&\\&&&k&&\\&&&&1&\\&&&&&\ddots&\\&&&&&&1\end{bmatrix}i$$

(3)以数 k 乘某行(列)加到另一行(列)上去

把 n 阶单位矩阵的第 j 行(第 i 列)所有元素乘以 k,加到第 i 行(第 j 列)所得初等矩阵可记作 $\boldsymbol{E}[i,j(k)]$。

$$\boldsymbol{E}\xrightarrow[(c_j+kc_i)]{r_i+kr_j}\boldsymbol{E}[i,j(k)]=\begin{bmatrix}1&&&&\\&\ddots&&&\\&&1&\cdots&k&\\&&&\ddots&\vdots&\\&&&&1&\\&&&&&\ddots&\\&&&&&&1\end{bmatrix}\begin{matrix}\\\\i\\\\j\\\\\\\end{matrix}$$

矩阵的初等变换与初等矩阵有下面关系:矩阵左乘一个初等矩阵,相当于对矩阵作一次与初等矩阵相应的同类型的初等行变换;矩阵右乘一个初等矩阵,相当于对矩阵作了一次与初等矩阵同类型的初等列变换。

初等矩阵都是可逆的,其逆矩阵仍是初等矩阵,且有

$$[\boldsymbol{E}(i,j)]^{-1}=\boldsymbol{E}(i,j)$$

$$[\boldsymbol{E}(i(k))]^{-1}=\boldsymbol{E}[i(\frac{1}{k})]$$

$$[\boldsymbol{E}(i,j(k))]^{-1}=\boldsymbol{E}[i,j(-k)]$$

任何矩阵都可以通过矩阵的行初等变换化为阶梯形,即所有零行都在矩阵的底部,每个阶梯只有一行,每一个阶梯的第一个非零元素在这一行的左边,而这个非零元素所在的列下方的其他元素全为零。

如

$$\begin{bmatrix}1&-2&-1&0&2\\0&3&2&2&-1\\0&0&0&-3&1\\0&0&0&0&0\end{bmatrix}$$

阶梯形中非零行向量的个数即为矩阵的秩,这样就可以利用初等行变换:①把满秩方阵化为单位矩阵;②求满秩矩阵 $\boldsymbol{A}$ 的逆矩阵 $\boldsymbol{A}^{-1}$;③利用初等行变换求矩阵 $\boldsymbol{A}$ 的秩。

利用初等行变换求矩阵的秩时,只需把矩阵化为阶梯形,非零行的个数即为矩阵的秩。

(三)等价矩阵的概念和性质,矩阵的标准形

如果矩阵 $\boldsymbol{A}$ 经有限次初等变换变成矩阵 $\boldsymbol{B}$,就称矩阵 $\boldsymbol{A}$ 与 $\boldsymbol{B}$ 等价,记作 $\boldsymbol{A}\cong\boldsymbol{B}$。

矩阵之间的等价关系具有下列性质:

(1)反身性,$\boldsymbol{A}\cong\boldsymbol{A}$;

(2)对称性，若 $\boldsymbol{A} \cong \boldsymbol{B}$，则 $\boldsymbol{B} \cong \boldsymbol{A}$；

(3)传递性，若 $\boldsymbol{A} \cong \boldsymbol{B}, \boldsymbol{B} \cong \boldsymbol{C}$，则 $\boldsymbol{A} \cong \boldsymbol{C}$

定义：形如$\begin{bmatrix} \boldsymbol{E}_r & \cdots & \boldsymbol{0} \\ \cdots & \cdots & \cdots \\ \boldsymbol{0} & \cdots & \boldsymbol{0} \end{bmatrix}$的矩阵，称为矩阵的标准形，其中 $\boldsymbol{E}_r = \begin{bmatrix} 1 & & \\ & 1 & \\ & & 1 \end{bmatrix}$为 r 阶单位矩阵。

任何矩阵都可经过一系列的初等行、列变换化为标准形，而对矩阵进行的行或列的初等变换不改变矩阵的秩，所以最后得到的矩阵的标准形和原矩阵等价。

每个矩阵都有一个唯一的等价标准形；反之，有相同矩阵标准形的矩阵是等价的。

矩阵标准形中单位矩阵 $\boldsymbol{E}_r$ 的阶数又称为矩阵的秩，利用这个性质可以求出矩阵的秩。

方法 1：利用矩阵的初等变换，将其化成标准形，得到的单位矩阵的阶数即为矩阵的秩。

方法 2：通过矩阵的初等行变换，将其化为行阶梯形，非零行的行数就是矩阵的秩。

零矩阵的秩规定为零。

矩阵的秩 $R(\boldsymbol{A}) \geqslant r$ 的充分必要条件：$\boldsymbol{A}$ 中有一个 r 阶子式不为零。

矩阵的秩 $R(\boldsymbol{A}) \leqslant r$ 的充分必要条件：$\boldsymbol{A}$ 中所有 $r+1$ 阶子式全为零。

若 $\boldsymbol{A}$ 为 $m \times n$ 矩阵，则 $\boldsymbol{A}$ 的秩不会大于它的行或列数，即 $R(\boldsymbol{A}) \leqslant \min\{m, n\}$。

对于矩阵的秩，常用到的性质有以下几个：

(1)$R(\boldsymbol{A}) = R(\boldsymbol{A}^{\mathrm{T}})$

(2)$R(\boldsymbol{A}+\boldsymbol{B}) \leqslant R(\boldsymbol{A}) + R(\boldsymbol{B})$

(3)$R(\boldsymbol{AB}) \leqslant \min[R(\boldsymbol{A}), R(\boldsymbol{B})]$

(4)若 $\boldsymbol{AB}=\boldsymbol{0}$，则 $R(\boldsymbol{A})+R(\boldsymbol{B}) \leqslant n$，其中 $\boldsymbol{A}$ 为 $m \times n$ 矩阵，$\boldsymbol{B}$ 为 $n \times s$ 矩阵。

(5)若 $\boldsymbol{A} \neq \boldsymbol{0}$，则 $R(\boldsymbol{A}) > 0$

(6)若 $\boldsymbol{A}$ 可逆，则 $R(\boldsymbol{AB}) = R(\boldsymbol{B})$，若 $\boldsymbol{B}$ 可逆，则 $R(\boldsymbol{AB}) = R(\boldsymbol{A})$

(7)若 $\boldsymbol{A}+\boldsymbol{B}=k\boldsymbol{E}(k \neq 0)$，则 $R(\boldsymbol{A})+R(\boldsymbol{B}) \geqslant n$，(其中 $\boldsymbol{A}, \boldsymbol{B}$ 为 n 阶方阵)。

(四)逆矩阵

1.定义

设 $\boldsymbol{A}$ 为 n 阶方阵，若存在 n 阶方阵 $\boldsymbol{B}$，使

$$\boldsymbol{AB} = \boldsymbol{BA} = \boldsymbol{E}$$

则称 $\boldsymbol{A}$ 是可逆矩阵，并称 $\boldsymbol{B}$ 为 $\boldsymbol{A}$ 的逆矩阵，记作 $\boldsymbol{A}^{-1} = \boldsymbol{B}$。

一般情况，只要验证：若 $\boldsymbol{A}$ 为 n 阶方阵，存在 n 阶方阵 $\boldsymbol{B}$，使 $\boldsymbol{AB}=\boldsymbol{E}$，则 $\boldsymbol{A}$ 可逆，$\boldsymbol{B}$ 为 $\boldsymbol{A}$ 的逆矩阵，即 $\boldsymbol{A}^{-1} = \boldsymbol{B}$。

可逆矩阵一定是方阵，并且它的逆矩阵也为同阶方阵。如果 $\boldsymbol{B}$ 是 $\boldsymbol{A}$ 的逆矩阵，那么 $\boldsymbol{B}$ 也是可逆矩阵，并且 $\boldsymbol{A}$ 是 $\boldsymbol{B}$ 的逆矩阵。

由正交矩阵的定义，若 $\boldsymbol{A}$ 为正交矩阵，满足 $\boldsymbol{A}^{\mathrm{T}}\boldsymbol{A} = \boldsymbol{A}\boldsymbol{A}^{\mathrm{T}} = \boldsymbol{E}$，可推出，$\boldsymbol{A}^{-1} = \boldsymbol{A}^{\mathrm{T}}$，即正交矩阵的逆矩阵为其转置矩阵。

设 $\boldsymbol{A}$ 为 $\boldsymbol{n}$ 阶方阵

$$\boldsymbol{A} = \begin{bmatrix} a_{11} & a_{12} & \cdots & a_{1n} \\ a_{21} & a_{22} & \cdots & a_{2n} \\ \vdots & \vdots & & \vdots \\ a_{n1} & a_{n2} & \cdots & a_{nn} \end{bmatrix}$$

$\boldsymbol{A}_{ij}$是方阵的行列式$|\boldsymbol{A}|$中元素a_{ij}的代数余子式，则称矩阵$\boldsymbol{A}^{*}=\begin{bmatrix} A_{11} & A_{21} & \cdots & A_{n1} \\ A_{12} & A_{22} & \cdots & A_{n2} \\ \vdots & \vdots & & \vdots \\ A_{1n} & A_{2n} & \cdots & A_{nn} \end{bmatrix}$为矩阵$\boldsymbol{A}$的伴随矩阵。

2. 伴随矩阵的性质

(1)$\boldsymbol{A}\boldsymbol{A}^{*}=\boldsymbol{A}^{*}\boldsymbol{A}=|\boldsymbol{A}|\boldsymbol{E}$。

(2)设$\boldsymbol{A}$为n阶方阵，则$|\boldsymbol{A}^{*}|=|\boldsymbol{A}|^{n-1}$。

(3)若$\boldsymbol{A}$可逆，则$\boldsymbol{A}^{*}=|\boldsymbol{A}|\boldsymbol{A}^{-1}$，$(\boldsymbol{A}^{*})^{-1}=\boldsymbol{A}/|\boldsymbol{A}|$，$(\boldsymbol{A}^{-1})^{*}=(\boldsymbol{A}^{*})^{-1}$。

(4)设$\boldsymbol{A}$、$\boldsymbol{B}$为n阶方阵，则　$(k\boldsymbol{A})^{*}=k^{n-1}A^{*}$，$(\boldsymbol{A}^{k})^{*}=(\boldsymbol{A}^{*})^{k}$

$(\boldsymbol{A}^{*})^{*}=|\boldsymbol{A}|^{n-2}\boldsymbol{A}$，$(\boldsymbol{A}\boldsymbol{B})^{*}=\boldsymbol{B}^{*}\boldsymbol{A}^{*}$

方阵$\boldsymbol{A}$的逆矩阵$\boldsymbol{A}^{-1}$存在的充要条件是$\boldsymbol{A}$为非奇异方阵。

方阵$\boldsymbol{A}$的逆矩阵$\boldsymbol{A}^{-1}$若存在，则必唯一。

3. 方阵的逆矩阵满足运算律

(1)若$\boldsymbol{A}$可逆，则$\boldsymbol{A}^{-1}$亦可逆，且$(\boldsymbol{A}^{-1})^{-1}=\boldsymbol{A}$。

(2)若$\boldsymbol{A}$可逆，数$\lambda\neq 0$则$\lambda\boldsymbol{A}$可逆，且$(\lambda\boldsymbol{A})^{-1}=\frac{1}{\lambda}\boldsymbol{A}^{-1}$。

(3)若$\boldsymbol{A}$、$\boldsymbol{B}$为同阶方阵且均可逆，则$\boldsymbol{A}\boldsymbol{B}$亦可逆，且$(\boldsymbol{A}\boldsymbol{B})^{-1}=\boldsymbol{B}^{-1}\boldsymbol{A}^{-1}$。

(4)若$\boldsymbol{A}$可逆，则$\boldsymbol{A}^{\mathrm{T}}$亦可逆，且$(\boldsymbol{A}^{\mathrm{T}})^{-1}=(\boldsymbol{A}^{-1})^{\mathrm{T}}$。

(5)$|\boldsymbol{A}^{-1}|=\frac{1}{|\boldsymbol{A}|}$。

(6)$\begin{bmatrix} \boldsymbol{A} & \\ & \boldsymbol{B} \end{bmatrix}^{-1}=\begin{bmatrix} \boldsymbol{A}^{-1} & \boldsymbol{0} \\ \boldsymbol{0} & \boldsymbol{B}^{-1} \end{bmatrix}$，$\begin{bmatrix} \boldsymbol{0} & \boldsymbol{A} \\ \boldsymbol{B} & \boldsymbol{0} \end{bmatrix}^{-1}=\begin{bmatrix} \boldsymbol{0} & \boldsymbol{B}^{-1} \\ \boldsymbol{A}^{-1} & \boldsymbol{0} \end{bmatrix}$。其中$\boldsymbol{A}$、$\boldsymbol{B}$为可逆矩阵。

4. 求逆矩阵的方法

(1)初等变换法

设$\boldsymbol{A}$为非奇异的n阶方阵，取一n阶单位矩阵$\boldsymbol{E}$构成下面的矩阵

$$(\boldsymbol{A}|\boldsymbol{E})=\left[\begin{array}{ccc|ccc} a_{11} & \cdots & a_{1n} & 1 & \cdots & 0 \\ a_{21} & \cdots & a_{2n} & 0 & \cdots & 0 \\ \vdots & & \vdots & \vdots & & \vdots \\ a_{n1} & \cdots & a_{nn} & 0 & \cdots & 1 \end{array}\right]$$

对$(\boldsymbol{A}|\boldsymbol{E})$进行“初等行变换”(即对$\boldsymbol{A}$和$\boldsymbol{E}$同时进行相同的行变换)，当$(\boldsymbol{A}|\boldsymbol{E})$中的$\boldsymbol{A}$变成$\boldsymbol{E}$时，$\boldsymbol{E}$便化为$\boldsymbol{A}^{-1}$

$$(\boldsymbol{A}|\boldsymbol{E})\xrightarrow{\text{初等行变换}}(\boldsymbol{E}|\boldsymbol{A}^{-1})$$

(2)用伴随矩阵求逆矩阵

设$\boldsymbol{A}$为非奇异矩阵，$\boldsymbol{A}$的伴随矩阵为$\boldsymbol{A}^{*}$，即

$$\boldsymbol{A}^{*}=\begin{bmatrix} A_{11} & A_{21} & \cdots & A_{n1} \\ A_{12} & A_{22} & \cdots & A_{n2} \\ \vdots & \vdots & & \vdots \\ A_{1n} & A_{2n} & \cdots & A_{nn} \end{bmatrix} \tag{1-8-3}$$

则$\boldsymbol{A}$的逆阵

$$A^{-1}=\frac{A^*}{|A|}$$

由 $A^*=|A|A^{-1}$ 可推出　　　　$AA^*=|A|E$

该公式包含了伴随矩阵、逆矩阵、单位矩阵以及行列式等众多因素，线性代数关于矩阵的符号运算几乎都可以从中导出，要灵活运用。

【例 1-8-6】 设 $A=\begin{bmatrix}2 & 5\\1 & 3\end{bmatrix}$，$B=\begin{bmatrix}4 & -6\\2 & 1\end{bmatrix}$，求解矩阵方程 $AZ=B$。

解 方程两边左乘 A^{-1}，得 $Z=A^{-1}B$

$$A^{-1}=\frac{1}{|A|}A^*=\frac{1}{6-5}\begin{bmatrix}3 & -1\\-5 & 2\end{bmatrix}^{T}=\frac{1}{6-5}\begin{bmatrix}3 & -5\\-1 & 2\end{bmatrix}=\begin{bmatrix}3 & -5\\-1 & 2\end{bmatrix}$$

所以 $$Z=\begin{bmatrix}3 & -5\\-1 & 2\end{bmatrix}\begin{bmatrix}4 & -6\\2 & 1\end{bmatrix}=\begin{bmatrix}2 & -23\\0 & 8\end{bmatrix}$$

【例 1-8-7】 设 A 为 4 阶矩阵，且 $|A|=2$，则 $\left|\frac{1}{2}A\right|$ 为：

A. $\frac{1}{8}$　　B. 4　　C. 1　　D. 0

解 由数乘矩阵的法则，$\frac{1}{2}A$，即用 $\frac{1}{2}$ 乘以矩阵 A 的每一个元素，利用行列式的性质计算得

$$\left|\frac{1}{2}A\right|=\left(\frac{1}{2}\right)^4\cdot|A|=\frac{1}{16}\times 2=\frac{1}{8}$$

答案：A

【例 1-8-8】 设 A 为 3 阶方阵，且 $|A|=\frac{1}{2}$，则 $|(2A^*)^{-1}|=$：

A. $\frac{1}{2}$　　B. $\frac{1}{4}$　　C. 1　　D. 2

解 因为 $(2A^*)(2A^*)^{-1}=E$，$|2A^*||(2A^*)^{-1}|=1$

所以 $$|(2A^*)^{-1}|=\frac{1}{|2A^*|}\xlongequal[\text{行列式}]{|A^*|\text{为三阶}}\frac{1}{8|A^*|}$$

$$\xlongequal{A^*=|A|A^{-1}}\frac{1}{8\left||A|A^{-1}\right|}\xlongequal[\text{矩阵}]{A^{-1}\text{为三阶}}\frac{1}{8}\frac{1}{|A|^3|A^{-1}|}$$

$$\xlongequal{|A^{-1}|=\frac{1}{|A|}}\frac{1}{8}\frac{1}{|A|^3}|A|=\frac{1}{8}\frac{1}{|A|^2}=\frac{1}{8}\times 4=\frac{1}{2}$$

答案：A

【例 1-8-9】 已知矩阵 $A=\begin{bmatrix}1 & 2 & -1\\3 & 4 & -2\\5 & -4 & 1\end{bmatrix}$，则 A^{-1} 为：

A. $\begin{bmatrix}-4 & 2 & 0\\-13 & 6 & -1\\-32 & 14 & -2\end{bmatrix}$　　B. $\begin{bmatrix}-4 & -13 & -32\\2 & 6 & 14\\0 & -1 & -2\end{bmatrix}$

C. $\begin{bmatrix} -2 & 1 & 0 \\ -13 & 3 & -\frac{1}{2} \\ -16 & 7 & -1 \end{bmatrix}$　　　D. $\begin{bmatrix} -2 & 1 & 0 \\ -\frac{13}{2} & 3 & -\frac{1}{2} \\ -16 & 7 & -1 \end{bmatrix}$

解　方法 1:$\boldsymbol{A}^{-1}=\frac{1}{|\boldsymbol{A}|}\boldsymbol{A}^{*}$

$$|\boldsymbol{A}|=\begin{vmatrix} 1 & 2 & -1 \\ 3 & 4 & -2 \\ 5 & -4 & 1 \end{vmatrix}=\begin{vmatrix} 1 & 2 & -1 \\ 0 & -2 & 1 \\ 0 & -14 & 6 \end{vmatrix}=2\neq 0$$

$$\boldsymbol{A}^{*}=\begin{bmatrix} -4 & -13 & -32 \\ 2 & 6 & 14 \\ 0 & -1 & -2 \end{bmatrix}^{\mathrm{T}}=\begin{bmatrix} -4 & 2 & 0 \\ -13 & 6 & -1 \\ -32 & 14 & -2 \end{bmatrix}$$

$$\boldsymbol{A}^{-1}=\frac{1}{2}\boldsymbol{A}^{*}=\begin{bmatrix} -2 & 1 & 0 \\ -\frac{13}{2} & 3 & -\frac{1}{2} \\ -16 & 7 & -1 \end{bmatrix}$$

方法 2:$(\boldsymbol{A}\mid\boldsymbol{E})=\left[\begin{array}{ccc|ccc} 1 & 2 & -1 & 1 & 0 & 0 \\ 3 & 4 & -2 & 0 & 1 & 0 \\ 5 & -4 & 1 & 0 & 0 & 1 \end{array}\right]\rightarrow\left[\begin{array}{ccc|ccc} 1 & 2 & -1 & 1 & 0 & 0 \\ 0 & -2 & 1 & -3 & 1 & 0 \\ 0 & -14 & 6 & -5 & 0 & 1 \end{array}\right]\rightarrow$

$$\left[\begin{array}{ccc|ccc} 1 & 2 & -1 & 1 & 0 & 0 \\ 0 & 1 & -\frac{1}{2} & \frac{3}{2} & -\frac{1}{2} & 0 \\ 0 & -14 & 6 & -5 & 0 & 1 \end{array}\right]\rightarrow\left[\begin{array}{ccc|ccc} 1 & 0 & 0 & -2 & 1 & 0 \\ 0 & 1 & -\frac{1}{2} & \frac{3}{2} & -\frac{1}{2} & 0 \\ 0 & 0 & -1 & 16 & -7 & 1 \end{array}\right]\rightarrow\left[\begin{array}{ccc|ccc} 1 & 0 & 0 & -2 & 1 & 0 \\ 0 & 1 & 0 & -\frac{13}{2} & 3 & -\frac{1}{2} \\ 0 & 0 & 1 & -16 & 7 & -1 \end{array}\right]$$

$$\boldsymbol{A}^{-1}=\begin{bmatrix} -2 & 1 & 0 \\ -\frac{13}{2} & 3 & -\frac{1}{2} \\ -16 & 7 & -1 \end{bmatrix}$$

方法 3:可利用题中已知的矩阵 $\boldsymbol{A}$ 分别与答案中给出的矩阵作乘积;乘积后若得到单位矩阵即为所求。如 $\boldsymbol{A}$ 乘选项 D 的矩阵得 $\boldsymbol{E}$,那么选项 D 为 $\boldsymbol{A}$ 的逆矩阵。方法 3 一般来说是比较适用的方法。

答案:D

【例 1-8-10】　已知矩阵 $\boldsymbol{A}=\begin{bmatrix} 1 & 2 & -1 \\ 3 & 4 & -2 \\ 5 & -4 & 1 \end{bmatrix}$,且 $\boldsymbol{A}^{2}-\boldsymbol{AB}=\boldsymbol{E}$,则矩阵 $\boldsymbol{B}$ 为:

A. $\begin{bmatrix} 3 & 1 & -1 \\ \frac{19}{2} & 1 & -\frac{3}{2} \\ 21 & -11 & 2 \end{bmatrix}$　　　B. $\begin{bmatrix} 3 & 1 & -1 \\ 4 & \frac{3}{2} & -3 \\ 21 & -11 & 2 \end{bmatrix}$

C. $\begin{bmatrix} 2 & 1 & -1 \\ \frac{19}{2} & 1 & -\frac{3}{2} \\ 21 & -11 & 2 \end{bmatrix}$　　　D. $\begin{bmatrix} 3 & 1 & -1 \\ \frac{19}{2} & 1 & -\frac{3}{2} \\ 12 & -11 & 2 \end{bmatrix}$

解 由上例可知$|\boldsymbol{A}|\neq 0$,$\boldsymbol{A}$可逆

$$\boldsymbol{A}^{-1}=\begin{bmatrix}-2 & 1 & 0\\ -\frac{13}{2} & 3 & -\frac{1}{2}\\ -16 & 7 & -1\end{bmatrix}$$

已知$\boldsymbol{A}^2-\boldsymbol{AB}=\boldsymbol{E}$,$\boldsymbol{A}(\boldsymbol{A}-\boldsymbol{B})=\boldsymbol{E}$

两边左乘$\boldsymbol{A}^{-1}$,即$\boldsymbol{A}^{-1}\boldsymbol{A}(\boldsymbol{A}-\boldsymbol{B})=\boldsymbol{A}^{-1}\boldsymbol{E}$,$\boldsymbol{A}-\boldsymbol{B}=\boldsymbol{A}^{-1}$

$$\boldsymbol{B}=\boldsymbol{A}-\boldsymbol{A}^{-1}=\begin{bmatrix}1 & 2 & -1\\ 3 & 4 & -2\\ 5 & -4 & 1\end{bmatrix}-\begin{bmatrix}-2 & 1 & 0\\ -\frac{13}{2} & 3 & -\frac{1}{2}\\ -16 & 7 & -1\end{bmatrix}$$

$$=\begin{bmatrix}3 & 1 & -1\\ \frac{19}{2} & 1 & -\frac{3}{2}\\ 21 & -11 & 2\end{bmatrix}$$

答案:A

【例 1-8-11】 设$\boldsymbol{A}$、$\boldsymbol{B}$均为三阶矩阵,且行列式$|\boldsymbol{A}|=1$,$|\boldsymbol{B}|=-2$,$\boldsymbol{A}^{\mathrm{T}}$为$\boldsymbol{A}$的转置矩阵,则行列式$|-2\boldsymbol{A}^{\mathrm{T}}\boldsymbol{B}^{-1}|$等于:

A. −1　　B. 1　　C. −4　　D. 4

解 本题考查矩阵和行列式的基本计算。

因为$\boldsymbol{A}$、$\boldsymbol{B}$均为三阶矩阵,则

$|-2\boldsymbol{A}^{\mathrm{T}}\boldsymbol{B}^{-1}|$

$=(-2)^3|\boldsymbol{A}^{\mathrm{T}}\boldsymbol{B}^{-1}|$

$=(-8)|\boldsymbol{A}^{\mathrm{T}}|\cdot|\boldsymbol{B}^{-1}|$(矩阵乘积的行列式性质)

$=(-8)|\boldsymbol{A}|\cdot\frac{1}{|\boldsymbol{B}|}$$\left(矩阵转置行列式性质,|\boldsymbol{BB}^{-1}|=\boldsymbol{E},|\boldsymbol{B}|\cdot|\boldsymbol{B}^{-1}|=1,|\boldsymbol{B}^{-1}|=\frac{1}{|\boldsymbol{B}|}\right)$

$=-8\times 1\times\frac{1}{-2}=4$

答案:D

【例 1-8-12】 设$\boldsymbol{A}$,$\boldsymbol{B}$为三阶方阵,且行列式$|\boldsymbol{A}|=-\frac{1}{2}$,$|\boldsymbol{B}|=2$,$\boldsymbol{A}^*$是$\boldsymbol{A}$的伴随矩阵,则行列式$|2\boldsymbol{A}^*\boldsymbol{B}^{-1}|$等于:

A. 1　　B. −1　　C. 2　　D. −2

解 $|2\boldsymbol{A}^*\boldsymbol{B}^{-1}|=2^3|\boldsymbol{A}^*\boldsymbol{B}^{-1}|=2^3|\boldsymbol{A}^*|\cdot|\boldsymbol{B}^{-1}|$

分别计算$|\boldsymbol{A}^*|$,$|\boldsymbol{B}^{-1}|$,$\boldsymbol{A}\cdot\boldsymbol{A}^{-1}=\boldsymbol{E}$,$|\boldsymbol{A}|\cdot|\boldsymbol{A}^{-1}|=1$,

$$|\boldsymbol{A}^{-1}|=\frac{1}{|\boldsymbol{A}|}=\frac{1}{-\frac{1}{2}}=-2$$

因为$\boldsymbol{A}^*=|\boldsymbol{A}|\cdot\boldsymbol{A}^{-1}$

所以$|\boldsymbol{A}^*|=\left||\boldsymbol{A}|\cdot\boldsymbol{A}^{-1}\right|=\left|-\frac{1}{2}\boldsymbol{A}^{-1}\right|=\left(-\frac{1}{2}\right)^3|\boldsymbol{A}^{-1}|=\left(-\frac{1}{2}\right)^3\times(-2)=\frac{1}{4}$

$\boldsymbol{B}\cdot\boldsymbol{B}^{-1}=\boldsymbol{E},|\boldsymbol{B}|\cdot|\boldsymbol{B}^{-1}|=1,|\boldsymbol{B}^{-1}|=\dfrac{1}{|\boldsymbol{B}|}=\dfrac{1}{2}$

因此，$|2\boldsymbol{A}^*\boldsymbol{B}^{-1}|=2^3\times\dfrac{1}{4}\times\dfrac{1}{2}=1$

答案：A

注：本题中利用的基本计算公式较多，如行列式、伴随矩阵、逆矩阵的一些性质和计算公式，应在计算前将相关的公式复习一下，并运用到计算中。

【例 1-8-13】 设 $\boldsymbol{A}$、$\boldsymbol{B}$ 是 n 阶矩阵，且 $\boldsymbol{B}\neq\boldsymbol{0}$，满足 $\boldsymbol{AB}=\boldsymbol{0}$，则以下选项中错误的是：

A. $R(\boldsymbol{A})+R(\boldsymbol{B})\leqslant n$　　B. $|\boldsymbol{A}|=0$ 或 $|\boldsymbol{B}|=0$

C. $0\leqslant R(\boldsymbol{A})<n$　　D. $\boldsymbol{A}=\boldsymbol{0}$

解 由矩阵乘法运算法则知，两个非零矩阵之积可以是零矩阵。所以由 $\boldsymbol{AB}=\boldsymbol{0}$，得 $\boldsymbol{A}=\boldsymbol{0}$ 是错误的，即选项 D 错误。

选项 A、B、C 可由矩阵的秩的性质判定。

若 $\boldsymbol{AB}=\boldsymbol{0}$，则 $R(\boldsymbol{A})+R(\boldsymbol{B})\leqslant n$，选项 A 正确。

已知 $\boldsymbol{AB}=\boldsymbol{0}$，$|\boldsymbol{AB}|=|\boldsymbol{0}|$，$|\boldsymbol{A}||\boldsymbol{B}|=0$，所以 $|\boldsymbol{A}|=0$ 或 $|\boldsymbol{B}|=0$，选项 B 正确。

另外，因 $\boldsymbol{AB}=\boldsymbol{0}$，所以 $R(\boldsymbol{A})+R(\boldsymbol{B})\leqslant n$ 成立，而 $\boldsymbol{B}\neq\boldsymbol{0}$，所以 $1\leqslant R(\boldsymbol{B})\leqslant n$，$0\leqslant R(\boldsymbol{A})<n$，选项 C 正确。

答案：D

【例 1-8-14】 设矩阵 $\boldsymbol{A}$ 中有一个 $(k-1)$ 阶子式不为零，且所有 $(k+1)$ 阶子式全为零，则 $\boldsymbol{A}$ 的秩 r 必为：

A. k　　B. $k-1$　　C. $k+1$　　D. $k-1$ 或 k

解 $\boldsymbol{A}$ 中所有 $(k+1)$ 阶子式全为零，故 $R(\boldsymbol{A})<\mathrm{k}+1$，又因为 $\boldsymbol{A}$ 中有一个 $(k-1)$ 阶子式不为零，故 $R(\boldsymbol{A})\geqslant k-1$，由此可知，$r=k-1$ 或 $r=k$。

答案：D

【例 1-8-15】 已知矩阵 $\boldsymbol{A}=\begin{bmatrix}1&0&0\\0&1&2\\0&2&4\end{bmatrix}$，则 $\boldsymbol{A}$ 的秩 $R(\boldsymbol{A})$ 等于：

A. 0　　B. 1　　C. 2　　D. 3

解 $\boldsymbol{A}=\begin{bmatrix}1&0&0\\0&1&2\\0&2&4\end{bmatrix}\xrightarrow{(-2)r_2+r_3}\begin{bmatrix}1&0&0\\0&1&2\\0&0&0\end{bmatrix}$

非零行向量的个数为 2，所以 $R(\boldsymbol{A})=2$。

答案：C

注：对于矩阵求秩这一类题目，都可以通过矩阵的初等行变换，把矩阵化为阶梯形，非零行的个数，即为矩阵的秩。

【例 1-8-16】 设 $\boldsymbol{A}$ 为 3 阶矩阵，且 $|\boldsymbol{A}|=\dfrac{1}{2}$，则 $\left|\dfrac{3}{2}\boldsymbol{A}^{-1}+7\boldsymbol{A}^*\right|$ 等于：

A. 10　　B. 125　　C. 500　　D. 250

解 因为 $\boldsymbol{A}^{-1}=\dfrac{1}{|\boldsymbol{A}|}\boldsymbol{A}^*$

$$\left|\frac{3}{2}\boldsymbol{A}^{-1}+7\boldsymbol{A}^*\right|=\left|\frac{3}{2}\,\frac{1}{|\boldsymbol{A}|}\boldsymbol{A}^*+7\boldsymbol{A}^*\right|=|3\boldsymbol{A}^*+7\boldsymbol{A}^*|=|10\boldsymbol{A}^*|\xlongequal[\text{三阶矩阵}]{\boldsymbol{A}^*\text{为}}10^3|\boldsymbol{A}^*|$$，求下面$|\boldsymbol{A}^*|$的值

又因
$$\boldsymbol{A}\boldsymbol{A}^{-1}=\boldsymbol{A}\cdot\frac{\boldsymbol{A}^*}{|\boldsymbol{A}|}=\boldsymbol{E},\boldsymbol{A}\boldsymbol{A}^*=|\boldsymbol{A}|\boldsymbol{E}$$
$$|\boldsymbol{A}\boldsymbol{A}^*|=||\boldsymbol{A}|\boldsymbol{E}|=|\boldsymbol{A}|^3|\boldsymbol{E}|=|\boldsymbol{A}|^3,\text{即}|\boldsymbol{A}||\boldsymbol{A}^*|=|\boldsymbol{A}|^3$$

所以
$$|\boldsymbol{A}^*|=|\boldsymbol{A}|^2$$

原式$=10^3|\boldsymbol{A}^*|=10^3|\boldsymbol{A}|^2=10^3\times\frac{1}{4}=250$

答案:D

【例 1-8-17】 设$\boldsymbol{A}=\begin{bmatrix}1&-1&2\\2&1&1\\-1&1&-2\end{bmatrix}$，$\boldsymbol{B}=\begin{bmatrix}2&a&1\\0&3&a\\0&0&-1\end{bmatrix}$，则秩$R(\boldsymbol{AB}-\boldsymbol{A})$等于：

A. 1　　B. 2　　C. 3　　D. 与a的取值有关

解　方法 1:$\boldsymbol{AB}-\boldsymbol{A}=\boldsymbol{AB}-\boldsymbol{AE}=\boldsymbol{A}(\boldsymbol{B}-\boldsymbol{E})$

$$=\begin{bmatrix}1&-1&2\\2&1&1\\-1&1&-2\end{bmatrix}\begin{bmatrix}1&a&1\\0&2&a\\0&0&-2\end{bmatrix}=\begin{bmatrix}1&a-2&-a-3\\2&2a+2&a\\-1&-a+2&a+3\end{bmatrix}$$

$$\boldsymbol{AB}-\boldsymbol{A}\xrightarrow[\text{行初等变换}]{r_1+r_3}\begin{bmatrix}1&a-2&-a-3\\2&2a+2&a\\0&0&0\end{bmatrix}$$

$$\xrightarrow[\text{行初等交换}]{-2r_1+r_2}\begin{bmatrix}1&a-2&-a-3\\0&6&3a+6\\0&0&0\end{bmatrix}$$

因$\begin{vmatrix}1&a-2\\0&6\end{vmatrix}=6\neq0$，$\begin{vmatrix}1&a-2&-a-3\\0&6&3a+6\\0&0&0\end{vmatrix}=0$

所以秩为2，即$R(\boldsymbol{AB}-\boldsymbol{A})=2$

方法 2:$\boldsymbol{AB}-\boldsymbol{A}=\boldsymbol{A}(\boldsymbol{B}-\boldsymbol{E})$，$R(\boldsymbol{AB}-\boldsymbol{A})=R[\boldsymbol{A}(\boldsymbol{B}-\boldsymbol{E})]$　　①

利用矩阵秩的性质：若$\boldsymbol{A}$可逆，则$R(\boldsymbol{AB})=R(\boldsymbol{B})$

①式中$\boldsymbol{B}-\boldsymbol{E}=\begin{bmatrix}1&a&1\\0&2&a\\0&0&-2\end{bmatrix}$，$|\boldsymbol{B}-\boldsymbol{E}|=-4\neq0$

所以矩阵$\boldsymbol{B}-\boldsymbol{E}$可逆

①式中$R[\boldsymbol{A}(\boldsymbol{B}-\boldsymbol{E})]=R(\boldsymbol{A})$

而$\boldsymbol{A}=\begin{bmatrix}1&-1&2\\2&1&1\\-1&1&-2\end{bmatrix}\to\begin{bmatrix}1&-1&2\\0&3&-3\\0&0&0\end{bmatrix}$

$R(\boldsymbol{A})=2$

所以$R(\boldsymbol{AB}-\boldsymbol{A})=2$

答案:B

【例 1-8-18】 已知矩阵 $A=\begin{bmatrix}1 & 1 & 2 & -2\\1 & 3 & -x & -2x\\1 & -1 & 6 & 0\end{bmatrix}$ 的秩为 2，则 $x=$：

A. 1　　B. 2　　C. 4　　D. −1

解　$R(A)=2$，说明矩阵 A 的一切三阶子式都为 0

故 $\begin{vmatrix}1 & 1 & 2\\1 & 3 & -x\\1 & -1 & 6\end{vmatrix}=0$

而 $\begin{vmatrix}1 & 1 & 2\\1 & 3 & -x\\1 & -1 & 6\end{vmatrix}\xlongequal[r_1\times(-1)+r_3]{r_1\times(-1)+r_2}\begin{vmatrix}1 & 1 & 2\\0 & 2 & -x-2\\0 & -2 & 4\end{vmatrix}=\begin{vmatrix}2 & -2-x\\-2 & 4\end{vmatrix}$

$=8-(4+2x)=4-2x=0$，即 $x=2$。

答案：B

四、向量组的线性相关性

(一) n 维向量

由 n 个数组成的有序数组 $(a_1,a_2,\cdots,a_n)$，称作一个 n 维向量，记作 $\boldsymbol{\alpha}=(a_1,a_2,\cdots,a_n)$，其中 a_i 称作 $\boldsymbol{\alpha}$ 的第 i 个坐标 $(i=1,2,\cdots,n)$。

设 $\boldsymbol{\alpha}=(a_1,a_2,\cdots,a_n)$，$\boldsymbol{\beta}=(b_1,b_2,\cdots,b_n)$，当 $a_i=b_i(i=1,2,\cdots,n)$ 时，称 $\boldsymbol{\alpha}$ 与 $\boldsymbol{\beta}$ 相等，记作 $\boldsymbol{\alpha}=\boldsymbol{\beta}$。

称 $\boldsymbol{\alpha}=(a_1,a_2,\cdots,a_n)$ 为 n 维行向量，$\boldsymbol{\alpha}^{\mathrm{T}}=\begin{bmatrix}a_1\\a_2\\\vdots\\a_n\end{bmatrix}$ 为 n 维列向量。

分量全为 0 的向量称为零向量，记作 $\mathbf{0}$，即 $\mathbf{0}=(0,0,\cdots,0)$

向量 $\boldsymbol{\alpha}=(a_1,a_2,\cdots a_n)$ 的各分量的相反数所组成的向量，称为 $\boldsymbol{\alpha}$ 的负向量，记作 $-\boldsymbol{\alpha}$，即 $-\boldsymbol{\alpha}=(-a_1,-a_2,\cdots-a_n)$

设 $\boldsymbol{\alpha}=(a_1,a_2,\cdots,a_n)$，$\boldsymbol{\beta}=(b_1,b_2,\cdots,b_n)$

向量加法定义：

$$\boldsymbol{\alpha}+\boldsymbol{\beta}=(a_1+b_1,a_2+b_2,\cdots,a_n+b_n)$$

向量减法定义：

$$\boldsymbol{\alpha}-\boldsymbol{\beta}=\boldsymbol{\alpha}+(-\boldsymbol{\beta})=(a_1-b_1,a_2-b_2,\cdots,a_n-b_n)$$

向量 $\boldsymbol{\alpha}$ 与数乘积定义：k 为任意实数，则 $k\boldsymbol{\alpha}=(k\alpha_1,k\alpha_2,\cdots,k\alpha_n)$

n 维向量的加法和数乘运算满足下面性质(设 α、β、γ 表示 n 维向量，k、l 表示数量)。

(1) $\boldsymbol{\alpha}+\boldsymbol{\beta}=\boldsymbol{\beta}+\boldsymbol{\alpha}$；

(2) $(\boldsymbol{\alpha}+\boldsymbol{\beta})+\boldsymbol{\gamma}=\boldsymbol{\alpha}+(\boldsymbol{\beta}+\boldsymbol{\gamma})$；

(3) $\boldsymbol{\alpha}+\mathbf{0}=\boldsymbol{\alpha}$；

(4) $\boldsymbol{\alpha}+(-\boldsymbol{\alpha})=\mathbf{0}$；

(5) $k(\boldsymbol{\alpha}+\boldsymbol{\beta})=k\boldsymbol{\alpha}+k\boldsymbol{\beta}$；

(6) $(k+l)\boldsymbol{\alpha}=k\boldsymbol{\alpha}+l\boldsymbol{\alpha}$。

(二)向量的线性表示

设 $\boldsymbol{\alpha}_1,\boldsymbol{\alpha}_2,\cdots,\boldsymbol{\alpha}_s,\boldsymbol{\beta}$ 均为 n 维向量,若存在一组数 $k_1,k_2,\cdots,k_s$,使得 $\boldsymbol{\beta}=k_1\boldsymbol{\alpha}_1+k_2\boldsymbol{\alpha}_2+\cdots+k_s\boldsymbol{\alpha}_s$,则称向量 $\boldsymbol{\beta}$ 是向量组 $\boldsymbol{\alpha}_1,\boldsymbol{\alpha}_2,\cdots,\boldsymbol{\alpha}_s$ 的一个线性组合,也称向量 $\boldsymbol{\beta}$ 可由向量组 $\boldsymbol{\alpha}_1,\boldsymbol{\alpha}_2,\cdots,\boldsymbol{\alpha}_s$ 线性表示。

(三)向量组的线性相关性

对于 m 个 n 维向量 $\boldsymbol{\alpha}_1,\boldsymbol{\alpha}_2,\cdots,\boldsymbol{\alpha}_m$,若存在不全为零的 m 个数 $k_1,k_2,\cdots,k_m$,使得

$$k_1\boldsymbol{\alpha}_1+k_2\boldsymbol{\alpha}_2+\cdots+k_m\boldsymbol{\alpha}_m=\mathbf{0}$$

则称这 m 个向量线性相关;否则,称它们线性无关。

通过线性相关和线性无关的定义可推出:

(1)单独一个零向量,线性相关;

(2)含有零向量的向量组,线性相关;

(3)单独一个非零向量,线性无关;

(4)由 n 个标准单位向量 $\boldsymbol{\varepsilon}_1=(1,0,0,\cdots,0),\boldsymbol{\varepsilon}_2=(0,1,0,\cdots,0),\cdots,\boldsymbol{\varepsilon}_n=(0,\cdots,0,1)$ 组成的向量组,线性无关。

判别向量组的线性相关性还有下面几个重要结论:

(1)若 $\boldsymbol{\alpha}_1,\boldsymbol{\alpha}_2,\cdots,\boldsymbol{\alpha}_s$ 线性无关,而 $\boldsymbol{\alpha}_1,\boldsymbol{\alpha}_2,\cdots,\boldsymbol{\alpha}_s,\boldsymbol{\beta}$ 线性相关,则 $\boldsymbol{\beta}$ 可由 $\boldsymbol{\alpha}_1,\boldsymbol{\alpha}_2,\cdots,\boldsymbol{\alpha}_s$ 线性表示,且表示法唯一。

(2)一个向量组中如果有一部分向量线性相关,那么这个向量组线性相关。

(3)如果一个向量组线性无关,那么它的任何一部分向量组也线性无关。

(4)如果向量组 $\boldsymbol{\alpha}_i=(a_{1i},a_{2i},a_{3i},\cdots,a_{ji}),i=1,2,\cdots,s$,线性无关,那么在每一个向量上添一个分量所得到的向量组 $\boldsymbol{\beta}_i=(a_{1i},a_{2i},a_{3i},\cdots,a_{ji},a_{(j+1)i}),i=1,2,\cdots,s$,也线性无关。

(5)$n+1$ 个 n 维向量 $\boldsymbol{\alpha}_i=(a_{i1},a_{i2},\cdots,a_{in}),i=1,2,\cdots,n,n+1$,一定线性相关。

(6)向量组 $\boldsymbol{\alpha}_1,\boldsymbol{\alpha}_2,\cdots,\boldsymbol{\alpha}_s(s\geqslant 2)$ 线性相关的充要条件,是其中至少有一个向量可由其余向量线性表示。

等价命题是向量组线性无关的充分必要条件,是向量组中任一向量都不能由其余向量线性表示。

(7)n 个 n 维向量 $\boldsymbol{\alpha}_i=(a_{i1},a_{i2},\cdots,a_{in}),i=1,2,\cdots,n$,线性无关的充要条件是

$$\begin{vmatrix} a_{11}, & a_{12}, & \cdots & a_{1n} \\ \vdots & \vdots & & \vdots \\ a_{n1} & a_{n2} & \cdots & a_{nn} \end{vmatrix} \neq 0$$

(8)n 个 n 维向量 $\boldsymbol{\alpha}_i=(a_{i1},a_{i2},\cdots,a_{in}),i=1,2,\cdots,n$,线性相关的充要条件是

$$\begin{vmatrix} a_{11} & a_{12} & \cdots & a_{1n} \\ \vdots & \vdots & & \vdots \\ a_{n1} & a_{n2} & \cdots & a_{nn} \end{vmatrix} = 0$$

如果把 $m\times n$ 矩阵 $\mathbf{A}$ 看作是由 $\mathbf{A}$ 的列(行)向量组成,则其列(行)向量的相关性与矩阵 $\mathbf{A}$ 的秩之间有以下关系:

当 $\mathbf{A}$ 的列(行)向量个数 $n(m)$ 大于 $\mathbf{A}$ 的秩时,即

$$n>R(\mathbf{A}) \quad [m>R(\mathbf{A})]$$

则列(行)向量组线性相关;

当列(行)向量个数等于矩阵 **A** 的秩时,即

$$n=R(\boldsymbol{A}) \quad [m=R(\boldsymbol{A})]$$

则列(行)向量组线性无关。以上结论可以作为判别向量组线性相关性的有效方法。

(四)最大线性无关组

定义 1,设有两个向量组,$\boldsymbol{A}:\boldsymbol{\alpha}_1,\boldsymbol{\alpha}_2,\cdots,\boldsymbol{\alpha}_s$,$\boldsymbol{B}:\boldsymbol{\beta}_1,\boldsymbol{\beta}_2,\cdots,\boldsymbol{\beta}_t$,如果向量组 **A** 中每个向量都能由向量组 **B** 线性表示,则称向量组 **A** 能由向量组 **B** 线性表示。

定义 2,如果向量组 **A** 能由向量组 **B** 线性表示,且向量组 **B** 也能由向量组 **A** 线性表示,则称两个向量组等价,记作 $\boldsymbol{A}\cong\boldsymbol{B}$。

向量组等价具有以下性质:

(1)反身性:$\boldsymbol{A}\cong\boldsymbol{A}$。

(2)对称性:若 $\boldsymbol{A}\cong\boldsymbol{B}$,则 $\boldsymbol{B}\cong\boldsymbol{A}$。

(3)传递性:若 $\boldsymbol{A}\cong\boldsymbol{B}$,$\boldsymbol{B}\cong\boldsymbol{C}$,则 $\boldsymbol{A}\cong\boldsymbol{C}$。

最大线性无关组定义:设有向量组 $\boldsymbol{A}:\boldsymbol{\alpha}_1,\boldsymbol{\alpha}_2,\cdots,\boldsymbol{\alpha}_s$,而向量组 $\boldsymbol{B}:\boldsymbol{\alpha}_{i1},\boldsymbol{\alpha}_{i2},\cdots,\boldsymbol{\alpha}_{ir}(r\leqslant s)$是向量组**A**的一个部分向量组。如果:①向量组**B**线性无关;②向量组**A**中的每一个向量都可由向量组 **B** 线性表示。则称向量组 **B** 是向量组 **A** 的一个最大线性无关组。

由定义可知,向量组的一个最大线性无关组与向量组本身是等价的。

一般地,向量组的最大线性无关组不是唯一的。一个向量组的任意两个极大线性无关组可以互相线性表示,因此它们是等价的。根据定理两个等价的线性无关的向量组各自所含的向量的个数必定相等。因而一个向量组的最大线性无关向量组所含向量的个数是个不变数,它由向量组本身确定。

【例 1-8-19】 设 $\boldsymbol{\beta}=(0,k,k^2)$能由 $\boldsymbol{\alpha}_1=(1+k,1,1)$,$\boldsymbol{\alpha}_2=(1,1+k,1)$,$\boldsymbol{\alpha}_3=(1,1,1+k)$唯一线性表示,则 k 的取值为:

A. $k\neq0$　　B. $k=0$ 或 1　　C. $k\neq1$　　D. $k\neq0,-3$

解 $\boldsymbol{\beta}$ 可由 $\boldsymbol{\alpha}_1,\boldsymbol{\alpha}_2,\boldsymbol{\alpha}_3$ 唯一线性表示,即存在一组数 x_1,x_2,x_3 使 $x_1\boldsymbol{\alpha}_1+x_2\boldsymbol{\alpha}_2+x_3\boldsymbol{\alpha}_3=\boldsymbol{\beta}$,即 $(\boldsymbol{\alpha}_1,\boldsymbol{\alpha}_2,\boldsymbol{\alpha}_3)\begin{pmatrix}x_1\\x_2\\x_3\end{pmatrix}=\boldsymbol{\beta}$ 方程组有唯一解。

那么 $|(\boldsymbol{\alpha}_1,\boldsymbol{\alpha}_2,\boldsymbol{\alpha}_3)|\neq0$

即　行列式 $\begin{vmatrix}1+k&1&1\\1&1+k&1\\1&1&1+k\end{vmatrix}\neq0$

计算行列式 $\begin{vmatrix}1+k&1&1\\1&1+k&1\\1&1&1+k\end{vmatrix}\xlongequal{r_1\leftrightarrow r_3}-\begin{vmatrix}1&1&1+k\\1&1+k&1\\1+k&1&1\end{vmatrix}$

$$=-\begin{vmatrix}1&1&1+k\\0&k&-k\\0&-k&-2k-k^2\end{vmatrix}=-(-2k^2-k^3-k^2)=k^3+3k^2=k^2(3+k)\neq0$$

即 $k\neq0,-3$。

答案:D

【例 1-8-20】 已知向量组 $\boldsymbol{\alpha}_1=(3,2,-5)^{\mathrm{T}}$,$\boldsymbol{\alpha}_2=(3,-1,3)^{\mathrm{T}}$,$\boldsymbol{\alpha}_3=\left(1,-\frac{1}{3},1\right)^{\mathrm{T}}$,$\boldsymbol{\alpha}_4=(6,-2,6)^{\mathrm{T}}$,则该向量组的一个极大线性无关组是:

A. $\boldsymbol{\alpha}_2,\boldsymbol{\alpha}_4$　　B. $\boldsymbol{\alpha}_3,\boldsymbol{\alpha}_4$　　C. $\boldsymbol{\alpha}_1,\boldsymbol{\alpha}_2$　　D. $\boldsymbol{\alpha}_2,\boldsymbol{\alpha}_3$

解 以 $\boldsymbol{\alpha}_1$、$\boldsymbol{\alpha}_2$、$\boldsymbol{\alpha}_3$、$\boldsymbol{\alpha}_4$ 为列向量作矩阵 $\boldsymbol{A}$

$$\boldsymbol{A}=\begin{bmatrix}3&3&1&6\\2&-1&-\frac{1}{3}&-2\\-5&3&1&6\end{bmatrix}\xrightarrow{-r_1+r_3}\begin{bmatrix}3&3&1&6\\2&-1&-\frac{1}{3}&-2\\-8&0&0&0\end{bmatrix}\xrightarrow{-\frac{1}{8}r_3}$$

$$\begin{bmatrix}3&3&1&6\\2&-1&-\frac{1}{3}&-2\\1&0&0&0\end{bmatrix}\xrightarrow[(-2)r_3+r_2]{(-3)r_3+r_1}\begin{bmatrix}0&3&1&6\\0&-1&-\frac{1}{3}&-2\\1&0&0&0\end{bmatrix}\xrightarrow{3r_2+r_1}\begin{bmatrix}0&0&0&0\\0&-1&-\frac{1}{3}&-2\\1&0&0&0\end{bmatrix}$$

$$\xrightarrow{r_1\leftrightarrow r_3}\begin{bmatrix}1&0&0&0\\0&-1&-\frac{1}{3}&-2\\0&0&0&0\end{bmatrix}$$

极大无关组为 $\boldsymbol{\alpha}_1$、$\boldsymbol{\alpha}_2$。

答案:C

【例 1-8-21】 若向量组 $\boldsymbol{\alpha}$、$\boldsymbol{\beta}$、$\boldsymbol{\gamma}_1$ 线性无关,$\boldsymbol{\alpha}$、$\boldsymbol{\beta}$、$\boldsymbol{\gamma}_2$ 线性相关,则:

A. $\boldsymbol{\alpha}$ 必可由向量组 $\boldsymbol{\beta},\boldsymbol{\gamma}_1,\boldsymbol{\gamma}_2$ 线性表示

B. $\boldsymbol{\beta}$ 必不可由 $\boldsymbol{\alpha},\boldsymbol{\gamma}_1,\boldsymbol{\gamma}_2$ 线性表示

C. $\boldsymbol{\gamma}_2$ 必可由 $\boldsymbol{\alpha},\boldsymbol{\beta},\boldsymbol{\gamma}_1$ 线性表示

D. $\boldsymbol{\gamma}_2$ 必不可由 $\boldsymbol{\alpha},\boldsymbol{\beta},\boldsymbol{\gamma}_1$ 线性表示

解 因为 $\boldsymbol{\alpha}$、$\boldsymbol{\beta}$、$\boldsymbol{\gamma}_1$ 线性无关,所以 $\boldsymbol{\alpha},\boldsymbol{\beta}$ 线性无关(性质),而 $\boldsymbol{\alpha}$、$\boldsymbol{\beta}$、$\boldsymbol{\gamma}_2$ 线性相关,故 $\boldsymbol{\gamma}_2$ 必可由 $\boldsymbol{\alpha},\boldsymbol{\beta}$ 线性表示,从而 $\boldsymbol{\gamma}_2$ 必可由 $\boldsymbol{\alpha}$、$\boldsymbol{\beta}$、$\boldsymbol{\gamma}_1$ 线性表示(性质)。

答案:C

【例 1-8-22】 设 $\boldsymbol{\alpha},\boldsymbol{\beta},\boldsymbol{\gamma},\boldsymbol{\delta}$ 是 n 维向量,已知 $\boldsymbol{\alpha},\boldsymbol{\beta}$ 线性无关,$\boldsymbol{\gamma}$ 可以由 $\boldsymbol{\alpha},\boldsymbol{\beta}$ 线性表示,$\boldsymbol{\delta}$ 不能由 $\boldsymbol{\alpha},\boldsymbol{\beta}$ 线性表示,则以下选项中正确的是:

A. $\boldsymbol{\alpha},\boldsymbol{\beta},\boldsymbol{\gamma},\boldsymbol{\delta}$ 线性无关　　B. $\boldsymbol{\alpha},\boldsymbol{\beta},\boldsymbol{\gamma}$ 线性无关

C. $\boldsymbol{\alpha},\boldsymbol{\beta},\boldsymbol{\delta}$ 线性相关　　D. $\boldsymbol{\alpha},\boldsymbol{\beta},\boldsymbol{\delta}$ 线性无关

解 已知 $\boldsymbol{\alpha},\boldsymbol{\beta}$ 线性无关,$\boldsymbol{\gamma}$ 可以由 $\boldsymbol{\alpha},\boldsymbol{\beta}$ 线性表示,可推出 $\boldsymbol{\alpha}$、$\boldsymbol{\beta}$、$\boldsymbol{\gamma}$ 线性相关,所以选项 B 错误。

由 $\boldsymbol{\alpha},\boldsymbol{\beta},\boldsymbol{\gamma}$ 相关,推出 $\boldsymbol{\alpha},\boldsymbol{\beta},\boldsymbol{\gamma},\boldsymbol{\delta}$ 也相关,所以选项 A 错误。

选项 C 可用反证法,证明它是错误的。设 $\boldsymbol{\alpha},\boldsymbol{\beta},\boldsymbol{\delta}$ 线性相关,已知 $\boldsymbol{\alpha},\boldsymbol{\beta}$ 线性无关,而 $\boldsymbol{\alpha},\boldsymbol{\beta},\boldsymbol{\delta}$ 线性相关,由向量组线性相关性的重要结论,推出 $\boldsymbol{\delta}$ 可由 $\boldsymbol{\alpha},\boldsymbol{\beta}$ 线性表示,与已知条件矛盾,所以 $\boldsymbol{\alpha},\boldsymbol{\beta},\boldsymbol{\delta}$ 线性无关,从而选项 C 错误。

答案:D

（五）向量组的秩

定义:向量组的最大线性无关组中所含向量的个数，称为这个向量组的秩。

向量组的秩有两个重要性质：

（1）设向量组$\boldsymbol{A}$的秩为r_1，向量组$\boldsymbol{B}$的秩为r_2，若向量组$\boldsymbol{A}$可以由向量组$\boldsymbol{B}$线性表示，则$r_1 \leqslant r_2$。若向量组$\boldsymbol{B}$可以由向量组$\boldsymbol{A}$线性表示，则$r_2 \leqslant r_1$。

（2）等价向量组有相同的秩。

（3）矩阵的行秩、列秩的定义

设$\boldsymbol{A}$是$m \times n$矩阵，将矩阵的每个行看作行向量，矩阵的m个行向量构成一个向量组，该向量组的秩称为矩阵的行秩。

将矩阵的每个列看作列向量，矩阵的n个列向量构成一个向量组，该向量组的秩称为矩阵的列秩。

定理:矩阵的行秩＝矩阵的列秩＝矩阵的秩。

五、线性方程组

（一）齐次线性方程组

$$\begin{cases} a_{11}x_1 + a_{12}x_2 + \cdots + a_{1n}x_n = 0 \\ a_{21}x_1 + a_{22}x_2 + \cdots + a_{2n}x_n = 0 \\ \qquad\qquad \cdots \\ a_{m1}x_1 + a_{m2}x_2 + \cdots + a_{mn}x_n = 0 \end{cases} \tag{1-8-4}$$

可用矩阵形式表示为

$$\boldsymbol{Ax}=\boldsymbol{0}$$

其中，$\boldsymbol{A}$为系数矩阵

$$\boldsymbol{A}=\begin{bmatrix} a_{11} & a_{12} & \cdots & a_{1n} \\ a_{21} & a_{22} & \cdots & a_{2n} \\ \vdots & \vdots & & \vdots \\ a_{m1} & a_{m2} & \cdots & a_{mn} \end{bmatrix}; \quad \boldsymbol{x}=\begin{bmatrix} x_1 \\ x_2 \\ \vdots \\ x_n \end{bmatrix}$$

若将$\boldsymbol{A}$的第j列元素看作是向量$\boldsymbol{\alpha}_j=\begin{bmatrix} a_{1j} \\ a_{2j} \\ \vdots \\ a_{mj} \end{bmatrix}(j=1,2,\cdots,n)$，则方程组(1-8-4)可用向量形式表示为

$$x_1\boldsymbol{\alpha}_1+x_2\boldsymbol{\alpha}_2+\cdots+x_n\boldsymbol{\alpha}_n=\boldsymbol{0}$$

若$\boldsymbol{\beta}_1,\boldsymbol{\beta}_2,\cdots,\boldsymbol{\beta}_l$是齐次方程组(1-8-4)的$l$个解向量，并且：

（1）$\boldsymbol{\beta}_1,\boldsymbol{\beta}_2,\cdots,\boldsymbol{\beta}_l$线性无关；

（2）方程组(1-8-4)的任意解向量都是$\boldsymbol{\beta}_1,\boldsymbol{\beta}_2,\cdots,\boldsymbol{\beta}_l$的线性组合，则称$\boldsymbol{\beta}_1,\boldsymbol{\beta}_2,\cdots,\boldsymbol{\beta}_l$是方程组(1-8-4)的基础解系。

方程组(1-8-4)的基础解系不唯一,但每个基础解系所含向量个数相同。

还有以下结论:

若 $\mathbf{A}$ 的秩 $R(\mathbf{A})=r$,则:①当 $r=n$ 时,方程组(1-8-4)只有零解。②当 $r<n$ 时,方程组(1-8-4)有无穷多解,这时基础解系含有 $n-r$ 个解向量。并可按下列方法求基础解系:

设 $\mathbf{A}$ 中的 r 阶子式

$$\begin{vmatrix} a_{11} & \cdots & a_{1r} \\ \vdots & & \vdots \\ a_{r1} & \cdots & a_{rr} \end{vmatrix} \neq 0$$

方程组(1-8-4)与下列方程组同解

$$\begin{cases} a_{11}x_1+\cdots+a_{1r}x_r=-a_{1r+1}x_{r+1}-\cdots-a_{1n}x_n \\ \cdots\cdots \\ a_{r1}x_1+\cdots+a_{rr}x_r=-a_{rr+1}x_{r+1}-\cdots-a_{rn}x_n \end{cases}$$

可以分别取

$$\begin{bmatrix} x_{r+1} \\ x_{r+2} \\ \vdots \\ x_n \end{bmatrix} = \begin{bmatrix} 1 \\ 0 \\ \vdots \\ 0 \end{bmatrix}, \begin{bmatrix} 0 \\ 1 \\ \vdots \\ 0 \end{bmatrix}, \cdots, \begin{bmatrix} 0 \\ 0 \\ \vdots \\ 1 \end{bmatrix}$$

$n-r$ 组数,由此可求得方程组的 $n-r$ 个解向量,即为方程组的基础解系。

若 $\boldsymbol{\xi}_1,\boldsymbol{\xi}_2,\cdots,\boldsymbol{\xi}_t$ 是齐次方程组 $\mathbf{A}\boldsymbol{x}=\mathbf{0}$ 的一个基础解系,则齐次线性方程组 $\mathbf{A}\boldsymbol{x}=\mathbf{0}$ 的通解是 $\boldsymbol{x}=k_1\boldsymbol{\xi}_1+k_2\boldsymbol{\xi}_2+\cdots+k_t\boldsymbol{\xi}_t$,其中 $k_1,k_2,\cdots,k_t$ 是任意常数。

由上面推导过程可知:

n(未知数个数)$-R(\mathbf{A})$(矩阵 $\mathbf{A}$ 的秩)$=$基础解系中解向量的个数

(二)非齐次线性方程组

$$\begin{cases} a_{11}x_1+a_{12}x_2+\cdots+a_{1n}x_n=b_1 \\ a_{21}x_1+a_{22}x_2+\cdots+a_{2n}x_n=b_2 \\ \cdots \\ a_{m1}x_1+a_{m2}x_2+\cdots+a_{mn}x_n=b_m \end{cases} \tag{1-8-5}$$

其中 $x_1,x_2,\cdots,x_n$ 表示 n 个未知量,m 是方程个数,a_{ij} 表示第 i 个方程中含 x_j 项的系数,$b_1,b_2,\cdots,b_m$,叫常数项。

当 $b_1,b_2,\cdots,b_m$ 不全为零时,称其为非齐次线性方程组。

用矩阵形式表示为

$$\mathbf{A}\boldsymbol{x}=\boldsymbol{b} \quad \boldsymbol{b}=(b_1,b_2,\cdots,b_m)^{\mathrm{T}}$$

或用向量形式表示为

$$x_1\boldsymbol{\alpha}_1+x_2\boldsymbol{\alpha}_2+\cdots+x_n\boldsymbol{\alpha}_n=\boldsymbol{b} \tag{1-8-6}$$

式中 $\mathbf{A}$ 为式(1-8-5)的系数矩阵,向量 $\boldsymbol{\alpha}_j=(a_{1j},a_{2j},\cdots,a_{mj})^{\mathrm{T}}$(其中,$j=1,2,\cdots,n$)。

若将一组数 $c_1,c_2,\cdots,c_n$ 代替未知量 $x_1,x_2,\cdots,x_n$,使方程组的 m 个等式都成立,就说($c_1,c_2,\cdots,c_n$)是方程组的一个解。方程组的全体解称为方程组的解集。解集相同的方程组称为同解方程组。

常用的非齐次线性方程组的解法有克莱姆法则和高斯消元法。

1. 克莱姆法则

设方程组① $\begin{cases} a_{11}x_1+a_{12}x_2+\cdots+a_{1n}x_n=b_1 \\ a_{21}x_1+a_{22}x_2+\cdots+a_{2n}x_n=b_2 \\ \cdots\cdots \\ a_{n1}x_1+a_{n2}x_2+\cdots+a_{nn}x_n=b_n \end{cases}$，用矩阵记为 $\boldsymbol{Ax}=\boldsymbol{b}$

若线性方程组①的系数行列式 $\boldsymbol{D}=|\mathbf{A}|\neq 0$，则该方程组有唯一解

$$x_j=\frac{\boldsymbol{D}_j}{\boldsymbol{D}}(j=1,2,\cdots,n)$$

其中 $\boldsymbol{D}_j$ 是将 $\boldsymbol{D}$ 中的第 j 列用方程组的常数列替换后得到的 n 阶行列式。

在变量个数较少且 $|\mathbf{A}|\neq 0$ 时，可用克莱姆法则求解。

2. 高斯消元法

解方程组 $\boldsymbol{Ax}=\boldsymbol{b}$，最基本的方法是高斯消元法。把方程组写成增广矩阵，矩阵 $\widetilde{\mathbf{A}}=(\mathbf{A}|\boldsymbol{b})$

即
$$\widetilde{\mathrm{A}}=\begin{pmatrix} a_{11} & a_{12} & \cdots & a_{1n} & b_1 \\ a_{21} & a_{22} & \cdots & a_{2n} & b_2 \\ \cdots & \cdots & \cdots & \cdots & \cdots \\ a_{m1} & a_{m2} & \cdots & a_{mn} & b_m \end{pmatrix}$$

为式(1-8-5)的增广矩阵，并对增广矩阵作行的初等变换，得到和原方程同解方程组，再求解。

将增广矩阵 $\widetilde{\mathbf{A}}=(\mathbf{A}|\boldsymbol{b})$ 施行矩阵的初等行变换化为行阶梯形。线性方程组(1-8-5)有解的充要 条件，是系数矩阵 $\mathbf{A}$ 与增广矩阵 $\widetilde{\mathbf{A}}$ 的秩相等：$R(\mathbf{A})=R(\widetilde{\mathbf{A}})$。在有解的情况下，如果 $R(\mathbf{A})=R(\widetilde{\mathbf{A}})<n$，则方程组(1-8-5)有无穷多解。若 $R(\mathbf{A})=R(\widetilde{\mathbf{A}})=n$，则方程组(1-8-5)有唯一解。具体解法如下

$$\widetilde{\mathbf{A}}=(\mathbf{A}\mid\boldsymbol{b})=\begin{bmatrix} \boldsymbol{a}_{11} & \boldsymbol{a}_{12} & \cdots & \boldsymbol{a}_{1n} & \boldsymbol{b}_1 \\ \boldsymbol{a}_{21} & \boldsymbol{a}_{22} & \cdots & \boldsymbol{a}_{2n} & \boldsymbol{b}_2 \\ \vdots & \vdots & & \vdots & \vdots \\ \boldsymbol{a}_{m1} & \boldsymbol{a}_{m2} & \cdots & \boldsymbol{a}_{mn} & \boldsymbol{b}_m \end{bmatrix}\xrightarrow[\text{初等行变换化为行阶梯形}]{\text{进行若干次}}\begin{bmatrix} c_{11} & c_{12} & c_{1r} & \boldsymbol{c}_{1n} & \boldsymbol{d}_1 \\ & \boldsymbol{c}_{22} & \boldsymbol{c}_{2r} & \boldsymbol{c}_{2n} & \boldsymbol{d}_2 \\ & \ddots & & & \\ & & \boldsymbol{c}_{rr} & \boldsymbol{c}_{rn} & \boldsymbol{d}_r \\ & & & & \boldsymbol{d}_{r+1} \\ & & & & 0 \\ & & & & \vdots \\ & & & & 0 \end{bmatrix}$$

根据行阶梯形矩阵的性质，方程组的解有如下的结论

(1)若 $d_{r+1}\neq 0$，方程组无解。即 $R(\mathbf{A})\neq R(\widetilde{\mathbf{A}})$ 无解。

(2)若 $d_{r+1}=0$，方程组有解。即 $R(\mathbf{A})=R(\widetilde{\mathbf{A}})$，方程组有解。若 $R(\mathbf{A})=R(\widetilde{\mathbf{A}})=r$，当 $r=n$ 时，方程组有唯一解；当 $r<n$ 时，方程组有无穷多解。

(三)线性方程组解的性质

1. 线性齐次方程组

(1)设 ξ_1,ξ_2 均为齐次线性方程组 $\boldsymbol{Ax}=\mathbf{0}$ 的解，则 $\xi_1+\xi_2$ 也是方程组 $\boldsymbol{Ax}=\mathbf{0}$ 的解。

(2)设 ξ 为齐次线性方程组 $\boldsymbol{Ax}=\mathbf{0}$ 的解，则 $k\boldsymbol{\xi}$(k 为任意常数)也是方程组 $\boldsymbol{Ax}=\mathbf{0}$ 的解。

(3)若 $\boldsymbol{\xi}_1,\boldsymbol{\xi}_2,\cdots,\boldsymbol{\xi}_t$ 均为方程组 $\boldsymbol{Ax}=\mathbf{0}$ 的解($k_1,k_2,\cdots,k_t$ 为任意常数)，则 $k_1\boldsymbol{\xi}_1+k_2\boldsymbol{\xi}_2+\cdots+k_t\boldsymbol{\xi}_t$ 也是方程组 $\boldsymbol{Ax}=\mathbf{0}$ 的解。

(4)设 $\mathbf{A}$ 是 $m\times n$ 矩阵，且 $R(\mathbf{A})=r<n$，则齐次线性方程组 $\boldsymbol{Ax}=\mathbf{0}$ 的基础解系由 $n-r$ 个向量构成。

(5)设 $\boldsymbol{\xi}_1,\boldsymbol{\xi}_2,\cdots,\boldsymbol{\xi}_{n-r}$ 为方程组 $\boldsymbol{Ax}=\boldsymbol{0}$ 的一组基础解系，则方程组的通解 $\boldsymbol{x}=k_1\boldsymbol{\xi}_1+k_2\boldsymbol{\xi}_2+\cdots+k_{n-r}\boldsymbol{\xi}_{n-r}$（其中 $k_1,k_2,\cdots,k_{n-r}$ 为任意常数）。

2.非齐次线性方程组

(1)若 $\boldsymbol{y}_1,\boldsymbol{y}_2$ 是方程组 $\boldsymbol{Ax}=\boldsymbol{b}$ 的解，则 $\boldsymbol{y}_1-\boldsymbol{y}_2$ 是对应齐次方程组 $\boldsymbol{Ax}=\boldsymbol{0}$ 的解。

(2)设 $\boldsymbol{A}$ 为 $m\times n$ 矩阵，且 $R(\boldsymbol{A}|\boldsymbol{b})=R(\boldsymbol{A})=n$，则非齐次线性方程组 $\boldsymbol{Ax}=\boldsymbol{b}$ 有唯一解。

(3)若 $\boldsymbol{y}$ 是方程组 $\boldsymbol{Ax}=\boldsymbol{b}$ 的解，$\boldsymbol{\xi}$ 是 $\boldsymbol{Ax}=\boldsymbol{0}$ 的解，则 $\boldsymbol{y}+\boldsymbol{\xi}$ 是方程组 $\boldsymbol{Ax}=\boldsymbol{b}$ 的解。

(4)若 $\boldsymbol{Ax}=\boldsymbol{b}$，当 $R(\boldsymbol{A})=R(\widetilde{\boldsymbol{A}})=r<n$ 时，有无穷多解，则其通解

$$\boldsymbol{x}=\boldsymbol{y}^*+k_1\boldsymbol{\xi}_1+k_2\boldsymbol{\xi}_2+\cdots+k_{n-r}\boldsymbol{\xi}_{n-r}$$

其中 $\boldsymbol{y}^*$ 为非齐次方程组一个解，$\boldsymbol{\xi}_1,\boldsymbol{\xi}_2,\cdots,\boldsymbol{\xi}_{n-r}$ 为 $\boldsymbol{Ax}=\boldsymbol{0}$ 的一组基础解系，$k_1,k_2,\cdots,k_{n-r}$ 为任意常数。

【例 1-8-23】 设 $y_1,y_2,\cdots,y_s$ 是方程组 $\boldsymbol{Ax}=\boldsymbol{b}$ 的解，若 $k_1y_1+k_2y_2+\cdots+k_sy_s$ 也是 $\boldsymbol{Ax}=\boldsymbol{b}$ 的解，则 $k_1+k_2+\cdots+k_s$ 等于：

A. 2　　B. 1　　C. -1　　D. 不存在

解 若 $k_1y_1+k_2y_2+\cdots+k_sy_s$ 是方程组的解，则 $\boldsymbol{A}(k_1y_1+k_2y_2+\cdots+k_sy_s)=\boldsymbol{b}$

即 $\boldsymbol{A}k_1y_1+\boldsymbol{A}k_2y_2+\cdots+\boldsymbol{A}k_sy_s$

$=k_1\boldsymbol{A}y_1+k_2\boldsymbol{A}y_2+\cdots+k_s\boldsymbol{A}y_s$

$=k_1\boldsymbol{b}+k_2\boldsymbol{b}+\cdots+k_s\boldsymbol{b}$

$=(k_1+k_2+\cdots+k_s)\cdot\boldsymbol{b}=\boldsymbol{b}$

所以 $k_1+k_2+\cdots+k_s=1$

答案：B

【例 1-8-24】 设方程组 $\begin{cases}x_1-x_2+6x_3=0\\4x_2-8x_3=-4\\x_1+3x_2-2x_3=a\end{cases}$，问 a 取何值时，方程组有解：

A. -4　　B. 2　　C. 1　　D. -1

解 $\widetilde{\boldsymbol{A}}=\begin{bmatrix}1&-1&6&0\\0&4&-8&-4\\1&3&-2&a\end{bmatrix}\xrightarrow{-r_1+r_3}\begin{bmatrix}1&-1&6&0\\0&4&-8&-4\\0&4&-8&a\end{bmatrix}\xrightarrow{-r_2+r_3}\begin{bmatrix}1&-1&6&0\\0&4&-8&-4\\0&0&0&a+4\end{bmatrix}$

$a=-4$ 时，$R(\boldsymbol{A})=R(\widetilde{\boldsymbol{A}})=2$，方程组有解。

答案：A

【例 1-8-25】 求线性齐次方程组 $\begin{cases}x_1-x_2-x_3+x_4=0\\x_1-x_2+x_3-3x_4=0\\x_1-x_2-2x_3+3x_4=0\end{cases}$ 的通解。

解 $\boldsymbol{A}=\begin{bmatrix}1&-1&-1&1\\1&-1&1&-3\\1&-1&-2&3\end{bmatrix}\xrightarrow[-r_1+r_3]{-r_1+r_2}\begin{bmatrix}1&-1&-1&1\\0&0&2&-4\\0&0&-1&2\end{bmatrix}\longrightarrow\begin{bmatrix}1&-1&-1&1\\0&0&1&-2\\0&0&-1&2\end{bmatrix}\longrightarrow$

$\begin{bmatrix}1&-1&-1&1\\0&0&1&-2\\0&0&0&0\end{bmatrix}\longrightarrow\begin{bmatrix}1&-1&0&-1\\0&0&1&-2\\0&0&0&0\end{bmatrix}$

同解方程组为$\begin{cases}x_1-x_2-x_4=0\\x_3-2x_4=0\end{cases}$，$\begin{cases}x_1=x_2+x_4\\x_3=2x_4\end{cases}$

$\begin{bmatrix}x_2\\x_4\end{bmatrix}$取$\begin{bmatrix}1\\0\end{bmatrix}$，$\begin{bmatrix}0\\1\end{bmatrix}$，则$\begin{bmatrix}x_1\\x_3\end{bmatrix}$为$\begin{bmatrix}1\\0\end{bmatrix}$，$\begin{bmatrix}1\\2\end{bmatrix}$

基础解系 $\boldsymbol{\xi}_1=\begin{bmatrix}1\\1\\0\\0\end{bmatrix}$，$\boldsymbol{\xi}_2=\begin{bmatrix}1\\0\\2\\1\end{bmatrix}$

通解 $\boldsymbol{x}=C_1\begin{bmatrix}1\\1\\0\\0\end{bmatrix}+C_2\begin{bmatrix}1\\0\\2\\1\end{bmatrix}$。（其中 C_1，C_2 为任意实数）

【例 1-8-26】 设非齐次线性方程组$\begin{cases}x_1-x_2-x_3+x_4=0\\x_1-x_2+x_3-3x_4=1\\x_1-x_2-2x_3+3x_4=-\dfrac{1}{2}\end{cases}$，求方程组通解。

解 $\widetilde{\boldsymbol{A}}=\begin{bmatrix}1&-1&-1&1&0\\1&-1&1&-3&1\\1&-1&-2&3&-\dfrac{1}{2}\end{bmatrix}\xrightarrow[(-1)r_1+r_3]{(-1)r_1+r_2}\begin{bmatrix}1&-1&-1&1&0\\0&0&2&-4&1\\0&0&-1&2&-\dfrac{1}{2}\end{bmatrix}$

$\xrightarrow{\frac{1}{2}r_2}\begin{bmatrix}1&-1&-1&1&0\\0&0&1&-2&\dfrac{1}{2}\\0&0&-1&2&-\dfrac{1}{2}\end{bmatrix}\xrightarrow{1\cdot r_2+r_3}\begin{bmatrix}1&-1&-1&1&0\\0&0&1&-2&\dfrac{1}{2}\\0&0&0&0&0\end{bmatrix}$

$\xrightarrow{1\cdot r_2+r_1}\begin{bmatrix}1&-1&0&-1&\dfrac{1}{2}\\0&0&1&-2&\dfrac{1}{2}\\0&0&0&0&0\end{bmatrix}$

$R(\boldsymbol{A})=R(\widetilde{\boldsymbol{A}})=2<4$，方程组有解且有无穷多组解。

同解方程组为 $\begin{cases}x_1-x_2-x_4=\dfrac{1}{2}\\x_3-2x_4=\dfrac{1}{2}\end{cases}$

变形 $\begin{cases}x_1=x_2+x_4+\dfrac{1}{2}\\x_3=2x_4+\dfrac{1}{2}\end{cases}$（$x_2$，$x_4$ 为自由未知量）

令 $x_2=C_1$，$x_4=C_2$

$$\begin{cases} x_1 = C_1 + C_2 + \dfrac{1}{2} \\ x_2 = C_1 \\ x_3 = 2C_2 + \dfrac{1}{2} \\ x_4 = C_2 \end{cases}$$

方程组通解 $\begin{bmatrix} x_1 \\ x_2 \\ x_3 \\ x_4 \end{bmatrix} = C_1 \begin{bmatrix} 1 \\ 1 \\ 0 \\ 0 \end{bmatrix} + C_2 \begin{bmatrix} 1 \\ 0 \\ 2 \\ 1 \end{bmatrix} + \begin{bmatrix} \frac{1}{2} \\ 0 \\ \frac{1}{2} \\ 0 \end{bmatrix}$

【例 1-8-27】 设 $\boldsymbol{B}$ 是 3 阶非零矩阵，已知 $\boldsymbol{B}$ 的每一列都是方程组 $\begin{cases} x_1 + 2x_2 - 2x_3 = 0 \\ 2x_1 - x_2 + tx_3 = 0 \\ 3x_1 + x_2 - x_3 = 0 \end{cases}$ 的解。则 t 等于：

A. 0　　B. 2　　C. -1　　D. 1

解 已知 $\boldsymbol{B}$ 是 3 阶非零矩阵，即在 $\boldsymbol{B}$ 中至少有一行或一列为非零向量。可知方程组应有非零解。因而方程组 $\begin{bmatrix} 1 & 2 & -2 \\ 2 & -1 & t \\ 3 & 1 & -1 \end{bmatrix} \begin{bmatrix} x_1 \\ x_2 \\ x_3 \end{bmatrix} = 0$ 中系数矩阵的行列式 $\begin{vmatrix} 1 & 2 & -2 \\ 2 & -1 & t \\ 3 & 1 & -1 \end{vmatrix} = 0$

由克莱姆法则知，齐次方程组 $\begin{cases} a_{11}x_1 + a_{12}x_2 + a_{13}x_3 = 0 \\ a_{21}x_1 + a_{22}x_2 + a_{23}x_3 = 0 \\ a_{31}x_1 + a_{32}x_2 + a_{33}x_3 = 0 \end{cases}$ 的系数行列式 $\boldsymbol{D} \neq 0$ 时，它仅有零解。齐次方程组有非零解，则它的系数行列式 $\boldsymbol{D} = 0$。

计算 $\begin{vmatrix} 1 & 2 & -2 \\ 2 & -1 & t \\ 3 & 1 & -1 \end{vmatrix} \xlongequal[(-3)r_1 + r_3]{(-2)r_1 + r_2} \begin{vmatrix} 1 & 2 & -2 \\ 0 & -5 & 4+t \\ 0 & -5 & 5 \end{vmatrix} \xlongequal{(-1)r_2 + r_3} \begin{vmatrix} 1 & 2 & -2 \\ 0 & -5 & 4+t \\ 0 & 0 & 1-t \end{vmatrix}$

$= -5(1-t) = 0 \Rightarrow t = 1$

答案：D

【例 1-8-28】 设 $\boldsymbol{A} = \begin{bmatrix} 1 & 2 & -2 \\ 4 & t & 3 \\ 3 & -1 & 1 \end{bmatrix}$，$\boldsymbol{B}$ 为三阶非零矩阵，且 $\boldsymbol{AB} = \boldsymbol{0}$，则参数 t 等于：

A. -3　　B. 1　　C. 4　　D. -1

解 因为 $\boldsymbol{B}$ 是三阶非零矩阵，故 $\boldsymbol{B}$ 的三个列向量中至少有一个非零，设 $\boldsymbol{B} = (\boldsymbol{b}_1, \boldsymbol{b}_2, \boldsymbol{b}_3)$，则 $\boldsymbol{b}_1, \boldsymbol{b}_2, \boldsymbol{b}_3$ 中至少有一个为非零向量，由 $\boldsymbol{AB} = \boldsymbol{0}$，有 $\boldsymbol{A}(\boldsymbol{b}_1, \boldsymbol{b}_2, \boldsymbol{b}_3) = \boldsymbol{0}$，即 $(\boldsymbol{Ab}_1, \boldsymbol{Ab}_2, \boldsymbol{Ab}_3) = \boldsymbol{0}$

从而有 $\boldsymbol{Ab}_1 = \boldsymbol{0}, \boldsymbol{Ab}_2 = \boldsymbol{0}, \boldsymbol{Ab}_3 = \boldsymbol{0}$，即方程组 $\boldsymbol{Ab}_1 = \boldsymbol{0}, \boldsymbol{Ab}_2 = \boldsymbol{0}, \boldsymbol{Ab}_3 = \boldsymbol{0}$ 有非零解。

由方程组 $\boldsymbol{Ax} = \boldsymbol{0}$ 有非零解的充分条件是 $|\boldsymbol{A}| = 0$，得：

$$|\boldsymbol{A}| = \begin{vmatrix} 1 & 2 & -2 \\ 4 & t & 3 \\ 3 & -1 & 1 \end{vmatrix} \xlongequal[r_1 \times (-3) + r_3]{r_1 \times (-4) + r_2} \begin{vmatrix} 1 & 2 & -2 \\ 0 & t-8 & 11 \\ 0 & -7 & 7 \end{vmatrix} = 7(t-8) + 77$$

$=7t-56+77=0, 7t+21=0, t=-3$

答案:A

【例 1-8-29】 设 $\boldsymbol{A}$ 为矩阵,$\boldsymbol{\alpha}_1=\begin{bmatrix}1\\0\\2\end{bmatrix}$,$\boldsymbol{\alpha}_2=\begin{bmatrix}0\\1\\-1\end{bmatrix}$都是线性方程组 $\boldsymbol{Ax}=\boldsymbol{0}$ 的解,则矩阵 $\boldsymbol{A}$ 为:

A. $\begin{bmatrix}0 & 1 & -1\\4 & -2 & -2\\0 & 1 & 1\end{bmatrix}$　　　B. $\begin{bmatrix}2 & 0 & -1\\0 & 1 & 1\end{bmatrix}$

C. $\begin{bmatrix}-1 & 0 & 2\\0 & 1 & -1\end{bmatrix}$　　　D. $(-2\quad 1\quad 1)$

解　方法 1:本题可将矩阵各选项分别代入矩阵方程 $\boldsymbol{Ax}=0$,得到对应的线性方程组。如选项 A 代入得到方程组$\begin{cases}x_2-x_3=0\\4x_1-2x_2-2x_3=0\\x_2+x_3=0\end{cases}$。把 $\boldsymbol{\alpha}_1=\begin{bmatrix}1\\0\\2\end{bmatrix}$,$\boldsymbol{\alpha}_2=\begin{bmatrix}0\\1\\-1\end{bmatrix}$逐一代入方程组检验,满足方程组的即为所求矩阵,反之则不是。选项 A 不满足方程组,舍去。同样选项 B、C 也不成立。

选项 D 代入得到的方程组为$(-2\quad 1\quad 1)\begin{bmatrix}x_1\\x_2\\x_3\end{bmatrix}=0$

即　$-2x_1+x_2+x_3=0, x_3=2x_1-x_2$

当 $x_1=1, x_2=0$ 时,$x_3=2$

当 $x_1=0, x_2=1$ 时,$x_3=-1$

解为 $\boldsymbol{\alpha}_1=\begin{bmatrix}1\\0\\2\end{bmatrix}$,$\boldsymbol{\alpha}_2=\begin{bmatrix}0\\1\\-1\end{bmatrix}$

方法 2:已知 $\boldsymbol{\alpha}_1$、$\boldsymbol{\alpha}_2$ 是方程组 $\boldsymbol{Ax}=0$ 的解,而 $\boldsymbol{\alpha}_1$、$\boldsymbol{\alpha}_2$ 线性无关,未知数个数是 3,$\boldsymbol{\alpha}_1$、$\boldsymbol{\alpha}_2$ 为 $\boldsymbol{Ax}=0$ 的一组基础解系,基础解系解向量的个数为 2。在方程组 $\boldsymbol{Ax}=0$ 中,有 n(未知量的个数)$-R(\boldsymbol{A})$(矩阵 $\boldsymbol{A}$ 的秩)=基础解系解向量的个数。

所以推出 $R(\boldsymbol{A})=3-2=1$。

答案:D

六、方阵的特征值与特征向量

(一)定义

对于 n 阶方阵 $\boldsymbol{A}$,如果数 λ 和 n 维非零列向量 $\boldsymbol{x}$ 满足

$$\boldsymbol{Ax}=\lambda\boldsymbol{x}$$

则数 λ 称为方阵 $\boldsymbol{A}$ 的特征值,非零向量 $\boldsymbol{x}$ 称为方阵 $\boldsymbol{A}$ 对应特征值 λ 的特征向量。

上式可写成

$$(\boldsymbol{A}-\lambda\boldsymbol{E})\boldsymbol{x}=0\quad 或\quad (\lambda\boldsymbol{E}-\boldsymbol{A})\boldsymbol{x}=0$$

该齐次线性方程组有非零解的充要条件是系数行列式

$$|\boldsymbol{A}-\lambda\boldsymbol{E}|=0 \quad 或 \quad |\lambda\boldsymbol{E}-\boldsymbol{A}|=0 \tag{1-8-7}$$

即

$$\begin{vmatrix} a_{11}-\lambda & a_{12} & \cdots & a_{1n} \\ a_{21} & a_{22}-\lambda & \cdots & a_{2n} \\ \vdots & \vdots & & \vdots \\ a_{n1} & a_{n2} & \cdots & a_{nn}-\lambda \end{vmatrix}=0 \text{ 或 } \begin{vmatrix} \lambda-a_{11} & -a_{12} & \cdots & -a_{1n} \\ -a_{21} & \lambda-a_{22} & \cdots & -a_{2n} \\ \cdots\cdots & & & \\ -a_{n1} & -a_{n2} & \cdots & \lambda-a_{nn} \end{vmatrix}=0$$

上式是以 λ 为未知数的一元 n 次方程，叫做方阵 $\boldsymbol{A}$ 的特征方程。其左端是关于 λ 的 n 次多项式 $|\lambda\boldsymbol{E}-\boldsymbol{A}|$ 称作方阵 $\boldsymbol{A}$ 的特征多项式。特征方程 $|\lambda\boldsymbol{E}-\boldsymbol{A}|=0$ 的解，称为方阵 $\boldsymbol{A}$ 的特征值，且 n 次方程有 n 个特征值。

设 $\lambda=\lambda_i$ 为 $\boldsymbol{A}$ 的一个特征值，则由方程

$$(\lambda_i\boldsymbol{E}-\boldsymbol{A})\boldsymbol{x}=0$$

可求得非零解 $\boldsymbol{x}=\boldsymbol{P}_i$，$\boldsymbol{P}_i$ 就是方阵 $\boldsymbol{A}$ 对应于特征值 λ_i 的特征向量。

（二）求 n 阶矩阵 $\boldsymbol{A}$ 的特征值与特征向量的步骤

(1)求 $\boldsymbol{A}$ 的特征方程 $\det(\lambda\boldsymbol{E}-\boldsymbol{A})=0$ 的全部根 $\lambda_1,\lambda_2,\cdots,\lambda_n$。

(2)将 $\lambda=\lambda_i(i=1,2,\cdots,n)$，分别代入 $(\lambda\boldsymbol{E}-\boldsymbol{A})\boldsymbol{x}=0$，得齐次线性方程组 $(\lambda_i\boldsymbol{E}-\boldsymbol{A})\boldsymbol{x}=0$。

(3)方程组 $(\lambda_i\boldsymbol{E}-\boldsymbol{A})\boldsymbol{x}=0$ 的基础解系，就是 $\boldsymbol{A}$ 对应于 λ_i 的特征向量，基础解系的线性组合($\boldsymbol{0}$ 除外)就是 $\boldsymbol{A}$ 对应于 $\lambda=\lambda_i$ 的全部特征向量。

若在计算特征值时，有 $\lambda=0$，那么 $\boldsymbol{Ax}=\boldsymbol{0}$ 的所有非零解向量，即为特征值 $\lambda=0$ 对应的特征向量。

（三）特征值和特征向量的几个重要性质

(1)若线性无关的非零向量 $\boldsymbol{x}_1,\boldsymbol{x}_2$ 都是矩阵 $\boldsymbol{A}$ 属于特征值 λ 的特征向量，对任意不全为零的数 k_1、k_2，向量 $k_1\boldsymbol{x}_1+k_2\boldsymbol{x}_2$ 也是矩阵 $\boldsymbol{A}$ 的属于特征值 λ 的特征向量。

(2)方阵 $\boldsymbol{A}$ 的属于不同特征值的特征向量是线性无关的。

(3)如果 $\lambda_1,\lambda_2,\cdots,\lambda_m$ 是方阵 $\boldsymbol{A}$ 的 m 个特征值，向量 $\boldsymbol{x}_1,\boldsymbol{x}_2,\cdots,\boldsymbol{x}_m$ 是依次与之对应的特征向量，如果 $\lambda_1,\lambda_2,\cdots,\lambda_m$ 是两两互不相同的，那么向量组 $\boldsymbol{x}_1,\boldsymbol{x}_2,\cdots,\boldsymbol{x}_m$ 一定线性无关。

(4)如果 n 阶方阵 A 的全部特征值是 $\lambda_1,\lambda_2,\cdots,\lambda_n$，那么

①$\lambda_1+\lambda_2+\cdots+\lambda_n=a_{11}+a_{22}+\cdots+a_{nn}$（其中 $a_{11},a_{22},\cdots,a_{nn}$ 为方阵 $\boldsymbol{A}$ 主对角线上的元素）。

②$\lambda_1\lambda_2\cdots\lambda_n=|\boldsymbol{A}|$。

(5)若 λ 为 $\boldsymbol{A}$ 的特征值，则矩阵 $k\boldsymbol{A}$，$a\boldsymbol{A}+b\boldsymbol{E}$、$\boldsymbol{A}^2$、$\boldsymbol{A}^m$、$\boldsymbol{A}^{-1}$、$\boldsymbol{A}^*$ 分别有特征值 $k\lambda$、$a\lambda+b$、λ^2、λ^m、$\frac{1}{\lambda}$、$\frac{|\boldsymbol{A}|}{\lambda}(\lambda\neq0)$，且特征向量相同。（式中字母 a,b 为不为零的常数）

【例 1-8-30】 求矩阵 $\boldsymbol{A}=\begin{bmatrix} -2 & 1 & 1 \\ 0 & 2 & 0 \\ -4 & 1 & 3 \end{bmatrix}$ 的特征值与特征向量。

解 求特征值，$|\lambda\boldsymbol{E}-\boldsymbol{A}|=0$

$$\begin{vmatrix} \lambda+2 & -1 & -1 \\ 0 & \lambda-2 & 0 \\ 4 & -1 & \lambda-3 \end{vmatrix}=(\lambda-2)\begin{vmatrix} \lambda+2 & -1 \\ 4 & \lambda-3 \end{vmatrix}=(\lambda-2)^2(\lambda+1)$$

所以 $\lambda_1=\lambda_2=2,\lambda_3=-1$

计算 $\lambda_1=\lambda_2=2$ 对应矩阵 $\boldsymbol{A}$ 的特征向量

将 $\lambda=2$ 代入得 $(2\boldsymbol{E}-\boldsymbol{A})\boldsymbol{x}=\boldsymbol{0}$

即 $\begin{bmatrix}4 & -1 & -1\\0 & 0 & 0\\4 & -1 & -1\end{bmatrix}\begin{bmatrix}x_1\\x_2\\x_3\end{bmatrix}=\begin{bmatrix}0\\0\\0\end{bmatrix}$

而 $\begin{bmatrix}4 & -1 & -1\\0 & 0 & 0\\4 & -1 & -1\end{bmatrix}\longrightarrow\begin{bmatrix}4 & -1 & -1\\0 & 0 & 0\\0 & 0 & 0\end{bmatrix}$

所以 $4x_1-x_2-x_3=0, 4x_1=x_2+x_3, x_1=\frac{1}{4}x_2+\frac{1}{4}x_3$

$\begin{bmatrix}x_2\\x_3\end{bmatrix}$ 取 $\begin{bmatrix}4\\0\end{bmatrix},\begin{bmatrix}0\\4\end{bmatrix}$

x_1 ： 1 1

对应 $\lambda=2$，矩阵 A 对应特征向量 $\boldsymbol{\xi}_1=\begin{bmatrix}1\\4\\0\end{bmatrix},\boldsymbol{\xi}_2=\begin{bmatrix}1\\0\\4\end{bmatrix}$

对应 $\lambda=2$ 的全部特征向量 $C_1\boldsymbol{\xi}_1+C_2\boldsymbol{\xi}_2=C_1\begin{bmatrix}1\\4\\0\end{bmatrix}+C_2\begin{bmatrix}1\\0\\4\end{bmatrix}$（$C_1,C_2$ 为不同时为零的任意常数）

计算 $\lambda_3=-1$ 对应矩阵 $\boldsymbol{A}$ 的特征向量，$(\lambda_3\boldsymbol{E}-\boldsymbol{A})\boldsymbol{x}=\boldsymbol{0}$

即 $\begin{bmatrix}1 & -1 & -1\\0 & -3 & 0\\4 & -1 & -4\end{bmatrix}\begin{bmatrix}x_1\\x_2\\x_3\end{bmatrix}=\begin{bmatrix}0\\0\\0\end{bmatrix}$

$$\begin{bmatrix}1 & -1 & -1\\0 & -3 & 0\\4 & -1 & -4\end{bmatrix}\longrightarrow\begin{bmatrix}1 & -1 & -1\\0 & -3 & 0\\0 & 3 & 0\end{bmatrix}\longrightarrow\begin{bmatrix}1 & -1 & -1\\0 & -3 & 0\\0 & 0 & 0\end{bmatrix}\longrightarrow\begin{bmatrix}1 & 0 & -1\\0 & 1 & 0\\0 & 0 & 0\end{bmatrix}$$

所以 $\begin{cases}x_1=x_3\\x_2=0\end{cases}$，当 $x_3=1$ 时，$x_2=0, x_1=1$，特征向量 $\boldsymbol{\xi}=\begin{bmatrix}1\\0\\1\end{bmatrix}$

$\lambda_3=-1$ 对应矩阵 A 的全部特征向量 $C\begin{bmatrix}1\\0\\1\end{bmatrix}$（其中 C 为不等于 0 的任意常数）。

【例 1-8-31】 设三阶方阵有 3 个特征值 $\lambda_1,\lambda_2,\lambda_3$，若 $|\boldsymbol{A}|=36, \lambda_1=2, \lambda_2=3$，则 λ_3 为：

A. 6　　B. 3　　C. 2　　D. 4

解 由方阵 $\boldsymbol{A}$ 的行列式与特征值的关系 $|\boldsymbol{A}|=\lambda_1\lambda_2\lambda_3$，得：

$$\lambda_1\lambda_2\lambda_3=36$$

又 $\lambda_1=2, \lambda_2=3$，所以 $\lambda_3=\frac{36}{\lambda_1\lambda_2}=\frac{36}{2\times3}=6$。

答案：A

【例 1-8-32】 设 $\boldsymbol{A}$ 是 3 阶矩阵，$\boldsymbol{\alpha}_1=(1,0,1)^T, \boldsymbol{\alpha}_2=(1,1,0)^T$ 是 $\boldsymbol{A}$ 的属于特征值为 1 的特征向量。$\boldsymbol{\alpha}_3=(0,1,2)^T$ 是 $\boldsymbol{A}$ 的属于特征值为 -1 的特征向量，则：

A. $\boldsymbol{\alpha}_1-\boldsymbol{\alpha}_2$ 是 $\boldsymbol{A}$ 的属于特征值为 1 的特征向量

B. $\boldsymbol{\alpha}_1-\boldsymbol{\alpha}_3$ 是 $\boldsymbol{A}$ 的属于特征值为 1 的特征向量

C. $\boldsymbol{\alpha}_1-\boldsymbol{\alpha}_3$ 是 $\boldsymbol{A}$ 的属于特征值为 2 的特征向量

D. $\boldsymbol{\alpha}_1+\boldsymbol{\alpha}_2+\boldsymbol{\alpha}_3$ 是 $\boldsymbol{A}$ 的属于特征值为 1 的特征向量

解 方法 1：根据矩阵的特征值和特征向量的定义 $\boldsymbol{\alpha}_1,\boldsymbol{\alpha}_2$ 是矩阵 $\boldsymbol{A}$ 特征值 1 对应的特征向量，就有 $\begin{cases}\boldsymbol{A}\,\alpha_1=1\cdot\boldsymbol{\alpha}_1 & ①\\ \boldsymbol{A}\,\alpha_2=1\cdot\boldsymbol{\alpha}_2 & ②\end{cases}$ 成立。

①式－②式得 $\boldsymbol{A}(\boldsymbol{\alpha}_1-\boldsymbol{\alpha}_2)=1\cdot(\boldsymbol{\alpha}_1-\boldsymbol{\alpha}_2)$，而 $\boldsymbol{\alpha}_1-\boldsymbol{\alpha}_2$ 为非零向量，由定义可知，$\boldsymbol{\alpha}_1-\boldsymbol{\alpha}_2$ 是 $\boldsymbol{A}$ 的属于特征值为 1 的特征向量，选项 B、C、D 均不成立。

方法 2：可通过特征值和特征向量的重要性质直接判定。

答案：A

【例 1-8-33】 设 $\lambda_1=6,\lambda_2=\lambda_3=3$ 为三阶实对称矩阵 $\boldsymbol{A}$ 的特征值，属于 $\lambda_2=\lambda_3=3$ 的特征向量为 $\xi_2=(-1,0,1)^{\mathrm{T}},\xi_3=(1,2,1)^{\mathrm{T}}$，则属于 $\lambda_1=6$ 的特征向量是：

A. $(1,-1,1)^{\mathrm{T}}$　　B. $(1,1,1)^{\mathrm{T}}$　　C. $(0,2,2)^{\mathrm{T}}$　　D. $(2,2,0)^{\mathrm{T}}$

解 实对称矩阵其不同特征值对应的特征向量之间必定互相正交[见下面实对称矩阵的特征值和特征向量的性质(3)]。由题意得，属于特征值 $\lambda_1=6$ 所对应的特征向量 ξ_1 必定和 λ_2 和 λ_3 所对应的特征向量即 ξ_2 和 ξ_3 分别正交，故有 $\xi_1\cdot\xi_2=\xi_1\cdot\xi_3=0$，代入选项只有 A 满足。

答案：A

【例 1-8-34】 已知 3 维列向量 $\boldsymbol{\alpha},\boldsymbol{\beta}$ 满足 $\boldsymbol{\beta}\neq k\,\boldsymbol{\alpha}$（$k$ 为常数），$\boldsymbol{\alpha}^{\mathrm{T}}\boldsymbol{\beta}=4$，设 3 阶矩阵 $\boldsymbol{A}=\boldsymbol{\beta}\,\boldsymbol{\alpha}^{T}$，则：

A. $\boldsymbol{\beta}$ 是 $\boldsymbol{A}$ 的属于特征值 0 的特征向量

B. $\boldsymbol{\alpha}$ 是 $\boldsymbol{A}$ 的属于特征值 0 的特征向量

C. $\boldsymbol{\beta}$ 是 $\boldsymbol{A}$ 的属于特征值 4 的特征向量

D. $\boldsymbol{\alpha}$ 是 $\boldsymbol{A}$ 的属于特征值 4 的特征向量

解 利用矩阵的特征值、特征向量的定义和题目给的条件判定。

$\boldsymbol{A\alpha}\xrightarrow[\boldsymbol{A}=\boldsymbol{\beta\alpha}^{\mathrm{T}}]{\text{代入}}\boldsymbol{\beta}\,\boldsymbol{\alpha}^{\mathrm{T}}\boldsymbol{\alpha}=\boldsymbol{\beta}|\boldsymbol{\alpha}|^2=|\boldsymbol{\alpha}|^2\boldsymbol{\beta}$，因为 $\boldsymbol{\beta}\neq k\boldsymbol{\alpha}$，所以 $|\boldsymbol{\alpha}|^2\boldsymbol{\beta}\neq|\boldsymbol{\alpha}|^2k\boldsymbol{\alpha}$，而 $|\boldsymbol{\alpha}|^2k\boldsymbol{\alpha}\neq\lambda\boldsymbol{\alpha}$（$\lambda=0$ 或 $\lambda=4$），从而 $\boldsymbol{A\alpha}\neq\lambda\boldsymbol{\alpha}$，选项 B、D 不成立。

而 $\boldsymbol{A\beta}=\boldsymbol{\beta}\,\boldsymbol{\alpha}^{\mathrm{T}}\boldsymbol{\beta}=\boldsymbol{\beta}(\boldsymbol{\alpha}^{\mathrm{T}}\boldsymbol{\beta})=4\boldsymbol{\beta}$，即 $\boldsymbol{A\beta}=4\boldsymbol{\beta}$ 成立，选项 C 成立。

答案：C

七、相似矩阵的概念和性质

（一）相似矩阵的概念

设 $\boldsymbol{A}$、$\boldsymbol{B}$ 都是 n 阶矩阵，若有可逆矩阵 $\boldsymbol{P}$，使 $\boldsymbol{P}^{-1}\boldsymbol{AP}=\boldsymbol{B}$，则称 $\boldsymbol{A}$ 和 $\boldsymbol{B}$ 相似，或说 $\boldsymbol{A}$ 相似于 $\boldsymbol{B}$，记作 $\boldsymbol{A}\sim\boldsymbol{B}$，可逆矩阵 $\boldsymbol{P}$ 称为相似变换矩阵。

（二）相似矩阵的性质

(1)$\boldsymbol{A}\sim\boldsymbol{A}$。

(2)$\boldsymbol{A}\sim\boldsymbol{B}$，则 $\boldsymbol{B}\sim\boldsymbol{A}$。

(3)$\boldsymbol{A}\sim\boldsymbol{B}$ 且 $\boldsymbol{B}\sim\boldsymbol{C}$，则 $\boldsymbol{A}\sim\boldsymbol{C}$。

(4)设 n 阶方阵 A 和 B 相似，则有：

①$R(\boldsymbol{A})=R(\boldsymbol{B})$；

②$|\boldsymbol{A}|=|\boldsymbol{B}|$；

③$\boldsymbol{A}$ 和 $\boldsymbol{B}$ 的特征多项式相同，即 $|\lambda\boldsymbol{E}-\boldsymbol{A}|=|\lambda\boldsymbol{E}-\boldsymbol{B}|$；

④$\boldsymbol{A}$ 和 $\boldsymbol{B}$ 的特征值相同。

八、矩阵的相似对角化

(1)对 n 阶方阵 $\boldsymbol{A}$，若存在可逆矩阵 $\boldsymbol{P}$，使

$$\boldsymbol{P}^{-1}\boldsymbol{A}\boldsymbol{P}=\begin{bmatrix}\lambda_1 & & & \\ & \lambda_2 & & \\ & & \ddots & \\ & & & \lambda_n\end{bmatrix}\text{（对角矩阵）} \tag{1-8-8}$$

则称 $\boldsymbol{A}$ 相似于对角矩阵，也称矩阵 $\boldsymbol{A}$ 可相似对角化。

(2)n 阶矩阵 $\boldsymbol{A}$ 相似于对角矩阵 $\boldsymbol{\Lambda}$ 的充要条件，是 $\boldsymbol{A}$ 有 n 个线性无关的特征向量。

若有可逆矩阵 $\boldsymbol{P}$，使得

$$\boldsymbol{P}^{-1}\boldsymbol{A}\boldsymbol{P}=\begin{bmatrix}\lambda_1 & & & \\ & \lambda_2 & & \\ & & \ddots & \\ & & & \lambda_n\end{bmatrix}$$

则 $\lambda_1,\lambda_2,\cdots,\lambda_n$ 为 $\boldsymbol{A}$ 的 n 个特征值，而矩阵 $\boldsymbol{P}$ 的 n 个列向量是矩阵 $\boldsymbol{A}$ 的对应于这些特征值 $\lambda_1,\lambda_2,\cdots,\lambda_n$ 的 n 个线性无关的特征向量。

还可以得到下面结论：

(1)如果 n 阶方阵 $\boldsymbol{A}$ 有 n 个不同的特征值，则 $\boldsymbol{A}$ 一定可以相似对角化。

(2)如果 $\boldsymbol{A}$ 有重特征值，且对每一个重特征值，其重数和对应的线性无关的特征向量的个数都相等，则 $\boldsymbol{A}$ 一定可以相似对角化。

(3)如果对应方阵 $\boldsymbol{A}$ 的特征值 λ 线性无关的特征向量的个数小于该特征值 λ 的重数，造成方阵 $\boldsymbol{A}$ 的线性无关的特征向量个数小于 n，从而 $\boldsymbol{A}$ 不可相似对角化。

(4)实对称矩阵的相似对角化：

如果 n 阶方阵 $\boldsymbol{A}$ 等于它的转置矩阵，即 $\boldsymbol{A}=\boldsymbol{A}^{\mathrm{T}}$，则称 $\boldsymbol{A}$ 为对称矩阵。所有元素为实数的对称矩阵，称为实对称矩阵。

实对称矩阵的特征值、特征向量有下列性质：

(1)实对称矩阵的特征值一定都是实数。

(2)在实数范围内 n 阶实对称矩阵有 n 个特征值(重根按重数计算)。

(3)实对称矩阵对应于不同特征值的特征向量必正交。

前面已讲 n 阶矩阵 $\boldsymbol{A}$ 满足 $\boldsymbol{A}^{\mathrm{T}}\boldsymbol{A}=\boldsymbol{A}\boldsymbol{A}^{\mathrm{T}}=\boldsymbol{E}$，则称 $\boldsymbol{A}$ 为正交矩阵。由此定义可见正交矩阵是可逆矩阵。若矩阵 $\boldsymbol{A}$ 是正交矩阵，那么 $\boldsymbol{A}^{-1}=\boldsymbol{A}^{\mathrm{T}}$。

定理：设 $\boldsymbol{A}$ 为 n 阶实对称矩阵，则必存在正交矩阵 $\boldsymbol{P}$，使

$$\boldsymbol{P}^{-1}\boldsymbol{A}\boldsymbol{P}=\boldsymbol{P}^{\mathrm{T}}\boldsymbol{A}\boldsymbol{P}=\boldsymbol{\Lambda}=\begin{bmatrix}\lambda_1 & & & \\ & \lambda_2 & & \\ & & \ddots & \\ & & & \lambda_n\end{bmatrix}$$

其中 $\lambda_1,\lambda_2,\cdots,\lambda_n$ 是 $\boldsymbol{A}$ 的特征值。

给定实对称矩阵 $\boldsymbol{A}$，求正交矩阵 $\boldsymbol{P}$ 使其相似对角化的步骤：

①设 $|\lambda\boldsymbol{E}-\boldsymbol{A}|=0$，解特征方程求出 $\boldsymbol{A}$ 的全部特征值 $\lambda_1,\lambda_2,\cdots,\lambda_n$（做完这一步，就已经求

出 $\boldsymbol{A}$ 的相似对角矩阵 $\boldsymbol{\Lambda}$）。

②对每个特征值 $\lambda_i(i=1,2,\cdots,n)$，代入 $(\lambda\boldsymbol{E}-\boldsymbol{A})\boldsymbol{x}=\boldsymbol{0}$，解齐次线性方程组 $(\lambda_i\boldsymbol{E}-\boldsymbol{A})\boldsymbol{x}=\boldsymbol{0}$，求出对应的特征向量。如果特征值是单根，就对应一个特征向量，如果特征值是 K 重根，就对应 K 个线性无关的特征向量。

③对于重的特征根，对它所对应的那组线性无关特征向量进行施密特正交化再单位化（或称正交规范化）。

④对特征值是单根，要对求出的这个特征向量单位化。

⑤所有经过单位化、正交规范化的特征向量 $\boldsymbol{q}_1,\boldsymbol{q}_2,\cdots,\boldsymbol{q}_n$（依次对应特征值 $\lambda_1,\lambda_2,\cdots\lambda_n$）构成一个正交向量组。

⑥将所有正交的特征向量按列排成一个矩阵，令其为 $\boldsymbol{P}=(\boldsymbol{q}_1,\boldsymbol{q}_2,\cdots,\boldsymbol{q}_n)$，那么 $\boldsymbol{P}$ 是正交矩阵，而且有 $\boldsymbol{P}^{-1}\boldsymbol{A}\boldsymbol{P}=\boldsymbol{P}^{\mathrm{T}}\boldsymbol{A}\boldsymbol{P}=\boldsymbol{\Lambda}=\begin{bmatrix}\lambda_1 & & & \\ & \lambda_2 & & \\ & & \ddots & \\ & & & \lambda_n\end{bmatrix}$。

即注意：$\boldsymbol{P}=(\boldsymbol{q}_1,\boldsymbol{q}_2,\cdots,\boldsymbol{q}_n)$ 中，$\boldsymbol{q}_1,\boldsymbol{q}_2,\cdots,\boldsymbol{q}_n$ 的排列顺序应和特征值 $\lambda_1,\lambda_2,\cdots,\lambda_n$ 的排列顺序一致，即 $\boldsymbol{q}_i(i=1,\cdots,n)$ 恰好是 λ_i 的特征向量。

【例 1-8-35】 已知矩阵 $\boldsymbol{A}=\begin{bmatrix}1 & -1 & 1\\ 2 & 4 & -2\\ -3 & -3 & 5\end{bmatrix}$ 与 $\boldsymbol{B}=\begin{bmatrix}\lambda & 0 & 0\\ 0 & 2 & 0\\ 0 & 0 & 2\end{bmatrix}$ 相似，则 λ 等于：

A. 6　　B. 5　　C. 4　　D. 14

解　矩阵相似有相同的特征多项式、有相同的特征值。

方法 1：

$$|\lambda\boldsymbol{E}-\boldsymbol{A}|=\begin{vmatrix}\lambda-1 & 1 & -1\\ -2 & \lambda-4 & 2\\ 3 & 3 & \lambda-5\end{vmatrix}\xrightarrow{(-3)r_1+r_3}\begin{vmatrix}\lambda-1 & 1 & -1\\ -2 & \lambda-4 & 2\\ -3\lambda+6 & 0 & \lambda-2\end{vmatrix}\xrightarrow{-(\lambda-4)r_1+r_2}$$

$$\begin{vmatrix}\lambda-1 & 1 & -1\\ -\lambda^2+5\lambda-6 & 0 & \lambda-2\\ -3\lambda+6 & 0 & \lambda-2\end{vmatrix}=(-1)^{1+2}\begin{vmatrix}-(\lambda-2)(\lambda-3) & \lambda-2\\ -3(\lambda-2) & \lambda-2\end{vmatrix}$$

$$=(\lambda-2)(\lambda-2)\begin{vmatrix}+(\lambda-3) & 1\\ 3 & 1\end{vmatrix}=(\lambda-2)(\lambda-2)[+(\lambda-3)-3]$$

$$=(\lambda-2)(\lambda-2)(\lambda-6)$$

特征值为 2,2,6；矩阵 $\boldsymbol{B}$ 中 $\lambda=6$。

方法 2：因为 $\boldsymbol{A}\sim\boldsymbol{B}$，所以 $\boldsymbol{A}$ 与 $\boldsymbol{B}$ 有相同特征值，设矩阵 $\boldsymbol{A}$ 的特征值为 $\lambda_1,\lambda_2,\lambda_3$，由性质可知：$\lambda_1+\lambda_2+\lambda_3=1+4+5=10$。故 $\lambda_1+\lambda_2+\lambda_3=\lambda+2+2=10$，得 $\lambda=6$。

答案：A

九、合同矩阵的概念和性质

（一）合同矩阵

设 $\boldsymbol{A}$、$\boldsymbol{B}$ 为 n 阶方阵，若存在 n 阶可逆矩阵 $\boldsymbol{P}$，使 $\boldsymbol{P}^{\mathrm{T}}\boldsymbol{A}\boldsymbol{P}=\boldsymbol{B}$，则称 $\boldsymbol{A}$ 合同于 $\boldsymbol{B}$，记作 $\boldsymbol{A}\simeq\boldsymbol{B}$。

(二)合同矩阵的性质

合同是方阵之间的又一个等价关系,它具有下列性质:

(1)自反性:$\boldsymbol{A}\simeq\boldsymbol{A}$。

(2)对称性:$\boldsymbol{A}\simeq\boldsymbol{B}$,则 $\boldsymbol{B}\simeq\boldsymbol{A}$。

(3)传递性:$\boldsymbol{A}\simeq\boldsymbol{B}$ 且 $\boldsymbol{B}\simeq\boldsymbol{C}$,则 $\boldsymbol{A}\simeq\boldsymbol{C}$。

合同变换不改变矩阵的秩。

(4)任何一个实对称矩阵 $\boldsymbol{A}$ 都合同于对角矩阵,即存在正交矩阵 $\boldsymbol{P}$,使得

$$\boldsymbol{P}^{\mathrm{T}}\boldsymbol{A}\boldsymbol{P}=\begin{bmatrix}\lambda_1 & & & \\ & \lambda_2 & & \\ & & \ddots & \\ & & & \lambda_n\end{bmatrix}\text{(其中 }\lambda_1,\lambda_2,\cdots,\lambda_n\text{ 为实对称矩阵 }\boldsymbol{A}\text{ 的特征值)} \tag{1-8-9}$$

十、二次型

(一)二次型定义

含有 n 个变量 $x_1,x_2,\cdots,x_n$ 的二次齐次函数(即每项都是二次的多项式)。

$f(x_1,x_2,\cdots,x_n)=a_{11}x_1^2+a_{22}x_2^2+\cdots+a_{nn}x_n^2+2a_{12}x_1x_2+2a_{13}x_1x_3+\cdots+2a_{n-1,n}x_{n-1}x_n$ 称为一个 n 元二次型,简称二次型。当 a_{ij} 都是实数时,称为实二次型。

(二)二次型的矩阵表示

$$\begin{aligned}f(x_1,x_2,\cdots,x_n)&=x_1(a_{11}x_1+a_{12}x_2+\cdots+a_{1n}x_n)+x_2(a_{21}x_1+a_{22}x_2+\cdots+a_{2n}x_n)+\cdots+\\&\quad x_n(a_{n1}x_1+a_{n2}x_2+\cdots+a_{nn}x_n)\\&=(x_1,x_2,\cdots,x_n)\begin{bmatrix}a_{11}x_1+a_{12}x_2+\cdots+a_{1n}x_n\\a_{21}x_1+a_{22}x_2+\cdots+a_{2n}x_n\\\vdots\\a_{n1}x_1+a_{n2}x_2+\cdots+a_{nn}x_n\end{bmatrix}\\&=(x_1,x_2,\cdots,x_n)\begin{bmatrix}a_{11}&a_{12}&\cdots&a_{1n}\\a_{21}&a_{22}&\cdots&a_{2n}\\\vdots&\vdots&&\vdots\\a_{n1}&a_{n2}&\cdots&a_{nn}\end{bmatrix}\begin{bmatrix}x_1\\x_2\\\vdots\\x_n\end{bmatrix}\end{aligned} \tag{1-8-10}$$

记 $$\boldsymbol{A}=\begin{bmatrix}a_{11}&a_{12}&\cdots&a_{1n}\\a_{21}&a_{22}&\cdots&a_{2n}\\\vdots&\vdots&&\vdots\\a_{n1}&a_{n2}&\cdots&a_{nn}\end{bmatrix},\boldsymbol{x}=\begin{bmatrix}x_1\\x_2\\\vdots\\x_n\end{bmatrix}$$

则二次型可记作

$$f=\boldsymbol{x}^{\mathrm{T}}\boldsymbol{A}\boldsymbol{x}$$

其中 $\boldsymbol{A}$ 为实对称矩阵。

对称矩阵 $\boldsymbol{A}$ 叫做二次型 f 的矩阵。$\boldsymbol{A}$ 的秩叫做二次型 f 的秩。

【例 1-8-36】 二次型 $f=x^2-3z^2-4xy+yz$ 用矩阵记号表示,就是

$$f=(x,y,z)\begin{bmatrix}1 & -2 & 0\\ -2 & 0 & \frac{1}{2}\\ 0 & \frac{1}{2} & -3\end{bmatrix}\begin{bmatrix}x\\ y\\ z\end{bmatrix}$$

任给一个实二次型,就唯一地确定一个实对称矩阵;反之,任给一个实对称矩阵,也可唯一地确定一个实二次型。一个实二次型和一个实对称矩阵是一一对应的。

(三)二次型的标准型

定义:形如 $f=\varphi_1x_1^2+\varphi_2x_2^2+\cdots+\varphi_nx_n^2$ 的二次型称为二次型的标准型。在标准型中,如果平方项的系数 $\varphi_i(i=1,2,\cdots,n)$ 为 1,−1 或 0,即 $f=x_1^2+x_2^2+\cdots+x_p^2-x_{p+1}^2-\cdots-x_r^2$,则称其为二次型的规范形。

正交变换定义:如果 $\boldsymbol{P}$ 为正交矩阵,则线性变换 $\boldsymbol{x}=\boldsymbol{P}\boldsymbol{y}$ 称为正交变换。

定理:任给实二次型 $f(x_1,x_2,\cdots,x_n)=\boldsymbol{x}^{\mathrm{T}}\boldsymbol{A}\boldsymbol{x}$(其中 $\boldsymbol{A}=\boldsymbol{A}^{\mathrm{T}}$),一定有正交变换 $\boldsymbol{x}=\boldsymbol{P}\boldsymbol{y}$($\boldsymbol{P}^{\mathrm{T}}=\boldsymbol{P}^{-1}$),使 $f=\lambda_1y_1^2+\lambda_2y_2^2+\cdots+\lambda_ny_n^2$。

其中 $\lambda_1,\lambda_2,\cdots,\lambda_n$ 是 $\boldsymbol{A}$ 的特征值,而 $\boldsymbol{P}$ 的列向量就是对应于 $\lambda_1,\lambda_2,\cdots,\lambda_n$ 的两两正交的单位特征向量。

用正交变换化实二次型为标准形的计算步骤:

(1)写出二次型的矩阵 $\boldsymbol{A}$。

(2)求出矩阵 $\boldsymbol{A}$ 的特征值 $\lambda_1,\lambda_2,\cdots,\lambda_n$。

(3)求特征值对应的特征向量。

(4)将 k 重特征值对应的 k 个线性无关的特征向量作施密特正交化再单位化(或说正交规范化),得到正交的 k 个单位特征向量。

(5)将单特征值对应的一个特征向量单位化。

(6)将这些向量按 $\lambda_1,\lambda_2,\cdots,\lambda_n$ 对应的顺序排列成矩阵,得到正交矩阵 $\boldsymbol{P}$,这时有 $\boldsymbol{P}^{\mathrm{T}}\boldsymbol{A}\boldsymbol{P}=\boldsymbol{P}^{-1}\boldsymbol{A}\boldsymbol{P}=\boldsymbol{\Lambda}$,其中 $\boldsymbol{\Lambda}$ 是对角矩阵,它由 $\boldsymbol{A}$ 的特征值构成,即 $\boldsymbol{\Lambda}=\begin{bmatrix}\lambda_1 & & & \\ & \lambda_2 & & \\ & & \ddots & \\ & & & \lambda_n\end{bmatrix}$。

(7)写出正交变换 $\boldsymbol{x}=\boldsymbol{P}\boldsymbol{y}$,代入二次型,得到 $f=\boldsymbol{x}^{\mathrm{T}}\boldsymbol{A}\boldsymbol{x}=(\boldsymbol{P}\boldsymbol{y})^{\mathrm{T}}\boldsymbol{A}\boldsymbol{P}\boldsymbol{y}=\boldsymbol{y}^{\mathrm{T}}\boldsymbol{P}^{\mathrm{T}}\boldsymbol{A}\boldsymbol{P}\boldsymbol{y}=\boldsymbol{y}^{\mathrm{T}}\boldsymbol{\Lambda}\boldsymbol{y}=\lambda_1y_1^2+\lambda_2y_2^2+\cdots+\lambda_ny_n^2$。

(四)惯性定理

设有实二次型 $f=\boldsymbol{x}^{\mathrm{T}}\boldsymbol{A}\boldsymbol{x}$,它的秩为 r,有两个实的可逆变换 $\boldsymbol{x}=\boldsymbol{P}\boldsymbol{y}$ 及 $\boldsymbol{x}=\boldsymbol{Q}\boldsymbol{z}$($\boldsymbol{P},\boldsymbol{Q}$ 为与 $\boldsymbol{A}$ 同阶的可逆阵),使

$$f=k_1y_1^2+k_2y_2^2+\cdots+k_ry_r^2 \qquad (k_i\neq 0)$$

及

$$f=\lambda_1z_1^2+\lambda_2z_2^2+\cdots+\lambda_rz_r^2 \qquad (\lambda_i\neq 0)$$

则 $k_1,\cdots,k_r$ 中正数的个数与 $\lambda_1,\cdots,\lambda_r$ 中正数的个数相等,这个定理称为惯性定理。

在二次型的标准形中,尽管实二次型 $f(x_1,x_2,\cdots,x_u)$ 的标准形不唯一,但标准形中正平方项的个数、负平方项的个数是唯一确定的,分别称为二次型的正惯性指数和负惯性指数。

在实二次型中,二次型的秩 r 可反映 f 通过可逆线性变换化为标准型或规范型后非零平方项的个数,正惯性指数的数量反映 f 通过可逆线性变换化为标准型或规范型后这些非零平

方项中正项的个数，负惯性指数反映负项的个数。

（五）二次型及其矩阵的正定性

（1）设有实二次型$f(\boldsymbol{x})=\boldsymbol{x}^{\mathrm{T}}\boldsymbol{A}\boldsymbol{x}$，如果对任何$\boldsymbol{x}\neq\boldsymbol{0}$，都有$f(\boldsymbol{x})>0$，则称$f$为正定二次型，并称实对称矩阵$\boldsymbol{A}$是正定矩阵；如果对任何$\boldsymbol{x}\neq\boldsymbol{0}$，都有$f(\boldsymbol{x})<0$，则称$f$为负定二次型，并称实对称矩阵$\boldsymbol{A}$是负定矩阵。

（2）判断二次型是正定的几个充要条件：

①实二次型$f=\boldsymbol{x}^{\mathrm{T}}\boldsymbol{A}\boldsymbol{x}$为正定的充分必要条件是正惯性指数等于未知数的个数。

②实二次型$f=\boldsymbol{x}^{\mathrm{T}}\boldsymbol{A}\boldsymbol{x}$为正定的充分必要条件是对称矩阵$\boldsymbol{A}$是正定的。

③实二次型$f=\boldsymbol{x}^{\mathrm{T}}\boldsymbol{A}\boldsymbol{x}$为正定的充分必要条件是对称矩阵$\boldsymbol{A}$的特征值全为正。

④实二次型$f=\boldsymbol{x}^{\mathrm{T}}\boldsymbol{A}\boldsymbol{x}$为正定的充分必要条件是对称矩阵$\boldsymbol{A}$合同于单位矩阵。

⑤实二次型$f=\boldsymbol{x}^{\mathrm{T}}\boldsymbol{A}\boldsymbol{x}$的对称矩阵$\boldsymbol{A}$为正定的充分必要条件是各阶顺序主子式都为正，即

$$a_{11}>0,\begin{vmatrix}a_{11}&a_{12}\\a_{21}&a_{22}\end{vmatrix}>0,\cdots,\begin{vmatrix}a_{11}&\cdots&a_{1n}\\\vdots&&\vdots\\a_{n1}&\cdots&a_{nn}\end{vmatrix}>0$$

实对称矩阵$\boldsymbol{A}$为负定的充分必要条件是：奇数阶主子式为负，而偶数阶主子式为正，即

$$(-1)^r\begin{vmatrix}a_{11}&\cdots&a_{1r}\\\vdots&&\vdots\\a_{r1}&\cdots&a_{rr}\end{vmatrix}>0\qquad(r=1,2,\cdots,n)$$

【例 1-8-37】 若实二次型$f(x_1,x_2,x_3)=x_1^2+4x_2^2+2x_3^2+2tx_1+2x_1x_3$是正定的，则$t$应满足：

A. $-2<t<2$　　B. $-\sqrt{2}<t<\sqrt{2}$　　C. $-\sqrt{2}<t<2$　　D. $-2<t<\sqrt{2}$

解　二次型f的矩阵为$\begin{bmatrix}1&t&1\\t&4&0\\1&0&2\end{bmatrix}$

要使二次型正定，其各阶顺序主子式应满足

$$|\boldsymbol{A}_1|=1>0,|\boldsymbol{A}_2|=\begin{vmatrix}1&t\\t&4\end{vmatrix}=4-t^2>0$$

$$|\boldsymbol{A}_3|=\begin{vmatrix}1&t&1\\t&4&0\\1&0&2\end{vmatrix}=4-2t^2>0$$

解不等式组$\begin{cases}4-t^2>0\Rightarrow t^2<4\Rightarrow-2<t<2\\4-2t^2>0\Rightarrow t^2<2\Rightarrow-\sqrt{2}<t<\sqrt{2}\end{cases}$

取公共部分得：$-\sqrt{2}<t<\sqrt{2}$。

答案：B

【例 1-8-38】 判别二次型$f_1=2x_1^2+3x_2^2+x_3^2+2\sqrt{2}x_1x_2$，$f_2=-x_1^2-x_2^2-3x_3^2-2x_1x_3-2x_2x_3$是正定的，还是负定的？

解　(1) $f_1=(x_1,x_2,x_3)\begin{bmatrix}2&\sqrt{2}&0\\\sqrt{2}&3&0\\0&0&1\end{bmatrix}\begin{bmatrix}x_1\\x_2\\x_3\end{bmatrix}$

$$D_1=2>0,D_2=\begin{vmatrix}2&\sqrt{2}\\\sqrt{2}&3\end{vmatrix}=6-2>0,D_3=\begin{vmatrix}2&\sqrt{2}&0\\\sqrt{2}&3&0\\0&0&1\end{vmatrix}=1\times\begin{vmatrix}2&\sqrt{2}\\\sqrt{2}&3\end{vmatrix}>0$$

f_1 是正定的。

(2) $f_2=(x_1,x_2,x_3)\begin{bmatrix}-1&0&-1\\0&-1&-1\\-1&-1&-3\end{bmatrix}\begin{bmatrix}x_1\\x_2\\x_3\end{bmatrix}$

$$D_1=-1<0,D_2=\begin{vmatrix}-1&0\\0&-1\end{vmatrix}=1>0,D_3=\begin{vmatrix}-1&0&-1\\0&-1&-1\\-1&-1&-3\end{vmatrix}=-1<0$$

f_2 是负定的。

【例 1-8-39】 实二次型 $f(x_1,x_2,x_3)=x_1^2+2x_1x_2+tx_2^2+3x_3^2$，当 $t=($　　$)$时，f 的秩为 2。

A. 0　　B. 1　　C. 2　　D. 3

解　实二次型对应的矩阵　$\boldsymbol{A}=\begin{bmatrix}1&1&0\\1&t&0\\0&0&3\end{bmatrix}$

对 $\boldsymbol{A}$ 施行初等行变换

$$\begin{bmatrix}1&1&0\\1&t&0\\0&0&3\end{bmatrix}\longrightarrow\begin{bmatrix}1&1&0\\0&t-1&0\\0&0&3\end{bmatrix}$$

因为 $\boldsymbol{R}(\mathbf{A})=2$，故 $t-1=0,t=1$

答案:B

【例 1-8-40】 已知三元二次型 $f=ax_1^2+ax_2^2+x_3^2-2ax_2x_3$，$a$ 满足以下哪个条件时，f 是正定二次型。

A. $a>1$　　B. $0<a<1$　　C. $-1<a<0$　　D. $a>0$

解

$$f=ax_1^2+ax_2^2+x_3^2-2ax_2x_3=(x_1\ x_2\ x_3)\begin{bmatrix}a&0&0\\0&a&-a\\0&-a&1\end{bmatrix}\begin{bmatrix}x_1\\x_2\\x_3\end{bmatrix}$$

二次型的矩阵　$\boldsymbol{A}=\begin{bmatrix}a&0&0\\0&a&-a\\0&-a&1\end{bmatrix}$

f 为正定的充要条件：

$$a>0,\begin{vmatrix}a&0\\0&a\end{vmatrix}>0,\begin{vmatrix}a&0&0\\0&a&-a\\0&-a&1\end{vmatrix}>0$$

即 $\begin{cases}a>0\\a^2>0\\a^2(1-a)>0\end{cases}$ $\Rightarrow$ 公共解　$0<a<1$

答案:B

习　题

1-8-1　行列式 $D_1=\begin{vmatrix}1&3&1\\2&2&3\\3&1&5\end{vmatrix}$，$D_2=\begin{vmatrix}\lambda&0&1\\0&\lambda-1&1\\1&0&\lambda\end{vmatrix}$，若 $D_1=D_2$，则 λ 的值为(　　)。

A. 0,1　　B. 0,2　　C. −1,1　　D. −1,2

1-8-2　已知行列式 $\begin{vmatrix} & & & \lambda_1\\ & & \lambda_2 & \\ & \iddots & & \\ \lambda_n & & & \end{vmatrix}$，其中 $\lambda_i\neq0(i=1,2,\cdots,n)$，则行列式的值为(　　)。

A. $\lambda_1\lambda_2\lambda_3\cdots\lambda_n$　　B. 0

C. $-\lambda_1\lambda_2\cdots\lambda_n$　　D. $(-1)^{\frac{n(n-1)}{2}}\lambda_1\lambda_2\cdots\lambda_n$

1-8-3　设 $\boldsymbol{A}$ 是 4×5 矩阵，$\boldsymbol{B}$ 是 5×4 矩阵，则下列结论中不正确的是(　　)。

A. $|\boldsymbol{AB}|\neq0$　　B. $|\boldsymbol{A}^{\mathrm{T}}\boldsymbol{B}^{\mathrm{T}}|$ 有意义　　C. $R(\boldsymbol{A})=R(\boldsymbol{A}^{\mathrm{T}})\leqslant4$　　D. $R(\boldsymbol{AB})\leqslant4$

1-8-4　已知 $\boldsymbol{\alpha}_1=\begin{bmatrix}2\\0\\0\end{bmatrix}$，$\boldsymbol{\alpha}_2=\begin{bmatrix}0\\0\\-3\end{bmatrix}$，下列向量中是 $\boldsymbol{\alpha}_1,\boldsymbol{\alpha}_2$ 的线性组合的是(　　)。

A. $\boldsymbol{\beta}=\begin{bmatrix}-3\\0\\4\end{bmatrix}$　　B. $\boldsymbol{\beta}=\begin{bmatrix}0\\1\\0\end{bmatrix}$　　C. $\boldsymbol{\beta}=\begin{bmatrix}1\\1\\0\end{bmatrix}$　　D. $\boldsymbol{\beta}=\begin{bmatrix}0\\-1\\1\end{bmatrix}$

1-8-5　设向量组的秩为 r，则(　　)。

A. 该向量组所含向量的个数必大于 r

B. 该向量组中任何 r 个向量必线性无关，任何 $r+1$ 个向量必线性相关

C. 该向量组中有 r 个向量线性无关，有 $r+1$ 个向量线性相关

D. 该向量组中有 r 个向量线性无关，任何 $r+1$ 个向量必线性相关

1-8-6　利用初等行变换求矩阵 $\begin{bmatrix}1&1&2&2&1\\0&2&1&5&-1\\2&0&3&-1&3\\1&1&0&4&-1\end{bmatrix}$ 的列向量组的一个最大无关组为(　　)。

A. 第 1、2 列　　B. 第 2、3 列　　C. 第 4、5 列　　D. 第 1、2、3 列

1-8-7　设 $\boldsymbol{A}=\begin{bmatrix}a_1b_1&a_1b_2&\cdots&a_1b_n\\a_2b_1&a_2b_2&\cdots&a_2b_n\\\vdots&\vdots&&\vdots\\a_nb_1&a_nb_2&\cdots&a_nb_n\end{bmatrix}$，其中 $a_i\neq0,b_i\neq0(i=1,2,\cdots,n)$，则矩阵 $\boldsymbol{A}$ 的秩等于(　　)。

A. n　　B. 0　　C. 1　　D. 2

1-8-8　设 $\boldsymbol{\alpha}_1,\boldsymbol{\alpha}_2,\boldsymbol{\alpha}_3$ 是四元非齐次线性方程组 $\boldsymbol{Ax}=\boldsymbol{b}$ 的三个解向量，且 $R(\boldsymbol{A})=3$，$\boldsymbol{\alpha}_1=(1,$

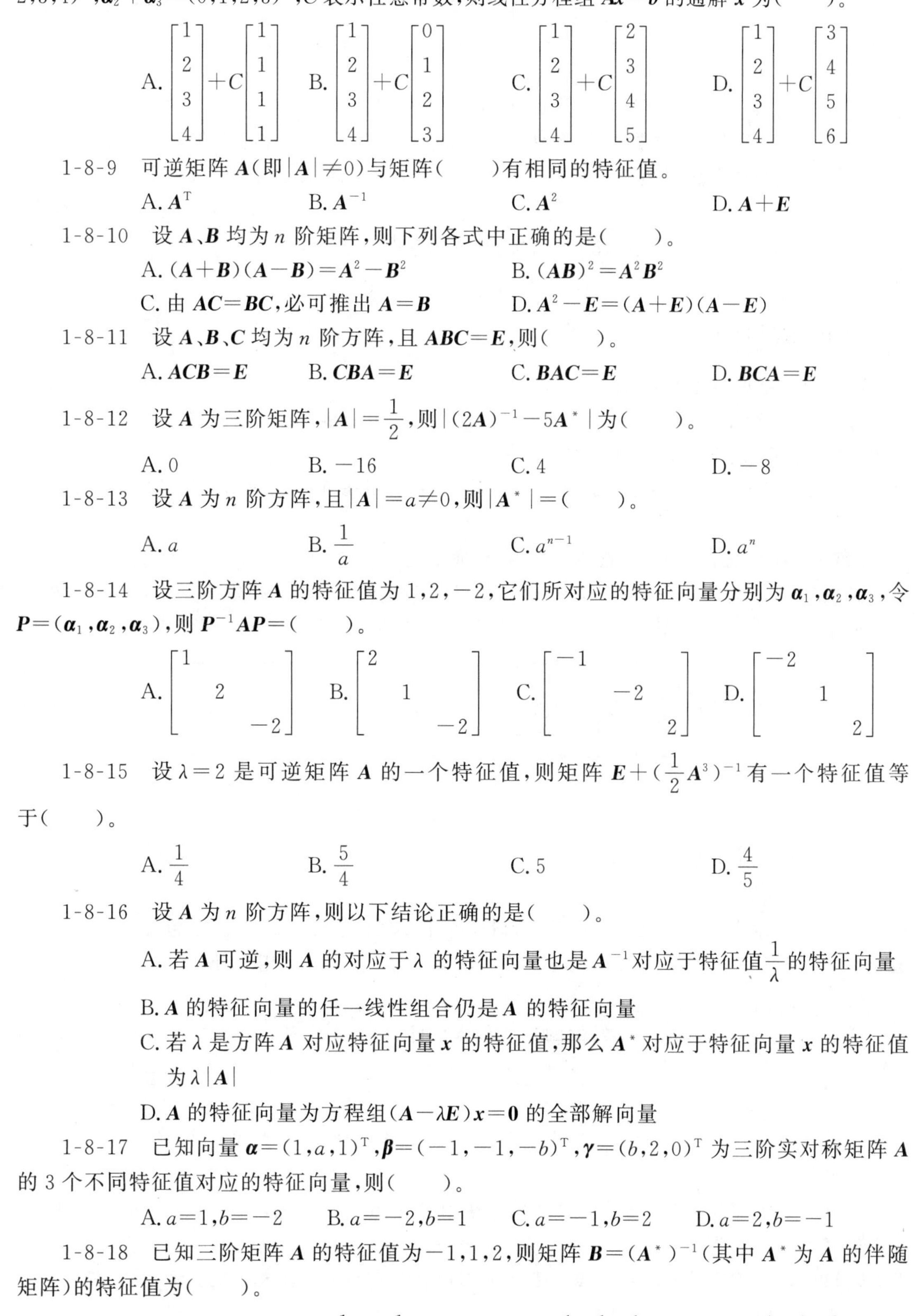

2,3,4)^{T},$\boldsymbol{\alpha}_2+\boldsymbol{\alpha}_3=(0,1,2,3)^{\mathrm{T}}$,$C$ 表示任意常数,则线性方程组 $\boldsymbol{Ax}=\boldsymbol{b}$ 的通解 $\boldsymbol{x}$ 为(　　)。

A. $\begin{bmatrix}1\\2\\3\\4\end{bmatrix}+C\begin{bmatrix}1\\1\\1\\1\end{bmatrix}$　　B. $\begin{bmatrix}1\\2\\3\\4\end{bmatrix}+C\begin{bmatrix}0\\1\\2\\3\end{bmatrix}$　　C. $\begin{bmatrix}1\\2\\3\\4\end{bmatrix}+C\begin{bmatrix}2\\3\\4\\5\end{bmatrix}$　　D. $\begin{bmatrix}1\\2\\3\\4\end{bmatrix}+C\begin{bmatrix}3\\4\\5\\6\end{bmatrix}$

1-8-9　可逆矩阵 $\boldsymbol{A}$(即 $|\boldsymbol{A}|\neq 0$)与矩阵(　　)有相同的特征值。

A. $\boldsymbol{A}^{\mathrm{T}}$　　B. $\boldsymbol{A}^{-1}$　　C. $\boldsymbol{A}^2$　　D. $\boldsymbol{A}+\boldsymbol{E}$

1-8-10　设 $\boldsymbol{A}$、$\boldsymbol{B}$ 均为 n 阶矩阵,则下列各式中正确的是(　　)。

A. $(\boldsymbol{A}+\boldsymbol{B})(\boldsymbol{A}-\boldsymbol{B})=\boldsymbol{A}^2-\boldsymbol{B}^2$　　B. $(\boldsymbol{AB})^2=\boldsymbol{A}^2\boldsymbol{B}^2$

C. 由 $\boldsymbol{AC}=\boldsymbol{BC}$,必可推出 $\boldsymbol{A}=\boldsymbol{B}$　　D. $\boldsymbol{A}^2-\boldsymbol{E}=(\boldsymbol{A}+\boldsymbol{E})(\boldsymbol{A}-\boldsymbol{E})$

1-8-11　设 $\boldsymbol{A}$、$\boldsymbol{B}$、$\boldsymbol{C}$ 均为 n 阶方阵,且 $\boldsymbol{ABC}=\boldsymbol{E}$,则(　　)。

A. $\boldsymbol{ACB}=\boldsymbol{E}$　　B. $\boldsymbol{CBA}=\boldsymbol{E}$　　C. $\boldsymbol{BAC}=\boldsymbol{E}$　　D. $\boldsymbol{BCA}=\boldsymbol{E}$

1-8-12　设 $\boldsymbol{A}$ 为三阶矩阵,$|\boldsymbol{A}|=\dfrac{1}{2}$,则 $|(2\boldsymbol{A})^{-1}-5\boldsymbol{A}^*|$ 为(　　)。

A. 0　　B. -16　　C. 4　　D. -8

1-8-13　设 $\boldsymbol{A}$ 为 n 阶方阵,且 $|\boldsymbol{A}|=a\neq 0$,则 $|\boldsymbol{A}^*|=$(　　)。

A. a　　B. $\dfrac{1}{a}$　　C. a^{n-1}　　D. a^n

1-8-14　设三阶方阵 $\boldsymbol{A}$ 的特征值为 1,2,-2,它们所对应的特征向量分别为 $\boldsymbol{\alpha}_1,\boldsymbol{\alpha}_2,\boldsymbol{\alpha}_3$,令 $\boldsymbol{P}=(\boldsymbol{\alpha}_1,\boldsymbol{\alpha}_2,\boldsymbol{\alpha}_3)$,则 $\boldsymbol{P}^{-1}\boldsymbol{AP}=$(　　)。

A. $\begin{bmatrix}1&&\\&2&\\&&-2\end{bmatrix}$　　B. $\begin{bmatrix}2&&\\&1&\\&&-2\end{bmatrix}$　　C. $\begin{bmatrix}-1&&\\&-2&\\&&2\end{bmatrix}$　　D. $\begin{bmatrix}-2&&\\&1&\\&&2\end{bmatrix}$

1-8-15　设 $\lambda=2$ 是可逆矩阵 $\boldsymbol{A}$ 的一个特征值,则矩阵 $\boldsymbol{E}+(\dfrac{1}{2}\boldsymbol{A}^3)^{-1}$ 有一个特征值等于(　　)。

A. $\dfrac{1}{4}$　　B. $\dfrac{5}{4}$　　C. 5　　D. $\dfrac{4}{5}$

1-8-16　设 $\boldsymbol{A}$ 为 n 阶方阵,则以下结论正确的是(　　)。

A. 若 $\boldsymbol{A}$ 可逆,则 $\boldsymbol{A}$ 的对应于 λ 的特征向量也是 $\boldsymbol{A}^{-1}$ 对应于特征值 $\dfrac{1}{\lambda}$ 的特征向量

B. $\boldsymbol{A}$ 的特征向量的任一线性组合仍是 $\boldsymbol{A}$ 的特征向量

C. 若 λ 是方阵 $\boldsymbol{A}$ 对应特征向量 $\boldsymbol{x}$ 的特征值,那么 $\boldsymbol{A}^*$ 对应于特征向量 $\boldsymbol{x}$ 的特征值为 $\lambda|\boldsymbol{A}|$

D. $\boldsymbol{A}$ 的特征向量为方程组 $(\boldsymbol{A}-\lambda\boldsymbol{E})\boldsymbol{x}=\boldsymbol{0}$ 的全部解向量

1-8-17　已知向量 $\boldsymbol{\alpha}=(1,a,1)^{\mathrm{T}}$,$\boldsymbol{\beta}=(-1,-1,-b)^{\mathrm{T}}$,$\boldsymbol{\gamma}=(b,2,0)^{\mathrm{T}}$ 为三阶实对称矩阵 $\boldsymbol{A}$ 的 3 个不同特征值对应的特征向量,则(　　)。

A. $a=1,b=-2$　　B. $a=-2,b=1$　　C. $a=-1,b=2$　　D. $a=2,b=-1$

1-8-18　已知三阶矩阵 $\boldsymbol{A}$ 的特征值为 -1,1,2,则矩阵 $\boldsymbol{B}=(\boldsymbol{A}^*)^{-1}$(其中 $\boldsymbol{A}^*$ 为 $\boldsymbol{A}$ 的伴随矩阵)的特征值为(　　)。

A. 1,-1,-2　　B. $\dfrac{1}{2},-\dfrac{1}{2},-1$　　C. $-\dfrac{1}{4},\dfrac{1}{4},\dfrac{1}{2}$　　D. $-\dfrac{1}{3},\dfrac{1}{3},\dfrac{2}{3}$

1-8-19　设 $\boldsymbol{A}$ 是一个三阶实矩阵，如果对于任一三维列向量 $\boldsymbol{x}$，都有 $\boldsymbol{x}^{\mathrm{T}}\boldsymbol{A}\boldsymbol{x}=0$，那么（　　）。

A. $|\boldsymbol{A}|=0$　　B. $|\boldsymbol{A}|>0$　　C. $|\boldsymbol{A}|<0$　　D. 以上都不成立

1-8-20　n 阶实对称矩阵 $\boldsymbol{A}$ 为正定矩阵，则下列不成立的是（　　）。

A. 所有 K 阶子式为正（$K=1,2,\cdots,n$）　　B. $\boldsymbol{A}$ 的所有特征值全为正

C. $\boldsymbol{A}^{-1}$ 为正定矩阵　　D. 秩（$\boldsymbol{A}$）$=n$

第九节　概率论与数理统计

一、随机事件与概率

（一）随机事件与样本空间

随机试验（记作 E）具有以下特点：每次试验结果不可能事先确定，但试验的全部可能结果是可知的，在相同条件下试验可以重复进行。

随机试验 E 的每个可能结果称为一个基本事件，试验 E 的所有可能结果的集合称为 E 的样本空间，记作 Ω。

随机事件可以由 E 的某些基本事件组成，通常用 $A,B,C,\cdots$ 表示。

每次试验必然发生的事件，称作必然事件，记作 Ω；每次试验必不发生的事件，称作不可能事件，记作 $\varnothing$。用图形表示事件，可使分析直观方便，图 1-9-1 中方形区域表示 Ω。

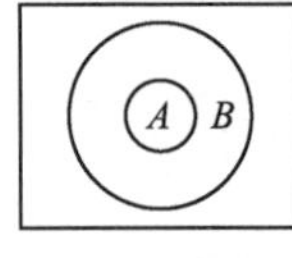

a)

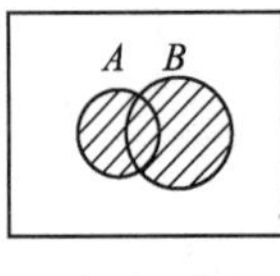

b)

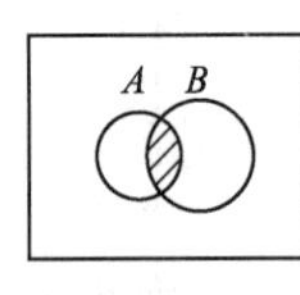

c)

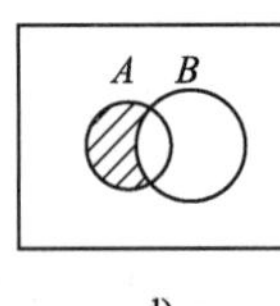

d)

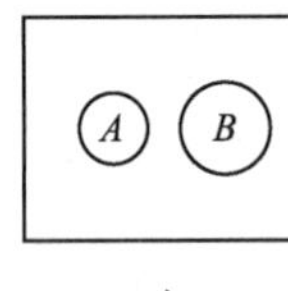

e)

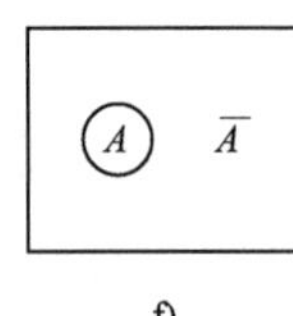

f)

图 1-9-1

（二）随机事件的关系及运算

1. 包含与相等

若事件 A 发生必然导致事件 B 发生，则称事件 B 包含事件 A 或 A 被 B 包含，记作 $B\supset A$ 或 $A\subset B$（图 1-9-1a）。若 $A\subset B$ 且 $B\subset A$，则称事件 A 与事件 B 相等，记作 $A=B$。

2. 和事件

事件 A 与 B 中至少有一个发生的事件称作事件 A 与 B 之和，记作 $A\cup B$ 或 $A+B$（图 1-9-1b）。

3. 积事件

事件 A 与 B 同时发生的事件称作事件 A 与 B 之积，记作 AB 或 $A\cap B$（图 1-9-1c）。

4. 差事件

事件 A 发生而事件 B 不发生，这样的事件称作事件 A 与 B 之差，记作 $A-B$（图 1-9-1d）。

5. 互不相容事件

若事件 A 与 B 不能同时发生，即 $AB=\varnothing$，则称事件 A 与 B 互不相容或互斥（图 1-9-1e）。

6. 对立事件

若事件 A 与 B 中必有且仅有一个发生，即 $A\cup B=\Omega$ 且 $AB=\varnothing$，则称 A 与 B 互为

对立事件(或逆事件)。A 的对立事件记为 $\overline{A}$,所以 $A\cup\overline{A}=\Omega,A\overline{A}=\varnothing$(图 1-9-1f)。注意"$A$ 不发生"即"$\overline{A}$ 发生",所以 $A-B=A\overline{B}$。

事件的运算律:

①$A\cup B=B\cup A$

②$A\cup(B\cup C)=(A\cup B)\cup C$

③$AB=BA$

④$(AB)C=A(BC)$

⑤$A(B\cup C)=(AB)\cup(AC)$

⑥$A\cup(BC)=(A\cup B)(A\cup C)$

⑦$\overline{A\cup B}=\overline{A}\,\overline{B}$

⑧$\overline{AB}=\overline{A}\cup\overline{B}$

【例 1-9-1】 已知事件 **A** 与 **B** 相互独立,且 $P(\overline{A})=0.4,P(\overline{B})=0.5$,则 $P(A\cup B)$等于:

A. 0.6　　B. 0.7　　C. 0.8　　D. 0.9

解 本题考查古典概型的基本计算,是概率论考查范围的基本题型,应重点掌握。

因为 A 与 B 独立,所以 $\overline{A}$ 与 $\overline{B}$ 独立。

$P(A\cup B)=1-P(\overline{A\cup B})=1-P(\overline{A}\,\overline{B})=1-P(\overline{A})P(\overline{B})$

或者 $P(A\cup B)=P(A)+P(B)-P(AB)$

由于 A 与 B 相互独立,则 $P(AB)=P(A)P(B)$

而 $P(A)=1-P(\overline{A})=0.6,P(B)=1-P(\overline{B})=0.5$

故 $P(A\cup B)=0.6+0.5-0.6\times0.5=0.8$

答案:C

【例 1-9-2】 有 A、B、C 三个事件,下列选项中与事件 A 互斥的是:

A. $\overline{B\cup C}$　　B. $\overline{A\cup B\cup C}$　　C. $\overline{A}B+AC$　　D. $A(B+C)$

解 $A(\overline{B\cup C})=A\overline{B}\,\overline{C}$ 可能发生,选项 A 错。

$A(\overline{A\cup B\cup C})=A\overline{A}\,\overline{B}\,\overline{C}=\varnothing$,选项 B 对。

或见解图:

图 a),$\overline{B\cup C}$(斜线区域)与 A 有交集。

图 b),$\overline{A\cup B\cup C}$(斜线区域)与 A 无交集。

答案:B

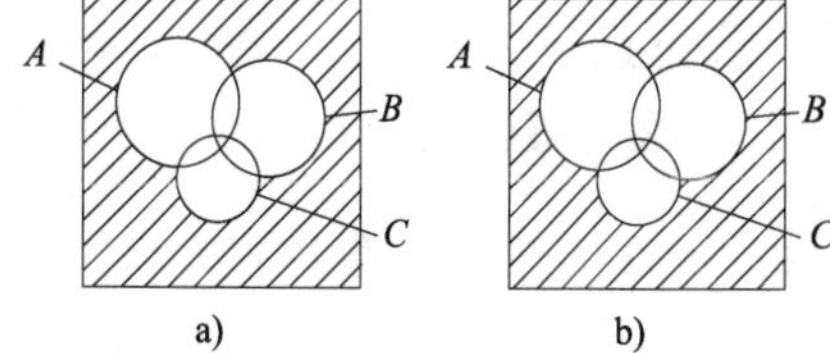

例 1-9-2 解图

(三)概率及其性质

1. 概率的统计定义

若在 n 次重复试验中事件 A 出现了 m 次,则比值$\frac{m}{n}$称为事件 A 在这 n 次试验中出现的频率,记为 $f_n(A)=\frac{m}{n}$。

当试验次数 n 无限增大时,$f_n(A)$就稳定于某个常数 p,则数 p 称为 A 的概率,记作 $P(A)$。$P(A)$表示事件 A 发生的可能性有多大,在图示法中,可把 $P(A)$看作 A 区域的面积(表示 Ω 的方形区域面积为 1)。

2. 概率的性质(公式)

(1)对任意事件 A,有 $0\leqslant P(A)\leqslant1$。$P(\Omega)=1,P(\varnothing)=0$。

(2)对任意两事件 A、B(图 1-9-1b),$P(A\cup B)=P(A)+P(B)-P(AB)$。

(3)对互不相容事件 A、B(图 1-9-1e),有 $P(A\cup B)=P(A)+P(B)$。

(4)$P(A)+P(\overline{A})=1$,$P(\overline{A})=1-P(A)$(图 1-9-1f)。

(5)$P(AB)+P(A\overline{B})=P(A)$,$P(A\overline{B})=P(A-B)=P(A)-P(AB)$(图 1-9-1d)。

当 $B\subset A$ 时,$AB=B$,$P(A-B)=P(A)-P(B)$。

【例 1-9-3】 若 $P(A)=0.8$,$P(A\overline{B})=0.2$,则 $P(\overline{A}\cup\overline{B})$等于:

A. 0.4　　B. 0.6　　C. 0　　D. 0.3

解 因
$$P(AB)+P(A\overline{B})=P(A)$$
所以
$$P(AB)=P(A)-P(A\overline{B})=0.6$$
$$P(\overline{A}\cup\overline{B})=P(\overline{AB})=1-P(AB)=1-0.6=0.4$$

答案:A

3. 概率的古典定义

设随机试验的全部可能结果是 n 个等可能发生的基本事件,其中有且仅有 m 个基本事件被随机事件 A 包含,则事件 A 的概率
$$P(A)=\frac{m}{n}$$

例如,在一批 N 个产品中有 M 个次品。设事件 A 是"从这批产品中任取 n 个产品,其中恰有 m 个次品",那么
$$P(A)=\frac{C_M^m\cdot C_{N-M}^{n-m}}{C_N^n}$$

【例 1-9-4】 袋中有 5 个球,其中 3 个是白球,2 个是红球,一次随机地取出 3 个球,其中恰有 2 个是白球的概率是:

A. $\left[\frac{3}{5}\right]^2\frac{2}{5}$　　B. $C_5^3\left[\frac{3}{5}\right]^2\frac{1}{5}$　　C. $\left[\frac{3}{5}\right]^2$　　D. $\frac{C_3^2C_2^1}{C_5^3}$

答案:D

(四)条件概率

1. 条件概率

设 A、B 为两个事件,$P(A)>0$,则称 $P(B|A)=\frac{P(AB)}{P(A)}$为事件 A 发生的条件下,事件 B 发生的条件概率。

设 A、B、C 为随机事件,$P(C)>0$,条件概率性质(公式):

(1)$0\leqslant P(A|C)\leqslant 1$;

(2)$P(A\cup B|C)=P(A|C)+P(B|C)-P(AB|C)$;

(3)$AB=\varnothing$ 时,$P(A\cup B|C)=P(A|C)+P(B|C)$;

(4)$P(A|C)+P(\overline{A}|C)=1$;

(5)$P(AB|C)+P(A\overline{B}|C)=P(A|C)$。

2. 乘法公式

$$P(A)>0\text{ 时},P(AB)=P(A)P(B|A) \tag{1-9-1}$$

或
$$P(B)>0\text{ 时},P(AB)=P(B)P(A|B)$$

3. 全概率公式

设事件组 $A_1, A_2, \cdots, A_n$ 互不相容，且 $A_1 \cup A_2 \cup \cdots \cup A_n = \Omega$，$P(A_i) > 0$，$i = 1, 2, \cdots, n$。则对任一事件 B 有

$$P(B) = \sum_{i=1}^{n} P(B|A_i)P(A_i) \tag{1-9-2}$$

4. 贝叶斯(Bayes)公式

在全概率公式条件下，且 $P(B) > 0$，则有

$$P(A_i|B) = \frac{P(A_i)P(B|A_i)}{\sum_{k=1}^{n} P(A_k)P(B|A_k)} \quad (i = 1, 2, \cdots, n) \tag{1-9-3}$$

【例 1-9-5】 设有一箱产品由三家工厂生产，第一家工厂生产总量的$\frac{1}{2}$，其他两厂各产总量的$\frac{1}{4}$，又知各厂次品率分别为 2%、2%、4%，现从此箱任取一件产品，(1)问取到正品的概率是多少？(2)如果已知取到的这件产品恰为正品，问它是由第二家工厂生产的概率是多少？

解 设 A_i 为"取到一件第 i 厂产品"，$i = 1, 2, 3$；B 为"取到一件正品"，$\overline{B}$ 为"取到一件次品"。

注意：$\frac{1}{2}$、$\frac{1}{4}$、$\frac{1}{4}$为概率，分别设对应的一个事件；2%、2%、4%为条件概率，分别设对应的两个事件。

(1)由全概率公式 $P(B) = \sum_{i=1}^{3} P(A_i)P(B|A_i)$

且 $P(B|A_i) = 1 - P(\overline{B}|A_i) \quad (i = 1, 2, 3)$

$$P(B) = \frac{1}{2} \times 0.98 + \frac{1}{4} \times 0.98 + \frac{1}{4} \times 0.96 = 0.975$$

或

$$P(\overline{B}) = \frac{1}{2} \times 0.02 + \frac{1}{4} \times 0.02 + \frac{1}{4} \times 0.04 = 0.025$$

$$P(B) = 1 - P(\overline{B}) = 0.975$$

(2)由贝叶斯公式可知 $P(A_2|B) = \dfrac{\frac{1}{4} \times 0.98}{\frac{1}{2} \times 0.98 + \frac{1}{4} \times 0.98 + \frac{1}{4} \times 0.96} \approx 0.2513$

(五)独立性

1. 相互独立

若事件 A、B 满足 $P(AB) = P(A)P(B)$，则称 A 与 B 相互独立。

如果 A、B 相互独立，则 A 与 $\overline{B}$、$\overline{A}$ 与 B、$\overline{A}$ 与 $\overline{B}$ 均相互独立。

如果 A、B 独立，$0 < P(A) < 1$，则 $P(B|A) = P(B|\overline{A}) = P(B)$($A$ 发生与否不影响 B 发生的概率)。A、B 独立的含意是"A 发生与否"同"B 发生与否"在概率上互不影响。

【例 1-9-6】 若 $P(A) > 0$，$P(B) > 0$，$P(\overline{B}) > 0$，$P(A|B) = P(A)$，则下列各式不成立的是：

A. $P(B|A) = P(B)$　　B. $P(A|\overline{B}) = P(A)$

C. $P(AB) = P(A)P(B)$　　D. $AB = \varnothing$

解 因 $P(AB) = P(B)P(A|B) = P(A)P(B) > 0$，而 $AB = \varnothing$ 时，$P(AB) = 0$。

或因 $P(AB) = P(B)P(A|B) = P(A)P(B)$，选项 C 成立；$A$、$B$ 相互独立，所以选项 A、B 也成立。

答案:D

对于三个事件 A、B、C,如果有

$$P(AB)=P(A)P(B)$$
$$P(AC)=P(A)P(C)$$
$$P(BC)=P(B)P(C)$$
$$P(ABC)=P(A)P(B)P(C)$$

则称三事件 A、B、C 相互独立。

对于 n 个事件 A_1、A_2、…、A_n,如果对任何整数 $k(2\leqslant k\leqslant n)$,任意 $1\leqslant i_1<i_2<\cdots<i_k\leqslant n$,有 $P(A_{i1}A_{i2}\cdots A_{ik})=P(A_{i1})P(A_{i2})\cdots P(A_{ik})$成立,则称 A_1、A_2、…、A_n 相互独立。

2. 独立重复试验

设一次试验中,事件 A 发生的概率为 $p(0<p<1)$,则在 n 次独立重复试验(n 重贝努利试验)中 A 发生 k 次的概率

$$P_k=C_n^k p^k q^{n-k} \quad (q=1-p;k=0,1,2,\cdots,n)$$

【例 1-9-7】 在一小时内一台车床不需要工人看管的概率为0.8,一个工人看管三台车床,三台车床工作相互独立,求在一小时内三台车床中至少有一台不需要人看管的概率。

解　方法 1:

设 A 表示"一小时内一台车床不需要看管",看管三台车床相当于 3 次独立重复试验。

B 表示"一小时内三台车床中至少有一台不需要看管";

B_k 表示"一小时内三台车床中恰有 k 台不需要看管",$k=0,1,2,3$。

由题意可知 $$p=P(A)=0.8$$

$$P(B_k)=C_3^k 0.8^k 0.2^{3-k} \qquad (k=0,1,2,3)$$

$$P(B)=P(B_1)+P(B_2)+P(B_3)$$

$$=\sum_{k=1}^{3}C_3^k 0.8^k 0.2^{3-k}=0.992$$

方法 2: $$P(B)=1-P(\overline{B})$$

$$P(\overline{B})=P(B_0)=0.2^3$$

$$P(B)=1-0.2^3=0.992$$

由此可见,借助性质 $P(A)=1-P(\overline{A})$有时可简化计算。

二、随机变量

为了进一步研究随机现象,需要将随机试验的结果数量化,为此先定义随机变量。

(一)随机变量及其分布函数

如果对于随机试验的每一个可能结果 ω,变量 X 都有一确定实数与它对应,则称 X 为随机变量。含随机变量的等式、不等式表示随机事件,如 $X=0$,$X\leqslant 2$ 等。对任意实数 x,称函数

$$F(x)=P\{X\leqslant x\} \qquad (-\infty<x<+\infty)$$

为随机变量 X 的分布函数。

分布函数性质：

(1)$0\leqslant F(x)\leqslant 1(-\infty<x<+\infty)$；$\lim\limits_{x\to+\infty}F(x)=1$，$\lim\limits_{x\to-\infty}F(x)=0$；

(2)$F(x)$是非减函数，即 $x_1<x_2$ 时，$F(x_1)\leqslant F(x_2)$；

(3)$F(x)$是右连续的，即 $\lim\limits_{x\to a^+}F(x)=F(a)$；

(4)$P\{a<X\leqslant b\}=F(b)-F(a)$，$P(X>a)=1-F(a)$。

(二)离散型随机变量

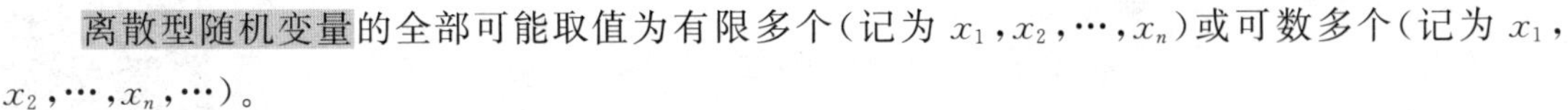

离散型随机变量的全部可能取值为有限多个（记为 $x_1,x_2,\cdots,x_n$）或可数多个（记为 $x_1,x_2,\cdots,x_n,\cdots$）。

离散型随机变量的分布律为

$$P\{X=x_k\}=P_k \qquad (k=1,2,\cdots,n,\cdots)$$

也可用表格表示

X	x_1	x_2	$\cdots$	x_n	$\cdots$
P_k	P_1	P_2	$\cdots$	P_n	$\cdots$

分布律的性质：

(1)非负性，$P_k\geqslant 0(k=1,2,\cdots)$；

(2)全部概率的和为 1，即 $\sum\limits_{k=1}^{\infty}P_k=1$。

(3)$P(a<X\leqslant b)=\sum\limits_{a<x_k\leqslant b}P_k$。

离散型随机变量的分布函数

$$F(x)=P\{X\leqslant x\}=\sum_{x_k\leqslant x}P\{X=x_k\}$$

【例 1-9-8】 离散型随机变量 X 的分布律为 $P(X=k)=C\lambda^k(k=0,1,2,\cdots)$，则下列不成立的是：

A. $C>0$　　B. $0<\lambda<1$　　C. $C=1-\lambda$　　D. $C=\dfrac{1}{1-\lambda}$

解 由分布律性质知 $C\lambda^k\geqslant 0(k=0,1,2,\cdots)$，$\sum\limits_{k=0}^{\infty}C\lambda^k=\dfrac{C}{1-\lambda}=1$。所以 $C>0,\lambda>0,|\lambda|<1,C=1-\lambda$。

答案：D

(三)连续型随机变量

对于随机变量 X，如果存在非负函数 $f(x)$，使对任意实数 x 有

$$F(x)=P\{X\leqslant x\}=\int_{-\infty}^{x}f(t)\mathrm{d}t$$

则称 X 为连续型随机变量，称 $f(x)$为 X 的概率密度。此时，$F(x)$为连续函数。

概率密度 $f(x)$性质：

(1) $\int_{-\infty}^{+\infty}f(x)\mathrm{d}x=1$；

(2)在 $f(x)$连续点有 $F'(x)=f(x)$；

(3) $P\{a<X\leqslant b\}=F(b)-F(a)=\int_{a}^{b}f(x)\mathrm{d}x$（等于曲边梯形面积）。

注意：连续型随机变量 X 取任一定值 a 的概率 $P\{X=a\}=0$，但“$X=a$”有时并非不可能事件。

【例 1-9-9】 下列函数中,可以作为连续型随机变量的分布函数的是:

A. $\Phi(x)=\begin{cases}0, & x<0\\ 1-e^{x}, & x\geqslant 0\end{cases}$　　B. $F(x)=\begin{cases}e^{x}, & x<0\\ 1, & x\geqslant 0\end{cases}$

C. $G(x)=\begin{cases}e^{-x}, & x<0\\ 1, & x\geqslant 0\end{cases}$　　D. $H(x)=\begin{cases}0, & x<0\\ 1+e^{-x}, & x\geqslant 0\end{cases}$

解 分布函数[记为 $Q(x)$]性质为:①$0\leqslant Q(x)\leqslant 1$,$Q(-\infty)=0$,$Q(+\infty)=1$;②$Q(x)$是非减函数;③$Q(x)$是右连续的。

$\Phi(+\infty)=-\infty$;$F(x)$满足分布函数的性质①、②、③;

$G(-\infty)=+\infty$;$x\geqslant 0$ 时,$H(x)>1$。

答案:B

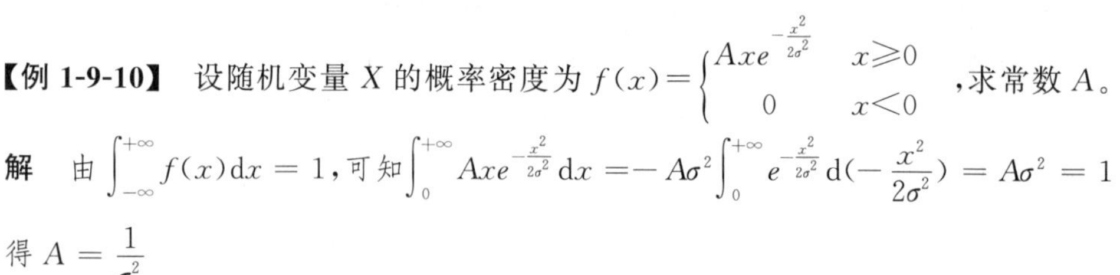

【例 1-9-10】 设随机变量 X 的概率密度为 $f(x)=\begin{cases}Axe^{-\frac{x^2}{2\sigma^2}} & x\geqslant 0\\ 0 & x<0\end{cases}$,求常数 A。

解 由 $\int_{-\infty}^{+\infty}f(x)\mathrm{d}x=1$,可知 $\int_{0}^{+\infty}Axe^{-\frac{x^2}{2\sigma^2}}\mathrm{d}x=-A\sigma^2\int_{0}^{+\infty}e^{-\frac{x^2}{2\sigma^2}}\mathrm{d}(-\frac{x^2}{2\sigma^2})=A\sigma^2=1$

得 $A=\dfrac{1}{\sigma^2}$

【例 1-9-11】 设连续型随机变量 X 的分布函数为

$$F(x)=A+B\arctan x\qquad(-\infty<x<+\infty)$$

求:(1) 常数 A 与 B;

(2) 随机变量 X 在$(-1,1)$内取值的概率;

(3) 随机变量 X 的概率密度。

解 (1) 因 $F(+\infty)=A+\dfrac{\pi}{2}B=1$,$F(-\infty)=A-\dfrac{\pi}{2}B=0$

所以 $A=\dfrac{1}{2}$,$B=\dfrac{1}{\pi}$,$F(x)=\dfrac{1}{2}+\dfrac{1}{\pi}\arctan x$

(2) $P\{-1<X<1\}=F(1)-F(-1)=\dfrac{1}{2}$

(3) $f(x)=F'(x)=\dfrac{1}{\pi(1+x^2)}\qquad(-\infty<x<+\infty)$

(四)常用概率分布

1. 二点分布(0—1 分布)

分布律

$$P\{X=k\}=p^kq^{1-k}\qquad(k=0,1)$$

或
$$\begin{array}{c|cc}X & 0 & 1\\ \hline P_k & q & p\end{array}\qquad(0<p<1,q=1-p)$$

2. 二项分布 $B(n,p)$

分布律

$$P\{X=k\}=C_n^kp^kq^{n-k}\qquad(0<p<1,q=1-p;k=0,1,2,\cdots,n)$$

说明:(1)0—1 分布就是 $B(1,p)$。

(2)当 X 表示"n 次独立重复试验中，事件 A 发生的次数"时，$X \sim B(n,p)$，$p=P(A)$。

3. 泊松分布 $P(\lambda)$

分布律

$$P\{X=k\}=\frac{e^{-\lambda}\lambda^{k}}{k!} \quad (\text{参数}\lambda\text{为正常数}, k=0,1,2,\cdots)$$

4. 均匀分布 $U(a,b)$

概率密度

$$f(x)=\begin{cases}\dfrac{1}{b-a} & a \leqslant x \leqslant b \\ 0 & \text{其他}\end{cases}$$

5. 指数分布 $E(\lambda)$

概率密度

$$f(x)=\begin{cases}\lambda e^{-\lambda x} & x \geqslant 0 \\ 0 & x<0\end{cases} \quad (\text{参数}\lambda\text{为正常数})$$

6. 正态分布 $N(\mu,\sigma^2)$

概率密度

$$f(x)=\frac{1}{\sqrt{2\pi}\sigma} e^{-\frac{(x-\mu)^2}{2\sigma^2}} \quad (-\infty<x<+\infty, \mu\text{为常数}, \sigma\text{为正常数})$$

标准正态分布 $N(0,1)$

概率密度

$$\varphi(x)=\frac{1}{\sqrt{2\pi}} e^{-\frac{x^2}{2}} \quad (-\infty<x<+\infty) \tag{1-9-4}$$

分布函数 $\Phi(x)=\dfrac{1}{\sqrt{2\pi}}\displaystyle\int_{-\infty}^{x} e^{-\frac{t^2}{2}}\,\mathrm{d}t$

$\Phi(x)$为图 1-9-2 斜线部分面积值。显然

$$\Phi(0)=0.5$$

$$\Phi(-a)=1-\Phi(a) \quad (\text{图 1-9-3})$$

$$a>0\text{ 时}, P\{|X|<a\}=2\Phi(a)-1 \quad (\text{图 1-9-3})$$

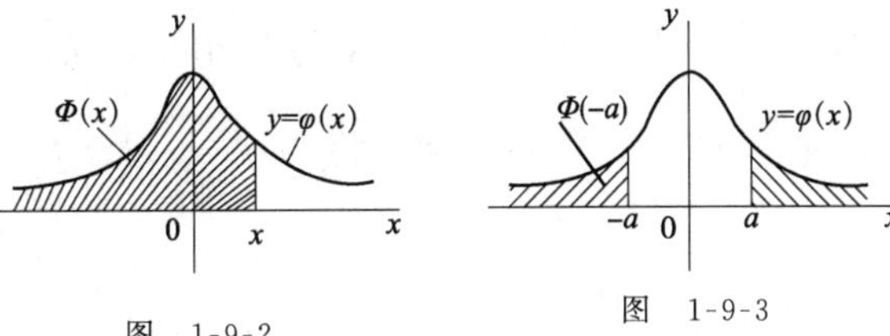

图 1-9-2　　　图 1-9-3

结论：设 $X \sim N(\mu,\sigma^2)$，则

(1) $\dfrac{X-\mu}{\sigma} \sim N(0,1)$

(2) $P(a<X \leqslant b)=P\left(\dfrac{a-\mu}{\sigma}<\dfrac{X-\mu}{\sigma} \leqslant \dfrac{b-\mu}{\sigma}\right)=\Phi\left(\dfrac{b-\mu}{\sigma}\right)-\Phi\left(\dfrac{a-\mu}{\sigma}\right)$

(3)当 a、b 为常数，$a \neq 0$ 时，$aX+b \sim N(a\mu+b, a^2\sigma^2)$。

【例 1-9-12】 设 $X \sim N(1,2^2)$，$\Phi(0.5)=0.69$，$\Phi(1)=0.84$，求 $P\{-1<X^3<8\}$。

解 $P\{-1<X^3<8\}=P\{-1<X<2\}$

$$=\Phi\left(\frac{2-1}{2}\right)-\Phi\left(\frac{-1-1}{2}\right)=\Phi(0.5)-\Phi(-1)$$

$$=\Phi(0.5)-[1-\Phi(1)]=0.69-(1-0.84)=0.53$$

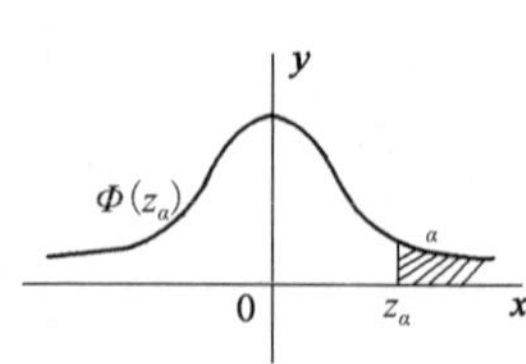

图 1-9-4

为了便于应用，对于标准正态分布，我们引入上 α 分位数的定义：设 $X\sim N(0,1)$，若数 z_α 满足条件（见图 1-9-4）

$$P\{X>z_\alpha\}=\alpha \qquad (0<\alpha<1) \qquad (1\text{-}9\text{-}5)$$

则称数 z_α 为标准正态分布上 α 分位数。$\Phi(z_\alpha)=P(X\leqslant z_\alpha)=1-\alpha$，由于概率密度 $\varphi(x)$ 为偶函数，所以 $z_{1-\alpha}=-z_\alpha$。（有的书不用 z_α 而用 u_α）

查表可知 $z_{0.05}=1.645$，$z_{0.025}=1.96$，$z_{0.95}=-1.645$。

7. 二维连续型随机变量

(1)二维连续型随机变量 X、Y 的联合概率密度 $f(x,y)$ 的性质

$f(x,y)\geqslant 0$ 且 $\int_{-\infty}^{+\infty}\int_{-\infty}^{+\infty} f(x,y)\mathrm{d}x\mathrm{d}y = 1$

(2)边缘概率密度

关于 X 的，$f_X(x) = \int_{-\infty}^{+\infty} f(x,y)\mathrm{d}y$

关于 Y 的，$f_Y(y) = \int_{-\infty}^{+\infty} f(x,y)\mathrm{d}x$

(3)X 与 Y 相互独立的充要条件

$f(x,y)=f_X(x)\cdot f_Y(y)$ 处处成立

如设 X、Y 的联合概率密度为：

$$f(x,y) = \begin{cases} 6xy^2, 0\leqslant x\leqslant 1, 0\leqslant y\leqslant 1 \\ 0, \text{其他} \end{cases}$$

则 $f_X(x) = \begin{cases} \int_0^1 6xy^2\mathrm{d}y = 2x\cdot y^3\Big|_0^1 = 2x, 0\leqslant x\leqslant 1 \\ 0, \text{其他} \end{cases}$

$f_Y(y) = \begin{cases} \int_0^1 6xy^2\mathrm{d}x = 3y^2\cdot x^2\Big|_0^1 = 3y^2, 0\leqslant y\leqslant 1 \\ 0, \text{其他} \end{cases}$

因为 $f(x,y)=f_X(x)\cdot f_Y(y)$ 处处成立，所以 X 与 Y 相互独立。

【例 1-9-13】 设二维随机变量(X,Y)的概率密度为 $f(x,y)=\begin{cases} e^{-2ax+by}, x>0, y>0 \\ 0, \text{其他} \end{cases}$，则常数 a，b 应满足的条件是：

A. $ab=-\frac{1}{2}$，且 $a>0$，$b<0$　　B. $ab=\frac{1}{2}$，且 $a>0$，$b>0$

C. $ab=-\frac{1}{2}$，$a<0$，$b<0$　　D. $ab=\frac{1}{2}$，且 $a<0$，$b<0$

解　利用联合概率密度的性质：$\int_{-\infty}^{+\infty}\int_{-\infty}^{+\infty} f(x,y)\mathrm{d}x\mathrm{d}y = 1$

方法 1： $\int_0^{+\infty}\int_0^{+\infty} e^{-2ax+by}\mathrm{d}y\mathrm{d}x = \int_0^{+\infty} e^{-2ax}\mathrm{d}x\cdot\int_0^{+\infty} e^{by}\mathrm{d}y = 1$

当 $a>0$ 时，$\int_0^{+\infty} e^{-2ax}\mathrm{d}x = \frac{-1}{2a}e^{2ax}\Big|_0^{+\infty} = \frac{1}{2a}$

当 $b<0$ 时，$\int_0^{+\infty} e^{by}\mathrm{d}y=\frac{1}{b}e^{by}\Big|_0^{+\infty}=\frac{-1}{b}$

$\frac{1}{2a}\times\frac{-1}{b}=1, ab=-\frac{1}{2}$

方法 2：$x>0, y>0$ 时

$f(x,y)=e^{-2ax+by}=2ae^{-2ax}\cdot(-b)e^{by}\cdot\frac{-1}{2ab}$

当 $\frac{-1}{2ab}=1$，即 $ab=-\frac{1}{2}$ 时，X 服从参数 $\lambda=2a(a>0)$ 的指数分布，Y 服从参数 $\lambda=-b(b<0)$ 的指数分布，X 与 Y 相互独立。

答案：A

(4)二维正态分布 $N(\mu_1,\mu_2,\sigma_1^2,\sigma_2^2,\rho)$

①若 X 与 Y 的联合概率密度为

$$f(x,y)=\frac{1}{2\pi\sigma_1\sigma_2\sqrt{1-\rho^2}}e^{-\frac{1}{2(1-\rho^2)}\left[\frac{(x-\mu_1)^2}{\sigma_1^2}-2\rho\frac{(x-\mu_1)(y-\mu_2)}{\sigma_1\sigma_2}+\frac{(y-\mu_2)^2}{\sigma_2^2}\right]}$$

(μ_1,μ_2 为常数，σ_1、σ_2 为正常数，$|\rho|<1$)

则称 (X,Y) 服从二维正态分布，记为 $(X,Y)\sim N(\mu_1,\mu_2,\sigma_1^2,\sigma_2^2,\rho)$

②设 $(X,Y)\sim N(\mu_1,\mu_2,\sigma_1^2,\sigma_2^2,\rho)$，则

a. $X\sim N(\mu_1,\sigma_1^2)$，$Y\sim N(\mu_2,\sigma_2^2)$

b. X 与 Y 相互独立的充要条件是 $\rho=0$(X,Y 不相关)，即

$$f(x,y)=\frac{1}{\sqrt{2\pi}\sigma_1}e^{-\frac{(x-\mu_1)^2}{2\sigma_1^2}}\cdot\frac{1}{\sqrt{2\pi}\sigma_2}e^{-\frac{(y-\mu_2)^2}{2\sigma_2^2}}$$

三、随机变量的数字特征

(一)随机变量的数字特征

1. 数学期望(均值)

设离散型随机变量 X 的分布律为 $P\{X=x_k\}=P_k(k=1,2,\cdots,n,\cdots)$。若 $\sum_{k=1}^{\infty}x_kP_k$ 绝对收敛，则称 $\sum_{k=1}^{\infty}x_kP_k$ 为 X 的数学期望，记作 $E(X)$，即 $E(X)=\sum_{k=1}^{\infty}x_kP_k$。

设连续型随机变量 X 的概率密度为 $f(x)$，若 $\int_{-\infty}^{+\infty}xf(x)\mathrm{d}x$ 绝对收敛，则称 $\int_{-\infty}^{+\infty}xf(x)\mathrm{d}x$ 为 X 的数学期望，记作 $E(X)$，即 $E(X)=\int_{-\infty}^{+\infty}xf(x)\mathrm{d}x$。

(1)数学期望性质

①$E(c)=c$　(c 为常数)；

②$E(kX)=kE(X)$　(k 为常数)；

③$E(kX+b)=kE(X)+b$　(k,b 均为常数)；

④$E(X_1+X_2)=E(X_1)+E(X_2)$；

⑤$E(X_1\cdot X_2)=E(X_1)\cdot E(X_2)$　(X_1,X_2 相互独立时)。

对 n 个随机变量 $X_1,\cdots,X_n$ 有类似结论。

(2)随机变量函数的数学期望：

①设 X 为离散型，分布律为 $P(X=x_i)=P_i(i=1,2,\cdots)$，$Y=g(X)$，则随机变量 Y 的数学期望为 $E(Y)=E[g(X)]=\sum_{i=1}^{\infty}g(x_i)P_i$（绝对收敛）。

②设 X 为连续型，概率密度为 $f(x)$，$Y=g(X)$，则随机变量 Y 的数学期望为 $E(Y)=E[g(X)]=\int_{-\infty}^{+\infty}g(x)f(x)\mathrm{d}x$（绝对收敛）。

③设 (X,Y) 的联合概率密度为 $f(x,y)$，$Z=g(X,Y)$，则 $E(Z)=E[g(X,Y)]=\int_{-\infty}^{+\infty}\int_{-\infty}^{+\infty}g(x,y)f(x,y)\mathrm{d}x\mathrm{d}y$。

2. 方差

称 $E[(X-E(X))^2]$ 为 X 的方差，记为 $D(X)$，即 $D(X)=E[(X-E(X))^2]$，方差用于刻画随机变量取值分散程度。称 $\sqrt{D(X)}$ 为 X 的标准差或均方差。

设离散型随机变量 X 的分布律为 $P(X=x_k)=P_k(k=1,2,\cdots)$，则

$$D(X)=\sum_{k=1}^{\infty}[x_k-E(X)]^2P_k$$

设连续型随机变量 X 的概率密度为 $f(x)$，则

$$D(X)=\int_{-\infty}^{+\infty}[x-E(X)]^2f(x)\mathrm{d}x$$

计算方差有时用公式

$$D(X)=E(X^2)-[E(X)]^2 \tag{1-9-6}$$

方差性质：

(1) $D(C)=0$ （C 为常数）；

(2) $D(CX)=C^2D(X)$，$D(X\pm C)=D(X)$ （C 为常数）；

(3) 设随机变量 X_1,X_2 相互独立，则

$$D(X_1\pm X_2)=D(X_1)+D(X_2)$$

设随机变量 $X_1,\cdots,X_n$ 相互独立，$C_1,C_2,\cdots,C_n$ 为常数，则 $D(\sum_{i=1}^{n}C_iX_i)=\sum_{i=1}^{n}C_i^2D(X_i)$。

特别对独立同分布的随机变量 $X_1,\cdots,X_n$，如果 $E(X_i)=\mu$，$D(X_i)=\sigma^2(i=1,2,\cdots,n)$，令 $\overline{X}=\frac{1}{n}\sum_{i=1}^{n}X_i$，则

$$E(\overline{X})=E\left(\frac{1}{n}\sum_{i=1}^{n}X_i\right)=\mu$$

$$D(\overline{X})=D\left(\frac{1}{n}\sum_{i=1}^{n}X_i\right)=\frac{1}{n}\sigma^2$$

【例 1-9-14】 已知 $E(X)=2$，$D(X)=1$，$Y=X^2$，求 $E(Y)$。

解 $E(Y)=E(X^2)=D(X)+[E(X)]^2=1+2^2=5$。

（二）常用概率分布的期望和方差（见表 1-9-1）

表 1-9-1

X 服从的分布	$E(X)$	$D(X)$
参数 p 的 0－1 分布，$q=1-p$	p	pq
二项分布 $B(n,p)$，$q=1-p$	np	npq
参数 λ 的泊松分布 $P(\lambda)$	λ	λ

续上表

X 服从的分布	E(X)	D(X)
(a,b)上的均匀分布$U(a,b)$	$\frac{a+b}{2}$	$\frac{(b-a)^2}{12}$
参数λ的指数分布$E(\lambda)$	$\frac{1}{\lambda}$	$\frac{1}{\lambda^2}$
正态分布$N(\mu,\sigma^2)$	μ	σ^2

【例 1-9-15】 设随机变量 X 服从参数为 2 的泊松分布，则随机变量 $Z=3X+2$ 的标准差是：

A. 18　　B. $3\sqrt{2}$　　C. 6　　D. 4

解 $\sqrt{D(Z)}=\sqrt{9D(X)}=\sqrt{9\times2}=3\sqrt{2}$

答案：B

(三)矩、协方差、相关系数及其性质

(1)设 k 为正整数，称 $E(X^k)$为 X 的k阶原点矩，$E(X)$存在时，称 $E[(X-E(X))^k]$为 X 的k阶中心矩。X 的方差 $D(X)$为 X 的二阶中心矩。

(2)设 X、Y 为随机变量，$E(X)$、$E(Y)$存在，则称 $E[(X-E(X))(Y-E(Y))]$为 X 与 Y 的协方差，记作 Cov$(X$、$Y)$，即 $\text{Cov}(X、Y)=E[(X-E(X))(Y-E(Y))]$。

因为$(X-E(X))(Y-E(Y))=XY-XE(Y)-YE(X)+E(X)E(Y)$，所以

$$\text{Cov}(X,Y)=E(XY)-E(X)\cdot E(Y)$$

协方差性质：

①$\text{Cov}(X,Y)=\text{Cov}(Y,X)$；

②$\text{Cov}(X_1+X_2,Y)=\text{Cov}(X_1,Y)+\text{Cov}(X_2,Y)$；

③$\text{Cov}(aX,bY)=ab\text{Cov}(X,Y)$，其中 a、b 为常数；

④若 X 与 Y 相互独立，则 $\text{Cov}(X,Y)=0$。

(3)设 $D(X)>0$，$D(Y)>0$，则称$\frac{\text{Cov}(X,Y)}{\sqrt{D(X)D(Y)}}$为 X 与 Y 的相关系数，记作 ρ_{XY}。

相关系数性质：

①$|\rho_{XY}|\leqslant1$；

②$|\rho_{XY}|=1$ 的充分必要条件是存在常数 a、$b(a\neq0)$，使 $P\{Y=aX+b\}=1$。

ρ_{XY}描述 X 和 Y 之间线性相关关系的密切程度。$|\rho_{XY}|$接近 1，说明 X、Y 之间有密切的线性相关关系；$\rho_{XY}=0$ 时称 X 与 Y 不相关，说明 X 与 Y 之间没有线性相关关系。

四、数理统计的基本概念

(一)总体与样本

在统计学中，我们把研究对象的全体(或某项指标 X)称为总体，组成总体的基本单元称为个体。总体可以用随机变量 X 表示。例如 X 表示钢筋强度、灯泡寿命等。

从一个总体 X 中，随机地抽取 n 个个体称为样本，记为 $X_1,X_2,\cdots,X_n$。若样本 $X_1,X_2,\cdots,X_n$ 相互独立，且与 X 有相同的概率分布，则称 $X_1,X_2,\cdots,X_n$ 是来自总体 X 的容量为 n 的(简单随机)样本。每次具体抽样，所得数据为样本观察值，用 $x_1,x_2,\cdots,x_n$ 表示。

如果总体的概率密度为 $f(x)$，则$(X_1,X_2,\cdots,X_n)$有联合密度 $f(x_1)f(x_2)\cdots f(x_n)$。

(二)统计量

设 $X_1,X_2,\cdots,X_n$ 是来自总体 X 的样本，则不含未知参数的连续函数 $g(X_1,X_2,\cdots,X_n)$ 称为统计量。

常用统计量有：

(1)样本均值 $\overline{X}=\frac{1}{n}\sum\limits_{i=1}^{n}X_i$；

(2)样本方差 $S^2=\frac{1}{n-1}\sum\limits_{i=1}^{n}(X_i-\overline{X})^2$；

(3)样本标准差 $S=\sqrt{\frac{1}{n-1}\sum\limits_{i=1}^{n}(X_i-\overline{X})^2}$。

如果 $E(X)=\mu,D(X)=\sigma^2$，则 $E(\overline{X})=\mu,D(\overline{X})=\frac{1}{n}\sigma^2$ 且 $E(S^2)=\sigma^2$。

(4)样本 k 阶原点矩　　　$A_k=\frac{1}{n}\sum\limits_{i=1}^{n}X_i^k,k=1,2,\cdots$

样本 k 阶中心矩　　　$B_k=\frac{1}{n}\sum\limits_{i=1}^{n}(X_i-\overline{X})^k,k=1,2,\cdots$

(三)正态总体样本均值与样本方差的分布

1. 数理统计中常用的分布

(1)χ^2 分布

图　1-9-5

设 $Z_1,Z_2,\cdots,Z_n$ 相互独立且都服从 $N(0,1)$分布，则称

$$Y=\sum_{i=1}^{n}Z_i^2$$

服从自由度为 n 的χ^2 分布，记作 $Y\sim\chi^2(n)$。

若数 $\chi^2_\alpha(n)$满足 $P\{Y>\chi^2_\alpha(n)\}=\alpha(0<\alpha<1)$，则称数 $\chi^2_\alpha(n)$为$\chi^2(n)$分布的上 α 分位数(见图 1-9-5)。

χ^2 分布的性质：

①设 $X\sim\chi^2(n)$，则 $E(X)=n,D(X)=2n$。

②可加性：设 $X\sim\chi^2(n_1),Y\sim\chi^2(n_2)$，且 X,Y 相互独立，则 $X+Y\sim\chi^2(n_1+n_2)$。

(2)t 分布

设 X、Y 相互独立，且 $X\sim N(0,1),Y\sim\chi^2(n)$，则称

$$T=\frac{X}{\sqrt{\frac{Y}{n}}}$$

服从自由度为 n 的t 分布，记作 $T\sim t(n)$。

若数 $t_\alpha(n)$满足

$$P\{T>t_\alpha(n)\}=\alpha\quad(0<\alpha<1)$$

则称数 $t_\alpha(n)$为 $t(n)$分布的上 α 分位数(见图 1-9-6)。

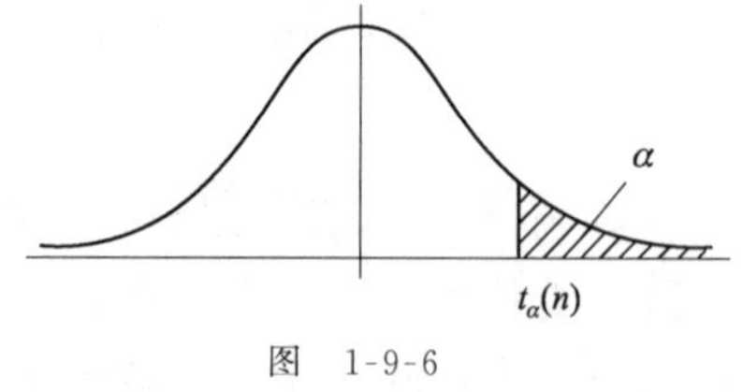

图　1-9-6

$t(n)$分布的概率密度 $f(x)$为偶函数，因而有

$t_{1-\alpha}(n)=-t_\alpha(n)$

(3)F 分布

设 X、Y 相互独立，且 $X\sim\chi^2(n_1)$、$Y\sim\chi^2(n_2)$，则称

$$F = \frac{X/n_1}{Y/n_2}$$

服从**F 分布**,记作 $F \sim F(n_1, n_2)$,n_1、n_2 分别为第一、第二自由度。

若数 $F_\alpha(n_1, n_2)$满足

$$P\{F > F_\alpha(n_1, n_2)\} = \alpha \quad (0 < \alpha < 1)$$

则称数 $F_\alpha(n_1, n_2)$为 $F(n_1, n_2)$分布的上 α 分位数(见图 1-9-7)。

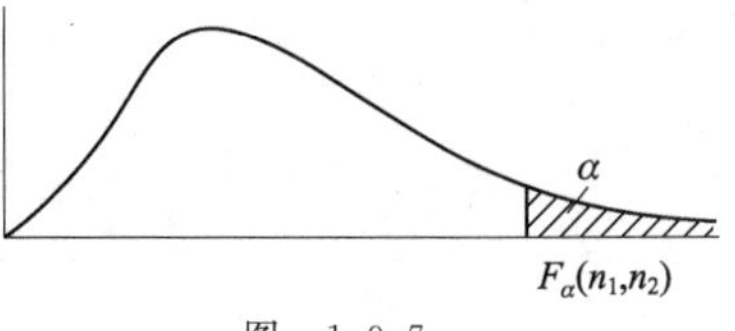

图 1-9-7

若 $F \sim F(n_1, n_2)$,则$\frac{1}{F} \sim F(n_2, n_1)$,由此可得 $F_{1-\alpha}(n_1, n_2) = \frac{1}{F_\alpha(n_2, n_1)}$。

若 $T \sim t(n)$,则 $T^2 \sim F(1, n)$,$\frac{1}{T^2} \sim F(n, 1)$。

2. 正态总体常用抽样分布

结论 1:设 $X_1, X_2, \cdots, X_n$ 是来自总体 $N(\mu, \sigma^2)$的样本,$\bar{x}$为样本均值,S^2 为样本方差,则

①$\overline{X}$ 与 S^2 相互独立。

② $\overline{X} \sim N\left(\mu, \frac{\sigma^2}{n}\right)$,$\frac{\overline{X} - \mu}{\frac{\sigma}{\sqrt{n}}} \sim N(0,1)$。

③$Y = \frac{(n-1)S^2}{\sigma^2} = \frac{\sum\limits_{i=1}^{n}(X_i - \overline{X})^2}{\sigma^2} \sim \chi^2(n-1)$。

④$T = \frac{\overline{X} - \mu}{\frac{S}{\sqrt{n}}} \sim t(n-1)$。

结论 2:设 $X_1, X_2, \cdots, X_{n1}$和 $Y_1, Y_2, \cdots, Y_{n2}$是分别来自总体 $N(\mu_1, \sigma_1^2)$和 $N(\mu_2, \sigma_2^2)$的样本,且 $X_1, X_2, \cdots, X_{n1}$;$Y_1, Y_2, \cdots, Y_{n2}$相互独立,$\overline{X}$,$\overline{Y}$ 分别为两样本均值,S_1^2、S_2^2 分别为两样本方差,则

①当 ${\sigma_1}^2 = {\sigma_2}^2 = \sigma^2$ 时,

记 $S_w = \sqrt{\frac{(n_1 - 1)S_1^2 + (n_2 - 1)S_2^2}{n_1 + n_2 - 2}}$,则

$$\frac{(\overline{X} - \overline{Y}) - (\mu_1 - \mu_2)}{\sqrt{\frac{n_1 + n_2}{n_1 n_2}} S_w} \sim t(n_1 + n_2 - 2)$$

② $\frac{\sigma_2^2 S_1^2}{\sigma_1^2 S_2^2} \sim F(n_1 - 1, n_2 - 1)$

【例 1-9-16】 设 $X_1, X_2, \cdots, X_n$ 与 $Y_1, Y_2, \cdots, Y_n$ 是来自正态总体 $X \sim N(\mu, \sigma^2)$的样本,并且相互独立,$\overline{X}$ 与 $\overline{Y}$ 分别是其样本均值,则$\frac{\sum\limits_{i=1}^{n}(X_i - \overline{X})^2}{\sum\limits_{i=1}^{n}(Y_i - \overline{Y})^2}$服从的分布是:

A. $t(n-1)$　　B. $F(n-1, n-1)$

C. $\chi^2(n-1)$　　D. $N(\mu, \sigma^2)$

解　设 $S_1^2 = \frac{1}{n-1}\sum\limits_{i=1}^{n}(X_i - \overline{X})^2$

因为总体 $X \sim N(\mu,\sigma^2)$

所以 $\dfrac{\sum\limits_{i=1}^{n}(X_i-\overline{X})^2}{\sigma^2}=\dfrac{(n-1)S_1^2}{\sigma^2}\sim\chi^2(n-1)$，同理 $\dfrac{\sum\limits_{i=1}^{n}(Y_i-\overline{Y})^2}{\sigma^2}\sim\chi^2(n-1)$

又因为两样本相互独立

所以 $\dfrac{\sum\limits_{i=1}^{n}(X_i-\overline{X})^2}{\sigma^2}$ 与 $\dfrac{\sum\limits_{i=1}^{n}(Y_i-\overline{Y})^2}{\sigma^2}$ 相互独立

$$\frac{\sum\limits_{i=1}^{n}(X_i-\overline{X})^2}{\sum\limits_{i=1}^{n}(Y_i-\overline{Y})^2}=\frac{\dfrac{\sum\limits_{i=1}^{n}(X_i-\overline{X})^2}{(n-1)\sigma^2}}{\dfrac{\sum\limits_{i=1}^{n}(Y_i-\overline{Y})^2}{(n-1)\sigma^2}}\sim F(n-1,n-1)$$

答案：B

注：如果知道 $\sum\limits_{i=1}^{n}(X_i-\overline{X})^2$ 与 χ^2 分布有关，则 $\dfrac{\sum\limits_{i=1}^{n}(X_i-\overline{X})^2}{\sum\limits_{i=1}^{n}(Y_i-\overline{Y})^2}$ 与 F 分布有关。

而本题只有一个选项是 F 分布，不用推导即可判定。

五、参数估计

用样本来估计总体的某些未知参数(主要是期望和方差)，这就是参数估计。参数估计有点估计和区间估计两种。

(一)点估计

设总体 X 的分布函数为 $F(x,\theta)$，θ 是未知参数，构造一个统计量 $g(X_1,X_2\cdots,X_n)$，用它的值 $g(x_1,x_2,\cdots,x_n)$ 估计参数 θ，称为参数的点估计问题。称统计量 $g(X_1,X_2,\cdots,X_n)$ 为 θ 的估计量，称 $g(x_1,x_2,\cdots,x_n)$ 为 θ 的估计值，θ 的估计量和估计值可记为 $\hat{\theta}$。

1. 矩估计法

设 $X_1,X_2,\cdots,X_n$ 是 X 的样本，X 的分布中含 k 个待估计参数 $\theta_1,\theta_2,\cdots,\theta_k$。如果总体矩 $\mu_l=E(X^l)(l=1,2,\cdots,k)$ 存在，相应的样本矩 $A_l=\dfrac{1}{n}\sum\limits_{i=1}^{n}X_i^l(l=1,2,\cdots,k)$，令 $\mu_l=A_l(l=1,2,\cdots,k)$，$\theta_1,\theta_2,\cdots,\theta_k$ 的解 $\hat{\theta}_1,\hat{\theta}_2,\cdots,\hat{\theta}_k$ 分别为 $\theta_1,\theta_2,\cdots,\theta_k$ 的矩估计量。

样本均值 $\overline{X}=\dfrac{1}{n}\sum\limits_{i=1}^{n}X_i$

样本二阶中心矩 $S_n^2=\dfrac{1}{n}\sum\limits_{i=1}^{n}(X_i-\overline{X})^2$

$\overline{X}$、S_n^2 分别是总体参数 $E(X)$、$D(X)$ 的矩估计量。

【例 1-9-17】 设总体 X 的概率密度 $f(x)=\begin{cases}(\theta+1)x^{\theta} & 0<x<1\\ 0 & \text{其他}\end{cases}$，其中 $\theta>-1$ 是未知参数，$X_1,X_2,\cdots,X_n$ 是来自总体 X 的样本，则 θ 的矩估计量是：

A. $\overline{X}$　　B. $\dfrac{2\overline{X}-1}{1-\overline{X}}$　　C. $2\overline{X}$　　D. $\overline{X}-1$

解 $E(X)=\int_0^1 x(\theta+1)x^{\theta}\mathrm{d}x=\frac{\theta+1}{\theta+2}$，$\theta=\frac{2E(X)-1}{1-E(X)}$，用 $\overline{X}$ 替换 $E(X)$，得 $\hat{\theta}=\frac{2\overline{X}-1}{1-\overline{X}}$。

答案：B

【例 1-9-18】 设总体 X 的概率分布为：

X	0	1	2	3
P	θ^2	$2\theta(1-\theta)$	θ^2	$1-2\theta$

其中 $\theta(0<\theta<\frac{1}{2})$ 是未知参数，利用样本值 3，1，3，0，3，1，2，3，所得 θ 的矩估计值是：

A. $\frac{1}{4}$　　B. $\frac{1}{2}$　　C. 2　　D. 0

解 $E(X)=1\times2\theta(1-\theta)+2\theta^2+3(1-2\theta)=3-4\theta$，$\theta=\frac{3-E(X)}{4}$，用 $\overline{X}$ 替换 $E(X)$，得估计量 $\hat{\theta}=\frac{3-\overline{X}}{4}$。

因为 $\overline{X}=\frac{3+1+3+3+1+2+3}{8}=2$，得估计值 $\hat{\theta}=\frac{3-2}{4}=\frac{1}{4}$。

答案：A

2. 最(极)大似然估计法

(1)似然函数

设总体 X 的分布律为 $P(X=x_k)=P_k(\theta)(k=1,2,\cdots)$，其中含有未知参数 θ，$x_1,x_2,\cdots,x_n$ 为一组样本值，则函数 $L(\theta)=\prod_{i=1}^{n}P(X=x_i)$ 称为似然函数。

设总体 X 的概率密度 $f(x,\theta)$ 已知，其中 θ 为未知参数，Θ 为 θ 的取值范围。对于样本 X_1，$X_2,\cdots,X_n$ 的一组样本值 $x_1,x_2,\cdots,x_n$，

则函数
$$L(\theta)=\prod_{i=1}^{n}f(x_i,\theta),\theta\in\Theta \tag{1-9-7}$$
称为似然函数。未知参数可以是一个也可以是多个。

(2)最(极)大似然估计

如果似然函数 $L(\theta)$ 在 $\hat{\theta}$ 上取得最大值，则称 $\hat{\theta}$ 为 θ 的最(极)大似然估计。一般来说，求 θ 的最(极)大似然估计 $\hat{\theta}$ 可以通过求解下面方程

$$\frac{\mathrm{d}L(\theta)}{\mathrm{d}\theta}=0 \quad 或 \quad \frac{\mathrm{d}}{\mathrm{d}\theta}\ln L(\theta)=0$$

求得，当概率密度中含多个未知参数 $\theta_1,\cdots,\theta_k$ 时，可用类似方法求得 $\hat{\theta}_1,\cdots,\hat{\theta}_k$。

【例 1-9-19】 设总体 X 服从指数分布，概率密度为

$$f(x)=\begin{cases}\lambda e^{-\lambda x} & x>0\\ 0 & x\leqslant0\end{cases}\quad(\lambda>0)$$

其中 λ 为未知数，如果取得样本观察值为 $x_1,x_2,\cdots,x_n$，求参数 λ 的极大似然估计。

解 似然函数

$$L(\lambda)=\prod_{i=1}^{n}\lambda e^{-\lambda x_i}=\lambda^n e^{-\lambda\sum_{i=1}^{n}x_i}\quad(\lambda>0)$$

$$\ln L(\lambda)=n\ln\lambda-\lambda\sum_{i=1}^{n}x_i$$

$$\frac{\mathrm{d}}{\mathrm{d}\lambda}\ln L(\lambda)=\frac{n}{\lambda}-\sum_{i=1}^{n}x_i=0$$

所以，λ 的极大似然估计为

$$\hat{\lambda}=\frac{n}{\sum\limits_{i=1}^{n}x_i}=\frac{1}{\bar{x}}(\text{估计值}),\hat{\lambda}=\frac{1}{\bar{X}}(\text{估计量})$$

（二）估计量的评选标准

1. 无偏性

设 $\hat{\theta}=\hat{\theta}(X_1,X_2,\cdots,X_n)$ 是参数 θ 的估计量，若 $E(\hat{\theta})=\theta$，则称 $\hat{\theta}$ 是 θ 的无偏估计量。例如，$\bar{X}$ 是 $E(X)$ 的无偏估计量，S^2 是 $D(X)$ 的无偏估计量。

【例 1-9-20】 设 $\hat{\theta}$ 是参数 θ 的一个无偏估计量，又方差 $D(\hat{\theta})>0$，下面结论中正确的是：

A. $\hat{\theta}^2$ 是 θ^2 的无偏估计量

B. $(\hat{\theta})^2$ 不是 θ^2 的无偏估计量

C. 不能确定 $(\hat{\theta})^2$ 是不是 θ^2 的无偏估计量

D. $(\hat{\theta})^2$ 不是 θ^2 的估计量

解 因为 $\hat{\theta}$ 是 θ 的一个无偏估计量，所以 $E(\hat{\theta})=\theta$。

$$E[(\hat{\theta})^2]=D(\hat{\theta})+[E(\hat{\theta})]^2=D(\hat{\theta})+\theta^2$$

又要 $D(\hat{\theta})>0$，所以 $E[(\hat{\theta})^2]>\theta^2$，$(\hat{\theta})^2$ 不是 θ^2 的无偏估计量。

答案：B

2. 有效性

设 $\hat{\theta}_1$、$\hat{\theta}_2$ 都是 θ 的无偏估计量，若 $D(\hat{\theta}_1)<D(\hat{\theta}_2)$，则称 $\hat{\theta}_1$ 比 $\hat{\theta}_2$ 有效。

例如，设 $\mu=E(X)$，$\sigma^2=D(X)>0$，X_1、X_2 为总体 X 的样本，μ 的两个估计量为

$$\hat{\mu}_1=\frac{1}{2}X_1+\frac{1}{2}X_2,\hat{\mu}_2=\frac{1}{3}X_1+\frac{2}{3}X_2$$

因为

$$E(\hat{\mu}_1)=\frac{1}{2}E(X_1)+\frac{1}{2}E(X_2)=\mu$$

$$E(\hat{\mu}_2)=\frac{1}{3}E(X_1)+\frac{2}{3}E(X_2)=\mu$$

所以 $\hat{\mu}_1$、$\hat{\mu}_2$ 都是 μ 的无偏估计量。

但是

$$D(\hat{\mu}_1)=\frac{1}{4}D(X_1)+\frac{1}{4}D(X_2)=\frac{1}{2}\sigma^2$$

$$D(\hat{\mu}_2)=\frac{1}{9}D(X_1)+\frac{4}{9}D(X_2)=\frac{5}{9}\sigma^2$$

$$D(\hat{\mu}_1)<D(\hat{\mu}_2)$$

所以 $\hat{\mu}_1$ 比 $\hat{\mu}_2$ 有效。

结论：设 $X_1,X_2,\cdots,X_n$ 是总体 X 的样本，$E(X)=\mu$，$D(X)=\sigma^2$

则：(1)$C_1\ C_2,\cdots,C_n$ 为常数，当$\sum_{i=1}^{n}C_i=1$ 时，$\hat{\mu}=\sum_{i=1}^{n}C_iX_i$ 是 μ 的无偏估计量。

(2)$\overline{X}=\frac{1}{n}\sum_{i=1}^{n}X_i$ 在(1)的所有无偏估计量当中最有效。

3. 一致性

设 $\hat{\theta}(X_1,X_2,\cdots,X_n)$是 θ 的估计量，若对任一给定的 $\varepsilon>0$ 和一切 $\theta\in\Theta$(Θ 为 θ 的可能取值范围，称为参数空间)，均有$\lim_{n\to\infty}P(|\hat{\theta}-\theta|>\varepsilon)=0$，则称 $\hat{\theta}$ 是 θ 的一致估计量。

结论：设$X_1,X_2,\cdots,X_n$是总体 X 的一个样本，$E(X)=\mu,D(X)>0$，则样本均值$\overline{X}$是 μ 的一致估计量。

(三)区间估计

点估计不能反映估计的可靠性和精确性，由此产生了区间估计。

设总体 X 的分布含有未知参数 θ。若由样本 $X_1,X_2,\cdots,X_n$ 确定的两个统计量 $\theta_1(X_1,X_2,\cdots,X_n)$及 $\theta_2(X_1,X_2,\cdots,X_n)$，对于给定的值 $\alpha(0<\alpha<1)$满足

$$P\{\theta_1(X_1,X_2,\cdots,X_n)<\theta<\theta_2(X_1,X_2,\cdots,X_n)\}=1-\alpha \tag{1-9-8}$$

则称随机区间(θ_1,θ_2)为 θ 的置信度为$(1-\alpha)$的置信区间。θ_1 和 θ_2 分别称为置信下限和置信上限。

式(1-9-8)的意义是：随机抽样得到的区间(θ_1,θ_2)包含 θ 真值的概率为$(1-\alpha)$，不含 θ 值的概率为 α。

置信度 $1-\alpha$ 就是区间估计的可靠性，α 小则置信度高。区间长度$\theta_2-\theta_1$反映区间估计的精确性，$\theta_2-\theta_1$小表示估计精度高。当 n 一定时，提高置信度(α 取值小)则降低估计精度($\theta_2-\theta_1$的值大)。

求置信区间的方法：

(1)先找一个与待估参数有关的统计量，一般找 θ 的一个良好的点估计量 $\hat{\theta}$。

(2)设法找出表达式中含此统计量 $\hat{\theta}$ 和待估参数 θ 的一个随机变量 U，其分布已知且与 θ 无关。

(3)对于给定的置信度$(1-\alpha)$，选取常数 a、b，使 $P(a<U<b)=1-\alpha$。一般取 b 为 U 的分布的上$\frac{\alpha}{2}$分位数，取 a 为 U 的分布的上$\left(1-\frac{\alpha}{2}\right)$分位数。

(4)把不等式 $a<U<b$ 改写为等价的形式$\theta_1<\theta<\theta_2$，其中 θ_1、θ_2 与 a、b 和样本 $X_1,X_2,\cdots X_n$ 有关，而与 θ 无关，于是有 $P(\theta_1<\theta<\theta_2)=1-\alpha$，随机区间$(\theta_1,\theta_2)$就是参数 θ 的一个置信度为$(1-\alpha)$的置信区间。

1. 正态总体均值 μ 的区间估计

设总体 $X\sim N(\mu,\sigma^2)$。

(1)σ^2 已知，求 μ 的置信区间

取 $\hat{\mu}=\overline{X}$，由于 $U=\frac{\overline{X}-\mu}{\sigma/\sqrt{n}}\sim N(0,1)$，$P\left\{-z_{\frac{\alpha}{2}}<\frac{\overline{X}-\mu}{\sigma}\sqrt{n}<z_{\frac{\alpha}{2}}\right\}=1-\alpha$

$$P\left\{\overline{X}-z_{\frac{\alpha}{2}}\frac{\sigma}{\sqrt{n}}<\overline{X}<\overline{X}+z_{\frac{\alpha}{2}}\frac{\sigma}{\sqrt{n}}\right\}=1-\alpha$$

总体均值 μ 的$(1-\alpha)$置信区间为

$$\left(\overline{X}-z_{\frac{\alpha}{2}}\frac{\sigma}{\sqrt{n}},\overline{X}+z_{\frac{\alpha}{2}}\frac{\sigma}{\sqrt{n}}\right) \tag{1-9-9}$$

说明：置信上下限为 $\overline{X}\pm z_{\frac{\alpha}{2}}\frac{\sigma}{\sqrt{n}}$。

(2)σ^2 未知，求 μ 的置信区间

$$S^2=\frac{1}{n-1}\sum_{i=1}^{n}(X_i-\overline{X})^2$$

取 $\hat{\mu}=\overline{X}$，由于 $U=\frac{\overline{X}-\mu}{S/\sqrt{n}}\sim t(n-1)$，$P\left\{-t_{\frac{\alpha}{2}}(n-1)<\frac{\overline{X}-\mu}{S}\sqrt{n}<t_{\frac{\alpha}{2}}(n-1)\right\}=1-\alpha$

总体均值 μ 的 $(1-\alpha)$ 置信区间为

$$\left(\overline{X}-t_{\frac{\alpha}{2}}(n-1)\frac{S}{\sqrt{n}},\overline{X}+t_{\frac{\alpha}{2}}(n-1)\frac{S}{\sqrt{n}}\right)\tag{1-9-10}$$

说明：置信上下限 $\overline{X}\pm t_{\frac{\alpha}{2}}(1-1)\frac{S}{\sqrt{n}}$ 与式(1-9-9)对比记。

2. 正态总体方差 σ^2 的区间估计

取 $\hat{\sigma}^2=S^2$，由于 $U=\frac{(n-1)S^2}{\sigma^2}\sim\chi^2(n-1)$，

$$P\left\{\chi^2_{1-\frac{\alpha}{2}}(n-1)<\frac{(n-1)S^2}{\sigma^2}<\chi_{\frac{\alpha}{2}}(n-1)\right\}=1-\alpha$$

总体方差 σ^2 的 $(1-\alpha)$ 置信区间为 $\left(\frac{(n-1)S^2}{\chi^2_{\frac{\alpha}{2}}(n-1)},\frac{(n-1)S^2}{\chi^2_{1-\frac{\alpha}{2}}(n-1)}\right)$ (1-9-11)

3. 两个正态总体均值差和方差比的区间估计

设 X_1、X_2、…、X_{n_1} 和 Y_1、Y_2、…、Y_{n_2} 分别是总体 $N(\mu_1,\sigma_1^2)$ 和 $N(\mu_2,\sigma_2^2)$ 的两个相互独立的样本。$\overline{X}$ 和 $\overline{Y}$ 为两样本均值，S_1^2 和 S_2^2 为两样本方差。

(1)σ_1^2 和 σ_2^2 已知时，$(\mu_1-\mu_2)$ 的置信区间

由于 $\quad\overline{X}-\overline{Y}\sim N\left(\mu_1-\mu_2,\frac{\sigma_1^2}{n_1}+\frac{\sigma_2^2}{n_2}\right),\frac{(\overline{X}-\overline{Y})-(\mu_1-\mu_2)}{\sqrt{\frac{\sigma_1^2}{n_1}+\frac{\sigma_2^2}{n_2}}}\sim N(0,1)$

$(\mu_1-\mu_2)$ 的 $(1-\alpha)$ 置信区间为

$$\left(\overline{X}-\overline{Y}-z_{\frac{\alpha}{2}}\sqrt{\frac{\sigma_1^2}{n_1}+\frac{\sigma_2^2}{n_2}},\overline{X}-\overline{Y}+z_{\frac{\alpha}{2}}\sqrt{\frac{\sigma_1^2}{n_1}+\frac{\sigma_2^2}{n_2}}\right)$$

(2)σ_1^2、σ_2^2 未知，但知 $\sigma_1^2=\sigma_2^2$ 时，$(\mu_1-\mu_2)$ 的置信区间

记
$$S_w=\sqrt{\frac{(n_1-1)S_1^2+(n_2-1)S_2^2}{n_1+n_2-2}}$$

由于
$$\frac{(\overline{X}-\overline{Y})-(\mu_1-\mu_2)}{\sqrt{\frac{n_1+n_2}{n_1n_2}}S_w}\sim t(n_1+n_2-2)$$

所以 $(\mu_1-\mu_2)$ 的 $(1-\alpha)$ 置信区间为

$$\left(\overline{X}-\overline{Y}-t_{\frac{\alpha}{2}}(n_1+n_2-2)\sqrt{\frac{n_1+n_2}{n_1n_2}}S_w,\overline{X}-\overline{Y}+t_{\frac{\alpha}{2}}(n_1+n_2-2)\sqrt{\frac{n_1+n_2}{n_1n_2}}S_w\right)$$

【例 1-9-21】 甲、乙两工人生产同一零件，甲 8 天的日产量是 628、583、510、554、612、523、530、615，乙 10 天的日产量是 535、433、398、470、567、480、498、560、503、426。

假定日产量均服从正态分布，且方差相同，试求两工人日平均产量之差的置信区间。($\alpha=0.05$)

解 记甲日产量为 X，乙日产量为 Y，$n_1=8$，$n_2=10$。

$$\overline{X}=569.38, S_1^2=2\,110.55$$
$$\overline{Y}=487.00, S_2^2=3\,256.22$$
$$S_w=\sqrt{\frac{(n_1-1)S_1^2+(n_2-1)S_2^2}{n_1+n_2-2}}=\sqrt{\frac{7\times 2\,110.55+9\times 3\,256.22}{16}}=52.488$$
$$t_{0.025}(16)=2.119\,9$$
$$t_{\frac{\alpha}{2}}(n_1+n_2-2)\sqrt{\frac{n_1+n_2}{n_1n_2}}S_w=2.119\,9\times\sqrt{\frac{18}{80}}\times 52.488=52.78$$

则$(\mu_1-\mu_2)$的 0.95 置信区间为(29.60,135.16)。

(3)σ_1^2/σ_2^2 的置信区间

由于
$$\frac{\sigma_2^2 S_1^2}{\sigma_1^2 S_2^2}\sim F(n_1-1,n_2-1)$$
$$P\left\{F_{1-\frac{\alpha}{2}}(n_1-1,n_2-1)<\frac{\sigma_2^2 S_1^2}{\sigma_1^2 S_2^2}<F_{\frac{\alpha}{2}}(n_1-1,n_2-1)\right\}=1-\alpha$$

所以 σ_1^2/σ_2^2 的$(1-\alpha)$置信区间为$\left(\frac{S_1^2}{S_2^2}\cdot\frac{1}{F_{\frac{\alpha}{2}}(n_1-1,n_2-1)},\frac{S_1^2}{S_2^2}\cdot\frac{1}{F_{1-\frac{\alpha}{2}}(n_1-1,n_2-1)}\right)$

六、假设检验

假设检验是根据样本信息,通过构造适当的统计量,对原假设是否为真作出统计推断,得出拒绝或接受的决定。假设检验的基本思想是:小概率事件(例如发生概率小于 0.01 的事件)在一次观察中可以认为几乎不可能发生。

(一)假设检验的一般步骤

(1)根据问题的要求,设立一个待检验的原假设 H_0(也称零假设)及对立假设 H_1(也称备择假设),这里 H_0、H_1 是首先必须明确给出的。假设检验分为参数假设检验(对总体未知参数提出假设)和非参数假设检验(如检验总体是否服从正态分布)。参数假设检验时,H_0 中一定有等号,H_1 中一定没有等号。设 θ 为未知参数,θ_0 为已知常数:①检验 θ 与 θ_0 是否有(显著)差异时,$H_0:\theta=\theta_0$,$H_1:\theta\neq\theta_0$;②检验 θ 是否比 θ_0(显著)大时,$H_0:\theta\leqslant\theta_0$(或 $\theta=\theta_0$),$H_1:\theta>\theta_0$;③检验 θ 是否比 θ_0(显著)小时,$H_0:\theta\geqslant\theta_0$(或 $\theta=\theta_0$),$H_1:\theta<\theta_0$。

(2)选一个检验统计量 $T(X_1,X_2,\cdots,X_n)$,在假设 H_0 成立(等号成立)的条件下,其分布是完全已知的。

(3)选一检验显著性水平 α(小概率值)并确定 H_0 的一个否定域(或拒绝域)W_α,使 H_0 成立时,$P(T\in W_\alpha)=\alpha$。

(4)由样本具体数据算出 $T(X_1,X_2,\cdots,X_n)$的实际值 $T(x_1,x_2,\cdots,x_n)$,若 $T\in W_\alpha$,则否定 H_0 接受 H_1,这时可能犯第一类错误(弃真),其概率为 α。若 $T\notin W_\alpha$,则接受 H_0。这时可能犯第二类错误(取伪)。

(二)正态总体参数的假设检验

设总体 $X\sim N(\mu,\sigma^2)$,$X_1,X_2,\cdots,X_n$ 是来自 X 的一个样本,$\overline{X}$ 为样本均值,S^2 为样本方差,显著性水平为 α。

1.σ^2 已知时,总体均值 μ 的假设检验(见表 1-9-2)

$H_0:\mu=\mu_0$ $H_1:\mu\neq\mu_0$ (μ_0 为已知常数)

H_0 成立时,统计量 $U=\frac{\overline{X}-\mu_0}{\sigma}\sqrt{n}\sim N(0,1)$

当$|U|=\frac{|\overline{X}-\mu_0|}{\sigma}\sqrt{n}>z_{\frac{\alpha}{2}}$时(用$\overline{X}$代替$\mu$与$\mu_0$比较,$\overline{X}$与$\mu_0$差别大,推断$\mu$与$\mu_0$差别大),否定$H_0$;当$|U|\leqslant I_{\frac{\alpha}{2}}$时,接受$H_0$。

表 1-9-2

H_0	H_1	统计量及其分布	拒绝(H_0)域
$\mu=\mu_0$	$\mu\neq\mu_0$	$U=\frac{\overline{X}-\mu_0}{\sigma}\sqrt{n}\sim N(0,1)$	$\lvert U\rvert>z_{\frac{\alpha}{2}}$
$\mu\leqslant\mu_1$	$\mu>\mu_0$		$U>z_\alpha$
$\mu\geqslant\mu_0$	$\mu<\mu_0$		$U<-z_\alpha$

2.σ^2未知时,总体均值μ的假设检验(见表 1-9-3)

$H_0:\mu=\mu_0$　$H_1:\mu>\mu_0$　(μ_0为已知常数)

H_0成立时,统计量$T=\frac{\overline{X}-\mu_0}{S}\sqrt{n}\sim t(n-1)$

当$T=\frac{\overline{X}-\mu_0}{S}\sqrt{n}>t_\alpha(n-1)$时($\overline{X}$比$\mu_0$显著大,推断$\mu$比$\mu_0$显著大),否定$H_0$;当$T\leqslant t_\alpha(n-1)$时,接受$H_0$。

表 1-9-3

H_0	H_1	统计量及其分布	拒绝(H_0)域
$\mu=\mu_0$	$\mu\neq\mu_0$	$T=\frac{\overline{X}-\mu_0}{S}\sqrt{n}\sim t(n-1)$	$\lvert T\rvert>t_{\frac{\alpha}{2}}(n-1)$
$\mu\leqslant\mu_1$	$\mu>\mu_0$		$T>t_\alpha(n-1)$
$\mu\geqslant\mu_0$	$\mu<\mu_0$		$T<-t_\alpha(n-1)$

3.μ未知时,总体方差σ^2的假设检验(见表 1-9-4)

$H_0:\sigma^2=\sigma_0^2$　$H_1:\sigma^2<\sigma_0^2$　(σ_0为已知常数)

H_0成立时,统计量

$$\chi^2=\frac{1}{\sigma_0^2}\sum_{i=1}^{n}(X_i-\overline{X})^2=\frac{(n-1)S^2}{\sigma_0^2}\sim\chi^2(n-1)$$

当$\chi^2<\chi^2_{1-\alpha}(n-1)$时,否定$H_0$($\sigma^2$比$\sigma_0^2$显著小);否则,接受$H_0$。

表 1-9-4

H_0	H_1	统计量及其分布	拒绝(H_0)域
$\sigma^2=\sigma_0^2$	$\sigma^2\neq\sigma_0^2$	$\chi^2=\frac{(n-1)S^2}{\sigma_0^2}\sim\chi^2(n-1)$	$\chi^2<\chi^2_{1-\frac{\alpha}{2}}(n-1)$或$\chi^2-\chi^2_{\frac{\alpha}{2}}(n-1)$
$\sigma^2\leqslant\sigma_0^2$	$\sigma^2>\sigma_0^2$		$\chi^2>\chi^2_\alpha(n-1)$
$\sigma^2\geqslant\sigma_0^2$	$\sigma^2<\sigma_0^2$		$\chi^2<\chi^2_{1-\alpha}(n-1)$

【例 1-9-22】 根据长期经验和资料的分析,某砖瓦厂所生产的砖的抗断强度X服从正态分布,方差$\sigma^2=1.21$,今从该厂生产的一批砖中随机抽取6块,测得抗断强度分别为(单位:kg/cm²):32.56,29.66,31.64,30.00,31.87,31.03。

问:这批砖的平均抗断强度可否认为是32.50kg/cm²?($\alpha=0.05$)

解 假设$H_0:\mu=32.50$,$H_1:\mu\neq32.50$

根据所给样本值,计算统计量U的值

$$U=\frac{\overline{x}-32.50}{\sigma/\sqrt{n}}=\frac{31.13-32.50}{\sqrt{1.21/6}}=\frac{-1.37}{1.1}\times\sqrt{6}\approx-3$$

$z_{0.025}=1.96$,而$|U|=3>1.96$,故应在显著性水平$\alpha=0.05$下否定H_0,即不能认为平均

抗断强度是 32.50kg/cm^2。

【例 1-9-23】 设 $X_1,X_2,\cdots,X_n$ 是来自总体 $N(\mu,\sigma^2)$ 的样本，μ、σ^2 未知，$\overline{x}=\frac{1}{n}\sum_{i=1}^{n}X_i$，$Q^2=\sum_{i=1}^{n}(X_i-\overline{X})^2$，$Q>0$。则检验假设 $H_0:\mu=0$ 时应选取的统计量是：

A. $\sqrt{n(n-1)}\frac{\overline{X}}{Q}$　　B. $\sqrt{n}\frac{\overline{X}}{Q}$

C. $\sqrt{n-1}\frac{\overline{X}}{Q}$　　D. $\sqrt{n}\frac{\overline{X}}{Q^2}$

解 当 σ^2 未知时检验假设 $H_0:\mu=\mu_0$，应选取统计量 $T=\frac{\overline{X}-\mu_0}{S}\sqrt{n}$，本题 $S^2=\frac{1}{n-1}\cdot\sum_{i=1}^{n}(X_i-\overline{X})^2=\frac{1}{n-1}Q^2$，$S=\frac{Q}{\sqrt{n-1}}$，取 $\mu_0=0$。

答案：A

习　题

1-9-1 设 A、B 为随机事件，$A\cup B=B$，则错误的是（　　）。

A. $A\subset B$　　B. $\overline{B}\subset\overline{A}$　　C. $A\overline{B}=\varnothing$　　D. $\overline{A}B=\varnothing$

1-9-2 设 $P(A)=P(B)=\frac{1}{2}$，则正确的是（　　）。

A. $P(A\cup B)=1$　　B. $P(\overline{A}\,\overline{B})=\frac{1}{4}$

C. $P(AB)=\frac{1}{2}$　　D. $P(AB)=P(\overline{A}\,\overline{B})$

1-9-3 设 $P(A)>0$，则 $P(B|A)=1$ 成立的充分条件是（　　）。

A. $A=\Omega$　　B. $B\subset A$　　C. $A\subset B$　　D. $P(B|\overline{A})=0$

1-9-4 两台机床加工同样的零件，第一台出现废品的概率是 0.03，第二台出现废品的概率是 0.02，第一台加工的零件比第二台加工的零件多一倍，将加工出来的零件放在一起，则任意取出一零件是合格品的概率是（　　）。

A. 0.027　　B. 0.973　　C. 0.954　　D. 0.982

1-9-5 两个小组生产同样的零件，第一组的废品率是 2%，第二组的产量是第一组的两倍而废品率是 3%。若两组生产的零件放在一起，从中任抽取一件，经检查是废品，则这件废品是第一组生产的概率为（　　）。

A. 15%　　B. 25%　　C. 35%　　D. 45%

1-9-6 设随机事件 A 与 B 相互独立，且 $P(A)=0.4$，$P(B)=0.3$，则 $P(A\cup B)$ 是（　　）。

A. 0.48　　B. 0.58　　C. 0.50　　D. 0.70

1-9-7 设 A、B 相互独立，$P(A)=0.2$，$P(B)=0.4$，则 $P(\overline{A}|B)$ 等于：

A. 0.2　　B. 0.4　　C. 0.6　　D. 0.8

1-9-8 设 A、B 相互独立，$P(A)>0$，$P(B)>0$，则一定有 $P(A\cup B)$ 等于：

A. $P(A)+P(B)$　B. $P(A)\ P(B)$　　C. $1-P(\overline{A})P(\overline{B})$　D. $1+P(\overline{A})P(\overline{B})$

1-9-9 设 $0<P(A)<1$，$0<P(B)<1$，$P(A|B)+P(\overline{A}|\overline{B})=1$，则正确的是（　　）。

A. A、B 互斥　　B. A、B 对立　　C. A、B 独立　　D. A、B 不独立

1-9-10　某人射击，每次击中目标的概率为 0.8，射击 3 次，至少击中 2 次的概率约为(　　)。

A. 0.7　　B. 0.8　　C. 0.5　　D. 0.9

1-9-11　设 X 的分布律为

X	0	1	2	3
P	0.4	a	b	0.1

，已知随机事件 $\{X\leqslant 1\}$ 与 $\{0<X<3\}$ 相互独立，则(　　)。

A. $a=0.2\quad b=0.3$　　B. $a=0.4\quad b=0.1$

C. $a=0.3\quad b=0.2$　　D. $a=0.1\quad b=0.4$

1-9-12　设随机变量 X 的概率密度 $f(x)$ 为偶函数，X 的分布函数为 $F(x)$，则对任意实数 a，有(　　)。

A. $F(-a)=1-\int_0^a f(x)\mathrm{d}x$　　B. $F(-a)=\frac{1}{2}-\int_0^a f(x)\mathrm{d}x$

C. $F(-a)=F(a)$　　D. $F(-a)=2F(a)-1$

1-9-13　下列 4 个函数中，(　　)可作为随机变量的概率密度。

A. $f(x)=\begin{cases} x & -1<x<1 \\ 0 & \text{其他} \end{cases}$　　B. $f(x)=\begin{cases} x^2 & -1<x<1 \\ 0 & \text{其他} \end{cases}$

C. $f(x)=\begin{cases} \frac{1}{2} & -1<x<1 \\ 0 & \text{其他} \end{cases}$　　D. $f(x)=\begin{cases} 2 & -1<x<1 \\ 0 & \text{其他} \end{cases}$

1-9-14　设 X 服从参数 $\lambda=3$ 的指数分布，其分布函数为 $F(x)$，则 $F\left(\frac{1}{3}\right)$ 等于：

A. $\frac{1}{3e}$　　B. $\frac{e}{3}$　　C. $1-e^{-1}$　　D. $1-\frac{1}{3}e^{-1}$

1-9-15　设 $X\sim N(\mu,\sigma^2)$，则 σ 增大时，$P(|X-\mu|<\sigma)$(　　)。

A. 增大　　B. 减小　　C. 不变　　D. 变化情况不确定

1-9-16　设随机变量 X 服从正态 $N(1,2^2)$，$a=P\{12<X\leqslant 16\}$，$b=P\{14<X\leqslant 18\}$，则 a 与 b 之间的关系是(　　)。

A. $a<b$　　B. $a>b$　　C. $a=b$　　D. $a\leqslant b$

1-9-17　设 X 的分布律为

X	-2	1	a
P	$\frac{1}{4}$	b	$\frac{1}{4}$

，$E(X)=1$，则常数 a、b 分别为：

A. $2,\frac{1}{2}$　　B. $4,\frac{1}{2}$　　C. $6,\frac{1}{4}$　　D. $8,\frac{1}{3}$

1-9-18　设 X 的分布函数 $F(x)=\frac{1}{2}+\frac{1}{\pi}\arctan x$，则 $E(X)=$(　　)。

A. 0　　B. $\frac{1}{2}$　　C. $\frac{1}{\pi}$　　D. 不存在

1-9-19　设 X 表示 4 次独立射击命中次数，已知 4 次射击至少命中一次的概率为 $\frac{15}{16}$，则 $E(X^2)=$(　　)。

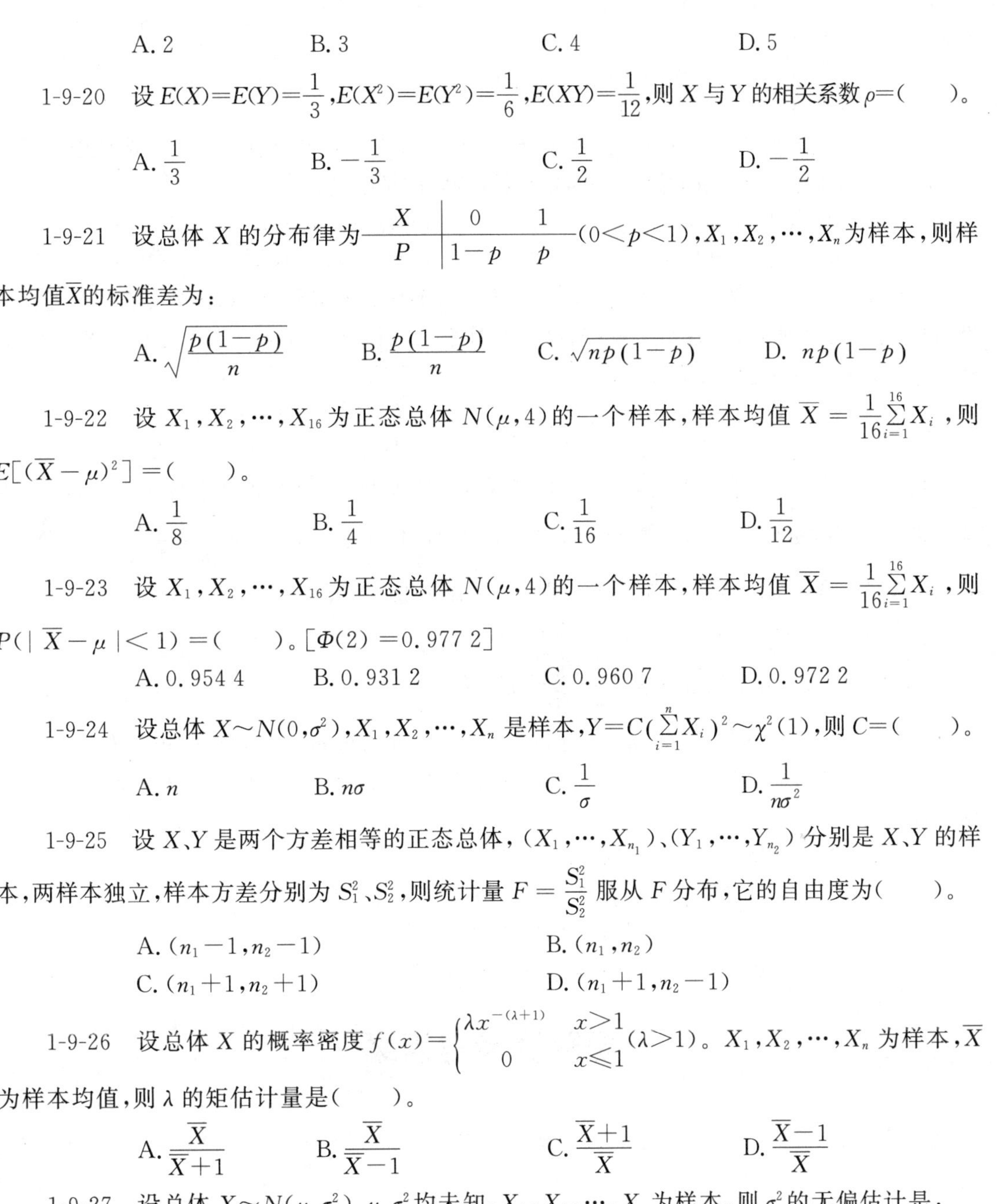

A. 2　　B. 3　　C. 4　　D. 5

1-9-20　设 $E(X)=E(Y)=\frac{1}{3}$，$E(X^2)=E(Y^2)=\frac{1}{6}$，$E(XY)=\frac{1}{12}$，则 X 与 Y 的相关系数 $\rho=$(　　)。

A. $\frac{1}{3}$　　B. $-\frac{1}{3}$　　C. $\frac{1}{2}$　　D. $-\frac{1}{2}$

1-9-21　设总体 X 的分布律为

X	0	1
P	$1-p$	p

$(0<p<1)$，$X_1,X_2,\cdots,X_n$ 为样本，则样本均值 $\overline{X}$ 的标准差为：

A. $\sqrt{\frac{p(1-p)}{n}}$　　B. $\frac{p(1-p)}{n}$　　C. $\sqrt{np(1-p)}$　　D. $np(1-p)$

1-9-22　设 $X_1,X_2,\cdots,X_{16}$ 为正态总体 $N(\mu,4)$ 的一个样本，样本均值 $\overline{X}=\frac{1}{16}\sum_{i=1}^{16}X_i$，则 $E[(\overline{X}-\mu)^2]=$(　　)。

A. $\frac{1}{8}$　　B. $\frac{1}{4}$　　C. $\frac{1}{16}$　　D. $\frac{1}{12}$

1-9-23　设 $X_1,X_2,\cdots,X_{16}$ 为正态总体 $N(\mu,4)$ 的一个样本，样本均值 $\overline{X}=\frac{1}{16}\sum_{i=1}^{16}X_i$，则 $P(|\overline{X}-\mu|<1)=$(　　)。[$\Phi(2)=0.977\,2$]

A. 0.954 4　　B. 0.931 2　　C. 0.960 7　　D. 0.972 2

1-9-24　设总体 $X\sim N(0,\sigma^2)$，$X_1,X_2,\cdots,X_n$ 是样本，$Y=C(\sum_{i=1}^{n}X_i)^2\sim\chi^2(1)$，则 $C=$(　　)。

A. n　　B. $n\sigma$　　C. $\frac{1}{\sigma}$　　D. $\frac{1}{n\sigma^2}$

1-9-25　设 X、Y 是两个方差相等的正态总体，$(X_1,\cdots,X_{n_1})$、$(Y_1,\cdots,Y_{n_2})$ 分别是 X、Y 的样本，两样本独立，样本方差分别为 S_1^2、S_2^2，则统计量 $F=\frac{S_1^2}{S_2^2}$ 服从 F 分布，它的自由度为(　　)。

A. (n_1-1,n_2-1)　　B. (n_1,n_2)

C. (n_1+1,n_2+1)　　D. (n_1+1,n_2-1)

1-9-26　设总体 X 的概率密度 $f(x)=\begin{cases}\lambda x^{-(\lambda+1)} & x>1\\ 0 & x\leqslant 1\end{cases}(\lambda>1)$。$X_1,X_2,\cdots,X_n$ 为样本，$\overline{X}$ 为样本均值，则 λ 的矩估计量是(　　)。

A. $\frac{\overline{X}}{\overline{X}+1}$　　B. $\frac{\overline{X}}{\overline{X}-1}$　　C. $\frac{\overline{X}+1}{\overline{X}}$　　D. $\frac{\overline{X}-1}{\overline{X}}$

1-9-27　设总体 $X\sim N(\mu,\sigma^2)$，μ，σ^2 均未知，$X_1,X_2,\cdots,X_n$ 为样本，则 σ^2 的无偏估计是：

A. $\frac{1}{n-1}\sum_{i=1}^{n}(X_i-\overline{X})^2$　　B. $\frac{1}{n-1}\sum_{i=1}^{n}(X_i-\mu)^2$

C. $\frac{1}{n}\sum_{i=1}^{n}(X_i-\overline{X})^2$　　D. $\frac{1}{n}\sum_{i=1}^{n}(X_i-\mu)^2$

1-9-28　设总体 $X\sim P(\lambda)$(参数 λ 的泊松分布)，λ 未知，$X_1,X_2,\cdots,X_n$ 是样本，$\overline{X}$ 是样本均值，S^2 是样本方差，$\hat{\lambda}=a\overline{X}+(2-3a)S^2$ 为 λ 的无偏估计，则 $a=$(　　)。

A. -1　　B. 0　　C. $\frac{1}{2}$　　D. 1

1-9-29　设 X_1、X_2 是总体 X 的样本，$E(X)=\mu$ 未知，$D(X)=\sigma^2$，则下列 μ 的估计量中最

有效的估计量是(　　)。

A. $\frac{2}{3}X_1+\frac{1}{3}X_2$　B. $\frac{1}{4}X_1+\frac{3}{4}X_2$　C. $\frac{2}{5}X_1+\frac{3}{5}X_2$　D. $\frac{1}{2}X_1+\frac{1}{2}X_2$

1-9-30　设总体 $X\sim N(\mu,\sigma^2)$，μ 未知，σ^2 已知，$X_1,X_2,\cdots,X_n$ 是样本，下列选项中能提高 μ 的区间估计精度(置信区间长度 L 小，估计精度高)的做法是(　　)。

A. 减小 α，增大 n　B. 减小 α，减小 n

C. 增大 α，增大 n　D. 增大 α，减小 n

1-9-31　某厂家广告宣称，饮用其产品一个月可平均减体重大于 3kg。为考察广告的真实性，检验部门随机抽取 30 名饮用者，测得一个月平均减体重 2.8kg。设月减体重 $X\sim N(\mu,\sigma^2)$，原假设 H_0 和对立假设应写成(　　)。

A. $H_0:\mu\leqslant 3,H_1:\mu>3$　B. $H_0:\mu\geqslant 3,H_1:\mu<3$

C. $H_0:\mu\leqslant 2.8,H_1:\mu>2.8$　D. $H_0:\mu\geqslant 2.8,H_1:\mu<2.8$

1-9-32　某厂生产合金弦线，其抗拉强度服从均值为 10560MPa 的正态分布 $N(\mu,\sigma^2)$。现从一批产品中随机抽出 10 根，得样本均值 $\overline{x}=10631.4$，样本方差 $S^2=\frac{1}{n-1}\sum_{i=1}^{n}(x_i-\overline{x})^2=6560.4$，现检验这批产品的平均抗拉强度有无显著变化($\alpha=0.05$)。

检验假设 $H_0:\mu=10560,H_1:\mu\neq 10560$

问：在 H_0 成立时采用统计量 $\frac{\overline{X}-10560}{S/\sqrt{10}}$ 服从(　　)。

A. $t(9)$分布　B. $t(10)$分布　C. 正态分布　D. $\chi^2(9)$分布

1-9-33　对单个正态总体 $N(\mu,\sigma^2)$ 作假设检验时，在下列(　　)情况下采用 t 检验法(检验统计量服从 t 分布)。

A. σ^2 已知，$H_0:\mu=\mu_0$(μ_0 为已知常数)

B. σ^2 未知，$H_0:\mu=\mu_0$(μ_0 为已知常数)

C. μ 已知，$H_0:\sigma^2=\sigma_0^2$(σ_0 为已知正常数)

D. μ 未知，$H_0:\sigma^2=\sigma_0^2$(σ_0 为已知正常数)

题解及参考答案

第一节

1-1-1　**解**：利用向量积求出与 $\vec{\alpha}$、$\vec{\beta}$ 都垂直的向量，$\vec{\alpha}\times\vec{\beta}=\begin{vmatrix}\vec{i} & \vec{j} & \vec{k}\\ 1 & 2 & 3\\ 1 & -3 & -2\end{vmatrix}=5(\vec{i}+\vec{j}-\vec{k})$，$|\vec{\alpha}\times\vec{\beta}|=5\sqrt{3}$，因单位的量 $\vec{\alpha}^0=\frac{\vec{\alpha}}{|a|}$，所以 $\vec{\alpha}^0=\pm\frac{1}{\sqrt{3}}(\vec{i}+\vec{j}-\vec{k})$。

答案：D

1-1-2　**解**：利用数量积计算公式 $\vec{a}\cdot\vec{a}=|\vec{a}|^2$，求出 $|\vec{a}|^2$，即得到 $|\vec{a}|$。$|\vec{a}+\vec{b}|^2=(\vec{a}+\vec{b})\cdot(\vec{a}+\vec{b})=\vec{a}\cdot\vec{a}+2\vec{a}\cdot\vec{b}+\vec{b}\cdot\vec{b}=5$，所以 $|\vec{a}+\vec{b}|=\sqrt{5}$。

答案：D

1-1-3 **解**:运用数量积和向量积的定义及它们的运算性质计算,$(\vec{a}+\vec{b})\cdot(\vec{a}-\vec{b})=\vec{a}\cdot\vec{a}+\vec{b}\cdot\vec{a}-\vec{a}\cdot\vec{b}-\vec{b}\cdot\vec{b}=|\vec{a}|^2-|\vec{b}|^2$,选项 A 成立。选项 B、C、D 均不成立。

答案:A

1-1-4 **解**:利用已知的两直线方程计算出它们各自的方向向量。

例如$\begin{cases}3x+z=4\\y+2z=9\end{cases}$,$\vec{S}_1=\vec{n_1}\times\vec{n_2}=\begin{vmatrix}i & j & k\\3 & 0 & 1\\0 & 1 & 2\end{vmatrix}=-\vec{i}-6\vec{j}+3\vec{k}$,同理求出 $\vec{S}_2=-6\vec{i}-36\vec{j}+18\vec{k}$。$\vec{S}_1$、$\vec{S}_2$ 对应坐标成比例,故 $\vec{S}_1/\!/\vec{S}_2$,则 $\vec{L}_1/\!/\vec{L}_2$ 或重合,在 L_1 上取一点(1,7,1),代入 L_2 方程,不满足 L_2 方程,因而 L_1、L_2 平行但不重合。

答案:A

1-1-5 **解**:直线 L 的方向向量 $\vec{S}=\{2,1,3\}$,平面 π 的法向量 $\vec{n}=\{4,-2,-2\}$,$\vec{S}\cdot\vec{n}=0$,则 $\vec{S}\perp\vec{n}$,直线与平面平行或重合,取 L 上一点(−3,−4,0)代入平面 π 方程得 $4\times(-3)-2\times(-4)+0=-4\neq3$,不满足平面方程,故直线//平面。

答案:A

1-1-6 **解**:见解图,取已知直线的方向向量为与其垂直平面的法向量,取 $\vec{n}=\vec{S}=\{3,2,-1\}$,$M_0(2,1,3)$。过 M_0 与 L 垂直的平面方程:$3(x-2)+2(y-1)-(z-3)=0$,化简得 $3x+2y-z-5=0$。求出已知直线和垂直平面的交点,L 的参数方程为 $x=3t-1$,$y=2t+1$,$z=-t$,代入平面方程 $3(3t-1)+2(2t+1)+t-5=0$,解出 $t=\frac{3}{7}$,交点为 $M_1(\frac{2}{7},\frac{13}{7},-\frac{3}{7})$。连接 M_0M_1,$\overline{M_0M_1}=\left\{-\frac{12}{7},\frac{6}{7},-\frac{24}{7}\right\}=-\frac{6}{7}\{2,-1,4\}$,取 $\vec{S}_{M_0M_1}=\{2,-1,4\}$,与已知直线垂直相交的直线方程为 $\frac{x-2}{2}=\frac{y-1}{-1}=\frac{z-3}{4}$。

题 1-1-6 解图

答案:C

1-1-7 **解**:利用给出的直线方程,求出直线方程的方向向量,$\vec{n}_1=\{1,-1,-1\}$,$\vec{n}_2=\{2,1,-3\}$,$\vec{n}_1\times\vec{n}_2=4\vec{i}+\vec{j}+3\vec{k}$,取 $\vec{S}=\{4,1,3\}$。利用 $\vec{S}=\{4,1,3\}$,点 $M(3,-2,1)$写出 L 的方程:$\frac{x-3}{4}=\frac{y+2}{1}=\frac{z-1}{3}$。

答案:D

1-1-8 **解**:通过方程组$\begin{cases}x^2+y^2+(z+3)^2=25\\z=1\end{cases}$消去 z,得 $x^2+y^2=9$,为空间曲线在 xOy 平面上的投影柱面。联立$\begin{cases}x^2+y^2=9\\z=1\end{cases}$,为球面与平面 $z=1$ 的交线。

答案:D

1-1-9 **解**:分别写出向量 $\overrightarrow{M_1M_2}=\{-1,-1,1\}$,$\overrightarrow{M_1M_3}=\{-1,0,1\}$,平面 π 的法向量 $\vec{n}=\overrightarrow{M_1M_2}\times\overrightarrow{M_1M_3}=-\vec{i}+0\vec{j}-\vec{k}$,取 $\vec{S}=\vec{n}=\{1,0,1\}$,点 $M(1,1,1)$,所求直线对

称式方程为：$\frac{x-1}{1}=\frac{y-1}{0}=\frac{z-1}{1}$。

答案：A

1-1-10 **解**：在 xOz 平面上的曲线 $f(x,z)=0$，绕 x 轴旋转一周，旋转曲面方程为 $f(x,\pm\sqrt{y^2+z^2})=0$。则旋转曲面方程为 $\frac{x^2}{9}+\frac{y^2+z^2}{4}=1$。

答案：C

1-1-11 **解**：$\begin{cases}2x^2+y^2+z^2=16 & ① \\ x^2-y^2+z^2=0 & ②\end{cases}$

消 x，由②×2 得 $2x^2-2y^2+2z^2=0$　③

①－③得　$3y^2-z^2=16$

答案：C

1-1-12 **解**：方法 1：点 $M_0(1,2,3)$，$\vec{S}\{3,2,1\}$

xOy 平面方程为 $z=0$，法向量 $\vec{n}=\{0,0,1\}$

设直线 L_0 在 xOy 平面上投影平面的法向量为 $\vec{n}_{投影平面}$

$$\vec{n}_{投影平面}=\vec{S}\times\vec{n}=\begin{vmatrix} i & j & k \\ 3 & 2 & 1 \\ 0 & 0 & 1\end{vmatrix}=\{2,-3,0\}$$

过点 M_0 在 xOy 平面上投影平面为 $2(x-1)-3(y-2)=0$

即 $2x-3y+4=0$

L_0 在 xOy 平面上投影直线方程为 $\begin{cases}2x-3y+4=0 \\ z=0\end{cases}$

方法 2：也可以用 L_0 方程中前面部分 $\frac{x-1}{3}=\frac{y-2}{2}$ 所表示的平面和 $z=0$ 所表示的平面表示 L_0 在 xOy 平面上的投影直线方程，即 $\begin{cases}\frac{x-1}{3}=\frac{y-2}{2} \\ z=0\end{cases}$

即 $\begin{cases}2x-3y+4=0 \\ z=0\end{cases}$

答案：B

第二节

1-2-1 **解**：$\lim\limits_{x\to\infty}\frac{3x^2+5}{5x+3}\sin\frac{2}{x}=\lim\limits_{x\to\infty}\frac{x\left(3x+\frac{5}{x}\right)}{5x+3}\sin\frac{2}{x}$

$$=\lim_{x\to\infty}\frac{3x+\frac{5}{x}}{5x+3}\times\frac{\sin\frac{2}{x}}{\frac{2}{x}}\times 2=\frac{3}{5}\times 1\times 2=\frac{6}{5}$$

答案：B

1-2-2 **解**：$x\to 0$ 利用等价无穷小计算，$\ln(1-tx^2)\sim -tx^2$，$x^2\sim x\sin x$，原式$=\lim\limits_{x\to 0}\frac{-tx^2}{x^2}=-t$。

答案：B

1-2-3 **解**：$\lim\limits_{x\to 0}\frac{x^2-\sin x}{x}=\lim\limits_{x\to 0}(x-\frac{\sin x}{x})=-1(\neq 1)$，为同阶无穷小，但不是等价无穷小。

答案:B

1-2-4 **解**:已知$\lim\limits_{x\to 1}f(x)=1$,$\lim\limits_{x\to 1^+}f(x)=\lim\limits_{x\to 1^-}f(x)=1$,而$\lim\limits_{x\to 1^+}f(x)=\lim\limits_{x\to 1^+}\cos(x-1)=1$,要求:$\lim\limits_{x\to 1^-}f(x)=1$,即$\lim\limits_{x\to 1^-}g(x)=1$,可验证当$g(x)=1+e^{\frac{1}{x-1}}$时极限为1,$\lim\limits_{x\to 1^-}(1+e^{\frac{1}{x-1}})=1+\lim\limits_{x\to 1^-}e^{\frac{1}{x-1}}=1$。

答案:D

1-2-5 **解**:$\lim\limits_{x\to 0}\dfrac{\sqrt{2-2\cos x}}{x}=\lim\limits_{x\to 0}\dfrac{\sqrt{4\sin^2\dfrac{x}{2}}}{x}=\lim\limits_{x\to 0}\dfrac{2\left|\sin\dfrac{x}{2}\right|}{x}$。

当$x\to 0^+$时,$\lim\limits_{x\to 0^+}\dfrac{2\left|\sin\dfrac{x}{2}\right|}{x}=\lim\limits_{x\to 0^+}\dfrac{2\sin\dfrac{x}{2}}{x}=1$;

当$x\to 0^-$时,$\lim\limits_{x\to 0^-}\dfrac{2\left|\sin\dfrac{x}{2}\right|}{x}=\lim\limits_{x\to 0^-}\dfrac{-2\sin\dfrac{x}{2}}{x}=-1$。

答案:A

1-2-6 **解**:在$x=0$处,当满足$\lim\limits_{x\to 0^+}f(x)=\lim\limits_{x\to 0^-}f(x)=f(0)$时,$f(x)$在$x=0$处连续。

计算:$x=0$,$f(0)=1$,$\lim\limits_{x\to 0^-}(\cos x+x\sin\dfrac{1}{x})=1$,$\lim\limits_{x\to 0^+}(x^2+1)=1$,所以在$x=0$处,$f(x)$连续。

答案:D

1-2-7 **解**:举列说明

①$\alpha(x)=x$,$\beta(x)=x^4$,在$x\to 0$时为无穷小,$\lim\limits_{x\to 0}\dfrac{x^2}{x^4}=\lim\limits_{x\to 0}\dfrac{1}{x^2}=\infty$

②$\alpha(x)=x^2$,$\beta(x)=x^4$,在$x\to 0$时为无穷小,$\lim\limits_{x\to 0}\dfrac{(x^2)^2}{x^4}=1$

答案 D

1-2-8 **解**:可以验证$f(x)=Cg(x)$错误,求导$f'(x)=Cg'(x)$。

答案:A

1-2-9 **解**:利用函数在一点可导的定义计算$f'(x_0)=\lim\limits_{\Delta x\to 0}\dfrac{f(x_0+\Delta x)-f(x_0)}{\Delta x}$

原式$=\lim\limits_{x\to 0}\dfrac{1}{\dfrac{f(x_0-2x)-f(x_0)}{x}}=\lim\limits_{x\to 0}\dfrac{1}{\dfrac{f(x_0-2x)-f(x_0)}{-2x}\times(-2)}=\dfrac{1}{-2f'(x_0)}=\dfrac{1}{4}$

求出$f'(x_0)=-2$

答案:C

1-2-10 **解**:验证$f(x)$在区间[1,2]上满足拉格朗日中值定理的条件,即有$f(2)-f(1)=f'(\xi)(2-1)$,$1<\xi<2$。$\dfrac{3}{2}-2=-\dfrac{1}{x^2}\Big|_{x=\xi}(2-1)$,$-\dfrac{1}{2}=-\dfrac{1}{\xi^2}$,$\xi^2=2$,$\xi=\sqrt{2}$。

答案:A

1-2-11 **解**:利用点(0,1)是曲线$y=ax^3+bx^2+c$拐点的条件,$y'=3ax^2+2bx$,$y''=6ax+2b$,令$y''=0$,$6ax+2b=0$,$x=\dfrac{-2b}{6a}=-\dfrac{1}{3}\dfrac{b}{a}$。

因拐点横坐标为0,即$x=0$,则$b=0$。

将 $b=0$ 代入曲线方程，$y=ax^3+C$，$y''=6ax$，当 $a\neq 0$ 时，$(-\infty,0)$，$(0,+\infty)$ 两侧 y'' 异号，再将拐点坐标 $x=0$，$y=1$ 代入 $y=ax^3+bx^2+c$，$c=1$，所以 $b=0$，$c=1$，a 为不等于 0 的任何实数。

答案：B

1-2-12　**解：**利用多元隐函数方法求导，$F(x,y)=0$，求出 F_x、F_y，则 $\frac{dy}{dx}=-\frac{F_x}{F_y}$，$F_x=3x^2+\cos\pi y$，$F_y=3y^2+(x+1)[-(\sin\pi y)\cdot\pi]$，$\frac{dy}{dx}=-\frac{F_x}{F_y}=-\frac{3x^2+\cos\pi y}{3y^2+(x+1)(-\pi\sin\pi y)}$，当 $x=-1$ 时，代入原方程 $y=-2$。

切线斜率 $K_{切}=\frac{dy}{dx}\Big|_{\substack{x=-1\\y=-2}}=-\frac{1}{3}$，法线斜率 $K_{法}=3$，法线方程 $y+2=3(x+1)$，即 $y-3x-1=0$。

答案：B

1-2-13　**解：**面积 $A=\int_a^{a+1}x^2dx=\frac{1}{3}[(a+1)^3-a^3]$，利用导数知识求在面积最小时的 a 值，$A'=\frac{1}{3}[3(a+1)^2-3a^2]=2a+1$，令 $A'=0$，$a=-\frac{1}{2}$，$A''=2>0$，所以当 $a=-\frac{1}{2}$ 取得面积最小。

题 1-2-13 解图

答案：B

1-2-14　**解：**用复合函数求导法则计算，$y'=\frac{1}{f(x)}\cdot f'(x)=\frac{f'(x)}{f(x)}$，再利用函数商的求导法则 $y''=\frac{f''\cdot f-f'\cdot f'}{f^2(x)}=\frac{f\cdot f''-(f')^2}{f^2}$。

答案：A

1-2-15　**解：**$\frac{dy}{dt}=f(t)+tf'(t)$，$\frac{dx}{dt}=f'(t)-\frac{f'(t)}{f(t)}$，$\frac{dy}{dx}=\frac{\frac{dy}{dt}}{\frac{dx}{dt}}=\frac{f^2(t)+tf(t)f'(t)}{f(t)f'(t)-f'(t)}$。

将 $t=0$，$f(0)=2$，$f'(0)=2$ 代入得：$\frac{dy}{dx}\Big|_{\substack{t=0\\f(0)=2\\f'(0)=2}}=\frac{2^2+0}{2\times 2-2}=2$。

答案：D

1-2-16　**解：**$\frac{dy}{dx}=\frac{2x}{1+x^2}$，已知直线 $y=x-1$，斜率 $k=1$，$\frac{2x}{1+x^2}=1$，$x^2-2x+1=0$，解出 $x=1$，二重根。当 $x=1$ 时，$y=\ln 2$。

答案：C

1-2-17　**解：**$f'(x)=g'(x)$，$f(x)$、$g(x)$ 可差一常数，即 $f(x)=g(x)+C$。

答案：D

1-2-18　**解：**已知 $f'(x)=f(1-x)$，两边求导，有：

$$f''(x)=-f'(1-x) \qquad ①$$

在式 $f'(x)=f(1-x)$ 中，当 x 取 $1-x$ 时，有：

$$f'(1-x)=f(x) \qquad ②$$

将②式代入①式：$f''(x)=-f(x)$，$f''(x)+f(x)=0$。

答案：C

1-2-19 **解:**已知 $f(x)$ 在 $x=0$ 可导,即左导 $f'_-(0)=$ 右导 $f'_+(0)$,则

$$f'_+(0)=\lim_{x\to0^+}\frac{f(x)-f(0)}{x-0}=\lim_{x\to0^+}\frac{ax+2-2}{x-0}=a$$

$$f'_-(0)=\lim_{x\to0^-}\frac{f(x)-f(0)}{x-0}=\lim_{x\to0^-}\frac{e^{-x}+1-2}{x}=\lim_{x\to0^-}\frac{e^{-x}-1}{x}$$

$$=\lim_{x\to0^-}\frac{-x}{x}=-1(\text{当 } x\to0 \text{ 时},e^{-x}-1\sim-x)$$

答案:D

1-2-20 **解:**$f(x)$ 在 $x=0$ 可导,所以在 $x=0$ 必连续,即 $\lim\limits_{x\to0^+}f(x)=\lim\limits_{x\to0^-}f(x)=f(0)$,$f(0)=b$,$\lim\limits_{x\to0^+}x^2\sin\dfrac{1}{x}=0$,$\lim\limits_{x\to0^-}(ax+b)=b$,得到 $b=0$,利用 $f(x)$ 在 $x=0$ 可导,$f'_+(0)=f'_-(0)$,而 $f'_+(0)=\lim\limits_{x\to0^+}\dfrac{x^2\sin\frac{1}{x}-b}{x-0}=0$,$f'_-(0)=\lim\limits_{x\to0^-}\dfrac{ax+b-b}{x}=a$,得到 $a=0$,$b=0$。

答案:C

1-2-21 **解:**$\dfrac{dx}{dt}=\dfrac{-4t}{(1+t^2)^2}$,$\dfrac{dy}{dt}=\dfrac{2-2t^2}{(1+t^2)^2}$,则 $\dfrac{dy}{dx}=\dfrac{\frac{dy}{dt}}{\frac{dx}{dt}}=\dfrac{t^2-1}{2t}$。

答案:A

1-2-22 **解:**$f(x)$ 为幂指函数,利用对数求导法计算,两边取对数,即 $\ln y=\dfrac{1}{x}\ln(1+x)$,求导 $\dfrac{1}{y}\dfrac{dy}{dx}=-\dfrac{1}{x^2}\ln(1+x)+\dfrac{1}{x(1+x)}$,

$$\frac{dy}{dx}=(1+x)^{\frac{1}{x}}\left[-\frac{1}{x^2}\ln(1+x)+\frac{1}{x(1+x)}\right],\left.\frac{dy}{dx}\right|_{x=1}=1-\ln4。$$

答案:D

1-2-23 **解:**定义域$(0,+\infty)$,$f'(x)=\dfrac{10}{1+x^2}-\dfrac{3}{x}=\dfrac{-3x^2+10x-3}{x(1+x^2)}$,令 $f'(x)=0$,$-3x^2+10x-3=0$,得到 $x=3$,$x=\dfrac{1}{3}$,分割定义域,判定 $x=\dfrac{1}{3}$,$x=3$ 时两侧一阶导数的符号,确定 $x=3$ 处取得极大值 $f(3)$。

答案:C

1-2-24 **解:**画示意图

已知当 $0<x<a$ 时,$f(x)<f(0)$,函数是连续偶函数,所以当 $-a<x<0$ 时,$f(0)>f(x)$,即 $f(0)$ 是 $f(x)$ 在$(-a,a)$上的极大值,也是最大值。

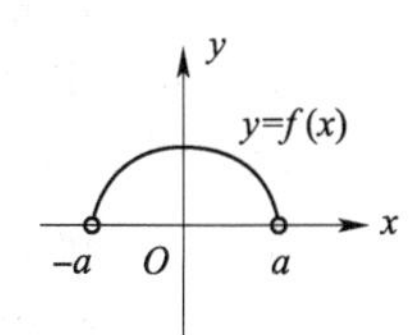

题 1-2-24 解图

答案:C

1-2-25 **解:**定义域$(-\infty,+\infty)$,求 $y'=4x^2(x-3)=0$,得到 $x=0$,$x=3$。则由 $y''=12(x-2)x=0$,得到 $x=0$,$x=2$。列表如下。

题 1-2-25 解表

x	$(-\infty,0)$	0	$(0,2)$	2	$(2,3)$	3	$(3,+\infty)$
y'	$-$	0	$-$	$-$	$-$	0	$+$
y''	$+$	0	$-$	0	$+$	$+$	$+$
y	↘	拐	↘	拐	↘	极值	↗

确定单增且向上凹的区间为$(3,+\infty)$。

答案:D

1-2-26 **解:**定义域$[-4,-1]$，$f'(x)=x+2+\dfrac{1}{x}=\dfrac{x^2+2x+1}{x}$，可作为公式记住$(\ln|x|)'=\dfrac{1}{x}$。令$f'(x)=0$，即$x^2+2x+1=0$，$x=-1$为驻点，端点$x=-4$，$x=-1$，比较$f(-1)$与$f(-4)$函数值的大小，确定最大值。

答案:C

1-2-27 **解:**将x_0代入方程$x_0f''(x_0)+3x_0(f'(x_0))^2=1-e^{-x_0}$，已知$x_0$是函数的一个驻点，则$f'(x_0)=0$，化简，得：

$$x_0f''(x_0)=1-e^{-x_0},f''(x_0)=\frac{1-e^{-x_0}}{x_0}=\frac{e^{x_0}-1}{x_0e^{x_0}}>0$$

答案:B

第三节

1-3-1 **解:**利用凑微分方法，即

$$\int f'(3-2x)\mathrm{d}x=\frac{-1}{2}\int f'(3-2x)\mathrm{d}(-2x+3)=-\frac{1}{2}f(3-2x)+C$$

答案:A

1-3-2 **解:**利用第一类换元积分法(凑微分法)，即

$$\int e^{-x}f(e^{-x})\mathrm{d}x=-\int f(e^{-x})\mathrm{d}e^{-x}=-F(e^{-x})+C$$

答案:B

1-3-3 **解:**凑微分，即

$$\int\frac{f'(\ln x)}{x\sqrt{f(\ln x)}}\mathrm{d}x=\int\frac{f'(\ln x)}{\sqrt{f(\ln x)}}\mathrm{d}\ln x=\int\frac{1}{\sqrt{f(\ln x)}}\mathrm{d}f(\ln x)=2\sqrt{f(\ln x)}+C$$

答案:C

1-3-4 **解:**利用函数原函数的定义计算。

$$(x^2)'=2x,g(x)=2x,(\cos x)'=-\sin x,f(x)=-\sin x$$

所以$f[g(x)]=-\sin[g(x)]=-\sin 2x$。

答案:D

1-3-5 **解:**计算函数的积分，即左$=\int f'(\ln x)\mathrm{d}\ln x=f(\ln x)+C$

而右$=x^2+C_2$，则$f(\ln x)+C_1=x^2+C_2$，设$t=\ln x$，$x=e^t$，代入得$f(t)+C_1=e^{2t}+C_2$；则$f(x)=e^{2x}+c$(其中$C=C_2-C_1$)。

答案:C

1-3-6 **解**:$\lim\limits_{x\to a}\dfrac{x}{x-a}\int_a^x f(t)\mathrm{d}t=\lim\limits_{x\to a}\dfrac{x\int_a^x f(t)\mathrm{d}t}{x-a}\xlongequal{\frac{0}{0}}\lim\limits_{x\to a}\dfrac{\int_a^x f(t)\mathrm{d}t+xf(x)}{1}=af(a)$(因 $\int_a^a f(t)\mathrm{d}t=0$)。

答案:C

1-3-7 **解**:$f(x)$在$[a,b]$连续,$f(x)$在$[a,b]$可积,定积分$\int_a^b f(x)\mathrm{d}x$为一确定常数。

答案:A

1-3-8 **解**:$\lim\limits_{x\to 0}\dfrac{\int_0^x f(t)\mathrm{d}t}{x^2}\xlongequal{\frac{0}{0}}\lim\limits_{x\to 0}\dfrac{f(x)}{2x}=\dfrac{1}{2}\lim\limits_{x\to 0}\dfrac{f(x)-f(0)}{x-0}=\dfrac{1}{2}f'(0)=\dfrac{2}{2}=1$。

答案:B

1-3-9 **解**:$I=\int_e^{+\infty}\dfrac{1}{x(\ln x)^2}\mathrm{d}x=\int_e^{+\infty}\dfrac{1}{(\ln x)^2}\mathrm{d}\ln x=-\dfrac{1}{\ln x}\Big|_e^{+\infty}=-\left(\lim\limits_{x\to+\infty}\dfrac{1}{\ln x}-\dfrac{1}{\ln e}\right)=1$。

答案:A

1-3-10 **解**:逐一计算选项A、B、C、D来确定。

选项A:$\int_2^{+\infty}\dfrac{1}{x\ln^3 x}\mathrm{d}x=\int_2^{+\infty}\dfrac{1}{\ln^3 x}\mathrm{d}(\ln x)=-\dfrac{1}{2}\dfrac{1}{\ln^2 x}\Big|_2^{+\infty}=-\dfrac{1}{2}(\lim\limits_{x\to+\infty}\dfrac{1}{\ln^2 x}-\dfrac{1}{\ln^2 2})=\dfrac{1}{2\ln^2 2}$,收敛。

选项B:$\int_0^{+\infty}e^{-x}\mathrm{d}x=-e^{-x}\Big|_0^{+\infty}=-(\lim\limits_{x\to+\infty}e^{-x}-1)=1$,收敛。

选项C:因$x=-1$为无穷不连续点,则$\int_{-1}^0\dfrac{2}{\sqrt{1-x^2}}\mathrm{d}x=2\arcsin x\Big|_{-1}^0=2(0-\lim\limits_{x\to-1^+}\arcsin x)=\pi$,收敛。

选项D:因$x=1$为函数的无穷不连续点,则$\int_1^e\dfrac{1}{x\ln x}\mathrm{d}x=\int_1^e\dfrac{1}{\ln x}\mathrm{d}\ln x=\ln\ln x\Big|_1^e=\ln\ln e-\lim\limits_{x\to 1^+}\ln\ln x=\infty$,发散。

答案:D

1-3-11 **解**:积分上限函数求导数,$Q'(x)=x^2e^{-x^2}\cdot 2x=2x^3e^{-x^2}$。

答案:C

1-3-12 **解**:$\int_0^a f(x)\mathrm{d}x=\int_0^{\frac{a}{2}}f(x)\mathrm{d}x+\int_{\frac{a}{2}}^a f(x)\mathrm{d}x$。

将$\int_{\frac{a}{2}}^a f(x)\mathrm{d}x$变形,设$x=a-t,\mathrm{d}x=-\mathrm{d}t$。当$x=a$时,$t=0$;当$x=\dfrac{a}{2}$时,$t=\dfrac{a}{2}$。

$\int_{\frac{a}{2}}^a f(x)\mathrm{d}x=\int_{\frac{a}{2}}^0 f(a-t)(-\mathrm{d}t)=\int_0^{\frac{a}{2}}f(a-t)\mathrm{d}t=\int_0^{\frac{a}{2}}f(a-x)\mathrm{d}x$。

答案:B

1-3-13 **解**:计算$\int_0^1 f(x)\mathrm{d}x=\int_0^{\frac{1}{2}}1\mathrm{d}x+\int_{\frac{1}{2}}^1 0\mathrm{d}x=\dfrac{1}{2}$,因此在$[0,1]$内不存在$\xi$,使等式

成立。

答案:B

1-3-14 **解**:可以验证选项 A、B、C 均成立,例如$\int_{-a}^{a}f(x^2)\mathrm{d}x=\int_{-a}^{0}f(x^2)\mathrm{d}x+\int_{0}^{a}f(x^2)\mathrm{d}x$,设 $x=-t,\mathrm{d}x=-\mathrm{d}t,\int_{-a}^{0}f(x^2)\mathrm{d}x=\int_{a}^{0}f[(-t)^2](-\mathrm{d}t)=\int_{0}^{a}f(t^2)\mathrm{d}t=\int_{0}^{a}f(x^2)\mathrm{d}x$,从而$\int_{-a}^{a}f(x)\mathrm{d}x=2\int_{0}^{a}f(x^2)\mathrm{d}x$。

选项 D:$\int_{0}^{1}10^x\mathrm{d}x=\frac{1}{\ln 10}10^x\Big|_0^1=\frac{1}{\ln 10}(10-1)=\frac{9}{\ln 10}$。

答案:D

1-3-15 **解**:$\varphi(-x)=\int_{0}^{-x}f(t)\mathrm{d}t$

设 $t=-u,\mathrm{d}t=-\mathrm{d}u$

当 $t=-x$ 时,$u=x$;当 $t=0$ 时,$u=0$

$\varphi(-x)=\int_{0}^{-x}f(t)\mathrm{d}t=\int_{0}^{x}f(-u)(-\mathrm{d}u)\xlongequal{f\text{ 为偶函数}}-\int_{0}^{x}f(u)\mathrm{d}u=-\int_{0}^{x}f(t)\mathrm{d}t=-\varphi(x)$,即 $\varphi(-x)=-\varphi(x)$,所以 $\varphi(x)$ 为奇函数。

答案:B

1-3-16 **解**:已知 $f(x)$ 在 $[0,+\infty)$ 连续,$f(x)$ 在 $[0,1]$ 上可积,定积分$\int_0^1 f(x)\mathrm{d}x$ 为一常数。设 $A=\int_0^1 f(x)\mathrm{d}x$,则 $f(x)=xe^{-x}+Ae^x$,两边在 $[0,1]$ 区间上作定积分,得$\int_0^1 f(x)\mathrm{d}x=\int_0^1 xe^{-x}\mathrm{d}x+\int_0^1 Ae^x\mathrm{d}x$,$A=\int_0^1 xe^{-x}\mathrm{d}x+A\int_0^1 e^x\mathrm{d}x$……①,而$\int_0^1 xe^{-x}\mathrm{d}x=-\int_0^1 x\mathrm{d}e^{-x}=-\left[xe^{-x}\Big|_0^1-\int_0^1 e^{-x}\mathrm{d}x\right]=-\left(\frac{2}{e}-1\right)$,$\int_0^1 e^x\mathrm{d}x=e-1$,代入①式 $A=-\left(\frac{2}{e}-1\right)+(e-1)A$,求出 $A=-\frac{1}{e}$,则 $f(x)=xe^{-x}-\frac{1}{e}e^x$。

答案:B

1-3-17 **解**:见解图,$y^2=4-x$,$x=4-y^2$ 当 $x=0$ 时,$y=\pm 2$

$S=\int_{-2}^{2}(4-y^2)\mathrm{d}y$。

题 1-3-17 解图

答案:A

1-3-18 **解**:画图

$x:\left[\frac{\pi}{4},\frac{5}{4}\pi\right]$

$A=\int_{\frac{1}{4}\pi}^{\frac{5}{4}\pi}(\sin x-\cos x)\mathrm{d}x$。

题 1-3-18 解图

答案:B

第四节

1-4-1 **解**:利用二元复合函数,求偏导的方法计算。

$$\frac{\partial z}{\partial y}=\frac{\partial z}{\partial u}\cdot\frac{\partial u}{\partial y}+\frac{\partial z}{\partial v}\cdot\frac{\partial v}{\partial y}=2u\varphi'_y\ln v+\frac{u^2}{v}\varphi'_y$$

答案:C

1-4-2 **解**:$xyz-e^{x+y}=0$,$F_x=yz-e^{x+y}$,$F_y=xz-e^{x+y}$。

$$\frac{\partial y}{\partial x}=-\frac{F_x}{F_y}=-\frac{yz-e^{x+y}}{xz-e^{x+y}}\xlongequal[xyz=e^{x+y}]{\text{由原方程可知}}-\frac{yz-xyz}{xz-xyz}=-\frac{z(y-xy)}{z(x-xy)}=-\frac{y(1-x)}{x(1-y)}$$

答案:A

1-4-3 **解**:$\frac{\partial z}{\partial x}=\frac{1}{y}\cdot\frac{1}{xy}\cdot y=\frac{1}{xy}$,　$\left.\frac{\partial z}{\partial x}\right|_{\substack{x=e\\y=e^{-1}}}=1$

$$\frac{\partial z}{\partial y}=\frac{\frac{1}{xy}xy-\ln(xy)}{y^2}=\frac{1-\ln xy}{y^2},\quad \left.\frac{\partial z}{\partial y}\right|_{\substack{x=e\\y=e^{-1}}}=e^2$$

$\mathrm{d}z=\mathrm{d}x+e^2\mathrm{d}y$

答案:C

1-4-4 **解**:曲线切线的方向向量 $\vec{s}=\{1,2t,3t^2\}$,平面法向量 $\vec{n}=\{1,2,1\}$,切线与平面平行,那么切线的方向向量应与平面的法向量垂直。

$\vec{s}\perp\vec{n}$,则 $\vec{s}\cdot\vec{n}=0$,即 $1+4t+3t^2=0$,解方程 $3t^2+4t+1=0$,$t_1=-\frac{1}{3}$,$t_2=-1$,得对应点$(-\frac{1}{3},\frac{1}{9},-\frac{1}{27})$,$(-1,1,-1)$。

答案:A

1-4-5 **解**:求曲面 $z=x^2-y^2$ 的切平面的法向量,$x^2-y^2-z=0$,$\vec{n}=\{F_x,F_y,F_z\}=\{2x,-2y,-1\}$,已知平面法向量 $\vec{n}_{\text{已知}}=\{1,-1,-1\}$,两平面平行,法向量平行,$\vec{n}/\!/\vec{n}_{\text{已知}}$,对应坐标成比例,有$\frac{2x}{1}=\frac{-2y}{-1}=\frac{-1}{-1}=1$,得 $x=\frac{1}{2}$,$y=\frac{1}{2}$,代入方程得 $z=0$,求出切点坐标 $M_0(\frac{1}{2},\frac{1}{2},0)$。$\vec{n}=\{1,-1,-1\}$,切平面方程 $(x-\frac{1}{2})-(y-\frac{1}{2})-(z-0)=0$,化简为 $x-y-z=0$。

答案:C

1-4-6 **解**:利用二元函数求极值的充分条件计算

$$\begin{cases}z'_x=3x^2+6x-9=0,\text{得 } x_1=-3,x_2=1\\ z'_y=-3y^2+6y=0,\text{得 } y_1=0,y_2=2\end{cases}$$

求出驻点 $M_1(-3,0)$,$M_2(-3,2)$,$M_3(1,0)$,$M_4(1,2)$,再求出 z_{xx},z_{xy},z_{yy} 逐一判定在哪一点取得极大值,如 $M_2(-3,2)$,$z_{xx}=6x+6$,$z_{xy}=0$,$z_{yy}=-6y+6$,代入 $A=-12$,$B=0$,$C=-6$,$AC-B^2>0$,$A<0$,在该点取得极大值。

答案:D

1-4-7 **解**:$xyz-1=0$,计算 F_x、F_y、F_z,即 $F_x=yz$,$F_y=xz$,$F_z=xy$,$\vec{n}=\{yz,xz,xy\}$。已知平面法向量 $\vec{n}=\{1,1,1\}$,因两平面平行,平面法向量平行,对应坐标成比例,即$\frac{yz}{1}=\frac{xz}{1}=\frac{xy}{1}$,解出 $y=x=z$,代入得 $x^3=1$,$x=1$,即 $x=y=z=1$。

M_0 点坐标(1,1,1),$\vec{n}=\{1,1,1\}$,切平面方程$(x-1)+(y-1)+(z-1)=0$,$x+y+z-3=0$。

答案:D

1-4-8 **解**:$z=x^2-y^2$,$M_0(\sqrt{2},-1,1)$,$x^2-y^2-z=0$,$\vec{n}=\{2x,-2y,-1\}\Big|_{(\sqrt{2},-1,1)}=\{2\sqrt{2},2,-1\}$,取$\vec{s}=\vec{n}=\{2\sqrt{2},2,-1\}$,$M_0(\sqrt{2},-1,1)$,法线方程

$$\frac{x-\sqrt{2}}{2\sqrt{2}}=\frac{y+1}{2}=\frac{z-1}{-1}$$

答案:C

1-4-9 **解**:可通过图 1-4-1 基本概念关系图得到答案 B。

答案:B

1-4-10 **解**:偏导数$\frac{\partial z}{\partial x}\Big|_{(x_0 y_0)}$存在,表示一元函数$z=f(x,y_0)$在点$x=x_0$处可导,所以$z=f(x,y_0)$在$P_0$点连续,即选项 B 正确。

选项 A 对于二元函数在某一点存在偏导数,即使是存在所有偏导,也不能推出函数在该点连续,所以 A 错误。

选项 C 对于二元函数在某一点存在所有偏导数也推不出函数在该点可微,所以 C 错误,D 也错误。

答案:B

第五节

题 1-5-1 解图

1-5-1 **解**:求交点$\begin{cases}y=x\\y=1\end{cases}$,(1,1),先对$y$积分,再对$x$积分

$D:\begin{cases}0\leqslant x\leqslant 1\\x\leqslant y\leqslant 1\end{cases}$

$$\iint_D e^{-y}\,dxdy=\int_0^1 dx\int_x^1 e^{-y}\,dy=-\int_0^1\left(\frac{1}{e}-e^{-x}\right)dx=-\left(\frac{1}{e}\cdot x+e^{-x}\right)_0^1$$

$$=-\left(\frac{2}{e}-1\right)=-\frac{2}{e}+1$$

答案:D

1-5-2 **解**:还原积分区域D,如图所示,D在极坐标下不等式组为:

$\begin{cases}0\leqslant\theta\leqslant\frac{\pi}{4}\\\tan x\sec\theta\leqslant r\leqslant\sec\theta\end{cases}$

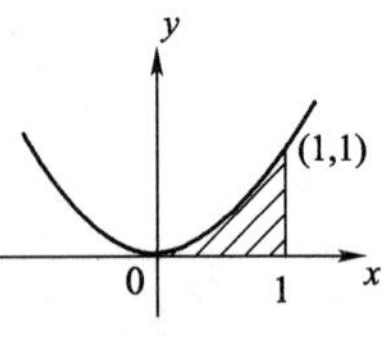

题 1-5-2 解图

其中$y=x^2$,化为$r\sin\theta=(r\cos\theta)^2$,$r=\frac{\sin\theta}{\cos^2\theta}=\tan\theta\sec\theta$。

$x=1$,化为$r\cos\theta=1$,$r=\sec\theta$,面积元素$dxdy=rdrd\theta$,

原式$=\int_0^{\frac{\pi}{4}}d\theta\int_{\tan\theta\sec\theta}^{\sec\theta}f(r\cos\theta,r\sin\theta)rdr$。

答案:D

1-5-3 **解**:G 为圆域 $\iint\limits_G \sin(x^2+y^2)\mathrm{d}x\mathrm{d}y$,用 $x=r\cos\theta, y=r\sin\theta, \mathrm{d}x\mathrm{d}y=r\mathrm{d}r\mathrm{d}\theta$ 代入积分式

原式 $=\iint\limits_G \sin r^2 \cdot r\mathrm{d}r\mathrm{d}\theta=\int_0^{2\pi}\mathrm{d}\theta\int_0^2 r\sin r^2\mathrm{d}r \qquad G:\begin{cases}0\leqslant\theta\leqslant 2\pi\\ 0\leqslant r\leqslant 2\end{cases}$

答案:C

1-5-4 **解**:求交点 $\begin{cases}y^2=x\\ y=x-2\end{cases}$,$(4,2)$,$(1,-1)$

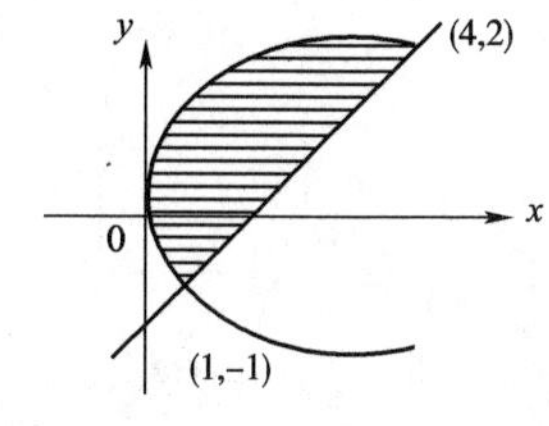

题 1-5-4 解图

先对 x 积分,后对 y 积分,D:$\begin{cases}-1\leqslant y\leqslant 2\\ y^2\leqslant x\leqslant y+2\end{cases}$

$I=\int_{-1}^{2}\mathrm{d}y\int_{y^2}^{y+2}xy\,\mathrm{d}x$。

答案:B

1-5-5 **解**:复原积分区域画出图形。

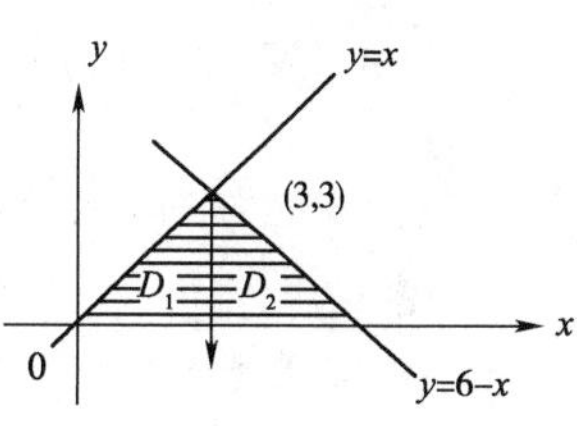

题 1-5-5 解图

求交点 $\begin{cases}y=6-x\\ y=x\end{cases}$, 交点为 $(3,3)$,因围成区域 D 的上面曲线由两个方程组成,因而分成两个部分计算。

D_1:$\begin{cases}0\leqslant x\leqslant 3\\ 0\leqslant y\leqslant x\end{cases}$,$D_2$:$\begin{cases}3\leqslant x\leqslant 6\\ 0\leqslant y\leqslant 6-x\end{cases}$

$$\begin{aligned}\text{原式}&=\iint\limits_D f(x,y)\mathrm{d}x\mathrm{d}y\\ &=\iint\limits_{D_1} f(x,y)\mathrm{d}x\mathrm{d}y+\iint\limits_{D_2} f(x,y)\mathrm{d}x\mathrm{d}y\\ &=\int_0^3\mathrm{d}x\int_0^x f(x,y)\mathrm{d}y+\int_3^6\mathrm{d}x\int_0^{6-x} f(x,y)\mathrm{d}y\end{aligned}$$

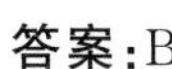

答案:B

1-5-6 **解**:L:$\begin{cases}y=\dfrac{2}{3}x^{\frac{3}{2}}\\ x=x\end{cases}$,$0\leqslant x\leqslant 1$,$\mathrm{d}s=\sqrt{1+[y'(x)]^2}\mathrm{d}x=\sqrt{1+x}\,\mathrm{d}x$,$S=\int_L 1\cdot\mathrm{d}s=\int_0^1\sqrt{1+x}\,\mathrm{d}x=\dfrac{2}{3}\left(2\sqrt{2}-1\right)$。

答案:C

1-5-7 **解**:此题为对坐标的曲线积分,$\int_{ABC}\dfrac{\mathrm{d}x+\mathrm{d}y}{|x|+|y|}=\int_{L_1}+\int_{L_2}$,

L_1:$\begin{cases}y=-x+1\\ x=x\end{cases}$, x:$1\to 0$

$\int_{L_1}=\int_1^0\dfrac{1+(-1)}{x+(-x+1)}\mathrm{d}x=0$;

L_2:$\begin{cases}y=x+1\\ x=x\end{cases}$, x:$0\to -1$

$\int_{L_2}=\int_0^{-1}\dfrac{1+1}{-x+(x+1)}\mathrm{d}x=\int_0^{-1}2\mathrm{d}x=-2\int_{-1}^{0}\mathrm{d}x=-2$。

题 1-5-7 解图

答案:B

1-5-8 **解**:画出公共部分图形,V 由八块相等的部分构成,只要求出一块即可。计算 V_1,体积 $V=8V_1$,D_1 由 $x^2+y^2=R^2$,$x=0$,$y=0$ 围成,由 $x^2+z^2=R^2$,得 $z=\sqrt{R^2-x^2}$,

$$V_1=\iint_{D_1}\sqrt{R^2-x^2}\,\mathrm{d}x\mathrm{d}y,\ D_1:\begin{cases}0\leqslant x\leqslant R\\0\leqslant y\leqslant\sqrt{R^2-x^2}\end{cases}$$

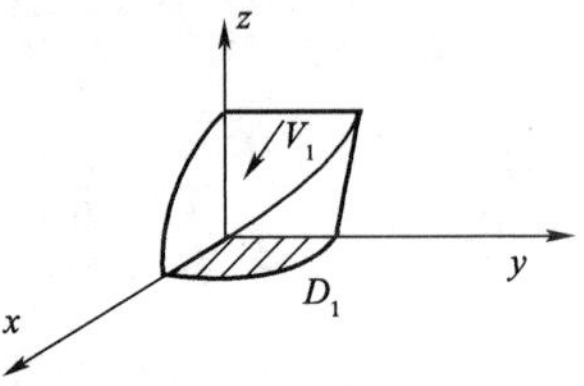

题 1-5-8 解图

$$V_1=\int_0^R\mathrm{d}x\int_0^{\sqrt{R^2-x^2}}\sqrt{R^2-x^2}\,\mathrm{d}y$$

则 $V=8\int_0^R\mathrm{d}x\int_0^{\sqrt{R^2-x^2}}\sqrt{R^2-x^2}\,\mathrm{d}y$

答案:B

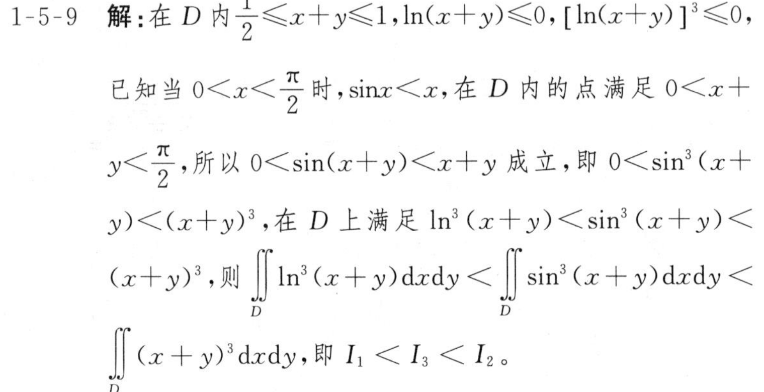

1-5-9 **解**:在 D 内 $\frac{1}{2}\leqslant x+y\leqslant 1$,$\ln(x+y)\leqslant 0$,$[\ln(x+y)]^3\leqslant 0$,已知当 $0<x<\frac{\pi}{2}$ 时,$\sin x<x$,在 D 内的点满足 $0<x+y<\frac{\pi}{2}$,所以 $0<\sin(x+y)<x+y$ 成立,即 $0<\sin^3(x+y)<(x+y)^3$,在 D 上满足 $\ln^3(x+y)<\sin^3(x+y)<(x+y)^3$,则 $\iint_D\ln^3(x+y)\mathrm{d}x\mathrm{d}y<\iint_D\sin^3(x+y)\mathrm{d}x\mathrm{d}y<\iint_D(x+y)^3\mathrm{d}x\mathrm{d}y$,即 $I_1<I_3<I_2$。

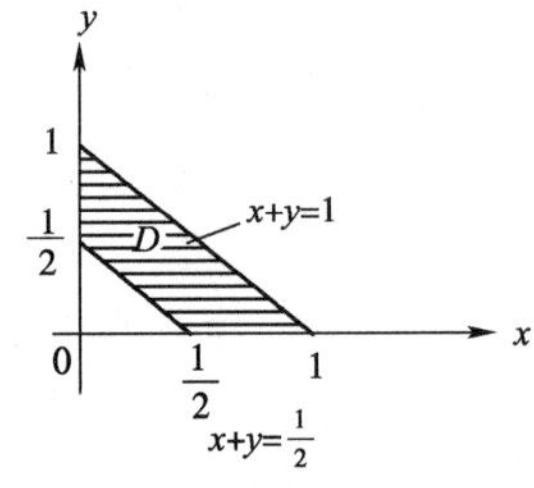

题 1-5-9 解图

答案:B

第六节

1-6-1 **解**:可验证选项 A、B、C 均收敛。

$\sum\limits_{n=1}^{\infty}(-1)^n\frac{1}{\sqrt{n}}$,因 $u_n\geqslant u_{n+1}$,$\lim\limits_{n\to\infty}u_n=0$,收敛。

$\sum\limits_{n=1}^{\infty}\frac{n}{2^n}$,因 $\lim\limits_{n\to\infty}\frac{u_{n+1}}{u_n}=\lim\limits_{n\to\infty}\frac{\frac{n+1}{2^{n+1}}}{\frac{n}{2^n}}=\lim\limits_{n\to\infty}\frac{n+1}{n}\cdot\frac{1}{2}=\frac{1}{2}<1$,收敛。

$\sum\limits_{n=1}^{\infty}\left(\frac{1}{n}-\frac{1}{n+1}\right)$,因 $\frac{1}{n}-\frac{1}{n+1}=\frac{1}{n(n+1)}<\frac{1}{n^2}$,而 $\sum\limits_{n=1}^{\infty}\frac{1}{n^2}$ 收敛,所以 $\sum\limits_{n=1}^{\infty}\left(\frac{1}{n}-\frac{1}{n+1}\right)$ 收敛。

$\sum\limits_{n=1}^{\infty}\sin\frac{n\pi}{3}$,因 $\lim\limits_{n\to\infty}u_n=\lim\limits_{n\to\infty}\sin\frac{n\pi}{3}\neq 0$,发散。

答案:D

1-6-2 **解**:$\sum\limits_{n=1}^{\infty}\left|(-1)^{n-1}\frac{1}{n}\right|=\sum\limits_{n=1}^{\infty}\frac{1}{n}$ 发散,而 $u_n\geqslant u_{n+1}$,且 $\lim\limits_{n\to\infty}u_n=0$,级数 $\sum\limits_{n=1}^{\infty}\frac{(-1)^{n-1}}{n}$ 收敛,所以级数 $\sum\limits_{n=1}^{\infty}(-1)^{n-1}\frac{1}{n}$ 条件收敛。

答案:B

1-6-3 **解**:$\sum\limits_{n=1}^{\infty}U_n$ 条件收敛,即 $\sum\limits_{n=1}^{\infty}|U_n|$ 发散,$\sum\limits_{n=1}^{\infty}U_n$ 收敛,所以 $\frac{1}{2}\sum\limits_{n=1}^{\infty}U_n$ 收敛,$\frac{1}{2}\sum\limits_{n=1}^{\infty}|U_n|$ 发散。

而 $U^{*}=\frac{1}{2}U_n+\frac{1}{2}|U_n|$,$\sum\limits_{n=1}^{\infty}U^{*}$ 发散。

$U^{**}=\frac{1}{2}U_n-\frac{1}{2}|U_n|$,$\sum\limits_{n=1}^{\infty}U^{**}$ 发散。

根据常数项级数的性质。

答案:B

1-6-4 **解**:$\lim\limits_{n\to\infty}\left|\frac{a_{n+1}}{a_n}\right|=\lim\limits_{n\to\infty}\frac{\frac{a^{n+1}-b^{n+1}}{a^{n+1}+b^{n+1}}}{\frac{a^n-b^n}{a^n+b^n}}=\lim\limits_{n\to\infty}\frac{a^{n+1}-b^{n+1}}{a^n-b^n}\cdot\frac{a^n+b^n}{a^{n+1}+b^{n+1}}$

$$=\lim_{n\to\infty}\frac{b^{n+1}\left[\left(\frac{a}{b}\right)^{n+1}-1\right]}{b^n\left[\left(\frac{a}{b}\right)^{n}-1\right]}\cdot\frac{b^{n}\left[\left(\frac{a}{b}\right)^{n}+1\right]}{b^{n+1}\left[\left(\frac{a}{b}\right)^{n+1}+1\right]}=b\cdot\frac{1}{b}=1$$

$R=\frac{1}{\rho}=1$

答案:D

1-6-5 **解**:$\sum\limits_{n=1}^{\infty}\left(x^n+\frac{1}{2^nx^n}\right)=\sum\limits_{n=1}^{\infty}x^n+\sum\limits_{n=1}^{\infty}\frac{1}{2^nx^n}$

级数 $\sum\limits_{n=1}^{\infty}x^n$ 为公比 $q=x$ 的等比级数,当 $|x|<1$ 时,级数收敛

级数 $\sum\limits_{n=1}^{\infty}\frac{1}{2^nx^n}=\sum\limits_{n=1}^{\infty}\left(\frac{1}{2x}\right)^n$ 为公比 $q=\frac{1}{2x}$ 的等比级数,

当 $\left|\frac{1}{2x}\right|<1$ 时,级数收敛,即 $|x|>\frac{1}{2}$ 时收敛

因此,级数 $\sum\limits_{n=1}^{\infty}x^n$,$\sum\limits_{n=1}^{\infty}\left(\frac{1}{2x}\right)^n$ 的和在 $\frac{1}{2}<|x|<1$ 收敛

答案:C

1-6-6 **解**:$f(x)=\begin{cases}x & -\pi\leqslant x<0\\ 1 & 0\leqslant x\leqslant\pi\end{cases}$,利用公式求出 a_3 的值。

$$a_3=\frac{1}{\pi}\int_{-\pi}^{\pi}f(x)\cos3x\mathrm{d}x=\frac{1}{\pi}\left(\int_{-\pi}^{0}x\cos3x\mathrm{d}x+\int_{0}^{\pi}\cos3x\mathrm{d}x\right)$$

$$=\frac{1}{\pi}\left(\frac{1}{3}\int_{-\pi}^{0}x\mathrm{d}\sin3x+0\right)=\frac{1}{\pi}\left[\frac{1}{3}\left(x\sin3x\Big|_{-\pi}^{0}-\int_{-\pi}^{0}\sin3x\mathrm{d}x\right)\right]$$

$$=\frac{1}{9\pi}\cos3x\Big|_{-\pi}^{0}=\frac{2}{9\pi}$$

答案:C

1-6-7 **解**:原级数$=x(x-\frac{1}{2}x^2+\frac{1}{3}x^3-\cdots+(-1)^{n+1}x^n+\cdots)$,已知 $\ln(1+x)=x-\frac{1}{2}x^2+\frac{1}{3}x^3-\cdots$,$-1<x\leqslant1$,幂级数和为 $x\ln(1+x)$。

答案:D

1-6-8　**解**:设 $x-1=z$,原幂级数$=\sum\limits_{n=0}^{\infty}C_nz^n$

因为$\lim\limits_{n\to\infty}\left|\frac{C_{n+1}}{C_n}\right|=\lim\limits_{n\to\infty}\left|\frac{\frac{1}{C_n}}{\frac{C_n}{C_{n+1}}}\right|=\frac{1}{3}$

所以 $R=3$,$\sum\limits_{n=0}^{\infty}C_nz^n$ 在$-3<z<3$ 收敛。即原幂级数在$-2<x<4$ 收敛。

只有选项 D 正确。

答案:D

1-6-9　**解**:利用 $f(x)=\frac{x}{(x-2)(x-3)}=\frac{A}{x-2}+\frac{B}{x-3}$,计算出 $A=-2,B=3$。

$f(x)=\frac{-2}{x-2}+\frac{3}{x-3}$,函数$\frac{-2}{x-2}=-2\frac{1}{x-5+3}=-\frac{2}{3}\frac{1}{1+\frac{x-5}{3}}$,展开成 $x-5$ 的幂级数后,收敛区间通过下式计算:由$-1<\frac{x-5}{3}<1$,解出 $2<x<8$。

同理,函数$\frac{3}{x-3}=3\times\frac{1}{x-5+2}=\frac{3}{2}\times\frac{1}{1+\frac{x-5}{2}}$,展开成 $x-5$ 的幂级数后,求出收敛区间 $3<x<7$。公共部分 $3<x<7$。

答案:C

1-6-10　**解**:奇延拓,周期延拓,由迪利克雷收敛定理可知。因 $x=-\frac{\pi}{2}$为间断点

$$s\left(-\frac{\pi}{2}\right)=-s\left(\frac{\pi}{2}\right)=-\frac{f\left(\frac{\pi}{2}-0\right)+f\left(\frac{\pi}{2}+0\right)}{2}=-\frac{\frac{\pi}{2}+\pi}{2}=-\frac{3}{4}\pi$$

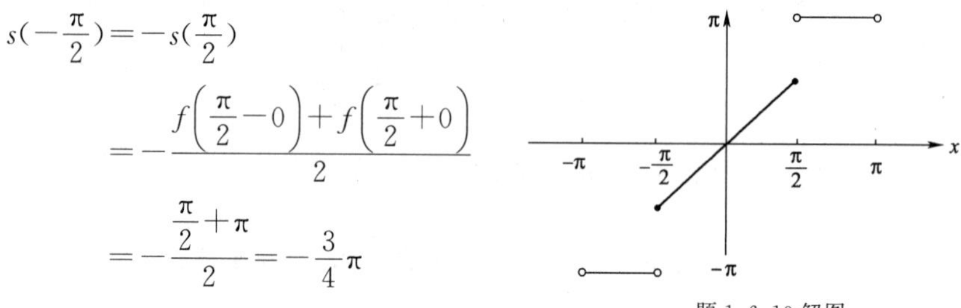

题 1-6-10 解图

答案:C

第七节

1-7-1　**解**:$\mathrm{d}y-e^x\mathrm{d}x=-2xy\mathrm{d}x$,$\frac{\mathrm{d}y}{\mathrm{d}x}-e^x=-2xy$,$\frac{\mathrm{d}y}{\mathrm{d}x}+2xy=e^x$。

答案:D

1-7-2　**解**:本题为一阶齐次方程。

设 $u=\frac{y}{x}$,$y=xu$,$\frac{\mathrm{d}y}{\mathrm{d}x}=u+x\frac{\mathrm{d}u}{\mathrm{d}x}$,

代入 $u+x\frac{\mathrm{d}u}{\mathrm{d}x}=\frac{1}{u}+u$,$x\frac{\mathrm{d}u}{\mathrm{d}x}=\frac{1}{u}$,$u\mathrm{d}u=\frac{1}{x}\mathrm{d}x$,$\frac{1}{2}u^2=\ln x+C$,

通解$\frac{1}{2}\frac{y^2}{x^2}=\ln x+C$,

代入初始条件$x=1$,$y=2$,$C=2$,特解 $y^2=2x^2(2+\ln x)$。

答案:C

1-7-3 **解:**方法 1,可将 $y=\cos 2x$ 代入原方程求出 $p(x)$,计算如下:$y=\cos 2x$,$y'=-2\sin 2x$,代入 $-2\sin 2x+p(x)\cos 2x=0$,则 $p(x)=2\tan 2x$。再把求出的 $p(x)$ 代入原方程得:$y'+2(\tan 2x)y=0$,$\frac{\mathrm{d}y}{\mathrm{d}x}=-2\tan 2x\cdot y$,$\frac{1}{y}\mathrm{d}y=-2\tan 2x\mathrm{d}x$,$\ln y=\ln\cos 2x+\ln C$,通解 $y=C\cos 2x$,代入初始条件 $x=0$,$y=2$,解出 $C=2$,选项 D 正确。

方法 2,因为一阶线性齐次方程 $y'+p(x)y=0$ 任意两个解只差一个常数因子,所以选项 A、B、C 都不是该方程的解。

答案:D

1-7-4 **解:**$y_1(x)$、$y_2(x)$ 为非齐次方程的解,$y_2(x)-y_1(x)$ 是对应齐次方程的解,

那么 $C[y_2(x)-y_1(x)]$ 为对应齐次方程的通解。

一阶线性非齐次方程的通解 $y=y^*$(非齐次的一特解)$+Y$(齐次的通解),

则通解为 $y_2(x)+C[y_2(x)-y_1(x)]$。

答案:D

1-7-5 **解:**方程是 $y''=f(x,y')$ 不显含字母 y,设 $y'=p(x)$,$y''=p'$,代入方程并分离变量得 $\frac{\mathrm{d}p}{p}=\frac{2x}{1+x^2}\mathrm{d}x$,两边积分,$\ln p=\ln(1+x^2)+\ln C_1$,$p=C_1(1+x^2)$,即 $p=y'=C_1(1+x^2)$,由条件 $y'|_{x=0}=3$,知 $C_1=3$,得 $y'=3(1+x^2)$,两边积分 $y=x^3+3x+c_2$,由条件 $y|_{x=0}=1$,得 $C_2=1$,特解 $y=x^3+3x+1$。

答案:C

1-7-6 **解:**$y''-2y'+y=0$。

方法 1,对应特征方程 $r^2-2r+1=0$,$r=1$,二重根。

通解 $y=(C_1+C_2x)e^x$,其中 C_1、C_2 为任意常数。

当 $C_1=0$,$C_2=1$ 时,解 $y=xe^x$,选项 C 成立。

当 $C_1=2$,$C_2=1$ 时,解为 $y=(x+2)e^x$,选项 D 成立。

当 $C_1=1$,$C_2=0$ 时,解为 $y=e^x$,选项 B 也成立,选项 A 不是方程的解。

方法 2,将选项 A、B、C、D 逐个代入方程检验,选项 A 代入后不满足方程,计算如下:

$y=x^2e^x$,$y'=(2x+x^2)e^x$,$y''=(2+4x+x^2)e^x$,

把 y、y'、y'' 代入原方程不成立,所以选项 A 不是方程的解函数。选项 B、C、D 代入均成立。

方法 3,在方程的通解 $y=(C_1+C_2x)e^x$ 中,常数 C_1、C_2 取任意数,选项 A 均不成立。

答案:A

1-7-7 **解:**已知 $r_1=3$,$r_2=-3$,从而可知二阶线性齐次方程对应的特征方程为 $(r-3)\cdot(r+3)=0$,即 $r^2-9=0$,反推知二阶常系数线性齐次方程为 $\frac{\mathrm{d}^2y}{\mathrm{d}x^2}-9y=0$。

答案:D

1-7-8 **解:**直接看出 $y^*=\frac{1}{2}$ 是线性非齐次方程的一个特解。求齐次方程通解,$r^2+2=0$,$r=\pm\sqrt{2}i$,$y=C_1\cos\sqrt{2}x+C_2\sin\sqrt{2}x$。对应齐次方程的通解 $Y=C_1\cos\sqrt{2}x+C_2\sin\sqrt{2}x$,则方程的通解 $y=\frac{1}{2}+C_1\cos\sqrt{2}x+C_2\sin\sqrt{2}x$。

答案:A

第八节

1-8-1 **解**:分别求出行列式 D_1,D_2 的值。

即 $D_1=0$,$D_2=(\lambda+1)(\lambda-1)^2$,从而 λ 值取 -1,1。

答案:C

1-8-2 **解**:利用行列式的性质将第一行按顺序与第二行、第三行互换,一直换到第 n 行,一共交换 $n-1$ 次,变号次数$(n-1)$次,再将原行列式第二行按顺序换到第 $n-1$ 行,交换$(n-2)$次,依次进行,最后将原行列式第 $n-1$ 行和第 n 行交换,得

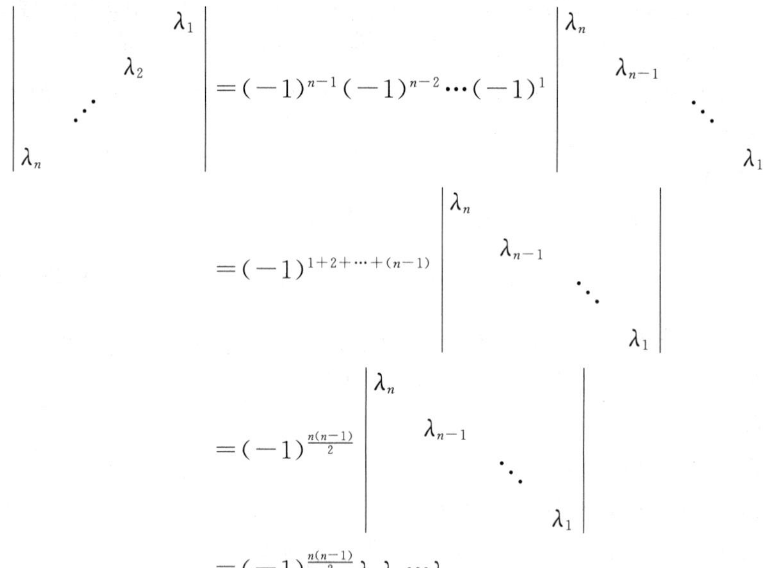

$$\begin{vmatrix} & & & \lambda_1 \\ & & \lambda_2 & \\ & \iddots & & \\ \lambda_n & & & \end{vmatrix}=(-1)^{n-1}(-1)^{n-2}\cdots(-1)^1\begin{vmatrix} \lambda_n & & & \\ & \lambda_{n-1} & & \\ & & \ddots & \\ & & & \lambda_1 \end{vmatrix}$$

$$=(-1)^{1+2+\cdots+(n-1)}\begin{vmatrix} \lambda_n & & & \\ & \lambda_{n-1} & & \\ & & \ddots & \\ & & & \lambda_1 \end{vmatrix}$$

$$=(-1)^{\frac{n(n-1)}{2}}\begin{vmatrix} \lambda_n & & & \\ & \lambda_{n-1} & & \\ & & \ddots & \\ & & & \lambda_1 \end{vmatrix}$$

$$=(-1)^{\frac{n(n-1)}{2}}\lambda_1\lambda_2\cdots\lambda_n$$

答案:D

1-8-3 **解**:矩阵 $\boldsymbol{AB}$ 可能为奇异矩阵,也可能为非奇异矩阵;若 $\boldsymbol{AB}$ 为奇异矩阵,则有 $|\boldsymbol{AB}|=0$,故选项 A 不成立。

答案:A

1-8-4 **解**:方法 1,$\boldsymbol{\beta}$ 是 $\boldsymbol{\alpha}_1$,$\boldsymbol{\alpha}_2$ 的线性组合,则 $\boldsymbol{\beta}$,$\boldsymbol{\alpha}_1$,$\boldsymbol{\alpha}_2$ 线性相关,于是 $|\boldsymbol{\beta},\boldsymbol{\alpha}_1,\boldsymbol{\alpha}_2|=0$,选项 A 计算如下:$\begin{vmatrix} -3 & 2 & 0 \\ 0 & 0 & 0 \\ 4 & 0 & -3 \end{vmatrix}=0$,其余选项计算行列式的值均不为 0,故选项 A 成立。

方法 2,由于 $\boldsymbol{\alpha}_1$ 与 $\boldsymbol{\alpha}_2$ 的第 2 个分量为 0,所以 $\boldsymbol{\alpha}_1$、$\boldsymbol{\alpha}_2$ 线性组合的第 2 个分量还为 0,选 A。

答案:A

1-8-5 **解**:设该向量组构成的矩阵为 $\boldsymbol{A}$,则有 $R(\boldsymbol{A})=r$,于是在 $\boldsymbol{A}$ 中有 r 阶子式 $D_r\neq0$,这 r 阶子式所在的列(行)向量组线性无关,又由 $\boldsymbol{A}$ 中所有 $r+1$ 阶子式均为零,可知 $\boldsymbol{A}$ 中任意 $r+1$ 列(行)向量都线性相关,故选 D。

答案:D

1-8-6 **解**:将矩阵作行的初等变换化为阶梯形,找出不为零的行列式的最高阶子式对应的列向量。

$$\begin{bmatrix}1&1&2&2&1\\0&2&1&5&-1\\2&0&3&-1&3\\1&1&0&4&-1\end{bmatrix}\xrightarrow[-r_1+r_4]{-2r_1+r_3}\begin{bmatrix}1&1&2&2&1\\0&2&1&5&-1\\0&-2&-1&-5&1\\0&0&-2&2&-2\end{bmatrix}\xrightarrow{r_2+r_3}$$

$$\begin{bmatrix}1&1&2&2&1\\0&2&1&5&-1\\0&0&0&0&0\\0&0&-2&2&-2\end{bmatrix}\xrightarrow{r_3\leftrightarrow r_4}\begin{bmatrix}1&1&2&2&1\\0&2&1&5&-1\\0&0&-2&2&-2\\0&0&0&0&0\end{bmatrix}$$，因为 $\begin{vmatrix}1&1&2\\0&2&1\\0&0&-2\end{vmatrix}\neq 0$。

答案:D

1-8-7 **解:**方法 1 $\boldsymbol{A}\xrightarrow[-\frac{a_n}{a_1}r_1+r_n]{-\frac{a_2}{a_1}r_1+r_2 \quad \cdots\cdots}\begin{bmatrix}a_1b_1&a_1b_2&\cdots&a_1b_n\\0&0&\cdots&0\\\cdots&\cdots&\cdots&\cdots\\0&0&\cdots&0\end{bmatrix}\longrightarrow a_1\begin{bmatrix}b_1&b_2&\cdots&b_n\\0&0&\cdots&0\\0&0&\cdots&0\end{bmatrix}$，

则 $R(\boldsymbol{A})=1$。

方法 2 令 $\boldsymbol{B}=\begin{bmatrix}a_1\\a_2\\\vdots\\a_n\end{bmatrix}_{n\times 1}$，$\boldsymbol{C}=(b_1,b_2,\cdots,b_n)_{1\times n}$，则 $\boldsymbol{A}=\boldsymbol{B}_{n\times 1}\cdot\boldsymbol{C}_{1\times n}$

因 $R(\boldsymbol{B}_{n\times 1})=1$，$R(\boldsymbol{C}_{1\times n})=1$，$R(\boldsymbol{A})=R(\boldsymbol{BC})\leqslant\min\{R(\boldsymbol{B})、R(\boldsymbol{C})\}$，则 $R(\boldsymbol{A})=1$。

答案:C

1-8-8 **解:**验证 $\boldsymbol{\alpha}=\dfrac{\boldsymbol{\alpha}_2+\boldsymbol{\alpha}_3}{2}$ 是非齐次方程组 $\boldsymbol{Ax}=\boldsymbol{b}$ 的解。

代入方程 $\boldsymbol{A\alpha}=\boldsymbol{A}\dfrac{\boldsymbol{\alpha}_2+\boldsymbol{\alpha}_3}{2}=\dfrac{1}{2}(\boldsymbol{A\alpha}_2+\boldsymbol{A\alpha}_3)=\dfrac{1}{2}(\boldsymbol{b}+\boldsymbol{b})=\boldsymbol{b}$，$\boldsymbol{\alpha}=\dfrac{\boldsymbol{\alpha}_2+\boldsymbol{\alpha}_3}{2}=\begin{bmatrix}0\\\frac{1}{2}\\1\\\frac{3}{2}\end{bmatrix}$，因

$\boldsymbol{\alpha}_1$ 是非齐次线性方程组的解，$\boldsymbol{\alpha}$ 也是非齐次线性方程组的解，可以验证 $\boldsymbol{\alpha}_1-\boldsymbol{\alpha}$ 是对应齐次方程组 $\boldsymbol{Ax}=\boldsymbol{0}$ 的解，代入方程组 $\boldsymbol{A}(\boldsymbol{\alpha}_1-\boldsymbol{\alpha})=\boldsymbol{A\alpha}_1-\boldsymbol{A\alpha}=\boldsymbol{b}-\boldsymbol{b}=\boldsymbol{0}$。

设 $\boldsymbol{\xi}=\boldsymbol{\alpha}_1-\boldsymbol{\alpha}=\begin{bmatrix}1\\\frac{3}{2}\\2\\\frac{5}{2}\end{bmatrix}$，而对应齐次线性方程组 $\boldsymbol{Ax}=\boldsymbol{0}$ 基础解系中向量个数 $=4$(未

知数个数)$-3[R(A)]=1$,所以对应齐次线性方程组的通解为 $c\boldsymbol{\xi}$(c 为任意常数),非齐次方程组 $\boldsymbol{Ax}=\boldsymbol{b}$ 的通解为:

$\boldsymbol{x}=\boldsymbol{\alpha}_1+C\boldsymbol{\xi}$(非齐次的一个特解+齐次的通解)

$$=\begin{bmatrix}1\\2\\3\\4\end{bmatrix}+C\begin{bmatrix}1\\\frac{3}{2}\\2\\\frac{5}{2}\end{bmatrix}=\begin{bmatrix}1\\2\\3\\4\end{bmatrix}+C\,\frac{1}{2}\begin{bmatrix}2\\3\\4\\5\end{bmatrix},$$

即 $\boldsymbol{x}=\begin{bmatrix}1\\2\\3\\4\end{bmatrix}+C_1\begin{bmatrix}2\\3\\4\\5\end{bmatrix},\left(C_1=\frac{C}{2}\right)$。

答案:C

1-8-9 **解:**矩阵对应的特征多项式相同,则有相同的特征值。

因 $|\lambda\boldsymbol{E}-\boldsymbol{A}^{\mathrm{T}}|=|(\lambda\boldsymbol{E}-\boldsymbol{A})^{\mathrm{T}}|=|\lambda\boldsymbol{E}-\boldsymbol{A}|$,所以 $|\lambda\boldsymbol{E}-\boldsymbol{A}^{\mathrm{T}}|=|\lambda\boldsymbol{E}-\boldsymbol{A}|$,特征多项式相同,因而有相同的特征值。

答案:A

1-8-10 **解:**运算中应注意矩阵的乘法不满足交换律,即 $\boldsymbol{AB}\neq\boldsymbol{BA}$,逐个验证选项 A、B、C、D,计算如下:

选项 A,$(\boldsymbol{A}+\boldsymbol{B})(\boldsymbol{A}-\boldsymbol{B})=\boldsymbol{A}^2+\boldsymbol{BA}-\boldsymbol{AB}+\boldsymbol{B}^2\neq\boldsymbol{A}^2-\boldsymbol{B}^2$。

选项 B,$(\boldsymbol{AB})^2=(\boldsymbol{AB})(\boldsymbol{AB})=\boldsymbol{ABAB}\neq\boldsymbol{A}^2\boldsymbol{B}^2$。

选项 C,$\boldsymbol{AC}=\boldsymbol{BC}$,只有当矩阵 $\boldsymbol{C}$ 可逆时,选项 C 才成立,但矩阵 $\boldsymbol{C}$ 是否可逆,未知。

选项 D,$(\boldsymbol{A}+\boldsymbol{E})(\boldsymbol{A}-\boldsymbol{E})=\boldsymbol{A}^2+\boldsymbol{EA}-\boldsymbol{AE}-\boldsymbol{E}^2=\boldsymbol{A}^2-\boldsymbol{E}$,成立。

答案:D

1-8-11 **解:**因 $\boldsymbol{A}$、$\boldsymbol{B}$、$\boldsymbol{C}$ 均为 n 阶方阵,且 $\boldsymbol{ABC}=\boldsymbol{E}$,取行列式 $|\boldsymbol{ABC}|=1$,即 $|\boldsymbol{A}||\boldsymbol{B}||\boldsymbol{C}|=1$,可知 $|\boldsymbol{A}|$、$|\boldsymbol{B}|$、$|\boldsymbol{C}|$ 均不为 0,所以 $\boldsymbol{A}$、$\boldsymbol{B}$、$\boldsymbol{C}$ 均可逆。

等式 $\boldsymbol{ABC}=\boldsymbol{E}$ 两边左乘 $\boldsymbol{A}^{-1}$,得 $\boldsymbol{BC}=\boldsymbol{A}^{-1}\boldsymbol{E}$,$\boldsymbol{BC}=\boldsymbol{EA}^{-1}$,等式两边再右乘 $\boldsymbol{A}$ 得 $\boldsymbol{BCA}=\boldsymbol{EA}^{-1}\boldsymbol{A}=\boldsymbol{E}$。

答案:D

1-8-12 **解:**将行列式中的第一项,利用数乘矩阵的逆的性质变形,$(2\boldsymbol{A})^{-1}=\frac{1}{2}\boldsymbol{A}^{-1}$,再将第二项 $\boldsymbol{A}^*$ 写成 $\boldsymbol{A}^{-1}$ 的形式,因 $\boldsymbol{A}^{-1}=\frac{1}{|\boldsymbol{A}|}\boldsymbol{A}^*$,所以 $\boldsymbol{A}^*=|\boldsymbol{A}|\boldsymbol{A}^{-1}$,代入行列式计算:

$$\begin{aligned}|(2\boldsymbol{A})^{-1}-5\boldsymbol{A}^*|&=\left|\frac{1}{2}\boldsymbol{A}^{-1}-5|\boldsymbol{A}|\boldsymbol{A}^{-1}\right|=\left|\frac{1}{2}\boldsymbol{A}^{-1}-\frac{5}{2}\boldsymbol{A}^{-1}\right|\\&=|-2\boldsymbol{A}^{-1}|=(-2)^3|\boldsymbol{A}^{-1}|=-8\times2=-16\end{aligned}$$

(因 $\boldsymbol{A}\cdot\boldsymbol{A}^{-1}=\boldsymbol{E}$,$|\boldsymbol{A}||\boldsymbol{A}^{-1}|=1$,$|\boldsymbol{A}^{-1}|=\frac{1}{|\boldsymbol{A}|}=2$)

在计算中还用到公式 $|k\boldsymbol{A}|=k^n|\boldsymbol{A}|$($k$ 为任意常数,$\boldsymbol{A}$ 为 n 阶方阵)

答案:B

1-8-13 **解:**利用 $\boldsymbol{A}^*=|\boldsymbol{A}|\boldsymbol{A}^{-1}$，两边取行列式，$|\boldsymbol{A}^*|=||\boldsymbol{A}|\boldsymbol{A}^{-1}|=|\boldsymbol{A}|^n|\boldsymbol{A}^{-1}|$，又因 $\boldsymbol{A}\boldsymbol{A}^{-1}=\boldsymbol{E}$，$|\boldsymbol{A}||\boldsymbol{A}^{-1}|=1$，从而 $|\boldsymbol{A}^{-1}|=\dfrac{1}{|\boldsymbol{A}|}$，推出 $|\boldsymbol{A}^*|=|\boldsymbol{A}|^n\cdot\dfrac{1}{|\boldsymbol{A}|}=|\boldsymbol{A}|^{n-1}=a^{n-1}$。

答案:C

1-8-14 **解:**已知三阶方阵 $\boldsymbol{A}$ 存在一可逆矩阵 $\boldsymbol{P}=(\boldsymbol{\alpha}_1,\boldsymbol{\alpha}_2,\boldsymbol{\alpha}_3)$，使 $\boldsymbol{P}^{-1}\boldsymbol{A}\boldsymbol{P}=\boldsymbol{\Lambda}$（$\boldsymbol{\Lambda}$ 为对角矩阵）。

若式子 $\boldsymbol{P}^{-1}\boldsymbol{A}\boldsymbol{P}=\begin{bmatrix}\lambda_1 & & \\ & \lambda_2 & \\ & & \lambda_3\end{bmatrix}$。则 $\boldsymbol{P}$ 列向量的排列与 $\boldsymbol{\Lambda}$ 矩阵中特征值的排列之间存在着对应关系。即可逆矩阵 $\boldsymbol{P}$ 中的 $\boldsymbol{\alpha}_1$ 对应 $\boldsymbol{\Lambda}$（对角矩阵）中的 λ_1，可逆矩阵 $\boldsymbol{P}$ 中的 $\boldsymbol{\alpha}_2$ 对应 $\boldsymbol{\Lambda}$（对角矩阵）中的 λ_2，可逆矩阵 $\boldsymbol{P}$ 中的 $\boldsymbol{\alpha}_3$ 对应 $\boldsymbol{\Lambda}$（对角矩阵）中的 λ_3，

所以当 $\boldsymbol{P}$ 的列向量排列顺序确定后，对角矩阵 $\boldsymbol{\Lambda}$ 中特征值的排列即可确定。

$\boldsymbol{\Lambda}=\begin{bmatrix}1 & & \\ & 2 & \\ & & -2\end{bmatrix}$。

答案:A

1-8-15 **解:**分别找出矩阵 $\boldsymbol{E}+\left(\dfrac{1}{2}\boldsymbol{A}^3\right)^{-1}$ 中，每一部分矩阵所对应的特征值，利用特征值和特征向量的重要性质得出对应特征值。设 λ 为 $\boldsymbol{A}$ 的特征值，矩阵 $a\boldsymbol{A}+b\boldsymbol{E}$ 对应特征值为 $a\lambda+b$（a,b 为常数）。利用 $\lambda=2$ 是可逆矩阵 $\boldsymbol{A}$ 的一个特征值，推出矩阵 $(\frac{1}{2}\boldsymbol{A}^3)^{-1}$ 对应的特征值，步骤如下：$\boldsymbol{A}^3$ 对应特征值 $\lambda^3=2^3$，$\dfrac{1}{2}\boldsymbol{A}^3$ 对应特征值为 $\dfrac{1}{2}\lambda^3=4$，$\left(\dfrac{1}{2}\boldsymbol{A}^3\right)^{-1}$ 对应特征值是 $\dfrac{1}{2}\boldsymbol{A}^3$ 对应特征值的倒数，即为 $\dfrac{1}{4}$。故 $\boldsymbol{E}+\left(\dfrac{1}{2}\boldsymbol{A}^3\right)^{-1}$ 对应特征值 $=1+\dfrac{1}{4}=\dfrac{5}{4}$。

答案:B

1-8-16 **解:**选项 A，设可逆阵 $\boldsymbol{A}$ 的特征值 λ 对应的特征向量为 $\boldsymbol{\alpha}$，则 $\boldsymbol{A}\boldsymbol{\alpha}=\lambda\boldsymbol{\alpha}$，$\lambda\neq0$，所以 $\boldsymbol{\alpha}=\boldsymbol{A}^{-1}\lambda\boldsymbol{\alpha}$，$\boldsymbol{\alpha}=\lambda\boldsymbol{A}^{-1}\boldsymbol{\alpha}$，$\boldsymbol{A}^{-1}\boldsymbol{\alpha}=\dfrac{1}{\lambda}\boldsymbol{\alpha}$，所以 $\dfrac{1}{\lambda}$ 是 $\boldsymbol{A}^{-1}$ 对应特征向量 $\boldsymbol{\alpha}$ 的特征值。

选项 B，设 λ_1,λ_2 为 n 阶方阵 $\boldsymbol{A}$ 的两个不相等特征值 $\lambda\neq0$，$(i=1,2)$。$\boldsymbol{x}_1,\boldsymbol{x}_2$ 分别为 λ_1,λ_2 对应的特征向量，则线性组合 $\boldsymbol{x}_1+\boldsymbol{x}_2$ 不是 $\boldsymbol{A}$ 的特征向量，选项 B 不成立。

选项 C，由方阵的特征值和特征向量的性质可知，若 λ 为方阵 $\boldsymbol{A}$ 对应特征向量 $\boldsymbol{x}$ 的特征值 $\lambda\neq0$，那么 $\boldsymbol{A}^*$ 对应于方阵 $\boldsymbol{A}$ 特征向量 $\boldsymbol{x}$ 的特征值为 $\dfrac{|\boldsymbol{A}|}{\lambda}$，$\lambda\neq0$。选项 C 不成立。

选项 D，由于 $\boldsymbol{A}$ 的特征向量为非零向量，故方程组 $(\lambda\boldsymbol{E}-\boldsymbol{A})\boldsymbol{x}=\boldsymbol{0}$ 的零向量不是 $\boldsymbol{A}$ 的特征向量，选项 D 不成立。

答案:A

1-8-17 **解:**实对称矩阵对应于不同特征值的特征向量必正交。

$\boldsymbol{\alpha}^{\mathrm{T}}\cdot\boldsymbol{\beta}=0$，即 $(1,a,1)\begin{bmatrix}-1\\ -1\\ -b\end{bmatrix}=-1-a-b=0$；

$\boldsymbol{\beta}^{\mathrm{T}}\boldsymbol{\gamma}=0$，即$(-1,-1,-b)\begin{bmatrix}b\\2\\0\end{bmatrix}=-b-2=0$；

$\boldsymbol{\alpha}^{\mathrm{T}}\boldsymbol{\gamma}=0$，即$(1,a,1)\begin{bmatrix}b\\2\\0\end{bmatrix}=b+2a=0$；

解方程组$\begin{cases}a+b+1=0\\b+2=0\\b+2a=0\end{cases}$，解出$a=1,b=-2$。

答案:A

1-8-18 **解**:利用相关知识可知$(\boldsymbol{A}^*)^{-1}=\frac{1}{|\boldsymbol{A}|}\boldsymbol{A}$。(因为$\boldsymbol{A}^{-1}=\frac{1}{|\boldsymbol{A}|}\boldsymbol{A}^*$，$\boldsymbol{A}^*=|\boldsymbol{A}|\boldsymbol{A}^{-1}$，$(\boldsymbol{A}^*)^{-1}=(|\boldsymbol{A}|\boldsymbol{A}^{-1})^{-1}$，$(\boldsymbol{A}^*)^{-1}=\frac{1}{|\boldsymbol{A}|}(\boldsymbol{A}^{-1})^{-1}$(利用数乘矩阵的逆的性质)，$(\boldsymbol{A}^*)^{-1}=\frac{\boldsymbol{A}}{|\boldsymbol{A}|}$)，又因方阵的行列式与方阵的特征值有如下关系：设$\boldsymbol{A}=(a_{ij})_{n\times n}$的$n$个特征值为$\lambda_1,\lambda_2,\cdots,\lambda_n$，则：①$\lambda_1+\lambda_2+\cdots+\lambda_n=a_{11}+a_{22}+\cdots+a_{nn}$；②$\lambda_1\cdot\lambda_2\cdots\lambda_n=|\boldsymbol{A}|$。得到$|\boldsymbol{A}|=\lambda_1\lambda_2\lambda_3=(-1)\times1\times2=-2$，所以$(\boldsymbol{A}^*)^{-1}=\frac{\boldsymbol{A}}{|\boldsymbol{A}|}=-\frac{1}{2}\boldsymbol{A}$。

若λ是$\boldsymbol{A}$的特征值，$k\boldsymbol{A}$的特征值为$k\lambda$，且特征向量相同。所以$(\boldsymbol{A}^*)^{-1}=-\frac{1}{2}\boldsymbol{A}$的特征值为$(-\frac{1}{2})\lambda$，即为$\frac{1}{2},-\frac{1}{2},-1$。

答案:B

1-8-19 **解**:已知对任一三维列向量$\boldsymbol{x}$有$\boldsymbol{x}^{\mathrm{T}}\boldsymbol{A}\boldsymbol{x}=0$成立 ①

对①式取转置$(\boldsymbol{x}^{\mathrm{T}}\boldsymbol{A}\boldsymbol{x})^{\mathrm{T}}=0$，$\boldsymbol{x}^{\mathrm{T}}\boldsymbol{A}^{\mathrm{T}}\boldsymbol{x}=0$ ②

则①式+②式：$\boldsymbol{x}^{\mathrm{T}}\boldsymbol{A}\boldsymbol{x}+\boldsymbol{x}^{\mathrm{T}}\boldsymbol{A}^{\mathrm{T}}\boldsymbol{x}=0$，$\boldsymbol{x}^{\mathrm{T}}(\boldsymbol{A}+\boldsymbol{A}^{\mathrm{T}})\boldsymbol{x}=0$ ③

在③式中，可证明$\boldsymbol{A}+\boldsymbol{A}^{\mathrm{T}}$为实对称矩阵，

因$(\boldsymbol{A}+\boldsymbol{A}^{\mathrm{T}})^{\mathrm{T}}=(\boldsymbol{A})^{\mathrm{T}}+(\boldsymbol{A}^{\mathrm{T}})^{\mathrm{T}}=\boldsymbol{A}^{\mathrm{T}}+\boldsymbol{A}=\boldsymbol{A}+\boldsymbol{A}^{\mathrm{T}}$，

设$\boldsymbol{A}+\boldsymbol{A}^{\mathrm{T}}=\boldsymbol{B}$，$\boldsymbol{B}=\begin{bmatrix}a_{11}&a_{12}&a_{13}\\a_{12}&a_{22}&a_{23}\\a_{13}&a_{23}&a_{33}\end{bmatrix}$，即有$(x_1,x_2,x_3)\begin{bmatrix}a_{11}&a_{12}&a_{13}\\a_{12}&a_{22}&a_{23}\\a_{13}&a_{23}&a_{33}\end{bmatrix}\begin{bmatrix}x_1\\x_2\\x_3\end{bmatrix}=0$ ④

也就是$a_{11}x_1^2+a_{22}x_2^2+a_{33}x_3^2+2a_{12}x_1x_2+2a_{13}x_1x_3+2a_{23}x_2x_3=0$，

由已知④式对任一三维列向量$\boldsymbol{x}$都成立，取一些特殊的三维列向量代入，可得$a_{11},a_{22},a_{33},\cdots a_{23}$皆为0，

所以$\boldsymbol{A}+\boldsymbol{A}^{\mathrm{T}}=\boldsymbol{0}$，$\boldsymbol{A}=-\boldsymbol{A}^{\mathrm{T}}$，所以$\boldsymbol{A}$为三阶反对称阵。 ⑤

⑤式取行列式：$|\boldsymbol{A}|=|-\boldsymbol{A}^{\mathrm{T}}|=(-1)^3|\boldsymbol{A}^{\mathrm{T}}|=-|\boldsymbol{A}^{\mathrm{T}}|=-|\boldsymbol{A}|$，

得$2|\boldsymbol{A}|=0$，则$|\boldsymbol{A}|=0$。

此题解题过程可以不记，理解即可，但应记住结论。

答案:A

1-8-20 **解**:已知 n 阶实对称矩阵 $\boldsymbol{A}$ 为正定矩阵,所以 $\boldsymbol{A}$ 的所有特征值皆正,选项 B 成立。

设 $\boldsymbol{A}$ 的特征值为 $\lambda_1,\lambda_2,\cdots,\lambda_n$,可知 $\boldsymbol{A}^{-1}$ 的特征值为 $\frac{1}{\lambda_1},\frac{1}{\lambda_2},\cdots,\frac{1}{\lambda_n}$。因 $\lambda_1,\lambda_2,\cdots,\lambda_n$ 均大于 0,则 $\frac{1}{\lambda_1},\frac{1}{\lambda_2},\cdots,\frac{1}{\lambda_n}$ 均大于 0,所以 $\boldsymbol{A}^{-1}$ 为正定矩阵,选项 C 成立。

又由于 $\boldsymbol{A}$ 为正定,其所有顺序主子式全大于零,因而矩阵 $\boldsymbol{A}$ 的行列式大于 0,$R(\boldsymbol{A})=n$,选项 D 成立,故选项 A 不成立。

答案:A

第九节

1-9-1 **解**:$A\subset(A\cup B)=B,\overline{B}=(\overline{A}\,\overline{B})\subset\overline{A},A\,\overline{B}=A(\overline{\overline{A}\cup B})=A\,\overline{A}\,\overline{B}=\varnothing$,选项 A、B、C 均正确。

答案:D

1-9-2 **解**:$P(A\cup B)=P(A)+P(B)-P(AB)=1-P(AB)\leqslant 1$

$P(\overline{A}\,\overline{B})=P(\overline{A\cup B})=1-P(A\cup B)=1-[P(A)+P(B)-P(AB)]=P(AB)$。

答案:D

1-9-3 **解**:$A=\Omega$ 时,$AB=B,P(B|A)=\frac{P(AB)}{P(A)}=\frac{P(B)}{P(\Omega)}=P(B)\leqslant 1$

$B\subset A$ 时,$AB=B$ 且 $P(B)\leqslant P(A),P(B|A)=\frac{P(AB)}{P(A)}=\frac{P(B)}{P(A)}\leqslant 1$

$A\subset B$ 时,$AB=A,P(B|A)=\frac{P(AB)}{P(A)}=\frac{P(A)}{P(A)}=1$。

答案:C

1-9-4 **解**:注意 0.03 和 0.02 是条件概率,作为条件的事件与不作条件的事件要分别设。设 A_i 为"第 i 台加工的零件",$i=1$、2,B 为"废品",则 $\overline{B}$ 为合格品。

$P(A_1)=\frac{2}{3},P(A_2)=\frac{1}{3},P(B|A_1)=0.03,P(B|A_2)=0.02$

$P(\overline{B})=1-P(B)=1-[P(A_1)P(B|A_1)+P(A_2)P(B|A_2)]$

答案:B

1-9-5 **解**:设 A_i 为"第 i 组生产的零件",$i=1$、2,B 为"废品",则 $P(A_1)=\frac{1}{3},P(A_2)=\frac{2}{3},P(B|A_1)=0.02,P(B|A_2)=0.03$,求 $P(A_1|B)$,显然可用贝叶斯公式,

$P(A_1|B)=\frac{P(A_1B)}{P(B)}=\frac{P(A_1)P(B|A_1)}{P(A_1)P(B|A_1)+P(A_2)P(B|A_2)}$。

答案:B

1-9-6 **解**:A 与 B 相互独立,即 $P(AB)=P(A)P(B),P(A\cup B)=P(A)+P(B)-P(AB)=P(A)+P(B)-P(A)P(B)$ 或 $P(A\cup B)=1-P(\overline{A\cup B})=1-P(\overline{A}\,\overline{B})=1-P(\overline{A})P(\overline{B})=1-[1-P(A)][1-P(B)]$。

答案:B

1-9-7 **解**:因为 A、B 相互独立,所以 $\overline{A}$、B 相互独立,则

$$P(\overline{A}|B)=P(\overline{A})=1-P(A)=0.8$$

答案:D

1-9-8 **解**:$P(A\cup B)=P(A)+P(B)-P(AB)=P(A)+P(B)-P(A)P(B)$,选项 A、B 错误;$1+P(\overline{A})P(\overline{B})\geqslant 1$,选项 D 错误。

$P(A\cup B)=1-P(\overline{A\cup B})=1-P(\overline{A}\overline{B})=1-P(\overline{A})P(\overline{B})$,选项 C 正确。

答案:C

1-9-9 **解**:注意选项 C 和 D 中必有一个对,一个错。

$P(A|B)+P(\overline{A}|\overline{B})=1,P(A|B)=1-P(\overline{A}|\overline{B})=P(A|\overline{B})$

$$\frac{P(AB)}{P(B)}=\frac{P(A\overline{B})}{P(\overline{B})}=\frac{P(A)-P(AB)}{1-P(B)}$$

$P(AB)-P(AB)P(B)=P(B)P(A)-P(B)P(AB),P(AB)=P(A)P(B)$。

答案:C

1-9-10 **解**:这是 3 次独立重复试验,设 A 为"每次命中目标",$P(A)=0.8$,至少击中两次的概率为:

$$P=C_3^2 0.8^2\times 0.2+C_3^3 0.8^3$$

或设 X 为"3 次射击命中的次数",则 $X\sim B(3,0.8)$,

$$P(X\geqslant 2)=P(X=2)+P(X=3)$$

答案:D

1-9-11 **解**:由分布律的性质可知 $0.4+a+b+0.1=1$,即 $a+b=0.5$,

$\{X\leqslant 1\}\cap\{0<X<3\}=\{X=1\}$,

由独立性 $P\{X=1\}=P\{X\leqslant 1\}\cdot P\{0<X<3\}$,

即 $a=(0.4+a)(a+b)$,得出 $a=0.4,b=0.1$。

答案:B

1-9-12 **解**:因 $f(-x)=f(x)$,

所以 $F(0)=\int_{-\infty}^{0}f(x)\mathrm{d}x=\int_{0}^{+\infty}f(t)\mathrm{d}t=0.5$,

$$F(-a)=\int_{-\infty}^{-a}f(x)\mathrm{d}x=-\int_{+\infty}^{a}f(-t)\mathrm{d}t=\int_{a}^{+\infty}f(t)\mathrm{d}t=\int_{0}^{+\infty}f(x)\mathrm{d}x-\int_{0}^{a}f(x)\mathrm{d}x$$
$$=0.5-\int_{0}^{a}f(x)\mathrm{d}x。$$

也可把 $f(x)$ 的积分值理解为曲边梯形面积(见解图)并利用图形对称性来判定。

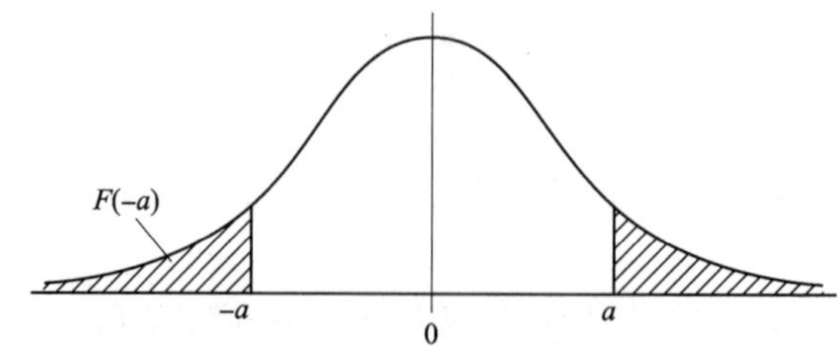

图 1-9-12 解图

答案:B

1-9-13 **解**:用概率密度性质 $f(x)\geqslant 0$ 且 $\int_{-\infty}^{+\infty}f(x)\mathrm{d}x=1$ 去核对。

选项 A 中 $f(x)$ 不满足 $f(x)\geqslant 0$。

选项 B、D 中 $f(x)$ 不满足$\int_{-\infty}^{+\infty}f(x)\mathrm{d}x=1$。

选项 C 中 $f(x)$ 满足 $f(x)\geqslant 0$，且$\int_{-\infty}^{+\infty}f(x)\mathrm{d}x=1$。

也可以由均匀分布的概率密度函数 $f(x)=\begin{cases}\dfrac{1}{b-a}, a<x<b\\ 0,其他\end{cases}$ 直接判定选项 C 正确。

答案：C

1-9-14 **解**：$F\left(\frac{1}{3}\right)=P\left(X\leqslant\frac{1}{3}\right)=\int_0^{\frac{1}{3}}3e^{-3x}\mathrm{d}x=-e^{-3x}\Big|_0^{\frac{1}{3}}=1-e^{-1}$

答案：C

1-9-15 **解**：$X\sim N(\mu,\sigma^2)$，$\frac{X-\mu}{\sigma}\sim N(0,1)$

$P(|X-\mu|<\sigma)=P\left(\left|\frac{X-\mu}{\sigma}\right|<1\right)=2\Phi(1)-1$。

答案：C

1-9-16 **解**：$f(x)>0$，且 $x>1$ 时，$f(x)$单调减少（见解图）。

$a=\int_{12}^{16}f(x)\mathrm{d}x$ 等于区间$[12,16]$上曲边梯形面积。

$b=\int_{14}^{18}f(x)\mathrm{d}x$ 等于区间$[14,18]$上曲边梯形面积。

显然 $a>b$

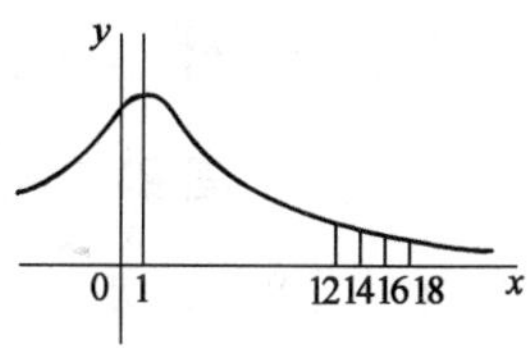

题 1-9-16 解图

或 $b=\int_{14}^{18}f(x)\mathrm{d}x\xlongequal{x=t+2}\int_{12}^{16}f(t+2)\mathrm{d}t=\int_{12}^{16}f(x+2)\mathrm{d}x$

$$a-b=\int_{12}^{16}f(x)\mathrm{d}x-\int_{12}^{16}f(x+2)\mathrm{d}x$$

$$=\int_{12}^{16}[f(x)-f(x+2)]\mathrm{d}x$$

因为 $x>1$ 时，$f(x)$ 严格单调减少，所以在$[12,16]$上 $f(x)-f(x+2)>0$

故 $a-b>0$，$a>b$。

答案：B

1-9-17 **解**：由$\frac{1}{4}+b+\frac{1}{4}=1$，得 $b=\frac{1}{2}$

由 $E(X)=-2\times\frac{1}{4}+1\times\frac{1}{2}+a\times\frac{1}{4}=1$，得 $a=4$。

答案：B

1-9-18 **解**：$f(x)=F'(x)=\frac{1}{\pi(1+x^2)}$

$E(X)=\int_{-\infty}^{+\infty}\frac{x}{\pi(1+x^2)}\mathrm{d}x=\frac{1}{2\pi}\int_{-\infty}^{+\infty}\frac{1}{1+x^2}\mathrm{d}(1+x^2)=\frac{1}{2\pi}\ln(1+x^2)\Big|_{-\infty}^{+\infty}$（发散）

答案:D

注意:如果根据 $f(x)$ 为偶函数,判定 $E(X)=0$ 就错了。

1-9-19 解:$X\sim B(4,p)$,$P(X\geqslant 1)=\frac{15}{16}$,$P(X=0)=(1-p)^4=\frac{1}{16}$,$p=\frac{1}{2}$,$E(X^2)=D(X)+[E(X)]^2=np(1-p)+(np)^2$。

答案:D

1-9-20 解:$D(X)=E(X^2)-[E(X)]^2=\frac{1}{18}$,$D(Y)=\frac{1}{18}$,

$\mathrm{Cov}(X,Y)=E(XY)-E(X)E(Y)=-\frac{1}{36}$,$\rho=\frac{\mathrm{Cov}(X,Y)}{\sqrt{D(X)D(Y)}}=-\frac{1}{2}$。

答案:D

1-9-21 解:X 服从 0—1 分布,$D(X)=p(1-p)$

$D(\overline{X})=\frac{D(X)}{n}=\frac{p(1-p)}{n}$

$\sqrt{D(\overline{X})}=\sqrt{\frac{p(1-p)}{n}}$。

答案:A

1-9-22 解:因为 $E(\overline{X})=\mu$,所以 $E[(\overline{X}-\mu)^2]=D(\overline{X})=\frac{\sigma^2}{n}=\frac{4}{16}=\frac{1}{4}$。

答案:B

1-9-23 解:$\overline{X}\sim N(\mu,\frac{\sigma^2}{n})$,$\frac{\overline{X}-\mu}{\frac{\sigma}{\sqrt{n}}}=2(\overline{X}-\mu)\sim N(0,1)$,

$P(|\overline{X}-\mu|<1)=P(|2(\overline{X}-\mu)|<2)=2\Phi(2)-1=0.954\ 4$。

答案:A

1-9-24 解:当 $W\sim N(0,1)$ 时,$W^2\sim\chi^2(1)$。

$Y=C(\sum\limits_{i=1}^{n}X_i)^2=(\sum\limits_{i=1}^{n}\sqrt{C}X_i)^2$

要使 $\sum\limits_{i=1}^{n}\sqrt{C}X_i\sim N(0,1)$

应使 $D(\sum\limits_{i=1}^{n}\sqrt{C}X_i)=1$,即 $\sum\limits_{i=1}^{n}CD(X_i)=nCD(X)=nC\sigma^2=1$,$C=\frac{1}{n\sigma^2}$。

答案:D

1-9-25 解:注意对两个正态总体的样本有 $\frac{\sigma_2^2S_1^2}{\sigma_1^2S_2^2}\sim F(n_1-1,n_2-1)$,两总体方差相等,即 $\sigma_1^2=\sigma_2^2$ 时,$\frac{\sigma_2^2S_1^2}{\sigma_1^2S_2^2}=\frac{S_1^2}{S_2^2}\sim F(n_1-1,n_2-1)$。

答案:A

1-9-26 解:$E(X)=\int_1^{+\infty}x\lambda x^{-(\lambda+1)}\mathrm{d}x=\frac{\lambda}{\lambda-1}$,$\lambda=\frac{E(X)}{E(X)-1}$,用 $\overline{X}$ 替换 $E(X)$,得 λ 的矩估计量 $\hat{\lambda}=\frac{\overline{X}}{\overline{X}-1}$。

答案:B

1-9-27 **解**:因为 $S^2=\frac{1}{n-1}\sum_{i=1}^{n}(X_i-\overline{X})^2$,$E(S^2)=D(X)=\sigma^2$

答案:A

说明:选项 B、D 中含有未知参数,不是统计量,因而不是估计量。选项 C 是σ^2的矩估计量,但不是无偏估计量。

1-9-28 **解**:$E(\hat{\lambda})=aE(\overline{X})+(2-3a)E(S^2)$

$=aE(X)+(2-3a)D(X)$

$=a\lambda+(2-3a)\lambda=(2-2a)\lambda=\lambda$

$2-2a=1,a=\frac{1}{2}$。

答案:C

1-9-29 **解**:用结论:当$\sum_{i=1}^{n}C_i=1$时,$\sum_{i=1}^{n}C_iX_i$是$E(X)$的无偏估计,在这些无偏估计中$\overline{X}$的方差最小,$\overline{X}$最有效。或仿有效性中的例子做。

答案:D

1-9-30 **解**:μ 的$(1-\alpha)$置信区间是$(\overline{X}-u_{\frac{\alpha}{2}}\frac{\sigma}{\sqrt{n}},\overline{X}+u_{\frac{\alpha}{2}}\frac{\sigma}{\sqrt{n}})$

区间长 $L=2u_{\frac{\alpha}{2}}\frac{\sigma}{\sqrt{n}}$

提高精度(应减小 L),应减小 $u_{\frac{\alpha}{2}}$,增大 n;而减小 $u_{\frac{\alpha}{2}}$应增大 α(见解图)。

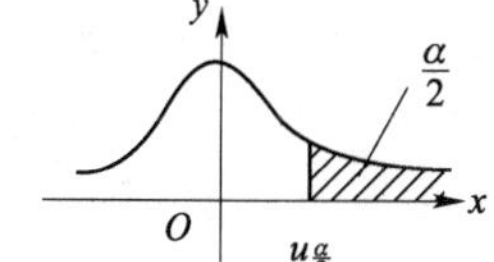

题 1-9-30 解图

答案:C

说明:标准正态分布上 α 分位数可记为 z_α,也可记为 u_α。

1-9-31 **解**:月减体重 $X\sim N(\mu,\sigma^2)$,μ 为月平均减体重。广告宣称的月平均减体重大于3kg,即 $\mu>3$。检验 $\mu>3$ 是真是伪(没有等号应作为 H_1),H_0 应写成 $\mu\leqslant3$ 或 $\mu=3$(2.8 是样本均值 $\overline{X}$)。

答案:A

1-9-32 **解**:总体 $X\sim N(\mu,\sigma^2)$时,$\frac{\overline{X}-\mu}{\frac{S}{\sqrt{n}}}\sim t(n-1)$,在 $H_0:\mu=\mu_0$ 成立时,检验统计量

$\frac{\overline{X}-\mu_0}{\frac{S}{\sqrt{n}}}\sim t(n-1)$。本题 $n=10$。

答案:A

1-9-33 **解**:选项 A,H_0成立时,统计量 $\mu=\frac{\overline{X}-\mu_0}{\sigma}\sqrt{n}\sim N(0,1)$(称为 μ 检验法);

选项 B,H_0成立时,统计量 $T=\frac{\overline{X}-\mu_0}{S}\sqrt{n}\sim t(n-1)$(称为 t 检验法);

选项 C、D,统计量服从χ^2分布(称为χ^2检验法)。

答案:B

第二章 普通物理

复习指导

一、考试大纲

2.1 热学

气体状态参量;平衡态;理想气体状态方程;理想气体的压强和温度的统计解释;自由度;能量按自由度均分原理;理想气体内能;平均碰撞频率和平均自由程;麦克斯韦速率分布律;方均根速率;平均速率;最概然速率;功;热量;内能;热力学第一定律及其对理想气体等值过程的应用;绝热过程;气体的摩尔热容量;循环过程;卡诺循环;热机效率;净功;制冷系数;热力学第二定律及其统计意义;可逆过程和不可逆过程。

2.2 波动学

机械波的产生和传播;一维简谐波表达式;描述波的特征量;波面,波前,波线;波的能量、能流、能流密度;波的衍射;波的干涉;驻波;自由端反射与固定端反射;声波;声强级;多普勒效应。

2.3 光学

相干光的获得;杨氏双缝干涉;光程和光程差;薄膜干涉;光疏介质;光密介质;迈克尔逊干涉仪;惠更斯-菲涅尔原理;单缝衍射;光学仪器分辨本领;衍射光栅与光谱分析;X 射线衍射;布拉格公式;自然光和偏振光;布儒斯特定律;马吕斯定律;双折射现象。

二、复习指导

(一)热学

热学包含两部分内容:气体分子运动论和热力学基础。

气体分子运动论主要是研究宏观热现象的本质,对大量分子运用统计平均方法揭示压强、温度的微观本质,进而讨论三个统计规律,即分子平均动能按自由度均分的统计规律,分子速率分布的统计规律,分子碰撞的统计规律。

其中,理想气体状态方程,气体的压强和温度公式及其推导,理想气体的内能,麦克斯韦分子速率分布为重点。本部分内容公式较多,但切不可死记公式,必须弄清公式的来龙去脉和公式的物理意义。

热力学部分的核心是热力学第一定律、热力学第二定律,尤以热力学第一定律及其在各等值过程、绝热过程中的应用为重点。此外,对循环过程(包括卡诺循环)热机效率也应予以足够的重视。

热力学部分习题主要是根据热力学第一定律来计算理想气体的几种典型过程的功、热量、内能变化以及循环过程的效率等问题。解题前应首先弄清是什么过程(等温、等压、等容、绝热)及这一过程的特点。因为功、热量都是过程量,其值与过程的性质有关。

(二)波动学

这一节主要讨论机械波的产生、描述、能量和干涉。其中平面简谐波的波动方程和波的干涉为本节重点。

理解波动方程 $y(x,t)$时要特别注意理解建立波动方程的思路,要从三个不同角度,即 $x=$常量,$t=$常量以及 x 和 t 都变化的三个方面去理解波动方程的物理意义。

学习波的干涉时,要注意掌握相干条件并运用相位差或波程差的概念分析相干波的叠加后振幅极大、极小问题。

此外,由于机械振动是产生机械波的根源,因此有必要复习机械振动的有关概念:谐振动方程、相位、同方向同频率谐振动的合成。

(三)光学

光学(波动光学)含有三部分内容:光的干涉、光的衍射、光的偏振。

光的干涉是波动光学的基础,在光的衍射、偏振中都要用到。

在光的干涉中,以分波阵面干涉(双缝)和分振幅干涉(薄膜、劈尖)为重点。但不管是分是分波阵面干涉还是分振幅干涉,最重要的是要善于分析光路,掌握好光程的概念及在垂直入射的情况下光程差的计算。此外在光程差的计算中,应注意因界面反射条件不同而产生的附加光程差 $\lambda/2$(半波损失)。

光的衍射以夫琅和费单缝衍射为重点。要特别注意不要把单缝衍射暗纹公式 $a\sin\theta=k\lambda$ 与双缝干涉明纹公式 $\delta=k\lambda$ 相混淆,二者形式相似而结果相反,前者表示单缝边缘光线的光程差,后者是两束相干光的光程差。

此外,式中 k 是一可变的整数,具体取值视问题的条件而定。

在光的偏振中,以马吕斯定律和布儒斯特定律为重点。理解马吕斯定律时应注意,定律中的光强 I_0 为入射偏振片前的偏振光的光强,而自然光通过偏振片后光强减半$\left(\frac{1}{2}I_0\right)$。

第一节 热 学

一、平衡态、气体状态参量

热学的研究对象是由大量原子、分子组成的宏观物质系统,称为热力学系统。关于分子数目的典型数量是阿伏伽德罗常数 $N_0=6.022\times10^{23}$ 个分子/mol,即 1 mol 的任何物质有 6.022×10^{23} 个分子。热学的研究内容:热现象所遵循的普遍规律,即热力学第一定律和热力学第二定律,以及(热力学)系统的物理性质与冷热现象的关系。热学的研究方法有两种:一是宏观方法,称为热力学方法;二是微观方法,称为分子运动论。

(一)平衡态

系统的宏观物理性质不随时间变化的状态,称系统处于平衡态,或称为静态。

(二)气体状态参量

系统的宏观物理性质,是由经过定义的物理量来描述。经长期研究发现,当一定量的气体处于平衡态时,用它的体积 V、压强 p、温度 T 来描述它的物理状态最好,这些描述气体状态的物理量,称为气体平衡状态参量,简称状态参量。

体积(V),指气体分子可到达的空间。在容器中气体的体积,也就是容器体积。体积的国际单位是立方米(m^3)。有时也用升(L),$1L=10^{-3}m^3$。

压强(p),是指气体作用于外界(例如容器壁)每单位面积上的正压力。压强的国际单位称为帕斯卡,简称帕(Pa),即牛顿/米^2(N/m^2)。应用中经常会出现大气压的压强单位,$1atm=1.013\times10^5Pa$。

温度(T),是热学中特有的表示系统冷热程度的物理量,温度的数值表示叫温标,采用热力学温标时,温度用 T 表示,而用摄氏温标时,温度用 t 表示,热力学温度 T 与摄氏温度 t 的关系为

$$T(K)=273.15+t(℃)$$

二、理想气体状态方程

严格遵守波义耳-马略特定律、盖吕萨克定律、查理定律和阿伏伽德罗定律的气体称为理想气体,与气体的化学成分无关。实际中的各种气体只是在压强较低(或稀薄气体)的情况下才能视为理想气体。

综合上述理想气体遵守的四条定律,可导出理想气体状态参量之间的一个在任何情况下都成立的关系式,叫理想气体状态方程。

$$pV=\frac{m}{M}RT \tag{2-1-1}$$

式中:m——气体的质量;

M——摩尔质量;

R——摩尔气体常量值为 8.31J/(mol·K)。

理想气体状态方程还可化为另一种形式,设质量为 m 的气体的分子数为 N,1 mol 气体的分子数为 N_0(阿伏伽德罗常数),$\left(\frac{m}{M}\right)$mol 气体的分子数为 $N=\frac{m}{M}N_0$。

即

$$\frac{m}{M}=\frac{N}{N_0} \tag{2-1-2}$$

把它代入式(2-1-1),有 $pV=\frac{N}{N_0}RT=N\frac{R}{N_0}T$,即

$$p=\frac{N}{V}\frac{R}{N_0}T \tag{2-1-3}$$

令

$$n=\frac{N}{V},k=\frac{R}{N_0} \tag{2-1-4}$$

于是

$$p=nkT \tag{2-1-5}$$

式中:n——单位体积内的分子数,称分子数密度;

k——$1.38\times10^{-23}J/K$,称玻尔兹曼常数。

三、理想气体的压强和温度的统计解释

(一)理想气体的微观图景

从微观图景来看,理想气体是由数目巨大的运动着的分子组成。各运动着的分子之间,以及分子与容器壁之间会发生频繁的碰撞,使每个分子的运动速率和方向发生频繁的变化,这样,从整体来看,理想气体是一个这样的群体:其中每一个分子都做杂乱无章的运动,或者说,分子做热运动。

（二）理想气体分子模型

最简单的分子模型是把分子看成一个直径可忽略不计的、具有一定质量（分子质量）m'的弹性小球。所谓直径可以忽略是指小球之间的距离远大于小球直径，这样，可把小球当作质点来处理。小球与器壁间碰撞，视为完全弹性碰撞。

（三）压强的统计解释

理想气体对容器壁产生的压强，是大量分子不断撞击器壁的结果。根据完全弹性碰撞的力学知识，以及处于平衡态的理想气体的压强特征——对容器各面施加的压强相等，可推导出一个重要的压强公式

$$p=\frac{2}{3}n\bar{\omega} \tag{2-1-6}$$

式中，$n=N/V$，即分子数密度，N 是分子总数，$\bar{\omega}$ 称为分子的平均平动动能，它等于全体分子的平动动能之和除以全体分子总数，即

$$\bar{\omega}=\left(\frac{1}{2}m'v_1^2+\frac{1}{2}m'v_2^2+\cdots+\frac{1}{2}m'v_N^2\right)/N=\frac{1}{2}m'\overline{v^2} \tag{2-1-7}$$

$\overline{v^2}$为分子速率平方的平均值。请注意，各分子间的频繁碰撞使每个分子的速率 v_1，v_2，…，v_N 在发生频繁的变化，但 $\overline{v^2}$ 及 $\bar{\omega}$ 却不随时间变化（因为压强 p 不随时间变化），这是大量做热运动分子集体的统计规律性的表现。所谓统计规律性，是指以平动动能为例，一个特定的分子，例如编号为 i 的分子，它的平动动能 $\omega_i=\frac{1}{2}m'v_i^2$ 是随时（或随机）变化的，而大量分子的平均平动动能 $\bar{\omega}$ 却表现出不变的规律性——统计规律性。

（四）温度的统计解释

联立理想气体状态方程（2-1-5）及压强公式（2-1-6）

$$\begin{cases}p=nkT\\ p=\frac{2}{3}n\bar{\omega}\end{cases}$$

由上两式消去 p 得

$$\bar{\omega}=\frac{3}{2}kT \tag{2-1-8}$$

上式把热学中特有的量——温度与大量分子的平均平动动能联系起来，这使我们摆脱了温度是冷热程度这种无法定量描述的经验之谈，而把温度看作是大量分子热运动强度的标志。温度越高，分子的总体表现是热运动越激烈。

四、能量按自由度均分原理

（一）自由度数目 i

气体中每一个分子可由单个原子或多个原子组成，称单原子分子或多原子分子，由单原子分子组成的气体如氦气（He）、氖气（Ne）等，由双原子分子组成的气体如氧气（O_2）、氮气（N_2）等，至于甲烷气（CH_4），自然是由五原子分子组成的气体了。

自由度数目 i 是指决定某物体在空间的位置所需要的独立坐标数目。

据此，把构成气体分子的每一个原子看成一质点，且各原子之间的距离固定不变（称刚性分子，即视为刚体）。那么，单原子分子的自由度 $i=3$，即有三个平动自由度；刚性双原子分子

的自由度 $i=5$，即有三个平动自由度和两个转动自由度；由三个以上原子组成的刚性多原子分子 $i=6$，有三个平动自由度和三个转动自由度。

（二）能量按自由度均分原理

它的内容是：在温度为 T 的平衡态下，每一个分子的每一个自由度都具有相同的平均动能，其值为 $\frac{1}{2}kT$（请特别注意“平均”两字）。

据此，一个单原子分子有三个平均自由度，单原子分子的平均（平动）动能 $\bar{\omega}=3\cdot\frac{1}{2}kT$，这正是式（2-1-8）。刚性双原子分子 $i=5$，它的平均动能 $\bar{\varepsilon}=\frac{5}{2}kT$（细说起来，即三个平动自由度对应平均平动动能为 $\frac{3}{2}kT$，两个转动自由度对应平均转动动能为 $\frac{2}{2}kT$）。一般说来，若一个分子的自由度数为 i，那么，据能量按自由度均分原理，该分子的平均动能为

$$\bar{\varepsilon}=\frac{i}{2}kT$$

五、理想气体内能

从微观上讲，理想气体是指分子之间相互作用势能小到可以忽略不计的气体，因为各分子的热运动动能远大于它们之间相互作用势能。这样，整个理想气体具有的机械能量，就等于每个分子热运动动能之和，设理想气体分子总数为 N，一个分子的动能用 ε 表示，则理想气体的内能 E 可表示为

$$E=\varepsilon_1+\varepsilon_2+\cdots+\varepsilon_N$$

$$=N\cdot\frac{(\varepsilon_1+\varepsilon_2+\cdots+\varepsilon_N)}{N}=N\bar{\varepsilon}$$

式中，$\bar{\varepsilon}$ 为每一分子的平均动能，应为 $\frac{i}{2}kT$，故

$$E=\frac{i}{2}NkT \tag{2-1-9}$$

$$N=\left(\frac{m}{M}\right)N_0$$

$$N_0k=R$$

$$E=\frac{i}{2}\left(\frac{m}{M}\right)RT \tag{2-1-10}$$

由于理想气体状态方程 $pV=(\frac{m}{M})RT$，E 还可表示为

$$E=\frac{i}{2}pV \tag{2-1-11}$$

理想气体每单位体积的内能，即内能密度为

$$E/V=\frac{i}{2}p \tag{2-1-12}$$

【例 2-1-1】 在标准状态下，当氢气和氦气的压强与体积都相等时，氢气和氦气的内能之比为：

A. $\frac{5}{3}$　　B. $\frac{3}{5}$　　C. $\frac{1}{2}$　　D. $\frac{3}{2}$

解 由 $E=\frac{m}{M}\frac{i}{2}RT=\frac{i}{2}pV$，注意到氢为双原子分子，氦为单原子分子，即 $i(H_2)=5$，$i(He)=3$，又 $p(H_2)=p(He)$，$V(H_2)=V(He)$，故 $\frac{E(H_2)}{E(He)}=\frac{i(H_2)}{i(He)}=\frac{5}{3}$。

答案：A

【例 2-1-2】 有两种理想气体，第一种的压强为 p_1，体积为 V_1，温度为 T_1，总质量为 M_1，摩尔质量为 μ_1；第二种的压强为 p_2，体积为 V_2，温度为 T_2，总质量为 M_2，摩尔质量为 μ_2。当 $V_1=V_2$，$T_1=T_2$，$M_1=M_2$ 时，则 $\frac{\mu_1}{\mu_2}$：

A. $\frac{\mu_1}{\mu_2}=\sqrt{\frac{p_1}{p_2}}$　　B. $\frac{\mu_1}{\mu_2}=\frac{p_1}{p_2}$　　C. $\frac{\mu_1}{\mu_2}=\sqrt{\frac{p_2}{p_1}}$　　D. $\frac{\mu_1}{\mu_2}=\frac{p_2}{p_1}$

解 理想气体状态方程 $pV=\frac{M}{\mu}RT$，因为 $V_1=V_2$，$T_1=T_2$，$M_1=M_2$，所以 $\frac{\mu_1}{\mu_2}=\frac{p_2}{p_1}$。

答案：D

六、麦克斯韦速率分布律

(一)速率分布函数

设理想气体分子总数为 N，各分子的速率自然有大有小，现以 dN 表示速率在 $v\to v+dv$ 区间内的分子数，定义速率分布函数为

$$f(v)=\frac{dN}{Ndv} \tag{2-1-13}$$

从速率分布函数的定义式可知，它的意义是在单位速率间隔内分子的百分数，当理想气体处于平衡态时，分布函数与时间无关，而与速率 v 有关。式(2-1-13)可改写为

$$dN=Nf(v)dv \tag{2-1-14}$$

如要表示速率在 $v_1\to v_2$ 区间内的分子数，可将上式积分

$$\int_{v_1}^{v_2}dN=\Delta N=\int_{v_1}^{v_2}Nf(v)dv$$

故

$$\int_{v_1}^{v_2}f(v)dv=\frac{\Delta N}{N} \tag{2-1-15}$$

表示速率在 $v_1\to v_2$ 区间内的分子数占总分子数的百分率。由于全体分子速率分布总在 $0\to\infty$ 区间内，把式(2-1-14)从 $v=0$ 到 $v\to\infty$ 积分得

$$\int_0^{\infty}f(v)dv=1 \tag{2-1-16}$$

上式说明，$\int_0^{\infty}f(v)dv=$ 分布曲线下总面积 $=1$，速率分布函数应满足归一化条件。

(二)麦克斯韦速率分布函数

理论和实践都证实，处于温度为 T 的理想气体，速率分布函数的具体数学形式是

$$f(v)=\left(\frac{m'}{2\pi kT}\right)^{3/2}e^{\frac{-m'v^2}{2kT}}4\pi v^2 \tag{2-1-17}$$

式中各文字的意义都已交代过。此式称为麦克斯韦速率分布函数。若以 v 为横坐标，以 $f(v)$ 为纵坐标，此函数的大致图形，如图 2-1-1 所示，温度越高，分布曲线的最高点越向速率大的方向移动。

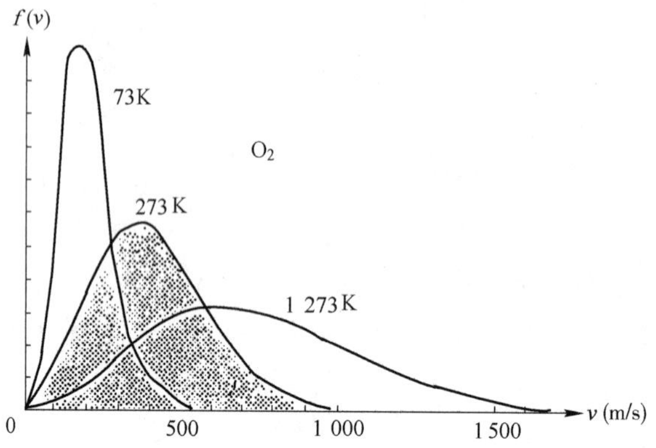

图 2-1-1 不同温度下速率分布曲线

(三)三种速率

知道了麦克斯韦速率分布函数后，可求出全体分子的三种速率。

1. 最可几速率 v_p(最概然速率)

由 $\dfrac{df(v)}{dv}=0$，得

$$v_p=\sqrt{\frac{2kT}{m'}}=\sqrt{\frac{2RT}{M}} \tag{2-1-18}$$

M 为气体的摩尔质量。

2. 平均速率 $\bar{v}$

$$\bar{v}=\frac{1}{N}\int_0^{\infty} v\mathrm{d}N=\int_0^{\infty} vf(v)\mathrm{d}v=\sqrt{\frac{8kT}{\pi m'}}=\sqrt{\frac{8RT}{\pi M}} \tag{2-1-19}$$

【例 2-1-3】 假定氧气的热力学温度提高一倍，氧分子全部离解为氧原子，则氧原子的平均速率是氧分子平均速率的：

A. 4 倍　　B. 2 倍　　C. $\sqrt{2}$倍　　D. $\dfrac{1}{\sqrt{2}}$

解 $\bar{v}=\sqrt{\dfrac{8RT}{\pi M}}$，$\bar{v}_{O_2}=\sqrt{\dfrac{8RT}{\pi M}}=\sqrt{\dfrac{8RT}{\pi\cdot 32}}$

氧气的热力学温度提高一倍，氧分子全部离解为氧原子，$T_O=2T_{O_2}$

$$\bar{v}_O=\sqrt{\frac{8RT_O}{\pi M_0}}=\sqrt{\frac{8R\cdot 2T}{\pi\cdot 16}}，则\ \frac{\bar{v}_O}{\bar{v}_{O_2}}=\frac{\sqrt{\dfrac{8R\cdot 2T}{\pi\cdot 16}}}{\sqrt{\dfrac{8RT}{\pi\cdot 32}}}=2$$

答案:B

3. 方均根速率 $\sqrt{\bar{v}^2}$

$$\bar{v}^2=\frac{1}{N}\int_0^{\infty} v^2 f(v)\mathrm{d}v=\frac{3kT}{m'} \tag{2-1-20}$$

$$\sqrt{\bar{v}^2}=\sqrt{\frac{3kT}{m'}}=\sqrt{\frac{3RT}{M}}$$

七、平均碰撞频率$\bar{Z}$和平均自由程$\bar{\lambda}$

气体分子间在做频繁的相互碰撞，一个分子在单位时间内的碰撞次数 Z 简称为碰撞次数，或称碰撞频率。由于分子热运动的无规则性，没有理由说各分子的 Z 是一样的，Z 对全体分子的平均值 $\bar{Z}$，称平均碰撞频率(次数)。

一个分子在相继的两次碰撞之间所飞行的路程，叫自由程。各分子的自由程各不相同，对全体分子取平均，叫平均自由程，以 $\bar{\lambda}$ 表示。对于一个分子平均来说，在单位时间内的飞行路程为平均速率 $\bar{v}$，所以下式成立

$$\bar{v}=\bar{Z}\bar{\lambda} \tag{2-1-21}$$

研究表明

$$\bar{Z}=\sqrt{2}\pi d^2 n\bar{v} \tag{2-1-22}$$

式中：n——分子数密度；

d——分子有效直径，不同分子有不同的有效直径。

$$\bar{\lambda}=\frac{\bar{v}}{\bar{Z}}=\frac{1}{\sqrt{2}\pi d^2 n}=\frac{kT}{\sqrt{2}\pi d^2 p} \tag{2-1-23}$$

上式中最后一等式利用了理想气体状态方程 $p=nkT$。式(2-1-23)表明在 T 一定时，$\bar{\lambda}$ 与 p 成反比。$\bar{\lambda}$ 在对气体内迁移现象(包括热传导、扩散、黏滞等)讨论时起重要作用。

【例 2-1-4】 容积恒定的容器内盛有一定量的某种理想气体，分子的平均自由程为 $\bar{\lambda}_0$，平均碰撞频率为 $\bar{Z}_0$，若气体的温度降低为原来的$\frac{1}{4}$倍，则此时分子的平均自由程 $\bar{\lambda}$ 和平均碰撞频率 $\bar{Z}$ 为：

A. $\bar{\lambda}=\bar{\lambda}_0,\bar{Z}=\bar{Z}_0$　　B. $\bar{\lambda}=\bar{\lambda}_0,\bar{Z}=\frac{1}{2}\bar{Z}_0$

C. $\bar{\lambda}=2\bar{\lambda}_0,\bar{Z}=2\bar{Z}_0$　　D. $\bar{\lambda}=\sqrt{2}\lambda_0,\bar{Z}=4\bar{Z}_0$

解 气体分子的平均碰撞频率 $Z_0=\sqrt{2}n\pi d^2\bar{v}=\sqrt{2}n\pi d^2\sqrt{\frac{8RT}{\pi M}}$，平均自由程 $\bar{\lambda}_0=\frac{\bar{v}}{\bar{Z}_0}=\frac{1}{\sqrt{2}n\pi d^2}$，$T'=\frac{1}{4}T$，$\bar{\lambda}=\bar{\lambda}_0,\bar{Z}=\frac{1}{2}\bar{Z}_0$。

答案：B

八、热力学第一定律

(一)准静态过程

热力学系统在与外界发生相互作用时，它(以及外界)的状态要发生变化，状态变化的过程，叫热力学过程。以理想气体为例，系统从初态(p_0,V_0,T_0)变化到终态(p_1,V_1,T_1)，可通过各种不同过程实现(参看示意图 2-1-2)，不同的过程体现了系统与外界的不同相互作用。

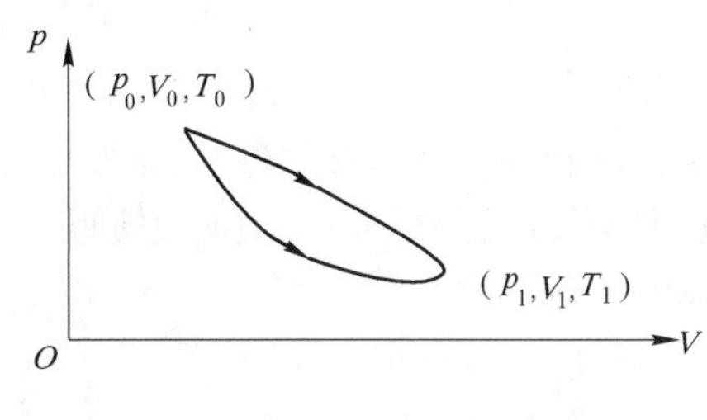

图 2-1-2

要使原先处于平衡态的理想气体状态发生变化，首先要破坏它原先的平衡态。也即系统要历经一非平衡态（非静态）情形。但若过程进行得如此缓慢，使过程进行中系统的状态都近似达到平衡态，这种理想化的过程叫准静态过程。在准静态过程中，气体的状态都可用平衡态（静态）参量（p，V，T）来描述。

（二）理想气体内能的改变 ΔE

一定量理想气体的内能 E 由式（2-1-10）确定。故理想气体经历任何过程从温度为 T_1 的状态变到温度为 T_2 的状态时，内能的增量为

$$\Delta E=E_2-E_1=\frac{m}{M}\ \frac{i}{2}\ R(T_2-T_1)=\frac{m}{M}\ \frac{i}{2}R\Delta T \tag{2-1-24}$$

显然，一定量理想气体的内能增量只取决于系统的初、终态，而与联系初、终态的过程无关，这一结论十分重要。或者可说，内能本身是状态的单值函数。

（三）功 A

利用力学中功的概念，计算气缸中气体在准静态过程中所做的功。设气体的压强为 p，活塞面积为 S，气体对活塞的压力 $f=pS$（见图 2-1-3），当活塞移动微小距离 $\mathrm{d}L$ 时，气体体积变化 $\mathrm{d}V=S\mathrm{d}L$，过程中所做微功 $\mathrm{d}A=f\mathrm{d}L=pS\mathrm{d}L=p\mathrm{d}V$。当气体体积从 V_1 膨胀到 V_2 时，气体对外（活塞）做功为

$$A=\int_{V_1}^{V_2}p\mathrm{d}V \tag{2-1-25}$$

当过程用 p-V 图上一条曲线表示时（见图 2-1-4），功 A 即表示曲边梯形的面积。可见，若以不同的曲线（代表不同的变化过程）连接相同的初态（V_1）、终态（V_2），功 A 不同，功与过程有关。注意，若 $V_2>V_1$，气体体积随过程膨胀，气体对外做正功（$A>0$）；反之，若 $V_2<V_1$，气体被压缩，气体对外做负功。还要注意，功 A 的表达式（2-1-25）只对准静态过程成立，对非准静态过程不成立。如气体向真空膨胀，对外做功 $A=0$。

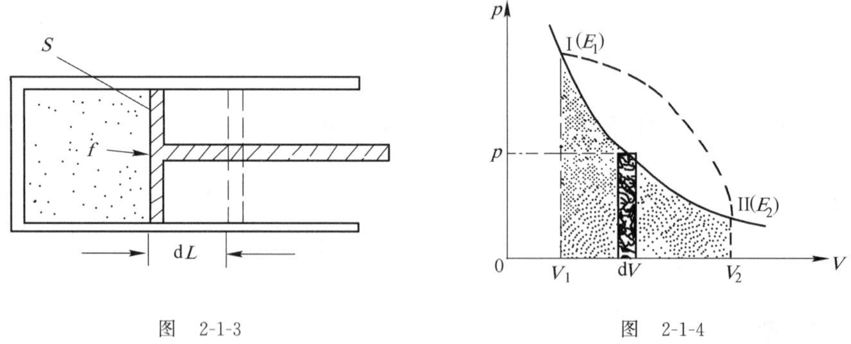

图 2-1-3　　图 2-1-4

（四）热量 Q

气体对外做正功或负功（外界对气体做正功），都会使气体（及外界）状态发生变化。改变系统状态，不仅可采取做功的方式，也可采取热量交换的方式。气体从外界吸收热量或放热给外界，都会使气体（及外界）状态发生变化。气体从外界吸收（或放热给外界）的热量多少，不仅取决于气体的初、终态，也取决于联系两态的变化过程，这一点在热力学第一定律中会清楚地看出。

（五）热力学第一定律

设一热力学系统与外界相互作用，使系统从某一初态 a 经过一个系统状态变化过程到达

终态 b，无数试验事实总结出下面的热力学第一定律（即能量守恒与转换定律）

$$Q_{a\to b}=E_b-E_a+A_{a\to b}$$

或简写为

$$Q=\Delta E+A \tag{2-1-26}$$

式中：Q——过程中系统从外界吸收的热量（若 $Q>0$ 为吸热，$Q<0$ 为放热）；

A——过程中系统对外界做功（可正可负，负功表示外界对系统做正功）；

ΔE——系统内能的增量，即系统终态内能与初态内能的差。

若过程的初、终态一定，则 ΔE 一定，而 A 与过程有关，故 Q 也与过程有关。

对于一个微小变化过程，热力学第一定律可写成微分形式

$$\mathrm{d}Q=\mathrm{d}E+\mathrm{d}A$$

热力学第一定律不仅适用于理想气体，而且还适用于液体、固体等一切热力学系统。

【例 2-1-5】 一定量的理想气体由 a 状态经过一过程到达 b 状态，吸热为 335J，系统对外做功 126J；若系统经过另一过程由 a 状态到达 b 状态，系统对外做功 42J，则过程中传入系统的热量为：

A. 530J　　B. 167J　　C. 251J　　D. 335J

解 两过程都是由 a 状态到达 b 状态，内能是状态量，内能增量 $\Delta E=\frac{m}{M}\frac{i}{2}R(T_b-T_a)$相同。

由热力学第一定律 $Q=(E_2-E_1)+W=\Delta E+W$，有 $Q_1-W_1=Q_2-W_2$，即 $335-126=Q_2-42$，可得 $Q_2=251$J。

答案：C

【例 2-1-6】 一定量的理想气体对外做了 500J 的功，如果过程是绝热的，气体内能的增量为：

A. 0　　B. 500J　　C. −500J　　D. 250J

解 由热力学第一定律 $Q=W+\Delta E$ 知，绝热过程做功等于内能增量的负值，$\Delta E=-W=-500$J。

答案：C

九、热力学第一定律对理想气体等值过程和绝热过程的应用

$(\frac{m}{M})$mol 的理想气体，从初态(p_1,V_1,T_1)经某一过程变化到终态(p_2,V_2,T_2)，如何计算热力学第一定律中的 Q、ΔE、A？

首先要注意 ΔE 与过程无关，它由式(2-1-24)确定

$$\Delta E=(\frac{m}{M})\frac{i}{2}R(T_2-T_1)$$

功 A 可通过式(2-1-25)计算，那么过程吸热 Q 可以从热力学第一定律算出。

（一）等容过程

过程方程：$V=$恒量，或 $p/T=$恒量

$$A=\int_{V_1}^{V_2}p\mathrm{d}V=0 \qquad (\mathrm{d}V=0)$$

$$Q_V = \Delta E + A = (\frac{m}{M})\ \frac{i}{2}R(T_2 - T_1) \qquad (2\text{-}1\text{-}27)$$

【例 2-1-7】 一定量的理想气体，经过等体过程，温度增量 ΔT，内能变化 ΔE_1，吸收热量 Q_1；若经过等压过程，温度增量也为 ΔT，内能变化 ΔE_2，吸收热量 Q_2，则一定是：

A. $\Delta E_2 = \Delta E_1, Q_2 > Q_1$　　B. $\Delta E_2 = \Delta E_1, Q_2 < Q_1$

C. $\Delta E_2 > \Delta E_1, Q_2 > Q_1$　　D. $\Delta E_2 < \Delta E_1, Q_2 < Q_1$

解 两过程温度增量均为 ΔT，内能增量 $\Delta E = \frac{m}{M}\frac{i}{2}R\Delta T$ 相同，即 $\Delta E_2 = \Delta E_1$。

由热力学第一定律，等体过程不做功，$W_1 = 0, Q_1 = \Delta E_1 = \frac{m}{M}\frac{i}{2}R\Delta T$；

对于等压过程，$Q_2 = \Delta E_2 + W_2 = \frac{m}{M}(\frac{i}{2}+1)R\Delta T$，所以 $Q_2 > Q_1$。

答案：A

（二）等压过程

过程方程：p＝恒量，或 T/V＝恒量

$$A = \int_{V_1}^{V_2} p\mathrm{d}V = p(V_2 - V_1)$$

利用状态方程 $pV = (\frac{m}{M})RT$，可将上式写成

$$A = (\frac{m}{M})R(T_2 - T_1) \qquad (2\text{-}1\text{-}28)$$

$$Q_p = \Delta E + A = (\frac{m}{M})(\frac{i+2}{2})R(T_2 - T_1) \qquad (2\text{-}1\text{-}29)$$

比较式(2-1-29)和式(2-1-27)可知，等压过程吸热量比等容过程吸热量多。

【例 2-1-8】 有 1mol 刚性双原子分子理想气体，在等压过程中对外做功 W，则其温度变化 ΔT 为：

A. $\frac{R}{W}$　　B. $\frac{W}{R}$　　C. $\frac{2R}{W}$　　D. $\frac{2W}{R}$

解 等压过程由 $W = p\Delta V = p(V_2 - V_1) = \frac{m}{M}R\Delta T$，今 $\frac{m}{M} = 1$，故 $\Delta T = \frac{W}{R}$。

答案：B

（三）等温过程

过程方程：T＝恒量，或 pV＝恒量

$$A = \int_{V_1}^{V_2} p\mathrm{d}V = \int_{V_1}^{V_2} \frac{(\frac{m}{M})RT}{V}\mathrm{d}V = (\frac{m}{M})RT\int_{V_1}^{V_2}\frac{\mathrm{d}V}{V}$$

$$A = (\frac{m}{M})RT\ln\frac{V_2}{V_1} = (\frac{m}{M})RT\ln\frac{p_1}{p_2} \qquad (2\text{-}1\text{-}30)$$

而 $\Delta E = 0$（因 $T_2 = T_1$）

$$Q_T = A = (\frac{m}{M})RT\ln\frac{V_2}{V_1} = (\frac{m}{M})RT\ln\frac{p_1}{p_2} \qquad (2\text{-}1\text{-}31)$$

可见等温过程中，理想气体从外界吸收的热量 Q，全部转化为气体对外做功。

【例 2-1-9】 一定量理想气体由初态(p_1, V_1, T_1)经等温膨胀到达终态(p_2, V_2, T_1)，则气

体吸收的热量 Q 为：

A. $Q=p_1V_1\ln\frac{V_2}{V_1}$　　B. $Q=p_1V_2\ln\frac{V_2}{V_1}$

C. $Q=p_1V_1\ln\frac{V_1}{V_2}$　　D. $Q=p_2V_1\ln\frac{p_2}{p_1}$

解　等温过程 $\Delta E=0$，吸收的热量等于对外做功，$Q=\frac{m}{M}RT\ln\frac{V_2}{V_1}=p_1V_1\ln\frac{V_2}{V_1}$。

答案：A

（四）绝热过程

$$Q=0$$
$$A=-\Delta E=-\left(\frac{m}{M}\right)\frac{i}{2}R(T_2-T_1) \tag{2-1-32}$$

绝热过程中，气体对外做功，是以减少自己的内能为代价的。绝热过程的方程将在第十一节中介绍。

十、热容量

（一）热容量定义

一系统每升高单位温度所吸收的热量，称为系统的热容量。即

$$C=\mathrm{d}Q/\mathrm{d}T \tag{2-1-33}$$

当系统为 1mol 时，它的热容量称摩尔热容量，单位为 J/(mol·K)。系统热容量 C 等于摩尔热容量乘以摩尔数。

（二）定容摩尔热容量 C_V 与定压摩尔热容量 C_p

1mol 系统在等容过程中，每升高单位温度所吸收的热量，称定容摩尔热容量 C_V。1mol 系统在等压过程中，每升高单位温度所吸收的热量，称定压摩尔热容量 C_p，即

$$C_V=\frac{\mathrm{d}Q}{\mathrm{d}T}\bigg|_{V=\text{恒量}},\quad C_p=\frac{\mathrm{d}Q}{\mathrm{d}T}\bigg|_{p=\text{恒量}} \tag{2-1-34}$$

对 1mol 理想气体而言，由式(2-1-27)及式(2-1-29)可得

$$C_V=\frac{Q}{T_2-T_1}=\frac{i}{2}R,C_p=\frac{Q}{T_2-T_1}=\frac{i+2}{2}R \tag{2-1-35}$$

由此可知

$$C_p-C_V=R \tag{2-1-36}$$

此式也称为迈耶公式。

令
$$\gamma=C_p/C_V=(i+2)/i \tag{2-1-37}$$

γ 为比热容比，亦为绝热系数。

对单原子分子，自由度 $i=3$，故 $\gamma=5/3$；对刚性双原子分子，$i=5$，故 $\gamma=7/5$。

引入 C_v 与 C_p 后，式(2-1-29)可表示为 $Q_V=\left(\frac{m}{M}\right)C_V(T_2-T_1)$，式(2-1-29)可表示为 $Q_p=\left(\frac{m}{M}\right)C_p(T_2-T_1)$。

十一、绝热过程方程

理想气体的绝热过程方程可由热力学第一定律式(2-1-26)通过积分求得，结果是

$$V^{\gamma-1}T=\text{恒量} \tag{2-1-38}$$

利用理想气体状态方程还可把上式改写为以下两种形式

$$pV^{\gamma}=\text{恒量},p^{\gamma-1}T^{-\gamma}=\text{恒量} \tag{2-1-39}$$

绝热过程做功已由式(2-1-32)给出。也可根据理想气体状态方程 $pV=\frac{m}{M}RT$ 改写为

$$A=\frac{i}{2}(p_1V_1-p_2V_2)$$

由式(2-1-37)知 $\frac{i}{2}=\frac{1}{(\gamma-1)}$,故

$$A=\frac{1}{\gamma-1}(p_1V_1-p_2V_2) \tag{2-1-40}$$

这是绝热过程做功的另一计算公式。此公式可直接由功的表达式得到

$$A=\int_{V_1}^{V_2}p\mathrm{d}V=p_1V_1\int_{V_1}^{V_2}\frac{\mathrm{d}V}{V^{\gamma}}=p_1V_1^{\gamma}\left(\frac{V_2^{1-\gamma}}{1-\gamma}-\frac{V_1^{1-\gamma}}{1-\gamma}\right)=\frac{1}{\gamma-1}(p_1V_1-p_2V_2)$$

十二、循环过程、热机效率、卡诺循环

(一)循环过程

系统从某一状态开始经一系列变化过程又回到原来状态,这个变化过程叫循环过程。在过程的 p-V 图上,循环过程必为一封闭曲线。系统经一循环后,由于返回原来状态,故系统内能不变,这是循环过程的重要特性。

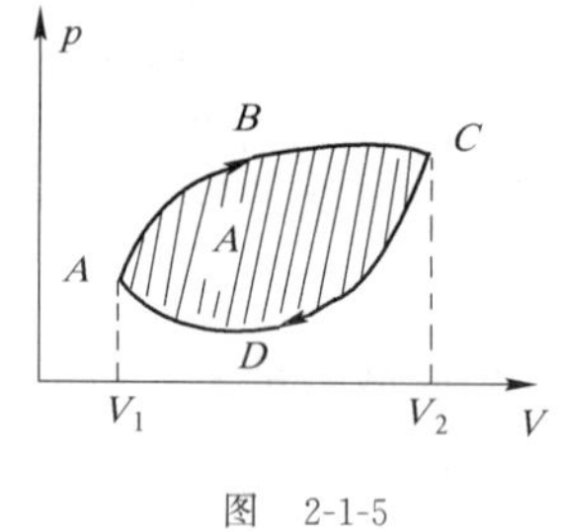

图 2-1-5

在如图 2-1-5 所示的循环过程中,系统从 A 态出发,在过程 $A\to B\to C$ 中,系统对外做正功;在过程 $C\to D\to A$ 中,系统对外做负功(外界对系统做正功)。因此,整个循环过程系统对外做的净功为循环过程曲线所包围的面积(图中阴影部分),把热力学第一定律应用于循环过程,因 $\Delta E=0$,故有

$$A=Q\text{(循环过程)} \tag{2-1-41}$$

即系统对外做的净功应等于系统从外界吸收的净热量。循环是顺时针的,则 $A>0$,称为热机。

(二)热机效率 η

式(2-1-41)中 Q 表示系统在循环过程中从外界吸收的净热量,可把它改写成 $Q=Q_1-Q_2$,Q_1 表示吸热,Q_2 表示放热,热机效率 η 被定义为

$$\eta=\frac{A}{Q_1}=\frac{Q_1-Q_2}{Q_1}=1-\frac{Q_2}{Q_1} \tag{2-1-42}$$

(三)致冷系数 ω

如果工作物质做逆循环,系统从低温热源吸收热量 Q_2,向高温热源放出热量 Q_1,而外界必须做功 A,这样的循环为制冷机,致冷系数定义为:

$$\omega=\frac{Q_2}{A}=\frac{Q_2}{Q_1-Q_2} \tag{2-1-43}$$

(四)卡诺循环

卡诺循环是在两个恒定的高温(T_1)热源和低温(T_2)热源之间工作的热机的一个特殊循

环过程。它由两个等温过程、两个绝热过程组成。以理想气体为工作物质的卡诺循环如图2-1-6所示。

过程 1→2 为等温吸热过程，系统从高温热源吸热 Q_1 由式(2-1-31)确定

$$Q_1=\frac{m}{M}RT_1\ln\frac{V_2}{V_1}$$

过程 3→4 为等温放热过程，系统放热给低温热源 Q_2 为

$$Q_2=\frac{m}{M}RT_2\ln\frac{V_3}{V_4}$$

又因 2→3 及 4→1 均为绝热过程，故有

$$T_1V_1^{\gamma-1}=T_2V_4^{\gamma-1}$$

$$T_1V_2^{\gamma-1}=T_2V_3^{\gamma-1}$$

$$\frac{V_2}{V_1}=\frac{V_3}{V_4}$$

于是，卡诺循环效率为

$$\eta=\frac{Q_1-Q_2}{Q_1}=\frac{T_1-T_2}{T_1}=1-\frac{T_2}{T_1} \tag{2-1-44}$$

若使卡诺循环逆时针方向进行：1→4→3→2→1，如图 2-1-7 所示。气体将从低温热源吸热 Q_2，又接受外界做功 A，向高温热源放热 $Q_1=A+Q_2$，这是卡诺制冷循环。

由致冷系数定义

$$\omega=\frac{Q_2}{A}=\frac{Q_2}{Q_1-Q_2}$$

因此卡诺制冷机的制冷系数为

$$\omega_{\text{卡诺}}=\frac{T_2}{T_1-T_2} \tag{2-1-45}$$

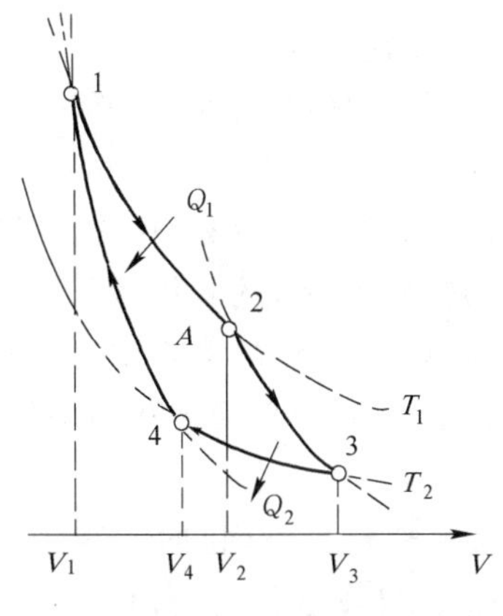

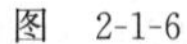
图 2-1-6

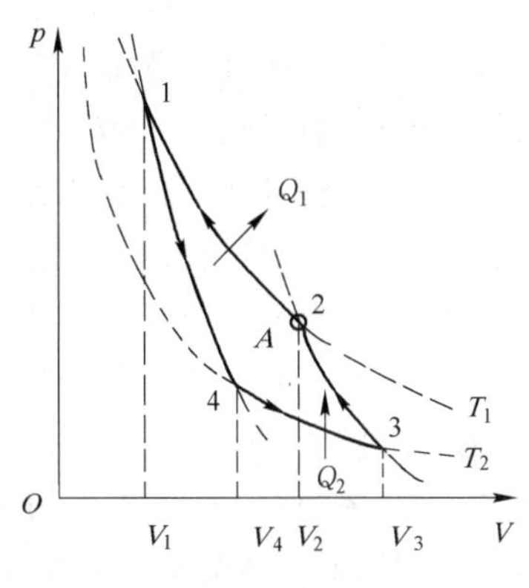

图 2-1-7

【例 2-1-10】 卡诺致冷机工作于温度为 300K 和 400K 的两个热源之间，此致冷机的致冷系数为：

A. 2　　B. 1/2　　C. 1/3　　D. 3

解 卡诺致冷机 $\omega=\dfrac{T_2}{T_1-T_2}=\dfrac{300}{400-300}=3$。

答案：D

十三、可逆过程和不可逆过程

系统在外界作用下经过一个过程从初态变到终态，外界同时要发生变化：也从初态变到终态，现使系统发生的变化过程逆向进行，即从终态到初态，若外界同时也从终态恢复到初态，那么系统（及外界）发生的过程叫可逆过程。所谓可逆过程是指逆过程可以抹去正过程所留下的一切变化，好像世界上什么事情都没有发生过一样，不满足可逆过程条件的一切过程，称为不可逆过程。

功、热转换过程是不可逆的：功可以完全转变成热量；但在不引起其他任何变化的条件下（外界也同时复原），热不能完全变化为功。热量可以自动地从高温物体传到低温物体。但在不引起其他任何变化的条件下（即不能自动地），热量不能从低温物体传到高温物体。气体分子可自动地从密度大处向密度小处扩散，而自动的逆过程不行。动、植物的生老病死等等都是不可逆过程。

十四、热力学第二定律及其统计意义

上节提到的许多不可逆过程实例，说明自然界所发生的千变万化的过程有单向性（不可逆性），可以证明，各种单向性过程是相互沟通的，即从某一过程的单向性可推得另一过程的单向性。因此，要说明这种单向性的变化规律，只要任选一实例即可。有以下两种典型表述，并称之为热力学第二定律。

（1）开尔文表述：不可能制造出一种循环工作的热机，它只从单一热源吸热使之完全变为功而不使外界发生任何变化。

（2）克劳修斯表述：热量不能自动地从低温物体传向高温物体而不引起外界变化。

人们把从单一热源吸热并使之全部变成功而不引起其他变化的机器叫第二类永动机。这种永动机不违背热力学第一定律，但违背热力学第二定律，故不能制成。

电冰箱是克劳修斯表述的很好注释。热量不是不能从低温物体（冰箱内部）传向高温物体（箱外），而是不能自动地进行。冰箱不插上电源就不会制冷。

自（动）发（生）过程的单向性可以用系统处于某一状态的几率予以解释，这称为热力学第二定律的统计意义（或统计解释）。我们举一个气体向真空膨胀（扩散）的具体例子，来说明热力学第二定律的统计意义。假定气体由 N 个分子组成，处在体积为 V 的容器中，但一开始全部气体被隔板挡在只占容器 $1/n$ 的空间中。当隔板被抽掉时，气体会自动扩散到均匀占满整个容器空间为止，这是个不可逆过程。

系统的初态几率为 $(1/n)^N$，扩散过程使气体分子占据越来越大空间，即 n 减小，几率变大，最后当 $n=1$ 时，即气体分布在整个容器中时，几率达最大，自发过程终止，系统达平衡态。系统内部进行的自发过程，总是由几率小的宏观状态向几率大的宏观状态进行，这就是热力学第二定律的统计意义。由于分子总数 N 极大，n 与 1 的任何有限偏离，例如 $n=1.1$，则此宏观态的概率为$(1/1.1)^N \to 0$，因此，要使系统自动返回初态的可能性几近乎零，即实际上过程是不可逆的。

习　题

2-1-1　两容器内分别装有氢气和氦气，若它们的温度和质量分别相等，则(　　)。

A. 两种气体分子的平均平动动能相等

B. 两种气体分子的平均动能相等

C. 两种气体分子的平均速率相等

D. 两种气体的内能相等

2-1-2　若理想气体的体积为V，压强为p，温度为T，一个分子的质量为m'，k为玻兹曼常量，R为摩尔气体常量，则该理想气体的分子数为(　　)。

A. pV/m'　　B. $pV/(kT)$　　C. $pV/(RT)$　　D. $pV/(m'T)$

2-1-3　一瓶氦气和一瓶氮气密度相同，分子平均平动动能相同，而且它们都处于平衡状态，则它们(　　)。

A. 温度相同、压强相同

B. 温度、压强都不相同

C. 温度相同，但氦气的压强大于氮气的压强

D. 温度相同，但氦气的压强小于氮气的压强

2-1-4　压强为p、体积为V的氦气(He，视为刚性分子理想气体)的内能为(　　)。

A. $\frac{3}{2}pV$　　B. $\frac{5}{2}pV$　　C. $\frac{1}{2}pV$　　D. $3pV$

2-1-5　在容积$V=8\times10^{-3}\text{m}^3$的容器中，装有压强$p=5\times10^2\text{Pa}$的理想气体，则容器中气体分子的平动动能总和为(　　)。

A. 2J　　B. 3J　　C. 5J　　D. 6J

2-1-6　某容器内储有1mol氢气和1mol氦气，设两种气体各自对器壁产生的压强分别为p_1和p_2，则两者的大小关系是(　　)。

A. $p_1>p_2$　　B. $p_1=p_2$　　C. $p_1<p_2$　　D. 不确定

2-1-7　两瓶不同的气体，一瓶是氧，另一瓶是一氧化碳，若它们的压强和温度相同，但体积不同，则下列量相同的是：①单位体积中的分子数，②单位体积的质量，③单位体积的内能，其中正确的是(　　)。

A. ①②　　B. ②③　　C. ①③　　D. ①②③

2-1-8　两种理想气体的温度相等，则它们的：①分子的平均动能相等，②分子的转动动能相等，③分子的平均平动动能相等，④内能相等，以上论断中，正确的是(　　)。

A. ①②③④　　B. ①②④　　C. ①④　　D. ③

2-1-9　一定量氢气和氧气，都可视为理想气体，它们分子的平均平动动能相同，那么它们分子的平均速率之比$\bar{v}_{H_2}:\bar{v}_{O_2}$为(　　)。

A. 1∶16　　B. 16∶1　　C. 1∶4　　D. 4∶1

2-1-10　一定量的理想气体，在容积不变的条件下，当温度升高时，分子平均碰撞次数$\bar{Z}$及平均自由程$\bar{\lambda}$的变化情况是(　　)。

A. $\overline{Z}$ 增大,$\overline{\lambda}$ 不变　　　　B. $\overline{Z}$ 不变,$\overline{\lambda}$ 增大

C. $\overline{Z}$ 增大,$\overline{\lambda}$ 增大　　　　D. $\overline{Z}$、$\overline{\lambda}$ 都不变

2-1-11　理想气体的密度 ρ 在某一过程中与绝对温度 T 成反比关系,则该过程为(　　)。

A. 等容过程　　B. 等压过程　　C. 等温过程　　D. 绝热过程

2-1-12　两个相同的容器,一个装氦气,一个装氧气(视为刚性分子),开始时它们的温度和压强都相同。现将 9J 的热量传给氦气,使之升高一定温度。若使氧气也升高同样的温度,则应向氧气传递的热量是(　　)。

A. 9J　　B. 15J　　C. 18J　　D. 6J

2-1-13　1mol 氧气和 1mol 水蒸气(均视为刚性分子理想气体),若在体积不变的情况下吸收相等的热量,则它们的(　　)。

A. 温度升高相同,压强增加相同　　B. 温度升高不同,压强增加不同

C. 温度升高相同,压强增加不同　　D. 温度升高不同,压强增加相同

2-1-14　在常温条件下,压强、体积、温度都相同的氮气和氦气在等压过程中吸收了相等的热量,则它们对外做功之比为(　　)。

A. 5∶9　　B. 5∶7

C. 1∶1　　D. 9∶5

2-1-15　如图所示,理想气体由初态 a 经 acb 过程变到终态 b。则(　　)。

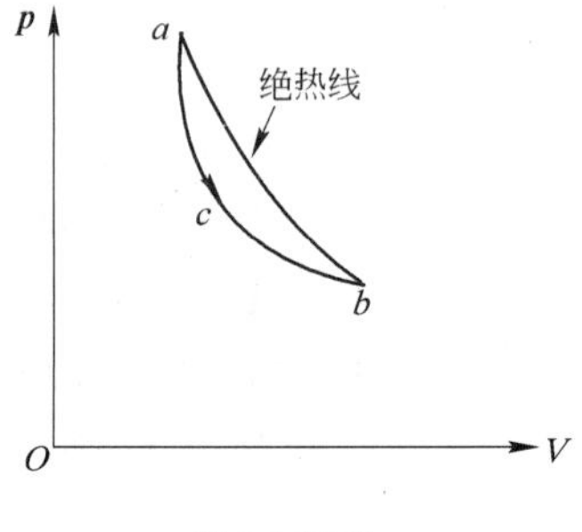

题 2-1-15 图

A. 内能增量为正,对外做功为正,系统吸热为正

B. 内能增量为负,对外做功为正,系统吸热为正

C. 内能增量为负,对外做功为正,系统吸热为负

D. 不能判断

2-1-16　一定量理想气体,从状态 A 开始,分别经历等压、等温、绝热三种过程(AB、AC、AD),其容积由 V_1 都膨胀到 $2V_1$,其中(　　)。

A. 气体内能增加的是等压过程,气体内能减少的是等温过程

B. 气体内能增加的是绝热过程,气体内能减少的是等压过程

C. 气体内能增加的是等压过程,气体内能减少的是绝热过程

D. 气体内能增加的是绝热过程,气体内能减少的是等温过程

2-1-17　一定量的理想气体,起始温度为 T,体积为 V_0,后经历绝热过程,体积变为 $2V_0$,再经过等压过程,温度回升到起始温度,最后再经过等温过程,回到起始状态,则在此循环过程中(　　)。

A. 气体从外界净吸的热量为负值

B. 气体对外界净做的功为正值

C. 气体从外界净吸的热量为正值

D. 气体内能减少

2-1-18　设高温热源的热力学温度是低温热源热力学温度的 n 倍,则理想气体在一次卡诺循环中,传给低温热源的热量是从高温热源吸取的热量的(　　)。

A. n 倍　　B. $n-1$ 倍　　C. $1/n$　　D. $(n+1)/n$ 倍

2-1-19　热力学第二定律可表述为(　　)。

A. 功可以全部转换为热,但热不能全部转换为功

B. 热量不能从低温物体传到高温物体

C. 热可以全部转换为功,但功不能全部转换为热

D. 热量不能自动地从低温物体传到高温物体

2-1-20 “理想气体和单一热源接触做等温膨胀时,吸收的热量全部用来对外做功。”对此说法,有如下几种评论,哪种是正确的?(   )。

A. 不违反热力学第一定律,但违反热力学第二定律

B. 不违反热力学第二定律,但违反热力学第一定律

C. 不违反热力学第一定律,也不违反热力学第二定律

D. 违反热力学第一定律,也违反热力学第二定律

第二节 波 动 学

一、机械波的产生和传播

(一)一些基本概念

振动(状态)的传播过程称为波动。机械振动在弹性媒质中的传播过程称为机械波。变化的电磁场在空间的传播过程称为电磁波。本节研究的是机械波,但许多基本规律都适用于电磁波。

产生波动要有两个条件:第一要有振动源,第二要有传播振动的弹性媒质。

如果质点振动方向与波的传播方向垂直,这种波叫横波(如手握长绳一端上下抖动,振动沿水平方向传播出去,绳上形成横波)。如果质点振动方向与波的传播方向一致,这种波叫纵波(如空气中传播的声波是纵波)。

波从波源出发,在媒质中向各个方向传播,那些振动相位相同的点的集合称为波(阵)面。波面为平面的称为平面波,波面为球面的称为球面波等。传到最前面的那个波面称为波前。波的传播方向称为波线。在各向同性的媒质中,波线与波面垂直。

(二)波速、波长、频率

波速是单位时间内振动状态传播的距离,以 u 表示。u 取决于媒质的物理性质,对机械波来说,取决于媒质的惯性与弹性,具体结论如下。

在弹性固体中,横波与纵波的速度分别是

$$u=\sqrt{G/\rho} \qquad (横波)$$

$$u=\sqrt{Y/\rho} \qquad (纵波)$$

式中,G 和 Y 分别为媒质的切变弹性模量和杨氏弹性模量,ρ 为媒质密度。

在气体和液体中,不能传播横波,因为它们的切变弹性模量为零。而纵波在气体和液体中的传播速度为

$$u=\sqrt{B/\rho} \quad (纵波)$$

式中,B 为媒质容变弹性模量。在理想气体中,声速为

$$u=\sqrt{\gamma p/\rho}=\sqrt{\gamma RT/M}$$

式中,$\gamma=C_p/C_V$,p 为压强,ρ 为密度,M 为摩尔质量。

波长 λ:波动传播时,同一波线上的两个相邻的相位相差为 2π 的质点,它们之间的距离称为波长 λ。

周期 T 和频率 ν:振动状态传播一个波长的距离所需的时间为一个周期 T。频率 $\nu=1/T$,

单位为 1/秒(1/s),或称赫兹(Hz)。

二、平面简谐波的波动方程

波面为平面、媒质中各点均做简谐振动(简谐振动的传播过程)的波,叫平面简谐波。

设在无吸收的均匀媒质中,有一平面简谐波沿 x 轴正向以波速 u 传播。各质点振动位移方向与 x 轴垂直(横波),即 y 方向,设在 $x=0$ 处质点的振动方程为

$$y=A\cos(\omega t+\varphi_0)$$

式中,A 为振幅,ω 为圆频率(角频率),y 是 $x=0$ 处的质点在 t 时刻偏离平衡位置的位移。设媒质中某点 P 的 x 坐标为 x_P,由于 P 点的振动是由 $x=0$ 处的振动以波速 u 传过来的,故应比 $x=0$ 处的质点晚振动 x_P/u 的时间,P 点的振动方程应为

$$y_P=A\cos[\omega(t-x_P/u)+\varphi_0]$$

略去 P,即媒质中任一坐标为 x 的质点,其振动方程,亦即平面简谐波的波动方程为

$$y=A\cos[\omega(t-\frac{x}{u})+\varphi_0] \tag{2-2-1}$$

利用 $\omega=2\pi\nu$,$\nu=1/T$,$u=\lambda/T$ 等,可将波动方程变为如下形式

$$y=A\cos(2\pi\nu t-\frac{2\pi x}{\lambda}+\varphi_0) \tag{2-2-2}$$

$$y=A\cos[2\pi(\frac{t}{T}-\frac{x}{\lambda})+\varphi_0] \tag{2-2-3}$$

$$y=A\cos[\frac{2\pi}{\lambda}(ut-x)+\varphi_0] \tag{2-2-4}$$

波动方程的意义:

(1)当 x 一定时(即波线上某一点),波动方程表示坐标为 x 的质点的振动方程。

(2)当 t 一定时(即某一瞬时),波动方程表示 t 时刻各质点的位移,即 t 时刻的波形。

(3)当 x、t 都变时,波动方程表示整个波形以波速 u 向 x 正方向传播。

如果波沿 x 轴负向传播,仍设 $x=0$ 处振动方程为

$$y=A\cos(\omega t+\varphi_0)$$

任一坐标为 x 的质点要比 $x=0$ 处的质点早振动 x/u 这么多时间,即相位超前 $\omega\frac{x}{u}$。因此,任一坐标为 x 的质点振动方程,即波动方程为

$$\begin{aligned} y&=A\cos[\omega(t+\frac{x}{u})+\varphi_0] \\ &=A\cos(2\pi\nu t+\frac{2\pi x}{\lambda}+\varphi_0) \\ &=A\cos[2\pi(\frac{t}{T}+\frac{x}{\lambda})+\varphi_0] \\ &=A\cos[\frac{2\pi}{\lambda}(ut+x)+\varphi_0] \end{aligned} \tag{2-2-5}$$

又若设 $x=x_0$ 处质点的振动方程为

$$y=A\cos(\omega t+\Phi)$$

则沿 x 正向传播,波速为 u 的波动方程为

$$y=A\cos[\omega(t-\frac{x-x_0}{u})+\Phi] \quad (2\text{-}2\text{-}6)$$

沿 x 轴负向传播的波动方程为

$$y=A\cos[\omega(t+\frac{x-x_0}{u})+\Phi] \quad (2\text{-}2\text{-}7)$$

【例 2-2-1】 一平面简谐波沿 x 轴正方向传播，振幅 $A=0.02\text{m}$，周期 $T=0.5\text{s}$，波长 $\lambda=100\text{m}$，原点处质元的初相位 $\varphi=0$，则波动方程的表达式为：

A. $y=0.02\cos 2\pi\left(\frac{t}{2}-0.01x\right)(\text{SI})$

B. $y=0.02\cos 2\pi(2t-0.01x)(\text{SI})$

C. $y=0.02\cos 2\pi\left(\frac{t}{2}-100x\right)(\text{SI})$

D. $y=0.02\cos 2\pi(2t-100x)(\text{SI})$

解 当初相位 $\varphi=0$ 时，波动方程的表达式为 $y=A\cos\left[\omega\left(t-\frac{x}{u}\right)+\varphi_0\right]$，利用 $\omega=2\pi\nu$，$\nu=\frac{1}{T}$，$u=\lambda\nu$，波动方程可写为 $y=A\cos\left[2\pi\left(\frac{t}{T}-\frac{x}{\lambda}\right)+\varphi_0\right]$，令 $A=0.02\text{m}$，$T=0.5\text{s}$，$\lambda=100\text{m}$，则得 $y=0.02\cos 2\pi(2t-0.01x)(\text{SI})$。

答案：B

【例 2-2-2】 一横波沿一根弦线传播，其方程为 $y=-0.02\cos\pi(4x-50t)$ (SI)，该波的振幅与波长分别为：

A. 0.02cm，0.5cm　　B. −0.02m，−0.5m

C. −0.02m，0.5m　　D. 0.02m，0.5m

解 ①波动方程标准式：$y=A\cos\left[\omega\left(t-\frac{x-x_0}{u}\right)+\varphi_0\right]$

②本题方程：$y=-0.02\cos\pi(4x-50t)=0.02\cos[\pi(4x-50t)+\pi]$

$$=0.02\cos[\pi(50t-4x)+\pi]=0.02\cos\left[50\pi(t-\frac{4x}{50})+\pi\right]$$

$$=0.02\cos\left[50\pi\left[t-\frac{x}{\frac{50}{4}}\right]+\pi\right]$$

故 $\omega=50\pi=2\pi\nu$，$\nu=25\text{Hz}$，$u=\frac{50}{4}$，波长 $\lambda=\frac{u}{\nu}=0.5\text{m}$，振幅 $A=0.02\text{m}$。

答案：D

【例 2-2-3】 已知平面简谐波的方程为 $y=A\cos(Bt-Cx)$，式中 A、B、C 为正常数，此波的波长和波速分别为：

A. $\frac{B}{C}$，$\frac{2\pi}{C}$　　B. $\frac{2\pi}{C}$，$\frac{B}{C}$　　C. $\frac{\pi}{C}$，$\frac{2B}{C}$　　D. $\frac{2\pi}{C}$，$\frac{C}{B}$

解 此题考查波动方程基本关系。

$y=A\cos(Bt-Cx)=A\cos B\left(t-\frac{x}{B/C}\right)$

$u=\frac{B}{C}$，$\omega=B$，$T=\frac{2\pi}{\omega}=\frac{2\pi}{B}$

$\lambda=u\cdot T=\frac{B}{C}\cdot\frac{2\pi}{B}=\frac{2\pi}{C}$

答案:B

【例 2-2-4】 一平面简谐波的波动方程为 $y=2\times10^{-2}\cos2\pi\left(10t-\frac{x}{5}\right)$(SI)。$t=0.25$s 时,处于平衡位置,且与坐标原点 $x=0$ 最近的质元的位置是:

A. ±5m　　B. 5m　　C. ±1.25m　　D. 1.25m

解　在 $t=0.25$s 时刻,处于平衡位置,$y=0$

由简谐波的波动方程 $y=2\times10^{-2}\cos2\pi(10\times0.25-\frac{x}{5})=0$,可知

$$\cos2\pi(10\times0.25-\frac{x}{5})=0$$

则 $2\pi(10\times0.25-\frac{x}{5})=(2k+1)\frac{\pi}{2}$,$k=0,\pm1,\pm2,\cdots$

由此可得 $x=\frac{5}{4}(9-2k)$

当 $x=0$ 时,$k=4.5$。所以 $k=4$,$x=1.25$ 或 $k=5$,$x=-1.25$ 时,与坐标原点 $x=0$ 最近。

答案:C

【例 2-2-5】 一横波的波动方程是 $y=2\times10^{-2}\cos2\pi(10t-\frac{x}{5})$(SI),$t=0.25$s 时,距离原点($x=0$)处最近的波峰位置为:

A. ±2.5m　　B. ±7.5m　　C. ±4.5m　　D. ±5m

解　所谓波峰,其纵坐标 $y=+2\times10^{-2}$m,亦即要求 $\cos2\pi(10t-\frac{x}{5})=1$,即 $2\pi(10t-\frac{x}{5})=\pm2k\pi$;当 $t=0.25$s 时,$20\pi\times0.25-\frac{2\pi x}{5}=\pm2k\pi$,$x=(12.5\mp5k)$。

距原点最近的点取 $x=0$,得 $k=2.5$。则当 $k=2$,$x=2.5$;$k=3$,$x=-2.5$。

答案:A

三、波的能量、能流密度

(一)波的能量

当弹性媒质中有振动传播时,各质元要发生振动,因而有动能。各质元也要发生弹性形变,因而有势能,振动传播时,媒质中各质元由近及远一层层振动起来,所以能量也逐层传播出去。能量随波动而传播,这是波动的重要特征。

设在质量密度为 ρ 的弹性媒质中,有一平面简谐波以速度 u 沿 x 轴正向传播,初相 $\varphi_0=0$,其波动方程设为式(2-2-1)[注:也可设为式(2-2-5),结果一样]

$$y=A\cos\omega(t-\frac{x}{u})$$

在 x 处取一小块媒质,体积为 ΔV,质量为 $\Delta m=\rho\Delta V$(质元),此质元做简谐振动,其动能 W_K 为

$$W_K=\frac{1}{2}\Delta mv^2=\frac{1}{2}\rho\Delta V(\frac{\partial y}{\partial t})^2=\frac{1}{2}\rho A^2\omega^2\sin^2[\omega(t-\frac{x}{u})]\Delta V$$

可以证明,质元的弹性形变势能 $W_p=W_K$,所以在质元(或体元)内总机械能为

$$W=W_K+W_p=\rho A^2\omega^2\sin^2[\omega(t-\frac{x}{u})]\Delta V \tag{2-2-8}$$

说明两点:

(1)由于 $\sin^2[\omega(t-\frac{x}{u})]=\sin^2[\frac{2\pi}{T}(t-\frac{x}{u})]$随时间 t 在 0～1 之间变化。当 ΔV 中机械能增加时,说明上一个邻近体元传给它能量;当 ΔV 中机械能减少时,说明它的能量传给下一个邻近体元。这正符合能量传播图。

(2)体元 ΔV 中动能与势能同时达最大值(当体元处在平衡位置 $y=0$ 时)及最小值(当体元处在最大位移 $y=A$ 时)。

(二)能量密度、能流密度

能量(体)密度是指媒质中每单位体积具有的机械能,按式(2-2-8),应为

$$w=W/\Delta V=\rho A^2\omega^2\sin^2[\omega(t-\frac{x}{u})] \tag{2-2-9}$$

可见 ω 也随时间而变化。能量密度在一个周期内的平均值叫平均能量密度,用 $\overline{w}$ 表示,即

$$\overline{w}=\frac{1}{T}\int_0^T\rho A^2\omega^2\sin^2[\omega(t-\frac{x}{u})]\mathrm{d}t=\frac{1}{2}\rho A^2\omega^2 \tag{2-2-10}$$

从上式可看出,对平面简谐波而言,$\overline{w}$ 与体元所在位置无关,是个恒量。它的单位是 $\mathrm{J/m^3}$。

为了定量地描述能量随波动而传播,引进能流密度这一物理量,它的定义是:单位时间内通过垂直于波传播方向每单位截面面积的平均能量,用 I 表示。

参见图 2-2-1,在垂直于波传播方向上取一截面积 S,并以波速 u 为高作一柱体,该柱体内含有能量平均为

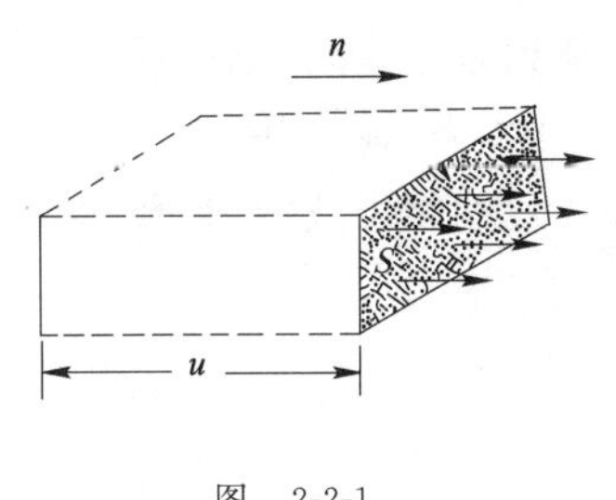

图 2-2-1

$$\overline{W}=\overline{w}\Delta V=\frac{1}{2}\rho A^2\omega^2 Su$$

在单位时间内,这些能量都应传过 S 面,根据能流密度 I 的定义应为

$$I=\overline{W}/S=\frac{1}{2}\rho A^2\omega^2 u \tag{2-2-11}$$

定义能流密度矢量 $\boldsymbol{I}$,它的方向为波的传播方向,即波速 $\boldsymbol{u}$ 的方向,故

$$\boldsymbol{I}=\frac{1}{2}\rho A^2\omega^2\boldsymbol{u} \tag{2-2-12}$$

能流密度又称为波强。它的单位是 $\mathrm{J/(m^2\cdot s)}$,或 $\mathrm{W/m^2}$(瓦/米^2)。

【例 2-2-6】 一平面简谐波的波动方程为 $y=2\times10^{-2}\cos2\pi(10t-\frac{x}{5})$(SI),对$x=2.5\mathrm{m}$ 处的质元,在 $t=0.25\mathrm{s}$ 时,它的:

A. 动能最大,势能最大　　B. 动能最大,势能最小

C. 动能最小,势能最大　　D. 动能最小,势能最小

解 简谐波在弹性媒质中传播时媒质质元的能量不守恒,任一质元 $W_p=W_k$,平衡位置时动能及势能均为最大,最大位移处动能及势能均为零。

将 $x=2.5\mathrm{m}$,$t=0.25\mathrm{s}$ 代入波动方程 $y=2\times10^{-2}\cos2\pi(10\times0.25-\frac{2.5}{5})=0.02\mathrm{m}$,为波峰位置,动能及势能均为零。

答案:D

四、波的衍射

波在传播过程中遇到障碍物时，能够绕过障碍物的边缘，在障碍物的阴影区内继续传播，这种现象称为波的衍射。

五、波的干涉

（一）波的叠加原理

从几个波源发出的波在同一媒质中传播时，不论相遇与否，都各自保持原有特性（频率、波长、振动方向、传播方向等），按各自原来的传播方向前进。在相遇区域中，各质点同时参与几种振动，各质点的振动位移等于各振动引起位移的矢量和。上述结论，称为波的叠加原理。

（二）波的干涉现象

由两个（或多个）频率相同、振动方向相同、相位差恒定的波源发出的波叫相干波。满足上述条件的波源叫相干波源。在相干波相遇的区域内，各质点（同时参与两种振动）的振动将有恒定的振幅，但有的质点振幅大，即振动加强；有的质点振幅小，即振动减弱。这种现象称为波的干涉现象。

（三）干涉条件

设两相干波源 S_1 及 S_2 的振动方程为

$$y_1=A_1\cos(\omega t+\Phi_1)$$

$$y_2=A_2\cos(\omega t+\Phi_2)$$

由两波源发出的两列平面简谐波在媒质中经 r_1、r_2 的波程分别传到 P 点相遇（参见图 2-2-2）。在 P 点引起的分振动分别为

$$y_{1P}=A_1\cos(\omega t+\Phi_1-\frac{2\pi r_1}{\lambda})$$

$$y_{2P}=A_2\cos(\omega t+\Phi_2-\frac{2\pi r_2}{\lambda})$$

图 2-2-2

P 点的合振动方程为

$$\begin{aligned}y_P&=y_{1P}+y_{2P}\\&=A\cos(\omega t+\Phi)\end{aligned} \tag{2-2-13}$$

其中

$$A=\sqrt{A_1^2+A_2^2+2A_1A_2\cos[\Phi_2-\Phi_1-\frac{2\pi(r_2-r_1)}{\lambda}]} \tag{2-2-14}$$

$$\tan\Phi=\frac{A_1\sin(\Phi_1-\frac{2\pi r_1}{\lambda})+A_2\sin(\Phi_2-\frac{2\pi r_2}{\lambda})}{A_1\cos(\Phi_1-\frac{2\pi r_1}{\lambda})+A_2\cos(\Phi_2-\frac{2\pi r_2}{\lambda})} \tag{2-2-15}$$

上面的结果由来，可参阅程守洙的《同方向简谐振动的合成》。

由式(2-2-14)可看出，当两分振动在 P 点的相位差 $\Delta\Phi=\Phi_2-\Phi_1-2\pi(r_2-r_1)/\lambda$ 为 2π 的整数倍时，合振幅最大，$A=A_1+A_2$；当 $\Delta\Phi$ 为 π 的奇数倍时，合振幅最小，$A=|A_1-A_2|$。即：

$\Delta\Phi=\pm 2k\pi$　　$(k=0,1,2,\cdots)$干涉加强条件。

$\Delta\Phi=\pm(2k+1)\pi$　　$(k=0,1,2,\cdots)$干涉减弱条件。

干涉加强及减弱条件也可用波程差 $\delta=r_2-r_1$ 来表示：

当 $\delta=r_2-r_1=\pm k\lambda-(\Phi_2-\Phi_1)\lambda/2\pi$ 时，干涉加强。

当 $\delta=r_2-r_1=\pm(2k+1)\lambda/2-(\Phi_2-\Phi_1)\lambda/2\pi$ 时，干涉减弱。

如果两相干波源的振动初相位相等，即 $\Phi_1=\Phi_2$，则：

当 $\delta=r_2-r_1=\pm k\lambda$ 时，干涉加强；

当 $\delta=r_2-r_1=\pm(2k+1)\lambda/2$ 时，干涉减弱。

波的干涉加强及减弱条件，在讨论光的干涉现象时会用到。

六、驻波

（一）驻波的形成

两频率相同、振动方向相同、振幅相同，沿相反方向传播的平面简谐波，叠加起来形成驻波，这是一种具体的干涉现象。

如图 2-2-3 所示，左边放一音叉，音叉末端系一水平细绳 AB，细绳经过滑轮悬一重物。音叉振动时，绳上产生波动向右传播到达 B 点，在 B 点反射产生反射波向左传播。这样入射波和反射波在同一绳子上沿相反方向传播，它们相互干涉产生驻波。这里波在绳子固定端 B 处反射，因而在反射处形成波节（振幅为零）。如果波在绳子自由端反射，那么反射处形成波腹（振幅最大）。

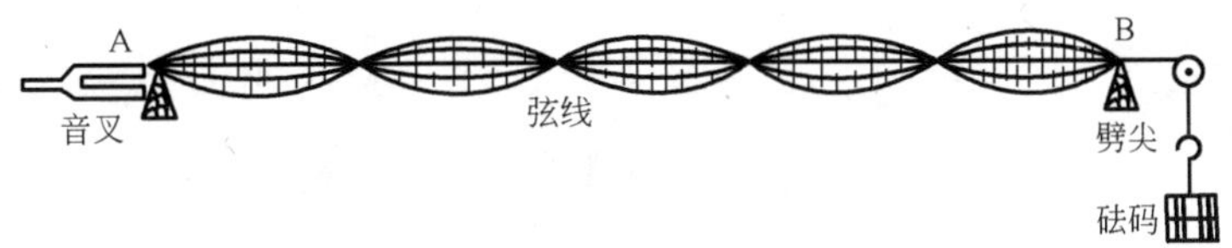

图 2-2-3　驻波试验

（二）驻波方程

设一列平面简谐波沿 x 正向传播，另一列沿 x 负向传播，波动方程分别设为

$$y_1=A\cos2\pi(\nu t-\frac{x}{\lambda})$$

$$y_2=A\cos2\pi(\nu t+\frac{x}{\lambda})$$

合成波的波动方程为

$$y=y_1+y_2=A\cos2\pi(\nu t-\frac{x}{\lambda})+A\cos2\pi(\nu t+\frac{x}{\lambda})$$

利用三角公式

$$\cos\alpha+\cos\beta=2\cos\frac{(\alpha+\beta)}{2}\cos\frac{(\alpha-\beta)}{2}$$

可得

$$y=2A\cos\frac{2\pi x}{\lambda}\cos2\pi\nu t \tag{2-2-16}$$

上式为驻波方程。

（三）驻波的特点

1. 振幅分布特点

驻波中各质点的振幅$|2A\cos 2\pi \frac{x}{\lambda}|$随各质点的位置 x 而变化。

当 $2\pi x/\lambda=k\pi(k=0,\pm 1,\pm 2,\cdots)$时，即

$$x=k\lambda/2 \qquad (k=0,\pm 1,\pm 2,\cdots)$$

各处的振幅最大(2A)，这些点称为波腹。

当 $2\pi x/\lambda=[(2k+1)\pi]/2(k=0,\pm 1,\pm 2,\cdots)$时，即

$$x=(2k+1)\lambda/4 \qquad (k=0,\pm 1,\pm 2,\cdots)$$

各处的振幅为零，即质点不动，这些点称为波节。可见，相邻两波节(或波腹)间距为半波长 $\lambda/2$。

2. 位相分布特点

从驻波方程式(2-2-16)看，有 $\cos 2\pi\nu t$，似乎各点相位都为 $2\pi\nu t$，即各点相位似乎相同。其实不然。因 $2A\cos(2\pi x/\lambda)$ 是随 x 的变化而有正、负之分，而在相邻两节点间各质点因为 $2A\cos(2\pi x/\lambda)$有相同的符号，所以各质点相位相同；在同一节点的两侧各质点因 $2A\cos(2\pi x/\lambda)$ 有相反的符号，故节点两侧的质点相位相反(即相位相关为 π)。也就是说，驻波被波节点分成若干长度为 $\lambda/2$ 的小段，每一小段上各质点相位相同；相邻两段上各质点相位相反。概貌见图 2-2-4。

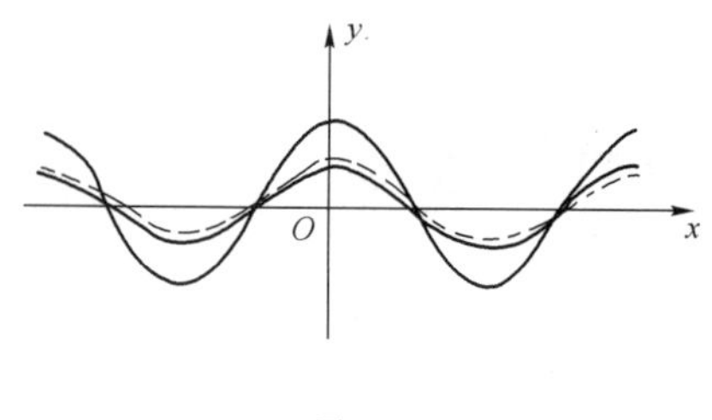

图 2-2-4

3. 能量传播特点

驻波是由方向相反的两列波叠加而成。由能流密度矢量 $\boldsymbol{I}=\frac{1}{2}\rho A^2\omega^2\boldsymbol{u}$ 知，驻波的能流密度矢量 $\boldsymbol{I}_1+\boldsymbol{I}_2=0$，故驻波不传播能量。

七、声波、声强级

在弹性媒质中传播的机械纵波，其频率在 20～20 000Hz之间，能引起人的听觉，这种波叫声波；频率高于 20 000Hz 的波叫超声波，低于 20Hz 的叫次声波。

(一)声强

声强就是声波的能流密度，即

$$I=\frac{1}{2}\rho A^2\omega^2 u \tag{2-2-17}$$

由上式可知，频率越高，越容易获得较大的声强。

(二)声强级

能引起听觉的声波，不仅有频率范围，而且还有声强范围。对于每个可闻频率，声强都有上下两个限值，低于下限的声强不能引起听觉，称为听阈声强，高于上限的声强也不能引起听觉，太高了只能引起痛觉，称为痛阈声强。在 1 000Hz 频率时，一般正常人听觉的最高声强为 10^{-4} W/m^2，最低声强为 10^{-12} W/m^2，规定声强 $I_0=10^{-12}$ W/m^2 作为测定声强的标准，由于声强的数量级相差悬殊，所以常用对数标度作为声强级的量度，声强级 I_L 定义为

$$I_L=\lg\frac{I}{I_0}(\mathrm{B}) \tag{2-2-18}$$

声强级单位为贝尔(B)，1 贝尔=10 分贝(dB)，故声强级也可定义为

$$I_L=10\lg\frac{I}{I_0}(\mathrm{dB}) \tag{2-2-19}$$

【例 2-2-7】 两人轻声谈话的声强级为 40dB,热闹市场上噪声的声强级为 80dB。市场上噪声的声强与轻声谈话的声强之比为:

A. 2　　B. 20　　C. 10^2　　D. 10^4

解　声强级为 $L=10\lg\frac{I}{I_0}$,其中 $I_0=10^{-12}\,\text{W/m}^2$ 为测定基准,I 的单位为 B(贝尔)。轻声谈话的声强级为 40dB(分贝),dB 为 B(贝尔)的 1/10,即为 4B(贝),则由 $4=\lg\frac{I_1}{I_0}$,得轻声谈话声强 $I_1=I_0\times10^4\,\text{W/m}^2$,同理可得热闹市场上声强 $I_2=I_0\times10^8\,\text{W/m}^2$,可知市场上噪声的声强与轻声谈话的声强之比 $\frac{I_2}{I_1}=\frac{I_0\times10^8}{I_0\times10^4}=10^4$。

答案:D

八、多普勒效应

当波源、观察者(接收器)相对媒质静止时,观察者接收到的频率是波源的频率 ν_0。

当波源或观察者相对媒质运动,或两者都相对媒质运动时,观察者接收到的频率 ν' 和声源频率 ν_0 不同,这种现象称为多普勒效应。

为简明计,设声源和观察者在同一直线上运动(这种限制并非必要,下面要说明的)。以 ν_S 表示波源(相对于媒质)的运动速度,v_B 表示观察者(相对于媒质)的运动速度,u 表示波在媒质中的传播速度,下面分三种情况讨论。

(一)声源不动,观察者以 v_B 运动

若观察者向着波源运动,表示 $v_B>0$(规定)。此时,相当于波以 $u+v_B$ 的速度通过观察者,所以单位时间内通过观察者的完整波数,即观察者接收到的波的频率为

$$\nu'=\frac{u+v_B}{\lambda}=(1+\frac{v_B}{u})\nu_0 \tag{2-2-20}$$

可见,若观察者向着波源运动,$\nu_B>0$,$\nu'>\nu_0$;反之若观察者背离波源运动,$v_B<0$,$\nu'<\nu_0$。

(二)观察者静止,波源以 v_S 运动

若波源向着观察者运动,表示 $v_S>0$。由于波速 u 与波源运动无关,波在一周期内传播距离总等于波长 λ,但在一周期内波源向前移动了 $v_S T$ 的距离,其效果相当于波长缩短为

$$\lambda'=\lambda-v_S T$$

因此,观察者接收到的频率 ν' 由于波长缩短而增大为

$$\nu'=\frac{u}{\lambda-v_S T}=\frac{u}{(u-v_S)T}=\frac{u}{u-v_S}\nu_0 \tag{2-2-21}$$

若波源背离观察者运动,$v_S<0$,$\nu'<\nu_0$。

(三)波源、观察者同时运动

综上(一)、(二)所述,此时观察者接收到的频率为

$$\nu'=\frac{u}{u-v_S}(1+\frac{v_B}{u})\nu_0=\frac{u+v_B}{u-v_S}\nu_0 \tag{2-2-22}$$

最后要说明,如果波源与观察者不在同一直线上运动,则以上公式中 v_B、v_S 代表观察者及波源速度在两者连线上的分量。

习　题

2-2-1　一横波沿绳子传播时的波动方程为 $y=0.05\cos(4\pi x-10\pi t)$(SI),则(　　)。

A. 波长为 0.05m　　　　B. 波长为 0.5m

C. 波速为 25m/s　　　　D. 波速为 5m/s

2-2-2　一平面简谐波在弹性媒质中传播,在某一瞬时,媒质中某质元正处于平衡位置,此时它的能量是(　　)。

A. 动能为零,势能为零　　　　B. 动能最大,势能最大

C. 动能为零,势能最大　　　　D. 动能最大,势能为零

2-2-3　一平面简谐波沿 x 轴正向传播,已知 $x=L(L<\lambda)$ 处质点的振动方程为 $y=A\cos\omega t$,波速为 u,那么 $x=0$ 处质点的振动方程为(　　)。

A. $y=A\cos(\omega t+L/u)$　　　　B. $y=A\cos(\omega t-L/u)$

C. $y=A\cos\omega(t+L/u)$　　　　D. $y=A\cos\omega(t-L/u)$

2-2-4　一振幅为 A、周期为 T、波长为 λ 的平面简谐波沿 x 轴负向传播,在 $x=\lambda/2$ 处,$t=T/4$ 时,振动相位为 π,则此平面简谐波的波动方程为(　　)。

A. $y=A\cos(2\pi t/T-2\pi x/\lambda-\pi/2)$

B. $y=A\cos(2\pi t/T+2\pi x/\lambda+\pi/2)$

C. $y=A\cos(2\pi t/T+2\pi x/\lambda-\pi/2)$

D. $y=A\cos(2\pi t/T-2\pi x/\lambda+\pi)$

2-2-5　在下面几种说法中,正确的说法是(　　)。

A. 波源不动时,波源的振动周期与波动周期在数值上是不同的

B. 波源振动的速度与波速相同

C. 在波传播方向上的任一质点的振动相位总是比波源的相位滞后

D. 在波传播方向上的任一质点的振动相位总是比波源的相位超前

2-2-6　一平面简谐波在媒质中沿 x 轴正方向传播,传播速度 $u=15$cm/s,波的周期 $T=2$s,沿波线上 A、B 两点相距 5.0cm,当波传播时,B 点的振动相位比 A 点落后(　　)。

A. $\pi/2$　　　B. $\pi/3$　　　C. $\pi/6$　　　D. $3\pi/2$

2-2-7　一平面简谐波在弹性媒质中传播,在媒质质元从最大位移处回到平衡位置的过程中(　　)。

A. 它的势能转换成动能

B. 它的动能转换成势能

C. 它从相邻一段媒质元获得能量,其能量逐渐增加

D. 它把自己的能量传给相邻的一段媒质元,其能量逐渐减少

2-2-8　在驻波中,两个相邻波节间各质点的振动(　　)。

A. 振幅相同,相位相同　　　　B. 振幅不同,相位相同

C. 振幅相同,相位不同　　　　D. 振幅不同,相位不同

2-2-9　两列相干平面简谐波振幅都是 4cm,两波源相距 30cm,相位差为 π,在两波源连线的中垂线上任意一点 P,两列波叠加后合振幅为(　　)。

A. 8cm　　B. 16cm　　C. 30cm　　D. 0

2-2-10　两振幅均为 A 的相干波源 S_1 和 S_2（见图）相距 $3\lambda/4$（λ 为波长），若在 S_1、S_2 的连线上，S_1 右侧的各点合振幅均为 $2A$，则两波的初相位差 $\Phi_{02}-\Phi_{01}$ 是（　　）。

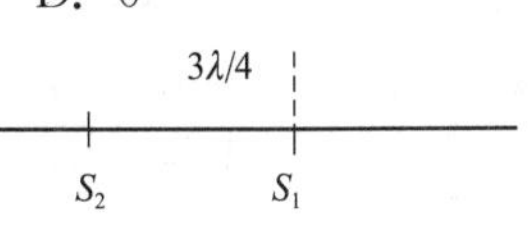

题 2-2-10 图

A. 0　　B. $\pi/2$

C. π　　D. $3\pi/2$

2-2-11　在波长为 λ 的驻波中两个相邻波节之间的距离为（　　）。

A. λ　　B. $\lambda/2$　　C. $3\lambda/4$　　D. $\lambda/4$

第三节　光　　学

光波是电磁波，是电磁量 $\boldsymbol{E}$、$\boldsymbol{H}$（$\boldsymbol{E}$ 为电场强度，$\boldsymbol{H}$ 为磁场强度）的扰动在空间的传播。它不依赖于空间是否存在媒质，光的传播速度为 $c=3.0\times10^8\,\text{m/s}$，在媒质中的传播速度为 $u=c/n$，n 为媒质的折射率。光波是横波，其中 $\boldsymbol{E}$、$\boldsymbol{H}$ 矢量的振动方向与光波的传播方向总是垂直的（图 2-3-1）。

由于对人眼和光学仪器起作用的主要是由矢量 $\boldsymbol{E}$，故称 $\boldsymbol{E}$ 为光矢量。

一、相干光波的叠加

几列光波在媒质中传播而相遇时，通常满足波的叠加原理。我们首先讨论的是同方向、同频率、有恒定初相差的两个单色光源（称相干光源）所发出的两列光波的叠加（即相干光的叠加）。

在场点 P，由相干光源 S_1、S_2（图 2-3-2）所发出的两列相干光波引起的光扰动分别为

$$y_1=A_1\cos(\omega t-2\pi\frac{r_1}{\lambda}+\varphi_1)$$

$$y_2=A_2\cos(\omega t-2\pi\frac{r_2}{\lambda}+\varphi_2)$$

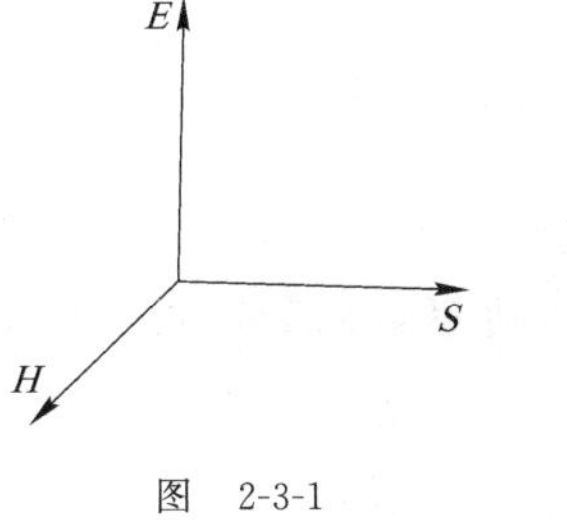

图　2-3-1

图　2-3-2

在 P 点合扰动的振幅满足

$$A^2=A_1^2+A_2^2+2A_1A_2\cos(\varphi_2-\varphi_1-2\pi\frac{r_2-r_1}{\lambda})$$

相应地，P 点的光强为

$$I=I_1+I_2+2\sqrt{I_1I_2}\cos\Delta\Phi \tag{2-3-1}$$

式中，$I_1=A_1^2$，$I_2=A_2^2$，$2\sqrt{I_1I_2}\cos\Delta\Phi$ 为干涉项，它决定了空间干涉场的光强分布。

当 $\Delta\Phi=\pm2k\pi$ 时（$k=0,1,2,\cdots$），有 $I_{\max}=I_1+I_2+2\sqrt{I_1I_2}$，此时场点光强最大、亮点。

当 $\Delta\Phi=\pm(2k+1)\pi$ 时（$k=0,1,2,\cdots$），则有 $I_{\min}=I_1+I_2-2\sqrt{I_1I_2}$，此时场点光强最小、暗点。

在干涉场中，凡具有相同相位差的所有亮点（或暗点）的轨迹，就形成同一 k 级的（或暗）条

纹，k 称干涉条纹的级次。

当 $\Delta\Phi$ 为其他值，该对应点光强介于 I_{max} 与 I_{min} 之间。

当 $I_1=I_2$ 时，则合光强为

$$I=2I_1+2I_1\cos\Delta\Phi=2I_1(1+\cos\Delta\Phi)=4I_1\cos^2\frac{\Delta\Phi}{2} \tag{2-3-2}$$

当 $\Delta\Phi=\pm2k\pi$ 时，$I_{max}=4I_1$；

当 $\Delta\Phi=\pm(2k+1)\pi$ 时，$I_{min}=0$。

若两相干光源的初相位相同，即 $\varphi_1=\varphi_2$，则

$$\Delta\Phi=2\pi\frac{r_1-r_2}{\lambda} \tag{2-3-3}$$

当波程差 $\delta=r_1-r_2$ 满足以下条件时，即

$$\delta=r_1-r_2=\begin{cases}\pm k\lambda & & \text{有最大光强}\\ & (k=0,1,2,\cdots) & \\ \pm(2k+1)\dfrac{\lambda}{2} & & \text{有最小光强}\end{cases} \tag{2-3-4}$$

二、光程与光程差

在实际问题中经常遇到相干的两束光在不同媒质中传播的情形，此时须引入光程的概念。

若两相干光分别在折射率为 n_1、n_2 的媒质中传播 r_1、r_2 的几何路程，因光在媒质中的传播速度 u 是真空中光速 c 的 $\dfrac{1}{n}$，而在媒质中的波长 λ_n 与真空中波长 λ 的关系为 $\lambda_n=\lambda/n$，一个波长对应 2π 的相位改变。故有

$$2\pi r_1/\lambda_1=2\pi n_1r_1/\lambda$$

$$2\pi r_2/\lambda_2=2\pi n_2r_2/\lambda$$

将媒质的折射率 n 与光在媒质中通过的几何路程 r 的乘积叫光程(nr)。于是

$$\Delta\Phi=\varphi_2-\varphi_1+\frac{2\pi}{\lambda}(n_1r_1-n_2r_2) \tag{2-3-5}$$

通常两束相干光源取自同一波阵面上，有 $\varphi_2=\varphi_1$，则两束相干光在空间各点的相位差仅取决于光程差 δ，即

$$\Delta\Phi=\frac{2\pi}{\lambda}(n_1r_1-n_2r_2)=\frac{2\pi}{\lambda}\delta \tag{2-3-6}$$

当

$$\Delta\Phi=\frac{2\pi}{\lambda}\delta=\begin{cases}\pm2k\pi & (k=0,1,2,\cdots) & \text{加强}\\ \pm(2k+1)\pi & & \text{减弱}\end{cases} \tag{2-3-7}$$

或

$$\delta=\begin{cases}\pm k\lambda & & \text{加强}\\ & (k=0,1,2,\cdots) & \\ \pm(2k+1)\dfrac{\lambda}{2} & & \text{减弱}\end{cases} \tag{2-3-8}$$

三、相干光的获得

前面提到通过分离光波，可得到相干光。有两种方法：分割波阵面及分割振幅。

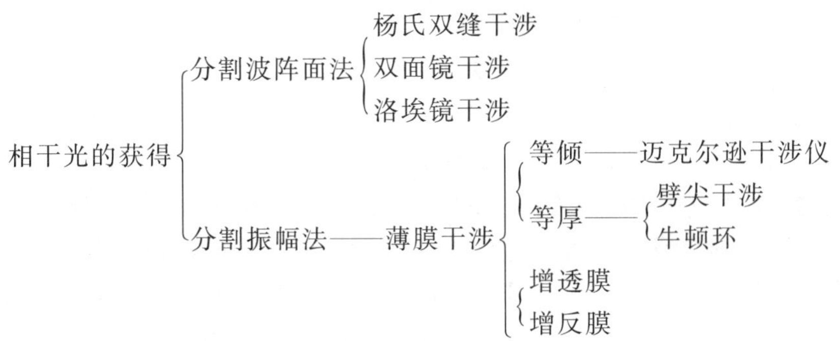

四、光的干涉

(一)杨氏双缝干涉

如图 2-3-3 所示，杨氏用单色光从 S 发出的光波波阵面到达离 S 等远的双缝 S_1、S_2 时，S_1、S_2 为同一波阵面上的两点，可视为两相干波源(称分波阵面法)，从 S_1、S_2 发出的两列波分别经 r_1、r_2 传到屏上 P 点，产生干涉条纹的明暗条件由光程差 δ 决定。

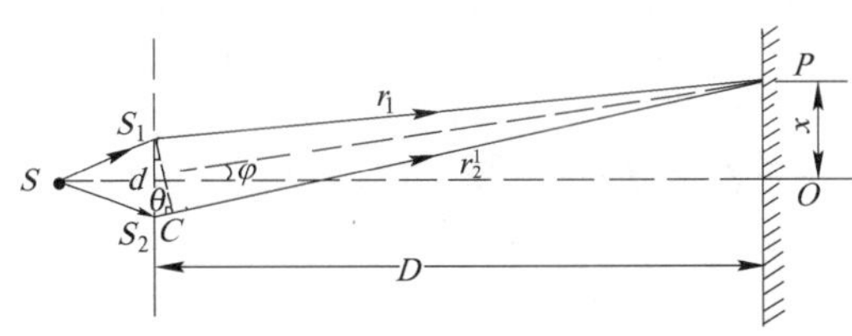

图 2-3-3　双狭缝干涉条纹分布计算用图

1. 干涉条纹分布的特点

(1)屏幕上出现的是平行、等距的明、暗相间的直条纹，条纹间距与 D 成正比，与缝距 d 成反比，条纹间距随入射波长的增大而变大。

(2)以白光入射，除中央条纹为白色外，两侧的干涉条纹将按波长从中间向两侧对称排列，对同级彩色条纹，紫光靠正中央明纹，红光远离中央明纹。

(3)由于不同波长与其相应的干涉条纹的间距不同，故当级次增加时，不同级的条纹可能发生重叠。

(4)干涉条纹不仅出现在屏幕上，凡是两束光重叠的区域都存在干涉场，场内均可观察到干涉条纹，故杨氏双缝干涉属于非定域干涉。

2. 明、暗纹条件、位置及间距

在折射率为 n 的媒质中，两束相干光在干涉场中任一点 P 的光程差为 $\delta=n(r_2-r_1)$

当

$$\delta=\begin{cases}\pm k\lambda & \text{出现明条纹}\\ \pm(2k+1)\dfrac{\lambda}{2} & \text{出现暗条纹}\end{cases}\qquad (k=0,1,2,\cdots)$$

式中：λ——光在真空中的波长。

由图 2-3-3 知　　$r_2-r_1\approx d\sin\theta\approx xd/D$

所以　　$\delta=nd\sin\theta=nxd/D$

故明、暗的位置为

$$x_{明}=\pm kD\lambda/(nd)$$
$$x_{暗}=\pm(2k+1)D\lambda/(2nd) \quad (k=0,1,2,\cdots) \qquad (2\text{-}3\text{-}9)$$

相邻明(或暗)纹的间距为

$$\Delta x=D\lambda/(nd) \qquad (2\text{-}3\text{-}10)$$

【例 2-3-1】 在空气中用波长为 λ 的单色光进行双缝干涉实验时，观测到相邻明条纹的间距为1.33mm，当把实验装置放入水中(水的折射率为 $n=1.33$)时，则相邻明条纹的间距变为：

A. 1.33mm B. 2.66mm C. 1mm D. 2mm

解 由杨氏双缝干涉条纹间距公式知，空气中 $\Delta x=\frac{D}{d}\lambda$，放入水中 $\Delta x_n=\frac{D}{d}\lambda_n=\frac{\Delta x}{n}=\frac{1.33}{1.33}=1$。

答案：C

(二)薄膜干涉

1. 等倾干涉

图 2-3-4 为厚度均匀，折射率为 n_2 的薄膜，置于折射率为 n_1 的媒质中，一单色光经薄膜上下表面反射后得到 1 和 2 两条光线，它们相互平行，并且是相干的。由反射、折射定律可得到两光束的光程差为

$$\delta=2d\sqrt{n_2^2-n_1^2\sin^2 i}=2n_2 d\cos\gamma$$

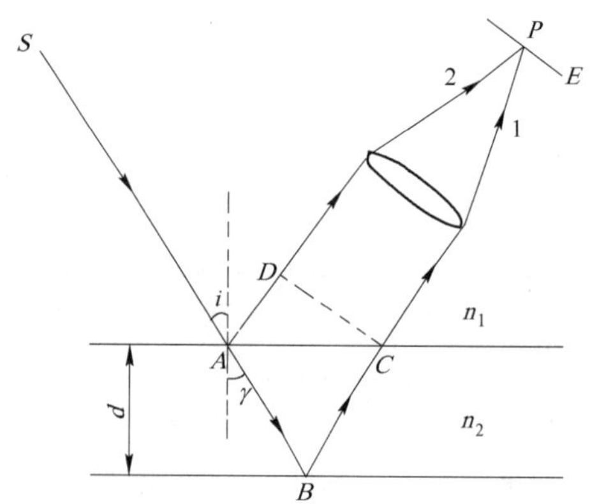

图 2-3-4

由上式可知，光程差取决于入射角 i 的大小，理论证明，当光从光疏媒质射向光密媒质，在分界面反射时有半波损失。在我们讨论的问题中，不论 $n_1<n_2$，还是 $n_1>n_2$，1 与 2 两条光线之一总有半波损失出现，因而在光程差中必须计及这个半波损失。1 与 2 两条光线的光程差最后应表示为

$$\delta=2n_2 d\cos\gamma+\frac{\lambda}{2} \qquad (2\text{-}3\text{-}11)$$

而光线的干涉图样由下式决定

$$\delta=2n_2 d\cos\gamma+\frac{\lambda}{2}=\begin{cases}2k\,\dfrac{\lambda}{2}(k=1,2,\cdots) & \text{相长干涉(明纹)}\\[2ex](2k+1)\dfrac{\lambda}{2}(k=0,1,2,\cdots) & \text{相消干涉(暗纹)}\end{cases} \qquad (2\text{-}3\text{-}12)$$

要注意的是，引时干涉图样不是在薄膜面上，而是在无穷远，若用透镜进行观察，在置于透

镜焦平面的屏上，可以看到干涉图样。因干涉图样中同一干涉条纹是来自膜面的等倾角光线经透镜聚焦后的轨迹，故称为等倾干涉条纹。

当 $i=0$ 时，光垂直入射，有

$$\delta=2n_2d+\frac{\lambda}{2}=\begin{cases}2k\frac{\lambda}{2}(k=1,2,\cdots) & \text{反射光加强，透射光减弱}\\(2k+1)\frac{\lambda}{2}(k=0,1,2,\cdots) & \text{反射光相消，透射光加强}\end{cases}\tag{2-3-13}$$

2.等厚干涉

劈尖薄膜的厚度不均匀而形成如图 2-3-5 所示的劈尖形的膜层，称之为劈尖。

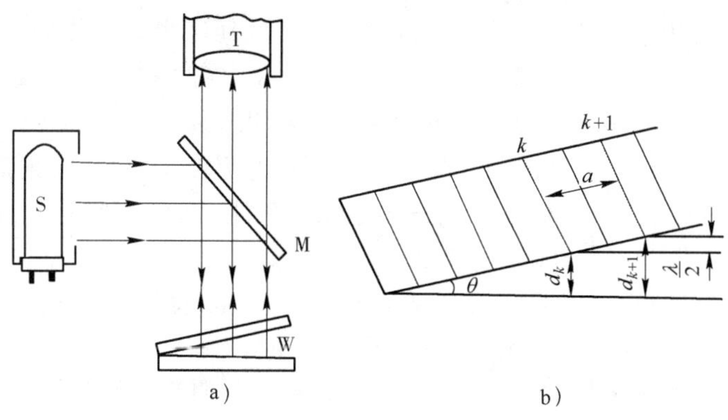

图 2-3-5

从单色光源 S 发出的光经光学系统成为平行光束，经平玻璃片 M 反射后垂直入射到空气壁尖 W，由劈尖上、下表面反射的光速进行相干叠加，形成干涉条纹，通过显微镜 T 进行观察、测量。

根据式(2-3-13)知

$$\delta=2d+\frac{\lambda}{2}=\begin{cases}2k\frac{\lambda}{2} & (k=1,2,\cdots) & \text{明条纹}\\(2k+1)\frac{\lambda}{2} & (k=0,1,2\cdots) & \text{暗条纹}\end{cases}\tag{2-3-14}$$

显然，同一明(或暗)条纹对应相同厚度的空气层，因而是等厚条纹。

由式(2-3-14)得，两相邻明(或暗)条纹对应的空气层厚度差都等于 $\lambda/2$，见图 2-3-5。

$$d_{k+1}-d_k=\frac{\lambda}{2}$$

设劈尖的夹角为 θ，则相邻明(或暗)纹之间距 a 应满足关系式

$$a\sin\theta=\lambda/2\tag{2-3-15}$$

从式(2-3-15)看出，θ 角越小，条纹分布越疏；反之，θ 角越大，条纹分布越密。当 θ 角大到一定程度，干涉条纹将密得无法分辨，这时将看不到干涉条纹。

从式(2-3-15)可知，如已知夹角 θ，测出条纹间距 a，就可算出波长 λ。反之，如 λ 已知，测出条纹，就可算出微小角度 θ。

【例 2-3-2】 波长为 λ 的单色光垂直照射在折射率为 n 的劈尖薄膜上，在由反射光形成的干涉条纹中，第五级明条纹与第三级明条纹所对应的薄膜厚度差为：

A. $\frac{\lambda}{2n}$　　B. $\frac{\lambda}{n}$　　C. $\frac{\lambda}{5n}$　　D. $\frac{\lambda}{3n}$

解 相邻两条纹的厚度差为介质中的半个波长，第五级明条纹与第三级明条纹所对应的薄膜厚度差为 $2 \cdot \frac{\lambda}{2n} = \frac{\lambda}{n}$ 。

答案：B

3. 迈克尔逊干涉仪

如图 2-3-6 所示迈克尔逊干涉仪结构示意图。M_1、M_2 为平面反射镜，G_1、G_2 为两块相同材料制成的等厚平行玻璃板，在 G_1 的一面镀有半透明的薄银层，称为分束板，G_2 为光路补偿板。G_1、G_2 与 M_1、M_2 均成 45°交角。

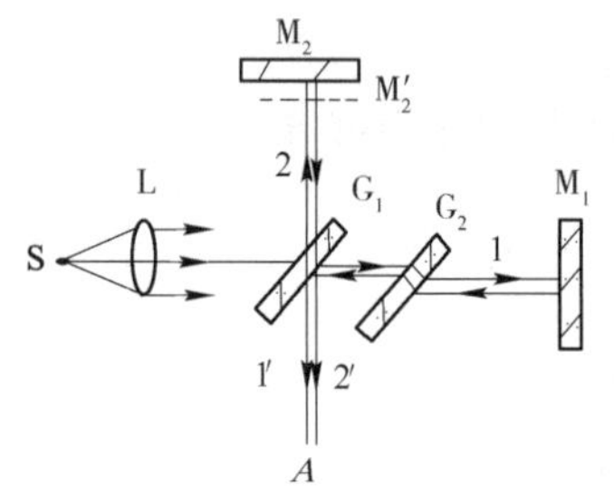

图 2-3-6 迈克尔逊干涉仪光路示意图

平行光束射入 G_1 后到达半透明银膜层，分成两束，其中一束 I_1 透过银层到达 G_2，穿过 G_2 传向 M_1，经 M_1 反射后又穿过 G_2，再经 G_1 的薄银层反射传向 A 处；另一束 I_2 经镀银层反射，经 G_1 射出向 M_2 传播，经 M_2 反射后再穿过 G_1 传向 A 处。I_1、I_2 满足相干条件，故在 A 处通过望远镜可以看到干涉条纹。

由图可知，从 M_1 上反射的光，可以看成是从 M_1 在 G_1 的薄银层产生的虚像 M' 处发出的，故 I_1、I_2 之间的光程差由 M_2 与 M'_1 之间距离 Δd 决定。

当 M_1 与 M_2 不严格垂直时，M'_1 与 M_2 构成劈尖，产生明暗相间的等厚干涉条纹。

当 M_1 与 M_2 严格垂直时，M'_1 与 M_2 平行，产生等倾干涉条纹。

当移动 M_2 时，Δd 改变，干涉条纹移动。当 M_2 移动 $\frac{\lambda}{2}$ 的距离，视场中看到干涉条纹移动 1 条，若条纹移动 ΔN 条，则 M_2 移动的距离为

$$\Delta d = \Delta N \frac{\lambda}{2} \tag{2-3-16}$$

依此可测光波波长；反之，若已知波长 λ，可测微小长度 Δd。

【例 2-3-3】 若在迈克尔逊干涉仪的可动反射镜 M 移动了 0.620mm 的过程中，观察到干涉条纹移动了 2 300 条，则所用光波的波长为：

A. 269nm　　B. 539nm　　C. 2 690nm　　D. 5 390nm

解 由迈克尔逊干涉仪公式 $\Delta d = k \cdot \frac{\lambda}{2}$，可得 $\lambda = \frac{2 \times 0.62 \times 10^6}{2\ 300} = 539\text{nm}$ 。

答案：B

注：此题由可见光范围(400～760nm)可不用计算直接得出结论。

【例 2-3-4】 在空气中做牛顿环实验，当平凸透镜垂直向上缓慢平移而远离平面镜时，可以观察到这些环状干涉条纹：

A. 向右平移　　B. 静止不动　　C. 向外扩张　　D. 向中心收缩

解 牛顿环的环状干涉条纹为等厚干涉条纹，当平凸透镜垂直向上缓慢平移而远离平面镜时，原 k 级条纹向环中心移动，故这些环状干涉条纹向中心收缩。

答案：D

五、光的衍射

光沿直线传播是建立几何光学的基本依据，在通常情况下，光表现出直线传播的性质。但

是，当光通过很窄的单缝时，却表现出与直线传播不同的现象，一部分光线绕过单缝的边缘到达偏离直线传播的区域在屏上出现明、暗相间的条纹，这种现象称为光的衍射现象。它与光的干涉现象一样，显示了光的波的特性。

（一）惠更斯-菲涅耳原理

惠更斯原理可以解释光偏离直线传播的现象，但它不能解释为什么在屏上会出现明、暗条纹。菲涅耳接受了惠更斯的次波概念，并提出各次波都是相干的，从而发展了惠更斯原理，后称惠更斯-菲涅耳原理。其要点可定性表述为：从同一波源上各点发出的次波是相干波，经过传播在空间某点相遇时的叠加是相干叠加。

（二）夫琅禾费单缝衍射

平行光线的衍射现象，叫夫琅禾费衍射。

在不透明的平面物体上开一条狭缝 K（缝长远大于缝宽），用一束平行光线垂直地照射在狭缝上，当缝宽 a 与入射光波长的数量级相近时，经单缝衍射的光线，通过透镜 L 会聚在屏幕 E 上，出现与狭缝平行的明暗相间的衍射条纹。

采用菲涅耳"半波带法"可以说明衍射图样的形成。如图 2-3-7a）所示，AB 为狭缝截面，缝宽为 a。一束平行单色光垂直狭缝平面入射，通过狭缝的光发生衍射，衍射角 φ 相同的平行光束经透镜 L_2 会聚于放置在透镜焦平面处的屏上，会聚点 P 的光强取决于同一衍射角 φ 的平行光束中各光线之间的光程差。

如图 2-3-7 b）所示，对应于某衍射角 φ，把缝上波前 S 沿着与狭缝平行方向分成一系列宽度相等的窄条 ΔS，并使从相邻 ΔS 各对应点发出的光线的光程差为半个波长，这样的 ΔS 称为半波带。由图2-3-7可知，对应于衍射角为 φ 的屏上 P 点，缝边缘两条光线之间的光程差为

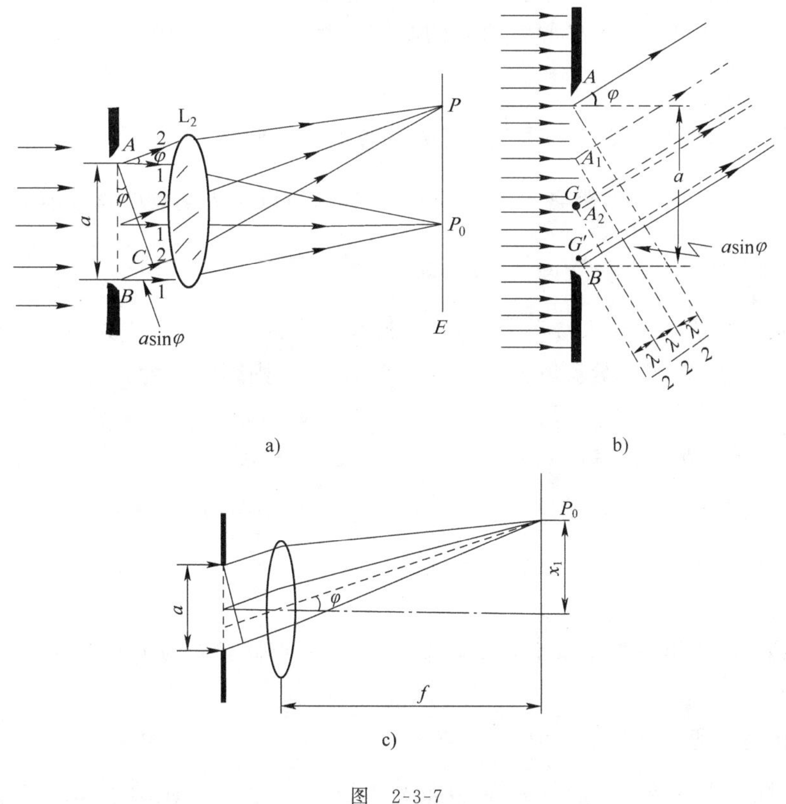

图 2-3-7

$$\delta=BC=a\sin\varphi$$

因而半波带的数目 N 为

$$N=2a\sin\varphi/\lambda$$

当 N 恰好为偶数时，因相邻半波带各对应点的光线的光线差都是 $\lambda/2$，即相位差为 π，因而两相邻半波带的光线在 P 点都干涉相消，P 点的光强为零，即 P 点为暗点；当 N 为奇数时，因相邻半波带发出的光两两干涉相消后，剩下一个半波带发出的光未被抵消，因此 P 点为明点。由此可得单缝夫琅和费衍射条纹的明暗纹条件为

$$a\sin\varphi=\begin{cases}\pm 2k\dfrac{\lambda}{2} \quad (k=1,2,\cdots) & \text{暗纹}\\ \pm(2k+1)\lambda/2 \quad (k=0,1,2,\cdots) & \text{明纹}\end{cases} \tag{2-3-17}$$

当 $\varphi=0$ 时，有

$$a\sin\varphi=0 \quad \text{中央明纹中心}$$

式中 k 为衍射级，中央明纹是零级明纹，因所有光线到达中央明纹中心 P_0 点的光程相同，光程差为零，故中央明纹中心 P_0 处光强最大。明暗以中央明纹为中心两边对称分布，依次是第一级($k=1$)，第二级($k=2$)，……暗纹和明纹。中央明纹宽度是由紧邻中央明纹两侧的暗纹($k=1$)决定，即

$$-\lambda<a\sin\varphi<\lambda$$

当半波带数 N 不是整数时，P 点的光强介于明暗之间，实际上屏上光强的分布是连续变化的。对一定波长的单色光，缝宽 a 越小，各级条纹的衍射角 φ 越大，在屏上相邻条纹的间隔也越大，即衍射效果越显著。反之，a 越大，φ 越小，各级衍射条纹向中央明纹靠拢；当 a 增大到分辨不清各级条纹时，衍射现象消失，此时相当于光直线传播的情况。

中央明纹的宽度由紧邻中央明纹两侧的暗纹($k=1$)决定。如图 2-3-7c)所示，通常衍射角 φ 很小。

由暗纹条件 $a\sin\varphi=1\times\lambda(k=1)$，得 $\varphi\approx\dfrac{\lambda}{a}$，$x_1=\varphi f$。

第一级暗纹距中心 P_0 的距离为 $x_1=\varphi f=\dfrac{\lambda}{a}f$，所以中央明纹的宽度 $l_0=2x_1=\dfrac{2\lambda f}{a}$。

其他明纹宽度是中央明纹宽度的一半，即 $l=\dfrac{l_0}{2}=\dfrac{\lambda f}{a}$。

【例 2-3-5】 在单缝夫琅禾费衍射实验中，波长为 λ 的单色光垂直入射到单缝上，对应衍射角为 30°的方向上，若单缝处波阵面可分成 3 个半波带，则缝宽 a 为：

A. λ　　B. 1.5λ　　C. 2λ　　D. 3λ

解 由单缝夫琅禾费衍射明纹条件，对应衍射角为 30°的方向上，

单缝处波面可分成 3 个半波带，即 $\delta=a\sin 30^\circ=(2k+1)\dfrac{\lambda}{2}=3\cdot\dfrac{\lambda}{2}$

可得 $a=3\lambda$。

答案：D

【例 2-3-6】 在单缝夫琅禾费衍射实验中，屏上第三级暗纹对应的单缝处波面可分成的半波带的数目为：

A. 3　　B. 4　　C. 5　　D. 6

解 由单缝夫琅禾费衍射暗纹条件，$a\sin\varphi=2k\cdot\dfrac{\lambda}{2}=6\cdot\dfrac{\lambda}{2}$，半波纹的数目为 6。

答案:D

【例 2-3-7】 在单缝夫琅禾费衍射实验中,单缝宽度 $a=1\times10^{-4}$ m,透镜焦距 $f=0.5$m。若用 $\lambda=400$nm 的单色平行光垂直入射,中央明纹的宽度为:

A. 2×10^{-3}m　　　　B. 2×10^{-4}m

C. 4×10^{-4}m　　　　D. 4×10^{-3}m

解　单缝夫琅禾费衍射中央明纹的宽度为:

$$l_0=\frac{2\lambda f}{a}=\frac{2\times400\times10^{-9}\times0.5}{1\times10^{-4}}=4\times10^{-3}\text{ m}$$

答案:D

(三)光学仪器的分辨本领

若夫琅和费单缝衍射中的狭缝用直径为 D 的圆孔代替,则衍射图样的中央是一明亮的圆斑,外围是一组同心暗环和明环,如图 2-3-8 所示。

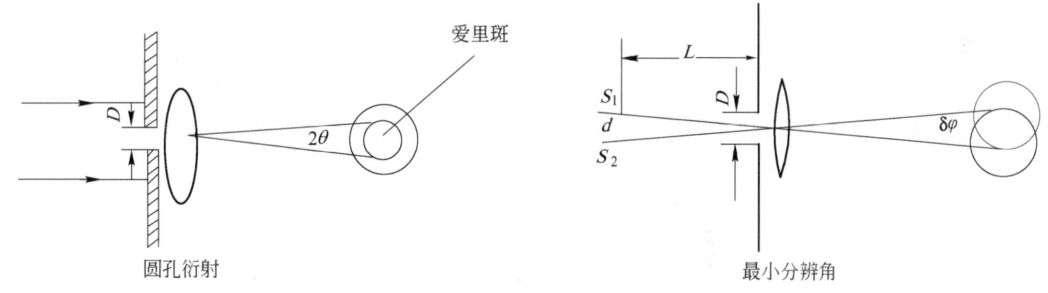

图　2-3-8

由第一暗环所包围的中央亮斑称爱里斑,其光强占整个入射光强的 84%,理论计算可得爱里斑的半角宽度为

$$\theta=1.22\lambda/D \tag{2-3-18}$$

通常,光学仪器中所用的光阑和透镜都是圆形的,点光源通过透镜所成的像因圆孔衍射其结果不是一个清晰的像点,而是一个衍射光斑。

当用光学仪器观察物体时,物体上靠得很近的两物点(或靠得很近的两物体)S_1、S_2 发出的光通过直径为 D 的透镜时,形成了两个一定大小的爱里斑,如图 2-3-8 所示。瑞利指出,若一个点光源的爱里斑中心恰好与另一点光源的爱里斑的第一暗环相重合,这两个点光源恰好能为光学仪器所分辨,这就是瑞利准则。

两物点的像的最小分辨角 $\delta\varphi$ 恰等于爱里斑的半角宽度,即

$$\delta\varphi=\theta=1.22\lambda/D \tag{2-3-19}$$

分辨角 $\delta\varphi$ 越小,说明光学仪器的分辨率越高,常取 $1/\delta\varphi$ 表示光学仪器的分辨本领 R,即

$$R=D/1.22\lambda \tag{2-3-20}$$

例如,人眼的瞳孔直径 $D\approx2$mm,入射光平均波长 $\lambda=550$nm,可算得最小分辨角 $\delta\varphi\approx3.4\times10^{-4}$rad,即约 1′;而世界上最大天文望远镜物镜的孔径有 6m,可算得 $\delta\varphi=1.12\times10^{-7}$rad,比人眼的分辨能力提高 3 000 倍。

【例 2-3-8】 通常亮度下，人眼睛瞳孔的直径约为 3mm，视觉感受到最灵敏的光波波长为 550nm（$1\text{nm}=1\times10^{-9}\text{m}$），则人眼睛的最小分辨角约为：

A. 2.24×10^{-3} rad　　B. 1.12×10^{-4} rad

C. 2.24×10^{-4} rad　　D. 1.12×10^{-3} rad

解 人眼睛的最小分辨角：

$$\theta = 1.22\,\frac{\lambda}{D} = \frac{1.22\times550\times10^{-6}}{3} = 2.24\times10^{-4}\text{rad}$$

答案：C

（四）衍射光栅

单缝衍射形成的明条纹尚不够理想，为使明纹本身既窄又亮且相邻明纹分得很开，通常都使用衍射光栅。例如我们在玻璃片上刻划出许多等距离等宽度的平行直线，刻痕处不透光，而两刻痕间可以透光，相当于一个单缝，这样就构成了透射式平面衍射光栅。由大量等宽、等间距的平行狭缝所组成的光学元件称衍射光栅。光栅和棱镜一样是一种分光装置，主要用来形成光谱（图 2-3-9）。

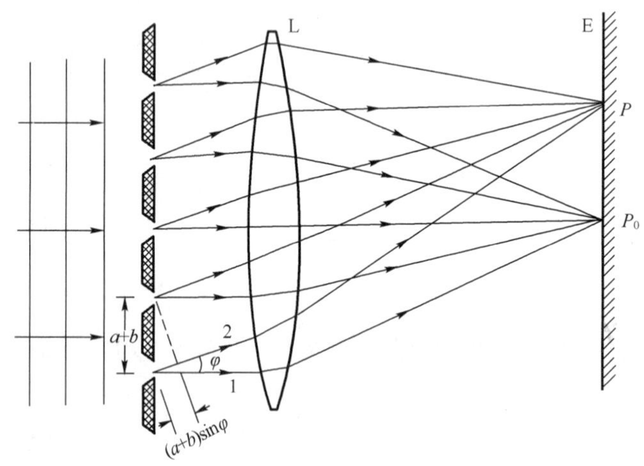

图 2-3-9　衍射光栅

缝的宽度 a 和刻痕（不透光）的宽度 b 之和，即 $a+b$ 称为光栅常数。

一束平行单色光垂直照射在光栅上，光线经过透镜 L 后将在屏幕 E 上呈现各级衍射条纹，如图 2-3-9 所示。

对光栅中每一条透光缝，由于衍射都将在屏幕上呈现衍射图样，而各缝发出的衍射光都是相干光，所以缝与缝之间的光波相互干涉，光栅衍射条纹是单缝衍射和多缝干涉的总效果。

$$(a+b)\sin\varphi = \pm k\lambda \qquad (k=0,1,2,\cdots) \tag{2-3-21}$$

当衍射角 φ 满足条件时，即形成明条纹。显然，光栅上狭缝的条数愈多，条纹就愈明亮。上式中整数 k 表示条纹的级数，上述明条纹称为光栅的衍射条纹。式（2-3-21）称为光栅公式。

一般来说，当 φ 满足式（2-3-21）时，是合成光强为最大的必要条件，这些明条纹，细窄而明亮，称为主极大。可以证明，各主极大明条纹之间充满大量的暗条纹，当光栅狭缝数很大时，在主极大明条纹之间实际上形成一片黑暗的背景。当多缝干涉明纹与单缝衍射暗纹位置重叠时，会产生缺级现象。

【例 2-3-9】 波长 $\lambda=550\text{nm}(1\text{nm}=10^{-9}\text{m})$ 的单色光垂直入射于光栅常数为 $2\times10^{-4}\text{cm}$ 的平面衍射光栅上，可能观察到光谱线的最大级次为：

A. 2　　B. 3　　C. 4　　D. 5

解 光栅公式　$d\sin\theta=\pm k\lambda \quad (k=1,2,3,\cdots)$

在波长、光栅常数不变的情况下，要使 k 最大，$\sin\theta$ 必最大，取 $\sin\theta=1$，此时，$d=\pm k\lambda$，$k=\pm\dfrac{d}{\lambda}=\pm\dfrac{2\times10^{-4}\times10^{-2}}{550\times10^{-9}}=3.636$，取整后可得最大级次为 3。

答案：B

（五）光谱分析

由式(2-3-21)可知，在给定光栅常数情况下，衍射角 φ 的大小和入射光的波长有关，白光通过光栅后，各单色光将产生相应的各自分开的条纹，形成光栅的衍射光谱。中央明纹(零级)仍为白色，而在中央条纹两侧，对称地排列着第一级、第二级等光谱，如图 2-3-10 所示。

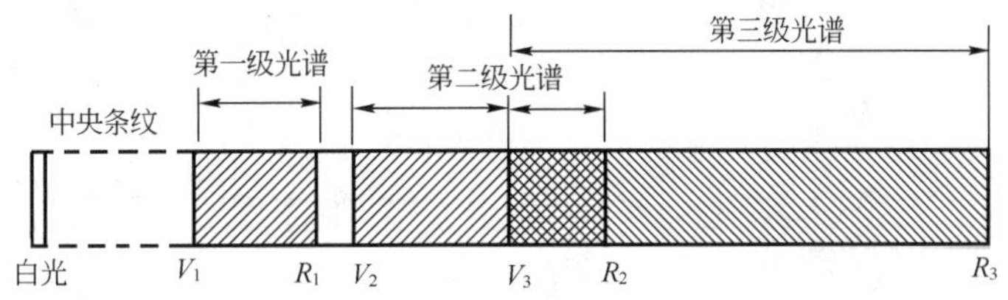

图 2-3-10　衍射光谱

由于不同元素(或化合物)各有自己特定的光谱，所以由谱线的成分可以分析出发光物质所含的元素和化合物，还可以从谱线的强度定量地分析出元素的含量，这种分析方法叫做光谱分析。

（六）伦琴射线的衍射

伦琴射线又叫 X 射线，它是一种波长为 0.1nm 数量级电磁波。1912 年德国物理学家劳厄用晶格常数 d(晶体中相邻原子间距)作衍射光栅，获得了 X 射线的衍射图样，开创了 X 射线作晶体结构分析的重要应用。

英国科学家布喇格把晶体中周期性排列的原子看成为一系列互相平行的原子层，如图 2-3-11所示，当一束平行的 X 射线照射到晶体上时，晶体中各原子都成为向各方向散射子波的波源，各层间的散射线相互叠加产生相干现象。

如图 2-3-11 所示，设原子层之间距离为 d，当一束平行的相干 X 射线以与晶面夹角 θ 入射时，相邻两层反射线的光程差为

$$AC+CB=2d\sin\theta$$

显然，当符合以下条件

$$2d\sin\theta=k\lambda \qquad (k=1,2,3,\cdots) \qquad (2\text{-}3\text{-}22)$$

时，各原子层的反射线都将相互加强，光强极大，上式就是著名的布喇格公式。

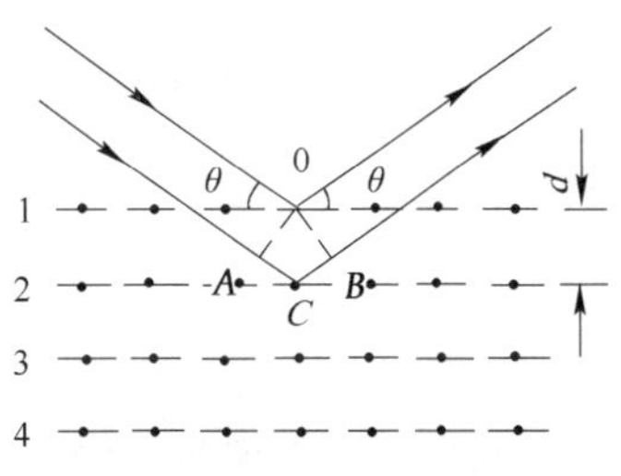

图 2-3-11　布喇格方法

晶体对 X 射线的衍射应用很广，若已知晶体的晶格常数，就可用来测定 X 射线的波长，这一方面的工作叫 X 射线的光谱分析；若用已知波长的 X 射线在晶体上衍射，就可测定晶体的晶格常数，这类工作叫 X 光结构分析。

六、光的偏振

(一)自然光和偏振光

光矢量只限于单一方向振动的光称线偏振光。一般光源(如电灯、太阳等)的发光机理是由为数众多的原子或分子等的自发辐射,它们之间,无论在发光的前后次序(相位),振动的取向和大小(偏振和振幅),以及发光的持续时间(波列的长短)都相互独立。所以从垂直光传播方向的平面上看,几乎各个方向都有大小不等、前后参差不齐而变化很快的光矢量的振动,按统计平均而言,无论哪一个方向的振动都不比其他方向占优势,这种光就是自然光。

自然光中任一方向的光振动,都可分解成某两个相互垂直方向的振动,它们在每个方向上的时间平均值相等,但无固定的相位关系,不能合成一个线偏振光。通常把自然光用两个相互独立的、等振幅的、振动方向互相垂直的线偏振光表示,如图 2-3-12 所示,这两个线偏振光的光强等于自然光光强度的一半。

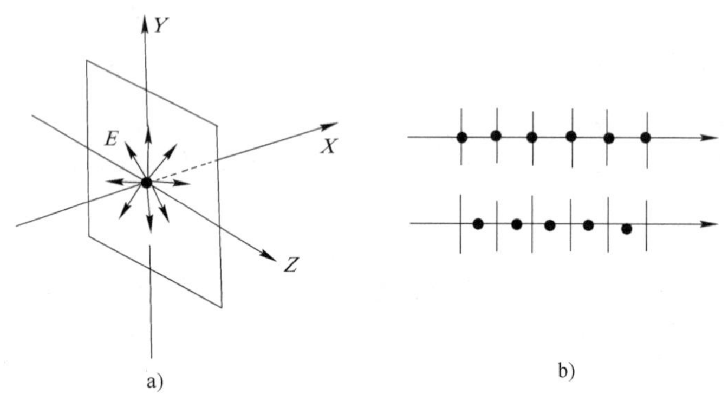

图 2-3-12

线偏振光传播方向与振动方向构成的平面叫振动面。由于线偏振光的 **E** 总在振动面内,故又称平面偏振光如图 2-3-13a)所示。

若光矢量 **E** 可取任意方向,但在各方向上振幅不同,这种光叫部分偏振光,如图2-3-13b)所示。

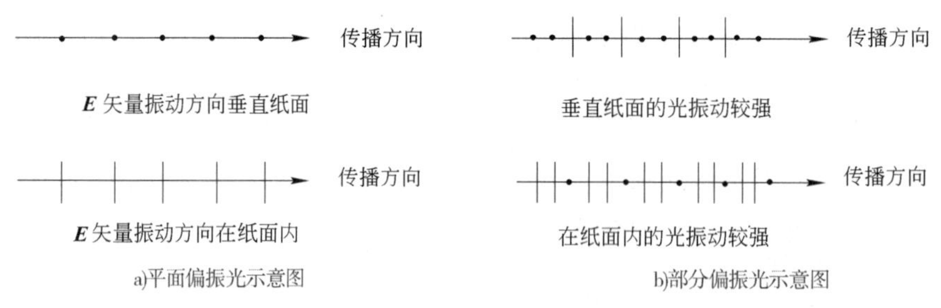

图 2-3-13

(二)起偏和检偏,马吕斯定律

1.偏振片的起偏和检偏

使自然光转变成偏振光叫起偏,能使自然光变成偏振光的装置叫偏振器。起偏器有多种,如利用光的反射和折射起偏的玻璃片堆,利用晶体的双折射特性起偏的尼科耳棱镜等,以及利用晶体的二向色性的各类起偏器。

起偏器只能透过沿某方向振动的光矢量或光矢量振动沿该方向的分量，而不能透过与该方向垂直振动的光矢量或光矢量振动与该方向垂直的分量。这个透光方向称为偏振化方向或起偏方向。自然光透过偏振片后，透光强变为入射光强的一半，透射光即变为偏振光。由偏振片的特性可知，它既可用作起偏器，也可用作检偏器，检验向它入射的光是否为线偏振光。

自然光透过偏振片后，透光强度变为入射光强的一半，逆着光的传播方向观察透射光的强弱，当转动偏振片时，光强不变。若线偏振光入射偏振片，则透射光的强弱在转动偏振片时要发生周期性变化。光矢量振动方向与偏振光方向平行时透射光量最强，垂直时最暗。

图 2-3-14 表示利用偏振片起偏与检偏的情况，图中 A、B 分别为起偏器和检偏器。

2. 马吕斯定律

若入射线偏振光的光强为 I_0，透过检偏器后，透射光强（不计检偏器对光的吸收）为 I，则

$$I=I_0\cos^2\alpha \tag{2-3-23}$$

式中，α 是线偏振光振动方向和检偏器偏振化方向之间的夹角。上式即为马吕斯定律（参见图 2-3-15）。

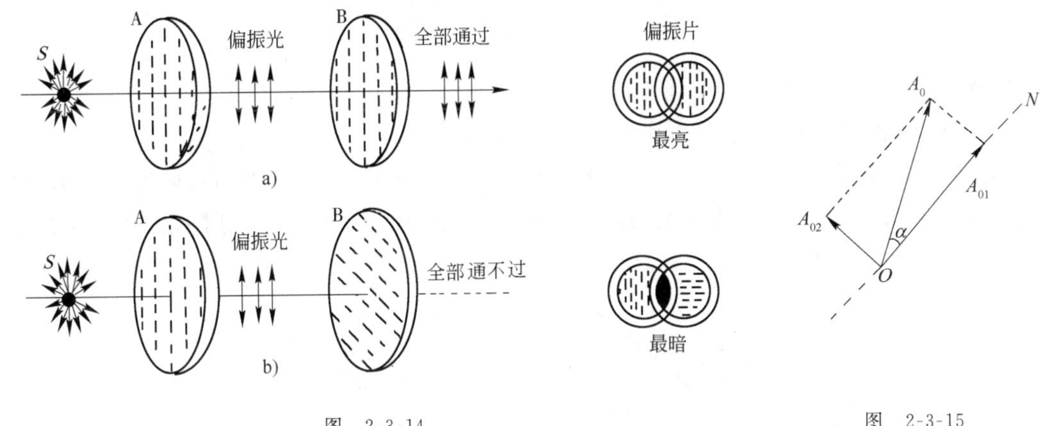

图 2-3-14　　图 2-3-15

由式上可知，当 $\alpha=0°$（或 180°）时，$I=I_0$；$\alpha=90°$（或 270°）时，$I=0$，此时无光从检偏器射出。

【例 2-3-10】 两偏振片叠放在一起，欲使一束垂直入射的线偏振光经过两个偏振片后振动方向转过 90°，且使出射光强尽可能大，则入射光的振动方向与前后两偏振片的偏振化方向夹角分别为：

A. 45°和 90°　　B. 0°和 90°　　C. 30°和 90°　　D. 60°和 90°

解　注意题目给定入射光为线偏振光，由马吕斯定律：

经过第一个偏振片后　$I=I_0\cos^2\alpha$

经过第二个偏振片后　$I'=I\cos^2\left(\frac{\pi}{2}-\alpha\right)=\frac{I_0}{4}\sin^2(2\alpha)$

出射光强最大 $I'=\frac{I_0}{4}\sin^2(2\alpha)=\frac{I_0}{4}$，$\sin(2\alpha)=1$，$\alpha=\frac{\pi}{4}$

答案：A

【例 2-3-11】 一束自然光垂直穿过两个偏振片，两个偏振片的偏振化方向成 45°。已知通过此两偏振片后光强为 I，则入射至第二个偏振片的线偏振光强度。

A. I　　B. $2I$　　C. $3I$　　D. $I/2$

解 注意题目的问题为入射至第二个偏振片的线偏振光强度。

由马吕斯定律：$I=I_0\cos^2\alpha=I_0\cos^2 45°$，则 $I_0=2I$。

答案:B

【例 2-3-12】 一束自然光通过两块叠放在一起的偏振片，若两偏振片的偏振化方向间夹角由 α_1 转到 α_2，则前后透射光强度之比为：

A. $\dfrac{\cos^2\alpha_2}{\cos^2\alpha_1}$　　B. $\dfrac{\cos\alpha_2}{\cos\alpha_1}$　　C. $\dfrac{\cos^2\alpha_1}{\cos^2\alpha_2}$　　D. $\dfrac{\cos\alpha_1}{\cos\alpha_2}$

解 此题考查马吕斯定律。

$$I=I_0\cos^2\alpha$$

光强为 I_0 的自然光通过第一个偏振片的光强为入射光强的一半，即 $I_1=\dfrac{1}{2}I_0\cos^2\alpha_1$，通过第二个偏振片的光强为 $I_2=\dfrac{I_0}{2}\cos^2\alpha_2$，则：

$$\frac{I_1}{I_2}=\frac{\frac{1}{2}I_0\cos^2\alpha_1}{\frac{1}{2}I_0\cos^2\alpha_2}=\frac{\cos^2\alpha_1}{\cos^2\alpha_2}$$

答案:C

(三)反射、折射产生的偏振、布儒斯特定律

当一束自然光在两种媒质 n_1、n_2 的分界面上反射和折射时，反射光和折射光都是部分偏振光。实验表明：反射光中垂直入射面的光振动较强，折射光中平行于入射面的光振动较强，它们随入射角的变化而变化，参见图 2-3-16。

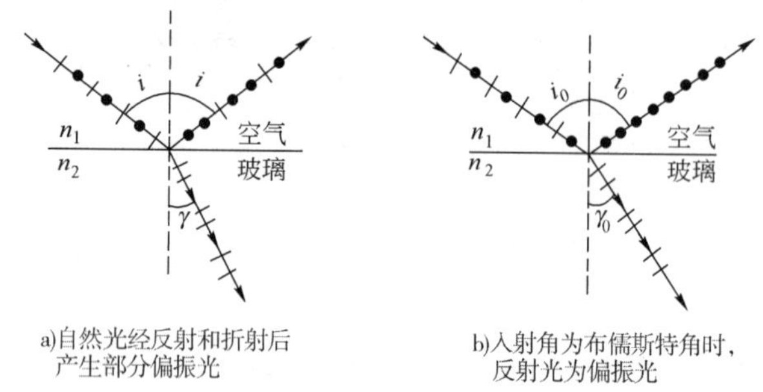

图 2-3-16 反射和折射时的偏振现象

1815 年，布儒斯特发现：当入射角 i 增大至某一特定值 i_0，且满足

$$\tan i_0=n_2/n_1=n_{21} \tag{2-3-24}$$

时，反射光为光振动垂直入射面的线偏振光，折射光仍为部分偏振光。i_0 称为布儒斯特角。上式即布儒斯特定律的数学表达式，式中，n_1、n_2 为媒质的折射率。

由折射定律，入射角 i_0 与折射角 γ 的关系

$$\frac{\sin i_0}{\sin r}=\frac{n_2}{n_1}=\tan i_0=\frac{\sin i_0}{\cos i_0}$$

故

$$i_0+\gamma=\pi/2 \tag{2-3-25}$$

【例 2-3-13】 一束自然光从空气投射到玻璃板表面上，当折射角为 30°时，反射光为完全偏振光，则此玻璃的折射率为：

A. 2　　B. 3　　C. $\sqrt{2}$　　D. $\sqrt{3}$

解 依据布儒斯特定律，折射角为 30°时，入射角为 60°，则 $\tan 60° = \frac{n_2}{n_1} = \sqrt{3}$。

答案：D

七、双折射现象

（一）概述

当一束自然光射向各向异性媒质时，在界面折入晶体内部的折射光线常分为传播方向不同的两束折射光线，如图 2-3-17 所示，这种现象称为晶体的双折射现象。

试验发现，两束折射光具有如下特性：

（1）两束折射光是光振动方向不同的线偏振光。

（2）其中一束折射光始终在入射面内，并遵守折射定律，称为寻常光，简称 o 光；另一束折射光一般不在入射面内，且不遵从折射定律，称为非常光，简称 e 光。在入射角 $i=0$ 时，寻常光沿原方向传播（$\gamma_0=0$），而非常光一般不沿原方向传播（$\gamma_0 \neq 0$），如图 2-3-18 所示，此时当以入射光为轴转动晶体时，o 光不动，而 e 光绕轴旋转。

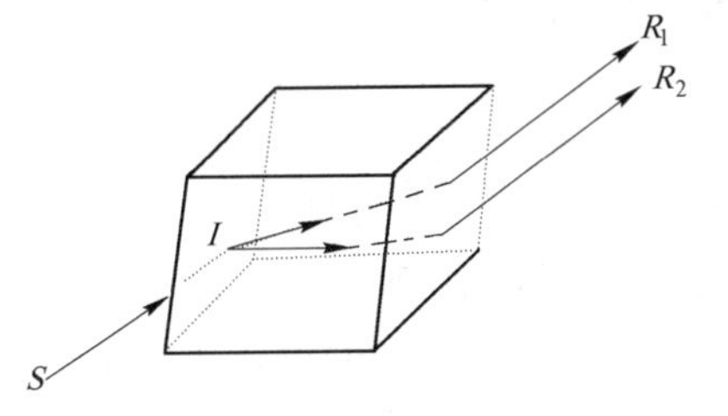

图 2-3-17

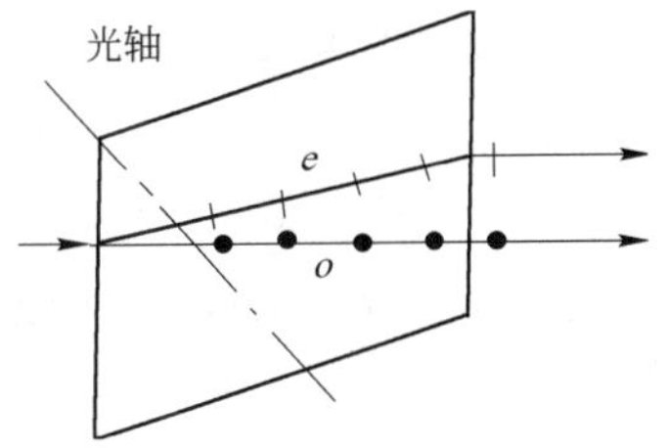

图 2-3-18

（3）在方解石一类晶体内存在一个特殊方向，光线沿该方向传播时，不产生双折射现象，这个特殊的方向称为晶体的光轴。光轴仅标志双折射晶体的一个特定方向，任何平行于这个方向的直线都是晶体的光轴。只有一个光轴方向的晶体，称为单轴晶体，为方解石、石英等；有两个光轴方向的晶体，称为双轴晶体，如云母、硫磺等。

当光线沿晶体的某一表面入射时，此表面的法线与晶体的光轴所构成的平面叫做主截面，方解石的主截面是一平行四边形，自然光沿如图 2-3-18 所示的方向入射时，入射面就是主截面，由检偏器可以检测到 o 光、e 光都是偏振光，o 光的光振动垂直于主截面，而 e 光的光振动则在主截面内。

（二）偏振光的干涉

振幅为 A 的偏振光通过晶体后形成 o、e 光，这两束光频率相同，存在一定相位差，只是由于振动方向相互垂直而不相干，于是利用偏振片 N 偏振化方向与偏振片 M 的偏振化方向正交，如图 2-3-19 所示把 o、e 光的振动方向引到同一方向，这样就成为两束相干的偏振光。

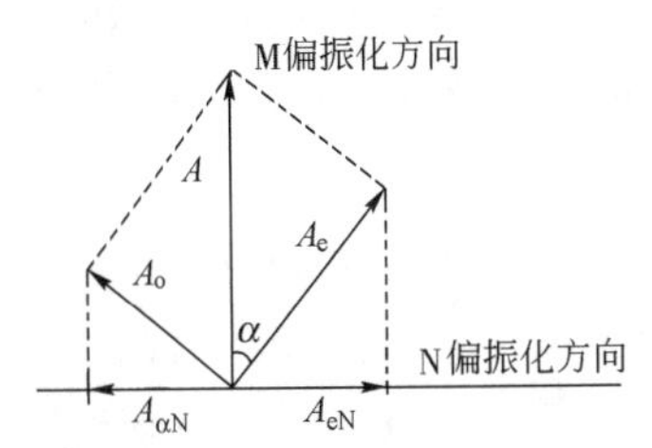

图 2-3-19　偏振光的干涉

习　题

2-3-1　在真空中波长为 λ 的单色光，在折射率为 n 的透明介质中从 A 沿某路径传播到 B，若 A、B 两点相位差为 3π，则此路径 AB 的光程为（　　）。

A. 1.5λ　　B. $1.5n\lambda$　　C. 3λ　　D. $1.5\lambda/n$

2-3-2　用白光光源进行双缝实验，若用一个纯红色的滤光片遮盖一条缝，用一个纯蓝色的滤光片遮盖另一条缝，则（　　）。

A. 干涉条纹的宽度将发生改变　　B. 产生红光和蓝光的两套彩色干涉条纹

C. 干涉条纹的亮度将发生改变　　D. 不产生干涉条纹

2-3-3　在双缝干涉实验中，若用透明的云母片遮住上面的一条缝，则（　　）。

A. 干涉图样不变　　B. 干涉图样下移

C. 干涉图样上移　　D. 不产生干涉条纹

2-3-4　双缝间距为 2mm，双缝与屏幕相距 300cm，用波长 600nm 的光照射时，屏幕上干涉条纹的相邻两明纹的距离是(单位：mm)（　　）。

A. 5.0　　B. 4.5　　C. 4.2　　D. 0.9

2-3-5　一束波长为 λ 的单色光从空气垂直入射到折射率为 n 的透明薄膜上，要使反射光线得到加强，薄膜最小厚度应为（　　）。

A. $\lambda/4$　　B. $\lambda/(4n)$　　C. $\lambda/2$　　D. $\lambda/(2n)$

2-3-6　真空中波长为 λ 的单色光，在折射率为 n 的均匀透明媒质中，从 A 点沿某一路径传播到 B 点，路径长度为 L，A、B 两点光振动相位差记为 $\Delta\Phi$，则（　　）。

A. $L=3\lambda/2$ 时，$\Delta\Phi=3\pi$　　B. $L=3\lambda/(2n)$时，$\Delta\Phi=3n\pi$

C. $L=3\lambda/(2n)$时，$\Delta\Phi=3\pi$　　D. $L=3n\lambda/2$ 时，$\Delta\Phi=3n\pi$

2-3-7　两块平玻璃构成空气壁尖，左边为棱边。用单色平行光垂直入射。若上面的玻璃慢慢向上平移，则干涉条纹（　　）。

A. 向棱边方向平移，条纹间隔变小　　B. 向棱边方向平移，条纹间隔变大

C. 向棱边方向平移，条纹间隔不变　　D. 向离开棱边方向平移，条纹间隔不变

2-3-8　用波长为 λ 的单色光垂直照射到空气劈尖上，从反射光中观察干涉条纹，距顶点 L 处是暗纹。使劈尖角 θ 连续增大，直到该处再次出现暗纹时(见图)，劈尖角的改变量 $\Delta\theta$ 是（　　）。

A. $\lambda/(2L)$　　B. λ/L　　C. $2\lambda/L$　　D. $\lambda/(4L)$

题 2-3-8 图

2-3-9　在单缝夫琅和费衍射实验中波长为 λ 的单色光垂直入射到单缝上，对应于衍射角 $\Phi=30°$的方向上，若单缝处波阵面可划分为 4 个半波带，则单缝的宽度 $a=$（　　）。

A. 6λ　　B. 4λ　　C. 3λ　　D. λ

2-3-10　在单缝夫琅和费衍射实验中，若将缝宽缩小一半，原来第三级暗纹处将是（　　）。

A. 第一级暗纹　　B. 第一级明纹

C. 第二级暗纹　　D. 第二级明纹

2-3-11　汽车两前灯相距约 1.2m，夜间人眼瞳孔直径为 5mm，车灯发出波长为 $0.5\mu m$ 的

光，则人眼夜间能区分两前车灯的最大距离为(　　)。

A. 10km　　B. 3km　　C. 2km　　D. 4km

2-3-12　在两个偏振化方向正交的偏振片 P_1 和 P_2 之间，平行地插入第三个偏振片 P，P_1 与 P 的偏振化方向间的夹角为 60°。若入射自然光的光强为 I_0，不考虑偏振片的吸收与反射，则出射光的光强为(　　)。

A. $I_0/4$　　B. $3I_0/32$　　C. $3I_0/8$　　D. $I_0/16$

2-3-13　一束自然光以布儒斯特角入射到平板玻璃上，则(　　)。

A. 反射光束垂直于入射面偏振，透射光束平行于入射面偏振且为完全偏振光

B. 反射光束平行于入射面偏振，透射光束为部分偏振光

C. 反射光束是垂直于入射面的线偏振光，透射光束是部分偏振光

D. 反射光束和透射光束都是部分偏振光

2-3-14　假设某一介质对于空气的临界角是 45°，则光从空气射向此介质时的布儒斯特角是(　　)。

A. 45°　　B. 90°　　C. 35.2°　　D. 54.7°

2-3-15　某单色光垂直入射到一个每一毫米有 800 条刻痕线的光栅上，如果第一级谱线的衍射角为 30°，则入射光的波长应为(　　)。

A. 0.625μm　　B. 1.25μm　　C. 2.5μm　　D. 5μm

2-3-16　波长 $\lambda=0.55\mu m$ 的单色光垂直入射于光栅常数 $(a+b)=2\times10^{-6}$ m 的平面衍射光栅上，可能观察到的光谱线的最大级次为(　　)。

A. 第二级　　B. 第三级　　C. 第四级　　D. 第五级

2-3-17　一束自然光从空气投射到玻璃表面上(空气折射率为 1)，当折射角为 30°时，反射光是完全偏振光，则此玻璃板的折射率等于(　　)。

A. 1.33　　B. $\sqrt{2}$　　C. $\sqrt{3}$　　D. 1.5

题解及参考答案

第一节

2-1-1　**解**：用 $\overline{\omega}=\frac{3}{2}kT$，平均动能 $=\frac{i}{2}kT$，平均速率 $\overline{v}\propto\sqrt{\frac{RT}{M}}$，$E_{内}=\frac{m}{M}\frac{i}{2}RT$ 分析，注意到 $M(H_2)\neq M(He)$，$i(H_2)\neq i(He)$。

答案：A

2-1-2　**解**：$p=nkT$，分子数密度 $n=\frac{N(分子数)}{V}$，即 $p=\frac{N}{V}kT$，则 $N=\frac{pV}{kT}$。

答案：B

2-1-3　**解**：由 $\overline{\omega}=\frac{3}{2}kT$ 知，若两气体分子平均平动动能相同，则 $T(He)=T(N_2)$，又根据 $pV=\frac{m}{M}RT$ 得 $p=\frac{\frac{m}{V}}{M}RT$，式中 $\frac{m}{V}$ 即气体密度，由于摩尔质量 $M(He)<M(N_2)$，

故 $p(\text{He})>p(\text{N}_2)$。

答案:C

2-1-4 **解**:$E=\frac{i}{2}\frac{m}{M}RT=\frac{i}{2}pV$。氦气自由度 $i=3$,则 $E=\frac{3}{2}pV$。

答案:A

2-1-5 **解**:气体分子的平动自由度 $i=3$,平动动能的总和即气体由平动产生的内能 $E=\frac{3}{2}\frac{m}{M}RT=\frac{3}{2}pV=\frac{3}{2}\times5\times10^2\times8\times10^{-3}=6\text{J}$。

答案:D

2-1-6 **解**:用 $p=nkT$ 或 $pV=\frac{m}{M}RT$ 分析。注意到氢气、氦气都在同一容器中,温度相同,单位体积的分子数相同。

答案:B

2-1-7 **解**:1. 用 $p=nkT$ 分析①,单位体积内分子数 n 应相同。

2. 用 $pV=\frac{m}{M}RT$ 分析②,单位体积内的质量$\frac{m}{V}=\frac{pM}{RT}$不同(摩尔质量 M 不同)。

3. 用内能 $E=\frac{i}{2}\frac{m}{M}RT=\frac{i}{2}pV$ 分析③,单位体积内的内能$\frac{E}{V}=\frac{i}{2}p$ 应相同,因为氧和一氧化碳都是双原子分子,自由度 i 相同。

答案:C

2-1-8 **解**:1. 平均动能=平均平动动能+平均转动动能$=\frac{3}{2}kT+\frac{i(\text{转动})}{2}kT$。

2. 内能 $E=\frac{i}{2}\frac{m}{M}RT$。温度相同,平均平动动能相等。

答案:D

2-1-9 **解**:由 $\bar{\omega}=\frac{3}{2}kT$,知:$T(\text{H}_2)=T(\text{O}_2)$

又平均速率 $\bar{v}\propto\sqrt{\frac{RT}{M}}$,$\frac{\bar{v}_{\text{H}_2}}{\bar{v}_{\text{O}_2}}=\sqrt{\frac{M(\text{O}_2)}{M(\text{H}_2)}}=\sqrt{\frac{32}{2}}=\frac{4}{1}$。

答案:D

2-1-10 **解**:平均碰撞次数$\bar{Z}=\sqrt{2}\pi d^2n\bar{v}$,平均速率 $\bar{v}=1.6\sqrt{\frac{RT}{M}}$,平均自由程$\bar{\lambda}=\frac{\bar{v}}{\bar{Z}}=\frac{1}{\sqrt{2}\pi d^2n}$。

答案:A

2-1-11 **解**:由 $pV=\frac{m}{M}RT$,可得 $p=\frac{\rho}{M}RT$;当 p 不变时,ρ 与 T 成反比。

答案:B

2-1-12 **解**:由 $pV=\frac{m}{M}RT$,知:$\frac{m}{M}(\text{He})=\frac{m}{M}(\text{O}_2)$,对 He,有$\frac{m}{M}\frac{3}{2}R\Delta T=9\text{J}$,即$\frac{m}{M}R\Delta T=6\text{J}$;对 O_2,有$\frac{m}{M}\frac{5}{2}R\Delta T=\frac{5}{2}\times6=15\text{J}$。

答案:B

2-1-13　解:$Q_V=\frac{m}{M}\frac{i}{2}R\Delta T$。在本题中,$Q_V=\frac{m}{M}\frac{i(O_2)}{2}R\Delta T(O_2)=\frac{m}{M}\frac{i(H_2O)}{2}R\Delta T(H_2O)$,因 $i(O_2)\neq i(H_2O)$,则 $\Delta T(H_2)\neq\Delta T(H_2O)$,又由 $pV=\frac{m}{M}RT$,知 V 不变时,$\Delta p(O_2)\neq\Delta p(H_2O)$。

答案:B

2-1-14　解:$Q_p=\frac{m}{M}(\frac{i}{2}+1)R\Delta T=(\frac{i}{2}+1)p\Delta V$,$A_p=p\Delta V$,$\frac{7}{2}p\Delta V(N_2)=\frac{5}{2}p\Delta V'(He)$,$\frac{A(N_2)}{A(He)}=\frac{p\Delta V}{p\Delta V'}=\frac{5}{7}$。

答案:B

2-1-15　解:①由图知 $T_a>T_b$,所以沿 acb 过程内能减少(内能增量为负)。

②由图知沿 acb 过程 $A>0$。

③$Q_{acb}=E_b-E_a+A_{acb}$,又 $E_b-E_a=-A_{绝热}=-$(绝热曲线下面积)。

比较 $A_{绝热}$ 和 A_{acb},知 $Q_{acb}<0$。

答案:C

2-1-16　解:画 p-V 图,当容积增加时,等压过程内能增加(T 增加),绝热过程内能减少。而等温过程内能不变。

答案:C

2-1-17　解:画 p-V 图,此循环为逆循环(致冷机,)Q(循环)$=A$(净),A(净)<0。

答案:A

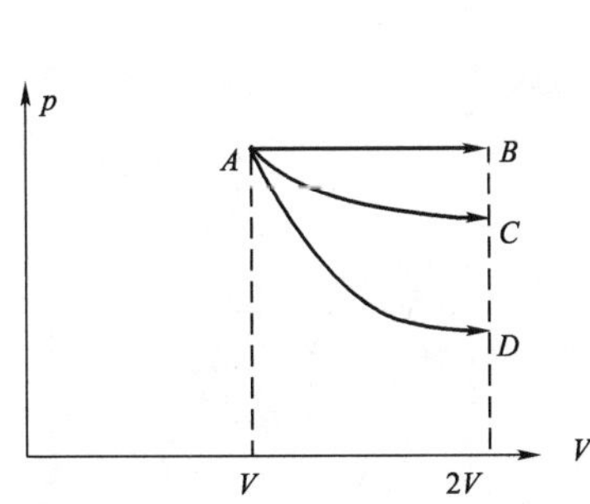

题 2-1-16 解图

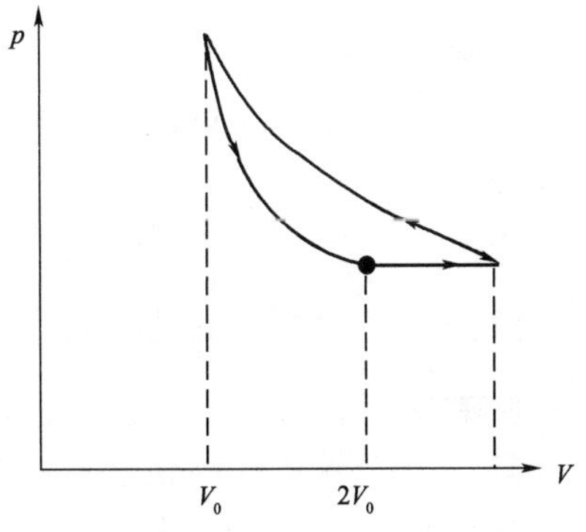

题 2-1-17 解图

2-1-18　解:$\eta_{卡诺}=1-\frac{T_2}{T_1}=1-\frac{Q_2}{Q_1}$

$T_1=nT_2$,$\frac{1}{n}=\frac{Q_2}{Q_1}$,$Q_2=\frac{1}{n}Q_1$

答案:C

2-1-19　解:注意对热力学第二定律的全面理解。

答案:D

2-1-20 **解:**热力学第二定律开尔文表述:不可能制成一种循环动作的热机,只从一个热源吸取热量,使之完全变为有用功……,而本题叙述的是单一的"等温过程",不违反热力学第二定律。

答案:C

第二节

2-2-1 **解:**将波动方程化为标准形式,再比较计算。并注意到 $\cos\varphi=\cos(-\varphi)$,$y=0.05\cos(4\pi x-10\pi t)=0.05\cos(10\pi t-4\pi x)=0.05\cos[10\pi(t-\frac{x}{2.5})]$,故 $\omega=10\pi=2\pi\nu$,波速 $u=2.5\text{m/s}$,波长 $\lambda=\frac{u}{\nu}=\frac{2.5}{5}=0.5\text{m}$。

答案:B

2-2-2 **解:**在波动中,质元的动能和势能变化是同相位的,它们同时达到最大值,又同时达到最小值。本题中"质元正处于平衡位置",此时速度最大。

答案:B

2-2-3 **解:**以 $x=L$ 处为原点,写出波动方程,$y_L=A\cos\omega(t-\frac{x}{u})$,再令 $x=-L$ 代入波动方程,得 $x=0$ 处质点的振动方程。

答案:C

2-2-4 **解:**设负向传播波动方程为 $y=A\cos(\omega t+\frac{\omega x}{u}+\varphi_0)=A\cos(\frac{2\pi}{T}t+\frac{2\pi x}{\lambda}+\varphi_0)$,因 $\frac{2\pi}{T}\times\frac{T}{4}+\frac{2\pi\times\frac{\lambda}{2}}{\lambda}+\varphi_0=\pi$,所以 $\varphi_0=-\frac{\pi}{2}$。

答案:C

2-2-5 **解:**波动周期等于波源的振动周期,沿波传播方向上任一点总是比波源的相位滞后。

答案:C

2-2-6 **解:**$\Delta\Phi=\frac{2\pi(\Delta x)}{\lambda}$,波速 $u=\lambda\nu=\lambda\frac{1}{T}$,$\Delta\Phi=\frac{2\pi}{u\cdot T}\cdot\Delta x=\frac{2\pi\cdot 5}{15\cdot 2}=\frac{\pi}{3}$。

答案:B

2-2-7 **解:**在波动中动能和势能的变化是同相位的,它们同时达到最大值,又同时达到最小值。对任意质元来说,它的机械能是不守恒的,即沿着波动的传播方向,该质元不断地从后面的质元获得能量(质元从一端点向平衡位置移动时),又不断地把能量传递给前面的质元(质元从平衡位置向端点移动时)。

答案:C

2-2-8 **解:**驻波两相邻波节间各点振幅不同,相位相同。

答案:B

2-2-9 **解:**由干涉减弱条件,$\Delta\Phi=\Phi_{02}-\Phi_{01}-\frac{2\pi(r_2-r_1)}{\lambda}=\pm(2k+1)\pi\quad(k=0,1,2,\cdots)$

现 $\varphi_{02}-\varphi_{01}=\pi$,$r_2-r_1=0$,故 $\Delta\varphi=\pi$,$A=|A_1-A_2|=0$。

答案:D

2-2-10 **解**:按题意作图,S_1 右侧任取 P 点,可见 $r_2-r_1=\frac{3\lambda}{4}$,又知 S_1 右侧的各点合振幅均为 $2A$,说明 S_1 右侧各点干涉加强,即 $\Delta\Phi=0$(取 $k=0$)。

$$\Delta\Phi=\Phi_{02}-\Phi_{01}-\frac{2\pi(r_2-r_1)}{\lambda}=0(k=0)$$

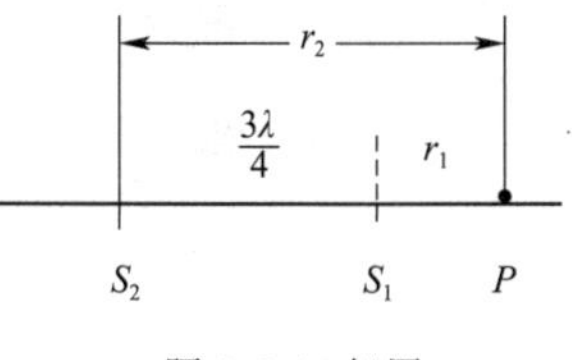

题 2-2-10 解图

得 $\Phi_{02}-\Phi_{01}=\frac{2\pi(\frac{3\lambda}{4})}{\lambda}=\frac{3}{2}\pi$。

答案:D

2-2-11 **解**:波节的位置 $x=(2k+1)\frac{\lambda}{4}\quad(k=0,\pm1,\pm2,\cdots)$

令 $k=0$ 和 $k=1$,相邻两波节之间距离 $x_1-x_0=\frac{\lambda}{2}$。

答案:B

第三节

2-3-1 **解**:$\Delta\Phi=\frac{2\pi\delta}{\lambda}$($\delta$ 指光程差)。

答案:A

2-3-2 **解**:考虑相干光源(波源)的条件,从两滤光片出来的光是不是相干光。

答案:D

2-3-3 **解**:考查零级明纹向哪一方向移动。

答案:C

2-3-4 **解**:$\Delta x=\frac{D}{d}\lambda=\frac{3000}{2}\times600\times10^{-6}=0.9\text{mm}$。

答案:D

2-3-5 **解**:$2ne+\frac{\lambda}{2}=k\lambda(k=1)$,式中 $\frac{\lambda}{2}$ 为附加光程差(半波损失)。

答案:B

2-3-6 **解**:$\Delta\Phi=\frac{2\pi\delta}{\lambda}$($\delta$ 指光程差),依本题题意 $\delta=nL$,即 $\Delta\Phi=\frac{2\pi nL}{\lambda}$。

答案:C

2-3-7 **解**:同一明纹(暗纹)对应相同厚度的空气层,间距为$\frac{\lambda}{2\sin\theta}$。

答案:C

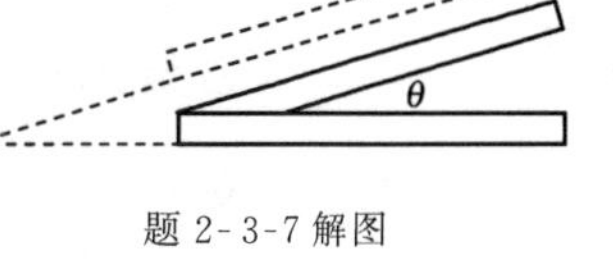

题 2-3-7 解图

2-3-8 **解**:$\theta\approx\frac{e}{L}$(e 为空气层厚度),$\Delta\theta=\frac{\Delta e}{L}$,又相邻两明(暗)纹对应的空气层厚度差 $\Delta e=e_{k+1}-e_k=\frac{\lambda}{2}$。

答案:A

2-3-9 **解**:$a\sin\varphi=k\lambda=2k\ \frac{\lambda}{2}$,今 $a\sin30°=4\times\frac{\lambda}{2}$。

答案:B

2-3-10 **解**:由 $a\sin\varphi=k\lambda$(暗纹),知 $a\sin\varphi=3\lambda$,现 $a'\sin\varphi=\frac{3}{2}\lambda(a'=\frac{a}{2})$,应满足明纹条件,即 $a'\sin\varphi=\frac{3}{2}\lambda=(2k+1)\frac{\lambda}{2}\Rightarrow k=1$。

答案:B

2-3-11 **解**:最小分辨角 $\delta\varphi=1.22\frac{\lambda}{D}$,两车灯对瞳孔中心张角为$\frac{\Delta x(\text{车灯距})}{L(\text{人车距离})}$,故

$$1.22\frac{\lambda}{D(\text{孔径})}=\frac{\Delta x}{L},L=\frac{D\times\Delta x}{1.22\times\lambda}=\frac{5\times10^{-3}\times1.2}{1.22\times0.5\times10^{-6}}\approx10\times10^{3}\,\text{m}$$

答案:A

2-3-12 **解**:由 $I=I_0\cos^2\alpha$,并注意到"自然光通过偏振片后,光强减半",则

$$I=\frac{I_0}{2}\cos^2 60^\circ\cos^2 30^\circ=\frac{3I_0}{32}$$

答案:B

2-3-13 **解**:自然光以布儒斯特角入射,反射光为垂直于入射面的线偏振光,折射光(透射光束)为部分偏振光。

答案:C

2-3-14 **解**:如解图所示,按临界角的概念,光必须从光密介质射向光疏介质才可能发生全反射,即$\frac{\sin45^\circ}{\sin90^\circ}=\frac{n_1}{n_2}$,而光从空气射向介质时,布儒斯特角应满足 $\tan i_0=\frac{n_2}{n_1}$,故 $\tan i_0=\frac{n_2}{n_1}=\frac{1}{\sin45^\circ}=\sqrt{2},i_0=54.7^\circ$。

空气 n_1

介质 n_2

题 2-3-14 解图

答案:D

2-3-15 **解**:注意到光栅常数 $a+b=\frac{1}{800}\text{mm}$,由 $(a+b)\sin\varphi=k\lambda,\frac{1}{800}\sin30^\circ=1\times\lambda,1\mu\text{m}=10^{-6}\text{m}$。

答案:A

2-3-16 **解**:由 $(a+b)\sin\varphi=k\lambda$,令 $2\times10^{-6}\sin90^\circ=k\times0.55\times10^{-6},k=3.6$,$k$ 只能取整数。

答案:B

2-3-17 **解**:由 $\tan i_0=\frac{n_2}{n_1}$,又 $i_0+\gamma_0=90^\circ,\tan60^\circ=n_2$。

答案:C

第三章 普通化学

复习指导

一、考试大纲

3.1 物质的结构和物质状态

原子结构的近代概念；原子轨道和电子云；原子核外电子分布；原子和离子的电子结构；原子结构和元素周期律；元素周期表；周期、族；元素性质及氧化物及其酸碱性。离子键的特征；共价键的特征和类型；杂化轨道与分子空间构型；分子结构式；键的极性和分子的极性；分子间力与氢键；理想气体状态方程；分压定律；晶体与非晶体；晶体类型与物质性质。

3.2 溶液

溶液的浓度；非电解质稀溶液通性；渗透压；弱电解质溶液的解离平衡；解离常数；同离子效应；缓冲溶液；水的离子积及溶液的 pH 值；盐类的水解及溶液的酸碱性；溶度积常数；溶度积规则。

3.3 化学反应速率及化学平衡

反应热与热化学方程式；化学反应速率；温度和反应物浓度对反应速率的影响；活化能的物理意义；催化剂；化学反应方向的判断；化学平衡的特征；化学平衡移动原理。

3.4 氧化还原反应与电化学

氧化还原的概念；氧化剂与还原剂；氧化还原电对；氧化还原反应方程式的配平；原电池的组成和符号；电极反应与电池反应；标准电极电势；电极电势的影响因素及应用；金属腐蚀与防护。

3.5 有机化学

有机物特点、分类及命名；官能团及分子构造式；同分异构；有机物的重要反应：加成、取代、消除、氧化、催化加氢、聚合反应、加聚与缩聚；基本有机物的结构、基本性质及用途：烷烃、烯烃、炔烃、芳烃、卤代烃、醇、苯酚、醛和酮、羧酸、酯；合成材料：高分子化合物、塑料、合成橡胶、合成纤维、工程塑料。

二、复习指导

普通化学中基本概念和基本理论较多，而计算方面的问题比较简单，所以在复习时应特别注意对基本概念及理论的理解。

（一）物质结构和物质状态

本节内容多、概念多，考生复习时不易掌握。若将其分类，可包括以下两个方面的内容。

1.原子结构

核外电子到底是如何运动的？它涉及原子轨道、波函数、量子数、电子云等基本概念。考生必须明确一个波函数就是一个原子轨道，它由三个量子数（n、l、m）正确组合来决定，在每个轨道上只能容纳二个自旋相反的电子(即 $m_s=\pm\frac{1}{2}$)，在此基础上才能进行包括原子、离子的核外电子排布，进一步了解原子核外电子的排布与周期表的关系，以及元素性质、元素氧化物及其水合物酸碱性的递变规律。

2. 化学键与晶体结构

$$
\text{化学键}\begin{cases}\text{离子键——离子晶体}\\ \text{共价键——}\begin{cases}\text{分子晶体}\\ \text{原子晶体}\end{cases}\\ \text{金属键——金属晶体}\end{cases}
$$

(1)不同的化学键有不同的形成和特征。例如共价键：①形成；②特征；③类型；④键的极性和分子的极性。

(2)不同的晶体结构有不同的物理特性。

(3)分子间力与氢键。

(4)杂化轨道理论，这部分内容是难点但不是重点，只要求对给出的分子能确定它的杂化类型和分子的空间构型即可。

本节其余部分作为一般了解。

(二)溶液

溶液中包括溶质和溶剂。

溶液的浓度是指一定量溶剂(或溶液)中含有的溶质量，常用的有“物质的量”浓度和质量摩尔浓度。

溶剂可以是水、乙醇、苯、四氯化碳等。

溶质按其在水中是否电离分电解质和非电解质，本节讨论非电解质稀溶液的通性。

电解质按其电离的程度分强电解质和弱电解质，本节讨论弱电解质的电离平衡及其移动。

电解质按其溶解的程度分易溶电解质和难溶电解质，本节讨论后者的溶解平衡及其移动。

1. 稀溶液的通性

稀溶液的通性是指难挥发非电解质的稀溶液的蒸气压下降、沸点升高、凝固点下降以及渗透压等。计算不是重点，但对浓溶液和电解质溶液要求会定性分析。

2. 电离平衡、溶解平衡及其移动

这是本节的重点。内容较多，但不难掌握，可按以下思路复习。

(1)电离平衡

①弱电解质的电离平衡；

②水的离子积及 pH 值；

③水解平衡。

以上要求掌握电离平衡常数的表达式，它与电离度的关系，溶液的 C_{H^+}、C_{OH^-} 和 pH 值的计算。

(2)电离平衡的移动

①单相同离子效应；

②缓冲溶液：缓冲溶液的组成、溶液 pH 值的计算。

(3)溶解平衡

①溶度积(K_{sp})；

②溶度积与溶解度(S)的关系；

③溶度积规则及应用。

(三)化学反应速率和化学平衡

本节讨论三个问题,重点是后两者。同时提出几个要点:

1.书写热化学方程式时注意物质的状态、反应条件、计量系数,$\Delta H<0$ 为放热;$\Delta H>0$ 为吸热。

2.平均速率与瞬时速率均能表示反应速率,但以不同物质的浓度变化表示反应速率时其数值不一定相等。

3.影响速率的因素主要有物质的本性(对给定反应体现在活化能上)、反应温度、反应物浓度及催化剂。

(1)浓度的影响

除必须掌握质量作用定律以外,还要明确基元反应,非基元反应、反应级数、速度常数等基本概念。

(2)温度的影响

主要反应在温度对速度常数的影响上,公式不用死记,但温度升高时速率常数升高、反应速度增加的结论必须掌握,而且这结论对吸热反应、放热反应、正反应的速率常数、逆反应的速率常数均适用。

(3)催化剂的影响

使用催化剂能降低活化能从而提高反应速率。明确活化能、活化分子等概念,反应热与正、逆反应活化能的关系。

4.化学平衡

除明确平衡时的特征外,还必须写出平衡时的特征常数——平衡常数表达式。掌握平衡常数物理意义、影响因素、特征和应用。

在化学平衡的移动方面,掌握浓度、温度、压强改变对移动的影响。

总之除掌握质量作用定律表达式和平衡常数表达式外,还要掌握浓度、温度、压力、催化剂对速率、速率常数、平衡常数及平衡移动的影响。

(四)氧化还原与电化学

本节没有难点,基本概念与要记忆的较多,要求掌握以下五个方面。

1.基本概念

如氧化数、氧化剂、还原剂、氧化反应、还原反应等,以及它们之间的关系。如:

氧化剂在发生还原反应过程中氧化数降低。

还原剂在发生氧化反应过程中氧化数升高。

2.原电池

自发的氧化还原反应(即原电池中的电池反应)可以组成原电池,原电池中有正、负极,两极上发生不同的电极反应。原电池的电动势 $E=\varphi_{正}-\varphi_{负}$,最后落实到原电池符号。

3.电极电势

影响电极电势的因素中,温度的影响一般不大,常将温度定在 298K;浓度、介质与物质的本性对电极电势的影响,可从能斯特方程看出。例如半反应

$$MnO_4^- + 8H^+ + 5e \rightleftharpoons Mn^{2+} + 4H_2O$$

能斯特方程为

$$\varphi_{MnO_4^-/Mn^{2+}} = \varphi^{\ominus}_{MnO_4^-/Mn^{2+}} + \frac{0.059}{5}\lg\frac{C_{MnO_4^-} \cdot C_{H^+}^8}{C_{Mn^{2+}}}$$

由上式可见氧化态的浓度升高、介质的酸度升高，能使电极电势升高。至于物质本性的影响体现在 $\varphi^{\ominus}$ 数值的大小上。

电极电势应用很广，可用来判断原电池的正、负极；氧化剂、还原剂的相对强弱；氧化还原反应的方向和进行的程度。

4. 电解

电解池中发生的氧化还原反应是不自发的，因此电解池中两极名称、两极反应不同于原电池，除要掌握这些之外，还要明确分解电压、超电势的概念及形成的原因，判断电解的产物。

5. 金属腐蚀及防止

了解电化学腐蚀的目的是如何防止金属的腐蚀。

（五）有机化合物

重点掌握：

(1)有机物的特点、分类和命名。

(2)有机物的重要反应包括取代、加成、消去、氧化还原、加聚、缩聚反应和定位效应、不对称加成规则及查氏规则。

(3)重要的高分子材料，如 PVC、ABS、环氧树脂、橡胶等。

第一节 物质结构和物质状态

物质结构与性质之间有着必然的联系，要深入了解物质的宏观性质，必须探究其微观性质。分子是保持物质化学性质的最小微粒，由原子组成。所以本节主要学习原子结构理论，在此基础上，讨论分子结构和晶体结构的基本内容。

一、原子核外电子排布

（一）核外电子运动的特性

核外电子运动具有两大特性，即量子化和波粒二象性，这也是一切实物微粒运动的共同特性。

1. 能量的量子化

实验证明，辐射能的吸收和发射只能是一小份一小份的，是不连续的。这一小份不连续能量的基本单位叫量子。物质吸收或发射能量只能是量子的整数倍。量子的能量 E 与频率 ν 成正比。即

$$E=h\nu \tag{3-1-1}$$

式中，h 为普朗克常数，等于 $6.626\times10^{-34}\,\mathrm{J\cdot s}$。

原子中电子的能量是量子化的，当电子从高能量状态 $E_{高}$ 跃迁到低能量状态 $E_{低}$ 时，就以光量子的形式发射能量；反之吸收能量，其频率为

$$\nu=\frac{E_{高}-E_{低}}{h} \tag{3-1-2}$$

由于电子的能量是量子化的，所以光量子的能量和波长也是不连续的，这就是原子光谱是线状的原因所在。

2. 波粒二象性

一切实物微粒（光子、电子、中子、质子等）运动时，既有粒子的性质又有波的性质，即为

波粒二象性。电子在核外运动也有波粒二象性。粒子性表现在电子与实物相互作用时有能量的吸收或发射，如能量 E 和动量 p；波动性表现在电子在传播过程中有干涉和衍射现象，如波长 λ 和频率 ν。

波粒二象性的内在联系是

$$E=h\nu \tag{3-1-3}$$

$$p=h/\lambda \tag{3-1-4}$$

$$\lambda=h/p=h/m\nu \tag{3-1-5}$$

式中，m 为实物粒子的质量；ν 为实物粒子的运动速度；p 为动量。

此式就是著名的德布罗意(de Broglie)关系式，它把微观粒子的粒子性和波动性统一起来。人们把这种与微观粒子相联系的波，叫做德布罗意波或物质波。

3. 测不准原理

宏观物体运动时，人们可以依据经典物理定律准确确定其在任何指定时刻的位置和速度。而对于微观粒子则不同，对运动中的微观粒子来说，不可能同时准确确定它的位置和动量。这就是海森堡(Heisenberg)不确定原理。其关系式为

$$\Delta p \cdot \Delta x \geqslant h/4\pi \tag{3-1-6}$$

式中，Δp 为微观粒子动量的不确定度；Δx 为微观粒子位置的不确定度。

它表明，微观粒子位置的不确定度 Δx 越小，相应它的动量的不确定度 Δp 就越大。对电子来说，当电子位置确定的误差越小，相应的动量的测定误差就越大，反之亦然。也就是说，电子的位置若能准确的测定，其动量就不可能准确的测定。电子运动有它特殊的规律。

(二)核外电子运动状态的描述

可用波函数和电子云来描述核外电子运动的状态。

1. 波函数与原子轨道

描述核外电子运动规律的方程叫薛定谔方程，对单电子体系该方程可写成下列形式

$$\frac{\partial^2 \psi}{\partial x^2}+\frac{\partial^2 \psi}{\partial y^2}+\frac{\partial^2 \psi}{\partial z^2}+\frac{8\pi^2 m}{h^2}(E-V)\psi=0 \tag{3-1-7}$$

式中，ψ 为描述电子运动情况的波函数，m 为电子质量，E 为电子的总能量，V 为电子的势能。

求解该方程，可得到波函数 ψ 和总能量 E。在求解过程中必须引入三种量子数 n、l、m，才能解出一系列符合量子数条件的波函数 ψ_1、ψ_2、…，以及相应的能量 E_1、E_2、…。

波函数是描述波的数学函数式，表示核外电子的运动状态；波函数是空间坐标的函数 $\psi(x,y,z)$ 或 $\psi(\gamma,\theta,\Phi)$。在量子力学里，将描述原子中单个电子运动状态的函数式称为波函数，习惯上又称为原子轨道。每一个波函数代表核外电子的一种运动状态，表示一个原子轨道。所以不同波函数 $\psi_{n、l、m}$ 就可以表示电子在核外出现的不同原子轨道或运动状态。

2. 量子数

波函数 ψ 是描述原子处于定态时电子运动状态的数学函数式。求解薛定谔方程时，要得到合理的波函数解，要求方程中的一些参数满足一定的条件，为此引进取分立值的三个参数(量子数)，即主量子数 n、角量子数 l、磁量子数 m。三个量子数取值不是任意的，有一定限制条件。一组允许的量子数 n、l、m 取值对应一个合理的波函数 $\psi_{n,l,m}$，即可以确定一个原子轨道。电子除轨道运动外，还有自旋运动，所以，描述一个电子的运动状态除以上三个量子数外，还需第四个量子数，即自旋量子数 m_s。量子数的物理意义及取值的限制描述如下：

(1)主量子数 n

n 的取值：$n=1,2,3,\cdots$，目前稳定原子中 n 最大为 7。

n 的意义：

①代表电子层，$n=1,2,\cdots$，分别为第一电子层，第二电子层，……，分别用 K，L，M，N，…表示；

②代表电子离核的平均距离（$r \propto n^2$）；

③决定原子轨道的能级（$E \propto n$）。

所以 n 越大能级越高（$E_1<E_2<E_3<\cdots$），电子离核的平均距离越远（$r_1<r_2<r_3<\cdots$）。

(2)角量子数 l

l 的取值：$l=0,1,2,\cdots,n-1$，目前 l 最大为 3。

n 与 l 的关系为：$n=1,l=0$；$n=2,l=0,1$；$n=3,l=0,1,2$；$n=4,l=0,1,2,3,\cdots$

l 的意义：

①表示电子亚层，$l=0,1,2,3$，分别为 s，p，d，f 亚层，其轨道分别叫 s，p，d，f 轨道，轨道上的电子分别叫 s，p，d，f 电子。

②确定轨道的形状：$l=0,1,2,\cdots$，轨道的形状分别为球形、双球形、四橄榄形……。

③在多电子原子中 l 还决定亚层的能量，当 n 一定时，l 越大亚层能量也越大，同一亚层的原子轨道能量相等，故叫等价（简并）轨道。

(3)磁量子数 m

m 的取值：$m=0,\pm1,\pm2,\pm3,\cdots,\pm l$，由于 l 最大为 3，所以 m 只有前 7 个取值。

l 与 m 的关系为：$l=0,m=0$；$l=1,m=0,\pm1$；$l=2,m=0,\pm1$、±2；$l=3,m=0,\pm1,\pm2,\pm3$。

m 的意义：

①确定轨道在空间的取向。

②确定亚层中轨道的数目。m 的每一个取值代表轨道在空间的一种取向，即一条轨道。如 $l=1$ 的 p 亚层，m 为 0，±1 三个取值，所以 p 亚层在空间有三种取向，有三条 p 轨道。

③在无外加磁场的情况下，轨道能量与 m 无关。

(4)自旋量子数 m_s

m_s 决定电子自旋方向，可取 $+\frac{1}{2}$ 和 $-\frac{1}{2}$ 两个值。每一套（n,l,m），m_s 可取 $\pm\frac{1}{2}$ 两个值。

量子数与核外电子运动状态列于表 3-1-1。

量子数与核外电子运动状态 表 3-1-1

主量子数 n	主层符号	角量子数 l	亚层符号	磁量子数 m	亚层轨道数	电子层中轨道数	自旋量子数 m_s	电子层中电子容量
1	K	0	1s	0	1	1	±1/2	2
2	L	0	2s	0	1	4	±1/2	8
		1	2p	0，±1	3		±1/2	
3	M	0	3s	0	1	9	±1/2	18
		1	3p	0，±1	3		±1/2	
		2	3d	0，±1，±2	5		±1/2	
4	N	0	4s	0	1	16	±1/2	32
		1	4p	0，±1	3		±1/2	
		2	4d	0，±1，±2	5		±1/2	
		3	4f	0，±1，±2，±3	7		±1/2	

【例 3-1-1】 下列量子数正确组合的是：

A. $n=1,l=1,m=0$　　B. $n=2,l=0,m=1$

C. $n=3,l=2,m=3$　　D. $n=4,l=3,m=2$

解　三个量子数取值不是任意的，一组正确的量子数 n、l、m 取值对应一个合理波函数，即可以确定一个原子轨道。n 的取值：$n=1,2,3,\cdots$，目前稳定原子中 n 最大为 7；l 的取值：$l=0,1,2,\cdots,n-1$，目前 l 最大为 3；m 的取值：$m=0,\pm1,\pm2,\pm3,\cdots,\pm l$，由于 l 最大为 3，所以 m 只有前 7 个取值。

答案：D

【例 3-1-2】 量子数 $n=4,l=2,m=0$ 的原子轨道数目是：

A. 1　　B. 2　　C. 3　　D. 4

解　一组允许的量子数 n、l、m 取值对应一个合理的波函数，即可以确定一个原子轨道。量子数 $n=4,l=2,m=0$ 为一组合理的量子数，确定一个原子轨道。

答案：A

【例 3-1-3】 决定原子轨道取向的量子数和确定原子轨道形状的量子数分别是：

A. 主量子数、角量子数　　B. 角量子数、磁量子数

C. 磁量子数、角量子数　　D. 自旋量子数、主量子数

解　三个量子数的物理意义分别为：

主量子数 n：①代表电子层；②代表电子离原子核的平均距离；③决定原子轨道的能量。

角量子数 l：①表示电子亚层；②确定原子轨道形状；③在多电子原子中决定亚层能量。

磁量子数 m：①确定原子轨道在空间的取向；②确定亚层中轨道数目。

答案：C

【例 3-1-4】 多电子原子中同一电子层原子轨道能级（量）最高的亚层是：

A. s 亚层　　B. p 亚层

C. d 亚层　　D. f 亚层

解　多电子原子中原子轨道的能级取决于主量子数 n 和角量子数 l：主量子数 n 相同时，l 越大，能量越高；角量子数 l 相同时，n 越大，能量越高。n 决定原子轨道所处的电子层数，l 决定原子轨道所处亚层（$l=0$ 为 s 亚层，$l=1$ 为 p 亚层，$l=2$ 为 d 亚层，$l=3$ 为 f 亚层）。同一电子层中的原子轨道 n 相同，l 越大，能量越高。

答案：D

3. 概率密度与电子云

概率是核外电子在空间出现的机会。概率密度是电子在核外空间某处单位体积内出现的概率。根据实验和理论的研究已经证实，电子的概率密度等于波函数的平方，即 ψ^2。为了形象地表示电子在原子中的概率密度分布情况，在化学上引入电子云的概念。电子云是用黑点的疏密度来表示核外空间各点电子概率密度大小的具体图像。例如基态氢原子的 1s 电子云呈球状。

4. 原子轨道和电子云的角度分布图

用数学方法把 $\psi(\gamma,\theta,\Phi)$ 分成两个函数的乘积，即

$$\psi(\gamma,\theta,\Phi)=R(r)\cdot Y(\theta,\Phi) \tag{3-1-8}$$

式中：$R(r)$——波函数的径向分布部分；

$Y(\theta,\Phi)$——波函数的角度分布部分。

角度分布图：波函数的角度分布部分（Y）随角度（θ,Φ）变化的图形。原子轨道和电子云的

角度分布平面示意图见图 3-1-1 和图 3-1-2。两图的作法、外形和空间取向相似，区别在于前者比后者“胖”些；前者有“＋”、“－”之分，后者则没有。

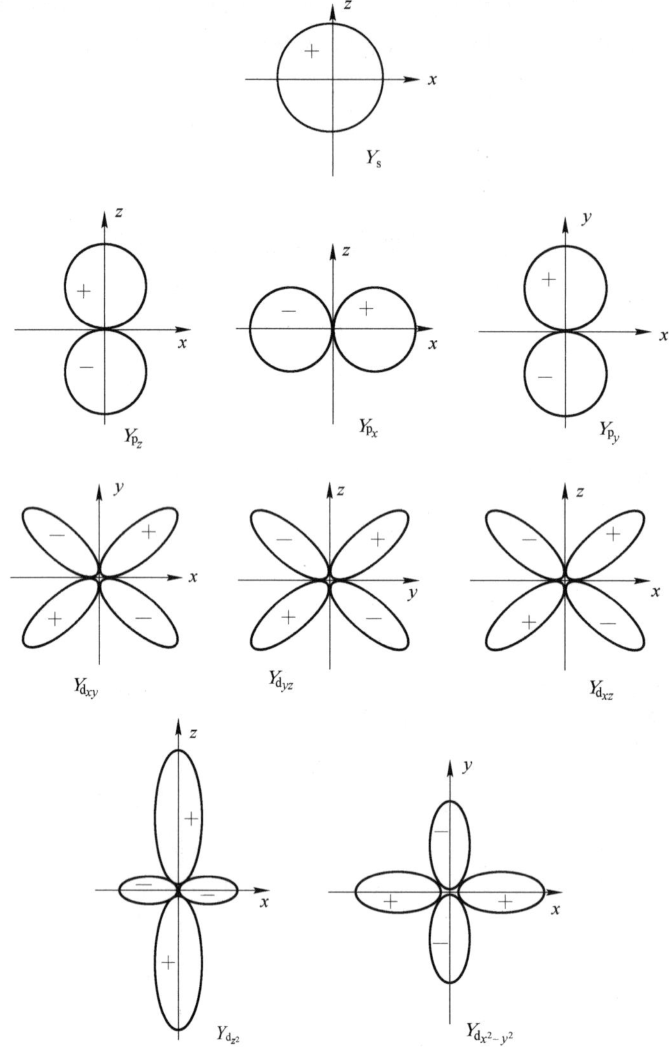

图 3-1-1　s、p、d 原子轨道角度分布平面示意图

(三)核外电子的分布

1. 原子轨道的近似能级顺序

在多电子原子中，原子轨道的能级不仅与主量子数有关，与角量子数也有关系。我国化学家徐光宪教授，根据光谱试验数据的结果归纳出一个近似规律：在多电子原子中各原子轨道的能量由 $n+0.7l$ 来决定，数值越大，能量越高，见表 3-1-2。

多电子原子的能级顺序　　表 3-1-2

轨道符号	1s	2s	2p	3s	3p	4s	3d	4p	5s	4d	5p	6s	4f	5d	6p	7s	5f	…
$n+0.7l$	1.0	2.0	2.7	3.0	3.7	4.0	4.4	4.7	5.0	5.4	5.7	6.0	6.1	6.4	6.7	7.0	7.1	
能级高低顺序	⟶ 从左到右、依次升高																	

由表 3-1-2 可知：

(1)当 l 不变时，E 随 n 增大而增大。如 $E_{1s}<E_{2s}<E_{3s}<\cdots$，$E_{2p}<E_{3p}<E_{4p}<\cdots$。

(2)当 n 不变时，E 随 l 增大而增大。如 $E_{4s}<E_{4p}<E_{4d}<E_{4f}$。

(3)当 n、l 均变化时，出现能级交错。如 $E_{4s}<E_{3d}<E_{4p}$，$E_{5s}<E_{4d}<E_{5p}$，$E_{6s}<E_{4f}<E_{5d}<E_{6p}$。

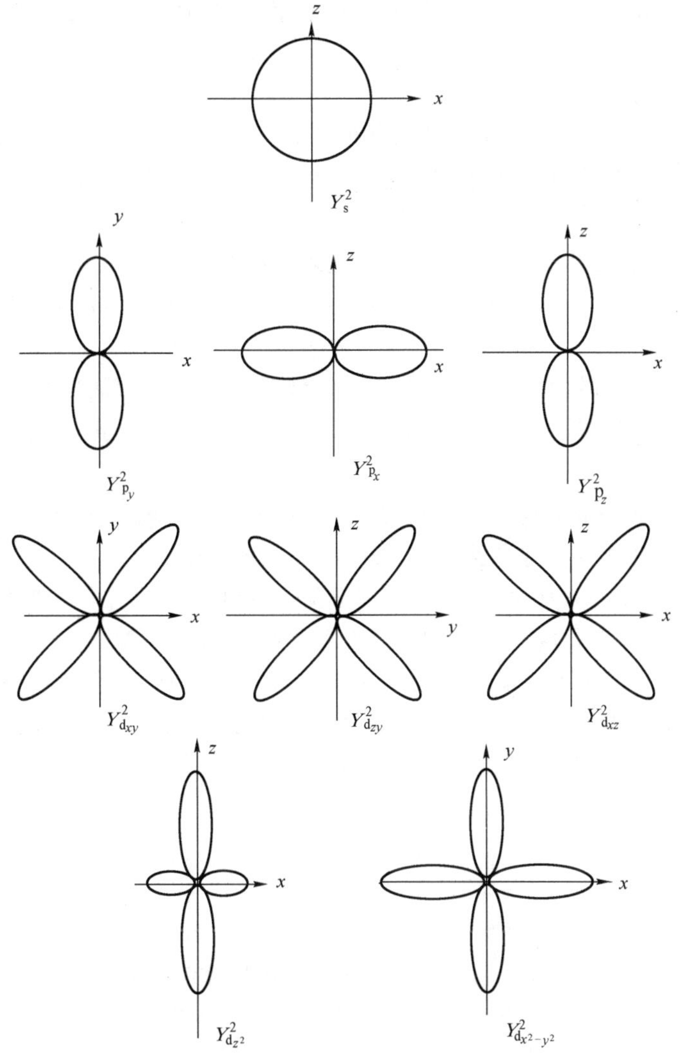

图 3-1-2　s、p、d 电子云角度分布平面示意图

2. 屏蔽效应

在多电子原子中，核电荷(Z)对某个电子的吸引力，由于其他电子对该电子的排斥而被削弱的作用称为屏蔽效应，若削弱部分为 σ(叫屏蔽常数)，则有效核电荷 $Z^*=Z-\sigma$。屏蔽作用越大，核电荷减小越多，核对电子的引力越小，电子能级越高，屏蔽作用的大小为 K>L>M>N…，所以当 l 相同时，能级随 n 增大而升高。

3. 钻穿效应

外层电子穿过内层钻入核附近，减少内层电子对它的屏蔽作用而使能级降低的现象称为钻穿效应。钻穿效应越大，轨道能级越低。钻穿效应的大小顺序为 ns>np>nd>nf，所以当 n 不变时，轨道能级随 l 增大而升高。

至于能量出现交错如 $E_{4s}<E_{3d}$，是因为 4s 电子钻穿效应比 3d 大，受其他电子的屏蔽作用小，故使得 4s 电子的能级比 3d 还低。同理可解释 $E_{6s}<E_{4f}<E_{5d}<E_{6p}$。

4. 核外电子排布的规则

原子中的电子按一定规则排布在各原子轨道上。人们根据原子光谱实验和量子力学理论，总结出三个排布原则：泡利不相容原理、能量最低原理和洪特规则。

(1)泡利不相容原理

在同一原子中，不可能有四个量子数完全相同的两个电子存在。每一个轨道上最多只能容纳两个自旋相反的电子。每个电子层中电子的最大容量为 $2n^2$。

(2)能量最低原理

电子总是尽先占据能级较低的轨道。电子进入轨道的先后顺序为：ns、($n-2$)f、($n-1$)d、np，即按 1s，2s、2p，3s、3p，4s、3d、4p，5s、4d、5p，6s、4f、5d、6p，7s、5f、6d、7p 的顺序填充。

(3)洪特规则

在等价轨道(如 3 个 p 轨道、5 个 d 轨道、7 个 f 轨道)上，电子尽可能分占不同的轨道，而且自旋方向相同。同一电子亚层，电子处于全充满(p^6、d^{10}、f^{14})、半充满(p^3、d^5、f^7)状态时较稳定。

5. 核外电子分布式和外层电子分布式

原子的核外电子分布式是电子按 n 和 l 增大的顺序在各个轨道上分布的式子。例如，25 号元素 Mn 原子的核外电子分布式为 $1s^2 2s^2 2p^6 3s^2 3p^6 3d^5 4s^2$。

外层电子(价电子)是指那些对元素性质有显著影响的电子，它们在各个轨道上分布的式子叫做外层电子分布式，或外层(价层)电子构型。例如，Mn 的外层电子构型为 $3d^5 4s^2$，又如 K 是 $4s^1$。

原子得到或失去电子后便是离子。应当指出，当原子失去电子而成为正离子时，一般是能量较高的最外层的电子先失去，而且往往引起电子层数的减少。原子成为负离子时，原子所得的电子总是分布在它的最外电子层上。Mo^{2+} 和 I^- 离子的核外电子分布式及外层电子分布式为：

离子	离子的核外电子分布式	离子的外层电子分布式
Mo^{2+}	$1s^2 2s^2 2p^6 3s^2 3p^6 3d^{10} 4s^2 4p^6 4d^4$	$4s^2 4p^6 4d^4$
I^-	$1s^2 2s^2 2p^6 3s^2 3p^6 3d^{10} 4s^2 4p^6 4d^{10} 5s^2 5p^6$	$5s^2 5p^6$

正确书写核外电子分布式，可先根据三个分布规则和近似能级顺序将电子依次填入相应轨道，再按电子层顺序整理一下分布式，按 n 由小到大自左向右排列各原子轨道，相同电子层的轨道排在一起。

例如，4s 轨道的能级比 3d 轨道低，在填入电子时，先填入 4s，后填入 3d，但 4s 是比 3d 更外层的轨道，因而在正确书写原子的电子分布式时，3d 总是写在 4s 前面。

例如，第 29 号元素铜，Cu $1s^2 2s^2 2p^6 3s^2 3p^6 3d^{10} 4s^1$。

对于核外电子比较多的元素，由光谱测定的核外电子分布，并不完全与理论预测的一致。对于这些特例，应以实验事实为准。

二、原子结构与元素周期律

原子核外电子分布的周期性是元素周期律的基础，元素周期表是周期律的表现形式。

(一)核外电子的排布与元素周期表的关系

首先分析周期表中各元素最后一个电子填充的电子亚层，见表 3-1-3。

电子填充与周期表的关系 表 3-1-3

周期	IA IIA	IIIB～VIIB、VIII、IB、IIB	IIIA～0	元素的数目	电子填充的亚层	最高主量子数 n	原子的电子层数
1	$1s^1$		$1s^2$	2	1s	1	1
2	$2s^{1\sim2}$		$2p^{1\sim6}$	8	2s、2p	2	2
3	$3s^{1\sim2}$		$3p^{1\sim6}$	8	3s、3p	3	3
4	$4s^{1\sim2}$	$3d^{1\sim10}4s^{1\sim2}$	$4p^{1\sim6}$	18	4s、3d、4p	4	4
5	$5s^{1\sim2}$	$4d^{1\sim10}5s^{1\sim2}$	$5p^{1\sim6}$	18	5s、4d、5p	5	5
6	$6s^{1\sim2}$	$4f^{1\sim14}5d^{1\sim10}6s^{1\sim2}$	$6p^{1\sim6}$	32	6s、4f、5d、6p	6	6

由表 3-1-3 可看到：

(1)在周期表中各同周期或同族元素的外层电子排布是有规律的。如同主族元素，原子的最外层电子数相等；同周期主族元素最外层电子数由 1 逐渐增加到 8 个电子。

(2)核外电子排布与划分周期有关。如元素所在周期数等于该元素原子的电子层数，等于原子中最高主量子数。

(3)核外电子排布与族的关系，由表 3-1-3 可见：

主族、IB 和 IIB 的族数等于($ns+np$)层上的电子数，n 为最高主量子数。

IIIB～VIIB 的族数等于[$(n-1)d+ns$]层上的电子数。

VIII 族元素的电子数为[$(n-1)d+ns$]层上的电子数，即 8～10 个电子。

(4)元素在周期表中的分区：

s 区：包括 IA、IIA 族元素。外层电子构型为 ns^1 和 ns^2(n 是最高主量子数)。

p 区：包括 IIIA 至 VIIA 和零族元素。外层电子构型为 ns^2np^1 至 ns^2np^6(He 为 $1s^2$)。

d 区：包括 IIIB 至 VIIB 和 VIII 族元素。外层电子构型一般为 $(n-1)d^1ns^2$ 至 $(n-1)d^8ns^2$，但有例外。

ds 区：包括 IB、IIB 族元素。外层电子构型为 $(n-1)d^{10}ns^1$ 和 $(n-1)d^{10}ns^2$。d 区和 ds 区元素叫过渡元素。

f 区：包括镧系中的 57～71 号元素和锕系中的 89～103 号元素。外层电子构型为 $(n-2)f^{0\sim14}(n-1)d^{0\sim2}ns^2$。

【例 3-1-5】 锰原子的核外电子排布式为 $1s^22s^22p^63s^23p^63d^54s^2$，锰所在的：(1)周期数为(　　)；(2)族数为(　　)。

(1)　A. 2　B. 4　C. 3　D. 5

(2)　A. VIIA　B. IIA　C. VIIB　D. IIB

解　周期数为最高主量子数；价电子构型 $3d^54s^2$，为 d 区副族元素，族数为价电子数。

答案：(1)B；(2)C

【例 3-1-6】 下列基态原子的核外电子分布式错误的是：

A. $1s^22s^22p^63s^23p^3$　B. $1s^22s^22p^63s^13p^1$

C. $1s^22s^22p^63s^23p^4$　D. $1s^22s^22p^63s^23p^5$

解　3s 轨道未满，不是基态分布。

答案：B

(二)周期表中元素性质的递变规律

元素的性质决定于原子结构。由于原子的电子层结构呈周期性变化，所以元素的基本性质如原子半径、电离能、电子亲和能、电负性等也呈周期性变化，元素的化合物如氧化物及其水合物的酸碱性也呈递变性规律变化。

1. 原子半径

原子半径包括共价半径、金属半径、范德华半径。共价半径是同种元素的两原子以共价单键结合时两原子核间距的一半；金属半径是金属晶体中相邻两原子核间距的一半；在分子晶体中，分子间是以范德华力结合的。例如稀有气体形成的单原子分子晶体中，两个同种原子核间距离的一半就是范德华半径。

在周期表中，原子半径的变化规律为：同一周期主族元素从左到右有效核电荷 E^* 依次增加，原子半径依次减小，副族元素的原子半径略有减小；同一族元素从上到下，主族元素原子半径递增，副族元素略有增大但不明显，特别是五、六周期的元素，由于镧系收缩使得它们的原子半径相差很小。

2. 电离能(I)

定义：基态的气态原子失去一个电子形成+1价气态离子所需要的最低能量为该原子的第一电离能(I_1)；从+1价气态离子再失去一个电子形成+2价气态离子时所需最低能量为第二电离能(I_2)；依此类推。随失去电子数的增加，电离能依次增加，即 $I_1 < I_2 < I_3 < \cdots$。通常所说的电离能是指 I_1，单位为 kJ/mol。

变化规律：同一周期从左到右，主族元素的有效核电荷数依次增加，原子半径依次减小，电离能依次增大；同一主族元素从上到下原子半径依次增大，电离能依次减小，副族元素的变化不如主族元素那样有规律。

意义：电离能可用来衡量单个气态原子失去电子的难易程度。元素的电离能越小，越易失去电子，金属性越强。

3. 电子亲和能(Y)

基态的气态原子得到一个电子形成-1价气态离子所放出的能量称为该元素的电子亲和能。电子亲和能越大，越容易获得电子，元素的非金属性越强。

4. 电负性(X)

为了衡量分子中各原子吸引电子的能力，泡利在1932年引入了电负性的概念。电负性数值越大，表明原子在分子中吸引电子的能力越强；电负性数值越小，表明原子在分子中吸引电子的能力越弱。元素的电负性较全面反映了元素的金属性和非金属性的强弱。

变化规律：同一周期从左到右，主族元素的电负性逐渐增大；同一主族从上到下元素的电负性逐渐减小。副族元素的电负性规律性较差。金属元素的电负性一般小于2.0(金和铂除外)；非金属元素的电负性一般大于2.0(硅除外)。

【例 3-1-7】 下列元素，电负性最大的是：

A. F　　B. Cl　　C. Br　　D. I

解 周期表中元素电负性的递变规律：同一周期从左到右，主族元素的电负性逐渐增大；同一主族从上到下元素的电负性逐渐减小。

答案：A

【例 3-1-8】 下列几种元素中原子半径最小的是：

A. Na　　B. Al　　C. F　　D. Bi

解 原子半径的变化规律为：同一周期主族元素从左到右原子半径依次减小，同一主族元素从上到下原子半径依次增加。Na、Al、P、Cl是同一周期主族元素，原子半径 Na > Al>P

>Cl;P 和 Bi 是同一主族元素，原子半径 Bi>P;F 和 Cl 是同一主族元素，原子半径 Cl>F。所以题中四个元素原子半径最小的是 F。

答案:C

5. 对角线规则和镧系收缩

在 s 区和 p 区元素中，除了同族元素的性质相似外，还有一些元素及其化合物的性质呈现出“对角线”相似性。所谓对角线相似，即 IA 族的 Li 与 IIA 族的 Mg、IIA 族的 Be 与 IIIA 族的 Al、IIIA 族的 B 与 IVA 族的 Si，这三对元素在周期表中处于对角线位置，相应的两元素及其化合物的性质有许多相似之处。这种相似性称为对角线规则。

镧系元素的原子半径和离子半径的递变趋势是随着原子序数的增大而缓慢的减小，这种现象称为镧系收缩。随着原子序数的增加，镧系元素的原子半径虽然只是缓慢的变小，但是经过从 La 到 Yb 的 14 种元素的原子半径递减的积累却减小了 14pm 之多，从而造成了镧系后边 Lu，Hf 和 Ta 的原子半径与同族的 Y，Zr 和 Nb 的原子半径极为接近。

(三)元素的氧化物及其水合物酸碱性递变规律

1. 分类

(1)碱性氧化物——活泼金属的氧化物。

(2)酸性氧化物——主要是非金属氧化物。

(3)两性氧化物——主要是 Be、Al、Pb、Sb 等对角线上元素的氧化物和一些金属氧化物，如 TiO_2、Cr_2O_3 等。

(4)惰性氧化物或称不成盐氧化物，即不与水、酸、碱反应的氧化物，如 CO、NO 等。

2. 一般规律

(1)同周期元素最高价态氧化物及其水合物从左到右酸性递增、碱性递减。例如第三周期主族元素的氧化物及其水合物的酸碱性变化规律如下：

氧化物	Na_2O	MgO	Al_2O_3	SiO_2	P_2O_5	SO_3	Cl_2O_7
氧化物的水合物	NaOH	$Mg(OH)_2$	$Al(OH)_3$	H_2SiO_3	H_3PO_4	H_2SO_4	$HClO_4$
酸碱性	强碱	中强碱	两性	弱酸	中强酸	强酸	最强酸

酸性递增、碱性递减 →

又如第四周期副族：

氧化物	Sc_2O_3	TiO_2	V_2O_5	CrO_3	Mn_2O_7
氧化物的水合物	$Sc(OH)_3$	$Ti(OH)_4$	HVO_3	H_2CrO_4	$HMnO_4$
酸碱性	碱性	两性	弱酸	中强酸	高强酸

酸性递增、碱性递减 →

(2)同一主族元素相同价态的氧化物及其水合物，从上至下酸性减弱、碱性增强。例如 VA 族：

碱性增强 ↓				酸性增强 ↑
碱	N_2O_3	HNO_2	中强酸	酸
性	P_2O_3	H_3PO_3	中强酸	性
增	As_2O_3	H_3AsO_3	两性偏酸	增
强	Sb_2O_3	$Sb(OH)_3$	两性偏碱	强
	Bi_2O_3	$Bi(OH)_3$	碱性	

又例如 VIB 族：

酸性 $H_2CrO_4 > H_2MoO_4 > H_2WO_4$

(3)同一元素不同价态的氧化物及其水合物,依价态升高的顺序酸性增强,碱性减弱。例如:

CrO	Cr_2O_3	CrO_3
$Cr(OH)_2$	$Cr(OH)_3$	H_2CrO_4
碱性	两性	酸性

酸性增强 →

3.氧化物及其水合物的酸碱性与结构的关系

(1)R—O—H 规则

以下分四点简要说明规则内容:

①氧化物的水合物不论是酸还是碱,其结构中均含有 R—O—H 部分。如:

$$Mg(OH)_2: HO—Mg—OH; H_2SO_4: HO—\overset{\overset{O}{\|}}{\underset{\underset{O}{\|}}{S}}—OH$$

②规则把 R、O、H 都看成离子,即 R^{n+}、O^{2-}、H^+。

③R—O—H 有两种电离方式,即:

R — O ┊ H 酸式电离,产生 H^+,则为酸

R ┊ O — H 碱式电离,产生 OH^-,则为碱

④采取何种方式电离取决于 R^{n+} 与 O^{2-} 和 O^{2-} 与 H^+ 之间作用力的大小。若 R^{n+} 的电荷多、半径小,则 R^{n+} 与 O^{2-} 的引力将大于 O^{2-} 与 H^+ 的引力,则发生酸式电离呈酸性;若 R^{n+} 电荷少,半径大,具有 8 电子构型,R^{n+} 与 O^{2-} 的引力将小于 O^{2-} 与 H^+ 的引力,则发生碱式电离呈碱性;如果 R^{n+} 与 O^{2-} 的引力近似等于 O^{2-} 与 H^+ 的引力,既可发生酸式电离,也可以发生碱式电离,该水合物具有两性。以第三周期氧化物之水合物的酸碱性递变规律说明如下:

R^{n+}	Na^+	Mg^{2+}	Al^{3+}	Si^{4+}	P^{5+}	S^{6+}	Cl^{7+}
R^{n+} 电荷数	+1	+2	+3	+4	+5	+6	+7
R^{n+} 半径(Pm)	90	65	50	41	34	29	26
$R(OH)_n$	$NaOH$	$Mg(OH)_2$	$Al(OH)_3$	H_2SiO_3	H_3PO_4	H_2SO_4	$HClO_4$
酸碱性	强碱	中强碱	两性	弱酸	中强酸	强酸	最强酸

R^{n+} 的电荷数递增,半径递减,R^{n+} 与 O^{2-} 引力递增,酸式电离递增,酸性增强。→

(2)鲍林规则

为了说明含氧酸酸性的相对强弱,鲍林将含氧酸写成 $(HO)_mRO_n$,n 为不与 H 结合的氧原子数。鲍林认为:n 值越大,酸性越强。例如:

$HClO_4$	写成 $HOClO_3$	$n=3$	↓ n 值下降 酸性减弱
H_2SO_4	写成 $(HO)_2SO_2$	$n=2$	
HNO_2	写成 $HONO$	$n=1$	
H_3BO_3	写成 $(HO)_3B$	$n=0$	

【例 3-1-9】 下列物质中酸性最弱的是:

A. H_3PO_4 B. $HClO_4$ C. H_3AsO_4 D. H_3AsO_3

解 同一周期元素最高价态氧化物及其水合物从左到右酸性递增、碱性递减，酸性 $HClO_4 > H_3PO_4$；同一主族元素相同价态的氧化物及其水合物，从上到下酸性减弱、碱性增强；同一元素不同价态的氧化物及其水合物，依价态升高的顺序酸性增强、碱性减弱。酸性 $H_3PO_4 > H_3AsO_4 > H_3AsO_3$。所以题中最弱酸是 H_3AsO_3。

答案：D

【例 3-1-10】 下列物质中酸性最强的是：

A. $HClO_4$　　B. $HClO_3$　　C. $HClO_2$　　D. HClO

解 同一元素不同价态的氧化物及其水合物，依价态升高的顺序酸性增强、碱性减弱。所以酸性 $HClO_4 > HClO_3 > HClO_2 > HClO$。

答案：A

三、化学键

化学键是分子或晶体中原子或离子间的强烈作用力。键能约为 100～800kJ/mol，是决定分子和晶体的化学性质的主要因素。一般分为共价键、离子键和金属键三大类。

（一）离子键

1. 离子键的形成和特性

电负性大的非金属原子（如 VIIA 元素）和电负性小的金属原子（如 IA 元素）相互靠近时发生电子转移形成正负离子，正负离子借静电作用形成离子键。由离子键结合而成的化合物或晶体叫离子型化合物或离子晶体。

离子键的特征是没有饱和性和方向性。离子键的实质是静电引力。离子的电荷数取决于形成离子时原子得失电子数。

2. 离子半径

离子半径是反映离子大小的一个物理量。在离子型化合物中，相邻两正、负离子的核间距也就是正、负离子半径之和。离子半径的导出以正、负离子半径之和等于相邻两正、负离子的核间距（离子键键长）这一原理为基础，从大量 X 射线晶体结构分析实测键长值中推引出离子半径。离子半径的大小主要取决于离子所带电荷和离子本身的电子分布，但还要受离子化合物结构类型的影响。其变化规律为：同周期不同元素离子的半径随离子电荷代数值增大而减小，如 $S^{2-} > Cl^- > Na^+ > Mg^{2+} > Al^{3+} > Si^{4+} > P^{5+}$。同族元素电荷数相同的离子半径随电子层数增加而增大，如 $Be^{2+} < Mg^{2+} < Ca^{2+} < Sr^{2+} < Ba^{2+}$，$F^- < Cl^- < Br^- < I^-$。同种元素的离子半径随电荷数的增大而减小，如 $Fe^{2+} > Fe^{3+}$，$Pb^{2+} > Pb^{4+}$ 等。

3. 离子的电子构型

在离子型化合物中，对简单的负离子来讲都具有稀有气体原子的稳定结构，如 $Cl^-(3s^2 3p^6)$、$O^{2-}(2s^2 2p^6)$ 等，对正离子来讲具有：

(1)2 电子构型，如 Li^+、$Be^{2+}(1s^2)$。

(2)8 电子构型，如 Na^+、Mg^{2+}、Al^{3+}、$Ca^{2+}(ns^2 np^6)$。

(3)9～17 电子构型，如 Fe^{2+}、Cr^{3+}、Cu^{2+}、$Mn^{2+}(ns^2 np^6 nd^{1\sim9})$。

(4)18 电子构型，如 Cu^+、Zn^{2+}、Ag^+、$Cd^{2+}(ns^2 np^6 nd^{10})$。

(5)18+2 电子构型，如 Sn^{2+}、Pb^{2+}、$Sb^{3+}[(n-1)s^2(n-1)p^6(n-1)d^{10}ns^2]$。

4. 晶格能(U)

在离子晶体中表示离子键的强度和晶格的牢固程度可用晶格能衡量。晶格能是指在 298K、100kPa 压力下，由气态正负离子生成 1 摩尔离子晶体时所放出的能量。由此可见晶格能值越大，放出的能量越大，离子晶体越稳定，破坏其晶格时耗费的能量也越大。

影响晶格能的因素主要有正负离子的电荷数和其半径，它们的关系可粗略表示为

$$U \propto \frac{|Z_{+} \cdot Z_{-}|}{r_{+} + r_{-}} \tag{3-1-9}$$

对于晶体构型相同的离子晶体，离子电荷越多，半径越小，晶格能越大，离子键越强，晶格越牢固。

5. 离子的极化

离子在外电场或另一离子作用下，发生变形产生诱导偶极的现象叫离子极化。正负离子相互极化的强弱取决于离子的极化力和变形性。

离子的极化力是指某离子使其他离子变形的能力，极化力取决于：

(1)离子的电荷。电荷数越多，极化力越强。

(2)离子的半径。半径越小，极化力越强。

(3)离子的电子构型。当电荷数相等、半径相近时，极化力的大小为：18 或 18+2 电子构型>9～17 电子构型>8 电子构型。

离子的变形性是指某离子在外电场作用下电子云变形的程度。影响变形性的因素有：

(1)离子的电荷。正离子电荷越多，变形性越小；负离子电荷越多，变形性越大，如

$$Si^{4+} < Al^{3+} < Mg^{2+} < Na^{+} < F^{-} < O^{2-}$$

(2)离子半径。半径越大，变形性越大。如

$$I^{-} > Br^{-} > Cl^{-} > F^{-}$$

(3)离子的电子构型。8 电子构型的离子其变形性小于其他电子构型。

每种离子都具有极化力与变形性，但在一般情况下，主要考虑正离子的极化力和负离子的变形性，只有当正离子也容易变形时才考虑正负离子间的相互极化作用。

由于离子的极化作用，使负离子的电子云向正离子偏移，导致电子云的重叠，键的极性减弱，使离子键向共价键过渡，离子晶体向分子晶体过渡。例如 d 区、ds 区、p 区金属元素的氯化物、氧化物等晶体的过渡就是离子极化作用的结果。

【例 3-1-11】 在 $NaCl$，$MgCl_2$，$AlCl_2$，$SiCl_4$ 四种物质中，离子极化作用最强的是：

A. $NaCl$　　B. $MgCl_2$　　C. $AlCl_2$　　D. $SiCl_4$

解　离子的极化作用是指离子的极化力，离子的极化力为某离子使其他离子变形的能力。极化力取决于：①离子的电荷，电荷数越多，极化力越强；②离子的半径，半径越小，极化力越强；③离子的电子构型，当电荷数相等、半径相近时，极化力的大小为：18 或 18+2 电子构型>9～17 电子构型>8 电子构型。每种离子都具有极化力和变形性，一般情况下，主要考虑正离子的极化力和负离子的变形性。离子半径的变化规律：同周期不同元素离子的半径随离子电荷代数值增大而减小。四个化合物的阳离子为同周期元素，离子半径逐渐减小，离子电荷的代数值逐渐增大，所以极化作用逐渐增大。

答案：D

(二)共价键

1. 共价键的形成

当非金属元素和电负性相差不大的原子之间相互靠近时，通过电子相互配对形成的化学键为共价键。由共价键形成的化合物叫共价型化合物。共价型化合物的晶体有原子晶体和分子晶体。

共价键理论包括价键理论和杂化轨道理论。

2.价键理论的要点

(1)两原子靠近时,自旋相反的未成对电子可以配对形成共价键(所以价键理论也称电子配对法)。

(2)成键电子的原子轨道必须发生最大限度的重叠。轨道重叠越多,共价键越牢固。

3.共价键的特征

(1)具有饱和性。一个原子含有 n 个未成对电子,只能和 n 个自旋方向相反的电子配对成键。如 :N· 可形成 3 个共价单键,或形成一个共价叁键; :O: 可形成 2 个共价单键,或形成一个共价双键, :F· 只能形成一个共价单键。

(2)具有方向性。轨道重叠时成键电子的原子轨道总是沿一定的方向进行重叠。

4.共价键的类型——σ 键和 π 键

σ 键:成键轨道沿键轴(两原子核间连线)方向以“头碰头”的方式重叠。重叠部分以键轴为对称轴呈圆柱形对称分布。故 σ 键重叠程度大、键能大、稳定性高。

π 键:成键轨道沿键轴方向以“肩并肩”方式重叠。重叠部分垂直于键轴镜面反对称。π 键重叠程度较 σ 键小,π 键没有 σ 键牢固,稳定性较差,易发生化学反应。共价单键一般为 σ 键,双键中含一个 σ 键一个 π 键,叁键中一个 σ 键两个 π 键。

5.杂化轨道理论要点

杂化轨道理论是在价键理论基础上发展起来的,能较好的解释多原子分子的空间构型。其主要论点为:

(1)原子轨道在成键过程中并不是一成不变的。原子(一般为中心原子)在成键时,受外力作用使原子中能级相近的原子轨道重新组合成新的原子轨道,这一过程称为轨道杂化,简称杂化。新组合成的原子轨道叫杂化轨道。

(2)杂化轨道的数目取决于参加杂化的轨道数(见表 3-1-4),即一个原子中能量相近的 n 个原子轨道,可以而且只能形成 n 个杂化轨道。

杂化类型与分子空间构型 表 3-1-4

杂化类型	sp	sp^2	sp^3	sp^3 不等性	
参加杂化轨道数	1 个 s、1 个 p	1 个 s、2 个 p	1 个 s、3 个 p	1 个 s、3 个 p	
杂化轨道数	2	3	4	4	
轨道间夹角	180°	120°	109°28′	<109°28′	<109°28′
空间构型	直线形	平面三角形	正四面体	三角锥形	“V”字形
实例	$BeCl_2$、$HgCl_2$	BF_3、BCl_3	CH_4、SiF_4	NH_3、PH_3	H_2O、H_2S

(3)杂化轨道的形状:杂化后使轨道的正瓣变大,更能满足最大重叠原理,从而提高成键能力,使分子更稳定。

(4)杂化轨道的空间构型决定分子的空间构型(见表 3-1-4)。sp^3 杂化轨道中含孤电子对数不同,分子的空间构型不同。

(5)杂化轨道分等性杂化轨道和不等性杂化轨道。凡能量相等、成分相同的杂化轨道叫等性杂化轨道;凡原子中有孤对电子占据杂化轨道而不成键的杂化叫不等性杂化,所形成的杂化轨道的成分不完全等同,故称不等性杂化轨道。

6. 杂化类型的确定

对于 AB_n 型的分子、离子,且限于只有 s、p 参与的杂化,下面介绍如何确定中心原子的杂化类型。

(1)确定 A 的价电子对数(x)

若 AB_n 为分子:$x=\frac{1}{2}$(A 的价电子数+B 提供的电子总数),见表 3-1-5。

表 3-1-5

族数	H	IIA、IIB	IIIA	IVA	VA	VIA	VIIA
A 的价电子数	—	2	3	4	5	6	7
B 提供的电子数	1	—	—	—	—	0	1

若 AB_n^{m+} 为正离子:$x=\frac{1}{2}$(A 的价电子数+B 提供的电子总数−离子的电荷数)

若 AB_n^{m-} 为负离子:$x=\frac{1}{2}$(A 的价电子数+B 提供的电子总数+离子的电荷数)

离子的电荷数即 m 值。

(2)确定杂化类型(见表 3-1-6)

表 3-1-6

价电子对数	2	3	4
杂化类型	sp 杂化	sp^2 杂化	sp^3 杂化

【例 3-1-12】 PCl_3 分子空间几何构型及中心原子杂化类型分别为:

A. 正四面体,sp^3 杂化　　B. 三角锥型,不等性 sp^3 杂化

C. 正方形,dsp^2 杂化　　D. 正三角形,sp^2 杂化

解 P 和 N 为同主族元素,PCl_3 中 P 的杂化类型与 NH_3 中的 N 原子杂化类型相同,为不等性 sp^3 杂化,四个杂化轨道呈四面体型,有一个杂化轨道被孤对电子占据,其余三个杂化轨道与三个 Cl 原子形成三个共价单键,分子为三角锥形。

答案:B

(三)金属键

金属中自由电子与原子(或正离子)之间的作用力称为金属键。

1. 金属键的形成

金属元素的原子半径一般较大,而最外层电子数又较少,因此,金属晶体中最外层电子易从金属原子上脱落,在晶体内自由运动,成为自由电子。原子脱落电子后形成正离子。在整个金属晶体中的原子(或离子)与自由电子所形成的化学键称为金属键。又称改性共价键,即将自由电子看成是金属原子或离子的共有电子,所有原子都参与的一种特殊的共价键。金属的一些特性,如传热性、导电性、延展性等,都与自由电子的存在与运动有关。

2. 金属键的特征

无方向性和无饱和性。

3. 金属键的强度

决定于金属的价电子数和原子半径。价电子数越多,原子半径越小,金属键越强。

离子键通常存在于离子晶体中，共价键存在于共价型单质或共价型化合物中，金属键存在于金属及合金中。

四、分子间的力和氢键

（一）共价键的极性

共价键有无极性取决于相邻两原子间共用电子对有无偏移。有偏移的是极性共价键；没有偏移的是非极性共价键。采用电负性差值来判别时：电负性差等于零为非极性共价键；电负性差不等于零为极性共价键。

（二）分子的极性

分子是否有极性取决于分子中正负电荷中心是否重合。重合的为非极性分子；不重合的为极性分子。分子是否有极性或分子极性的大小也可用分子的偶极矩来判断。

偶极矩 μ 等于极上电荷 q 乘以偶极长度 l。μ 等于零为非极性分子；μ 不等于零为极性分子，而且 μ 值越大，分子的极性越大。

对双原子分子，分子的极性决定于键的极性。对于多原子分子，分子的极性决定于键的极性和分子的空间构型，若键有极性，而分子空间构型对称，则分子无极性，如 CO_2、$HgCl_2$、BF_3、CCl_4 等；若键有极性，而分子空间构型不对称，则分子有极性，如 NH_3、H_2O、$SiHCl_3$ 等。

多原子分子（AB_n 型）极性的判断：

A 的氧化数的绝对值与 A 的价电子数是否相等，相等为非极性分子，不等为极性分子。

总之，共价键是否有极性，取决于相邻两原子间共用电子对是否偏移；而分子是否有极性，取决于整个分子中正、负电荷中心是否重合。

上述讨论分子极性时，只是考虑孤立分子中电荷的分布情况。如果把分子置于外加电场中，由于同性相斥，异性相吸，非极性分子原来重合的正、负电荷中心被分开，极性分子原来不重合的正、负电荷中心也被进一步分开。这种正、负两“极”（即电中心）分开的过程叫极化。由此产生的偶极叫诱导偶极。分子被极化的难易程度用分子的极化率来表示，极化率由试验测定，它反映分子在外电场作用下变形的性质。分子的变形性与分子大小有关，分子越大，包含的电子越多，就会有较多的电子被吸引的较松，分子的变形性也越大。

分子以原子核为骨架，电子受到骨架的吸引。但是，原子核和电子无时无刻不在运动。所谓分子构型其实只表现了在一段时间内的大体情况，每一瞬间都是不平衡的。因此，所谓的正、负电荷中心的位置只是在一段时间的统计结果。在某一瞬间，正、负电荷中心可能离开它的平衡位置，由此产生的偶极叫瞬时偶极。

（三）分子间力

在分子与分子之间存在的作用力称分子间力，也称范德华力。分子间力是分子间一种较弱的相互作用力，比化学键小 1～2 个数量级。

1. 分子间力的产生

任何分子都有正、负电荷中心，非极性分子也有正、负电荷中心，不过是重合在一起。任何分子都有变形的性能。分子的极性和变形性是当分子互相靠近时分子间产生吸引作用的根本原因。

（1）色散力

色散力是瞬时偶极与瞬时偶极之间产生的作用力。瞬时偶极是由于每一瞬间分子的正、负电荷中心不重合产生的偶极。分子量越大,产生的瞬时偶极也越大,色散力越大。色散力存在于非极性分子与非极性分子之间,也存在于非极性分子与极性分子、极性分子与极性分子之间。

(2)诱导力

诱导力是由诱导偶极和固有偶极之间产生的作用力。诱导偶极是由于在极性分子的固有偶极的影响下产生的偶极。固有偶极越大,产生的诱导偶极也越大,诱导力也就越大。诱导力存在于非极性分子与极性分子之间,也存在于极性分子与极性分子之间。

诱导偶极也可在外电场的作用下产生。

(3)取向力

取向力是由固有偶极和固有偶极之间产生的作用力。固有偶极即极性分子原有的偶极。分子的极性越大,取向力越大。取向力存在于极性分子与极性分子之间。

分子间力是色散力、诱导力、取向力的总称。

2.影响分子间力的因素

分子间力以色散力为主,只有当分子的极性特别大时(如 H_2O)才以取向力为主。

在同类型分子中,色散力正比于分子的摩尔质量,正比于分子半径。所以分子间力正比于分子的摩尔质量,正比于分子半径。

3.分子间力的特征

(1)没有方向性和饱和性;

(2)分子间力比化学键小 1~2 个数量级;

(3)分子间力的作用范围 0.3~0.5nm。

分子间力主要影响物质的熔点、沸点和硬度等。对同类型分子,分子量越大,色散力越大,分子间力越大,物质的熔、沸点相对要高,硬度要大。

(四)氢键

氢原子与电负性大、半径小、有孤对电子的原子 X(如 F、O、N)形成强极性共价键(H—X)后,还能吸引另一个电负性较大的原子 Y(如 F、O、N)中的孤对电子而形成氢键(X—H…Y),点线表示氢键。氢键具有饱和性和方向性,其键能比共价键的键能小得多,与分子间力更为接近些。氢键分为分子内氢键和分子间氢键,分子间氢键使物质熔点、沸点升高,分子内氢键使物质溶、沸点降低。若溶质分子与溶剂分子之间可以形成氢键,则溶质的溶解度增大。

【例 3-1-13】 下列分子中属极性分子的是:

A. $SiCl_4$　　B. NH_3　　C. CO_2　　D. BF_3

解　对于多原子分子,分子的极性取决于键的极性和分子的空间构型,若键有极性,而分子的空间构型对称,则分子无极性;若键有极性,而分子的空间构型不对称,则分子有极性。$SiCl_4$、NH_3、CO_2、BF_3 四个分子中的共价键都是极性键,但 $SiCl_4$、CO_2、BF_3 三个分子空间构型对称,为非极性分子,而 NH_3 是三角锥形分子,为极性分子。

答案:B

【例 3-1-14】 下列每组分子中只存在色散力的是:

A. H_2 和 CO_2　　B. HCl 和 SO_3　　C. H_2O 和 O_2　　D. SO_2 和 H_2S

解　非极性分子与非极性分子间只存在色散力,极性分子与非极性分子间存在色散力和诱导力;极性分子与极性分子间存在色散力、诱导力和取向力。H_2 和 CO_2 都为非极性分子,只存在色散力。

答案:A

【例 3-1-15】 下列分子中存在氢键的是:

A. CO_2　　B. HBr　　C. NH_3　　D. CH_4

解 当分子中的氢原子与电负性大、半径小、有孤对电子的原子(如 N、O、F)形成强极性共价键后,还能吸引另一个电负性较大原子(如 N、O、F)中的孤对电子而形成氢键。

答案:C

【例 3-1-16】 下列分子中键的极性最大的是:

A. HF　　B. HCl　　C. HBr　　D. HI

解 两个原子间形成共价键时,两原子电负性差值越大,共价键极性越大。F 原子电负性最大。

答案:A

【例 3-1-17】 下列化合物中,含极性键的非极性分子是:

A. Cl_2　　B. H_2S　　C. CH_4　　D. H_2O

解 不同原子间形成的共价键为极性共价键。对于多原子分子,分子的极性取决于键的极性和分子的空间构型,若键有极性,而分子的空间构型对称,则分子无极性。CH_4 为正四面体构型,为非极性分子。

答案:C

五、理想气体定律

气体的基本特征是它的扩散性和压缩性。

气体的密度小,分子之间的空隙很大,这正是气体具有较大压缩性的原因,也是不同气体可以任何比例混合成为均匀混合物的原因。

温度与压力对气体体积的影响很大,联系体积、压力和温度之间关系的方程式称为状态方程。

(一)理想气体状态方程

理想气体体积、温度和压力之间的关系式为理想气体状态方程式,即为

$$pV=nRT \tag{3-1-10}$$

式中,R 称为摩尔气体常数。在国际单位制中,p 以 Pa、V 以 m^3、T 以 K 为单位,则 $R=8.314J/(mol\cdot K)$。

对真实气体,该式实际上是一个近似方程式,只有在分子本身体积极小(接近于没有体积)和分子间相互作用力极小(可忽略)的情况下,上述方程式才是准确的。真实气体分子本身有体积,分子之间有相互作用力,但在较高温度(不低于 0℃)、较低压强(不高于 101.3kPa)的情况下,这两个因素可忽略不计,用上式进行计算的结果能接近实际情况。

(二)混合气体分压定律

(1)分体积:指相同温度下,组分气体 i 具有和混合气体相同压强时所占的体积 V_i。若混合气体中有组分 1、2、3、…、i 种气体,则混合气体的体积 $V_总=V_1+V_2+\cdots+V_i$。

(2)体积分数:指某组分 i 的分体积 V_i 与总体积 $V_总$ 之比,即 $X_i=V_i/V_总$。

(3)分压强:在恒温时,某组分气体 i 占据与混合气体相同体积时,对容器所产生的压强,即为该组分气体的分压强 p_i,也称分压。

(4)分压定律:

由实验结果得出:混合气体的总压强 $p_总$ 为各组分气体的分压之和,即

$$p_总=p_1+p_2+\cdots+p_i \tag{3-1-11}$$

混合气体中每一种气体都分别遵守理想气体状态方程式，即

$$p_i V_{总} = n_i RT \tag{3-1-12}$$

由以上两点可引出两条重要推论，即

$$p_i = p_{总} \times \frac{V_i}{V_{总}} \tag{3-1-13}$$

$$p_i = p_{总} \times \frac{n_i}{n_{总}} \tag{3-1-14}$$

所以混合气体分压定律为：混合气体的总压强 $p_{总}$ 等于组分气体分压之和；某组分气体分压 p_i 的大小和它在气体混合物中的体积分数 $V_i/V_{总}$（或摩尔分数 $n_i/n_{总}$）成正比。

（三）有关计算

根据分压定律，可以计算混合气体的总压，也可根据总压和体积分数计算组分气体的分压。

【例 3-1-18】 在 298K 时，将压强为3.33×10^4Pa的氮气 0.2L 和压强为 4.67×10^4Pa 的氧气0.3L移入 0.3L 的真空容器，问混合气体中各组分气体的分压强、分体积和总压强各为多少？从答案中可得到什么结论？

解 由题意可知，两气体混合过程中温度不变，又知两气体在 298K 时不发生化学反应，混合前后物质的量不变。所以

$$(pV)_{混合前} = (pV)_{混合后}$$

对氮气 $$3.33\times10^4\times0.2 = P_{N_2}\times0.3$$

$$p_{N_2} = 2.22\times10^4\,\text{Pa}$$

对氧气 $$4.67\times10^4\times0.3 = p_{O_2}\times0.3$$

$$p_{O_2} = 4.67\times10^4\,\text{Pa}$$

$$p_{总} = (2.22+4.67)\times10^4 = 6.89\times10^4\,\text{Pa}$$

根据分压定律 $$p_i = p_{总}\times V_i/V_{总}$$

$$V_i = p_i\times V_{总}/P_{总}$$

对氮气 $$V_{N_2} = 2.22\times10^4\times0.3\div(6.89\times10^4) = 0.097\text{L}$$

对氧气 $$V_{O_2} = 4.67\times10^4\times0.3\div(6.89\times10^4) = 0.203\text{L}$$

则氮气和氧气的分压分别为 2.22×10^4Pa 和 4.67×10^4Pa，分体积分别为 0.097L 和 0.203L，总压强为 6.89×10^4Pa。可见分体积并不一定是混合前气体的体积。

【例 3-1-19】 将 1 体积氮气和 3 体积氢气的混合物放入反应器中，在总压强为 1.42×10^6Pa 的压强下开始反应，当原料气有 9%反应时，各组分的分压和混合气体的总压各为多少？

解 ①先求反应前各物质的分压，根据

$$p_i = p_{总}\times\frac{V_i}{V_{总}}$$

对氮气 $$p_{N_2} = 1.42\times10^6\times\frac{1}{1+3} = 3.55\times10^5\,\text{Pa}$$

对氢气 $$p_{H_2} = 1.42\times10^6\times\frac{3}{1+3} = 1.065\times10^6\,\text{Pa}$$

②求反应后各物质的分压，由于氮气和氢气已有 9%起了反应，故它们的分压比反应前减小 9%，即：

对氮气 $$p_{N_2} = 3.55\times10^5\times(1-9\%) = 3.23\times10^5\,\text{Pa}$$

对氢气 $$p_{H_2} = 1.065\times10^6\times(1-9\%) = 9.69\times10^5\,\text{Pa}$$

对氨气：根据化学反应方程式

$$N_2+3H_2=2NH_3$$

氨的生成量为氮消耗量的2倍，因此生成的氨的分压为氮分压减少值的2倍，即

$$p_{NH_3}=2\times(3.55-3.23)\times10^5=6.40\times10^4\,\text{Pa}$$

因此混合气体的总压强

$$p_{总}=p_{H_2}+p_{N_2}+p_{NH_3}=(3.23+9.69+0.64)\times10^5=1.36\times10^6\,\text{Pa}$$

则氮的分压为 3.23×10^5 Pa，氢的分压为 9.69×10^5 Pa，氨的分压 6.40×10^4 Pa；混合气体的总压为 1.36×10^6 Pa。

六、液体蒸气压、沸点、汽化热

同气体相比，液体是不可压缩的；液体分子的扩散也比气体分子缓慢得多。

(一)液体的蒸气压

蒸气压是饱和蒸气压的简称，指在一定温度下与液体相互平衡的蒸气所具有的压强。

在某温度下，若将某液体放置在密封的容器中，液体分子将迅速蒸发，随气相中蒸气分子的浓度增加，凝聚速度 V_1 逐渐增加而接近蒸发速度 V_2

$$液体\underset{凝聚}{\overset{蒸发}{\rightleftharpoons}}蒸气$$

当 $V_1=V_2$ 时，液气之间达成动态平衡，此时蒸气分子的浓度和蒸气压均达到某一恒定值。只要有液体与蒸气共存，蒸气压与容器的体积无关。当温度升高时，蒸气压升高。如80℃时水的蒸气压为47.4kPa，100℃时为101.3kPa。

(二)液体的沸点

液体在其蒸气压与液面上压强相等时的温度下沸腾，如果此压强为一个标准大气压(101.3kPa)，液体沸腾时的温度就为该液体的正常沸点。即一种液体的正常沸点就是它的平衡蒸气压恰好等于101.3kPa时的温度。在101.3kPa下的水，正常沸点是100℃，苯的正常沸点是80℃。若液面上的压强降低，液体的沸点低于正常沸点，如水面压强降到3.2kPa，水在25℃就沸腾，水的沸点为25℃。反之，水面压强高于101.3kPa，水的沸点高于正常沸点100℃，如高压锅中沸水的温度就高于100℃。

(三)液体的汽化热

为使一种液体能在恒温下蒸发，必须向此液体供给充分的热量。所以把在恒温下使单位质量的液体蒸发所必须供给的热能叫做汽化热。如水的汽化热在100℃时为40.6kJ/mol，50℃时为42.7kJ/mol。

七、晶体类型与物质的性质

(一)晶体的基本类型及物理性质

大多数固体物质都是晶体。晶体是具有规则几何多面体外形的固体。由于晶格结点上的粒子不同，粒子间作用力不同，可将晶体分为离子晶体、原子晶体、分子晶体和金属晶体四种基本类型。

1.离子晶体

在离子晶体中，组成晶格的微粒是正、负离子，它们交错地排列在晶格结点上，彼此以离子

键相结合，离子键的键能较大，因此离子晶体具有较高的熔点、沸点，硬而较脆，易溶于极性溶剂，固态时不导电，熔融状态或水溶液中能导电。

绝大多数盐类（如 NaCl、CaF_2、K_2SO_4 等）、强碱（如 NaOH、KOH 等）和许多金属氧化物（如 MgO、CaO、Na_2O 等）都属于离子晶体的结构类型。

离子晶体的熔点、硬度与晶格的牢固程度与晶格能的大小有关。晶格能是指在 298.15K 和标准压力下，由气态正、负离子生成 1mol 离子晶体所释放出来的能量。

离子电荷与离子半径对离子晶体熔点和硬度的影响：晶格能的大小与正、负离子的电荷（分别以 q^+、q^- 表示）及正、负离子的半径（分别用 r^+、r^- 表示）有关。离子电荷数越多、离子半径越小时，产生的静电强度越大，与相反电荷离子的结合力就越强，相应离子的晶格能就越大，熔点就越高，硬度也越大。

2. 原子晶体

在原子晶体中，组成晶格的粒子是原子。原子间以共价键相结合，由于共价键的结合力极强，所以这类晶体的熔点极高，硬度极大，延展性差，不能导电，不溶于大多数溶剂中。

周期表中第 IVA 族元素碳（金刚石）、硅、锗、灰锡等单质的晶体是原子晶体。周期表中第 IIIA、IVA、VA 族元素彼此组成的化合物如碳化硅（SiC）、氮化铝（AlN）等化合物也是原子晶体。

3. 分子晶体

在分子晶体中，组成晶格的粒子是分子，分子内部虽以共价键相结合，但分子之间则仅靠分子间作用力结合成晶体。由于分子间力比化学键力弱得多，因此，分子晶体的熔点、沸点都很低，在常温下多为气体、液体或低熔点固体。

在分子晶体中，不存在离子或自由电子，所以无论是固态、还是液态都不导电。

分子晶体的物种极多，许多单质如 H_2、O_2、N_2、I、硫（S_3）、白磷（P_4）等和数以万计的化合物如冰（H_2O）、氨（NH_3）、氯化氢（HCl）等在一定条件下形成的固体都属于分子晶体。

4. 金属晶体

在金属晶体的晶格结点上排列着金属的原子和正离子，在它们之间存在着从金属原子脱落下来的自由电子。由于自由电子的存在使金属具有导电性。它的导电性随着温度的升高而降低，它还具有良好的传热性和延展性。

以上四种晶体的结构特征及物理特性，归纳于表 3-1-7。

四种晶体的结构特征与物理特性 表 3-1-7

晶体类型		离子晶体	原子晶体	分子晶体	金属晶体
晶格结点上粒子		正、负离子	原子	分子	原子、正离子
粒子间作用力		离子键	共价键	分子间力（氢键）	金属键
物理特性	熔点	较高	高	低	多数高、少数低
	硬度	较硬	大	小	多数大、少数小
	导电性	熔融或溶解后导电	差	差	良
	延展性	差	差	差	良
实例		NaCl、MgO、KNO_3、CsCl	金刚石、Si、SiC、GaAs、BN	CO_2、H_2、I_2、H_2O、SO_2	金属及合金

（二）过渡型晶体

过渡型晶体又叫混合型晶体。晶体内部质点间有多种作用力。

1. 层状结构晶体

如石墨，层内碳原子间作用力是 sp^2-sp^2 σ 键和大 π 键，层与层之间是分子间力。故石墨耐高温，有金属光泽和良好的传热性、导电性及润滑性。

2. 链状结构晶体

如石棉，链内原子之间是共价键，链与链之间作用力是弱静电引力。故石棉易撕裂成纤维状。

（三）推测晶体某些物理特性的一般方法

1. 根据元素的性质确定键型和晶型

(1)绝大多数金属为金属键，属金属晶体。

(2)在共价化合物中，先区分原子晶体。原子晶体为数不多，如金刚石(C)、Si、Ge、灰 Sn，化合物有 SiC、SiO_2、GaAs、AlN、BN 等。

(3)区分离子晶体和分子晶体。位于周期表左下角的金属元素与右上角的非金属元素形成的晶体是典型的离子晶体；一般金属元素与非金属元素形成的晶体是过渡型晶体；非金属元素的单体及其化合物除少数为原子晶体外，其余都是分子晶体。

2. 根据各类晶体的特性预测其物理性能

注意区分分子晶体中原子间作用力(即化学键力)和分子间作用力(包括分子间力和氢键)，同类型分子晶体随摩尔质量增大，分子间力增大，熔沸点升高。有氢键的分子晶体，熔沸点有所升高但仍低于离子晶体、原子晶体和金属晶体。

不同的金属晶体金属键强度差别较大，IA 族金属原子半径较大、价电子最小，因此金属键较弱，金属晶体熔点低，硬度小，VIB 族原子未成对的外电子数多，原子半径小，金属键较强，元素单质的熔沸点最高。

【例 3-1-20】 下列物质中熔点最高的是：

A. NaCl　　B. NaF　　C. NaBr　　D. NaI

解 四个化合物都是离子晶体，离子晶体晶格能越大，熔点越高。晶格能大小与正、负离子电荷和半径有关，离子电荷数越多、离子半径越小，晶格能越大。四个化合物正、负离子电荷数相同，氟离子半径最小，NaF 的晶格能最大，熔点最高。

答案：B

【例 3-1-21】 下列物质中熔点最高的是：

A. $AlCl_3$　　B. $SiCl_4$　　C. SiO_2　　D. H_2O

解 四种晶体类型中，原子晶体熔点最高。题中四种物质，SiO_2 是原子晶体，熔点最高。

答案：C

习　题

3-1-1 下列各套量子数中不合理的是(　　)。

A. $n=2, l=1, m=-1$　　B. $n=3, l=1, m=0$

C. $n=2, l=2, m=-2$　　D. $n=4, l=3, m=3$

3-1-2 下列原子或离子的外层电子分布式中不正确的是(　　)。

A. V^{2+} $3s^2 3p^6 3d^3$　　B. Fe^{2+} $3d^4 4s^2$

C. Cu^{2+} $3s^2 3p^6 3d^9$　　D. Cl $3s^2 3p^5$

3-1-3 属于第五周期的某一元素的原子失去三个电子后，在角量子数为 2 的外层轨道上电子恰好处于半充满状态，该元素的原子序数为(　　)。

A. 26　　B. 41　　C. 76　　D. 44

3-1-4　量子数 $n=4$、$l=2$ 的轨道上允许容纳的最多电子数是(　　)。

A. 8　　B. 10　　C. 18　　D. 32

3-1-5　下列各组原子和离子半径变化的顺序中，不正确的一组是(　　)。

A. $P^{3-}>S^{2-}>Cl^{-}>F^{-}$　　B. $K^{+}>Ca^{2+}>Fe^{2+}>Ni^{2+}$

C. $Al>Si>Mg>Ca$　　D. $V>V^{2+}>V^{3+}>V^{4+}$

3-1-6　下列元素电负性大小顺序中正确的是(　　)。

A. $Be>B>Al>Mg$　　B. $B>Al>Be\approx Mg$

C. $B>Be\approx Al>Mg$　　D. $B\approx Al<Be<Mg$

3-1-7　下列含氧酸中酸性最弱的是(　　)。

A. $HClO_3$　　B. $HBrO_3$　　C. H_2SO_4　　D. H_2CO_3

3-1-8　下列氢氧化物中碱性最强的是(　　)。

A. $Sr(OH)_2$　　B. $Fe(OH)_3$　　C. $Ca(OH)_2$　　D. $Sc(OH)_3$

3-1-9　下列共价型化合物中键有极性、分子没有极性的是(　　)。

A. H_2O　　B. $CHCl_3$　　C. BF_3　　D. PCl_3

3-1-10　OF_2 分子中氧原子的杂化轨道是(　　)。

A. sp^3 杂化　　B. dsp^2 杂化

C. sp^2 杂化　　D. sp^3 不等性杂化

3-1-11　下列各组判断中不正确的是(　　)。

A. $SiCl_4$、CH_4、CO_2、BCl_3 均为非极性分子

B. H_2O、H_2S、OF_2、SO_2 均为非极性分子

C. $SnCl_2$、HCl、H_2S、PCl_3 均为极性分子

D. CO、HI、NH_3、HF 均为极性分子

3-1-12　SO_2 分子之间存在着(　　)。

A. 色散力　　B. 色散力、诱导力

C. 色散力、取向力　　D. 取向力、诱导力、色散力

3-1-13　下列化合物中，分子间具有氢键的是(　　)。

A. SiH_4　　B. HF　　C. H_2S　　D. C_2H_6

3-1-14　下列晶体熔化时要破坏共价键力的是(　　)。

A. SiC　　B. MgO　　C. CO_2　　D. Cu

第二节　溶　　液

溶液是由一种或几种物质以分子、原子或离子状态分散到另一种物质中形成均匀而稳定的体系。后者称溶剂，一般为液体；前者为溶质，可为固体、液体、气体。

一、溶液的浓度及计算

溶液的浓度是指一定量的溶剂(或溶液)中含有的溶质量。

（一）质量百分比浓度（A%）

溶液中组分 A 的质量百分比浓度可表示为

$$A\%=\frac{A\text{的质量}}{\text{溶液总质量}}\times 100\% \tag{3-2-1}$$

例如，36%的浓盐酸即为 100g 浓盐酸中含 36g 氯化氢和 64g 水。

（二）"物质的量"浓度（C_A）

在溶液的单位体积 V 中，含有溶质 A 的"物质的量"n_A。表达式为

$$C_A=\frac{n_A(\mathrm{mol})}{V(\mathrm{L})} \tag{3-2-2}$$

（三）物质的量分数（或摩尔分数）（X_A）

溶液中组分 A 的"物质的量"（或组分 A 的摩尔数）n_A，与各组分的"物质的量"总和（或各组分的总摩尔数）n_A+n_B 之比，可表达为

$$X_A=\frac{n_A}{n_A+n_B} \tag{3-2-3}$$

（四）质量摩尔浓度（m_A）

1 000g 溶剂中溶质 A 的"物质的量"为 n_A，则 m_A 可表示为

$$m_A=n_A/1\,000\mathrm{g} \tag{3-2-4}$$

【例 3-2-1】 现有 100mL 浓硫酸，测得其质量分数为 98%，密度为 1.84g·mL^{-1}，其物质的量浓度为：

A. 18.4mol·L^{-1}　　B. 18.8mol·L^{-1}

C. 18.0mol·L^{-1}　　D. 1.84mol·L^{-1}

解　100mL 浓硫酸中 H_2SO_4 的物质的量 $n=\dfrac{100\times 1.84\times 0.98}{98}=1.84\mathrm{mol}$

物质的量浓度 $C=\dfrac{1.84}{0.1}=18.4\mathrm{mol}\cdot\mathrm{L}^{-1}$

答案：A

二、稀溶液通性

稀溶液的通性是指溶液的蒸气压降低、沸点升高、凝固点下降以及渗透压等。这些性质只与溶质的粒子数有关，与溶质本性无关，所以又叫依数性。

（一）溶液的蒸气压下降

蒸气压是指在一定温度下，液体与它的蒸气处于平衡时蒸气所具有的压强。所谓溶液的蒸气压，实际上是指溶液中溶剂的蒸气压。在相同温度下，溶液的蒸气压总是低于纯溶剂的蒸气压。纯溶剂的蒸气压 p^* 与溶液蒸气压 $p_{溶液}$ 之差叫溶液蒸气压的降低 Δp。

$$\Delta p=p^*-p_{溶液} \tag{3-2-5}$$

其定量关系为拉乌尔定律

$$\Delta p=\frac{n_A}{n_A+n_B}\times p^* \quad 或 \quad \Delta p=\frac{n_A}{n_B}\times p^* \tag{3-2-6}$$

式中，n_A、n_B 分别表示溶质、溶剂物质的量。$\dfrac{n_A}{n_A+n_B}$（或 n_A/n_B）称溶质 A 的物质的量分数。该式表示：难挥发非电解质稀溶液的蒸气压下降与溶质的物质的量分数成正比。

（二）溶液的沸点上升和凝固点下降

沸点就是液相蒸气压等于外压时的温度，而凝固点则是固相蒸气压等于液相蒸气压时的温度。一切纯物质都有一定的沸点和凝固点。例如当纯水的蒸气压等于 101.325kPa 时，它的沸点（正常沸点）就是 100℃，而 0℃即为水的凝固点，此时 $p_{H_2O}(s)=p_{H_2O}(L)=0.611kPa$，冰水共存。

由于溶液的蒸气压下降，使得它的沸点高于纯溶剂的沸点。而溶液的凝固点都低于纯溶剂的凝固点。溶液沸点上升和凝固点下降的定量关系为拉乌尔定律。

$$\Delta T_{bp}=k_{bp}\cdot m \tag{3-2-7}$$

$$\Delta T_{fp}=k_{fp}\cdot m \tag{3-2-8}$$

上述式中：ΔT_{bp}、ΔT_{fp}——分别表示沸点升高度数和凝固点降低度数；

k_{bp}、k_{fp}——分别表示溶剂的沸点上升常数和凝固点下降常数；

m——质量摩尔浓度，在近似计算中也可用物质的量浓度（C）代替。

沸点升高用于热处理，凝固点下降一般作制冷剂的防冻剂。

【例 3-2-2】 将 3.0g 尿素 $CO(NH_2)_2$ 溶于 200g 水中，计算此溶液的沸点和凝固点。已知水的 $k_{bp}=0.52$，$k_{fp}=1.86$。

解 尿素的摩尔质量为 60g/mol，尿素的 $n=3.0/60=0.05$mol。

质量摩尔浓度 $$m=\frac{0.05}{200}\times 1\,000=0.25\text{mol/kg}$$

$$\Delta T_{bp}=k_{bp}\cdot m=0.52\times 0.25=0.13℃$$

此溶液的沸点为 $$100+0.13=100.13℃$$

$$\Delta T_{fp}=k_{fp}\cdot m=1.86\times 0.25=0.47℃$$

此溶液的凝固点为 $$0.00-0.47=-0.47℃$$

（三）渗透压

只允许溶剂分子通过，不允许溶质分子通过的薄膜叫半透膜。溶剂分子透过半透膜进入溶液的现象叫渗透。阻止溶剂分子通过半透膜进入溶液所施加于溶液的最小额外压力叫渗透压。渗透压的大小可用范托夫公式表示

$$p_{渗}=\frac{n}{V}RT=CRT \tag{3-2-9}$$

式中：R——取值为 8.31[Pa·m³/(mol·K)]；

T——绝对温度(K)。

难挥发非电解质稀溶液的性质（Δp、ΔT_{bp}、ΔT_{fp}、$p_{渗}$）与一定量溶剂中所溶解溶质的物质的量成正比，与溶质本性无关。

稀溶液定律并不适用于浓溶液和电解质溶液，但可做到定性比较。例如下列水溶液的凝固点，由高到低的排列顺序为：0.1mol/L $C_6H_{12}O_6$ > 0.1mol/L HAc > 0.1mol/L NaCl > 0.1mol/L $CaCl_2$ > 1mol/L $C_6H_{12}O_6$ > 1mol/L HAc > 1mol/L NaCl > 1mol/L H_2SO_4。

【例 3-2-3】 下列溶液凝固点最高的是：

A. 1mol/L HAc　　B. 0.1mol/L $CaCl_2$

C. 1mol/L H_2SO_4　　D. 0.1mol/L HAc

解 根据拉乌尔定律，溶液凝固点下降的度数与溶液中所有溶质粒子的质量摩尔浓度（近似等于物质量浓度）成正比。四种溶液中溶质粒子浓度大小顺序为：C>A>B>D，所以选项

D 溶液凝固点下降最小，凝固点最高。

答案：D

【例 3-2-4】 下列溶液中渗透压最高的是：

A. 0.1mol/L C_2H_5OH　　B. 0.1mol/L NaCl

C. 0.1mol/L HAc　　D. 0.1mol/L Na_2SO_4

解 根据范托夫公式 $p_{渗}=CRT$，四种溶液中粒子浓度顺序为：D>B>C>A，所以选项 D 溶液的渗透压最大。

答案：D

三、电解质溶液

在水溶液中或在熔融状态下能形成离子，因而能导电的物质称电解质。在水溶液中能完全电离的电解质称为强电解质；仅能部分电离的称为弱电解质。

（一）一元弱酸、弱碱的电离平衡

$$AB \rightleftharpoons A^+ + B^-$$

平衡时 $$K_i=\frac{[C_{A^+}/C^\ominus][C_{B^-}/C^\ominus]}{[C_{AB}/C^\ominus]} \quad 或 \quad K_i=\frac{C_{A^+}\cdot C_{B^-}}{C_{AB}} \qquad (3\text{-}2\text{-}10)$$

式中：K_i——电离常数，K_i 是温度的函数，与物质的浓度无关；对类型相同的酸或碱可用 K_i 值的大小衡量它们电离程度的大小，并比较其酸性或碱性的相对强弱。

当弱电解质在溶液中达到电离平衡时，已电离的分子数占溶质分子总数的百分比叫做电离度（解离度），常用 α 表示，即

$$\alpha=\frac{已电离的溶质分子数}{溶质的分子总数}\times 100\% \qquad (3\text{-}2\text{-}11)$$

α 与 K_i 都能表示弱电解质的电离能力，都可用来比较弱电解质的相对强弱，不同的是电离度受温度和浓度的影响。

电离度 α 与 K_i 的关系

$$K_i=\frac{C\alpha^2}{1-\alpha} \qquad (3\text{-}2\text{-}12)$$

式中：C——AB 的起始浓度。

当 $C/K_i \geqslant 500$ 时，α 很小，上式可改写为

$$K_i=C\alpha^2 \quad 或 \quad \alpha=\sqrt{K_i/C} \quad （稀释定律） \qquad (3\text{-}2\text{-}13)$$

它表明浓度越稀，电离度越大。

当 AB 为弱酸时　　$K_i=K_a$ ；$C_{A^+}=C_{H^+}$

$$C_{H^+}=C\cdot\alpha=\sqrt{K_a\cdot C} \qquad (3\text{-}2\text{-}14)$$

当 AB 为弱碱时　　$K_i=K_b$ ；$C_{B^-}=C_{OH^-}$

$$C_{OH^-}=C\cdot\alpha=\sqrt{K_b\cdot C} \qquad (3\text{-}2\text{-}15)$$

当 AB 是 H_2O 时　　$C_{H^+}=C_{A^+}$ ；$C_{OH^-}=C_{B^-}$

则 $$C_{H^+}\cdot C_{OH^-}=K_i\cdot C_{H_2O}=K_w \qquad (3\text{-}2\text{-}16)$$

K_w 为 H_2O 的离子积，298K 纯水中 $C_{H^+}=C_{OH^-}=1\times10^{-7}$ mol/L，所以 $K_w=1\times10^{-14}$。

令 $$-\lg C_{H^+}=pH \quad （酸度） \qquad (3\text{-}2\text{-}17)$$

$$-\lg C_{OH^-}=pOH \quad (碱度) \tag{3-2-18}$$

则
$$-\lg C_{H^+}-\lg C_{OH^-}=-\lg K_w$$
$$pH+pOH=14 \tag{3-2-19}$$

【例 3-2-5】 已知 $K_b^{\ominus}(NH_3 \cdot H_2O)=1.8\times10^{-5}$，0.1mol·L^{-1}的 $NH_3 \cdot H_2O$ 溶液的 pH 为：

A. 2.87　　B. 11.13　　C. 2.37　　D. 11.63

解　$NH_3 \cdot H_2O$ 为一元弱碱，

$$C_{OH^-}=\sqrt{K_b \cdot C}=\sqrt{1.8\times10^{-5}\times0.1}\approx1.34\times10^{-3}\text{mol/L}$$

$$C_{H^+}=10^{-14}/C_{OH^-}\approx7.46\times10^{-12}, pH=-\lg C_{H^+}\approx11.13$$

答案：B

（二）多元弱酸的电离平衡

多元弱酸的电离是分级进行的，每一级有一个电离常数，且 $K_{a1}>K_{a2}$，以硫化氢为例：

一级电离　$H_2S \rightleftharpoons H^+ + HS^-$　　$K_{a1}=C_{H^+} \cdot C_{HS^-}/C_{H_2S}=1.0\times10^{-7}$

二级电离　$HS^- \rightleftharpoons H^+ + S^{2-}$　　$K_{a2}=C_{H^+} \cdot C_{S^{2-}}/C_{HS^-}=1.3\times10^{-13}$

计算溶液中 C_{H^+} 时，可采用与一元弱酸计算 C_{H^+} 相似的计算方法，如 H_2S 水溶液中

$$C_{H^+}=C_{HS^-}=\sqrt{K_{a1} \cdot C} \tag{3-2-20}$$

因此比较多元弱酸的强弱时，或与一元弱酸比较强弱时，只需比较 K_{a1} 的大小即可。

计算 $C_{S^{2-}}$ 时用 K_{a2}
$$C_{S^{2-}}=K_{a2} \cdot \frac{C_{HS^-}}{C_{H^+}}=K_{a2} \tag{3-2-21}$$

以上两级电离平衡符合多重平衡规则：两电离平衡方程式相加得总平衡式，总式的 K_a 等于 $K_{a1} \cdot K_{a2}$，即

$$H_2S \rightleftharpoons 2H^+ + S^{2-} \qquad K_a=K_{a1} \cdot K_{a2}=\frac{C_{H^+}^2 \cdot C_{S^{2-}}}{C_{H_2S}}$$

或
$$C_{S^{2-}}=K_{a1} \cdot K_{a2} \cdot \frac{C_{H_2S}}{C_{H^+}^2} \tag{3-2-22}$$

该关系式表明：只要调节 H_2S 饱和溶液中的 pH 值就可以控制 S^{2-} 的浓度。室温时 H_2S 饱和溶液的浓度可视为 0.1mol/L。

（三）单相同离子效应

在弱电解质溶液中，加入与其具有共同离子的强电解质时，导致弱电解质电离度降低的现象称为单相同离子效应。它是离子浓度的改变引起电离平衡移动的结果。例如在 HAc 溶液中加入 NaAc，由于增加了 Ac^- 离子的浓度，使 HAc 电离平衡向左移动，从而降低了 HAc 的电离度。

（四）缓冲溶液

缓冲溶液是弱酸及弱酸盐（或弱碱及弱碱盐）的混合液，其 pH 值能在一定范围内不受少量酸或碱或稀释的影响而发生显著的变化。缓冲溶液的缓冲原理就是单相同离子效应。

【例 3-2-6】 下列各组溶液能作缓冲溶液的是：

A. KOH 溶液—KNO_3 溶液

B. 0.1mol/L 20mL $NH_3 \cdot H_2O$—0.1mol/L 30mL HCl 溶液

C. 0.5mol/L 50mL HAc 溶液—0.5mol/L 25mL NaOH 溶液

D. 0.5mol/L 50mL HCl 溶液—0.5mol/L 25mL NaOH 溶液

解 缓冲溶液是由弱酸及弱酸盐(或弱碱及弱碱盐)的混合液。选项 C 中 HAc 的物质的量是 NaOH 的 2 倍,两种溶液混合后反应生成 NaAc,形成 HAc—NaAc 缓冲溶液。

答案:C

缓冲溶液 pH 值的计算方法:

酸性缓冲溶液 $C_{H^+}=K_a\cdot C_{酸}/C_{盐}$

$$pH=pK_a-\lg\frac{C_{酸}}{C_{盐}} \qquad (3\text{-}2\text{-}23)$$

式中 $pK_a=-\lg K_a$

碱性缓冲溶液 $C_{OH^-}=K_b\cdot\frac{C_{碱}}{C_{盐}}$

$$pH=14-pK_b+\lg\frac{C_{碱}}{C_{盐}} \qquad (3\text{-}2\text{-}24)$$

式中 $pK_b=-\lg K_b$

【例 3-2-7】 20mL 0.1mol/L 氨水与 10mL 0.1mol/L HCl 混合。求 pH 值($K_b=1.77\times10^{-5}$)。

解 两种溶液混合后,生成 NH_4Cl,其浓度为 $C_{NH_4^+}=10\times0.1/30=\frac{1}{30}$mol/L,剩余的氨浓度为 $C_{NH_3}=(20\times0.1-10\times0.1)/30=\frac{1}{30}$mol/L。所以该体系为 NH_3—NH_4^+ 体系,其 pH 值为 $pH=14-pK_b+\lg C_{碱}/C_{盐}=14-4.75=9.25$。

【例 3-2-8】 计算 0.2mol/L 50mL $NH_3\cdot H_2O$ 和 0.2mol/L 30mL HCl 溶液的 pH 值时,应用的公式为:

A. $pH=14-pK_b+\lg\frac{C_{碱}}{C_{盐}}$　　B. $pH=\frac{1}{2}(pK_a-\lg C)$

C. $pH=\frac{1}{2}(pK_b-\lg C)$　　D. $pH=pK_a-\lg\frac{C_{酸}}{C_{盐}}$

解 两种溶液混合后形成 $NH_3\cdot H_2O$—NH_4Cl 缓冲溶液,是弱碱和弱碱盐形成的缓冲溶液。pH 值计算公式为 A。

答案:A

缓冲溶液的选择与配制:

缓冲溶液的 pH 值首先取决于 pK_a 或 pK_b,其次是 $C_{酸}/C_{盐}$ 或 $C_{碱}/C_{盐}$ 的比值。在配制一定 pH 值的缓冲溶液时,所选择弱酸的 pK_a(或弱碱的 pK_b)要尽可能与要求的 pH 值(或pOH值)接近,然后调节 $C_{酸}/C_{盐}$(或 $C_{碱}/C_{盐}$)的比值,当比值为 1 时缓冲能力最大。这时溶液的 $pH=pK_a$ ($pOH=pK_b$)。例如配制 pH 值为 5 的缓冲溶液时,可选择 HAc－NaAc(因 $pK_{HAc}=4.75$),然后再确定 HAc 和 NaAc 的用量。

【例 3-2-9】 将 0.2mol/L 的醋酸与 0.2mol/L 的醋酸钠溶液混合,为使溶液的 pH 维持在 4.05,则加入酸和盐的体积比为($K_a=1.76\times10^{-5}$):

A. 6∶1　　B. 4∶1　　C. 5∶1　　D. 10∶1

解 弱酸和弱酸盐组成的缓冲溶液 $pH=pK_a-\lg\frac{C_{酸}}{C_{盐}}$

所以 $4.05=-\lg1.76\times10^{-5}-\lg\frac{C_{酸}}{C_{盐}}$

$$\lg\frac{C_{酸}}{C_{盐}}=-\lg 1.76\times10^{-5}-4.05\approx0.704\text{ , }\frac{C_{酸}}{C_{盐}}\approx5.0$$

设加入酸的体积为$V_{酸}$,加入盐的体积为$V_{盐}$,则

$$\frac{(0.2\times V_{酸})\div(V_{酸}+V_{盐})}{(0.2\times V_{盐})\div(V_{酸}+V_{盐})}=5$$

即$\frac{V_{酸}}{V_{盐}}=5:1$

答案:C

(五)盐类的水解

盐类的水解是指盐类的离子与水作用生成弱酸或弱碱的反应。由于这个反应的发生,破坏了水的电离平衡,使溶液具有酸性或碱性。

盐类的水解由水的电离平衡和弱电解质的电离平衡组成。其水解常数K_h可由多重平衡规则导出。如NaAc的水解平衡,可由下列两个电离平衡相减得到

$$H_2O \rightleftharpoons H^+ + OH^- \qquad K_w$$
$$HAc \rightleftharpoons H^+ + Ac^- \qquad K_a$$
$$H_2O + Ac^- \rightleftharpoons HAc + OH^- \qquad K_h$$

$$K_h=\frac{C_{HAc}\cdot C_{OH^-}}{C_{Ac^-}}=\frac{K_w}{K_a} \tag{3-2-25}$$

同理可推导出一元弱碱强酸盐、弱酸弱碱盐及多元弱酸强碱盐的水解常数(见表3-2-1)。

各类盐的水解常数、C_{H^+}或C_{OH^-}及溶液的酸碱性 表3-2-1

盐的种类	水解平衡实例	水解常数	C_{H^+}或C_{OH^-}	酸碱性
强碱弱酸盐	$Ac^- + H_2O \rightleftharpoons HAc + OH^-$	K_w/K_a	$C_{OH^-}=\sqrt{C\cdot K_w/K_a}$	碱性
强酸弱碱盐	$NH_4^+ + H_2O \rightleftharpoons NH_3\cdot H_2O + H^+$	K_w/K_b	$C_{H^+}=\sqrt{C\cdot K_w/K_b}$	酸性
弱酸弱碱盐	$NH_4^+ + Ac^- + H_2O \rightleftharpoons NH_3\cdot H_2O + HAc$	$K_w/K_a\cdot K_b$	$C_{H^+}=\sqrt{K_a\cdot K_w/K_b}$	$K_a=K_b$ 中性 $K_a>K_b$ 酸性 $K_a<K_b$ 碱性
多元弱酸盐	$CO_3^{2-} + H_2O \rightleftharpoons HCO_3^- + OH^-$	K_w/K_{a2}	$C_{OH^-}=\sqrt{\frac{K_w\cdot C}{K_{a2}}}$	碱性
	$HCO_3^- + H_2O \rightleftharpoons H_2CO_3 + OH^-$	K_w/K_{a1}		

盐类水解的程度可用水解常数来衡量,K_h越大(或K_a或K_b越小),盐类的水解程度越大;也可用水解度h来衡量。

$$h=\frac{\text{已水解盐的物质的量(或浓度)}}{\text{起始盐物质的量(或浓度)}}\times100\% \tag{3-2-26}$$

多元弱酸强碱盐的水解是分级进行的。如Na_2CO_3按下面两级进行水解:

一级水解 $CO_3^{2-} + H_2O \rightleftharpoons HCO_3^- + OH^-$ $K_{h1}=1.8\times10^{-4}$

二级水解 $HCO_3^- + H_2O \rightleftharpoons H_2CO_3 + OH^-$ $K_{h2}=2.3\times10^{-8}$

由于$K_{h1}\geqslant K_{h2}$,所以计算该类盐溶液的pH值时,一般只考虑一级水解即可。

影响水解平衡移动的因素有:水解离子的本性、温度、盐的浓度、溶液的酸度等。

【例3-2-10】 已知$K_b(NH_3\cdot H_2O)=1.8\times10^{-5}$,将$0.2mol\cdot L^{-1}$的$NH_3\cdot H_2O$溶液和$0.2mol\cdot L^{-1}$的HCl溶液等体积混合,其混合溶液pH为:

A. 5.12　　B. 8.87　　C. 1.63　　9.73

解 将 0.2 mol·L^{-1} 的 $NH_3 \cdot H_2O$ 与 0.2 mol·L^{-1} 的 HCl 溶液等体积混合生成 0.1mol·L^{-1} 的 NH_4Cl 溶液，NH_4Cl 为强酸弱碱盐，可以水解，

溶液 $C_{H^+} = \sqrt{C \cdot K_W / K_b} = \sqrt{0.1 \times \frac{10^{-14}}{1.8 \times 10^{-5}}} \approx 7.5 \times 10^{-6}$，$pH = -\lg C_{H^+} = 5.12$

答案：A

【例 3-2-11】 浓度均为 0.1mol·L^{-1} 的 NH_4Cl、NaCl、NaOAc、Na_3PO_4 溶液，其 pH 值从小到大顺序正确的是：

A. NH_4Cl，NaCl，NaOAc，Na_3PO_4　　B. Na_3PO_4，NaOAc，NaCl，NH_4Cl

C. NH_4Cl，NaCl，Na_3PO_4，NaOAc　　D. NaOAc，Na_3PO_4，NaCl，NH_4Cl

解 NH_4Cl 为强酸弱碱盐，水解显酸性；NaCl 不水解；NaOAc 和 Na_3PO_4 均为强碱弱酸盐，水解显碱性，因为 $K_a(HAc) > K_{a3}(H_3PO_4)$，所以 Na_3PO_4 的水解程度更大，碱性更强。

答案：A

（六）多相离子平衡

一定温度下的难溶电解质饱和溶液中未溶解的固体与溶液中离子之间的平衡叫多相离子平衡，简称溶解平衡。平衡时离子浓度的乘积为一常数，称溶度积。

1. 溶度积（K_{sp}）

$$A_nB_m(s) \rightleftharpoons nA^{m+} + mB^{n-}$$

溶度积的表达式为

$$K_{sp(A_nB_m)} = C^n_{A^{m+}} \cdot C^m_{B^{n-}} \tag{3-2-27}$$

溶度积和溶解度 S（单位：mol/L）都可表示物质的溶解能力。如用 K_{sp} 直接比较，仅限于同类型的难溶电解质。K_{sp} 与 S 的关系如下：

对 AB 型物质：如 AgX、$BaSO_4$、$CaCO_3$ 等。

$$S = \sqrt{K_{sp(AB)}} \tag{3-2-28}$$

对 A_2B（或 AB_2）型物质：如 Ag_2CrO_4、$Mg(OH)_2$ 等。

$$S = \sqrt[3]{\frac{K_{sp(A_2B)}}{4}} \tag{3-2-29}$$

对同类型的难溶物质，其溶度积大，则溶解度也一定大。但对于不同类型的难溶物质，溶度积大的，溶解度不一定大，所以要求出溶解度方可比较溶解能力的大小。

【例 3-2-12】 能正确表示 $HgCl_2$ 的 S 与 K_{sp} 之间的关系式是：

A. $S = \sqrt{\frac{K_{sp}}{2}}$　　B. $S = \sqrt{K_{sp}}$

C. $S = \sqrt[3]{K_{sp}}$　　D. $S = \sqrt[3]{\frac{K_{sp}}{4}}$

解 $HgCl_2$ 为 AB_2 型物质，S 与 K_{sp} 的关系为 D 式。

答案：D

2. 溶度积规则

对于难溶电解质 A_nB_m，在任意状态时

$$C^n_{A^{m+}} \cdot C^m_{B^{n-}} = Q\text{（离子积）} \tag{3-2-30}$$

若 $Q > K_{sp}$　为过饱和溶液，有沉淀析出；

若 $Q=K_{sp}$　为饱和溶液，处于平衡状态；

若 $Q<K_{sp}$　为不饱和溶液，无沉淀析出。

3. 多相同离子效应

在难溶电解质饱和溶液中加入含有相同离子的强电解质，使难溶电解质溶解度降低的现象称多相同离子效应。利用同离子效应可使某些离子沉淀更完全。离子沉淀完全的条件是被沉淀离子的浓度≤10^{-5}mol/L。

4. 沉淀的溶解

根据溶度积规则，沉淀溶解的必要条件是 $Q<K_{sp}$。因此，一切能降低离子浓度的方法都会促使溶解平衡向溶解的方向移动，沉淀就会溶解。通常采用的方法有酸碱溶解法、氧化还原法、配合溶解法等。

5. 沉淀的转化

由一种沉淀向另一种沉淀转化的过程称沉淀的转化。向沉淀物中加入另一沉淀剂后，沉淀转化的可能性和限度，由平衡常数 K 确定。

例如　$$Ag_2CrO_4(s)+2Cl^- \rightleftharpoons 2AgCl(s)+CrO_4^{2-}$$

$$K=\frac{C_{CrO_4^{2-}}}{C_{Cl^-}^2}=\frac{C_{CrO_4^{2-}}\cdot C_{Ag^+}^2}{C_{Cl^-}^2\cdot C_{Ag^+}^2}=\frac{K_{sp(Ag_2CrO_4)}}{K_{sp(AgCl)}^2}$$

$$K=\frac{9\times10^{-12}}{(1.56\times10^{-10})^2}=3.7\times10^8>1\times10^7$$

K 值较大，沉淀转化可以实现。对同一类型的难溶电解质，反应物的 K_{sp} 与生成物的 K_{sp} 的比值越大，沉淀转化越完全。

6. 分步沉淀

若溶液中含有多种离子，加入沉淀剂时，离子积先超过 K_{sp} 的离子先沉淀，后超过者后沉淀。这种先后沉淀的现象叫分步沉淀。分步沉淀不仅与 K_{sp} 有关，而且还与被沉淀的离子浓度有关。当离子浓度相同时，对同类型难溶电解质，K_{sp} 越小者越先沉淀。

分步沉淀可用来分离或提纯物质。如果被分离的几种物质 K_{sp} 相差越大，则分离就越完全。

【例 3-2-13】　在 $BaSO_4$ 饱和溶液中，加入 $BaCl_2$，利用同离子效应使 $BaSO_4$ 的溶解度降低，体系中$C(SO_4^{2-})$的变化是：

A. 增大　　B. 减小

C. 不变　　D. 不能确定

解　在 $BaSO_4$ 饱和溶液中，存在 $BaSO_4=Ba^{2+}+SO_4^{2-}$ 平衡，加入 $BaCl_2$，溶液中 Ba^{2+} 增加，平衡向左移动，SO_4^{2+} 的浓度减小。

答案：B

【例 3-2-14】　AgCl 固体在下列哪一种溶液中的溶解度最大：

A. 0.01mol/L 氨水溶液　　B. 0.01mol/L 氯化钠溶液

C. 纯水　　D. 0.01mol/L 硝酸银溶液

解　AgCl 溶液中存在如下沉淀溶解平衡：$AgCl(s)\rightleftharpoons Ag^++Cl^-$。加入氯化钠和硝酸银溶液都会使 AgCl 的溶解度降低(多相同离子效应)；加入纯水对 AgCl 溶解度没影响；加入氨水后，Ag^+ 与 NH_3 形成配合物，使平衡向右移动，从而使 AgCl 溶解度增大。

答案：A

【例 3-2-15】　下列水溶液中 pH 值最大的是：

A. 0.1mol/dm^3 HCN

B. 0.1mol/dm^3 NaCN

C. 0.1mol/dm^3 HCN+0.1mol/dm^3 NaCN

D. 0.1mol/dm^3 NaAc

解 HCN 和 HAc 两个弱酸的解离常数分别为 5.8×10^{-10} 和 1.76×10^{-5}

选题 A 溶液为一元弱酸，$C_{H^+}=\sqrt{K_a\cdot C}=\sqrt{5.8\times10^{-11}}\approx7.6\times10^{-6}\text{mol}\cdot L^{-1}$

选项 C 溶液为缓冲溶液，$C_{H^+}=K_a\times\frac{C_{酸}}{C_{盐}}=K_a=5.8\times10^{-10}\text{mol}\cdot L^{-1}$

选项 B、D 均为强碱弱酸盐，可以水解，溶液显碱性。

选项 B 溶液的 $C_{OH^-}=\sqrt{C\times\frac{K_W}{K_a}}=\sqrt{0.1\times\frac{10^{-14}}{5.8\times10^{-10}}}\approx1.3\times10^{-3}\text{mol}\cdot L^{-1}$

则 $C_{H^+}=\frac{K_W}{C_{OH^-}}\approx7.7\times10^{-12}\text{mol}\cdot L^{-1}$

选项 D 溶液的 $C_{OH^-}=\sqrt{C\times\frac{K_w}{K_a}}=\sqrt{0.1\times\frac{10^{-14}}{1.76\times10^{-5}}}\approx7.5\times10^{-6}\text{mol}\cdot L^{-1}$

则 $C_{H^+}=\frac{K_W}{C_{OH^-}}\approx1.3\times10^{-9}\text{mol}\cdot L^{-1}$

总结：一元弱酸溶液显酸性；一元弱酸及弱酸盐组成的缓冲溶液显酸性；强碱弱酸盐显碱性，弱酸的解离常数越小，强碱弱酸盐的碱性越强。

答案：B

7. 多相离子平衡计算举例

【例 3-2-16】 计算 $Mg(OH)_2$：①在纯水中；②在 0.01mol/L $MgCl_2$ 溶液中；③在 0.2mol/L NH_4Cl 和 0.5mol/L 氨水混合溶液中的溶解度。已知 $K_{sp[Mg(OH)_2]}=1.8\times10^{-11}$，$K_{b[NH_3\cdot H_2O]}=1.77\times10^{-5}$。

解 设 $Mg(OH)_2$ 的溶解度为 $x$mol/L

①在纯水中

$$Mg(OH)_2(s)\rightleftharpoons Mg^{2+}+2OH^-$$

平衡浓度(mol/L)　　x　　$2x$

$$K_{sp}=C_{Mg^{2+}}\cdot C_{OH^-}^2=4x^3$$

$$x=\sqrt[3]{\frac{K_{sp[Mg(OH)_2]}}{4}}=\sqrt[3]{\frac{1.8\times10^{-11}}{4}}=1.65\times10^{-4}\text{mol/L}$$

②在 $MgCl_2$ 溶液中

$$Mg(OH)_2(s)\rightleftharpoons Mg^{2+}+2OH^-$$

平衡浓度(mol/L)　　$0.01+x$　　$2x$

$$K_{sp}=(0.01+x)(2x)^2=1.8\times10^{-11}$$

按近似计算，$0.01+x\approx0.01$，则 $x=2.12\times10^{-5}$mol/L

③在混合溶液中

$$Mg(OH)_2(s)+2NH_4^+\rightleftharpoons Mg^{2+}+2NH_3\cdot H_2O$$

平衡浓度(mol/L)　　$0.2-2x$　　x　　$0.5+2x$

该式的 K　　$K=K_{sp[Mg(OH)]_2}/K_b^2$

$$=1.8\times10^{-11}/(1.77\times10^{-5})^2$$
$$=0.057$$
$$K=C_{Mg^{2+}}\cdot C^2_{NH_3\cdot H_2O}/C^2_{NH_4^+}$$
$$=x(0.5+2x)^2/(0.2-2x)^2=0.057$$

按近似计算，$0.5+2x\approx0.5$，则 $x=9.12\times10^{-3}$ mol/L

因 $2x$ 远小于 0.2，故可忽略 $2x$。

【例 3-2-17】 向含有 0.1mol/L $CuSO_4$ 和 1.0mol/L HCl 混合液中不断通入 H_2S 气体，计算溶液中残留的 Cu^{2+} 离子浓度。已知 $K_{a1}=1.1\times10^{-7}$，$K_{a2}=1.3\times10^{-13}$，$K_{sp(CuS)}=6.3\times10^{-36}$，$H_2S$ 饱和溶液的浓度为 0.1mol/L。

解 设反应后溶液中残留的 Cu^{2+} 浓度为 $x$mol/L

$$Cu^{2+}+H_2S \rightleftharpoons CuS(s)+2H^+$$

平衡浓度(mol/L) $\quad x \quad 0.1 \quad 1.2-2x$

$$K=\frac{K_{a1}\cdot K_{a2}}{K_{sp}}=\frac{1.1\times10^{-7}\times1.3\times10^{-13}}{6.3\times10^{-36}}=2.27\times10^{15}$$
$$2.27\times10^{15}=C^2_{H^+}/C_{Cu^{2+}}\cdot C_{H_2S}=(1.2-2x)^2/x\times0.1$$

按近似计算，$1.2-2x\approx1.2$

$$x=1.2^2/(0.1\times2.27\times10^{15})=6.3\times10^{-15}\text{ mol/L}$$

【例 3-2-18】 在 0.1mol/L $FeCl_3$ 溶液中加入等体积 0.2mol/L 氨水和 2.0mol/L NH_4Cl 混合液，能否产生 $Fe(OH)_3$ 沉淀？已知 $K_{sp[Fe(OH)_3]}=4.0\times10^{-38}$，$K_{b(NH_3\cdot H_2O)}=1.77\times10^{-5}$。

解 加入等体积的 $NH_3\cdot H_2O$ 和 NH_4Cl 溶液后，各物质浓度将降低一半。即

$C_{Fe^{3+}}=0.05$mol/L，$C_{NH_3\cdot H_2O}=0.1$mol/L，$C_{NH_4Cl}=1.0$mol/L

$$C_{OH^-}=K_b\cdot\frac{C_{碱}}{C_{盐}}=1.77\times10^{-5}\times\frac{0.1}{1.0}=1.77\times10^{-6}\text{ mol/L}$$
$$Q=C_{Fe^{3+}}\cdot C^3_{OH^-}=0.05\times(1.77\times10^{-6})^3=2.8\times10^{-19}>4.8\times10^{-38}$$

所以有 $Fe(OH)_3$ 沉淀析出。

习　题

3-2-1　在 120cm^3 的水溶液中含糖($C_{12}H_{22}O_{11}$)15.0g，溶液密度为 1.047g/cm^3，该溶液的质量百分比浓度(%)、物质的量浓度(mol/L)、质量摩尔浓度(mol/kg)、物质的量分数分别为(　　)。

A. 11.1%、0.366mol/L、0.347mol/kg，7.09×10^{-3}

B. 11.9%、0.366mol/L、0.397mol/kg，7.09×10^{-3}

C. 11.9%、0.044mol/L、0.347mol/kg，7.09×10^{-3}

D. 11.1%、0.044mol/L、0.397mol/kg，6.20×10^{-3}

3-2-2　在 20℃时，将 15.0g 葡萄糖($C_6H_{12}O_6$)溶于 200g 水中，该溶液的冰点($K_{fp}=1.86$℃)、正常沸点($K_{bp}=0.52$℃)、渗透压(设 $C=m$)分别是(　　)。

A. −0.776℃、100.22℃、1.02×10^3 Pa

B. 0.776℃、99.78℃、1.02×10^3 kPa

C. −0.776℃、100.22℃、1.02×10^3 kPa

D. 273.93℃、72.93℃、1.02×10^{6}Pa

3-2-3 下列酸溶液的 C_{H^+}、电离度分别为(　　)。

(1)0.25mol/L 氢溴酸；(2)0.25mol/L 次氯酸($K_a=3.2\times10^{-8}$)。

A. (1)0.25mol/L,0%；(2)8.9×10^{-5}mol/L,0.036

B. (1)0.25mol/L,50%；(2)8.0×10^{-9}mol/L,3.2×10^{-6}

C. (1)0.25mol/L,100%；(2)8.0×10^{-9}mol/L,3.2×10^{-6}%

D. (1)0.25mol/L,100%；(2)8.9×10^{-5}mol/L,0.036%

3-2-4 H_2S 饱和溶液浓度为 0.1mol/L,已知 $K_{a1}=1.32\times10^{-7}$,$K_{a2}=7.1\times10^{-15}$,该溶液的 C_{H^+}、C_{HS^-}、$C_{S^{2-}}$ 和 pH 值分别为(　　)。

A. 1.15×10^{-4}、1.15×10^{-4}、7.1×10^{-15}、3.94

B. 1.15×10^{-4}、7.1×10^{-15}、2.3×10^{-4}、3.94

C. 3.6×10^{-15}、0、7.1×10^{-15}、14.4

D. 2.3×10^{-4}、1.15×10^{-4}、1.15×10^{-4}、3.64

3-2-5 在 0.1mol/L 醋酸溶液中,下列说法不正确的是(　　)。

A. 加入少量氢氧化钠溶液,醋酸的电离平衡向右移动

B. 加入水稀释后,醋酸的电离度增加

C. 加入浓醋酸,由于增加反应物的浓度,使醋酸的电离平衡向右移动,电离度增加

D. 加入少量盐酸,使醋酸电离度减小

3-2-6 在含有 0.1mol/L 氨水与 0.1mol/L NH_4Cl 的溶液中,C_{H^+} 为(　　)(已知 $K_{bNH_3\cdot H_2O}=1.8\times10^{-5}$)。

A. 1.34×10^{-3}mol/L　　B. 9.46×10^{-12}mol/L

C. 1.8×10^{-5}mol/L　　D. 5.56×10^{-10}mol/L

3-2-7 50mL、0.1mol/L 的某一元弱酸 HA 溶液与 20mL、0.10mol/L 的 KOH 溶液混合,并加水稀释至 100mL,测得该溶液的 pH=5.25。此一元弱酸的电离常数为(　　)。

A. 5.6×10^{-6}　　B. 3.7×10^{-6}

C. 8.4×10^{-6}　　D. 6.3×10^{-6}

3-2-8 AgCl 在(1)纯水中；(2)NaCl 溶液中；(3)$Na_2S_2O_3$ 溶液中的溶解度大小的顺序是(　　)。

A. (1)>(2)>(3)　　B. (3)>(2)>(1)

C. (3)>(1)>(2)　　D. (1)>(3)>(2)

3-2-9 0.025mol/L NaAc 溶液的 pH 值及水解度分别为(　　)($K_a=1.76\times10^{-5}$)。

A. 5.42,1.06×10^{-4}　　B. 8.58,0.015%

C. 8.58,1.06×10^{-4}　　D. 5.42,0.015%

第三节　化学反应速率与化学平衡

一、热化学

(一)系统和环境、状态和状态函数

1.系统和环境

系统：人们将其作为研究对象的那部分物质世界，即被研究的物质和它们所占有的空间。

环境：系统之外并与系统有密切联系的其他物质或空间。

系统和环境之间可以有物质和能量的传递。按传递情况不同，将系统分为：

(1)敞开系统：与环境之间既有物质交换又有能量交换的系统。

(2)封闭系统：与环境之间没有物质交换，但有能量交换的系统。

(3)隔离系统：与环境之间既无物质交换又无能量交换的系统。

2.状态和状态函数

状态：即系统的物理和化学性质的综合表现。系统的状态由状态量进行描述。状态量就是描述系统有确定值的物理量。如以气体为系统时，n、p，V、T 等。

状态函数：确定体系状态的物理量。

状态函数的特点：状态函数是状态的单值函数。当系统的状态发生变化时，状态函数的变化量只与系统的始、末态有关，而与变化的实际途径无关。

(二)化学反应计量式和反应进度

根据质量守恒定律，用规定的化学符号和化学式来表示化学反应的式子，叫做化学反应方程式或化学反应计量式。

书写化学反应计量式时应做到：

(1)根据实验事实，正确写出反应物和产物的化学式；

(2)反应前后原子的种类和数量保持不变，即满足原子守恒，如果是离子方程式还要满足电荷守恒；

(3)要表明物质的聚集状态，g 表示气态，l 表示液态，s 表示固态，aq 表示水溶液。

一般用化学反应计量式表示化学反应中的质量守恒关系，通式为

$$0=\sum_{B}\nu_{B}B \tag{3-3-1}$$

ν_B称为 B 的化学计量数，量纲为一。并规定，反应物的化学计量数为负，产物的化学计量数为正。对任一反应

$$aA+bB=yY+zZ$$

$$\nu_A=-a;\nu_B=-b;\nu_Y=y;\nu_Z=z$$

例如，合成氨的化学反应计量式为

$$N_2+3H_2=2NH_3$$

则 $\nu(N_2)=-1;\nu(H_2)=-3;\nu(NH_3)=2$

化学计量数与化学反应方程式的写法有关，如合成氨的化学反应计量式写为

$$1/2N_2+3/2H_2=NH_3$$

则 $\nu(N_2)=-1/2;\nu(H_2)=-3/2;\nu(NH_3)=1$

ν_B的物理意义：表示按计量反应方程式反应时各物质转化的比例数。

反应进度：为了描述化学反应进行的程度，引入一个新物理量——反应进度。反应进度 ξ 的定义为式

$$d\xi=\nu_B{}^{-1}dn_B \tag{3-3-2}$$

式中，n_B为物质 B 的物质的量，ν_B为 B 的化学计量数。反应进度 ξ 的单位为 mol。

对于有限的变化，有 $\Delta\xi=\Delta n_B/\nu_B$

对于化学反应，一般选尚未反应时，$\xi=0$，因此

$$\xi=[n_B(\xi)-n_B(0)]/\nu_B \tag{3-3-3}$$

式中，$n_B(0)$为$\xi=0$时物质B的物质的量，$n_B(\xi)$为$\xi=\xi$时物质B的物质的量。

引入反应进度这个量的最大优点，是在反应进行到任意时刻时，可用任一反应物或产物来表示反应进行的程度，所得的值总是相等的。

应用反应进度时应注意：

(1)反应进度与化学计量式匹配；

(2)对于同一化学反应计量式，用任何物质的物质的量的变化量来计算反应进度都是相等的。

$\xi=1mol$的物理意义：反应按所给反应式的系数比例进行了一个单位的化学反应。

(三)热和功

热和功是系统发生变化时与环境进行能量交换的两种形式。

(1)热。体系与环境之间因温度不同而交换或传递的能量称为热，表示为Q。规定：体系从环境吸热时，Q为正值；体系向环境放热时，Q为负值。Q与具体的变化途径有关，不是状态函数。

(2)功。除了热之外，其他被传递的能量叫做功，表示为W。规定：环境对体系做功时，W为正值；体系对环境做功时，W为负值。功与途径有关，不是状态函数。功分体积功和非体积功(表面功、电功等)。

等外压过程中，体积功为

$$W_{体}=-p_{外}(V_2-V_1)=-p_{外}\Delta V \tag{3-3-4}$$

(四)热力学能

热力学能为系统内部运动能量的总和。内部运动包括分子的平动、转动、振动以及电子运动和核运动，用U表示。

由于分子内部运动的相互作用十分复杂，因此目前尚无法测定内能的绝对数值。

内能的特征：状态函数、无绝对数值、广度性质。

(五)热力学第一定律

当系统由始态变化到终态时，系统与环境间传递的热量Q和功W之和等于系统的热力学能的变化量ΔU。即

$$\Delta U=Q+W \tag{3-3-5}$$

这就是热力学第一定律的数学表达式。

例如，某封闭体系在某一过程中从环境中吸收了50kJ的热量，对环境做了30kJ的功，则体系在过程中热力学能的变化为：$\Delta U_{体系}=(+50kJ)+(-30kJ)=20kJ$。体系热力学能净增为20kJ。

(六)化学反应的反应热

化学反应热是指等温过程热，即当反应发生后，使反应产物的温度回到反应前始态的温度，化学反应过程中吸收或放出的热量，简称反应热。

根据反应条件的不同，反应热又可分为恒容反应热和恒压反应热两种。

1.恒容反应热

恒容过程，体积功$W_{体}=0$，不做非体积功$W'=0$时，所以

$$W=W_{体}+W'=0, Q_V=\Delta U \tag{3-3-6}$$

2.恒压反应热

恒压过程，不做非体积功时，$W_{体}=-p(V_2-V_1)$，所以$Q_p=\Delta U+p(V_2-V_1)$

(七)焓和焓变

在封闭体系中等压反应条件下进行化学反应时，反应热为

$$Q_p=\Delta U+p(V_2-V_1)=(U_2-U_1)+p(V_2-V_1)=(U_2+p_2V_2)-(U_1+p_1V_1) \quad (3\text{-}3\text{-}7)$$

定义：$H=U+pV$，H 称为焓。则 $Q_p=H_2-H_1=\Delta H$。

H 是一个重要的热力学函数，是状态函数，但不能知道它的绝对数值。

公式 $Q_p=\Delta H$ 的意义：

(1)等压热效应即为焓的增量，故 Q_p 也只取决于始终态，而与途径无关；

(2)可以通过 ΔH 的计算求出的 Q_p 值。

通常，许多化学反应是在"敞口"容器中进行的，系统压力与环境压力相等，这时的反应热称为定压反应热。定压反应热以 ΔH 表示，单位：kJ/mol。并规定，当反应放出热量时(放热反应)，$\Delta H<0$；当反应吸收热量时(吸热反应)，$\Delta H>0$。

(八)热化学方程式

热化学方程式：表示化学反应与其热效应关系的化学方程式。

如：$2H_2(g)+O_2(g)=2H_2O(g)$；$\Delta_r H_m^{\ominus}(298)=-483.6$kJ/mol

表示在298K、100kPa下，当反应进度为1mol时，放出483.6kJ的热量。

r表示反应(reaction)，$\Delta_r H_m$ 表示反应的摩尔焓变，m表示反应进度为1mol，$^{\ominus}$ 表示热力学标准态。

热力学中对标准态($^{\ominus}$)的规定：气态物质的标准态是标准压力 $p^{\ominus}=100$kPa时表现出理想气体性质的纯气体物质的状态；液体、固体物质的标准态是指处于标准压力下纯液体或纯固体的状态；溶液中溶质的标准态是在标准压力下，质量摩尔浓度为1mol/kg时的状态。标准状态时温度不作规定。

书写热化学方程式时应注意以下几个问题：

(1)注明反应物与生成物的聚集状态。g表示气态，l表示液态，s表示固态。

$$2H_2(g)+O_2(g)=2H_2O(g),\Delta_r H_m^{\ominus}=-483.6\text{kJ/mol}$$

$$2H_2(g)+O_2(g)=2H_2O(l),\Delta_r H_m^{\ominus}=-571.68\text{kJ/mol}$$

(2)不同计量系数的同一反应，其摩尔反应热不同。

$$H_2(g)+1/2O_2(g)=H_2O(g),\Delta_r H_m^{\ominus}(298)=-241.8\text{kJ/mol}$$

$$2H_2(g)+O_2(g)=2H_2O(g),\Delta_r H_m^{\ominus}(298)=-483.6\text{kJ/mol}$$

(3)正逆反应的反应热效应数值相等，符号相反。

$$2H_2(g)+O_2(g)=2H_2O(g),\Delta_r H_m^{\ominus}(298)=-483.6\text{kJ/mol}$$

$$2H_2O(g)=2H_2(g)+O_2(g),\Delta_r H_m^{\ominus}(298)=+483.6\text{kJ/mol}$$

(4)注明反应的温度和压力。

(九)盖斯定律

盖斯定律，即化学反应的恒压或恒容反应热只与物质的始态或终态有关而与变化的途径无关。换句话说，一个化学反应如果分几步完成，则总反应的反应热等于各步反应的反应热之和。

应用盖斯定律通过计算不仅可以得到某些恒压反应热，从而减少大量实验测定工作，而且可以计算出难以或无法用实验直接测定的某些反应的反应热。

【例3-3-1】 已知反应 $C+O_2=CO_2$ 和 $CO+\frac{1}{2}O_2=CO_2$ 的反应热，计算 $C+\frac{1}{2}O_2=CO$ 的反应热。

解 (1)$C+O_2=CO_2$，$\Delta_r H_{m,1}=-393.5$kJ/mol

(2)$CO+\frac{1}{2}O_2=CO_2$，$\Delta_r H_{m,2}=-283.0$kJ/mol

式(1)－(2)为 $C+\frac{1}{2}O_2=CO$

所以　$C+\frac{1}{2}O_2=CO$ 的 $\Delta_r H_{m,3}=\Delta_r H_{m,1}-\Delta_r H_{m,2}$

$$=[-393.5-(-283)]\text{kJ/mol}$$

$$=-110.5\text{kJ/mol}$$

(十)标准摩尔生成焓

标准状态时,由指定单质生成单位物质的量的纯物质B时反应的焓变,称为标准摩尔生成焓,记作 $\Delta_f H_m^{\ominus}$。上标$^{\ominus}$ 表示标准状态,下标"f"(formation 的词头)表示生成。$\Delta_f H_m^{\ominus}$ 的单位为 kJ/mol,通常使用的是 298.15K 的摩尔生成焓数据。

指定单质通常指标准压力和该温度下最稳定的单质。如 C:石墨(s);Hg:Hg(l)等。但 P 为白磷(s),即 P(s,白)。

显然,标准态指定单质的标准生成焓为0。生成焓的负值越大,表明该物质键能越大,对热越稳定。

由标准摩尔生成焓($\Delta_f H_m^{\ominus}$)计算标准摩尔反应焓变($\Delta_r H_m^{\ominus}$):根据标准摩尔生成焓的定义,应用盖斯定律可以导出,化学反应的标准摩尔反应焓变等于生成物的标准摩尔生成焓的总和减去反应物的标准摩尔生成焓的总和。

二、化学反应速率

(一)化学反应速率的表示方法

化学反应速率通常是用单位时间内反应物或生成物浓度的变化量来表示。时间单位常用 s(秒)、min(分)或 h(小时),浓度单位一般用 mol/L。

$$\bar{v}_i=\Delta C_i/\Delta t(\text{平均速率}) \quad (3\text{-}3\text{-}8)$$

对同一反应,用不同物质的浓度变化表示 $\bar{v}$ 时,其数值不一定相等。如

$$N_2(g)+3H_2(g)\rightleftharpoons 2NH_3(g)$$

当 $\bar{v}_{NH_3}=0.2\text{mol/(L·s)}$ 时,$\bar{v}_{H_2}=0.3\text{mol/(L·s)}$,而 $\bar{v}_{N_2}=0.1\text{mol/(L·s)}$。它们的比值恰好等于反应方程中各物质的化学计量数之比,即

$$\bar{v}_{N_2}:\bar{v}_{H_2}:\bar{v}_{NH_3}=0.1:0.3:0.2=1:3:2$$

所以当反应速率以数值表达时应注明以哪种物质的浓度变化为标准。

实际速率为瞬时速率 v_i,即

$$v_i=\lim_{\Delta t\to 0}\frac{\Delta C_i}{\Delta t}=\frac{dC_i}{dt} \quad (3\text{-}3\text{-}9)$$

瞬时速率可通过试验,并经作图法求得。

用反应进度定义的反应速率:单位体积内反应进度随时间的变化率。即

$$v=\frac{1}{V}\frac{d\xi}{dt} \quad (3\text{-}3\text{-}10)$$

因为 $d\xi=v_B^{-1}dn_B$,对于恒容反应 $dC_B=dn_B/V$,上式可写成反应速率的常用定义式

$$v=\frac{1}{v_B}\cdot\frac{dC_B}{dt} \quad (3\text{-}3\text{-}11)$$

v 的 SI 单位:$\text{mol/(dm}^3\text{·s)}$。

例如,对于合成氨反应　$N_2(g)+3H_2(g)=2NH_3(g)$

其反应速率:

$$v=\frac{1}{2}\frac{dC(NH_3)}{dt}=-\frac{dC(N_2)}{dt}=-\frac{1}{3}\frac{dC(H_2)}{dt}$$

显然,用反应进度定义的反应速率的量值与表示速率物质的选择无关,亦即一个反应就只有一个反应速率值,但与计量系数有关,所以在表示反应速率时,必须写明相应的化学计量方程式。

(二)反应速率方程

浓度是影响反应速率的重要因素之一,表明反应物浓度与反应速率之间的定量关系的方程称为反应速率方程,简称速率方程。

1. 基元反应的速率方程——质量作用定律

实验证明,浓度越大,速率越快,对基元反应(一步完成的反应)

$$aA+bB \rightarrow C$$

其反应速率方程或质量作用定律表达式为

$$v=kC_A^a \cdot C_B^b \tag{3-3-12}$$

即基元反应的反应速率与以化学计量数为方次的反应物浓度的乘积成正比,这就是质量作用定律,也叫速率定律。

a、b 分别是反应物 A、B 的化学计量数,表示反应级数。对于 A 是 a 级反应,对于 B 是 b 级反应,对整个反应或总反应的级数为$(a+b)$级。一个一级反应就是 $a+b=1$ 的反应,依此类推。

k 为速率常数,它表示反应物均为单位浓度时的反应速率。k 的大小取决于反应物的本质及反应温度,而与浓度无关。

质量作用定律只适用于基元反应。

2. 非基元反应的速率方程

非基元反应即由几个基元反应组成的复杂反应,质量作用定律虽适用于其中每一个基元反应,但往往不适用于总的反应,其速率方程必须由试验测得反应速度才能确定。对于反应式

$$aA+bB \longrightarrow cC+dD$$

其速率方程为

$$v=kC_A^x \cdot C_B^y$$

式中,x、y 的值通常由试验测定,可为零、整数或小数。

上述定量关系式,除适用于气体反应外,也适用于溶液中的反应。液态和固态纯物质由于浓度不变,在式中通常不表达出来。气体压力的改变相当于浓度的影响。

【例 3-3-2】 某基元反应的速率方程为 $v=kC_A \cdot C_B^2$,当 $C'_A=2C_A$;$C'_B=2C_B$ 时,其速率方程为:

A. $v'=v$　　B. $v'=4v$　　C. $v'=8v$　　D. $v'=16v$

解 $v'=k(2C_A)(2C_B)^2=8kC_A \cdot C_B^2=8v$

答案:C

(三)温度对速率的影响——阿仑尼乌斯公式

温度对化学反应速率的影响主要体现在速率常数 k 上。温度升高,k 值增大。两者的定量关系可用阿仑尼乌斯公式表示

$$k=Ze^{\frac{-\varepsilon}{RT}}$$

或 $$\lg k=-\frac{\varepsilon}{2.303RT}+\lg Z \tag{3-3-13}$$

式中：ε——给定的反应活化能；

Z——给定的指前因子。

由公式可知：

(1)对某反应温度越高，速率常数就越大，所以速率也越大；温度一定时，活化能越大，速率常数就越小，速率也越小。

(2)以 $\lg k$ 对 $\frac{1}{T}$ 作图可得一直线，其斜率为 $-\varepsilon/2.303R$，截距为 $\lg Z$。因此，由作图法可求给定反应的活化能和指前因子，以及给定温度下的速率常数值。ε 也可由下式求得

$$\lg\frac{k_2}{k_1}=\frac{\varepsilon}{2.303R}\left(\frac{T_2-T_1}{T_1\cdot T_2}\right) \tag{3-3-14}$$

(四)催化剂对速率的影响

化学反应过程的实质是旧的化学键断裂，新的化学键建立的过程，在此过程中必定伴随着能量的变化。首先需足够的能量使旧的化学键断裂。

1. 化学反应活化能和活化分子

根据气体运动理论，只有具有足够能量的分子(或原子)的碰撞才有可能发生反应。这种能够发生反应的碰撞叫有效碰撞。这种具有足够能量可以发生有效碰撞而发生反应的分子叫做活化分子。活化分子所具有的平均能量与反应物分子的平均能量之差称为活化能。活化能的大小，由反应物自身性质所决定。活化分子占反应分子总数的百分比叫活化分子百分数。反应的活化能越高，活化分子百分数越小，反应越慢，反之反应越快。

2. 催化剂

催化剂是一种能改变反应速率而本身在反应前后的质量和化学性质都不改变的物质。催化剂之所以加快反应的速率，是因为它改变了反应的历程，降低了反应活化能，增加了活化分子百分数，如图 3-3-1 所示。

图 3-3-1 表明有催化剂时和无催化剂时活化能的差别。图中 A 和 B 分别为反应物分子和生成物分子的平均能量；C 和 C' 分别表示无催化剂和有催化剂时活化分子的平均能量；ε_1 和 ε_2 分别为无催化剂和有催化剂时的活化能，显然 $\varepsilon_1>\varepsilon_2$。

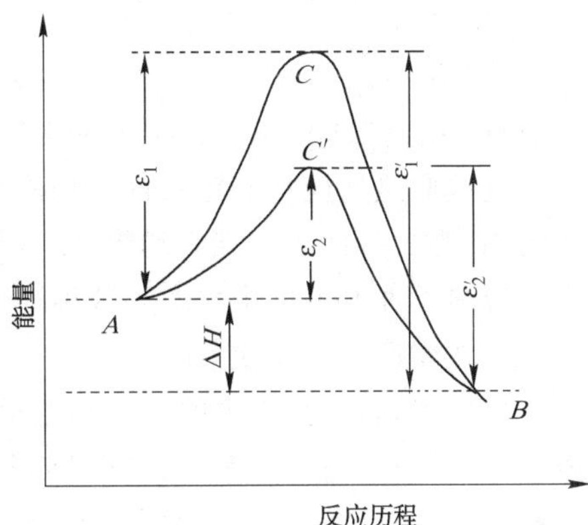

图 3-3-1 有催化与无催化的反应活化能比较

一般化学反应的活化能在 40～420kJ/mol 之间，大多数反应在 60～240kJ/mol 之间。

对可逆反应，ε_1 为正反应活化能，ε'_1 为逆反应活化能，则正反应的热效应 ΔH 和逆反应的热效应 $-\Delta H$ 可表示为

$$\Delta H=\varepsilon_1-\varepsilon'_1=-\Delta H \tag{3-3-15}$$

由以上讨论可见：浓度、温度、催化剂对反应速率的影响都可归结为活化分子数的改变，但改变的原因各不相同。浓度的影响是通过增加单位体积内的分子总数；温度的影响是通过能量的变化改变活化分子百分数；而催化剂是通过改变反应机理，降低反应活化能增加活化分子的百分数。

【例 3-3-3】 催化剂可加快反应速率的原因，下列叙述正确的是：

A. 降低了反应的 $\Delta_r H_m^\ominus$　　B. 降低了反应的 $\Delta_r G_m^\ominus$

C. 降低了反应的活化能　　D. 使反应的平衡常数 $K^\ominus$ 减小

解　催化剂之所以加快反应的速率，是因为它改变了反应的历程，降低了反应的活化能，增加了活化分子百分数。

答案：C

三、化学反应的方向

（一）化学反应的自发性

在给定条件下能自动进行的反应或过程叫自发反应或自发过程。

自发过程具有以下共同特征：

（1）具有不可逆性——单向性；

（2）有一定的限度；

（3）可由一定物理量判断变化的方向和限度。

化学反应在指定条件下自发进行的方向和限度问题，是科学研究和生产实践中极为重要的理论问题之一。

（二）化学反应方向的判据

1. 化学反应方向和焓变

化学反应中，许多放热反应都能自发的进行。例如：

$H_2(g)+1/2O_2(g)=H_2O(l)$，$\Delta_r H_m^\ominus(298K)=-285.83kJ/mol$

$H^+(aq)+OH^-(aq)=H_2O(l)$，$\Delta_r H_m^\ominus(298K)=-55.84kJ/mol$

显然，能量越低，体系的状态就越稳定。化学反应一般也符合上述能量最低原理。的确，很多化学反应自发朝着放热的方向进行。据此，有人曾试图以反应的焓变（$\Delta_r H_m$）作为反应自发性的判据。认为，在等温等压条件下，当 $\Delta_r H_m<0$ 时，化学反应自发进行。

但是，试验表明，有些吸热过程（$\Delta_r H_m>0$）也能自发进行。例如：

$NH_4Cl(s)=NH_4^+(aq)+Cl^-(aq)$，$\Delta_r H_m^\ominus(298K)=9.76kJ/mol$

$CaCO_3(s)=CaO(s)+CO_2(g)$，$\Delta_r H_m^\ominus(1123K)=178.32kJ/mol$

$H_2O(l)=H_2O(g)$，$\Delta_r H_m^\ominus(298K)=44kJ/mol$

这些吸热反应在一定条件下均能自发进行。说明放热（$\Delta_r H_m<0$）只是有助于反应自发进行的因素之一，而不是唯一的因素。当温度升高时，另外一个因素变得更重要，热力学上，将决定反应自发性的另一个状态函数称为熵。

2. 化学反应与熵变

研究发现，自然界中的物理和化学的自发过程一般都朝着混乱程度增大的方向进行。热力学上，用一个新的状态函数“熵”来表示体系的混乱度。熵是系统内部质点混乱程度或无序程度的量度，以“S”表示。系统的混乱度愈大，熵愈大。熵是状态函数。熵的变化只与始态、终态有关，而与途径无关。

热力学第二定律的统计表达：在隔离系统中发生的自发进行的反应必伴随着熵的增加，或隔离系统的熵总是趋向于极大值。这就是自发过程的热力学准则，称为熵增加原理。这就是隔离系统的熵判据。

热力学第三定律：系统内物质微观粒子的混乱度与物质的聚集状态和温度等有关。在绝对零度时，理想晶体内分子的各种运动都将停止，物质微观粒子处于完全整齐有序的状态。人们根据一系列低温实验事实和推测，总结出一个经验定律——热力学第三定律。

在绝对零度时，一切纯物质的完美晶体的熵值都等于零，即 $S(0K)=0$。

知道某一物质从绝对零度到指定温度下的一些化学数据，就可以求出此温度的熵值，称为这一物质的规定熵。

标准摩尔熵：单位物质的量的纯物质在标准状态下的规定熵叫做该物质的标准摩尔熵，以 S_m（或简写为 S）表示。注意 S_m 的 SI 单位为 J/(mol·K)。

根据上述讨论并比较物质的标准熵值，可以得出下面一些规律：对于同一种物质，$S_g > S_l > S_s$；同一物质在相同的聚集状态时，其熵值随温度的升高而增大，$S_{高温} > S_{低温}$。对于不同种物质，$S_{复杂分子} > S_{简单分子}$。对于混合物和纯净物，$S_{混合物} > S_{纯物质}$。

熵变的计算：熵是状态函数，反应或过程的熵变 $\Delta_r S$，只跟始态和终态有关，而与变化的途径无关。反应的标准摩尔熵变 $\Delta_r S_m^\ominus$（或简写为 $\Delta S^\ominus$），其计算及注意点与 $\Delta_r H_m$ 的相似。

$$\Delta_r S_m^\ominus = \sum v_i S_m^\ominus(生成物) - \sum v_i S_m^\ominus(反应物)$$

应当指出，虽然物质的标准熵随温度的升高而增大，但只要温度升高没有引起物质聚集状态的改变时，则可忽略温度的影响，近似认为反应的熵变基本不随温度而变。

虽然熵增加有利于反应的自发进行，但与反应焓变一样，一般情况不能仅用熵变作为反应自发进行的判据。要判断反应自发进行的方向，必须将这两个因素综合考虑。

3. 反应自发性的判据——反应的吉布斯函数变

为了确定反应自发性的判据，1875 年，美国化学家吉布斯（Gibbs）首先提出一个把焓和熵归并在一起的热力学函数——G（现称吉布斯自由能或吉布斯函数），并定义：$G=H-TS$。

对于等温过程：
$$\Delta G = \Delta H - T\Delta S \qquad (3\text{-}3\text{-}16)$$

ΔG 表示反应和过程的吉布斯函数变，简称吉布斯函数变，式(3-3-16)称为吉布斯等温方程。

反应自发性的判据：根据热力学推导得出，对于恒温、恒压不做非体积功的一般反应，其自发性的判断标准（称为最小自由能原理）为：

$\Delta G<0$，自发过程，过程能向正方向进行。

$\Delta G=0$，平衡状态。

$\Delta G>0$，非自发过程，过程能向逆方向进行。

这一规律表明：等温、等压的封闭体系内，不做非体积功的条件下，任何自发过程总是朝着吉布斯函数减小的方向进行。系统不会自发地从吉布斯函数小的状态向吉布斯函数大的状态进行。

恒温、恒压下化学反应自发进行方向的判据是化学反应的 ΔG，ΔG 的大小取决于反应的 ΔH、ΔS 和温度 T。表 3-3-1 给出了 ΔH、ΔS 和 T 对反应自发性的影响。

ΔH、ΔS 和 T 对反应自发性的影响 表 3-3-1

反应实例	ΔH	ΔS	$\Delta G=\Delta H-T\Delta S$	反应情况
$H_2(g)+Cl_2(g)=2HCl(g)$	−	+	−	自发（任何温度）
$2CO(g)=2C(s)+O_2(g)$	+	−	+	非自发（任何温度）
$CaCO_3(s)=CaO(s)+CO_2(s)$	+	+	升高至某温度时由正值变为负值	升高温度有利于反应自发进行
$N_2(g)+3H_2(g)=2NH_3(g)$	−	−	降低至某温度时由正值变为负值	降低温度有利于反应自发进行

4. 反应的摩尔吉布斯函数变的计算及应用

(1)标准状态下摩尔吉布斯函数变的计算

标准摩尔生成吉布斯函数：在标准状态时，由指定单质生成单位物质的量的纯物质时反应的吉布斯函数变，叫做该物质的标准摩尔生成吉布斯函数，用 $\Delta_f G_m^\ominus$ 表示，常用单位为 kJ/mol。

任何指定单质(注意磷为白磷)：$\Delta_f G_m^\ominus = 0$

298.15K 时的物质的 $\Delta_f G_m^\ominus$ 可以查到。

反应的标准摩尔吉布斯函数变以 $\Delta_r G_m^\ominus$ 表示。

298.15K 时，反应的标准摩尔吉布斯函数变的计算公式为

$$\Delta_r G_m^\ominus(298.15\text{K}) = \sum v_i \Delta_f G_m^\ominus(\text{生成物}) - \sum v_i \Delta_f G_m^\ominus(\text{反应物})$$

利用物质的 $\Delta_f H_m^\ominus$(298.15K)和 $S_m^\ominus$(298.15K)的数据求算：先计算得到反应的 $\Delta_r H_m^\ominus$ 和 $\Delta_r S_m^\ominus$，然后利用下列公式计算反应的 $\Delta_r G_m^\ominus$(298.15K)

$$\Delta_r G_m^\ominus(298.15\text{K}) = \Delta_r H_m^\ominus(298.15\text{K}) - 298.15\Delta_r S_m^\ominus(298.15\text{K})$$

需要指出，上式计算得到的 $\Delta_r G_m^\ominus$ 为 298.15K 时的值，而 $\Delta_r G_m^\ominus$ 值随温度不同而改变。但由于温度对大多数反应的焓变和熵变影响较小，对这些反应可看作：$\Delta_r H_m^\ominus(T) \approx \Delta_r H_m^\ominus$(298.15K)，$\Delta_r S_m^\ominus(T) \approx \Delta_r S_m^\ominus$(298.15K)，所以任一温度 T 时的标准摩尔吉布斯函数变可按下式近似计算

$$\begin{aligned}\Delta_r G_m^\ominus(T) &= \Delta_r H_m^\ominus(T) - T\Delta_r S_m^\ominus(T) \\ &\approx \Delta_r H_m^\ominus(298.15\text{K}) - T\Delta_r S_m^\ominus(298.15\text{K})\end{aligned}$$

(2)非标准状态下摩尔吉布斯函数变的计算

许多化学反应是在等温等压非标准状态下进行的，此时反应的 $\Delta_r G_m$ 可根据实际条件用热力学等温方程进行计算

$$\Delta_r G_m(T) = \Delta_r G_m^\ominus(T) + RT\ln Q \tag{3-3-17}$$

式中，Q 为反应熵。

【例 3-3-4】 已知反应 $N_2(g) + 3H_2(g) \rightarrow 2NH_3(g)$ 的 $\Delta_r H_m < 0$，$\Delta_r S_m < 0$，则该反应为：

A. 低温易自发，高温不易自发　　B. 高温易自发，低温不易自发

C. 任何温度都易自发　　D. 任何温度都不易自发

解　由公式 $\Delta G = \Delta H - T\Delta S$ 可知，当 ΔH 和 ΔS 均小于零时，ΔG 在低温时小于零，所以低温自发，高温非自发。

答案：A

【例 3-3-5】 某化学反应在任何温度下都可以自发进行，此反应需满足的条件是：

A. $\Delta_r H_m < 0$，$\Delta_r S_m > 0$　　B. $\Delta_r H_m > 0$，$\Delta_r S_m < 0$

C. $\Delta_r H_m < 0$，$\Delta_r S_m < 0$　　D. $\Delta_r H_m > 0$，$\Delta_r S_m > 0$

解　由公式 $\Delta G = \Delta H - T\Delta S$ 可知，当 $\Delta H < 0$ 和 $\Delta S > 0$ 时，ΔG 在任何温度下都小于零，都能自发进行。

答案：A

【例 3-3-6】 金属钠在氯气中燃烧生成氯化钠晶体，其反应的熵变是：

A. 增大　　B. 减少　　C. 不变　　D. 无法判断

解　反应方程式为 $2Na(s) + Cl_2(g) = 2NaCl(s)$。气体分子数增加的反应，其熵值增大；气体分子数减小的反应，熵值减小。

答案：B

四、化学平衡

(一)化学平衡时的特征

当 $v_{正}$ 等于 $v_{逆}$ 时,化学反应达到平衡状态。化学平衡的特征:

(1)外观上反应“停顿”了,实质是动态平衡;

(2)当外界条件不变时,反应物和生成物浓度不再随时间改变;

(3)平衡状态可以从正逆两方向到达。

(二)化学平衡常数表达式

1.经验平衡常数(或实验平衡常数)

对任何可逆反应

$$aA+bB \rightleftharpoons dD+gG$$

在一定温度下,反应达到平衡时生成物浓度的乘积与反应物浓度乘积之比是一个常数

$$\frac{C_G^g \cdot C_D^d}{C_A^a \cdot C_B^b}=K_c \tag{3-3-18}$$

K_c 叫浓度平衡常数,简称平衡常数。上式为化学平衡常数表达式。

对气体反应,平衡常数既可用浓度表示,也可用平衡时各气体的分压表示。

$$K_p=\frac{p_G^g \cdot p_D^d}{p_A^a \cdot p_B^b} \tag{3-3-19}$$

K_p 叫分压平衡常数(或压力平衡常数)。K_p 与 K_c 的关系为

$$K_p=K_c(RT)^{\Delta n} \tag{3-3-20}$$

式中,$\Delta n=(g+d)-(a+b)$,$R=8.314\text{Pa}\cdot\text{m}^3/(\text{K}\cdot\text{mol})$。注意计算时 p、C 与 R 的单位一致。

2.标准平衡常数 $K^\ominus$

在 K_c 与 K_p 表达式中,浓度或分压均为用平衡时物质的绝对浓度或绝对分压来表示的;而标准平衡常数,则是用平衡时物质的相对浓度或相对分压来表示。如

$$Zn(s)+2H^+ \rightleftharpoons H_2(g)+Zn^{2+}$$

$$K^\theta=\frac{[C_{Zn^{2+}}/C^\ominus][p_{H_2}/p^\ominus]}{[C_{H^+}/C^\ominus]^2} \tag{3-3-21}$$

式中:$C^\ominus$——标准浓度,$C^\ominus=1.0\text{mol/L}$;

$p^\ominus$——标准压强,$p^\ominus=100\text{kPa}$。

热力学上,标准平衡常数简称平衡常数,是一无量纲的量。平衡常数是表征化学反应进行到最大程度时反应进行程度的一个常数。对于同一类型的反应,在给定反应条件下,$K^\ominus$ 值越大,表明正反应进行得越完全。在一定温度下,不同反应,各有其特定的 $K^\ominus$ 值。对于指定反应,其平衡常数 $K^\ominus$ 的值只是温度的函数,而与参与平衡的物质的量无关。

书写平衡常数表达式时应注意:

(1)平衡常数表达式与反应历程无关,但必须是平衡时的相对浓度或相对压力,化学计量数为其指数;

(2)纯固体、纯液体的浓度不列入表达式;

(3)平衡常数表达式与反应方程的书写形式有关，例如在 373K 时

$$N_2O_4 \rightleftharpoons 2NO_2 \qquad K_1=\frac{[C_{NO_2}/C^\Theta]^2}{C_{N_2O_4}/C^\Theta}=0.36$$

$$\frac{1}{2}N_2O_4 \rightleftharpoons NO_2 \qquad K_2=\frac{C_{NO_2}/C^\Theta}{[C_{N_2O_4}/C^\Theta]^{\frac{1}{2}}}=\sqrt{K_1}=0.6$$

$$2NO_2 \rightleftharpoons N_2O_4 \qquad K_3=[C_{N_2O_4}/C^\Theta]/[C_{NO_2}/C^\Theta]^2=1/K_1=2.8$$

【例 3-3-7】 下列反应的标准平衡常数可用 p^Θ/p_{H_2} 表示的是：

A. $H_2(g)+S(g) \rightleftharpoons H_2S(g)$　　B. $H_2(g)+S(s) \rightleftharpoons H_2S(g)$

C. $H_2(g)+S(s) \rightleftharpoons H_2S(l)$　　D. $H_2(l)+S(s) \rightleftharpoons H_2S(s)$

解 选项 A、B、C、D 的标准平衡常数分别为：

$$K_1^\Theta=\frac{p_{H_2S}/p^\Theta}{p_{H_2}/p^\Theta \cdot p_S/p^\Theta}=\frac{p_{H_2S}\cdot p^\Theta}{p_{H_2}\cdot p_S}$$

$$K_2^\Theta=\frac{p_{H_2S}/p^\Theta}{p_{H_2}/p^\Theta}=\frac{p_{H_2S}}{p_{H_2}}$$

$$K_3^\Theta=\frac{1}{p_{H_2}/p^\Theta}=\frac{p^\Theta}{p_{H_2}}$$

$$K_4^\Theta=\frac{1}{1}=1$$

答案:C

3.平衡常数的物理意义和特征

(1)平衡常数是可逆反应进行程度的特征常数，其值越大，表明正反应趋势越大，反应物的平衡转化率也越高，如表 3-3-2 所示。

(2)平衡常数只是温度的函数。表 3-3-2 中，反应 I 的 K 值，随温度的升高而减少，此反应为放热反应，$\Delta H<0$；反应 II 的 K 值，随温度的升高而增大，此反应为吸热反应，$\Delta H>0$。

平衡常数与转化率　　表 3-3-2

反应 I：$SO_2(g)+\frac{1}{2}O_2(g) \rightleftharpoons SO_3(g)$				反应 II：$CH_4(g)+H_2O(g) \rightleftharpoons CO(g)+3H_2(g)$			
T(K)	400	500	600	T(K)	600	700	900
K	442.4	50.5	9.37	K	0.38	7.4	1.3×10^3
SO_2 转化率(%)	99.2	93.5	73.6	CH_4 转化率(%)	65	92	99

(3)符合多重平衡规则。当 n 个反应相加(或相减)得总反应时，总反应的 K 等于各个反应平衡常数的乘积(或商)。如

$$\begin{array}{ll} FeO(s)+CO(g) \rightleftharpoons Fe(s)+CO_2(g) & K_1 \\ -)FeO(s)+H_2(g) \rightleftharpoons Fe(s)+H_2O(g) & K_2 \\ \hline CO(g)+H_2O(g)=CO_2(g)+H_2(g) & K_3=K_1/K_2 \end{array}$$

【例 3-3-8】 已知反应(1)$H_2(g)+S(s) \rightleftarrows H_2S(g)$，其平衡常数为 K_1^Θ，

(2)$S(s)+O_2(g) \rightleftarrows SO_2(g)$，其平衡常数为 K_2^Θ，则反应

(3)$H_2(g)+SO_2(s) \rightleftarrows O_2(g)+H_2S(g)$ 的平衡常数为 K_3^Θ 是：

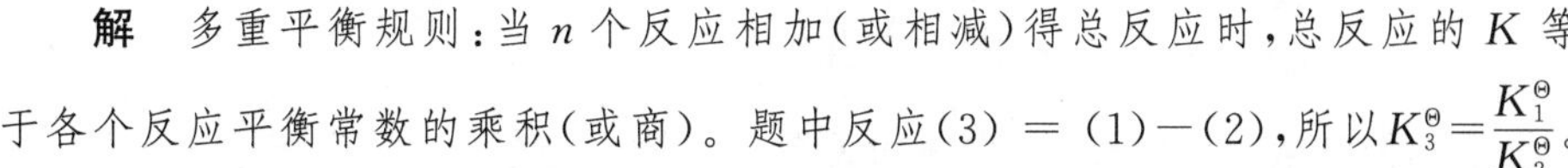

A. $K_1^\ominus + K_2^\ominus$　　B. $K_1^\ominus \cdot K_2^\ominus$

C. $K_1^\ominus - K_2^\ominus$　　D. $K_1^\ominus / K_2^\ominus$

解　多重平衡规则：当 n 个反应相加(或相减)得总反应时，总反应的 K 等于各个反应平衡常数的乘积(或商)。题中反应(3) = (1)−(2)，所以$K_3^\ominus = \dfrac{K_1^\ominus}{K_2^\ominus}$。

答案：D

4. 平衡常数的应用

(1)判断反应进行的方向

对于反应　　$a\text{A} + b\text{B} \rightleftharpoons g\text{G} + d\text{D}$

体系处于任意状态，浓度熵和分压熵分别为

$$Q_c = \frac{[C_G/C^\ominus]^g \cdot [C_D/C^\ominus]^d}{[C_A/C^\ominus]^a \cdot [C_B/C^\ominus]^b} \qquad Q_p = \frac{[p_G/p^\ominus]^g \cdot [p_D/p^\ominus]^d}{[p_A/p^\ominus]^a \cdot [p_B/p^\ominus]^b} \tag{3-3-22}$$

Q_c 与 Q_p 总称反应熵 Q。

当 $Q=K$ 时　　处于平衡状态

当 $Q<K$ 时　　反应正向进行

当 $Q>K$ 时　　反应逆向进行

(2)进行有关的计算

①已知 K 和各反应物的起始浓度，可求各物质的平衡浓度及某反应物的转化率。平衡转化率为

$$\alpha = \frac{\text{某物已转化浓度}}{\text{该物起始浓度}} \times 100\% \tag{3-3-23}$$

②已知某温度下各物质的平衡浓度(分压)或各反应物的起始浓度(分压)和某一物质的转化率，求 K。

③用多重平衡规则求另一平衡的 K。

【例 3-3-9】　在 313K 时，$N_2O_4 \rightleftharpoons 2NO_2$ 反应的压力为 506.625kPa，$K=0.9$，求该温度下 N_2O_4 的平衡转化率。

解　设 N_2O_4 的起始量为 $n$mol，平衡转化率为 α。

	N_2O_4	$\rightleftharpoons 2NO_2$
起始物质的量(mol)	n	0
平衡物质的量(mol)	$n-n\alpha$	$2n\alpha$
平衡时总物质的量(mol)	$n-n\alpha+2n\alpha=n(1+\alpha)$	
平衡时物质的分量	$\dfrac{1-\alpha}{1+\alpha}$	$\dfrac{2\alpha}{1+\alpha}$
平衡时分压(Pa)	$\dfrac{1-\alpha}{1+\alpha} \cdot p$	$\dfrac{2\alpha}{1+\alpha} \cdot p$

$$K = \frac{[p_{NO_2}/p^\ominus]^2}{[p_{N_2O_4}/p^\ominus]} = \frac{4\alpha^2 p}{(1-\alpha^2)p^\ominus} = 0.9$$

$$\frac{20\alpha^2}{1-\alpha^2} = 0.9 \Rightarrow \alpha = 0.208 = 20.8\%$$

标准平衡常数可由吉布斯等温方程式导出。

在化学热力学中，推导出了 $\Delta_r G_m$ 与系统组成间的关系

$$\Delta_r G_m(T) = \Delta_r G_m^\ominus(T) + RT\ln Q \tag{3-3-24}$$

当反应达到平衡时 $\Delta_r G_m = 0, Q = K^\ominus$

$$\Delta_r G_m^\ominus(T) = -RT\ln K^\ominus$$

$$\ln K^\ominus = \frac{\Delta_r G_m^\ominus}{-RT} \tag{3-3-25}$$

上式反映了标准平衡常数 $K^\ominus$ 与 $\Delta_r G_m^\ominus$ 之间的关系。

（三）化学平衡的移动

化学平衡是相对的、暂时的、有条件的。当外界条件（浓度、压强、温度）改变时，可逆反应从一个平衡状态向另一个平衡状态转化的过程称化学平衡的移动。

1. 浓度对平衡的影响

对处于平衡状态的可逆反应，若保持其他条件不变，则增加反应物浓度或减少生成物浓度，使 $Q<K$，平衡向右移动；同理减少反应物浓度或增加生成物浓度，使 $Q>K$，平衡向左移动。

2. 压强对平衡的影响

对有气体参加的反应，改变总压强（各气体反应物和生成物分压之和）时，如果反应前后气体分子数相等，平衡不移动；如果反应前后气体分子总数不等，平衡就会移动。例如

$$N_2 + 3H_2 \rightleftharpoons 2NH_3$$

平衡时各气体分压（Pa） a b c

$$K = \frac{c^2}{a \cdot b^3}(p^0)^2$$

总压增大 2 倍时（Pa） $2a$ $2b$ $2c$

$$Q = \frac{c^2}{4a \cdot b^3}(p^0)^2$$

$Q<K$，平衡向右移动

所以增加总压强时，平衡向气体分子总数减少的方向移动；降低总压强时，平衡向气体分子数增加的方向移动。

【例 3-3-10】 在一容器中，反应 $2SO_2(g) + O_2(g) \rightleftharpoons 2SO_3(g)$ 达平衡后，在恒温下加入一定量氮气，并保持总压不变，平衡将会：

A. 正向移动　　B. 逆向移动

C. 无明显变化　　D. 不能判断

解 加入氮气，总压不变，各气体分压减小，平衡向气体分子数增加方向移动，逆向移动。

答案：B

3. 温度对平衡的影响

温度对平衡的影响与反应的热效应有关。对放热反应（$\Delta H<0$），升高温度，K 下降（使 $K<Q$），平衡向吸热方向移动；对吸热反应（$\Delta H>0$），升高温度，K 升高（使 $K>Q$），平衡向吸热反应方向移动。总之，温度升高，平衡向吸热方向移动；温度降低，平衡向放热方向移动。正反应为放热反应，则逆反应为吸热反应；若正反应为吸热反应，则逆反应为放热反应。

4. 吕查德原理

如果改变平衡体系的条件之一（浓度、压强和温度），平衡就向着削弱这种改变的方向移动（见表 3-3-3）。

外界条件对反应速率、平衡常数和平衡移动的影响 表 3-3-3

影 响 因 素	v	k	K	平衡移动方向
增加反应物浓度	增加	不变	不变	向正反应方向移动
增加气体分子总压强	增加	不变	不变	向气体分子总数减小方向移动
升高反应温度	增加	增大	正反应吸热 K 增大， 正反应放热 K 减小	向吸热方向移动
加催化剂	增加	增大	不变	不移动

【例 3-3-11】 已知反应 $C_2H_2(g)+2H_2(g) \rightleftharpoons C_2H_6(g)$ 的 $\Delta_r H_m<0$，当反应达平衡后，欲使反应向右进行，可采取的方法是：

A. 升温，升压　　B. 升温，减压

C. 降温，升压　　D. 降温，减压

解 此反应为气体分子数减小的反应，升压，反应向右进行；反应的 $\Delta_r H_m<0$，为放热反应，降温，反应向右进行。

答案：C

【例 3-3-12】 反应 $A(S)+B(g) \rightleftharpoons C(g)$ 的 $\Delta H<0$，欲增大其平衡常数，可采取的措施是：

A. 增大 B 的分压　　B. 降低反应温度

C. 使用催化剂　　D. 减小 C 的分压

解 此反应为放热反应。平衡常数只是温度的函数，对于放热反应，平衡常数随着温度升高而减小。相反，对于吸热反应，平衡常数随着温度的升高而增大。

答案：B

习　　题

3-3-1 升高温度可以增加反应速率的主要原因是(　　)。

A. 增加了分子总数　　B. 降低了活化能

C. 增加了活化分子百分数　　D. 分子平均动能增加

3-3-2 某放热反应的正反应活化能为 15kJ/mol，逆反应的活化能是(　　)。

A. －15kJ/mol　　B. 大于 15kJ/mol

C. 小于 15kJ/mol　　D. 无法判断

3-3-3 对于一个给定条件下的反应，随着反应的进行(　　)。

A. 正反应速率降低　　B. 速率常数变小

C. 平衡常数变大　　D. 逆反应速率降低

3-3-4 下列不正确的说法是(　　)。

A. 质量作用定律只适用于基元反应

B. 对吸热反应温度升高，平衡常数减小

C. 非基元反应是由若干个基元反应组成

D. 反应速率常数的大小取决于反应物的本性及反应温度

3-3-5 某温度下，下列反应的平衡常数的关系是(　　)。

$$2SO_2(g)+O_2(g) \rightleftharpoons 2SO_3(g) \qquad K_1$$

$$SO_3(g) \rightleftharpoons SO_2(g) + \frac{1}{2}O_2(g) \qquad K_2$$

A. $K_1 = K_2$　　B. $K_1 = \frac{1}{(K_2)^2}$　　C. $(K_2)^2 = K_1$　　D. $K_2 = 2K_1$

3-3-6　在 298K，总压强为 101 325Pa 的混合气体中，含有 N_2、H_2、He、CO_2 四种气体，其质量均为 1g，它们分压的大小顺序是（　　）。

A. $H_2 > He > N_2 > CO_2$　　B. $CO_2 > N_2 > He > H_2$

C. $He > N_2 > CO_2 > H_2$　　D. $CO_2 > He > N_2 > H_2$

3-3-7　某气相反应 $2NO(g) + O_2(g) \rightleftharpoons 2NO_2(g)$ 是放热反应，反应达到平衡时，使平衡向右移动的条件是（　　）。

A. 升高温度和增加压力　　B. 降低温度和压力

C. 降低温度和增加压力　　D. 升高温度和降低压力

3-3-8　已知在一定温度下

$$SO_3(g) \rightleftharpoons SO_2(g) + \frac{1}{2}O_2(g) \qquad K = 0.050$$

$$NO_2(g) \rightleftharpoons NO(g) + \frac{1}{2}O_2(g) \qquad K = 0.012$$

则反应 $SO_2(g) + NO_2(g) \rightleftharpoons SO_3(g) + NO(g)$ 的 K 为（　　）。

A. 4.2　　B. 0.038　　C. 0.24　　D. 0.062

第四节　氧化还原反应与电化学

一、氧化还原反应的基本概念

化学反应中有电子转移的反应称氧化还原反应，反应前后反应物和生成物的氧化数发生了变化。

（一）氧化数（又称氧化值）

元素的氧化数是划分氧化还原反应和非氧化还原反应的主要依据，也是定义氧化剂、还原剂的重要概念。

1. 氧化数的概念

氧化数是某元素一个原子的电荷数，这种电荷数可由假设把每个键中的电子指定给电负性更大的原子而求得。

2. 确定氧化数的规则

(1)在离子型化合物中，氧化数等于离子电荷。

(2)在共价化合物中，把共用电子对指定给电负性大的原子后，原子的表观电荷数就是该原子的氧化数。

(3)分子或离子的总电荷数等于各元素氧化数的代数和。分子的总电荷数为零。

3. 一些已知元素氧化数的习惯规定

(1)在单质中，元素的氧化数均为零。

(2)除在金属氢化物中 H 的氧化数为－1 外，氢在其他化合物中的氧化数均为＋1。

(3)除在过氧化物中氧的氧化数为－1，在氟化物中氧的氧化数为＋1 或＋2（分别如 O_2F_2 和 OF_2）外，氧的氧化数一般为－2。

(4)在化合物中，碱金属的氧化数为+1，碱土金属的氧化数为+2，F 的氧化数为−1。

(二)氧化剂和还原剂

在氧化还原反应中，某元素的原子失去电子，使该元素的氧化数增加；相反，某元素的原子得到电子，其氧化数减少。

失去电子的物质为还原剂，在反应中被氧化；得到电子的物质为氧化剂，在反应中被还原。例如

失电子，氧化数升高（氧化）

$$Zn + Cu^{2+} = Zn^{2+} + Cu$$

得电子，氧化数降低（还原）

还原剂　　氧化剂

氧化、还原是指反应过程。

(三)氧化还原方程的配平

1.配平原则

还原剂失电子总数等于氧化剂得电子总数，反应前后各元素原子总数相等。

2.配平的步骤

(1)写出未配平的离子方程，如 $MnO_4^- + SO_3^{2-} + H^+ \rightarrow Mn^{2+} + SO_4^{2-} + H_2O$

(2)将离子方程写成氧化、还原半反应式，并配平，即

还原反应　　$MnO_4^- + 8H^+ + 5e^- = Mn^{2+} + 4H_2O$

氧化反应　　$SO_3^{2-} + H_2O - 2e^- = SO_4^{2-} + 2H^+$

(3)将两个半反应式各乘以适当系数，使得失电子数相等，然后将两个半反应式合并得到一个配平的氧化还原方程，即

$$\begin{array}{rr|l} & 2\times & MnO_4^- + 8H^+ + 5e^- = Mn^{2+} + 4H_2O \\ + & 5\times & SO_3^{2-} + H_2O - 2e^- = SO_4^{2-} + 2H^+ \\ \hline \end{array}$$

$$2MnO_4^- + 5SO_3^{2-} + 6H^+ = 2Mn^{2+} + 5SO_4^{2-} + 3H_2O$$

二、原电池

原电池是借助氧化还原反应产生电流的装置。

(一)原电池的组成、电极反应和电池反应

1.原电池的组成

原电池由三部分组成。

(1)半电池或称电极(包括导体)。

(2)金属导线:组成外电路。

(3)盐桥:盐桥的作用为沟通内电路，保持溶液电中性，使电流持续产生，例如铜锌原电池是由两个半电池组成，一个为锌半电池或叫锌电极；另一个为铜半电池或叫铜电极。

2.电极反应和电池反应

对于铜锌原电池：

锌电极上发生的电极反应为

$$Zn(s) - 2e = Zn^{2+}(aq) \qquad (氧化反应)$$

铜电极上发生的电极反应为

$$Cu^{2+}(aq)+2e=Cu(s) \qquad (\text{还原反应})$$

原电池中发生的电池反应为

$$Zn(s)+Cu^{2+}(aq)=Zn^{2+}(aq)+Cu(s) \qquad (\text{氧化还原反应})$$

电极反应也称**半反应**，每一个半反应都有两类物质：一类可作还原剂的物质，称为还原态物质，如 Cu、Zn 等；另一类可作氧化剂的物质，称为氧化态物质，如 Cu^{2+}、Zn^{2+} 等。氧化态和相应的还原态物质组成电对，称氧化还原电对，可表示为氧化态/还原态，如 Cu^{2+}/Cu 和 Zn^{2+}/Zn。一些电极反应，电极符号见表 3-4-1。

电极种类和电极符号 表 3-4-1

电极种类	电极反应	电极符号	
		负极	正极
I. 金属—金属离子	$Zn^{2+}+2e^- \rightleftharpoons Zn$	$Zn \mid Zn^{2+}$	$Zn^{2+} \mid Zn$
II. 同种金属不同价态离子	$Fe^{3+}+e^- \rightleftharpoons Fe^{2+}$	$Pt \mid Fe^{3+},Fe^{2+}$	$Fe^{2+},Fe^{3+} \mid Pt$
III. 非金属—非金属离子	$2H^++2e^- \rightleftharpoons H_2$	$Pt \mid H_2 \mid H^+$	$H^+ \mid H_2 \mid Pt$
IV. 金属—金属难溶盐—负离子	$AgCl(s)+e^- \rightleftharpoons Ag+Cl^-$	$Ag \mid AgCl(s) \mid Cl^-$	$Cl^- \mid AgCl(s) \mid Ag$

在铜半电池中，氧化剂 Cu^{2+} 发生还原反应，所以是**正极**；在锌半电池中，还原剂 Zn 发生氧化反应，所以是**负极**。原电池中电子流动方向由负极流向正极，电流方向刚好相反。原电池电动势为

$$E=\varphi_{\text{正}}-\varphi_{\text{负}}=\varphi_{\text{氧化剂}}-\varphi_{\text{还原剂}} \tag{3-4-1}$$

(二)原电池的符号(图式)

原电池的装置可用符号表示，如铜锌原电池表示为

$$(-)Zn \mid ZnSO_4(C_1) \mid\mid CuSO_4(C_2) \mid Cu(+)$$

按规定负极写在左边，正极写在右边，以双垂线(||)表示盐桥，单线(|)表示两相之间的界面，盐桥两边应是半电池组成中的溶液，若离子浓度不是标准浓度(1mol/L)，则需标明。除金属及其对应的金属盐溶液组成的半电池外，其余几种电极在组成半电池时需外加导电体材料如铂、石墨等。

【例 3-4-1】 两个电极组成原电池，下列叙述正确的是：

A. 作正极的电极的 $E(+)$ 值必须大于零

B. 作负极的电极的 $E(-)$ 值必须小于零

C. 必须是 $E^0(+)>E^0(-)$

D. 电极电势 E 值大的是正极，E 值小的是负极

解 电对的电极电势越大，其氧化态的氧化能力越强，越易得电子发生还原反应，做正极；电对的电极电势越小，其还原态的还原能力越强，越易失电子发生氧化反应，做负极。

答案：D

【例 3-4-2】 将下列反应组成原电池，并用原电池符号表示

$$FeCl_3+KI \rightarrow I_2+FeCl_2+KCl$$

解 ①由氧化数变化确定氧化剂和还原剂

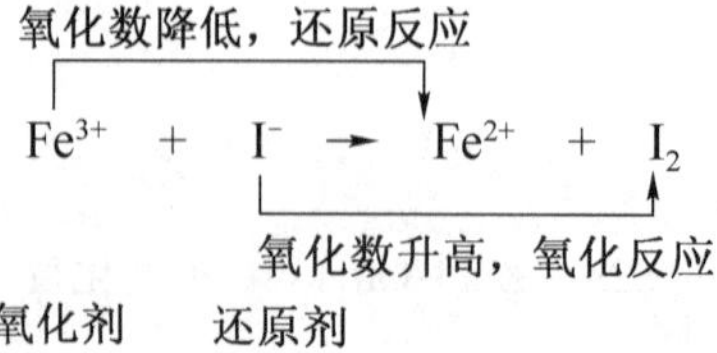

②确定正负极，并选择电极

氧化剂发生还原反应为正极；还原剂发生氧化反应为负极。正极选择第Ⅱ类电极；负极选择第Ⅲ类电极。

③组成原电池并用原电池符号表示

$$(-)Pt|I_2(s)|I^-(C_1)\parallel Fe^{2+}(C_2),Fe^{3+}(C_3)|Pt(+)$$

三、电极电势

(一)标准电极电势

当温度为298K，离子浓度为1mol/L，气体的分压为100kPa，固体为纯固体，液体为纯液体，此状态称标准状态。标准状态时的电极电势称标准电极电势，用$\varphi^\ominus$表示，非标准状态下的电势就称电极电势，用φ表示。标准电极电势标志着物质氧化还原能力的大小，是判断氧化剂、还原剂强弱以及氧化还原反应方向的基本依据。$\varphi^\ominus$值的大小只取决于物质的本性，与物质的数量和电极反应的方向无关。例如

$$Zn^{2+}+2e^- \rightleftharpoons Zn \qquad \varphi^\ominus=-0.76V$$

$$2Zn^{2+}+4e^- \rightleftharpoons 2Zn \qquad \varphi^\ominus=-0.76V$$

$$Zn \rightleftharpoons Zn^{2+}+2e^- \qquad \varphi^\ominus=-0.76V$$

电极电势的物理意义和注意事项：

(1)$\varphi^\ominus$代数值越大，表明电对的氧化态越易得电子，即氧化态就是越强的氧化剂；$\varphi^\ominus$代数值越小，表明电对的还原态越易失电子，即还原态就是越强的还原剂。如：$\varphi^\ominus(Cl_2/Cl^-)=1.3583V$，$\varphi^\ominus(Br_2/Br^-)=1.066V$，$\varphi^\ominus(I_2/I^-)=0.5355V$。可知：$Cl_2$氧化性较强，而$I^-$还原性较强。

(2)$\varphi^\ominus$代数值与电极反应中化学计量数的选配无关。如$Zn^{2+}+2e^-=Zn$与$2Zn^{2+}+4e=2Zn$，$\varphi^\ominus$数值相同。

(3)$\varphi^\ominus$代数值与半反应的方向无关。无论电对物质在实际反应中的转化方向如何，其$\varphi^\ominus$代数值不变。如$Cu^{2+}+2e=Cu$与$Cu=Cu^{2+}+2e$，$\varphi^\ominus$数值相同。

(二)浓度对电极电势的影响——能斯特方程

电极电势与物质的本性、物质的浓度、温度有关，一般温度的影响较小，对某一电对而言，浓度的影响可用能斯特方程表示

$$a\text{氧化型}+ne^- \rightleftharpoons b\text{还原型}$$

在25℃时
$$\varphi=\varphi^\ominus+\frac{0.059}{n}\lg\frac{C^a_{\text{氧化型}}}{C^b_{\text{还原型}}} \qquad (3\text{-}4\text{-}2)$$

式中，φ为指定浓度下的电极电势；$\varphi^\ominus$为标准电极电势；n为电极反应中得失电子数；$C_{\text{还原型}}$为还原态物质的浓度；$C_{\text{氧化型}}$为氧化态物质的浓度。

利用该方程可计算不同离子浓度或不同分压时的φ值，但使用时须注意：

(1)纯固体、纯液体不列入方程；

(2)电极反应式中，化学计量数为浓度或分压的指数；

(3)参加电极反应的H^+或OH^-或其他离子的浓度也应列入方程；水的浓度不必写入式中。

【例3-4-3】 计算当H^+浓度为3.0mol/L，其他离子浓度为1mol/L时，电对$Cr_2O_7^{2-}/Cr^{3+}$的电极电势。已知$\varphi^\ominus_{Cr_2O_7^{2-}/Cr^{3+}}=1.33V$。

解
$$Cr_2O_7^{2-}+14H^++6e^- \rightleftharpoons 2Cr^{3+}+7H_2O$$

能斯特方程 $\varphi_{Cr_2O_7^{2-}/Cr^{3+}} = \varphi^{\ominus}_{Cr_2O_7^{2-}/Cr^{3+}} + \frac{0.059}{n}\lg\frac{C_{Cr_2O_7^{2-}} \cdot C^{14}_{H^+}}{C^2_{Cr^{3+}}}$

$$= 1.33 + \frac{0.059}{6}\lg 3^{14}$$

$$= 1.40V$$

【例 3-4-4】 向原电池(－)Ag,AgCl|Cl⁻ ‖ Ag⁺|Ag(＋)的负极中加入 NaCl,则原电池电动势的变化是：

A. 变大　　B. 变小　　C. 不变　　D. 不能确定

解 负极 氧化反应：$Ag + Cl^- = AgCl + e$

正极 还原反应：$Ag^+ + e = Ag$

电池反应：$Ag^+ + Cl^- = AgCl$

原电池负极能斯特方程式为：$\varphi_{AgCl/Ag} = \varphi^{\ominus}_{AgCl/Ag} + 0.059\lg\frac{1}{C_{(Cl^-)}}$。

由于负极中加入 NaCl,Cl^- 浓度增加,则负极电极电势减小,正极电极电势不变,因此电池的电动势增大。

答案：A

【例 3-4-5】 有原电池(－)Zn|$ZnSO_4(c_1)$||$CuSO_4(c_2)$|Cu(＋),如向铜半电池中通入硫化氢,则原电池电动势变化趋势是：

A. 变大　　B. 变小　　C. 不变　　D. 无法判断

解 铜电极通入 H_2S,生成 CuS 沉淀,Cu^{2+} 浓度减小。

铜半电池反应为：$Cu^{2+} + 2e^- = Cu$,根据电极电势的能斯特方程式

$$\varphi = \varphi^{\ominus} + \frac{0.059}{2}\lg\frac{C_{氧化型}}{C_{还原型}} = \varphi^{\ominus} + \frac{0.059}{2}\lg C_{cu^{2+}}$$

$C_{cu^{2+}}$ 减小,电极电势减小。原电池的电动势 $E = \varphi_{正} - \varphi_{负}$,$\varphi_{正}$ 减小,$\varphi_{负}$ 不变,则电动势 E 减小。

答案：B

【例 3-4-6】 下列各电对的电极电势与 H^+ 浓度有关的是：

A. Zn^{2+}/Zn　　B. Br_2/Br

C. Agl/Ag　　D. MnO_4^-/Mn^{2+}

解 四个电对的电极反应分别为：

$$Zn^{2+} + 2e^- = Zn; Br_2 + 2e^- = 2Br^-$$

$$AgI + e^- = Ag + I^-$$

$$MnO_4^- + 8H^+ + 5e = Mn^{2+} + 4H_2O$$

只有 MnO_4^-/Mn^{2+} 电对的电极反应与 H^+ 的浓度有关。

根据电极电势的能斯特方程式,MnO_4^-/Mn^{2+} 电对的电极电势与 H^+ 的浓度有关。

答案：D

(三)电极电势的应用

(1)判断原电池正负极,计算原电池电动势,φ 值较大的为正极,φ 值较小的为负极。当两极处于标准状态时,直接用 $\varphi^{\ominus}$ 来判断和计算。

(2)判断氧化剂和还原剂的相对强弱。$\varphi^{\ominus}$ 值或 φ 值越大,表示电对中氧化态的氧化能力

越强，是强氧化剂；$\varphi^{\ominus}$ 值或 φ 值越小，表示电对中还原态的还原能力越强，是强还原剂。

(3)判断氧化还原反应的方向

$E=\varphi_{氧化剂}-\varphi_{还原剂}>0$　　反应正向进行

$E=\varphi_{氧化剂}-\varphi_{还原剂}=0$　　处于平衡状态

$E=\varphi_{氧化剂}-\varphi_{还原剂}<0$　　反应逆向进行

(4)判断反应进行的程度

氧化还原反应达到平衡时，平衡常数 $K^{\ominus}$ 与标准电动势 $E^{\ominus}$ 之间的关系为

$$\lg K^{\ominus}=\frac{nE^{\ominus}}{0.059}=\frac{n(\varphi^{\ominus}_{氧化剂}-\varphi^{\ominus}_{还原剂})}{0.059} \tag{3-4-3}$$

式中，n 为氧化还原反应中转移的电子数。K 越大，反应进行的程度越大。

【例 3-4-7】 在 298K 时，对反应

$$2Fe^{3+}(1.0mol/L)+Cu \rightleftharpoons 2Fe^{2+}(0.2mol/L)+Cu^{2+}(0.01mol/L)$$

已知 $\varphi^{\ominus}_{Cu^{2+}/Cu}=0.34V$，$\varphi^{\ominus}_{Fe^{3+}/+Fe^{2+}}=0.77V$。

①将该反应设计成原电池，并用符号表示；

②写出两极反应；

③判断反应进行方向；

④计算 298K 时反应的平衡常数 $K^{\ominus}$。

解 ①设计原电池

$$\varphi_{Fe^{3+}/Fe^{2+}}=0.77+\frac{0.059}{1}\lg\frac{1.0}{0.2}=0.81V$$

$$\varphi_{Cu^{2+}/Cu}=0.34+\frac{0.059}{2}\lg 0.01=0.28V$$

原电池符号：(－)Cu|Cu^{2+}(0.01mol/L) ‖ Fe^{2+}(0.2mol/L)，Fe^{3+}(1.0mol/L)|Pt(＋)

②写出两极反应

正极电极反应　　$Fe^{3+}+e^{-} \rightleftharpoons Fe^{2+}$

负极电极反应　　$Cu-2e^{-} \rightleftharpoons Cu^{2+}$

③判断反应方向

$$E=\varphi_{氧化剂}-\varphi_{还原剂}=0.81-0.28=0.53V>0\text{(反应正向进行)}$$

④计算平衡常数

$$\lg K^{\ominus}=\frac{nE^{\ominus}}{0.059}=\frac{2\times(0.77-0.34)}{0.059}=14.58$$

$$K^{\ominus}=3.80\times10^{14}$$

【例 3-4-8】 已知：$\varphi^{\ominus}_{Fe^{3+}/Fe^{2+}}=0.77V$；$\varphi^{\ominus}_{Zn^{2+}/Zn}=-0.76V$；$\varphi^{\ominus}_{Cu^{2+}/Cu}=0.34V$。

氧化型物质的氧化能力由强到弱的排列次序正确的是：

A. $Fe^{3+}>Zn^{2+}>Cu^{2+}$　　B. $Zn^{2+}>Fe^{3+}>Cu^{2+}$

C. $Cu^{2+}>Fe^{3+}>Zn^{2+}$　　D. $Fe^{3+}>Cu^{2+}>Zn^{2+}$

解 $\varphi^{\ominus}$ 值或 φ 值越大，表示电对中氧化态的氧化能力越强；$\varphi^{\ominus}$ 值或 φ 值越小，表示电对中还原态的还原能力越强。三个电对中氧化型物质的氧化能力由强到弱的顺序为：$Fe^{3+}>Cu^{2+}$

$>Zn^{2+}$。

答案:D

【例 3-4-9】 反应 $Zn^{2+}(1.0mol/L)+Fe \rightleftharpoons Zn+Fe^{2+}(0.1mol/L)$ 自发进行的方向是:

A. 正向　　B. 逆向

C. 平衡状态　　D. 不能判断

解 $\varphi_{Zn^{2+}/Zn}=\varphi^{\ominus}_{Zn^{2+}/Zn}+\frac{0.059}{2}\lg C_{Zn^{2+}}=-0.76V$

$\varphi_{Fe^{2+}/Fe}=\varphi^{\ominus}_{Fe^{2+}/Fe}+\frac{0.059}{2}\lg C_{Fe^{2+}}=-0.44-0.0295\approx-0.47V$

$E=\varphi_{Zn^{2+}/Zn}-\varphi^{\ominus}_{Fe^{2+}/Fe}=-0.76+0.47=-0.29V<0$(反应逆向进行)

答案:B

【例 3-4-10】 上题反应的 $\lg K^{\ominus}$ 是:

A. $\frac{-2\times0.32}{0.059}$　　B. $\frac{2\times0.32}{0.059}$

C. $\frac{-2\times0.29}{0.059}$　　D. $\frac{2\times0.29}{0.059}$

解 $\lg K^{\ominus}=\frac{nE^{\ominus}}{0.059}=\frac{2\times(-0.76+0.44)}{0.059}=\frac{-2\times0.32}{0.059}$

答案:A

(四)元素电势图

当某元素可以形成三种或三种以上氧化值的物质时,这些物质可以组成多种不同的电对,各电对的标准电极电势可用图的形式表示出来,这种图叫做元素电势图。元素电势图一般按元素的氧化值由高到低的顺序,把各物质的化学式从左到右写出来,各不同氧化值物质之间用直线连接起来,在直线上表明两种不同氧化值物质所组成的电对的标准电极电势。例如氧元素在酸性溶液中的电势图为:$O_2 \xrightarrow{0.6945} H_2O_2 \xrightarrow{1.763} H_2O$(O₂ 至 H₂O 连线上标 1.229)

元素电势图的应用:

(1)判断歧化反应。对于元素电势图 $A \xrightarrow{\varphi^{\ominus}_{左}} B \xrightarrow{\varphi^{\ominus}_{右}} C$,若 $\varphi^{\ominus}_{右}>\varphi^{\ominus}_{左}$,B 即是电极电势大的电对的氧化型,可作氧化剂,又是电极电势小的电对的还原型,也可作还原剂,B 的歧化反应能够发生;若 $\varphi^{\ominus}_{右}<\varphi^{\ominus}_{左}$,B 的歧化反应不能发生。

(2)计算标准电极电势。根据元素电势图,可以从已知某些电对的标准电极电势计算出另一电对的标准电极电势。假如有一元素电势图为:$A \xrightarrow[(z_1)]{\varphi^{\ominus}_1} B \xrightarrow[(z_2)]{\varphi^{\ominus}_2} C$(A 至 C 连线上标 $\varphi^{\ominus}_x$、(z_x)),则 $\varphi^{\ominus}_x=\frac{z_1\varphi^{\ominus}_1+z_2\varphi^{\ominus}_2}{z_x}$($z$ 为电对中具有变价的元素的一个原子氧化值的变化数)。

如在酸性溶液中,铜元素的电势图为 $Cu^{2+} \xrightarrow{0.16V} Cu^{+} \xrightarrow{0.52V} Cu$,则计算得:$\varphi^{\ominus}_{Cu^{2+}/Cu}=\frac{\varphi^{\ominus}_{Cu^{2+}/Cu^{+}}+\varphi^{\ominus}_{Cu^{+}/Cu}}{2}=\frac{0.16+0.52}{2}=0.34V$。

四、电解

电流通过电解液在电极上引起氧化还原反应的过程叫电解。

（一）电解池的组成和电极反应

电解池是将电能转变成化学能的装置。电解池中有两极，与外电源负极相连的极叫阴极，与外电源正极相连的极叫阳极。电解时阴极上发生还原反应，阳极上发生氧化反应。

（二）分解电压与超电压

使电解顺利进行时所需最小外加电压叫实际分解电压，理论分解电压是电解产物形成原电池时所产生的电动势，它与外加电压方向相反。一般情况下实际分解电压总是大于理论分解电压。主要原因是电极的极化。电极极化又分浓差极化和电化学极化两类。

浓差极化是由电极反应速度快，而离子扩散速度慢，使电极表面离子浓度低于整体的离子浓度所造成的极化现象。阴极表面离子浓度降低将使阴极电势更负，阳极表面离子浓度降低将使阳极电势更正，分解电压将增大。浓差极化可用加热和搅拌等方法消除。

电化学极化是电极反应速度慢所引起的极化现象。其结果也是使阴极电势变得更负，阳极电势更正。实际析出电势与理论析出电势之差叫超电势（η 表示），统一规定超电势取正值。即

$$\eta_{阴}=\varphi_{阴、理}-\varphi_{阴、实} \tag{3-4-4}$$

$$\eta_{阳}=\varphi_{阳、实}-\varphi_{阳、理} \tag{3-4-5}$$

阴极超电势与阳极超电势之和等于超电压，即

$$E_{超}=\eta_{阴}+\eta_{阳} \tag{3-4-6}$$

（三）电解产物的一般规律

电解产物析出的先后顺序由它们的析出电势来决定。而析出电势又与标准电极电势、离子浓度、超电势等有关。但总的原则是：析出电势代数值较大的氧化型物质首先在阴极还原；析出电势代数值较小的还原型物质首先在阳极氧化。一般规律是：

阴极　　当 $\varphi^{\ominus}>\varphi^{\ominus}_{Al^{3+}/Al}$ 时　$M^{n+}+ne^{-}\rightleftharpoons M$

　　　　当 $\varphi^{\ominus}<\varphi^{\ominus}_{Al^{3+}/Al}$ 时　$2H^{+}+2e^{-}\rightleftharpoons H_2$

阳极　可溶性电极　　$M-ne^{-}\rightleftharpoons M^{n+}$

　　　惰性电极　简单负离子，如 Cl^-、Br^-、I^-、S^{2-} 分别析出 Cl_2、Br_2、I_2、S。

　　　　　　　　复杂离子，如 $4OH^{-}-4e^{-}\rightleftharpoons O_2+2H_2O$。

【例 3-4-11】 电解 NaCl 水溶液时，阴极上放电的离子是：

A. H^+　　B. OH^-　　C. Na^+　　D. Cl^-

解 电解产物析出顺序由它们的析出电势决定。析出电势与标准电极电势、离子浓度、超电势有关。总的原则：析出电势代数值较大的氧化型物质首先在阴极还原，析出电势代数值较小的还原型物质首先在阳极氧化。

阴极：当 $\varphi^{\ominus}>\varphi^{\ominus}_{Al^{3+}/Al}$ 时，$M^{n+}+ne^{-}=M$

　　　当 $\varphi^{\ominus}<\varphi^{\ominus}_{Al^{3+}/Al}$ 时，$2H^{+}+2e^{-}=H_2$

因 $\varphi^{\ominus}_{Na^{+}/Na}<\varphi^{\ominus}_{Al^{3+}/Al}$ 时，所以 H^+ 首先放电析出。

答案：A

五、金属的腐蚀及其防止

（一）金属的腐蚀

金属腐蚀是指金属表面与周围介质发生化学或电化学作用而遭受的破坏。金属腐蚀分化学腐蚀和电化学腐蚀两大类。

单纯由化学作用引起的腐蚀叫化学腐蚀。其特点是腐蚀过程中没有水气的参与。如

金属与干燥的 O_2、H_2S、Cl_2、SO_2 等气体和石油中的有机硫化物作用生成相应的化合物，高温时尤为显著。

金属与电解质溶液接触时发生电化学腐蚀。在腐蚀过程中形成许多微小的腐蚀电池。杂质等电极电势较大的物质作为阴极发生还原反应，电极电势较小的物质在阳极上发生氧化反应而被腐蚀。由于腐蚀介质的不同，电化学腐蚀又可分为下列三种类型。

1. 析氢腐蚀

在酸性介质中(以 Fe 为例)

阳极 $$Fe-2e^- \rightleftharpoons Fe^{2+}$$

阴极(导电杂质) $$2H^+ + 2e^- = H_2$$

电池反应 $$Fe+2H^+ \rightleftharpoons Fe^{2+} + H_2$$

或 $$Fe+2H_2O \rightleftharpoons Fe(OH)_2 + H_2$$

2. 吸氧腐蚀

在弱碱性或中性介质中(以 Fe 为例)：

阳极 $$Fe-2e^- \rightleftharpoons Fe^{2+}$$

阴极(导电杂质) $$\frac{1}{2}O_2 + H_2O + 2e^- \rightleftharpoons 2OH^-$$

总反应 $$Fe + H_2O + \frac{1}{2}O_2 \rightleftharpoons Fe(OH)_2$$

$Fe(OH)_2$ 在空气中进一步氧化脱水成为铁锈 Fe_2O_3，钢铁在大气中的腐蚀主要是吸氧腐蚀。

3. 差异充气腐蚀

当金属表面氧气分布不均时发生差异充气腐蚀，实际上是吸氧腐蚀的一种。

$$O_2 + 2H_2O + 4e^- \rightleftharpoons 4OH^-$$

$$\varphi = \varphi^\ominus + \frac{0.059}{4}\lg\frac{p_{O_2}}{C_{OH^-}^4}$$

可见，p_{O_2} 小的部位，φ 值小，作为阳极被腐蚀。这种腐蚀的危害极大，多发生在金属表面不光滑或加工的接口处等。

【例 3-4-12】 在差异充气腐蚀中，氧气浓度大和小部分的名称分别为：

A. 阳极和阴极　　B. 阴极和阳极

C. 正极和负极　　D. 负极和正极

解 差异充气腐蚀中，$\varphi = \varphi^\ominus + \frac{0.059}{4}\lg\frac{p_{O_2}}{C_{OH^-}^4}$，所以，$p_{O_2}$ 大的部分，φ 值大，为阴极；p_{O_2} 小的部分，φ 值小，为阳极，被腐蚀。

答案：B

(二)金属腐蚀的防止

防止金属腐蚀的方法很多，常用的有组成合金法、表面涂层法、缓蚀剂法、阴极保护法等。

缓蚀剂法是在腐蚀介质中加入少量物质来延缓腐蚀速率的方法，所加的物质叫缓蚀剂。缓蚀剂分为无机缓蚀剂和有机缓蚀剂两大类，在中性或碱性介质中常加无机缓蚀剂，如亚硝酸盐、铬酸盐、重铬酸盐、磷酸盐等；在酸性介质中加入有机缓蚀剂，如乌洛托品[六次甲基四胺 $(CH_2)_6N_4$]、若丁(其主要成分为苯基硫脲)等来减缓钢铁的腐蚀。

阴极保护法分为两种。

1. 牺牲阳极保护法

将活泼金属与被保护金属组成原电池，使活泼金属作为腐蚀电池的阳极而被腐蚀，被保护的金属作为阴极得到保护。此法常用于保护海轮外壳、锅炉及海底设备。

2. 外加电流法

这是在直流电源作用下，将被保护的金属与另一附加电极组成电解池，被保护金属作为电解池的阴极而达到保护的目的。这种方法用于防止土壤、河水和海水中的金属设备被腐蚀。

【例 3-4-13】 下列防止金属腐蚀的方法中错误的是：

A. 在金属表面涂刷油漆

B. 在外加电流保护法中，被保护金属直接与电源正极相连

C. 在外加电流保护法中，被保护金属直接与电源负极相连

D. 为了保护铁制管道，可使其与锌片相连

解 在外加电流保护法中，被保护金属作为电解池的阴极得到保护，与电源负极相连。

答案：B

六、原电池、电解池、腐蚀电池的比较

(一)原电池中发生自发的氧化还原反应(表 3-4-2)

表 3-4-2

电极名称	电势	电极反应
正极	高	还原反应
负极	低	氧化反应

(二)电解池中发生强制的氧化还原反应(表 3-4-3)

表 3-4-3

电极名称	电势	电极反应
阳极	高	氧化反应
阴极	低	还原反应

(三)腐蚀电池中发生自发的氧化还原反应(表 3-4-4)

表 3-4-4

电极名称	电势	电极反应
阴极	高	还原反应
阳极	低	氧化反应

习　题

3-4-1 在 $KMnO_4 + HCl \rightarrow KCl + MnCl_2 + Cl_2 + H_2O$ 反应中，配平后各物种前的化学计量数从左到右依次为(　　)。

A. 2、8、2、2、3、8　　B. 2、16、2、2、5、8

C. 2、4、1、2、3、8　　D. 2、16、2、2、5、4

3-4-2 在上题反应中，作为氧化剂的是(　　)。

A. HCl　　B. $MnCl_2$　　C. Cl_2　　D. $KMnO_4$

3-4-3 下列两电极反应

$$Cu^{2+}+2e^- \rightleftharpoons Cu$$

$$I_2+2e^- \rightleftharpoons 2I^-$$

当离子浓度增大时，电极电势变化正确的是(　　)。

A. $\varphi_{Cu^{2+}/Cu}$变小，φ_{I_2/I^-}变大　　B. $\varphi_{Cu^{2+}/Cu}$变大，φ_{I_2/I^-}变大

C. $\varphi_{Cu^{2+}/Cu}$变小，φ_{I_2/I^-}变大　　D. $\varphi_{Cu^{2+}/Cu}$变大，φ_{I_2/I^-}变小

3-4-4 已知 $\varphi^{\ominus}_{MnO_4^-/Mn^{2+}}=1.51V$，$\varphi^{\ominus}_{MnO_4^-/MnO_2}=1.68V$，$\varphi^{\ominus}_{MnO_4^-/MnO_4^{2-}}=0.56V$，则还原型物质的还原性由强到弱排列的次序是(　　)。

A. $MnO_4^{2-}>MnO_2>Mn^{2+}$　　B. $Mn^{2+}>MnO_4^{2-}>MnO_2$

C. $MnO_4^{2-}>Mn^{2+}>MnO_2$　　D. $MnO_2>MnO_4^{2-}>Mn^{2+}$

3-4-5 下列两反应能自发进行

$$2Fe^{3+}+Cu \rightleftharpoons 2Fe^{2+}+Cu^{2+};\quad Cu^{2+}+Fe \rightleftharpoons Fe^{2+}+Cu$$

由此比较 a：$\varphi_{Fe^{3+}/Fe^{2+}}$，b：$\varphi_{Cu^{2+}/Cu}$，c：$\varphi_{Fe^{2+}/Fe}$的代数值大小顺序为(　　)。

A. a>b>c　　B. c>b>a　　C. b>a>c　　D. a>c>b

3-4-6 反应 $A+B^{2+}=A^{2+}+B$ 的标准平衡常数是 10^4，则该反应组成原电池时，该原电池的电动势是(　　)。

A. 0.118V　　B. 1.20V　　C. 0.07V　　D. 0.236V

3-4-7 用铜作电极电解 $CuCl_2$ 水溶液时，阳极的主要反应是(　　)。

A. $4OH^- -4e^- \rightleftharpoons 2H_2O+O_2$　　B. $2Cl^- -2e^- = Cl_2$

C. $2H^+ +2e^+ \rightleftharpoons H_2$　　D. $Cu-2e^- = Cu^{2+}$

3-4-8 将钢管一部分埋在沙土中，另一部分埋在黏土中，埋入黏土中的钢管成为腐蚀电池的(　　)。

A. 正极　　B. 负极　　C. 阴极　　D. 阳极

第五节　有机化合物

一、有机化合物的特点、分类及命名

有机化合物在结构和性质上的特点如下：

(一)结构特点

(1)碳原子之间可以形成 C—C 单键、C=C 双键和 C≡C 叁键。碳原子的连接方式有长短不等的直链、支链和首尾相连的环链。例如

$CH_3-C\equiv CH$　　$CH_3(CH_2)_{16}CH_3$　　（环状结构式：HC=CH—CH₂—CH₂—CH₂—CH₂ 成环）

丙炔　　正十八烷　　环己烯

(2)普遍存在同分异构现象。一种分子式往往可以表示几种性能完全不同的化合物，这些化合物叫同分异构体。例如正丁烷与异丁烷的分子式都是 C_4H_{10}，而它们的结构式分别为

$$CH_3—CH_2—CH_2—CH_3$$

正丁烷

$$\begin{array}{c} \quad CH_3 \\ \quad | \\ CH_3—CH—CH_3 \end{array}$$

异丁烷

这种由于碳原子的连接方式不同形成的异构体叫碳骼异构体。又如分子式都是 C_2H_6O 的乙醇和甲醚结构式分别为

$$CH_3—CH_2—OH \qquad CH_3—O—CH_3$$

乙醇　　　　甲醚

这种由于官能团的不同形成的异构体叫官能团异构体。因此，为了准确地表示一个有机化合物，通常采用结构式而不用分子式。

(二)性质特点

(1)容易燃烧。除 CCl_4 外都可以燃烧，目前所用的固体、液体、气体燃料几乎都是有机物。

(2)熔点、沸点低。绝大多数有机化合物都是共价化合物，晶体类型属分子晶体，分子间作用力较弱。故大多数有机物的熔点、沸点较低，一般熔点在 573K 以下。

(3)难溶于水，易溶于有机溶剂。大多数有机化合物是非极性或弱极性的分子，根据“相似相溶”原则，都可溶于酒精、乙醚、丙酮、煤油、汽油等有机溶剂。

(4)反应速率慢、产物种类多。有机物之间的反应速率慢，常要用加热加压或加催化剂的方法来加速反应。有机反应进行时，常有副反应发生，产物种类多。

(5)绝缘性能好。绝大多数有机物是非电解质，在溶解和熔融状态下不导电，是优良的绝缘材料。

(三)有机物的分类

1.按碳原子的连接方式分类

(1)开链化合物

碳原子相互连接成两端张开的链，开链化合物又叫脂肪类化合物。如

$$CH_3—CH_2—OH \qquad \begin{array}{c} O \\ \| \\ CH_3—C—CH_3 \end{array} \qquad H_2C═CH—CH═CH_2$$

乙醇　　　　丙酮　　　　1,3-丁二烯

(2)碳环化合物

碳原子相互连接成环状。碳环化合物又分三类：

①脂环化合物，性质与链状化合物相似，主要存在于石油和煤焦油中，如：

环戊烷（C_5H_{10}，五个 CH_2 成环）　　1,3-环己二烯（CH_2、CH_2、CH=CH、CH=CH 成环）　　环己酮（C=O 与五个 CH_2 成环）

②芳香族化合物，这类化合物分子中都含有苯环结构，如：

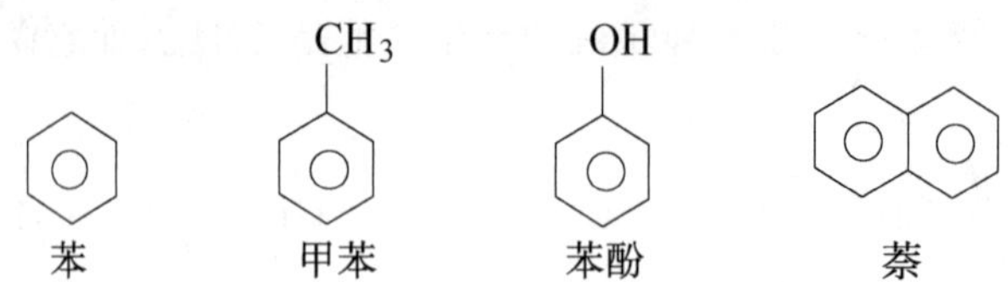

③杂环化合物，环上除有碳原子外，还有其他原子(如 O、N、S)，如：

2. 按官能团分类

将含有相同官能团和化学性质基本相似的化合物划分为一类。表 3-5-1 列出了一些主要化合物的类别、官能团的名称及通式等。表中 R、R′表示烷基，Ar 表示芳烃基，X 表示卤素。

一些主要有机物的类型　　表 3-5-1

类　别	通　式	官 能 团	名　称	例　　子
烷烃	C_nH_{2n+2}			CH_4　甲烷
烯烃	C_nH_{2n}	$\gt C{=}C\lt$	双键	$CH_2{=}CH_2$　乙烯
炔烃	C_nH_{2n-2}	$—C{\equiv}C—$	叁键	$CH{\equiv}CH$　乙炔
卤代烃	R—X	—X	卤素原子	C_6H_5Br　溴苯
醇或酚	R—OH 或 Ar—OH	—OH	羟基	CH_3CH_2OH　乙醇，C_6H_5OH　苯酚
醚	R—O—R′	—O—	醚键	$C_2H_5—O—C_2H_5$　乙醚
醛	R—CHO	$—\overset{H}{\overset{\mid}{C}}{=}O$	醛基	$CH_3—\overset{O}{\overset{\Vert}{C}}—H$ 乙醛
酮	$R—\overset{O}{\overset{\Vert}{C}}—R'$	$—\overset{O}{\overset{\Vert}{C}}—$	羰基	$CH_3—\overset{O}{\overset{\Vert}{C}}—CH_3$　丙酮
羧酸	RCOOH	$—\overset{O}{\overset{\Vert}{C}}—OH$	羧基	CH_3COOH　乙酸
酯	RCOOR′	$—\overset{O}{\overset{\Vert}{C}}—O—R'$	烷氧羰基	$CH_3COOCH_2CH_3$　乙酸乙酯
胺	$R—NH_2$	$—NH_2$	氨基	$H_2NCH_2CH_2NH_2$　乙二胺
酰胺	$R—\overset{O}{\overset{\Vert}{C}}—NH_2$	$—\overset{O}{\overset{\Vert}{C}}—NH_2$	氨基甲酰基	$CH_3—\overset{O}{\overset{\Vert}{C}}—NH_2$　乙酰胺
腈	R—CN	—CN	氰基	$H_2C{=}CHCN$　丙烯腈
硝基化合物	$R—NO_2$ 或 $Ar—NO_2$	$—NO_2$	硝基	$C_6H_5NO_2$　硝基苯
磺酸	$R—SO_3H$	$—SO_3H$	磺酸基	$C_6H_5SO_3H$　苯磺酸

(四)有机物的命名

有机物的命名方法有习惯命名法、衍生物命名法、系统命名法。重点介绍系统命名法。

1.链烃及其衍生物的命名原则

(1)选择主链

选择最长碳链或含有官能团的最长碳链为主链,以主链作为母体,主链中的碳原子数用甲、乙、……壬、癸、十一、十二……表示,称某烷、某烯、某炔、某醇、某醛、某酸等,支链、卤原子、硝基则视为取代基。

(2)主链编号

从距取代基或官能团最近的一端开始,对碳原子依次用 1,2,3,…进行编号,来表明取代基或官能团的位置。但要尽可能采用最小数目。有 n 个取代基时,简单的在前,复杂的在后,相同的取代基和官能团的数目,用二、三、…表示。

(3)写出全称

将取代基的位置编号、数目和名称写在前面,将母体化合物的名称写在后面,例如

$$\overset{6}{C}H_3-\overset{5}{C}H_2-\overset{4}{C}H(CH_2CH_3)-\overset{3}{C}H_2-\overset{2}{C}(=CH_2)-CH_3$$

2- 甲基 -4- 乙基 -1- 己烯

$$\overset{7}{C}H_3-\overset{6}{C}(CH_3)_2-\overset{5}{C}H(CH_2CH_3)-\overset{4}{C}\equiv\overset{3}{C}-\overset{2}{C}(CH_3)_2-\overset{1}{C}H_3$$

2,2,6,6-四甲基-5-乙基-3-庚炔

$$\overset{6}{C}H_3-\overset{5}{C}H=\overset{4}{C}H-\overset{3}{C}(=O)-\overset{2}{C}(CH_3)(Cl)-\overset{1}{C}H_3$$

2-氯-2-甲基-4-己烯-3-酮

2.芳香烃及其衍生物的命名原则

(1)选择母体

选择苯环上所连官能团($-OR$、$-NH_2$、$-OH$、$-\overset{O}{\overset{\|}{C}}-$、$-CN$、$-\overset{O}{\overset{\|}{C}}-H$、$-\overset{O}{\overset{\|}{C}}-NH_2$、$-\overset{O}{\overset{\|}{C}}-X$、$-SO_3H$、$-\overset{O}{\overset{\|}{C}}-OR$、$-\overset{O}{\overset{\|}{C}}-OH$、$\gt C=C\lt$、$-C\equiv C-$)或带官能团最长的碳链为母体,把苯环视为取代基。当苯环上有简单的烃基(分子量较小的烃基)、卤原子、硝基时,把苯环当做母体。

(2)编号

将母体中碳原子依次用 1,2,…编号,使官能团或取代基位次具有最小值。当苯环上含有两个或三个取代基时,可分别用邻-、间-、对-或连-、均-、偏-等词头表示。例如:

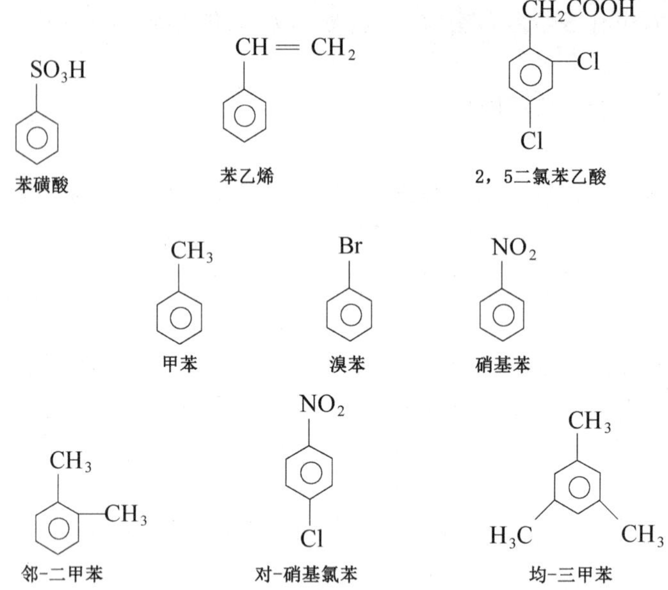

【例 3-5-1】 下列物质中，不属于醇类的是：

A. C_4H_9OH　　B. 甘油　　C. $C_6H_5CH_2OH$　　D. C_6H_5OH

解 羟基与烷基直接相连为醇，通式为 R—OH(R 为烷基)；羟基与芳香基直接相连为酚，通式为 Ar—OH(Ar 为芳香基)。

答案：D

【例 3-5-2】 下列有机物中，对于可能处在同一平面上的最多原子数目的判断，正确的是：

A. 丙烷最多有 6 个原子处于同一平面上

B. 丙烯最多有 9 个原子处于同一平面上

C. 苯乙烯($C_6H_5-CH=CH_2$)最多有 16 个原子处于同一平面上

D. $CH_3CH=CH-C\equiv C-CH_3$ 最多有 12 个原子处于同一平面上

解 丙烷最多 5 个原子处于一个平面，丙烯最多 7 个原子处于一个平面，苯乙烯最多 16 个原子处于一个平面，$CH_3CH=CH-C\equiv C-CH_3$ 最多 10 个原子处于一个平面。

答案：C

二、有机物的重要反应

(一)裂化反应

有机化合物在高温下分解叫热解，烷烃的热解叫裂化反应，裂化反应的实质是 C—C 键和C—H 键的断裂。反应产物是混合物，碳原子越多的有机物热解时产物越复杂。丁烷的裂化反应如下

$$CH_3CH_2CH_2CH_3 \longrightarrow \begin{cases} CH_3-CH=CH_2+CH_4 \\ CH_2=CH_2+CH_3-CH_3 \\ CH_3-CH_2-CH=CH_2+H_2 \end{cases}$$

在催化裂化下，除有 C—C 键的断裂外还伴随着异构化、环化、芳香化、聚合、缩合等反应发生。

(二)取代反应

在反应中，反应物分子的一个原子或原子团被其他原子或原子团替代的反应。例如：在日

光或加热下，CH_4 与 Cl_2 发生的取代反应生成 HCl 和氯甲烷（CH_3Cl）、二氯甲烷（CH_2Cl_2）、三氯甲烷（$CHCl_3$）、四氯化碳（CCl_4）。

芳香烃有以下几种重要取代反应：

（1）氯化

$$C_6H_6 + Cl_2 \xrightarrow{\text{Fe 或 }FeCl_3} C_6H_5Cl + HCl$$

（2）硝化

$$C_6H_6 + HNO_3 \xrightarrow{\text{浓 }H_2SO_4} C_6H_5NO_2 + H_2O$$

（3）磺化

$$C_6H_6 + H_2SO_4(\text{浓}) \longrightarrow C_6H_5SO_3H + H_2O$$

当苯环上已有一个取代基，再进入第二个取代基时，按苯环的结构可以进入邻位、间位和对位形成三种异构体。但事实上这三个不同的位置取代的机会是不均等的，第二个取代基进入的位置决定于苯环上原有取代基，与新进入的取代基关系不大，把苯环上原有取代基对新进入取代基的定位作用叫取代基的定位效应。根据实验结果一般把定位基分为两类：

（1）邻位、对位定位基

定位效应的大小顺序：$-NH_2 > -OH > -CH_3 > Cl > Br > I > -C_6H_5$，同时使苯环活化。例如：

$$C_6H_5CH_3 + HNO_3(\text{浓}) \xrightarrow{\text{浓 }H_2SO_4} \underset{58\%}{o\text{-}CH_3C_6H_4NO_2} + \underset{38\%}{p\text{-}CH_3C_6H_4NO_2} + \underset{4\%}{m\text{-}CH_3C_6H_4NO_2}$$

（2）间位定位基

其定位效应大小顺序：$-NO_2 > -CN > -SO_3H > -CHO > -COOH$，同时使苯环钝化。例如：

$$C_6H_5NO_2 + HNO_3(\text{发烟}) \xrightarrow[368\sim373K]{\text{浓 }H_2SO_4} \underset{93.2\%}{m\text{-}C_6H_4(NO_2)_2} + \underset{6.5\%}{o\text{-}C_6H_4(NO_2)_2} + \underset{0.3\%}{p\text{-}C_6H_4(NO_2)_2}$$

（三）加成反应

不饱和分子中的双键、叁键打开，即分子中的π键断裂，两个一价的原子或原子团加到不饱和键的两个碳原子上，这种反应叫加成反应，重要的加成反应有以下两种类型。

1. 不饱和烃的加成反应

如烯烃的加成反应

$$CH_3CH{=}CH_2+HOH{=}CH_3\underset{\displaystyle OH}{\underset{|}{CH}}{-}\underset{\displaystyle H}{\underset{|}{CH_2}}$$

像这种结构不对称的烯烃与水、卤化氢等极性试剂加成时，主要是试剂中带负电荷的部分加到双键含氢较少的或不含氢的碳原子上，而带正电荷部分加到双键含氢较多的碳原子上，这一规律称不对称加成规则，此经验规律也称马尔可夫尼克夫规则，简称马氏规则。合成高分子的原料如氯乙烯、乙酸乙烯酯、丙烯腈等都是通过加成反应得到的。例如：乙炔与 HCl 的加成得氯乙烯

$$CH{\equiv}CH+HCl\xrightarrow{HgCl_2}CH_2{=}CHCl$$

乙炔与乙酸的加成得乙酸乙烯酯

$$CH{\equiv}CH+CH_3COOH\xrightarrow[150\times10^5\sim180\times10^5Pa]{碱}H_2C{=}CH{-}O{-}\overset{\displaystyle O}{\overset{\|}{C}}{-}CH_3$$

乙炔与 HCN 的加成得丙烯腈

$$CH{\equiv}CH+HCN\xrightarrow[353\sim363K]{CuCl_2+NH_4Cl}CH_2{=}CHCN$$

2. 醛和酮的加成反应

醛和酮的分子中都含有羰基（$-\overset{\displaystyle O}{\overset{\|}{C}}-$），羰基中 $C{=}O$ 双键也能发生加成反应。当醛酮与结构对称的试剂加成时，反应情况类似烯烃加成；当与结构不对称的试剂加成时，由于

$$>\overset{\delta+}{C}{=}\overset{\delta-}{O}$$

试剂分子中带负电荷的部分加到碳原子上，带正电荷部分加到氧原子上。如醛、酮与 HCN 的加成反应

$$\begin{matrix}R\\ & \diagdown\\ & & \overset{\delta+}{C}{=}\overset{\delta-}{O}\\ & \diagup\\ H\end{matrix}+\overset{\delta+}{H}\overset{\delta-}{CN}\longrightarrow\begin{matrix}R & & & & OH\\ & \diagdown & & \diagup\\ & & C\\ & \diagup & & \diagdown\\ H & & & & CN\end{matrix}$$

$$\begin{matrix}R'\\ & \diagdown\\ & & C{=}O\\ & \diagup\\ R\end{matrix}+HCN\longrightarrow\begin{matrix}R' & & & & OH\\ & \diagdown & & \diagup\\ & & C\\ & \diagup & & \diagdown\\ R & & & & CN\end{matrix}$$

（四）消去反应

从有机化合物分子中消去一个小分子化合物如 HX、H_2O 等的作用叫消去反应，重要的消去反应有卤代烷的消去反应和醇的消去反应等。

1. 卤代烷的消去反应

卤代烷与 NaOH 的乙醇溶液共热时，可发生消去反应

$$R-\underset{\mid}{\overset{}{C}}H-\underset{\mid}{C}H_2 + NaOH \xrightarrow{C_2H_5OH} RCH{=}CH_2 + NaX + H_2O$$
$$\quad\ H \qquad\ X$$

叔卤代烷最容易脱卤化氢，仲卤代烷次之，伯卤代烷最难。仲、叔卤代烷脱卤化氢时，氢原子主要是从含氢较少的碳原子上脱去，如 2-溴丁烷的消去反应

$$\underset{\substack{|\\H}}{CH_3-CH}-\underset{\substack{|\\Br}}{CH}-\underset{\substack{|\\H}}{CH_2} + KOH \xrightarrow{C_2H_5OH} \underset{81\%}{CH_3CH{=}CHCH_3} + \underset{19\%}{CH_3CH_2CH{=}CH_2}$$

2. 醇的消去反应

醇在有催化剂和一定高温下能发生消去反应，使醇分子脱去水而变成烯烃，例如

$$\underset{\substack{|\\H}}{CH_2}-\underset{\substack{|\\OH}}{CH_2} \xrightarrow[\text{(或 }Al_2O_3\text{,360℃)}]{\text{浓 }H_2SO_4\text{,170℃}} H_2C{=}CH_2 + H_2O$$

醇脱水时主要从含氢较少的碳原子上脱去氢原子，这样形成的烯烃比较稳定，此规律叫做查依采夫规律，简称**查氏规则**，例如

$$CH_3-CH_2-CH_2-\underset{\substack{|\\OH}}{CH}-CH_3 \xrightarrow[-H_2O]{\text{酸}} \begin{cases} CH_3CH_2-CH{=}CH-CH_3 \\ \text{2-戊烯(主要产物)} \\ CH_3-CH_2-CH_2-CH{=}CH_2 \\ \text{1-戊烯(次要产物)} \end{cases}$$

(五) 氧化还原反应

有机化学中把分子中加入氧或失去氢的反应叫**氧化反应**，把分子中失去氧或加入氢的反应叫**还原反应**。

1. 烷烃的氧化

烷烃在常温下是稳定的，但在高温催化下可氧化成醇、醛、酮、酸，例如甲烷氧化可得到甲醛、甲酸

$$CH_4 + O_2 \xrightarrow[873K]{N_i} HCHO + H_2O$$

2. 不饱和烃的氧化

烯烃分子中由于存在双键，比烷烃容易氧化，冷的稀高锰酸钾碱性溶液能使烯烃氧化为二元醇

$$3CH_2{=}CH_2 + 2KMnO_4 + 4H_2O = 3\underset{\substack{|\\OH}}{CH_2}-\underset{\substack{|\\OH}}{CH_2} + 2KOH + 2MnO_2$$

在较强的氧化剂作用下(如酸性高锰酸钾溶液)，可进一步氧化而使碳链在原双键处完全断裂，氧化结果可简单表示如下

$$RCH{=}CH_2 \xrightarrow{[O]} R\overset{O}{\overset{\|}{C}}-OH + H\overset{O}{\overset{\|}{C}}-OH,\quad H\overset{O}{\overset{\|}{C}}-OH \xrightarrow{[O]} CO_2 + H_2O$$

$$\begin{matrix}R\\ \ \end{matrix}\!\!\!\!\!\!\begin{matrix}\diagdown\\ \diagup\end{matrix}\!C{=}CH-R' \xrightarrow{[O]} \begin{matrix}R\\ \ \end{matrix}\!\!\!\!\!\!\begin{matrix}\diagdown\\ \diagup\end{matrix}\!C{=}O + R'-\overset{O}{\overset{\|}{C}}-OH \quad (\text{两个 }R\text{ 取代基})$$

即当原双键碳原子上连有两个氢原子时，氧化后 $CH_2\langle$ 就变成甲酸或进一步氧化成 CO_2 和 H_2O；当原双键碳原子上连有一个氢原子和一个烷基时，氧化后 $RCH\langle$ 就变成 RCOOH（羧酸）；当原双键碳原子上连有两个烷基时，氧化后 $R_2C\langle$ 就变成 $R-\overset{\overset{O}{\|}}{C}-R$（酮）。

炔烃最易被氧化，一般叁键完全断裂，如乙炔被 $KMnO_4$ 氧化

$$3CH\equiv CH+10KM_nO_4+2H_2O=6CO_2+10KOH+10MnO_2\downarrow$$

3. 芳烃的氧化

芳香烃中苯环较稳定，普通情况下与氧化剂不作用。但苯环带有侧链时，不论侧链长短如何，都是侧链中直接与苯环连接的碳原子被氧化变为羧基（—COOH），例如

$$C_6H_5-CH_2-CH_3 \xrightarrow{[O]} C_6H_5-COOH$$

4. 醇的氧化

醇的氧化随分子中—OH 的位置不同而难易程度不同：伯醇（R—OH）氧化最初得到醛，继续氧化可得到羧酸，例如

$$CH_3CH_2OH \xrightarrow{[O]} CH_3CHO \xrightarrow{[O]} CH_3COOH$$

仲醇（$\begin{matrix}R\\ \\R\end{matrix}\rangle CH-OH$）氧化得到酮，一般不再被氧化，例如

$$\underset{\text{(异丙醇)}}{CH_3-\underset{\underset{OH}{|}}{CH}-CH_3} \xrightarrow{[O]} \underset{\text{(丙酮)}}{CH_3-\underset{\underset{O}{\|}}{C}-CH_3}$$

5. 醛的氧化

醛非常容易氧化成酸。弱氧化剂（$CuSO_4$ 及酒石酸钾钠的碱溶液）可将醛氧化成酸，但与酮不能反应。

（六）加聚反应

由低分子化合物（单体）通过加成反应，相互结合成为高聚物的反应叫加聚反应。在此反应过程中，没有产生其他副产物，因此高聚物具有与单体相同的成分。发生加聚反应的单体必须含有不饱和键，乙烯类单体的加聚反应如下

$$\underset{\text{乙烯类单体}}{n\,CH_2=\underset{\underset{X}{|}}{CH}} \rightarrow \underset{\text{乙烯类高聚物}}{\left[CH_2-\underset{\underset{X}{|}}{CH}\right]_n}$$

反应式中 $\left[CH_2-\underset{\underset{X}{|}}{CH}\right]$ 为链节，n 为聚合度，X 可以是 H、R、Cl、CN、Ar 等。

常见的单体和加聚而成的高聚物见表 3-5-2。

常见单体和高聚物 表 3-5-2

单　体	高　聚　物
$CH_2=CH_2$　乙烯	$\text{+}CH_2-CH_2\text{+}_n$　聚乙烯
$CH_2=CH-CH_3$　丙烯	$\text{+}CH_2-CH(CH_3)\text{+}_n$　聚丙烯
$CH_2=CHCl$　氯乙烯	$\text{+}CH_2-CHCl\text{+}_n$　聚氯乙烯
$CH_2=CH-CH=CH_2$　1,3-丁二烯	$\text{+}CH_2-CH=CH-CH_2\text{+}_n$　聚丁二烯
$CH_2=CHCN$　丙烯腈	$\text{+}CH_2-CH(CN)\text{+}_n$　聚丙烯腈
$CF_2=CF_2$　四氟乙烯	$\text{+}CF_2-CF_2\text{+}_n$　聚四氟乙烯
$CH_2=CH-C_6H_5$　苯乙烯	$\text{+}CH(C_6H_5)-CH_2\text{+}_n$　聚苯乙烯
$CH_2=C(CH_3)-COOCH_3$　2-甲基丙烯酸甲酯	$\text{+}CH_2-C(CH_3)(COOCH_3)\text{+}_n$　聚 2-甲基丙烯酸甲酯（有机玻璃）
$CH_2=CH-O-C(=O)-CH_3$　乙酸乙烯酯	$\text{+}CH_2-CH(O-C(=O)-CH_3)\text{+}_n$　聚乙酸乙烯酯

（七）缩聚反应

由一种或多种单体互相缩合成为高聚物，同时析出其他低分子物质（如水、氨、醇、卤化氢等）的反应叫缩聚反应，所生成的高聚物的成分与单体不同，例如

$$nHO-\underset{\underset{O}{\|}}{C}\text{+}CH_2\text{+}_4\underset{\underset{O}{\|}}{C}-OH + nH-\underset{\underset{H}{|}}{N}\text{+}CH_2\text{+}_6\underset{\underset{H}{|}}{N}-H \longrightarrow$$

（己二酸）　　　　（己二胺）

$$\text{+}\underset{\underset{O}{\|}}{C}\text{+}CH_2\text{+}_4\underset{\underset{O}{\|}}{C}-\underset{\underset{H}{|}}{N}\text{+}CH_2\text{+}_6\underset{\underset{H}{|}}{N}\text{+}_n + (2n-1)H_2O$$

（聚酰胺 66，即尼龙 66）

一般而言，含有两个官能团的单体缩聚形成线型高聚物，如聚酰胺 66；含有三个官能团的单体缩聚形成体型高聚物，如丙三醇与邻苯二甲酸酐缩聚形成醇酸树脂，反应如下

$$n\,\underset{OH}{CH_2}-\underset{OH}{CH}-\underset{OH}{CH_2} + n\,C_6H_4(CO)_2O \xrightarrow{-H_2O}$$

（丙三醇）

$$\cdots O—\underset{\|}{C}\ \underset{\|}{C}—O—CH_2—CH—CH_2—O—\underset{\|}{C}\ \underset{\|}{C}—O—CH_2—CH—CH_2—O\cdots$$

$$\cdots O—\underset{\|}{C}\ \underset{\|}{C}—O—CH_2—CH—CH_2—O—\overset{\|}{C}\ \overset{\|}{C}—O—CH_2—CH—CH_2—O\cdots$$

(八)催化加氢

催化加氢是指在催化剂作用下,还原剂氢等与不饱和化合物的加成反应。

1.碳-碳重键的加氢反应

催化加氢方法几乎能使各种类型的碳-碳双键或叁键,无论是孤立的还是共轭的,以不同的难易程度加氢成为饱和键(示例如下)。常用的催化剂有钯、铂、镍等。该方法具有成本低、操作简单、收率高、产品质量好和选择性好等优点,因此它在精细有机合成和工业生产中成为广泛采用的方法。

$$CH_2 = CH_2 \xrightarrow[\text{催化剂}]{H_2} CH_3—CH_3$$

2.芳香环系的加氢反应

芳香族化合物也能进行催化加氢,转变成饱和的脂肪族环系。但它要比脂肪族化合物中的烯键加氢困难得多。例如,异丙烯基苯在很温和的条件下(常温、常压),侧链上的烯键就能够被加氢,而苯环保持不变。

$$\text{异丙烯基苯} \xrightarrow{H_2} \text{异丙苯}$$

芳香环系催化加氢示例

$$\text{苯} \xrightarrow[170\sim230℃]{H_2(4MPa)/Ni} \text{环己烷}$$

三、典型有机物的分子式、性质和用途

(一)烷烃

烷烃是只有碳-碳单键的饱和链烃。烷烃的通式为 C_nH_{2n+2}。随着相对分子质量的增加,烷烃的熔沸点有规律地升高,它们的密度也由小变大。烷烃都不溶于水,易溶于有机溶剂。烷烃的化学性质较稳定,常温下与强酸、强碱、强氧化剂及还原剂都不易反应,所以除作为燃料外,还常用作溶剂、润滑油。在较特殊的条件下,烷烃也显示一定的反应能力,而这些化学性质在基本有机原料工业及石油化工中都非常重要。

甲烷(CH_4)是最简单的烷烃。甲烷是无色、无味的可燃性气体,比空气轻,微溶解于水,燃烧热 $3.97\times10^4 kJ/m^3$,可被液化和固化;性质稳定,在适当条件下能发生氧化、卤化、热解等反应;甲烷与空气的混合气体在点燃时会发生爆炸,爆炸极限 5.3%~14.0%(体积)。

甲烷在工业上主要用于制造乙炔以及经转化制成氢气或合成氨和有机合成的原料气，也用于制备炭黑、硝基甲烷、一氯甲烷、二氯甲烷、三氯甲烷(氯仿)、二硫化碳、四氯化碳和氢氰酸等，也可直接用作燃料。

(二)烯烃

烯烃是指含碳-碳双键(烯键)的碳氢化合物，属于不饱和烃。烯烃的通式为 C_nH_{2n}。随着相对分子质量的增加，烯烃的熔沸点逐渐升高。烯烃最重要的反应是双键上的亲电加成反应。不饱和烯烃通过聚合反应可以形成聚合物。烯烃双键两边 C 原子均通过共价键与不同基团连接时，有顺反异构体。

(三)炔烃

炔烃是含碳-碳叁键的一类不饱和脂肪烃。炔烃的通式为 C_nH_{2n-2}。炔烃的熔沸点低，密度小，难溶于水，易溶于有机溶剂。炔烃的化学活性比烯烃弱，能被高锰酸钾氧化，产物为羧酸。

(四)芳烃

芳烃是芳香烃的简称，是指分子结构中含有一个或者多个苯环的烃类化合物。最简单和最重要的芳烃是苯及其同系物甲苯、二甲苯、乙苯等。芳烃的物理性质和其他烃类类似，它们都没有极性，不溶于水，密度比水小。

苯(⌬)是无色、易挥发、易燃烧的液体，有芳香气味；有毒，比水轻；熔点 5.5℃，沸点80.1℃，溶于乙醇、乙醚等许多有机溶剂；苯蒸气与空气形成爆炸性混合物，爆炸极限 1.5%～8.0%(体积)；在适当情况下，分子中的氢能被卤素、硝基、磺酸基等置换；也能与氯、氢等起加成反应。

苯是染料、塑料、合成橡胶、合成树脂、合成纤维、合成药物和农药等的重要原料，也可用作动力燃料以及涂料、橡胶、胶水等的溶剂。

苯的来源：工业上由焦炉气(煤气)和炼焦油的轻油部分中回收，近年来随石油化工的发展，将由石油产品的芳构化得到。

甲苯(⌬—CH_3)是无色易挥发的液体，有芳香气味，比水轻，熔点 −95℃，沸点 110.8℃，不溶于水，溶于乙醇、乙醚和丙酮，化学性质与苯相似；蒸气与空气形成爆炸性混合物，爆炸极限 1.2%～7.0%(体积)；用于制造糖精、染料、药物和炸药等，并用作溶剂；由分馏煤焦油的轻油部分或由催化重整轻汽油馏分而制得。

(五)卤代烃

卤代烃是指烃分子中的氢原子被卤素(氟、氯、溴、碘)取代后生成的化合物。绝大多数卤代烃不溶于水或在水中溶解度很小，但能溶于很多有机溶剂，有些可以直接作为溶剂使用。卤代烃大都具有一种特殊气味，多卤代烃一般都难燃或不燃。卤代烃是一类重要的有机合成中间体，是许多有机合成的原料。

(六)醇

醇的官能团是羟基。醇的沸点比含同数碳原子的烷烃、卤代烷高。在同系列中醇的沸点也是随着碳原子数的增加而有规律地上升。低级的醇能溶于水，相对分子质量增加，溶解度就降低。含有三个以下碳原子的一元醇，可以和水混溶。醇也能溶于强酸。醇在强酸水溶液中溶解度要比在纯水中大。醇的用途极广，是有机合成工业的原料，也是用得最多最普遍的溶剂。

乙醇为无色透明易挥发的液体，比水轻，熔点 −117.3℃，沸点 78.4℃，能溶于水、甲醇、乙醚和氯仿等溶剂，也能作为溶剂溶解有机化合物和若干无机化合物；乙醇与水能形成共沸混合物，普通的酒精中含乙醇 95.57%（质量）在 78.10℃时馏出；乙醇是易燃的液体，其蒸气与空气混合能形成爆炸性混合物，爆炸极限 3.5%～18%（体积）。

乙醇的用途很广，是一种重要的溶剂，并用于制染料、涂料、药物、合成橡胶、洗涤剂等。

长期以来乙醇是由淀粉、纤维素以及某些植物的糖通过发酵来制取的。

$$\underset{\text{葡萄糖}}{C_6H_{12}O_6} \xrightarrow{\text{酵素中的酶}} \underset{\text{乙醇}}{2C_2H_5OH} + 2CO_2\uparrow$$

由发酵得来的醇溶液含有 8%～12%的乙醇，通过分馏可得 95%的乙醇。在 CaO 或 BaO 上进行蒸馏可除去残余水而得到绝对酒精，即无水酒精。

大量乙醇是由乙烯按直接或间接方法生产的

$$CH_2 = CH_2 + H_2O \xrightarrow{H^+} CH_3CH_2OH$$

（七）酚

酚是—OH 基与芳烃基直接连接的化合物，通式为 Ar—OH（Ar 为芳烃基）。根据分子中所含羟基的数目可分为一元酚：分子中含一个羟基，如苯酚 C_6H_5OH；二元酚：分子中含二个羟基，如苯二酚 $C_6H_4(OH)_2$；多元酚：分子中含三个或三个以上羟基，如苯三酚 $C_6H_3(OH)_3$ 和苯六酚 $C_6(OH)_6$。

酚类大多数是无色晶体，难溶于水，易溶于乙醇和乙醚，和醇相比，酚有显著酸性，能和碱直接作用形成酚盐（如苯酚钠 C_6H_5ONa），大多能与三氯化铁溶液作用而发生特殊颜色，可资鉴别。

苯酚 ⌬—OH（俗名石碳酸），无色或白色晶体，有特殊气味，有毒，具有腐蚀性，在空气中变成粉红色，比水重，熔点 42～43℃，沸点 182℃，在室温时稍溶于水，65℃以上时能与水混溶，易溶于乙醇、乙酸、氯仿、甘油、二硫化碳等溶剂，苯酚的水溶液与三氯化铁溶液作用呈紫色；苯酚与醛类缩聚生成酚醛树脂，商业上称电木。

苯酚除用作防腐剂、医药品、增塑剂外，还用于制染料、合成树脂、塑料、合成纤维和农药等。

（八）醛和酮

醛和酮是含有羰基的化合物。一般来说，醛和酮比烯烃的沸点高，比醇和羧酸的沸点低。小于或等于 5 个碳原子的低级醛和酮在水中的溶解度较高，醛和酮一般能溶于有机溶剂。很大程度上，醛和酮都有芳香性气味，是芬芳气味天然物质中的主要活性成分。基于此，一些醛和酮被用作香水和香料。

乙醛（CH_3CHO）为无色流动的液体，有辛辣刺激性的气味，比水轻，熔点 −123.5℃，沸点 20.2℃；能与水、乙醇、乙醚、氯仿相混合，易燃、易挥发，蒸气与空气形成爆炸性混合物，爆炸极限 4.0%～57.0%（体积），易氧化成乙酸，与碱作用时发生许多复杂的变化，于浓硫酸或盐酸存在下聚合成三聚乙醛。

乙醛用于制造醋酸、乙酸乙酯、正丁醇、合成树脂等。

（九）羧酸

羧酸是一类通式为 RCOOH 或 R(COOH)n 的化合物，式中 R 为脂烃基或芳烃基，分别称为脂肪（族）酸或芳香（族）酸。羧酸的沸点比多数相对分子质量相近的烃、卤代烃都要高，甚至比相对分子质量相当的醇、醛、酮的沸点还要高。羧酸在水中可以电离出氢离子，它的酸性比醇和酚要强得多。羧酸在自然界中分布广泛，在有机合成中有着重要的作用。

（十）酯

酯是指由酸（羧酸或无机含氧酸）与醇起反应生成的一类有机化合物。酯类都难溶于水，易溶于乙醇和乙醚等有机溶剂，密度一般比水小。低级酯是具有芳香气味的液体。在有酸或有碱存在的条件下，酯能发生水解反应生成相应的酸或醇。相对分子质量小的酯可用作溶剂，相对分子质量较大的酯是良好的增塑剂。

乙酸乙酯（$CH_3COOC_2H_5$）为无色可燃性液体，有果子香味，熔点－83.6℃，沸点 77.1℃；易着火，微溶于水，溶于乙醇、乙醚、氯仿和苯等溶剂，易起水解和皂化作用，蒸气与空气形成爆炸性混合物，爆炸极限2.2%～11.2%（体积）。

乙酸乙酯用作清漆、稀薄剂、人造革、硝酸纤维素塑料等的溶剂，也用作制染料、药物、香料等的原料。

四、几种重要的高分子合成材料

高分子合成材料的主要成分是合成树脂，其次为增强和改善材料的某些性能，还常加入一些填料、增塑剂、固定剂、润滑剂、抗静电剂等。主要的合成树脂有聚乙烯、聚苯乙烯、聚氯乙烯、聚酰胺、环氧树脂、ABS 树脂、聚碳酸酯等，下面简要介绍：

（一）聚乙烯 $\text{+}CH_2-CH_2\text{+}_n$

聚乙烯是由单体乙烯加聚而成的加聚物，有低分子量和高分子量两种。

低分子量聚乙烯一般为无色、无臭、无味、无毒的液体；比水轻；不溶于水，微溶于松节油、甲苯等溶剂；耐水和大多数化学品；可用作高级润滑油和涂料等。

高分子量聚乙烯的纯品是乳白色蜡状固体粉末，经加入稳定剂后可加工成粒状；在常温下不溶于已知溶剂中，但在脂肪烃、芳香烃、卤代烃中长期接触时能溶胀；在 70℃以上时可稍溶于甲苯、醋酸、戊酯等溶剂中，具热塑性；在空气中加热和受日光影响，发生氧化作用；能耐大多数酸碱的侵蚀，吸水性小；在低温时可保持柔软性，电绝缘性高。

聚乙烯主要用于制造塑料制品，如包装薄膜、容器、管道、日用品、电视和雷达的高频电绝缘材料，也用于抽丝成纤维，以及用作金属、木材和织物的涂层等。

（二）聚氯乙烯 $\text{+}CH_2-CHCl\text{+}_n$

聚氯乙烯是由单体氯乙烯 $CH_2=CHCl$ 经加聚而成的高聚物。

聚氯乙烯有热塑性；工业品是白色或浅黄色粉末；相对密度约 1.4，含氯量 56%～58%；低分子量的易溶于酮类、酯类、氯化烃类溶剂，高分子量的则难溶解；具有极好的耐化学腐蚀性，但热稳定性和耐光性较差，在 140℃开始分解出氯化氢，在制造塑料时需加稳定剂；电绝缘性优良，不会燃烧。

聚氯乙烯用于制造塑料、涂料、合成纤维等。根据所加增塑剂的多少，可制得软质和硬质塑料，前者可用于制成薄膜（如雨衣、台布、包装材料、农业用薄膜等）、人造革和电线套层等，后者可用于制板材、管道和阀等。

（三）聚丙烯腈 $\text{+}CH_2-\underset{\displaystyle CN}{\underset{|}{CH}}\text{+}_n$

聚丙烯腈是由单体丙烯腈 $CH_2=CH-CN$ 经加聚而成的高分子化合物。

聚丙烯腈为白色粉末，溶于二甲基甲酰胺或硫氰酸盐等溶液；耐老化强度高，绝热性能好。

聚丙烯腈主要用于制造合成纤维（如人造羊毛）。

(四)聚酰胺(尼龙)

聚酰胺树脂是具有许多重复的酰胺基 $-\overset{\overset{\displaystyle O}{\|}}{C}-\overset{\overset{\displaystyle H}{|}}{N}-$ 的高聚物的总称，商品名尼龙。它是由二元胺与二元酸缩聚而成或由内酰胺聚合而成的，例如尼龙 66(聚己二酰己二胺)是由己二胺 $H_2N-(CH_2)_6-NH_2$ 和己二酸[$HOOC(CH_2)_4COOH$]缩聚而成的。

尼龙 6(聚己内酰胺)是由氨基酸或其内酰胺缩聚而成的，尼龙 1010(聚癸二酰癸二胺)则是癸二酸与癸二胺的缩聚物。

聚酰胺为白色至淡黄色的不透明固体，熔点 180～280℃；不溶于乙醇、丙酮、醋酸乙酯等普通溶剂，但溶于酚类、硫酸、甲酸、醋酸和某些无机盐溶液；有良好的韧性、耐油和耐溶剂性、优异的机械性能、耐磨性，一定的吸水性和耐温性。

主要用于制合成纤维、工程塑料、涂料和胶黏剂等。

(五)聚碳酸酯

聚碳酸酯的结构式为 $\left[O-C_6H_4-\underset{\underset{\displaystyle CH_3}{|}}{\overset{\overset{\displaystyle CH_3}{|}}{C}}-C_6H_4-O-\overset{\overset{\displaystyle O}{\|}}{C} \right]_n$，它是由二酚基丙烷 $HO-C_6H_4-\underset{\underset{\displaystyle CH_3}{|}}{\overset{\overset{\displaystyle CH_3}{|}}{C}}-C_6H_4-OH$ 的钠盐与光气 $Cl-\underset{\underset{\displaystyle O}{\|}}{C}-Cl$ 在常温常压下缩聚而成的。或由二酚基丙烷与碳酸二苯酯 $C_6H_5-O-\underset{\underset{\displaystyle O}{\|}}{C}-O-C_6H_5$ 经酯交换和缩聚而制得。

聚碳酸酯是透明几乎无色或淡黄色的固体，相对密度为 1.2，熔点等于或大于 220℃，软化点高；能耐低温；溶于二氯甲烷，稍溶于芳香烃和酮等；吸水性小；熔化与冷却后变成透明的玻璃状物；能耐盐类、无机稀酸、有机稀酸、弱碱等，但被碱破坏、在甲醇中溶胀。聚碳酸酯可用作工程塑料，特别适用于制造外形复杂的摩擦件，如齿轮和其他机械零件、电子元件、精密仪器零件等；可用作医疗用具、光学仪器、家具日用品等，还可用作薄膜、泡沫体和玻璃纤维增强塑料等。

(六)ABS 树脂

ABS 树脂又称丙丁苯树脂，学名丙烯腈-丁二烯-苯乙烯共聚物。即它是由丙烯腈(A)与丁二烯(B)、苯乙烯(S)共聚而制成。其结构式为

$$\left[CH_2-\underset{\underset{\displaystyle CN}{|}}{CH} \right]_x \left[CH_2-CH=CH-CH_2 \right]_y \left[CH_2-\underset{\underset{\displaystyle C_6H_5}{|}}{CH} \right]_n$$

ABS 树脂兼有丙烯腈较高的强度、耐热和耐油性；苯乙烯的透明、坚硬、良好的电绝缘性和机械加工性；以及丁二烯的弹性和抗冲击性等优良的综合性能。

ABS 树脂可用作工程塑料，制造齿轮、轴承、仪表壳、冰箱门框衬里、汽车零件、电话机、行李箱、水管、煤气管、工具零件等。

（七）橡胶

天然橡胶是由异戊二烯互相结合起来而成的高聚物。

$$nCH_2=\underset{\text{异戊二烯}}{\overset{CH_3}{\overset{|}{C}}-CH=CH_2} \rightarrow \underset{\text{聚异戊二烯}}{\left[CH_2-\overset{CH_3}{\overset{|}{C}}=CH-CH_2\right]_n}$$

合成橡胶是由1,3-丁二烯或与其他单体聚合而成的丁二烯类高聚物。

1.丁二烯类合成橡胶

在催化剂作用下，1,3-丁二烯可聚合成顺丁橡胶。

$$n\;CH_2=CH-CH=CH_2 \rightarrow \left[CH_2-CH=CH-CH_2\right]_n$$

顺丁橡胶的弹性虽好，但抗拉强度和塑性都不如天然橡胶。

由1,3-丁二烯与苯乙烯共聚可得丁苯橡胶，一般可用下式表示

$$\left[CH_2-CH=CH-CH_2-CH_2-\underset{C_6H_5}{\underset{|}{CH}}\right]_n$$

丁苯橡胶的机械性能和耐磨性接近天然橡胶，绝缘性较好，但不耐油和有机溶剂。

由丁二烯与丙烯腈共聚则可得丁腈橡胶，可用下式表示

$$\left[CH_2-CH=CH-CH_2-CH_2-\underset{CN}{\underset{|}{CH}}\right]_n$$

丁腈橡胶的最大优点是耐油，抗拉强度比丁苯橡胶好，耐磨性、耐热性比天然橡胶好，但塑性低，加工较难。

顺丁橡胶用于制造胶鞋、胶管、胶板、胶布和模型等制品；丁苯橡胶主要用于制造轮胎和其他橡胶等工业制品，苯乙烯含量约10%的丁苯橡胶用于制造耐寒橡胶制品；丁腈橡胶用于制造耐油胶管、飞机油箱、密封热圈、胶黏剂等橡胶制品。

2.硅橡胶

硅橡胶是含有硅原子的特种合成橡胶的总称，结构式示意如下

$$\left[\underset{R}{\underset{|}{\overset{R}{\overset{|}{Si}}}}-O\right]_n$$

式中，R主要是甲基CH_3，部分是乙基C_2H_5、乙烯基$CH=CH_2$、苯基C_6H_5或其他有机基团，以改进胶的性能。

硅橡胶是一种线形的聚硅氧烷，它是由有机硅单体部分水解后缩聚而成的。例如：

$$\underset{\text{二甲基二氯硅烷}}{(CH_3)_2SiCl_2}+2H_2O \rightarrow \underset{\text{二甲基硅二醇}}{(CH_3)_2Si(OH)_2}+2HCl$$

$$n(CH_3)_2Si(OH)_2 \longrightarrow \left[\underset{CH_3}{\underset{|}{\overset{CH_3}{\overset{|}{Si}}}}-O\right]_n+nH_2O$$

硅橡胶的种类很多，具有不同技术性能和用途。一般在－60～250℃仍能保持良好的弹性，耐热、耐油、防水、不易老化、绝缘性能好，但机械性能较差，耐碱性不及其他橡胶。

硅橡胶用于制造火箭、导弹、飞机的零件和绝缘材料，也用于制造高温和低温下使用的垫圈，密封零件，高温高压设备的衬垫、油管衬里等。

（八）环氧树脂

环氧树脂是含有环氧基团 $-\overset{|}{\underset{|}{C}}\overset{O}{—}\overset{|}{\underset{|}{C}}-$ 的树脂的总称。环氧树脂品种很多，目前应用较广的是由环氧氯丙烷 $-\overset{|}{\underset{|}{C}}\overset{O}{—}\overset{|}{\underset{|}{C}}-$ 和双酚A即二酚基丙烷 $HO-C_6H_4-C(CH_3)_2-C_6H_4-OH$，在碱性催化作用下缩聚而成的线形高聚物，结构简示如下

$$\underset{\backslash O /}{CH_2—CH}—CH_2\!\left[O—C_6H_4—\underset{CH_3}{\overset{CH_3}{\overset{|}{\underset{|}{C}}}}—C_6H_4—O—CH_2—\underset{OH}{\underset{|}{CH}}—CH_2\right]_n$$

根据不同配比和制法，可得不同相对分子质量的产品。相对分子质量小的是黄色或琥珀色高黏度透明液体，相对分子质量大的是固体，熔点一般在145～155℃；溶于丙酮、乙二醇、甲苯和苯乙烯等溶剂；无臭无味，耐碱和大部分溶剂；与多元胺、有机酸酐、其他固化剂反应变成坚硬的体型高聚物；耐热性、绝缘性、硬度和柔韧性都好；对金属和非金属具有优异的黏合力。

环氧树脂是目前广泛使用的黏合剂，俗称万能胶，可作金属和非金属材料（如陶瓷、玻璃、木材等）的黏合剂，也可用以制造涂料、增强塑料或浇铸成绝缘制品等，还可用于处理纺织品，起防皱、防缩、防水等作用。

【例 3-5-3】 某液体烃与溴水发生加成反应生成2，3-二溴-2-甲基丁烷，该液体烃是：

A. 2-丁烯　　B. 2-甲基-1-丁烷

C. 3-甲基-1-丁烷　　D. 2-甲基-2-丁烯

解　加成反应生成2，3-二溴-2-甲基丁烷，所以在2，3位碳碳间有双键，所以该烃为2-甲基-2-丁烯。

答案：D

【例 3-5-4】 下列各组物质在一定条件下反应，可以制得比较纯净的1，2-二氯乙烷的是：

A. 乙烯通入浓盐酸中　　B. 乙烷与氯气混合

C. 乙烯与氯气混合　　D. 乙烯与卤化氢气体混合

解　乙烯与氯气混合，可以发生加成反应：$C_2H_4+Cl_2=CH_2Cl-CH_2Cl$。

答案：C

【例 3-5-5】 下列有机物中，既能发生加成反应和酯化反应，又能发生氧化反应的化合物是：

A. $CH_3CH=CHCOOH$　　B. $CH_3CH=CHCOOC_2H_5$

C. $CH_3CH_2CH_2CH_2OH$　　D. $HOCH_2CH_2CH_2CH_2OH$

解　选项A为丙烯酸，烯烃能发生加成反应和氧化反应，酸可以发生酯化反应。

答案：A

【例 3-5-6】　人造象牙的主要成分是$\mathrm{\left[CH_2-O\right]_n}$，它是经加聚反应制得的。合成此高聚物的单体是：

A. $(CH_3)_2O$　　B. CH_3CHO

C. HCHO　　D. HCOOH

解　由低分子化合物(单体)通过加成反应，相互结合成高聚物的反应称为加聚反应。加聚反应没有产生副产物，高聚物成分与单体相同，单体含有不饱和键。HCHO为甲醛，加聚反应为：$nH_2C=O \rightarrow \mathrm{\left[CH_2-O\right]_n}$。

答案：C

【例 3-5-7】　人造羊毛的结构简式为：$\mathrm{\left[CH_2-\underset{\underset{CN}{|}}{CH}\right]_n}$，它属于：

①共价化合物　②无机化合物　③有机化合物

④高分子化合物　⑤离子化合物

A. ②④⑤　　B. ①④⑤

C. ①③④　　D. ③④⑤

解　人造羊毛为聚丙烯腈，由单体丙烯腈通过加聚反应合成，为高分子化合物。分子中存在共价键，为共价化合物，同时为有机化合物。

答案：C

习　题

3-5-1　下列化合物属于芳香族化合物的是(　　)。

A. 环状结构：CH_2—CH═CH—CH═CH—CH_2—（成环）　　B. 苯环—CH_3

C. $CH_2═CH—CH═CH_2$　　D. 呋喃环（含O五元环）

3-5-2　下列化合物属于醛类的有机物是(　　)。

A. RCHO　　B. $R-\underset{\underset{O}{\|}}{C}-R'$　　C. R—OH　　D. RCOOH

3-5-3　下列化合物叫2,4-二氯苯乙酸的物质是(　　)。

A. CH_2COOH（苯环上2,3位Cl）　　B. CH_2COOH（苯环上2,4位Cl）

C. CH_2COOH

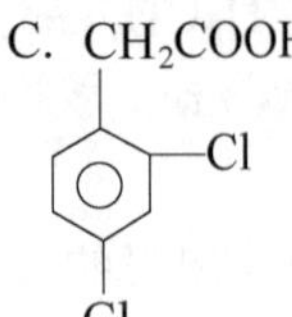

D. CH_2COOH

Cl　Cl

3-5-4　下列反应属于取代反应的是(　　)。

A. $C_6H_6 + H_2SO_4$(浓)$\longrightarrow C_6H_5SO_3H + H_2O$

B. $CH_3—CH═CH_2 + H_2O \longrightarrow CH_3—CH(OH)—CH_3$

C. $CH_3—CH_2—CH(Br)—CH_3 \xrightarrow[KOH]{C_2H_5OH} CH_3—CH═CH—CH_3$

D. $3CH_2═CH_2 + 2KMnO_4 + 4H_2O ═ 3CH_2(OH)—CH_2(OH) + 2KOH + 2MnO_2$

3-5-5　苯乙烯与丁二烯反应后的产物是(　　)。

A. 尼龙 66　　B. 丁苯橡胶　　C. 环氧树脂　　D. 聚苯乙烯

3-5-6　ABS 是下列哪一组单体的共聚物(　　)。

A. 苯乙烯、氯丁烯、丙烯腈　　B. 丁二烯、氯乙烯、苯烯腈

C. 苯烯腈、丁二烯、苯乙烯　　D. 丁二烯、苯乙烯、丙烯腈

3-5-7　聚酰胺树脂中含有下列哪种结构(　　)。

A. $\text{-[}CH_2—CH(CN)\text{]-}$　　B. $CH_2—C(CH_3)═CH—CH_2\text{]-}$

C. $\text{-[}C(=O)—N(H)\text{]-}$　　D. $\text{-[}Si(R)(R)—O\text{]-}$

3-5-8　双酚 A 与环氧氯丙烷作用后的产物为(　　)。

A. 尼龙 66　　B. 聚碳酸酯

C. 顺丁橡胶　　D. 环氧树脂

题解及参考答案

第一节

3-1-1　**解:**三个量子数取值不是任意的。n 的取值:$n=1,2,3,\cdots$,目前稳定原子中 n 最大为 7;l 的取值:$l=0,1,2,\cdots,n-1$,目前 l 最大为 3;m 的取值:$m=0,\pm1,\pm2,\pm3,\cdots,\pm l$,由于 l 最大为 3,所以 m 只有前 7 个取值。n 取 2 时,l 可以取 0,1。

答案:C

3-1-2　**解:**原子得到或失去电子后便是离子。当原子失去电子而成为正离子时,一般是

能量较高的最外层的电子先失去，而且往往引起电子层数的减小。Fe 原子基态时外层电子分布式为 $3d^6 4s^2$，Fe^{2+} 的外层电子分布式为 $3s^2 3p^6 3d^6$。

答案:B

3-1-3 **解**:据题意该元素三价正离子的外层电子分布式为 $4s^2 4p^6 4d^5$，故该元素原子基态外层电子分布式为 $4d^6 5s^2$。所以该元素原子序数为 44。

答案:D

3-1-4 **解**:$n=4$，$l=2$ 为 4d 轨道，d 轨道为 5 个等价的原子轨道，每个轨道可以容纳两个自旋相反的电子，所以 4d 轨道最大容纳 10 个电子。

答案:B

3-1-5 **解**:原子半径变化规律：同一周期从左到右，主族元素的有效核电荷数依次增加，原子半径依次减小；同一主族元素从上到下原子半径依次增加。

离子半径变化规律：同周期不同元素离子的半径随离子电荷代数值增大而减小，同族元素电荷数相同的离子半径随电子层数增加而增大，同种元素的离子半径随电荷数代数值增大而减小。

答案:C

3-1-6 **解**:同一周期从左到右，主族元素的电负性逐渐增大；同一主族元素从上到下电负性逐渐减小。

答案:C

3-1-7 **解**:元素氧化物及其水合物酸碱性变化规律：同周期元素最高价态氧化物及其水合物从左到右酸性递增、碱性递减；同一主族元素相同价态的氧化物及其水合物，从上至下酸性减弱、碱性增强；同一元素不同价态的氧化物及其水合物，依价态升高的顺序酸性增强，碱性减弱。

答案:D

3-1-8 **解**:根据元素氧化物及其水合物酸碱性变化规律。

答案:A

3-1-9 **解**:不同元素原子间形成的共价键为极性共价键。分子的极性取决于键的极性和分子的空间构型。若键有极性，而分子的空间构型对称，则分子无极性；若键有极性，而分子空间构型不对称，则分子有极性。BF_3 中 B 与 F 间为极性共价键，而分子为平面三角形分子，为非极性分子。

答案:C

3-1-10 **解**:OF_2 中 O 原子的价电子对数 $x=\frac{1}{2}(6+2)=4$，中心原子 O 的杂化类型与 H_2O 中的氧原子类似，为 sp^3 不等性杂化。

答案:D

3-1-11 **解**:分子的极性取决于键的极性和分子的空间构型。若键有极性，而分子的空间构型对称，则分子无极性；若键有极性，而分子空间构型不对称，则分子有极性。B 项中四个化合物均为极性分子。

答案:B

3-1-12 **解**:分子间力包括色散力、诱导力和取向力。非极性分子与非极性分子间只有色散力，极性分子与非极性分子间存在诱导力和色散力，极性分子间存在取向力、诱导力和色散力。SO_2 为极性分子，极性分子间存在取向力、诱导力和色散力。

答案:D

3-1-13 **解**:氢键形成条件:当分子中的氢原子与电负性大、半径小、有孤对电子的原子(如 N、O、F)形成强极性共价键后,还能吸引另一个电负性较大原子(如 N、O、F)中的孤对电子而形成氢键。

答案:B

3-1-14 **解**:原子晶体融化时要破坏共价键。SiC 为原子晶体。

答案:A

第二节

3-2-1 **解**:糖水溶液质量 $= 120 \times 1.047 \approx 125.6\text{g}$

糖水中水的质量 $= 125.6 - 15.0 = 110.6\text{g}$

糖水中糖和水的物质的量 $n_{糖} = \dfrac{15.0}{342} \approx 0.0439\text{mol}$,$n_{水} = \dfrac{110.6}{18} \approx 6.14\text{mol}$

质量百分比浓度 $= \dfrac{15.0}{125.6} \times 100\% \approx 11.9\%$

物质的量浓度 $C_{糖} = \dfrac{0.0439}{0.12} \approx 0.366\text{mol/L}$

质量摩尔浓度 $m_{糖} = \dfrac{0.0439}{110.6} \times 1000 \approx 0.397\text{mol/kg}$

物质的量分数 $x_{糖} = \dfrac{0.0439}{0.0439 + 6.14} \approx 7.09 \times 10^{-3}$

答案:B

3-2-2 **解**:葡萄糖水溶液的质量摩尔浓度 $m = \dfrac{\frac{15.0}{180}}{200} \times 1000 \approx 0.417\text{mol/kg}$

根据拉乌尔定律,$\Delta T_{fp} = k_{fp} \cdot m = 1.86 \times 0.417 \approx 0.776℃$

则溶液冰点为$-0.776℃$

$\Delta T_{bp} = k_{bp} \cdot m = 0.52 \times 0.417 \approx 0.220℃$

则溶液沸点为 100.22℃

溶液渗透压 $p_{渗} = CRT \approx mRT = 0.417 \times 8.31 \times 293 \approx 1.02 \times 10^3\text{kPa}$

答案:C

3-2-3 **解**:氢溴酸是强酸,水溶液中完全电离,所以 0.25mol/L 氢溴酸的氢离子浓度和电离度分别为 0.25mol/L、100%。

次氯酸为一元弱酸,0.25mol/L 次氯酸的 $C_{H^+} = \sqrt{K_a \cdot C} = \sqrt{3.2 \times 10^{-8} \times 0.25} \approx 8.9 \times 10^{-5}\text{mol/L}$

电离度 $\alpha = \dfrac{8.9 \times 10^{-5}}{0.25} \times 100\% \approx 0.036\%$

答案:D

3-2-4 **解**:因为 H_2S 的 $K_{a1} \gg K_{a2}$,计算 C_{H^+} 时,按一元弱酸处理,

所以 $C_{H^+} = C_{HS^-} = \sqrt{K_{a1} \cdot C} = \sqrt{1.32 \times 10^{-7} \times 0.1} \approx 1.15 \times 10^{-4}\text{mol/L}$

计算 $C_{S^{2-}}$ 时用二级电离 $HS^- \rightleftharpoons H^+ + S^{2-}$

$C_{S^{2-}} = K_{a2} \cdot \dfrac{C_{HS^-}}{C_{H^+}} = 7.1 \times 10^{-15}\text{mol/L}$

$\text{pH} = -\lg 1.15 \times 10^{-4} \approx 3.94$

答案:A

3-2-5 **解**:根据公式 $\alpha = \sqrt{\frac{K_a}{C}}$,加入冰醋酸,浓度增大,电离度减小。

答案:C

3-2-6 **解**:氨水和氯化铵组成缓冲溶液

$$C_{OH^-} = K_b \cdot \frac{C_{碱}}{C_{盐}} = 1.8 \times 10^{-5} \times \frac{0.1}{0.1} = 1.8 \times 10^{-5} mol/L$$

$$C_{H^+} = \frac{K_W}{C_{OH^-}} = \frac{10^{-14}}{1.8 \times 10^{-5}} \approx 5.56 \times 10^{-10} mol/L$$

答案:D

3-2-7 **解**:HA 过量,反应后形成 HA—KA 缓冲溶液,溶液中 HA 和 KA 的浓度分别为:

$$C_{HA} = \frac{(0.05 - 0.02) \times 0.1}{0.1} = 0.03 mol/L$$

$$C_{KA} = \frac{0.02 \times 0.1}{0.1} = 0.02 mol/L$$

pH = 5.25 ,则 $C_{H^+} = 5.62 \times 10^{-6} mol/L$

根据公式 $C_{H^+} = K_a \times \frac{C_{酸}}{C_{盐}}$

则 $K_a = \frac{C_{H^+} \times C_{盐}}{C_{酸}} = \frac{5.62 \times 10^{-6} \times 0.02}{0.03} \approx 3.7 \times 10^{-6}$

答案:B

3-2-8 **解**:在 NaCl 溶液中由于同离子效应,AgCl 溶解度降低;在 $Na_2S_2O_3$ 溶液中,由于形成 $Ag_2S_2O_3$ 沉淀,AgCl 溶解度增大。

答案:C

3-2-9 **解**:NaAc 为强碱弱酸盐,发生水解

$$C_{OH^-} = \sqrt{C \times \frac{K_W}{K_a}} = \sqrt{0.025 \times \frac{10^{-14}}{1.76 \times 10^{-5}}} \approx 3.77 \times 10^{-6} mol/L$$

$$C_{H^+} = \frac{K_W}{C_{OH^-}} = \frac{10^{-14}}{3.77 \times 10^{-6}} \approx 2.65 \times 10^{-9} mol/L$$

$$pH = -\lg 2.65 \times 10^{-9} \approx 8.58$$

水解度 $\alpha = \frac{C_{OH^-}}{C_{盐}} = \frac{3.77 \times 10^{-6}}{0.025} \approx 0.015\%$

答案:B

第三节

3-3-1 **解**:升高温度,分子获得能量,活化分子百分数增加。

答案:C

3-3-2 **解**: $\Delta H = \varepsilon - \varepsilon'$, ΔH 为正反应热效应,ε 为正反应活化能,ε′ 为逆反应活化能。正反应为放热反应, $\Delta H < 0$,则 $\varepsilon - \varepsilon' < 0$, $\varepsilon' > \varepsilon = 15kJ/mol$。

答案:B

3-3-3 **解**:随着反应进行,反应物浓度降低,生成物浓度升高,正反应速度降低,逆反应速度升高,速率常数和平衡常数不变。

答案:A

3-3-4 **解**:对放热反应,温度升高,平衡常数减小;对吸热反应,温度升高,平衡常数增大。

答案:B

3-3-5 **解**:反应方程式 1 为反应方程式 2 的逆反应乘以 2。

根据多重平衡规则,$K_1 = (\frac{1}{K_2})^2 = \frac{1}{(K_2)^2}$

答案:B

3-3-6 **解**:四种气体质量相等,分子量越小,物质的量越大。四种气体分子量大小顺序为:$H_2 < He < N_2 < CO_2$,所以物质的量的大小顺序为:$CO_2 < N_2 < He < H_2$。根据分压定律可知分压大小顺序为:$H_2 > He > N_2 > CO_2$。

答案:A

3-3-7 **解**:放热反应,降低温度,平衡向右移动;气体分子数减小的反应,增大压力,平衡向右移动。

答案:C

3-3-8 **解**:反应 3 为反应 2 减反应 1 得到的。

根据多重平衡规则,$K_3 = \frac{K_2}{K_1} = \frac{0.012}{0.050} = 0.24$

答案:C

第四节

3-4-1 **解**:按氧化还原配平法配平。

答案:B

3-4-2 **解**:Mn 的氧化数由+7(反应物 $KMnO_4$)降低到+2(生成物 $MnCl_2$),得电子,$KMnO_4$为氧化剂。

答案:D

3-4-3 **解**:两个电极的电极电势分别为:

$$\varphi_{Cu^{2+}/Cu} = \varphi^{\ominus}_{Cu^{2+}/cu} + \frac{0.059}{2}\lg C_{Cu^{2+}}$$

$$\varphi_{I_2/I^-} = \varphi^{\ominus}_{I_2/I^-} + \frac{0.059}{2}\lg\frac{1}{(C_{I^-})^2} = \varphi^{\ominus}_{I_2/I^-} - 0.059\lg C_{I^-}$$

所以,当离子浓度增大时,$\varphi_{Cu^{2+}/Cu}$变大,φ_{I_2/I^-}变小。

答案:D

3-4-4 **解**:$\varphi^{\ominus}$ 值或 φ 值越大,表示电对中氧化态的氧化能力越强,$\varphi^{\ominus}$ 值或 φ 值越小,表示电对中还原态的还原能力越强。三个电对中还原型物质的还原能力由强到弱的顺序为选项 C。

答案:C

3-4-5 **解**:两个反应能自发进行,所以两个反应的电动势都大于零,即正极电极电势大于负极电极电势。由反应 1 可知:$\varphi_{Fe^{3+}/Fe^{2+}} > \varphi_{Cu^{2+}/Cu}$;由反应 2 可知:$\varphi_{Cu^{2+}/Cu} > \varphi^{\ominus}_{Fe^{2+}/Fe}$。

答案:A

3-4-6 **解**:根据 $\lg K^{\ominus} = \frac{nE^{\ominus}}{0.059}$,知 $E^{\ominus} = \frac{0.059 \times \lg K^{\ominus}}{n} = \frac{0.059 \times \lg 10^4}{2} = 0.118\text{V}$。

答案:A

3-4-7 **解:**电解池中,与外电源负极相连的极叫阴极,与外电源正极相连的极叫阳极。电解时阴极发生还原反应,阳极发生氧化反应。析出电势代数值较大的氧化型物质首先在阴极还原,析出电势代数值较小的还原型物质首先在阳极氧化。电解时,阳极如果是可溶性电极,可溶性电极首先被氧化,阳极如果是惰性电极,简单负离子被氧化,如 Cl^-、Br^-、I^-、S^{2-} 分别析出 Cl_2、Br_2、I_2、S。

答案:D

3-4-8 **解:**为差异充气腐蚀,埋在黏土中的钢管表面氧气浓度小,作为阳极。

答案:D

第五节

3-5-1 **解:**芳香族类化合物分子中含有苯环结构。选项 A 为脂环化合物,选项 D 为杂环化合物。

答案:B

3-5-2 **解:** 选项 A 为醛,选项 B 为酮,选项 C 为醇,选项 D 为酸。

答案:A

3-5-3 **解:**根据芳香烃及其衍生物命名原则,选项 A 为 2,3-二氯苯乙酸,选项 B 为 3,4-二氯苯乙酸,选项 C 为 2,4-二氯苯乙酸,选项 D 为 3,5-二氯苯乙酸。

答案:C

3-5-4 **解:** 选项 A 为苯环上的磺化反应,相当于苯环上的氢被磺酸基取代;选项 B 为加成反应;选项 C 为消去反应;选项 D 为氧化反应。

答案:A

3-5-5 **解:** 1,3-丁二烯与苯乙烯共聚可得丁苯橡胶。

答案:B

3-5-6 **解:** ABS 树脂又称丙丁苯树脂,学名丙烯腈-丁二烯-苯乙烯共聚物。

答案:D

3-5-7 **解:**聚酰胺树脂,商品名尼龙,是具有许多重复的酰胺基的高聚物。

答案:C

3-5-8 **解:**环氧树脂是含有环氧基团的树脂,品种很多,目前应用较广的是双酚 A 与环氧氯丙烷在碱性催化作用下缩聚而成的线性高聚物。

答案:D

第四章 理论力学

复习指导

一、考试大纲

4.1 静力学

平衡；刚体；力；约束及约束力；受力图；力矩；力偶及力偶矩；力系的等效和简化；力的平移定理；平面力系的简化；主矢；主矩；平面力系的平衡条件和平衡方程式；物体系统（含平面静定桁架）的平衡；摩擦力；摩擦定律；摩擦角；摩擦自锁。

4.2 运动学

点的运动方程；轨迹；速度；加速度；切向加速度和法向加速度；平动和绕定轴转动；角速度；角加速度；刚体内任一点的速度和加速度。

4.3 动力学

牛顿定律；质点的直线振动；自由振动微分方程；固有频率；周期；振幅；衰减振动；阻尼对自由振动振幅的影响——振幅衰减曲线；受迫振动；受迫振动频率；幅频特性；共振；动力学普遍定理；动量；质心；动量定理及质心运动定理；动量及质心运动守恒；动量矩；动量矩定理；动量矩守恒；刚体定轴转动微分方程；转动惯量；回转半径；平行轴定理；功；动能；势能；动能定理及机械能守恒；达朗贝尔原理；惯性力；刚体作平动和绕定轴转动（转轴垂直于刚体的对称面）时惯性力系的简化；动静法。

二、基本要求

（一）静力学

熟练掌握并能灵活运用静力学中的基本概念及公理分析相关问题，特别是对物体的受力分析；掌握不同力系的简化方法和简化结果；能够根据各种力系和滑动摩擦的特性，定性或定量地分析和解决物体系统的平衡问题。

（二）运动学

熟练运用直角坐标法和自然法求解点的各运动量；能根据刚体的平行移动（平动）、绕定轴转动和平面运动的定义及其运动特征，求解刚体的各运动量；掌握刚体上任一点的速度和加速度的计算公式及刚体上各点速度和加速度的分布规律。

（三）动力学

能应用动力学基本定律列出质点运动微分方程；能正确理解并熟练地计算动力学普遍定理中各基本物理量（如动量、动量矩、动能、功、势能等），熟练掌握动力学普遍定理（包括动量定理、质心运动定理、动量矩定理、刚体定轴转动微分方程、动能定理）及相应的守恒定理；掌握刚体转动惯量的计算公式及方法，熟记杆、圆盘及圆环的转动惯量，并会利用平行移轴定理计算简单组合形体的转动惯量；能正确理解惯性力的概念，并能正确表示出各种不同运动状态的刚体上惯性力系主矢和主矩的大小、方向、作用点，能应用动静法求解质点、质点系的动力学问题；能应用质点运动微分方程列出单自由度系统线性振动的微分方程，并会求其周期、频率和振幅。掌握阻尼对自由振动振幅的影响及受迫振动的幅频特性和共振的概念。

三、重点难点分析

（一）静力学

静力学所研究的是物体受力作用后的平衡规律，重点包括以下三部分内容：

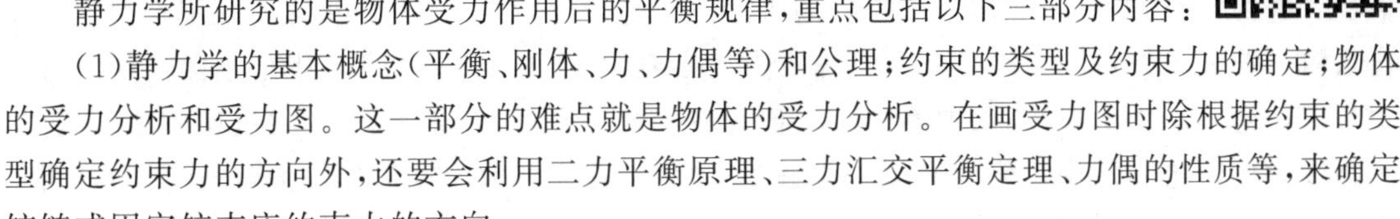

（1）静力学的基本概念（平衡、刚体、力、力偶等）和公理；约束的类型及约束力的确定；物体的受力分析和受力图。这一部分的难点就是物体的受力分析。在画受力图时除根据约束的类型确定约束力的方向外，还要会利用二力平衡原理、三力汇交平衡定理、力偶的性质等，来确定铰链或固定铰支座约束力的方向。

（2）各种力系的简化方法及简化结果。其难点在于主矢和主矩的概念及计算。可通过力的平移定理加深对主矢、主矩、合力、合力偶的认识，通过熟练掌握力的投影，力对点之矩和力对轴之矩的计算，来得到主矢和主矩的正确结果。

（3）各种力系的平衡条件及与之相对应的平衡方程，平衡方程的不同形式及对应的附加条件。难点在于物体及物体系统（包括考虑摩擦）平衡问题的求解。解题时要灵活选取合适的研究对象进行受力分析，列平衡方程时要选取适当的投影轴和矩心（矩轴），使问题能够得到快速准确的解答。

（二）运动学

运动学研究物体运动的几何性质。重点是：

（1）描述点的运动的矢量法、直角坐标法和自然法。要明确用不同的方法所表示的同一个点的运动量，形式不同，但不同形式的结果之间是相互有关系的，要熟练掌握这些关系，并将这些关系应用到解题当中去。

（2）刚体的平动及其运动特征（尤其是作曲线平动的刚体）；作定轴转动刚体的转动方程、角速度和角加速度及刚体内各点速度、加速度的计算方法。这是运动学的基本内容，在物理学中都学习过，正是这些看似简单的问题，却往往容易出现概念性错误且不能熟练应用。解决的方法是在认真分析刚体运动形式的基础上，根据其运动特征，选择相应的计算公式。

（3）点的复合运动。解题时首先要明确一个动点、两个坐标系以及与之相应的三种运动，合理选择动点、动系，其原则是相对运动轨迹易于判断。这一部分的难点是牵连点的概念，以及牵连速度、牵连加速度的判断与计算。要把动系看成是 $O'x'y'$ 平面，在此平面上与所选动点相重合的点，即为牵连点，该点相对于定参考系的速度、加速度，称为牵连速度和牵连加速度，解题时一定要深刻理解这一定义。

（4）刚体的平面运动。要会正确判断机构中作平面运动的刚体，熟练掌握并能灵活运用求平面运动刚体上点的速度的三种方法——基点法、瞬心法和速度投影法；会应用基点法求平面运动刚体上点的加速度。特别要熟悉刚体瞬时平动时的运动特征为：刚体的角速度为零，角加速度不为零；刚体上各点的速度相同，加速度不同，但其上任意两点的加速度在该两点连线上的投影相等。

（三）动力学

动力学研究物体受力作用后的运动规律。重点是：

(1)会应用动力学基本定律(牛顿第二定律)和动力学普遍定理(动量定理、动量矩定理和动能定理)列出质点和质点系(包括平动、定轴转动、平面运动的刚体)的运动微分方程,解微分方程时要注意初始条件只能用于确定微分方程解中的积分常数;要熟练掌握动量、动量矩、动能、势能、功的概念与计算方法,正确选择及综合应用动力学普遍定理求解质点系动力学问题;动力学普遍定理的综合应用,大体上包含两方面含义:一是对几个定理,即动量定理、质心运动定理、动量矩定理、定轴转动微分方程、平面运动微分方程和动能定理的特点、应用条件、可求解何类问题等有透彻的了解,能根据不同类型问题的已知条件和待求量,选择适当的定理,包括各种守恒情况的判断,相应守恒定理的应用。二是对比较复杂的问题,应能采用多个定理联合求解。此外,求解动力学问题,往往需要进行运动分析,以提供运动学补充方程。因而对动力学普遍定理的综合应用,须熟悉有关定理及应用范围和条件,多做练习,通过比较总结(包括一题多解的讨论),从中摸索出规律。其解题步骤是:首先选取研究对象,对其进行受力分析和运动分析;其次是根据分析的结果,针对物体不同的运动选择不同的定理,通常可先应用动能定理求解系统的各运动量(速度、加速度、角速度和角加速度),再应用质心运动定理或动量矩定理(定轴转动微分方程)求解未知力。

(2)刚体系统惯性力系的简化及达朗贝尔原理的应用。这一部分的关键是要分析物体的运动形式,并根据其运动形式确定惯性力并将其画在受力图上,根据受力图列平衡方程,求解未知量。要注意的是:因为达朗贝尔原理是采用静力平衡方程求解未知量,故未知量的数目不能超过独立的平衡方程数。未知量中包括速度、加速度、角速度、角加速度、约束力等,若未知量数目超过了独立的平衡方程数,则需要建立补充方程,在多数情况下,是建立运动学的补充方程。当单独使用达朗贝尔原理解题出现计算上的困难(如需解微分方程)时,由于质点系的达朗贝尔原理实际是动量定理、动量矩定理的另一种表达形式,故可联合应用达朗贝尔原理与动能定理求解质点系的动力学问题。

第一节 静 力 学

静力学研究物体在力作用下的平衡规律,主要包括物体的受力分析、力系的等效简化、力系的平衡条件及其应用。

一、静力学的基本概念及基本原理

(一)基本概念

1. 力的概念

力是物体间相互的机械作用,这种作用将使物体的运动状态发生变化——运动效应,或使物体的形状发生变化——变形效应。力的量纲为牛顿(N)。力的作用效果取决于力的三要素:力的大小、方向、作用点。力是矢量,满足矢量的运算法则。当求共点二力之合力时,采用力的平行四边形法则:其合力可由两个共点力为边构成的平行四边形的对角线确定,见图 4-1-1a)。或者说,合力矢等于此二力的几何和,即

$$\boldsymbol{F}_R = \boldsymbol{F}_1 + \boldsymbol{F}_2 \tag{4-1-1}$$

显然,求 $\boldsymbol{F}_R$ 时,只需画出平行四边形的一半就够了,即以力矢 $\boldsymbol{F}_1$ 的尾端 B 作为力矢 $\boldsymbol{F}_2$ 的起点,连接 AC 所得矢量即为合力 $\boldsymbol{F}_R$。如图 4-1-1b)所示三角形 ABC 称为力三角形。这种求合力的方法称为力的三角形法则。

多个共点力的合成可采用力的多边形规则:若有汇交于点 A 的四个力 $\boldsymbol{F}_1$、$\boldsymbol{F}_2$、$\boldsymbol{F}_3$、$\boldsymbol{F}_4$,如图 4-1-2a)所示,求合力时可任取一点 a,先作力三角形求出 $\boldsymbol{F}_1$ 与 $\boldsymbol{F}_2$ 的合力 $\boldsymbol{F}_{R1}$,再作力三角形求出 $\boldsymbol{F}_{R1}$ 与 $\boldsymbol{F}_3$ 的合力 $\boldsymbol{F}_{R2}$,最后作力三角形合成 $\boldsymbol{F}_{R2}$ 与 $\boldsymbol{F}_4$ 即得合力 $\boldsymbol{F}_R$,如图 4-1-2b)所示。多边形 $abcde$ 称为此汇交力系的力多边形,而封闭边 ae 则表示此汇交力系合力 $\boldsymbol{F}_R$ 的大小和方向,显然 $\boldsymbol{F}_R$ 的作用线必过汇交点 A。利用力多边形法简化力系时,求 $\boldsymbol{F}_{R1}$ 和 $\boldsymbol{F}_{R2}$ 的中间过程可略去,只需将组成力多边形的各分力首尾相连,而合力则由第一个分力的起点指向最后一个分力的终点(矢端)即可。根据矢量相加的交换率,任意变换各分力矢的作图次序,可得形状不同的力多边形,但其合力矢仍然不变,如图 4-1-2c)所示。

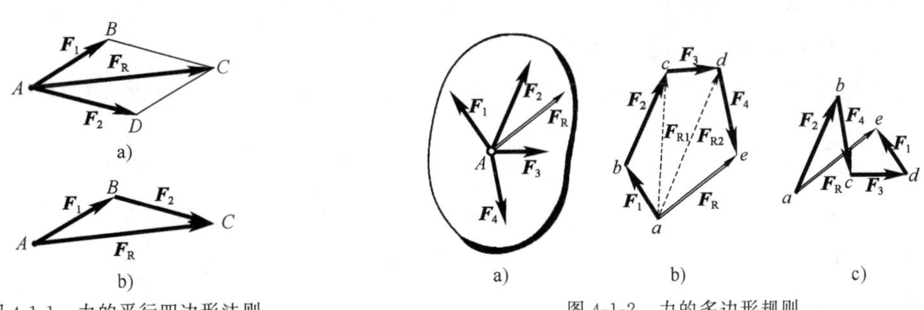

图 4-1-1　力的平行四边形法则

图 4-1-2　力的多边形规则

【例 4-1-1】 平面汇交力系($\boldsymbol{F}_1$,$\boldsymbol{F}_2$, $\boldsymbol{F}_3$,$\boldsymbol{F}_4$,$\boldsymbol{F}_5$)的力多边形如图所示,则该力系的合力 $\boldsymbol{F}_R$ 等于:

A. $\boldsymbol{F}_3$　　B. $-\boldsymbol{F}_3$　　C. $\boldsymbol{F}_2$　　D. $-\boldsymbol{F}_2$

解 根据力的多边形规则,当 $\boldsymbol{F}_1$、$\boldsymbol{F}_2$、$\boldsymbol{F}_3$、$\boldsymbol{F}_4$、$\boldsymbol{F}_5$ 各分力首尾相连时,合力应由第一个分力 $\boldsymbol{F}_1$ 的起点指向最后一个分力 $\boldsymbol{F}_5$ 的终点(矢端)。

答案:B

(1)力对点之矩

力使物体绕某支点(或矩心)转动的效果可用力对点之矩度量。设力 $\boldsymbol{F}$ 作用于刚体上的 A 点,如图 4-1-3 所示,用 $\boldsymbol{r}$ 表示空间任意点 O 到 A 点的矢径,于是,力 $\boldsymbol{F}$ 对 O 点的力矩定义为矢径 $\boldsymbol{r}$ 与力矢 $\boldsymbol{F}$ 的矢量积,记为 $\boldsymbol{M}_O(\boldsymbol{F})$。即

$$\boldsymbol{M}_O(\boldsymbol{F})=\boldsymbol{r}\times\boldsymbol{F} \tag{4-1-2}$$

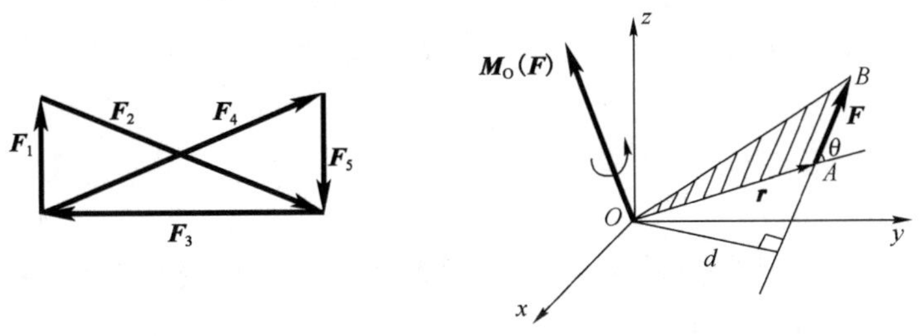

例 4-1-1 图

图 4-1-3　力对点之矩

式(4-1-2)中点 O 称作力矩中心,简称矩心。力 $\boldsymbol{F}$ 使刚体绕 O 点转动效果的强弱取决于:①力矩的大小;②力矩的转向;③力和矢径所组成平面的方位。因此,力矩是一个矢量,矢量的模即力矩的大小为

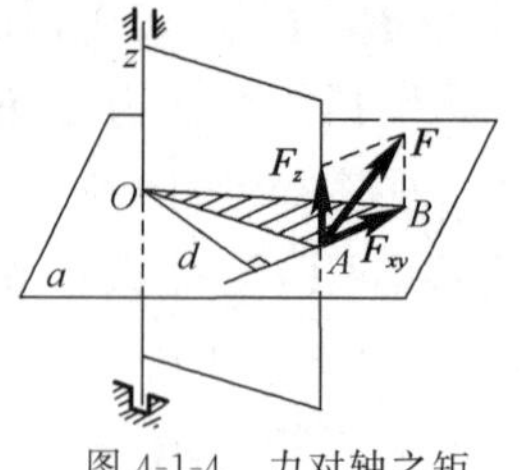

图 4-1-4　力对轴之矩

$$|M_O(F)| = |r \times F| = rF\sin\theta = Fd \quad (4\text{-}1\text{-}3)$$

矢量的方向与 OAB 平面的法线 $\boldsymbol{n}$ 一致，按右手螺旋法则来确定。力矩的单位为 N・m 或 kN・m。

(2)力对轴之矩

如图 4-1-4 所示，力 $\boldsymbol{F}$ 对任意轴 z 的矩用 $M_z(\boldsymbol{F})$ 表示，称为力对轴之矩。其值为

$$M_z(\boldsymbol{F}) = M_O(\boldsymbol{F}_{xy}) = \pm F_{xy}d \quad (4\text{-}1\text{-}4)$$

力对轴的矩是力使刚体绕某轴转动效果的度量，是代数量。其正负号按右手螺旋法则确定。从力对轴之矩的定义可得其性质：

①当力沿其作用线移动时，力对轴之矩不变。

②当力的作用线与某轴平行(如与 z 轴平行，则 $F_{xy} = 0$)或相交($d = 0$)时，力对该轴之矩为零。

(3)力矩关系定理

力对任意点的矩矢在通过该点的任一轴上的投影，等于此力对该轴的矩。即

$$[\boldsymbol{M}_O(\boldsymbol{F})]_z = M_z(\boldsymbol{F}) \quad (4\text{-}1\text{-}5)$$

(4)合力矩定理

汇交力系的合力对某点(或某轴)之矩等于力系中各分力对同一点(或同一轴)之矩的矢量和(或代数和)。即

$$\boldsymbol{M}_O(\boldsymbol{F}_R) = \sum \boldsymbol{M}_O(\boldsymbol{F}_i) \quad (4\text{-}1\text{-}6a)$$

或

$$M_z(\boldsymbol{F}_R) = \sum M_z(\boldsymbol{F}_i) \quad (4\text{-}1\text{-}6b)$$

【例 4-1-2】 如图所示结构直杆 BC，受荷载 $\boldsymbol{F}$、q 作用，$BC = L$，$F = qL$，其中 q 为均布荷载，单位 N/m，集中力以 N 计，长度以 m 计。则该主动力系对 O 点的合力矩为：

A. $M_O = 0$

B. $M_O = \frac{qL^2}{2}$ N・m(↶)

C. $M_O = \frac{3qL^2}{2}$ N・m(↶)

D. $M_O = qL^2$ N・m(↷)

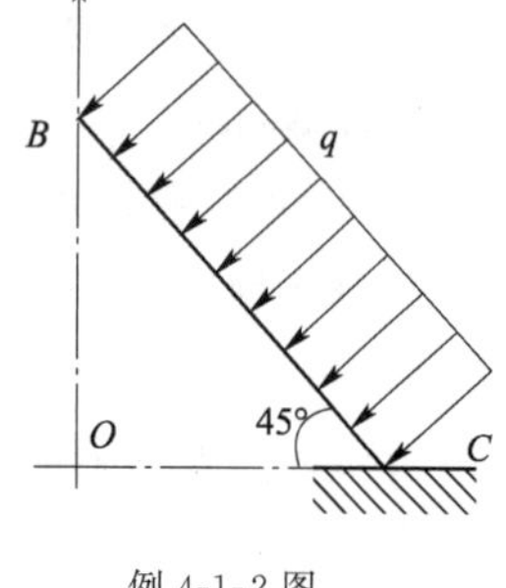

例 4-1-2 图

解　根据合力矩定理，主动力系对 O 点的合力矩等于各分力对 O 点的力矩之代数和，即：$M_O(\boldsymbol{F}_R) = M_O(\boldsymbol{F}) + M_O(qL)$。由于 $\boldsymbol{F}$ 力和均布荷载 q 的合力作用线均通过 O 点，故合力矩为零。

答案：A

2. 力偶的概念

大小相等、方向相反、作用线互相平行但不重合的两个力所组成的力系(见图 4-1-5)，称为力偶，记为$(\boldsymbol{F}, \boldsymbol{F}')$，且 $\boldsymbol{F} = -\boldsymbol{F}'$。力偶与力同是力学中的基本元素。力偶没有合力，故只能使物体产生转动并将改变其转动状态。力偶对物体的转动效果取决于力偶矩矢 $\boldsymbol{M}$。$\boldsymbol{M}$ 定义为组成力偶的两个力对任一点之矩的矢量和，即

$$\begin{aligned}\boldsymbol{M} &= \boldsymbol{M}_O(\boldsymbol{F}) + \boldsymbol{M}_O(\boldsymbol{F}') \\ &= \boldsymbol{r}_A \times \boldsymbol{F} + \boldsymbol{r}_B \times \boldsymbol{F}' = \boldsymbol{r}_{BA} \times \boldsymbol{F}\end{aligned} \quad (4\text{-}1\text{-}7)$$

力偶矩矢与矩心 O 无关。力偶的三要素为：

(1)力偶矩的大小；

(2)力偶的转向；

(3)力偶作用面的方位。

力偶矩矢的大小为

$$|\boldsymbol{M}|=Fd \tag{4-1-8}$$

其中，d 为力偶中两个力之间的垂直距离，称为力偶臂。方向按右手螺旋法则确定。

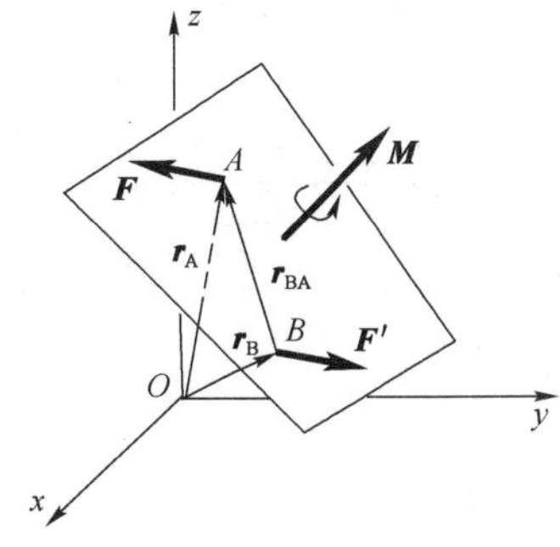

图 4-1-5　力偶矩矢量

力偶的作用效果仅取决于力偶矩矢，故只要保持力偶矩矢不变，力偶可在其作用面内任意移动和转动，或同时改变力偶中力的大小和力偶臂的长短，或在平行平面内移动，都不改变力偶对同一刚体的作用效果。

3.刚体的概念

在物体受力以后的变形对其运动和平衡的影响小到可以忽略不计的情况下，便可把物体抽象成为不变形的力学模型——刚体。

4.平衡的概念

平衡是指物体相对惯性参考系静止或作匀速直线平行移动的状态。

(二)基本原理

1.二力平衡原理

不计自重的刚体在二力作用下平衡的必要和充分条件是：二力沿着同一作用线，大小相等，方向相反。仅受两个力作用且处于平衡状态的物体，称为二力体，又称二力构件。

2.加减平衡力系原理

在作用于刚体的力系中，加上或减去任意一个平衡力系，不改变原力系对刚体的作用效应。

推论Ⅰ：力的可传性。作用于刚体上的力可沿其作用线滑移至刚体内任意点而不改变力对刚体的作用效应。

推论Ⅱ：三力平衡汇交定理。作用于刚体上三个相互平衡的力，若其中两个力的作用线汇交于一点，则此三力必在同一平面内，且第三个力的作用线通过汇交点。

【例 4-1-3】　作用在一个刚体上的两个力 $\boldsymbol{F}_1$、$\boldsymbol{F}_2$，满足 $\boldsymbol{F}_1=-\boldsymbol{F}_2$ 的条件，则该二力可能是：

A. 作用力和反作用力或一对平衡的力

B. 一对平衡的力或一个力偶

C. 一对平衡的力或一个力和一个力偶

D. 作用力和反作用力或一个力偶

解　因为作用力和反作用力分别作用在两个不同的刚体上，故选项 A、D 是错误的；而当 $\boldsymbol{F}_1=-\boldsymbol{F}_2$ 时，两个力不可能合成为一个力，选项 C 也不正确。

答案：B

注：作用力与反作用力、一对平衡的力和一个力偶中的两个力均可用矢量表达式 $\boldsymbol{F}_1=-\boldsymbol{F}_2$ 表示，一定要分清三者的不同之处。

(三)约束与约束力

阻碍物体运动的限制条件称为约束，约束对被约束物体的机械作用称为约束力。

工程中常见的几种典型约束的性质以及相应约束力的确定方法见表 4-1-1。

几种典型约束的性质及相应约束力的确定方法 表 4-1-1

约束的类型	约束的性质	约束力的确定
柔体约束(如绳索、胶带、链条等)	柔体约束只能限制物体沿着柔体的中心线伸长方向的运动,而不能限制物体沿其他方向的运动	约束力必定沿柔体的中心线,且背离被约束的物体
光滑接触约束	光滑接触约束只能限制物体沿接触面的公法线指向支承面的运动,而不能限制物体沿接触面或离开支承面的运动	光滑接触面的约束力通过接触点,沿接触面的公法线并指向被约束的物体
圆柱铰链与铰链支座	铰链约束只能限制物体在垂直于销钉轴线的平面内任意方向的运动,而不能限制物体绕销钉的转动	约束力作用在垂直于销钉轴线平面内,通过销钉中心,而方向待定
可动铰支座(辊轴支座)	可动铰支座不能限制物体绕销钉的转动和沿支承面的运动,而只能限制物体在支承面垂直方向的运动	可动铰支座的约束力通过销钉中心且垂直于支承面,指向待定
固定端约束	固定端约束既能限制物体移动,又能限制物体绕固定端转动	约束力可表示为两个互相垂直的分力和一个约束力偶,指向均待定

(四)受力分析与受力图

分析力学问题时,往往必须首先根据问题的性质、已知量和所要求的未知量,选择某一物体(或几个物体组成的系统)作为研究对象,并假想地将所研究的物体从与之接触或连接的物体中分离出来,即解除其所受的约束而代之以相应的约束力。解除约束后的物体,称为分离体。分析作用在分离体上的全部主动力和约束力,画出分离体的受力简图——受力图。这一过程即为受力分析。

受力分析是求解静力学和动力学问题的重要基础,具体步骤如下:

(1)选定合适的研究对象,确定分离体;

(2)画出所有作用在分离体上的主动力(一般皆为已知力);

(3)在分离体的所有约束处,根据约束的性质画出约束力。

【例 4-1-4】 如图所示构架由 AC、BD、CE 三杆组成,A、B、C、D 处为铰接,E 处光滑接触。已知:$F_{\mathrm{p}}=2\mathrm{kN}$,$\theta=45°$,杆及轮重均不计,则 E 处约束力的方向与 x 轴正向所成的夹角为:

A. 0°　　B. 45°　　C. 90°　　D. 225°

解 E 处为光滑接触面约束,根据约束的性质,约束力应垂直于支撑面,指向被约束物体。

答案:B

【例 4-1-5】 结构如图所示,杆 DE 的点 H 由水平闸拉住,其上的销钉 C 置于杆 AB 的光滑直槽中,各杆自重均不计,已知 $F_{\mathrm{P}}=10\mathrm{kN}$。销钉 C 处约束力的作用线与 x 轴正向所成的夹角为:

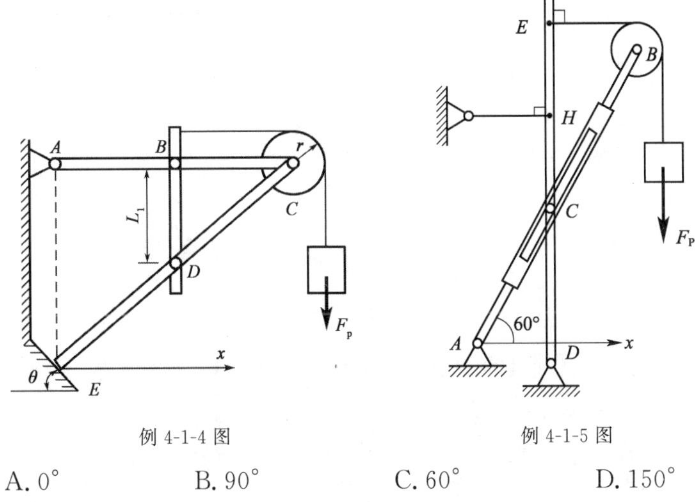

例 4-1-4 图　　例 4-1-5 图

A. 0°　　B. 90°　　C. 60°　　D. 150°

解 销钉 C 处为光滑接触约束,约束力应垂直于 AB 光滑直槽,由于 $\boldsymbol{F}_{\mathrm{P}}$ 的作用,直槽的左上侧与销钉接触,故其约束力的作用线与 x 轴正向所成的夹角为 150°。

答案:D

【例 4-1-6】 在如图 a)所示结构中,如果将作用于构件 AC 上的力偶 M 搬移到构件 BC 上,则根据力偶的性质(力偶可在其作用面内任意移动和转动,不改变力偶对同一刚体的作用效果),A、B、C 三处的约束力:

A. 都不变　　B. 仅 C 处改变

C. 都改变　　D. 仅 C 处不变

解 若力偶 M 作用于构件 AC 上,则 BC 为二力构件,AC 满足力偶的平衡条件,受力图如图 b)所示；若力偶 M 作用于构件 BC 上，则 AC 为二力构件，BC 满足力偶的平衡条件，受力图如图 c)所示。从图中看出，两种情况下 A、B、C 三处约束力的方向都发生了变化，这与力偶的性质并不矛盾，因为力偶在其作用面内移动后（从构件 AC 移至构件 BC），并未改变其使系统整体（ACB）产生顺时针转动趋势的作用效果。

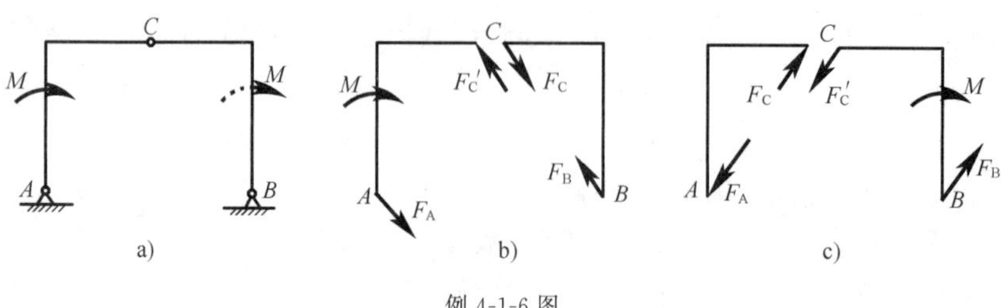

例 4-1-6 图

答案:C

【例 4-1-7】 如图 a)所示将大小为 100N 的力 $\boldsymbol{F}$ 沿 x、y 方向分解，若 $\boldsymbol{F}$ 在 x 轴上的投影为 50N，而沿 x 方向的分力的大小为 200N，则 $\boldsymbol{F}$ 在 y 轴上的投影为：

A. 0　　B. 50N　　C. 200N　　D. 100N

解 如图 b)所示，根据力的投影公式，$F_x = F\cos\alpha = 50\text{N}$，故 $\alpha = 60°$。而分力 $\boldsymbol{F}'_x$ 的大小是力 $\boldsymbol{F}$ 大小的 2 倍，因此力 $\boldsymbol{F}$ 与 y 轴垂直，在 y 轴的投影为零。

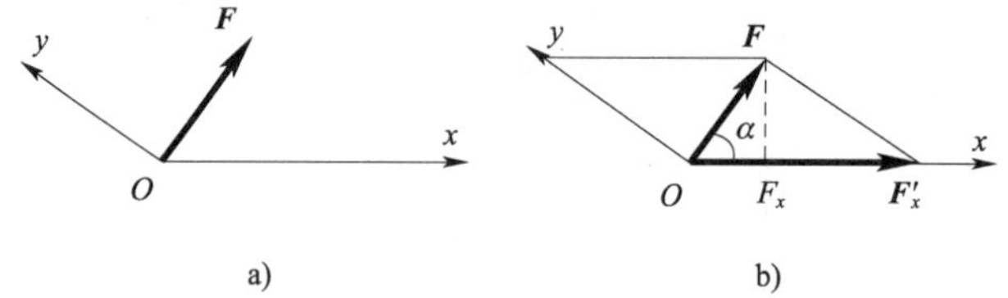

例 4-1-7 图

答案:A

【例 4-1-8】 试确定如图 a)、b)所示系统中 A、B 处约束力的方向。

解 在图 a)中，BC 为二力杆，根据二力平衡原理，B 处约束力 $\boldsymbol{F}_B$ 必沿杆 BC 方向；因为系统整体受三个力作用，由三力平衡汇交定理知，A 处约束力 $\boldsymbol{F}_A$ 与力 $\boldsymbol{F}_B$、$\boldsymbol{F}$ 汇交于一点，见图 c)。

在图 b)中，AC 为二力杆（只在 A、C 处受力），根据二力平衡原理，A 处约束力 $\boldsymbol{F}_A$ 必沿杆 AC 方向；由力偶的性质（力偶只能与力偶平衡）知，B 处约束力 $\boldsymbol{F}_B$ 应与力 $\boldsymbol{F}_A$ 组成一力偶，与 m 平衡，其受力如图 d)所示。

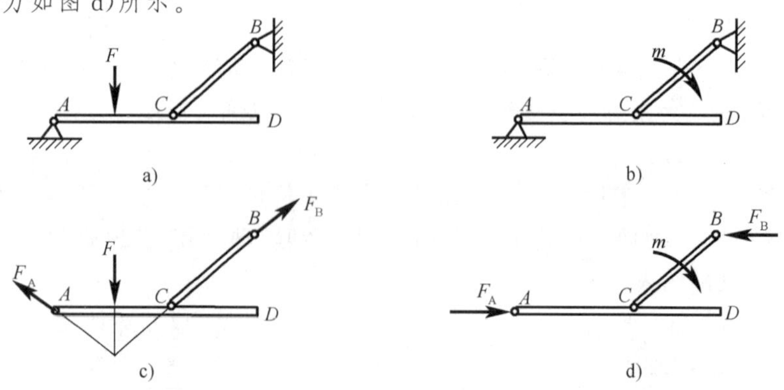

例 4-1-8 图

【例 4-1-9】 图示结构由直杆 AC,DE 和直角弯杆 BCD 所组成,自重不计,受载荷 $\boldsymbol{F}$ 与 $M=Fa$ 作用。则 A 处约束力的作用线与 x 轴正向所成的夹角为:

A. 135° B. 90°

C. 0° D. 45°

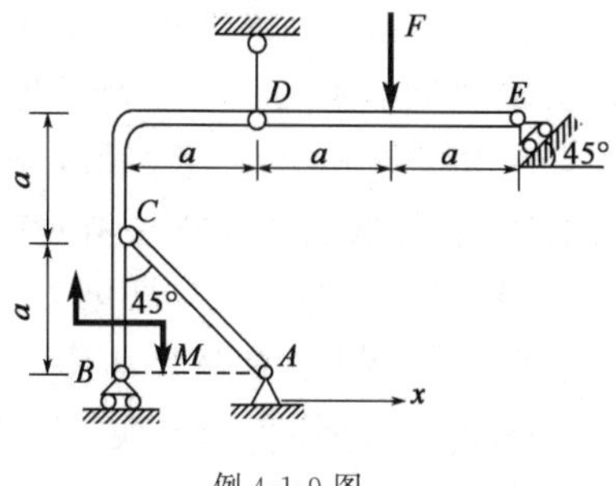

例 4-1-9 图

解 首先分析杆 DE,E 处为活动铰链支座,约束力垂直于支撑面如解图 a)所示,杆 DE 的铰链 D 处的约束力可按三力汇交原理确定;其次分析铰链 D,D 处铰接了杆 DE、直角弯杆 BCD 和连杆,连杆的约束力 $\boldsymbol{F}_{\mathrm{D}}$ 沿杆为铅垂方向,杆 DE 作用在铰链 D 上的力为 $\boldsymbol{F}'_{\mathrm{D右}}$,按照铰链 D 的平衡,其受力图如解图 b)所示;最后分析直杆 AC 和直角弯杆 BCD,直杆 AC 为二力杆,A 处约束力沿杆方向,根据力偶的平衡,由 $\boldsymbol{F}_{\mathrm{A}}$ 与 $\boldsymbol{F}'_{\mathrm{D左}}$ 组成的逆时针转向力偶与顺时针转向的主动力偶 M 组成平衡力系,故 A 处约束力的指向如解图 c)所示。

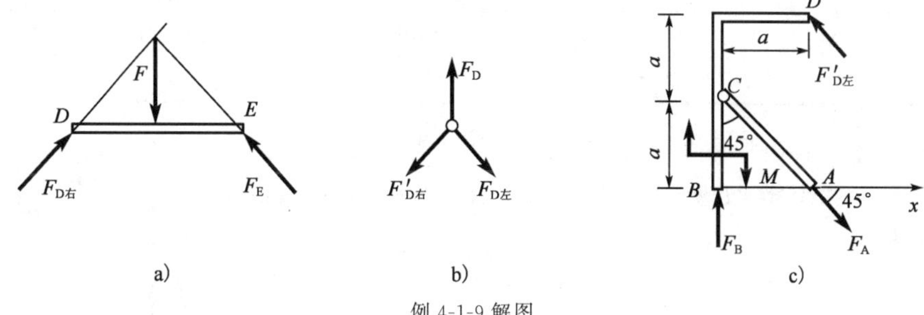

例 4-1-9 解图

答案:D

二、力系的简化

将作用在物体上的一个力系用另一个与其对物体作用效果相同的力系来代替,则这两个力系互为等效力系。若用一个简单力系等效地替换一个复杂力系,则称为力系的简化。

(一)力的平移定理

作用在刚体上的力可以向任意点 O 平移,但必须同时附加一个力偶,这一附加力偶的力偶矩等于平移前的力对平移点 O 之矩。

(二)任意力系的简化

考察作用在刚体上的任意力系($\boldsymbol{F}_1,\boldsymbol{F}_2,\cdots,\boldsymbol{F}_n$),如图 4-1-6a)所示。若在刚体上任取一点 O(简化中心),应用力的平移定理,将力系中的各力 $\boldsymbol{F}_1,\boldsymbol{F}_2,\cdots,\boldsymbol{F}_n$ 逐个向简化中心平移,最后得到汇交于O 点的,由 $\boldsymbol{F}'_1,\boldsymbol{F}'_2,\cdots,\boldsymbol{F}'_n$组成的汇交力系,以及由所有附加力偶 $\boldsymbol{M}_1,\boldsymbol{M}_2,\cdots,\boldsymbol{M}_n$ 组成的力偶系,如图 4-1-6b)所示。

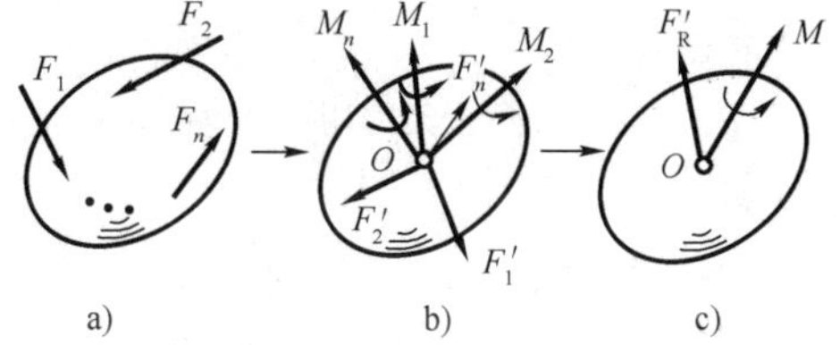

图 4-1-6 任意力系的简化

平移后得到的汇交力系和力偶系,可以分别合成一个作用于 O 点的合力 $\boldsymbol{F}'_{\mathrm{R}}$,以及合力偶 $\boldsymbol{M}_{\mathrm{O}}$,如图 4-1-6c)所示。其中

$$\left.\begin{aligned}\boldsymbol{F}'_{\mathrm{R}}&=\sum_{i=1}^{n}\boldsymbol{F}_i\\ \boldsymbol{M}_{\mathrm{O}}&=\sum_{i=1}^{n}\boldsymbol{M}_i=\sum_{i=1}^{n}\boldsymbol{M}_{\mathrm{O}}(\boldsymbol{F}_i)\end{aligned}\right\}\tag{4-1-9}$$

任意力系中所有各力的矢量和 $\boldsymbol{F}'_{\mathrm{R}}$，称为该力系的主矢；而诸力对于任选简化中心 O 之矩的矢量和 $\boldsymbol{M}_{\mathrm{O}}$，称为该力系对简化中心的主矩。

上述结果表明：任意力系向任选一点 O 简化，可得一个力和一个力偶，这个力等于该力系的主矢，作用线通过简化中心；简化所得力偶的力偶矩矢等于该力系对简化中心 O 的主矩。注意：任意力系的主矢与简化中心的选择无关，而其主矩与简化中心的选择有关。

(三)平面力系的简化结果

平面力系的简化结果见表 4-1-2。

平面力系简化的最后结果 表 4-1-2

$\boldsymbol{F}'_{\mathrm{R}}$(主矢)	$\boldsymbol{M}_{\mathrm{O}}$(主矩)	最后结果	说明
$\boldsymbol{F}'_{\mathrm{R}}\neq\boldsymbol{0}$	$\boldsymbol{M}_{\mathrm{O}}\neq 0$	合力	合力作用线到简化中心 O 的距离为 $d=\dfrac{\lvert \boldsymbol{M}_{\mathrm{O}}\rvert}{F'_{\mathrm{R}}}$
	$\boldsymbol{M}_{\mathrm{O}}=0$	合力	合力作用线通过简化中心
$\boldsymbol{F}'_{\mathrm{R}}=\boldsymbol{0}$	$\boldsymbol{M}_{\mathrm{O}}\neq 0$	合力偶	此时主矩与简化中心无关
	$\boldsymbol{M}_{\mathrm{O}}=0$	平衡	

【例 4-1-10】 如图所示边长为 a 的正方形物块 $OABC$。已知：各力的大小 $=F$，力偶矩 $M_1=M_2=Fa$。该力系向 O 点简化后的主矢及主矩应为：

A. $F_{\mathrm{R}}=0\mathrm{N}, M_{\mathrm{O}}=4Fa$(↷)

B. $F_{\mathrm{R}}=0\mathrm{N}, M_{\mathrm{O}}=3Fa$(↶)

C. $F_{\mathrm{R}}=0\mathrm{N}, M_{\mathrm{O}}=2Fa$(↶)

D. $F_{\mathrm{R}}=0\mathrm{N}, M_{\mathrm{O}}=2Fa$(↷)

例 4-1-10 图

解 四个分力构成自行封闭的四边形(F_1 与 F_3 等值反向、F_2 与 F_4 等值反向)，故主矢为零：$F_{\mathrm{R}}=0\mathrm{N}$；$M_1$ 与 M_2 等值反向，$\boldsymbol{F}_1$ 与 $\boldsymbol{F}_3$、$\boldsymbol{F}_2$ 与 $\boldsymbol{F}_4$ 构成顺时针转向的两个力偶，每个力偶的力偶矩大小均为 Fa，故主矩为：$M_{\mathrm{O}}=M_2-M_1-Fa-Fa=-2Fa$(顺时针)。

答案：D

【例 4-1-11】 平面力系不平衡，其简化的最后结果为：

A. 合力　B. 合力偶　C. 合力或合力偶　D. 合力和合力偶

解 对于平面力系，若主矢为零，力系简化的最后结果为合力偶；若主矢不为零，无论主矩是否为零，力系简化的最后结果均为合力。

答案：C

注：平面力系若不平衡，简化的最后结果只可能是合力或合力偶。

【例 4-1-12】 图示平面力系中，已知 $q=10\mathrm{kN/m}$，$M=20\mathrm{kN\cdot m}$，$a=2\mathrm{m}$。则该主动力系对 B 点的合力矩为：

A. $M_{\mathrm{B}}=0$

B. $M_{\mathrm{B}}=20\mathrm{kN\cdot m}$(↶)

C. $M_{\mathrm{B}}=40\mathrm{kN\cdot m}$(↶)

D. $M_{\mathrm{B}}=40\mathrm{kN\cdot m}$(↷)

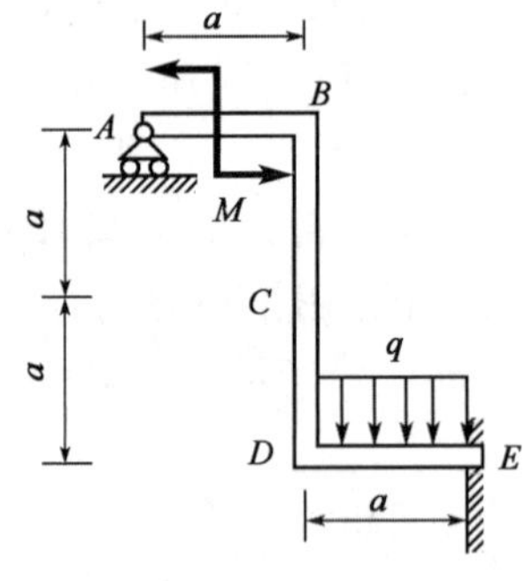

例 4-1-12 图

解 将主动力系对 B 点取矩求代数和：

$$M_B = M - qa^2/2 = 20 - 10 \times 2^2/2 = 0$$

答案：A

三、力系的平衡

力系平衡的充分必要条件是力系的主矢与主矩同时等于零。

（一）平面力系的平衡

1. 平面力系的平衡方程

根据平衡条件 $\boldsymbol{F}'_R=0$，$\boldsymbol{M}_O=0$，可得平面任意力系和平面特殊力系的几种不同形式的平衡方程（见表 4-1-3）。

平面力系的平衡方程 表 4-1-3

力（偶）系	平面任意力系	平面汇交力系	平面平行力系（取 y 轴与各力作用线平行）	平面力偶系
平衡条件	主矢、主矩同时为零 $\boldsymbol{F}'_R=0$，$\boldsymbol{M}_O=0$	合力为零 $\boldsymbol{F}_R=0$	主矢、主矩同时为零 $\boldsymbol{F}'_R=0$，$\boldsymbol{M}_O=0$	合力偶矩为零 $\boldsymbol{M}=0$
基本形式平衡方程	$\sum F_x=0$ $\sum F_y=0$ $\sum m_O(\boldsymbol{F})=0$	$\sum F_x=0$ $\sum F_y=0$	$\sum F_y=0$ $\sum m_O(\boldsymbol{F})=0$	$\sum m=0$
二力矩形式平衡方程	$\sum F_x=0$（或 $\sum F_y=0$） $\sum m_A(\boldsymbol{F})=0$ $\sum m_B(\boldsymbol{F})=0$ A、B 两点连线不垂直于 x 轴（或 y 轴）	$\sum m_A(\boldsymbol{F})=0$ $\sum m_B(\boldsymbol{F})=0$ A、B 两点与力系的汇交点不在同一直线上	$\sum m_A(\boldsymbol{F})=0$ $\sum m_B(\boldsymbol{F})=0$ A、B 两点连线不与各力平行	无
三力矩形式平衡方程	$\sum m_A(\boldsymbol{F})=0$ $\sum m_B(\boldsymbol{F})=0$ $\sum m_C(\boldsymbol{F})=0$ A、B、C 三点不在同一直线上	无	无	无

【例 4-1-13】 平面平行力系处于平衡，应有独力平衡方程的个数为：

A. 1 个　　B. 2 个　　C. 3 个　　D. 4 个

解 对于平面平行力系，向一点简化的结果仍为一主矢和一主矩，但主矢的作用线与平行力系中的力平行，若要令其等于零，只需一个平衡方程。而主矩为零应和任意力系一样需要一个平衡方程。

答案：B

【例 4-1-14】 如图 a）所示平面构架，不计各杆自重。已知：物块 M 重力的大小为 F_P，悬挂如图所示，不计小滑轮 D 的尺寸与重量，A、E、C 均为光滑铰链，$L_1=1.5\text{m}$，$L_2=2\text{m}$。则支座 B 的约束力为：

A. $F_B=\frac{3}{4}F_P(\rightarrow)$　　B. $F_B=\frac{3}{4}F_P(\leftarrow)$

C. $F_B=F_P(\leftarrow)$　　　　　　　　　D. $F_B=0$

解　取构架整体为研究对象，根据约束的性质，B 处为活动铰链支座，约束力为水平方向（图 b）。列平衡方程：$\sum M_A(F)=0, F_B\cdot 2L_2-F_P\cdot 2L_1=0, F_B=\frac{3}{4}F_P$。

答案：A

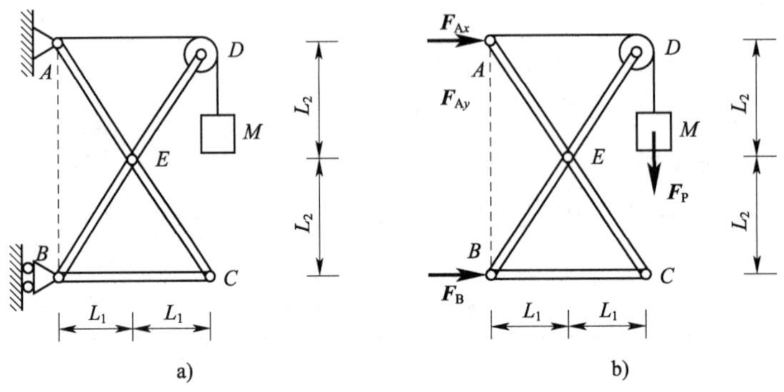

例 4-1-14 图

【例 4-1-15】　重力为 $\boldsymbol{W}$ 的圆球置于光滑的斜槽内，如图所示。右侧斜面 B 处对球的约束力 $\boldsymbol{F}_{NB}$ 的大小为：

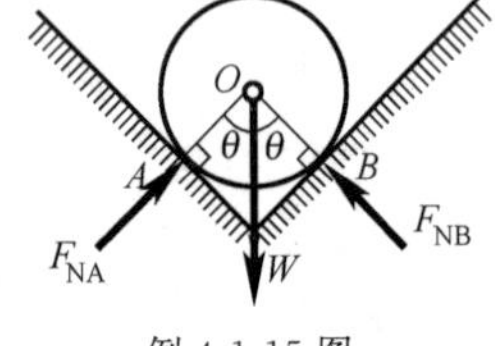

例 4-1-15 图

A. $F_{NB}=\dfrac{W}{2\cos\theta}$　　　　　B. $F_{NB}=\dfrac{W}{\cos\theta}$

C. $F_{NB}=W\cos\theta$　　　　　D. $F_{NB}=\dfrac{W}{2}\cos\theta$

解　以圆球为研究对象，沿 OA、OB 方向有约束力 $\boldsymbol{F}_{NA}$ 和 $\boldsymbol{F}_{NB}$，由对称性可知两约束力大小相等，对圆球列铅垂方向的平衡方程

$$\sum F_y=0=F_{NA}\cos\theta+F_{NB}\cos\theta-W=0\Rightarrow F_{NB}=\frac{W}{2\cos\theta}$$

答案：A

2. 物体系统的平衡

由两个或两个以上的物体（构件）通过一定的约束方式连接在一起而组成的系统，称为物体系统，简称物系。

当物系整体平衡时，系统中每一个物体也都平衡。系统内各物体间相互的作用力，称为内力；系统以外的物体作用于系统的力，称为外力。

通常情况下，每一个处于平衡状态的物体在平面力系作用下，具有三个独立的平衡方程，若物体系统由 n 个物体组成，则系统便具有 $3n$ 个独立的平衡方程（在特殊力系作用下，物系中独立的平衡方程数目可由表 4-1-3 确定），可解 $3n$ 个未知量。若物系中实际存在的未知量数目为 k，则当 $k=3n$ 时，应用全部独立的平衡方程就可求得全部未知量，此类问题称为静定问题；当 $k>3n$ 时，应用全部独立的平衡方程不能求出全部未知量，此类问题称为静不定问题，或称为超静定问题。

求解物体系统平衡问题的方法及步骤：

（1）首先判断物系的静定性。只有肯定了所给物系是静定的，才着手求解。

（2）选取研究对象。尽可能通过整体平衡，求得某些未知约束力，再根据具体所要求的未知量，选择合适的局部或单个物体作为研究对象。

(3)进行受力分析。根据约束的性质及作用与反作用定律，严格区分施力体与受力体，内力与外力(只分析所选研究对象受到的外力)，画出研究对象的受力图。

(4)建立平衡方程，求解未知量。

【例 4-1-16】 在如图 a)所示结构中，已知 q、L，设力偶逆时针转向为正。则固定端 B 处约束力的值为：

A. $F_{Bx}=qL$，$F_{By}=qL$，$M_B=-\dfrac{3}{2}qL^2$

B. $F_{Bx}=-qL$，$F_{By}=qL$，$M_B=\dfrac{3}{2}qL^2$

C. $F_{Bx}=qL$，$F_{By}=-qL$，$M_B=\dfrac{3}{2}qL^2$

D. $F_{Bx}=-qL$，$F_{By}=-qL$，$M_B=\dfrac{3}{2}qL^2$

解 选 AC 为研究对象，受力如图 b)所示，列平衡方程

$$\sum m_C(\boldsymbol{F})=0: qL\cdot\frac{L}{2}-F_A\cdot\frac{L}{2}=0,F_A=qL$$

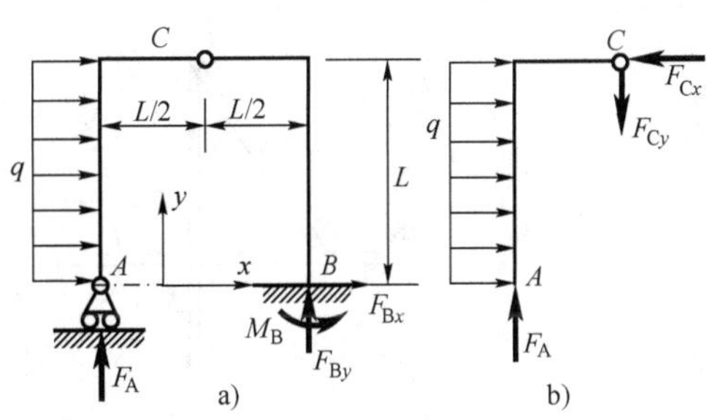

例 4-1-16 图

再选结构整体为研究对象，受力如图 a)所示，列平衡方程

$$\sum F_x=0: F_{Bx}+qL=0,\ F_{Bx}=-qL$$

$$\sum F_y=0: F_A+F_{By}=0,\ F_{By}=-qL$$

$$\sum m_B(\boldsymbol{F})=0: M_B-qL\cdot\frac{L}{2}-F_A\cdot L=0,\ M_B=\frac{3}{2}qL^2$$

答案：D

【例 4-1-17】 如图 a)所示水平梁 AB 由铰 A 与杆 BD 支撑。在梁上 O 处用小轴安装滑轮，轮上跨过软绳，绳一端水平地系于墙上，另一端悬挂重力为 $\boldsymbol{W}$ 的物块。构件均不计自重。铰 A 的约束力大小为：

A. $F_{Ax}=\dfrac{5}{4}W,F_{Ay}=\dfrac{3}{4}W$　　B. $F_{Ax}=W,F_{Ay}=\dfrac{1}{2}W$

C. $F_{Ax}=\dfrac{3}{4}W,F_{Ay}=\dfrac{1}{4}W$　　D. $F_{Ax}=\dfrac{1}{2}W,F_{Ay}=W$

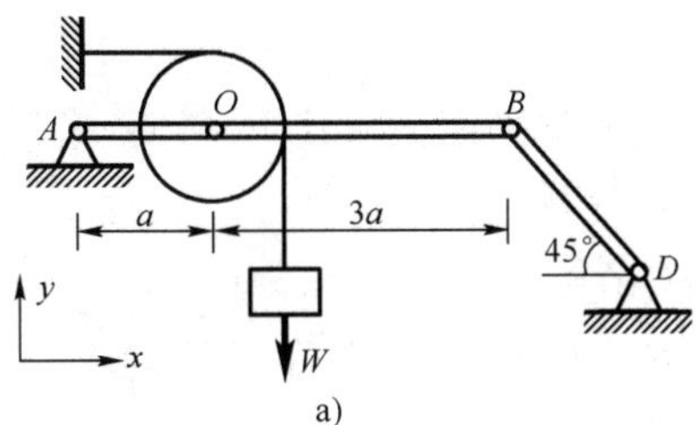

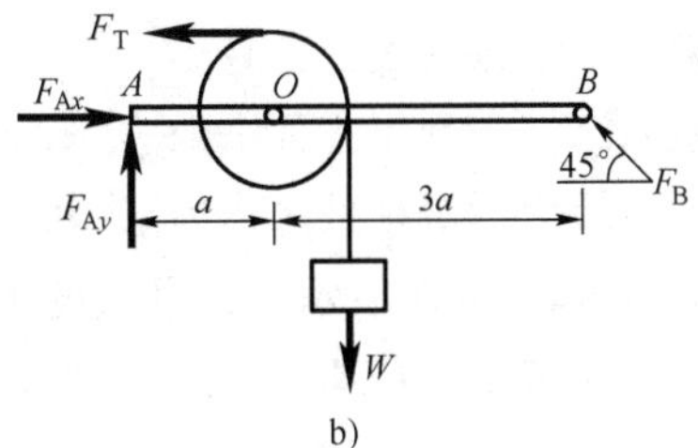

例 4-1-17 图

解 取杆 AB 及滑轮为研究对象，受力如图b)所示。

列平衡方程

$$\sum m_A(\boldsymbol{F})=0: F_B\cos45°\times4a+F_T\cdot r-W(a+r)=0$$

因为 $F_T=W$，$F_B\cos45°=F_B\sin45°=\dfrac{W}{4}$

$\sum F_x=0$：$F_{Ax}-F_T-F_B\cos45°=0$，$F_{Ax}=\dfrac{5}{4}W$

$\sum F_y=0$：$F_{Ay}-W+F_B\sin45°=0$，$F_{Ay}=\dfrac{3}{4}W$

答案：A

【例 4-1-18】 在如图 a)所示机构中，已知：F_P，$L=2\text{m}$，$r=0.5\text{m}$，$q=30°$，$BE=EG$，$CE=EH$。则支座 A 的约束力为：

A. $F_{Ax}=F_P(\leftarrow)$，$F_{Ay}=1.75F_P(\downarrow)$　　B. $F_{Ax}=0$，$F_{Ay}=0.75F_P(\downarrow)$

C. $F_{Ax}=0$，$F_{Ay}=0.75F_P(\uparrow)$　　D. $F_{Ax}=F_P(\rightarrow)$，$F_{Ay}=1.75F_P(\uparrow)$

解 对系统进行整体分析，外力有主动力 $\boldsymbol{F}_P$，A、H 处约束力，由于 $\boldsymbol{F}_P$ 与 H 处约束力均为铅垂方向，故 A 处也只有铅垂方向约束力（图 b)，列平衡方程 $\sum M_H(\boldsymbol{F})=0$，$F_{Ay}\cdot L-F_P(0.5L+r)=0$，$F_{Ay}=0.75F_P$。

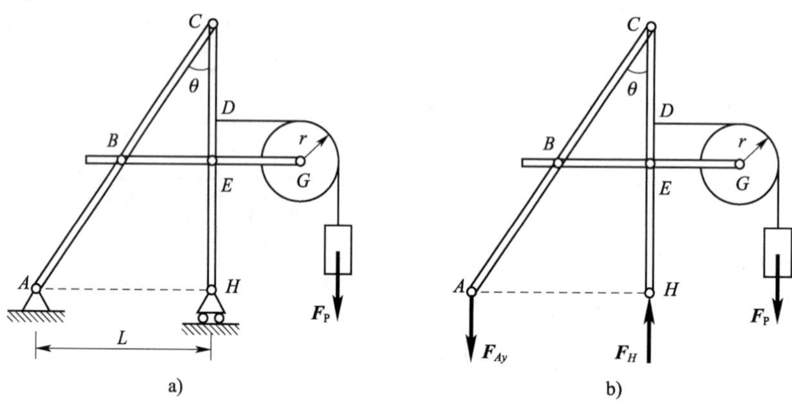

例 4-1-18 图

答案：B

（二）平面静定桁架

桁架是一种由若干直杆在两端彼此用铰链连接而成的杆系结构，其特点是受力后几何形状不变。若桁架所有的杆件都在同一平面内，称其为平面桁架，各杆间的铰接点称作节点；各杆自重不计，所受荷载均作用于节点上，或平均分配在杆件两端的节点上。所以桁架中的各杆均为二力杆。

平面静定桁架的内力计算方法：

（1）节点法——利用平面汇交力系的平衡方程，选取各节点为研究对象，计算桁架中各杆之内力；常用于结构的设计计算。

（2）截面法——利用平面一般力系的平衡方程，用假想平面截取其中一部分桁架作为研究对象，计算桁架中指定杆件之内力；常用于结构的校核计算。

【例 4-1-19】 如图所示不计自重的水平梁与桁架在 B 点铰接。已知：荷载 $\boldsymbol{F}_1$、$\boldsymbol{F}$ 均与 BH 垂直，$F_1=8\text{kN}$，$F=4\text{kN}$，$M=6\text{kN}\cdot\text{m}$，$q=1\text{kN/m}$，$L=2\text{m}$。则杆件 1 的内力为：

A. $F_1=0$

B. $F_1=8\text{kN}$

C. $F_1=-8\text{kN}$

D. $F_1=-4\text{kN}$

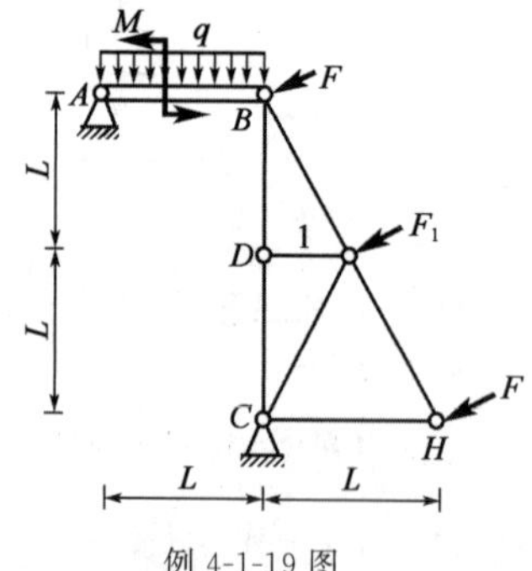

例 4-1-19 图

解 取节点 D 分析其平衡，可知 1 杆为零杆。

答案:A

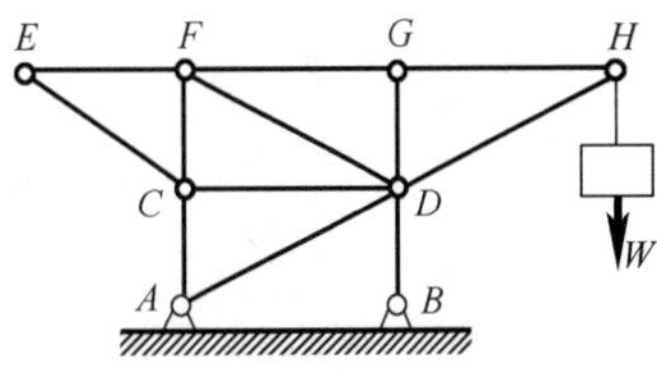

例 4-1-20 图

【例 4-1-20】 不经计算，通过直接判定得出如图所示桁架中内力为零的杆数为：

A. 2 根　　B. 3 根

C. 4 根　　D. 5 根

解 根据节点法，由节点 E 的平衡，可判断出杆 EC、EF 为零杆，再由节点 C 和 G，可判断出杆 CD、GD 为零杆；由系统的整体平衡可知：支座 A 处只有铅垂方向的约束力，故通过分析节点 A，可判断出杆 AD 为零杆。

答案:D

注：判断零杆时，首先分析无外荷载作用的两杆节点和其中两杆在同一直线上的三杆节点。

(三)滑动摩擦

在主动力作用下，当两物体接触处有相对滑动或有相对滑动趋势时，在接触处的公切面内将受到一定的阻力阻碍其相对滑动，这种现象称为滑动摩擦。

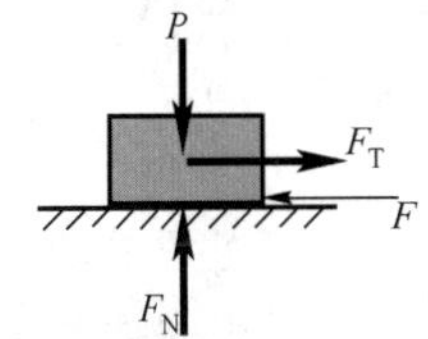

图 4-1-7　滑动摩擦

1. 各种摩擦力的计算公式

图 4-1-7 中所示力 $\boldsymbol{P}$、$\boldsymbol{F}_T$ 为主动力，摩擦力 $\boldsymbol{F}$ 可根据物体的运动状态分为三类。其计算公式见表 4-1-4。

摩擦力计算一览表　　表 4-1-4

类　别	静摩擦力 $\boldsymbol{F}_s$	最大静摩擦力 $\boldsymbol{F}_{max}$	动摩擦力 $\boldsymbol{F}_d$
产生条件	物体接触面之间有相对滑动趋势，但物体仍保持静止	物体接触面之间有相对滑动趋势，但物体处于要滑而未滑的临界平衡状态	物体接触面之间开始相对滑动
方向	与相对滑动趋势方向相反	与相对滑动趋势方向相反	与相对滑动方向相反
大小	$0 \leqslant F_s \leqslant F_{max}$ F_s 之值由平衡方程确定 $F_s = F_T$	$F_{max} = f_s F_N$ 式中，F_N 为接触面的法向约束力(也称法向正压力)；f_s 称作静滑动摩擦因数，其值可从工程手册中查找	$F_d = f_d F_N$ 式中，F_N 为接触面法向反力；f_d 为动滑动摩擦因数

2. 摩擦曲线

摩擦力 $\boldsymbol{F}$ 与主动力 $\boldsymbol{F}_T$ 之间的关系以及物体的运动状态，可用如图 4-1-8 所示的摩擦曲线来表示。

3. 摩擦角与自锁

静摩擦力 $\boldsymbol{F}_s$ 与法向约束力 $\boldsymbol{F}_N$ 的合力 $\boldsymbol{F}_{RA}$ 称为全约束力，其作用线与接触面的公法线成一偏角 φ，见图 4-1-9a)。当物块处于平衡的临界状态时，静摩擦力达到最大值 $\boldsymbol{F}_{max}$，偏角 φ 也达到最大值 φ_f，见图 4-1-9b)。全约束力与法线间夹角的最大值 φ_f 称为摩擦角。由图可得

$$\tan\varphi_f = \frac{F_{max}}{F_N} = \frac{f_s F_N}{F_N} = f_s \tag{4-1-10}$$

即摩擦角的正切等于静摩擦因数。

因静摩擦力 $\boldsymbol{F}_s$ 总是小于或等于最大静摩擦力 $\boldsymbol{F}_{max}$，故全约束力与支承面法线间的夹角 φ，总是小于或等于摩擦角 φ_f，其变化范围为

$$0 \leqslant \varphi \leqslant \varphi_f \tag{4-1-11}$$

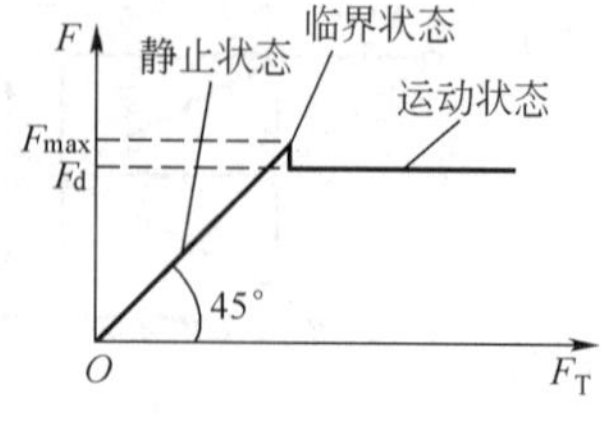

图 4-1-8 摩擦曲线

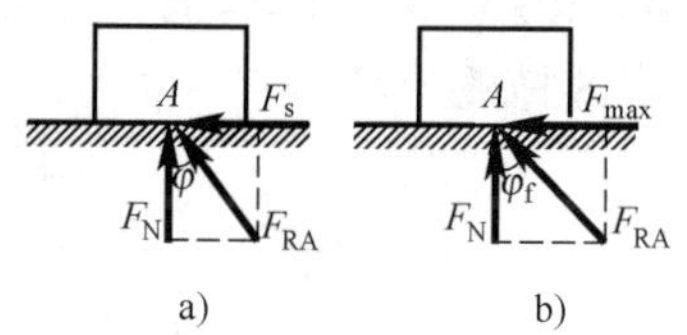

图 4-1-9 摩擦角

如图 4-1-10a)所示，若设作用于物块上主动力的合力 $\boldsymbol{F}_R$ 与接触面法线的夹角为 θ，全约束力 $\boldsymbol{F}_{RA}$ 与接触面法线间的夹角为 φ，则当 $\boldsymbol{F}_R$ 的作用线在摩擦角之内($\theta < \varphi_f$)时，无论这个力怎样大，都会产生与之满足二力平衡条件的全约束力 $\boldsymbol{F}_{RA}$($\varphi = \theta < \varphi_f$)，使物块保持静止，这种现象称为自锁现象。

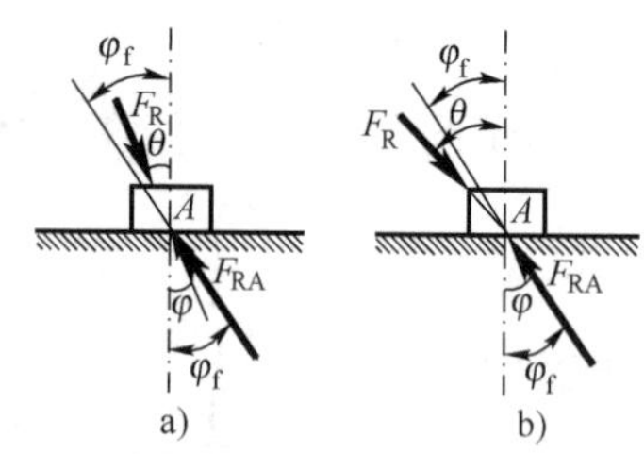

图 4-1-10 自锁现象

反之，如图 4-1-10b)所示，当 $\boldsymbol{F}_R$ 的作用线在摩擦角之外($\theta > \varphi_f$)时，无论这个力怎样小，物块一定会滑动。$\theta = \varphi_f$ 时，物块处于临界平衡状态。

4.考虑滑动摩擦时物体系统的平衡

考虑摩擦时平衡问题的特点是：在受力分析时必须考虑摩擦力。考虑摩擦力后，物体系统除满足力系的平衡条件(平衡方程)外，还需满足物理条件，即

$$F_s \leqslant f_s F_N \quad \text{或} \quad \theta \leqslant \varphi_f$$

【例 4-1-21】 重力大小为 W 的物块自由地放在倾角为 α 的斜面上，如图 a)所示。且 $\sin\alpha = \frac{3}{5}$，$\cos\alpha = \frac{4}{5}$。物块上作用一水平力 $\boldsymbol{F}$，且 $F = W$。若物块与斜面间的静摩擦系数 $f = 0.2$，则该物块的状态为：

A.静止状态　　B.临界平衡状态

C.滑动状态　　D.条件不足，不能确定

解 如图 b)所示，若物块平衡，沿斜面方向有 $F_f = F\cos\alpha - W\sin\alpha = 0.2F$

而最大静摩擦力 $F_{fmax} = f \cdot F_N = f(F\sin\alpha + W\cos\alpha) = 0.28F$

因 $F_{fmax} > F_f$，所以物块静止。

答案：A

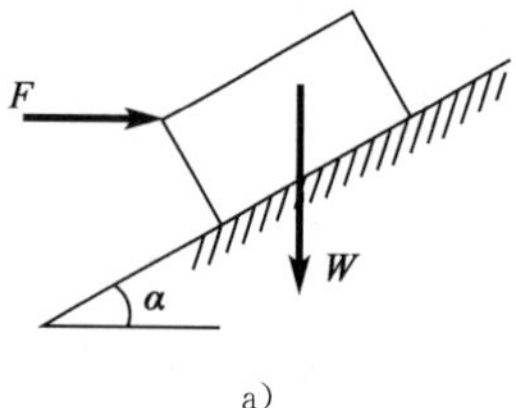

a)

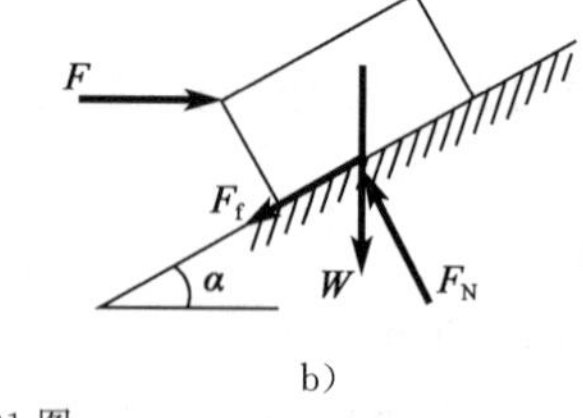

b)

例 4-1-21 图

【例 4-1-22】 杆 AB 的 A 端置于光滑水平面上，AB 与水平面夹角为 30°，杆重力大小为 P 如图所示。B 处有摩擦，则杆 AB 平衡时，B 处的摩擦力与 x 方向的夹角为：

A. 90°　　B. 30°

C. 60°　　D. 45°

例 4-1-22 图

解　在重力作用下，杆 A 端有向左侧滑动的趋势，故 B 处摩擦力应沿杆指向右上方向。

答案：B

【例 4-1-23】　如图 a)所示结构中，已知：B 处光滑，杆 AC 与墙间的静摩擦因数 $f_s=1$，$\theta=60°$，$BC=2AB$，杆自重不计。试问在垂直于杆 AC 的力 $\boldsymbol{F}$ 作用下，杆能否平衡？为什么？

解　本例已知静摩擦因数以及外加力方向，求保持静止的条件，因此需用平衡方程与物理条件联合求解，现用解析法与几何法分别求解。

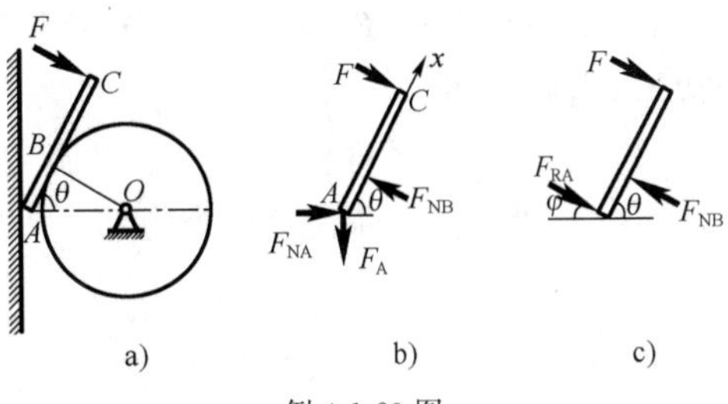

例 4-1-23 图

(1)解析法

以杆 AC 为研究对象，其受力图如图 b)所示。注意到，杆在 A 处有摩擦，B 处光滑。应用平面力系平衡方程和 A 处摩擦力的物理方程，有

$$\sum \boldsymbol{F}_x=0:F_{NA}\cos60°-F_A\sin60°=0 \qquad ①$$

$$F_A\leqslant f_sF_{NA} \qquad ②$$

由①式得

$$\frac{F_A}{F_{NA}}=\frac{\cos60°}{\sin60°}=\cot60°=0.577 \qquad ③$$

由②式得

$$\frac{F_A}{F_{NA}}\leqslant f_s=1 \qquad ④$$

比较③式和④式，满足平衡条件，所以系统平衡。

(2)几何法

因为杆 AC 在 C、B 两处的力均垂直于杆，故杆若平衡，A 处的全反力 $\boldsymbol{F}_{RA}$ 必与杆垂直，见图 c)，其中 $\boldsymbol{F}_{RA}=\boldsymbol{F}_A+\boldsymbol{F}_{NA}$。由于 $\boldsymbol{F}_{RA}$ 与 $\boldsymbol{F}_{NA}$ 的夹角 $\varphi=30°$，而 A 处的摩擦角为

$$\varphi_f=\arctan f_s=\arctan1=45°$$

由此可得

$$\varphi<\varphi_f$$

满足自锁条件，所以系统平衡。

注：若已知条件为摩擦角而非摩擦因数时，尽量应用自锁条件求解摩擦问题。

习　　题

4-1-1　如图所示三力矢 $\boldsymbol{F}_1$、$\boldsymbol{F}_2$、$\boldsymbol{F}_3$ 的关系是(　　)。

A. $\boldsymbol{F}_1+\boldsymbol{F}_2+\boldsymbol{F}_3=0$

B. $\boldsymbol{F}_3=\boldsymbol{F}_1+\boldsymbol{F}_2$

C. $\boldsymbol{F}_2=\boldsymbol{F}_1+\boldsymbol{F}_3$

D. $\boldsymbol{F}_1=\boldsymbol{F}_2+\boldsymbol{F}_3$

题 4-1-1 图

4-1-2　作用在一个刚体上的两个力 $\boldsymbol{F}_A$、$\boldsymbol{F}_B$，满足 $\boldsymbol{F}_A=-\boldsymbol{F}_B$ 的条件，则该二力可能是(　　)。

A. 作用力和反作用力或一对平衡的力

B. 一对平衡的力或一个力偶

C. 一对平衡的力或一个力和一个力偶

D. 作用力和反作用力或一个力偶

4-1-3 两直角刚杆 AC、CB 支承如图所示，在铰 C 处受力 $\boldsymbol{P}$ 作用，则 A、B 两处约束反力与 x 轴正向所成的夹角 α＝(　　)，β＝(　　)。

A. 30°，45°　　B. 45°，135°　　C. 90°，30°　　D. 135°，90°

4-1-4 已知 $\boldsymbol{F}_1$、$\boldsymbol{F}_2$、$\boldsymbol{F}_3$、$\boldsymbol{F}_4$ 为作用于刚体上的平面共点力系，其力矢关系如图所示为平行四边形，由此可知(　　)。

A. 力系可合成为一个力偶　　B. 力系可合成为一个力

C. 力系简化为一个力和一力偶　　D. 力系的合力为零，力系平衡

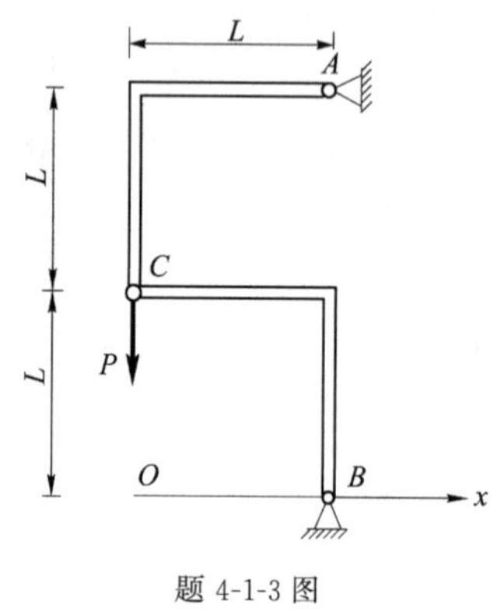

题 4-1-3 图

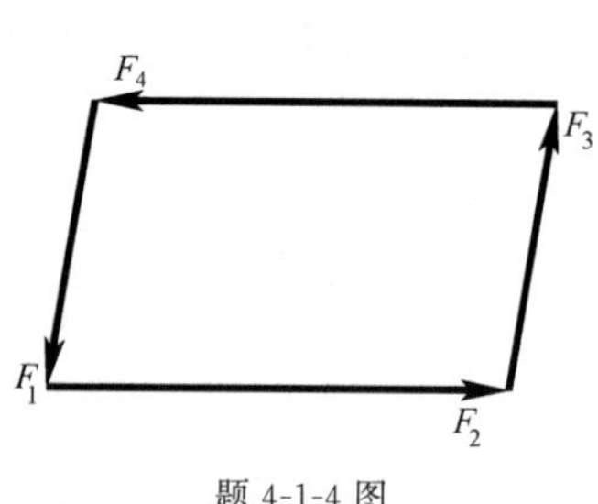

题 4-1-4 图

4-1-5 设力 $\boldsymbol{F}$ 在 x 轴上的投影为 F，则该力在与 x 轴共面的任一轴上的投影(　　)。

A. 一定不等于零　　B. 不一定等于零

C. 一定等于零　　D. 等于 F

4-1-6 如图所示结构受力 $\boldsymbol{P}$ 作用，杆重不计，则 A 支座约束力的大小为(　　)。

A. $P/2$　　B. $\sqrt{3}P/2$

C. $\dfrac{P}{\sqrt{3}}$　　D. 0

4-1-7 如图所示一等边三角形板，边长为 a，沿三边分别作用有力 $\boldsymbol{F}_1$、$\boldsymbol{F}_2$ 和 $\boldsymbol{F}_3$，且 $F_1=F_2=F_3$，则此三角形板处于(　　)状态。

A. 平衡　　B. 移动

C. 转动　　D. 既移动又转动

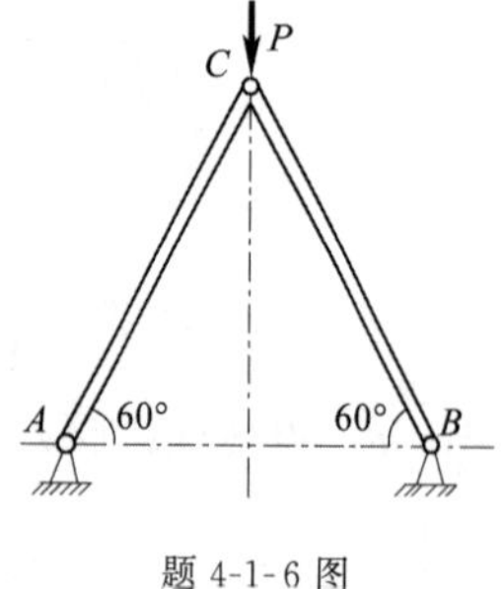

题 4-1-6 图

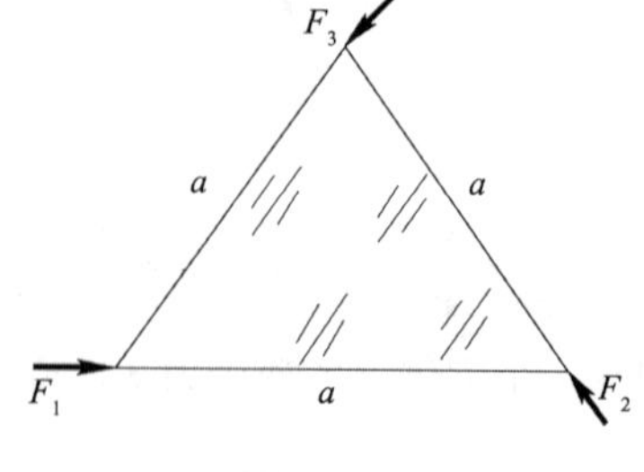

题 4-1-7 图

4-1-8 在如图所示结构中，如果将作用于构件 AC 上的力偶 m 搬移到构件 BC 上，则 A、B、C 三处的反力(　　)。

A. 都不变　　B. A、B 处反力不变，C 处反力改变

C. 都改变　　D. A、B 处反力改变，C 处反力不变

4-1-9　杆 AF、BE、EF、CD 相互铰接，并支承如图所示，今在 AF 杆上作用一力偶（**P**、**P′**），若不计各杆自重，则 A 支座反力的作用线（　　）。

A. 过 A 点平行力 **P**　　B. 过 A 点平行 BG 连线

C. 沿 AG 直线　　D. 沿 AH 直线

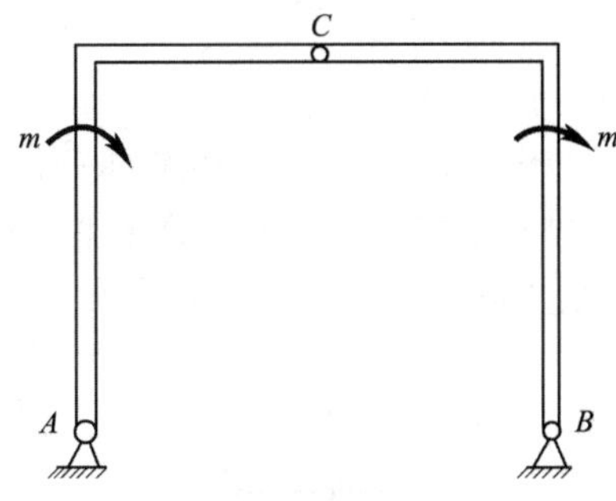

题 4-1-8 图

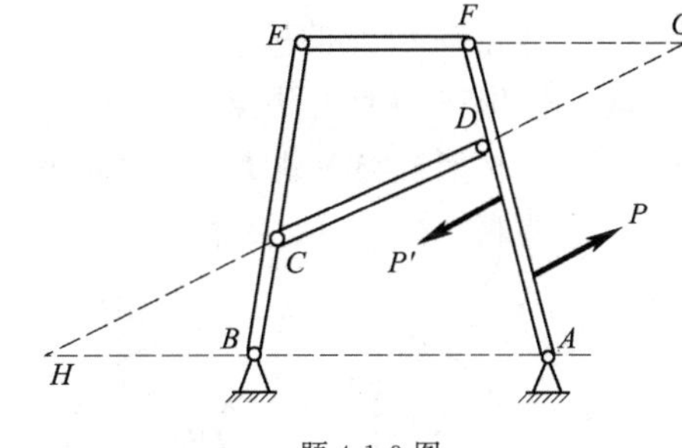

题 4-1-9 图

4-1-10　力 $\boldsymbol{F}_1$，$\boldsymbol{F}_2$ 共线且方向相反，大小为 $F_1=2F_2$，其合力为 $\boldsymbol{F}_R$ 可表示为（　　）。

A. $\boldsymbol{F}_R=\boldsymbol{F}_1-\boldsymbol{F}_2$　　B. $\boldsymbol{F}_R=\boldsymbol{F}_2-\boldsymbol{F}_1$

C. $\boldsymbol{F}_R=\frac{1}{2}\boldsymbol{F}_1$　　D. $\boldsymbol{F}_R=\boldsymbol{F}_2$

4-1-11　平面力系向点 1 简化时，主矢 $\boldsymbol{R}'=0$，主矩 $\boldsymbol{M}_1\neq0$，如将该力系向另一点 2 简化，则（　　）。

A. $\boldsymbol{R}'\neq0$，$\boldsymbol{M}_2\neq0$　　B. $\boldsymbol{R}'=0$，$\boldsymbol{M}_2\neq\boldsymbol{M}_1$

C. $\boldsymbol{R}'=0$，$\boldsymbol{M}_2=\boldsymbol{M}_1$　　D. $\boldsymbol{R}'\neq0$，$\boldsymbol{M}_2=\boldsymbol{M}_1$

4-1-12　五根等长的细直杆铰接成图所示杆系结构，各杆重量不计，若 $P_A=P_C=P$，且垂直 BD，则杆 BD 的内力 S_{BD} 为（　　）。

A. $-P$(压)　　B. $-\sqrt{3}P$(压)　　C. $-\sqrt{3}P/3$(压)　　D. $-\sqrt{3}P/2$(压)

4-1-13　在如图所示系统中，绳 DE 能承受的最大拉力为 10kN，杆重不计，则力 **P** 的最大值为（　　）。

A. 5kN　　B. 10kN　　C. 15kN　　D. 20kN

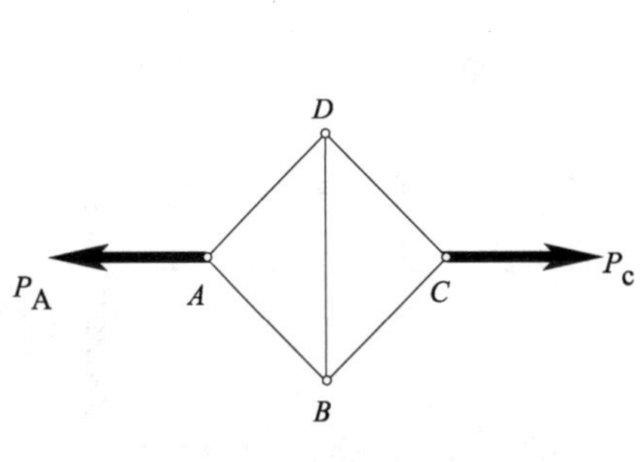

题 4-1-12 图

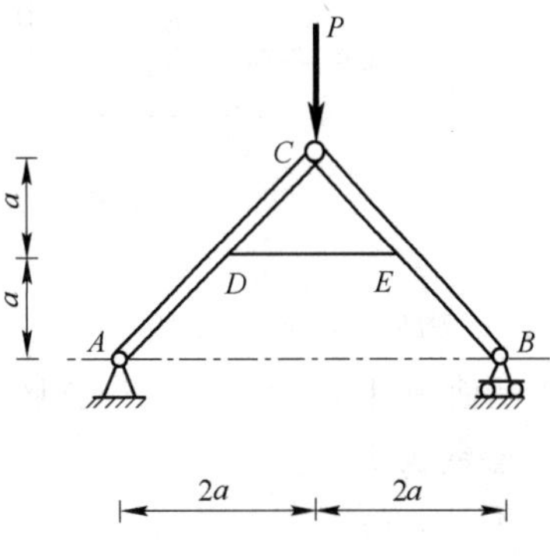

题 4-1-13 图

4-1-14　力系简化时若取不同的简化中心，则(　　)。

A. 力系的主矢、主矩都会改变

B. 力系的主矢不会改变，主矩一般会改变

C. 力系的主矢会改变、主矩一般不改变

D. 力系的主矢、主矩都不会改变，力系简化时与简化中心无关

4-1-15　某平面任意力系向 O 点简化后，得到如图所示的一个力 $\boldsymbol{R}$ 和一个力偶矩为 $\boldsymbol{M}_O$ 的力偶，则该力系的最后合成结果是(　　)。

A. 作用在 O 点的一个合力　　B. 合力偶

C. 作用在 O 点左边某点的一个合力　D. 作用在 O 点右边某点的一个合力

4-1-16　桁架结构形式与荷载 $\boldsymbol{F}_P$ 均已知(见图)。结构中杆件内力为零的杆件数为(　　)。

A. 零根　　B. 2 根　　C. 4 根　　D. 6 根

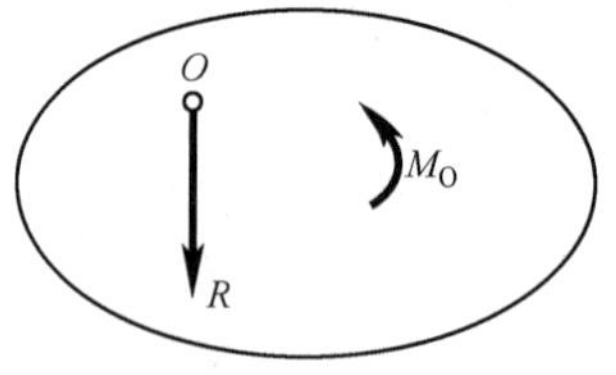

题 4-1-14 图

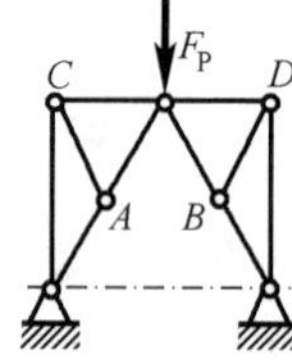

题 4-1-16 图

4-1-17　两直角刚杆 ACD，BEC 在 C 处铰接，并支承如图所示。若各杆重不计，则支座 A 处约束力的方向为(　　)。

A. $\boldsymbol{F}_A$ 的作用线沿水平方向　　B. $\boldsymbol{F}_A$ 的作用线沿铅垂方向

C. $\boldsymbol{F}_A$ 的作用线平行于 B、C 连线　D. $\boldsymbol{F}_A$ 的作用线方向无法确定

4-1-18　带有不平行两槽的矩形平板上作用一力偶 M，如图所示。今在槽内插入两个固定于地面的销钉，若不计摩擦则有(　　)。

A. 平板保持平衡　　B. 平板不能平衡

C. 平衡与否不能判断　　D. 上述三种结果都不对

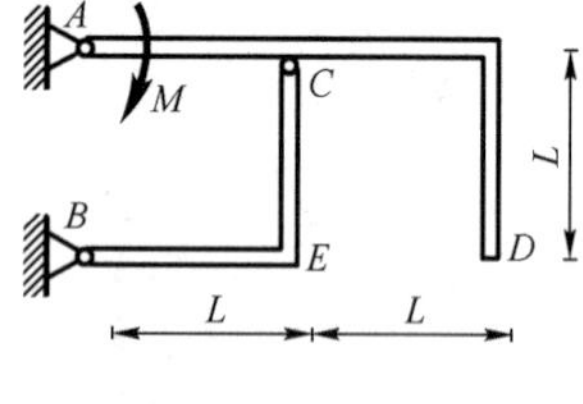

题 4-1-17 图

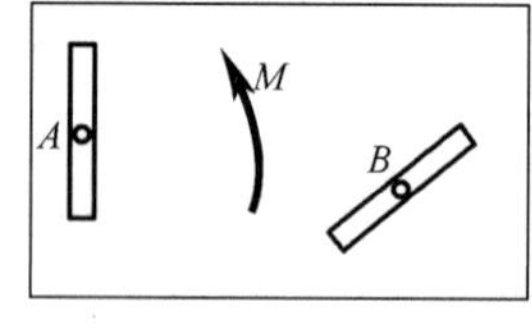

题 4-1-18 图

4-1-19　物块 A 的重力 $W=10\text{N}$，被大小为 $F_P=50\text{N}$ 的水平力挤压在粗糙的铅垂墙面 B 上，且处于平衡(见图)。物块与墙间的摩擦系数 $f=0.3$。A 与 B 间的摩擦力大小为(　　)。

A. $F=15\text{N}$

B. $F=10\text{N}$

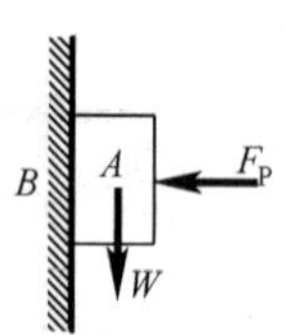

题 4-1-19 图

C. $F=3N$

D. 只依据所给条件则无法确定

4-1-20 物块重力的大小为 5kN，与水平面间的摩擦角为 $\varphi_m=35°$，今用与铅垂线成 60°角的力 $\boldsymbol{P}$ 推动物块，如图所示，若 $P=5kN$，则物块将（　　）。

A. 不动　　B. 滑动

C. 处于临界状态　　D. 滑动与否无法确定

4-1-21 物块重力的大小为 $G=20N$，用 $P=40N$ 的力按如图所示方向把物块压在铅直墙上，物块与墙之间的摩擦系数 $f=\sqrt{3}/4$，则作用在物块上的摩擦力等于（　　）。

A. 20N　　B. 15N

C. 0　　D. $10\sqrt{3}N$

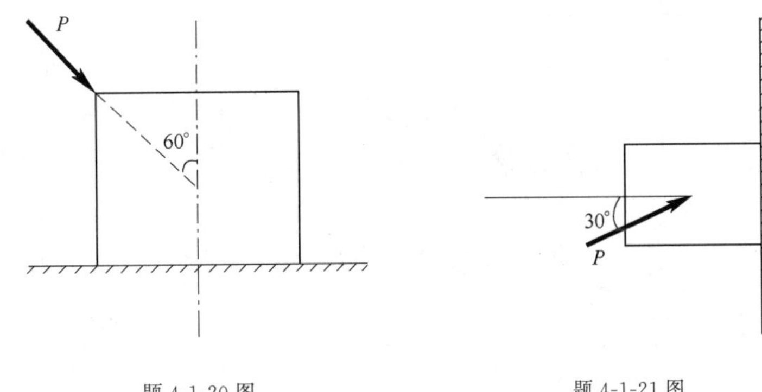

题 4-1-20 图　　题 4-1-21 图

4-1-22 重力 $W=80kN$ 的物体自由地放在倾角为 30°的斜面上，如图所示，若物体与斜面间的静摩擦系数 $f=\sqrt{3}/4$，动摩擦系数 $f'=0.4$，则作用在物体上的摩擦力的大小为（　　）。

A. 30kN　　B. 40kN　　C. 27.7kN　　D. 0

4-1-23 物 A 重力的大小为 100kN，物 B 重力的大小为 25kN，A 物与地面摩擦系数为 0.2，滑轮处摩擦不计，如图所示，则物体 A 与地面间的摩擦力为（　　）。

A. 20kN　　B. 16kN　　C. 15kN　　D. 12kN

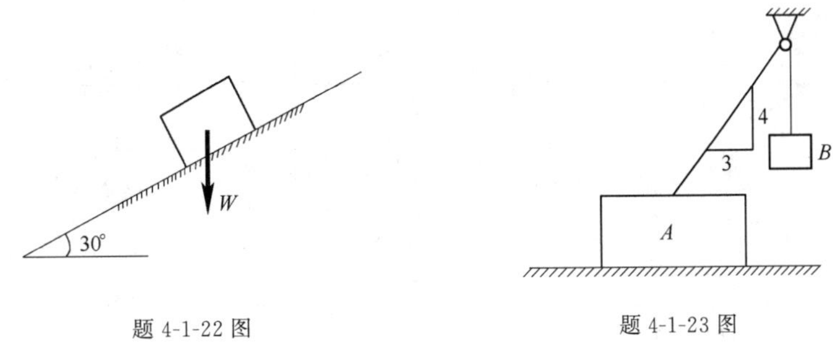

题 4-1-22 图　　题 4-1-23 图

第二节　运　动　学

运动学是用几何学的观点来研究物体的运动规律，即物体运动的描述（其在空间的位置随时间变化的规律）、运动的速度和加速度，而不涉及引起物体运动的物理原因。

一、点的运动学

点的运动学主要研究点相对于某一参考系的运动量随时间的变化规律，包括：点的运动方程的建立，运动轨迹的描述，速度和加速度的确定。

（一）描述点的运动的基本方法与基本公式

描述点的运动常用的基本方法有矢量法、直角坐标法、自然法。现将这三种方法及其应用范围归纳于表 4-2-1 中。

研究点的运动的基本方法 表 4-2-1

方 法	矢 量 法	直角坐标法	自 然 法
特点与用途	简明、直观，常用于理论推导	便于代数及微积分运算，常用于轨迹未知的情况	速度、切向加速度、法向加速度的算式简单、物理意义明确，常用于轨迹已知的情况
参考系			
参考系	以参考体上任一固定点 O 为参考点	以直角坐标系的三个坐标轴为参考坐标轴	在轨迹上任选一点 O 为参考点
运动方程	$\boldsymbol{r}=\boldsymbol{r}(t)$	$x=f_1(t), y=f_2(t), z=f_3(t)$	$s=f(t)$
轨迹	矢径 $\boldsymbol{r}$ 的矢端曲线	从上式中消去时间"t"即可得轨迹方程：$F_1(x,y)=0, F_2(y,z)=0$	事先已知

用上述三种方法描述的点的速度、加速度的基本公式见表 4-2-2。

速度、加速度计算公式 表 4-2-2

基本方法	速 度	加速度分量	全 加 速 度	备注
矢量法	$\boldsymbol{v}=\frac{d\boldsymbol{r}}{dt}=\dot{\boldsymbol{r}}$		$\boldsymbol{a}=\frac{d\boldsymbol{v}}{dt}=\frac{d^2\boldsymbol{r}}{dt^2}=\ddot{\boldsymbol{r}}$	
直角坐标法	$v_x=\frac{dx}{dt}, v_y=\frac{dy}{dt}, v_z=\frac{dz}{dt}$ $v=\sqrt{v_x^2+v_y^2+v_z^2}$ $\cos(\boldsymbol{v},\boldsymbol{i})=\frac{v_x}{v}$ $\cos(\boldsymbol{v},\boldsymbol{j})=\frac{v_y}{v}$ $\cos(\boldsymbol{v},\boldsymbol{k})=\frac{v_z}{v}$	$a_x=\frac{dv_x}{dt}=\ddot{x}$ $a_y=\frac{dv_x}{dt}=\ddot{y}$ $a_z=\frac{dv_z}{dt}=\ddot{z}$	$a=\sqrt{a_x^2+a_y^2+a_z^2}$ $\cos(\boldsymbol{a},\boldsymbol{i})=\frac{a_x}{a}$ $\cos(\boldsymbol{a},\boldsymbol{j})=\frac{a_y}{a}$ $\cos(\boldsymbol{a},\boldsymbol{k})=\frac{a_z}{a}$	
自然法	$v=\frac{ds}{dt}=\dot{s}$ 或 $\boldsymbol{v}=\dot{s}\boldsymbol{\tau}$	$a_\tau=\frac{dv}{dt}=\ddot{s}$ 沿切线方向 $a_n=\frac{v^2}{\rho}=\frac{(\dot{s})^2}{\rho}$ 恒指向曲率中心	$a=\sqrt{a_\tau^2+a_n^2}, \tan\beta=\frac{\lvert a_\tau \rvert}{a_n}$ β 为 $\boldsymbol{a}$ 与法线轴 n 正向间的夹角	加速度恒指向曲线凹的一侧

(二)三种基本方法之间的相互关系(见表 4-2-3)

三种基本方法之间的相互关系　　表 4-2-3

运动方程	速度	加速度
$\boldsymbol{r}=x\boldsymbol{i}+y\boldsymbol{j}+z\boldsymbol{k}$	$\boldsymbol{v}=v_x\boldsymbol{i}+v_y\boldsymbol{j}+v_z\boldsymbol{k}=\dot{s}\boldsymbol{\tau}$ $v=\dot{s}=\sqrt{v_x^2+v_y^2+v_z^2}$	$\boldsymbol{a}=a_x\boldsymbol{i}+a_y\boldsymbol{j}+a_z\boldsymbol{k}=\ddot{s}\boldsymbol{\tau}+\frac{\dot{s}^2}{\rho}\boldsymbol{n}$ $a=\sqrt{a_x^2+a_y^2+a_z^2}=\sqrt{\ddot{s}^2+\frac{\dot{s}^4}{\rho^2}}$

【例 4-2-1】 如图所示点 P 沿螺线自外向内运动。它走过的弧长与时间的一次方成正比。关于该点的运动,有以下 4 种答案,请判断哪一个答案是正确的:

A. 速度越来越快　　B. 速度越来越慢

C. 加速度越来越大　　D. 加速度越来越小

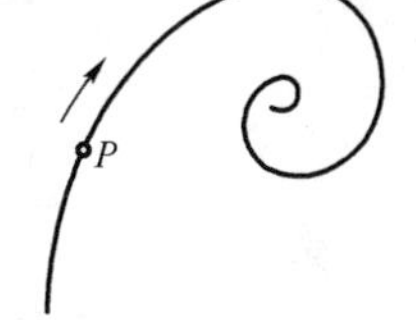

例 4-2-1 图

解 因为运动轨迹的弧长与时间的一次方成正比,所以有

$$s=kt$$

其中 k 为比例常数。对时间求一次导数后得到点的速度

$$v=\dot{s}=k$$

可见该点做匀速运动。但这只是指速度的大小。由于运动的轨迹为曲线,速度的方向不断改变,所以,还需要作加速度分析。于是,有

$$a_\tau=\frac{\mathrm{d}v}{\mathrm{d}t}=0, a_n=\frac{v^2}{\rho}$$

总加速度

$$a=\sqrt{a_\tau^2+a_n^2}=a_n=\frac{v^2}{\rho}$$

当点由外向内运动时,运动轨迹的曲率半径 ρ 逐渐变小,所以加速度 a 越来越大。

答案:C

【例 4-2-2】 点在铅垂平面 Oxy 内的运动方程为$\begin{cases}x=v_0t\\ y=\frac{1}{2}gt^2\end{cases}$,式中,$t$ 为时间,v_0、g 为常数。点的运动轨迹应为:

A. 直线　　B. 圆弧曲线

C. 抛物线　　D. 直线与圆连线

解 由第一个方程可得 $t=\frac{x}{v_0}$,将其代入第二个方程,可得抛物线方程 $y=\frac{g}{2v_0^2}x^2$。

答案:C

【例 4-2-3】 点沿直线运动,其速度 $v=20t+5$,已知:当 $t=0$ 时,$x=5\mathrm{m}$,则点的运动方程为:

A. $x=10t^2+5t+5$　　B. $x=20t+5$

C. $x=10t^2+5t$　　D. $x=20t^2+5t+5$

解 因为速度 $v=\frac{\mathrm{d}x}{\mathrm{d}t}$,积一次分,即:$\int_5^x\mathrm{d}x=\int_0^t(20t+5)\mathrm{d}t$,$x-5=10t^2+5t$。

答案:A

【例 4-2-4】 已知动点的运动方程为 $x=t$,$y=2t^2$,则其轨迹方程为:

A. $x=t^2-t$　　B. $y=2t$

C. $y-2x^2=0$　　　　D. $y+2x^2=0$

解　将运动方程中的参数 t 消去：$t=x$，$y=2x^2$。

答案：C

【例 4-2-5】　一炮弹以初速度和仰角 α 射出。对于如图所示直角坐标的运动方程为 $x=v_0\cos\alpha t$，$y=v_0\sin\alpha t-\frac{1}{2}gt^2$，则当 $t=0$时，炮弹的速度和加速度的大小分别为：

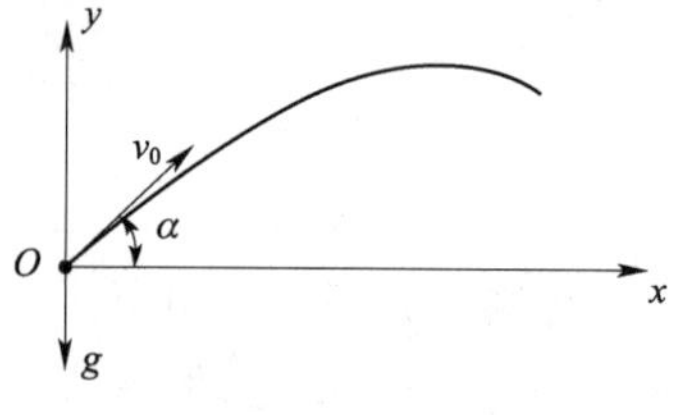

例 4-2-5 图

A. $v=v_0\cos\alpha$，$a=g$

B. $v=v_0$，$a=g$

C. $v=v_0\sin\alpha$，$a=-g$

D. $v=v_0$，$a=-g$

解　分别对运动方程 x 和 y 求时间 t 的一阶、二阶导数，即：$\dot{x}=v_0\cos\alpha$，$\dot{y}=v_0\sin\alpha-gt$；$\ddot{x}=0$，$\ddot{y}=-g$；当 $t=0$ 时，速度的大小 $v=\sqrt{\dot{x}^2+\dot{y}^2}=v_0$，加速度的大小 $a=|\ddot{y}|=g$。

答案：B

【例 4-2-6】　动点 A 和 B 在同一坐标系中的运动方程分别为 $\begin{cases}x_A=t\\y_A=2t^2\end{cases}$，$\begin{cases}x_B=t^2\\y_B=2t^4\end{cases}$，其中 x、y 以 cm 计，t 以 s 计，则两点相遇的时刻为：

A. $t=1$s　　B. $t=0.5$s　　C. 2s　　D. $t=1.5$s

解　两点相遇时应具有相同的坐标，即 $x_A=x_B$，$y_A=y_B$，根据运动方程有 $t=t^2$，$2t^2=2t^4$，解得 $t=1$s。

答案：A

【例 4-2-7】　一动点沿直线轨道按照 $x=3t^3+t+2$ 的规律运动(x 以 m 计，t 以 s 计)，则当 $t=4$s时，动点的位移、速度和加速度分别为：

A. $x=54$m，$v=145$m/s，$a=18$m/s^2　　B. $x=198$m，$v=145$m/s，$a=72$m/s^2

C. $x=198$m，$v=49$m/s，$a=72$m/s^2　　D. $x=192$m，$v=145$m/s，$a=12$m/s^2

解　将 x 对时间 t 求一阶导数为速度，即：$v=9t^2+1$；再对时间 t 求一阶导数为加速度，即 $a=18t$，将 $t=4$s 代入，可得：$x=198$m，$v=145$m/s，$a=72$m/s^2。

答案：B

二、刚体的基本运动

刚体的基本运动包括刚体的平行移动和刚体绕定轴转动这两种简单的运动形式。

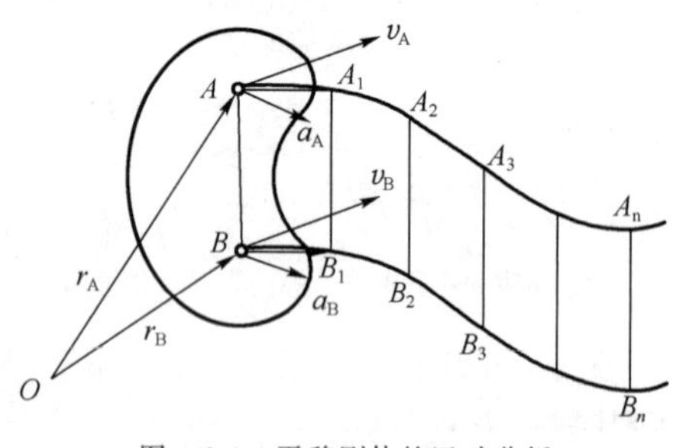

图 4-2-1　平移刚体的运动分析

(一)刚体的平行移动

1. 定义

刚体运动时，其上任意直线始终平行于其初始位置，刚体的这种运动称为平行移动，简称平移。

2. 平移刚体的运动分析

若在平移刚体内任选两点 A、B(见图 4-2-1)，其矢径分别为 $\boldsymbol{r}_A$ 和 $\boldsymbol{r}_B$，则两条矢端曲线就是这两点的轨迹。根据图中的几何关系，有：$\boldsymbol{r}_A=\boldsymbol{r}_B+\boldsymbol{r}_{BA}$，且 $\boldsymbol{r}_{BA}$ 为常矢量，则类似地，有

$$\dot{\boldsymbol{r}}_A = \dot{\boldsymbol{r}}_B \text{，即 } \boldsymbol{v}_A = \boldsymbol{v}_B \tag{4-2-1}$$

$$\dot{\boldsymbol{v}}_A = \dot{\boldsymbol{v}}_B \text{，即 } \boldsymbol{a}_A = \boldsymbol{a}_B \tag{4-2-2}$$

式(4-2-1)和式(4-2-2)表明：刚体平移时，其上各点的运动轨迹形状相同；同一瞬时，刚体上各点的速度、加速度均相同。因此平移时，可以用刚体上任一点(如质心)的运动表示刚体的运动。于是，研究平移刚体的运动可归结为研究点的运动。

(二)刚体绕定轴转动

1.定义

刚体运动时，若其上(或其扩展部分)有一条直线始终保持不动，则称这种运动为绕定轴转动，简称转动。这条固定的直线称为转轴(见图 4-2-2)。轴线上各点的速度和加速度均恒为零，其他各点均围绕轴线做圆周运动。

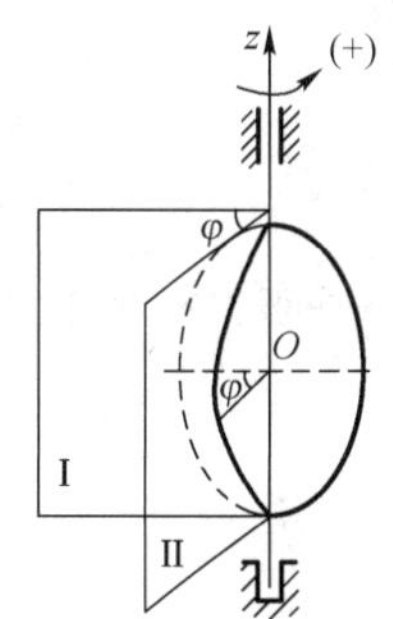

图 4-2-2　刚体绕定轴转动

2.转动刚体的运动分析

(1)转动方程

如图 4-2-2 所示绕定轴 z 转动的刚体，设通过转轴 z 所作的平面 I 固定不动(称为定平面)，平面 II 与刚体固连随刚体一起转动(称为动平面)。任一瞬时刚体的位置，可由动平面 II 与定平面 I 的夹角 φ 确定。角 φ 称为转角，单位是弧度(rad)，为代数量。当刚体转动时，转角 φ 随时间 t 变化，它是时间的单值连续函数，即

$$\varphi = f(t) \tag{4-2-3}$$

上式称为刚体的转动方程，它反映了刚体绕定轴转动的规律。

(2)角速度

刚体的转角对时间的一阶导数，称为角速度，用于度量刚体转动的快慢和转动方向，用字母 ω 表示。即

$$\omega = \frac{d\varphi}{dt} = \dot{\varphi} \tag{4-2-4}$$

角速度的单位是弧度/秒(rad/s)。在工程中很多情况还用转速 n(转/分)来表示刚体转动的快慢。此时，ω 与 n 之间的换算关系为

$$\omega = \frac{2n\pi}{60} = \frac{n\pi}{30} \tag{4-2-5}$$

(3)角加速度

刚体的角速度对时间的一阶导数，称为角加速度，用于度量角速度的快慢和转动方向，用字母 α 表示。即

$$\alpha = \frac{d\omega}{dt} = \dot{\omega} = \ddot{\varphi} \tag{4-2-6}$$

角加速度的单位为弧度/秒^2(rad/s^2)。角速度和角加速度都是描述刚体整体运动的物理量。

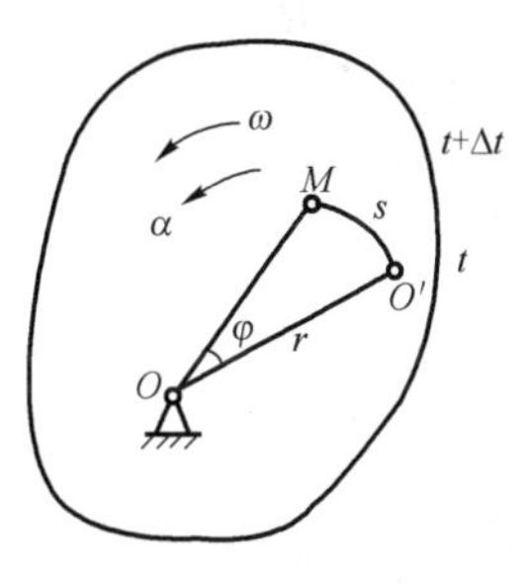

图 4-2-3　转动刚体上 M 点的运动分析

3.定轴转动刚体上各点的速度和加速度

在转动刚体上任取一点 M，设其到转轴 O 的垂直距离为 r 称为转动半径，如图 4-2-3 所示。显然，M 点的运动是以 O 为圆心、r 为半径的圆周运动。若转动刚体的角速度为 ω，角加速度为 α，弧坐标原点为 O'，则当刚体转过角度 φ 时，点 M 的弧坐标为

$$s=r\varphi \tag{4-2-7}$$

点 M 速度的大小为

$$v=\frac{\mathrm{d}s}{\mathrm{d}t}=\frac{\mathrm{d}}{\mathrm{d}t}(r\varphi)=r\frac{\mathrm{d}\varphi}{\mathrm{d}t}=r\cdot\omega \tag{4-2-8}$$

点 M 的切向加速度和法向加速度的大小分别为

$$a_\tau=\frac{\mathrm{d}v}{\mathrm{d}t}=\frac{\mathrm{d}}{\mathrm{d}t}(r\omega)=r\frac{\mathrm{d}\omega}{\mathrm{d}t}=r\cdot\alpha \tag{4-2-9}$$

$$a_n=\frac{v^2}{\rho}=\frac{(r\omega)^2}{\rho}=r\cdot\omega^2 \tag{4-2-10}$$

所以刚体上任一 M 点的加速度大小为

$$\left.\begin{aligned}a&=\sqrt{a_\tau^2+a_n^2}=r\sqrt{\alpha^2+\omega^4}\\ \text{方向}\qquad \tan\theta&=\frac{|a_\tau|}{a_n}=\frac{|\alpha|}{\omega^2}\end{aligned}\right\} \tag{4-2-11}$$

式中：θ——加速度 $\boldsymbol{a}$ 与法向加速度的夹角。

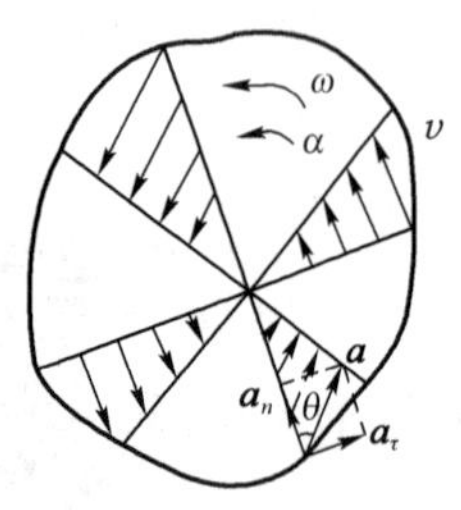

图 4-2-4 转动刚体上各点速度、加速度分布

由公式(4-2-8)与式(4-2-11)可得以下结论：

①在任意瞬时，转动刚体内各点的速度、切向加速度、法向加速度和全加速度的大小与各点的转动半径成正比。

②在任意瞬时，转动刚体内各点的速度方向与各点的转动半径垂直，各点的全加速度的方向与各点转动半径的夹角全部相同。所以，刚体内任一条通过且垂直于轴的直线上各点的速度和加速度呈线性分布，如图 4-2-4 所示。

【例 4-2-8】 二摩擦轮如图所示。则两轮的角速度与半径关系的表达式为：

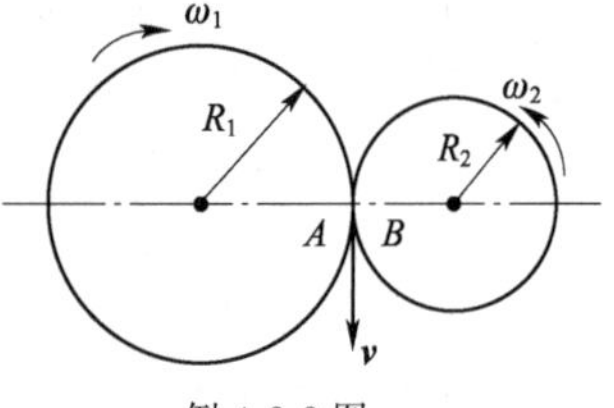

例 4-2-8 图

A. $\frac{\omega_1}{\omega_2}=\frac{R_1}{R_2}$　　B. $\frac{\omega_1}{\omega_2}=\frac{R_2}{R_1^2}$

C. $\frac{\omega_1}{\omega_2}=\frac{R_1}{R_2^2}$　　D. $\frac{\omega_1}{\omega_2}=\frac{R_2}{R_1}$

解 两轮啮合点 A、B 的速度相同，且 $v_A=R_1\omega_1=v_B=R_2\omega_2$。所以有 $\frac{\omega_1}{\omega_2}=\frac{R_2}{R_1}$。

答案：D

【例 4-2-9】 刚体作平动时，某瞬时体内各点的速度与加速度为：

A. 体内各点速度不相同，加速度相同

B. 体内各点速度相同，加速度不相同

C. 体内各点速度相同，加速度也相同

D. 体内各点速度不相同，加速度也不相同

解 根据平行移动刚体的定义，平行移动刚体内各点速度和加速度均相同。

答案：C

【例 4-2-10】 杆 $OA=l$，绕固定轴 O 转动，某瞬时杆端 A 点的加速度 $\boldsymbol{a}$ 如图所示，则该瞬时杆 OA 的角速度及角加速度为：

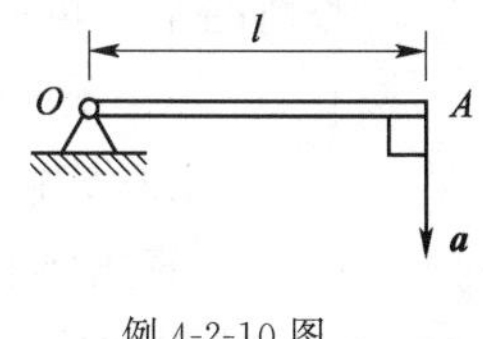

例 4-2-10 图

A. $0,\frac{a}{l}$　　　　B. $\sqrt{\frac{a\cos\alpha}{l}},\frac{a\sin\alpha}{l}$

C. $\sqrt{\frac{a}{l}},0$　　　　D. $0,\sqrt{\frac{a}{l}}$

解 根据定轴转动刚体上一点加速度与转动角速度、角加速度的关系：$a_n=\omega^2 l$，$a_\tau=\alpha l$，而题中 $a_n=0=\omega^2 l$，$a_\tau=a=\alpha l$，所以有杆的角速度 $\omega=0$，角加速度 $\alpha=\frac{a}{l}$。

答案：A

【例 4-2-11】 一绳缠绕在半径为 r 的鼓轮上，绳端系一重物 M，重物 M 以速度 v 和加速度 a 向下运动(如图所示)。则绳上两点 A、D 和轮缘上两点 B、C 的加速度是：

A. A、B 两点的加速度相同，C、A 两点的加速度相同

B. A、B 两点的加速度不相同，C、D 两点的加速度不相同

C. A、B 两点的加速度相同，C、D 两点的加速度不相同

D. A、B 两点的加速度相同，C、D 两点的加速度相同

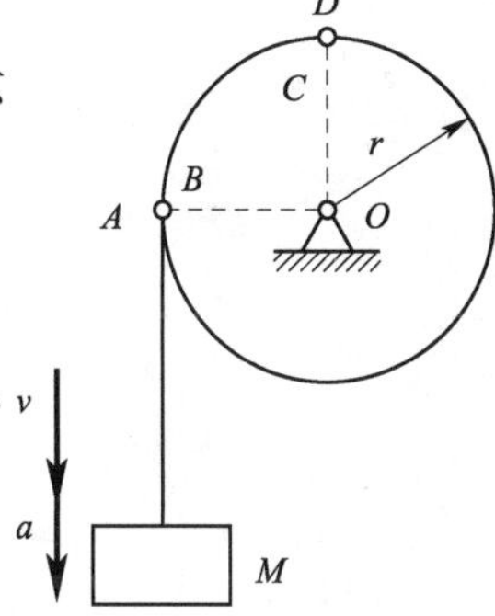

例 4-2-10 图

解 绳上各点的加速度大小均为 a，而轮缘上各点的加速度大小为 $\sqrt{a^2+(\frac{v^2}{r})^2}$。

答案：B

【例 4-2-12】 图示机构中，三杆长度相同，且 $AC//BD$，则 AB 杆的运动形式为：

A. 绕点 C 的定轴转动　　B. 平行移动

C. 绕点 O 的定轴转动　　D. 圆周运动

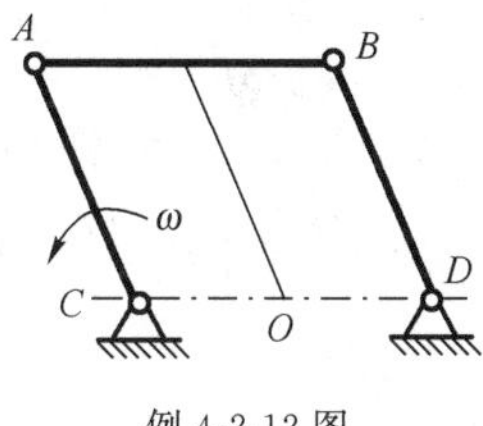

例 4-2-12 图

解 因为 A、B 两点的速度方向相同，大小相等，根据刚体作平行移动时的特性，可作判断。

答案：B

习　题

4-2-1　点 M 沿半径为 R 的圆周运动，其速度的大小为 $v=kt$，k 是有量纲的常数，则点 M 的全加速度的大小为(　　)。

A. $(k^2t^2/R)+k^2$　　　　B. $[(k^2t^2/R^2)+k^2]^{1/2}$

C. $[(k^4t^4/R^2)+k^2]^{1/2}$　　　　D. $[(k^4t^2/R^2)+k^2]^{1/2}$

4-2-2　已知点 P 在 Oxy 平面内的运动方程为 $\begin{cases}x=4\sin\frac{\pi}{3}t\\y=4\cos\frac{\pi}{3}t\end{cases}$，则点的运动轨迹为(　　)。

A. 直线运动　　B. 圆周运动　　C. 椭圆运动　　D. 不能确定

4-2-3　圆轮绕固定轴 O 转动，某瞬时轮缘上一点的速度 $\boldsymbol{v}$ 和加速度 $\boldsymbol{a}$ 如图所示，试问

(　　)情况是不可能的。

A. 图 a)、图 b)的运动是不可能的　　B. 图 a)、图 c)的运动是不可能的

C. 图 b)、图 c)的运动是不可能的　　D. 均不可能

4-2-4　直角刚杆 OAB 在如图所示瞬时有 $\omega=2\text{rad/s}$，$\alpha=5\text{rad/s}^2$，若 $OA=40\text{cm}$，$AB=30\text{cm}$，则 B 点的速度大小为(　　)cm/s。

A. 100　　B. 160　　C. 200　　D. 250

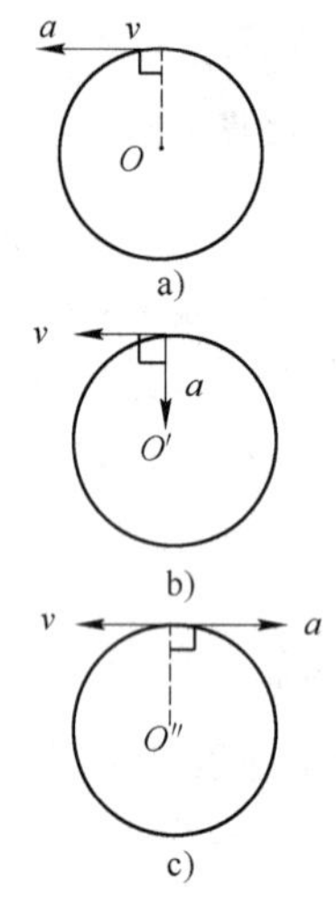

题 4-2-3 图

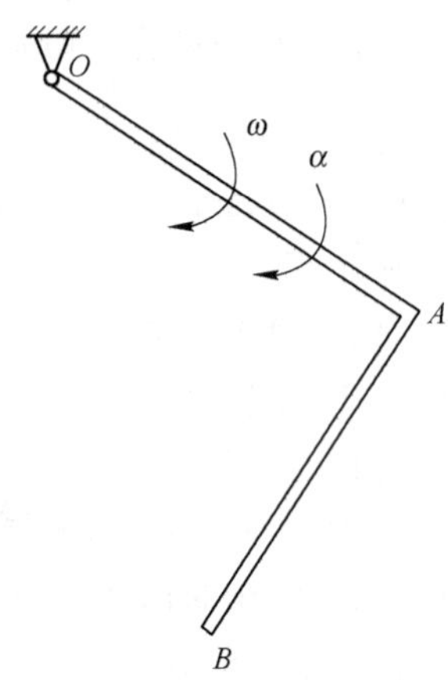

题 4-2-4 图

4-2-5　直角刚杆 $AO=2\text{m}$，$BO=3\text{m}$，已知某瞬时 A 点速度的大小 $v_A=6\text{m/s}$，而 B 点的加速度与 BO 成 $\theta=60°$角，如图所示，则该瞬时刚杆的角加速度 α 为(　　)rad/s²。

A. 3　　B. $\sqrt{3}$　　C. $5\sqrt{3}$　　D. $9\sqrt{3}$

4-2-6　直角刚杆 OAB 可绕固定轴 O 在图示平面内转动，已知 $OA=40\text{cm}$，$AB=30\text{cm}$，$\omega=2\text{rad/s}$，$\alpha=1\text{rad/s}^2$，则如图所示瞬时，B 点加速度在 y 方向的投影为(　　)cm/s²。

A. 40　　B. 200　　C. 50　　D. −200

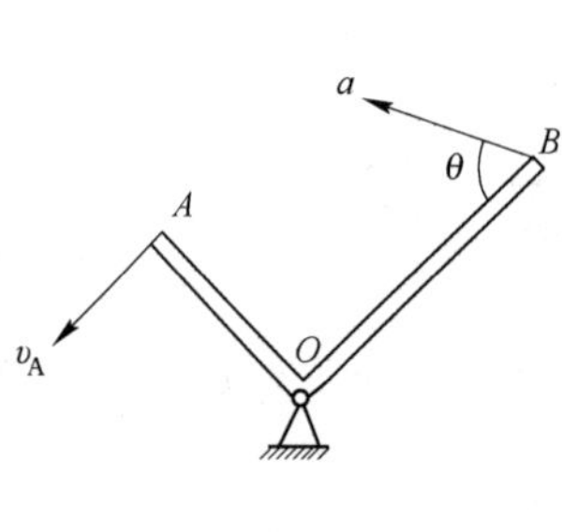

题 4-2-5 图

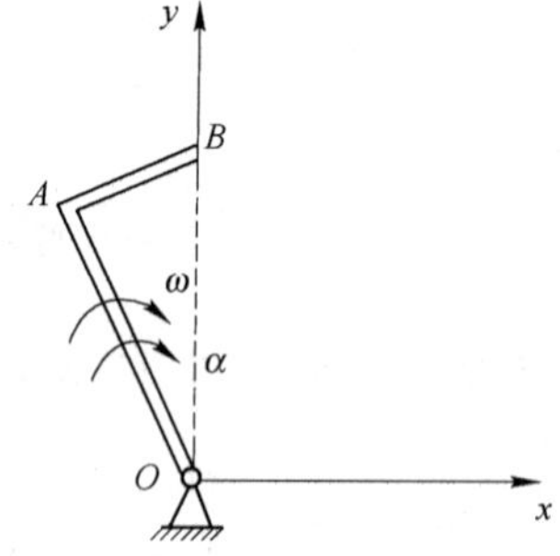

题 4-2-6 图

4-2-7　绳子的一端绕在滑轮上，另一端与置于水平面上的物块 B 相连，如图所示，若物 B 的运动方程为 $x=kt^2$，其中 k 为常数，轮子半径为 R，则轮缘上 A 点的加速度的大小为(　　)。

A. $2k$　　B. $(4k^2t^2/R)^{\frac{1}{2}}$

C. $(4k^2+16k^4t^4/R^2)^{\frac{1}{2}}$　　D. $2k+4k^2t^2/R$

4-2-8　圆盘某瞬时以角速度 ω，角加速度 α 绕 O 轴转动，其上 A、B 两点的加速度分别为 $\boldsymbol{a}_{\mathrm{A}}$ 和 $\boldsymbol{a}_{\mathrm{B}}$，与半径的夹角分别为 θ 和 φ，如图所示，若 $OA=R$，$OB=R/2$，则(　　)。

A. $a_{\mathrm{A}}=a_{\mathrm{B}}, \theta=\varphi$　　　　B. $a_{\mathrm{A}}=a_{\mathrm{B}}, \theta=2\varphi$

C. $a_{\mathrm{A}}=2a_{\mathrm{B}}, \theta=\varphi$　　　　D. $a_{\mathrm{A}}=2a_{\mathrm{B}}, \theta=2\varphi$

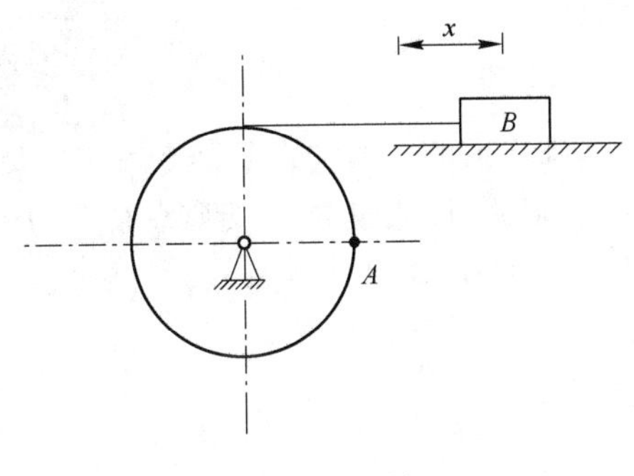

题 4-2-7 图

题 4-2-8 图

4-2-9　两个相啮合的齿轮，A、B 分别为齿轮 O_1、O_2 上的啮合点(见图)，则 A、B 两点的加速度关系是(　　)。

A. $a_{\mathrm{A}\tau}=a_{\mathrm{B}\tau}, a_{\mathrm{A}n}=a_{\mathrm{B}n}$　　　　B. $a_{\mathrm{A}\tau}=a_{\mathrm{B}\tau}, a_{\mathrm{A}n}\neq a_{\mathrm{B}n}$

C. $a_{\mathrm{A}\tau}\neq a_{\mathrm{B}\tau}, a_{\mathrm{A}n}=a_{\mathrm{B}n}$　　　　D. $a_{\mathrm{A}\tau}\neq a_{\mathrm{B}\tau}, a_{\mathrm{A}n}\neq a_{\mathrm{B}n}$

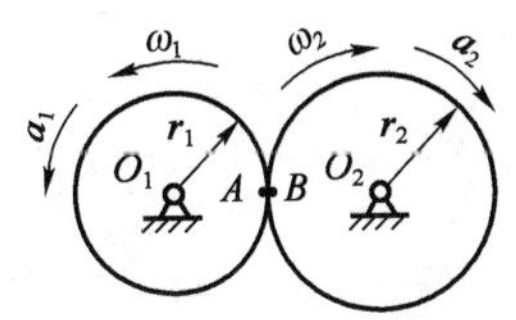

题 4-2-9 图

4-2-10　单摆由长 l 的摆杆与摆锤 A 组成(见图)，其运动规律 $\varphi=\varphi_0\sin\omega t$ 。锤 A 在 $t=\dfrac{\pi}{4\omega}$ s 时的速度、切向加速度与法向加速度的大小分别为(　　)。

A. $v=\dfrac{1}{2}l\varphi_0\omega, a_\tau=-\dfrac{1}{2}l\varphi_0\omega^2, a_n=\dfrac{\sqrt{2}}{2}l\varphi_0^2\omega^2$

B. $v=\dfrac{1}{2}l\varphi_0\omega, a_\tau=\dfrac{1}{2}l\varphi_0\omega^2, a_n=-\dfrac{\sqrt{2}}{2}l\varphi_0^2\omega^2$

C. $v=\dfrac{\sqrt{2}}{2}l\varphi_0\omega, a_\tau=-\dfrac{\sqrt{2}}{2}l\varphi_0\omega^2, a_n=\dfrac{1}{2}l\varphi_0^2\omega^2$

D. $v=\dfrac{\sqrt{2}}{2}l\varphi_0\omega, a_\tau=\dfrac{\sqrt{2}}{2}l\varphi_0\omega^2, a_n=-\dfrac{1}{2}l\varphi_0^2\omega^2$

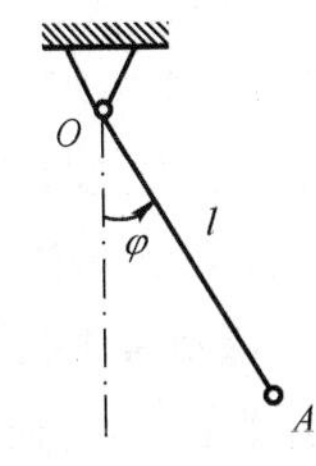

题 4-2-10 图

4-2-11　每段长度相等的直角折杆在图示的平面内绕 O 轴转动，角速度 ω 为顺时针转向，M 点的速度方向应是图中的(　　)。

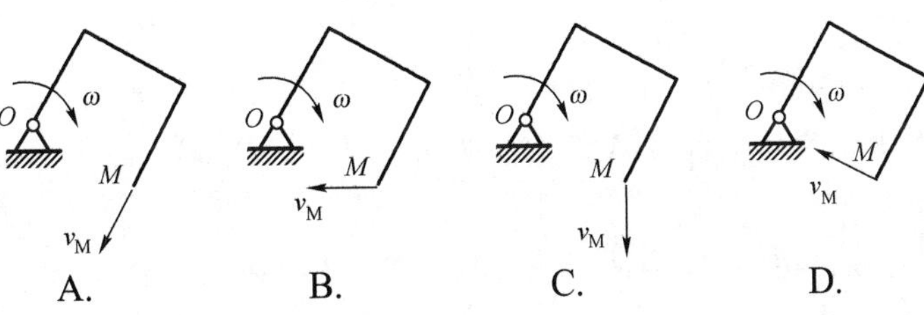

第三节　动　力　学

动力学所研究的是物体的运动与其所受力之间的关系。

一、动力学基本定律及质点运动微分方程

(一)动力学基本定律

动力学的全部理论都是建立在动力学基本定律基础之上的。而动力学基本定律就是牛顿运动定律,或曰牛顿三定律。其中最重要的是牛顿第二定律,即质量为 m 的质点在合力 $\boldsymbol{F}_{\mathrm{R}}$ 的作用下所产生的加速度 $\boldsymbol{a}$ 满足下列关系式

$$\boldsymbol{F}_{\mathrm{R}} = m\boldsymbol{a} \tag{4-3-1}$$

式(4-3-1)称为动力学基本方程。

(二)质点运动微分方程

若将式(4-3-1)中的加速度表示为矢径对时间的二阶导数,便得质点运动微分方程为

$$m\frac{\mathrm{d}^2\boldsymbol{r}}{\mathrm{d}t^2} = \boldsymbol{F}_{\mathrm{R}} \quad 或 \quad m\ddot{\boldsymbol{r}} = \boldsymbol{F}_{\mathrm{R}} \tag{4-3-2}$$

将式(4-3-2)投影到固定的直角坐标轴上,得到直角坐标形式的质点运动微分方程为

$$m\ddot{x} = F_{\mathrm{R}x}, m\ddot{y} = F_{\mathrm{R}y}, m\ddot{z} = F_{\mathrm{R}z} \tag{4-3-3}$$

将式(4-3-2)投影到质点轨迹的自然轴系上,得到质点自然形式的运动微分方程为

$$m\ddot{s} = F_{\mathrm{R}\tau}, m\frac{\dot{s}^2}{\rho} = F_{\mathrm{R}n}, 0 = F_{\mathrm{R}b} \tag{4-3-4}$$

应用式(4-3-3)和式(4-3-4)可求解质点动力学的两类问题。第一类问题是:已知质点的运动,求作用于该质点的力;第二类问题是:已知作用于质点的力,求该质点的运动。由式(4-3-2)可知,第一类问题只需进行微分运算,而第二类问题则需要解微分方程(进行积分运算),借已知的运动初始条件确定积分常数后,才能完全确定质点的运动。

【例 4-3-1】 在如图 a)所示圆锥摆中,球 M 的质量为 m,绳长 l,若 α 角保持不变,则小球的法向加速度为:

A. $g\sin\alpha$　　　B. $g\cos\alpha$

C. $g\tan\alpha$　　　D. $g\cot\alpha$

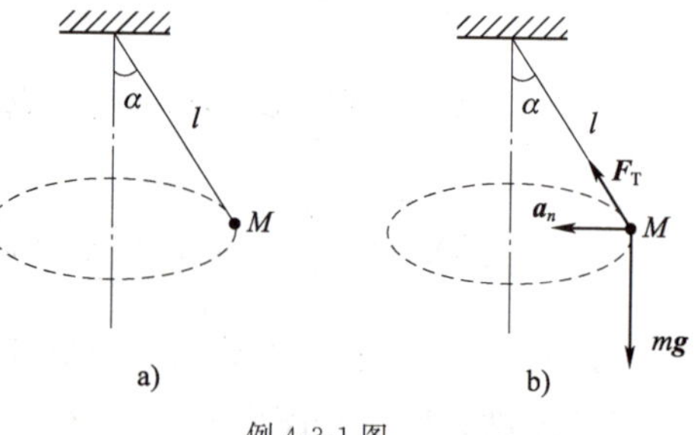

例 4-3-1 图

解 小球受力如图 b)所示。在铅垂平面内垂直于绳的方向列质点运动微分方程(牛顿第二定律),有:$ma_n\cos\alpha = mg\sin\alpha$,所以,$a_n = g\tan\alpha$。

答案:C

【例 4-3-2】 放在弹簧平台上的物块 A,重力为 $\boldsymbol{W}$,做上下往复运动,当经过图示位置的 1、0、2 时(0 为静平衡位置),平台对 A 的约束力分别为 $\boldsymbol{P}_1$、$\boldsymbol{P}_2$、$\boldsymbol{P}_3$,它们之间的大小关系为:

A. $P_1 = P_2 = W = P_3$　　　B. $P_1 > P_2 = W > P_3$

C. $P_1 < P_2 = W < P_3$　　　D. $P_1 < P_3 = W > P_2$

例 4-3-2 图

解 物块 A 在位置 1 时，其加速度向下，应用牛顿第二定律，$\frac{W}{g}a = W - P_1$，则 $P_1 = W\left(1-\frac{a}{g}\right)$；而在静平衡位置 0 时，物块 A 的加速度为零，即 $P_2 = W$；同理，物块 A 在位置 2 时，其加速度向上，故 $P_3 = W\left(1+\frac{a}{g}\right)$。

答案： C

【例 4-3-3】 质量为 m 的物块 A，置于与水平面成 θ 角的斜面 B 上，如图 a)所示，A 与 B 间的摩擦系数为 f，为保持 A 与 B 一起以加速度 $\boldsymbol{a}$ 水平向右运动，则所需的加速度 $\boldsymbol{a}$ 至少是：

A. $a=\dfrac{g(f\cos\theta+\sin\theta)}{\cos\theta+f\sin\theta}$

B. $a=\dfrac{gf\cos\theta}{\cos\theta+f\sin\theta}$

C. $a=\dfrac{g(f\cos\theta-\sin\theta)}{\cos\theta+f\sin\theta}$

D. $a=\dfrac{gf\sin\theta}{\cos\theta+f\sin\theta}$

例 4-3-3 图

解 物块 A 的受力如图 b)所示，应用牛顿第二定律，沿斜面方向有：$ma\cos\theta = F - mg\sin\theta$，垂直于斜面方向有：$ma\sin\theta = mg\cos\theta - F_N$；所以当摩擦力 $F = ma\cos\theta + mg\sin\theta \leqslant F_N f$ 时可保证 A 与 B 一起以加速度 $\boldsymbol{a}$ 水平向右运动。式中 $F_N = mg\cos\theta - ma\sin\theta$，代入后可求：$a=\dfrac{g(f\cos\theta-\sin\theta)}{\cos\theta+f\sin\theta}$。

答案： C

二、动力学普遍定理

由有限个或无限个质点通过约束联系在一起的系统，称为质点系。工程实际中的机械和结构物以及刚体均为质点系。对于质点系，没有必要研究其中每个质点的运动。

动力学普遍定理（包括动量定理、动量矩定理、动能定理）建立了表明质点系整体运动的物理量（如动量、动量矩、动能）与表明力作用效果的量（如冲量、力、力矩、力的功）之间的关系。应用动力学普遍定理能够有效地解决质点系的动力学问题。

（一）动力学普遍定理中各物理量的概念及定义

1. 质心

质心为质点系的质量中心，其位置可通过下列公式确定

$$x_C=\frac{\sum m_i x_i}{\sum m_i}=\frac{\sum m_i x_i}{m},\ y_C=\frac{\sum m_i y_i}{\sum m_i}=\frac{\sum m_i y_i}{m},\ z_C=\frac{\sum m_i z_i}{\sum m_i}=\frac{\sum m_i z_i}{m} \tag{4-3-5}$$

若令质点系质心的矢径为 $\boldsymbol{r}_C = x_C\boldsymbol{i} + y_C\boldsymbol{j} + z_C\boldsymbol{k}$，第 i 个质点的矢径为 $\boldsymbol{r}_i = x_i\boldsymbol{i} + y_i\boldsymbol{j} + z_i\boldsymbol{k}$；则质点系质心坐标的公式还可表示为

$$\boldsymbol{r}_C=\frac{\sum m_i \boldsymbol{r}_i}{\sum m_i}=\frac{\sum m_i \boldsymbol{r}_i}{m} \tag{4-3-6}$$

2. 转动惯量

转动惯量的定义、计算公式及常用简单形体的转动惯量见表 4-3-1 及表 4-3-2。

转动惯量的定义及计算公式 表 4-3-1

名称	定　义	计算公式
转动惯量	刚体内各质点的质量与质点到轴的垂直距离平方的乘积之和，是刚体转动惯性的度量	$J_z=\sum_{i=1}^{n} m_i r_i^2$
	刚体的质量与回转半径平方的乘积	$J_z=m\rho_z^2$
平行移轴定理	刚体对任一轴的转动惯量等于其对通过质心并与该轴平行的轴的转动惯量，加上刚体质量与两轴间距离平方的乘积	$J_z=J_{Cz}+md^2$

常用简单均质物体的转动惯量及回转半径 表 4-3-2

物体形状	简　图	转动惯量	回转半径
细直杆	y; l/2; l/2	$J_y=\frac{1}{12}ml^2$	$\rho_y=\frac{1}{\sqrt{12}}l$
细圆环	y; O; r; x	$J_x=J_y=\frac{1}{2}mr^2$ $J_z=J_O=mr^2$	$\rho_x=\rho_y=\frac{1}{\sqrt{2}}r$ $\rho_z=r$
薄圆盘	y; O; r; x	$J_x=J_y=\frac{1}{4}mr^2$ $J_z=J_O=\frac{1}{2}mr^2$	$\rho_x=\rho_y=\frac{1}{2}r$ $\rho_z=\frac{1}{\sqrt{2}}r$

3. 其他基本物理量

动力学普遍定理中各基本物理量（如动量、动量矩、动能、冲量、功、势能等）的概念、定义及表达式见表 4-3-3。

动力学普遍定理中各物理量的概念、定义及表达式 表 4-3-3

物理量	概念及定义	表达式		量纲及单位
		质点	质点系	
动量	物体的质量与其速度的乘积，是物体机械运动强弱的一种度量	mv	$\boldsymbol{p}=\sum m_i\boldsymbol{v}_i=m\boldsymbol{v}_C$	$[M][L][T]^{-1}$ kg・m/s
冲量	力与其作用时间的乘积，用以度量作用于物体的力在一段时间内对其运动所产生的累计效应	$\boldsymbol{I}=\int_{t_1}^{t_2}\boldsymbol{F}\mathrm{d}t$	$\boldsymbol{I}=\sum\int_{t_1}^{t_2}\boldsymbol{F}_i\mathrm{d}t=\sum\boldsymbol{I}^i$	$[M][L][T]^{-1}$ kg・m/s

续上表

<table>
<tr><th colspan="2" rowspan="2">物 理 量</th><th rowspan="2">概 念 及 定 义</th><th colspan="2">表 达 式</th><th rowspan="2">量纲及单位</th></tr>
<tr><th>质 点</th><th>质点系</th></tr>
<tr><td rowspan="4">动量矩</td><td>质点</td><td>质点的动量对任选固定点 O 之矩，用以度量质点绕该点运动的强弱</td><td colspan="2">$\boldsymbol{M}_O(m\boldsymbol{v})=\boldsymbol{r}\times m\boldsymbol{v}$
$[\boldsymbol{M}_O(m\boldsymbol{v})]_z=M_z(m\boldsymbol{v})$</td><td rowspan="4">$[M][L]^2[T]^{-1}$
$kg\cdot m^2/s$ 或
$N\cdot m\cdot s$</td></tr>
<tr><td>质系</td><td>质点系中所有各质点的动量对于任选固定点 O 之矩的矢量和</td><td colspan="2">$\boldsymbol{L}_O=\sum\boldsymbol{M}_O(m_i\boldsymbol{v}_i)=\sum\boldsymbol{r}_i\times m_i\boldsymbol{v}_i$</td></tr>
<tr><td>平移刚体</td><td>刚体的动量对于任选固定点 O 之矩</td><td colspan="2">$\boldsymbol{L}_O=\boldsymbol{M}_O(m\,\boldsymbol{v}_C)=\boldsymbol{r}_C\times m\boldsymbol{v}_C$</td></tr>
<tr><td>转动刚体</td><td>刚体的转动惯量与角速度的乘积</td><td colspan="2">$L_z=J_z\omega$</td></tr>
<tr><td rowspan="5">动能</td><td>质点</td><td>质点的质量与速度平方的乘积之半，是由于物体的运动而具有的能量</td><td colspan="2">$T=\frac{1}{2}mv^2$</td><td rowspan="5">$[M][L]^2[T]^{-2}$
J 或 $N\cdot m$ 或
$kg\cdot m^2/s^2$</td></tr>
<tr><td>质系</td><td>质点系中所有各质点动能之和</td><td colspan="2">$T=\sum\frac{1}{2}m_iv_i^2$</td></tr>
<tr><td>平移刚体</td><td>刚体的质量与质心速度的平方之半</td><td colspan="2">$T=\frac{1}{2}mv_C^2$</td></tr>
<tr><td>转动刚体</td><td>刚体的转动惯量与角速度的平方之半</td><td colspan="2">$T=\frac{1}{2}J_z\cdot\omega^2$</td></tr>
<tr><td>平面运动刚体</td><td>随质心平移的动能与绕质心转动的动能之和</td><td colspan="2">$T=\frac{1}{2}mv_C^2+\frac{1}{2}J_C\omega^2$</td></tr>
<tr><td colspan="2" rowspan="4">功</td><td>力在其作用点的运动路程中对物体作用的累积效应，功是能量变化的度量</td><td colspan="2">$W_{12}=\int_{M_1}^{M_2}\boldsymbol{F}\cdot d\boldsymbol{r}$
$=\int_{M_1}^{M_2}(\boldsymbol{F}_x dx+\boldsymbol{F}_y dy+\boldsymbol{F}_z dz)$</td><td rowspan="4">$[M][L]^2[T]^{-2}$
J 或 $N\cdot m$ 或
$kg\cdot m^2/s^2$</td></tr>
<tr><td>重力的功只与质点起、止位置有关</td><td colspan="2">$W_{12}=mg(z_1-z_2)$</td></tr>
<tr><td>弹性力的功只与质点起、止位置的变形量有关</td><td colspan="2">$W_{12}=\frac{k}{2}(\delta_1^2-\delta_2^2)$</td></tr>
<tr><td>定轴转动刚体上作用力的功
若 $m_z(\boldsymbol{F})=$ 常量，则表达式表示如右栏</td><td colspan="2">$W_{12}=\int_{\varphi_1}^{\varphi_2}m_z(\boldsymbol{F})d\varphi$
$W_{12}=m_z(\boldsymbol{F})(\varphi_2-\varphi_1)$</td></tr>
<tr><td colspan="2" rowspan="3">势能</td><td>质点从某位置至零势点有势力所做的功</td><td colspan="2">$V=\int_{M}^{M_0}\boldsymbol{F}\cdot d\boldsymbol{r}$</td><td rowspan="3">$[M][L]^2[T]^{-2}$
J 或 $N\cdot m$ 或
$kg\cdot m^2/s^2$</td></tr>
<tr><td>重力势能：空间直角坐标系原点为零势点</td><td colspan="2">$V=mgz_C$</td></tr>
<tr><td>弹性势能：弹簧原长为零势点</td><td colspan="2">$V=\frac{1}{2}k\delta^2$</td></tr>
</table>

（二）动力学三大普遍定理

动力学普遍定理（包括动量定理、质心运动定理，对固定点和相对质心的动量矩定理、动能定理）及相应的守恒定理的表达式及适用范围见表 4-3-4。

动力学普遍定理的表达式及适用范围 表 4-3-4

<table>
<tr><th>定理</th><th colspan="3">表 达 式</th><th>守 恒 情 况</th><th>说 明</th></tr>
<tr><td rowspan="3">动量定理</td><td>质点</td><td colspan="2">$\frac{\mathrm{d}}{\mathrm{d}t}(m\boldsymbol{v})=\boldsymbol{F}$</td><td>若$\sum \boldsymbol{F}^{(e)}=0$,则$\boldsymbol{p}=$恒量
若$\sum F_x^{(e)}=0$,则$\boldsymbol{p}_x=$恒量</td><td rowspan="3">主要阐明了刚体作平动或质系随质心平动部分的运动规律,常用于研究平动部分、质心的运动及约束力的求解</td></tr>
<tr><td>质系</td><td colspan="2">$\frac{\mathrm{d}}{\mathrm{d}t}\boldsymbol{p}=\sum \boldsymbol{F}^{(e)}$</td><td rowspan="2">若$\sum \boldsymbol{F}^{(e)}=0$,则$\boldsymbol{v}_C=$恒量;当$\boldsymbol{v}_{C0}=0$时,$\boldsymbol{r}_C=$恒量,即质心位置不变
若$\sum F_x^{(e)}=0$,则$v_{Cx}=$恒量;当$v_{Cx0}=0$时,$x_C=$恒量,即质心x坐标不变</td></tr>
<tr><td>质心运动定理</td><td colspan="2">$m\boldsymbol{a}_C=\sum \boldsymbol{F}^{(e)}$</td></tr>
<tr><td rowspan="4">动量矩定理</td><td>质点</td><td colspan="2">$\frac{\mathrm{d}}{\mathrm{d}t}\boldsymbol{M}_O(m\boldsymbol{v})=\boldsymbol{M}_O(\boldsymbol{F})$
$\frac{\mathrm{d}}{\mathrm{d}t}M_z(m\boldsymbol{v})=M_z(\boldsymbol{F})$</td><td>若$\boldsymbol{M}_O(\boldsymbol{F})=0$,则$\boldsymbol{M}_O(m\boldsymbol{v})=$恒量
若$M_z(\boldsymbol{F})=0$,则$M_z(m\boldsymbol{v})=$恒量</td><td rowspan="4">主要阐明了刚体作定轴转动或质系绕质心转动部分的运动规律,常用于研究定轴转动及绕质心转动部分的运动</td></tr>
<tr><td>质系</td><td colspan="2">$\frac{\mathrm{d}\boldsymbol{L}_O}{\mathrm{d}t}=\boldsymbol{M}_O^{(e)}=\sum \boldsymbol{M}_O(\boldsymbol{F}^{(e)})$
$\frac{\mathrm{d}L_z}{\mathrm{d}t}=M_z^{(e)}=\sum M_z(\boldsymbol{F}^{(e)})$
注:矩心O可以是任意固定点,亦可是质心</td><td>若$\sum \boldsymbol{M}_O(\boldsymbol{F}^{(e)})=0$,则$\boldsymbol{L}_O=$恒量
若$\sum M_z(\boldsymbol{F}^{(e)})=0$,则$L_z=$恒量</td></tr>
<tr><td>定轴转动刚体</td><td colspan="2">$J_z\alpha=\sum M_z(\boldsymbol{F}^{(e)})$</td><td rowspan="2">若$\sum M_z(\boldsymbol{F}^{(e)})=0$,则$\alpha=0$,$\omega=$恒量,刚体绕$z$轴作匀角速度转动
若$\sum M_z(\boldsymbol{F}^{(e)})=$恒量,则$\alpha=$恒量,刚体绕$z$轴作匀变速度转动</td></tr>
<tr><td>平面运动刚体</td><td colspan="2">$m\boldsymbol{a}_C=\sum \boldsymbol{F}^{(e)}$
$J_C\alpha=\sum M_C(\boldsymbol{F}^{(e)})$</td></tr>
<tr><td rowspan="3">动能定理</td><td></td><td>微分形式</td><td>积分形式</td><td rowspan="3">若质点或质系只在有势力作用下运动,则机械能守恒
$E=T+V=$常值</td><td rowspan="3">由于能量的概念更为广泛,所以此定理能阐明平动、转动、平面运动等运动规律,故常用于解各物体有关的运动量($\boldsymbol{v}$、$\boldsymbol{a}$、ω、α)</td></tr>
<tr><td>质点</td><td>$\mathrm{d}\left(\frac{1}{2}mv^2\right)=\delta W$</td><td>$\frac{1}{2}mv_2^2-\frac{1}{2}mv_1^2=W_{12}$</td></tr>
<tr><td>质系</td><td>$\mathrm{d}T=\sum \delta W_i$</td><td>$T_2-T_1=\sum W_{12i}$</td></tr>
</table>

【例 4-3-4】 如图所示丁字杆$OABD$的OA及BD段质量均为m,且$AD=AB=OA/2=l/2$,已知丁字杆在图示位置的角速度为ω,求此瞬时丁字杆的动量,对O轴的动量矩及动能。

例 4-3-4 图

解 丁字杆作定轴转动,按照定义可求如下物理量。

(1)动量

根据公式$\boldsymbol{p}=\sum m_i\boldsymbol{v}_i=\sum \boldsymbol{p}_i=m\boldsymbol{v}_C$,可将丁字杆分为$OA$和$BD$两部分,则整体的动量大小为

$$p=p_{OA}+p_{BD}=mv_E+mv_A=m\frac{l}{2}\omega+ml\omega=\frac{3}{2}ml\omega\text{(方向铅垂向下)}$$

亦可求出丁字杆质心C的位置,即

$$x_C = \frac{m\frac{l}{2} + ml}{2m} = \frac{3}{4}l$$

丁字杆的动量为

$$p = 2mv_C = 2m \cdot \frac{3}{4}l\omega = \frac{3}{2}ml\omega$$

(2)对 O 轴的动量矩

$$L_O = J_O\omega$$

其中转动惯量 J_O 为

$$J_O = \frac{1}{3}ml^2 + \frac{1}{12}ml^2 + ml^2 = \frac{17}{12}ml^2$$

所以对 O 轴的动量矩为

$$L_O = \frac{17}{12}ml^2\omega$$

(3)动能

$$T = \frac{1}{2}J_O\omega^2 = \frac{17}{24}ml^2\omega^2$$

注:求解刚体的动量时,主要是求出刚体质心的速度;而求解刚体的动量矩和动能时,则首先需要判断刚体的运动形式,再应用相应的公式求解。

【例 4-3-5】 图示均质圆轮,质量 m,半径 R,由挂在绳上的重力大小为 W 的物块使其绕 O 运动。设物块速度为 v,不计绳重,则系统动量、动能的大小为:

A. $\frac{W}{g} \cdot v$; $\frac{1}{2} \cdot \frac{v^2}{g}\left(\frac{1}{2}mg + W\right)$

B. mv ; $\frac{1}{2} \cdot \frac{v^2}{g}\left(\frac{1}{2}mg + W\right)$

C. $\frac{W}{g} \cdot v + mv$; $\frac{1}{2} \cdot \frac{v^2}{g}\left(\frac{1}{2}mg - W\right)$

D. $\frac{W}{g} \cdot v - mv$; $\frac{W}{g} \cdot v + mv$

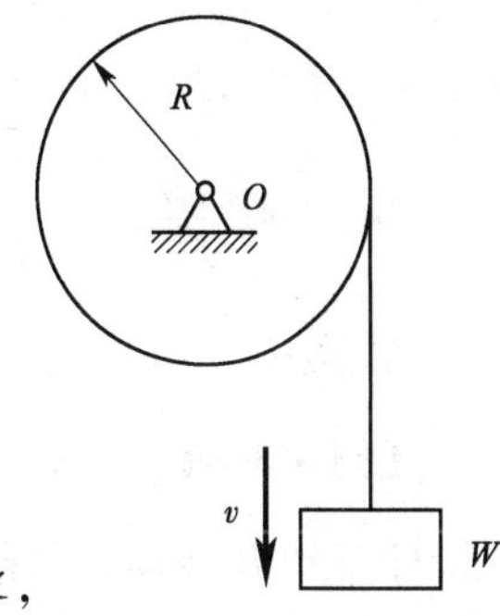

例 4-3-5 图

解 根据动量的公式:$p = mv_C$,则圆轮质心速度为零而动量为零,故系统的动量只有物块的 $\frac{W}{g} \cdot v$

又根据动能的公式:圆轮的动能为 $\frac{1}{2} \cdot \frac{1}{2}mR^2\omega^2 = \frac{1}{4}mR^2\left(\frac{v}{R}\right)^2 = \frac{1}{4}mv^2$,物块的动能为 $\frac{1}{2} \cdot \frac{W}{g}v^2$

二者相加为 $\frac{1}{2} \cdot \frac{v^2}{g}\left(\frac{1}{2}mg + W\right)$

答案:A

【例 4-3-6】 A 块与 B 块叠放如图所示,各接触面处均考虑摩擦。当 B 块受力 $\boldsymbol{F}$ 作用沿水平面运动时,A 块仍静止于 B 块上,于是:

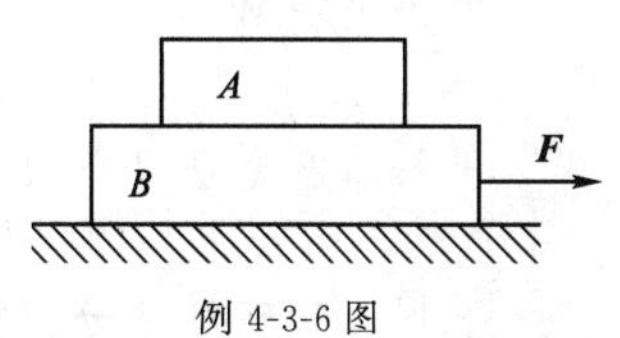

例 4-3-6 图

A. 各接触面处的摩擦力均做负功

B. 各接触面处的摩擦力均做正功

C. A 块上的摩擦力做正功

D. B 块上的摩擦力做正功

解 作用在物块 B 上下两面的摩擦力均水平向左，而物块 B 向右运动，其摩擦力做负功；而作用在物块 A 上的摩擦力水平向右，使其向右运动，做正功。

答案：C

【例 4-3-7】 质量 m_1 与半径 r 均相同的三个均质滑轮，在绳端作用有力或挂有重物，如图所示。已知均质滑轮的质量为 $m_1=2\text{kN}\cdot\text{s}^2/\text{m}$，重物的质量分别为 $m_2=0.2\text{kN}\cdot\text{s}^2/\text{m}$，$m_3=0.1\text{kN}\cdot\text{s}^2/\text{m}$，重力加速度按 $g=10\text{m/s}^2$ 计算，则各轮转动的角加速度 α 间的关系是：

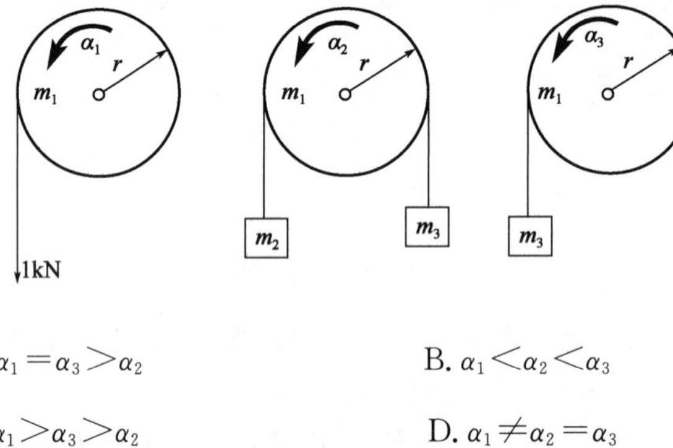

A. $\alpha_1=\alpha_3>\alpha_2$　　　　B. $\alpha_1<\alpha_2<\alpha_3$

C. $\alpha_1>\alpha_3>\alpha_2$　　　　D. $\alpha_1\neq\alpha_2=\alpha_3$

解 根据动量矩定理：$J\alpha_1=1\times r$（J 为滑轮的转动惯量）；$J\alpha_2+m_2r^2\alpha_2+m_3r^2\alpha_2=(m_2g-m_3g)r=1\times r$；$J\alpha_3+m_3r^2\alpha_3=m_3gr=1\times r$。

则 $\alpha_1=\dfrac{1\times r}{J}$；$\alpha_2=\dfrac{1\times r}{J+m_2r^2+m_3r^2}$；$\alpha_3=\dfrac{1\times r}{J+m_3r^2}$

答案：C

【例 4-3-8】 质量为 m，长为 $2l$ 的均质细杆初始位于水平位置，如图 a）所示。A 端脱落后，杆绕轴 B 转动，当杆转到铅垂位置时，AB 杆 B 处的约束力大小为：

A. $F_{Bx}=0$；$F_{By}=0$　　　　B. $F_{Bx}=0$，$F_{By}=\dfrac{mg}{4}$

C. $F_{Bx}=l$，$F_{By}=mg$　　　　D. $F_{Bx}=0$，$F_{By}=\dfrac{5mg}{2}$

解 根据动能定理，当杆从水平位置转动到铅垂位置时（图 b），

初动能 $T_1=0$；末动能 $T_2=\dfrac{1}{2}J_B\omega^2=\dfrac{1}{2}\cdot\dfrac{1}{3}m(2l)^2\omega^2=\dfrac{2}{3}ml^2\omega^2$；

重力的功 $W_{12}=mgl$。

代入动能定理 $T_2-T_1=W_{12}$，得 $\omega^2=\dfrac{3g}{2l}$，$\omega=\sqrt{\dfrac{3g}{2l}}$。

根据定轴转动微分方程：$J_B\alpha=M_B(F)=0$，$\alpha=0$。

杆质心的加速度 $a_{C\tau}=l\alpha=0$，$a_{Cn}=l\omega^2=\frac{3g}{2}$；

由质心运动定理：$m\boldsymbol{a}_C=\sum\boldsymbol{F}$，

可得：$ml\omega^2=F_{By}-mg$，则 $F_{By}=\frac{5}{2}mg$，$F_{Bx}=0$。

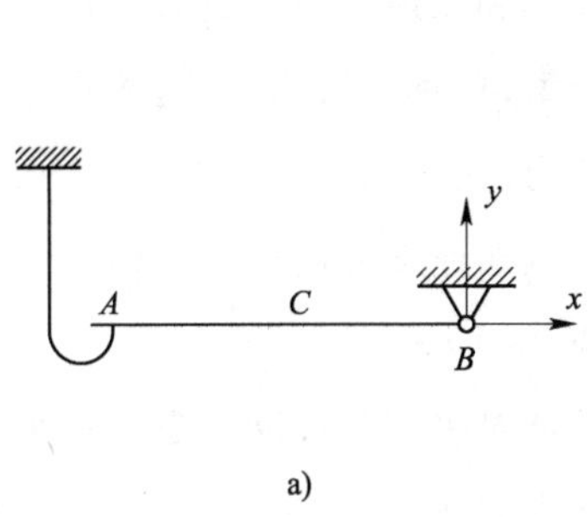

例 4-3-8 图

答案：D

【例 4-3-9】 如图所示均质链条传动机构的大齿轮以角速度 ω 转动，已知大齿轮半径为 R，质量为 m_1，小齿轮半径为 r，质量为 m_2，链条质量不计，则此系统的动量为：

A. $(m_1+2m_2)v\rightarrow$　　B. $(m_1+m_2)v\rightarrow$

C. $(2m_2-m_1)v\rightarrow$　　D. 0

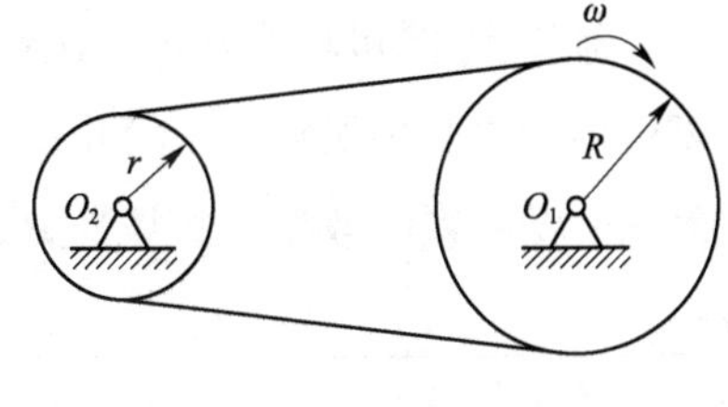

例 4-3-9 图

解 根据动量的定义，系统的动量 $p=m_iv_i$，而两轮质心的速度均为零，故动量为零，链条不计质量，所以此系统的动量为零。

答案：D

【例 4-3-10】 均质圆柱体半径为 R，质量为 m，绕关于对纸面垂直的固定水平轴自由转动，初瞬时静止（质心 G 在 O 轴的铅垂线上，$\theta=0$），如图所示。则圆柱体在位置 $\theta=90°$时的角速度是：

A. $\sqrt{\frac{g}{3R}}$　B. $\sqrt{\frac{2g}{3R}}$　C. $\sqrt{\frac{4g}{3R}}$　D. $\sqrt{\frac{g}{2R}}$

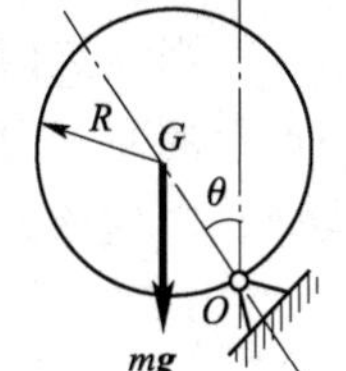

例 4-3-10 图

解 根据动能定理：$T_2-T_1=W_{12}$，其中 $T_1=0$（初瞬时静止），$T_2=\frac{1}{2}\cdot\frac{3}{2}mR^2\omega^2$，$W_{12}=mgR$，代入动能定理：$\frac{3}{4}mR^2\omega^2-0=mgR$，可得 $\omega=\sqrt{\frac{4g}{3R}}$。

答案：C

三、达朗贝尔原理

达朗贝尔原理提供了研究非自由质点系动力学问题的一种普遍方法，即通过引入惯性力，将动力学问题在形式上转化为静力学问题，用静力学中求解平衡问题的方法求解动力学问题，故亦称动静法。

(一)惯性力的概念

当质点受到力的作用而要其改变运动状态时，由于质点具有保持其原有运动状态不变的惯性，将会体现出一种抵抗能力，这种抵抗力，就是质点给予施力物体的反作用力，而这个反作用力称为惯性力，用 $\boldsymbol{F}_{\mathrm{I}}$ 表示。质点惯性力的大小等于质点的质量与加速度的乘积，方向与质点加速度方向相反。即

$$\boldsymbol{F}_{\mathrm{I}}=-m\boldsymbol{a} \tag{4-3-7}$$

需要特别指出的是，质点的惯性力是质点对改变其运动状态的一种抵抗，它并不作用于质点上，而是作用在使质点改变运动状态的施力物体上，但由于惯性力反映了质点本身的惯性特征，所以其大小、方向又由质点的质量和加速度来度量。

(二)刚体惯性力系的简化

对于刚体，可以将其细分而作为无穷多个质点的集合。如果我们研究刚体整体的运动，可以运用静力学中所述力系简化的方法，将刚体无穷多质点上虚加的惯性力向一点简化，并利用简化的结果来等效原来的惯性力系。其简化结果见表 4-3-5。

刚体惯性力系的简化结果 表 4-3-5

刚体的运动形式	表达式	备注	
平移刚体	$\boldsymbol{F}_{\mathrm{I}}=-m\boldsymbol{a}_{C}, M_{\mathrm{IC}}=0$	惯性力合力的作用点在质心，适用于任意形状的刚体	
定轴转动刚体	$\boldsymbol{F}_{\mathrm{I}}=-m\boldsymbol{a}_{C}, M_{\mathrm{IO}}=-J_{O}\alpha$	惯性力的作用点在转动轴 O 处	只适用于转动轴垂直于质量对称平面的刚体
	$\boldsymbol{F}_{\mathrm{I}}=-m\boldsymbol{a}_{C}, M_{\mathrm{IC}}=-J_{C}\alpha$	惯性力的作用点在质心 C 处	
平面运动刚体	$\boldsymbol{F}_{\mathrm{I}}=-m\boldsymbol{a}_{C}, M_{\mathrm{IC}}=-J_{C}\alpha$	惯性力的作用点在质心 C 处	

(三)达朗贝尔原理的含义

当质点(系)上施加了恰当的惯性力后，从形式上看，质点(系)运动的任一瞬时，作用于质点上的主动力、约束力，以及质点的惯性力构成一平衡力系。这就是质点(系)的达朗贝尔原理。应用该原理求解动力学问题的方法，称为动静法。达朗贝尔原理的方程见表 4-3-6。

达朗贝尔原理基本方程 表 4-3-6

方法	方程	备注
质点的达朗贝尔原理	$\boldsymbol{F}+\boldsymbol{F}_{\mathrm{N}}+\boldsymbol{F}_{\mathrm{I}}=0$	由牛顿第二定律推出，只具有平衡方程的形式，而没有平衡的实质。特别适用于已知质点(系)的运动求约束力的情形。对质点系的动静法，只需考虑外力的作用
质点系的达朗贝尔原理	$\sum\limits_{i=1}^{n}\boldsymbol{F}_{i}+\sum\limits_{i=1}^{n}\boldsymbol{F}_{\mathrm{N}i}+\sum\limits_{i=1}^{n}\boldsymbol{F}_{\mathrm{I}i}=0$ $\sum\limits_{i=1}^{n}\boldsymbol{M}_{O}(\boldsymbol{F}_{i})+\sum\limits_{i=1}^{n}\boldsymbol{M}_{O}(\boldsymbol{F}_{\mathrm{N}i})+\sum\limits_{i=1}^{n}\boldsymbol{M}_{O}(\boldsymbol{F}_{\mathrm{I}i})=0$	

【例 4-3-11】 图所示均质圆盘作定轴转动，其中图 a)、图 c)的转动角速度为常量，而图 b)、图 d)的角速度不为常量。则(　　)的惯性力系简化结果为平衡力系。

A. 图 a)　　B. 图 b)　　C. 图 c)　　D. 图 d)

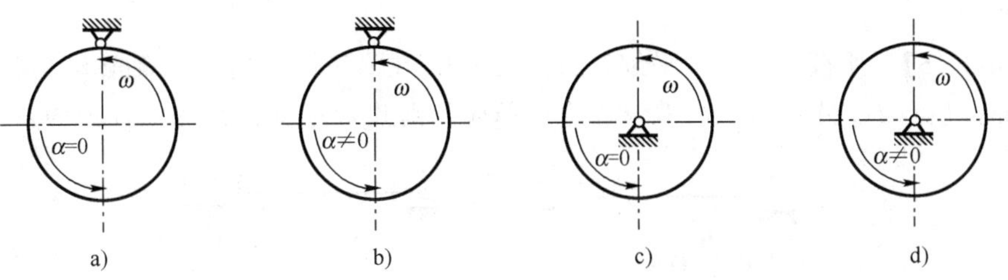

例 4-3-11 图

解　根据定轴转动刚体惯性力系的简化结果，上述圆盘的惯性力系均可简化为作用于质心的一个力 $\boldsymbol{F}_{\mathrm{I}}$ 和一力偶矩为 M_{IC} 的力偶，且

$$\boldsymbol{F}_{\mathrm{I}}=-m\boldsymbol{a}_{\mathrm{C}},M_{\mathrm{IC}}=-J_{\mathrm{C}}\alpha$$

在图 c)中，$\boldsymbol{a}_{\mathrm{C}}=0,\alpha=0$，故 $\boldsymbol{F}_{\mathrm{I}}=0,M_{\mathrm{IC}}=0$，惯性力系成为平衡力系。

答案：C

【例 4-3-12】 质量为 m 的物体 M 在地面附近自由降落，它所受的空气阻力的大小为 $F_{\mathrm{R}}=Kv^2$，其中 K 为阻力系数，v 为物体速度，该物体所能达到的最大速度为：

A. $v=\sqrt{\dfrac{mg}{K}}$　　B. $v=\sqrt{mgK}$　　C. $v=\sqrt{\dfrac{g}{K}}$　　D. $v=\sqrt{gK}$

解　按照牛顿第二定律，在铅垂方向有 $ma=F_{\mathrm{R}}-mg=Kv^2-mg$，当 $a=0$(速度 v 的导数为零)时有速度最大，为 $v=\sqrt{\dfrac{mg}{K}}$。

答案：A

【例 4-3-13】 质量为 m，半径为 R 的均质圆盘，绕垂直于图面的水平轴 O 转动，其角速度为 ω，在图示瞬时，角加速度为零，盘心 C 在其最低位置，此时将圆盘的惯性力系向 O 点简化，其惯性力主矢和惯性力主矩的大小分别为：

A. $m\dfrac{R}{2}\omega^2$；0　　B. $mR\omega^2$；0

C. 0；0　　D. 0；$\dfrac{1}{2}mR^2\omega^2$

例 4-3-13 图

解　根据定轴转动刚体惯性力系的简化结果，求惯性力主矢和主矩大小的公式分别为 $F_{\mathrm{I}}=ma_{\mathrm{C}},M_{\mathrm{IO}}=J_{\mathrm{O}}\alpha$，此题中：$a_{\mathrm{C}}=\dfrac{1}{2}R\omega^2,a=0$，代入公式可得：$F_{\mathrm{I}}=m\dfrac{R}{2}\omega^2,M_{\mathrm{I}}=0$。

答案：A

【例 4-3-14】 均质直杆 OA 的质量为 m，长为 l，以匀角速度 ω 绕 O 轴转动如图示。此时将 OA 杆的惯性力系向 O 点简化，其惯性力主矢和惯性力主矩的大小分别为：

A. 0，0　　B. $\dfrac{1}{2}ml\omega^2$，$\dfrac{1}{3}ml^2\omega^2$

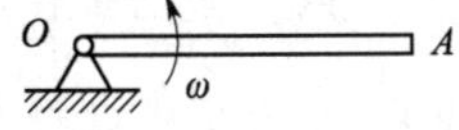

例 4-3-14 图

C. $ml\omega^2$ ，$\frac{1}{2}ml^2\omega^2$　　　　D. $\frac{1}{2}ml\omega^2$ ，0

解　根据定轴转动刚体惯性力系的简化结果分析，匀角速度转动($\alpha=0$)刚体的惯性力主矢和主矩的大小分别为：$F_{\rm I}=ma_{\rm C}=\frac{1}{2}ml\omega^2$ ，$M_{\rm IO}=J_{\rm O}\alpha=0$。

答案：D

【例 4-3-15】　质量不计的水平细杆 AB 长为 L，在沿垂图面内绕 A 轴转动，其另一端固连质量为 m 的质点 B，在图 a)示水平位置静止释放。则此瞬时质点 B 的惯性力为：

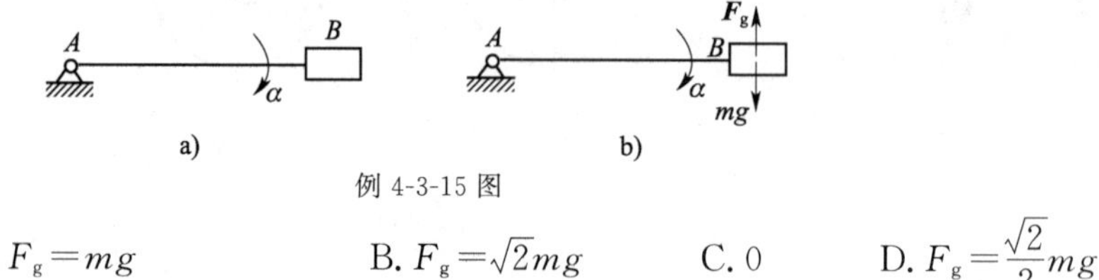

例 4-3-15 图

A. $F_{\rm g}=mg$　　　B. $F_{\rm g}=\sqrt{2}mg$　　　C. 0　　　D. $F_{\rm g}=\frac{\sqrt{2}}{2}mg$

解　杆水平瞬时，其角速度为零，加在物块上的惯性力铅垂向上(图 b)，列平衡方程$\sum M_{\rm O}(\boldsymbol{F})=0$，则有 $(F_{\rm g}-mg)l=0$ ，所以$F_{\rm g}=mg$。

答案：A

【例 4-3-16】　三角形物块沿水平地面运动的加速度为 $\boldsymbol{a}$，方向如图 a)所示。物块倾斜角为 θ。重力大小为 W 的小球在斜面上用细绳拉住，绳另端固定在斜面上。设物块运动中绳不松软，则小球对斜面的压力 $\boldsymbol{F}_{\rm N}$ 的大小为：

A. $F_{\rm N}<W\cos\theta$

B. $F_{\rm N}>W\cos\theta$

C. $F_{\rm N}=W\cos\theta$

D. 只根据所给条件则不能确定

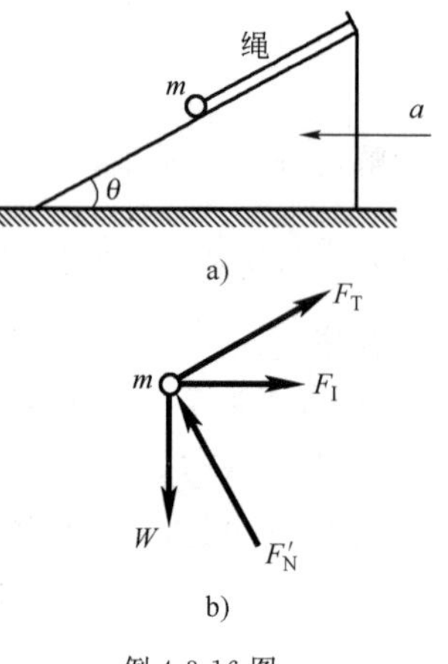

例 4-3-16 图

解　应用达朗贝尔原理，在小球上加一水平向右的惯性力 $\boldsymbol{F}_{\rm I}$，使其与重力 $\boldsymbol{W}$、绳的拉力 $\boldsymbol{F}_{\rm T}$ 及斜面的约束力 $\boldsymbol{F}'_{\rm N}$形成形式上的平衡状态，受力如图 b)所示。将小球所受之力沿垂直于斜面的方向列力的投影平衡方程，有

$$F'_{\rm N}-F_{\rm I}\sin\theta-W\cos\theta=0$$

则　$$F'_{\rm N}=F_{\rm N}=F_{\rm I}\sin\theta+W\cos\theta$$

答案：B

【例 4-3-17】　如图所示圆环以角速度 ω 绕铅直轴 AC 自由转动，圆环的半径为 R，对转轴 z 的转动惯量为 I。在圆环中的 A 点放一质量为 m 的小球，设由于微小的干扰，小球离开 A 点。忽略一切摩擦，则当小球达到 B 点时，圆环的角速度为：

A. $\frac{mR^2\omega}{I+mR^2}$　　　B. $\frac{I\omega}{I+mR^2}$

C. ω　　　D. $\frac{2I\omega}{I+mR^2}$

例 4-3-17 图

解　系统在转动中对转动轴 z 的动量矩守恒，即：$I\omega=(I+mR^2)\omega_{\rm t}$ (设 $\omega_{\rm t}$ 为小球达到 B 点时圆环的角速度)，则 $\omega_{\rm t}=\frac{I\omega}{I+mR^2}$。

答案:B

四、质点的直线振动

物体在某一位置附近作往复运动,这种运动称为振动。常见的振动有钟摆的运动、汽缸中活塞的运动等。

(一)自由振动微分方程

质量块受初始扰动,仅在恢复力作用下产生的振动称为自由振动。考察如图 4-3-1 所示之弹簧振子,设物块的质量为 m,弹簧的刚度为 k,由牛顿定律

$$m\frac{\mathrm{d}^2x}{\mathrm{d}t^2}=-kx$$

令 $\omega_0^2=\dfrac{k}{m}$,则有

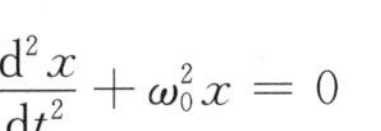

$$\frac{\mathrm{d}^2x}{\mathrm{d}t^2}+\omega_0^2x=0 \tag{4-3-8}$$

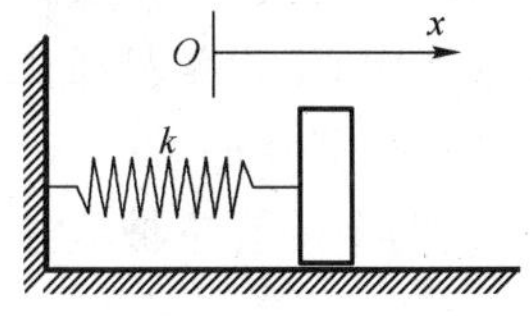

图 4-3-1 单自由度系统自由振动模型

此式称为无阻尼自由振动微分方程的标准形式。其解为

$$x=A\sin(\omega_0t+\varphi) \tag{4-3-9}$$

(二)振动周期、固有频率和振幅

若初始 $t=0$ 时,$x=x_0$,$v=v_0$,则式(4-3-9)中各参数的物理意义及计算公式列于表 4-3-7 中。

自由振动的参数 表 4-3-7

	振　幅	初　相　角	固有圆频率	周　期
公式	$A=\sqrt{x_0^2+\dfrac{v_0^2}{\omega_0^2}}$	$\varphi=\arctan\dfrac{\omega_0x_0}{v_0}$	$\omega_0=\sqrt{\dfrac{k}{m}}$	$T=\dfrac{2\pi}{\omega_0}$
定义	相对于振动中心的最大位移	初相角决定质点运动的起始位置	2π 秒内的振动次数	振动一次所需要的时间

(三)求固有频率的方法

1. 列微分方程

化振动微分方程为标准形式(4-3-8)后,取位移坐标 x 前的系数,即为固有频率 ω_0 的平方。

2. 利用弹簧的静变形 δ_{st}

在静平衡位置,刚度为 k 的弹簧产生的弹性力与物块的重力 mg 相等,即 $k\delta_{st}=mg$,将其代入表 4-3-7 中固有圆频率的表达式,有

$$\omega_0=\sqrt{\frac{k}{m}}=\sqrt{\frac{mg}{m\delta_{st}}}=\sqrt{\frac{g}{\delta_{st}}} \tag{4-3-10}$$

3. 等效弹簧刚度

图 4-3-2a)为两个弹簧并联的模型,图 4-3-2b)为弹簧串联模型,这两种模型均可简化为如图 4-3-2c)所示弹簧-质量系统。

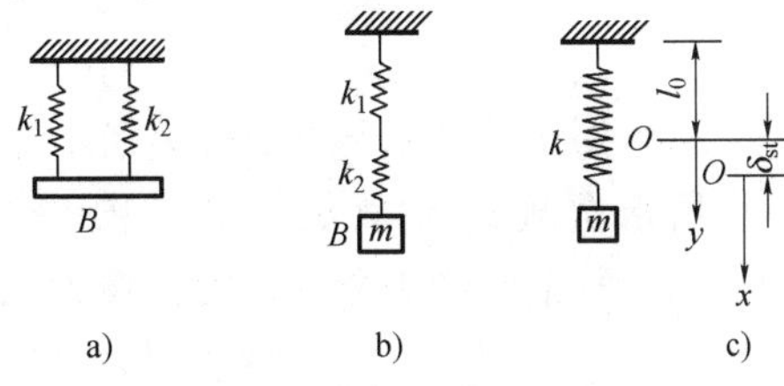

图 4-3-2 弹簧的并联和串联模型

弹簧并联 $$k = k_1 + k_2 \tag{4-3-11}$$

系统的固有频率 $$\omega_0 = \sqrt{\frac{k}{m}} = \sqrt{\frac{k_1 + k_2}{m}}$$

弹簧串联 $$k = \frac{k_1 k_2}{k_1 + k_2} \tag{4-3-12}$$

系统的固有频率 $$\omega_0 = \sqrt{\frac{k}{m}} = \sqrt{\frac{k_1 k_2}{m(k_1 + k_2)}}$$

4.能量法

因为自由振动系统为保守系统,故运动过程中,系统的机械能守恒。若设系统的静平衡位置(振动中心)为零势能位置,则在此位置,物块的速度达到最大,系统具有最大动能,势能为零;当物块偏离振动中心极端位置时,位移最大,速度为零,系统具有最大势能,动能为零。因此在这两个位置机械能守恒,有

$$T_{\max} = V_{\max} \tag{4-3-13}$$

根据式(4-3-9),可得

$$T_{\max} = \frac{1}{2}m\dot{x}^2_{\max} = \frac{1}{2}mA^2\omega_0^2, V_{\max} = \frac{1}{2}kx^2_{\max} = \frac{1}{2}kA^2$$

则有

$$\omega_0 = \sqrt{\frac{k}{m}}$$

所得结果与表 4-3-7 中固有频率的公式相同。

(四)衰减振动

振动中的阻力,习惯上称为阻尼。这里仅考虑阻力的大小与运动速度成正比,阻力的方向与速度矢量的方向相反这种类型的阻力,即

$$\boldsymbol{F}_{\mathrm{d}} = -c\boldsymbol{v} \tag{4-3-14}$$

如图 4-3-3 所示为弹簧振子的有阻尼自由振动的力学模型,根据牛顿定律

$$m\frac{\mathrm{d}^2 x}{\mathrm{d}t^2} = -kx - c\frac{\mathrm{d}x}{\mathrm{d}t}$$

令 $n = \frac{c}{2m}$,上述方程可以整理成

$$\frac{\mathrm{d}^2 x}{\mathrm{d}t^2} + 2n\frac{\mathrm{d}x}{\mathrm{d}t} + \omega_0^2 x = 0 \tag{4-3-15}$$

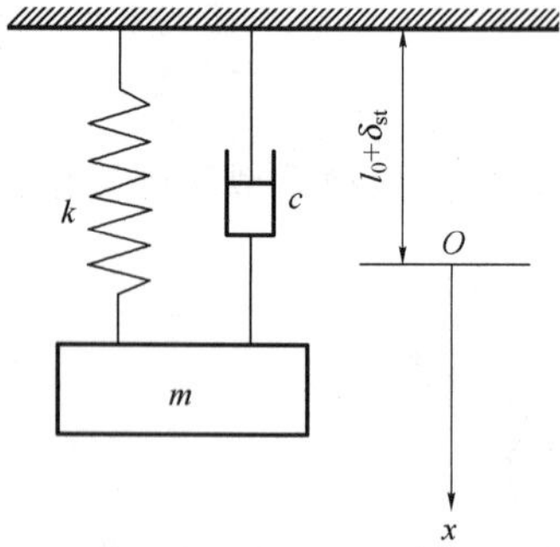

图 4-3-3 弹簧振子的有阻尼自由振动模型

对于不同的 n 值,上述方程的解有以下三种不同形式。

1.弱阻尼状态(或欠阻尼状态)

此时,$n < \omega_0$,方程(4-3-15)的解为

$$x = Ae^{-nt}\sin(\sqrt{\omega_0^2 - n^2}\,t + \varphi) \tag{4-3-16}$$

式中,A、φ 为积分常数,由初始条件决定。如图 4-3-4 所示为振子的位移与时间的关系。此时振子的运动是一种振幅按指数规律衰减的振动。图中振幅的包络线的表达式为 Ae^{-nt},相邻的两个振幅之比称为减缩系数,记作 η。

$$\eta = \frac{A_m}{A_{m+1}} = \frac{Ae^{-nt_{\mathrm{m}}}}{Ae^{-n(t_{\mathrm{m}}+T_{\mathrm{d}})}} = e^{nT_{\mathrm{d}}} \tag{4-3-17}$$

其中 $T_d = \frac{2\pi}{\omega_d} = \frac{2\pi}{\sqrt{\omega_0^2 - n^2}}$ 为阻尼振动的周期。为应用方便，常引入对数减缩率，记作 Λ 。

$$\Lambda = \ln\left(\frac{A_m}{A_{m+1}}\right) = nT_d \tag{4-3-18}$$

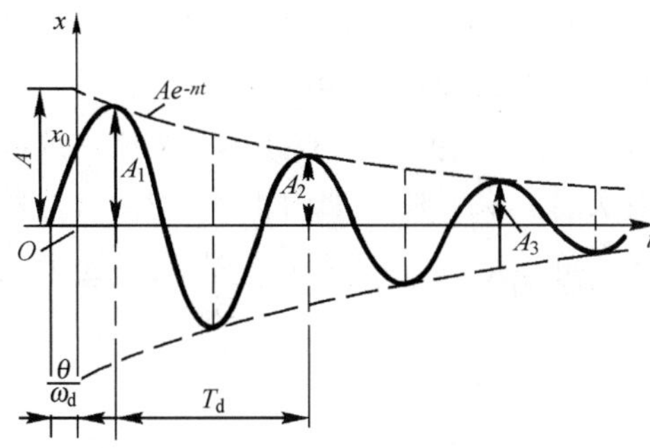

图 4-3-4　弱阻尼状态振子的位移与时间的关系

2. 过阻尼状态

此时 $n > \omega_n$ ，方程(4-3-15)的解为

$$x = C_1 e^{\lambda_1 t} + C_2 e^{\lambda_2 t} \tag{4-3-19}$$

式中，C_1、C_2 为积分常数，由初始条件决定。此时已不能振动，系统缓慢回到平衡状态。

3. 临界阻尼状态

此时 $n = \omega_n$ ，方程(4-3-15)的解为

$$x = e^{-nt}(C_1 + C_2 t) \tag{4-3-20}$$

系统也不能振动，较快地回到平衡位置。

(五)受迫振动

受迫振动是系统在外界激励下所产生的振动，如图 4-3-5 所示为强迫振动的力学模型，系统在激振力 **F** 作用下发生振动。

外激振力一般为时间的函数，最简单的形式是简谐激振力

$$F = H\sin\omega t \tag{4-3-21}$$

对质点应用牛顿第二定律，有

$$m\frac{d^2x}{dt^2} = -kx - c\frac{dx}{dt} + H\sin\omega t$$

令 $h = \frac{H}{m}$ ，上述方程变为

$$\frac{d^2x}{dt} + 2n\frac{dx}{dt} + \omega_0^2 x = h\sin\omega t \tag{4-3-22}$$

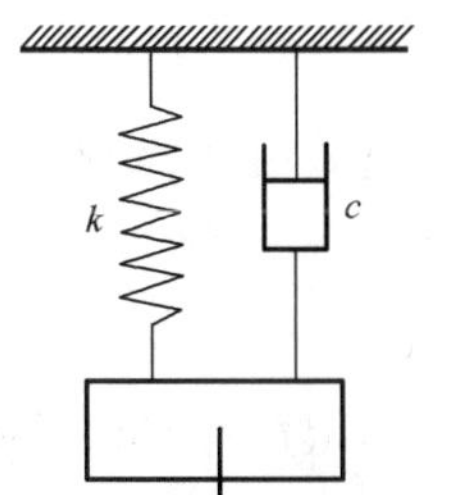

图 4-3-5　弹簧振子的强迫振动模型

这一方程称为有阻尼受迫振动微分方程的标准形式，若其中第二项(即阻尼项)为零，则为无阻尼受迫振动。方程(4-3-20)的通解为

$$x = Ae^{-nt}\sin(\sqrt{\omega_0^2 - n^2}t + \varphi) + B\sin(\omega t - \varepsilon) \tag{4-3-23}$$

其中 A 和 φ 为积分常数，由运动初始条件确定；B 为受迫振动的振幅，ε 为受迫振动的相位差，可由下列公式表示

$$B = \frac{h}{\sqrt{(\omega_0^2 - \omega^2)^2 + 4n^2\omega^2}} \tag{4-3-24}$$

$$\tan\varepsilon = \frac{2n\omega}{\omega_0^2 - \omega^2} \tag{4-3-25}$$

可见有阻尼受迫振动的解由两部分组成，第一部分是衰减振动，第二部分是受迫振动。通常将第一部分称为瞬态过程，第二部分称为稳态过程，稳态过程是研究的重点。

受迫振动的振幅达到极大值的现象称为共振。

在稳态过程中，受迫振动的一个重要特征是：振幅、相位差的取值与激振力的频率、系统的自由振动固有频率和阻尼有关。其关系曲线如图 4-3-6、图 4-3-7 所示。采用量纲为 1 的形式，图中横轴表示频率比 $s = \frac{\omega}{\omega_0}$，纵轴表示振幅比 $\beta = \frac{B}{B_0}\left(B_0 = \frac{H}{k}\right)$，阻尼的改变用阻尼比 $\zeta = \frac{n}{\omega_0}$ 的改变来表示。

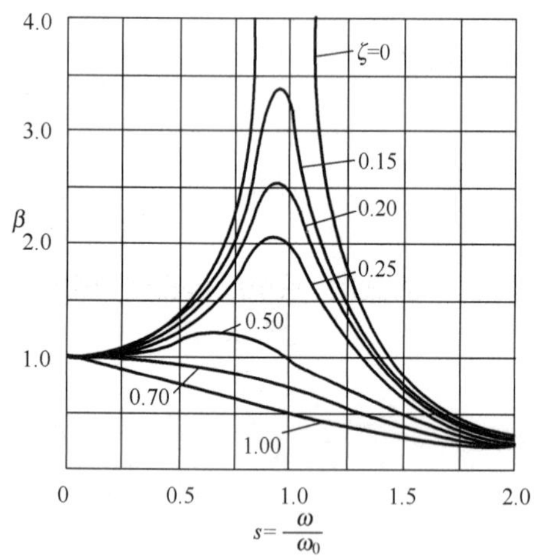

图 4-3-6 幅频特性曲线

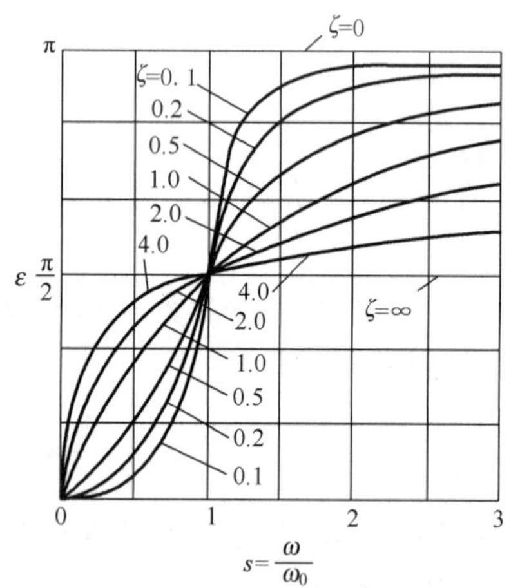

图 4-3-7 相频特性曲线

将式(4-3-24)对 ω 求一次导数并令其等于零，可以发现，此时振幅 B 有极大值，即共振固有圆频率 ω_r 为

$$\omega_r = \sqrt{\omega_0^2 - 2n^2} \tag{4-3-26}$$

当阻尼为零时，共振固有圆频率为

$$\omega_r = \omega_0 \tag{4-3-27}$$

即无阻尼强迫振动时，只要激振力频率与自由振动频率相等，便发生共振，由式(4-3-20)可知，此时的振幅 B 为无穷大。

共振是受迫振动中常见的现象，共振时，振幅随时间的增加不断增大，有时会引起系统的破坏，应设法避免；利用共振也可制造各种设备，如超声波发生器、核磁共振仪等，造福于人类。实际问题中，由于阻尼的存在，振幅不会无限增大。

【例 4-3-18】 如图所示，弹簧-物块直线振动系统位于铅垂面内。弹簧刚度系数为 k，物块质量为 m。若已知物块的运动微分方程为 $m\ddot{x} + kx = 0$，则描述运动坐标 Ox 的坐标原点应为：

A. 弹簧悬挂处之点 O_1

B. 弹簧原长 l_0 处之点 O_2

C. 弹簧由物块重力引起静伸长 δ_{st} 之点 O_3

D. 任意点皆可

例 4-3-18 图

解 列振动微分方程时，把坐标原点设在物体静平衡的位置处，列出的方程才是齐次微分方程。

答案：C

【例 4-3-19】 单摆作微幅摆动的周期与质量 m 和摆长 l 的关系是：

A. $\frac{1}{2\pi}\sqrt{\frac{g}{l}}$　　B. $\frac{1}{2\pi}\sqrt{\frac{l}{g}}$　　C. $2\pi\sqrt{\frac{g}{l}}$　　D. $2\pi\sqrt{\frac{l}{g}}$

解 单摆的运动微分方程为

$$ml\ddot{\varphi} = -mg\sin\varphi$$

因为是微幅摆动，$\sin\varphi \approx \varphi$，则有

$$\ddot{\varphi} + \frac{g}{l}\varphi = 0$$

所以，单摆的圆频率 $\omega = \sqrt{\frac{g}{l}}$，而周期 $T = \frac{2\pi}{\omega} = 2\pi\sqrt{\frac{l}{g}}$。

答案：D

【例 4-3-20】 图示振动系统中 $m=200\text{kg}$，弹簧刚度 $k=10\,000\text{N/m}$，设地面振动可表示为 $y=0.1\sin(10t)$（y 以 cm、t 以 s 计）。则：

A. 装置 a 振幅最大

B. 装置 b 振幅最大

C. 装置 c 振幅最大

D. 三种装置振动情况一样

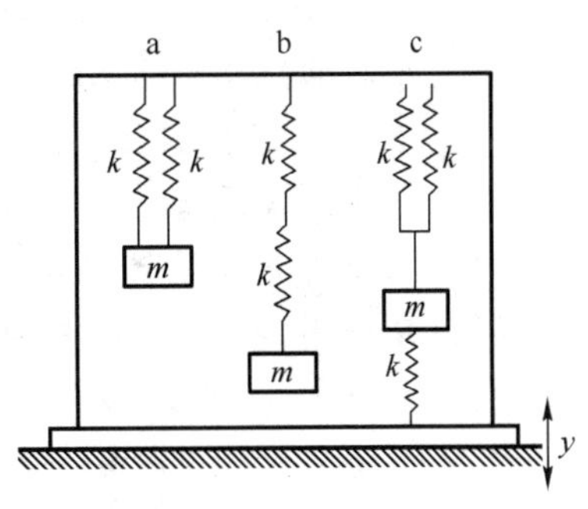

例 4-3-20 图

解 此系统为无阻尼受迫振动，装置 a、b、c 的自由振动频率分别为

$$\omega_{0a} = \sqrt{\frac{2k}{m}} = \sqrt{\frac{20\,000}{200}} = 10\text{rad/s}$$

$$\omega_{0b} = \sqrt{\frac{k}{2m}} = \sqrt{\frac{10\,000}{400}} = 5\text{rad/s}$$

$$\omega_{0c} = \sqrt{\frac{3k}{m}} = \sqrt{\frac{30\,000}{200}} = 12.25\text{rad/s}$$

由于外加激振 y 的频率为 10rad/s，与 ω_{0a} 相等，故装置 a 会发生共振，从理论上讲振幅将无穷大。

答案：A

【例 4-3-21】 质量为 110kg 的机器固定在刚度为 $2\times10^6\text{N/m}$ 的弹性基础上，当系统发生共振时，机器的工作频率为：

A. 66.7rad/s　　B. 95.3rad/s　　C. 42.6rad/s　　D. 134.8rad/s

解 发生共振时，系统的工作频率与其固有频率相等，为 $\sqrt{\frac{k}{m}} = \sqrt{\frac{2\times10^6}{110}} = 134.8\text{rad/s}$

答案：D

【例 4-3-22】 如图所示系统中，当物块振动的频率比为 1.27 时，k 的值是：

A. 1×10^5 N/m

B. 2×10^5 N/m

C. 1×10^4 N/m

D. 1.5×10^5 N/m

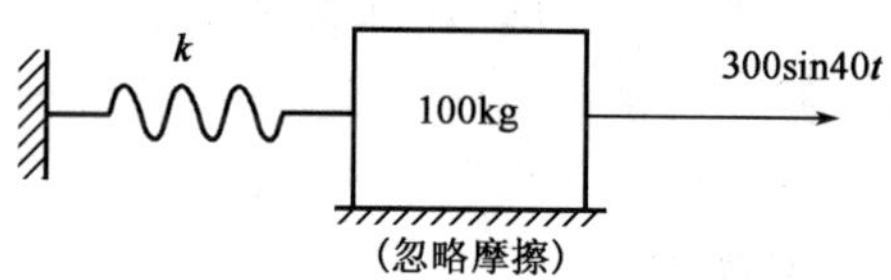

例 4-3-22 图

解 已知频率比 $\frac{\omega}{\omega_0}=1.27$，且 $\omega=40\text{rad/s}$，$\omega_0=\sqrt{\frac{k}{m}}(m=100\text{kg})$，所以，$k=(\frac{40}{1.27})^2\times100=9.9\times10^4\approx1\times10^5$ N/m。

答案：A

习 题

4-3-1 已知 A 物重力的大小 $P=20$N，B 物重力的大小 $Q=30$N，滑轮 C、滑轮 D 不计质量，并略去各处摩擦，如图所示，则绳水平段的拉力为（ ）。

A. 30N B. 20N C. 16N D. 24N

4-3-2 求解质点动力学问题时，质点的初条件是用来（ ）。

A. 分析力的变化规律 B. 建立质点运动微分方程

C. 确定积分常数 D. 分离积分变量

4-3-3 质量为 m 的物体自高 H 处水平抛出，如图所示，运动中受到与速度一次方成正比的空气阻力 $\boldsymbol{R}$ 作用，$\boldsymbol{R}=-km\boldsymbol{v}$，$k$ 为常数。则其运动微分方程为（ ）。

A. $m\ddot{x}=-km\dot{x}, m\ddot{y}=-km\dot{y}-mg$ B. $m\ddot{x}=km\dot{x}, m\ddot{y}=km\dot{y}-mg$

C. $m\ddot{x}=-km\dot{x}, m\ddot{y}=km\dot{y}-mg$ D. $m\ddot{x}=-km\dot{x}, m\ddot{y}=-km\dot{y}+mg$

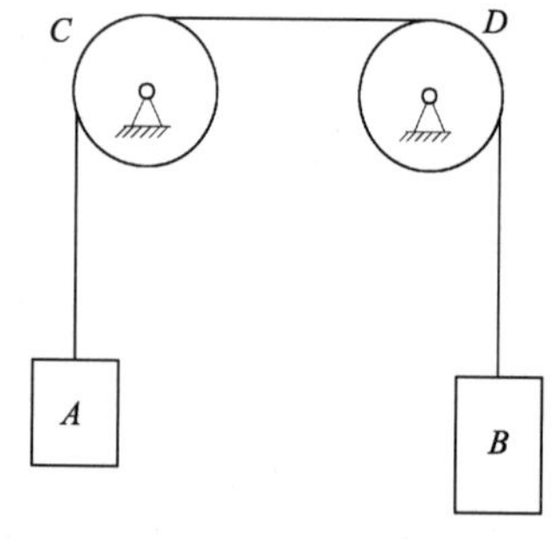

题 4-3-1 图

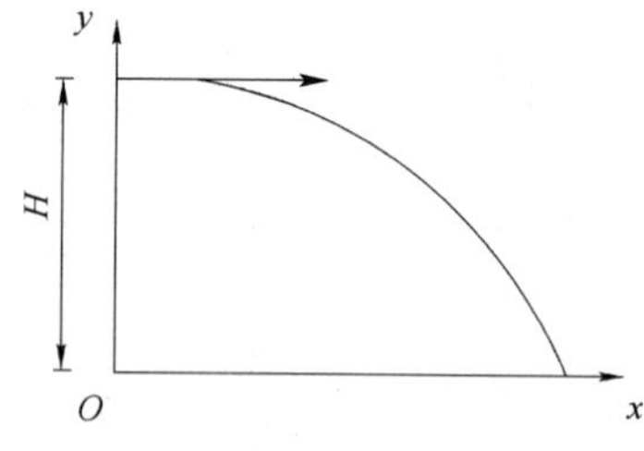

题 4-3-3 图

4-3-4 汽车以匀速率 v 在不平的道路上行驶，如图所示，当汽车通过 A、B、C 三个位置时，汽车对路面的压力分别为 $\boldsymbol{N}_A$、$\boldsymbol{N}_B$、$\boldsymbol{N}_C$，则下述关系式（ ）成立。

A. $N_A=N_B=N_C$ B. $N_A<N_B<N_C$

C. $N_A>N_B>N_C$ D. $N_A=N_B>N_C$

4-3-5 质量分别为 $m_1=m$，$m_2=2m$ 的两个小球 M_1，M_2 用长为 L 而重量不计的刚杆相连，现将 M_1 置于光滑水平面上，且 M_1M_2 与水平面成 60°角，如图所示，则当无初速释放、M_2 球落地时，M_1 球移动的水平距离为(　　)。

A. $L/3$　　B. $L/4$　　C. $L/6$　　D. 0

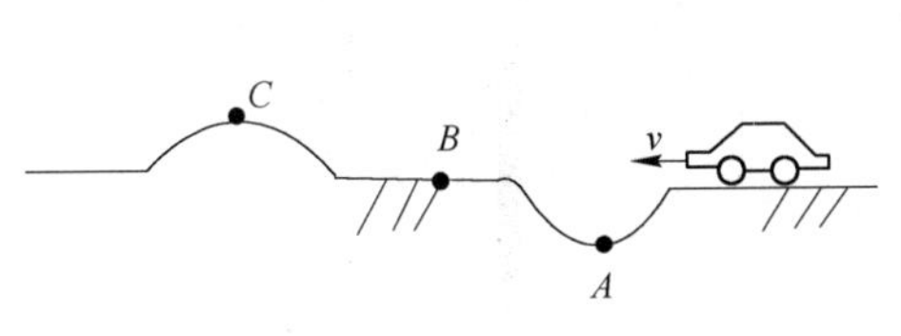

题 4-3-4 图

题 4-3-5 图

4-3-6　设有质量相等的两物体 A、B，在同一段时间内，A 物发生水平移动，而 B 物发生铅直移动，则此两物体的重力在这段时间内的冲量(　　)。

A. 不同　　B. 相同

C. A 物重力的冲量大　　D. B 物重力的冲量大

4-3-7　匀质杆质量为 m，长 $OA=l$，在铅垂面内绕定轴 O 转动。杆质心 C 处连接刚度系数 k 较大的弹簧，弹簧另端固定。图示位置为弹簧原长，当杆由此位置逆时针方向转动时，杆上 A 点的速度为 v_A，若杆落至水平位置的角速度为零，则 v_A 的大小应为(　　)。

A. $\sqrt{\frac{1}{2}(2-\sqrt{2})^2\frac{k}{m}l^2-2gl}$

B. $\sqrt{\frac{1}{4}(2-\sqrt{2})^2\frac{k}{m}l^2-gl}$

C. $\sqrt{\frac{1}{2}(2-\sqrt{2})^2\frac{k}{m}l^2-8gl}$

D. $\sqrt{\frac{3}{4}(2-\sqrt{2})^2\frac{k}{m}l^2-3gl}$

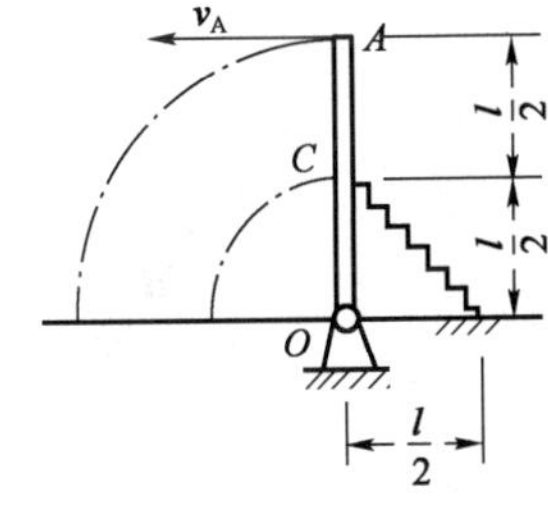

题 4-3-7 图

4-3-8　在光滑的水平面上，放置一静止的均质直杆 AB，当 AB 上受一力偶 m 作用时，如图所示，AB 将绕(　　)点转动。

A. A 点　　B. B 点

C. C 点　　D. 先绕 A 点转动，然后绕 C 点转动

4-3-9　如图所示，两种不同材料的均质细长杆焊接成直杆 ABC，AB 段为一种材料，长度为 a，质量为 m_1，BC 段为另一种材料，长度为 b，质量为 m_2，杆 ABC 以匀角速度 ω 转动，则其对 A 轴的动量矩大小为(　　)。

A. $L_A=(m_1+m_2)(a+b)^2\omega/3$

B. $L_A=[m_1a^2/3+m_2b^2/12+m_2(b/2+a)^2]\omega$

C. $L_A=(m_1a^2/3+m_2b^2/3+m_2a^2)\omega$

D. $L_A=m_1a^2\omega/3+m_2b^2\omega/3$

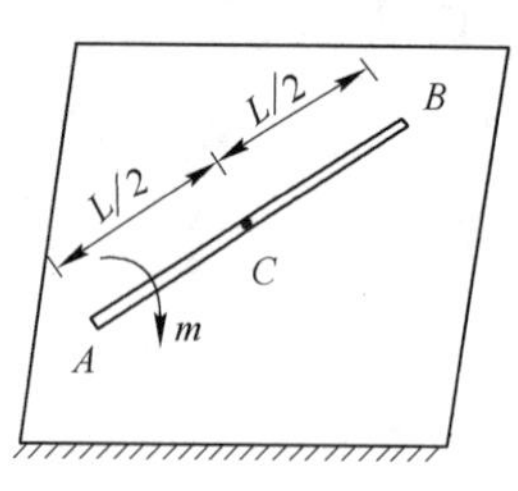

题 4-3-8 图

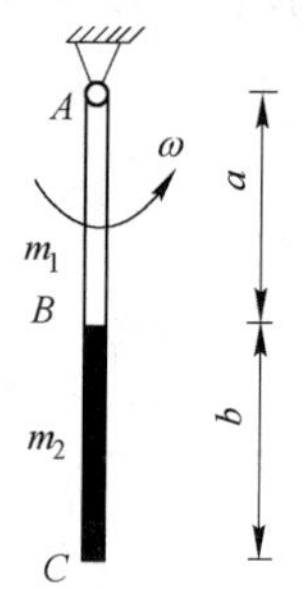

题 4-3-9 图

4-3-10 如图所示，直角均质弯杆 ABC，$AB=BC=L$，每段质量记作 M_{AB}、M_{BC}，则弯杆对过 A 且垂直于图平面的 A 轴的转动惯量为（ ）。

A. $J_A=M_{AB}L^2/3+M_{BC}L^2/3+M_{BC}L^2$

B. $J_A=M_{AB}L^2/3+M_{BC}L^2/3+M_{BC}\sqrt{2}L^2$

C. $J_A=M_{AB}L^2/3+M_{BC}L^2/12+M_{BC}L^2/4$

D. $J_A=M_{AB}L^2/3+M_{BC}L^2/12+5M_{BC}L^2/4$

4-3-11 如图所示，刚体的质量 m，质心为 C，对定轴 O 的转动惯量为 J_O，对质心的转动惯量为 J_C，若转动角速度为 ω，则刚体对 O 轴的动量矩 H_O 为（ ）。

A. $mv_C\cdot OC$　　B. $J_O\omega$　　C. $J_C\omega$　　D. $J_O\omega^2$

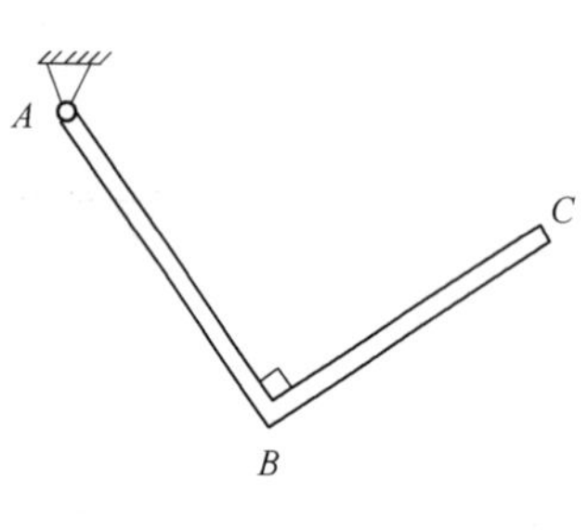

题 4-3-10 图

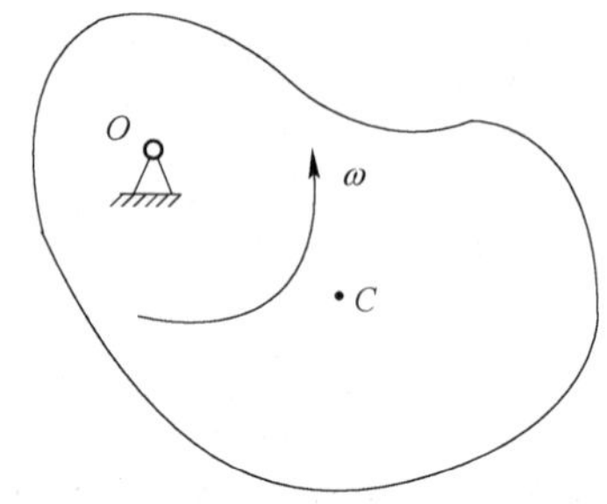

题 4-3-11 图

4-3-12 一端固结于 O 点的弹簧，如图所示，另一端可自由运动，弹簧的原长 $L_0=2b/3$，弹簧的弹性系数为 k，若以 B 点处为零势能面，则 A 处的弹性势能为（ ）。

A. $kb^2/24$　　B. $5kb^2/18$　　C. $3kb^2/8$　　D. $-3kb^2/8$

4-3-13 某弹簧的弹性系数为 k，在 I 位置弹簧的变形为 δ_1，在 II 位置弹簧的变形为 δ_2。若取 II 位置为零势能位置，则在 I 位置弹性力的势能为（ ）。

A. $k(\delta_1^2-\delta_2^2)$　　B. $k(\delta_2^2-\delta_1^2)$　　C. $\frac{1}{2}k(\delta_1^2-\delta_2^2)$　　D. $\frac{1}{2}k(\delta_2^2-\delta_1^2)$

4-3-14 半径为 R，质量为 m 的均质圆盘在其自身平面内作平面运动。在如图所示位置时，若已知图形上 A、B 两点的速度方向如图所示，$\alpha=45°$，且知 B 点速度大小为 v_B。则圆轮的动能为（ ）。

A. $mv_B^2/16$　　B. $3mv_B^2/16$　　C. $mv_B^2/4$　　D. $3mv_B^2/4$

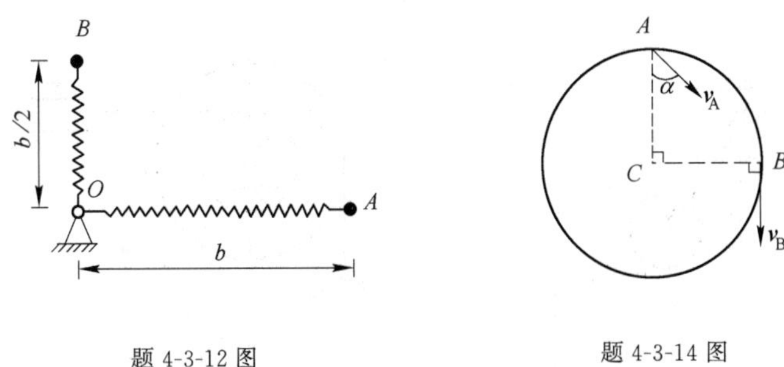

题 4-3-12 图　　题 4-3-14 图

4-3-15　已知曲柄 OA 长 r，以角速度 ω 转动，均质圆盘半径为 R，质量为 m，在固定水平面上作纯滚动，则如图所示瞬时圆盘的动能为（　　）。

A. $2mr^2\omega^2/3$　　B. $mr^2\omega^2/3$　　C. $4mr^2\omega^2/3$　　D. $mr^2\omega^2$

4-3-16　如图所示，一弹簧常数为 k 的弹簧下挂一质量为 m 的物体，若物体从静平衡位置（设静伸长为 δ）下降 Δ 距离，则弹性力所做的功为（　　）。

A. $\frac{1}{2}k\Delta^2$　　B. $\frac{1}{2}k(\delta+\Delta)^2$

C. $\frac{1}{2}k[(\Delta+\delta)^2-\delta^2]$　　D. $\frac{1}{2}k[\delta^2-(\Delta+\delta)^2]$

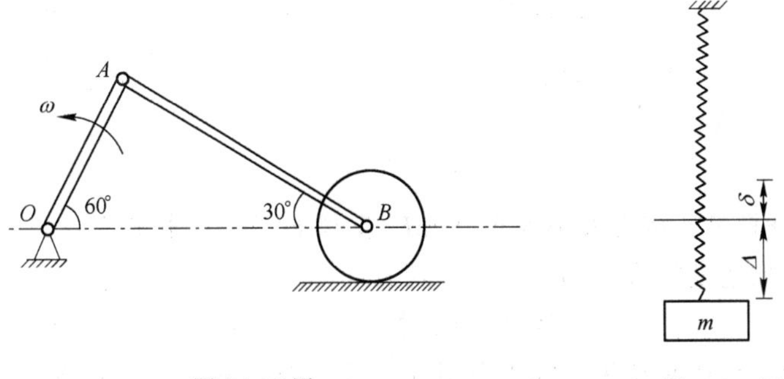

题 4-3-15 图　　题 4-3-16 图

4-3-17　如图所示，忽略质量的细杆 $OC=l$，其端部固结均质圆盘，杆上点 C 为圆盘圆心，盘质量为 m，半径为 r，系统以角速度 ω 绕轴 O 转动，系统的动能是（　　）。

A. $T=\frac{1}{2}m(l\omega)^2$　　B. $T=\frac{1}{2}m[(l+r)\omega^2]$

C. $T=\frac{1}{2}(\frac{1}{2}mr^2)\omega^2$　　D. $T=\frac{1}{2}\left(\frac{1}{2}mr^2+ml^2\right)\omega^2$

4-3-18　两重物的质量均为 m，分别系在两软绳上（见图）。此两绳又分别绕在半径各为 r 与 $2r$ 并固结一起的两圆轮上。两圆轮构成之鼓轮的质量亦为 m，对轴 O 的回转半径为 ρ_0。两重物中一铅垂悬挂，一置于光滑平面上。当系统在左重物重力作用下运动时，鼓轮的角加速度 α 为（　　）。

A. $\alpha=\frac{2gr}{5r^2+\rho_0^2}$　　B. $\alpha=\frac{2gr}{3r^2+\rho_0^2}$　　C. $\alpha=\frac{2gr}{\rho_0^2}$　　D. $\alpha=\frac{gr}{5r^2+\rho_0^2}$

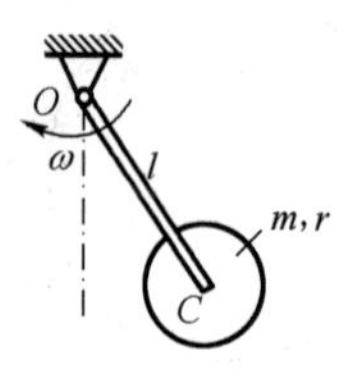

题 4-3-17 图

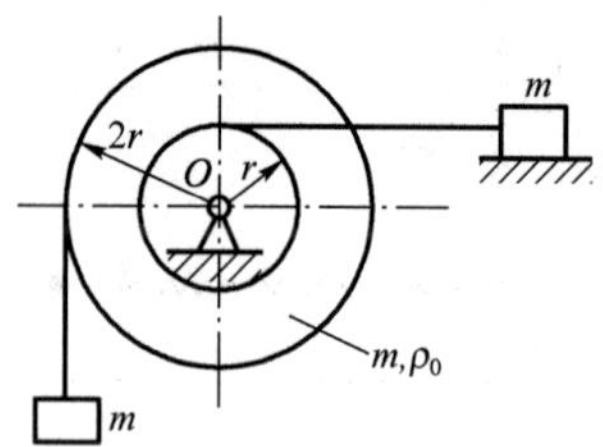

题 4-3-18 图

4-3-19 如图所示，均质圆盘作定轴转动，其中图 a)、图 c)的转动角速度为常数($\omega=C$)，而图 b)、图 d)的角速度不为常数($\omega\neq C$)，则(　　)的惯性力系简化的结果为平衡力系。

A. 图 a)　　B. 图 b)　　C. 图 c)　　D. 图 d)

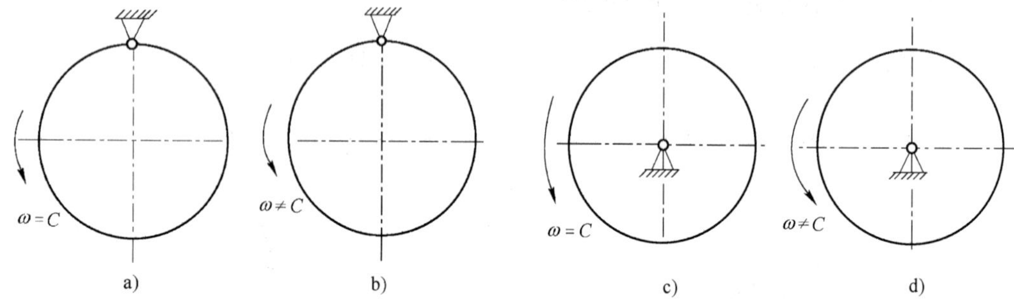

题 4-3-19 图

4-3-20 均质细杆 AB 重力大小为 P、长 $2L$，支承如图所示水平位置。当 B 端细绳突然剪断瞬时，AB 杆的角加速度的大小为(　　)。

A. 0　　B. $3g/(4L)$　　C. $3g/(2L)$　　D. $6g/L$

4-3-21 如图所示，在倾角为 α 的光滑斜面上置一弹性系数为 k 的弹簧，一质量为 m 的物块沿斜面下滑 s 距离与弹簧相碰，碰后弹簧与物块不分离并发生振动，则自由振动的固有圆频率为(　　)。

A. $(k/m)^{1/2}$　　B. $[k/(ms)]^{1/2}$

C. $[k/(m\sin\alpha)]^{1/2}$　　D. $(k\sin\alpha/m)^{1/2}$

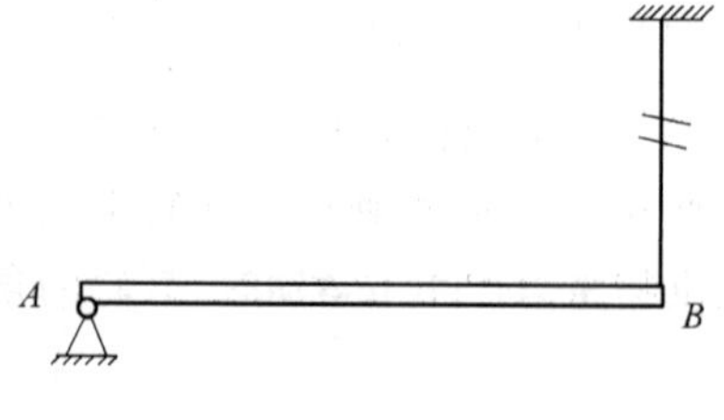

题 4-3-20 图

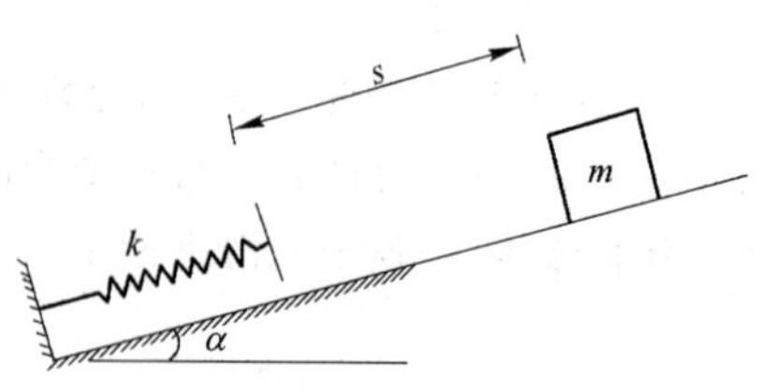

题 4-3-21 图

4-3-22 设如图所示 a)、b)、c)三个质量弹簧系统的固有频率分别为 ω_1、ω_2、ω_3，则它们之间的关系是(　　)。

A. $\omega_1<\omega_2=\omega_3$　　B. $\omega_2<\omega_3=\omega_1$　　C. $\omega_3<\omega_1=\omega_2$　　D. $\omega_1=\omega_2=\omega_3$

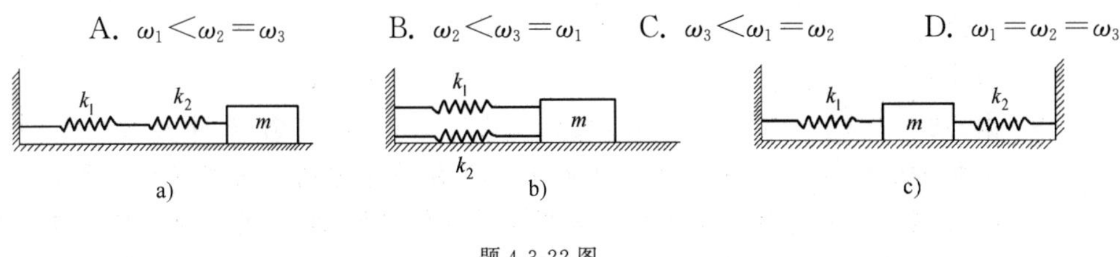

题 4-3-22 图

题解及参考答案

第一节

4-1-1　**解:**根据力多边形法则:各分力首尾相连,而合力则由第一个分力的起点指向最后一个分力的终点(矢端),题中 $\boldsymbol{F}_2$、$\boldsymbol{F}_3$ 首尾相连为分力,而 $\boldsymbol{F}_1$ 由 $\boldsymbol{F}_2$ 的起点指向 $\boldsymbol{F}_3$ 的终点为两分力的合力,所以表达式为:$\boldsymbol{F}_1=\boldsymbol{F}_2+\boldsymbol{F}_3$。

答案:D

4-1-2　**解:**作用力与反作用力分别作用在两个不同的物体上,所以选项 A、D 不对。而由于一个刚体上的两个力满足 $\boldsymbol{F}_A=-\boldsymbol{F}_B$,故无合力,选项 C 亦错。

答案:B

4-1-3　**解:**AC 与 BC 均为二力构件,故 A 处约束力沿 AC 方向,B 处约束力沿 BC 方向;分析铰链 C 的平衡,其受力如解图所示。

答案:B

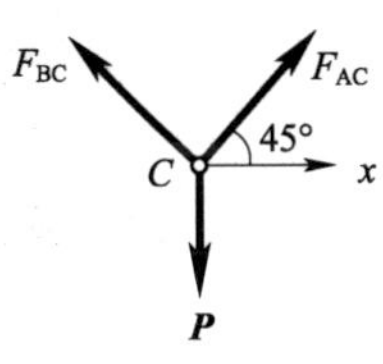

题 4-1-3 解图

4-1-4　**解:**题中四个力为作用于同一刚体上的平面共点力系,其力矢关系图构成了首尾相连自行封闭的平行四边形,满足平面共点力系平衡的几何条件,所以力系平衡。

答案:D

4-1-5　**解:**因为 $\boldsymbol{F}$ 与 x 轴平行,故 $\boldsymbol{F}$ 除在与 x 轴垂直的轴上投影为零外,在其他轴上的投影均不为零。

答案:B

4-1-6　**解:**AC 与 BC 均为二力杆,铰链 C 的受力图见解图,列平衡方程:$\sum F_x=0$,可得 $F_A=F_B$;$\sum F_y=0$,$F_A\sin60°+F_B\sin60°-P=0$,解得:$F_A=\dfrac{P}{\sqrt{3}}$。

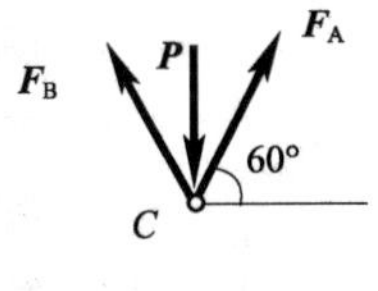

题 4-1-6 解图

答案:C

4-1-7　**解:**将各力向 $\boldsymbol{F}_1$ 力作用点平移进行简化,简化后的主矢为零(各力首尾相连),$\boldsymbol{F}_2$ 平移后将附加一力偶($\boldsymbol{F}_1$ 不动 $\boldsymbol{F}_3$ 沿作用线移动),使三角形板转动。

答案:C

4-1-8　**解:**力偶作用 在 AC 杆时,BC 杆是二力构件,B、C 处约束力沿 BC 连线方向;再考虑整体平衡,A、B 处约束力应组成一力偶与主动力偶 m 平衡,故 A 处约束力的方向与 B 处约束力反向平行。若将外力偶搬移至 BC 杆,则 AC 杆是二力构件,同理:A、B、C 处约束力的方向均沿 AC 连线方向。由此可知,力偶作用在不同的刚体上,约束力的作用线方向都改变了。

答案:C

4-1-9 **解**:题中杆 CD、EF 为二力杆,故 C 处约束力沿 CD 方向,E 处约束力沿 EF 方向,分析 BE 杆,应用三力平衡汇交定理得 B 处约束力的作用线应汇交于 G 点(也是 C、E 两处约束力的汇交点);再分析结构整体平衡,A、B 处约束力应组成一力偶与主动力偶(P,P')平衡,故 A 处约束力的方向与 B 处约束力反向平行(平行于 BG 连线)。

答案:B

4-1-10 **解**:按矢量的表达式应该表示为:$\boldsymbol{F}_R=\boldsymbol{F}_1+\boldsymbol{F}_2$,如图所示,合力的方向应与 $\boldsymbol{F}_1$ 相同,大小等于 $\boldsymbol{F}_1$ 的一半。

题 4-1-10 解图

答案:C

4-1-11 **解**:根据平面任意力系的简化结果分析,主矢为零时,力系简化的最后结果为一合力偶,合力偶矩与简化中心的位置无关。

答案:C

4-1-12 **解**:截面法(见题解图):设 y 轴与 BC 垂直,则

$\sum F_y=0$

$P_C\cos60°+F_{DB}\cos30°=0$

$F_{DB}=-\dfrac{\sqrt{3}P}{3}$(压)

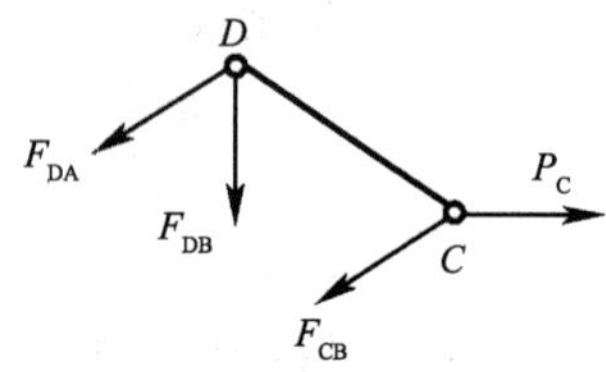

题 4-1-12 解图

答案:C

4-1-13 **解**:根据整体的对称性,A、B 处的约束力均垂直向上,大小为 $F_A=F_B=\dfrac{P}{2}$。以 BC 为研究对象,受力如解图所示,列平衡方程:$\sum M_C(F)=0$,$F_B\cdot 2a-T_E\cdot a=0$,

将 $T_E=10\text{kN}$ 代入,得:$P=10\text{kN}$。

题 4-1-13 解图

答案:B

4-1-14 **解**:根据主矢和主矩的性质,主矢与简化中心无关,主矩一般与简化中心有关。

答案:B

4-1-15 **解**:根据力的平移定理,若主矢 $\boldsymbol{F}_R'$ 向 O 点左边某点 O' 平移后,将附加一顺时针转向的力偶。

答案:C

4-1-16 **解**:应用桁架零杆判断的方法,先分析 A、B 节点,可知 AC、BD 杆为零杆,再分析 C、D 节点,两节点分别连接的是两根互相垂直的杆件,若要节点平衡,则两节点连接的杆均为零杆。

答案:D

4-1-17 **解**:因为 BEC 为二力构件,故 B 处约束力的方向应是沿 BC 连线,对结构整体分析,A、B 处的约束力必须组成一力偶,才能与作用在结构上的外力偶 M 组成平衡力系。

答案:C

4-1-18 **解**:A、B 槽均为光滑接触面约束,其约束力均垂直于槽壁,由于两约束力的作用

线不平行，无法组成力偶与外力偶 M 平衡，故平板不能平衡。

答案：B

4-1-19 **解**：物块平衡，受力如图所示，最大摩擦力为 $F_{max}=f\cdot F_N=0.3\times50=15N$，而主动力 $W=10N$，所以摩擦力可按铅垂方向力的平衡来计算，即：$F=W=10N$。

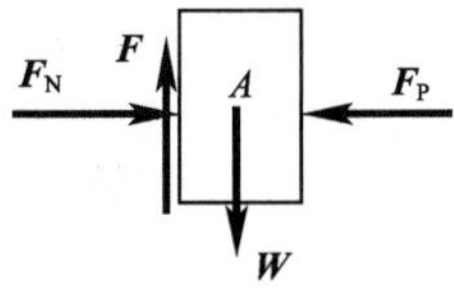

题 4-1-19 解图

答案：B

4-1-20 **解**：主动力（大小相等的重力与 **P** 力）合力的作用线与接触面法线的夹角为 30°，小于摩擦角 35°，故物块自锁。

答案：A

4-1-21 **解**：在铅垂方向主动力合力为：$P\sin30°-G=40\times0.5-20=0$，物块无滑动趋势，故摩擦力为零。

答案：C

4-1-22 **解**：摩擦角 $\varphi_m=\arctan f=23.4°<30°$（斜面的倾角）故物块不自锁而滑动，摩擦力为 $F=W\cos30°f'=80\times0.866\times0.4=27.7kN$。

答案：C

4-1-23 **解**：物 A 所受正压力 $F_N=100-25\times\frac{4}{5}=80kN$，$F_{max}=F_N\cdot f=16kN$，而水平方向的主动力为 $2.5\times\frac{3}{5}=15kN$，故物体处于平衡状态，摩擦力按平衡方程来计算。

答案：C

第二节

4-2-1 **解**：因为 $a_\tau=\frac{dv}{dt}=k$，$a_n=\frac{v^2}{R}=\frac{(kt)^2}{R}$，所以 $a=\sqrt{a_\tau^2+a_n^2}=\sqrt{k^2+(k^4t^4/R^2)}$。

答案：C

4-2-2 **解**：将两个运动方程平方相加，有 $x^2+y^2=4^2(\sin^2\frac{\pi}{3}t+\cos^2\frac{\pi}{3}t)=4^2$。

答案：B

4-2-3 **解**：轮缘上一点做圆周运动，必有法向加速度，所以图 a)、c) 的运动是不可能的。

答案：B

4-2-4 **解**：曲杆 OAB 为定轴转动刚体，点 B 的速度为转动半径 OB 与角速度的乘积，即：$v_B=OB\cdot\omega=50\times2=100cm/s$。

答案：A

4-2-5 **解**：由 $v_A=w\cdot OA$，所以 $\omega=6/2=3rad/s$；再由 $\tan\theta=\frac{\alpha}{\omega^2}$，求得 $a=3^2\times\tan60°=9\sqrt{3}\ rad/s^2$。

答案：D

4-2-6 **解**：曲杆 OAB 为定轴转动刚体，点 B 的加速度在 y 轴上的投影即为其法向加速度，点 B 的转动半径为 OB，故 $a_{By}=-\omega^2\cdot OB$。

答案：D

4-2-7 **解**:轮缘点 A 的速度与物块 B 的速度相同,即:$v_A=v_B=\dfrac{dx}{dt}=2kt$;轮缘点 A 的切向加速度与物块 B 的加速度相同,即:$a_{A\tau}=a_B=\dfrac{dv_B}{dt}=2k$。所以,$a_{An}=\dfrac{v_A^2}{R}=\dfrac{4k^2t^2}{R}$,而 $a_A=\sqrt{a_{A\tau}^2+a_{An}^2}=\sqrt{4k^2+(16k^4t^4/R^2)}$。

答案:C

4-2-8 **解**:定轴转动刚体内各点加速度的分布为 $a=r\sqrt{\alpha^2+\omega^4}$,其中 r 为点到转动轴的距离;而各点加速度与转动半径的夹角均相同,即 $\tan\theta=\tan\varphi=\dfrac{\alpha}{\omega^2}$,所以,$a_A=2a_B$,$\theta=\varphi$。

答案:C

4-2-9 **解**:根据两啮合齿轮运动的性质,A、B 两点无相对滑动,故两点速度和切向加速度相同,而法向加速度分别为 $a_{An}=\dfrac{v_A^2}{r_1}$,$a_{Bn}=\dfrac{v_B^2}{r_2}$,由于 $v_A=v_B$,$r_1\neq r_2$,所以两点法向加速度不同。

答案:B

4-2-10 **解**:摆杆的角速度为 $\dot{\varphi}=\varphi_0\omega\cos\omega t$,角加速度为 $\ddot{\varphi}=-\varphi_0\omega^2\sin\omega t$

将 $t=\dfrac{\pi}{4\omega}$s 代入,则有:$\dot{\varphi}=\dfrac{\sqrt{2}}{2}\varphi_0\omega$,$\ddot{\varphi}=-\dfrac{\sqrt{2}}{2}\varphi_0\omega^2$

摆锤 A 的速度为 $v=\dot{\varphi}l=\dfrac{\sqrt{2}}{2}l\varphi_0\omega$,

切向加速度为 $a_\tau=\ddot{\varphi}l=-\dfrac{\sqrt{2}}{2}l\varphi_0\omega^2$,法向加速度为 $a_n=l\dot{\varphi}^2=\dfrac{1}{2}l\varphi_0^2\omega^2$

答案:C

4-2-11 **解**:根据定轴转动刚体内点的速度分析,M 点速度的方向应垂直于转动半径 OM。

答案:A

第三节

4-3-1 **解**:设绳的拉力为 $\boldsymbol{F}_T$ 且处处相等(因为滑轮质量及各处摩擦不计),对 A、B 物块分别使用牛顿第二定律:$\dfrac{P}{g}a_A=F_T-P$;$\dfrac{Q}{g}a_B=Q-F_T$,且 $a_A=a_B$。

答案:D

4-3-2 **解**:初始条件反映的是质点某一时刻的运动,只能用来确定解质点运动微分方程时出现的积分常数。

答案:C

4-3-3 **解**:质点在运动过程中受重力和阻力作用,应用直角坐标形式的质点运动微分方程,而阻力在直角坐标系中可表示为:$\boldsymbol{R}=-km\dot{x}\boldsymbol{i}-km\dot{y}\boldsymbol{j}$。
请注意:质点竖向运动向下,与 Y 轴反向,故 $\dot{y}$ 为负值。空气阻力向上,为正值,所以为 $-km\dot{y}$。

答案:A

4-3-4 **解**:汽车匀速行驶,切向加速度为零,途经 A、B、C 三点时的法向加速度分别为铅垂向上、零、铅垂向下,可加惯性力用达朗贝尔原理进行分析,在 A、B、C 三点所加惯性力别为铅垂向下、零、铅垂向上,由此可知,汽车对路面的压力 $N_A > N_B > N_C$。

答案:C

4-3-5 **解**:系统在水平方向受力为零,且初始为静止,故质心在水平方向守恒,其运动为铅垂线,而系统质心到 M_1 的距离为 $2L/3$。

答案:A

4-3-6 **解**:同样力的冲量只取决于作用时间,与位移无关。

答案:B

4-3-7 **解**:应用动能定理 $T_2 - T_1 = W_{12}$

其中:$T_2 = 0$, $T_1 = \dfrac{1}{2}J_O\omega^2 = \dfrac{1}{2}\cdot\dfrac{1}{3}ml^2\dfrac{v_A^2}{l^2} = \dfrac{1}{6}mv_A^2$

$$W_{12} = mg\frac{l}{2} - \frac{k}{2}\left(l - \frac{\sqrt{2}}{2}l\right)^2 = mg\frac{l}{2} - \frac{k}{8}\left(2-\sqrt{2}\right)^2 l^2$$

答案:D

4-3-8 **解**:根据质心运动定理,在水平面上直杆受力为零,故质心不运动,且动量矩定理 $J_C\alpha = m$。

答案:C

4-3-9 **解**:$L_A = J_A\omega$

其中:$J_A = J_{(AB)A} + J_{(BC)A}$

求 $J_{(BC)A}$ 时要使用平行移轴定理

即:$J_{(BC)A} = \dfrac{1}{12}m_2b^2 + m_2\left(a + \dfrac{b}{2}\right)^2$。

答案:B

4-3-10 **解**:$J_A = J_{(AB)A} + J_{(BC)A}$

求 $J_{(BC)A}$ 时要使用平行移轴定理

即:$J_{(BC)A} = \dfrac{1}{12}M_{BC}L^2 + M_{BC}\left(L^2 + \dfrac{L^2}{4}\right)$。

答案:D

4-3-11 **解**:根据定轴转动刚体动量矩的定义 $H_0 = J_0\cdot\omega$。

答案:B

4-3-12 **解**:根据势能的定义 $U = \dfrac{k}{2}(\delta_A^2 - \delta_B^2)$,式中 δ_A、δ_B 分别为 A、B 位置弹簧的变形量。

答案:A

4-3-13 **解**:根据势能的定义,弹性力从 I 位置到 II 位置所做的功即为弹性力在 I 位置的势能。

答案:C

4-3-14 **解**:根据 v_A、v_B 的方向可求出圆盘的瞬时速度中心在 BC 延长线与轮缘左侧的交点，故圆盘的角速度为：$\omega=\frac{v_B}{2R}$，质心的速度为：$v_C=\frac{v_B}{2}$，再由动能的定义 $T=\frac{1}{2}mv_C^2+\frac{1}{2}J_C\omega^2$ 求解，其中：$J_C=\frac{1}{2}mR^2$。

答案：B

4-3-15 **解**：应用速度投影定理通过 A 点速度求出 B 点速度，即：$v_A=r\omega=v_B\cos30°$，进而求出圆轮的角速度 $\omega=\frac{v_B}{R}$，并由 $T=\frac{1}{2}mv_B^2+\frac{1}{2}J_B\omega^2$ 求动能，其中：$J_B=\frac{1}{2}mR^2$。

答案：D

4-3-16 **解**：弹性力的功 $W_{12}=\frac{k}{2}(\delta_1^2-\delta_2^2)$。

答案：D

4-3-17 **解**：圆盘绕轴 O 作定轴转动，其动能为 $T=\frac{1}{2}J_O\omega^2$，其中：$J_O=\frac{1}{2}mr^2+ml^2$。

答案：D

4-3-18 **解**：应用动能定理：$T_2-T_1=W_{12}$。若设重物 A 下降 h 时鼓轮的角速度为 ω_O，则系统的动能为 $T_2=\frac{1}{2}mv_A^2+\frac{1}{2}mv_B^2+\frac{1}{2}J_O\omega_O^2$，$T_1=$常量。其中 $v_A=2r\omega_O$，$v_B=r\omega_O$，$J_O=m\rho_O^2$。力所做的功为 $W_{12}=mgh$。

答案：A

4-3-19 **解**：因为质心的加速度和轮的角加速度均为零，故惯性力系的主矢和主矩皆为零。

答案：C

4-3-20 **解**：将惯性力系向 A 点简化，其运动和受力分析如图所示，图中 $M_{IA}=J_A\alpha=\frac{1}{3}\frac{P}{g}(2L)^2\alpha$，通过平衡方程 $\sum M_A(F)=0$，$M_{IA}-PL=0$ 可求出角加速度。

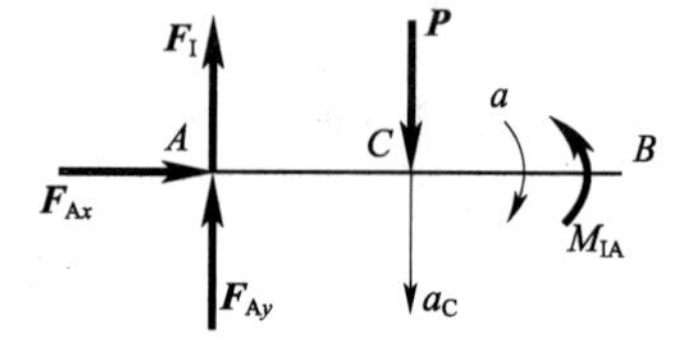

题 4-3-20 解图

答案：B

4-3-21 **解**：物块的自由振动固有圆频率为$\sqrt{\frac{k}{m}}$，与其他条件无关。

答案：A

4-3-22 **解**：因为 $\omega=\sqrt{\frac{k}{m}}$，所以只要系统等效的弹簧刚度大，固有频率就大。按弹簧的串、并联计算其等效的弹簧刚度 。图 a)两弹簧为串联，$k=\frac{k_1k_2}{k_1+k_2}$；图 b)和 c)两弹簧均为并联，$k=k_1+k_2$。

答案：A

第五章　材料力学

复习指导

一、考试大纲

5.1　材料在拉伸、压缩时的力学性能

低碳钢、铸铁拉伸、压缩试验的应力-应变曲线；力学性能指标。

5.2　拉伸和压缩

轴力和轴力图；杆件横截面和斜截面上的应力；强度条件；虎克定律；变形计算。

5.3　剪切和挤压

剪切和挤压的实用计算；剪切面；挤压面；剪切强度；挤压强度；剪切虎克定律。

5.4　扭转

扭矩和扭矩图；圆轴扭转切应力；切应力互等定理；圆轴扭转的强度条件；扭转角计算及刚度条件。

5.5　截面几何性质

静矩和形心；惯性矩和惯性积；平行轴公式；形心主轴及形心主惯性矩概念。

5.6　弯曲

梁的内力方程；剪力图和弯矩图；分布荷载、剪力、弯矩之间的微分关系；正应力强度条件；切应力强度条件；梁的合理截面；弯曲中心概念；求梁变形的积分法、叠加法。

5.7　应力状态

平面应力状态分析的解析法和应力圆法；主应力和最大切应力；广义虎克定律；四个常用的强度理论。

5.8　组合变形

拉/压-弯组合、弯-扭组合情况下杆件的强度校核；斜弯曲。

5.9　压杆稳定

压杆的临界荷载；欧拉公式；柔度；临界应力总图；压杆的稳定校核。

二、复习指导

根据“考试大纲”的要求，结合以往的考试，考生在复习材料力学部分时，应注意以下几点。

(1)轴向拉伸和压缩部分的内容重点考察基本概念，考试题以概念类、记忆类、简单计算类为主。

(2)剪切和挤压实用计算部分，受力分析和破坏形式是重点，剪切面和挤压面的区分是难点，挤压面面积的计算容易混淆，考试题以概念题、比较判别题和简单计算题为主。

(3)扭转部分考试题以概念、记忆和一般计算为主，对于实心圆截面和空心圆截面两种情形，截面上剪应力的分布、极惯性矩与抗扭截面系数计算要严格区分。

(4)截面的几何性质部分的考试题，侧重于平行移轴公式的应用，形心主轴概念的理解和有一对称轴的组合截面惯性矩的计算步骤与计算方法。

(5)弯曲内力部分考试题主要考察作 Q、M 图的熟练程度，熟练掌握用简便法计算指定截面的 Q、M 和用简便法作 Q、M 图是这部分的关键所在。

(6)弯曲应力部分考试题重点考察：①正应力最大的危险截面，剪应力最大的危险截面的确定；②梁受拉侧、受压侧的判断，对于 U 形、T 形等截面中性轴为非对称轴的情形尤其重要；③焊接工字形截面梁三类危险点的确定，即除了正应力危险点，剪应力危险点外，还有一类危险点，即在 M、Q 均较大的截面上腹板与翼缘交界处的点，但该类危险点处于复杂应力状态，需要用强度理论进行强度计算。题型以分析、计算为主。

(7)弯曲变形部分考试题重点考察给定梁的边界条件和连续条件的正确写法和用叠加法求梁的位移的灵活应用。叠加法有三方面的应用：①荷载分解，变形或位移叠加，这是叠加法的直接应用；②计算梁不变形部分的位移的叠加法，就是变形部分的位移叠加上不变形部分的位移；③逐段刚化法，是上面两种方法的进一步延拓。

(8)应力状态与强度理论部分考试题重点测试：①应力状态的有关概念；②主应力、最大剪应力的计算；③主应力、最大剪应力计算与强度理论的综合应用；④在各种应力状态下尤其是单向应力状态、纯剪切应力状态下材料的破坏原因分析。考试题多属于概念理解、分析计算类。

(9)组合变形部分考试题重点考察：①各种基本变形组合时的分析方法；②对于有两根对称轴、四个角点的截面杆，在斜弯曲、拉(压)-弯曲、偏心拉(压)时最大正应力计算；③用强度理论解决弯-扭组合变形的强度计算问题。

(10)压杆稳定部分考试题重点测试：①压杆稳定性的概念。压杆的极限应力不但与材料有关，而且与 λ 有关，而 λ 又与长度、支承情况、截面形状和尺寸有关；②压杆临界应力的计算思路，即先计算压杆在两个形心主惯性平面内的柔度，取其中最大的一个作为依据，再根据该最大柔度的范围选择适当的临界应力计算公式计算临界应力。考试题多属概念类和比较判别类。

本章的重点是弯曲内力、弯曲应力、应力状态与强度理论，其他各部分均有考题，覆盖了全部内容。

材料力学本身概念性很强，基本内容要求相当熟练，少部分内容如应力状态分析和压杆稳定则还要求能深入进行分析，一般来说，计算都不复杂。尤其是注册结构工程师基础考试，题量大，时间紧，更不会涉及很复杂的计算。

第一节　概　　论

材料力学是研究各种类型构件(主要是杆)的强度、刚度和稳定性的学科，它提供了有关的基本理论、计算方法和试验技术，使我们能合理地确定构件的材料、尺寸和形状，以达到安全与经济的设计要求。

一、材料力学的基本思路

(一)理论公式的建立

理论公式的建立思路如图 5-1-1 所示。

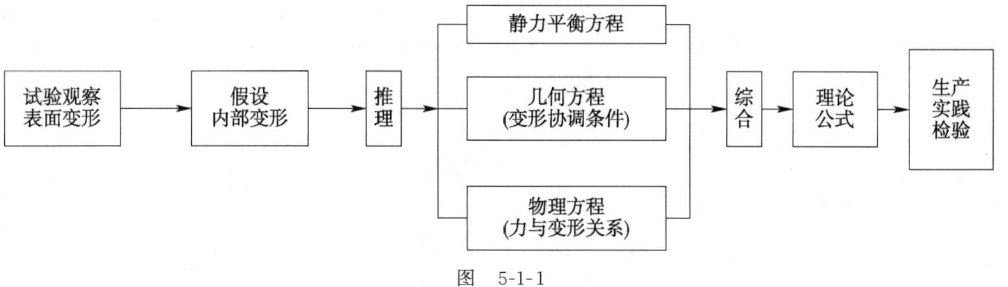

图 5-1-1

(二)分析问题和解决问题

分析问题和解决问题思路如图 5-1-2 所示。

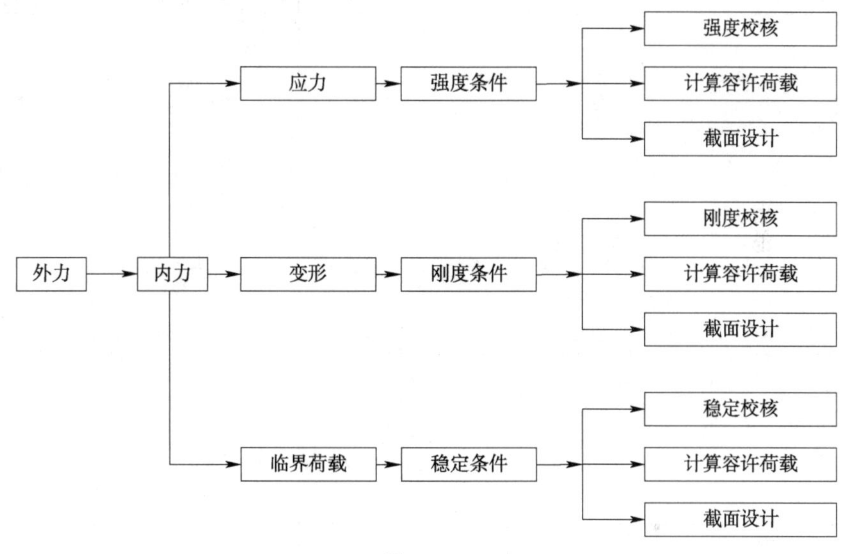

图 5-1-2

二、杆的四种基本变形

杆的四种基本变形见表 5-1-1。

杆的四种基本变形 表 5-1-1

类型	轴向拉伸(压缩)	剪　切	扭　转	平面弯曲	
外力特点					
横截面内力	轴力 N 等于截面一侧所有轴向外力代数和	剪力 Q 等于 P	扭矩 T 等于截面一侧对 x 轴外力偶矩代数和	弯矩 M 等于截面一侧外力对截面形心力矩代数和	剪力 Q 等于截面一侧所有竖向外力代数和

类型	轴向拉伸(压缩)	剪 切	扭 转	平面弯曲	
应力分布情况	均布	假设均布	线性分布	线性分布	抛物线分布
应力公式	$\sigma=\frac{N}{A}$	$\tau=\frac{Q}{A_s}$ $\sigma_{bs}=\frac{P_{bs}}{A_{bs}}$	$\tau_\rho=\frac{T}{I_p}\rho$	$\sigma=\frac{M}{I_z}y$	$\tau=\frac{QS_z^*}{bI_z}$
强度条件	$\sigma_{max}=\frac{N_{max}}{A}\leqslant[\sigma]$	$\tau=\frac{Q}{A_s}\leqslant[\tau]$ $\sigma_{bs}=\frac{P_{bs}}{A_{bs}}\leqslant[\sigma_{bs}]$	$\tau_{max}=\frac{T_{max}}{W_p}\leqslant[\tau]$	$\sigma_{max}=\frac{M_{max}}{W_z}\leqslant[\sigma]$	$\tau_{max}=\frac{Q_{max}S_{zmax}^*}{bI_z}\leqslant[\tau]$
变形公式	$\Delta l=\frac{Nl}{EA}$		$\Phi=\frac{Tl}{GI_p}$	$f_c=\frac{5ql^4}{384EI_z}$	$\theta_A=\frac{ql^3}{24EI_z}$
刚度条件			$\varphi_{max}=\frac{T_{max}}{GI_p}\leqslant[\varphi]$	$\frac{f_{max}}{l}\leqslant\left[\frac{f}{l}\right]$	$\theta_{max}\leqslant[\theta]$
应变能	$U=\frac{N^2l}{2EA}$		$U=\frac{T^2l}{2GI_p}$	纯弯 $U=\frac{M^2l}{2EI_z}$	非纯弯 $U=\int_l\frac{M^2(x)}{2EI_z}dx$

三、材料的力学性质

在表 5-1-1 所列的强度条件中，为确保构件不致因强度不足而破坏，应使其最大工作应力 σ_{max} 不超过材料的某个限值。显然，该限值应小于材料的极限应力 σ_u，可规定为极限应力 σ_u 的若干分之一，并称之为材料的许用应力，以[σ](或[τ])表示，即

$$[\sigma]=\frac{\sigma_u}{n} \tag{5-1-1}$$

式中，n 是一个大于 1 的系数，称为安全系数，其数值通常由设计规范规定；而极限应力 σ_u 则要通过材料的力学性能试验才能确定。这里主要介绍典型的塑性材料——低碳钢和典型的脆性材料——铸铁在常温、静载下的力学性能。

(一)低碳钢材料拉伸和压缩时的力学性质

低碳钢(通常将含碳量在 0.3%以下的钢称为低碳钢，也叫软钢)材料拉伸和压缩时的 σ-ε 曲

线如图 5-1-3 所示。

从图 5-1-3 中拉伸时的 σ-ε 曲线可看出，整个拉伸过程可分为以下四个阶段。

1. 弹性阶段（Ob 段）

在该段中的直线段（Oa）称线弹性段，其斜率即为弹性模量 E，对应的最高应力值 σ_p 为比例极限。在该段应力范围（即 $\sigma \leqslant \sigma_p$）内，虎克定律 $\sigma = E\varepsilon$ 成立。而 ab 段，即为非线性弹性段，在该段内所产生的应变仍是弹性的，但它与应力已不成正比。b 点相对应的应力 σ_e 称为弹性极限。

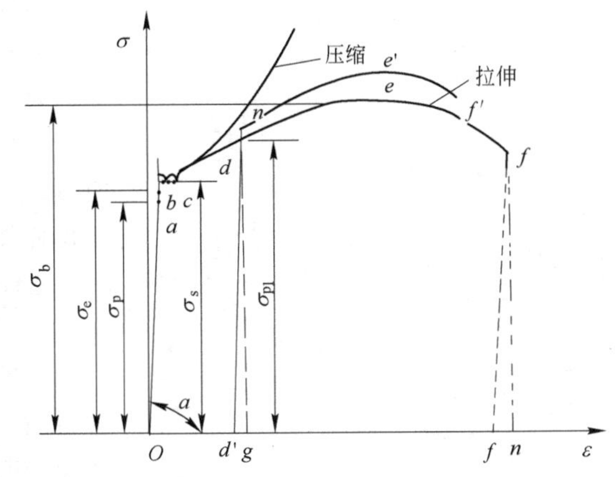

图 5-1-3　低碳钢拉伸、压缩的力学性质

2. 屈服阶段（bc 段）

该段内应力基本上不变，但应变却在迅速增长，而且在该段内所产生的应变成分，除弹性应变外，还包含了明显的塑性变形，该段的应力最低点 σ_s 称为屈服极限。这时，试件上原光滑表面将会出现与轴线大致成 45°的滑移线，这是由于试件材料在 45°的斜截面上存在着最大剪应力而引起的。对于塑性材料来说，由于屈服时所产生的显著的塑性变形将会严重地影响其正常工作，故 σ_s 是衡量塑性材料强度的一个重要指标。对于无明显屈服阶段的其他塑性材料，工程上将产生 0.2%塑性应变时的应力作为名义屈服极限，并用 $\sigma_{0.2}$ 表示。

3. 强化阶段（ce 段）

在该段，应力又随应变增大而增大，故称强化。该段中的最高点 e 所对应的应力乃材料所能承受的最大应力 σ_b，称为强度极限，它是衡量材料强度（特别是脆性材料）的另一重要指标。在强化阶段中，绝大部分的变形是塑性变形，并发生“冷作硬化”的现象。

4. 局部变形阶段（ef 段）

在应力到达 e 点之前，试件标距内的变形是均匀的；但当到达 e 点后，试件的变形就开始集中于某一较弱的局部范围内进行，该处截面纵向急剧伸长，横向显著收缩，形成“颈缩”；最后至 f 点试件被拉断。

试件拉断后，可测得以下两个反映材料塑性性能的指标。

（1）延伸率

$$\delta = \frac{l_1 - l_0}{l_0} \times 100\% \tag{5-1-2}$$

式中：l_0——试件原长；

l_1——试件拉断后的长度。

工程上规定 $\delta \geqslant 5\%$的材料称为塑性材料，$\delta < 5\%$的称为脆性材料。

（2）截面收缩率

$$\psi = \frac{A_0 - A_1}{A_0} \times 100\% \tag{5-1-3}$$

式中：A_0——变形前的试件横截面面积；

A_1——试件拉断后的最小截面积。

对比低碳钢压缩时与拉伸时的 σ-ε 曲线可知，低碳钢压缩时的弹性模量 E、比例极限 σ_p 和

屈服极限 σ_s 与拉伸时大致相同。

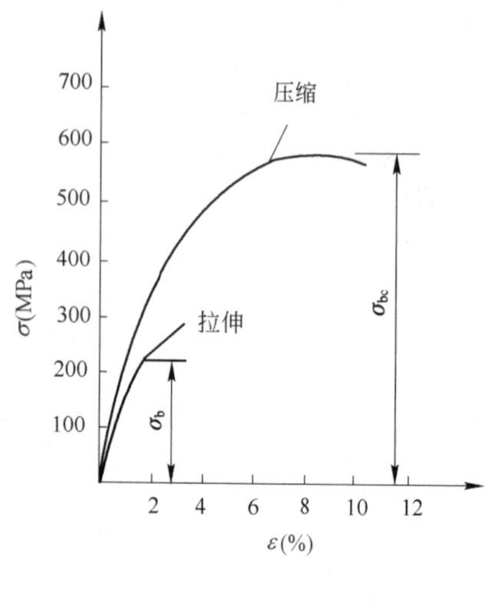

图 5-1-4

（二）铸铁拉伸与压缩时的力学性质

铸铁拉伸与压缩时的 σ-ε 曲线如图 5-1-4 所示。

从铸铁拉伸时的 σ-ε 曲线中可以看出，它没有明显的直线部分。因其拉断前的应变很小，因此工程上通常取其 σ-ε 曲线的一条割线的斜率，作为其弹性模量。它没有屈服阶段，也没有颈缩现象（故衡量铸铁拉伸强度的唯一指标就是它被拉断时的最大应力 σ_b），在较小的拉应力作用下即被拉断，且其延伸率很小，故铸铁是一种典型的脆性材料。

铸铁压缩时的 σ-ε 曲线与拉伸相比，可看出这类材料的抗压能力要比抗拉能力强得多，其塑性变形也较为明显。破坏断口为斜断面，这表明试件是因 τ_{max} 的作用而剪坏的。

综上所述，对于塑性材料制成的杆，通常取屈服极限 σ_s（或名义屈服极限 $\sigma_{0.2}$）作为极限应力 σ_u 的值；而对脆性材料制成的杆，应该取强度极限 σ_b 作为极限应力 σ_u 的值。

习　题

5-1-1　在低碳钢拉伸实验中，冷作硬化现象发生在（　　）。

A. 弹性阶段

B. 屈服阶段

C. 强化阶段

D. 局部变形阶段

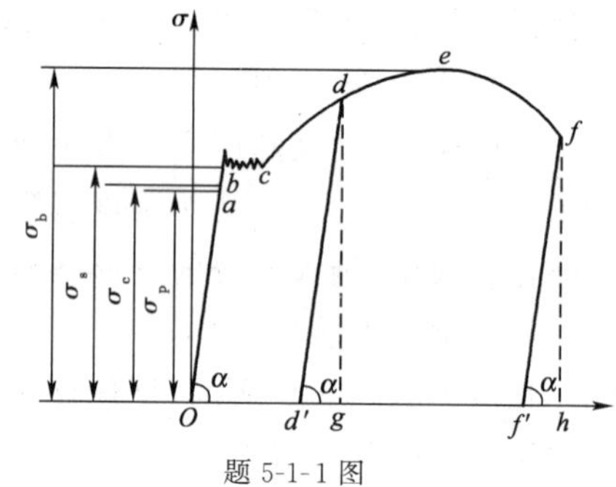

题 5-1-1 图

第二节　轴向拉伸与压缩

一、轴向拉伸与压缩的概念

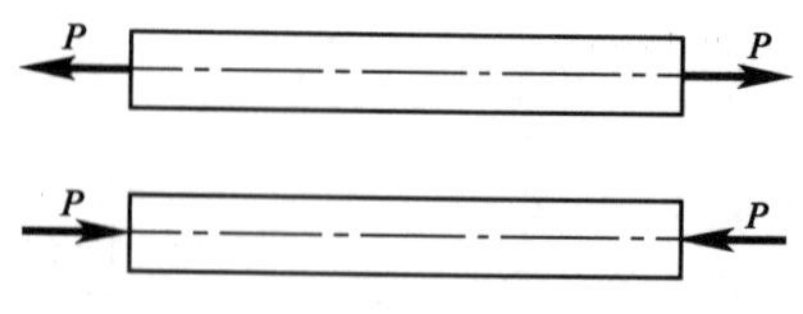

图 5-2-1　轴向拉压杆的力学模型

P-轴向拉力或压力

（一）力学模型

轴向拉压杆的力学模型如图 5-2-1 所示。

（二）受力特征

作用于杆两端外力的合力，大小相等、方向相反，并沿杆件轴线作用。

（三）变形特征

杆件主要产生轴线方向的均匀伸长（缩短）。

二、轴向拉伸(压缩)杆横截面上的内力

(一)内力

由外力作用而引起的构件内部各部分之间的相互作用力。

(二)截面法

截面法是求内力的一般方法,用截面法求内力的步骤如下。

(1)截开。在需求内力的截面处,假想地沿该截面将构件截分为二。

(2)代替。任取一部分为研究对象,称为脱离体。用内力代替弃去部分对脱离体的作用。

(3)平衡。对脱离体列写平衡条件,求解未知内力。

截面法示意图如图 5-2-2 所示。

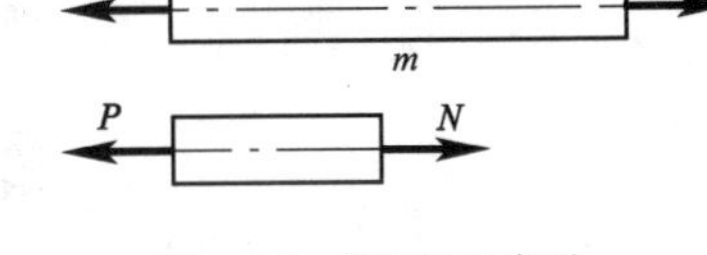

图 5-2-2 截面法示意图

(三)轴力

轴向拉压杆横截面上的内力,其作用线必定与杆轴线相重合,称为轴力,以 N 表示。轴力 N 规定以拉力为正,压力为负。

(四)轴力图

轴力图表示沿杆件轴线各横截面上轴力变化规律的图线。

【例 5-2-1】 试作如图 a)所示等直杆的轴力图。

解 先考虑外力平衡,求出支反力 $R=10\text{kN}$

显然 $N_{AB}=10\text{kN}$, $N_{BC}=50\text{kN}$, $N_{CD}=-5\text{kN}$, $N_{DE}=20\text{kN}$

由图 b)可见,某截面上外力的大小等于该截面两侧内力的变化。

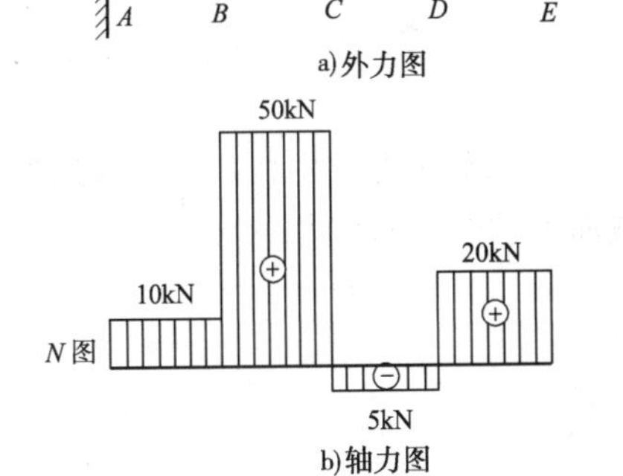

例 5-2-1 图

三、轴向拉压杆横截面上的应力

分布规律:轴向拉压杆横截面上的应力垂直于截面,为正应力,且正应力在整个横截面上均匀分布,如图 5-2-3 所示。

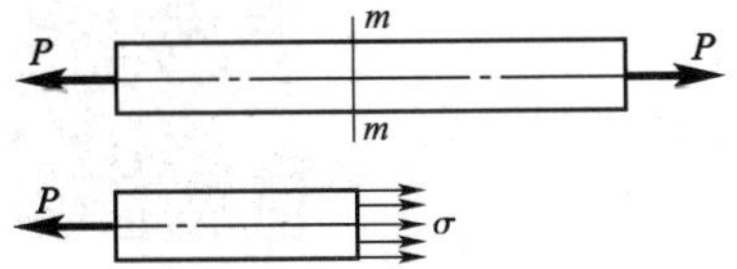

图 5-2-3 正应力在整个横截面上均匀分布

正应力公式

$$\sigma=\frac{N}{A} \tag{5-2-1}$$

式中:N——轴力(N);

A——横截面面积(m^2)。

应力单位为 N/m^2,即 Pa,也常用 MPa,$1\text{MPa}=10^6\text{Pa}=1\text{N/mm}^2$。

四、轴向拉压杆斜截面上的应力

斜截面上的应力均匀分布,如图 5-2-4 所示,其总应力及应力分量如下。

总应力

$$p_\alpha=\frac{N}{A_\alpha}=\sigma_0\cos\alpha \tag{5-2-2}$$

正应力

$$\sigma = p_\alpha \cos\alpha = \sigma_0 \cos^2\alpha \tag{5-2-3}$$

剪应力

$$\tau_\alpha = p_\alpha \sin\alpha = \frac{\sigma_0}{2}\sin 2\alpha \tag{5-2-4}$$

上述式中：α——由横截面外法线转至斜截面外法线的夹角，以逆时针转动为正；

A_α——斜截面 m-m 的截面积；

σ_0——横截面上的正应力。

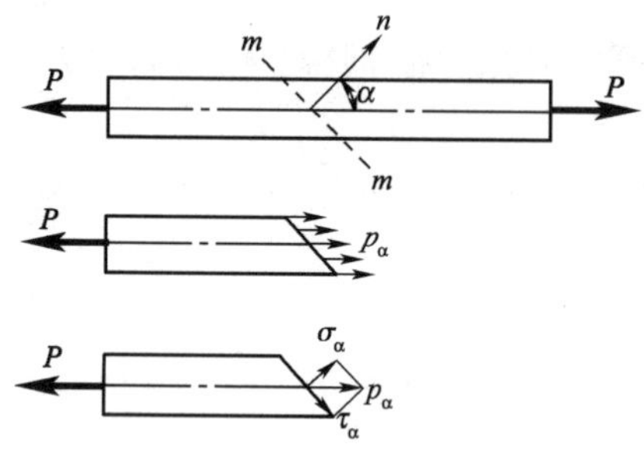

图 5-2-4　斜截面上的应力均匀分布

σ_α 拉应力为正，压应力为负。τ_α 以其对截面内一点产生顺时针力矩时为正，反之为负。

轴向拉压杆中最大正应力发生在 $\alpha=0°$ 的横截面上，最小正应力发生在 $\alpha=90°$ 的纵截面上，其值分别为

$$\sigma_{\alpha\max} = \sigma_0$$

$$\sigma_{\alpha\min} = 0$$

最大剪应力发生在 $\alpha=\pm45°$ 的斜截面上，最小剪应力发生在 $\alpha=0°$ 的横截面和 $\alpha=90°$ 的纵截面上，其值分别为

$$|\tau_\alpha|_{\max} = \frac{\sigma_0}{2}$$

$$|\tau_\alpha|_{\min} = 0$$

五、强度条件

（一）许用应力

材料正常工作容许采用的最高应力，由极限应力除以安全系数求得。

1. 塑性材料

$$[\sigma] = \frac{\sigma_s}{n_s} \tag{5-2-5}$$

2. 脆性材料

$$[\sigma] = \frac{\sigma_b}{n_b} \tag{5-2-6}$$

上两式中：σ_s——屈服极限；

σ_b——抗拉强度；

n_s、n_b——安全系数。

（二）强度条件

构件的最大工作应力不得超过材料的许用应力。轴向拉压杆的强度条件为

$$\sigma_{max}=\frac{N_{max}}{A}\leqslant[\sigma] \tag{5-2-7}$$

强度计算的三类问题：

(1)强度校核：

$$\sigma_{max}=\frac{N_{max}}{A}\leqslant[\sigma]$$

(2)截面设计：

$$A\geqslant\frac{N_{max}}{[\sigma]}$$

(3)确定许可荷载 $N_{max}\leqslant[\sigma]A$，再根据平衡条件，由 N_{max} 计算$[P]$。

【例 5-2-2】 图示结构的两杆许用应力均为$[\sigma]$，杆 1 的面积为 A，杆 2 的面积为 $2A$，则该结构的许用载荷是：

A. $[F]=A[\sigma]$

B. $[F]=2A[\sigma]$

C. $[F]=3A[\sigma]$

D. $[F]=4A[\sigma]$

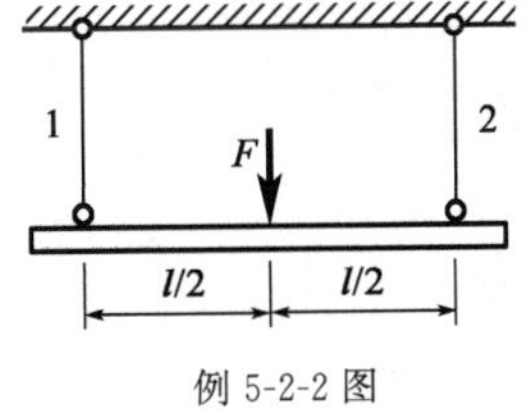

例 5-2-2 图

解 此题受力是对称的，故 $F_1=F_2=\frac{F}{2}$

由杆 1，得 $\sigma_1=\frac{F_1}{A_1}=\frac{\frac{F}{2}}{A}=\frac{F}{2A}\leqslant[\sigma]$，故 $F\leqslant2A[\sigma]$

由杆 2，得 $\sigma_2=\frac{F_2}{A_2}=\frac{\frac{F}{2}}{2A}=\frac{F}{4A}\leqslant[\sigma]$，故 $F\leqslant4A[\sigma]$

从两者取最小的，所以$[F]=2A[\sigma]$。

答案：B

六、轴向拉压杆的变形——虎克定律

(一)轴向拉压杆的变形

杆件在轴向拉伸时，轴向伸长，横向缩短，见图 5-2-5；而在轴向压缩时，轴向缩短，横向伸长。

轴向变形

$$\Delta L=L'-L \tag{5-2-8}$$

轴向线应变

$$\varepsilon=\frac{\Delta L}{L} \tag{5-2-9}$$

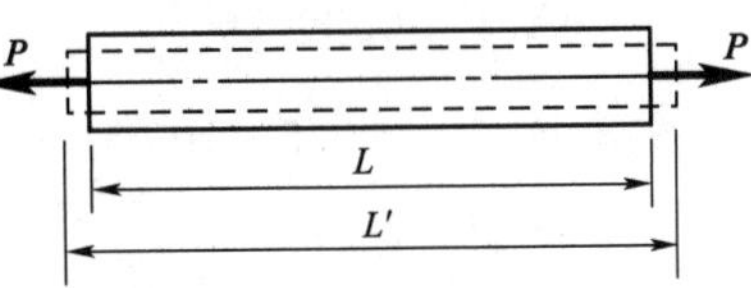

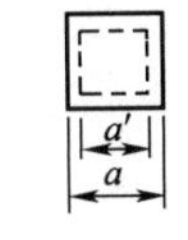

图 5-2-5 轴向拉杆的变形

横向变形

$$\Delta a=a'-a \tag{5-2-10}$$

横向线应变

$$\varepsilon'=\frac{\Delta a}{a} \tag{5-2-11}$$

(二)虎克定律

当应力不超过材料比例极限时，应力与应变成正比，即

$$\sigma=E\varepsilon \tag{5-2-12}$$

式中：E——材料的弹性模量。

或用轴力及杆件变形量表示为

$$\Delta L=\frac{NL}{EA} \tag{5-2-13}$$

式中：EA——杆的抗拉(压)刚度，表示杆件抵抗拉、压弹性变形的能力。

【例 5-2-3】 变截面杆 AC 受力如图所示。已知材料弹性模量为 E，杆 BC 段的截面积为 A，杆 AB 段的截面积为 $2A$，则杆 C 截面的轴向位移是：

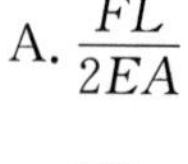

A. $\frac{FL}{2EA}$

B. $\frac{FL}{EA}$

C. $\frac{2FL}{EA}$

D. $\frac{3FL}{EA}$

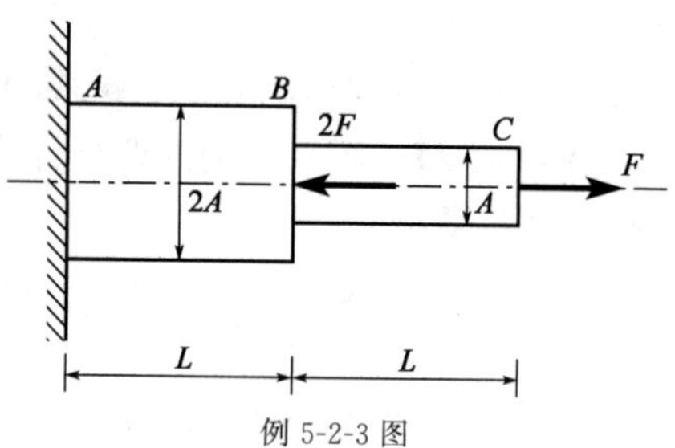

例 5-2-3 图

解 用直接法求轴力，可得：$N_{AB}=-F, N_{BC}=F$

杆 C 截面的位移是 $\delta_C=\Delta l_{AB}+\Delta l_{BC}=\frac{-F\cdot l}{E\cdot 2A}+\frac{Fl}{EA}=\frac{Fl}{2EA}$。

答案：A

(三)泊松比

当应力不超过材料的比例极限时，横向线应变 ε' 与纵向线应变 ε 之比的绝对值，即为泊松比，即

$$\mu=\left|\frac{\varepsilon'}{\varepsilon}\right|=-\frac{\varepsilon'}{\varepsilon} \tag{5-2-14}$$

泊松比 μ 是材料的弹性常数之一，无量纲。

【例 5-2-4】 已知拉杆横截面积，弹性模量，横向变形系数，轴向拉力，拉杆的横向应变是：

A. $\varepsilon'=0.3\times10^{-3}$

B. $\varepsilon'=-0.3\times10^{-3}$

C. $\varepsilon'=10^{-3}$

D. $\varepsilon'=-10^{-3}$

例 5-2-4 图

解 $\varepsilon'=-\mu\varepsilon=-\mu\frac{\sigma}{E}=-\mu\frac{F_N}{AE}$

$$=-0.3\frac{20\times10^3\,N}{100mm^2\times200\times10^3\,MPa}=-0.3\times10^{-3}$$

答案：B

习　题

5-2-1　等截面杆轴向受力如图所示。杆的最大轴力是(　　)kN。

A. 8　　B. 5　　C. 3　　D. 13

5-2-2　如图所示，拉杆承受轴向拉力 **P** 的作用，设斜截面 $m-m$ 的面积为 A，则 $\sigma=P/A$ 为(　　)。

A. 横截面上的正应力　　B. 斜截面上的正应力

C. 斜截面上的应力　　D. 斜截面上的剪应力

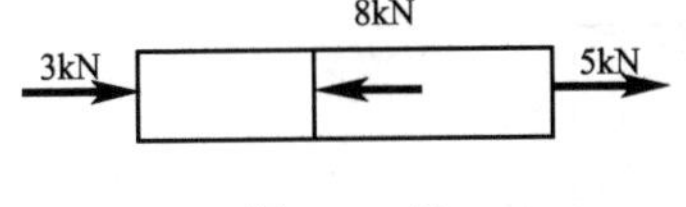

题 5-2-1 图

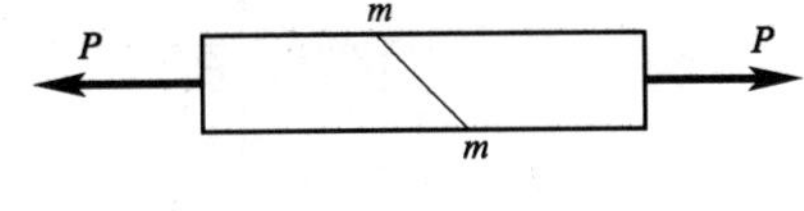

题 5-2-2 图

5-2-3　两拉杆的材料和所受拉力都相同，且均处在弹性范围内，若两杆长度相等，横截面面积 $A_1>A_2$，则(　　)。

A. $\Delta l_1<\Delta l_2$，$\varepsilon_1=\varepsilon_2$　　B. $\Delta l_1=\Delta l_2$，$\varepsilon_1<\varepsilon_2$

C. $\Delta l_1<\Delta l_2$，$\varepsilon_1<\varepsilon_2$　　D. $\Delta l_1=\Delta l_2$，$\varepsilon_1=\varepsilon_2$

5-2-4　等直杆的受力情况如图所示，则杆内最大拉力 N_1 和最大压力 N_2 分别为(　　)。

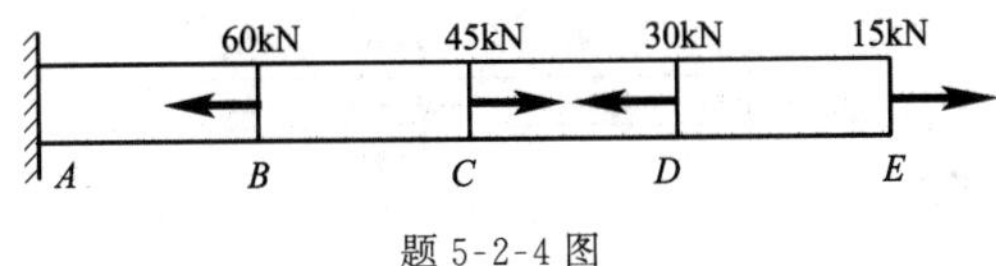

题 5-2-4 图

A. $N_1=60\text{kN}$，$N_2=15\text{kN}$　　B. $N_1=60\text{kN}$，$N_2=-15\text{kN}$

C. $N_1=30\text{kN}$，$N_2=-30\text{kN}$　　D. $N_1=90\text{kN}$，$N_2=-60\text{kN}$

5-2-5　如图所示，刚梁 AB 由杆 1 和杆 2 支承。已知两杆的材料相同，长度不等，横截面面积分别为 A_1 和 A_2，若荷载 **P** 使刚梁平行下移，则其截面面积为(　　)。

A. $A_1<A_2$　　B. $A_1=A_2$

C. $A_1>A_2$　　D. A_1、A_2 为任意

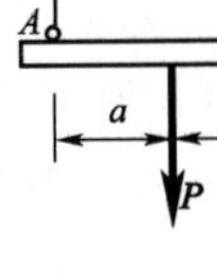

题 5-2-5 图

5-2-6　如图所示变截面杆中，AB 段、BC 段的轴力为(　　)。

A. $N_{AB}=-10\text{kN}$，$N_{BC}=4\text{kN}$

B. $N_{AB}=6\text{kN}$，$N_{BC}=4\text{kN}$

C. $N_{AB}=-6\text{kN}$，$N_{BC}=4\text{kN}$

D. $N_{AB}=10\text{kN}$，$N_{BC}=4\text{kN}$

5-2-7　变形杆如图所示，其中在 BC 段内(　　)。

A. 有位移，无变形　　B. 有变形，无位移

C. 既有位移，又有变形　　D. 既无位移，又无变形

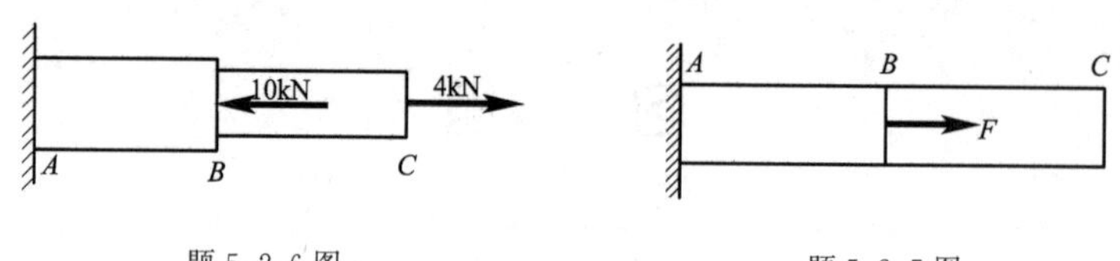

题 5-2-6 图　　　　　　　　　　　　　　题 5-2-7 图

5-2-8　已知如图所示等直杆的轴力图（N 图），则该杆相应的荷载图如（　　）所示。（图中集中荷载单位均为 kN，分布荷载单位均为 kN/m）

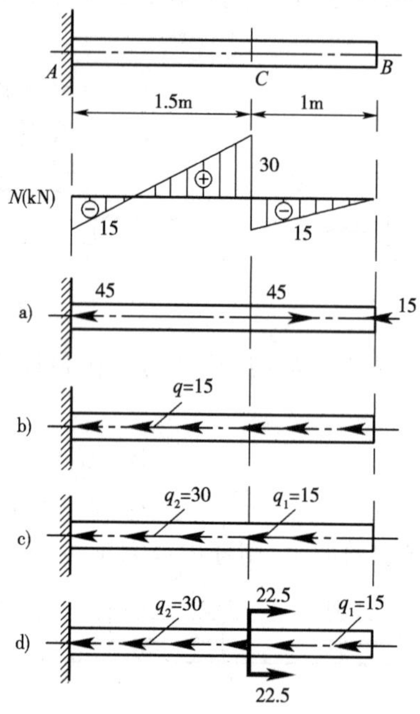

题 5-2-8 图

A. 图 a)　　　　B. 图 b)　　　　C. 图 c)　　　　D. 图 d)

5-2-9　有一横截面面积为 A 的圆截面杆件受轴向拉力作用，在其他条件不变时，若将其横截面改为面积仍为 A 的空心圆，则杆为（　　）。

A. 内力、应力、轴向变形均增大　　B. 内力、应力、轴向变形均减少

C. 内力、应力、轴向变形均不变　　D. 内力、应力不变、轴向变形增大

5-2-10　如图所示桁架，在结点 C 沿水平方向受 P 力作用。各杆的抗拉刚度相等。若结点 C 的铅垂位移以 V_C 表示，BC 杆的轴力以 N_{BC} 表示，则（　　）。

A. $N_{BC}=0, V_C=0$　　B. $N_{BC}=0, V_C\neq0$

C. $N_{BC}\neq0, V_C=0$　　D. $N_{BC}\neq0, V_C\neq0$

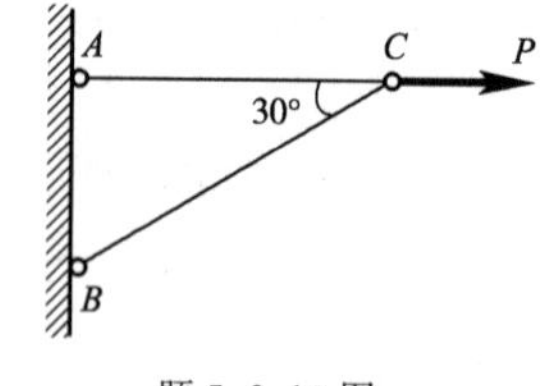

题 5-2-10 图

第三节　剪切和挤压

一、剪切的实用计算

（一）剪切的概念

力学模型如图 5-3-1 所示。

(1)受力特征。构件上受到一对大小相等、方向相反,作用线相距很近,且与构件轴线垂直的力作用。

(2)变形特征。构件沿两力的分界面有发生相对错动的趋势。

(3)剪切面。构件将发生相对错动的面。

(4)剪力 Q。剪切面上的内力,其作用线与剪切面平行。

(二)剪切实用计算

(1)名义剪应力。假定剪应力沿剪切面是均匀分布的,若 A_Q 为剪切面面积,Q 为剪力,则

$$\tau=\frac{Q}{A_Q} \tag{5-3-1}$$

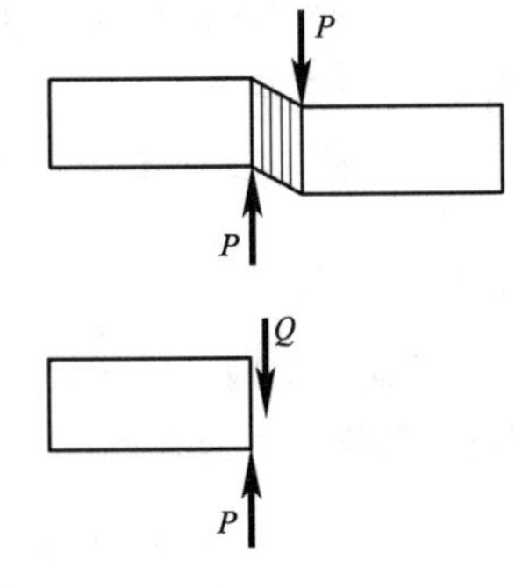

图 5-3-1　剪切的力学模型

(2)许用剪应力。按实际构件的受力方式,用试验的方法求得名义剪切极限应力 τ^0,再除以安全系数 n。

(3)剪切强度条件。剪切面上的工作剪应力不得超过材料的许用剪应力

$$\tau=\frac{Q}{A_Q}\leqslant[\tau] \tag{5-3-2}$$

【例 5-3-1】 冲床在钢板上冲一圆孔(见图),圆孔直径 $d=100$mm,钢板的厚度 $t=10$mm 钢板的剪切强度极限 $\tau_b=300$MPa,需要的冲压力 F 是:

A. $F=300\pi$kN

B. $F=3\ 000\pi$kN

C. $F=2\ 500\pi$kN

D. $F=7\ 500\pi$kN

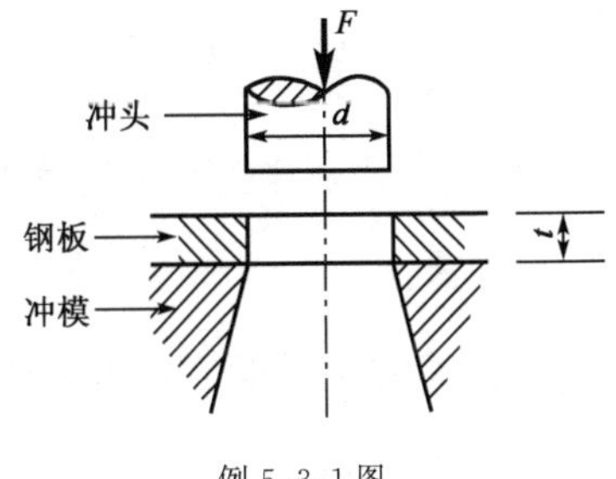

例 5-3-1 图

解　被冲断的钢板的剪切面是一个圆柱面,其面积 $A_Q=\pi dt$,根据钢板破坏的条件:

$$\tau_Q=\frac{Q}{A_Q}=\frac{F}{\pi dt}=\tau_b$$

可得 $F=\pi dt\tau_b=\pi\times100\text{mm}\times10\text{mm}\times300\text{MPa}=300\pi\times10^3\text{N}=300\pi\text{kN}$

答案:A

二、挤压的实用计算

(一)挤压的概念

(1)挤压。两构件相互接触的局部承压作用。

(2)挤压面。两构件间相互接触的面。

(3)挤压力 P_{bs}。承压接触面上的总压力。

(二)挤压实用计算

(1)名义挤压应力。假设挤压力在名义挤压面上均匀分布,即

$$\sigma_{bs}=\frac{P_{bs}}{A_{bs}} \tag{5-3-3}$$

式中:A_{bs}——名义挤压面面积。

当挤压面为平面时,名义挤压面面积等于实际的承压接触面面积;当挤压面为曲面时,则名义挤压面面积取为实际承压接触面在垂直挤压力方向的投影面积。

(2)许用挤压应力。根据直接试验结果，按照名义挤压应力公式计算名义极限挤压应力，再除以安全系数。

(3)挤压强度条件。挤压面上的工作挤压应力不得超过材料的许用挤压应力，即

$$\sigma_{bs}=\frac{P_{bs}}{A_{bs}}\leqslant[\sigma_{bs}] \tag{5-3-4}$$

【例 5-3-2】 已知铆钉的许用切应力为$[\tau]$，许用挤压应力为$[\sigma_{bs}]$，钢板的厚度为 t，则图示铆钉直径 d 与钢板厚度 t 的合理关系是：

A. $d=\frac{8t[\sigma_{bs}]}{\pi[\tau]}$　　B. $d=\frac{4t[\sigma_{bs}]}{\pi[\tau]}$

C. $d=\frac{\pi[\tau]}{8t[\sigma_{bs}]}$　　D. $d=\frac{\pi[\tau]}{4t[\sigma_{bs}]}$

例 5-3-2 图

解 由铆钉的剪切强度条件：$\tau=\frac{F_s}{A_s}=\frac{F}{\frac{\pi}{4}d^2}=[\tau]$，

可得：

$$\frac{4F}{\pi d^2}=[\tau] \tag{①}$$

由铆钉的挤压强度条件：

$$\sigma_{bs}=\frac{F_{bs}}{A_{bs}}=\frac{F}{dt}=[\sigma_{bs}]\text{，可得：}\frac{F}{dt}=[\sigma_{bs}] \tag{②}$$

d 与 t 的合理关系应使两式同时成立，②式除以①式，得到$\frac{\pi d}{4t}=\frac{[\sigma_{bs}]}{[\tau]}$，即 $d=\frac{4t[\sigma_{bs}]}{\pi[\tau]}$。

答案：B

三、剪应力互等定理与剪切虎克定律

(一)纯剪切

若单元体各个侧面上只有剪应力而无正应力，称为纯剪切。

纯剪切引起剪应变 γ，即相互垂直的两线段间角度的改变。

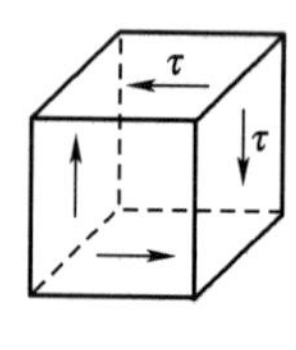

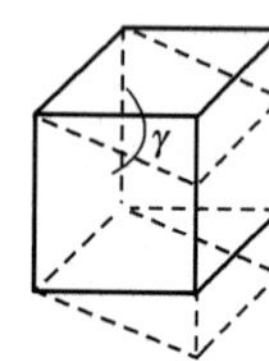

图 5-3-2　纯剪切单元体

(二)剪应力互等定理

在互相垂直的两个平面上，垂直于两平面交线的剪应力，总是大小相等，且共同指向或背离这一交线(见图 5-3-2)，即

$$\tau=-\tau' \tag{5-3-5}$$

(三)剪切虎克定律

当剪应力不超过材料的剪切比例极限时，剪应力 τ 与剪应变 γ 成正比，即

$$\tau=G\gamma \tag{5-3-6}$$

式中：G——材料的剪切弹性模量。

对各向同性材料，E、G、μ 间只有两个独立常数，即

$$G=\frac{E}{2(1+\mu)} \tag{5-3-7}$$

习　题

5-3-1　钢板用两个铆钉固定在支座上，铆钉直径为 d，在图示荷载下，铆钉的最大切应力

是(　　)。

A. $\tau_{\max}=\dfrac{4F}{\pi d^2}$　　　　B. $\tau_{\max}=\dfrac{8F}{\pi d^2}$

C. $\tau_{\max}=\dfrac{12F}{\pi d^2}$　　　　D. $\tau_{\max}=\dfrac{2F}{\pi d^2}$

5-3-2　螺钉受力如图所示,一直螺钉和钢板的材料相同,拉伸许用应力$[\sigma]$是剪切许可应力$[\tau]$的2倍,即$[\sigma]=2[\tau]$,钢板厚度t是螺钉头高度h的1.5倍,则螺钉直径d的合理值为(　　)。

A. $d=2h$　　　　B. $d=0.5h$

C. $d^2=2Dt$　　　　D. $d^2=Dt$

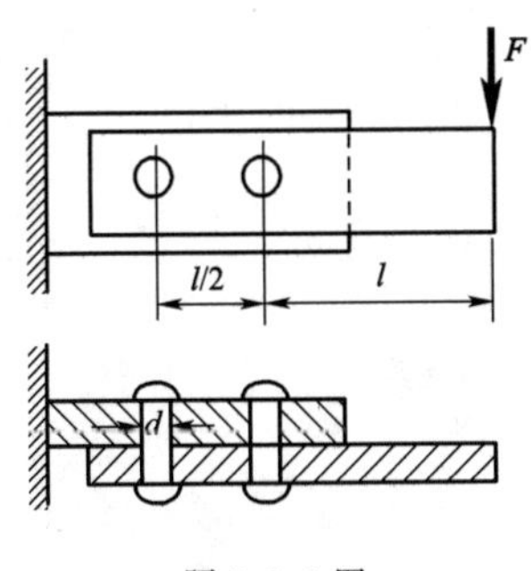

题5-3-1图

题5-3-2图

5-3-3　图示连接件,两端受拉力$\boldsymbol{P}$作用,接头的挤压面积为(　　)。

A. ab　　B. cb　　C. lb　　D. lc

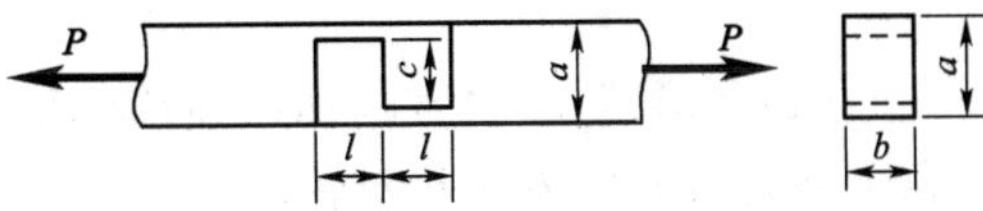

题5-3-3图

5-3-4　如图所示,在平板和受拉螺栓之间垫上一个垫圈,可以提高(　　)。

A. 螺栓的拉伸强度　　　　B. 螺栓的剪切强度

C. 螺栓的挤压强度　　　　D. 平板的挤压强度

5-3-5　图示铆接件,设钢板和铝铆钉的挤压应力分别为$\sigma_{jy,1}$、$\sigma_{jy,2}$,则两者的大小关系是(　　)。

A. $\sigma_{jy,1}<\sigma_{jy,2}$　　B. $\sigma_{jy,1}=\sigma_{jy,2}$　　C. $\sigma_{jy,1}>\sigma_{jy,2}$　　D. 不确定的

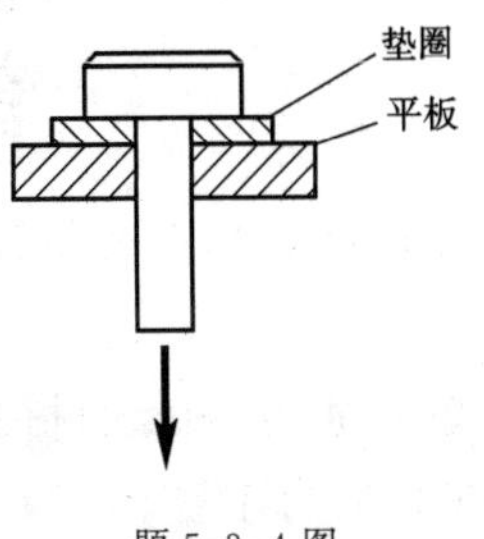

题5-3-4图

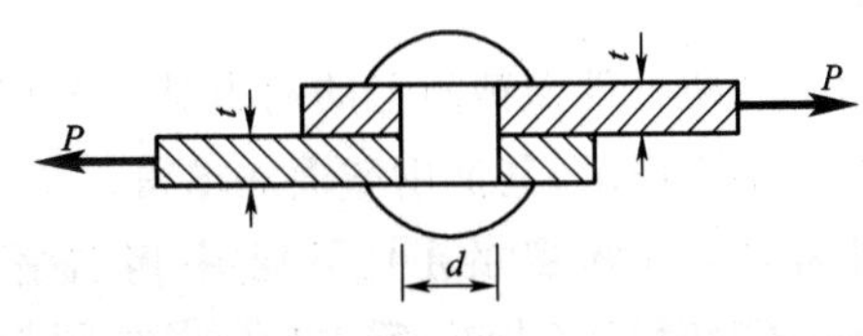

题5-3-5图

5-3-6　如图所示,插销穿过水平放置平板上的圆孔,在其下端受有一拉力$\boldsymbol{P}$,该插销的剪

切面积和挤压面积分别为(　　)。

A. $\pi dh,\frac{1}{4}\pi D^2$

B. $\pi dh,\frac{1}{4}\pi(D^2-d^2)$

C. $\pi Dh,\frac{1}{4}\pi D^2$

D. $\pi Dh,\frac{1}{4}\pi(D^2-d^2)$

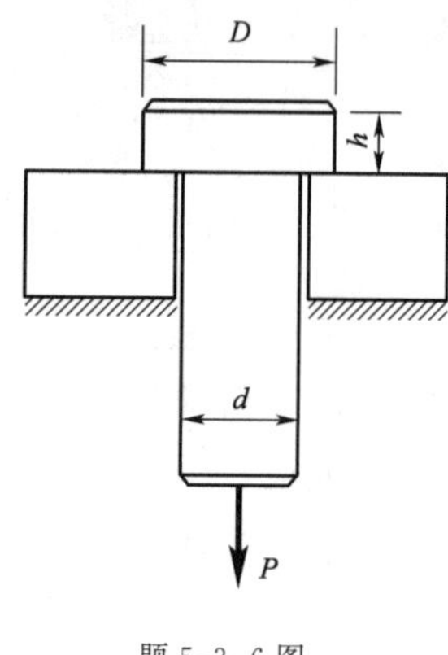

题 5-3-6 图

5-3-7　要用冲床在厚度为 t 的钢板上冲出一圆孔,则冲力大小(　　)。

A. 与圆孔直径的平方成正比

B. 与圆孔直径的平方根成正比

C. 与圆孔直径成正比

D. 与圆孔直径的三次方成正比

第四节　扭　　转

一、扭转的概念

(一)扭转的力学模型

扭转的力学模型,如图 5-4-1 所示。

(1)受力特征。杆两端受到一对力偶矩相等,转向相反,作用平面与杆件轴线相垂直的外力偶作用。

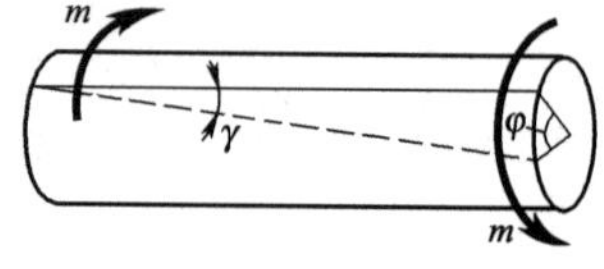

图 5-4-1　扭转力学模型

(2)变形特征。杆件表面纵向线变成螺旋线,即杆件任意两横截面绕杆件轴线发生相对转动。

(3)扭转角 φ。杆件任意两横截面间相对转动的角度。

(二)外力偶矩的计算

轴所传递的功率、转速与外力偶矩(kN · m)间有如下关系

$$m=9.55\frac{P}{n} \tag{5-4-1}$$

式中:P——传递功率(kW);

n——转速(r/min)。

二、扭矩及扭矩图

(1)扭矩。受扭杆件横截面上的内力是一个在截面平面内的力偶,其力偶矩称为扭矩,用 T 表示,如图 5-4-2 所示,其值用截面法求得。

(2)扭矩符号。扭矩 T 的正负号规定,以右手法则表示扭矩矢量,若矢量的指向与截面外向法线的指向一致时扭矩为正,反之为负。如图 5-4-2 所示,扭矩均为正号。

(3)扭矩图。表示沿杆件轴线各横截面上扭矩变化规律的图线。扭矩图实例见本节后习题 5-4-6。

三、圆杆扭转时的剪应力与强度条件

(一)横截面上的剪应力

(1)剪应力分布规律。横截面上任一点的剪应力,其方向垂直于该点所在的半径,其值与该点到圆心的距离成正比,如图 5-4-3 所示。

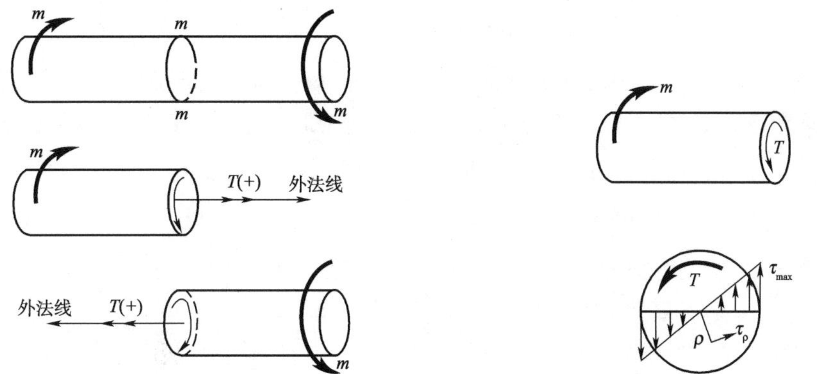

图 5-4-2　扭矩及其正负号规定

图 5-4-3　圆杆扭转时横截面上的剪应力

(2)剪应力计算公式。横截面上距圆心为 ρ 的任一点的剪应力 τ_ρ 为

$$\tau_\rho=\frac{T}{I_p}\rho \qquad (5\text{-}4\text{-}2)$$

横截面上的最大剪应力发生在横截面周边各点处,其值为

$$\tau_{\max}=\frac{T}{I_p}R=\frac{T}{W_p} \qquad (5\text{-}4\text{-}3)$$

(3)剪应力公式的讨论:

①公式适用于线弹性范围($\tau_{\max}\leqslant\tau_p$),小变形条件下的等截面实心或空心圆直杆。

②T 为所求截面上的扭矩。

③I_p 称为极惯性矩,W_p 称为抗扭截面系数,其值与截面尺寸有关。

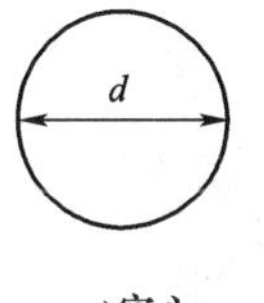

a)实心

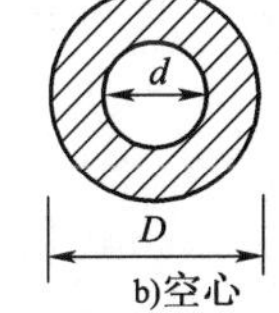

b)空心

图 5-4-4　圆截面

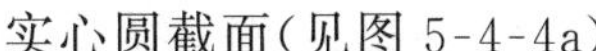

实心圆截面(见图 5-4-4a)

$$\left.\begin{aligned}I_p&=\frac{\pi d^4}{32}\\W_p&=\frac{\pi d^3}{16}\end{aligned}\right\} \qquad (5\text{-}4\text{-}4)$$

空心圆截面(见图 5-4-4b)

$$\left.\begin{aligned}I_p&=\frac{\pi D^4}{32}(1-\alpha^4)\\W_p&=\frac{\pi D^3}{16}(1-\alpha^4)\end{aligned}\right\} \qquad (5\text{-}4\text{-}5)$$

其中

$$\alpha=\frac{d}{D}$$

【**例 5-4-1**】 图示两根圆轴，横截面积相同，但分别为实心圆和空心圆。在相同的扭矩 T 作用下，两轴最大切应力的关系是：

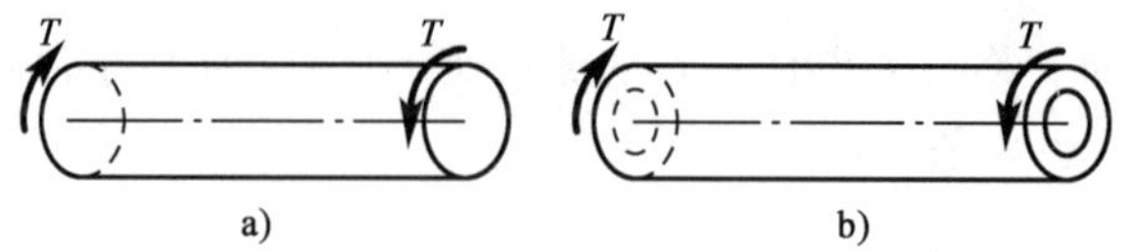

例 5-4-1 图

A. $\tau_a<\tau_b$　　B. $\tau_a=\tau_b$　　C. $\tau_a>\tau_b$　　D. 不能确定

解 设实心圆直径为 d，空心圆外径为 D，空心圆内外径之比为 α，因两者横截面积相同，故有 $\frac{\pi}{4}d^2=\frac{\pi}{4}D^2(1-\alpha^2)$，即 $d=D(1-\alpha^2)^{\frac{1}{2}}$。

$$\frac{\tau_a}{\tau_b}=\frac{\dfrac{T}{\dfrac{\pi}{16}d^3}}{\dfrac{T}{\dfrac{\pi}{16}D^3(1-\alpha^4)}}=\frac{D^3(1-\alpha^4)}{d^3}=\frac{D^3(1-\alpha^2)(1+\alpha^2)}{D^3(1-\alpha^2)(1-\alpha^2)^{\frac{1}{2}}}=\frac{1+\alpha^2}{\sqrt{1-\alpha^2}}>1$$

答案：C

（二）圆杆扭转时的强度条件

强度条件：圆杆扭转时横截面上的最大剪应力不得超过材料的许用剪应力，即

$$\tau_{max}=\frac{T_{max}}{W_p}\leqslant[\tau] \tag{5-4-6}$$

由强度条件可对受扭杆进行强度校核、截面设计和确定许可荷载三类问题的计算。

四、圆杆扭转时的变形及刚度条件

（一）圆杆的扭转变形计算

单位长度扭转角 θ(rad/m)

$$\theta=\frac{d\varphi}{dx}=\frac{T}{GI_p} \tag{5-4-7}$$

扭转角 φ(rad)

$$\varphi=\int_L\frac{T}{GI_p}dx \tag{5-4-8}$$

若在长度 L 内，T、G、I_p 均为常量时

$$\varphi=\frac{TL}{GI_p} \tag{5-4-9}$$

式(5-4-9)适用于线弹性范围，小变形下的等直圆杆。GI_p 表示圆杆抵抗扭转弹性变形的能力，称为抗扭刚度。

（二）圆杆扭转时的刚度条件

即刚度条件：圆杆扭转时的最大单位长度扭转角不得超过规定的许可值$[\theta]$(°/m)，即

$$\theta_{max}=\frac{T_{max}}{GI_p}\times\frac{180^\circ}{\pi}\leqslant[\theta] \tag{5-4-10}$$

由刚度条件，同样可对受扭圆杆进行刚度校核、截面设计和确定许可荷载三类问题的计算。

习　题

5-4-1　直径为 d 的实心圆轴受扭，为使扭转最大切应力减少一半，圆轴的直径应改为(　　)。

A. $2d$　　B. $0.5d$　　C. $\sqrt{2}d$　　D. $\sqrt[3]{2}d$

5-4-2　圆轴直径为 d，剪切弹性模量为 G，在外力作用下发生扭转变形，现测得单位长度扭转角为 θ，圆轴的最大切应力是(　　)。

A. $\tau=\frac{16\theta G}{\pi d^3}$　　B. $\tau=\theta G\frac{\pi d^3}{16}$　　C. $\tau=\theta Gd$　　D. $\tau=\frac{\theta Gd}{2}$

5-4-3　图 a)所示圆轴抗扭截面模量为 W_p，切变模量为 G，扭转变形后，圆轴表面 A 点处截取的单元体互相垂直的相邻边线改变了 γ 角，如图 b)所示。圆轴承受的扭矩 T 为(　　)。

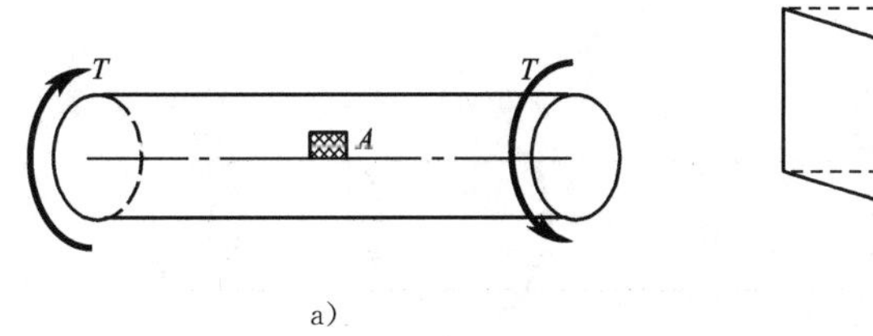

题 5-4-3 图

A. $T=G\gamma W_p$　　B. $T=\frac{G\gamma}{W_p}$

C. $T=\frac{\gamma}{G}W_p$　　D. $T=\frac{W_p}{G\gamma}$

5-4-4　直径为 d 的实心圆轴受扭，若使扭转角减小一半，圆轴的直径需变为(　　)。

A. $\sqrt[4]{2}d$　　B. $\sqrt[3]{\sqrt{2}}d$　　C. $0.5d$　　D. $2d$

5-4-5　如图所示，左端固定的直杆受扭转力偶作用，在截面 1-1 和 1-2 处的扭矩为(　　)。

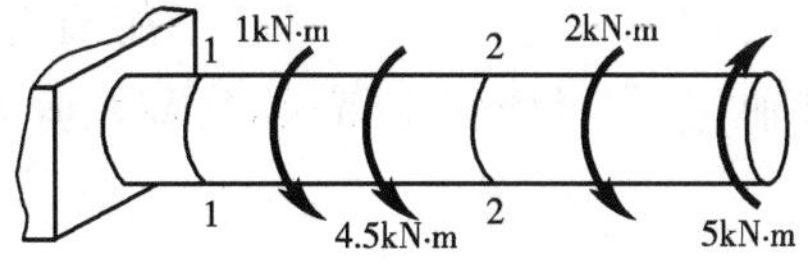

题 5-4-5 图

A. 12.5kN・m，−3kN・m　　B. −2.5kN・m，−3kN・m

C. −2.5kN・m，3kN・m　　D. 2.5kN・m，−3kN・m

5-4-6　如图所示，圆轴的扭矩图为(　　)。

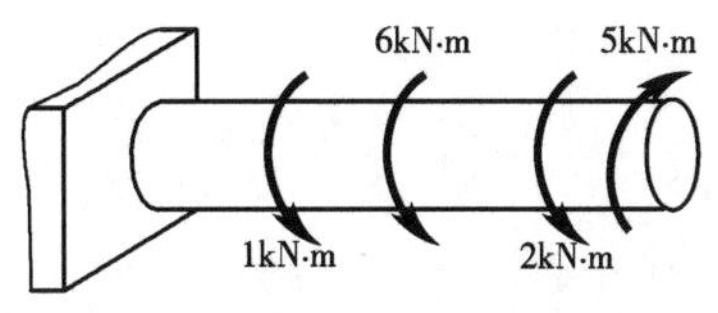

题 5-4-6 图

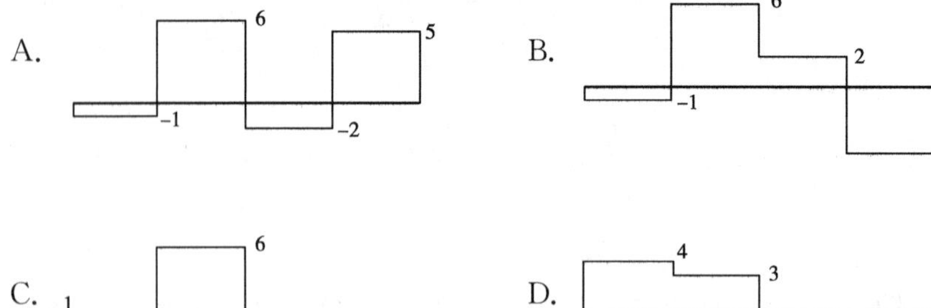

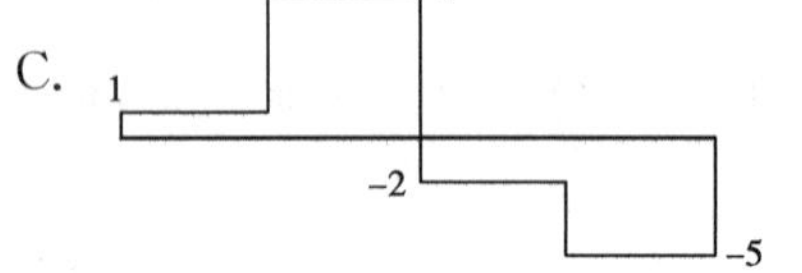

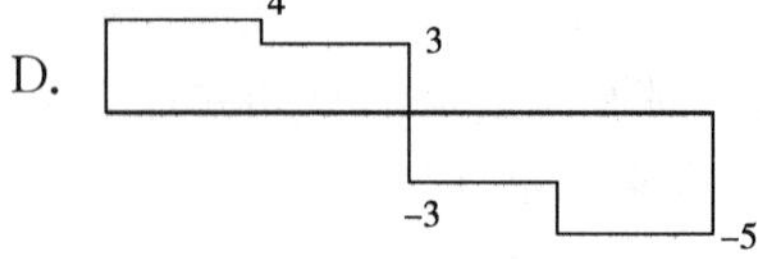

5-4-7 直径为 D 的实心圆轴，两端受扭转力矩作用，轴内最大剪应力为 τ。若轴的直径改为 $D/2$，则轴内的最大剪应力应为(　　)。

A. 2τ　　B. 4τ　　C. 8τ　　D. 16τ

5-4-8 如图所示，直杆受扭转力偶作用，在截面 1-1 和 2-2 处的扭矩为(　　)。

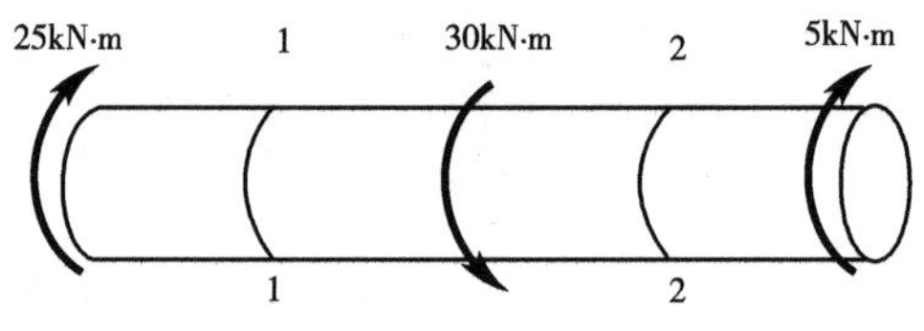

题 5-4-8 图

A. 5kN·m，5kN·m　　B. 25kN·m，−5kN·m

C. 35kN·m，−5kN·m　　D. −25kN·m，25kN·m

5-4-9 两端受扭转力偶矩作用的实心圆轴，不发生屈服的最大许可荷载为 M_0，若将其横截面面积增加 1 倍，则最大许可荷载为(　　)。

A. $\sqrt{2}M_0$　　B. $2M_0$　　C. $2\sqrt{2}M_0$　　D. $4M_0$

5-4-10 空心圆轴和实心圆轴的外径相同时，截面的抗扭截面模量较大的是(　　)。

A. 空心轴　　B. 实心轴

C. 一样大　　D. 不能确定

5-4-11 受扭实心等直圆轴，当直径增大 1 倍时，其最大剪应力 $\tau_{2\max}$ 和两端相对扭转角 φ_2 与原来的 $\tau_{1\max}$ 和 φ_1 的比值为(　　)。

A. $\tau_{2\max}:\tau_{1\max}=1:2, \varphi_2:\varphi_1=1:4$　　B. $\tau_{2\max}:\tau_{1\max}=1:4, \varphi_2:\varphi_1=1:8$

C. $\tau_{2\max}:\tau_{1\max}=1:8, \varphi_2:\varphi_1=1:16$　　D. $\tau_{2\max}:\tau_{1\max}=1:4, \varphi_2:\varphi_1=1:16$

第五节　截面图形的几何性质

一、静矩与形心

对图 5-5-1 所示截图

$$\left.\begin{aligned} S_z &= \int_A y\,\mathrm{d}A \\ S_y &= \int_A z\,\mathrm{d}A \end{aligned}\right\} \tag{5-5-1}$$

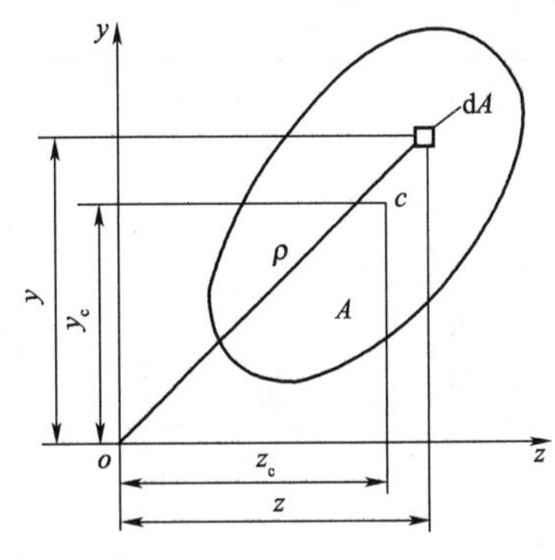

图 5-5-1 截面图形

静矩的量纲为长度的三次方。

对于由几个简单图形组成的组合截面

$$\left.\begin{aligned} S_z &= A_1 y_1 + A_2 y_2 + A_3 y_3 + \cdots = A \cdot y_c \\ S_y &= A_1 z_1 + A_2 z_2 + A_3 z_3 + \cdots = A \cdot z_c \end{aligned}\right\} \tag{5-5-2}$$

形心坐标

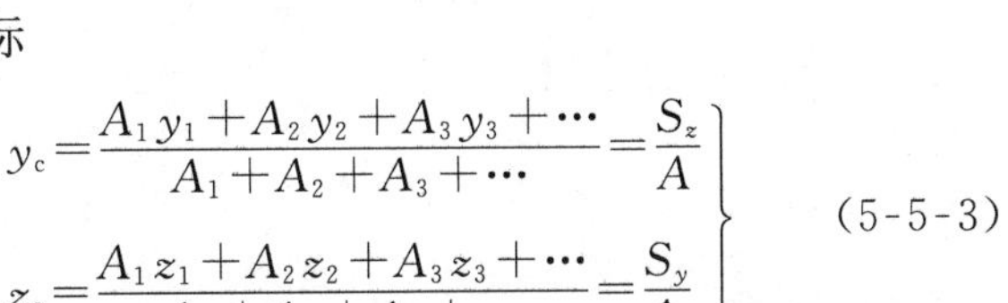

$$\left.\begin{aligned} y_c &= \frac{A_1 y_1 + A_2 y_2 + A_3 y_3 + \cdots}{A_1 + A_2 + A_3 + \cdots} = \frac{S_z}{A} \\ z_c &= \frac{A_1 z_1 + A_2 z_2 + A_3 z_3 + \cdots}{A_1 + A_2 + A_3 + \cdots} = \frac{S_y}{A} \end{aligned}\right\} \tag{5-5-3}$$

显然，若 z 轴过形心，$y_c=0$，则有 $S_z=0$，反之亦然；若 y 轴过形心，$z_c=0$，则有 $S_y=0$，反之亦然。

二、惯性矩、惯性半径、极惯性矩、惯性积

对图 5-5-1 所示截面，对 z 轴和 y 轴的惯性矩为

$$\left.\begin{aligned} I_z &= \int_A y^2\,\mathrm{d}A \\ I_y &= \int_A z^2\,\mathrm{d}A \end{aligned}\right\} \tag{5-5-4}$$

惯性矩总是正值，其量纲为长度的四次方，亦可写成

$$\left.\begin{aligned} I_z &= A i_z^2 \\ I_y &= A i_y^2 \end{aligned}\right\} \tag{5-5-5}$$

$$\left.\begin{aligned} i_z &= \sqrt{\frac{I_z}{A}} \\ i_y &= \sqrt{\frac{I_y}{A}} \end{aligned}\right\} \tag{5-5-6}$$

i_z、i_y 称为截面对 z、y 轴的惯性半径，其量纲为长度的 1 次方。

截面对 o 点的极惯性矩为

$$I_p = \int_A \rho^2\,\mathrm{d}A \tag{5-5-7}$$

因 $\rho^2=y^2+z^2$，故有 $I_p=I_z+I_y$，显然 I_p 也恒为正值，其量纲为长度的 4 次方。

截面对 y、z 轴的惯性积为

$$I_{yz} = \int_A yz\,\mathrm{d}A \tag{5-5-8}$$

I_{yz} 可以为正值，也可以为负值，也可以是零，其量纲为长度的 4 次方。若 y、z 两坐标轴中有一个为截面的对称轴，则其惯性积 I_{yz} 恒等于零。

常用截面的几何性质见表 5-5-1。

常用截面的几何性质 表 5-5-1

项目	矩 形	图 形	空心圆	箱 形
截面图形	y, c, z, h, b	y, c, z, D	y, c, z, d, D	y, c, z, H, h, b, B
截面的几何性质	$A=bh$ $I_z=\frac{bh^3}{12}$ $I_y=\frac{hb^3}{12}$ $I_{yz}=0$ $i_z=\frac{h}{2\sqrt{3}}$ $i_y=\frac{b}{2\sqrt{3}}$ $W_z=\frac{bh^2}{6},W_y=\frac{hb^2}{6}$	$A=\frac{\pi}{4}D^2$ $I_z=I_y=\frac{\pi}{64}D^4$ $I_p=\frac{\pi}{32}D^4$ $I_{yz}=0$ $i_z=i_y=\frac{D}{4}$ $W_z=W_y=\frac{\pi}{32}D^3$ $W_p=\frac{\pi}{16}D^3$	$A=\frac{\pi}{4}D^2(1-\alpha^2)$ $I_z=I_y=\frac{\pi}{64}D^4(1-\alpha^4)$ $I_p=\frac{\pi}{32}D^4(1-\alpha^4)$ $I_{yz}=0,\alpha=\frac{d}{D}$ $i_z=i_y=\frac{\sqrt{D^2+d^2}}{4}$ $W_z=W_y=\frac{\pi}{32}D^3(1-\alpha^4)$ $W_p=\frac{\pi}{16}D^3(1-\alpha^4)$	$A=BH-bh$ $I_z=\frac{BH^3-bh^3}{12}$ $I_y=\frac{HB^3-hb^3}{12}$ $I_{yz}=0$

注：图形中的 c 为截面形心；公式中 W_z、W_y 为抗弯截面系数，W_p 为抗扭截面系数。

三、平行移轴公式

若已知任一截面图形（见图 5-5-2）形心为 c，面积为 A，对形心轴 z_c 和 y_c 的惯性矩为 I_{zc} 和 I_{yc}、惯性积为 I_{yczc}，则该图形对于与 z_c 轴平行且相距为 a 的 z 轴，及与 y_c 轴平行且相距为 b 的 y 轴的惯性矩和惯性积分别为

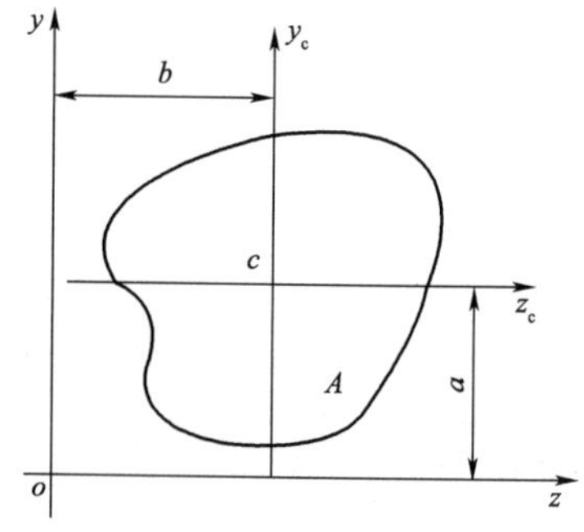

图 5-5-2 具有平行轴的截面图形

$$\left.\begin{aligned} I_z&=I_{zc}+a^2A\\ I_y&=I_{yc}+b^2A\\ I_{yz}&=I_{yczc}+abA \end{aligned}\right\} \qquad (5\text{-}5\text{-}9)$$

显然，在图形对所有互相平行的惯性矩中，以形心轴的惯性矩为最小。

四、主惯性轴和主惯性矩、形心主（惯性）轴和形心主（惯形）矩

若截面图形对通过某点的某一对正交坐标轴的惯性积为零，则称这对坐标轴为图形在该点的主惯性轴，简称主轴。图形对主惯性轴的惯性矩称为主惯性矩。显然，当任意一对正交坐标轴中之一轴为图形的对称轴时，图形对该两轴的惯性积必为零，故这对轴必为主轴。

过截面形心的主惯性轴，称为形心主轴。截面对形心主轴的惯性矩称为形心主矩。杆件的轴线与横截面形心主轴所组成的平面，称为形心主惯性平面。

习　题

5-5-1　图示矩形截面对 z_1 轴的惯性矩 I_{z_1} 为(　　)。

A. $I_{z_1}=\frac{bh^3}{12}$　　B. $I_{z_1}=\frac{bh^3}{3}$　　C. $I_{z_1}=\frac{7bh^3}{6}$　　D. $I_{z_1}=\frac{13bh^3}{12}$

5-5-2　矩形截面挖去一个边长为 a 的正方形，如图所示，该截面对 z 轴的惯性矩 I_z 为(　　)。

A. $I_z=\frac{bh^3}{12}-\frac{a^4}{12}$　B. $I_z=\frac{bh^3}{12}-\frac{13a^4}{12}$　C. $I_z=\frac{bh^3}{12}-\frac{a^4}{3}$　D. $I_z=\frac{bh^3}{12}-\frac{7a^4}{12}$

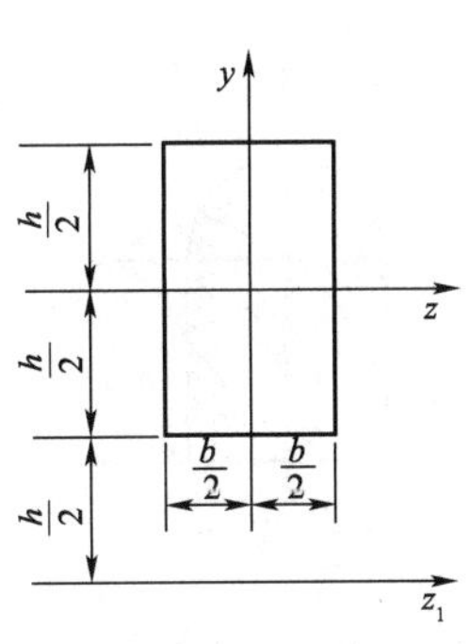

题 5-5-1 图

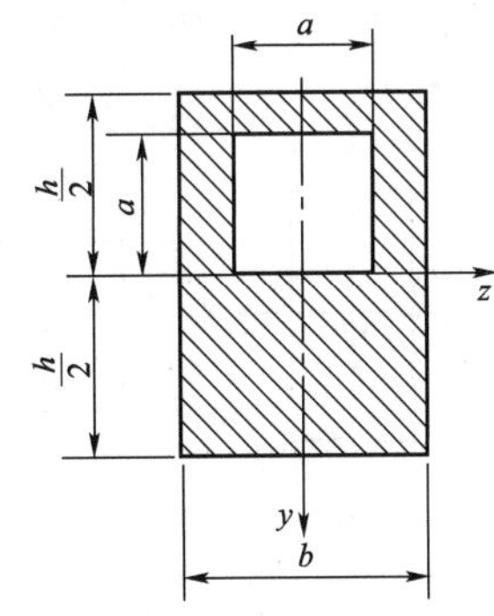

题 5-5-2 图

5-5-3　面积相等的两个图形分别如图所示。它们与对称轴 y、z 的惯性矩之间的关系为(　　)。

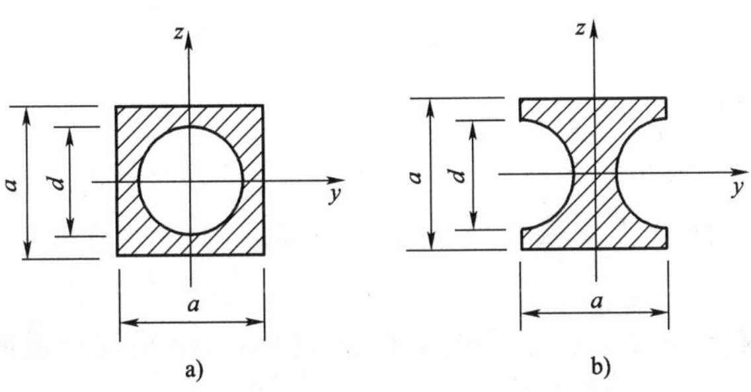

题 5-5-3 图

A. $I_z^a<I_z^b, I_y^a=I_y^b$　B. $I_z^a>I_z^b, I_y^a=I_y^b$　C. $I_z^a=I_z^b, I_y^a=I_y^b$　D. $I_z^a=I_z^b, I_y^a>I_y^b$

5-5-4　在 yoz 正交坐标系中，设图形对 y、z 轴的惯性矩分别为 I_y 和 I_z，则图形对坐标原点极惯性矩为(　　)。

A. $I_p=0$　　B. $I_p=I_z+I_y$　　C. $I_p=\sqrt{I_z^2+I_y^2}$　　D. $I_p=I_z^2+I_y^2$

5-5-5　图示矩形截面，$m-m$ 线以上部分和以下部分对形心轴 z 的两个静矩(　　)。

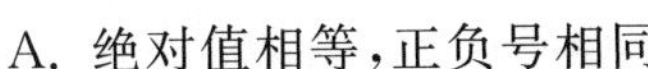

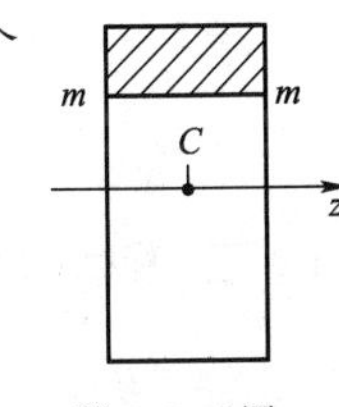

题 5-5-5 图

A. 绝对值相等，正负号相同

B. 绝对值相等，正负号不同

C. 绝对值不等，正负号相同

D. 绝对值不等，正负号不同

5-5-6　直径为 d 的圆形对其形心轴的惯性半径 i 等于(　　)。

A. $d/2$　　B. $d/4$　　C. $d/6$　　D. $d/8$

5-5-7　图示的矩形截面和正方形截面具有相同的面积。设它们对对称轴 y 的惯性矩分别为 I_y^a、I_y^b,对对称轴 z 的惯性分别为 I_z^a、I_z^b,则(　　)。

A. $I_z^a > I_z^b, I_y^a < I_y^b$　　B. $I_z^a > I_z^b, I_y^a > I_y^b$

C. $I_z^a < I_z^b, I_y^a > I_y^b$　　D. $I_z^a < I_z^b, I_y^a < I_y^b$

5-5-8　在图形对通过某点的所有轴的惯性矩中,图形对主惯性轴的惯性矩一定(　　)。

A. 最大　　B. 最小　　C. 最大或最小　　D. 为零

5-5-9　如图所示的截面,其轴惯性矩的关系为(　　)。

A. $I_{z_1} = I_{z_2}$　　B. $I_{z_1} > I_{z_2}$　　C. $I_{z_1} < I_{z_2}$　　D. 不能确定

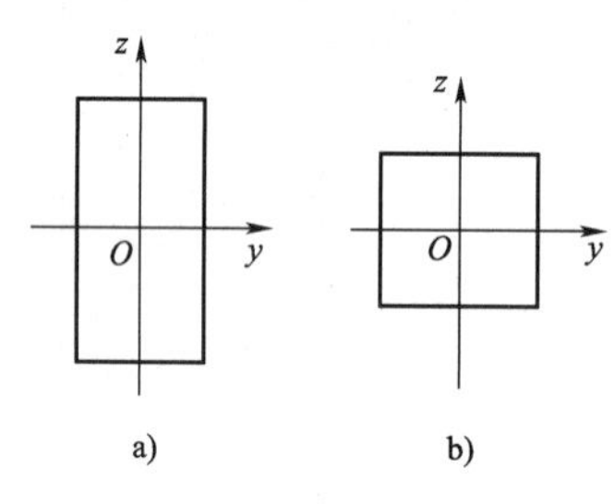

题 5-5-7 图

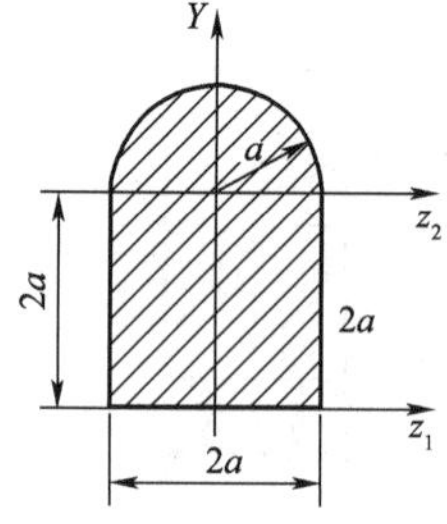

题 5-5-9 图

第六节　弯曲梁的内力、应力和变形

一、平面弯曲的概念

弯曲变形是杆件的基本变形之一。以弯曲为主要变形的杆件通常为梁。

(1)弯曲变形特征。任意两横截面绕垂直杆轴线的轴做相对转动,同时杆的轴线也弯成曲线。

(2)平面弯曲。荷载作用面(外力偶作用面或横向力与梁轴线组成的平面)与弯曲平面(即梁轴线弯曲后所在平面)相平行或重合的弯曲。

产生平面弯曲的条件:

(1)梁具有纵对称面时,只要外力(横向力或外力偶)都作用在此纵对称面内。

(2)非对称截面梁。

纯弯曲时,只要外力偶作用在与梁的形心主惯平面(即梁的轴线与其横截面的形心主惯性轴所构成的平面)平行的平面内。

横力弯曲时,横向力必须通过截面的弯曲中心,并在与梁的形心主惯性平面平行的平面内。

二、梁横截面上的内力分量——剪力与弯矩

(一)剪力与弯矩

(1)剪力。梁横截面上切向分布内力的合力,称为剪力,以 Q 表示。

(2)弯矩。梁横截面上法向分布内力形成的合力偶矩,称为弯矩,以 M 表示。

(3)剪力与弯矩的符号。考虑梁微段 dx,使右侧截面对左侧截面产生向下相对错动的剪力为正,反之为负;使微段产生凹向上的弯曲变形的弯矩为正,反之为负,如图 5-6-1 所示。

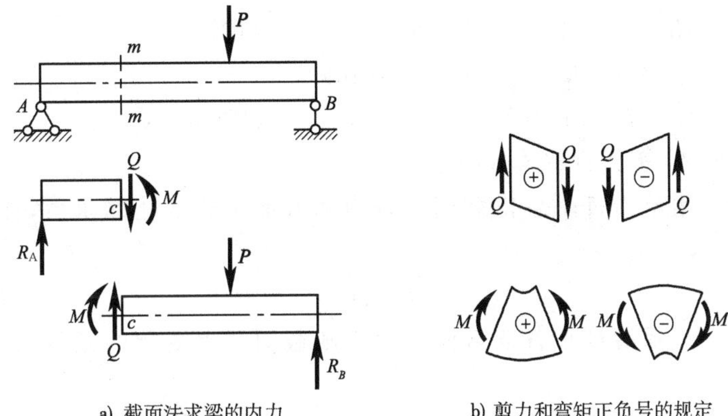

图 5-6-1 梁的内力

(4)剪力与弯矩的计算。由截面法可知,梁的内力可用直接法求出:

①横截面上的剪力,其值等于该截面左侧(或右侧)梁上所有外力在横截面方向的投影代数和,且左侧梁上向上的外力或右侧梁上向下的外力引起正剪力,反之则引起负剪力。

②横截面上的弯矩,其值等于该截面左侧(或右侧)梁上所有外力对该截面形心的力矩代数和,且向上外力均引起正弯矩,左侧梁上顺时针转向的外力偶及右侧梁上逆时针转向的外力偶引起正弯矩,反之则产生负弯矩,如图 5-6-2 所示。

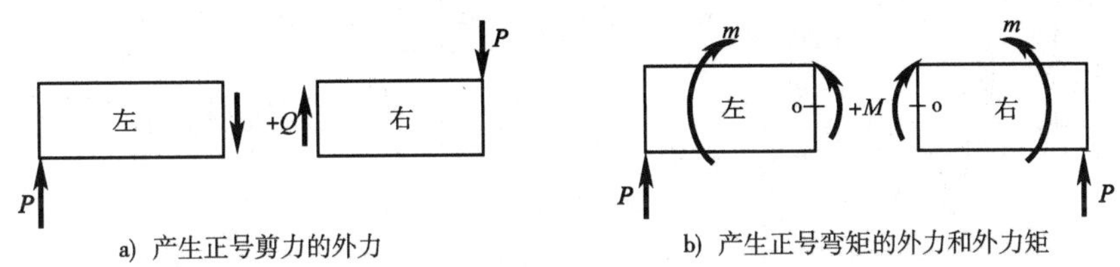

图 5-6-2 直接法求梁的内力

【例 5-6-1】 如图所示,求 1-1 截面和 2-2 截面的内力。

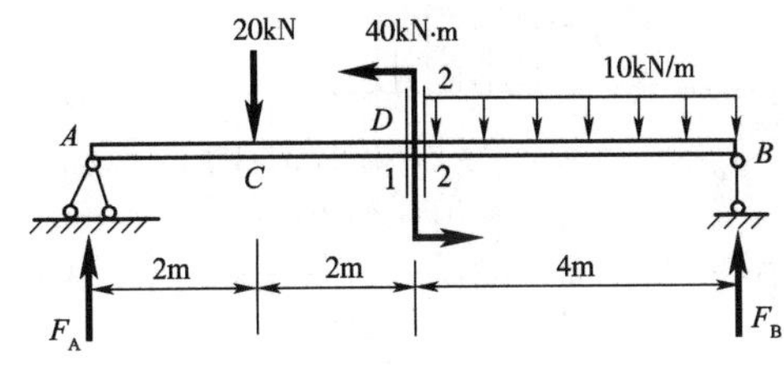

例 5-6-1 图

解 先求支反力,$\sum M_B=0$

$$F_A\times(2+2+4)=20\times6+40+(10\times4)\times2$$

$F_A = 30\text{kN}$

$\sum F_y = 0, F_A + F_B = 20 + 10 \times 4$

$F_B = 30\text{kN}$

直接法求内力，$Q_1 = F_A - 20 = 30 - 20 = 10\text{kN}$

$M_1 = F_A \times 4 - 20 \times 2 = 30 \times 4 - 40 = 80\text{kN} \cdot \text{m}$

$Q_2 = 10 \times 4 - F_B = 40 - 30 = 10\text{kN}$

$M_2 = F_B \times 4 - (10 \times 4) \times 2 = 30 \times 4 - 80 = 40\text{kN} \cdot \text{m}$

（二）内力方程——剪力方程与弯矩方程

（1）剪力方程。表示沿杆轴各横截面上剪力随截面位置变化的函数，称为剪力方程，表示为

$$Q = Q(x)$$

（2）弯矩方程。表示沿杆轴各横截面上弯矩随截面位置变化的函数，称为弯矩方程，表示为

$$M = M(x)$$

（三）剪力图与弯矩图

（1）剪力图。表示沿杆轴和横截面上剪力随截面位置变化的图线，称为剪力图。

（2）弯矩图。表示沿杆轴各横截面上弯矩随截面位置变化的图线，称为弯矩图。

图 5-6-3 给出了常用梁的剪力图和弯矩图。

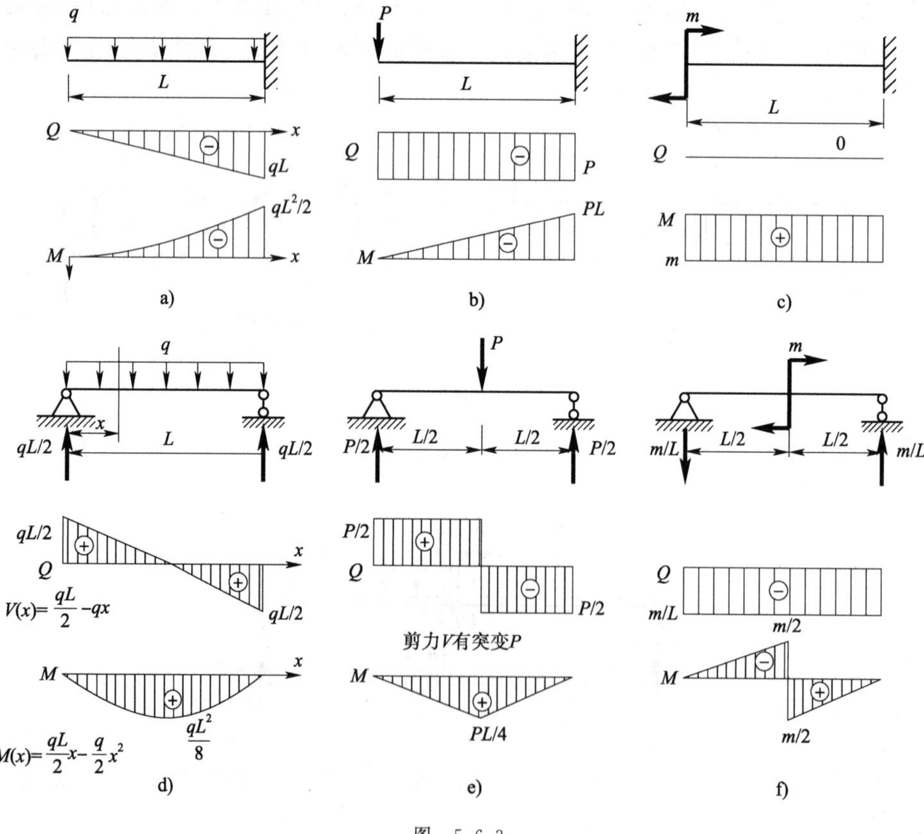

图 5-6-3

三、荷载集度与剪力、弯矩间的关系及应用

(一)微分关系

若规定荷载集度 q 向上为正,则梁任一横截面上的剪力、弯矩与荷载集度间的微分关系

$$\left.\begin{aligned}\frac{\mathrm{d}Q}{\mathrm{d}x}&=q\\ \frac{\mathrm{d}M}{\mathrm{d}x}&=Q\\ \frac{\mathrm{d}^2M}{\mathrm{d}x^2}&=q\end{aligned}\right\}\tag{5-6-1}$$

当以梁的左端为 x 轴原点,且以向右为 x 正轴,并规定剪力图以向上为正轴,而弯矩图则取向下为正轴时,可将工程上常见的外力与剪力图和弯矩图之间的关系列在表 5-6-1 中。

几种常见外力与剪力图和弯矩图间的关系　表 5-6-1

梁上外力情况	$q=0$ (无外力段)	q= 常量<0 水平直线	q= 常量>0 水平直线	集中力 P	集中力偶 m	特殊点
剪力图 Q	Q= 常量 水平直线	下斜直线 $Q=0$	上斜直线 $Q=0$	在集中力作用处发生突变,突变方向、大小与 P 相同	无影响	无集中力作用的端点 $Q=0$
弯矩图 M	斜直线	M_{max} 抛物线	M_{min} 抛物线	在集中力作用处发生转折(斜率改变)	在 m 作用处发生突变,突变大小与 m 相同	无集中偶作用的简支端、自由端、中间铰 $M=0$

利用表 5-6-1 可以快速地作出剪力图和弯矩图。

(二)快速作图法

(1)求支反力,并校核。

(2)根据外力不连续点分段。

(3)定形:根据各段梁上的外力,确定其 Q、M 图的形状。

(4)定量:用直接法计算各分段点、极值点的 Q、M 值。

【例 5-6-2】 作图 a)所示悬臂梁的剪力图、弯矩图。

解　见图 b)、c)。

【例 5-6-3】 由图 b)所示梁的剪力图,画出梁的荷载图和弯矩图。(梁上无集中力偶作用)

解　见图 a)、c)。

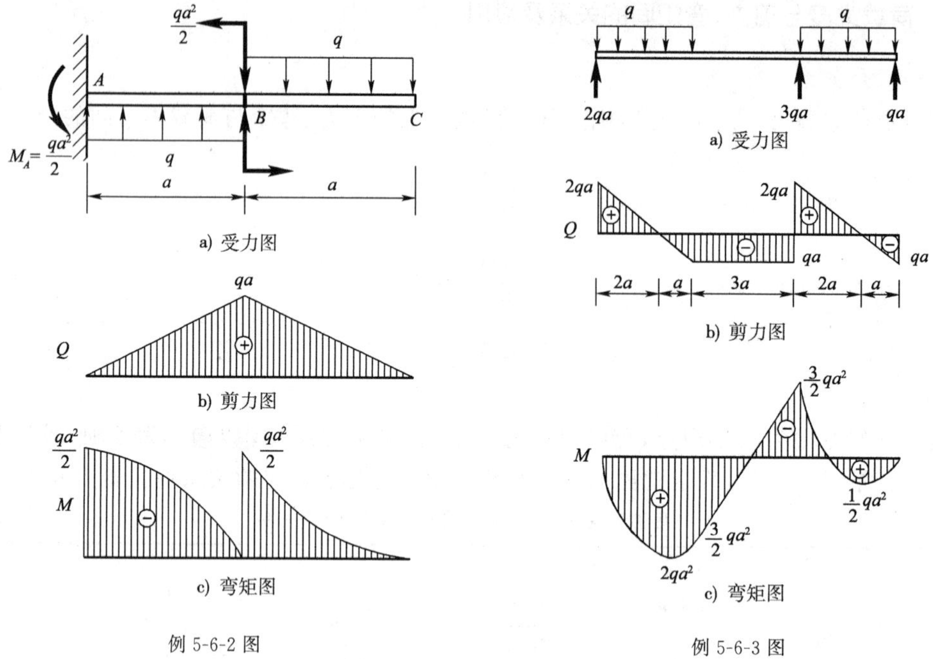

例 5-6-2 图

例 5-6-3 图

【例 5-6-4】 简支梁 AB 的剪力图和弯矩图如图所示。该梁正确的受力图是：

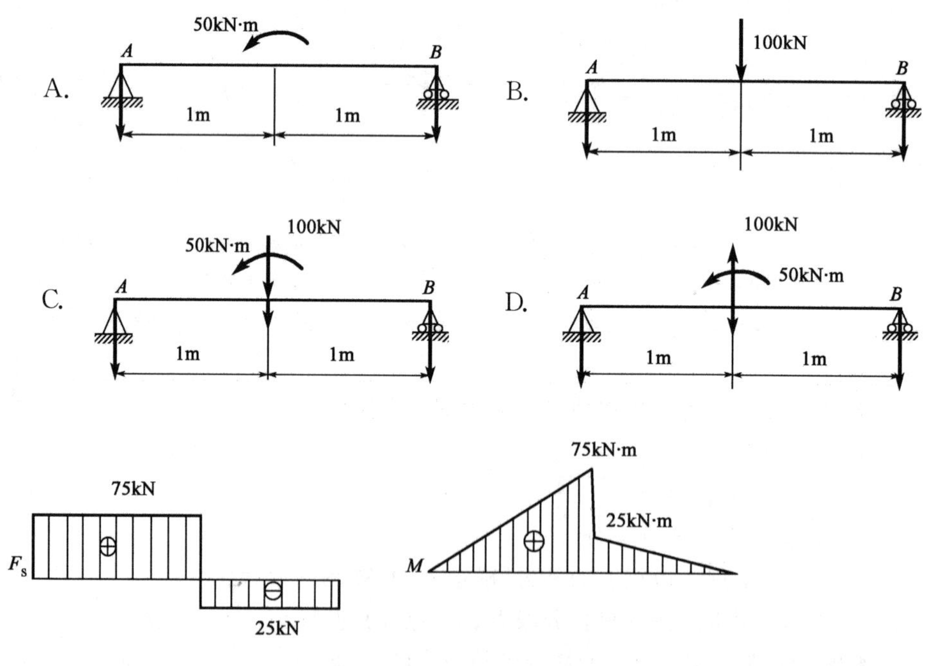

例 5-6-4 图

解 从剪力图看梁跨中有一个向下的突变，对应于一个向下的集中力，其值等于突变值 100kN；从弯矩图看梁的跨中有一个突变值 50kN·m，对应于一个外力偶矩 50kN·m，所以只能选 C 图。

答案：C

【例 5-6-5】 梁 AB 的弯矩图如图所示，梁上荷载 F、m 的值为：

A. $F=8\text{kN}, m=14\text{kN}\cdot\text{m}$

B. $F=8\text{kN}, m=6\text{kN}\cdot\text{m}$

C. $F=6\text{kN}, m=8\text{kN}\cdot\text{m}$

D. $F=6\text{kN}, m=14\text{kN}\cdot\text{m}$

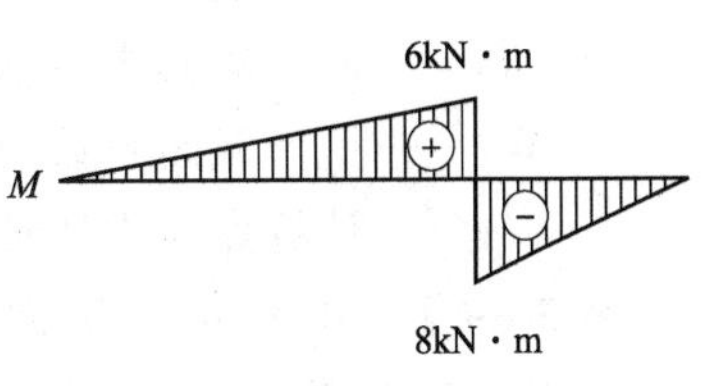

例 5-6-5 图

解 由最大负弯矩为 8kN · m，可以反推：$M_{\max}=F\times 1\text{m}$，故 $F=8\text{kN}$

再由支座 C 处（即外力偶矩 m 作用处）两侧的弯矩的突变值是 14kN · m，可知外力偶矩 $m=14\text{kN}\cdot\text{m}$

答案：A

四、弯曲正应力、正应力强度条件

（一）纯弯曲

梁的横截面上只有弯矩而无剪力时的弯曲，称为纯弯曲。

（二）中性层与中性轴

（1）中性层。杆件弯曲变形时既不伸长也不缩短的一层。

（2）中性轴。中性层与横截面的交线，即横截面上正应力为零的各点的连线。

（3）中性轴位置。当杆件发生平面弯曲，且处于线弹性范围时，中性轴通过横截面形心，且垂直于荷载作用平面。

（4）中性层的曲率。杆件发生平面弯曲，中性层（或杆轴）的曲率与弯矩间的关系为

$$\frac{1}{\rho}=\frac{M}{EI_z} \qquad (5\text{-}6\text{-}2)$$

式中：ρ——变形后中性层（或杆轴）的曲率半径；

EI_z——杆的抗弯刚度，轴 z 为横截面的中性轴。

（三）平面弯曲杆件横截面上的正应力

分布规律：正应力与大小与该点至中性轴的垂直距离成正比，中性轴一侧为拉应力，另一侧为压应力，如图 5-6-4 所示。

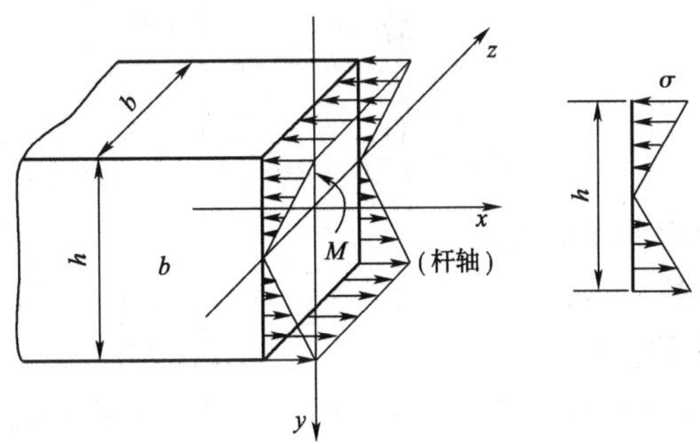

图 5-6-4 弯曲梁横截面上正应力分布

计算公式如下，任一点应力

$$\sigma=\frac{M}{I_z}y \qquad (5\text{-}6\text{-}3)$$

最大应力

$$\sigma_{max}=\frac{M}{I_z}y_{max}=\frac{M}{W_z} \tag{5-6-4}$$

其中

$$W_z=\frac{I_z}{y_{max}} \tag{5-6-5}$$

上述式中：M——截面上的弯矩；

I_z——截面对其中性轴的惯性矩；

W_z——抗弯截面系数，其量纲为长度的三次方，常用截面 W_z 的计算公式，见表 5-2；

y——计算点与中性轴间的距离。

【例 5-6-6】 图示矩形截面简支梁中点承受集中力 $F=100\text{kN}$。若 $h=200\text{mm}$，$b=100\text{mm}$，梁的最大弯曲正应力是：

A. 75MPa　　B. 150MPa　　C. 300MPa　　D. 50MPa

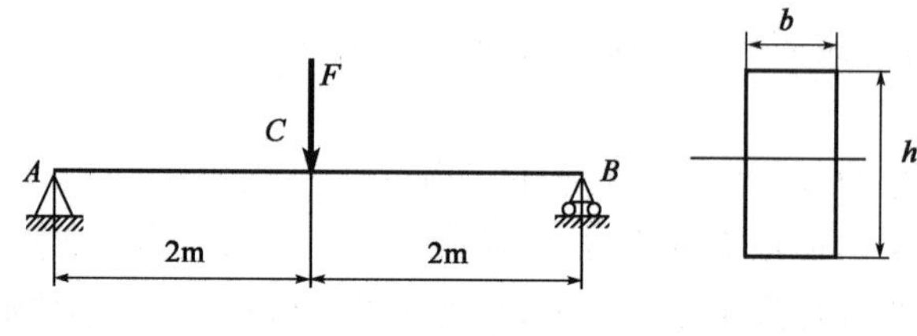

例 5-6-6 图

解 梁两端的支座反力为 $\frac{F}{2}=50\text{kN}$，梁中点最大弯矩 $M_{max}=50\times2=100\text{kN}\cdot\text{m}$

最大弯曲正应力 $\sigma_{max}=\frac{M_{max}}{W_z}=\frac{M_{max}}{\frac{bh^2}{6}}=\frac{100\times10^6\text{N}\cdot\text{mm}}{\frac{1}{6}\times100\times200^2\text{mm}^3}=150\text{MPa}$

答案：B

（四）梁的正应力强度条件

在危险截面上

$$\sigma_{max}=\frac{M}{W_z}\leqslant[\sigma] \tag{5-6-6}$$

或

$$\left.\begin{aligned}\sigma_{max}^{+}=\frac{M}{I_z}y_{max}^{+}\leqslant[\sigma_t]\\ \sigma_{max}^{-}=\frac{M}{I_z}y_{max}^{-}\leqslant[\sigma_c]\end{aligned}\right\} \tag{5-6-7}$$

式中：$[\sigma]$——材料的许用弯曲正应力；

$[\sigma_t]$——材料的许用拉应力；

$[\sigma_c]$——材料的许用压应力；

y_{max}^{+}、y_{max}^{-}——分别为最大拉应力 σ_{max}^{+} 和最大压应力 σ_{max}^{-} 所在的截面边缘到中性轴 z 的距离。

【例 5-6-7】 图示悬臂梁 AB，由三根相同的矩形截面直杆胶合而成，材料的许可应力为 $[\sigma]$。若胶合面开裂，假设开裂后三根杆的挠曲线相同，接触面之间无摩擦力，则开裂后的梁承载能力是原来的：

A. 1/9　　B. 1/3

C. 两者相同　　D. 3 倍

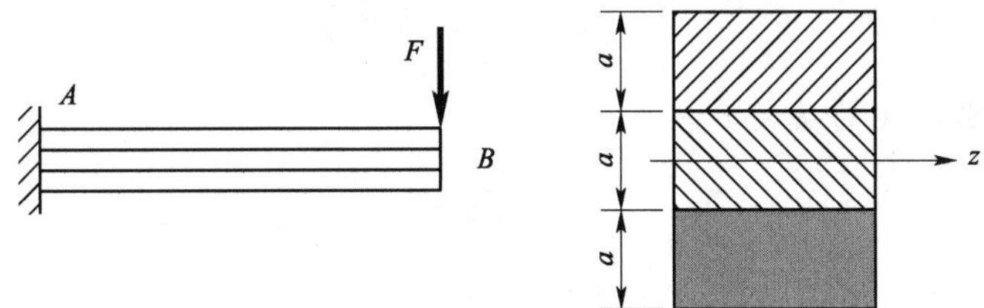

例 5-6-7 图

解 开裂前，由整体梁的强度条件 $\sigma_{\max}=\dfrac{M}{W_{\mathrm{g}}}\leqslant[\sigma]$，可知 $M\leqslant[\sigma]W_{\mathrm{g}}=[\sigma]\dfrac{b(3a)^2}{6}=\dfrac{3}{2}ba^2[\sigma]$

胶合面开裂后，每根梁承担总弯矩 M_1 的 $\dfrac{1}{3}$，由单根梁的强度条件 $\sigma_{1\max}=\dfrac{M_1}{W_{\mathrm{g1}}}=\dfrac{\frac{M_1}{3}}{W_{\mathrm{g1}}}=\dfrac{M_1}{3W_{\mathrm{g1}}}\leqslant[\sigma]$，可知 $M_1\leqslant3[\sigma]W_{\mathrm{g1}}=3[\sigma]\dfrac{ba^2}{6}=\dfrac{1}{2}ba^2[\sigma]$

故开裂后每根梁的承载能力是原来的 $\dfrac{1}{3}$

答案：B

五、弯曲剪应力与剪应力强度条件

(一)矩形截面梁的剪应力

两个假设：

(1)剪应力方向与截面的侧边平行。

(2)沿截面宽度剪应力均匀分布(见图 5-6-5)。

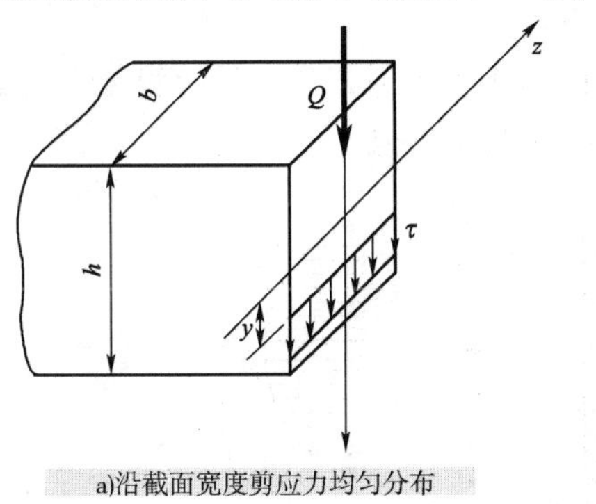

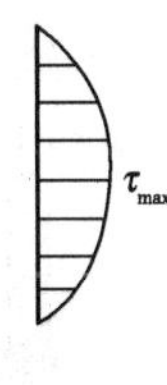

a)沿截面宽度剪应力均匀分布　　b)沿截面高度剪应力抛物线分布

图 5-6-5　矩形截面梁剪应力的分布

计算公式

$$\tau=\frac{QS_z^*}{bI_z} \tag{5-6-8}$$

式中：Q——横截面上的剪力；

b——横截面的宽度；

I_z——整个横截面对中性轴的惯性矩；

S_z^*——横截面上距中性轴为 y 处横线一侧的部分截面对中性轴的静矩。

最大剪应力发生在中性轴处

$$\tau_{\max}=\frac{3}{2}\frac{Q}{bh}=\frac{3}{2}\frac{Q}{A} \quad (5\text{-}6\text{-}9)$$

（二）其他常用截面梁的最大剪应力

工字形截面

$$\tau_{\max}=\frac{QS_{z\max}^{*}}{I_z d} \quad (5\text{-}6\text{-}10)$$

其中，d 为腹板厚度，工字型钢中，$I_z/S_{z\max}^{*}$ 可查型钢表。

圆形截面

$$\tau_{\max}=\frac{4}{3}\frac{Q}{A} \quad (5\text{-}6\text{-}11)$$

环形截面

$$\tau_{\max}=2\frac{Q}{A} \quad (5\text{-}6\text{-}12)$$

最大剪应力均发生在中性轴上。

（三）剪应力强度条件

梁的最大工作剪应力不得超过材料的许用剪应力，即

$$\tau_{\max}=\frac{Q_{\max}S_{z\max}^{*}}{bI_z}\leqslant[\tau] \quad (5\text{-}6\text{-}13)$$

式中：$Q_{\max}$——全梁的最大剪力；

$S_{z\max}^{*}$——中性轴一边的横截面面积对中性轴的静矩；

b——横截面在中性轴处的宽度；

I_z——整个横截面对中性轴的惯矩。

【例 5-6-8】 梁的横截面是由狭长矩形构成的工字形截面，如图 a)所示，z 轴为中性轴，截面上的剪力竖直向下，该截面上的最大切应力在：

A. 腹板中性轴处　　B. 腹板上下缘延长线与两侧翼缘相交处

C. 截面上下缘　　D. 腹板上下缘

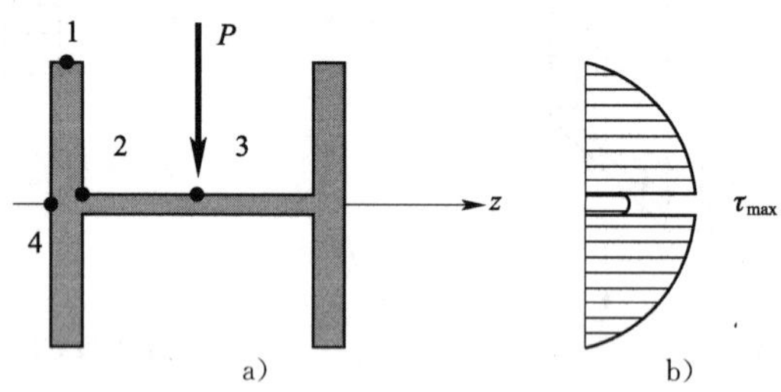

例 5-6-8 图

解 矩形截面切应力的分布是一个抛物线形状（见图 b)，最大切应力在中性轴子上，图 a)示梁的横截面可以看作是一个中性轴，附近梁的宽度 b 突然变大的矩形截面。根据弯曲切应力的计算公式：

$$\tau=\frac{QS_g^{*}}{gI_g}$$

在 b 突然变大的情况下，中性轴附近的 τ 突然变小，切应力分布图沿 y 方向的分布如图 b)所示。所以最大切应力该在 2 点。

答案：B

六、梁的合理截面

梁的强度通常是由横截面上的正应力控制的。由弯曲正应力强度条件 $\sigma_{max}=\frac{M_{max}}{W_z}\leqslant[\sigma]$ 可知，在截面积 A 一定的条件下，截面图形的抗弯截面系数越大，梁的承载能力就越大，故截面就越合理。因此就 W_z/A 而言，对工字形、矩形和圆形三种形状的截面，工字形最为合理，矩形次之，圆形最差。此外对于$[\sigma_t]=[\sigma_c]$的塑性材料，一般采用对称于中性轴的截面，使截面上、下边缘的最大拉应力和最大压应力同时达到许用应力。对于$[\sigma_t]\neq[\sigma_c]$的脆性材料，一般采用不对称于中性轴的截面，如 T 形、冂形等，使最大拉应力 σ_{tmax} 和最大压应力 σ_{cmax} 同时达到$[\sigma_t]$和$[\sigma_c]$，如图 5-6-6 所示。

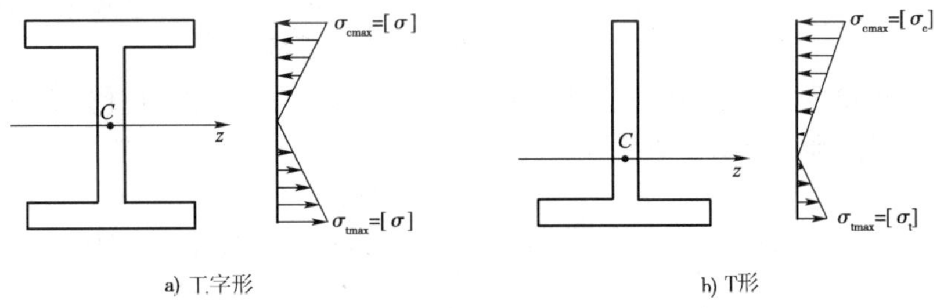

a) 工字形　　b) T形

图 5-6-6　横截面上正应力的分布

七、弯曲中心的概念

在横向力作用下，梁分别在两个形心主惯性平面 xy 和 xz 的内弯曲时，横截面上剪力 Q_y 和 Q_z 作用线的交点，称为截面的弯曲中心，也称为剪切中心。

当梁上的横向力不能过截面的弯曲中心时，梁除了发生弯曲变形外还要发生扭转变形。

弯曲中心的位置仅取决于截面的几何形状和大小，它与外力的大小和材料的力学性质无关。弯曲中心实际上是截面上弯曲剪应力的合力作用点，见表 5-6-2。

几种薄壁截面的弯心位置　　表 5-6-2

项次	1	2	3	4	5	6	7
截面形状							
弯心A的位置	与形心重合	$e=\frac{b_1^2<h_1^2<2t}{4I_z}$	$e=r_0$	在两个狭长矩形中线的交点			与形心重合

因此，弯曲中心的位置有以下特点。

(1)具有两个对称轴或反对称轴的截面，其弯曲中心与形心重合。

(2)有一个对称轴的截面,其弯曲中心必在此对称轴上。

(3)若薄壁截面的中心线是由相交于一点的若干直线段所组成,则此交点就是截面的弯曲中心。

八、梁的变形——挠度与转角

(一)挠曲线

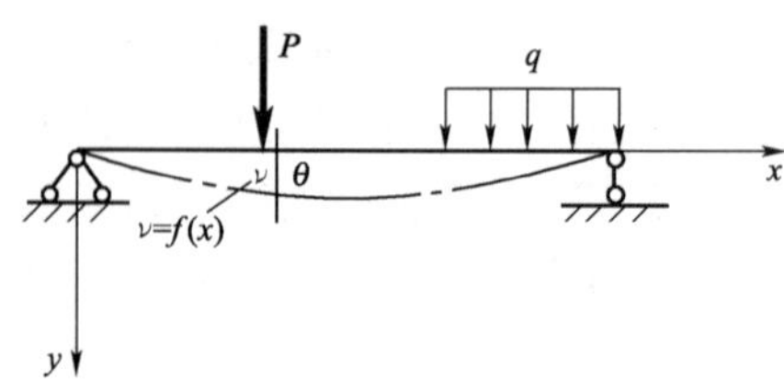

图 5-6-7 梁的挠度与转角

在外力作用下,梁的轴线由直线变为光滑的弹性曲线,梁弯曲后的轴线称为挠曲线。在平面弯曲下,挠曲线为梁形心主惯性平面内的一条平面曲线 $\nu=f(x)$,如图 5-6-7 所示。

(二)挠度与转角

梁弯曲变形后,梁的每一个横截面都要产生位移,它包括挠度和转角两部分。

(1)挠度。梁横截面形心在垂直于轴线方向的线位移,称为挠度,记作 ν。沿梁轴各横截面挠度的变化规律,即为梁的挠曲线方程,即

$$\nu=f(x)$$

(2)转角。横截面相对原来位置绕中性轴所转过的角度,称为转角,记作 θ。小变形情况下

$$\theta\approx\tan\theta=\frac{\mathrm{d}\nu}{\mathrm{d}x}=\nu'$$

此外,横截面形心沿梁轴线方向的位移,小变形条件下可忽略不计。

(三)挠曲线近似微分方程

在线弹性范围、小变形条件下,挠曲线近似微分方程为

$$\frac{\mathrm{d}^2\nu}{\mathrm{d}x^2}=-\frac{M(x)}{EI_z} \tag{5-6-14}$$

挠度 ν 向下为正,转角 θ 顺时针转为正。

九、积分法计算梁的变形

根据挠曲线近似微分方程(5-6-14),积分两次,即得梁的转角方程和挠度方程

$$\theta=\frac{\mathrm{d}\nu}{\mathrm{d}x}=-\int\frac{M(x)}{EI_i}\mathrm{d}x+C$$

$$\nu=-\iint\frac{M(x)}{EI_z}\mathrm{d}x\mathrm{d}x+Cx+D$$

其中,积分常数 C、D 可由梁的边界条件来确定。当梁的弯矩方程需分段列出时,挠曲线微分方程也需分段建立、分段积分。于是全梁的积分常数数目将为分段数目的两倍。为了确定全部积分常数,除利用边界条件外,还需利用分段处挠曲线的连续条件(在分界点处左、右两段梁的转角和挠度均应相等)。

十、用叠加法求梁的变形

(一)叠加原理

几个荷载同时作用下梁的任一截面的挠度或转角,等于各个荷载单独作用下同一截面挠度或转角的总和。

(二)叠加原理的适用条件

叠加原理仅适用于线性函数。要求挠度、转角为梁上荷载的线性函数,必须满足以下条件:

(1)材料为线弹性材料。

(2)梁的变形为小变形。

(3)结构为几何线性。

(三)叠加法的特征

(1)各荷载同时作用下的挠度、转角等于各荷载单独作用下挠度、转角的总和,应该是几何和,同一方向的几何和即为代数和。

(2)梁的简单荷载作用下的挠度、转角应为已知或可查手册,见表 5-6-3。

(3)叠加法适宜于求梁某一指定截面的挠度和转角。

几种常用梁在简单荷载作用下的变形　　表 5-6-3

序号	支承和荷载作用情况	梁端转角	最大挠度
1		$\theta_B=\frac{ml}{EI}$	$f_B=\frac{ml^2}{2EI}$
2		$\theta_B=\frac{Pl^2}{2EI}$	$f_B=\frac{Pl^3}{3EI}$
3		$\theta_B=\frac{ql^3}{6EI}$	$f_B=\frac{ql^4}{8EI}$
4		$\theta_A=\frac{Ml}{3EI}$ $\theta_B=-\frac{Ml}{6EI}$	在 $x=\left(1-\frac{1}{\sqrt{3}}\right)l$ 处,$f_{max}=\frac{Ml^2}{9\sqrt{3}EI}$ $x=\frac{l}{2}$ 处,$f_C=\frac{Ml^2}{16EI}$
5		$\theta_A=-\theta_B=\frac{Pl^2}{16EI}$	$x=\frac{l}{2}$ 处 $f_C=\frac{Pl^3}{48EI}$
6		$\theta_A=-\theta_B=\frac{ql^3}{24EI}$	$x=\frac{l}{2}$ 处 $f_C=\frac{5ql^4}{384EI}$

【例 5-6-9】 图示悬臂梁自由端承受集中力偶 M_g。若梁的长度减少一半，梁的最大挠度是原来的：

A. 1/2　　　　B. 1/4

C. 1/8　　　　D. 1/16

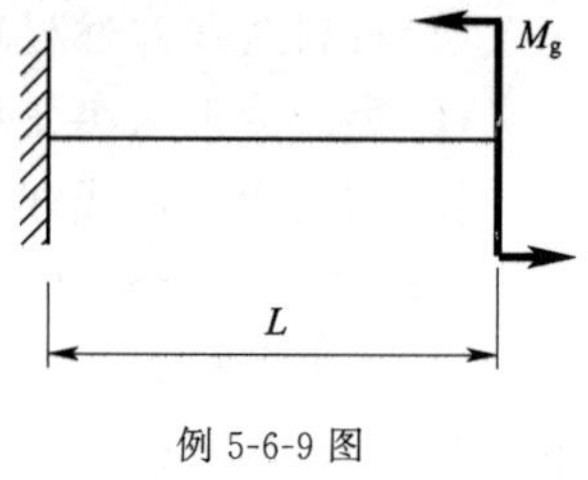

例 5-6-9 图

解 由悬臂梁的最大挠度计算公式 $f_{\max}=\dfrac{M_gL^2}{2EI}$，可知 $f_{\max}$ 与 L^2 成正比，故有：

$$f_{1\max}=\frac{M_g\left(\frac{L}{2}\right)^2}{2EI}=\frac{1}{4}f_{max}$$

答案：B

习　题

5-6-1 图示外伸梁，在 C、D 处作用相同的集中力 F，截面 A 的剪力和截面 C 的弯矩分别是(　　)。

A. $F_{SA}=0, M_C=0$　　　　B. $F_{SA}=F, M_C=Fl$

C. $F_{SA}=\dfrac{F}{2}, M_C=\dfrac{Fl}{2}$　　　　D. $F_{SA}=0, M_C=2Fl$

5-6-2 图示悬臂梁自由端承受集中力偶 M_e，若梁的长度减少一半，梁的最大挠度是原来的(　　)。

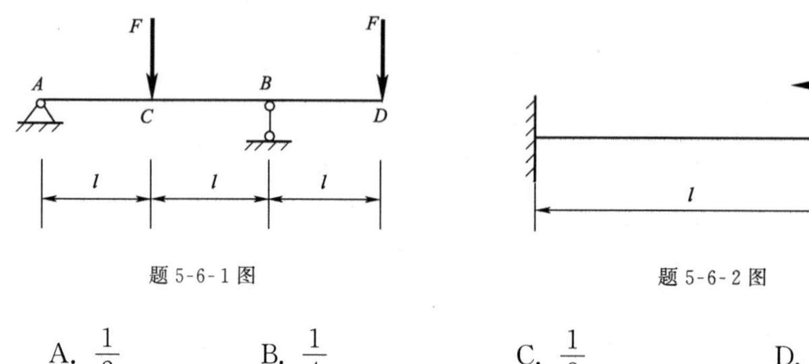

题 5-6-1 图　　　　题 5-6-2 图

A. $\dfrac{1}{2}$　　B. $\dfrac{1}{4}$　　C. $\dfrac{1}{8}$　　D. $\dfrac{1}{16}$

5-6-3 如图所示，悬臂梁 AB 由两根相同的矩形截面梁胶合而成。若胶合面全部开裂，假设开裂后两杆的弯曲变形相同，接触面之间无摩擦力，则开裂后梁的最大挠度是原来的(　　)。

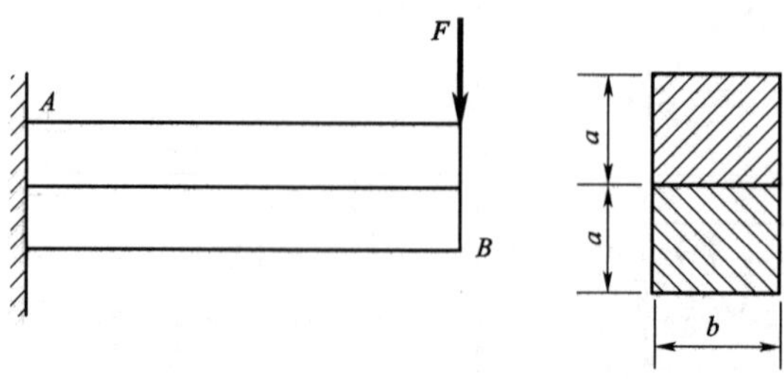

题 5-6-3 图

A. 两者相同　　B. 2 倍　　C. 4 倍　　D. 8 倍

5-6-4　图示外伸梁，A 截面的剪力为(　　)。

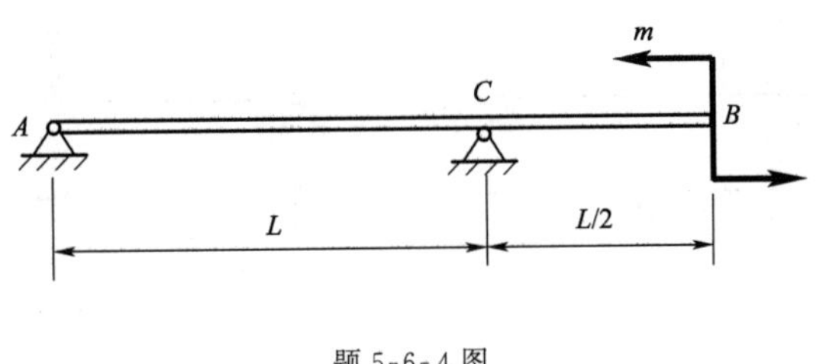

题 5-6-4 图

A. 0　　B. $\frac{3m}{2L}$　　C. $\frac{m}{L}$　　D. $-\frac{m}{L}$

5-6-5　两根梁长度、截面形状和约束条件完全相同，一根材料为钢，另一根为铝。在相同的外力作用下发生弯曲形变，两者不同之处为(　　)。

A. 弯曲内力　　B. 弯曲正应力

C. 弯曲切应力　　D. 挠曲线

5-6-6　图示四个悬臂梁中挠曲线是圆弧的(　　)。

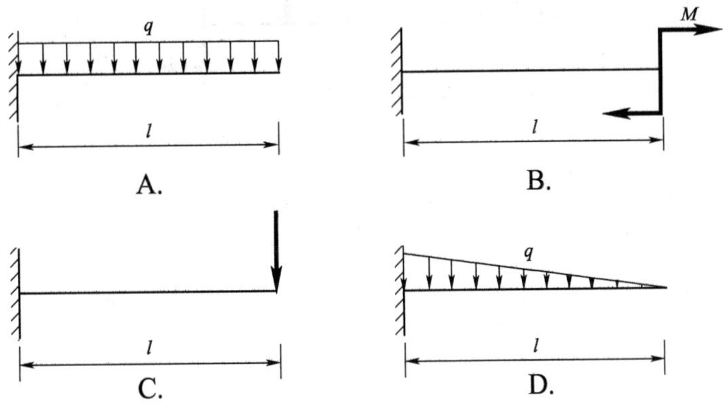

5-6-7　带有中间铰的静定梁受载情况如图所示，则(　　)。

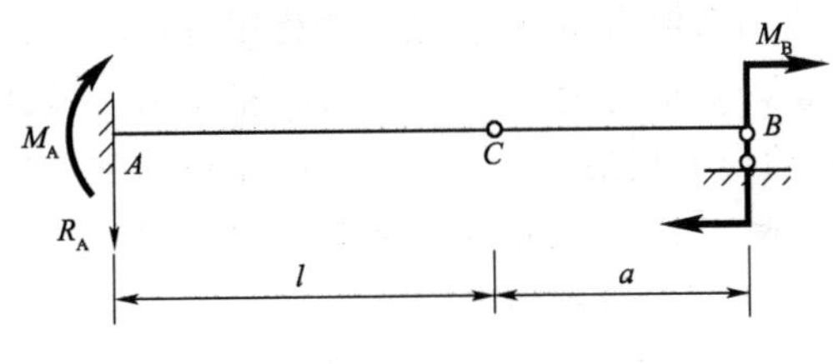

题 5-6-7 图

A. a 越大，则 M_A 越大　　B. l 越大，M_A 则越大

C. a 越大，则 R_A 越大　　D. l 越大，R_A 则越大

5-6-8　设图示两根圆截面梁的直径分别为 d 和 $2d$，许可荷载分别为$[P_1]$和$[P_2]$。若两梁的材料相同，则$[P_1]/[P_2]$等于(　　)。

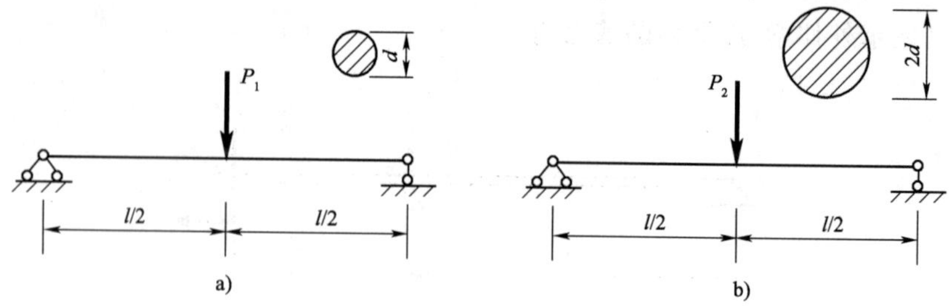

题 5-6-8 图

A. 2　　B. 4　　C. 8　　D. 16

5-6-9　悬臂梁受截情况如图所示，在截面 C 上(　　)。

A. 剪力为零，弯矩不为零

B. 剪力不为零，弯矩为零

C. 剪力和弯矩均为零

D. 剪力和弯矩不为零

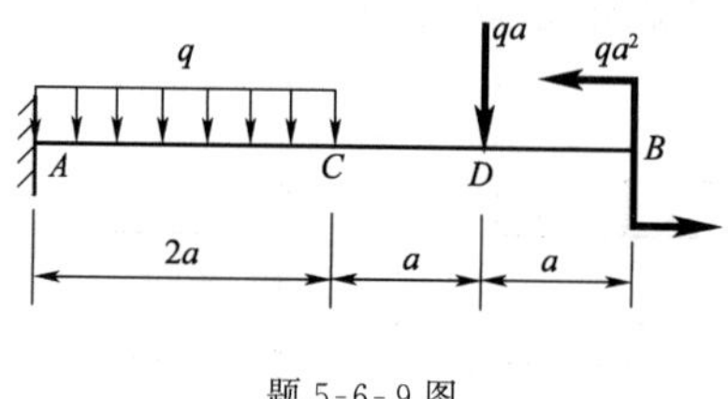

题 5-6-9 图

5-6-10　已知图示两梁的抗弯截面刚度 EI 相同，若两者自由端的挠度相等，则 P_1/P_2 等于(　　)。

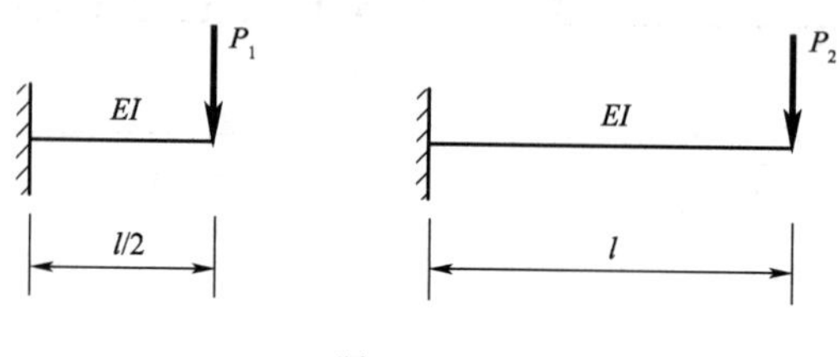

题 5-6-10 图

A. 2　　B. 4　　C. 8　　D. 16

5-6-11　矩形截面梁横力弯曲时，在横截面的中性轴处(　　)。

A. 正应力最大，剪应力为零　　B. 正应力为零，剪应力最大

C. 正应力和剪应力均最大　　D. 正应力和剪应力均为零

5-6-12　一跨度为 l 的简支架，若仅承受一个集中力 P，当 P 在梁上任意移动时，梁内产生的最大剪力 Q_{max} 和最大弯矩 M_{max} 分别满足(　　)。

A. $Q_{max} \leqslant P, M_{max} = Pl/4$　　B. $Q_{max} \leqslant P/2, M_{max} \leqslant Pl/4$

C. $Q_{max} \leqslant P, M_{max} \leqslant Pl/4$　　D. $Q_{max} \leqslant P/2, M_{max} = Pl/2$

5-6-13　图示梁的剪力等于零的截面位置 x 之值为(　　)。

A. $\frac{5a}{6}$　　B. $\frac{6a}{5}$　　C. $\frac{6a}{7}$　　D. $\frac{7a}{6}$

5-6-14　梁的横截面形状如图所示，则截面对 z 轴的抗弯截面模量 W_z 为(　　)。

A. $\frac{1}{12}(BH^3-bh^3)$　　B. $\frac{1}{6}(BH^2-bh^2)$

C. $\frac{1}{6H}(BH^3-bh^3)$　　D. $\frac{1}{6h}(BH^3-bh^3)$

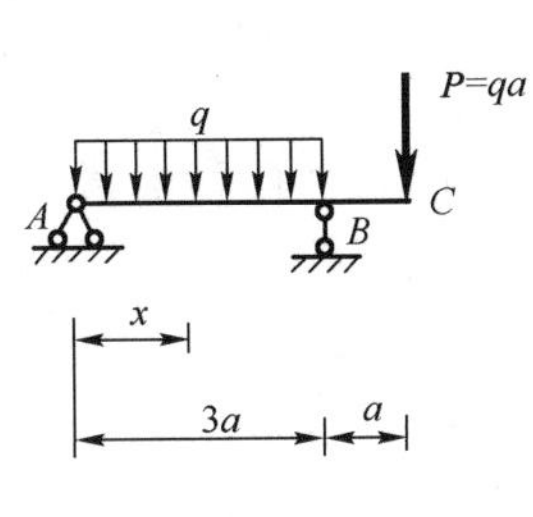

题 5-6-13 图

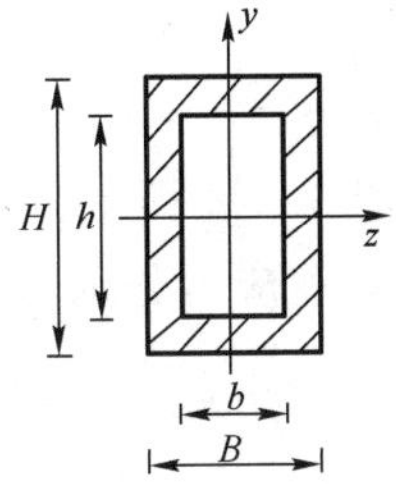

题 5-6-14 图

5-6-15　就正应力强度而言，如图所示的梁，以下列哪个图所示的加载方式最好？(　　)

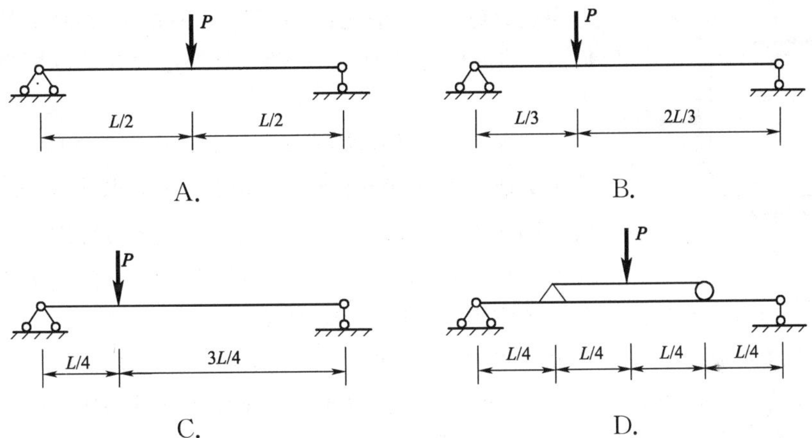

5-6-16　在等直梁平面弯曲的挠曲线上，曲率最大值发生在(　　)的截面上。

A. 挠度最大　B. 转角最大　C. 弯矩最大　D. 剪力最大

第七节　应力状态与强度理论

一、点的应力状态及其分类

(1)定义：受力后构件上任一点沿各个不同方向上应力情况的集合，称为一点的应力状态。

(2)单元体选取方法：

①分析构件的外力和支座反力；

②过研究点取横截面，分析其内力；

③确定横截面上该点的 σ、τ 的大小和方向。

(3)主平面：过某点的无数多个截面中，最大(或最小)正应力所在的平面称为主平面，主平面上剪应力必为零。

(4)主应力：主平面上的最大(或最小)正应力。

(5)点的应力状态分类：对任一点总可找到三对互相垂直的主平面，相应地存在三个互相垂直的主应力，按代数值大小排列为 $\sigma_1 \geqslant \sigma_2 \geqslant \sigma_3$。若这三个主应力中，仅一个不为零，则该应力状态称为单向应力状态；如有两个不为零，称为二向应力状态；当三个主应力均不为零时，称为三向应力状态。

二、二向应力状态

（一）斜截面上的应力

平面应力状态如图 5-7-1 所示，设其 σ_x、σ_y、τ_x 为已知，则任意斜截面（其外法线 n 与 x 轴夹角为 α）上的正应力和剪应力分别为

$$\left.\begin{aligned}\sigma_\alpha &= \frac{\sigma_x+\sigma_y}{2}+\frac{\sigma_x-\sigma_y}{2}\cos 2\alpha-\tau_x\sin 2\alpha \\ \tau_\alpha &= \frac{\sigma_x-\sigma_y}{2}\sin 2\alpha+\tau_x\cos 2\alpha\end{aligned}\right\} \tag{5-7-1}$$

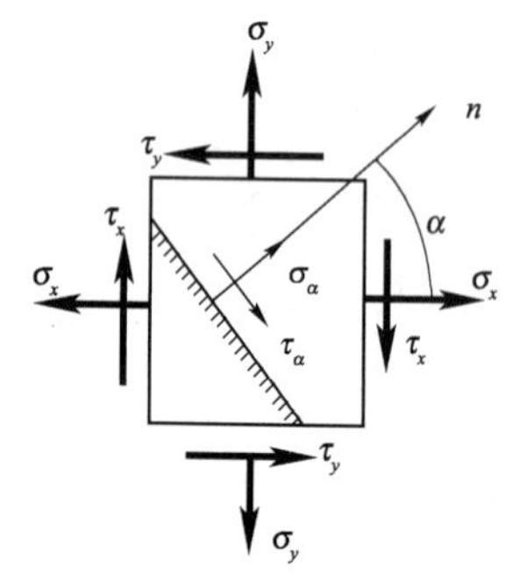

图 5-7-1　平面应力状态单元体

式(5-7-1)中应力的符号规定为：正应力以拉应力为正，压应力为负；剪应力对单元体内任意点的矩为顺时针者为正，反之为负。α 的符号规定为：由 x 轴转到外法线 n 为逆时针者为正，反之为负。

首先，按下列方法画应力圆，如图 5-7-2 所示。按一定比例尺在 σ 轴上取横坐标 $\overline{OF}=\sigma_x$，在 τ 轴上取纵坐标 $\overline{FD}=\tau_x$，得 D 点；量取 $\overline{OH}=\sigma_y$，$\overline{HE}=\tau_y$，得 E 点；连接 D、E 两点的直线，与 x 轴交于 C 点（此点即为应力圆的圆心）；以 C 点为圆心，$\overline{CD}$ 或 $\overline{CE}$ 为半径作圆，此圆即为应力圆。

然后，以 CD 为单元体 x 轴的基准线，沿逆时针方向量 2α 角度，画其射线，此射线与应力圆的交点 G 的横坐标和纵坐标，即为单元体 α 斜截面上的正应力 σ_α 和剪应力 τ_α。

图解法的步骤可以用 16 个字概括如下：点面对应，先找基准，转向相同，夹角两倍。

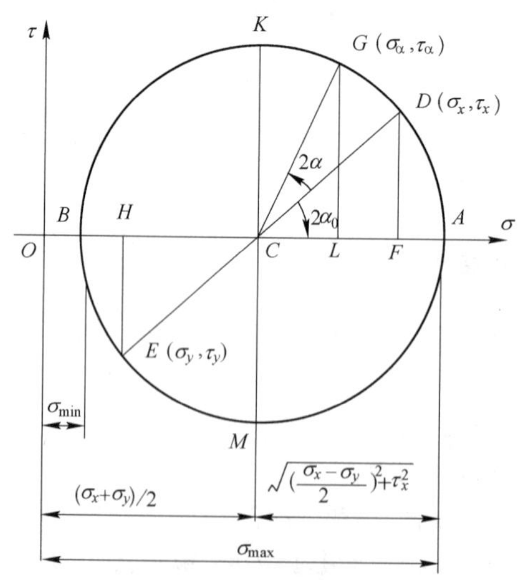

图 5-7-2　应力圆

（二）主应力、主平面

根据理论推导，平面应力状态（见图 5-7-2）的主应力计算公式为

$$\frac{\sigma_{max}}{\sigma_{min}}=\frac{\sigma_x+\sigma_y}{2}\pm\sqrt{\left(\frac{\sigma_x-\sigma_y}{2}\right)^2+\tau_x^2} \tag{5-7-2}$$

主平面所在截面的方位 α_0 可由下式确定

$$\tan 2\alpha_0=\frac{-2\tau_x}{\sigma_x-\sigma_y} \tag{5-7-3}$$

同时满足该式的两个角度 α_1 和 α_3 相差 90°，其中 α_1 和 α_3 分别对应于主应力 α_1 和 α_3（设 $\alpha_2=0$，则 $\sigma_1=\sigma_{max}$，$\sigma_3=\sigma_{min}$，否则按代数值排列）。若式(5-7-2)中的负号放在分子上，按 $\tan 2\alpha_0$ 的定义确定 $2\alpha_0$ 的象限，即设 $\theta=\arctan\left(\frac{-2\tau_x}{\sigma_x-\sigma_y}\right)$，则 $2\alpha_0$ 分别为 θ(第 I 象限)，$180°-\theta$(第 II 象限)，$180°+\theta$(第 III 象限)和 $-\theta$(第 IV 象限)，这样得到的 α_0 即为 α_1 的值。

在图 5-7-2 中，$\overline{OA}=\sigma_{max}$，$\overline{OB}=\sigma_{min}$，由图可见，在应力圆上 D 点（代表法线为 x 轴的平面）到 A 点所对的圆心角为 $2\alpha_0$（顺时针方向），相应地，在单元体上由 x 轴顺时针方向量取 α_0，就是 σ_{max} 所在平面的法线位置。

（三）最大（最小）剪应力

图 5-7-2 中应力圆上 K、M 点的纵坐标即分别为 τ_{max} 和 τ_{min}

$$\frac{\tau_{max}}{\tau_{min}}=\pm\sqrt{\left(\frac{\sigma_x-\sigma_y}{2}\right)^2+\tau_x^2} \tag{5-7-4}$$

显然，最大（最小）剪应力所在平面与主平面夹角为 45°。

三、三向应力状态、广义虎克定律

（一）斜截面上应力、最大剪应力

在 σ-τ 直角坐标系下，代表单元体任何截面上应力的点，必定在由 σ_1 和 σ_2、σ_2 和 σ_3、σ_3 和 σ_1 所组成的三个应力圆（见图 5-7-3）的圆周上，或由它们所围成的阴影范围内。

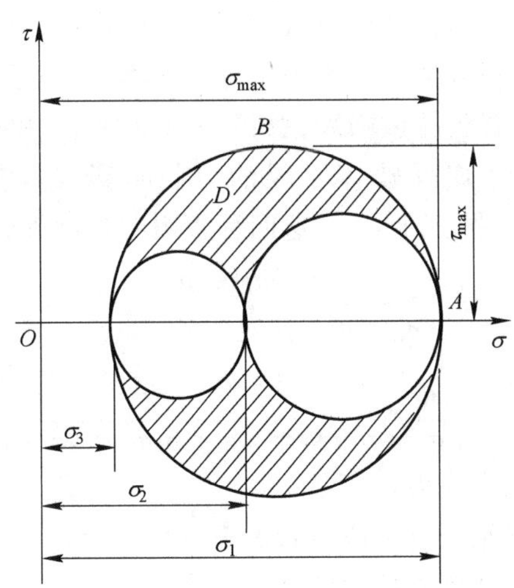

图 5-7-3　三向应力状态的应力圆

理论分析证明了在三向应力状态中，最大剪应力的作用面与最大主应力 σ_1 和最小主应力 σ_3 所在平面成 45°，而与 σ_2 所在平面垂直，其值为

$$\tau_{max}=\frac{\sigma_1-\sigma_3}{2} \tag{5-7-5}$$

(二)广义虎克定律

对各向同性材料，在线弹性范围内，复杂应力状态下的应力与应变之间存在着如下的关系，这种关系称为广义虎克定律，即

$$\left.\begin{aligned}\varepsilon_x&=\frac{1}{E}[\sigma_x-\mu(\sigma_y+\sigma_z)]\\\varepsilon_y&=\frac{1}{E}[\sigma_y-\mu(\sigma_z+\sigma_x)]\\\varepsilon_z&=\frac{1}{E}[\sigma_z-\mu(\sigma_x+\sigma_y)]\end{aligned}\right\}\tag{5-7-6}$$

以及

$$\tau_{xy}=G\gamma_{xy}\quad\tau_{yz}=G\gamma_{yz}\quad\tau_{zx}=G\gamma_{zx}\tag{5-7-7}$$

在平面应力状态下，$\sigma_z=0$，式(5-7-5)成为

$$\left.\begin{aligned}\varepsilon_x&=\frac{1}{E}(\sigma_x-\mu\sigma_y)\\\varepsilon_y&=\frac{1}{E}(\sigma_y-\mu\sigma_x)\\\varepsilon_z&=-\frac{\mu}{E}(\sigma_x+\sigma_y)\end{aligned}\right\}\tag{5-7-8}$$

由式(5-7-7)可以反解出

$$\left.\begin{aligned}\sigma_x&=\frac{E}{1-\mu^2}(\varepsilon_x+\mu\varepsilon_y)\\\sigma_y&=\frac{E}{1-\mu^2}(\varepsilon_y+\mu\varepsilon_x)\end{aligned}\right\}\tag{5-7-9}$$

四、强度理论

强度理论实质上是利用简单拉压的试验结果，建立复杂应力状态下的强度条件的一些假说。这些假说认为，复杂应力状态下的危险准则，是某种决定因素达到单向拉伸时同一因素的极限值。强度理论分为两类：一类是解释材料发生脆性断裂破坏原因的，例如，最大拉应力理论（第一强度理论）和最大伸长线应变理论（第二强度理论）；另一类是解释塑性屈服破坏原因的，例如，最大剪应力理论（第三强度理论）和最大形状改变比能理论（第四强度理论）。这四种常用的强度理论的强度条件为

$$\sigma_{r1}=\sigma_1\leqslant[\sigma]\tag{5-7-10}$$

$$\sigma_{r2}=\sigma_1-\mu(\sigma_2+\sigma_3)\leqslant[\sigma]\tag{5-7-11}$$

$$\sigma_{r3}=\sigma_1-\sigma_3\leqslant[\sigma]\tag{5-7-12}$$

$$\sigma_{r4}=\sqrt{\sigma_1^2+\sigma_2^2+\sigma_3^2-\sigma_1\sigma_2-\sigma_2\sigma_3-\sigma_3\sigma_1}\leqslant[\sigma]\tag{5-7-13}$$

式中：$\sigma_{ri}(i=1,2,3,4)$——相当应力；

σ_1、σ_2、σ_3——分别为复杂应力状态下的主应力；

$[\sigma]$——材料单向拉伸的许用应力。

在平面应力状态下（如 $\sigma_2=0$），第四强度理论可简化为

$$\sigma_{r4}=\sqrt{\sigma_1^2+\sigma_3^2-\sigma_1\sigma_3}\leqslant[\sigma]\tag{5-7-14}$$

若平面应力状态如图 5-7-4 所示，即 $\sigma_x=\sigma,\sigma_y=0,\tau_x=\tau_y=\tau$ 时

$$\sigma_{r3}=\sqrt{\sigma^2+4\tau^2}\leqslant[\sigma]\tag{5-7-15}$$

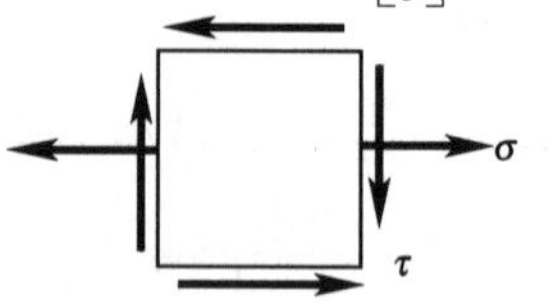

图 5-7-4　$\sigma_y=0$ 时的平面应力状态

$$\sigma_{r4}=\sqrt{\sigma^2+3\tau^2}\leqslant[\sigma] \tag{5-7-16}$$

梁中任一点的应力状态，以及弯扭组合或拉扭组合变形时危险点的应力状态都可以归结为上述情况。

此外，对于抗拉和抗压强度不等的材料，还有根据综合试验结果建立的莫尔强度理论，其强度条件为

$$\sigma_m=\sigma_1-\frac{[\sigma_t]}{[\sigma_c]}\sigma_3\leqslant[\sigma_t] \tag{5-7-17}$$

式中：σ_m——莫尔强度理论的相当应力；

$[\sigma_t]$、$[\sigma_c]$——分别为材料的单向拉伸和单向压缩时的许用拉应力和许用压应力。

【例 5-7-1】 已知某点的应力状态如图 a)所示，求该点的主应力大小及方位。

解

$$\begin{aligned}\left.\begin{matrix}\sigma_{max}\\ \sigma_{min}\end{matrix}\right\}&=\frac{\sigma_x+\sigma_y}{2}\pm\sqrt{\left(\frac{\sigma_x-\sigma_y}{2}\right)^2+\tau_x^2}\\&=\frac{-120+0}{2}\pm\sqrt{\left(\frac{-120-0}{2}\right)^2+60^2}\\&=\begin{matrix}24.85\text{MPa}\\-144.85\text{MPa}\end{matrix}\end{aligned}$$

$$\sigma_1=24.85\text{MPa},\sigma_2=0\text{MPa},\sigma_3=-144.85\text{MPa}$$

$$\tan2\alpha_1=\frac{-2\tau_x}{\sigma_x-\sigma_y}=\frac{-2\times60}{-120-0}=1$$

$$2\alpha_1=180°+45°=225°$$

$$\alpha_1=112.5°,\alpha_3=112.5°-90°=22.5°$$

主应力方位如图 b)所示。

思考：主应力方向位能否用观察法确定。

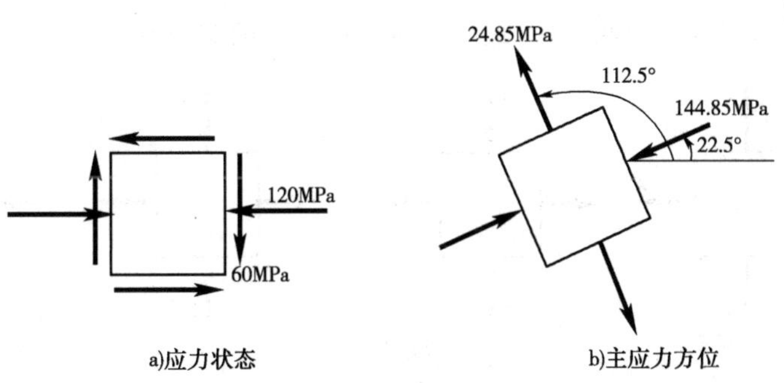

例 5-7-1 图

【例 5-7-2】 按照第三强度理论，图示两种应力状态的危险程度是：

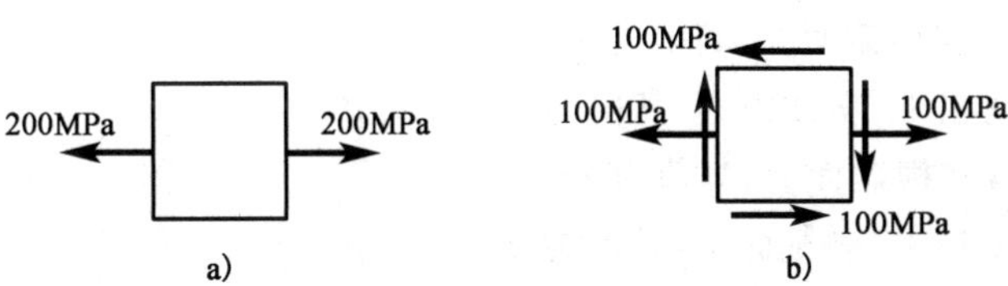

例 5-7-2 图

A. 无法判断　　B. 两者相同　　C. a)更危险　　D. b)更危险

解　图 a)中 $\sigma_1=200\text{MPa},\sigma_2=0,\sigma_3=0$

$\sigma_{r3}^{a}=\sigma_1-\sigma_3=200\text{MPa}$

图 b)中 $\sigma_1=\frac{100}{2}+\sqrt{(\frac{100}{2})^2+100^2}=161.8\text{MPa},\sigma_2=0$

$\sigma_3=\frac{100}{2}-\sqrt{(\frac{100}{2})^2+100^2}=-61.8\text{MPa}$

$\sigma_{r3}^{b}=\sigma_1-\sigma_3=223.6\text{MPa}$

故图 b)更危险。

答案:D

【例 5-7-3】　在图示 xy 坐标系下,单元体的最大主应力 σ_1 大致指向:

A. 第一象限,靠近 x 轴

B. 第一象限,靠近 y 轴

C. 第二象限,靠近 x 轴

D. 第二象限,靠近 y 轴

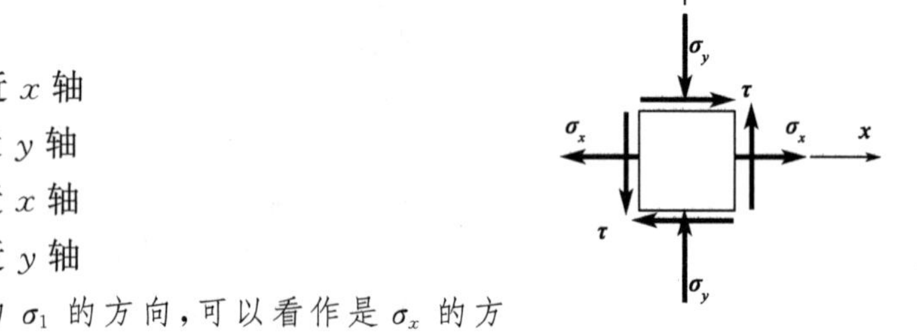

例 5-7-3 图

解　图示单元体的最大主应力 σ_1 的方向,可以看作是 σ_x 的方向(沿 x 轴)和纯剪切单元体的最大拉应力的主方向(在第一象限沿45°向上),叠加后的合应力的指向。

答案:A

习　　题

5-7-1　在图示四种应力状态中,最大切应力值最大的应力状态是(　　)。

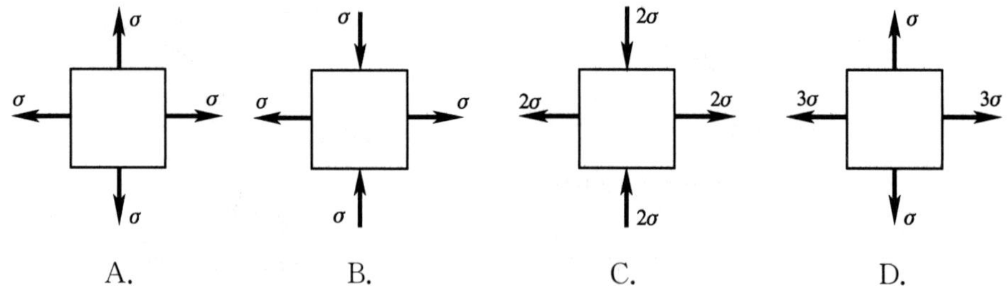

5-7-2　受力体一点处的应力状态如图所示,该点的最大主应力 σ_1 为(　　)MPa。

A. 70　　B. 10　　C. 40　　D. 50

5-7-3　设受扭圆轴中的最大剪应力为 τ,则最大正应力(　　)。

A. 出现在横截面上,其值为 τ

B. 出现在 45°斜截面上,其值为 2τ

C. 出现在横截面上,其值为 2τ

D. 出现在 45°斜截面上,其值为 τ

5-7-4　图示为三角形单元体,已知 ab、ca 两斜布的正应力为 σ,剪应力为零。在竖直面 bc 上有(　　)。

A. $\sigma_x=\sigma, \tau_{xy}=0$

B. $\sigma_x=\sigma, \tau_{xy}=\sigma\sin60^\circ-\sigma\sin45^\circ$

C. $\sigma_x=\sigma\cos60^\circ+\sigma\cos45^\circ, \tau_{xy}=0$

D. $\sigma_x=\sigma\cos60^\circ+\sigma\cos45^\circ, \tau_{xy}=\sigma\sin60^\circ-\sigma\sin45^\circ$

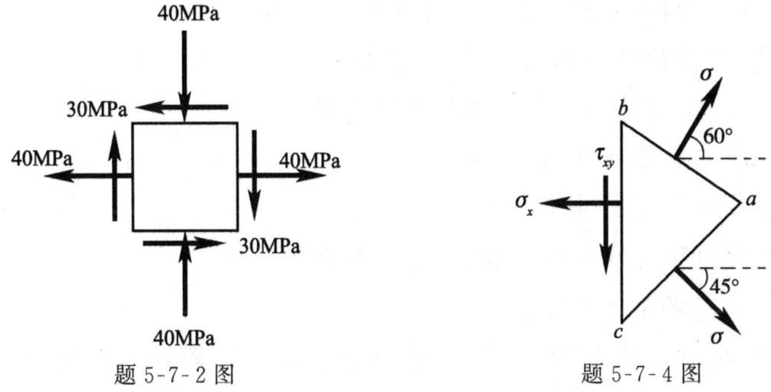

题 5-7-2 图　　　　题 5-7-4 图

5-7-5　四种应力状态分别如图所示,按照第三强度理论,其相当应力最大的是(　　)。

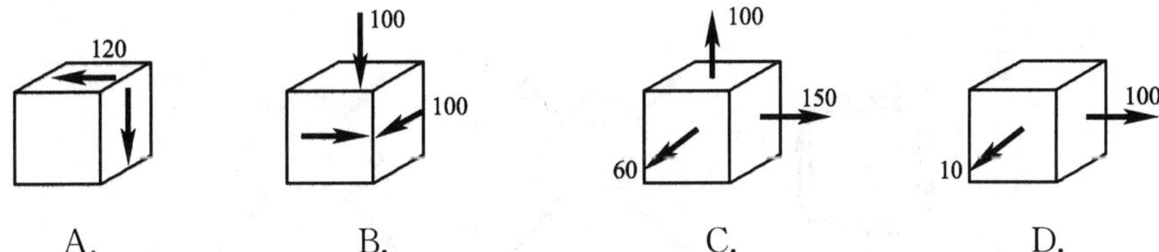

5-7-6　图示为等腰直角三角形单元体,已知两直角边表示的截面上只有剪应力,且等于τ_0,则底边表示的截面上的正应力σ和剪应力τ分别为(　　)。

A. $\sigma=\tau_0, \tau=\tau_0$　　　　B. $\sigma=\tau_0, \tau=0$

C. $\sigma=\sqrt{2}\tau_0, \tau=\tau_0$　　　　D. $\sigma=\sqrt{2}\tau_0, \tau=0$

5-7-7　单元体的应力状态如图所示,若已知其中一个主应力为 5MPa,则另一个主应力为(　　)MPa。

A. -85　　B. 85　　C. -75　　D. 75

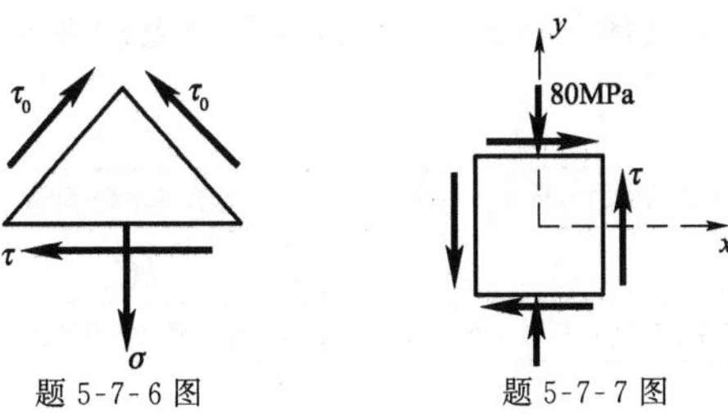

题 5-7-6 图　　　　题 5-7-7 图

5-7-8　如图所示悬臂梁,给出了 1、2、3、4 点处的应力状态如图所示,其中应力状态错误的位置点是(　　)。

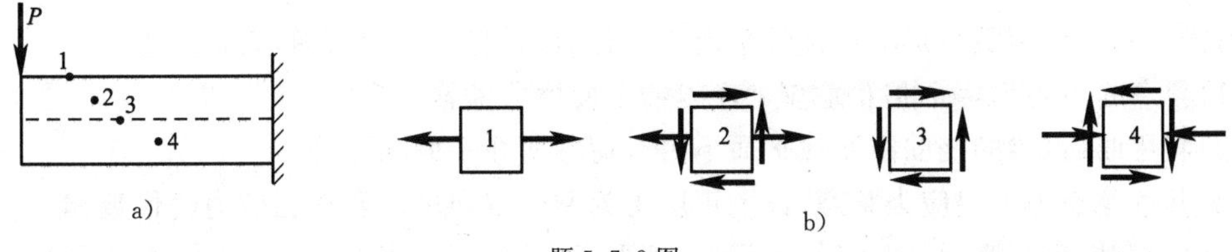

题 5-7-8 图

A. 1 点　　B. 2 点　　C. 3 点　　D. 4 点

5-7-9　单元体的应力状态如图所示，其 σ_1 的方向(　　)。

A. 在第一、三象限内，且与 x 轴成小于 45°的夹角

B. 在第一、三象限内，且与 y 轴成小于 45°的夹角

C. 在第二、四象限内，且与 x 轴成小于 45°的夹角

D. 在第二、四象限内，且与 y 轴成小于 45°的夹角

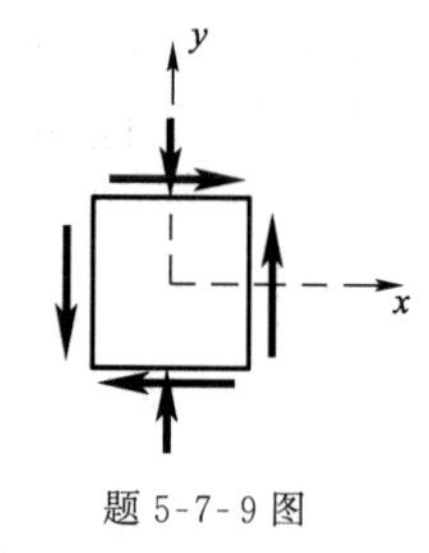

题 5-7-9 图

5-7-10　对于平面应力状态，以下说法正确的是(　　)。

A. 主应力就是最大正应力

B. 主平面上无剪应力

C. 最大剪应力作用的平面上正应力必为零

D. 主应力必不为零

5-7-11　三种平面应力状态如图所示(图中用 σ 和 τ 分别表示正应力和剪应力)，它们之间的关系是(　　)。

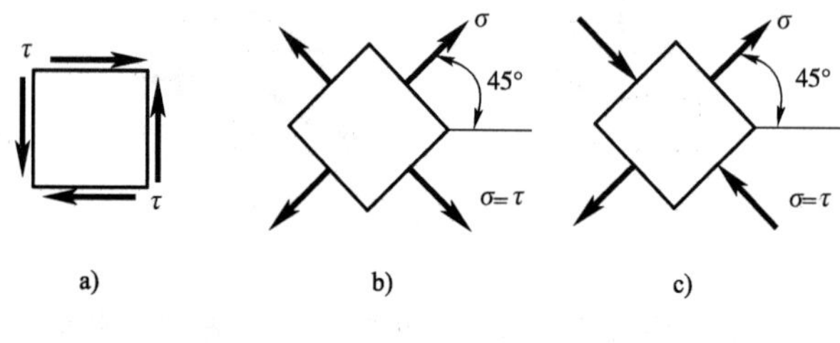

题 5-7-11 图

A. 全部等价　　B. a)与 b)等价

C. a)与 c)等价　　D. 都不等价

第八节　组 合 变 形

在小变形和材料服从虎克定律的前提下，组合变形问题的解法思路如图 5-8-1 所示。

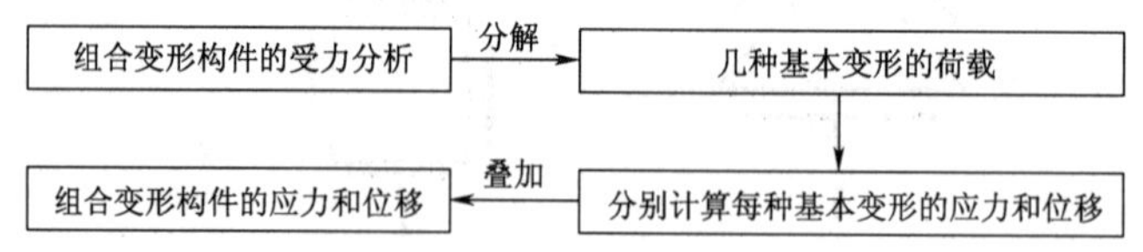

图 5-8-1　组合变形问题的解法思路

一、斜弯曲

当梁上的横向荷载与形心主惯性平面不平行时，梁将发生斜弯曲，其特点为：

(1)斜弯曲可看作两个相互垂直平面内的平面弯曲的叠加。

(2)斜弯曲后，梁的挠曲线所在平面不再与荷载所在平面相重合。

(3)其危险点为单向应力状态，最大正应力为两个方向平面弯曲正应力的代数和。

①对于有棱角的截面，如矩形、工字形、槽形等，危险点在凸角处，具体位置可用观察法确

定。其强度条件为

$$\sigma_{\max}=\frac{M_{y\max}}{W_y}+\frac{M_{z\max}}{W_z}\leqslant[\sigma] \tag{5-8-1}$$

式中：$M_{y\max}$、$M_{z\max}$——分别为危险截面上两个表心主惯性平面内的弯矩；

W_y、W_z——分别为截面对 y 轴、z 轴的抗弯截面模量。

②对没有凸角的截面，则必须先确定中性轴的位置，斜弯曲梁的中性轴是一条过截面形心的斜线，其与 z 轴的夹角 α 可根据下式确定

$$\tan\alpha=\frac{I_z M_y}{I_y M_z} \tag{5-8-2}$$

式中：M_y、M_z——分别为梁危险截面上两个形心主惯性平面内的弯矩；

I_y、I_z——分别为危险截面对 y 轴、z 轴的惯性矩。

设截面上距中性轴最远的危险点 a 的坐标为 y_a、z_a，则其强度条件为

$$\sigma_{\max}=\frac{M_{y\max}}{I_y}z_a+\frac{M_{z\max}}{I_z}y_a\leqslant[\sigma] \tag{5-8-3}$$

③对圆轴截面（或正多边形截面），因为任一形心轴均为形心主轴，所以最大弯矩的方向即为最大应力的方向，其强度条件为

$$\sigma_{\max}=\frac{M_{\max}}{W}=\frac{32\sqrt{M_y^2+M_z^2}}{\pi d^3}\leqslant[\sigma] \tag{5-8-4}$$

二、拉（压）弯组合变形

当构件同时受到轴向力和横向力作用，或构件上仅作用有轴向力，但其作用线未与轴线重合，即偏心拉伸（压缩）时，都会产生拉（压）弯组合变形。其强度条件都可用式(5-8-5)表示

$$\begin{matrix}\sigma_{t\max}\\ \sigma_{c\max}\end{matrix}=\frac{N}{A}\pm\frac{M_y}{W_y}\pm\frac{M_z}{W_z}\leqslant\begin{matrix}[\sigma_t]\\ [\sigma_c]\end{matrix} \tag{5-8-5}$$

式中：N、M_y、M_z——分别为危险截面上的轴力、弯矩；

$[\sigma_t]$、$[\sigma_c]$——分别为材料的许用拉应力、许用压应力。

其危险点在危险截面的上、下边缘，为单向应力状态，最大拉应力和最大压应力为轴向拉压正应力和两个方向平面弯曲正应力的代数和。式(5-8-5)中各项的正负号可由观察法确定。

对于有棱角的截面，危险点在凸角处；对没有凸角的截面，则必须先确定中性轴的位置。偏心压缩构件危险截面上的中性轴是一条不通过截面形心的斜直线，它在 y 轴、z 轴上的截距分别为

$$a_y=-\frac{i_z^2}{y_P}\quad a_z=-\frac{i_y^2}{z_P} \tag{5-8-6}$$

式中：i_z、i_y——分别为截面对 z 轴、y 轴的惯性半径；

z_P、y_P——分别为轴向力 P 的作用点距 y 轴、z 轴的偏心距。

【例 5-8-1】 如图 a)所示正方形截面杆中间开有 $\frac{a}{2}$ 宽的槽，求杆中的 $\sigma_{\max}^{+}$ 和 $\sigma_{\max}^{-}$，并在危险截面上标明其所在位置。

解 显然，在开槽部位的横截面为危险截面，其剖面图如图 b)所示，角点 A、B、C、D 的应力情况用观察法，见表，其中 A 点为 σ_{max}^{+}，C 点为最大压应力 σ_{max}^{-}，其值分别为

$$\begin{matrix}\sigma_{max}^{+}\\ \sigma_{max}^{-}\end{matrix}=\frac{P}{A}\pm\frac{M_z}{W_z}\pm\frac{M_y}{W_y}=\frac{P}{\frac{a^2}{2}}\pm\frac{P\frac{a}{2}}{\frac{1}{6}\left(\frac{a}{2}\right)a^2}\pm\frac{P\frac{3}{4}a}{\frac{a}{6}\left(\frac{a}{2}\right)^2}$$

$$=2\frac{P}{a^2}\pm6\frac{P}{a^2}\pm18\frac{P}{a^2}=\begin{matrix}26\frac{P}{a^2}\\ -22\frac{P}{a^2}\end{matrix}$$

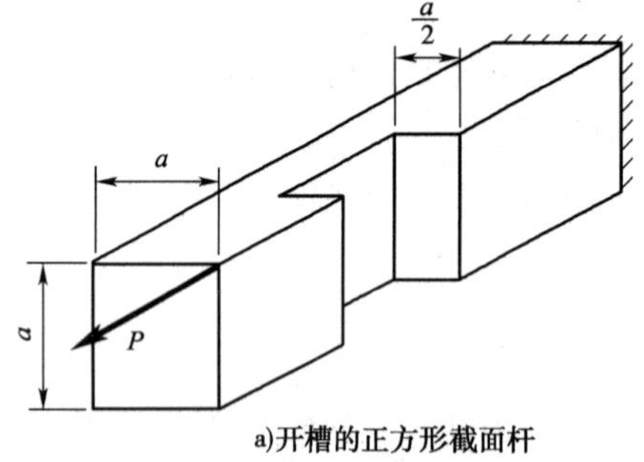

a)开槽的正方形截面杆

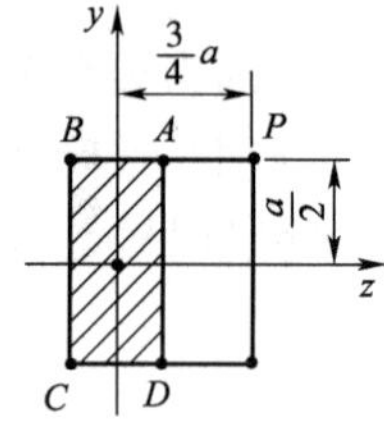

b)危险截面的剖面图

例 5-8-1 图

例 5-8-1 图中各点的应用情况 例 5-8-1 解表

点	P	M_y	M_z	应力	点	P	M_y	M_z	应力
A	+	+	+	σ_{max}^{+}	C	+	−	−	σ_{max}^{-}
B	+	−	+		D	+	+	−	

【例 5-8-2】 图示正方形截面杆 AB，力 F 作用在 xOy 平面内，与 x 轴夹角 α，杆距离 B 端为 a 的横截面上最大正应力在 $\alpha=45°$ 时的值是 $\alpha=0$ 时值的：

A. $\frac{7\sqrt{2}}{2}$倍

B. $3\sqrt{2}$倍

C. $\frac{5\sqrt{2}}{2}$倍

D. $\sqrt{2}$倍

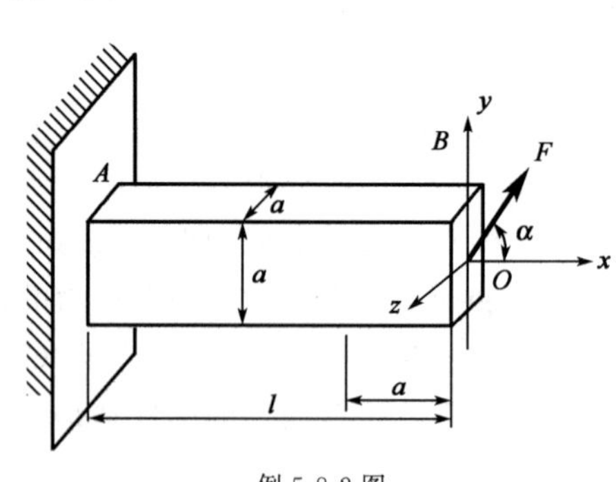

例 5-8-2 图

解 当 $\alpha=0°$ 时，杆是轴向受位：

$$\sigma_{max}^{0°}=\frac{F_N}{A}=\frac{F}{a^2}$$

当 $\alpha=45°$ 时，杆是轴向受拉与弯曲组合变形：

$$\sigma_{max}^{45°}=\frac{F_N}{A}+\frac{M_g}{W_g}=\frac{\frac{\sqrt{2}}{2}F}{a^2}+\frac{\frac{\sqrt{2}}{2}F\cdot a}{\frac{a^3}{6}}=\frac{7\sqrt{2}}{2}\frac{F}{a^2}$$

可得$\dfrac{\sigma_{\max}^{45°}}{\sigma_{\max}^{0°}}=\dfrac{\dfrac{7\sqrt{2}}{2}\dfrac{F}{a^2}}{\dfrac{F}{a^2}}=\dfrac{7\sqrt{2}}{2}$。

答案：A

三、弯扭组合变形

弯扭组合变形（或拉压、弯、扭组合变形）时的危险截面是最大弯矩 $M_{\max}$（或最大轴力 $N_{\max}$）与最大扭矩同时作用的截面，危险点是 $\sigma_{\max}$（弯曲正应力或拉压应力）和 $\tau_{\max}$（扭转剪应力）同时作用的点。该点属复杂应力状态，因此其第三和第四强度理论的强度条件仍可由式(5-7-15)、式(5-7-16)来表示

$$\sigma_{r3}=\sqrt{\sigma^2+4\tau^2}$$

$$\sigma_{r4}=\sqrt{\sigma^2+3\tau^2}$$

式中：σ、τ——分别在危险点处的最大弯曲（或拉压）正应力、最大扭转剪应力。

对于圆截面杆，在弯扭组合变形时，可以用下式计算

$$\sigma_{r3}=\frac{\sqrt{M^2+T^2}}{W}\leqslant[\sigma] \tag{5-8-7}$$

其中

$$W=\frac{\pi d^3}{32}；\sigma_{r4}=\frac{\sqrt{M^2+0.75T^2}}{W}\leqslant[\sigma] \tag{5-8-8}$$

式中：M——危险截面上的弯矩或合成弯矩，$M=\sqrt{M_y^2+M_z^2}$；

T——危险截面上的扭矩；

W——抗弯截面系数。

习　题

5-8-1　矩形截面杆 AB，A 端固定，B 端自由，B 端右下角处承受力与轴线平行的集中力 F（见图），杆的最大正应力是（　　）。

A. $\sigma=\dfrac{3F}{bh}$　　B. $\sigma=\dfrac{4F}{bh}$　　C. $\sigma=\dfrac{7F}{bh}$　　D. $\sigma=\dfrac{13F}{bh}$

5-8-2　图示圆轴固定端最上缘 A 点的单元体的应力状态是（　　）。

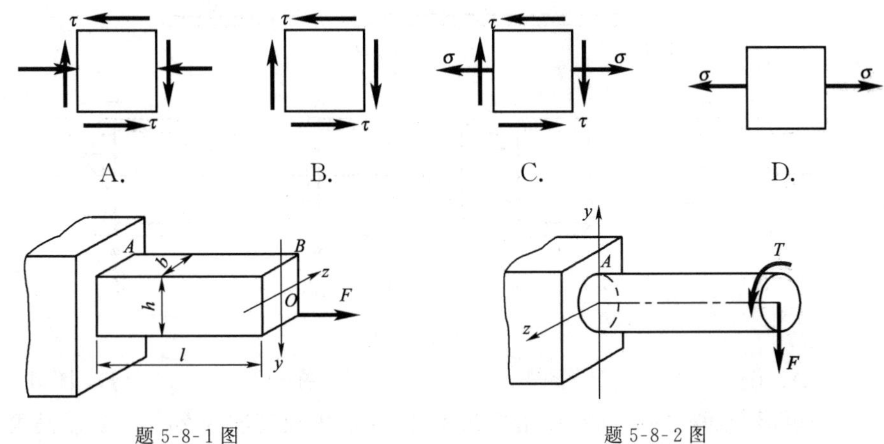

题 5-8-1 图　　题 5-8-2 图

5-8-3　图示为 T 形截面杆，一端固定、一端自由，自由端的集中力 $\boldsymbol{F}$ 作用在截面的左下角点，并与杆件的轴线平行。该杆发生的变形为(　　)。

A. 绕 y 和 z 轴的双向弯曲

B. 轴向拉伸和绕 y、z 轴的双向弯曲

C. 轴向拉伸和绕 z 轴弯曲

D. 轴向拉伸和绕 y 轴弯曲

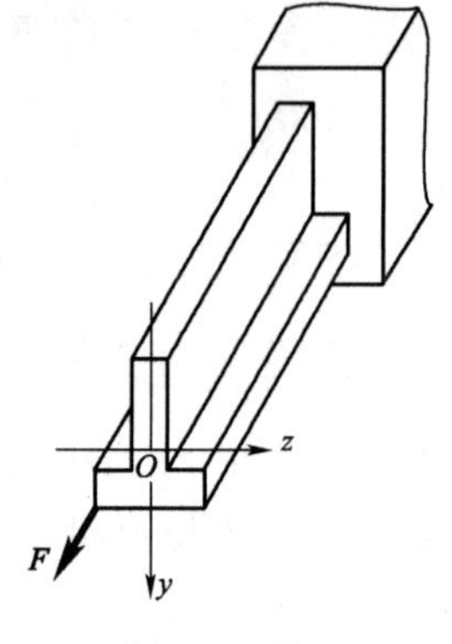

题 5-8-3 图

5-8-4　图示圆轴，在自由端圆周边界承受竖直向下的集中力 $\boldsymbol{F}$，按第三强度理论，危险截面的相当力 σ_{r3} 为(　　)。

A. $\sigma_{r3}=\dfrac{16}{\pi d^3}\sqrt{(FL)^2+4\left(\dfrac{Fd}{2}\right)^2}$

B. $\sigma_{r3}=\dfrac{16}{\pi d^3}\sqrt{(FL)^2+\left(\dfrac{Fd}{2}\right)^2}$

C. $\sigma_{r3}=\dfrac{32}{\pi d^3}\sqrt{(FL)^2+4\left(\dfrac{Fd}{2}\right)^2}$

D. $\sigma_{r3}=\dfrac{32}{\pi d^3}\sqrt{(FL)^2+\left(\dfrac{Fd}{2}\right)^2}$

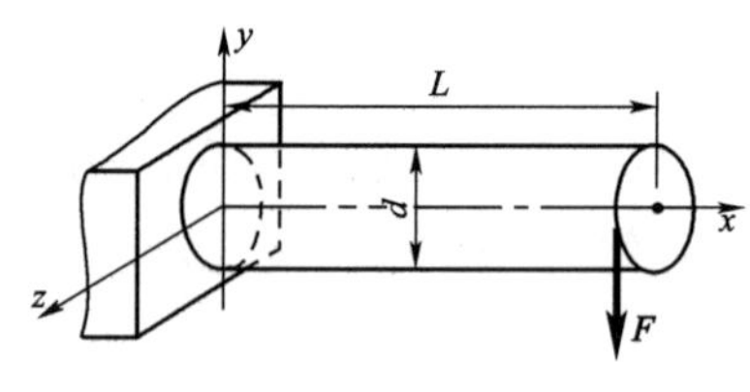

题 5-8-4 图

5-8-5　图示为正方形截面等直杆，抗弯截面模量为 W，在危险截面上，弯矩为 M，扭矩为 M_n，A 点处有最大正应力 σ 和最大剪应力 τ。若材料为低碳钢，则其强度条件为(　　)。

A. $\sigma\leqslant[\sigma]$，$\tau\leqslant[\tau]$

B. $\dfrac{1}{W}\sqrt{M^2+M_n^2}\leqslant[\sigma]$

C. $\dfrac{1}{W}\sqrt{M^2+0.75M_n^2}\leqslant[\sigma]$

D. $\sqrt{\sigma^2+4_\tau^2}\leqslant[\sigma]$

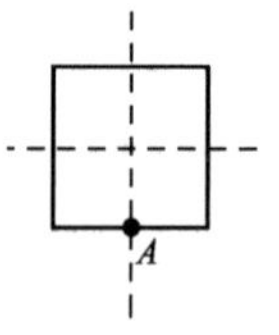

题 5-8-5 图

5-8-6　工字形截面梁在图示荷载作用下，截面 m-m 上的正应力分布为(　　)。

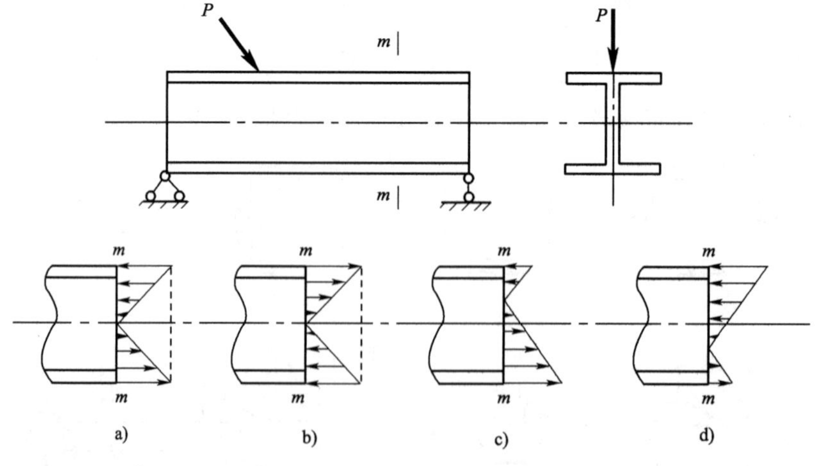

题 5-8-6 图

A. 图 a)　　B. 图 b)　　C. 图 c)　　D. 图 d)

5-8-7　矩形截面杆的截面宽度沿杆长不变，杆的中段高度为 2α，左、右段高度为 3α，在图

示三角形分布荷载作用下，杆的截面 m-m 和截面 n-n 分别发生（　　）。

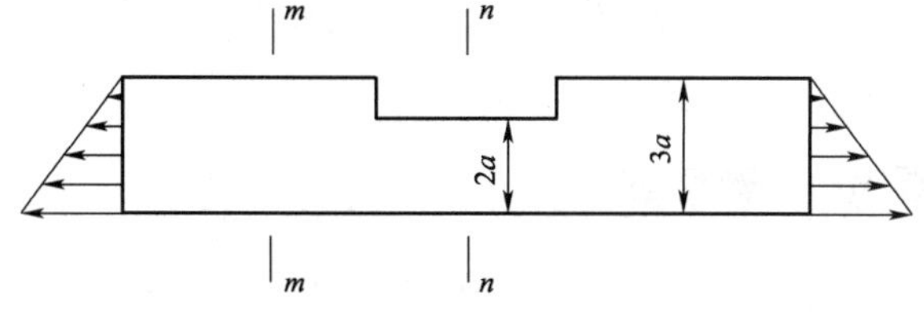

题 5-8-7 图

A. 单向拉伸、拉弯组合变形　　B. 单向拉伸、单向拉伸变形

C. 拉弯组合、单向拉伸变形　　D. 拉弯组合、拉弯组合变形

5-8-8　一正方形截面短粗立柱（图 a），若将其底面加宽 1 倍（图 b），原厚度不变，则该立柱的强度（　　）。

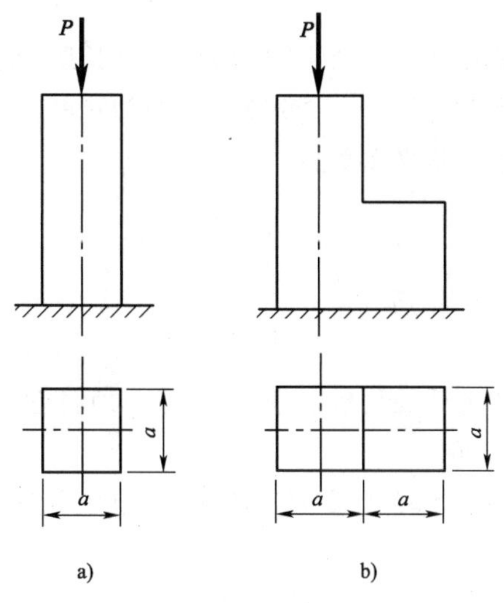

题 5-8-8 图

A. 提高 1 倍　B. 提高不到 1 倍　C. 不变　D. 降低

5-8-9　图示应力状态为其危险点的应力状态，则杆件为（　　）。

A. 斜弯曲变形　　B. 偏心拉弯变形

C. 拉弯组合变形　　D. 弯扭组合变形

5-8-10　折杆受力如图所示，以下结论中错误的为（　　）。

A. 点 B 和 D 处于纯剪状态

B. 点 A 和 C 处为二向应力状态，两点处 $\sigma_1>0$，$\sigma_2=0$，$\sigma_3<0$

C. 按照第三强度理论，点 A 及 C 比点 B 及 D 危险

D. 点 A 及 C 的最大主应力 σ_1 数值相同

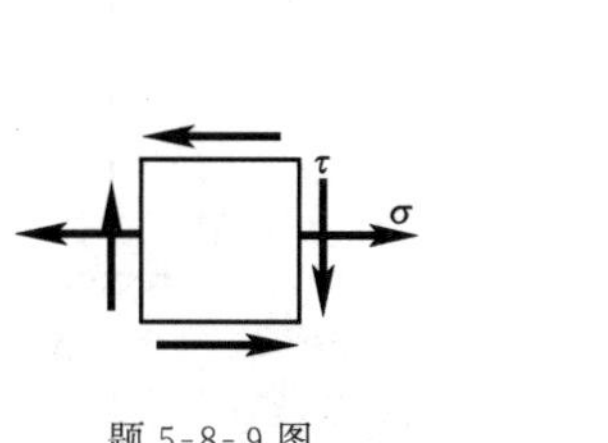

题 5-8-9 图

题 5-8-10 图

第九节　压杆稳定

一、细长压杆的临界力——欧拉公式

欧拉公式如下

$$P_{cr}=\frac{\pi^2 EI}{(\mu l)^2} \tag{5-9-1}$$

式中：P_{cr}——压杆的临界力；

E——压杆材料的弹性模量；

I——截面的主惯性矩；

μ——长度系数；

μl——压杆失稳时挠曲线中一个“半波正弦曲线”的长度，称为相当长度，此相当长度等于压杆失稳时挠曲线上两个弯矩零点之间的长度。

常用的四种杆端约束压杆的长度系数 μ：

(1)一端固定、一端自由，$\mu=2$；

(2)两端铰支，$\mu=1$；

(3)一端固定、一端铰支，$\mu=0.7$；

(4)两端固定，$\mu=0.5$。

工程实际中压杆的杆端约束往往比较复杂，不能简单地将它归于哪一类，要对其作具体分析，从而定出与实际较接近的 μ 值。

【例 5-9-1】　图示细长压杆 AB 的 A 端自由，B 端固定在简支梁上。该压杆的长度系数 μ 是：

A. $\mu>2$　　B. $2>\mu>1$

C. $1>\mu>0.7$　　D. $0.7>\mu>0.5$

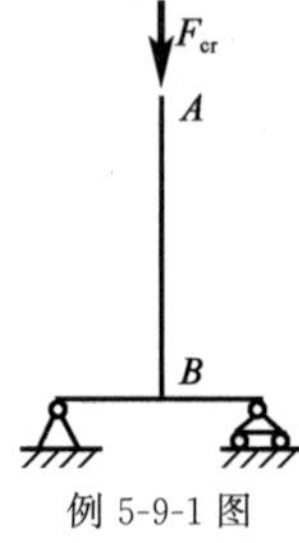

例 5-9-1 图

解　杆端约束越弱，μ 越大，在两端固定($\mu=0.5$)，一端固定、一端铰支($\mu=0.7$)，两端铰支($\mu=1$)和一端固定、一端自由($\mu=2$)这四种杆端约束中，一端固定、一端自由的约束最弱，μ 最大。而图示细长压杆 AB 一端自由、一端固定在简支梁上，其杆端约束比一端固定、一端自由($\mu=2$)时更弱，故 μ 比 2 更大。

答案：A

【例 5-9-2】　一端固定另端自由的细长(大柔度)压杆，长度为 L(图 a)，当杆的长度减少一半时(图 b)，其临界载荷是原来的：

A. 4 倍　　B. 3 倍

C. 2 倍　　D. 1 倍

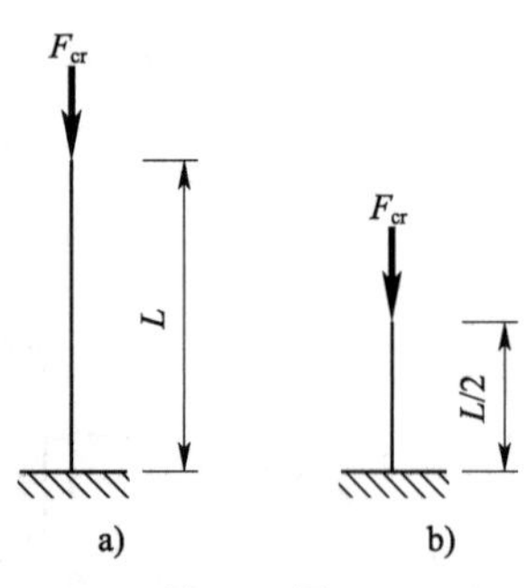

例 5-9-2 图

解　由一端固定、另端自由的细长压杆的临界力计算公式 $F_{cr}=\frac{\pi^2 EI}{(2l)^2}$，可知 F_{cr} 与 L^2 成反比。故有：

$$F_{cr1}=\frac{\pi^2 EI}{\left(2\cdot\frac{L}{2}\right)^2}=4\frac{\pi^2 EI}{(2L)^2}=4F_{cr}$$

答案：A

二、临界应力、柔度、欧拉公式的适用范围

（一）临界应力、柔度

$$\sigma_{cr}=\frac{P_{cr}}{A}=\frac{\pi^2 EI}{(\mu l)^2 A}=\frac{\pi^2 Ei^2}{(\mu l)^2}=\frac{\pi^2 E}{\left(\frac{\mu l}{i}\right)^2}=\frac{\pi^2 E}{\lambda^2} \tag{5-9-2}$$

其中

$$i=\sqrt{\frac{I}{A}},\lambda=\frac{\mu l}{i}$$

式中：i——惯性半径，它是反映截面形状和尺寸的一个几何量；

λ——压杆的柔度，又称为长细比，它是一个无量纲量，综合地反映了杆长、杆端约束以及截面形状和尺寸对临界应力的影响。

可见，柔度 λ 是一个极其重要的量。

（二）临界应力总图、欧拉公式的适用范围

根据压杆的柔度值可将所有压杆分为三类：$\lambda\geqslant\lambda_p$ 的压杆为细长杆或大柔度杆，其临界应力可按欧拉公式计算；$\lambda_s<\lambda<\lambda_p$ 的压杆为中长杆或中柔度杆，其临界应力可按经验公式 $\sigma_{cr}=a-b\lambda$ 计算；$\lambda\leqslant\lambda_s$ 的压杆则为短杆或小柔度杆，应按强度问题处理，用 $\sigma_{cr}=\sigma_s$ 来计算其临界应力。图 5-9-1 表示出这三种压杆的临界应力 σ_{cr} 随柔度 λ 的变化关系，称为临界应力总图，由图 5-9-1 中可以看到欧拉公式的使用条件是 $\sigma_{cr}=\frac{\pi^2 E}{\lambda^2}\leqslant\sigma_p$，亦即

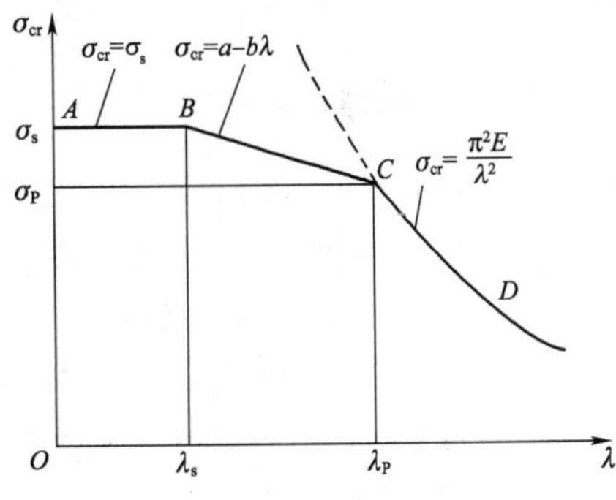

图 5-9-1　压杆临界应力总图

$$\lambda\geqslant\sqrt{\frac{\pi^2 E}{\sigma_p}}=\lambda_p \tag{5-9-3}$$

中长杆与短杆的柔度分界值为（a、b 是由试验得到的材料常数）

$$\lambda_s=\frac{a-\sigma_s}{b} \tag{5-9-4}$$

三、压杆的稳定计算

（一）安全系数法

$$P\leqslant\frac{P_{cr}}{[n_{st}]}\quad 或 \quad n_{st}=\frac{P_{cr}}{P}\geqslant[n_{st}] \tag{5-9-5}$$

式中：P——压杆所受的实际轴向压力；

P_{cr}——压杆的临界力；

n_{st}——压杆的工作稳定安全系数；

$[n_{st}]$——规定的稳定安全系数。

（二）折减系数法（土建结构规范中常用）

$$\sigma=\frac{P}{A}\leqslant[\sigma_{st}]=\varphi[\sigma]\quad 或 \quad \frac{P}{\varphi A}\leqslant[\sigma] \tag{5-9-6}$$

式中：$[\sigma]$——强度许用应力；

A——压杆横截面面积；

$[\sigma_{st}]$——稳定许用应力；

φ——$[\sigma_{st}]$与$[\sigma]$的比值，称为折减系数，是一个小于1的系数，其值可根据有关材料的φ-λ关系曲线或折减系数表查得，或由经验公式算得。

对折减系数表中没有的非整数λ所对应值的φ值，可用线性插值公式计算

$$\varphi=\varphi_1-\frac{\lambda-\lambda_1}{\lambda_2-\lambda_1}(\varphi_1-\varphi_2) \tag{5-9-7}$$

式中：λ_1、λ_2——整数的柔度；

φ_1、φ_2——分别为λ_1、λ_2所对应的折减系数。

利用式(5-9-5)、式(5-9-6)两个稳定条件，除了可用来对压杆的稳定性进行校核，确定压杆的允许荷载外，还可用试算法确定压杆的截面尺寸。

若压杆横截面上两个形心主惯性轴方向μ和i各不相同，则应用公式$\lambda=\frac{\mu l}{i}$分别计算λ_y和λ_z，求出最大柔度λ_{max}作为计算的依据。

四、提高压杆稳定性的措施

(1)减小压杆长度l，或在压杆的中间增加支承。

(2)改善杆端约束，使长度系数μ值减小。

(3)选择合理的截面形状：

①尽可能将材料分布的离截面形心较远，以增大惯性矩I；

②尽可能使压杆在两个形心主惯性平面内有相等或相近的稳定性，即$\lambda_z\approx\lambda_y$。

(4)合理选用材料。

对大柔度杆，在弹性模量E值相同或相近的材料中，没有必要选用高强度钢。对中柔度杆和小柔度杆，选用高强度钢能提高其稳定性。

习　题

5-9-1　图示三根压杆均为细长(大柔度)，且弯曲刚度均为EI。三根压杆的临界荷载F_{cr}的关系为(　　)。

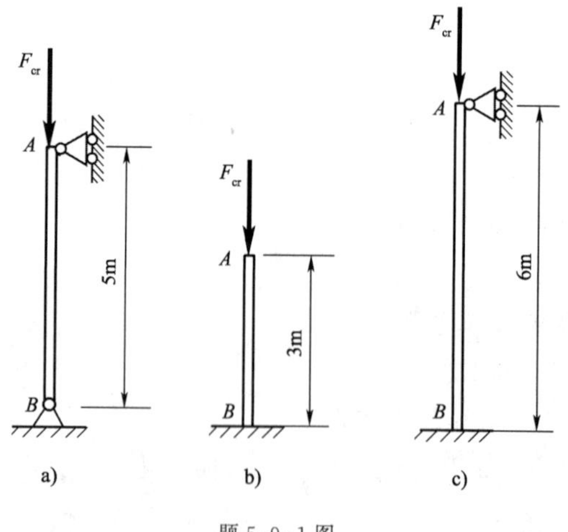

题5-9-1图

A. $F_{cra} > F_{crb} > F_{crc}$　　B. $F_{crb} > F_{cra} > F_{crc}$

C. $F_{crc} > F_{cra} > F_{crb}$　　D. $F_{crb} > F_{crc} > F_{cra}$

5-9-2 两根安全相同的细长(大柔度)压杆 AB 和 CD 如图所示,杆的下端为固定铰链约束,上端与刚性水平杆固结。两杆的弯曲刚度均为 EI,其临界荷载 F_a 为(　　)。

A. $2.04\times\frac{\pi^2 EI}{L^2}$　B. $4.08\times\frac{\pi^2 EI}{L^2}$　C. $8\times\frac{\pi^2 EI}{L^2}$　D. $2\times\frac{\pi^2 EI}{L^2}$

5-9-3 圆截面细长压杆的材料和杆端约束保持不变,若将其直径缩小一半,则压杆的临界压力的原压杆的(　　)。

A. 1/2　B. 1/4　C. 1/8　D. 1/16

5-9-4 压杆下端固定,上端与水平弹簧相连,如图所示,该杆长度系数 μ 值为(　　)。

A. $\mu<0.5$　B. $0.5<\mu<0.7$　C. $0.7<\mu<2$　D. $\mu>2$

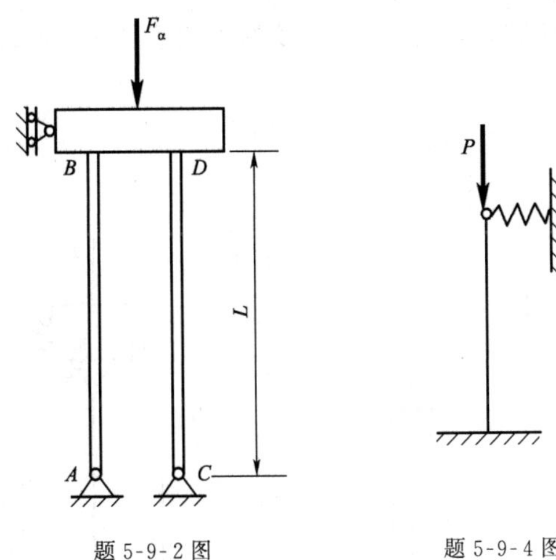

题 5-9-2 图　　题 5-9-4 图

5-9-5 压杆失稳是指压杆在轴向压力作用下(　　)。

A. 局部横截面的面积迅速变化

B. 危险截面发生屈服或断裂

C. 不能维持平衡状态而突然发生运动

D. 不能维持直线平衡状态而突然变弯

5-9-6 假设图示三个受压结构失稳时临界压力分别为 P_{cr}^{a}、P_{cr}^{b}、P_{cr}^{c},比较三者的大小,则(　　)。

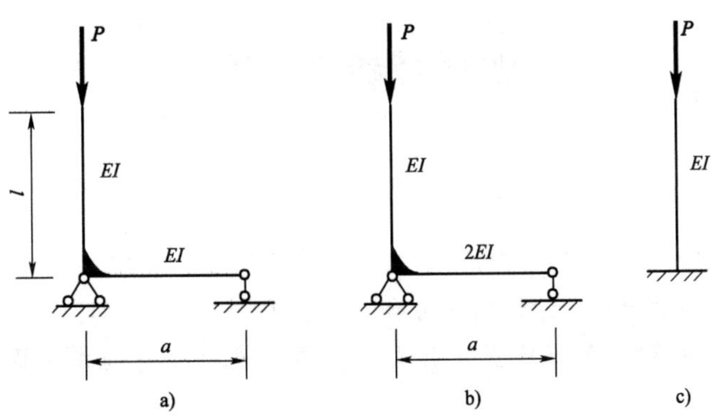

题 5-9-6 图

A. P_{cr}^{a}最小　　B. P_{cr}^{b}最小　　C. P_{cr}^{c}最小　　D. $P_{cr}^{a}=P_{cr}^{b}=P_{cr}^{c}$

5-9-7　图示两端铰支压杆的截面为矩形，当其失稳时，(　　)。

A. 临界压力 $P_{cr}=\pi^2 EI_y/l^2$，挠曲线位于 xy 面内

B. 临界压力 $P_{cr}=\pi^2 EI_y/l^2$，挠曲线位于 xz 面内

C. 临界压力 $P_{cr}=\pi^2 EI_z/l^2$，挠曲线位于 xy 面内

D. 临界压力 $P_{cr}=\pi^2 EI_z/l^2$，挠曲线位于 xz 面内

5-9-8　在材料相同的条件下，随着柔度的增大(　　)。

A. 细长杆的临界应力是减小的，中长杆不是

B. 中长杆的临界应力是减小的，细长杆不是

C. 细长杆和中长杆的临界应力均是减小的

D. 细长杆和中长杆的临界应力均不是减小的

5-9-9　如图所示，一端固定，一端为球形铰的大柔度压杆，横截面为矩形，则该杆临界力 P_{cr} 为(　　)。

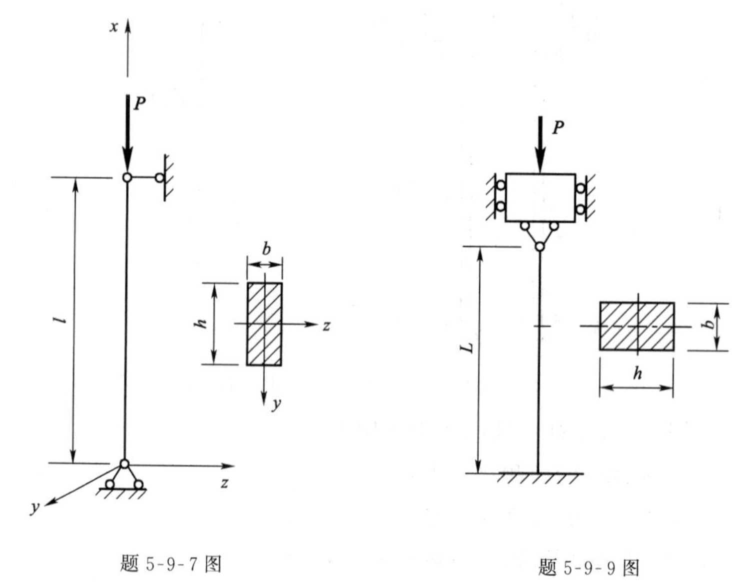

题 5-9-7 图　　　　题 5-9-9 图

A. $1.68\dfrac{Ebh^3}{L^2}$　　B. $3.29\dfrac{Ebh^3}{L^2}$　　C. $1.68\dfrac{Eb^3h}{L^2}$　　D. $0.82\dfrac{Eb^3h}{L^2}$

题解及参考答案

第一节

5-1-1　**解**：低碳钢拉伸试验时的应力-应变曲线如图 5-1-3 所示。当材料拉伸到强化阶段(ce 段)后，卸除荷载时，应力和应变按直线规律变化，如图 5-1-3 中直线 dd'。当再次加载时，沿 $d'd$ 直线上升，材料的比例极限提高到 d 而塑性减少，此现象称为冷作硬化。

答案：C

第二节

5-2-1　**解:**用直接法求轴力,可得左段轴力为-3kN,而右段轴力为5kN。

答案:B

5-2-2　**解:**由于A是斜截面m-m的面积,轴向拉力P沿斜截面是均匀分布的,所以$\sigma=\frac{P}{A}$应为斜截面上沿轴线方向的总应力,而不是垂直于斜截面的正应力。

答案:C

5-2-3　**解:**$\Delta l_1=\frac{F_N l}{EA_1}l$,$\Delta l_2=\frac{F_N l}{EA_2}$,因为$A_1>A_2$,所以$\Delta l_1<\Delta l_2$。又$\varepsilon_1=\frac{\Delta l_1}{l}$,$\varepsilon_2=\frac{\Delta l_2}{l}$,故$\varepsilon_1<\varepsilon_2$。

答案:C

5-2-4　**解:**用直接法求轴力,可得$N_{AB}=-30$kN,$N_{BC}=30$kN,$N_{CD}=-15$kN,$N_{DE}=15$kN。

答案:C

5-2-5　**解:**$N_1=N_2=\frac{P}{2}$,若使刚梁平行下移,则应使两杆位移相同,即$\Delta l_2=\frac{2}{E}\frac{l_1}{A_1}=\Delta l_2\frac{\frac{P}{2}l_2}{EA_2}$,则$\frac{A_1}{A_2}=\frac{l_1}{l_2}>1$。

答案:C

5-2-6　**解:**用直接法求轴力,可得$N_{AB}=-6$kN,$N_{BC}=4$kN。

答案:C

5-2-7　**解:**用直接法求内力,可得AB段轴力为F,既有变形,又有位移;BC段没有轴力,所以没有变形,但是由于AB段的位移使BC段有一个向右的位移。

答案:A

5-2-8　**解:**由轴力图(N图)可见,轴力沿轴线是线性渐变的,所以杆上必有沿轴线分布的均布荷载,同时在C截面两侧轴力的突变值是45kN,故在C截面上一定对应有集中力45kN。

答案:D

5-2-9　**解:**受轴向拉力作用杆件的内力$F_N=\sum F_x$(截面一侧轴向外力代数和),应力$\sigma=\frac{F_N}{A}$,轴向变形$\Delta l=\frac{F_N l}{EA}$,若横截面面积$A$和其他条件不变,则内力、应力、轴向变形均不变。

答案:C

5-2-10　**解:**由零杆判别法可知BC杆为零杆,$N_{BC}=0$。但是AC杆受拉伸长后与BC杆仍然相连,由杆的小变形的威利沃特法(williot)可知变形后C点移到C'点,如解图所示。

答案:B

题 5-2-10 解图

第三节

5-3-1 **解：**把 F 平移到铆钉群中心 O 点，并加一个附加力偶 m，如解图所示。

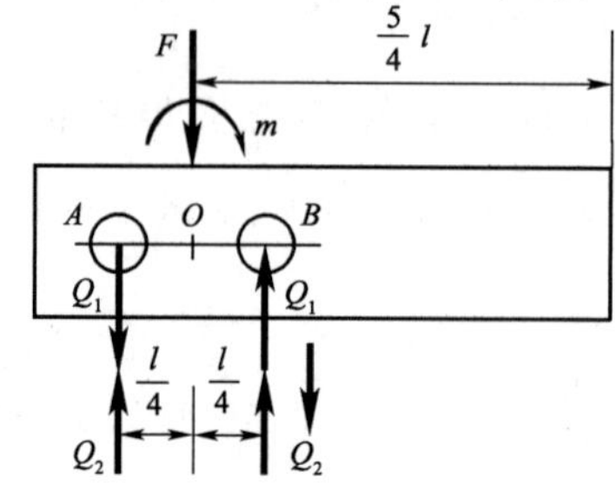

题 5-3-1 解图

$\sum M_O=0$：$Q_1\cdot\frac{1}{2}=F\cdot\frac{5}{4}l=m$，$Q_1=\frac{5}{2}F$

$\sum M_y=0$：$Q_2=\frac{F}{2}$

式中，Q_1 为力偶 m 产生的剪力，Q_2 为平移后的 F 力产生的剪力。显然铆钉 B 比铆钉 A 受的剪力大，$F_{smax}=Q_1+Q_2=3F$，$\tau_{max}=\frac{F_{smax}}{A_S}=\frac{3F}{\frac{\pi}{4}d^2}=\frac{12F}{\pi d^2}$。

答案：C

5-3-2 **解：**由螺杆的拉伸强度条件，得

$$\sigma=\frac{F_N}{A}=\frac{F}{\frac{\pi}{4}d^2}=\frac{4F}{\pi d^2}=[\sigma]$$

由螺母的剪切强度条件，得

$$\tau=\frac{F_s}{A_s}=\frac{F}{\pi dh}=[\tau]$$

把以上两式代入$[\sigma]=2\tau$，得$\frac{4F}{\pi d^2}=2\ \frac{F}{\pi dh}$，即 $d=2h$。

答案：A

5-3-3 **解：**当挤压的接触面为平面时，接触面面积 cb 就是挤压面积。

答案：B

5-3-4 **解：**加垫圈后，螺栓的剪切面、挤压面、拉伸面积都无改变，只有平板的挤压面积增加了，平板的挤压强度提高了。

答案：D

5-3-5 **解：**挤压应力等于挤压力除以挤压面积。钢板和铝铆钉的挤压力互为作用力和反作用力，大小相等、方向相反；而挤压面积就是相互接触面的正投影面积，也相同。

答案：B

5-3-6 **解：**插销中心部分有向下的趋势，插销帽周边部分受平板支撑有向上的趋势，故插销的剪切面积是一个圆柱面积 πdh，而插销帽与平板的接触面积就是挤压面积，为一个圆环面积$\frac{\pi}{4}(D^2-d^2)$。

答案：B

5-3-7 **解:** 在钢板上冲断的圆孔板，如解图所示。设冲力为 F，剪力为 Q，钢板的剪切强度极限为 τ_b，圆孔直径为 d。则有 $\tau=\dfrac{Q}{\pi dt}=\tau_b$，故冲力 $F=Q=\tau dt\tau_b$。

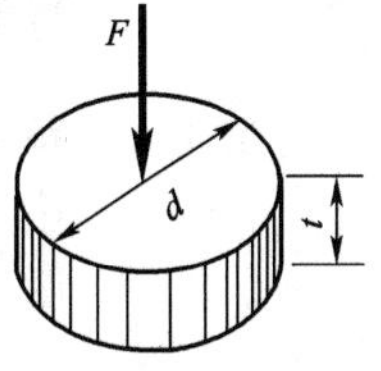

题 5-3-7 解图

答案: C

第四节

5-4-1 **解:** 为使 $\tau_1=\dfrac{1}{2}\tau$，应使 $\dfrac{T}{\dfrac{\pi}{16}d_1^3}=\dfrac{1}{2}\dfrac{T}{\dfrac{\pi}{16}d^3}$，即 $d_1^3=2d^3$，$d_1=\sqrt[3]{2}d$。

答案: D

5-4-2 **解:** 由 $\theta=\dfrac{T}{GI_p}$，得 $\dfrac{T}{I_p}=\theta G$，故 $\tau_{max}=\dfrac{T}{I_p}\dfrac{d}{2}=\dfrac{\theta Gd}{2}$。

答案: D

5-4-3 **解:** 根据剪应力计算公式 $\tau=\dfrac{T}{W_p}$，可得 $T=\tau W_p$，又由剪切胡克定律 $\tau=G\gamma$，有 $T=G\gamma W_p$。

答案: A

5-4-4 **解:** 设圆轴的直径变为 d_1，则有 $\phi_1=\dfrac{\phi}{2}$，即 $\dfrac{Tl}{GI_{p1}}=\dfrac{1}{2}\dfrac{Tl}{GI_p}$，所以 $I_{p1}=2I_p$，则 $\dfrac{\pi}{64}d_1^4=2\times\dfrac{\pi}{64}d^4$，得到 $d_1=\sqrt[4]{2}d$。

答案: A

5-4-5 **解:** 首先考虑整体平衡，设左端反力偶 m 由外向里转，则有

$\sum M_x=0$：$m-1-4.5-2+5=0$

所以 $m=2.5\text{kN}\cdot\text{m}$

再由截面法平衡求出：$T_1=m=2.5\text{kN}\cdot\text{m}$，$T_2=2-5=-3\text{kN}\cdot\text{m}$

答案: D

5-4-6 **解:** 首先考虑整体平衡，设左端反力偶 m 在外表面由外向里转，则有

$\sum M_x=0$：$m-1-6-2+5=0$

所以 $m=4\text{kN}\cdot\text{m}$。

再由直接法求出各段扭矩，从左至右各段扭矩分别为 4kN·m、3kN·m、−3kN·m、−5kN·m，在各集中力偶两侧截面上扭矩的变化量就等于集中力偶矩的大小。显然符合这些规律的扭矩图只有 D 图。

答案: D

5-4-7 **解:** 设直径为 D 的实心圆轴最大剪应力 $\tau=\dfrac{T}{\dfrac{\pi}{16}D^3}$，则直径为 $\dfrac{D}{2}$ 的实心圆轴最大剪应力 $\tau_1=\dfrac{T}{\dfrac{\pi}{16}\left(\dfrac{D}{2}\right)^3}=8\dfrac{T}{\dfrac{\pi}{16}D^3}=8\tau$。

答案: C

5-4-8 **解:** 用截面法（或直接法）可求出截面 1-1 处的扭矩为 25kN·m，截面 2-2 处的扭矩为 −5kN·m。

答案:B

5-4-9 **解**:设实心圆原来横截面面积为 $A=\frac{\pi}{4}d^2$,增大后面积 $A_1=\frac{\pi}{4}d_1^2$,则有:$A_1=2A$,即 $\frac{\pi}{4}d_1^2=2\ \frac{\pi}{4}d^2$,所以 $d_1=\sqrt{2}d$。原面积不发生屈服时,$\tau_{\max}=\frac{M_0}{W_p}=\frac{M_0}{\frac{\pi}{16}d^3}\leqslant\tau_s$,$M_0\leqslant\frac{\pi}{16}d^3\tau_s$,将面积增大后,$\tau_{\max 1}=\frac{M_1}{W_{p1}}=\frac{M_1}{\frac{\pi}{16}d_1^3}\leqslant\tau_s$,最大许可荷载 $M_1\leqslant\frac{\pi}{16}d_1^3\tau_s=2\sqrt{2}\frac{\pi}{16}d^3\tau_s=2\sqrt{2}M_0$。

答案:C

5-4-10 **解**:实心圆轴截面的抗扭截面模量 $W_{p1}=\frac{\pi}{16}D^3$,空心圆轴截面的抗扭截面模量 $W_{p2}=\frac{\pi}{16}D^3\left(1-\frac{d^4}{D^4}\right)$,当外径 D 相同时,显然 $W_{p1}>W_{p2}$。

答案:B

5-4-11 **解**:$\tau_{2\max}=\frac{T}{\frac{\pi}{16}(2d)^3}=\frac{1}{8}\ \frac{T}{\frac{\pi}{16}d^3}=\frac{1}{8}\tau_{1\max}$

$$\phi_2=\frac{Tl}{G\ \frac{\pi}{32}(2d)^4}=\frac{1}{16}\frac{Tl}{G\ \frac{\pi}{32}d^4}=\frac{1}{16}\phi_1$$

答案:C

第五节

5-5-1 **解**:图示矩形截面形心轴为 z 轴,z_1 轴到 z 轴距离是 h,由移轴定理可得

$$I_{z1}=I_z+a^2A=\frac{bh^3}{12}+h^2\cdot bh=\frac{13}{12}bh^3$$

答案:D

5-5-2 **解**:正方形的形心轴矩 z 轴的距离是 $\frac{a}{2}$,如解图所示。用移轴定理得 $I_z^{方}=I_{zc}+\left(\frac{a}{2}\right)^2A=\frac{a^4}{12}+\frac{a^2}{4}\cdot a^2=\frac{a^4}{3}$,整个组合截面的惯性矩为

$$I_z=I_z^{矩}-I_z^{方}=\frac{bh^3}{12}-\frac{a^4}{3}$$

题 5-5-2 解图

答案:C

5-5-3 **解**:由定义 $I_z=\int_A y^2\mathrm{d}A$ 和 $I_y=\int_A z^2\mathrm{d}A$,可知 a)、b) 两图图形面积相同,但图 a) 中的面积距离 z 轴较远,因此 $I_z^a>I_z^b$;而两图面积距离 y 轴远近相同,故 $I_y^a=I_y^b$。

答案:B

5-5-4 **解**:由定义 $I_p=\int_A\rho^2\mathrm{d}A$,$I_z=\int_A y^2\mathrm{d}A$,$I_y=\int_A z^2\mathrm{d}A$,以及勾股定理 $\rho^2=y^2+z^2$,

两边积分就可得 $I_p = I_z + I_y$。

答案:B

5-5-5 **解**:根据静矩定义 $S_z = \int_A y\mathrm{d}A$,图示矩形截面的静矩等于 m-m 线以上部分和以下部分静矩之和,即 $S_z = S_z^{上} + S_z^{下}$,又由于 z 轴是形心轴,$S_z = 0$,故 $S_z^{上} + S_z^{下} = 0$,$S_z^{上} = -S_z^{下}$。

答案:B

5-5-6 **解**:$i=i_y=i_z=\sqrt{\dfrac{I_z}{A}}=\sqrt{\dfrac{\dfrac{\pi}{64}d^4}{\dfrac{\pi}{4}d^2}}=\dfrac{d}{4}$。

答案:B

5-5-7 **解**:**解**:根据惯性矩的定义 $I_z = \int_A y^2\mathrm{d}A$,$I_y = \int_A z^2\mathrm{d}A$,可知惯性矩的大小与面积到轴的距离有关。面积分布离轴越远,其惯性矩越大;面积分布离轴越近,其惯性矩越小。可见 I_y^a 最大,I_z^a 最小。

答案:C

5-5-8 **解**:图形对主惯性轴的惯性积为零,对主惯性轴的惯性矩是对通过某点的所有轴的惯性矩中的极值,也就是最大或最小的惯性矩。

答案:C

5-5-9 **解**:由移轴定理 $I_z=I_{zc}+a^2A$ 可知,在所有与形心轴平行的轴中,距离形心轴越远,其惯性矩越大。图示截面为一个正方形与一半圆形的组合截面,其形心轴应在正方形形心和半圆形形心之间。所以 z_1 轴距离截面形心轴较远,其惯性矩较大。

答案:B

第六节

5-6-1 **解**:对 B 点取力矩:$\sum M_B=0$,$F_A=0$。应用直接法求剪力和弯矩,得 $F_{SA}=0$,$M_C=0$。

答案:A

5-6-2 **解**:原来 $f=\dfrac{Ml^2}{2EI}$

梁长减半后 $f_1=\dfrac{M\left(\dfrac{l}{2}\right)^2}{2EI}=\dfrac{1}{4}f$

答案:B

5-6-3 **解**:开裂前 $f=\dfrac{Fl^3}{3EI}$,其中 $I=\dfrac{b(2a)^3}{12}=8\,\dfrac{ba^3}{12}=8I_1$

开裂后 $f_1=\dfrac{\dfrac{F}{2}l^3}{3EI_1}=\dfrac{\dfrac{1}{2}Fl^3}{3E\cdot\dfrac{I}{8}}=4\,\dfrac{Fl^3}{3EI}=4f$

答案:C

5-6-4 **解**：设 F_A 向上，取整体平衡：$\sum M_C=0, m-F_AL=0$，所以 $F_A=\dfrac{m}{l}$。用直接法求 A 截面剪力 $F_{SA}=F_A=\dfrac{m}{l}$。

答案：C

5-6-5 **解**：因为钢和铝的弹性模量不同，而只有挠度涉及弹性模量，所以选挠曲线。

答案：D

5-6-6 **解**：由挠曲线方程 $\nu=\dfrac{Mx^2}{2EI}$ 可以得到正确答案。

答案：B

5-6-7 **解**：由中间铰链 C 处断开，分别画出 AC 和 BC 的受力图(见图)。

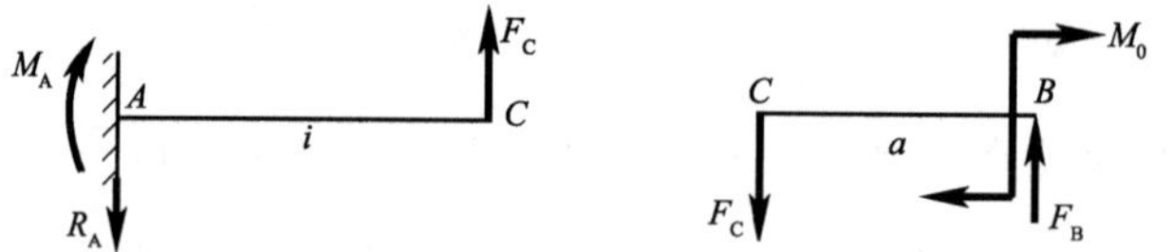

题 5-6-7 解图

先取 BC 杆，$\sum M_B=0: F_Ca=M_0, F_C=\dfrac{M_O}{a}$

再取 AC 杆，$\sum M_y=0: R_A=F_C=\dfrac{M_O}{a}$

$$\sum M_A=0: M_A=F_Cl=\frac{M_O}{a}l$$

可见只有选项 B 是正确的。

答案：B

5-6-8 **解**：从题图 a) 可知，$M_{max}=\dfrac{P_1l}{4}, \sigma_{max}=\dfrac{M_{max}}{W_z}=\dfrac{\frac{P_1l}{4}}{\frac{\pi}{32}d^3}=\dfrac{8P_1l}{\pi d^3}\leqslant[\sigma]$，所以 $P_1\leqslant\dfrac{\pi d^3[\sigma]}{8l}$。

从题图 b) 可知，$M_{max}=\dfrac{P_2l}{4}$，同理，$P_2\leqslant\dfrac{\pi(2d)^3[\sigma]}{8l}$，可见 $\dfrac{P_2}{P_1}=\dfrac{(2d)^3}{d^3}=8$。

答案：C

5-6-9 **解**：用直接法，取截面 C 右侧计算比较简单：$F_{SC}=qa, M_C=qa^2-qa\cdot a=0$。

答案：B

5-6-10 **解**：设 $f_1=\dfrac{P_1\left(\frac{l}{2}\right)^3}{3EI}, f_2=\dfrac{P_2l^3}{3EI}$，令 $f_1=f_2$，则有 $P_1\left(\dfrac{l}{2}\right)^3=P_2l^3, \dfrac{P_1}{P_2}=8$。

答案：C

5-6-11 **解**：矩形截面梁横力弯曲时，横截面上的正应力 σ 沿截面高度线性分布，如解图 a) 所示，在上下边缘 σ 最大，在中性轴上正应力为零。横截面上的剪应力 τ 沿截面高度呈

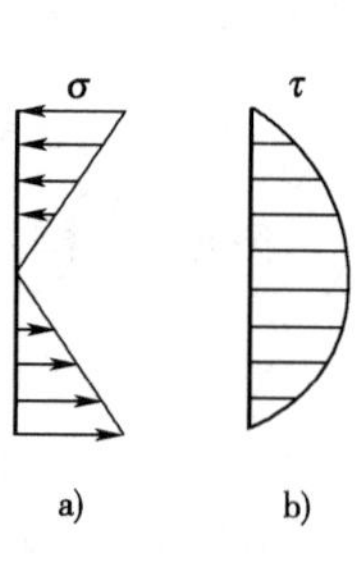

题 5-6-11 解图

抛物线分布，如解图 b)所示，在上下边缘 τ 为零，在中性轴处剪应力最大。

答案：B

5-6-12 **解**：经分析可知，移动荷载作用在跨中$\dfrac{l}{2}$处时，有最大弯矩 $M_{max}=\dfrac{Pl}{4}$，支反力和弯矩图如解图 a)所示。当移动荷载作用在支座附近、无限接近支座时，见解图 b)有最大剪力 Q_{max} 趋近于 P 值。

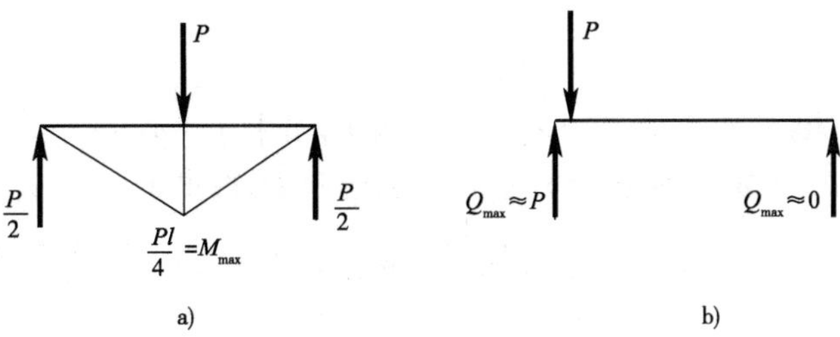

题 5-6-12 解图

答案：A

5-6-13 **解**：首先求支反力，设 F_A 向上，取整体平衡：

$\sum M_B=0, F_A \cdot 3a+qa \cdot a=3qa \cdot \dfrac{3}{2}a$，所以 $F_A=\dfrac{7}{6}qa$

由 $F_S(x)=F_A=qx=0$，得 $x=\dfrac{F_A}{q}=\dfrac{7}{6}a$

答案：D

5-6-14 **解**：根据定义，$W_z=\dfrac{I_z}{y_{max}}=\dfrac{\dfrac{BH^3}{12}-\dfrac{bh^3}{12}}{\dfrac{H}{2}}=\dfrac{BH^3-bh^3}{6H}$。

答案：C

5-6-15 **解**：题图所示四个梁，其支反力和弯矩图如解图所示。

就梁的正应力强度条件而言，$\sigma_{max}=\dfrac{M_{max}}{W_z}\leqslant[\sigma]$，$M_{max}$越小，$\sigma_{max}$越小，梁就越安全。上述四个弯矩图中显然 D 图的 M_{max} 最小。

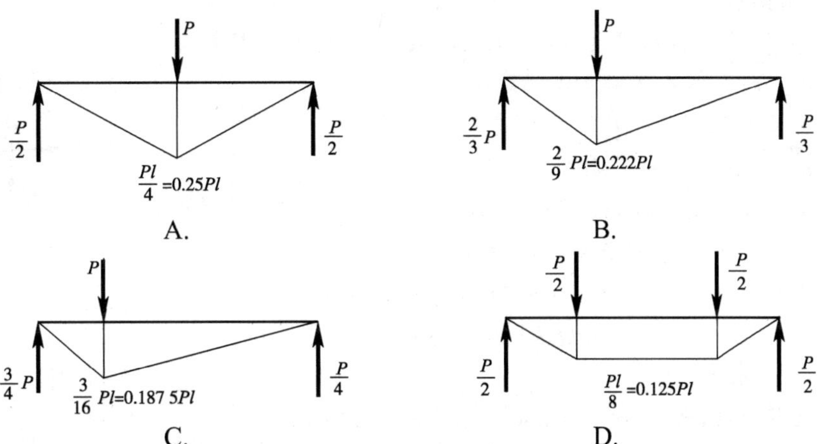

题 5-6-15 解图

答案:D

5-6-16 **解**:根据公式梁的弯曲曲率$\frac{1}{\rho}=\frac{M}{EI}$与弯矩成正比,故曲率的最大值发生在弯矩最大的截面上。

答案:C

第七节

5-7-1 **解**:

选项A,图中$\sigma_1=\sigma,\sigma_2=\sigma,\sigma_3=0$;选项B,图中$\sigma_1=\sigma,\sigma_2=0,\sigma_3=-\sigma$

选项C,图中$\sigma_1=2\sigma,\sigma_2=0,\sigma_3=-2\sigma$;选项D,图中$\sigma_1=3\sigma,\sigma_2=\sigma,\sigma_3=0$

根据最大切应力公式$\tau_{\max}=\frac{\sigma_1-\sigma_3}{2}$,显然C图$\tau_{\max}=\frac{2\sigma-(-2\sigma)}{2}=2\sigma$最大。

答案:C

5-7-2 **解**:图中,$\sigma_x=40\text{MPa},\sigma_y=-40\text{MPa},\tau_x=30\text{MPa}$,由公式$\sigma_{\max}=\frac{\sigma_x+\sigma_y}{2}+\sqrt{\left(\frac{\sigma_x-\sigma_y}{2}\right)^2+\tau_x^2}=\frac{40+(-40)}{2}+\sqrt{\left[\frac{40-(-40)}{2}\right]^2+30^2}=50\text{MPa}$,故$\sigma_1=50\text{MPa}$。

答案:D

5-7-3 **解**:受扭圆轴最大剪应力τ发生在圆轴表面,是纯剪切应力状态(解图a),而其主应力$\sigma_1=\tau$出现在45°斜截面上(解图b),其值为τ。

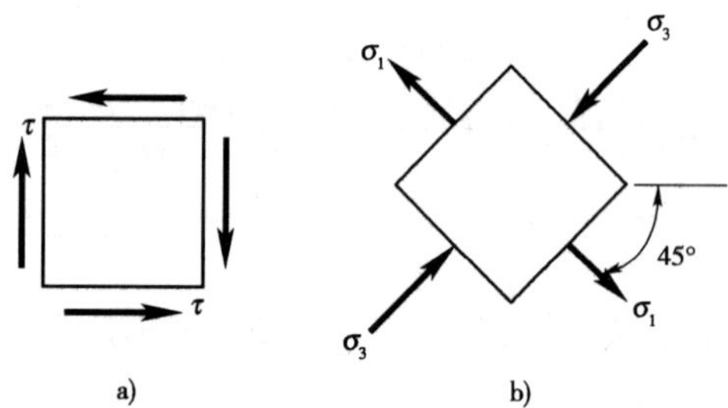

题5-7-3解图

答案:D

5-7-4 **解**:设单元体厚度为1,则ab、bc、ac三个面的面积就等于ab、bc、ac;在单元体图上作辅助线ad,则

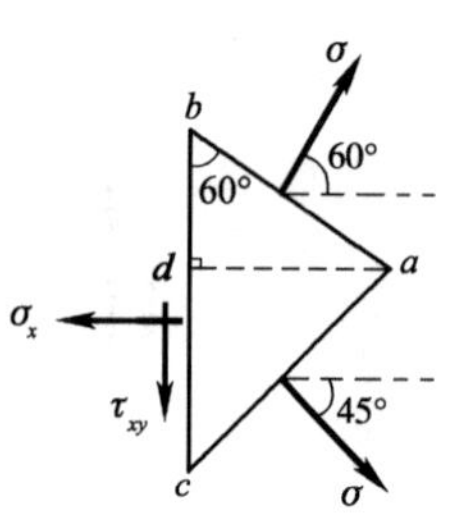

题5-7-4解图

从图中可以看出如下几何关系:

$ad=ab\sin60°=ac\sin45°$

$bc=bd+dc=ac\cos60°+ac\cos45°$

由单元体的整体平衡方程,可得:

$$\sum F_x=0,\sigma_x\cdot bc=\sigma\cos60°\cdot ab+\sigma\cos45°\cdot ac$$
$$=\sigma(bd+dc)=\sigma\cdot bc$$

$$\sigma_x=\sigma$$

$$\sum F_y=0,\tau_{xy}\cdot bc=\sigma\sin60°\cdot ab-\sigma\sin45°\cdot ac$$
$$=\sigma(ad-ad)=0$$

$\tau_{xy}=0$

答案:A

5-7-5 **解**:

状态 A,$\sigma_{r3}=\sigma_1-\sigma_3=120-(-120)=240$

状态 B,$\sigma_{r3}=\sigma_1-\sigma_3=100-(-100)=200$

状态 C,$\sigma_{r3}=\sigma_1-\sigma_3=150-60=90$

状态 D,$\sigma_{r4}=\sigma_1-\sigma_3=100-0=100$

显然状态 A 相当应力 σ_{r3} 最大。

答案:A

5-7-6 **解**:该题有两种解法。

方法 1:对比法

把图示等腰三角形单元体与纯剪切应力状态对比。把两上直角边看作是纯剪切应力状态中单元体的两个边,则 σ 和 τ 所在截面就相当于纯剪切单元体的主平面,故 $\sigma=\tau_0$,$\tau=0$。

方法 2:小块平衡法

设两个直角边截面面积为 A,则底边截面面积为$\sqrt{2}A$。由平衡方程

$\sum F_y=0$:$\sigma\cdot\sqrt{2}A=2\tau_0 A\cdot\sin45°$,所以 $\sigma=\tau_0$;

$\sum F_x=0$:$\tau\cdot\sqrt{2}A+\tau_0 A\cos45°=\tau_0 A\cdot\cos45°$,所以 $\tau=0$。

答案:B

5-7-7 **解**:图示单元体应力状态类同于梁的应力状态:$\sigma_2=0$ 且 $\sigma_x=0$(或 $\sigma_y=0$),故其主应力的特点与梁相同,即有如下规律

$$\sigma_1=\frac{\sigma}{2}+\sqrt{\left(\frac{\sigma}{2}\right)^2+\tau^2}>0;\sigma_3=\frac{\sigma}{2}-\sqrt{\left(\frac{\sigma}{2}\right)^2+\tau^2}<0$$

已知其中一个主应力为 5MPa>0,即 $\sigma_1=\frac{-80}{2}+\sqrt{\left(\frac{-80}{2}\right)^2+\tau^2}=5\text{MPa}$,所以 $\sqrt{\left(\frac{-80}{2}\right)^2+\tau^2}=45\text{MPa}$,则另一个主应力必为 $\sigma_3=\frac{-80}{2}-\sqrt{\left(\frac{-80}{2}\right)^2+\tau^2}=-85\text{MPa}$。

答案:A

5-7-8 **解**:首先分析各横截面上的内力——剪力 Q 和弯矩 M,如解图 a)所示。再分析各横截面上的正应力 σ 和剪应力 τ 沿高度的分布,如解图 b)和图 c)所示。可见 4 点的剪应力方向不对。

答案:D

5-7-9 **解**:题图单元体的主方向可用叠加法判断。把图中单元体看成是单向压缩和纯剪切两种应力状态的叠加,如解图 a)、b)所示。

其中解图 a)主压应力 σ_3'的方向即为 σ_y 的方向(沿 y 轴),而解图 b)与解图 c)等价,其主压应力 σ_3'的方向沿与 y 轴成 45°的方向。因此题中单元体主压应力 σ_3 的方向应为σ_3'和 σ_3''的合力方向。根据求合力的平行四边形法则,σ_3 与 y 轴的夹角 α 必小于 45°,而 σ_1 与 σ_3 相互垂直,故 σ_1 与 x 轴夹角也是 $\alpha<45°$,如解图 d)所示。

答案:A

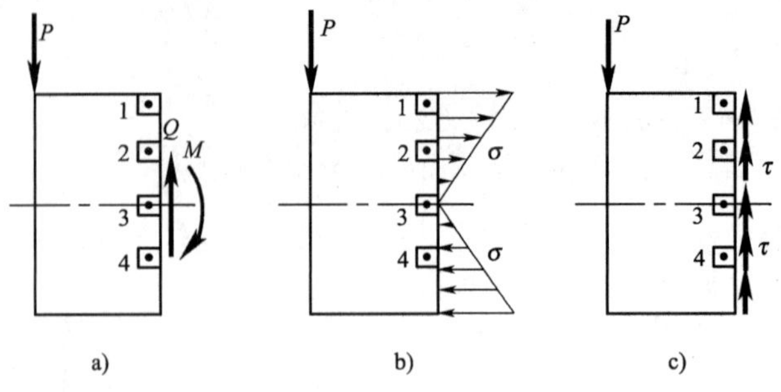

题 5-7-8 解图

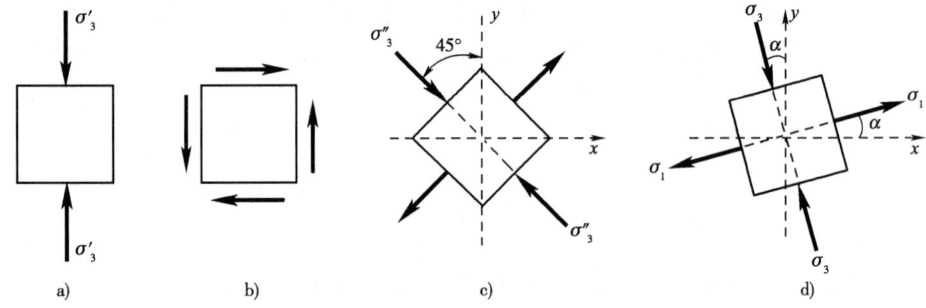

题 5-7-9 解图

5-7-10　**解**:根据定义,剪应力等于零的平面为主平面,主平面上的正应力为主应力。可以证明,主应力为该点各平面中的最大或最小正应力。主应力可以是零。

答案:B

5-7-11　**解**:图 a)为纯剪切应力状态,经分析可知其主应力为 $\sigma_1=\tau,\sigma_2=0,\sigma_3=-\tau$,方向如图 c)所示。

答案:C

第八节

5-8-1　**解**:把力 F 平移到截面形心,加两个附加力偶 M_y 和 M_z,AB 杆的变形为轴向拉伸和对 y、z 轴双向弯曲。最大拉应力

$$\sigma_{\max}^{+}=\frac{F_N}{A}+\frac{M_z}{W_z}+\frac{M_y}{W_y}=\frac{F}{bh}+\frac{F\dfrac{h}{2}}{\dfrac{bh^2}{6}}+\frac{F\dfrac{b}{2}}{\dfrac{hb^2}{6}}=7\frac{F}{bh}$$

答案:C

5-8-2　**解**:图示圆轴为弯扭组合变形。力 F 产生的弯矩引起 A 点的拉应力 σ,力偶 T 产生的扭矩引起 A 点的切应力 τ。

答案:C

5-8-3　**解**:这显然是偏心拉伸,而且对 y、z 轴都有偏心。把 F 力平移到截面形心 O 点,要加两个附加力偶矩,该杆要发生轴向拉伸和绕 y、z 轴的双向弯曲。

答案:B

5-8-4　**解**:把 F 力向轴线 x 平移并加一个附加力偶,则使圆轴产生弯曲和扭转组合变

形。最大弯矩 $M=Fl$，最大扭矩 $T=F\dfrac{d}{2}$。

由公式 $\sigma_{r3}=\dfrac{\sqrt{M^2+T^2}}{W_z}=\dfrac{\sqrt{(Fl)^2+\left(\dfrac{Fd}{2}\right)^2}}{\dfrac{\pi}{32}d^3}$，可知正确答案为 D。

答案：D

5-8-5 **解**：在弯扭组合变形情况下，A 点属于复杂应力状态，既有最大正应力，又有最大剪应 τ(见解图)。和梁的应力状态相同：$\sigma_y=0$，$\sigma_2=0$，$\sigma_1=\dfrac{\sigma}{2}+\sqrt{\left(\dfrac{\sigma}{2}\right)^2+\tau^2}$，$\sigma_3=\dfrac{\sigma}{2}-\sqrt{\left(\dfrac{\sigma}{2}\right)^2+\tau^2}$，$\sigma_{r3}=\sigma_1-\sigma_3=\sqrt{\sigma^2+4\tau^2}$。

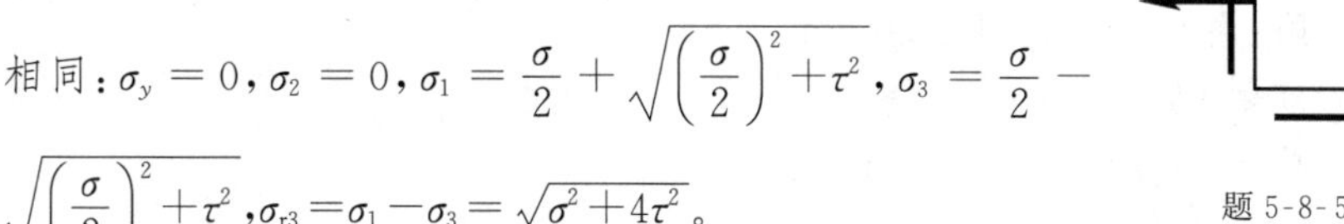

题 5-8-5 解图

选项中 A 为单向应力状态，B、C 只适用于圆截面。

答案：D

5-8-6 **解**：从截面 m-m 截开后取右侧部分分析可知，右边只有一个铅垂的反力，只能在 m-m 截面上产生题图 a)所示的弯曲正应力。

答案：A

5-8-7 **解**：图中三角形分布荷载可简化为一个合力，其作用线距离杆的截面下边缘的距离为 $\dfrac{3a}{3}=a$，所以这个合力对 m-m 截面是一个偏心拉力，m-m 截面要发生拉弯组合变形，而这个合力作用线正好通过 n-n 截面发生单向拉伸变形。

答案：C

5-8-8 **解**：题图 a)是轴向受压变形，最大压应力 $\sigma_{max}^{a}=-\dfrac{P}{a^2}$；题图 b)底部是偏心受压变形，偏心矩为 $\dfrac{a}{2}$，最大压应力 $\sigma_{max}^{b}=\dfrac{F_N}{A}-\dfrac{M_z}{Wz}=-\dfrac{P}{2a^2}-\dfrac{P\cdot\dfrac{a}{2}}{\dfrac{a}{6}(2a)^2}=-\dfrac{5P}{4a^2}$。

显然题图 b)最大压应力大于题图 a)，该立柱的强度降低了。

答案：D

5-8-9 **解**：斜弯曲、偏心拉弯和拉弯组合变形中单元体上只有正应力没有剪应力，只有弯扭组合变形中才既有正应力 σ，又有剪应力 τ。

答案：D

5-8-10 **解**：把力 P 平移到圆轴轴线上，再加一个附加力偶，可见圆轴为弯扭组合变形。其中 A 点的应力状态如解图 a)所示，C 点的应力状态如解图 b)所示。A、C 两点的应力状态与梁中各点相同，而 B、D 两点位于中性轴上，为纯剪切应力状态。但由于 A 点的正应力为拉应力，而 C 点的正应力为压应力，所以最大拉力 $\sigma_1=\dfrac{\sigma}{2}+\sqrt{\left(\dfrac{\sigma}{2}\right)^2+\tau^2}$ 计算中，σ 的正负号不同，σ_1 的数值也不相同。

答案：D

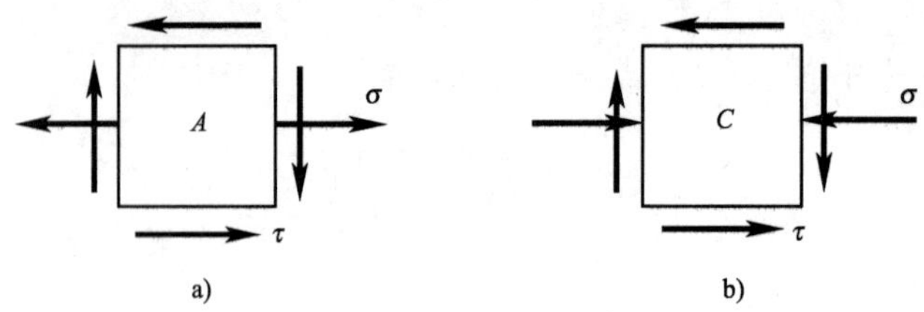

题 5-8-10 解图

第九节

5-9-1 **解**:题图 a):$\mu l=1\times5=5\text{m}$

题图 b):$\mu l=2\times3=6\text{m}$

题图 c):$\mu l=0.7\times6=4.2\text{m}$

由公式 $F_{cr}=\frac{\pi^2EI}{(\mu l)^2}$,可知题图 b)中 F_{crb} 最小,题图 c)中 F_{crc} 最大。

答案:C

5-9-2 **解**:题图所示结构的临界荷载应该是使压杆 AB 和 CD 同时到达临界荷载,也就是压杆 AB(或 CD)临界荷载的 2 倍,故有

$$F_a=3F_{cr}=2\times\frac{\pi^2EI}{(0.7l)^2}=4.08\times\frac{\pi^2EI}{l^2}$$

答案:B

5-9-3 **解**:细长压杆临界力 $P_{cr}=\frac{\pi^2EI}{(\mu l)^2}$,对圆截面 $I=\frac{\pi}{64}d^4$,当直径 d 缩小一半,变为 $\frac{d}{2}$ 时,压杆的临界力 P_{cr} 为压杆的 $\left(\frac{1}{2}\right)^4=\frac{1}{16}$。

答案:D

5-9-4 **解**:从常用的四种杆端约束压杆的长度系数 μ 的值变化规律中可看出,杆端约束越强,μ 值越小(压杆的临界力越大)。图示压杆的杆端约束一端固定、一端弹性支承,比一端固定、一端自由时($\mu=2$)强,但又比一端固定、一端铰支时($\mu=0.7$)弱,故 $0.7<\mu<2$,即为选项 C 的范围内。

答案:C

5-9-5 **解**:根据压杆稳定的概念,压杆稳定是指压杆直线平衡的状态在微小外力干扰去除后自我恢复的能力,因此只有选项 D 是正确的。

答案:D

5-9-6 **解**:根据压杆临界压力的公式 $P_{cr}=\frac{\pi^2EI}{(\mu l)^2}$ 可知,当 EI 相同时,杆端约束越强,μ 值越小,压杆的临界压力越大。题图 a)中压杆下边杆端约束最弱(刚度为 EI),题图 c)中杆端约束最强(刚度为无穷大),故 P_{cr}^a 最小。

答案:A

5-9-7 **解**:临界压力是指压杆由稳定开始转化为不稳定的最小轴向压力。由公式 $P_{cr}=\frac{\pi^2EI}{(\mu l)^2}$ 可知,当压杆截面对某轴惯性矩最小时,则压杆截面绕该轴转动并发生弯曲最省力,即这时的轴向压力最小。显然图示矩形截面中 I_y 是最小惯性矩,而挠曲

线应位于 xz 面内。

答案:B

5-9-8 **解**:不同压杆的临界应力总图如解图所示。解图中 AB 段表示短杆的临界应力,BC 段表示中长杆的临界应力,CD 段表示细长杆的临界应力。从解图中可以看出,在材料相同的条件下,随着柔度的增大,细长杆和中长杆的临界应力均是减小的。

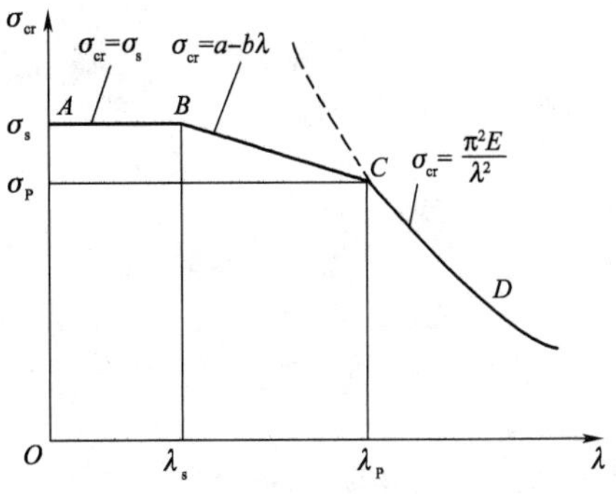

题 5-9-8 解图

答案:C

5-9-9 **解**:压杆临界力公式中的惯性矩应取压杆横截面上的最小惯性矩 I_{max},故

$$P_{cr}=\frac{\pi^2 EI_{min}}{(\mu l)^2}=\frac{\pi^2 E\,\frac{1}{12}hb^3}{(0.7L)^2}=1.68\,\frac{Eb^3 h}{L^2}$$

答案:C

第六章 流体力学

复习指导

一、考试大纲

6.1 流体的主要物性与流体静力学

流体的压缩性与膨胀性；流体的黏性与牛顿内摩擦定律；流体静压强及其特性；重力作用下静水压强的分布规律；作用于平面的液体总压力的计算。

6.2 流体动力学基础

以流场为对象描述流动的概念；流体运动的总流分析；恒定总流连续性方程、能量方程和动量方程的运用。

6.3 流动阻力和能量损失

沿程阻力损失和局部阻力损失；实际流体的两种流态——层流和紊流；圆管中层流运动；紊流运动的特征；减小阻力的措施。

6.4 孔口、管嘴管道流动

孔口自由出流、孔口淹没出流；管嘴出流；有压管道恒定流；管道的串联和并联。

6.5 明渠恒定流

明渠均匀水流特性；产生均匀流的条件；明渠恒定非均匀流的流动状态；明渠恒定均匀流的水力计算。

6.6 渗流、井和集水廊道

土壤的渗流特性；达西定律；井和集水廊道。

6.7 相似原理和量纲分析

力学相似原理；相似准数；量纲分析法。

二、复习指导

注册工程师基础课程考试的特点是题型固定(均为单项选择题)，每题做题时间短(平均每2分钟应做完一道题)，知识覆盖面宽且侧重于基本概念、基本理论、基本公式的应用，较少涉及艰深复杂的理论和数量大的计算。根据以上特点，在复习时应注意对基本概念的准确理解，以提高分析判断能力。例如，下面节后习题6-2-1，其中的B项中有“剪切变形”，而D项中有“剪切变形速度”，两者只差“速度”两字，如果对牛顿内摩擦定律有准确的理解，可立刻判断出D项为正确答案。在单选题中有一部分是数字答案供选择，这部分题是需要经过计算后确定的，所以在复习时应记住重要的基本公式，并掌握其运用方法，结合第四节提供的复习题灵活运用，勤加练习，例如习题6-3-2，就是应用静水压强基本方程和压强的三种表示方法解答的。在单选题中有一部分题是要靠记住一些基本结论去回答的，例如习题6-5-2、习题6-5-4，是要记住层流与紊流核心区的流速分布图才能正确选择。所以复习时对一些重要结论应该加强记忆。在单选题中，还有一部分题是要用基本原理或基本方程去分析的题，例如圆柱形外管嘴流量增加的原因，就是要用能量方程去分析，证明管内收缩断面处存在真空值，产生吸力，增加了作用水头，从而使流量增加。如果理解了能量方程的物理意义，就能解释在位能不变的条件下，流速增加的地方，压强将减小。所以在复习基本方程时，不仅要记住其表达式，更重要的是应理解其物理意义，并学会应用这些方程分析问题。

下面按考试大纲的顺序列出一部分需要准确理解、熟练掌握、灵活运用的基本概念、基本理论和基本方程，供复习时参考。

连续介质，流体的黏性及牛顿内摩擦定律，$\tau=\mu\dfrac{\mathrm{d}u}{\mathrm{d}y}$。

静水压强及其特性；静水压强的基本方程：$p=p_0+\rho gh$；压强分布图；测管水头 $z+\dfrac{p}{\rho g}$ 的物理意义；等压面的性质和画法以及运用等压面求解压力计算题的方法；平面总压力的大小、方向和作用点（公式 $P=\gamma h_c A$，$y_D=y_c+\dfrac{J_c}{y_c A}$，或图解法公式 $P=\Omega b$）；曲面总压力水平分力和垂直分力的计算公式 $P_x=\gamma h_c A_z$，$P_z=\gamma V$，$\theta=\arctan\dfrac{P_z}{P_x}$。

流线、元流、总流的性质，过流断面及水力要素；流量、平均流速关系式：$Q=VA$；连续性方程：$v_1A_1=v_2A_2$；能量方程：$z_1+\dfrac{p_1}{\gamma}+\dfrac{\alpha_1 v_1^2}{2g}=z_2+\dfrac{p_2}{\gamma}+\dfrac{\alpha_2 v_2^2}{2g}+h_w$ 的物理意义，应用范围，应用方法（选断面、基准面、选点）；动量方程 $\sum F=\rho Q(\alpha_{02}v_2-\alpha_{01}v_1)$ 的物理意义，应用范围和应用方法（选控制体、选坐标），总水头线、测压管水头线的画法和变化规律。

层流与紊流的判别标准，圆管层流的流速分布和沿程损失的基本公式（$h_f=\lambda\dfrac{L}{d}\dfrac{v^2}{2g}$）；紊流的流速分布和紊流沿程阻力系数的变化规律（尼古拉兹图）；局部水头损失产生的原因及计算公式（$h_m=\zeta\dfrac{v^2}{2g}$），突然放大局部阻力系数公式；边界层及边界层的分离现象，绕流阻力。

孔口及管嘴出流的流速、流量公式（$v=\phi\sqrt{2gH_0}$，$Q=\mu A\sqrt{2gH_0}$）；流速系数、收缩系数、流量系数之间的相互关系；原柱形外管嘴流量增加的原因；串联管路总水头；并联管路水头损失相等、流量与阻抗平方根成反比等概念。

明渠均匀流水力坡度、水面坡度、渠底坡度相等的概念，发生明渠均匀流的条件；谢才公式 $v=C\sqrt{Ri}$ 与曼宁公式 $C=\dfrac{1}{n}R^{1/6}$ 公式的联合运用；梯形断面水力要素的计算，水力最佳断面概念。

渗流模型必须遵循的条件；达西定律（$v=KJ$，$Q=KAJ$）的物理意义，应用范围；潜水井、承压井、廊道的流量计算。

基本量纲与导出量纲，量纲和谐原理的应用，无量纲量的组合方法，π 定理；两个流动力学相似的条件；重力、黏性力、压力相似准则的物理意义；在何种情况下选用何种相似准则。

流速、压强、流量的量测仪器和量测方法。

第一节　流体力学定义及连续介质假设

流体力学是研究流体宏观机械运动规律及其在工程上应用方法的科学。本章所研究的流体仅限于不可压缩流体，即以水为代表的液体和密度变化较小的低流速气体。

流体力学原理在水利、土木、环保、航天、化工、机械等工程上均有广泛的应用，是土木工程师、结构工程师所应具有的基础理论知识。

流体是由大量的分子所组成，分子间具有一定的空隙，每个分子都在不断地作不规则运动，因此流体的微观结构和运动，在空间和时间上都是不连续的。由于流体力学是研究流体的宏观运动，没有必要对流体进行以分子为单元的微观研究，因而假设流体为连续介质，即认为流体是由微观上充分大而宏观上充分小的质点所组成，质点之间没有空隙，连续地充满流体所占有的空间。将流体运动作为由无数个流体质点所组成的连续介质的运动，它们的物理量在空间和时间上都是连续的。这样就可以摆脱研究分子运动的复杂性，运用数学分析中的连续函数这一有力工具。根据连续介质假设所得的理论结果，在很多情况下与相应的实验结果很符合，因此这一假设已普遍地被采用，只是在某些特殊情况，例如高空的稀薄气体不能作为连续介质来处理。此外，在深入探讨流体黏滞性产生机理时，仍不能不考虑到流体实际存在着分子运动。

习　题

6-1-1　连续介质假设既可摆脱研究流体分子运动的复杂性，又可(　　)。

A. 不考虑流体的压缩性

B. 不考虑流体的黏性

C. 运用数学分析中的连续函数理论分析流体运动

D. 不计及流体的内摩擦力

第二节　流体的主要物理性质

流体运动的外因是流体所受到的外力和外部边界的作用，流体运动的内因则是流体自身的物理性质。为了研究流体的运动规律，必须对两方面有所探讨，本节首先介绍流体所具有的主要的物理性质。

一、易流动性

固体在静止时，可以承受切应力，流体在静止时不能承受切应力，只要在微小切应力作用下，就发生流动而变形。流体在静止时不能承受切应力、抵抗剪切变形的性质称为易流动性。这是因为流体分子之间距离远大于固体，流体也被认为不能承受拉力，而只能承受压力。

二、质量、密度

物体中所含物质数量，称为质量，单位体积流体中所含流体的质量称为密度，以 ρ 表示。对于均质流体，设体积为 V 的流体具有的质量为 m，则其密度为

$$\rho = \frac{m}{V} \tag{6-2-1}$$

对于非均质流体，由连续介质假设可得

$$\rho = \lim_{\Delta V \to 0} \frac{\Delta m}{\Delta V} \tag{6-2-2}$$

密度的国际单位为 kg/m^3。

流体密度随温度与压强而变，但变化甚微，对液体和低流速气体，可认为密度是一个常数。在一个标准大气压下，不同温度的水和空气的物理性质分别见表 6-2-1 及表 6-2-2。4℃左右水的密度 $\rho=1\ 000kg/m^3$，可以作为标准状态下水的密度，一般的冷水也可采用此值，温度较高的热水要考虑密度的变化。

水的物理特性（在一个标准大气压下） 表 6-2-1

温度 (℃)	重度 γ (kN/m^3)	密度 ρ (kg/m^3)	黏度 $\mu\times10^3$ ($N\cdot s/m^2$)	运动黏度 $\nu\times10^6$ (m^2/s)	表面张力 σ (N/m)	汽化压强 p_v (kN/m^2)，绝对	体积模量 $K\times10^{-6}$ (kN/m^2)
0	9.805	999.8	1.781	1.785	0.075 6	0.61	2.02
5	9.807	1000.0	1.518	1.519	0.074 9	0.87	2.06
10	9.804	999.7	1.307	1.396	0.074 2	1.23	2.10
15	9.798	999.1	1.139	1.139	0.073 5	1.70	2.15
20	9.789	998.2	1.002	1.003	0.072 8	2.34	2.18
25	9.777	997.0	0.890	0.893	0.072 0	3.17	2.22
30	9.764	995.7	0.798	0.800	0.071 2	4.24	2.25
40	9.730	992.2	0.653	0.658	0.069 6	7.38	2.28
50	9.689	988.0	0.547	0.553	0.067 9	12.33	2.29
60	9.642	983.2	0.466	0.474	0.066 2	19.92	2.28
70	9.589	977.8	0.404	0.413	0.064 4	31.16	2.25
80	9.530	971.8	0.354	0.364	0.062 6	46.34	2.20
90	9.466	965.3	0.315	0.326	0.060 8	70.10	2.14
100	9.399	958.4	0.282	0.294	0.058 9	101.33	2.07

空气的物理特性（在一个标准大气压下） 表 6-2-2

温度 (℃)	密度 ρ (kg/m^3)	重度 γ (N/m^3)	黏度 $\mu\times10^5$ ($N\cdot s/m^2$)	运动黏度 $\nu\times10^5$ (m^2/s)
−40	1.515	14.86	1.49	0.98
−20	1.395	13.68	1.61	1.15
0	1.293	12.68	1.71	1.32
10	1.248	12.24	1.76	1.41
20	1.205	11.82	1.81	1.50
30	1.165	11.43	1.86	1.60
40	1.128	11.06	1.90	1.68
60	1.060	10.40	2.00	1.87
80	1.000	9.81	2.09	2.09
100	0.946	9.28	2.18	2.31
200	0.747	7.33	2.58	3.45

三、重力、重度

地球对流体的引力，即为重力，单位体积流体内所具有的重力称为容重或重度，以 γ 表示。

对于均质流体，设体积为V的流体具有的重力为G，则重度

$$\gamma = \frac{G}{V} \tag{6-2-3}$$

对于非均质流体，由连续介质假设可得

$$\gamma = \lim_{\Delta V \to 0} \frac{\Delta G}{\Delta V} \tag{6-2-4}$$

由牛顿运动定律知：$G=mg$，g为重力加速度，一般采用$g=9.8\text{m/s}^2$，由式(6-2-3)可得

$$\gamma = \rho g \tag{6-2-5}$$

重度亦随压力和温度而变，在一个标准大气压下水的重度随温度而变化的值见表6-1。一般冷水的重度可视为常数，可用$\gamma=9\ 800\text{N/m}^3$（重度$\gamma$均可用$\rho g$代替）。

四、黏性

流体在运动时，具有抵抗剪切变形速度的性质，称为黏性，它是由于流体内部分子的黏聚力及分子运动的动量输运所引起。当某流层对其邻流层发生相对位移而引起剪切变形时，在流层间产生的切力（即流层间内摩擦力）就是黏性的表现。由实验知，在二维平行直线流动中，流层间切力（即内摩擦力）T的大小与流体的黏性有关，并与速度梯度$\frac{\mathrm{d}u}{\mathrm{d}y}$（即剪切变形速度）和接触面积$A$成正比，而与接触面上压力无关，即

$$T = \mu A \frac{\mathrm{d}u}{\mathrm{d}y} \tag{6-2-6}$$

单位面积上的切力称为切应力，以τ表示，有

$$\tau = \mu \frac{\mathrm{d}u}{\mathrm{d}y} \tag{6-2-7}$$

上式为牛顿内摩擦定律的表达式，式中μ称为动力黏度（或动力黏性系数），单位为Pa·s（帕·秒）或$\frac{\text{N}\cdot\text{s}}{\text{m}^2}$，动力黏度与密度的比值称为运动黏度（或运动黏性系数），以ν表示，即

$$\nu = \frac{\mu}{\rho} \tag{6-2-8}$$

ν的单位为m^2/s，或cm^2/s，动力黏度μ与运动黏度ν的值均随温度t和流体种类而变，水、空气的μ及ν值随温度t的变化可查表6-2-1和表6-2-2。水的运动黏度ν可用下列经验公式求得

$$\nu = \frac{0.017\ 75}{1 + 0.033\ 7t + 0.000\ 221t^2} \tag{6-2-9}$$

式中：ν——运动黏度（cm^2/s）；

t——水温（℃）。

由上式可知水的运动黏度随温度升高而减少，而空气的运动黏度随温度升高而增加。

【例 6-2-1】 水的运动黏性系数随温度的升高而：

A. 增大　　B. 减小　　C. 不变　　D. 先减小然后增大

解 水的运动黏性系数随温度的升高而减小。

答案：B

式(6-2-6)中的速度梯度$\frac{\mathrm{d}u}{\mathrm{d}y}$也就是剪切变形速度$\frac{\mathrm{d}\alpha}{\mathrm{d}t}$，可证明如下：

从图 6-2-1 可看出，原为正方形的微元体，由于速度梯度的存在，上边运动快于下边，经时间 dt后，正方形变为平行四边形，直角变形为锐角，产生一剪切变形角 dα，当 dα 角度很小时，$\mathrm{d}\alpha \approx \tan \mathrm{d}\alpha = \frac{\mathrm{d}u\mathrm{d}t}{\mathrm{d}y}$。

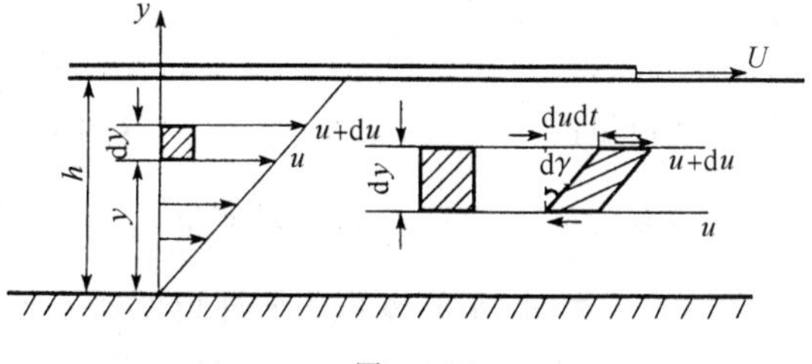

图 6-2-1

即

$$\frac{\mathrm{d}u}{\mathrm{d}y} = \frac{\mathrm{d}\alpha}{\mathrm{d}t}$$

$\frac{\mathrm{d}\alpha}{\mathrm{d}t}$为单位时间内的剪切变形角度，故称为剪切变形速度，或剪切变形率。

凡是符合牛顿内摩擦定律的流体称为牛顿流体，例如水、酒精和一般气体。凡 τ 与$\frac{\mathrm{d}u}{\mathrm{d}y}$不成线性关系的流体称为非牛顿流体，例如泥浆、血液、胶溶液、聚合物液体等。本章主要讨论牛顿流体。

【例 6-2-2】 某固定不动平板水平放置，其上有一层厚度为 10mm 的油层，油的黏度 $\mu = 9.81 \times 10^{-2}$ Pa · s，油层液面上漂浮一水平滑移平板，已知其水平移动速度 $u - 1$m/s，试求作用在移动平板上单位面积的切应力 τ；又若油层厚度增加至 80mm，且沿铅直方向油层断面上的流速分布式为：$u = 4y - y^2$，式中 y 为从固定平板起算的铅直坐标，此时平板移动速度改变，再求移动平板单位面积切应力 τ(参见图 6-2-1)。

解 (1)当油层厚度为 10mm 时，由于厚度小流速分布可近似为直线分布，此时沿铅直方向的流速梯度

$$\frac{\mathrm{d}u}{\mathrm{d}y} \approx \frac{u}{y} = \frac{1\mathrm{m/s}}{0.01\mathrm{m}} = 100\mathrm{s}^{-1}$$

切应力

$$\tau = \mu \frac{\mathrm{d}u}{\mathrm{d}y} = 9.81 \times 10^{-2} \times 100 = 9.81\mathrm{Pa}$$

(2)当厚度增至 80mm，流速分布为 $u = 4y - y^2$，则有

$$\tau = \mu \frac{\mathrm{d}u}{\mathrm{d}y} = \mu(4 - 2y) = 9.81 \times 10^{-2} \times (4 - 2 \times 0.08) = 0.376\ 7\mathrm{Pa}$$

五、压缩性与热胀性

当作用在流体上的压力增大时，流体的体积减小；压力减小时，体积增大的性质称为流体的压缩性或流体的弹性。液体的压缩性一般以体积压缩系数 β 或弹性系数 K 来量度，设液体体积为 V，压强增加 dp 后，体积减少 dV，则压缩系数

$$\beta = -\frac{\frac{\mathrm{d}V}{V}}{\mathrm{d}p} \tag{6-2-10}$$

式中，负号表示压强增大，体积减小；β 的单位为 m^2/N。

压缩系数的倒数称为体积弹性模量 K，即

$$K = \frac{1}{\beta} = -V\frac{dp}{dV} \tag{6-2-11}$$

体积弹性模量的单位为 N/m^2 或 Pa。不同的液体有不同的 β 及 K 值，水的体积弹性模量 K 可近似地取为 2×10^9Pa。若压强增量 dp 为一个大气压，则体积的相对变化 $\frac{\Delta V}{V}$ 约为 1/20 000，因此在 dp 不大时，水的体积压缩性可忽略不计，此种液体称为不可压缩流体。

气体的压缩性较大，对于理想气体体积与压强、温度的关系，一般遵循理想气体的状态方程式

$$\frac{p}{\rho} = RT \tag{6-2-12}$$

式中：p——压强；

ρ——密度；

T——流体温度(K)；

R——气体常数[m·N/(kg·K)]，与气体的分子量有关，对空气 R=287m·N/(kg·K)。

当气体的流速小于 50m/s 时，密度变化为 1%，可作为未压缩气体来处理。

流体温度升高体积膨胀的性质称为热胀性，可用热胀系数 α 来量度，$\alpha=\frac{dV}{VdT}$。

六、表面张力特性

在流体自由液面的分子作用半径范围内，由于分子的引力大于斥力，在表层沿表面产生张力，称为表面张力。其大小可用表面张力系数 σ 来量度，σ 是自由液面单位长度上所受到的张力，单位为 N/m。

由于表面张力的作用，如果把细管竖立在液体中，液体就会在细管中上升(如水)或下降(如水银)，这种现象称为毛细管现象。毛细管内外液面高差 h 与液体的种类及毛细管直径 d 有关。对于水，由于黏聚力小于水与管壁的附着力，因此毛细管内液面上升，实验得知

$$h = \frac{29.8}{d} \tag{6-2-13}$$

式中，d 以 mm 计。

对于水银，黏聚力大于附着力，管中水面下降，其液面差

$$h = \frac{10.15}{d} \tag{6-2-14}$$

后文将要介绍的玻璃测压管，为了避免表面张力毛细现象的影响，其管径 d 应大于 10mm。

七、汽化压强与空蚀现象

液体分子逸出液面，向空间扩散的过程称汽化，液体汽化为蒸气；汽化的逆过程为凝结，蒸气凝结为液体。在液体中，汽化与凝结同时存在，当这两个过程达到平衡时，宏观的汽化现象停止，此时液面压强称为饱和蒸气压强或汽化压强，水的汽化压强列于表 6-2-3。当液体某处的压强低于汽化压时，该处即产生汽化。液体汽化处，将发生空泡，当空泡流入高压区时，会突然破裂溃灭，周围水则以极高速度充填其间并产生很高的冲击压力。如空泡在固壁处溃灭，则使壁面承受很高的冲压，使壁面受到破坏，同时汽化时逸出的活泼气体，也有化学腐蚀的作用，因此液体在汽化时易引起固壁的所谓空蚀现象。水泵或建筑物中发生空蚀时，往往伴有振动、噪声、断流等现象，应尽量避免。

水的汽化压强 表 6-2-3

水温(℃)	0	5	10	15	20	25	30
汽化压强(kN/m^2)	0.61	0.87	1.23	1.70	2.34	3.17	4.21
水温(℃)	40	50	60	70	80	90	100
汽化压强(kN/m^2)	7.38	12.33	19.92	31.16	47.34	70.10	101.33

【例 6-2-3】 半径为 R 的圆管中,横截面上流速分布为 $u=2\left(1-\frac{r^2}{R^2}\right)$,其中 r 表示到圆管轴线的距离,则在 $r_1=0.2R$ 处的黏性切应力与 $r_2=R$ 处的黏性切应力大小之比为:

A. 5　　B. 25　　C. 1/5　　D. 1/25

解 切应力 $\tau=\mu\frac{\mathrm{d}u}{\mathrm{d}y}$,而 $y=R-r$,$\mathrm{d}y=-\mathrm{d}r$,故 $\frac{\mathrm{d}u}{\mathrm{d}y}=-\frac{\mathrm{d}u}{\mathrm{d}r}$

题设流速 $u=2\left(1-\frac{r^2}{R^2}\right)$,故 $\frac{\mathrm{d}u}{\mathrm{d}y}=-\frac{\mathrm{d}u}{\mathrm{d}r}=\frac{2\times 2r}{R^2}=\frac{4r}{R^2}$

题设 $r_1=0.2R$,故切应力 $\tau_1=\mu\left(\frac{4\times 0.2R}{R^2}\right)=\mu\left(\frac{0.8}{R}\right)$

题设 $r_2=R$,则切应力 $\tau_2=\mu\left(\frac{4R}{R^2}\right)=\mu\left(\frac{4}{R}\right)$

切应力大小之比 $\frac{\tau_1}{\tau_2}=\frac{\mu\left(\frac{0.8}{R}\right)}{\mu\left(\frac{4}{R}\right)}=\frac{0.8}{4}=\frac{1}{5}$

答案:C

习　　题

6-2-1　与牛顿内摩擦定律直接有关的因素是(　　)。

A. 压强、速度和黏度

B. 压强、黏度、剪切变形

C. 切应力、温度和速度

D. 黏度、切应力与剪切变形速度

6-2-2　水的动力黏度随温度的升高而(　　)。

A. 增大　　B. 减小　　C. 不变　　D. 不定

第三节　流体静力学

一、作用在流体上的力

作用在流体上的力可分为两大类。

(一)质量力

作用于每一个流体质点上与流体质量成正比的力,称质量力;在均质流体中它与体积成正比,又称为体积力。常见的质量力有重力和惯性力,重力等于质量 m 与重力加速度 g 的乘积,惯性力则等于质量与加速度的乘积，方向与加速度方向相反。在分析流体运动时，常引用单位质量流体所受质量力，称为单位质量力，以$\frac{\boldsymbol{F}}{m}$表示，具有加速度 $\boldsymbol{a}$ 的量纲。设单位质量在直角坐标系三个轴上的分量，以 X、Y、Z 表示，则仅受重力作用的流体，其单位质量力在三个轴上的分量分别为

$$X = 0 \quad Y = 0 \quad Z = -g$$

（二）表面力

作用于流体的表面，与作用的面积成比例的力称表面力。表面力又可以分为垂直于作用面的压力和沿作用面切线方向的切力；表面力既可以是作用于流体边界面上的压力、切力，例如大气压力、活塞压力，也可以是一部分流体质点作用于另一部分流体质点上的压力和切力；表面力的单位为 N。

作用在单位面积上的表面力称为表面应力，例如压应力和切应力，在连续介质中可用下式表示

$$p = \lim_{\Delta A \to 0} \frac{\Delta p}{\Delta A} \tag{6-3-1}$$

$$\tau = \lim_{\Delta A \to 0} \frac{\Delta T}{\Delta A} \tag{6-3-2}$$

式中：p——压应力或压强（Pa）；

τ——切应力（Pa）。

在静止流体中，没有切应力，只有压强。静水压强有两个特性：垂直于作用面，且同一点上的静水压强在各个方向上相等，与作用面的方位无关。

二、欧拉平衡微分方程

1755 年，欧拉（Euler）以平衡流体中取出的正六面体作为隔离体，经过微元分析，在外力平衡条件下得出了欧拉平衡微分方程

$$\begin{cases} X - \dfrac{1}{\rho}\dfrac{\partial p}{\partial x} = 0 \\ Y - \dfrac{1}{\rho}\dfrac{\partial p}{\partial y} = 0 \\ Z - \dfrac{1}{\rho}\dfrac{\partial p}{\partial z} = 0 \end{cases} \tag{6-3-3}$$

式中：X、Y、Z——分别代表 x、y、z 方向上流体所受的单位质量力；

ρ——流体密度；

$\frac{1}{\rho}\frac{\partial p}{\partial x}$、$\frac{1}{\rho}\frac{\partial p}{\partial y}$、$\frac{1}{\rho}\frac{\partial p}{\partial z}$——分别为 x、y、z 三个方向上的单位质量表面力，$\frac{\partial p}{\partial x}$、$\frac{\partial p}{\partial y}$、$\frac{\partial p}{\partial z}$分别为三个轴向的压强变化率。

改写欧拉平衡微分方程可得

$$\begin{cases} X = \dfrac{1}{\rho}\dfrac{\partial p}{\partial x} \\ Y = \dfrac{1}{\rho}\dfrac{\partial p}{\partial y} \\ Z = \dfrac{1}{\rho}\dfrac{\partial p}{\partial z} \end{cases}$$

对于不可压缩流体，其密度 ρ 为常数，上式表明质量力与压强变化率同号，即质量力作用的方向即为压强增加的方向。仅受重力作用的静水中，压强沿地心引力的方向增加，所以静水中越往下，水深越大压强也越大。上式还表明，如果任两个轴向的单位质量力为零，则此两轴构成的面为等压面；等压面上压强不变。例如仅受重力作用的静水，$X=0$、$Y=0$，则 X,Y 轴构成的面为等压面，即仅受重力作用的静水中，等压面是与重力垂直的面，在小范围内是水平面。将欧拉平衡方程(6-3-3)各式分别乘以 dx、dy、dz 相加后可得

$$dp = \rho(Xdx + Ydy + Zdz) \tag{6-3-4}$$

式中：dp——压强的全微分；

其余符号意义同前。

上式是欧拉平衡微分方程的又一形式。

三、仅受重力作用时静水压强基本方程

将欧拉平衡微分方程(6-3-4)对仅受重力作用的静水积分即可得静水压强基本方程。

以 $X=Y=0$,$Z=-g$ 代入上式得

$$dp = -\rho g\,dz = -\gamma dz$$

两边作不定积分得

$$p = -\gamma z + C$$

或

$$z + \frac{p}{\gamma} = C \tag{6-3-5}$$

式中：C——积分常数，可根据边界条件定出。

以如图 6-3-1 所示静水容器中表面压强为 p_0，自液面向下计算的水深为 $h=z_0-z$，则由式(6-3-5)

$$z + \frac{p}{\gamma} = z_0 + \frac{p_0}{\gamma}$$

则有

$$p = p_0 + \gamma(z_0 - z)$$

或

$$p = p_0 + \gamma h = p_0 + \rho g h \tag{6-3-6}$$

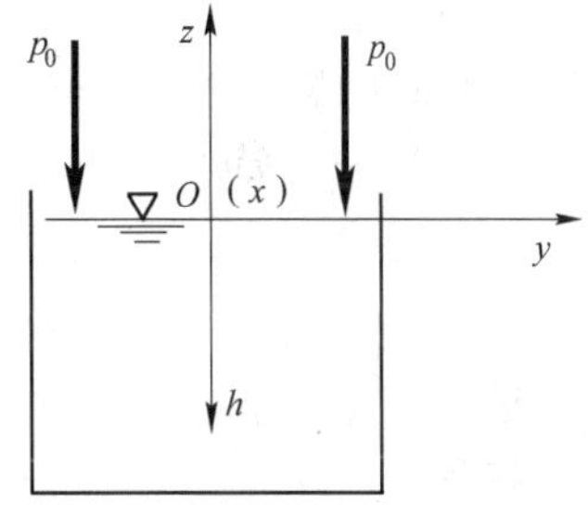

图 6-3-1

式(6-3-6)称为静水压强基本方程，可用来计算液面下某一水深处的流体静压强 p。

式中表面压强 p_0 在敞口容器中为大气压强 p_a，大气压强 p_a 的值与海拔标高有关，通常海拔高度不大处，一般采用 $p_a=98$kPa，即为一个工程大气压(用 at 表示)，1at=98kPa。这不同于海平面处的标准大气压，一个标准大气压为 101.325kPa(以 atm 表示)。

式(6-3-6)表明水下任一点静压强由表面压强 p_0 与水柱重力所构成的压强 γh 两部分组成，且水面压强 p_0 均匀传播到水中所有各点，与水深无关，这正是读者熟知的帕斯卡原理。

四、压强的两种基准和三种表示方法

(一)两种基准

压强的基准是指压强的起算点，如以绝对真空为零点起算的压强称为绝对压强 p'；绝对压强最小为零，无负压强。

如以当地大气压为零起算则称为相对压强 p，它与绝对压强 p' 只相差一当地大气压 p_a，即

$$p = p' - p_a \tag{6-3-7}$$

相对压强可正可负，当相对压强小于当地大气压时则出现负压，此时称为出现部分真空现象，真空值用 p_v 表示，其大小可用下式求出

$$p_v = p_a - p' \tag{6-3-8}$$

或

$$p_v = -p \tag{6-3-9}$$

真空值所对应的液柱高度为 h_v，称真空度，即

$$h_v = \frac{p_v}{\gamma} \tag{6-3-10}$$

（二）压强的三种表示方法[1]

第一种表示压强的方法是从压强的基本定义出发，以单位面积上的压力来表示，在国际单位制中为 N/m^2 或 Pa，$1N/m^2 = 1Pa$。第二种表示方法是用工程大气压的倍数表示，$1at = 9.8 \times 10^4 Pa = 98kPa$。第三种表示方法是用液柱高度 h 来表示，常用水柱高度或水银柱高度来表示，其单位是 mH_2O 或 mmHg。与压强 p 的关系可用 $h = \frac{p}{\gamma}$ 确定，例如一个工程大气压所对应的水柱高度 h 应为

$$h = \frac{p}{\gamma} = \frac{9.8 \times 10^4}{9.8 \times 10^3} = 10mH_2O$$

记住下面一组数据，有助于以心算法进行压强单位的换算，即 $1mH_2O = 0.1$ 个工程大气压 $= 9.8kPa$。

【例 6-3-1】 密闭水箱如图所示，已知水深 $h = 1m$，自由面上的压强 $p_0 = 90kN/m^2$，当地大气压 $p_a = 101kN/m^2$，则水箱底部 A 点的真空度为：

A. $-1.2kN/m^2$　　B. $9.8kN/m^2$

C. $1.2kN/m^2$　　D. $-9.8kN/m^2$

解　真空度 $p_v = p_a - p' = 101 - (90 + 9.8) = 1.2kN/m^2$

答案：C

例 6-3-1 图

五、静水压强基本方程的物理意义

（一）几何意义

z——位置高度，即计算点距基准面的铅直高度，以 m 计；

$\frac{p}{\gamma}$——压强高度或测压管高度，即计算点至测压管中液面的铅直高度，以 m 计，见图 6-3-2；

$z + \frac{p}{\gamma}$——测压管水头，即从基准面到测压管中液面的高度，以 m 计。在静止液体中 $z + \frac{p}{\gamma} = C$，即静水中各点的测压管水头相等，各点测压管水头上端构成的线或面称为测压管水头线（或面）。静水中测压管水头线是一水平线。

[1]《中华人民共和国法定计量单位》中规定，标准大气压和毫米汞（水）柱两种压强的表示方法（即本款所述的第二、第三种方法），属于废除单位。但在目前工程实用上，仍有大量资料应用后两种单位，故此处仍编入。

（二）能量意义

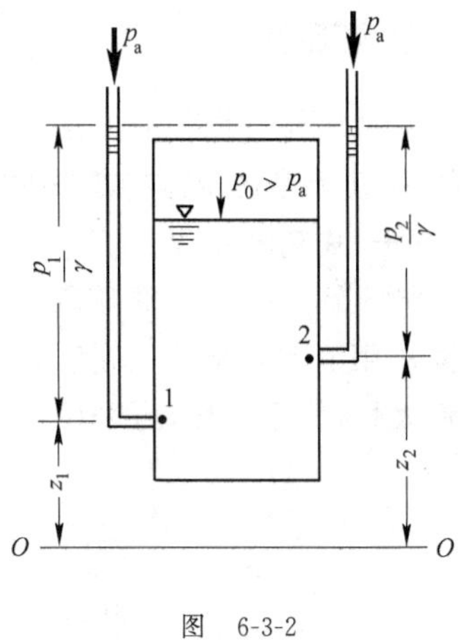

图 6-3-2

z——单位重量流体的位能，因为 $z=\frac{mg\cdot z}{mg}$，简称单位位能；

$\frac{p}{\gamma}$——单位重量流体的压能，简称单位压能，因为 $\frac{p}{\gamma}=\frac{mg\cdot\frac{p}{\gamma}}{mg}$；

$z+\frac{p}{\gamma}$——单位重量流体的势能，简称单位势能。在静水中 $z+\frac{p}{\gamma}=C$，表明静水中各点单位势能相等，为能量守恒定律的一种反映。

此外，在水力学中习惯上将高度称为水头，所以 z 又可称为位置水头，$\frac{p}{\gamma}$ 称为压强水头。

六、压强分布图

在实际工程中常把静压强的分布用作图法表示出来，便于形象直观地分析问题。从静压强基本方程 $p=p_0+\gamma h$ 可知，当容器为敞口时，表面压强 $p_0=p_a$，容器外壁同时作用着大气压强 p_a，两者抵消后，容器所受到的有效压强为相对压强。此外 $p=\gamma h$，即与水深 h 为一线性关系，所以压强沿水深的变化为一直线，在液面处 $\gamma h=0$，在水深为 H 处为 γH，此两点连一直线，即为压强分布图。作图时应注意力矢的方向要与作用面成直角，因为静水压强的特性之一是与作用面垂直，各种情况下的压强分布如图 6-3-3 所示。如在密闭容器中 $p_0\neq p_a$ 时，则要计及 p_0 的作用，但因 p_0 在传递时是等值的，与 h 无关，所以只要几何地叠加即可。

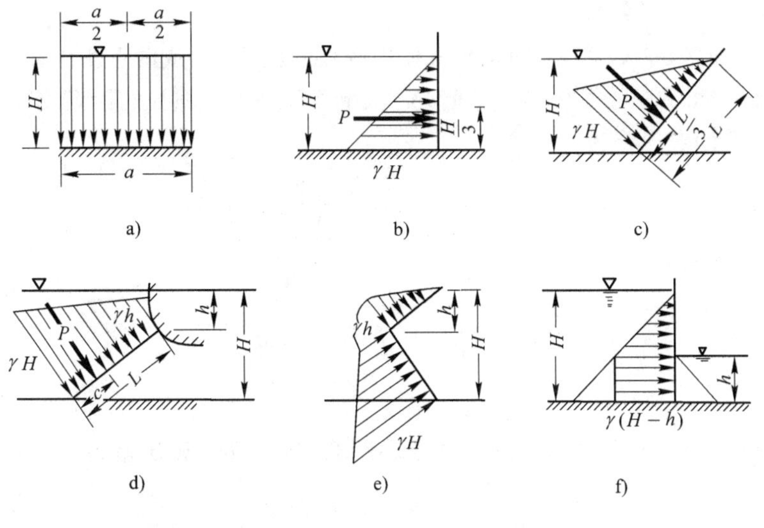

图 6-3-3

七、测压计

测量流体静压强的方法、仪器种类很多，并日趋现代化。下面介绍常用的液柱式测压计及其原理，其余将在流体参数的量测一节中再讲。

(一)玻璃测压管

测压管是一根两端开口的玻璃管，一端与所测流体连通，另一端与大气连通，管内液体在压强作用下上升至某一高度 h_A，见图 6-3-4a)，则被测点流体压强 $p_A=\gamma h_A$。当压强较大时，测压管太长，使用不便，可采用 U 形水银压力计测压。

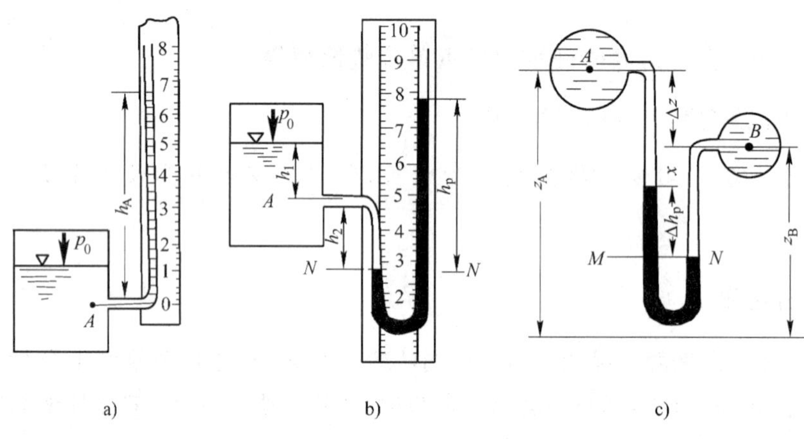

图 6-3-4

(二)U 形水银压力计

此种压力计如图 6-3-4b)所示，在 U 形玻璃管中盛以与水不相混掺的某种液体，例如水银。在测量气体压强时，可盛水或酒精。被测点压强 $p_A=\gamma_{Hg}h_p-\gamma h_2$，液面压强 $p_0=\gamma_{Hg}h_p-\gamma(h_1+h_2)$。

(三)压差计

水银压差计如图 6-3-4c)所示，可测出液体中两点的压差 Δp 或两点测压管水头差。仅受重力作用的等压面为水平面如图 6-3-4 中的 MN 平面，等压面上压强处处相等。利用等压面原理可导出图中 A、B 两点压差为

$$p_B-p_A=\Delta p=\gamma\Delta z+\left(\frac{\gamma_{Hg}}{\gamma}-1\right)\gamma\Delta h_p$$

两点测压管水头差为

$$\left(z_B+\frac{p_B}{\gamma}\right)-\left(z_A+\frac{p_A}{\gamma}\right)=\left(\frac{\gamma_{Hg}}{\gamma}-1\right)\Delta h_p$$

若水的重度 $\gamma=9.8\text{kN/m}^3$，水银的重度 $\gamma_{Hg}=133.28\text{kN/m}^3$，则压差为

$$\Delta p=\gamma\Delta z+12.6\gamma\Delta h_p$$

两点测压管水头差为

$$\left(z_B + \frac{p_B}{\gamma}\right) - \left(z_A + \frac{p_A}{\gamma}\right) = 12.6\Delta h_p$$

八、液体的相对平衡

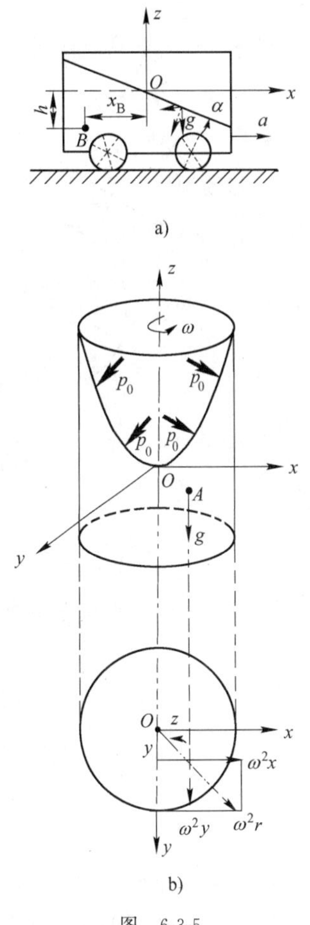

图 6-3-5

液体相对于地球运动，但液体质点之间及液体与容器壁之间无相对运动时，称为液体的相对平衡或相对静止状态。例如相对于地面作等加速直线运动的洒水车和容器中的液体绕中心轴作等角速旋转运动，在运动经历一定时间后就会达到这种相对平衡状态。

现来用达伦伯原理，把坐标系取在运动容器上，液体相对于这一坐标系是静止的，这样便使这种运动问题作为静止问题来处理。如图 6-3-5a)所示为一水平等加速运动的洒水车，取直角坐标系 x、y、z 在自由液面上，此时车中液体在重力及水平惯性力共同作用处于相对平衡状态，作用在液体质点上的单位质量力在各个轴向的分量分别为

$$X = -a \qquad Y = 0 \qquad Z = -g$$

代入 Euler 平衡方程 $\mathrm{d}p = \rho(X\mathrm{d}x + Y\mathrm{d}y + Z\mathrm{d}z)$，有

$$\mathrm{d}p = \rho(-a\mathrm{d}x - g\mathrm{d}z)$$

积分后得

$$p = -(\rho a x + \rho g z) + C$$

或

$$p = -\gamma\left(\frac{a}{g}x + z\right) + C$$

当 $x=0$，$z=0$ 时，$p=p_0$ 代入上式可得 $C=p_0$，最后得

$$p = p_0 - \gamma\left(\frac{a}{g}x + z\right)$$

其中，p_0 为液面压强，$\gamma=\rho g$ 为液体重度。自由液面上 $p=p_0$，即 $\frac{a}{g}x + z = 0$，或 $ax + gz = 0$，液面倾角为 α，则 $\tan\alpha = -\frac{z}{x} = \frac{a}{g}$，当水平加速度增加时，液面倾角增大。

又如图 6-3-5b)为绕容器纵轴作等角速旋转之相对平衡，此时各轴向的单位质量力分别为

$$X = \omega^2 x \qquad Y = \omega^2 y \qquad Z = -g$$

代入 Euler 平衡方程后积分得

$$p = p_0 + \gamma\left(\frac{\omega^2 r^2}{2g} - z\right)$$

式中：ω——旋转角速度；

r——质点距轴心的旋转半径。

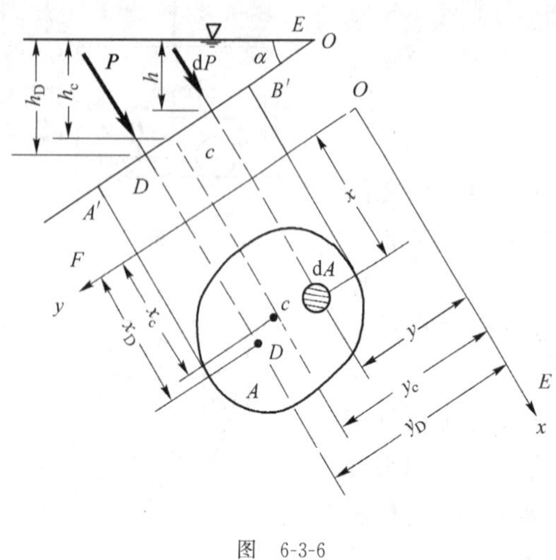

图 6-3-6

自由液面上 $p=p_0$，由上式可得自由液面方程为

$$z=\frac{\omega^2 r^2}{2g}$$

所以自由液面为一旋转抛物面，旋转越快，液面上高度越大。在同一转速下，边壁处液面上升最高。

九、作用在平面上的液体总压力

（一）平面静水总压力的大小

如图 6-3-6 所示一倾斜置于水下的任意形状平面，总面积为 A，与水平线的交角为 α，围绕面上 M 点取一微小面积 $\mathrm{d}A$，淹没深度为 h，作用在 $\mathrm{d}A$ 上的静水总压力为 $\mathrm{d}P$，则

$$\mathrm{d}P=p\mathrm{d}A=\gamma h\,\mathrm{d}A$$

而全面积 A 上的静水总压为 P，则

$$\begin{aligned}P&=\int_A \mathrm{d}P=\int_A \gamma h\,\mathrm{d}A\\&=\int_A \gamma y\sin\alpha \mathrm{d}A=\gamma\sin\alpha\int_A y\,\mathrm{d}A\\&=\gamma\sin\alpha y_c A=\gamma h_c A=p_c A\end{aligned}$$

即

$$P=\gamma h_c A=p_c A \tag{6-3-11}$$

式中：h_c——面积 A 形心点 c 处的水深；

p_c——形心点 c 处的静压强。

上式表明平面总压力的大小等于形心点压强乘以平面受压面积。

（二）平面总压力的方向和作用点

由静水压强特性知，总压力垂直于受压平面，总压力作用点可根据合力对某一轴的力矩等于各分力对同一轴力矩之和求得。设总压力对 x 轴的力矩为 $P\cdot y_D$，y_D 为总压力作用点 D 至 x 轴的距离，则有

$$\begin{aligned}P\cdot y_D&=\int y\mathrm{d}P=\int_A y\gamma y\sin\alpha \mathrm{d}A=\gamma\sin\alpha\int_A y^2\,\mathrm{d}A\\&=\gamma\sin\alpha J_x=\gamma\sin\alpha(J_c+y_c^2 A)\end{aligned}$$

又因为 $P=\gamma y\sin\alpha A$，代入上式后求得 y_D

$$y_D=y_c+\frac{J_c}{y_c A} \tag{6-3-12}$$

式中：y_c——面积形心 c 点至 x 轴的距离；

J_c——过形心 c 轴的受压面积 A 的惯性矩，可查有关表格，例如矩形面积 $J_c=\frac{b\,h^3}{12}$，圆形面积 $J_c=\frac{\pi r^4}{4}$。

（三）平面总压力的图解法

对于垂直置于水中的矩形平面，见图 6-3-3b)，总压力可应用图解法求得，其大小等于压强

分布图的面积 S 乘以受压面的宽度 b，即 $p=b\cdot s$。总压力的作用线通过压强分布图的形心，作用线与受压面的交点，即为总压力的作用点。

十、作用在曲面上的液体总压力

如图 6-3-7 所示一受压曲面，取曲面上一点 M 并绕 M 取微小面积 dA，作用在微小面积 dA 上的总压力为 $dP=pdA=\gamma h dA$，dP 垂直于 dA，与水平方向成 θ 角，将 dP 分解为水平分力 dP_x 及铅垂分力 dP_z，分别为

$$dP_x = dP\cos\theta = \gamma h\,dA\cos\theta = \gamma h dA_x$$

$$dP_z = dP\sin\theta = \gamma h\,dA\sin\theta = \gamma h dA_z$$

作用在全部曲面上的水平总分力为

$$P_x = \int dP_x = \int_A \gamma h\,dA\cos\theta$$

$$= \int_{A_x} \gamma h\,dA_x = \gamma h_c A_x$$

即
$$P_x = \gamma h_c A_x \tag{6-3-13}$$

式中：h_c——曲面在铅垂面上投影面积 A_x 的形心点水深。

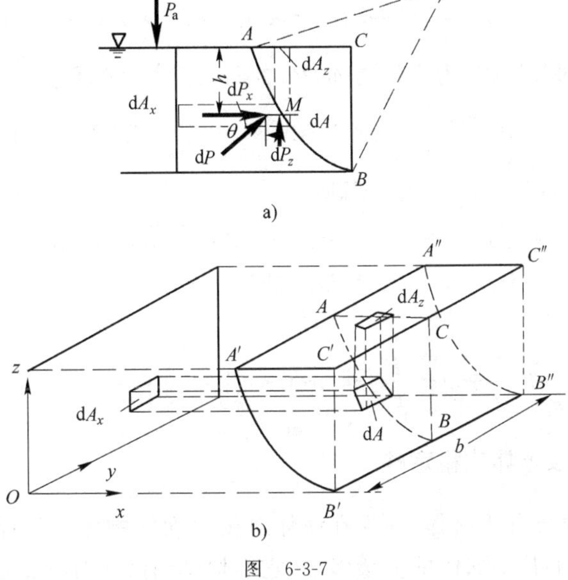

图 6-3-7

作用在全部曲面上的铅垂总分力为

$$P_z = \int dP_z = \int_A \gamma h\,dA\sin\theta = \int_{A_z} \gamma h\,dA_z = \gamma\int_{A_z} h\,dA_z$$

积分式 $\int_{A_z} h\,dA_z$ 为曲面以上与自由液面（或其延长面）以下铅垂柱体的体积，称为压力体的体积 V，如图 6-3-7 所示 $A'B'C'A''B''C''$ 的体积，所以曲面总压力的铅垂分力为

$$P_z = \gamma V \tag{6-3-14}$$

即铅垂分力 $\boldsymbol{P}_z$ 等于压力体内液体的重力 γV。若压力体内有液体压力体与液体在曲面同一侧则为实压力体，$\boldsymbol{P}_z$ 方向向下，若压力体内无液体，液体在曲面的另一侧，则为虚压力体，此时 $\boldsymbol{P}_z$

的方向向上，称为浮力。曲面总压力的合力 $\boldsymbol{P}$ 可用 $\boldsymbol{P}_x$ 及 $\boldsymbol{P}_z$ 求得

$$P = \sqrt{P_x^2 + P_z^2} \tag{6-3-15}$$

曲面总压力与水平线的夹角 θ

$$\theta = \arctan\frac{P_z}{P_x} \tag{6-3-16}$$

对于对称的几何图形，总压力作用点均应在水平对称轴上。

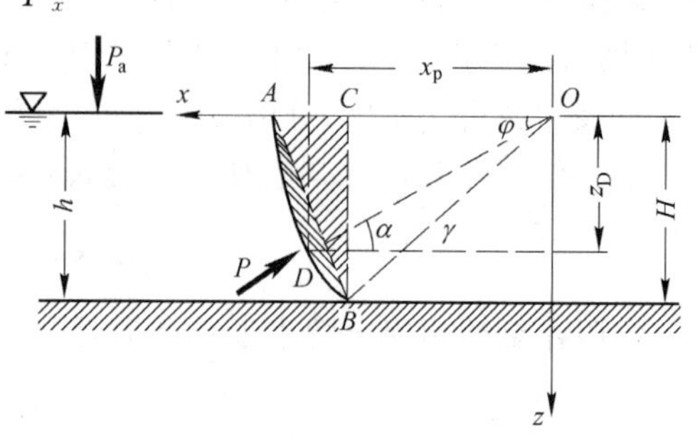

例 6-3-2 图

【例 6-3-2】 设有一弧形闸门，如图所示，已知闸门宽度 $b=3\text{m}$，半径 $r=2.828\text{m}$，$\varphi=45°$，闸门转动轴 O 点距底面高度 $H=2\text{m}$，门轴 O 在水面延长线上，试求当闸门前水深 $h=2\text{m}$ 时，作用在闸门上的静水总压力。

解 水平分力

$$\begin{aligned}P_x &= \gamma h_c A_x = 9.8\times10^3\times\frac{1}{2}\times2\times2\times3\\ &=58.8\times10^3\text{N} = 58.8\text{kN}\end{aligned}$$

铅直分力

$$P_z = \gamma V = \gamma\left(\frac{\varphi}{360°}\times\pi\times r^2 - \frac{1}{2}h\times r\cos\varphi\right)\times b$$

V 是图中阴影线部分体积，为虚压力体，$\boldsymbol{P}_z$ 方向向上，为浮力。

$$\begin{aligned}P_z&=9.8\times10^3\left(\frac{45°}{360°}\times\pi\times2.828^2-\frac{1}{2}\times2\times2.828\times\cos45°\right)\times2\\ &=33.52\times10^3\text{N}=33.52\text{kN}\end{aligned}$$

合力

$$\begin{aligned}P&=\sqrt{P_x^2+P_z^2}=\sqrt{(58.8\times10^3)^2+(33.52\times10^3)^2}\\ &=67.68\times10^3\text{N}=67.68\text{kN}\end{aligned}$$

与水平线夹角为

$$\theta = \arctan\frac{P_z}{P_x} = \arctan\frac{33.52\times10^3}{58.8\times10^3} = 30°$$

十一、浮力和潜体及浮体的稳定性

浸没于液体中的物体称为潜体，漂浮在液体自由表面的物体称为浮体。无论是潜体还是浮体，也无论物体表面形状是如何的复杂多变，它们均受到液体对其施加的铅直向上的托举力的作用，此力称为浮力或浮托力。浮力的大小可用上述曲面总压力铅垂分力计算法计算。如图 6-3-8 所示一浸没于水中的潜体沿潜体表面作铅直切线 AA'、BB'……，这些切线组成切于潜体表面的垂直向上的柱状体，该柱面与潜体表面的交线，把潜体表面分为 AFB、AHB 上下两部分，上半部分 AFB 表面所受到静水总压力铅垂分力 $\boldsymbol{P}_z$，应等于曲面 AFB 上压力体内液体的重力，方向向下，下半部分 AHB 表面所受到的静水总压力铅垂分力 $\boldsymbol{P}_{z2}$ 等于曲面 AHB 以上压力体的重力，方向向上为浮力。作用在整个潜体表面上的铅垂分力 $P_z=P_{z2}-P_{z1}$，亦即等于潜体自身体积大小的液体重力，所以潜体所受浮力应等于潜体所排开的同体积的液体重力。潜体所受的水平分力 $\boldsymbol{P}_x$，左右前后均大小相等方向相反，水平分力的合力 $\boldsymbol{P}_x=0$，故潜体所受总压力的合力，只有铅垂向上的浮力。计算潜体浮力的原理就是人们熟知的阿基米德(Archimeds)原理，此

原理对浮体也同样适用。

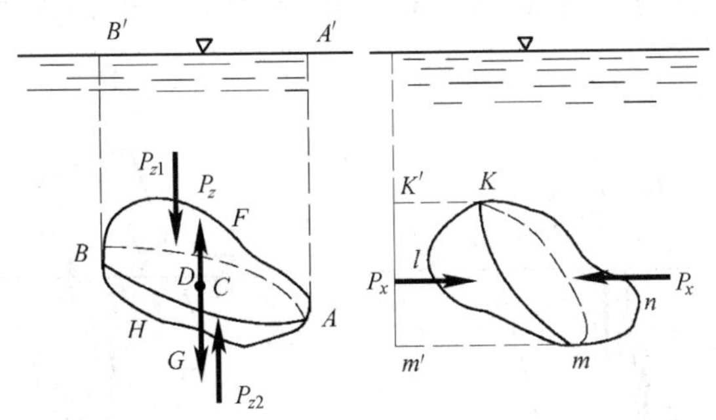

图 6-3-8

浮力的作用点称为浮心，浮心显然与所排开液体体积的形心重合。

潜体除了浮力作用外，还同时受到重力的作用，当潜体重力 $\boldsymbol{G}$ 大于浮力 $\boldsymbol{P}_z$ 时，物体下沉；当 $G=P_z$ 时，物体可在液体中任意深度保持平衡。当 $G<P_z$ 时，物体上升，减少在液体中浸没体积，从而减小浮力，直至浮力与重力相等时为止，此时潜体就变为浮体了。

现探讨潜体的稳定性。潜体在倾斜后恢复其原来平衡位置的能力，称为潜体的稳定性。按照重心 C 与浮心 D 在同一铅垂线上的相对位置，有三种可能性：①重心 C 位于浮心 D 之下，如图 6-3-9a)所示，潜体如有倾斜，重力 $\boldsymbol{G}$ 与浮力 $\boldsymbol{P}_z$ 形成一个使潜体恢复原来平衡位置的转动力矩，使潜体能恢复原位，称为稳定平衡。②重心 C 位于浮心 D 之上，如图 6-3-9b)所示，潜体如有倾斜，重力 $\boldsymbol{G}$ 与浮力 $\boldsymbol{P}_z$ 将产生一个使潜体继续倾斜的转动力矩，潜体不能恢复其原位，称为不稳定平衡。③重心 C 与浮心 D 相重合，如图 6-3-9c)所示，潜体如有倾斜，重力 $\boldsymbol{G}$ 与浮力 $\boldsymbol{P}_z$ 不产生转动力矩，潜体处于随遇平衡状态。即潜体在任意位置均可随意平衡，不需恢复原有状态。

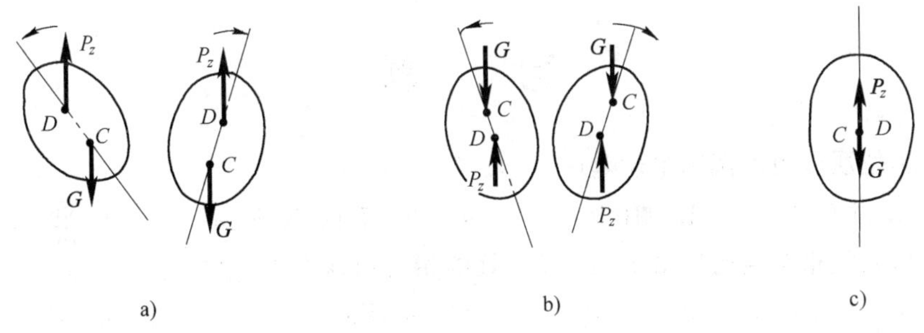

图 6-3-9

浮体平衡的稳定性要求与潜体有所不同，浮体重心 C 在浮心 D 之上时，其平衡仍有可能是稳定的。设有两浮体如图 6-3-10 所示，浮体处于平衡位置时重心 C 与浮心 D 的连线垂直于浮面（浮体在平衡位置时与自由液面交线），称为浮轴，浮心与重心均在浮轴上；倾斜后重心 C 位置一般不改变，但浮心及浮力和浮轴不重合，改变了位置。设浮力与浮轴的交点为 M，称定倾中心，定倾中心到原浮心 D 的距离称定倾半径，以 ρ 表示。重心 C 和原浮心 D 的距离称为偏心距，以 e 表示。浮体倾斜后能否恢复其原平衡位置，取决于重心 C 与定倾中心 M 的相对位置，有三种可能性：①$\rho>e$，即 M 点高于 C 点，如图 6-3-10a)所示，这时重力 $\boldsymbol{G}$ 与倾斜后的浮力 $\boldsymbol{P}'_z$ 构成一扶正力矩，使浮体恢复到原位，浮体处于稳定平衡；②$\rho<e$，即 M 点低于 C 点，如

图 6-3-10b)所示，这时重力 **G** 与倾斜后浮力 $\boldsymbol{P}_z'$ 构成一倾覆力矩，使浮体继续倾斜，浮体处于不稳定平衡；③$\rho=e$，即 M 与 C 重合，这时 **G** 与 $\boldsymbol{P}_z'$ 不产生力矩，浮体处于随遇平衡。

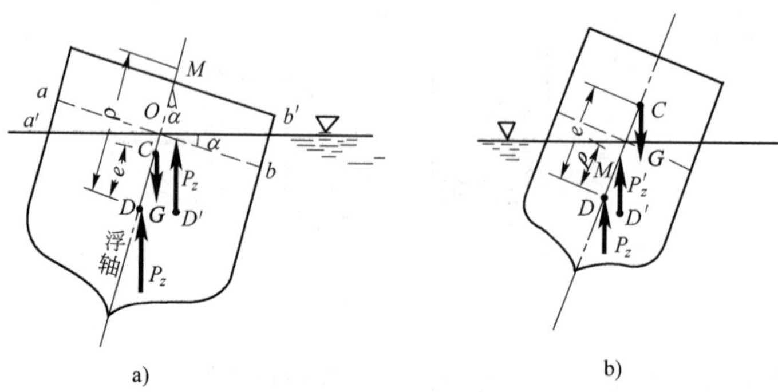

图 6-3-10

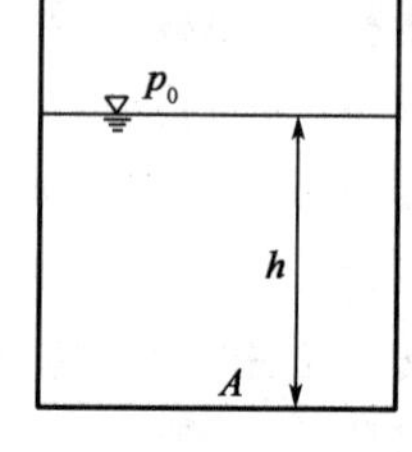

例 6-3-3 图

【例 6-3-3】 密闭水箱如图所示，已知水深 $h=2\text{m}$，自由面上的压强 $p_0=88\text{kN/m}^2$，当地大气压强 $p_a=101\text{kN/m}^2$，则水箱底部 A 点的绝对压强与相对压强分别为：

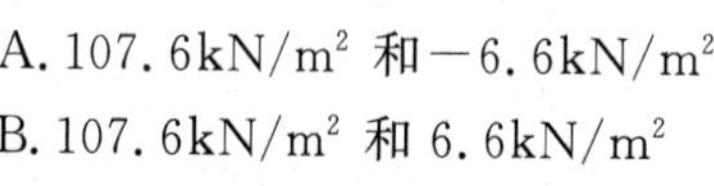

A. 107.6kN/m^2 和 -6.6kN/m^2

B. 107.6kN/m^2 和 6.6kN/m^2

C. 120.6kN/m^2 和 -6.6kN/m^2

D. 120.6kN/m^2 和 6.6kN/m^2

解 A 点绝对压强 $p_A'=p_0+\rho gh=88+1\times9.8\times2=107.6\text{kPa}$

A 点相对压强 $p_A=p_A'-p_a=107.6-101=6.6\text{kPa}$。

答案：B

习 题

6-3-1 单位质量力的国际单位是（ ）。

A. 牛(N) B. 帕(Pa) C. 牛/千克(N/kg) D. 米/秒^2(m/s^2)

6-3-2 与大气相连通的自由水面下 5m 处的相对压强为（ ）。

A. 5at B. 0.5at C. 98kPa D. 40kPa

6-3-3 某点的相对压强为 -39.2kPa，则该点的真空值与真空高度分别为（ ）。

A. 39.2kPa，$4\text{mH}_2\text{O}$ B. 58.8kPa，$6\text{mH}_2\text{O}$

C. 34.3kPa，$3.5\text{mH}_2\text{O}$ D. 19.6kPa，$2\text{mH}_2\text{O}$

6-3-4 密闭容器内自由表面压强 $p_0=9.8\text{kPa}$ 液面下水深 2m 处的绝对压强为（ ）。

A. 19.6kPa B. 29.4kPa C. 205.8kPa D. 117.6kPa

6-3-5 用 U 形水银压力计测容器中某点水的相对压强，如已知水和水银的重度分别为 γ 及 γ'，压力计中液面差为 Δh，被测点至内侧低水银液面的高差为 h_1，则被测点的相对压强为（ ）。

A. $\gamma'\times\Delta h$ B. $(\gamma'-\gamma)\Delta h$ C. $\gamma'(h_1+\Delta h)$ D. $\gamma'\Delta h-\gamma h_1$

6-3-6 圆形木桶，顶部与底部用环箍紧，桶内盛满液体，顶箍与底箍所受张力之比为（ ）。

A. 2　　　　B. 1/2　　　　C. 2/3　　　　D. 1/4

6-3-7　一垂直立于水中的矩形平板闸门，门宽 4m，门前水深 2m，该闸门所受静水总压强为（　　），压力中心距自由液面的铅直距离为（　　）。

A. 60kPa，1m　　　　B. 78.4kN，$\frac{4}{3}$m

C. 85kN，1.2m　　　　D. 70kN，1m

第四节　流体动力学

一、流体运动学基本概念

表征流体运动的各种物理量，如速度、加速度、压强、密度、动量、能量等，称为运动要素。流体运动学就是要研究流体运动要素随时间、空间而变化的规律。由于描述流体运动的方法不同，运动要素的表示式也有不同。在流体力学中，有两种描述流体运动方法，即拉格朗日(Largange)法和欧拉(Euler)法。

拉格朗日是从分析流体质点的运动着手，设法描述出每一个流体质点自始至终的运动过程，即它们的位置随时间变化的规律。如所有流体质点的运动轨迹均知道了，则整个流体运动的状况也就清楚了。为了区分不同的流体质点，拉格朗日采用起始时刻 $t=t_0$ 时每个质点的空间坐标(a,b,c)作为标志，然后表达出每一流体质点在任意时刻 t 在空间的坐标位置，在直角坐标系它们皆是拉格朗日变量 a、b、c 和时间 t 的连续函数，即

$$\begin{cases} x = x(a,b,c,t) \\ y = y(a,b,c,t) \\ z = z(a,b,c,t) \end{cases}$$

由上式可知，若 a，b，c 为常数，t 为变数，可得某个指定质点运动轨迹方程；如果 t 为常数，a、b、c 为变数，可得某一瞬时不同质点在空间分布位置。如 a、b、c、t 全都是变量时，则方程所表达的是任意质点的运动轨迹。流体质点在任何时刻的速度，可从上式对时间取偏导数得到，即

$$u_x = \frac{\partial x}{\partial t} = \frac{\partial x(a,b,c,t)}{\partial t}$$

$$u_y = \frac{\partial y}{\partial t} = \frac{\partial y(a,b,c,t)}{\partial t}$$

$$u_z = \frac{\partial z}{\partial t} = \frac{\partial z(a,b,c,t)}{\partial t}$$

任意流体质点在任何时刻的加速度，可从上式对时间取偏导数得到，即

$$a_x = \frac{\partial u_x}{\partial t} = \frac{\partial^2 x(a,b,c,t)}{\partial t^2}$$

$$a_y = \frac{\partial u_y}{\partial t} = \frac{\partial^2 y(a,b,c,t)}{\partial t^2}$$

$$a_z = \frac{\partial u_z}{\partial t} = \frac{\partial^2 z(a,b,c,t)}{\partial t^2}$$

当加速度确定后，可通过牛顿第二定律，建立运动和作用于该点上力的关系，反之亦然。

由于流体不同于固体，流体微团运动中有线变形、角变形，互相间位置不固定，因此运动轨迹极其复杂多变，要想求出这些函数，常导致数学上的困难；其次，在实际工程上，多数情况下

并不需要知道每一质点的运动轨迹及其速度等要素的变化；再次，测量流体运动要素，要跟着流体质点移动测量仪器，以测出不同瞬时的数值，这种测量方法是很难实现的。因此不常采用拉格朗日方法，而多采用欧拉方法。

欧拉方法是从分析通过流场中某固定空间点上流体质点的运动着手，设法描述出每一个空间点上流体质点的运动随时间变化的规律。如果知道了所有空间点上质点的运动规律，那么整个流动情况也就清楚了。至于流体质点在到达某空间点之前是从哪里来的，到达某空间点后又将到那里去，则不予研究。在直角坐标系中，选取坐标(x,y,z)将每一空间点区分开来。在一般情况下，同一时刻，不同空间点上流体质点的速度也是不同的，所以任意时刻任意空间点在流体质点的速度u将是空间坐标和时间的函数，写成向量形式为

$$u=u(x,y,z,t)$$

投影到x,y,z各个轴向的速度分量为

$$u_x=u_x(x,y,z,t)$$
$$u_y=u_y(x,y,z,t)$$
$$u_z=u_z(x,y,z,t)$$

同样，其他运动要素如压强p和密度ρ可写为

$$p=p(x,y,z,t)$$
$$\rho=\rho(x,y,z,t)$$

由上式可知，当t为常数，(x,y,z)为变数，则可得同一瞬时，通过不同空间点各流体质点速度分布情况，是某瞬时空间的流速向量场。若(x,y,z)为常数，t为变量，则可得不同瞬时，通过空间某固定点流体质点速度变化的情况。

现讨论流体质点加速度的表达式。从欧拉法的观点来看，在流动中不仅处于不同空间点上的质点可以具有不同的速度，就是同一空间点上的质点，也因时间先后的不同可以有不同的速度。所以流体质点的加速度由两部分组成，一是由于时间过程而使空间点上的质点速度发生变化的加速度，称当地加速度（或时变加速度），另一是流动中质点位置移动而引起的速度变化所形成的加速度，称为迁移加速度（或位变加速度）。以欧拉法求加速度时，x,y,z,t均看成是自变量，以复合函数求导法则，求流速u的全导数，各轴加速度的分量为

$$a_x=\frac{\mathrm{d}u_x}{\mathrm{d}t}=\frac{\partial u_x}{\partial t}+\frac{\partial u_x}{\partial x}\frac{\mathrm{d}x}{\mathrm{d}t}+\frac{\partial u_x}{\partial y}\frac{\mathrm{d}y}{\mathrm{d}t}+\frac{\partial u_x}{\partial z}\frac{\mathrm{d}z}{\mathrm{d}t}$$
$$a_y=\frac{\mathrm{d}u_y}{\mathrm{d}t}=\frac{\partial u_y}{\partial t}+\frac{\partial u_y}{\partial x}\frac{\mathrm{d}x}{\mathrm{d}t}+\frac{\partial u_y}{\partial y}\frac{\mathrm{d}y}{\mathrm{d}t}+\frac{\partial u_y}{\partial z}\frac{\mathrm{d}z}{\mathrm{d}t}$$
$$a_z=\frac{\mathrm{d}u_z}{\mathrm{d}t}=\frac{\partial u_z}{\partial t}+\frac{\partial u_z}{\partial x}\frac{\mathrm{d}x}{\mathrm{d}t}+\frac{\partial u_z}{\partial y}\frac{\mathrm{d}y}{\mathrm{d}t}+\frac{\partial u_z}{\partial z}\frac{\mathrm{d}z}{\mathrm{d}t}$$

上式中$\mathrm{d}x$、$\mathrm{d}y$、$\mathrm{d}z$是流体质点在$\mathrm{d}t$时段内在空间的位移在各个轴的投影，因此

$$\frac{\mathrm{d}x}{\mathrm{d}t}=u_x \qquad \frac{\mathrm{d}y}{\mathrm{d}t}=u_y \qquad \frac{\mathrm{d}z}{\mathrm{d}t}=u_z$$

代入上式得欧拉法流体质点加速度的表达式

$$\left.\begin{aligned}a_x&=\frac{\partial u_x}{\partial t}+u_x\frac{\partial u_x}{\partial x}+u_y\frac{\partial u_x}{\partial y}+u_z\frac{\partial u_x}{\partial z}\\a_y&=\frac{\partial u_y}{\partial t}+u_x\frac{\partial u_y}{\partial x}+u_y\frac{\partial u_y}{\partial y}+u_z\frac{\partial u_y}{\partial z}\\a_z&=\frac{\partial u_z}{\partial t}+u_x\frac{\partial u_z}{\partial x}+u_y\frac{\partial u_z}{\partial y}+u_z\frac{\partial u_z}{\partial z}\end{aligned}\right\}\tag{6-4-1}$$

工程上大多采用欧拉法，因多数情况下，感兴趣的只是某些固定位置上流体质点的运动情况，并不一定要知道流体质点运动情况的历史演变。其次，测量流体的运动要素，用欧拉法时可将测试仪表固定在指定的空间点上即可，较易进行量测。

二、迹线、流线、元流、总流等基本概念

(一)迹线

迹线是一个流体质点在一段连续时间内在空间运动的轨迹线，它是拉格朗日法研究流体的几何表示。

(二)流线

流线是这样的曲线，对于某一固定时刻而言，曲线上任一点的速度方向与曲线在该点的切线方向重合；流线描绘出同一时刻不同位置上流体质点的速度方向。可以把流体运动想象为流线族构成的几何图像，如图 6-4-1 所示。这是欧拉法研究流体运动的几何表示方式。

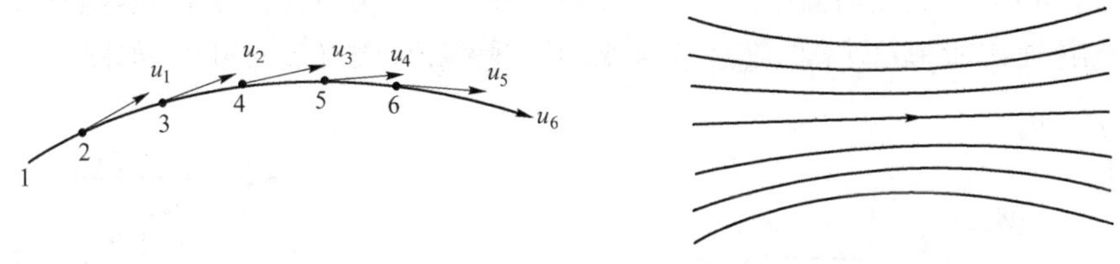

图 6-4-1

由流线的定义可知，流线有这样一些性质：过空间某点在同一时刻只能作一根流线；流线不能转折，因为折点处会有两个流速向量，流线只能是光滑的连续曲线；对流速不随时间变化的恒定流动，流线形状不随时间改变，与迹线重合，对非恒定流流线形状随时间而改变；流线密处流速快，流线疏处流速慢。

由于流速向量与切线向量重合，两向量方向余弦相同，方向平行，所以两向量的向量积

$$u \times ds = 0$$

从而可得

$$\frac{dx}{u_x} = \frac{dy}{u_y} = \frac{dz}{u_z} = \frac{ds}{u} \tag{6-4-2}$$

上式称为流线微分方程，式中，dx、dy、dz 为流线上微小长度 ds 在三个坐标轴上的投影，u_x、u_y、u_z 为相应的流速分量，解上式可得到流线方程。

【例 6-4-1】 关于流线，下列说法错误的是：

A. 流线不能相交

B. 流线可以是一条直线，也可以是光滑的曲线，但不可能是折线

C. 在恒定流中，流线与迹线重合

D. 流线表示不同时刻的流动趋势

解 流线表示同一时刻的流动趋势。

答案：D

(三)流管、流束、过流断面、元流、总流

在流场中，任意取一非流线且不自相交的封闭曲线，从这封闭曲线上各点绘出流线，组成管状曲面，称为流管，如图 6-4-2 所示的虚线所示流管内的流体称为流束。在流束上取一横断面，使它与流线正交，这一断面称为过流断面，当流体为水时称为过水断面。过流断面为无限

小的流束称为元流，元流同一断面上各点的运动要素如流速，压强等可以认为是相等的。过流断面面积有一定大小的流束称为总流，总流可以看成是由无限多个元流所组成，总流断面上各点的流速、压强不一定相等。

（四）流量、断面平均流速

单位时间内流过过流断面的流体数量称为流量，它可以用体积流量 Q、质量流量 Q_m、重力流量 Q_G 表示，单位分别为 m^3/s、kg/s、N/s 等。对不可压缩流体，一般均用体积流量 Q 表示；对于元流而言，流速为 u，断面上各点相等，断面积为 dA，则体积流量为

$$dQ = u dA \tag{6-4-3}$$

对于总流而言，通过断面积为 A 的体积流量为

$$Q = \int_A dQ = \int_A u dA \tag{6-4-4}$$

当点流速 u 在断面上的分布函数已知时，可用上式直接积分求出流量。当总流断面各点流速 u 的变化未知时，需利用断面平均流速 v 来计算总流量。断面平均流速 v 是假想的，在断面上均匀分布的流速，以此流速计算的流量，应与各点以实际流速通过的流量相等。如图6-4-3所示。

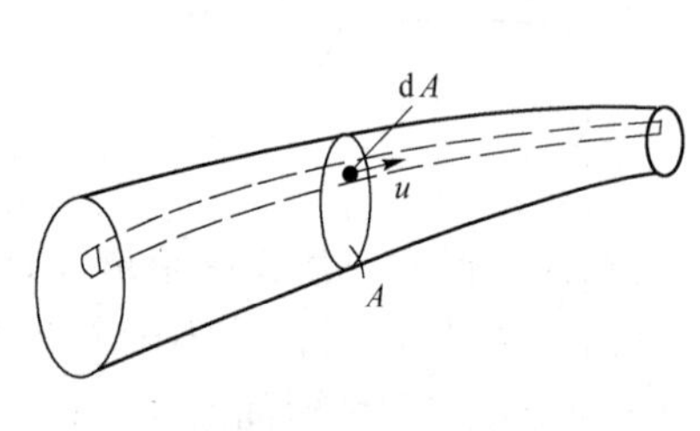

图 6-4-2

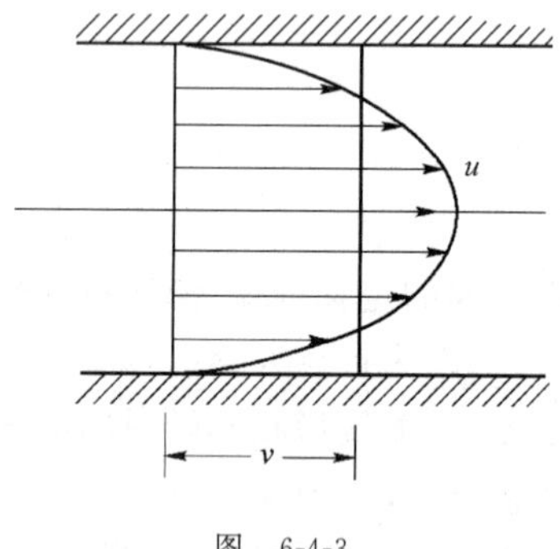

图 6-4-3

将平均流速代入式(6-4-4)中可求得总流的流量 Q，即

$$Q = \int_A dQ = \int_A u dA = \int_A v dA = v\int_A dA = vA$$

即

$$Q = vA \tag{6-4-5}$$

或

$$v = \frac{Q}{A} \tag{6-4-6}$$

已知体积流量 Q，可以用下面式子求出质量流量 Q_m 和重力流量 Q_G

$$Q_m = \rho Q \tag{6-4-7}$$

$$Q_G = \gamma Q \tag{6-4-8}$$

式中：ρ、γ——分别为流体的密度和重度。

（五）流体运动的分类

按各点运动要素（流速、压强等）是否随时间而变化，可将流体运动分为恒定流和非恒定流。各点运动要素不随时间而变化的流体运动称为恒定流，例如常水头孔口出流即是恒定流的一种。各点运动要素随时间而变化的流体运动称为非恒定流，变水头孔口出流即是一例。

按各点运动要素是否随位置而变化，可将流体运动分成均匀流和非均匀流。在给定的某一时刻，各点流速都不随位置而变的流动称为均匀流；反之，则称为非均匀流。按此严格定义的均匀流，工程上甚少出现。在经常使用的管道渠道中，一般定义均匀流是按各断面相应点流速相等为均匀流，或流线为平行直线的流动为均匀流，例如直径不变的长直管道内离进口较远处的流动，即是实际均匀流的一种。反之如流线不平行或相应点流速不相等的流动为非均匀流。

按流线是否接近于平行直线，又可将非均匀流分成渐变流和急变流。各流线之间的夹角很小，即各流线几乎是平行的，且各流线曲率半径很大，即各流线几乎是直线的流体运动称为渐变流；反之，则称为急变流。顶角很小的渐变圆锥形管道中的流动，可视为渐变流。

按限制总流的边界情况，可将流体运动分为有压流、无压流和射流。边界全部为固体所限没有自由液面的流动称为有压流，例如水泵的压水管道中的流动。边界部分为固体、部分为大气，具有自由液面的流体运动称为无压流，例如河流、引水明渠中的流动。流体经由孔口或管嘴喷射到某一空间，在充满气体或其他流体的空间继续喷射流动，其边界不受固体限制而与其他流体接触，这种流动称为射流，例如消防水枪的喷射流动即是射流的一种。

按决定流体的运动要素所需空间坐标的维数，可将流动分为一维、二维、三维流动，或称一元、二元、三元流动。长管、明渠以断面平均运动要素而言，主流方向只有一个，故可视为平均意义上的一维流动。

三、恒定流连续方程

连续性方程是根据质量守恒定理与连续介质假设推导而得。取一元流如图 6-4-4 所示，设为恒定流，流管形状不变，在 dt 时间内由 dA_1 流入的质量为 $\rho_1 u_1 dA_1 dt$，从 dA_2 流出的质量为 $\rho_2 u_2 dA_2 dt$，由于流体为连续介质，流管内充满无空隙的流体，根据质量守恒原理，流入的质量必与流出的质量相等，可得

$$\rho_1 u_1 dA_1 dt = \rho_2 u_2 dA_2 dt$$

消去 dt 得

$$\rho_1 u_1 dA_1 = \rho_2 u_2 dA_2 \tag{6-4-9}$$

对于不可压缩流体 $\rho_1 = \rho_2 = \rho$，有

$$u_1 dA_1 = u_2 dA_2 \tag{6-4-10}$$

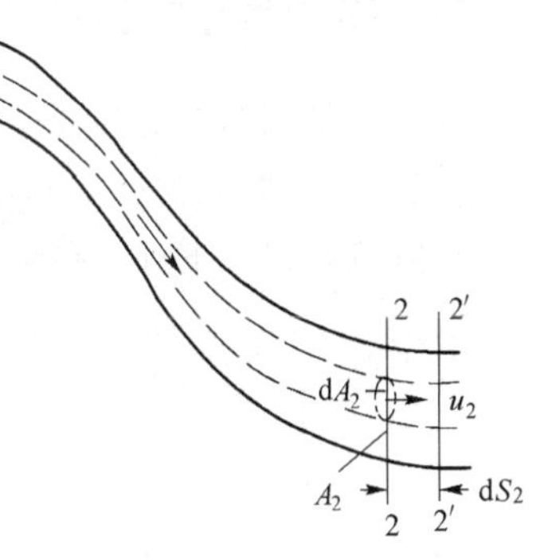

图 6-4-4

式(6-4-9)、式(6-4-10)为元流连续性方程。将式(6-4-10)积分，可得不可压缩流体总流连续性方程。即

$$\int_{A_1} u_1 dA_1 = \int_{A_2} u_2 dA_2$$

$$Q_1 = Q_2$$

$$v_1 A_1 = v_2 A_2 \tag{6-4-11}$$

将式(6-4-9)对总流积分可得

$$\rho_1 v_1 A_1 = \rho_2 v_2 A_2 \tag{6-4-12}$$

由式(6-4-11)可写出

$$\frac{v_1}{v_2}=\frac{A_2}{A_1}$$

上式表明在同一总流上，各断面的断面平均流速 v 与断面面积成反比，即断面增大时流速减少，反之亦然。

四、欧拉运动微分方程

由牛顿第二运动定律：$F=ma$，两边除以质量 m，对单位质量而言，有

$$\frac{F}{m}=a$$

即单位质量的外力合力等于加速度，比拟欧拉平衡方程的形式，将上式写成应用于流体微元的三维表达式

$$\left.\begin{aligned}X-\frac{1}{\rho}\frac{\partial p}{\partial x}=\frac{\mathrm{d}u_x}{\mathrm{d}t}\\Y-\frac{1}{\rho}\frac{\partial p}{\partial y}=\frac{\mathrm{d}u_y}{\mathrm{d}t}\\Z-\frac{1}{\rho}\frac{\partial p}{\partial z}=\frac{\mathrm{d}u_z}{\mathrm{d}t}\end{aligned}\right\}\qquad(6\text{-}4\text{-}13)$$

上式即为欧拉运动微分方程，仅适用于理想流体，因为没有计及流体的黏性切应力。

欧拉方程有四个未知数 u_x、u_y、u_z、p，它与连续性微分方程一起有四个方程式，所以从原则上讲欧拉方程是可解的，但因为它是一阶非线性偏微分方程，至今仍未找到一般解，只是在几种特殊情况下得到了它的解，水力学中最常见的是在重力场中的伯诺里(Bernoulli)积分。

五、恒定流能量方程(或伯努利方程)

(一)理想流体元流的能量方程

理想流体，即无黏性流体，无内摩擦力和能量损失。

将欧拉方程在下列条件下积分：

恒定流：$\frac{\partial u}{\partial t}=0$，$\frac{\partial p}{\partial t}=0$，则

$$\mathrm{d}p=\frac{\partial p}{\partial x}\mathrm{d}x+\frac{\partial p}{\partial y}\mathrm{d}y+\frac{\partial p}{\partial z}\mathrm{d}z$$

不可压缩流体：$\rho=$常数

仅受重力作用：$X=Y=0$，$Z=-g$

沿流线积分：$\mathrm{d}x=u_x\mathrm{d}t$，$\mathrm{d}y=u_y\mathrm{d}t$，$\mathrm{d}z=u_z\mathrm{d}t$

将式(6-4-13)分别乘以 $\mathrm{d}x$，$\mathrm{d}y$，$\mathrm{d}z$，相加后得

$$(X\mathrm{d}x+Y\mathrm{d}y+Z\mathrm{d}z)-\frac{1}{\rho}(\frac{\partial p}{\partial x}\mathrm{d}x+\frac{\partial p}{\partial y}\mathrm{d}y+\frac{\partial p}{\partial x}\mathrm{d}z)$$

$$=\frac{\mathrm{d}u_x}{\mathrm{d}t}\mathrm{d}x+\frac{\mathrm{d}u_y}{\mathrm{d}t}\mathrm{d}y+\frac{\mathrm{d}u_z}{\mathrm{d}t}\mathrm{d}z$$

利用上述积分条件可得

$$-g\mathrm{d}z-\frac{1}{\rho}\mathrm{d}p=u_x\mathrm{d}u_x+u_y\mathrm{d}u_y+u_z\mathrm{d}u_z$$

$$=\frac{1}{2}\mathrm{d}(u_x^2+u_y^2+u_z^2)=\mathrm{d}\left(\frac{u^2}{2}\right)$$

因为 ρ=常数，上式变为

$$\mathrm{d}\left(gz+\frac{p}{\rho}+\frac{u^2}{2}\right)=0$$

积分得

$$gz+\frac{p}{\rho}+\frac{u^2}{2}=\text{常数}$$

两边除以重力加速度 g，并且因 $\rho g=\gamma$ 得

$$z+\frac{p}{\gamma}+\frac{u^2}{2g}=\text{常数} \tag{6-4-14}$$

上式即为伯诺里积分或理想流体元流伯诺里方程，对同一元流的任意二断面可将式(6-4-14)写成

$$z_1+\frac{p_1}{\gamma}+\frac{u_1^2}{2g}=z_2+\frac{p_2}{\gamma}+\frac{u_2^2}{2g} \tag{6-4-15a}$$

上式以 $\gamma=\rho g$ 代入，可写成

$$z_1+\frac{p_1}{\rho g}+\frac{u_1^2}{2g}=z_2+\frac{p_2}{\rho g}+\frac{u_2^2}{2g} \tag{6-4-15b}$$

（二）理想流体元流能量方程的物理意义

z——位置高度或位置水头，单位位能；

$\frac{p}{\gamma}$——压强高度或压强水头，单位压能；

$\frac{u^2}{2g}$——流速水头，单位动能，因为单位动能等于动能 $\frac{1}{2}mu^2$ 除以流体重力 mg，即单位动能 $=\frac{\frac{1}{2}mu^2}{mg}=\frac{u^2}{2g}$；

$z+\frac{p}{\gamma}$——测压管水头，单位势能，各断面测压管水头的连线称测管水头线，如图 6-4-5 所示，测压管水头线沿流向可升、可降、可水平；

$z+\frac{p}{\gamma}+\frac{u^2}{2g}$——总水头，单位重力流体的总机械能，简称单位能，沿流各断面总水头的连线为总水头线，理想流体的总水头线是一水平线，反映了理想流体运动时各断面单位能守恒，是能量守恒定律在流体运动中的一种体现。因任一断面三种单位能之和为一常数，如果其中某一种单位能发生变化，则另两种必定也会跟着转变。例如对一水平管道，单位位能 z 各断面

相同，当管道断面变小处，该处流速加快（连续性方程），单位动能$\frac{u^2}{2g}$加大，则该处压强水头或单位压能$\frac{p}{\gamma}$必然降低，当动能加大到一定程度，该处将出现负压，可将气体或其他流体吸入，这就是喷射器（或射流泵）能抽水的原因。这也表明流体运动过程中，不仅遵循能量守恒原理，同时能量也可从一种形式转化为另一种形式，体现了能量转化原理。

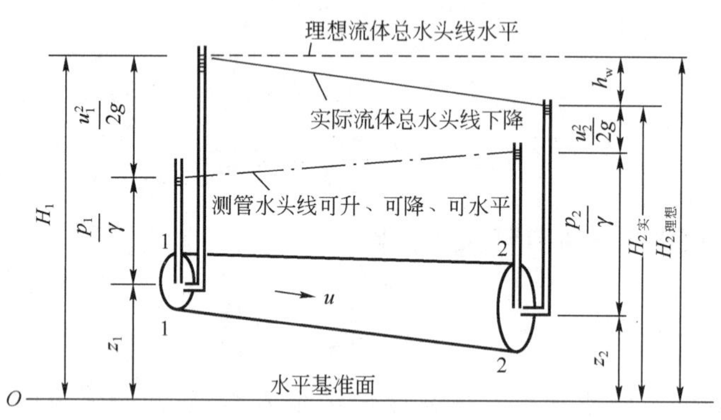

图 6-4-5

人们利用元流能量方程原理，制造出简便的测量流体某处流速 u 的仪器，这就是工程上常用的毕托(Pitot)管，毕托管构造示意于图 6-4-6。毕托管是一有 90°弯曲的细管，其顶端开孔截面正对迎面液流，放在测定点 A 处，在来流势能、动能共同作用下，流体沿弯管上升至一定高度$\frac{p'}{\gamma}$后保持稳定，此时 A 点的运动质点由于受到测速管的阻滞，流速变为零。测压管置于和 A 同一断面的壁上，其液柱高度为$\frac{p}{\gamma}$。未放测速毕托管前 A 处的总单位能为 $z+\frac{p}{\gamma}+\frac{u^2}{2g}$，放入测速毕托管后，动能全部转化为压能，故总单位能为 $z+\frac{p'}{\gamma}$。

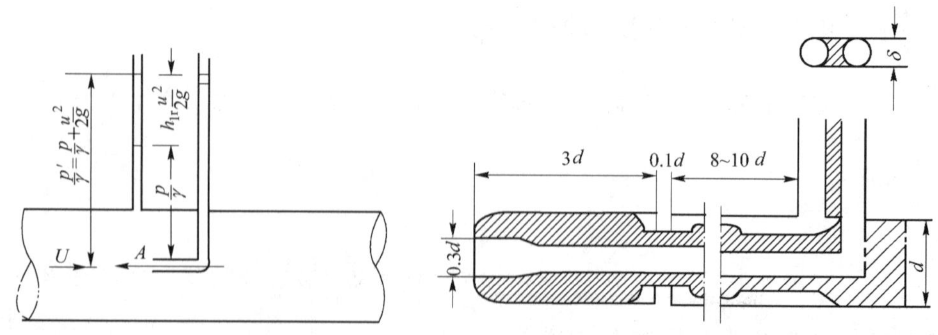

图 6-4-6

对于恒定流，当测管很少影响流场时，A 点的单位能应保持不变，故

$$z+\frac{p}{\gamma}+\frac{u^2}{2g}=z+\frac{p'}{\gamma}$$

$$\frac{u^2}{2g}=\frac{p'}{\gamma}-\frac{p}{\gamma}=h_u$$

式中，h_u 为测速管与测压管二者水头差，反映了被测点的流速水头大小，而流速 u 可按下式求得

$$u=\sqrt{2gh_u}=\sqrt{2g(\frac{p'-p}{\gamma})} \tag{6-4-16}$$

毕托管细部构造亦示意于图 6-4-6 中，由于放入毕托管后流场受到干扰，而实际流体的黏性亦有影响，所以使用式(6-4-16)时需加一修正系数 C，称毕托管修正系数。由实验确定，$C=1\sim1.04$，近似可取 $C=1.0$。此时流速为

$$u=C\sqrt{2g(\frac{p'-p}{\gamma})} \tag{6-4-17}$$

(三)实际流体元流能量方程

对于实际流体，黏性切应力阻碍流体运动，为克服阻力将损失机械能，单位重量流体损失的机械能称为单位能损失，所对应的水柱高度称为水头损失。令元流断面 1 至断面 2 的水头损失为 $h'_{w_{1-2}}$，则实际流体元流的能量方程为

$$z_1+\frac{p_1}{\gamma}+\frac{u_1^2}{2g}=z_2+\frac{p^2}{\gamma}+\frac{u_2^2}{2g}+h'_{w_{1-2}} \tag{6-4-18}$$

实际流体元流的总水头线是一条沿流下降的斜坡线，又称为水力坡度线。总水头线的坡度称为水力坡度 J，水力坡度可用单位长度上的水头损失计算，对线性变化的水力坡度

$$J=\frac{h'_w}{L} \tag{6-4-19}$$

L 为发生水头损失流段的流长，当非线性变化时，水力坡度为

$$J=\frac{\mathrm{d}h'_w}{\mathrm{d}L} \tag{6-4-20}$$

(四)实际流体总流的能量方程

根据实际流体元流的能量方程(6-4-18)对总流过水断面积分，即可得到实际流体总流的能量方程。在积分时需作一些假设，除了要满足伯诺里积分时的四个假设之外，还需满足无能量输入或输出总流之中和所取过水断面处满足渐变流条件。由于渐变流中加速度很小，加速度形成的惯性力可不计，质量力仅为重力，因而同一过水断面上动压按静压分布，即同一断面上的 $z+\frac{p}{\gamma}=$常数，即同一断面的各点测压管水头相等。

根据式(6-4-18)，单位时间内通过元流两过水断面的总能量的关系式为

$$(z_1+\frac{p_1}{\gamma}+\frac{u_1^2}{2g})\gamma\mathrm{d}Q=(z_2+\frac{p_2}{\gamma}+\frac{u_2^2}{2g})\gamma\mathrm{d}Q+h'_{w_{1-2}}\gamma\mathrm{d}Q$$

而由连续性方程知 $\mathrm{d}Q=u_1\mathrm{d}A_1=u_2\mathrm{d}A_2$，代入上式后并对总流两断面进行积分

$$\int_{A_1}(z_1+\frac{p_1}{\gamma}+\frac{u_1^2}{2g})\gamma u_1\mathrm{d}A_1=\int_{A_2}(z_2+\frac{p_2}{\gamma}+\frac{u_2^2}{2g})\gamma u_2\mathrm{d}A_2+\int_Q h'_{w_{1-2}}\gamma\mathrm{d}Q$$

上式中第一种形式的积分为

$$\int_A(z+\frac{p}{\gamma})\gamma\mathrm{d}Q=\gamma(z+\frac{p}{\gamma})\int_A\mathrm{d}Q=\gamma Q(z+\frac{p}{\gamma})$$

第二种形式的积分为

$$\int_A \gamma \frac{u^3}{2g}\mathrm{d}A = \frac{\gamma}{2g}\int_A u^3 \mathrm{d}A = \frac{\gamma}{2g}\int_A (v+\Delta u)^3 \mathrm{d}A$$

$$= \frac{\gamma}{2g}\int_A (v^3 + 3v^2\Delta u + 3v\Delta u^2 + \Delta u^3)\mathrm{d}A$$

$$= \frac{\gamma}{2g}(v^3 A + 3v^2\int_A \Delta u \mathrm{d}A + 3v\int_A \Delta u^2 \mathrm{d}A + \int_A \Delta u^3 \mathrm{d}A)$$

$$= \frac{\gamma}{2g}(v^3 A + 3v\int \Delta u^2 \mathrm{d}A) = \frac{\gamma}{2g}(\alpha v^3 A) = \gamma Q \frac{\alpha v^2}{2g}$$

因为 $\int_A \Delta u \mathrm{d}A = 0$，而 $\int_A \Delta u^3 \mathrm{d}A$ 可略去，括号内 $3v\int \Delta u^2 \mathrm{d}A$ 项为正值，故 $\int_A u^3 \mathrm{d}A > v^3 A$。

令 $\alpha = \dfrac{\int u^3 \mathrm{d}A}{v^3 A}$，则知 $\alpha>1$，称为动能改正系数，由试验知 $\alpha=1.0\sim1.1$，通常取 $\alpha=1.0$。第三种积分为 $\int_Q h'_{\mathrm{w}}\gamma \mathrm{d}Q$，若令 h_{w} 为单位质量流体从断面 1 流至断面 2 能量损失的平均值，上积分可写成

$$\int_Q h'_{\mathrm{w}}\gamma \mathrm{d}Q = \gamma Q h_{\mathrm{w}}$$

将上述三种积分结果汇总化简后可得

$$(z_1 + \frac{p_1}{\gamma})\gamma Q + \frac{\alpha_1 v_1^2}{2g}\gamma Q = (z_2 + \frac{p_2}{\gamma})\gamma Q + \frac{\alpha_2 v_2^2}{2g}\gamma Q + h_{\mathrm{w}}\gamma Q$$

以重量流量 γQ 除以各项，得到以单位重量流体表示的总流能量方程

$$z_1 + \frac{p_1}{\gamma} + \frac{\alpha_1 v_1^2}{2g} = z_2 + \frac{p_2}{\gamma} + \frac{\alpha_2 v_2^2}{2g} + h_{\mathrm{w}_{1\text{-}2}} \tag{6-4-21a}$$

以 $\gamma=\rho g$ 代入，上式亦可写为

$$z_1 + \frac{p_1}{\rho g} + \frac{\alpha_1 v_1^2}{2g} = z_2 + \frac{p_2}{\rho g} + \frac{\alpha_2 v_2^2}{2g} + h_{\mathrm{w}_{1\text{-}2}} \tag{6-4-21b}$$

与元流能量方程比较可见，以平均流速流速水头与动能改正系数乘积 $\frac{\alpha v^2}{2g}$ 代替了 $\frac{u^2}{2g}$，又以总流的水头损失 h_{w} 代替了元流的水头损失 h'_{w}，其余各项不变。

（五）总流能量方程的应用范围和应用举例

由能量方程推导过程可知，能量方程必须满足这些条件方可应用，即恒定流、不可压缩流体、仅受重力作用、所取断面必须是渐变流、两断面间无机械能的输入或输出、也无流量的汇入或分出。

如果欲用于有机械能的输入或输出，则可修正如下

$$z_1 + \frac{p_1}{\gamma} + \frac{\alpha_1 v_1^2}{2g} \pm H = z_2 + \frac{p_2}{\gamma} + \frac{\alpha_2 v_2^2}{2g} + h_{\mathrm{w}} \tag{6-4-22}$$

上式中 H 为输入或输出的单位机械能以液柱高度表示的水头，输入时用正号，输出时用负号。如果欲用于有流量分出或汇入的情况，则按单位能的意义作如下处理，对于如图 6-4-7a）所示的情况有

$$
\left.\begin{aligned}
&z_1+\frac{p_1}{\gamma}+\frac{\alpha_1 v_1^2}{2g}=z_2+\frac{p_2}{\gamma}+\frac{\alpha_2 v_2^2}{2g}+h_{w_{1-2}}\\
&z_1+\frac{p_1}{\gamma}+\frac{\alpha_1 v_1^2}{2g}=z_3+\frac{p_3}{\gamma}+\frac{\alpha_3 v_3^2}{2g}+h_{w_{1-3}}\\
&Q_1=Q_2+Q_3
\end{aligned}\right\} \tag{6-4-23}
$$

对于如图 6-4-7b)所示的情况有

$$
\left.\begin{aligned}
&z_1+\frac{p_1}{\gamma}+\frac{\alpha_1 v_1^2}{2g}=z_3+\frac{p_3}{\gamma}+\frac{\alpha_3 v_3^3}{2g}+h_{w_{1-3}}\\
&z_2+\frac{p_2}{\gamma}+\frac{\alpha_2 v_2^2}{2g}=z_3+\frac{p_3}{\gamma}+\frac{\alpha_3 v_3^2}{2g}+h_{w_{2-3}}\\
&Q_1+Q_2=Q_3
\end{aligned}\right\} \tag{6-4-24}
$$

在使用能量方程时，应注意配合应用连续方程。

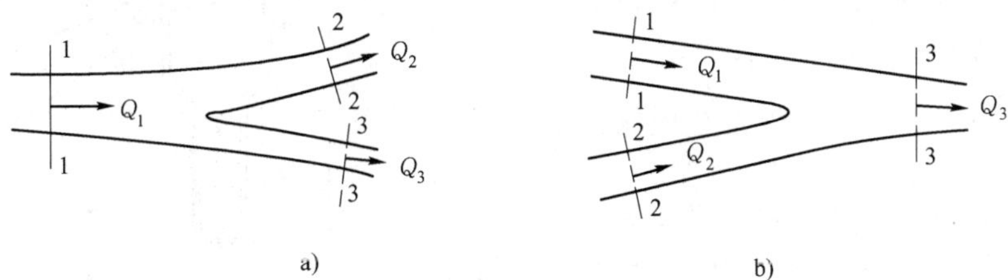

图 6-4-7

【例 6-4-2】 用一根直径 d 为 100mm 的管道从恒定水位的水箱引水，如图所示。若所需引水流量 Q 为 30L/s，水箱至管道出口的总水头损失 $h_w=3\text{m}$，水箱水面流速很小可忽略不计，试求水面至出口中心点的水头 H。

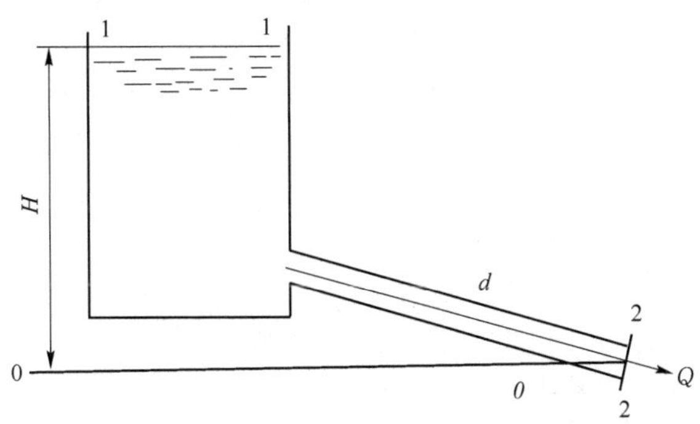

例 6-4-2 图

解 选水箱水面为断面 1-1，管道出口断面为断面 2-2，过断面 2-2 中点取一水平面为基准面 0-0，对此二断面写能量方程

$$z_1+\frac{p_1}{\gamma}+\frac{\alpha_1 v_1^2}{2g}=z_2+\frac{p_2}{\gamma}+\frac{\alpha_2 v_2^2}{2g}+h_{w_{1-2}}$$

$$H+0+0=0+0+\frac{\alpha_2 v_2^2}{2g}+h_{w_{1-2}}$$

因两断面均与大气相连，压强为当地大气压，所以 $p_1=p_2=0$，水面流速 $v_1\approx 0$，现取 $\alpha_2=1.0$，则有

$$H=\frac{v_2^2}{2g}+h_{w_{1-2}}$$

管道出口流速 $v_2=\frac{Q}{A_2}=\frac{Q}{\frac{\pi}{4}d^2}=3.82\text{m/s}$，所以水头 H 为

$$H=\frac{3.82^2}{2\times9.8}+3=3.74\text{m}$$

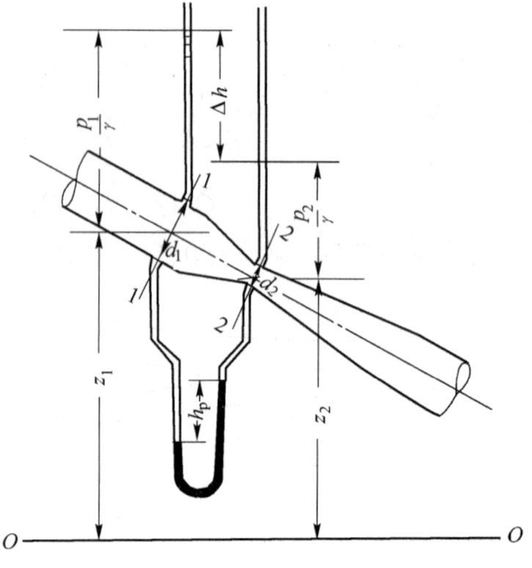

例 6-4-3 图

【例 6-4-3】 试导出如图所示的文丘里(Venturi)流量计的流量公式，若已测出测压管水头差 $\Delta h=0.5\text{mH}_2\text{O}$，流量系数 $\mu=0.98$；管道直径 $d_1=100\text{mm}$，文丘里管的喉管直径 $d_2=50\text{mm}$，求此时管内通过的流量 Q。

解 如图在测压管所在位置选取与流线垂直的断面 1-1 及 2-2，基准面选在管道下方任一位置。对断面 1-1 及 2-2 写能量方程，则

$$z_1+\frac{p_1}{\gamma}+\frac{\alpha_1 v_1^2}{2g}=z_2+\frac{p_2}{\gamma}+\frac{\alpha_2 v_2^2}{2g}+h_{w_{1-2}}$$

令 $\alpha_1=\alpha_2\approx1.0$，因文丘里管两断面相距很近且很光滑，阻力很小，$h_w$ 可先忽略不计，再用实验得到的流量系数校正。

$$(z_1+\frac{p_1}{\gamma})-(z_2+\frac{p_2}{\gamma})=\frac{v_2^2-v_1^2}{2g}$$

等号左端为断面 1-1 与断面 2-2 测压管水头差 Δh，所以

$$v_2^2-v_1^2=2g\Delta h$$

利用连续方程 $v_1A_1=v_2A_2$ 可将 v_2 换算成 v_1

$$v_2=v_1\frac{A_1}{A_2}=v_1(\frac{d_1}{d_2})^2$$

代入上式

$$v_1^2(\frac{d_1}{d_2})^4-v_1^2=2g\Delta h$$

故

$$v_1=\sqrt{\frac{2g\Delta h}{(\frac{d_1}{d_2})^4-1}}$$

流量

$$Q=v_1A_1=\frac{\pi}{4}d_1^2\sqrt{\frac{2g\Delta h}{(\frac{d_1}{d_2})^4-1}} \tag{6-4-25}$$

对某一已知的文丘里流量计，直径 d_1 及 d_2 为已定常数，$g=9.8\text{m/s}^2$ 也是常数，所以 $\frac{\pi}{4}d_1^2\times\sqrt{\frac{2g}{(\frac{d_1}{d_2})^4-1}}$ 也是一常数，令 $K=\frac{\pi}{4}d_1^2\sqrt{\frac{2g}{(\frac{d_1}{d_2})^4-1}}$，则有

$$Q = K\sqrt{\Delta h} \tag{6-4-26}$$

代入本题数据得

$$K = \frac{\pi}{4}(0.1)^2\sqrt{\frac{2\times 9.8}{(\frac{0.1}{0.05})^4 - 1}} \approx 0.008\ 97\mathrm{m}^{\frac{5}{2}}/\mathrm{s}$$

$$Q = \mu K\sqrt{\Delta h} = 0.98 \times 0.008\ 97 \times \sqrt{0.5} = 0.006\ 22\mathrm{m}^3/\mathrm{s}$$

【例 6-4-4】 设在供水管路中有一水泵，如图所示，已知吸水池水面与水塔水面高差 $z=30\mathrm{m}$，从断面 1-1 流至断面 2-2 的总水头损失 $h_{w_{1-2}}$ 为 5m。求水泵所需要的水头或水泵扬程需要多少。

解 因为在流程中有水泵的机械能输入，所以采用式(6-4-21)，选断面 1 及 2 写能量方程

$$z_1 + \frac{p_1}{\gamma} + \frac{\alpha_1 v_1^2}{2g} + H = z_2 + \frac{p_2}{\gamma} + \frac{\alpha_2 v_2^2}{2g} + h_{w_{1-2}}$$

水泵扬程 H 为

$$H = (z_2 - z_1) + (\frac{p_2 - p_1}{\gamma}) + \frac{\alpha_2 v_2^2 - \alpha_1 v_1^2}{2g} + h_{w_{1-2}}$$

$z_2 - z_1 = z$ 为两水面高差，1-1 及 2-2 液面均为当地大气压，相对压强为零，$p_1 = p_2 = 0$，令 $\alpha_1 = \alpha_2 = 1.0$，且因水面流速很小可不计，$v_1 = v_2 \approx 0$，所以

$$H = z + h_{w_{1-2}}$$

例 6-4-4 图

代入本题数据后得

$$H = 30 + 5 = 35\mathrm{m}$$

六、恒定流动量方程

流体像其他物体一样遵循动量定律，即动量对于时间的变化率 $\frac{\mathrm{d}K}{\mathrm{d}t}$ 等于作用于物体上各外力的合力 $\boldsymbol{F}$。现将此定理运用于如图 6-4-8 所示的元流和总流推导出恒定流动量方程，取过流断面 1-1 及 2-2，作为控制面，流体由 1-1 向 2-2 流动，先取一条元流(图中虚线所示)分析。经过时间 $\mathrm{d}t$ 后断面从 1-1 移至 $1'$-$1'$，2-2 移至 $2'$-$2'$，元流的动量增量应为 1-$1'$ 段和 2-$2'$ 段的动量之差，即等于流出控制面的动量减去流入控制面的动量，因为中间一段 $1'$-2 动量无变化，所以

$$\mathrm{d}\boldsymbol{K} = \rho\mathrm{d}S_2\mathrm{d}A_2\boldsymbol{u}_2 - \rho\mathrm{d}S_1\mathrm{d}A_1\boldsymbol{u}_1$$

$$= \rho\mathrm{d}Q\mathrm{d}t(\boldsymbol{u}_2 - \boldsymbol{u}_1)$$

动量的变化率 $\frac{\mathrm{d}\boldsymbol{K}}{\mathrm{d}t} = \rho\mathrm{d}Q(\boldsymbol{u}_2 - \boldsymbol{u}_1)$，按动量定律

$$\rho\mathrm{d}Q(\boldsymbol{u}_2 - \boldsymbol{u}_1) = \boldsymbol{F}$$

将上式对总流积分，即可得总流动量方程

$$\int_{A_2}\rho\boldsymbol{u}_2 u_2\mathrm{d}A_2 - \int_{A_1}\rho\boldsymbol{u}_1 u_1\mathrm{d}A_1 = \sum\boldsymbol{F}$$

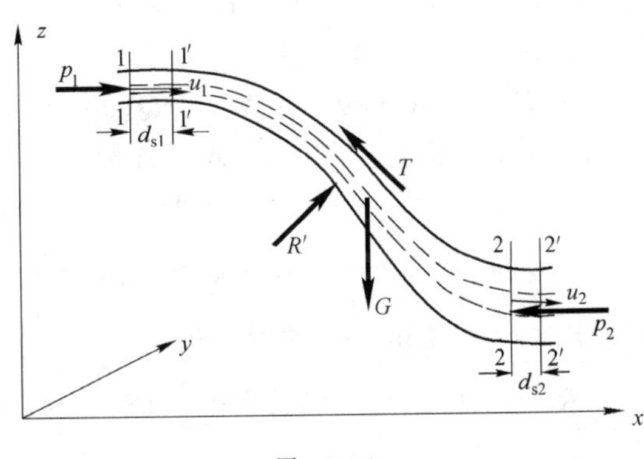

图 6-4-8

现分析$\int_A u^2 \mathrm{d}A$积分形式

$$\int_A u^2 \mathrm{d}A = \int_A (v+\Delta u)^2 \mathrm{d}A$$
$$= \int_A (v^2 + 2v\Delta u + \Delta u^2)\mathrm{d}A$$
$$= v^2 A + \int_A \Delta u^2 dA = \alpha_0 v^2 A$$

因为$\int_A \Delta u \mathrm{d}A = 0$，且$\int \Delta u^2 \mathrm{d}A$为正数，故$\int_A u^2 \mathrm{d}A > v^2 A$，$\alpha_0 > 1$，$\alpha_0 = \dfrac{\int_A u^2 \mathrm{d}A}{v^2 A}$称动量改正系数，由试验确定，$\alpha_0 = 1.0 \sim 1.05$，一般可取$\alpha_0 \approx 1.0$。将此代入原积分式后有

$$\alpha_{02}\rho v_2 v_2 A_2 - \alpha_{01}\rho v_1 v_1 A_1 = \sum F$$

因

$$v_2 A_2 = v_1 A_1 = Q$$

得

$$\sum F = \rho Q(\alpha_{02} v_2 - \alpha_{01} v_1) \tag{6-4-27}$$

上式即为以向量形式表示的动量方程，如果投影到三个坐标轴上分别计算则有

$$\begin{cases} \sum F_x = \rho Q(\alpha_{02} v_{2x} - \alpha_{01} v_{1x}) \\ \sum F_y = \rho Q(\alpha_{02} v_{2y} - \alpha_{01} v_{1y}) \\ \sum F_z = \rho Q(\alpha_{02} v_{2z} - \alpha_{01} v_{1z}) \end{cases} \tag{6-4-28}$$

动量方程中的力F和速度$\boldsymbol{v}$均是向量，即使应用式(6-4-27)，应注意方向和正负号。并且牢记脚标“2”代表流出控制体的断面，脚标“1”代表流入控制体的断面，且动量的增量要用“2”减去“1”，次序不能颠倒。

动量方程主要用于求流体与固体边界的相互作用力。

【例 6-4-5】 求水平放置的等截面弯头所受到的水流推力，如图所示，弯管直径$d = 200\text{mm}$，管中流速$v = 4\text{m/s}$，压强为$p = 98\text{kPa}$，不计水头损失。

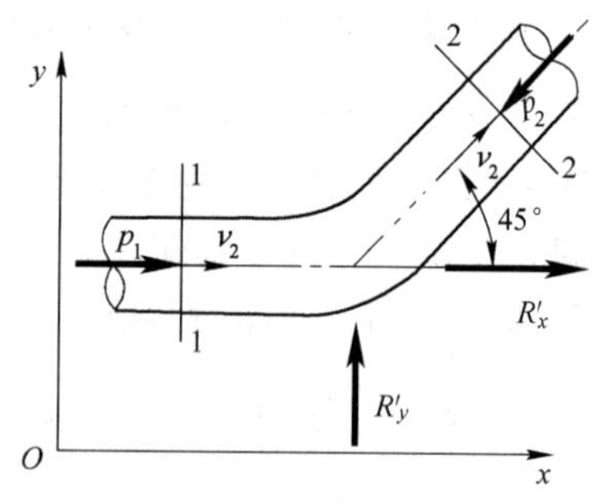

例 6-4-5 图

解 取二维坐标x、y如图所示，选控制面为1-1、2-2，令管壁对水流的反力在两个轴上投影分别为R'_x、R'_y，先对x轴应用式(6-4-28)

$$\sum F_x = \rho Q(\alpha_{02} v_{2x} - \alpha_{01} v_{1x})$$

设$\alpha_{02} = \alpha_{01} = 1.0$

$$-R'_x - p_2 A_2 \cos\theta + p_1 A_1 = \rho Q(v_2 \cos\theta - v_1)$$

由于是等截面，所以$A_1 = A_2 = A$，得

$$R'_x = A(p_1 - p_2\cos\theta) - \rho Q(v_2\cos\theta - v_1)$$

由于等截面，又不计水头损失，所$v_1 = v_2 = v = 4\text{m/s}$，$p_1 = p_2 = p = 98\text{kPa}$，$Q = \dfrac{\pi}{4}d^2 v = \dfrac{\pi}{4}(0.2)^2 \times 4 = 0.126\text{m}^3/\text{s}$。将数字代入求得

$$R'_x = \frac{\pi}{4}(0.2)^2 \times (98\times 10^3 - 98\times 10^3 \cos 45°) - 1\,000 \times 0.126 \times (4\times\cos 45° - 4)$$
$$= 1\,049.7\text{N}$$

再对 y 轴应用式(6-4-28)

$$\sum F_y=\rho Q(\alpha_{02}v_{2y}-\alpha_{01}v_{1y})$$

$$R'_y-p_2A_2\sin\theta=\rho Q(v_2\sin\theta-0)$$

$$R'_y=p_2A_2\sin\theta+\rho Qv_2\sin45^\circ$$

$$=98\times10^3\times\frac{\pi}{4}(0.2)^2\times\sin45^\circ+1\ 000\times0.126\times4\sin45^\circ=2\ 533\text{N}$$

合力 $$R=\sqrt{R_x^2+R_y^2}=\sqrt{1\ 049.7^2+2\ 533^2}=2\ 741.9\text{N}$$

管道所受推力 $\boldsymbol{P}$ 与此大小相等方向相反,$\boldsymbol{P}=-\boldsymbol{R}$。

习 题

6-4-1 理想流体是指( )的流体。

A. 密度为常数　　B. 黏度不变

C. 不可压缩　　D. 无黏性

6-4-2 恒定流是指( )。

A. 当地加速度$\frac{\partial \boldsymbol{u}}{\partial t}=0$　　B. 迁移加速度$\frac{\partial \boldsymbol{u}}{\partial S}=0$

C. 当地加速度$\frac{\partial \boldsymbol{u}}{\partial t}\neq0$　　D. 迁移加速度$\frac{\partial \boldsymbol{u}}{\partial S}\neq0$

6-4-3 均匀流是指( )。

A. 当地加速度为零　　B. 合加速度为零

C. 流线为平行直线　　D. 流线为平行曲线

6-4-4 伯努利方程中 $z+\frac{p}{\gamma}+\frac{\alpha v^3}{2g}$表示( )。

A. 单位重量流体的势能　　B. 单位重量流体的动能

C. 单位重量流体的机械能　　D. 单位质量流体的机械能

6-4-5 毕托管测速比压计中的水头差是( )。

A. 单位动能与单位压能之差

B. 单位动能与单位势能之差

C. 测压管水头与流速水头之差

D. 总水头与测压管水头之差

6-4-6 黏性流体测压管水头线的沿程变化是( )。

A. 沿程下降　　B. 沿程上升

C. 保持水平　　D. 前三种情况都有可能

6-4-7 变直径有压圆管流动,上游断面 1 的直径 $d_1=150$mm,下游断面 2 的直径 $d_2=300$mm,断面 1 的平均流速 $v_1=6$m/s,断面 2 的平均流速 v_2 为( )。

A. 3m/s　　B. 2m/s　　C. 1.5m/s　　D. 1m/s

6-4-8 已知倾斜放置的文丘里流量计的测压管水头差 $\Delta h=0.6\text{mH}_2\text{O}$,如例 6-4-2 图所示,收缩前粗管直径 $d_1=100$mm,喉管直径 $d_2=50$mm,流量校正系数 $\mu=0.98$,流量 Q 为( )。

A. $0.008\text{m}^3/\text{s}$　　B. $0.006\ 51\text{m}^3/\text{s}$　　C. $0.007\ 5\text{m}^3/\text{s}$　　D. $0.006\ 81\text{m}^3/\text{s}$

第五节　流动阻力和能量损失

本节主要研究由于流体黏性的作用而产生的流动阻力和由于克服阻力而消耗的能量损失。对于液体，常用单位重量液体的能量损失即水头损失 h_w 来表示；对于气体，常用单位体积的能量损失即压强损失 $p_w=\gamma h_w$ 来表示。

水头损失可分为沿程水头损失和局部水头损失两种类型。当流体作流线平行的均匀流动时，水流阻力只有沿程不变的切应力，称为沿程阻力，由于克服沿程阻力消耗能量而产生的水头损失称为沿程水头损失 h_f，如图 6-5-1 所示直管段部分的水头损失即是此种水头损失；当限制流体的固体边界急剧改变，从而引起流体流速分布、内部结构变化、形成漩涡等一系列现象，因此产生的阻力称为局部阻力，由于克服局部阻力消耗能量而产生的水头损失称为局部水头损失 h_m，如图 6-5-1 所示流经"弯头"、"缩小"、"放大"及"闸门"等处的水头损失即为局部损失。

图 6-5-1 流段两断面间的全部水头损失 h_w 可以表示为两断面间所有沿程损失和所有局部损失的总和，即

$$h_w=\sum h_f+\sum h_m$$

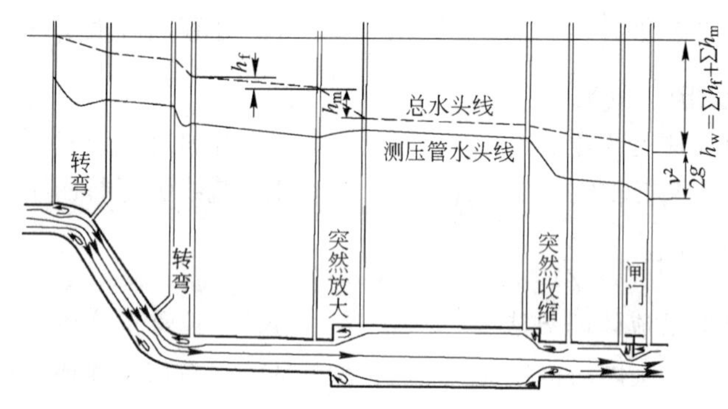

图　6-5-1

一、两种流态——层流和紊流

1883 年英国物理学家奥斯本·雷诺(Osborne Reynotds)经实验研究发现，水头损失和流体流动状态有关，而流动状态又可分为层流和紊流两种类型。

(一)层流

流体呈层状流动，各层的质点互不混掺；层流时水头损失 h_f 与平均流速的一次方成比例，即 $h_f=k_1v$；层流一般发生在低流速、细管径、高黏性的流体流动中。

(二)紊流

流体的质点互相混掺，迹线紊乱的流动；紊流时水头损失 h_f 与平均流速的 1.75～2 次方成比例，即$h_f=k_2v^{1.75\sim2}$；紊流发生在流速较快、断面较大、黏性小的流体流动中。

(三)层流与紊流的判别标准

雷诺经大量实验研究后提出用一个无量纲数$\frac{vd}{\nu}$来区别流态。后人为纪念他，称之为下临

界雷诺数，并以雷诺名字的头两个字母表示，即

$$\mathrm{Re}_k = \frac{v_k d}{\nu} = 2\ 300 \tag{6-5-1}$$

若管道中实际的雷诺数 $\mathrm{Re}=\frac{vd}{\nu}<2\ 300$ 为层流，$\mathrm{Re}>2\ 300$ 为紊流。

【例 6-5-1】 直径为 20mm 的管流，平均流速为 9m/s，已知水的运动黏性系数 $\nu=0.011\ 4\mathrm{cm^2/s}$，则管中水流的流态和水流流态转变的层流流速分别是：

A. 层流，19cm/s　　B. 层流，13cm/s

C. 紊流，19cm/s　　D. 紊流，13cm/s

解 管中雷诺数 $\mathrm{Re}=\frac{v\cdot d}{\nu}=\frac{2\times 900}{0.011\ 4}=157894.74\gg \mathrm{Re}_k$，为紊流。

欲使流态转变为层流时的流速 $v_k=\frac{\mathrm{Re}_k\cdot\nu}{d}=\frac{2\ 300\times 0.011\ 4}{2}=13.1\mathrm{cm/s}$。

答案：D

二、均匀流基本方程

在均匀流条件下可导出切应力 τ 与水力坡度 J 的关系式

$$\tau = \rho g R J = \rho g \frac{r}{2} J$$

上式表明圆管中切应力与半径 r 成正比，为线性分布，如图 6-5-2a)所示。

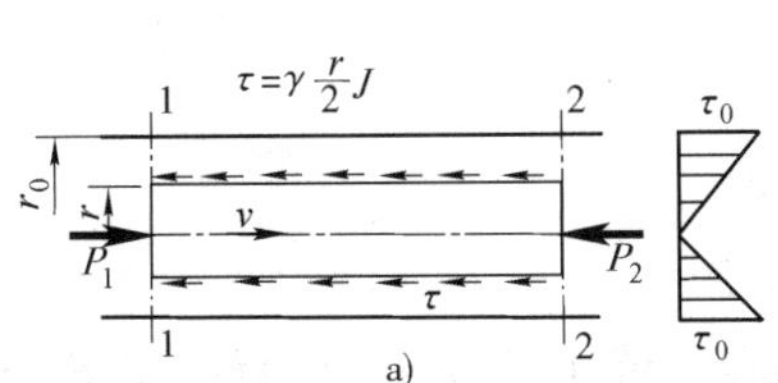

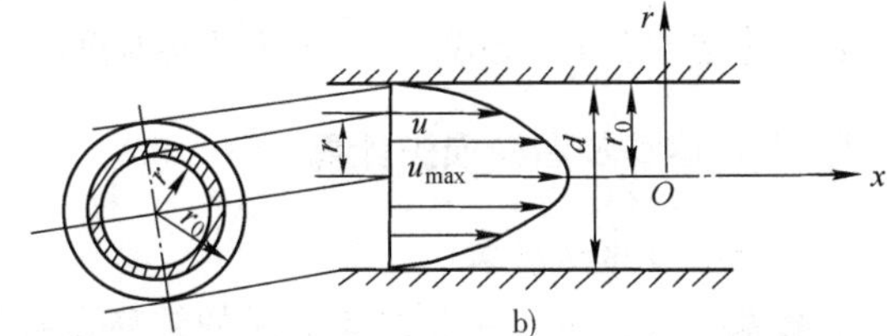

图 6-5-2

三、圆管中的层流运动及沿程损失计算

当圆管中的流态为层流时，断面上各点的流速 u 可用下式计算

$$u = \frac{\gamma J}{4\mu}(r_0^2 - r^2) \tag{6-5-2}$$

式中：γ——重度；

J——水力坡度；

μ——动力黏度；

r_0——水管内半径；

r——断面上任一点半径。

由上式可知，层流时圆管断面流速分布为二次抛物线，如图 6-5-2b)所示。最大流速 u_{max} 发生在 $r=0$ 的管轴心处，$u_{max}=\frac{\gamma J}{4\mu}r_0^2$；断面平均流速 $v=\frac{Q}{A}=\frac{\int_A u\mathrm{d}A}{A}$ 经积分计算后可得 $v=\frac{\gamma J}{8\mu}r_0^2$，所以 $v=\frac{1}{2}u_{max}$，即平均流速是最大流速的一半。而动能改正系数 $\alpha=2$，动量改正系数 $\alpha_0=1.33$。

若以 $u_m=\frac{\gamma J}{4\mu}r_0^2$ 代入式(6-5-2)中可得：$u=u_m\left[1-\left(\frac{r}{r_0}\right)^2\right]$。

圆管层流时水头损失 h_f 的计算公式可导出为

$$h_f=\lambda\frac{L}{d}\frac{v^2}{2g} \tag{6-5-3}$$

上式称达西-魏斯巴赫(Darcy-Weisbach)，公式中 L 为流长，d 为管内径，v 为断面平均流速，g 为重力加速度，λ 为沿程阻力系数，在圆管层流时可按下式计算

$$\lambda=\frac{64}{\mathrm{Re}} \tag{6-5-4}$$

上式只能在 $\mathrm{Re}<2\,300$ 时应用。

对于非圆断面的管道，可以用水力半径 R 来代替式中的管径 d，水力半径为断面面积 A 与湿周 x 之比，即

$$R=\frac{A}{x} \tag{6-5-5}$$

对有压圆管其水力半径按式(6-5-5)可求得为

$$R=\frac{\frac{\pi}{4}d^2}{\pi d}=\frac{d}{4}$$

将此关系代入式(6-5-3)可得

$$h_f=\lambda\frac{L}{4R}\frac{v^2}{2g} \tag{6-5-6}$$

上式称达西公式，比式(6-5-3)应用范围更广。

四、紊流运动及沿程损失计算

(一)紊流的脉动现象

在紊流中由于质点的混掺及旋涡的转移，使紊流中某点的流速、压强均随时间 t 而围绕某一时间平均值上下跳动，此现象称为脉动现象。图 6-5-3a)表示紊流流速 u_x 随时间 t 而脉动的情况，由于紊流脉动是一个随机过程，从瞬时来看没有规律，给研究带来困难。但从较长的时间过程来看，它又有一定规律，它可以看成是一个时间平均流动和脉动的叠加，而时均流动是恒定的。例如时均流速 $\overline{u}_x=\frac{1}{T}\int u_x\mathrm{d}t$，在图 6-5-3 中 $\overline{u}_x$ 是一条水平线。

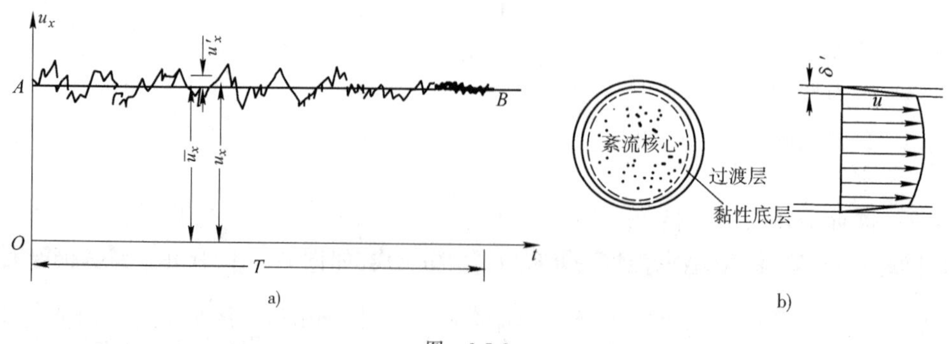

图 6-5-3

(二)紊流的阻力

紊流除由于黏性而产生的黏性切应力之外，更主要的是由于质点混掺、动量交换而形成的

惯性切应力$\overline{\tau_2}=-\rho\overline{u_x^{\prime}u_y^{\prime}}$。根据普朗德(Prandtl)混掺长度半经验理论，惯性切应力

$$\tau_2=\rho l^2(\frac{\mathrm{d}u_x}{\mathrm{d}y})^2$$

式中，l 为混掺长度。据卡门(Kazman)的研究：$l=ky$，$k=0.36\sim0.435$，平均值取 $k=0.4$。所以紊流阻力由两部分叠加，得

$$\tau=\mu\frac{\mathrm{d}u_x}{\mathrm{d}y}+\rho l^2(\frac{\mathrm{d}u_x}{\mathrm{d}y})^2$$

根据上述紊流阻力公式，可导出紊流核心区紊流速分布公式为

$$u=\frac{1}{k}v^{*}\cdot\ln y+C \tag{6-5-7}$$

由上式知紊流核心区流速分布为对数分布，远较层流均匀，如图 6-5-3b)所示，式中 $v_*=\sqrt{\frac{\tau_0}{\rho}}$称为切应力流速，$y$ 为距壁面的距离。式中积分常数与固壁壁面的粗糙度 Δ 高低有关，所以紊流的阻力、流速分布、水头损失，不仅与黏性有关，与雷诺数 Re 有关，而且还与边壁粗糙度 Δ 和相对粗糙度$\frac{\Delta}{d}$有关。

在壁面附近的黏性底层中，紊流流速分布为直线分布。

(三)紊流的沿程阻力系数

紊流与层流一样，计算沿程损失的公式仍可用达西公式(6-5-3)或公式(6-5-6)，但沿程阻力系数随流态不同及所在流区不同而用不同公式计算。根据尼柯拉兹(Nikuradse)在人工粗糙(黏沙粒)管中的试验，流区可划分如下：

1. 层流区

$Re<2\ 000$，$\lambda=\frac{64}{Re}$，参见图 6-5-4。

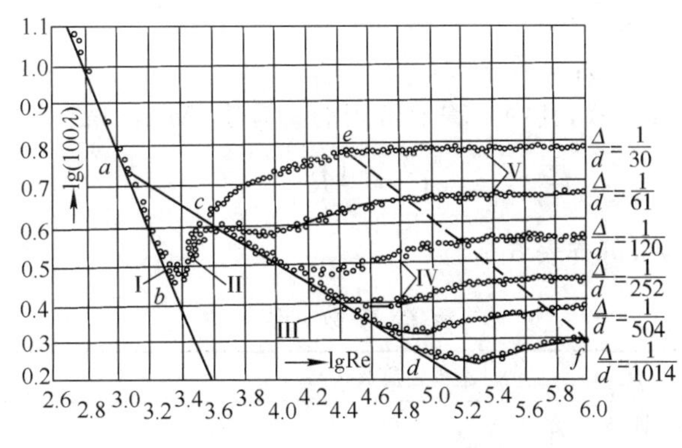

图 6-5-4

2. 紊流光滑区

$4\ 000<Re<10^5$，管壁绝对粗糙度 $\Delta<0.4\delta$，而黏性底层厚度 $\delta=\frac{32.8d}{Re\sqrt{\lambda}}$，此时黏性底层厚度遮盖了边壁粗糙度，沿程阻力系数仅随雷诺数而变，$\lambda=\lambda(Re)$，可用伯拉休斯(Blasince)公式计算

$$\lambda=\frac{0.316\ 4}{Re^{0.25}} \tag{6-5-8}$$

也可用尼柯拉兹光滑管公式计算

$$\frac{1}{\sqrt{\lambda}} = 2\lg(\mathrm{Re}\sqrt{\lambda}) - 0.8 \tag{6-5-9}$$

3.紊流过渡区

由水力光滑区向水力粗糙区的过渡，此时 $0.4\delta<\Delta<6\delta$，沿程阻力系数 λ 可按柯列布洛克(Colebrook)公式计算，此时 λ 与 Re、$\frac{\Delta}{d}$ 均有关，即

$$\frac{1}{\sqrt{\lambda}} = -2\lg\left(\frac{\Delta}{3.7d} + \frac{2.51}{\mathrm{Re}\sqrt{\lambda}}\right) \tag{6-5-10}$$

本流区的沿程阻力系数也可用阿尔特苏尔经验公式计算：$\lambda=0.11\left(\frac{\Delta}{d}+\frac{68}{\mathrm{Re}}\right)^{0.25}$。

4.紊流粗糙区(或称阻力平方区)

因为此时阻力系数 λ 只与相对粗糙度 $\frac{\Delta}{d}$ 有关，与 Re 无关，h_f 与 v^2 成正比。阻力系数有多种计算公式，最著名的有尼柯拉兹粗糙区公式和谢才(Chegy)公式。尼氏公式如下

$$\lambda = \frac{1}{\left(2\lg 3.7\frac{d}{\Delta}\right)^2} \tag{6-5-11}$$

应用范围为 $\Delta>6\delta$。

谢才公式如下

$$v = C\sqrt{RJ} \tag{6-5-12}$$

式中：v——平均流速；

C——谢才系数；

R——水力半径，$R=\frac{A}{x}$；

J——水力坡度 $J=h_f/L$，或者 $h_f=LJ$。

谢才系数有多种计算公式，其中工程上常用的有曼宁(Manning)公式

$$C = \frac{1}{n}R^{\frac{1}{6}} \tag{6-5-13}$$

式中：n——边壁粗糙系数，可查表 6-5-1。

粗糙系数 n 值 表 6-5-1

序号	壁面性质及状况	n
1	特别光滑的黄铜管、玻璃管	0.009
2	精致水泥浆抹面，安装及连接良好的新制的清洁铸铁管及钢管，精刨木板	0.011
3	正常情况下无显著水锈的给水管，非常清洁的排水管，最光滑的混凝土面	0.012
4	正常情况的排水管，略有积污的给水管，良好的砖砌体	0.013
5	积污的给水管和排水管，中等情况下渠道的混凝土砌面	0.014
6	良好的块石圬工，旧的砖砌体，比较粗制的混凝土砌面，特别光滑、仔细开挖的岩石面	0.017
7	坚实黏土的渠道，不密实淤泥层(有的地方是中断的)覆盖的黄土、砾石及泥土的渠道，良好养护情况下的大土渠	0.022 5

续上表

序号	壁面性质及状况	n
8	良好的干砌圬工，中等养护情况的土渠，情况极良好的河道（河床清洁、顺直、水流畅通、无塌岸深潭）	0.025
9	养护情况中等标准以下的土渠	0.027 5
10	情况较坏的土渠（如部分渠底有杂草、卵石或砾石、部分岸坡崩塌等），情况良好的天然河道	0.030
11	情况很坏的土渠（如断面不规则，有杂草、块石、水流不畅等），情况较良好的天然河道，但有不多的块石和野草	0.035
12	情况特别坏的土渠（如有不少深潭及塌岸，杂草丛生，渠底有大石块等），情况不大良好的天然河道（如杂草、块石较多，河床不甚规则而有弯曲，有不少深潭和塌岸）	0.040

比较达西公式与谢才公式，可得

$$C=\sqrt{\frac{8g}{\lambda}}$$

和

$$\lambda=\frac{8g}{C^2} \qquad (6\text{-}5\text{-}14)$$

谢才公式对水力粗糙区的明渠、管道均可用，对明渠应用尤为方便。

5.第一过渡区（流态过渡区）

由层流向紊流过渡，该区域很窄，且 λ 无定量公式。

此后，柯列布洛克（Co Lebrook）等人，对工业上实用管道进行研究，得出了计算紊流过渡区的阻力系数公式[式(6-5-10)]，式中 Δ 为实用管道的当量粗糙度，所谓当量粗糙度，就是指和 实用管道紊流粗糙区 λ 值相等的、管径相同的尼古拉兹人工粗糙管的砂粒粒径高度。见表 6-5-2。1944 年莫迪（Moody L. F）在式(6-5-10)的基础上绘制了实用管道的 λ 与 Re、$\frac{\Delta}{d}$ 之间关系图，称莫迪图，如图 6-5-5 所示。根据已知的 Re 与 $\frac{\Delta}{d}$ 可由莫迪图查出沿程阻力系数 λ 值。

实用管道当量粗糙度 Δ 值 表 6-5-2

序　号	边 界 种 类	当量粗糙度 Δ 值(mm)
1	钢板制风管	0.15（引自全国通用通风管道计算表）
2	塑料板制风管	0.10（引自全国通用通风管道计算表）
3	表面光滑砖风道	4.0（引自采暖通风设计手册）
4	矿渣混凝土板风道	1.5（引自采暖通风设计手册）
5	钢丝网抹灰风道	10～15（引自采暖通风设计手册）
6	胶合板风道	1.0（引自采暖通风设计手册）
7	铅管、铜管、玻璃管	0.01（引自莫迪当量粗糙度图等）
8	镀锌钢管	0.15（引自莫迪当量粗糙度图等）
9	铸铁管	0.25（引自莫迪当量粗糙度图等）
10	混凝土管	0.3～3（引自莫迪当量粗糙度图等）
11	旧的生锈金属管	0.60（引自莫迪当量粗糙度图等）
12	污秽的金属管	0.75～0.97（引自莫迪当量粗糙度图等）

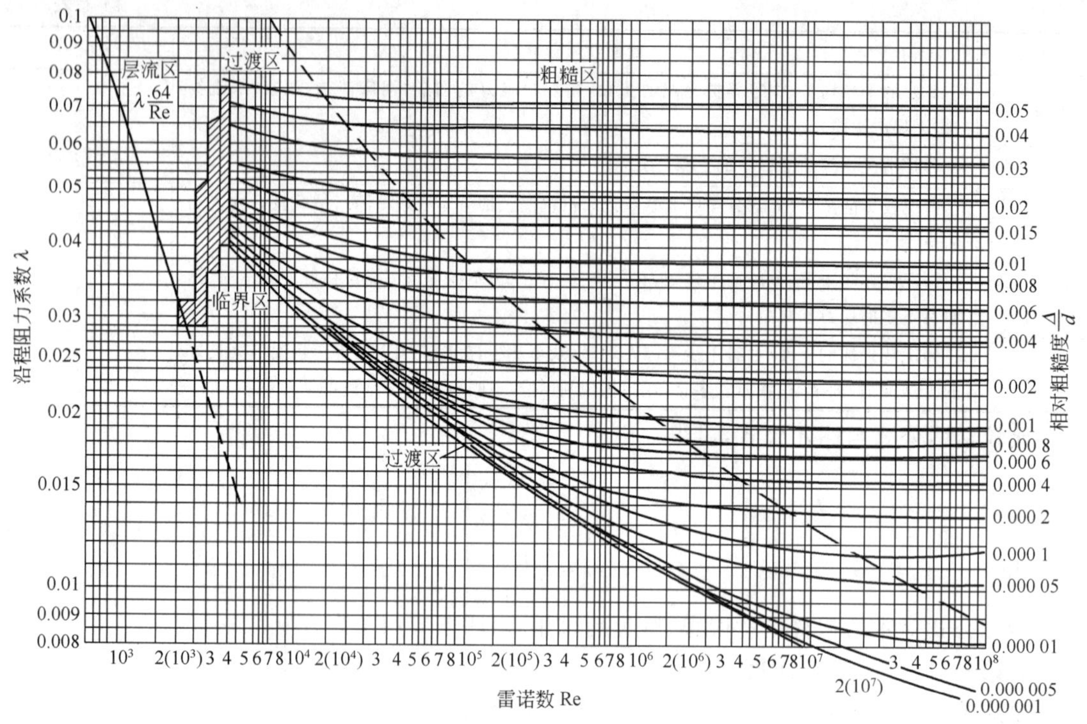

图 6-5-5

五、局部水头损失

局部水头损失计算的普遍公式为

$$h_m = \zeta \frac{v^2}{2g} \tag{6-5-15}$$

式中：ζ——局部阻力系数，视局部阻力形式而定，其数值由试验确定，可查局部阻力系数图表。

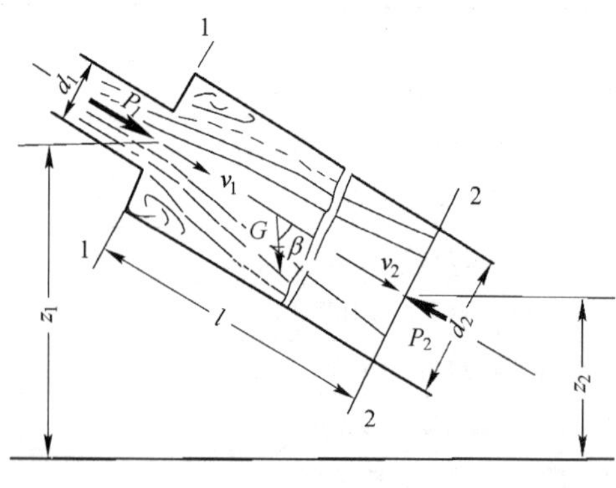

图 6-5-6

但对突然放大的局部损失(见图 6-5-6)，可用理论导出局部阻力系数。

$$\zeta_1 = (1-\frac{A_1}{A_2})^2, h_m = \zeta_1 \frac{v_1^2}{2g}$$

相应于放大前流速 v_1。

$$\zeta_2 = (\frac{A_2}{A_1}-1)^2, h_m = \zeta_2 \frac{v_2^2}{2g}$$

相应于放大后流速 v_2。

【例 6-5-2】 设有一恒定均匀有压管流，管径 $d=200\text{mm}$，绝对粗糙度 $\Delta=0.2\text{mm}$，水的运动黏度 $\nu=0.15\times10^{-5}\text{m}^2/\text{s}$，流量 $Q=5\text{L/s}$，试求该管的沿程阻力系数 λ 及每米管长沿程损失 h_f。

解 为判别流态，先求断面平均流速 v

$$v=\frac{Q}{A}=\frac{4Q}{\pi d^2}=\frac{4\times0.005}{\pi\times(0.2)^2}=0.16\text{m/s}$$

雷诺数 $Re=\frac{vd}{\nu}=\frac{0.16\times0.2}{0.15\times10^{-5}}=21\ 333>2\ 000$ 紊流，但 $Re<10^5$。

设紊流处于水力光滑区，按伯拉休斯公式求沿程阻力的系数 $\lambda=\frac{0.316\ 4}{Re^{0.25}}=\frac{0.316\ 4}{21\ 333^{0.25}}=0.026$。验证是否在水力光滑区，为此先求黏性底层厚度

$$\delta=\frac{32.8d}{Re\sqrt{\lambda}}=\frac{32.8\times0.2}{21\ 333\ \sqrt{0.026}}=1.95\text{mm}$$

$$0.4\delta=0.4\times1.95=0.78\text{mm}>0.2\text{mm}$$

是光滑区，假设正确。

$$h_f=\lambda\frac{L}{d}\cdot\frac{v^2}{2g}=0.026\times\frac{1}{0.2}\times\frac{0.16^2}{19.6}=1.7\times10^{-4}\text{m}$$

【例 6-5-3】 略有积污的给水管，管径 d 为 600mm，通过流量 Q 为 352L/s，管长 7.5km，绝对粗糙度 $\Delta=1.5$mm，平均水温 10℃，求沿程损失 h_f。

解 流速

$$v=\frac{4Q}{\pi d^2}=\frac{4\times0.352}{\pi(0.6)^2}=1.245\text{m/s}$$

雷诺数

$$Re=\frac{vd}{\nu}=\frac{1.245\times0.6}{1.306\times10^{-6}}=571\ 950>2\ 000$$

因 Re 较大且粗糙度较大，设在水力粗糙区用尼氏粗糙公式(6-5-11)求沿程阻力系数 λ

$$\lambda=\frac{1}{(2\lg3.7\frac{d}{\Delta})^2}=\frac{1}{(2\lg3.7\times\frac{600}{1.5})^2}=0.024\ 9$$

验证是否在水力粗糙区，求黏性底层厚度

$$\delta=\frac{32.8d}{Re\sqrt{\lambda}}=\frac{32.8\times0.6}{571\ 950\times\sqrt{0.024\ 9}}=0.218\text{mm}$$

$$6\delta=6\times0.218=1.308\text{mm}$$

$\Delta=1.5\text{mm}>6\delta$，是在水力粗糙区。

$$h_f=\lambda\frac{L}{d}\frac{v^2}{2g}=0.024\ 9\times\frac{7\ 500}{0.6}\times\frac{1.245^2}{2\times9.8}=24.61\text{m}$$

用谢才公式再求一次，按略有积污的给水管查表 6-5-1 得粗糙系数 $n=0.013$，代入曼宁公式

$$C=\frac{1}{n}R^{1/6}=\frac{1}{0.013}(\frac{0.6}{4})^{1/6}=56.071\ \sqrt{\text{m}}/\text{s}$$

$$\lambda=\frac{8g}{C^2}=\frac{8\times9.8}{56.071^2}=0.024\ 94$$

与用尼氏式计算基本相同，在以上计算中关键是要把粗糙系数及绝对粗糙度选好，其次选用流区公式要正确。

六、边界层基本概念和线流阻力

(一)边界层的定义和分类

当应用理想流体运动微分方程即欧拉运动方程来求解低黏性大雷诺数的实际流动时与实验结果出现有较大的差别，在圆柱绕流问题上甚至出现谬误，但完全应用黏性流体运动方程，即纳维-斯托克司(Navier-Stokes)方程求解整个流场时又有数学上的困难。直到 1904 年普朗德(L. Prandtl)提出了边界层理论，为解决实际流体的流动开拓了新的境界，现以如图 6-5-7 所示的平板边界层为例加以说明。当实际流体以某一速度 u_0 流向平板时，不论其雷诺数多么

大，由于黏性作用紧贴固定边界上的流速必为零，但沿边界法线方向（图中 y 方向）流速迅速增大，这样，在边界附近的流区存在着相当大的流速梯度，此区内的黏性切应力就不能忽略，边界附近的这一流体层就称为边界层。边界层外的流区，因流速梯度小，黏性作用可略去，按理想流体处理。普朗德又根据边界层内流动的具体条件，运用量级对比法，把实际流体运动微分方程（N-S）方程加以简化，成为边界层方程，为解决边界层内的流动创造了条件。

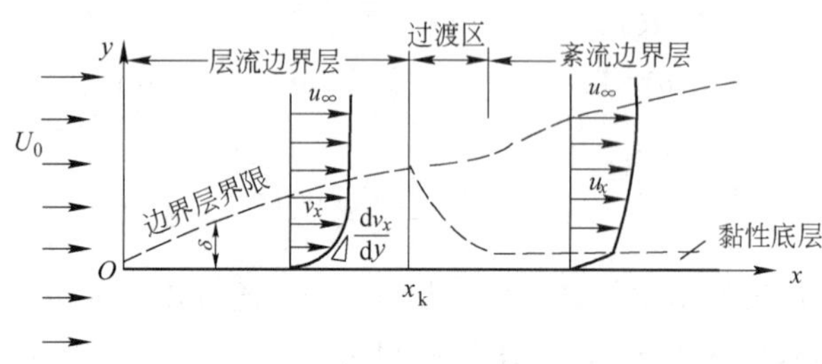

图 6-5-7

边界层的厚度 δ 从理论上讲，应该是由平板的表面流速为零处沿平板外法线方向一直到流速达到来流流速 u_0 的地方，这样厚度 δ 将是无穷大。实际观察发现，在离平板法向很小距离内流速就恢复到接近来流的速度。因此，一般规定当 $u_x=0.99U_0$ 时的地方，即是边界层的外边界，所以边界层的厚度 δ 是随距平板前端 0 点处的水平距离 x 而变的，在 $x=0$ 即平板前端处 $\delta=0$，然后随 x 之增大 δ 也随之增大；在 $x=x_k$ 以前为层流边界层，在 $x>x_k$ 以后经一很短的过渡段就发展为紊流边界层。层流边界层转变为紊流边界层的转变点称为转捩点，转捩点的雷诺数为 $Re_k=u_0x_k/\nu$，对于光滑平板 Re_k 的范围为$3\times10^5<Re_k<3\times10^6$。在紊流边界层内紧靠壁面处，流速较小，黏性仍起作用，近于层流运动，这一极薄层称为黏性底层（或近壁层流层）。

伯拉休斯（Blasiuce）于 1908 年求得边界层方程在层流边界时的精确解，边界层厚度 δ 与 x 坐标的关系如下

$$\delta=5\sqrt{\frac{Lx}{Re_L}}=5\frac{x}{\sqrt{Re_x}} \tag{6-5-16}$$

式中：L——平板长度；

x——水平距离；

Re_L——平板末端断面的雷诺数，$Re_L=\frac{u_0L}{\nu}$；

Re_x——距起点 x 距离断面的雷诺数，$Re_x=\frac{u_0x}{\nu}$。

由式（6-5-16）可知平板末端层流边界层的厚度

$$\delta=5\frac{L}{\sqrt{Re_L}} \tag{6-5-17}$$

当平板边界层已发展为紊流边界层时，则需用冯·卡门（V. Kazman）动量积分方程求近似解。

（二）边界层的分离现象

当流体不是流经平板，而是流向曲面物体时，可能产生边界层分离现象。现以圆柱绕流为例加以分析，如图 6-5-8a）所示一圆柱绕流的平面图。流体由 A 至 B 流动时，断面收缩，流速

加快，压强减少($\frac{\partial P}{\partial x}<0$)是加速减压段，此顺流的压差足以克服边界层内的阻力和主流动能的增加，边界层内流速不会减至零。但在流过 B 点以后，由于断面扩大，流体处于减速增压段($\frac{\partial p}{\partial x}>0$)，这时动能部分恢复为压能，为克服边界层内的阻力，也消耗了动能，此双重原因，使边界层内质点流速迅速降低，到一定地点，如图 6-5-8b)所示的贴近柱面的 C 点流速降到了零，流体质点将在 C 点停滞下来，继续流来的流体质点被迫脱离原来的流线，沿 CE 方向流去，从而使边界层脱离了柱面，这种现象即为边界层分离现象。C 点称为分离点，它不是指柱面上流速为零的点而是指贴近柱面流速为零的点。由于分离点下游的逆流向压差，使边界层分离后的液体反向回流，形成旋涡区。绕流物体边界层分离后的旋涡区称为绕流物体的尾流区，尾流区是充斥旋涡体的负压力，这使绕流体上下游形成"压差阻力"。尾流区的大小取决于边界层分离点的位置，而分离点的位置又取决于绕流物体的形状、粗糙度、雷诺数等。如流体遇到绕流体的锐缘时，分离点就在锐缘，如遇到流线形状的绕流体，则尾流区大大减小，所以"压差阻力"又称为"形状阻力"。

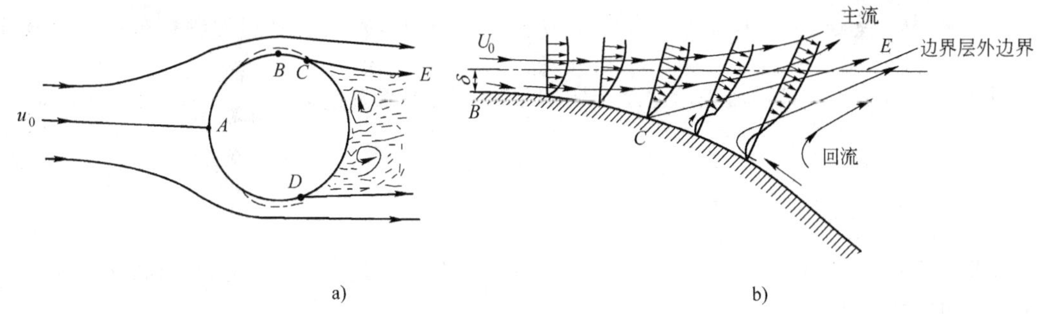

图 6-5-8

(三)绕流阻力

绕流阻力是指物体受到的绕其流过的流体所给予的阻力，绕流阻力由摩擦阻力和压差阻力(或称形状阻力)两部分所组成。1726 年牛顿提出绕流阻力计算公式为

$$D = C_D A \frac{\rho u_0^2}{2} \tag{6-5-18}$$

式中：D——绕流阻力；

ρ——流体密度；

u_0——来流流体未受物体影响前相对于物体的流速；

A——绕流物体与流体流向正交的断面投影面积；

C_D——绕流阻力系数，主要取决于被绕流体的形状、流体雷诺数、物面粗糙度及来流紊流强度，依靠试验来确定(参见图 6-5-9)。

1851 年斯托克司(Stokes)研究了微小圆球形颗粒在流体中极慢流动(蠕动)时的阻力，它利用黏性流体运动微分方程(N-S 方程)忽略了惯性项，进行理论分析，得到了绕流阻力公式

$$D = 3\pi\mu v d \tag{6-5-19}$$

式中：D——圆球绕流阻力；

μ——流体动力黏度；

d——圆球颗粒直径；

v——颗粒与流体的相对流速。

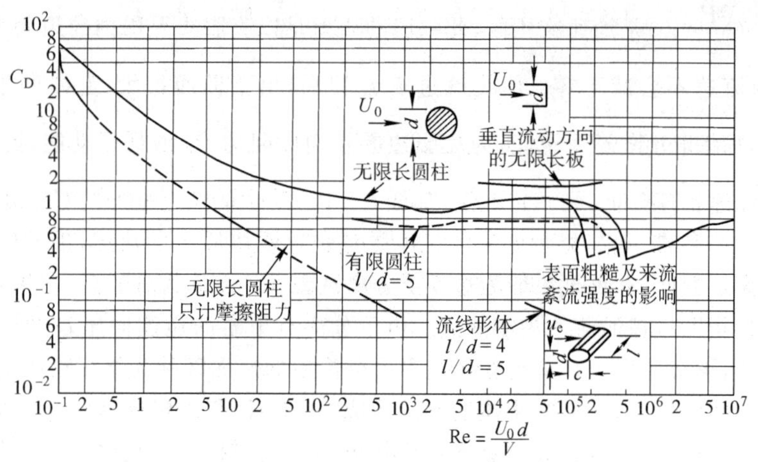

图 6-5-9

当泥沙颗粒在水中下沉时，重力与浮力及绕流阻力三者达到平衡，颗粒将均匀下沉，此时相对速度即为沉降速度 v，重力与浮力之差为 $\frac{\pi}{6}d^3(\gamma'-\gamma)$，$\gamma'$ 与 γ 分别为颗粒重度与流体重度。此两力差与式(6-5-19)所表示之绕流阻力平衡后可求得沉速 $v=\frac{1}{3\pi\mu d}\frac{\pi}{6}d^3(\gamma'-\gamma)$，即

$$v=\frac{d^2}{18\mu}(\gamma'-\gamma) \tag{6-5-20}$$

上式在 Re<1 时适用。

将圆球阻力公式(6-5-19)与牛顿提出的绕流阻力普遍公式(6-5-18)比较，可得圆球阻力系数 C_D 的理论公式为

$$C_D A\frac{\rho u_0^2}{2}=3\pi\mu u_0 d$$

$$C_D\times\frac{\pi}{4}d^2\ \frac{\rho u_0^2}{2}=3\pi\mu u_0 d$$

化简后得

$$C_D=\frac{24}{\mathrm{Re}} \tag{6-5-21}$$

式中：$\mathrm{Re}=\frac{u_0 d}{\nu}$——雷诺数。

上式在 Re<1 时与实验符合很好。在 $\mathrm{Re}=10\sim10^3$ 时，$C_D\approx\frac{13}{\sqrt{\mathrm{Re}}}$，当 $\mathrm{Re}=10^3\sim2\times10^5$ 时，可采用平均值 $C_D=0.45$。而且当 Re>1 时，沉降速度用下式计算

$$v=\sqrt{\frac{4}{3C_D}\left(\frac{\gamma'-\gamma}{\gamma}\right)gd} \tag{6-5-22}$$

为了减小绕流阻力可将物体设计成流线型使边界层分离点后移，尾流区缩小，减少形状阻力；使物体表面光滑平顺及吸走边界层停滞点处的流体，也可达到减阻的目的。

七、减小阻力的措施

长期以来，减小阻力就是工程流体力学中的一个重要的研究课题。这方面的研究成果，对

国民经济和国防建设的很多部门都有十分重大的意义。例如，对于在流体中航行的各种运载工具(飞机、轮船等)，减小阻力就意味着减小发动机的功率和节省燃料消耗，或者在可能提供的动力条件下提高航行速度。这一点在军事上具有更大的意义。长距离输送像原油这类黏性很大的液体，需要消耗巨大的能量，如能将原油的管输摩阻大幅度降低，会给国民经济带来很大好处。对于经常运转的其他管道系统，减阻在节约能源上的意义也是不容忽视的。因此近年来减阻问题的研究，日益引起各有关领域的重视。

减小管中流体运动的阻力有两条完全不同的途径：一是改进流体外部的边界，改善边壁对流动的影响；另一是在流体内部投加极少量的添加剂，使其影响流体运动的内部结构来实现减阻。

添加剂减阻是近二十年才迅速发展起来的减阻技术。虽然到目前为止，它在工业技术中还没有得到广泛的应用，但就当前了解的试验研究成果和少数生产使用情况来看，它的减阻效果是很突出的。此外，添加剂减阻又和紊流机理这个流体力学中的基本理论问题密切相关。通过对添加剂减阻机理的研究，必将推动紊流理论的进一步发展。添加剂减阻已成为流体力学中一项富有生命力的研究课题。

下面介绍改善边壁的减阻措施。

要降低粗糙区或过渡区内的紊流沿程阻力，最容易想到的减阻措施是减小管壁的粗糙度。此外，用柔性边壁代替刚性边壁也可能减少沿程阻力。水槽中的拖曳试验表明，高雷诺数下的柔性平板的摩擦阻力比刚性平板小 50%。对安放在另一管道中间的弹性软管进行过阻力试验，两管间的环形空间充满液体，结果比同样条件的刚性管道的沿程阻力小 35%。环形空间内液体的黏性愈大，软管的管壁愈薄，减阻效果愈好。

减小紊流局部阻力的着眼点在于防止或推迟流体与壁面的分离，避免旋涡区的产生或减小旋涡区的大小和强度。下面选几种典型的常用配件为例来说明这个问题。

(一)管道进口

图 6-5-10 表明，平顺的管道进口可以减小局部损失系数 90%以上。

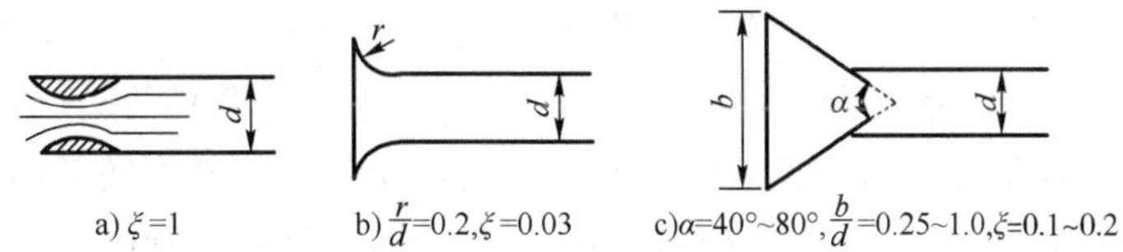

图 6-5-10 几种进口阻力系数

(二)渐扩管和突扩管

扩散角大的渐扩管阻力系数较大，如制成图 6-5-11a)示的形式，阻力系数约减小一半。突扩管如制成图 6-5-11b)示的台阶式，阻力系数也可能有所减小。

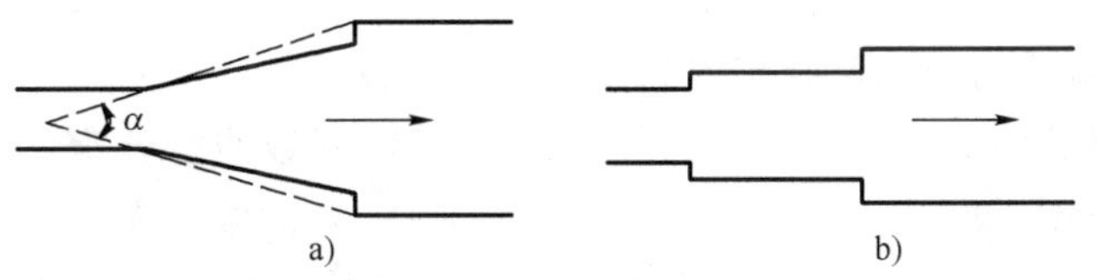

图 6-5-11 复合式渐扩管和台阶式突扩管

(三)弯管

弯管的阻力系数在一定范围内随曲率半径 R 的增大而减小。表 6-5-3 给出了 90°弯管在不同 R/d 时的 ξ 值。

不同 R/d 时 90°弯管的 ξ 值($Re=10^6$)　　表 6-5-3

R/d	0	0.5	1	2	3	4	6	10
ξ	1.14	1.00	0.246	0.159	0.145	0.167	0.20	0.24

由表可知,如 $R/d<1$,ξ 值随 R/d 的减小而急剧增加,这与旋涡区的出现和增大有关。如 $R/d>3$,ξ 值又随 R/d 的加大而增加,这是由于弯管加长后,摩阻增大造成的。因此弯管的 R 最好在(1～4)d 的范围内。

断面大的弯管,往往只能采用较小的 R/d,可在弯管内部布置一组导流叶片,以减小旋涡区和二次流,降低弯管的阻力系数。愈接近内侧,导流叶片应布置得愈密些。如图 6-5-12 所示的弯管,装上圆弧形导流叶片后,阻力系数由 1.0 减小到 0.3 左右。

(四)三通

尽可能地减小支管与合流管之间的夹角,或将支管与合流管连接处的折角改缓,都能改进三通的工作,减小局部阻力系数。例如将 90°T 形三通的折角切割成如图 6-5-13 所示的 45°斜角,则合流时的 ξ_{1-3} 和 ξ_{2-3} 减小 30%～50%,分流时的 ξ_{3-1} 减小 20%～30%。但对分流的 ξ_{3-2} 影响不大。如将切割的三角形加大,阻力系数还能显著下降。

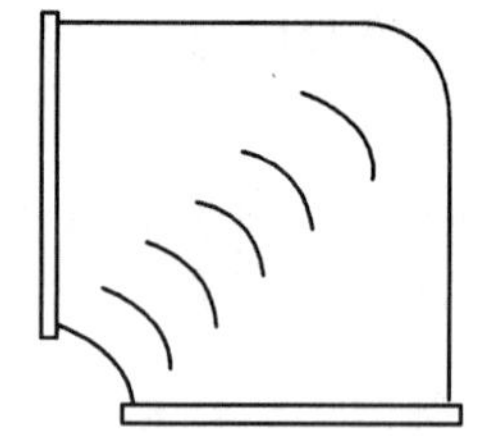

图 6-5-12　装有导叶的弯管

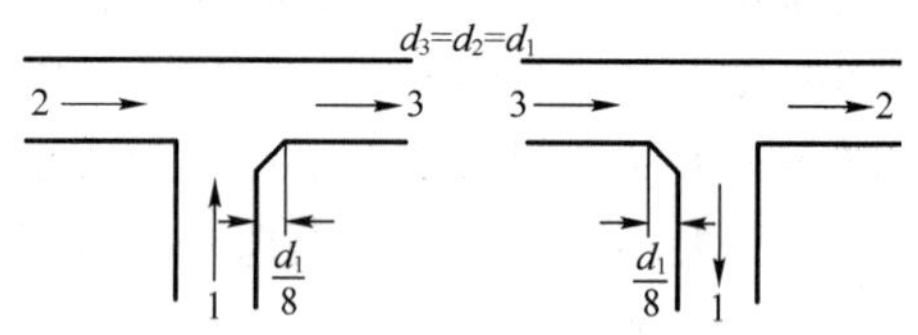

图 6-5-13　切割折角的 T 形三通

配件之间的不合理衔接,也会使局部阻力加大。例如在既要转 90°,又要扩大断面的流动中,如均选用 $R/d=1$ 的弯管和 $A_2/A_1=2.28$、$l_d/r_1=4.1$ 的渐扩管,在直接连接($l_s=0$)的情况下,先弯后扩的水头损失为先扩后弯的水头损失的 4 倍。即使中间都插入一段 $l_0=4d$ 的短管,也仍然大 2.4 倍。因此,如果没有其他原因,先弯后扩是不合理的。

习　　题

6-5-1　有压圆管均匀流切应力 τ 沿断面的分布为(　　)。

A. 断面上各点 τ 相等　　B. 管壁处是零,向管轴线性增大

C. 管轴处是零,与半径成正比　　D. 按抛物线分布

6-5-2　圆管层流运动的流速分布图是(　　)。

A. 直线分布　　B. 对数曲线分布

C. 抛物线分布　　D. 双曲线分布

6-5-3　圆管层流运动,轴心处最大流速与断面平均流速的比值是(　　)。

A. 1　　B. 2　　C. 3/2　　D. 3

6-5-4　圆管紊流核心区的流速分布是(　　)。

A. 直线分布　　B. 抛物线分布　　C. 对数曲线分布　　D. 双曲线分布

6-5-5　有压圆管流动，若断面1的直径是其下游断面2直径的2倍，则断面1与断面2雷诺数的关系是(　　)。

A. $Re_1=0.5Re_2$　　B. $Re_1=Re_2$　　C. $Re_1=1.5Re_2$　　D. $Re_1=2Re_2$

6-5-6　有压圆管层流的沿程阻力系数 λ 在莫迪图上随着雷诺数 Re 的增加而(　　)。

A. 增加　　B. 线性的减少

C. 不变　　D. 以上答案均不对

6-5-7　层流的沿程损失与平均流速的(　　)成正比。

A. 2次方　　B. 1.75次方　　C. 1次方　　D. 1.85次方

6-5-8　有压圆管流动，紊流粗糙区的沿程阻力系数 λ(　　)。

A. 与相对粗糙度有关　　B. 与雷诺数有关

C. 与相对粗糙度及雷诺数均有关　　D. 与雷诺数及管长有关

6-5-9　谢才公式仅适用于(　　)。

A. 水力光滑区　　B. 水力粗糙区或阻力平方区

C. 紊流过渡区　　D. 第一过渡区

6-5-10　若一管道的绝对粗糙度 Δ 不改变，只要改变管中流动参数，也能使其由水力粗糙管变成水力光滑管，这是(　　)。

A. 因为加大流速后，黏性底层变厚了

B. 减小管中雷诺数，黏性底层变厚遮住了绝对粗糙度

C. 流速加大后，把管壁冲得光滑了

D. 其他原因

6-5-11　流体绕固体流动时所形成的绕流阻力，除了黏性摩擦力外，更主要的是因为(　　)形成的形状阻力。

A. 流速和密度的加大

B. 固体表面粗糙

C. 雷诺数加大，表面积加大

D. 有尖锐边缘的非流线形物体，产生边界层的分离和漩涡区

6-5-12　如例6-4-4图所示的水泵供水管路，水池与水塔液面高差 $z=15$m，两液面间吸水管及压水管系统总阻力系数 $\zeta_s=\sum\lambda\frac{L}{d}+\sum\zeta=65$，管中流速 $v=1$m/s，水泵所需的最小扬程 H 为(　　)。

A. $16mH_2O$　　B. $20mH_2O$　　C. $17.31mH_2O$　　D. $18.32mH_2O$

第六节　孔口、管嘴及有压管流

一、孔口出流

(一)孔口出流的分类

容器壁上开一孔口有液体流出称孔口出流。如壁厚对出流现象无影响，孔壁

与液流仅在一条周线上接触，这种孔口称为薄壁孔口，反之称为非薄壁孔口。当孔口高度 $e<\frac{H}{10}$ 时称为小孔口，式中 H 为孔口形心上的水头，小孔口断面上各点水头近似相等可用形心点水头代表。若孔口高度 $e\geqslant\frac{H}{10}$就称为大孔口。孔口前水头 H 恒定不变时，称为常水头孔口，如孔口前水头随时间而改变时称为变水头孔口出流。液体经孔口流入大气称自由出流孔口，液体经孔口流入液面以下称为淹没出流孔口。

（二）常水头薄壁小孔口自由出流

如图 6-6-1 所示，取基准面 0-0 过孔口中心，并取上游自由液面为断面 1-1，孔口外收缩断面（距壁 $e/2$ 处）c-c 为下游断面，写能量方程

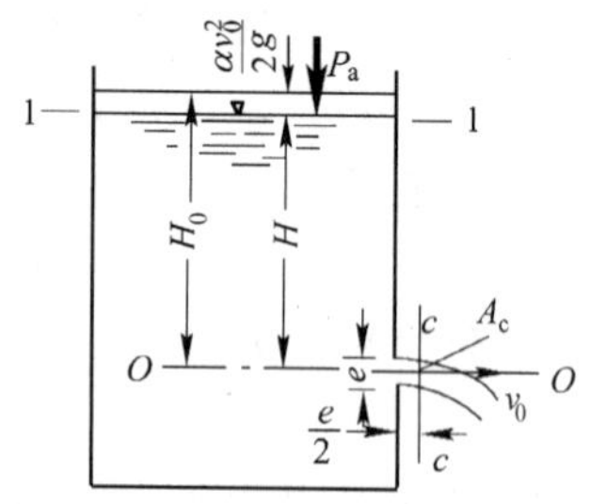

图 6-6-1

$$H+0+\frac{\alpha_1 v_0^2}{2g}=0+0+\frac{\alpha_2 v_c^2}{2g}+h_w$$

令 $H_0=H+\frac{\alpha_1 v_0^2}{2g}$，$v_0$ 为上游水面流速，H_0 称自由出流小孔口水头。当 v_0 很小时 $H_0\approx H$，孔口水头损失 $h_w=\zeta_c\frac{v_c^2}{2g}$，$\zeta_c$ 为小孔口阻力系数由试验确定。代入上式后得 $H=(\alpha_c+\zeta_c)\frac{v_c^2}{2g}$，故收缩断面平均流速

$$v_c=\frac{1}{\sqrt{\alpha_c+\zeta_c}}\sqrt{2gH_0}=\varphi\sqrt{2gH_0} \tag{6-6-1}$$

式中，$\varphi=\frac{1}{\sqrt{\alpha_c+\zeta_c}}$为小孔口流速系数，可用试验确定，据前人研究 $\varphi=0.97$，$\zeta_c=0.06$，$\alpha_c=1.0$。

设收缩断面面积与孔口断面面积比值为 $\varepsilon=\frac{A_c}{A}$，称为收缩系数，小孔口的收缩系数 $\varepsilon=0.64$（当收缩为充分、完善圆形时），故小孔口的出流流量

$$Q=V_cA_c=\varphi\sqrt{2gH_0}\times\varepsilon A=\varepsilon\varphi A\sqrt{2gH_0}$$

令 $\mu=\varepsilon\varphi$，称小孔口流量系数，则有

$$Q=\mu A\sqrt{2gH_0} \tag{6-6-2}$$

对充分收缩的圆形小孔口，$\mu=0.97\times0.64\approx0.62$，收缩是否充分和完善与孔口至容器壁的距离有关，当孔口距壁的距离大于相应的孔口边长的 3 倍时，为充分完善收缩，否则为不充分完善收缩。

（三）常水头薄壁小孔口淹没出流

如图 6-6-2 所示，取上游自由液面为断面 1-1，下游过水断面 2-2，能量方程为

$$H_1+0+\frac{\alpha_1 v_0^2}{2g}=H_2+0+\frac{\alpha_2 v_2^2}{2g}+h_w$$

水头损失包括水流经孔口的局部损失及经收缩面后放大的损失两项，即 $h_w=(\zeta_1+\zeta_2)\frac{v_c^2}{2g}$。

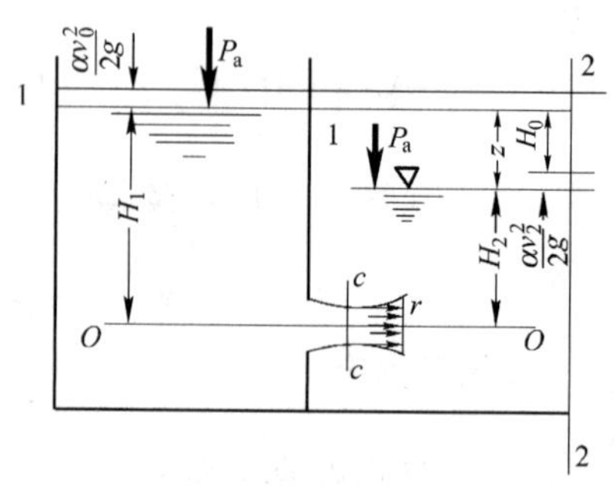

图 6-6-2

令 $H_0=(H_1-H_2)+\frac{\alpha_1 v_0^2}{2g}-\frac{\alpha_2 v_2^2}{2g}$，代入上式可得

$$H_0=(\zeta_1+\zeta_2)\frac{v_c^2}{2g}$$

因 A_2 远大于 A_c，故 $\zeta_2=1$，所以流速

$$v_c=\frac{1}{\sqrt{1+\zeta_1}}\sqrt{2gH_0}=\varphi\sqrt{2gH_0}$$

孔口流量

$$Q=\varepsilon\varphi A\sqrt{2gH_0}=\mu A\sqrt{2gH_0}$$

上式与小孔口自由出流形式完全相同，但应注意孔口的水头 H_0 的意义有所不同，此处的 H_0 是孔口上下游断面总水头之差，当上下游断面流速水头可不计时，即为上下游液面高差 Z。

（四）薄壁大孔口出流

上述关于小孔口出流的公式可以用于大孔口，只是流量系数 μ 值要大于小孔口，随孔口型式而变，大约为 $\mu=0.65\sim0.9$，详见水力学手册有关表格。

二、管嘴出流

管嘴出流是在孔口处连接长为 3～4 倍孔口直径的短管后形成的液体出流，与孔口类似可以分为常水头、变水头、自由出流、淹没出流等，并根据外形可以将管嘴分为如图 6-6-3 所示的圆柱形、圆锥形和流线型管嘴等类型。

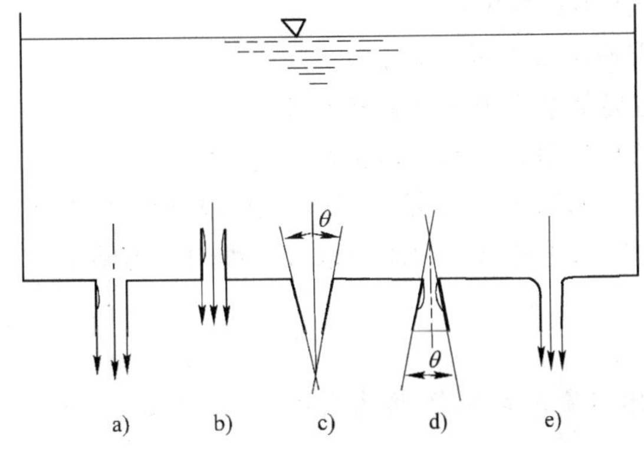

图 6-6-3

管嘴出流很多地方与孔口类似，故流速流量公式可应用与孔口相同的公式，但流速系数 φ 及流量系数 μ 与孔口不同，现以圆柱形外管嘴为例加以说明。圆柱形管嘴进口处先收缩，形成一收缩断面，收缩断面后流线扩张至出口处充满断面，无收缩，故出口断面的收缩系数 $\varepsilon=1$，流速系数 φ 与流量系数相等，其值为 $\varphi=\mu=0.82$，远大于小孔口的流量系数。与相同直径、水头的小孔口相比较，其出流量约为小孔口的 $\frac{0.82}{0.62}=1.32$ 倍。流量增加的原因是在收缩断面处存在真空，其真空度 $\frac{p_v}{\gamma}=0.75H_0$，这就使管嘴比孔口的作用总水头加大，从而加大了出流量。圆柱形管嘴必须满足的工作条件是：$H<9\text{mH}_2\text{O}$，管嘴长度 $L=3\sim4\text{d}$。

其余各种管嘴的 φ、μ、ε 值均可查有关水力计算手册确定。

三、有压管流

(一)有压管流的分类及简单短管水力计算

按水头损失所占比例不同可将有压管分为长管和短管。长管是指该管流中的能量损失以沿程损失为主,局部损失和流速水头所占比重很小,可以忽略不计的管道;短管是指局部损失和流速水头所占比重较大,计算时不能忽略的管道。根据管道布置与连接情况又可将有压管道分为简单管道与复杂管道两类,前者指没有分支的等直径管道,后者指由两条以上的管道组成的管系。复杂管又可分为串联、并联管道和枝状、环状管网,如图 6-6-4 所示。

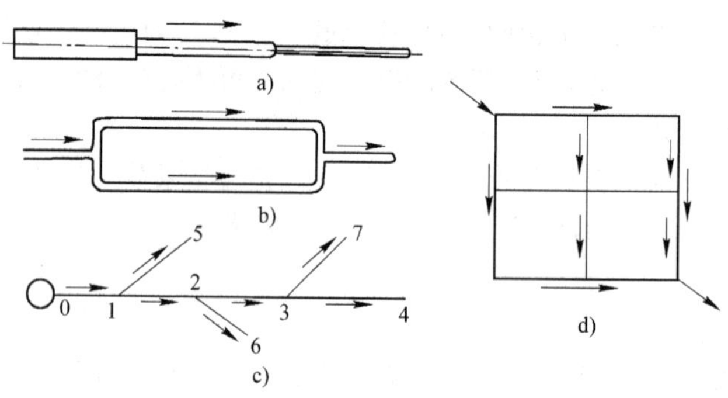

图 6-6-4

【例 6-6-1】 在长管水力计算中:

A. 只有速度水头可忽略不计

B. 只有局部水头损失可忽略不计

C. 速度水头和局部水头损失均可忽略不计

D. 两断面的测压管水头差并不等于两断面间的沿程水头损失

解 在长管水力计算中,速度水头和局部水头损失均可忽略不计。

答案:C

1. 短管自由出流

若短管中的液体经出口流入大气中,称为自由出流,如图 6-6-5 所示。

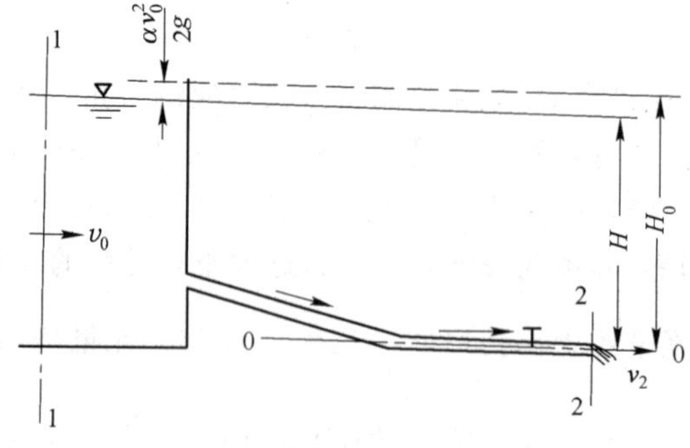

图 6-6-5

选上游过流断面 1-1 和管道出口过流断面 2-2,其能量方程为

$$H + 0 + \frac{\alpha_1 v_0^2}{2g} = 0 + 0 + \frac{\alpha_2 v_0^2}{2g} + h_{w1\text{-}2}$$

令 $H_0 = H + \frac{\alpha_1 v_0^2}{2g}$,称作用水头,则

$$H_0 = \frac{\alpha v_2}{2g} + h_w \tag{6-6-3}$$

水头损失 $h_w = \sum h_f + \sum h_m = \sum\lambda \frac{L}{d}\frac{v^2}{2g} + \sum\zeta\frac{v^2}{2g} = \zeta_c\frac{v^2}{2g}$,$\zeta_c = \sum\lambda\frac{L}{d} + \sum\zeta$ 为短管的总阻力系数,代入式(6-6-3)中得

$$H_0 = (\alpha + \zeta_c)\frac{v^2}{2g} \tag{6-6-4}$$

取 $\alpha = 1$ 得

$$v = \frac{1}{\sqrt{1+\zeta_c}}\sqrt{2gH_0} = \varphi_c\sqrt{2gH_0} \tag{6-6-5}$$

$\varphi_c = \frac{1}{\sqrt{1+\zeta_c}}$称为短管的流速系数。

短管的流量为

$$Q = vA = \varphi_c A\sqrt{2gH_0} = \mu_c A\sqrt{2gH_0} \tag{6-6-6}$$

式中:A——短管过流断面积;

$\varphi_c = \mu_c$——短管流量系数。

2.短管淹没出流

若短管中流体经出口流入下游自由液面之下的液体中,则称为淹没出流,如图 6-6-6 所示。以下游自由液面为基准面,对断面 1-1 及 2-2 写能量方程,即

$$H + 0 + \frac{\alpha_0 v_0^2}{2g} = 0 + 0 + \frac{\alpha_2 v_2^2}{2g} + h_w$$

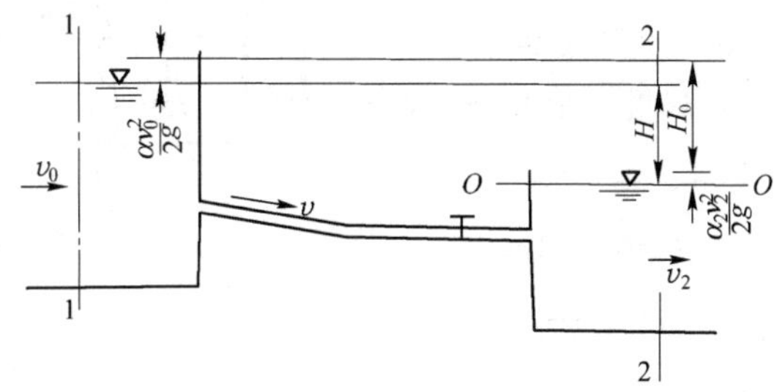

图 6-6-6

令 $H_0 = z + \frac{\alpha_0 v_0^2}{2g} - \frac{\alpha_2 v_2^2}{2g}$,则得

$$H_0 = h_w = h_f + h_m \tag{6-6-7}$$

H_0 为淹没出流短管上下游断面总水头之差,式中的水头损失可按 $h_w = \zeta_c\frac{v^2}{2g}$计算,$\zeta_c = \sum\lambda\frac{L}{d} + \sum\zeta$,式中$\sum\zeta$ 比自由出流多一出口,损失 $\zeta_{出口} = 1.0$ 代入式(6-6-7)中,有

$$H_0 = \zeta_c \frac{v^2}{2g}$$

或

$$v = \frac{1}{\sqrt{\zeta_c}} \sqrt{2gH_0} = \varphi_c \sqrt{2gH_0} \tag{6-6-8}$$

短管的流量

$$Q = vA = \varphi_c A \sqrt{2gH_0} = \mu_c A \sqrt{2gH_0} \tag{6-6-9}$$

式中，$\mu_c = \varphi_c = \frac{1}{\sqrt{\zeta_c}}$。比较与自由出流短管的差别主要在于总水头不同，淹没出流用的是总水头之差。当上下游水面流速很小时，$H_0 = H$，即可用液面高差代替总水头之差。

3. 简单短管水力计算几类问题

应用简单短管基本公式于工程实际的水力计算，一般有以下几类问题。

(1)已知水头、管径、管长、管道壁面性质和局部阻力的组成，求流量和流速。这类问题多属校核性质，可直接代入短管的流量、流速公式求解。

(2)已知流量、管径、管长、管壁性质及局部阻力组成，求作用水头。

(3)已知流量、水头、管长、管壁性质及局部阻力组成，求管径。这类问题直接用前述各短管公式求解有一定困难，因为式中阻力系数及断面面积中均包含有管径，所以一般用试算法求解。解得的管径尺寸，与标准管径的规格可能不一致，要选用相近的且稍大的标准管径。

(4)计算各过流断面的压强。对于位置固定的管道，绘制测压管水头线，便可解决此类问题。有时为了防止短管最高点处，由于真空而产生汽蚀、汽化，需求出短管最高点允许的安装高度。

【例 6-6-2】 离心泵管道系统如图所示。已知水泵流量 $Q=25\text{m}^3/\text{h}$，吸水管长 $L_1=5\text{m}$，压水管长 $L_2=20\text{m}$，水泵提水高度 $z=18\text{m}$，最大允许的真空度不超过 $\frac{p_v}{\gamma}=6\text{mH}_2\text{O}$。试确定吸水管直径 d_a、压水管直径 d_p 和水泵允许的安装高度 h_s 以及水泵的总扬程 H。

例 6-6-2 图

解 由给排水设计手册查得水泵吸水管允许的经济流速 $v_a=1\sim1.6\text{m/s}$，现采用 $v_a=1.6\text{m/s}$，则吸水管径：

$$d_a = \frac{4Q}{\pi v_a} = \frac{4\times25}{\pi\times1.6\times3\ 600} = 0.074\text{m}$$

$$=74\text{mm}$$

选取标准管径 $d_a=75\text{mm}$，相应的 v_a 为

$$v_a = \frac{4\times25}{\pi\times0.075^2\times3\ 600} = 1.57\text{m/s}$$

对吸水池液面 1-1 及水泵吸入口断面 2-2 写能量方程，得水泵吸水管最高点安装高度(水泵轴线高度)，即

$$h_s = \frac{p_v}{\gamma} - \frac{\alpha_2 v_2^2}{2g} - h_{w_{1-2}}$$

给水管粗糙系数 $n=0.012\ 5$，用曼宁公式求谢才系数 $C=\frac{1}{n}R^{\frac{1}{6}}=\frac{1}{0.012\ 5}\times\left(\frac{0.075}{4}\right)^{\frac{1}{6}}=$

41.23$\sqrt{m}$/s，沿程阻力系数 $\lambda=\frac{8g}{C^2}=\frac{8\times9.8}{41.23^2}=0.0461$。吸水管的局部阻力系数有滤水网底阀 $\zeta_1=8.5$，弯头 $\zeta_2=0.29$。水泵入口前的渐缩管 $\zeta_3=0.1$，将数据代入求安装高度，即

$$h_s=6-\frac{1.57^2}{2\times9.8}-\left(0.0461\times\frac{5}{0.075}+8.5+0.29+0.1\right)\times\frac{1.57^2}{2\times9.8}=4.37\text{m}$$

如压水管选取相同的经济流速，可得相同的管径，即 $d_p=0.075\text{m}=75\text{mm}$，$v_p=1.57\text{m/s}$，$\lambda=0.0461$。压水管的局部阻力系数有两个弯头，一个出口即 $\zeta_{弯头}=0.29$，$\zeta_{出口}=1.0$。压水管水头损失

$$h_{wp}=\left(0.046\times\frac{20}{0.075}+2\times0.29+1\right)\times\frac{1.57^2}{2\times9.8}=1.74\text{m}$$

吸水管水头损失

$$h_{wa}=\left(0.0461\times\frac{5}{0.075}+8.5+0.29+0.1\right)\times\frac{1.57^2}{2\times9.8}=1.5\text{m}$$

水泵总扬程

$$H=z+h_w=z+h_{wp}+h_{wa}=18+1.74+1.5=21.24\text{m}$$

（二）有压长管中的恒定流

1. 简单长管

图 6-6-7 为一简单长管示意图。由于不考虑流速水头，总水头线与测管水头线重合。又因不计局部损失，对断面 1-1 及 2-2 写能量方程可得

$$H=h_f=\lambda\frac{L}{d}\frac{v^2}{2g}=\lambda\frac{L}{d}\frac{\left(\frac{4Q}{\pi d^2}\right)^2}{2g}$$
$$=\frac{8\lambda}{\pi^2 gd^5}LQ^2$$

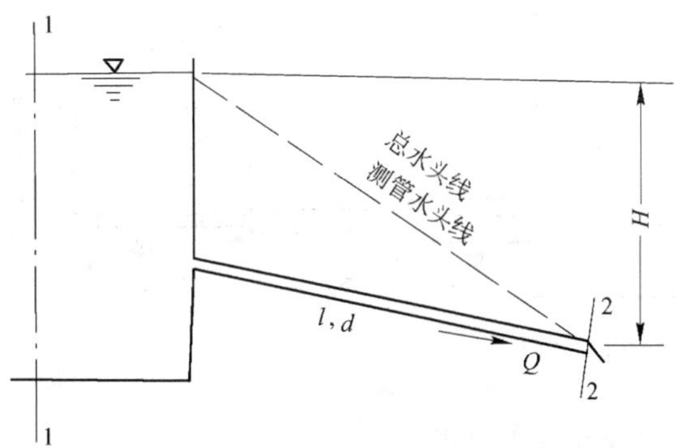

图 6-6-7

令 $S_0=\frac{8\lambda}{\pi^2 gd^5}$，称为管道的比阻，为单位流量通过单位长度管道所损失的水头。S_0 的单位为 s^2/m^6，$S_0=f(\lambda,d)$，当管壁性质已知时，S_0 仅与 d 有关，可制成表格备查。将比阻代入长管公式可得

$$H=h_f=S_0LQ^2=SQ^2 \tag{6-6-10}$$

上式即为简单长管的基本公式，它可解 Q、H、d 各类问题，式中 $S=S_0L$ 称为管道的阻抗。S

的单位为 s^2/m^5。

【例 6-6-3】 如图所示由大体积水箱供水，且水位恒定，水箱顶部压力表读数 19 600Pa，水深 $H=2m$，水平管道长 $l=100m$，直径 $d=200mm$，沿程损失系数 0.02，忽略局部损失，则管道通过流量是：

A. 83.8L/s　　B. 196.5L/s

C. 59.3L/s　　D. 47.4L/s

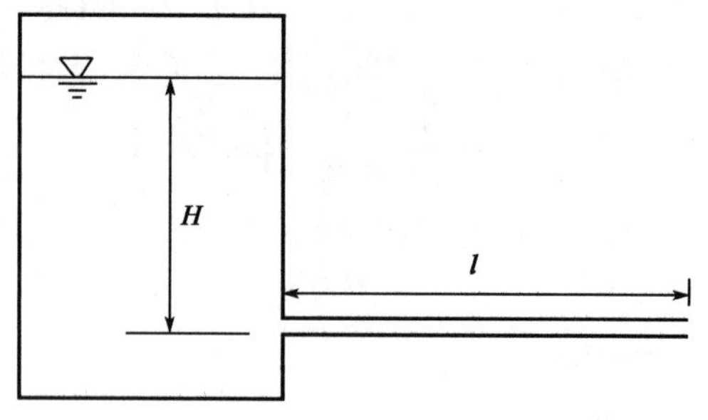

例 6-6-3 图

解 对水箱自由液面与管道出口写能量方程：

$$H+\frac{p}{\rho g}=\frac{v^2}{2g}+h_f=\frac{v^2}{2g}\left(1+\lambda\frac{L}{d}\right)$$

代入题设数据并化简：

$$2+\frac{19\ 600}{9\ 800}=\frac{v^2}{2g}\left(1+0.02\times\frac{100}{0.2}\right)$$

计算得流速 $v=2.67m/s$

流量 $Q=v\times\frac{\pi}{4}d^2=2.67\times\frac{\pi}{4}(0.2)^2=0.083\ 84m^3/s=83.84L/s$

答案：A

2. 串联管道

由不同直径的管段顺次联结而成的管道系统称为串联管系，如图 6-6-8 所示。

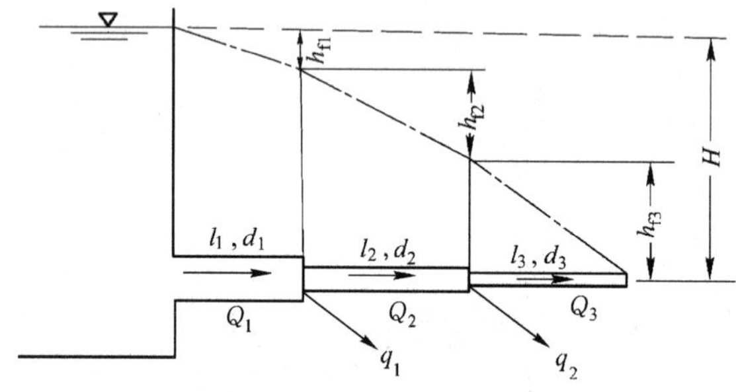

图 6-6-8

各管段流量关系，由连续性方程可得

$$Q_i=Q_{i+1}+q_i \tag{6-6-11}$$

总水头

$$H=\sum h_f=\sum_{i=1}^{n}S_{0i}L_iQ_i^2=\sum_{i=1}^{n}S_iQ^2 \tag{6-6-12}$$

将上两式联立可解 Q、H、d 等问题。

3. 并联管道

两条以上的管道在一处分流，以后又在另一处汇流，这样组成的管系称为并联管系，如图 6-6-9所示。

并联管道分流点与汇流点之间各管段水头损失皆相等，即

$$h_{f1}=h_{f2}=h_{f3}=\cdots=h_f$$

或

$$h_f=S_1Q_1^2=S_2Q_2^2=S_3Q_3^2=\cdots=S_iQ_i^2 \tag{6-6-13}$$

而每一并联管段中的流量

$$Q_i=\sqrt{\frac{h_f}{S_i}} \tag{6-6-14}$$

分流点 A 之前的总流量

$$Q=Q_1+Q_2+Q_3+\cdots+Q_n+q_A$$

或

$$Q=\sum_{i=1}^{n}Q_i+q_A \tag{6-6-15}$$

当已知总流量 Q，欲求各并联管流量时可用下式

$$Q_i=(Q-q_A)\sqrt{\frac{S_p}{S_i}} \tag{6-6-16}$$

式中，S_p 可按下式求解

$$\frac{1}{\sqrt{S_p}}=\frac{1}{\sqrt{S_1}}+\frac{1}{\sqrt{S_2}}+\cdots+\frac{1}{\sqrt{S_n}}$$

由式(6-6-13)可看出任两分路流量之比，等于该两管段阻抗反比之平方根，即

$$\frac{Q_1}{Q_2}=\sqrt{\frac{S_2}{S_1}}$$

(三)沿程均匀泄流长管

沿程均匀泄流管道如图 6-6-10 所示。

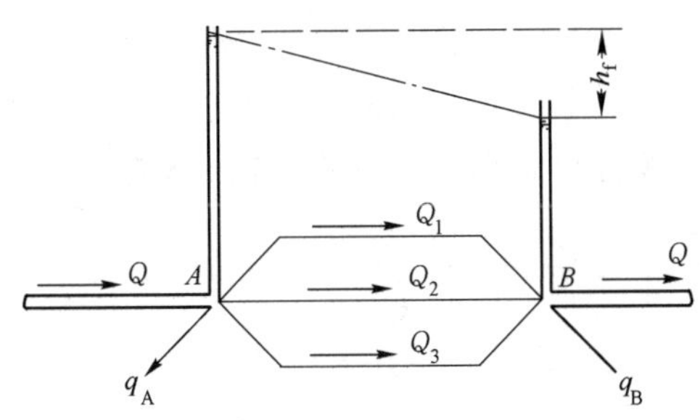

图 6-6-9

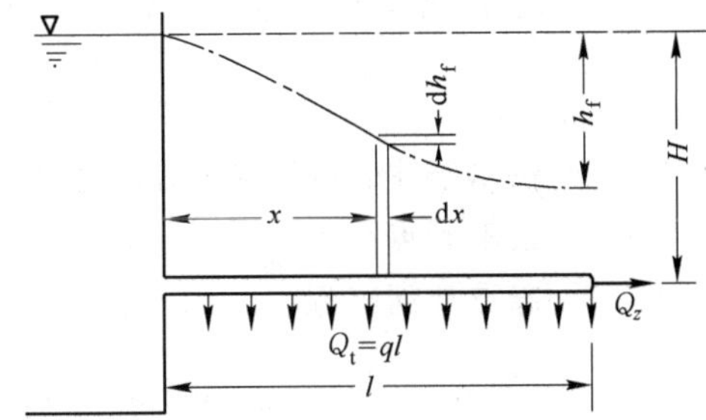

图 6-6-10

距进口 x 距离处的通过流量 Q_x 与转输流 Q_z 及途泄流量 Q_t 的关系如下

$$Q_x=Q_z+Q_t-\frac{Q_t}{L}x$$

在 dx 长度上的沿程损失为 $dh_f=SdxQ_x^2$，即 $dh_f=S_0(Q_z+Q_t-\frac{Q_t}{L}x)^2dx$，全长水头损失

$$h_f=\int_0^L dh_f=S_0L(Q_z^2+Q_zQ_t+\frac{1}{3}Q_t^2) \tag{6-6-17}$$

当转输流量 $Q_z=0$，即仅有途泄流量时，则

$$h_f = \frac{1}{3}S_0 L Q_t^2 \tag{6-6-18}$$

表明当全程均匀泄流时的水头损失，等于全部流量在末端泄出时的水头损失的$\frac{1}{3}$。式(6-6-17)还可用下列近似公式代替

$$h_f = S_0 L(Q_z + 0.55Q_t)^2 = S_0 L Q_c^2 \tag{6-6-19}$$

Q_c 称为计算流量，而

$$Q_c = Q_z + 0.55Q_t \tag{6-6-20}$$

(四)枝状管网

枝状管网是由多条管段串联而成的干管和与干管相连的多条支管组成，如图 6-6-11 所示。

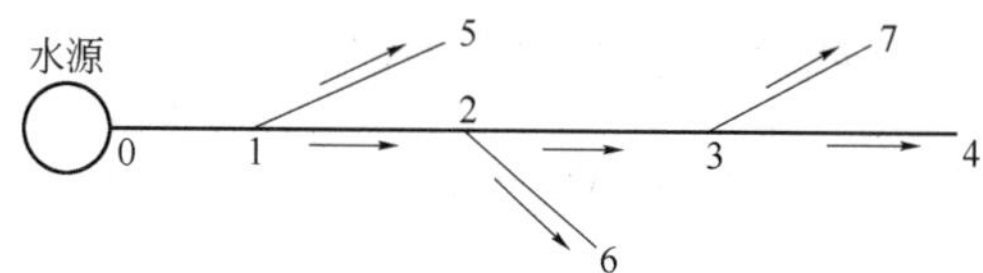

图 6-6-11

枝状管网水力计算主要是求干管起点水头及管径。计算顺序是先由经济流速求干管管径，再求干线起点水头和各节点水头，最后由各节点水头和支管流量求支管管径。经济流速可查设计手册求得，在初步计算时，可参考下列数值：管径 $d=100\sim200$mm，流速 $v=0.6\sim1.0$m/s，管径 $d=200\sim400$mm，流速 $v=1.0\sim1.4$m/s。

干管是指从水源开始到供水条件最不利点的管道，其余则为支线。供水条件最不利点一般是指距水源远、地形高、建筑物层数多、需用流量大的供水点。为克服沿途阻力和满足供水的其他要求，在水流到达最不利点之后，应保留一定的剩余水头(或称自由水头)，由图 6-6-12 可推得干管起点水塔水面距地面的总水头 H 为

$$H = \sum h_f + H_z + z - z_0 \tag{6-6-21}$$

式中：H_z——供水条件最不利点所需自由水头，由用户提出需要，对于楼房建筑可参考表 6-6-1；

z——最不利点高程；

z_0——起点地面高程。

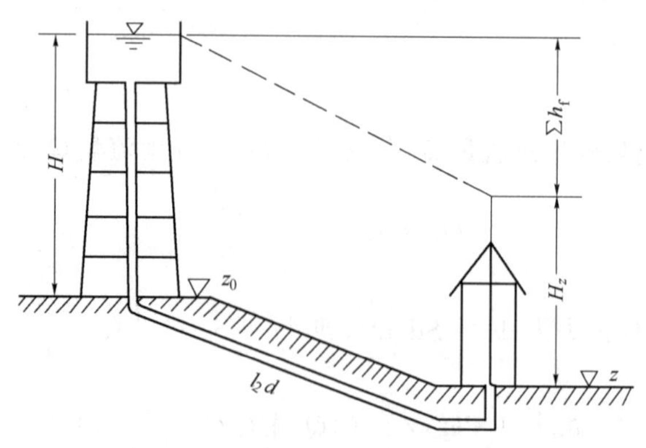

图 6-6-12

表 6-6-1

建筑物层数	1	2	3	4	5	6	7	8
自由水头(m)	10	12	16	20	24	28	32	36

（五）环状管网

环状管网是由多条管段互相连接成为闭合形状的管道系统，其优点是增加了供水的可靠性，缺点是增加了管长从而也增加了造价。将有两个环的管网示意于图 6-6-13。

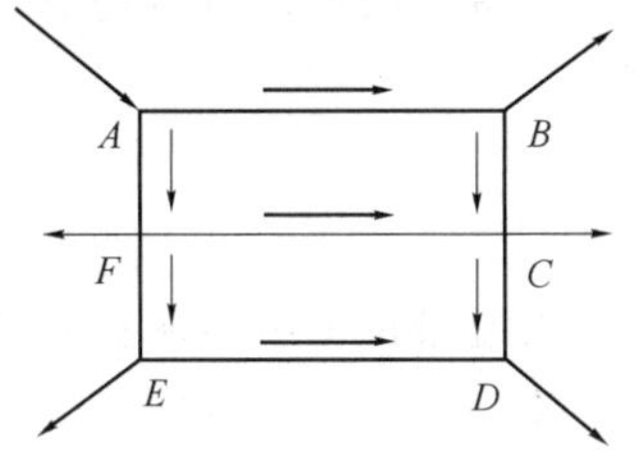

图 6-6-13

根据工程要求先进行管线布置，管长和各节点流量均是已知的。环网计算主要求各管段通过流量、管径和管段水头损失，管径当通过流量已知时可用选定的经济流速求出，与管段数相等的通过流量是待求的未知数，管段数、节点数与环数有下列关系

$$n_p = n_j + n_c - 1 \tag{6-6-22}$$

式中：n_p——管段总数；

n_j——节点数；

n_c——环数。

如图 6-6-13 所示两个环网的管段数

$$n_p = 6 + 2 - 1 = 7$$

下面探讨一下是否能列 n_p 个方程求解 n_p 个未知流量。由环网特性，必须满足下列两个水力计算原则。

(1)节点流量的代数和为零，即

$$\sum Q_{节点} = 0 \tag{6-6-23}$$

因为流入某一节点的流量必须等于同时流出该节点的流量(连续性要求)。如以流入为正流出为负，则节点流量正负相消代数和为零。

(2)沿任一闭合环路水头损失的代数和为零，即

$$\sum h_{f沿环} = 0 \tag{6-6-24}$$

任一闭合环路均可视为分流点与汇流点两边的并联管道，因此沿分流点两个方向至汇流点的水头损失应相等，如以顺时针方向为正，逆时针方向为负，则沿环一周水头损失代数和为零。就以图 6-6-13 中的上一环为例有

$$h_{fABC} - h_{fAFC} = 0$$

根据水力计算第一原则可列出$(n_j - 1)$个方程，根据第二原则可列出 n_c 个方程，共可列出 $n_j + n_c - 1 = n_p$ 个方程，方程数与管段数相等，正好求解 n_p 个未知数。但当环数增多，方程个数很多时手工计算工作量很大，目前多用电脑辅助计算。对于环数较少的简单环网，可用哈代-克罗斯(Hardy-Cross)逐步渐近法求解较好，该法实质上是解环方程方法，其计算步骤如下。

(1)初步拟定水流方向，并按 $\sum Q_{节} = 0$ 分配各管段通过流量。

(2)按初分流量和所选经济流速求管径 d，$d = \sqrt{\dfrac{4Q}{\pi v}}$，选接近的标准直径。

(3)根据 d、n 或 λ 求比阻 S_0，再求出各段水头损失 $h_f=S_0LQ^2=SQ^2$，S 为阻抗。

(4)求每一环的水头损失代数和 $\sum h_{沿环}$，视其是否满足 $\sum h_{沿环}=0$，如不满足，则其值 $\sum h_{沿环}=\Delta h$ 为闭合差；然后看 $|\Delta h|$ 是否小于允许的误差 ε，如 $|\Delta h|>\varepsilon$，则需校正初步分配的流量。

(5)求各环的校正流量。

设各环的校正流量为 ΔQ，则

$$\Delta Q=-\frac{\sum h_f}{2\sum\dfrac{h_f}{Q}}=\frac{-\Delta h}{2\sum\dfrac{h_f}{Q}} \tag{6-6-25}$$

当流量校正后需从步骤(3)开始重复计算，直到每一环的闭合差 Δh 均趋于零或小于允许的误差。

(六)有压管路中的水击(水锤)

1.水击现象

在有压管道中，由于某种原因(如迅速关闭或开启阀门、水泵机组突然停机等)使得管中水流速度发生突然变化，从而引起管内压强急剧升高和降低的交替变化及水体、管壁压缩与膨胀的交替变化，并以波的形式在管中往返传播的现象称为水击(或水锤)，因其声音犹如用锤锤击管道的声音一样。水击可能导致强烈的振动、噪声和气穴，有时甚至引起管道的变形、爆裂或阀门的损坏。因此水击问题，影响工程的安全与经济，应给予足够的重视。

水击现象产生的外因是边界条件的突然变化，内因则是水流运动的惯性和水体的压缩性以及管壁的弹性。

2.水击波的发展过程

水击波的发展过程如图 6-6-14 所示，约为四个过程，现以关闭阀门水击为例加以说明。

(1)升压波向上游传播

如图 6-6-14a)所示，在 $0<t<\frac{L}{c}$ 时间段，水击压力升高水头 $\Delta H=\frac{\Delta p}{\gamma}$，以很高波速 c(钢管中约 1 000m/s)从阀门处开始逆流而上，在 $t=\frac{L}{c}$ 时传到水箱处。

(2)降压反射波向下游传播

如图 6-6-14c)所示，当 $t=\frac{L}{c}$ 时，升压波到达水箱，由于水箱水位不变，管中压力大于水箱水位，使高压水向水箱流去产生一反向流速 $\boldsymbol{v}$，即产生一降压反射波使管中压力恢复正常；在 $\frac{2L}{c}<t<\frac{3L}{c}$ 时段一直持续着；当 $t=\frac{2L}{c}$ 时到达阀门。

(3)降压波向上游传播

如图 6-6-14e)所示，当 $t=\frac{2L}{c}$ 时，降压反射波到达阀门后，因惯性使阀门处水流反向流动，在阀门处形成一降压波向上游传播；在 $\frac{2L}{c}<t<\frac{3L}{c}$ 时段一直持续着；当 $t=\frac{3L}{c}$ 时，降压波到达水箱，并且压力低于水箱中水位，这使水箱中水向阀门流动，流速由零变为 $\boldsymbol{v}$，这就开始了第四过程。

(4)升压反射波向下游传播

如图 6-6-14g)所示，在 $\frac{3L}{c}<t<\frac{4L}{c}$ 过程中，升压反射波一直向阀门传播，反射波传到处，压

强即由负压恢复到正常；在 $t=\frac{4L}{c}$，传到了阀门处，完成了一个传播周期，此后又重复上述过程，直到能量消耗殆尽为止。

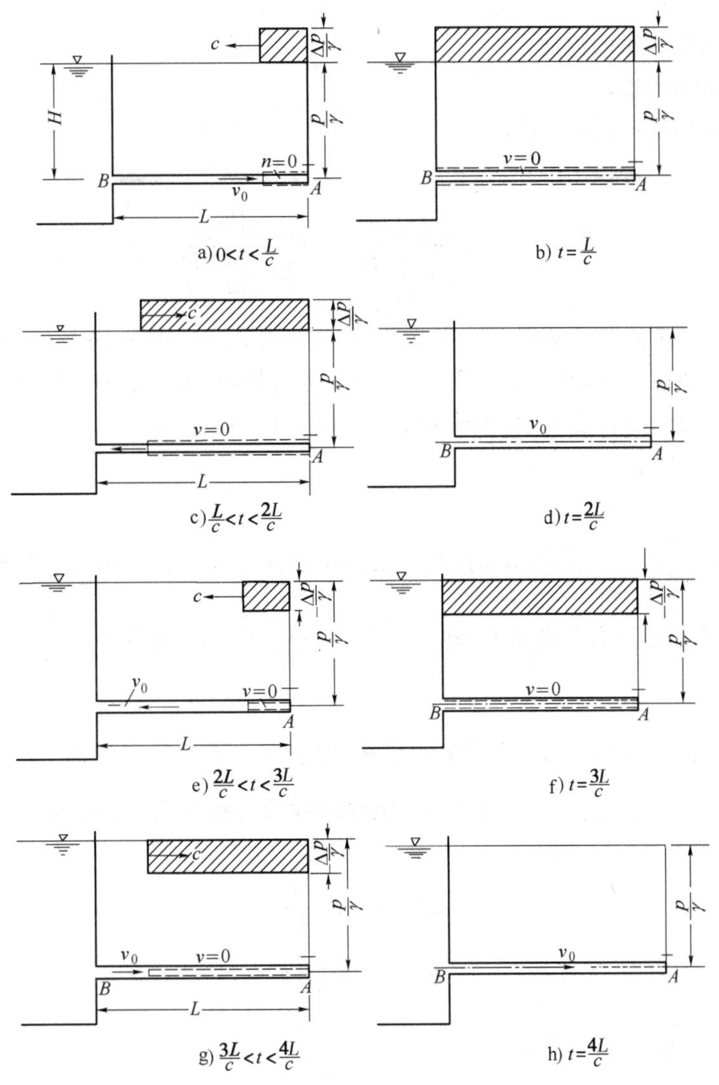

图 6-6-14

水击波往返传播一次的时间称为相长，$\frac{2L}{c}$为半周期，周期为$\frac{4L}{c}$。

3. 水击的分类和直接水击压强的计算

水击按关闭阀门时间 T_s 与相长$\frac{2L}{c}$比较可以分为直接水击和间接水击两种。

(1)直接水击

$T_s<\frac{2L}{c}$，此时降压反射波尚未回到阀门处，水击压力升高已经完成，所以未受到降压的抵消作用，因此直接水击压力升高大，最为危险，须尽量避免和防止。直接水击压力升高计算式已于 1898 年被儒柯夫斯基导出，即

$$\Delta p = \rho c v_0 \tag{6-6-26}$$

或以水头表示

$$\Delta H = \frac{c v_0}{g} \tag{6-6-27}$$

式中：v_0——阀门全开时的流速；

g——重力加速度；

c——水击传播速度(m/s)。

而

$$c = \frac{c_0}{\sqrt{1+\frac{K}{E}\frac{D}{\delta}}} = \frac{1\ 435}{\sqrt{1+\frac{K}{E}\frac{D}{\delta}}} \tag{6-6-28}$$

式中：c_0——液体中声波传播速度，在1～25个大气压时，$c_0 = 1\ 435\text{m/s}$；

K——水的弹性模量，在水温10℃，1个标准大气压时，$K = 2.10\times10^5\text{N/cm}^2$；

E——管壁材料的弹性模量，钢管的$E = 2.06\times10^7\text{N/cm}^2$；

D——管内直径；

δ——壁厚。

对于一般钢管$\frac{D}{\delta}\approx100$，$\frac{K}{E}\approx0.01$，代入式(6-6-27)，得$c\approx1\ 000\text{m/s}$。如管内关阀前流速$v_0 = 1\text{m/s}$，则直接水击压力升高水头$\Delta H = \frac{c v_0}{g} = \frac{1\ 000\times1}{9.8} = 102\text{mH}_2\text{O}$。

(2)间接水击

$T_\text{S}\geqslant\frac{2L}{c}$，此时降压反射波已回到阀门处，抵消了部分压力升高值，此种水击称间接水击，间接水击压力小于直接水击。间接水击压力的精确计算，涉及水击波的叠加，较为复杂，但可按下式作近似的估算

$$\Delta p = \rho c v_0 \frac{T}{T_\text{S}} \tag{6-6-29}$$

$$\Delta H = \frac{c v_0}{g}\frac{T}{T_\text{S}} \tag{6-6-30}$$

式中：T——水击波相长，$T = \frac{2L}{c}$；

T_S——阀门关闭的时间；

其余符号意义同前。

4.水击危害的预防

一般来说，可从延长关闭阀门时间，缩短水击波传播长度，减小管内流速，以及在管路上设置减压、缓冲装置等方面着手。

【例6-6-4】 主干管在A、B间是由两条支管组成的一个并联管路，两支管的长度和管径分别为$l_1 = 1800\text{m}$，$d_1 = 150\text{mm}$，$l_2 = 3000\text{m}$，$d_2 = 200\text{mm}$，两支管的沿程阻力系数λ均为0.01，若主干管流量$Q = 39\text{L/s}$，则两支管流量分别为：

A. $Q_1 = 12\text{L/s}$，$Q_2 = 27\text{L/s}$　　B. $Q_1 = 15\text{L/s}$，$Q_2 = 24\text{L/s}$

C. $Q_1 = 24\text{L/s}$，$Q_2 = 15\text{L/s}$　　D. $Q_1 = 27\text{L/s}$，$Q_2 = 12\text{L/s}$

解　$Q_1 + Q_2 = 39\text{L/s}$

$$\frac{Q_1}{Q_2}=\sqrt{\frac{S_2}{S_1}}=\sqrt{\frac{8\lambda L_2}{\pi^2 g d_2^5}\Big/\frac{8\lambda L_1}{\pi^2 g d_1^5}}=\sqrt{\frac{L_2\cdot d_1^5}{L_1\cdot d_2^5}}=\sqrt{\frac{3000}{1800}\times\left(\frac{0.15}{0.20}\right)^5}=0.629$$

即 $0.629Q_2+Q_2=39\text{L/s}$，得 $Q_2=24\text{L/s}$，$Q_1=15\text{L/s}$

答案：B

习　题

6-6-1　环状管网水力计算的原则是(　　)。

A. 各节点的流量与各管段流量代数和为零，水头损失相等

B. 各管段水头损失代数和为零，流量相等

C. 流入为正、流出为负，每一节点流量的代数和为零；顺时针为正，逆时针为负，沿环一周水头损失的代数和为零

D. 其他

6-6-2　水头与直径均相同的圆柱形外管嘴和小孔口，前者的通过流量是后者的(　　)倍，原因是(　　)。

A. 1.75，前者收缩断面处有真空存在

B. 0.75，后者的阻力比前者小

C. 1.82，前者过流面积大

D. 1.32，前者收缩断面处有真空存在

6-6-3　某常水头薄壁小孔口的水头 $H_0=5\text{m}$，孔口直径 $d=10\text{mm}$，流量系数 $\mu=0.62$，该小孔口的出流量 Q 为(　　)。

A. 0.61L/s　　　　B. $7.82\times10^{-4}\text{m}^3/\text{s}$

C. 0.58L/s　　　　D. $4.82\times10^{-4}\text{m}^3/\text{s}$

第七节　明渠恒定流

一、明渠均匀流特性及其发生条件

明渠均匀流是水深、断面平均流速、断面流速分布均沿流程不变的具有自由液面的明渠流，如图6-7-1所示。

由于河底坡度线与水面线及水力坡度线三条线平行，所以三线的坡度相等，即

$$J=J_z=i \tag{6-7-1}$$

式中：J——水力坡度，$J=\dfrac{h_f}{L}$；

J_z——水面坡度，$J_z=\dfrac{(z_1+h_1)-(z_2+h_2)}{L}$；

i——河底坡度，$i=\dfrac{z_1-z_2}{L}$，$i=\sin\theta$，当 $\theta<6°$

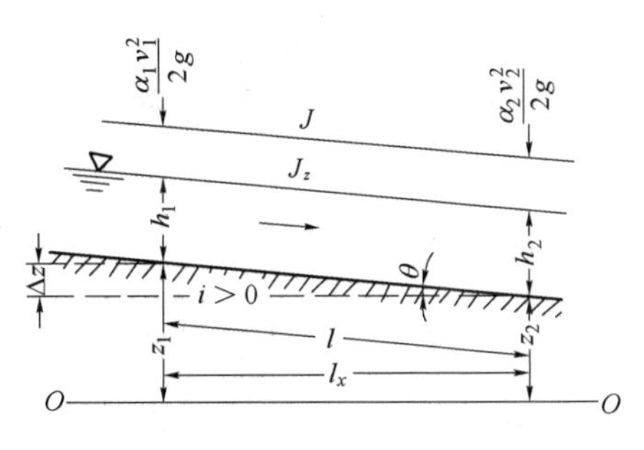

图　6-7-1

时，$\sin\theta \approx \tan\theta, i=\dfrac{\Delta z}{Lx}$。

水力坡度＝水面坡度＝河底坡度，是明渠均匀流的特性。产生明渠均匀流必须满足以下这些条件：渠中流量保持不变；渠道为长直棱柱体；顺坡渠道（即河底高程沿水流方向降低）；渠壁粗糙系数沿程不变，没有局部损失，以及底坡不变、断面形状与面积不变等。所以均匀流多在人工明渠中产生，天然河流的顺直渠段，可近似作为均匀流来处理。

二、明渠均匀流基本公式及断面水力要素

明渠流断面尺寸大，流速快，壁面粗糙，一般均属于大雷诺数的水力粗糙区，其水力计算的基本公式用谢才公式

$$v = C\sqrt{RJ}$$

但在均匀流时由明渠均匀流特性知 $J=i$，可用渠底坡度 i 代替 J，应用更加方便，此时

$$\left.\begin{aligned} v &= C\sqrt{Ri} \\ Q &= CA\sqrt{Ri} = K\sqrt{i} \\ K &= CA\sqrt{R} \end{aligned}\right\} \tag{6-7-2}$$

式中，K 称为流量模数，单位为 m^3/s，与流量同。为了使用谢才公式，必须配合断面水力要素的计算公式和谢才系数 C 的计算公式，例如前面介绍的 $C=\dfrac{1}{n}R^{\frac{1}{6}}$ 的曼宁公式。

断面水力要素的计算公式常用的有矩形、梯形和未充满的圆形断面以及复式断面几种，如图 6-7-2 所示，现分别介绍。

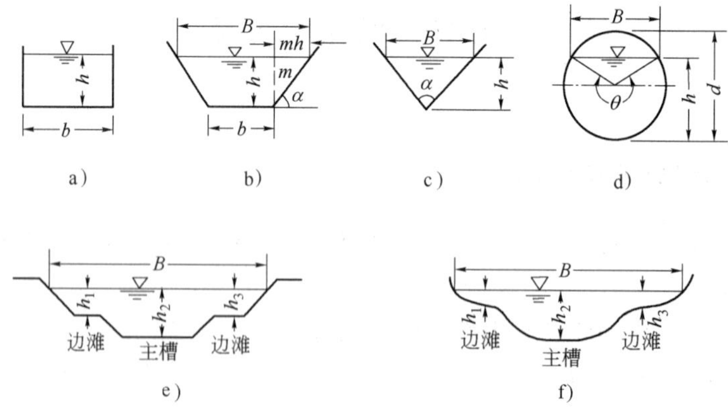

图 6-7-2

（一）矩形断面水力要素

$$\left.\begin{aligned} A &= bh \\ \chi &= b + 2h \\ R &= \frac{A}{\chi} \end{aligned}\right\} \tag{6-7-3}$$

(二)梯形断面水力要素

$$\left.\begin{aligned} A &= (b+mh)h \\ \chi &= b+2h\sqrt{1+m^2} \\ R &= \frac{A}{\chi} \\ B &= b+2mh \end{aligned}\right\} \tag{6-7-4}$$

上式中 $m=\cot\alpha$,称为边坡系数,α 为边坡角,见图 6-7-2b),当 $\alpha=90°$时,$m=0$,梯形变为矩形,式(6-7-3)是式(6-7-4)的一个特例。

【例 6-7-1】 一梯形断面明渠,水力半径 $R=1\text{m}$,底坡 $i=0.0008$,粗糙系数 $n=0.02$,则输水流速度为:

A. 1m/s　　B. 1.4m/s　　C. 2.2m/s　　D. 0.84m/s

解 由明渠均匀流谢才公式知流速 $v=C\sqrt{Ri}$,$C=\frac{1}{n}R^{\frac{1}{6}}$

代入题设数据,得:$C=\frac{1}{0.02}(1)^{\frac{1}{6}}=50\sqrt{\text{m}}/\text{s}$

流速 $v=50\sqrt{1\times0.0008}=1.41\text{m/s}$

答案:B

(三)未充满的圆形断面水力要素

$$\left.\begin{aligned} A &= \frac{d^2}{8}(\theta-\sin\theta) \\ \chi &= \frac{d}{2}\theta \\ R &= \frac{d}{4}\left(1-\frac{\sin\theta}{\theta}\right) \\ B &= d\sin\frac{\theta}{2} \end{aligned}\right\} \tag{6-7-5}$$

上式中 θ 为圆心角,与管内液体的充满度$\frac{h}{d}$有关,h 为充水深度,见图 6-7-2d)。因此

$$\frac{h}{d}=\sin^2\frac{\theta}{4} \tag{6-7-6}$$

当已知充满度 h/d 后可用上式求出 θ,再由直径 d 和 θ 用式(6-7-5)求各种水力要素。

(四)复式断面水力要素

可将其分解为几个简单的几何图形叠加求解,注意湿周只计入固体与液体接触的边长,液体与液体接触部分不计入。断面各部分水力坡度 J 不变,则

$$Q=(K_1+K_2+\cdots)\sqrt{J}$$

【例 6-7-2】 两条明渠过水断面面积相等,断面形状分别为(1)方形,边长为 a;(2)矩形,底边宽为 $2a$,水深为 $0.5a$,它们的底坡与粗糙系数相同,则两者的均匀流流量关系式为:

A. $Q_1>Q_2$　　B. $Q_1=Q_2$　　C. $Q_1<Q_2$　　D. 不能确定

解 由明渠均匀流谢才-曼宁公式 $Q=\frac{1}{n}R^{\frac{2}{3}}i^{\frac{1}{2}}A$ 可知:在题设条件下面积 A,粗糙系数 n,底坡 i 均相同,则流量 Q 的大小取决于水力半径 R 的大小。对于方形断面,其水力半径 $R_1=$

$\frac{a^2}{3a}=\frac{a}{3}$，对于矩形断面，其水力半径为 $R_2=\frac{2a\times0.5a}{2a+2\times0.5a}=\frac{a^2}{3a}=\frac{a}{3}$，即 $R_1=R_2$。故 $Q_1=Q_2$。

答案：B

三、明渠的水力最佳断面和允许流速

（一）水力最佳断面

当过水断面积 A、粗糙系数 n、底坡 i 一定时，通过流量 Q 或过水能力最大时的断面形状，称为水力最佳断面。由谢才公式和曼宁公式可得

$$Q=CA\sqrt{Ri}=\frac{1}{n}R^{1/6}AR^{1/2}i^{1/2}=\frac{1}{n}(\frac{A}{\chi})^{2/3}Ai^{1/2}=\frac{1}{n}R^{2/3}Ai^{1/2}$$

即

$$Q=\frac{i^{1/2}}{n}A^{5/3}\chi^{-2/3} \tag{6-7-7}$$

由式(6-7-7)可知，当 A、n、i 一定时，湿周 χ 最小，Q 才最大，故圆形是最佳的形状。但在明渠中，圆形施工不便，往往用梯形。梯形的边坡系数取决于土壤的性质，当边坡系数 m 按土壤性质已确定时，梯形的水力最佳断面条件，可由 $\frac{\mathrm{d}\chi}{\mathrm{d}h}=0$ 求 χ 极小值的办法求出。

$$\chi=\frac{A}{h}-mh+2h\sqrt{1+m^2}$$

$$\frac{\mathrm{d}\chi}{\mathrm{d}h}=-\frac{A}{h^2}-m+2\sqrt{1+m^2}=0$$

将 $A=(b+mh)h$ 代入上式并整理后可得

$$\beta=\frac{b}{h}=2(\sqrt{1+m^2}-m) \tag{6-7-8}$$

式中，$\beta=\frac{b}{h}$ 为水力最佳宽深比。将式(6-7-8)依次代入 A 及 χ 公式，最后求得水力最佳的水力半径为

$$R=\frac{h}{2} \tag{6-7-9}$$

对于矩形断面 $m=0$，代入式(6-7-8)得水力最佳矩形断面宽深比为 $\beta=2$，即 $b=2h$ 的扁矩形。对于小型土渠，工程造价主要取决于土方量，因此水力最佳断面，可能是经济实用的。对于大型渠道，按水力最佳梯形决定的断面，往往是太过窄而深，深挖高填式施工，未必是经济合理的，就不一定采用水力最佳断面。

（二）明渠的允许流速

明渠中流速过大会引起渠道的冲刷，过小又会导致水中悬浮泥沙在渠中淤积，且易使河滩上滋生杂草，从而影响渠道的输水能力。因此，在设计渠道时，应使其断面平均流速 v 在允许范围内，即

$$v_{\max}>v>v_{\min}$$

式中：$v_{\max}$——渠道最大不冲刷流速或最大允许流速；

$v_{\min}$——渠道最小不淤积流速或最小允许流速。

最大允许流速取决于渠道土壤或加固材料性质，最小允许流速取决于悬浮泥沙颗粒大小，

可查有关手册或用经验公式计算。

四、明渠均匀流水力计算的几类问题

(一)已知 b、h、m、n、i 要求渠道的通过流量 Q

这类问题往往是对已建成渠道进行的校核验算,可直接代入谢才公式求解。

(二)已知 Q、b、h、m、i,求粗糙系数 n

可联合用谢才、曼宁两式解出 n

$$n=\frac{A}{Q}R^{2/3}i^{1/2}$$

直接代入数据即可。

(三)已知 Q、b、h、m、n,设计渠道底坡 i

先求出流量模数 $K=AC\sqrt{R}$,之后再代入谢才公式求底坡 $i=\frac{Q^2}{K^2}$,或求出流速再用 $i=\frac{v^2}{C^2R}$求底坡。在实际工程中,由此计算而得的底坡数值,只是一个参考值,还要综合考虑地形、地质、施工等因素后才能确定。

(四)已知 Q、m、n、i,设计渠道过水断面的尺寸 b 和 h

此时,在基本公式中出现两个未知数,解答不确定。为了使问题有唯一确定的解,须结合工程要求和经济条件,先定出其中的一个 b 或 h 值,或是宽深比 β 值,再行设计,现分述如下。

1. 设定渠道底宽 b,求均匀流水深 h_0

首先由已知的流量 Q 及底坡 i,算出所设计的渠道断面应具有的流量模数 $K_0=\frac{Q}{\sqrt{i}}$;然后根据 $K=AC\sqrt{R}=(b+mh)h\frac{1}{n}\left[\frac{(b+mh)h}{b+2h\sqrt{1+m^2}}\right]^{2/3}=f(h)$公式,用试算法或图解法求解。以试算为例,就要多次设定一系列的 h,求对应的 K,当此 K 值恰好等于 K_0 时,此时的 h 就是所要求的水深 h_0。如以所设定的一系列的水深 h 为纵标,以所对应的 K 作为横标,可绘出 $K=f(h)$曲线;再以 $K_0=\frac{Q}{\sqrt{i}}$为横坐标,作垂线交 $K=f(h)$曲线于一点,由交点引水平线截取纵坐标于一点,此点的 h 值即为所求的均匀流水深 h_0。

2. 设定渠道水深 h_0,求相应的渠道底宽 b

这种情况与上面的相似,可用试算法或图解法求解。设定一系列 b,求对应的 K,作出 $K=f(b)$曲线;再求出 $K_0=\frac{Q}{\sqrt{i}}$,在 $K=f(b)$曲线上找出对应于此 K_0 的 b 值,即为所求的底宽 b。

3. 设定渠道宽深比 β,求相应的 h_0 和 b 值

由于补充了一个条件,设定了 β,使 h_0 和 b 转变成互相依赖的一个变量,使方程有确定的解。按上面介绍的方法,求得 h_0 或 b 后,即可由 $\beta=\frac{b}{h_0}$求得另一个。

4. 根据允许流速求断面尺寸

先求面积 $A=\frac{Q}{v_{\max}}$,再求水力半径 $R=\left(\frac{nv_{\max}}{\sqrt{i}}\right)^{3/2}$。

五、圆形断面无压排水管水力计算

现行《室外排水设计规范》(GB 50014—2006)(2016 年版)规定，雨水管道与合流管道，可按满流设计。而污水管道应按不满流设计，其最大设计充满度 $\alpha=\frac{h}{d}$ 按表 6-7-1 规定采用。

最大设计充满度 表 6-7-1

管径 d(mm)	最大设计充满度 $\alpha\left(\frac{h}{d}\right)$	管径 d(mm)	最大设计充满度 $\alpha\left(\frac{h}{d}\right)$
150～300	0.60	500～900	0.75
350～450	0.70	≥1 000	0.80

在进行排水管水力计算时，首先确定其充满度 $\alpha=\frac{h}{d}$ 值，然后由 $\frac{h}{d}=\sin^2\frac{\theta}{4}$，解出圆心角 θ，再由 d 及 θ 用式(6-7-5)求出水力要素，最后由谢才公式求解所要解的问题。

排水管水力计算问题的类型，与明渠均匀流相似，也是求流量 Q、粗糙系数 n、底坡 i 和管径 d 或水深 h。现举例说明。

【例 6-7-3】 某圆形污水管管径 $d=600$mm，管壁粗糙系数 $n=0.014$，管道底坡 $i=0.0024$，求最大设计充满度时的流速和流量。

解 由表 6-7-1 查出当 $d=600$ 时最大设计充满度 $\alpha=\frac{h}{d}=0.75$，代入式(6-7-6)，解出

$$\theta=\frac{4}{3}\pi$$

由式(6-7-5)可得

面积 $$A=\frac{d^2}{8}(\theta-\sin\theta)=\frac{0.6^2}{8}\times\left(\frac{4}{3}\pi-\sin\frac{4}{3}\pi\right)=0.2275\text{m}^2$$

湿周 $$\chi=\frac{d}{2}\theta=\frac{0.6}{2}\times\frac{4}{3}\pi=1.2566\text{m}$$

水力半径 $$R=\frac{A}{\chi}=\frac{0.2275}{1.2566}=0.1810\text{m}$$

谢才系数 $$C=\frac{1}{n}R^{\frac{1}{6}}=\frac{1}{0.014}\times(0.181)^{\frac{1}{6}}=53.722\ \sqrt{\text{m}}/\text{s}$$

流速 $$v=C\sqrt{Ri}=53.722\times\sqrt{0.181\times0.0024}=1.12\text{m/s}$$

流量 $$Q=vA=1.12\times0.2275=0.2548\text{m}^3/\text{s}$$

在实际工作中，为了简便，还制定了各种图表，载于各种手册中，此处就省略了。

排水管水力最优充满度为 $h/d=0.95$，$\theta=308°$，此时流量最大；当 $h/d=0.81$ 时，流速最快。但这两个充满度均大于最大设计充满度，不宜作为设计充满度采用。

六、明渠非均匀流基本概念

(一)明渠非均匀流发生的条件

无论是天然河流或人工渠道，由于地形、地质情况复杂多变，河槽本身的边界条件是不断变化的，而且在河渠上往往有各种形式的水工建筑物(如闸、坝、跌水、桥、涵等)。在河槽边界发生变化的地方和有水工建筑物的地方，破坏了均匀流形成的条件，就会产生非均匀流的水流现象。例如闸、坝挡水后使上游水位壅高，水深增加，流速变小；而在陡坡或跌水的上游则水位

降低，水深逐渐减小，流速变大。

对非均匀流现象进行研究具有重要的实际意义，如计算壅水曲线，可正确估计闸、坝壅水对上游淹没影响的范围；对水跃现象的研究，有助于正确设计下游消能防冲措施。

（二）明渠非均流的特点和几类现象

明渠非均匀流的特点是水深、流速不断地沿程变化，而在此变化中又可分为渐变流和急变流。

属于渐变流的有以下两类水力现象：

1.壅水现象

如在河流或渠道中的水流遇到闸、坝等挡水建筑物时，上游水位壅高，水深沿流增加，流速逐渐减少，这种现象称为壅水现象，其水面曲线称为壅水曲线，如图 6-7-3 所示。

2.降水现象

如在河底坡度突然变陡的陡坡上游或河底高程突然下降的跌水上游，水深沿流不断减小，水面高程逐渐下降的现象称为降水现象，其水面曲线，如图 6-7-4 所示。

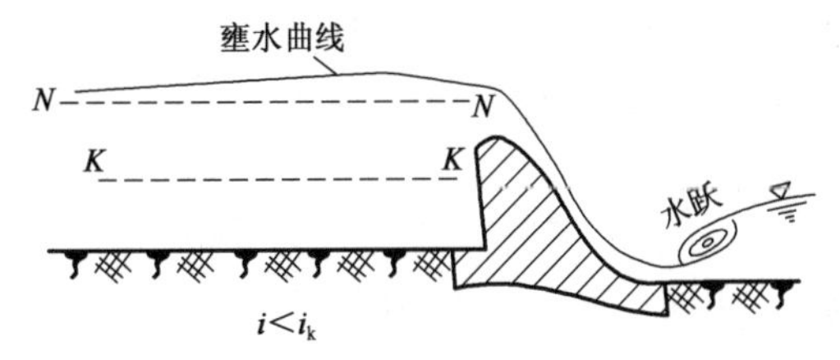

图 6-7-3 壅水曲线

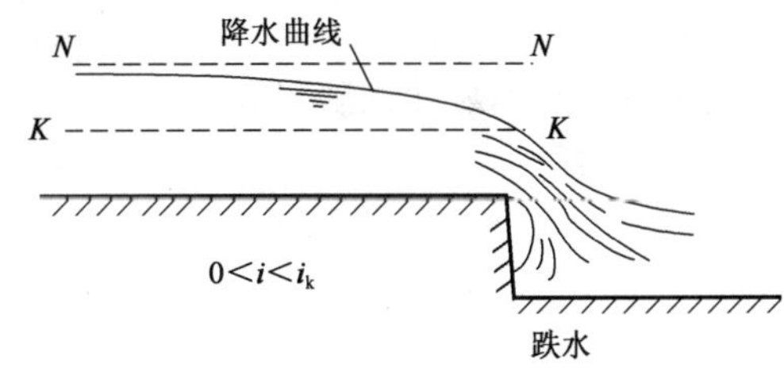

图 6-7-4 降水曲线与跌水

属于急变流的有以下两类水力现象：

1.水跃现象

当水流由水深小、流速大的急流状态急剧转变为水深大、流速小的缓流时，将发生强烈的旋滚和消耗巨大的能量，这就是水跃现象，如图 6-7-5 所示。

图 6-7-5 水跃现象

2.跌水现象

在底坡突然下降或由缓坡变陡处，水面骤然下降，流速剧增的现象称为跌水现象，如图 6-7-4 所示。

（三）明渠非均匀流的流态（急流、缓流、临界流）

本段所讨论的是以微弱扰动波在水中传播的速度为判别标准的一种流动分类。这种流态的划分，对明渠非均匀流运动规律的分析，很有帮助。

1.明渠中弱扰动波传播速度

由于明渠的自由液面没有固体边界的限制，受扰动后可改变水面标高以适应扰动，因而能在水面形成一微微隆起的波（简称微幅波），此波形成后将以某一速度向四周传播，称为微幅波的传播波速 c，它的快慢与水流深度有关。现在我们对矩形断面渠道中静止水中的波速 c 的计算方法进行分析（见图 6-7-6）。

将平板 N 向左拨动到 N' 时，水面将产生一隆起的微幅波，并以波速 c 向左传播。设波高 Δh 很小，与水深相比可以忽略不计，波移动时的摩擦阻力也可忽略不计，呈非恒定流。现取移动坐标，以速度 c 与波一起向左移动，此时波就固定不动，而渠中的水则有了向右的速度 c，呈恒定流。由伯努利方程可知

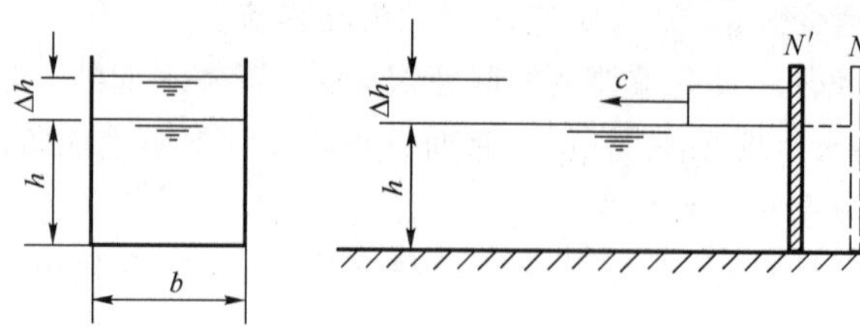

图 6-7-6　微幅波的传播

$$h+\frac{c^2}{2g}=常数$$

另一方面，对单位宽度而言，连续性方程可写成

$$ch=常数$$

将上两式微分后为

$$\begin{cases}\mathrm{d}h+\dfrac{c\mathrm{d}c}{g}=0\\ c\mathrm{d}h+h\mathrm{d}c=0\end{cases}$$

将上述方程组联立求解，得

$$\frac{c^2\mathrm{d}c}{g}-h\mathrm{d}c=0$$

$$\left(\frac{c^2}{g}-h\right)\mathrm{d}c=0$$

$$\frac{c^2}{g}=h$$

故

$$c=\pm\sqrt{gh}\tag{6-7-10}$$

对梯形等棱柱形断面，可用平均水深 $\bar{h}=\dfrac{A}{B}$ 代入，式中 A 为过水断面面积，B 为水面宽度，则上式变为

$$c=\pm\sqrt{g\bar{h}}$$

如果在明渠流中，水流流速为 v，则波的传递速度与水流流速叠加后即为波的实际传播速度 c'，即

$$c'=v\pm\sqrt{g\bar{h}}$$

当微波顺水流方向传播时，上式右端第二项取正号；逆水流方向传播时，取负号。

2. 急流、缓流、临界流

我们以波速 c 与流速 v 的相互关系来区分明渠中水流的缓急。

当明渠中水流流速较大而波速较小，满足不等式 $v>c$ 或 $v>\sqrt{g\bar{h}}$ 时，则微幅波速与流速叠加后的波速为正值，说明干扰只能顺水流方向向下游传播，不能逆水流方向朝上游传播，这种流动称为急流。

当明渠中水流流速较小而波速较大，满足不等式 $v<c$ 或 $v<\sqrt{g\bar{h}}$ 时，则叠加后的波速值可能有正有负。说明干扰既能向下游传播，也能向上游传播，这种流动称为缓流。

当明渠中水流流速 v 正好等于波速 c 时，即满足等式 $v=c$ 时，干扰向上游传播的速度为零，正是急流与缓流的分界，称为临界流。此时的水流流速称为临界流速 $v_c=\sqrt{g\bar{h}}$，可用来判别流态的缓急。$v>v_c$ 为急流，$v<v_c$ 为缓流，$v=v_c$ 为临界流。

3.弗劳德数

如果把流态判别式的等号两边都除以 $\sqrt{gh}$ 可得

$$\left.\begin{array}{ll}\dfrac{v}{\sqrt{gh}}>1 & \text{急流}\\[2ex] \dfrac{v}{\sqrt{gh}}=1 & \text{临界流}\\[2ex] \dfrac{v}{\sqrt{gh}}<1 & \text{缓流}\end{array}\right\} \tag{6-7-11}$$

等号左边为无量纲数，称为弗劳德数，以符号 Fr 表示，Fr 可作为判断流态缓急的判别准则。

$$\left.\begin{array}{ll}\mathrm{Fr}>1 & \text{急流}\\ \mathrm{Fr}=1 & \text{临界流}\\ \mathrm{Fr}<1 & \text{缓流}\end{array}\right\} \tag{6-7-12}$$

4.临界水深和临界底坡

为了区别渠中流态的缓、急，还可以运用临界水深和临界底坡的概念。

(1)临界水深 h_k 是断面比能$(h+\frac{\alpha v^2}{2g})$最小时的水深，对矩形断面可用下式计算

$$h_k=\sqrt[3]{\frac{\alpha q^2}{g}} \tag{6-7-13}$$

式中，q 为单宽流量；α 为动能改正系数，一般取 1～1.1。

设明渠中产生均匀流的水深为正常水深 h_0，则有

$$\left.\begin{array}{ll}h_0<h_k & \text{急流}\\ h_0=h_k & \text{临界流}\\ h_0>h_k & \text{缓流}\end{array}\right\} \tag{6-7-14}$$

(2)临界底坡 i_k，当通过一定流量时的正常水深恰好等于临界水深，此时的底坡称为临界底坡。临界底坡可用下式计算

$$i_k=\frac{Q^2}{K_k^2} \tag{6-7-15}$$

式中，Q 为通过流量；K_k 为临界流时的流量模数，$K_k=C_kA_k\sqrt{R_k}$。

设明渠中形成均匀流时的底坡为 i，则有

$$\left.\begin{array}{ll}i>i_k & \text{急流}\\ i=i_k & \text{临界流}\\ i<i_k & \text{缓流}\end{array}\right\} \tag{6-7-16}$$

习　题

6-7-1　明渠均匀流的特征是(　　)。

A. 断面面积、壁面粗糙度沿流程不变

B. 流量不变的长直渠道

C. 底坡不变、粗糙度不变的长渠

D. 水力坡度、水面坡度、河底坡度皆相等

6-7-2 某梯形断面明渠均匀流，渠底宽度 $b=2.0$m，水深 $h=1.2$m，边坡系数 $m=1.0$，渠道底坡 $i=0.000\ 8$，粗糙系数 $n=0.025$，则渠中的通过流量 Q 应为(　　)。

A. 5.25m^3/s　　B. 3.43m^3/s　　C. 2.52m^3/s　　D. 1.95m^3/s

第八节　渗流定律、井和集水廊道

一、渗流及渗流模型

流体在孔隙介质中的流动称为渗流，水在土壤孔隙中的流动是渗流典型的例子。工程中水源井、集水廊道出水量的计算，以滤池为代表的各种过滤设备中流经多孔介质的渗流速度、渗流系数的确定，地下水资源、油气资源的开发利用等方面，均需应用渗流理论的有关知识。在土木工程上，主要是研究以水为代表的液体，在土壤孔隙中的流动。水在土壤孔隙中的流动，是极不规则的迂回曲折运动，要详细考察每一孔隙中的流动状况是非常困难的，一般也无此必要。工程中所关心的主要是宏观的平均效果，为了研究方便，常用简化的渗流模型来代替实际的渗流运动。所谓渗流模型，是设想流体作为连续介质连续地充满渗流区的全部空间，包括土壤颗粒骨架所占据的空间；渗流的运动要素可作为渗流区全部空间的连续函数来研究。以渗流模型取代实际渗流，必须要遵循这几个原则：①通过渗流模型某一断面的流量必须与实际渗流通过该断面的流量相等；②渗流模型某一确定作用面上的压力，要与实际渗流在该作用面上的真实压力相等；③渗流模型的阻力与实际渗流的阻力相等，即能量损失相等。

渗流模型中的渗流流速 u 为渗流模型中微小过流断面面积 ΔA 除通过该面积的真实渗流量 ΔQ，即

$$u=\frac{\Delta Q}{\Delta A}$$

因为上式中 ΔA 内有一部分面积为土粒所占据，所以孔隙的过流断面面积 $\Delta A'$ 要比 ΔA 小，$\Delta A'=n\Delta A$，n 为土壤孔隙率(为孔隙体积与土壤总体积之比)。因此孔隙中真实渗流速度为

$$u'=\frac{\Delta Q}{\Delta A'}=\frac{\Delta Q}{n\Delta A}=\frac{u}{n}$$

由于孔隙率 $n<1$，所以 $u'>u$。引入渗流模型之后，把渗流视为连续介质运动，前面各章关于分析连续介质空间场运动要素的各种方法和概念就可直接应用于渗流中。例如按运动要素是否随时间变化，可分为恒定渗流和非恒定渗流；按运动要素是否沿流程变化，可分为均匀渗流和非均匀渗流等。非均匀渗流又可分为渐变渗流和急变渗流；从有无地下水自由浸润面可分为无压渗流和有压渗流等。

二、渗流基本定律——达西定律

1852～1855 年，达西对均质沙土中的渗流，做了大量的试验研究，总结得

出了渗流能量损失与渗流流速、流量之间的关系式为

$$Q = kAJ \tag{6-8-1}$$

式中：Q——渗流流量；

k——渗透系数，表示土壤在透水方面的物理性质，具有速度的量纲；

J——水力坡度，$J=\frac{h_w}{L}\approx\frac{H_1-H_2}{L}$；

H_1、H_2——分别为渗流上、下游断面的测压管水头。

因渗流速极小，流速水头可忽略不计，测压管水头差就可代替总水头差。$J=-\frac{\mathrm{d}H}{\mathrm{d}L}$，所以用负号是因 H 沿 L 减少。

渗流断面平均流速为

$$v=\frac{Q}{A}=kJ \tag{6-8-2}$$

上式表明渗流速度与水力坡度一次方成正比，亦即与水头损失一次方成正比，并与土壤的透水性有关。由此得知渗流遵循层流运动的规律，所以达西渗流定律也称为渗流线性定律。

对于均质土壤试样，其中产生的是均匀渗流，可认为各点的流动状态相同，点流速 u 与断面平均流速 v 相同，所以达西定律也可写为

$$u = kJ \tag{6-8-3}$$

对于非均质土壤，u 与 J 均与位置有关，u 与 v 不一定相同，达西定律只能以式(6-8-3)的形式表示。

对于渐变渗流，裘皮幼(Dupuit)认为流线曲率很小，两断面间任一流线长度近似相等，水力坡度相同，断面上各点流速均匀分布，即

$$u=v=kJ=-k\frac{\mathrm{d}H}{\mathrm{d}S}$$

也可以应用达西定律。

达西定律的适用范围为线性渗流，其雷诺数 $\mathrm{Re}=\frac{vd}{\nu}<1\sim10$。式中，$d$ 为土壤颗粒有效粒径，可用 d_{10} 代表，d_{10} 表示筛分后占 10%质量的土粒所能通过的筛孔直径。

三、集水廊道

集水廊道既是采集地下水作水源的给水建筑物，又是排泄地下水降低附近地下水位的排水建筑物。如图 6-8-1 所示一水平底的集水廊道，底部为不透水层，侧面为透水性均质土壤，上为地面，在廊道未取水前土壤中天然无压地下水水面(称浸润面)，为一水平线，如图中虚线所示，取水后水面降落为曲率极小的缓降曲线，为一渐变渗流，可以用达西定律。

集水廊道主要要解决两类问题：一是求出每一侧面单位长度的出流量 q、总流量 Q；另一是求出地下水降落曲面的坐标 x 及 z 的关系式，以便确定取水后各处的水位 z 值。x 为距廊道侧壁的水平距离，z 为从廊道底部算起的水面铅垂高度，即地下水水位。设 h 为廊道内水深，根据达西定律，$Q=kAJ$，单位长流量

$$q=kz\frac{\mathrm{d}z}{\mathrm{d}x}$$

$$\frac{q}{k}\int_0^x \mathrm{d}x=\int_h^z z\,\mathrm{d}z$$

$$\frac{q}{k}x = \frac{1}{2}(z^2 - h^2)$$

或

$$z^2 - h^2 = \frac{2q}{k}x \tag{6-8-4}$$

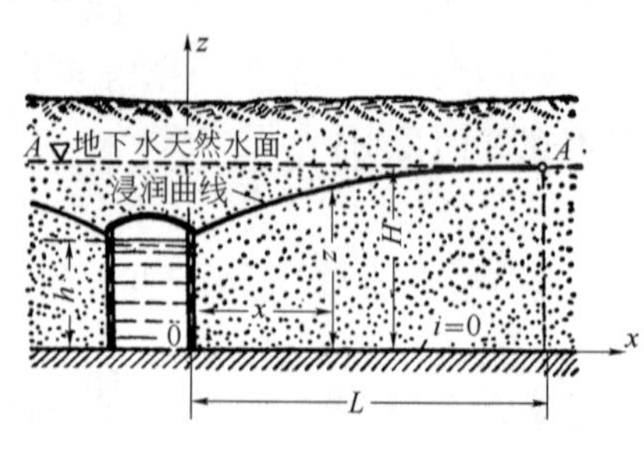

图 6-8-1

上式为地下廊道采水后地下水浸润线方程，若 q 及 h 已知，k 是渗流系数，为常数，则任一距离 x 处的水位 z 可求得，并可绘出水面曲线。

为了求单长流量 q，可利用其边界条件，当水平距离 $x \to L$ 时，地下水位 $z \to H$，H 为取水前地下水天然水平面到不透水层的高度，亦称含水层厚度，代入式(6-8-4)可得

$$q = \frac{k(H^2 - h^2)}{2L} \tag{6-8-5}$$

式中，L 称为集水廊道的影响长度(沿 x 方向)，即在 L 之外水面不再降落，恢复天然地下水位，不受取水的影响。

集水廊道两侧的总流量为 Q，则

$$Q = 2qL_0 \tag{6-8-6}$$

式中：L_0——垂直于纸面的廊道纵向长度。

四、管井涌水量的计算

(一)潜水井(普通完全井)

具有自由液面的无压地下水称潜水。潜水井用来汲取无压地下水，井的断面通常为圆形，水由透水的井壁渗入井中。潜水井又可分为完全井与不完全井两类，井底深达不透水层的称为完全井，如图 6-8-2 所示，按达西定律其流量为

$$Q = kAJ$$

$$= k2\pi rz \frac{\mathrm{d}z}{\mathrm{d}r}$$

分离变量后积分上式，得

$$\int z\mathrm{d}z = \frac{Q}{2\pi k}\int \frac{\mathrm{d}r}{r}$$

$$z^2 = \frac{Q}{\pi k}\ln r + c$$

式中：c——积分常数。

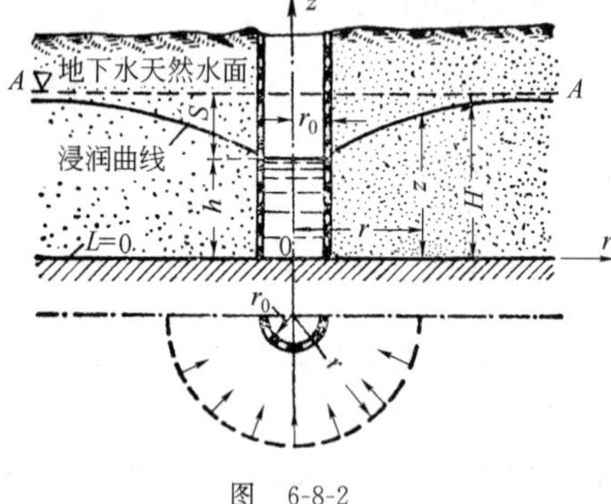

图 6-8-2

当 $r = r_0$ 时，$z = h$，代入上式得积分常数 $c = h^2 - \frac{Q}{\pi k}\ln r_0$，将积分常数 c 再代回原式有

$$z^2 - h^2 = \frac{Q}{\pi k}\ln \frac{r}{r_0} \tag{6-8-7}$$

换成常用对数后得

$$z^2 - h^2 = \frac{0.73Q}{k}\lg \frac{r}{r_0} \tag{6-8-8}$$

式中：h——井中水深；

r_0——井的半径。

上式表明潜水井取水时井外地下水浸润线方程，即 r 与 z 的关系式。从理论上说，当某井取水，四周形成漏斗状浸润面后，水面降落的影响应该延伸到无穷远处。但从工程实用观点来看，当水面降落的浸润线延伸到某一距离 R 之后，水面即接近含水层原有的厚度。即当 $r \to R$ 后，$z \to H$，R 称为井的影响半径，将此边界条件代入式(6-8-8)中，可求出潜水井涌水量公式

$$Q = 1.366 \frac{k(H^2 - h^2)}{\lg \dfrac{R}{r_0}} \tag{6-8-9}$$

式中的影响半径 R 可由试验方法求得。当无试验资料，初步计算时可用经验公式估算

$$R = 3\,000 S \sqrt{k} \tag{6-8-10}$$

式中，$S = H - h$，为抽水稳定后，井中水面降落深度以米(m)计。k 为渗流系数，以m/s计。

【例 6-8-1】 潜水完全井抽水量大小与相关物理量的关系是：

A. 与井半径成正比　　B. 与井的影响半径成正比

C. 与含水层厚度成正比　　D. 与土体渗透系数成正比

解 根据公式(6-8-9)可知，潜水完全井抽水量与渗透系数 k 和含水层厚度 H 有关，且与渗透系数 k 成正比。

答案：D

（二）自流井（承压井）

如含水层位于两不透水层之间，其中渗流所受的压强大于大气压强，这样的含水层称为自流层，由自流层供水的井为自流井。设一井底直至不透水层的完全自流井如图 6-8-3 所示。在未抽水时，井中水位将升高至 H 高度处，此 H 值即为天然状态下含水层的测压管水头，它大于含水层的厚度 t，有时甚至高出地面，使水从井口中自动流出。当抽水经过相当长的时间后，井四周的测管水头线，将形成一稳定的轴对称的漏斗状曲线，如图 6-8-3 所示。取距井中心轴为 r 处的渗流过水断面，该面面积 $A = 2\pi rt$，它与测管水头无关，该处水力坡度 $J = \dfrac{dz}{dr}$，为该处测管水头线的坡度，则该断面渗流流量 Q 按达西公式，有

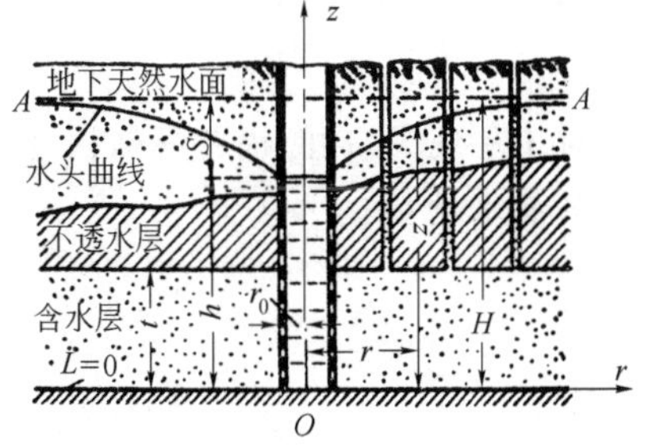

图 6-8-3

$$Q = k 2\pi rt \frac{dz}{dr}$$

分离变量并积分得

$$z = \frac{Q}{2\pi kt} \ln r + c$$

式中，c 为积分常数，由边界条件确定。当 $r = r_0$ 时，$z = h$，代入上式得 $c = h - \dfrac{Q}{2\pi kt} \ln r_0$，将 c

代入原式有

$$z-h=\frac{Q}{2\pi kt}\ln\frac{r}{r_0} \tag{6-8-11}$$

或转换成常用对数

$$z-h=0.366\frac{Q}{kt}\lg\frac{r}{r_0} \tag{6-8-12}$$

此即自流井水头曲线方程。引入井的影响半径概念，令上式中的 $r=R$ 时，$z=H$，就可得到自流井的涌水量公式

$$Q=2.73\frac{kt(H-h)}{\lg\frac{R}{r_0}} \tag{6-8-13}$$

井中水面降落深度 $S=H-h$，上式可写成

$$Q=2.73\frac{ktS}{\lg\frac{R}{r_0}} \tag{6-8-14}$$

五、大口井涌水量

大口井是汲取浅层地下水的一种井，井径较大，大致为 2～10m 或更大些。大口井一般是不完全井，下接含水量丰富的透水层，底部进水成为涌水量的重要部分。如图 6-8-4 所示一底部为半球形，井壁四周为不透水层，主要由底部进水的大口井，利用达西公式可推得其流量 Q 的计算公式

$$Q=\frac{2\pi kS}{\frac{1}{r_0}-\frac{1}{R}} \tag{6-8-15}$$

因 $R\gg r_0$，所以上式近似为

$$Q=2\pi kr_0S \tag{6-8-16}$$

对于平底大口井，福希海梅认为过流断面是半椭球面，渗流流线是双曲线，如图 6-8-5 所示。其涌水量 Q 的公式为

$$Q=4kr_0S \tag{6-8-17}$$

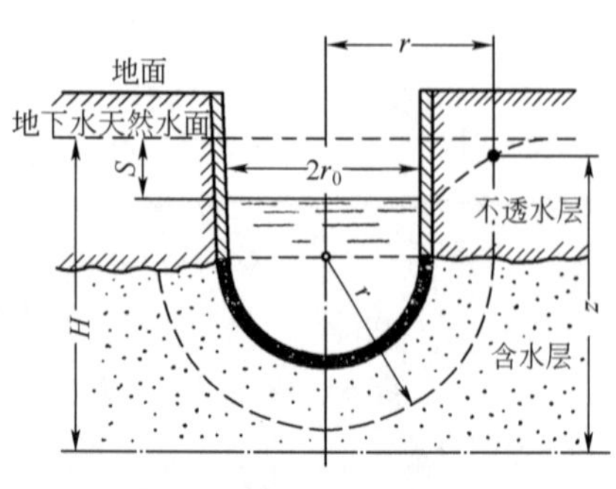

图 6-8-4

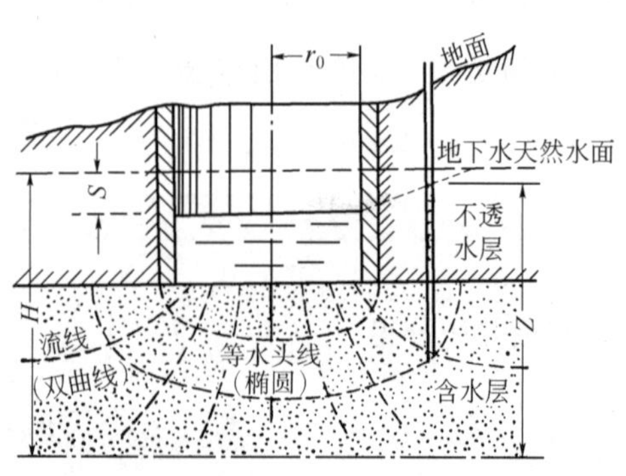

图 6-8-5

六、井群的涌水量

(一)潜水井井群

如图 6-8-6 所示一潜水井井群平面图,在水平不透水层上有 n 个完全潜水井,由于各井之间距离较近,因此各井的出水量和浸润曲线的形状均相互影响,所以井群计算与单井不同,需应用势流叠加原理。经分析推导得潜水井井群的浸润线方程为

$$z^2 = H^2 - 0.732\frac{Q}{k}\left[\lg R - \frac{1}{n}\lg(r_1 r_2 r_3 \cdots r_n)\right] \quad (6\text{-}8\text{-}18)$$

式中: z——潜水井井群影响范围内某点的浸润线水头;

H——未抽水时含水层水位;

Q——井群总流量;

n——井的总数;

$r_1、r_2、r_3、\cdots、r_n$——各个井到计算点的半径;

R——井群的影响半径可用经验公式(6-8-19)计算或做抽水试验确定。

图 6-8-6

$$R = 575S\sqrt{Hk} \quad (6\text{-}8\text{-}19)$$

井群的总流量公式为

$$Q = 1.366\frac{k(H^2 - z^2)}{\lg R - \frac{1}{n}\lg(r_1 r_2 r_3 \cdots r_n)} \quad (6\text{-}8\text{-}20)$$

(二)自流井井群

与潜水井类似,用势流叠加原理可导出自流井井群的水头线方程和流量公式。水头线方程为

$$z = H - \frac{0.366Q}{kt}\left[\lg R - \frac{1}{n}(r_1 r_2 r_3 \cdots r_n)\right] \quad (6\text{-}8\text{-}21)$$

自流井井群的流量为

$$Q = 2.73\frac{kt(H - z)}{\lg R - \frac{1}{n}\lg(r_1 r_2 r_3 \cdots r_n)} \quad (6\text{-}8\text{-}22)$$

【例 6-8-2】 设某圆形基坑,其周围布置了 6 个潜水完全井,如图所示。各井距基坑中心点距离 r 为 30m,含水层厚度 H 为 15m,渗流系数 $k=0.000\,8\text{m/s}$,井群影响半径 $R=300\text{m}$,欲使基坑中心点水位下降 $S=5\text{m}$,求各井的抽水量。

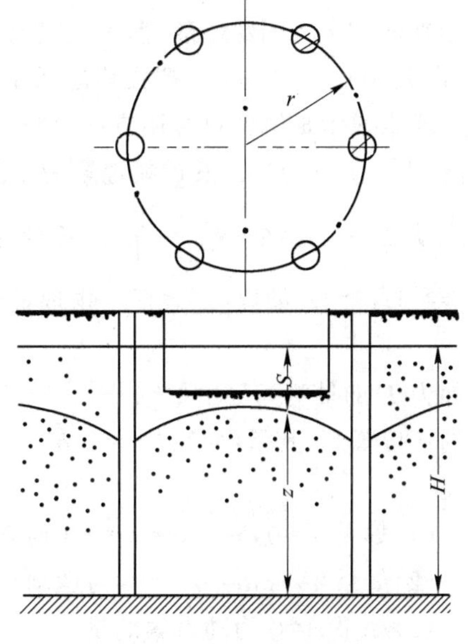

例 6-8-2 图

解 $r_1=r_2=r_3=\cdots=r_n=30\text{m}$,代入式(6-8-16)得总流

$$Q = 1.366\frac{0.000\,8\times(15^2 - 10^2)}{\lg 300 - \frac{1}{6}\lg(30^6)} = 0.136\text{m}^3/\text{s}$$

每口井抽出量为

$$\frac{Q}{n} = \frac{0.136}{6} = 0.022\,7\text{m}^3/\text{s} = 22.7\text{L/s}$$

习　题

6-8-1　达西渗透定律表明渗流量与(　　)成正比，与(　　)有关。

A. 过流面积、流速，介质颗粒大小

B. 过流面积、水力坡度，水的黏性

C. 过流面积、水头损失，土壤均匀程度

D. 过流面积、水力坡度一次方，渗透系数

6-8-2　潜水井是指(　　)。

A. 全部潜没在地下水中的井

B. 从有自由表面潜水含水层中开凿的井

C. 井底直达不透水层的井

D. 从两不透水层之间汲取有压地下水的井

6-8-3　某一井底直达不透水层的潜水井，井的半径 $r_0=0.2\text{m}$，含水层的水头 $H=10\text{m}$，渗透系数 $k=0.0006\text{m/s}$，影响半径 $R=294\text{m}$，抽水稳定后井中水深为 $h=6\text{m}$，此时该井的出水流量 Q 为(　　)。

A. 20.51L/s　　B. 18.5L/s　　C. 16.56L/s　　D. 14.55L/s

第九节　量纲分析和相似原理

一、量纲分析

(一)量纲和单位

描述流体运动的物理量如长度、时间、质量、速度、加速度等，都可按其性质不同而加以分类，表征各种物理量性质和类别的标志称为物理量的量纲(或因次)。例如长度、时间、质量是三个性质完全不同的物理量，因而具有三种不同的量纲。我们注意到这三种量纲是互不依赖的，即其中任一量纲，不能从其他两个推导出来，这种互不依赖，互相独立的量纲称为基本量纲。通常表示量纲的符号用方括号将字母括起来，这三个基本量纲可分别表示为：长度[L]、时间[T]、质量[M]。其他物理量的量纲，均可用基本量纲推导出来，称为导出量纲，例如速度量纲就是导出量纲，$[\text{v}]=\frac{[\text{L}]}{[\text{T}]}$。各种导出量纲，一般可用基本量纲指数乘积的形式来表示，$[\text{v}]=[\text{LT}^{-1}]$。如以[x]表任一物理量的导出量纲，则

$$[\text{x}]=[\text{L}^a\text{T}^b\text{M}^c] \tag{6-9-1}$$

例如力 F 的量纲为导出量纲 $[\text{F}]=[\text{LT}^{-2}\text{M}]$，则其量纲指数 $a=1,b=-2,c=1$；又如前面导出的速度量纲，其量纲指数 $a=1,b=-1,c=0$。导出量纲按照其基本量纲的指数可分成以下三类：

(1)如果 $a\neq0,b=0,c=0$ 为几何学的量；

(2)如果 $a\neq0,b\neq0,c=0$ 为运动学的量；

(3)如果 $c\neq0$ 为动力学的量。

除现在所选择的三种基本量纲[L]、[T]、[M](国际单位制 SI)之外，以往在工程上曾广泛

使用过工程单位制，其基本量纲的选择为[L]、[T]、[F]，质量反而成为导出量纲。

为了比较同一类物理量的大小，可以选择与其同类的标准量加以比较，此标准量称为单位。例如要比较长度的大小，可以选择 m、cm 或市尺为单位。但由于选择的单位不同，同一长度可以用不同的数值表示，可以是 1(以 m 为单位)，也可以是 100(以 cm 为单位)，也可以是 3(以市尺为单位)。可见有量纲量的数值大小是不确定的，随所选用单位不同而变化的。当基本量纲指数 $a=b=c=0$ 时，则

$$[\mathrm{x}] = [\mathrm{L}^0 \mathrm{T}^0 \mathrm{M}^0] = [1]$$

[x]为无量纲纯数，或量纲为 1 的量，它的数值大小，与所选用单位无关。使实验成果无量纲化，往往更具普遍意义。例如要反映沿程机械能减少情况，用水力坡度 $J=hw/L$ 这一无量纲值 ($[J]=[LL^{-1}]=[1]$) 要比用水头损失值更能反映其普遍性。因为后者随所选单位不同而变化，而前者不论所选择的是何种长度单位，只要形成该水力坡度的物理条件不变，则 J 的值也不会变。又如判别流态的雷诺数 $\mathrm{Re}=\dfrac{vd}{\nu}$，其量纲式为

$$[\mathrm{Re}] = \frac{[\mathrm{LT}^{-1}][\mathrm{L}]}{[\mathrm{L}^2\mathrm{T}^{-1}]} = [\mathrm{L}^0 \mathrm{T}^0 \mathrm{M}^0] = [1]$$

为无量纲数。

前已指出下临界雷诺数 $\mathrm{Re}_k=2\ 000$，就是判别流态的普适性常数，不论单位是英制还是国际单位制 $\mathrm{Re}_k=2\ 000$ 不变，均是判别流态是层流还是紊流的标准数值。

(二)量纲和谐原理

一个正确的、完整的反映客观规律的物理方程中，各项的量纲是一致的，这就是量纲一致性原理，或称量纲和谐原理。

量纲和谐原理用途广泛，是量纲分析的基础，它首先可以判断物理方程是否正确。人们熟知水动力学三大方程是正确的，这三个方程的量纲每一个均是和谐的。连续方程等号前后是流量的量纲，能量方程每一项皆为长度量纲，动量方程每一项皆为力的量纲。

量纲和谐原理还可用来确定方程式中系数的量纲以及分析经验公式的结构是否合理。

量纲和谐原理还表明，量纲相同的量才可以相加减；量纲不同的量不能相加减，也不能相等，但可以相乘除。

量纲和谐原理最主要的用途还在于将各有关的物理量的函数关系，以各物理量指数乘积的形式表达出来，并确定其指数，以便将实验结果建立起一个结构合理、正确反映客观规律的力学方程或物理方程，此种分析方法称为量纲分析法。

(三)量纲分析法

量纲分析法有两种：一种适用于影响因素间的关系为单项指数形式的场合，称瑞利(Ray-Leigh)法；另一种为具有普遍性的方法，称 π 定理。下面分别介绍。

1. 瑞利法

首先列出影响该物理过程的主要因素 x_1、x_2、x_3、…、x_n 之间待定的函数关系

$$y = f(x_1, x_2, x_3, \cdots, x_n)$$

由于各因素的量纲只能由基本量纲的积和商导出而不能相加减，因此函数关系式可写成指数乘积的形式为

$$y = kx_1^{a_1} x_2^{a_2} x_3^{a_3} \cdots x_n^{a_n}$$

式中：　　k——无量纲系数；

x_1、x_2、…、x_n——待定指数。

再将上式用基本量纲表示为

$$[L^a T^b M^c] = [L^{a_1} T^{b_1} M^{c_1}]\alpha_1 [L^{a_2} T^{b_2} M^{c_2}]\alpha_2 \cdots [L^{a_n} T^{b_n} M^{c_n}]\alpha_n$$

由量纲和谐原理可得

[L]　　$a = a_1\alpha_1 + a_2\alpha_2 + \cdots a_n\alpha_n$

[T]　　$b = b_1\alpha_1 + b_2\alpha_2 + \cdots b_n\alpha_n$

[M]　　$c = c_1\alpha_1 + c_2\alpha_2 + \cdots c_n\alpha_n$

解上述联立方程组，可求出待定 α_1、α_2、…、α_n，从而确定函数关系。但因方程组中的方程数只有三个，当待定指数个数 $n>3$ 时，则有$(n-3)$个指数需用其他指数的函数来表示。

【例 6-9-1】 实验指出判别层流、紊流的下临界流速 v_k 与管径 d、流体密度 ρ、流体黏度 μ 有关，试用量纲分析法求出它们间的函数关系。

解　　$v_k = f(d, \rho, \mu)$

或　　$v_k = kd^{a_1} \rho^{a_2} \mu^{a_3}$

再写成量纲式

$$[LT^{-1}M^0] = [LT^0M^0]\alpha_1 [L^{-3}T^0M]\alpha_2 [L^{-1}T^{-1}M]\alpha_3$$

由量纲和谐得

$$\left.\begin{array}{ll} [L] & 1 = \alpha_1 - 3\alpha_2 - \alpha_3 \\ [T] & -1 = -\alpha_3 \\ [M] & 0 = \alpha_2 + \alpha_3 \end{array}\right\} \text{解得 } \alpha_3 = 1, \alpha_2 = -1, \alpha_1 = -1$$

将指数 α_1、α_2、α_3 回代入指数乘积函数关系式，有

$$v_k = k\frac{\mu}{\rho d} = k\frac{v}{d}$$

上式化为无量纲形式后有

$$k = \frac{v_k d}{\nu}$$

此无量纲数 k 即为下临界雷诺数

$$Re_k = \frac{v_k d}{\nu}$$

2. π 定理

π 定理在 1915 年由布金汉(E. Buckingham)首先提出，所以又称为布金汉原理。

设有 n 个变量的物理方程式

$$f(x_1, x_2, x_3, \cdots, x_n) = 0$$

其中可选出 m 个变量在量纲上是互相独立的，那么此方程式必然可以表示为$(n-m)$个无量纲数(以 π 表示)的物理方程，即

$$F(\pi_1, \pi_2, \pi_3, \cdots, \pi_{n-m}) = 0$$

在应用 π 定理时，要注意所选取的 m 个量纲独立的物理量，应使它们不能组成一个无量纲数。设所选择的物理量为 x_1、x_2、x_3，它们的量纲式可用基本量纲表示为

$$\left.\begin{aligned}[x_1] &= [L^{a_1} T^{b_1} M^{c_1}] \\ [x_2] &= [L^{a_2} T^{b_2} M^{c_2}] \\ [x_3] &= [L^{a_3} T^{b_3} M^{c_3}]\end{aligned}\right\} \tag{6-9-2}$$

为使 x_1、x_2、x_3 互相独立、不能组合成无量纲数，就要使它们的指数乘积不能为零，也就要求式(6-9-2)中的指数行列式不等于零(证明略去)，即

$$\begin{vmatrix} a_1 & b_1 & c_1 \\ a_2 & b_2 & c_2 \\ a_3 & b_3 & c_3 \end{vmatrix} \neq 0 \tag{6-9-3}$$

现以 x_1 为长度，x_2 为时间，x_3 为质量，即 $a_1=1, b_2=1, c_3=1$，其余均为零代入式(6-9-3)

$$\begin{vmatrix} 1 & 0 & 0 \\ 0 & 1 & 0 \\ 0 & 0 & 1 \end{vmatrix} = 1 \neq 0$$

所以上述三个基本物理量的量纲是互相独立的。如果我们所选择的物理量分别属于此三种类型，则容易满足相互独立的条件。在实践中常分别选几何学的量(管径 d，水头 H 等)、运动学的量(速度 v，加速度 g 等)和动力学的量(密度 ρ，黏度 μ 等)各一个，作为独立的变量。

无量纲的 π 项的组成，可以从所选用的独立变量之外的其余变量中，每次轮取一个，与所选的独立变量组合而成，即

$$\left.\begin{aligned}\pi_1 &= x_1^{\alpha_1} x_2^{\beta_1} x_3^{\gamma_1} x_4 \\ \pi_2 &= x_1^{\alpha_2} x_2^{\beta_2} x_3^{\gamma_2} x_5 \\ &\cdots\cdots \\ \pi_{n-m} &= x_1^{\alpha(n-m)} x_2^{\beta(n-m)} x_3^{\gamma(n-m)} x_n\end{aligned}\right\} \tag{6-9-4}$$

式中：α_i、β_i、γ_i——待定指数。

根据量纲和谐原理，可以求出式(6-9-4)中的指数 α_i、β_i、γ_i，因左端各 π 项的指数为零(π 为无量纲数)。

二、流动相似的概念

为了能用模型试验的结果去预测原型流将要发生的情况，必须使模型流动与原型流动满足力学相似条件，所谓力学相似包括几何相似、运动相似、动力相似、初始条件与边界条件相似几个方面。在下面的讨论中，原型中的物理量标以下标 p，模型中的物理量标以下标 m。

(一)几何相似

几何相似是指两个流动的对应线段长度成比例，对应角度相等，对应的边界性质相同或边界条件相似(指固体边界的粗糙度和自由液面等)，亦即原型和模型两个流动的几何形状相似。两个流动的长度比尺、面积比尺、体积比尺可分别表示为

$$\left.\begin{aligned}\lambda_L &= \frac{L_p}{L_m} \\ \lambda_A &= \frac{A_p}{A_m} = \lambda_L^2 \\ \lambda_V &= \frac{V_p}{V_m} = \lambda_L^3\end{aligned}\right\} \tag{6-9-5}$$

长度比尺视试验场地大小，试验要求不同而取不同的值，通常水工模型 $\lambda_L=10\sim100$。当长、宽、高三个方向长度比尺相同时称为正态模型，否则称为变态模型。几何相似是力学相似的前提。

（二）运动相似

运动相似是指两个流场对应点上同名的运动学的量成比例，主要是流速场、加速度场相似。时间比尺、速度比尺、加速度比尺可分别表示为

$$\left.\begin{aligned}\lambda_t &= \frac{t_p}{t_m} \\ \lambda_v &= \frac{v_p}{v_m} \\ \lambda_a &= \frac{a_p}{a_m}\end{aligned}\right\} \tag{6-9-6}$$

作为特例，重力加速度比尺 $\lambda_g=\frac{g_p}{g_m}$，如果原型与模型均在同一星球上，$\lambda_g\approx1$。

（三）动力相似

动力相似是指两个流场对应点上同名的动力学的量成比例，即力场相似。密度比尺、动力黏度比尺、作用力比尺可分别表示为

$$\left.\begin{aligned}\lambda_\rho &= \frac{\rho_p}{\rho_m} \\ \lambda_\mu &= \frac{\mu_p}{\mu_m} \\ \lambda_F &= \frac{F_p}{F_m}\end{aligned}\right\} \tag{6-9-7}$$

作用在流体上的外力通常有重力 G、黏性切力 T、压力 P、弹性力 E、表面张力 S 等，其比尺为

$$\lambda_F=\frac{G_p}{G_m}=\frac{T_p}{T_m}=\frac{P_p}{P_m}=\frac{E_p}{E_m}=\frac{S_p}{S_m}$$

对非恒定流还应满足初始条件相似。

（四）边界条件与初始条件相似

（五）牛顿一般相似原理

设作用在流体上的外力合力 F，使流体产生的加速度为 a，流体的质量为 m，则由牛顿第二定律惯性力 $F=ma$ 可知，力的比尺 λ_F 也可表示为

$$\lambda_F=\frac{F_p}{F_m}=\frac{M_p a_p}{M_m a_m}=\frac{\rho_p L_p^2 v_p^2}{\rho_m L_m^2 v_m^2} \tag{6-9-8}$$

或

$$\frac{F_p}{\rho_p L_p^2 v_p^2}=\frac{F_m}{\rho_m L_m^2 v_m^2} \tag{6-9-9}$$

式中，$\frac{F}{\rho L^2 v^2}$为一无量纲数，以 Ne 表示有

$$\mathrm{Ne} = \frac{F}{\rho L^2 v^2} \tag{6-9-10}$$

Ne 称为牛顿数。式(6-9-10)可表示为

$$(\mathrm{Ne})_p = (\mathrm{N_e})_m$$

两流动动力相似，归结为牛顿数相等。以比尺表示可得

$$\frac{\lambda_F}{\lambda_\rho \lambda_L^2 \lambda_v^2} = 1 \tag{6-9-11}$$

三、相似准则

要使流动完全满足牛顿相似准则，牛顿数相等，就要求相应点上所有的同名力均有同一比尺，实际上很难做到。在某一具体流动中，占主导地位的作用力往往只有一种，因此在做模型试验时，只要让主要作用力满足相似条件即可。下面介绍只考虑一种主要作用力的相似准则。

(一)重力相似准则

当外力只有重力 G 时，则牛顿数中的外力合力 $F=G$，考虑式(6-9-8)有

$$\lambda_F = \frac{G_p}{G_m} = \frac{\rho_p L_p^3 g_p}{\rho_m L_m^3 g_m} = \frac{\rho_p L_p^2 v_p^2}{\rho_m L_m^2 v_m^2}$$

化简后得

$$\frac{v_p^2}{g_p L_p} = \frac{v_m^2}{g_m L_m} \tag{6-9-12}$$

上式中$\frac{v^2}{gL}$为一无量纲数，称为弗劳德(Fraude)数，以 Fr 表示，则重力相似，归结为弗劳德数相等，即

$$(\mathrm{Fr})_p = (\mathrm{Fr})_m \tag{6-9-13}$$

以相似比尺表示

$$\frac{\lambda_v^2}{\lambda_g \lambda_L} = 1 \tag{6-9-14}$$

一般 $\lambda_g=1$，所以在重力相似时，流速比尺与长度比尺的关系为

$$\lambda_v = \lambda_L^{\frac{1}{2}} \tag{6-9-15}$$

据此，可推得流量比尺 λ_Q

$$\lambda_Q = \lambda_v \lambda_A = \lambda_L^{\frac{1}{2}} \lambda_L^2$$

所以

$$\lambda_Q = \lambda_L^{\frac{5}{2}} \tag{6-9-16}$$

同理可导出

$$\lambda_t = \frac{\lambda_L}{\lambda_v} = \lambda_L^{\frac{1}{2}} \tag{6-9-17}$$

弗劳德数的物理意义为惯性力与重力之比。

（二）黏性切力相似准则

当主要作用力为黏性切力 T 时，$F=T$，代入式(6-9-8)有

$$\lambda_{F}=\frac{T_{p}}{T_{m}}=\frac{\mu_{p}L_{p}v_{p}}{\mu_{m}L_{m}v_{m}}=\frac{\rho_{p}L_{p}^{2}v_{p}^{2}}{\rho_{m}L_{m}^{2}v_{m}^{2}}$$

化简后得

$$\frac{v_{p}L_{p}}{\nu_{p}}=\frac{v_{m}L_{m}}{\nu_{m}} \tag{6-9-18}$$

式中$\frac{vL}{\nu}$为一无量纲数，为雷诺数，以 Re 表示，则黏性切力相似准则归结为雷诺数相等，即

$$(Re)_{p}=(Re)_{m} \tag{6-9-19}$$

以比尺表示为

$$\frac{\lambda_{v}\lambda_{L}}{\lambda_{\nu}}=1 \tag{6-9-20}$$

如原型与模型均用同一种流体且温度也相近，则黏度比尺 $\lambda_{r}=1$，所以黏性力相似时，速度比尺与长度比尺有以下关系

$$\left.\begin{aligned}\lambda_{v}&=\frac{1}{\lambda_{L}}\\ \lambda_{Q}&=\lambda_{L}\\ \lambda_{t}&=\lambda_{L}^{2}\end{aligned}\right\} \tag{6-9-21}$$

雷诺数的物理意义为惯性力与黏性力之比。

一般来说，当影响流速的主要因素是黏滞力时，就可用雷诺准则设计模型，例如有压管流，当其阻力处于层流区、水力光滑区，主要考虑使原型与模型的雷诺数相等，在紊流过渡区，既要雷诺数相等，又要相对粗糙度$\frac{\Delta}{d}$相似。但在紊流粗糙区或称阻力平方区时，阻力主要取决于相对粗糙度$\frac{\Delta}{d}$，而与黏性关系很少，故只要保持原型与模型几何相似、相对糙度相似即可达到力学相似，而不需要雷诺数相等，这一区域称为自动模型区。在阻力平方区的明渠也只要考虑重力相似准则和几何相似准则，而不必考虑雷诺准则。

若要同时满足弗劳德准则和雷诺准则是很困难的，因为必须使这两个准则等价，即

$$\frac{\lambda_{v}^{2}}{\lambda_{g}\lambda_{L}}=\frac{\lambda_{v}\lambda_{L}}{\lambda_{\nu}}$$

$\lambda_{g}=1$，代入上式有

$$\lambda_{\nu}=\frac{\lambda_{L}^{2}}{\lambda_{v}}=\frac{\lambda_{L}^{2}}{\lambda_{L}^{1/2}}=\lambda_{L}^{3/2}$$

要使流体的黏度正好满足上式很难做到。

（三）压力相似准则

$$\lambda_{F}=\frac{P_{p}}{P_{m}}=\frac{p_{p}L_{P}^{2}}{p_{m}L_{m}^{2}}=\frac{\rho_{p}L_{p}^{2}v_{p}^{2}}{\rho_{m}L_{m}^{2}v_{m}^{2}}$$

化简后得

$$\frac{p_{p}}{\rho_{p}v_{p}^{2}}=\frac{p_{m}}{\rho_{m}v_{m}^{2}} \tag{6-9-22}$$

式中：$\frac{p}{\rho v^{2}}$——无量纲数，称欧拉(Euler)数，以 Eu 表示，则压力相似归结为欧拉数相等。

$$(\mathrm{Eu})_{\mathrm{p}} = (\mathrm{Eu})_{\mathrm{m}} \tag{6-9-23}$$

写成比尺形式

$$\frac{\lambda_{\mathrm{p}}}{\lambda_{\rho}\lambda_{\mathrm{v}}^{2}} = 1 \tag{6-9-24}$$

欧拉准则不是独立准则，当佛劳德准则与雷诺准则满足时，欧拉准则自动满足。Eu 也可用压差形式表示为

$$\mathrm{Eu} = \frac{\Delta p}{\rho v^{2}} \tag{6-9-25}$$

（四）其他各种准则

除上述三种主要的相似准数外，尚有柯西（Canchy）数、马赫（Mach）数、韦伯（Weber）数和斯特鲁哈（Strohae）数等准数，分别表示弹性力、高速气流弹性力、表面张力、惯性力（非恒定性）等起的作用。土木工程上较少应用，此处不再详述。

【例 6-9-2】 烟气在加热炉回热装置中流动，拟用空气介质进行实验。已知空气黏度 $\nu_{空气}=15\times10^{-6}\mathrm{m^2/s}$，烟气运动黏度 $\nu_{烟气}=60\times10^{-6}\mathrm{m^2/s}$，烟气流速 $v_{烟气}=3\mathrm{m/s}$，如若实际长度与模型长度的比尺 $\lambda_{\mathrm{L}}=5$，则模型空气的流速应为：

A. 3.75m/s　　B. 0.15m/s　　C. 2.4m/s　　D. 60m/s

解 按雷诺模型，$\frac{\lambda_{\mathrm{v}}\lambda_{\mathrm{L}}}{\lambda_{\nu}}=1$，流速比尺 $\lambda_{\mathrm{v}}=\frac{\lambda_{\nu}}{\lambda_{\mathrm{L}}}$

按题设 $\lambda_{\nu}=\frac{60\times10^{-6}}{15\times10^{-6}}=4$，长度比尺 $\lambda_{\mathrm{L}}=5$，因此流速比尺 $\lambda_{\mathrm{v}}=\frac{4}{5}=0.8$

$\lambda_{\mathrm{v}}=\frac{v_{烟气}}{v_{空气}}$，$v_{空气}=\frac{v_{烟气}}{\lambda_{\mathrm{v}}}=\frac{3\mathrm{m/s}}{0.8}=3.75\mathrm{m/s}$

答案：A

习　题

6-9-1　量纲和谐原理用途很多，其中最重要的一种是（　　）。

A. 判断物理方程是否正确

B. 确定经验公式中系数的量纲

C. 分析经验公式结构是否合理

D. 作为量纲分析原理探求物理量间的函数关系

6-9-2　模型设计中的自动模型区是指（　　）。

A. 只要原型与模型雷诺数相等，即自动相似的区域

B. 只要模型与原型弗劳德数相等，即自动相似的区域

C. 处于水力光滑区时，两个流场雷诺数不需要相等即自动相似

D. 在紊流粗糙区，只要满足几何相似，即可自动满足力学相似

题解及参考答案

第一节

6-1-1　**解：**运用高等数学中连续函数理论分析流体运动。

答案:C

第二节

6-2-1 **解**:与牛顿内摩擦定律直接有关的因素是黏度、切应力、与剪切变形速度。

答案:D

6-2-2 **解**:水的动力黏度随温度的升高而减少。

答案:B

第三节

6-3-1 **解**:单位质量力具有加速度的量纲。

答案:D

6-3-2 **解**:与大气连通的自由液面下5m水深处的相对压强为0.5at。

答案:B

6-3-3 **解**:真空高度$h_v=\frac{p_v}{\rho g}=\frac{39.2\text{kPa}}{9.8\text{kN/m}^3}=4\text{m H}_2\text{O}$,真空值$p_v=39.2\text{kPa}$。

答案:A

6-3-4 **解**:绝对压强$p'=p_0+\rho gh=9.8\text{kPa}+9.8\times2\text{kPa}=29.4\text{kPa}$。

答案:B

6-3-5 **解**:被测点的相对压强为$r'\Delta h-rh_1$。

答案:D

6-3-6 **解**:设桶顶部所受张力为T_1,底部所受张力为T_2,总压力p作用于距底部1/3水深h处,由静力矩原量可知:$T_1\cdot\frac{2}{3}h=T_2\cdot\frac{1}{3}h$,则有$T_1/T_2=\frac{1}{2}$,则张力之比为1/2。

答案:B

6-3-7 **解**:总压力$p=\rho gh_cA=9.8\text{kN/m}^3\times1\text{m}\times4\text{m}\times\pi\text{m}=78.4\text{kN}$

压力中心距液面为$2/3h=\frac{2}{3}\times2\text{m}=\frac{4}{3}\text{m}$。

答案:B

第四节

6-4-1 **解**:理想流体是指无黏性流体。

答案:D

6-4-2 **解**:恒定流是指当地加速度$\frac{\partial u}{\partial t}=0$的流动。

答案:A

6-4-3 **解**:均匀流指流线为平行直线的流动。

答案:C

6-4-4 **解**:伯努利方程中$z+\frac{p}{r}+\frac{\alpha v^2}{2g}$表示单位重量流体的机械能。

答案:C

6-4-5 **解**:毕托管比压计中的水头差是总水头与测压管水头之差。

答案:D

6-4-6 **解**:黏性流体测压管水头线的沿程变化:可升、可降、可水平。

答案:D

6-4-7 **解**:由连续方程可得:$v_2=v_1\left(\frac{A_1}{A_2}\right)=v_1\left(\frac{d_1}{d_2}\right)^2=6\text{m/s}\left(\frac{150\text{mm}}{300\text{mm}}\right)^2$

$v_2=\frac{6}{4}\text{m/s}=1.5\text{m/s}$。

答案:C

6-4-8 **解**:文丘里流量计的流量:$Q=\mu\ \frac{\pi}{4}d_1^2\ \sqrt{\frac{2g\Delta h}{\left(\frac{d_1}{d_2}\right)^4-1}}$

代入数据后:

$$Q=0.98\ \frac{\pi}{4}(0.1)^2\ \sqrt{\frac{2\times 9.8\times 0.6}{\left(\frac{0.1}{0.05}\right)^4-1}}=0.006\ 81\text{m}^3/\text{s}$$

答案:D

第五节

6-5-1 **解**:有压圆管均匀流切应力 τ 沿断面的分布为管轴处是 0,与半径成正比。

答案:C

6-5-2 **解**:圆管层流的流速分布是抛物线分布。

答案:C

6-5-3 **解**:圆管层流轴心处最大流速是断面平均流速的 2 倍。

答案:B

6-5-4 **解**:圆管紊流核心区的流速分布为对数分布曲线。

答案:C

6-5-5 **解**:由题设条件得:$d_1=2d_2$

根据连续方程知:

$$v_1=v_2\left(\frac{d_2}{d_1}\right)^2=v_2\left(\frac{d_2}{2d_2}\right)^2=\frac{v_2}{4}$$

代入雷诺数公式:

$$\text{Re}_1=\frac{v_1d_1}{\nu}=\frac{\frac{v_2}{4}\cdot 2d_2}{\nu}=\frac{1}{2}\ \frac{v_2d_2}{\nu}=\frac{1}{2}\text{Re}_2=0.5\text{Re}_2$$

答案:A

6-5-6 **解**:有压圆管层流的沿程阻力系数:$\lambda=\frac{64}{\text{Re}}$,随 Re 的增加阻力系数 λ 线性减少。

答案:B

6-5-7 **解**:层流的沿程损失与平均流速的 1 次方成正比。

答案:C

6-5-8 **解**:有压圆管流动,紊流粗糙区的沿程阻力系数与相对粗糙度有关。

答案:A

6-5-9 **解**:谢才公式仅适用于水力粗糙区即阻力平方区。

答案:B

6-5-10 **解**:随雷诺数的减少,黏性底层变厚,遮住了绝对粗糙度。

答案:B

6-5-11 **解**:由于边界层分离形成漩涡区,增大了压差阻力。

答案:D

6-5-12 **解**:水泵所需扬程 $H=z+hw=15\text{m}+65\times\frac{1^2}{2\times9.8}\text{m}=18.33\text{m}$。

答案:D

第六节

6-6-1 **解**:每一节点流量代数和为 0,即 $\sum Q_{节点}=0$;沿环一周水头损失的代数和为 0,即 $\sum h_{w沿环}=0$。

答案:C

6-6-2 **解**:水头与直径均相同的圆柱形外管嘴过流量是小孔口过流量的 1.32 倍。

答案:D

6-6-3 **解**:小孔口出流量:

$$Q=\mu A\sqrt{2gH_0}=0.62\times\frac{\pi}{4}(0.01)^2\sqrt{2\times9.8\times5}=4.82\times10^{-4}\text{m}^3/\text{s}。$$

答案:D

第七节

6-7-1 **解**:明渠均匀流的特征是:水力坡度=水面坡度=河底坡度。

答案:D

6-7-2 **解**:明渠均匀流的流量:$A=CA\sqrt{Ri}$,$C=\frac{1}{n}R^{\frac{1}{6}}$,其中:

面积 $A=(b+mh)h-(2+1\times1.2)\times1.2=3.84\text{m}^2$

湿周 $\chi=b+2h\sqrt{1+m^2}=2+2\times1.2\sqrt{1+1^2}=5.394\text{m}$

水力半径 $R=\frac{A}{\chi}=\frac{3.84}{5.394}=0.7119\text{m}$

谢才系数 $C=\frac{1}{n}R^{\frac{1}{6}}=\frac{1}{0.025}\times0.7119^{\frac{1}{6}}=37.8\sqrt{\text{m}}/\text{s}$

代入流量公式:

$Q=CA\sqrt{Ri}=37.8\times3.84\sqrt{0.7119\times0.0008}$

$Q=3.463\text{m}^3/\text{s}$。

答案:B

第八节

6-8-1 **解**:渗流量与过流面积 A、水力坡度 J 的一次方成正比,与土壤的渗透系数 k 有关。

答案:D

6-8-2 **解**:潜水井是指从有自由液面的潜水含水层中开凿的井。

答案:B

6-8-3 **解**:潜水井流量公式:$Q=1.366\dfrac{k(H^2-h^2)}{\lg\dfrac{R}{r_0}}$

代入数据:$Q=1.366\dfrac{0.0006\times(10^2-6^2)}{\lg\dfrac{294}{0.2}}=0.01656\text{m}^3/\text{s}=16.56\text{l/s}$

答案:C

第九节

6-9-1 **解**:纲和谐原量最重要一种用途是:探求物理量间的函数关系。

答案:D

6-9-2 **解**:紊流粗糙区为自动模型区。

答案:D

第七章 电工电子技术

复习指导

一、考试大纲

7.1 电磁学概念

电荷与电场；库仑定律；高斯定理；电流与磁场；安培环路定律；电磁感应定律；洛仑兹力。

7.2 电路知识

电路组成；电路的基本物理过程；理想电路元件及其约束关系；电路模型；欧姆定律；基尔霍夫定律；支路电流法；等效电源定理；叠加原理；正弦交流电的时间函数描述；阻抗；正弦交流电的相量描述；复数阻抗；交流电路稳态分析的相量法；交流电路功率；功率因数；三相配电电路及用电安全；电路暂态；R-C、R-L 电路暂态特性；电路频率特性；R-C、R-L 电路频率特性。

7.3 电动机与变压器

理想变压器；变压器的电压变换、电流变换和阻抗变换原理；三相异步电动机接线、起动、反转及调速方法；三相异步电动机运行特性；简单继电-接触控制电路。

7.5 模拟电子技术

晶体二极管；极型晶体三极管；共射极放大电路；输入阻抗与输出阻抗；射极跟随器与阻抗变换；运算放大器；反相运算放大电路；同相运算放大电路；基于运算放大器的比较器电路；二极管单相半波整流电路；二极管单相桥式整流电路。

7.6 数字电子技术

与、或、非门的逻辑功能；简单组合逻辑电路；D 触发器；JK 触发器数字寄存器；脉冲计数器。

二、复习指导

本章内容可以分为电场与磁场、电路分析方法、电机及拖动基础、模拟电子技术和数字电子技术五个部分。复习重点及要点如下。

(一)电场与磁场

该部分属于物理学中电学部分的内容，是分析电学现象的基础，主要包括库仑定律、高斯定律、安培环路定律、电磁感应定律。利用这些定理分析电磁场问题时物理概念一定要清楚，要注意所用公式、定律的使用条件和公式中各物理量的意义。

(二)电路分析方法

1. 直流电路重点

重点内容包括电路的基本元件、欧姆定律、基尔霍夫定律、叠加原理、戴维南定理。

电路分析的任务是分析线性电路的电压、电流及功率关系。重点是要弄清有源源件(电压源和电流源)和无源元件(电阻、电感和电容)在电路中的作用;电路中电压、电流受克希霍夫电压定律和电流定律约束,欧姆定律控制了电路元件中电压电流关系;使用公式时必须注意电路图中电压、电流正方向和实际方向的关系。叠加原理和戴维南定理是分析线性电路重要定理,必须通过大量的练习灵活地处理电路问题。

2.正弦交流电路重点

重点内容包括正弦量的表示方法、单相和三相电路计算、功率及功率因数、串联与并联谐振的概念。

交流电路与直流电路的分析方法相同,关键是建立正弦交流电路大小、相位和频率的概念和正确地表示正弦量的最大值、有效值、初相位、相位差和角频率,熟悉各种表示方法间的关系并进行转换;能用相量法和复数法计算正弦交流电路。

交流电路的无功功率反映电路中储能元件与电源进行能量交换的规模,有功功率才是电路中真正消耗掉的功率,它不仅与电路中电压和电流的大小有关,还与功率因数 $\cos\phi$ 有关。

谐振是交流电路中电压的相位与电流的相位相同时的特殊现象。此时电路对外呈电阻性质,注意掌握串联谐振和并联谐振的条件和电压电流特征。

三相电路中负载连接的原则是保证负载上得到额定电压,分清对称性负载和非对称性负载的条件,并会计算对称性负载三相电路中电压电流和有功功率的大小;注意星形接法中中线的作用。

3.一阶电路的暂态过程

理解暂态过程出现的条件和物理意义。含有储能元件 C、L 的电路中,电容电压和电感电流不会发生跃变。电路换路(如开关动作)时必须经过一段时间,各物理量才会从旧的稳态过渡到新的稳态。重点是建立电路暂态的概念,用一阶电路三要素法分析电路换路时,电路的电压电流的变化规律。关键在于确定电压电流的初始值、稳态值和时间常数,并用典型公式计算。

(三)电机及拖动基础

主要内容:变压器、三相异步电动机的基本工作原理和使用方法、常用继电器-接触器控制电路、安全用电常识。

了解变压器的基本结构、工作原理,单相变压器原副边电压、电流、阻抗关系及变压器额定值的意义,经济运行条件。了解三相交流异步电动机中转速、转矩、功率关系、名牌数据的意义,特别是电动机的常规使用方法。例如,对三相交流异步电动机启动进行控制的目的是为了限制电动机的起动电流。正常运行为三角形接法的电动机,起动时采用星型接法,起动电流减少的程度可根据三相电路理论,将三相电动机视为一个三相对称形负载便可确定。

掌握常用低压电气控制电路的绘图方法,必须明确,控制电路图中控制电器符号是按照电器未动作的状态表示的。阅读继电接触器控制电路图时要特别注意自锁、联锁的作用,了解过载,短路和失压保护的方法。

安全用电属于基本用电知识,重点是了解接零、接地的区别和应用场合。

(四)模拟电子技术

主要内容:二极管及二极管整流电路、电容电感滤波原理、稳压电路的基本结构;三极管及单管电压放大电路,能够确定三极管电压放大电器的主要技术指标。

了解半导体器件结构、原理、伏安特性、主要参数及使用方法。学习半导体器件的重点是要掌握 PN 结的单向导电性,难点是正确理解和应用二极管的非线性、三极管的电流控制关系。

能正确计算二极管整流电路中输入电压的有效值和整流输出电压平均值的大小关系,理解电容滤波电路的滤波原理和稳压管稳压电路的原理和对电路输出电压的影响。

分析分离元件放大电路的基础在于正确读懂放大电路图（静态偏置、交流耦合、反馈环节的主要特点），正确计算放大电路的静态参数，并会用微变等效电路分析放大器的动态指标（放大倍数、输入电阻、输出电阻）。

分析理想运算放大器组成的线性运算电路（比例、加法、减法和积分运算电路）的基础是正确理解应用运算放大器的理想条件（虚短路——同相输入端和反向输入端的电位相同，虚断路——运放的输入电流为零，输出电阻很小——恒压输出），然后根据线性电路理论分析输出电压（电流）与输入电压（电流）的关系。

（五）数字电子技术

数字电路是利用晶体管的开关特性工作的，分析数字电路时要注意输入和输出信号的逻辑关系，而不是大小关系。复习要点是正确对电路进行化简，并会用波形图和逻辑代数式表示电路输出和输入逻辑关系。基础元件是与门、或门、与非门和异或门电路。学员必需熟练地应用这些器件的逻辑功能，组合逻辑电路就是这些元件的逻辑组合，组合电路没有记忆功能，输出只与当前的输入逻辑有关。

时序逻辑电路有保持、记忆和计数功能，这种触发器主要有三种：R-S、D、J-K 型触发器。分析时序电路时必须注意时钟作用时刻，复习时必须记住这三种触发器的逻辑状态表，会分析时序电路输入、输出信号的时序关系。

第一节　电场与磁场

（一）库仑定律

库仑定律是研究两个静止的点电荷在真空中相互作用规律的，内容如下：

在真空中两个静止点电荷间的相互作用力，方向沿两个点电荷的连线，同种电荷相斥，异种电荷相吸；大小正比于两点电荷电量大小的乘积，反比于两点电荷间距离的平方。

该定律可用矢量公式表示为

$$\boldsymbol{F}_{21}=-\boldsymbol{F}_{12}=\frac{1}{4\pi\varepsilon_0}\frac{q_1q_2}{r_{12}^3}\boldsymbol{r}_{12} \tag{7-1-1}$$

式中：$\boldsymbol{F}_{12}$——点电荷 2 作用于点电荷 1 上的力（N）；

$\boldsymbol{F}_{21}$——点电荷 1 作用于点电荷 2 上的力（N）；

r_{12}——点电荷 1 和 2 之间的距离（m）；

$\boldsymbol{r}_{12}$——点电荷 1 指向点电荷 2 的矢量（m）；

q_1、q_2——分别为点电荷 1 和 2 的电量（C），含正负；

ε_0——真空的介电常数，大小为 $8.85\times10^{-12}\mathrm{C^2/(N\cdot m^2)}$。

（二）电场强度

传递电力的中介物质是电场。置于电场中某点的试验电荷 q_0 将受到源电荷作用的电力 $\boldsymbol{F}$，定义该点电场强度（简称场强）

$$\boldsymbol{E}=\frac{\boldsymbol{F}}{q_0}(\mathrm{N/C}) \tag{7-1-2}$$

作为描写电场的场量。$\boldsymbol{E}$ 是矢量，可以叠加。

若场源是电量为 q(含正负)的点电荷,由计算可知,在观察点 P 的电场强度为

$$\boldsymbol{E}=\frac{q}{4\pi\varepsilon_0 r^3}\boldsymbol{r} \tag{7-1-3}$$

式中:$\boldsymbol{E}$——点电荷 q 产生的电场强度(N/C);

r——点电荷 q 至观察点 P 的距离(m);

$\boldsymbol{r}$——点电荷 q 指向 P 的矢径(m)。

【例 7-1-1】 真空中,点电荷 q_1 和 q_2 的空间位置如图所示,q_1 为正电荷,且 $q_2=-q_1$,则 A 点的电场强度的方向是:

A. 从 A 点指向 q_1

B. 从 A 点指向 q_2

C. 垂直于 q_1q_2 连线,方向向上

D. 垂直于 q_1q_2 连线,方向向下

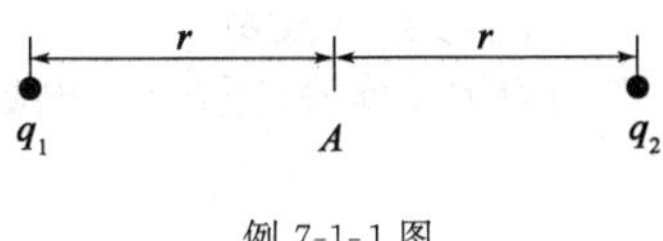

例 7-1-1 图

解 点电荷 q_1、q_2 电场作用的方向分布为:始于正电荷(q_1),终止于负电荷(q_2)。

答案:B

【例 7-1-2】 两个等量异号的点电荷 $+q$ 和 $-q$,间隔为 l,求如图所示考察点 P 在两点电荷连线的中垂线上时,P 点的电场强度。

解 正负电荷单独在 P 点产生的电场的场强分别为

$$E_+=\frac{1}{4\pi\varepsilon_0}\frac{q}{r^2+\left(\frac{l}{2}\right)^2}$$

$$E_-=\frac{1}{4\pi\varepsilon_0}\frac{q}{r^2+\left(\frac{l}{2}\right)^2}$$

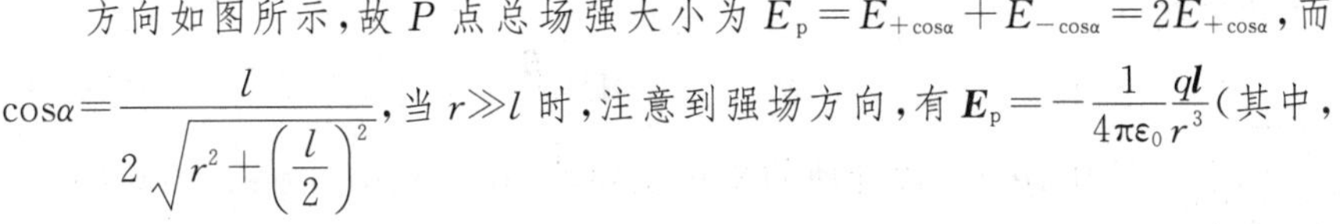

方向如图所示,故 P 点总场强大小为 $E_p=E_{+\cos\alpha}+E_{-\cos\alpha}=2E_{+\cos\alpha}$,而 $\cos\alpha=\frac{l}{2\sqrt{r^2+\left(\frac{l}{2}\right)^2}}$,当 $r\gg l$ 时,注意到强场方向,有 $\boldsymbol{E}_p=-\frac{1}{4\pi\varepsilon_0}\frac{q\boldsymbol{l}}{r^3}$(其中,$\boldsymbol{l}$ 为负电荷指向正电荷的矢量)。

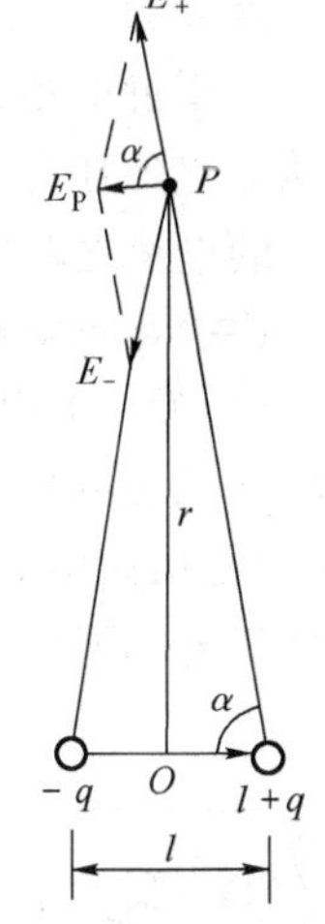

例 7-1-2 图

(三)高斯定理

高斯定理指出了电场强度的分布与场源之间的关系:静电场对任意封闭曲面的电通量只决定于被包围在该曲面内部的电量,且等于被包围在该曲面内的电量代数和除以 ε_0,即

$$\oint_A \boldsymbol{E}\cdot \mathrm{d}\boldsymbol{A}=\frac{1}{\varepsilon_0}\sum q \tag{7-1-4}$$

式中:$\boldsymbol{E}$——电场强度(N/C);

$\mathrm{d}\boldsymbol{A}$——面积元矢量,大小等于 $\mathrm{d}A$(A 为封闭曲面),方向是 $\mathrm{d}A$ 的正法线方向(由内指向外);

ε_0——真空介电常数;

$\sum q$——封闭曲面内电量代数和(C)。

【例 7-1-3】 用高斯定理计算场强。如图所示,无限长带电直导线,电荷密度为 η,求其电场。

解 任取一考查点 P,到导线距离为 R,过 P 作一封闭圆柱面,柱面高 l,底面半径 R,轴线

与导线重合。由对称性知，P 点场强方向沿半径方向，设其大小为 E，按高斯定理，有

$$2\pi Rl \cdot E=\frac{1}{\varepsilon_0}\eta \cdot l$$

所以

$$E=\frac{1}{\varepsilon_0}\eta \cdot \frac{1}{2\pi R}$$

考虑方向，有 $\boldsymbol{E}=\frac{1}{2\pi\varepsilon_0}\frac{\eta}{R}<\boldsymbol{R}^0$（$\boldsymbol{R}^0$ 为由 O 点指向 P 的单位矢量）。

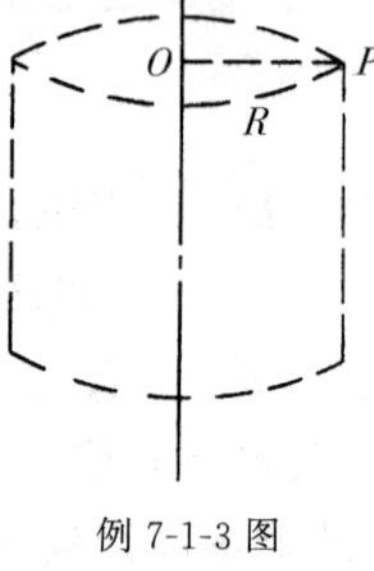

例 7-1-3 图

（四）电场力做功

电荷从 a 点移至 b 点，电场力做功

$$A_{ab}=\int_a^b \boldsymbol{F} \cdot \mathrm{d}\boldsymbol{l} \tag{7-1-5}$$

式中：$\boldsymbol{F}$——电场对电荷的作用力。

可以证明，A_{ab} 的大小仅与试验电荷电量以及 a、b 点的位置有关，而与路径无关，即静电场力是保守力。

基于静电场是保守力场，可以定义电场空间位置的标量函数：电势，其量值等于单位正电荷从该点经任意路径到无穷远处时电场力所做的功，单位为伏特（V）。静电场中，任意两点 a 和 b 的电势之差叫电势差，也叫电压。

（五）磁感应强度，磁场强度，磁通

（1）静止的电荷产生静电场；而运动电荷周围不仅存在电场，也存在磁场。对于电场曾以作用在试验电荷上的电力定义了场强 $\boldsymbol{E}$，仿此，研究作用在运动电荷上的磁力来引入描写磁场的物理量：磁感应强度（又称磁通密度）$\boldsymbol{B}$，单位为特斯拉（T）。在各向同性的磁介质中，再定义辅助量磁场强度 $\boldsymbol{H}$（A/m），即

$$\boldsymbol{H}=\frac{\boldsymbol{B}}{\mu} \tag{7-1-6}$$

式中：μ——磁介质的相对磁导率，在空气中 $\mu=\mu_0=4\pi\times10^{-7}$ H/m。

举例来说，如图 7-1-1 所示无限长直导线电流强度大小为 I，方向向上，则距导线 a 处磁感应强度大小为 $\frac{I\mu}{2\pi a}$，磁场强度大小为 $H=\frac{I}{2\pi a}$，两者方向皆垂直半径，与电流方向成右手螺旋。

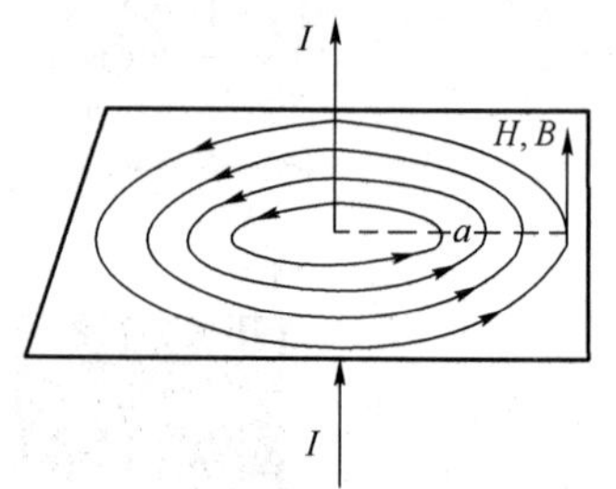

图 7-1-1　无限长直导线的磁感应强度与磁场强度

【例 7-1-4】 由图示长直导线上的电流产生的磁场：

A. 方向与电流方向相同

B. 方向与电流方向相反

C. 顺时针方向环绕长直导线（自上向下俯视）

D. 逆时针方向环绕长直导线（自上向下俯视）

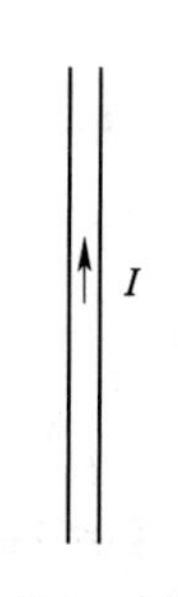

例 7-1-4 图

解　电流与磁场的方向可以根据右手螺旋定则确定，即让右手大拇指指向电流的方向，那么四指的指向就是磁感线的环绕方向。

答案：D

（2）定义通过有限曲面 S 的磁通量（Wb）为

$$\Phi_m = \int_S \boldsymbol{B} \cdot d\boldsymbol{S} \tag{7-1-7}$$

（六）安培力

磁场中的载流导体会受到磁场力的作用，称为安培力，考查电流元所受安培力，有

$$d\boldsymbol{F} = Id\boldsymbol{l} \times \boldsymbol{B} \tag{7-1-8}$$

式中：$Id\boldsymbol{l}$——电流元；

$\boldsymbol{B}$——磁感应强度。

至于任意形状载流导体在磁场中所受安培力，应等于各电流元所受安培力之和（矢量和）

$$\boldsymbol{F} = \int_L d\boldsymbol{F} = \int Id\boldsymbol{l} \times \boldsymbol{B} \tag{7-1-9}$$

显然，长为 l 的直线电流在匀强磁场 $\boldsymbol{B}$ 中所受安培力为

$$\boldsymbol{F} = I\boldsymbol{l} \times \boldsymbol{B} \tag{7-1-10}$$

【例 7-1-5】 一载流直导线 AB 如图所示放置，电流大小为 i_0，方向从 A 至 B，磁感应强度 $\boldsymbol{B}_0$ 方向沿 x 轴正向，大小为 B_0，求 AB 导线受力。

解 $\boldsymbol{F} = i_0 \overrightarrow{AB} \times \boldsymbol{B}_0$

$$|\vec{\boldsymbol{F}}| = i_0 B |\overrightarrow{AB}| \sin\theta = i_0 B_0 \sqrt{5} \cdot \frac{1}{\sqrt{5}} = i_0 B_0$$

$\boldsymbol{F}$ 方向可以用左手判定，垂直纸面向内。

例 7-1-5 图

（七）安培环路定理

在稳恒电流产生的磁场中，不管载流回路形状如何，对任意闭合路径，磁感应强度的线积分（即环流）仅取决于被闭合路径所圈围的电流的代数和

$$\oint_L \boldsymbol{B} \cdot d\boldsymbol{l} = \mu_0 \sum I \tag{7-1-11}$$

式中：$\boldsymbol{B}$——磁感应强度（T）；

μ_0——真空磁导率（H/m）；

$\sum I$——被闭合路径圈围的电流代数和（A）。

亦可表示成

$$\oint_L \boldsymbol{H} \cdot d\boldsymbol{l} = \sum I \tag{7-1-12}$$

式中：$\boldsymbol{H}$——磁场强度。

电流的正负，由积分时在闭合曲线上所取绕行方向按右手螺旋法则决定。

【例 7-1-6】 磁场由若干互相平行的无限长载流直导线产生，各导线电流分别记为 I_1、I_2、I_3、I_4、I_5、I_6，大小分别为 i_1、i_2、i_3、i_4、i_5、i_6，方向如图所示，求磁感应强度 $\boldsymbol{B}$ 对闭合回路 C 的线积分，绕行方向如图所示。

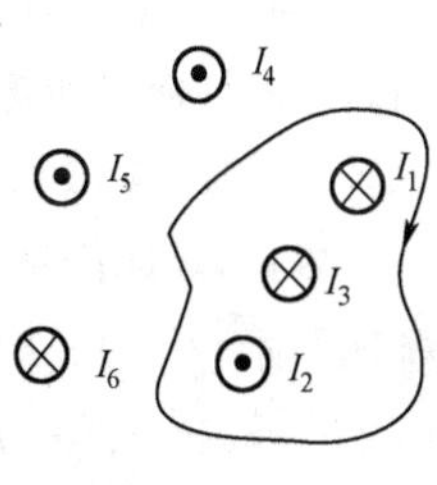

例 7-1-6 图

解 根据安培环路定理

$$\oint_C \boldsymbol{B}\cdot \mathrm{d}\boldsymbol{l}=\mu_0(i_1-i_2+i_3)$$

（八）电磁感应定律

当空间磁场随时间发生变化时，就在周围空间激起感应电场，这个感应电场作用于导体回路，在导体回路中产生感应电动势，并形成感应电流。

法拉第电磁感应定律指出：不论任何原因，使通过回路面积的磁通量发生变化时，回路中产生的感应电动势与磁通量对时间的变化率成正比，即

$$\varepsilon=-\frac{\mathrm{d}\Phi}{\mathrm{d}t} \tag{7-1-13}$$

如果感应回路不止一匝，而是 N 匝，则有：

任意规定回路"绕行正方向"如下

$$\varepsilon=-N\frac{\mathrm{d}\Phi}{\mathrm{d}t} \tag{7-1-14}$$

使用式(7-1-13)及式(7-1-14)时，要先在回路上任意规定一个绕行方向作为回路正方向，再用右手螺旋法则确定回路面积正法线方向。

【例 7-1-7】 如图所示，均匀磁场中，磁感应强度方向向上，大小为5T，圆环半径 0.5m，电阻 5Ω，现磁感应强度以 1T/s 速度均匀减小，问圆环内电流的大小及方向。

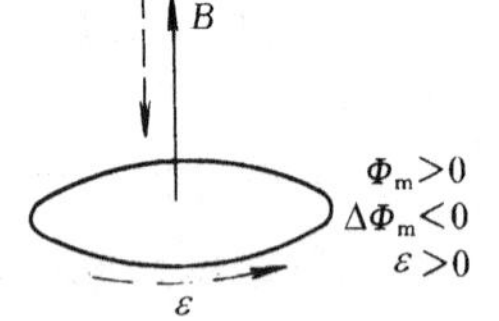

例 7-1-7 图

解 确定绕行方向如图所示，则

$$\boldsymbol{\Phi}=\int_S \boldsymbol{B}\cdot \mathrm{d}S=B\cdot \pi r^2$$

$$\varepsilon=-\frac{\mathrm{d}\Phi}{\mathrm{d}t}=-\frac{\mathrm{d}B}{\mathrm{d}t}\cdot \pi r^2=\frac{\pi}{4}$$

所以圆环内电流大小 $i=\frac{\varepsilon}{R}=\frac{\pi}{20}$，方向与绕行方向一致。

习 题

7-1-1 无限大平行板电容器，两极板相隔 5cm，板上均匀带电，$\sigma=3\times10^{-6}\,\mathrm{c/m^2}$，若将负极板接地，则正极板的电势为（　　）。

A. $\frac{7.5}{\varepsilon_0}\times10^{-8}\,\mathrm{V}$　B. $\frac{15}{\varepsilon_0}\times10^{-8}\,\mathrm{V}$　C. $\frac{30}{\varepsilon_0}\times10^{-6}\,\mathrm{V}$　D. $\frac{7.5}{\varepsilon_0}\times10^{-6}\,\mathrm{V}$

7-1-2 如图所示导体回路处在一均匀磁场中，$B=0.5\mathrm{T}$，$R=2\Omega$，ab 边长 $L=0.5\mathrm{m}$，可以滑动，$\alpha=60°$，现以速度 $v=4\mathrm{m/s}$ 将 ab 边向右匀速平行移动，通过 R 的感应电流为（　　）。

A. 0.5A　B. −1A　C. −0.86A　D. 0.43A

7-1-3 如图所示电路中，磁性材料上绕有两个导电线圈，若上方线圈加的是 100V 的直流电压，则（　　）。

A. 下方线圈两端不会产生磁感应电动势

B. 下方线圈两端产生方向为左"−"右"+"的磁感应电动势

C. 下方线圈两端产生方向为左“+”右“−”的磁感应电动势

D. 磁性材料内部的磁通取逆时针方向

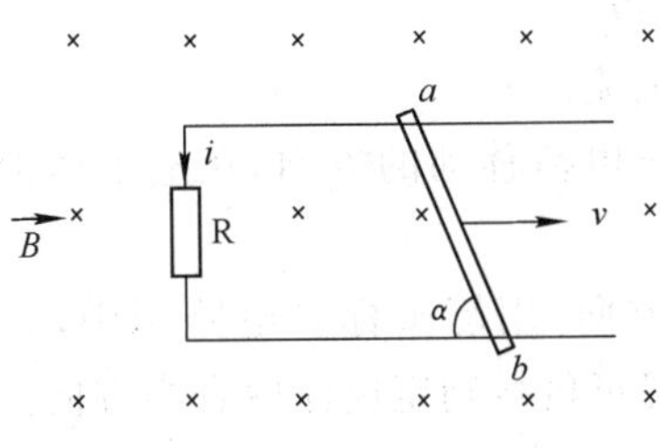

题 7-1-2 图

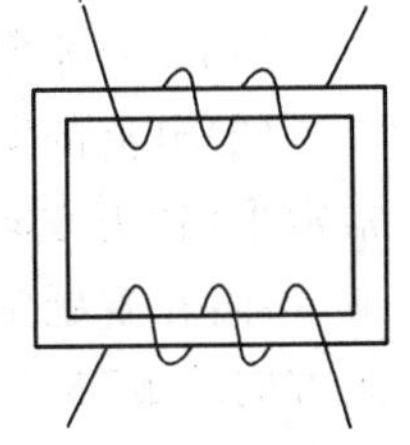

题 7-1-3 图

7-1-4 在图中，线圈 a 的电阻为 R_a，线圈 b 的电阻为 R_b，两者彼此靠近如图示，若外加激励 $u=U_M\sin\omega t$，则(　　)。

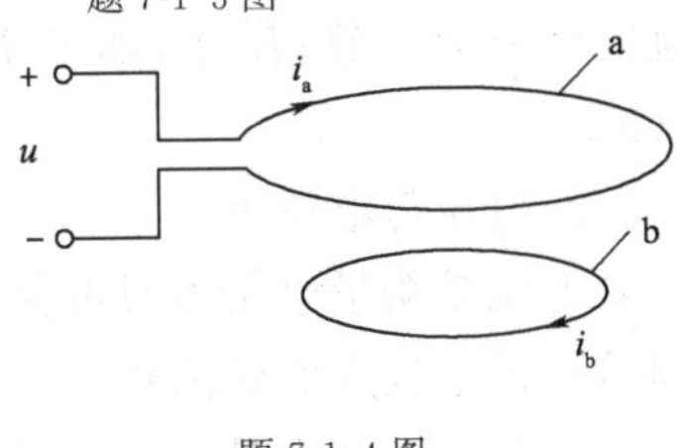

题 7-1-4 图

A. $i_a=\dfrac{u}{R_a}, i_b=0$　　B. $i_a\neq\dfrac{u}{R_a}, i_b\neq 0$

C. $i_a=\dfrac{u}{R_a}, i_b\neq 0$　　D. $i_a\neq\dfrac{u}{R_a}, i_b=0$

第二节　电路的基本概念和基本定律

一、电路的作用和基本物理量

(一)电路的作用

电路是电流流通的路径。它是人们为实现某种要求，将必要的元件、设备按一定的方式组合起来的物理系统。

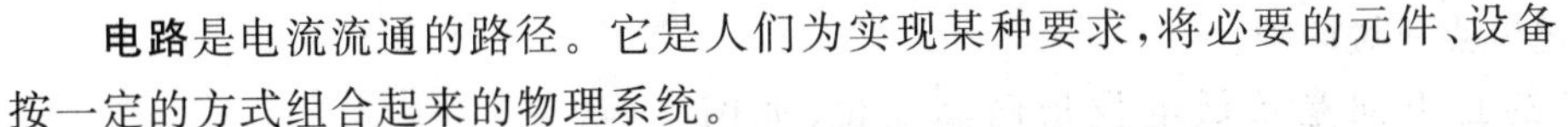

电路的作用大体上可以分为两类：实现能量的传输与分配和传递并处理信息。但无论电路的作用属于前者或是后者，从电路的具体结构中都可以分为电源、负载和中间环节这三部分。

电源：将非电能转变为电能的物理装置(如发电机、电池、传感器等)，作用是为电路提供电能或信号。

负载：将电能转变为非电能的物理装置(如电炉、电动机、扬声器等)。

中间环节：对电能量进行传输，分配和控制的部分(如开关等)。

为便于对实际电路进行分析，可以用数学语言来说明电路现象，根据问题要求，突出电路的电、磁性质，用电路符号和连线组合起来的图形就是电路模型，如图 7-2-1 所示。

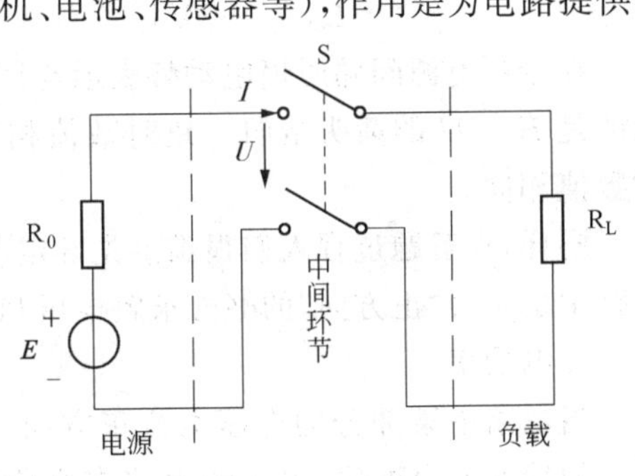

图 7-2-1　电路模型

(二)电路的基本物理量

1. 电流

反映电荷定向流动的物理现象。

(1)电流的大小用**电流强度**表示，简称**电流**，单位是安培(A)。

电流用公式表示为：

$$i=\frac{\mathrm{d}q}{\mathrm{d}t} \tag{7-2-1}$$

当 $i=I$(常数)时，称为直流电流。

(2)电流的实际方向定义为正电荷移动的方向，在电工理论中为解题方便常常采用“正方向”的概念。

即：在解题中先人为假定正方向，用箭头标在电路图中，然后根据假定的正方向求解，最后根据电流数值的正负号判定电流的真实方向。

图 7-2-2 电路图

如图 7-2-2 所示电路中，求解电流为 $I=3\text{A}>0$，说明假定电流正方向与电流实际方向一致；反之，如果 $I=-3\text{A}<0$，说明假设的电流正方向与实际的电流方向是相反的。

2. 电压与电位差

电压是衡量电场力对电荷做功的物理量，其大小用电场力将单位正电荷从高电位点移动到另一低电位点所做的功。

电位是电路中某一点对于参考点之间的电压，电路中由 a 点到 b 点之间的电压 U_{ab} 可以表示为：

$$U_{\mathrm{ab}}=U_{\mathrm{a}}-U_{\mathrm{b}} \tag{7-2-2}$$

式中，U_{a}，U_{b} 分别表示电路中 a，b 两点的电位。

电压、电位的基本单位是伏特(V)。

3. 电动势

电动势是反映电源内部非电力做功的物理量，在数值上等于非静电力将单位正电荷从低电位点推向高电位点所做的功。

电动势 E 的正方向是从低电位指向高电位，如图 7-2-3 所示。

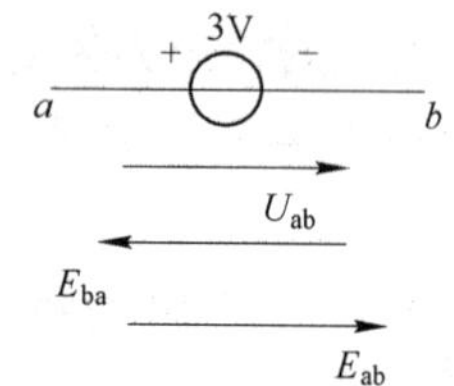

图 7-2-3 电压与电动势方向

$$\left.\begin{array}{l}E_{\mathrm{ba}}=3\mathrm{V}\\U_{\mathrm{ab}}=3\mathrm{V}\end{array}\right\}U_{\mathrm{ab}}=E_{\mathrm{ba}}$$

$$\left.\begin{array}{l}U_{\mathrm{ab}}=3\mathrm{V}\\E_{\mathrm{ab}}=-3\mathrm{V}\end{array}\right\}U_{\mathrm{ab}}=-E_{\mathrm{ab}}$$

在分析电源问题时用电动势表示与用电压表示是一样的，注意的是 E 与 U 的箭头指向一致时数值相反，两者箭头指向相反时数值相同。

同样，在解题过程人们很难事先确定电压、电动势的实际方向。因此，与电流一样，在实际电路中也是用“正方向”的概念求解电压和电动势的。

4. 电功率

当电路中某部分的电压电流正方向一致时，根据 $P=UI$ 计算出的功率若为正值，表示该电路在吸收功率；若计算出的功率为负值，则认为该电路是发出功率的，起电源的作用。

【例 7-2-1】 分析如图所示电路的功率分配情况。

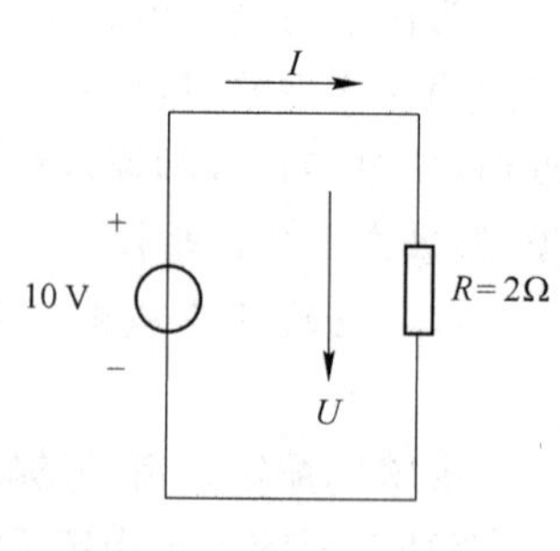

例 7-2-1 图

解 根据

$$I=\frac{U}{R}=\frac{10}{2}=5\text{A}$$

且

$$P_R = RI^2 = 2 \times 5^2 = 50\text{W} > 0$$

可见负载 R 消耗功率。

10V 电源功率为：

$$P_s = -UI = -10 \times 5 = -50\text{W} < 0$$

可见，该电压源发出功率。

全部电路的功率关系：

$$\sum P = P_R + P_s = 50 + (-50) = 0\text{W}$$

说明该电路的功率平衡。

【例 7-2-2】 图示电路消耗电功率 2W，则下列表达式中正确的是：

A. $(8+R)I^2=2,(8+R)I=10$

B. $(8+R)I^2=2,-(8+R)I=10$

C. $-(8+R)I^2=2,-(8+R)I=10$

D. $-(8+R)I=10,(8+R)I=10$

例 7-2-2 图

解 电路的功率关系 $P=UI=I^2R$ 以及欧姆定律 $U=RI$，是在电路的电压、电流的正方向一致时成立；当方向不一致时，前面增加“－”号。

答案：B

二、基本电路元件

电路中的元件必须能正确反映电路的两种性质：电源性质和负载性质。

(一)电源元件

电源的作用是满足负载要求的电压、电流和功率。电源的外特性(电压、电流关系)称为电源的“V-A 特性”，它可以表示电源的端电压和端电流关系。实际电源的物理结构可以不同，但是对外电路的作用都可以用电压源模型或者是电流源模型来表示。

1. 电压源模型

电动势(U_s)与电阻(R_0)串联组成如图 7-2-4a)所示，电压源端电压可用下式计算

$$U = U_s - R_0 I \tag{7-2-3}$$

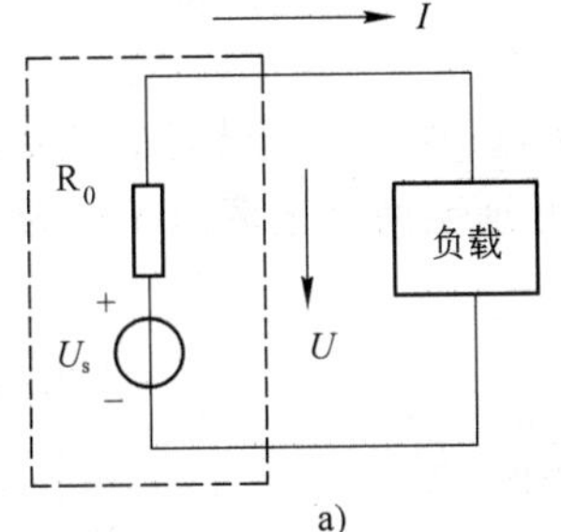

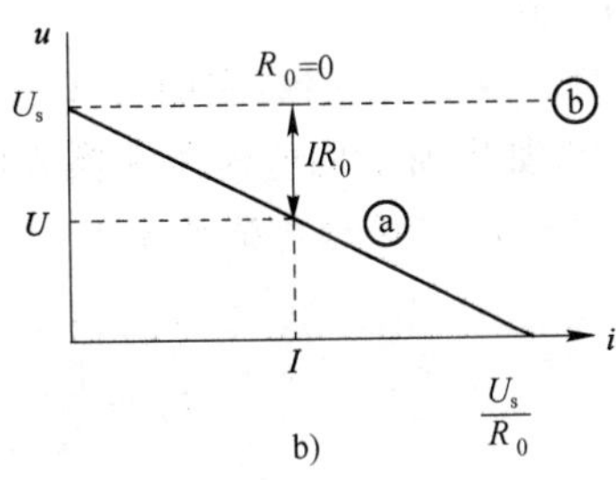

图 7-2-4 电源模型与 V-A 特性

可以得出如图 7-2-4b)所示的“V-A 特性”。可见，负载电流增加时电源端电压减少的过程，并且电压减少的程度与 R_0 的大小有关。为减少电源内部的能量消耗，我们希望实际电压源的内阻 R_0 越小越好。

$R_0=0$ 的电压源称为理想电压源，如图 7-2-4b)所示曲线ⓑ，理想电压源的特点是：$U=E_s=$ 常数，与负载电流的大小无关，理想电压源供出电流大小是由负载控制的：$I=U_s/R$。

2. 电流源模型

电流源(I_s)与电源内阻(R_0)并联组成。如图 7-2-5a)所示，电流源输出电流的大小可以用下式表示：

$$I=I_s-\frac{U}{R_0} \tag{7-2-4}$$

“V-A 特性”如图 7-2-5b)所示，可见实际电流源的电流随负载电压的增加而减少，为减少电流源内部损耗，电流源内阻 R_0 越大越好。

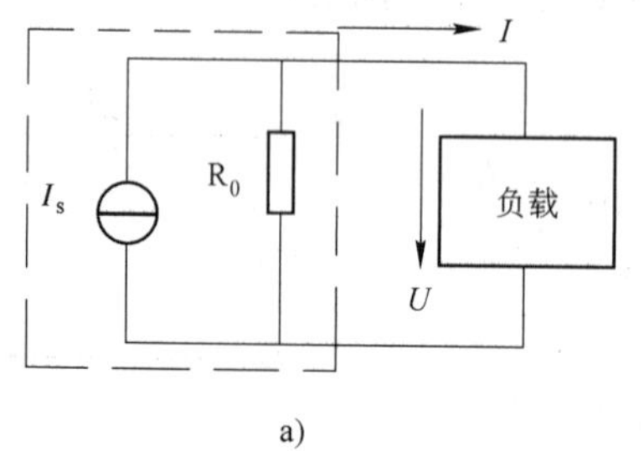

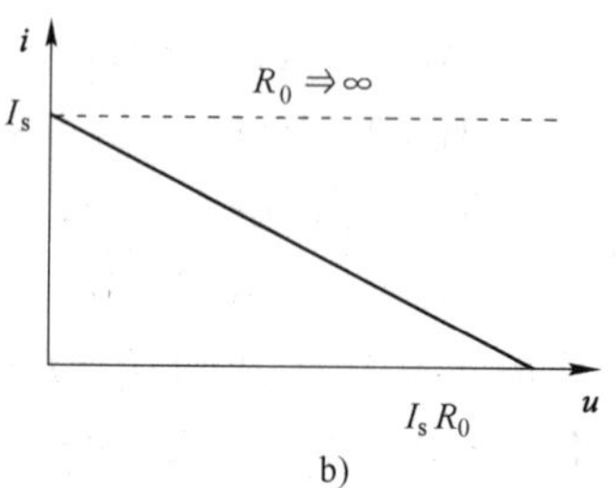

图 7-2-5 电流源模型及外特性

$R_0=\infty$ 的电流源称为理想电流源，如图 7-2-5b)所示曲线。

理想电流源的特点是 $I=I_s=$ 常数，即输出电流与负载的大小无关；而理想电流源两端的电压大小由负载电阻决定：$U=R\cdot I_s$。

3. 两种电源的等效变换

在实际中，用电压源或电流源符号表示电源的作用没有本质的区别，因为两种电源模型对外部(负载)作用是完全等效的。

电压源与电流源的变换方法：电压源和电流源中电阻 R_0 的数值相同。

且 $U_s=R_0I_s$，则公式(7-2-3)可改写为

$$U=R_0I_s-R_0I \tag{7-2-5}$$

进而可改写为

$$I=I_s-\frac{U}{R_0}$$

与式(7-2-4)一致。

两种电源的外特性方程一致，它们对外电路的作用是一样的，这就是等效变换的概念。

【例 7-2-3】 将如图所示的电压源变换为电流源，并证明两个电源对负载 R_L 的作用相同。

解 将电压源图 a)转换为电流源图 b)，其中

$$R_0=1\Omega$$

$$I_s=\frac{U_s}{R_0}=\frac{5}{1}=5\text{A}$$

$$I=\frac{U_s}{R_0+R_L}=1\text{A} \qquad I=I_s\frac{R_0}{R_0+R_L}=1\text{A}$$

$$U = R_L I = 4\mathrm{V} \qquad U = R_L I = 4\mathrm{V}$$

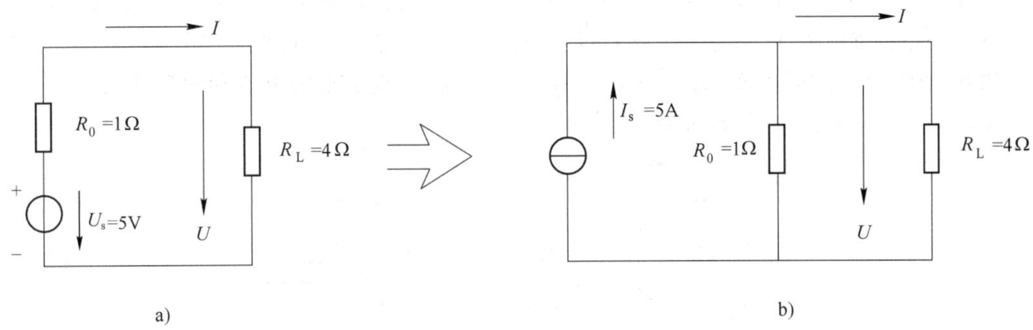

例 7-2-3 图　电压源转变为电流源

可见两个电源在电阻 R_L 上产生的电压、电流相同，$P_R = UI = 4 \times 1 = 4\mathrm{W}$。

这里有三点需要注意：

(1)理想电压源与理想电流源不能等效变换；

(2)所谓等效变换是指端电压 U、端电流 I 的等效，即对外部负载等效，不对内部电路等效；

(3)变换以后电流源 I_s 正方向与电源 U_s 的方向相反。

(二)负载元件

1. 电阻元件

电阻元件是反映电路中消耗电能多少的元件，其端电压 u 的大小与流过该电阻电流 i 的大小成比例。

线性电阻：$\frac{u}{i} = r = R =$ 常数(见图 7-2-6 中曲线 ⓐ)；非线性电阻：$\frac{u}{i} = r \neq$ 常数(见图 7-2-6 中曲线 ⓑ)。

2. 电感元件

电感元件是反映储存磁场能量多少的元件，由物理学中电磁感应定律(Ψ 为电感元件中的磁通量)，即

$$e_1 = -\frac{\mathrm{d}\Psi}{\mathrm{d}t} = -\left(\frac{\mathrm{d}\Psi}{\mathrm{d}i}\right)\frac{\mathrm{d}i}{\mathrm{d}t}$$

当 $\frac{\mathrm{d}\Psi}{\mathrm{d}t} =$ 常数 $= L$，称为线性电感(见图 7-2-7 中曲线ⓐ)，可写出电压电流关系式

$$u = -e = L\frac{\mathrm{d}i}{\mathrm{d}t}\left(\text{或 } i = \frac{1}{L}\int u\mathrm{d}t\right)$$

当 $\frac{\mathrm{d}\Psi}{\mathrm{d}t} \neq$ 常数，称为非线性电感(见图 7-2-7 中曲线ⓑ)。

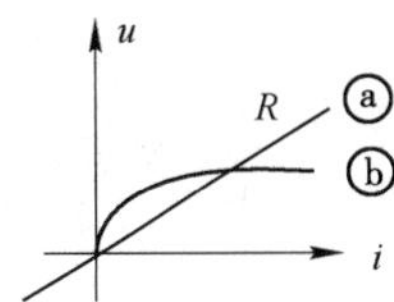

图 7-2-6　电阻元件

3. 电容元件

电容元件是反映储存电场能量多少的元件。

根据 $i = \mathrm{d}q/\mathrm{d}t = \frac{\mathrm{d}q}{\mathrm{d}u} \cdot \frac{\mathrm{d}u}{\mathrm{d}t}$，当 $\frac{\mathrm{d}q}{\mathrm{d}u} = C =$ 常数时，为线性电容，见图 7-2-8 中曲线 ⓐ，即

$$i = C\frac{\mathrm{d}u}{\mathrm{d}t} \quad \text{或} \quad u = \frac{1}{C}\int i\mathrm{d}t$$

当 $\frac{\mathrm{d}q}{\mathrm{d}u} \neq$ 常数时，为非线性电容，见图 7-2-8 中曲线ⓑ。

电路基础部分是以分析线性电路为主。

线性电路是由独立电源和线性元件构成的。即使在后边遇到非线性元件(二极管、三极管……),也是将非线性元件线性化以后,用线性电路的解题方法处理。

独立电源——电压源 E_s、电流源 I_s 的数值为常数,与其供出的电流和电压无关。

线性元件——R、L、C 线性元件。

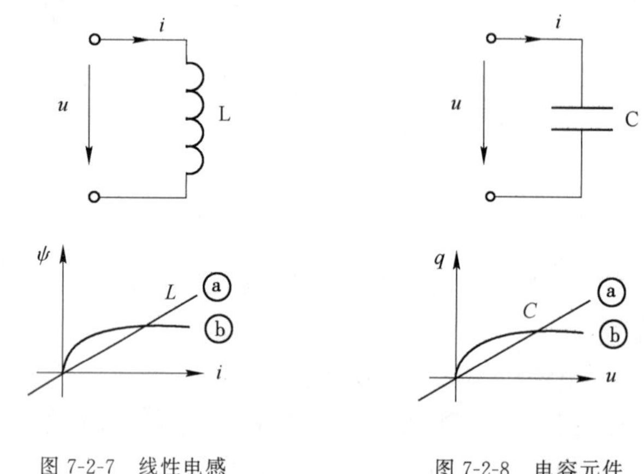

图 7-2-7 线性电感　　图 7-2-8 电容元件

三、电路的工作状态

如图 7-2-9 所示为最简单的电源向负载供电路:通过开关 S_1、S_2 的适当组合,电路将工作于三种状态(有载工作状态、开路和短路工作状态)。

电源端电压关系　　$U = U_s - R_0 I$　[得图 7-2-9b)中曲线①]　　(7-2-6)

负载电压关系　　$U = R_L I$　[得图 7-2-9b)中曲线②]　　(7-2-7)

图 7-2-9b)中①、②曲线交点 I_Q、U_Q 是实际电路的工作电压和工作电流。

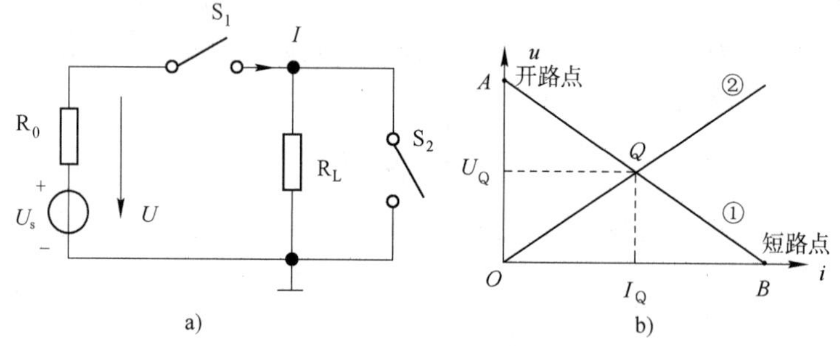

图 7-2-9 工作电路

(一)有载工作状态(S_1 合,S_2 分)

这时电源与负载接通向负载供电,供电的多少与负载电阻 R_L 有关。

由式(7-2-6)和式(7-2-7)可知　　$U_s - R_0 I = R_L I$

变为功率方程　　$U_s I - R_0 I^2 = R_L I^2$

即　　$P_s - \Delta P = P_L$　　(7-2-8)

电源电动势发出的功率 P_s 减去电源内阻 R_0 上消耗的功率 ΔP 以后,才是负载上实际得到的功率 P_L。

当电源或负载电压、电流、功率都达到规定值(生产厂家规定的标称值)时,称电源或负载运行为额定工作状态。

（二）开路状态

指电源与负载断开（S_1 分），即

$$I=0, U=U_s, P_L=0$$

此时称电路的开路状态，电源不向负载供电（空载）。

（三）短路状态

指电源电流不流经负载，直接由导线返回电源的情况。对电压源来说短路时，$U=0$，$I=\frac{U_s}{R_0}$，$P_L=0$（图7-2-9中 B 点）。但电源电动势产生的功率很大（$P_s=IU_s$），该功率全部消耗在电源内阻 R_0 上，使电源严重发热。电压源短路是一种事故状态，实际中必须避免。

四、电路的基本定律

电路一旦构成，应注意如何分析电路中的电压、电流和功率的大小。分析电路的依据有两个：一是元件本身的规律；二是这些元件组成电路以后，电路中电压、电流的规律（即基尔霍夫电压、电流定律）。

（一）基尔霍夫电流定律

根据电流连续性质，基尔霍夫电流定律是用来处理节点（三条或三条以上通电导线汇合点）电流关系的定律。

定义：任一电路，任何时刻，任一节点电流的代数和为0，即

$$\sum i=0 \tag{7-2-9}$$

一般流入节点电流为正，流出节点电流为负。

如图 7-2-10 所示电路中，节点 a 的电流关系为

$$I_1+I_2-I_3=0$$

基尔霍夫电流定律也可以用来分析闭合曲面的电流关系，如图 7-2-11 所示电路，$I'=I$。当 S 打开时，$I=0$。

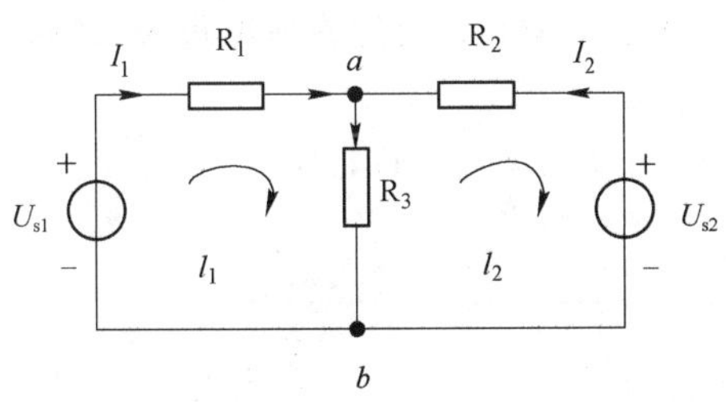

图 7-2-10

图 7-2-11

（二）基尔霍夫电压定律

根据能量守衡性质，基尔霍夫电压定律可以确定回路中各部分电压关系。

定义：任一电路，任何时刻，任一回路电压降的代数和为0，即

$$\sum u=0 \tag{7-2-10}$$

如图 7-2-10 所示电路 l_1、l_2 回路（取顺时针方向），有

$$l_1:\quad -U_{s1}+I_1R_1+I_3R_3=0$$

$$l_2:\quad -I_3R_3-I_2R_2+U_{s2}=0$$

同样基尔霍夫定律也可以从闭合回路推广应用于开路的情况。

【例 7-2-4】 已知电路如图 a)所示，其中电流 I 等于：

A. 0.1A　　B. 0.2A　　C. −0.1A　　D. −0.2A

解 见图 b)，设 2V 电压源电流为 I'，则：$I=I'+0.1$

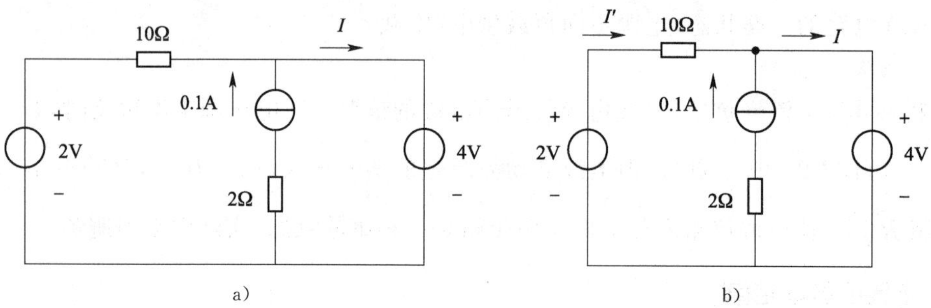

例 7-2-4 图

$10I'=2-4=-2\text{V}$

$I'=-0.2\text{A}$

$I=-0.2+0.1=-0.1\text{A}$

答案：C

习　题

7-2-1 如图所示电阻电路中 a、b 端的等效电阻为(　　)。

A. 6Ω　　B. 12Ω　　C. 3Ω　　D. 9Ω

7-2-2 某电热器的额定功率为 2W，额定电压为 100V。拟将它串联一电阻后接在额定电压为 200V 的直流电源上使用，则该串联电阻 R 的阻值和额定功率 P_N 分别应为(　　)。

A. $R=5\text{k}\Omega$，$P_N=1\text{W}$　　B. $R=5\text{k}\Omega$，$P_N=2\text{W}$

C. $R=10\text{k}\Omega$，$P_N=2\text{W}$　　D. $R=10\text{k}\Omega$，$P_N=1\text{W}$

7-2-3 在如图所示的电路中，用量程为 10V、内阻为 20kΩ/V 级的直流电压表，测得 A、B 两点间的电压 U_{AB} 为(　　)。

A. 6V　　B. 5V　　C. 4V　　D. 3V

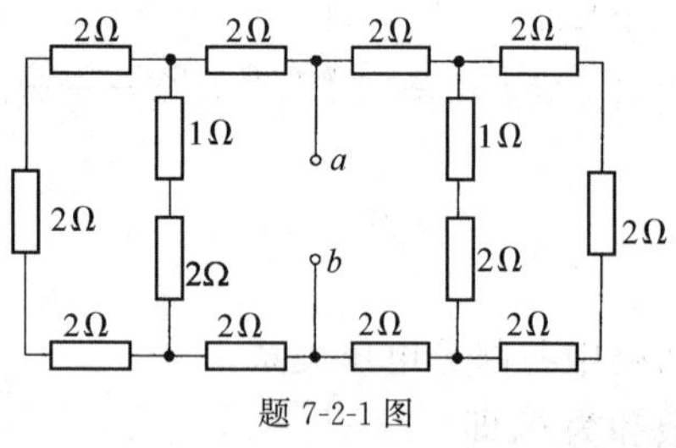

题 7-2-1 图

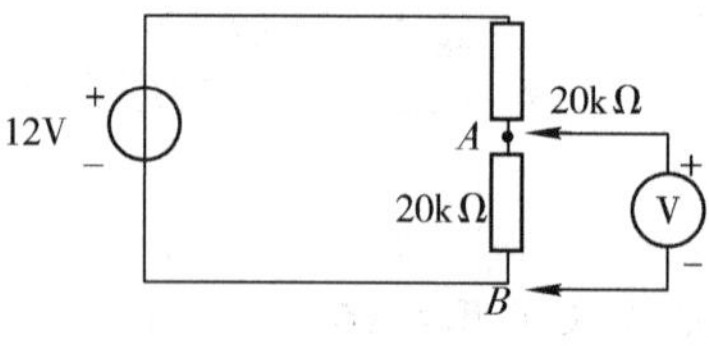

题 7-2-3 图

7-2-4 如图所示电路中，已知：$U_1=U_2=12\text{V}$，$R_1=R_2=4\text{k}\Omega$，$R_3=16\text{k}\Omega$。S 断开后 A 点电位 U_{AO} 和 S 闭合后 A 点电位 U_{As} 分别是(　　)。

A. −4V，3.6V　　B. 6V，0V

C. 4V，−2.4V　　D. −4V，2.4V

7-2-5 在如图所示的电路中，$I_{s1}=3\text{A}$，$I_{s2}=6\text{A}$。当电流源 I_{s1} 单独作用时，流过 $R=1\Omega$

电阻的电流 $I'=1\text{A}$，则流过电阻 R 的实际电流 I 值为(　　)。

A. -1A　　　　B. $+1\text{A}$

C. -2A　　　　D. $+2\text{A}$

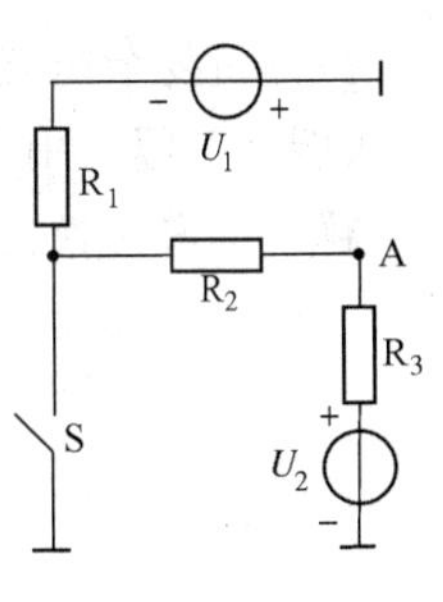

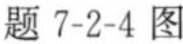
题 7-2-4 图

7-2-6　观察如图所示的直流电路，可知，在该电路中(　　)。

A. I_s 和 R_1 形成一个电流源模型，U_s 和 R_2 形成一个电压源模型

B. 理想电流源 I_s 的端电压为 0

C. 理想电流源 I_s 的端电压由 U_1 和 U_2 共同决定

D. 流过理想电压源的电流与 I_s 无关

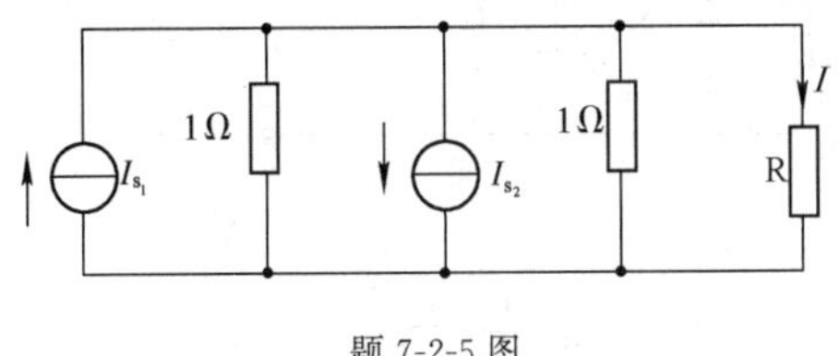

题 7-2-5 图

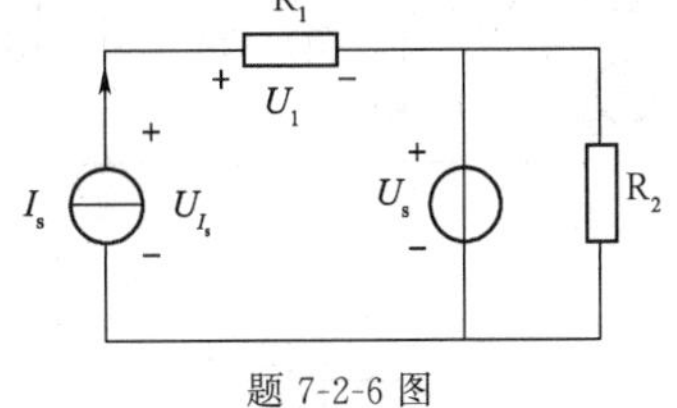

题 7-2-6 图

第三节　直流电路的解题方法

电路分析的目的是找出电路中 U、I、P 的关系。在线性电路中解决问题的常用方法是叠加原理和戴维南定理。

对于不能用简单串并联方法求解的复杂电路，要根据电路的特点去寻找更合适的求解方法。本部分总结几种最常用的电路分析方法：电源变换法、支路电流法、叠加原理和戴维南定理。

一、电源等效变换法

由上节电源元件的介绍，可知电压源模型的外特性和电流源模型的外特性是相同的。因此，电源的两种模型互相等效，可以进行等效变换。但是，电压源模型和电流源模型的等效关系只是对外电路而言的，对电源内部则不等效。

例如在图 7-3-1a) 中，当电压源开路时，$I=0$，电源内阻 R_0 上不损耗功率；但在图 7-3-1b) 中电流源开路时，电源内部仍有电流，内阻 R_0 上有功率损耗。

电源等效电阻不限于电源内部内阻 R_0，只要一个电动势为 E 的理想电压源和某个电阻 R 串联的电路，都可以化为一个电流为 I_s 的理想电流源和这个电阻并联的电路图 7-3-2，两者是等效的。

其中
$$I_s=\frac{E}{R}\quad \text{或}\quad E=RI_s \tag{7-3-1}$$

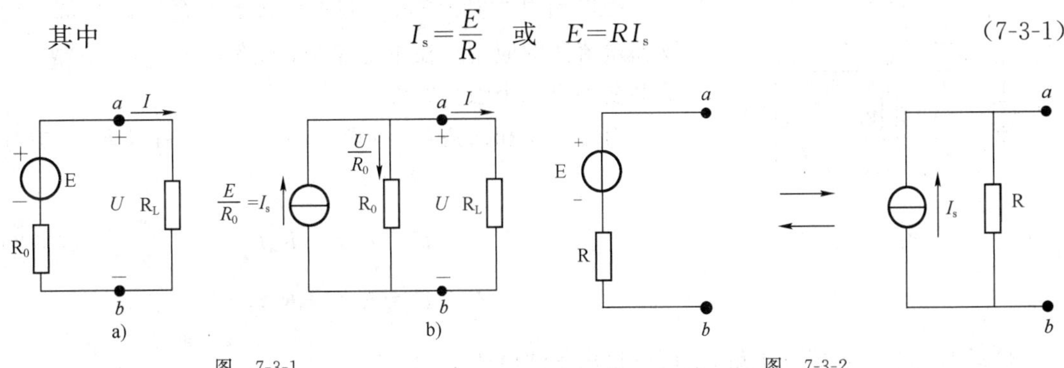

图　7-3-1　　　　图　7-3-2

在分析复杂电路时，也可以用电源等效变换的方法。

【例 7-3-1】 用电源变换法求如图所示电路中的电流。

解 电源变换过程如图 b)、c)、d)所示，由图 d)得出

$$I=\frac{9-4}{1+2+7}=0.5\mathrm{A}$$

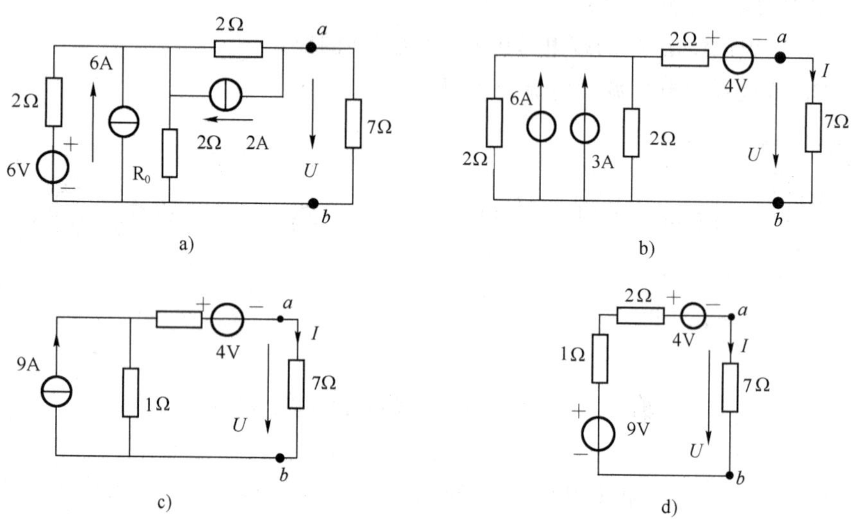

例 7-3-1 图

二、支路电流法

在计算复杂电路的各种方法中，支路电流法是最基本的。它是应用基尔霍夫电流定律和电压定律分别对结点和回路列出所需要的方程组，而后解出各未知支路电流。

支路电流法的解题步骤：

(1)选定支路并标出各支路电流的参考方向，并对选定的回路标出回路循行方向。

(2)应用 KCL 列出 $(n-1)$个独立的结点电流方程。

(3)应用 KVL 列出 $b-(n-1)$个独立的回路电压方程。

(4)联立求解 b 个方程，求出各支路电流。

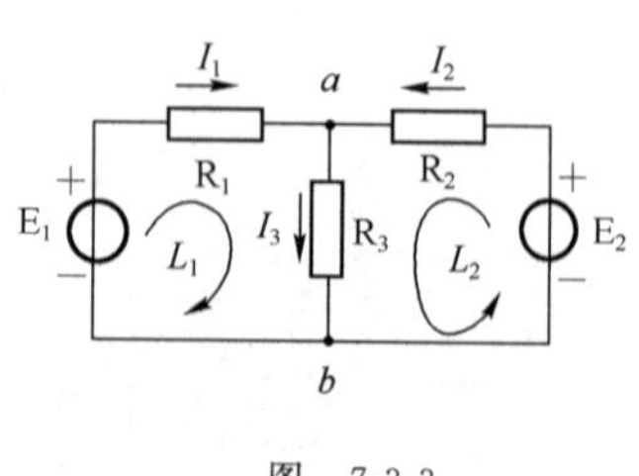

图 7-3-3

今以如图 7-3-3 所示的两个电源并联的电路为例说明支路电流法的应用。在本电路中，支路数 $b=3$，结点数 $n=2$，共要列出三个独立方程。

对结点 a 和回路 L_1、回路 L_2 列 KCL 方程及 KVL 方程

$$\begin{aligned} &I_1+I_2-I_3=0 \\ &E_1=R_1I_1+R_3I_3 \\ &E_2=R_2I_2+R_3I_3 \end{aligned} \qquad (7\text{-}3\text{-}2)$$

最后对三个方程联立求解，就可以得出支路电流 I_1、I_2、I_3。

三、叠加原理

1. 内容

在有多个电源共同作用的线性电路中，各支路电流（或元件的端电压）等于各个电源单独作用时，在该支路中产生电流（或电压）的代数和。

2. 方法

当一个电源单独作用时，其他不作用的电源令其数值为 0。即不作用的电压源电压 $E_s=0$（短路），不作用的电流源 $I_s=0$（断路）。电路其他部分结构参数不变的情况下求其响应。

对单个电源作用的响应求代数和时，要注意各电源单独作用时支路电流（或电压）的方向是否与原图一致，一致时此项取"+"号，相反时该项为"−"号。

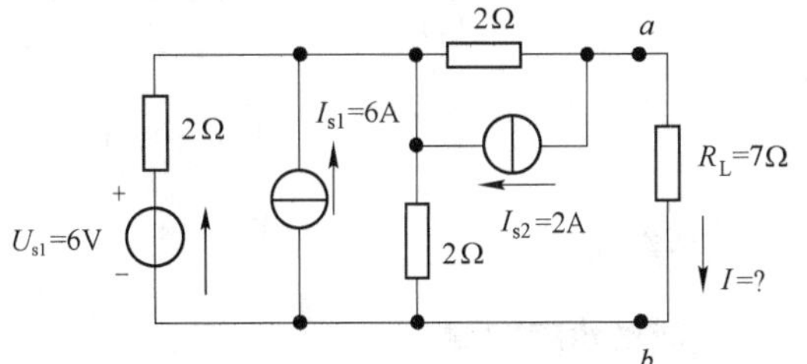

例 7-3-2 图　电路图（叠加原理）

【例 7-3-2】 用叠加原理求图中的电流 I。

分析　该图有三个独立电源共同作用，且为线性电阻，该电路为线性电路，可以用叠加原理求。

解　第一步：将原图改画为单一电源作用的简单电路，如解图所示。

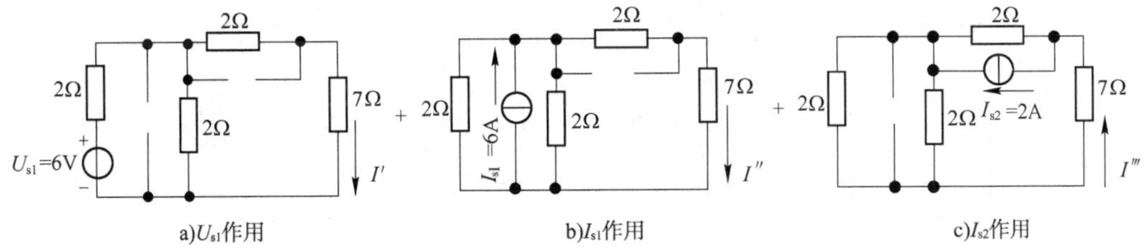

例 7-3-2 解图　简单电路图

第二步：求分电路中电流 I'、I''和 I'''。

$$I'=\frac{U_{s1}}{2+2\ /\!/\ (2+7)}\cdot\frac{2}{2+(7+2)}$$

$$=\frac{6}{2+(2\ /\!/\ 9)}\cdot\frac{2}{11}=0.3\text{A}$$

$$I''=I_{s1}\frac{2}{2+2\ /\!/\ (2+7)}\cdot\frac{2}{2+(7+2)}$$

$$=\frac{6\times2}{2+(2\ /\!/\ 9)}\cdot\frac{2}{2+9}=0.6\text{A}$$

$$I'''=I_{s2}\frac{2}{[(2\ /\!/\ 2)+7]+2}$$

$$=2\times\frac{2}{1+7+2}=0.4\text{A}$$

（这里"$/\!/$"为电阻并联符号，如 $2/\!/9=\frac{2\times9}{2+9}$）

第三步：求各电源单独作用时响应的代数和。

$$I=I'+I''-I'''=0.3+0.6-0.4=0.5\text{A}$$

【例 7-3-3】 已知电路如图 a)所示，其中，响应电流 I 在电压源单独作用时的分量为：

A. 0.375A　　B. 0.25A

C. 0.125A　　D. 0.1875A

解 根据叠加原理，写出电压源单独作用时的电路模型，如图 b)所示。

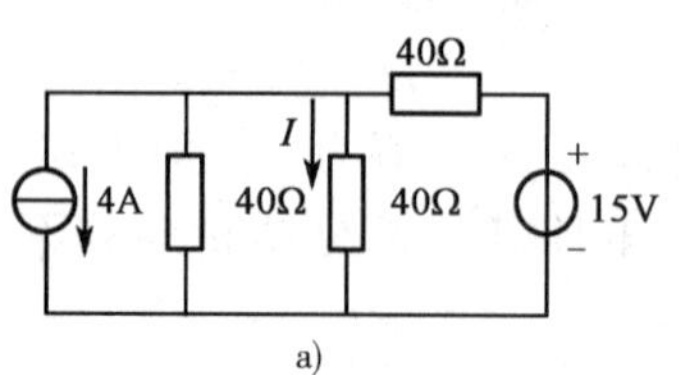

a)

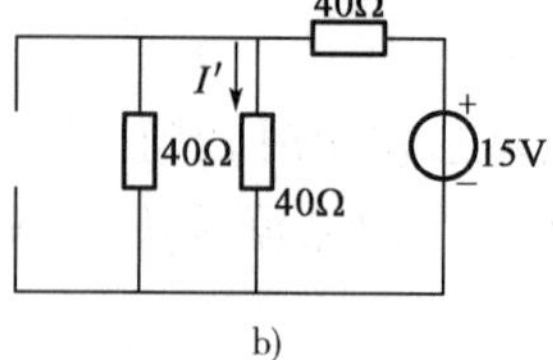

b)

例 7-3-3 图

$$I' = \frac{15}{40+20} \times \frac{40}{40+40} = 0.125\text{A}$$

答案：C

四、戴维南定理

1. 内容

任何一个线性有源二端网络，对外部电路来说总可以用一个电压为 U_s 的理想电压源和一个电阻 R_0 串联的电路表示，如图 7-3-4 所示。

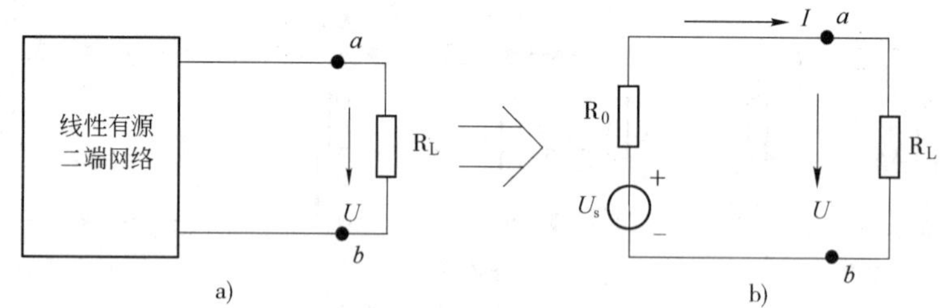

a)　　b)

图 7-3-4　线性有源二端网络简化

2. 方法

理想电压源电压为原来电路在图 7-3-4a)中 a、b 点断开的开路电压

$$U_s = U_{oc}$$

等效电阻 R_0 的数值：由电路开路端口(图 7-3-4 中 a、b 点)向线性有源二端网络内部看过去的除源电阻(除源——去除电源作用，将电压源短路、电流源断路即可)。

【例 7-3-4】 用戴维南定理求图中 7Ω 电阻中的电流 I。

解 第一步：移去待求电流支路，将图中 a、b 点断开，构成线性有源二端网络。

第二步：求等效电压源电压 U_s 和内阻 R_0。

(1)用叠加原理求 U_{oc}(见图 a)

$$U_{oc} = U_{s1}\frac{2}{2+2} + I_1(2 \mathbin{//} 2) - I_2 \cdot 2$$

$$= 6 \times \frac{2}{4} + 6 \times 1 - 2 \times 2 = 5\text{V}$$

(2)求 R_0

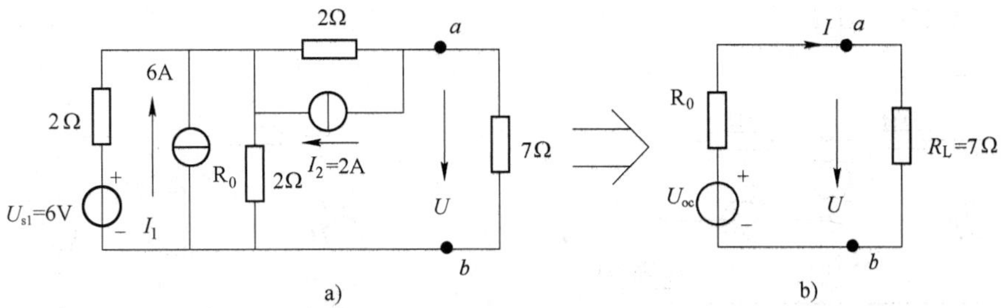

例 7-3-4 图　电路图(戴维南定理)

将有源二端网络除源后，求端口电阻 R_{ab}，见解图。

$$R_{ab} = 2 + (2 /\!/ 2) = 3\Omega$$

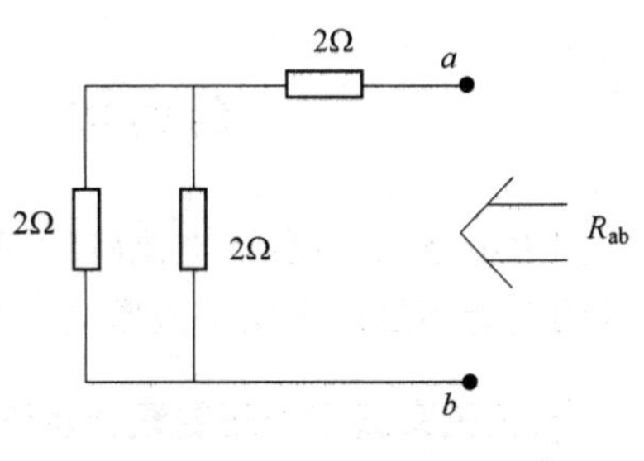

例 7-3-4 解图　等效电阻

第三步：画等效电路图，如图 b)所示，求 I。

$$R_0 = R_{ab} = 3\Omega$$

$$U_s = U_{oc} = 5V$$

$$I = \frac{U_s}{R_0 + R_L} = \frac{5}{3+7} = 0.5A$$

习　题

7-3-1　在如图 a)所示电路中的电流为 I 时，可将图 a)等效为图 b)，其中等效电压源电动势 E_s 和等效电源内阻 R_0 分别为(　　)。

A. −1V，5.143Ω　　B. 1V，5Ω　　C. −1V，5Ω　　D. 1V，5.143Ω

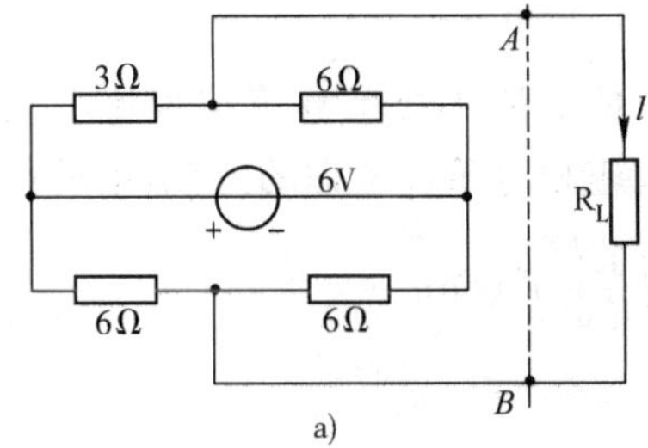

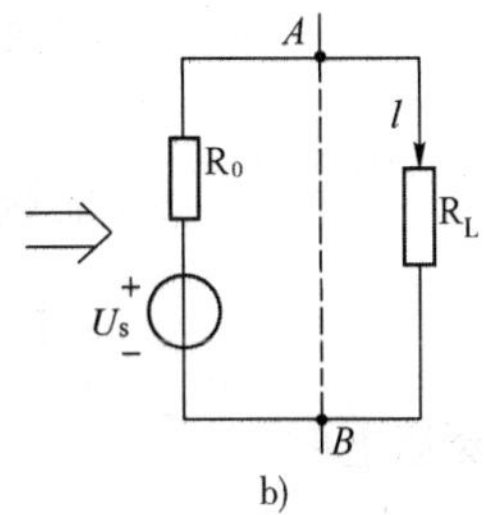

题 7-3-1 图

7-3-2　如图所示电路中，已知：$U_{s1} = 100V$，$U_{s2} = 80V$，$R_2 = 2\Omega$，$I = 4A$，$I_2 = 2A$，则可用基尔霍夫定律求得电阻 R_1 和供给负载 N 的功率分别为(　　)。

A. 16Ω，304W　　B. 16Ω，272W

C. 12Ω，304W　　D. 12Ω，0W

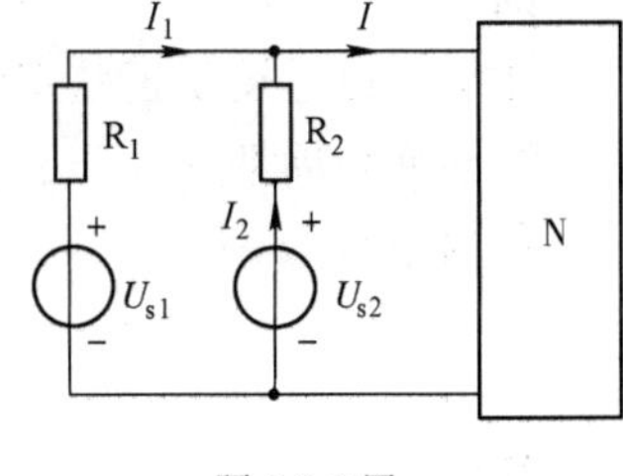

题 7-3-2 图

7-3-3　电路如图所示，用叠加定理求得电阻 R_L 消耗的功率为(　　)。

A. 1/24W　　B. 3/8W

C. 1/8W　　D. 12W

7-3-4　如图所示电路中，电压源 U_{s2} 单独作用时，电流源端电压分量 U'_{I_s} 为(　　)。

A. $U_{s2}-I_sR_2$ B. U_{s2}

C. 0 D. I_sR_2

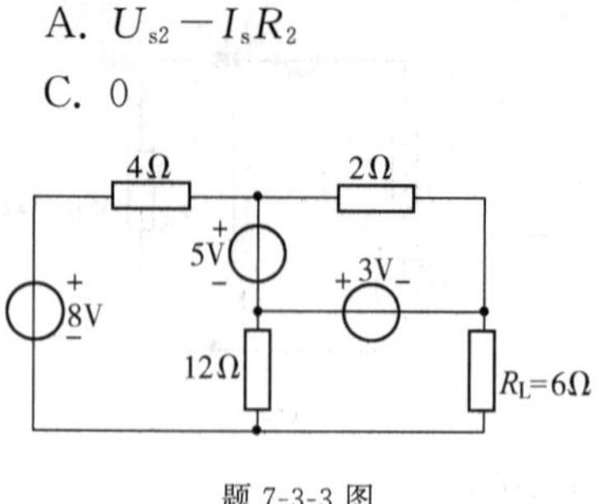

题 7-3-3 图

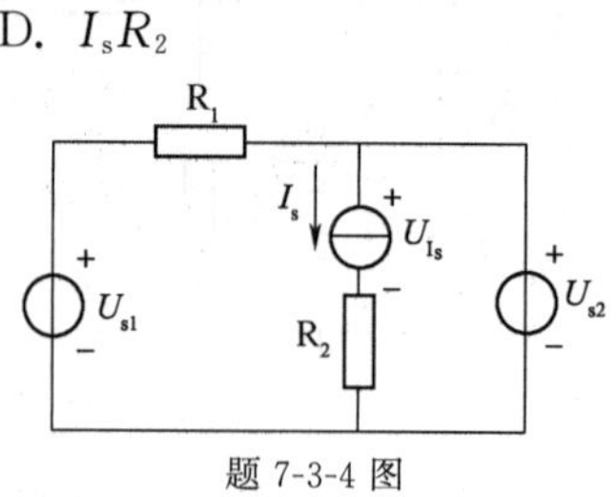

题 7-3-4 图

第四节　正弦交流电路的解题方法

如果电路中的电压、电流随时间按正弦规律变化，该电路便称为“正弦交流电路”，电网上输送的电能都是以正弦交流形式工作的。

一、正弦交流电的三要素表示法

(一)正弦交流电的三要素

已知正弦电流随时间的变化规律如图 7-4-1 所示，写成瞬时值表达式为

$$i(t)=I_m\sin(\omega t+\psi_i)\quad (A)$$

图 7-4-1　正弦电流电压随时间变化规律

其中，I_m、ω 和 ψ_i 分别表示正弦电流的大小、变化速度和在时间轴上的位置，称为正弦交流电的三要素。

1. 幅值与有效值

幅值 I_m 表示正弦量在变化的过程中可能出现的最高峰值。

有效值 I 是从交流电流与直流电流在同一元件上产生的热效应相等条件考虑的，交流电的有效值为

$$I=\sqrt{\frac{1}{T}\int_0^T i^2(t)\mathrm{d}t}$$

当 $i(t)$ 是正弦交流电时

$$i(t)=I_m\sin(\omega t+\psi_i)$$

则

$$I=I_m/\sqrt{2}=0.707I_m \qquad (7\text{-}4\text{-}1)$$

此结论也适用于正弦交流电压，电动势的有效值计算。

2. 频率与周期

角频率

$$\omega=\frac{2\pi}{T}(\text{rad/s})$$

其中

$$T=\frac{1}{f} \qquad (7\text{-}4\text{-}2)$$

式中：f(频率)——反映正弦量每秒钟变化的次数(Hz)；

T(周期)——反映正弦量变化一次所用的时间(s)。

对于工频率电源 $f=50\text{Hz}$

$$T=1/f=0.02\text{s}$$

$$\omega=2\pi f=314\text{rad/s}$$

3.初相位和相位差

ψ 叫做正弦量的初相位(当时间 $t=0$ 时正弦量的相位)。

相位差是两个正弦量的相位之差,反映正弦量在时间上的先后关系,当两个正弦量的频率相同时,相位差也就是初相位之差。

相位差

$$\varphi=(\omega t+\psi_u)-(\omega t+\psi_i)=\psi_u-\psi_i \tag{7-4-3}$$

如图 7-4-1 所示

$$i(t)=I_m\sin\left(\omega t+\frac{\pi}{3}\right)$$

$$u(t)=U_m\sin\left(\omega t-\frac{\pi}{2}\right)$$

$$\varphi=\left(-\frac{\pi}{2}\right)-\frac{\pi}{3}=-\frac{5}{6}\pi$$

$\varphi<0$ 说明电压 $u(t)$ 滞后于 $i(t)\frac{5}{6}\pi$。正弦量的初相位 ψ 与计时点有关,而相位差 φ 与计时起点无关;并且只有同频率的正弦量才有相位差可言。

(二)正弦量的表示法

有四种方法可以表示正弦量:

(1)三角函数,$i(t)=I_m\sin(\omega t+\psi_i)$;

(2)波形图,如图 7-4-1 所示;

(3)相量表示法;

(4)复数表示法。

前面两种方法都直观地表示了正弦量的三要素,但是对电路进行定量分析时很不方便,后面两种方法是定量求解正弦交流电路的常用方法。

可以证明,线性电路中各部分电压电流的频率与电源频率相同。因此在计算时,只要解出各正弦量的大小关系(幅值或有效值)和相对位置(初相位或相位差)即可。

1.相量表示法

相量是一个特殊矢量,与空间矢量不同的是相量表示的是在特定时刻正弦量的大小和位置,即幅值(或有效值)与初相位关系。线性电路中的 u,i 频率已由电源频率确定,利用相量法求解线性交流电路将使计算大大简化。

当 $t=0$ 时

$$i(t)=I_m\sin\psi_i$$

写成相量式为

$$\dot{I}_m=I_m\angle\psi_i$$

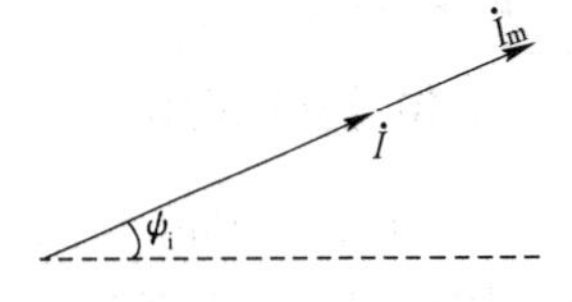

图 7-4-2 相量图

相量图如图 7-4-2 所示。

频率相同的正弦量可以画在同一张相量图上,这样可以直观地反映多个正弦量之间的大小及其相位关系。

相量也可用有效值表示

$$\dot{I}=I\angle\psi_i$$

即 $$\dot{I}=\dot{I}_m/\sqrt{2}$$

2.复数表示法

在数学中,可以用复数来表示矢量,既然正弦量表示为特殊矢量(相量),那么正弦相量就可用复数表示。

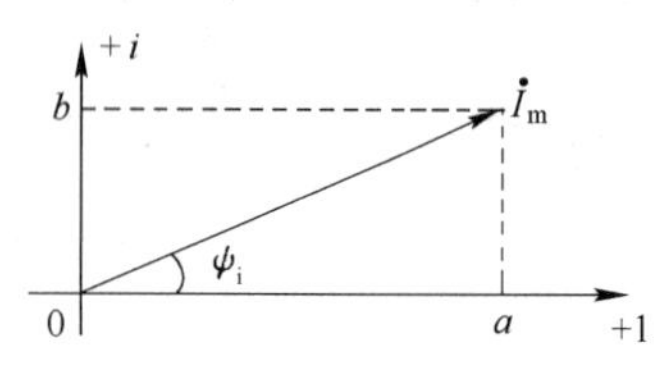

图 7-4-3 复数图

对于如图 7-4-3 所示的电流相量用复数坐标表示后,如图 7-4-3 所示,可以写为三种对应的复数表达式。

代数式

$$\dot{I}_m=a+jb \tag{7-4-4}$$

极坐标式

$$\dot{I}_m=I_m\angle\psi_i \tag{7-4-5}$$

指数式

$$\dot{I}_m=I_m e^{j\psi_i} \tag{7-4-6}$$

变换公式如下

$$\left.\begin{aligned}I_m&=\sqrt{a^2+b^2}\\ \psi_i&=\arctan\frac{b}{a}\end{aligned}\right\} \tag{7-4-7}$$

$$\left.\begin{aligned}a&=I_m\cos\psi_i\\ b&=I_m\sin\psi_i\end{aligned}\right\} \tag{7-4-8}$$

【例 7-4-1】 已知有效值为 10V 的正弦交流电压的相量图如图所示,则它的时间函数形式是:

A. $u(t)=10\sqrt{2}\sin(\omega t-30°)$V

B. $u(t)=10\sin(\omega t-30°)$V

C. $u(t)=10\sqrt{2}\sin(-30°)$V

D. $u(t)=10\cos(-30°)+10\sin(-30°)$V

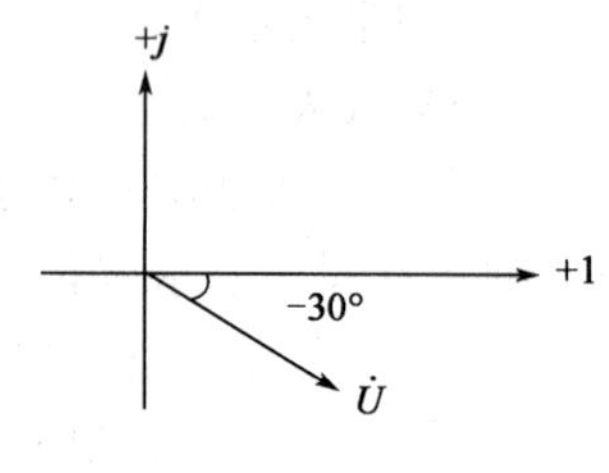

例 7-4-1 图

解 本题注意正弦交流电的三个特征(大小、相位、速度)和描述方法。

由相量图可分析,电压最大值为 $10\sqrt{2}$V,初相位为−30°,角频率用 ω 表示,正确描述为:

$$u(t)=10\sqrt{2}\sin(\omega t-30°)\text{V}$$

答案:A

二、单相交流电路

在交流电路中由于电压、电流随时间变化,那么电路中储存的电磁场能量也都是随时间变化的,因此交流电路分析时不仅要分析电阻(R)元件的消耗电能情况,还要注意电感(L)元件和电容(C)元件对电场磁场储能的变化情况。

(一)纯电阻电路(见图 7-4-4)

1. u_R-i 关系

由 $$u_R=Ri$$

设 $$i(t)=I_m\sin(\omega t+\psi_i)$$
$$u_R=RI_m\sin(\omega t+\psi_i)=U_{Rm}\sin(\omega t+\psi_u)$$

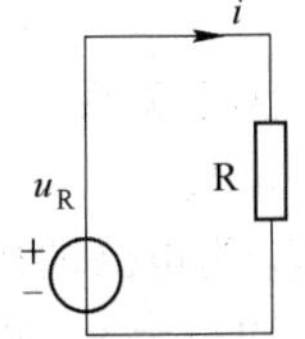

图 7-4-4 纯电阻电路

大小关系

$$U_{Rm}=RI_m(\text{或 } U_R=RI)$$

相位关系

$$\psi_u=\psi_i,\varphi=\psi_u-\psi_i=0$$

纯电阻元件中电压电流的相位相同。

复数表达式 $$\dot{I}_m=I_m\angle\psi_i$$

$$\dot{U}_{Rm}=U_{Rm}\angle\psi_u=RI_m\angle\psi_i=R\dot{I}_m$$

即

$$\dot{U}_{Rm}=R\dot{I}_m(\text{或 } \dot{U}_R=R\dot{I})$$

相量图(设 $\psi_i=0$)如图 7-4-5a)所示,波形图如图 7-4-5b)所示。

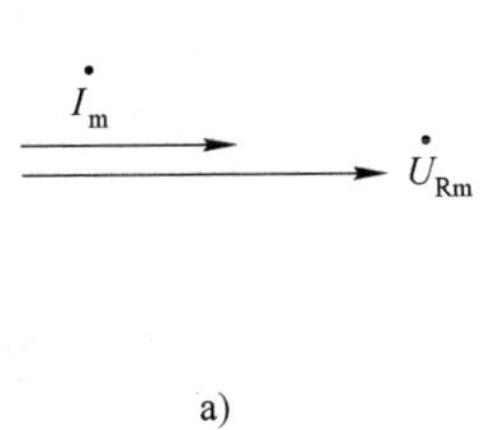

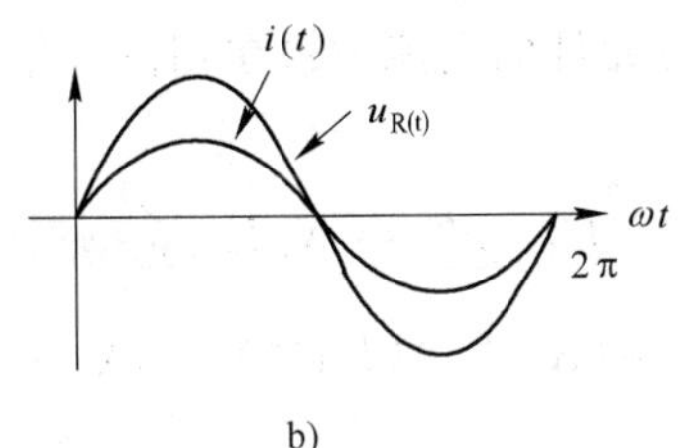

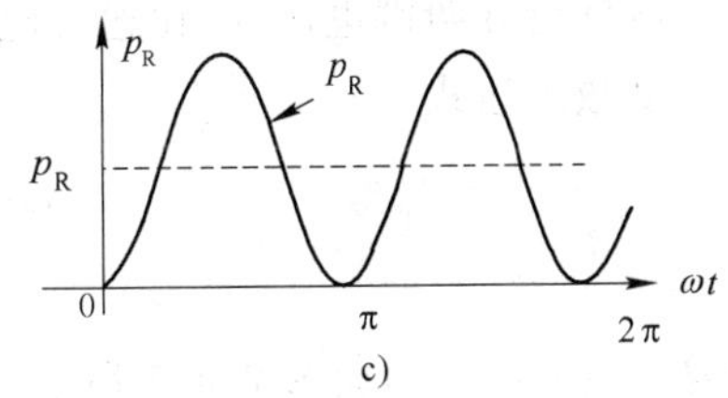

图 7-4-5 纯电阻电路中 u_R-i 关系

2. 功率关系

瞬时功率

$$p_R=u_Ri=U_{Rm}\sin(\omega t+\psi_u)I_m\sin(\omega t+\psi_i)$$

令

$$\psi_i=0$$

则

$$\psi_u=0$$
$$p_R=U_{Rm}I(1-\cos2\omega t)$$

图 7-4-5c)表示瞬时功率波形图,$p_R>0$ 电阻元件任何瞬时都在消耗功率。

瞬时功率形象反映任意时刻电阻消耗功率情况,但我们平时用功率表测量的功率是电路中平均消耗功率的多少,定为平均功率(有功功率)。

平均功率

$$P_R=\frac{1}{T}\int_0^T p_R\mathrm{d}t=U_RI=RI^2=U_R^2/R \tag{7-4-9}$$

(二)纯电感电路(见图 7-4-6)

1. u_L-i 关系

$$u_L=L\frac{\mathrm{d}}{\mathrm{d}t}i(t) \tag{7-4-10}$$

设 $$i(t)=I_m\sin(\omega t+\psi_i)$$

$$u_L=L\frac{\mathrm{d}}{\mathrm{d}t}[I_m\sin(\omega t+\psi_i)]$$

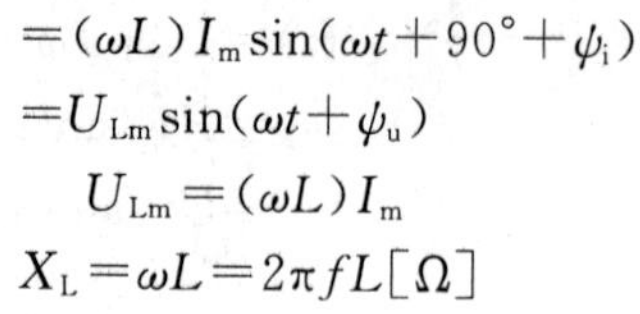

$$=(\omega L)I_m\sin(\omega t+90°+\psi_i)$$

$$=U_{Lm}\sin(\omega t+\psi_u)$$

大小关系　　$U_{Lm}=(\omega L)I_m$

定义　　$X_L=\omega L=2\pi fL[\Omega]$

称 X_L 为电路的感抗。

相位关系(见图 7-4-7)　　$\psi_u=\psi_i+90°$

$$\varphi=\psi_u-\psi_i=90°$$

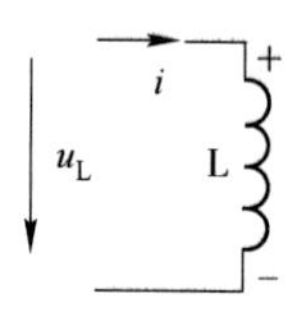

图 7-4-6　纯电感电路

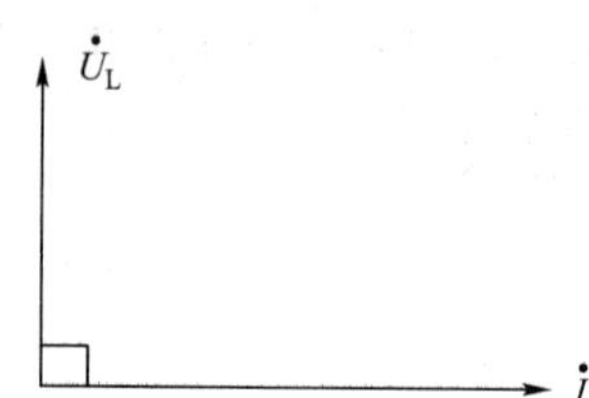

图 7-4-7　纯电感电路相量图

电感元件两端电压 u_L 比通过电感元件的电流 $i(t)$在相位上超前 90°。

复数表达式

$$\dot{U}_{Lm}=U_{Lm}\angle\psi_u=X_LI_m\angle\psi_i+90°$$

$$=(X_Le^{j90°})(I_me^{j\psi_i})=jX_L\cdot\dot{I}_m \qquad (7\text{-}4\text{-}11)$$

相量图(设 $\psi_i=0°$)如图 7-4-7 所示。

电感元件的电压 $u_L(t)$和电流 $i(t)$波形图如图 7-4-8a)所示。

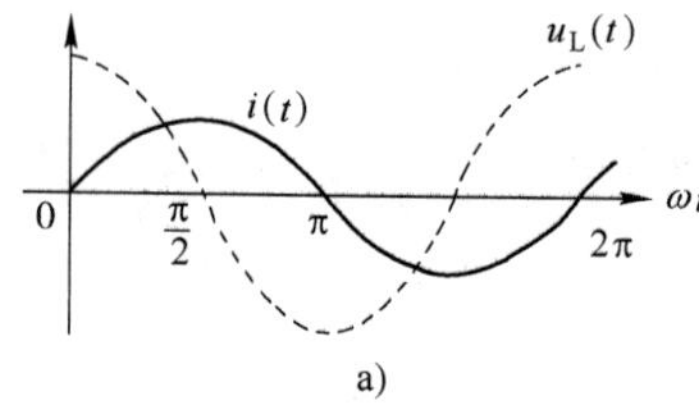

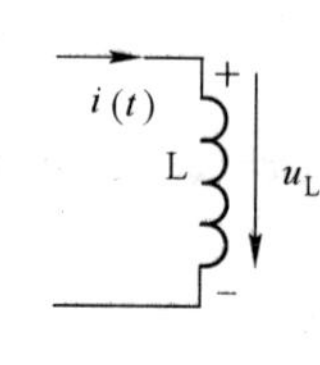

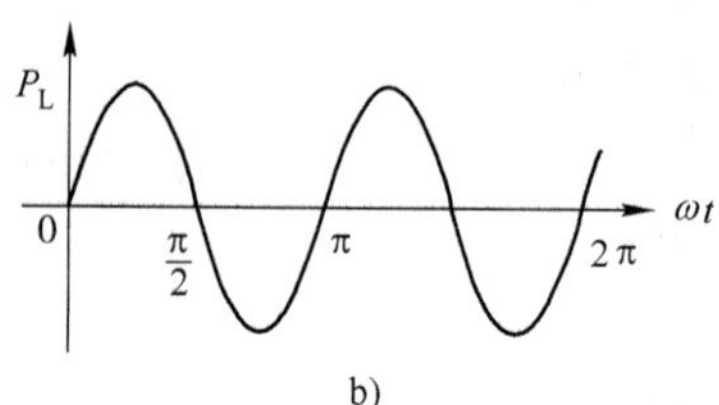

图 7-4-8　纯电感电路中各电量关系

2. 功率关系

瞬时功率　　$p_L=u_Li=U_{Lm}\sin(\omega t+90°)I_m\sin(\omega t)$

$$=U_LI\sin(2\omega t)$$

得到波形如图 7-4-8b)所示。

下面分析电感元件中磁场能量转化情况。

在图 7-4-8a)中 $0\sim\frac{\pi}{2}$：$u_L(t)>0$，且$i(t)>0$，说明此时间内电感元件的实际电压、电流方向就是假定的正方向。

$$p_L(t)=u_L(t)i(t)>0$$

电感元件的作用相当于负载，它将电源能量吸收后变成磁场能量储存。

$\frac{\pi}{2}\sim\pi$：$u_L(t)<0$，但 $i(t)>0$

$$p_L(t)=u_L(t)\cdot i(t)<0$$

电感元件的作用相当于电源，它是把已经储存的磁场能量还给电源。

在 0～π 内，纯电感元件吸收的能量与发出的能量相等。

平均功率
$$P_L=\frac{1}{T}\int_0^T p_L(t)\mathrm{d}t=0 \tag{7-4-12}$$

可见，理想电感元件不消耗能量。

为了衡量电感元件与电源之间进行能量交换的规模，定义无功功率用符号“Q_L”表示，单位为“乏”，记为 var，即
$$Q_L=U_LI=I^2X_L=U_L^2/X_L(\text{var}) \tag{7-4-13}$$

（三）纯电容电路（见图 7-4-9）

1. u_C-i 关系

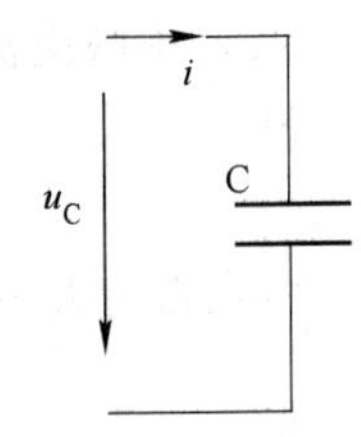

图 7-4-9 纯电容电路

$$i=C\frac{\mathrm{d}u_C}{\mathrm{d}t}$$

设
$$u_C=U_{Cm}\sin(\omega t+\psi_u)$$

则
$$\begin{aligned}i&=C\frac{\mathrm{d}}{\mathrm{d}t}[U_{Cm}\sin(\omega t+\psi_u)]\\&=(\omega C)U_{Cm}\sin(\omega t+\psi_u+90^\circ)\\&=I_m\sin(\omega t+\psi_i)\end{aligned}$$

大小关系
$$I_m=U_{Cm}\Big/\left(\frac{1}{\omega C}\right)$$

定义“$X_C=\frac{1}{\omega C}$”为电路的“容抗”，单位为 Ω。

则
$$I_m=U_{Cm}/X_C$$
或
$$I=U_C/X_C$$
相位关系
$$\psi_i=\psi_u+90^\circ$$
$$\varphi=\psi_u-\psi_i=-90^\circ$$

即：电容元件中的电流 $i(t)$ 比电压 u_C 超前 90°[或元件的端电压 $u_C(t)$ 滞后电流 $i(t)$90°]。

用复数表示电容元件电压、电流的大小和相位关系。

$$\dot{I}_m=I_m\angle\psi_i=\frac{U_{Cm}}{X_C}\angle\psi_U+90^\circ=\left(\frac{1}{X_C}e^{j90^\circ}\right)\cdot U_{Cm}=\frac{1}{-jX_C}\dot{U}_{cm}$$

$$\dot{U}_{Cm}=-jX_C\dot{I}_m(\text{或 }\dot{I}_C=-jX_C\dot{I})$$

相量图和波形图如图 7-4-10 所示，其中 $\psi_u=0^\circ$。

图 7-4-10 纯电容电路的相量图和波形图

2. 功率关系

瞬时功率
$$p_C(t)=u_C(t)i(t)=U_{Cm}\sin(\omega t)I_m\sin(\omega t+90^\circ)=U_CI\sin2(\omega t)$$

平均功率

$$P_C = \frac{1}{T}\int_0^T p_C(t)\mathrm{d}t$$
$$=0$$

无功功率

$$Q_C = U_C I = I^2 X_C$$
$$= U_C^2 / X_C$$

为将 P 与 Q 对应,平均功率 P 又称为电路的“有功功率”。

(四)RLC 串联的正弦交流电路

1. u-i 关系

RLC 串联交流电路如图 7-4-11 所示。

设

$$i = I_m \sin\omega t$$

由克希荷夫电压定律可知

$$\begin{aligned} u &= u_R + u_L + u_C \\ &= Ri + L\frac{\mathrm{d}i}{\mathrm{d}t} + \frac{1}{C}\int i\mathrm{d}t \\ &= RI_m \sin\omega t + L\omega I_m \sin(\omega t + 90°) + \frac{I_m}{\omega C}\sin(\omega t - 90°) \\ &= U_m \sin(\omega t + \psi_u) \end{aligned} \tag{7-4-14}$$

相量关系

$$\begin{aligned} U &= \dot{U}_R + \dot{U}_L + \dot{U}_C \\ &= R\dot{I} + jX_L\dot{I} - jX_C\dot{I} \\ &= [R + j(X_L - X_C)]\dot{I} = Z\dot{I} \end{aligned} \tag{7-4-15}$$

假设:$X_L > X_C$,作出相量图如图 7-4-12 所示。

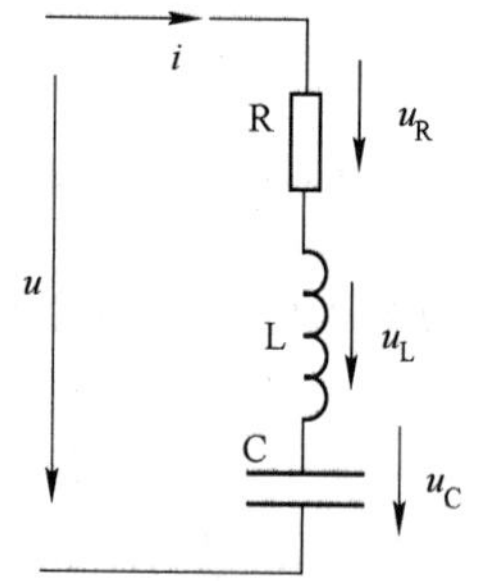

图 7-4-11 RLC 串联电路

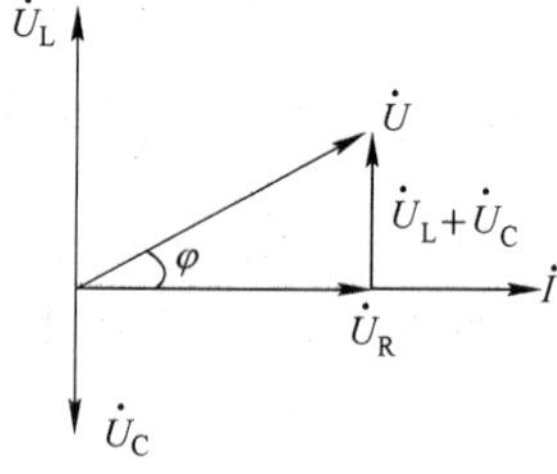

图 7-4-12 RLC 串联电路的相量图

可见,$\dot{U}$、$\dot{U}_R$、$\dot{U}_L + \dot{U}_C$ 组成一个直角三角形,称为电压三角形,利用它可知 $\dot{U}$ 的大小和相位关系

$$\begin{aligned} U &= \sqrt{U_R^2 + (U_L - U_C)^2} \\ &= \sqrt{(IR)^2 + (IX_L - IX_C)^2} \\ &= I\sqrt{R^2 + (X_L - X_C)^2} \end{aligned}$$

$\frac{U}{I}=\sqrt{R^2+(X_L-X_C)^2}$为"欧姆"单位，称为电路的阻抗，用$|Z|$表示。

相位差φ可以用下式分析

$$\varphi=\arctan\frac{U_L-U_C}{U_R}=\arctan\frac{X_L-X_C}{R}$$

已知X_L、X_C、R参数后，完全可以确定u、i的大小和相位关系，即可以将$\dot{U}$、$\dot{I}$表示如下

$$\frac{\dot{U}}{\dot{I}}=Z=|Z|\angle\varphi=\sqrt{R^2+(X_L-X_C)^2} \quad (7\text{-}4\text{-}16)$$

定义：$Z=|Z|\angle\varphi$为电路的复阻抗，由此作出的三角形称为**阻抗三角形**，如图7-4-13a)所示(注意：Z并不是表示正弦量的相量，阻抗三角形各边只能用直线段表示不要画"箭头")。

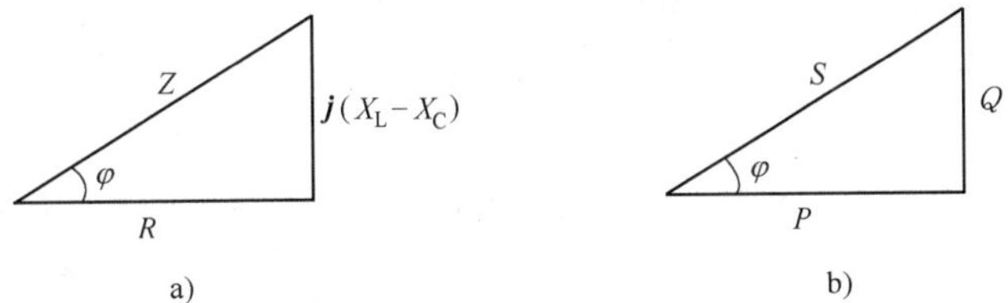

图7-4-13　阻抗三角形和功率三角形

交流电路中欧姆定律的复数表达式为

$$\dot{U}=Z\dot{I} \quad (7\text{-}4\text{-}17)$$

$$\varphi=\psi_u-\psi_i$$

φ表示电压超前电流的角度。

当$X_L>X_C$时，$\varphi>0$电压超前于电流，该电路具有感性性质，称**感性电路**。

当$X_L<X_C$时，$\varphi<0$电压滞后于电流，该电路具有容性性质，称**容性电路**。

当$X_L=X_C$时，$\varphi=0$电压与电流同相位，该电路具有阻性性质，称**阻性电路**。

2. 功率关系

在RLC串联的交流电路中，有耗能元件R又有储能元件L和C，即在消耗能量的过程中又与电源不断进行能量交换，既有有功功率，又有无功功率。

有功功率(平均功率)

$$P=U_R I=UI\cos\varphi(\mathrm{W}) \quad (7\text{-}4\text{-}18)$$

无功功率

$$Q=(U_L-U_C)I=Q_L-Q_C=UI\sin\varphi(\mathrm{var}) \quad (7\text{-}4\text{-}19)$$

视在功率

$$S=UI=UI\sqrt{\cos^2\varphi+\sin^2\varphi}$$
$$=\sqrt{(UI\cos\varphi)^2+(UI\sin\varphi)^2}$$
$$S=\sqrt{P^2+Q^2} \quad (7\text{-}4\text{-}20)$$

由此形成的功率关系用功率三角形表示(见图7-4-13b)，其中$S=UI$表示电源做功能力，消耗的功率为$P=S\cos\varphi$，这里$\cos\varphi$称为电路的功率因数，在交流电路中是个重要概念。

(五)交流电路的计算

计算交流电路的方法与直流电路的计算方法相同，以叠加原理和戴维南定理为主要解题方法。注意的是由于交流电路中电压电流相位不同，我们不仅要注意电压电流的大小关系，也

同样要注意它们之间的相位关系，所以交流电路的计算是采用相量图和复数运算相结合的办法。

简单地说，在计算交流电路时只要把直流电路中的 R,U,I,P 参数分别改写为相应的 Z，$\dot{U},\dot{I}$，S 即可。

欧姆定律

$$\dot{U}=Z\dot{I} \tag{7-4-21}$$

基尔霍夫电压定律

$$\sum\dot{U}=0$$

基尔霍夫电流定律

$$\sum\dot{I}=0$$

视在功率

$$S=UI \tag{7-4-22}$$

有功功率

$$P=UI\cos\varphi \tag{7-4-23}$$

无功功率

$$Q=UI\sin\varphi \tag{7-4-24}$$

【例 7-4-2】 电路如图所示，已知：$u(t)=220\sqrt{2}\sin 314t$(V)，求 i,i_1,i_2，并分析功率关系。

解 (1)相量分析

i_1 支路为感性，i_1 滞后 u，i_2 支路为容性，i_2 超前 u，将 u 写为复数 $\dot{U}=220\angle 0^\circ$(V)。

定性作相量图如解图所示。

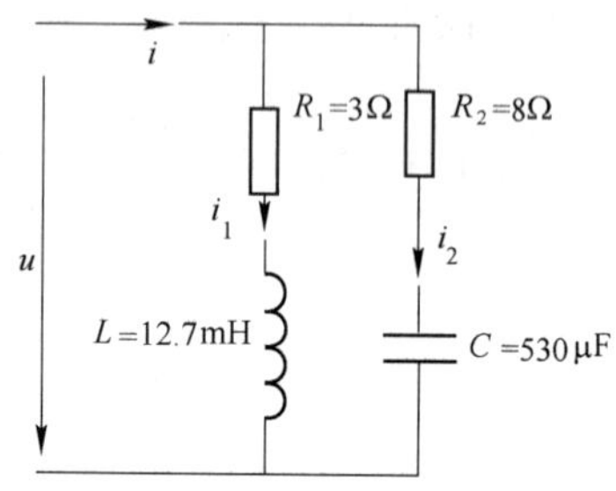

例 7-4-2 图 电路图

例 7-4-2 解图 相量图

(2)复数计算

$$Z_1=R_1+jX_{L1}=3+j(314\times 1.27\times 10^{-3})$$
$$=3+j4=5\angle 53.1^\circ\ \Omega$$

$$Z_2=R_2-jX_{C1}=8-j\frac{10^6}{314\times 530}=8-j6=10\angle -36.9^\circ\ \Omega$$

$$\dot{I}_1=\dot{U}/Z_1=220\angle 0^\circ/5\angle 53.1^\circ=44\angle -53.1^\circ\ \mathrm{A}$$

$$\dot{I}_2=\dot{U}/Z_2=220\angle 0^\circ/10\angle -36.9^\circ=22\angle 36.9^\circ\ \mathrm{A}$$

$$\dot{I}=\dot{I}_1+\dot{I}_2=44\angle -53.1^\circ+22\angle 36.9^\circ$$

$=44\cos(-53.1°)+j44\sin(-53.1°)+22\cos36.9°+j22\sin36.9°$

$=49.2\angle{-26.5°}$

电流计算结果可见与相量图的分析是一致的。

【例 7-4-3】 用仪表测得图示电路的电压 $u(t)$ 和电流 $i(t)$ 的结果是 10V 和 0.2A，设电流 $i(t)$ 的初相位为 10°，电压与电流呈反相关系，则如下关系成立的是：

A. $\dot{U}=10\angle-10°\text{V}$　　B. $\dot{U}=-10\angle-10°\text{V}$

C. $\dot{U}=10\sqrt{2}\angle-170°\text{V}$　　D. $\dot{U}=10\angle-170°\text{V}$

解 画相量图分析(见解图)，电压表和电流表读数为有效值。

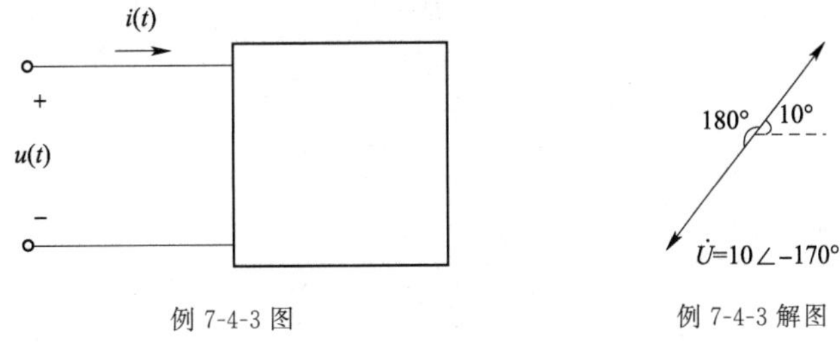

例 7-4-3 图　　例 7-4-3 解图

答案：D

【例 7-4-4】 一交流电路由 R、L、C 串联而成，其中，$R=10\Omega$，$X_L=8\Omega$，$X_C=6\Omega$。通过该电路的电流为 10A，则该电路的有功功率、无功功率和视在功率分别为：

A. 1kW，1.6kvar，2.6kV·A

B. 1kW，200var，1.2kV·A

C. 100W，200var，223.6V·A

D. 1kW，200var，1.02kV·A

解 交流电路的功率关系为：

$$S^2=P^2+Q^2$$

式中：S——视在功率反映设备容量；

P——耗能元件消耗的有功功率；

Q——储能元件交换的无功功率。

本题中：$P=I^2R=1000\text{W}$，$Q=I^2(X_L-X_C)=200\text{var}$

$S=\sqrt{P^2+Q^2}=1019\approx1020\text{V}\cdot\text{A}$

答案：D

(六)交流电路的谐振

在有 R、L、C 三种元件存在的交流电路中，电压电流的大小和相位关系除了与这三个参数有关以外，还与电源频率有关，即

$$\frac{\dot{U}}{\dot{I}}=Z=F(R,L,C,W)$$

如果调节电路参数使 $\varphi=0$(电路出现纯电阻性质)，我们就说该电路出现**谐振**。这是交流电的特殊现象，在电子技术中非常有用，而在强电系统中要防止电路中出现过高电压，过大电流必须避免电路出现谐振。因此我们必须充分认识电路的谐振现象，对它进行合理的应用和控制。

1.串联谐振(见图 7-4-14)

(1)串联谐振条件

根据 $Z=R+j(X_L-X_C)=\sqrt{R^2+(X_L-X_C)^2}\angle\arctan\frac{X_L-X_C}{R}$

可知:当 $X_L=X_C$ 时 $\varphi=0$ 电路出现纯电阻性质,即

$$\omega_0 L=(\omega_0 C)^{-1}$$

$$\omega_0=\frac{1}{\sqrt{LC}} \quad 或 \quad f_0=\frac{1}{2\pi\sqrt{LC}} \tag{7-4-25}$$

(2)串联电路谐振特点

阻抗最小

$$Z_0=R=Z_{min}$$

电流最大

$$I_0=\frac{U}{|Z_0|}=\frac{U}{Z_{min}}=I_{max}$$

电压谐振

因 $$U_C=I_0X_C=\frac{U}{R}X_C=\left(\frac{X_C}{R}\right)\cdot U$$

定义品质因数 $$Q=\frac{X_C}{R}$$

所以 $$U_C=QU$$

$$U_L=U_C=QU \tag{7-4-26}$$

当 $Q\gg1$ 时,分电压(U_L 或 U_C)可能比总电压大许多倍,故称为电压谐振。

2.并联谐振

这里主要分析电感线圈与电容器并联的实际情况,一般电容器的漏电流很小,可以设电容器为纯电容元件,得如图 7-4-15 所示电路图。

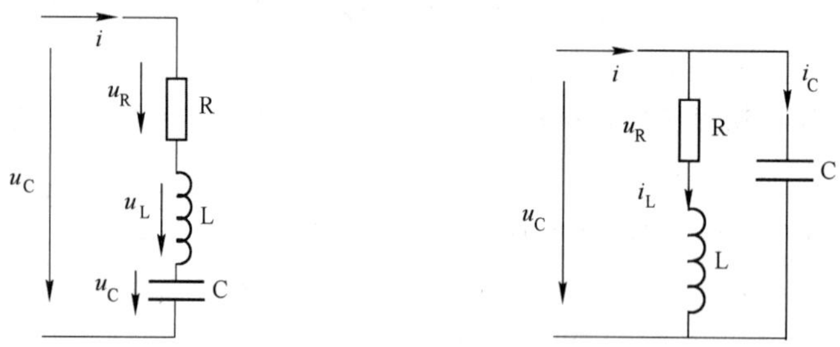

图 7-4-14 RLC 串联电路　　图 7-4-15 LC 并联电路

同样,当 $u(t)$ 和 $i(t)$ 的相位相同时($\varphi=0$),电路谐振。

(1)并联谐振条件

根据

$$\frac{\dot{I}}{\dot{U}}=\frac{1}{Z}=\frac{1}{R+jX_L}+\frac{1}{-jX_C}=\frac{R-jX_L}{R^2+X_L^2}+j\frac{1}{X_C}$$

$$=\frac{R}{R^2+X_L^2}+j\left(\frac{1}{X_C}-\frac{X_2}{R^2+X_L^2}\right)$$

令：上式的虚部为 0，则可实现 $\varphi=0$ 的要求（且设电感线圈的电阻 R 比其感抗 X_L 小许多）。

$$\frac{1}{X_C}=\frac{X_L}{R^2+X_L{}^2}\approx\frac{1}{X_L}$$

可得并联电路谐振条件为：

$$\omega_0 C=\frac{1}{\omega_0 L}$$

$$\omega_0=\frac{1}{\sqrt{LC}} \quad 或 \quad f_0=\frac{1}{2\pi\sqrt{LC}}$$

（2）并联电路谐振特点

阻抗最大

$$Z_0=\frac{R^2+X_L^2}{R}=Z_{max}$$

电流最小

$$I_0=\frac{U}{|Z_0|}=\frac{U}{|Z_{max}|}=I_{min}$$

电流谐振

$$I_0=\frac{U}{(Z_0)}=\frac{UR}{R^2+X_L^2}\approx\frac{UR}{X_L^2}=\frac{U}{X_C}\cdot\frac{R}{X_L}=\frac{I_C}{Q}$$

$$I_C=QI_0$$

当 $Q=\dfrac{X_C}{R}\gg 1$ 时，电路中电容支路的分电流 I_C 可能会比总电流大许多，这就是“电流谐振”的含义。

三、三相交流电路

（一）三相交流电源（见图 7-4-16）

三相交流电是目前广泛使用的输、配电方式，其原因是三相电源应用方便，且经济性能也比较理想。在用电方面三相电的负载主要是三相交流电动机。

三相交流电源是三相交流发电机产生的，三相发电机内部有三相定子绕组，电机中每套绕组电动势分别为

$$\left.\begin{aligned} e_A &= E_m\sin(\omega t) \\ e_B &= E_m\sin(\omega t-120^\circ) \\ e_C &= E_m\sin(\omega t+120^\circ) \end{aligned}\right\} \qquad (7\text{-}4\text{-}27)$$

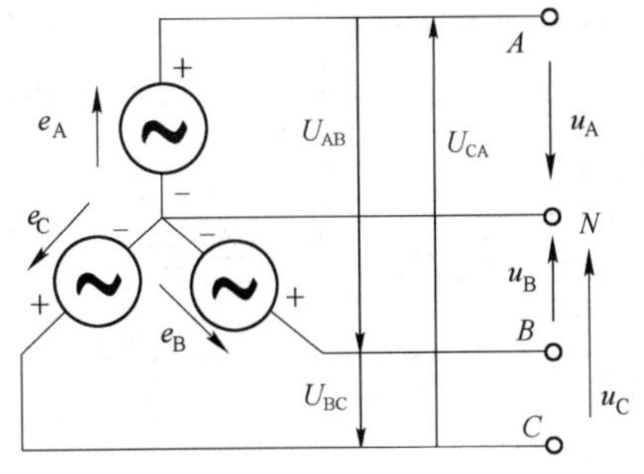

图 7-4-16　三相交流电源

这种具有有效值（或幅值）相等、频率相等、相位上互差 120°的三相电动势，称为对称三相电动势，具有这一性质的电源就是我们常说的三相电源。

1. 两种端线

（1）火线：各电动势的正向（绕组首端）引出线（A，B，C）；

（2）中线：各相电动势的尾端公共线（N）。

2. 两种端电压

（1）相电压：火线与中线之间的电压（U_A，U_B，U_C），简记为“U_P”；

(2)线电压：火线与火线间的电压(U_{AB},U_{BC},U_{CA})，简记为“U_L”。

一般相电压的有效值可以用 U_P 表示。两种电压之间的关系分析如下

$$\left.\begin{aligned}\dot{U}_A&=\dot{E}_A=U_p\angle 0^\circ\\ \dot{U}_B&=U_P\angle -120^\circ\\ \dot{U}_C&=U_P\angle 120^\circ\end{aligned}\right\}\tag{7-4-28}$$

同理

$$\left.\begin{aligned}\dot{U}_{AB}&=\dot{U}_A-\dot{U}_B=(\sqrt{3}U_P\angle 30^\circ)\\ \dot{U}_{BC}&=(\sqrt{3}\angle 30^\circ)\dot{U}_B\\ \dot{U}_{BA}&=(\sqrt{3}\angle 30^\circ)\dot{U}_C\end{aligned}\right\}\tag{7-4-29}$$

通常，三相交流电器的电压标称值是线电压 U_L。

(二)三相交流负载

负载与电源之间的接线原则是：使负载上得到额定电压，具体接法分为两种。

(1)星形接法：负载上得到电源的相电压。

(2)三角形接法：负载上得到电源的线电压。

就负载本身性质分析，又可以将负载划分为两类，对称性负载($Z_A=Z_B=Z_C$)和不对称负载(不符合对称关系的负载)。三相电动机和三相变压器是属于三相对称性负载，使用时必须接在三相电源上方能工作。而白炽灯、日光灯及普通家用电器为单相用电器，使用时是接在三相源的其中一相上，在分析三相电路时，这类负载对三相电源的关系为不对称负载。

1. 三相负载的星形(Y)连接

由图 7-4-17 可知，星形连接时负载上得到的电压是电源的相电压，数值为 $U_{Load}=U_P=U_L/\sqrt{3}$，流过负载的电流 i_a、i_b、i_c 叫做相电流，用 I_P 表示相电流的有效值；在输电线流过的电流 i_A、i_B、i_C 叫做线电流，用 I_L 表示线电流的有效值。

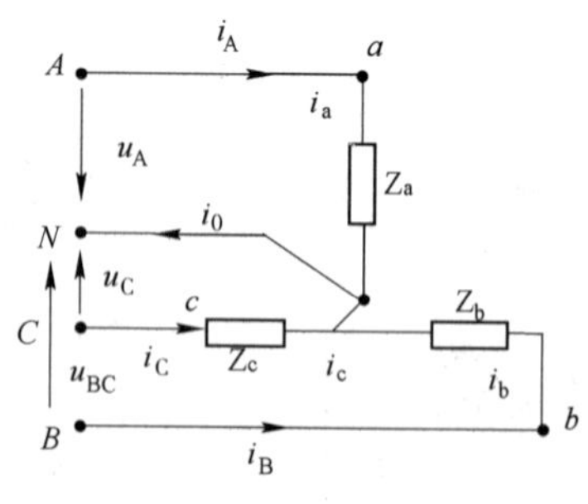

图 7-4-17　三相负载星形连接

在负载为星形接法的三相电路中，各个相电流与线电流相等，即

$$I_P=I_L\tag{7-4-30}$$

如果是三相对称性电路，则只取一相计算即可，如

$$I_L=I_P=I_A=\frac{U_A}{|Z_A|}$$

可以证明：采用三相四线制(有中线)星形连接的三相对称性负载，中线电流 $I_N=0$；此时使中线断开，负载的相电压仍旧保持三相对称关系，也就是说星形接法的对称性三相电路中，可以采用三相三线制(无中线)供电体系。但是当负载不对称时中线电流不为零($I_N\neq 0$)，为了保证负载的电压对称，中线不允许断开，所以在不对称负载、星形接法的三相电路中，中线上不许接熔断器或刀闸开关，并且中线应选用强度较好的钢线。

2. 三相负载的三角形(△)连接

当三相负载采用三角形接法时，负载上得到的电压是电源的线电压：

$$U_{\text{Load}}=U_{\text{L}} \tag{7-4-31}$$

如果负载是对称的，三角形接法的线电流是相电流的$\sqrt{3}$倍：

$$I_{\text{L}}=\sqrt{3}I_{\text{P}}=\sqrt{3}\frac{U_{\text{AB}}}{|Z_{\text{AB}}|} \tag{7-4-32}$$

三角形接法(见图 7-4-18)的负载不能引中线，因此，它只有一种三相三线制供电体系。

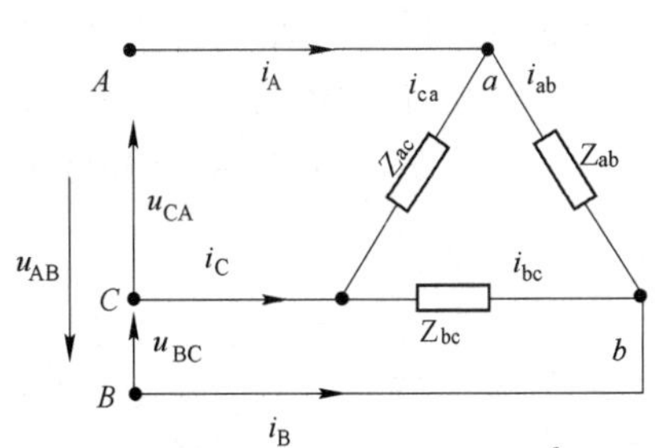

图 7-4-18 三相负载三角形连接

在实际中应采用何种方法将负载与三相电源连接，主要取决于负载额定电压的大小。例如：三个额定电压为 220V 的负载，接入 380V 的三相电源中，必须以星形连接方式与电源接通，并且应使三个负载分别接在电源的三相中，以便保证三相电源平衡分配。

三相电路的有功功率 P 和无功功率 Q 可以分相计算，对称式三相电路的功率关系为

有功功率

$$P=3U_{\text{P}}I_{\text{P}}\cos\varphi=\sqrt{3}U_{\text{L}}I_{\text{L}}\cos\varphi$$

无功功率

$$Q=3U_{\text{P}}I_{\text{P}}\sin\varphi=\sqrt{3}U_{\text{L}}I_{\text{L}}\sin\varphi$$

视在功率

$$S=3U_{\text{P}}I_{\text{P}}=\sqrt{3}U_{\text{L}}I_{\text{L}}$$

习　　题

7-4-1　如图所示正弦交流电路中，各电压表读数均为有效值。已知电压表 V、V_1 和 V_2 的读数分别为 10V、6V 和 3V，则电压表 V_3 读数为(　　)。

A. 1V　　B. 5V　　C. 4V　　D. 11V

7-4-2　如图所示电路中，已知 Z_1 是纯电阻负载，电流表 A、A_1、A_2 的读数分别为 5A、4A、3A，那么 Z_2 负载一定是(　　)。

A. 电阻性的　　B. 纯电感性或纯电容性质

C. 电感性的　　D. 电容性的

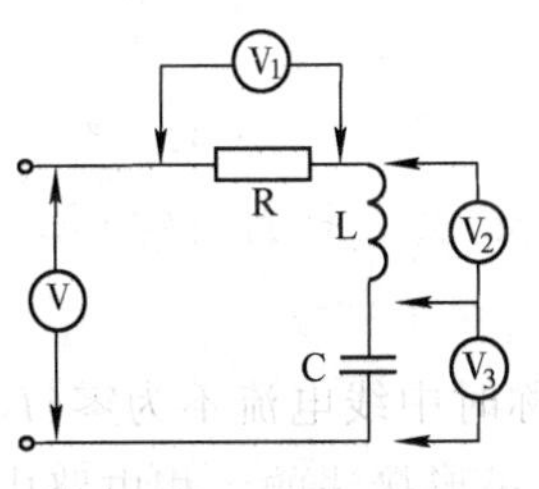

题 7-4-1 图

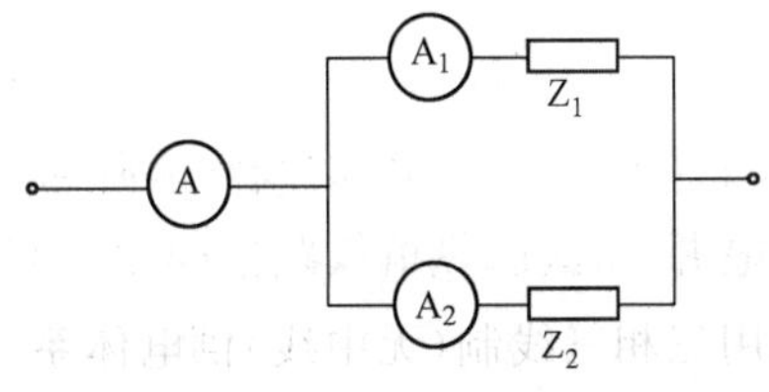

题 7-4-2 图

7-4-3　已知无源二端网络如图所示，输入电压和电流按下式计算

$$u(t)=220\sqrt{2}\sin(314t+30°)(\mathrm{V})$$

$$i(t)=4\sqrt{2}\sin(314t-25°)(\mathrm{V})$$

则该网络消耗的电功率为(　　)。

A. 721W　　B. 880W　　C. 505W　　D. 850W

7-4-4　如图所示正弦交流电路中，已知 $u=100\sin(10t+45°)\mathrm{V}$，$i_1=i=10\sin(10t+45°)\mathrm{A}$，$i_2=20\sin(10t+135°)\mathrm{A}$，元件 1、2、3 的等效参数值分别为(　　)。

A. $R=5\Omega, L=0.5\mathrm{H}, C=0.02\mathrm{F}$　　B. $L=0.5\mathrm{H}, C=0.02\mathrm{F}, R=20\Omega$

C. $R_1=10\Omega, R_2=10\mathrm{H}, C=5\mathrm{F}$　　D. $R=10\Omega, C=0.02\mathrm{F}, L=0.5\mathrm{H}$

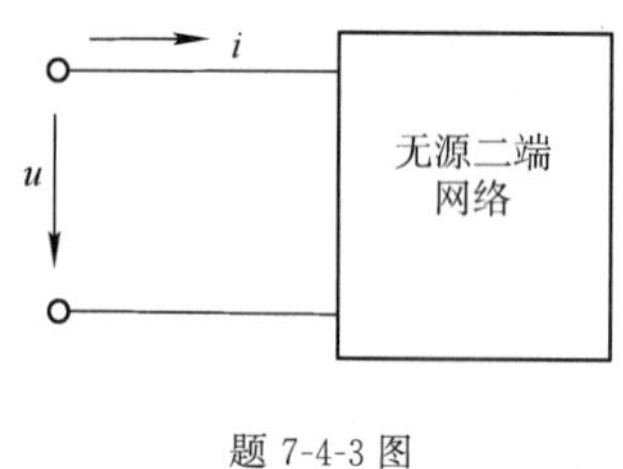

题 7-4-3 图

题 7-4-4 图

7-4-5　某三相电路中，三个线电流分别为

$$i_{\mathrm{A}}=18\sin(314t+23°)(\mathrm{A})$$

$$i_{\mathrm{R}}=18\sin(314t-97°)(\mathrm{A})$$

$$i_{\mathrm{C}}=18\sin(314t+143°)(\mathrm{A})$$

当 $t=10\mathrm{s}$ 时，三个电流之和为(　　)。

A. 18A　　B. 0A　　C. $18\sqrt{2}\mathrm{A}$　　D. $18\sqrt{3}\mathrm{A}$

7-4-6　如图所示 RLC 串联电路原处于感性状态，今保持频率不变欲调节可变电容使其进入谐振状态，则电容 C 值(　　)。

A. 必须增大　　B. 必须减小

C. 不能预知其增减　　D. 先增大后减小

题 7-4-6 图

7-4-7　在三相对称电路中，负载每相的复阻抗为 Z，且电源电压保持不变。若负载接成 Y 形时消耗的有功功率为 P_{Y}，接成△形时消耗的有功功率为 $P_{\triangle}$，则两种连接法的有功功率关系为(　　)。

A. $P_{\triangle}=3P_{\mathrm{Y}}$　　B. $P_{\triangle}=1/3P_{\mathrm{Y}}$　　C. $P_{\triangle}=P_{\mathrm{Y}}$　　D. $P_{\triangle}=1/2P_{\mathrm{Y}}$

7-4-8　有三个 100Ω 的线性电阻接成△形三相对称负载，然后挂接在电压为 220V 的三相对称电源上，这时供电线路上的电流应为(　　)A。

A. 6.6　　B. 3.8　　C. 2.2　　D. 1.3

7-4-9　中性点接地的三相五线制电路中，所有单相电气设备电源插座的正确接线是图中的(　　)。

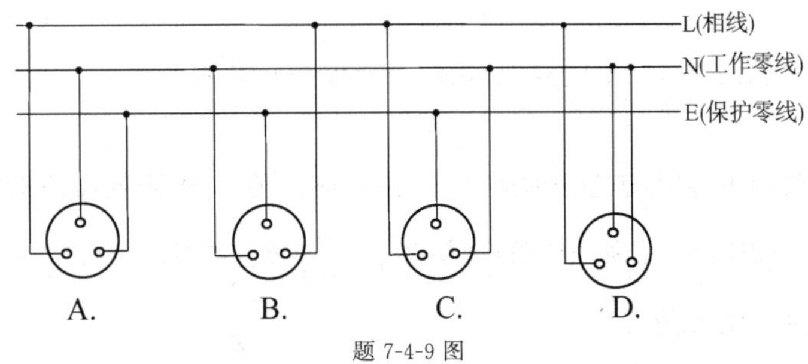

题 7-4-9 图

7-4-10　在如图所示的三相四线制低压供电系统中，如果电动机 M_1 采用保护接中线，电动机 M_2 采用保护接地。当电动机 M_2 的一相绕组的绝缘破坏导致外壳带电，则电动机 1 的外壳与地的电位（　　）。

A. 相等或不等　　B. 不相等　　C. 不能确定　　D. 相等

7-4-11　当如图所示电路的激励电压 $u_i=\sqrt{2}U_i\sin(\omega t+\varphi)$ 时，电感元件上的响应电压 u_L 的初相位为（　　）。

A. $90°-\arctan\frac{\omega L}{R}$　　B. $90°-\arctan\frac{\omega L}{R}+\varphi$

C. $\arctan\frac{\omega L}{R}$　　D. $\varphi-\arctan\frac{\omega L}{R}$

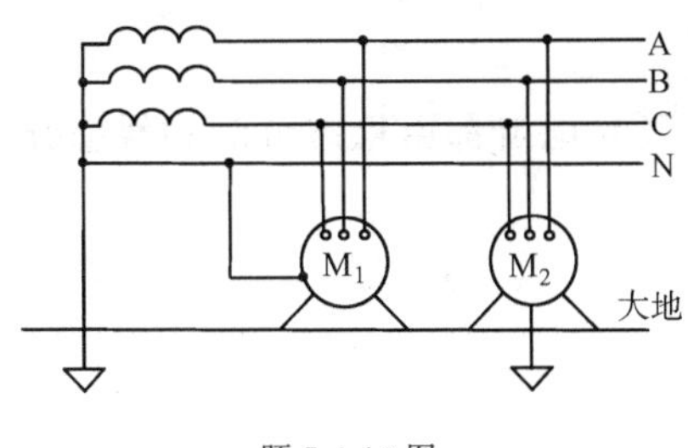

题 7-4-10 图

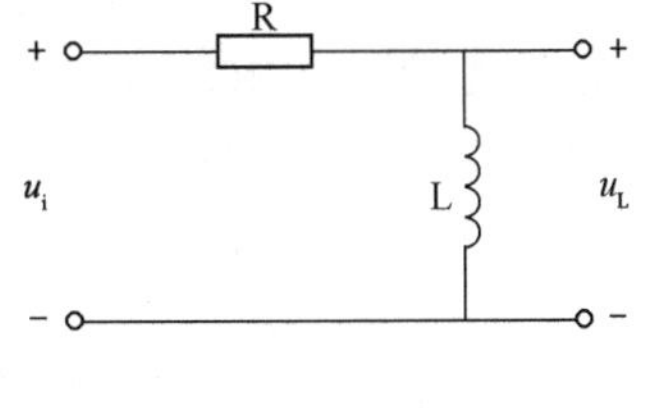

题 7-4-11 图

第五节　电路的暂态过程

电路的结构发生变化（如开关动作），电路就要从一种稳定状态向另一种稳定状态过渡。在有储能元件的电路中（有 L、C 元件），转换需要有一定的时间才能完成，这种物理过程就是电路的暂态过程。

如果电路中只有一个储能元件（L 或 C），而元件的伏安关系为积分或微分关系，那么描述这一电路的方程就是一阶微分方程，我们将这种电路的暂态过程称为"一阶电路的暂态过程"。

（一）电路的响应

电路中的电源（电压源或电流源）称为电路的激励，它推动电路工作；由激励作用在电路中各部分产生的电压和电流称为电路的响应。

根据电路储能元件的不同分为 RC 电路响应和 RL 电路响应，同时每种响应都可以化分为三种基本响应方式。

1. 零输入响应

电路换路以后，无外加激励，暂态过程仅由初始能量产生。

2. 零状态响应

电路的初始能量为零，仅由外加激励产生响应。

3. 全响应

电路的响应由储能元件(L、C)的初始能量和外加激励共同产生。

(二)换路定则

换路定则用来确定电路暂态过程的电压、电流的初始值。根据能量不跃变原则,能量的积累和衰减都要经过一段时间,否则相应的电功率 $p=\frac{\mathrm{d}w}{\mathrm{d}t}$ 就趋向无限大(即 $\mathrm{d}t\to 0$,而 $\mathrm{d}w\neq 0$)一般电路是做不到功率无限大的。

已知

$$\text{磁场能量} \qquad W_L=\frac{1}{2}Li_L^2$$

$$\text{电场能量} \qquad W_C=\frac{1}{2}Cu_C^2$$

既然能量(W_L、W_C)不会跃变,i_L 和 u_C 也不能出现跃变,由此可得出换路定则的两个公式

$$I_{L(t_0+)}=I_{L(t_0-)} \tag{7-5-1}$$

$$U_{C(t_0+)}=U_{C(t_0-)} \tag{7-5-2}$$

(三)求解一阶电路的三要素法

对于一阶电路(RL 或 RC),响应不论是电压还是电流都由稳态分量和暂态分量两部分合成,即

$$f(t)=f(\infty)+[f(t_0+)-f(\infty)]e^{-t/\tau} \tag{7-5-3}$$

式中: $f(t)$——电压、电流的全响应;

$f(\infty)$——电压、电流的稳分量;

$[f(t_0+)-f(\infty)]e^{-t/\tau}$——电压、电流的暂态分量。

τ——暂态过程的时间常数。

可见,只要能解出 $f(\infty)$、$f(t_0+)$ 和 τ 这三个要素,就可以求出暂态过程中的电压或电流响应。下面通过一个具体例子加以说明。

【例 7-5-1】 如图所示电路中已知 $U_s=4\text{V}$,$R_1=2\text{k}\Omega$,$R_2=2\text{k}\Omega$,$R_3=1\text{k}\Omega$,$C=1\mu\text{F}$。开关 S 在 t_0 时刻突然闭合,电容电压的初始值为 $U_{C(0-)}=1\text{V}$,试求 $i_2(t)$,$u_C(t)$,并画出 $U_C(t)$ 的暂态过程曲线。

解 (1)确定初始值 $f(0+)$

根据换路定则 $U_{C(0+)}=U_{C(0-)}=1\text{V}$

将 $t=0+$ 的电路表示为如解图 1 所示,这时 $U_{C(0+)}$ 的作用与独立电源的作用相同(其数值与当前电路结构无关,仅由 $U_{C(0-)}$ 决定)。

求 $I_{2(0+)}$ 时可以用戴维南定理,具体做法是:将 R_2 电阻两端 a、b 点分开,求除去 R_2 以后,a、b 两端除源电阻 R_0,即

$$R_0=R_1/\!/R_3=\frac{1\times 2}{1+2}=\frac{2}{3}\text{k}\Omega$$

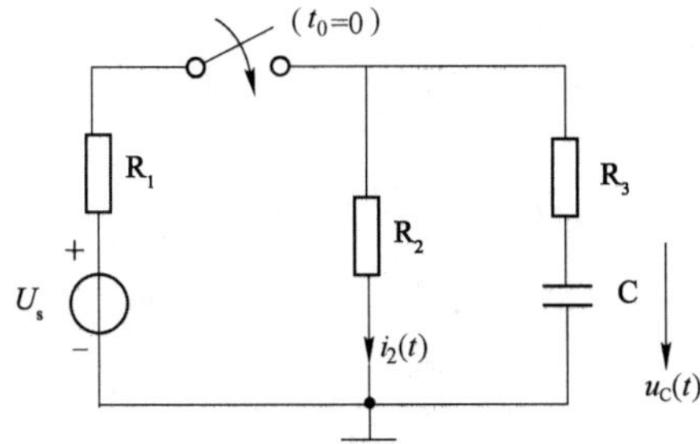

例 7-5-1 图　电路图

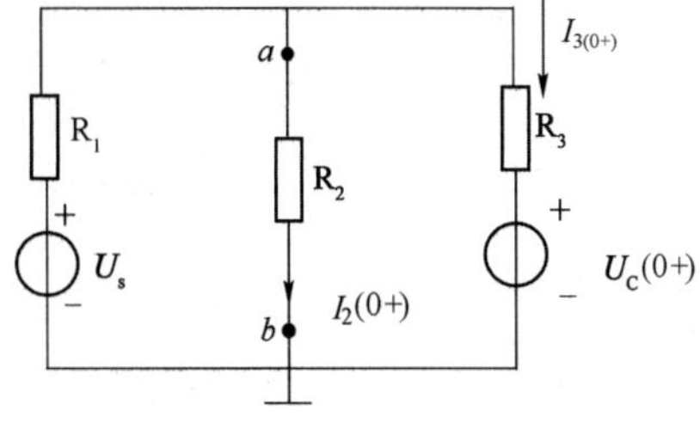

例 7-5-1 解图 1　$t=0+$时的电路图

求 ab 端的开路电压 U_{ab0}，即

$$U_{ab0}=U_{C(0+)}+I_{3(0+)}R_3=U_{C(0+)}+\frac{U_s-U_{C(0+)}}{R_1+R_3}\cdot R_3$$

$$=1+\frac{4-1}{2+1}\times 1=2\text{V}$$

R_2 电阻与等效电压源接通以后（见解图 2），求实际 R_2 电阻中通过的电流 $I_{2(0+)}$，即：

$$I_{2(0+)}=\frac{U_{2ab0}}{R_0+R_2}=\frac{2}{\frac{2}{3}+2}=0.75\text{mA}$$

(2)确定稳态值 $f(\infty)$

在稳态时，电容元件相当于开路，电路如解图 3 所示。

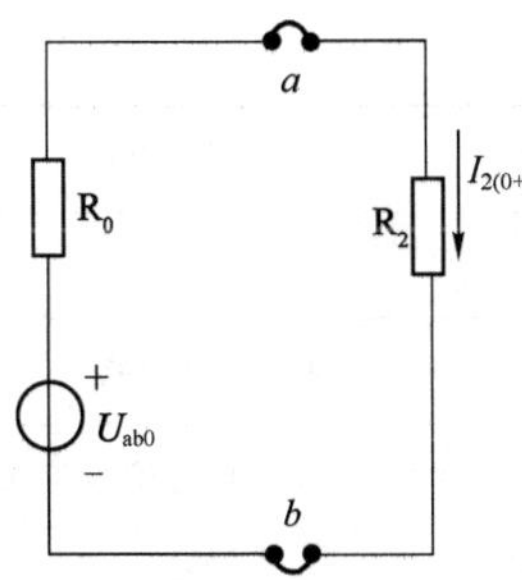

例 7-5-1 解图 2　R_2 等效电路

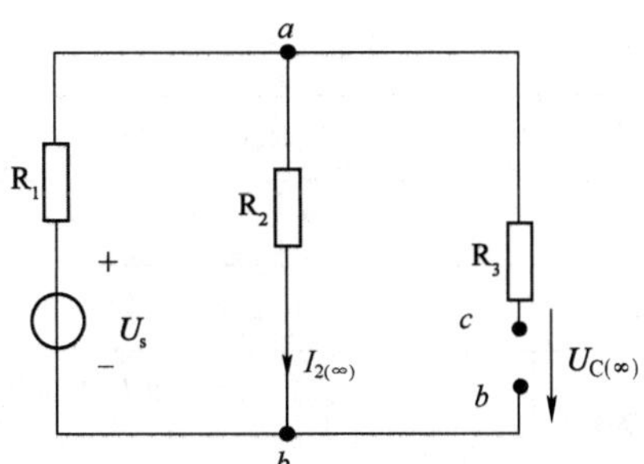

例 7-5-1 解图 3　$t\to\infty$稳态电路

$$I_{2(\infty)}=\frac{U_s}{R_1+R_2}=\frac{4}{2+2}=1\text{mA}$$

$$U_{2(\infty)}=R_2I_{2(\infty)}=2\times 1=2\text{V}$$

$$U_{C(\infty)}=U_{2(\infty)}=2\text{V}$$

(3)确定时间常数 τ

$$\tau=R\cdot C \tag{7-5-4}$$

R 是由电容 C 两端向电路其他部分看的除源等效电阻，如解图 4 所示。

$$R=R_3+(R_1/\!/R_2)=1+(2/\!/2)=2\text{k}\Omega$$

$$\tau=R\cdot C=2\times1\times10^{-3}=2\text{ms}$$

(4)将三要素参数代入公式

$$u_C(t)=U_{C(\infty)}+(U_{C(0+)}-U_{C(\infty)})e^{-t/\tau}$$

$$=2+(1-2)e^{-t/2\times10^{-3}}\ (\text{V})$$

$$i_2(t)=I_{2(\infty)}+(I_{2(0+)}-I_{2(\infty)})e^{-t/\tau}$$

$$=1+(0.75-1)e^{-t/2\times10^{-3}}\ (\text{mA})$$

(5)绘制 $u_C(t)$ 的暂态过程曲线(见解图 5)

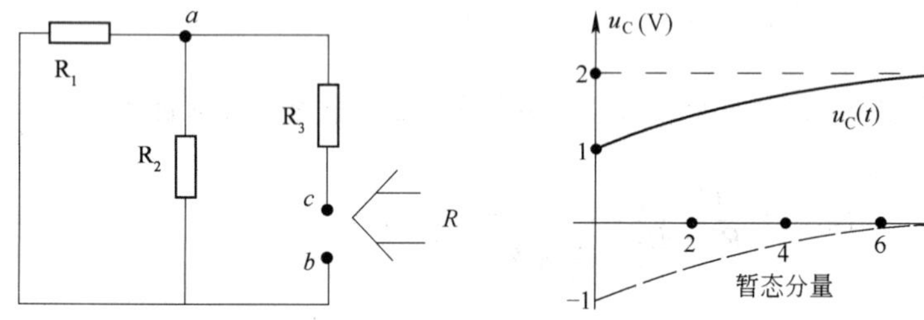

例 7-5-1 解图 4　等效电阻

例 7-5-1 解图 5　电容电压 $u_C(t)$ 的波形图

这里，我们只分析了 RC 电路，RL 电路的暂态过程分析方法不变，但有如表 7-5-1 所示三点区别。

表 7-5-1

序号	区　别	RC 电路	RL 电路
1	时间常数	$\tau=RC$	$\tau=L/R$
2	在稳态电路中	电容元件开路	电感元件短路
3	在 t_0+ 电路中	$U_{C(t_0+)}=U_{C(t_0-)}$ 电容初始电压按理想电压源处理	$I_{L(t_0+)}=I_{L(t_0-)}$ 电感初始电流按理想电流源处理

【例 7-5-2】 已知电路如图所示，设开关在 $t=0$ 时刻断开，那么：

A. 电流 i_C 从 0 逐渐增长，再逐渐衰减为 0

B. 电压从 3V 逐渐衰减到 2V

C. 电压从 2V 逐渐增长到 3V

D. 时间常数 $\tau=4C$

解　开关未动作前，$u=U_{C(0-)}$

在直流稳态电路中，电容为开路状态时，$U_{C(0-)}=\dfrac{1}{2}\times6=3\text{V}$

电源充电进入新的稳压时

$$U_{C(\infty)}=\frac{1}{3}\times 6=2\text{V}$$

因此换路电器电压逐步衰减到 2V。

答案:B

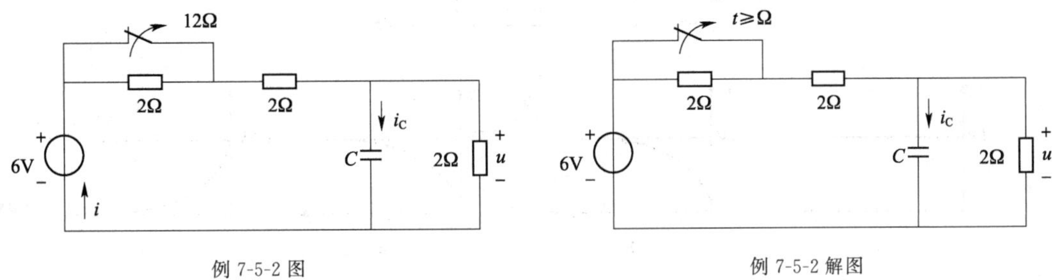

例 7-5-2 图　　　　例 7-5-2 解图

习　题

7-5-1　在开关 S 闭合瞬间，如图所示电路中的 i_R、i_L、i_C 和 i 这四个量中，发生跃变的量是(　　)。

A. i_R 和 i_C　　B. i_C 和 i

C. i_C 和 i_L　　D. i_R 和 i

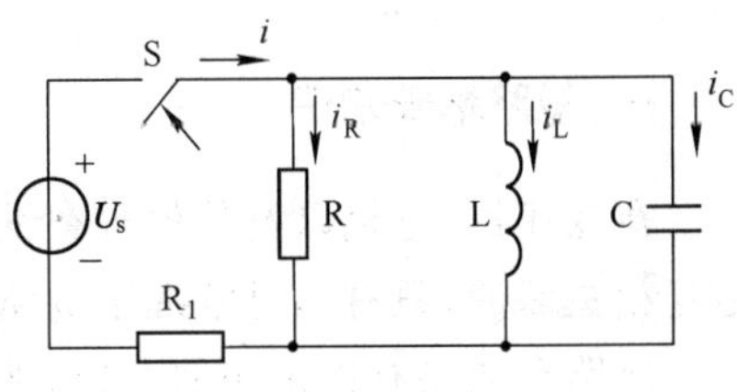

题 7-5-1 图

7-5-2　如图所示电路在开关 S 闭合后的时间常数 τ 值为(　　)。

A. 0.1s　　B. 0.2s

C. 0.3s　　D. 0.5s

7-5-3　如图所示电路当开关 S 在位置“1”时已达稳定状态。在 $t=0$ 时将开关 S 瞬间合到位置“2”，则在 $t>0$ 后电流 i_e 应(　　)。

A. 与图示方向相同且逐渐增大　　B. 与图示方向相反且逐渐衰减到零

C. 与图示方向相同且逐渐减少　　D. 与图示方向相同且逐渐衰减到零

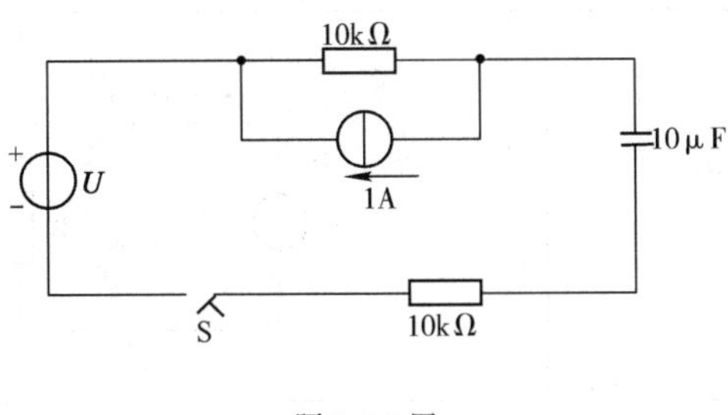

题 7-5-2 图

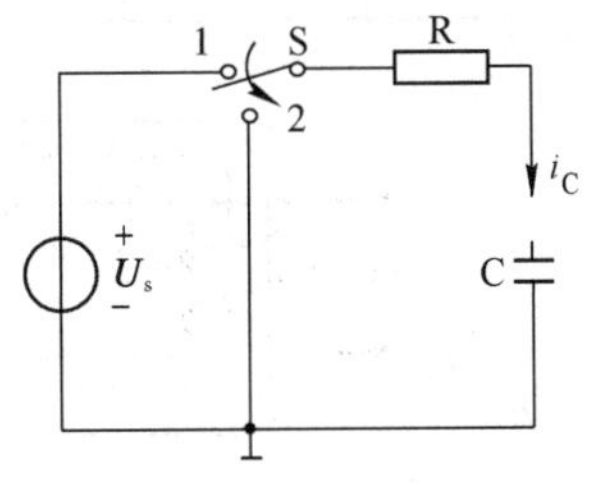

题 7-5-3 图

7-5-4　如图所示电路中，$R=1\text{k}\Omega$，$C=1\mu\text{F}$，$U_1=1\text{V}$，电容无初始储能，如果开关 S 在 $t=0$ 时刻闭合，则给出输出电压波形的是(　　)。

A. a)　　B. b)　　C. c)　　D. d)

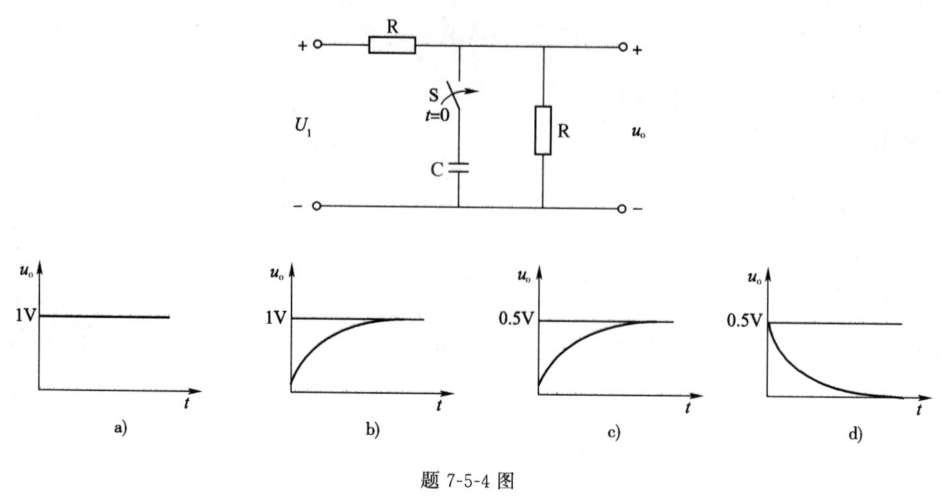

题 7-5-4 图

第六节　变压器、电动机及继电接触控制

一、磁路基础知识

在变压器、电机以及其他含有铁磁元件的电路中，不仅有电路问题，而且有磁路问题，两者是互相关联的，只有同时掌握了电路和磁路的基本知识，才能对这些元件或电路进行分析。

磁路和电路有许多相似之处，现在将两者的情况对照于表 7-6-1。

磁路与电路对照图　　　　表 7-6-1

	磁　路	电　路
物理量	磁动势 $F=NI$ 磁通 Φ 磁感应强度 $B=\dfrac{\Phi}{S}$ 磁阻 $R_m=\dfrac{l}{\mu S}$	电动势 E 电流 I 电流密度 J 电阻 $R=\dfrac{l}{\rho S}$
模型		
计算公式	$\Phi=\dfrac{F}{R_m}=\dfrac{NI}{R_m}$	$I=\dfrac{E}{R}$

分析磁路的一般做法是将磁路关系转化为电路关系，这就要用到磁场电流定律——安培环路定律

$$\oint \boldsymbol{H} d\boldsymbol{l} = \sum I \qquad (7\text{-}6\text{-}1)$$

由此可以得出两个关系式

$$\Phi=\frac{NI}{\frac{l}{\mu s}}=\frac{F}{R_m} \quad (7\text{-}6\text{-}2)$$

该式在形式上与电路的欧姆定律相似，称为“磁路欧姆定律”。由于磁导率 μ 不是常数（与电流 I 有关），则该公式不作为定量公式，只能用来定性分析。

$$\sum I=NI=H_1l_1+H_2l_2+\cdots=\sum(Hl)$$

式中，H_1l_1，H_2l_2，…是磁路各段的磁压降，从形式看，它可以称为磁路的克希荷夫定律，可以直接计算磁路。

本课程的重点在于用磁路基础分析电动机和变压器的性质。

二、变压器

变压器是一种常用的交流电气设备，在电力系统和电子线路中应用广泛。

变压器的一般构造包括闭合铁芯和高压、低压绕组等主要部分，其中绕组是变压器的电路部分，铁芯是变压器的磁路部分。对于绕组来说，与电源相连的称为原绕组（或称初级绕组、一次绕组），与负载相连的称为副绕组（或称次级绕组、二次绕组）。变压器的工作基于电磁感应原理，图 7-6-1 为变压器的原理示意图。

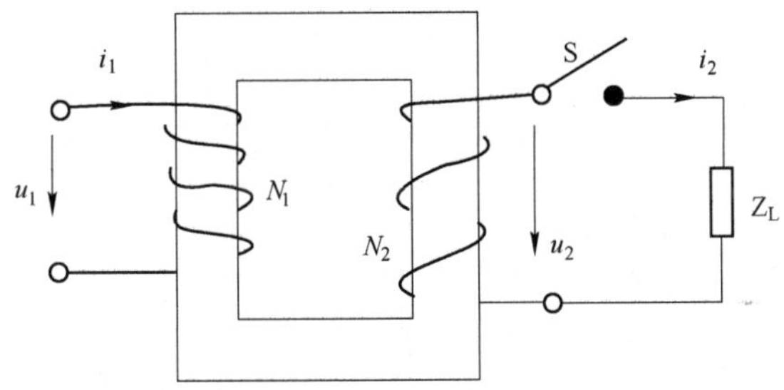

图 7-6-1　变压器原理示意图

（一）电压变换

若原绕组接交流电源，电压有效值为 U_1，则副绕组空载电压为 U_{2o}。

则：

$$\frac{U_1}{U_{2o}}=\frac{N_1}{N_2}=K \quad (7\text{-}6\text{-}3)$$

式中，K 为变压器的变化，亦即原绕组匝数 N_1 与副绕组匝数 N_2 的比。

式(7-6-3)说明，空载时，变压器原、副绕组的电压之比等于匝数比。当电源电压 U_1 一定时，只要改变匝数比，就可以得到不同的输出电压 U_{2o}，这就是变压器的电压变换作用。当变压器有载工作时，负载电压 U_2 与空载电压 U_{2o} 近似相等。

（二）电流变换

若原绕组的电流为 I_1，副绕组的电流为 I_2，则

$$\frac{I_1}{I_2}=\frac{N_2}{N_1}=\frac{1}{K} \quad (7\text{-}6\text{-}4)$$

式(7-6-4)说明，变压器原、副绕组电流有效值之比近似等于它们匝数比的倒数，这就是变压器的电流变换作用。

(三)阻抗变换

当把阻抗为 Z_L 的负载接到变压器副边,则

$$|Z_L|=\frac{U_2}{I_2}$$

对电源来说,它所接的负载等效阻抗为

$$|Z_L'|=\frac{U_1}{I_1}=\frac{KU_2}{I_2/K}=K^2\frac{U_2}{I_2}=K^2|Z_L| \tag{7-6-5}$$

式(7-6-5)说明,当把阻抗为$|Z_L|$的负载接到变压器副边,对电源来说,相当于接上一个阻抗为$|Z_L'|=K^2|Z_L|$的负载。这就是变压器的阻抗变换作用,在电子电路中就可以根据这一功能实现阻抗"匹配"。

【例 7-6-1】 图示变压器为理想变压器,且 $N_1=100$ 匝,若希望 $I_1=1\text{A}$ 时,$P_{R2}=40\text{W}$,则 N_2 应为:

A. 50 匝　　B. 200 匝　　C. 25 匝　　D. 400 匝

解 如解图所示,根据理想变压器关系有

$$I_2=\sqrt{\frac{P_2}{R_2}}=\sqrt{\frac{40}{10}}=2\text{A}$$

$$K=\frac{I_2}{I_1}=2$$

$$N_2=\frac{N_1}{K}=\frac{100}{2}=50\text{ 匝}$$

答案:A

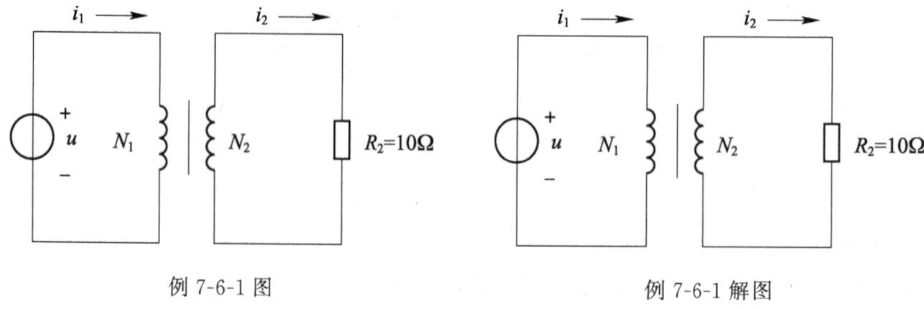

例 7-6-1 图　　例 7-6-1 解图

三、三相交流异步电动机

电动机是一种能将电能转化为机械能的旋转机械,电动机按照电源的种类不同,可分为交流电动机和直流电动机。交流电动机又分为异步电动机(或称感应电动机)和同步电动机。异步电动机按结构又分为鼠笼式异步电动机和绕线异式步电动机。三相异步电动机是在工农业生产、科研和国防等部门得到最广泛应用的一种电动机。

三相异步电动机主要由固定不动的定子和可转动的转子以及其他零部件组成。无论是定子还是转子,都包括绕组和铁芯两个主要部分。

(一)三相异步电动机基本关系

1. 转速和转向

三相异步电动机的转速 n 是转子转速,其大小取决于定子绕组通以三相交流电后产生的旋转磁场的转速 n_0(称为同步转速),同步转速可用下式计算

$$n_0=\frac{60f_1}{P}\quad(\text{转 / 分,r/min}) \tag{7-6-6}$$

式中：f_1——电源频率；

P——电动机的磁极对数。

异步电动机的转速 $n<n_0$，转差率 s 是用来表示 n 与 n_0 相差程度的量，即

$$s=\frac{n_0-n}{n_0} \tag{7-6-7}$$

一般异步电动机在额定负载时的转差率为 1%～9%，而在起动开始瞬间由于 $n=0$ 而 $s=1$ 为最大，式(7-6-7)也可写成

$$n=(1-s)n_0 \tag{7-6-8}$$

表 7-6-2 为三相异步电动机的磁极对数 P 与同步转速 n_0 以及电动机转速 n(当 $s=3\%$)之间的数量关系。

P 与 n_0 及 n 的关系　　表 7-6-2

P(极对数)	1	2	3	4	5	6
n_0(r/min)	3 000	1 500	1 000	750	600	500
n(r/min)	2 910	1 455	970	728	582	485

三相异步电动机的型号中，最后一位数字是表示磁极数的，例如 Y132-4 型号说明了该电动机为 4 极(即 $P=2$)电机。根据这个数字就可以判断电动机的转速，反过来也可以根据转速确定磁极数。

异步机的转向与旋转磁场的转向相同。要改变电动机转向，只要任意对调两根定子绕组连接电源的导线即可。

2.机械特性曲线和电磁转矩

(1)机械特性曲线

在一定的电源电压和转子电阻下，转速与电磁转矩的关系曲线 $n=f(T)$ 称为电动机的机械特性曲线。如图 7-6-2 所示。

机械特性曲线上的 AB 段是电动机的稳定工作段。在 AB 段，当负载有所变动，电动机能自动调节转速和转矩来适应负载的变化。例如当负载增大，电动机会沿着 AB 段下行，降低转速(仍高于临界转速)而发出更大的电磁转矩来满足负载，电动机仍能稳定工作。AB 段较平坦，电动机从空载到额定负载转速下降很少，也就是说异步电动机的机械特性是硬特性。

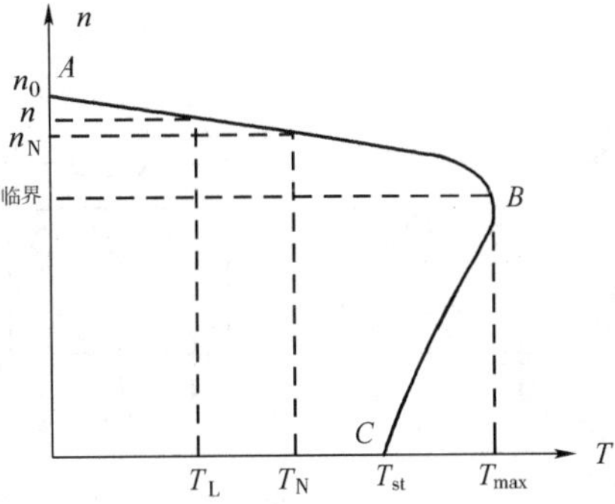

图 7-6-2　电动机的机械特性曲线和电磁转矩

BC 段则是不稳定段。假如负载转矩增大到超过电动机的最大转矩，那么电动机的转速下降超过临界转速，于是它发出的电磁转矩也减小，直至电动停转发生堵转(闷车)，时间一长则电动机烧毁。

(2)电磁转矩

异步电动机的电磁转矩是由旋转磁场的每极磁通与转子电流相互作用而产生的。转矩与定子电压的平方成正比，并与转子回路的电阻和感抗、转差率以及电动机的结构有关。

①额定转矩 T_N

电动机在额定负载时的转矩

$$T_N = 9\ 550\,\frac{P_{2N}}{n_N} \qquad (牛 \cdot 米, \mathrm{N \cdot m}) \tag{7-6-9}$$

式中：P_{2N}——电动机的额定输出功率(kW)；

n_N——电动机的额定转速(r/min)。

②负载转矩 T_L

电动机在实际负载下发出的实际转矩

$$T_L = 9\ 550\,\frac{P_2}{n} \qquad (\mathrm{N \cdot m}) \tag{7-6-10}$$

式中：P_2——电动机的实际输出功率(kW)；

n——电动机的实际转速(rad/min)。

③最大转矩 T_{max}

电动机能发出的最大转矩

$$T_{max} = \lambda T_N \tag{7-6-11}$$

式中，λ 为电动机的过载系数，一般为 1.8～2.2。电动机发出最大转矩时对应的转速为临界转速 $n_{临界}$。

④起动转矩 T_{st}

电动机刚起动时发出的转矩，一般有

$$T_{st} = (1.0 \sim 2.2)\,T_N \tag{7-6-12}$$

3.星形接法和三角形接法

鼠笼式异步电动机接线盒内有 6 根引出线，分别标以 U_1、U_2、V_1、V_2、W_1 和 W_2。其中 U_1 和 U_2 是定子第一相绕组的首末端，V_1 和 V_2、W_1 和 W_2 分别是第二相和第三相绕组的首末端。定子三相绕组的连接法有星形和三角形两种，见图 7-6-3。

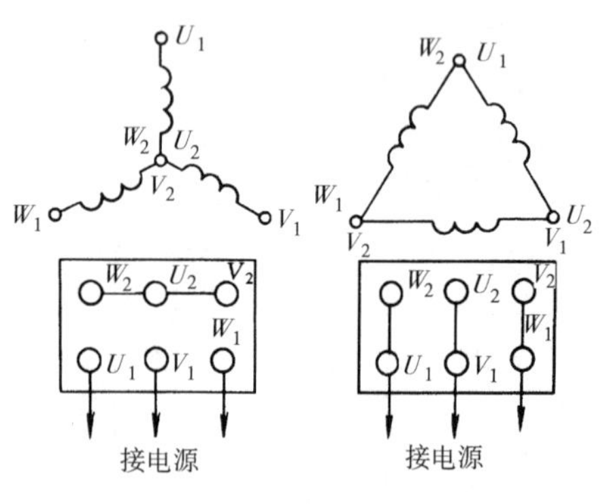

图 7-6-3 定子绕组的星形连接和三角形连接

4.功率、效率和功率因数

电动机的输入功率

$$P_1 = \sqrt{3} U_L I_L \cos\varphi \tag{7-6-13}$$

式中：U_L、I_L——分别为线电压、线电流；

$\cos\varphi$——电动机的功率因数。

电动机的输出功率 $P_2 < P_1$，其差值为电动机本身的功率损耗，包括铜损、铁损以及机械损耗，电动机的效率

$$\eta = \frac{P_2}{P_1} \tag{7-6-14}$$

一般为 72%～93%。

电动机的功率因数在额定负载时为 0.7～0.9，轻载和空载时为 0.2～0.3。故应适当选用电动机容量，避免“大马拉小车”，更要缩短空载运行时间。

(二)三相异步电动机的应用

1.起动

将三相异步电动机接到三相电源上，它的转速从零开始，直到匀速转动的过程为起动。三相异步电动机起动转矩的大小与定子电压 U_1 和转子电阻 R_2 有关，当定子电压减小时起动转矩减小，在一定条件下转子电阻 R_2 增加时起动转矩增加。

三相异步电动机起动时的电流很大，定子边的起动电流为额定电流的5～7倍，但起动转矩却较小。因此，为了减小异步电动机的起动电流(有时也为了提高起动转矩)必须采用适当的起动方法。

(1)直接起动

直接起动(也称全压起动)是得用闸刀开关或接触器，将电动机直接接到具有额定电压的电源上，这种起动方法最为简单经济。电动机能否直接起动，应按各地区电业部门的规定执行，30kW以下的异步电动机一般都可以采用直接起动。

(2)降压起动

在不允许直接起动的场合，可以采用降低定子绕组电压的方法来减小起动电流称为降压起动，主要有以下几种方法。

①星形-三角形换接起动

正常工作时采用三角形接法的异步电动机，起动时先接成星形，待转速上升到接近额定转速时，再换接成三角形，这种方法叫星-角(Y-△)换接起动。

由于电动机的转矩与电压的平方成正比，所以采用Y-△换接起动时，起动电流、起动转矩都减小到直接起动时的$(1/\sqrt{3})^2=1/3$。

这种方法虽然使起动电流受到控制，但也使起动转矩减小很多，故只适应于空载或轻载起动的电动机。

②自耦变压器降压起动

对于容量较大，且正常运行时做星形连接的鼠笼式异步电动机，可利用三相自耦变压器来降压起动，称为自耦变压器降压起动。

这种方法适用于起动不频繁的场合。由于起动设备较笨重且费用高，故本方法仅适用于较大容量的鼠笼式异步电动机。

自耦变压器起动时电动机的起动电流和起动转矩均为直接起动时的$1/K^2$，其中K为自耦变压器的变比。

③转子串电阻起动

由于绕线式异步电动机的结构特点，绕线式异步电动机可采用在转子电路中串入附加电阻的方法来起动。

起动时，转子电路串入附加电阻，起动完毕后，将附加电阻短接。这种方法不仅可以减小起动电流，还可以使起动转矩提高，因此，广泛应用于要求起动转矩较大的生产机械，如起重机、卷扬机等。

2.调速

调速就是在同一负载下得到不同转速，以满足生产过程的要求。改变电动机的转速有三种可能，即改变电源的频率调速，改变电动机极对数调速，以及改变电动机转差率调速，前两者是鼠笼式异步电动机的调速方法，后者是绕线式异步电动机的调速方法。随着近年来电子技术的迅速发展，变频调速技术发展很快。

3.制动

因为电动机的转动部分有惯性，所以把电源切断后，电动机还继续转动一定时间，然后停止。为了缩短辅助工时，提高生产机械的生产率，并为了安全起见，往往要求电动机能够迅速停车，这就需要对电动机制动。电动机制动，也就是要求它产生一个与转子转动方向相反的制动转矩。

异步电动机的制动常用下列几种方法。

(1)能耗制动

这种制动方法就是在切断三相电源的同时,接通直流电源,使直流通入定子绕组从而生产制动转矩。

因为这种方法是用消耗转子的动能来进行制动的,所以称为能耗制动。这种制动能量消耗小,制动平稳,但需要直流电源。

(2)反接制动

在电动机停车时,可将定子绕组接到电源的三根导线中的任意两根对调位置,从而产生制动转矩的制动方法。

这种制动比较简单,效果较好,但能量消耗较大,且当转速接近零时,应利用某种控制电器将电源自动切断,否则电动机将反转。

(3)发电反馈制动

当转子的转速超过旋转磁场的转速时,这时的转矩也是制动的。例如,当起重机快速下放重物时,就会发生这种情况。实际上这时电动机已转入发电机运行,将重物的位能转换为电能而反馈到电网里去,所以称为发电反馈制动。

四、电动机的继电接触器控制

采用继电器、接触器及按钮等控制电器来实现对电动机的自动控制称为电动机的继电器、接触器控制。

(一)常用控制电器

1.组合开关

组合开关有单极、双极、三极和四极几种,额定持续电流有10A、25A、60A和100A等多种。可以用作电源的引入开关,也可以用它来直接起动和停止小容量的电动机或使电动机正反转等。

2.按钮

按钮通常用来接通或断开控制电路,从而控制电动机的运行。

按钮的特点是靠外力(手按)动作(常闭断开或常开闭合),但当外力消失时可以自己复位,按钮结构原理图及符号如图7-6-4所示。

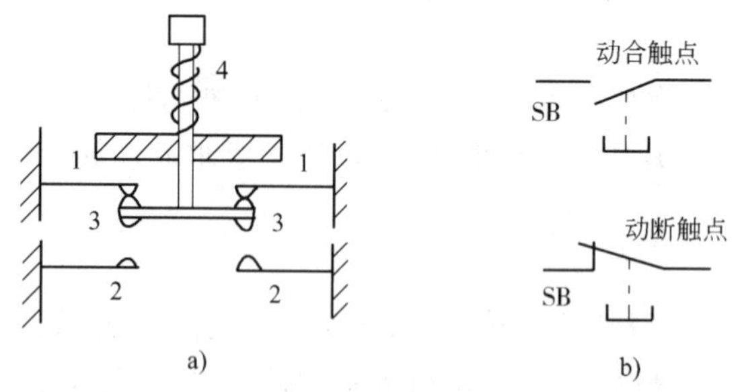

图7-6-4　按钮结构原理及符号

3.行程开关

行程开关(即限位开关)是利用生产机械的某些运动部件碰撞而使其动作,从而接通或断开控制电路的一种电器,行程开关结构及符号如图7-6-5所示。

4.交流接触器

交流接触器常用来接通或断开电动机的主电路。

接触器是利用电磁吸力来工作的,主要由电磁铁和触点两部分组成,其结构原理图及电器符号如图 7-6-6 所示。当线圈 1 得电产生电磁吸力使触点 2、3 动作(常开闭合,或常闭断开);当线圈失电,触点靠弹簧 4 拉力而复位。图 7-6-6b)为交流接触器的电器符号。

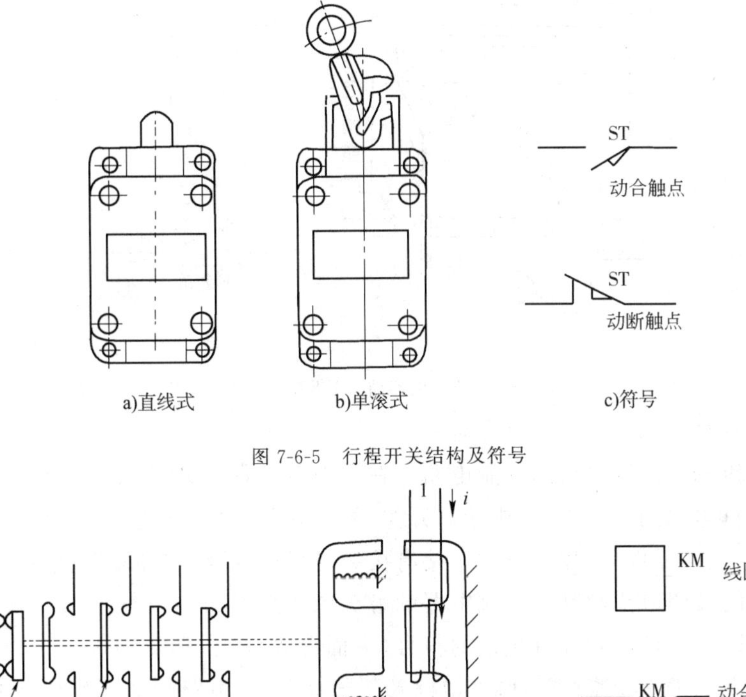

图 7-6-5　行程开关结构及符号

图 7-6-6　接触器结构图及电器符号

5. 热继电器

热继电器是用于电动机过载保护的一种电器,它的动作原理基于电流的热效应,其结构图及符号如图 7-6-7 所示。发热元件串接在电动机的主电路中,当电动机长期过载时,发热元件通过电流大于容许值,其热量使双金属片受热弯曲,从而脱扣,使动断(常闭)触点断开,切断电路达到保护电器的目的。

由于热惯性,热继电器不能立即动作,因此不能作短路保护。

6. 熔断器

熔断器(常说的"保险丝")是最常用的简便有效的保护电器,熔断器的熔体用电阻率较高的易熔合金制成。

7. 自动空气断路器

自动空气断路器又名自动空气开关。它兼有刀开关和熔断器的功能,其特点是动作后不要更换元件,动作电流可整定,切断电流大,断开时间短,工作安全可靠。

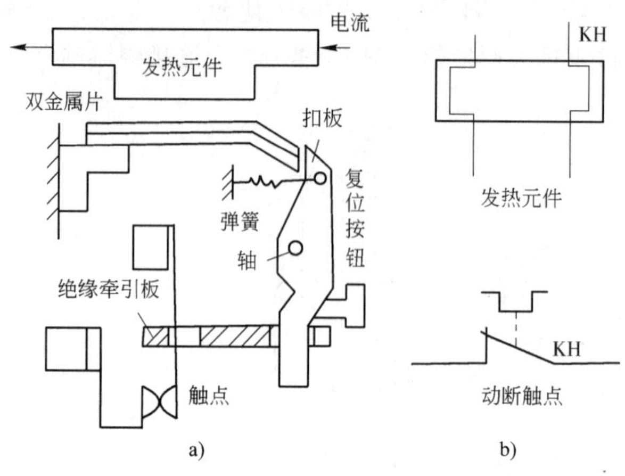

图 7-6-7 热继电器结构图及电器符号

（二）三相异步电动机的基本控制电路

这里主要分析的是鼠笼电机的控制电路。在看电气控制原理图时，要分清主电路和控制电路。主电路是从电源到电动机，其中接有开关（闸门开关、组合开关等）、熔断器、接触器的主触头、热断电器的发热元件等；控制电路中接有按钮、接触器的线圈和辅助触头（如自锁和互锁触头）、热继电器的常闭触头和其他控制电器的触头和线圈。

在电气原理图中各种电器都有规定的符号（下面分别介绍）和文字表示。为读图方便，同一电器的线圈和触点虽然按需要分画在电路的不同部分（主电路和辅电路），但必须用同一符号说明；另外还要说明的是各种触点的状态全表示在电气未通电的状态。

1. 直接起动控制电路

控制原理图如图 7-6-8 所示。

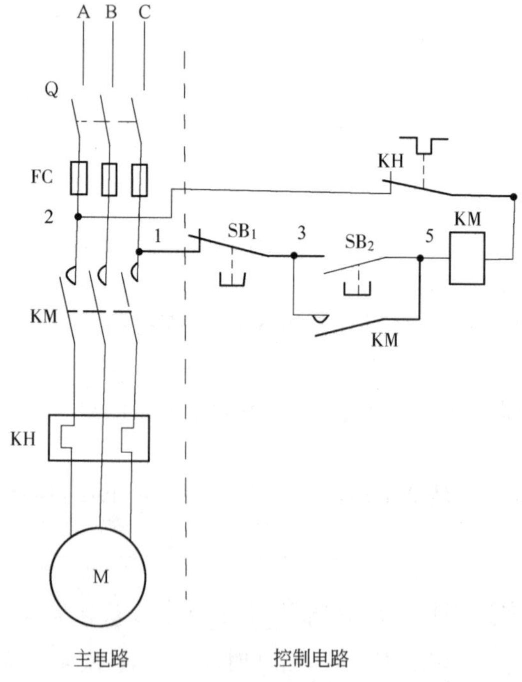

图 7-6-8 直接起动控制电路

电路的工作过程：先将组合开关 Q 闭合，为电动机起动作准备。当按下起动钮 SB_2 时，交流接触器 KM 的线圈得电，动铁心被吸合而将三个主触点闭合，电动机 M 起动。当松开 SB_2 时，起动按钮复位，但是由于与起动按钮并联的辅助触点和主触点同时闭合，因此接触器线圈的电路仍然接通，而使接触器触点保持在闭合的位置，这个辅助触点称为自锁触点。如将停止按钮 SB_1 按下，则将线圈的电路切断，动铁心和触点恢复到断开的位置而使电动机停机。

上述控制线路中，熔断器 FU 起短路保护，热继电器 KH 起过载保护，交流接触器 KM 起零压和失压保护作用。

2. 正反转控制电路

控制电路原理图如图 7-6-9 所示。

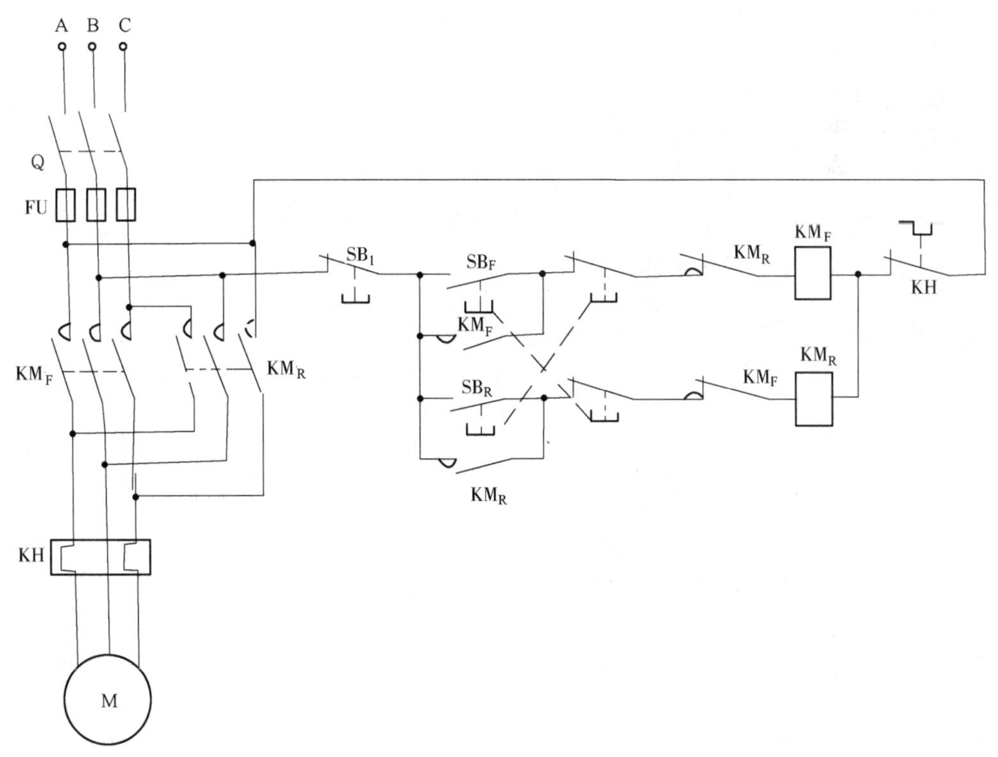

图 7-6-9　鼠笼式电动机正反转的控制电路

按下正转起动按钮 SB_F，正转接触器 KM_F 通电，电动机 M 正转；按下反转起动按钮 SB_R，反转接触器 KM_R 通电，电动机 M 反转。按下停机按钮 SB_1，正反转接触器 KM_F 和 KM_R 均失电，电动机停止运行。

上述控制电路中，正转接触器 KM_F 的一个常闭辅助触点串接在反转接触器 KM_R 的线圈电路中，而反转接触器的一个常闭辅助触点串接在正转接触器的线圈电路中，这两个常闭触点称为联锁触点。联锁触点可防止正反转两个接触器同时闭合，以免造成电源短路。

【例 7-6-2】　为实现对电动机的过载保护，除了将热继电器的热元件串接在电动机的供电电路中外，还应将其：

A. 常开触点串接在控制电路中　　　　B. 常闭触点串接在控制电路中

C. 常开触点串接在主电路中　　　　　D. 常闭触点串接在主电路中

解　实现对电动机的过载保护，除了将热继电器的热元件串联在电动机的主电路的解，还应将热继电器的常闭触点串接在控制电路中。

当电机过载时，这个常闭触点断开，控制电路供电通路断开。

答案：B

五、安全用电

为了人身安全和电力系统工作的需要，要求电气设备采取接地措施。

（一）工作接地

将电力系统的中性点接地，如图 7-6-10 所示，这种接地方式称为工作接地。

工作接地有下列目的：

（1）降低触电电压；

（2）迅速切断故障设备；

（3）降低电气设备对地的绝缘水平。

（二）保护接地

保护接地就是将电气设备正常情况下不带电的金属外壳接地，如图 7-6-11 所示，保护接地适用于中性点不接地的低压系统。

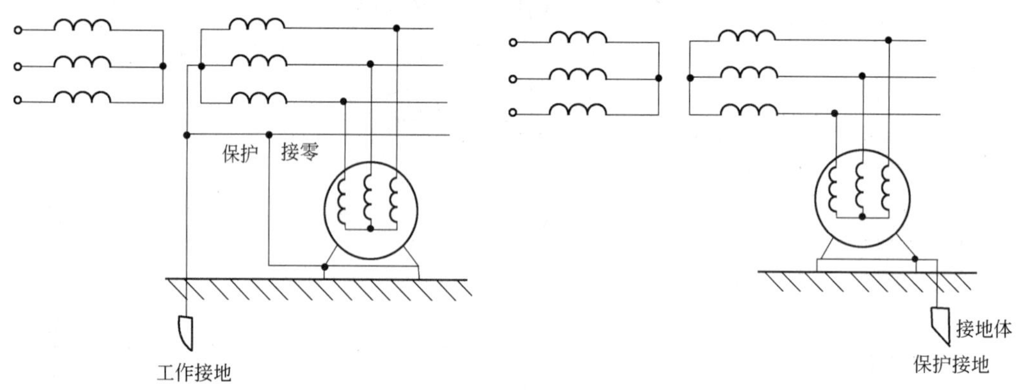

图 7-6-10　工作接地、保护接零　　　　图 7-6-11　保护接地

（三）保护接零

保护接零就是将电气设备的金属外壳接到零线（或称中线）上，如图 7-6-11 所示，保护接零宜用于中性点接地的低压系统中。

习　题

7-6-1　有一容量为 10kV·A 的单相变压器，电压为 3 300/220V，变压器在额定状态下运行。在理想的情况下副边可接 40W、220V、功率因数 $\cos\varphi=0.44$ 的日光灯（　　）盏。

A. 110　　B. 200　　C. 250　　D. 50

7-6-2　三相异步电动机的转动方向由（　　）决定。

A. 电源电压的大小　　B. 电源频率

C. 定子电流相序　　D. 起动瞬间定转子相对位置

7-6-3　三相异步电动机空载起动与满载起动时的起动转矩关系是(　　)。

A. 二者相等　　B. 满载起动转矩大

C. 空载起动转矩大　　D. 无法估计

7-6-4　针对三相异步电动机起动的特点,采用 Y-△换接起动可减小起动电流和起动转矩,以下说法中正确的是(　　)。

A. Y 连接的电动机采用 Y-△换接起动,起动电流和起动转矩都是直接起动的$\frac{1}{3}$

B. Y 连接的电动机采用 Y-△换接起动,起动电流是直接起动的$\frac{1}{3}$,起动转矩是直接起动的$\frac{1}{\sqrt{3}}$

C. △连接的电动机采用 Y-△换接起动,起动电流是直接起动的$\frac{1}{\sqrt{3}}$,起动转矩是直接起动的$\frac{1}{\sqrt{3}}$

D. △连接的电动机采用 Y-△换接起动,起动电流和起动转矩都是直接起动的$\frac{1}{3}$

7-6-5　三相异步电动机在额定负载下,欠压运行,定子电流将(　　)。

A. 小于额定电流　B. 大于额定电流　C. 等于额定电流　D. 不变

7-6-6　如图所示的控制电路中,SB 为按钮,KM 为接触器,若按动 SB_2,试判断下述哪个结论正确?(　　)

A. 接触器 KM_2 通电动作后 KM_1 跟着动作

B. 只有接触器 KM_2 动作

C. 只有接触器 KM_1 动作

D. 以上答案都不对

7-6-7　如图所示为两台电动机 M_1、M_2 的控制电路,两个交流接触器 KM_1、KM_2 的主常开触头分别接入 M_1、M_2 的主电路,该控制电路所起的作用是(　　)。

A. 必须 M_1 先起动,M_2 才能起动,然后两机连续运转

B. M_1、M_2 可同时起动,必须 M_1 先停机,M_2 才能停机

C. 必须 M_1 先起动、M_2 才能起动,M_2 起动后,M_1 自动停机

D. 必须 M_2 先起动,M_1 才能起动,M_1 起动后,M_2 自动停机

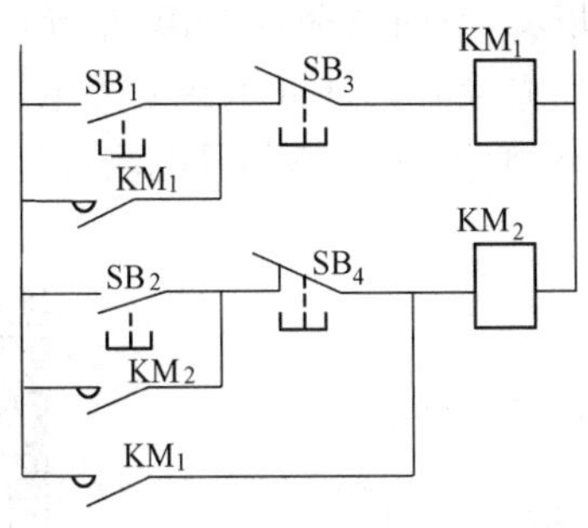

题 7-6-6 图

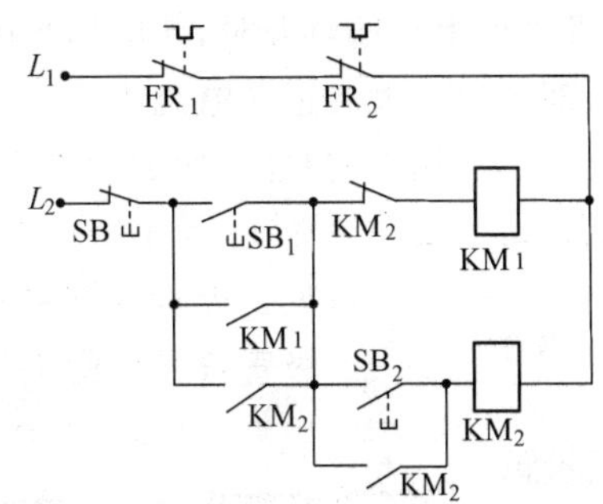

题 7-6-7 图

7-6-8　额定转速为 1 450r/min 的三相异步电动机，空载运行时转差率为（　　）。

A. $s=\frac{1\,500-1\,450}{1\,500}=0.033$　　B. $s=\frac{1\,500-1\,450}{1\,450}=0.035$

C. $0.033<s<0.035$　　D. $s<0.033$

7-6-9　在电动机的继电接触控制电路中，具有短路保护、过载保护、欠压保护和行程保护，其中，需要同时接在主电路和控制电路中的保护电器是（　　）。

A. 热继电器和行程开关　　B. 熔断器和行程开关

C. 接触哭和行程开关　　D. 接触器和热继电器

第七节　二极管及其应用

半导体材料与导体、绝缘体最大的不同之处在于它的导电能力在一定条件下可以转化，当温度变化或掺入杂质以后它的导电能力会发生明显的改变。

常用的半导体材料是硅(Si)和锗(Ge)，它们都是四价元素，我们称纯净的半导体材料为本征半导体。如果我们在本征半导体的一侧掺入五价元素（如磷）将生成大量的自由电子，构成 N 型半导体；在另一侧掺入三价元素（如硼）就会产生大量的空穴。这样在 P 型区和 N 型区的交界处就形成 PN 结，PN 结是构成各种半导体器件的基础。

当不加电源时，在半导体内部由于 P 型区和 N 型区的浓度差别出现扩散过程。扩散的结果在 PN 结交界处形成“空间电荷区”，这个空间电荷区产生一个内电场，内电场的方向由 N 区指向 P 区。

二极管的核心就是 PN 结，由 P 区引出的电极叫做阳极，N 区引出的电极叫做阴极。我们把阳极电位高于阴极电位的情况叫做二极管的正向偏置状态，简称“正偏”，如图 7-7-1a)所示，而把阳极电位低于阴极电位的状态叫做二极管的反向偏置状态，如图 7-7-1b)所示。

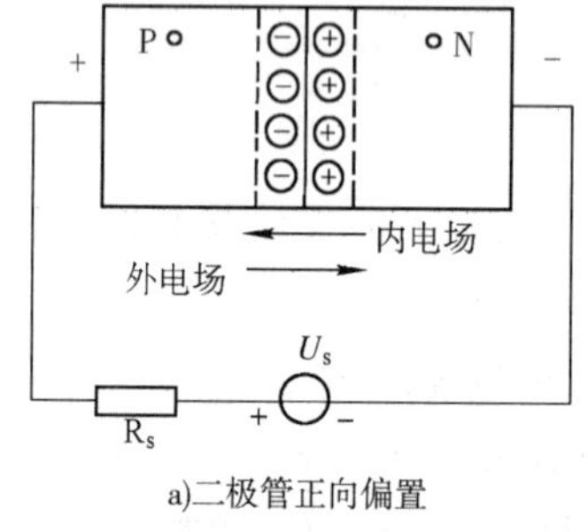

a)二极管正向偏置

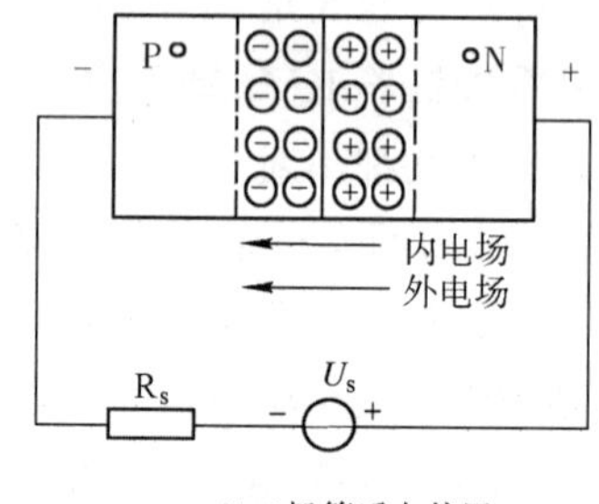

b)二极管反向偏置

图　7-7-1

当二极管加上正偏电源时，外电场与内电场方向相反，空间电荷区变薄，半导体的导电能力增加，外部产生较大的正向电流 I_F。当二极管加上反向偏置的外部电源时外电场与内部电场方向相同，使 PN 结处的空间电荷区加宽，半导体的导电能力削弱，产生的反向电流 I_R 远小于正向电流 I_F。

D

图 7-7-2　二极管符号

可见二极管具有单向导电性。

二极管符号如图 7-7-2 所示。

一、二极管

二极管的伏安特性如图 7-7-3 所示。

由图可见，当外加正向电压很低时，正向电流很小，几乎为零。当正向电压超过一定数值后，电流增长很快，这个一定数值的正向电压称为死区电压，死区电压 U_T 的大小与材料及环境温度有关。通常，硅管的死区电压约为 0.5V，锗管约为 0.2V；二极管正常工作电压 U_F 硅管为 0.6～1V，锗管工作电压为 0.2～0.3V。

当外加反向电压时，只有很小的反向电流。反向电流随温度的上升增长很快；在反向电压不超过某一范围时基本恒定，而与反向电压的高低无关，故通常称它为反向饱和电流。当外加反向电压过高时，反向电流将突然增加，二极管失去单向导电性，这种现象称为击穿，二极管被击穿后，一般不能恢复原来的性能而损坏。

二、稳压管

稳压管是一种特殊的面接触型半导体硅二极管，由于它在电路中与适当数值的电阻配合后能起稳定电压的作用，故称为稳压管。

稳压管的伏安特性曲线与普通二极管类似，如图 7-7-4 所示。其差异是稳压管的反向特性曲线比较陡，且电压较低。

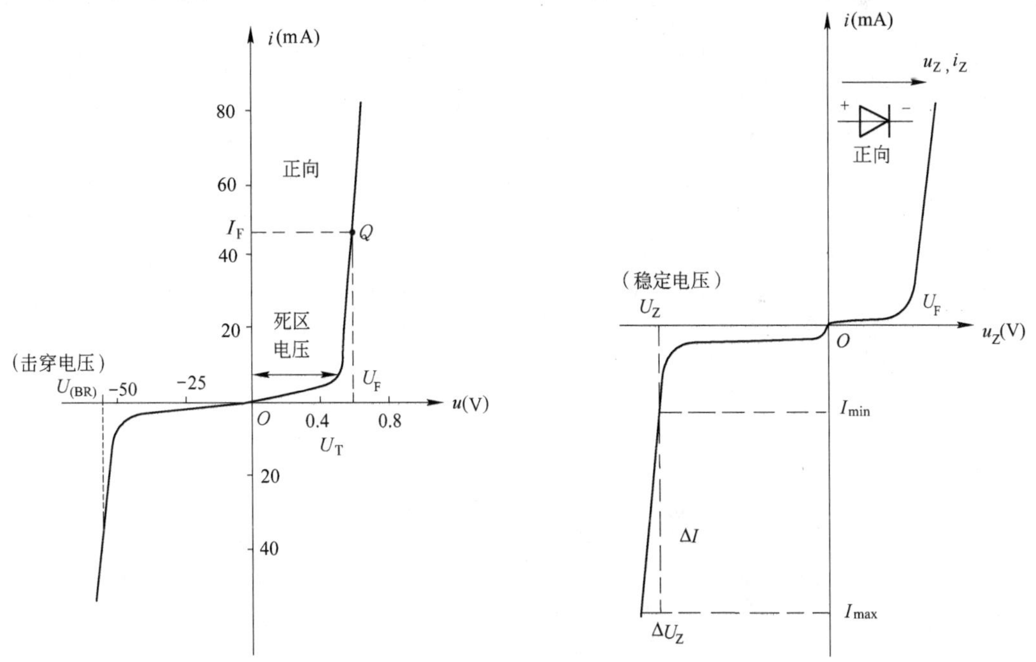

图 7-7-3　2CP10 硅二极管的伏安特性曲线

图 7-7-4　稳压管的伏安特性曲线

稳压管工作于反向击穿区，从反向特性曲线上可见，在反向击穿区，虽然电流在很大范围内变化，但稳压管两端的电压变化很小，正是利用这一特性实现稳压。稳压管与普通二极管不同的是反向击穿是可逆的，去掉反向电压之后，稳压管可恢复正常。当然，如果反向电流超过允许范围，稳压管也将会发生热击穿而损坏。

三、二极管应用电路

（一）整流电路

整流电路的作用是将交流电变为单方向变化的直流电，目前主要采用单相半波整流电路和桥式整流电路。

1.单相半波整流电路

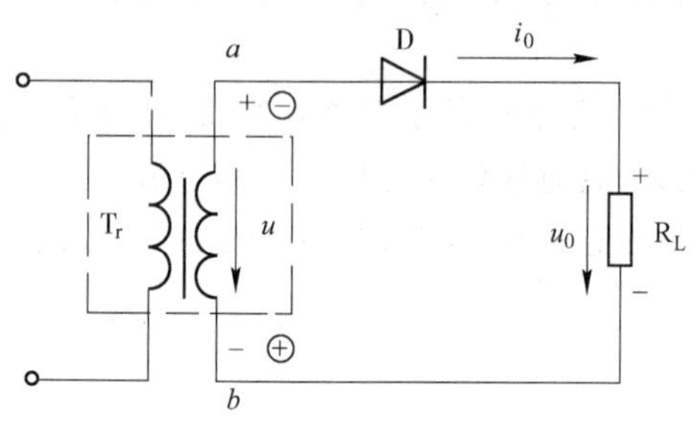

图 7-7-5 单相半波整流电路

如图 7-7-5 所示为单相半波整流电路,由整流变压器 T_r、整流元件 D(二极管)及负载电阻 R_L 组成。

设整流变压器副边的电压为

$$u=\sqrt{2}U\sin\omega t$$

其波形如图 7-7-6a)所示。

由于二极管具有单向导电性,只有当它的阳极电位高于阴极电位时才能导通。在变压器副边电压 u 的正半周,a 点的电位高于 b 点,二极管因承受正向电压而导通,二极管的正向压降可以忽略不计,这时负载电阻 R_L 上的电压 u_0 的正半波和 u 的正半波是相同的,通过的电流为 i_0。在电压 u 的负半周,a 点的电位低于 b 点,二极管因承受反向电压而截止,负载电阻 R_L 上没有电压,因此,在负载电阻 R_L 上得到的是半波整流电压 u_0,如图 7-7-6 负载上整流电压的平均值

$$U_0=\frac{1}{2\pi}\int_0^{\pi}\sqrt{2}U\sin\omega t\mathrm{d}(\omega t)=\frac{\sqrt{2}}{\pi}U=0.45U \qquad (7\text{-}7\text{-}1)$$

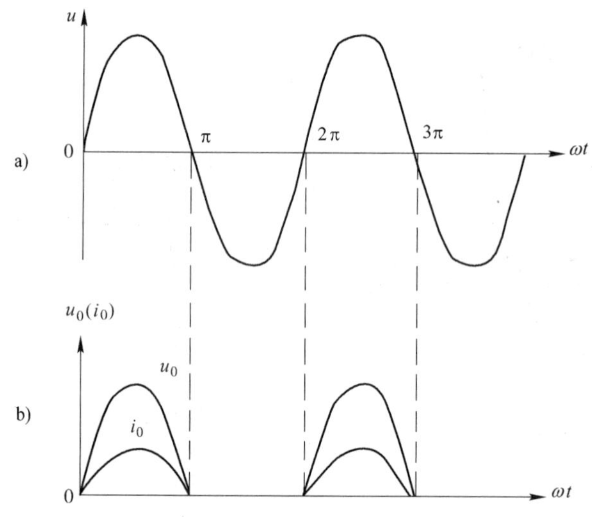

图 7-7-6 单相半波整流电路的电压与电流的波形

负载上整流电流平均值

$$I_0=\frac{U_0}{R_L}=0.45\frac{U}{R_L} \qquad (7\text{-}7\text{-}2)$$

二极管不导通时,承受的最高反向电压和平均电流为

$$\left.\begin{aligned}U_{DRM}&=U_m=\sqrt{2}U\\ I_D&=I_0=0.45\frac{U}{R_L}\end{aligned}\right\} \qquad (7\text{-}7\text{-}3)$$

这样,根据 U_0、I_0 和 U_{DRM}、I_D 就可确定整流电路输出电压、电流的大小,并可以选择合适的整流元件。

2. 单相桥式整流电路

单相桥式整流电路如图 7-7-7 所示。

在变压器副边电压 u 的正半周，a 点的电位高于 b 点，二极管 D_1 和 D_3 导通，D_2 和 D_4 截止；电流 i_1 的通路是 $a \longrightarrow D_1 \longrightarrow R_L \longrightarrow D_3 \longrightarrow b$。这时，负载电阻 R_L 上得到一个半波电压，如图 7-7-8b)所示的 0～π 段所示。

在电压 u 的负半周，b 点的电位高于 a 点；因此，D_1 和 D_3 截止，D_2 和 D_4 导通，电流 i_2 的通路是 $b \longrightarrow D_2 \longrightarrow R_L \longrightarrow D_4 \longrightarrow a$；同样，在负载电阻上得到一个半波电压，如图 7-7-8b)所示的 π～2π 段所示。

因此，单相桥式整流电路的整流电压的平均值 U_o 比半波整流时增加了 1 倍，即

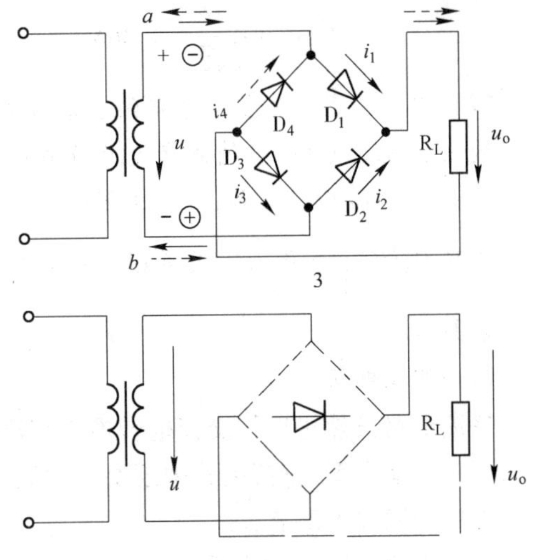

图 7-7-7 单相桥式整流电路

$$U_o = 2 \times 0.45U = 0.9U \tag{7-7-4}$$

负载电阻中的直流电流为：

$$I_o = \frac{U_o}{R_L} = 0.9\frac{U}{R_L} \tag{7-7-5}$$

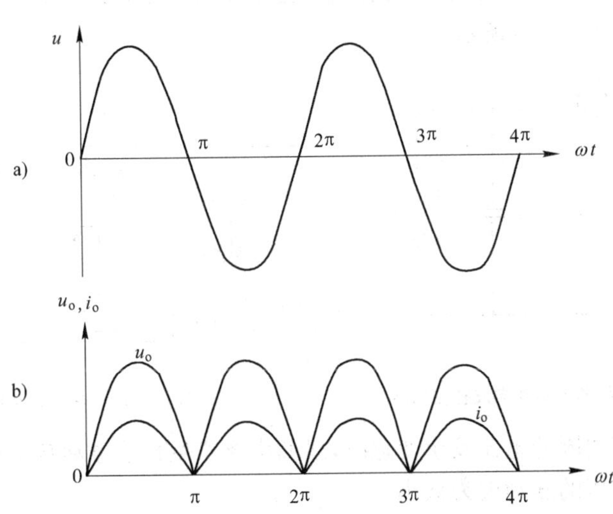

图 7-7-8 单相桥式整流电路的电压与电流的波形

由于四个二极管是交替导通的，故每个二极管中流过的平均电流只有负载电流的一半，即

$$I_D = \frac{1}{2}I_o = 0.45\frac{U}{R_L} \tag{7-7-6}$$

二极管截止时所承受的最高反向电压就是电源电压的最大值，即

$$U_{DRM} = \sqrt{2}U \tag{7-7-7}$$

【例 7-7-1】 二极管应用电路如图所示，设二极管为理想器件，当 $u_1 = 10\sin\omega t$V 时，输出电压 u_o 的平均值 U_o 等于：

A. 10V　　　　B. 0.9×10=9V

C. $0.9\times\frac{10}{\sqrt{2}}=6.36\text{V}$　　　　D. $-0.9\times\frac{10}{\sqrt{2}}=-6.36\text{V}$

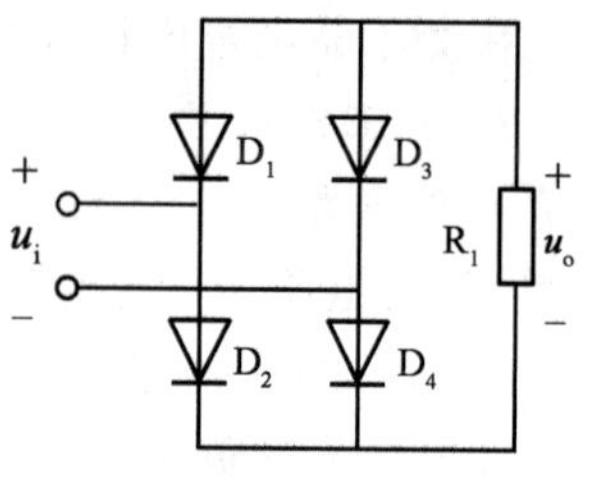

例 7-7-1 图

解　本题采用全波整流电路结合二极管连接方式分析。

输出直流电压 U_o 与输入交流有效值 U_i 的关系为：

$$U_o=-0.9U_i$$

本题 $U_i=\frac{10}{\sqrt{2}}\text{V}$，代入上式得 $U_o=-0.9\times\frac{10}{\sqrt{2}}=-6.36\text{V}$。

答案：D

（二）滤波电路

整流电路虽然可以把交流电转换为直流电，但是这种直流电压是脉动电压。为了改善输出电压的脉动程度，整流电路中还要接滤波器。

常用的滤波电路有：

1. 电容滤波器（C 滤波器）

负载两端并联电容器就是一个最简单的滤波器，如图 7-7-9 所示。电容滤波器是根据电容器的端电压在电路状态改变时不能跃变的原理制成的。

电容滤波器电路简单，一般用于输出电压 U_o 较高，并且负载变化较小的场合。

2. 电感电容滤波器（LC 滤波器）

为了减小输出电压的脉动程度，在滤波电容之前串接一个铁芯电感线圈 L，这样就组成了电感电容滤波器，如图 7-7-10 所示。

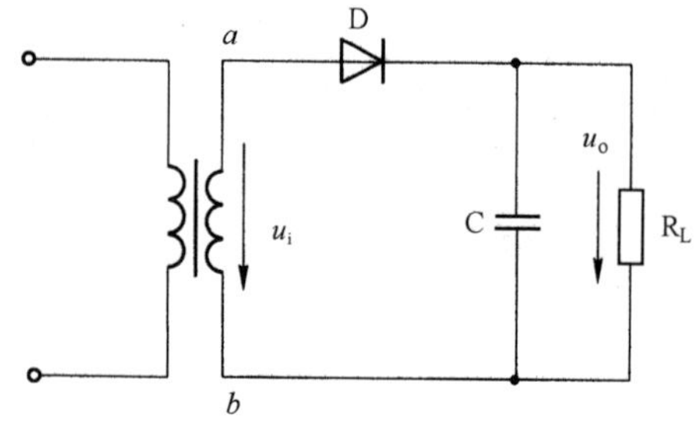

图 7-7-9　接有电容滤波器的单相半波整流电路

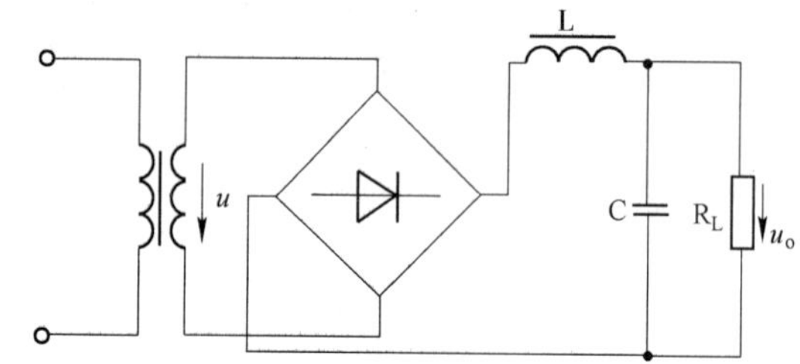

图 7-7-10　电感电容滤波电路

由于当通过电感线圈的电流发生变化时，线圈中要产生自感电动势阻碍电流的变化，因而使负载电流和负载电压的脉动大为减小。

具有 LC 滤波器的整流电路适用于电流较大，要求输出电压脉动很小的场合。

3. π 形滤波器

如果要求输出电压的脉动更小，可以在 LC 滤波器的前面再并联一滤波电容，这样便构成 π 形 LC 滤波器。它的滤波效果比 LC 滤波器更好，但整流二极管冲击电流较大。

π 形滤波电路主要适用于负载电流较小而又要求输出电压脉动很小的场合。

（三）稳压电路

经整流和滤波后的电压往往会随交流电源电压的波动和负载的变化而变化，因此需要设置稳压电路。最简单的直流稳压电路是采用稳压管的稳压电路，如图 7-7-11 所示。

引起电压不稳定的原因是交流电源电压的波动和负载电流的变化。通过稳压管与电阻 R 的调整作用，可以维持输出电压的稳定。

稳压管稳压电路的稳压效果不够理想，它一般适用于稳压性能要求不高，并且负载电流较小的场合。串联型晶体管稳压电路是性能较好的一种稳压电路，目前广泛采用的集成稳压电路也都是以晶体管串联稳压电路为基础的。

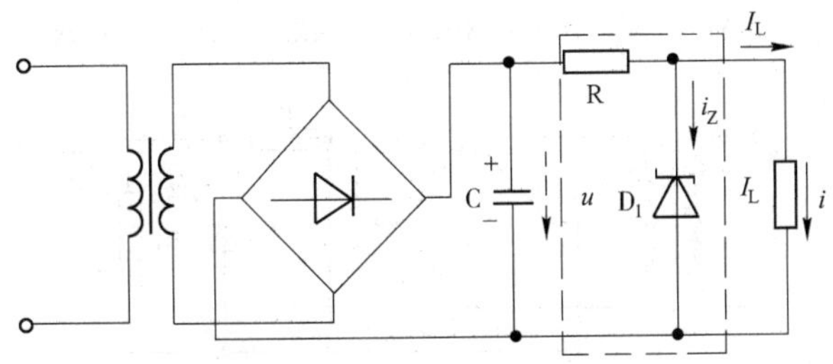

图 7-7-11 稳压管稳压电路

习 题

7-7-1 如果把一个小功率二极管直接同一个电源电压为 1.5V、内阻为零的电池实行正向连接，电路如图所示，则后果是该管(　　)。

A. 击穿　　B. 电流为零　　C. 电流正常　　D. 电流过大使管子烧坏

7-7-2 在如图所示的二极管电路中，设二极管 D 是理想的(正向电压为 0V，反向电流为 0A)，且电压表内阻为无限大，则电压表的读数为(　　)。

A. 15V　　B. 3V　　C. −18V　　D. −15V

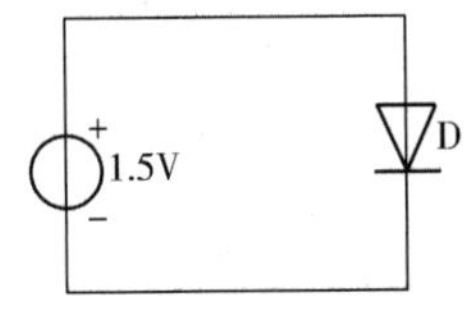

题 7-7-1 图

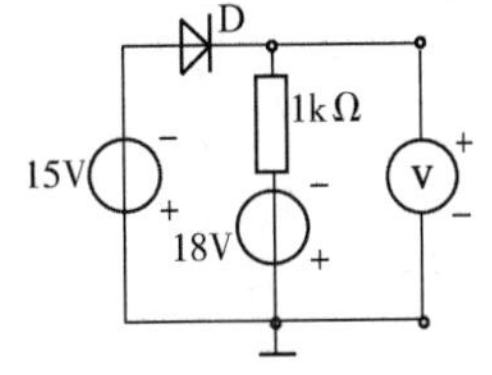

题 7-7-2 图

7-7-3 如图所示电路中，A 点和 B 点的电位分别是(　　)。

A. 2V，−1V　　B. −2V，1V　　C. 2V，1V　　D. 1V，2V

7-7-4 单相桥式整流电路如图 a)所示，变压器副边电压 u_2 的波形如图 b)所示，设四个二极管均为理想元件，则二极管 D_1 两端的电压 u_{D_1} 的波形为图 c)中的(　　)图。

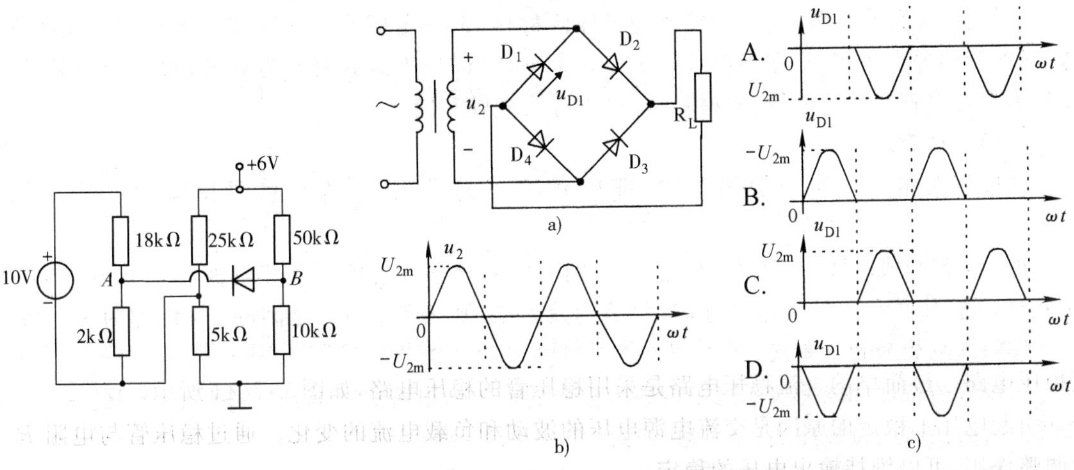

题 7-7-3 图

题 7-7-4 图

7-7-5　整流滤波电路如图所示，已知 $U_1=30\text{V}$，$U_0=12\text{V}$，$R=2\text{k}\Omega$，$R_L=4\text{k}\Omega$，稳压管的稳定电流 $I_{zmin}=5\text{mA}$ 与 $I_{zmax}=18\text{mA}$，通过稳压管的电流和通过二极管的平均电流分别是(　　)。

A. 5mA，2.5mA　　B. 8mA，8mA　　C. 6mA，2.5mA　　D. 6mA，4.5mA

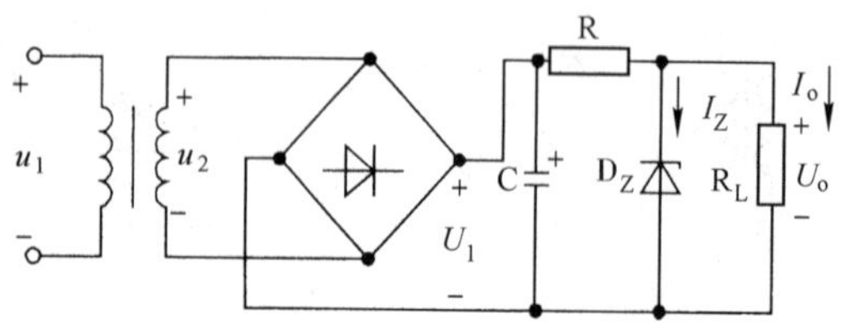

题 7-7-5 图

7-7-6　如图所示电路中，若输入电压 $U_i=10\sin(\omega t+30°)\text{V}$，则输出电压的平均值 U_L 为(　　)V。

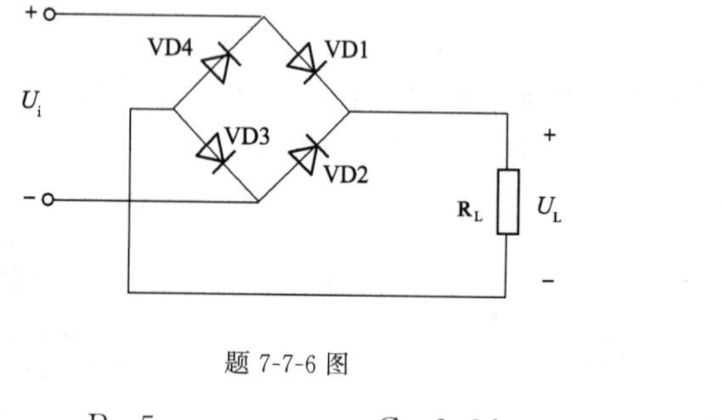

题 7-7-6 图

A. 3.18　　B. 5　　C. 6.36　　D. 10

第八节　三极管及其基本放大电路

一、晶体三极管

三极管（又称晶体管）是一种重要的半导体材料，它的出现使半导体技术出现了重大的飞越，三极管的种类很多，根据三极管的工作频率分，可以分为高频管和低频管；根据功率分，可以分为大功率管和小功率管；按材料分，可以分为硅管和锗管。

（一）三极管结构

三极管在结构上可以分为 NPN 型和 PNP 型两类，其结构示意图和符号如图 7-8-1 所示。

每一类都分成基区、发射区和集电区，分别引出基极 B、发射极 E 和集电极 C；三极管内部有两个 PN 结，基区和发射区之间的 PN 结称为发射结，基区和集电区之间的 PN 结称为集电结。

（二）三极管的特性曲线

三极管的特性曲线反映了三极管各电极上的电压和电流之间的函数关系。常用的是三极管共发射极接法的特性曲线，分为输入特性曲线和输出特性曲线。

NPN 管的特性曲线分析如下，见图 7-8-2 晶体管试验电路。

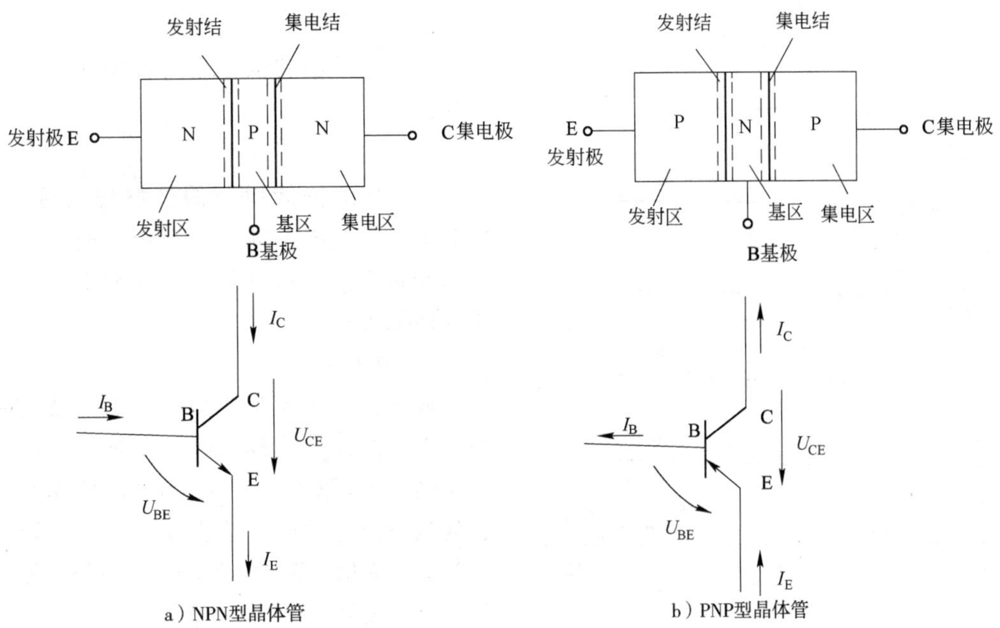

图 7-8-1 三极管的结构示意图和表示符号

1. 输入特性曲线

三极管的输入特性曲线是指当集-射极电压 U_{CE} 为常数时，输入电路中基极电流 i_B 与基-射极电压 u_{BE} 之间的关系曲线，其表达式为

$$i_B = f(u_{BE})|U_{CE=常数} \tag{7-8-1}$$

如图 7-8-3 所示，三极管输入特性曲线与二极管的伏安特性一样。

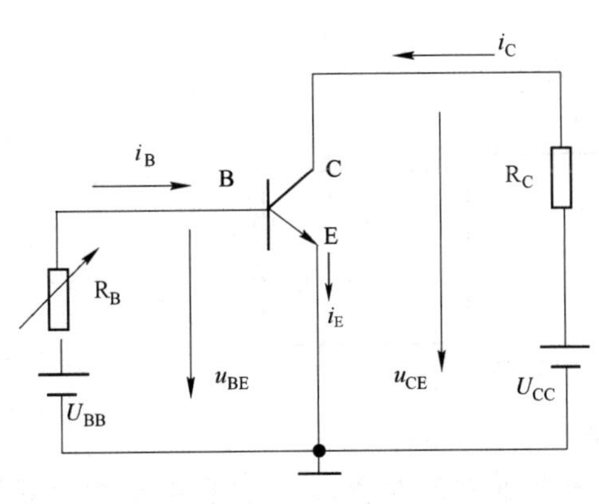

图 7-8-2 晶体管实验电路

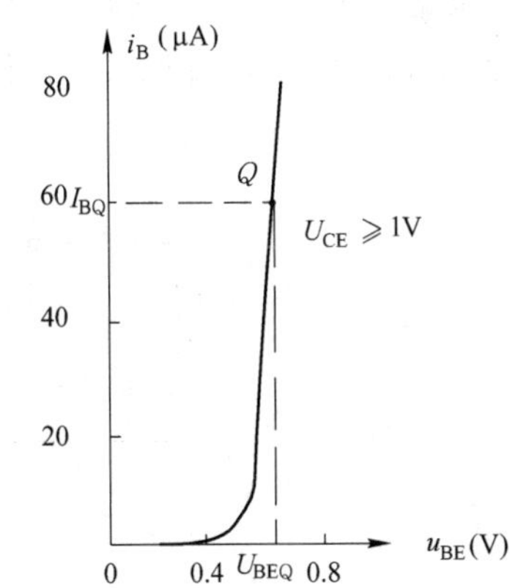

图 7-8-3 3DG6 三极管的输入特性曲线

2. 输出特性曲线

输出特性曲线是指基极电流 I_B 为常数时，集电极电流 i_C 与集-射极电压 u_{CE} 之间的关系曲线，其表达式为

$$i_C = f(u_{CE})|I_B = 常数 \tag{7-8-2}$$

如图 7-8-4 所示，不同的 I_B 下，可得出不同的曲线，所以三极管的输出特性曲线是一族

曲线。

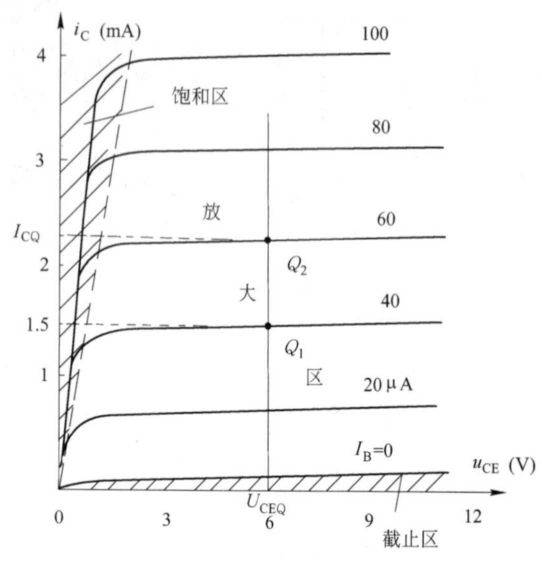

图 7-8-4　3DG6 三极管的输出特性曲线

通常把三极管的输出特性曲线分为三个工作区。

(1)截止区

$I_B=0$ 的曲线以下的区域称为截止区。此时 $I_B=0$、$I_C\approx0$，相当于三极管的三个极处于断开状态。其特点是发射结和集电结均处于反向偏置状态。

(2)放大区

输出特性曲线近似水平，且各曲线之间又相互平行的部分是放大区。此时，I_C 和 I_B 成正比例关系，即 $I_C=\beta I_B$(β 为电流放大系数)，这就是三极管的电流放大作用。三极管工作于放大状态时，发射结处于正向偏置，集电结处于反向偏置。

(3)饱和区

当 $U_{CE}<U_{BE}$时，集电结处于正向偏置，三极管工作于饱和区，此时 I_B 的变化对 I_C 的影响较小。其特点是发射结和集电结均处于正向偏置状态。

二、基本放大电路

三极管放大电路是将模拟信号进行放大的电路系统，对放大电路的基本要求是能够不失真地放大信号。

放大电路的框图，如图 7-8-5 所示。

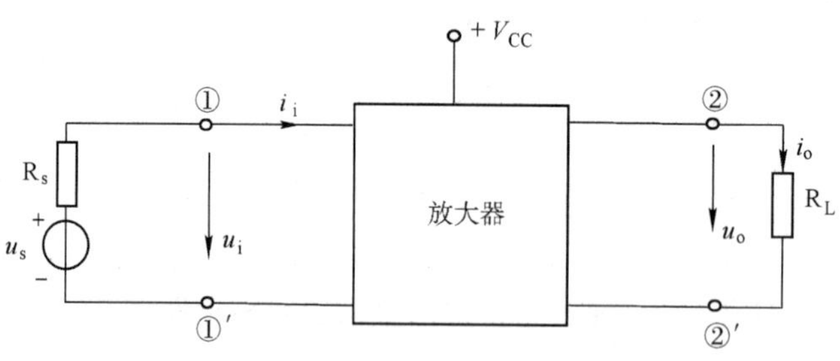

图　7-8-5

图 7-8-5 中①-①′左端是等效信号源，是放大器处理的对象，②-②′右端是放大器的负载。放大器的基本任务是：在输入信号的控制下把电源的能量无失真地传递给负载。

放大器内的三极管是主要控制元件，它必须工作在放大状态。

这部分内容的复习要求是能确定放大器在没有信号输入时三极管的静态工作点(I_{BQ}，I_{CQ}，V_{CEQ})，并能正确估算放大器的动态指标(电压放大倍数 A_u，输入电阻 r_i，输出电阻 r_o)。

(一)放大电路的组成

利用三极管的电流放大作用，可以组成多种类型的放大电路，常见的有共射极接法的单管电压放大电路，如图 7-8-6 所示。

需要放大的输入电压 u_i 接在三极管的基极和发射极之间，负载电阻 R_L 接在三极管的集电极和发射极之间，被放大的输出电压 u_o 从 R_L 两端取出。

（二）放大电路的静态分析

静态是指放大电路输入信号为零时的工作状态。静态分析是要确定放大电路的静态值（直流值）I_B、I_C、U_{BE}和 U_{CE}，以保证三极管工作在放大区。

因为静态值是直流，故用放大电路的直流通路分析计算。绘制放大电路直流通路的原则是电路中的电容视为开路，图 7-8-6 电路的直流通路如图 7-8-7 所示。

由图 7-8-7 的直流通路，可得出

$$I_B=\frac{U_{CC}-U_{BE}}{R_B}\approx\frac{U_{CC}}{R_B} \tag{7-8-3}$$

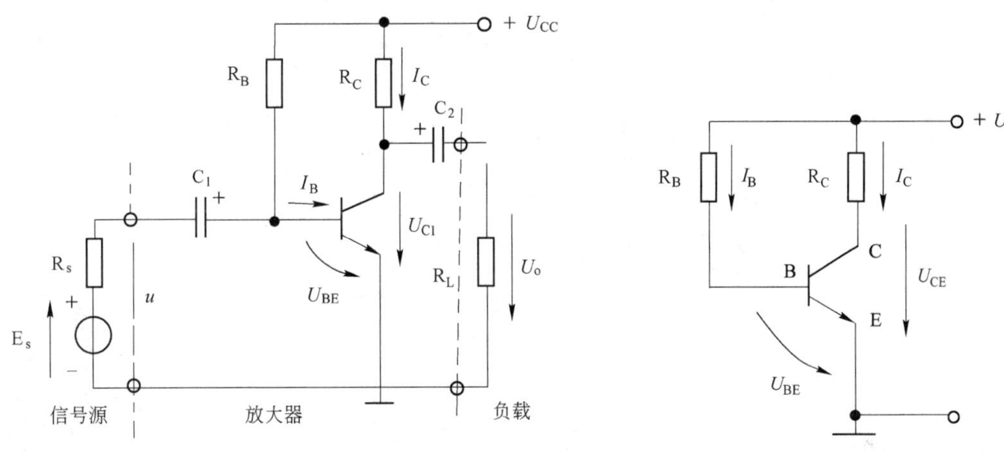

图 7-8-6　基本交流放大电路

图 7-8-7　图 7-8-5 示交流放大器的直流通路

硅管的 U_{BE} 为 0.6～0.7V，相对于 U_{CC} 较小，计算时可以将 U_{BE} 忽略。

$$I_C=\beta I_B \tag{7-8-4}$$

$$U_{CE}=U_{CC}-I_CR_C \tag{7-8-5}$$

（三）放大电路的动态分析

动态是放大电路有输入信号时的工作状态，动态分析要确定放大电路的电压放大倍数 A_u、输入电阻 r_i 和输出电阻 r_o 等。它是在静态值确定后分析动态信号的传输情况，考虑的只是电流和电压的动态信号分量，常用的分析方法是微变等效电路法。

1. 微变等效电路

所谓放大电路的微变等效电路，是把非线性电路等效为一个线性电路，即把三极管线性化，图 7-8-8a）示三极管的微变等效电路如图 7-8-8b）所示。

其中输入电阻 r_{be} 的估算公式为

$$r_{be}=300(\Omega)+(\beta+1)\frac{26(\mathrm{mV})}{I_E(\mathrm{mA})} \tag{7-8-6}$$

将三极管用微变等效电路代替后可得出放大电路的微变等效电路。画放大器的微变等效电路时要把电路中的电容及直流电源视为短路，如图 7-8-9b）所示。

2. 电压放大倍数 A_u

根据图 7-8-9b），当放大电路输入正弦交流信号时，可将电压和电流用相量表示，分析

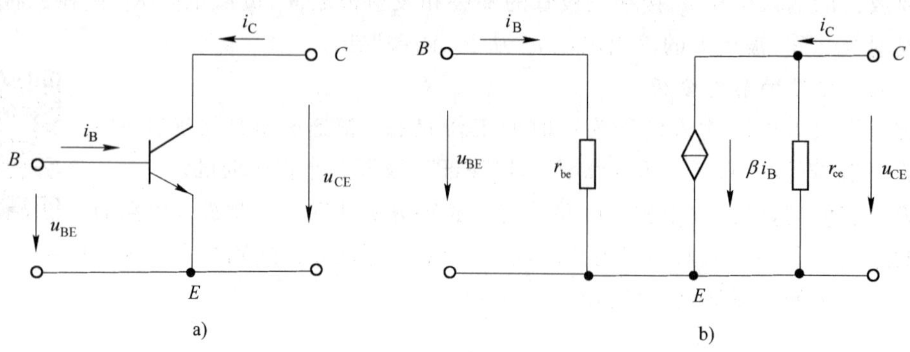

图 7-8-8 三极管及其微变等效电路

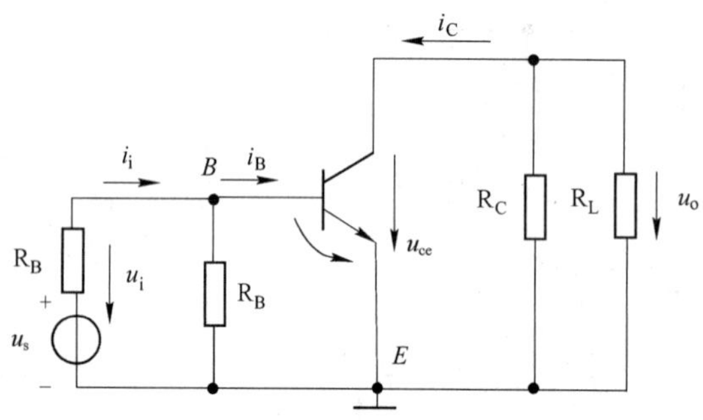

a）图7-8-5所示放大器的交流通路

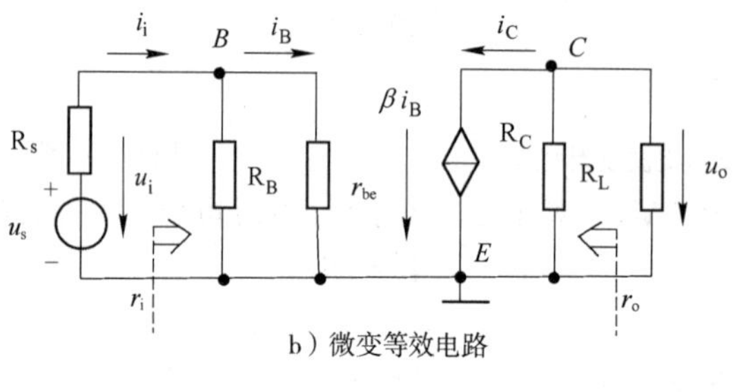

b）微变等效电路

图 7-8-9

如下

$$\dot{U}_i = \dot{I}_B r_{be}$$

$$\dot{U}_o = -\dot{I}_C R_L' = -\beta \dot{I}_B R_L'$$

式中

$$R_L' = R_C // R_L$$

整理后可知放大电路的电压放大倍数

$$\dot{A}_u = \frac{\dot{U}_o}{\dot{U}_i} = -\beta \frac{R_L'}{r_{be}} \qquad (7\text{-}8\text{-}7)$$

3. 输入电阻 r_i

放大电路的输入电阻 r_i 是从信号源 u_i 向放大器看进去的电阻

$$r_i = \frac{\dot{U}_i}{\dot{I}_i} = R_B // r_{be} \approx r_{be} \tag{7-8-8}$$

通常放大器的基极电阻 R_B 远大于三极管输入电阻 r_{be}（约 1kΩ），分析时可认为放大器的输入电阻就是 r_{be}的数值。

r_i 是对交流而言的动态电阻，通常希望电压放大电路的输入电阻能高一些。

4. 输出电阻 r_o

放大电路的输出电阻就是放大电路的输出端向左看的等效电阻

$$r_o \approx R_c \tag{7-8-9}$$

通常，希望放大电路的输出电阻 r_o 越小越好。

（四）静态工作点和静态工作点稳定的放大电路

放大电路应有合适的静态工作点，以保证有较好的放大效果，否则将引起非线性失真。

在图 7-8-6 的基本交流放大电路中

$$I_B = \frac{U_{CC} - U_{BE}}{R_B} \approx \frac{U_{CC}}{R_B}$$

当 R_B 一经选定后，I_B 也就固定下来，故该电路称为固定偏置电路。

固定偏置电路虽然简单和容易调整，但在外部因素的影响下，将引起静态工作点的变动，严重时使放大电路不能正常工作，其中影响最大的是温度变化。

为使静态工作点稳定，常采用图 7-8-10 所示的分压偏置式放大电路。

分压偏置放大电路的特点有两个：第一是在输入端用 R_{B1}、R_{B2} 两分压电阻使 B 点电位 U_B 不变；第二是用了 R_E 电阻使温度发生变化时，U_E 电位变化，从而 U_{BE} 改变，调节 I_B 后，使 I_C 稳定。

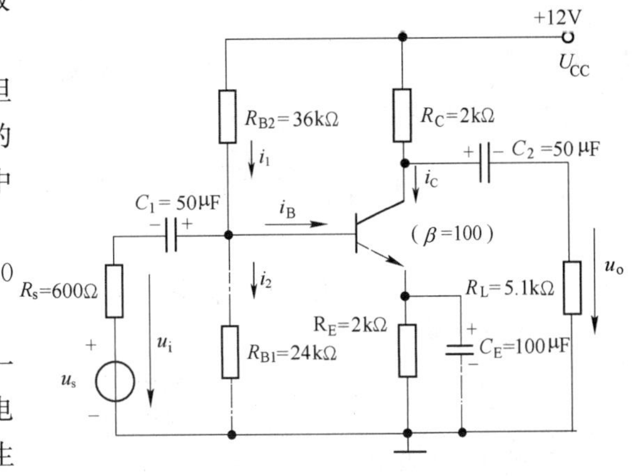

图 7-8-10 分压式偏置放大电路

当温度变化时，导致放大电路的 I_C 变化，只要稳定了 I_C，也就稳定了静态工作点。分压式偏置电路稳定静态工作点的物理过程如下

$$T(℃)\uparrow \rightarrow I_C \uparrow \rightarrow I_E \uparrow \xrightarrow{R_E} U_E \uparrow \xrightarrow{U_B \text{不变}} U_{BE} \downarrow \rightarrow I_B \downarrow \rightarrow I_C \downarrow$$

【例 7-8-1】 设如图所示放大电路的输入信号 u_i 为正弦信号，可见，该电路具有稳定 I_C 的作用。电路参数如图上所注。试求：(1)放大电路的输入电阻和输出电阻；(2)放大电路的电压放大倍数。

解 因放大器的动态参数与静态工作点有关，故应先分析放大器的静态工作点，先画出放大电路的直流通路，如解图 1a)所示。从三极管基极端与接地端往左看，R_{B1}、R_{B2} 和电源 U_{CC} 组成一个有源两端网络。应用戴维南定理，此有源两端网络可用一个等效电压源表示，如解图 1b)所示。其中 U_0 为有源两端网络的开路电压，即

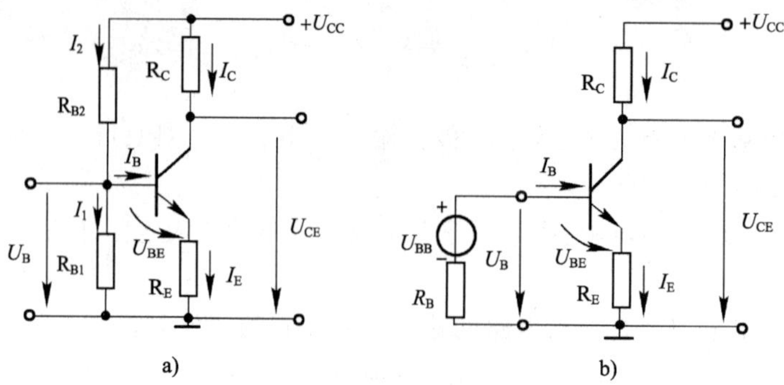

例 7-8-1 解图 1　放大电路的直流通路

$$U_B=\frac{R_{B1}}{R_{B1}+R_{B2}}U_{CC}=\frac{24\times10^3}{(24+36)\times10^3}\times12=4.8\text{V}$$

R_0 为除源网络的等效电阻，将电压源短路（除源）得

$$R_B=\frac{R_{B1}R_{B2}}{R_{B1}+R_{B2}}=\frac{24\times10^3\times36\times10^3}{(24+36)\times10^3}=14.4\text{k}\Omega$$

由此，列出基极回路的 KVL 方程

$$U_B=I_BR_B+U_{BE}+I_ER_E$$

$$=I_BR_B+U_{BE}+(1+\beta)I_BR_E$$

所以，基极电流

$$I_B=\frac{U_{BB}-U_{BE}}{R_B+(1+\beta)R_E}=\frac{4.8-0.7}{14.4\times10^3+(1+100)\times2\times10^3}=19\mu\text{A}$$

发射极电流

$$I_E=(1+\beta)I_B=(1+100)\times19\times10^{-6}=1.92\text{mA}$$

三极管的输入电阻

$$r_{be}=300+(\beta+1)\frac{26(\text{mV})}{I_E(\text{mA})}=300+(100+1)\times\frac{26}{1.92}=1.668\text{k}\Omega$$

在实际放大电路中，一般取 $I_1\gg I_B[I_1\geqslant(5\sim10)I_B]$，用以保证 U_B 不随 I_B 而变，所以 $I_1\approx I_2$。在近似估算时，可认为基极对地电压

$$U_B\approx\frac{R_{B1}}{R_{B1}+R_{B2}}U_{CC}=4.8\text{V}$$

发射极电流

$$I_E=\frac{U_B-U_{BE}}{R_E}=\frac{4.8-0.7}{2\times10^3}=2\text{mA}$$

三极管的输入电阻

$$r_{be}=300+(\beta+1)\times\frac{26(\text{mV})}{I_E(\text{mA})}=300+(100+1)\times\frac{26}{2}=1.6\text{k}\Omega$$

从上可见，应用估算法与应用戴维南定理的精确计算法相比，r_{be} 稍小些（本例小于 4%），这在工程计算中是允许的。

（1）为了求出放大电路的输入电阻和输出电阻，画出其微变等效电路如解图 2 所示。可以看出，放大电路的输入电阻 r_i 是 R_{B1}、R_{B2} 和 r_{be} 三者的并联，即

$$r_i=R_{B1}/\!/R_{B2}/\!/r_{be}=24/\!/36/\!/1.6=1.44\text{k}\Omega$$

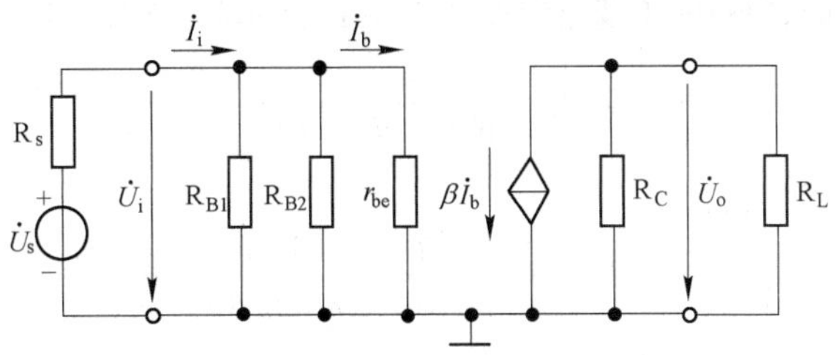

例 7-8-1 解图 2　微变等效电路图

由解图 2 可知，输出电阻 r_o 等于集电极负载电阻 R_C，即

$$r_o = R_C = 2\text{k}\Omega$$

(2)如果考虑信号源内阻 R_s 的影响时，放大电路的电压放大倍数应该是

$$\dot{A}_{us} = \frac{\dot{U}_o}{\dot{U}_s} = \frac{\dot{U}_o}{\dot{U}_i} \times \frac{\dot{U}_i}{\dot{U}_s} = -\beta \frac{R'_L}{r_{be}} \times \frac{r_i}{R_s + r_i} \tag{7-8-10}$$

从上式可见，当 $r_i \gg R_s$ 时，R_s 对电压放大倍数的影响就很小。因此，一般要求电压放大电路的输入电阻 r_i 值较大。

对于本例题，电压放大倍数

$$\dot{A}_{us} = -100 \times \frac{1.44 \times 10^3}{1.6 \times 10^3} \times \frac{1.44 \times 10^3}{(0.6 + 1.44) \times 10^3}$$
$$= -89 \times 0.71 = -63$$

式(7-8-10)中 $R'_L = R_C /\!/ R_L = 2 /\!/ 5.1 = 1.44\text{k}\Omega$

(五)射极输出器

1.射极输出器的工作原理

共发射极电路能获得较高的电压放大倍数，但其输入电阻较小，输出电阻较大。因此，共发射极电路常用作多级放大电路的中间级，用来获得较高的电压放大倍数。射极输出器具有较高的输入电阻和较低的输出电阻，可用作多级放大电路的输入级或输出级，以适应信号源或负载对放大电路的要求。

如图 7-8-11 所示是射极输出器的电路，从图可见，这种电路的负载电阻 R_L 经过耦合电容 C_2 接在三极管的发射极上，即输出电压 u_o 从三极管的发射极取出，所以称为射极输出器。它的直流和交流通路如图 7-8-12、图 7-8-13 所示，由交流通路可见，这种电路以三极管的集电极作为输入回路和输出回路的公共端，所以是属共集电极电路。

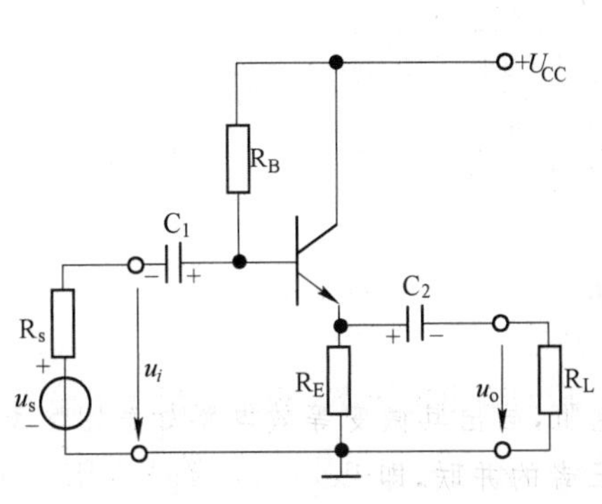

图 7-8-11　射极输出器

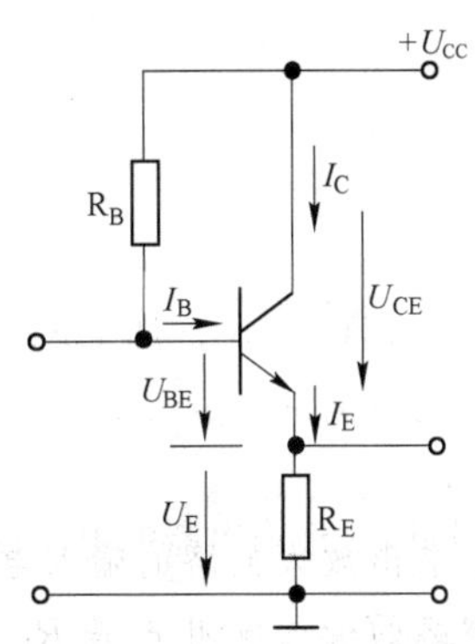

图 7-8-12　射极输出器的直流通路

当没有输入信号(静态)时,射极输出器可用如图 7-8-12 所示的直流通路来分析,此时基极电流

$$I_B=\frac{U_{CC}-U_{BE}}{R_B+(\beta+1)R_E}$$

静态时的集电极电流

$$I_C=\beta I_B=\frac{\beta(U_{CC}-U_{BE})}{R_B+(\bar{\beta}+1)R_E}$$

静态时的集电极-发射极间电压

$$U_{CE}=U_{CC}-I_E R_E\approx U_{CC}-I_C R_E$$

2.射极输出器的电压放大倍数

为了分析射极输出器的电压放大倍数,图 7-8-14 中画出射极输出器的微变等效电路。图中假设输入为正弦信号,放大电路没有非线性失真,即电压和电流的交流分量也是正弦信号,所以均用相量表示。

从图 7-8-14 可列出输入回路的电压方程

$$\begin{aligned}\dot{U}_i&=\dot{I}_b r_{be}+\dot{I}_e(R_E/\!/R_L)\\&=\dot{I}_b r_{be}+(\beta+1)\dot{I}_b(R_E/\!/R_L)\\&=\dot{I}_b[r_{be}+(\beta+1)R_L']\end{aligned}$$

式中,$R_L'=R_E/\!/R_L$ 为等效负载电阻。

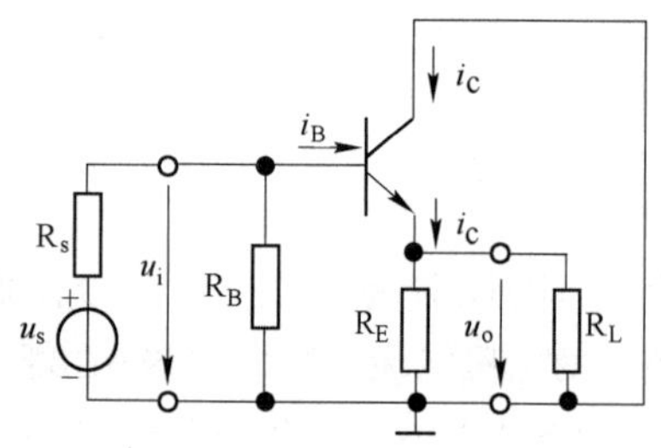

图 7-8-13　射极输出器的交流通路

图 7-8-14　射极输出器的微变等效电路

输出电压

$$\dot{U}_o=\dot{I}_e(R_E/\!/R_L)=(\beta+1)\dot{I}_b R_L'$$

所以,电压放大倍数

$$\begin{aligned}\dot{A}_u=\frac{\dot{U}_o}{\dot{U}_i}&=\frac{(\beta+1)\dot{I}_b R_L'}{\dot{I}_b[r_{be}+(\beta+1)R_L']}\\&=\frac{(\beta+1)R_L'}{r_{be}+(\beta+1)R_L'}\end{aligned}\qquad(7\text{-}8\text{-}11)$$

一般 $\beta\gg1$,且 r_{be} 小于 R_L',所以

$$\dot{A}_u\approx\frac{\beta R_L'}{r_{be}+\beta R_L'}\leqslant1\qquad(7\text{-}8\text{-}12)$$

从上式可见,射极输出器的电压放大倍数小于 1,即输出电压 U_o 的大小接近于输入电压 U_i 的大小。同时从式(7-8-9)还可看到 $\dot{A}_u$ 为正,即射极输出器的输出电压 $\dot{U}_o$ 和输入电压 $\dot{U}_i$ 同相位。

综上所述,射极输出器不但输出电压 U_o 的大小与输入电压 U_i 的大小相等,而且两者的相

位相同。也就是说，输出电压 U_o 总是跟随输入电压 U_i 作相应变化，因此，射极输出器又称为电压跟随器。

应该指出，虽然射极输出器没有电压放大作用，但是，由于射极输出器的发射极电流 I_e 比基极电流 I_b 要大$(\beta+1)$倍，所以它具有一定的电流放大和功率放大作用。

3. 射极输出器的输入电阻和输出电阻

射极输出器的输入电阻可以从如图 7-8-14 所示的微变等效电路中求得，同时可以看出，输入电流

$$\dot{I}_i=\dot{I}_{RB}+\dot{I}_b=\frac{\dot{U}_i}{R_B}+\frac{\dot{U}_i}{r_{be}+(\beta+1)R_L'}$$
$$=\left[\frac{1}{R_B}+\frac{1}{r_{be}+(\beta+1)R_L'}\right]\dot{U}_i$$

所以，射极输出器的输入电阻

$$r_i=\frac{\dot{U}_i}{\dot{I}_i}=\frac{1}{\frac{1}{R_B}+\frac{1}{r_{be}+(\beta+1)R_L'}}$$
$$=R_B/\!/[r_{be}+(\beta+1)R_L'] \tag{7-8-13}$$

可见，射极输出器的输入电阻 r_i 由两部分电阻并联而成：一个是偏置电阻 R_B；另一个是基极回路电阻$[r_{be}+(\beta+1)R_L']$。在一般情况下，R_B 的阻值很大(几十千欧到几百千欧)，并且基极回路电阻$[r_{be}+(\beta+1)R_L']$要比共发射极放大电路的输入电阻大得多。所以，射极输出器的输入电阻比共发射极放大电路的输入电阻提高几十倍到几百倍。

射极输出器的输出电阻，按定义可用求等效电源内电阻的方法求得。其方法之一是除源法，即将信号源 u_s 短路(除独立源)，在输出端(断开负载电阻 R_L)加一交流电压 $\dot{U}_o$，如图 7-8-15 所示。

按输出电阻的定义

$$r_0=\frac{\dot{U}_o}{\dot{I}_o}\bigg|_{\substack{R_L=\infty\\u_s=0}}$$

由图 7-8-15 可得

$$\dot{I}_o=\dot{I}_{RE}+\beta\dot{I}_b+\dot{I}_b=\dot{I}_{RE}+(\beta+1)\dot{I}_b$$
$$=\frac{\dot{U}_o}{R_E}+(\beta+1)\frac{\dot{U}_o}{r_{be}+(R_s/\!/R_B)}$$
$$=\left(\frac{1}{R_E}+\frac{\beta+1}{r_{be}+R_s'}\right)\dot{U}_o$$

式中，$R_s'=R_s/\!/R_B$。

所以，输出电阻

$$r_o=\frac{\dot{U}_o}{\dot{I}_o}=\frac{1}{\frac{1}{R_E}+\frac{\beta+1}{r_{be}+R_s'}}$$
$$=R_E/\!/\frac{r_{be}+R_s'}{\beta+1} \tag{7-8-14}$$

图 7-8-15 求射极输出器的输出电阻

上式说明，射极输出器的输出电阻 r_o 是 R_E 和$\frac{r_{be}+R_s'}{\beta+1}$两部分电阻并联的结果。在一般情况下，$(r_{be}+R_s')$较小，$\beta\gg1$，而 R_E 通常为几千欧，因此射极输出器的输出电阻 r_o 很低。

习　题

7-8-1　如图所示电路，能实现交流放大的是图(　　)。

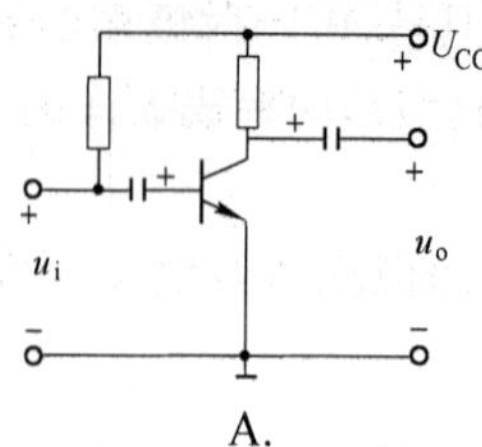

A.

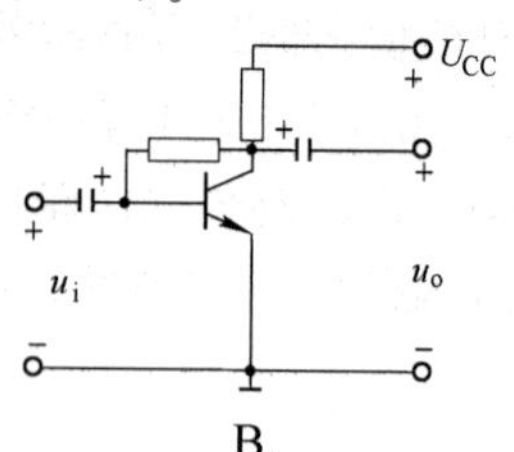

B.

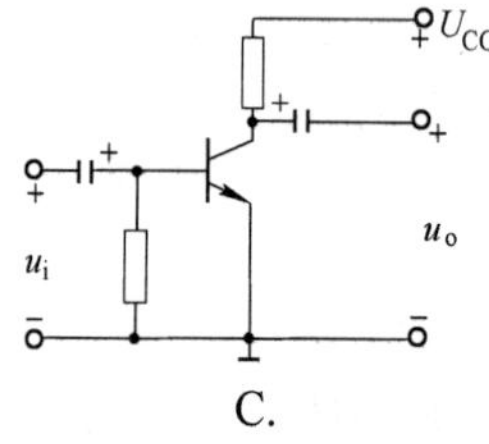

C.

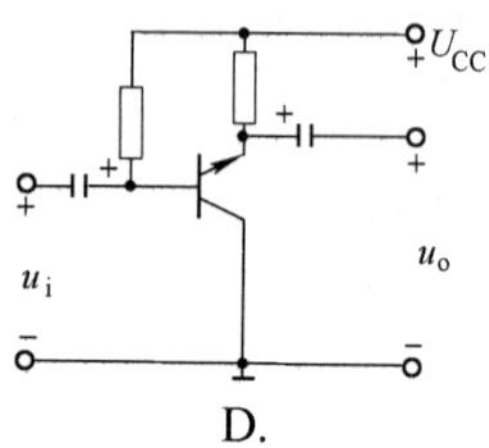

D.

7-8-2　如图所示电路中的晶体管，当输入信号为 3V 时，工作状态是(　　)。

A. 饱和　　B. 截止　　C. 放大　　D. 不确定

7-8-3　如图所示为共发射极单管电压放大电路，估算静态点 I_B、I_C、V_{CE}分别为(　　)。

A. 57μA，2.8mA，3.5V　　B. 57μA，2.8mA，8V

C. 57μA，4mA，0V　　D. 30μA，2.8mA，3.5V

7-8-4　如图所示放大器的输入电阻 r_i、输出电阻 r_o 和电压放大倍数 A_u 分别为(　　)。

A. 200kΩ，3kΩ，47.5 倍　　B. 1.25kΩ，3kΩ，47.5 倍

C. 1.25kΩ，3kΩ，−47.5 倍　　D. 1.25kΩ，1.5kΩ，−47.5 倍

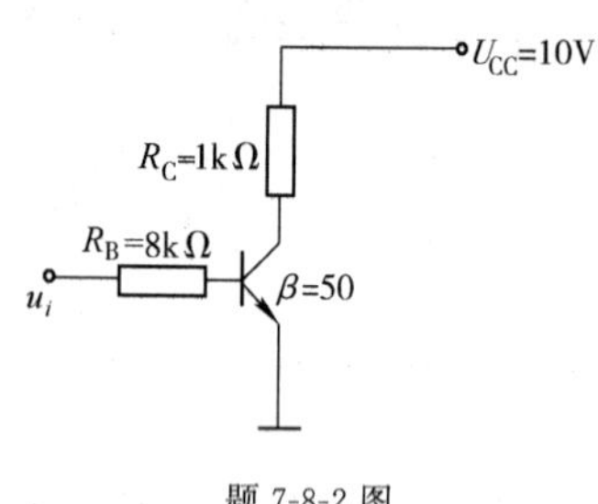

题 7-8-2 图

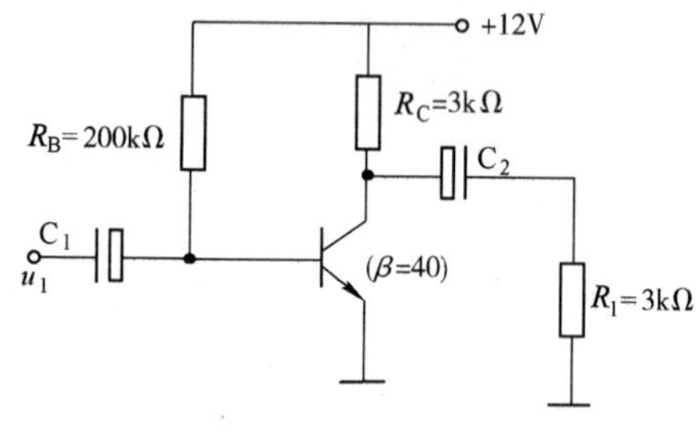

题 7-8-3、题 7-8-4 图

7-8-5　某晶体管放大电路的空载放大倍数 $A_k=-80$、输入电阻 $r_i=1k\Omega$ 和输出电阻 $r_o=3k\Omega$，将信号源($u_s=10\sin\omega t$ mV，$R_s=1k\Omega$)和负载($R=5k\Omega$)接于该放大电路之后(见图)，负载电压 u_o 将为(　　)。

A. $-0.8\sin\omega t$V　　B. $-0.5\sin\omega t$V　　C. $-0.4\sin\omega t$V　　D. $-0.25\sin\omega t$V

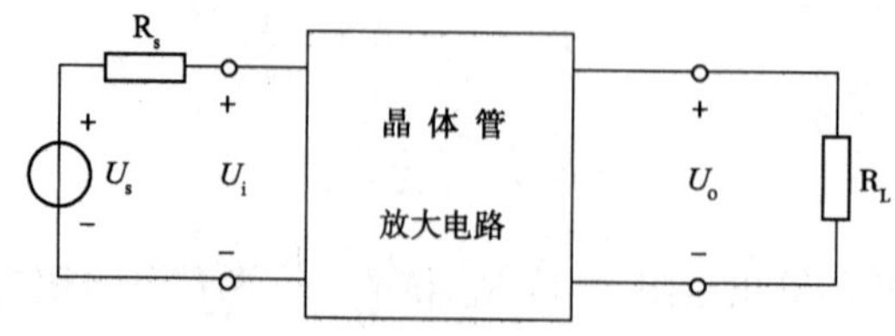

题 7-8-5 图

7-8-6　将放大倍数为 1，输入电阻为 100Ω，输出电阻为 50Ω 的射级输出器插接在信号源（u_s，R_s）与负载（R_L）之间，形成图 b）电路，与图 a）电路相比，负载电压的有效值（　　）。

A. $U_{L2}>U_{L1}$　　　　B. $U_{L2}=U_{L1}$

C. $U_{L2}<U_{L1}$　　　　D. 因为 U_2 未知，不能确定 U_{L1} 和 U_{L2} 之间的关系

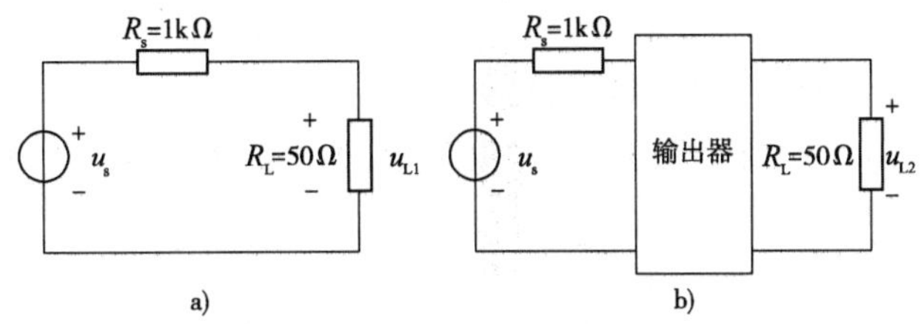

题 7-8-6 图

第九节　集成运算放大器

一、集成运算放大器简介

集成运算放大器是具有高开环放大倍数并带有深度负反馈的多级直接耦合放大电路，它不仅可以放大直流信号，也可以放大交流信号。集成运算放大器具有开环放大倍数高、输入电阻高、输出电阻低、可靠性高、体积小等主要特点。

为了使集成运算放大器（简称运算放大器）电路分析得以简化，一般将实际运算放大器进行理想化，理想化的条件是：

开环电压放大倍数　$A_u \longrightarrow \infty$

输入电阻　$r_i \longrightarrow \infty$

输出电阻　$r_o \longrightarrow 0$

如图 7-9-1 所示是理想运算放大器的图形符号，它有两个输入端和一个输出端。反相输入端标上“－”号，同相输入端和输出端标上“＋”号。它们对“地”的电位分别用 u_-、u_+ 和 u_o 表示反相输入信号 u_- 的电位变化极性与输出信号 u_o 的极性相反；同反相输入信号 u_+ 的电位变化极性与输出信号 u_o 的极性相同。当运算放大器工作在线性区时，u_o、u_+ 和 u_- 之间关系为

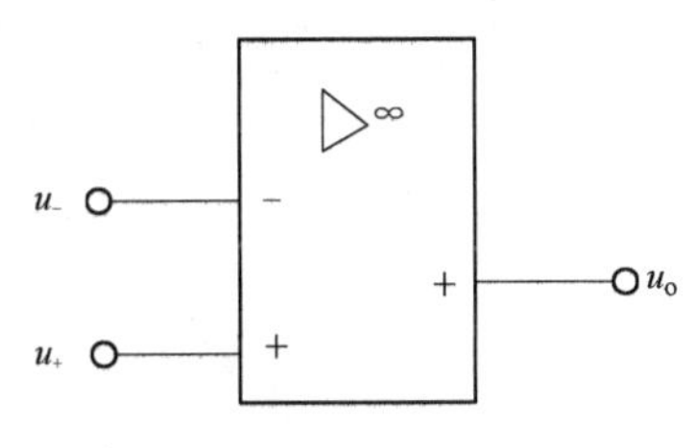

图 7-9-1　运算放大器的图形符号

$$u_o = A_u(u_+ - u_-) \qquad (7\text{-}9\text{-}1)$$

由于 $r_i=\infty$，故可认为两个输入端的输入电流为零；由于运算放大器的开环电压放大倍数 $A_u \longrightarrow \infty$，而输出电压 u_o 是一个有限值，则

$$u_+ - u_- = \frac{u_o}{A_u} \approx 0$$

即

$$u_+ \approx u_- \qquad (7\text{-}9\text{-}2)$$

如果反相端有输入时，同相端接“地”，即 $u_+=0$，则 $u_- \approx 0$。这就是说反相输入端的电位接近于“地”电位，通常称为“虚地”。

由于 $r_o \Rightarrow 0$，可以认为输出端电压恒定，仅受输入信号控制，与负载 R_L 的变化无关：

$$u_o = A_u(u_+ - u_-)$$

二、基本运算电路

（一）比例运算

1. 反相输入

如图 7-9-2 所示，输入信号从反相输入端引入。

由于 $i_1 \approx i_f$，$u_- \approx u_+ = 0$（流过图 7-9-2 中电阻 R_2 的电流基本为 0），则

$$i_1 = \frac{u_i - u_-}{R_1} = \frac{u_i}{R_1}$$

$$i_f = \frac{u_- - u_o}{R_F} = -\frac{u_o}{R_F}$$

由此得出

$$u_o = -\frac{R_F}{R_1}u_i \tag{7-9-3}$$

闭环电压放大倍数为

$$A_{uf} = \frac{u_o}{u_i} = -\frac{R_F}{R_1} \tag{7-9-4}$$

上式表明，输出电压与输入电压是反相比例运算关系。

2. 同相输入

如图 7-9-3 所示，输入信号从同相输入端引入。

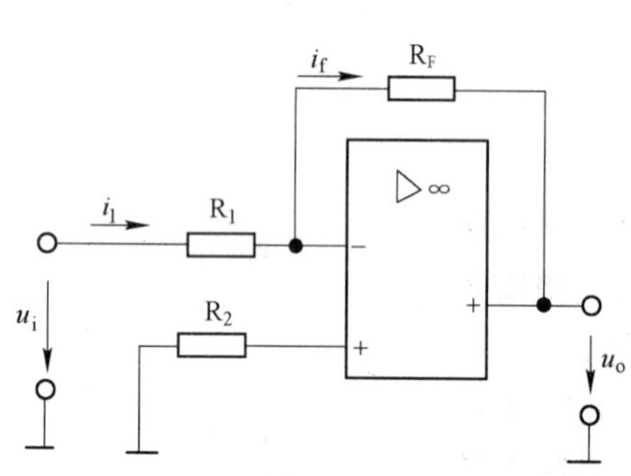

图 7-9-2　反相比例运算电路

图 7-9-3　同相比例运算电路

由于

$$u_- \approx u_+ = u_i$$

则

$$i_1 = \frac{0 - u_-}{R_1} = \frac{-u_i}{R_1}$$

$$i_f = \frac{u_- - u_o}{R_F} = \frac{u_i - u_o}{R_F}$$

由于 $i_1 = i_f$，可得出

$$-\frac{u_i}{R_i} = \frac{u_i - u_o}{R_F}$$

则

$$u_o=\left(1+\frac{R_F}{R_1}\right)u_i \qquad (7\text{-}9\text{-}5)$$

闭环电压放大倍数则为

$$A_{uf}=\frac{u_o}{u_i}=1+\frac{R_F}{R_1} \qquad (7\text{-}9\text{-}6)$$

可见，输出电压与输入电压是同相比例运算关系。

【例 7-9-1】 运算放大器应用电路如图所示，设运算放大器输出电压的极限值为±11V。如果将－2.5V 电压接入“A”端，而“B”端接地后，测得输出电压为 10V，如果将－2.5V电压接入“B”端，而“A”端接地，则该电路的输出电压 u_o 等于：

A. 10V

B. －10V

C. －11V

D. －12.5V

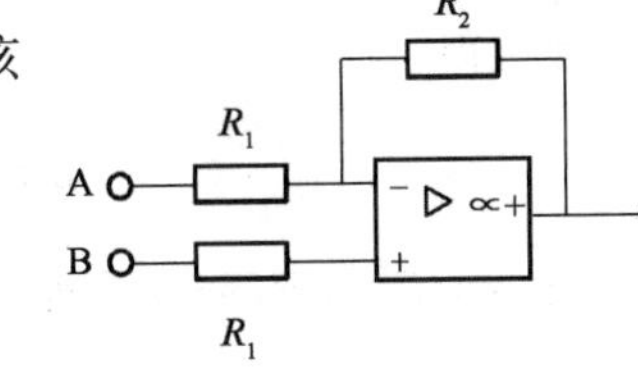

例 7-9-1 图

解 将电路“A”端接入－2.5V 的信号电压，“B”端接地，则构成反相比例运算电路。输出电压与输入的信号电压关系为：

$$u_o=-\frac{R_2}{R_1}u_i$$

可知：

$$\frac{R_2}{R_1}=-\frac{u_o}{u_i}=4$$

当“A”端接地，“B”端接信号电压，就构成同相比例电路，则输出 u_o 与输入电压 u_i 的关系为：

$$u_o=\left(1+\frac{R_2}{R_1}\right)u_i=-12.5\text{V}$$

考虑到运算放大器输出电压在－11～11V 之间，可以确定放大器已经工作在负饱和状态，输出电压为负的极限值－11V。

答案：C

（二）加法运算

如果在反相输入端增加若干输入电路，则构成反相加法运算电路，如图 7-9-4 所示。

由图可列出

$$i_{11}=\frac{u_{i1}}{R_{11}} \quad i_{12}=\frac{u_{i2}}{R_{12}} \quad i_{13}=\frac{u_{i3}}{R_{13}} \quad i_f=\frac{-u_o}{R_F}$$

$$i_f=i_{11}+i_{12}+i_{13}$$

整理可得

$$u_o=-\left(\frac{R_F}{R_{11}}u_{i1}+\frac{R_F}{R_{12}}u_{i2}+\frac{R_F}{R_{13}}u_{i3}\right) \qquad (7\text{-}9\text{-}7)$$

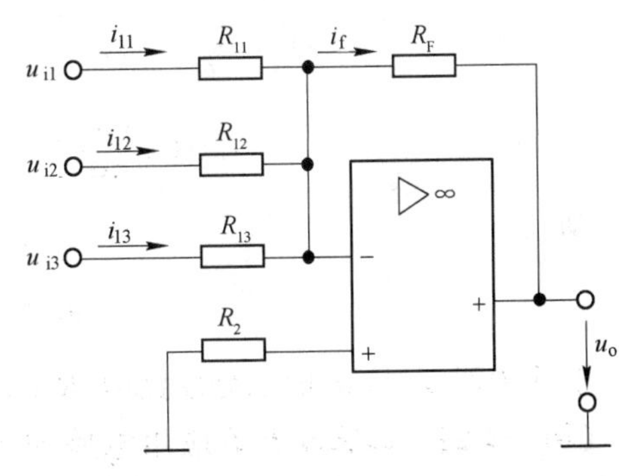

图 7-9-4　反相加法运算电路

当 $R_{11}=R_{12}=R_{13}=R_F$ 时，则上式为

$$u_o=-(u_{i1}+u_{i2}+u_{i3}) \qquad (7\text{-}9\text{-}8)$$

（三）减法电路

减法运算电路如图 7-9-5 所示。两个输入端都有信号输入，为差动输入方式。

由图 7-9-5 可列出

$$u_- = u_{i1} - i_1 R_1 = u_{i1} - \frac{u_{i1} - u_o}{R_1 + R_F} R_1$$

$$u_+ = \frac{u_{i2}}{R_2 + R_3} R_3$$

因为

$$u_- \approx u_+$$

整理可得

$$u_o = \left(1 + \frac{R_F}{R_1}\right) \frac{R_3}{R_2 + R_3} u_{i2} - \frac{R_F}{R_1} u_{i1} \qquad (7\text{-}9\text{-}9)$$

当 $R_1 = R_2 = R_3 = R_F$，则

$$u_o = u_{i2} - u_{i1} \qquad (7\text{-}9\text{-}10)$$

可见，输出电压 u_o 是两个输入电压的差值，实现了减法运算。

（四）积分运算

积分运算电路如图 7-9-6 所示。

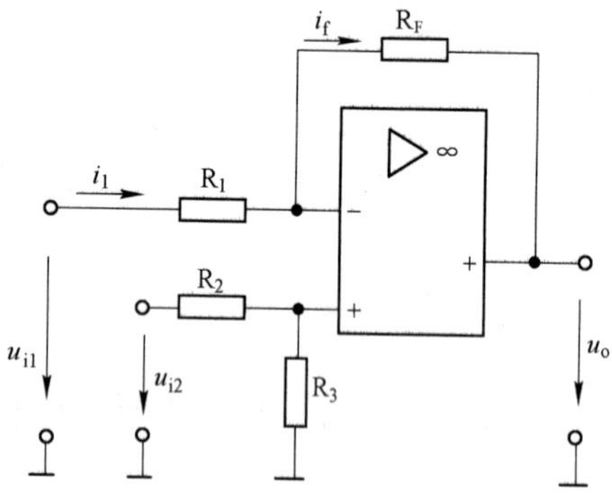

图 7-9-5　减法运算电路

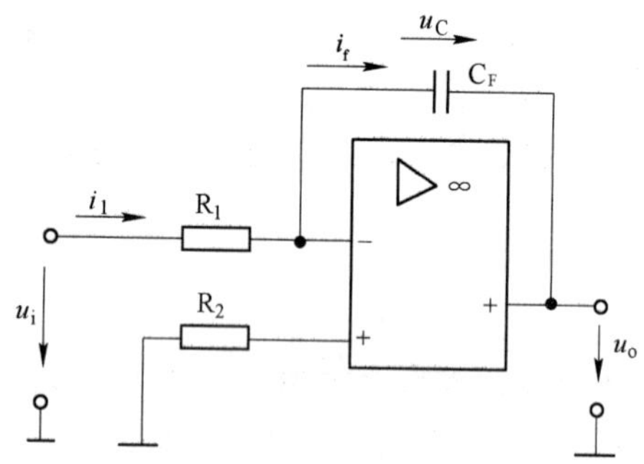

图 7-9-6　积分运算电路

由于反相输入 $u_- = u_+ \approx 0$，故

$$i_1 = \frac{u_i}{R_1}$$

$$i_f = C_F \frac{du_C}{dt} = C_F \frac{d(u_- - u_o)}{dt} = -C_F \frac{du_o}{dt}$$

则

$$u_0 = -\frac{1}{R_1 C_F} \int u_i dt \qquad (7\text{-}9\text{-}11)$$

上式表明 u_o 与 u_i 的积分成比例，$R_1 C_F$ 称为积分时间常数。

【例 7-9-2】 运算放大器应用电路如图所示，其中 $C = 1\mu F$，$R = 1M\Omega$，$U_{OM} = \pm 10V$，若 $u_1 = 1V$，则 u_o：

A. 等于 0V　　B. 等于 1V

C. 等于 10V　　D. $t < 10s$ 时，为 $-t$；$t \geqslant 10s$ 后，为 $-10V$

解 该电路为运算放大器的积分运算电路。

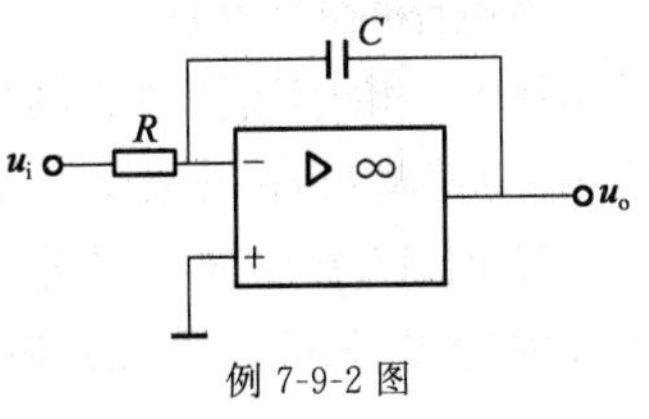

例 7-9-2 图

$$u_o=-\frac{1}{RC}\int u_i \mathrm{d}t$$

当 $u_i=1\mathrm{V}$ 时，$u_o=-\frac{1}{RC}t$

当 $t<10\mathrm{s}$ 时，$u_o=-t$

$t\geqslant 10\mathrm{s}$ 后，电路出现反向饱和，$u_o=-10\mathrm{V}$

答案：D

实例：仪表测量电路

如图 7-9-7 所示为三运放构成的仪用放大器，A_1，A_2 均为同相放大电路。

其中

$$u_a=\left(1+\frac{R_1}{\frac{R_P}{2}}\right)u_{i1}$$

$$u_b=(1+\frac{R_1}{\frac{R_P}{2}})u_{i2}$$

$$u_{ab}=u_a-u_b=(1+\frac{2R_1}{R_P})(u_{i1}-u_{i2})$$

A_3 为差动放大电路，输出电压

$$u_o=-\frac{R_3}{R_2}u_{ab}=\frac{R_3}{R_2}(1+\frac{2R_1}{R_P})(u_{i2}-u_{i1})$$

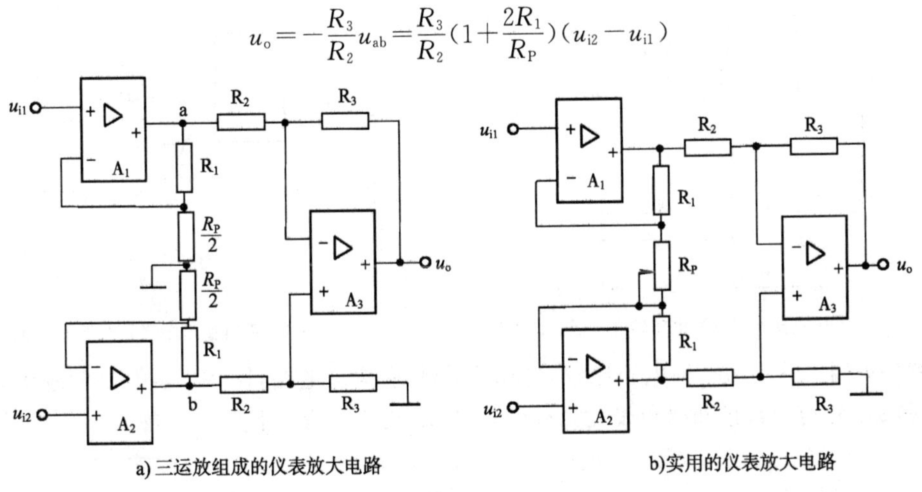

图 7-9-7

当输出电压需要调节时可以采用图 7-9-7b)所示电路，调节可变电阻 R_P 即可改变电路的电压放大倍数。该电路的特点为电压放大倍数容易调整，输入电阻较大。在 LH0036 系列仪表中电路的输入电阻可达到 300MΩ 以上。

三、电压比较器电路

电压比较器的作用是用来比较输入电压和参考电压，图 7-9-8a)是一种基本电压比较器电路和输入、输出电压的传输特性。

该电路的参考电压 U_R 加在同相输入端，输入电压 u_i 加在反相输入端，运算放大器工作于开环状态。由于运算放大器的开环电压放大倍数很高，即使输入端有一个非常微小的差值信号，也会使输出电压饱和。因此，用作比较器时，运算放大器工作在饱和区(即非线性区)。当 $u_i < U_R$ 时，$U_o = +U_{o(sat)}$；当 $u_i > U_R$ 时，$U_o = -U_{o(sat)}$。当参考电压 $U_R = 0$ 时，电压比较器又叫做过零比较器，图 7-9-9b)是过零比较器的电压传输特性。

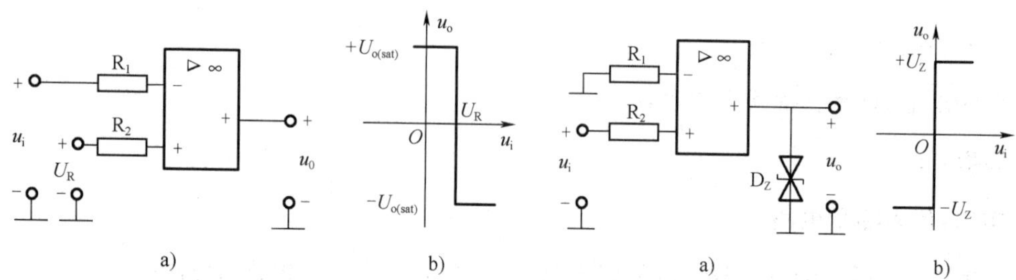

图 7-9-8　电压比较器

图 7-9-9　过零比较器电路和电压传输特性

图 7-9-10 为过零比较器将正弦波电压转变为矩形波电压。

当电压比较器的输入端进行模拟信号大小的比较时，在输出端则以高电平或低电平[即为数字信号(1 或 0)]来反映比较结果。当 $U_R = 0$ 时，输入电压 u_i 与零电平比较，成为过零比较器。

有时为了将输出电压限制在某一特定值，与接在输出端的数字电路的电平配合，可在比较器的输出端与“地”之间跨接一个双向稳压二极管 D_Z，作双向限幅用。稳压二极管的电压为 U_Z，电路和传输特性如图 7-9-11 所示。U_i 与零电平比较，输出电压 u 被限制在 $+U_Z$ 或 $-U_Z$。

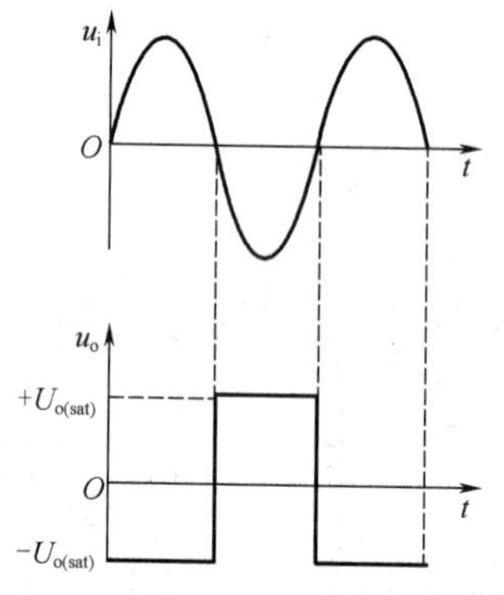

图 7-9-10　过零比较器将正弦波电压转变为矩形波电压

图 7-9-11　带有输出限幅的电压比较电路

【例 7-9-3】　图示为一种电压比较电路，用作电平检测电路，图中 U_R 为参考电压且为正值，D_R 和 D_G 分别为红色和绿色发光二极管，试判断在什么情况下它们会亮？

解　当 $u_i < U_R$ 时($U_+ < U_-$)，$u_o = -U_{o(sat)}$，二极管 D_G 导通，D_R 截止，绿灯亮；

当 $u_i > U_R$ 时($U_+ < U_-$)，$u_o = +U_{o(sat)}$，二极管 D_G 截止，D_R 导通，红灯亮。

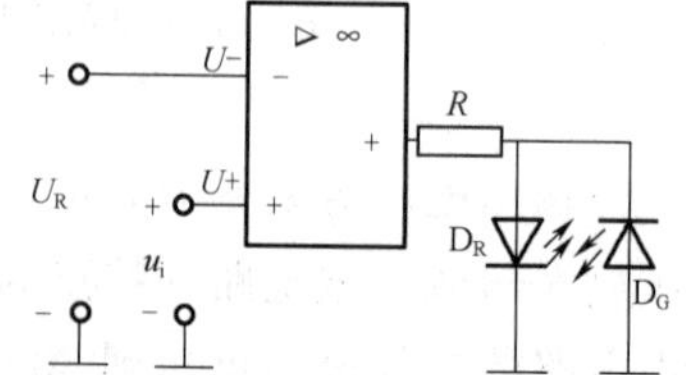

例 7-9-3 图　电压比较电路用作电平检测电路

四、滤波电路的基础知识

(一)滤波电路分类

通常，按照滤波电路的工作频带为其命名，分为低通滤波器(LPF)、高通滤波器(HPF)、带通滤波器(BPF)、带阻滤波器(BEF)和全通滤波器(AF)。设截止频率为 f_p，频率低于 f_p 的信号可以通过，高于 f_p 的信号被衰减的滤波电路称为低通滤波器；反之，频率高于 f_p 的信号可以通过，而频率低于 f_p 的信号被衰减的滤波电路称为高通滤波器。前者可以作为直流电源整流后的滤波电路，以便得到平滑的直流电压；后者可以作为交流放大电路的耦合电路，隔离直流成分，削弱低频信号，只放大频率高于 f_p 的信号。

设低频段的截止频率为 f_{p1}，高频段的截止频率为 f_{p2}，频率为 f_{p1} 到 f_{p2} 之间的信号可以通过，低于 f_{p1} 或高于 f_{p2} 的信号被衰减的滤波电路称为带通滤波器；反之，频率低于 f_{p1} 和高于 f_{p2} 的信号可以通过，而频率是 f_{p1} 到 f_{p2} 之间的信号被衰减的滤波电路称为带阻滤波器。前者常用于载波通信或弱信号提取等场合，以提高信噪比；后者用于在已知干扰或噪声频率的情况下，阻止其通过。

全通滤波器对于频率从零到无穷大的信号具有同样的比例系数，但对于不同频率的信号将产生不同的相移。

（二）典型滤波电路

实际上，任何滤波器均不可能具备如图 7-9-12 所示的幅频特性，在通带和阻带之间存在着过渡带。称通带中输出电压与输入电压之比 $\dot{A}_{up}$ 为通带放大倍数。如图 7-9-13 所示为低通滤波器电路和幅频特性。

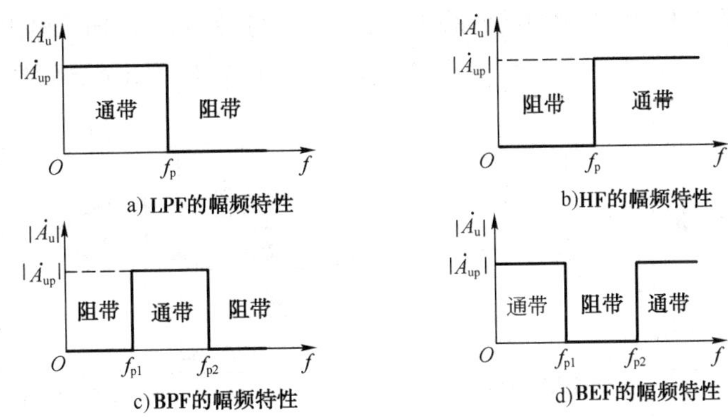

图 7-9-12　理想滤波电路的幅频特性

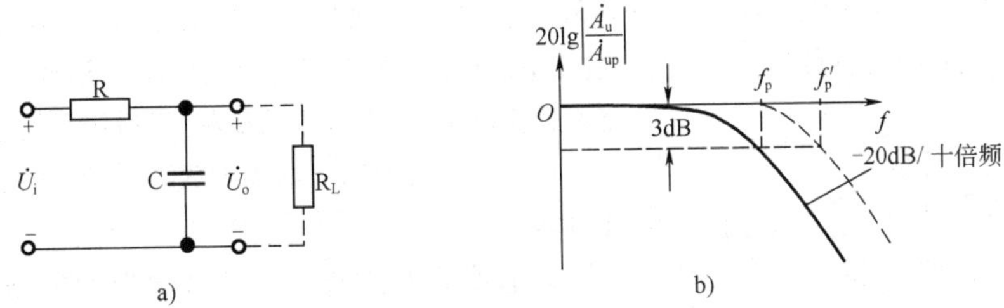

图 7-9-13　低通滤波器电路和幅频特性

使 $|\dot{A}_u| \approx 0.707|\dot{A}_{up}|$ 的频率为通带截止频率 f_p。从 f_p 到 $|\dot{A}_u|$ 接近零的频段称为过渡带。使 $|\dot{A}_u|$ 趋近于零的频段称为阻带。过渡带愈窄，电路的选择性愈好，滤波特性愈理想。

分析滤波电路，就是求解电路的频率特性。若滤波电路仅由无源元件（电阻、电容、电感）组成，则称为无源滤波电路。若滤波电路不仅有无源元件，还有有源元件（双极型管、单极型管、集成运放）组成，则称为有源滤波电路。

1. 无源低通滤波器

如图 7-9-13 所示为 RC 低通滤波器，当信号频率趋于零时，电容的容抗趋于无穷大，通带

放大倍数计算如下

$$\dot{A}_u = \frac{\dot{U}_o}{\dot{U}_i} = \frac{R_L // \frac{1}{j\omega C}}{R + R_L // \frac{1}{j\omega C}} = \frac{\frac{R_L}{R+R_L}}{1 + j\omega (R//R_L) C}$$

$$\dot{A}_u = \frac{\dot{U}_o}{\dot{U}_i} = \frac{\dot{A}_{up}}{1 + j\frac{f}{f'_p}}$$

$$f'_p = \frac{1}{2\pi (R//R_L) C}$$

结果表明负载电阻 R_L 对放大倍数的影响：负载电阻 R_L 减小，通带放大倍数的数值减小，通带截止频率升高。可见，无源滤波电路的通带放大倍数及其截止频率都随负载而变化，这一缺点不符合信号处理的要求，因而产生有源滤波电路。

2. 有源滤波电路

为了使负载不影响滤波特性，可在无源滤波电路和负载之间加一个高输入电阻低输出电阻的隔离电路，最简单的方法是加一个电压跟随器，即构成一阶有源低通滤波电路，如图 7-9-14a)所示，这样就构成了有源滤波电路。在理想运放的条件下，由于电压跟随器的输入电阻为无穷大，输出电阻为零，电路的负载能力提高。负载变化，放大倍数的表达式不变，因此频率特性不变。

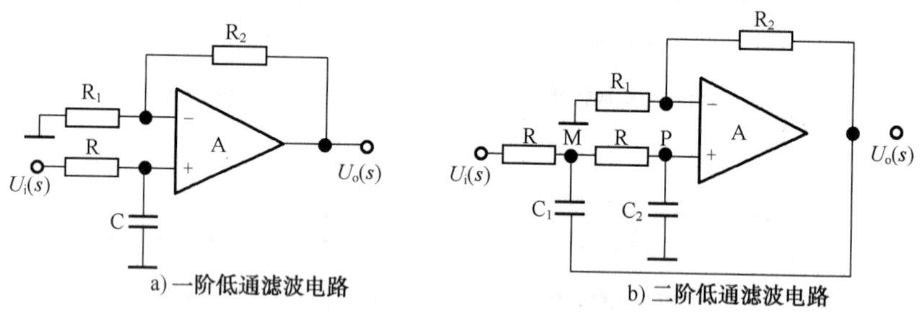

图 7-9-14　低通滤波电路

有源滤波电路一般由 RC 网络和集成运放组成，因而必须在合适的直流电源供电的情况下才能起滤波作用，与此同时，还可以进行放大。组成电路时，应选用带宽合适的集成运放。有源滤波电路不适于高电压、大电流的负载，只适用于信号处理。

图 7-9-14b)为用运算放大器构成的一阶、二阶低通滤波电路。

高通滤波电路与低通滤波电路具有对偶性，如果将如图 7-9-14b)所示二阶低通滤波电路中滤波环节的电容替换成电阻，电阻替换成电容，就可得如图 7-9-15 所示的高通滤波电路。

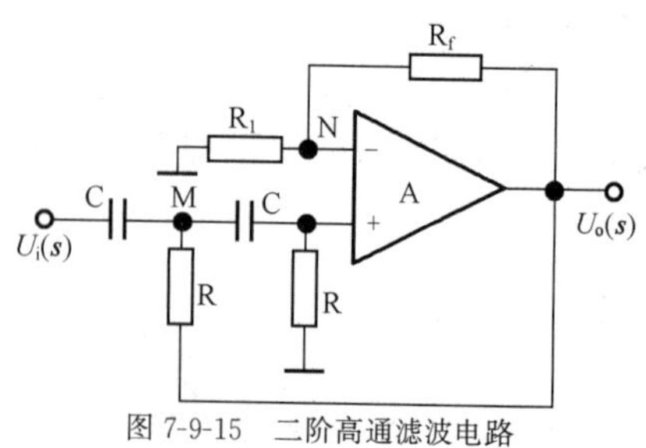

图 7-9-15　二阶高通滤波电路

习　题

7-9-1　如图所示电路中，输出电压的表达式是(　　)。

A. $-\frac{R_{F2}}{R_2}u_{i1} + \left(1 + \frac{R_{F2}}{R_2}\right)u_{i2}$　　B. $-\frac{R_{F1}}{R_2}u_{i1} + \left(1 + \frac{R_{F2}}{R_2}\right)u_{i2}$

C. $u_{i1}\dfrac{R_{F1}\cdot R_{F2}}{R_1R_2}+u_{i2}\dfrac{R_2+R_{F2}}{R_2}$　　D. $u_{i1}\dfrac{R_{F1}\cdot R_{F2}}{R_1R_2}-u_{i2}\dfrac{R_2+R_{F2}}{R_2}$

7-9-2　电路如图所示，负载电流 i_L 与负载电阻 R_L 的关系为(　　)。

A. R_L 增加，i_L 减小　　B. i_L 的大小与 R_L 的阻值无关

C. i_L 随 R_L 增加而增大　　D. R_L 减小，i_L 减小

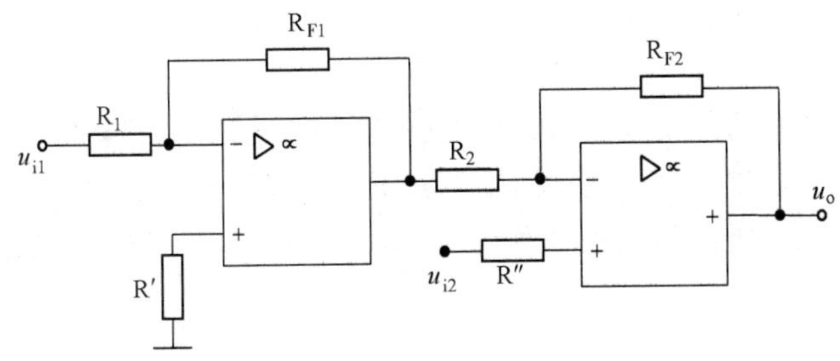

题 7-9-1 图

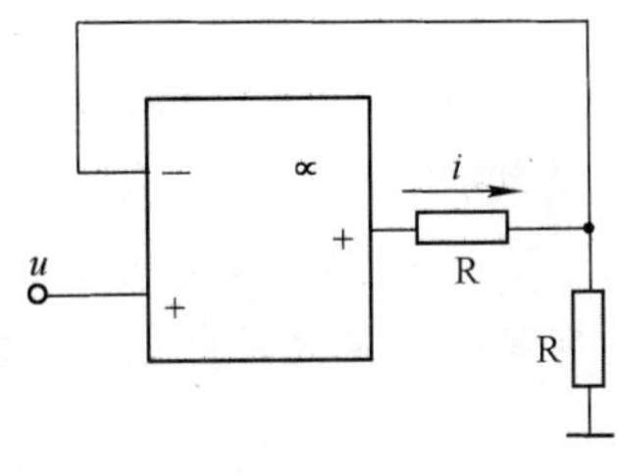

题 7-9-2 图

7-9-3　如图所示为可变电压放大器，当输入 $u_i=\frac{1}{2}$V 时，调节范围为(　　)。

A. −5.5～5.5V

B. −1～+1V

C. −0.5～−1V

D. −0.5～+0.5V

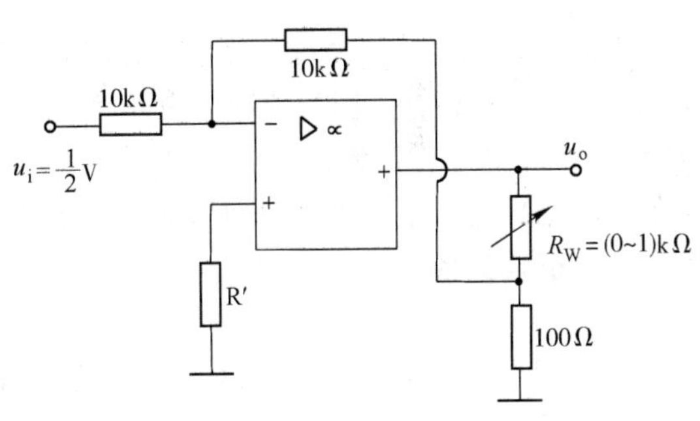

题 7-9-3 图

7-9-4　将运算放大器直接用于两信号的比较，如图 a)所示，其中：$u_{i2}=-1$V，u_{i1} 的波形由图 b)给出，则输出电压 u_o 等于(　　)。

A. u_{i1}　　B. $-u_{i2}$　　C. 正的饱和值　　D. 负的饱和值

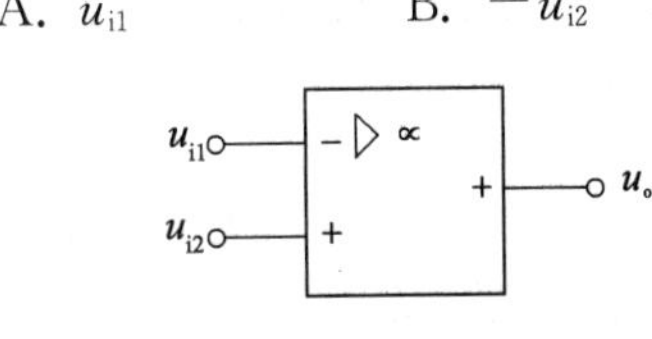

a)

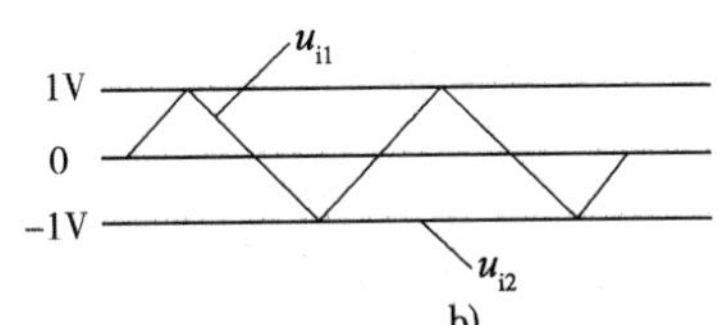

b)

题 7-9-4 图

7-9-5　运算放大器应用电路如图所示，在运算放大器线性工作区，输出电压与输入电压之间的运算关系是(　　)。

A. $u_o=-\dfrac{1}{R_1C}\int u_i\mathrm{d}t$　　B. $u_o=\dfrac{1}{R_1C}\int u_i\mathrm{d}t$

C. $u_o=-\dfrac{1}{(R_1+R_2)C}\int u_i\mathrm{d}t$　　D. $u_o=\dfrac{1}{(R_1+R_2)C}\int u_i\mathrm{d}t$

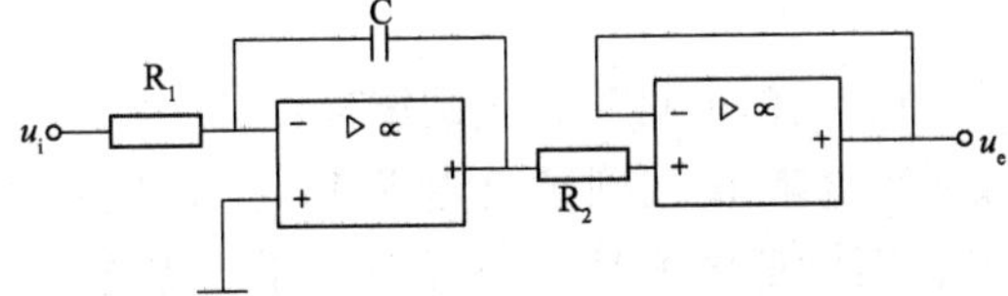

题 7-9-5 图

第十节　数字电路

一、门电路

(一)门电路的基本概念

在数字电路中,门电路是组合逻辑电路的最基本逻辑元件,它的应用极为广泛。所谓门,就是一个开关,在一定的条件下允许信号通过,条件不满足,信号就不能通过。门电路的输入信号与输出信号之间存在一定的逻辑关系,所以门电路又称为逻辑门电路。基本逻辑门电路有与门、或门和非门电路。

(二)基本门电路

1. 与门电路

如图 7-10-1a)所示为二极管与门电路,其中 A、B 为输入逻辑变量,F 为输出端。设二极管 D_A、D_B 为理想元件,即导通时端电压为 0V。由图 7-10-1 可见,在 A、B 中只要有一个输入为低电平时,输出端 F 就是低电平,只有当 A、B 端全为高电平时,F 端才有可能出现高电平。现在我们把高电平定义为逻辑“1”,而把低电平定义为逻辑“0”,则 F 与输入端 A、B 的逻辑关系符合与逻辑关系。

$$F = A \cdot B \tag{7-10-1}$$

逻辑功能表见表 7-10-1。

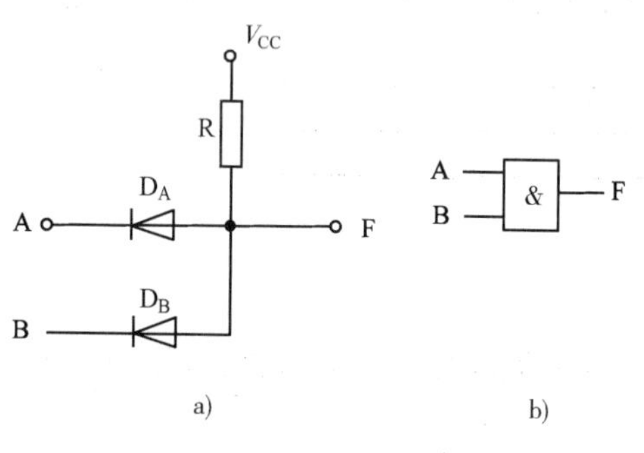

图 7-10-1　二极管与门电路及符号

与门逻辑状态表　　表 7-10-1

A	B	F
0	0	0
0	1	0
1	0	0
1	1	1

通常在进行逻辑电路的分析时,人们只关心输出和输入之间的逻辑关系,而不关心其内部结构,因此可以把与门用图 7-10-1b)的逻辑符号表示。

2. 或门电路

如图 7-10-2a)所示为二极管或门电路和它的逻辑符号。

两个二极管的负极同时经电阻 R 接到了负电源 V_{EE} 上,只要 A、B 中有一个是高电平;F 就是高电平;只有在 A、B 同时为低电平时,F 才是低电平。因此 F 与 A、B 之间为或的逻辑关系,逻辑状态表见表 7-10-2。

$$F=A+B \tag{7-10-2}$$

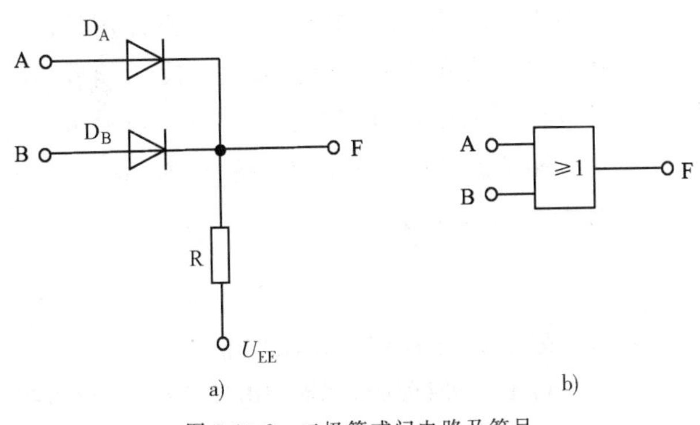

图 7-10-2　二极管或门电路及符号

或门逻辑状态表 表 7-10-2

A	B	F
0	0	0
0	1	1
1	0	1
1	1	1

3.三极管非门电路

(1)半导体三极管的开关特性

三极管有截止、饱和、放大三个工作区，在如图 7-10-3 所示的三极管电路中，$U_i \leqslant 0$ 时，$V_{BE} \leqslant 0$，因而三极管工作在截止区。截止区的工作特点是 $i_B \approx 0$，集电极电流 $i_C = i_{CEO} \approx 0$，所以三极管的集射极之间如同一个断开的开关一样，这时输出电压 $u_o \approx V_{CC}$。

当 u_i 为正，并且使 $i_B \geqslant i_{Bs} = \dfrac{V_{CC}}{\beta R_C}$ 时，V_{BE} 和 V_{BC} 同时为正向偏置，三极管工作在饱和区。饱和区的工作特点是 C-E 间的饱和压降 $V_{CES} \approx 0$，而 i_C 不再随 i_B 的增加而增加，此时 C-E 间如同开关短路一样，故三极重集电极电位 $V_C = 0$。

可见，只要用 u_i 的高低电平控制三极管分别工作在饱和导通和截止状态，就可控制它的开关状态，并在输出端得到对应的高、低电平。而与之相反的电平，即符合“非”的逻辑关系。

电路中通常满足 $V_{CC} \gg V_{CES}$，$i_{CEO} \approx 0$，所以在分析三极管开关电路时经常使用图 7-10-4 给出的三极管开关等效电路。

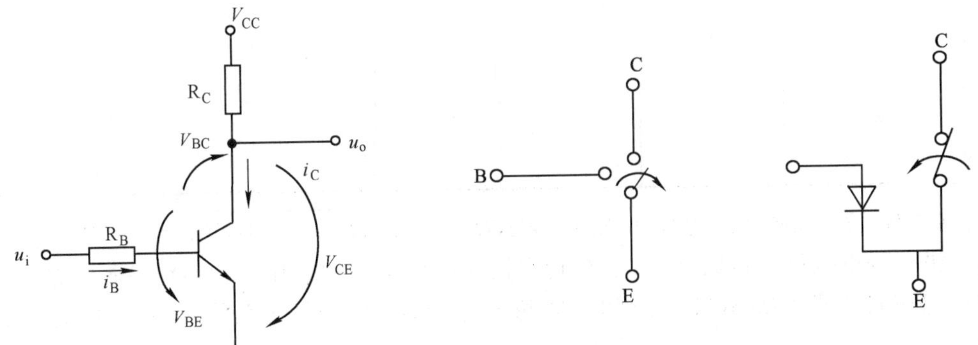

图 7-10-3　三极管非门电路

图 7-10-4　三极管开关等效电路

(2)非门

从以上分析的三极管开关特性可以发现，当输入 u_i 为低电平时，输出 u_o 为高电平；而输入 u_i 为高电平时输出 u_o 为低电平，因此输入与输出之间具有反相关系，即非逻辑，因此我们可以把它当作非门使用。

在实用的非门电路中，为保证输入为低电平时三极管能可靠截止，通常将电路接成如

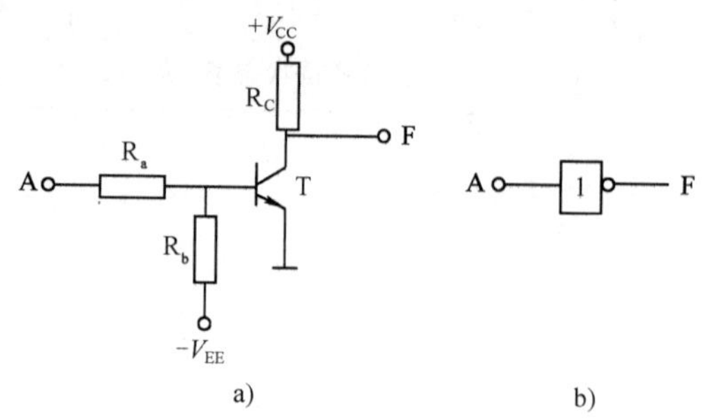

图 7-10-5

图 7-10-5所示的形式。由于增加了电阻 R_a 和负电源 V_{EE}，当输入低电平信号为 0V 时三极管的基极电位为负电位，发射结处于反向偏置，从而可以保证三极管可靠截止。

图 7-10-5b)是非门的逻辑符号，其中 F 与 A 的逻辑关系式为

$$F=\overline{A} \tag{7-10-3}$$

表 7-10-3 是非门逻辑状态表。

以上三种是基本逻辑门电路，有时还可以把它们组合成为组合门电路，以丰富逻辑功能。常用的一种是与非门电路，其图形符号如图 7-10-6 所示。

非门逻辑状态表 表 7-10-3

A	F
0	1
1	0

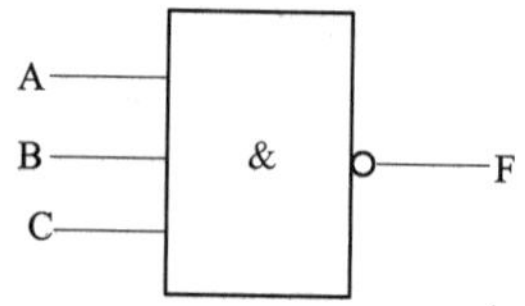

图 7-10-6 与非门电路的图形符号

与非门的逻辑功能是：当输入端全为 1 时，输出为 0；当输入端有一个或几个为 0 时，输出为 1。与非逻辑关系可用下式表示

$$F=\overline{A\cdot B\cdot C} \tag{7-10-4}$$

表 7-10-4 是与非门逻辑状态表。

与非门逻辑状态 表 7-10-4

A	B	C	F	A	B	C	F
0	0	0	1	1	0	0	1
0	0	1	1	1	0	1	1
0	1	0	1	1	1	0	1
0	1	1	1	1	1	1	0

【例 7-10-1】 如图所示电路中 $R_C=1\text{k}\Omega$，$R_1=12\text{k}\Omega$，$R_2=12\text{k}\Omega$，$V_{CC}=12\text{V}$，$V_{EE}=12\text{V}$，晶体三极管的电流放大倍数 $\beta=30$。分析在输入电位 $V_A=0\text{V}$ 和 $V_A=3\text{V}$ 时此电路是否符合“非”门逻辑要求？如不符合应如何调整？输出端与 +3V 电源相连的二极管起什么作用？

解 ①当输入端 A 为“0”时，$V_A=0\text{V}$，此时 V_B 电位可按下式计算(此时晶体三极管设为截止状态，$I_B=0\text{A}$)

$$V_B=V_A-\frac{V_A-(-V_{EE})}{R_1+R_2}R_1$$

$$=0-\frac{0-(-12)}{12+2}\times 2=-1.71\text{V}$$

此时 $V_B=V_{BE}<0.5V$，三极管可靠截止，输出状态为“1”。

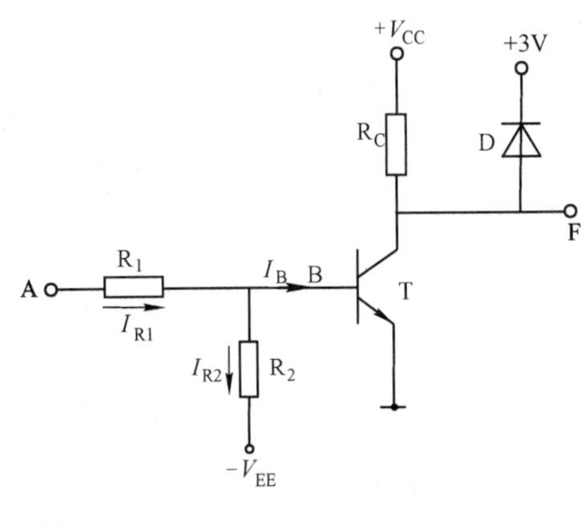

例 7-10-1 图

②当输入端 A 为“1”，即 $V_A=3V$ 时，设三极管为导通状态，$V_{BE}=0.7V$，则

$$I_B=I_{R1}-I_{R2}=\frac{V_A-V_B}{R_1}-\frac{V_B-V_{EE}}{R_2}$$

$$=\frac{3-0.7}{2}-\frac{0.7-(-12)}{12}$$

$$=1.15-1.06=0.09mA$$

$I_{BS}=\dfrac{I_{CS}}{\beta}\approx\dfrac{V_{CC}/R_C}{\beta}=\dfrac{12/1}{30}=0.4mA$（$I_{CS}$ 为三极管集电极最大允许电流）

故 $$I_B\leqslant I_{BS}$$

I_B 不足以使三极管饱和，必须调整。若使 $R_1=1.5k\Omega$，$R_2=18k\Omega$，则

$$I_B=\frac{3-0.7}{1.5}-\frac{0.7-(-12)}{18}=0.83mA>I_{BS}$$

此时 $I_B>I_{BS}$，三极管处于饱和状态，$V_{CE}=V_{CES}=0.3V$，即为逻辑“0”。通常逻辑电路中的电平高于 2.4V 时，设为逻辑“1”状态；逻辑“0”的电平小于 0.4V，此电路接入二极管是使输出高电平时二极管导通，使输出电位不超过 3V 太多（实际为 3.3V 左右）。符合“1”电平要求。

【例 7-10-2】 试分析图示逻辑电路的逻辑功能。

解 根据逻辑图，可写出其逻辑表达式为

$$F=\overline{\overline{\overline{ABC}\cdot A}\cdot\overline{\overline{ABC}\cdot B}\cdot\overline{\overline{ABC}\cdot C}}$$

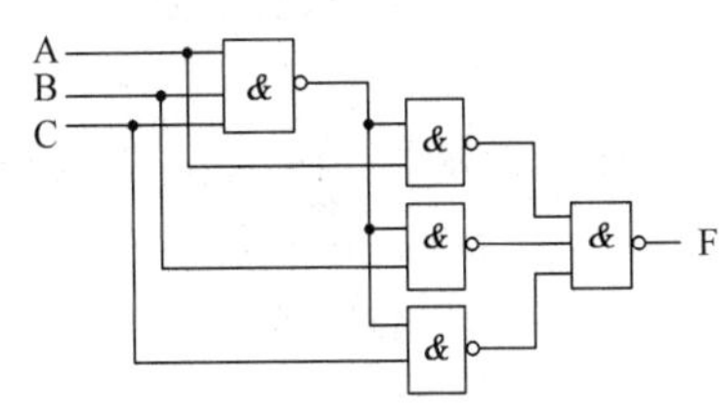

例 7-10-2 图 逻辑电路

利用逻辑代数的反演定理，上式可化简为

$$F=\overline{ABC}\cdot A+\overline{ABC}\cdot B+\overline{ABC}\cdot C$$

$$=\overline{ABC}(A+B+C)$$

$$=\overline{ABC}\cdot\overline{\overline{A}\cdot\overline{B}\cdot\overline{C}}$$

$$=\overline{ABC+\overline{A}\cdot\overline{B}\cdot\overline{C}}$$

其逻辑状态表见表 7-10-5。由表可知，该电路的逻辑功能是：当三个输入端的电平一致时（A、B、C 均为“1”或均为“0”），输出为“0”；当三个输入电平不一致时，输出为“1”。因此有时把它称为“不一致”电路，可以用这个逻辑电路来识别输入电平是否一致。

例题 7-10-2 的逻辑状态表 表 7-10-5

A	B	C	F	A	B	C	F
0	0	0	0	1	0	0	1
0	0	1	1	1	0	1	1
0	1	0	1	1	1	0	1
0	1	1	1	1	1	1	0

【例 7-10-3】 已知数字信号 A 和数字信号 B 的波形如图所示，则数字信号 $F=\overline{AB}$ 的波形

为：

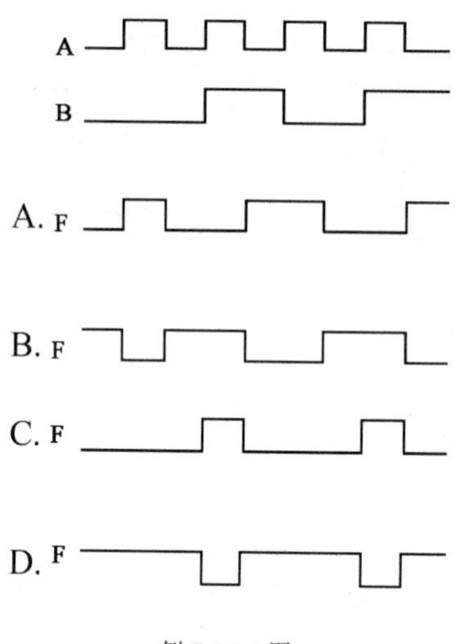

例 7-10-3 图

解 “与非门”电路遵循输入有“0”输出则“1”的原则，利用输入信号 A、B 的对应波形分析即可。

答案：D

二、触发器

触发器是时序逻辑电路的基本单元，常见的 RS 触发器、D 触发器和 JK 触发器都是具有两个稳定状态的双稳态触发器。

（一）RS 触发器

RS 触发器又分基本 RS 触发器和可控 R-S 触发器。

1. 基本 RS 触发器

基本 RS 触发器可由两个与非门交叉连接而成，如图 7-10-7a）所示。

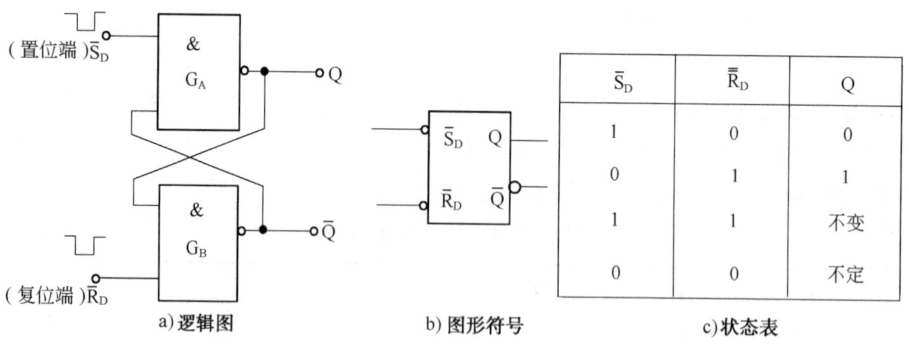

$\overline{S}_D$	$\overline{R}_D$	Q
1	0	0
0	1	1
1	1	不变
0	0	不定

图 7-10-7　基本 RS 触发器

Q 与 $\overline{Q}$ 是基本 RS 触发器的输出端，两者的逻辑状态在正常条件下保持相反。这种触发器有两种稳定状态：Q=1、Q=0，称为置位状态（“1”态）；Q=0、Q=1，称为复位状态（“0”态）。相应的输入端分别为直接置位端或直接置 1 端（S_D）和直接复位端或直接置 0 端（R_D）。

基本 RS 触发器输入对应有四种不同的状态，可以得出输出与输入的逻辑关系如

图 7-10-7c)所示状态表。从而可知，基本 RS 触发器有两个稳定的状态，它可以直接置位或复位。在直接置位端加负脉冲($S_D=0$)即可置位，在直接复位端加负脉冲($R_D=0$)即可复位。负脉冲除去以后，直接置位端和直接复位端都处于“1”态高电平(平时固定接高电平)，此时触发器保持原状态不变，实现存储或记忆功能。但是，负脉冲不可同时加直接置位端和直接复位端。

图 7-10-7b)是基本 RS 触发器的图形符号，图中输入端引线上靠近方框的小圆圈是表示触发器用负脉冲(0 电平)来置位或复位，即代表低电平有效；输出端 $\overline{Q}$ 的小圆圈表示在正常情况下 $\overline{Q}$ 与 Q 的状态相反。

2. 可控 RS 触发器

图 7-10-8a)是可控 RS 触发器的逻辑图。其中，与非门 G_A 和 G_B 构成基本触发器，与非门 G_C 和 G_D 构引导电路，R 和 S 是信号输入端。cp 是时钟脉冲输入端，通过引导电路来实现脉冲对输入端 R 和 S 的控制，故称为可控 RS 触发器。

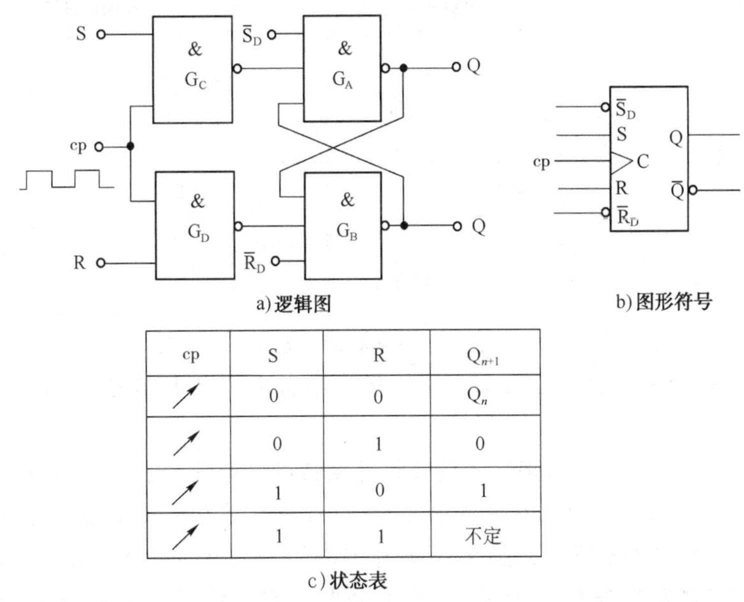

a)逻辑图

b)图形符号

cp	S	R	Q_{n+1}
↗	0	0	Q_n
↗	0	1	0
↗	1	0	1
↗	1	1	不定

c)状态表

图 7-10-8 可控 RS 触发器

当时钟脉冲来到之前，即 cp=0 时，不论 R 和 S 端的电平如何变化，G_C 门和 G_D 门的输出均为 1，基本触发器保持原状态不变。只有 cp=1 时，触发器才按 R、S 端的输入状态来决定其输出状态。时钟脉冲过去后，CP 恢复为“0”状态，输出状态不变。

R_D 和 S_D 是直接复位端和直接置位端，即不经过时钟脉冲 cp 的控制可以直接使基本触发器置 0 或置 1。一般用在工作之初，预先使触发器处于某一给定状态，在不用时让它们处于高电平。触发器的输出状态与 R、S 输入状态的关系如图 7-10-8c)所示的状态表。Q_n 表示时钟脉冲来到之前触发器的输出状态，Q_{n+1} 表示时钟脉冲来到之后的状态。

(二)JK 触发器

如图 7-10-9a)所示是 JK 触发器的逻辑图，它由两个可控 RS 触发器组成，分别称为主触发器和从触发器。此外，还通过一个非门将两个触发器联系起来。这就是触发器的主从器结构，时钟脉冲先使主触发器翻转，然后使从触发器翻转，“主从”之名由此而来。

当时钟脉冲来到后，即 cp=1 时，非门的输出为 0，从触发器的状态不变；至于这时主触发器是否翻转，要看触发器当前输出的状态以及 J、K 输入端所处状态而定（$S=J\overline{Q}$、$R=KQ$）。当 cp 从 1 变为 0 时，主触发器的状态保持；由于这时非门的输出为 1，从触发器打开，主触发器就可以将信号送到从触发器，使两者状态一致。

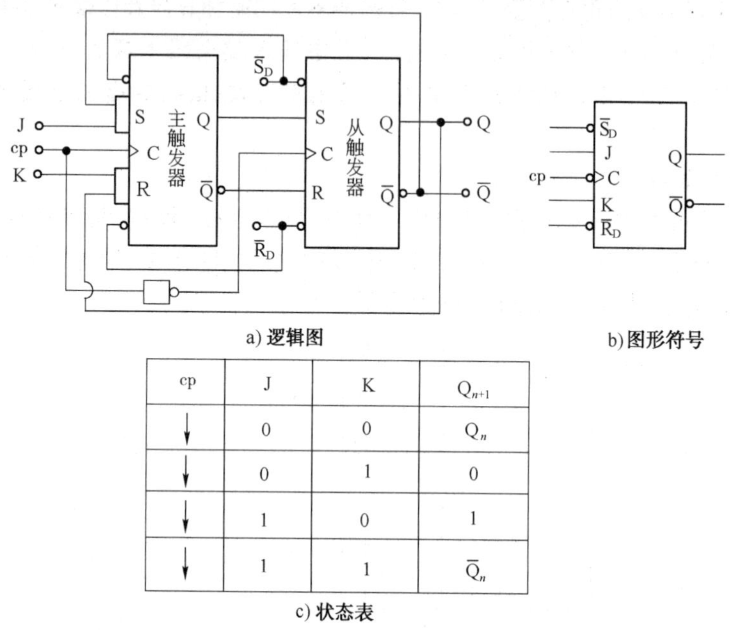

cp	J	K	Q_{n+1}
↓	0	0	Q_n
↓	0	1	0
↓	1	0	1
↓	1	1	$\overline{Q}_n$

c) 状态表

图 7-10-9　主从型 JK 触发器

可见，在时钟脉冲来到之前（即 cp=0 时），触发器的状态（即从触发器的状态）与主触发器的状态是一致的。

由于 JK 触发器在 cp=1 时，把输入信号暂时存储在主触发器中，为从触发器翻转或保持原态做好准备；到 cp 下跳为 0 时，存储的信号起作用，或者触发从触发器使之翻转，或者使之保持原态。此外，主从型触发器具有在 cp 下跳为 0 时翻转的特点，也就是具有在时钟脉冲后沿触发的特点。后沿触发在图形符号中 cp 输入端靠近方框处用小圆圈表示，如图 7-10-9b）所示。

JK 触发器的状态表如图 7-10-9c）所示。

（三）D 触发器

D 触发器的逻辑功能是：它的输出端 Q 的状态随输入端 D 的状态而变化，但总比输入端状态的变化晚一步。

即

$$Q_{n+1}=D_n \tag{7-10-5}$$

如图 7-10-10a）所示为 JK 触发器转换为 D 触发器的逻辑电路图。

D 触发器和 JK 触发器都是常用的寄存器和计数器等时序逻辑电路的逻辑部件。

D 触发器的状态表如图 7-10-10b）所示。

【例 7-10-4】 图示为单脉冲输出电路，输入信号 J_1、P_1 和时钟 cp 的信号如图所示，试画出 Q_1、Q_2 和 M 端的工作波形（设触发器的初始状态为“0”）。

解 触发器 F_1 和 F_2 在同一时钟脉冲作用下，为同步触发方式。分析时，应先确定 Q_1、Q_2 的波形；

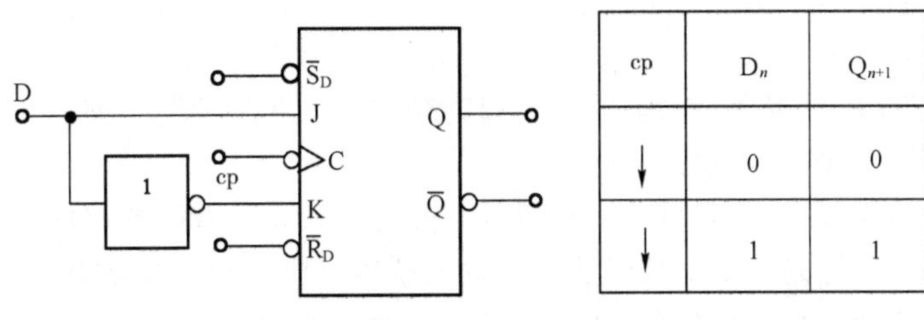

cp	D_n	Q_{n+1}
↓	0	0
↓	1	1

a) 逻辑图　　　　b) 触发器的状态表

图 7-10-10　将 JK 触发器转换为 D 触发器

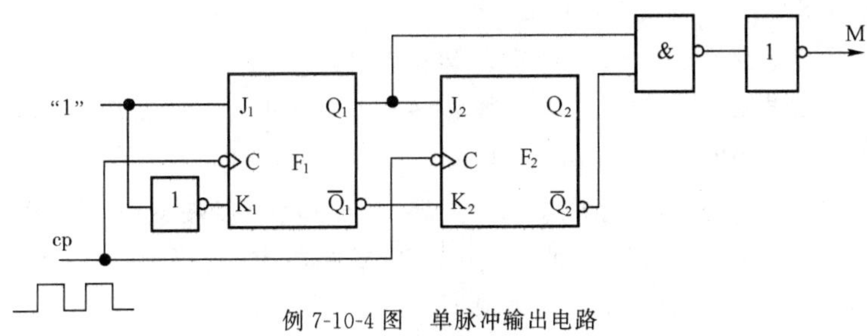

例 7-10-4 图　单脉冲输出电路

输出端 M 与 Q_1、Q_2 的输出为组合逻辑关系，$M=Q_1\cdot\overline{Q}_2$。绘制的 Q_1、Q_2 和 M 的波形如解图所示。

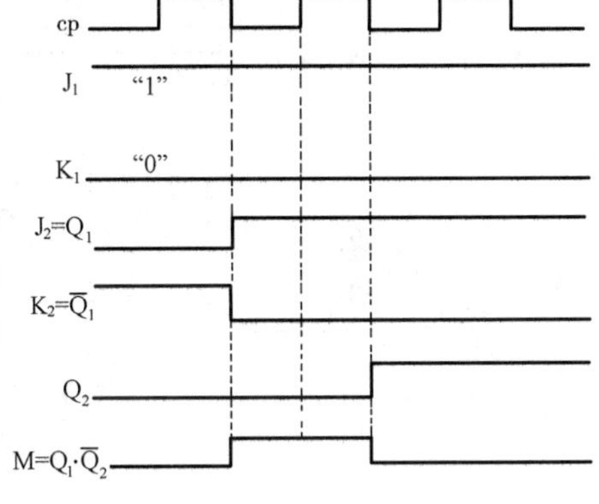

例 7-10-4 解图　波形图

触发器具有时序逻辑的特征，可以由它组成各种时序逻辑电路。其中，寄存器和计数器是最典型的时序逻辑电路。

【例 7-10-5】　如图 a）所示电路中，复位信号、数据输入及时钟脉冲信号如图 b）所示，经分析可知，在第一个和第二个时钟脉冲的下降沿过后，输出 Q 先后等于：

A. 0，0　　　B. 0，1

C. 1，0　　　D. 1，1

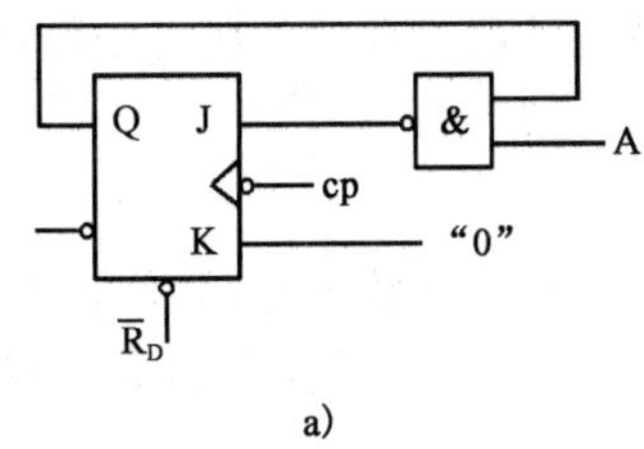

a)

b)

例 7-10-5 图

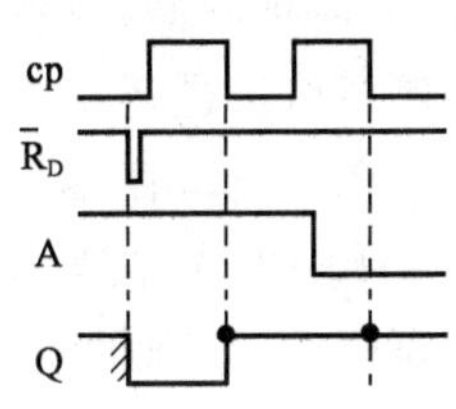

例 7-10-5 解图

解　图示为 JK 触发器和与非门的组合，触发时刻为 cp 脉冲的下降沿，触发器输入信号为：$J=\overline{Q\cdot A}$，K="0"。

输出波形为解图 Q 所示。两个脉冲的下降沿后 Q 为高电平。

答案：D

三、寄存器

寄存器用来暂时存放参与运算的数据和运算结果。一个触发器只能寄存一位二进制数，要存多位数时就得用多个触发器。

寄存器存放数码的方式有并行和串行两种。并行方式就是数码各位从各对应位输入端同时输入到寄存器中，串行方式就是数码从一个输入端逐位输入到寄存器中。

寄存器取出数码的方式也有并行和串行两种。在并行方式中，被取出的数码各位在对应于各位的输出端上同时出现；而在串行方式中，被取出的数码仅在一个输出端逐位出现。

寄存器常分为数码寄存器和移位寄存器两种，其区别在于有无移位的功能。

(一)数码寄存器

这种寄存器只有寄存数码和清除原有数码的功能。图 7-10-11 是一种四位数码寄存器。输入端是四个与门，如果要输入四位二进制数 $d_3 \sim d_0$ 时，可使与门的寄存控制信号 IE=1，把与非打开 $d_3 \sim d_0$ 便输入。当时钟脉冲 cp=1 时，$d_3 \sim d_0$ 以反量形式寄存在四个 D 触发器 $FF_3 \sim FF_0$ 的 Q 端。输出端是四个三态非门(当取出信号 OE=0 时 $Q_3 \sim Q_0$ 端悬空，当 OE=1 时 $Q_3 \sim Q_0$ 取触发器 $FF_3 \sim FF_0$ 端悬空输出的反量)。这样，如果要取出时，可使三态门的输出控制信号 OE=1，$d_3 \sim d_0$ 便可从三态门的 $Q_3 \sim Q_0$ 端输出。

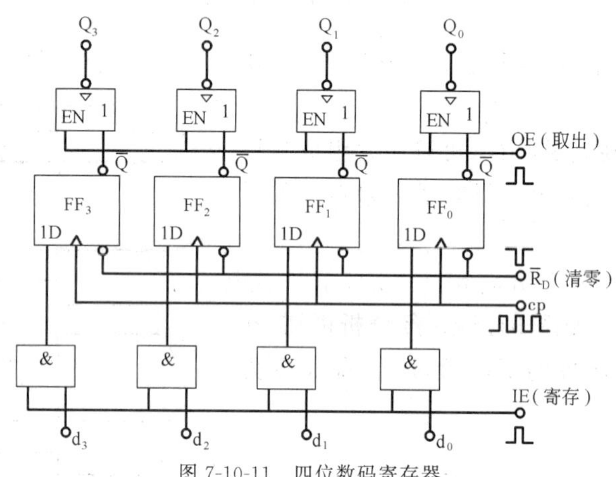

图 7-10-11　四位数码寄存器

(二)移位寄存器

移位寄存器除了有存放数码的功能以外，还有将存储的数据移位的功能，即每当来一个移位正脉冲(时钟脉冲)，触发器的状态便向右或向左移一位，也就是指寄存的数码可以在移位脉冲的控制下依次进行左右移位。

1. 单向移位寄存器

图 7-10-12 是由 JK 触发器组成的四位移位寄存器。FF_0 接成 D 触发器，数码由 D 端输入。设寄存的二进制数为 1011，按移位脉冲的工作节拍从高位到低位依次串行送到 D 端。

工作之初各触发器清零。

首先 D=1，第一个移位脉冲的下降沿来到时使触发器 FF_0 翻转 $Q_0=1$，其他仍保持0 态。接着 D=0，第二个移位脉冲的下降沿来到时使 FF_0 和 FF_1 同时翻转，由于 FF_1 的 J 端为 1，FF_0 的 J 端为 0，所以 $Q_1=1, Q_0=0$，Q_2 和 Q_3 仍为 0。

以后的过程见表 7-10-6，移位一次存入一个新的数码。直到第四个脉冲的下降沿来到时，存数结束，这时可以在四个触发器的输出端得到并行的数码输出。

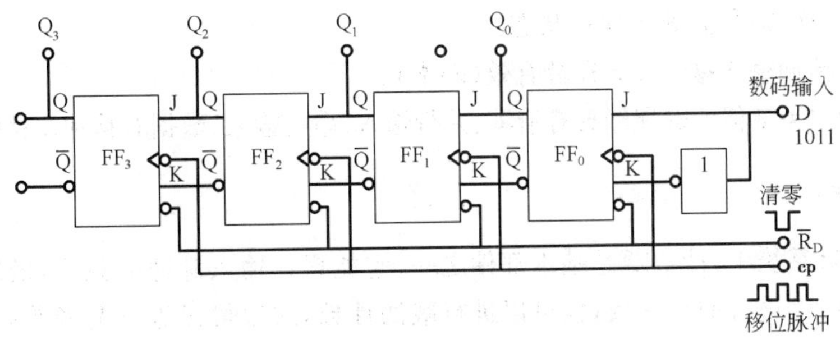

图 7-10-12 四位移位寄存器

移位寄存器状态表

表 7-10-6

移位脉冲数	寄存器中的数码				移动过程
	Q_3	Q_2	Q_1	Q_0	
0	0	0	0	0	清零
1	0	0	0	1	左移一位
2	0	0	1	0	左移二位
3	0	1	0	1	左移三位
4	1	0	1	1	左移四位

2. 双向移位寄存器

74LS194 是双向移位寄存器，其外引线排列和逻辑符号如图 7-10-13 所示，各引线说明如下：

1 为数据清零端，R_D 是清零线，低电平有效。

3～6 为并行数据输入端 D_3～D_0。

12～15 位数据输出端 Q_3～Q_0。

2 为右移的串行数据输入端 D_{SR}。

7 为左移的串行数据输入端 D_{SL}。

9、10 位工作方式控制端：当 $S_1=S_0=1$ 时，数据并行输入；

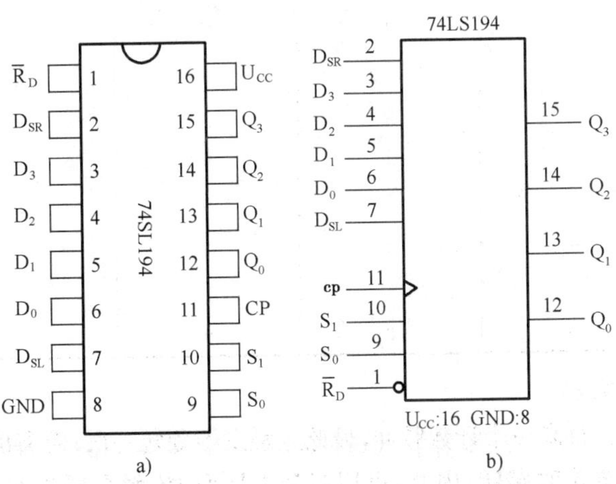

图 7-10-13 74LS194 引线排列和逻辑符号

$S_1=0$，$S_0=1$ 时，右移数据输入；

$S_1=1,S_0=0$ 时,左移数据输入;

$S_1=S_0=0$ 时,寄存器处于保持状态。

11 为时钟脉冲输入端 cp,上升沿有效(cp↑)。

可见,74LS194 型移位寄存器具有清零、并行输入、串行输入、数据右移和左移的移位功能。

四、计数器

在数字逻辑系统中,计数器是基本部件之一,它能累计输入脉冲的数目,最后给出累计的总数。计数器可以进行加法计数,也可以进行减法计数,或者可以进行两者兼有的可逆计数。若从进位制来分,有二进制计数器、十进制计数器等多种。

(一)二进制计数器

二进制只有 0 和 1 两个数码。当本位是 1,再加 1 时,本位变为 0,而向高位进位。由于双稳态触发器有 1 和 0 两个状态,所以一个触发器可以表示一位二进制数。如果要表示 n 位二进制数,就得用 n 个触发器。

根据上述,可以列出四位二进制加法计数器的状态表 7-10-7,表中还列出对应的十进制数。要实现四位二进制加法计数,必须用四个双稳态触发器。

四位二进制加法计数器的状态 表 7-10-7

计数脉冲数	二进制数				十进制数
	Q_3	Q_2	Q_1	Q_0	
0	0	0	0	0	0
1	0	0	0	1	1
2	0	0	1	0	2
3	0	0	1	1	3
4	0	1	0	0	4
5	0	1	0	1	5
6	0	1	1	0	6
7	0	1	1	1	7
8	1	0	0	0	8
9	1	0	0	1	9
10	1	0	1	0	10
11	1	0	1	1	11
12	1	1	0	0	12
13	1	1	0	1	13
14	1	1	1	0	14
15	1	1	1	1	15
16	0	0	0	0	0

1. 异步二进制计数器

由表 7-10-14 可见,每来一个计数脉冲,最低位触发器翻转一次;而高位触发器是在相邻的低位触发器从 1 变为 0 进位时翻转。因此,可用四个主从型 JK 触发器来组成四位异步二进制加法计数器图 7-10-14 所示,触发器的 J、K 端悬空相当于 1,有计数功能。触发器的进位脉冲从 Q 端输出送到相邻高位触发器的 cp 端,这符合主从型触发器在输入正脉冲的下降沿触发的特点。

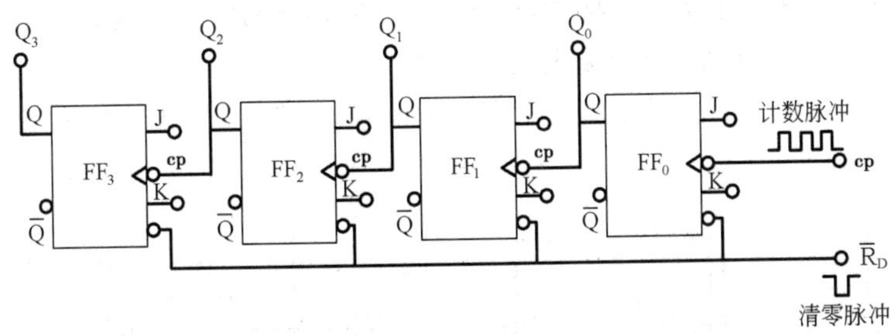

图 7-10-14　四位异步二进制加法计数器

图 7-10-15 是四位异步二进制加法计数器的波形图。

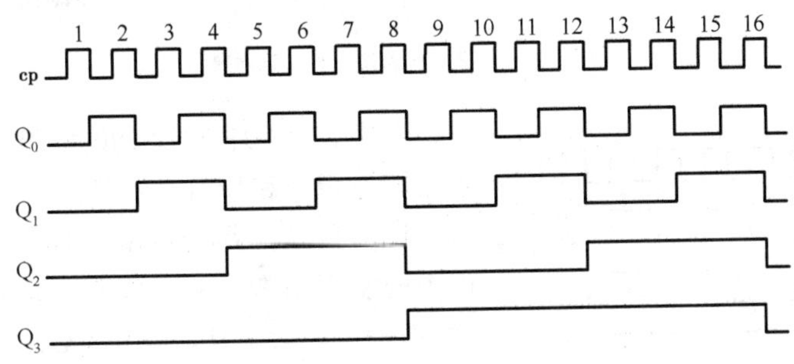

图 7-10-15　四位异步二进制加法计数器波形图

2.同步二进制计数器

如果计数器还是用四个主从型 JK 触发器组成，根据表 7-10-7 可得出各位触发器的 J、K 端的逻辑关系式：

(1)第一位触发器 FFo，每来一个计数脉冲就翻转一次，故 $J_0=K_0=1$；

(2)第二位触发器 FF_1，在 $Q_0=1$ 时再来一个脉冲才翻转，故 $J_1=K_1=Q_0$；

(3)第三位触发器 FF_2，在 $Q_1=Q_0=1$ 时再来一个脉冲才翻转，故 $J_2=K_2=Q_1Q_0$；

(4)第四位触发器 FF_3，在 $Q_2=Q_1=Q_0=1$ 时再来一个脉冲才翻转，故 $J_3=K_3=Q_2Q_1Q_0$。

由上述逻辑关系式可得出如图 7-10-16 所示的四位同步二进制加法计数器的逻辑电路图。由于计数脉冲同时加到各位触发器的 cp 端，各触发器输出端的状态变换和计数脉冲同步，这是“同步”名称的由来，并与“异步”相区别。同步计数器的计数速度较异步为快。

四位二进制加法计数器，能记的最大十进制数为 $2^4-1=15$。n 位二进制加法计数器，能记的最大十进制数为 2^n-1。

(二)十进制计数器

二进制计数器结构简单，但是读数不习惯，所以在有些场合采用十进制计数器较为方便。

十进制计数器是在二进制计数器的基础上得出的，用四位二进制数来代表十进制的每一位数所以也称为二-十进制计数器。如采用最常用的 8421 编码方式，是取四位二进制数前面的 0000～1001 来表示十进制的 0～9 十个数码，而去掉后面的 1010～1111 六个数。也就是计数器计到第九个脉冲时再来一个脉冲，即由 1001 变为 0000，经过十个脉冲循环一次。同步十进制计数器与二进制加法计数器相比，同步十进制计数器来第十个脉冲不是由 1001 变为 1010，而是恢复 0000，即要求第二位触发器 FF_1 不得翻转，保持 0 态，第四位触发器 FF_3 应翻转为 0。图 7-10-17 是十进制加法计数器的波形图。

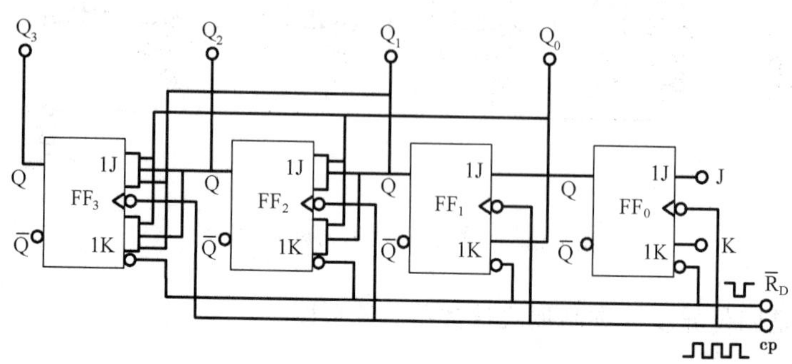

图 7-10-16　四位同步二进制加法计数器

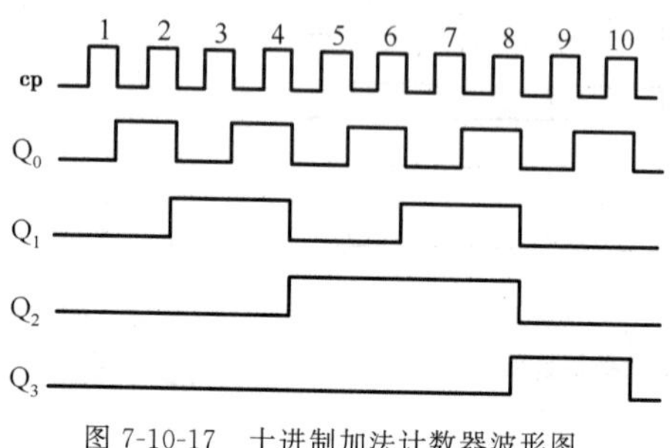

图 7-10-17　十进制加法计数器波形图

图 7-10-18 是 74LS290 型异步二-五-十进制计数器的逻辑图和外引线列图。

$R_{0(1)}$ 和 $R_{0(2)}$ 是清零输入端，当两端全为 1 时，将四个触发器清零；$S_{9(1)}$ 和 $S_{9(2)}$ 是置"9"输入端。同样，当两端全为 1 时，$Q_3Q_2Q_1Q_0=1001$，即表示十进制数 9。清零时，$S_{9(1)}$ 和 $S_{9(2)}$ 中至少有一端为 0，不使置 1，以保证清零可靠进行。它有两个时钟脉冲输入端 cp_0 和 cp_1。

(1)只输入计数脉冲 cp_0，由 Q_0 输出，$FF_1 \sim FF_3$ 三位触发器不用，为二进制计数器。

(2)只输入计数脉冲 cp_1，由 $Q_3Q_2Q_1$ 输出，为五进制计数器。

(3)将 Q_0 端与 FF_1 的 cp_1 端连接，输入计数脉冲 cp_0。

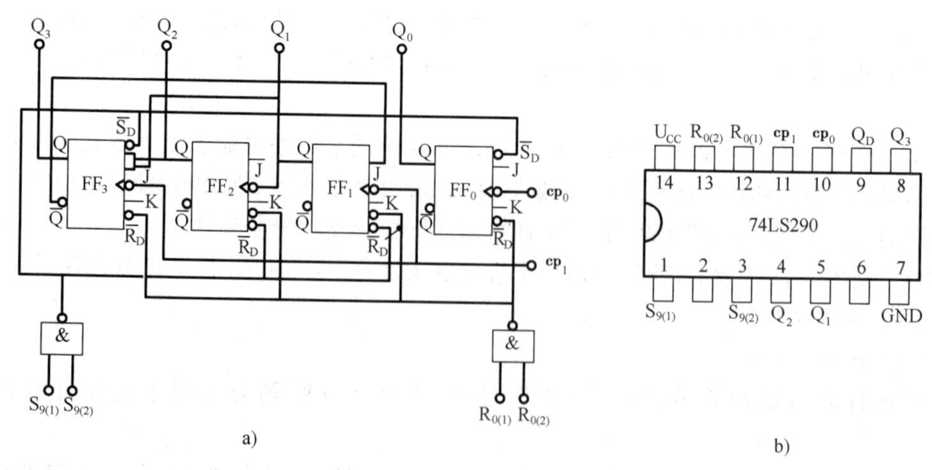

图 7-10-18　74LS290 型计数器的逻辑图和外引线列图

（三）任意进制计数器

当需要任意进制的计数器时，将现有的计数器改接即可。如利用清零端进行反馈置 0，可得出小于原进制的多种进制的计数器。将图 7-10-19a)中的 74LS290 型十进制计数器改接成图 7-10-19 所示的两个电路，就分别成为六进制计数器和九进制计数器。以图 7-10-19 为例，它从 0000 开始计数，来五个脉冲 cp 后变为 0101。

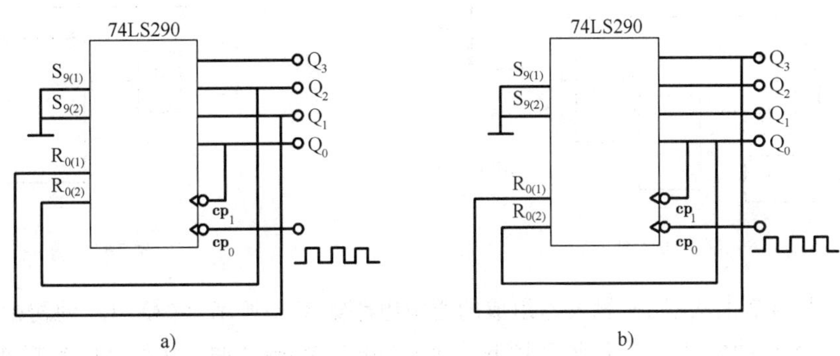

图 7-10-19　六进制计数器和九进制计数器

当第六个脉冲来到后，出现 0110 的状态，由于 Q_0 和 Q_1 端分别接到 $R_{0(1)}$ 和 $R_{0(2)}$ 清零端强迫清零，0110 这一状态转瞬即逝，立即回到 0000。它经过六个脉冲循环一次，故为六进制计数器，状态循环如图 7-10-20 所示。

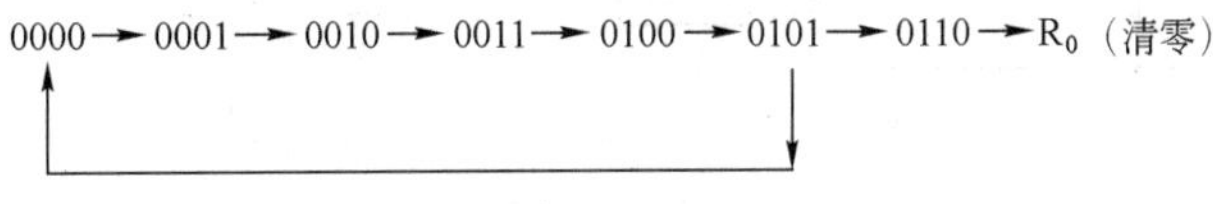

图 7-10-20　进制计数器状态循环图

当需要十以上进制的计数时，可以采用多片 74LS290 来实现。

习　　题

7-10-1　由三个二极管和电阻 R 组成一个基本逻辑门电路，如图所示，输入二极管的高电平和低电平分别是 3V 和 0V，电路的逻辑关系式是（　　）。

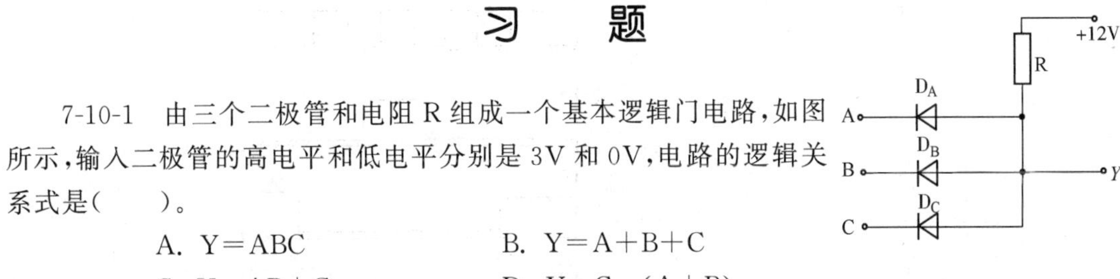

A. Y＝ABC　　B. Y＝A＋B＋C

C. Y＝AB＋C　　D. Y＝C·(A＋B)

题 7-10-1 图

7-10-2　现有一个三输入端与非门，需要把它用作反相器（非门），请问如图所示电路中哪种接法正确（　　）。

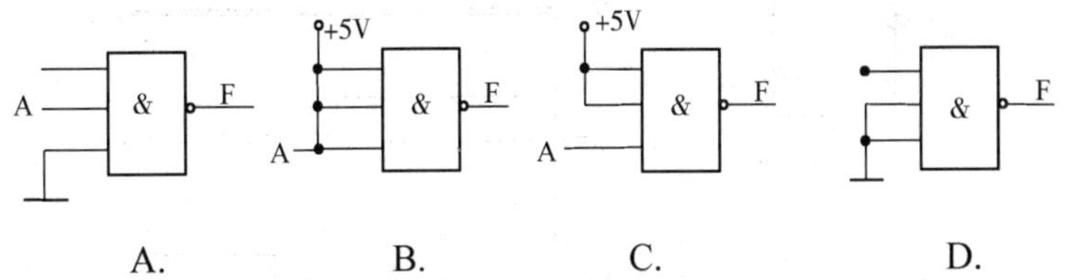

A.　B.　C.　D.

7-10-3　如图所示电路的逻辑式是（　　）。

A. $Y=AB(\overline{A}+\overline{B})$　　B. $Y=A\overline{B}+B\overline{A}$

C. $Y=(A+B)\overline{AB}$　　　　D. $Y=AB+\overline{A}\,\overline{B}$

7-10-4　逻辑电路如图所示，A=“1”时，C 脉冲来到后 D 触发器(　　)。

A. 具有计数器功能　　B. 置“0”　　C. 置“1”　　D. 无法确定

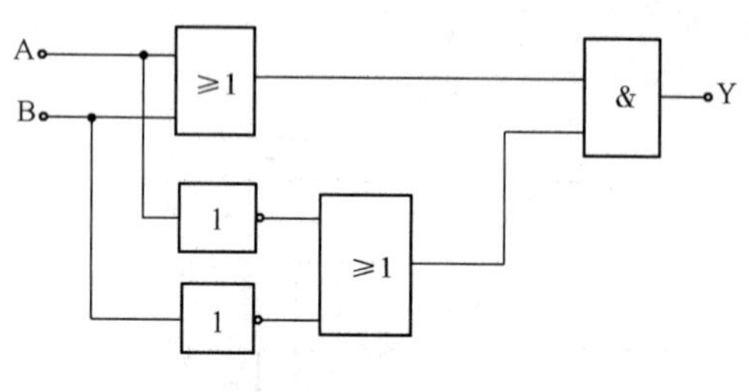

题 7-10-3 图

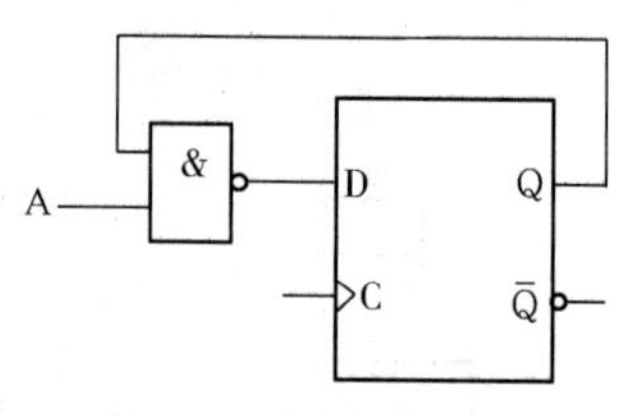

题 7-10-4 图

7-10-5　由两个主从型 JK 触发器组成的逻辑电路如图 a)所示，设 Q_1、Q_2 的初始态是 00，已知输入信号 A 和脉冲信号 cp 的波形如图 b)所示，当第二个 cp 脉冲作用后，Q_1Q_2 将变为(　　)。

A. 11　　B. 10　　C. 01　　D. 保持 00 不变

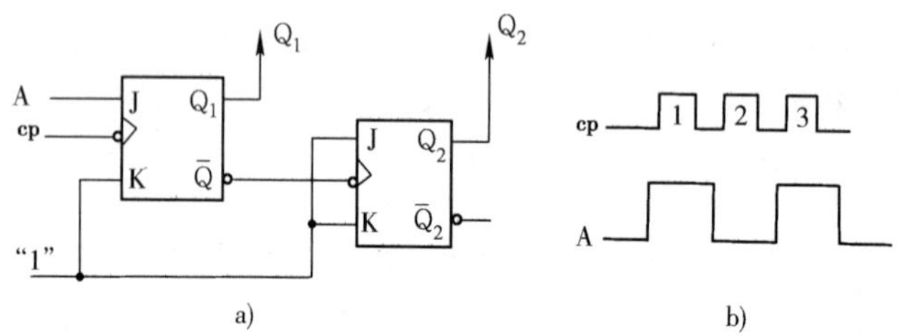

题 7-10-5 图

7-10-6　已知 RS 触发器，R、S、C 端的信号如图所示，请问输出端 Q 的几种波形中，正确的是(　　)(设触发器初始状态为“0”)。

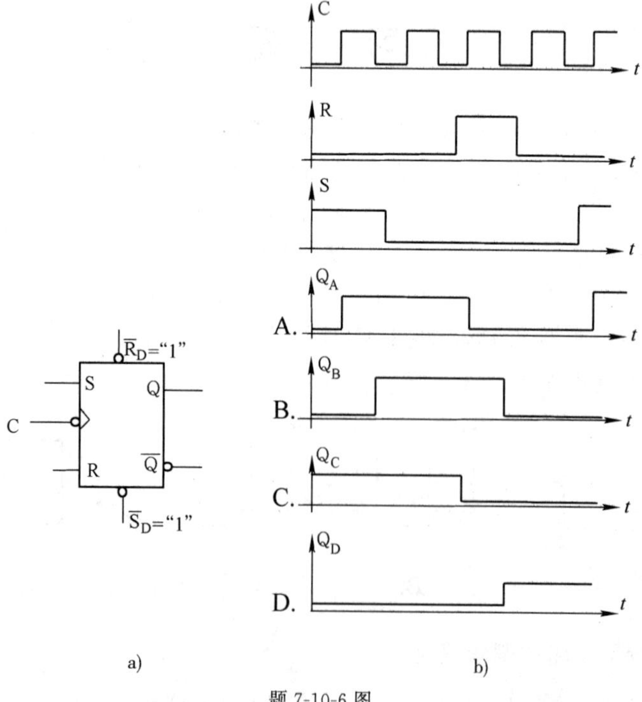

题 7-10-6 图

题解及参考答案

第一节

7-1-1 **解**:σ 为电荷密度,对于无限大平行板电容器而言,极板间的电势差为$\frac{\sigma l}{\varepsilon_0}$。

答案:B

7-1-2 **解**:感应电动势的大小与磁感应强度 $\boldsymbol{B}$、导体切割磁场的速度以及磁场中有效导体的长度成正比。

答案:D

7-1-3 **解**:根据电磁感应定律 $e=-\frac{\mathrm{d}\varphi}{\mathrm{d}t}$,当外加电压为直流量时,$\frac{\mathrm{d}\varphi}{\mathrm{d}t}=0$,则 $e=0$,则下方线圈中无感应电动势。

答案:A

7-1-4 **解**:a 线圈中加上变化的电源 u,则产生变化的电流和磁通 ϕ(在线圈中产生感应电动势 e_a,影响电流 i_a);该磁通又与线圈 b 交链,在线圈 b 中产生感应电动势,并由此产生电流 i_b。

答案:B

第二节

7-2-1 **解**:注意所求电阻的端口位置,用简单电阻串、并联方法求解。

答案:C

7-2-2 **解**:根据题意可知,电热器的额定电阻为 $R_N=\frac{U_N{}^2}{P_N}=\frac{100^2}{2}=5\text{k}\Omega$。

答案:B

7-2-3 **解**:电压表内阻与 20kΩ 电阻为并联法。

答案:C

7-2-4 **解**:当开关 S 开时,电阻 R_1、R_2、R_3 为串联,当开关 S 闭合时,电位可以 R_1、R_2 电阻分压决定。

答案:D

7-2-5 **解**:用线性电路的叠加原理分析。

答案:A

7-2-6 **解**:理想电流源 I_s 两端的电压由其以外电路决定。$U_{I_s}=U_1+U_s$。

答案:C

第三节

7-3-1 **解**:用戴维南定理。U_s 为原电路的负载 R_L 开路电压,R_0 为除源(6V 电压源短路)的电阻。

答案:B

7-3-2 **解**:根据节点电流关系求出电流 I_1 后,确定网络 N 的端口电压。

答案:C

7-3-3 解:用叠加原理求出 R_L 上的电压 U_L 后,再用公式 $P_L=\frac{U_L^2}{R_L}$ 计算功率。

答案:A

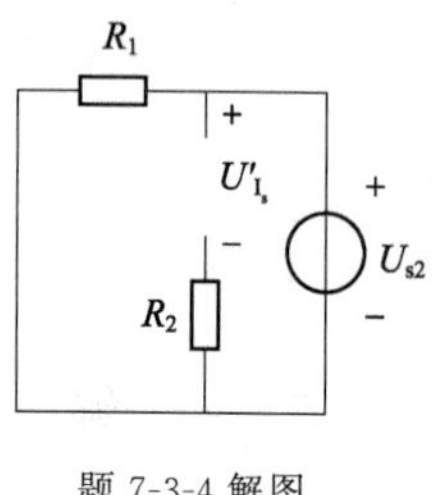

题 7-3-4 解图

7-3-4 解:当电压源 U_{s2} 单独作用时需将 U_{s1} 短路,电流源 I_s 断路处理。题图的电路应等效为解图所示电路,即 $U'_{I_s}=U_{s2}$。

答案:B

第四节

7-4-1 解:交流电压表读数为交流电压的有效值,回路电压关系为相量关系:$\dot{U}=\dot{U}_1+\dot{U}_2+\dot{U}_3$。

答案:D

7-4-2 解:交流电路中电流为相量关系:$\dot{I}=\dot{I}_1+\dot{I}_2$。

答案:B

7-4-3 解:电路中消耗的功率为:$P=UI\cos\varphi$,$\varphi=\varphi_u-\varphi_i$。

答案:C

7-4-4 解:由给定条件 $i_1=i$ 可见该电路为谐振电路,1 为电阻性电路,2、3 分别为纯电容电路和纯电感电路(或反之)。

答案:D

7-4-5 解:三相对称电路中三相电流之和为 0,即:

$$i_A+i_B+i_C=0$$

答案:B

7-4-6 解:串联电路中 $z=R+j(w_L-\frac{1}{w_c})$,感性电路中 $w_L>\frac{1}{w_c}$,而处于谐振状态的电路 $w_L=\frac{1}{w_c}$。

答案:B

7-4-7 解:三相对称电路中负载消耗的功率与每相负载电压有关,当电源线电压一定时,三角形连接负载电压是星形连接负载电压的$\sqrt{3}$倍。

答案:A

7-4-8 解:三角形连接的对称三相电路中,线电流是相电流的$\sqrt{3}$倍。

答案:B

7-4-9 解:三相供电系统中对于单相供电的负载一般要用到火线 L(相线),电源的中性点线 N(或工作零线),以及保护零线 E。电源插座对这三根线位置有明确的规定。

答案:B

7-4-10 解:此题分析时应考虑接地电阻对电路的影响。

答案:B

7-4-11 解:用交流电路的复数符号法分析。

电感上的电压相量：$\dot{U}_L=\dfrac{jwL}{R+jwL}\dot{U}_i$。

答案:B

第五节

7-5-1 **解**:根据储能元件的换路关系,电容电压不跃变,电感元件的电流不跃变。

答案:B

7-5-2 **解**:一阶 R-C 电路的暂态过程中,时间常数 $\tau=RC$,其中 R 的数值是在电容 C 两端等效的电阻。

答案:B

7-5-3 **解**:开关动作以后,电容进入放电过程。电流是由电容电压释放形成的,应与图示电流 i 的参考方向相反。

答案:B

7-5-4 **解**:根据一阶电路暂态过程的三要素公式:$u_{0(t)}=U_{c(\infty)}+[U_{e(0+)}-U_{c(\infty)}]e^{-t/\tau}$。

答案:C

第六节

7-6-1 **解**:变压器的容量为视在功率 $S=10\text{kV}\cdot\text{A}$,理想情况下负载上得到的总的有功功率 $P=S\cos\varphi=N\times40$,"N"为所求日光灯数量。

答案:A

7-6-2 **解**:电动机转子的转向与旋转磁场转向一致,旋转磁场的转向由定子电流的相序决定。

答案:C

7-6-3 **解**:三相异步电动机的起动转矩由定子电压和转子电阻决定,与负载无关。

答案:A

7-6-4 **解**:Y-△换接起动方法仅用于正常运行时△连接的电机,起动时由于绕组电压降低,使得电流和起动转矩都是直接起动的$\dfrac{1}{3}$。

答案:D

7-6-5 **解**:根据电动机的功率平衡关系即可分析。

答案:B

7-6-6 **解**:控制电路中电器符号均为设有动作的状态,且同电器采用同标号。读图时一般采用自上而下的顺序。

答案:B

7-6-7 **解**:同上题。

答案:C

7-6-8 **解**:由三相交流异步电动机的转差率关系 $S_N=\dfrac{n_0-n_N}{n_0}\times100\%=0.033$,可以判断电动机为 4 极电机,旋转磁场的转速 $n_0=1500\text{r/min}$,电机空载时转差率应小于额定转差率。

答案:D

7-6-9　**解**：根据继电器工作原理分析，其线圈在控制电路中，接触点分别在主辅电路中。

答案：D

第七节

7-7-1　**解**：二极管为非线性元件。当它正向偏置时，电流-电压关系成指数关系，正向电压一般为0.3V或0.7V左右。

答案：D

7-7-2　**解**：由电路分析可见，该图中的二极管工作于正向偏置，处于导通状态。

答案：D

7-7-3　**解**：首先设二极管处于截止状态，判断二极管的偏置状态。

答案：C

7-7-4　**解**：该电路为桥式的全波整流电路，当 u_2 的瞬时电压为负时，D_1 二极管正向偏置；当 u_2 的瞬时电压为正时，二极管反向偏置。

答案：B

7-7-5　**解**：该电路为全波整流、稳压电路，其中电容C上的电压为直流量，可以认为电容电流为零；整流二极管中的电流为电阻R中电流的1/2。

答案：D

7-7-6　**解**：该电路为二极管桥式全波整流电路，电压关系为 $U_L=0.9U_i$。

答案：C

第八节

7-8-1　**解**：图示电路中三极管发射极电压反偏时为截止状态，$i_B=0$。集电结反偏时为放大状态，$i_c=\beta i_B$；集电结正偏（$V_C<V_B$）时，放大器工作在饱和状态。

答案：A

7-8-2　**解**：分为放大电路的静态和动态两部分电路分析。静态时，要求工作点合适（在线性工作区）。动态时，信号能正常输出。

答案：B

7-8-3　**解**：画放大器的直流通道分析。

答案：A

7-8-4　**解**：画放大器的交流微变等效电路图分析。

答案：C

7-8-5　**解**：考虑放大器输入、输出电阻影响时，可以将电路等效为：

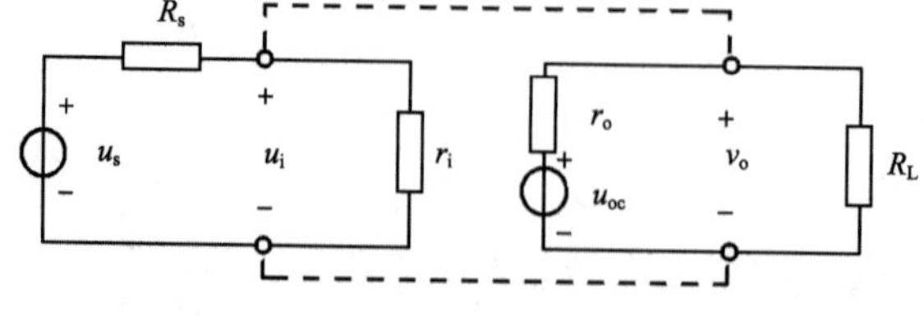

题7-8-5解图

答案：D

7-8-6　**解**：图b）的等效电路与上题的提示电路相仿。R_s 与输入电阻 r_i 串联，输出电阻

r_o与负载电阻串联。

答案:C

第九节

7-9-1 **解**:两极的运算放大电路分析,可以拆成两个单级放大电路分析,负载电阻的大小不影响各级的放大倍数。

答案:C

7-9-2 **解**:用线性运算电路的三个理想条件分析。题中电阻 R 的电流与 R_L 中的电流相同,R 上的电压就是输入电压 u_i。

答案:B

7-9-3 **解**:结合运算放大器的理想化条件,列方程分析即可。

答案:D

7-9-4 **解**:图示为电压比较电路。当 $u_+ > u_-$ 时,输出正饱和值;当 $u_+ < u_-$ 时,输出为负饱和值。

答案:D

7-9-5 **解**:电路为集成运算放大器构成的二级线性放大电路,第一级为积分电路,第二级是电压跟随电路。

答案:A

第十节

7-10-1 **解**:输出信号 y 与输入信号按逻辑分析,当某点电压 $u \geqslant 2.4$V 时,为逻辑"1";当某点电压 $u \leqslant 0.4$V 时,为逻辑"0"。分析时可以设二极管为理想二极管。

答案:A

7-10-2 **解**:当与非门的输入端接 5V 为逻辑"1",接地为逻辑"0",悬空为逻辑"1"处理。

答案:C

7-10-3 **解**:用逻辑代数公式计算。

答案:B

7-10-4 **解**:D 触发器的逻辑关系式为 $Q_{n+1}=D$,$Q_{n+1}=\overline{Q}_n$ 时为计数功能。

答案:A

7-10-5 **解**:根据触发器符号可见输出信号在 CP 脉冲的下降沿动作。

答案:C

7-10-6 **解**:利用 R-S 触发器的功能表分析,输出信号在脉冲 C 的下降沿动作。

答案:B

第八章　信号与信息技术

复习指导

一、考试大纲

7.4　信号与信息

信号；信息；信号的分类；模拟信号与信息；模拟信号描述方法；模拟信号的频谱；模拟信号增强；模拟信号滤波；模拟信号变换；数字信号与信息；数字信号的逻辑编码与逻辑演算；数字信号的数值编码与数值运算。

二、复习指导

目前，信号与信息技术正处于快速发展阶段，内容涉及面广，主要包括：计算机基础知识、电路电子技术、信息通信技术等。但是，就其具体内容来讲，该部分内容正是目前工程技术人员在工作中经常用到的问题。复习的重点是信息技术应用的系统化、规范化。

根据考试大纲的要求，本次复习应该注意以下几项内容：

(一)信息、消息与信号的概念

信息、消息和信号关系是借助于信号形式，传送消息，使受信者从所得到的消息中的获取信息。

(二)信号的分类

要搞清楚信号的概念：什么是确定性信号、随机信号、连续信号和离散信号，特别要搞清楚模拟信号和数字信号形式上的不同，并区别它们的不同表示方法。

(三)模拟信号的描述

在信号分析中不仅可以从时域考虑，而且可以从频域考虑问题。在复习本部分内容时，一般是以正弦函数为基本信号，分析常用的周期和非周期信号的一些基本特性以及信号在系统中的传输问题。抓住基本概念，即周期信号频谱的离散性、谐波性和收敛性。

频谱分析是模拟信号分析的重要方法，也是模拟信号处理的基础，在工程上有着重要的应用。

要了解模拟信号滤波、模拟信号变换、模拟信号识别的知识。

数字电子信号的处理采用了与模拟信号不同的方式，电子器件的工作状态也不同。数字电路的工作信号是二值信号，要用它来表示数并进行数的运算，就必须采取二进制形式表示。复习内容主要包括：

(1)了解数字信号的数制和代码，掌握几种常用进制表示，数制转换、数字信号的常用代码。

(2)搞清楚算术运算和逻辑运算的特点和区别，逻辑函数化简处理后能凸显其内在的逻辑关系，通常还可以使硬件电路结构简单。

(3)了解数字信号的符号信息处理方法,数字信号的存储技术,模拟信号与数字信号的互换知识。

数字信号是信息的编码形式,可以用电子电路或电子计算机方便、快速地对它进行传输、存储和处理。因此,将模拟信号转换为数字信号,或者说用数字信号对模拟信号进行编码,从而将模拟信号问题转化为数字信号问题加以处理,是现代信息技术中的重要内容。

第一节　基本概念

一、信息、消息与信号

信息、消息和信号三者的关系是借助于某种信号形式,传送消息,使受信者从所得到的消息中获取信息。具体可以概括为:

信息(information)——受信者预先不知道的新内容。一般是指人的大脑通过感官直接或间接接收的关于客观事物的存在形式和变化情况。

消息(message) ——信息的物理形式(如声音、文字、图像等),一般是指传递信息的媒体。

信号(signal)——消息的表现形式。信号是运载消息的工具,是可以直接观测到的物理现象(如电、光、声、电磁波等)。通常说"信号是信息的表现形式"。

在现代技术中信息表现为有特点的数据。数据是一种符号代码,用来描述信息。广义地讲,数据包括一切可以用来描述信息的符号体系,如文字、数字、图表、曲线等。在信息工程中,数据是一种以二进制数数字"0"和"1"为代码的符号体系。应当指出,任何符号本身都不具有特定的含义,只有当它们按照确定的编码规则,被用来表示特定的信息时才可以称为数据。因此。正是由此在信息技术中通常认为数据就是信息。信号是具体的,可以对它进行加工、处理和传输;信息和数据都是抽象的,它们都必须借助信号才能得以加工、处理和传送。有些教材中把信息、消息和信号比喻成货物、道路(媒体)和交通工具(车)的关系,即信息是货,媒体是路,信号是车。"货"是利用"车"通过"路"来传送的。

除了人的大脑,任何物理系统都不能直接处理抽象的信息或数据,因此在以计算机为核心的信息系统中以数字信号来表示、存储、处理、传送信息或数据。从这个意义上讲,数字信号是信息的物理代码,亦可称为代码信号。

人们通过两个渠道从信号获取信息:一个是直接观测对象;另一个是通过人与人之间的交流。前者是借助对象发出的真实信号直接获取信息。例如,观测化学反应器中的温度、压力、流量、浓度等信号随时间变化的情况,获取化工过程的信息,观测机械零件和建筑结构中的应力、变形等信号,获取机械或建筑物的状态信息等;后者则用符号对信息进行编码后再以信号的形式传送出去,人们在收到这种编码信号并对它进行必要的翻译处理(译码)之后,间接获取信息,例如书籍、报刊用的是文字符号编码,口头报告、演讲用的是语音信号编码,数字通信系统中使用的是数字信号编码等,它们传递的都是预先编制好的信息。

二、信号的分类

直接观测对象所获取的信号是在现实世界的时间域里进行的,是随时间变化的,称为时间信号;人为生成并按照既定的编码规则对信息进行编码的信号是代码信号。时间信号可以用时间函数、时间曲线或时间序列来描述,在波形图上时间信号是按照时间的变化反映的。但是代码信号与时间信号不同，只能用它的序列式波形图或自身所代表的符号代码序列表示。

图 8-1-1a)表示的是实际观测到的时间信号-压力信号 $p(t)$ 的时间曲线描述形式，它的时间函数描述形式为 $p=f(t)$；

图 8-1-1b)是一个二进制数代码信号的波形表示形式，它的符号代码序列描述形式是 0101100。

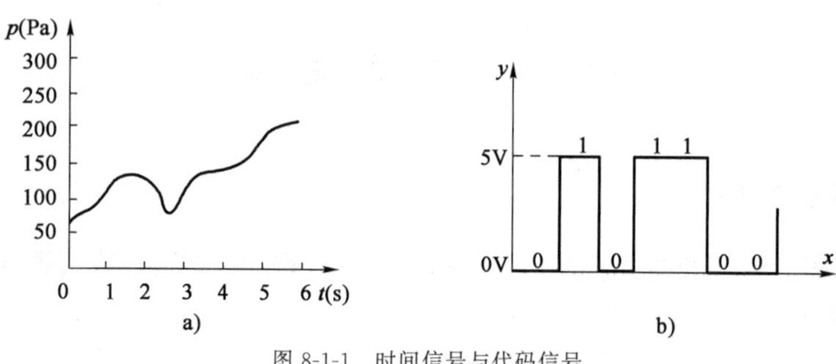

图 8-1-1 时间信号与代码信号

文字、图像、语言、数据等消息的复杂性，导致传送的信号也是多种多样的，但无论信号多么复杂，终归可以表示成时间的函数，因此“信号”与“函数”常常相互通用。信号随时间变化的规律是多种多样的，可以大致分类如下：

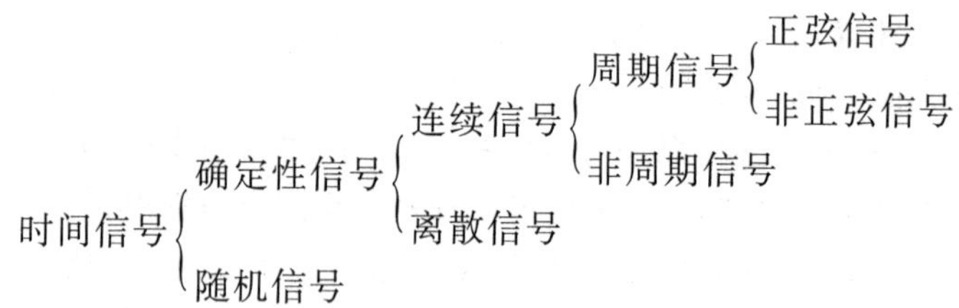

1. 确定性信号和随机信号

按信号是否可以预知划分，可以将其分为确定性信号和随机信号。

(1)确定性信号，是可以表示成确定时间函数的信号，即对于给定的时刻，信号都有一个确定的函数值与之对应，如 $f(t)=2\cos 2\pi t$ 等。

(2)随机信号，是只能知道在某时刻取某一数值的概率，不能表示成确定时间函数的信号。由于随机信号带有“不确定性”和“不可预知性”，通常使用概率统计的方法进行研究。

例如电力系统的运行中难免受到其他信号的干扰，这些干扰信号是不可预知的，是随机出现的，那么该系统中负荷变化的信号属于随机信号。

严格来讲，除了实验室专用设备发出的有规律的信号外，电子信息系统中传输的信号都是随机信号。

2. 连续信号和离散信号

按信号是否是时间连续的函数划分，可以将其分为连续时间信号和离散时间信号，简称连续信号和离散信号。

(1)连续信号，是指在某一时间范围内，对于一切时间值除了有限个间断点外都有确定的函数值的信号 $f(t)$。连续时间信号的时间一定是连续的，但是幅值不一定是连续的(存在有限个间断点)。

连续信号与通常所说的模拟信号不同，模拟信号是幅值随时间连续变化的连续时间信号。由观测所得到的各种原始形态的时间信号(光的、热的、机械的、化学的，等等)都必须转换成电信号(电压或电流信号)之后才能加以处理。通常，由原始时间信号转换而来的电信号就称为模拟信号。

为了保证模拟转换不丢信息，模拟信号的变化规律必须与原始信号相同；而为了便于处理，模拟信号的幅值变化区间又必须控制在一定的范围之内，在电气与信息工程中，模拟信号的幅值范围为0～5V(电压信号)或0～20mA(电流信号)。

从技术上讲，由于"模拟"转换在观测过程中就已实际完成，所以通常指时间信号为模拟信号；而离散的时间信号通常是运用模-数(AD)转换技术变换为数字代码信号之后再加以处理的，所以在电气与信息工程中，实际处理的模拟信号都是连续的时间信号。因此，"模拟信号"一词实际上是指连续时间信号。

(2)离散信号，是指在某些不连续时间(也称离散时刻)定义函数值的信号，在离散时刻以外的时间，信号是无定义的。离散信号的时间不连续，幅值可连续也可不连续。在离散信号中相邻离散时刻的间隔可以是相等的，也可以是不相等的。

为了方便研究或处理信号，人们常常将连续信号进行采样，即只取有代表性的离散时刻的信号数值，抽样后得到离散的采样信号。将幅值量化后并以二进制代码表示的离散信号(也就是时间和幅值均离散的信号)称为数字信号。

数字信号通常是指以二进制数字符号"0"和"1"为代码对信息进行编码的信号。在实际应用中，数字信号是一种电压信号，它通常取0V和+5V两个离散值，这两个具体的离散值分别用来表示两个抽象的代码"0"和"1"。一个数字信号序列表示一串代码，只要确定某种编码规则，这种数字代码串就可以用来对任何信息进行编码。

模拟信号具体、直观，便于人的理解和运用；数字信号则便于计算机处理。所以，在实际应用中经常将两者互相转换，以发挥各自的优点。

模拟信号数字化的过程如图8-1-2所示。时间、幅值均连续的模拟信号如图8-1-2a)所示，经过等间距采样变成时间离散、幅值连续的抽样信号如图8-1-2b)所示，再经过量化后的离散信号如图8-1-2c)所示，以二进制对量化的幅度编码得到的数字信号如图8-1-2d)所示。

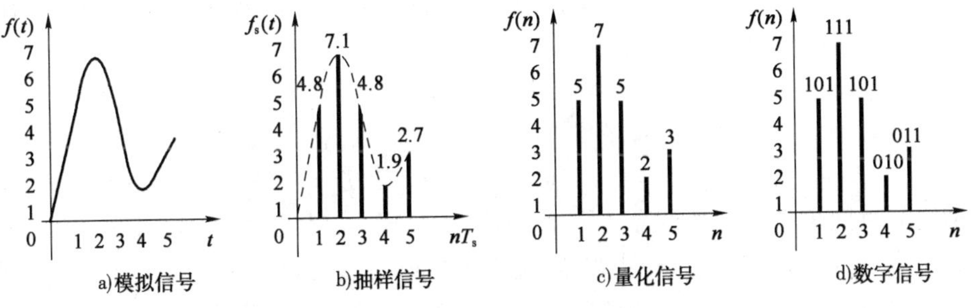

图8-1-2 模拟信号数字化的过程

3.周期信号和非周期信号

按信号是否具有重复性，可以将其划分为周期信号和非周期信号。

(1)周期信号，是按一定时间间隔 T 或 N 重复着某一变化规律的连续或离散信号。最典型的连续周期信号是正弦函数的信号。除正弦函数信号以外的连续周期函数信号称为非正弦周期信号。

连续周期信号 $f(t)$ 满足

$$f(t)=f(t+mT) \qquad (m=0,\pm 1,\pm 2,\cdots) \tag{8-1-1}$$

时间间隔 T 称为最小正周期，简称连续周期信号的周期。

离散周期信号 $f(k)$ 满足

$$f(k)=f(k+mN) \qquad (m=0,\pm1,\pm2,\cdots) \tag{8-1-2}$$

时间间隔 N 称为最小正周期,简称离散周期信号的周期。

(2)非周期信号,是不满足周期信号特性的、不具有重复性的连续或离散信号。当周期信号的周期为无穷大时,周期信号就变成了非周期信号。

4.采样信号

按等时间间隔读取连续信号某一时刻的数值叫做采样(或抽样),采样所得到的信号称为采样(抽样)信号。显然,采样信号是一种离散信号,它是连续信号的离散化形式。或者说,通过采样,连续信号被转换为离散信号。

采样的更深一层意义在于通过模拟-数字转换装置,可以将采样信号进一步转换为数字描述形式,并进而采用数值分析与计算方法高效地处理模拟信号,例如,采用数值运算方法实现模拟信号的放大、变换、滤波等(见图 8-1-3)。

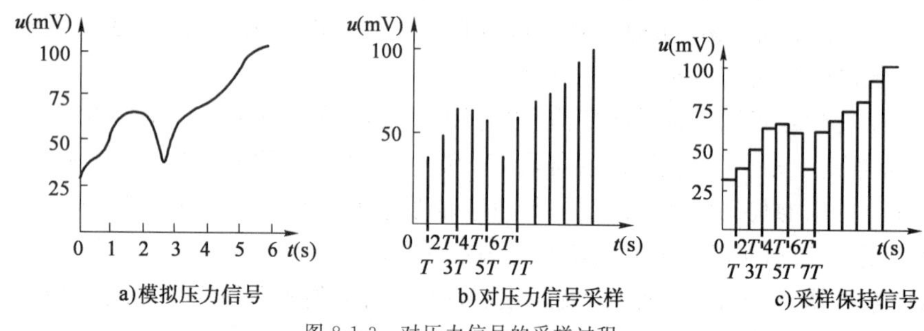

图 8-1-3 对压力信号的采样过程

图 8-1-3b)的电压信号是图 8-1-3a)压力信号的采样信号。不难看出,在每个采样点上,采样信号的值与连续信号在该点上的瞬间值相等,而在整个采样区间里,采样信号的变化规律与连续信号相同。

由于如图 8-1-3b)所示的离散时间信号是如图 8-1-3a)所示的连续时间信号的采样信号,所以,若连续时间信号的连续时间函数描述为

$$u=f(t)$$

则该离散时间信号的离散时间序列描述形式为

$$u^*=\{f(0),f(T),f(2T),f(3T),\cdots,f(nT),f[(n+1)T],\cdots\} \tag{8-1-3}$$

所谓离散时间信号是指只在特定的时间点上才出现的信号。例如图 8-1-3b)所示的信号,它只在时间点 0、T、$2T$、$3T$、$4T$、…上出现,而在这些时间点之间的任何瞬间,信号的值是没有定义的。所以,在离散时间信号的描述中,时间轴上是不能连续取值的。

令采样的时间间隔为采样周期 T,每秒采样次数为采样频率 f,那么采样频率越高,采样信号越接近原来的连续信号。但是过于频繁的采样,势必会降低系统的整体工作效率。按照著名的采样定理,取采样频率为信号中最高谐波频率的 2 倍以上时,采样信号即可保留原始信号的全部信息。在实际应用中,往往将采样得到的每一个瞬间信号在其采样周期内予以保持,生成所谓的采样保持信号如图 8-1-3c)所示。采样保持信号是一种特殊信号形式,它兼有离散和连续的双重性质,在数字控制系统中有着广泛应用。

三、模拟信号与信息

模拟信号是通过观测,直接从对象获取的信号。模拟信号是连续的时间信号,它提供对象

原始形态的信息。

在时间域里，它的瞬间量值表示对象的状态信息，比如某一时刻对象中的温度有多高，压力是多强；它随时间变化的情况提供对象的过程信息，比如对象中的温度或压力是在增加还是在减小，它们以什么样的规律在变化等。通过时间函数的描述，可以借助相关的数学运算对模拟信号进行各种处理和变换，实现信息分析、综合、评价等各种复杂的处理。

在频率域里，模拟信号是由诸多频率不同、大小不同、相位不同的信号叠加组成的，具有自身特定的频谱结构。所以从频域的角度看，信息被装载于模拟信号的频谱结构之中，通过频域分析可以从中提取更加丰富、更加细微的信息，进行更为简洁、更为精细的信息分析和处理。

(一)常用模拟信号的描述

在信号分析中，常用一些基本函数表示复杂信号。

1. 直流信号

直流信号定义为

$$f(t) = A \qquad (-\infty < t < \infty) \tag{8-1-4}$$

即在全时间域上等于恒值的信号，波形如图 8-1-4 所示。

2. 正弦信号

如图 8-1-5 所示为大家所熟知的正弦信号，表示为

$$f(t) = A\sin(\omega t + \varphi) \tag{8-1-5}$$

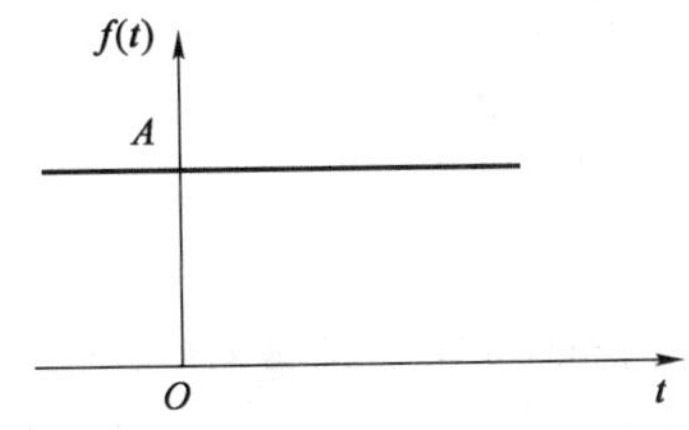

图 8-1-4　直流信号

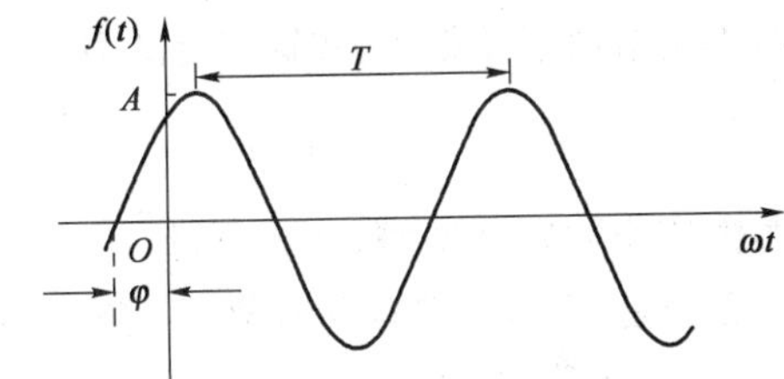

图 8-1-5　正弦信号

3. 单位阶跃信号

单位阶跃信号用 $\varepsilon(t)$ 表示，其定义为

$$\varepsilon(t) = \begin{cases} 1 & (t > 0) \\ 0 & (t < 0) \end{cases} \tag{8-1-6}$$

该函数在 $t=0$ 处发生跃变，数值 1 为阶跃的幅度，若阶跃幅度为 A，则可记为 $A\varepsilon(t)$。延迟 t_0 后发生跃变的单位阶跃函数可表示为

$$\varepsilon(t - t_0) = \begin{cases} 1 & (t > t_0) \\ 0 & (t < t_0) \end{cases} \tag{8-1-7}$$

在负时间域幅值恒定为 1，而在 $t=0$ 发生跃变到零的阶跃信号可表示为

$$\varepsilon(-t) = \begin{cases} 1 & (t < 0) \\ 0 & (t > 0) \end{cases} \tag{8-1-8}$$

$\varepsilon(t)$、$\varepsilon(t-t_0)$和 $\varepsilon(-t)$的波形分别如图 8-1-6 所示。

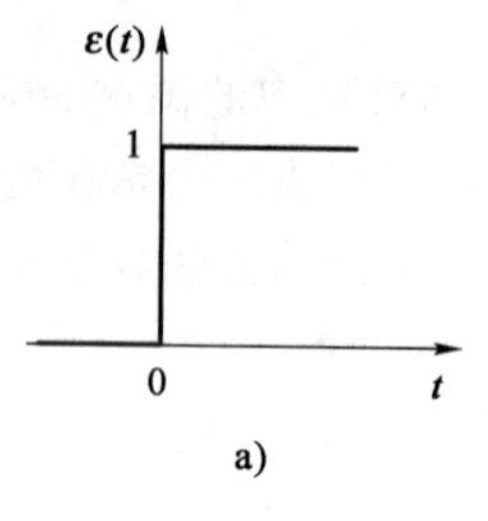

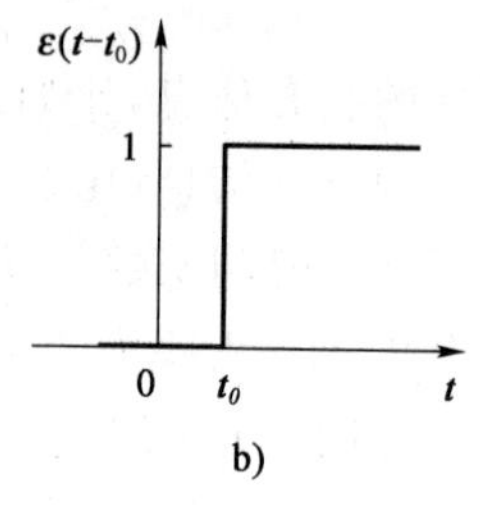

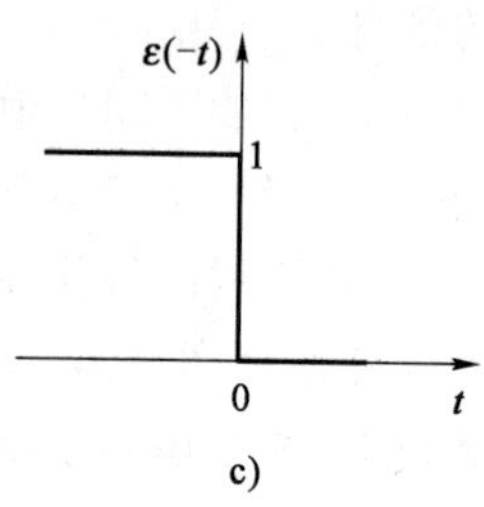

图 8-1-6　波形图

4. 斜坡信号

斜坡信号常用 $r(t)$ 表示，其定义为

$$r(t)=\begin{cases} t & (t \geqslant 0) \\ 0 & (t<0) \end{cases} \tag{8-1-9}$$

也可以借助阶跃信号简洁地表示为

$$r(t)=t\varepsilon(t) \tag{8-1-10}$$

斜坡信号的波形如图 8-1-7 所示。

5. 实指数信号

常用的实指数信号是单边的，其定义为

$$f(t)=Ae^{-\alpha t} \qquad (\alpha>0, t>0) \tag{8-1-11}$$

实指数信号的波形如图 8-1-8 所示。

要注意的是，引入单位阶跃函数后，信号 $f(t)$ 和 $f(t)\varepsilon(t)$ 的波形有时是不同的。例如，信号 e^{-t} 和 $e^{-t}\varepsilon(t)$ 的波形如图 8-1-9 所示，图 8-1-9a) 在整个时间域均按 e^{-t} 规律变化，而图 8-1-9b) 仅在正时间域按规律 e^{-t} 变化，它在负时间域全为零。

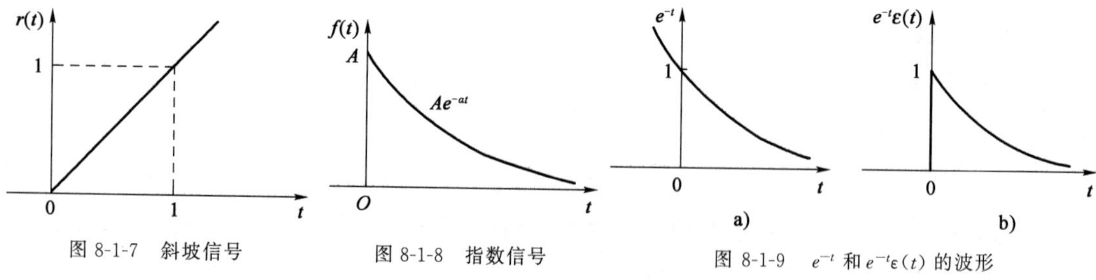

图 8-1-7　斜坡信号　　图 8-1-8　指数信号　　图 8-1-9　e^{-t} 和 $e^{-t}\varepsilon(t)$ 的波形

6. 复指数信号

设 α 为任意实数，则复指数信号可表示为

$$f(t)=Ae^{(\alpha+j\omega)t} \tag{8-1-12}$$

式中，若 $\alpha=0$，则 $f(t)$ 成为虚指数信号；若 $\omega=0$，则 $f(t)$ 成为实指数信号。根据欧拉公式，复指数信号可以表示为

$$f(t)=Ae^{\alpha t}(\cos\omega t+j\sin\omega t) \tag{8-1-13}$$

$\alpha<0$，$t\geqslant 0$ 时，实部和虚部波形如图 8-1-10 所示。

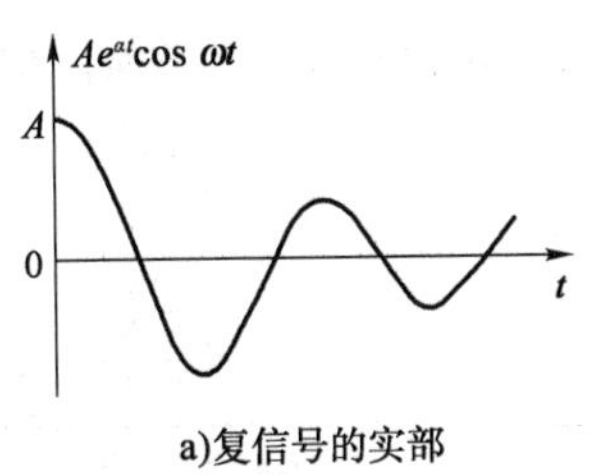

a)复信号的实部

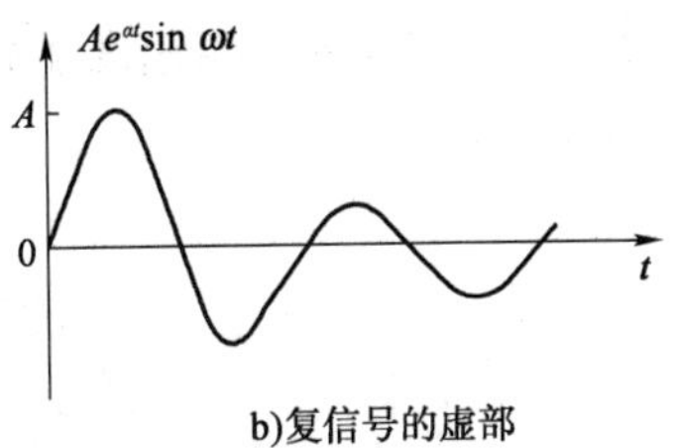

b)复信号的虚部

图 8-1-10　复指数信号

（二）模拟信号的时域处理

在信号的时域分析中，复杂信号可以通过对简单信号进行加（减）、延时、反转、尺度展缩、微分、积分等运算获得。

1. 相加与相乘

设有信号 $f_1(t)=\varepsilon(t)$，$f_2(t)=-\varepsilon(t-t_0)$，则两者之和为 $f(t)=\varepsilon(t)-\varepsilon(t-t_0)$。

$f(t)$ 在任意时刻的值是两信号在该时刻值的和，$f(t)$ 的波形如图 8-1-11 所示。

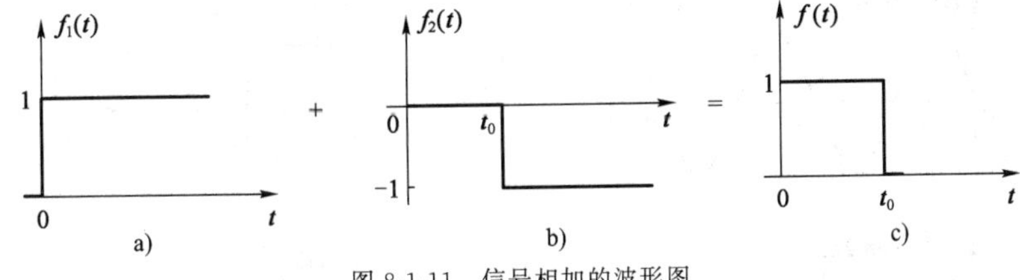

图 8-1-11　信号相加的波形图

信号 $f_1(t)$ 和 $f_2(t)$ 相乘所得的新函数 $f(t)=f_1(t)f_2(t)$ 在任意时刻的值等于两个信号在该时刻的值之积，图 8-1-12 为信号相乘的波形。

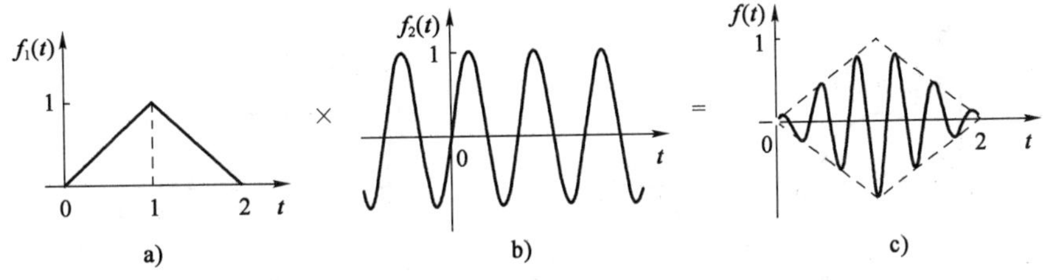

图 8-1-12　信号相乘后的波形图

2. 反转与延时

将信号 $f_1(t)$ 的自变量 t 换为 $-t$，可得到另一个信号 $f_1(-t)$，这称为信号的反转。作图时将 $f_1(t)$ 的波形以纵坐标为轴反转 180°即成为 $f_1(-t)$，图 8-1-13a) 是其示意图。

将信号 $f_2(t)$ 的自变量 t 换为 $(t\pm t_0)$，t_0 为正的实常数，则可得一个新的信号 $f_2(t\pm t_0)$。这就意味着把 $f(t)$的波形沿时间轴整体平移（延时）t_0 个单位，$f_2(t+t_0)$ 表示向右平移 t_0 个单位，$f(t-t_0)$ 表示向左平移 t_0 个单位。图 8-1-13b)为其示意图。

3. 压缩与扩展

若将信号 $f(t)$ 的自变量 t 换为 at（a 为正实数），则信号 $f(\alpha t)$ 将在时间尺度上压缩或扩展，这称为信号的尺度变换。若 $0<\alpha<1$，就意味着原信号从原点沿 t 轴扩展；若 $\alpha>1$，就意味着原信号沿 t 轴压缩（幅值不变）。如图 8-1-14 中 $f(t)$和 $x(t)$ 所示。

信号的尺度展缩应用在信息的存储、压缩和解压缩技术方面。如 $f(t)$是已录制好的音乐信号磁带，则 $f(2t)$ 是以原声的 2 倍速度播放，$f\left(\frac{t}{2}\right)$ 是将原声降低一半速度播放。

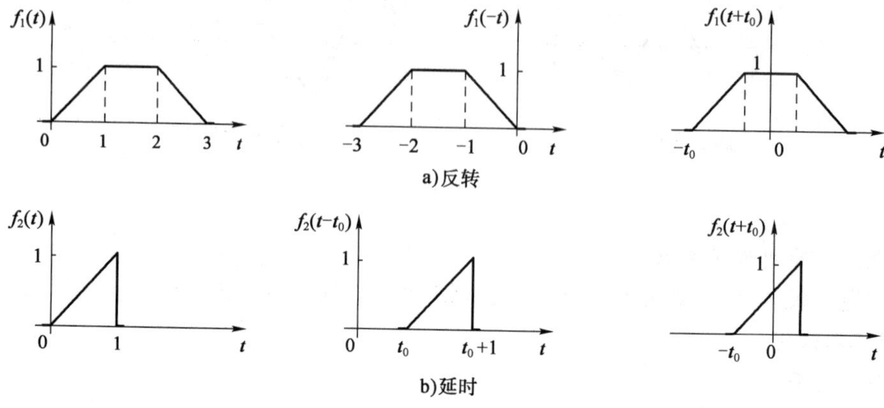

图 8-1-13　信号反转与延时后波形图

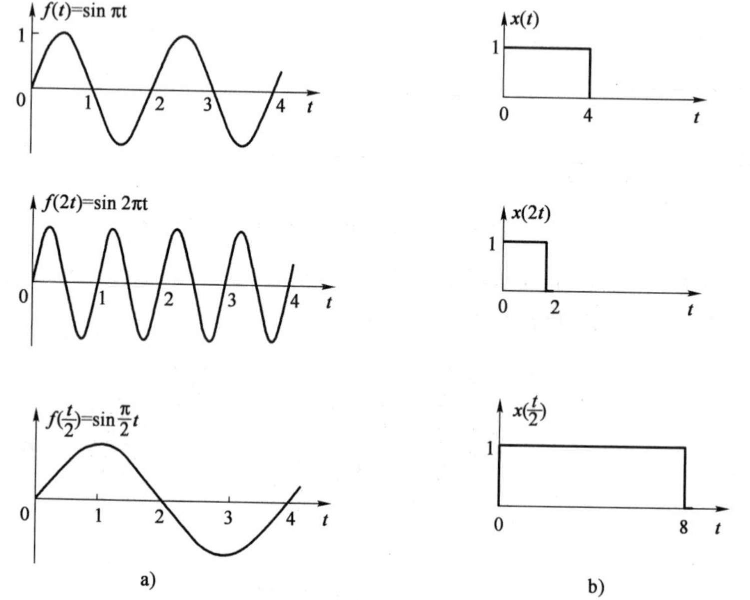

图 8-1-14　信号压缩与扩展后的波形图

4. 微分与积分

设信号 $f(t)$ 的微分表示为

$$y(t)=\frac{\mathrm{d}f(t)}{\mathrm{d}t}=f'(t)=f^{(1)}(t) \tag{8-1-14}$$

$f(t)$ 的积分表示为

$$y(t)=\int_{-\infty}^{t}f(\tau)\mathrm{d}\tau=f^{(-1)}(t) \tag{8-1-15}$$

式中 τ 为积分变量，以区别于积分上限 t。

对于斜坡函数，其导数为阶跃函数，即 $r'(t)=\varepsilon(t)$；反之，单位阶跃函数的积分为斜坡函数，即

$$r(t)=\int_{-\infty}^{t}\varepsilon(\tau)\mathrm{d}\tau=t\varepsilon(t) \qquad (8\text{-}1\text{-}16)$$

例如,对于如图 8-1-15 所示信号 $f(t)$,可表示为

$$f(t)=\begin{cases}\dfrac{1}{2}t+1 & (-2\leqslant t\leqslant 0)\\ -\dfrac{1}{2}t+1 & (0\leqslant t\leqslant 2)\end{cases} \qquad (8\text{-}1\text{-}17)$$

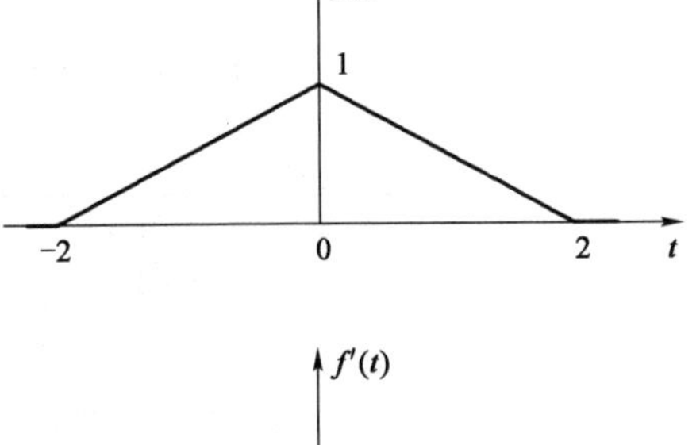

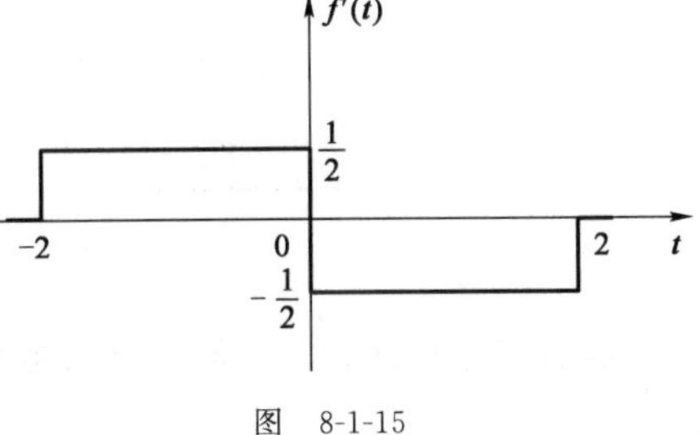

图 8-1-15

5. 单位冲激函数

冲激函数的提出有着广泛的物理基础。RC 串联电路接通直流电源的情形。如图 8-1-16a)所示,设电容电压初始状态为零,当 $t=0$ 时电路接通,充电电流从起始值开始按指数规律下降,即

$$i_c(t)=\frac{1}{R}e^{-\frac{t}{rc}} \qquad (t>0) \qquad (8\text{-}1\text{-}18)$$

若电路中 $R\to 0$,则充电时间常数 $\tau=RC=0$,这意味着在 $t=0$ 瞬间电源以无穷大电流给电容充电,即

$$i_c(t)=\begin{cases}\infty & (t=0)\\ 0 & (t\neq 0)\end{cases} \qquad (8\text{-}1\text{-}19)$$

电容上的电荷应是电流的积分值,即

$$q=\int_{-\infty}^{\infty}i_c\mathrm{d}t=CU_s=1\mathrm{C} \qquad (8\text{-}1\text{-}20)$$

这 1C 的电荷恰是图 8-1-16b)中 i_c 曲线下的面积。

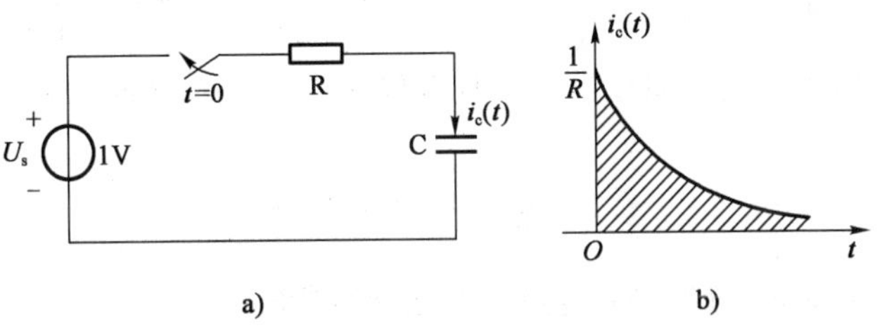

图 8-1-16 电容充电波形

再观察图 8-1-17 中的函数 $f(t)$,当其缓升宽度 $\tau\to 0$ 时,它就变成了阶跃信号 $\varepsilon(t)$;而对 $f(t)$ 求导后,则变为高度为 $\frac{1}{\tau}$、宽度为 τ 的矩形脉冲,即 $f'(t)=f_\tau(t)$,注意 $f_\tau(t)$ 的面积为 1。当 $\tau\to 0$ 时 $f_\tau(t)$ 的高度变为无穷大,但此面积仍为 1,此时变为冲激函数,用 $\delta(t)$ 表示。对应来看,即有 $\varepsilon'(t)=\delta(t)$。可见,$\delta(t)$ 只在 $t=0$ 出现,其余时间均为零。

由上可知,单位冲激函数 $\delta(t)$ 可以看作是一个宽度为无穷小,高度为无穷大,但面积为 1 的极窄矩形脉冲。该函数是一个不同于一般信号的奇异函数,其定义为

$$\begin{cases}\delta(t)=0 & (t\neq 0)\\ \int_{-\infty}^{0}\delta(t)\mathrm{d}t=1\end{cases} \qquad (8\text{-}1\text{-}21)$$

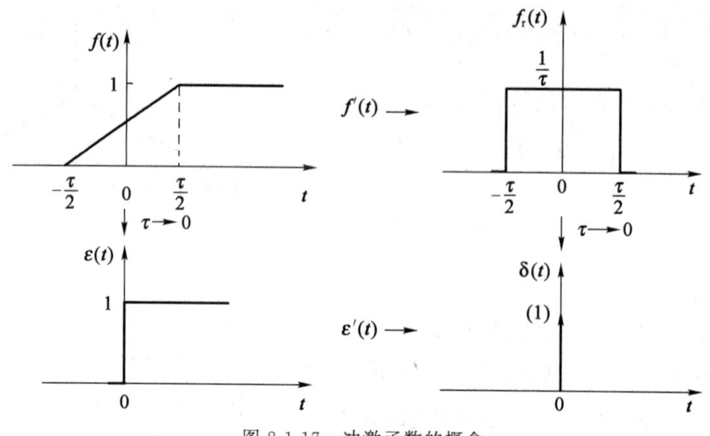

图 8-1-17 冲激函数的概念

上述定义表明，$\delta(t)$ 是在 $t=0$ 瞬间出现又立即消失的信号，且幅值为无限大；在 $t\neq 0$ 处，它始终为零，而积分 $\int_{-\infty}^{\infty}\delta(t)\mathrm{d}t=1$ 是该函数的面积，通常称为 $\delta(t)$ 的强度。强度为 A 的冲激信号可记为 $A\delta(t)$，延迟 t_0 出现的冲激信号可记为 $A\delta(t-t_0)$，它们的波形如图 8-1-18 所示，符号(A)表示其强度。

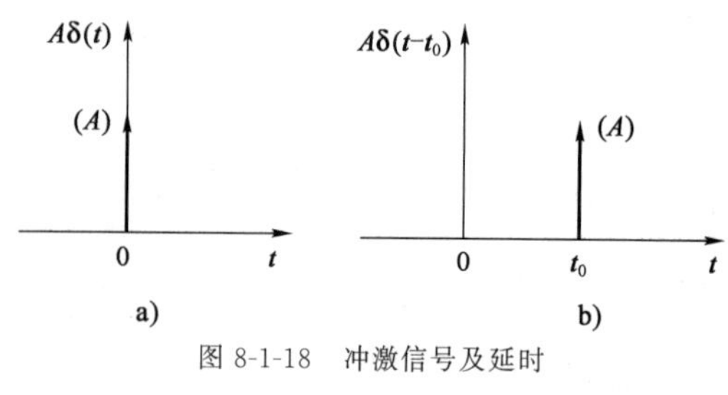

图 8-1-18 冲激信号及延时

根据 $\delta(t)$ 的定义，可以建立单位阶跃函数与单位冲击函数的确切关系，由于 $\delta(t)$ 只在 $t=0$ 时刻存在，所以

$$\int_{-\infty}^{\infty}\delta(t)\mathrm{d}t=\int_{0-}^{0+}\delta(t)\mathrm{d}t=1 \quad (8\text{-}1\text{-}22)$$

则
$$\int_{-\infty}^{\infty}\delta(t)\mathrm{d}t=\begin{cases}1 & (t>0)\\ 0 & (t<0)\end{cases} \quad (8\text{-}1\text{-}23)$$

上式表明：单位冲激信号的积分为单位阶跃信号；反过来，单位阶跃信号的导数应为单位冲激信号，即

$$\delta(t)=\frac{\mathrm{d}\varepsilon(t)}{\mathrm{d}t} \quad (8\text{-}1\text{-}24)$$

在引入 $\delta(t)$ 的前提下，函数在不连续点处也有导数值。

【例 8-1-1】 已知 $f(t)$ 的波形如图 a)所示，试求其一阶导数并画出波形。

解 首先用 $\varepsilon(t)$ 的组合表示 $f(t)$，即 $f(t)=\varepsilon(t)+\varepsilon(t-t_1)-2\varepsilon(t-t_2)$

对上式求导，得 $f'(t)=\delta(t)+\delta(t-t_1)-2\delta(t-t_2)$

其波形如图 b)所示。

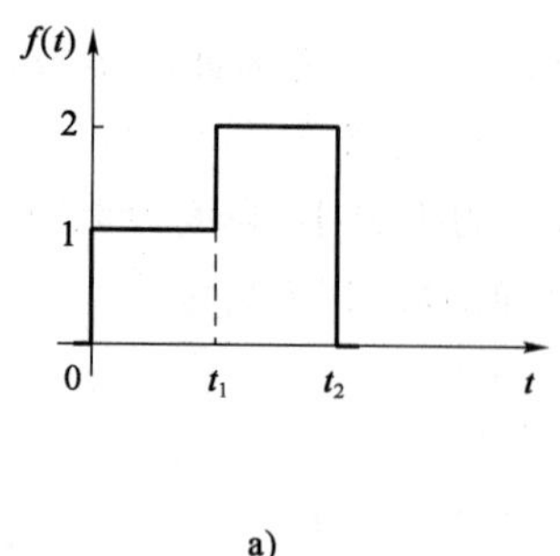

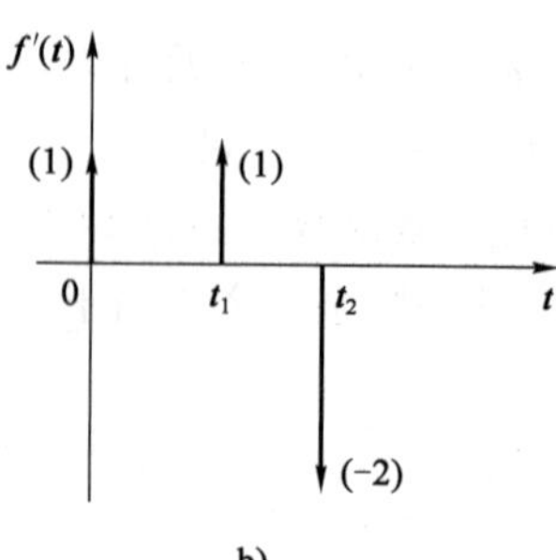

例 8-1-1 图

【例 8-1-2】 给出如图 a)所示非周期信号的时域描述形式：

A. $u(t)=10\times1(t-3)-10\times1(t-6)$V

B. $u(t)=3\times1(t-3)-10\times1(t-6)$V

C. $u(t)=3\times1(t-3)-6\times1(t-6)$V

D. $u(t)=10\times1(t-3)-1(t-6)$V

解 将图 a)中的信号 $u(t)$分解为图 b)所示信号 $u_1(t)$和图 c)所示信号 $u_2(t)$的叠加 $u(t)=u_1(t)+u_2(t)$。

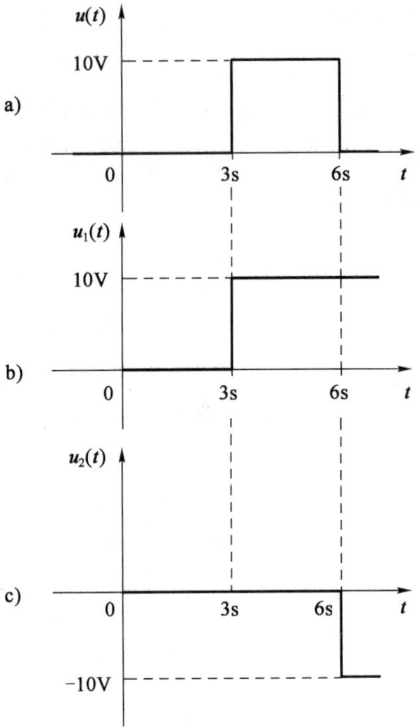

例 8-1-2 图

答案：A

(三)模拟信号的频谱

本部分以正弦函数(余弦函数亦统称为正弦函数)为基本信号，分析常用的周期和非周期信号的一些基本特性以及信号在系统中的传输问题。由数学上的欧拉公式可知

$$\left.\begin{aligned}\sin\omega t&=\frac{1}{2j}(e^{j\omega t}-e^{-j\omega t})\\ \cos\omega t&=\frac{1}{2}(e^{j\omega t}+e^{-j\omega t})\end{aligned}\right\}\qquad(8\text{-}1\text{-}25)$$

可把虚指数函数 $e^{j\omega t}$ 作为基本信号，将任意周期信号和非周期信号分解为一系列虚指数函数的和。分解工具是傅里叶级数(针对周期信号)和傅里叶积分(针对非周期信号)。利用信号的正弦分解思想，系统的响应可看作各不同频率正弦信号产生响应的叠加。由于在信号分析中所用的独立变量是频率，故称为频域分析。

1. 周期信号的频谱

周期信号是定义在$(-\infty,\infty)$区间内，每隔一定周期 T 按相同规律重复变化的信号，它们一般可表示为

$$f(t)=f(t+mT)\qquad(m=0,\pm1,\pm2,\cdots)\qquad(8\text{-}1\text{-}26)$$

当周期信号 $f(t)$ 满足狄里赫利条件时，则可用傅里叶级数表示为三角函数

$$f(t)=a_0+\sum_{n=1}^{\infty}(a_n\cos n\omega_1 t+b_n\sin n\omega_1 t)\qquad(8\text{-}1\text{-}27)$$

式中，$\omega_1=\frac{2\pi}{T}$ 称为 $f(t)$ 的基波角频率，$n\omega_1$ 称为 n 次谐波的频率；a_0 为 $f(t)$ 的直流分量，a_n 和 b_n 分别为各余弦分量和正弦分量的幅度。当函数给定以后，系数 a_0、a_n 和 b_n 可以由下式确定

$$\left.\begin{aligned}a_0&=\frac{1}{T}\int_0^T f(t)\mathrm{d}t\\ a_n&=\frac{2}{T}\int_0^T f(t)\cos n\omega t\,\mathrm{d}t\\ b_n&=\frac{2}{T}\int_0^T f(t)\sin n\omega t\,\mathrm{d}t\end{aligned}\right\}\qquad(8\text{-}1\text{-}28)$$

傅里叶级数还可以写成

$$f(t)=A_0+\sum_{n=1}^{\infty}A_n\cos(n\omega_1 t+\varphi_n) \tag{8-1-29}$$

这里

$$A_n = \sqrt{a_n^2+b_n^2} \qquad \varphi_n = -\arctan\frac{b_n}{a_n} \tag{8-1-30}$$

可见,模拟信号为一个直流信号和一系列正弦信号的叠加。由于直流信号可表示为0次谐波信号,$A_n\cos(n\omega_1 t+\varphi_n)$ 称为函数 $f(t)$ 的第 n 次谐波分量,这种将一个周期函数展开成一系列谐波之和的傅里叶级数的方法叫做谐波分析。谐波分析中,我们认为模拟信号是由一系列谐波信号叠加而成的。我们用典型模拟信号分析:不同周期信号的谐波构成情况是不相同的,例如如图 8-1-19 所示的几种常见周期信号经过傅里叶级数分解后的谐波分量描述形式分别为

$$u_1(t) = \frac{4U_{1m}}{\pi}\left(\frac{1}{2}-\frac{1}{3}\cos2\omega t-\frac{1}{15}\cos4\omega t-\cdots\right) \tag{8-1-31}$$

$$u_2(t) = \frac{4U_{2m}}{\pi}(\sin\omega t+\frac{1}{3}\sin3\omega t+\frac{1}{5}\sin5\omega t+\cdots) \tag{8-1-32}$$

$$u_3(t) = U_{3m}\left[\frac{1}{2}-\frac{1}{\pi}\left(\sin\omega t+\frac{1}{2}\sin2\omega t+\frac{1}{3}\sin3\omega t+\cdots\right)\right] \tag{8-1-33}$$

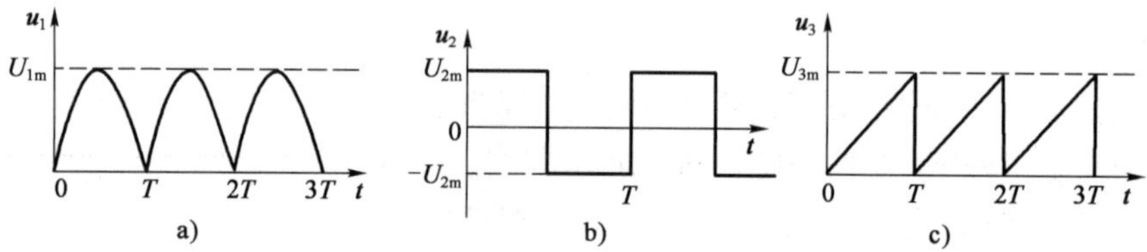

图 8-1-19 典型非正弦信号的时域波形图

显然,周期信号的波形不同,其谐波组成的成分情况也不同。信号的谐波组成情况通常用频谱的形式来表示。

(1)周期信号波形的谐波叠加

图 8-1-20 表示了图 8-1-19b)信号谐波叠加的情况。其中,图 8-1-20b)、c)表示的是 1、3 次谐波叠加的波形与原始方波波形的比较;图 8-1-20c)表示的是 1、3、5 次谐波叠加后的波形与原始方波的比较。不难看出,随着更多谐波成分的加入,叠加后的波形将越来越趋近于原始的方波波形。

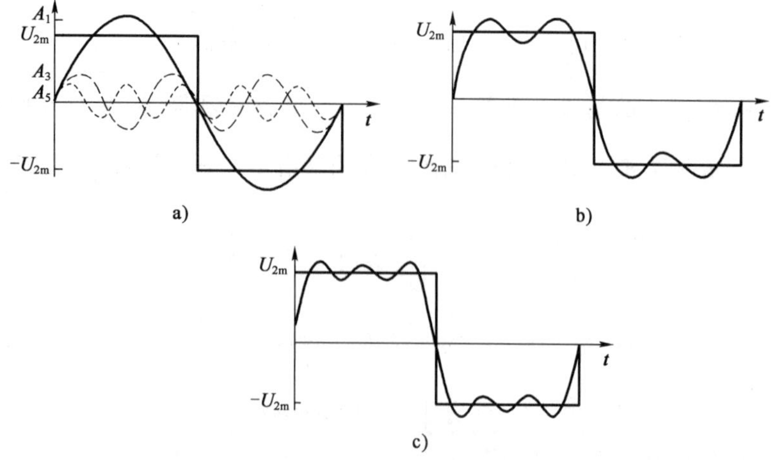

图 8-1-20 方波信号的谐波叠加

(2)周期信号的频谱

仔细考查式(8-1-32)可以发现:随着谐波次数 k 的增加,方波信号各个谐波的幅值按照 $\frac{4}{k\pi}$ 的规律衰减(其中,$k=1,3,5,7,\cdots$),而它们的初相位却保持 0°不变。将方波信号谐波成分的这种特性用图形的形式表达出来,就形成了如图 8-1-21 所示的谱线形式。这种表示方波信号性质的谱线称为频谱。图 8-1-21a)所表示的谐波幅值谱线随频率的分布状况称为幅度频谱;图 8-1-21b)则称为相位频谱,它表示谐波的初相与频率的关系。谱线顶点的连线称为频谱的包络线(图中以虚线表示),它形象地表示了频谱的分布状况。借助数学工具分析可知,周期信号频谱的谱线只出现在周期信号频率 ω 整数倍的地方,是离散的频谱。周期信号的幅度频谱随着谐波次数的增高而迅速减小。

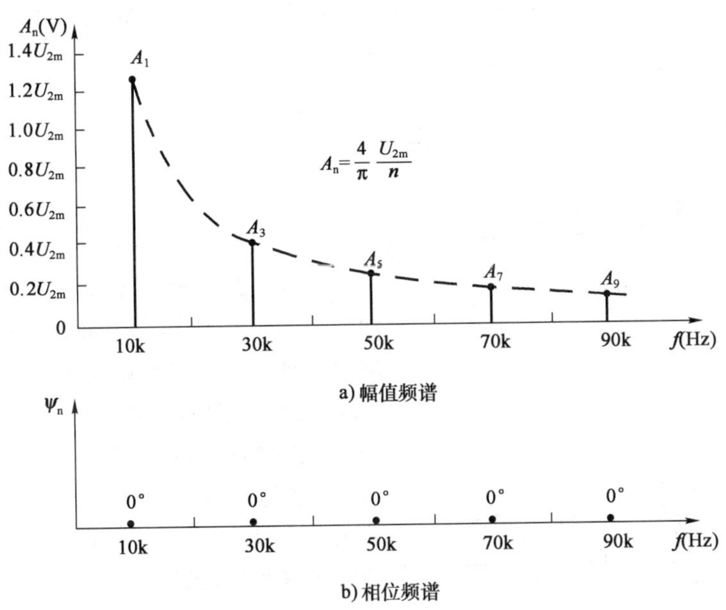

图 8-1-21 方波信号的频谱

【例 8-1-3】 设周期信号 $u(t)$ 的幅值频谱如图所示,则该信号:

A. 是一个离散时间信号

B. 是一个连续时间信号

C. 在任意瞬间均取正值

D. 最大瞬时值为 1.5V

U(V) 1.5 1 0.9 0.4 0.1 0 1 2 5 7 f(kHz)

例 8-1-3 图

解 周期信号的幅值频谱是离散且收敛的。这个周期信号一定是时间上的连续信号。

本题给出的图形是周期信号的频谱图。频谱图是非正弦信号中不同正弦信号分量的幅值按频率变化排列的图形,其大小是表示各次谐波分量的幅值,用正值表示。例如本题频谱图中出现的 1.5V 对应于 1kHz 的正弦信号分量的幅值,而不是这个周期信号的幅值。因此本题选项 C 或 D 都是错误的。

答案:B

【例 8-1-4】 求如图所示周期信号 $f(t)$ 的傅里叶级数展开式,并画出频谱图。

解 $f(t)$在第一个周期内的表达式为

$$\begin{cases} f(t)=U_{\mathrm{m}} & 0\leqslant t\leqslant \dfrac{T}{2} \\ f(t)=-U_{\mathrm{m}} & \dfrac{T}{2}\leqslant t\leqslant T \end{cases}$$

例 8-1-4 图 矩形波

根据式(8-1-28)求得所需要的系数为

$$a_n=\frac{1}{T}\int_0^T f(t)\mathrm{d}t=0$$

$$a_k=\frac{1}{\pi}\int_0^{2\pi} f(t)\cos(k\omega_1 t)\mathrm{d}(\omega_1 t)=\frac{2U_{\mathrm{m}}}{\pi}\int_0^{\pi}\cos(k\omega_1 t)\mathrm{d}(\omega_1 t)=0$$

$$b_k=\frac{1}{\pi}\int_0^{2\pi} f(t)\sin(k\omega_1 t)\mathrm{d}(\omega_1 t)=\frac{2U_{\mathrm{m}}}{k\pi}[1-\cos(k\pi)]$$

当 k 为偶数时，$\cos(k\pi)=1, b_k=0$

当 k 为奇数时，$\cos(k\pi)=-1, b_k=\dfrac{4U_{\mathrm{m}}}{k\pi}$

由此求得

$$f(t)=\frac{4U_{\mathrm{m}}}{\pi}\left[\sin(\omega_1 t)+\frac{1}{3}\sin(3\omega_1 t)+\frac{1}{5}\sin(5\omega_1 t)+\cdots\right]$$

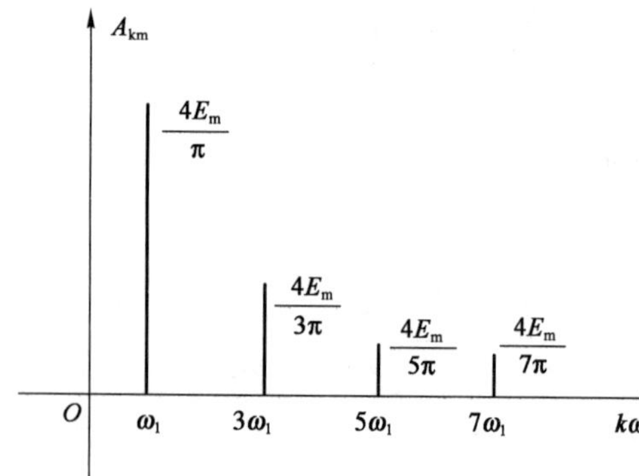

图 8-1-22 矩形波函数的频谱图

图 8-1-22 是矩形波函数的频谱图，由上例方波信号的频谱图中，每根垂直线称为谱线，其所在频率位置 $n\omega_1$ 为该次谐波的角频率。每根谱线的高度为该次谐波的振幅值。观察可知，周期信号的振幅谱具有下列特点：

①离散性。频谱图由频率离散的谱线组成，每根谱线代表一个谐波分量。这样的频谱称为不连续频谱或离散频谱。

②谐波性。谱中的谱线只能在基波频率 ω_1 的整数倍频率上出现。

③收敛性。频谱中各谱线的高度，随谐波次数的增高而逐渐减小。当谐波次数无限增多时，谐波分量的振幅趋于无穷小。

这些特点虽然是从具体的信号得出的，但除了少数特例外，许多信号的频谱都具有这些特点。

【例 8-1-5】 若某周期信号的一次谐波分量为 $5\sin10^3 t\mathrm{V}$，则它的三次谐波分量可表示为：

A. $U\sin3\times10^3 t, U>5\mathrm{V}$　　B. $U\sin3\times10^3 t, U<5\mathrm{V}$

C. $U\sin10^6 t, U>5\mathrm{V}$　　D. $U\sin10^6 t, U<5\mathrm{V}$

解 周期信号频谱是离散的频谱，信号的幅度随谐波次数的增高而减小。针对本题情况可知该周期信号的一次谐波分量为：

$u_1=U_{1\mathrm{m}}\sin\omega_1 t=5\sin10^3 t$

$U_{1\mathrm{m}}=5\mathrm{V}, \omega_1=10^3$

$u_3=U_{3\mathrm{m}}\sin3\omega t$

$\omega_3=3\omega_1=3\times10^3$

$U_{3m}<U_{1m}$

答案:B、C(因功率因数$|\lambda|_{C_1}|=|\lambda|_{C_2}|$,所以这两种方案均可采用)

2.非周期信号的频谱

非周期信号是模拟信号的普遍形式,所以本节所讨论的非周期信号描述问题实质上是模拟信号描述的一般性问题。

从直观的角度看,非周期信号可以定义为周期 $T\to\infty$(或频率 $f=0$)的周期信号,即:当周期信号的周期趋向无穷大时,这个周期信号就转化成了非周期信号。当周期 T 趋向无穷大时,各次谐波之间的谱线距离趋于消失,信号的频谱也从离散形式变成了连续形式。因此在非周期信号的分析中,可以先把这种非周期函数看作一种周期函数,在周期趋于无限大的条件下,求出其极限形式的傅氏级数展开式,就得到了表示这种非周期函数的傅氏积分公式。得到

$$f(t)=\sum_{k=-\infty}^{\infty}c_k e^{jk\omega_1 t} \tag{8-1-34}$$

其中
$$c_k=\frac{1}{T}\int_{-\frac{T}{2}}^{\frac{T}{2}}f(t)e^{-jk\omega_1 t}\mathrm{d}t \qquad (k=0,\pm1,\pm2\cdots) \tag{8-1-35}$$

c_k 的频谱是 $k\omega_1$ 的函数,且为线状的,其相邻间隔(频率差)为

$$\Delta\omega_k=(k+1)\omega_1-k\omega_1=\omega_1=\frac{2\pi}{T} \tag{8-1-36}$$

当 T 越来越大时,c_k 的值及相邻谱线的间隔就越来越小,谱线就变成连续的,而其幅度 $|k\omega_1|$ 将趋于无限小,这样我们可以定义一个新的函数

$$F(jk\omega_1)=Tc_k=\frac{2\pi c_k}{\Delta\omega_k}=\int_{-\frac{T}{2}}^{\frac{T}{2}}f(t)e^{-jk\omega_1 t}\mathrm{d}t \tag{8-1-37}$$

当 $T\to\infty$时,$\omega_1=\dfrac{2\pi}{T}\to\mathrm{d}\omega$,而相邻谐波之间的频率差也越来越小,这时可以把 $k\omega_1$ 看作是一个连续变量 ω 并取极限时,式(8-1-37)可以写成

$$F(j\omega)=\int_{-\infty}^{\infty}f(t)e^{-jk\omega t}\mathrm{d}t \tag{8-1-38}$$

上式称为傅里叶积分或傅里叶变换。它把一个时间函数变成了一个频率函数。另外,由式(8-1-37)知

$$c_k=\frac{F(jk\omega_1)}{T}=\frac{\Delta\omega_k F(jk\omega_1)}{2\pi} \tag{8-1-39}$$

将 c_k 代入式(8-1-34),当 $T\to\infty$时,上式的求和变成积分,可以将式(8-1-34)改写成

$$f(t)=\frac{1}{2\pi}\int_{-\infty}^{\infty}F(j\omega)e^{jk\omega t}\mathrm{d}\omega \tag{8-1-40}$$

式(8-1-40)称为傅氏反变换。频谱函数 $F(j\omega)$一般为 ω 的复函数,有时把 $F(j\omega)$简记为 $F(\omega)$。将非周期信号的频谱表示为傅里叶积分,当然,时域信号 $f(t)$要满足绝对可积。凡满足绝对可积条件的信号,它的变换 $F(\omega)$必然存在。对非周期函数进行傅氏变换就可以得到非周期函数的频谱。

下面给出几个常用非周期信号的频谱:

(1)门函数 $g_\tau(t)$ 的频谱

幅度为 1、宽度为 τ 的单个矩形脉冲常称为门函数,记为 $g_\tau(t)$,它可表示

$$g_\tau(t)=\begin{cases}1 & \left(|t|<\dfrac{\tau}{2}\right)\\ 0 & \left(|t|>\dfrac{\tau}{2}\right)\end{cases} \tag{8-1-41}$$

其波形如图 8-1-23a)所示。

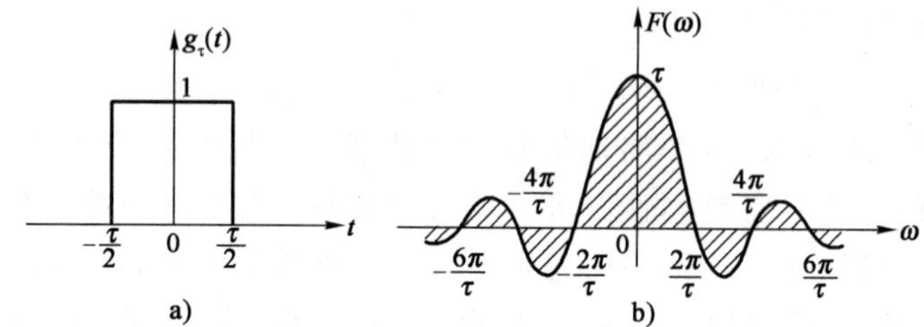

图 8-1-23 门函数的频谱图

(2)冲击函数 $\delta(t)$的频谱

由定义式(8-1-38),并应用 $\delta(t)$的取样性质,得

$$F(\omega)=\int_{-\infty}^{\infty}\delta(t)e^{-j\omega t}\mathrm{d}t=1 \tag{8-1-42}$$

即有变换对

$$\delta(t)\leftrightarrow 1 \tag{8-1-43}$$

图 8-1-24 为它们的图示。可见,冲激信号的频谱是均匀谱。

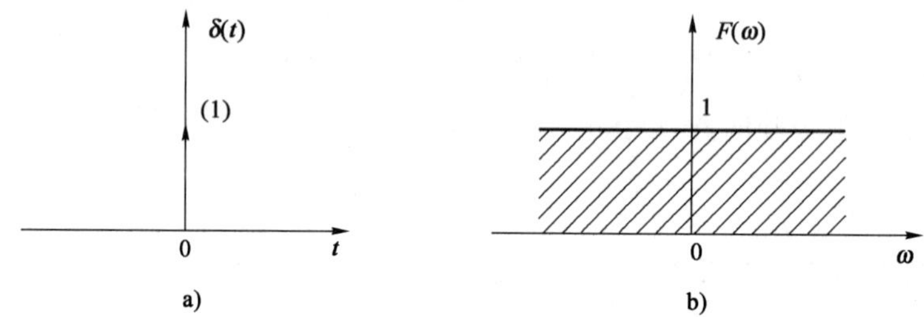

图 8-1-24 冲击函数的频谱图

(3)直流信号的频谱

设直流信号

$$f(t)=1 \qquad (-\infty,\infty) \tag{8-1-44}$$

经傅氏反变换,且 $\delta(t)$为 t 的偶函数,则 $\delta(t)$可表示为

$$\delta(t)=\delta(-t)=\frac{1}{2\pi}\int_{-\infty}^{\infty}1\cdot e^{-j\omega t}\mathrm{d}\omega \tag{8-1-45}$$

将上式中 ω 换为 t,t 换为 ω,有

$$2\pi\delta(\omega)=\int_{-\infty}^{\infty}1\cdot e^{-j\omega t}\mathrm{d}t \tag{8-1-46}$$

上式表明单位直流信号的傅里叶变换(频谱)为 $2\pi\delta(\omega)$,即

$$1\leftrightarrow 2\pi\delta(\omega) \tag{8-1-47}$$

它们的图形如图 8-1-25 所示。这表明,直流仅由 $\omega=0$ 的分量组成。

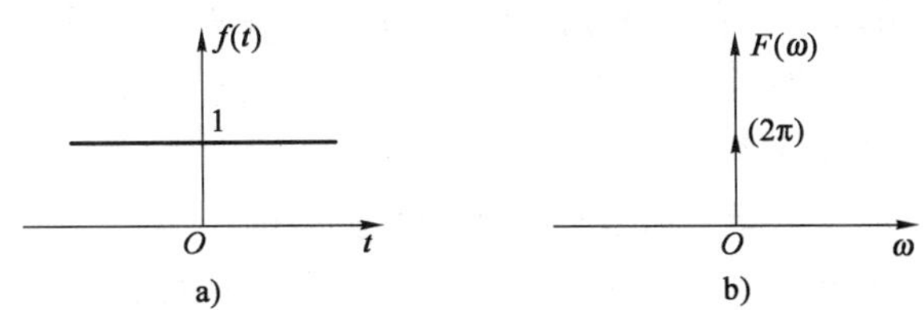

图 8-1-25　直流信号的频谱图

归纳以上分析，对于非周期信号可以得到如下重要结论：

①非周期信号的频谱是连续频谱；

②若信号在时域中持续时间有限，则其频谱在频域将延伸到无限，这可简单地称为时间有限，频域无限。

③信号的脉冲宽度越窄，则信号的带宽越宽。

频谱分析是模拟信号分析的重要方法，也是模拟信号处理的基础，在工程上有着重要的应用。这种分析方法实质上是对信号特征的更为细致的提取，在信号处理中，根据频谱的特征可以进行信号的识别和信息的提取。

在实际运用中，根据问题性质和分析目标的不同，可以采用不同方式来描述模拟信号。例如，在电路稳态分析中采用时域描述方式以求分析过程直观并便于理解；在电路动态过程分析中，则采用频域描述方式以求分析简便和透彻。

【例 8-1-6】 周期信号中的谐波信号是：

A. 离散时间信号　　B. 数字信号

C. 采样信号　　D. 连续时间信号

解 周期信号中的谐波信号是从傅里叶级数分解中得到的，它是正弦交流信号，是连续时间信号。

答案：D

【例 8-1-7】 周期信号的频谱是：

A. 离散的

B. 连续的

C. 高频谐波部分是离散的，低频谐波部分是连续的

D. 有离散的，也有连续的，无规律可循

解 周期信号的谐波是按照级数形式分解出来的，所以频谱是离散的频谱。

答案：A

四、模拟信号的处理

信号是信息的载体。在电子系统中，信号的处理服从于信息处理的需要，如信号的放大处理为的是信息的增强，信号之间的算术运算、微分积分运算等是信息的变换，信号的滤波、整形等则通常是为了信息的识别和提取。

（一）模拟信号增强

将微弱的信号放大到可以方便观测和利用是模拟信号最基本的一种处理方式。信号的放大包含信号幅度的放大和信号带载能力的增强两个目标，前者称为电压放大，后者称为功率放大，这是模拟电子电路的重点内容。实际上，电压放大和功率放大都涉及信号本身能量的增强，所以，信号的放大过程可以理解为一种能量转换过程，电子电路的放大理论就是在较微弱

的信号控制下把电源的能量转换成具有较大能量的信号。模拟信号放大的核心问题是保证放大前后的信号是同一个信号，即经过放大处理后的信号不能失真、信号的形状或频谱结构保持不变，即信号所携带的信息保持不变。

针对这些基本要求，电子电路中所要处理的问题主要有：

(1)非线性问题。电子器件本身的非线性特性无法严格保持信号放大过程的线性变换关系，这导致信号放大之后出现波形的畸变。

(2)频率特性问题。由于电路中储能元件(电容、电感)的影响，电子电路不能保证信号中的各次谐波成分获得同等比例的放大效果，这导致放大后信号的谐波组分或频谱结构发生改变。

(3)噪声与干扰问题。放大电路内部的电子噪声和外部的干扰信号导致放大后的信号中夹杂着其他的信号，在情况严重时，这些夹杂信号会淹没放大信号本身，导致无法对信号进行识别和应用。

(二)模拟信号滤波

从信号中滤除部分谐波信号叫做滤波。滤波是从模拟信号中去除伪信息，提取有用信息的一种重要技术手段。

滤波电路通常是按照滤波电路的工作频带命名的，分为低通滤波器(LPF)、高通滤波器(HPF)、带通滤波器(BPF)、带阻滤波器(BEF)等。

各种滤波器的理想幅频特性如图 8-1-26 所示。允许通过的频段称为通带，将信号的幅值衰减到零的频段称为阻带。

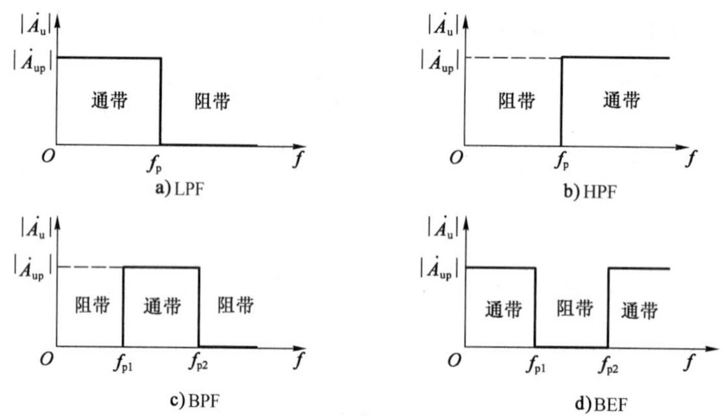

图 8-1-26 理想滤波电路的幅频特性

幅频特性通常用来描述放大器的电压放大倍数与频率变化之间的关系，如图 8-1-26 描述了典型滤波器的幅频特性。在图 8-1-26a)中，设截止频率为 f_p，低于频率 f_p 的信号可以通过，高于 f_p 的信号被衰减的滤波电路称为低通滤波器；反之，频率高于 f_p 的信号可以通过，而频率低于 f_p 的信号被衰减的滤波电路称为高通滤波器。低通和高通滤波器的理想频率特性分别如图 8-1-26a)、b)所示。

对于带通电路，设低频段的截止频率为 f_{p1}，高频段的截止频率为 f_{p2}，频率在 f_{p1} 到 f_{p2} 之间的信号可以通过，低于 f_{p1} 或高于 f_{p2} 的信号被衰减的滤波电路称为带通滤波器，如图 8-1-26c)所示；对于频率低于 f_{p1} 和高于 f_{p2} 的信号可以通过，频率是 f_{p1} 到 f_{p2} 之间的信号被衰减的滤波电路称为带阻滤波器，如图 8-1-26d)所示。

滤波是模拟信号处理的一项核心技术，在信号识别和信息提取中有着重要应用，通常信号在传输和处理过程中会受到干扰信号的影响，干扰信号的谐波与有用信号的谐波往往分布在频谱不同的频段上，所以通常采用滤波手段来排除或削弱干扰信号。例如，在观测到的大型汽轮发电机组的振动信号中，包含有正常运转的振动信号和因机械故障所引起的附加振动信号，这通常用信号和干扰信号谐波组分分布在频谱中的不同区间里，利用适当的滤波手段即可从总的振动信号中识别出故障信号，借以判断系统有无故障、故障类型及故障程度等信息；另外，各个广播电台和电视台采用不同的载波频率播送节目，它们分布在天线所接收到的信号频谱中的不同频段上，利用带通滤波即可将它们提取出来收听或观看。

（三）模拟信号变换

将一种信号变换为另一种信号是模拟信号处理的一项主要内容。在模拟系统中，信号的相加、相减、比例、微分及积分变换是常见的几种信号变换。从信息处理的角度看，信号变换是从信号中提取信息的重要手段，例如通过信号相加提取求和信息，从相减提取差异信息，通过比例变换提取增强后的信息，从微分变换提取信号时间变化率信息，从积分变换提取信号对时间的累积信息等。

信号变换的主要问题是：由于难以找到一种理想的运算装置，所以，信号变换都只能近似地实现，这为信息的提取带来不便。实际上，在模拟系统中，为了准确提取信息，往往还要增加许多额外的处理过程，如反馈技术。

图 8-1-27 给出一个模拟信号微分-积分变换的理想波形图。从图中可知，一个三角波模拟信号描述函数为 $f_1(t)$，经过微分变换

$$f_2(t) = \frac{\mathrm{d}f_1(t)}{\mathrm{d}t} \tag{8-1-48}$$

被变换为一个方波信号 $f_2(t)$，这个方波信号承载的是三角波信号的时间变化率信息；反之，一个方波信号 $f_2(t)$ 经过积分变换

$$f_1(t) = \int f_2(t)\mathrm{d}t \tag{8-1-49}$$

被变换为一个三角波 $f_1(t)$ 信号，它承载的是方波信号时间累积信息。

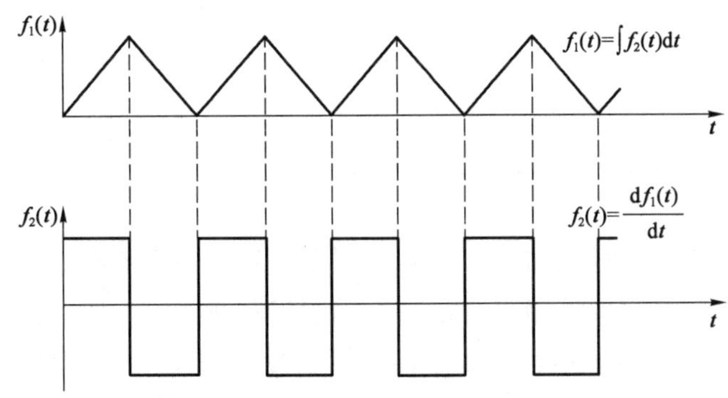

图 8-1-27　模拟信号微分-积分变换波形

（四）模拟信号识别

从一种不干净的、夹杂着许多无用信号的混合信号中把所需要的信号提取出来，这是信号识别问题。从信息的角度讲，信号识别是信息提取的一种前期处理过程，它剔除夹杂在信号中的各种伪信息，并保留原来的信息。利用频率的差异，采用滤波器滤除夹杂信号是信号识别的主要方法，但是，由于各种滤波器的特性都是非理想的，所以对于与信号频率相近的夹杂信号，滤波方法是无能为力的。增强有用信号自身的强度，也是一种信号识别的常用方法。但是，对

于微弱信号，由于电子噪声信号也随着信号的增强而增强，这种方法的效果是有限的。

图 8-1-28 表示的是从调幅信号中识别出一个正弦波信号的过程。图 8-1-28a)表示原始的调幅信号 $u_1(t)$，图 8-1-28b)表示经过单向导电器件处理后的调幅信号 $u_2(t)$，图 8-1-28c)表示采用滤波器滤除高频载波信号后的信号 $u_3(t)$，图 8-1-28d)表示滤除直流信号后所提取出来的真实信号 $u_4(t)$。

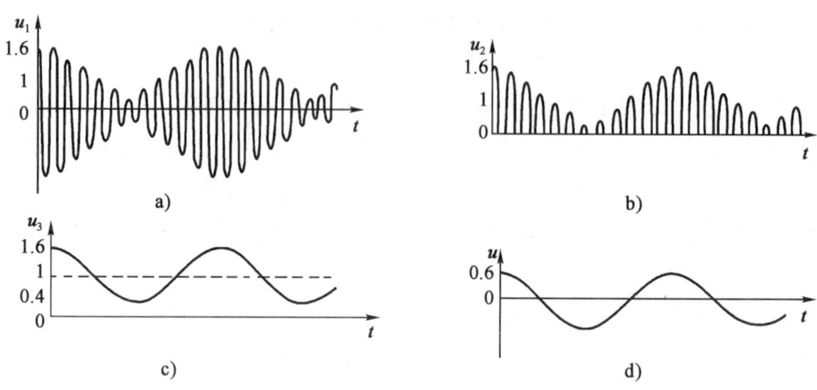

图 8-1-28　从调制信号中识别出模拟信号的过程

【例 8-1-8】 设放大器的输入信号为 $u_1(t)$，放大器的幅频特性如图所示，令 $u_1(t)=\sqrt{2}u_1\sin 2\pi ft$，且 $f>f_H$，则：

A. $u_2(t)$的出现频率失真

B. $u_2(t)$的有效值 $U_2=AU_1$

C. $u_2(t)$的有效值 $U_2<AU_1$

D. $u_2(t)$的有效值 $U_2>AU_1$

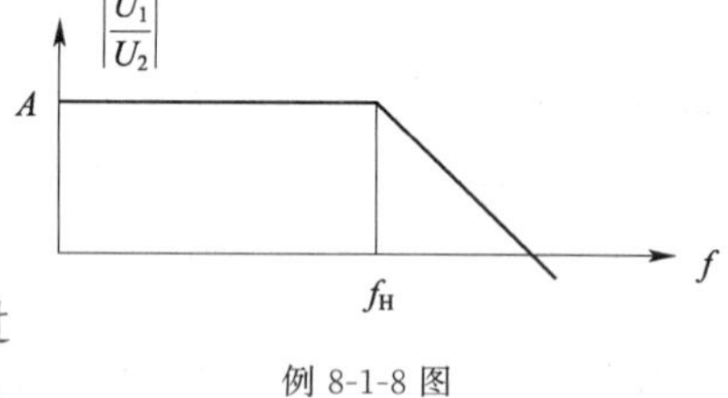

例 8-1-8 图

解　放大器的输入为正弦交流信号。但 $u_1(t)$的频率过高，超出了上限频率 f_H，放大倍数小于 A，因此输出信号 u_2 的有效值 $U_2<AU_1$。

答案：C

第二节　数字信号与信息

对电子信号的处理，针对数字信号与模拟信号的不同采用了不同的处理方式，电子器件的工作状态也不同。数字电路的工作信号是二值信号，要用它来表示数并进行数的运算，就必须采取二进制形式表示。在电子电路中，信号往往表现为突变的电压或电流，并且只有两个可能的状态。正如我们所知，数字电路中的二极管和三极管工作在开关状态。利用导通和截止两种不同的工作状态，代表不同的数字信息，完成信号的传递和处理任务。由于一个 n 位的二进制数字代码序列可以有多种不同的排列方式，所以数字代码具有极强的表达能力。采用适当长度的数字脉冲序列数字信号就可以用来对各种复杂信息进行编码，并借助数字计算机的强大处理能力实现信息的处理，这就是数字信号得以广泛应用的根本所在。

数字信号可以用来对“数”进行编码，实现数值信息的表示、运算、传送和处理；号也可以用来对文字和其他符号进行编码，实现符号信息的表达、传送和处理；数字信号可以用来表示逻辑关系，实现逻辑演算、逻辑控制等。因此，在数字电路中，重点研究的是输入信号与输出信号之间的逻辑关系。为了分析这些逻辑关系，必须了解信号的编码规则，使用一套科学的代码和数学工具来处理数字信号，即逻辑代码和逻辑代数。

一、数字信号的数制和代码

(一)几种常用进制

1. 十进制

十进制是我们所熟悉的计数体制，它用0～9十个数字符号，按照一定的规律排列起来，表示数值的大小。

例如，$123.45 = 1\times10^2 + 2\times10^1 + 3\times10^0 + 4\times10^{-1} + 5\times10^{-2}$

十进制数的特点：它的基数是10，其中低位和相邻高位之间的关系是“逢十进一”，故称为十进制。任意一个十进制数D均可展开为

$$D=\sum k_i \times 10^i \qquad (8\text{-}2\text{-}1)$$

式中，k_i是第i位的系数，它可以是0～9这十个数码中的任何一个。

若整数部分的位数是n，小数部分的位数是m，则i包含从$n-1$到0的所有正整数和从-1到$-m$的所有负整数。

若以N取代式(8-2-1)中的10，即可得到任意进制(N进制)数展开式的普遍形式

$$D=\sum k_i \times N^i \qquad (8\text{-}2\text{-}2)$$

式中i的取值与式(8-2-1)的规定相同，N称为计数的基数，k_i为第i位的系数，N^i为第i位的权。

2. 二进制

目前在数字电路中应用最广的是二进制。在二进制数中，每一位仅有0和1两个可能的数字符号，所以计数的基数为2。低位和相邻高位间的进位关系是“逢二进一”，故称为二进制。

根据式(8-2-2)，任何一个二进制数均可展开为

$$D=\sum k_i \times 2^i \qquad (8\text{-}2\text{-}3)$$

并由此计可算出它表示的十进制数的数值。

例如，$(101.11)_2 = 1\times2^2+0\times2^1+1\times2^0+1\times2^{-1}+1\times2^{-2} = (5.75)_{10}$

上式中分别使用下脚注的2和10表示括号里的数是二进制和十进制数。有时也用B(Binary)和D(Decimal)代替2和10这两个脚注。

3. 十六进制

十六进制数用0～9、A、B、C、D、E、F等16个符号表示。任意一个十六进制数均可表示为

$$D=\sum k_i \times 16^i \qquad (8\text{-}2\text{-}4)$$

例如，$(2B.6F)_{16} = 2\times16^1 + 11\times16^0 + 6\times16^{-1} + 15\times16^{-2} = (43.433\,59)_{10}$

式中的下脚注16表示括号里的数是十六进制，有时也用H(Hexadecimal)标注。

由于目前在微型计算机中普遍采用8位、16位和32位二进制并行运算，而8位、16位和32位的二进制数可以用2位、4位和8位的十六进制数表示。为了应用方便，通常用十六进制符号书写程序。

(二)数制转换

1. 二～十转换

把二进制数转换为等值的十进制数称为二～十转换。转换时只要将二进制数按式

(8-2-3)展开，然后把所有各项的数值按十进制数相加，就可以得到等值的十进制数了。

例如，$(1\,101.01)_2 = 1\times2^3 + 1\times2^2 + 0\times2^1 + 1\times2^0 + 0\times2^{-1} + 1\times2^{-2} = (13.25)_{10}$

2. 十～二转换

把十进制数转换为二进制数，整数部分用“除 2 取余法”，小数部分用“乘 2 取整法”，具体操作举例如下。

【例 8-2-1】 分别将$(25)_{10}$和$(0.8125)_{10}$转换为二进制数。

解

```
2 |2 5  | 1   ↑ 低位         0.8125      高    0.25
2 |1 2  | 0   |            ×      2      位  ×    2
  2 |6  | 0   |            ---------     |   ------
  2 |3  | 1   | 高位         (1).6250    |   (0).50
     1                       0.6250      |     0.5
                           ×      2      |   ×   2
                           ---------     ↓   ------   ↓ 低位
                             (1).250          (1).0
```

因此 $(25)_{10}=(11001)_2$ $(0.8125)_{10}=(0.1101)_2$

3. 二～十六转换

把二进制数转换为等值的十六进制数，称为二～十六转换。

由于 4 位二进制数恰好有 16 个状态，而把这 4 位二进制数看作一个整体时，它的进位输出又正好是逢十六进一，所以只要从低位到高位将每 4 位二进制数分为一组，并代之以等值的十六进制数，即可得到对应的十六进制数。

例如，将$(01101010.11010010)_2$化为十六进制数时可得

$$
\begin{array}{cccccc}
(0110, & 1010 & . & 1101, & 0010)_2 \\
\downarrow & \downarrow & & \downarrow & \downarrow \\
=(6 & A & . & D & 2)_{16}
\end{array}
$$

4. 十六～二转换

十六～二转换是指把十六进制数转换成等值的二进制数。转换时只需将十六进制数的每一位用等值的 4 位二进制数代替就行了。

例如，将$(8FB.C5)_{16}$化为二进制数时可得

$$
\begin{array}{cccccc}
(8 & F & B & . & C & 5)_{16} \\
\downarrow & \downarrow & \downarrow & & \downarrow & \downarrow \\
=(1000 & 1111 & 1011 & . & 1100 & 0101)_2
\end{array}
$$

5. 十六进制数与十进制数的转换

在将十六进制数转换为十进制数时，可根据式(8-2-4)将各位数按权展开后相加求得。在将十进制数转换为十六进制数时，可以先转换成二进制数，然后再将得到的二进制数转换为等值的十六进制数。

(三)代码

不同的数码不仅可以表示不同的数量大小，而且还能用来表示不同的事物。在后一种情况下，这些数码已没有表示数量大小的含义，只是表示不同事物的代号而已。这些数码称为代码。为了便于记忆和处理，在编制代码时总要遵循一定的规则，这些规则就叫做“码制”。

例如，在用 4 位二进制数码表示 1 位十进制数的 0 ～9 这十个状态时，就有多种不同的码制。通常将这些代码称为二～十进制代码，简称 BCD(Binary Coded Decimal)代码。表 8-2-1 列出了几种常见的 BCD 代码，它们的码制规则各不相同。

几种常见的 BCD 代码 表 8-2-1

十进制数＼编码种类	8421 码	余 3 码	2421 码	5211 码	余 3 循环码
0	0000	0011	0000	0000	0010
1	0001	0100	0001	0001	0110
2	0010	0101	0010	0100	0111
3	0011	0110	0011	0101	0101
4	0100	0111	0100	0111	0100
5	0101	1000	1011	1000	1100
6	0110	1001	1100	1001	1101
7	0111	1010	1101	1100	1111
8	1000	1011	1110	1101	1110
9	1001	1100	1111	1111	1010
权	8421		2421	5211	

下面分别介绍不同码制的特点：

(1)8421 码是 BCD 代码中最常用的一种。在这种编码方式中，每一位二值代码的 1 都代表一个固定的数值，把每一位的 1 代表的十进制数加起来，得到的结果就是它所代表的十进制数码。由于代码中从左到右每一位的 1 分别表示 8、4、2、1 ，所以把这种代码叫做 8421 码。每一位的 1 代表的十进制数称为这一位的权。8421 码中每一位的权是固定不变的，它属于恒权代码。

(2)余 3 码的编码规则与 8421 码不同，如果把每一个余 3 码看作 4 位二进制数，则它的数值要比它所表示的十进制数码多 3，故而将这种代码叫做余 3 码。

如果将两个余 3 码相加，所得的和将比十进制数和所对应的二进制数多 6。因此，在用余 3 码作十进制加法运算时，若两数之和为 10，则余 3 码正好等于二进制数的 16，便从高位自动产生进位信号。

此外，从表 8-1 还可以看出，0 和 9、1 和 8、2 和 7、3 和 6、4 和 5 的余 3 码互为反码，这对于求取对 10 的补码是很方便的。

余 3 码不是恒权代码。如果试图把每个代码视为二进制数，并使它所等效的十进制数与所表示的代码相等，那么代码中每一位的 1 所代表的十进制数在各个代码中不是固定的。

(3)2421 码是一种恒权代码。它的 0 和 9、1 和 8、2 和 7、3 和 6、4 和 5 也互为反码，这个特点和余 3 码相仿。

(4)5211 码是另一种恒权代码。学了计数器的分频作用后可以发现，如果按 8421 码接成十进制计数器，则连续输入计数脉冲的 4 个触发器输出脉冲对于计数脉冲的分频比从低位到高位依次为 5：2：1：1。可见，5211 码每一位的权正好与 8421 码十进制计数器 4 个触发器输出脉冲的分频比相对应。这种对应关系在构成某些数字系统时很有用。

(5)余 3 循环码是一种变权码，每一位的 1 在不同代码中并不代表固定的数值。它的主要特点是相邻的两个代码之间仅有一位的状态不同。因此，按余 3 循环码接成计数器时，每次状态转换过程中只有一个触发器翻转，译码时不会发生竞争冒险现象。

实际上，包括文字在内的任何抽象的符号，以及诸如图像、语音等任何具体的物理符号都可以用“0”和“1”代码进行编码，并以数字信号的形式进行信息的传输和处理。为此，诞生了许多国际通用的编码标准或协议，以便于信息的交流和应用。通用的符号为美国标准信息代码 ASCII(America Standard Code for Information Interchange)的一些基本的示例，它规范了全球抽象符号的编码形式。相应地，还有图像编码标准、语音编码标准等。按照这些标准进行编码的信息都可以用数字信号来描述，从而可以实现诸如文字信息、图像信息、语音信息等复杂的数字处理，并且可以在世界范围内自由地通信和交流。

【例 8-2-2】 十进制数 65 的八位二进制代码是：

A. 01100101　　B. 01000001　　C. 10000000　　D. 10000001

解 根据二进制数规则，数 65 需要用 7 位二进制数表示，最高位的权重是 $2^6=64$，习惯上可以用八位二进制数表示，所以它的二进制代码是 01 000 001。

答案：B

【例 8-2-3】 十进制数 65 的 BCD 码是：

A. 01100101　　B. 01000001　　C. 10000000　　D. 10000001

解 BCD 码用 4bit 二进制代码表示十进制数的 1 个位，所以 BCD 码是 $6_{10}=0110_2$ 和 $5_{10}=0101_2$ 的组合，即 $65_{10}=01100101_2$。

答案：A

【例 8-2-4】 十进制数字 32 的 BCD 码为：

A. 00110010　　B. 00100000

C. 100000　　D. 00100011

解 BCD 码是用二进制数表示的十进制数，属于无权码，此题的 BCD 码是用四位二进制数表示的。

答案：A

二、算术运算

(一)基本算术运算

在数字电路中，1 位二进制数码的 0 和 1 不仅可以表示数量的大小，而且可以表示两种不同的逻辑状态。例如，可以用 1 和 0 分别表示一件事情的是和非、真和伪、有和无、好和坏，或者表示电路的通和断、电灯的亮和暗等。这种只有两种对立逻辑状态的逻辑关系称为二值逻辑。当两个二进制数码表示两个数量的大小时，它们之间可以进行数值运算，这种运算称为算术。二进制的算术运算和十进制的算术运算的规则基本相同，唯一区别是二进制运算是逢二进一，而十进制数的加法逢十进一；当然，结合信号处理上的一些硬件电路的特殊要求，还要了解二进制运算中的特殊方法。事实上，二进制数的运算都是用代码的“移位”和“相加”(相减也转换为补码相加)两种操作来实现。

1. 加减运算

(1)加法。和十进制加法规则一样，二进制的加法也是从低位开始加，逢二进一。

(2)减法。为简化逻辑运算过程，在数字电路中减法的运算是用它们的补码来完成的。

二进制的补码定义：最高位是符号位(正数为 0，负数为 1)；正数的补码与原码相同；负数的补码可以通过将原码的数值逐位求反，然后将结果加 1 实现的(即求反加一)。

例如，数 1010 的反码是 0101，而它的补码就是它的反码加 1：

$$(1010)_{补码}=0101+0001=0110$$

【例 8-2-5】 计算$(+1001)_2-(0101)_2$

解 根据二进制的运算规则可知

$$(+1001-0101)_{补}=(+1001)_{补}+(-0101)_{补}$$

```
        0 1 0 0 1
      + 1 1 0 1 1
  溢出 →1 0 0 1 0 0
        ↑  └真值
      符号位
```

因此，+1001－0101＝00100（正数），真值为$(4)_{10}$。

说明：在采取补码运算时，首先求出$(+1001)_2$和$(-0101)_2$的补码，它们是：

```
[+1001]补 = [0]1001
             └正数，符号位为0
[-1001]补 = [1]1001
             └负数，符号位为1
```

然后两个补码相加并舍去进位，则得到与前面一样的结果。这样就把减法运算转化成了加法运算。

2.乘除运算

(1)乘法。与十进制数的乘法相同，二进制数的乘法也是从右向左逐位操作的，下面是二进制数乘法操作的示例。

【例 8-2-6】

$$(7\times 6)_{10}=(111)_2\times(110)_2$$
$$=(101010)_2=(42)_{10}$$

因

```
      111
    × 110
    -----
      000
     111
    111
   ------
   101010
```

所以$(111)_2\times(110)_2=(101010)_2$

仔细考查例题中的乘法运算可以发现，它实际上是由一系列"移位"和"相加"操作组成的，即被乘数逐步左移并逐步相加即可完成乘法运算。被乘数左移的位数与乘数中取值"1"所处的位数相同，而在乘数取值"0"的位置上则不进行任何操作。这样，示例中的乘法运算步骤转变成：

①乘数第0位为"0"，不做任何操作；

②乘数第1位为"1"，乘数左移1位，得数1110；

③乘数第2位为"1"，乘数左移2位，得数11100；

④将前面两数相加：1110＋11100＝ 101010。

乘法的原义是被乘数自身相加若干次（乘数规定了相加的次数），一个数与自身每相加一次，其值加倍，对二进制数而言，这意味着这个数向左移动一个位。从这个角度看，二进制数的乘法运算等价为"移位加"的操作就不难理解了。

(2)除法。与十进制数相同，二进制数除法运算也是从左向右操作的，下面是二进制数除法运算的一个示例。

【例 8-2-7】

$$42\div 6=(42)_{10}\div(6)_{10}$$
$$=(101010)_2\div(110)_2=(111)_2$$

$$=(7)_{10}$$

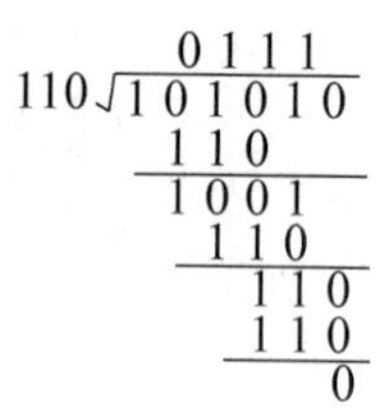

分析可知，二进制的除法运算实际上是由一系列"移位"和"相减"操作组成的，即以被除数逐步右移并逐步和被除数相减的方式完成除法运算的。当被除数大于除数时，进行相减，完成一次比较，该位的商置1，接着除数右移一位（减半）再和前面相减的余数比较，这样逐位进行，若被除数小于除数，则不操作，相应位的商置0，则接着将除数减半（右移1位）再行比较，如此逐位进行。因为除法的本意是"求解一数（被除数）是另一数（除数）的多少倍"，这实质上是一个两个数的比较问题。上述"移位减"操作的含义是这样的：

①将除数倍增到和被除数相同的位数，先进行大数比较，求得商的高位值(0或1)；

②然后将除数减半（右移1位），再和前面的余数比较，求得低一位的商值(0或1)；

③如此进行，直到除尽为止。

不难发现，乘法运算可以用加法和移位两种操作实现，而除法运算可以用减法和移位操作实现。因此，二进制数的加、减、乘、除运算都可以用加法运算电路完成，这就大大简化了运算电路的结构。

3.微分与积分运算

在数值计算中，微分运算被转换为差分运算，积分运算则被转换为数值的逐步累积即所谓的数值积分运算，它们都可以用上述基本的算术运算来实现。

这为通过数字信号处理来实现数值信息处理提供了方便。当然，还有二进制小数的表示及运算等其他问题，这里不再作进一步介绍，读者可参阅相关计算机课程的教材。

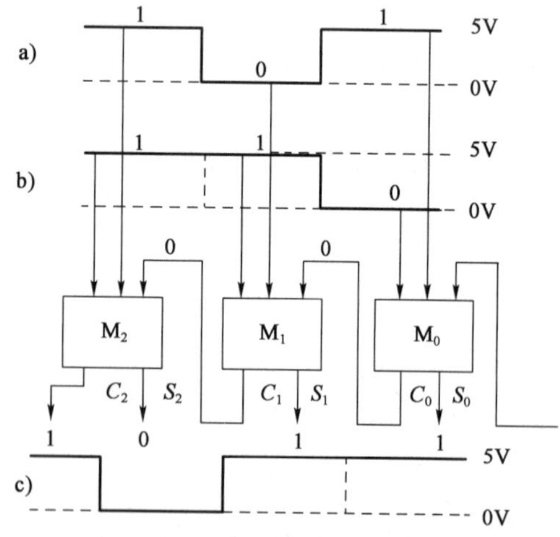

图8-2-1　三位数相加的数字系统原理图

（二）用数字电路实现数值运算

在数字系统中，数字信号的"移位"操作由移位寄存器电路来实现；数字信号的"相加"则由相应的逻辑电路即所谓的加法器电路来完成。数字电子电路加法器就是根据"异或"原理设计的。图8-2-1是实现两个三位数(101和110)相加的数字系统原理图。图8-2-1中的数字信号分别表示这两个数以及这两个数之"和"。M_2、M_1、M_0分别表示三个加法器。C_2、C_1、C_0表示各位相加后的进位值，在电路的接法上是与前级串联，表示进位。S_2、S_1、S_0是每一位相加后的输出值，显然，这个系统的输出信号是两个输入信号之和信号的移位由数字移位寄存器来完成。

三、逻辑运算

当两个二进制数码表示不同的逻辑状态时，它们之间可以按照指定的某种因果关系进行逻辑运算。这种逻辑运算和算术运算有着本质的不同。下面介绍逻辑运算的各种规律。

(一)逻辑变量与逻辑函数

事物的发展和变化通常是按照一定的因果关系进行的。例如,照明电路中电灯是否能亮取决于电源是否接通和灯泡的好坏。后两者是因,前者是果。这种因果关系一般称为逻辑关系。逻辑代数正是反映这种逻辑关系的数学工具。

为了描述事物两种对立的逻辑状态,采用的是仅有两个取值的变量。这种变量称为逻辑变量。和普通代数变量一样,逻辑变量都是用字母表示。但是,它又和普通代数变量有着本质区别,研究的逻辑变量的取值只有 0 和 1 两种可能,而且这里的 0 和 1 不是表示数值大小,而是代表逻辑变量的两种对立状态。

如果以逻辑变量作为输入,以运算结果作为输出,那么当输入变量的取值确定之后,输出的取值便随之而定。因此,输出与输入之间乃是一种函数关系,这种函数关系称为逻辑函数,其逻辑关系用逻辑代数(布尔代数)讨论。下面就逻辑代数体系作一简要介绍:

1.符号

(1)变量。逻辑变量用大写英文字母(ABC…XYZ)表示。

(2)数值。"0"和"1"表示逻辑变量的取值,"0"表示"假"(F),"1"表示"真"(T)。

(3)运算符。"+"、"×"分别表示由逻辑连接词"或"和"与"所定义的逻辑"或"和逻辑"与"运算,称为逻辑"加"和逻辑"乘";逻辑求反运算用变量上方加一横杆表示,如$\overline{A}$、$\overline{B}$等。符号"="是逻辑演绎推理的演算符。和代数运算一样,逻辑"乘"运算符"×"通常不写出来。

2.函数(表达式)

如前所述,逻辑变量表示事物或事件的状态,逻辑函数或逻辑表达式表示事物或事件之间的关系,即事物运动演化的规律性描述。逻辑函数是由逻辑变量符和运算符组成,它表述变量之间的逻辑关系,例如,C=A+B、D=(A+B)+AB 等。

3.逻辑函数化简

直接由逻辑变量写出的逻辑函数表达式往往不是简洁的表达式,简化处理后逼近能凸显其内在的逻辑关系,通常还可以使硬件电路结构简单。表 8-2-2 中列出了逻辑代数运算中的基本公式。

逻辑代数运算中的基本公式 表 8-2-2

范　围	名　称	逻　辑　与	逻　辑　或
变量与常量的关系	01 律	(1)A·1=A (3)A·0=0	(2)A+0=A (4)A+1=1
和普通代数相似的定律	交通律 结合律 分配律	(5)A·B=B·A (7)A·(B·C)=(A·B)·C (9)A·(B+C)=A·B+A·C	(6)A+B=B+A (8)A+(B+C)=(A+B)+C (10)A+(B·C)=(A+B)·(A+C)
逻辑代数特殊规律	互补律 重叠律 反演律 (摩根定理)对合律	(11)$A\cdot\overline{A}=0$ (13)A·A=A (15)$\overline{A\cdot B}=\overline{A}+\overline{B}$ (17)$\overline{\overline{A}}=A$	(12)$A+\overline{A}=1$ (14)A+A=A (16)$\overline{A+B}=\overline{A}\cdot\overline{B}$

【例 8-2-8】 逻辑表达式(A+B)(A+C)的化简结果是:

A. A　　　　B. A^2+AB+AC+BC

C. A+BC　　　　D. (A+B)(A+C)

解　根据逻辑代数公式分析如下：

$$(A+B)(A+C)=A\cdot A+A\cdot B+A\cdot C+B\cdot C=A(1+B+C)+BC=A+BC$$

答案：C

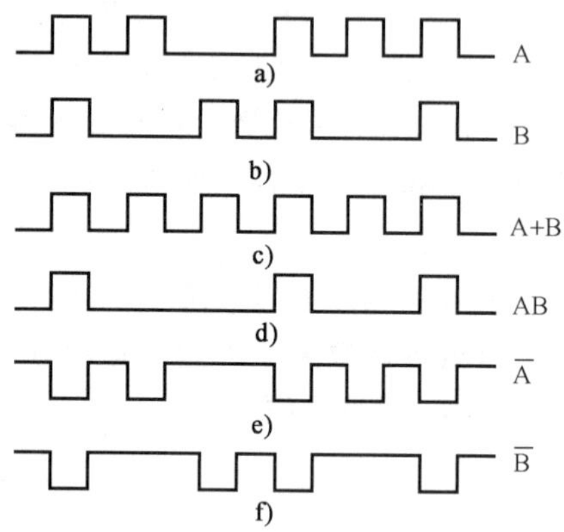

图 8-2-2　数字信号的基本逻辑运算

这是常用的逻辑电路分析方法，需要熟练掌握和灵活运用。从工程的角度看，逻辑函数的运算是借助数字逻辑系统完成的。逻辑器件按照逻辑表达式的要求组合起来构成数字逻辑系统，因此，逻辑表达式的简化形式还需要考虑数字逻辑系统组建的技术因素，这种化简并不意味着"越简越好"。经验丰富的电气工程师能够恰当地处理这个问题。

4. 数字信号的逻辑演算

用数字信号表示逻辑变量的取值情况，逻辑函数的演算即可以用数字信号处理的方法来实现。

图 8-2-2 说明用数字信号表示逻辑变量、逻辑函数以及实现基本逻辑演算的情况。其中的数字信号 a 和 b 分别表示逻辑变量 A 和 B 的输入情况，信号中的高位 5V 代表"真"(逻辑"I"状态)，低位 0V 代表"假"(逻辑"0"状态)；而数字信号 c、d、e、f 分别表示 A+B、AB、$\overline{A}$、$\overline{B}$则表示"或"、"与"、"非"三种简单逻辑函数的演算结果。

在数字系统中使用专门制作的各种逻辑门电路来自动、快速地完成数字信号之间按位的逻辑"与"、"或"、"非"演算操作，将这些基本的演算逻辑门电路组合起来组成所谓的组合逻辑系统，就可以完成任意复杂的逻辑函数的演算。有关技术细节请参阅本书第 7 章关于数字电路问题的讨论。

【例 8-2-9】　已知数字信号 A 和数字信号 B 的波形如图所示，则数字信号 F=$\overline{A+B}$的波形为：

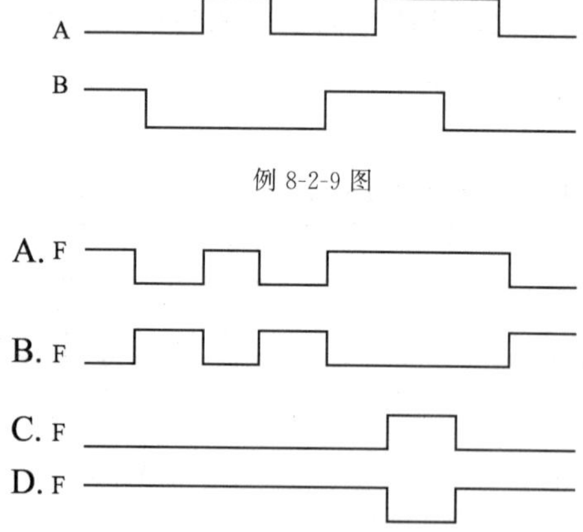

例 8-2-9 图

解　$\overline{A+B}=F$

F 是个或非关系，可以用"有 1 则 0"的口诀处理。

答案：B

(二)数字信号的符号信息处理

符号的处理主要体现为符号代码转换。在数字技术中，各种符号信息都是按照 ASCII 标准编码的。当符号被具体应用时，这些符号的标准代码往往需要转换为便于处理的其他形式，如在汉字处理中，以拼音方式从键盘输入计算机的是 ASCII 代码，在计算机内部，这个代码要转换为汉字编码(即所谓的汉字内码)才能进一步进行汉字处理。又如,在符号显示中,数字的、文字的或其他符号的ASCII代码都必须转换为显示装置所要求的代码形式才能在显示器中显示这些符号。

四、数字信号的存储

数字电路处理数字信号的存储问题,简单来说,就是只要将0V或5V信号电压按原来的顺序保持在一个电路中即可,这在电子电路中是容易实现的。如图8-2-3所示的原理电路可以确切地表示数字信号存储的方法,它由双位置开关和5V电源组成。开关合到电源侧,对应位置给出的是5V电压;开关投到接地侧,对应位置则给出0V电压。只要开关位置不变,信号就被永久保存。图中的开关所处的位置表示存储的是数字信号110(即5V、5V、0V信号),开关链的长度和数字信号的位数相同。数字信号中的每一位电压被用来触发对应位置上的开关动作,完成信号的存储。

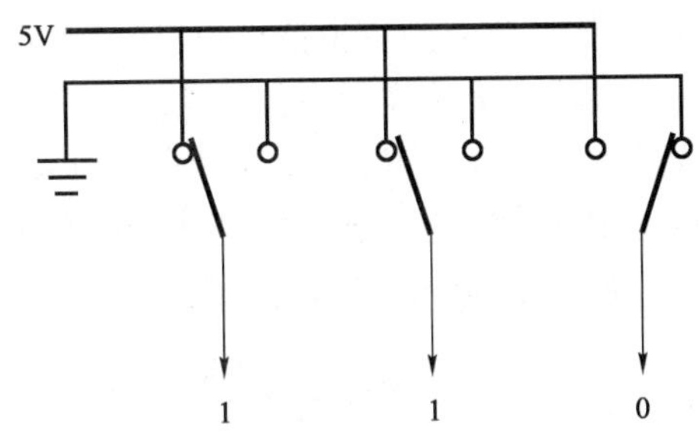

图8-2-3 数字信号存储原理

显然,图8-2-3电路是一种通用的存储器设计方案,它可以存储任何数字信号。当前数字系统中普遍采用的信息存储器正是根据这种简单的方案设计制作的。便于存储是数字信号得到广泛应用的一个重要原因。相比之下,模拟信号由于是连续取值的信号,它的存储在技术上十分困难,这个问题尚未得到理想的解决方法。

五、模拟信号与数字信号的相互转换

我们已经知道模拟信号真实反映原始形式的物理信号,是人类感知外部世界的主要信息来源,也是信息处理的主要对象,而数字信号是信息的编码形式,可以用电子电路或电子计算机方便、快速地对它进行传输、存储和处理。因此,将模拟信号转换为数字信号,或者说用数字信号对模拟信号进行编码,从而将模拟信号问题转化为数字信号问题加以处理,是现代信息技术中的一项重要内容。

图8-2-4表示的是现代数字化信息系统的基本组成。模拟信号通过采样和模拟/数字(Analog to Digital,简记为A/D)转换完成数字编码,数字编码信号经过处理、存储、传输后,再由数字/模拟(Digital to Analog,简记为D/A)转换为模拟信号的形式输出。例如,在数字化的广播系统中,连续的声音信号经过采样、A/D变换后,以数字信号的形式发送和传输,在接收端经过D/A变换将数字信号还原成连续的声音信号。在控制系统中,对象状态和过程的连续信号经过采样和A/D变换被转换为数字信号,数字信号经过控制系统模型的运算和处理后输出数字控制信号,再经过D/A变换,将数字控制信号转换成模拟控制信号,完成对象的控制和调节等。

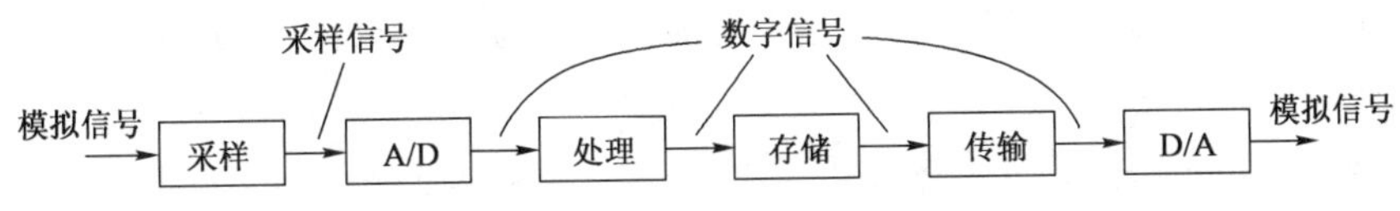

图8-2-4 现代数字信息系统组成

(一)信号的采样与采样定理

对模拟信号进行采样可获得采样信号,采样信号是一种可连续取值的离散时间信号。采样过程在采样脉冲的控制下进行,它的基本原理如图 8-2-5a)所示。采样脉冲控制开关 k 的通断,从而将连续的模拟信号(见图 8-2-5b)转换成离散的采样信号,如图 8-2-5c)所示。采样脉冲的频率称为采样频率。从直观上看,采样频率越高,采样信号就越接近模拟信号,采样所造成的信息损失也就越小。但是,这种采样方法将占用大量的系统有效工作时间,降低系统的运行速度。从理论上讲,只要采样频率保持在被采样信号带宽(最高谐波频率)的 2 倍以上,就可以保证采样处理不会丢失原来的信息。这就是著名的采样定理。

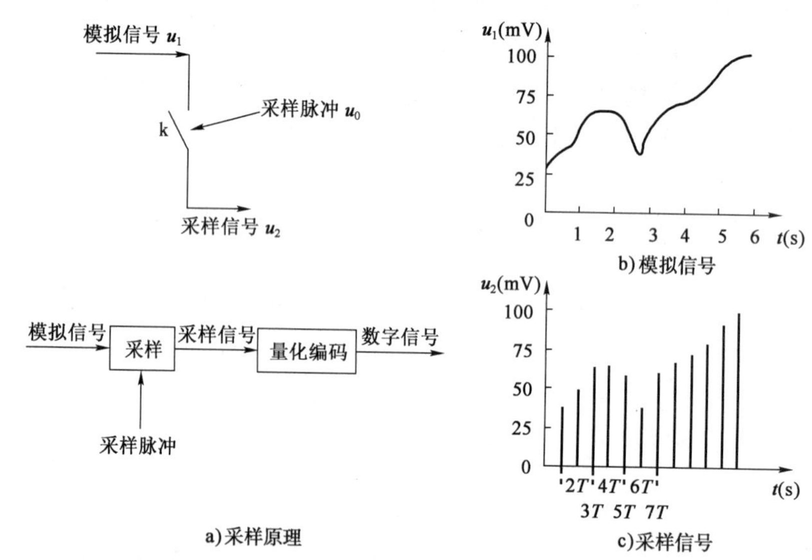

图 8-2-5 信号采样

当然,在采样之前需要对模拟信号进行预处理,包括滤波、放大等,以消除经过传感器变换或其他系统噪声带来的干扰,并增强模拟信号的幅值;在采样之后还要对离散的采样信号进行滤波处理,以保证采样后的信号不丢失有用的信息。

(二)数字/模拟转换(D/A)

D/A 转换过程和 A/D 相反,它将数字信号转换为模拟信号。从信息处理的角度讲,A/D 转换是对模拟信号进行编码,D/A 转换则是对数字信号进行解码。从技术的角度看,D/A 转换只要用简单的电阻网络即可实现,这要比 A/D 转换容易得多。

图 8-2-6 表示的是一种 4 位 D/A 转换器的原理图,它是一个由 4 个电阻构成的网络,每个电阻转换一位数字信号。电阻的阻值按二进制设置,其中 D_3 位电阻为 R、D_2 位电阻为 $2R$、D_1 位电阻为 $4R$、D_0 位电阻为 $8R$。电流/电压转换器通常用运算放放大器电路实现,它将输入电流转换为电压输出,其传递特性为 $U_A = R_A I$。电压/电流转换器输入端保持在零电位,因此,D_3,…,D_0 端上的信号电压就分别加到了电阻 R、$2R$、$4R$、$8R$ 上,所以,各个电阻上的电流为

$I_3 = D_3/R$

$I_2 = D_2/2R$

$I_1 = D_1/4R$

$I_0 = D_0/8R$

$I = I_3 + I_2 + I_1 + I_0$

$U_A = IR$

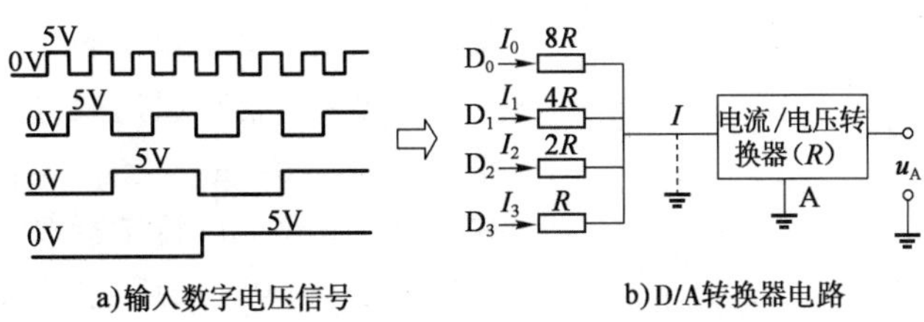

图 8-2-6 D/A 转换原理图

表 8-2-3 给出该 4 位 D/A 转换器按图8-2-6b)的顺序输入数字信号时的转换关系。从表 8-2-3中可以看出，D/A 转换过程将数字信号转换成逐级增长的阶梯形模拟信号，信号代码不同，阶梯高度也就不同。在前面关于 A/D 转换问题的讨论中，我们已经利用了 D/A 转换器作为阶梯信号发生器来产生模拟比较电压。图 8-2-7 表示的是一个 4 应数字信号的所有代码从 0000 开始，以逐 1 增长的顺序转换成模拟信号的情况。不同的代码对应不同的阶梯电压高度。

D/A 转换器中主要数据关系 表 8-2-3

数字信号(V)				数字代码				各电阻电流				电流	模拟信号
D_3	D_2	D_1	D_0	D_3	D_2	D_1	D_0	I_3	I_2	I_1	I_0	$I=I_3+I_2+I_1+I_0$	u_A
0	0	0	0	0	0	0	0	0	0	0	0	0	0
0	0	0	5	0	0	0	1	0	0	0	5/8R	I_0	I_0R_A
0	0	5	0	0	0	1	0	0	0	5/4R	0	$2I_0$	$2I_0R_A$
0	0	5	5	0	0	1	1	0	0	5/4R	5/8R	$3I_0$	$3I_0R_A$
0	5	0	0	0	1	0	0	0	5/2R	0	0	$4I_0$	$4I_0R_A$
0	5	0	5	0	1	0	1	0	5/2R	0	5/8R	$5I_0$	$5I_0R_A$
0	5	5	0	0	1	1	0	0	5/2R	5/4R	0	$6I_0$	$6I_0R_A$
0	5	5	5	0	1	1	1	0	5/2R	5/4R	5/8R	$7I_0$	$7I_0R_A$
5	0	0	0	1	0	0	0	5/R	0	0	0	$8I_0$	$8I_0R_A$
5	0	0	5	1	0	0	1	5/R	0	0	5/8R	$9I_0$	$9I_0R_A$
5	0	5	0	1	0	1	0	5/R	0	5/4R	0	$10I_0$	$10I_0R_A$
5	0	5	5	1	0	1	1	5/R	0	5/4R	5/8R	$11I_0$	$11I_0R_A$
5	5	0	0	1	1	0	0	5/R	5/2R	0	0	$12I_0$	$12I_0R_A$
5	5	0	5	1	1	0	1	5/R	5/2R	0	5/8R	$13I_0$	$13I_0R_A$
5	5	5	0	1	1	1	0	5/R	5/2R	5/4R	0	$14I_0$	$14I_0R_A$
5	5	5	5	1	1	1	1	5/R	5/2R	5/4R	5/8R	$15I_0$	$15I_0R_A$

(三)模拟/数字转换(A/D)

采样信号在离散的采样点上或采样期间(采样脉冲宽度)里表示模拟信号的值。而 A/D

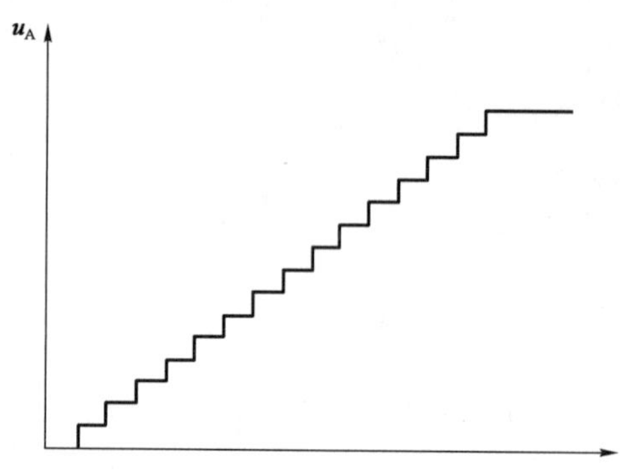

图 8-2-7　D/A 转换器输出电压波形

转换则对采样信号进行幅值量化处理，即用二进制代码来表示采样瞬间信号的值，或者说，用“0”、“1”代码对采样信号的值进行编码，从而将采样信号进一步转换为数字信号。

有多种方法可以用来将模拟信号转换为数字信号，图 8-2-8a)是数字电路中典型的基于逐次比较原理的 8 位 AD 转换原理图。图中的阶梯信号发生器在一个 8 位的数字信号(D_0，…，D_7，代码形式是从 0000 0000 到 1111 1111)驱动下工作，它从 0000000 开始，以每次加 1 的顺序产生 $2^8=256$ 个数字信号。相应地，阶梯波发生器从 0 开始，以每次增加一个台阶的顺序生成阶梯形式的模拟输出电压。对 8 位 A/D 转换器而言，阶梯信号发生器最多可以产生 255 个阶梯的模拟电压。不难看出，阶梯信号发生器将数字信号转换成了模拟信号，所以它实质上是一个 D/A 转换器。

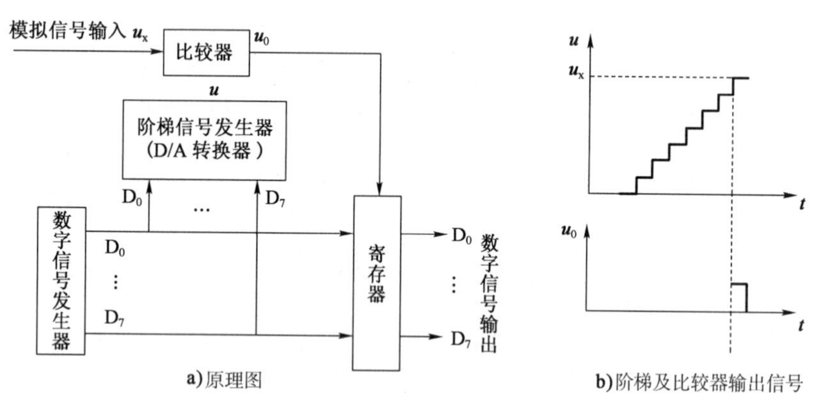

图 8-2-8　A/D 变换器工作原理

A/D 转换的主要过程叙述如下(见图 8-2-8a)：数字发生器发出信号 D_0，…，D_7 按二进制计数方式从 0 开始逐次加 1 生成数字信号序列，并驱动阶梯信号发生器输出电压逐次上升一个阶梯，同时将驱动数字信号送入寄存器中暂存；阶梯信号发生器输出电压 u 在比较器上与待转换的模拟信号电压 u_x 进行比较，当 $u \geqslant u_x$ 时，比较器送出一个脉冲信号 u_0，并控制寄存器将此时的数字信号输出，变换过程至此结束。

在实际测量中，阶梯信号电压与被测电压的逐次比较过程不可能正好以整数次结束。由于系统误差和外界干扰的影响，在被测值附近会发生一个阶梯电压的差异，即有时多一个字，有时少一个字的测量误差。数字电压表在使用中所发生的最后一位数字跳动的现象也是来源于此。所以，通常以字误差表示数字电压表的测量误差。本例中一个字误差等于

$$\Delta u = \frac{5v}{2^8 - 1} = 19.61\text{mV} \approx 20\text{mV}$$

即电压表的误差字约为 20mV，所以 8 位转换器组成的 5V 量程数字电压表只能用 3 位数来表示测量值，即整数 1 位，小数 2 位。显然，由于该表无法分辨 20mV 以下的电压，所以更长位数的显示对它是没有意义的。

习 题

8-2-1 信息与消息和信号的意义不同,但三者又是互相关联的概念,信息指受信者预先不知道的新内容。下列对于信息的描述正确的是( )。

A. 信号用来表示信息的物理形式,消息是运载消息的工具

B. 信息用来表示消息的物理形式,信号是运载消息的工具

C. 消息用来表示信号的物理形式,信息是运载消息的工具

D. 消息用来表示信息的物理形式,信号是运载消息的工具

8-2-2 信息可以以编码的方式载入( )。

A. 数字信号之中　　B. 模拟信号这中

C. 离散信号之中　　D. 采样保持信号之中

8-2-3 下述信号中哪一种属于时间信号( )。

A. 数字信号　　B. 模拟信号

C. 数字信号和模拟信号　　D. 数字信号和采样信号

8-2-4 模拟信号是( )。

A. 从对象发出的原始信号

B. 从对象发出并由人的感官所接收的信号

C. 从对象发出的原始信号的采样信号

D. 从对象发出的原始信号的电模拟信号

8-2-5 下列信号中哪一种是代码信号( )。

A. 模拟信号　　B. 模拟信号的采样信号

C. 采样保持信号　　D. 数字信号

8-2-6 下述哪种说法是错误的( )。

A. 在时间域中,模拟信号是信息的表现形式,信息装载于模拟信号的大小和变化之中

B. 在频率域中,信息装载于模拟信号特定的频谱结构之中

C. 模拟信号可描述为时间的函数,在一定条件下也可以用频率函数表示

D. 信高级息装载于模拟信号的传输媒体之中

8-2-7 用传感器对某管道中流动的液体流量 $x(t)$ 进行测量,测量结果为 $u(t)$,用采样器对 $u(t)$ 采样后得到信号 $u^*(t)$,那么( )。

A. $x(t)$ 和 $u(t)$ 均随时间连续变化,因此均是模拟信号

B. $u^*(t)$ 仅在采样点上有定义,因此是离散信号

C. $u^*(t)$ 仅在采样点上有定义,因此是数字信号

D. $u^*(t)$ 是 $x(t)$ 的模拟信号

8-2-8 模拟信号 $u(t)$ 的波形图如图所示,它的时间域描述形式是( )。

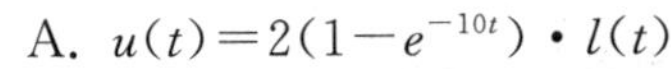

A. $u(t)=2(1-e^{-10t})\cdot l(t)$

B. $u(t)=2(1-e^{-0.1t})\cdot l(t)$

C. $u(t)=[2(1-e^{-10t})-2]\cdot l(t)$

D. $u(t)=2(1-e^{-10t})\cdot l(t)-2\cdot l(t-2)$

题 8-2-8 图

8-2-9 周期信号中的谐波信号频率是(　　)。

A. 固定不变的　　B. 连续变化的

C. 按周期信号频率的整倍数变化　　D. 按指数规律变化

8-2-10 非周期信号的频谱是(　　)。

A. 离散的

B. 连续的

C. 高频谐波部分是离散的,低频谐波部分是连续的

D. 有离散的有连续的,无规律可循

8-2-11 如图所示为电报信号、温度信号、触发脉冲信号和高频脉冲信号的波形,其中是连续信号的是(　　)。

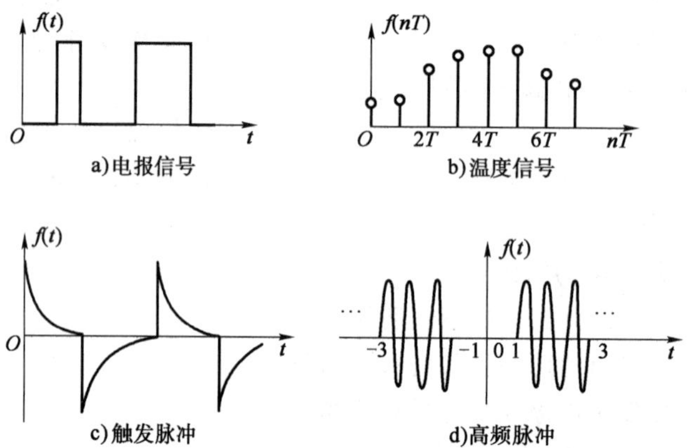

题 8-2-11 图

A. a)c)d)　　B. b)c)d)　　C. a)b)c)　　D. a)b)d)

8-2-12 图 a)所示电压信号波形经电路 A 变换成图 b)波形,在经电路 B 变换成图 c)波形,那么,电路 A 和电路 B 应依次选用(　　)。

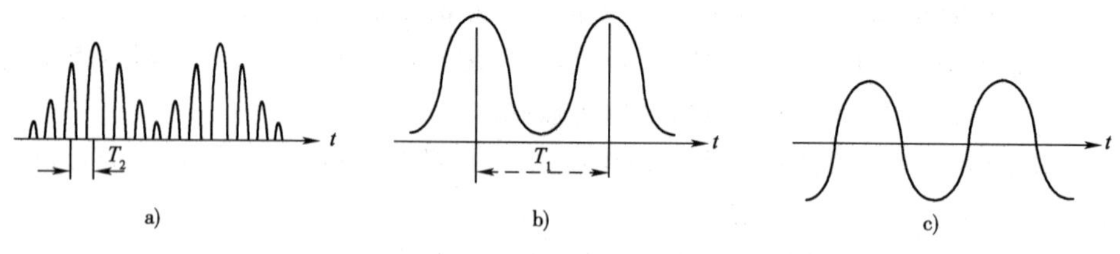

题 8-2-12 图

A. 低通滤波器和高通滤波器　　B. 高通滤波器和低通滤波器

C. 低通滤波器和带通滤波器　　D. 高通滤波器和带通滤波器

8-2-13 模拟信号经过(　　),才能转化为数字信号。

A. 信号幅度的量化　　B. 信号时间上的量化

C. 幅度和时间的量化　　D. 抽样

8-2-14 连续时间信号与通常所说的模拟信号的关系(　　)。

A. 完全不同　　B. 是同一个概念

C. 不完全相同　　D. 无法回答

8-2-15 根据如图所示信号 $f(t)$ 画出的 $f(2t)$ 波形图是(　　)。

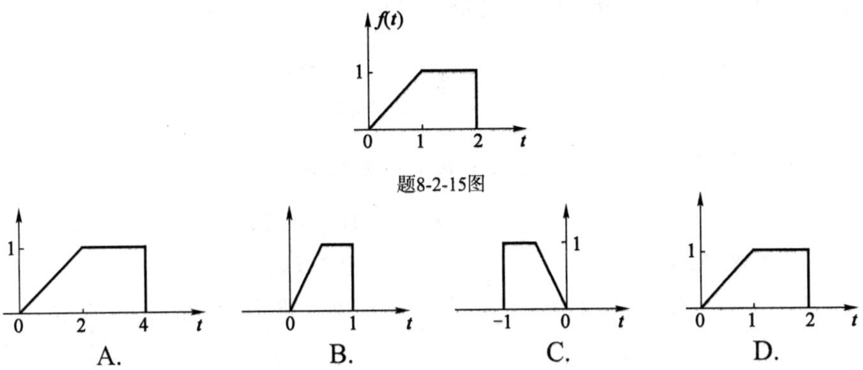

8-2-16　单位冲激信号 $\delta(t)$ 是(　　)。

A. 奇函数　　B. 偶函数

C. 非奇非偶函数　　D. 奇异函数，无奇偶性

8-2-17　单位阶跃函数信号 $\varepsilon(t)$ 具有(　　)。

A. 周期性　　B. 抽样性

C. 单边性　　D. 截断性

8-2-18　单位阶跃信号 $\varepsilon(t)$ 是物理量单位跃变现象，而单位冲激信号 $\delta(t)$ 是物理量产生单位跃变(　　)的现象。

A. 速度　　B. 幅度

C. 加速度　　D. 高度

8-2-19　如图所示的周期为 T 的三角波信号，在用傅氏级数分析周期信号时，系数 a_0、a_n 和 b_n 判断正确的是(　　)。

A. 该信号是奇函数且在一个周期的平均值为零，所以傅里叶系数 a_0 和 b_n 是零

B. 该信号是偶函数且在一个周期的平均值不为零，所以傅里叶系数 a_0 和 a_n 不是零

C. 该信号是奇函数且在一个周期的平均值不为零，所以傅里叶系数 a_0 和 b_n 不是零

D. 该信号是偶函数且在一个周期的平均值为零，所以傅里叶系数 a_0 和 b_n 是零

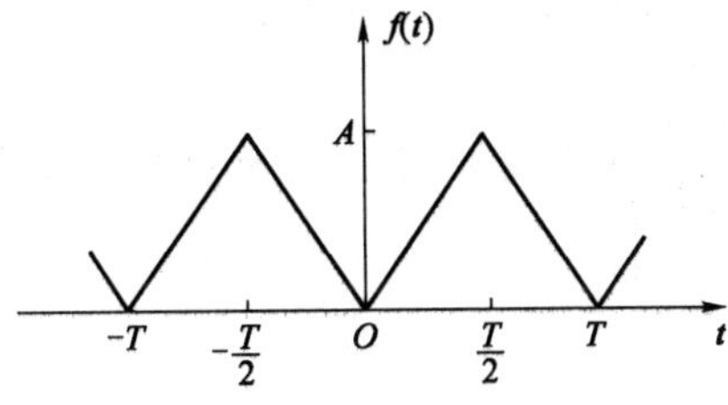

题 8-2-19 图

8-2-20　$(70)_{10}$ 的二进制数是(　　)。

A. $(0011100)_2$　　B. $(1000110)_2$

C. $(1110000)_2$　　D. $(0111001)_2$

8-2-21　将$(10010.0101)_2$转换成十进制数是(　　)。

A. 36.1875　　B. 18.1875

C. 18.3125　　D. 36.3125

8-2-22　将$(11010010.01010100)_2$表示成十六进制数是(　　)。

A. $(D2.54)_H$　　B. D2.54

C. $(D2.A8)_H$　　D. $(D2.54)_B$

8-2-23　数字信号如图所示，如果用其表示数值，那么，该数字信号表示的数量是(　　)。

A. 3个0和3个1

B. 一万零一十一

C. 3

D. 19

0 1 0 0 1 1

题 8-2-23 图

8-2-24　某逻辑问题的真值表见表，由此可以得到，该逻辑问题的输入输出之间的关系为(　　)。

A. F=0+1=1

B. $F=\overline{A}\overline{B}C+ABC$

C. $F=A\overline{B}C+ABC$

D. $F=\overline{A}\overline{B}+AB$

题 8-2-24 表

C A B	F
1 0 0	1
1 0 1	0
1 1 0	0
1 1 1	1

题解及参考答案

第二节

8-2-1　**解**:信息、消息与信号的关系是借助某种信号的形式传送消息，受信者可以从所得到的消息中提取信息。

答案:D

8-2-2　**解**:信息是以编码方式载入数字信号中的。

答案:A

8-2-3　**解**:模拟信号是连续的时间信号，是实际物理对象随时间变化的真实过程。

答案:B

8-2-4　**解**:同上题。

答案:D

8-2-5　**解**:模拟信号是连续的时间信号，它的采样信号是离散的时间信号，采样保持信号是采样信号的特殊形式，只有数字信号是代码信号。

答案:D

8-2-6　**解**:传输媒体是一种介质，它可以传送信号但不表示信息。

答案:D

8-2-7 **解**:由原始形态(光、热等物理量)转换而来的连续时间信号,通常是指电信号,称作模拟信号。

答案:B

8-2-8 **解**:本题可以用信号的叠加关系分析。将原图分解为指数函数和阶跃函数,将结果求和即可。

答案:D

8-2-9 **解**:周期信号中的谐波信号是由傅里叶级数分解得到的,它的频率是同期信号频率的整数倍。

答案:C

8-2-10 **解**:非周期信号的傅里叶变换形式是频率的连续函数,它的频谱是连续频谱。

答案:B

8-2-11 **解**:图示中的温度信号是采样以后的信号,$f(nt)$只是在n为整数点上有值,因此它是个离散信号。

答案:A

8-2-12 **解**:该电路是通过频率选择器,根据信号频率的不同来处理信号的。

答案:A

8-2-13 **解**:模拟信号不仅要经过抽样过程,还要在信号的幅度上进行量化才能成为数字信号。

答案:C

8-2-14 **解**:模拟信号定义为在时间和数值都连续的信号,通常指的是电信号。

答案:C

8-2-15 **解**:图 b)所示的信号是原图信号的压缩信号。

答案:B

8-2-16 **解**:单位中激信号符合偶数特性,关于y轴对称。

答案:B

8-2-17 **解**:单位阶跃信号有单边性质。$\varepsilon(t)=\begin{cases}0 & t<0\\1 & t>0\end{cases}$

答案:C

8-2-18 **解**:单位中激函数和单位阶跃信号的关系为$\delta(t)=\frac{\mathrm{d}}{\mathrm{d}t}[\varepsilon(t)]$。

答案:A

8-2-19 **解**:当函数在一个周期里的正、负面积相等时,a_0等于零;函数关于$f(t)$轴对称,为偶函数,$a_n=0$;如果函数对称于原点时,$b_n=0$。

答案:B

8-2-20 **解**:根据$D=\sum k_i\times N^i$展开,进制中$k_i=0,1$。

答案:B

8-2-21 **解**:将十进制转换为二进制数时,整数部分用除法,小数部分用乘法。

答案:C

8-2-22 **解**:将二进制转换为十六进制数时,以小数点为界,将二进制4位一组,左右两边分开写。注意只有十进制数的脚标才能省去。

答案:A

8-2-23 **解**:通常数字信号是二进制数。数字电路中的高电位表示“1”,低电位表示“0”。

答案:D

8-2-24 **解**:本题为数字信号中的编码问题,输入信号 CAB 相互之间是与逻辑关系,输出 F 的对应关系是或逻辑关系。

答案:B

第九章　计算机应用基础

复 习 指 导

一、考试大纲

7.7　计算机系统

计算机系统组成；计算机的发展；计算机的分类；计算机系统特点；计算机硬件系统组成；CPU；存储器；输入/输出设备及控制系统；总线；数模/模数转换；计算机软件系统组成；系统软件；操作系统；操作系统定义；操作系统特征；操作系统功能；操作系统分类；支撑软件；应用软件；计算机程序设计语言。

7.8　信息表示

信息在计算机内的表示；二进制编码；数据单位；计算机内数值数据的表示；计算机内非数值数据的表示；信息及其主要特征。

7.9　常用操作系统

Windows 发展；进程和处理器管理；存储管理；文件管理；输入/输出管理；设备管理；网络服务。

7.10　计算机网络

计算机与计算机网络；网络概念；网络功能；网络组成；网络分类；局域网；广域网；因特网；网络管理；网络安全；Windows 系统中的网络应用；信息安全；信息保密。

二、复习指导

在计算机系统这一章中要求掌握以下几部分内容。

（一）计算机基础知识

计算机的分类、计算机系统的组成（硬件和软件的组成及功能）、操作系统，在这部分中重点掌握以下内容：

（1）计算机按年代的分类；

（2）CPU 的组成及功能、存储器的种类、输入/输出设备；

（3）软件的组成；

（4）操作系统的功能。

（二）计算机程序设计语言

计算机语言的分类，发展趋势及计算机常用的高级程序设计语言。

（三）信息表示

数制、二进制、数值转换、信息的表示及存储，并要求重点掌握以下内容：

（1）信息的表示方法；

（2）数制的定义；

（3）二进制；

(4)数制的转换；

(5)非数值数据在计算机内的表示；

(6)多媒体数据在计算机内的表示。

(四)常用操作系统

Windows 的发展、操作系统管理，并要求重点掌握以下内容：

(1)进程和处理器管理；

(2)存储资源管理；

(3)文件管理；

(4)输入/输出管理；

(5)设备管理；

(6)网络服务。

(五)计算机网络

网络的功能、组成及分类、网络安全、网络应用，并要求重点掌握以下内容：

(1)网络的概念；

(2)网络的功能；

(3)网络的组成；

(4)网络的分类；

(5)TCP/IP 协议的作用；

(6)IP 地址和域名的作用；

(7)如何防止病毒的攻击；

(8)网络应用；

(9)网络管理。

第一节　计算机基础知识

一、计算机的发展

1946 年 2 月，人类历史上第一台数字电子计算机 ENIAC 诞生了，它标志着人类社会计算机时代的开始。ENIAC 由 18 000 多个电子管和 1 500 多个继电器组成，占地达 170m^2，重 30t，每秒钟可执行 5 000 次加法运算，应用于当时军事指挥中的弹道计算。它的严重缺陷在于不能存储程序。

为了解决存储程序问题，1946 年 6 月，著名数学家冯・诺依曼提出了“存储程序”和“程序控制”的概念，为现代计算机的体系结构奠定了理论基础。它的主要思想是：

(1)采用二进制形式表示数据和指令。

(2)计算机应包括运算器、控制器、存储器、输入设备和输出设备等五大基本部件。

(3)采用存储程序和程序控制的工作方式。

存储程序是指把解决问题的程序和需要加工处理的原始数据存入存储器中，这是计算机能够自动、连续工作的先决条件。

程序控制是指由控制器从存储器中逐条地读出指令，并发出各条指令相应的控制信号，指挥和控制计算机的各个组成部件自动、协调地执行指令所规定的操作，直至得到最终的结果，即整个信息处理过程是在程序的控制下自动实现的。因此，计算机的工作过程实际上是周而复始地取指令，执行指令的过程。

半个多世纪以来，尽管计算机技术的发展速度是惊人的，但至今广泛使用的绝大部分计算机，就其基本组成而言，仍遵循冯·诺依曼提出的这种设计思想，均属于冯·诺依曼体系的计算机。

计算机与信息处理技术的广泛应用，推动了集成电路技术与制造工艺的迅猛发展。自ENIAC诞生以来直至多年后的今天，微型计算机上使用的 Pentium（奔腾）CPU 芯片，集成了上亿个晶体管，而面积只有几个平方毫米，时钟工作频率可达 3G 以上，总功率几十瓦。1981年美国 IBM 公司推出的个人计算机（PC，Personal Computer），最终导致了计算机应用的社会化与家庭化。

【例 9-1-1】 当前计算机的发展趋势是向多个方向发展，下面四个选项中不正确的一项是：

A. 高性能、人性化、网络化　　B. 多极化、多媒体、智能化

C. 高性能、多媒体、智能化　　D. 高集成、低噪声、低成本

答案：D

二、现代计算机的分类

（一）按年代分类

1. 大型主机阶段

20 世纪 40～50 年代，是第一代电子管计算机。经历了电子管数字计算机、晶体管数字计算机、集成电路数字计算机和大规模集成电路数字计算机的发展历程，计算机技术逐渐走向成熟。

2. 小型计算机阶段

20 世纪 60～70 年代，是对大型主机进行的第一次“缩小化”，可以满足中小企业事业单位的信息处理要求，成本较低，价格可被接受。

3. 微型计算机阶段

20 世纪 70～80 年代，是对大型主机进行的第二次“缩小化”，1976 年美国苹果公司成立，1977 年就推出了 Apple II 计算机，大获成功。1981 年 IBM 推出 IBM-PC，此后它经历了若干代的演进，占领了个人计算机市场，使得个人计算机得到了很大的普及。

4. 客户机/服务器阶段

该阶段即 C/S 阶段。随着 1964 年 IBM 与美国航空公司建立了第一个全球联机订票系统，把美国当时 2 000 多个订票的终端用电话线连接在了一起，标志着计算机进入了客户机/服务器阶段，这种模式至今仍在大量使用。在客户机/服务器网络中，服务器是网络的核心，而客户机是网络的基础，客户机依靠服务器获得所需要的网络资源，而服务器为客户机提供网络必需的资源。C/S 结构的优点是能充分发挥客户端 PC 的处理能力，很多工作可以在客户端处理后再提交给服务器，大大减轻了服务器的压力。

5. Internet 阶段

Internet 阶段也称互联网、因特网、网际网阶段。互联网即广域网、局域网及单机按照一定的通信协议组成的国际计算机网络。互联网始于 1969 年，是在 ARPA（美国国防部研究计划署）将美国西南部的大学[UCLA（加利福尼亚大学洛杉矶分校）、StanfordResearchInstitute（史坦福大学研究学院）、UCSB（加利福尼亚大学）和 University of Utah（犹他州大学）]的四台主要的计算机连接起来。此后经历了文本到图片，到现在语音、视频等阶段，带宽越来越快，功

能越来越强。互联网的特征是：全球性，交互性，成长性，即时性，多媒体性。

6.云计算时代

从2008年起，云计算(Cloud Computing)概念逐渐流行起来，它正在成为一个通俗和大众化(Popular)的词语。云计算被视为“革命性的计算模型”，因为它使得超级计算能力通过互联网自由流通成为可能。企业与个人用户无需再投入昂贵的硬件购置成本，只需要通过互联网来购买或租赁计算力，用户只需为自己需要的功能付钱，同时消除传统软件在硬件、软件、专业技能方面的花费。云计算让用户脱离技术与部署上的复杂性而获得应用。云计算囊括了开发、架构、负载平衡和商业模式等，是软件业的未来模式。它基于Web的服务，以互联网为中心。

(二)按硬件分类

将计算机按硬件分类，分为服务器、工作站、台式机、笔记本计算机、手持设备五大类。

1.服务器

服务器的英文名为Server，专指某些高性能计算机，能通过网络对外提供服务。相对于普通电脑来说，稳定性、安全性、性能等方面都要求更高，因此在CPU、芯片组、内存、磁盘系统、网络等硬件上和普通电脑有所不同。服务器是网络的节点，存储、处理网络上80%的数据、信息，在网络中起到举足轻重的作用。它们是为客户端计算机提供各种服务的高性能的计算机，其高性能主要表现在高速度的运算能力，长时间的可靠运行，强大的外部数据吞吐能力等方面。服务器的构成与普通电脑类似，也有处理器、硬盘、内存、系统总线等，但因为它是针对具体的网络应用特别制定的，因而服务器与微机在处理能力、稳定性、可靠性、安全性、可扩展性、可管理性等方面差异很大。

2.工作站

工作站的英文名为Workstation，是一种以个人计算机和分布式网络计算为基础，主要面向专业应用领域，具备强大的数据运算与图形、图像处理能力，为满足工程设计、动画制作、科学研究、软件开发、金融管理、信息服务、模拟仿真等专业领域而设计开发的高性能计算机。它属于一种高档的电脑，一般拥有较大屏幕显示器和大容量的内存和硬盘，也拥有较强的信息处理功能和高性能的图形、图像处理功能以及联网功能。

3.台式机

台式机的英文名为Desktop，也叫桌面机，为现在非常流行的微型计算机，多数家用和办公用的机器都是台式机。台式机的性能相对较笔记本电脑要强。

4.笔记本电脑

笔记本电脑的英文名为Notebook Computer(简称NB)，也称手提电脑或膝上型电脑，笔记本电脑可以大体分为4类：

(1)商务型。商务型笔记本电脑一般可以概括为移动性强、电池续航时间长、商务软件多。

(2)时尚型。时尚型外观主要针对时尚女性。

(3)多媒体应用型。多媒体应用型笔记本电脑则有较强的图形、图像处理功能和多媒体功能，尤其是播放功能。

(4)特殊用途。

5.手持设备

手持设备英文名为Handhold，种类较多，如PDA，SmartPhone，智能手机，3G手机，Netbook，EeePC等，它们的特点是体积小。随着3G时代的到来，手持设备将会获得更大的发展，其功能也会越来越强。

三、计算机系统的特点及组成(硬件和软件部分)

(一)计算机系统的特点

(1)使用单一的处理部件来完成计算、存储以及通信的工作;

(2)存储单元是定长的线性组织;

(3)存储空间的单元是直接寻址的;

(4)使用低级机器语言,指令通过操作码来完成简单的操作;

(5)对计算进行集中的顺序控制;

(6)计算机硬件系统由运算器、存储器、控制器、输入设备、输出设备五大部件组成并规定了它们的基本功能;

(7)采用二进制形式表示数据和指令;

(8)在执行程序和处理数据时必须将程序和数据从外存储器装入主存储器中,然后才能使计算机在工作时能够自动地从存储器中取出指令并加以执行。

【例 9-1-2】 根据冯·诺依曼结构原理,计算机的硬件由:

A. 运算器、存储器、打印机组成

B. 寄存器、存储器、硬盘存储器组成

C. 运算器、控制器、存储器、I/O 设备组成

D. CPU、显示器、键盘组成

解 根据冯·诺依曼结构原理,计算机硬件是由运算器、控制器、存储器、I/O 设备组成。

答案:C

【例 9-1-3】 计算机系统拥有非常突出的特点,在下面有关计算机系统特点的四个选项中不正确的一项是:

A. 计算能力、判断能力、存储能力　　B. 精确计算能力、通俗易用

C. 价格低廉、操作方便、界面友好　　D. 联网功能、快速操作能力、通用性

解 选项 C 属于没有抓住重点,表述不当。

答案:C

【例 9-1-4】 计算器按用途可分为:

A. 专业计算器和通用计算器　　B. 专业计算器和数字计算器

C. 通用计算器和模拟计算器　　D. 数字计算器和现代计算器

解 计算机按用途可分为专业计算机和通用计算机。专业计算机是为解决某种特殊问题而设计的计算机,针对具体问题能显示出有效、快速和经济的特性,但它的适应性较差,不适用于其他方面的应用。在导弹和火箭上使用的计算机很大部分就是专业计算机。通用计算机适应性很强,应用范围很广,如应用于科学计算、数据处理和实时控制等领域。

答案:A

(二)计算机系统的组成

计算机系统由硬件和软件两大部分组成。其中,硬件是指构成计算机系统的物理实体(或物理装置),如主板、机箱、键盘、显示器和打印机等。软件是指为运行、维护、管理和应用计算机所编制的所有程序的集合。图 9-1-1 给出了计算机硬件系统组成框图。

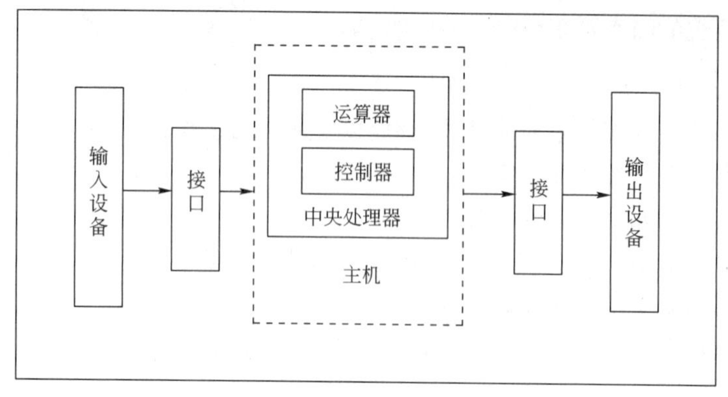

图 9-1-1 计算机硬件系统组成

1.硬件部分

(1)输入装置。将程序和数据的信息转换成相应的电信号,让计算机能接收的装置,如键盘、鼠标、光笔、扫描仪、图形板、外存储器等。

(2)输出装置。能将计算机内部处理后的信息传递出来的设备,如显示器、打印机、绘图仪、外存储器等。

(3)存储器。计算机在处理数据的过程中或在处理数据之后把程序和数据存储起来的装置。存储器分为主存储器和辅助存储器。主存储器与中央处理器组装在一起构成主机,直接受 CPU 控制,因此也被称为内存储器,简称内存。存储器由内存、高速缓存、外存和管理这些存储器的软件组成,以字节为单位,是用来存放正在执行的程序、待处理数据及运算结果的部件。内存分为只读存储器(ROM)、随机存储器(RAM)、高速缓冲存储器(Cache)。

①只读存储器(ROM):是一种只能读不能写入的存储器,最大特点是电源断电后信息不会丢失,经常用来存放监控和诊断程序。

②随机存储器(RAM):可随机读出和写入信息,用来存放用户的程序和数据,关机后 RAM 中的内容自动消失,并不可恢复。

③高速缓冲存储器(Cache):在逻辑上位于 CPU 和内存之间,其运算速度高于内存而低于 CPU,其作用是减少 CPU 的等待时间,提高 CPU 的读写速度,而不会改变内存的容量。辅助存储器也称外存储器,存储容量大,外存分为磁表面存储器和光存储器两大类。

(4)运算器。它是计算机的核心部件,对信息或数据进行加工和处理,主要由逻辑运算单元(ALU)组成,在控制器的指挥下可以完成各种算术运算、逻辑运算和其他操作。

(5)控制器。它是计算机的神经中枢和指挥中心,计算机的硬件系统由控制器控制其全部动作。运算器和控制器一起称为中央处理器。主存、运算器和控制器统称为主机。输入装置和输出装置统称为输入、输出装置。通常把输入、输出装置和外存一起称为外围设备。外存既是输入设备又是输出设备。

(6)中央处理器(CPU)。CPU 主要由运算器、控制器、寄存器等组成。运算器按控制器发出的命令来完成各种操作。控制器规定计算机执行指令的顺序,并根据指令的信息控制计算机各部分协同动作。

(7)计算机总线。在计算机系统中,各个部件之间传送信息的公共通路叫总线。总线是一种内部结构,它是 CPU、内存、输入、输出设备传递信息的公用通道,主机的各个部件通过总线相连接,外部设备通过相应的接口电路再与总线相连接,从而形成了计算机硬件系统。微型计算机是以总线结构来连接各个功能部件的。总线分为主板总线、硬盘总线及其他总线。

(8)数模/模数转换。数模转换器是将数字信号转换为模拟信号的系统，一般用低通滤波即可以实现。模数转换器是将模拟信号转换成数字信号的系统，是一个滤波、采样保持和编码的过程。模拟信号经带限滤波、采样保持电路，变为阶梯形状信号，然后通过编码器，使得阶梯状信号中的各个电平变为二进制码。

【例 9-1-5】 总线中的控制总线传输的是：

A. 程序和数据　　B. 主存储器的地址码

C. 控制信息　　D. 用户输入的数据

解 计算机的总线可以划分为数据总线、地址总线和控制总线。数据总线用来传输数据，地址总线用来传输数据地址，控制总线用来传输控制信息。

答案：C

【例 9-1-6】 微处理器与存储器以及外围设备之间的数据传送操作通过：

A. 显示器和键盘进行　　B. 总线进行

C. 输入/输出设备进行　　D. 控制命令进行

解 当要对存储器中的内容进行读写操作时，来自地址总线的存储器地址经地址译码器译码之后，选中指定的存储单元，而读写控制电路根据读写命令实施对存储器的存取操作，数据总线则用来传送写入内存储器或从内存储器读出的信息。

答案：B

2. 软件部分(见图 9-1-2)

(1)系统软件。它是生成、准备和执行其他软件所需要的一组程序，通常负责管理、监督和维护计算机各种软硬件资源。给用户提供一个友好的操作界面。

系统软件主要有操作系统、程序设计语言[机器语言、汇编语言、高级语言、非过程语言(不必关心问题的解法和处理过程的描述，只要说明所要完成的加工和条件，指明输入数据以及输出形式，就能得到所要的结果。如 Visual C＋＋、Java 语言等)、智能性语言(应用于抽象问题求解、数据逻辑、公式处理、自然语言理解、专家系统和人工智能的许多领域)]。

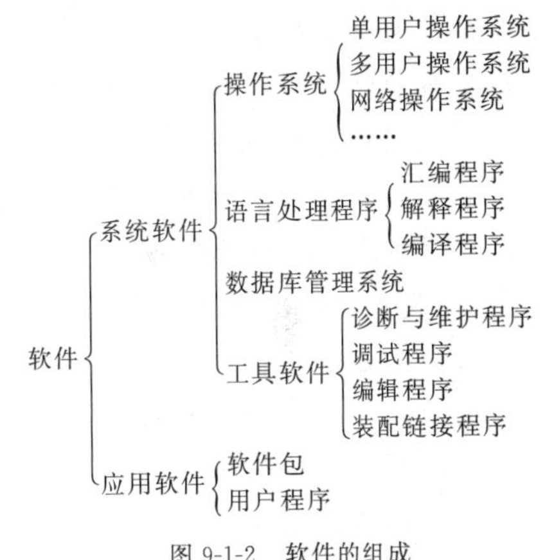

图 9-1-2　软件的组成

(2)应用软件。它是用户为了解决某些特定具体问题而开发或外购的各种程序，如 Word，Excel 等。

【例 9-1-7】 目前常用的计算机辅助设计软件是：

A. Microsoft Word　　B. Auto CAD

C. Visual BASIC　　D. Microsoft Access

解 Microsoft Word 是文字处理软件。Visual BASIC 简称 VB，是 Microsoft 公司推出的一种 Windows 应用程序开发工具。Microsoft Access 是小型数据库管理软件。Auto CAD 是专业绘图软件，主要用于工业设计中，被广泛用于民用、军事等各个领域。CAD 是 Computer Aided Design 的缩写，意思为计算机辅助设计。加上 Auto，指它可以应用于几乎所有跟绘图有关的行业，比如建筑、机械、电子、天文、物理、化工等。

答案：B

【例 9-1-8】 根据软件的功能和特点，计算机软件一般分为：

A. 系统软件和非系统软件　　　　B. 应用软件和非应用软件
C. 系统软件和应用软件　　　　D. 系统软件和管理软件

答案:C

四、操作系统

(一)操作系统定义

操作系统是控制其他程序运行,管理系统资源并为用户提供操作界面的系统软件的集合。

(二)操作系统功能及特征

操作系统(Operating System,简称 OS)是一种管理电脑硬件与软件资源的程序,同时也是计算机系统的内核与基石。操作系统身负诸如管理与配置内存,决定系统资源供需的优先次序,控制输入与输出设备,操作网络与管理文件系统等基本事务。操作系统管理计算机系统的全部硬件资源,包括软件资源及数据资源,控制程序运行,改善人机界面,为其他应用软件提供支持等,使计算机系统所有资源最大限度地发挥作用,为用户提供方便的、有效的、友善的服务界面。操作系统是一个庞大的管理控制程序,大致包括五个方面的管理功能:进程与处理机管理,作业管理,存储管理,设备管理,文件管理。目前微机上常见的操作系统有 DOS、OS/2、UNIX、XENIX、LINUX、Windows、Netware 等。但所有的操作系统都具有并发性、共享性、虚拟性和不确定性这四个基本特征。

(三)操作系统的分类

操作系统大致可分为六种类型。

1. 简单操作系统

它是计算机初期所配置的操作系统,如 IBM 公司的磁盘操作系统 DOS/360 和微型计算机的操作系统 CP/M 等。这类操作系统的功能主要是操作命令的执行,文件服务,支持高级程序设计语言编译程序和控制外部设备等。

2. 分时系统

它支持位于不同终端的多个用户同时使用一台计算机,彼此独立互不干扰,用户感到好像一台计算机全为他所用。

3. 实时操作系统

它是为实时计算机系统配置的操作系统。其主要特点是资源的分配和调度,首先要考虑实时性,然后才是效率。此外,实时操作系统应有较强的容错能力。

4. 网络操作系统

它是为计算机网络配置的操作系统。在其支持下,网络中的各台计算机能互相通信和共享资源。其主要特点是与网络的硬件相结合来完成网络的通信任务。

5. 分布操作系统

它是为分布计算系统配置的操作系统。它在资源管理、通信控制和操作系统的结构等方面都与其他操作系统有较大的区别。由于计算机系统的资源分布于系统的不同计算机上,操作系统对用户的资源需求不能像一般的操作系统那样等待有资源时直接分配的简单做法,而是要在系统的各台计算机上搜索,找到所需资源后才可进行分配。对于有些资源,如具有多个副本的文件,还必须考虑一致性。所谓一致性,是指若干个用户对同一个文件所同时读出的数据是一致的。为了保证一致性,操作系统须控制文件的读、写、操作,使得多个用户可同时读一个文件,而任一时刻最多只能有一个用户在修改文件。分布操作系统的通信功能类似于网络操作系统。由于分布计算机系统不像网络分布得很广,同时分布操作系统还要支持并行处理,因此它提供的通信机制和网络操作系统提供的有所不同,它要求通信速度高。分布操作系统的结构也不同于其他操作系统,它分布于系统的各台计算机上,能并行地处理用户的各种需求,有较强的容错能力。

6. 智能操作系统

现在很多智能操作系统应用在手机上,如 Symbian 操作系统在智能移动终端上拥有强大的应用程序以及通信能力,它有一个非常健全的核心——强大的对象导向系统、企业用标准通信传输协议以及完美的 sunjava 语言。Symbian 认为无线通信装置除了要提供声音沟通的功能外,同时也应具有其他多种沟通方式,如触笔、键盘等。在硬件设计上,它可以提供许多不同风格的外形,像使用真实或虚拟的键盘,在软件功能上可以容纳许多功能,包括和他人互相分享信息,浏览网页,传输、接收电子信件,传真以及个人生活行程管理等。此外,Symbian 操作系统在扩展性方面为制造商预留了多种接口,而且操作系统还可以细分成三种类型:Pearl、Quartz、Crystal,分别对应普通手机、智能手机、HandHeld PC 场合的应用。

习　题

9-1-1　微型计算机的硬件包括(　　)。

A. 微处理器、存储器、外部设备、外围设备

B. 微处理器、RAM、MS 系统、FORTRAN 语言

C. ROM 和键盘、显示器

D. 软盘驱动器和微处理器、打印机

9-1-2　微型计算机的软件包括(　　)。

A. MS-DOS 系统、Super SAP　　B. dBASE 数据库、FORTRAN 语言

C. 机器语言和通用软件　　D. 系统软件、程序语言和通用软件

9-1-3　对磁盘写保护后,对磁盘(　　)。

A. 只能读取数据,不能写入数据　　B. 只能写入数据,不能读取数据

C. 不能读取数据,也不能写入数据　　D. 既能读取数据,又能写入数据

9-1-4　既可做输入设备,又可做输出设备的是(　　)。

A. 显示器　　B. 打印机　　C. 硬盘　　D. 光盘

9-1-5　软件中(　　)是非系统软件。

A. DOS 系统　　B. FORTRAN 77　　C. BASIC　　D. TBSA

9-1-6　计算机的中央处理器包括(　　)。

A. 整个计算机主板　　B. CPU 的运算器部分

C. CPU 的控制器部分　　D. 运算器和控制器

9-1-7　计算机中 CPU 中央处理器的功能是(　　)。

A. 完成输入输出操作　　B. 进行数据处理

C. 协调计算机各种操作　　D. 负责各种运算和控制工作

9-1-8　在工作中,若微型计算机的电源突然中断,则只有(　　)不会丢失。

A. RAM 和 ROM 中的信息　　B. ROM 中的信息

C. RAM 中的信息　　D. RAM 中部分信息

9-1-9　在“我的电脑”窗口中,如果要整理磁盘上的碎片,应选择磁盘“属性”对话框的

(　　)选项卡。

A. 常规　　　B. 硬件　　　C. 共享　　　D. 工具

第二节　计算机程序设计语言

一、计算机语言

计算机语言(Computer Language)指用于人与计算机之间通讯的语言。计算机语言是人与计算机之间传递信息的媒介。计算机系统的最大特征是指令通过一种语言传达给机器。为了使电子计算机进行各种工作,就需要有一套用以编写计算机程序的数字、字符和语法规则,由这些字符和语法规则组成对计算机的各种指令(或各种语句),就是计算机能接受的语言。

(一)计算机语言的分类

计算机语言的种类非常的多,总的来说可以分成机器语言、汇编语言、高级语言三大类。

1. 机器语言

机器语言是用二进制代码表示的计算机能直接识别和执行的一种机器指令的集合。它是计算机的设计者通过计算机的硬件结构赋予计算机的操作功能。机器语言具有灵活、直接执行和速度快等特点。

用机器语言编写程序,编程人员要首先熟记所用计算机的全部指令代码和代码的含义。手编程序时,程序员得自己处理每条指令和每一数据的存储分配和输入输出,还得记住编程过程中每步所使用的工作单元处在何种状态。这是一件十分繁琐的工作,编写程序花费的时间往往是实际运行时间的几十倍或几百倍。而且,编出的程序全是些 0 和 1 的指令代码。直观性差,还容易出错。除了计算机生产厂家的专业人员外,绝大多数程序员已经不再去学习机器语言了。

2. 汇编语言

为了克服机器语言难读、难编、难记和易出错的缺点,人们就用与代码指令实际含义相近的英文缩写词、字母和数字等符号来取代指令代码(如用 ADD 表示运算符号"+"的机器代码),于是就产生了汇编语言。所以说,汇编语言是一种用助记符表示的仍然面向机器的计算机语言。汇编语言亦称符号语言。汇编语言由于是采用了助记符号来编写程序,比用机器语言的二进制代码编程要方便些,在一定程度上简化了编程过程。汇编语言的特点是用符号代替了机器指令代码。而且助记符与指令代码一一对应,基本保留了机器语言的灵活性。使用汇编语言能面向机器并较好地发挥机器的特性,得到质量较高的程序。

汇编语言中由于使用了助记符号,用汇编语言编制的程序送入计算机,计算机不能像用机器语言编写的程序一样直接识别和执行,必须通过预先放入计算机的"汇编程序"的加工和翻译,才能变成能够被计算机识别和处理的二进制代码程序。用汇编语言等非机器语言书写好的符号程序称源程序,运行时汇编程序要将源程序翻译成目标程序。目标程序是机器语言程序,它一经被安置在内存的预定位置上,就能被计算机的 CPU 处理和执行。

汇编语言像机器指令一样,是硬件操作的控制信息,因而仍然是面向机器的语言,使用起来还是比较繁琐费时,通用性也差。汇编语言是低级语言。但是,汇编语言用来编制系统软件和过程控制软件,其目标程序占用内存空间少,运行速度快,有着高级语言不可替代的用途。

3. 高级语言

不论是机器语言还是汇编语言都是面向硬件具体操作的,语言对机器过分依赖,要求使用者必须对硬件结构及其工作原理都十分熟悉，这对非计算机专业人员是难以做到的，对于计算机的推广应用是不利的。计算机事业的发展，促使人们去寻求一些与人类自然语言相接近且能为计算机所接受的语意确定、规则明确、自然直观和通用易学的计算机语言。这种与自然语言相近并为计算机所接受和执行的计算机语言称高级语言。高级语言是面向用户的语言。无论何种机型的计算机，只要配备上相应的高级语言的编译或解释程序，则用该高级语言编写的程序就可以通用。

如今被广泛使用的高级语言有 BASIC、PASCAL、C、COBOL、FORTRAN、LOGO 以及 VC、VB 等。这些语言都是属于系统软件。

计算机并不能直接地接受和执行用高级语言编写的源程序，源程序在输入计算机时，通过“翻译程序”翻译成机器语言形式的目标程序，计算机才能识别和执行。这种“翻译”通常有两种方式，即编译方式和解释方式。编译方式是：事先编好一个称为编译程序的机器语言程序，作为系统软件存放在计算机内，当用户由高级语言编写的源程序输入计算机后，编译程序便把源程序整个地翻译成用机器语言表示的与之等价的目标程序，然后计算机再执行该目标程序，以完成源程序要处理的运算并取得结果。解释方式是：源程序进入计算机时，解释程序边扫描边解释并逐句输入逐句翻译，计算机一句句执行，并不产生目标程序。PASCAL、FORTRAN、COBOL 等高级语言执行编译方式；BASIC 语言则以执行解释方式为主；而 PASCAL、C 语言是能书写编译程序的高级程序设计语言。每一种高级（程序设计）语言，都有自己人为规定的专用符号、英文单词、语法规则和语句结构（书写格式）。高级语言与自然语言（英语）更接近，而与硬件功能相分离（彻底脱离了具体的指令系统），便于广大用户掌握和使用。高级语言的通用性强，兼容性好，便于移植。

（二）计算机语言的发展趋势

面向对象程序设计以及数据抽象在现代程序设计思想中占有很重要的地位，未来语言的发展将不再是一种单纯的语言标准，将会以一种完全面向对象，更易表达现实世界，更易为人编写，其使用将不再只是专业的编程人员，人们完全可以用订制真实生活中一项工作流程的简单方式来完成编程。

二、计算机程序设计语言

1. C 语言

C 语言是 Dennis Ritchie 在 20 世纪 70 年代创建的，它功能更强大且与 ALGOL 保持更连续的继承性，而 ALGOL 则是 COBOL 和 FORTRAN 的结构化继承者。C 语言被设计成一个比它的前辈更精巧、更简单的版本，它适于编写系统级的程序，比如操作系统。在此之前，操作系统是使用汇编语言编写的，而且不可移植。C 语言是第一个使得系统级代码移植成为可能的编程语言。

2. C++

C++语言是具有面向对象特性的 C 语言的继承者。面向对象编程，或称 OOP（Object Oriented Programming）是结构化编程的下一步。OOP 程序由对象组成，其中的对象是数据和函数离散集合。有许多可用的对象库存在，这使得编程简单得只需要将一些程序堆在一起。比如说，有很多的 GUI（Graphical User Interface）和数据库的库实现为对象的集合。

3. 汇编语言

汇编是第一个计算机语言。汇编语言实际上是你对计算机处理器实际运行的指令的命令形式表示法。这意味着你将与处理器的底层打交道，比如寄存器和堆栈。如果你要找的是类英语且有相关的自我说明的语言，这不是你想要的。特别注意：语言的名字叫“汇编”。把汇编语言翻译成真实的机器码的工具叫“汇编程序”。把这门语言叫做“汇编程序”这种用词不当相当普遍，因此，请从这门语言的正确称呼作为起点出发。

4. Pascal 语言

Pascal 语言是由 NicolasWirth 在 20 世纪 70 年代早期设计的，Pascal 被设计来强行使用结构化编程。最初的 Pascal 被严格设计成教学之用，最终，大量的拥护者促使它闯入了商业编程中。当 Borland 发布 IBMPC 上的 TurboPascal 时，Pascal 辉煌一时。集成的编辑器，闪电般的编译器加上低廉的价格使之变得不可抵抗，Pascal 编程成为 MS－DOS 编写小程序的首选语言。然而时日不久，C 编译器变得更快，并具有优秀的内置编辑器和调试器。Pascal 在 1990 年 Windows 开始流行时走到了尽头，Borland 放弃了 Pascal 而把目光转向了为 Windows 编写程序的 C++ 。TurboPascal 很快被人遗忘。

5. Java

Java 是由 Sun 最初设计用于嵌入程序的可移植性“小 C++”。在网页上运行小程序的想法着实吸引了不少人的目光，于是，这门语言迅速崛起。事实证明，Java 不仅仅适于在网页上内嵌动画，它是一门极好的完全的软件编程的小语言。“虚拟机”机制、垃圾回收以及没有指针等使它很容易成为不易崩溃且不会泄漏资源的可靠程序。

虽然不是 C_{++} 的正式续篇，Java 从 C_{++} 中借用了大量的语法。它丢弃了很多 C_{++} 的复杂功能，从而形成一门紧凑而易学的语言。不像 C_{++}，Java 强制面向对象编程，要在 Java 里写非面向对象的程序就像要在 Pascal 里写“空心粉式代码”一样困难。

6. C＃

C＃是一种精确、简单、类型安全、面向对象的语言。其是. Net 的代表性语言。什么是. Net 呢？按照微软总裁兼首席执行官 Steve Ballmer 把它定义为：. Net 代表一个集合，一个环境，它可以作为平台支持下一代 Internet 的可编程结构。

7. FORTRAN

FORTRAN 语言是世界上第一个被正式推广使用的高级语言。它是 1954 年被提出来的，1956 年开始正式使用，至今已有五十多年的历史，但仍历久不衰，它始终是数值计算领域所使用的主要语言。FORTRAN 语言是 Formula Translation 的缩写，意为“公式翻译”。它是为科学、工程问题或企事业管理中的那些能够用数学公式表达的问题而设计的，其数值计算的功能较强。

习　题

9-2-1　根据计算机语言的发展过程，它们出现的顺序为（　　）。

A. 机器语言、汇编语言、高级语言

B. 汇编语言、机器语言、高级语言

C. 高级语言、汇编语言、机器语言

D. 机器语言、高级语言、汇编语言

9-2-2　汇编语言是（　　）。

A. 机器语言　　B. 低级语言

C. 高级语言　　D. 自然语言

第三节　信 息 表 示

一、计算机中的信息表示方法

计算机采用二进制，用 0 和 1 存储信息。

数据的存储单位有位、字节和字等。

1. 位

比特，记为 bit，是计算机最小的存储信息单位，是用 0 或 1 来表示的一个二进制位数。

2. 字节

拜特，记为 Byte，是数据存储中最常用的基本单位。8 位二进制构成一个字节，从最小的 00000000 到最大的 11111111。

3. 字符

以一个字节表示的信息称为一个字符。一个英文字符占一个字节的位置，一个中文占两个字节的位置。

4. 字

由若干个字节组成一个存储单元，称为“字”(Word)。一个存储单元中存放一条指令或一个数据。

【例 9-3-1】 计算机的信息数量的单位常用 kB、MB、GB、TB 表示，它们中表示信息数量最大的一个是：

A. kB　　B. MB　　C. GB　　D. TB

解 $1\text{kB}=2^{10}\text{B}=1024\text{B}$

$1\text{MB}=2^{20}\text{B}=1024\text{kB}$

$1\text{GB}=2^{30}\text{B}=1024\text{MB}$

$1\text{TB}=2^{40}\text{B}=1024\text{GB}$

答案：D

【例 9-3-2】 计算机存储器是按字节进行编址的，一个存储单元是：

A. 8 个字节　　B. 1 个字节

C. 16 个二进制数位　　D. 32 个二进制数位

解 计算机内的存储器是由一个个存储单元组成的，每一个存储单元的容量为 8 位二进制信息，称 1 个字节。

答案：B

二、信息的表示及存储

信息是人们表示一定意义的符号的集合，可以是数字、文字、图形、图像、动画、声音等。数据是信息在计算机内部的表现形式。数据本身就是一种信息。

（一）数制

1. 数制的定义

用一种固定的数字(数码符号)和一套统一的规则来表示数值的方法，即为数制。

(1)数制的种类，如十进制、二进制、八进制、十六进制、六十进制、十二进制等。

(2)数制的规则，如 R 进制的规则是逢 R 进 1。

2. 权

权是指指数位上的数字乘上一个固定的数值。

3. 基数

十进制的基数是十，二进制的基数是二，八进制的基数是八。

进位计数制中的三个要素：数位（数字在一个数中所处的位置）、权、基数。

4. 二进制数

二进制是“逢二进一”的计数方法，计算机中的数据如文字、数字、声音、图像、动画、色彩等信息都是用二进制数来表示的。

采用二进制记数的原因，主要是由于二进制数在技术操作上的可行性、可靠性、简易性及通用性。

(1)可行性。二进制数只有 0、1 两个数码，要表示这两个状态，在物理技术上很容易实现，如电灯的亮和灭、晶体管门电路的导通和截止等。

(2)可靠性。因二进制只有两个状态，数字转移和处理抗干扰能力强，不易出错。

(3)简易性。二进制数的运算法则简单，使计算机运算器结构大大简化。

(4)通用性。因为二进制数只有 0、1 两个数码，与逻辑代数中的“真”和“假”两个值对应，从而为计算机实现逻辑运算和逻辑判断提供了方便。

(二)数制的转换

日常生活中使用的进位制很多，如一年等于十二个月（十二进制），一斤等于十两（十进制），一分钟等于六十秒（六十进制）等。在计算机系统中经常使用十进制、八进制、十六进制、二进制。

1. 十进制数转换二进制数

十进制数转换为二进制数步骤：

(1)将十进制整数转换为二进制整数。

(2)将十进制小数转换为二进制小数。

(3)合成一个二进制数。

【例 9-3-3】 信息与数据之间存在着固有的内在联系，信息是：

A. 由数据产生的　　B. 信息就是数据

C. 没有加工过的数据　　D. 客观地记录事物的数据

解 数据是反映客观事物属性的原始事实。信息是由原始数据经过处理加工，按特定的方式组织起来的，对人们有价值的数据的集合。

答案：A

【例 9-3-4】 把十进制数 29.125 转换为二进制数。

解 ①先将十进制整数 29 转换成二进制（除 2 取余数法）

十进制数	余数	
2 | 29	……1	转换结果的最低位
2 | 14	……0	↑
2 | 7	……1	↑
2 | 3	……1	↑
1	……1	转换结果的最高位

转换后结果：$(29)_{10}=(11101)_2$

②把十进制小数 0.125 转换成二进制(乘 2 取整法)

	取整数部分	
0.125		
× 2		
0.250	0	……………………转换结果的最高位
× 2		
0.50	0	
× 2		
1.0	1	……………………转换结果的最低位

转换后结果:$(0.125)_{10}=(0.001)_2$

③将整数部分与小数部分合在一起。

$$(29)_{10}+(0.125)_{10}=(11101)_2+(0.001)_2$$

$$(29.125)_{10}=(11101.001)_2$$

2.二进制数转换成十进制数

【例 9-3-5】 将二进制数$(11101.001)_2$转换成十进制数(按权展开法)。

解 $(11101.001)_2=1\times2^4+1\times2^3+1\times2^2+0\times2^1+1\times2^0+0\times2^{-1}+0\times2^{-2}+1\times2^{-3}$

$=16+8+4+0+1+0.0+0.0+0.125$

$=(29.125)_{10}$

3.八进制数与十六进制数

计算机中经常使用八进制数与十六进制数,因为二进制数写起来太长,不便于比较和记忆。而八进制数、十六进制数与二进制数有简单的对应规则,可方便地写成二进制数的形式。它们的对应关系如表 9-3-1、表 9-3-2 所示。

表 9-3-1

十六进制数	0	1	2	3	…	8	9	A	B	…	E	F
二进制数	0000	0001	0010	0011	…	1000	1001	1010	1011	…	1110	1111

表 9-3-2

八进制数	0	1	2	3	4	5	6	7
二进制数	000	001	010	011	100	101	110	111

例如,十进制数 345 可表示为表 9-3-3 所列的其他制数。

表 9-3-3

<table>
<tr><td>八进制数</td><td>531</td><td colspan="2">5</td><td colspan="2">3</td><td>1</td></tr>
<tr><td>二进制数</td><td>101011001</td><td colspan="2">1 0 1</td><td colspan="2">0 1 1</td><td>0 0 1</td></tr>
<tr><td>十六进制数</td><td>159</td><td>1</td><td colspan="2">5</td><td colspan="2">9</td></tr>
</table>

4.十进制数转换为 R 进制数

对于十进制数转换为 R 进制数仍可采用除 R 取余法和乘 R 取整法。

5.R 进制数转换为十进制数

对于 R 进制数转换为十进制仍可采用按权(R^i)展开算法。

(三)非数值数据在计算机内的表示

计算机中数据的概念是广义的。计算机内除了有数值的信息之外,还有数字、字母、通用符号、控制符号等字符信息,还有逻辑信息、图形、图像、语音等信息,这些信息进入计算机都转变成 0、1 表示的编码，所以称为非数值数据。

1. 字符的表示方法

字符主要是指数字、字母、通用符号等，在计算机内它们都被转换成计算机能够识别的十进制编码形式。这些字符编码方式有很多种，国际上广泛采用的是美国国家信息交换标准代码(American Standard Code for Information Interchange)，简称 ASCII 码，如表 9-3-4 所示。

ASCII 字符编码表

表 9-3-4

	000	001	010	011	100	101	110	111
0000	NUL	DLE	SP	0	@	P	、	p
0001	SOH	DC1	!	1	A	Q	a	q
0010	STX	DC2	“	2	B	R	b	r
0011	ETX	DC3	#	3	C	S	c	s
0100	EOT	DC4	$	4	D	T	d	t
0101	ENQ	NAK	%	5	E	U	e	u
0110	ACK	SYN	&	6	F	V	f	v
0111	BEL	ETB	‘	7	G	W	g	w
1000	BS	CAN	(	8	H	X	h	x
1001	HT	EM	)	9	I	Y	i	y
1010	LF	SUB	*	:	J	Z	j	z
1011	VT	ESC	+	;	K	]	k	{
1100	FF	FS	,	<	L	\	l	|
1101	CR	GS	—	=	M	]	m	}
1110	SO	RS	.	>	N	ˆ	n	～
1111	SI	US	/	?	O	—	o	del

ASCII 规定每个字符用 7 位二进制编码表示，表中的横坐标是第 6、5、4 位的二进制编码值，纵坐标是第 3、2、1、0 位的十进制编码值，两坐标的交点则是指定的字符，7 位二进制可以给出 128 个编码，表示 128 个常用的字符。其中 95 个编码，对应着计算机终端能输入并可以显示的 95 个字符，打印机设备也能打印这 95 个字符，如大小写各 26 个英文字母，0～9 这 10 个数字符，通用的运算符和标点符号＝、－、＊、/、＜、＞、,、{、}等。

【例 9-3-6】 查表写出字母 A，字母 1 的 ASCII 码。

解 根据字母 A 在表中的位置，行指示了 ASCII 码第 3、2、1、0 位的状态，列指示第 6、5、4 位的状态，因此字母 A 的 ASCII 码是 1000001B = 41H。同理可以查到数字 1 的 ASCII 码是 0110001B = 31H。

2. 汉字编码

我国制定了《信息交换用汉字编码字符集——基本集》(GB 2312—80)。这种编码称为国标码。在国标码的字符集中共收录了汉字和图形符 7 445 个，其中一级汉字 3 755 个，二级汉字 3 008 个，图形符号 682 个。

国标 GB 2312—80 规定，全部国标汉字及符号组成 94×94 的矩阵。在这矩阵中，每一行称为一个“区”，每一列称为一个“位”。这样，就组成了 94 个区(01～94 区)，每个区内有 94 个位(01～94)的汉字字符集。区码和位码简单地组合在一起(即两位区码居高位,两位位码居低位)就形成了“区位码”。区位码可唯一确定某一个汉字或汉字符号,反之,一个汉字或汉字符号都对应唯一的区位码,如汉字“玻”的区位码为“1803”(即在18区的第3位)。

所有汉字及符号的94个区划分成如下四个组:

(1)1～15区为图形符号区,其中,1～9区为标准区,10～15区为自定义符号区。

(2)16～55区为一级常用汉字区,共有3 755个汉字,该区的汉字按拼音排序。

(3)56～87区为二级非常用汉字区,共有3 008个汉字,该区的汉字按部首排序。

(4)88～94区为用户自定义汉字区。

汉字的内码是从上述区位码的基础上演变而来的。它是在计算机内部进行存储、传输所使用的汉字代码。

区码和位码的范围都在01～94内,如果直接用它作为内码就会与基本ASCII码发生冲突,因此汉字的内码采用如下的运算规定:

高位内码＝区码＋20H＋80H

低位内码＝位码＋20H＋80H

在上述运算规则中加20H应理解为基本ASCII的控制码;加80H意在把最高二进制位置“1”与基本ASCII码相区别,或者说是识别是否汉字的标志位。

例:将汉字“玻”的区位码转换成机内码:

$$
\begin{aligned}
\text{高位内码} &= (18)_{10}+(20)_{16}+(80)_{16} \\
&= (00010010)_2+(00100000)_2+(10000000)_2 \\
&= (10110010)_2 \\
&= (B2)_{16}=B2H
\end{aligned}
$$

$$
\begin{aligned}
\text{低位内码} &= (3)_{10}+(20)_{16}+(80)_{16} \\
&= (00000011)_2+(00100000)_2+(10000000)_2 \\
&= (10100011)_2 \\
&= (A3)_{16}=A3H
\end{aligned}
$$

$$
\begin{aligned}
\text{内码} &= \text{区码}+20H+80H+\text{位码}+20H+80H \\
&= (1011001010100011)_2=B2A3H
\end{aligned}
$$

(四)多媒体数据在计算机内的表示

1.多媒体技术

多媒体信息都是以数字形式而不是以模拟信号的形式存储和传输的。传播信息的媒体的种类很多,如文字、声音、图形、图像、动画等。多媒体技术是指能对多种载体(媒介)的信息和多种存储体(媒质)上的信息进行处理的技术,是一种将文字、图形、图像、视频、动画和声音等表现信息的媒体结合在一起,并通过计算机进行综合处理和控制,将多媒体各个要素进行有机组合,完成一系列随机性交互式操作的技术。

2.媒体的分类

按照国际电联的定义,媒体分为五类:

(1)感觉媒体,如图形、图像、语言、音乐等。

(2)表示媒体,如图像编码、声音编码、电报码、条形码等。

(3)显示媒体,如显示器、打印机、鼠标、摄像机等。

(4)存储媒体,如软盘、硬盘、光盘等。

(5)传输媒体,如同轴电缆、光纤、无线链路等。

3.多媒体的特性

(1)多样性。多媒体强调的是信息媒体的多样化和媒体处理方式的多样化,它将文字、声音、图形、图像甚至视频集成进入了计算机,使得信息的表现有声有色,图文并茂。

(2)交互性。其指任何计算机能对话,以便进行人工干预控制。交互性是多媒体技术的关键特征,也就是可与使用者作交互性沟通的特征,这也正是它与传统媒体的最大不同。

(3)集成性。将计算机、声像、通信技术合为一体,即把多种媒体如文本、声音、图形、图像、视频等信息有机地组织在一起,共同表达一个完整的多媒体信息。

(4)数字化。其指多媒体中各个多媒体信息都以数字形式存放在计算机中。

(5)实时性。声音、图像是与时间密切相关的,这就决定了多媒体技术必须要支持实时处理。

4.矢量图形的表示

矢量图(vector),也叫向量图,简单地说,就是缩放不失真的图像格式。矢量图是通过多个对象的组合生成的,对其中每一个对象的记录方式,都是以数学函数来实现的,也就是说,矢量图实际上并不是相位图那样记录画面上每一点的信息,而是记录了元素形状及颜色的算法,当你打开一副矢量图的时候,软件对图像对应的函数进行运算,将运算结果(图形的形状和颜色)显示给你看。无论显示画面是大还是小,画面上的对象对应的算法是不变的,所以,即使对画面进行倍数相当大的缩放,其显示效果仍然相同(不失真)。举例来说,矢量图就好比画在质量非常好的橡胶膜上的图,不管对橡胶膜怎样的长宽等比成倍拉伸,画面依然清晰,不管你离得多么近去看,也不会看到图形的最小单位。

矢量图的好处是轮廓的形状更容易修改和控制,但是对于单独的对象,色彩上变化的实现不如位图来得方便直接。另外,支持矢量格式的应用程序也远远没有支持位图的多,很多矢量图形都需要专门设计的程序才能打开浏览和编辑。

常用的矢量绘制软件有 adobe illustrator、coreldraw、freehand、flash 等,对应的文件格式为“.ai”、“.eps”、“.cdr”、“.fh”等,另外还有“.dwg”、“.wmf”、“.emf”等。

5.位图的表示

位图(bitmap),也叫点阵图、删格图像、像素图,简单地说,就是最小单位由像素构成的图,缩放会失真。构成位图的最小单位是像素,位图就是由像素阵列的排列来实现其显示效果的,每个像素有自己的颜色信息,在对位图图像进行编辑操作的时候,可操作的对象是每个像素,可以改变图像的色相、饱和度、明度,从而改变图像的显示效果。举个例子,位图图像就好比在巨大的沙盘上画好的画,当你从远处看的时候,画面细腻多彩,但是当你靠得非常近的时候,你就能看到组成画面的每粒沙子以及每个沙粒单纯的不可变化的颜色。

位图的好处是色彩变化丰富,编辑上可以改变任何形状区域的色彩显示效果,相应的,要实现的效果越复杂,需要的像素数越多,图像文件的大小(长宽)和体积(存储空间)越大。

常用的位图绘制软件有 adobe photoshop、corel painter 等,对应的文件格式为“.psd”、“tif”、“.rif”等,另外还有“.jpg”、“.gif”、“.png”、“.bmp”等。

6.声音的表示

声音是一种连续变化的模拟量。我们可以通过“模/数”转换器对声音信号按固定的时间进行采样,把它变成数字量,一旦转变成数字形式,便可把声音存储在计算机中并进行处理了。声音是一种物理信号,计算机要对它进行处理,其前提是必须用二进制数字的编码形式来表示声音。最常用的声音信号数字化方法是取样—量化法，它分成如下三个步骤：

取样(Sampling)→量化→编码(Encoding)。

计算机中的数字声音有两种不同的表示方法。一种称为“波形声音”，通过对实际声音的波形信号进行数字化(取样和量化)处理而获得，它可表示任何种类的声音。另一种是“合成声音”，它使用符号(参数)对声音进行描述，然后通过合成(synthesize)的方法生成声音，合成语音(用声母、韵母或清音、浊音、基音频率等参数描述的语音)等。

计算机中使用最广泛的波形声音文件采用 wav 作为扩展名，称为波形文件格式(wave file format)，wav 文件格式能支持多种取样频率和样本精度，并支持压缩的声音数据。

习　题

9-3-1　二进制数 10110101111 的八进制数和十进制数分别为(　　)。

A. 2657,1455　　B. 2657,1554　　C. 2657,1545　　D. 2567,1455

9-3-2　计算机能直接接收的数为(　　)。

A. 二进制　　B. 十六进制　　C. 十进制　　D. 其他进制

9-3-3　下列数据中，有可能是八进制数的是(　　)。

A. 488　　B. 317　　C. 597　　D. 189

9-3-4　信息与数据之间存在着固有的内在联系，信息是(　　)。

A. 由数据产生的　　B. 信息就是数据

C. 没有加工过的数据　　D. 客观地记录事物的数据

9-3-5　标准的 ASCII 编码采用(　　)。

A. 7 位编码，在存储时点用一个字节　　B. 8 位编码，在存储时占用一个字节

C. 16 位编码，在存储时占用二个字节　　D. 24 位编码，在存储时占用三个字节

9-3-6　由于计算机采用了多媒体技术，使计算机具有处理(　　)。

A. 文字与数据的能力　　B. 文字、图形、声音、视频和动画的能力

C. 照片与图形的能力　　D. 文互性的能力

第四节　常用操作系统

操作系统就是管理电脑硬件与软件的程序，所有的软件都是在基于操作系统程序的基础上去开发的。操作系统种类很多，有工业用的，商业用的，个人用的，涉及的范围很广，电脑常用的操作系统有以下几种。

一、常用操作系统

(一)Windows 操作系统

Windows 操作系统由微软公司开发，大多数用于我们平时的台式电脑和笔记本电脑。Windows 操作系统有着良好的用户界面和简单的操作。我们最熟悉的莫过于 Windows XP 和现在很流行的 Windows 7，还有比较新的 Windows 10。Windows 之所以取得成功，主要在于它具有以下优点：直观、高效的面向对象的图形用户界面，易学易用。Windows 是一个多任务的操作环境，它允许用户同时运行多个应用程序，或在一个程序中同时做几件事情。每个程

序在屏幕上占据一块矩形区域,这个区域称为窗口,窗口是可以重叠的。用户可以移动这些窗口,或在不同的应用程序之间进行切换,并可以在程序之间进行手工和自动的数据交换和通信。虽然同一时刻计算机可以运行多个应用程序,但仅有一个是处于活动状态的,其标题栏呈现高亮颜色。一个活动的程序是指当前能够接收用户键盘输入的程序。

(二)UNIX 操作系统

UNIX 操作系统是一个强大的多用户、多任务操作系统,支持多种处理器架构,最早由 Ken Thompson、Dennis Ritchie 和 Douglas Mcllroy 于 1969 年在 AT&T 的贝尔实验室开发。经过长期的发展和完善,目前已成长为一种主流的操作系统技术和基于这种技术的产品大家族。由于 UNIX 具有技术成熟、可靠性高、网络和数据库功能强、伸缩性突出和开放性好等特色,可满足各行各业的实际需要,特别能满足企业重要业务的需要,已经成为主要的工作站平台和重要的企业操作平台。

(三)Lillux 操作系统

Linux 继承了 UNIX 的许多特性,还加入自己的一些新的功能。Linux 是开放源代码的,免费的。谁都可以拿去做修改,然后开发出有自己特色的操作系统。做的比较好的有红旗、Ubntu、Fedora、Debian 等。这些都可以装在台式机或笔记本上。

(四)苹果操作系统

Mac OS X 是全球领先的操作系统。基于 UNIX 基础,设计简单直观,让处处创新的 mac 安全易用,兼容 mac 软件,不支持其他软件。Mac OS X 以稳定可靠著称。由于系统不兼容任何非 mac 软件,因此在开发 Snow Leopard 的过程中,Apple 工程师们只能开发 mac 系列软件。所以他们可以不断寻找可供完善、优化和提速的地方,即从简单的卸载外部驱动到安装操作系统。只专注一样,所以品质非凡。

二、操作系统管理

(一)进程和处理器管理

进程和处理器管理或称处理器调度,是操作系统资源管理功能的另一个重要内容。在一个允许多道程序同时执行的系统里,操作系统会根据一定的策略将处理器交替地分配给系统内等待运行的程序。一道等待运行的程序只有在获得了处理器后才能运行。一道程序在运行中若遇到某个事件,如启动外部设备而暂时不能继续运行下去,或一个外部事件的发生等,操作系统就要来处理相应的事件,然后将处理器重新分配。

(二)存储管理

系统的设备资源和信息资源都是操作系统根据用户需求按一定的策略来进行分配和调度的。操作系统的存储管理就负责把内存单元分配给需要内存的程序以便让它执行,在程序执行结束后将它占用的内存单元收回以便再使用。对于提供虚拟存储的计算机系统,操作系统还要与硬件配合做好页面调度工作,根据执行程序的要求分配页面,在执行中将页面调入和调出内存以及回收页面等。

(三)文件管理

文件管理是操作系统的一个重要的功能,主要是向用户提供一个文件系统。一般来说,一个文件系统向用户提供创建文件、撤销文件、读写文件、打开和关闭文件等功能。有了文件系统后,用户可按文件名存取数据而无需知道这些数据存放在哪里。这种做法不仅便于用户使用而且还有利于用户共享公共数据。此外,由于文件建立时允许创建者规定使用权限,这就可以保证数据的安全性。

（四）输入/输出管理

操作系统的人机交互功能是决定计算机系统“友善性”的一个重要因素。人机交互功能主要靠可输入输出的外部设备和相应的软件来完成。可供人机交互使用的设备主要有键盘显示、鼠标、各种模式识别设备等。与这些设备相应的软件就是操作系统提供人机交互功能的部分。人机交互部分的主要作用是控制有关设备的运行和理解并执行通过人机交互设备传来的有关的各种命令和要求。早期的人机交互设施是键盘显示器。操作员通过键盘输入命令，操作系统接到命令后立即执行并将结果通过显示器显示。输入的命令可以有不同方式，但每一条命令的解释是清楚的、唯一的。随着计算机技术的发展，操作命令也越来越多，功能也越来越强。随着模式识别，如语音识别、汉字识别等输入设备的发展，操作员和计算机在类似于自然语言或受限制的自然语言这一级上进行交互成为可能。此外，通过图形进行人机交互也吸引着人们去进行研究。这些人机交互可称为智能化的人机交互。

（五）设备管理

操作系统的设备管理功能主要是分配和回收外部设备以及控制外部设备按用户程序的要求进行操作等。对于非存储型外部设备，如打印机、显示器等，它们可以直接作为一个设备分配给一个用户程序，在使用完毕后回收以便给另一个需求的用户使用。对于存储型的外部设备，如磁盘、磁带等，则是提供存储空间给用户，用来存放文件和数据。存储性外部设备的管理与信息管理是密切结合的。

（六）网络服务

网络服务（Web Services）是指一些在网络上运行的、面向服务的、基于分布式程序的软件模块，网络服务采用 HTTP 和 XML 等互联网通用标准，使人们可以在不同的地方通过不同的终端设备访问 WEB 上的数据，如网上订票、查看订座情况。网络服务在电子商务、电子政务、公司业务流程电子化等领域有广泛的应用，被业内人士奉为互联网的下一个重点，据估计，未来网络服务将占领软件行业的半壁江山，特别是在目前 IT 领域衰退的情况下，网络服务更被认为是软件行业的一个新的增长点。

【例 9-4-1】 在下面四条有关进程特征的叙述中，其中正确的一条是：

A. 静态性、并发性、共享性、同步性

B. 动态性、并发性、共享性、异步性

C. 静态性、并发性、独立性、同步性

D. 动态性、并发性、独立性、异步性

解 进程与程序的概念是不同的，进程有以下四个特征。

动态性：进程是动态的，它由系统创建而产生，并由调度而执行。

并发性：用户程序和操作系统的管理程序等，在它们运行过程中，产生的进程在时间上是重叠的，它们同存在于内存储器中，并共同在系统中运行。

独立性：进程是一个能独立运行的基本单位，同时也是系统中独立获得资源和独立调度的基本单位，进程根据其获得的资源情况可独立地执行或暂停。

异步性：由于进程之间的相互制约，使进程具有执行的间断性。各进程按各自独立的、不可预知的速度向前推进。

答案：D

【例 9-4-2】 一幅图像的分辨率为 640×480 像素，这表示该图像中：

A. 至少由 480 个像素组成

B. 总共由 480 个像素组成

C. 每行由 640×480 个像素组成

D. 每列由 480 个像素组成

解 点阵中行数和列数的乘积称为图像的分辨率，若一个图像的点阵总共有 480 行，每行 640 个点，则该图像的分辨率为 640×480＝307 200 个像素。每一条水平线上包含 640 个像素点，共有 480 条线，即扫描列数为 640 列，行数为 480 行。

答案：D

【例 9-4-3】 操作系统的设备管理功能是对系统中的外围设备：

A. 提供相应的设备驱动程序，初始化程序和设备控制程序等

B. 直接进行操作

C. 通过人和计算机的操作系统对外围设备直接进行操作

D. 既可以由用户干预，也可以直接执行操作

解 操作系统的设备管理功能是负责分配、回收外部设备，并控制设备的运行，是人与外部设备之间的接口。

答案：C

【例 9-4-4】 操作系统中的进程与处理器管理的主要功能是：

A. 实现程序的安装、卸载

B. 提高主存储器的利用率

C. 使计算机系统中的软硬件资源得以充分利用

D. 优化外部设备的运行环境

解 进程与处理器调度负责把 CPU 的运行时间合理地分配给各个程序，以使处理器的软硬件资源得以充分的利用。

答案：C

【例 9-4-5】 操作系统的随机性指的是：

A. 操作系统的运行操作室多层次的

B. 操作系统与单个用户程序共同系统资源

C. 操作系统的运行是在一个随机的环境中进行的

D. 在计算机系统中同时存在多个操作系统，且同时进行操作

解 操作系统的运行是在一个随机的环境中进行的，也就是说，人们不能对于所运行的程序的行为以及硬件设备的情况做任何的假定，一个设备可能在任何时候向微处理器发出中断请求。人们也无法知道运行着的程序会在什么时候做了些什么事情，也无法确切的知道操作系统正处于什么样的状态之中，这就是随机性的含义。

答案：C

习　题

9-4-1　操作系统在计算机中是哪部分的接口？（　　）

A. 软件与硬件的接口　　　　B. 主机与外设的接口

C. 计算机与用户的接口　　D. 高级语言与机器的接口

9-4-2　运行中的Windows应用程序名，列在桌面任务栏的(　　)中。

A. 地址工具栏　　B. 系统区

C. 活动任务区　　D. 快捷启动工具栏

9-4-3　在“资源管理器”右窗口中，若希望显示文件的名称、类型、大小、修改时间等信息，则应该选择“查看”等菜单的(　　)命令。

A. 平铺　　B. 详细信息　　C. 图标　　D. 列表

9-4-4　Windows XP中，操作具有(　　)的特点。

A. 先选择操作命令，再选择操作对象

B. 先选择操作对象，再选择操作命令

C. 需同时选择操作命令和操作对象

D. 允许用户任意选择

9-4-5　操作系统的功能是(　　)。

A. 管理和控制计算机系统的所有资源　　B. 管理存储器

C. 管理微处理机存储程序和数据　　D. 管理输入/输出设备

9-4-6　Windows XP的许多应用程序的“文件”菜单中，都有“保存”和“另存为”两个命令，下列说法中正确的是(　　)。

A. “保存”命令只能用原文件名存盘，“另存为”不能用原文件名

B. “保存”命令不能用原文件名存盘，“另存为”只能用原文件名

C. “保存”命令只能用原文件名存盘，“另存为”也能用原文件名

D. “保存”和“另存为”命令都能用任意文件名存盘

9-4-7　下列说法中不正确的是(　　)。

A. 在同一台PC机上可以安装多个操作系统

B. 在同一台PC机上可以安装多个网卡

C. 在PC机的一个网卡上可以同时绑定多个IP地址

D. 一个IP地址可以同时绑定到多个网卡上

9-4-8　操作系统功能不包括(　　)。

A. 提供用户操作界面　　B. 管理系统资源

C. 提供应用程序接口　　D. 提供HTML

第五节　计算机网络

一、网络的概念

计算机发展到现在，已经不再是单机使用，而是进入了计算机网络时代。网络已是无处不在。数据通信就是将数据从某端传送到另一端，达到信息交换的目的。从计算机与计算机之间的数据传送，乃至于无线广播、卫星通信等，均属于数据通信的范畴。利用通信设备联结多台计算机及外设而成的系统，就称为计算机网络(Computer Network)。

二、计算机网络的功能

计算机网络的功能主要有硬件资源共享、软件资源共享和用户间信息交换。

（一）硬件资源共享

可以在全网范围内提供对处理资源、存储资源、输入输出资源等设备的共享，使用户节省投资，也便于集中管理和均衡分担负荷。

（二）软件资源共享

允许互联网上的用户远程访问各类大型数据库，可以得到网络文件传送服务、远地进程管理服务和远程文件访问服务，从而避免软件研制上的重复劳动以及数据资源的重复存储，也便于集中管理。

（三）用户间信息交换

计算机网络为分布在各地的用户提供了强有力的通信手段。用户可以通过计算机网络传送电子邮件，发布新闻消息和进行电子商务活动。

【例 9-5-1】 计算机网络的主要功能包括：

A. 软、硬件资源共享，数据通信，提高可靠性，增强系统处理功能

B. 计算机计算功能、通信功能和网络功能

C. 信息查询功能、快速通信功能、修复系统软件功能

D. 发送电报、拨打电话、进行微波通信等功能

答案：A

三、计算机网络的组成及分类

计算机网络，通俗地讲，就是将分散的多台计算机、终端和外部设备用通信线路互联起来，彼此间实现互相通信。总的来说，计算机网络的组成基本上包括计算机、网络操作系统、传输介质以及相应的应用软件四部分。按照地理范围划分，可以把各种网络类型划分为局域网、城域网、广域网和互联网四种。

（一）计算机网络的组成

网络硬件是计算机网络系统的物质基础。要构成一个计算机网络系统，首先要将计算机及其附属硬件设备与网络中的其他计算机系统连接起来。不同的计算机网络系统，在硬件方面是有差别的。随着计算机技术和网络技术的发展，网络硬件日趋多样化，功能更加强大，更加复杂。下面是一些常见的网络硬件。

(1)主机。在网络上提供资源和服务的主机被称为服务器，使用资源和接受服务的计算机被称为客户机。

(2)传输介质。传输介质是传输数据信号的物理通道，将网络中各种设备连接起来。常用的有线传输介质有双绞线、同轴电缆、光缆等。

(3)网络互联设备。用于连接计算机与传输介质、连接网络与网络的设备，如网卡、交换机、路由器、网关等。

网络软件是实现网络功能不可缺少的软件环境。在网络系统中，网络上的每个用户，都可享有系统中的各种资源，系统必须对用户进行控制。否则，就会造成系统混乱、信息数据的破坏和丢失。为了协调系统资源，系统需要通过软件工具对网络资源进行全面的管理、调度和分配，并采取一系列的安全保密措施，防止用户不合理的数据和信息访问，以防数据和信息的破坏与丢失。网络软件主要包括网络协议和网络操作系统。

(4)网络协议。网络协议是实现计算机之间、网络之间相互识别并正确进行通信的一组标准规则，它是计算机网络工作的基础。如 TCP、IP、HTTP、FTP 协议等。

(5)网络操作系统。网络操作系统是网络系统管理和通信控制软件的集合,它负责整个网络的软、硬件资源的管理以及网络通信和任务的调度,并提供用户与网络之间的接口。目前,常用的网络操作系统有 Windows 2000 Server、Windows XP、UNIX 和 Linux 等。

从另一种角度来看,计算机网络可以分为资源子网和通信子网两个组成部分,如图 9-5-1 所示。

资源子网主要负责全网的信息处理,为网络用户提供网络服务和资源共享功能等。它主要包括网络中所有的主计算机、I/O 设备、终端,各种网络协议、网络软件和数据库等。

通信子网主要负责全网的数据通信,为网络用户提供数据传输、转接、加工和变换等通信处理工作。它主要包括通信线路(即传输介质)、网络连接设备(如网络接口设备、通信控制处理器、网桥、路由器、交换机、网关、调制解调器、卫星地面接收站等)、网络通信协议和通信控制软件等。

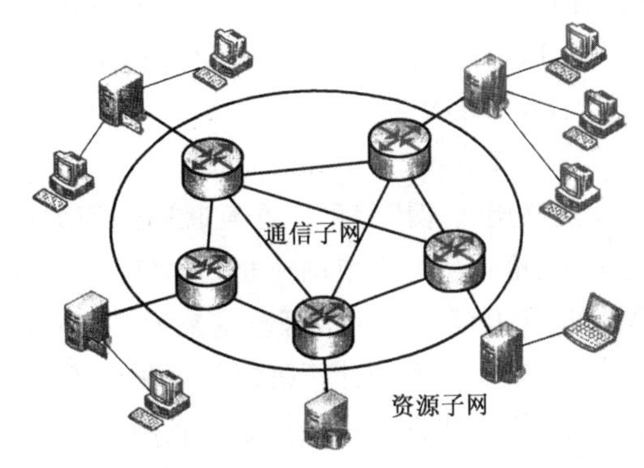

图 9-5-1 资源子网和通信子网

值得一提的是,资源子网和通信子网的概念是针对计算机广域网而言的,对局域网来讲,没有通信子网和资源子网之分。

(二)局域网(LAN)

LAN 就是指局域网,这是最常见、应用最广的一种网络。现在,随着整个计算机网络技术的发展和提高,局域网得到了充分的应用和普及,几乎每个单位都有自己的局域网,甚至有的家庭都有自己的小型局域网。很明显,所谓局域网,就是在局部地区范围内的网络,它所覆盖的地区范围较小。局域网在计算机数量配置上没有太多的限制,少的可以只有两台,多的可达几百台。一般来说,在企业局域网中,工作站的数量在几十到两百台左右。在网络所涉及的地理距离上,一般来说,可以是几米至 10km 以内。局域网一般位于一个建筑物或一个单位内,不存在寻径问题,不包括网络层的应用。这种网络的特点就是:联结范围窄,用户数少,配置容易,联结速率高。目前,局域网最快的速率要算现今的 10G 以太网了。IEEE 的 802 标准委员会定义了多种主要的 LAN 网:以太网(Ethernet)、令牌环网(Token Ring)、光纤分布式接口网络(FDDI)、异步传输模式网(ATM)以及最新的无线局域网(WLAN)。

(三)城域网(MAN)

这种网络的地理范围一般是一座城市,其联结距离在 10~100km 之间,采用的是 IEEE 802.6 标准。MAN 与 LAN 相比,扩展的距离更长,连接的计算机数量更多,在地理范围上可以说是 LAN 网络的延伸。在一个大型城市或都市地区,一个 MAN 网络通常联结着多个 LAN 网,如联结政府机构的 LAN、医院的 LAN、电信的 LAN、公司企业的 LAN 等。由于光纤联结的引入,使 MAN 中高速的 LAN 互联成为可能。

城域网多采用 ATM 技术做骨干网。ATM 是一个用于数据、语音、视频以及多媒体应用程序的高速网络传输方法。ATM 包括一个接口和一个协议,该协议能够在一个常规的传输信道上,在比特率不变及变化的通信量之间进行切换。ATM 也包括硬件、软件以及与 ATM 协议标准一致的介质。ATM 提供一个可伸缩的主干基础设施,以便能够适应不同规模、速度以及寻址技术的网络。ATM 的最大缺点就是成本太高,所以一般在政府城域网中应用,如邮政、银行、医院等。

（四）广域网(WAN)

这种网络也称为远程网，所覆盖的范围比城域网(MAN)更广，它一般是在不同城市之间的LAN或者MAN网络互联，地理范围可从几百公里到几千公里。因为距离较远，信息衰减比较严重，所以这种网络一般是要租用专线，通过IMP(接口信息处理)协议和线路联结起来，构成网状结构，解决寻径问题。这种城域网因为所联结的用户多，总出口带宽有限，所以用户的终端联结速率一般较低，通常为9.6Kb/s～45Mb/s，如邮电部的CHINANET、CHINAPAC和CHINADDN网。

（五）互联网(Internet)

互联网又称因特网。在互联网应用如此发展的今天，它已是我们每天都要打交道的一种网络，无论是从地理范围还是从网络规模来讲它都是最大的一种网络，就是我们常说的Web、WWW和万维网。从地理范围来说，它可以是全球计算机的互联，这种网络最大的特点就是不定性，整个网络的计算机每时每刻随着人们网络的接入在不变地变化。当你联在互联网上的时候，你的计算机可以算是互联网的一部分，但一旦断开与互联网的联结时，你的计算机就不属于互联网了。它的优点是信息量大，传播广，无论你身处何地，只要联上互联网，就可以对任何可以联网用户发出你的信函和广告。

【例9-5-2】 一个典型的计算机网络系统主要是由：

A. 网络硬件系统和网络软件系统组成

B. 主机和网络软件系统组成

C. 网络操作系统和若干计算机组成

D. 网络协议和网络操作系统组成

解 一个典型的计算机网络系统主要是由网络硬件系统和网络软件系统组成。网络硬件是计算机网络系统的物质基础，网络软件是实现网络功能不可缺少的软件环境。

答案：A

（六）网络体系结构与协议

1. 网络协议概念

计算机网络是由多种计算机和各类终端，通过通信线路连接起来组成的一个复合系统，要实现资源共享、数据传输、均衡负载、分布处理等网络功能，都离不开信息交换（即通信），而通信双方交流什么，怎样交流，以及何时交流，都必须遵循某种互相都能接受的一组规则，这些规则的集合称为协议(Protocol)，它可以定义为在两实体间控制数据交换的规则的集合。

一般来说，网络协议主要由语法、语义和同步（定时）三个要素组成。

(1)语法。即数据与控制信息的结构或格式。例如在某个协议中，第一个字节表示源地址，第二个字节表示目的地址，其余字节为要发送的数据等。

(2)语义。定义数据格式中每一个字段的含义。例如发出何种控制信息，完成何种动作以及做出何种应答等。

(3)同步。收发双方或多方在收发时间和速度上的严格匹配，即事件实现顺序的详细说明。

由此可见，网络协议是计算机网络不可缺少的组成部分。

2. 分层原则

由于不同系统中的实体间通信的任务十分复杂，很难想象制定一个完整的规则来描述所有的问题。为了简化计算机网络设计复杂程度，一般将网络功能分成若干层，每一层关注和解决通信中的某一方面的规则。

一般来说，层次划分应遵循以下原则。

(1)每层的功能应是明确的，并且是相互独立的。当某一层具体实现方法更新时，只要保持与上、下层的接口不变，那么就不会对邻层产生影响。

(2)同一节点相邻层之间通过接口通信，层间接口必须清晰，跨越接口的信息量应尽可能少。

(3)层数应适中。若层数太少，则层间功能的划分会不明确，多种功能混杂在一层中，造成每一层的协议太复杂。若层次太多，则体系过于复杂，各层组装时的任务要变得困难。

(4)每一层都使用下层的服务，并为上层提供服务。

(5)在需要不同的通信服务时，可在一层内再设置两个或更多的子层次，当不需要该服务时，也可绕过这些子层次。

3. 网络的体系结构

所谓网络的体系结构(Architecture)，就是计算机网络各层次及其协议的集合。层次结构一般以垂直分层模型来表示。如果两个网络的体系结构不完全相同就称为异构网络。异构网络之间的通信需要相应的连接设备进行协议的转换。

网络的体系结构具有以下特点。

(1)以功能作为划分层次的基础。

(2)第 n 层的实体在实现自身定义的功能时，只能使用第 $n-1$ 层提供的服务。

(3)第 n 层向第 $n+l$ 层提供和服务不仅包含第 n 层本身的功能，还包含由下层服务提供的功能。

(4)仅在相邻层间有接口，且所提供的服务的具体实现细节对上一层完全屏蔽。

(5)不同层次根据本层数据单元格式对数据进行封装。

应该注意的是，网络体系结构中层次的划分是人为的，有多种划分的方法。每一层功能也可以有多种协议实现。因此伴随网络的发展产生了多种体系结构模型。

4. 接口和服务

接口和服务是分层体系结构中十分重要的概念。实际上，正是通过接口和服务将各个层次的协议连接为整体，完成网络通信的全部功能。

对于一个层次化的网络体系结构，每一层中活动的元素被称为实体(Entity)。实体可以是软件实体，如一个进程；也可以是硬件实体，如智能芯片等。不同系统的同一层实体称为对等实体。同一系统中的下层实体向上层实体提供服务。经常称下层实体为服务提供者，上层实体为服务用户。

服务是通过接口完成的。接口就是上层实体和下层实体交换数据的地方，被称为服务访问点(Service Access Point，SAP)。例如 n 层实体和 $n-1$ 层实体之间的接口就是 n 层实体和 $n-1$ 层实体之间交换数据的 SAP。为了找到这个 SAP，每一个 SAP 都有一个唯一的标志，称为端口(Port)或套接字(Socket)。

通过上述分析可以看出，协议和服务是两个不同的概念。协议好像是“水平方向”的，即协议是不同系统对等层实体之间的通信规则。而服务则是在“垂直方向”上的，即服务是同一系统中下层实体向上层实体通过层间的接口提供的。网络通信协议是实现不同系统对等层之间的逻辑连接，而服务则是通过接口实现同一个系统中不同层之间的物理连接，并最终通过物理介质实现不同系统之间的物理传输过程。

上下层实体之间交换的数据传输单位称为数据单元，数据单元分为三种：协议数据单元、接口数据单元和服务数据单元。

5. 开放系统互联参考模型 OSI/RM

从 20 世纪 70 年代起，世界许多著名计算机公司都纷纷推出自己的网络体系结构，如 IBM 公司的 SNA(System Network Architecture)，Digital 公司的 DNA(Digital Network Architecture)等。有了网络体系结构，满足同一体系结构的计算机系统能够很容易地互连在一起。然而，已建立的网络系统结构很不一致，互不相容，难于相互连接。为了建立一个国际统一标准的网络体系结构，国际标准化组织(International Organization for Standardization，ISO)从 1978 年 2 月开始研究开放系统互联参考模型(Open Systems Interconnection Reference Model，OSI/RM)，1982 年 4 月形成国际标准草案。

7	应用层
6	表示层
5	会话层
4	传输层
3	网络层
2	数据链路层
1	物理层

图 9-5-2 OSI 参考模型

所谓开放系统，是指一个系统在它和其他系统进行通信时，能够遵循 OSI 标准的系统。按 OSI 标准研制的系统，均可实现互连。OSI/RM 采用分层描述的方法，将整个网络的通信功能划分为七个层次，每层各自完成一定的功能。由低层至高层分别称为物理、数据链路层、网络层、传输层、会话层、表示层和应用层。OSI 参考模型如图 9-5-2 所示。

OSI 参考模型包括 7 层功能及其对应的协议，每完成一个明确定义的功能集合，并按协议相互通信。每层向上层提供所需的服务，在完成本层协议时使用下层提供的服务。各层的功能是相对独立的，层间的相互作用通过层接口实现。只要保证层接口不变，那么任何一层实现技术的变更均不影响其余各层。

下面简单介绍一下各层的主要功能。

(1)物理层(Physical Layer)。物理层的功能及其特性物理层是网络通信协议的最低层，它建立在通信媒体的基础上，规定通信双方相互连接的机械、电气、功能和规程特性。物理层提供在两个物理通信实体之间的透明的位流传输，过程中的传输状态进行检测，出现故障时，即通知相关的通信实体。

关于物理上互联的问题，国际上已有许多标准可用。其中主要有美国电子工业协会(EIA)的 RS-232-C、RS-366-A、RS-449，CCITT 建议的 X.21，IEEE 802 系列标准等。

(2)数据链路层(Data Link Layer)。数据链路层负责在数据链路上无差错地传送。数据链路层将传输的数据组织的数据链路协议数据单元(Protocol Data Unit，PDU)，称为数据帧(Frame)。数据帧中包含地址、控制、数据及校验码等信息。这样，数据链路层就把一条有可能出差错的实际链路，转变成让其上一层(网络层)看起来好像是一条不出差错的链路。

数据链路层的主要作用是，确定目的节点的物理地址并实现接收方和发送方数据帧的时钟同步：通过校验、确认和重等手段，将不可靠的物理链路改造成对网络层来说是无差错的数据链路；数据链路层还要协调收发双方的数据传输速率，即进行流量控制，以防止接收方因来不及处理发送方来的高速数据而导致溢出或阻塞。

(3)网络层(Network Layer)。网络层的基本工作是接收来自源主机的报文，把它转换成报文分组或称数据包括(Packet)，而后送到指定目标主机。报文分组在源主机与目标主机之间建立起的网络连接上传送，当它到达目标主机后再还原为报文。

网络层关心的是通信子网的运行控制，需要在通信子网中进行路由选择。如果同时在通信子网中出现过多的分组，会造成阻塞，因而要对其进行控制。当分组要跨越多个通信子网才能到达目的地时，还要解决网际互联的问题。此外，网络层因为要涉及不同网络之间的数据传送，所以如何表示和确定网络地址和主机地址也是网络层协议的重要内容之一。

(4)传输层(Transport Layer)。传输层为上一层(会话层)提供一个可靠的端到端的服务，实现端到端的透明数据传输服务。该层的目的是提供一种独立于通信子网的数据传输服务，即对高层隐藏通信子网的结构，使高层用户不必关心通信子网的存在。由此用统一的传输原语书写的高层软件便可运行于任何通信子网上。传输层传输信息的单位称为报文(Message)。当报文较长时，先分成几个分组(称为段)，然后再交给下一层(网络层)进行传输。

传输层的具体工作是负责是建立和管理两个端点中应用程序(或进程)之间的连接，实现端到端的数据传输、差错控制和流量控制；服务访问点寻址；传输层数据在源端分段和在目的端重新装配；连接控制问题。

传输层是一个端对端，也就是主机到主机的层，负责端到端的通信。其上各层面向应用，是属于资源子网的问题；其下各层面向通信，主要解决通信子网的问题。显然，传输层是七层协议中很重要一个中间过渡层，实现了数据通信中由通信子网向资源子网的过渡，和两种不同类型问题的转换。

(5)会话层(Session Layer)。将进程之间的数据通信称为会话。会话层的主要功能是组织和同步不同的主机上各种进程间的通信，控制和管理会话过程的有效进行。会话层负责在两个会话层实体之间进行会话连接的建立和拆除。

会话层不参与具体的数据传输，但对数据传输的同步进行管理。会话层在两个不同系统互相通信的应用进程之间建立、组织和协调其交互。在会话层及以上更高层次中，数据传送的单位一般都称为报文。

(6)表示层(Presentation Layer)。表示层为上层用户提供共同需要的数据或信息语法表示变换。大多数用户间并非仅交换随机的比特数据，而是要交换诸如人名、日期、货币数量和商业凭证之类的信息。它们是通过字符、整型数、浮点数以及由简单类型组合成的各种数据结构来表示的。不同的机器采用不同的编码方法来表示这些数据类型和数据结构(如 ASCII 或 EBCDIC、反码或补码等)。为了让采用不同编码方法的计算机通信交换后能相互理解数据的值，可以采用抽象的标准方法来定义数据结构，并采用标准的编码表示形式。管理这些抽象的数据结构，并把计算机内部的表示形式，转换成网络通信中采用的标准表示形式，是由表示层来完成的。数据压缩和加密也是表示层可提供的表示变换功能。

(7)应用层(Application Layer)。应用层是开放系统互联环境中的最高层。不同的应用层为特定类型的网络应用提供访问 OSI 环境的手段。例如因特网中使用的支持 Web 应用的 HTTP 协议，支持收发电子邮件的 SMTP 协议等都属于应用层的范畴。

开放系统互联参考模型 OSI/RM 在网络技术发展中起了主导作用，促进了网络技术的发展和标准化。但是应该指出的是，OSI 参考模型只是定义了分层结构中每一层向其高层所提供的服务，并没有为准确地定义互连结构的服务和协议提供分的细节。OSI 参考模型并非具体实现的协议描述，它只是一个为制定标准而提供的概念性框架，仅仅是功能参考模型。对于学习者，通过 OSI 的七层参考模型比较容易对网络通信的功能和实现过程建立起具体形象的概念。

但是 OSI 参考模型是在其协议开发之前设计出来的。这就意味着 OSI 模型在协议实现方面存在某些不足。实际上，OSI 协议过于复杂，这也是 OSI 从未真正流行开来的原因所在。

虽然 OSI 模型和协议并未获得巨大的成功，但是 OSI 参考模型在计算机网络的发展过程中仍然起了非常重要的指导作用，作为一种参考模型和完整体系，它仍对今后计算机网络技术朝标准化、规范化方向发展具有指导意义。

【例 9-5-3】 在 OSI 参考模型中，处于数据链路层与传输层之间的是：

A. 物理层　　B. 表示层　　C. 会话层　　D. 网络层

答案：D

6. TCP/IP 体系结构

TCP/IP 是运行在 Internet 上的一个网络通信协议，实际上 TCP/IP 是一个协议集，目前已包含了 100 多个协议，TCP 和 IP 是其中的两个协议，也是最基本、最重要的两个协议，因此通常用 TCP/IP 来代表整个协议集。

TCP/IP 最早的起源可以追溯到 1969 年由美国国防部开发的 ARPANET，它是为该网络制定的网络体系结构和体系标准，其目的是为了能无缝隙地连接多个网络。TCP/IP 可用于任何互联网系统间的通信。它既能用于局域网中，也能用于广域网中。在 TCP/IP 协议出现之后，出现了 TCP/IP 参考模型。

TCP/IP 使各种单独的网络有了一个共同的可参考的网络协议，实现了不同设备间互操作。虽然 TCP/IP 不是 OSI 的标准，但由于 TCP/IP 能够用来连接异构机环境，得到了工业界很多公司的支持，而且 TCP/IP 已经成为 UNIX 实现的一部分，特别是 TCP/IP 是 Internet 的连接协议，使得它已被公认为当前的网络互联标准。

TCP/IP 协议之所以能够迅速发展，是因为它适应了世界范围内数据通信的需要。TCP/IP 协议具有以下几个特点。

(1)协议标准具有开放性，它独立于特定的计算机硬件与操作系统，可以免费使用。

(2)统一分配网络地址，使得整个 TCP/IP 设备在网络中都具有唯一的 IP 地址。

(3)实现了高层协议的标准化，能为用户提供多种可靠的服务。

在 TCP/IP 参考模型的各层中定义了不同的协议，这些分层的协议形成了一组从上到下单项依赖关系的协议栈，也称为协议簇。TCP/IP 参考模型与 TCP/IP 协议簇之间的关系如图 9-5-3 所示。

应用层	SMTP	DNS	NFS	FTP	TELNET	Others
传输层	TCP			UDP		
互联层	ICMP IP ARP　RARP					
主机－网络层	Ethernet	ARPANET		PDN		Others

图 9-5-3　TCP/IP 参考模型与 TCP/IP 协议簇

(1)主机网络层。TCP/IP 参考模型允许主机联入网络使用多种现成的、流行的协议，如局域网协议或其他一些协议。在 TCP/IP 的主机—网络层中，它包括各种物理网协议，例如局域网的 Ethernet、Token Ring、分组交换网的 X. 25、FDDI、ISDN 等。当某种物理网被用作传送 IP 数据的通道时，就可以认为是这一层的内容。这体现了 TCP/IP 协议的兼容性与适应性。TCP/IP 还用于多种传输介质，如在 Ethernet 中可以支持同轴电缆、双绞线和光纤等。

(2)互联层。

①IP 协议。互联层的核心协议是互联网协议 IP。IP 协议的基本任务是通过互联网传输数据报，各个 IP 数据报之间是相互独立的。IP 协议是提供无连接数据服务，这是 Internet 和 Intranet 上最主要的服务。IP 并不保证正确的传递数据报。分组可能丢失、重复、延迟以及次序颠倒，系统既不能检测这些情况，也不通知发送者和接收者。一系统的 IP 数据报从一台计算机传送到另一台计算机可以通过不同的路径。

IP 提供了三个基本功能：一是基本数据单元的传送，规定了通过 TCP/IP 网的数据的确切格式；二是 IP 软件执行路功能，选择传递数据的路径；三是 IP 包括了一些其他规则以确定主机和路由器如何处理分组、差错报文产生的处理等。

除 IP 协议之外，互联层还包括以下协议：互联网络控制报文协议 ICMP、正向地址解析协议 ARP、反向地址解析协议 RARP。

②ICMP 协议。ICMP 协议是 IP 的一部分，随同 IP 一起使用。ICMP 允许路由器向其他路由器或主机发送差错或控制报文，ICMP 在两台机器上的 Internet 协议软件之间提供了通信。另外，ICMP 还用来检测报文差错，根据 ICMP 协议数据单元格式规定的代码可确定差错类型。

③ARP 协议。地址解析协议 ARP 是将 IP 地址转换成相应物理地址的协议。只需给出目的主机的互联网地址，它可以找出同一物理网络中任一主机的物理地址。这样，网络的物理编址可以对网络层服务透明。

④RARP 协议。反向地址解析协议 RARP 是将物理地址转换成 IP 地址的协议。当节点只有自己的物理地址而没有 IP 地址时，则可能通过 RARP 协议发出广播请求，征寻自己的 IP 地址，这样，无 IP 地址的节点可通过 RARP 协议取得自己的 IP 地址。

(3)传输层。TCP/IP 模型在传输层提供了两个协议，即传输控制协议 TCP 和用户数据报协议 UDP。

①TCP 协议。TCP 是一种建立在 IP 协议之上的可靠的、面向连接的、端到端的通信协议，它保证将一台主机的字节流无差错地传送到目的主机。TCP 协议将来自应用层的字节流分成多个字节段，然后将一个个的字节段传送到互联层，发送到目的主机。当互联层将接收到的字节段传送给传输层时，传输层再将多个字节还原成字节流传送到应用层。为了保障数据的可靠传输，TCP 对从应用层传送来的数据进行监控管理，提供重发机制。TCP 协议同时要完成流量控制功能，协调收发双方的发送与接收速度，达到正确传输的目的。

②UDP 协议。UDP 协议是建立在 IP 协议之上的不可靠的、无法连接的端到端的通信协议。它没有重发和纠错功能，不能保障数据传输的可靠性。因此 UDP 适用于不要求分组顺序到达的传输过程，分组传输顺序的检查与排序由应用层完成。UDP 增加了多端口机制，发送方使用这种机制可以区分一台主机上的多个接收者的问题。

(4)应用层。TCP/IP 模型的应用层包括了所有的高层协议，并且总是不断有新的协议加入。目前，应用层协议主要有以下几种：

①网络终端协议 Telnet，用于实现互联网中的远程登录功能，它允许一台本地机器登录到远程服务器上作为服务器的终端，以共享远程服务器的所有资源和功能。

②文件传输协议 FTP，用于实现互联网中交互式文件传输功能，它允许授权用户登录到

文件服务器中，通过远程服务器传输文件，也可向远程服务器下载或上载文件。

③简单邮件传输协议 SMTP，用于实现互联网中电子邮件传送功能，它解决如何通过一条链路把电子邮件传送到接收者。

④域名系统 DNS，用于实现网络设备名到 IP 地址映射的网络服务，它采用层次结构的域名系统，为用户提供了高效、可靠的查询方式。

⑤简单网络管理协议 SNMP，用于管理与监视网络设备，它定义了一种在工作站或微机等典型的管理平台与设备之间使用 SNMP 命令进行网络设备管理的标准。

⑥超文本传输协议 HTTP，用于 WWW（World Wide Web）服务。通过它可以将 WWW 服务器中的用超文本标注语言 HTML 制作的网页传送到客户机中，用户便可以用浏览器浏览网页。

应用层协议可以分为三类：一类依赖于 TCP 协议，如网络终端协议 Telnet、简单电子邮件协议 SMTP、文件传输协议 FTP 等；另一类依赖于 UDP 协议，如简单网络管理协议 SNMP、简单文件传输协议 TFTP；再一类则既依赖于 TCP 协议，也依赖于 UDP 协议，如域名系统 DNS。

（七）IP 地址和域名

1. IP 地址

Internet 上有几百上万台主机，那么各主机是如何标志自己的呢？原来，Internet 中的每台主机都分配一个地址，叫 IP 地址。IP 地址相当于计算机主机在互联网上的门牌号码。网络上每台主机都必须拥有一个独一无二的 IP 地址，每一笔通过网络传送的信息都会清楚表明发出信息的主机及终点主机的地址，以确保传送无误。IP 地址的表示方法是以 4 组 0～255 的数字，中间用“.”符号隔开，如 198.137.240.92 是美国白宫的 IP 地址，198.116.14.34 是美国太空总署的 IP 地址等。

IP 地址是由一个 32 位的二进制数组成的号码，并将 32 位的二进制数分为 4 段，每段 8 位。IP 地址的表示方法为：nnn.hhh.hhh.hhh。IP 地址由两部分组成，即网络地址和收信主机（收信主机指网络中的计算机主机或通信设备如路由器、网关等）地址。

Internet 网委员会定义了五类地址，即 A、B、C、D、E 类地址，以适应不同网络规模的要求。每类地址规定了网络地址、收信主机地址各使用多少位，也就定义了可能有的网络数目和每个网络中可能有的收信主机数，下面以 A、B、C 三类地址为例分别定义如下：

（1）A 类地址（表 9-5-1）

表 9-5-1

1 位	7 位	24 位
0	网络地址	主机地址

A 类地址有效网络数为 126 个，每个网络主机数为 16 777 214，这类地址一般分配给具有大量主机的网络使用。

（2）B 类地址（表 9-5-2）

表 9-5-2

2 位	14 位	16 位
10	网络地址	主机地址

B 类地址有效网络数为 16 348 个，每个网络主机数为 65 534，这类地址一般分配给具有中等规模主机数的网络使用。

(3)C 类地址(表 9-5-3)

表 9-5-3

3 位	21 位	8 位
110	网络地址	主机地址

C 类地址有效网络数为 2 097 154 个，每个网络主机数为 254，这类地址一般分配给小型的局域网络使用。

2. 域名

域是指局域网或互联网所涵盖的范围中，某些计算机及网络设备的集合。而域名则是指某一区域的名称，它可以用来当作互联网上一台主机的代称，而且域名要比 IP 地址便于记忆。一般来说，域名可以分解为三部分，分别为：

(1)主机名称。主机名称通常是按照主机所提供的服务种类来命名，如提供 WWW 服务的主机，其主机名称为 WWW，而提供 FTP 服务的主机，其主机名称就会是 FTP。WWW 是 World Wide Web 的缩写，中文意思是“全球网络信息查询系统”，简称为“环球网”或“万维网”，用户可以通过“IE”等浏览器查询 WWW 系统中的信息。

(2)机构名称及类别。机构名称通常是指公司、政府机构的英文名称或简称，如 sina 为新浪网络公司，sohu 为搜狐网络公司等；而类别则是指机构的性质，如 com 为公司，gov 为政府机关，edu 为教育机构等。

(3)地理名称。地理名称用以指出服务器主机的所在地，一般只有在美国以外的地区才会使用地理名称，如中国 cn，日本 jp，英国 uk 等。

(八)URL

URL(Uniform Resource Locator)用来指示某一项资源(或信息)的所在位置及访问方法，URL 的格式——访问方法://主机地址/路径文件名。例如，http://www.bta.net.cn/index.htm。

1. 访问方法

它用来表示该 URL 所链接的网络服务性质，如“http”为 www 的访问方式，“ftp”为文件传输服务的访问方式等。

2. 主机地址

它用来表示该项资源所在服务器主机的域名，如 www.bta.net.cn 及 www.sohu.com 等。

3. 路径文件名

它用来表示该项资源所在服务器主机中的路径及文件名，如 index.htm。

四、网络安全

目前计算机病毒及各类“黑客”软件多如牛毛，一台没有进行任何安全设置的 Windows 系统(不安装各种系统补丁、不安装病毒防火墙)，在 Internet 中很快就会被攻陷，致使人们在使用网络提供的各种高效工作方式的同时，不得不时刻提防来自计算机病毒、黑客等诸多方面的潜在威胁。所以，掌握 Windows 系列产品的安全防范技术十分重要，可以说这是每个计算机用户必须掌握的基本技术。各种用于网络安全防范的设置方法和工具软件，可以在很大程度上帮助用户提高计算机抵抗外来侵害的能力，能方便地检查和堵塞可能存在的各种安全漏洞。美国微软公司的 Windows 系列操作系统以其简便、易用的特点占据了较大的市场份额，自然也成为被攻击的主要对象。

（一）安装 Windows 系统补丁

对于一个新安装完毕的 Windows 操作系统，首先要做的事情就是立即安装系统补丁程序。微软公司为了方便用户使用，专门开设有“Windows Update”网站，随时发布各种新系统漏洞的补丁程序。一般情况下，能够及时安装补丁程序并进行安全设置的计算机不会受到病毒的侵袭。

（二）启用 Windows 防火墙

启用 Windows 防火墙可以有效地防止来自网络中其他计算机的访问，提高系统的安全性。

（三）用户账户安全设置

通过设置适当的用户账户，禁止不必要的用户账户来加强 Windows 的安全性。

（四）设置 TCP/IP 筛选

如果计算机在使用时有非常固定的用途，如某 Web 服务器工作时仅需要对外开放用户 HTTP 联结的 TCP80 端口和用户站点维护的 FTP 端口（默认为 TCP21 端口），此时可使用 Windows 的 TCP/IP 筛选器关闭所有其他端口。

（五）使用安全系数高的密码

提高安全性的最简单有效的方法之一就是使用一个不会轻易被暴力攻击所猜到的密码。

暴力攻击就是攻击者使用一个自动化系统来尽可能快地猜测密码，以希望不久可以发现正确的密码。因此，设置密码时应使用包含特殊字符和空格，同时使用大小写字母，避免使用从字典中能找到的单词。每使你的密码长度增加一位，就会以倍数级别增加由你的密码字符所构成的组合。一般来说，小于 8 个字符的密码被认为是很容易被破解的。可以用 10 个、12 个字符作为密码，16 个当然更好了。在不会因为过长而难于键入的情况下，让你的密码尽可能的更长会更加安全。

（六）升级软件

在很多情况下，在安装部署生产性应用软件之前，对系统进行补丁测试工作是至关重要的，最终安全补丁必须安装到你的系统中。如果很长时间没有进行安全升级，可能会导致你使用的计算机非常容易成为不道德黑客的攻击目标。因此，不要把软件安装在长期没有进行安全补丁更新的计算机上。同样的情况也适用于任何基于特征码的恶意软件保护工具，诸如防病毒应用程序，如果不对它进行及时的更新，从而不能得到当前的恶意软件特征定义，防护效果会大打折扣。

（七）使用数据加密

对于那些有安全意识的计算机用户或系统管理员来说，有不同级别的数据加密范围可以使用，根据需要选择正确级别的加密通常是根据具体情况来决定的。数据加密的范围很广，从使用密码工具来逐一对文件进行加密，到文件系统加密，最后到整个磁盘加密。

（八）通过备份保护你的数据

备份数据是在面对灾难的时候把损失降到最低的重要方法之一。数据冗余策略既可以包括简单、基本的定期拷贝数据到 CD 上，也包括复杂的定期自动备份到一个服务器上。

【例 9-5-4】 在对网络安全问题的解决上，采用了多项技术，在下面四个叙述中不正确的是：

A. 加密的目的是为防止信息的非授权泄漏

B. 鉴别的目的是验明用户或信息的正身

C. 访问控制的目的是防止非法访问

D. 防火墙的目的是防止火灾的发生

答案:D

【例 9-5-5】 现在全国都在开发三网合一的系统工程,即:

A. 将电信网、计算机网、通信网合为一体

B. 将电信网、计算机网、无线电视网合为一体

C. 将电信网、计算机网、有线电视网合为一体

D. 将电信网、计算机网、电话网合为一体

解 "三网合一"是指在未来的数字信息时代,当前的数据通信网(俗称数据网、计算机网)将与电视网(含有线电视网)以及电信网合三为一,并且合并的方向是传输、接收和处理全部实现数字化。

答案:C

【例 9-5-6】 下面四个选项中,不属于数字签名技术的是:

A. 权限管理

B. 接收者能够核实发送者对报文的签名

C. 发送者事后不能对报文的签名进行抵赖

D. 接收者不能伪造对报文的签名

解 数字签名机制提供了一种鉴别方法,以解决伪造、抵赖、冒充和篡改等安全问题。接收方能够鉴别发送方所宣称的身份,发送方事后不能否认他曾经发送过数据这一事实。

答案:A

【例 9-5-7】 下列选项中,不是计算机病毒特点的是:

A. 非授权执行性、复制传播性　　B. 感染性、寄生性

C. 潜伏性、破坏性、依附性　　D. 人机共患性、细菌传播性

解 计算机病毒特点包括非授权执行性、复制传染性、依附性、寄生性、潜伏性、破坏性、隐蔽性、可触发性。

答案:D

五、网络服务与应用

(一)网上订票、订旅馆

在网上订购飞机票、火车票及旅馆,既方便,又节省时间。例如,在 IE 浏览器的地址栏中,输入首铁在线的网址"http://www.036.com.cn",打开网站首页,就可以在网上订票。

(二)查询公交线路

有时出门不知道如何乘车到达目的地,利用 8684 公交网,可以方便地查到最佳乘车方案。例如,在 IE 浏览器的地址栏中,输入 8684 公交网的网址"http://www.8684.cn",打开网站首页,而后选择城市即可查询。

(三)利用 Outlook Express 进行邮件收发

Outlook Express 是 Office 组件之一,它是一个桌面信息管理系统,可以处理许多办公日常事务。使用它,可以收发电子邮件,管理邮件,安排约会,建立联系人和任务等,从而提高日

常工作效率。

(四)IE浏览器和搜索引擎

要获取网络信息,浏览器和搜索引擎是必不可少的。浏览器是用于显示网页信息的软件,目前最常用的是 Windows 自带的 Internet Explorer。搜索引擎运用特定的计算机程序搜索网络信息,并对信息进行组织和处理,为人们提供检索服务,常用的搜索引擎有百度、Google、Hao123 等。

(五)电子商务、电子政务

如利用网络购书、购物,还可以在网上查看政府的规章制度及网上申请注册填表等。

六、网络管理

(一)网络管理的概念

网络管理是指网络管理员通过网络管理程序对网络上的资源进行集中化管理的操作,包括配置管理、性能和记账管理、问题管理、操作管理和变化管理等。一台设备所支持的管理程度反映了该设备的可管理性及可操作性。

(二)网络管理软件的划分

网络管理技术是伴随着计算机、网络和通信技术的发展而发展的,两者相辅相成。从网络管理范畴来分类,可分为对网“路”的管理,即针对交换机、路由器等主干网络进行管理;对接入设备的管理,即对内部 PC、服务器、交换机等进行管理;对行为的管理,即针对用户的使用进行管理;对资产的管理,即统计 IT 软硬件的信息等。根据网管软件的发展历史,可以将其划分为三代:

第一代网管软件就是最常用的命令行方式,并结合一些简单的网络监测工具,它不仅要求使用者精通网络的原理及概念,还要求使用者了解不同厂商的不同网络设备的配置方法。

第二代网管软件有良好的图形化界面。用户无须过多了解设备的配置方法,就能图形化地对多台设备同时进行配置和监控,大大提高了工作效率。但仍然存在人为因素造成的设备功能使用不全面或不正确的问题,容易引发误操作。

第三代网管软件相对来说比较智能,是真正将网络和管理进行有机结合的软件系统,具有“自动配置”和“自动调整”功能。对网管人员来说,只要把用户情况、设备情况以及用户与网络资源之间的分配关系输入网管系统,系统就能自动地建立图形化的人员与网络的配置关系,并自动鉴别用户身份,分配用户所需的资源(如电子邮件、Web、文档服务等)。

(三)网络管理的五大功能

根据国际标准化组织定义的网络管理有五大功能:故障管理、配置管理、性能管理、安全管理、计费管理。依据网络管理软件产品功能的不同,又可细分为五类,即网络故障管理软件、网络配置管理软件、网络性能管理软件、网络服务/安全管理软件、网络计费管理软件。

1. 故障管理

故障管理是网络管理中最基本的功能之一。用户都希望有一个可靠的计算机网络。当网络中某个组成失效时,网络管理器必须迅速查找到故障并及时排除。通常不大可能迅速隔离某个故障,因为网络故障的产生原因往往相当复杂,特别是当故障由多个网络组成共同引起的。在此情况下,一般先将网络修复,然后再分析网络故障的原因。分析故障原因对于防止类似故障的再发生相当重要。网络故障管理包括故障检测、隔离和纠正三方面,应包括以下典型功能:

(1)故障监测。主动探测或被动接收网络上的各种事件信息，并识别出其中与网络和系统故障相关的内容，对其中的关键部分保持跟踪，生成网络故障事件记录。

(2)故障报警。接收故障监测模块传来的报警信息，根据报警策略驱动不同的报警程序，以报警窗口/振铃(通知一线网络管理人员)或电子邮件(通知决策管理人员)发出网络严重故障警报。

(3)故障信息管理。依靠对事件记录的分析，定义网络故障并生成故障卡片，记录排除故障的步骤和与故障相关的值班员日志，构造排错行动记录，将事件—故障—日志构成逻辑上相互关联的整体，以反映故障产生、变化、消除的整个过程的各个方面。

(4)排错支持工具。向管理人员提供一系列的实时检测工具，对被管设备的状况进行测试并记录下测试结果以供技术人员分析和排错。根据已有的排错经验和管理员对故障状态的描述给出对排错行动的提示。

(5)检索/分析故障信息。浏阅并且以关键字检索查询故障管理系统中所有的数据库记录，定期收集故障记录数据，在此基础上给出被管网络系统、被管线路设备的可靠性参数。

(6)对网络故障的检测是对网络组成部件状态监测的依据。不严重的简单故障通常被记录在？错误日志中，并不作特别处理；而严重一些的故障则需要通知网络管理器，即所谓的"警报"。一般网络管理器应根据有关信息对警报进行处理，排除故障。当故障比较复杂时，网络管理器应能执行一些诊断测试来辨别故障原因。

2.计费管理

计费管理记录网络资源的使用，目的是控制和监测网络操作的费用和代价。它对一些公共商业网络尤为重要。它可以估算出用户使用网络资源可能需要的费用和代价，以及已经使用的资源。网络管理员还可规定用户可使用的最大费用，从而控制用户过多占用和使用网络资源。这也从另一方面提高了网络的效率。另外，当用户为了一个通信目的需要使用多个网络中的资源时，计费管理应可计算总计费用。

(1)计费数据采集。计费数据采集是整个计费系统的基础，但计费数据采集往往受到采集设备硬件与软件的制约，而且也与进行计费的网络资源有关。

(2)数据管理与数据维护。计费管理人工交互性很强，虽然有很多数据维护系统自动完成，但仍然需要人为管理，包括交纳费用的输入、联网单位信息维护，以及账单样式决定等。

(3)计费政策制定。由于计费政策经常灵活变化，因此实现用户自由制定输入计费政策尤其重要。这样需要一个制定计费政策的友好人机界面和完善的实现计费政策的数据模型。

(4)政策比较与决策支持。计费管理应该提供多套计费政策的数据比较，为政策制定提供决策依据。

(5)数据分析与费用计算。利用采集的网络资源使用数据，联网用户的详细信息以及计费政策计算网络用户资源的使用情况，并计算出应交纳的费用。

(6)数据查询。提供给每个网络用户关于自身使用网络资源情况的详细信息，网络用户根据这些信息可以计算、核对自己的收费情况。

3.配置管理

配置管理同样相当重要。它初始化网络并配置网络，以使其提供网络服务。配置管理是一组对辨别、定义、控制和监视组成一个通信网络的对象所必要的相关功能，目的是为了实现某个特定功能或使网络性能达到最优。

(1)配置信息的自动获取。在一个大型网络中，需要管理的设备是比较多的，如果每个设备的配置信息都完全依靠管理人员的手工输入，工作量则相当大，而且还存在出错的可能性。对于不熟悉网络结构的人员来说，这项工作甚至无法完成，因此，一个先进的网络管理系统应该具有配置信息自动获取功能。即使在管理人员不是很熟悉网络结构和配置状况的情况下，也能通过有关的技术手段来完成对网络的配置和管理。在网络设备的配置信息中，根据获取手段大致可以分为三类：第一类是网络管理协议标准的 MIB 中定义的配置信息（包括 SNMP 和 CMIP 协议）；第二类是不在网络管理协议标准中有定义，但是对设备运行比较重要的配置信息；第三类就是用于管理的一些辅助信息。

（2）自动配置、自动备份及相关技术。配置信息自动获取功能相当于从网络设备中"读"信息，相应的，在网络管理应用中还有大量"写"信息的需求。同样，根据设置手段对网络配置信息进行分类：第一类是可以通过网络管理协议标准中定义的方法（如 SNMP 中的 set 服务）进行设置的配置信息；第二类是可以通过自动登录到设备进行配置的信息；第三类就是需要修改的管理性配置信息。

（3）配置一致性检查。在一个大型网络中，由于网络设备众多，而且由于管理的原因，这些设备很可能不是由同一个管理人员进行配置的。实际上，即使是同一个管理员对设备进行的配置，也会由于各种原因导致发生配置一致性问题。因此，对整个网络的配置情况进行一致性检查是必需的。在网络的配置中，对网络正常运行影响最大的，主要是路由器端口配置和路由信息配置，因此，要进行一致性检查的也主要是这两类信息。

（4）用户操作记录功能。配置系统的安全性是整个网络管理系统安全的核心。因此，必须对用户进行的每一配置操作进行记录。在配置管理中，需要对用户操作进行记录，并保存下来。管理人员可以随时查看特定用户在特定时间内进行的特定配置操作。

4. 性能管理

性能管理估价系统资源的运行状况及通信效率等系统性能。其能力包括监视和分析被管网络及其所提供服务的性能机制。性能分析的结果可能会触发某个诊断测试过程或重新配置网络以维持网络的性能。性能管理收集分析有关被管网络当前状况的数据信息，并维持和分析性能日志。一些典型的功能包括：

（1）性能监控。由用户定义被管对象及其属性。被管对象类型包括线路和路由器，被管对象属性包括流量、延迟、丢包率、CPU 利用率、温度、内存余量。对于每个被管对象，定时采集性能数据，自动生成性能报告。

（2）阈值控制。可对每一个被管对象的每一条属性设置阈值，对于特定被管对象的特定属性，可以针对不同的时间段和性能指标进行阈值设置。可通过设置阈值检查开关控制阀值检查和告警，提供相应的阈值管理和溢出告警机制。

（3）性能分析。对历史数据进行分析、统计和整理，计算性能指标，对性能状况作出判断，为网络规划提供参考。

（4）可视化的性能报告。对数据进行扫描和处理，生成性能趋势曲线，以直观的图形反映性能分析的结果。

（5）实时性能监控。提供一系列实时数据采集、分析和可视化工具，用以对流量、负载、丢包、温度、内存、延迟等网络设备和线路的性能指标进行实时检测，可任意设置数据采集间隔。

（6）网络对象性能查询。可通过列表或按关键字检索被管网络对象及其属性的性能记录。

5. 安全管理

安全性一直是网络的薄弱环节之一，而用户对网络安全的要求又相当高，因此网络安全管理非常重要。网络中主要有以下几大安全问题：

网络数据的私有性(保护网络数据不被侵入者非法获取)，授权(防止侵入者在网络上发送错误信息)，访问控制(控制对网络资源的访问)。

相应的，网络安全管理应包括对授权机制、访问控制 、加密和加密关键字的管理，另外还要维护和检查安全日志，包括网络管理过程中，存储和传输的管理及控制信息对网络的运行和管理至关重要，一旦泄密、被篡改和伪造，将给网络造成灾难性的破坏。

(1)网络管理本身的安全由以下机制来保证：

①管理员身份认证，采用基于公开密钥的证书认证机制。为提高系统效率，对于信任域内(如局域网)的用户，可以使用简单口令认证。

②管理信息存储和传输的加密与完整性。Web 浏览器和网络管理服务器之间采用安全套接字层(SSL)传输协议，对管理信息加密传输并保证其完整性；内部存储的机密信息，如登录口令等，也是经过加密的。

③网络管理用户分组管理与访问控制。网络管理系统的用户(即管理员)按任务的不同分成若干用户组，不同的用户组中有不同的权限范围，对用户的操作由访问控制检查，保证用户不能越权使用网络管理系统。

④系统日志分析、记录用户所有的操作，使系统的操作和对网络对象的修改有据可查，同时也有助于故障的跟踪与恢复。

(2)网络对象的安全管理有以下功能：

①网络资源的访问控制。通过管理路由器的访问控制链表，完成防火墙的管理功能，即从网络层和传输层控制对网络资源的访问，保护网络内部的设备和应用服务，防止外来的攻击。

②告警事件分析。接收网络对象所发出的告警事件，分析与安全相关的信息(如路由器登录信息、SNMP 认证失败信息)，实时地向管理员告警，并提供历史安全事件的检索与分析机制，及时地发现正在进行的攻击或可疑的攻击迹象。

③主机系统的安全漏洞检测。实时地监测主机系统的重要服务(如 WWW、DNS 等)的状态，提供安全监测工具，以搜索系统可能存在的安全漏洞或安全隐患，并给出弥补的措施。

(四)网络管理协议

随着网络的不断发展，规模增大，复杂性增加，简单的网络管理技术已不能适应网络迅速发展的要求。以往的网络管理系统往往是厂商在自己的网络系统中开发的专用系统，很难对其他厂商的网络系统、通信设备软件等进行管理，这种状况很不适应网络异构互联的发展趋势。20 世纪 80 年代初期 Internet 的出现和发展使人们进一步意识到了这一点。研究开发者们迅速展开了对网络管理的研究，并提出了多种网络管理方案，包括 HEMS、SGMP、CMIS/CMIP 等。

1. SNMP

简单网络管理协议 SNMP 的前身是 1987 年发布的简单网关监控协议 SGMP。SGMP 给出了监控网关 OSI 第三层路由器的直接手段，SNMP 则是在其基础上发展而来。最初，SNMP 是作为一种可提供最小网络管理功能的临时方法开发的，它具有以下两个优点：

(1)与 SNMP 相关的管理信息结构(SMI)以及管理信息库(MIB)非常简单，从而能够迅速、简便地实现。

(2)SNMP 是建立在 SGMP 基础上的，而对于 SGMP 人们积累了大量的操作经验。

SNMP 经历了两次版本升级，现在的最新版本是 SNMP－V3。在前两个版本中 SNMP 功能都得到了极大的增强，而在最新的版本中，SNMP 在安全性方面有了很大的改善，SNMP 缺乏安全性的弱点正逐渐得到克服。

2. CMIS/CMIP

公共管理信息服务/公共管理信息协议 CMIS/CMIP 是 OSI 提供的网络管理协议簇。CMIS 定义了每个网络组成部分提供的网络管理服务，这些服务在本质上是很普通的，CMIP 则是实现 CMIS 服务的协议。

OSI 网络协议旨在为所有设备在 ISO 参考模型的每一层提供一个公共网络结构，而 CMIS/CMIP 正是这样一个用于所有网络设备的完整网络管理协议簇。出于通用性的考虑，CMIS/CMIP 的功能与结构跟 SNMP 很不相同，SNMP 是按照简单和易于实现的原则设计的，而 CMIS/CMIP 则能够提供支持一个完整网络管理方案所需的功能。

3. CMOT

公共管理信息服务与协议 CMOT 是在 TCP/IP 协议簇上实现 CMIS 服务，这是一种过渡性的解决方案，直到 OSI 网络管理协议被广泛采用。

4. LMMP

局域网个人管理协议 LMMP 试图为 LAN 环境提供一个网络管理方案。LMMP 以前被称为 IEEE802 逻辑链路控制上的公共管理信息服务与协议 CMOL。由于该协议直接位于 IEEE802 逻辑链路层 LLC 上，它可以不依赖于任何特定的网络层协议进行网络传输。由于不要求任何网络层协议，LMMP 比 CMIS/CMIP 或 CMOT 都易于实现。然而没有网络层提供路由信息，LMMP 信息不能跨越路由器，从而限制了它只能在局域网中发展。但是，跨越局域网传输局限的 LMMP 信息转换代理可能会克服这一问题。

习　题

9-5-1　下列域名中，表示教育机构的是（　　）。

A. ftp. btu. net　　B. ftp. cnc. ac. cn

C. www. ioa. ac. cn　　D. www. nefu. edu. cn

9-5-2　用 IE 浏览上网时，要进入某一页，可在 IE 的 URL 栏中输入该网页的（　　）。

A. IP 地址或域名　　B. 只能是域名

C. 实际的文件名称　　D. 只能是 IP 地址

9-5-3　下列邮件地址格式中，正确的是（　　）。

A. 用户名@主机域名　　B. 主机域名@用户名

C. 用户名. 主机域名　　D. 主机域名. 用户名

9-5-4　建立计算机网线路和主要目的是（　　）。

A. 资源共享　　B. 速度快　　C. 内存增大　　D. 可靠性高

9-5-5　合法的 IP 地址是（　　）。

A. 202:196:112:50　　B. 202、196、112、50

C. 202,196,112,50　　D. 202.196.112.50

9-5-6　校园网属于（　　）。

A. 远程网　　B. 局域网　　C. 广域网　　D. 城域网

9-5-7 计算机系统安全与保护计算机系统的全部资源具有(　　)、完备性和可用性。

A. 秘密性　　B. 公开性　　C. 系统性　　D. 先进性

9-5-8 计算机病毒主要是通过(　　)传播的。

A. 硬盘　　B. 键盘　　C. 软盘　　D. 显示器

9-5-9 目前计算机病毒对计算机造成的危害主要是通过(　　)实现的。

A. 腐蚀计算机的电源　　B. 破坏计算机程序和数据

C. 破坏计算机的硬件设备　　D. 破坏计算机的软件和硬件

9-5-10 下列哪一个不能防病毒(　　)。

A. KV300　　B. KILL　　C. WPS　　D. 防病毒卡

9-5-11 计算机病毒种类繁多,按计算机病毒的类型来分,下面四条有关病毒的表述中,不属于计算机病毒的一条叙述是(　　)。

A. 文件型计算机病毒、引导区型计算病毒、混合型计算机病毒

B. 引导区型计算机病毒、宏病毒、特洛伊木马病毒

C. 蠕虫病毒、混合型计算机病毒、时间炸弹和逻辑炸弹

D. 在人畜间流行的病毒、人畜混合型病毒

9-5-12 给信息实施保密可供选择的方法有两种(　　)。

A. 给计算机系统加密,给用户个人账户加密

B. 为计算机配置杀毒软件,每天进行杀毒操作

C. 计算机系统使用正版软件,不使用盗版软件

D. 给信息加密,把信息藏起来

9-5-13 用于解域名的协议是(　　)。

A. HTTP　　B. DNS　　C. FTP　　D. SMTP

9-5-14 TCP 协议称为(　　)。

A. 网际协议　　B. 传输控制协议

C. Network 内部协议　　D. 中转控制协议

9-5-15 IP 地址能唯一地确定 Internet 上每台计算机与每个用户的(　　)。

A. 距离　　B. 费用　　C. 位置　　D. 时间

题解及参考答案

第一节

9-1-1 **解**:一个完整的计算机系统包括硬件与软件部分。硬件包括中央处理器、存储器、外部设备等。

答案:A

9-1-2 **解**:计算机的软件系统包括系统软件和应用软件两个部分,如操作系统、程序语言及通用办公软件等。

答案:D

9-1-3 **解**:在对磁盘进行保护后,可以读出数据,但不能写入数据。

答案:A

9-1-4 **解**:可以从硬盘读出数据,也可以往硬盘上写入数据,因此它既可是输入设备,又可是输出设备。

答案:C

9-1-5 **解**:DOS属于操作系统软件,FORTRAN 77和BASIC属于程序设计语言,而TBSA是应用软件。

答案:D

9-1-6 **解**:从计算机硬件系统组成,我们可以看到中央处理器包括运算器和控制器。

答案:D

9-1-7 **解**:在中央处理器中,运算器按控制器发出的指令来完成各种操作。控制器规定计算机执行指令的顺序,并根据指令的信息控制计算机各部分协同动作。

答案:D

9-1-8 **解**:ROM是只读存储器,程序固化在芯片上,当电源断电时,上面的信息是不会丢失的。

答案:B

9-1-9 **解**:在"我的电脑"窗口中,可以实施驱动器、文件夹、文件等管理功能。当磁盘使用时间比较长,用户存放新文件、删除文件、修改文件时,都会使文件在磁盘上被分成多块不连续的碎片,碎片多了,系统读写文件的时间就会加长,降低系统性能。"属性"对话框有"常规"、"工具"、"共享"等选项卡。利用"常规"选项卡可设置或修改磁盘的卷标,查看磁盘容量、已使用字节和可用字节数以及清理磁盘;利用"共享"选项卡可以设置驱动器是否共享,如果选择了共享,还可以设置访问的类型:"只读"、"完全"或"根据密码访问";利用"工具"选项卡可以检查磁盘、做磁盘备份和整理磁盘碎片。

答案:D

第二节

9-2-1 **解**:计算机语言发展经历了由最初的机器语言发展到使用符号表示的汇编语言,继而开发出人们使用方便的高级语言。

答案:A

9-2-2 **解**:机器语言和汇编语言都属于计算机低级语言。

答案:B

第三节

9-3-1 **解**:二进制最后一位为1,所对应的十进制数一定是个奇数,二进制数转为十进制数,按权展开法得到1455。将二进制从后往前每3位为一组,所对应的八进制为2657 。

答案:A

9-3-2 **解**:计算机能接收的语言为机器语言,而机器语言是由二进制编码组成的。

答案:A

9-3-3 **解**:八进制数是由0、1、2、3、4、5、6、7八个数码组成,采用的是逢八进一的规则。

答案:B

9-3-4 **解**:数据是信息的符号表示或称为载体,信息是数据的内涵,是对数据语义的解释。采用数据这种形势来表示信息，更加易于人们的理解和接受。

答案:A

9-3-5 **解**:在 ASCII 编码中，每个字符用 7 位二进制数表示。一个字符的 ASCII 码通常占用一个字节，由 7 位二进制数编码组成，所以 ASCII 码最多可表示 128 个不同的字符。

答案:A

9-3-6 **解**:计算机的多媒体技术，使计算机不仅具有处理文字与数字的能力，而且还有处理文字、图形、声音、视频和动画的能力，使计算机拥有了处理多媒体信息的能力。

答案:B

第四节

9-4-1 **解**:计算机操作系统是计算机的系统软件。在计算机内，操作系统管理计算机系统的各种资源，扩充硬件的功能，它提供良好的人机界面，方便用户使用计算机。它在整个计算机系统中具有承上启下的作用，是计算机与用户的接口。

答案:C

9-4-2 **解**:运行中的 Windows 应用程序名，是列在桌面任务栏的活动任务区，作用主要是方便程序打开和管理，比如可以把多个窗口最小化到任务栏中。

答案:C

9-4-3 **解**:在资源管理器查看菜单下有缩略图、平铺、图标、列表、详细信息等子菜单，如果希望查看文件的名称、类型、大小、修改时间等信息，要进入详细信息子菜单。

答案:B

9-4-4 **解**:在 Windows XP 中，要想进行操作，首先要选择操作对象。

答案:B

9-4-5 **解**:操作系统(Operating System，简称 OS)的功能为：管理计算机系统的全部硬件资源，包括软件资源及数据资源；控制程序运行；改善人机界面；为其他应用软件提供支持等，使计算机系统所有资源最大限度地发挥作用，为用户提供方便的、有效的、友善的服务界面。

答案:A

9-4-6 **解**:在 Windows 操作系统中，“保存”文件和“另存为”文件都可以使用原文件名。

答案:C

9-4-7 **解**:操作系统是管理计算机系统的各种软、硬件资源，以及提供人机交互的界面。为了使用不同的操作系统，常常在同一台 PC 机上安装多个操作系统。若某一台 PC 机连接了两个网络，便需要为该计算机配置两个 IP 地址，这两个 IP 地址可以配置在同一个网卡上，也可以配置在不同的网卡上(前提条件为该 PC 机安装多个网卡)。但一个 IP 地址却不可以同时绑定到多个网卡上。

答案:D

9-4-8 **解**:操作系统有两个重要的作用：

(1)通过资源管理，提高计算机系统的效率。操作系统是计算机系统的资源管理者，它含有对系统软、硬件资源实施管理的一组程序。其首要作用就是通过 CPU 管理、存储管理、设备管理和文件管理，对各种资源进行合理的分配，改善资源的共享和利用程度,最大限度地发挥计算机系统的工作效率,提高计算机系统在单位时间内处理工作的能力。

(2)改善人机界面,向用户提供友好的工作环境。操作系统不仅是计算机硬件和各种软件之间的接口,也是用户与计算机之间的接口。试想如果不安装操作系统,用户将要面对的是01代码和一些难懂的机器指令,通过按钮或开关来操作计算机,这样既笨拙又费时。安装操作系统后,用户面对的不再是笨拙的裸机,而是操作便利、服务周到的操作系统,从而明显改善了用户界面,提高了用户的工作效率。

HTML代表的意义是超文本标记语言,它是全球广域网上描述网页内容和外观的标准。所以,HTML不是由操作系统提供的。

答案:D

第五节

9-5-1 **解:**域名(Domain Name)是由一串用点分隔的名字组成的Internet上某一台计算机或计算机组的名称,用于在数据传输时标记计算机的电子方位(有时也指地理位置)。education,教育机构,edu是它的缩写。

答案:D

9-5-2 **解:**当要浏览某一网页时,IP地址就等于域名。

答案:A

9-5-3 **解:**邮件地址格式,不允许把用户名放在@后面。

答案:A

9-5-4 **解:**建立网络的目的主要是数据、信息、资源共享。

答案:A

9-5-5 **解:**IP地址在数据之间是用点来分割的。

答案:D

9-5-6 **解:**局域网地域范围小,用于办公室、机关、学校、工厂等内部联网。其范围没有严格的定义,一般认为距离为0.1～25km。

答案:B

9-5-7 **解:**计算机系统安全与保护指计算机系统的全部资源具有系统性、完备性和可用性。

答案:C

9-5-8 **解:**通过使用外界被感染的软盘,如不同渠道来的系统盘,来历不明的软件、游戏盘等是最普遍的传染途径。

答案:C

9-5-9 **解:**大部分病毒在激发的时候直接破坏计算机的重要信息数据,所利用的手段有格式化磁盘、改写文件分配表和目录区、删除重要文件或者用无意义的"垃圾"数据改写文件等。引导型病毒的一般侵占方式是由病毒本身占据磁盘引导扇区,而把原来的引导区转移到其他扇区,也就是引导型病毒要覆盖一个磁盘扇区。被覆盖的扇区数据永久性丢失,无法恢复。

答案:D

9-5-10 **解**:WPS 是一个应用软件,用于文档的编辑与处理。

答案:C

9-5-11 **解**:计算机病毒是破坏计算机功能或者破坏数据,影响计算机使用的一组计算机指令或者程序代码,是一种功能比较特殊的、具有破坏性的计算机程序,并非真的是医学上的病毒。

答案:D

9-5-12 **解**:给信息加密,即隐蔽信息的可读性,将可读的信息数据转换为不可读的信息数据,即密文,也称密码。这样就可以使非法者不能直接了解数据内容,从而达到给信息加密的目的。把信息藏起来,即隐蔽信息的存在性,将信息隐藏在一个容量更大的信息载体之中,形成隐秘载体,做到使非法者难于察觉出其中隐藏有某些数据,从而实现给信息加密的目的。

答案:D

9-5-13 **解**:DNS 就是将各个网页的 IP 地址转换成人们常见的网址。

答案:B

9-5-14 **解**:TCP 为 Transmission Control Protocol 的简写,译为传输控制协议,又名网络通信协议,是 Internet 最基本的协议。

答案:B

9-5-15 **解**:IP 地址能唯一地确定 Internet 上每台计算机与每个用户的位置。

答案:C

第十章　工程经济

复　习　指　导

一、考试大纲

9.1　资金的时间价值

资金时间价值的概念；利息及计算；实际利率和名义利率；现金流量及现金流量图；资金等值计算的常用公式及应用；复利系数表的应用。

9.2　财务效益与费用估算

项目的分类；项目计算期；财务效益与费用；营业收入；补贴收入；建设投资；建设期利息；流动资金；总成本费用；经营成本；项目评价涉及的税费；总投资形成的资产。

9.3　资金来源与融资方案

资金筹措的主要方式；资金成本；债务偿还的主要方式。

9.4　财务分析

财务评价的内容；盈利能力分析（财务净现值、财务内部收益率、项目投资回收期、总投资收益率、项目资本金净利润率）；偿债能力分析（利息备付率、偿债备付率、资产负债率）；财务生存能力分析；财务分析报表（项目投资现金流量表、项目资本金现金流量表、利润与利润分配表、财务计划现金流量表）；基准收益率。

9.5　经济费用效益分析

经济费用和效益；社会折现率；影子价格；影子汇率；影子工资；经济净现值；经济内部收益率；经济效益费用比。

9.6　不确定性分析

盈亏平衡分析（盈亏平衡点、盈亏平衡分析图）；敏感性分析（敏感度系数、临界点、敏感性分析图）。

9.7　方案经济比选

方案比选的类型；方案经济比选的方法（效益比选法、费用比选法、最低价格法）；计算期不同的互斥方案的比选。

9.8　改扩建项目的经济评价特点

改扩建项目的经济评价特点。

9.9　价值工程

价值工程原理；实施步骤。

二、复习指导

（一）资金的时间价值

复习本节时应注意掌握资金时间价值的概念，熟悉现金流量和现金流量图。重点掌握资金等值计算,应会利用公式和复利系数表进行计算,掌握实际利率和名义利率的概念及计算公式。

对于资金等值计算公式,应该注意等额系列计算公式中 F、P、A 发生的时点,应用时注意它的应用条件。

应会查复利系数表,掌握 $(F/P,i,n)$ 、$(P/F,i,n)$、$(F/A,i,n)$、$(A/F,i,n)$、$(P/A,i,n)$、$(A/P,i,n)$几个符号的含义,如$(P/A,i,n)$是表示已知 A 求 P 的等额支付现值系数。

(二)财务效益与费用估算

本节应了解项目的分类和项目的计算期,熟悉财务效益与费用所包含的内容,重点掌握建设投资的构成、建设期利息的计算、经营成本的概念、项目评价涉及的税费以及总投资形成的资产。

(三)资金来源与融资方案

本节应了解资金筹措的主要方式,掌握资金成本的概念及计算,熟悉债务偿还的主要方式。

(四)财务分析

本节应了解财务评价的内容,熟练掌握盈利能力分析的相关指标的概念和计算,重点掌握净现值、内部收益率、净年值、费用现值、费用年值、投资回收期的含义和计算方法,熟悉利用这些指标评价方案盈利能力时的判别标准。如采用净现值、净年值指标时要根据其是否大于或等于零进行判断,采用内部收益率指标要根据其是否大于或等于基准收益率进行判断等。应用时注意它们的应用条件,如内部收益率可用于单个方案自身的经济性评价,两个方案比选时就要用差额内部收益率等。熟悉偿债能力分析、财务生存能力的概念,熟悉相关财务分析报表。

(五)经济费用效益分析

本节应理解社会折现率、影子价格、影子汇率、影子工资的概念,复习时应注意经济净现值、经济内部收益率指标与财务净现值、财务内部收益率的区别。了解效益费用比的概念。掌握经济净现值、经济内部收益率、效益费用比的判别标准。

(六)不确定性分析

对于盈亏平衡分析,应熟悉固定成本、可变成本的概念,熟练掌握盈亏平衡分析的计算,了解盈亏平衡点的含义。

对于单因素敏感性分析,应了解该方法的概念、敏感度系数和临界点的含义,看懂敏感性分析图。

(七)方案经济比选

本节应熟悉独立型方案与互斥型方案的区别,掌握互斥方案比选的效益比选法、费用比选法和判别标准,了解最低价格法的概念;熟悉计算期不同的互斥方案的比选可采用的方法和指标。

(八)改扩建项目的经济评价特点

对于改扩建项目,应了解其与新建项目在经济评价上的不同特点。

(九)价值工程

应掌握价值工程的基本概念,包括价值工程中价值、功能及成本的概念,掌握价值的公式,根据公式可知提高价值的途径。

了解价值工程的实施步骤,掌握价值系数、功能系数、成本系数的计算。应掌握价值工程的核心。

本章的复习,应注重掌握相关的基本概念、基本公式和计算方法。在复习的同时,应该通过做习题训练,进一步巩固考试大纲要求掌握的内容。做习题时,应注意掌握习题考核的知识点。

第一节　资金的时间价值

一、资金时间价值的概念

随着时间的推移，资金的价值是会发生变化的。通过资金运动可以使资金增值。不同时间发生的等额资金在价值上的差别称为资金的时间价值，也称为货币的时间价值。

应该指出，资金的时间价值不是资金本身或时间产生的，而是在资金运动中产生的。把资金作为生产要素，经过生产与交换，会给投资者带来资金的增值。当然，资金的增值也不可能没有资金和时间，资金是其增值的基础，而生产与交换，需要经历一定的时间过程。

二、利息与利率

(一)利息的计算

利息是在一定时期内占用资金所付出的代价，用下式表示

利息＝目前应付(收)总金额－原来借(贷)款金额

原来的借(贷)款金额称为本金。

计算利息的时间单位称为计息周期，通常为年、季、月、周或日。

利率是一个计息周期中单位资金所产生的利息(即单位时间里所得到的利息额)与本金之比，通常用百分数表示

$$i = \frac{I}{P} \times 100\% \tag{10-1-1}$$

式中：i——利率；

P——本金；

I——单位时间所得利息。

计算利息有单利计息和复利计息两种方法。

1.单利计息

这种计息方法是指计算利息时，只考虑本金计算利息，而利息本身不再另外计算利息。

单利计息的计算公式为

$$I = P \cdot i \cdot n \tag{10-1-2}$$

$$F = P(1 + i \cdot n) \tag{10-1-3}$$

式中：I——利息；

P——本金；

i——利率；

n——计息周期；

F——本金与利息之和，简称本利和。

由于单利计息没有考虑利息本身的时间价值，在工程经济分析中的应用较少，一般只适合于不超过一年的短期投资或短期贷款。

2.复利计息

复利计息是指在计算利息时，将上一计息期产生的利息，累加到本金中去，以本利和的总

额进行计息。即不仅本金要计算利息，而且上一期利息在下一计息期中仍然要计算利息。

复利计息公式为

$$F = P(1+i)^n \tag{10-1-4}$$

式中符号含义同前。应该注意，上式中的 i 和 n 所反映的时段应该是一致的，如 i 为年利率，则 n 为计息年数；如 i 为月利率，则 n 为计息月数。

（二）实际利率与名义利率

计息期通常以一年为计算单位，但有时借贷双方也可以商定每年分几次按复利计息，这时计息周期短于一年，如按月、按季或按半年计息等。比如，设月度为计息期，每月利率为 1%，则一年要计息 12 次，1%×12=12%称为名义利率，即名义利率是周期利率与每年计息周期数的乘积。这种计息方式习惯上表述为"年利率为12%，按月计息"。

需要注意的是，名义利率为 12%时的实际利息额比年利率为 12%时的利息额要高，比如借款 1 000 元，年利率 12%，按月计息，则第 1 年年末的本利和为

$$F = 1\,000 \times \left(1 + \frac{12\%}{12}\right)^{12} = 1\,126.83 \text{ 元}$$

若按年利率 12%复利计息，则第 1 年年末本利和为

$$F = 1\,000 \times (1 + 12\%) - 1120 \text{ 元}$$

比按月计息少了 6.83 元。由此可见，一年内复利计息次数不同。其年末的本利和也不同。对于相同的名义利率，如果一年内计息次数增加，则年末的本利和也会增加。

实际利息多少可以用实际利率计算。为了避免不同语言表述方式不同可能造成的混乱，1973 年通过的国际"借贷真实性法"规定：年实际利率是一年利息额与本金之比。

例如上面的例子，年名义利率都是 12%，计息期不同，则按年计息的实际利率为

$$\text{年实际利率} = \frac{F-P}{P} = \frac{1\,120 - 1\,000}{1\,000} = 12\%$$

按月计息的年实际利率为

$$\text{年实际利率} = \frac{F-P}{P} = \frac{1\,126.83 - 1\,000}{1\,000} = 12.68\%$$

这意味着"名义利率 12%，按月计息"与按年利率 12.68%计息，两者是一致的。

设名义利率为 r，一年中的计息周期数为 m，则一个计息周期的利率为 $\frac{r}{m}$，根据复利计息公式，由名义利率求年实际利率的公式为

$$i = \left(1 + \frac{r}{m}\right)^m - 1 \tag{10-1-5}$$

【例 10-1-1】 某企业向银行借款，按季度计息，年名义利率为 8%，则年实际利率为：

A. 8%　　B. 8.16%　　C. 8.24%　　D. 8.3%

解 利用由年名义利率求年实际利率的公式计算：

$$i = \left(1 + \frac{r}{m}\right)^m - 1 = \left(1 + \frac{8\%}{4}\right)^4 - 1 = 8.24\%$$

答案：C

【例 10-1-2】 某项目借款 2000 万元，借款期限 3 年，年利率为 6%，若每半年计复利一次，则实际年利率会高出名义利率多少：

A. 0.16%　　B. 0.25%　　C. 0.09%　　D. 0.06%

解　年实际利率为：

$$i=\left(1+\frac{r}{m}\right)^{m}-1=\left(1+\frac{6\%}{2}\right)^{2}-1=6.09\%$$

年实际利率高出名义利率：6.09%－6%＝0.09%

答案：C

三、现金流量及现金流量图

一个投资建设项目在其整个计算期内各个时间点上有货币的收入和支出，其中货币收入称现金流入(CI)，记为“＋”；货币支出称现金流出(CO)，记为“－”。

现金流入和现金流出统称为现金流量。现金流入与现金流出之差称为净现金流量，记为NCF或(CI－CO)，即

净现金流量＝现金流入－现金流出

现金流量有三个要素：流向、大小、时间。现金流量可以用表格或图形表示。在工程经济分析中，经常用图形表示现金流量。用于表示现金流量与时间对应关系的图形称为现金流量图，如图10-1-1所示。

在现金流量图中，横轴是时间标度，每一格代表一个时间单位(如年、季、月等)，即一期。0点为计算期的起始时刻，也称为零期。横轴上任意一时点 t 表示第 t 期期末，同时也是第 $t+1$ 期的期初。

各时间点上箭头向上表示现金流入，向下表示现金流出，其箭线的长短与现金流入和现金流出的大小成比例，箭头处一般要标注出现金流量的数值。

在工程经济分析中，对投资与收益发生的时间点有两种处理方法。一种是年初投资年末收益法，即将投资计入发生年的年初，收益计入发生年的年末；一种是年(期)末习惯法，即将投资和收益均计入发生年的年(期)末。两种处理方法的计算结果稍有差别，但一般不会引起本质的变化。

当实际问题的现金流量发生的时点未说明是期末还是期初时，一般可将投资画在期初，经营费用和销售收入画在期末。

借方的现金流量就是贷方的现金流出，对于借贷双方，其财务活动的现金流量图正好相反。例如，张某现在从银行贷款10 000元，3年后需还本付息共11 500元，其现金流量图如图10-1-2a)所示，而对于银行，该项财务活动的现金流量图如图10-1-2b)所示。

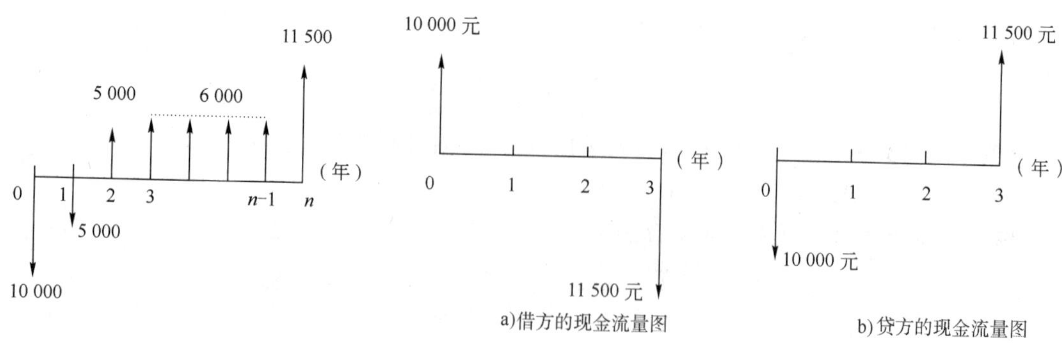

图10-1-1　现金流量图

图10-1-2　某项财务活动的现金流量图

四、资金等值计算的常用公式及应用

在工程经济分析中，常常需要将发生在某一时点上的资金换算到另一时点，以便进行计算分析和比较。

在不同时点上发生的资金，其绝对数额不等但价值可能相等。如果我们考虑反映资金时间价值的尺度复利率 i，将某一时点发生的资金按利率 i 换算到另一时点，则二者绝对数额不等，但它们的价值相等，这就是资金的等值。这种资金金额的换算称为资金等值计算。

若把将来某一时点的资金金额换算成该时点之前某一时点的等值金额，称之为“贴现”或“折现”，计算中所采用的反映资金时间价值尺度的参数 i 称为“贴现率”或“折现率”，折现率一般采用银行利率进行计算。

(一)一次支付系列

一次支付系列是指在期初借款 P，当借款到期时，将本利和 F 一次还清。一次支付的现金流量图如图 10-1-3 所示。

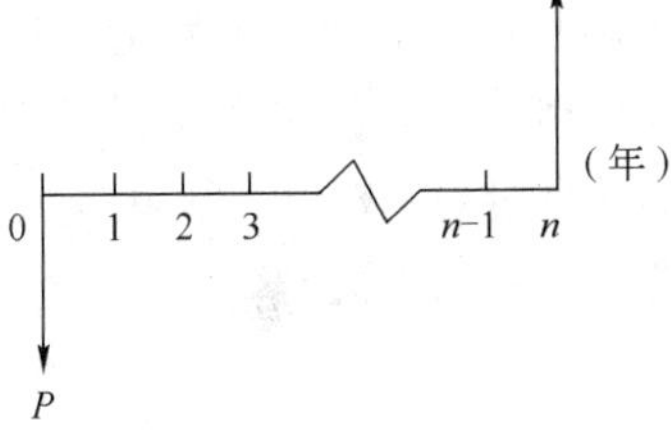

图 10-1-3　一次支付现金流量图

1. 一次支付终值公式(已知 P 求 F)

一次支付终值公式为

$$F = P(1+i)^n \tag{10-1-6}$$

上式称为一次支付终值公式，式中 P 称为本金或现值；F 称为本利和，也称为终值或将来值；i 为利率；n 为计息期数；$(1+i)^n$ 称为一次支付终值系数(一次支付终值因子)，可用 $(F/P,i,n)$ 表示，含义为利率 i、计息期数 n，已知 P 求 F。上式可写成

$$F = P(1+i)^n = P(F/P,i,n)$$

为计算方便，可将 $(F/P,i,n)$ 按不同的利率 i 和不同的计息期数 n 制成复利系数表格以便于应用。

应用上式时应注意，期数为 n 时，P 发生在第一个计息期的期初，F 发生在第 n 期的期末。如图 10-1-2 所示，借款 10 000 元发生在第一年年初(0 年末)，还款 11 500 元发生在第 3 年年末。

【例 10-1-3】 某工程贷款 1 000 万元，合同规定 3 年后偿还，年利率为 5%，问 3 年后应偿还贷款的本利和是多少？

解 绘出现金流量图如解图所示。

查复利系数表(参见表 10-1-1)，可得

$$(F/P,5,3)=1.158$$

3 年后本利和为

$$F=P(F/P,5,3)=1\,000\times1.158=1\,158 \text{ 万元}$$

也可按一次支付终值公式计算，即

$$F = P(1+i)^n = 1\,000\times(1+5\%)^3 = 1\,158 \text{ 万元}$$

也即 3 年后应偿还本利和 1 158 万元。

例 10-1-3 解图　某工程贷款现金流量图

2. 一次支付现值公式(已知 F 求 P)

当需要将期末一次性偿还的本利和折算成现值时，即已知将来值 F 求现值 P，可由一次支付终值公式得到

$$P=\frac{F}{(1+i)^n}=F(P/F,i,n) \tag{10-1-7}$$

式中，$\frac{1}{(1+i)^n}$称为一次支付现值系数，记为$(P/F,i,n)$。

【例 10-1-4】 为了 5 年后得到 500 万元，年利率为 8%，问现在应投资多少？

解 绘出现金流量图，如解图所示。

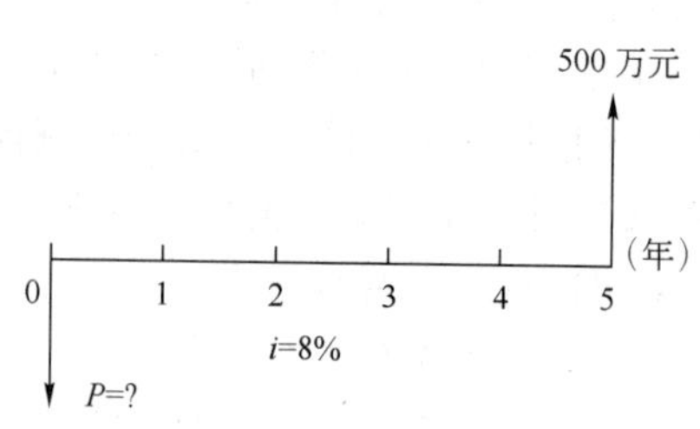

例 10-1-4 解图 现金流量图

查表可得$(P/F,8,5)=0.680\,6$，现在应投资额为

$$P=F(P/F,8,5)=500\times0.680\,6=340.3\text{ 万元}$$

或 $P=F/(1+i)^n=500/(1+8\%)^5=340.3$ 万元

(二)等额多次支付系列

等额多次支付是指所分析系统中的现金流入或现金流出在多个时点上发生，其现金流量每期均发生，且数额相等。等额多次支付情况下，共有 4 个参数：i、n、A，再加上 F 或 P。等额多次支付有 4 个等值计算公式，在各个计算公式中，i、n 均为已知。

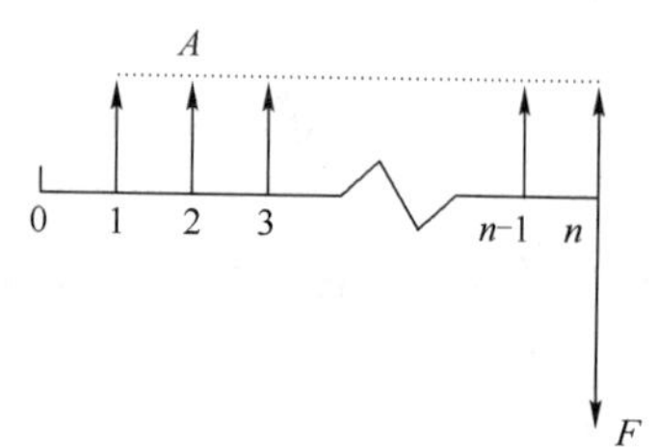

图 10-1-4 多次支付现金流量图

1. 等额支付终值公式(已知 A 求 F)

假设某人连续每期期末从银行贷款，数额均为 A，连续贷款 n 期，则 n 期后应一次还贷多少？该问题的现金流量图如图 10-1-4 所示。

如图 10-1-4 所示的现金流量图，等额资金为 A，利率 i，计息期数 n，将来值为 F，计算公式为

$$F=A\left[\frac{(1+i)^n-1}{i}\right]=A(F/A,i,n) \tag{10-1-8}$$

上式称为等额支付终值公式，$\frac{(1+i)^n-1}{i}$称为等额支付终值系数，记为$(F/A,i,n)$。

【例 10-1-5】 若连续 6 年每年年末投资 1 000 万元，年复利利率 $i=5\%$，问 6 年后可得本利和多少？

解 绘出现金流量图，见解图。

根据上式，可得

$$\begin{aligned}F&=A\left[\frac{(1+i)^n-1}{i}\right]\\&=1\,000\times\left[\frac{(1+5\%)^6-1}{5\%}\right]\\&=6\,802\text{ 万元}\end{aligned}$$

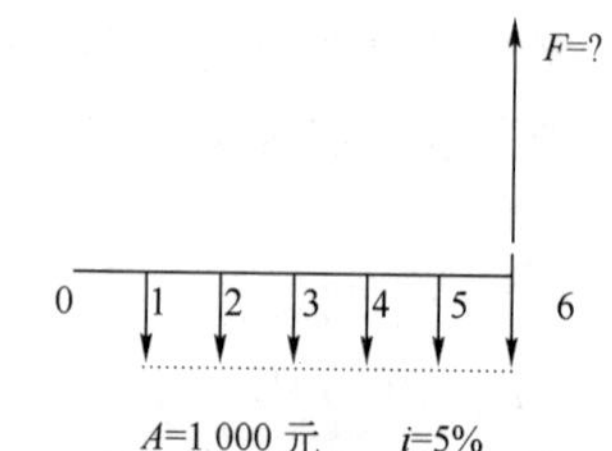

例 10-1-5 解图 等额投资现金流量图

或利用复利系数表

$$F=A(F/A,i,n)=1\,000\times6.802=6\,802\text{ 万元}$$

即 6 年后可得本利和 6 802 万元。

2. 等额支付偿债基金公式(已知 F 求 A)

等额支付偿债基金是指为了未来偿还一笔债务 F，每期期末预先准备的年金。

由等额支付终值公式可得

$$A=F\left[\frac{i}{(1+i)^n-1}\right]=F(A/F,i,n) \tag{10-1-9}$$

上式称为等额支付偿债基金公式，式中$\frac{i}{(1+i)^n-1}$称为等额支付偿债基金系数，记为$(A/F,i,n)$。

应用上面等额支付系列终值公式和等额支付偿债基金公式时应注意，等额支付的第一个A发生在第1期期末，最后一个A与F同时发生在第n期期末。

【例10-1-6】 某企业预计4年后需要资金100万元，$i=5\%$，复利计息，问每年年末应存款多少？

解 绘出现金流量图，见解图。

根据上面公式，可得

$$A=F\left[\frac{i}{(1+i)^n-1}\right]=100\times\left[\frac{5\%}{(1+5\%)^4-1}\right]=23.20\text{ 万元}$$

或利用复利系数表 $A=F(A/F,i,n)=100\times0.232\,01=23.20$ 万元

即每年年末应存款23.20万元。

3. 等额支付资金回收公式(已知P求A)

等额支付资金回收是指以利率i投入一笔资金，希望今后n期内以每期等额A的方式回收，其A值应为多少？这类问题的现金流量图如图10-1-5所示。

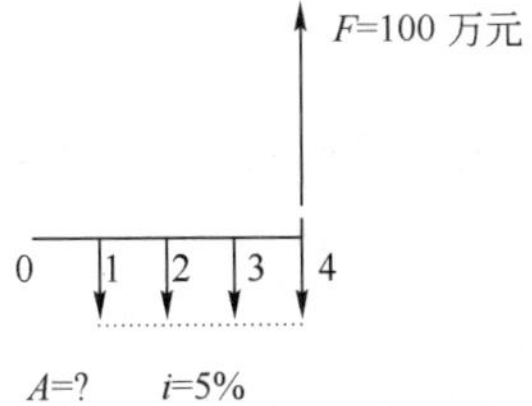

例10-1-6解图 某企业等额支付现金流量图

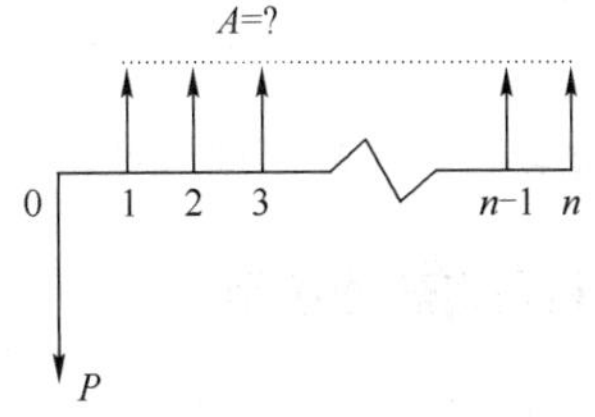

图10-1-5 等额支付资金回收现金流量图

等额支付资金回收公式为

$$A=P\left[\frac{i(1+i)^n}{(1+i)^n-1}\right]=P(A/P,i,n) \tag{10-1-10}$$

式中，$\frac{i(1+i)^n}{(1+i)^n-1}$称为等额支付资金回收系数，记为$(A/P,i,n)$。

【例10-1-7】 如现在投资100万元，预计年利率为10%，分5年等额回收，每年可回收：[已知：$(A/P,10\%,5)=0.2638$，$(A/F,10\%,5)=0.1638$]

A. 16.38万元　　B. 26.38万元　　C. 62.09万元　　D. 75.82万元

解 根据等额支付资金回收公式，每年可回收：

$$A=P(A/P,10\%,5)=100\times0.2638=26.38\text{ 万元}$$

答案：B

4. 等额支付现值公式(已知A求P)

每年收益(或支付)等额年金，求其现值，现金流量图如图10-1-6所示。

等额支付现值公式为

$$P=A\left[\frac{(1+i)^n-1}{i(1+i)^n}\right]=A(P/A,i,n) \tag{10-1-11}$$

式中 $\frac{(1+i)^n-1}{i(1+i)^n}$ 称为等额支付现值系数，记为$(P/A,i,n)$。

应用等额支付资金回收公式和等额支付现值公式时应注意，P 发生在第 0 年年末，即第 1 期期初，A 发生在各期期末，P 和 A 不在同一时间发生。

【例 10-1-8】 某企业利用银行贷款建设，年复利率 8%，当年建成并投产，预计每年可获得净利润 100 万元，要求 10 年内收回全部贷款，问投资额应控制在多少以内？

解 绘出现金流量图，如解图所示。

根据上式，可得

$$P=A\left[\frac{(1+i)^n-1}{i(1+i)^n}\right]=100\times\left[\frac{(1+8\%)^{10}-1}{8\%\times(1+8\%)^{10}}\right]=671.0\text{ 万元}$$

或利用复利系数表　　$P=A(P/A,i,n)=100\times 6.710=671.0$ 万元

即投资额应控制在 671.0 万元以内。

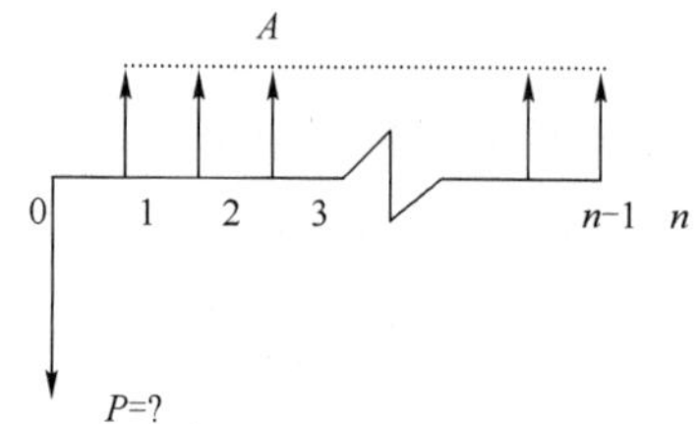

图 10-1-6　等额支付现值现金流量图

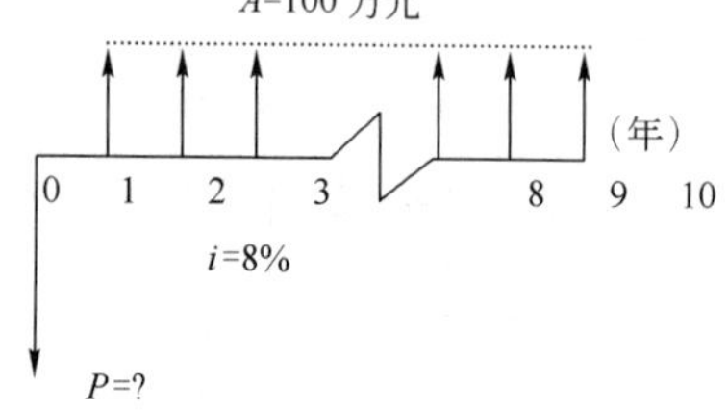

例 10-1-8 解图　等额支付现金流量图

五、复利系数表的应用

资金等值计算时，可以利用相应的公式计算，也可以应用复利系数表进行计算。复利系数表的形式见表 10-1-1 所列。表 10-1-1 是利率为 5%的复利系数表。

复利系数表(利率为 5%)　　表 10-1-1

年份 n	一次支付		等额支付			
	终值系数 $(1+i)^n$ $(F/P,i,n)$	现值系数 $\frac{1}{(1+i)^n}$ $(P/F,i,n)$	终值系数 $\frac{(1+i)^n-1}{i}$ $(F/A,i,n)$	偿债基金系数 $\frac{i}{(1+i)^n-1}$ $(A/F,i,n)$	资金回收系数 $\frac{i(1+i)^n}{(1+i)^n-1}$ $(A/P,i,n)$	现值系数 $\frac{(1+i)^n-1}{i(1+i)^n}$ $(P/A,i,n)$
1	1.050	0.952 4	1.000	1.000 00	1.050 00	0.952
2	1.103	0.907 0	2.050	0.487 80	0.537 80	1.859
3	1.158	0.868 8	3.153	0.317 21	0.367 21	2.723
4	1.216	0.827 7	4.310	0.232 01	0.282 01	3.546
5	1.276	0.783 5	5.526	0.180 97	0.230 97	4.329
6	1.340	0.746 2	6.802	0.147 02	0.197 02	5.076
7	1.407	0.710 7	8.142	0.122 82	0.172 82	5.788
8	1.477	0.676 8	9.549	0.104 72	0.154 72	6.463
9	1.551	0.644 6	11.027	0.090 69	0.140 69	7.108
10	1.629	0.613 9	12.578	0.079 50	0.129 50	7.722

【例 10-1-9】 某项目建设期 2 年，前 2 年年初分别投资 1 000 万元和 800 万元，2 年建成并投产，从第 3 年开始每年净收益 300 万元，项目生产期为 10 年，年利率为 5%，试计算该项目的净现值（净现值：按设定的折现率，将项目计算期内各年的净现金流量折现到建设期初的现值之和）。

解 该项目的现金流量图如解图所示，净现值为

$$\begin{aligned}NPV &= -1\,000-800(P/F,5,1)+300(P/A,5,10)(P/F,5,2)\\ &= -1\,000-800\times0.952\,4+300\times7.722\times0.907\,0\\ &= 339.24 \text{ 万元}\end{aligned}$$

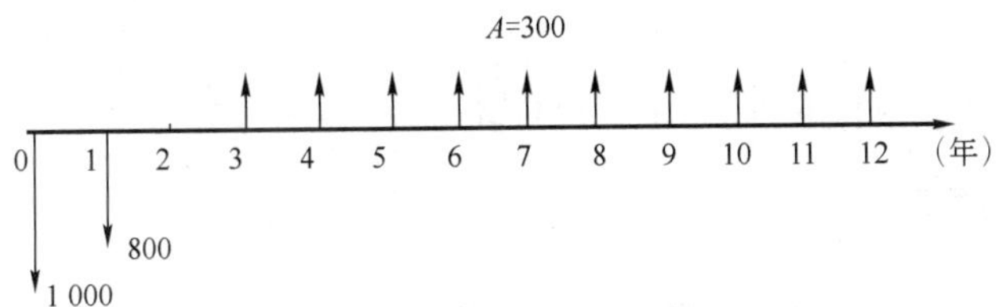

例 10-1-9 解图　某投资项目的现金流量图

习　题

10-1-1　某公司购买设备，有三家银行可提供贷款，甲银行年利率 18%，半年计息一次；乙银行年利率 17%，每月计息一次；丙银行年利率 18.2%，每年计息一次。均按复利计息，若其他条件相同，公司应向（　　）。

A. 向甲银行借款　　B. 向乙银行借款

C. 向丙银行借款　　D. 向甲银行、丙银行借款都一样

10-1-2　某公司从银行贷款，年利率 11%，每年年末贷款金额 10 万元，按复利计息，到第 5 年年末需偿还本利和（　　）。

A. 54.4 万元　　B. 55.5 万元　　C. 61.051 万元　　D. 62.278 万元

10-1-3　某公司从银行贷款，年利率 8%，按复利计息，借贷期限 5 年，每年年末偿还等额本息 50 万元。到第 3 年年初，企业已经按期偿还 2 年本息，现在企业有较充裕资金，与银行协商，计划第 3 年年初一次偿还贷款，需还款金额为（　　）。

A. 89.2 万元　　B. 128.9 万元　　C. 150 万元　　D. 199.6 万元

10-1-4　某学生从银行贷款上学，贷款年利率 5%，上学期限 3 年，与银行约定从毕业工作的第 1 年年末开始，连续 5 年以等额本息还款方式还清全部贷款，预计该生每年还款能力为 6 000元。该学生上学期间每年年初可从银行得到等额贷款是（　　）。

A. 7 848 元　　B. 8 240 元　　C. 9 508 元　　D. 9 539 元

第二节　财务效益与费用估算

一、项目的分类与项目计算期

对建设项目可以从不同的角度进行分类，通常有以下分类方法：

(1)按项目的目标，可分为经营性项目和非经营性项目；

(2)按项目的产出属性(产品或服务),可分为公共项目和非公共项目;

(3)按项目的投资管理形式,可分为政府投资项目和企业投资项目;

(4)按项目与企业原有资产的关系,可分为新建项目和改扩建项目;

(5)按项目的融资主体,可分为新设法人项目和既有法人项目。

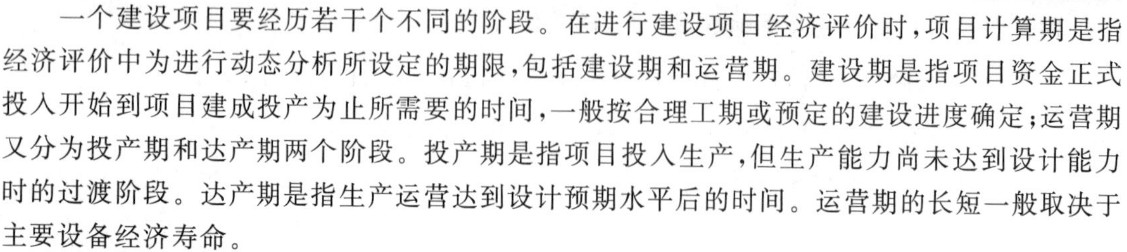

一个建设项目要经历若干个不同的阶段。在进行建设项目经济评价时,项目计算期是指经济评价中为进行动态分析所设定的期限,包括建设期和运营期。建设期是指项目资金正式投入开始到项目建成投产为止所需要的时间,一般按合理工期或预定的建设进度确定;运营期又分为投产期和达产期两个阶段。投产期是指项目投入生产,但生产能力尚未达到设计能力时的过渡阶段。达产期是指生产运营达到设计预期水平后的时间。运营期的长短一般取决于主要设备经济寿命。

项目计算期的长短与行业特点、主要设备经济寿命等有关。

二、财务效益与费用

财务效益与费用是对项目进行财务分析的基础,这里的财务效益与费用是指项目实施后所获得的收入和费用支出。

(一)收入

项目的收入包括营业收入和补贴收入。

1. 营业收入

营业收入是指销售产品或提供服务获得的收入。对于生产销售产品的项目,营业收入就是销售收入。销售收入是指企业向社会出售商品或提供劳务的货币收入。

销售收入=产品销售量×产品单价

在项目经济评价中需要对营业收入进行估算,根据市场预测分析数据、产品或服务价格、各期的运营负荷(产品或服务的数量)等因素估算。

2. 补贴收入

补贴收入是企业从政府或某些国际组织得到的补贴。

对于适用增值税的经营性项目,除营业收入外,可得到的增值税返还也作为补贴收入计入财务效益;对于非经营性项目,财务效益包括可能获得的各种补贴收入。

3. 利润

利润是企业在一定期间的经营成果。

营业利润=营业收入-营业成本-营业税金及附加-销售费用-管理费用-财务费用-资产减值损失-公允价值变动损失(+收益)+投资收益(-损失)

利润总额=营业利润+营业外收入-营业外支出

净利润=利润总额-所得税费用=利润总额×(1-所得税率)

(二)项目的费用支出

建设项目所支出的费用主要包括投资、成本费用和税金等。

1. 建设投资

建设投资是指项目筹建和建设期间所需的建设费用。建设投资由工程费用(包括建筑工程费、设备购置费、安装工程费)、工程建设其他费用和预备费(包括基本预备费和涨价预备费)所组成。

其中工程建设其他费用是指建设投资中除建筑工程费、设备购置费和安装工程费之外的,为保证项目顺利建成并交付使用的各项费用，包括建设用地费用、与项目建设有关的费用（如建设管理费、可行性研究费、勘察设计费等）及与项目运营有关的费用（如专利使用费、联合试运转费、生产准备费等）。

建设项目的总投资包括建设投资、建设期利息和流动资金之和。建设期利息包括银行借款和其他债务资金的利息，以及其他融资费用。流动资金是指项目运营期内长期占用并周转使用的营运资金。建设项目投资构成如图 10-2-1 所示。

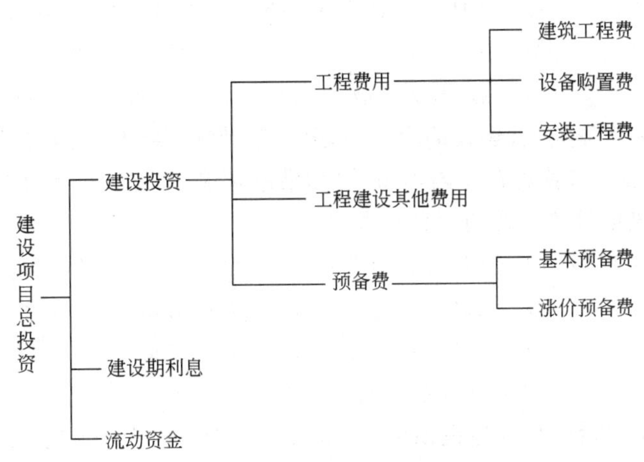

图 10-2-1　建设项目投资构成

【例 10-2-1】 在下列费用中，应列入项目建设投资的是：

A. 项目经营成本　　B. 流动资金

C. 预备费　　D. 建设期利息

解　建设项目评价中的总投资包括建设投资、建设期利息和流动资金之和。建设投资由工程费用（建筑工程费、设备购置费、安装工程费）、工程建设其他费用和预备费（基本预备费和涨价预备费）组成。

答案：C

2. 建设期利息

建设期利息是指为建设项目所筹措的债务资金在建设期内发生并按规定允许在投产后计入固定资产原值的利息，即资本化利息。估算建设期利息一般按年计算。

根据借款是在建设期各年年初发生还是在各年年内均衡发生，估算建设期利息应采用不同的计算公式。

（1）借款在建设期各年年初发生，建设期利息为

$$Q=\sum[(P_{t-1}+A_t)\cdot i] \tag{10-2-1}$$

式中：Q——建设期利息；

P_{t-1}——按单利计算时为建设期第 $t-1$ 年末借款累计，按复利计息时为建设期第 $t-1$ 年末借款本息累计；

A_t——建设期第 t 年借款额；

i——借款年利率；

t——年份。

（2）借款在建设期各年年内均衡发生，建设期利息为

$$Q=\sum\left[\left(P_{t-1}+\frac{A_t}{2}\right)\cdot i\right] \tag{10-2-2}$$

【例 10-2-2】 某新建项目，建设期为 3 年，第 1 年年初借款 500 万元，第 2 年年初借款 800 万元，第 3 年年初借款 400 万元，借款年利率 8%，按年计息，建设期内不支付利息。试问该项目的建设期利息是多少？

解 第 1 年借款利息 $Q_1=(P_{1-1}+A_1)\times i=500\times 8\%=40$ 万元

第 2 年借款利息 $Q_2=(P_{2-1}+A_2)\times i=(540+800)\times 8\%=107.2$ 万元

第 3 年借款利息 $Q_3=(P_{3-1}+A_3)\times i=(540+907.2+400)\times 8\%=147.78$ 万元

建设期利息为 $Q=Q_1+Q_2+Q_3=40+107.2+147.78=294.98$ 万元

【例 10-2-3】 某新建项目，建设期为 3 年，第 1 年借款 500 万元，第 2 年借款 800 万元，第 3 年借款 400 万元，各年借款均在年内均衡发生，借款年利率 8%，每年计息一次，建设期内按期支付利息。试问该项目的建设期利息是多少？

解 第 1 年借款利息 $Q_1=(P_{1-1}+A_1/2)\times i=500\div 2\times 8\%=20$ 万元

第 2 年借款利息 $Q_2=(P_{2-1}+A_2/2)\times i=(500+800\div 2)\times 8\%=72$ 万元

第 3 年借款利息 $Q_3=(P_{3-1}+A_3/2)\times i=(500+800+400\div 2)\times 8\%=120$ 万元

建设期利息为 $Q=Q_1+Q_2+Q_3=20+72+120=212$ 万元

【例 10-2-4】 某建设项目的建设期为 2 年，第一年贷款额为 400 万元，第二年贷款额 800 万元，贷款在年内均衡发生，贷款年利率为 6%，建设期内不支付利息，计算建设期贷款利息为：

A. 12 万元　　B. 48.72 万　　C. 60 万元　　D. 60.72 万元

解 第一年贷款利息：400/2×6%=12 万元

第二年贷款利息：(400+800/2+12)×6%=48.72 万元

建设期贷款利息：12+48.72=60.72 万元

答案：D

3. 流动资金

流动资金是指运营期内长期占用并周转使用的营运资金，不包括运营中需要的临时性营运资金。建设项目投资期垫支的营运资金一般默认在营业终结期（项目寿命期满）收回。营运资金垫支一般发生在投资期，垫支时做现金流出，在项目寿命期满收回时做现金流入。流动资金估算的基础是营业收入、经营成本和商业信用等。在估算营业收入和经营成本后估算流动资金。按行业或前期研究阶段的不同，估算流动资金的方法可选用扩大指标法或分项详细估算法。

(1) 扩大指标法

扩大指标法是参照同类企业流动资金占营业收入或经营成本的比例，或者单位产品占用营运资金的数额估算流动资金，计算公式如下

流动资金＝年营业收入额×营业收入资金率

或　　流动资金＝年经营成本×经营成本资金率

或　　流动资金＝单位产品占用流动资金额×年产量

(2) 分项详细估算法

分项详细估算法是利用流动资产与流动负债估算项目占用的流动资金。流动资产的构成要素一般包括存货、库存现金、应收账款和预付账款，流动负债的构成要素一般只考虑应付账

款和预收账款。计算公式如下

流动资金＝流动资产－流动负债

流动资产＝存货＋现金＋应收账款＋预付账款

流动负债＝应付账款＋预收账款

流动资金本年增加额＝本年流动资金－上年流动资金

4.总成本费用

费用是指企业在日常活动中发生的、会导致所有者权益减少的、与向所有者分配利润无关的经济利益的总流出。成本通常是指企业为生产产品或提供服务所进行经营活动的耗费。

总成本费用是指在运营期内为生产产品或提供服务所发生的全部费用，等于经营成本与折旧费、摊销费和财务费用之和。

总成本费用可按以下两种方法计算：

(1)生产成本加期间费用估算法

总成本费用＝生产成本＋期间费用

其中　生产成本＝直接材料费＋直接燃料和动力费＋直接工资＋其他直接支出＋制造费用

期间费用＝管理费用＋营业费用＋财务费用

生产成本是企业为生产产品或提供服务而发生的各项生产费用，包括各项直接支出和制造费用。其中，直接支出包括直接材料、直接燃料和动力、直接工资、其他直接支出(如福利费)；制造费用是指企业内的车间为组织和管理生产所发生的各项费用，包括车间管理人员工资、折旧费、修理费及其他制造费用(办公费、差旅费、劳保费等)。

管理费用是指企业行政管理部门为组织和管理生产经营活动而发生的各项费用，包括企业管理人员的工资、福利费及公司一级的折旧费、修理费、无形资产摊销费、长期待摊费用、其他管理费用(如办公费、差旅费、技术转让费、咨询费等)。

营业费用是指企业在销售产品和提供服务等经营过程中发生的各项费用以及专设销售机构的各项经费。

财务费用是指企业在生产经营过程中为筹集资金而发生的各项费用，包括企业生产经营期间发生的利息支出、汇兑净损失、金融机构手续费等。在项目评价中一般只考虑其中的利息支出。

(2)生产要素估算法

总成本费用＝外购原材料、燃料和动力费＋工资及福利费＋折旧费＋摊销费＋修理费＋财务费用(利息支出)＋其他费用

5.固定资产折旧

固定资产是指使用期限超过一年，单位价值在规定标准以上，并在使用过程中保持原有物质形态的资产。固定资产在使用过程中，其价值量会不断变化。

建设项目建成或者设备购置投入使用时发生并核定的固定资产完全原始价值总量，称为固定资产原值。固定资产在使用过程中会发生损耗，这种损耗称为固定资产损耗，产生的损耗，包括有形损耗和无形损耗。有形损耗也称为物理损耗，是由于使用或者自然力的作用而引起的固定资产物质上的损耗。无形损耗也称为精神损耗，是由于科学技术进步、社会劳动生产率提高而引起原来的固定资产贬值。

固定资产原值或者重置价值减去累计折旧额后的余额称为固定资产净值，它反映了固定资产现存的价值。

固定资产达到规定的使用期限或者报废清理时可以回收的价值称为固定资产残值。

固定资产折旧简称折旧，是指固定资产在使用过程中由于逐渐磨损和贬值而转移到产品中去的那部分价值。固定资产在使用过程中，虽然其实物形态不变，但是由于磨损和贬值其价值会发生变化。折旧是固定资产价值补偿的一种方式，通过从销售收入中提取折旧费对固定资产进行价值形态的补偿，提取的折旧费积累起来可以用作固定资产的更新。

在项目投产前一次性支付的无形资产的费用，如技术转让费（包括专利费、许可证费等），在项目投产后分次摊入成本的金额，称为摊销费。摊销费是无形资产转移到成本的那部分价值。同样，摊销费也在销售收入中回收，其性质与折旧费类似，所以也可以把它列入计算折旧的栏目中，一并计算现金流量。

折旧常用的方法有年限平均法、工作量法、双倍余额递减法、年数总和法等。其中，双倍余额递减法属于加速折旧法，对企业较为有利，一方面可以避免承担固定资产无形损耗带来的风险；另一方面可以冲减企业的利润，减少同期的纳税额。各种折旧方法计算公式如下：

(1)年限平均法

$$\text{年折旧额}=\frac{\text{固定资产原值}-\text{残值}}{\text{折旧年限}} \tag{10-2-3}$$

残值与固定资产原值之比称为净残值率，将上式两边同除以固定资产原值，可以得到年折旧率，所以年折旧额也可以按以下两式计算

$$\text{年折旧率}=\frac{1-\text{预计净残值率}}{\text{折旧年限}}\times 100\% \tag{10-2-4}$$

$$\text{年折旧额}=\text{固定资产原值}\times\text{年折旧率} \tag{10-2-5}$$

按这种折旧方法计算，折旧率不变，每年折旧额也相等。

【例 10-2-5】 某企业以 15 万元购入一种测试仪器，按规定使用年限为 10 年，残值率为 3%，求各年的折旧额。

解 根据式(10-2-4)和式(10-2-5)，可知

$$\text{年折旧率}=\frac{1-3\%}{10}=9.7\%$$

$$\text{年折旧额}=15\times 9.7\%=1.455\text{ 万元}$$

(2)工作量法

这种方法根据固定资产实际完成的工作量计算折旧额。一些专业设备，如汽车、机床等一般用这种方法计提折旧。工作量法分为两种，一种是按照行驶里程计算折旧，另一种是按照工作小时计算折旧。

按行驶里程计算折旧的公式如下

$$\text{单位里程折旧额}=\frac{\text{原值}\times(1-\text{预计净产值率})}{\text{总行驶里程}} \tag{10-2-6}$$

$$\text{年折旧额}=\text{单位里程折旧额}\times\text{年行驶里程}$$

按照工作小时计算折旧的公式为

$$\text{每工作小时折旧额}=\frac{\text{原值}\times(1-\text{预计净产值率})}{\text{总工作小时}} \tag{10-2-7}$$

$$\text{年折旧额}=\text{每工作小时折旧额}\times\text{年工作小时}$$

采用工作量法折旧，若每年的工作量不同，则每年的折旧额不等。

【例 10-2-6】 同例 10-2-5，各年该测试仪器工作小时见表，用工作量法计算各年的折旧额。

某测试仪器各年的工作小时 例 10-2-6 表

年　份	1	2	3	4	5	6	7	8	9	10	合计
工作小时	420	450	460	500	510	500	530	550	540	540	5 000

解 根据公式(10-2-7)，可知

$$第1年折旧额=(15-15\times3\%)\times\frac{420}{5\,000}=1.222\ 万元$$

$$第2年折旧额=(15-15\times3\%)\times\frac{450}{5\,000}=1.310\ 万元$$

同样，可求得其余各年折旧额。

(3)双倍余额递减法

双倍余额递减法属于加速折旧法，是一种加快回收折旧金额的方法。此法初始年折旧额大，随着固定资产使用年数的增加，年折旧额逐年降低，但每年的折旧率是相同的。

$$年折旧率=\frac{2}{折旧年限}\times100\% \tag{10-2-8}$$

$$第\ n\ 年折旧额=第\ n\ 年固定资产净值\times年折旧率 \tag{10-2-9}$$

采用此法计算折旧额，应在固定资产折旧年限到期的前 2 年内，将固定资产净值扣除预计残值后的净额平均摊销。

【例 10-2-7】 同例 10-2-5，但用双倍余额递减法计算各年的折旧额。

解 根据公式(10-2-8)和公式(10-2-9)可得

$$年折旧率=\frac{2}{10}\times100\%=20\%$$

第 1 年折旧额$=15\times20\%=3$ 万元

第 2 年折旧额$=(15-3)\times20\%=2.4$ 万元

第 3 年折旧额$=15\times(1-20\%)^2\times20\%=1.92$ 万元

……

第 8 年折旧额$=15\times(1-20\%)^7\times20\%=0.629$ 万元

第 9 年和第 10 年的折旧额：

(固定资产净值－预计残值)÷2

$=[15\times(1-20\%)^8-15\times3\%]\div2$

$=1.033$ 万元

(4)年数总和法

$$年折旧率=\frac{折旧年限-已使用年限}{折旧年限\times(折旧年限+1)\div2}\times100\% \tag{10-2-10}$$

$$年折旧额=(固定资产原值-残值)\times年折旧率 \tag{10-2-11}$$

年数总和法也是一种加速折旧的方法，前几种方法每年的折旧率是不变的，而采用这种方法折旧，折旧额和折旧率都是逐年减小的。

【例 10-2-8】 同例 10-2-5，但用年数总和法计算各年的折旧额。

解 根据公式(10-2-10)和公式(10-2-11)可得

$$第1年折旧率=\frac{10-0}{10\times(10+1)\div2}\times100\%=18.18\%$$

第 1 年折旧额 =(15－15×3%)×18.18%=2.645 万元

$$第2年折旧率=\frac{10-1}{10\times(10+1)\div2}\times100\%=16.36\%$$

第 2 年折旧额=(15－15×3%)×16.36%=2.380 万元

同理可计算出各年的折旧率及折旧额。

各年折旧额累计之和应等于固定资产原值减去残值。

6.经营成本

经营成本是指建设项目总成本费用扣除折旧费、摊销费和财务费用以后的全部费用。

经营成本是项目评价中所使用的特定概念，是从投资方案本身考察的，在一定期间(一般为一年)内由于生产和销售产品或提供服务而实际发生的现金支出。经营成本不包括虽已经计入产品成本费用中但实际没有发生现金支出的费用项目。

经营成本与项目的融资方案无关，在完成建设投资和营业收入的估算后就可以估算经营成本，为项目融资之前的现金流量分析提供依据。

经营成本按下式计算

经营成本＝外购原材料、燃料和动力费＋工资及福利费＋修理费＋其他费用

经营成本与总成本费用之间的关系是

经营成本＝总成本费用－折旧费－摊销费－财务费用

7.固定成本和可变成本

总成本费用按成本与产量的关系可分为固定成本和可变成本。

固定成本是指产品总成本中，在一定产量范围内不随产量变动而变动的费用，如固定资产折旧费、管理费用等。固定成本一般包括折旧费、摊销费、修理费、工资、福利费(计件工资除外)及其他费用等。通常把运营期间发生的全部利息也作为固定成本。

可变成本也称为变动成本，是指产品总成本中随产量变动而变动的费用，如产品外购原材料、燃料及动力费、计件工资等。

固定成本总额在一定时期和一定业务范围内不随产量的增加而变动。但在单位产品成本中，固定成本部分与产量的增加成反比，即产量增加，单位产品的固定成本减少。

变动成本总额随产量增加而增加，但单位产品成本中，产量增加，单位可变成本不变。

8.机会成本和沉没成本

机会成本是指将有限资源投入某种经济活动时所放弃的投入到其他经济活动所能带来的最高收益。

沉没成本是指过去已经支出而现在已无法得到补偿的成本。

【例 10-2-9】 某项目投资中有部分资金源于银行贷款，该贷款在整个项目期间将等额偿还本息。项目预计年经营成本为 5 000 万元，年折旧费和摊销为 2 000 万元，则该项目的年总成本费用应：

A. 等于 5 000 万元　　B. 等于 7 000 万元

C. 大于 7 000 万元　　D. 在 5 000 万元与 7 000 万元之间

解 经营成本是指项目总成本费用扣除固定资产折旧费、摊销费和利息支出以后的全部费用。即，经营成本＝总成本费用－折旧费－摊销费－利息支出。本题经营成本与折旧费、摊销费之和为7 000万元，再加上利息支出，则该项目的年总成本费用大于7 000万元。

答案：C

（三）项目评价涉及的税费

项目评价涉及的税费主要包括关税、增值税、营业税、消费税、所得税、资源税、城市维护建设税和教育费附加等，有的行业还涉及土地增值税。

我国目前的工商税制分为流转税、资源税、收益税、财产税、特定行为税等几类。其中项目评价所涉及的主要税费有从销售收入中扣除的增值税、营业税及附加，计入总成本费用的房产税、土地使用税、车船使用税、印花税等，计入建设投资的引进技术、设备材料的关税和固定资产投资方向调节税等，以及从利润中扣除的所得税等。以下简述几种主要的税种。

1. 增值税

增值税是就商品生产、商品流通和劳务服务各个环节的增值额征收的一种流转税（流转税是指以商品生产、商品流通和劳务服务的流转额为征税对象的各种税，包括增值税、消费税和营业税）。增值税设基本税率、低税率和零税率三档。计税公式为

$$应纳税额=当期销项税额-当期进项税额$$

其中

$$销项税额=销售额\times适用增值税率$$

销项税额是按照销售额和规定税率计算并向购买方收取的增值税额。进项税额是指纳税人购进货物或者应税劳务所支付或者负担的增值税额。准予从销项税额中抵扣的进项税额，是指从销售方取得增值税专用发票上注明的增值税额或从海关取得的完税凭证上注明的增值税额。

财务分析应按税法规定计算增值税。当采用含（增值）税价格计算销售收入和原材料、燃料动力成本时，利润和利润分配表以及现金流量表中应单列增值税科目；采用不含（增值）税价格计算时，利润表和利润分配表以及现金流量表中不包括增值税科目。

2. 营业税

营业税是对在我国境内提供应税劳务、转让无形资产、销售不动产的单位和个人，就其营业额征收的一种税。凡在我国境内从事交通运输、建筑业、金融保险业、邮电通信业、文化体育业、娱乐业、服务业、转让无形资产、销售不动产等业务，都属于营业税的征收范围。其计算公式为

$$应纳营业税税额=营业额\times适用税率$$

营业税是价内税，包含在营业收入之内。

3. 资源税

资源税是对在我国境内从事开采特定矿产品和生产盐的单位和个人征收的税种，通常按矿产的产量计征。

4. 消费税

消费税是以特定消费品为纳税对象的税种。

5. 关税

关税是以进出口应税货物为纳税对象的税种。

6. 土地增值税

土地增值税是按照转让房地产所取得的增值额征收的一种税。房地产开发项目应按规定

计算土地增值税。

7. 城乡维护建设税

城乡维护建设税是对一切有经营收入的单位和个人，就其经营收入征收的一种税。城市维护建设税是一种地方附加税，目前以流转税额（包括增值税、营业税和消费税）为计税依据。

8. 教育费附加

教育费附加是向缴纳增值税、消费税、营业税的单位和个人征收的一种专项费用。

9. 企业所得税

企业所得税是企业应纳税所得额征收的税种，其计算公式为

$$\text{应纳所得税额} = \text{应纳税所得额} \times \text{所得税税率}$$

$$\text{应纳税所得额} = \text{利润总额} \pm \text{税收项目调整项目金额}$$

10. 固定资产投资方向调节税

固定资产投资方向调节税是以投资行为为征税对象的一种税。按国家规定，自 2000 年 1 月起新发生的投资额，暂停征收固定资产投资方向调节税。

在财务现金流量表中所列的"营业税及附加"，是指在项目运营期内各年销售产品或提供服务所发生的应从营业收入中缴纳的税金，包括营业税、资源税、消费税、土地增值税、城市维护建设税和教育费附加。

（四）总投资形成的资产

建设项目评价中的总投资，是指项目建设和投入运营所需要的全部投资，为建设投资、建设期利息和流动资金之和。应注意项目评价中的总投资区别于目前国家考核建设规模的总投资，后者包括建设投资和 30％的流动资金（又称铺底流动资金）。

按现行财务会计制度的规定，固定资产是指为生产商品、提供劳务、出租或经营管理而持有的，使用寿命超过一个会计年度的有形资产。

无形资产是指企业拥有或控制的没有实物形态的可辨认非货币性资产。

其他资产，原称递延资产，是指除流动资产、长期投资、固定资产、无形资产以外的其他资产，如长期待摊费用。

项目评价中总投资形成的资产可划分为：

1. 固定资产

构成固定资产原值的费用包括：

(1)工程费用，即建筑工程费、设备购置费和安装工程费；

(2)工程建设其他费用；

(3)预备费，可含基本预备费和涨价预备费；

(4)建设期利息。

2. 无形资产

构成无形资产原值的费用，主要包括技术转让费或技术使用费（含专利权和非专利技术）、商标权和商誉等。

3. 其他资产

构成其他资产原值的费用，主要包括生产准备费、开办费、出国人员费、来华人员费、图纸资料翻译复制费、样品样机购置费和农业开荒费等。

建设项目经济评价中，应按有关规定将建设投资中的各分项分别形成固定资产原值、无形资产原值和其他资产原值。形成的固定资产原值可用于计算折旧费，形成的无形资产原值和

其他资产原值可用于计算摊销费。建设期利息应计入固定资产原值。

总投资中的流动资金与流动负债共同构成流动资产。

习 题

10-2-1 构成建设项目的总投资的三部分费用是(　　)。

A. 工程费用、预备费、流动资金

B. 建设投资、建设期利息、流动资金

C. 建设投资、建设期利息、预备费

D. 建筑安装工程费、工程建设其他费用、预备费

10-2-2 建设项目总投资中,形成固定资产原值的费用包括(　　)。

A. 工程费用、工程建设其他费用、预备费、建设期利息

B. 工程费用、专利费、预备费、建设期利息

C. 建筑安装工程费、设备购置费、建设期利息、商标权

D. 建筑安装工程费、预备费、流动资金、技术转让费

10-2-3 某新建项目,建设期2年,第1年年初借款1 500万元,第2年年初借款1 000万元,借款按年计息,利率为7%,建设期内不支付利息,第2年借款利息为(　　)。

A. 70万元　　B. 77.35万元　　C. 175万元　　D. 182.35万元

10-2-4 某企业购置一台设备,固定资产原值为20万元,采用双倍余额递减法折旧,折旧年限为10年,则该设备第2年折旧额为(　　)。

A. 2万元　　B. 2.4万元　　C. 3.2万元　　D. 4.0万元

10-2-5 某工业企业预计今年销售收入可达8 000万元,总成本费用为8 200万元,则该企业今年可以不缴纳(　　)。

A. 企业所得税　　B. 营业税金及附加

C. 企业自有车辆的车船税　　D. 企业自有房产的房产税

10-2-6 在建设项目总投资中,以下应计入固定资产原值的是(　　)。

A. 建设期利息　　B. 外购专利权

C. 土地使用权　　D. 开办费

第三节 资金来源与融资方案

一、资金筹措的主要方式

一个项目的建设,需要通过融资筹集建设项目所需的资金,资金筹措方式是指项目获得资金的具体方式。按照融资主体不同,项目的融资可分为既有法人融资和新设法人融资两种融资方式;按融资的性质,可以分为权益融资和债务融资。权益融资形成项目的资本金,债务融资形成项目的债务资金。

(一)资本金筹措

项目资本金是指在建设项目总投资中,由投资者认缴的出资额,对项目来说是非债务资金,投资者按出资比例依法享有所有者权益,可转让其出资,但不得抽回。项目法人不承担资

本金的任何利息和债务，没有按期还本付息的压力。股利的支付依投产后的经营状况而定，项目法人的财务负担较小。由于股利从税后利润中支付，没有抵税作用，且发行费用较高，故资金成本较高。

项目资本金(即项目权益资金)的来源和筹措方式根据融资主体的特点有不同筹措方式。

既有法人融资项目新增资本金，可通过原有股东增资扩股、吸收新股东投资、发行股票、政府投资等方式筹措；新设法人融资项目的资本金，可通过股东直接投资、发行股票、政府投资等方式筹措。

(二)债务资金筹措

债务资金是项目投资中以负债方式从金融机构、证券市场等资本市场取得的资金。债务资金的特点是：使用上有时间性限制，到期必须偿还；不管企业经营好坏，均得按期还本付息，形成企业的财务负担；资金成本一般比权益资金低；不会分散投资者对企业的控制权。

目前，我国项目债务资金的来源和筹措方式有：

1.商业银行贷款

国内商业银行贷款手续简单、成本较低，适用于有偿债能力的项目。

2.政策性银行贷款

政策性银行贷款一般期限较长，利率较低。

3.外国政府贷款

外国政府贷款在经济上有援助性质，期限长、利率低。

4.国际金融组织贷款

国际金融组织贷款，如国际货币基金组织、世界银行、亚洲开发银行等。国际金融组织有自己的贷款政策，符合该组织认为应当支持的项目才能获得贷款。

5.出口信贷

出口信贷是设备出口国政府为促进本国设备出口，鼓励本国银行向本国出口商或外国进口商(或进口方银行)提供的贷款。贷款的使用条件是购买贷款国的设备，其利率通常低于国际上商业银行的利率，但需要支付一定的附加费用(管理费、承诺费、信贷保险费等)。

6.银团贷款

银团贷款是指多家银行组成一个集团，由一家或几家银行牵头，采用同一贷款协议，按照共同约定的贷款计划，向借款人提供贷款的贷款方式。它主要适用于资金需要量大、偿债能力较强的项目。

7.企业债券

企业债券是企业以自身的财务状况和信用条件为基础，按有关法律、法规规定的条件和程序发行的、约定在一定期限内还本付息的债券。企业债券的特点是筹资对象广，但发债条件严格、手续复杂；其利率虽低于贷款利率，但发行费用较高。它适用于资金需求量大、偿债能力较强的项目。

8.国际债券

国际债券是在国际金融市场上发行的、以外国货币为面值的债券。

9.融资租赁

租赁筹资是指出租人以租赁方式将出租物租给承租人，承租人以交纳租金的方式取得租赁物的使用权，在租赁期间出租人仍保持出租物的所有权，并于租赁期满收回出租物的一种经济行为。

企业筹集资金除了受到宏观经济、法律、政策及行业特点等因素制约外，还受到企业或项目自身因素的影响，包括：拟建项目的规模、拟建项目的速度、控制权、资金结构、资金成本等因素的影响。

（三）准股本资金筹措

准股本资金是一种既具有资本金性质，又具有债务资金性质的资金。主要包括优先股股票和可转换债券。

（1）优先股股票：是一种兼具资本金和债务资金性质的有价证券。从普通股股东的立场看，优先股可视同一种负债；但从债权人的立场看，优先股可视同资本金。

在项目评价中，优先股股票应视为项目资本金。

（2）可转换债券：兼有债券和股票的特性。有债权性、股权性和可转换性三个特点。在项目评价中，可转换债券应视为项目债务资金。

二、资金成本

资金成本是企业为筹措资金和使用资金而付出的代价，由资金筹集费和资金占用费所组成。资金筹集费是筹集资金过程中发生的费用，如律师费、证券印刷费、发行手续费、资信评估费等；资金占用费是使用资金过程中向提供资金者所支付的费用，如借款利息、债券利息、优先股股息、普通股股息等。

资金成本一般用资金成本率表示。资金成本率是指筹集的资金与筹资发生的各种费用等值时的贴现率。考虑了资金时间价值的资金成本率的一般计算公式为

$$\sum_{t=0}^{n}\frac{F_t - C_t}{(1+K)^n} = 0 \qquad (10\text{-}3\text{-}1)$$

式中：F_t——各年实际筹措资金流入额；

C_t——各年实际资金筹集费和资金占用费；

K——资金成本率；

n——资金占用期限。

若不考虑资金的时间价值，资金成本可按下式计算

$$K = \frac{D}{I-C} = \frac{D}{I(1-f)} \qquad (10\text{-}3\text{-}2)$$

式中：K——资金成本；

D——资金占用费；

I——筹集资金总额；

C——资金筹集费；

f——筹资费率。

（一）各种资金来源的资金成本

1. 银行借款成本

借贷、债券等的融资费用和利息支出均在缴纳所得税之前支付，因此作为股权投资者可以获得所得税抵减的好处，所得税后资金成本可根据下式计算

所得税后资金成本＝所得税前资金成本×（1－所得税税率）

借款成本主要是利息支出，在筹资的时候也有一些费用，但这些费用一般较少，进行财务评价时可以忽略不计。考虑到利息在所得税前支付，可少交一部分所得税。其资金成本计算

公式为

$$K_e = R_e(1-T) \tag{10-3-3}$$

式中：K_e——借款成本；

R_e——借款利率；

T——所得税税率。

如果考虑筹资费用，计算公式为

$$K_e = R_e(1-T)/(1-f) \tag{10-3-4}$$

式中：f——筹资费率。

【例 10-3-1】 某项目从银行贷款 500 万元，年利率为 8%，在借款期间每年支付利息 2 次，所得税税率为 25%，手续费忽略不计，问该借款的资金成本是多少？

解 将名义利率折算为实际利率，即

$$R_e = \left(1+\frac{r}{m}\right)^m - 1 = \left(1+\frac{8\%}{2}\right)^2 - 1 = 8.16\%$$

借款资金成本 $K_e = R_e(1-T) = 8.16\% \times (1-25\%) = 6.12\%$

2. 债券成本

与借款类似，企业发行债券筹集成本所支付的利息计入税前成本费用，同样可以少交一部分所得税。企业发行债券的筹资费用较高，计算其资金成本时应予以考虑。债券成本的计算公式为

$$K_b = R_b(1-T)/[B(1-f_b)] \tag{10-3-5}$$

式中：K_b——债券成本；

R_b——债券每年实际利息；

B——债券每年发行总额；

f_b——债券筹资费用率。

3. 优先股资金成本

优先股是一种兼有资本金和债务资金特点的融资方式，优先股股东不参与公司经营管理，对公司无控制权。发行优先股通常不需要还本，但需要支付固定股息，股息一般高于银行贷款利息。从债权人的立场看，优先股可视为资本金；从普通股股东的立场看，优先股可视为一种负债。在项目评价中，优先股股票应视为资本金。优先股资金成本的计算公式为

优先股资金成本＝优先股股息/(优先股发行价格－发行成本)

【例 10-3-2】 某优先股面值 100 元，发行价格 99 元，发行成本为面值的 3%，每年支付利息 1 次，固定股息率为 8%，问该优先股的资金成本是多少？

解 该优先股的资金成本＝8/(99－3)×100%＝8.33%

4. 普通股资金成本

普通股资金成本属于权益资金成本。其计算方法有资本资产定价模型法、税前债务成本加风险溢价法、股利增长模型法等。

(1)资本资产定价模型法

资本资产定价模型法的计算公式为

$$K_c = R_f + \beta(R_m - R_f) \tag{10-3-6}$$

式中：K_c——普通股资金成本；

R_m——市场投资组合预期收益率；

R_f——无风险投资收益率；

β——项目的投资风险系数。

(2)股利增长模型法

该模型是一种假定股票投资收益以固定的增长率递增的计算股票资金成本的方法，计算公式为

$$K_s=\frac{D_i}{P_0(1-f)}+g \tag{10-3-7}$$

式中：K_s——普通股资金成本；

D_i——第 i 期支付的股利；

P_0——普通股现值；

f——筹资费率；

g——期望股利增长率。

由于股利必须在企业税后利润中支付，因而不能抵减所得税的缴纳。

5.保留盈余资金成本

保留盈余又称留存收益，是指企业从历年实现的利润中提取或形成的留存于企业内部的积累。保留盈余包括盈余公积和未分配利润。由于企业保留盈余资金不仅可以用来追加本企业的投资，也可把资金放入银行或者投资到别的企业。因此，使用保留盈余资金意味着要承受机会成本。

(二)扣除通货膨胀影响的资金成本

借贷资金利息等通常包含通货膨胀因素的影响，扣除通货膨胀因素影响的资金成本计算公式为

$$扣除通货膨胀因素影响的资金成本=\frac{1+未扣除通货膨胀因素影响的资金成本}{1+通货膨胀率}-1 \tag{10-3-8}$$

如果需要计算扣除所得税和扣除通货膨胀因素影响的资金成本，应当先计算扣除所得税影响的资金成本，然后再计算扣除通货膨胀因素影响的资金成本。

【例 10-3-3】 如果通货膨胀率为 2%，试计算例 10-3-1 的借款资金成本。

解 例 10-3-1 的计算结果已扣除了所得税的影响，则扣除通货膨胀因素影响的借款资金成本为

$$(1+6.12\%)\div(1+2\%)-1=4.04\%$$

(三)加权平均资金成本

项目的资金有不同来源，其成本一般是不同的。对项目进行评价时，需要计算整个融资方案的综合资金成本，一般是以各种资金所占全部资金的比重为权重，对个别资金成本进行加权计算，即加权平均资金成本，其计算公式为

$$K_w=\sum_{t=1}^{n}K_tW_t$$

式中：K_w——加权平均资金成本；

K_t——第 t 种融资的资金成本；

W_t——第 t 种融资金额占总融资金额的比重，有 $\sum W_t=1$。

【例 10-3-4】 某项目资金来源包括普通股、长期借款和短期借款，其融资金额分别为 500 万元、400 万元和 200 万元，资金成本分别为 15%、6%和 8%。试计算该项目融资的加权平均资金成本。

解 该项目融资总金额为 500+400+200=1 100 万元，其加权平均资金成本为

$$\frac{500}{1\,100}\times15\%+\frac{400}{1\,100}\times6\%+\frac{200}{1\,100}\times8\%=10.45\%$$

从以上例子可以看出，个别资金成本、税收、通货膨胀等因素会影响企业的平均资金成本。

三、债务偿还的主要方式

(一)等额利息法

等额利息法，即每期付息额相等，期中不还本金，最后一期归还本金和当期利息。

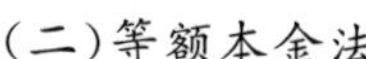

(二)等额本金法

等额本金法，即每期偿还相等的本金和相应的利息。

假定每年还款，等额本金法的计算公式为

$$A_t=\frac{I_c}{n}+I_c\cdot\left(1-\frac{t-1}{n}\right)\cdot i \tag{10-3-9}$$

式中：A_t——第 t 期的还本付息额；

I_c——还款开始的期初借款余额；

$\frac{I_c}{n}$——每年偿还的本金；

n——约定的还款期；

i——借款的年利率。

(三)等额本息法

等额本息法，即每期偿还本利额相等。

可利用等额支付资金回收公式(10-1-10)计算，即

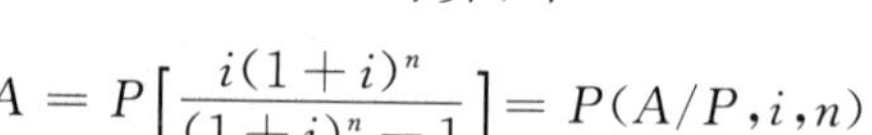

$$A=P\left[\frac{i(1+i)^n}{(1+i)^n-1}\right]=P(A/P,i,n)$$

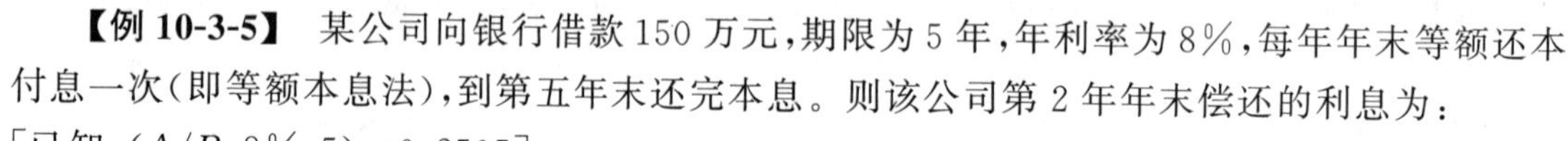

【例 10-3-5】 某公司向银行借款 150 万元，期限为 5 年，年利率为 8%，每年年末等额还本付息一次(即等额本息法)，到第五年末还完本息。则该公司第 2 年年末偿还的利息为：[已知：$(A/P,8\%,5)=0.2505$]

A. 9.954 万元　　B. 12 万元

C. 25.575 万元　　D. 37.575 万元

解 注意题目问的是第 2 年年末偿还的利息(不包括本金)。

等额本息法每年还款的本利和相等，根据等额支付资金回收公式(已知 P 求 A)，每年年末还本付息金额为：

$$A=P\left[\frac{i(1+i)^n}{(1+i)^n-1}\right]$$

$$=P(A/P,8\%,5)=150\times0.2505=37.575\text{ 万元}$$

则第 1 年年末偿还利息为 150×8%=12 万元，偿还本金为 37.575−12=25.575 万元；

第 1 年已经偿还本金 25.575 万元，尚未偿还本金为 150−25.575=124.425 万元；

第 2 年年末应偿还利息为(150−25.575)×8%=9.954 万元

答案：A

(四)“气球法”(任意法)

“气球法”，即期中任意偿还本利，到期末全部还清。

（五）一次偿付法

一次偿付法，即最后一期偿还本利。

（六）偿债基金法

偿债基金法，即每期偿还贷款利息，同时向银行存入一笔等额现金，到期末存款正好偿付贷款本金。

【例 10-3-6】 某公司向银行借款 2400 万元，期限为 6 年，年利率为 8%，每年年末付息一次，每年等额还本，到第 6 年年末还完本息。请问该公司第 4 年年末应还的本息和是：

A. 432 万元　　B. 464 万元　　C. 496 万元　　D. 592 万元

解　该公司借款的偿还方式为等额本金法。

每年应偿还的本金均为：2400/6＝400 万元

前 3 年已经偿还本金：400×3＝1200 万元

尚未还款本金：2400－1200＝1200 万元

第 4 年年末应还利息为：$I_4=1200\times8\%=96$ 万元

第 4 年年末应还本息和：$A_4=400+96=496$ 万元

或按等额本金法公式计算：

$$A_t=\frac{I_c}{n}+I_c\cdot\left(1-\frac{t-1}{n}\right)\cdot i=\frac{2400}{6}+2400\times\left(1-\frac{4-1}{6}\right)\times8\%=496\text{ 万元}$$

答案：C

习　题

10-3-1　某企业发行债券筹集资金，发行总额 500 万元，债券年利率为 5%，发行时的筹资费用率 1%，所得税税率 25%，该债券筹资成本为（　　）。

A. 3%　　B. 3.8%　　C. 5%　　D. 6%

10-3-2　某扩建项目总投资 1 000 万元，筹集资金的来源为：原有股东增资 400 万元，资金成本为 15%；银行长期借款 600 万元，年实际利率为 6%。该项目年初投资当年获利，所得税税率 25%，该项目所得税后加权平均资金成本为（　　）。

A. 7.2%　　B. 8.7%　　C. 9.6%　　D. 10.5%

10-3-3　某项目从银行贷款 500 万元，期限 5 年，年利率 5%，采取等额还本利息照付方式还本付息，每年末还本付息一次，第 2 年应付利息是（　　）万元。

A. 5　　B. 20　　C. 23　　D. 25

第四节　财 务 分 析

建设项目经济评价包括财务评价（也称财务分析）和国民经济评价（也称经济分析）。

财务评价（财务分析）是在国家现行财税制度和价格体系的前提下，从项目的角度进行经济分析，评价项目的盈利能力和借款偿还能力，评价项目在财务上的可行性。对于经营性项目，应分析项目的盈利能力、偿债能力和财务生存能力，判断项目的财务可接受性；对于非经营性项目，财务分析主要分析项目的财务生存能力。

一、财务评价的内容

(1)根据项目的性质和目标选择适当的方法。

(2)收集、预测财务分析的数据,进行财务效益和费用的估算。

(3)进行财务分析。通过编制财务报表,计算财务指标,分析项目的盈利能力、偿债能力和财务生存能力。

(4)进行不确定性分析,估计项目可能承担的风险。

二、盈利能力分析

财务分析可分为融资前分析和融资后分析,一般先进行融资前分析,在满足条件的基础上,考虑融资方案进行融资后分析。

融资前分析应以动态分析(折现现金流量分析)为主,静态分析为辅。融资前动态分析,不考虑债务融资方案,通过编制项目投资现金流量表,计算项目投资内部收益率和净现值等指标,从项目投资总获利能力的角度,考察项目方案的合理性。

根据分析的角度不同,融资前分析可选择计算所得税前指标和(或)所得税后指标。

融资前分析也可计算静态投资回收期指标,以反映收回项目投资所需要的时间。

融资后的盈利能力分析包括动态分析和静态分析,其中动态分析包括项目资本金现金流量分析和投资各方现金流量分析。项目资本金现金流量分析考虑了融资方案的影响,通过编制项目资本金现金流量表,计算项目资本金财务内部收益率,考察项目资本金的收益水平。投资各方现金流量分析通过编制投资各方现金流量表,计算投资各方的财务内部收益率指标,考察投资各方的收益水平。静态分析不考虑资金的时间价值,依据利润和利润分配表计算项目资本金净利润率和总投资收益率指标。

按照是否考虑资金的时间价值,项目经济评价指标可分为静态评价指标和动态评价指标;按照指标的性质,项目经济评价指标可分为时间性指标、价值性指标和比率性指标;国家发改委、建设部发布的《建设项目经济评价方法与参数》(第三版)按照分析的角度不同,将项目经济评价分为财务分析和经济分析,对应的指标为财务分析指标和经济分析指标。

以下介绍常用的评价指标。

(一)净现值

净现值是考察项目在计算期内盈利能力的主要动态评价指标,是采用最为普遍的指标之一。

净现值是指按行业的基准收益率或设定的折现率,将项目计算期内各年的净现金流量折现到建设期初的现值之和。基准收益率也称基准折现率,是企业或行业或投资者以动态的观点所确定的、可接受的投资项目最低标准的受益水平。

净现值的计算公式为

$$\mathrm{NPV}=\sum_{t=0}^{n}(\mathrm{CI}-\mathrm{CO})_t(1+i_c)^{-t} \tag{10-4-1}$$

式中:NPV——净现值;

CI——现金流入量;

CO——现金流出量;

$(\mathrm{CI}-\mathrm{CO})_t$——第 t 年的净现金流量;

n——项目计算期;

i_c——基准收益率(折现率)。

确定基准收益率应考虑年资金费用率、机会成本、投资风险和通货膨胀等因素，一般可按下式确定：

$$i_c=(1+i_1)(1+i_2)(1+i_3)-1\approx i_1+i_2+i_3 \tag{10-4-2}$$

式中：i_1——资金费用率与机会成本中较高者；

i_2——风险贴补率；

i_3——通货膨胀率。

利用净现值指标时，首先确定一个基准收益率 i_c，然后确定计算现值的基准年，计算时将各年发生的净现金流量等值换算到基准年，最后根据计算结果进行评价。

根据净现值的计算结果进行评价，NPV≥0 表示项目的投资方案可以接受。

【例 10-4-1】 某项目寿命期为 5 年，各年投资额及收支情况见表，基准投资收益率为 10%，试用净现值指标判断该项目财务上的可行性。

某项目的现金流量表(单位：万元)　　例 10-4-1 表

年 末	0	1	2	3	4	5
投资支出	40	20				
收入			30	45	45	45
经营成本			15	20	20	20
净现金流量	−40	−20	15	25	25	25

解 绘出该项目的现金流量图，见解图。

项目方案的净现值为

$$NPV=-40-20(P/F,10,1)+[15+25(P/A,10,3)](P/F,10,2)$$

$$=-40-20\times0.9091+(15+25\times2.4869)\times0.8264$$

$$=5.59\text{ 万元}>0$$

由于 NPV>0，故从盈利的角度上看，该项目可取。

例 10-4-1 解图　某项目的现金流量图

净现值指标是最常用的动态指标之一，其优点是只要设定了收益率，可以根据 NPV 是否大于零判断方案财务上的可行性，概念清晰。对于单方案的经济评价，可以直接采用净现值指标进行评价。其缺点在于多方案比较时，该指标一是有利于投资额大的方案，二是有利于寿命期长的方案。因此，当进行投资额相差较大的方案比较，或是寿命期不等的方案比较时，可采用其他评价指标作为净现值的辅助评价指标。

净现值用于项目的财务分析时，计算时采用设定的折现率一般为基准收益率，其结果称为财务净现值，记为 FNPV；净现值用于项目的经济分析时，设定的折现率为社会折现率，其结果称为经济净现值，记为 ENPV。

(二)净年度等值(净年值)

净年度等值也可以简称净年值 NAV、等额年值 AW。它是通过资金的等值计算，将项目净现值分摊到寿命期内各年年末的等额年值。其计算公式为

$$\begin{aligned}NAV&=NPV(A/P,i_c,n)\\&=\sum_{t=0}^{n}(CI-CO)_t(1+i_c)^{-t}(A/P,i_c,n)\end{aligned} \tag{10-4-3}$$

式中：NPV——净现值，$NPV=\sum_{t=0}^{n}(CI-CO)_t(1+i_c)^{-t}$；

$(A/P,i_c,n)$——等额支付资金回收系数，$(A/P,i_c,n)=\dfrac{i_c(1+i_c)^n}{(1+i_c)^n-1}$；

其余符号含义同前。

对于单一方案，NAV≥0时，表示方案在经济上可行。从等值计算公式可知，由于等额支付资金回收系数$(A/P,i,n)$为正数，因此NAV与NPV符号相同，即若NPV≥0，则NAV也一定不小于0，采用NPV指标和NAV指标评价同一方案的经济性时，得出的结论是一致的。

在项目投资方案比选时，常用净年值指标作为净现值指标的补充。比如对一些寿命期不等的方案比选，采用净现值指标一般有利于寿命期长的方案，这时可采用净年值指标进行项目方案的经济评价，净年值大的方案较优。

当方案的收益相同或者收益难以直接计算时(如教育、环保、国防等项目)，进行方案比较也可以用年度费用等值AC(费用年值)指标，其计算公式为

$$\begin{aligned}AC&=NPV(A/P,i_c,n)\\&=\sum_{t=0}^{n}CO_t(1+i_c)^{-t}(A/P,i_c,n)\end{aligned}\tag{10-4-4}$$

采用年度费用等值指标进行方案比选时，年度费用等值小的方案较优。

如果采用基准收益率计算费用的净现值，称为费用现值。费用现值小的方案较优。

【例10-4-2】 某项目的净现金流量见表，已知设定的折现率为10%，试用净年值指标评价方案的可行性。

某项目的净现金流量(单位：万元)　　例10-4-2表

年末	0	1～10
净现金流量	−400	80

解　该项目的净年度等值为

$$\begin{aligned}NAV&=-400(A/P,10\%,10)+80\\&=-400\times0.1627+80\\&=14.92\text{万元}\end{aligned}$$

由于NAV>0，故该项目经济上可行。

(三)内部收益率IRR

内部收益率也是考查项目在计算期内盈利能力的主要动态评价指标。内部收益率是使项目净现值为零时的折现率，其表达式为

$$\sum_{t=0}^{n}(CI-CO)_t(1+IRR)^{-t}=0$$

式中：IRR——内部收益率；

其余符号意义同前面公式。

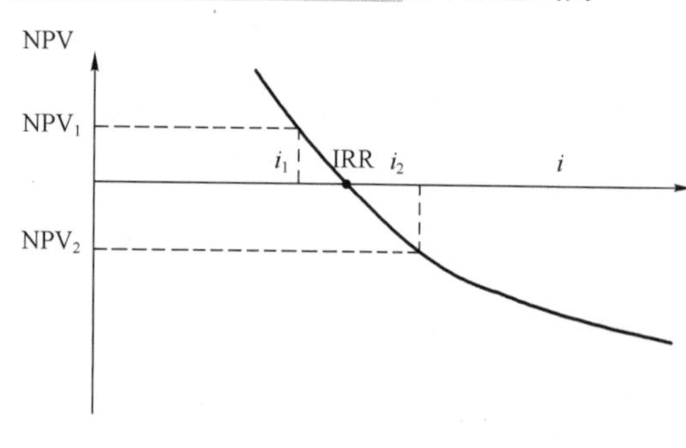

图10-4-1　某项目的净现值函数

前面介绍净现值指标时，需要事先给出基准收益率或者设定一个折现率i，对于一个具体的项目，采用不同的折现率i计算净现值NPV，可以得出不同的NPV值。NPV与i之间的函数关系称为净现值函数。图10-4-1为某项目的净现值函数，图中净现值曲线与横坐标的交点所对应的利率就是内部收益率IRR。

内部收益率的经济内涵可以这样理解：资金投入项目后，通过项目各年的净收益回收投资，各年尚未回收的资金以内部收益率IRR为利率增值，则到项目寿命期末时，正好可以全部

收回投资。

采用内部收益率指标评价项目方案时，其判定准则为：设基准收益率为 i_c，若 $IRR \geq i_c$，则方案在经济效果上可以接受；反之，则不能接受。内部收益率用于财务分析时，称为财务内部收益率，记为 FIRR；用于经济分析时，称为经济内部收益率，记为 EIRR。

可采用线性插值试算法求得 IRR 的近似解，其计算步骤为：

(1)作出方案的现金流量图或现金流量表，列出净现值计算公式。

(2)选择一个初始的收益率代入净现值计算公式，计算净现值。若 NPV＞0，说明试算的收益率较小，应增大收益率；若 NPV＜0，说明试算的收益率偏大，应减小。

(3)重复步骤(2)。

(4)当试算的两个净现值的绝对值较小，且符号相反时，可用线性插值公式求得内部收益率的近似解。其计算公式为

$$IRR = i_1 + \frac{NPV_1}{NPV_1 + |NPV_2|}(i_2 - i_1) \tag{10-4-5}$$

式中：i_1——试算较小的收益率；

i_2——试算较大的收益率；

NPV_1——用 i_1 计算的净现值，$NPV_1>0$；

NPV_2——用 i_2 计算的净现值，$NPV_2<0$。

【例 10-4-3】 某项目 A 的现金流量见表，已知基准收益率 $i_c=15\%$，试用内部收益率指标判断该项目的经济性。

某项目 A 的现金流量表(单位：万元) 例 10-4-3 表

年份	0	1	2	3	4	5
净现金流量	－120	30	40	40	40	40

解 项目 A 的净现值计算公式为

$$NPV=-120+30(P/F,i,1)+40(P/A,i,4)(P/F,i,1)$$

现在分别设 $i_1=15\%$，$i_2=18\%$，计算相应的净现值 NPV_1 和 NPV_2 如下。

$$NPV_1=-120+30\times0.869\,6+40\times2.855\,0\times0.869\,6=5.396\,3 \text{ 万元}$$

$$NPV_2=-120+30\times0.847\,5+40\times2.690\,1\times0.847\,5=-3.380\,6 \text{ 万元}$$

利用公式(10-36)可求得 IRR 的近似解

$$IRR=i_1+\frac{NPV_1}{NPV_1+|NPV_2|}(i_2-i_1)$$

$$=15\%+\frac{5.396\,3}{5.396\,3+3.380\,6}\times(18\%-15\%)=16.8\%$$

因为该项目 $IRR=16.8\%>i_c=15\%$，所以该项目在经济效果上可以接受。

(四)差额内部收益率

由于 IRR 并不是初始投资的收益率，实际上是未收回投资的增值率，所以在互斥方案比较排序时，不能用 IRR 进行排序和选优，而应该采用差额投资内部收益率指标。差额投资内部收益率(增量投资内部收益率)是两个方案各年净现金流量差额的现值之和等于零时的折现率，其表达式为

$$\sum_{t=0}^{n}[(CI-CO)_2-(CI-CO)_1]_t(1+\Delta IRR)^{-t}=0 \tag{10-4-6}$$

式中：$(CI-CO)_1$——投资小的方案的年净现金流量；

$(CI-CO)_2$——投资大的方案的年净现金流量；

ΔIRR——差额投资内部收益率；

n——计算期。

采用 ΔIRR 进行方案比较时，应将 ΔIRR 与基准收益率 i_c 比较，其评价准则是：

若 $\Delta IRR > i_c$，投资大的方案为优；

若 $\Delta IRR < i_c$，投资小的方案为优。

（五）动态投资回收期

动态投资回收期 T^* 是指在给定的基准收益率（基准折现率）i_c 的条件下，用项目的净收益回收总投资所需要的时间。动态投资回收期的表达式为：

$$\sum_{t=0}^{T^*}(CI-CO)_t(1+i_c)^{-t}=0 \tag{10-4-7}$$

式中：T^*——动态投资回收期；

其余符号含义同前。

【例 10-4-4】 某项目动态投资回收期刚好等于项目计算期，则以下说法中正确的是：

A. 该项目动态回收期小于基准回收期

B. 该项目净现值大于零

C. 该项目净现值小于零

D. 该项目内部收益率等于基准收益率

解 动态投资回收期 T^* 是指在给定的基准收益率（基准折现率）i_c 的条件下，用项目的净收益回收总投资所需要的时间。动态投资回收期的表达式为：

$$\sum_{t=0}^{T^*}(CI-CO)_t(1+i_c)^{-t}=0$$

式中，i_c 为基准收益率。

内部收益率 IRR 是使一个项目在整个计算期内各年净现金流量的现值累计为零时的利率，表达式为：

$$\sum_{t=0}^{n}(CI-CO)_t(1+IRR)^{-t}=0$$

式中，n 为项目计算期。如果项目的动态投资回收期正好等于计算期，则该项目的内部收益率 IRR 等于基准收益率 i_c。

答案：D

（六）静态投资回收期

静态投资回收期指在不考虑资金时间价值的条件下，以项目的净收益（包括利润和折旧）回收全部投资所需要的时间。投资回收期通常以"年"为单位，一般从建设年开始计算。其表达式为

$$\sum_{t=0}^{P_t}(CI-CO)_t=0 \tag{10-4-8}$$

式中：CI——现金流入量；

CO——现金流出量；

$(CI-CO)_t$——第 t 年的净现金流量；

P_t——投资回收期。

通常按下式计算

$$P_t=\text{累计净现金流量开始出现正值的年份数}-1+\frac{\text{上年累计净现金流量的绝对值}}{\text{当年净现金流量}} \quad (10\text{-}4\text{-}9)$$

计算出投资回收期 P_t 后，应与部门或行业的基准投资回收期 P_c 进行比较，当 $P_t \leqslant P_c$ 时，表明项目投资在规定的时间内可以回收，该项目在投资回收能力上是可以接受的。

【例 10-4-5】 某建设项目 A 的各年净现金流量见表，项目计算期 10 年，基准投资回收期 P_c 为 6 年。试使用投资回收期法评价项目经济上的可行性。

项目 A 的投资及各年纯收入表(单位：万元)　　例 10-4-5 表

年份	0	1	2	3	4～10
净现金流量	−100	−200	−500	175	275

解 该项目的累计净现金流量表见解表。

项目 A 的累计净现金流量(单位：万元)　　例 10-4-5 解表

序号	0	1	2	3	4	5	6	7	8	9	10
净现金流量	−100	−200	−500	175	275	275	275	275	275	275	275
累计净现金流量	−100	−300	−800	−625	−350	−75	200	475	750	1 025	1 300

根据上表和公式(10-4-8)，可得该项目的投资回收期为

$$P_t=6-1+\frac{|-75|}{275}=5.3\text{ 年}$$

由于 $P_t<P_c$，所以该项目的投资方案可以接受。

(七)总投资收益率(ROI)

总投资收益率表示总投资的盈利水平，是指项目达到设计能力后，正常年份的年息税前利润或运营期内年平均息税前利润(EBIT)与项目总投资(TI)的比率。其计算公式为

$$\text{总投资收益率}=\frac{\text{正常年份的年息税前利润或运营期内年平均息税前利润}}{\text{项目总投资}}\times 100\%$$

息税前利润是指企业支付利息和缴纳所得税之前的利润。

总投资收益率高于同行业的收益率参考值，说明用总投资收益率表示的盈利能力满足要求。

(八)项目资本金利润率

项目资本金利润率表示项目资本金的盈利水平，是指项目达到设计能力后，正常年份的年净利润或运营期内年平均净利润与项目资本金的比率。其计算公式为

$$\text{项目资本金利润率}=\frac{\text{正常年份的年净利润或运营期内年平均净利润}}{\text{项目资本金}}\times 100\% \quad (10\text{-}4\text{-}10)$$

如果项目资本金利润率高于同行业的资本金利润率参考值，说明用项目资本金利润率表示的盈利能力满足要求。

【例 10-4-6】 某新建项目的资本金为 2 000 万元，建设投资为 4 000 万元，需要投入流动资金 700 万元，项目建设获得银行贷款 3 000 万元，年利率为 10%。项目一年建成并投产，预计达产期年利润总额为 800 万元，正常运营期每年支付银行利息 100 万元，所得税率为 25%，试计算该项目的总投资收益率和项目资本金净利润率。

解 该项目的总投资为

$$\begin{aligned}\text{总投资}&=\text{建设投资}+\text{建设期利息}+\text{流动资金}\\&=4\,000+3\,000\times 10\%+700=5\,000\text{ 万元}\end{aligned}$$

息税前利润 = 利润总额 + 利息支出 = 800 + 100 = 900 万元

总投资收益率 = 900 ÷ 5 000 × 100% = 18%

年净利润 = 利润总额 ×(1 − 所得税率) = 800 ×(1 − 25%) = 600 万元

项目资本金净利润率 = 600 ÷ 2 000 × 100% = 30%

三、偿债能力分析和财务生存能力分析

(一)偿债能力分析

偿债能力分析是通过编制相关报表，计算利息备付率、偿债备付率和资产负债率等指标，考察财务主体的偿债能力。

1. 利息备付率

利息备付率是指在借款偿还期内的息税前利润与应付利息的比值。该指标从付息资金来源的充裕性角度，反映偿付债务利息的保障程度和支付能力。其计算公式为

$$利息备付率=\frac{息税前利润}{应付利息} \tag{10-4-11}$$

利息备付率应分年计算。利息备付率越高，利息偿付的保障程度越高，利息备付率应大于1，一般不宜低于2，并结合债权人的要求确定。

2. 偿债备付率

偿债备付率是指在借款偿还期内，用于计算还本付息的资金与应还本付息金额之比。该指标从还本付息资金来源的充裕性角度，反映偿付债务本息的保障程度和支付能力。其计算公式为

$$偿债备付率=\frac{用于计算还本付息的资金}{应还本付息金额} \tag{10-4-12}$$

式中用于还本付息的资金按下式计算

$$用于计算还本付息的资金=息税前利润+折旧和摊销-所得税$$

偿债备付率应分年计算。偿债备付率越高，可用于还本付息的资金保障程度越高，偿债备付率应大于1，一般不宜低于1.3，并结合债权人的要求确定。

3. 资产负债率

资产负债率是指各期末负债总额同资产总额的比率，按下式计算

$$资产负债率=\frac{期末负债总额}{期末资产总额} \tag{10-4-13}$$

适度的资产负债率，表明企业经营安全、有较强的筹资能力，企业和债权人的风险较小。

(二)财务生存能力分析

财务生存能力分析是通过编制财务计划现金流量表，计算项目在计算期内的净现金流量和累计盈余资金，分析项目是否有足够的净现金流量维持正常经营，实现财务的可持续性，从而判断项目在财务上的生存能力。

可通过以下两个方面具体判断项目的财务生存能力：

(1)拥有足够的经营净现金流量是财务可持续性的基本条件。

(2)各年累计盈余资金不出现负值是财务生存的必要条件。

四、财务分析报表

进行财务分析需要编制相关的财务分析报表。财务分析报表主要包括项目投资现金流量

表、项目资本金现金流量表、投资各方现金流量表、利润与利润分配表、财务计划现金流量表、资产负债表和借款还本付息计划表等。

(一)项目投资现金流量表

现金流量表是反映项目计算期内各年现金收支的报表,用以计算各项静态和动态指标,进行项目的财务盈利能力分析。

项目投资现金流量表原称为全部投资现金流量表,是以项目建设所需总投资为计算基础,不考虑融资方案的影响,反映计算期内各年的现金流入和流出的财务报表。该表用于项目投资现金流量分析,通过计算项目投资内部收益率和净现值等指标来评价项目在财务上的可行性。项目投资现金流量分析属于融资前分析,排除了融资方案的影响,从项目投资总的获利能力的角度,考察项目方案设计本身的合理性。项目投资现金流量表的构成见表 10-4-1。

项目投资现金流量表 表 10-4-1

序号	项目	合计	计算期				
			1	2	3	…	n
1	现金流入						
1.1	营业收入						
1.2	补贴收入						
1.3	回收固定资产余值						
1.4	回收流动资金						
2	现金流出						
2.1	建设投资						
2.2	流动资金						
2.3	经营成本						
2.4	营业税金及附加						
2.5	维持运营投资						
3	所得税前净现金流量(1－2)						
4	累计所得税前净现金流量						
5	调整所得税						
6	所得税后净现金流量(3－5)						
7	累计所得税后净现金流量						

计算指标:项目投资财务内部收益率(%)(所得税前),项目投资财务内部收益率(%)(所得税后)

项目投资财务净现值(所得税前)(i_c= %),项目投资财务净现值(所得税后)(i_c= %)

项目投资回收期(所得税前),项目投资回收期(所得税后)

表中的调整所得税为以息税前利润为基数计算的所得税。

(二)项目资本金现金流量表

项目资本金现金流量表从项目资本金出资者整体的角度,以项目资本金为计算的基础,根据拟定的融资方案和项目其他数据,确定项目各年的现金流入和现金流出,用于进行项目资本金现金流量分析。项目资本金现金流量表考虑了融资,属于融资后分析。根据项目资本金现金流量表计算的指标,可以反映项目权益投资者整体在该投资项目上的盈利能力。项目资本金现金流量表见表 10-4-2。

项目资本金现金流量表

表 10-4-2

序号	项　　目	合计	计　算　期				
			1	2	3	…	n
1	现金流入						
1.1	营业收入						
1.2	补贴收入						
1.3	回收固定资产余值						
1.4	回收流动资金						
2	现金流出						
2.1	项目资本金						
2.2	借款本金偿还						
2.3	借款利息支付						
2.4	经营成本						
2.5	营业税金及附加						
2.6	所得税						
2.7	维持运营投资						
3	净现金流量(1－2)						
计算指标：项目财务内部收益率(%)							

项目资本金现金流量分析考察的是项目资本金整体的获利能力，有时为了考察投资各方的收益，还需要编制投资各方现金流量表。

(三)投资各方现金流量表

此表是在项目融资后的财务盈利能力分析中，以项目投投资者的出资额作为计算基础。把股权投资、租赁资产支出和其他现金流出作为现金流出；而现金流入包括股利分配、资产处置收益分配、租赁费收入、技术转让收入和其他现金流入，用以计算项目投资各方的财务内部收益率和财务净现值等评价指标，反映项目投资各方可能获得的收益水平。

(四)利润与利润分配表

利润与利润分配表反映项目计算期内各年利润总额、所得税及税后利润的分配情况，用以计算投资利润率、投资利税率和资本金利润率等指标。利润与利润分配表见表 10-4-3。

利润与利润分配表

表 10-4-3

序　号	项　　目	合　　计	计　算　期				
			1	2	3	…	n
1	营业收入						
2	营业税金及附加						
3	总成本费用						
4	补贴收入						
5	利润总额(1－2－3＋4)						
6	弥补以前年度亏损						
7	应纳税所得额(5－6)						
8	所得税						
9	净利润(5－8)						

续上表

序号	项目	合计	计算期				
			1	2	3	…	n
10	期初未分配利润						
11	可供分配利润(9+10)						
12	提取法定盈余公积金						
13	可供投资者分配的利润(11－12)						
14	应付优先股股利						
15	提取任意盈余公积金						
16	应付普通股股利(13－14－15)						
17	各投资方利润分配						
	其中:××方 …						
18	未分配利润(13－14－15－17)						
19	息税前利润(利润总额+利息支出)						
20	息税折旧摊销前利润(息税前利润+折旧+摊销)						

(五)财务计划现金流量表

财务计划现金流量表反映项目计算期内各年经营活动、投资活动和筹资活动的现金流入和流出,用于计算各年的累计盈余资金,分析项目是否有足够的净现金流量维持正常运营,即项目的财务生存能力。

(六)资产负债表

资产负债表反映项目计算期内各年年末资产、负债和所有者权益的增减变化及对应关系,用以考察项目的资产、负债、所有者权益的结构是否合理,通过计算资产负债率,进行偿债能力分析。

(七)借款还本付息计划表

借款还本付息计划表用于计算利息备付率和偿债备付率指标,用于偿债能力分析。

习　题

10-4-1　某项目第1、2年年初分别投资800万元、400万元,第3年开始每年年末净收益300万元,项目运营期8年,残值30万元。设折现率为10%,已知$(P/F,10\%,1)=0.909\ 1$、$(P/F,10\%,2)=0.826\ 4$、$(P/F,10\%,10)=0.385\ 5$、$(P/A,10\%,8)=5.334\ 9$。则该项目的财务净现值为(　　)。

A. 158.99万元　　B. 170.55万元　　C. 448.40万元　　D. 1 230万元

10-4-2　已知某项目投资方案一次投资12 000元,预计每年净现金流量为4 300元,项目寿命5年,$(P/A,18\%,5)=3.127$,$(P/A,20\%,5)=2.991$,$(P/A,25\%,5)=2.689$,则该方案的内部收益率为(　　)。

A. <18%　　B. 18%~20%　　C. 20%~25%　　D. >25%

10-4-3　某投资项目一次性投资200万元，当年投产并收益，评价该项目的财务盈利能力时，计算财务净现值选取的基准收益率为i_c，若财务内部收益率小于i_c，则有(　　)。

A. i_c低于贷款利率　　B. 内部收益率低于贷款利率

C. 净现值大于零　　D. 净现值小于零

10-4-4　某小区建设一块绿地，需一次性投资20万元，每年维护费用5万元，设基准折现率10%，绿地使用10年，则费用年值为(　　)万元。

A. 4.750　　B. 5　　C. 7.250　　D. 8.255

10-4-5　某项目的净现金流量见题表，则该项目的静态投资回收期为(　　)。

题10-4-5表

年份	1	2	3	4	5	6	7
净现金流量(万元)	−400	−100	100	200	200	200	200

A. 4.5年　　B. 5年　　C. 5.5年　　D. 6年

10-4-6　某项目建设投资400万元，建设期贷款利息40万元，流动资金60万元。投产后正常运营期每年净利润为60万元，所得税为20万元，利息支出为10万元。则该项目的总投资收益率为(　　)。

A. 19.6%　　B. 18%　　C. 16%　　D. 12%

10-4-7　某项目总投资16 000万元，资本金5 000万元。预计项目运营期总投资收益率为20%，年利息支出为900万元，所得税率为25%，则该项目的资本金利润率为(　　)。

A. 30%　　B. 32.4%　　C. 34.5%　　D. 48%

10-4-8　某企业去年利润总额300万元，上缴所得税75万元，在成本中列支的利息100万元，折旧和摊销费30万元，还本金额120万元，该企业去年的偿债备付率为(　　)。

A. 1.34　　B. 1.55　　C. 1.61　　D. 2.02

10-4-9　下列关于现金流量表的表述中，正确的是(　　)。

A. 项目资本金现金流量表排除了融资方案的影响

B. 通过项目投资现金流量表计算的评价指标反映投资者各方权益投资的获利能力

C. 通过项目投资现金流量表可计算财务内部收益、财务净现值和投资回收期等评价指标

D. 通过项目资本金现金流量表进行的分析反映了项目投资总体的获利能力

10-4-10　为了从项目权益投资者整体角度考查盈利能力，应编制(　　)。

A. 项目资本金现金流量表　　B. 项目投资现金流量表

C. 借款还本付息计划表　　D. 资产负债表

第五节　经济费用效益分析

经济费用效益分析是在合理配置社会资源的前提下，分析项目投资的经济效益和对社会福利所作出的贡献，评价项目的经济合理性。经济费用效益分析强调从资源配置效率的角度分析项目的外部效果，考察项目对国民经济的贡献。

对于以下类型的项目应作经济费用效益分析：①有垄断特征的项目；②产出有公共产品特征的项目；③外部效果显著的项目；④资源开发项目；⑤涉及国家经济安全的项目；⑥受过度行

政干预的项目。

一、经济费用效益分析参数

进行项目的经济费用效益分析，首先需要对项目的经济效益和费用进行识别。项目对提高社会福利和社会经济所作的贡献都记为项目的经济效益，包括项目的直接效益和间接效益；整个社会为项目所付出的代价记为项目的经济费用。经济效益的计算应遵循支付意愿原则和接受补偿意愿原则(项目产出物的正面效果的计算遵循支付意愿原则；项目产生物的负面效果的计算遵循接受补偿意愿原则)，经济费用的计算(项目投入物的经济价值计算)应遵循机会成本的原则。计算经济费用效益指标采用的参数有社会折现率、影子价格、影子汇率和影子工资等。

经济费用效益分析应按照“有无对比，增量分析”的原则，不应考虑沉没成本和已实现的效益，“转移支付”不作为经济分析中的效益和费用。

(一)社会折现率

社会折现率是社会对资金时间价值的估量，是从整个国民经济角度所要求的资金投资收益率标准。社会折现率代表社会投资所应获得的最低收益率水平，代表资金占用的机会成本，在建设项目国民经济评价中是衡量经济内部收益率的基准值，也是计算项目经济净现值、用作不同年份之间资金换算的折现率。

(二)影子价格

影子价格是计算经济费用效益分析中投入物或产出物所使用的计算价格，是社会处于某种最优状态下，能够反映社会劳动消耗、资源稀缺程度和最终产品需求状况的一种计算价格。影子价格应能够反映项目投入物和产出物的真实经济价值。

对于市场定价货物的影子价格，可按下述公式计算：

(1)可外贸货物影子价格

直接进口投入物的影子价格(到厂价)＝到岸价(CIF)×影子汇率＋进口费用 (10-5-1)

直接出口产出物的影子价格(出厂价)＝离岸价(FOB)×影子汇率－出口费用 (10-5-2)

(2)市场定价的非外贸货物影子价格

投入物影子价格(到厂价)＝市场价格＋国内运杂费 (10-5-3)

产出物的影子价格(出厂价)＝市场价格－国内运杂费 (10-5-4)

(三)影子汇率

影子汇率是指单位外汇的经济价值，是能正确反映国家外汇经济价值的汇率，即外汇的影子价格。建设项目国民经济评价中，项目的进口投入物、出口产出物均应采用影子汇率以正确反映外汇的真实经济价值。影子汇率换算系数是影子汇率与外汇牌价的比值。影子汇率按下式计算

影子汇率＝外汇牌价×影子汇率换算系数 (10-5-5)

(四)影子工资

影子工资是指建设项目使用劳动力资源而使社会付出的代价，按下式计算

影子工资＝劳动力机会成本×新增资源消耗 (10-5-6)

式中，劳动力机会成本是指劳动力在本单位使用，而不能在其他项目中使用而被迫放弃的劳动收益；新增资源消耗是指劳动力在本项目新就业或由其他就业岗位转移来本项目而发生的社会资源消耗。影子工资与财务分析中的劳动力工资之间的比值称为影子工资换算系数，影子工资可按下式计算

$$影子工资=财务工资\times影子工资换算系数 \tag{10-5-7}$$

【例 10-5-1】 某项目要从国外进口一种原材料，原始材料的 CIF（到岸价格）为 150 美元/t，美元的影子汇率为 6.5，进口费用为 240 元/t，请问这种原材料的影子价格是：

A. 735 元人民币　　B. 975 元人民币

C. 1 215 元人民币　　D. 1 710 元人民币

解 直接进口原材料的影子价格（到厂价）＝到岸价（CIF）×影子汇率＋进口费用

＝150×6.5＋240＝1 215 元人民币/t

答案：C

二、经济费用效益指标

（一）经济净现值

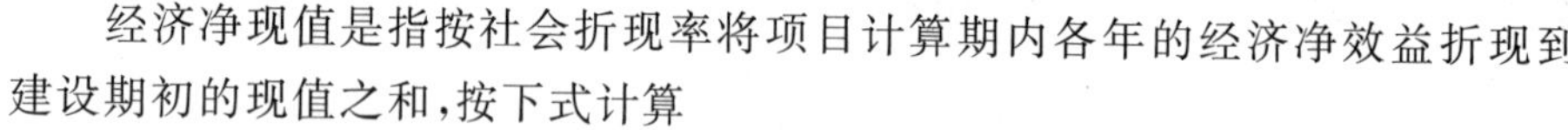

经济净现值是指按社会折现率将项目计算期内各年的经济净效益折现到建设期初的现值之和，按下式计算

$$ENPV=\sum_{t=1}^{n}(B-C)_t(1+i_s)^{-t} \tag{10-5-8}$$

式中：ENPV——经济净现值；

B——经济效益流量；

C——经济费用流量；

$(B-C)_t$——第 t 年的经济净效益流量；

n——项目计算期；

i_s——社会折现率。

经济净现值是反映项目对社会经济贡献的绝对值，是经济效益分析的主要指标。如果经济净现值等于或大于 0，则表明项目可达到符合社会折现率的效率水平，从经济资源配置的角度可以接受该项目。

（二）经济内部收益率

经济内部收益率是指项目在计算期内经济净效益流量的现值累计等于 0 时的折现率。其表达式为

$$\sum_{t=1}^{n}(B-C)_t(1+EIRR)^{-t}=0 \tag{10-5-9}$$

式中：EIRR——经济内部收益率；

其余符号意义同前面公式。

经济内部收益率是经济费用效益分析的辅助评价指标，如果经济内部收益率等于或者大于社会折现率，则表明项目资源配置的效率达到了可以被接受的水平。

（三）效益费用比

效益费用比是指项目在计算期内效益流量的现值与费用流量的现值之比，计算公式为

$$R_{BC}=\frac{\sum_{t=1}^{n}B_t(1+i_s)^{-t}}{\sum_{t=1}^{n}C_t(1+i_s)^{-t}} \tag{10-5-10}$$

式中：R_{BC}——效益费用比；

B_t——第 t 期的经济效益；

C_t——第 t 期的经济费用。

效益费用比也是经济费用效益分析的辅助评价指标，如果效益费用比大于1，说明项目资源配置的经济效益达到了可以被接受的水平。

【例 10-5-2】 交通部门拟修建一条公路，预计建设期为一年，建设期初投资为 100 万元，建设后即投入使用，预计使用寿命为 10 年，每年将产生的效益为 20 万元，每年需投入保养费 8000 元。若社会折现率为 10%，则该项目的效益费用比为：

A. 1.07　　B. 1.17　　C. 1.85　　D. 1.92

解 项目建设期 1 年、使用寿命 10 年，则项目计算期为 11 年，现金流量图如解图所示：

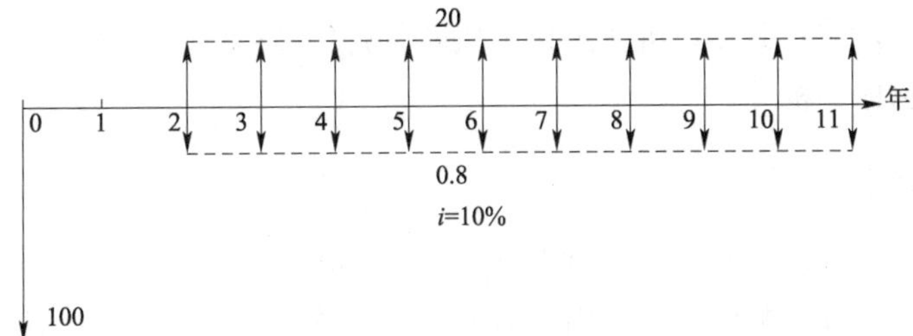

例 10-5-2 解图　现金流量图

项目计算期内效益流量的现值为：

$$B=20\times(P/A,10\%,10)\times(P/F,10\%,1)=20\times6.1446\times0.9091=111.72\text{ 万元}$$

费用流量的现值为：

$$C=0.8\times(P/A,10\%,10)\times(P/F,10\%,1)+100$$
$$=0.8\times6.1446\times0.9091+100=104.47\text{ 万元}$$

该项目的效益费用比为：

$$R_{BC}=B/C=111.72/104.47=1.07$$

答案：A

习　题

10-5-1　对建设项目进行经济费用效益分析所使用的影子价格的正确含义是(　　)。

A. 政府为保证国计民生为项目核定的指导价格

B. 使项目产出品具有竞争力的价格

C. 项目投入物和产出物的市场最低价格

D. 反映项目投入物和产出物真实经济价值的价格

10-5-2　计算经济效益净现值采用的折现率应是(　　)。

A. 企业设定的折现率　　B. 国债平均利率

C. 社会折现率　　D. 银行贷款利率

10-5-3　从经济资源配置的角度判断建设项目可以被接受的条件是(　　)。

A. 经济内部收益率等于或大于社会折现率

B. 财务内部收益率等于或大于社会折现率

C. 经济内部收益率等于或大于银行利率

D. 财务内部收益率等于或大于银行利率

10-5-4　某地区为减少水灾损失，拟建水利工程。项目投资预计 500 万元，计算期按无限年考虑，年维护费 20 万元。项目建设前每年平均损失 300 万元。若利率 5%，则该项目的费用效益比为(　　)。

A. 6.11　　B. 6.67　　C. 7.11　　D. 7.22

第六节　不确定性分析

不确定性分析是对影响项目的不确定性因素进行分析，测算不确定性因素变化对经济评价指标的影响程度，从而判断项目可能承担的风险，为投资决策提供依据。不确定分析方法有盈亏平衡分析、敏感性分析等。

一、盈亏平衡分析

通过分析产品产量、成本和盈利之间的关系，找出项目方案在产量、单价、成本等方面的临界点，进而判断不确定因素对方案经济效果的影响程度。这个临界点称为盈亏平衡点(BEP)。盈亏平衡点是企业盈利与亏损的转折点，在该点上销售收入(扣除销售税金及附加)正好等于总成本费用，达到盈亏平衡。盈亏平衡分析就是通过计算项目达产年的盈亏平衡点，分析项目收入与成本费用的平衡关系，判断项目对产品数量变化的适应能力和抗风险能力。盈亏平衡分析只用于财务分析。

盈亏平衡分析可分为线性盈亏平衡分析和非线性盈亏平衡分析，对建设项目评价仅进行线性盈亏平衡分析。线性盈亏平衡分析的基本假定有：

(1)产量等于销售量；

(2)产量变化，单位可变成本不变，从而总成本费用是产量的线性函数；

(3)产量变化，产品售价不变，从而销售收入是产量的线性函数；

(4)按单一产品计算，生产多种产品的应换算成单一产品，不同产品的生产负荷率变化保持一致。

如果营业收入和成本费用都是按含税价格计算的，还应减去增值税。

为了便于进行盈亏平衡分析，可将项目投产后的总成本费用分为固定成本和可变成本(变动成本)两部分。固定成本指在一定生产规模限度内不随产量变动而变动的费用；可变成本是指随产品产量变动而变动的费用。总成本费用是固定成本与可变成本之和。对于线性盈亏平衡分析，收入与销售量、费用与销售量的关系可以在同一坐标图上表示出来，即盈亏平衡分析图，见图 10-6-1。

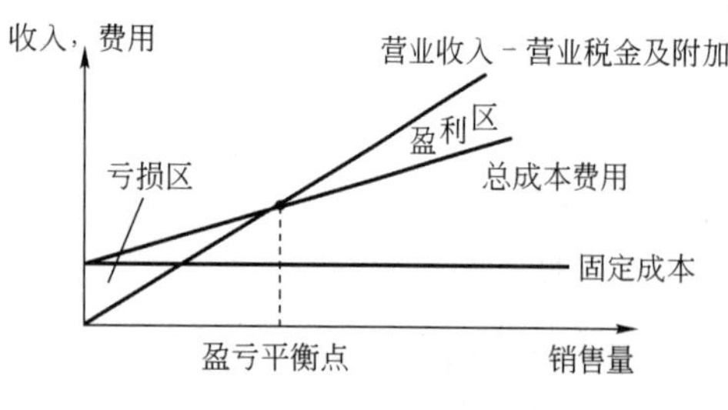

图 10-6-1　盈亏平衡分析图

图中纵坐标为销售收入和成本费用，横坐标为产品销售量。销售收入线与总成本费用线的交点称作盈亏平衡点(BEP)，该点是项目盈利与亏损的临界点。在 BEP 右边，销售收入大于总成本费用，项目盈利；在 BEP 左边，销售收入小于总成本费用，项目亏损；在 BEP 上，销售收入等于总成本费用，项目不盈不亏。盈亏平衡点对应的产量称为盈亏平衡产量。盈亏平衡点可以用产量、生产能力利用率或产品售价等表示。盈亏平衡点可采用以下公式计算

$$BEP_{\text{生产能力利用率}}=\frac{\text{年固定总成本}}{\text{年营业收入}-\text{年可变成本}-\text{年营业税金及附加}}\times 100\% \quad (10\text{-}6\text{-}1)$$

生产能力利用率是盈亏平衡产量与设计生产能力的比率。

$$BEP_{产量}=\frac{年固定总成本}{单位产品销售价格-单位产品可变成本-单位产品营业税金及附加}=BEP_{生产能力利用率}\times 设计生产能力 \tag{10-6-2}$$

在其他条件不变的前提下，盈亏平衡产量与年固定总成本成正比。

$$BEP_{单位产品售价}=\frac{年固定总成本}{设计生产能力}+单位产品可变成本+单位产品营业税金及附加 \tag{10-6-3}$$

盈亏平衡点越低，项目盈利可能性越大，抗风险能力越强。

【例 10-6-1】 某工业项目生产的产品年设计生产能力为 200t，达产第一年销售收入为 4 000 万元，营业收入及附加为 240 万元，固定成本 1 300 万元，可变成本 1 200 万元。销售收入和成本费用均以不含税价格表示，求以生产能力利用率、产量及销售价格表示的盈亏平衡点。

解 首先计算单位产品变动成本

$$BEP_{生产能力利用率}=1\ 300\div(4\ 000-1\ 200-240)\times 100\%=50.78\%$$

$$BEP_{产量}=1\ 300\div(4\ 000\div 200-1\ 200\div 200-240\div 200)=101.56t$$

或

$$BEP_{产量}=200\times 50.78\%=101.56t$$

$$BEP_{产品售价}=1\ 300\div 200+1\ 200\div 200+240\div 200=13.7\ 万元$$

计算结果表明，该项目的生产负荷达到设计能力的 50.78%即可实现盈亏平衡，产量达到 101.56t 则可实现盈亏平衡，产品售价最低降至 13.7 万元/t 即可维持盈亏平衡。

二、敏感性分析

敏感性分析是通过测定一个或者多个不确定因素的变化所导致财务或经济评价指标的变化幅度，了解各种因素变化对实现预期目标的影响程度，从而对外部因素发生变化时项目投资方案的承受能力作出判断。通常只进行单因素敏感性分析。单因素敏感性分析在计算敏感因素对经济效果指标影响时，假定只有一个因素变动，其他因素不变。

（一）单因素敏感性分析的步骤和内容

1. 选择需要分析的不确定性因素，并设定这些因素的变动范围

对于一般工业投资项目，常从以下因素中选取需要作为敏感性分析的因素：

(1)投资额，包括固定资产投资和流动资金占用；

(2)项目建设期限、投产期限、投产时产出能力及达到设计能力所需时间；

(3)产品产量及销售量；

(4)产品价格；

(5)经营成本，特别是其中的变动成本；

(6)项目寿命期；

(7)项目寿命期的资产残值；

(8)折现率；

(9)外汇汇率。

选择需要分析的不确定因素时，应根据实际情况设定其可能的变动范围，一般选择不确定性因素变化的百分率为±5%、±10%、±15%、±20%等。

2. 确定分析指标

敏感性分析可选用前述各种评价指标，如内部收益率、净现值、投资回收期等。一般进行

敏感性分析的指标应与确定性分析采用的指标一致。通常财务分析与评价中的敏感性分析必选的指标是项目投资财务内部收益率。

3. 计算各不确定性因素在不同幅度变化下，所导致的评价指标变动结果

建立起一一对应的关系，一般用图或表的形式表示。

4. 确定敏感因素，对方案的风险情况作出判断

通过计算敏感度系数和临界点，找出敏感因素，可粗略预测项目可能承担的风险。

敏感因素是指其数值变动能显著影响方案经济效果的因素。

（二）敏感性指标的计算

1. 敏感度系数

敏感度系数是指项目评价指标变化的百分率与不确定性因素变化的百分率之比。敏感度系数高，表示项目效益对该不确定性因素的敏感程度高。敏感度系数的计算公式为

$$S_{AF}=\frac{\Delta A/A}{\Delta F/F} \tag{10-6-4}$$

式中：S_{AF}——评价指标 A 对于不确定性因素 F 的敏感度系数；

$\Delta F/F$——不确定性因素 F 的变化率；

$\Delta A/A$——不确定性因素 F 发生 ΔF 变化率时，评价指标 A 的相应变化率。

$S_{AF}>0$，表示评价指标与不确定性因素同方向变化；$S_{AF}<0$，表示评价指标与不确定性因素反方向变化。S_{AF} 绝对值较大者敏感度系数高，$|S_{AF}|$ 越大，说明评价指标 A 对不确定性因素 F 越敏感。

2. 临界点（转换值）

临界点是指不确定性因素的变化使项目由可行变为不可行的临界数值。即当不确定性因素达到某一变化率时，正好使内部收益率等于基准收益率（或者使净现值等于零），该变化率就是临界点。

临界点的高低与计算临界点的指标的初始值有关，如果选取基准收益率为计算临界点的指标，则对于同一个项目，随着设定的基准收益率的提高，临界点就会变低；而在一定的基准收益率下，临界点越低，说明该因素对项目评价指标的影响就越大，项目对该因素就越敏感。敏感性分析的结果通常采用敏感性分析表和敏感性分析图表示。

【例 10-6-2】 某项目以内部收益率作为项目评价指标，选取投资额、产品价格和主要原材料成本作为敏感性因素对项目进行敏感性分析，计算基本方案的内部收益率为 17.5%，当投资额增加 10%时，内部收益率降为 14.5%，试计算其敏感度系数。

解 投资额增加 10%时，内部收益率的变化率为

$$\Delta A=(14.5\%-17.5\%)\div 17.5\%=-0.171$$

敏感度系数 $$S_{AF}=-0.171\div 0.1=-1.71$$

图 10-6-2 是单因素敏感性分析的一个例子，该例选取的分析指标为净现值 NPV，考虑投资额、产品价格、经营成本的变动（按一定百分比变动）对净现值指标的影响。

由图可以看出，本方案的净现值对产品价格最敏感，不确定性因素产品价格的临界点约为 10%，产品价格降低 10%左右，净现值将为 0，项目对三个不确定性因素的敏感程度由高到低依次为产品价格、经营成本、投资额。

【例 10-6-3】 某项目在进行敏感性分析时，得到以下结论：产品价格下降 10%，可使 NPV=0；经营成本上升 15%，NPV=0；寿命期缩短 20%，NPV=0；投资增加 25%，NPV=0。则下列

因素中，最敏感的是：

A. 产品价格　　B. 经营成本　　C. 寿命期　　D. 投资

解　题目中影响因素中，产品价格变化幅度较小就使得项目净现值为零，故该因素最敏感。

答案：A

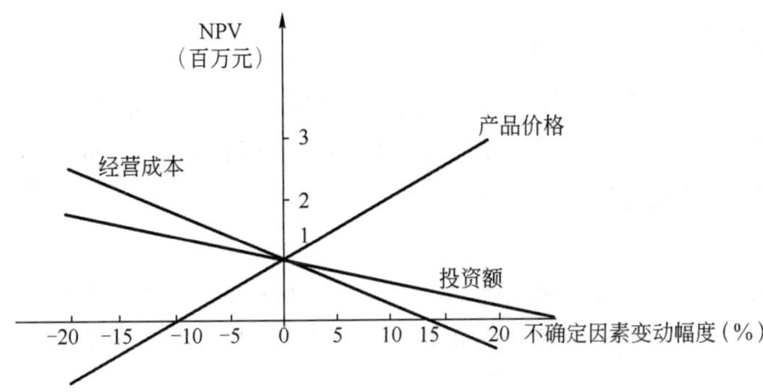

图 10-6-2　敏感性分析图

习　　题

10-6-1　某项目设计生产能力为年产 5 000 台，每台销售价格 500 元，单位产品可变成本 350 元，每台产品税金 50 元，年固定成本 265 000 元，则该项目的盈亏平衡产量为（　　）。

A. 2 650 台　　B. 3 500 台　　C. 4 500 台　　D. 5 000 台

10-6-2　某企业拟投资生产一种产品，设计生产能力为 15 万件/年，单位产品可变成本 120 元，总固定成本 1 500 万元，达到设计生产能力时，保证企业不亏损的单位产品售价最低为（　　）。

A. 150 元　　B. 200 元　　C. 220 元　　D. 250 元

10-6-3　对某项目进行敏感性分析，采用的评价指标为内部收益，基本方案的内部收益率为 15%，当不确定性因素原材料价格增加 10%时，内部收益率为 13%，则原材料的敏感度系数为（　　）。

A. －1.54　　B. －1.33　　C. 1.33　　D. 1.54

10-6-4　对某项目投资方案进行单因素敏感性分析，基准收益率 15%，采用内部收益率作为评价指标，投资额、经营成本、销售收入为不确定性因素，计算其变化对 IRR 的影响见表。

不确定性因素变化对 IRR 的影响　　题 10-6-4 表

变化幅度	－20%	0	＋20%
投资额	22.4	18.2	14
经营成本	23.2	18.2	13.2
销售收入	4.6	18.2	31.8

则敏感性因素按对评价指标影响的程度从大到小排列依次为（　　）。

A. 投资额、经营成本、销售收入　　B. 销售收入、经营成本、投资额

C. 经营成本、投资额、销售收入　　D. 销售收入、投资额、经营成

第七节　方案经济比选

方案经济比选是对不同的项目方案从技术和经济相结合的角度进行多方面分析论证，比较、择优的过程。

一、方案比选的类型

对项目方案的经济评价中除了要计算各种评价指标，分析指标是否达到了标准的要求(如$P_t \leqslant P_c$，NPV≥0，IRR≥i_c等)，往往还需要对多个方案进行比选，进而从中选择较优方案。项目的备选方案根据其相互之间的关系可分为三种类型：

(一)独立型

独立型是指各个方案的现金流量是独立的，不具有相关性，任一方案的采用与否不影响是否采用其他方案的决策。其特点是具有可加性。方案采用与否取决于方案自身的经济性。

(二)互斥型

互斥型是指方案具有排他性，选择了一个方案，就不能选择另外的方案。只能在不同方案中选择其一。对于同一地域土地的利用方案、厂址选择方案、建设规模方案等都是互斥方案。

(三)混合型

混合型是指独立方案和互斥方案混合的情况。

二、方案经济比选的方法

独立方案的采用与否，取决于方案自身的经济性，可用净现值、净年值或内部收益率作为方案的评价指标，当净现值 NPV≥0，或净年值 NAW≥0，或内部收益率 IRR≥i_c 时，则方案在财务上是可行的。

对于互斥型方案，在多个方案进行比较选择时，有方案的计算期相等和计算期不等两种情况。

(一)计算期相等的方案比较

方案比选可以采用效益比选法、费用比选法和最低价格法。

1.效益比选法

比较备选方案的效益，从中择优，具体方法有净现值法、净年值法、差额内部收益率法等。

(1)净现值法

分别计算各方案的净现值，以净现值较大的方案为优。

(2)净年值法

比较各方案的净收益的等额年值，以净年值较大的方案为优。

(3)差额投资内部收益率法

对于若干个互斥方案，可两两比较，分别计算两个方案的差额内部收益率 $\Delta IRR_{A\text{-}B}$，若差额内部收益率 $\Delta IRR_{A\text{-}B}$大于基准收益率 i_c，则投资大的方案较优。

差额内部收益率只反映两方案增量现金流的经济性(相对经济性)，不能反映各方案自身的经济效果。

注意：互斥方案的比较，不能直接用内部收益率 IRR 进行比较。

如果选取相同的基准收益率，对于计算期相同的互斥方案，采用净现值法或差额内部收益率法，其评价结果是一致的。

2. 费用比选法

通过比较备选方案的费用现值或年值，从中择优。费用比选法包括费用现值法和费用年值法。

(1)费用现值法

计算备选方案的费用现值并进行比较，费用现值较低的方案较优。

(2)费用年值法

计算备选方案的费用年值并进行比较，费用年值较低的方案较优。

3. 最低价格(服务收费标准)法

最低价格法是在相同产品方案比选中，按净现值为 0 推算备选方案的产品价格，以最低产品价格较低的方案为优。

(二)计算期不同的互斥方案的比选

当方案的计算期不同时，不能直接采用净现值法、净现值率法、差额内部收益率等方法进行方案比较，可采用年值法、最小公倍数法或研究期法等进行方案比较。

1. 年值法

计算备选方案的等额年值，以等额年值不小于 0 且等额年值最大者为最优方案。由此可见，年值法既可用于寿命期相等的方案比较，也可用于寿命期不等的方案比较。

2. 最小公倍数法

这种方法是先求出两个方案计算期的最小公倍数，然后以最小公倍数作为方案比较的计算期(寿命期)，即假定方案重复实施，将计算期不等的方案转化为计算期相等的方案，然后可采用上述计算期相等的方案比较方法进行指标计算，从中择优。

3. 研究期法

研究期法是通过研究分析，直接选取一个适当的计算期作为备选方案共同的计算期，计算各个方案在该计算期内的净现值，以净现值较大的为优。通常选取各方案中最短的计算期作为共同的计算期。

【例 10-7-1】 已知甲、乙为两个寿命期相同的互斥项目，其中乙项目投资大于甲项目。通过测算得出甲、乙两项目的内部收益率分别为 17%和 14%，增量内部收益 ΔIRR(乙－甲)＝13%，基准收益率为 14%，以下说法中正确的是：

A. 应选择甲项目　　B. 应选择乙项目

C. 应同时选择甲、乙两个项目　　D. 甲、乙两项目均不应选择

解 两个寿命期相同的互斥项目的选优应采用增量内部收益率指标，ΔIRR(乙－甲)为 13%，小于基准收益率 14%，应选择投资较小的方案。

答案：A

习　题

10-7-1　某项目有甲乙丙丁 4 个投资方案，寿命期都是 8 年，设定的折现率为 8%，$(A/P, 8\%, 8)=0.174$，各方案各年的净现金流量见题表。

各方案各年的净现金流量表(单位:万元)　　题 10-7-1 表

年　份	0	1～8
甲	－500	92
乙	－500	90
丙	－420	76
丁	－400	77

采用年值法应选用(　　)。

A. 甲方案　　B. 乙方案　　C. 丙方案　　D. 丁方案

10-7-2　有甲乙丙丁 4 个互斥方案,投资额分别为 1 000 万元、800 万元、700 万元、600 万元,方案计算期均为 10 年,基准收益率为 15%,计算差额内部收益率结果 $\Delta IRR_{甲-乙}$、$\Delta IRR_{乙-丙}$、$\Delta IRR_{丙-丁}$分别为 14.2%、16%、15.1%,应选择(　　)。

A. 甲方案　　B. 乙方案　　C. 丙方案　　D. 丁方案

10-7-3　在几个产品相同的备选方案比选中,最低价格法是(　　)。

A. 按主要原材料推算成本,其中原材料价格较低的方案为优

B. 按净现值为 0 计算方案的产品价格,其中产品价格较低的方案为优

C. 按市场风险最低推算产品价格,其中产品价格较低的方案为优

D. 按市场需求推算产品价格,其中产品价格较低的方案为优

10-7-4　既可用于计算期相等的方案比较,也可用于计算期不等的方案比较方法是(　　)。

A. 年值法　　B. 内部收益率法

C. 投资回收期法　　D. 净现值率法

第八节　改扩建项目的经济评价特点

改扩建项目是在企业原有基础上建设的。对于新建项目,所发生的费用和收益都可归于项目;而改扩建和技改项目的费用和收益既涉及新投资部分,又涉及原有基础部分,因此对项目经济效果的评价与新建项目有所不同。

一、改扩建项目的主要特点

(1)项目的活动与既有企业有联系但在一定程度上又有区别。

(2)项目的融资主体和还款主体都是既有企业。

(3)项目一般要利用既有企业的部分或全部资产、资源,但不发生产权转移。

(4)建设期内企业生产经营与项目建设一般同时进行。

二、改扩建项目的经济评价特点

由于改扩建项目的特点,其经济评价往往比较复杂。改扩建项目经济评价主要有以下特点:

(1)需要正确识别和估算"有项目"、"无项目"、"现状"、"新增"、"增量"等五种状态(五套数据)下的资产、资源、效益和费用,"无项目"和"有项目"的计算口径和范围要一致。应遵循"有无对比"的原则。

(2)应明确界定项目的效益和费用范围。

(3)财务分析采用一般建设项目财务分析的基本原理和分析指标。一般要按项目和企业两个层次进行财务分析。

(4)应分析项目对既有企业的贡献。

(5)改扩建项目的经济费用效益分析采用一般建设项目的经济费用效益分析原理。

(6)需要根据项目目的、项目和企业两个层次的财务分析结果和经济费用效益分析结果,结合不确定性分析、风险分析结果等进行多指标投融资决策。

(7)需要合理确定计算期、原有资产利用、停产损失和沉没成本等问题。

【例 10-8-1】 以下关于改扩建项目财务分析的说法中正确的是:

A. 应以财务生存能力分析为主

B. 应以项目清偿能力分析为主

C. 应以企业层次为主进行财务分析

D. 应遵循“有无对比”原则

解 改扩建项目财务分析要进行项目层次和企业层次两个层次的分析。项目层次应进行盈利能力分析、清偿能力分析和财务生存能力分析,应遵循“有无对比”的原则。

答案:D

习　　题

10-8-1 对于改扩建项目的经济评价,以下表述中正确的是(　　)。

A. 仅需要估算“有项目”、“无项目”、“增量”三种状态下的效益和费用

B. 只对项目本身进行经济性评价,不考虑对既有企业的影响

C. 财务分析一般只按项目一个层次进行财务分析

D. 需要合理确定原有资产利用、停产损失和沉没成本

10-8-2 价值工程的“价值(V)”对于产品来说,可以表示为 $V=F/C$,式中 C 是指(　　)。

A. 产品的寿命周期成本　　B. 产品的开发成本

C. 产品的制造成本　　D. 产品的销售成本

第九节　价 值 工 程

一、价值工程的基本概念

(一)价值、功能和寿命周期成本

1. 功能

功能是指产品或作业的功用和效能。它实质上也是产品或作业的使用价值。

2. 寿命周期成本

寿命周期成本是指产品或服务在寿命期内所花费的全部费用。其费用不仅包括产品生产工程中的费用,也包括使用过程中的费用和残值。

3. 价值

价值工程中的“价值”,是指产品或作业的功能与实现其功能的总成本的比值。它是对所研究的对象的功能和成本的综合评价。其表达式为

$$\text{价值}(V)=\frac{\text{功能}(F)}{\text{成本}(C)} \tag{10-9-1}$$

这里的成本是指实现产品或作业的寿命周期成本。

（二）价值工程的定义

价值工程，也可称为价值分析，是指以产品或作业的功能分析为核心，以提高产品或作业的价值为目的，力求以最低寿命周期成本实现产品或作业使用所要求的必要功能的一项有组织的创造性活动。

价值工程是一种以提高产品和作业价值为目标的管理技术。其主要特点是：

(1)价值工程着眼于寿命周期成本，把研究的重点放在对产品的功能研究上，核心是功能分析。

(2)价值工程将保证产品功能和降低成本作为一个整体考虑。

(3)价值工程强调创新。

(4)价值工程要求将功能定量化。

(5)价值工程是一种有计划、有组织的活动。

（三）提高价值的途径

从上面价值的表达式可知，在成本不变的情况下，价值与功能成正比；功能不变的情况下，价值与成本成反比。由此可以得出提高产品或作业的5种主要途径：

(1)成本不变，提高功能；

(2)功能不变，降低成本；

(3)成本略有增加，功能较大幅度提高；

(4)功能略有下降，成本大幅度降低；

(5)成本降低，功能提高，则价值更高。

二、价值工程的实施步骤

价值工程活动过程一般包括准备阶段、功能分析阶段、方案创造阶段和方案实施阶段。

（一）准备阶段

(1)对象选择；

(2)组成价值工程领导小组；

(3)制订工作计划。

（二）功能分析阶段

(1)收集整理信息资料；

(2)功能系统分析；

(3)功能评价。

（三）创新阶段

(1)方案创新；

(2)方案评价；

(3)提案编写。

（四）实施阶段

(1)审批；

(2)实施与检查；

(3)成果鉴定。

三、价值工程研究对象的选择

（一）选择研究对象的原则

研究对象的选择，应选择对国计民生影响大的、需要量大的、正在研制准备投放市场的、质量功能急需改进的、市场竞争激烈的、成本高利润低的、需提高市场占有率的、改善价值有较大潜力的产品等。

（二）选择研究对象的方法

常用方法有 ABC 分析法、价值系数法、百分比法、最合适区域法等。

1. ABC 分析法

应用数理统计分析的方法选择对象。按产品零部件成本大小由高到低排列，绘出费用累计曲线，一般规律如下。

A 类部件：占部件的 5%～10%，占总成本的 70%～75%（数量较少，但占总成本比重较大）；

B 类部件：占部件的 20%左右，占总成本的 20%左右；

C 类部件：占部件的 70%～75%，占总成本的 5%～10%（数量较多，但占总成本比重不大）。

通常可以把 A 类部件作为分析对象。

2. 价值系数法

（1）价值系数法的步骤

①用 01 评分法（强制确定法）或其他评分法计算功能系数。即将零件排列起来，一一进行重要性对比，重要的得 1 分，不重要的得 0 分，求出各零件得分累计分数，其功能系数按下式计算

$$功能系数(f_i)=\frac{零件得分累计}{总分} \tag{10-9-2}$$

②求出每一零件成本与各零件成本总和之比，即成本系数

$$成本系数(C_i)=\frac{零部件成本}{各零部件成本总和} \tag{10-9-3}$$

③求出各零件的价值系数

$$价值系数(V_i)=\frac{功能系数}{成本系数} \tag{10-9-4}$$

（2）计算结果存在的三种情况

①价值系数小于 1，表明该零件相对不重要且费用偏高，应作为价值分析的对象；

【例 10-9-1】 某产品共有五项功能 F_1、F_2、F_3、F_4、F_5，用强制确定法确定零件功能评价体系时，其功能得分分别为 3、5、4、1、2，则 F_5 的功能评价系数为：

A. 0.20　　B. 0.13　　C. 0.27　　D. 0.33

解　F_3 的功能系数为：$F_3=4/(3+5+4+1+2)=0.27$

答案：C

②价值系数大于 1，即功能系数大于成本系数，表明该零件较重要而成本偏低，是否需要提高费用视具体情况而定；

③价值系数接近或等于 1，表明该零件重要性与成本适应，较为合理。

表 10-9-1 给出了价值系数计算的例子，显然，该表中 D 零件的价值系数远小于 1，为 0.463，可考虑作为价值分析的对象。

价值系数计算表　　表 10-9-1

零部件代号	一对一比较结果				积分	成本（元）	功能系数 f_i	成本系数 C_i	价值系数 V_i
	A	B	C	D					
A	×	1	0	1	2	115	0.333	0.319	1.044
B	0	×	0	1	1	50	0.167	0.139	1.201
C	1	1	×	0	2	65	0.333	0.181	1.840
D	0	0	1	×	1	130	0.167	0.361	0.463
小计					6	360	1	1	

四、功能分析

功能分析是价值工程的核心。功能是某个产品或零件在整体中所担负的职能或所起的作用。功能分析的目的是用最少的成本实现同一功能。

功能分析一般有功能定义、功能整理、功能评价三个步骤。

（一）功能定义

功能定义就是用简明准确的语言表达功能的本质内容。

根据功能的不同特性，功能可以按以下标志分类：

（1）按功能的重要程度分为基本功能和辅助功能。基本功能是必不可少的功能，辅助功能属于次要功能。

（2）按功能的性质可分为使用功能和美学功能。使用功能有使用目的，如手机的通话功能；美学功能也称为外观功能，具有外观的艺术特征，如手机的造型、色彩款式等。

（3）按目的和手段功能可分为上位功能和下位功能。上位功能是目的性功能，下位功能是实现上位功能的手段性功能。这种上位与下位、目的与手段是相对的。

（4）按总体和局部，功能可分为总体功能和局部功能。总体功能体现出整体性的特征，是以局部功能为基础的。

（5）按功能的有用性可分为必要功能和不必要功能。使用功能、美学功能、基本功能、辅助功能等都是必要功能。多余功能、过剩功能都属于不必要功能。

（二）功能整理

功能整理就是要明确功能之间的逻辑关系，确定必要功能，剔除不必要功能。

功能整理有功能分析系统技术和功能卡片排列法两种方法。

功能分析系统技术的主要步骤：

（1）分析出基本功能，列在最左侧，称为上位功能，其余的是辅助功能。

（2）确定功能之间的关系，是并列关系还是上下位关系。

（3）绘出功能系统图。

（三）功能评价

功能评价主要解决功能的定量化问题，以便进行比较分析。功能评价的方法有 01 评分法、04 评分法、DARE 法等。

【例 10-9-2】 下面关于价值工程的论述中正确的是：

A. 价值工程中的价值是指成本与功能的比值

B. 价值工程中的价值是指产品消耗的必要劳动时间

C. 价值工程中的成本是指寿命周期成本，包括产品在寿命期内发生的全部费用

D. 价值工程中的成本就是产品的生产成本，它随着产品功能的增加而提高

解 根据价值工程中价值公式中成本的概念。

答案:C

习　题

10-9-1 价值工程的核心是(　　)。

A. 尽可能降低产品成本　　B. 降低成本提高产品价格

C. 功能分析　　D. 有组织的活动

10-9-2 价值工程的工作目标是(　　)。

A. 尽可能提高产品的功能　　B. 尽可能降低产品的成本

C. 提高产品价值　　D. 延长产品的寿命周期

10-9-3 某企业原采用甲工艺生产某种产品，现采用新技术乙工艺生产，不仅达到甲工艺相同的质量，而且成本降低了15%。根据价值工程原理，该企业提高产品价值的途径是(　　)。

A. 功能不变，成本降低　　B. 功能和成本都降低，但成本降幅较大

C. 功能提高，成本降低　　D. 功能提高，成本不变

题解及参考答案

第一节

10-1-1 **解**:利用名义利率求实际利率公式计算、比较，或用一次支付终值公式计算、比较。

答案:C

10-1-2 **解**:已知 A，求 F，用等额支付系列终值公式计算。

答案:D

10-1-3 **解**:已知 A，求 P，用等额支付系列现值公式计算。第三年年初已经偿还2年等额本息，还有3年等额本息没有偿还。所以 $n=3$，$A=50$。

答案:B

10-1-4 **解**:可绘出现金流量图，利用资金等值计算公式，将借款和还款等值计算折算到同一年，求 A。

$A(P/A,5\%,3)(1+i)=6\,000(P/A,5\%,5)(P/F,5\%,3)$

$A\times 2.723\,2\times 1.05=6\,000\times 4.329\,5\times 0.863\,8$

或:$A(P/A,5\%,3)(F/P,5\%,4)=6\,000(P/A,5\%,5)$，$A\times 2.723\,2\times 1.215\,5=6\,000\times 4.329\,5$。

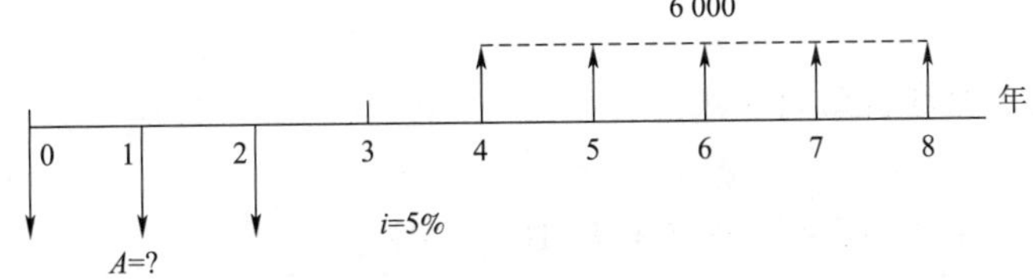

题 10-1-4 解图

解得:$A=7\ 848$

答案:A

第二节

10-2-1 **解:**建设项目总投资由建设投资、建设期利息、流动资金三部分构成。

答案:B

10-2-2 **解:**总投资形成的资产包括工程费用、工程建设其他费用、预备费、建设期利息。

答案:A

10-2-3 **解:**按借款在年初发生的建设利息计算公式计算。第一年借款利息:1 500×7%=105 万元,第二年借款利息:[(1 500+105)+1 000]×7%=182.35 万元。

答案:D

10-2-4 **解:**用双倍余额递减法公式计算,注意计算第二年折旧额时,要用固定资产净值计算。

答案:C

10-2-5 **解:**无营业利润可以不缴纳所得税。

答案:A

10-2-6 **解:**按规定,建设期利息应计入固定资产原值。

答案:A

第三节

10-3-1 **解:**按债券筹资成本公式计算,即(500×5%)×(1−25%)/[500×(1−1%)]=38%。

答案:B

10-3-2 **解:**权益资金成本不能抵减所得税。15%×(400/1 000)+6%×(1−25%)×(600/1 000)=8.7%

答案:B

10-3-3 **解:**等额还本则每年还本 100 万元,次年以未还本金为基数计算利息。

答案:B

第四节

10-4-1 **解:**可先绘出现金流量图再计算。$P=-800-400(P/F,10\%,1)+300(P/A,10\%,8)(P/F,10\%,2)+30(P/F,10\%,10)=170.55$。

答案:B

10-4-2 **解:**用不同的等额支付系列现值系数计算净现值,根据净现值的正负判断内部收益率位于那个区间。

答案:C

10-4-3 **解:**根据净现值函数曲线可判断。

答案:D

10-4-4 **解:**费用年值 $AC=5+20(A/P,10\%,10)$。

答案:D

10-4-5 **解:**根据静态投资回收期公式计算。

答案:B

10-4-6 **解:**项目总投资为建设投资、建设期利息和流动资金之和,计算总投资收益率要用息税前利润。

答案:B

10-4-7 **解:**先根据总投资收益率计算息税前利润,然后计算总利润、净利润,最后计算资本金利润率。项目总投资为建设投资、建设期利息和流动资金之和,计算总投资收益率要用息税前利润。息税前利润=16 000×20%=3 200 万元,总利润=3 200−900=2 300 万元,净利润=2 300×(1−25%)=1 725 万元,资本金利润率=1 725÷5 000×100%=34.5%。

答案:C

10-4-8 **解:**按偿债备付率公式计算。

答案:C

10-4-9 **解:**项目投资现金流量表反映了项目投资总体的获利能力,主要用来计算财务内部收益、财务净现值和投资回收期等评价指标。

答案:C

10-4-10 **解:**项目资本金现金流量表从项目权益投资者的整体角度考察盈利能力。

答案:A

第五节

10-5-1 **解:**影子价格反映项目投入物和产出物的真实经济价值。

答案:D

10-5-2 **解:**进行经济费用效益分析采用社会折现率。

答案:C

10-5-3 **解:**从国民经济效率的角度看,经济内部收益率等于或大于社会折现率,表明项目的经济盈利性达到或超过了经济效益要求。

答案:A

10-5-4 **解:**项目建成每年减少损失,视为经济效益。若 $n \to \infty$,则 $(P/A,i,n)=1/i$。按效益费用比公式计算:

$$B=300\times\frac{1}{i}=6000,c=500+20\times\frac{1}{i}=900$$

$R_{BC}=6000/900=6.67$。

答案:B

第六节

10-6-1 **解:**用盈亏平衡分析公式计算,考虑每台产品的税金。

答案:A

10-6-2 **解:**用盈亏平衡分析公式计算。

答案:C

10-6-3 **解:**按敏感度系数公式计算。[(13%−15%)/15%]/10%=−1.33。

答案:B

10-6-4 **解**:变化幅度的绝对值相同时(如变化幅度为±20%),敏感性系数较大者对应的因素较敏感。

答案:B

第七节

10-7-1 **解**:甲乙方案年投资相等,但甲方案年收益较大,所以淘汰乙方案;丙乙方案比较,丙方案投资大但年收益值较小,淘汰丙方案,比较甲丁方案净年值。

答案:D

10-7-2 **解**:ΔIRR 大于基准收益率时,应选投资额较大的方案;反之,应选投资额较小的方案。

答案:B

10-7-3 **解**:最低价格法是在相同产品方案比选中,按净现值为0推算备选方案的产品价格,以最低产品价格较低的方案为优。

答案:B

10-7-4 **解**:计算期相等和计算期不等的方案比较均可以用年值法。

答案:A

第八节

10-8-1 **解**:改扩建项目的经济评价应考虑原有资产的利用、停产损失和沉没成本等问题。

答案:D

10-8-2 **解**:依据价值工程定义。

答案:A

第九节

10-9-1 **解**:价值工程的核心是功能分析。

答案:C

10-9-2 **解**:价值工程以提高价值为工作目标。

答案:C

10-9-3 **解**:质量相同,功能上没有变化。

答案:A

第十一章 法律法规

复习指导

一、"法律法规"考试大纲

8.1 中华人民共和国建筑法

总则；建筑许可；建筑工程发包与承包；建筑工程监理；建筑安全生产管理；建筑工程质量管理；法律责任。

8.2 中华人民共和国安全生产法

总则；生产经营单位的安全生产保障；从业人员的权利和义务；安全生产的监督管理；生产安全事故的应急救援与调查处理。

8.3 中华人民共和国招标投标法

总则；招标；投标；开标；评标和中标；法律责任。

8.4 中华人民共和国合同法

一般规定；合同的订立；合同的效力；合同的履行；合同的变更和转让；合同的权利义务终止；违约责任；其他规定。

8.5 中华人民共和国行政许可法

总则；行政许可的设定；行政许可的实施机关；行政许可的实施程序；行政许可的费用。

8.6 中华人民共和国节约能源法

总则；节能管理；合理使用与节约能源；节能技术进步；激励措施；法律责任。

8.7 中华人民共和国环境保护法

总则；环境监督管理；保护和改善环境；防治环境污染和其他公害；法律责任。

8.8 建设工程勘察设计管理条例

总则；资质资格管理；建设工程勘察设计发包与承包；建设工程勘察设计文件的编制与实施；监督管理。

8.9 建设工程质量管理条例

总则；建设单位的质量责任和义务；勘察设计单位的质量责任和义务；施工单位的质量责任和义务；工程监理单位的质量责任和义务；建设工程质量保修。

8.10 建设工程安全生产管理条例

总则；建设单位的安全责任；勘察设计工程监理及其他有关单位的安全责任；施工单位的安全责任；监督管理；生产安全事故的应急救援和调查处理。

二、复习指导

与工程建设有关的法规应当是重点复习的内容，尤其是建筑法、招投标法中的内容。

法规中与设计工作有关的规定要给予特别注意。

第一节 我国法规的基本体系

按现行立法权限，我国的法规可分为五个层次。即：全国人大及其常委会通过的法律；国务院发布的行政规定；国务院各部委发布的规章制度；地方人大制定的地方法律；地方行政部门制定并发布的地方规章制度。

举例如下：

一、法律

中华人民共和国建筑法	1998 年 3 月 1 日起实施，2011 年 4 月 22 日修改
中华人民共和国安全生产法	2002 年 11 月 1 日起实施，2014 年 8 月 31 日修改
中华人民共和国招标投标法	2000 年 1 月 1 日起实施，2017 年 12 月 28 日修正
中华人民共和国合同法	1999 年 10 月 1 日起实施
中华人民共和国行政许可法	2004 年 7 月 1 日起实施
中华人民共和国节约能源法	1997 年 1 月 1 日颁布，2007 年 10 月修改，2008 年 4 月 1 日起实施修订版
中华人民共和国环境保护法	1989 年 12 月 26 日起实施，2014 年 4 月 24 日修改，2015 年 1 月 1 日起实施修订版

二、行政规定

建设工程勘察设计管理条例	2000 年 9 月 20 日起实施，2015 年 6 月 12 日修改
建设工程质量管理条例	2000 年 1 月 30 日起实施，2017 年 10 月 7 日修改
建设工程安全生产管理条例	2004 年 2 月 1 日起实施

三、部门规章

建设工程勘察设计资质管理规定	2007 年 9 月 1 日起实施
工程监理企业资质管理规定	2007 年 8 月 1 日起实施
建筑企业资质管理规定	2007 年 9 月 1 日起实施

地方法律、规章不再举例。

第二节 中华人民共和国建筑法

第一章 总 则

第一条 为了加强对建筑活动的监督管理，维护建筑市场秩序，保证建筑工程的质量和安全，促进建筑业健康发展，制定本法。

第二条 在中华人民共和国境内从事建筑活动，实施对建筑活动的监督管理，应当遵守本法。

本法所称建筑活动，是指各类房屋建筑及其附属设施的建造和与其配套的线路、管道、设备的安装活动。

第三条　建筑活动应当确保建筑工程质量和安全，符合国家的建筑工程安全标准。

第四条　国家扶持建筑业的发展，支持建筑科学技术研究，提高房屋建筑设计水平，鼓励节约能源和保护环境，提倡采用先进技术、先进设备、先进工艺、新型建筑材料和现代管理方式。

第五条　从事建筑活动应当遵守法律、法规，不得损害社会公共利益和他人的合法权益。

任何单位和个人都不得妨碍和阻挠依法进行的建筑活动。

第六条　国务院建设行政主管部门对全国的建筑活动实施统一监督管理。

第二章　建筑许可

第一节　建筑工程施工许可

第七条　建筑工程开工前，建设单位应当按照国家有关规定向工程所在地县级以上人民政府建设行政主管部门申请领取施工许可证；但是，国务院建设行政主管部门确定的限额以下的小型工程除外。

按照国务院规定的权限和程序批准开工报告的建筑工程，不再领取施工许可证。

第八条　申请领取施工许可证，应当具备下列条件：

（一）已经办理该建筑工程用地批准手续；

（二）在城市规划区的建筑工程，已经取得规划许可证；

（三）需要拆迁的，其拆迁进度符合施工要求；

（四）已经确定建筑施工企业；

（五）有满足施工需要的施工图纸及技术资料；

（六）有保证工程质量和安全的具体措施；

（七）建设资金已经落实；

（八）法律、行政法规规定的其他条件。

建设行政主管部门应当自收到申请之日起十五日内，对符合条件的申请颁发施工许可证。

第九条　建设单位应当自领取施工许可证之日起三个月内开工。因故不能按期开工的，应当向发证机关申请延期；延期以两次为限，每次不超过三个月。既不开工又不申请延期或者超过延期时限的，施工许可证自行废止。

第十条　在建的建筑工程因故中止施工的，建设单位应当自中止施工之日起一个月内，向发证机关报告，并按照规定做好建筑工程的维护管理工作。

建筑工程恢复施工时，应当向发证机关报告；中止施工满一年的工程恢复施工前，建设单位应当报发证机关核验施工许可证。

第十一条　按照国务院有关规定批准开工报告的建筑工程，因故不能按期开工或者中止施工的，应当及时向批准机关报告情况。因故不能按期开工超过六个月的，应当重新办理开工报告的批准手续。

第二节　从业资格

第十二条　从事建筑活动的建筑施工企业、勘察单位、设计单位和工程监理单位，应当具备下列条件：

（一）有符合国家规定的注册资本；

（二）有与其从事的建筑活动相适应的具有法定执业资格的专业技术人员；

（三）有从事相关建筑活动所应有的技术装备；

（四）法律、行政法规规定的其他条件。

第十三条　从事建筑活动的建筑施工企业、勘察单位、设计单位和工程监理单位，按照其拥有的注册资本、专业技术人员、技术装备和已完成的建筑工程业绩等资质条件，划分为不同的资质等级，经资质审查合格，取得相应等级的资质证书后，方可在其资质等级许可的范围内从事建筑活动。

第十四条　从事建筑活动的专业技术人员，应当依法取得相应的执业资格证书，并在执业资格证书许可的范围内从事建筑活动。

第三章　建筑工程发包与承包

第一节　一般规定

第十五条　建筑工程的发包单位与承包单位应当依法订立书面合同，明确双方的权利和义务。

发包单位和承包单位应当全面履行合同约定的义务。不按照合同约定履行义务的，依法承担违约责任。

第十六条　建筑工程发包与承包的招标投标活动，应当遵循公开、公正、平等竞争的原则，择优选择承包单位。

建筑工程的招标投标，本法没有规定的，适用有关招标投标法律的规定。

第十七条　发包单位及其工作人员在建筑工程发包中不得收受贿赂、回扣或者索取其他好处。

承包单位及其工作人员不得利用向发包单位及其工作人员行贿、提供回扣或者给予其他好处等不正当手段承揽工程。

第十八条　建筑工程造价应当按照国家有关规定，由发包单位与承包单位在合同中约定。公开招标发包的，其造价的约定，须遵守招标投标法律的规定。

发包单位应当按照合同的约定，及时拨付工程款项。

第二节　发　　包

第十九条　建筑工程依法实行招标发包，对不适于招标发包的可以直接发包。

第二十条　建筑工程实行公开招标的，发包单位应当依照法定程序和方式，发布招标公告，提供载有招标工程的主要技术要求、主要的合同条款、评标的标准和方法以及开标、评标、定标的程序等内容的招标文件。

开标应当在招标文件规定的时间、地点公开进行。开标后应当按照招标文件规定的评标标准和程序对标书进行评价、比较，在具备相应资质条件的投标者中，择优选定中标者。

第二十一条　建筑工程招标的开标、评标、定标由建设单位依法组织实施，并接受有关行政主管部门的监督。

第二十二条　建筑工程实行招标发包的，发包单位应当将建筑工程发包给依法中标的承包单位。建筑工程实行直接发包的，发包单位应当将建筑工程发包给具有相应资质条件的承包单位。

第二十三条　政府及其所属部门不得滥用行政权力，限定发包单位将招标发包的建筑工程发包给指定的承包单位。

第二十四条　提倡对建筑工程实行总承包，禁止将建筑工程肢解发包。

建筑工程的发包单位可以将建筑工程的勘察、设计、施工、设备采购一并发包给一个工程总承包单位，也可以将建筑工程勘察、设计、施工、设备采购的一项或者多项发包给一个工程总承包单位;但是,不得将应当由一个承包单位完成的建筑工程肢解成若干部分发包给几个承包单位。

第二十五条 按照合同约定,建筑材料、建筑构配件和设备由工程承包单位采购的,发包单位不得指定承包单位购入用于工程的建筑材料、建筑构配件和设备或者指定生产厂、供应商。

第三节 承 包

第二十六条 承包建筑工程的单位应当持有依法取得的资质证书,并在其资质等级许可的业务范围内承揽工程。

禁止建筑施工企业超越本企业资质等级许可的业务范围或者以任何形式用其他建筑施工企业的名义承揽工程。禁止建筑施工企业以任何形式允许其他单位或者个人使用本企业的资质证书、营业执照,以本企业的名义承揽工程。

第二十七条 大型建筑工程或者结构复杂的建筑工程,可以由两个以上的承包单位联合共同承包。共同承包的各方对承包合同的履行承担连带责任。

两个以上不同资质等级的单位实行联合共同承包的,应当按照资质等级低的单位的业务许可范围承揽工程。

第二十八条 禁止承包单位将其承包的全部建筑工程转包给他人,禁止承包单位将其承包的全部建筑工程肢解以后以分包的名义分别转包给他人。

第二十九条 建筑工程总承包单位可以将承包工程中的部分工程发包给具有相应资质条件的分包单位;但是,除总承包合同中约定的分包外,必须经建设单位认可。施工总承包的,建筑工程主体结构的施工必须由总承包单位自行完成。

建筑工程总承包单位按照总承包合同的约定对建设单位负责;分包单位按照分包合同的约定对总承包单位负责。总承包单位和分包单位就分包工程对建设单位承担连带责任。

禁止总承包单位将工程分包给不具备相应资质条件的单位。禁止分包单位将其承包的工程再分包。

第四章 建筑工程监理

第三十条 国家推行建筑工程监理制度。

国务院可以规定实行强制监理的建筑工程的范围。

第三十一条 实行监理的建筑工程,由建设单位委托具有相应资质条件的工程监理单位监理。建设单位与其委托的工程监理单位应当订立书面委托监理合同。

第三十二条 建筑工程监理应当依照法律、行政法规及有关的技术标准、设计文件和建筑工程承包合同,对承包单位在施工质量、建设工期和建设资金使用等方面,代表建设单位实施监督。

工程监理人员认为工程施工不符合工程设计要求、施工技术标准和合同约定的,有权要求建筑施工企业改正。

工程监理人员发现工程设计不符合建筑工程质量标准或者合同约定的质量要求的,应当报告建设单位要求设计单位改正。

第三十三条 实施建筑工程监理前,建设单位应当将委托的工程监理单位、监理的内容及监理权限,书面通知被监理的建筑施工企业。

第三十四条 工程监理单位应当在其资质等级许可的监理范围内,承担工程监理业务。

工程监理单位应当根据建设单位的委托,客观、公正地执行监理任务。

工程监理单位与被监理工程的承包单位以及建筑材料、建筑构配件和设备供应单位不得有隶属关系或者其他利害关系。

工程监理单位不得转让工程监理业务。

第三十五条　工程监理单位不按照委托监理合同的约定履行监理义务，对应当监督检查的项目不检查或者不按照规定检查，给建设单位造成损失的，应当承担相应的赔偿责任。

工程监理单位与承包单位串通，为承包单位谋取非法利益，给建设单位造成损失的，应当与承包单位承担连带赔偿责任。

第五章　建筑安全生产管理

第三十六条　建筑工程安全生产管理必须坚持安全第一、预防为主的方针，建立健全安全生产的责任制度和群防群治制度。

第三十七条　建筑工程设计应当符合按照国家规定制定的建筑安全规程和技术规范，保证工程的安全性能。

第三十八条　建筑施工企业在编制施工组织设计时，应当根据建筑工程的特点制定相应的安全技术措施；对专业性较强的工程项目，应当编制专项安全施工组织设计，并采取安全技术措施。

第三十九条　建筑施工企业应当在施工现场采取维护安全、防范危险、预防火灾等措施；有条件的，应当对施工现场实行封闭管理。

施工现场对毗邻的建筑物、构筑物和特殊作业环境可能造成损害的，建筑施工企业应当采取安全防护措施。

第四十条　建设单位应当向建筑施工企业提供与施工现场相关的地下管线资料，建筑施工企业应当采取措施加以保护。

第四十一条　建筑施工企业应当遵守有关环境保护和安全生产的法律、法规的规定，采取控制和处理施工现场的各种粉尘、废气、废水、固体废物以及噪声、振动对环境的污染和危害的措施。

第四十二条　有下列情形之一的，建设单位应当按照国家有关规定办理申请批准手续：

（一）需要临时占用规划批准范围以外场地的；

（二）可能损坏道路、管线、电力、邮电通讯等公共设施的；

（三）需要临时停水、停电、中断道路交通的；

（四）需要进行爆破作业的；

（五）法律、法规规定需要办理报批手续的其他情形。

第四十三条　建设行政主管部门负责建筑安全生产的管理，并依法接受劳动行政主管部门对建筑安全生产的指导和监督。

第四十四条　建筑施工企业必须依法加强对建筑安全生产的管理，执行安全生产责任制度，采取有效措施，防止伤亡和其他安全生产事故的发生。

建筑施工企业的法定代表人对本企业的安全生产负责。

第四十五条　施工现场安全由建筑施工企业负责。实行施工总承包的，由总承包单位负责。分包单位向总承包单位负责，服从总承包单位对施工现场的安全生产管理。

第四十六条　建筑施工企业应当建立健全劳动安全生产教育培训制度，加强对职工安全生产的教育培训；未经安全生产教育培训的人员，不得上岗作业。

第四十七条　建筑施工企业和作业人员在施工过程中，应当遵守有关安全生产的法律、法规和建筑行业安全规章、规程，不得违章指挥或者违章作业。作业人员有权对影响人身健康的作业程序和作业条件提出改进意见，有权获得安全生产所需的防护用品。作业人员对危及生命安全和人身健康的行为有权提出批评、检举和控告。

第四十八条　建筑施工企业应当依法为职工参加工伤保险缴纳工伤保险费。鼓励企业为从事危险作业的职工办理意外伤害保险，支付保险费。

第四十九条　涉及建筑主体和承重结构变动的装修工程，建设单位应当在施工前委托原设计单位或者具有相应资质条件的设计单位提出设计方案；没有设计方案的，不得施工。

第五十条　房屋拆除应当由具备保证安全条件的建筑施工单位承担，由建筑施工单位负责人对安全负责。

第五十一条　施工中发生事故时，建筑施工企业应当采取紧急措施减少人员伤亡和事故损失，并按照国家有关规定及时向有关部门报告。

第六章　建筑工程质量管理

第五十二条　建筑工程勘察、设计、施工的质量必须符合国家有关建筑工程安全标准的要求，具体管理办法由国务院规定。

有关建筑工程安全的国家标准不能适应确保建筑安全的要求时，应当及时修订。

第五十三条　国家对从事建筑活动的单位推行质量体系认证制度。从事建筑活动的单位根据自愿原则可以向国务院产品质量监督管理部门或者国务院产品质量监督管理部门授权的部门认可的认证机构申请质量体系认证。经认证合格的，由认证机构颁发质量体系认证证书。

第五十四条　建设单位不得以任何理由，要求建筑设计单位或者建筑施工企业在工程设计或者施工作业中，违反法律、行政法规和建筑工程质量、安全标准，降低工程质量。

建筑设计单位和建筑施工企业对建设单位违反前款规定提出的降低工程质量的要求，应当予以拒绝。

第五十五条　建筑工程实行总承包的，工程质量由工程总承包单位负责，总承包单位将建筑工程分包给其他单位的，应当对分包工程的质量与分包单位承担连带责任。分包单位应当接受总承包单位的质量管理。

第五十六条　建筑工程的勘察、设计单位必须对其勘察、设计的质量负责。勘察、设计文件应当符合有关法律、行政法规的规定和建筑工程质量、安全标准、建筑工程勘察、设计技术规范以及合同的约定。设计文件选用的建筑材料、建筑构配件和设备，应当注明其规格、型号、性能等技术指标，其质量要求必须符合国家规定的标准。

第五十七条　建筑设计单位对设计文件选用的建筑材料、建筑构配件和设备，不得指定生产厂、供应商。

第五十八条　建筑施工企业对工程的施工质量负责。

建筑施工企业必须按照工程设计图纸和施工技术标准施工，不得偷工减料。工程设计的修改由原设计单位负责，建筑施工企业不得擅自修改工程设计。

第五十九条　建筑施工企业必须按照工程设计要求、施工技术标准和合同的约定，对建筑材料、建筑构配件和设备进行检验，不合格的不得使用。

第六十条　建筑物在合理使用寿命内，必须确保地基基础工程和主体结构的质量。

建筑工程竣工时，屋顶、墙面不得留有渗漏、开裂等质量缺陷；对已发现的质量缺陷，建筑施工企业应当修复。

第六十一条　交付竣工验收的建筑工程，必须符合规定的建筑工程质量标准，有完整的工程技术经济资料和经签署的工程保修书，并具备国家规定的其他竣工条件。

建筑工程竣工经验收合格后，方可交付使用；未经验收或者验收不合格的，不得交付使用。

第六十二条　建筑工程实行质量保修制度。

建筑工程的保修范围应当包括地基基础工程、主体结构工程、屋面防水工程和其他土建工程，以及电气管线、上下水管线的安装工程，供热、供冷系统工程等项目；保修的期限应当按照保证建筑物合理寿命年限内正常使用，维护使用者合法权益的原则确定。具体的保修范围和最低保修期限由国务院规定。

第六十三条　任何单位和个人对建筑工程的质量事故、质量缺陷都有权向建设行政主管部门或者其他有关部门进行检举、控告、投诉。

第七章　法律责任

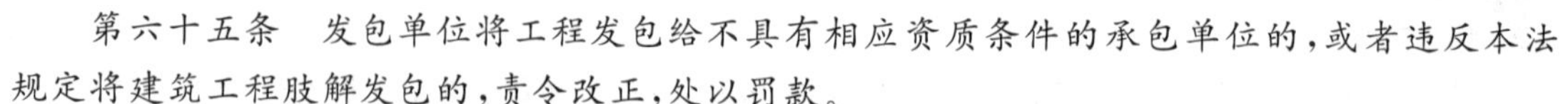

第六十四条　违反本法规定，未取得施工许可证或者开工报告未经批准擅自施工的，责令改正，对不符合开工条件的责令停止施工，可以处以罚款。

第六十五条　发包单位将工程发包给不具有相应资质条件的承包单位的，或者违反本法规定将建筑工程肢解发包的，责令改正，处以罚款。

超越本单位资质等级承揽工程的，责令停止违法行为，处以罚款，可以责令停业整顿，降低资质等级；情节严重的，吊销资质证书；有违法所得的，予以没收。

未取得资质证书承揽工程的，予以取缔，并处罚款；有违法所得的，予以没收。

以欺骗手段取得资质证书的，吊销资质证书，处以罚款；构成犯罪的，依法追究刑事责任。

第六十六条　建筑施工企业转让、出借资质证书或者以其他方式允许他人以本企业的名义承揽工程的，责令改正，没收违法所得，并处罚款，可以责令停业整顿，降低资质等级；情节严重的，吊销资质证书。对因该项承揽工程不符合规定的质量标准造成的损失，建筑施工企业与使用本企业名义的单位或者个人承担连带赔偿责任。

第六十七条　承包单位将承包的工程转包的，或者违反本法规定进行分包的，责令改正，没收违法所得，并处罚款，可以责令停业整顿，降低资质等级；情节严重的，吊销资质证书。

承包单位有前款规定的违法行为的，对因转包工程或者违法分包的工程不符合规定的质量标准造成的损失，与接受转包或者分包的单位承担连带赔偿责任。

第六十八条　在工程发包与承包中索贿、受贿、行贿，构成犯罪的，依法追究刑事责任；不构成犯罪的，分别处以罚款，没收贿赂的财物，对直接负责的主管人员和其他直接责任人员给予处分。

对在工程承包中行贿的承包单位，除依照前款规定处罚外，可以责令停业整顿，降低资质等级或者吊销资质证书。

第六十九条　工程监理单位与建设单位或者建筑施工企业串通，弄虚作假、降低工程质量的，责令改正，处以罚款，降低资质等级或者吊销资质证书；有违法所得的，予以没收；造成损失的，承担连带赔偿责任；构成犯罪的，依法追究刑事责任。

工程监理单位转让监理业务的，责令改正，没收违法所得，可以责令停业整顿，降低资质等级；情节严重的，吊销资质证书。

第七十条　违反本法规定，涉及建筑主体或者承重结构变动的装修工程擅自施工的，责令改正，处以罚款；造成损失的，承担赔偿责任；构成犯罪的，依法追究刑事责任。

第七十一条　建筑施工企业违反本法规定，对建筑安全事故隐患不采取措施予以消除的，责令改正，可以处以罚款；情节严重的，责令停业整顿，降低资质等级或者吊销资质证书；构成犯罪的，依法追究刑事责任。

建筑施工企业的管理人员违章指挥、强令职工冒险作业，因而发生重大伤亡事故或者造成其他严重后果的，依法追究刑事责任。

第七十二条　建设单位违反本法规定，要求建筑设计单位或者建筑施工企业违反建筑工程质量、安全标准，降低工程质量的，责令改正，可以处以罚款；构成犯罪的，依法追究刑事责任。

第七十三条　建筑设计单位不按照建筑工程质量、安全标准进行设计的，责令改正，处以罚款；造成工程质量事故的，责令停业整顿，降低资质等级或者吊销资质证书，没收违法所得，并处罚款；造成损失的，承担赔偿责任；构成犯罪的，依法追究刑事责任。

第七十四条　建筑施工企业在施工中偷工减料的，使用不合格的建筑材料、建筑构配件和设备的，或者有其他不按照工程设计图纸或者施工技术标准施工的行为的，责令改正，处以罚款；情节严重的，责令停业整顿，降低资质等级或者吊销资质证书；造成建筑工程质量不符合规定的质量标准的，负责返工、修理，并赔偿因此造成的损失；构成犯罪的，依法追究刑事责任。

第七十五条　建筑施工企业违反本法规定，不履行保修义务或者拖延履行保修义务的，责令改正，可以处以罚款，并对在保修期内因屋顶、墙面渗漏、开裂等质量缺陷造成的损失，承担赔偿责任。

第七十六条　本法规定的责令停业整顿、降低资质等级和吊销资质证书的行政处罚，由颁发资质证书的机关决定；其他行政处罚，由建设行政主管部门或者有关部门依照法律和国务院规定的职权范围决定。

依照本法规定被吊销资质证书的，由工商行政管理部门吊销其营业执照。

第七十七条　违反本法规定，对不具备相应资质等级条件的单位颁发该等级资质证书的，由其上级机关责令收回所发的资质证书，对直接负责的主管人员和其他直接责任人员给予行政处分；构成犯罪的，依法追究刑事责任。

第七十八条　政府及其所属部门的工作人员违反本法规定，限定发包单位将招标发包的工程发包给指定的承包单位的，由上级机关责令改正；构成犯罪的，依法追究刑事责任。

第七十九条　负责颁发建筑工程施工许可证的部门及其工作人员对不符合施工条件的建筑工程颁发施工许可证的，负责工程质量监督检查或者竣工验收的部门及其工作人员对不合格的建筑工程出具质量合格文件或者按合格工程验收的，由上级机关责令改正，对责任人员给予行政处分；构成犯罪的，依法追究刑事责任；造成损失的，由该部门承担相应的赔偿责任。

第八十条　在建筑物的合理使用寿命内，因建筑工程质量不合格受到损害的，有权向责任者要求赔偿。

第八章　附　　则

第八十一条　本法关于施工许可、建筑施工企业资质审查和建筑工程发包、承包、禁止转包，以及建筑工程监理、建筑工程安全和质量管理的规定，适用于其他专业建筑工程的建筑活动，具体办法由国务院规定。

第八十二条　建设行政主管部门和其他有关部门在对建筑活动实施监督管理中，除按照国务院有关规定收取费用外，不得收取其他费用。

第八十三条　省、自治区、直辖市人民政府确定的小型房屋建筑工程的建筑活动，参照本法执行。

依法核定作为文物保护的纪念建筑物和古建筑等的修缮，依照文物保护的有关法律规定执行。

抢险救灾及其他临时性房屋建筑和农民自建低层住宅的建筑活动，不适用本法。

第八十四条　军用房屋建筑工程建筑活动的具体管理办法，由国务院、中央军事委员会依据本法制定。

第八十五条　本法自1998年3月1日起施行。

【例11-2-1】 某工程项目甲建设单位委托乙监理单位对丙施工总承包单位进行监理，有关监理单位的行为符合规定的是：

A. 在监理合同规定的范围内承揽监理业务

B. 按建设单位委托，客观公正地执行监理任务

C. 与施工单位建立隶属关系或者其他利害关系

D. 将工程监理业务转让给具有相应资质的其他监理单位

解　《中华人民共和国建筑法》第三十四条规定，工程监理单位应当根据建设单位的委托，客观、公正地执行监理任务。

选项C和D明显错误。选项A也是错误的，因为监理单位承揽监理业务的范围是根据其单位资质决定的，而不是和甲方签订的合同所决定的。

答案：B

【例11-2-2】 根据《中华人民共和国建筑法》的规定，有关工程发包的规定，下列理解错误的是：

A. 关于对建筑工程进行肢解发包的规定，属于禁止性规定

B. 可以将建筑工程的勘察、设计、施工、设备采购一并发包给一个工程总承包单位

C. 建筑工程实行直接发包的，发包单位可以将建筑工程发包给具有资质证书的承包单位

D. 提倡对建筑工程实行总承包

解　《中华人民共和国建筑法》第二十二条规定，发包单位应当将建筑工程发包给具有资质证书的承包单位。

答案：C

【例11-2-3】 根据《中华人民共和国建筑法》规定，施工企业矿业将部分工程分包给其他具有相应资质的分包单位施工，下列情形中不违反有关承包的禁止性规定的是：

A. 建筑施工企业超越本企业资质等级许可的业务范围或者以任何形式用其他建筑施工企业的名义承揽工程

B. 承包单位将其承包的全部建筑工程转包给他人

C. 承包单位将其承包的全部建筑工程肢解以后以分包的名义分别转包给他人

D. 两个不同资质等级的承包单位联合共同承包

解　《中华人民共和国建筑法》第二十七条规定：大型建筑工程或者结构复杂的建筑工程，可以由两个以上的承包单位联合共同承包。共同承包的各方对承包合同的履行承担连带责任。

两个以上不同资质等级的单位实行联合共同承包的，应当按照资质等级低的单位的业务许可范围承揽工程。

答案：D

【例11-2-4】 根据《中华人民共和国建筑法》规定，某建设单位领取了施工许可证，下列情节中，可能不导致施工许可证废止的是：

A. 领取施工许可证之日起三个月内因故不能按期开工,也未申请延期

B. 领取施工许可证之日起按期开工后又中止施工

C. 向发证机关申请延期开工一次,延期之日起三个月内,因故仍不能按期开工,也未申请延期

D. 向发证机关申请延期开工两次,超过六个月因故不能按期开工,继续申请延期

解 《中华人民共和国建筑法》第九条规定,建设单位应当自领取施工许可证之日起三个月内开工。因故不能按期开工的,应当向发证机关申请延期;延期以两次为限,每次不超过三个月。既不开工又不申请延期或者超过延期时限的,施工许可证自行废止。

答案:B

习　　题

11-2-1　施工许可证的申请者是(　　)。

A. 监理单位　　B. 设计单位　　C. 施工单位　　D. 建设单位

11-2-2　建设单位在领取开工证之后,应当在(　　)个月内开工。

A. 3　　B. 6　　C. 10　　D. 12

11-2-3　违法分包是指以下哪几种情况?(　　)

①总承包单位将建设工程分包给不具备相应资质条件的单位　②总承包单位将建设工程主体分包给其他单位　③分包单位将其承包的工程再分包的　④分包单位多于3个以上的

A. ①　　B. ①②③④　　C. ①②③　　D. ②③④

11-2-4　《中华人民共和国建筑法》中所指的建筑活动是(　　)。

A. 各类房屋建筑

B. 各类房屋建筑其附属设施的建造和与其配套的线路、管道、设备的安装活动

C. 在国内的所有建筑工程

D. 国内所有工程包括中国企业在境外承包的工程。

11-2-5　我国推行建筑工程监理制度的项目范围应该是(　　)。

A. 由国务院规定实行强制监理的建筑工程的范围

B. 所有工程必须强制接受监理

C. 由业主自行决定是否聘请监理

D. 只有国家投资的项目才需要监理

11-2-6　《中华人民共和国建筑法》中规定了申领开工证的必备条件,下列条件中哪项不符合建筑法的要求?(　　)

A. 已办理用地手续材料　　B. 已确定施工企业

C. 已有了方案设计图　　D. 资金已落实

第三节　中华人民共和国安全生产法

第一章　总　　则

第一条　为了加强安全生产工作,防止和减少生产安全事故,保障人民群众生命和财产安

全，促进经济社会持续健康发展，制定本法。

第二条　在中华人民共和国领域内从事生产经营活动的单位（以下统称生产经营单位）的安全生产，适用本法；有关法律、行政法规对消防安全和道路交通安全、铁路交通安全、水上交通安全、民用航空安全以及核与辐射安全、特种设备安全另有规定的，适用其规定。

第三条　安全生产工作应当以人为本，坚持安全发展，坚持安全第一、预防为主、综合治理的方针，强化和落实生产经营单位的主体责任，建立生产经营单位负责、职工参与、政府监管、行业自律和社会监督的机制。

第四条　生产经营单位必须遵守本法和其他有关安全生产的法律、法规，加强安全生产管理，建立、健全安全生产责任制和安全生产规章制度，改善安全生产条件，推进安全生产标准化建设，提高安全生产水平，确保安全生产。

第五条　生产经营单位的主要负责人对本单位的安全生产工作全面负责。

第六条　生产经营单位的从业人员有依法获得安全生产保障的权利，并应当依法履行安全生产方面的义务。

第七条　工会依法对安全生产工作进行监督。

生产经营单位的工会依法组织职工参加本单位安全生产工作的民主管理和民主监督，维护职工在安全生产方面的合法权益。生产经营单位制定或者修改有关安全生产的规章制度，应当听取工会的意见。

第八条　国务院和县级以上地方各级人民政府应当根据国民经济和社会发展规划制定安全生产规划，并组织实施。安全生产规划应当与城乡规划相衔接。

国务院和县级以上地方各级人民政府应当加强对安全生产工作的领导，支持、督促各有关部门依法履行安全生产监督管理职责，建立健全安全生产工作协调机制，及时协调、解决安全生产监督管理中存在的重大问题。

乡、镇人民政府以及街道办事处、开发区管理机构等地方人民政府的派出机关应当按照职责，加强对本行政区域内生产经营单位安全生产状况的监督检查，协助上级人民政府有关部门依法履行安全生产监督管理职责。

第九条　国务院安全生产监督管理部门依照本法，对全国安全生产工作实施综合监督管理；县级以上地方各级人民政府安全生产监督管理部门依照本法，对本行政区域内安全生产工作实施综合监督管理。

国务院有关部门依照本法和其他有关法律、行政法规的规定，在各自的职责范围内对有关行业、领域的安全生产工作实施监督管理；县级以上地方各级人民政府有关部门依照本法和其他有关法律、法规的规定，在各自的职责范围内对有关行业、领域的安全生产工作实施监督管理。

安全生产监督管理部门和对有关行业、领域的安全生产工作实施监督管理的部门，统称负有安全生产监督管理职责的部门。

第十条　国务院有关部门应当按照保障安全生产的要求，依法及时制定有关的国家标准或者行业标准，并根据科技进步和经济发展适时修订。

生产经营单位必须执行依法制定的保障安全生产的国家标准或者行业标准。

第十一条　各级人民政府及其有关部门应当采取多种形式，加强对有关安全生产的法律、法规和安全生产知识的宣传，增强全社会的安全生产意识。

第十二条　有关协会组织依照法律、行政法规和章程，为生产经营单位提供安全生产方面的信息、培训等服务，发挥自律作用，促进生产经营单位加强安全生产管理。

第十三条　依法设立的为安全生产提供技术、管理服务的机构，依照法律、行政法规和执业准则，接受生产经营单位的委托为其安全生产工作提供技术、管理服务。

生产经营单位委托前款规定的机构提供安全生产技术、管理服务的，保证安全生产的责任仍由本单位负责。

第十四条　国家实行生产安全事故责任追究制度，依照本法和有关法律、法规的规定，追究生产安全事故责任人员的法律责任。

第十五条　国家鼓励和支持安全生产科学技术研究和安全生产先进技术的推广应用，提高安全生产水平。

第十六条　国家对在改善安全生产条件、防止生产安全事故、参加抢险救护等方面取得显著成绩的单位和个人，给予奖励。

第二章　生产经营单位的安全生产保障

第十七条　生产经营单位应当具备本法和有关法律、行政法规和国家标准或者行业标准规定的安全生产条件；不具备安全生产条件的，不得从事生产经营活动。

第十八条　生产经营单位的主要负责人对本单位安全生产工作负有下列职责：

（一）建立、健全本单位安全生产责任制；

（二）组织制定本单位安全生产规章制度和操作规程；

（三）组织制定并实施本单位安全生产教育和培训计划；

（四）保证本单位安全生产投入的有效实施；

（五）督促、检查本单位的安全生产工作，及时消除生产安全事故隐患；

（六）组织制定并实施本单位的生产安全事故应急救援预案；

（七）及时、如实报告生产安全事故。

第十九条　生产经营单位的安全生产责任制应当明确各岗位的责任人员、责任范围和考核标准等内容。

生产经营单位应当建立相应的机制，加强对安全生产责任制落实情况的监督考核，保证安全生产责任制的落实。

第二十条　生产经营单位应当具备的安全生产条件所必需的资金投入，由生产经营单位的决策机构、主要负责人或者个人经营的投资人予以保证，并对由于安全生产所必需的资金投入不足导致的后果承担责任。

有关生产经营单位应当按照规定提取和使用安全生产费用，专门用于改善安全生产条件。安全生产费用在成本中据实列支。安全生产费用提取、使用和监督管理的具体办法由国务院财政部门会同国务院安全生产监督管理部门征求国务院有关部门意见后制定。

第二十一条　矿山、金属冶炼、建筑施工、道路运输单位和危险物品的生产、经营、储存单位，应当设置安全生产管理机构或者配备专职安全生产管理人员。

前款规定以外的其他生产经营单位，从业人员超过一百人的，应当设置安全生产管理机构或者配备专职安全生产管理人员；从业人员在一百人以下的，应当配备专职或者兼职的安全生产管理人员。

第二十二条　生产经营单位的安全生产管理机构以及安全生产管理人员履行下列职责：

（一）组织或者参与拟订本单位安全生产规章制度、操作规程和生产安全事故应急救援预案；

（二）组织或者参与本单位安全生产教育和培训，如实记录安全生产教育和培训情况；

（三）督促落实本单位重大危险源的安全管理措施；

（四）组织或者参与本单位应急救援演练；

（五）检查本单位的安全生产状况，及时排查生产安全事故隐患，提出改进安全生产管理的建议；

（六）制止和纠正违章指挥、强令冒险作业、违反操作规程的行为；

（七）督促落实本单位安全生产整改措施。

第二十三条　生产经营单位的安全生产管理机构以及安全生产管理人员应当恪尽职守，依法履行职责。

生产经营单位作出涉及安全生产的经营决策，应当听取安全生产管理机构以及安全生产管理人员的意见。

生产经营单位不得因安全生产管理人员依法履行职责而降低其工资、福利等待遇或者解除与其订立的劳动合同。

危险物品的生产、储存单位以及矿山、金属冶炼单位的安全生产管理人员的任免，应当告知主管的负有安全生产监督管理职责的部门。

第二十四条　生产经营单位的主要负责人和安全生产管理人员必须具备与本单位所从事的生产经营活动相应的安全生产知识和管理能力。

危险物品的生产、经营、储存单位以及矿山、金属冶炼、建筑施工、道路运输单位的主要负责人和安全生产管理人员，应当由主管的负有安全生产监督管理职责的部门对其安全生产知识和管理能力考核合格。考核不得收费。

危险物品的生产、储存单位以及矿山、金属冶炼单位应当有注册安全工程师从事安全生产管理工作。鼓励其他生产经营单位聘用注册安全工程师从事安全生产管理工作。注册安全工程师按专业分类管理，具体办法由国务院人力资源和社会保障部门、国务院安全生产监督管理部门会同国务院有关部门制定。

第二十五条　生产经营单位应当对从业人员进行安全生产教育和培训，保证从业人员具备必要的安全生产知识，熟悉有关的安全生产规章制度和安全操作规程，掌握本岗位的安全操作技能，了解事故应急处理措施，知悉自身在安全生产方面的权利和义务。未经安全生产教育和培训合格的从业人员，不得上岗作业。

生产经营单位使用被派遣劳动者的，应当将被派遣劳动者纳入本单位从业人员统一管理，对被派遣劳动者进行岗位安全操作规程和安全操作技能的教育和培训。劳务派遣单位应当对被派遣劳动者进行必要的安全生产教育和培训。

生产经营单位接收中等职业学校、高等学校学生实习的，应当对实习学生进行相应的安全生产教育和培训，提供必要的劳动防护用品。学校应当协助生产经营单位对实习学生进行安全生产教育和培训。

生产经营单位应当建立安全生产教育和培训档案，如实记录安全生产教育和培训的时间、内容、参加人员以及考核结果等情况。

第二十六条　生产经营单位采用新工艺、新技术、新材料或者使用新设备，必须了解、掌握其安全技术特性，采取有效的安全防护措施，并对从业人员进行专门的安全生产教育和培训。

第二十七条　生产经营单位的特种作业人员必须按照国家有关规定经专门的安全作业培训，取得相应资格，方可上岗作业。

特种作业人员的范围由国务院安全生产监督管理部门会同国务院有关部门确定。

第二十八条　生产经营单位新建、改建、扩建工程项目(以下统称建设项目)的安全设施,必须与主体工程同时设计、同时施工、同时投入生产和使用。安全设施投资应当纳入建设项目概算。

第二十九条　矿山、金属冶炼建设项目和用于生产、储存、装卸危险物品的建设项目,应当按照国家有关规定进行安全评价。

第三十条　建设项目安全设施的设计人、设计单位应当对安全设施设计负责。

矿山、金属冶炼建设项目和用于生产、储存、装卸危险物品的建设项目的安全设施设计应当按照国家有关规定报经有关部门审查,审查部门及其负责审查的人员对审查结果负责。

第三十一条　矿山、金属冶炼建设项目和用于生产、储存、装卸危险物品的建设项目的施工单位必须按照批准的安全设施设计施工,并对安全设施的工程质量负责。

矿山、金属冶炼建设项目和用于生产、储存危险物品的建设项目竣工投入生产或者使用前,应当由建设单位负责组织对安全设施进行验收;验收合格后,方可投入生产和使用。安全生产监督管理部门应当加强对建设单位验收活动和验收结果的监督核查。

第三十二条　生产经营单位应当在有较大危险因素的生产经营场所和有关设施、设备上,设置明显的安全警示标志。

第三十三条　安全设备的设计、制造、安装、使用、检测、维修、改造和报废,应当符合国家标准或者行业标准。

生产经营单位必须对安全设备进行经常性维护、保养,并定期检测,保证正常运转。维护、保养、检测应当作好记录,并由有关人员签字。

第三十四条　生产经营单位使用的危险物品的容器、运输工具,以及涉及人身安全、危险性较大的海洋石油开采特种设备和矿山井下特种设备,必须按照国家有关规定,由专业生产单位生产,并经具有专业资质的检测、检验机构检测、检验合格,取得安全使用证或者安全标志,方可投入使用。检测、检验机构对检测、检验结果负责。

第三十五条　国家对严重危及生产安全的工艺、设备实行淘汰制度,具体目录由国务院安全生产监督管理部门会同国务院有关部门制定并公布。法律、行政法规对目录的制定另有规定的,适用其规定。

省、自治区、直辖市人民政府可以根据本地区实际情况制定并公布具体目录,对前款规定以外的危及生产安全的工艺、设备予以淘汰。

生产经营单位不得使用应当淘汰的危及生产安全的工艺、设备。

第三十六条　生产、经营、运输、储存、使用危险物品或者处置废弃危险物品的,由有关主管部门依照有关法律、法规的规定和国家标准或者行业标准审批并实施监督管理。

生产经营单位生产、经营、运输、储存、使用危险物品或者处置废弃危险物品,必须执行有关法律、法规和国家标准或者行业标准,建立专门的安全管理制度,采取可靠的安全措施,接受有关主管部门依法实施的监督管理。

第三十七条　生产经营单位对重大危险源应当登记建档,进行定期检测、评估、监控,并制定应急预案,告知从业人员和相关人员在紧急情况下应当采取的应急措施。

生产经营单位应当按照国家有关规定将本单位重大危险源及有关安全措施、应急措施报有关地方人民政府安全生产监督管理部门和有关部门备案。

第三十八条　生产经营单位应当建立健全生产安全事故隐患排查治理制度,采取技术、管理措施，及时发现并消除事故隐患。事故隐患排查治理情况应当如实记录，并向从业人员通报。

县级以上地方各级人民政府负有安全生产监督管理职责的部门应当建立健全重大事故隐患治理督办制度，督促生产经营单位消除重大事故隐患。

第三十九条　生产、经营、储存、使用危险物品的车间、商店、仓库不得与员工宿舍在同一座建筑物内，并应当与员工宿舍保持安全距离。

生产经营场所和员工宿舍应当设有符合紧急疏散要求、标志明显、保持畅通的出口。禁止锁闭、封堵生产经营场所或者员工宿舍的出口。

第四十条　生产经营单位进行爆破、吊装以及国务院安全生产监督管理部门会同国务院有关部门规定的其他危险作业，应当安排专门人员进行现场安全管理，确保操作规程的遵守和安全措施的落实。

第四十一条　生产经营单位应当教育和督促从业人员严格执行本单位的安全生产规章制度和安全操作规程；并向从业人员如实告知作业场所和工作岗位存在的危险因素、防范措施以及事故应急措施。

第四十二条　生产经营单位必须为从业人员提供符合国家标准或者行业标准的劳动防护用品，并监督、教育从业人员按照使用规则佩戴、使用。

第四十三条　生产经营单位的安全生产管理人员应当根据本单位的生产经营特点，对安全生产状况进行经常性检查；对检查中发现的安全问题，应当立即处理；不能处理的，应当及时报告本单位有关负责人，有关负责人应当及时处理。检查及处理情况应当如实记录在案。

生产经营单位的安全生产管理人员在检查中发现重大事故隐患，依照前款规定向本单位有关负责人报告，有关负责人不及时处理的，安全生产管理人员可以向主管的负有安全生产监督管理职责的部门报告，接到报告的部门应当依法及时处理。

第四十四条　生产经营单位应当安排用于配备劳动防护用品、进行安全生产培训的经费。

第四十五条　两个以上生产经营单位在同一作业区域内进行生产经营活动，可能危及对方生产安全的，应当签订安全生产管理协议，明确各自的安全生产管理职责和应当采取的安全措施，并指定专职安全生产管理人员进行安全检查与协调。

第四十六条　生产经营单位不得将生产经营项目、场所、设备发包或者出租给不具备安全生产条件或者相应资质的单位或者个人。

生产经营项目、场所发包或者出租给其他单位的，生产经营单位应当与承包单位、承租单位签订专门的安全生产管理协议，或者在承包合同、租赁合同中约定各自的安全生产管理职责；生产经营单位对承包单位、承租单位的安全生产工作统一协调、管理，定期进行安全检查，发现安全问题的，应当及时督促整改。

第四十七条　生产经营单位发生生产安全事故时，单位的主要负责人应当立即组织抢救，并不得在事故调查处理期间擅离职守。

第四十八条　生产经营单位必须依法参加工伤保险，为从业人员缴纳保险费。

国家鼓励生产经营单位投保安全生产责任保险。

第三章　从业人员的安全生产权利义务

第四十九条　生产经营单位与从业人员订立的劳动合同，应当载明有关保障从业人员劳动安全、防止职业危害的事项，以及依法为从业人员办理工伤保险的事项。

生产经营单位不得以任何形式与从业人员订立协议，免除或者减轻其对从业人员因生产安全事故伤亡依法应承担的责任。

第五十条 生产经营单位的从业人员有权了解其作业场所和工作岗位存在的危险因素、防范措施及事故应急措施，有权对本单位的安全生产工作提出建议。

第五十一条 从业人员有权对本单位安全生产工作中存在的问题提出批评、检举、控告；有权拒绝违章指挥和强令冒险作业。

生产经营单位不得因从业人员对本单位安全生产工作提出批评、检举、控告或者拒绝违章指挥、强令冒险作业而降低其工资、福利等待遇或者解除与其订立的劳动合同。

第五十二条 从业人员发现直接危及人身安全的紧急情况时，有权停止作业或者在采取可能的应急措施后撤离作业场所。

生产经营单位不得因从业人员在前款紧急情况下停止作业或者采取紧急撤离措施而降低其工资、福利等待遇或者解除与其订立的劳动合同。

第五十三条 因生产安全事故受到损害的从业人员，除依法享有工伤保险外，依照有关民事法律尚有获得赔偿的权利的，有权向本单位提出赔偿要求。

第五十四条 从业人员在作业过程中，应当严格遵守本单位的安全生产规章制度和操作规程，服从管理，正确佩戴和使用劳动防护用品。

第五十五条 从业人员应当接受安全生产教育和培训，掌握本职工作所需的安全生产知识，提高安全生产技能，增强事故预防和应急处理能力。

第五十六条 从业人员发现事故隐患或者其他不安全因素，应当立即向现场安全生产管理人员或者本单位负责人报告；接到报告的人员应当及时予以处理。

第五十七条 工会有权对建设项目的安全设施与主体工程同时设计、同时施工、同时投入生产和使用进行监督，提出意见。

工会对生产经营单位违反安全生产法律、法规，侵犯从业人员合法权益的行为，有权要求纠正；发现生产经营单位违章指挥、强令冒险作业或者发现事故隐患时，有权提出解决的建议，生产经营单位应当及时研究答复；发现危及从业人员生命安全的情况时，有权向生产经营单位建议组织从业人员撤离危险场所，生产经营单位必须立即作出处理。

工会有权依法参加事故调查，向有关部门提出处理意见，并要求追究有关人员的责任。

第五十八条 生产经营单位使用被派遣劳动者的，被派遣劳动者享有本法规定的从业人员的权利，并应当履行本法规定的从业人员的义务。

第四章 安全生产的监督管理

第五十九条 县级以上地方各级人民政府应当根据本行政区域内的安全生产状况，组织有关部门按照职责分工，对本行政区域内容易发生重大生产安全事故的生产经营单位进行严格检查。

安全生产监督管理部门应当按照分类分级监督管理的要求，制定安全生产年度监督检查计划，并按照年度监督检查计划进行监督检查，发现事故隐患，应当及时处理。

第六十条 负有安全生产监督管理职责的部门依照有关法律、法规的规定，对涉及安全生产的事项需要审查批准（包括批准、核准、许可、注册、认证、颁发证照等，下同）或者验收的，必须严格依照有关法律、法规和国家标准或者行业标准规定的安全生产条件和程序进行审查；不符合有关法律、法规和国家标准或者行业标准规定的安全生产条件的，不得批准或者验收通过。对未依法取得批准或者验收合格的单位擅自从事有关活动的，负责行政审批的部门发现或者接到举报后应当立即予以取缔，并依法予以处理。对已经依法取得批准的单位，负责行政审批的部门发现其不再具备安全生产条件的，应当撤销原批准。

第六十一条　负有安全生产监督管理职责的部门对涉及安全生产的事项进行审查、验收，不得收取费用；不得要求接受审查、验收的单位购买其指定品牌或者指定生产、销售单位的安全设备、器材或者其他产品。

第六十二条　安全生产监督管理部门和其他负有安全生产监督管理职责的部门依法开展安全生产行政执法工作，对生产经营单位执行有关安全生产的法律、法规和国家标准或者行业标准的情况进行监督检查，行使以下职权：

（一）进入生产经营单位进行检查，调阅有关资料，向有关单位和人员了解情况；

（二）对检查中发现的安全生产违法行为，当场予以纠正或者要求限期改正；对依法应当给予行政处罚的行为，依照本法和其他有关法律、行政法规的规定作出行政处罚决定；

（三）对检查中发现的事故隐患，应当责令立即排除；重大事故隐患排除前或者排除过程中无法保证安全的，应当责令从危险区域内撤出作业人员，责令暂时停产停业或者停止使用相关设施、设备；重大事故隐患排除后，经审查同意，方可恢复生产经营和使用；

（四）对有根据认为不符合保障安全生产的国家标准或者行业标准的设施、设备、器材以及违法生产、储存、使用、经营、运输的危险物品予以查封或者扣押，对违法生产、储存、使用、经营危险物品的作业场所予以查封，并依法作出处理决定。

监督检查不得影响被检查单位的正常生产经营活动。

第六十三条　生产经营单位对负有安全生产监督管理职责的部门的监督检查人员（以下统称安全生产监督检查人员）依法履行监督检查职责，应当予以配合，不得拒绝、阻挠。

第六十四条　安全生产监督检查人员应当忠于职守，坚持原则，秉公执法。

安全生产监督检查人员执行监督检查任务时，必须出示有效的监督执法证件；对涉及被检查单位的技术秘密和业务秘密，应当为其保密。

第六十五条　安全生产监督检查人员应当将检查的时间、地点、内容、发现的问题及其处理情况，作出书面记录，并由检查人员和被检查单位的负责人签字；被检查单位的负责人拒绝签字的，检查人员应当将情况记录在案，并向负有安全生产监督管理职责的部门报告。

第六十六条　负有安全生产监督管理职责的部门在监督检查中，应当互相配合，实行联合检查；确需分别进行检查的，应当互通情况，发现存在的安全问题应当由其他有关部门进行处理的，应当及时移送其他有关部门并形成记录备查，接受移送的部门应当及时进行处理。

第六十七条　负有安全生产监督管理职责的部门依法对存在重大事故隐患的生产经营单位作出停产停业、停止施工、停止使用相关设施或者设备的决定，生产经营单位应当依法执行，及时消除事故隐患。生产经营单位拒不执行，有发生生产安全事故的现实危险的，在保证安全的前提下，经本部门主要负责人批准，负有安全生产监督管理职责的部门可以采取通知有关单位停止供电、停止供应民用爆炸物品等措施，强制生产经营单位履行决定。通知应当采用书面形式，有关单位应当予以配合。

负有安全生产监督管理职责的部门依照前款规定采取停止供电措施，除有危及生产安全的紧急情形外，应当提前二十四小时通知生产经营单位。生产经营单位依法履行行政决定、采取相应措施消除事故隐患的，负有安全生产监督管理职责的部门应当及时解除前款规定的措施。

第六十八条　监察机关依照行政监察法的规定，对负有安全生产监督管理职责的部门及其工作人员履行安全生产监督管理职责实施监察。

第六十九条　承担安全评价、认证、检测、检验的机构应当具备国家规定的资质条件，并对其作出的安全评价、认证、检测、检验的结果负责。

第七十条　负有安全生产监督管理职责的部门应当建立举报制度，公开举报电话、信箱或者电子邮件地址，受理有关安全生产的举报；受理的举报事项经调查核实后，应当形成书面材料；需要落实整改措施的，报经有关负责人签字并督促落实。

第七十一条　任何单位或者个人对事故隐患或者安全生产违法行为，均有权向负有安全生产监督管理职责的部门报告或者举报。

第七十二条　居民委员会、村民委员会发现其所在区域内的生产经营单位存在事故隐患或者安全生产违法行为时，应当向当地人民政府或者有关部门报告。

第七十三条　县级以上各级人民政府及其有关部门对报告重大事故隐患或者举报安全生产违法行为的有功人员，给予奖励。具体奖励办法由国务院安全生产监督管理部门会同国务院财政部门制定。

第七十四条　新闻、出版、广播、电影、电视等单位有进行安全生产公益宣传教育的义务，有对违反安全生产法律、法规的行为进行舆论监督的权利。

第七十五条　负有安全生产监督管理职责的部门应当建立安全生产违法行为信息库，如实记录生产经营单位的安全生产违法行为信息；对违法行为情节严重的生产经营单位，应当向社会公告，并通报行业主管部门、投资主管部门、国上资源主管部门、证券监督管理机构以及有关金融机构。

第五章　生产安全事故的应急救援与调查处理

第七十六条　国家加强生产安全事故应急能力建设，在重点行业、领域建立应急救援基地和应急救援队伍，鼓励生产经营单位和其他社会力量建立应急救援队伍，配备相应的应急救援装备和物资，提高应急救援的专业化水平。

国务院安全生产监督管理部门建立全国统一的生产安全事故应急救援信息系统，国务院有关部门建立健全相关行业、领域的生产安全事故应急救援信息系统。

第七十七条　县级以上地方各级人民政府应当组织有关部门制定本行政区域内生产安全事故应急救援预案，建立应急救援体系。

第七十八条　生产经营单位应当制定本单位生产安全事故应急救援预案，与所在地县级以上地方人民政府组织制定的生产安全事故应急救援预案相衔接，并定期组织演练。

第七十九条　危险物品的生产、经营、储存单位以及矿山、金属冶炼、城市轨道交通运营、建筑施工单位应当建立应急救援组织；生产经营规模较小的，可以不建立应急救援组织，但应当指定兼职的应急救援人员。

危险物品的生产、经营、储存、运输单位以及矿山、金属冶炼、城市轨道交通运营、建筑施工单位应当配备必要的应急救援器材、设备和物资，并进行经常性维护、保养，保证正常运转。

第八十条　生产经营单位发生生产安全事故后，事故现场有关人员应当立即报告本单位负责人。

单位负责人接到事故报告后，应当迅速采取有效措施，组织抢救，防止事故扩大，减少人员伤亡和财产损失，并按照国家有关规定立即如实报告当地负有安全生产监督管理职责的部门，不得隐瞒不报、谎报或者迟报，不得故意破坏事故现场、毁灭有关证据。

第八十一条　负有安全生产监督管理职责的部门接到事故报告后，应当立即按照国家有关规定上报事故情况。负有安全生产监督管理职责的部门和有关地方人民政府对事故情况不得隐瞒不报、谎报或者迟报。

第八十二条　有关地方人民政府和负有安全生产监督管理职责的部门的负责人接到生产安全事故报告后，应当按照生产安全事故应急救援预案的要求立即赶到事故现场，组织事故抢救。

参与事故抢救的部门和单位应当服从统一指挥，加强协同联动，采取有效的应急救援措施，并根据事故救援的需要采取警戒、疏散等措施，防止事故扩大和次生灾害的发生，减少人员伤亡和财产损失。

事故抢救过程中应当采取必要措施，避免或者减少对环境造成的危害。

任何单位和个人都应当支持、配合事故抢救，并提供一切便利条件。

第八十三条　事故调查处理应当按照科学严谨、依法依规、实事求是、注重实效的原则，及时、准确地查清事故原因，查明事故性质和责任，总结事故教训，提出整改措施，并对事故责任者提出处理意见。事故调查报告应当依法及时向社会公布。事故调查和处理的具体办法由国务院制定。

事故发生单位应当及时全面落实整改措施，负有安全生产监督管理职责的部门应当加强监督检查。

第八十四条　生产经营单位发生生产安全事故，经调查确定为责任事故的，除了应当查明事故单位的责任并依法予以追究外，还应当查明对安全生产的有关事项负有审查批准和监督职责的行政部门的责任，对有失职、渎职行为的，依照本法第八十七条的规定追究法律责任。

第八十五条　任何单位和个人不得阻挠和干涉对事故的依法调查处理。

第八十六条　县级以上地方各级人民政府安全生产监督管理部门应当定期统计分析本行政区域内发生生产安全事故的情况，并定期向社会公布。

第六章　法律责任

第八十七条　负有安全生产监督管理职责的部门的工作人员，有下列行为之一的，给予降级或者撤职的处分；构成犯罪的，依照刑法有关规定追究刑事责任：

（一）对不符合法定安全生产条件的涉及安全生产的事项予以批准或者验收通过的；

（二）发现未依法取得批准、验收的单位擅自从事有关活动或者接到举报后不予取缔或者不依法予以处理的；

（三）对已经依法取得批准的单位不履行监督管理职责，发现其不再具备安全生产条件而不撤销原批准或者发现安全生产违法行为不予查处的；

（四）在监督检查中发现重大事故隐患，不依法及时处理的。

负有安全生产监督管理职责的部门的工作人员有前款规定以外的滥用职权、玩忽职守、徇私舞弊行为的，依法给予处分；构成犯罪的，依照刑法有关规定追究刑事责任。

第八十八条　负有安全生产监督管理职责的部门，要求被审查、验收的单位购买其指定的安全设备、器材或者其他产品的，在对安全生产事项的审查、验收中收取费用的，由其上级机关或者监察机关责令改正，责令退还收取的费用；情节严重的，对直接负责的主管人员和其他直接责任人员依法给予处分。

第八十九条　承担安全评价、认证、检测、检验工作的机构，出具虚假证明的，没收违法所得；违法所得在十万元以上的，并处违法所得二倍以上五倍以下的罚款；没有违法所得或者违法所得不足十万元的，单处或者并处十万元以上二十万元以下的罚款；对其直接负责的主管人员和其他直接责任人员处二万元以上五万元以下的罚款；给他人造成损害的，与生产经营单位承担连带赔偿责任；构成犯罪的，依照刑法有关规定追究刑事责任。

对有前款违法行为的机构，吊销其相应资质。

第九十条　生产经营单位的决策机构、主要负责人或者个人经营的投资人不依照本法规定保证安全生产所必需的资金投入，致使生产经营单位不具备安全生产条件的，责令限期改正，提供必需的资金；逾期未改正的，责令生产经营单位停产停业整顿。

有前款违法行为，导致发生生产安全事故的，对生产经营单位的主要负责人给予撤职处分，对个人经营的投资人处二万元以上二十万元以下的罚款；构成犯罪的，依照刑法有关规定追究刑事责任。

第九十一条　生产经营单位的主要负责人未履行本法规定的安全生产管理职责的，责令限期改正；逾期未改正的，处二万元以上五万元以下的罚款，责令生产经营单位停产停业整顿。

生产经营单位的主要负责人有前款违法行为，导致发生生产安全事故的，给予撤职处分；构成犯罪的，依照刑法有关规定追究刑事责任。

生产经营单位的主要负责人依照前款规定受刑事处罚或者撤职处分的，自刑罚执行完毕或者受处分之日起，五年内不得担任任何生产经营单位的主要负责人；对重大、特别重大生产安全事故负有责任的，终身不得担任本行业生产经营单位的主要负责人。

第九十二条　生产经营单位的主要负责人未履行本法规定的安全生产管理职责，导致发生生产安全事故的，由安全生产监督管理部门依照下列规定处以罚款：

（一）发生一般事故的，处上一年年收入百分之三十的罚款；

（二）发生较大事故的，处上一年年收入百分之四十的罚款；

（三）发生重大事故的，处上一年年收入百分之六十的罚款；

（四）发生特别重大事故的，处上一年年收入百分之八十的罚款。

第九十三条　生产经营单位的安全生产管理人员未履行本法规定的安全生产管理职责的，责令限期改正；导致发生生产安全事故的，暂停或者撤销其与安全生产有关的资格；构成犯罪的，依照刑法有关规定追究刑事责任。

第九十四条　生产经营单位有下列行为之一的，责令限期改正，可以处五万元以下的罚款；逾期未改正的，责令停产停业整顿，并处五万元以上十万元以下的罚款，对其直接负责的主管人员和其他直接责任人员处一万元以上二万元以下的罚款：

（一）未按照规定设置安全生产管理机构或者配备安全生产管理人员的；

（二）危险物品的生产、经营、储存单位以及矿山、金属冶炼、建筑施工、道路运输单位的主要负责人和安全生产管理人员未按照规定经考核合格的；

（三）未按照规定对从业人员、被派遣劳动者、实习学生进行安全生产教育和培训，或者未按照规定如实告知有关的安全生产事项的；

（四）未如实记录安全生产教育和培训情况的；

（五）未将事故隐患排查治理情况如实记录或者未向从业人员通报的；

（六）未按照规定制定生产安全事故应急救援预案或者未定期组织演练的；

（七）特种作业人员未按照规定经专门的安全作业培训并取得相应资格，上岗作业的。

第九十五条　生产经营单位有下列行为之一的，责令停止建设或者停产停业整顿，限期改正；逾期未改正的，处五十万元以上一百万元以下的罚款，对其直接负责的主管人员和其他直接责任人员处二万元以上五万元以下的罚款；构成犯罪的，依照刑法有关规定追究刑事责任：

（一）未按照规定对矿山、金属冶炼建设项目或者用于生产、储存、装卸危险物品的建设项目进行安全评价的；

（二）矿山、金属冶炼建设项目或者用于生产、储存、装卸危险物品的建设项目没有安全设施设计或者安全设施设计未按照规定

报经有关部门审查同意的；

（三）矿山、金属冶炼建设项目或者用于生产、储存、装卸危险物品的建设项目的施工单位未按照批准的安全设施设计施工的；

（四）矿山、金属冶炼建设项目或者用于生产、储存危险物品的建设项目竣工投入生产或者使用前，安全设施未经验收合格的。

第九十六条　生产经营单位有下列行为之一的，责令限期改正，可以处五万元以下的罚款；逾期未改正的，处五万元以上二十万元以下的罚款，对其直接负责的主管人员和其他直接责任人员处一万元以上二万元以下的罚款；情节严重的，责令停产停业整顿；构成犯罪的，依照刑法有关规定追究刑事责任：

（一）未在有较大危险因素的生产经营场所和有关设施、设备上设置明显的安全警示标志的；

（二）安全设备的安装、使用、检测、改造和报废不符合国家标准或者行业标准的；

（三）未对安全设备进行经常性维护、保养和定期检测的；

（四）未为从业人员提供符合国家标准或者行业标准的劳动防护用品的；

（五）危险物品的容器、运输工具，以及涉及人身安全、危险性较大的海洋石油开采特种设备和矿山井下特种设备未经具有专业资质的机构检测、检验合格，取得安全使用证或者安全标志，投入使用的；

（六）使用应当淘汰的危及生产安全的工艺、设备的。

第九十七条　未经依法批准，擅自生产、经营、运输、储存、使用危险物品或者处置废弃危险物品的，依照有关危险物品安全管理的法律、行政法规的规定予以处罚；构成犯罪的，依照刑法有关规定追究刑事责任。

第九十八条　生产经营单位有下列行为之一的，责令限期改正，可以处十万元以下的罚款；逾期未改正的，责令停产停业整顿，并处十万元以上二十万元以下的罚款，对其直接负责的主管人员和其他直接责任人员处二万元以上五万元以下的罚款；构成犯罪的，依照刑法有关规定追究刑事责任：

（一）生产、经营、运输、储存、使用危险物品或者处置废弃危险物品，未建立专门安全管理制度、未采取可靠的安全措施的；

（二）对重大危险源未登记建档，或者未进行评估、监控，或者未制定应急预案的；

（三）进行爆破、吊装以及国务院安全生产监督管理部门会同国务院有关部门规定的其他危险作业，未安排专门人员进行现场安全管理的；

（四）未建立事故隐患排查治理制度的。

第九十九条　生产经营单位未采取措施消除事故隐患的，责令立即消除或者限期消除；生产经营单位拒不执行的，责令停产停业整顿，并处十万元以上五十万元以下的罚款，对其直接负责的主管人员和其他直接责任人员处二万元以上五万元以下的罚款。

第一百条　生产经营单位将生产经营项目、场所、设备发包或者出租给不具备安全生产条件或者相应资质的单位或者个人的，责令限期改正，没收违法所得；违法所得十万元以上的，并处违法所得二倍以上五倍以下的罚款；没有违法所得或者违法所得不足十万元的，单处或者并

处十万元以上二十万元以下的罚款;对其直接负责的主管人员和其他直接责任人员处一万元以上二万元以下的罚款;导致发生生产安全事故给他人造成损害的,与承包方、承租方承担连带赔偿责任。

生产经营单位未与承包单位、承租单位签订专门的安全生产管理协议或者未在承包合同、租赁合同中明确各自的安全生产管理职责,或者未对承包单位、承租单位的安全生产统一协调、管理的,责令限期改正,可以处五万元以下的罚款,对其直接负责的主管人员和其他直接责任人员可以处一万元以下的罚款;逾期未改正的,责令停产停业整顿。

第一百零一条　两个以上生产经营单位在同一作业区域内进行可能危及对方安全生产的生产经营活动,未签订安全生产管理协议或者未指定专职安全生产管理人员进行安全检查与协调的,责令限期改正,可以处五万元以下的罚款,对其直接负责的主管人员和其他直接责任人员可以处一万元以下的罚款;逾期未改正的,责令停产停业。

第一百零二条　生产经营单位有下列行为之一的,责令限期改正,可以处五万元以下的罚款,对其直接负责的主管人员和其他直接责任人员可以处一万元以下的罚款;逾期未改正的,责令停产停业整顿;构成犯罪的,依照刑法有关规定追究刑事责任:

(一)生产、经营、储存、使用危险物品的车间、商店、仓库与员工宿舍在同一座建筑内,或者与员工宿舍的距离不符合安全要求的;

(二)生产经营场所和员工宿舍未设有符合紧急疏散需要、标志明显、保持畅通的出口,或者锁闭、封堵生产经营场所或者员工宿舍出口的。

第一百零三条　生产经营单位与从业人员订立协议,免除或者减轻其对从业人员因生产安全事故伤亡依法应承担的责任的,该协议无效;对生产经营单位的主要负责人、个人经营的投资人处二万元以上十万元以下的罚款。

第一百零四条　生产经营单位的从业人员不服从管理,违反安全生产规章制度或者操作规程的,由生产经营单位给予批评教育,依照有关规章　制度给予处分;构成犯罪的,依照刑法有关规定追究刑事责任。

第一百零五条　违反本法规定,生产经营单位拒绝、阻碍负有安全生产监督管理职责的部门依法实施监督检查的,责令改正;拒不改正的,处二万元以上二十万元以下的罚款;对其直接负责的主管人员和其他直接责任人员处一万元以上二万元以下的罚款;构成犯罪的,依照刑法有关规定追究刑事责任。

第一百零六条　生产经营单位的主要负责人在本单位发生生产安全事故时,不立即组织抢救或者在事故调查处理期间擅离职守或者逃匿的,给予降级、撤职的处分,并由安全生产监督管理部门处上一年年收入百分之六十至百分之一百的罚款;对逃匿的处十五日以下拘留;构成犯罪的,依照刑法有关规定追究刑事责任。

生产经营单位的主要负责人对生产安全事故隐瞒不报、谎报或者迟报的,依照前款规定处罚。

第一百零七条　有关地方人民政府、负有安全生产监督管理职责的部门,对生产安全事故隐瞒不报、谎报或者迟报的,对直接负责的主管人员和其他直接责任人员依法给予处分;构成犯罪的,依照刑法有关规定追究刑事责任。

第一百零八条　生产经营单位不具备本法和其他有关法律、行政法规和国家标准或者行业标准规定的安全生产条件,经停产停业整顿仍不具备安全生产条件的,予以关闭;有关部门应当依法吊销其有关证照。

第一百零九条　发生生产安全事故，对负有责任的生产经营单位除要求其依法承担相应的赔偿等责任外，由安全生产监督管理部门依照下列规定处以罚款：

（一）发生一般事故的，处二十万元以上五十万元以下的罚款；

（二）发生较大事故的，处五十万元以上一百万元以下的罚款；

（三）发生重大事故的，处一百万元以上五百万元以下的罚款；

（四）发生特别重大事故的，处五百万元以上一千万元以下的罚款；情节特别严重的，处一千万元以上二千万元以下的罚款。

第一百一十条　本法规定的行政处罚，由安全生产监督管理部门和其他负有安全生产监督管理职责的部门按照职责分工决定。予以关闭的行政处罚由负有安全生产监督管理职责的部门报请县级以上人民政府按照国务院规定的权限决定；给予拘留的行政处罚由公安机关依照治安管理处罚法的规定决定。

第一百一十一条　生产经营单位发生生产安全事故造成人员伤亡、他人财产损失的，应当依法承担赔偿责任；拒不承担或者其负责人逃匿的，由人民法院依法强制执行。

生产安全事故的责任人未依法承担赔偿责任，经人民法院依法采取执行措施后，仍不能对受害人给予足额赔偿的，应当继续履行赔偿义务；受害人发现责任人有其他财产的，可以随时请求人民法院执行。

第七章　附　　则

第一百一十二条　本法下列用语的含义：

危险物品，是指易燃易爆物品、危险化学品、放射性物品等能够危及人身安全和财产安全的物品。

重大危险源，是指长期地或者临时地生产、搬运、使用或者储存危险物品，且危险物品的数量等于或者超过临界量的单元（包括场所和设施）。

第一百一十三条　本法规定的生产安全一般事故、较大事故、重大事故、特别重大事故的划分标准由国务院规定。

国务院安全生产监督管理部门和其他负有安全生产监督管理职责的部门应当根据各自的职责分工，制定相关行业、领域重大事故隐患的判定标准。

第一百一十四条　本法自2002年11月1日起施行。

【例11-3-1】 根据《中华人民共和国安全生产法》规定，从业人员享有权利并承担义务，下列情形中属于从业人员履行义务的是：

A. 张某发现直接危及人身安全的紧急情况时禁止作业撤离现场

B. 李某发现事故隐患或者其他不安全因素，立即向现场安全生产管理人员或者本单位负责人报告

C. 王某对本单位安全生产工作中存在的问题提出批评、检举、控告

D. 赵某对本单位的安全生产工作提出建议

解　选项B属于义务，其他几个选项属于权利。

答案：B

【例11-3-2】 某生产经营单位使用危险性较大的特种设备，根据《中华人民共和国安全生产法》规定，该设备投入使用的条件不包括：

A. 该设备应由专业生产单位生产

B. 该设备应进行安全条件论证和安全评价

C. 该设备须经取得专业资质的检测、检验机构检测、检验合格

D. 该设备须取得安全使用证或者安全标志

解 《中华人民共和国安全生产法》第三十四条规定，生产经营单位使用的危险物品的容器、运输工具，以及涉及人身安全、危险性较大的海洋石油开采特种设备和矿山井下特种设备，必须按照国家有关规定，由专业生产单位生产，并经具有专业资质的检测、检验机构检测、检验合格，取得安全使用证或者安全标志，方可投入使用。检测、检验机构对检测、检验结果负责。

答案:B

【例 11-3-3】 国家规定的安全生产责任制度中，对单位主要负责人、施工项目经理、专职人员与从业人员的共同规定是：

A. 报告生产安全事故

B. 确保安全生产费用有效使用

C. 进行工伤事故统计、分析和报告

D. 由有关部门考试合格

解 《中华人民共和国安全生产法》第八十条规定，生产经营单位发生生产安全事故后，事故现场有关人员应当立即报告本单位负责人。

单位负责人接到事故报告后，应当迅速采取有效措施，组织抢救，防止事故扩大，减少人员伤亡和财产损失，并按照国家有关规定立即如实报告当地负有安全生产监督管理职责的部门，不得隐瞒不报、谎报或者迟报，不得故意破坏事故现场、毁灭有关证据。

答案:A

【例 11-3-4】 某超高层建筑施工中，一个塔吊分包商的施工人员因没有佩戴安全带加上作业疏忽而从高处坠落死亡。按我国《建筑工程安全生产管理条例》的规定，除工人本身的责任外，请问此意外的责任应：

A. 由分包商承担所有责任，总包商无需负责

B. 由总包商与分包商承担连带责任

C. 由总包商承担所有责任，分包商无需负责

D. 视分包合约的内容确定

解 《建设工程安全生产管理条例》第二十四条规定，建设工程实行施工总承包的，由总承包单位对施工现场的安全生产负总责。

总承包单位依法将建设工程分包给其他单位的，分包合同中应当明确各自的安全生产方面的权利、义务。总承包单位和分包单位对分包工程的安全生产承担连带责任。

分包单位应当服从总承包单位的安全生产管理，分包单位不服从管理导致生产安全事故的，由分包单位承担主要责任。

答案:B

习　题

11-3-1　重点工程建设项目应当坚持(　　)。

A. 安全第一的原则　　　　B. 为保证工程质量不怕牺牲

C. 确保进度不变的原则　　D. 投资不超过预算的原则

11-3-2　对本单位的安全生产工作全面负责的人员应当是(　　)。

A. 生产经营单位的主要负责人　　　B. 主管安全生产工作的副手

C. 项目经理　　　　　　　　　　　D. 专职安全员

第四节　中华人民共和国招标投标法

第一章　总　　则

第一条　为了规范招标投标活动，保护国家利益、社会公共利益和招标投标活动当事人的合法权益，提高经济效益，保证项目质量，制定本法。

第二条　在中华人民共和国境内进行招标投标活动，适用本法。

第三条　在中华人民共和国境内进行下列工程建设项目包括项目的勘察、设计、施工、监理以及与工程建设有关的重要设备、材料等的采购，必须进行招标：

（一）大型基础设施、公用事业等关系社会公共利益、公众安全的项目；

（二）全部或者部分使用国有资金投资或者国家融资的项目；

（三）使用国际组织或者外国政府贷款、援助资金的项目。

前款所列项目的具体范围和规模标准，由国务院发展计划部门会同国务院有关部门制订，报国务院批准。

法律或者国务院对必须进行招标的其他项目的范围有规定的，依照其规定。

第四条　任何单位和个人不得将依法必须进行招标的项目化整为零或者以其他任何方式规避招标。

第五条　招标投标活动应当遵循公开、公平、公正和诚实信用的原则。

第六条　依法必须进行招标的项目，其招标投标活动不受地区或者部门的限制。任何单位和个人不得违法限制或者排斥本地区、本系统以外的法人或者其他组织参加投标，不得以任何方式非法干涉招标投标活动。

第七条　招标投标活动及其当事人应当接受依法实施的监督。

有关行政监督部门依法对招标投标活动实施监督，依法查处招标投标活动中的违法行为。

对招标投标活动的行政监督及有关部门的具体职权划分，由国务院规定。

第二章　招　　标

第八条　招标人是依照本法规定提出招标项目、进行招标的法人或者其他组织。

第九条　招标项目按照国家有关规定需要履行项目审批手续的，应当先履行审批手续，取得批准。

招标人应当有进行招标项目的相应资金或者资金来源已经落实，并应当在招标文件中如实载明。

第十条　招标分为公开招标和邀请招标。

公开招标，是指招标人以招标公告的方式邀请不特定的法人或者其他组织投标。

邀请招标，是指招标人以投标邀请书的方式邀请特定的法人或者其他组织投标。

第十一条　国务院发展计划部门确定的国家重点项目和省、自治区、直辖市人民政府确定的地方重点项目不适宜公开招标的，经国务院发展计划部门或者省、自治区、直辖市人民政府批准，可以进行邀请招标。

第十二条　招标人有权自行选择招标代理机构，委托其办理招标事宜。任何单位和个人不得以任何方式为招标人指定招标代理机构。

招标人具有编制招标文件和组织评标能力的，可以自行办理招标事宜。任何单位和个人不得强制其委托招标代理机构办理招标事宜。依法必须进行招标的项目，招标人自行办理招标事宜的，应当向有关行政监督部门备案。

第十三条　招标代理机构是依法设立、从事招标代理业务并提供相关服务的社会中介组织。

招标代理机构应当具备下列条件：

（一）有从事招标代理业务的营业场所和相应资金；

（二）有能够编制招标文件和组织评标的相应专业力量；

第十四条　招标代理机构与行政机关和其他国家机关不得存在隶属关系或者其他利益关系。

第十五条　招标代理机构应当在招标人委托的范围内办理招标事宜，并遵守本法关于招标人的规定。

第十六条　招标人采用公开招标方式的，应当发布招标公告。依法必须进行招标的项目的招标公告，应当通过国家指定的报刊、信息网络或者其他媒介发布。

招标公告应当载明招标人的名称和地址、招标项目的性质、数量、实施地点和时间以及获取招标文件的办法等事项。

第十七条　招标人采用邀请招标方式的，应当向三个以上具备承担招标项目的能力、资信良好的特定的法人或者其他组织发出投标邀请书。

投标邀请书应当载明本法第十六条第二款规定的事项。

第十八条　招标人可以根据招标项目本身的要求，在招标公告或者投标邀请书中，要求潜在投标人提供有关资质证明文件和业绩情况，并对潜在投标人进行资格审查；国家对投标人的资格条件有规定的，依照其规定。

招标人不得以不合理的条件限制或者排斥潜在投标人，不得对潜在投标人实行歧视待遇。

第十九条　招标人应当根据招标项目的特点和需要编制招标文件。招标文件应当包括招标项目的技术要求、对投标人资格审查的标准、投标报价要求和评标标准等所有实质性要求和条件以及拟签订合同的主要条款。

国家对招标项目的技术、标准有规定的，招标人应当按照其规定在招标文件中提出相应要求。

招标项目需要划分标段、确定工期的，招标人应当合理划分标段、确定工期，并在招标文件中载明。

第二十条　招标文件不得要求或者标明特定的生产供应者以及含有倾向或者排斥潜在投标人的其他内容。

第二十一条　招标人根据招标项目的具体情况，可以组织潜在投标人踏勘项目现场。

第二十二条　招标人不得向他人透露已获取招标文件的潜在投标人的名称、数量以及可能影响公平竞争的有关招标投标的其他情况。

招标人设有标底的，标底必须保密。

第二十三条　招标人对已发出的招标文件进行必要的澄清或者修改的，应当在招标文件要求提交投标文件截止时间至少十五日前，以书面形式通知所有招标文件收受人。该澄清或者修改的内容为招标文件的组成部分。

第二十四条　招标人应当确定投标人编制投标文件所需要的合理时间；但是，依法必须进行招标的项目，自招标文件开始发出之日起至投标人提交投标文件截止之日止，最短不得少于二十日。

第三章 投　　标

第二十五条　投标人是响应招标、参加投标竞争的法人或者其他组织。

依法招标的科研项目允许个人参加投标的，投标的个人适用本法有关投标人的规定。

第二十六条　投标人应当具备承担招标项目的能力；国家有关规定对投标人资格条件或者招标文件对投标人资格条件有规定的，投标人应当具备规定的资格条件。

第二十七条　投标人应当按照招标文件的要求编制投标文件。投标文件应当对招标文件提出的实质性要求和条件作出响应。

招标项目属于建设施工的，投标文件的内容应当包括拟派出的项目负责人与主要技术人员的简历、业绩和拟用于完成招标项目的机械设备等。

第二十八条　投标人应当在招标文件要求提交投标文件的截止时间前，将投标文件送达投标地点。招标人收到投标文件后，应当签收保存，不得开启。投标人少于三个的，招标人应当依照本法重新招标。在招标文件要求提交投标文件的截止时间后送达的投标文件，招标人应当拒收。

第二十九条　投标人在招标文件要求提交投标文件的截止时间前，可以补充、修改或者撤回已提交的投标文件，并书面通知招标人。补充、修改的内容为投标文件的组成部分。

第三十条　投标人根据招标文件载明的项目实际情况，拟在中标后将中标项目的部分非主体、非关键性工作进行分包的，应当在投标文件中载明。

第三十一条　两个以上法人或者其他组织可以组成一个联合体，以一个投标人的身份共同投标。

联合体各方均应当具备承担招标项目的相应能力；国家有关规定或者招标文件对投标人资格条件有规定的，联合体各方均应当具备规定的相应资格条件。由同一专业的单位组成的联合体，按照资质等级较低的单位确定资质等级。

联合体各方应当签订共同投标协议，明确约定各方拟承担的工作和责任，并将共同投标协议连同投标文件一并提交招标人。联合体中标的，联合体各方应当共同与招标人签订合同，就中标项目向招标人承担连带责任。

招标人不得强制投标人组成联合体共同投标，不得限制投标人之间的竞争。

第三十二条　投标人不得相互串通投标报价，不得排挤其他投标人的公平竞争，损害招标人或者其他投标人的合法权益。

投标人不得与招标人串通投标，损害国家利益、社会公共利益或者他人的合法权益。

禁止投标人以向招标人或者评标委员会成员行贿的手段谋取中标。

第三十三条　投标人不得以低于成本的报价竞标，也不得以他人名义投标或者以其他方式弄虚作假，骗取中标。

第四章 开标、评标和中标

第三十四条　开标应当在招标文件确定的提交投标文件截止时间的同一时间公开进行；开标地点应当为招标文件中预先确定的地点。

第三十五条　开标由招标人主持，邀请所有投标人参加。

第三十六条　开标时，由投标人或者其推选的代表检查投标文件的密封情况，也可以由招标人委托的公证机构检查并公证；经确认无误后，由工作人员当众拆封，宣读投标人名称、投标价格和投标文件的其他主要内容。

招标人在招标文件要求提交投标文件的截止时间前收到的所有投标文件，开标时都应当当众予以拆封、宣读。

开标过程应当记录，并存档备查。

第三十七条　评标由招标人依法组建的评标委员会负责。

依法必须进行招标的项目，其评标委员会由招标人的代表和有关技术、经济等方面的专家组成，成员人数为五人以上单数，其中技术、经济等方面的专家不得少于成员总数的三分之二。

前款专家应当从事相关领域工作满八年并具有高级职称或者具有同等专业水平，由招标人从国务院有关部门或者省、自治区、直辖市人民政府有关部门提供的专家名册或者招标代理机构的专家库内的相关专业的专家名单中确定；一般招标项目可以采取随机抽取方式，特殊招标项目可以由招标人直接确定。

与投标人有利害关系的人不得进入相关项目的评标委员会；已经进入的应当更换。

评标委员会成员的名单在中标结果确定前应当保密。

第三十八条　招标人应当采取必要的措施，保证评标在严格保密的情况下进行。

任何单位和个人不得非法干预、影响评标的过程和结果。

第三十九条　评标委员会可以要求投标人对投标文件中含义不明确的内容作必要的澄清或者说明，但是澄清或者说明不得超出投标文件的范围或者改变投标文件的实质性内容。

第四十条　评标委员会应当按照招标文件确定的评标标准和方法，对投标文件进行评审和比较；设有标底的，应当参考标底。评标委员会完成评标后，应当向招标人提出书面评标报告，并推荐合格的中标候选人。

招标人根据评标委员会提出的书面评标报告和推荐的中标候选人确定中标人。招标人也可以授权评标委员会直接确定中标人。

国务院对特定招标项目的评标有特别规定的，从其规定。

第四十一条　中标人的投标应当符合下列条件之一：

（一）能够最大限度地满足招标文件中规定的各项综合评价标准；

（二）能够满足招标文件的实质性要求，并且经评审的投标价格最低；但是投标价格低于成本的除外。

第四十二条　评标委员会经评审，认为所有投标都不符合招标文件要求的，可以否决所有投标。

依法必须进行招标的项目的所有投标被否决的，招标人应当依照本法重新招标。

第四十三条　在确定中标人前，招标人不得与投标人就投标价格、投标方案等实质性内容进行谈判。

第四十四条　评标委员会成员应当客观、公正地履行职务，遵守职业道德，对所提出的评审意见承担个人责任。

评标委员会成员不得私下接触投标人，不得收受投标人的财物或者其他好处。

评标委员会成员和参与评标的有关工作人员不得透露对投标文件的评审和比较、中标候选人的推荐情况以及与评标有关的其他情况。

第四十五条　中标人确定后，招标人应当向中标人发出中标通知书，并同时将中标结果通知所有未中标的投标人。

中标通知书对招标人和中标人具有法律效力。中标通知书发出后，招标人改变中标结果的，或者中标人放弃中标项目的，应当依法承担法律责任。

第四十六条　招标人和中标人应当自中标通知书发出之日起三十日内，按照招标文件和中标人的投标文件订立书面合同。招标人和中标人不得再行订立背离合同实质性内容的其他协议。

招标文件要求中标人提交履约保证金的，中标人应当提交。

第四十七条　依法必须进行招标的项目，招标人应当自确定中标人之日起十五日内，向有关行政监督部门提交招标投标情况的书面报告。

第四十八条　中标人应当按照合同约定履行义务，完成中标项目。中标人不得向他人转让中标项目，也不得将中标项目肢解后分别向他人转让。

中标人按照合同约定或者经招标人同意，可以将中标项目的部分非主体、非关键性工作分包给他人完成。接受分包的人应当具备相应的资格条件，并不得再次分包。

中标人应当就分包项目向招标人负责，接受分包的人就分包项目承担连带责任。

第五章　法律责任

第四十九条　违反本法规定，必须进行招标的项目而不招标的，将必须进行招标的项目化整为零或者以其他任何方式规避招标的，责令限期改正，可以处项目合同金额千分之五以上千分之十以下的罚款；对全部或者部分使用国有资金的项目，可以暂停项目执行或者暂停资金拨付；对单位直接负责的主管人员和其他直接责任人员依法给予处分。

第五十条　招标代理机构违反本法规定，泄露应当保密的与招标投标活动有关的情况和资料的，或者与招标人、投标人串通损害国家利益、社会公共利益或者他人合法权益的，处五万元以上二十五万元以下的罚款，对单位直接负责的主管人员和其他直接责任人员处单位罚款数额百分之五以上百分之十以下的罚款；有违法所得的，并处没收违法所得；情节严重的，禁止其一年至二年内代理依法必须进行招标的项目并予以公告，直至工商机关吊销营业执照。

前款所列行为影响中标结果的，中标无效。

第五十一条　招标人以不合理的条件限制或者排斥潜在投标人的，对潜在投标人实行歧视待遇的，强制要求投标人组成联合体共同投标的，或者限制投标人之间竞争的，责令改正，可以处一万元以上五万元以下的罚款。

第五十二条　依法必须进行招标的项目的招标人向他人透露已获取招标文件的潜在投标人的名称、数量或者可能影响公平竞争的有关招标投标的其他情况的，或者泄露标底的，给予警告，可以并处一万元以上十万元以下的罚款；对单位直接负责的主管人员和其他直接责任人员依法给予处分；构成犯罪的，依法追究刑事责任。

前款所列行为影响中标结果的，中标无效。

第五十三条　投标人相互串通投标或者与招标人串通投标的，投标人以向招标人或者评标委员会成员行贿的手段谋取中标的，中标无效，处中标项目金额千分之五以上千分之十以下的罚款，对单位直接负责的主管人员和其他直接责任人员处单位罚款数额百分之五以上百分之十以下的罚款；有违法所得的，并处没收违法所得；情节严重的，取消其一年至二年内参加依法必须进行招标的项目的投标资格并予以公告，直至由工商行政管理机关吊销营业执照；构成犯罪的，依法追究刑事责任。给他人造成损失的，依法承担赔偿责任。

第五十四条　投标人以他人名义投标或者以其他方式弄虚作假，骗取中标的，中标无效，给招标人造成损失的，依法承担赔偿责任；构成犯罪的，依法追究刑事责任。

依法必须进行招标的项目的投标人有前款所列行为尚未构成犯罪的，处中标项目金额千分之五以上千分之十以下的罚款，对单位直接负责的主管人员和其他直接责任人员处单位罚款数额百分之五以上百分之十以下的罚款；有违法所得的，并处没收违法所得；情节严重的，取消其一年至三年内参加依法必须进行招标的项目的投标资格并予以公告，直至由工商行政管理机关吊销营业执照。

第五十五条　依法必须进行招标的项目，招标人违反本法规定，与投标人就投标价格、投标方案等实质性内容进行谈判的，给予警告，对单位直接负责的主管人员和其他直接责任人员依法给予处分。

前款所列行为影响中标结果的，中标无效。

第五十六条　评标委员会成员收受投标人的财物或者其他好处的，评标委员会成员或者参加评标的有关工作人员向他人透露对投标文件的评审和比较、中标候选人的推荐以及与评标有关的其他情况的，给予警告，没收收受的财物，可以并处三千元以上五万元以下的罚款，对有所列违法行为的评标委员会成员取消担任评标委员会成员的资格，不得再参加任何依法必须进行招标的项目的评标；构成犯罪的，依法追究刑事责任。

第五十七条　招标人在评标委员会依法推荐的中标候选人以外确定中标人的，依法必须进行招标的项目在所有投标被评标委员会否决后自行确定中标人的，中标无效。责令改正，可以处中标项目金额千分之五以上千分之十以下的罚款；对单位直接负责的主管人员和其他直接责任人员依法给予处分。

第五十八条　中标人将中标项目转让给他人的，将中标项目肢解后分别转让给他人的，违反本法规定将中标项目的部分主体、关键性工作分包给他人的，或者分包人再次分包的，转让、分包无效，处转让、分包项目金额千分之五以上千分之十以下的罚款；有违法所得的，并处没收违法所得；可以责令停业整顿；情节严重的，由工商行政管理机关吊销营业执照。

第五十九条　招标人与中标人不按照招标文件和中标人的投标文件订立合同的，或者招标人、中标人订立背离合同实质性内容的协议的，责令改正；可以处中标项目金额千分之五以上千分之十以下的罚款。

第六十条　中标人不履行与招标人订立的合同的，履约保证金不予退还，给招标人造成的损失超过履约保证金数额的，还应当对超过部分予以赔偿；没有提交履约保证金的，应当对招标人的损失承担赔偿责任。

中标人不按照与招标人订立的合同履行义务，情节严重的，取消其二年至五年内参加依法必须进行招标的项目的投标资格并予以公告，直至由工商行政管理机关吊销营业执照。

因不可抗力不能履行合同的，不适用前两款规定。

第六十一条　本章规定的行政处罚，由国务院规定的有关行政监督部门决定。本法已对实施行政处罚的机关作出规定的除外。

第六十二条　任何单位违反本法规定，限制或者排斥本地区、本系统以外的法人或者其他组织参加投标的，为招标人指定招标代理机构的，强制招标人委托招标代理机构办理招标事宜的，或者以其他方式干涉招标投标活动的，责令改正；对单位直接负责的主管人员和其他直接责任人员依法给予警告、记过、记大过的处分，情节较重的，依法给予降级、撤职、开除的处分。

个人利用职权进行前款违法行为的，依照前款规定追究责任。

第六十三条　对招标投标活动依法负有行政监督职责的国家机关工作人员徇私舞弊、滥用职权或者玩忽职守，构成犯罪的，依法追究刑事责任；不构成犯罪的，依法给予行政处分。

第六十四条　依法必须进行招标的项目违反本法规定,中标无效的,应当依照本法规定的中标条件从其余投标人中重新确定中标人或者依照本法重新进行招标。

第六章　附　则

第六十五条　投标人和其他利害关系人认为招标投标活动不符合本法有关规定的,有权向招标人提出异议或者依法向有关行政监督部门投诉。

第六十六条　涉及国家安全、国家秘密、抢险救灾或者属于利用扶贫资金实行以工代赈、需要使用农民工等特殊情况,不适宜进行招标的项目,按照国家有关规定可以不进行招标。

第六十七条　使用国际组织或者外国政府贷款、援助资金的项目进行招标,贷款方、资金提供方对招标投标的具体条件和程序有不同规定的,可以适用其规定,但违背中华人民共和国的社会公共利益的除外。

第六十八条　本法自2000年1月1日起施行。

【例11-4-1】　根据《中华人民共和国招标投标法》规定,某工程项目委托监理服务的招投标活动,应当遵循的原则是:

A.公开、公平、公正、诚实信用　　B.公开、平等、自愿、公平、诚实信用

C.公正、科学、独立、诚实信用　　D.全面、有效、合理、诚实信用

解　《中华人民共和国招标投标法》第五条规定,招标投标活动应当遵循公开、公平、公正和诚实信用的原则。

答案:A

【例11-4-2】　下列属于《中华人民共和国招标投标法》规定的招标方式是:

A.公开招标和直接招标　　B.公开招标和邀请招标

C.公开招标和协议招标　　D.公开招标和不公开招标

解　《中华人民共和国招标投标法》第十条规定,招标分为公开招标和邀请招标。

答案:B

【例11-4-3】　有关我国招投标的一般规定,下列理解错误的是:

A.采用书面合同　　B.禁止行贿受贿

C.承包商必须有相应资质　　D.可肢解分包

解　《中华人民共和国建筑法》第二十四条规定,提倡对建筑工程实行总承包,禁止将建筑工程肢解发包。

答案:D

【例11-4-4】　下列不属于招标人必须具备的条件是:

A.招标人须有法可依的项目

B.招标人有充足的专业人才

C.招标人有与项目相应的资金来源

D.招标人为法人或其他基本组织

解　《中华人民共和国招标投标法》第八条:招标人是依照本法规定提出招标项目、进行招标的法人或者其他组织。所以选项A、D对。

第九条:招标项目按照国家有关规定需要履行项目审批手续的,应当先履行审批手续,取得批准。招标人应当有进行招标项目的相应资金或者资金来源已经落实,并应当在招标文件中如实载明。所以选项C对。

第十二条:……招标人具有编制招标文件和组织评标能力的,可以自行办理招标事宜。

选项B中“充足人才”和《中华人民共和国招标投标法》的第十二条表述不一致，何为充足？很难界定，所以选项B的表述不合适。

答案：B

【例11-4-5】 有关评标方法的描述，错误的是：

A. 最低投标价法适合没有特殊要求的招标项目

B. 综合评估法可用打分的方法或货币的方法评估各项标准

C. 最低投标价法通常用来恶性削价竞争，反而工程质量更为低落

D. 综合评估法适合没有特殊要求的招标项目

解 《评标委员会和评标方法暂行规定》第三十条：经评审的最低投标价法一般适用于具有通用技术、性能标准或者招标人对其技术、性能没有特殊要求的招标项目。所以选项A对。

第三十五条：根据综合评估法，最大限度地满足招标文件中规定的各项综合评价标准的投标，应当推荐为中标候选人。

衡量投标文件是否最大限度地满足招标文件中规定的各项评价标准，可以采取折算为货币的方法、打分的方法或者其他方法。需量化的因素及其权重应当在招标文件中明确规定。所以选项B也对。

选项D的说法和上述第三十条矛盾。

答案：D

【例11-4-6】 有关招标的叙述，错误的是：

A. 邀请招标，又称优先性招标

B. 邀请招标中，招标人应向三个以上的潜在招标人发出邀请

C. 国家重点项目应公开招标

D. 公开招标适合专业性较强的项目

解 《中华人民共和国招标投标法》第十七条规定，招标人采用邀请招标方式的，应当向三个以上具备承担招标项目的能力、资信良好的特定的法人或者其他组织发出投标邀请书。所以选项B对。

《中华人民共和国招标投标法实施条例》第八条规定，国有资金占控股或者主导地位的依法必须进行招标的项目，应当公开招标；但有下列情形之一的，可以邀请招标：

（一）技术复杂、有特殊要求或者受自然环境限制，只有少量潜在投标人可供选择；

（二）采用公开招标方式的费用占项目合同金额的比例过大。

从上述条文可见：只有在特殊情况下才能邀请招标，一般情况下均应公开招标。所以选项C对。

答案：D

习　题

11-4-1 建设单位工程招标应具备下列哪些条件？（　　）

①有与招标工程相适应的经济技术管理人员 ②必须是一个经济实体，注册资金不少于一百万元人民币 ③有编制招标文件的能力 ④有审查投标单位资质的能力 ⑤具有组织开标、评标、定标的能力

A. ①②③④⑤　　B. ①②③④　　C. ①②④⑤　　D. ①③④⑤

11-4-2 施工招标的形式有以下哪几种？（　　）

①公开招标 ②邀请招标 ③议标 ④指定招标

A. ①②　　B. ①②④　　C. ①④　　D. ①②③

11-4-3　招标委员会的成员中，技术、经济等方面的专家不得少于(　　)。

A. 3人　　B. 5人

C. 成员总数的2/3　　D. 成员总数的1/2

11-4-4　建筑工程的评标活动应当由(　　)负责。

A. 建设单位　　B. 市招标办公室

C. 监理单位　　D. 评标委员会

11-4-5　在中华人民共和国境内进行下列工程建设项目必须要招标的条件，下面哪一条是不准确的说法？(　　)

A. 大型基础设施、公用事业等关系社会公共利益、公众安全的项目

B. 全部或者部分使用国有资金投资或者国家融资的项目

C. 使用国际组织或者外国政府贷款、援助资金的项目

D. 所有住宅项目

11-4-6　招标人和中标人应当自中标通知书发出之日起(　　)之内，按照招标文件和中标人的投标文件订立书面合同。

A. 15天　　B. 30天　　C. 60天　　D. 90天

第五节　中华人民共和国合同法

总　　则

第一章　一般规定

第一条　为了保护合同当事人的合法权益，维护社会经济秩序，促进社会主义现代化建设，制定本法。

第二条　本法所称合同是平等主体的自然人、法人、其他组织之间设立、变更、终止民事权利义务关系的协议。

婚姻、收养、监护等有关身份关系的协议，适用其他法律的规定。

第三条　合同当事人的法律地位平等，一方不得将自己的意志强加给另一方。

第四条　当事人依法享有自愿订立合同的权利，任何单位和个人不得非法干预。

第五条　当事人应当遵循公平原则确定各方的权利和义务。

第六条　当事人行使权利、履行义务应当遵循诚实信用原则。

第七条　当事人订立、履行合同，应当遵守法律、行政法规，尊重社会公德，不得扰乱社会经济秩序，损害社会公共利益。

第八条　依法成立的合同，对当事人具有法律约束力。当事人应当按照约定履行自己的义务，不得擅自变更或者解除合同。

依法成立的合同，受法律保护。

第二章　合同的订立

第九条　当事人订立合同，应当具有相应的民事权利能力和民事行为能力。

当事人依法可以委托代理人订立合同。

第十条　当事人订立合同，有书面形式、口头形式和其他形式。

法律、行政法规规定采用书面形式的，应当采用书面形式。当事人约定采用书面形式的，应当采用书面形式。

第十一条　书面形式是指合同书、信件和数据电文(包括电报、电传、传真、电子数据交换和电子邮件)等可以有形地表现所载内容的形式。

第十二条　合同的内容由当事人约定，一般包括以下条款：

(一)当事人的名称或者姓名和住所；

(二)标的；

(三)数量；

(四)质量；

(五)价款或者报酬；

(六)履行期限、地点和方式；

(七)违约责任；

(八)解决争议的方法。

当事人可以参照各类合同的示范文本订立合同。

第十三条　当事人订立合同，采取要约、承诺方式。

第十四条　要约是希望和他人订立合同的意思表示，该意思表示应当符合下列规定：

(一)内容具体确定；

(二)表明经受要约人承诺，要约人即受该意思表示约束。

第十五条　要约邀请是希望他人向自己发出要约的意思表示。寄送的价目表、拍卖公告、招标公告、招股说明书、商业广告等为要约邀请。

商业广告的内容符合要约规定的，视为要约。

第十六条　要约到达受要约人时生效。

采用数据电文形式订立合同，收件人指定特定系统接收数据电文的，该数据电文进入该特定系统的时间，视为到达时间；未指定特定系统的，该数据电文进入收件人的任何系统的首次时间，视为到达时间。

第十七条　要约可以撤回。撤回要约的通知应当在要约到达受要约人之前或者与要约同时到达受要约人。

第十八条　要约可以撤销。撤销要约的通知应当在受要约人发出承诺通知之前到达受要约人。

第十九条　有下列情形之一的，要约不得撤销：

(一)要约人确定了承诺期限或者以其他形式明示要约不可撤销；

(二)受要约人有理由认为要约是不可撤销的，并已经为履行合同作了准备工作。

第二十条　有下列情形之一的，要约失效：

(一)拒绝要约的通知到达要约人；

(二)要约人依法撤销要约；

(三)承诺期限届满，受要约人未作出承诺；

(四)受要约人对要约的内容作出实质性变更。

第二十一条　承诺是受要约人同意要约的意思表示。

第二十二条　承诺应当以通知的方式作出，但根据交易习惯或者要约表明可以通过行为作出承诺的除外。

第二十三条　承诺应当在要约确定的期限内到达要约人。

要约没有确定承诺期限的，承诺应当依照下列规定到达：

(一)要约以对话方式作出的，应当即时作出承诺，但当事人另有约定的除外；

(二)要约以非对话方式作出的，承诺应当在合理期限内到达。

第二十四条　要约以信件或者电报作出的，承诺期限自信件载明的日期或者电报交发之日开始计算。信件未载明日期的，自投寄该信件的邮戳日期开始计算。要约以电话、传真等快速通讯方式作出的，承诺期限自要约到达受要约人时开始计算。

第二十五条　承诺生效时合同成立。

第二十六条　承诺通知到达要约人时生效。承诺不需要通知的，根据交易习惯或者要约的要求作出承诺的行为时生效。

采用数据电文形式订立合同的，承诺到达的时间适用本法第十六条第二款的规定。

第二十七条　承诺可以撤回。撤回承诺的通知应当在承诺通知到达要约人之前或者与承诺通知同时到达要约人。

第二十八条　受要约人超过承诺期限发出承诺的，除要约人及时通知受要约人该承诺有效的以外，为新要约。

第二十九条　受要约人在承诺期限内发出承诺，按照通常情形能够及时到达要约人，但因其他原因承诺到达要约人时超过承诺期限的，除要约人及时通知受要约人因承诺超过期限不接受该承诺的以外，该承诺有效。

第三十条　承诺的内容应当与要约的内容一致。受要约人对要约的内容作出实质性变更的，为新要约。有关合同标的、数量、质量、价款或者报酬、履行期限、履行地点和方式、违约责任和解决争议方法等的变更，是对要约内容的实质性变更。

第三十一条　承诺对要约的内容作出非实质性变更的，除要约人及时表示反对或者要约表明承诺不得对要约的内容作出任何变更的以外，该承诺有效，合同的内容以承诺的内容为准。

第三十二条　当事人采用合同书形式订立合同的，自双方当事人签字或者盖章时合同成立。

第三十三条　当事人采用信件、数据电文等形式订立合同的，可以在合同成立之前要求签订确认书。签订确认书时合同成立。

第三十四条　承诺生效的地点为合同成立的地点。

采用数据电文形式订立合同的，收件人的主营业地为合同成立的地点；没有主营业地的，其经常居住地为合同成立的地点。当事人另有约定的，按照其约定。

第三十五条　当事人采用合同书形式订立合同的，双方当事人签字或者盖章的地点为合同成立的地点。

第三十六条　法律、行政法规规定或者当事人约定采用书面形式订立合同，当事人未采用书面形式但一方已经履行主要义务，对方接受的，该合同成立。

第三十七条　采用合同书形式订立合同，在签字或者盖章之前，当事人一方已经履行主要义务，对方接受的，该合同成立。

第三十八条　国家根据需要下达指令性任务或者国家订货任务的，有关法人、其他组织之间应当依照有关法律、行政法规规定的权利和义务订立合同。

第三十九条　采用格式条款订立合同的，提供格式条款的一方应当遵循公平原则确定当事人之间的权利和义务，并采取合理的方式提请对方注意免除或者限制其责任的条款，按照对方的要求，对该条款予以说明。

格式条款是当事人为了重复使用而预先拟定，并在订立合同时未与对方协商的条款。

第四十条　格式条款具有本法第五十二条和第五十三条规定情形的，或者提供格式条款一方免除其责任、加重对方责任、排除对方主要权利的，该条款无效。

第四十一条　对格式条款的理解发生争议的，应当按照通常理解予以解释。对格式条款有两种以上解释的，应当作出不利于提供格式条款一方的解释。格式条款和非格式条款不一致的，应当采用非格式条款。

第四十二条　当事人在订立合同过程中有下列情形之一，给对方造成损失的，应当承担损害赔偿责任：

（一）假借订立合同，恶意进行磋商；

（二）故意隐瞒与订立合同有关的重要事实或者提供虚假情况；

（三）有其他违背诚实信用原则的行为。

第四十三条　当事人在订立合同过程中知悉的商业秘密，无论合同是否成立，不得泄露或者不正当地使用。泄露或者不正当地使用该商业秘密给对方造成损失的，应当承担损害赔偿责任。

第三章　合同的效力

第四十四条　依法成立的合同，自成立时生效。

法律、行政法规规定应当办理批准、登记等手续生效的，依照其规定。

第四十五条　当事人对合同的效力可以约定附条件。附生效条件的合同，自条件成就时生效。附解除条件的合同，自条件成就时失效。

当事人为自己的利益不正当地阻止条件成就的，视为条件已成就；不正当地促成条件成就的，视为条件不成就。

第四十六条　当事人对合同的效力可以约定附期限。附生效期限的合同，自期限届至时生效。附终止期限的合同，自期限届满时失效。

第四十七条　限制民事行为能力人订立的合同，经法定代理人追认后，该合同有效，但纯获利益的合同或者与其年龄、智力、精神健康状况相适应而订立的合同，不必经法定代理人追认。

相对人可以催告法定代理人在一个月内予以追认。法定代理人未作表示的，视为拒绝追认。合同被追认之前，善意相对人有撤销的权利。撤销应当以通知的方式作出。

第四十八条　行为人没有代理权、超越代理权或者代理权终止后以被代理人名义订立的合同，未经被代理人追认，对被代理人不发生效力，由行为人承担责任。

相对人可以催告被代理人在一个月内予以追认。被代理人未作表示的，视为拒绝追认。合同被追认之前，善意相对人有撤销的权利。撤销应当以通知的方式作出。

第四十九条　行为人没有代理权、超越代理权或者代理权终止后以被代理人名义订立合同，相对人有理由相信行为人有代理权的，该代理行为有效。

第五十条　法人或者其他组织的法定代表人、负责人超越权限订立的合同，除相对人知道或者应当知道其超越权限的以外，该代表行为有效。

第五十一条　无处分权的人处分他人财产，经权利人追认或者无处分权的人订立合同后取得处分权的，该合同有效。

第五十二条　有下列情形之一的，合同无效：

（一）一方以欺诈、胁迫的手段订立合同，损害国家利益；

（二）恶意串通，损害国家、集体或者第三人利益；

（三）以合法形式掩盖非法目的；

（四）损害社会公共利益；

（五）违反法律、行政法规的强制性规定。

第五十三条　合同中的下列免责条款无效：

（一）造成对方人身伤害的；

（二）因故意或者重大过失造成对方财产损失的。

第五十四条　下列合同，当事人一方有权请求人民法院或者仲裁机构变更或者撤销：

（一）因重大误解订立的；

（二）在订立合同时显失公平的。

一方以欺诈、胁迫的手段或者乘人之危，使对方在违背真实意思的情况下订立的合同，受损害方有权请求人民法院或者仲裁机构变更或者撤销。

当事人请求变更的，人民法院或者仲裁机构不得撤销。

第五十五条　有下列情形之一的，撤销权消灭：

（一）具有撤销权的当事人自知道或者应当知道撤销事由之日起一年内没有行使撤销权；

（二）具有撤销权的当事人知道撤销事由后明确表示或者以自己的行为放弃撤销权。

第五十六条　无效的合同或者被撤销的合同自始没有法律约束力。合同部分无效，不影响其他部分效力的，其他部分仍然有效。

第五十七条　合同无效、被撤销或者终止的，不影响合同中独立存在的有关解决争议方法的条款的效力。

第五十八条　合同无效或者被撤销后，因该合同取得的财产，应当予以返还；不能返还或者没有必要返还的，应当折价补偿。有过错的一方应当赔偿对方因此所受到的损失，双方都有过错的，应当各自承担相应的责任。

第五十九条　当事人恶意串通，损害国家、集体或者第三人利益的，因此取得的财产收归国家所有或者返还集体、第三人。

第四章　合同的履行

第六十条　当事人应当按照约定全面履行自己的义务。

当事人应当遵循诚实信用原则，根据合同的性质、目的和交易习惯履行通知、协助、保密等义务。

第六十一条　合同生效后，当事人就质量、价款或者报酬、履行地点等内容没有约定或者约定不明确的，可以协议补充；不能达成补充协议的，按照合同有关条款或者交易习惯确定。

第六十二条　当事人就有关合同内容约定不明确，依照本法第六十一条的规定仍不能确定的，适用下列规定：

（一）质量要求不明确的，按照国家标准、行业标准履行；没有国家标准、行业标准的，按照通常标准或者符合合同目的的特定标准履行。

（二）价款或者报酬不明确的，按照订立合同时履行地的市场价格履行；依法应当执行政府定价或者政府指导价的，按照规定履行。

（三）履行地点不明确，给付货币的，在接受货币一方所在地履行；交付不动产的，在不动产所在地履行;其他标的,在履行义务一方所在地履行。

(四)履行期限不明确的,债务人可以随时履行,债权人也可以随时要求履行,但应当给对方必要的准备时间。

(五)履行方式不明确的,按照有利于实现合同目的的方式履行。

(六)履行费用的负担不明确的,由履行义务一方负担。

第六十三条 执行政府定价或者政府指导价的,在合同约定的交付期限内政府价格调整时,按照交付时的价格计价。逾期交付标的物的,遇价格上涨时,按照原价格执行;价格下降时,按照新价格执行。逾期提取标的物或者逾期付款的,遇价格上涨时,按照新价格执行;价格下降时,按照原价格执行。

第六十四条 当事人约定由债务人向第三人履行债务的,债务人未向第三人履行债务或者履行债务不符合约定,应当向债权人承担违约责任。

第六十五条 当事人约定由第三人向债权人履行债务的,第三人不履行债务或者履行债务不符合约定,债务人应当向债权人承担违约责任。

第六十六条 当事人互负债务,没有先后履行顺序的,应当同时履行。一方在对方履行之前有权拒绝其履行要求。一方在对方履行债务不符合约定时,有权拒绝其相应的履行要求。

第六十七条 当事人互负债务,有先后履行顺序,先履行一方未履行的,后履行一方有权拒绝其履行要求。先履行一方履行债务不符合约定的,后履行一方有权拒绝其相应的履行要求。

第六十八条 应当先履行债务的当事人,有确切证据证明对方有下列情形之一的,可以中止履行:

(一)经营状况严重恶化;

(二)转移财产、抽逃资金,以逃避债务;

(三)丧失商业信誉;

(四)有丧失或者可能丧失履行债务能力的其他情形。

当事人没有确切证据中止履行的,应当承担违约责任。

第六十九条 当事人依照本法第六十八条的规定中止履行的,应当及时通知对方。对方提供适当担保时,应当恢复履行。中止履行后,对方在合理期限内未恢复履行能力并且未提供适当担保的,中止履行的一方可以解除合同。

第七十条 债权人分立、合并或者变更住所没有通知债务人,致使履行债务发生困难的,债务人可以中止履行或者将标的物提存。

第七十一条 债权人可以拒绝债务人提前履行债务,但提前履行不损害债权人利益的除外。

债务人提前履行债务给债权人增加的费用,由债务人负担。

第七十二条 债权人可以拒绝债务人部分履行债务,但部分履行不损害债权人利益的除外。

债务人部分履行债务给债权人增加的费用,由债务人负担。

第七十三条 因债务人怠于行使其到期债权,对债权人造成损害的,债权人可以向人民法院请求以自己的名义代位行使债务人的债权,但该债权专属于债务人自身的除外。

代位权的行使范围以债权人的债权为限。债权人行使代位权的必要费用,由债务人负担。

第七十四条 因债务人放弃其到期债权或者无偿转让财产,对债权人造成损害的,债权人可以请求人民法院撤销债务人的行为。债务人以明显不合理的低价转让财产，对债权人造成损害，并且受让人知道该情形的，债权人也可以请求人民法院撤销债务人的行为。

撤销权的行使范围以债权人的债权为限。债权人行使撤销权的必要费用，由债务人负担。

第七十五条　撤销权自债权人知道或者应当知道撤销事由之日起一年内行使。自债务人的行为发生之日起五年内没有行使撤销权的，该撤销权消灭。

第七十六条　合同生效后，当事人不得因姓名、名称的变更或者法定代表人、负责人、承办人的变动而不履行合同义务。

第五章　合同的变更和转让

第七十七条　当事人协商一致，可以变更合同。

法律、行政法规规定变更合同应当办理批准、登记等手续的，依照其规定。

第七十八条　当事人对合同变更的内容约定不明确的，推定为未变更。

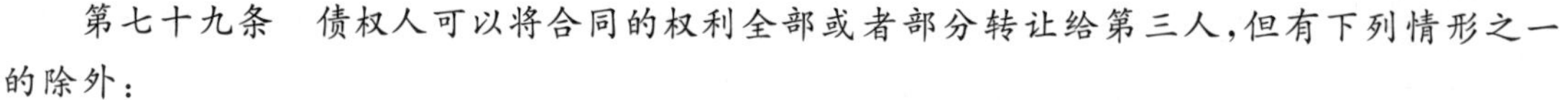

第七十九条　债权人可以将合同的权利全部或者部分转让给第三人，但有下列情形之一的除外：

(一)根据合同性质不得转让；

(二)按照当事人约定不得转让；

(三)依照法律规定不得转让。

第八十条　债权人转让权利的，应当通知债务人。未经通知，该转让对债务人不发生效力。

债权人转让权利的通知不得撤销，但经受让人同意的除外。

第八十一条　债权人转让权利的，受让人取得与债权有关的从权利，但该从权利专属于债权人自身的除外。

第八十二条　债务人接到债权转让通知后，债务人对让与人的抗辩，可以向受让人主张。

第八十三条　债务人接到债权转让通知时，债务人对让与人享有债权，并且债务人的债权先于转让的债权到期或者同时到期的，债务人可以向受让人主张抵销。

第八十四条　债务人将合同的义务全部或者部分转移给第三人的，应当经债权人同意。

第八十五条　债务人转移义务的，新债务人可以主张原债务人对债权人的抗辩。

第八十六条　债务人转移义务的，新债务人应当承担与主债务有关的从债务，但该从债务专属于原债务人自身的除外。

第八十七条　法律、行政法规规定转让权利或者转移义务应当办理批准、登记等手续的，依照其规定。

第八十八条　当事人一方经对方同意，可以将自己在合同中的权利和义务一并转让给第三人。

第八十九条　权利和义务一并转让的，适用本法第七十九条、第八十一条至第八十三条、第八十五条至第八十七条的规定。

第九十条　当事人订立合同后合并的，由合并后的法人或者其他组织行使合同权利，履行合同义务。当事人订立合同后分立的，除债权人和债务人另有约定的以外，由分立的法人或者其他组织对合同的权利和义务享有连带债权，承担连带债务。

第六章　合同的权利义务终止

第九十一条　有下列情形之一的，合同的权利义务终止：

(一)债务已经按照约定履行；

（二）合同解除；

（三）债务相互抵销；

（四）债务人依法将标的物提存；

（五）债权人免除债务；

（六）债权债务同归于一人；

（七）法律规定或者当事人约定终止的其他情形。

第九十二条　合同的权利义务终止后，当事人应当遵循诚实信用原则，根据交易习惯履行通知、协助、保密等义务。

第九十三条　当事人协商一致，可以解除合同。

当事人可以约定一方解除合同的条件。解除合同的条件成就时，解除权人可以解除合同。

第九十四条　有下列情形之一的，当事人可以解除合同：

（一）因不可抗力致使不能实现合同目的；

（二）在履行期限届满之前，当事人一方明确表示或者以自己的行为表明不履行主要债务；

（三）当事人一方迟延履行主要债务，经催告后在合理期限内仍未履行；

（四）当事人一方迟延履行债务或者有其他违约行为致使不能实现合同目的；

（五）法律规定的其他情形。

第九十五条　法律规定或者当事人约定解除权行使期限，期限届满当事人不行使的，该权利消灭。

法律没有规定或者当事人没有约定解除权行使期限，经对方催告后在合理期限内不行使的，该权利消灭。

第九十六条　当事人一方依照本法第九十三条第二款、第九十四条的规定主张解除合同的，应当通知对方。合同自通知到达对方时解除。对方有异议的，可以请求人民法院或者仲裁机构确认解除合同的效力。

法律、行政法规规定解除合同应当办理批准、登记等手续的，依照其规定。

第九十七条　合同解除后，尚未履行的，终止履行；已经履行的，根据履行情况和合同性质，当事人可以要求恢复原状、采取其他补救措施，并有权要求赔偿损失。

第九十八条　合同的权利义务终止，不影响合同中结算和清理条款的效力。

第九十九条　当事人互负到期债务，该债务的标的物种类、品质相同的，任何一方可以将自己的债务与对方的债务抵销，但依照法律规定或者按照合同性质不得抵销的除外。

当事人主张抵销的，应当通知对方。通知自到达对方时生效。抵销不得附条件或者附期限。

第一百条　当事人互负债务，标的物种类、品质不相同的，经双方协商一致，也可以抵销。

第一百零一条　有下列情形之一，难以履行债务的，债务人可以将标的物提存：

（一）债权人无正当理由拒绝受领；

（二）债权人下落不明；

（三）债权人死亡未确定继承人或者丧失民事行为能力未确定监护人；

（四）法律规定的其他情形。

标的物不适于提存或者提存费用过高的，债务人依法可以拍卖或者变卖标的物，提存所得的价款。

第一百零二条　标的物提存后，除债权人下落不明的以外，债务人应当及时通知债权人或者债权人的继承人、监护人。

第一百零三条　标的物提存后，毁损、灭失的风险由债权人承担。提存期间，标的物的孳息归债权人所有。提存费用由债权人负担。

第一百零四条　债权人可以随时领取提存物，但债权人对债务人负有到期债务的，在债权人未履行债务或者提供担保之前，提存部门根据债务人的要求应当拒绝其领取提存物。

债权人领取提存物的权利，自提存之日起五年内不行使而消灭，提存物扣除提存费用后归国家所有。

第一百零五条　债权人免除债务人部分或者全部债务的，合同的权利义务部分或者全部终止。

第一百零六条　债权和债务同归于一人的，合同的权利义务终止，但涉及第三人利益的除外。

第七章　违约责任

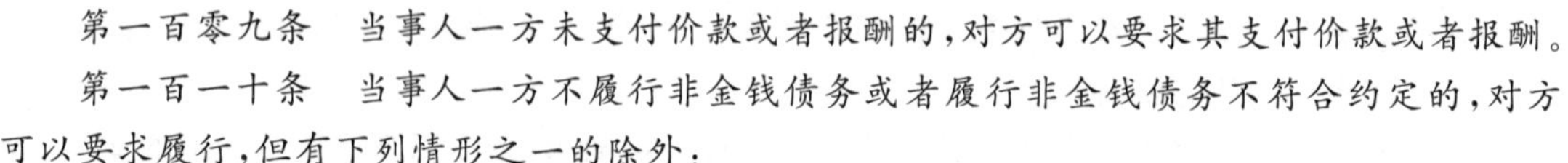

第一百零七条　当事人一方不履行合同义务或者履行合同义务不符合约定的，应当承担继续履行、采取补救措施或者赔偿损失等违约责任。

第一百零八条　当事人一方明确表示或者以自己的行为表明不履行合同义务的，对方可以在履行期限届满之前要求其承担违约责任。

第一百零九条　当事人一方未支付价款或者报酬的，对方可以要求其支付价款或者报酬。

第一百一十条　当事人一方不履行非金钱债务或者履行非金钱债务不符合约定的，对方可以要求履行，但有下列情形之一的除外：

（一）法律上或者事实上不能履行；

（二）债务的标的不适于强制履行或者履行费用过高；

（三）债权人在合理期限内未要求履行。

第一百一十一条　质量不符合约定的，应当按照当事人的约定承担违约责任。对违约责任没有约定或者约定不明确，依照本法第六十一条的规定仍不能确定的，受损害方根据标的的性质以及损失的大小，可以合理选择要求对方承担修理、更换、重作、退货、减少价款或者报酬等违约责任。

第一百一十二条　当事人一方不履行合同义务或者履行合同义务不符合约定的，在履行义务或者采取补救措施后，对方还有其他损失的，应当赔偿损失。

第一百一十三条　当事人一方不履行合同义务或者履行合同义务不符合约定，给对方造成损失的，损失赔偿额应当相当于因违约所造成的损失，包括合同履行后可以获得的利益，但不得超过违反合同一方订立合同时预见到或者应当预见到的因违反合同可能造成的损失。

经营者对消费者提供商品或者服务有欺诈行为的，依照《中华人民共和国消费者权益保护法》的规定承担损害赔偿责任。

第一百一十四条　当事人可以约定一方违约时应当根据违约情况向对方支付一定数额的违约金，也可以约定因违约产生的损失赔偿额的计算方法。

约定的违约金低于造成的损失的，当事人可以请求人民法院或者仲裁机构予以增加；约定的违约金过分高于造成的损失的，当事人可以请求人民法院或者仲裁机构予以适当减少。

当事人就迟延履行约定违约金的，违约方支付违约金后，还应当履行债务。

第一百一十五条　当事人可以依照《中华人民共和国担保法》约定一方向对方给付定金作为债权的担保。债务人履行债务后，定金应当抵作价款或者收回。给付定金的一方不履行约定的债务的，无权要求返还定金；收受定金的一方不履行约定的债务的，应当双倍返还定金。

第一百一十六条　当事人既约定违约金，又约定定金的，一方违约时，对方可以选择适用违约金或者定金条款。

第一百一十七条　因不可抗力不能履行合同的，根据不可抗力的影响，部分或者全部免除责任，但法律另有规定的除外。当事人迟延履行后发生不可抗力的，不能免除责任。

本法所称不可抗力，是指不能预见、不能避免并不能克服的客观情况。

第一百一十八条　当事人一方因不可抗力不能履行合同的，应当及时通知对方，以减轻可能给对方造成的损失，并应当在合理期限内提供证明。

第一百一十九条　当事人一方违约后，对方应当采取适当措施防止损失的扩大；没有采取适当措施致使损失扩大的，不得就扩大的损失要求赔偿。

当事人因防止损失扩大而支出的合理费用，由违约方承担。

第一百二十条　当事人双方都违反合同的，应当各自承担相应的责任。

第一百二十一条　当事人一方因第三人的原因造成违约的，应当向对方承担违约责任。当事人一方和第三人之间的纠纷，依照法律规定或者按照约定解决。

第一百二十二条　因当事人一方的违约行为，侵害对方人身、财产权益的，受损害方有权选择依照本法要求其承担违约责任或者依照其他法律要求其承担侵权责任。

第八章　其他规定

第一百二十三条　其他法律对合同另有规定的，依照其规定。

第一百二十四条　本法分则或者其他法律没有明文规定的合同，适用木法总则的规定，并可以参照本法分则或者其他法律最相类似的规定。

第一百二十五条　当事人对合同条款的理解有争议的，应当按照合同所使用的词句、合同的有关条款、合同的目的、交易习惯以及诚实信用原则，确定该条款的真实意思。

合同文本采用两种以上文字订立并约定具有同等效力的，对各文本使用的词句推定具有相同含义。各文本使用的词句不一致的，应当根据合同的目的予以解释。

第一百二十六条　涉外合同的当事人可以选择处理合同争议所适用的法律，但法律另有规定的除外。涉外合同的当事人没有选择的，适用与合同有最密切联系的国家的法律。

在中华人民共和国境内履行的中外合资经营企业合同、中外合作经营企业合同、中外合作勘探开发自然资源合同，适用中华人民共和国法律。

第一百二十七条　工商行政管理部门和其他有关行政主管部门在各自的职权范围内，依照法律、行政法规的规定，对利用合同危害国家利益、社会公共利益的违法行为，负责监督处理；构成犯罪的，依法追究刑事责任。

第一百二十八条　当事人可以通过和解或者调解解决合同争议。

当事人不愿和解、调解或者和解、调解不成的，可以根据仲裁协议向仲裁机构申请仲裁。涉外合同的当事人可以根据仲裁协议向中国仲裁机构或者其他仲裁机构申请仲裁。当事人没有订立仲裁协议或者仲裁协议无效的，可以向人民法院起诉。当事人应当履行发生法律效力的判决、仲裁裁决、调解书；拒不履行的，对方可以请求人民法院执行。

第一百二十九条　因国际货物买卖合同和技术进出口合同争议提起诉讼或者申请仲裁的期限为四年，自当事人知道或者应当知道其权利受到侵害之日起计算。因其他合同争议提起诉讼或者申请仲裁的期限，依照有关法律的规定。

分　则

第九章　买卖合同

第一百三十条　买卖合同是出卖人转移标的物的所有权于买受人，买受人支付价款的合同。

第一百三十一条　买卖合同的内容除依照本法第十二条的规定以外，还可以包括包装方式、检验标准和方法、结算方式、合同使用的文字及其效力等条款。

第一百三十二条　出卖的标的物，应当属于出卖人所有或者出卖人有权处分。

法律、行政法规禁止或者限制转让的标的物，依照其规定。

第一百三十三条　标的物的所有权自标的物交付时起转移，但法律另有规定或者当事人另有约定的除外。

第一百三十四条　当事人可以在买卖合同中约定买受人未履行支付价款或者其他义务的，标的物的所有权属于出卖人。

第一百三十五条　出卖人应当履行向买受人交付标的物或者交付提取标的物的单证，并转移标的物所有权的义务。

第一百三十六条　出卖人应当按照约定或者交易习惯向买受人交付提取标的物单证以外的有关单证和资料。

第一百三十七条　出卖具有知识产权的计算机软件等标的物的，除法律另有规定或者当事人另有约定的以外，该标的物的知识产权不属于买受人。

第一百三十八条　出卖人应当按照约定的期限交付标的物。约定交付期间的，出卖人可以在该交付期间内的任何时间交付。

第一百三十九条　当事人没有约定标的物的交付期限或者约定不明确的，适用本法第六十一条、第六十二条第四项的规定。

第一百四十条　标的物在订立合同之前已为买受人占有的，合同生效的时间为交付时间。

第一百四十一条　出卖人应当按照约定的地点交付标的物。

当事人没有约定交付地点或者约定不明确，依照本法第六十一条的规定仍不能确定的，适用下列规定：

（一）标的物需要运输的，出卖人应当将标的物交付给第一承运人以运交给买受人；

（二）标的物不需要运输，出卖人和买受人订立合同时知道标的物在某一地点的，出卖人应当在该地点交付标的物；不知道标的物在某一地点的，应当在出卖人订立合同时的营业地交付标的物。

第一百四十二条　标的物毁损、灭失的风险，在标的物交付之前由出卖人承担，交付之后由买受人承担，但法律另有规定或者当事人另有约定的除外。

第一百四十三条　因买受人的原因致使标的物不能按照约定的期限交付的，买受人应当自违反约定之日起承担标的物毁损、灭失的风险。

第一百四十四条　出卖人出卖交由承运人运输的在途标的物，除当事人另有约定的以外，毁损、灭失的风险自合同成立时起由买受人承担。

第一百四十五条　当事人没有约定交付地点或者约定不明确，依照本法第一百四十一条第二款第一项的规定标的物需要运输的，出卖人将标的物交付给第一承运人后，标的物毁损、灭失的风险由买受人承担。

第一百四十六条　出卖人按照约定或者依照本法第一百四十一条第二款第二项的规定将标的物置于交付地点，买受人违反约定没有收取的，标的物毁损、灭失的风险自违反约定之日起由买受人承担。

第一百四十七条　出卖人按照约定未交付有关标的物的单证和资料的，不影响标的物毁损、灭失风险的转移。

第一百四十八条　因标的物质量不符合质量要求，致使不能实现合同目的的，买受人可以拒绝接受标的物或者解除合同。买受人拒绝接受标的物或者解除合同的，标的物毁损、灭失的风险由出卖人承担。

第一百四十九条　标的物毁损、灭失的风险由买受人承担的，不影响因出卖人履行债务不符合约定，买受人要求其承担违约责任的权利。

第一百五十条　出卖人就交付的标的物，负有保证第三人不得向买受人主张任何权利的义务，但法律另有规定的除外。

第一百五十一条　买受人订立合同时知道或者应当知道第三人对买卖的标的物享有权利的，出卖人不承担本法第一百五十条规定的义务。

第一百五十二条　买受人有确切证据证明第三人可能就标的物主张权利的，可以中止支付相应的价款，但出卖人提供适当担保的除外。

第一百五十三条　出卖人应当按照约定的质量要求交付标的物。出卖人提供有关标的物质量说明的，交付的标的物应当符合该说明的质量要求。

第一百五十四条　当事人对标的物的质量要求没有约定或者约定不明确，依照本法第六十一条的规定仍不能确定的，适用本法第六十二条第一项的规定。

第一百五十五条　出卖人交付的标的物不符合质量要求的，买受人可以依照本法第一百一十一条的规定要求承担违约责任。

第一百五十六条　出卖人应当按照约定的包装方式交付标的物。对包装方式没有约定或者约定不明确，依照本法第六十一条的规定仍不能确定的，应当按照通用的方式包装，没有通用方式的，应当采取足以保护标的物的包装方式。

第一百五十七条　买受人收到标的物时应当在约定的检验期间内检验。没有约定检验期间的，应当及时检验。

第一百五十八条　当事人约定检验期间的，买受人应当在检验期间内将标的物的数量或者质量不符合约定的情形通知出卖人。买受人怠于通知的，视为标的物的数量或者质量符合约定。

当事人没有约定检验期间的，买受人应当在发现或者应当发现标的物的数量或者质量不符合约定的合理期间内通知出卖人。买受人在合理期间内未通知或者自标的物收到之日起两年内未通知出卖人的，视为标的物的数量或者质量符合约定，但对标的物有质量保证期的，适用质量保证期，不适用该两年的规定。

出卖人知道或者应当知道提供的标的物不符合约定的，买受人不受前两款规定的通知时间的限制。

第一百五十九条　买受人应当按照约定的数额支付价款。对价款没有约定或者约定不明确的，适用本法第六十一条、第六十二条第二项的规定。

第一百六十条　买受人应当按照约定的地点支付价款。对支付地点没有约定或者约定不明确，依照本法第六十一条的规定仍不能确定的，买受人应当在出卖人的营业地支付，但约定支付价款以交付标的物或者交付提取标的物单证为条件的，在交付标的物或者交付提取标的物单证的所在地支付。

第一百六十一条　买受人应当按照约定的时间支付价款。对支付时间没有约定或者约定不明确，依照本法第六十一条的规定仍不能确定的，买受人应当在收到标的物或者提取标的物单证的同时支付。

第一百六十二条　出卖人多交标的物的，买受人可以接收或者拒绝接收多交的部分。买受人接收多交部分的，按照合同的价格支付价款；买受人拒绝接收多交部分的，应当及时通知出卖人。

第一百六十三条　标的物在交付之前产生的孳息，归出卖人所有，交付之后产生的孳息，归买受人所有。

第一百六十四条　因标的物的主物不符合约定而解除合同的，解除合同的效力及于从物。因标的物的从物不符合约定被解除的，解除的效力不及于主物。

第一百六十五条　标的物为数物，其中一物不符合约定的，买受人可以就该物解除，但该物与他物分离使标的物的价值显受损害的，当事人可以就数物解除合同。

第一百六十六条　出卖人分批交付标的物的，出卖人对其中一批标的物不交付或者交付不符合约定，致使该批标的物不能实现合同目的的，买受人可以就该批标的物解除。

出卖人不交付其中一批标的物或者交付不符合约定，致使今后其他各批标的物的交付不能实现合同目的的，买受人可以就该批以及今后其他各批标的物解除。

买受人如果就其中一批标的物解除，该批标的物与其他各批标的物相互依存的，可以就已经交付和未交付的各批标的物解除。

第一百六十七条　分期付款的买受人未支付到期价款的金额达到全部价款的五分之一的，出卖人可以要求买受人支付全部价款或者解除合同。

出卖人解除合同的，可以向买受人要求支付该标的物的使用费。

第一百六十八条　凭样品买卖的当事人应当封存样品，并可以对样品质量予以说明。出卖人交付的标的物应当与样品及其说明的质量相同。

第一百六十九条　凭样品买卖的买受人不知道样品有隐蔽瑕疵的，即使交付的标的物与样品相同，出卖人交付的标的物的质量仍然应当符合同种物的通常标准。

第一百七十条　试用买卖的当事人可以约定标的物的试用期间。对试用期间没有约定或者约定不明确，依照本法第六十一条的规定仍不能确定的，由出卖人确定。

第一百七十一条　试用买卖的买受人在试用期内可以购买标的物，也可以拒绝购买。试用期间届满，买受人对是否购买标的物未作表示的，视为购买。

第一百七十二条　招标投标买卖的当事人的权利和义务以及招标投标程序等，依照有关法律、行政法规的规定。

第一百七十三条　拍卖的当事人的权利和义务以及拍卖程序等，依照有关法律、行政法规的规定。

第一百七十四条　法律对其他有偿合同有规定的，依照其规定；没有规定的，参照买卖合同的有关规定。

第一百七十五条　当事人约定易货交易，转移标的物的所有权的，参照买卖合同的有关规定。

第十章　供用电、水、气、热力合同

第一百七十六条　供用电合同是供电人向用电人供电，用电人支付电费的合同。

第一百七十七条　供用电合同的内容包括供电的方式、质量、时间，用电容量、地址、性质，计量方式，电价、电费的结算方式，供用电设施的维护责任等条款。

第一百七十八条　供用电合同的履行地点，按照当事人约定；当事人没有约定或者约定不明确的，供电设施的产权分界处为履行地点。

第一百七十九条　供电人应当按照国家规定的供电质量标准和约定安全供电。供电人未按照国家规定的供电质量标准和约定安全供电，造成用电人损失的，应当承担损害赔偿责任。

第一百八十条　供电人因供电设施计划检修、临时检修、依法限电或者用电人违法用电等原因，需要中断供电时，应当按照国家有关规定事先通知用电人。未事先通知用电人中断供电，造成用电人损失的，应当承担损害赔偿责任。

第一百八十一条　因自然灾害等原因断电，供电人应当按照国家有关规定及时抢修。未及时抢修，造成用电人损失的，应当承担损害赔偿责任。

第一百八十二条　用电人应当按照国家有关规定和当事人的约定及时交付电费。用电人逾期不交付电费的，应当按照约定支付违约金。经催告用电人在合理期限内仍不交付电费和违约金的，供电人可以按照国家规定的程序中止供电。

第一百八十三条　用电人应当按照国家有关规定和当事人的约定安全用电。用电人未按照国家有关规定和当事人的约定安全用电，造成供电人损失的，应当承担损害赔偿责任。

第一百八十四条　供用水、供用气、供用热力合同，参照供用电合同的有关规定。

第十一章　赠与合同

第一百八十五条　赠与合同是赠与人将自己的财产无偿给予受赠人，受赠人表示接受赠与的合同。

第一百八十六条　赠与人在赠与财产的权利转移之前可以撤销赠与。

具有救灾、扶贫等社会公益、道德义务性质的赠与合同或者经过公证的赠与合同，不适用前款规定。

第一百八十七条　赠与的财产依法需要办理登记等手续的，应当办理有关手续。

第一百八十八条　具有救灾、扶贫等社会公益、道德义务性质的赠与合同或者经过公证的赠与合同，赠与人不交付赠与的财产的，受赠人可以要求交付。

第一百八十九条　因赠与人故意或者重大过失致使赠与的财产毁损、灭失的，赠与人应当承担损害赔偿责任。

第一百九十条　赠与可以附义务。

赠与附义务的，受赠人应当按照约定履行义务。

第一百九十一条　赠与的财产有瑕疵的，赠与人不承担责任。附义务的赠与，赠与的财产有瑕疵的，赠与人在附义务的限度内承担与出卖人相同的责任。

赠与人故意不告知瑕疵或者保证无瑕疵，造成受赠人损失的，应当承担损害赔偿责任。

第一百九十二条　受赠人有下列情形之一的，赠与人可以撤销赠与：

（一）严重侵害赠与人或者赠与人的近亲属；

（二）对赠与人有扶养义务而不履行；

（三）不履行赠与合同约定的义务。

赠与人的撤销权，自知道或者应当知道撤销原因之日起一年内行使。

第一百九十三条　因受赠人的违法行为致使赠与人死亡或者丧失民事行为能力的，赠与人的继承人或者法定代理人可以撤销赠与。

赠与人的继承人或者法定代理人的撤销权，自知道或者应当知道撤销原因之日起六个月内行使。

第一百九十四条　撤销权人撤销赠与的，可以向受赠人要求返还赠与的财产。

第一百九十五条 赠与人的经济状况显著恶化,严重影响其生产经营或者家庭生活的,可以不再履行赠与义务。

第十二章 借款合同

第一百九十六条 借款合同是借款人向贷款人借款,到期返还借款并支付利息的合同。

第一百九十七条 借款合同采用书面形式,但自然人之间借款另有约定的除外。

借款合同的内容包括借款种类、币种、用途、数额、利率、期限和还款方式等条款。

第一百九十八条 订立借款合同,贷款人可以要求借款人提供担保。担保依照《中华人民共和国担保法》的规定。

第一百九十九条 订立借款合同,借款人应当按照贷款人的要求提供与借款有关的业务活动和财务状况的真实情况。

第二百条 借款的利息不得预先在本金中扣除。利息预先在本金中扣除的,应当按照实际借款数额返还借款并计算利息。

第二百零一条 贷款人未按照约定的日期、数额提供借款,造成借款人损失的,应当赔偿损失。

借款人未按照约定的日期、数额收取借款的,应当按照约定的日期、数额支付利息。

第二百零二条 贷款人按照约定可以检查、监督借款的使用情况。借款人应当按照约定向贷款人定期提供有关财务会计报表等资料。

第二百零三条 借款人未按照约定的借款用途使用借款的,贷款人可以停止发放借款、提前收回借款或者解除合同。

第二百零四条 办理贷款业务的金融机构贷款的利率,应当按照中国人民银行规定的贷款利率的上下限确定。

第二百零五条 借款人应当按照约定的期限支付利息。对支付利息的期限没有约定或者约定不明确,依照本法第六十一条的规定仍不能确定,借款期间不满一年的,应当在返还借款时一并支付;借款期间一年以上的,应当在每届满一年时支付,剩余期间不满一年的,应当在返还借款时一并支付。

第二百零六条 借款人应当按照约定的期限返还借款。对借款期限没有约定或者约定不明确,依照本法第六十一条的规定仍不能确定的,借款人可以随时返还;贷款人可以催告借款人在合理期限内返还。

第二百零七条 借款人未按照约定的期限返还借款的,应当按照约定或者国家有关规定支付逾期利息。

第二百零八条 借款人提前偿还借款的,除当事人另有约定的以外,应当按照实际借款的期间计算利息。

第二百零九条 借款人可以在还款期限届满之前向贷款人申请展期。贷款人同意的,可以展期。

第二百一十条 自然人之间的借款合同,自贷款人提供借款时生效。

第二百一十一条 自然人之间的借款合同对支付利息没有约定或者约定不明确的,视为不支付利息。

自然人之间的借款合同约定支付利息的,借款的利率不得违反国家有关限制借款利率的规定。

第十三章　租赁合同

第二百一十二条　租赁合同是出租人将租赁物交付承租人使用、收益，承租人支付租金的合同。

第二百一十三条　租赁合同的内容包括租赁物的名称、数量、用途、租赁期限、租金及其支付期限和方式、租赁物维修等条款。

第二百一十四条　租赁期限不得超过二十年。超过二十年的，超过部分无效。

租赁期间届满，当事人可以续订租赁合同，但约定的租赁期限自续订之日起不得超过二十年。

第二百一十五条　租赁期限六个月以上的，应当采用书面形式。当事人未采用书面形式的，视为不定期租赁。

第二百一十六条　出租人应当按照约定将租赁物交付承租人，并在租赁期间保持租赁物符合约定的用途。

第二百一十七条　承租人应当按照约定的方法使用租赁物。对租赁物的使用方法没有约定或者约定不明确，依照本法第六十一条的规定仍不能确定的，应当按照租赁物的性质使用。

第二百一十八条　承租人按照约定的方法或者租赁物的性质使用租赁物，致使租赁物受到损耗的，不承担损害赔偿责任。

第二百一十九条　承租人未按照约定的方法或者租赁物的性质使用租赁物，致使租赁物受到损失的，出租人可以解除合同并要求赔偿损失。

第二百二十条　出租人应当履行租赁物的维修义务，但当事人另有约定的除外。

第二百二十一条　承租人在租赁物需要维修时可以要求出租人在合理期限内维修。出租人未履行维修义务的，承租人可以自行维修，维修费用由出租人负担。因维修租赁物影响承租人使用的，应当相应减少租金或者延长租期。

第二百二十二条　承租人应当妥善保管租赁物，因保管不善造成租赁物毁损、灭失的，应当承担损害赔偿责任。

第二百二十三条　承租人经出租人同意，可以对租赁物进行改善或者增设他物。

承租人未经出租人同意，对租赁物进行改善或者增设他物的，出租人可以要求承租人恢复原状或者赔偿损失。

第二百二十四条　承租人经出租人同意，可以将租赁物转租给第三人。承租人转租的，承租人与出租人之间的租赁合同继续有效，第三人对租赁物造成损失的，承租人应当赔偿损失。

承租人未经出租人同意转租的，出租人可以解除合同。

第二百二十五条　在租赁期间因占有、使用租赁物获得的收益，归承租人所有，但当事人另有约定的除外。

第二百二十六条　承租人应当按照约定的期限支付租金。对支付期限没有约定或者约定不明确，依照本法第六十一条的规定仍不能确定，租赁期间不满一年的，应当在租赁期间届满时支付；租赁期间一年以上的，应当在每届满一年时支付，剩余期间不满一年的，应当在租赁期间届满时支付。

第二百二十七条　承租人无正当理由未支付或者迟延支付租金的，出租人可以要求承租人在合理期限内支付。承租人逾期不支付的，出租人可以解除合同。

第二百二十八条　因第三人主张权利，致使承租人不能对租赁物使用、收益的，承租人可以要求减少租金或者不支付租金。

第三人主张权利的，承租人应当及时通知出租人。

第二百二十九条　租赁物在租赁期间发生所有权变动的，不影响租赁合同的效力。

第二百三十条　出租人出卖租赁房屋的，应当在出卖之前的合理期限内通知承租人，承租人享有以同等条件优先购买的权利。

第二百三十一条　因不可归责于承租人的事由，致使租赁物部分或者全部毁损、灭失的，承租人可以要求减少租金或者不支付租金；因租赁物部分或者全部毁损、灭失，致使不能实现合同目的的，承租人可以解除合同。

第二百三十二条　当事人对租赁期限没有约定或者约定不明确，依照本法第六十一条的规定仍不能确定的，视为不定期租赁。当事人可以随时解除合同，但出租人解除合同应当在合理期限之前通知承租人。

第二百三十三条　租赁物危及承租人的安全或者健康的，即使承租人订立合同时明知该租赁物质量不合格，承租人仍然可以随时解除合同。

第二百三十四条　承租人在房屋租赁期间死亡的，与其生前共同居住的人可以按照原租赁合同租赁该房屋。

第二百三十五条　租赁期间届满，承租人应当返还租赁物。返还的租赁物应当符合按照约定或者租赁物的性质使用后的状态。

第二百三十六条　租赁期间届满，承租人继续使用租赁物，出租人没有提出异议的，原租赁合同继续有效，但租赁期限为不定期。

第十四章　融资租赁合同

第二百三十七条　融资租赁合同是出租人根据承租人对出卖人、租赁物的选择，向出卖人购买租赁物，提供给承租人使用，承租人支付租金的合同。

第二百三十八条　融资租赁合同的内容包括租赁物名称、数量、规格、技术性能、检验方法、租赁期限、租金构成及其支付期限和方式、币种、租赁期间届满租赁物的归属等条款。

融资租赁合同应当采用书面形式。

第二百三十九条　出租人根据承租人对出卖人、租赁物的选择订立的买卖合同，出卖人应当按照约定向承租人交付标的物，承租人享有与受领标的物有关的买受人的权利。

第二百四十条　出租人、出卖人、承租人可以约定，出卖人不履行买卖合同义务的，由承租人行使索赔的权利。承租人行使索赔权利的，出租人应当协助。

第二百四十一条　出租人根据承租人对出卖人、租赁物的选择订立的买卖合同，未经承租人同意，出租人不得变更与承租人有关的合同内容。

第二百四十二条　出租人享有租赁物的所有权。承租人破产的，租赁物不属于破产财产。

第二百四十三条　融资租赁合同的租金，除当事人另有约定的以外，应当根据购买租赁物的大部分或者全部成本以及出租人的合理利润确定。

第二百四十四条　租赁物不符合约定或者不符合使用目的的，出租人不承担责任，但承租人依赖出租人的技能确定租赁物或者出租人干预选择租赁物的除外。

第二百四十五条　出租人应当保证承租人对租赁物的占有和使用。

第二百四十六条　承租人占有租赁物期间，租赁物造成第三人的人身伤害或者财产损害的，出租人不承担责任。

第二百四十七条　承租人应当妥善保管、使用租赁物。

承租人应当履行占有租赁物期间的维修义务。

第二百四十八条　承租人应当按照约定支付租金。承租人经催告后在合理期限内仍不支付租金的，出租人可以要求支付全部租金；也可以解除合同，收回租赁物。

第二百四十九条　当事人约定租赁期间届满租赁物归承租人所有，承租人已经支付大部分租金，但无力支付剩余租金，出租人因此解除合同收回租赁物的，收回的租赁物的价值超过承租人欠付的租金以及其他费用的，承租人可以要求部分返还。

第二百五十条　出租人和承租人可以约定租赁期间届满租赁物的归属。对租赁物的归属没有约定或者约定不明确，依照本法第六十一条的规定仍不能确定的，租赁物的所有权归出租人。

第十五章　承揽合同

第二百五十一条　承揽合同是承揽人按照定作人的要求完成工作，交付工作成果，定作人给付报酬的合同。

承揽包括加工、定作、修理、复制、测试、检验等工作。

第二百五十二条　承揽合同的内容包括承揽的标的、数量、质量、报酬、承揽方式、材料的提供、履行期限、验收标准和方法等条款。

第二百五十三条　承揽人应当以自己的设备、技术和劳力，完成主要工作，但当事人另有约定的除外。

承揽人将其承揽的主要工作交由第三人完成的，应当就该第三人完成的工作成果向定作人负责；未经定作人同意的，定作人也可以解除合同。

第二百五十四条　承揽人可以将其承揽的辅助工作交由第三人完成。承揽人将其承揽的辅助工作交由第三人完成的，应当就该第三人完成的工作成果向定作人负责。

第二百五十五条　承揽人提供材料的，承揽人应当按照约定选用材料，并接受定作人检验。

第二百五十六条　定作人提供材料的，定作人应当按照约定提供材料。承揽人对定作人提供的材料，应当及时检验，发现不符合约定时，应当及时通知定作人更换、补齐或者采取其他补救措施。

承揽人不得擅自更换定作人提供的材料，不得更换不需要修理的零部件。

第二百五十七条　承揽人发现定作人提供的图纸或者技术要求不合理的，应当及时通知定作人。因定作人怠于答复等原因造成承揽人损失的，应当赔偿损失。

第二百五十八条　定作人中途变更承揽工作的要求，造成承揽人损失的，应当赔偿损失。

第二百五十九条　承揽工作需要定作人协助的，定作人有协助的义务。定作人不履行协助义务致使承揽工作不能完成的，承揽人可以催告定作人在合理期限内履行义务，并可以顺延履行期限；定作人逾期不履行的，承揽人可以解除合同。

第二百六十条　承揽人在工作期间，应当接受定作人必要的监督检验。定作人不得因监督检验妨碍承揽人的正常工作。

第二百六十一条　承揽人完成工作的，应当向定作人交付工作成果，并提交必要的技术资料和有关质量证明。定作人应当验收该工作成果。

第二百六十二条　承揽人交付的工作成果不符合质量要求的，定作人可以要求承揽人承担修理、重作、减少报酬、赔偿损失等违约责任。

第二百六十三条　定作人应当按照约定的期限支付报酬。对支付报酬的期限没有约定或者约定不明确，依照本法第六十一条的规定仍不能确定的，定作人应当在承揽人交付工作成果时支付;工作成果部分交付的,定作人应当相应支付。

第二百六十四条 定作人未向承揽人支付报酬或者材料费等价款的,承揽人对完成的工作成果享有留置权,但当事人另有约定的除外。

第二百六十五条 承揽人应当妥善保管定作人提供的材料以及完成的工作成果,因保管不善造成毁损、灭失的,应当承担损害赔偿责任。

第二百六十六条 承揽人应当按照定作人的要求保守秘密,未经定作人许可,不得留存复制品或者技术资料。

第二百六十七条 共同承揽人对定作人承担连带责任,但当事人另有约定的除外。

第二百六十八条 定作人可以随时解除承揽合同,造成承揽人损失的,应当赔偿损失。

第十六章 建设工程合同

第二百六十九条 建设工程合同是承包人进行工程建设,发包人支付价款的合同。

建设工程合同包括工程勘察、设计、施工合同。

第二百七十条 建设工程合同应当采用书面形式。

第二百七十一条 建设工程的招标投标活动,应当依照有关法律的规定公开、公平、公正进行。

第二百七十二条 发包人可以与总承包人订立建设工程合同,也可以分别与勘察人、设计人、施工人订立勘察、设计、施工承包合同。发包人不得将应当由一个承包人完成的建设工程肢解成若干部分发包给几个承包人。

总承包人或者勘察、设计、施工承包人经发包人同意,可以将自己承包的部分工作交由第三人完成。第三人就其完成的工作成果与总承包人或者勘察、设计、施工承包人向发包人承担连带责任。承包人不得将其承包的全部建设工程转包给第三人或者将其承包的全部建设工程肢解以后以分包的名义分别转包给第三人。

禁止承包人将工程分包给不具备相应资质条件的单位。禁止分包单位将其承包的工程再分包。建设工程主体结构的施工必须由承包人自行完成。

第二百七十三条 国家重大建设工程合同,应当按照国家规定的程序和国家批准的投资计划、可行性研究报告等文件订立。

第二百七十四条 勘察、设计合同的内容包括提交有关基础资料和文件(包括概预算)的期限、质量要求、费用以及其他协作条件等条款。

第二百七十五条 施工合同的内容包括工程范围、建设工期、中间交工工程的开工和竣工时间、工程质量、工程造价、技术资料交付时间、材料和设备供应责任、拨款和结算、竣工验收、质量保修范围和质量保证期、双方相互协作等条款。

第二百七十六条 建设工程实行监理的,发包人应当与监理人采用书面形式订立委托监理合同。发包人与监理人的权利和义务以及法律责任,应当依照本法委托合同以及其他有关法律、行政法规的规定。

第二百七十七条 发包人在不妨碍承包人正常作业的情况下,可以随时对作业进度、质量进行检查。

第二百七十八条 隐蔽工程在隐蔽以前,承包人应当通知发包人检查。发包人没有及时检查的,承包人可以顺延工程日期,并有权要求赔偿停工、窝工等损失。

第二百七十九条 建设工程竣工后,发包人应当根据施工图纸及说明书、国家颁发的施工验收规范和质量检验标准及时进行验收。验收合格的,发包人应当按照约定支付价款,并接收该建设工程。建设工程竣工经验收合格后，方可交付使用；未经验收或者验收不合格的，不得交付使用。

第二百八十条　勘察、设计的质量不符合要求或者未按照期限提交勘察、设计文件拖延工期，造成发包人损失的，勘察人、设计人应当继续完善勘察、设计，减收或者免收勘察、设计费并赔偿损失。

第二百八十一条　因施工人的原因致使建设工程质量不符合约定的，发包人有权要求施工人在合理期限内无偿修理或者返工、改建。经过修理或者返工、改建后，造成逾期交付的，施工人应当承担违约责任。

第二百八十二条　因承包人的原因致使建设工程在合理使用期限内造成人身和财产损害的，承包人应当承担损害赔偿责任。

第二百八十三条　发包人未按照约定的时间和要求提供原材料、设备、场地、资金、技术资料的，承包人可以顺延工程日期，并有权要求赔偿停工、窝工等损失。

第二百八十四条　因发包人的原因致使工程中途停建、缓建的，发包人应当采取措施弥补或者减少损失，赔偿承包人因此造成的停工、窝工、倒运、机械设备调迁、材料和构件积压等损失和实际费用。

第二百八十五条　因发包人变更计划，提供的资料不准确，或者未按照期限提供必需的勘察、设计工作条件而造成勘察、设计的返工、停工或者修改设计，发包人应当按照勘察人、设计人实际消耗的工作量增付费用。

第二百八十六条　发包人未按照约定支付价款的，承包人可以催告发包人在合理期限内支付价款。发包人逾期不支付的，除按照建设工程的性质不宜折价、拍卖的以外，承包人可以与发包人协议将该工程折价，也可以申请人民法院将该工程依法拍卖。建设工程的价款就该工程折价或者拍卖的价款优先受偿。

第二百八十七条　本章没有规定的，适用承揽合同的有关规定。

第十七章　运输合同

第一节　一般规定

第二百八十八条　运输合同是承运人将旅客或者货物从起运地点运输到约定地点，旅客、托运人或者收货人支付票款或者运输费用的合同。

第二百八十九条　从事公共运输的承运人不得拒绝旅客、托运人通常、合理的运输要求。

第二百九十条　承运人应当在约定期间或者合理期间内将旅客、货物安全运输到约定地点。

第二百九十一条　承运人应当按照约定的或者通常的运输路线将旅客、货物运输到约定地点。

第二百九十二条　旅客、托运人或者收货人应当支付票款或者运输费用。承运人未按照约定路线或者通常路线运输增加票款或者运输费用的，旅客、托运人或者收货人可以拒绝支付增加部分的票款或者运输费用。

第二节　客运合同

第二百九十三条　客运合同自承运人向旅客交付客票时成立，但当事人另有约定或者另有交易习惯的除外。

第二百九十四条　旅客应当持有效客票乘运。旅客无票乘运、超程乘运、越级乘运或者持失效客票乘运的，应当补交票款，承运人可以按照规定加收票款。旅客不交付票款的，承运人可以拒绝运输。

第二百九十五条　旅客因自己的原因不能按照客票记载的时间乘坐的，应当在约定的时间内办理退票或者变更手续。逾期办理的，承运人可以不退票款，并不再承担运输义务。

第二百九十六条　旅客在运输中应当按照约定的限量携带行李。超过限量携带行李的，应当办理托运手续。

第二百九十七条　旅客不得随身携带或者在行李中夹带易燃、易爆、有毒、有腐蚀性、有放射性以及有可能危及运输工具上人身和财产安全的危险物品或者其他违禁物品。

旅客违反前款规定的，承运人可以将违禁物品卸下、销毁或者送交有关部门。旅客坚持携带或者夹带违禁物品的，承运人应当拒绝运输。

第二百九十八条　承运人应当向旅客及时告知有关不能正常运输的重要事由和安全运输应当注意的事项。

第二百九十九条　承运人应当按照客票载明的时间和班次运输旅客。承运人迟延运输的，应当根据旅客的要求安排改乘其他班次或者退票。

第三百条　承运人擅自变更运输工具而降低服务标准的，应当根据旅客的要求退票或者减收票款；提高服务标准的，不应当加收票款。

第三百零一条　承运人在运输过程中，应当尽力救助患有急病、分娩、遇险的旅客。

第三百零二条　承运人应当对运输过程中旅客的伤亡承担损害赔偿责任，但伤亡是旅客自身健康原因造成的或者承运人证明伤亡是旅客故意、重大过失造成的除外。

前款规定适用于按照规定免票、持优待票或者经承运人许可搭乘的无票旅客。

第三百零三条　在运输过程中旅客自带物品毁损、灭失，承运人有过错的，应当承担损害赔偿责任。

旅客托运的行李毁损、灭失的，适用货物运输的有关规定。

第三节　货运合同

第三百零四条　托运人办理货物运输，应当向承运人准确表明收货人的名称或者姓名或者凭指示的收货人，货物的名称、性质、重量、数量，收货地点等有关货物运输的必要情况。

因托运人申报不实或者遗漏重要情况，造成承运人损失的，托运人应当承担损害赔偿责任。

第三百零五条　货物运输需要办理审批、检验等手续的，托运人应当将办理完有关手续的文件提交承运人。

第三百零六条　托运人应当按照约定的方式包装货物。对包装方式没有约定或者约定不明确的，适用本法第一百五十六条的规定。

托运人违反前款规定的，承运人可以拒绝运输。

第三百零七条　托运人托运易燃、易爆、有毒、有腐蚀性、有放射性等危险物品的，应当按照国家有关危险物品运输的规定对危险物品妥善包装，作出危险物标志和标签，并将有关危险物品的名称、性质和防范措施的书面材料提交承运人。

托运人违反前款规定的，承运人可以拒绝运输，也可以采取相应措施以避免损失的发生，因此产生的费用由托运人承担。

第三百零八条　在承运人将货物交付收货人之前，托运人可以要求承运人中止运输、返还货物、变更到达地或者将货物交给其他收货人，但应当赔偿承运人因此受到的损失。

第三百零九条　货物运输到达后，承运人知道收货人的，应当及时通知收货人，收货人应当及时提货。收货人逾期提货的，应当向承运人支付保管费等费用。

第三百一十条　收货人提货时应当按照约定的期限检验货物。对检验货物的期限没有约定或者约定不明确，依照本法第六十一条的规定仍不能确定的，应当在合理期限内检验货物。收货人在约定的期限或者合理期限内对货物的数量、毁损等未提出异议的，视为承运人已经按照运输单证的记载交付的初步证据。

第三百一十一条　承运人对运输过程中货物的毁损、灭失承担损害赔偿责任，但承运人证明货物的毁损、灭失是因不可抗力、货物本身的自然性质或者合理损耗以及托运人、收货人的过错造成的，不承担损害赔偿责任。

第三百一十二条　货物的毁损、灭失的赔偿额，当事人有约定的，按照其约定；没有约定或者约定不明确，依照本法第六十一条的规定仍不能确定的，按照交付或者应当交付时货物到达地的市场价格计算。法律、行政法规对赔偿额的计算方法和赔偿限额另有规定的，依照其规定。

第三百一十三条　两个以上承运人以同一运输方式联运的，与托运人订立合同的承运人应当对全程运输承担责任。损失发生在某一运输区段的，与托运人订立合同的承运人和该区段的承运人承担连带责任。

第三百一十四条　货物在运输过程中因不可抗力灭失，未收取运费的，承运人不得要求支付运费；已收取运费的，托运人可以要求返还。

第三百一十五条　托运人或者收货人不支付运费、保管费以及其他运输费用的，承运人对相应的运输货物享有留置权，但当事人另有约定的除外。

第三百一十六条　收货人不明或者收货人无正当理由拒绝受领货物的，依照本法第一百零一条的规定，承运人可以提存货物。

第四节　多式联运合同

第三百一十七条　多式联运经营人负责履行或者组织履行多式联运合同，对全程运输享有承运人的权利，承担承运人的义务。

第三百一十八条　多式联运经营人可以与参加多式联运的各区段承运人就多式联运合同的各区段运输约定相互之间的责任，但该约定不影响多式联运经营人对全程运输承担的义务。

第三百一十九条　多式联运经营人收到托运人交付的货物时，应当签发多式联运单据。按照托运人的要求，多式联运单据可以是可转让单据，也可以是不可转让单据。

第三百二十条　因托运人托运货物时的过错造成多式联运经营人损失的，即使托运人已经转让多式联运单据，托运人仍然应当承担损害赔偿责任。

第三百二十一条　货物的毁损、灭失发生于多式联运的某一运输区段的，多式联运经营人的赔偿责任和责任限额，适用调整该区段运输方式的有关法律规定。货物毁损、灭失发生的运输区段不能确定的，依照本章规定承担损害赔偿责任。

第十八章　技术合同

第一节　一般规定

第三百二十二条　技术合同是当事人就技术开发、转让、咨询或者服务订立的确立相互之间权利和义务的合同。

第三百二十三条　订立技术合同，应当有利于科学技术的进步，加速科学技术成果的转化、应用和推广。

第三百二十四条　技术合同的内容由当事人约定，一般包括以下条款：

(一)项目名称;

(二)标的的内容、范围和要求;

(三)履行的计划、进度、期限、地点、地域和方式;

(四)技术情报和资料的保密;

(五)风险责任的承担;

(六)技术成果的归属和收益的分成办法;

(七)验收标准和方法;

(八)价款、报酬或者使用费及其支付方式;

(九)违约金或者损失赔偿的计算方法;

(十)解决争议的方法;

(十一)名词和术语的解释。

与履行合同有关的技术背景资料、可行性论证和技术评价报告、项目任务书和计划书、技术标准、技术规范、原始设计和工艺文件,以及其他技术文档,按照当事人的约定可以作为合同的组成部分。

技术合同涉及专利的,应当注明发明创造的名称、专利申请人和专利权人、申请日期、申请号、专利号以及专利权的有效期限。

第三百二十五条　技术合同价款、报酬或者使用费的支付方式由当事人约定,可以采取一次总算、一次总付或者一次总算、分期支付,也可以采取提成支付或者提成支付附加预付入门费的方式。

约定提成支付的,可以按照产品价格、实施专利和使用技术秘密后新增的产值、利润或者产品销售额的一定比例提成,也可以按照约定的其他方式计算。提成支付的比例可以采取固定比例、逐年递增比例或者逐年递减比例。

约定提成支付的,当事人应当在合同中约定查阅有关会计帐目的办法。

第三百二十六条　职务技术成果的使用权、转让权属于法人或者其他组织的,法人或者其他组织可以就该项职务技术成果订立技术合同。法人或者其他组织应当从使用和转让该项职务技术成果所取得的收益中提取一定比例,对完成该项职务技术成果的个人给予奖励或者报酬。法人或者其他组织订立技术合同转让职务技术成果时,职务技术成果的完成人享有以同等条件优先受让的权利。

职务技术成果是执行法人或者其他组织的工作任务,或者主要是利用法人或者其他组织的物质技术条件所完成的技术成果。

第三百二十七条　非职务技术成果的使用权、转让权属于完成技术成果的个人,完成技术成果的个人可以就该项非职务技术成果订立技术合同。

第三百二十八条　完成技术成果的个人有在有关技术成果文件上写明自己是技术成果完成者的权利和取得荣誉证书、奖励的权利。

第三百二十九条　非法垄断技术、妨碍技术进步或者侵害他人技术成果的技术合同无效。

第二节　技术开发合同

第三百三十条　技术开发合同是指当事人之间就新技术、新产品、新工艺或者新材料及其系统的研究开发所订立的合同。

技术开发合同包括委托开发合同和合作开发合同。

技术开发合同应当采用书面形式。

当事人之间就具有产业应用价值的科技成果实施转化订立的合同，参照技术开发合同的规定。

第三百三十一条　委托开发合同的委托人应当按照约定支付研究开发经费和报酬；提供技术资料、原始数据；完成协作事项；接受研究开发成果。

第三百三十二条　委托开发合同的研究开发人应当按照约定制定和实施研究开发计划；合理使用研究开发经费；按期完成研究开发工作，交付研究开发成果，提供有关的技术资料和必要的技术指导，帮助委托人掌握研究开发成果。

第三百三十三条　委托人违反约定造成研究开发工作停滞、延误或者失败的，应当承担违约责任。

第三百三十四条　研究开发人违反约定造成研究开发工作停滞、延误或者失败的，应当承担违约责任。

第三百三十五条　合作开发合同的当事人应当按照约定进行投资，包括以技术进行投资；分工参与研究开发工作；协作配合研究开发工作。

第三百三十六条　合作开发合同的当事人违反约定造成研究开发工作停滞、延误或者失败的，应当承担违约责任。

第三百三十七条　因作为技术开发合同标的的技术已经由他人公开，致使技术开发合同的履行没有意义的，当事人可以解除合同。

第三百三十八条　在技术开发合同履行过程中，因出现无法克服的技术困难，致使研究开发失败或者部分失败的，该风险责任由当事人约定。没有约定或者约定不明确，依照本法第六十一条的规定仍不能确定的，风险责任由当事人合理分担。

当事人一方发现前款规定的可能致使研究开发失败或者部分失败的情形时，应当及时通知另一方并采取适当措施减少损失。没有及时通知并采取适当措施，致使损失扩大的，应当就扩大的损失承担责任。

第三百三十九条　委托开发完成的发明创造，除当事人另有约定的以外，申请专利的权利属于研究开发人。研究开发人取得专利权的，委托人可以免费实施该专利。

研究开发人转让专利申请权的，委托人享有以同等条件优先受让的权利。

第三百四十条　合作开发完成的发明创造，除当事人另有约定的以外，申请专利的权利属于合作开发的当事人共有。当事人一方转让其共有的专利申请权的，其他各方享有以同等条件优先受让的权利。

合作开发的当事人一方声明放弃其共有的专利申请权的，可以由另一方单独申请或者由其他各方共同申请。申请人取得专利权的，放弃专利申请权的一方可以免费实施该专利。

合作开发的当事人一方不同意申请专利的，另一方或者其他各方不得申请专利。

第三百四十一条　委托开发或者合作开发完成的技术秘密成果的使用权、转让权以及利益的分配办法，由当事人约定。没有约定或者约定不明确，依照本法第六十一条的规定仍不能确定的，当事人均有使用和转让的权利，但委托开发的研究开发人不得在向委托人交付研究开发成果之前，将研究开发成果转让给第三人。

第三节　技术转让合同

第三百四十二条　技术转让合同包括专利权转让、专利申请权转让、技术秘密转让、专利实施许可合同。

技术转让合同应当采用书面形式。

第三百四十三条　技术转让合同可以约定让与人和受让人实施专利或者使用技术秘密的范围，但不得限制技术竞争和技术发展。

第三百四十四条　专利实施许可合同只在该专利权的存续期间内有效。专利权有效期限届满或者专利权被宣布无效的，专利权人不得就该专利与他人订立专利实施许可合同。

第三百四十五条　专利实施许可合同的让与人应当按照约定许可受让人实施专利，交付实施专利有关的技术资料，提供必要的技术指导。

第三百四十六条　专利实施许可合同的受让人应当按照约定实施专利，不得许可约定以外的第三人实施该专利；并按照约定支付使用费。

第三百四十七条　技术秘密转让合同的让与人应当按照约定提供技术资料，进行技术指导，保证技术的实用性、可靠性，承担保密义务。

第三百四十八条　技术秘密转让合同的受让人应当按照约定使用技术，支付使用费，承担保密义务。

第三百四十九条　技术转让合同的让与人应当保证自己是所提供的技术的合法拥有者，并保证所提供的技术完整、无误、有效，能够达到约定的目标。

第三百五十条　技术转让合同的受让人应当按照约定的范围和期限，对让与人提供的技术中尚未公开的秘密部分，承担保密义务。

第三百五十一条　让与人未按照约定转让技术的，应当返还部分或者全部使用费，并应当承担违约责任；实施专利或者使用技术秘密超越约定的范围的，违反约定擅自许可第三人实施该项专利或者使用该项技术秘密的，应当停止违约行为，承担违约责任；违反约定的保密义务的，应当承担违约责任。

第三百五十二条　受让人未按照约定支付使用费的，应当补交使用费并按照约定支付违约金；不补交使用费或者支付违约金的，应当停止实施专利或者使用技术秘密，交还技术资料，承担违约责任；实施专利或者使用技术秘密超越约定的范围的，未经让与人同意擅自许可第三人实施该专利或者使用该技术秘密的，应当停止违约行为，承担违约责任；违反约定的保密义务的，应当承担违约责任。

第三百五十三条　受让人按照约定实施专利、使用技术秘密侵害他人合法权益的，由让与人承担责任，但当事人另有约定的除外。

第三百五十四条　当事人可以按照互利的原则，在技术转让合同中约定实施专利、使用技术秘密后续改进的技术成果的分享办法。没有约定或者约定不明确，依照本法第六十一条的规定仍不能确定的，一方后续改进的技术成果，其他各方无权分享。

第三百五十五条　法律、行政法规对技术进出口合同或者专利、专利申请合同另有规定的，依照其规定。

第四节　技术咨询合同和技术服务合同

第三百五十六条　技术咨询合同包括就特定技术项目提供可行性论证、技术预测、专题技术调查、分析评价报告等合同。

技术服务合同是指当事人一方以技术知识为另一方解决特定技术问题所订立的合同，不包括建设工程合同和承揽合同。

第三百五十七条　技术咨询合同的委托人应当按照约定阐明咨询的问题，提供技术背景材料及有关技术资料、数据；接受受托人的工作成果，支付报酬。

第三百五十八条　技术咨询合同的受托人应当按照约定的期限完成咨询报告或者解答问

题;提出的咨询报告应当达到约定的要求。

第三百五十九条　技术咨询合同的委托人未按照约定提供必要的资料和数据,影响工作进度和质量,不接受或者逾期接受工作成果的,支付的报酬不得追回,未支付的报酬应当支付。

技术咨询合同的受托人未按期提出咨询报告或者提出的咨询报告不符合约定的,应当承担减收或者免收报酬等违约责任。

技术咨询合同的委托人按照受托人符合约定要求的咨询报告和意见作出决策所造成的损失,由委托人承担,但当事人另有约定的除外。

第三百六十条　技术服务合同的委托人应当按照约定提供工作条件,完成配合事项;接受工作成果并支付报酬。

第三百六十一条　技术服务合同的受托人应当按照约定完成服务项目,解决技术问题,保证工作质量,并传授解决技术问题的知识。

第三百六十二条　技术服务合同的委托人不履行合同义务或者履行合同义务不符合约定,影响工作进度和质量,不接受或者逾期接受工作成果的,支付的报酬不得追回,未支付的报酬应当支付。

技术服务合同的受托人未按照合同约定完成服务工作的,应当承担免收报酬等违约责任。

第三百六十三条　在技术咨询合同、技术服务合同履行过程中,受托人利用委托人提供的技术资料和工作条件完成的新的技术成果,属于受托人。委托人利用受托人的工作成果完成的新的技术成果,属于委托人。当事人另有约定的,按照其约定。

第三百六十四条　法律、行政法规对技术中介合同、技术培训合同另有规定的,依照其规定。

第十九章　保管合同

第三百六十五条　保管合同是保管人保管寄存人交付的保管物,并返还该物的合同。

第三百六十六条　寄存人应当按照约定向保管人支付保管费。

当事人对保管费没有约定或者约定不明确,依照本法第六十一条的规定仍不能确定的,保管是无偿的。

第三百六十七条　保管合同自保管物交付时成立,但当事人另有约定的除外。

第三百六十八条　寄存人向保管人交付保管物的,保管人应当给付保管凭证,但另有交易习惯的除外。

第三百六十九条　保管人应当妥善保管保管物。

当事人可以约定保管场所或者方法。除紧急情况或者为了维护寄存人利益的以外,不得擅自改变保管场所或者方法。

第三百七十条　寄存人交付的保管物有瑕疵或者按照保管物的性质需要采取特殊保管措施的,寄存人应当将有关情况告知保管人。寄存人未告知,致使保管物受损失的,保管人不承担损害赔偿责任;保管人因此受损失的,除保管人知道或者应当知道并且未采取补救措施的以外,寄存人应当承担损害赔偿责任。

第三百七十一条　保管人不得将保管物转交第三人保管,但当事人另有约定的除外。

保管人违反前款规定,将保管物转交第三人保管,对保管物造成损失的,应当承担损害赔偿责任。

第三百七十二条　保管人不得使用或者许可第三人使用保管物,但当事人另有约定的除外。

第三百七十三条　第三人对保管物主张权利的，除依法对保管物采取保全或者执行的以外，保管人应当履行向寄存人返还保管物的义务。

第三人对保管人提起诉讼或者对保管物申请扣押的，保管人应当及时通知寄存人。

第三百七十四条　保管期间，因保管人保管不善造成保管物毁损、灭失的，保管人应当承担损害赔偿责任，但保管是无偿的，保管人证明自己没有重大过失的，不承担损害赔偿责任。

第三百七十五条　寄存人寄存货币、有价证券或者其他贵重物品的，应当向保管人声明，由保管人验收或者封存。寄存人未声明的，该物品毁损、灭失后，保管人可以按照一般物品予以赔偿。

第三百七十六条　寄存人可以随时领取保管物。

当事人对保管期间没有约定或者约定不明确的，保管人可以随时要求寄存人领取保管物；约定保管期间的，保管人无特别事由，不得要求寄存人提前领取保管物。

第三百七十七条　保管期间届满或者寄存人提前领取保管物的，保管人应当将原物及其孳息归还寄存人。

第三百七十八条　保管人保管货币的，可以返还相同种类、数量的货币。保管其他可替代物的，可以按照约定返还相同种类、品质、数量的物品。

第三百七十九条　有偿的保管合同，寄存人应当按照约定的期限向保管人支付保管费。

当事人对支付期限没有约定或者约定不明确，依照本法第六十一条的规定仍不能确定的，应当在领取保管物的同时支付。

第三百八十条　寄存人未按照约定支付保管费以及其他费用的，保管人对保管物享有留置权，但当事人另有约定的除外。

第二十章　仓储合同

第三百八十一条　仓储合同是保管人储存存货人交付的仓储物，存货人支付仓储费的合同。

第三百八十二条　仓储合同自成立时生效。

第三百八十三条　储存易燃、易爆、有毒、有腐蚀性、有放射性等危险物品或者易变质物品，存货人应当说明该物品的性质，提供有关资料。

存货人违反前款规定的，保管人可以拒收仓储物，也可以采取相应措施以避免损失的发生，因此产生的费用由存货人承担。

保管人储存易燃、易爆、有毒、有腐蚀性、有放射性等危险物品的，应当具备相应的保管条件。

第三百八十四条　保管人应当按照约定对入库仓储物进行验收。保管人验收时发现入库仓储物与约定不符合的，应当及时通知存货人。保管人验收后，发生仓储物的品种、数量、质量不符合约定的，保管人应当承担损害赔偿责任。

第三百八十五条　存货人交付仓储物的，保管人应当给付仓单。

第三百八十六条　保管人应当在仓单上签字或者盖章。仓单包括下列事项：

（一）存货人的名称或者姓名和住所；

（二）仓储物的品种、数量、质量、包装、件数和标记；

（三）仓储物的损耗标准；

（四）储存场所；

（五）储存期间；

（六）仓储费；

（七）仓储物已经办理保险的，其保险金额、期间以及保险人的名称；

（八）填发人、填发地和填发日期。

第三百八十七条　仓单是提取仓储物的凭证。存货人或者仓单持有人在仓单上背书并经保管人签字或者盖章的，可以转让提取仓储物的权利。

第三百八十八条　保管人根据存货人或者仓单持有人的要求，应当同意其检查仓储物或者提取样品。

第三百八十九条　保管人对入库仓储物发现有变质或者其他损坏的，应当及时通知存货人或者仓单持有人。

第三百九十条　保管人对入库仓储物发现有变质或者其他损坏，危及其他仓储物的安全和正常保管的，应当催告存货人或者仓单持有人作出必要的处置。因情况紧急，保管人可以作出必要的处置，但事后应当将该情况及时通知存货人或者仓单持有人。

第三百九十一条　当事人对储存期间没有约定或者约定不明确的，存货人或者仓单持有人可以随时提取仓储物，保管人也可以随时要求存货人或者仓单持有人提取仓储物，但应当给予必要的准备时间。

第三百九十二条　储存期间届满，存货人或者仓单持有人应当凭仓单提取仓储物。存货人或者仓单持有人逾期提取的，应当加收仓储费；提前提取的，不减收仓储费。

第三百九十三条　储存期间届满，存货人或者仓单持有人不提取仓储物的，保管人可以催告其在合理期限内提取，逾期不提取的，保管人可以提存仓储物。

第三百九十四条　储存期间，因保管人保管不善造成仓储物毁损、灭失的，保管人应当承担损害赔偿责任。因仓储物的性质、包装不符合约定或者超过有效储存期造成仓储物变质、损坏的，保管人不承担损害赔偿责任。

第三百九十五条　本章没有规定的，适用保管合同的有关规定。

第二十一章　委托合同

第三百九十六条　委托合同是委托人和受托人约定，由受托人处理委托人事务的合同。

第三百九十七条　委托人可以特别委托受托人处理一项或者数项事务，也可以概括委托受托人处理一切事务。

第三百九十八条　委托人应当预付处理委托事务的费用。受托人为处理委托事务垫付的必要费用，委托人应当偿还该费用及其利息。

第三百九十九条　受托人应当按照委托人的指示处理委托事务。需要变更委托人指示的，应当经委托人同意；因情况紧急，难以和委托人取得联系的，受托人应当妥善处理委托事务，但事后应当将该情况及时报告委托人。

第四百条　受托人应当亲自处理委托事务。经委托人同意，受托人可以转委托。转委托经同意的，委托人可以就委托事务直接指示转委托的第三人，受托人仅就第三人的选任及其对第三人的指示承担责任。转委托未经同意的，受托人应当对转委托的第三人的行为承担责任，但在紧急情况下受托人为维护委托人的利益需要转委托的除外。

第四百零一条　受托人应当按照委托人的要求，报告委托事务的处理情况。委托合同终止时，受托人应当报告委托事务的结果。

第四百零二条　受托人以自己的名义，在委托人的授权范围内与第三人订立的合同，第三人在订立合同时知道受托人与委托人之间的代理关系的，该合同直接约束委托人和第三人，但有确切证据证明该合同只约束受托人和第三人的除外。

第四百零三条　受托人以自己的名义与第三人订立合同时，第三人不知道受托人与委托人之间的代理关系的，受托人因第三人的原因对委托人不履行义务，受托人应当向委托人披露第三人，委托人因此可以行使受托人对第三人的权利，但第三人与受托人订立合同时如果知道该委托人就不会订立合同的除外。

受托人因委托人的原因对第三人不履行义务，受托人应当向第三人披露委托人，第三人因此可以选择受托人或者委托人作为相对人主张其权利，但第三人不得变更选定的相对人。

委托人行使受托人对第三人的权利的，第三人可以向委托人主张其对受托人的抗辩。第三人选定委托人作为其相对人的，委托人可以向第三人主张其对受托人的抗辩以及受托人对第三人的抗辩。

第四百零四条　受托人处理委托事务取得的财产，应当转交给委托人。

第四百零五条　受托人完成委托事务的，委托人应当向其支付报酬。因不可归责于受托人的事由，委托合同解除或者委托事务不能完成的，委托人应当向受托人支付相应的报酬。当事人另有约定的，按照其约定。

第四百零六条　有偿的委托合同，因受托人的过错给委托人造成损失的，委托人可以要求赔偿损失。无偿的委托合同，因受托人的故意或者重大过失给委托人造成损失的，委托人可以要求赔偿损失。

受托人超越权限给委托人造成损失的，应当赔偿损失。

第四百零七条　受托人处理委托事务时，因不可归责于自己的事由受到损失的，可以向委托人要求赔偿损失。

第四百零八条　委托人经受托人同意，可以在受托人之外委托第三人处理委托事务。因此给受托人造成损失的，受托人可以向委托人要求赔偿损失。

第四百零九条　两个以上的受托人共同处理委托事务的，对委托人承担连带责任。

第四百一十条　委托人或者受托人可以随时解除委托合同。因解除合同给对方造成损失的，除不可归责于该当事人的事由以外，应当赔偿损失。

第四百一十一条　委托人或者受托人死亡、丧失民事行为能力或者破产的，委托合同终止，但当事人另有约定或者根据委托事务的性质不宜终止的除外。

第四百一十二条　因委托人死亡、丧失民事行为能力或者破产，致使委托合同终止将损害委托人利益的，在委托人的继承人、法定代理人或者清算组织承受委托事务之前，受托人应当继续处理委托事务。

第四百一十三条　因受托人死亡、丧失民事行为能力或者破产，致使委托合同终止的，受托人的继承人、法定代理人或者清算组织应当及时通知委托人。因委托合同终止将损害委托人利益的，在委托人作出善后处理之前，受托人的继承人、法定代理人或者清算组织应当采取必要措施。

第二十二章　行纪合同

第四百一十四条　行纪合同是行纪人以自己的名义为委托人从事贸易活动，委托人支付报酬的合同。

第四百一十五条　行纪人处理委托事务支出的费用，由行纪人负担，但当事人另有约定的除外。

第四百一十六条　行纪人占有委托物的，应当妥善保管委托物。

第四百一十七条　委托物交付给行纪人时有瑕疵或者容易腐烂、变质的，经委托人同意，行纪人可以处分该物；和委托人不能及时取得联系的，行纪人可以合理处分。

第四百一十八条　行纪人低于委托人指定的价格卖出或者高于委托人指定的价格买入的，应当经委托人同意。未经委托人同意，行纪人补偿其差额的，该买卖对委托人发生效力。

行纪人高于委托人指定的价格卖出或者低于委托人指定的价格买入的，可以按照约定增加报酬。没有约定或者约定不明确，依照本法第六十一条的规定仍不能确定的，该利益属于委托人。

委托人对价格有特别指示的，行纪人不得违背该指示卖出或者买入。

第四百一十九条　行纪人卖出或者买入具有市场定价的商品，除委托人有相反的意思表示的以外，行纪人自己可以作为买受人或者出卖人。

行纪人有前款规定情形的，仍然可以要求委托人支付报酬。

第四百二十条　行纪人按照约定买入委托物，委托人应当及时受领。经行纪人催告，委托人无正当理由拒绝受领的，行纪人依照本法第一百零一条的规定可以提存委托物。

委托物不能卖出或者委托人撤回出卖，经行纪人催告，委托人不取回或者不处分该物的，行纪人依照本法第一百零一条的规定可以提存委托物。

第四百二十一条　行纪人与第三人订立合同的，行纪人对该合同直接享有权利、承担义务。

第三人不履行义务致使委托人受到损害的，行纪人应当承担损害赔偿责任，但行纪人与委托人另有约定的除外。

第四百二十二条　行纪人完成或者部分完成委托事务的，委托人应当向其支付相应的报酬。委托人逾期不支付报酬的，行纪人对委托物享有留置权，但当事人另有约定的除外。

第四百二十三条　本章没有规定的，适用委托合同的有关规定。

第二十三章　居间合同

第四百二十四条　居间合同是居间人向委托人报告订立合同的机会或者提供订立合同的媒介服务，委托人支付报酬的合同。

第四百二十五条　居间人应当就有关订立合同的事项向委托人如实报告。

居间人故意隐瞒与订立合同有关的重要事实或者提供虚假情况，损害委托人利益的，不得要求支付报酬并应当承担损害赔偿责任。

第四百二十六条　居间人促成合同成立的，委托人应当按照约定支付报酬。对居间人的报酬没有约定或者约定不明确，依照本法第六十一条的规定仍不能确定的，根据居间人的劳务合理确定。因居间人提供订立合同的媒介服务而促成合同成立的，由该合同的当事人平均负担居间人的报酬。

居间人促成合同成立的，居间活动的费用，由居间人负担。

第四百二十七条　居间人未促成合同成立的，不得要求支付报酬，但可以要求委托人支付从事居间活动支出的必要费用。

附　　则（略）

【例 11-5-1】 根据《中华人民共和国合同法》规定，要约可以撤回和撤销。下列要约，不得撤销的是：

A. 要约到达受要约人　　B. 要约人确定了承诺期限

C. 受要约人未发出承诺通知　　D. 受要约人即将发出承诺通知

解 《中华人民共和国合同法》第十九条规定，有下列情形之一的，要约不得撤销：

（一）要约人确定了承诺期限或者以其他形式明示要约不可撤销。

答案:B

【例 11-5-2】 根据《中华人民共和国合同法》规定,下列行为不属于要约邀请的是:

A. 某建设单位发布招标公告　　B. 某招标单位发出中标通知书

C. 某上市公司发出招标说明书　　D. 某商场寄送的价目表

解 《中华人民共和国合同法》第十五条规定,要约邀请是希望他人向自己发出要约的意思表示。寄送的价目表、拍卖公告、招标公告、招股说明书、商业广告等为要约邀请。商业广告的内容符合要约规定的,视为要约。

答案:B

习　　题

11-5-1　经济合同的无效与否由(　　)确认。

A. 人民政府　　B. 公安机关

C. 人民检察院　　D. 人民法院或仲裁机构

11-5-2　《中华人民共和国合同法》规定,当事人一方可向对方给付定金,给付定金的一方不履行合同的,无权请求返回定金,接受定金的一方不履行合同的应当返还定金的(　　)倍。

A. 2　　B. 5　　C. 8　　D. 10

11-5-3　当事人的(　　)即是要约邀请。

A. 招标公告　　B. 投标书　　C. 投标担保书　D. 中标函

11-5-4　《中华人民共和国合同法》规定,签订合同的当事人应当是下列中的哪几种人?(　　)

①自然人、法人及其他组织　②不包括自然人　③只能是法人　④只能是中国公民

A. ①　　B. ①②③④　　C. ①②③　　D. ②③④

11-5-5　撤销要约时,撤销要约的通知应当在受要约人发出承诺通知前后的什么时间到达受要约人?(　　)

A. 之前　　B. 当日　　C. 后五日　　D. 后十日

11-5-6　有关合同标的数量、质量、价款或者报酬、履行期限、履行地点和方式、违约责任和解决争议方法等的变更,是对要约内容什么性质的变更?(　　)

A. 重要性　　B. 必要性　　C. 实质性　　D. 一般性

11-5-7　签订建筑工程合同如何有效?(　　)

A. 必须同时盖章和签字才有效　　B. 签字或盖章均可有效

C. 只有盖章才有效　　D. 必须签字才有效

11-5-8　两个以上不同资质等级的单位如何联合共同承包工程?(　　)

A. 应当按照资质等级低的单位的业务许可范围承揽工程

B. 按任何一个单位的资质承包均可

C. 应当按照资质等级高的单位的业务许可范围承揽工程

D. 不允许联合承包

第六节　中华人民共和国行政许可法

第一章　总　　则

第一条　为了规范行政许可的设定和实施,保护公民、法人和其他组织的合法权益,维护

公共利益和社会秩序，保障和监督行政机关有效实施行政管理，根据宪法，制定本法。

第二条　本法所称行政许可，是指行政机关根据公民、法人或者其他组织的申请，经依法审查，准予其从事特定活动的行为。

第三条　行政许可的设定和实施，适用本法。

有关行政机关对其他机关或者对其直接管理的事业单位的人事、财务、外事等事项的审批，不适用本法。

第四条　设定和实施行政许可，应当依照法定的权限、范围、条件和程序。

第五条　设定和实施行政许可，应当遵循公开、公平、公正的原则。

有关行政许可的规定应当公布；未经公布的，不得作为实施行政许可的依据。行政许可的实施和结果，除涉及国家秘密、商业秘密或者个人隐私的外，应当公开。

符合法定条件、标准的，申请人有依法取得行政许可的平等权利，行政机关不得歧视。

第六条　实施行政许可，应当遵循便民的原则，提高办事效率，提供优质服务。

第七条　公民、法人或者其他组织对行政机关实施行政许可，享有陈述权、申辩权；有权依法申请行政复议或者提起行政诉讼；其合法权益因行政机关违法实施行政许可受到损害的，有权依法要求赔偿。

第八条　公民、法人或者其他组织依法取得的行政许可受法律保护，行政机关不得擅自改变已经生效的行政许可。

行政许可所依据的法律、法规、规章修改或者废止，或者准予行政许可所依据的客观情况发生重大变化的，为了公共利益的需要，行政机关可以依法变更或者撤回已经生效的行政许可。由此给公民、法人或者其他组织造成财产损失的，行政机关应当依法给予补偿。

第九条　依法取得的行政许可，除法律、法规规定依照法定条件和程序可以转让的外，不得转让。

第十条　县级以上人民政府应当建立健全对行政机关实施行政许可的监督制度，加强对行政机关实施行政许可的监督检查。

行政机关应当对公民、法人或者其他组织从事行政许可事项的活动实施有效监督。

第二章　行政许可的设定

第十一条　设定行政许可，应当遵循经济和社会发展规律，有利于发挥公民、法人或者其他组织的积极性、主动性，维护公共利益和社会秩序，促进经济、社会和生态环境协调发展。

第十二条　下列事项可以设定行政许可：

（一）直接涉及国家安全、公共安全、经济宏观调控、生态环境保护以及直接关系人身健康、生命财产安全等特定活动，需要按照法定条件予以批准的事项；

（二）有限自然资源开发利用、公共资源配置以及直接关系公共利益的特定行业的市场准入等，需要赋予特定权利的事项；

（三）提供公众服务并且直接关系公共利益的职业、行业，需要确定具备特殊信誉、特殊条件或者特殊技能等资格、资质的事项；

（四）直接关系公共安全、人身健康、生命财产安全的重要设备、设施、产品、物品，需要按照技术标准、技术规范，通过检验、检测、检疫等方式进行审定的事项；

（五）企业或者其他组织的设立等，需要确定主体资格的事项；

（六）法律、行政法规规定可以设定行政许可的其他事项。

第十三条　本法第十二条所列事项，通过下列方式能够予以规范的，可以不设行政许可：

（一）公民、法人或者其他组织能够自主决定的；

（二）市场竞争机制能够有效调节的；

（三）行业组织或者中介机构能够自律管理的；

（四）行政机关采用事后监督等其他行政管理方式能够解决的。

第十四条　本法第十二条所列事项，法律可以设定行政许可。尚未制定法律的，行政法规可以设定行政许可。

必要时，国务院可以采用发布决定的方式设定行政许可。实施后，除临时性行政许可事项外，国务院应当及时提请全国人民代表大会及其常务委员会制定法律，或者自行制定行政法规。

第十五条　本法第十二条所列事项，尚未制定法律、行政法规的，地方性法规可以设定行政许可；尚未制定法律、行政法规和地方性法规的，因行政管理的需要，确需立即实施行政许可的，省、自治区、直辖市人民政府规章可以设定临时性的行政许可。临时性的行政许可实施满一年需要继续实施的，应当提请本级人民代表大会及其常务委员会制定地方性法规。

地方性法规和省、自治区、直辖市人民政府规章，不得设定应当由国家统一确定的公民、法人或者其他组织的资格、资质的行政许可；不得设定企业或者其他组织的设立登记及其前置性行政许可。其设定的行政许可，不得限制其他地区的个人或者企业到本地区从事生产经营和提供服务，不得限制其他地区的商品进入本地区市场。

第十六条　行政法规可以在法律设定的行政许可事项范围内，对实施该行政许可作出具体规定。

地方性法规可以在法律、行政法规设定的行政许可事项范围内，对实施该行政许可作出具体规定。

规章可以在上位法设定的行政许可事项范围内，对实施该行政许可作出具体规定。

法规、规章对实施上位法设定的行政许可作出的具体规定，不得增设行政许可；对行政许可条件作出的具体规定，不得增设违反上位法的其他条件。

第十七条　除本法第十四条、第十五条规定的外，其他规范性文件一律不得设定行政许可。

第十八条　设定行政许可，应当规定行政许可的实施机关、条件、程序、期限。

第十九条　起草法律草案、法规草案和省、自治区、直辖市人民政府规章草案，拟设定行政许可的，起草单位应当采取听证会、论证会等形式听取意见，并向制定机关说明设定该行政许可的必要性、对经济和社会可能产生的影响以及听取和采纳意见的情况。

第二十条　行政许可的设定机关应当定期对其设定的行政许可进行评价；对已设定的行政许可，认为通过本法第十三条所列方式能够解决的，应当对设定该行政许可的规定及时予以修改或者废止。

行政许可的实施机关可以对已设定的行政许可的实施情况及存在的必要性适时进行评价，并将意见报告该行政许可的设定机关。

公民、法人或者其他组织可以向行政许可的设定机关和实施机关就行政许可的设定和实施提出意见和建议。

第二十一条　省、自治区、直辖市人民政府对行政法规设定的有关经济事务的行政许可，根据本行政区域经济和社会发展情况，认为通过本法第十三条所列方式能够解决的，报国务院批准后，可以在本行政区域内停止实施该行政许可。

第三章 行政许可的实施机关

第二十二条 行政许可由具有行政许可权的行政机关在其法定职权范围内实施。

第二十三条 法律、法规授权的具有管理公共事务职能的组织,在法定授权范围内,以自己的名义实施行政许可。被授权的组织适用本法有关行政机关的规定。

第二十四条 行政机关在其法定职权范围内,依照法律、法规、规章的规定,可以委托其他行政机关实施行政许可。委托机关应当将受委托行政机关和受委托实施行政许可的内容予以公告。

委托行政机关对受委托行政机关实施行政许可的行为应当负责监督,并对该行为的后果承担法律责任。

受委托行政机关在委托范围内,以委托行政机关名义实施行政许可;不得再委托其他组织或者个人实施行政许可。

第二十五条 经国务院批准,省、自治区、直辖市人民政府根据精简、统一、效能的原则,可以决定一个行政机关行使有关行政机关的行政许可权。

第二十六条 行政许可需要行政机关内设的多个机构办理的,该行政机关应当确定一个机构统一受理行政许可申请,统一送达行政许可决定。

行政许可依法由地方人民政府两个以上部门分别实施的,本级人民政府可以确定一个部门受理行政许可申请并转告有关部门分别提出意见后统一办理,或者组织有关部门联合办理、集中办理。

第二十七条 行政机关实施行政许可,不得向申请人提出购买指定商品、接受有偿服务等不正当要求。

行政机关工作人员办理行政许可,不得索取或者收受申请人的财物,不得谋取其他利益。

第二十八条 对直接关系公共安全、人身健康、生命财产安全的设备、设施、产品、物品的检验、检测、检疫,除法律、行政法规规定由行政机关实施的外,应当逐步由符合法定条件的专业技术组织实施。专业技术组织及其有关人员对所实施的检验、检测、检疫结论承担法律责任。

第四章 行政许可的实施程序

第一节 申请与受理

第二十九条 公民、法人或者其他组织从事特定活动,依法需要取得行政许可的,应当向行政机关提出申请。申请书需要采用格式文本的,行政机关应当向申请人提供行政许可申请书格式文本。申请书格式文本中不得包含与申请行政许可事项没有直接关系的内容。

申请人可以委托代理人提出行政许可申请。但是,依法应当由申请人到行政机关办公场所提出行政许可申请的除外。

行政许可申请可以通过信函、电报、电传、传真、电子数据交换和电子邮件等方式提出。

第三十条 行政机关应当将法律、法规、规章规定的有关行政许可的事项、依据、条件、数量、程序、期限以及需要提交的全部材料的目录和申请书示范文本等在办公场所公示。

申请人要求行政机关对公示内容予以说明、解释的,行政机关应当说明、解释,提供准确、可靠的信息。

第三十一条 申请人申请行政许可,应当如实向行政机关提交有关材料和反映真实情况,并对其申请材料实质内容的真实性负责。行政机关不得要求申请人提交与其申请的行政许可事项无关的技术资料和其他材料。

第三十二条　行政机关对申请人提出的行政许可申请，应当根据下列情况分别作出处理：

（一）申请事项依法不需要取得行政许可的，应当即时告知申请人不受理；

（二）申请事项依法不属于本行政机关职权范围的，应当即时作出不予受理的决定，并告知申请人向有关行政机关申请；

（三）申请材料存在可以当场更正的错误的，应当允许申请人当场更正；

（四）申请材料不齐全或者不符合法定形式的，应当当场或者在五日内一次告知申请人需要补正的全部内容，逾期不告知的，自收到申请材料之日起即为受理；

（五）申请事项属于本行政机关职权范围，申请材料齐全、符合法定形式，或者申请人按照本行政机关的要求提交全部补正申请材料的，应当受理行政许可申请。

行政机关受理或者不予受理行政许可申请，应当出具加盖本行政机关专用印章和注明日期的书面凭证。

第三十三条　行政机关应当建立和完善有关制度，推行电子政务，在行政机关的网站上公布行政许可事项，方便申请人采取数据电文等方式提出行政许可申请；应当与其他行政机关共享有关行政许可信息，提高办事效率。

第二节　审查与决定

第三十四条　行政机关应当对申请人提交的申请材料进行审查。

申请人提交的申请材料齐全、符合法定形式，行政机关能够当场作出决定的，应当当场作出书面的行政许可决定。

根据法定条件和程序，需要对申请材料的实质内容进行核实的，行政机关应当指派两名以上工作人员进行核查。

第三十五条　依法应当先经下级行政机关审查后报上级行政机关决定的行政许可，下级行政机关应当在法定期限内将初步审查意见和全部申请材料直接报送上级行政机关。上级行政机关不得要求申请人重复提供申请材料。

第三十六条　行政机关对行政许可申请进行审查时，发现行政许可事项直接关系他人重大利益的，应当告知该利害关系人。申请人、利害关系人有权进行陈述和申辩。行政机关应当听取申请人、利害关系人的意见。

第三十七条　行政机关对行政许可申请进行审查后，除当场作出行政许可决定的外，应当在法定期限内按照规定程序作出行政许可决定。

第三十八条　申请人的申请符合法定条件、标准的，行政机关应当依法作出准予行政许可的书面决定。

行政机关依法作出不予行政许可的书面决定的，应当说明理由，并告知申请人享有依法申请行政复议或者提起行政诉讼的权利。

第三十九条　行政机关作出准予行政许可的决定，需要颁发行政许可证件的，应当向申请人颁发加盖本行政机关印章的下列行政许可证件：

（一）许可证、执照或者其他许可证书；

（二）资格证、资质证或者其他合格证书；

（三）行政机关的批准文件或者证明文件；

（四）法律、法规规定的其他行政许可证件。

行政机关实施检验、检测、检疫的，可以在检验、检测、检疫合格的设备、设施、产品、物品上加贴标签或者加盖检验、检测、检疫印章。

第四十条　行政机关作出的准予行政许可决定，应当予以公开，公众有权查阅。

第四十一条　法律、行政法规设定的行政许可，其适用范围没有地域限制的，申请人取得的行政许可在全国范围内有效。

第三节　期　　限

第四十二条　除可以当场作出行政许可决定的外，行政机关应当自受理行政许可申请之日起二十日内作出行政许可决定。二十日内不能作出决定的，经本行政机关负责人批准，可以延长十日，并应当将延长期限的理由告知申请人。但是，法律、法规另有规定的，依照其规定。

依照本法第二十六条的规定，行政许可采取统一办理或者联合办理、集中办理的，办理的时间不得超过四十五日；四十五日内不能办结的，经本级人民政府负责人批准，可以延长十五日，并应当将延长期限的理由告知申请人。

第四十三条　依法应当先经下级行政机关审查后报上级行政机关决定的行政许可，下级行政机关应当自其受理行政许可申请之日起二十日内审查完毕。但是，法律、法规另有规定的，依照其规定。

第四十四条　行政机关作出准予行政许可的决定，应当自作出决定之日起十日内向申请人颁发、送达行政许可证件，或者加贴标签、加盖检验、检测、检疫印章。

第四十五条　行政机关作出行政许可决定，依法需要听证、招标、拍卖、检验、检测、检疫、鉴定和专家评审的，所需时间不计算在本节规定的期限内。行政机关应当将所需时间书面告知申请人。

第四节　听　　证

第四十六条　法律、法规、规章规定实施行政许可应当听证的事项，或者行政机关认为需要听证的其他涉及公共利益的重大行政许可事项，行政机关应当向社会公告，并举行听证。

第四十七条　行政许可直接涉及申请人与他人之间重大利益关系的，行政机关在作出行政许可决定前，应当告知申请人、利害关系人享有要求听证的权利；申请人、利害关系人在被告知听证权利之日起五日内提出听证申请的，行政机关应当在二十日内组织听证。

申请人、利害关系人不承担行政机关组织听证的费用。

第四十八条　听证按照下列程序进行：

（一）行政机关应当于举行听证的七日前将举行听证的时间、地点通知申请人、利害关系人，必要时予以公告；

（二）听证应当公开举行；

（三）行政机关应当指定审查该行政许可申请的工作人员以外的人员为听证主持人，申请人、利害关系人认为主持人与该行政许可事项有直接利害关系的，有权申请回避；

（四）举行听证时，审查该行政许可申请的工作人员应当提供审查意见的证据、理由，申请人、利害关系人可以提出证据，并进行申辩和质证；

（五）听证应当制作笔录，听证笔录应当交听证参加人确认无误后签字或者盖章。

行政机关应当根据听证笔录，作出行政许可决定。

第五节　变更与延续

第四十九条　被许可人要求变更行政许可事项的，应当向作出行政许可决定的行政机关提出申请；符合法定条件、标准的，行政机关应当依法办理变更手续。

第五十条　被许可人需要延续依法取得的行政许可的有效期的，应当在该行政许可有效期届满三十日前向作出行政许可决定的行政机关提出申请。但是，法律、法规、规章另有规定的，依照其规定。

行政机关应当根据被许可人的申请，在该行政许可有效期届满前作出是否准予延续的决定；逾期未作决定的，视为准予延续。

第六节　特别规定

第五十一条　实施行政许可的程序，本节有规定的，适用本节规定；本节没有规定的，适用本章其他有关规定。

第五十二条　国务院实施行政许可的程序，适用有关法律、行政法规的规定。

第五十三条　实施本法第十二条第二项所列事项的行政许可的，行政机关应当通过招标、拍卖等公平竞争的方式作出决定。但是，法律、行政法规另有规定的，依照其规定。

行政机关通过招标、拍卖等方式作出行政许可决定的具体程序，依照有关法律、行政法规的规定。

行政机关按照招标、拍卖程序确定中标人、买受人后，应当作出准予行政许可的决定，并依法向中标人、买受人颁发行政许可证件。

行政机关违反本条规定，不采用招标、拍卖方式，或者违反招标、拍卖程序，损害申请人合法权益的，申请人可以依法申请行政复议或者提起行政诉讼。

第五十四条　实施本法第十二条第三项所列事项的行政许可，赋予公民特定资格，依法应当举行国家考试的，行政机关根据考试成绩和其他法定条件作出行政许可决定；赋予法人或者其他组织特定的资格、资质的，行政机关根据申请人的专业人员构成、技术条件、经营业绩和管理水平等的考核结果作出行政许可决定。但是，法律、行政法规另有规定的，依照其规定。

公民特定资格的考试依法由行政机关或者行业组织实施，公开举行。行政机关或者行业组织应当事先公布资格考试的报名条件、报考办法、考试科目以及考试大纲。但是，不得组织强制性的资格考试的考前培训，不得指定教材或者其他助考材料。

第五十五条　实施本法第十二条第四项所列事项的行政许可的，应当按照技术标准、技术规范依法进行检验、检测、检疫，行政机关根据检验、检测、检疫的结果作出行政许可决定。

行政机关实施检验、检测、检疫，应当自受理申请之日起五日内指派两名以上工作人员按照技术标准、技术规范进行检验、检测、检疫。不需要对检验、检测、检疫结果作进一步技术分析即可认定设备、设施、产品、物品是否符合技术标准、技术规范的，行政机关应当当场作出行政许可决定。

行政机关根据检验、检测、检疫结果，作出不予行政许可决定的，应当书面说明不予行政许可所依据的技术标准、技术规范。

第五十六条　实施本法第十二条第五项所列事项的行政许可，申请人提交的申请材料齐全、符合法定形式的，行政机关应当当场予以登记。需要对申请材料的实质内容进行核实的，行政机关依照本法第三十四条第三款的规定办理。

第五十七条　有数量限制的行政许可，两个或者两个以上申请人的申请均符合法定条件、标准的，行政机关应当根据受理行政许可申请的先后顺序作出准予行政许可的决定。但是，法律、行政法规另有规定的，依照其规定。

第五章　行政许可的费用

第五十八条　行政机关实施行政许可和对行政许可事项进行监督检查，不得收取任何费用。但是，法律、行政法规另有规定的，依照其规定。

行政机关提供行政许可申请书格式文本，不得收费。

行政机关实施行政许可所需经费应当列入本行政机关的预算，由本级财政予以保障，按照批准的预算予以核拨。

第五十九条　行政机关实施行政许可，依照法律、行政法规收取费用的，应当按照公布的法定项目和标准收费；所收取的费用必须全部上缴国库，任何机关或者个人不得以任何形式截留、挪用、私分或者变相私分。财政部门不得以任何形式向行政机关返还或者变相返还实施行政许可所收取的费用。

第六章　监督检查

第六十条　上级行政机关应当加强对下级行政机关实施行政许可的监督检查，及时纠正行政许可实施中的违法行为。

第六十一条　行政机关应当建立健全监督制度，通过核查反映被许可人从事行政许可事项活动情况的有关材料，履行监督责任。

行政机关依法对被许可人从事行政许可事项的活动进行监督检查时，应当将监督检查的情况和处理结果予以记录，由监督检查人员签字后归档。公众有权查阅行政机关监督检查记录。

行政机关应当创造条件，实现与被许可人、其他有关行政机关的计算机档案系统互联，核查被许可人从事行政许可事项活动情况。

第六十二条　行政机关可以对被许可人生产经营的产品依法进行抽样检查、检验、检测，对其生产经营场所依法进行实地检查。检查时，行政机关可以依法查阅或者要求被许可人报送有关材料；被许可人应当如实提供有关情况和材料。

行政机关根据法律、行政法规的规定，对直接关系公共安全、人身健康、生命财产安全的重要设备、设施进行定期检验。对检验合格的，行政机关应当发给相应的证明文件。

第六十三条　行政机关实施监督检查，不得妨碍被许可人正常的生产经营活动，不得索取或者收受被许可人的财物，不得谋取其他利益。

第六十四条　被许可人在作出行政许可决定的行政机关管辖区域外违法从事行政许可事项活动的，违法行为发生地的行政机关应当依法将被许可人的违法事实、处理结果抄告作出行政许可决定的行政机关。

第六十五条　个人和组织发现违法从事行政许可事项的活动，有权向行政机关举报，行政机关应当及时核实、处理。

第六十六条　被许可人未依法履行开发利用自然资源义务或者未依法履行利用公共资源义务的，行政机关应当责令限期改正；被许可人在规定期限内不改正的，行政机关应当依照有关法律、行政法规的规定予以处理。

第六十七条　取得直接关系公共利益的特定行业的市场准入行政许可的被许可人，应当按照国家规定的服务标准、资费标准和行政机关依法规定的条件，向用户提供安全、方便、稳定和价格合理的服务，并履行普遍服务的义务；未经作出行政许可决定的行政机关批准，不得擅自停业、歇业。

被许可人不履行前款规定的义务的，行政机关应当责令限期改正，或者依法采取有效措施督促其履行义务。

第六十八条　对直接关系公共安全、人身健康、生命财产安全的重要设备、设施，行政机关应当督促设计、建造、安装和使用单位建立相应的自检制度。

行政机关在监督检查时，发现直接关系公共安全、人身健康、生命财产安全的重要设备、设施存在安全隐患的，应当责令停止建造、安装和使用，并责令设计、建造、安装和使用单位立即改正。

第六十九条　有下列情形之一的，作出行政许可决定的行政机关或者其上级行政机关，根据利害关系人的请求或者依据职权，可以撤销行政许可：

（一）行政机关工作人员滥用职权、玩忽职守作出准予行政许可决定的；

（二）超越法定职权作出准予行政许可决定的；

（三）违反法定程序作出准予行政许可决定的；

（四）对不具备申请资格或者不符合法定条件的申请人准予行政许可的；

（五）依法可以撤销行政许可的其他情形。

被许可人以欺骗、贿赂等不正当手段取得行政许可的，应当予以撤销。

依照前两款的规定撤销行政许可，可能对公共利益造成重大损害的，不予撤销。

依照本条第一款的规定撤销行政许可，被许可人的合法权益受到损害的，行政机关应当依法给予赔偿。依照本条第二款的规定撤销行政许可的，被许可人基于行政许可取得的利益不受保护。

第七十条　有下列情形之一的，行政机关应当依法办理有关行政许可的注销手续：

（一）行政许可有效期届满未延续的；

（二）赋予公民特定资格的行政许可，该公民死亡或者丧失行为能力的；

（三）法人或者其他组织依法终止的；

（四）行政许可依法被撤销、撤回，或者行政许可证件依法被吊销的；

（五）因不可抗力导致行政许可事项无法实施的；

（六）法律、法规规定的应当注销行政许可的其他情形。

第七章　法律责任

第七十一条　违反本法第十七条规定设定的行政许可，有关机关应当责令设定该行政许可的机关改正，或者依法予以撤销。

第七十二条　行政机关及其工作人员违反本法的规定，有下列情形之一的，由其上级行政机关或者监察机关责令改正；情节严重的，对直接负责的主管人员和其他直接责任人员依法给予行政处分：

（一）对符合法定条件的行政许可申请不予受理的；

（二）不在办公场所公示依法应当公示的材料的；

（三）在受理、审查、决定行政许可过程中，未向申请人、利害关系人履行法定告知义务的；

（四）申请人提交的申请材料不齐全、不符合法定形式，不一次告知申请人必须补正的全部内容的；

（五）未依法说明不受理行政许可申请或者不予行政许可的理由的；

（六）依法应当举行听证而不举行听证的。

第七十三条　行政机关工作人员办理行政许可、实施监督检查，索取或者收受他人财物或者谋取其他利益，构成犯罪的，依法追究刑事责任；尚不构成犯罪的，依法给予行政处分。

第七十四条　行政机关实施行政许可，有下列情形之一的，由其上级行政机关或者监察机关责令改正，对直接负责的主管人员和其他直接责任人员依法给予行政处分；构成犯罪的，依法追究刑事责任：

（一）对不符合法定条件的申请人准予行政许可或者超越法定职权作出准予行政许可决定的；

（二）对符合法定条件的申请人不予行政许可或者不在法定期限内作出准予行政许可决定的；

（三）依法应当根据招标、拍卖结果或者考试成绩择优作出准予行政许可决定，未经招标、拍卖或者考试，或者不根据招标、拍卖结果或者考试成绩择优作出准予行政许可决定的。

第七十五条 行政机关实施行政许可，擅自收费或者不按照法定项目和标准收费的，由其上级行政机关或者监察机关责令退还非法收取的费用；对直接负责的主管人员和其他直接责任人员依法给予行政处分。

截留、挪用、私分或者变相私分实施行政许可依法收取的费用的，予以追缴；对直接负责的主管人员和其他直接责任人员依法给予行政处分；构成犯罪的，依法追究刑事责任。

第七十六条 行政机关违法实施行政许可，给当事人的合法权益造成损害的，应当依照国家赔偿法的规定给予赔偿。

第七十七条 行政机关不依法履行监督职责或者监督不力，造成严重后果的，由其上级行政机关或者监察机关责令改正，对直接负责的主管人员和其他直接责任人员依法给予行政处分；构成犯罪的，依法追究刑事责任。

第七十八条 行政许可申请人隐瞒有关情况或者提供虚假材料申请行政许可的，行政机关不予受理或者不予行政许可，并给予警告；行政许可申请属于直接关系公共安全、人身健康、生命财产安全事项的，申请人在一年内不得再次申请该行政许可。

第七十九条 被许可人以欺骗、贿赂等不正当手段取得行政许可的，行政机关应当依法给予行政处罚；取得的行政许可属于直接关系公共安全、人身健康、生命财产安全事项的，申请人在三年内不得再次申请该行政许可；构成犯罪的，依法追究刑事责任。

第八十条 被许可人有下列行为之一的，行政机关应当依法给予行政处罚；构成犯罪的，依法追究刑事责任：

（一）涂改、倒卖、出租、出借行政许可证件，或者以其他形式非法转让行政许可的；

（二）超越行政许可范围进行活动的；

（三）向负责监督检查的行政机关隐瞒有关情况、提供虚假材料或者拒绝提供反映其活动情况的真实材料的；

（四）法律、法规、规章规定的其他违法行为。

第八十一条 公民、法人或者其他组织未经行政许可，擅自从事依法应当取得行政许可的活动的，行政机关应当依法采取措施予以制止，并依法给予行政处罚；构成犯罪的，依法追究刑事责任。

第八章 附 则

第八十二条 本法规定的行政机关实施行政许可的期限以工作日计算，不含法定节假日。

第八十三条 本法自2004年7月1日起施行。

本法施行前有关行政许可的规定，制定机关应当依照本法规定予以清理；不符合本法规定的，自本法施行之日起停止执行。

【例11-6-1】 根据《中华人民共和国行政许可法》的规定，除可以当场作出行政许可决定的外，行政机关应当自受理行政可之日起作出行政许可决定的时限是：

A. 5日之内 B. 7日之内 C. 15日之内 D. 20日之内

解 《中华人民共和国行政许可法》第四十二条规定，除可以当场作出行政许可决定的外，行政机关应当自受理行政许可申请之日起二十日内做出行政许可决定。二十日内不能做出决定的，经本行政机关负责人批准，可以延长十日，并应当将延长期限的理由告知申请人。但是，法律、法规另有规定的，依照其规定。

答案：D

习　题

11-6-1　行政机关实施行政许可和对行政许可事项进行监督检查（　　）。

A. 不得收取任何费用　　B. 应当收取适当费用

C. 收费必须上缴　　D. 收费必须开收据

11-6-2　行政机关应当自受理行政许可申请之日起（　　）作出行政许可决定。

A. 二十日内　　B. 三十日内

C. 十五日内　　D. 四十五日之内

第七节　中华人民共和国节约能源法

（2016年7月修订）

第一章　总　　则

第一条　为了推动全社会节约能源，提高能源利用效率，保护和改善环境，促进经济社会全面协调可持续发展，制定本法。

第二条　本法所称能源，是指煤炭、石油、天然气、生物质能和电力、热力以及其他直接或者通过加工、转换而取得有用能的各种资源。

第三条　本法所称节约能源（以下简称节能），是指加强用能管理，采取技术上可行、经济上合理以及环境和社会可以承受的措施，从能源生产到消费的各个环节，降低消耗、减少损失和污染物排放、制止浪费，有效、合理地利用能源。

第四条　节约资源是我国的基本国策。国家实施节约与开发并举、把节约放在首位的能源发展战略。

第五条　国务院和县级以上地方各级人民政府应当将节能工作纳入国民经济和社会发展规划、年度计划，并组织编制和实施节能中长期专项规划、年度节能计划。

国务院和县级以上地方各级人民政府每年向本级人民代表大会或者其常务委员会报告节能工作。

第六条　国家实行节能目标责任制和节能考核评价制度，将节能目标完成情况作为对地方人民政府及其负责人考核评价的内容。

省、自治区、直辖市人民政府每年向国务院报告节能目标责任的履行情况。

第七条　国家实行有利于节能和环境保护的产业政策，限制发展高耗能、高污染行业，发展节能环保型产业。

国务院和省、自治区、直辖市人民政府应当加强节能工作，合理调整产业结构、企业结构、产品结构和能源消费结构，推动企业降低单位产值能耗和单位产品能耗，淘汰落后的生产能力，改进能源的开发、加工、转换、输送、储存和供应，提高能源利用效率。

国家鼓励、支持开发和利用新能源、可再生能源。

第八条　国家鼓励、支持节能科学技术的研究、开发、示范和推广，促进节能技术创新与进步。

国家开展节能宣传和教育，将节能知识纳入国民教育和培训体系，普及节能科学知识，增强全民的节能意识，提倡节约型的消费方式。

第九条　任何单位和个人都应当依法履行节能义务，有权检举浪费能源的行为。

新闻媒体应当宣传节能法律、法规和政策，发挥舆论监督作用。

第十条　国务院管理节能工作的部门主管全国的节能监督管理工作。国务院有关部门在各自的职责范围内负责节能监督管理工作，并接受国务院管理节能工作的部门的指导。

县级以上地方各级人民政府管理节能工作的部门负责本行政区域内的节能监督管理工作。县级以上地方各级人民政府有关部门在各自的职责范围内负责节能监督管理工作，并接受同级管理节能工作的部门的指导。

第二章　节能管理

第十一条　国务院和县级以上地方各级人民政府应当加强对节能工作的领导，部署、协调、监督、检查、推动节能工作。

第十二条　县级以上人民政府管理节能工作的部门和有关部门应当在各自的职责范围内，加强对节能法律、法规和节能标准执行情况的监督检查，依法查处违法用能行为。

履行节能监督管理职责不得向监督管理对象收取费用。

第十三条　国务院标准化主管部门和国务院有关部门依法组织制定并适时修订有关节能的国家标准、行业标准，建立健全节能标准体系。

国务院标准化主管部门会同国务院管理节能工作的部门和国务院有关部门制定强制性的用能产品、设备能源效率标准和生产过程中耗能高的产品的单位产品能耗限额标准。

国家鼓励企业制定严于国家标准、行业标准的企业节能标准。

省、自治区、直辖市制定严于强制性国家标准、行业标准的地方节能标准，由省、自治区、直辖市人民政府报经国务院批准；本法另有规定的除外。

第十四条　建筑节能的国家标准、行业标准由国务院建设主管部门组织制定，并依照法定程序发布。

省、自治区、直辖市人民政府建设主管部门可以根据本地实际情况，制定严于国家标准或者行业标准的地方建筑节能标准，并报国务院标准化主管部门和国务院建设主管部门备案。

第十五条　国家实行固定资产投资项目节能评估和审查制度。不符合强制性节能标准的项目，建设单位不得开工建设；已经建成的，不得投入生产、使用。政府投资项目不符合强制性节能标准的，依法负责项目审批的机关不得批准建设。具体办法由国务院管理节能工作的部门会同国务院有关部门制定。

第十六条　国家对落后的耗能过高的用能产品、设备和生产工艺实行淘汰制度。淘汰的用能产品、设备、生产工艺的目录和实施办法，由国务院管理节能工作的部门会同国务院有关部门制定并公布。

生产过程中耗能高的产品的生产单位，应当执行单位产品能耗限额标准。对超过单位产品能耗限额标准用能的生产单位，由管理节能工作的部门按照国务院规定的权限责令限期治理。

对高耗能的特种设备，按照国务院的规定实行节能审查和监管。

第十七条　禁止生产、进口、销售国家明令淘汰或者不符合强制性能源效率标准的用能产品、设备；禁止使用国家明令淘汰的用能设备、生产工艺。

第十八条 国家对家用电器等使用面广、耗能量大的用能产品，实行能源效率标识管理。实行能源效率标识管理的产品目录和实施办法，由国务院管理节能工作的部门会同国务院产品质量监督部门制定并公布。

第十九条 生产者和进口商应当对列入国家能源效率标识管理产品目录的用能产品标注能源效率标识，在产品包装物上或者说明书中予以说明，并按照规定报国务院产品质量监督部门和国务院管理节能工作的部门共同授权的机构备案。

生产者和进口商应当对其标注的能源效率标识及相关信息的准确性负责。禁止销售应当标注而未标注能源效率标识的产品。

禁止伪造、冒用能源效率标识或者利用能源效率标识进行虚假宣传。

第二十条 用能产品的生产者、销售者，可以根据自愿原则，按照国家有关节能产品认证的规定，向经国务院认证认可监督管理部门认可的从事节能产品认证的机构提出节能产品认证申请；经认证合格后，取得节能产品认证证书，可以在用能产品或者其包装物上使用节能产品认证标志。

禁止使用伪造的节能产品认证标志或者冒用节能产品认证标志。

第二十一条 县级以上各级人民政府统计部门应当会同同级有关部门，建立健全能源统计制度，完善能源统计指标体系，改进和规范能源统计方法，确保能源统计数据真实、完整。

国务院统计部门会同国务院管理节能工作的部门，定期向社会公布各省、自治区、直辖市以及主要耗能行业的能源消费和节能情况等信息。

第二十二条 国家鼓励节能服务机构的发展，支持节能服务机构开展节能咨询、设计、评估、检测、审计、认证等服务。

国家支持节能服务机构开展节能知识宣传和节能技术培训，提供节能信息、节能示范和其他公益性节能服务。

第二十三条 国家鼓励行业协会在行业节能规划、节能标准的制定和实施、节能技术推广、能源消费统计、节能宣传培训和信息咨询等方面发挥作用。

第三章 合理使用与节约能源

第一节 一般规定

第二十四条 用能单位应当按照合理用能的原则，加强节能管理，制定并实施节能计划和节能技术措施，降低能源消耗。

第二十五条 用能单位应当建立节能目标责任制，对节能工作取得成绩的集体、个人给予奖励。

第二十六条 用能单位应当定期开展节能教育和岗位节能培训。

第二十七条 用能单位应当加强能源计量管理，按照规定配备和使用经依法检定合格的能源计量器具。

用能单位应当建立能源消费统计和能源利用状况分析制度，对各类能源的消费实行分类计量和统计，并确保能源消费统计数据真实、完整。

第二十八条 能源生产经营单位不得向本单位职工无偿提供能源。任何单位不得对能源消费实行包费制。

第二节 工业节能

第二十九条 国务院和省、自治区、直辖市人民政府推进能源资源优化开发利用和合理配置，推进有利于节能的行业结构调整，优化用能结构和企业布局。

第三十条 国务院管理节能工作的部门会同国务院有关部门制定电力、钢铁、有色金属、建材、石油加工、化工、煤炭等主要耗能行业的节能技术政策，推动企业节能技术改造。

第三十一条 国家鼓励工业企业采用高效、节能的电动机、锅炉、窑炉、风机、泵类等设备，采用热电联产、余热余压利用、洁净煤以及先进的用能监测和控制等技术。

第三十二条 电网企业应当按照国务院有关部门制定的节能发电调度管理的规定，安排清洁、高效和符合规定的热电联产、利用余热余压发电的机组以及其他符合资源综合利用规定的发电机组与电网并网运行，上网电价执行国家有关规定。

第三十三条 禁止新建不符合国家规定的燃煤发电机组、燃油发电机组和燃煤热电机组。

第三节 建筑节能

第三十四条 国务院建设主管部门负责全国建筑节能的监督管理工作。

县级以上地方各级人民政府建设主管部门负责本行政区域内建筑节能的监督管理工作。

县级以上地方各级人民政府建设主管部门会同同级管理节能工作的部门编制本行政区域内的建筑节能规划。建筑节能规划应当包括既有建筑节能改造计划。

第三十五条 建筑工程的建设、设计、施工和监理单位应当遵守建筑节能标准。

不符合建筑节能标准的建筑工程，建设主管部门不得批准开工建设；已经开工建设的，应当责令停止施工、限期改正；已经建成的，不得销售或者使用。

建设主管部门应当加强对在建建筑工程执行建筑节能标准情况的监督检查。

第三十六条 房地产开发企业在销售房屋时，应当向购买人明示所售房屋的节能措施、保温工程保修期等信息，在房屋买卖合同、质量保证书和使用说明书中载明，并对其真实性、准确性负责。

第三十七条 使用空调采暖、制冷的公共建筑应当实行室内温度控制制度。具体办法由国务院建设主管部门制定。

第三十八条 国家采取措施，对实行集中供热的建筑分步骤实行供热分户计量、按照用热量收费的制度。新建建筑或者对既有建筑进行节能改造，应当按照规定安装用热计量装置、室内温度调控装置和供热系统调控装置。具体办法由国务院建设主管部门会同国务院有关部门制定。

第三十九条 县级以上地方各级人民政府有关部门应当加强城市节约用电管理，严格控制公用设施和大型建筑物装饰性景观照明的能耗。

第四十条 国家鼓励在新建建筑和既有建筑节能改造中使用新型墙体材料等节能建筑材料和节能设备，安装和使用太阳能等可再生能源利用系统。

第四节 交通运输节能

第四十一条 国务院有关交通运输主管部门按照各自的职责负责全国交通运输相关领域的节能监督管理工作。

国务院有关交通运输主管部门会同国务院管理节能工作的部门分别制定相关领域的节能规划。

第四十二条 国务院及其有关部门指导、促进各种交通运输方式协调发展和有效衔接，优化交通运输结构，建设节能型综合交通运输体系。

第四十三条 县级以上地方各级人民政府应当优先发展公共交通，加大对公共交通的投入，完善公共交通服务体系，鼓励利用公共交通工具出行；鼓励使用非机动交通工具出行。

第四十四条　国务院有关交通运输主管部门应当加强交通运输组织管理，引导道路、水路、航空运输企业提高运输组织化程度和集约化水平，提高能源利用效率。

第四十五条　国家鼓励开发、生产、使用节能环保型汽车、摩托车、铁路机车车辆、船舶和其他交通运输工具，实行老旧交通运输工具的报废、更新制度。

国家鼓励开发和推广应用交通运输工具使用的清洁燃料、石油替代燃料。

第四十六条　国务院有关部门制定交通运输营运车船的燃料消耗量限值标准；不符合标准的，不得用于营运。

国务院有关交通运输主管部门应当加强对交通运输营运车船燃料消耗检测的监督管理。

第五节　公共机构节能

第四十七条　公共机构应当厉行节约，杜绝浪费，带头使用节能产品、设备，提高能源利用效率。

本法所称公共机构，是指全部或者部分使用财政性资金的国家机关、事业单位和团体组织。

第四十八条　国务院和县级以上地方各级人民政府管理机关事务工作的机构会同同级有关部门制定和组织实施本级公共机构节能规划。公共机构节能规划应当包括公共机构既有建筑节能改造计划。

第四十九条　公共机构应当制定年度节能目标和实施方案，加强能源消费计量和监测管理，向本级人民政府管理机关事务工作的机构报送上年度的能源消费状况报告。

国务院和县级以上地方各级人民政府管理机关事务工作的机构会同同级有关部门按照管理权限，制定本级公共机构的能源消耗定额，财政部门根据该定额制定能源消耗支出标准。

第五十条　公共机构应当加强本单位用能系统管理，保证用能系统的运行符合国家相关标准。

公共机构应当按照规定进行能源审计，并根据能源审计结果采取提高能源利用效率的措施。

第五十一条　公共机构采购用能产品、设备，应当优先采购列入节能产品、设备政府采购名录中的产品、设备。禁止采购国家明令淘汰的用能产品、设备。

节能产品、设备政府采购名录由省级以上人民政府的政府采购监督管理部门会同同级有关部门制定并公布。

第六节　重点用能单位节能

第五十二条　国家加强对重点用能单位的节能管理。

下列用能单位为重点用能单位：

（一）年综合能源消费总量一万吨标准煤以上的用能单位；

（二）国务院有关部门或者省、自治区、直辖市人民政府管理节能工作的部门指定的年综合能源消费总量五千吨以上不满一万吨标准煤的用能单位。

重点用能单位节能管理办法，由国务院管理节能工作的部门会同国务院有关部门制定。

第五十三条　重点用能单位应当每年向管理节能工作的部门报送上年度的能源利用状况报告。能源利用状况包括能源消费情况、能源利用效率、节能目标完成情况和节能效益分析、节能措施等内容。

第五十四条　管理节能工作的部门应当对重点用能单位报送的能源利用状况报告进行审查。对节能管理制度不健全、节能措施不落实、能源利用效率低的重点用能单位，管理节能工作的部门应当开展现场调查，组织实施用能设备能源效率检测，责令实施能源审计，并提出书面整改要求，限期整改。

第五十五条　重点用能单位应当设立能源管理岗位，在具有节能专业知识、实际经验以及中级以上技术职称的人员中聘任能源管理负责人，并报管理节能工作的部门和有关部门备案。

能源管理负责人负责组织对本单位用能状况进行分析、评价，组织编写本单位能源利用状况报告，提出本单位节能工作的改进措施并组织实施。

能源管理负责人应当接受节能培训。

第四章　节能技术进步

第五十六条　国务院管理节能工作的部门会同国务院科技主管部门发布节能技术政策大纲，指导节能技术研究、开发和推广应用。

第五十七条　县级以上各级人民政府应当把节能技术研究开发作为政府科技投入的重点领域，支持科研单位和企业开展节能技术应用研究，制定节能标准，开发节能共性和关键技术，促进节能技术创新与成果转化。

第五十八条　国务院管理节能工作的部门会同国务院有关部门制定并公布节能技术、节能产品的推广目录，引导用能单位和个人使用先进的节能技术、节能产品。

国务院管理节能工作的部门会同国务院有关部门组织实施重大节能科研项目、节能示范项目、重点节能工程。

第五十九条　县级以上各级人民政府应当按照因地制宜、多能互补、综合利用、讲求效益的原则，加强农业和农村节能工作，增加对农业和农村节能技术、节能产品推广应用的资金投入。

农业、科技等有关主管部门应当支持、推广在农业生产、农产品加工储运等方面应用节能技术和节能产品，鼓励更新和淘汰高耗能的农业机械和渔业船舶。

国家鼓励、支持在农村大力发展沼气，推广生物质能、太阳能和风能等可再生能源利用技术，按照科学规划、有序开发的原则发展小型水力发电，推广节能型的农村住宅和炉灶等，鼓励利用非耕地种植能源植物，大力发展薪炭林等能源林。

第五章　激 励 措 施

第六十条　中央财政和省级地方财政安排节能专项资金，支持节能技术研究开发、节能技术和产品的示范与推广、重点节能工程的实施、节能宣传培训、信息服务和表彰奖励等。

第六十一条　国家对生产、使用列入本法第五十八条规定的推广目录的需要支持的节能技术、节能产品，实行税收优惠等扶持政策。

国家通过财政补贴支持节能照明器具等节能产品的推广和使用。

第六十二条　国家实行有利于节约能源资源的税收政策，健全能源矿产资源有偿使用制度，促进能源资源的节约及其开采利用水平的提高。

第六十三条　国家运用税收等政策，鼓励先进节能技术、设备的进口，控制在生产过程中耗能高、污染重的产品的出口。

第六十四条　政府采购监督管理部门会同有关部门制定节能产品、设备政府采购名录，应当优先列入取得节能产品认证证书的产品、设备。

第六十五条　国家引导金融机构增加对节能项目的信贷支持，为符合条件的节能技术研究开发、节能产品生产以及节能技术改造等项目提供优惠贷款。

国家推动和引导社会有关方面加大对节能的资金投入，加快节能技术改造。

第六十六条　国家实行有利于节能的价格政策，引导用能单位和个人节能。

国家运用财税、价格等政策，支持推广电力需求侧管理、合同能源管理、节能自愿协议等节能办法。

国家实行峰谷分时电价、季节性电价、可中断负荷电价制度，鼓励电力用户合理调整用电负荷；对钢铁、有色金属、建材、化工和其他主要耗能行业的企业，分淘汰、限制、允许和鼓励类实行差别电价政策。

第六十七条　各级人民政府对在节能管理、节能科学技术研究和推广应用中有显著成绩以及检举严重浪费能源行为的单位和个人，给予表彰和奖励。

第六章　法律责任

第六十八条　负责审批政府投资项目的机关违反本法规定，对不符合强制性节能标准的项目予以批准建设的，对直接负责的主管人员和其他直接责任人员依法给予处分。

固定资产投资项目建设单位开工建设不符合强制性节能标准的项目或者将该项目投入生产、使用的，由管理节能工作的部门责令停止建设或者停止生产、使用，限期改造；不能改造或者逾期不改造的生产性项目，由管理节能工作的部门报请本级人民政府按照国务院规定的权限责令关闭。

第六十九条　生产、进口、销售国家明令淘汰的用能产品、设备的，使用伪造的节能产品认证标志或者冒用节能产品认证标志的，依照《中华人民共和国产品质量法》的规定处罚。

第七十条　生产、进口、销售不符合强制性能源效率标准的用能产品、设备的，由产品质量监督部门责令停止生产、进口、销售，没收违法生产、进口、销售的用能产品、设备和违法所得，并处违法所得一倍以上五倍以下罚款；情节严重的，由工商行政管理部门吊销营业执照。

第七十一条　使用国家明令淘汰的用能设备或者生产工艺的，由管理节能工作的部门责令停止使用，没收国家明令淘汰的用能设备；情节严重的，可以由管理节能工作的部门提出意见，报请本级人民政府按照国务院规定的权限责令停业整顿或者关闭。

第七十二条　生产单位超过单位产品能耗限额标准用能，情节严重，经限期治理逾期不治理或者没有达到治理要求的，可以由管理节能工作的部门提出意见，报请本级人民政府按照国务院规定的权限责令停业整顿或者关闭。

第七十三条　违反本法规定，应当标注能源效率标识而未标注的，由产品质量监督部门责令改正，处三万元以上五万元以下罚款。

违反本法规定，未办理能源效率标识备案，或者使用的能源效率标识不符合规定的，由产品质量监督部门责令限期改正；逾期不改正的，处一万元以上三万元以下罚款。

伪造、冒用能源效率标识或者利用能源效率标识进行虚假宣传的，由产品质量监督部门责令改正，处五万元以上十万元以下罚款；情节严重的，由工商行政管理部门吊销营业执照。

第七十四条　用能单位未按照规定配备、使用能源计量器具的，由产品质量监督部门责令限期改正；逾期不改正的，处一万元以上五万元以下罚款。

第七十五条　瞒报、伪造、篡改能源统计资料或者编造虚假能源统计数据的，依照《中华人民共和国统计法》的规定处罚。

第七十六条　从事节能咨询、设计、评估、检测、审计、认证等服务的机构提供虚假信息的，由管理节能工作的部门责令改正，没收违法所得，并处五万元以上十万元以下罚款。

第七十七条　违反本法规定，无偿向本单位职工提供能源或者对能源消费实行包费制的，由管理节能工作的部门责令限期改正；逾期不改正的，处五万元以上二十万元以下罚款。

第七十八条　电网企业未按照本法规定安排符合规定的热电联产和利用余热余压发电的机组与电网并网运行，或者未执行国家有关上网电价规定的，由国家电力监管机构责令改正；造成发电企业经济损失的，依法承担赔偿责任。

第七十九条　建设单位违反建筑节能标准的，由建设主管部门责令改正，处二十万元以上五十万元以下罚款。

设计单位、施工单位、监理单位违反建筑节能标准的，由建设主管部门责令改正，处十万元以上五十万元以下罚款；情节严重的，由颁发资质证书的部门降低资质等级或者吊销资质证书；造成损失的，依法承担赔偿责任。

第八十条　房地产开发企业违反本法规定，在销售房屋时未向购买人明示所售房屋的节能措施、保温工程保修期等信息的，由建设主管部门责令限期改正，逾期不改正的，处三万元以上五万元以下罚款；对以上信息作虚假宣传的，由建设主管部门责令改正，处五万元以上二十万元以下罚款。

第八十一条　公共机构采购用能产品、设备，未优先采购列入节能产品、设备政府采购名录中的产品、设备，或者采购国家明令淘汰的用能产品、设备的，由政府采购监督管理部门给予警告，可以并处罚款；对直接负责的主管人员和其他直接责任人员依法给予处分，并予通报。

第八十二条　重点用能单位未按照本法规定报送能源利用状况报告或者报告内容不实的，由管理节能工作的部门责令限期改正；逾期不改正的，处一万元以上五万元以下罚款。

第八十三条　重点用能单位无正当理由拒不落实本法第五十四条规定的整改要求或者整改没有达到要求的，由管理节能工作的部门处十万元以上三十万元以下罚款。

第八十四条　重点用能单位未按照本法规定设立能源管理岗位，聘任能源管理负责人，并报管理节能工作的部门和有关部门备案的，由管理节能工作的部门责令改正；拒不改正的，处一万元以上三万元以下罚款。

第八十五条　违反本法规定，构成犯罪的，依法追究刑事责任。

第八十六条　国家工作人员在节能管理工作中滥用职权、玩忽职守、徇私舞弊，构成犯罪的，依法追究刑事责任；尚不构成犯罪的，依法给予处分。

第七章　附　　则

第八十七条　本法自 2008 年 4 月 1 日起施行。

习　　题

11-7-1　用能产品的生产者、销售者，提出节能产品认证申请(　　)。

A. 可以根据自愿原则　　B. 必须在产品上市前申请

C. 不贴节能标志不能生产销售　　D. 必须取得节能证书后销售

11-7-2　建筑工程的建设、设计、施工和监理单位应当遵守建筑节能标准，对于(　　)。

A. 不符合建筑节能标准的建筑工程，建设主管部门不得批准开工建设

B. 已经开工建设的除外

C. 已经售出的房屋除外

D. 不符合建筑节能标准的建筑工程必须降价出售

第八节　中华人民共和国环境保护法

第一章　总　则

第一条　为保护和改善环境，防治污染和其他公害，保障公众健康，推进生态文明建设，促进经济社会可持续发展，制定本法。

第二条　本法所称环境，是指影响人类生存和发展的各种天然的和经过人工改造的自然因素的总体，包括大气、水、海洋、土地、矿藏、森林、草原、湿地、野生生物、自然遗迹、人文遗迹、自然保护区、风景名胜区、城市和乡村等。

第三条　本法适用于中华人民共和国领域和中华人民共和国管辖的其他海域。

第四条　保护环境是国家的基本国策。

国家采取有利于节约和循环利用资源、保护和改善环境、促进人与自然和谐的经济、技术政策和措施，使经济社会发展与环境保护相协调。

第五条　环境保护坚持保护优先、预防为主、综合治理、公众参与、损害担责的原则。

第六条　一切单位和个人都有保护环境的义务。

地方各级人民政府应当对本行政区域的环境质量负责。

企业事业单位和其他生产经营者应当防止、减少环境污染和生态破坏，对所造成的损害依法承担责任。

公民应当增强环境保护意识，采取低碳、节俭的生活方式，自觉履行环境保护义务。

第七条　国家支持环境保护科学技术研究、开发和应用，鼓励环境保护产业发展，促进环境保护信息化建设，提高环境保护科学技术水平。

第八条　各级人民政府应当加大保护和改善环境、防治污染和其他公害的财政投入，提高财政资金的使用效益。

第九条　各级人民政府应当加强环境保护宣传和普及工作，鼓励基层群众性自治组织、社会组织、环境保护志愿者开展环境保护法律法规和环境保护知识的宣传，营造保护环境的良好风气。

教育行政部门、学校应当将环境保护知识纳入学校教育内容，培养学生的环境保护意识。

新闻媒体应当开展环境保护法律法规和环境保护知识的宣传，对环境违法行为进行舆论监督。

第十条　国务院环境保护主管部门，对全国环境保护工作实施统一监督管理；县级以上地方人民政府环境保护主管部门，对本行政区域环境保护工作实施统一监督管理。

县级以上人民政府有关部门和军队环境保护部门，依照有关法律的规定对资源保护和污染防治等环境保护工作实施监督管理。

第十一条　对保护和改善环境有显著成绩的单位和个人，由人民政府给予奖励。

第十二条　每年6月5日为环境日。

第二章　监督管理

第十三条　县级以上人民政府应当将环境保护工作纳入国民经济和社会发展规划。

国务院环境保护主管部门会同有关部门，根据国民经济和社会发展规划编制国家环境保护规划，报国务院批准并公布实施。

县级以上地方人民政府环境保护主管部门会同有关部门，根据国家环境保护规划的要求，编制本行政区域的环境保护规划，报同级人民政府批准并公布实施。

环境保护规划的内容应当包括生态保护和污染防治的目标、任务、保障措施等，并与主体功能区规划、土地利用总体规划和城乡规划等相衔接。

第十四条　国务院有关部门和省、自治区、直辖市人民政府组织制定经济、技术政策，应当充分考虑对环境的影响，听取有关方面和专家的意见。

第十五条　国务院环境保护主管部门制定国家环境质量标准。

省、自治区、直辖市人民政府对国家环境质量标准中未作规定的项目，可以制定地方环境质量标准；对国家环境质量标准中已作规定的项目，可以制定严于国家环境质量标准的地方环境质量标准。地方环境质量标准应当报国务院环境保护主管部门备案。

国家鼓励开展环境基准研究。

第十六条　国务院环境保护主管部门根据国家环境质量标准和国家经济、技术条件，制定国家污染物排放标准。

省、自治区、直辖市人民政府对国家污染物排放标准中未作规定的项目，可以制定地方污染物排放标准；对国家污染物排放标准中已作规定的项目，可以制定严于国家污染物排放标准的地方污染物排放标准。地方污染物排放标准应当报国务院环境保护主管部门备案。

第十七条　国家建立、健全环境监测制度。国务院环境保护主管部门制定监测规范，会同有关部门组织监测网络，统一规划国家环境质量监测站（点）的设置，建立监测数据共享机制，加强对环境监测的管理。

有关行业、专业等各类环境质量监测站（点）的设置应当符合法律法规规定和监测规范的要求。

监测机构应当使用符合国家标准的监测设备，遵守监测规范。监测机构及其负责人对监测数据的真实性和准确性负责。

第十八条　省级以上人民政府应当组织有关部门或者委托专业机构，对环境状况进行调查、评价，建立环境资源承载能力监测预警机制。

第十九条　编制有关开发利用规划，建设对环境有影响的项目，应当依法进行环境影响评价。

未依法进行环境影响评价的开发利用规划，不得组织实施；未依法进行环境影响评价的建设项目，不得开工建设。

第二十条　国家建立跨行政区域的重点区域、流域环境污染和生态破坏联合防治协调机制，实行统一规划、统一标准、统一监测、统一的防治措施。

前款规定以外的跨行政区域的环境污染和生态破坏的防治，由上级人民政府协调解决，或者由有关地方人民政府协商解决。

第二十一条　国家采取财政、税收、价格、政府采购等方面的政策和措施，鼓励和支持环境保护技术装备、资源综合利用和环境服务等环境保护产业的发展。

第二十二条　企业事业单位和其他生产经营者，在污染物排放符合法定要求的基础上，进一步减少污染物排放的，人民政府应当依法采取财政、税收、价格、政府采购等方面的政策和措施予以鼓励和支持。

第二十三条　企业事业单位和其他生产经营者，为改善环境，依照有关规定转产、搬迁、关闭的，人民政府应当予以支持。

第二十四条　县级以上人民政府环境保护主管部门及其委托的环境监察机构和其他负有

环境保护监督管理职责的部门，有权对排放污染物的企业事业单位和其他生产经营者进行现场检查。被检查者应当如实反映情况，提供必要的资料。实施现场检查的部门、机构及其工作人员应当为被检查者保守商业秘密。

第二十五条　企业事业单位和其他生产经营者违反法律法规规定排放污染物，造成或者可能造成严重污染的，县级以上人民政府环境保护主管部门和其他负有环境保护监督管理职责的部门，可以查封、扣押造成污染物排放的设施、设备。

第二十六条　国家实行环境保护目标责任制和考核评价制度。县级以上人民政府应当将环境保护目标完成情况纳入对本级人民政府负有环境保护监督管理职责的部门及其负责人和下级人民政府及其负责人的考核内容，作为对其考核评价的重要依据。考核结果应当向社会公开。

第二十七条　县级以上人民政府应当每年向本级人民代表大会或者人民代表大会常务委员会报告环境状况和环境保护目标完成情况，对发生的重大环境事件应当及时向本级人民代表大会常务委员会报告，依法接受监督。

第三章　保护和改善环境

第二十八条　地方各级人民政府应当根据环境保护目标和治理任务，采取有效措施，改善环境质量。

未达到国家环境质量标准的重点区域、流域的有关地方人民政府，应当制定限期达标规划，并采取措施按期达标。

第二十九条　国家在重点生态功能区、生态环境敏感区和脆弱区等区域划定生态保护红线，实行严格保护。

各级人民政府对具有代表性的各种类型的自然生态系统区域，珍稀、濒危的野生动植物自然分布区域，重要的水源涵养区域，具有重大科学文化价值的地质构造、著名溶洞和化石分布区、冰川、火山、温泉等自然遗迹，以及人文遗迹、古树名木，应当采取措施予以保护，严禁破坏。

第三十条　开发利用自然资源，应当合理开发，保护生物多样性，保障生态安全，依法制定有关生态保护和恢复治理方案并予以实施。

引进外来物种以及研究、开发和利用生物技术，应当采取措施，防止对生物多样性的破坏。

第三十一条　国家建立、健全生态保护补偿制度。

国家加大对生态保护地区的财政转移支付力度。有关地方人民政府应当落实生态保护补偿资金，确保其用于生态保护补偿。

国家指导受益地区和生态保护地区人民政府通过协商或者按照市场规则进行生态保护补偿。

第三十二条　国家加强对大气、水、土壤等的保护，建立和完善相应的调查、监测、评估和修复制度。

第三十三条　各级人民政府应当加强对农业环境的保护，促进农业环境保护新技术的使用，加强对农业污染源的监测预警，统筹有关部门采取措施，防治土壤污染和土地沙化、盐渍化、贫瘠化、石漠化、地面沉降以及防治植被破坏、水土流失、水体富营养化、水源枯竭、种源灭绝等生态失调现象，推广植物病虫害的综合防治。

县级、乡级人民政府应当提高农村环境保护公共服务水平，推动农村环境综合整治。

第三十四条　国务院和沿海地方各级人民政府应当加强对海洋环境的保护。向海洋排放污染物、倾倒废弃物，进行海岸工程和海洋工程建设，应当符合法律法规规定和有关标准，防止和减少对海洋环境的污染损害。

第三十五条　城乡建设应当结合当地自然环境的特点，保护植被、水域和自然景观，加强城市园林、绿地和风景名胜区的建设与管理。

第三十六条　国家鼓励和引导公民、法人和其他组织使用有利于保护环境的产品和再生产品，减少废弃物的产生。

国家机关和使用财政资金的其他组织应当优先采购和使用节能、节水、节材等有利于保护环境的产品、设备和设施。

第三十七条　地方各级人民政府应当采取措施，组织对生活废弃物的分类处置、回收利用。

第三十八条　公民应当遵守环境保护法律法规，配合实施环境保护措施，按照规定对生活废弃物进行分类放置，减少日常生活对环境造成的损害。

第三十九条　国家建立、健全环境与健康监测、调查和风险评估制度；鼓励和组织开展环境质量对公众健康影响的研究，采取措施预防和控制与环境污染有关的疾病。

第四章　防治污染和其他公害

第四十条　国家促进清洁生产和资源循环利用。

国务院有关部门和地方各级人民政府应当采取措施，推广清洁能源的生产和使用。

企业应当优先使用清洁能源，采用资源利用率高、污染物排放量少的工艺、设备以及废弃物综合利用技术和污染物无害化处理技术，减少污染物的产生。

第四十一条　建设项目中防治污染的设施，应当与主体工程同时设计、同时施工、同时投产使用。防治污染的设施应当符合经批准的环境影响评价文件的要求，不得擅自拆除或者闲置。

第四十二条　排放污染物的企业事业单位和其他生产经营者，应当采取措施，防治在生产建设或者其他活动中产生的废气、废水、废渣、医疗废物、粉尘、恶臭气体、放射性物质以及噪声、振动、光辐射、电磁辐射等对环境的污染和危害。

排放污染物的企业事业单位，应当建立环境保护责任制度，明确单位负责人和相关人员的责任。

重点排污单位应当按照国家有关规定和监测规范安装使用监测设备，保证监测设备正常运行，保存原始监测记录。

严禁通过暗管、渗井、渗坑、灌注或者篡改、伪造监测数据，或者不正常运行防治污染设施等逃避监管的方式违法排放污染物。

第四十三条　排放污染物的企业事业单位和其他生产经营者，应当按照国家有关规定缴纳排污费。排污费应当全部专项用于环境污染防治，任何单位和个人不得截留、挤占或者挪作他用。

依照法律规定征收环境保护税的，不再征收排污费。

第四十四条　国家实行重点污染物排放总量控制制度。重点污染物排放总量控制指标由国务院下达，省、自治区、直辖市人民政府分解落实。企业事业单位在执行国家和地方污染物排放标准的同时，应当遵守分解落实到本单位的重点污染物排放总量控制指标。

对超过国家重点污染物排放总量控制指标或者未完成国家确定的环境质量目标的地区，省级以上人民政府环境保护主管部门应当暂停审批其新增重点污染物排放总量的建设项目环境影响评价文件。

第四十五条　国家依照法律规定实行排污许可管理制度。

实行排污许可管理的企业事业单位和其他生产经营者应当按照排污许可证的要求排放污染物；未取得排污许可证的，不得排放污染物。

第四十六条　国家对严重污染环境的工艺、设备和产品实行淘汰制度。任何单位和个人不得生产、销售或者转移、使用严重污染环境的工艺、设备和产品。

禁止引进不符合我国环境保护规定的技术、设备、材料和产品。

第四十七条　各级人民政府及其有关部门和企业事业单位，应当依照《中华人民共和国突发事件应对法》的规定，做好突发环境事件的风险控制、应急准备、应急处置和事后恢复等工作。

县级以上人民政府应当建立环境污染公共监测预警机制，组织制定预警方案；环境受到污染，可能影响公众健康和环境安全时，依法及时公布预警信息，启动应急措施。

企业事业单位应当按照国家有关规定制定突发环境事件应急预案，报环境保护主管部门和有关部门备案。在发生或者可能发生突发环境事件时，企业事业单位应当立即采取措施处理，及时通报可能受到危害的单位和居民，并向环境保护主管部门和有关部门报告。

突发环境事件应急处置工作结束后，有关人民政府应当立即组织评估事件造成的环境影响和损失，并及时将评估结果向社会公布。

第四十八条　生产、储存、运输、销售、使用、处置化学物品和含有放射性物质的物品，应当遵守国家有关规定，防止污染环境。

第四十九条　各级人民政府及其农业等有关部门和机构应当指导农业生产经营者科学种植和养殖，科学合理施用农药、化肥等农业投入品，科学处置农用薄膜、农作物秸秆等农业废弃物，防止农业面源污染。

禁止将不符合农用标准和环境保护标准的固体废物、废水施入农田。施用农药、化肥等农业投入品及进行灌溉，应当采取措施，防止重金属和其他有毒有害物质污染环境。

畜禽养殖场、养殖小区、定点屠宰企业等的选址、建设和管理应当符合有关法律法规规定。从事畜禽养殖和屠宰的单位和个人应当采取措施，对畜禽粪便、尸体和污水等废弃物进行科学处置，防止污染环境。

县级人民政府负责组织农村生活废弃物的处置工作。

第五十条　各级人民政府应当在财政预算中安排资金，支持农村饮用水水源地保护、生活污水和其他废弃物处理、畜禽养殖和屠宰污染防治、土壤污染防治和农村工矿污染治理等环境保护工作。

第五十一条　各级人民政府应当统筹城乡建设污水处理设施及配套管网，固体废物的收集、运输和处置等环境卫生设施，危险废物集中处置设施、场所以及其他环境保护公共设施，并保障其正常运行。

第五十二条　国家鼓励投保环境污染责任保险。

第五章　信息公开和公众参与

第五十三条　公民、法人和其他组织依法享有获取环境信息、参与和监督环境保护的权利。

各级人民政府环境保护主管部门和其他负有环境保护监督管理职责的部门，应当依法公开环境信息、完善公众参与程序，为公民、法人和其他组织参与和监督环境保护提供便利。

第五十四条　国务院环境保护主管部门统一发布国家环境质量、重点污染源监测信息及其他重大环境信息。省级以上人民政府环境保护主管部门定期发布环境状况公报。

县级以上人民政府环境保护主管部门和其他负有环境保护监督管理职责的部门,应当依法公开环境质量、环境监测、突发环境事件以及环境行政许可、行政处罚、排污费的征收和使用情况等信息。

县级以上地方人民政府环境保护主管部门和其他负有环境保护监督管理职责的部门,应当将企业事业单位和其他生产经营者的环境违法信息记入社会诚信档案,及时向社会公布违法者名单。

第五十五条　重点排污单位应当如实向社会公开其主要污染物的名称、排放方式、排放浓度和总量、超标排放情况,以及防治污染设施的建设和运行情况,接受社会监督。

第五十六条　对依法应当编制环境影响报告书的建设项目,建设单位应当在编制时向可能受影响的公众说明情况,充分征求意见。

负责审批建设项目环境影响评价文件的部门在收到建设项目环境影响报告书后,除涉及国家秘密和商业秘密的事项外,应当全文公开;发现建设项目未充分征求公众意见的,应当责成建设单位征求公众意见。

第五十七条　公民、法人和其他组织发现任何单位和个人有污染环境和破坏生态行为的,有权向环境保护主管部门或者其他负有环境保护监督管理职责的部门举报。

公民、法人和其他组织发现地方各级人民政府、县级以上人民政府环境保护主管部门和其他负有环境保护监督管理职责的部门不依法履行职责的,有权向其上级机关或者监察机关举报。

接受举报的机关应当对举报人的相关信息予以保密,保护举报人的合法权益。

第五十八条　对污染环境、破坏生态,损害社会公共利益的行为,符合下列条件的社会组织可以向人民法院提起诉讼:

(一)依法在设区的市级以上人民政府民政部门登记;

(二)专门从事环境保护公益活动连续五年以上且无违法记录。

符合前款规定的社会组织向人民法院提起诉讼,人民法院应当依法受理。

提起诉讼的社会组织不得通过诉讼牟取经济利益。

第六章　法律责任

第五十九条　企业事业单位和其他生产经营者违法排放污染物,受到罚款处罚,被责令改正,拒不改正的,依法作出处罚决定的行政机关可以自责令改正之日的次日起,按照原处罚数额按日连续处罚。

前款规定的罚款处罚,依照有关法律法规按照防治污染设施的运行成本、违法行为造成的直接损失或者违法所得等因素确定的规定执行。

地方性法规可以根据环境保护的实际需要,增加第一款规定的按日连续处罚的违法行为的种类。

第六十条　企业事业单位和其他生产经营者超过污染物排放标准或者超过重点污染物排放总量控制指标排放污染物的,县级以上人民政府环境保护主管部门可以责令其采取限制生产、停产整治等措施;情节严重的,报经有批准权的人民政府批准,责令停业、关闭。

第六十一条　建设单位未依法提交建设项目环境影响评价文件或者环境影响评价文件未经批准,擅自开工建设的,由负有环境保护监督管理职责的部门责令停止建设,处以罚款,并可以责令恢复原状。

第六十二条　违反本法规定，重点排污单位不公开或者不如实公开环境信息的，由县级以上地方人民政府环境保护主管部门责令公开，处以罚款，并予以公告。

第六十三条　企业事业单位和其他生产经营者有下列行为之一，尚不构成犯罪的，除依照有关法律法规规定予以处罚外，由县级以上人民政府环境保护主管部门或者其他有关部门将案件移送公安机关，对其直接负责的主管人员和其他直接责任人员，处十日以上十五日以下拘留；情节较轻的，处五日以上十日以下拘留：

（一）建设项目未依法进行环境影响评价，被责令停止建设，拒不执行的；

（二）违反法律规定，未取得排污许可证排放污染物，被责令停止排污，拒不执行的；

（三）通过暗管、渗井、渗坑、灌注或者篡改、伪造监测数据，或者不正常运行防治污染设施等逃避监管的方式违法排放污染物的；

（四）生产、使用国家明令禁止生产、使用的农药，被责令改正，拒不改正的。

第六十四条　因污染环境和破坏生态造成损害的，应当依照《中华人民共和国侵权责任法》的有关规定承担侵权责任。

第六十五条　环境影响评价机构、环境监测机构以及从事环境监测设备和防治污染设施维护、运营的机构，在有关环境服务活动中弄虚作假，对造成的环境污染和生态破坏负有责任的，除依照有关法律法规规定予以处罚外，还应当与造成环境污染和生态破坏的其他责任者承担连带责任。

第六十六条　提起环境损害赔偿诉讼的时效期间为三年，从当事人知道或者应当知道其受到损害时起计算。

第六十七条　上级人民政府及其环境保护主管部门应当加强对下级人民政府及其有关部门环境保护工作的监督。发现有关工作人员有违法行为，依法应当给予处分的，应当向其任免机关或者监察机关提出处分建议。

依法应当给予行政处罚，而有关环境保护主管部门不给予行政处罚的，上级人民政府环境保护主管部门可以直接作出行政处罚的决定。

第六十八条　地方各级人民政府、县级以上人民政府环境保护主管部门和其他负有环境保护监督管理职责的部门有下列行为之一的，对直接负责的主管人员和其他直接责任人员给予记过、记大过或者降级处分；造成严重后果的，给予撤职或者开除处分，其主要负责人应当引咎辞职：

（一）不符合行政许可条件准予行政许可的；

（二）对环境违法行为进行包庇的；

（三）依法应当作出责令停业、关闭的决定而未作出的；

（四）对超标排放污染物、采用逃避监管的方式排放污染物、造成环境事故以及不落实生态保护措施造成生态破坏等行为，发现或者接到举报未及时查处的；

（五）违反本法规定，查封、扣押企业事业单位和其他生产经营者的设施、设备的；

（六）篡改、伪造或者指使篡改、伪造监测数据的；

（七）应当依法公开环境信息而未公开的；

（八）将征收的排污费截留、挤占或者挪作他用的；

（九）法律法规规定的其他违法行为。

第六十九条　违反本法规定，构成犯罪的，依法追究刑事责任。

第七章　附　　则

第七十条　本法自 2015 年 1 月 1 日起施行。

【例 11-8-1】 根据《中华人民共和国环境保护法》的规定，下列关于建设项目中防治污染的设施的说法中，不正确的是：

A. 防治污染的设施，必须与主体工程同时设计、同时施工、同时投入使用

B. 防治污染的设施不得擅自拆除

C. 防治污染的设施不得擅自闲置

D. 防治污染的设施经建设行政主管部门验收合格后方可投入生产或者使用

解　选项 D，应经环保部门验收，非建设行政主管部门验收，参见《中华人民共和国环境保护法》。

第十条　国务院环境保护主管部门，对全国环境保护工作实施统一监督管理；县级以上地方人民政府环境保护主管部门，对本行政区域环境保护工作实施统一监督管理。

县级以上人民政府有关部门和军队环境保护部门，依照有关法律的规定对资源保护和污染防治等环境保护工作实施监督管理。

第四十一条　建设项目中防治污染的设施，应当与主体工程同时设计、同时施工、同时投产使用。防治污染的设施应当符合经批准的环境影响评价文件的要求，不得擅自拆除或者闲置。

（旧《中华人民共和国环境保护法》第二十六条　建设项目中防治污染的措施，必须与主体工程同时设计、同时施工、同时投产使用。防治污染的设施必须经原审批环境影响报告书的环境保护行政主管部门验收合格后，该建设项目方可投入生产或者使用。）

答案：D

【例 11-8-2】 建设项目对环境可能造成轻度影响的，应当编制：

A. 环境影响报告书　　B. 环境影响报告表

C. 环境影响分析表　　D. 环境影响登记表

解　见《中华人民共和国环境影响评价法》第十六条。

国家根据建设项目对环境的影响程度，对建设项目的环境影响评价实行分类管理。

建设单位应当按照下列规定组织编制环境影响报告书、环境影响报告表或者填报环境影响登记表（以下统称环境影响评价文件）：

（一）可能造成重大环境影响的，应当编制环境影响报告书，对产生的环境影响进行全面评价；

（二）可能造成轻度环境影响的，应当编制环境影响报告表，对产生的环境影响进行分析或者专项评价；

（三）对环境影响很小、不需要进行环境影响评价的，应当填报环境影响登记表。

建设项目的环境影响评价分类管理名录，由国务院环境保护行政主管部门制定并公布。

答案：B

习　　题

11-8-1　按照新修订后的环境保护法的规定，下列说法正确的选项是（　　）。

A. 排污单位必须事先取得排污许可证

B. 排污单位应当事先在环保部门登记备案

C. 污染物超出排放限量的必须交罚款后才能继续使用

D. 罚款必须用于本单位的污染治理

11-8-2 建设项目防治污染的设施必须与主体工程做到几个同时，下列说法中哪个是不必要的？（ ）

A. 同时设计　　B. 同时施工

C. 同时投产使用　　D. 同时备案登记

11-8-3 建设项目未进行环境影响评价，被责令停止建设，拒不执行的（ ）。

A. 可移交公安机关拘留直接负责的主管人员

B. 交罚款后才能继续建设

C. 经县级以上领导批准后可以继续建设

D. 可向法院起诉直接责任人

第九节 建设工程勘察设计管理条例

第一章 总 则

第一条 为了加强对建设工程勘察、设计活动的管理，保证建设工程勘察、设计质量，保护人民生命和财产安全，制定本条例。

第二条 从事建设工程勘察、设计活动，必须遵守本条例。

本条例所称建设工程勘察，是指根据建设工程的要求，查明、分析、评价建设场地的地质地理环境特征和岩土工程条件，编制建设工程勘察文件的活动。

本条例所称建设工程设计，是指根据建设工程的要求，对建设工程所需的技术、经济、资源、环境等条件进行综合分析、论证，编制建设工程设计文件的活动。

第三条 建设工程勘察、设计应当与社会、经济发展水平相适应，做到经济效益、社会效益和环境效益相统一。

第四条 从事建设工程勘察、设计活动，应当坚持先勘察、后设计、再施工的原则。

第五条 县级以上人民政府建设行政主管部门和交通、水利等有关部门应当依照本条例的规定，加强对建设工程勘察、设计活动的监督管理。

建设工程勘察、设计单位必须依法进行建设工程勘察、设计，严格执行工程建设强制性标准，并对建设工程勘察、设计的质量负责。

第六条 国家鼓励在建设工程勘察、设计活动中采用先进技术、先进工艺、先进设备、新型材料和现代管理方法。

第二章 资质资格管理

第七条 国家对从事建设工程勘察、设计活动的单位，实行资质管理制度。具体办法由国务院建设行政主管部门商国务院有关部门制定。

第八条 建设工程勘察、设计单位应当在其资质等级许可的范围内承揽建设工程勘察、设计业务。

禁止建设工程勘察、设计单位超越其资质等级许可的范围或者以其他建设工程勘察、设计单位的名义承揽建设工程勘察、设计业务。禁止建设工程勘察、设计单位允许其他单位或者个人以本单位的名义承揽建设工程勘察、设计业务。

第九条　国家对从事建设工程勘察、设计活动的专业技术人员，实行执业资格注册管理制度。

未经注册的建设工程勘察、设计人员，不得以注册执业人员的名义从事建设工程勘察、设计活动。

第十条　建设工程勘察、设计注册执业人员和其他专业技术人员只能受聘于一个建设工程勘察、设计单位；未受聘于建设工程勘察、设计单位的，不得从事建设工程的勘察、设计活动。

第十一条　建设工程勘察、设计单位资质证书和执业人员注册证书，由国务院建设行政主管部门统一制作。

第三章　建设工程勘察设计发包与承包

第十二条　建设工程勘察、设计发包依法实行招标发包或者直接发包。

第十三条　建设工程勘察、设计应当依照《中华人民共和国招标投标法》的规定，实行招标发包。

第十四条　建设工程勘察、设计方案评标，应当以投标人的业绩、信誉和勘察、设计人员的能力以及勘察、设计方案的优劣为依据，进行综合评定。

第十五条　建设工程勘察、设计的招标人应当在评标委员会推荐的候选方案中确定中标方案。但是，建设工程勘察、设计的招标人认为评标委员会推荐的候选方案不能最大限度满足招标文件规定的要求的，应当依法重新招标。

第十六条　下列建设工程的勘察、设计，经有关主管部门批准，可以直接发包：

（一）采用特定的专利或者专有技术的；

（二）建筑艺术造型有特殊要求的；

（三）国务院规定的其他建设工程的勘察、设计。

第十七条　发包方不得将建设工程勘察、设计业务发包给不具有相应勘察、设计资质等级的建设工程勘察、设计单位。

第十八条　发包方可以将整个建设工程的勘察、设计发包给一个勘察、设计单位；也可以将建设工程的勘察、设计分别发包给几个勘察、设计单位。

第十九条　除建设工程主体部分的勘察、设计外，经发包方书面同意，承包方可以将建设工程其他部分的勘察、设计再分包给其他具有相应资质等级的建设工程勘察、设计单位。

第二十条　建设工程勘察、设计单位不得将所承揽的建设工程勘察、设计转包。

第二十一条　承包方必须在建设工程勘察、设计资质证书规定的资质等级和业务范围内承揽建设工程的勘察、设计业务。

第二十二条　建设工程勘察、设计的发包方与承包方，应当执行国家规定的建设工程勘察、设计程序。

第二十三条　建设工程勘察、设计的发包方与承包方应当签订建设工程勘察、设计合同。

第二十四条　建设工程勘察、设计发包方与承包方应当执行国家有关建设工程勘察费、设计费的管理规定。

第四章　建设工程勘察设计文件的编制与实施

第二十五条　编制建设工程勘察、设计文件，应当以下列规定为依据：

（一）项目批准文件；

（二）城乡规划；

（三）工程建设强制性标准；

（四）国家规定的建设工程勘察、设计深度要求。

铁路、交通、水利等专业建设工程，还应当以专业规划的要求为依据。

第二十六条　编制建设工程勘察文件，应当真实、准确，满足建设工程规划、选址、设计、岩土治理和施工的需要。

编制方案设计文件，应当满足编制初步设计文件和控制概算的需要。

编制初步设计文件，应当满足编制施工招标文件、主要设备材料订货和编制施工图设计文件的需要。

编制施工图设计文件，应当满足设备材料采购、非标准设备制作和施工的需要，并注明建设工程合理使用年限。

第二十七条　设计文件中选用的材料、构配件、设备，应当注明其规格、型号、性能等技术指标，其质量要求必须符合国家规定的标准。

除有特殊要求的建筑材料、专用设备和工艺生产线等外，设计单位不得指定生产厂、供应商。

第二十八条　建设单位、施工单位、监理单位不得修改建设工程勘察、设计文件；确需修改建设工程勘察、设计文件的，应当由原建设工程勘察、设计单位修改。经原建设工程勘察、设计单位书面同意，建设单位也可以委托其他具有相应资质的建设工程勘察、设计单位修改。修改单位对修改的勘察、设计文件承担相应责任。

施工单位、监理单位发现建设工程勘察、设计文件不符合工程建设强制性标准、合同约定的质量要求的，应当报告建设单位，建设单位有权要求建设工程勘察、设计单位对建设工程勘察、设计文件进行补充、修改。

建设工程勘察、设计文件内容需要作重大修改的，建设单位应当报经原审批机关批准后，方可修改。

第二十九条　建设工程勘察、设计文件中规定采用的新技术、新材料，可能影响建设工程质量和安全，又没有国家技术标准的，应当由国家认可的检测机构进行试验、论证，出具检测报告，并经国务院有关部门或者省、自治区、直辖市人民政府有关部门组织的建设工程技术专家委员会审定后，方可使用。

第三十条　建设工程勘察、设计单位应当在建设工程施工前，向施工单位和监理单位说明建设工程勘察、设计意图，解释建设工程勘察、设计文件。

建设工程勘察、设计单位应当及时解决施工中出现的勘察、设计问题。

第五章　监督管理

第三十一条　国务院建设行政主管部门对全国的建设工程勘察、设计活动实施统一监督管理。国务院铁路、交通、水利等有关部门按照国务院规定的职责分工，负责对全国的有关专业建设工程勘察、设计活动的监督管理。

县级以上地方人民政府建设行政主管部门对本行政区域内的建设工程勘察、设计活动实施监督管理。县级以上地方人民政府交通、水利等有关部门在各自的职责范围内，负责对本行政区域内的有关专业建设工程勘察、设计活动的监督管理。

第三十二条　建设工程勘察、设计单位在建设工程勘察、设计资质证书规定的业务范围内跨部门、跨地区承揽勘察、设计业务的，有关地方人民政府及其所属部门不得设置障碍，不得违反国家规定收取任何费用。

第三十三条　县级以上人民政府建设行政主管部门或者交通、水利等有关部门应当对施工图设计文件中涉及公共利益、公众安全、工程建设强制性标准的内容进行审查。

施工图设计文件未经审查批准的，不得使用。

第三十四条　任何单位和个人对建设工程勘察、设计活动中的违法行为都有权检举、控告、投诉。

第六章　罚　　则

第三十五条　违反本条例第八条规定的，责令停止违法行为，处合同约定的勘察费、设计费1倍以上2倍以下的罚款，有违法所得的，予以没收；可以责令停业整顿，降低资质等级；情节严重的，吊销资质证书。

未取得资质证书承揽工程的，予以取缔，依照前款规定处以罚款；有违法所得的，予以没收。

以欺骗手段取得资质证书承揽工程的，吊销资质证书，依照本条第一款规定处以罚款；有违法所得的，予以没收。

第三十六条　违反本条例规定，未经注册，擅自以注册建设工程勘察、设计人员的名义从事建设工程勘察、设计活动的，责令停止违法行为，没收违法所得，处违法所得2倍以上5倍以下罚款；给他人造成损失的，依法承担赔偿责任。

第三十七条　违反本条例规定，建设工程勘察、设计注册执业人员和其他专业技术人员未受聘于一个建设工程勘察、设计单位或者同时受聘于两个以上建设工程勘察、设计单位，从事建设工程勘察、设计活动的，责令停止违法行为，没收违法所得，处违法所得2倍以上5倍以下的罚款；情节严重的，可以责令停止执行业务或者吊销资格证书；给他人造成损失的，依法承担赔偿责任。

第三十八条　违反本条例规定，发包方将建设工程勘察、设计业务发包给不具有相应资质等级的建设工程勘察、设计单位的，责令改正，处50万元以上100万元以下的罚款。

第三十九条　违反本条例规定，建设工程勘察、设计单位将所承揽的建设工程勘察、设计转包的，责令改正，没收违法所得，处合同约定的勘察费、设计费25%以上50%以下的罚款，可以责令停业整顿，降低资质等级；情节严重的，吊销资质证书。

第四十条　违反本条例规定，勘察、设计单位未依据项目批准文件，城乡规划及专业规划，国家规定的建设工程勘察、设计深度要求编制建设工程勘察、设计文件的，责令限期改正；逾期不改正的，处10万元以上30万元以下的罚款；造成工程质量事故或者环境污染和生态破坏的，责令停业整顿，降低资质等级；情节严重的，吊销资质证书；造成损失的，依法承担赔偿责任。

第四十一条　违反本条例规定，有下列行为之一的，依照《建设工程质量管理条例》第六十三条的规定给予处罚：

（一）勘察单位未按照工程建设强制性标准进行勘察的；

（二）设计单位未根据勘察成果文件进行工程设计的；

（三）设计单位指定建筑材料、建筑构配件的生产厂、供应商的；

（四）设计单位未按照工程建设强制性标准进行设计的。

第四十二条　本条例规定的责令停业整顿、降低资质等级和吊销资质证书、资格证书的行政处罚，由颁发资质证书、资格证书的机关决定；其他行政处罚，由建设行政主管部门或者其他有关部门依据法定职权范围决定。

依照本条例规定被吊销资质证书的，由工商行政管理部门吊销其营业执照。

第四十三条　国家机关工作人员在建设工程勘察、设计活动的监督管理工作中玩忽职守、滥用职权、徇私舞弊，构成犯罪的，依法追究刑事责任；尚不构成犯罪的，依法给予行政处分。

第七章　附　　则

第四十四条　抢险救灾及其他临时性建筑和农民自建两层以下住宅的勘察、设计活动，不适用本条例。

第四十五条　军事建设工程勘察、设计的管理，按照中央军事委员会的有关规定执行。

第四十六条　本条例自公布之日起施行。

第十节　建设工程质量管理条例

第一章　总　　则

第一条　为了加强对建设工程质量的管理，保证建设工程质量，保护人民生命和财产安全，根据《中华人民共和国建筑法》，制定本条例。

第二条　凡在中华人民共和国境内从事建设工程的新建、扩建、改建等有关活动及实施对建设工程质量监督管理的，必须遵守本条例。

本条例所称建设工程，是指土木工程、建筑工程、线路管道和设备安装工程及装修工程。

第三条　建设单位、勘察单位、设计单位、施工单位、工程监理单位依法对建设工程质量负责。

第四条　县级以上人民政府建设行政主管部门和其他有关部门应当加强对建设工程质量的监督管理。

第五条　从事建设工程活动，必须严格执行基本建设程序，坚持先勘察、后设计、再施工的原则。

县级以上人民政府及其有关部门不得超越权限审批建设项目或者擅自简化基本建设程序。

第六条　国家鼓励采用先进的科学技术和管理方法，提高建设工程质量。

第二章　建设单位的质量责任和义务

第七条　建设单位应当将工程发包给具有相应资质等级的单位。

建设单位不得将建设工程肢解发包。

第八条　建设单位应当依法对工程建设项目的勘察、设计、施工、监理以及与工程建设有关的重要设备、材料等的采购进行招标。

第九条　建设单位必须向有关的勘察、设计、施工、工程监理等单位提供与建设工程有关的原始资料。

原始资料必须真实、准确、齐全。

第十条　建设工程发包单位，不得迫使承包方以低于成本的价格竞标，不得任意压缩合理工期。

建设单位不得明示或者暗示设计单位或者施工单位违反工程建设强制性标准，降低建设工程质量。

第十一条　施工图设计文件审查的具体办法，由国务院建设行政主管部门会同国务院其他有关部门制定。

施工图设计文件未经审查批准的，不得使用。

第十二条　实行监理的建设工程，建设单位应当委托具有相应资质等级的工程监理单位进行监理，也可以委托具有工程监理相应资质等级并与被监理工程的施工承包单位没有隶属关系或者其他利害关系的该工程的设计单位进行监理。

下列建设工程必须实行监理：

（一）国家重点建设工程；

（二）大中型公用事业工程；

（三）成片开发建设的住宅小区工程；

（四）利用外国政府或者国际组织贷款、援助资金的工程；

（五）国家规定必须实行监理的其他工程。

第十三条　建设单位在领取施工许可证或者开工报告前，应当按照国家有关规定办理工程质量监督手续。

第十四条　按照合同约定，由建设单位采购建筑材料、建筑构配件和设备的，建设单位应当保证建筑材料、建筑构配件和设备符合设计文件和合同要求。

建设单位不得明示或者暗示施工单位使用不合格的建筑材料、建筑构配件和设备。

第十五条　涉及建筑主体和承重结构变动的装修工程，建设单位应当在施工前委托原设计单位或者具有相应资质等级的设计单位提出设计方案；没有设计方案的，不得施工。

房屋建筑使用者在装修过程中，不得擅自变动房屋建筑主体和承重结构。

第十六条　建设单位收到建设工程竣工报告后，应当组织设计、施工、工程监理等有关单位进行竣工验收。

建设工程竣工验收应当具备下列条件：

（一）完成建设工程设计和合同约定的各项内容；

（二）有完整的技术档案和施工管理资料；

（三）有工程使用的主要建筑材料、建筑构配件和设备的进场试验报告；

（四）有勘察、设计、施工、工程监理等单位分别签署的质量合格文件；

（五）有施工单位签署的工程保修书。

建设工程经验收合格的，方可交付使用。

第十七条　建设单位应当严格按照国家有关档案管理的规定，及时收集、整理建设项目各环节的文件资料，建立、健全建设项目档案，并在建设工程竣工验收后，及时向建设行政主管部门或者其他有关部门移交建设项目档案。

第三章　勘察、设计单位的质量责任和义务

第十八条　从事建设工程勘察、设计的单位应当依法取得相应等级的资质证书，并在其资质等级许可的范围内承揽工程。

禁止勘察、设计单位超越其资质等级许可的范围或者以其他勘察、设计单位的名义承揽工程。禁止勘察、设计单位允许其他单位或者个人以本单位的名义承揽工程。

勘察、设计单位不得转包或者违法分包所承揽的工程。

第十九条　勘察、设计单位必须按照工程建设强制性标准进行勘察、设计，并对其勘察、设计的质量负责。

注册建筑师、注册结构工程师等注册执业人员应当在设计文件上签字，对设计文件负责。

第二十条　勘察单位提供的地质、测量、水文等勘察成果必须真实、准确。

第二十一条　设计单位应当根据勘察成果文件进行建设工程设计。

设计文件应当符合国家规定的设计深度要求，注明工程合理使用年限。

第二十二条 设计单位在设计文件中选用的建筑材料、建筑构配件和设备，应当注明规格、型号、性能等技术指标，其质量要求必须符合国家规定的标准。

除有特殊要求的建筑材料、专用设备、工艺生产线等外，设计单位不得指定生产厂、供应商。

第二十三条 设计单位应当就审查合格的施工图设计文件向施工单位作出详细说明。

第二十四条 设计单位应当参与建设工程质量事故分析，并对因设计造成的质量事故，提出相应的技术处理方案。

第四章 施工单位的质量责任和义务

第二十五条 施工单位应当依法取得相应等级的资质证书，并在其资质等级许可的范围内承揽工程。

禁止施工单位超越本单位资质等级许可的业务范围或者以其他施工单位的名义承揽工程。禁止施工单位允许其他单位或者个人以本单位的名义承揽工程。

施工单位不得转包或者违法分包工程。

第二十六条 施工单位对建设工程的施工质量负责。

施工单位应当建立质量责任制，确定工程项目的项目经理、技术负责人和施工管理负责人。

建设工程实行总承包的，总承包单位应当对全部建设工程质量负责；建设工程勘察、设计、施工、设备采购的一项或者多项实行总承包的，总承包单位应当对其承包的建设工程或者采购的设备的质量负责。

第二十七条 总承包单位依法将建设工程分包给其他单位的，分包单位应当按照分包合同的约定对其分包工程的质量向总承包单位负责，总承包单位与分包单位对分包工程的质量承担连带责任。

第二十八条 施工单位必须按照工程设计图纸和施工技术标准施工，不得擅自修改工程设计，不得偷工减料。

施工单位在施工过程中发现设计文件和图纸有差错的，应当及时提出意见和建议。

第二十九条 施工单位必须按照工程设计要求、施工技术标准和合同约定，对建筑材料、建筑构配件、设备和商品混凝土进行检验，检验应当有书面记录和专人签字；未经检验或者检验不合格的，不得使用。

第三十条 施工单位必须建立、健全施工质量的检验制度，严格工序管理，作好隐蔽工程的质量检查和记录。隐蔽工程在隐蔽前，施工单位应当通知建设单位和建设工程质量监督机构。

第三十一条 施工人员对涉及结构安全的试块、试件以及有关材料，应当在建设单位或者工程监理单位监督下现场取样，并送具有相应资质等级的质量检测单位进行检测。

第三十二条 施工单位对施工中出现质量问题的建设工程或者竣工验收不合格的建设工程，应当负责返修。

第三十三条 施工单位应当建立、健全教育培训制度，加强对职工的教育培训；未经教育培训或者考核不合格的人员，不得上岗作业。

第五章 工程监理单位的质量责任和义务

第三十四条 工程监理单位应当依法取得相应等级的资质证书，并在其资质等级许可的范围内承担工程监理业务。

禁止工程监理单位超越本单位资质等级许可的范围或者以其他工程监理单位的名义承担工程监理业务。禁止工程监理单位允许其他单位或者个人以本单位的名义承担工程监理业务。

工程监理单位不得转让工程监理业务。

第三十五条　工程监理单位与被监理工程的施工承包单位以及建筑材料、建筑构配件和设备供应单位有隶属关系或者其他利害关系的，不得承担该项建设工程的监理业务。

第三十六条　工程监理单位应当依照法律、法规以及有关技术标准、设计文件和建设工程承包合同，代表建设单位对施工质量实施监理，并对施工质量承担监理责任。

第三十七条　工程监理单位应当选派具备相应资格的总监理工程师和监理工程师进驻施工现场。

未经监理工程师签字，建筑材料、建筑构配件和设备不得在工程上使用或者安装，施工单位不得进行下一道工序的施工。未经总监理工程师签字，建设单位不拨付工程款，不进行竣工验收。

第三十八条　监理工程师应当按照工程监理规范的要求，采取旁站、巡视和平行检验等形式，对建设工程实施监理。

第六章　建设工程质量保修

第三十九条　建设工程实行质量保修制度。

建设工程承包单位在向建设单位提交工程竣工验收报告时，应当向建设单位出具质量保修书。质量保修书中应当明确建设工程的保修范围、保修期限和保修责任等。

第四十条　在正常使用条件下，建设工程的最低保修期限为：

(一)基础设施工程、房屋建筑的地基基础工程和主体结构工程，为设计文件规定的该工程的合理使用年限；

(二)屋面防水工程、有防水要求的卫生间、房间和外墙面的防渗漏，为 5 年；

(三)供热与供冷系统，为 2 个采暖期、供冷期；

(四)电气管线、给排水管道、设备安装和装修工程，为 2 年。

其他项目的保修期限由发包方与承包方约定。

建设工程的保修期，自竣工验收合格之日起计算。

第四十一条　建设工程在保修范围和保修期限内发生质量问题的，施工单位应当履行保修义务，并对造成的损失承担赔偿责任。

第四十二条　建设工程在超过合理使用年限后需要继续使用的，产权所有人应当委托具有相应资质等级的勘察、设计单位鉴定，并根据鉴定结果采取加固、维修等措施，重新界定使用期。

第七章　监督管理

第四十三条　国家实行建设工程质量监督管理制度。

国务院建设行政主管部门对全国的建设工程质量实施统一监督管理。国务院铁路、交通、水利等有关部门按照国务院规定的职责分工，负责对全国的有关专业建设工程质量的监督管理。

县级以上地方人民政府建设行政主管部门对本行政区域内的建设工程质量实施监督管理。县级以上地方人民政府交通、水利等有关部门在各自的职责范围内，负责对本行政区域内的专业建设工程质量的监督管理。

第四十四条　国务院建设行政主管部门和国务院铁路、交通、水利等有关部门应当加强对有关建设工程质量的法律、法规和强制性标准执行情况的监督检查。

第四十五条　国务院发展计划部门按照国务院规定的职责，组织稽察特派员，对国家出资的重大建设项目实施监督检查。

国务院经济贸易主管部门按照国务院规定的职责，对国家重大技术改造项目实施监督检查。

第四十六条　建设工程质量监督管理，可民由建设行政主管部门或者其他有关部门委托的建设工程质量监督机构具体实施。

从事房屋建筑工程和市政基础设施工程质量监督的机构，必须按照国家有关规定经国务院建设行政主管部门或者省、自治区、直辖市人民政府建设行政主管部门考核；从事专业建设工程质量监督的机构，必须按照国家有关规定经国务院有关部门或者省、自治区、直辖市人民政府有关部门考核。经考核合格后，方可实施质量监督。

第四十七条　县级以上地方人民政府建设行政主管部门和其他有关部门应当加强对有关建设工程质量的法律、法规和强制性标准执行情况的监督检查。

第四十八条　县级以上人民政府建设行政主管部门和其他有关部门履行监督检查职责时，有权采取下列措施：

（一）要求被检查的单位提供有关工程质量的文件和资料；

（二）进入被检查单位的施工现场进行检查；

（三）发现有影响工程质量的问题时，责令改正。

第四十九条　建设单位应当自建设工程竣工验收合格之日起15日内，将建设工程竣工验收报告和规划、公安消防、环保等部门出具的认可文件或者准许使用文件报建设行政主管部门或者其他有关部门备案。

建设行政主管部门或者其他有关部门发现建设单位在竣工验收过程中有违反国家有关建设工程质量管理规定行为的，责令停止使用，重新组织竣工验收。

第五十条　有关单位和个人对县级以上人民政府建设行政主管部门和其他有关部门进行的监督检查应当支持与配合，不得拒绝或者阻碍建设工程质量监督检查人员依法执行职务。

第五十一条　供水、供电、供气、公安消防等部门或者单位不得明示或者暗示建设单位、施工单位购买其指定的生产供应单位的建筑材料、建筑构配件和设备。

第五十二条　建设工程发生质量事故，有关单位应当在24小时内向当地建设行政主管部门和其他有关部门报告。对重大质量事故，事故发生地的建设行政主管部门和其他有关部门应当按照事故类别和等级向当地人民政府和上级建设行政主管部门和其他有关部门报告。

特别重大质量事故的调查程序按照国务院有关规定办理。

第五十三条　任何单位和个人对建设工程的质量事故、质量缺陷都有权检举、控告、投诉。

第八章　罚　　则

第五十四条　违反本条例规定，建设单位将建设工程发包给不具有相应资质等级的勘察、设计、施工单位或者委托给不具有相应资质等级的工程监理单位的，责令改正，处50万元以上100万元以下的罚款。

第五十五条　违反本条例规定，建设单位将建设工程肢解发包的，责令改正，处工程合同价款0.5%以上1%以下的罚款；对全部或者部分使用国有资金的项目，并可以暂停项目执行或者暂停资金拨付。

第五十六条 违反本条例规定，建设单位有下列行为之一的，责令改正，处20万元以上50万元以下的罚款：

(一)迫使承包方以低于成本的价格竞标的；

(二)任意压缩合理工期的；

(三)明示或者暗示设计单位或者施工单位违反工程建设强制性标准，降低工程质量的；

(四)施工图设计文件未经审查或者审查不合格，擅自施工的；

(五)建设项目必须实行工程监理而未实行工程监理的；

(六)未按照国家规定办理工程质量监督手续的；

(七)明示或者暗示施工单位使用不合格的建筑材料、建筑构配件和设备的；

(八)未按照国家规定将竣工验收报告、有关认可文件或者准许使用文件报送备案的。

第五十七条 违反本条例规定，建设单位未取得施工许可证或者开工报告未经批准，擅自施工的，责令停止施工，限期改正，处工程合同价款1%以上2%以下的罚款。

第五十八条 违反本条例规定，建设单位有下列行为之一的，责令改正，处工程合同价款2%以上4%以下的罚款；造成损失的，依法承担赔偿责任：

(一)未组织竣工验收，擅自交付使用的；

(二)验收不合格，擅自交付使用的；

(三)对不合格的建设工程按照合格工程验收的。

第五十九条 违反本条例规定，建设工程竣工验收后，建设单位未向建设行政主管部门或者其他有关部门移交建设项目档案的，责令改正，处1万元以上10万元以下的罚款。

第六十条 违反本条例规定，勘察、设计、施工、工程监理单位超越本单位资质等级承揽工程的，责令停止违法行为，对勘察、设计单位或者工程监理单位处合同约定的勘察费、设计费或者监理酬金1倍以上2倍以下的罚款；对施工单位处工程合同价款2%以上4%以下的罚款，可以责令停业整顿，降低资质等级；情节严重的，吊销资质证书；有违法所得的，予以没收。

未取得资质证书承揽工程的，予以取缔，依照前款规定处以罚款；有违法所得的，予以没收。

以欺骗手段取得资质证书承揽工程的，吊销资质证书，依照本条第一款规定处以罚款；有违法所得的，予以没收。

第六十一条 违反本条例规定，勘察、设计、施工、工程监理单位允许其他单位或者个人以本单位名义承揽工程的，责令改正，没收违法所得，对勘察、设计单位和工程监理单位处合同约定的勘察费、设计费和监理酬金1倍以上2倍以下的罚款；对施工单位处工程合同价款2%以上4%以下的罚款；可以责令停业整顿，降低资质等级；情节严重的，吊销资质证书。

第六十二条 违反本条例规定，承包单位将承包的工程转包或者违法分包的，责令改正，没收违法所得，对勘察、设计单位处合同约定的勘察费、设计费25%以上50%以下的罚款；对施工单位处工程合同价款0.5%以上1%以下的罚款；可以责令停业整顿，降低资质等级；情节严重的，吊销资质证书。

工程监理单位转让工程监理业务的，责令改正，没收违法所得，处合同约定的监理酬金25%以上50%以下的罚款；可以责令停业整顿，降低资质等级；情节严重的，吊销资质证书。

第六十三条 违反本条例规定，有下列行为之一的，责令改正，处10万元以上30万元以下的罚款：

(一)勘察单位未按照工程建设强制性标准进行勘察的；

(二)设计单位未根据勘察成果文件进行工程设计的；

(三)设计单位指定建筑材料、建筑构配件的生产厂、供应商的；

(四)设计单位未按照工程建设强制性标准进行设计的。

有前款所列行为，造成重大工程质量事故的，责令停业整顿，降低资质等级；情节严重的，吊销资质证书；造成损失的，依法承担赔偿责任。

第六十四条　违反本条例规定，施工单位在施工中偷工减料的，使用不合格的建筑材料、建筑构配件和设备的，或者有不按照工程设计图纸或者施工技术标准施工的其他行为的，责令改正，处工程合同价款2%以上4%以下的罚款；造成建设工程质量不符合规定的质量标准的，负责返工、修理，并赔偿因此造成的损失；情节严重的，责令停业整顿，降低资质等级或者吊销资质证书。

第六十五条　违反本条例规定，施工单位未对建筑材料、建筑构配件、设备和商品混凝土进行检验，或者未对涉及结构安全的试块、试件以及有关材料取样检测的，责令改正，处10万元以上20万元以下的罚款；情节严重的，责令停业整顿，降低资质等级或者吊销资质证书；造成损失的，依法承担赔偿责任。

第六十六条　违反本条例规定，施工单位不履行保修义务或者拖延履行保修义务的，责令改正，处10万元以上20万元以下的罚款，并对在保修期内因质量缺陷造成的损失承担赔偿责任。

第六十七条　工程监理单位有下列行为之一的，责令改正，处50万元以上100万元以下的罚款，降低资质等级或者吊销资质证书；有违法所得的，予以没收；造成损失的，承担连带赔偿责任：

(一)与建设单位或者施工单位串通，弄虚作假、降低工程质量的；

(二)将不合格的建设工程、建筑材料、建筑构配件和设备按照合格签字的。

第六十八条　违反本条例规定，工程监理单位与被监理工程的施工承包单位以及建筑材料、建筑构配件和设备供应单位有隶属关系或者其他利害关系承担该项建设工程的监理业务的，责令改正，处5万元以上10万元以下的罚款，降低资质等级或者吊销资质证书；有违法所得的，予以没收。

第六十九条　违反本条例规定，涉及建筑主体或者承重结构变动的装修工程，没有设计方案擅自施工的，责令改正，处50万元以上100万元以下的罚款；房屋建筑使用者在装修过程中擅自变动房屋建筑主体和承重结构的，责令改正，处5万元以上10万元以下的罚款。

有前款所列行为，造成损失的，依法承担赔偿责任。

第七十条　发生重大工程质量事故隐瞒不报、谎报或者拖延报告期限的，对直接负责的主管人员和其他责任人员依法给予行政处分。

第七十一条　违反本条例规定，供水、供电、供气、公安消防等部门或者单位明示或者暗示建设单位或者施工单位购买其指定的生产供应单位的建筑材料、建筑构配件和设备的，责令改正。

第七十二条　违反本条例规定，注册建筑师、注册结构工程师、监理工程师等注册执业人员因过错造成质量事故的，责令停止执业1年；造成重大质量事故的，吊销执业资格证书，5年以内不予注册；情节特别恶劣的，终身不予注册。

第七十三条　依照本条例规定，给予单位罚款处罚的，对单位直接负责的主管人员和其他直接责任人员处单位罚款数额5%以上10%以下的罚款。

第七十四条　建设单位、设计单位、施工单位、工程监理单位违反国家规定，降低工程质量标准，造成重大安全事故，构成犯罪的，对直接责任人员依法追究刑事责任。

第七十五条　本条例规定的责令停业整顿，降低资质等级和吊销资质证书的行政处罚，由颁发资质证书的机关决定；其他行政处罚，由建设行政主管部门或者其他有关部门依照法定职权决定。

依照本条例规定被吊销资质证书的，由工商行政管理部门吊销其营业执照。

第七十六条　国家机关工作人员在建设工程质量监督管理工作中玩忽职守、滥用职权、徇私舞弊，构成犯罪的，依法追究刑事责任；尚不构成犯罪的，依法给予行政处分。

第七十七条　建设、勘察、设计、施工、工程监理单位的工作人员因调动工作、退休等原因离开该单位后，被发现在该单位工作期间违反国家有关建设工程质量管理规定，造成重大工程质量事故的，仍应当依法追究法律责任。

第九章　附　　则

第七十八条　本条例所称肢解发包，是指建设单位将应当由一个承包单位完成的建设工程分解成若干部分发包给不同的承包单位的行为。

本条例所称违法分包，是指下列行为：

（一）总承包单位将建设工程分包给不具备相应资质条件的单位的；

（二）建设工程总承包合同中未有约定，又未经建设单位认可，承包单位将其承包的部分建设工程交由其他单位完成的；

（三）施工总承包单位将建设工程主体结构的施工分包给其他单位的；

（四）分包单位将其承包的建设工程再分包的。

本条例所称转包，是指承包单位承包建设工程后，不履行合同约定的责任和义务，将其承包的全部建设工程转给他人或者将其承包的全部建设工程肢解以后以分包的名义分别转给其他单位承包的行为。

第七十九条　本条例规定的罚款和没收的违法所得，必须全部上缴国库。

第八十条　抢险救灾及其他临时性房屋建筑和农民自建低层住宅的建设活动，不适用本条例。

第八十一条　军事建设工程的管理，按照中央军事委员会的有关规定执行。

第八十二条　本条例自发布之日起施行。

附　刑法有关条款

第一百三十七条　建设单位、设计单位、施工单位、工程监理单位违反国家规定，降低工程质量标准，造成重大安全事故的，对直接责任人员处五年以下有期徒刑或者拘役，并处罚金；后果特别严重的，处五年以上十年以下有期徒刑，并处罚金。

【例 11-10-1】　根据《建设工程质量管理条例》的规定，监理单位代表建设单位对施工质量实施监理，并对施工质量承担监理责任，其监理的依据不包括：

A. 有关技术标准　　B. 设计文件

C. 工程承包合同　　D. 建设单位指令

解　《中华人民共和国建筑法》第三十二条规定，建筑工程监理应当依照法律、行政法规及有关的技术标准、设计文件和建筑工程承包合同，对承包单位在施工质量、建设工期和建设资金使用等方面，代表建设单位实施监督。

答案:D

【例 11-10-2】 有关建设单位的工程质量责任与义务，下列理解错误的是：

A. 可将一个工程的各部位分包给不同的设计或施工单位

B. 发包给具有相应资质登记的单位

C. 领取施工许可证或者开工前，办理工程质量监督手续

D. 委托具有相应资质等级的工程监理单位进行监理

解 《中华人民共和国建筑法》第二十四条规定，提倡对建筑工程实行总承包，禁止将建筑工程肢解发包。

答案:A

习 题

11-10-1 工程勘察设计单位超越其资质等级许可的范围承揽建设工程勘察设计业务的，将责令停止违法行为，处罚款额为合同约定的勘察费、设计费的多少倍？( )

A. 1 倍以下　　B. 1 倍以上，2 倍以下

C. 2 倍以上，5 倍以下　　D. 5 倍以上，10 倍以下

11-10-2 《建设工程质量管理条例》规定，建设单位拨付工程款必须经( )签字。

A. 总经理　　B. 总经济师

C. 总工程师　　D. 总监理工程师

第十一节 建设工程安全生产管理条例

第一章 总 则

第一条 为了加强建设工程安全生产监督管理，保障人民群众生命和财产安全，根据《中华人民共和国建筑法》、《中华人民共和国安全生产法》，制定本条例。

第二条 在中华人民共和国境内从事建设工程的新建、扩建、改建和拆除等有关活动及实施对建设工程安全生产的监督管理，必须遵守本条例。

本条例所称建设工程，是指土木工程、建筑工程、线路管道和设备安装工程及装修工程。

第三条 建设工程安全生产管理，坚持安全第一、预防为主的方针。

第四条 建设单位、勘察单位、设计单位、施工单位、工程监理单位及其他与建设工程安全生产有关的单位，必须遵守安全生产法律、法规的规定，保证建设工程安全生产，依法承担建设工程安全生产责任。

第五条 国家鼓励建设工程安全生产的科学技术研究和先进技术的推广应用，推进建设工程安全生产的科学管理。

第二章 建设单位的安全责任

第六条 建设单位应当向施工单位提供施工现场及毗邻区域内供水、排水、供电、供气、供热、通信、广播电视等地下管线资料，气象和水文观测资料，相邻建筑物和构筑物、地下工程的有关资料，并保证资料的真实、准确、完整。

建设单位因建设工程需要，向有关部门或者单位查询前款规定的资料时，有关部门或者单位应当及时提供。

第七条　建设单位不得对勘察、设计、施工、工程监理等单位提出不符合建设工程安全生产法律、法规和强制性标准规定的要求，不得压缩合同约定的工期。

第八条　建设单位在编制工程概算时，应当确定建设工程安全作业环境及安全施工措施所需费用。

第九条　建设单位不得明示或者暗示施工单位购买、租赁、使用不符合安全施工要求的安全防护用具、机械设备、施工机具及配件、消防设施和器材。

第十条　建设单位在申请领取施工许可证时，应当提供建设工程有关安全施工措施的资料。

依法批准开工报告的建设工程，建设单位应当自开工报告批准之日起 15 日内，将保证安全施工的措施报送建设工程所在地的县级以上地方人民政府建设行政主管部门或者其他有关部门备案。

第十一条　建设单位应当将拆除工程发包给具有相应资质等级的施工单位。

建设单位应当在拆除工程施工 15 日前，将下列资料报送建设工程所在地的县级以上地方人民政府建设行政主管部门或者其他有关部门备案：

(一)施工单位资质等级证明；

(二)拟拆除建筑物、构筑物及可能危及毗邻建筑的说明；

(三)拆除施工组织方案；

(四)堆放、清除废弃物的措施。

实施爆破作业的，应当遵守国家有关民用爆炸物品管理的规定。

第三章　勘察、设计、工程监理及其他有关单位的安全责任

第十二条　勘察单位应当按照法律、法规和工程建设强制性标准进行勘察，提供的勘察文件应当真实、准确，满足建设工程安全生产的需要。

勘察单位在勘察作业时，应当严格执行操作规程，采取措施保证各类管线、设施和周边建筑物、构筑物的安全。

第十三条　设计单位应当按照法律、法规和工程建设强制性标准进行设计，防止因设计不合理导致生产安全事故的发生。

设计单位应当考虑施工安全操作和防护的需要，对涉及施工安全的重点部位和环节在设计文件中注明，并对防范生产安全事故提出指导意见。

采用新结构、新材料、新工艺的建设工程和特殊结构的建设工程，设计单位应当在设计中提出保障施工作业人员安全和预防生产安全事故的措施建议。

设计单位和注册建筑师等注册执业人员应当对其设计负责。

第十四条　工程监理单位应当审查施工组织设计中的安全技术措施或者专项施工方案是否符合工程建设强制性标准。

工程监理单位在实施监理过程中，发现存在安全事故隐患的，应当要求施工单位整改；情况严重的，应当要求施工单位暂时停止施工，并及时报告建设单位。施工单位拒不整改或者不停止施工的，工程监理单位应当及时向有关主管部门报告。

工程监理单位和监理工程师应当按照法律、法规和工程建设强制性标准实施监理，并对建设工程安全生产承担监理责任。

第十五条　为建设工程提供机械设备和配件的单位，应当按照安全施工的要求配备齐全有效的保险、限位等安全设施和装置。

第十六条　出租的机械设备和施工机具及配件，应当具有生产(制造)许可证、产品合格证。

出租单位　应当对出租的机械设备和施工机具及配件的安全性能进行检测，在签订租赁协议时，应当出具检测合格证明。

禁止出租检测不合格的机械设备和施工机具及配件。

第十七条　在施工现场安装、拆卸施工起重机械和整体提升脚手架、模板等自升式架设设施，必须由具有相应资质的单位承担。

安装、拆卸施工起重机械和整体提升脚手架、模板等自升式架设设施，应当编制拆装方案、制定安全施工措施，并由专业技术人员现场监督。

施工起重机械和整体提升脚手架、模板等自升式架设设施安装完毕后，安装单位应当自检，出具自检合格证明，并向施工单位进行安全使用说明，办理验收手续并签字。

第十八条　施工起重机械和整体提升脚手架、模板等自升式架设设施的使用达到国家规定的检验检测期限的，必须经具有专业资质的检验检测机构检测。经检测不合格的，不得继续使用。

第十九条　检验检测机构对检测合格的施工起重机械和整体提升脚手架、模板等自升式架设设施，应当出具安全合格证明文件，并对检测结果负责。

第四章　施工单位的安全责任

第二十条　施工单位从事建设工程的新建、扩建、改建和拆除等活动，应当具备国家规定的注册资本、专业技术人员、技术装备和安全生产等条件，依法取得相应等级的资质证书，并在其资质等级许可的范围内承揽工程。

第二十一条　施工单位主要负责人依法对本单位的安全生产工作全面负责。施工单位应当建立健全安全生产责任制度和安全生产教育培训制度，制定安全生产规章制度和操作规程，保证本单位安全生产条件所需资金的投入，对所承担的建设工程进行定期和专项安全检查，并做好安全检查记录。

施工单位的项目负责人应当由取得相应执业资格的人员担任，对建设工程项目的安全施工负责，落实安全生产责任制度、安全生产规章制度和操作规程，确保安全生产费用的有效使用，并根据工程的特点组织制定安全施工措施，消除安全事故隐患，及时、如实报告生产安全事故。

第二十二条　施工单位对列入建设工程概算的安全作业环境及安全施工措施所需费用，应当用于施工安全防护用具及设施的采购和更新、安全施工措施的落实、安全生产条件的改善，不得挪作他用。

第二十三条　施工单位应当设立安全生产管理机构，配备专职安全生产管理人员。

专职安全生产管理人员负责对安全生产进行现场监督检查。发现安全事故隐患，应当及时向项目负责人和安全生产管理机构报告；对违章指挥、违章操作的，应当立即制止。

专职安全生产管理人员的配备办法由国务院建设行政主管部门会同国务院其他有关部门制定。

第二十四条　建设工程实行施工总承包的，由总承包单位对施工现场的安全生产负总责。

总承包单位应当自行完成建设工程主体结构的施工。

总承包单位依法将建设工程分包给其他单位的，分包合同中应当明确各自的安全生产方面的权利、义务。总承包单位和分包单位对分包工程的安全生产承担连带责任。

分包单位应当服从总承包单位的安全生产管理，分包单位不服从管理导致生产安全事故的，由分包单位承担主要责任。

第二十五条　垂直运输机械作业人员、安装拆卸工、爆破作业人员、起重信号工、登高架设作业人员等特种作业人员，必须按照国家有关规定经过专门的安全作业培训，并取得特种作业操作资格证书后，方可上岗作业。

第二十六条　施工单位应当在施工组织设计中编制安全技术措施和施工现场临时用电方案，对下列达到一定规模的危险性较大的分部分项工程编制专项施工方案，并附具安全验算结果，经施工单位技术负责人、总监理工程师签字后实施，由专职安全生产管理人员进行现场监督：

（一）基坑支护与降水工程；

（二）土方开挖工程；

（三）模板工程；

（四）起重吊装工程；

（五）脚手架工程；

（六）拆除、爆破工程；

（七）国务院建设行政主管部门或者其他有关部门规定的其他危险性较大的工程。

对前款所列工程中涉及深基坑、地下暗挖工程、高大模板工程的专项施工方案，施工单位还应当组织专家进行论证、审查。

本条第一款规定的达到一定规模的危险性较大工程的标准，由国务院建设行政主管部门会同国务院其他有关部门制定。

第二十七条　建设工程施工前，施工单位负责项目管理的技术人员应当对有关安全施工的技术要求向施工作业班组、作业人员作出详细说明，并由双方签字确认。

第二十八条　施工单位应当在施工现场入口处、施工起重机械、临时用电设施、脚手架、出入通道口、楼梯口、电梯井口、孔洞口、桥梁口、隧道口、基坑边沿、爆破物及有害危险气体和液体存放处等危险部位，设置明显的安全警示标志。安全警示标志必须符合国家标准。

施工单位应当根据不同施工阶段和周围环境及季节、气候的变化，在施工现场采取相应的安全施工措施。施工现场暂时停止施工的，施工单位应当做好现场防护，所需费用由责任方承担，或者按照合同约定执行。

第二十九条　施工单位应当将施工现场的办公、生活区与作业区分开设置，并保持安全距离；办公、生活区的选址应当符合安全性要求。职工的膳食、饮水、休息场所等应当符合卫生标准。施工单位不得在尚未竣工的建筑物内设置员工集体宿舍。

施工现场临时搭建的建筑物应当符合安全使用要求。施工现场使用的装配式活动房屋应当具有产品合格证。

第三十条　施工单位对因建设工程施工可能造成损害的毗邻建筑物、构筑物和地下管线等，应当采取专项防护措施。

施工单位应当遵守有关环境保护法律、法规的规定，在施工现场采取措施，防止或者减少粉尘、废气、废水、固体废物、噪声、振动和施工照明对人和环境的危害和污染。

在城市市区内的建设工程，施工单位应当对施工现场实行封闭围挡。

第三十一条　施工单位应当在施工现场建立消防安全责任制度，确定消防安全责任人，制定用火、用电、使用易燃易爆材料等各项消防安全管理制度和操作规程，设置消防通道、消防水源，配备消防设施和灭火器材，并在施工现场入口处设置明显标志。

第三十二条　施工单位应当向作业人员提供安全防护用具和安全防护服装，并书面告知危险岗位的操作规程和违章操作的危害。

作业人员有权对施工现场的作业条件、作业程序和作业方式中存在的安全问题提出批评、检举和控告，有权拒绝违章指挥和强令冒险作业。

在施工中发生危及人身安全的紧急情况时，作业人员有权立即停止作业或者在采取必要的应急措施后撤离危险区域。

第三十三条　作业人员应当遵守安全施工的强制性标准、规章制度和操作规程，正确使用安全防护用具、机械设备等。

第三十四条　施工单位采购、租赁的安全防护用具、机械设备、施工机具及配件，应当具有生产(制造)许可证、产品合格证，并在进入施工现场前进行查验。

施工现场的安全防护用具、机械设备、施工机具及配件必须由专人管理，定期进行检查、维修和保养，建立相应的资料档案，并按照国家有关规定及时报废。

第三十五条　施工单位在使用施工起重机械和整体提升脚手架、模板等自升式架设设施前，应当组织有关单位进行验收，也可以委托具有相应资质的检验检测机构进行验收；使用承租的机械设备和施工机具及配件的，由施工总承包单位、分包单位、出租单位和安装单位共同进行验收。验收合格的方可使用。

《特种设备安全监察条例》规定的施工起重机械，在验收前应当经有相应资质的检验检测机构监督检验合格。

施工单位应当自施工起重机械和整体提升脚手架、模板等自升式架设设施验收合格之日起30日内，向建设行政主管部门或者其他有关部门登记。登记标志应当置于或者附着于该设备的显著位置。

第三十六条　施工单位的主要负责人、项目负责人、专职安全生产管理人员应当经建设行政主管部门或者其他有关部门考核合格后方可任职。

施工单位应当对管理人员和作业人员每年至少进行一次安全生产教育培训，其教育培训情况记入个人工作档案。安全生产教育培训考核不合格的人员，不得上岗。

第三十七条　作业人员进入新的岗位或者新的施工现场前，应当接受安全生产教育培训。未经教育培训或者教育培训考核不合格的人员，不得上岗作业。

施工单位在采用新技术、新工艺、新设备、新材料时，应当对作业人员进行相应的安全生产教育培训。

第三十八条　施工单位应当为施工现场从事危险作业的人员办理意外伤害保险。

意外伤害保险费由施工单位支付。实行施工总承包的，由总承包单位支付意外伤害保险费。意外伤害保险期限自建设工程开工之日起至竣工验收合格止。

第五章　监督管理

第三十九条　国务院负责安全生产监督管理的部门依照《中华人民共和国安全生产法》的规定，对全国建设工程安全生产工作实施综合监督管理。

县级以上地方人民政府负责安全生产监督管理的部门依照《中华人民共和国安全生产法》的规定，对本行政区域内建设工程安全生产工作实施综合监督管理。

第四十条　国务院建设行政主管部门对全国的建设工程安全生产实施监督管理。国务院铁路、交通、水利等有关部门按照国务院规定的职责分工，负责有关专业建设工程安全生产的监督管理。

县级以上地方人民政府建设行政主管部门对本行政区域内的建设工程安全生产实施监督管理。县级以上地方人民政府交通、水利等有关部门在各自的职责范围内，负责本行政区域内的专业建设工程安全生产的监督管理。

第四十一条　建设行政主管部门和其他有关部门应当将本条例第十条、第十一条规定的有关资料的主要内容抄送同级负责安全生产监督管理的部门。

第四十二条　建设行政主管部门在审核发放施工许可证时，应当对建设工程是否有安全施工措施进行审查，对没有安全施工措施的，不得颁发施工许可证。

建设行政主管部门或者其他有关部门对建设工程是否有安全施工措施进行审查时，不得收取费用。

第四十三条　县级以上人民政府负有建设工程安全生产监督管理职责的部门在各自的职责范围内履行安全监督检查职责时，有权采取下列措施：

（一）要求被检查单位提供有关建设工程安全生产的文件和资料；

（二）进入被检查单位施工现场进行检查；

（三）纠正施工中违反安全生产要求的行为；

（四）对检查中发现的安全事故隐患，责令立即排除；重大安全事故隐患排除前或者排除过程中无法保证安全的，责令从危险区域内撤出作业人员或者暂时停止施工。

第四十四条　建设行政主管部门或者其他有关部门可以将施工现场的监督检查委托给建设工程安全监督机构具体实施。

第四十五条　国家对严重危及施工安全的工艺、设备、材料实行淘汰制度。具体目录由国务院建设行政主管部门会同国务院其他有关部门制定并公布。

第四十六条　县级以上人民政府建设行政主管部门和其他有关部门应当及时受理对建设工程生产安全事故及安全事故隐患的检举、控告和投诉。

第六章　生产安全事故的应急救援和调查处理

第四十七条　县级以上地方人民政府建设行政主管部门应当根据本级人民政府的要求，制定本行政区域内建设工程特大生产安全事故应急救援预案。

第四十八条　施工单位应当制定本单位生产安全事故应急救援预案，建立应急救援组织或者配备应急救援人员，配备必要的应急救援器材、设备，并定期组织演练。

第四十九条　施工单位应当根据建设工程施工的特点、范围，对施工现场易发生重大事故的部位、环节进行监控，制定施工现场生产安全事故应急救援预案。实行施工总承包的，由总承包单位统一组织编制建设工程生产安全事故应急救援预案，工程总承包单位和分包单位按照应急救援预案，各自建立应急救援组织或者配备应急救援人员，配备救援器材、设备，并定期组织演练。

第五十条　施工单位发生生产安全事故，应当按照国家有关伤亡事故报告和调查处理的规定，及时、如实地向负责安全生产监督管理的部门、建设行政主管部门或者其他有关部门报告；特种设备发生事故的，还应当同时向特种设备安全监督管理部门报告。接到报告的部门应当按照国家有关规定，如实上报。

实行施工总承包的建设工程，由总承包单位负责上报事故。

第五十一条　发生生产安全事故后，施工单位应当采取措施防止事故扩大，保护事故现场。需要移动现场物品时，应当做出标记和书面记录，妥善保管有关证物。

第五十二条　建设工程生产安全事故的调查、对事故责任单位和责任人的处罚与处理，按照有关法律、法规的规定执行。

第七章 法律责任

第五十三条 违反本条例的规定，县级以上人民政府建设行政主管部门或者其他有关行政管理部门的工作人员，有下列行为之一的，给予降级或者撤职的行政处分；构成犯罪的，依照刑法有关规定追究刑事责任：

（一）对不具备安全生产条件的施工单位颁发资质证书的；

（二）对没有安全施工措施的建设工程颁发施工许可证的；

（三）发现违法行为不予查处的；

（四）不依法履行监督管理职责的其他行为。

第五十四条 违反本条例的规定，建设单位未提供建设工程安全生产作业环境及安全施工措施所需费用的，责令限期改正；逾期未改正的，责令该建设工程停止施工。

建设单位未将保证安全施工的措施或者拆除工程的有关资料报送有关部门备案的，责令限期改正，给予警告。

第五十五条 违反本条例的规定，建设单位有下列行为之一的，责令限期改正，处20万元以上50万元以下的罚款；造成重大安全事故，构成犯罪的，对直接责任人员，依照刑法有关规定追究刑事责任；造成损失的，依法承担赔偿责任：

（一）对勘察、设计、施工、工程监理等单位提出不符合安全生产法律、法规和强制性标准规定的要求的；

（二）要求施工单位压缩合同约定的工期的；

（三）将拆除工程发包给不具有相应资质等级的施工单位的。

第五十六条 违反本条例的规定，勘察单位、设计单位有下列行为之一的，责令限期改正，处10万元以上30万元以下的罚款；情节严重的，责令停业整顿，降低资质等级，直至吊销资质证书；造成重大安全事故，构成犯罪的，对直接责任人员，依照刑法有关规定追究刑事责任；造成损失的，依法承担赔偿责任：

（一）未按照法律、法规和工程建设强制性标准进行勘察、设计的；

（二）采用新结构、新材料、新工艺的建设工程和特殊结构的建设工程，设计单位未在设计中提出保障施工作业人员安全和预防生产安全事故的措施建议的。

第五十七条 违反本条例的规定，工程监理单位有下列行为之一的，责令限期改正；逾期未改正的，责令停业整顿，并处10万元以上30万元以下的罚款；情节严重的，降低资质等级，直至吊销资质证书；造成重大安全事故，构成犯罪的，对直接责任人员，依照刑法有关规定追究刑事责任；造成损失的，依法承担赔偿责任：

（一）未对施工组织设计中的安全技术措施或者专项施工方案进行审查的；

（二）发现安全事故隐患未及时要求施工单位整改或者暂时停止施工的；

（三）施工单位拒不整改或者不停止施工，未及时向有关主管部门报告的；

（四）未依照法律、法规和工程建设强制性标准实施监理的。

第五十八条 注册执业人员未执行法律、法规和工程建设强制性标准的，责令停止执业3个月以上1年以下；情节严重的，吊销执业资格证书，5年内不予注册；造成重大安全事故的，终身不予注册；构成犯罪的，依照刑法有关规定追究刑事责任。

第五十九条 违反本条例的规定，为建设工程提供机械设备和配件的单位，未按照安全施工的要求配备齐全有效的保险、限位等安全设施和装置的，责令限期改正，处合同价款1倍以上3倍以下的罚款;造成损失的,依法承担赔偿责任。

第六十条　违反本条例的规定,出租单位出租未经安全性能检测或者经检测不合格的机械设备和施工机具及配件的,责令停业整顿,并处5万元以上10万元以下的罚款;造成损失的,依法承担赔偿责任。

第六十一条　违反本条例的规定,施工起重机械和整体提升脚手架、模板等自升式架设设施安装、拆卸单位有下列行为之一的,责令限期改正,处5万元以上10万元以下的罚款;情节严重的,责令停业整顿,降低资质等级,直至吊销资质证书;造成损失的,依法承担赔偿责任:

(一)未编制拆装方案、制定安全施工措施的;

(二)未由专业技术人员现场监督的;

(三)未出具自检合格证明或者出具虚假证明的;

(四)未向施工单位进行安全使用说明,办理移交手续的。

施工起重机械和整体提升脚手架、模板等自升式架设设施安装、拆卸单位有前款规定的第(一)项、第(三)项行为,经有关部门或者单位职工提出后,对事故隐患仍不采取措施,因而发生重大伤亡事故或者造成其他严重后果,构成犯罪的,对直接责任人员,依照刑法有关规定追究刑事责任。

第六十二条　违反本条例的规定,施工单位有下列行为之一的,责令限期改正;逾期未改正的,责令停业整顿,依照《中华人民共和国安全生产法》的有关规定处以罚款;造成重大安全事故,构成犯罪的,对直接责任人员,依照刑法有关规定追究刑事责任:

(一)未设立安全生产管理机构、配备专职安全生产管理人员或者分部分项工程施工时无专职安全生产管理人员现场监督的;

(二)施工单位的主要负责人、项目负责人、专职安全生产管理人员、作业人员或者特种作业人员,未经安全教育培训或者经考核不合格即从事相关工作的;

(三)未在施工现场的危险部位设置明显的安全警示标志,或者未按照国家有关规定在施工现场设置消防通道、消防水源、配备消防设施和灭火器材的;

(四)未向作业人员提供安全防护用具和安全防护服装的;

(五)未按照规定在施工起重机械和整体提升脚手架、模板等自升式架设设施验收合格后登记的;

(六)使用国家明令淘汰、禁止使用的危及施工安全的工艺、设备、材料的。

第六十三条　违反本条例的规定,施工单位挪用列入建设工程概算的安全生产作业环境及安全施工措施所需费用的,责令限期改正,处挪用费用20%以上50%以下的罚款;造成损失的,依法承担赔偿责任。

第六十四条　违反本条例的规定,施工单位有下列行为之一的,责令限期改正;逾期未改正的,责令停业整顿,并处5万元以上10万元以下的罚款;造成重大安全事故,构成犯罪的,对直接责任人员,依照刑法有关规定追究刑事责任:

(一)施工前未对有关安全施工的技术要求作出详细说明的;

(二)未根据不同施工阶段和周围环境及季节、气候的变化,在施工现场采取相应的安全施工措施,或者在城市市区内的建设工程的施工现场未实行封闭围挡的;

(三)在尚未竣工的建筑物内设置员工集体宿舍的;

(四)施工现场临时搭建的建筑物不符合安全使用要求的;

(五)未对因建设工程施工可能造成损害的毗邻建筑物、构筑物和地下管线等采取专项防护措施的。

施工单位有前款规定第(四)项、第(五)项行为,造成损失的,依法承担赔偿责任。

第六十五条　违反本条例的规定,施工单位有下列行为之一的,责令限期改正;逾期未改正的,责令停业整顿,并处10万元以上30万元以下的罚款;情节严重的,降低资质等级,直至吊销资质证书;造成重大安全事故,构成犯罪的,对直接责任人员,依照刑法有关规定追究刑事责任;造成损失的,依法承担赔偿责任:

(一)安全防护用具、机械设备、施工机具及配件在进入施工现场前未经查验或者查验不合格即投入使用的;

(二)使用未经验收或者验收不合格的施工起重机械和整体提升脚手架、模板等自升式架设设施的;

(三)委托不具有相应资质的单位承担施工现场安装、拆卸施工起重机械和整体提升脚手架、模板等自升式架设设施的;

(四)在施工组织设计中未编制安全技术措施、施工现场临时用电方案或者专项施工方案的。

第六十六条　违反本条例的规定,施工单位的主要负责人、项目负责人未履行安全生产管理职责的,责令限期改正;逾期未改正的,责令施工单位停业整顿;造成重大安全事故、重大伤亡事故或者其他严重后果,构成犯罪的,依照刑法有关规定追究刑事责任。

作业人员不服管理、违反规章制度和操作规程冒险作业造成重大伤亡事故或者其他严重后果,构成犯罪的,依照刑法有关规定追究刑事责任。

施工单位的主要负责人、项目负责人有前款违法行为,尚不够刑事处罚的,处2万元以上20万元以下的罚款或者按照管理权限给予撤职处分;自刑罚执行完毕或者受处分之日起,5年内不得担任任何施工单位的主要负责人、项目负责人。

第六十七条　施工单位取得资质证书后,降低安全生产条件的,责令限期改正;经整改仍未达到与其资质等级相适应的安全生产条件的,责令停业整顿,降低其资质等级直至吊销资质证书。

第六十八条　本条例规定的行政处罚,由建设行政主管部门或者其他有关部门依照法定职权决定。

违反消防安全管理规定的行为,由公安消防机构依法处罚。

有关法律、行政法规对建设工程安全生产违法行为的行政处罚决定机关另有规定的,从其规定。

第八章　附　　则

第六十九条　抢险救灾和农民自建低层住宅的安全生产管理,不适用本条例。

第七十条　军事建设工程的安全生产管理,按照中央军事委员会的有关规定执行。

第七十一条　本条例自2004年2月1日起施行。

【例11-11-1】 根据《建设工程安全生产管理条例》的规定,施工单位实施爆破、起重吊装等施工时,应当安排现场的监督人员是:

A. 项目管理技术人员　　　　B 应急救援人员

C. 专职安全生产管理人员　　　　D. 专职质量管理人员

解　《中华人民共和国安全法》第四十条规定,生产经营单位进行爆破、吊装以及国务院安全生产监督管理部门会同国务院有关部门规定的其他危险作业,应当安排专门人员进行现场安全管理,确保操作规程的遵守和安全措施的落实。

答案:C

【例 11-1-2】 根据《建设工程安全生产管理条例》规定,建设单位确定建设工程安全作业环境及安全施工措施所需费用的时间是:

A. 编制工程概算时　　B. 编制设计预算时

C. 编制施工预算时　　D. 编制投资估算时

解 《建设工程安全生产管理条例》第八条规定:建设单位在编制工程概算时,应当确定建设工程安全作业环境及安全施工措施所需费用。

答案:A

习　题

11-11-1 深基坑支护与降水工程、模板工程、脚手架工程的施工专项方案必须经下列哪些人员签字后实施?(　　)

①经施工单位技术负责人　②总监理工程师　③结构设计人　④施工方法人代表

A. ①②　　B. ①②③　　C. ①②③④　　D. ①④

11-11-2 施工现场及毗邻区域内的各种管线及地下工程的有关资料(　　)。

A. 应由建设单位向施工单位提供　　B. 施工单位必须在开工前自行查清

C. 应由监理单位提供　　D. 应由政府有关部门提供

题解及参考答案

第二节

11-2-1 **解:**《中华人民共和国建筑法》第七条规定,建筑工程开工前,建设单位应当按照国家有关规定向工程所在地县级以上人民政府建设行政主管部门申请领取施工许可证;但是,国务院建设行政主管部门确定的限额以下的小型工程除外。按照国务院规定的权限和程序批准开工报告的建筑工程,不再领取施工许可证。

答案:D

11-2-2 **解:**《中华人民共和国建筑法》第九条规定,建设单位应当自领取施工许可证之日起三个月内开工。因故不能按期开工的,应当向发证机关申请延期;延期以两次为限,每次不超过三个月。既不开工又不申请延期或者超过延期时限的,施工许可证自行废止。

答案:A

11-2-3 **解:**《中华人民共和国建筑法》第三节。

答案:C

11-2-4 **解:**《中华人民共和国建筑法》第二条规定,在中华人民共和国境内从事建筑活动,实施对建筑活动的监督管理,应当遵守本法。本法所称建筑活动,是指各类房屋建筑及其附属设施的建造和与其配套的线路、管道、设备的安装活动。

答案:B

11-2-5 **解:**《中华人民共和国建筑法》第三十条规定,国家推行建筑工程监理制度。国务院可以规定实行强制监理的建筑工程的范围。

答案:A

11-2-6 **解:**见《中华人民共和国建筑法》第八条第(一)、(四)、(七)款规定,可知 A、B、D 项符合要求。

答案:C

第三节

11-3-1 **解:**《中华人民共和国安全生产法》第三条规定,安全生产工作,坚持安全第一、预防为主、综合治理的方针。

答案:A

11-3-2 **解:**《中华人民共和国安全生产法》第五条规定,生产经营单位的主要负责人对本单位的安全生产工作全面负责。

答案:A

第四节

11-4-1 **解:**《中华人民共和国招标投标法》第十二条规定,招标人具有编制招标文件和组织评标能力的,可以自行办理招标事宜。任何单位和个人不得强制其委托招标代理机构办理招标事宜。

答案:D

11-4-2 **解:**见《中华人民共和国招标投标法》第十条。

答案:A

11-4-3 **解:**见《中华人民共和国招标投标法》第三十七条。

答案:C

11-4-4 **解:**《中华人民共和国招标投标法》第三十七条规定,评标由招标人依法组建的评标委员会负责。依法必须进行招标的项目,其评标委员会由招标人的代表和有关技术、经济等方面的专家组成,成员人数为五人以上单数,其中技术、经济等方面的专家不得少于成员总数的三分之二。

答案:D

11-4-5 **解:**《中华人民共和国招标投标法》第三条规定,不是所有住宅项目,都要监理。

答案:D

11-4-6 **解:**《中华人民共和国招标投标法》第四十六条规定,招标人和中标人应当自中标通知书发出之日起三十日内,按照招标文件和中标人的投标文件订立书面合同。招标人和中标人不得再行订立背离合同实质性内容的其他协议。

答案:B

第五节

11-5-1 **解:**《中华人民共和国合同法》第五十四条规定,下列合同,当事人一方有权请求人民法院或者仲裁机构变更或者撤销:

(一)因重大误解订立的;

(二)在订立合同时显失公平的。

一方以欺诈、胁迫的手段或者乘人之危,使对方在违背真实意思的情况下订立的合同,受损害方有权请求人民法院或者仲裁机构变更或者撤销。当事人请求变更的,人民法院或者仲裁机构不得撤销。

答案:D

11-5-2 **解:**《中华人民共和国合同法》第一百一十五条规定,当事人可以依照《中华人民共和国担保法》约定一方向对方给付定金作为债权的担保。债务人履行债务后,定金应当抵作价款或者收回。给付定金的一方不履行约定的债务的,无权要求返还定金;收受定金的一方不履行约定的债务的,应当双倍返还定金。

答案:A

11-5-3 **解:**《中华人民共和国合同法》第十五条规定,要约邀请是希望他人向自己发出要约的意思表示。寄送的价目表、拍卖公告、招标公告、招股说明书、商业广告等为要约邀请。

答案:A

11-5-4 **解:**见《中华人民共和国合同法》第二条。

答案:A

11-5-5 **解:**《中华人民共和国合同法》第十八条规定,要约可以撤销。撤销要约的通知应当在受要约人发出承诺通知之前到达受要约人。

答案:A

11-5-6 **解:**《中华人民共和国合同法》第三十条规定,承诺的内容应当与要约的内容一致。受要约人对要约的内容作出实质性变更的,为新要约。有关合同标的、数量、质量、价款或者报酬、履行期限、履行地点和方式、违约责任和解决争议方法等的变更,是对要约内容的实质性变更。

答案:C

11-5-7 **解:**《中华人民共和国合同法》第三十二条规定,当事人采用合同书形式订立合同的,自双方当事人签字或者盖章时合同成立。

答案:B

11-5-8 **解:**《中华人民共和国建筑法》第二十七条规定,大型建筑工程或者结构复杂的建筑工程,可以由两个以上的承包单位联合共同承包。共同承包的各方对承包合同的履行承担连带责任。两个以上不同资质等级的单位实行联合共同承包的,应当按照资质等级低的单位的业务许可范围承揽工程。

答案:A

第六节

11-6-1 **解:**《中华人民共和国行政许可法》第五十八条规定,行政机关实施行政许可和对行政许可事项进行监督检查,不得收取任何费用。但是法律、行政法规另有规定的,依照其规定。

答案:A

11-6-2 **解:**《中华人民共和国行政许可法》第四十二条规定,除可以当场作出行政许可决定的外,行政机关应当自受理行政许可申请之日起二十日内作出行政许可决定。

二十日内不能作出决定的，经本行政机关负责人批准，可以延长十日，并应当将延长期限的理由告知申请人。但是法律、法规另有规定的，依照其规定。

答案：A

第七节

11-7-1 **解**：《中华人民共和国节约能源法》第二十条规定，用能产品的生产者、销售者，可以根据自愿原则，按照国家有关节能产品认证的规定，向经国务院认证认可监督管理部门认可的从事节能产品认证的机构提出节能产品认证申请；经认证合格后，取得节能产品认证证书，可以在用能产品或者其包装物上使用节能产品认证标志。

答案：A

11-7-2 **解**：《中华人民共和国节约能源法》第三十五条规定，建筑工程的建设、设计、施工和监理单位应当遵守建筑节能标准。不符合建筑节能标准的建筑工程，建设主管部门不得批准开工建设；已经开工建设的，应当责令停止施工、限期改正；已经建成的，不得销售或者使用。

答案：A

第八节

11-8-1 **解**：《中华人民共和国环境保护法》第四十五条规定，国家依照法律规定实行排污许可管理制度。实行排污许可管理的企业事业单位和其他生产经营者，应当按照排污许可证的要求排放污染物；未取得排污许可证的，不得排放污染物。

答案：A

11-8-2 **解**：《中华人民共和国环境保护法》第四十一条规定，建设项目中防治污染的设施，应当与主体工程同时设计、同时施工、同时投产使用。防治污染的设施应当符合经批准的环境影响评价文件要求，不得擅自拆除或闲置。

答案：D

11-8-3 **解**：《中华人民共和国环境保护法》第六十三条规定，企业事业单位和其他生产经营者有下列行为之一，尚不构成犯罪的，除依照有关法律法规规定予以处罚外，由县级以上人民政府环境保护主管部门或者其他有关部门将案件移送公安机关，对其直接负责的主管人员和其他直接责任人员，处十日以上十五日以下拘留；情节较轻的，处五日以上十日以下拘留：

（一）建设项目未依法进行环境影响评价，被责令停止建设，拒不执行的；

……

答案：A

第十节

11-10-1 **解**：《建设工程质量管理条例》第六十条规定，违反本条例规定，勘察、设计、施工、工程监理单位超越本单位资质等级承揽工程的，责令停止违法行为，对勘察、设计单位或者监理单位处合同约定的勘察费、设计费或者监理酬金1倍以上2倍以下的罚款；对施工单位处工程合同价款2%以上4%以下的罚款，可以责令停业整顿，降低资质等级；情节严重的，吊销资质证书；有违法所得的，予以没收。未取得资质证书承揽工程的，予以取缔，依照前款规定处以罚款；有违法所得的，予以没收。

答案：B

11-10-2 **解**：《建设工程质量管理条例》第三十七条规定，工程监理单位应当选派具备相应资格的总监理工程师和监理工程师进驻施工现场。未经监理工程师签字，建筑材料、建筑构配件和设备不得在工程上使用或者安装，施工单位不得进行下一道工序的施工。未经总监理工程师签字，建设单位不拨付工程款，不进行竣工验收。

答案：D

第十一节

11-11-1 **解**：《中华人民共和国安全生产法》第二十六条规定，施工单位应当在施工组织设计中编制安全技术措施和施工现场临时用电方案，对下列达到一定规模的危险性较大的分部分项工程编制专项施工方案，并附具安全验算结果，经施工单位技术负责人、总监理工程师签字后实施，由专职安全生产管理人员进行现场监督：

(一)基坑支护与降水工程；

(二)土方开挖工程；

(三)模板工程；

(四)起重吊装工程；

(五)脚手架工程；

(六)拆除、爆破工程。

答案：A

11-11-2 **解**：《建设工程安全生产管理条例》第六条规定，建设单位应当向施工单位提供施工现场及毗邻区域内供水、排水、供电、供气、供热、通信、广播电视等地下管线资料，气象和水文观测资料，相邻建筑物和构筑物、地下工程的有关资料，并保证资料的真实、准确、完整。

答案：A

附录一

全国勘察设计注册工程师资格考试
公共基础考试大纲

Ⅰ.工程科学基础

一、数学

1.1 空间解析几何

向量的线性运算;向量的数量积、向量积及混合积;两向量垂直、平行的条件;直线方程;平面方程;平面与平面、直线与直线、平面与直线之间的位置关系;点到平面、直线的距离;球面、母线平行于坐标轴的柱面、旋转轴为坐标轴的旋转曲面的方程;常用的二次曲面方程;空间曲线在坐标面上的投影曲线方程。

1.2 微分学

函数的有界性、单调性、周期性和奇偶性;数列极限与函数极限的定义及其性质;无穷小和无穷大的概念及其关系;无穷小的性质及无穷小的比较极限的四则运算;函数连续的概念;函数间断点及其类型;导数与微分的概念;导数的几何意义和物理意义;平面曲线的切线和法线;导数和微分的四则运算;高阶导数;微分中值定理;洛必达法则;函数的切线及法平面和切平面及法线;函数单调性的判别;函数的极值;函数曲线的凹凸性、拐点;偏导数与全微分的概念;二阶偏导数;多元函数的极值和条件极值;多元函数的最大、最小值极其简单应用。

1.3 积分学

原函数与不定积分的概念;不定积分的基本性质;基本积分公式;定积分的基本概念和性质(包括定积分中值定理);积分上限的函数及其导数;牛顿-莱布尼兹公式;不定积分和定积分的换元积分法与分部积分法;有理函数、三角函数的有理式和简单无理函数的积分;广义积分;二重积分与三重积分的概念、性质、计算和应用;两类曲线积分的概念、性质和计算;求平面图形的面积、平面曲线的弧长和旋转体的体积。

1.4 无穷级数

数项级数的敛散性概念;收敛级数的和;级数的基本性质与级数收敛的必要条件;几何级数与 p 级数及其收敛性;正项级数敛散性的判别法;任意项级数的绝对收敛与条件收敛;幂级数及其收敛半径、收敛区间和收敛域;幂级数的和函数;函数的泰勒级数展开;函数的傅里叶系数与傅里叶级数。

1.5 常微分方程

常微分方程的基本概念;变量可分离的微分方程;齐次微分方程;一阶线性微分方程;全微分方程;可降阶的高阶微分方程;线性微分方程解的性质及解的结构定理;

二阶常系数齐次线性微分方程。

1.6 线性代数

行列式的性质及计算;行列式按行展开定理的应用;矩阵的运算;逆矩阵的概念、性质及求法;矩阵的初等变换和初等矩阵;矩阵的秩;等价矩阵的概念和性质;向量的线性表示;向量组的线性相关和线性无关;线性方程组有解的判定;线性方程组求解;矩阵的特征值和特征向量的概念与性质;相似矩阵的概念和性质;矩阵的相似对角化;二次型及其矩阵表示;合同矩阵的概念和性质;二次型的秩;惯性定理;二次型及其矩阵的正定性。

1.7 概率与数理统计

随机事件与样本空间;事件的关系与运算;概率的基本性质;古典型概率;条件概率;概率的基本公式;事件的独立性;独立重复试验;随机变量;随机变量的分布函数;离散型随机变量的概率分布;连续型随机变量的概率密度;常见随机变量的分布;随机变量的数学期望、方差、标准差及其性质;随机变量函数的数学期望;矩、协方差、相关系数及其性质;总体;个体;简单随机样本;统计量;样本均值;样本方差和样本矩;χ^2 分布;t 分布;F 分布;点估计的概念;估计量与估计值;矩估计法;最大似然估计法;估计量的评选标准;区间估计的概念;单个正态总体的均值和方差的区间估计;两个正态总体的均值差和方差比的区间估计;显著性检验;单个正态总体的均值和方差的假设检验。

二、物理学

2.1 热学

气体状态参量;平衡态;理想气体状态方程;理想气体的压强和温度的统计解释;自由度;能量按自由度均分原理;理想气体内能;平均碰撞频率和平均自由程;麦克斯韦速率分布律;方均根速率;平均速率;最概然速率;功;热量;内能;热力学第一定律及其对理想气体等值过程的应用;绝热过程;气体的摩尔热容量;循环过程;卡诺循环;热机效率;净功;制冷系数;热力学第二定律及其统计意义;可逆过程和不可逆过程。

2.2 波动学

机械波的产生和传播;一维简谐波表达式;描述波的特征量;波面,波前,波线;波的能量、能流、能流密度;波的衍射;波的干涉;驻波;自由端反射与固定端反射;声波;声强级;多普勒效应。

2.3 光学

相干光的获得;杨氏双缝干涉;光程和光程差;薄膜干涉;光疏介质;光密介质;迈克尔逊干涉仪;惠更斯-菲涅尔原理;单缝衍射;光学仪器分辨本领;衍射光栅与光谱分析;X 射线衍射;布拉格公式;自然光和偏振光;布儒斯特定律;马吕斯定律;双折射现象。

三、化学

3.1 物质的结构和物质状态

原子结构的近代概念;原子轨道和电子云;原子核外电子分布;原子和离子的电子结

构；原子结构和元素周期律；元素周期表；周期族；元素性质及氧化物及其酸碱性。离子键的特征；共价键的特征和类型；杂化轨道与分子空间构型；分子结构式；键的极性和分子的极性；分子间力与氢键；晶体与非晶体；晶体类型与物质性质。

3.2 溶液

溶液的浓度；非电解质稀溶液通性；渗透压；弱电解质溶液的解离平衡；分压定律；解离常数；同离子效应；缓冲溶液；水的离子积及溶液的 pH 值；盐类的水解及溶液的酸碱性；溶度积常数；溶度积规则。

3.3 化学反应速率与化学平衡

反应热与热化学方程式；化学反应速率；温度和反应物浓度对反应速率的影响；活化能的物理意义；催化剂；化学反应方向的判断；化学平衡的特征；化学平衡移动原理。

3.4 氧化还原反应与电化学

氧化还原的概念；氧化剂与还原剂；氧化还原电对；氧化还原反应方程式的配平；原电池的组成和符号；电极反应与电池反应；标准电极电势；电极电势的影响因素及应用；金属腐蚀与防护。

3.5 有机化学

有机物特点、分类及命名；官能团及分子构造式；同分异构；有机物的重要反应：加成、取代、消除、氧化、催化加氢、聚合反应、加聚与缩聚；基本有机物的结构、基本性质及用途：烷烃、烯烃、炔烃、芳烃、卤代烃、醇、苯酚、醛和酮、羧酸、酯；合成材料：高分子化合物、塑料、合成橡胶、合成纤维、工程塑料。

四、理论力学

4.1 静力学

平衡；刚体；力；约束及约束力；受力图；力矩；力偶及力偶矩；力系的等效和简化；力的平移定理；平面力系的简化；主矢；主矩；平面力系的平衡条件和平衡方程式；物体系统（含平面静定桁架）的平衡；摩擦力；摩擦定律；摩擦角；摩擦自锁。

4.2 运动学

点的运动方程；轨迹；速度；加速度；切向加速度和法向加速度；平动和绕定轴转动；角速度；角加速度；刚体内任一点的速度和加速度。

4.3 动力学

牛顿定律；质点的直线振动；自由振动微分方程；固有频率；周期；振幅；衰减振动；阻尼对自由振动振幅的影响——振幅衰减曲线；受迫振动；受迫振动频率；幅频特性；共振；动力学普遍定理；动量；质心；动量定理及质心运动定理；动量及质心运动守恒；动量矩；动量矩定理；动量矩守恒；刚体定轴转动微分方程；转动惯量；回转半径；平行轴定理；功；动能；势能；动能定理及机械能守恒；达朗贝尔原理；惯性力；刚体作平动和绕定轴转动（转轴垂直于刚体的对称面）时惯性力系的简化；动静法。

五、材料力学

5.1 材料在拉伸、压缩时的力学性能

低碳钢、铸铁拉伸、压缩试验的应力-应变曲线；力学性能指标。

5.2　拉伸和压缩

轴力和轴力图；杆件横截面和斜截面上的应力；强度条件；虎克定律；变形计算。

5.3　剪切和挤压

剪切和挤压的实用计算；剪切面；挤压面；剪切强度；挤压强度。

5.4　扭转

扭矩和扭矩图；圆轴扭转切应力；切应力互等定理；剪切虎克定律；圆轴扭转的强度条件；扭转角计算及刚度条件。

5.5　截面几何性质

静矩和形心；惯性矩和惯性积；平行轴公式；形心主轴及形心主惯性矩概念。

5.6　弯曲

梁的内力方程；剪力图和弯矩图；分布荷载、剪力、弯矩之间的微分关系；正应力强度条件；切应力强度条件；梁的合理截面；弯曲中心概念；求梁变形的积分法、叠加法。

5.7　应力状态

平面应力状态分析的解析法和应力圆法；主应力和最大切应力；广义虎克定律；四个常用的强度理论。

5.8　组合变形

拉/压-弯组合、弯-扭组合情况下杆件的强度校核；斜弯曲。

5.9　压杆稳定

压杆的临界荷载；欧拉公式；柔度；临界应力总图；压杆的稳定校核。

六、流体力学

6.1　流体的主要物性与流体静力学

流体的压缩性与膨胀性；流体的黏性与牛顿内摩擦定律；流体静压强及其特性；重力作用下静水压强的分布规律；作用于平面的液体总压力的计算。

6.2　流体动力学基础

以流场为对象描述流动的概念；流体运动的总流分析；恒定总流连续性方程、能量方程和动量方程的运用。

6.3　流动阻力和能量损失

沿程阻力损失和局部阻力损失；实际流体的两种流态——层流和紊流；圆管中层流运动；紊流运动的特征；减小阻力的措施。

6.4　孔口、管嘴管道流动

孔口自由出流、孔口淹没出流；管嘴出流；有压管道恒定流；管道的串联和并联。

6.5　明渠恒定流

明渠均匀水流特性；产生均匀流的条件；明渠恒定非均匀流的流动状态；明渠恒定均匀流的水力计算。

6.6　渗流、井和集水廊道

土壤的渗流特性；达西定律；井和集水廊道。

6.7　相似原理和量纲分析

力学相似原理；相似准数；量纲分析法。

II. 现代技术基础

七、电气与信息

7.1 电磁学概念

电荷与电场；库仑定律；高斯定理；电流与磁场；安培环路定律；电磁感应定律；洛仑兹力。

7.2 电路知识

电路组成；电路的基本物理过程；理想电路元件及其约束关系；电路模型；欧姆定律；基尔霍夫定律；支路电流法；等效电源定理；叠加原理；正弦交流电的时间函数描述；阻抗；正弦交流电的相量描述；复数阻抗；交流电路稳态分析的相量法；交流电路功率；功率因数；三相配电电路及用电安全；电路暂态；R-C、R-L 电路暂态特性；电路频率特性；R-C、R-L 电路频率特性。

7.3 电动机与变压器

理想变压器；变压器的电压变换、电流变换和阻抗变换原理；三相异步电动机接线、启动、反转及调速方法；三相异步电动机运行特性；简单继电-接触控制电路。

7.4 信号与信息

信号；信息；信号的分类；模拟信号与信息；模拟信号描述方法；模拟信号的频谱；模拟信号增强；模拟信号滤波；模拟信号变换；数字信号与信息；数字信号的逻辑编码与逻辑演算；数字信号的数值编码与数值运算。

7.5 模拟电子技术

晶体二极管；极型晶体三极管；共射极放大电路；输入阻抗与输出阻抗；射极跟随器与阻抗变换；运算放大器；反相运算放大电路；同相运算放大电路；基于运算放大器的比较器电路；二极管单相半波整流电路；二极管单相桥式整流电路。

7.6 数字电子技术

与、或、非门的逻辑功能；简单组合逻辑电路；D 触发器；JK 触发器数字寄存器；脉冲计数器。

7.7 计算机系统

计算机系统组成；计算机的发展；计算机的分类；计算机系统特点；计算机硬件系统组成；CPU；存储器；输入/输出设备及控制系统；总线；数模/模数转换；计算机软件系统组成；系统软件；操作系统；操作系统定义；操作系统特征；操作系统功能；操作系统分类；支撑软件；应用软件；计算机程序设计语言。

7.8 信息表示

信息在计算机内的表示；二进制编码；数据单位；计算机内数值数据的表示；计算机内非数值数据的表示；信息及其主要特征。

7.9 常用操作系统

Windows 发展；进程和处理器管理；存储管理；文件管理；输入/输出管理；设备管理；网络服务。

7.10 计算机网络

计算机与计算机网络;网络概念;网络功能;网络组成;网络分类;局域网;广域网;因特网;网络管理;网络安全;Windows 系统中的网络应用;信息安全;信息保密。

III. 工程管理基础

八、法律法规

8.1 中华人民共和国建筑法

总则;建筑许可;建筑工程发包与承包;建筑工程监理;建筑安全生产管理;建筑工程质量管理;法律责任。

8.2 中华人民共和国安全生产法

总则;生产经营单位的安全生产保障;从业人员的权利和义务;安全生产的监督管理;生产安全事故的应急救援与调查处理。

8.3 中华人民共和国招标投标法

总则;招标;投标;开标;评标和中标;法律责任。

8.4 中华人民共和国合同法

一般规定;合同的订立;合同的效力;合同的履行;合同的变更和转让;合同的权利义务终止;违约责任;其他规定。

8.5 中华人民共和国行政许可法

总则;行政许可的设定;行政许可的实施机关;行政许可的实施程序;行政许可的费用。

8.6 中华人民共和国节约能源法

总则;节能管理;合理使用与节约能源;节能技术进步;激励措施;法律责任。

8.7 中华人民共和国环境保护法

总则;环境监督管理;保护和改善环境;防治环境污染和其他公害;法律责任。

8.8 建设工程勘察设计管理条例

总则;资质资格管理;建设工程勘察设计发包与承包;建设工程勘察设计文件的编制与实施;监督管理。

8.9 建设工程质量管理条例

总则;建设单位的质量责任和义务;勘察设计单位的质量责任和义务;施工单位的质量责任和义务;工程监理单位的质量责任和义务;建设工程质量保修。

8.10 建设工程安全生产管理条例

总则;建设单位的安全责任;勘察设计工程监理及其他有关单位的安全责任;施工单位的安全责任;监督管理;生产安全事故的应急救援和调查处理。

九、工程经济

9.1 资金的时间价值

资金时间价值的概念;利息及计算;实际利率和名义利率;现金流量及现金流量图;资金等值计算的常用公式及应用;复利系数表的应用。

9.2 财务效益与费用估算

项目的分类;项目计算期;财务效益与费用;营业收入;补贴收入;建设投资;建设期利息;流动资金;总成本费用;经营成本;项目评价涉及的税费;总投资形成的资产。

9.3 资金来源与融资方案

资金筹措的主要方式;资金成本;债务偿还的主要方式。

9.4 财务分析

财务评价的内容;盈利能力分析(财务净现值、财务内部收益率、项目投资回收期、总投资收益率、项目资本金净利润率);偿债能力分析(利息备付率、偿债备付率、资产负债率);财务生存能力分析;财务分析报表(项目投资现金流量表、项目资本金现金流量表、利润与利润分配表、财务计划现金流量表);基准收益率。

9.5 经济费用效益分析

经济费用和效益;社会折现率;影子价格;影子汇率;影子工资;经济净现值;经济内部收益率;经济效益费用比。

9.6 不确定性分析

盈亏平衡分析(盈亏平衡点、盈亏平衡分析图);敏感性分析(敏感度系数、临界点、敏感性分析图)。

9.7 方案经济比选

方案比选的类型;方案经济比选的方法(效益比选法、费用比选法、最低价格法);计算期不同的互斥方案的比选。

9.8 改扩建项目的经济评价特点

改扩建项目经济评价特点。

9.9 价值工程

价值工程原理;实施步骤。

全国勘察设计注册工程师资格考试
公共基础试题配置说明

I. 工程科学基础(共78题)

数学基础	24题	理论力学基础	12题
物理基础	12题	材料力学基础	12题
化学基础	10题	流体力学基础	8题

II. 现代技术基础(共28题)

电气技术基础	12题	计算机基础	10题
信号与信息基础	6题		

III. 工程管理基础(共14题)

工程经济基础	8题	法律法规	6题

注:试卷题目数量合计120题,每题1分,满分为120分。考试时间为4小时。

2019 全国勘察设计注册工程师执业资格考试用书

Zhuce Gongyong Shebei Gongchengshi (Nuantong Kongtiao、Dongli) Zhiye Zige Kaoshi Jichu Kaoshi Fuxi Jiaocheng

注册公用设备工程师（暖通空调、动力）执业资格考试

基础考试复习教程

（下册）

注册工程师考试复习用书编委会 / 编

李洪欣　曹纬浚 / 主　编

人民交通出版社股份有限公司
China Communications Press Co.,Ltd.

内 容 提 要

本书编写人员全部是多年从事注册公用设备工程师基础考试培训工作的专家、教授。书中内容紧扣现行考试大纲并覆盖了考试大纲的全部内容，着重于对概念的理解运用，重点突出，全书分“考试大纲”“必备基础知识”“经典练习”等模块。其中，“必备基础知识”除包含考试须知须会的内容以外，还配有“典型例题解析”。

由于本书篇幅较大，特分为上、下两册，上册为公共基础考试内容，下册为专业基础考试内容，以便于携带和翻阅。

本书可供参加2019年注册公用设备工程师（暖通空调、动力专业）执业资格考试基础考试的考生复习使用。

图书在版编目(CIP)数据

2019注册公用设备工程师（暖通空调、动力）执业资格考试基础考试复习教程 / 李洪欣，曹纬浚主编. —北京：人民交通出版社股份有限公司，2019.3

ISBN 978-7-114-15310-5

Ⅰ.①2… Ⅱ.①李… ②曹… Ⅲ.①建筑工程—供热系统—资格考试—自学参考资料②建筑工程—通风系统—资格考试—自学参考资料③建筑工程—空气调节系统—资格考试—自学参考资料 Ⅳ.①TU8

中国版本图书馆CIP数据核字(2019)第002427号

书　　名：2019注册公用设备工程师（暖通空调、动力）执业资格考试基础考试复习教程
著 作 者：李洪欣　曹纬浚
责任编辑：刘彩云　李　梦
出版发行：人民交通出版社股份有限公司
地　　址：（100011）北京市朝阳区安定门外外馆斜街3号
网　　址：http://www.ccpress.com.cn
销售电话：（010）59757973
总 经 销：人民交通出版社股份有限公司发行部
经　　销：各地新华书店
印　　刷：北京鑫正大印刷有限公司
开　　本：787×1092　1/16
印　　张：81
字　　数：2036千
版　　次：2019年3月　第1版
印　　次：2019年3月　第1次印刷
书　　号：ISBN 978-7-114-15310-5
定　　价：158.00元（含上、下两册）

前　言

原建设部(现住房和城乡建设部)和原人事部(现人力资源和社会保障部)从 2003 年起实施注册公用设备工程师(暖通空调、动力)执业资格考试制度。

本教程的编写老师都是本专业有较深造诣的教授和高级工程师，分别来自北京建筑大学、北京工业大学、北京交通大学、北京工商大学、郑州大学及北京市建筑设计研究院。为了帮助公用设备工程师们准备考试，教师们根据多年教学实践经验和考生的回馈意见，依据考试大纲和现行教材、规范，为学员们编写了这本教程。本教程的目的是为了指导复习，因此力求简明扼要，联系实际，着重对概念和规范的理解应用，并注意突出重点，是一套值得考生信赖的考前辅导和培训用书。

本教程严格按现行考试大纲编写，并在多年教学实践中不断加以改进。为方便考生复习，本教程分上、下册出版，上册第 1 至第 11 章为上午段公共基础考试内容，下册第 12 至第 18 章为下午段专业基础考试内容，所选例题及练习题大多来自真题，并注有年号，考生做题时，可对此部分题多加关注。

本教程可与《2019 注册公用设备工程师(暖通空调、动力)执业资格考试基础考试历年真题详解(2005～2018)》配套使用。

(1)在结构设置上，首先对大纲要求的知识点进行精炼阐述，然后辅以典型例题并进行解析，每一小节后附经典练习，并在每一章后提供提示及参考答案。

(2)例题、练习题、模拟题等试题多来自历年真题，考生可在复习、练习过程中熟悉本考试的深度和广度。

(3)全书是对考试大纲内容的精炼，考生通过本书的复习和练习，可在较短时间内完成对考试大纲的理解和掌握。

特别提醒，《中华人民共和国城乡规划法》(2015 年版)对原第二十四条第二款第二项作了修订，本书已更新。《中华人民共和国环境保护法》(自 2015 年 1 月 1 日起施行)，本书也已更新。

本书中的部分知识点和试题配有视频讲解，考生可扫描书中“二维码”在线学习，或者扫描封面“二维码”，登录“注考大师”，获取更多学习资源。

本书由李洪欣、曹纬浚担任主编。参与或协助本书编写的老师有王连俊、王健、冯东、刘燕、刘世奎、乔春生、孙惠镐、许小重、许怡生、杨松林、李兆年、李魁元、吴昌泽、陈向东、陈璐、范元玮、侯云芬、赵知敬、钱民刚、谢亚勃、穆静波、魏京花、朱强、卢纪富、沈超、蒋全科、贾玲华、毛怀珍、刘宝生、张翠兰、毛元钰、李平、邓华、陈庆年、李广秋、郭虹、曹京、楼香林、杨守俊、王志刚、何承奎、曹铎、罗滨、吴莎莎、张文革、罗金标、徐华萍、栾彩虹、孙国樑、张炳珍。

由于考试涉及面广，书中难免存在疏漏和不足，真诚地希望读者批评指正，提出宝贵意见，以便本书再版时改进。

最后，祝愿各位考生取得好的成绩！

李洪欣

2019 年 1 月

主编致考生

一、注册公用设备工程师(暖通空调、动力)在专业考试之前进行基础考试是和国外接轨的做法。通过基础考试并达到职业实践年限后就可以申请参加专业考试。基础考试是考大学中的基础课程,按考试大纲的安排,上午考试段考11科,120道题,4个小时,每题1分,共120分;下午考试段考7科,60道题,4个小时,每题2分,共120分;上、下午共240分。试题均为4选1的单选题,平均每题时间上午2分钟,下午4分钟,因此不会有复杂的论证和计算,主要是检验考生的基本概念和基本知识。考生在复习时不要偏重难度大或过于复杂的知识,而应将复习的注意力主要放在弄清基本概念和基本知识方面。

二、考生在复习本教程之前,应认真阅读“考试大纲”,清楚地了解考试的内容和范围,以便合理制订自己的复习计划。复习时一定要紧扣“考试大纲”的内容,将全面复习与突出重点相结合。着重对“考试大纲”要求掌握的基本概念、基本理论、基本计算方法、计算公式和步骤,以及基本知识的应用等内容有系统、有条理地重点掌握,明白其中的道理和关系,掌握分析问题的方法。同时还应会使用为减少计算工作量或简化、方便计算所制作的表格等。本教程中每章前均有一节“复习指导”,具体说明本章的复习重点、难点和复习中要注意的问题,建议考生认真阅读每章的“复习指导”,参考“复习指导”的意见进行复习。在对基本概念、基本原理和基本知识有一个整体把握的基础上,对每章节的重点、难点进行重点复习和重点掌握。

三、注册公用设备工程师(暖通空调、动力)基础考试上、下午试卷共计240分,上、下午不分段计算成绩,这几年及格线都是55%,也就是说,上、下午试卷总分达到132分就可以通过。因此,考生在准备考试时应注意扬长避短。从道理上讲,自己较弱的科目更应该努力复习,但毕竟时间和精力有限,如2009年新增加的“信号与信息技术”,据了解,非信息专业的考生大多未学过,短时间内要掌握好比较困难,而“信号与信息技术”总共只有6道题,6分,只占总分的2.5%,也就是说,即使“信号与信息技术”1分未得,其他科目也还有234分,从234分中考132分是完全可以做到的。因此考生可以根据考试分科题量、分数分配和自己的具体情况,计划自己的复习重点和主要得分科目。当然一些主要得分科目是不能放松的,如“高等数学”24题(上午段)24分,“工程热力学”10题(下午段)20分,“传热学”10题(下午段)20分,都是不能放松的;其他科目则可根据自己过去对课程的掌握情况有所侧重,争取在自己过去学得好的课程中多得分。

四、在考试拿到试卷时,建议考生不要顺着题序顺次往下做。因为有的题会比较难,有的题不很熟悉,耽误的时间会比较多,以致到最后时间不够,题做不完,有些题会做但时间来不及,这就太得不偿失了。建议考生将做题过程分为四遍:

(1)首先用15～20分钟将题从头到尾看一遍,一是首先解答出自己很熟悉很有把握的题;

二是将那些需要稍加思考估计能在平均答题时间里做出的题做个记号。这里说的平均答题时间,是指上午段 4 个小时考 120 道题,平均每题 2 分钟;下午段 4 个小时考 60 道题,平均每题 4 分钟,这个 2 分钟(上午)、4 分钟(下午)就是平均答题时间。将估计在这个时间里能做出来的题做上记号。

(2)第二遍做这些做了记号的题,这些题应该在考试时间里能做完,做完了这些题可以说就考出了考生的基本水平,不管考生基础如何,复习得怎么样,考得如何,至少不会因为题没做完而遗憾了。

(3)这些会做或基本会做的题做完以后,如果还有时间,就做那些需要稍多花费时间的题,能做几个算几个,并适当抽时间检查一下已答题的答案。

(4)考试时间将近结束时,比如还剩 5 分钟要收卷了,这时你就应看看还有多少道题没有答,这些题确实不会了,建议考生也不要放弃。既然是单选,那也不妨估个答案,答对了也是有分的。建议考生回头看看已答题目的答案,A、B、C、D 各有多少,虽然整个卷子四种答案的数量并不一定是平均的,但还是可以这样考虑,看看已答的题 A、B、C、D 中哪个答案最少,然后将不会做没有答的题按这个前边最少的答案通填,这样其中会有 1/4 可能还会多于 1/4 的题能得分,如果考生前边答对的题离及格正好差几分,这样一补充就能及格了。

五、基础考试是不允许带书和资料的,2012 年前,考试时会给每位考生发一本"考试手册",载有公式和一些数据,考后收回。但从 2012 年起,取消了"考试手册"的配发。据说原因是考生使用不多,事实上也没有更多时间去翻手册。因此一些重要的公式、规定,考生一定要自己记住。

六、本教程每节后均附有习题,并在每章后附有提示及参考答案。建议考生在复习好本教程内容的基础上,多做习题。多做习题能帮助巩固已学的概念、理论、方法和公式等,并能发现自己的不足,哪些地方理解得不正确,哪些地方没有掌握好;同时熟能生巧,提高解题速度。本教程在最后提供了两套模拟试题,建议考生在复习完本教程以后,集中时间,排除干扰,模拟考试气氛,将模拟试题全部做一遍,以接近实战地检验一下自己的复习效果。

注册公用设备工程师考试已经进行了十多年,分析这些年的考题,特别是近两年的考题,可以总结出考题考查的一些新趋势。一个趋势就是考试题目考查点越来越细,越来越深入;另一个趋势就是有的题目考查得更加综合,一个题目可能涉及几个知识点,考题难度加大。这都对考生的备考提出了更高的要求。因此,考生需要对大纲涉及的考点做到真正理解,并在此基础上能够灵活应用。

复习中若遇到疑问,可写清楚问题发邮件至 caowj0818@126.com(上册问题)、466362436@qq.com(下册问题),我们会尽快回复解答。相信这本教程能帮助大家准备好考试。

最后,祝愿各位考生取得好成绩!

曹纬浚

2019 年 1 月

目　录

下　册

12　工程热力学

考题配置　单选,10 题

分数配置　每题 2 分,共 20 分

复 习 指 导

工程热力学要求掌握热力学基本定律和基本理论,熟悉工质的基本性质和实际热工装置的基本原理,学会对工程实际问题进行抽象、简化和以能量方程、熵方程、可用能方程为基础的分析方法。

12.1　基本概念

考试大纲☞:热力学系统　状态　平衡状态　状态参数　状态公理　状态方程　热力参数及坐标图　功和热量　热力过程　热力循环　单位制

必备基础知识

12.1.1　热力学系统

1)定义

根据研究问题的需要,人为地选取一定范围内的物质作为研究对象,称其为热力学系统,简称系统。系统以外的物质称为外界。系统与外界的交界面称为边界。边界面的选取可以是真实的、假想的、固定的、运动的,也可以是这几种边界面的组合。

2)分类

按热力系统与外界进行质量和能量交换的情况可将热力学系统分为:

(1)闭口系:热力学系统与外界无物质交换的系统。由于系统所包含的物质质量保持不变,亦称之为控制质量系统。对于闭口系,常用控制质量法来研究。

(2)开口系:热力学系统与外界之间有物质交换的系统。开口系统总是取一相对固定的空间,又称为控制容积系统,对其常用控制容积法进行研究。

(3)绝热系:热力学系统与外界无热量交换的系统。

(4)孤立系:热力学系统与外界既无能量交换又无物质交换的系统。

典型例题解析

【例 12.1-1】　闭口热力系统与开口热力系统的区别在于:

A. 在界面上有、无物质进出热力系

B. 在界面上与外界有无热量传递

C. 对外界是否做功

D. 在界面上有无功和热量的传递及转换

解 本题主要考查热力学系统的基本概念。按系统与外界有无物质交换,系统可分为闭口系统和开口系统。闭口系统:系统内外无物质交换;开口系统:系统内外有物质交换。选 A。

【例 12.1-2】 如果由工质和环境组成的系统,只在系统内发生热量和质量交换关系,而与外界没有任何其他关系或影响,该系统称为:

A. 孤立系统　　B. 开口系统　　C. 刚体系统　　D. 闭口系统

解 孤立系是与外界既无能量交换又无物质交换的系统。选 A。

12.1.2 状态

热力学系统在某一瞬间所呈现的宏观物理状况称为系统的状态。热力状态反映着工质大量分子热运动的平均特点,系统与外界之间能够进行能量交换的根本原因在于两者之间的热力状态存在差异。从热力学的观点出发,状态可以分为平衡状态和非平衡状态两种。

12.1.3 平衡状态

1)定义

平衡状态是指在没有外界影响(重力场除外)的条件下,系统的宏观性质不随时间变化的状态。

2)实现平衡的充要条件

系统内部及系统与外界之间各种不平衡势差(力差、温差、化学势差)的消失是系统实现热力平衡状态的充要条件。

在平衡状态时,参数不随时间改变只是现象,不能作为判断是否平衡的条件,只有系统内部及系统与外界之间的一切不平衡势差的消失,才是实现平衡的本质,也是实现平衡的充要条件。

平衡状态具有确定的状态参数,这是平衡状态的特点。

典型例题解析

【例 12.1-3】 热力学系统的平衡状态是指:

A. 系统内部作用力的合力为零,内部均匀一致

B. 所有广义作用力的合力为零

C. 无任何不平衡势差,系统参数处处均匀一致,且不随时间变化

D. 边界上有作用力,系统内部参数均匀一致,且保持不变

解 本题主要考查平衡状态的概念及实现条件。平衡状态是指在没有外界影响(重力场除外)的条件下,系统的宏观性质不随时间变化的状态。实现平衡的充要条件是系统内部及系统与外界之间不存在各种不平衡势差(力差、温差、化学势差)。因此热力系统的平衡状态应该是无任何不平衡势差,系统参数处处均匀一致而且是稳态的状态。选 C。

12.1.4 状态参数

描述系统工质状态的客观物理量称为状态参数。

状态参数的特征如下。

(1)状态确定,则状态参数也确定;反之,亦然。

(2)状态参数的积分特征:状态参数的变化量与路径无关,只与初终态有关,而且状态函数的循环积分为零。

$$\int_{1}^{2} \mathrm{d}z = \int_{1,a}^{2} \mathrm{d}z = \int_{1,b}^{2} \mathrm{d}z = z_2 - z_1 \tag{12.1-1}$$

$$\oint \mathrm{d}z = 0 \tag{12.1-2}$$

典型例题解析

【例 12.1-4】 状态参数用来描述热力系统状态特性,此热力系统应满足:

A. 系统内部处于热平衡和力平衡

B. 系统与外界处于热平衡

C. 系统与外界处于力平衡

D. 不需要任何条件

解 本题主要考查状态参数以及平衡状态的基本概念。状态参数的一个重要特征是:状态确定,则状态参数也确定,反之亦然。平衡状态的特点是具有确定的状态参数,而系统必须达到热平衡和力平衡时才称为平衡状态。选 A。

12.1.5 状态公理

状态公理提供了确定热力系统平衡状态所需的独立参数数目的经验规则,即对于组成一定的物质系统,若存在几种可逆功(系统进行可逆过程时和外界交换的功量)的作用,则决定该系统平衡状态的独立状态参数有 $n+1$ 个,其中“1”是考虑了系统与外界的热交换作用。

根据状态公理,简单可压缩系统平衡状态的独立参数只有 2 个。原则上,可以选取可测量参数 p、v 和 T 中的任意两个独立参数作为自变量,其余参数(u、h、s 等)则为 p、v 和 T 的因变量。

12.1.6 状态方程

对于平衡状态下基本状态参数之间,可以写成 $v=v(p,T)$ 或 $f(p,v,T)=0$ 之间的关系,称为状态方程式。状态方程式的具体形式取决于工质的性质。

12.1.7 热力参数及坐标图

在热力学中,常用的有压力(p)、温度(T)、比体积(也称质量体积)(v)、内能(U)、焓(H)和熵(S)6 个状态参数。状态参数分为广延参数和强度参数。其中,广延参数是指与系统的质量成正比且可相加的一类状态参数,如 U、H、S 等。强度参数是指与系统的质量无关且不可相加的一类状态参数,如 p、T 等。单位质量的广延参数具有强度参数的性质,称作比参数。

在常用的 6 个状态参数中,压力 p、比体积 v 和温度 T 可以直接用仪表测定,称为基本状态参数。其他的状态参数可以依据这些基本状态参数之间的关系间接导出。

(1)比体积(也称质量体积)v:比体积是单位质量的工质所占有的体积,即 $v=\frac{V}{m}$,单位为 m^3/kg。

(2)压力 p:压力 p 是指单位面积上承受的垂直作用力。对于气体,实质上是气体分子运动撞击容器壁面,在单位面积的容器壁面上所呈现的平均作用力。压力的单位是帕(斯卡)(Pa),以及千帕(kPa)和兆帕(MPa)。流体的压力常用压力表或真空表来测量。压力表测量的压力为表压力 p_g,真空表测量的压力为真空度 p_v,工质的真实压力 p 称为绝对压力。p_g、p_v 及大气压力 p_b 之间的关系为

$$p = p_g + p_b \qquad (\text{当 } p > p_b \text{ 时}) \tag{12.1-3}$$

$$p = p_b - p_v \qquad (\text{当 } p < p_b \text{ 时}) \tag{12.1-4}$$

(3)温度 T:温度是确定一个系统是否与其他系统处于热平衡的状态函数。温度是热平衡的唯一判据。温度的数量表示法称为温标。温标的建立一般需要选定测温物质及其某一物理性质,规定基准点及分度方法。热力学温标,是建立在热力学第二定律基础上而完全不依赖测温物质性质的温标。它采用开尔文(K)作为度量温度的单位,规定水的气、液、固三相平衡共存的状态点(三相点)为基准点,并规定此点的温度为273.16K。与热力学温度并用的有摄氏温度,以符号 t 表示,其单位为摄氏度(℃)。摄氏温度与热力学温度之间的关系为 $t=T-273.15K$。摄氏温度的零点相当于热力学温度的273.15K,而且这两种温标的温度间隔完全相同。

对于只有两个独立参数的热力系,可以任选两个参数组成二维平面坐标图来描述被确定的平衡状态,这种坐标图称为状态参数坐标图。经常用到的状态参数坐标图有压容图(p-v 图)和温熵图(T-s 图)等。利用坐标图进行热力分析,具有直观清晰、简单明了的优点。

典型例题解析

【例 12.1-5】 热力学中常用的状态参数有:

A. 温度、大气压力、比热容、内能、焓、熵等

B. 温度、表压力、比体积、内能,焓、熵、热量等

C. 温度、绝对压力、比体积、内能、焓、熵等

D. 温度、绝对压力、比热容、内能、功等

解 本题主要考查热力学中常用的状态参数。在热力学中,常用的有压力(p)、温度(T)、比体积(v)、内能(U)、焓(H)和熵(S)6个状态参数。选 C。

【例 12.1-6】 表压力、大气压力、真空度和绝对压力中只有:

A. 大气压力是状态参数　　B. 表压力是状态参数

C. 绝对压力是状态参数　　D. 真空度是状态参数

解 本题主要考查热力学中常用的状态参数的概念。只有绝对压力才是真实的压力,因此只有绝对压力才是系统的状态参数。选 C。

【例 12.1-7】 大气压力为 B,系统中工质真空压力读数为 p_1 时,系统的真实压力 p 为:

A. p_1　　B. $B+p_1$　　C. $B-p_1$　　D. p_1-B

解 本题主要考查大气压力、真空度以及系统真实压力的关系。选 C。

【例 12.1-8】 压力的常用国际单位表达中不正确的是：

A. N/m^2　　B. kPa　　C. MPa　　D. bar

解　压力的基本国际单位为 Pa，即 N/m^2。bar 是工程中经常用到的压力单位，但不是国际单位。选 D。

12.1.8 功和热量

功量和热量是在热力过程中系统与外界发生的能量交换量，即通过不同的方式交换的能量。能量转换的方式有两种，即做功和传热。

功是系统与外界之间在力差的推动下，通过宏观的有序运动的方式传递的能量。也即是，借做功来传递能量总是和物体的宏观位移有关。

热量是系统与外界之间在温差的推动下，通过微观粒子的无序运动的方式传递的能量，也即是，借传热来传递能量，不需要有物体的宏观移动。

功和热量不是状态参数。只有当系统状态参数发生变化时，才可能有功和热量的传递。所以功和热量的大小不仅与过程的初、终状态有关，而且与过程的性质有关，功和热量都是过程量。热力学中规定，系统对外做功时功取为正，外界对系统做功时功取为负；系统吸热时热量取为正，放热时取为负。

可逆过程的功量和热量分别用 p-v 图和 T-s 图上的相应面积表示。

12.1.9 热力过程

热力过程是指热力系统从一个状态向另一个状态变化时所经历的全部状态的综合。经典热力学可以描述的是两种理想化的过程：准平衡过程与可逆过程。

12.1.10 热力循环

工质由某一状态出发，经历一系列热力状态变化后，又回到原来初态的封闭热力过程称为热力循环，简称循环。系统实施热力循环的目的是为了实现预期连续的能量转换。按照循环的性质可以分为可逆循环（全部过程均可逆）和不可逆循环（还有不可逆过程的循环）。按照利用目的来分，有正向循环（动力循环）和逆向循环（制冷或热泵循环）。

循环的经济指标用工作系数来表示

$$\text{工作系数} = \frac{\text{得到的收益}}{\text{花费的代价}}$$

动力循环的经济性用循环热效率 η_t 来衡量，即

$$\eta_t = \frac{w}{q_1} = \frac{q_1 - q_2}{q_1} = 1 - \frac{q_2}{q_1} \tag{12.1-5}$$

制冷循环的经济性用制冷系数 ε 表示

$$\varepsilon = \frac{q_2}{w} = \frac{q_2}{q_1 - q_2}$$

热泵循环的经济性用供热系数 ε' 表示

$$\varepsilon' = \frac{q_1}{w} = \frac{q_1}{q_1 - q_2} \tag{12.1-6}$$

典型例题解析

【例 12.1-9】 图 12-1 为一热力循环 1—2—3—1 的 T-s 图，该循环的热效率可表示为：

A. $1-\dfrac{2b}{a+b}$　　B. $1-\dfrac{2b}{a-b}$

C. $1-\dfrac{b}{a+b}$　　D. $1-\dfrac{2a}{a+b}$

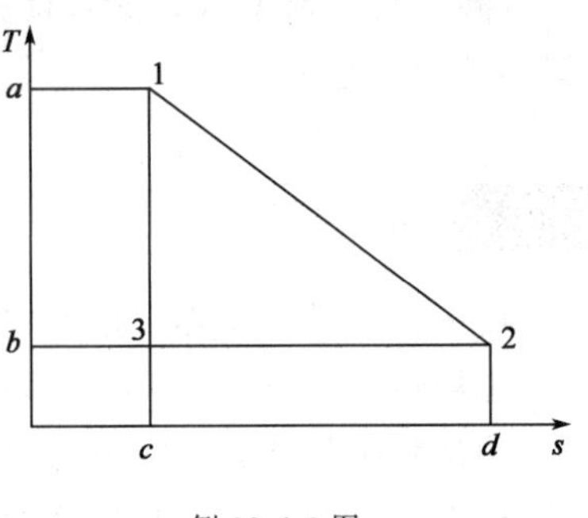

例 12.1-9 图

解　本题主要考查动力循环热效率的概念以及在 T-s 图上的标示方法。动力循环热效率计算表达式在 T-s 图上面积关系为：

$$\eta_t=\frac{w}{q_1}=\frac{q_1-q_2}{q_1}=1-\frac{q_2}{q_1}=\frac{A_{1231}}{A_{12dc1}}$$

经过几何关系计算两个面积，并推导可得正确答案为 A。

【例 12.1-10】 例 12.1-9 图所示循环中工质的吸热量是：

A. $(a-b)(d-c)/2$　　B. $(a+b)(d-c)/2$

C. $(a-b)(d+c)/2$　　D. $(a+b)(d+c)/2$

解　本题主要考查动力循环吸热量在 T-s 图上的标示方法。动力循环吸热量在 T-s 图上为 12dc1 所包含的面积，通过计算可知正确答案为 B。

12.1.11 单位制

热工学中涉及的物理量比较多，采用的单位制有工程单位制、国际单位制等。目前我国国家标准中统一采用国际单位制(SI)。

经典练习

12.1-1　若已知工质的绝对压力 $p=0.18$MPa，环境压力 $p_a=0.1$MPa，则测得的压差为(　　)。

A. 真空 $p_v=0.08$MPa　　B. 表压力 $p_g=0.08$MPa

C. 真空 $p_v=0.28$MPa　　D. 表压力 $p_g=0.28$MPa

12.1-2　可以通过测量直接得到数值的状态参数是(　　)。

A. 焓　　B. 热力学能　　C. 温度　　D. 熵

12.1-3　无质量交换的热力系统称为(　　)。

A. 孤立系统　　B. 闭口系统　　C. 绝热系统　　D. 开口系统

12.1-4　若工质经历一可逆过程和一不可逆过程，且其初终状态相同，则两过程中工质与外界交换的热量(　　)。

A. 相同　　B. 不相同　　C. 不确定　　D. 与状态无关

12.1-5　熵是(　　)量。

A. 广延状态参数　　B. 强度状态参数　　C. 过程量　　D. 无法确定

12.2　准静态过程、可逆过程与不可逆过程

考试大纲☞：准静态过程　可逆过程　不可逆过程

必备基础知识

12.2.1 准静态过程

(1)定义:由一系列连续的平衡状态组成的过程称为准静态过程,也称为准平衡过程。

(2)特点:准静态过程是实际过程进行的足够缓慢的极限情况。这里的"缓慢"是热力学意义上的缓慢,即由不平衡到平衡的弛豫时间远小于过程进行所用的时间,就可以认为足够缓慢。因此,工程上的大多数过程由于热力系统恢复平衡的速度很快,仍可以看作是准静态过程进行分析。

(3)实现条件:推动过程进行的势差无限小,从而保证系统在任意时刻皆无限接近于平衡态。

(4)建立准静态过程的优点:①可以用确定的状态参数变化描述过程;②可以在参数坐标图上用一条连续曲线表示过程。

典型例题解析

【例 12.2-1】 准静态是一种热力参数和作用力都有变化的过程,具有下列哪项特性?

A. 内部和边界是一起快速变化

B. 边界上已经达到平衡

C. 内部状态参数随时处于均匀

D. 内部参数变化远快于外部作用力变化

解 本题主要考查准静态过程的特点。准静态过程是在系统与外界的压力差、温差无限小的条件下,系统变化足够缓慢,系统经历一系列无限接近于平衡状态的过程。热力学意义上的"缓慢"是指由不平衡到平衡的弛豫时间远小于过程进行所用的时间,因此内部状态参数均匀,没有势差。选 C。

12.2.2 可逆过程与不可逆过程

(1)定义:如果系统完成某一热力过程后,再沿原来路径逆向进行时,能使系统和外界都返回原来状态而不留下任何变化,则这一过程称为可逆过程,否则称为不可逆过程。

(2)可逆过程实现条件:过程应为准平衡过程且过程中无任何耗散效应(摩擦、阻力等),这是实现可逆过程的充要条件。也就是说,无耗散的准平衡过程为可逆过程。准静态过程与可逆过程的区别在于有无耗散损失。一个可逆过程必须同时也是一个准静态过程,反之则不然。

典型例题解析

【例 12.2-2】 完成一个热力过程后,满足下述哪个条件时过程可逆?

A. 沿原路径逆向进行,系统和环境都恢复初态而不留下任何影响

B. 沿原路径逆向进行,中间可以存在温差和压差,系统和环境都恢复初态

C. 只要过程反向进行,系统和环境都恢复初态而不留下任何影响

D. 任意方向进行过程,系统和环境都恢复初态而不留下任何影响

解 可逆过程的定义"如果系统完成某一热力过程后,再沿原来路径逆向进行时,能使系统和外界都返回原来状态而不留下任何变化,则这一过程称为可逆过程"。选 A。

经 典 练 习

12.2-1 经过一个可逆过程，工质不会恢复原来状态，该说法（ ）。

A. 正确 B. 错误 C. 有一定道理 D. 不定

12.2-2 准静态过程中，系统经历的所有状态都接近于（ ）。

A. 相邻状态 B. 初状态 C. 平衡态 D. 终状态

12.2-3 系统进行一个过程后，如能使（ ）沿着与原过程相反的方向恢复初态，则这样的过程为可逆过程。

A. 系统 B. 外界 C. 系统和外界 D. 系统或外界

12.2-4 当热能和机械能发生转变时，能获得最大可用功的过程是（ ）。

A. 准静态过程 B. 平衡过程 C. 绝热过程 D. 可逆过程

12.3 热力学第一定律

考试大纲☞：热力学第一定律的实质 热力学能 焓 热力学第一定律在开口系统和闭口系统的表达式 储存能 稳定流动能量方程及其应用

必备基础知识

12.3.1 热力学第一定律的实质

热力学第一定律实质上就是能量守恒与转换定律在热现象中的应用。它确定了热力过程中各种能量在数量上的相互关系。

热力学第一定律表述为：当热能与其他形式的能量相互转换时，能量的总量保持不变。

热力学第一定律是热力学的基本定律，其适用于一切工质和一切热力过程。对于任何系统，各项能量之间的平衡关系一般表示为：

进入系统的能量－离开系统的能量＝系统储能的变化

典型例题解析

【例 12.3-1】 热力学第一定律是关于热能与其他形式的能量相互转换的定律，适用于：

A. 一切工质和一切热力过程 B. 量子级微观粒子的运动过程

C. 工质的可逆或准静态过程 D. 热机循环的一切过程

解 热力学第一定律是能量守恒定律在热现象中的应用。能量守恒定律适用于一切工质和一切热力过程。选 A。

12.3.2 热力学能

能量是物质运动的量度，运动有各种不同形式，相应地应有各种不同的能量，系统储存的能量称为储存能，它有内部储存能和外部储存能。而储存在系统内部的能量叫做内能，又叫做热力学能。它与系统内工质粒子的运动和粒子空间位置有关，是下列各种能量的总和：

(1)分子热运动形成的内动能,它是温度的函数。

(2)分子间相互作用形成的内位能,它是质量体积的函数。

(3)维持一定分子结构的化学能,原子核内部的原子能及电磁场作用下的电磁能等。

热力学能是状态参数,也就是说,若工质从初态1变化到终态2,其内能的变化ΔU只与初态、终态有关,而与过程路径无关。工质经循环变化后,内能的变化为零。

典型例题解析

【例 12.3-2】 内能是储存于系统物质内部的能量,有多种形式,下列哪一项不属于内能?

A. 分子热运动能　　B. 在重力场中的高度势能

C. 分子相互作用势能　　D. 原子核内部原子能

解 本题主要考查内能的定义。重力场中的高度势能是外部能。选B。

12.3.3 焓

在流动过程中,工质携带的能量除内能外,总伴有推动功,所以为工程应用方便起见,把U和pV组合起来,我们就把这些工质流经一个开口系统时的能量总和叫做焓,用大写字母H表示,其表达式为

$$H = U + pV \tag{12.3-1}$$

在分析开口系统时,因有工质流动,热力学能U和推动功pV必然同时出现,在此特定情况下,焓可以理解为由于工质流动而携带的,并取决于热力状态参数的能量,即热力学能与推动功之和。在分析闭口系统时,焓只是一个复合状态参数,无明确的物理意义。

12.3.4 热力学第一定律在开口系统和闭口系统的表达式

热力学第一定律应用于控制质量时,其一般表达式为

$$q = \Delta e + w \tag{12.3-2}$$

对于控制质量闭口系统来说,比较常见的情况是在状态变化过程中,系统的动能和位能的变化为零,或动能和位能的变化与过程中参与能量转换的其他各项能量相比,可以忽略不计。因此,上式中系统总能的变化,也就是热力学能的变化。

闭口系统能量方程的表达式有以下几种形式。

1kg 工质经历有限过程　$q=\Delta u+w$　(12.3-3)

1kg 工质经历微元过程　$\delta q=\mathrm{d}u+\delta w$　(12.3-4)

$m$kg 工质经历有限过程　$Q=\Delta U+W$　(12.3-5)

$m$kg 工质经历微元过程　$\delta Q=\mathrm{d}U+\delta W$

上述各式,对于闭口系统各种过程(可逆或不可逆过程)及各种工质都适用。

对于可逆过程,因$\delta w=p\mathrm{d}v$,$w=\int_1^2 p\mathrm{d}v$,则以上各式又可表达为以下形式。

1kg 工质经历有限过程　$q = \Delta u + \int_1^2 p\mathrm{d}v$　(12.3-6)

1kg 工质经历微元过程　$\delta q=\mathrm{d}u+p\mathrm{d}v$　(12.3-7)

$m$kg 工质经历有限过程 $$Q = \Delta U + \int_1^2 p\mathrm{d}V \tag{12.3-8}$$

$m$kg 工质经历微元过程 $$\delta Q = \mathrm{d}U + p\mathrm{d}V$$

闭口系统经历一个循环时，由于 $\oint \mathrm{d}U = 0$，所以

$$\oint \delta Q = \oint \delta W \tag{12.3-9}$$

式(12.3-9)是系统经历循环时的能量方程，即任一循环的净吸热量与净功量相等。

典型例题解析

【例 12.3-3】 某物质的内能只是温度的函数，且遵守关系式：$U=(12.5+0.125t)$kJ，此物质的温度由100℃升高到200℃。温度每变化1℃所做的功 $\delta W/\mathrm{d}t=0.46$kJ/℃，此过程中该物质与外界传递的热量是：

A. 57.5kJ　　B. 58.5kJ　　C. 39.5kJ　　D. 59.5kJ

解 本题主要考查热力学第一定律应用于控制质量时的表达式 $\Delta U=Q-W$，以及式中各项正负号的规定。在该过程中内能的变化 $\Delta U=U_2-U_1=(12.5+0.125t_2)-(12.5+0.125t_1)=0.125(t_2-t_1)=12.5$kJ，过程中功的变化为 $W=\int_{t_1}^{t_2}0.46\mathrm{d}t=\int_{100}^{200}0.46\mathrm{d}t=46$kJ。

由公式 $Q=\Delta U+W=12.5+46=58.5$kJ。选 B。

【例 12.3-4】 系统经一热力过程，放热 9kJ，对外做功 27kJ。为使其返回原状态，若对系统做功加热 6kJ，需对系统做功：

A. 42kJ　　B. 27kJ　　C. 30kJ　　D. 12kJ

解 因内能是状态参数，其变化与路径无关，其变化量：

$$\Delta U_{12}=U_2-U_1=-(U_1-U_2)=-\Delta U_{21} \quad ①$$

闭口系统能量方程 $Q=\Delta U+W$

对应 12 和 21 两个过程有：

$$Q_{12}=\Delta U_{12}+W_{12}\rightarrow \Delta U_{12}=Q_{12}-W_{12} \quad ②$$

$$Q_{21}=\Delta U_{21}+W_{21}\rightarrow \Delta U_{21}=Q_{21}-W_{21} \quad ③$$

将式②、式③代入式①，有：

$$Q_{12}-W_{12}=-(Q_{21}-W_{21})$$

因此，$W_{21}=Q_{12}-W_{12}+Q_{21}=-9-27+6=-30$kJ，负号表明外界对系统做功。选 B。

【例 12.3-5】 气体在某一过程放出热量 100kJ，对外界做功 50kJ，其能量变化量是：

A. −150kJ　　B. 150kJ　　C. 50kJ　　D. −50kJ

解 热力学第一定律应用于控制质量时，其表达式为 $\Delta U=Q-W$，式中，Q、W 符号规定为：工质吸热为正，放热为负，工质对外做功为正，外界对工质做功为负；ΔU 的符号为：系统的热力学能增加为正，反之为负。按照上述规定，气体能量变化 $\Delta U=-100-50=-150$kJ。选 A。

【例 12.3-6】 (2014)由热力学第一定律，开口系能量方程为 $\delta q = dh - \delta w$，闭口系能量方程为 $\delta q = du - \delta w$，经过循环后，可得出相同结果形式 $\oint \delta q = \oint \delta w$，正确的解释是：

A. 两系统热力过程相同　　B. 同样热量下可以做相同数量的功

C. 结果形式相同但内涵不同　D. 除去 q 和 w，其余参数含义相同

解 表达式 $\delta q = dh - \delta w$ 中 δw 为技术功，而 $\delta q = du - \delta w$ 中 δw 为膨胀功，因此经过循环后两式虽得出了相同的结果 $\oint q = \oint w$，但是对于两者其内涵是不同。选 C。

12.3.5 储存能

能量是物质运动的量度，运动有各种不同的形式，相应的就有各种不同的能量。系统储存的能量称为储存能 E，它为系统的内部储存能 U 和外部储存能 $E_k + E_p$ 之和，即

$$E = U + E_k + E_p \tag{12.3-10}$$

功的种类很多，主要的功有以下几种。

1)体积变化功(又称膨胀功)W

系统体积变化所完成的膨胀功或压缩功统称为体积变化功。由于热能和机械能的可逆转换总是和工质的膨胀和压缩联系在一起，所以体积变化功是热变功的源泉，而体积变化功和其他形式能量间的关系，则属于机械能的转换。

2)轴功 W_s

系统通过轴与外界交换的功量称为轴功。

3)推动功和流动功 W_f

开口系统因工质流动而传递的功称为推动功。相当于一个假想的活塞把前方的工质推进(或推出)系统所做的功 pV，此量随工质进入(或离开)系统而称为带入(或带出)系统的能量。推动功只有在工质流动时才有，当工质不流动时，虽然工质也具有一定的状态参数 p 和 V，但这时的 pV 并不代表推动功。

工质在流动时，总是从后面获得推动功，而对前面做出推动功，进出质量的推动功之差称为流动功。它可理解为在流动过程中，系统与外界由于物质的进出而传递的机械功。

4)技术功 W_t

工程技术上将技术上可以利用的功称为技术功。对于开口系统来讲，其包括轴功、进出口的宏观动能差和宏观位能差。

技术功为膨胀功与流动功之和，即

$$\text{技术功} = \text{膨胀功} + \text{流动功}$$

$$W_t = W + p_1V_1 - p_2V_2 \tag{12.3-11}$$

对于可逆过程

$$W_t = -\int_1^2 V dp \tag{12.3-12}$$

几种功及在稳定流动过程中的关系汇总于表 12.3-1。

几种功及相互之间的关系　　表 12.3-1

名　　称	含　　义	说　　明
体积变化功(或膨胀功)W	系统体积变化所完成的功	(1)当过程可逆时,$W=\int_1^2 V\mathrm{d}p$ (2)膨胀功是简单可压缩系统热变功的源泉 (3)膨胀功往往对应闭口系统所求的功
轴功 W_s	系统通过轴与外界交换的功	(1)轴功是开口系统所求的功 (2)当工质进出口间的动、位能差被忽略时,$W_t=W_s$,所以此时开口系统所求的功也是技术功
流动功 W_f	开口系统付诸于质量迁移所做的功	流动功是进出口推动功之差,即 $W_f=p_2V_2-p_1V_1$
技术功 W_t	技术上可资利用的功	(1)W_t 与 W_s 的关系:$W_t=\frac{1}{2}m\Delta c_f^2+mg\Delta z+W_s$ (2)W_t 与 W、W_f 的关系:$W_t=W-\Delta(pV)$ (3)当过程可逆时,$W_t=-\int_1^2 V\mathrm{d}p$,这也是动、位能差不计时的最大轴功

典型例题解析

【例 12.3-7】 热能转换成机械能的唯一途径是通过工质的体积膨胀,此种功称为体积变化功,它可分为:

A. 膨胀功和压缩功　　B. 技术功和流动功

C. 轴功和流动功　　D. 膨胀功和流动功

解　本题主要考查体积变化功的定义,即“热力系统体积变化所完成的膨胀功或压缩功统称为体积变化功”。选 A。

【例 12.3-8】 系统的总储存能包括内储存能和外储存能,其中外储存能是指:

A. 宏观动能+重力位能　　B. 宏观动能+流动功

C. 宏观动能+体积变化功　　D. 体积变化功+流动功

解　根据热力学能的分类,外部储存能包括宏观动能 E_k 和重力位能 E_p 两种。选 A。

【例 12.3-9】 系统的储存能 E 的表达式:

A. $E=U+pV$　　B. $E=U+pV+E_k+E_p$

C. $E=U+E_k+E_p$　　D. $E=U+H+E_k+E_p$

解　本题主要考查储存能的概念。能量是物质运动的量度,运动有各种不同形式,相应的应有各种不同的能量,系统储存的能量称为储存能,它有内部储存能和外部储存能。选 C。

12.3.6 稳定流动能量方程及其应用

稳定流动:在流动过程中,热力系内部及热力系界面上每一点的所有特征参数都不随时间而变化,则该流动过程为稳定流动。实现稳定流动的必要条件是,系统与外界进行物质和能量的交换不随时间而变,即:①进、出口截面的参数不随时间而变;②系统与外界交换的功量和热量不随时间而变;③工质的质量流量不随时间而变,且进、出口处的质量流量相等。

稳定流动能量方程的表达式有以下几种形式。

1kg 工质流过开口系，经过有限过程和微元过程时

$$\left.\begin{aligned} q &= \Delta h + \frac{1}{2}\Delta c^2 + g\Delta z + w_s = \Delta h + w_t \\ \delta q &= dh + \frac{1}{2}dc^2 + g dz + \delta w_s = dh + \delta w_t \end{aligned}\right\} \tag{12.3-13}$$

m kg 工质流过开口系，经过有限过程和微元过程时

$$\left.\begin{aligned} Q &= \Delta H + \frac{1}{2}m\Delta c^2 + mg\Delta z + W_s = \Delta H + W_t \\ \delta Q &= dH + \frac{1}{2}m dc^2 + mg dz + \delta W_s = dH + \delta W_t \end{aligned}\right\} \tag{12.3-14}$$

稳态稳流能量方程式在工程上有着广泛的应用，在不同条件下可适当简化为不同的形式，下面列举几种工程应用实例。

(1)透平机械：利用工质在机器中膨胀获得机械功的设备，如汽轮机。因进出口的高度差一般很小，进出口的流速变化也不大，工质在汽轮机中停留的时间很短，系统与外界热量的交换可以忽略，由稳态稳流能量方程得：$w_s = H_2 - H_1$。即在汽轮机中所做的轴功等于工质的焓降。

(2)压缩机械：消耗轴功使气体压缩以升高其压力的设备称为压气机。同样得：$-w_s = h_2 - h_1$，即压气机绝热压缩消耗的轴功等于压缩气体焓的增加。

(3)换热设备：应用稳态稳流能量方程式，可以解决如锅炉、空气加热(或冷却)器、蒸发器、冷凝器等各种热交换器在正常运行时的热量计算问题。在热交换器中，系统与外界没有功量交换，由稳态稳流能量方程得：$q = H_2 - H_1$。即在锅炉等换热设备中，工质所吸收的热量等于焓的增加。

(4)喷管：喷管是一种使气流加速的设备。工质流经喷管时与外界没有功量交换，位能差很小可以忽略，又因为工质流过喷管时速度很快，与外界的热交换也可以不考虑，有稳态稳流能量方程得：$\frac{c_2^2 - c_1^2}{2} = H_2 - H_1$，即在喷管注气流动能值增量等于工质的焓降。

(5)流体的混合：两股流体的混合，取混合室为控制体，混合为稳态稳流工况，在绝热条件下进行，且忽略流体动能、位能变化，则控制体的能量方程为

$$\dot{m}_1 h_1 + \dot{m}_2 h_2 = (\dot{m}_1 + \dot{m}_2) h_3 \tag{12.3-15}$$

(6)绝热节流：流体在管道内流动，遇到突然变窄的断面，由于存在阻力使流体压力降低的现象称为节流。稳态稳流的流体快速流过狭窄断面来不及与外界换热也没有功量的传递，可理想化为绝热节流。如果忽略流体进、出口截面的动能、位能变化，则控制体能量方程可简化为：$H_1 = H_2$。这表明绝热节流前后焓值相等，但是不能把整个节流过程当作定焓过程。

经 典 练 习

12.3-1　热力学第一定律的实质是(　　)。

A. 质量守恒定律　　　　B. 机械守恒定律

C. 能量转换和守恒定律　　D. 卡诺定律

12.3-2　开口系统的工质在可逆流动过程中，如压力降低，则(　　)。

A. 系统对外做技术功　　B. 外界对系统做技术功

C. 系统与外界无技术功的交换　　D. 无法确定

12.3-3　热力学第一定律阐述了能量转换的(　　)。

A. 方向　　B. 速度　　C. 限度　　D. 数量关系

12.3-4　热力学一般规定，系统从外界吸热为(　　)，外界对系统做功为(　　)。

A. 正，负　　B. 负，负　　C. 正，正　　D. 负，正

12.3-5　理想气体的内能包括分子具有的(　　)。

A. 移动动能　　B. 转动动能　　C. 振动动能　　D. A+B+C

12.3-6　在 p-v 图上，一个比体积减少的理想气体可逆过程线下的面积表示该过程中系统(　　)。

A. 吸热　　B. 放热　　C. 对外做功　　D. 消耗外界功

12.3-7　理想气体放热过程中，若工质温度上升，则其膨胀功一定(　　)。

A. 小于零　　B. 大于零　　C. 等于零　　D. 不一定

12.3-8　满足 $q=\Delta u$ 关系的热力工程是(　　)。

A. 任意气体任意过程　　B. 任意气体定压过程

C. 理想气体定压过程　　D. 理想气体可逆过程

12.3-9　工质状态变化，因其比体积变化而做的功称为(　　)。

A. 内部功　　B. 推动功　　C. 技术功　　D. 容积功

12.3-10　一封闭系统与外界之间由于温差而产生的系统内能变化量大小，取决于(　　)。

A. 密度差　　B. 传递的热量　　C. 熵变　　D. 功

12.4　气体性质

考试大纲☞：理想气体模型及其状态方程　实际气体模型及其状态方程　压缩因子　临界参数　对比态及其定律　理想气体比热容　混合气体的性质

必备基础知识

12.4.1　理想气体模型及其状态方程

能量的转换和传递必定伴随工质状态的变化，所以研究热能转变为机械能或其他形式能量的转换必定要涉及工质的性质。工程热力学研究的工质是气态和液态物质，主要是气态。不同的物质有其共性也有个性，这些个性常常造成能量转换的设备、过程不同，所以要分清所讨论的工质的性质。工程热力学常把气体工质分为理想气体和实际气体。

理想气体是一种假想的气体，即气体分子是一些弹性的、忽略分子相互作用力、不占有体积的质点；当实际气体达到 $p\to0$，$v\to\infty$ 的极限状态时，称为理想气体。它是远离液态的实际气体的近似模型。在实际中，有许多气体，如常温常压下的 H_2、O_2、N_2、CO_2、CO、He 及其混合物空气、燃气、烟气等，计算时可作为理想气体处理。

理想气体状态方程如下。

适用于 1kg 气体 $$pv=R_g T \quad (12.4\text{-}1)$$

适用于 $m$kg 气体 $$pV=mR_g T \quad (12.4\text{-}2)$$

适用于 1mol 气体 $$pv_m=RT \quad (12.4\text{-}3)$$

适用于 $n$mol 气体 $$pV=nRT \quad (12.4\text{-}4)$$

其中,R_g 为气体常数,与气体所处状态无关,随气体种类而异;R 为通用气体常数,不仅与气体所处状态无关,而且与气体种类无关,任何气体都是相同的。当采用国际单位制时,$R=8.314$kJ/(mol·K)。通用气体常数与气体常数之间的关系为 $R_g=R/M$。

典型例题解析

【例 12.4-1】 某电厂有三台锅炉合用一个烟囱,每台锅炉每秒钟产生烟气量为 73m^3(已折算到标准状态下的容积)。烟囱出口处的烟气温度为 100℃,压力近似等于 1.0133×10^5Pa,烟气流速为 30m/s,烟囱的出口直径是:

A. 3.56m　　B. 1.75m　　C. 1.66m　　D. 2.55m

解 本题主要考查理想气体状态方程的应用。根据理想气体状态方程 $pV=nRT$,可知本题中压力近似不变,气体状态方程简化为$\frac{V_1}{T_1}=\frac{V_2}{T_2}$,已知 V_1 为 3×73m^3,可以求得 V_2 为 299.22m^3。烟气的流速已知,通过圆柱体体积公式 $V_2=\pi r^2 l$,可以求得烟囱直径为 3.56m。选 A。

【例 12.4-2】 在煤气表上读得煤气消耗量为 668.5 m^3,若煤气消耗期间煤气压力表的平均值为 456.3 Pa,温度平均值为 17℃,当地大气压力为 100.1kPa,标准状态下煤气消耗量为:

A. 642 m^3　　B. 624 m^3　　C. 10 649 m^3　　D. 14 550 m^3

解 本题属于综合性考题,考查内容包括各种压力的关系以及理想气体状态方程的应用。题中已知煤气在 17℃时的体积和压力,求解标准状态(273K,101.325kPa)下煤气的体积。根据理想气体状态方程 $pV=nRT$ 即可求得,需要注意的是代入的压力均为绝对压力,温度为热力学温度。选 B。

【例 12.4-3】 理想气体的 p-v-T 关系式可表示成微分形式:

A. $\mathrm{d}p/p+\mathrm{d}v/v=\mathrm{d}T/T$　　B. $\mathrm{d}p/p-\mathrm{d}v/v=\mathrm{d}T/T$

C. $\mathrm{d}v/v-\mathrm{d}p/p=\mathrm{d}T/T$　　D. $\mathrm{d}T/T+\mathrm{d}v/v=\mathrm{d}p/p$

解 本题主要考查理想气体状态方程式的微分推导过程。在一定状态下,p、v、T 三个变量中只有两个是独立的,也就是当压力和温度确定之后,体系的体积也随之确定,即 $V=f(p,T)$,其微分为“全微分”,即:

$$\mathrm{d}v=\left(\frac{\partial v}{\partial p}\right)_T\mathrm{d}p+\left(\frac{\partial v}{\partial T}\right)_p\mathrm{d}T$$

理想气体状态方程式的实验基础是三个实验定律:①波义耳(Boyle)定律;②查理士-盖·吕萨克(Charles-Gay-Lussac)定律;③阿伏伽德罗(Avogadro)定律。由以上三个实验定律可得出上式中有关的偏微系数。

由波耳耳定律可得:

$$\left(\frac{\partial v}{\partial p}\right)_T=-\frac{v}{p}$$

由查理士-盖·吕萨克定律可得：

$$\left(\frac{\partial v}{\partial T}\right)_{\mathrm{p}}=\frac{v}{T}$$

由阿伏伽德罗定律：

$$\left(\frac{\partial v}{\partial n}\right)_{\mathrm{p,T}}=\frac{v}{n}$$

因此 $v=f(p,T)$ 的全微分可表示为：$\mathrm{d}v=-\frac{v}{p}\mathrm{d}p+\frac{v}{T}\mathrm{d}T$ 或 $\frac{\mathrm{d}v}{v}=-\frac{\mathrm{d}p}{p}+\frac{\mathrm{d}T}{T}$

上述两边不定积分的结果为：$\ln v=-\ln p+\ln T+\ln R_{\mathrm{g}}$

式中积分常数 $\ln R_{\mathrm{g}}$ 为一与气体性质无关的常数，称为"摩尔气体常量"。上式移项并除去对数符号，可得：$pv=R_{\mathrm{g}}T$。选 A。

【例 12.4-4】 已知氧气的表压为 0.15MPa，环境压力为 0.1MPa，温度为 123℃，钢瓶体积为 0.3m^3，则计算该钢瓶质量的计算式 $m=0.15\times10^6\times0.3/(123\times8\ 314)$ 中有：

A. 一处错误　　B. 两处错误　　C. 三处错误　　D. 无错误

解 本题主要考查适合 m kg 理想气体状态方程 $pV=mR_{\mathrm{g}}T$ 的应用。公式中的压力和温度分别为绝对压力和热力学温度，R_{g} 应为氧气的气体常数，而不是通用气体常数，故计算式中有三处错误。选 C。

12.4.2 实际气体模型及其状态方程

实际气体是真实气体，在工程使用范围内离液态较近，分子间作用力及分子本身体积不可忽略，因此热力性质复杂，工程计算主要靠图表。

按照理想气体状态方程式，在给定温度下，一定质量的气体，$pV=$常数，与压力无关。而实际气体则或多或少有偏差，即在定温下 $pV\neq$常数，而随压力变化。

实际气体对理想气体的偏差，主要由于实际气体分子之间相互作用力与分子本身体积的影响。如在一定温度下，气体被压缩，分子间的平均距离缩短，分子间引力作用变大，气体容积就会在分子引力作用下进一步缩小，气体的实际容积要比按理想气体计算所得的值小；但当气体被压缩到一定程度，气体分子本身的体积不能忽略时，分子之间的斥力作用不断增强，把气体压缩到一定容积所需的压力就要大于按理想气体计算之值。

范德瓦尔方程是一个形式简单而又有理论考虑的实际气体状态方程，其方程式为

$$p=\frac{R_{\mathrm{g}}T}{v-b}-\frac{a}{v^2}\qquad(12.4\text{-}5)$$

式中：a——气体分子间作用力强弱的特性常数；

b——气体分子体积影响的修正值。

12.4.3 压缩因子

工程上，在近似计算时常采用对理想气体性质引入修正项而得到实际气体性质的简便方法。实际气体的体积与同温度和同压力下理想气体的体积之比，称为压缩因子，压缩因子表示实际气体偏离理想气体的程度，用符号 z 表示，其表达式为

$$z = \frac{v}{v_{id}} = \frac{pv}{R_g T} \qquad (12.4\text{-}6)$$

引入压缩因子 z 后，实际气体方程为

$$pv = zR_g T \qquad (12.4\text{-}7)$$

对于理想气体 $z=1$；对于实际气体 z 是状态函数，可能大于或小于 1。压缩因子是气体温度和压力的函数，通常采用对比态定律建立的通用性图表——压缩因子图来确定。

典型例题解析

【例 12.4-5】 z 压缩因子法是依据理想气体计算参数修正后得出实际气体近似参数，下列说法中不正确的是：

A. $z=f(p,T)$

B. z 是状态的参数，可能大于 1 或小于 1

C. z 表明实际气体偏离理想气体的程度

D. z 是同样压力下实际气体体积与理想气体体积的比值

解 本题主要考查压缩因子的概念。压缩因子是在给定状态下(相同压力和温度)，实际气体的质量体积(比体积)和理想气体的质量体积的比值。选 D。

【例 12.4-6】 实际气体分子间有作用力且分子有体积，因此同样温度和体积下，若压力不太高，分别采用理想气体状态方程式计算得到的压力 $p_{理}$ 和实际气体状态方程式计算得到的压力 $p_{实}$ 之间关系为：

A. $p_{实} \approx p_{理}$　　B. $p_{实} > p_{理}$　　C. $p_{实} < p_{理}$　　D. 不确定

解 若考虑存在分子间作用力，气体对容器壁面所施加的压力要比理想气体的小；而存在分子体积，会使分子可自由活动的空间减小，气体体积减小压力相应稍有增大，因此综合考虑得出 $p_{实} \approx p_{理}$。选 A。

12.4.4 临界参数

自然界绝大多数物质都有气、液、固三态，而在气、液相变时存在临界状态。实验表明，各种气体都在一定程度上显示出热力学相似的性质。我们把各种状态与临界状态的同名参数的比值称为对比参数，如对比温度、对比压力和对比比体积。对比参数都是无因次量，它表明物质所处状态偏离其本身临界状态的程度。

12.4.5 对比态定律

用对比参数表示的状态方程称为对比状态方程。凡是含有两个常数(不包括气体常数 R)的实际气体状态方程式，根据物质特性常数与临界参数之间的关系，可以消去方程中的常数项而转换成具有通用性的对比状态方程式。

如果不同气体所处状态的对比状态参数都各自相同，则可称这些气体处于对应状态。例如临界状态，各种物质的对比参数都相同，且都等于 1，即处在对应状态。由对比态方程式可以推得：对于满足同一对比态方程式的各种气体，对比参数中若有两个相等，则第三个对比参数就一定相等，物质也就处于对应状态中，这一规律称为对比态定律。范德瓦尔斯对比态方程为

$$p_r = \frac{8T_r}{3v_r - 1} - \frac{3}{v_r^2} \qquad (12.4\text{-}8)$$

12.4.6 理想气体的比热容、内能及焓

1)理想气体比热容的计算

比热(比热容):单位质量的物体,当其温度变化 1K(或 1℃)时,物体和外界交换的热量。

根据所采用的物质量单位的不同,以及所经历的过程不同,比热可以有质量比热 c[单位:J/(kg·K)]、摩尔比热 c_m[单位:J/(mol·K)]及容积比热 c_v[单位:J/(m^3·K)]。每种比热又有定压比热 c_p。它们之间的关系为

$$\left.\begin{aligned} c_m &= Mc = 22.41c_v \\ c_p - c_v &= R_g \\ c_{p,m} - c_{v,m} &= R \end{aligned}\right\} \tag{12.4-9}$$

比热容的处理有如下几种方法。

(1)真实比热容:将实验测得的不同气体的比热容随温度的变化关系,表示为多项式形式,称之为真实比热容。

(2)平均比热容:评价比热容表示 $t_1 \sim t_2$ 间隔内比热容的积分平均值。

(3)定值比热容:当气体温度不太高且变化范围不大,或计算精度要求不高时,可将比热容近似看作不随温度而变的定值,称为定值比热容,见表 12.4-1。

定值比热容 表 12.4-1

气体种类	c_v[J/(kg·K)]	c_p[J/(kg·K)]	k
单原子	$3R_g/2$	$5R_g/2$	1.67
双原子	$5R_g/2$	$7R_g/2$	1.4
多原子	$7R_g/2$	$9R_g/2$	1.3

2)理想气体内能变化的计算

由 $\delta q_v = du_v = c_v dT$ 得

$$du = c_v dT, \Delta u = \int_1^2 c_v dT \text{ 或 } \Delta u = c_v(T_2 - T_1) \tag{12.4-10}$$

适用于理想气体一切过程或者实际气体定容过程。

3)理想气体焓变化的计算

对于理想气体

$$h = u + RT = f(T)$$

$$du = c_p dT, \Delta u = \int_1^2 c_p dT \text{ 或 } \Delta h = c_p(T_2 - T_1) \tag{12.4-11}$$

适用于理想气体的一切热力过程或者实际气体的定压过程。

12.4.7 混合气体

热力工程中常用到由几种气体组成的混合物,即混合气体。例如,燃气主要是由 H_2、N_2、CO_2、H_2O 和 O_2 等组成的混合气体;空气也是常见的混合气体,主要由 N_2、O_2、CO_2、惰性气体及少量水蒸气等气体组成。这些混合气体成分稳定,不发生化学反应且远离液态,因此可视为理想气体。

1)混合气体的压力和分容积

体积为 V 的容器中盛有压力为 p、温度为 T 的混合气体,若将每一种组成气体分离出来

后，且具有与混合气体相同的温度和体积时，给予容器的压力称为组成气体的分压力，用 p_i 表示。根据道尔顿分压定律，混合气体的总压力 p 应等于每一组成分气体分压力 p_i 之和，即

$$p = p_1 + p_2 + \cdots + p_n = \sum_{i=1}^{n} p_i \tag{12.4-12}$$

若将混合气体中每一组成气体分离出来，并且具有与混合气体相同的温度和压力时，所占据的体积称为组成气体的分体积，用 V_i 表示。根据阿密盖特分体积定律，混合气体的总体积应等于每一组成气体的分体积 V_i 之和，即

$$V = V_1 + V_2 + \cdots + V_n = \sum_{i=1}^{n} V_i \tag{12.4-13}$$

2）混合气体的成分及其换算关系

混合气体的成分指各组成气体的含量占混合气体总量的百分数。按物理量单位的不同通常有三种表示方法：质量分数、体积分数和摩尔分数。

（1）质量分数：混合气体中各组成气体的质量与混合气体总质量的比值，用 g_i 表示。

（2）体积分数：混合气体中各组成气体的分体积与混合气体总体积的比值，用 r_i 表示。

（3）摩尔分数：混合气体中各组成气体的摩尔数与混合气体总摩尔数的比值，用 x_i 表示。即

$$\left.\begin{aligned} g_i &= \frac{m_i}{m} \\ r_i &= \frac{V_i}{V} \\ x_i &= \frac{n_i}{n} \end{aligned}\right\} \tag{12.4-14}$$

并且，混合气体中各组成气体的质量分数之和、体积分数之和及摩尔分数之和均等于 1。三者的换算关系为

$$\left.\begin{aligned} r_i &= x_i \\ x_i &= \frac{M}{M_i} g_i = \frac{R_{g,i}}{R_g} g_i \end{aligned}\right\} \tag{12.4-15}$$

3）混合气体的折合摩尔质量与折合气体常数

由于混合气体不是单一气体，因而无法用一个分子式来表示其化学组成，可以假设某种单一气体，某分子数和总质量恰好与混合气体的相等，这种假设单一气体的摩尔质量和气体常数即为混合气体的折合摩尔质量 M 和折合气体常数 R_g。

$$\left.\begin{aligned} R_g &= \frac{R}{M} = \frac{nR}{m} = \frac{\sum_{i=1}^{n} n_i R}{m} = \frac{\sum_{i=1}^{n} m_i \dfrac{R}{M_i}}{m} = \sum_{i=1}^{n} g_i R_{g,i} \\ M &= \frac{R}{R_g} = \frac{8.314}{R_g} \end{aligned}\right\} \tag{12.4-16}$$

或

$$\left.\begin{aligned} R_g &= \frac{m}{n} = \frac{\sum_{i=1}^{n} n_i M_i}{n} = \sum_{i=1}^{n} x_i M_i = \sum_{i=1}^{n} r_i M_i \\ R_g &= \frac{R}{M} = \frac{8.314}{M} \end{aligned}\right\} \tag{12.4-17}$$

4）混合气体的比热容

混合气体的比热容与它的组成气体有关，混合气体温度升高所需的热量，等于各组成气体

相同温升所需的热量之和。由此可以推得混合气体比热容的计算公式分别如下。

混合气体的比热容 $c=g_1c_1+g_2c_2+\cdots+g_nc_n=\sum_{i=1}^{n}g_ic_i$

混合气体的容积比热容 $c'=r_1c'_1+r_2c'_2+\cdots+r_nc'_n=\sum_{i=1}^{n}r_ic'_i$

混合气体的摩尔比热容 $Mc=M\sum_{i=1}^{n}g_ic_i=\sum_{i=1}^{n}x_iM_ic_i$

典型例题解析

【例 12.4-7】 把空气作为理想气体，当其中 O_2 的质量分数为 21%，N_2 的质量分数为 78%，其他气体的质量分数为 1%，则其定压比热容 c_p 为：

A. 707J/(kg·K) B. 910J/(kg·K)

C. 1 010J/(kg·K) D. 1 023J/(kg·K)

解 本题主要考查混合气体比热容计算公式的应用。选 C。

经 典 练 习

12.4-1 理想混合气体的压力为各组成气体在具有与混合气体相同温度、相同容积时的分压力（ ）。

A. 之差 B. 之积 C. 之和 D. 之中最大的一个

12.4-2 理想混合气体的密度为各组成气体在具有与混合气体相同温度、相同压力时的密度（ ）。

A. 之差 B. 之积 C. 之和 D. 之中最大的一个

12.4-3 空气或燃气的定压比热是定容比热的（ ）倍。

A. 1.2 B. 1.3 C. 1.4 D. 1.5

12.4-4 物体的热容量与下列（ ）无关。

A. 组成该物体的物质 B. 物体的质量

C. 加热过程 D. 物体的密度

12.4-5 理想气体的比热容（ ）。

A. 与压力和温度有关 B. 与压力无关而与温度有关

C. 与压力和温度都无关 D. 与压力有关而与温度无关

12.5 理想气体基本热力过程及气体压缩

考试大纲☞： 定压 定容 定温和绝热过程 多变过程 气体压缩轴功 余隙 多级压缩和中间冷却

必备基础知识

12.5.1 定压、定容、定温和绝热过程

理想气体在闭口系统中进行的四个基本可逆过程为定容过程、定压过程、定温过程和可逆绝热过程，它们有一个共同的特征，就是过程进行中有一个状态参数（v，T 或 s）保持不变。因

此，保持一个参数不变的过程仅有上述四种，这四种过程称为基本过程。

1)定容过程

工质比体积保持不变的过程称为定容过程。气体在刚性容器内进行的加热过程即为定容过程。定容过程中加给气体的热量并未转变为机械能，而是全部用于增加气体的内能。

2)定压过程

压力保持不变时系统状态发生变化所经历的过程称为定压过程。定压过程中系统获得或放出的热量等于初、终状态的焓差。

3)定温过程

温度保持不变时系统状态发生变化所经历的过程称为定温过程。定温膨胀时吸热量全部转换为膨胀功，定温压缩时消耗的压缩功全部转换为放热量。

4)绝热过程

系统与外界不发生热量交换时所经历的过程称为绝热。对于无功耗散的准静态绝热过程(可逆绝热过程)即为定熵过程。绝热过程中工质与外界无热量交换。绝热膨胀时，膨胀功等于工质内能的减量；绝热压缩时，消耗的压缩功等于工质内能的增量。

图 12.5-1 为基本过程的 p-v 图和 T-s 图。

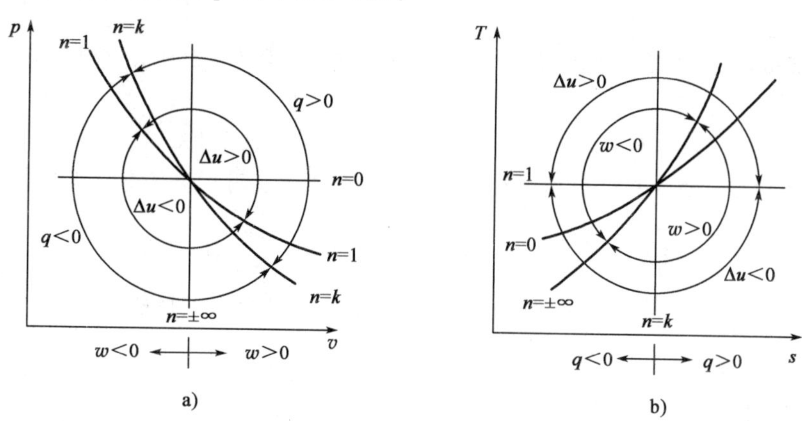

图 12.5-1　基本过程的 p-v 图和 T-s 图

典型例题解析

【例 12.5-1】　一容积为 $2m^3$ 的储气罐内盛有 $t_1=20℃$，$p_1=500kPa$ 的空气[已知：$c_p=1.005kJ/(kg·K)$，$R=0.287kJ/(kg·K)$]。若使压力提高到 $p_2=1MPa$，空气的温度将升高到：

A. 313℃　　B. 40℃　　C. 400℃　　D. 350℃

解　本题主要考查定容过程中的温度变化及理想气体状态方程的应用。本题提供了大量的信息，但真正在计算中用到的是初始压力、初始温度和终止压力，利用理想气体状态方程可以计算出定容过程的终止温度是 313℃。选 A。

【例 12.5-2】　0.3 标准立方米的氧气，在温度 $t_1=45℃$ 和压力 $p_1=103.2kPa$ 下盛于一个具有可移动活塞的圆筒中，先在定压下对氧气加热，热力过程为 2—2，然后在定容下冷却到初温 45℃，过程为 2—3。已知终态压力 $p_3=58.8kPa$。若氧气的气体常数 $R=259.8J/(kg·K)$，在这两个过程中氧气与外界净交换热量为：

A. 56.56kJ　　B. 24.2kJ　　C. 26.68kJ　　D. 46.52kJ

解　这两个过程包括定压加热和定容冷却两个过程，两个过程中氧气与外界净交换热量为两个过程中氧气与外界交换热量之和，即 $Q=Q_1+Q_2$。

0.3 标准立方米的氧气的质量 $m=\dfrac{p_0V_0}{RT_0}$

2—2 定压过程中的吸热量 $Q_1=mc_p\Delta t=\dfrac{p_0V_0}{RT_0}\times\dfrac{7}{2}R(T_2-T_1)$

2—3 定容过程中的吸热量 $Q_2=mc_v\Delta t=\dfrac{p_0V_0}{RT_0}\times\dfrac{5}{2}R(T_3-T_2)$

由于 2—2 过程为定压过程，因此 $p_1=p_2=103.2\text{kPa}$，2—3 过程为定容过程，已知状态点 3 的压力和温度，可以求得状态点 2 的温度 T_2：

$$T_2=\frac{p_2}{p_3}T_3=\frac{103.2}{58.8}\times(273+45)=558.1\text{K}$$

$$Q=Q_1+Q_2=\frac{p_0V_0}{RT_0}\times\frac{7}{2}R(T_2-T_1)+\frac{p_0V_0}{RT_0}\times\frac{5}{2}R(T_3-T_2)=26.68\text{kJ}$$

选 C。

【例 12.5-3】　空气进行可逆绝热压缩，压缩比为 6.5，初始温度为 27℃，则终了时气体温度可达：

A. 512K　　B. 430K　　C. 168℃　　D. 46℃

解　本题主要考查定熵过程中的状态参数变化公式的应用。由多变过程公式得：

$$\frac{T_2}{T_1}=\left(\frac{v_1}{v_2}\right)^{k-1}=\left(\frac{p_2}{p_1}\right)^{\frac{k-1}{k}}=6.5^{\frac{1.4-1}{1.4}}=1.707$$

$$T_2=1.707T_1=1.707\times(27+273)=512\text{K}$$

选 A。

【例 12.5-4】　理论上认为，水在工业锅炉内的吸热过程为：

A. 定容过程　　B. 定压过程

C. 多变过程　　D. 定温过程

解　水在工业蒸汽锅炉中被定压加热变为过热水蒸气。选 B。

12.5.2 多变过程

多变过程比四种基本热力过程更为一般化，是按一定规律变化的热力过程。

1) 多变过程方程式

在工程上，大部分实际过程可近似地用 $pv^n=$定值的多变过程来描述，n 是常数，称为多变指数。原则上 n 可以为 $-\infty\sim+\infty$ 之间的任一数值，但工程中遇到的过程 n 一般都为正值。

四种基本过程，实际上也都是多变过程的特例，即：

$n=0$，$p=$定值，为定压过程；

$n=1$，$pv=$定值，为定温过程；

$n=k$，$pv^k=$定值，为定熵过程；

$n=\pm\infty$，$v=$定值，为定容过程。

多变指数 n 的计算公式为：

$$n=\frac{\ln(p_2/p_1)}{\ln(v_1/v_2)} \tag{12.5-1}$$

2)过程中 q、w、Δu 的判断

(1)q 的判断：以绝热线为基准。

(2)w 的判断：以定容线为基准。

(3)Δu 的判断：以定温线为基准。

3)初、终状态参数关系式及内能、焓和熵的变化公式

$$\left.\begin{aligned} p_1v_1^n &= p_2v_2^n \\ T_1v_2^{n-1} &= T_2v_1^{n-1} \\ T_1p_1^{-\frac{n-1}{n}} &= T_2p_2^{-\frac{n-1}{n}} \end{aligned}\right\} \tag{12.5-2}$$

$$\left.\begin{aligned} \Delta u &= c_v\Big|_{t_1}^{t_2}(T_2-T_1) \\ \Delta h &= c_p\Big|_{t_1}^{t_2}(T_2-T_1) \\ \Delta s &= c_p\ln\frac{T_2}{T_1}-R_g\ln\frac{p_2}{p_1} \\ &= c_v\ln\frac{T_2}{T_1}+R_g\ln\frac{v_1}{v_2} \\ &= c_v\ln\frac{p_2}{p_1}+c_p\ln\frac{v_1}{v_2} \end{aligned}\right\} \tag{12.5-3}$$

为了应用方便，将常用的基本热力过程的主要计算公式汇总于表 12.5-1 中。

气体主要热力过程的基本计算公式 表 12.5-1

过程	定容过程	定压过程	定温过程	定熵过程	多变过程
过程指数 n	∞	0	1	κ	n
过程方程	v=常数	p=常数	pv=常数	pv^{κ}=常数	pv^n=常数
p、v、T 关系	$\frac{T_2}{T_1}=\frac{p_2}{p_1}$	$\frac{T_2}{T_1}=\frac{v_2}{v_1}$	$p_1v_1=p_2v_2$	$p_1v_1^k=p_2v_2^k$ $\frac{T_2}{T_1}=\left(\frac{v_1}{v_2}\right)^{k-1}$ $=\left(\frac{p_2}{p_1}\right)^{\frac{k-1}{k}}$	$p_1v_1^n=p_2v_2^n$ $\frac{T_2}{T_1}=\left(\frac{v_1}{v_2}\right)^{n-1}$ $=\left(\frac{p_2}{p_1}\right)^{\frac{n-1}{n}}$
Δu、Δh、Δs 计算式	$\Delta u=c_v(T_2-T_1)$ $\Delta h=c_p(T_2-T_1)$ $\Delta s=c_v\ln\frac{T_2}{T_1}$	$\Delta u=c_v(T_2-T_1)$ $\Delta h=c_p(T_2-T_1)$ $\Delta s=c_p\ln\frac{T_2}{T_1}$	$\Delta u=0$ $\Delta h=0$ $\Delta s=R\ln\frac{v_2}{v_1}$ $=R\ln\frac{p_1}{p_2}$	$\Delta u=c_v(T_2-T_1)$ $\Delta h=c_p(T_2-T_1)$ $\Delta s=0$	$\Delta u=c_v(T_2-T_1)$ $\Delta h=c_p(T_2-T_1)$ $\Delta s=c_v\ln\frac{T_2}{T_1}+R_g\ln\frac{v_2}{v_1}$ $=c_p\ln\frac{T_2}{T_1}-R_g\ln\frac{p_2}{p_1}$ $=c_p\ln\frac{v_2}{v_1}+c_v\ln\frac{p_2}{p_1}$
膨胀功 $w=\int_1^2 p\mathrm{d}v$	$w=0$	$w=p(v_2-v_1)$ $=R(T_2-T_1)$	$w=RT\ln\frac{v_2}{v_1}$ $=RT\ln\frac{p_1}{p_2}$	$w=-\Delta u=\frac{1}{k-1}(p_1v_1-p_2v_2)$ $=\frac{1}{k-1}R\times(T_1-T_2)$ $=\frac{RT_1}{k-1}\left[1-\left(\frac{p_2}{p_1}\right)^{\frac{k-1}{k}}\right]$	$w=\frac{1}{n-1}(p_1v_1-p_2v_2)$ $=\frac{1}{n-1}R\times(T_1-T_2)$ $=\frac{RT_1}{n-1}\left[1-\left(\frac{p_2}{p_1}\right)^{\frac{n-1}{n}}\right]$

续上表

过程	定容过程	定压过程	定温过程	定 熵 过 程	多 变 过 程
热量 $q=\int_1^2 c\mathrm{d}T$ $=\int_1^2 T\mathrm{d}s$	$q=\Delta u$ $=c_v(T_2-T_1)$	$q=\Delta h$ $=c_p(T_2-T_1)$	$q=T\Delta s$ $=w$	$q=0$	$q=\frac{n-k}{n-1}\times c_v(T_2-T_1)$ $(n\neq 1)$
比热容	c_v	c_p	∞	0	$c_n=\frac{n-k}{n-1}c_v$

注:表中比热容为定值比热容。

典型例题解析

【例 12.5-5】 空气的初始容积 $V_1=2\text{m}^3$,压力 $p_1=0.2\text{MPa}$,温度 $t_1=40℃$,经某一过程被压缩为 $V_2=0.5\text{m}^3$,$p_2=1\text{MPa}$,该过程的多变指数是:

A. 0.8　　B. 1.16　　C. 1.0　　D. −1.3

解 本题考查多变过程中一些常用公式的应用。利用多变过程公式 $p_1v_1^n=p_2v_2^n$ 可以推导出 $n=\ln(p_2/p_1)/\ln(V_1/V_2)$,代入压力和体积的数据后,可以求得多变指数 $n=1.16$。选 B。

【例 12.5-6】 1kg 空气初态压力为 3MPa、温度为 800K,进行一不可逆膨胀过程到终态,其终态压力为 1.5MPa、温度为 700K。若空气的气体常数为 0.287kJ/(kg·K),绝热指数为 1.4,此过程中空气的熵变化量是:

A. 64.8kJ/(kg·K)　　B. 64.8 J/(kg·K)

C. 52.37 kJ/(kg·K)　　D. 102.3 J/(kg·K)

解 本题属于复合型考题,主要考查理想气体比热容的计算 $c_p=\frac{kR}{(k-1)}$ 以及多变过程的熵产计算公式 $\Delta s=c_p\ln\frac{T_2}{T_1}-R\ln\frac{p_2}{p_1}$。代入数据可以求得答案为 B。

【例 12.5-7】 某理想气体吸收 3 349kJ 的热量而做定压变化。设定容比热容为 0.741kJ/(kg·K),气体常数为 0.297kJ/(kg·K),此过程中气体对外界做容积功:

A. 858kJ　　B. 900kJ　　C. 245kJ　　D. 958kJ

解 本题主要考查理想气体定容比热容与定压比热容的换算公式 $c_p-c_v=R$ 和定压过程容积功计算式 $w=p(v_2-v_1)=R(T_2-T_1)$,以及定压过程内能变化公式 $\Delta H=mc_p(T_2-T_1)$。已知气体的定容比热容,由公式 $c_p-c_v=R$ 可以求得定压比热容 c_p 为 1.038 kJ/(kg·K),由公式 $\Delta H=mc_p(T_2-T_1)=3\,349\text{kJ}$ 可以计算出温度变化 $m(T_2-T_1)=3\,226.4\text{kg}\cdot\text{K}$,则此过程对外界做的容积功为 $W=mR(T_2-T_1)=958\text{kJ}$。选 D。

【例 12.5-8】 理想气体初态 $v_1=1.5\text{m}^3$、$p_1=0.2\text{MPa}$,终态 $v_2=0.5\text{m}^3$、$p_2=1.0\text{MPa}$,则多变指数为:

A. 1.46　　B. 1.35　　C. 1.25　　D. 1.10

解 本题主要考查多变过程多变指数计算公式 $n=\ln(p_2/p_1)/\ln(v_1/v_2)$。将相应数据代入公式后可以求得 $n=1.46$。选 A。

【例 12.5-9】 某热力过程中，氮气初态为 $v_1=1.2\text{m}^3/\text{kg}$ 和 $p_1=0.1\text{MPa}$，终态为 $v_2=0.4\text{m}^3/\text{kg}$ 和 $p_2=0.6\text{MPa}$，该过程的多变比热容 c_n 为：

A. 271J/(kg·K)　　B. 297J/(kg·K)

C. 445J/(kg·K)　　D. 742J/(kg·K)

解 多变指数 $n=\dfrac{\ln(p_2/p_1)}{\ln(v_1/v_2)}=\dfrac{\ln(0.6/0.1)}{\ln(1.2/0.4)}=1.631$

双原子气体的 $k=1.4$，氮气的 $c_v=742\text{J}/(\text{kg}\cdot\text{K})$

多变比热容 $c_n=\dfrac{n-k}{n-1}c_v=\dfrac{1.631-1.4}{1.631-1}\times742=271\text{J}/(\text{kg}\cdot\text{K})$

选 A。

12.5.3 气体压缩轴功

用来压缩气体的设备称为压气机。压气机按其工作原理及构造形式，可分为活塞式、叶轮式(离心式、轴流式、回转容积式)及引射式压缩器等；以其产生压缩气体压力的高低，大致可分为通气机(<115kPa)、鼓风机(115～350kPa)和压气机(>350kPa)三类。

压缩过程可出现三种情况：第一种是过程中对气体未采取冷却措施，过程可视为绝热压缩；第二种是气体被充分冷却，过程接近定温压缩；第三种是压气机的实际压缩过程，虽采用了一定的冷却措施，但气体又未能充分冷却，所以压缩过程为定温与绝热之间的多变过程，如图 12.5-2 所示。

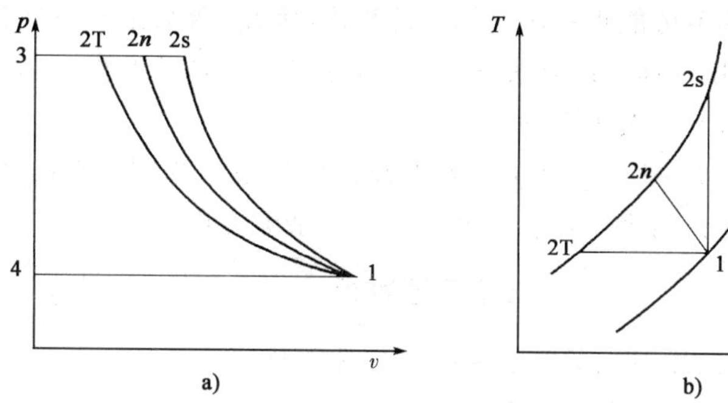

图 12.5-2 压缩过程

不同压缩过程的排气温度的计算为

$$\left.\begin{aligned}&\text{定熵过程} && T_{2s}=T_1\left(\frac{p_2}{p_1}\right)^{\frac{k-1}{k}}\\&\text{多变过程} && T_{2n}=T_1\left(\frac{p_2}{p_1}\right)^{\frac{n-1}{n}}\\&\text{定温压缩} && T_{2T}=T_1\end{aligned}\right\}\tag{12.5-4}$$

不同压缩过程的压气机耗功的计算为

$$\left.\begin{aligned}&\text{定熵过程} && w_{t,s}=\frac{k}{k-1}R_gT_1\left[1-\left(\frac{p_2}{p_1}\right)^{\frac{k-1}{k}}\right]\\&\text{多变过程} && w_{t,n}=\frac{n}{n-1}R_gT_1\left[1-\left(\frac{p_2}{p_1}\right)^{\frac{n-1}{n}}\right]\\&\text{定温过程} && w_{t,T}=R_gT_1\ln\frac{v_2}{v_1}=-R_gT_1\ln\frac{p_2}{p_1}\end{aligned}\right\}\tag{12.5-5}$$

由此得出，从同一初态压缩到某一预定压力，定温过程的耗功量最省，压缩终了的排气温度也最低，所以定温过程最好而绝热过程最差，多变过程介于两者之间。

典型例题解析

【例 12.5-10】 采用任何类型的压气机对气体进行压缩，所消耗的功都可用下式计算：

A. $w_c = q - \Delta h$　　B. $w_c = \Delta h$　　C. $w_c = q - \Delta u$　　D. $w_c = -\int v \mathrm{d}p$

解 选项 B 适用于绝热压缩，选项 C 适用于闭口系统的压缩过程，选项 D 适用于可逆压缩过程。选 A。

【例 12.5-11】 压气机最理想的压缩过程是采用：

A. $n=k$ 的绝热压缩过程　　B. $n=1$ 的定温压缩过程

C. $1<n<k$ 的多变压缩过程　　D. $n>k$ 的多变压缩过程

解 由不同压缩过程的 p-v 图可知，压缩机不同压缩过程中所消耗的功 $W_{s,t}<W_{s,n}<W_{s,s}$，故压缩机最理想的过程应采用定温过程。选 B。

12.5.4 余隙

实际的活塞式压气机，为了运转平稳，避免活塞与气缸盖撞击以及便于安装进气阀和排气阀等，当活塞处于左死点时，活塞顶面与缸盖之间须留有一定的空隙，称为余隙(余隙容积)。由于余隙容积的存在，活塞不可能将高压气体全部排出，因此，活塞在下一个吸气过程中，必须等待余隙容积中残留的高压气体膨胀到进气压力时，才能从外界吸入新气，余隙使一部分气缸容积不能被有效利用，压力比越大越不利。

不论压气机有无余隙，压缩 1kg 气体所需得理论压气轴功相同。然而有余隙容积时，进气量减少，气缸容积不能充分利用，因此，应该尽量减少余隙容积。

典型例题解析

【例 12.5-12】 活塞式压缩机留有余隙的主要目的是：

A. 减少压缩制气过程耗功

B. 运行平稳和安全

C. 增加产气量

D. 避免高温

解 活塞式压缩机留有余隙的主要目的，是保证压缩机的安全平稳运行，防止活塞撞击气缸底部。而留有余隙容积后会使得压缩机容积效率减小，实际输气量低于理论输气量。选 B。

12.5.5 多级压缩及中间冷却

由

$$\frac{T_2}{T_1} = \left(\frac{p_2}{p_1}\right)^{\frac{k-1}{k}} \tag{12.5-6}$$

即压力比越大，其压缩终了温度越高，气体压缩终了温度过高将影响气缸润滑油的性能，并可能造成运行事故。因此，各种气体的压气机对气体压缩终了温度都有限定数值。例如，空气压缩机的排气温度一般不允许超过160～180℃。另外，压缩终了温度过高还会影响压气机的容积效率。因此，要获得较高压力的压缩气体时，常采用具有中间冷却设备的多级压气机。

多级压气机是将气体依次在几个气缸中连续压缩，同时，为了避免过高温和减少气体的质量体积，以降低下一级所消耗的压缩功，在前一级压缩之后，将气体引入一个中间冷却器进行定压冷却，然后再进入下一级气缸继续压缩直至达到所要求的压力。

采用多级压缩和中间冷却具有降低排气温度和节省功耗的优点。多级压缩用中间冷却器的目的是，对从低压级出来的压缩气体及时进行冷却，让其温度降低到被压缩前的温度，然后再进入高压汽缸，以减少消耗压缩功。如果不用中间冷却器，让从低压汽缸出来的压缩气体直接进入高压汽缸，就达不到减少消耗压缩功的目的。

级间压力不同，所需的总轴功也不同，最有利的级间压力的确定原则应为使所需的总轴功最小。

压气机的增压比：压气机的出口压力与进口压力之比，称为压气机的增压比。

最佳增压比：使多级压缩中间冷却压气机耗功最小时，各级的增压比称为最佳增压比。

以两级压缩为例，得到

$$\frac{p_2}{p_1}=\frac{p_3}{p_2}$$

结论：两级压力比相等，功耗最小。

推广为 z 级压缩，即

$$\beta_1=\beta_2=\cdots=\sqrt[z]{\frac{p_{z+1}}{p_1}} \tag{12.5-7}$$

推论：

(1)每级进口、出口温度相等。

(2)各级压气机消耗功相等。

(3)各级气缸及各中间冷却放出和吸收热量相等。

经 典 练 习

12.5-1　理想气体过程方程 pv^n = 常数，当 $n=k$ 时，该过程为(　　)过程，外界对工质做的功(　　)。

A. 定压，用于增加系统内能和对外放热　B. 绝热，用于增加系统内能

C. 定容，用于增加系统内能和对外做功　D. 定温，用于对外做功

12.5-2　理想气体过程方程 pv^n = 常数，当 $n=\pm\infty$ 时，其热力过程是(　　)。

A. 等容过程　B. 等压过程　C. 等温过程　D. 绝热过程

12.5-3　对定容过程，外界加入封闭系统的热量全部用来增加系统内能，反之，封闭系统向外界放的热量全部由系统内能的减少来补充。这句话(　　)成立。

A. 仅对理想气体　B. 仅对实际气体

C. 对理想气体和实际气体都　D. 对理想气体和实际气体都不

12.5-4　在 p-v 图上，(　　)更陡一些，在 T-s 图上，(　　)更陡一些。

A. 绝热线，定容线　B. 绝热线，定压线

C. 定温线，定容线　D. 定温线，定压线

12.5-5　理想气体放热过程，当温度不变时，其膨胀功 W(　　)。

A. 大于0　B. 小于0　C. 等于0　D. 大于0或小于0

12.5-6　在绝热过程中，技术功是膨胀功的(　　)倍。

A. 0　　B. 1　　C. k　　D. 2

12.5-7　理想气体绝热过程的比热容为(　　)。

A. c_v　　B. c_p　　C. ∞　　D. 0

12.5-8　一台单级活塞式空气压缩机，余隙比为5%。若压缩前空气的压力为0.1MPa，温度为20℃，压缩后空气的压力为0.6MPa，设两个多变过程的多变指数均为1.25，该压缩机的容积温度为(　　)。

A. 146　　B. 305　　C. 419　　D. 578

12.5-9　活塞式空气压缩机的余隙比降低时，其容积效率将(　　)。

A. 提高　　B. 降低　　C. 不变　　D. 不定

12.6　热力学第二定律

考试大纲☞：热力学第二定律的实质及表述　卡诺循环和卡诺定理　熵　孤立系统熵增原理

必备基础知识

12.6.1 热力学第二定律的实质及表述

热力学第一定律，解释了在热力过程中参与转换与传递的各种能量在数量上的守恒。但满足能量守恒的过程是否都能实现？热力过程的方向、条件与限度是热力学第二定律给出的。只有同时满足热力学第一定律和热力学第二定律的过程才是能实现的过程。热力学第二定律与热力学第一定律共同组成了热力学的理论基础。

热力过程具有方向性这一客观规律，归根结底是由于不同类型或不同状态下的能量具有质的差别，而过程的方向性正缘于较高位能质向较低位能质的转化。例如，热量由高温传至低温。机械能转化为热能，按热力学第一定律能量的数值保持不变，但是，以做功能力为标志的能质却降低了，称之为能质的退化或贬值。因此，热力学第二定律的实质便是论述热力过程的方向性及能质退化或贬值的客观规律。所谓过程的方向性，除指明自发生过程进行的方向外，还包括对实现非自发过程所需的条件，以及过程进行的最大限度等内容。热力学第二定律告诫我们，自然界的物质和能量只能沿着一个方向转换，即从可利用到不可利用，从有效到无效，这说明了节能与节物的必要性。

热力学第二定律的两种经典描述：

克劳修斯从热量传递方向性的角度表述为："不可能把热从低温物体传到高温物体而不引起其他变化"。

开尔文从热功转换的角度表述为："不可能从单一热源取热，使之完全变为功而不引起其他变化"。

12.6.2 卡诺循环和卡诺定理

意义：解决了热变功最大限度的转换效率问题。

1)卡诺循环

(1)正循环组成：两个可逆定温过程、两个可逆绝热过程，如图12-4所示。

过程 $a—b$：工质从热源(T_1)可逆定温吸热；

过程 $b—c$：工质可逆绝热(定熵)膨胀；

过程 $c—d$：工质向冷源(T_2)可逆定温放热；

过程 $d—a$：工质可逆绝热(定熵)压缩回复到初始状态。

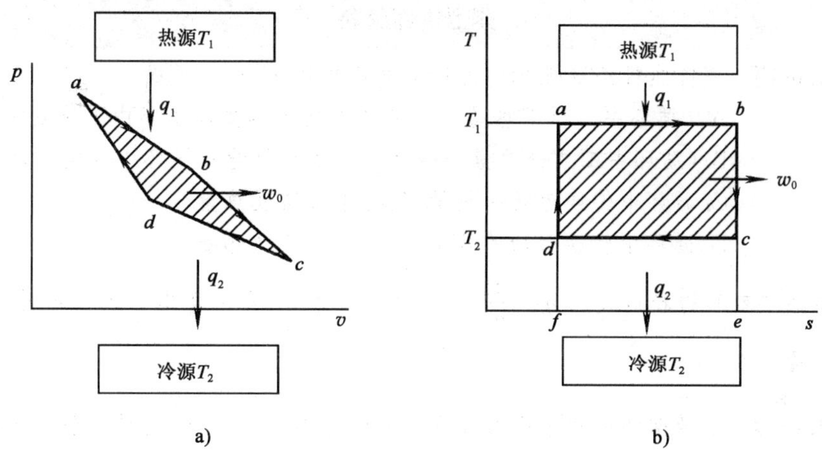

图 12.6 1　正循环

循环热效率：

$$\eta_t = \frac{w_0}{q_1} = 1 - \frac{q_2}{q_1}$$

$$q_1 = T_1(s_b - s_a) = \text{面积 } abefa \qquad q_2 = T_2(s_c - s_d) = \text{面积 } cdfec$$

因为
$$s_b - s_a = s_c - s_d$$

得到
$$\eta_{t_c} = 1 - \frac{T_2}{T_1} \tag{12.6-1}$$

分析：

①卡诺循环热效率仅取决于两热源的温度 T_1、T_2，与工质无关；

②由于 $T_1 \neq \infty$、$T_2 \neq 0$，因此热效率不能为 1；

③若 $T_1 = T_2$，热效率为零，即单一热源，热机不能实现。

(2)逆循环：卡诺循环是可逆循环，如果使循环沿反方向进行，就成为逆卡诺循环。由于使用的目的不同，分为制冷循环和热泵循环。包括绝热压缩、定温放热、定温吸热、绝热膨胀。

制冷系数
$$\varepsilon_c = \frac{q_2}{w_0} = \frac{q_2}{q_1 - q_2} = \frac{T_2}{T_1 - T_2} \tag{12.6-2}$$

供热系数
$$\varepsilon_c' = \frac{q_1}{w_0} = \frac{q_1}{q_1 - q_2} = \frac{T_1}{T_1 - T_2} \tag{12.6-3}$$

两者关系
$$\varepsilon_c' = \varepsilon_c + 1 \tag{12.6-4}$$

分析：通常 $T_2 > T_1 - T_2$，所以 $\varepsilon_c > 1$。

2)卡诺定理

所有工作于同温热源、同温冷源之间的一切热机，以可逆热机的热效率为最高。

在同温热源与同温冷源之间的一切可逆热机，其热效率均相等。

卡诺定理有重要的实用价值和理论价值，主要是：

(1)卡诺定理指出了热效率的极限值，这一极限值仅与热源及冷源的温度有关。热机热效率恒小于1。

(2)提高热效率的根本途径在于提高热源温度,降低冷源温度,以及尽可能减少不可逆因素。

(3)由于不花代价的低温热源的温度以大气环境温度 T_0 为限,而 T_0 比较稳定,视为定值,那么温度为 T 的热源放出的热量 Q 最多只能有部分可以转变为功,提示了热变功极限。

典型例题解析

【例 12.6-1】 评价热机经济性能的指标是循环热效率,它可写成:

A.(循环中工质吸热量-循环中工质放热量)/循环中工质吸热量

B.(循环中工质吸热量-循环中工质放热量)/循环中转换为功的热量

C. 循环中转换为功的热量/循环中工质吸热量

D. 循环中转换为功的热量/循环中工质放热量

解 循环热效率的表达式为 $\eta_t=\dfrac{w_0}{q_1}=\dfrac{q_1-q_2}{q_1}$,其中 q_1 为循环中工质吸热量,q_2 为循环中工质放热量。选A。

【例 12.6-2】 卡诺循环由两个等温过程和两个绝热过程组成,过程的条件是:

A. 绝热过程必须可逆,而等温过程可以任意

B. 所有过程均是可逆的

C. 所有过程均可以是不可逆的

D. 等温过程必须可逆,而绝热过程可以任意

解 由卡诺循环的定义可知,卡诺循环由两个可逆定温过程、两个可逆绝热过程组成,因此过程的条件应是所有过程均是可逆的。选B。

【例 12.6-3】 (2014)进行逆卡诺循环制热时,其供热系数 ε_c' 将随着冷热源温差的减小而:

A. 减小　　B. 增大　　C. 不变　　D. 不确定

解 热泵供热系数 $\varepsilon_c'=1+\varepsilon_c$,式中 $\varepsilon_c=\dfrac{T_0}{T_k-T_0}$,为逆卡诺循环制冷系数,当冷热源温差 T_k-T_0 减小时,逆卡诺循环制冷系数 ε_c 增大,故热泵供热系数 ε_c' 增大。选B。

12.6.3 熵

熵是表征系统微观粒子无序程度的一个宏观状态参数。

熵的变化量
$$\Delta S=S_2-S_1=\int_1^2\left(\frac{\partial q}{T}\right)_{re} \tag{12.6-5}$$

对微元过程的熵变化
$$dS=\left(\frac{\delta q}{T}\right)_{re} \tag{12.6-6}$$

不可逆过程熵变化
$$S_2-S_1>\int_1^2\left(\frac{\partial q}{T}\right)_{irr}$$

因此有
$$\Delta S=S_2-S_1\geqslant\int_1^2\frac{\delta q}{T} \tag{12.6-7}$$

对于微元过程,则
$$dS\geqslant\frac{\delta q}{T} \tag{12.6-8}$$

其中,等号适用于可逆过程,不等号适用于不可逆过程。

工质在完成一个循环后熵变为零，即

$$\oint dS = 0 \tag{12.6-9}$$

固体或液体熵变化的计算：$\Delta S = mc\ln\dfrac{T_2}{T_1}$。

其中，c 为固体或液体的比热容，一般情况下有 $c_v = c_p = c$。

热源熵变计算

恒温热源
$$\Delta S = \frac{Q}{T} \tag{12.6-10}$$

变温热源
$$\Delta S = \int \frac{\delta Q}{T} \tag{12.6-11}$$

孤立系统熵变
$$\Delta S = \sum_i \Delta S_i \tag{12.6-12}$$

12.6.4 孤立系统熵增原理

孤立系统熵增原理：若孤立系统所有的内部以及彼此间的作用都经历可逆变化，则孤立系统的总熵保持不变；若在任何一部分内发生不可逆过程或各部分间的相互作用中伴有不可逆性，则其总熵必定增加。即

$$\Delta S_{iso} \geqslant 0 \tag{12.6-13}$$

意义：

(1)可判断过程进行的方向。

(2)熵达到最大时，系统处于平衡态。

(3)系统不可逆程度越大，熵增越大。

(4)可作为热力学第二定律的数学表达式。

引起系统熵变化的因素有两类：一是由于与外界发生热交换由热流引起的熵流，记为 ΔS_f；二是由于不可逆因素的存在，而引起熵的增加 ΔS_g，称为熵产。熵流 $\Delta S_f = \int \dfrac{\delta Q}{T}$，可为正、负或为零，应视热流方向和情况而定(系统吸热为正，系统放热为负，绝热为零)；$\Delta S_g \geqslant 0$(不可逆过程为正，可逆过程为 0)，不可逆性越大，熵产越大。若过程中熵产为零，则不可逆性消失，即成为可逆过程。据此，不可逆过程的熵产可作为过程不可逆性大小的度量。

熵方程的一般形式为(输入熵－输出熵)＋熵产＝系统熵变

得到
$$\Delta S_{sys} = \Delta S_f + \Delta S_g \tag{12.6-14}$$

开口系统熵方程

$$(S_1 \partial m_1 - S_2 \partial m_2) + \partial S_f + \partial S_g = dS_{cv} \tag{12.6-15}$$

因此，热力学系统熵的变化都可以用熵流与熵产的代数和表示，即 $\Delta S = \Delta S_f + \Delta S_g$

其微分形式表示为 $dS = dS_f + dS_g$

对于孤立系统，$dS_f = 0$，因此有 $dS_{iso} = dS_g \geqslant 0$

$$\Delta S_{iso} = \Delta S_g \geqslant 0 \tag{12.6-16}$$

其中，不等号适用于不可逆过程；等号适用于可逆过程。说明在孤立系统内，一切实际过程(不可逆过程)都朝着使系统熵增加的方向进行，在极限情况下(可逆过程)维持系统的熵不变，而任何使系统熵减少的过程是不可能发生的，这一原理即为孤立系统熵增原理。孤立系统熵增原理同样揭示了自然过程方向性的客观规律。任何自发过程都是使孤立系统熵增加的过程。

经典练习

12.6-1　热力学第二定律指出(　　)。

A. 能量只能转换不能增加或消灭　　B. 能量只能增加或转换不能消灭

C. 能量在转换中是有方向性的　　D. 能量在转换中是无方向性的

12.6-2　能量在传递和转换过程进行的方向、条件及限度时热力学第二定律所研究的问题,其中(　　)是根本问题。

A. 方向　　B. 条件　　C. 限度　　D. 转换量

12.6-3　单一热源的热机,又称为第二类永动机,它违反了(　　)。

A. 能量守很定律　　B. 物质不变定律　　C. 热力学第一定律　　D. 热力学第二定律

12.6-4　热力学第二定律可以这样表述(　　)。

A. 热能可以百分之百的转变成功

B. 热能可以从低温物体自动的传递到高温物体

C. 使热能全部而且连续地转变为机械功是不可能的

D. 物体的热能与机械功既不能创造也不能消灭

12.6-5　关于热力学第二定律的表述,下列(　　)是正确的。

A. 不可能从热源吸取热量使之完全转变为有用功

B. 不可能把热量从低温物体传到高温物体而不产生其他变化

C. 不可能从单一热源吸取热量使之完全转变为有用功

D. 热量可从高温物体传到低温物体而不产生其他变化

12.6-6　制冷压缩机及其系统的最理想循环是(　　)。

A. 卡诺循环　　B. 逆卡诺循环　　C. 回热循环　　D. 奥拓循环

12.6-7　由等温放热过程、绝热压缩过程、等温加热过程和绝热膨胀过程所组成的循环是(　　)。

A. 混合加热循环　　B. 定容加热循环　　C. 定压加热循环　　D. 卡诺循环

12.6-8　工质经卡诺循环后又回到初始状态,其内能(　　)。

A. 增加　　B. 减少　　C. 不变　　D. 增加或减少

12.6-9　卡诺循环的热效率仅与下面(　　)有关。

A. 高温热源的温度

B. 低温热源的温度

C. 高温热源的温度和低温热源的温度

D. 高温热源的温度和低温热源的温度及工作性质

12.6-10　某封闭系统经历了一不可逆过程后,系统向外界放热 20kJ,同时对外界做功为 10kJ,则系统的熵变化量为(　　)。

A. 0　　B. 正　　C. 负　　D. 无法确定

12.7　水蒸气和湿空气

考试大纲☞:蒸发　冷凝　沸腾　气化　定压发生过程　水蒸气图表　水蒸气基本热力过程　湿空气性质　湿空气焓湿图　湿空气基本热力过程

必备基础知识

12.7.1 蒸发、冷凝、沸腾和气化

水蒸气是由液态水经汽化而来的一种气体，离液态较近，不是理想气体，是实际气体，水蒸气不能作为理想气体来处理，因此理想气体的计算公式不适用于水蒸气，只能通过查热力学性质图表进行各种热力过程的计算。工程应用水蒸气的热力计算，通常使用水蒸气热力性质表和图确定其热物性。

气化：使水由液相转变为气相的过程，相反的过程叫做冷凝。

气化有蒸发和沸腾两种形式。蒸发是指液体表面的气化过程，通常在任何温度下都可以发生；沸腾是指液体内部的气化过程，它只能在达到沸点时才会发生。

饱和状态：指气化和凝结的动态平衡状况。

饱和压力与饱和温度：当气液两相达到平衡时，蒸气所具有的压力称为饱和压力；在一定压力下，当气液两相达到平衡时，液体所具有的温度称为饱和温度。

处于饱和状态下的蒸气和液体分别称为饱和蒸气和饱和水。饱和蒸气和饱和水的混合物称为湿饱和蒸气，简称湿蒸气；不含饱和水的饱和蒸气称为干饱和蒸气。饱和温度和饱和压力必存在单值的对应关系。饱和压力与饱和温度关系为 $t_s=f(p_s)$。

12.7.2 水蒸气的定压发生过程

水蒸气的产生过程可分为预热、气化和过热三个阶段。在一定压力下的未饱和液态工质，受外界加热温度升高到该压力所对应的饱和温度时，称为饱和液体。工质继续吸热，饱和液开始沸腾，在定温下，产生水蒸气而形成饱和液体和饱和水蒸气的混合物，称为湿饱和蒸气，简称湿蒸气。继续吸热直至液体全部汽化为水蒸气，这时称为过热蒸气，如图 12.7-1 所示。在某一定压力下，过热蒸气的温度与压力下饱和温度的差值称为过热蒸气的过热度。

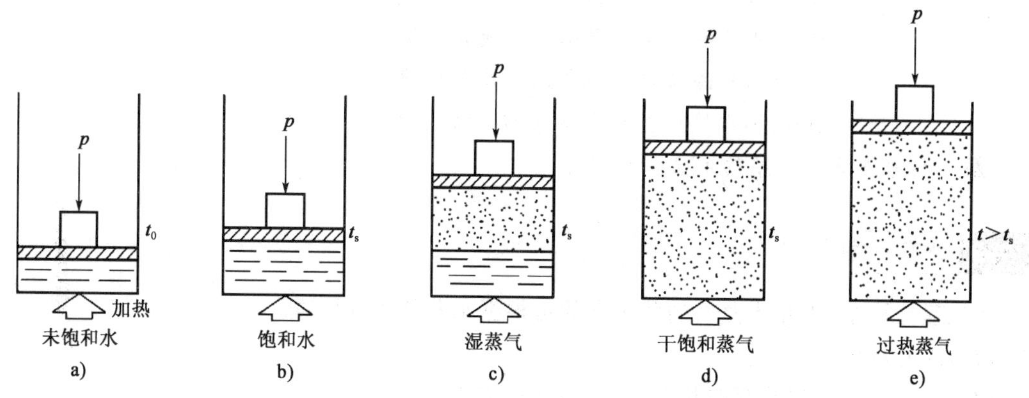

图 12.7-1　过热蒸气

水蒸气的定压发生过程在热力状态图上(图12.7-2)所标示的特征归纳起来为：

(1)一点：临界点 C，在状态参数坐标图上，饱和液体线与干饱和蒸气线相交的点，称为临界点。

(2)两线：饱和液体线、饱和蒸气线。

(3)三区：未饱和液体区、湿饱和蒸气区、过热蒸气区。

(4)五种状态：未饱和水状态、饱和水状态、湿饱和蒸气状态、干饱和蒸气状态和过热蒸气状态。在湿饱和蒸气区，湿蒸气的成分用干度 x 表示：

$$x = \frac{湿蒸气中含干蒸气的质量}{湿蒸气的总质量} \tag{12.7-1}$$

则 $(1-x)$ 称为湿度，它表示湿蒸气中饱和水的含量。饱和液体线为 $x=0$ 的定干度线，饱和蒸气线为 $x=1$ 的定干度线。

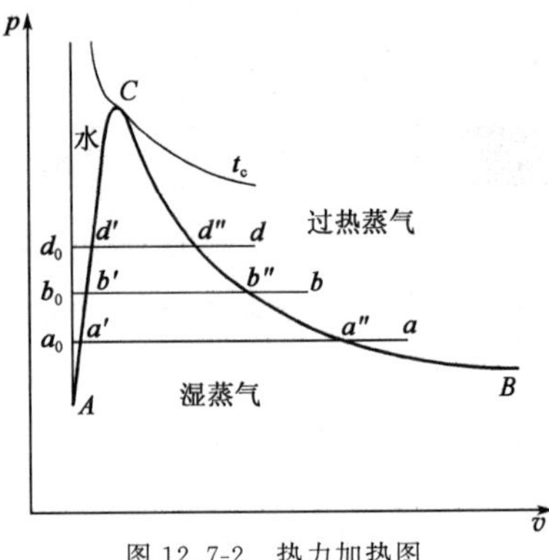

图 12.7-2　热力加热图

典型例题解析

【例 12.7-1】 水在定压下被加热可从未饱和水变成过热蒸气，此过程可分为三个阶段，其中包含的状态有：

A. 3 种　　B. 4 种　　C. 5 种　　D. 6 种

解　从水的 T-s 图上可以看出水从未饱和水变成过热蒸气的过程中经历五种状态：未饱和水状态、饱和水状态、湿饱和蒸气状态、干饱和蒸气状态、过热蒸气状态。选 C。

【例 12.7-2】 湿饱和蒸气是由饱和水和干饱和蒸气组成的混合物，表示湿饱和蒸气的成分的是：

A. 干度　　B. 含湿量　　C. 容积成分　　D. 绝对湿度

解　在湿饱和蒸气区中，湿蒸气的成分用干度 x 表示：

$$x = \frac{湿蒸气中含干蒸气的质量}{湿蒸气的总质量}$$

选 A。

【例 12.7-3】 水蒸气的干度被定义为：

A. 饱和水的质量与湿蒸气的质量之比

B. 干蒸气的质量与湿蒸气的质量之比

C. 干蒸气的质量与饱和水的质量之比

D. 饱和水的质量与干蒸气的质量之比

解　参考水蒸气干度的定义。选 B。

12.7.3 水蒸气图表

在工程计算中，水和水蒸气的状态参数可根据水蒸气表和图查。

1)零点的规定

物质气、液、固三相共存的状态点，称为该物质的三相点。

以水在三相(纯水的冰、水和气)平衡共存状态下的饱和水作为基准点。规定在三相态时饱和水的内能和熵为零。当压力低于三相点压力时，液相也不可能存在，而只可能是气相或固相。各种物质在三相点的温度和压力分别为定值。水的三相点温度和压力值为 $t_0=0.01$℃，$p_0=611.2$Pa。

2)临界点

当温度超过一定值 t_c 时，液相不可能存在，而只可能是气相。t_c 称为临界温度，与临界温度相对应的饱和压力 p_c 称为临界压力。所以，临界温度和压力是液相与气相能够平衡共存时的最高值临界参数，是物质的固有常数，不同物质其值是不同的。水的临界参数值为：t_c＝374.15℃，p_c＝22.129MPa，v_c＝0.003 26m^3/kg，h_c＝2 100kJ/kg，s_c＝4.429kJ/(kg·K)。

水蒸气表有三种：

(1)按温度排列的饱和水与干饱和蒸气表。

(2)按压力排列的饱和水与干饱和蒸气表。

(3)未饱和水与过热蒸气表。已知压力和温度这两个独立的参数，可从表中查出 v、h、s（表中参数角标为′表示饱和水的参数，角标为″表示干饱和蒸气的参数）。

水蒸气的焓熵 h-s 图如图 12.7-3 所示，以 h 为纵坐标，s 为横坐标。图中 C 为临界点，粗线为界限曲线，其下方为湿蒸气区，其右上方为过热蒸气区，图中共有以下六种线簇：

(1)定压线簇。在湿蒸气区内，定压线是一组倾斜的直线。由于饱和温度与压力是对应关系，所以定压线也是定温线。在过热蒸气区内，定压线为一组倾斜向上的曲线，其斜率随温度的升高而增大。

(2)定温线簇。在湿蒸气区内，定温线即定压线。在过热蒸气区内，定温线是一组比较平坦的自左向右延伸的曲线，且越往右越平坦，接近水平线。

(3)定干度线簇。定干度线只在湿蒸气区内才有，是一组自临界点 C 起向右下方发散的曲线。

(4)定容线簇。定容线的延伸方向与定压线一致，只是比定压线稍陡的倾斜线，为了便于识别常用红线标出。

(5)定焓线簇。定焓线是一组水平线。

(6)定熵线簇。定熵线是一组垂直线。

应用水蒸气的 h-s 图，可根据已知的两个独立的状态参数确定状态点在图上的位置，然后查出其余的状态参数，并进行水蒸气热力过程的分析计算。

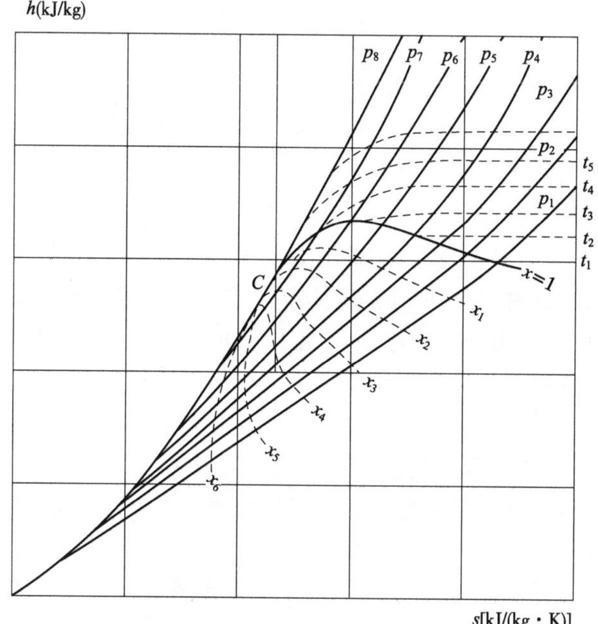

图 12.7-3 水蒸气的 h-s 图

典型例题解析

【例 12.7-4】 水蒸气的干度为 x，从水蒸气表中查得饱和水的焓为 h'，湿饱和蒸气的焓为 h''，计算湿蒸气焓的表达式是：

A. $hx = h' + x(h'' - h')$　　B. $hx = x(h'' - h')$

C. $hx = h' - x(h'' - h')$　　D. $hx = h'' + x(h'' - h')$

解　如果有 1kg 湿蒸气，干度为 x，即有 $x$kg 饱和蒸气，$(2-x)$kg 饱和水。则湿蒸气的一些参数计算公式如下：

$$h = xh'' + (1-x)h'$$
$$v = xv'' + (1-x)v'$$
$$s = xs'' + (1-x)s'$$

选 A。

【例 12.7-5】 确定水蒸气两相区域焓熵等热力参数需要给定参数：

A. x　　B. p 和 T　　C. p 和 v　　D. p 和 x

解　在水蒸气的两相区除 p 或 T 外，其他参数与两相比例有关，即在已知 p 或 T(h'，v'，s'，h''，v''，s'')和干度 x 的情况下，可以确定 h，v，s 等状态参数。选 D。

12.7.4 水蒸气的基本热力过程

水蒸气的基本热力过程为定温、定压、定容、定熵过程。

根据已知求得的初、终态参数，应用热力学第一、第二定律的基本方程及参数定义式计算。

定容过程，v=定值　　$w = \int p\mathrm{d}v = 0, q = \Delta u = \Delta h - v\Delta p$

定压过程，p=定值　　$w = \int p\mathrm{d}v = p(v_2 - v_1), q = \Delta h, \Delta u = \Delta h - p\Delta v$

定温过程，T=定值　　$q = \int T\mathrm{d}s = T(s_2 - s_1), w = q - \Delta u, \Delta u = \Delta h - \Delta(pv)$

定熵过程(可逆绝热过程)，s=定值

$$q = 0, w = \Delta u, w_t = -\Delta h \tag{12.7-2}$$

12.7.5 湿空气的性质

自然界中的空气是一种混合气体，它是由干空气和水蒸气所组成，也称为湿空气。其中干空气主要是由 N_2，O_2，CO_2 和微量的稀有气体所组成。在常温常压下，大气中的水蒸气分压力很低，且远离液态，可以视为理想气体，所以湿空气可以作为理想气体看待。

湿空气是定组元、变成分的混合气体。由于水蒸气份额很少，故湿空气中的水蒸气可以作为理想气体对待，但同时水蒸气又具有饱和、过热、冷凝等水蒸气特征，因此湿空气中的水蒸气具有两重性。由于湿空气中的水蒸气会随状态变化而增加或减少，故湿空气的成分会随状态变化而改变，水蒸气的状态变化是湿空气问题讨论的要点。

1)湿空气成分及分压力

$$\text{湿空气} = \text{干空气} + \text{水蒸气}$$
$$B = p = p_a + p_v \tag{12.7-3}$$

湿空气的总压力 p 等于干空气分压力 p_a 与水蒸气分压力 p_v 之和。

2)饱和空气与未饱和空气

$$未饱和空气 = 干空气 + 过热水蒸气$$

$$饱和空气 = 干空气 + 饱和水蒸气$$

注意:由未饱和空气到饱和空气的途径有等压降温、等温加压。

露点温度:维持水蒸气含量不变,冷却使未饱和湿空气的温度降至水蒸气的饱和状态所对应的温度。

想一想:冬季,室内玻璃窗内侧为何会结霜?

3)湿空气的分子量及气体常数(湿空气的折合摩尔质量和折合气体常数)

$$M = r_a M_a + r_v M_v = 28.97 - 10.95 \frac{p_v}{B}$$

$$R = \frac{287}{1 - 0.378 \frac{p_v}{B}} \tag{12.7-4}$$

结论:湿空气的气体常数随水蒸气分压力的提高而增大。

4)绝对湿度和相对湿度

绝对湿度:每立方米湿空气所含水蒸气的质量。

相对湿度:湿空气的绝对湿度与同温度下饱和空气的饱和绝对湿度的比值。

$$\varphi = \frac{\rho_v}{\rho_s} \tag{12.7-5}$$

相对湿度反应湿空气中水蒸气含量接近饱和的程度。相对湿度的范围:$0<\varphi<1$。

应用理想气体状态方程,相对湿度又可表示为:

$$\varphi = \frac{p_v}{p_s} \tag{12.7-6}$$

湿空气中可容纳水蒸气的数量是有限度的,在一定的温度下,水蒸气分压力越大,则湿空气中水蒸气数量越多,湿空气越潮湿。所以,湿空气中水蒸气分压力的大小直接反映了湿空气的干湿程度。

φ 值越小,表明湿空气越干燥,吸收水蒸气能力越强;φ 值越大,表明湿空气越潮湿,吸收水蒸气的能力越弱。当 $\varphi=0$ 时,即为干空气;当 $\varphi=1$ 时,即为饱和湿空气;φ 介于 0~1 之间的湿空气都是未饱和湿空气。

5)含湿量

湿空气中只有干空气的质量不会随湿空气的温度和湿度而改变。

含湿量(或称比湿度):在含有 1kg 干空气的湿空气中,所混有的水蒸气质量。

$$d = 622 \frac{p_v}{B - p_v} \tag{12.7-7}$$

6)焓

(1)定义:1kg 干空气的焓和 $0.001d$kg 水蒸气的焓总和。

$$h = h_a + 0.001 d h_v \tag{12.7-8}$$

湿空气的焓值以 0℃的干空气和水为基准点,以定值比热容计算时:

①干空气的比焓为

$$h_a = c_p t = 1.01t$$

②水蒸气的比焓由经验公式为

$$h_v = 2\,501 + 1.85t$$

式中：2 501——0℃时饱和水的气化潜热(kJ/kg)；

1.85——常温下水蒸气的平均质量定压热容[kJ/(kg·K)]。

(2)代入公式：

$$h = 1.01t + 0.001d(2\,501 + 1.85t)(\text{g/kg}) \tag{12.7-9}$$

7)湿球温度

用湿纱布包裹温度计的水银头部，由于空气是未饱和空气，湿球纱布上的水分将蒸发，水分蒸发所需的热量来自两部分：

(1)降低湿布上水分本身的温度而放出热量。

(2)由于空气温度 t 将高于湿纱布表面温度，通过对流换热空气将热量传给湿球。

当达到热湿平衡时，纱布上水分蒸发的热量全部来自空气的对流换热，纱布上水分温度不再降低，此时湿球温度计的度数就是湿球温度。

湿球加湿过程中的热平衡关系式

$$h_1 + c_p t_w (d_2 - d_1) 10^{-3} = h_2$$

由于湿纱布上水分蒸发量只有几克，而湿球温度计的度数又较低，在一般的通风空调工程中可以忽略不计。

因此

$$h_1 = h_2 \tag{12.7-10}$$

结论：通过湿球的湿空气在加湿过程中，湿空气是一个等焓过程。

若干湿球温度差越大，说明空气越干燥。若空气达到饱和状态，则湿球温度等于干球温度。

典型例题解析

【例 12.7-6】 湿空气是：

A. 饱和蒸气与干空气组成的混合物　B. 干空气与过热燃气组成的混合物

C. 干空气与水蒸气组成的混合物　D. 湿蒸气与过热蒸气组成的混合物

解 湿空气是定组元、变成分的混合气体。湿空气成分组成为干空气＋水蒸气。选 C。

【例 12.7-7】 4m^3 湿空气的质量是 4.55kg，其中干空气 4.47kg，此时湿空气的绝对湿度是：

A. 1.14kg/m^3　B. $1.12\ \text{kg/m}^3$　C. $0.02\ \text{kg/m}^3$　D. $0.03\ \text{kg/m}^3$

解 绝对湿度为每立方米湿空气所含水蒸气的质量。因为湿空气总质量是4.55kg，干空气质量为 4.47kg，因此其中的水蒸气的质量为 0.08kg，则绝对湿度为 $0.02\ \text{kg/m}^3$。选 C。

【例 12.7-8】 如果湿空气的总压力为 0.1MPa，水蒸气分压为 2.3kPa，则湿空气的含湿量约为：

A. 5g/kg(a)　B. 10g/kg(a)　C. 15g/kg(a)　D. 20g/kg(a)

解 $d = 0.622\dfrac{p_w}{p - p_w} = 0.622 \times \dfrac{2.3}{100 - 2.3} = 0.014\,6\text{kg/kg(a)} = 14.6\text{g/kg(a)}$，选 C。

【例 12.7-9】 湿空气的含湿量是指：

A. 1kg 干空气中所含有的水蒸气质量

B. $1m^3$ 干空气中所含有的水蒸气质量

C. 1kg 湿空气中所含有的水蒸气质量

D. 1kg 湿空气中所含有的干空气质量

解 湿空气的含湿量是在含有 1kg 干空气的湿空气中，所混有的水蒸气质量。选 A。

【例 12.7-10】 湿空气的焓可用 $h=1.01t+0.001d(2\,501+1.85t)$ 来计算，其中给定数字 1.85 是：

A. 干空气的定压平均质量比热容　　B. 水蒸气的定容平均质量比热容

C. 干空气的定容平均质量比热容　　D. 水蒸气的定压平均比热容

解 湿空气的焓值以 0℃的干空气和水为基准点，1kg 干空气的焓和 $0.001d$kg 水蒸气的焓总和，即 $h=h_a+0.001dh_v$，其中水蒸气的焓值为 $h_v=2\,501+1.85t$，式中 2 501 是 0℃时饱和水的汽化潜热，1.85 为常温下水蒸气的平均质量定压热容[kJ/(kg·K)]。选 D。

【例 12.7-11】 湿空气的焓可用 $h=1.01t+0.001d(2501+1.85t)$ 来计算，其中温度 t 是指：

A. 湿球温度　　B. 干球温度　　C. 露点温度　　D. 任意给定温度

解 湿空气的包括干空气的焓值以及水蒸气的焓值两部分。式中的 t 为湿空气的干球温度。选 B。

【例 12.7-12】 确定湿空气的热力状态需要的独立参数为：

A. 1 个　　B. 2 个　　C. 3 个　　D. 4 个

解 根据相律公式 $r=k-f+2$，其中 r 为需要的独立参数，k 为组元数，f 为相数。湿空气是由干空气与水蒸气组合而成的二元单相混合工质，因此 $k=2$，$f=1$，则 $r=3$。因此，要确定湿空气的热力状态需要的独立参数为 3 个。选 C。

12.7.6 湿空气的焓湿图

湿空气的 h-d 图如图 12.7-1 所示，是以 1kg 干空气量的湿空气为基准，在 0.1MPa 的大气压力下，以焓(h)为纵坐标，含湿量(d)为横坐标绘制而成的。利用 h-d 图不仅可以确定湿空气的状态，查出其状态参数，还可以用来分析湿空气的热力过程。

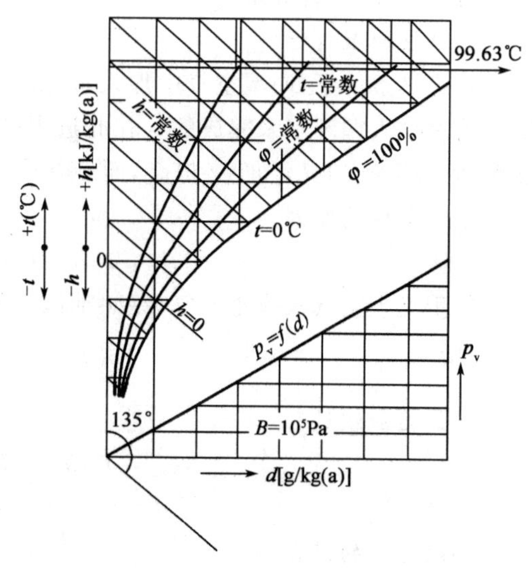

图 12.7-1　湿空气的 h-d 图

湿空气 h-d 图的构成如图 12.7-1 所示，为使图面展开，采用了两坐标夹角为 135℃的坐标系，图中共有下列五种线簇：

1) 定焓线

定焓线是一组与纵坐标成 135℃的平行线。湿空气的湿球温度 t_w 是定焓冷却至饱和湿空气($\varphi=100\%$)时的温度。因此，不同状态

的湿空气只要其 h 相同，则具有相同的湿球温度。

2)定含湿量线

定含湿量线是一组与纵坐标轴平行的直线。露点 t_d 是湿空气定湿冷却至饱和湿空气($\varphi=100\%$)时的温度。因此不同状态的湿空气，只要其含湿量 d 相同，则具有相同的露点。

3)定温线

定温线是一组互不平行的直线，随着 t 的增高，定温线的斜率增大。

4)定相对湿度线

定相对湿度线 φ 是一组曲线。$\varphi=0$ 的线就是干空气线，此时，$d=0$，即与纵坐标轴重合。$\varphi=100\%$线是饱和空气线，它将图面分成两部分。左上部是未饱和空气，$\varphi<1$，其中水蒸气为过热状态；右下部无实用意义，湿空气中多余的水蒸气会以水滴的形式析出，湿空气本身仍保持饱和状态($\varphi=100\%$)。

5)水蒸气分压力线

一个 d 值就可得到相应的 p_v 值，所以可绘出 d 与 p_v 的变换线，在 $\varphi=100\%$曲线下方，把与 d 相对应的 p_v 值表示在图右下方的纵坐标轴上，也有的表示在图的正上方。

图 12.7-1 中还绘出了一组定比体积(v)线。

12.7.7 湿空气的基本热力过程

1)加热过程

是干燥工程中不可缺少的组成过程之一。

状态参数：$t_2>t_1, h_2>h_1, \varphi_2>\varphi_1, \Delta d=0$

$$q = h_2 - h_1 (\text{kJ/kg})(\text{a}) \tag{12.7-11}$$

2)冷却过程

$$t_2 < t_1, h_2 < h_1, \varphi_2 > \varphi_1$$

$$q = h_2 - h_1 (\text{负值})\ (\text{kJ/kg})(\text{a}) \tag{12.7-12}$$

若 $\Delta d=0$，等含湿量冷却。

3)绝热加湿过程

在绝热条件下，向湿空气中加入水分以增加其含湿量称为绝热加湿过程。一般是在喷淋室中通过喷入循环水来完成的。在此过程中，湿空气的 h 值基本不变，可视为定焓过程。绝热加湿后，湿空气的 d 增加，φ 提高，而 t 降低了，这是由于绝热过程水分蒸发所吸收的汽化潜热取自空气本身的原因。

$$t_2 < t_1, h_2 = h_1, \varphi_2 > \varphi_1, d_2 > d_1$$

每千克干空气吸收水蒸气(绝热加湿过程中的喷水量)：

$$\Delta d = d_2 - d_1 (\text{g/kg})(\text{a}) \tag{12.7-13}$$

4)定温加湿过程

$$t_2 = t_1, h_2 > h_1, \varphi_2 > \varphi_1, d_2 > d_1$$

$$q = h_2 - h_1 0.001 \Delta d h_v (\text{kJ/kg})(\text{a}) \tag{12.7-14}$$

5)湿空气的混合

将两股或多股状态不同的湿空气混合，以得到温度和湿度符合一定要求的空气，是空气调节装置中经常采用的方法。如果混合过程中气流与外界无热量交换，则称为绝热混合。绝热混合得到的湿空气状态，取决于混合前各股空气的状态和它们的流量比例。

两股湿空气混合前分别处于状态 1 和 2，其质量流量分别为 m_1 和 m_2，焓值分别为 h_1 和 h_2，含湿量分别为 d_1 和 d_2。两股湿空气混合后的空气状态用 3 表示，参数分别为 m_3、h_3、d_3。

由于混合前后遵守质量守恒原理，则有 $m_3 = m_1 + m_2$；

同时，混合前后能量守恒，则有 $m_3 h_3 = m_1 h_1 + m_2 h_2$；

湿量守恒，则有 $m_3 d_3 = m_1 d_1 + m_2 d_2$。

如果已知混合前的两股湿空气的状态参数，可由上述三个守恒方程，求得混合后的湿空气状态参数：

混合后的焓值：
$$h_3 = \frac{m_1 h_1 + m_2 h_2}{m_1 + m_2} \tag{12.7-15}$$

混合后的含湿量：
$$d_3 = \frac{m_1 d_1 + m_2 d_2}{m_1 + m_2} \tag{12.7-16}$$

6)湿空气的蒸发冷却过程

$$\left.\begin{aligned} m_a(h_2 - h_1) &= m_{w3} h_{w3} - m_{w4} h_{w4} \\ m_{w3} - m_{w4} &= m_a(d_2 - d_1)10^{-3} \end{aligned}\right\} \tag{12.7-17}$$

典型例题解析

【例 12.7-13】 两股湿空气混合，其流量为 $m_1 = 2\text{kg/s}$ 和 $m_2 = 1\text{kg/s}$，含湿量分别为 $d_1 = 12\text{g/kg(a)}$ 和 $d_2 = 2\text{g/kg(a)}$，混合后的含湿量为：

A. 18g/kg(a)　　B. 16g/kg(a)

C. 15g/kg(a)　　D. 13g/kg(a)

解 两股湿空气混合前后湿量是守恒的，所以有：

$$d = \frac{m_{a1} d_1 + m_{a2} d_2}{m_{a1} + m_{a2}} = \frac{2 \times 12 + 1 \times 21}{2 + 1} = 15\text{g/kg(a)}$$

选 C。

经 典 练 习

12.7-1 当气体的压力越(　　)或温度越(　　)，它就越接近理想气体。

A. 高，高　B. 低，低　C. 高，低　D. 低，高

12.7-2 水的定压气化过程经历了除(　　)以外的三个阶段。

A. 定压升温阶段　B. 定压预热阶段　C. 定压气化阶段　D. 定压过热阶段

12.7-3 湿蒸气的状态由(　　)决定。

A. 压力与温度　B. 压力与干度　C. 过热度与压力　D. 过冷度与温度

12.7-4 在水蒸气的 p-v 图中，零度水线左侧的区域称为(　　)。

A. 过冷水状态区　B. 湿蒸气状态区　C. 过热蒸气状态区　D. 固体状态区

12.7-5 水在锅炉内加热蒸气化，所吸收的热量等于水的初状态的(　　)。

A. 温度变化　B. 压力变化　C. 熵的变化　D. 焓的变化

12.7-6 如果湿空气为未饱和蒸气，空气中的水蒸气处于(　　)。

A. 饱和状态　B. 过热状态　C. 临界状态　D. 任意状态

12.7-7　当湿空气定压降温时，若含湿量保持不变，则湿空气露点(　　)。

A. 增大　　B. 减少　　C. 不变　　D. 减少或不变

12.7-8　下列说法不正确的是(　　)。

A. 未饱和空气中的水蒸气是过热蒸气

B. 对饱和空气而言，干球温度、湿球温度和露点是相等的

C. 湿空气的含湿量相同，其相对湿度一定相同

D. 湿空气的温度不变，相对湿度变化时，其含湿量和露点也随之改变

12.7-9　对于未饱和空气，干球温度、湿球温度及露点中(　　)最高。

A. 干球温度　　B. 湿球温度　　C. 露点　　D. 三者相等

12.7-10　一定容积的湿空气中水蒸气的质量与干空气的质量之比称为(　　)。

A. 相对湿度　　B. 绝对湿度　　C. 含湿量　　D. 含水率

12.8　气体和蒸气的流动

考试大纲☞：喷管和扩压管　流动的基本特性和基本方程　流速　音速　流量　临界状态　绝热节流

必备基础知识

12.8.1　稳定流动基本方程

1)稳定流动

工质以恒定的流量连续不断地进出系统，系统内部及界面上每个工质的状态参数和宏观运动参数都保持一定，不随时间变化。

2)基本方程

气体和蒸气在管道中的一维稳定流动可通过以下三个基本方程来描述。

(1)连续性方程

由稳定流动特点

$$m_1 = m_2 = \cdots = m = \text{const} \tag{12.8-1}$$

而

$$m = \frac{fc}{v} \tag{12.8-2}$$

得

$$\frac{\mathrm{d}c}{c} + \frac{\mathrm{d}f}{f} - \frac{\mathrm{d}v}{v} = 0 \tag{12.8-3}$$

该式适用于任何工质可逆与不可逆过程。

(2)绝热稳定流动能量方程

$$\mathrm{d}h = \partial q - \frac{1}{2}\mathrm{d}c^2 - g\mathrm{d}z - \partial w_s \tag{12.8-4}$$

对绝热、不做功、忽略位能的稳定流动过程，得

$$\mathrm{d}\frac{c^2}{2} = -\mathrm{d}h \tag{12.8-5}$$

说明：增速以降低本身储能为代价。

(3)定熵过程方程

由可逆绝热过程方程 $pv^k = \text{const}$，得

$$\frac{dp}{p} + k\frac{dv}{v} = 0 \tag{12.8-6}$$

3)音速与马赫数

音速：微小扰动在流体中的传播速度。

定义式
$$a = \sqrt{\left(\frac{\delta p}{\delta \rho}\right)_s} \tag{12.8-7}$$

注意：压力波的传播过程作定熵处理。

特别的，对理想气体：$a=\sqrt{kRT}$只随绝对温度而变。

马赫数(无因次量)：流速与当地音速的比值。

$$M_a = \frac{c}{a}\begin{cases}M_a > 1\text{，超音速}\\ M_a = 1\text{，临界音速}\\ M_a < 1\text{，亚音速}\end{cases} \tag{12.8-8}$$

12.8.2 定熵流动的基本特性

1)气体流速变化与状态参数间的关系

对定熵过程，由 $dh=vdp$，得到：$cdc=-vdp$，适用于定熵流动过程。

分析：

(1)气体流速增加($dc>0$)，必导致气体的压力下降($dp<0$)。

(2)气体速度下降($dc<0$)，则将导致气体压力的升高($dp>0$)。

2)管道截面变化的规律

联立 $cdc=-vdp$、连续性方程、可逆绝热过程方程，得到

$$\frac{df}{f} = (M_a^2 - 1)\frac{dc}{c} \tag{12.8-9}$$

工程装置中为了改变流体流动，获取高速气流或者是气体流速降低，通常是采用改变其流动截面积的手段来实现的。

喷管是一种使流动工质加速从而增加其动能的管道。在喷管中，气体流速是增大的($dc>0$)。

扩压管是一种使工质沿流动方向增压的管道。在扩压管中，气流速度是减小的($dc<0$)。

对喷管：当 $M_a<1$，因为 $dc>0$，则喷管截面缩小 $df<0$，称渐缩喷管；$M_a>1$ 的超音速气流时，必须 $df>0$，称渐扩喷管；若将 $M_a<1$ 增大到 $M_a>1$，则喷管截面积由 $df<0$ 转变为 $df>0$，称为渐缩渐扩喷管，称拉伐尔(Laval)喷管。称 $M_a=1$、$df=0$ 为喉部，此处的截面称临界截面。对扩压管反之。

喷管和扩压管的种类见图 12.8-1。

12.8.3 喷管中流速及流量计算

1)定熵滞止参数

绝热滞止：工质在绝热流动中，因遇着障碍物或某种原因而受阻，使速度降低直至变为零，这种过程称为绝热滞止。

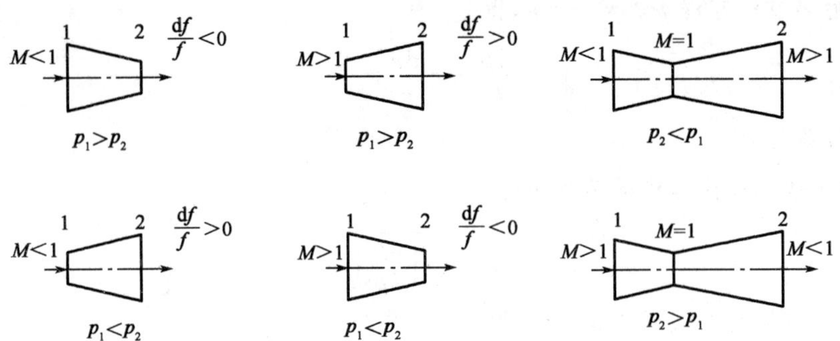

图 12.8-1 喷管和扩压管的种类

将具有一定速度的气流在定熵条件下扩压，使流速降低为零。

由 $$\left.\begin{aligned} h_0 &= h_1 + \frac{c_1^2}{2} \\ T_0 &= T_1 + \frac{c_1^2}{2c_p} \end{aligned}\right\} \tag{12.8-10}$$

应用等熵过程参数间的关系式得

$$\frac{p_0}{p_1} = \left(\frac{T_0}{T_1}\right)^{\frac{k}{k-1}}$$

得 $$p_0 = p_1\left(\frac{T_0}{T_1}\right)^{\frac{k}{k-1}} \tag{12.8-11}$$

2)喷管的出口流速

对理想气体 $$c_2 = \sqrt{\frac{2k}{k-1}RT_0\left[1-\left(\frac{p_2}{p_0}\right)^{\frac{k-1}{k}}\right]} \tag{12.8-12}$$

对实际气体 $$c_2 = 44.72\sqrt{c_p(T_0 - T_2)} \tag{12.8-13}$$

3)临界压力比及临界流速

临界状态：工质在喷管中流动时，在喷管的最小截面处，若工质的流动速度等于当地音速，则此时工质所处的状态称为临界状态。

临界压力比：临界状态时工质压力与滞止压力之比称为临界压力比。

$$\beta = \frac{p_c}{p_0} = \left(\frac{2}{k+1}\right)^{\frac{k}{k-1}} \tag{12.8-14}$$

特别的，对双原子气体：$\beta = 0.528$。

4)流量与临界流量

$$m = \frac{f_2 c_2}{v_2}(\mathrm{kg/s}) \tag{12.8-15}$$

5)喷管的计算

(1)喷管的设计计算。出发点：$p_2 = p_b$，当流体流过喷管，已知 p_0、T_0、k、p_b、f。

①当$\frac{p_b}{p_0} \geqslant \beta = \frac{p_c}{p_0}$，即 $p_b > p_c$：采用渐缩喷管。

②当$\frac{p_b}{p_0}\leqslant\beta=\frac{p_c}{p_0}$，即 $p_b<p_c$：采用渐扩喷管。

(2)渐缩喷管的校核计算。当流体流过渐缩喷管，已知 p_0、T_0、k、p_b、f。

①当$\frac{p_b}{p_0}\geqslant\beta=\frac{p_c}{p_0}$，即 $p_b>p_c$：$p_2=p_b$。

②当$\frac{p_b}{p_0}\leqslant\beta=\frac{p_c}{p_0}$，即 $p_b<p_c$：$p_2=p_c$。

喷管的最大流量 $m_{max}=\frac{f_c c_c}{v_c}$(kg/s)。

想一想：渐缩喷管中气流速度能否超过音速？缩放喷管中气流出口速度能否低于音速？

典型例题解析

【例 12.8-1】 理想气体流经喷管后会使：

A. 流速增加、压力增加、温度降低、比体积减小

B. 流滴增加、压力降低、温度降低、比体积增大

C. 流速增加、压力降低、温度升高、比体积增大

D. 流速增加、压力增加、温度升高、比体积均大

解 喷管的目的是使流体降压增速($dp<0, dc>0$)，同时经过喷管后比体积增大，温度降低，参照教材中温度、比体积计算公式。选 B。

【例 12.8-2】 理想气体流经一渐缩形喷管，若在入口截面上的参数为 c_1、T_1、p_1，测出出口截面处的温度和压力分别为 p_2、T_2，其流动速度 c_2 等于：

A. $\sqrt{c_1^2+2\frac{kR}{k-1}(T_1-T_2)}$　　B. $\sqrt{c_1+2\frac{kR}{k-1}(T_1-T_2)}$

C. $\sqrt{c_1^2-2\frac{kR}{k-1}(T_1-T_2)}$　　D. $\sqrt{c_1-2\frac{kR}{k-1}(T_1-T_2)}$

解 当初速为 c_1 的流体经过渐缩喷管时，出口流动速度 c_2 的计算式为：

$$c_2=\sqrt{c_1^2+2(h_1-h_2)}=\sqrt{c_1^2+2c_p(T_1-T_2)}=\sqrt{c_1^2+2\frac{kR}{k-1}(T_1-T_2)}$$

选 A。

【例 12.8-3】 设空气进入喷管的初始压力为 1.2MPa，初始温度 $T_1=350$K，背压为 0.1MPa，空气 $R_g=287$J/(kg·K)，采用渐缩喷管时可以达到的最大流速为：

A. 343m/s　　B. 597m/s　　C. 650m/s　　D. 725m/s

解 对于空气 $k=1.4$，临界压比为

$$\varepsilon_{cr}=\left(\frac{2}{k+1}\right)^{\frac{k}{k-1}}=\left(\frac{2}{1.4+1}\right)^{\frac{1.4}{1.4-1}}=0.528$$

采用渐缩喷管时所能达到的最大流速为其临界流速，即压比为临界压比时的出口流速，即为

$$c_{f,cr}=\sqrt{2\frac{k}{k+1}R_g T_1}=\sqrt{2\times\frac{1.4}{1.4+1}\times 287\times 350}=342.33\text{m/s}$$

题目虽然给出背压为0.1MPa，但很显然，若使喷嘴出口工质达到0.1MPa，则压比已经小于了临界压比0.521，这对于渐缩喷管是不能实现的。

选A。

【例12.8-4】 对于喷管内理想气体的一维定熵流动，流速 c、压力 p、比焓 h 及比体积 v 的变化，正确的是：

A. $dc>0, dp>0, dh<0, dv>0$　　B. $dc>0, dp<0, dh<0, dv<0$

C. $dc>0, dp<0, dh>0, dv>0$　　D. $dc>0, dp<0, dh<0, dv>0$

解 气体流经喷管时，速度逐渐升高即 $dc>0$；实现压力能向速度能的转变，根据 $cdc=-vdp$ 可知 $dc>0$ 时 $dp<0$；由 $Tds=dh-vdp$，对于喷管内的等熵过程有 $dh=vdp$，可知 $dp<0$ 时有 $dh<0$；根据过程方程 $pv^k=C$，可知压力降低时比容增大，即 $dv>0$。选D。

12.8.4 绝热节流

工质在管内绝热流动时，由于通道截面突然缩小，使工质压力降低，这种现象称为绝热节流。

特点：绝热节流过程的焓相等，但不是等焓过程，如图12.8-2所示。

因为在缩孔附近，由于流速增加，焓下降，流体在通过缩孔时动能增加，压力下降并产生强烈扰动和摩擦。扰动和摩擦的不可逆性，使节流后的压力却不能回复到节流前。

绝热节流前后状态参数的变化：

对理想气体，节流后 $h_1=h_2$、$T_1=T_2$、$p_1>p_2$、$v_1<v_2$、$s_2>s_1$。

对于实际气体，节流后焓值不变，压力下降，比体积增大，比熵增大，但其温度是可以变化的。若节流后温度升高，称为热效应；若节流后的温度不变，称为零效应；若节流后温度降低，则称为冷效应。大多数气体节流后温度是降低的，因此利用这一特性可使气体通过节流获得低温和使气体液化。

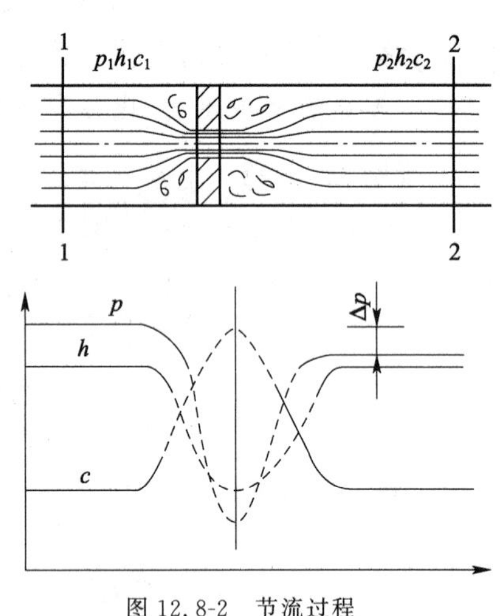

图12.8-2　节流过程

典型例题解析

【例12.8-5】 流体节流前后其焓保持不变，其温度将：

A. 减小　　B. 不变　　C. 增大　　D. 不确定

解 绝热节流前后状态参数的变化：

对理想气体：$h_1=h_2$、$T_1=T_2$、$p_1>p_2$、$v_1<v_2$、$s_2>s_1$；对于实际气体，节流后，焓值不变，压力下降，比体积增大，比熵增大，但其温度是可以变化的。若节流后温度升高，称为热效应；若节流后的温度不变，称为零效应；若节流后温度降低，则称为冷效应。因此流体节流前后期温度变化是不确定的。选D。

【例 12.8-6】 空气以 150m/s 的速度在管道内流动,用水银温度计测量空气的温度。若温度计上的读数为 70℃,空气的实际温度是:

A. 56℃　　B. 70℃　　C. 59℃　　D. 45℃

解 工质在绝热流动中,因遇着障碍物或某种原因而受阻,使速度降低直至变为零,这种过程称为绝热滞止。水银温度计在管道中测得的温度是流体的滞止温度。而对于理想气体滞止参数的计算公式为:

$$\left.\begin{aligned} h_0 &= h_1 + \frac{c_1^2}{2} \\ T_0 &= T_1 + \frac{c_1^2}{2c_p} \end{aligned}\right\}$$

因此空气的实际温度是 $T_1 = T_0 - \frac{c_1^2}{2c_p} = 70 - \frac{150\times150}{2\times1\,001} = 59$℃,选 C。

【例 12.8-7】 压力为 9.807×10^5Pa、温度为 30℃的空气,流经阀门时产生绝热节流作用,使压力降为 6.865×10^5Pa,此时的温度为:

A. 10℃　　B. 30℃　　C. 27℃　　D. 78℃

解 绝热节流前后温度的变化是,对理想气体:温度不变;对于实际气体,其温度可能升高、可能降低也可能保持不变。本题中的空气可以近似认为是理想气体,因此绝热节流后温度保持不变,为 30℃。选 B。

【例 12.8-8】 理想气体绝热节流过程中节流热效应为:

A. 零　　B. 热效应

C. 冷效应　　D. 热效应和冷效应均可能有

解 选 A。

【例 12.8-9】 关于孤立系统熵增原理,下述说法中错误的是:

A. 孤立系统中进行过程 $dS_{iso}\geqslant0$

B. 自发过程一定是不可逆过程

C. 孤立系统中所有过程一定都是不可逆过程

D. 当 S 达到最大值 S_{max} 时系统达到平衡

解 根据孤立系统熵增原理有 $dS_{iso}\geqslant0$。当 $dS_{iso}>0$ 时系统内部进行的为不可逆过程,而当 $dS_{iso}=0$ 时,系统内部为可逆过程。选 C。

经 典 练 习

12.8-1 喷管是用来将流体的压力能转化为(　　)。

A. 功　　B. 热量　　C. 动能　　D. 内能

12.8-2 当流道截面积变小时,气体的流速(　　)。

A. 增大　　B. 减小　　C. 不变　　D. 不一定

12.8-3 在缩放形扩压管的最小截面处,马赫数为(　　)。

A. 大于 1　　B. 小于 1　　C. 等于 1　　D. 等于 0

12.8-4 气体流动中,当渐缩喷管出口截面压力与进口压力之比达到临界压力比,如此时出口截面压力继续下降，它们的流量将(　　)。

A. 增加　　B. 减小　　C. 不变　　D. 不一定

12.8-5　任何压力下的理想气体经节流后，其温度将(　　)。

A. 降低　　B. 升高　　C. 不变　　D. 不一定

12.8-6　湿蒸气经绝热节流后，(　　)不变。

A. 压力　　B. 比焓　　C. 比熵　　D. 都不对

12.9　动力循环

考试大纲☞：朗肯循环　回热和再热循环　热电循环　内燃机循环

必备基础知识

12.9.1　朗肯循环(Rankine Cycle)

朗肯循环是最简单的蒸气动力理想循环，热力发电厂的各种较复杂的蒸气动力循环都是在朗肯循环的基础上予以改进而得到的。

1)装置与流程

(1)蒸气动力装置：主要设备为锅炉、汽轮机、冷凝器、给水泵，如图 12.9-1 所示。

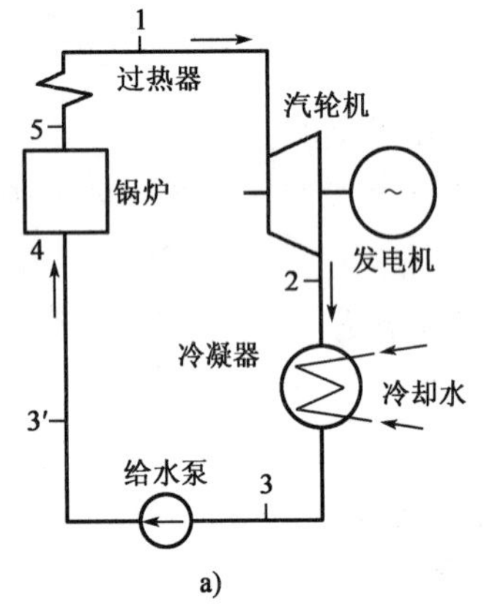

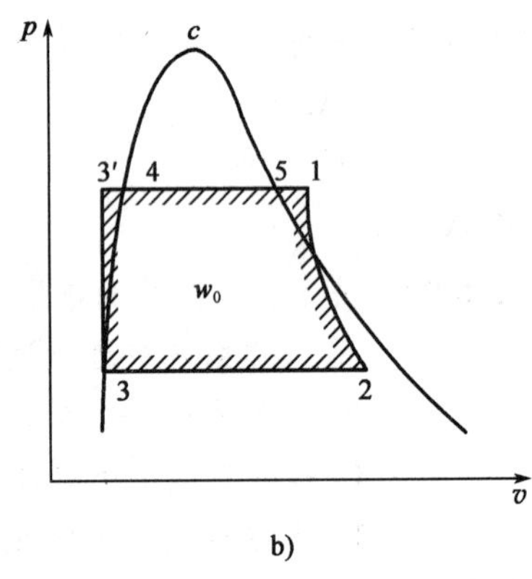

图 12.9-1　蒸气动力装置

(2)工作原理：朗肯循环可理想化为两个定压过程和两个定熵过程。

3′—4—5—1 水在蒸气锅炉中定压加热变为过热水蒸气，2—2 过热水蒸气在汽轮机内定熵膨胀，2—3 湿蒸气在凝汽器内定压(也定温)冷却凝结放热，3—3′凝结水在水泵中的定熵压缩。

2)朗肯循环的能量分析及热效率

汽耗率：蒸气动力循环装置每输出 1kW・h 功量时所消耗的蒸气量称为汽耗率。

取汽轮机为控制体，建立能量方程，朗肯循环的能量分析与计算如下。

循环吸热量　　$$q_1 = h_1 - h_3 \tag{12.9-1}$$

循环放热量　　$$q_1 = h_2 - h_3 \tag{12.9-2}$$

水蒸气流经汽轮机时，对外做功为

$$w_1 = h_1 - h_2 \tag{12.9-3}$$

水在水泵中升压所消耗的功为

$$w_p = h_4 - h_3 \tag{12.9-4}$$

由于水泵耗功相对于汽轮机做出的功极小，这样热效率可近似表示为

$$\eta = \frac{h_1 - h_2}{h_1 - h_3} \tag{12.9-5}$$

3）提高朗肯循环热效率的基本途径

依据：卡诺循环热效率。

（1）平均吸热温度。直接方法是提高蒸气压力和温度。

（2）降低排气温度。

典型例题解析

【例 12.9-1】 有一流体以 3m/s 的速度通过直径 7.62cm 的管路进入动力机。进口处的焓为 2 558.6kJ/kg，内能为 2 326kJ/kg，压力为 $p_1 = 689.48$kPa，而在动力机出口处的焓为 1 395.6kJ/kg。若过程为绝热过程，忽略流体动能和重力位能的变化，该动力机所发出的功率是：

A. 4.65kW　　B. 46.5kW　　C. 1 163kW　　D. 233kW

解 根据焓与内能的关系 $h=u+pv$，已知压力入口处内能、焓及压力，可以求得进口处的比体积 $v=(h-u)/p=0.337\text{m}^3/\text{kg}$，进口处的质量流量 $m-V/v-c\pi r^2/v=0.04$kg/s，单位质量流体经过动力机所做的功 $w=h_1-h_2=2\ 558.6-1\ 395.6=1\ 163$kJ/kg，则该动力机所发出的功 $W=m\cdot w=1\ 163\times0.04=46.5$kW。选 B。

【例 12.9-2】 最基本的蒸气动力朗肯循环，组成该循环的四个热力过程分别是：

A. 定温吸热、定熵膨胀、定温放热、定熵压缩

B. 定压吸热、定熵膨胀、定压放热、定熵压缩

C. 定压吸热、定温膨胀、定压放热、定温压缩

D. 定温吸热、定熵膨胀、定压发热、定熵压缩

解 郎肯循环是最简单的蒸气动力理想循环，郎肯循环可理想化为两个定压过程和两个定熵过程，即定压吸热、定熵膨胀、定压放热、定熵压缩。选 B。

【例 12.9-3】 组成蒸汽朗肯动力循环基本过程的是：

A. 等温加热，绝热膨胀，定温凝结，定熵压缩

B. 等温加热，绝热膨胀，定温凝结，绝热压缩

C. 定压加热，绝热膨胀，定温膨胀，定温压缩

D. 定压加热，绝热膨胀，定压凝结，定熵压缩

解 朗肯循环可理想化为两个定压过程和两个定熵过程。水在蒸汽锅炉中定压加热变为过热水蒸气，过热水蒸气在汽轮机内定熵膨胀，湿蒸汽在凝汽器内定压（也定温）冷却凝结放热，凝结水在水泵中的定熵压缩。选 D。

12.9.2 回热、再热循环

目的：提高等效卡诺循环的平均吸热温度。

1）回热循环

具有回热过程的热力循环称为回热循环。这里，回热是指在热力循环中不同温度水平的

工质之间产生的内部传热工程。蒸气功力的回热循环是指分次从汽轮机中抽出的一些做过功的蒸气。用其逐级对锅炉给水加热的热力循环。这样的回热循环也称为分级抽气回热循环。蒸气动力循环采用回热后，由于锅炉给水可从回热器中吸收一部分热量，使给水温度提高，这样可提高循环平均加热温度，从而提高循环的热效率。

抽气回热循环：用分级抽气来加热给水的实际回热循环。

利用一部分做过功的蒸气来加热给水，消除或减少平均吸热温度不高导致朗肯循环热效率不高这一不利因素的影响，即采用抽气回热的办法回热给水。一级抽气、混合式给水加热器的回热循环，如图 12.9-2 所示。由于采用了抽气回热，工质在热源（锅炉）中吸热，使平均吸热温度得到了提高。

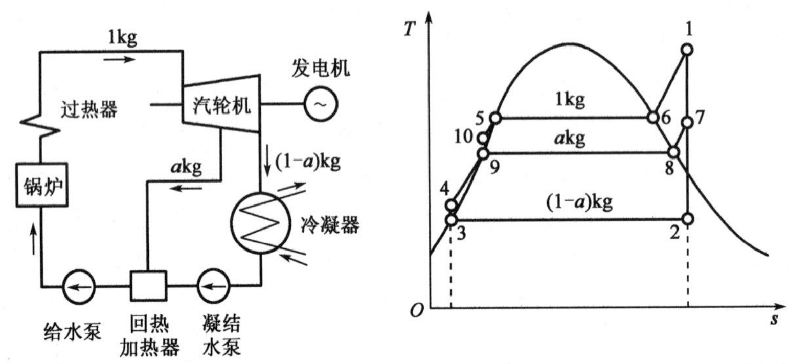

图 12.9-2　一级抽气、混合式给水加热器的回循环

2）再热循环

再热的目的是克服汽轮机尾部蒸气适度太大造成的危害。

将汽轮机高压段中膨胀到一定压力的蒸气重新引导锅炉的中间加热器（称为再热器）加热升温，然后再送入汽轮机使之继续膨胀做功。如图 12.9-3 所示。选择合适的再热压力，不仅可以使乏汽干度得到提高，而且由于附加循环提高了整个循环的平均吸热温度，因此还可以使循环热效率得到提高。

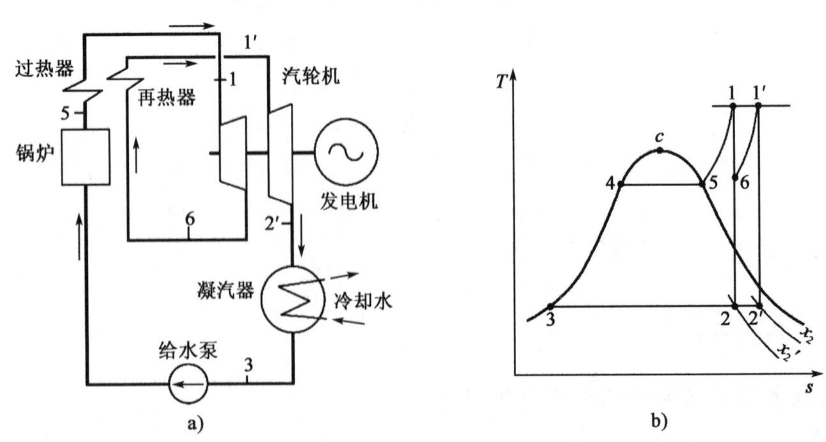

图 12.9-3　再热循环

12.9.3 热电循环

热电循环的实质:利用汽轮机中间抽气来供热。蒸气动力循环,通过凝汽器冷却水带走而排放到大气中去的能量约占总能量的50%以上。这部分热能数量很大,但温度不高(例如排气压力为4kPa时,其饱和温度仅为29℃),难以利用。利用发电厂中做了一定数量功的蒸气作供热热源,用房屋采暖和生活用热,可大大提高利用率,这种既发电又供热的动力循环称为热电循环,如图12.9-4所示。

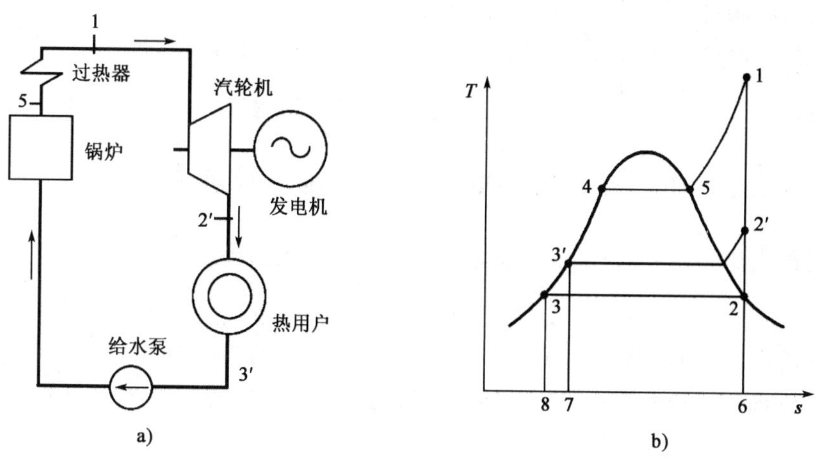

图12.9-4 热电循环

排气压力高于大气压力的汽轮机称为背压式汽轮机。这种系统没有凝汽器,蒸气在汽轮机内做功后仍具有一定的压力,通过管路送给热用户作为热源,放热后,全部或部分凝结水再回到热电厂。由于提高了汽轮机的排气压力,蒸气中用于做功(发电)的热能相应减少,所以背压式热电循环的循环热效率比单纯供电的凝汽式朗肯循环有所降低。由于热电循环中乏汽的热量得到了利用,所以热能利用率 K(所利用的能量与外热源提供的总能量的比值)提高了。背压式热电循环,热能利用率最高为 $K=1$(普通朗肯循环热能利用率最低,调节抽气式热电循环的热能利用率介于两者之间)。但其缺点是热负荷和电负荷不能调节。

典型例题解析

【例12.9-4】 热电循环是指:

A. 既发电又供热的动力循环　　B. 靠消耗热来发电的循环

C. 靠电炉作为热源产生蒸气的循环　　D. 蒸气轮机装置循环

解 热电循环是利用汽轮机中间抽气来供热。蒸气动力循环,通过凝汽器冷却水带走而排放到大气中去的能量约占总能量的50%以上。这部分热能数量很大,但温度不高难以利用。利用发电厂中做了一定数量功的蒸气做供热热源,用房屋采暖和生活用热,可大大提高利用率,这种既发电又供热的动力循环称为热电循环。选A。

12.9.4 内燃机循环

内燃机循环是指内燃机的燃烧过程在热机的气缸中进行。

内燃机是一个开口系统，每一个循环都要从外界吸入工质、循环结束时又将废气排于外界。同时，活塞在移动时与气缸壁不断发生摩擦，高温工质也可能通过气缸壁向外界少量放热，因此，实际的汽油机循环并不是闭合循环，也不是可逆循环。

图 12.9-5a)是一个四冲程汽油机的实际工作循环图。实际循环可简化为理想化情况。

(1)空气与燃气理想化为定比热容的理想气体。

(2)开式循环理想化为闭式循环。

(3)燃烧、排气过程理想化为工质的吸、放热过程。

(4)压缩与膨胀过程理想化为可逆绝热过程。

在对内燃机理论循环进行分析之前，首先引入三个特性参数：

(1)压缩比 $\varepsilon=\frac{v_1}{v_2}$，表示压缩过程中工质体积被压缩的程度。

(2)定容升压比 $\lambda=\frac{p_3}{p_2}$，表示定容加热过程中工质压力升高的程度。

(3)定压预胀比 $\rho=\frac{v_4}{v_3}$，表示定压加热时工质体积膨胀的程度。

理想循环如图 12.9-5b)、c)所示。工质首先被定熵压缩(过程 1—2)，接着从热源定容吸热(2—3)，然后进行定熵膨胀做功(3—4)，最后向冷源定容放热(4—1)，完成一个可逆循环。经过上述抽象和概括，汽油机的实际循环被理想化为定容加热循环，也即奥拓循环。

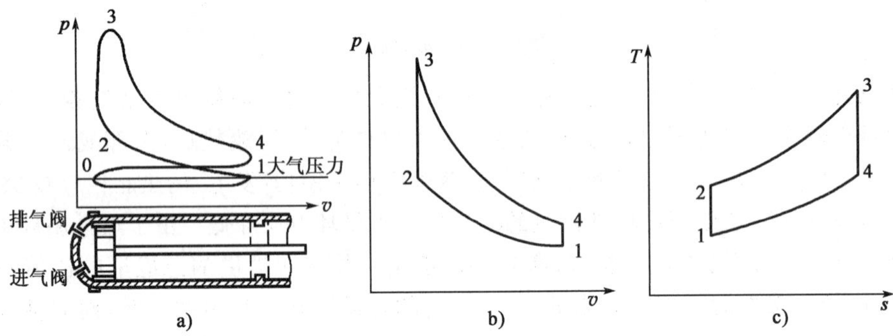

图 12.9-5　汽油机循环

定容加热理论循环的计算

$$\left.\begin{aligned}&\text{吸热量}\quad q_1=c_v(T_3-T_2)\\&\text{放热量}\quad q_2=c_v(T_4-T_1)\\&\text{循环净功}\quad \omega_0=q_1-q_2\end{aligned}\right\}$$

循环热效率　$\eta_t=\frac{\omega_0}{q_1}=1-\frac{q_2}{q_1}, \eta_{tv}=1-\frac{T_4-T_1}{T_3-T_2}=1-\frac{T_1(T_4/T_1-1)}{T_2(T_3/T_2-1)}$

因 $\Delta s_{23}=\Delta s_{14}$，即

$$c_v\ln\frac{T_3}{T_2}=c_v\ln\frac{T_4}{T_1}$$

有

$$\frac{T_3}{T_2}=\frac{T_4}{T_1}$$

代入上式 $\eta_{tv}=1-\frac{T_1}{T_2}=1-\frac{1}{T_2/T_1}=1-\frac{1}{(v_2/v_1)^{k-1}}$

得

$$\eta_{tv}=1-\frac{1}{\varepsilon^{k-1}} \tag{12.9-6}$$

其中，ε 为压缩比，是个大于 1 的数，表示工质在燃烧前被压缩的程度。

可知，压缩比越高，内燃机的热效率也越高。但是 ε 值并不能任意提高，因为压缩比过大，压缩终了温度过高，容易产生爆燃，对活塞和气缸造成损害。压缩比要根据所用燃料的性质而定。对于一般的汽油机，$\varepsilon=7\sim9$。

典型例题解析

【例 12.9-5】 组成四冲程内燃机定压加热循环的四个过程是：

A. 绝热压缩、定压吸热、绝热膨胀、定压放热

B. 绝热压缩、定压吸热、绝热膨胀、定容放热

C. 定温压缩、定压吸热、绝热膨胀、定容放热

D. 绝热压缩、定压吸热、定温膨胀、定压放热

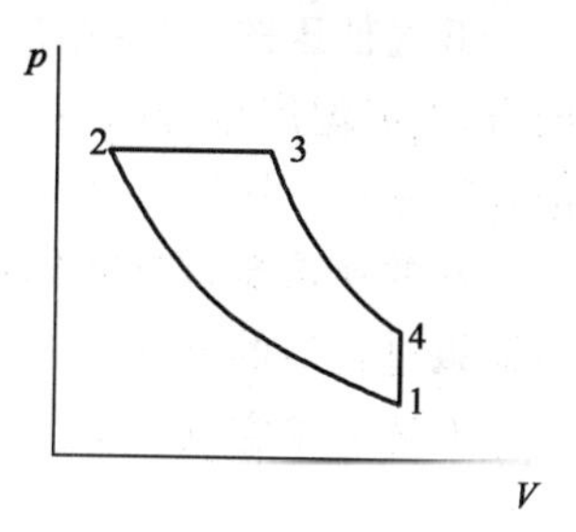

例 12.9-5 图

解 四冲程内燃机实际循环可简化为理想化情况，在 p-v 图上的表示如图所示。选 B。

【例 12.9-6】 在内燃机循环计算中，$m$kg 气体放热量的计算式是：

A. $mc_p(T_2-T_1)$　　B. $mc_v(T_2-T_1)$

C. $mc_p(T_2+T_1)$　　D. $mc_v(T_1-T_2)$

解 在内燃机循环中气体的放热过程为定容过程，因此计算放热量时应采用定容比热。选 D。

经 典 练 习

12.9-1 内燃机定压加热理想循环的组成依次为：绝热压缩过程、定压加热过程、绝热膨胀过程和（　　）。

A. 定容放热过程　B. 定压放热过程　C. 定容排气过程　D. 定压排气过程

12.9-2 内燃机定容加热理想循环的组成依次为：绝热压缩过程、定容加热过程、（　　）和定容放热过程。

A. 绝热压缩过程　B. 定容排气过程　C. 定温加热过程　D. 绝热膨胀过程

12.9-3 柴油机的理想循环中加热过程为（　　）过程。

A. 绝热　B. 定压　C. 定温　D. 多变

12.9-4 某内燃机混合加热理想循环，从外界吸热 1 000kJ/kg，向外界放热 400kJ/kg，其热效率为（　　）。

A. 0.3　B. 0.4　C. 0.6　D. 4

12.9-5 某热机在一个循环中，吸热 Q_1，放热 Q_2，则热效率为（　　）。

A. $Q_1/(Q_1-Q_2)$　B. $Q_2/(Q_1-Q_2)$　C. $(Q_1-Q_2)/Q_2$　D. $(Q_1-Q_2)/Q_1$

12.9-6 柴油机理想循环的热效率总是随压缩比的降低而（　　）。

A. 增大　B. 减小　C. 无关　D. 不定

12.10 制冷循环

考试大纲☞:空气压缩制冷循环　蒸气压缩制冷循环　吸收式制冷循环　热泵　气体的液化

必备基础知识

12.10.1 空气压缩制冷循环

空气压缩式制冷原理:将常温下较高压力的空气进行绝热膨胀,会获得低温低压的空气。原则是实现逆卡诺循环。

低温低压的空气(制冷剂)在冷室的盘管中定压吸热升温后进入压缩机,被绝热压缩提高压力,同时温度也升高,然后进入冷却器,被大气或水冷却到接近常温(即大气环境温度)后再进入膨胀机。压缩空气在膨胀机内进行绝热膨胀,压力降低同时温度也降低。将低温空气引入冷室的换热器,在换热器盘管内定压吸热,从而降低冷室的温度。空气吸热升温后又被吸入压缩机进行新的循环。

上述简单空气压缩制冷循环又称为布雷顿制冷循环,如图 12.10-1 所示。其中:

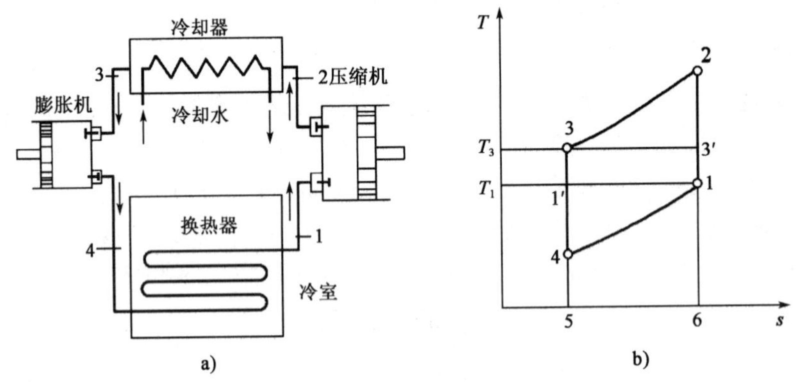

图 12.10-1　布雷顿制冷循环

1—2 是空气在压缩机内定熵压缩过程;

2—3 是空气在冷却器中定压放热过程;

3—4 是空气在膨胀机中定熵膨胀过程;

4—1 是空气在冷室换热器中定压吸热过程。

注意:空气的热物性决定了空气压缩制冷循环的制冷系数低和单位供职的制冷能力小。

制冷系数

$$\varepsilon_1 = \frac{1}{\dfrac{T_2}{T_1} - 1} = \frac{1}{\left(\dfrac{p_2}{p_1}\right)^{\frac{k}{k-1}} - 1} \tag{12.10-1}$$

或

$$\varepsilon_1 = \frac{T_1}{T_2 - T_1} \tag{12.10-2}$$

式(12.10-1)中$\dfrac{p_2}{p_1}$为压缩比。减小压缩比可提高制冷系数。

比较相同温度范围内的制冷系数,空气压缩制冷循环的制冷系数要比逆向卡诺循环的制冷系数小。

典型例题解析

【例 12.10-1】 图示为卡诺制冷循环的 T-S 图，从图中可知，表示制冷量的是：

A. 面积 $efghe$

B. 面积 $hgdch$

C. 面积 $efghe$＋面积 $hgdch$

D. 面积 $aehba$＋面积 $efghe$

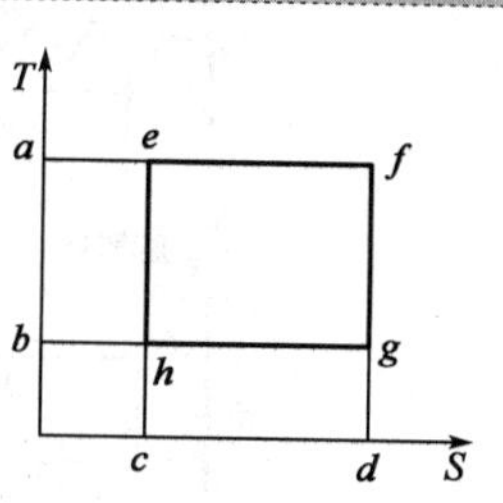

例 12.10-1 图

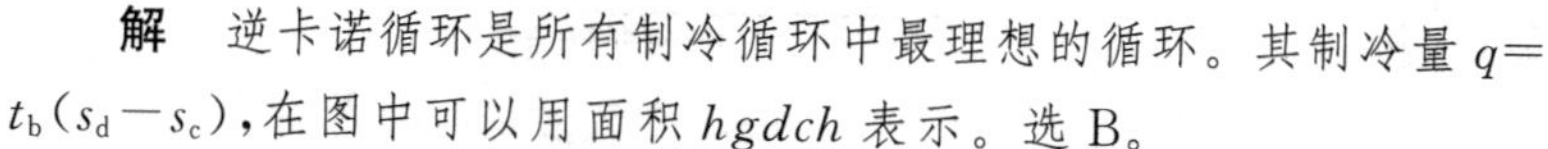

解 逆卡诺循环是所有制冷循环中最理想的循环。其制冷量 $q=t_b(s_d-s_c)$，在图中可以用面积 $hgdch$ 表示。选 B。

【例 12.10-2】 对于空气压缩式制冷理想循环，由两个可逆定压过程和两个可逆绝热过程，则提高该循环制冷系数的有效措施是：

A. 增加压缩机功率

B. 增大压缩比 p_2/p_1

C. 增加膨胀机功率

D. 提高冷却器和吸热换热器的传热能力

解 根据制冷循环的特点，循环中两个可逆定压过程和两个可逆绝热过程，分别为可逆定压冷凝、可逆定压蒸发、可逆绝热压缩、可逆绝热膨胀，通过提高冷却器和吸热换热器的传热能力，能够降低传热温差，从而减小冷凝温度和蒸发温度间的传热温差，以提高循环的制冷系数。选 D。

12.10.2 蒸气压缩制冷循环

1）实际压缩式制冷循环

（1）蒸气压缩制冷装置：由压缩机、冷凝器、膨胀阀及蒸发器组成。

（2）原理：从蒸发器出来的制冷剂的干饱和蒸气被吸入压缩机，绝热压缩后成为过热蒸气（过程 1→2），蒸气进入冷凝器，在定压下冷却（过程 2→3），进一步在定压定温下凝结成饱和液体（过程 3→4）。饱和液体继而经过一个膨胀阀（又称节流阀或减压阀），经绝热节流降压降温而变成低干度的湿蒸气，如图 12.10-2 所示。

注意：蒸气压缩制冷采用节流阀降压降温，是因为被节流的工质在饱和区域内，由于饱和温度和饱和压力互为函数，因此在节流降压的同时可以降温；而空气压缩制冷中的制冷工质空气，在一般使用温度范围内可视为理想气体，而理想气体经节流后，尽管其压力降低，但温度保持不变，所以不能通过节流达到降压降温的目的，因而，对空气压缩制冷必须用膨胀机而不能用节流阀。

2）制冷剂的压焓图（$\lg p$-h 图）

（1）原理：以制冷剂焓作为横坐标，以压力对数为纵坐标，共绘出制冷剂的六种状态参数线簇：定焓(h)、定压力(p)、定温度(T)、定比体积(v)、定熵(S)及定干度(x)线。

（2）在 $\lg p$-h 图（图 12.10-3）中，饱和液体线（$x=0$）与干饱和蒸气线（$x=1$）相交于临界点 c。整个图面分成三个区，下界线（$x=0$）左侧为过冷液体（或未饱和液体）区；下界线

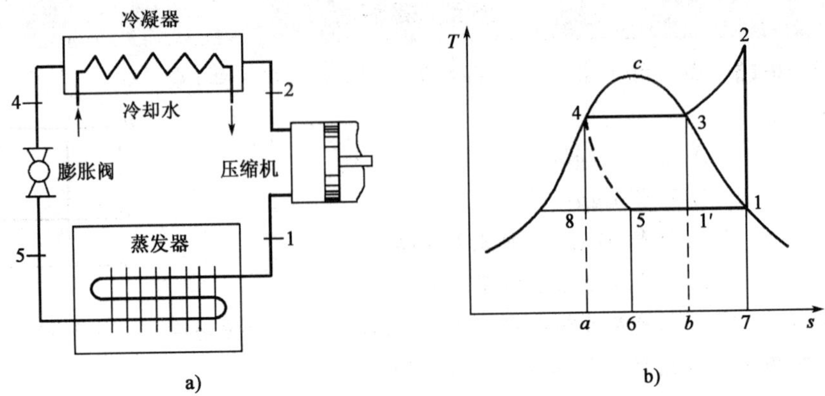

图 12.10-2　蒸气压缩制冷循环

与上界线($x=1$)之间是湿蒸气区;上界线右侧是过热蒸气区。图中共绘有六组等状态参数线簇:

①定压线簇:定压线是一组水平线;

②定焓线簇:定焓线是一组垂直线;

③定温线簇:定温线在过冷液体区是一组近似垂直线,在湿蒸气区是一组水平线,与相应的定压线重合,在过热蒸气区是一组斜向下的曲线;

④定比体积线簇:定比体积线在湿蒸气区是一组向右上方倾斜的曲线,在过热蒸气区,向右上方倾斜的幅度更大;

⑤定熵线簇:定熵线是一组向右上方倾斜的曲线,其倾斜比定比体积线的斜率大;

⑥定干度线:只在湿蒸气区内绘出,是一组自临界点向下发散的曲线,由 $x=0$ 线逐渐增大至 $x=1$ 线。

蒸气压缩式制冷循环各热力过程在 lg$p$-h 图上的表示如图 12.10-4 所示。状态 1 为压缩机的吸汽状态点,状态点 2 为压缩机的排汽状态点,状态点 4 为冷凝器的出口状态点,状态点 5 为蒸发器进口状态点。

1→2 表示压缩机中的绝热压缩过程,2→3→4 是冷凝器中的定压冷却过程,4→5 为膨胀阀中的绝热节流过程,5→1 表示蒸发器内的定压蒸发过程。

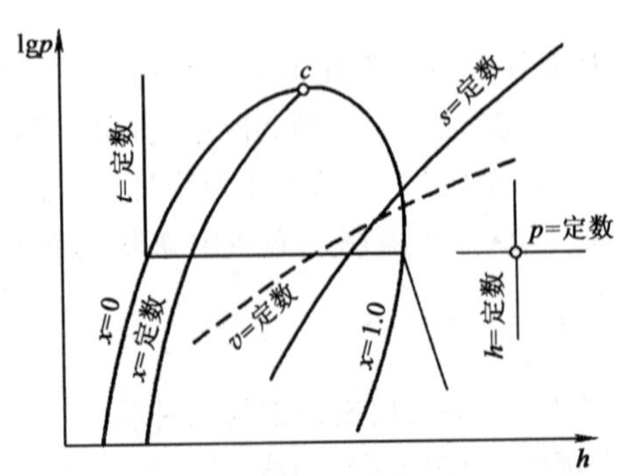

图 12.10-3　lg$p$-h 的典型曲线

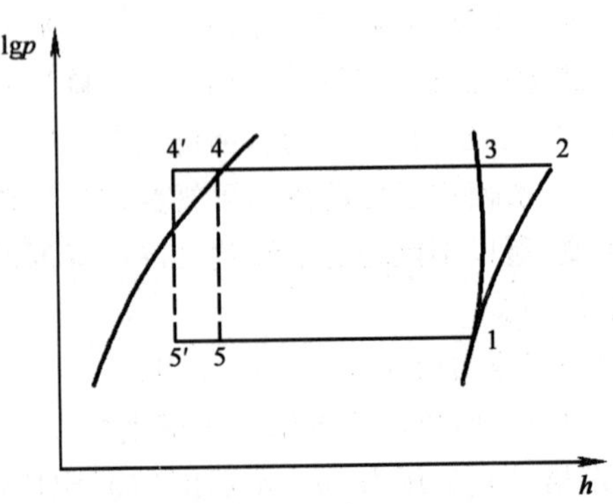

图 12.10-4　蒸气压缩式制冷循环各热力过程

3)制冷循环能量分析及制冷系数

(1)制冷剂在蒸发器内吸收低温物体的热量

$$q_0 = h_1 - h_5 \tag{12.10-3}$$

(2)制冷剂在冷凝器内向外界排出的热量

$$q_1 = h_2 - h_4 \tag{12.10-4}$$

(3)循环净功

$$\omega_0 = h_2 - h_1 \tag{12.10-5}$$

(4)制冷系数

$$\varepsilon_1 = \frac{q_2}{\omega_2} = \frac{h_1 - h_5}{h_2 - h_1} = \frac{\text{收获}}{\text{消耗}} \tag{12.10-6}$$

制冷剂质量流量

$$m = \frac{Q_2}{q_2} \tag{12.10-7}$$

压缩机所需功率

$$p = \frac{m\omega_0}{3\ 600} \tag{12.10-8}$$

冷凝器热负荷

$$Q = m(h_2 - h_1) \tag{12.10-9}$$

4)影响制冷系数的主要因素

(1)制冷剂的冷凝温度。

(2)蒸发温度。

典型例题解析

【例 12.10-3】 评价制冷循环优劣的经济性能指标为制冷系数，它可表示为：

A. 耗净功/制冷量　　B. 压缩机耗功/向环境放出的热量

C. 制冷量/耗净功　　D. 向环境放出的热量/从冷藏室吸收的热量

解　制冷系数 $\varepsilon_1 = \frac{q_2}{\omega_2} = \frac{\text{收获}}{\text{消耗}}$，在制冷系统中收获的是制冷机产生的制冷量，而消耗的是机械功。选 C。

【例 12.10-4】 靠消耗功来实现制冷的循环有：

A. 蒸气压缩式制冷，空气压缩式制冷

B. 吸收式制冷，空气压缩式制冷

C. 蒸气压缩式制冷，吸收式制冷

D. 所有的制冷循环都是靠消耗功来实现的

解　吸收式制冷是利用某些具有特殊性质的工质对，通过一种物质对另一种物质的吸收和释放，产生物质的状态变化，从而伴随吸热和放热过程。吸收式制冷机可用电或煤油加热，无运动部件，不消耗机械功。选 A。

【例 12.10-5】 制冷循环中的制冷量是指：

A. 制冷剂从冷藏室中吸收的热量

B. 制冷剂向环境放出的热量

C. 制冷剂从冷藏室中吸收的热量－制冷剂向环境放出的热量

D. 制冷剂从冷藏室中吸收的热量＋制冷剂向环境放出的热量

解 制冷量是指空调进行制冷运行时，单位时间内从密闭空间、房间或区域内去除的热量总和。选 A。

【例 12.10-6】 冬天用一热泵向室内供热，使室内温度保持在 20℃。已知房屋的散热损失是 120 000kJ/h，室外环境温度为 −10℃，则带动该热泵所需的最小功率是：

A. 8.24kW　　B. 3.41kW　　C. 3.14kW　　D. 10.67kW

解 带动该热泵所需要的最小功率应满足使房间满足热平衡的条件，即对应的最小制热量应等于房屋的散热损失，同时系统还需按照逆卡诺循环运行以期有最高的制热系数。按照逆卡诺循环系统的制热系数。

$$\varepsilon=\frac{q}{\omega}=\frac{T_1}{T_1-T_2}=\frac{273+20}{(273+20)-(273-10)}=9.77$$

所需最小功率

$$\omega=\frac{q}{\varepsilon}=\frac{120\ 000/3\ 600}{9.77}=3.41\text{kW}$$

选 B。

12.10.3 吸收式制冷循环

吸收式制冷是利用制冷剂液体气化吸热实现制冷，它是直接利用热能驱动，以消耗热能为补偿，将热量从低温物体转移到高温物体中去。吸收式制冷采用的工质是用两种沸点低的物质为制冷剂，沸点高的物质为吸收剂。

例如，氨吸收式制冷循环，如图 12.10-5 所示，其中氨用作制冷剂、水为吸收剂。冷凝器、膨胀阀和蒸发器与蒸气压缩制冷完全相同，区别是用吸收器、发生器、溶液泵及减压阀取代了压缩机。

吸收式制冷循环是利用溶液在不同温度下具有不同溶解的特性，使制冷剂（氨）在较低温度下被吸收剂（水）吸收，并在较高温度下蒸发起到升压的作用。因此，吸收器相当于压缩机的低压吸气侧，而发生器则相当于压缩机的高压排气侧，其中吸收剂（水）充当了将制冷剂（氨）从低压侧输运到高压侧的运载液体的角色。所以，吸收式制冷剂中为实现制冷目的工质进行了两个循环，即制冷剂循环和溶液循环。

12.10.4 热泵

将热量由大气送至高温暖室所用的机械装置称为热泵。热泵实质上是一种能源采掘机械，它以消耗一部分高质能（机械能、电能或高温热能等）为补偿，通过热力循环，把环境介质（水、空气、土地）中储存的低质能量加以发掘进行利用。在每一次供热循环中，1kg 工质放给暖室的热量称为供热量。它的工作原理与制冷机相同，都按逆循环工作，所不同的是它们工作的温度范围和要求的效果不同。

制冷装置是将低温物体的热量传给自然环境，以造成低温环境；热泵则是从自然环境中吸取热量，并将它输送到人们所需要温度较高的物体中去。

在蒸发器中，制冷剂蒸发吸取自然水源或环境大气中的热能，经压缩后的制冷剂在冷凝器中放出热量加热供热系统的回水，然后由循环泵送到热用户用作采暖或热水供应等；在冷凝器中，制冷剂凝结成饱和液体，经节流降压降温进入蒸发器，蒸发吸热，气化为干饱和蒸气，从而完成一个循环。

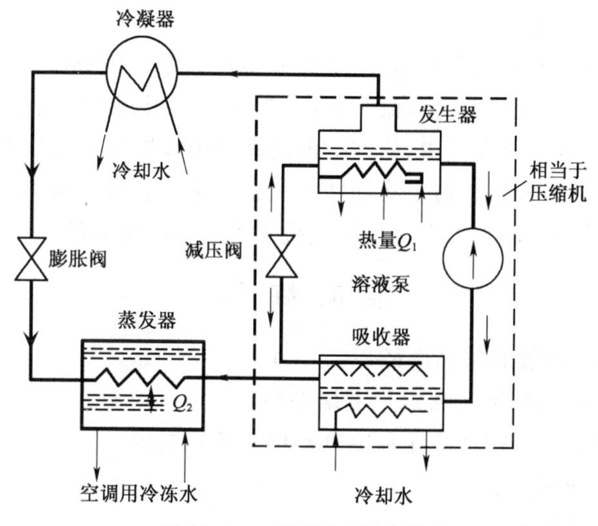

图 12.10-5　氨吸收式制冷循环

热泵循环的经济性以消耗单位功量所得到的供热量来衡量，称为供热系数。循环制冷系数越高，供热系数也越高。

典型例题解析

【例 12.10-7】 有一热泵用来冬季采暖和夏季降温。室内要求保持 20℃，室内外温度每相差 1℃，每小时通过房屋围护结构的热损失是 1 200kJ，热泵按逆向卡诺循环工作，当冬季室外温度为 0℃时，带动该热泵所需的功率是：

A. 4.55kW　　B. 0.455kW　　C. 5.55kW　　D. 6.42kW

解　选 B。

【例 12.10-8】 热泵与制冷机的工作原理相同，但是：

A. 它们工作的温度范围和要求的效果不同

B. 它们采用的工作物质和压缩机的形式不同

C. 它们消耗能量的方式不同

D. 它们吸收热量的多少不同

解　本题主要考查热泵供热循环与制冷循环的异同。热泵循环是通过消耗机械功，从大气中吸收热量，然后将其送入温度高于大气温度的暖室；而制冷循环是通过消耗机械功，从冷藏室吸收热量，然后将其送入大气环境。两者的相同之处在于都是消耗机械功的循环，不同之处在于热泵循环是从大气环境吸收热量，而制冷循环是把热量排入大气环境。热泵是将环境作为低温热源；而制冷是将环境作为高温热源。选 A。

12.10.5 气体的液化

气体可经液化得到相应的液态物质。任何气体只要使其经历适当的热力过程，将其温度降低至临界温度以下，并保持其压力大于对应温度下的饱和压力，便都可以从气体转化为液体。可以看出，为了使气体液化，最重要的是解决降温问题。最基本的气体液化循环——林德-汉普森(Linde-Hampson)循环。林德-汉普森系统工作原理主要是利用焦耳-汤姆逊效应，使气体通过节流阀而降温液化。

被液化的气体进入定温压气机压缩，然后进入换热器，在其中被定压冷却，使温度降低至最大回转温度下。这时，使气体通过节流阀，由于焦耳-汤姆逊效应，气体的压力和温度均大大降低，节流后为湿蒸气，流入分离器中，使空气的饱和液体和饱和蒸气分离开来，液体空气留在分离器中，而饱和蒸气被引入换热器去冷却从压气机出来的高压气体而自身被加热升温到状态点，然后与补充的新鲜空气混合，再进入压气机重新进行液化循环。

经典练习

12.10-1 提高制冷系数的正确途径是(　　)。

A. 尽量使实际循环接近逆卡诺循环

B. 尽量增大冷剂在冷库和冷凝器中的传热温度

C. 降低冷库温度

D. 提高冷却水温度

12.10-2 其他条件不变，蒸气压缩制冷循环的制冷系数随蒸发温度的提高、冷凝温度的提高、过冷度的加大而(　　)。

A. 升高　　B. 降低　　C. 不变　　D. 无法确定

12.10-3 某蒸气压缩制冷循环，向冷凝器放热 240kJ/kg，消耗外界功 60kJ/kg，其制冷系数为(　　)。

A. 1.33　　B. 0.75　　C. 4　　D. 3

12.10-4 一台热机带动一台热泵，热机和热泵排出的热量均用于加热暖气散热器的热水。若热机的热效率为 50%，热泵的供热系数为 10，则输给散热器的热量是输给热机热量的(　　)倍。

A. 5.5　　B. 9.5　　C. 10　　D. 10.5

12.10-5 以 R12 为工质的制冷循环，工质在压缩机进口为饱和蒸气状态($h_1=573.6$kJ/kg)，同压力下饱和液体的焓值为 $h_5=405.1$kJ/kg。若工质在压缩机出口处 $h_2=598$kJ/kg，在绝热节流阀进口处 $h_3=443.8$kJ/kg，则单位质量工质的制冷量为(　　)kJ/kg。

A. 24.4　　B. 129.8　　C. 154.2　　D. 168.5

参考答案及提示

12.1-1　B　由公式 $p=p_g+p_b$(当 $p>p_b$ 时)，可知表压 $p_g=p-p_b$，因此测得的压差为表压，数值为 0.08MPa。

12.1-2　C　题中几个状态参数只有温度能够通过直接测量获得。

12.1-3　B　闭口系统是指系统与外界没有任何质量交换的热力系统。

12.1-4　C

12.1-5　A

12.2-1　B　如果系统完成某一热力过程后，再沿原来路径逆向进行时，能使系统和外界都返回原来状态而不留下任何变化，则这一过程称为可逆过程。因此经过可逆过程工质必然恢复原来状态。

12.2-2　C

12.2-3　C

12.2-4　D　可逆过程中没有任何耗散，效率最高，因此获得的最大可用功最多。

12.3-1　C　热力学第一定律实质上就是能量守恒与转换定律在热现象中的应用。它确定了热力过程中各种能量在数量上的相互关系。

12.3-2　B

12.3-3　D　热力学第一定律阐述了能量的转换在数量上的守恒关系。

12.3-4　A

12.3-5　D　理想气体的内能包括分子具有的移动动能、转动动能以及振动动能。

12.3-6　D

12.3-7　A

12.3-8　B

12.3-9　D　由于工质的比体积发生变化而做的功称为容积功。

12.3-10　B

12.4-1　C　参考混合气体分压力定律。

12.4-2　C　参考混合气体分容积定律。

12.4-3　C　理想气体的定压比体积与定容比热的比值为比热容比，对空气为1.4。

12.4-4　D

12.4-5　B

12.5-1　B　pv^n=常数，当$n=k$时，为绝热过程，没有热量的交换，外界做功用于增加系统的内能。

12.5-2　A

12.5-3　C　该描述为热力学第一定律在定容过程中的具体描述，适用于任何气体。

12.5-4　A

12.5-5　B

12.5-6　C

12.5-7　D

12.5-8　A

12.5-9　A　当活塞处于左死点时，活塞顶面与缸盖之间须留有一定的空隙，称为余隙（余隙容积）。由于余隙容积的存在，活塞不可能将高压气体全部排出，因此余隙比减小，容积效率提高。

12.6-1　C　热力学第二定律的实质便是论述热力过程的方向性及能质退化或贬值的客观规律。

12.6-2　A

12.6-3　D　第二类永动机是指从单一热源中取热，由热力学第二定律可知该类热机不能实现。

12.6-4　C

12.6-5　B

12.6-6　B　制冷循环是逆向循环，在所有逆向循环中逆卡诺循环效率最高。

12.6-7　D

12.6-8　C　卡诺循环为理想可逆循环，经卡诺循环恢复到初始态时，没有任何变化。

12.6-9　C　影响卡诺循环效率的因素是高低温热源的温度。

12.6-10　D

12.7-1　D　气体压力越低，温度越高，则越远离液化状态，也越接近理想气体。

12.7-2　A

12.7-3　B　可以用压力和干度两个参数确定两相区内的湿蒸气的状态。

12.7-4　D

12.7-5　D　由热力学第一定律可知水在锅炉中的吸热量为水在锅炉进出口的焓差。

12.7-6　B　未饱和的湿空气的组成成分为干空气和过热蒸气。

12.7-7　C

12.7-8　C　含湿量与相对湿度是表征湿空气干湿情况的两个参数，但其物理意义不同。

12.7-9　A

12.7-10　C

12.8-1　C　喷管是通过改变流道截面面积，提升流体流速的装置，即将压力能转变为流体的动能。

12.8-2　D　流体速度变化情况不仅与流动截面面积变化有关，还与马赫数有关。

12.8-3　C

12.8-4　C　气体节流过程可以认为是一绝热过程，节流前后焓不变，而理想气体的焓是温度的单值函数，故理想气体节流后温度不变。

12.8-5　C

12.8-6　B　湿蒸气为实际气体，节流前后焓不变。

12.9-1　A

12.9-2　D

12.9-3　B

12.9-4　C

12.9-5　D

12.9-6　B　内燃机的效率 $\eta_{tv}=1-\frac{1}{\varepsilon^{k-1}}$，其中 ε 为内燃机压缩比，可见压缩比越大内燃机效率越高。

12.10-1　A　制冷循环越接近理想的逆卡诺循环效率越高。

12.10-2　D　蒸气压缩制冷循环的制冷系数分别随蒸发温度的提高而提高、随冷凝温度的提高而降低、过冷度的加大而增大。

12.10-3　D　由能量守恒定律可知，蒸发器的制冷量为 180kJ，按照制冷系数的定义可知答案为 D。

12.10-4　A

12.10-5　C

13 传 热 学

考题配置　单选，10 题
分数配置　每题 2 分，共 20 分

复 习 指 导

传热学是研究热量传递过程规律的一门科学，研究内容包括传热的三种基本方式（热传导、热对流、热辐射），实际传热过程的规律及控制。要求学生能够熟练掌握热量传递的三种基本方式及传热过程所遵循的基本规律，能运用传热学理论分析计算实际的热量传递过程，掌握控制实际传热过程的基本途经。

13.1　导热理论基础

考试大纲☞：导热基本概念　温度场　温度梯度　傅里叶定律　导热系数　导热微分方程　导热过程的单值性条件

必备基础知识

13.1.1 导热基本概念

传热的基本方式有热传导、热对流和热辐射三种。

热传导是指在不涉及物质转移的情况下，热量从物体中温度较高的部位传递给相邻的温度较低的部位，或从高温物体传递给相接触的低温物体的过程，简称导热。导热是物质的属性，可在固体、液体和气体中发生；单纯的导热发生在固体中。

1）温度场

温度场是指在各个时刻物体内各点温度分布的总称。一般地，物体的温度分布是坐标和时间的函数，即

$$t = f(x, y, z, \tau)$$

其中 x, y, z 为空间坐标，τ 为时间坐标。

稳态温度场（定常温度场）：是指在稳态条件下物体各点的温度分布不随时间的改变而变化的温度场。

$$t = f(x, y, z)$$

2）温度梯度

系统中某一点所在的等温面与相邻等温面之间的温差，与其法线间的距离之比的极限为该点的温度梯度，记为 grad$t$。它是一个矢量，其正方向指向温度升高的方向。

$$\text{grad}t = \frac{\partial t}{\partial n} n$$

直角坐标系：

$$\text{grad}t = \frac{\partial t}{\partial x}\bar{i} + \frac{\partial t}{\partial y}\bar{j} + \frac{\partial t}{\partial z}\bar{k}$$

显然，温度梯度表明了温度在空间上的最大变化率及其方向。

典型例题解析

【例 13.1-1】 关于传热的基本方式说法正确的是：

A. 导热、对流和辐射换热　　B. 导热、对流换热和辐射

C. 热传导、热对流和热辐射　　D. 导热、对流换热和辐射换热

解　对流换热和辐射换热都是复合换热，而不是基本传热方式。选 C。

13.1.2 傅里叶定律

傅里叶（Fourier）于 1822 年提出了著名的导热基本定律——傅里叶定律，指出了导热热流密度矢量与温度梯度之间的关系。

$$\vec{q} = -\lambda \text{grad}t = -\lambda \frac{\partial t}{\partial n}\vec{n}$$

式中：λ——比例常数，导热率（导热系数）；负号表示热量传递的方向同温度升高的方向相反。

在直角坐标系中的向量表达式为：$\vec{q} = -\lambda\left(\frac{\partial t}{\partial x}\bar{i} + \frac{\partial t}{\partial y}\bar{j} + \frac{\partial t}{\partial z}\bar{k}\right)$

对一维稳态导热可写为：$\vec{q}_x = -\lambda \frac{\mathrm{d}t}{\mathrm{d}x}\bar{i}$

傅里叶定律的适用条件：适用于各向同性物体。对于各向异性物体，热流密度矢量的方向不仅与温度梯度有关，还与热导率的方向性有关，因此热流密度矢量与温度梯度不一定在同一条直线上。

13.1.3 导热系数（导热率、比例系数）

导热系数的定义由傅里叶定律给出：

$$\lambda = \frac{q}{-\text{grad}t}$$

影响材料导热系数最主要的因素是温度。绝大多数材料的导热系数都可以近似表示为温度的线性函数形式，即：$\lambda = \lambda_0(1 + bt)$。

1）气体的导热系数

气体导热靠分子热运动时的相互碰撞，气体的导热系数一般在 0.006～0.6W/(m·℃)范围内变化。所有气体的导热系数均随温度升高而增大，氢和氦的导热系数比其他气体高得多。

2）液体导热系数

迄今为止对液体导热机理仍不是很清楚，液体导热系数大致在 0.07～0.7 W/(m·℃)范围，主要依靠弹性波的传递作用。多数液体的导热系数随温度升高而降低，但水例外。液态金属和电解液是一类特殊的液体。

3）固体（金属与保温材料）导热系数

固体中的热量传递是自由电子的迁移和晶格振动相叠加这两种作用的结果，合金的导热

系数一般比纯金属低，金属材料的导热系数和电导率的排列顺序完全相同。金属的导热系数一般随温度升高呈下降趋势。各类物质的导热系数数值的大致范围及随温度变化的情况如图 13.1-1所示。

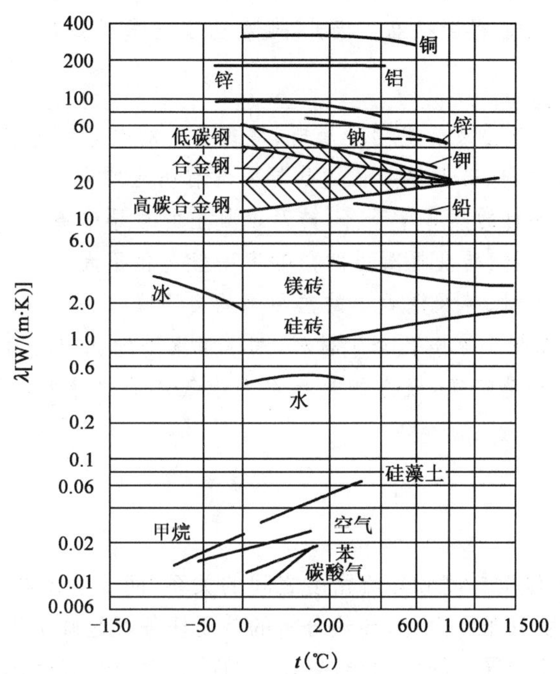

图 13.1-1　各种物质导热系数范围

我国规定：平均温度不高于 350℃时的导热系数不大于 0.12W/(m·℃)的材料称为保温材料。保温材料的特点是它们经常呈多孔状，或者具有纤维结构。

典型例题解析

【例 13.1-2】 下列物质的导热系数，排列正确的是：

A. 铝＜钢铁＜混凝土＜木材　　B. 木材＜钢铁＜铝＜混凝土

C. 木材＜钢铁＜混凝土＜铝　　D. 木材＜混凝土＜钢铁＜铝

解　根据物质导热系数的机理及图 13-1，各种物质种类导热系数一般为 $\lambda_{金}>\lambda_{液}>\lambda_{气}$；金属导热系数一般为 12～418W/(m·℃)，液体导热系数一般为 12～418W/(m·℃)，气体导热系数为 0.006～0.6W/(m·℃)。

可知金属的导热系数要大于混凝土和木材；而钢铁和铝两种金属相比较，铝的导热系数更大一些。选 D。

【例 13.1-3】 如果室内外温差不变，则用以下材料砌成的厚度相同的四种外墙中，热阻最大的是：

A. 干燥的红砖　　B. 潮湿的红砖

C. 干燥的空心红砖　　D. 潮湿且水分冻结的红砖

解　多孔保温材料受湿度的影响很大。因为水分的渗入替代了相当一部分空气，而且更重要的是，当潮湿材料有温度梯度时，水和湿汽顺热流方向迁移(即从高温区向低温区迁移),同时携带很多热量。例如,干砖的导热系数为 0.35W/(m·K);水的导热系数为 0.6W/(m·K);而湿砖的导热系数可达 1.0W/(m·K)。空气为热的不良导体,导热系数 λ 非常小;多孔保温材料受湿度的影响很大,干燥的红砖肯定比潮湿的红砖热阻大,同时空心砖含一定的空气,保温性能得到提高。因此,现在为了建筑节能的需要,很多建筑结构都采用空心砖。选 C。

【例 13.1-4】 当天气由潮湿变为干燥时,建筑材料的热导率可能会出现:

A. 木材、砖及混凝土的热导率均有明显增大

B. 木材的热导率下降,砖及混凝土的热导率不变

C. 木材、砖及混凝土的热导率一般变化不大

D. 木材、砖及混凝土的热导率均会下降

解 像木材、砖、混凝土等多孔介质材料,潮湿情况下细孔中会有大量的液态水出现,而干燥以后细孔中则完全是空气,液态的热导率大于气态的热导率,因此整体的热导率会下降。选 D。

13.1.4 导热微分方程

傅里叶定律确定了温度梯度和热流密度之间的关系,而要确定物体的温度梯度就必须知道物体的温度场,即温度分布。因此,导热分析的首要任务就是确定物体内部的温度场。解决导热问题,应首先建立关于导热问题的导热微分方程,其次求解温度场。

导热微分方程在直角坐标系中的基本表达式为

$$\rho c = \frac{\partial t}{\partial \tau} = \lambda\left(\frac{\partial^2 t}{\partial x^2} + \frac{\partial^2 t}{\partial y^2} + \frac{\partial^2 t}{\partial z^2}\right) + q_v$$

上式亦可写为

$$\frac{\partial t}{\partial \tau} = a\left(\frac{\partial^2 t}{\partial x^2} + \frac{\partial^2 t}{\partial y^2} + \frac{\partial^2 t}{\partial z^2}\right) + \frac{q_v}{\rho c} = a\nabla^2 t + \frac{q_v}{\rho c}$$

其中,∇^2 为拉普拉斯算子;$a = \frac{\lambda}{\rho c}$ 为热扩散系数,单位为 m^2/s。

它表述了导热系统内温度场随时间和空间的变化规律,是导热温度场的场方程。

对于物性参数为常数,稳态温度场,$\frac{\partial t}{\partial \tau} = 0$,则方程变为

$$\frac{\partial^2 t}{\partial x^2} + \frac{\partial^2 t}{\partial y^2} + \frac{\partial^2 t}{\partial z^2} + \frac{q_v}{\lambda} = 0$$

如果无内热源稳态温度场,则方程变为

$$\frac{\partial^2 t}{\partial x^2} + \frac{\partial^2 t}{\partial y^2} + \frac{\partial^2 t}{\partial z^2} = 0$$

对于圆柱坐标系

$$\frac{\partial t}{\partial \tau} = a\left(\frac{\partial^2 t}{\partial r^2} + \frac{1}{r}\frac{\partial t}{\partial r} + \frac{1}{r^2}\frac{\partial^2 t}{\partial \varphi^2}\frac{\partial^2 t}{\partial z^2}\right) + \frac{q_v}{\rho c}$$

对于球坐标系

$$\frac{\partial t}{\partial \tau}=a\left[\frac{1}{r^2}\frac{\partial}{\partial r}\left(r^2\frac{\partial t}{\partial r}\right)+\frac{1}{r^2\sin\theta}\frac{\partial}{\partial \theta}\left(\sin\theta\frac{\partial t}{\partial \theta}\right)+\frac{1}{r^2\sin^2\theta}\frac{\partial^2 t}{\partial \varphi^2}\right]+\frac{q_v}{\rho c}$$

13.1.5 导热过程的单值性条件

单值性条件是导热微分方程式确定唯一解的附加补充说明条件。导热问题的完整数学描述包括导热微分方程式和单值性条件两部分。导热问题的单值性条件通常包括如下四项。

(1)几何条件:表征导热系统的几何形状和大小(属于三维、二维或一维问题)。

(2)物理条件:说明导热系统的物理特性(即物性量和内热源的情况)。

(3)初始条件:又称时间条件,反映导热系统的初始状态。

$$t_{\tau=0}=f(x,y,z)$$

稳态导热过程无时间条件。

(4)边界条件:反映导热系统在界面上的特征,也可理解为系统与外界环境之间的关系。

①第一类边界条件:已知任何时刻物体边界上的温度分布,即:$t|_s=t_w$。

②第二类边界条件:给出导热物体边界面上的热流密度(包括大小、方向)分布及其随时间的变化规律。

$$q=q_w$$

或

$$\left.\frac{\partial t}{\partial n}\right|_w=-\frac{q_w}{\lambda}$$

绝热边界条件:当边界面绝热时,可看作恒热流边界条件的特例。

$$q_w=0$$

③第三类边界条件:给出导热体边界面与周围流体进行对流换热的流体温度 t_f 及表面换热系数 h。

$$-\lambda\left.\frac{dt}{dn}\right|_w=h(t_w-t_f)$$

说明:本节首先介绍了传热学的概貌,为以后分章复习创造条件。本章涉及各种导热问题的基本概念,重点阐述了导热的基本定律,导出了描述物体温度分布规律的导热微分方程,并简述了导热微分方程的单值性条件。要求读者对于导热过程及其数学描写有一个基本了解,复习本章内容应注意以下几个方面:

(1)掌握热量传递三种基本方式和基本过程的物理概念,对于常见的一些实际热量传递问题,能直觉地判明其中有关的基本方式和基本过程。

(2)傅里叶定律是导热的基本定律,要深刻理解它的含义,了解它的应用。

(3)导热系数表征物质的导热能力,它是用于导热分析的一个重要热物性参数。要了解影响导热系数的诸因素,对各种材料导热系数的大小有一个数量级概念。

(4)导热微分方程是用数学形式表达出导热物体内温度场的内在规律性,亦即导热过程的共性;而单值性条件则是说明一个具体导热过程的个性。从内因与外因的关系来说,物体温度场的内在规律性即为导热现象的内因,而边界条件则是体现外因对内因的影响。因此,导热微分方程和单值性条件,提供了导热过程的共性和个性、内因和外因的完整的数学描写。读者对于一个给定的导热过程应能构造出完整的数学模型。

典型例题解析

【例 13.1-5】 求解导热微分方程需要给出单值性条件，下列选项中哪一组不属于单值性条件？

A. 边界上对流换热时空气的相对湿度及压力

B. 几何尺寸及物性系数

C. 物体中的初始温度分布及内热源

D. 边界上温度梯度分布

解 单值性条件包含几何条件、物理条件、边界条件和时间条件。其中，边界条件有三类，第一类边界条件给出任何时刻物体边界上的温度值。第二类边界条件给出任何时刻物体边界上的热流密度值，根据傅里叶定律，第二类边界条件相当于已知任何时刻物体边界面法向的温度梯度值。第三类边界条件即对流换热边界条件，当物体壁面与流体相接触进行对流换热时，给出边界面周围流体温度 t_f 及边界面与流体之间的表面传热系数 h。

所以，选项 B、C、D 都对，而选项 A 不属于单值性条件。选 A。

经典练习

13.1-1 一般而言，液体的导热系数与气体的导热系数值相比是(　　)。

A. 较高的　　B. 较低的

C. 相等的　　D. 接近的

13.1-2 当物性参数为常数且无内热源时的导热微分方程式可写为(　　)。

A. $v^2 t+\frac{qv}{\lambda}=0$　　B. $\frac{\partial t}{\partial \tau}=\alpha\Delta^2 t$

C. $\Delta^2 t=0$　　D. $\frac{\mathrm{d}^2 t}{\mathrm{d}x^2}=0$

13.1-3 下列说法中正确的是(　　)。

A. 空气热导率随温度升高而增大

B. 空气热导率随温度升高而下降

C. 空气热导率随温度升高保持不变

D. 空气热导率随温度升高可能增大也可能减小

13.1-4 温度梯度的方向是指向温度(　　)。

A. 增加方向　　B. 降低方向　　C. 不变方向　　D. 趋于零方向

13.2 稳态导热

考试大纲☞：通过单平壁和复合平壁的导热　通过单圆筒壁和复合圆筒壁的导热　临界热绝缘直径　通过肋壁的导热　肋片效率　通过接触面的导热　二维稳态导热问题

必备基础知识

稳态导热：$\partial t/\partial\tau=0$，微分方程：$\nabla^2 t+\frac{q_v}{\lambda}=0$

13.2.1 通过平壁的导热

1)第一类边界条件

(1)无限大平壁,见图 13.2-1,厚度为 δ,无内热源,材料的导热系数 λ 为常数。平壁两侧表面分别保持均匀稳定的温度 t_{w_1} 和 t_{w_2},$t_{w_1}>t_{w_2}$。温度分布为线性,即

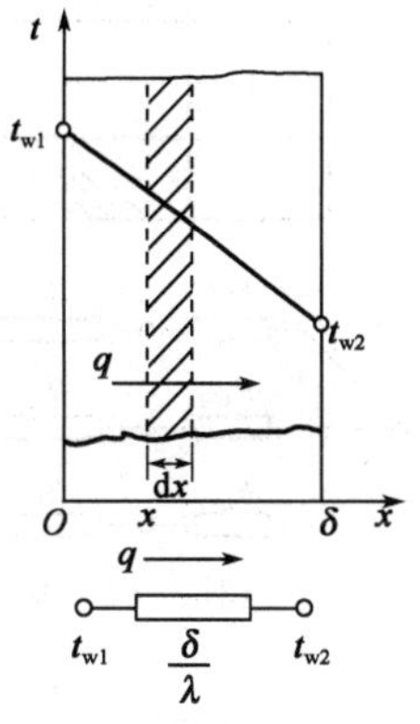

图 13.2-1 单层平壁的导热

$$t=t_{w_1}-\frac{t_{w_1}-t_{w_2}}{\delta}x$$

热流密度为

$$q=-\lambda\frac{\mathrm{d}t}{\mathrm{d}x}=\frac{\lambda}{\delta}(t_{w_1}-t_{w_2})\qquad (\mathrm{W/m^2})$$

(2)对于导热系数随温度线形变化,即 $\lambda=\lambda_0(1+bt)$,温度分布为

$$t+\frac{1}{2}bt^2=\left(t_{w_1}+\frac{1}{2}bt_{w_1}^2\right)+\frac{t_{w_2}-t_{w_1}}{\delta}x\left[1+\frac{1}{2}b(t_{w_1}+t_{w_2})\right]$$

说明:壁内温度不再是直线规律,而是按曲线变化。

$$b>0\Rightarrow\frac{\mathrm{d}^2t}{\mathrm{d}x^2}<0\rightarrow 曲线是向上凸的$$

$$b<0\Rightarrow\frac{\mathrm{d}^2t}{\mathrm{d}x^2}>0\Rightarrow 曲线是向上凹的$$

热流密度为

$$q=\frac{t_{w_1}-t_{w_2}}{\delta}\lambda_0\left[1+\frac{1}{2}b(t_{w_1}+t_{w_2})\right]$$

(3)热阻概念。

类比电学欧姆定律,热流密度为

$$q=\frac{t_{w_1}-t_{w_2}}{\frac{\delta}{\lambda}}=\frac{\Delta t}{R_\lambda}$$

其中,$R_\lambda=\delta/\lambda$ 为单位面积的导热热阻。

通过整个平壁的热流量为

$$\Phi=\frac{t_{w_1}-t_{w_2}}{\frac{\delta}{A\lambda}}=\frac{\Delta t}{R_{\lambda A}}$$

其中,$R_{\lambda A}=\delta/(\lambda A)$是面积为 A 的导热热阻。

(4)多层平壁(复合壁)的导热问题。

对于 n 层多层平壁,热流密度

$$q=\frac{t_{w_1}-t_{w_{n+1}}}{\sum\limits_{i=1}^{n}R_{\lambda,i}}$$

2)第三类边界条件

厚度为 δ 的无限大平壁,无内热源,材料的导热系数 λ 为常数。给出第三类边界条件,即:在 $x=0$ 处,界面外侧流体的温度为 t_{f_1},对流换热表面传热系数为 h_1;在 $x=\delta$ 处,界面外侧流体的温度为 t_{f_2},对流换热表面传热系数为 h_2,热流密度为

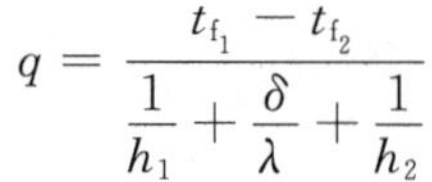

$$q=\frac{t_{f_1}-t_{f_2}}{\frac{1}{h_1}+\frac{\delta}{\lambda}+\frac{1}{h_2}}$$

多层平壁
$$q=\frac{t_{f_1}-t_{f_2}}{\frac{1}{h_1}+\sum_{i=1}^{n}\frac{\delta_i}{\lambda_i}+\frac{1}{h_2}}$$

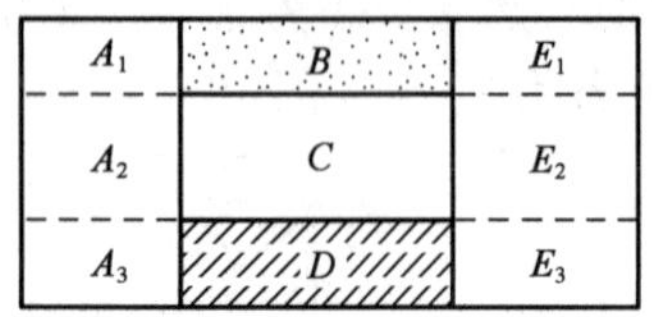

图 13.2-2　复合平壁的导热

3）通过复合平壁的导热

当组成复合平壁的各种不同材料的导热系数相差不大时，可近似当作一维导热问题处理。

复合平壁的导热量

$$\Phi=\frac{\Delta t}{\sum R_\lambda}$$

如图 13.2-2 所示，总导热热阻为

$$\sum R_\lambda=\frac{1}{\frac{1}{R_{\lambda A_1}+R_{\lambda B}+R_{\lambda E_1}}+\frac{1}{R_{\lambda A_2}+R_{\lambda C}+R_{\lambda E_2}}+\frac{1}{R_{\lambda A_3}+R_{\lambda D}+R_{\lambda E_3}}}$$

典型例题解析

【例 13.2-1】　有一砖砌墙壁，厚为 0.25m。已知内外壁面的温度分别为 25℃和 30℃。试计算墙壁内的温度分布和通过的热流密度。

解　由平壁导热的温度分布$\frac{t-t_1}{t_2-t_1}=\frac{x}{\delta}$代入已知数据可以得出墙壁内 $t=25+20x$ 的温度分布表达式。再从附录查得红砖的 $\lambda=0.87\text{W/(m·℃)}$，于是可以计算出通过墙壁的热流密度 $q=\frac{\lambda}{\delta}(t_1-t_2)=-17.4\text{W/m}^2$。

【例 13.2-2】　采用稳态平板法测量材料的导热系数时，依据的是无限大平板的一维稳态导热问题的解。已知测得材料两侧的温度分别是 60℃和 30℃，通过材料的热流量为 1W。若被测材料的厚度为 30mm，面积为 0.02m^2，则该材料的导热系数为：

A. 5.0W/(m·K)　　B. 0.5W/(m·K)

C. 0.05W/(m·K)　　D. 1.0W/(m·K)

解　$\Phi=Aq=A\lambda(t_{w_1}-t_{w_2})/\delta=0.02\lambda(60-30)/0.03$，$\lambda=0.05\text{W/(m·K)}$。选 C。

13.2.2　通过圆筒壁的导热

工程中常用圆管作为换热壁面，如锅筒、传热管、热交换器及其外壳。圆筒受力均匀、强度高、制造方便。

1）第一类边界条件

单层圆筒壁面，见图 13.2-3，内半径为 r_1，外半径为 r_2，长度为 l，长度 l 远大于壁厚，无内热源，圆筒壁材料的导热系数 λ 为常数，圆筒壁内、外表面分别维持均匀稳定的温度 t_{w_1} 和 t_{w_2}，且 $t_{w_1}>t_{w_2}$。

则圆筒壁的温度分布为

$$t = t_{w_1} - \frac{t_{w_1} - t_{w_2}}{\ln \dfrac{r_2}{r_1}} \ln \frac{r}{r_1}$$

或

$$t = t_{w_1} - \frac{t_{w_1} - t_{w_2}}{\ln \dfrac{d_2}{d_1}} \ln \frac{d}{d_1}$$

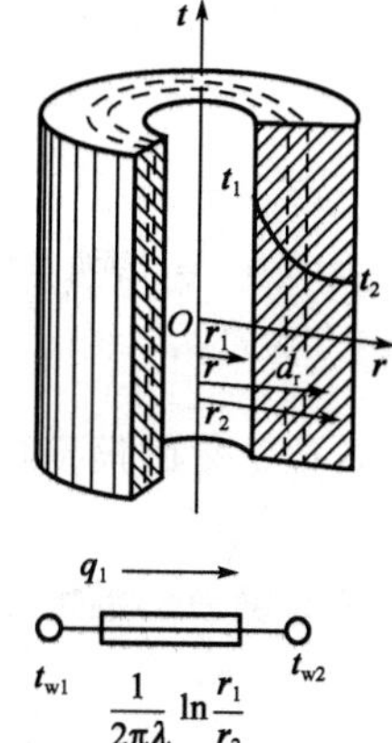

图 13.2-3　复合平壁的导热

由此可见，圆筒壁中的温度分布呈对数曲线，而平壁中的温度分布呈线性分布。

圆筒壁的导热量

$$\Phi = 2\pi\lambda l \cdot \frac{t_{w_1} - t_{w_2}}{\ln \dfrac{r_2}{r_1}}$$

可见，Φ 与 r 无关，通过整个圆筒壁面的热流量不随半径的变化而变化，在不同的 r 处，通过的热流量是相等的。

将 Φ 写成热阻形式，则

$$\Phi = \frac{t_{w_1} - t_{w_2}}{\dfrac{1}{2\pi\lambda l} \ln \dfrac{r_2}{r_1}} \qquad (\text{W})$$

其中，$\dfrac{1}{2\pi\lambda l} \ln \dfrac{r_2}{r_1}$ 是长度为 l 的圆筒壁的导热热阻(K/W)。

通过每米长圆筒壁的热流量为

$$q_l = \frac{\Phi}{l} = \frac{t_{w_1} - t_{w_2}}{\dfrac{1}{2\pi\lambda} \ln \dfrac{r_2}{r_1}} \qquad (\text{W/m})$$

单位长度圆筒壁的导热热阻为

$$R_{\lambda l} = \frac{1}{2\pi\lambda} \ln \frac{r_2}{r_1} \qquad (\text{m} \cdot \text{K/W})$$

多层圆筒壁的单位长度导热量为

$$q_l = \frac{t_{w_1} - t_{w,n+1}}{\sum\limits_{i=1}^{n} R_{\lambda l,i}} = \frac{t_{w_1} - t_{w,n+1}}{\sum\limits_{i=1}^{n} \dfrac{1}{2\pi\lambda_i} \ln \dfrac{d_{i+1}}{d_i}}$$

注意：求各层直径时，应是 $d+2\delta$。对于圆管外，用几层材料进行保温时，应将导热系数少的材料设置在内侧。对平壁有这种要求吗？

2)第三类边界条件

单位长度圆筒壁的导热量为：

$$q_l = \frac{t_{f_1} - t_{f_2}}{\dfrac{1}{h_1 \cdot 2\pi r_1} + \dfrac{1}{2\pi\lambda} \ln \dfrac{r_2}{r_1} + \dfrac{1}{h_2 \cdot 2\pi r_2}} \qquad (\text{W/m})$$

或

$$q_l = \frac{t_{f_1} - t_{f_2}}{\frac{1}{h_1 \cdot \pi d_1} + \frac{1}{2\pi\lambda}\ln\frac{d_2}{d_1} + \frac{1}{h_2 \cdot \pi d_2}} \quad (\text{W/m})$$

也可表示为 $q_l = k_l \cdot (t_{f_1} - t_{f_2})$

式中，k_l 为传热系数，表示冷、热流体之间温差为1℃时，单位时间通过单位长度圆筒壁的传热量[W/(m·K)]。

单位长度圆筒壁传热热阻 $R_l = \frac{1}{k_l} = \frac{1}{h_1 \cdot \pi d_1} + \frac{1}{2\pi\lambda} \cdot \ln\frac{d_2}{d_1} + \frac{1}{h_2 \cdot \pi d_2} \quad (\text{m} \cdot \text{K/W})$

圆筒壁中的温度分布 $t = t_{w_1} - \frac{t_{w_1} - t_{w_2}}{\ln\frac{r_2}{r_1}}\ln\frac{r}{r_1}$

对多层圆筒壁，热流体通过圆筒壁传给冷流体的热流量为：

$$q_l = \frac{t_{f_1} - t_{f_2}}{\frac{1}{h_1 \cdot \pi d_1} + \sum_{i=1}^{n}\frac{1}{2\pi\lambda_i}\ln\frac{d_{i+1}}{d_i} + \frac{1}{h_2 \cdot \pi d_{i+1}}}$$

典型例题解析

【例 13.2-3】 在一条蒸汽管道外敷设厚度相同的两层保温材料，其中材料A的导热系数小于材料B的导热系数。若不计导热系数随温度的变化，仅从减小传热量的角度考虑，哪种材料应敷在内层？

A. 材料A　　B. 材料B　　C. 无所谓　　D. 不确定

解 对于圆筒形保温材料而言，内侧的温度变化率比较大，故将导热系数小的保温材料放于内侧，将充分发挥保温材料的保温作用。选A。

13.2.3 临界热绝缘直径

工程上，为减少管道的散热损失，常在管道外侧覆盖热绝缘层或称隔热保温层。

覆盖热绝缘层不是在任何情况下都能减少热损失，应正确选择热绝缘材料，分析热流体通过管壁和热绝缘层传给冷流体传热过程的热阻，即

$$R_{总,l} = \frac{1}{\alpha_1 \pi d_1} + \frac{1}{2\pi\lambda_1}\ln\frac{d_2}{d_1} + \frac{1}{2\pi\lambda_1}\ln\frac{d_x}{d_2} + \frac{1}{\alpha_2 \pi d_x}$$

$$\frac{dR_{总,l}}{dd_x} = \frac{1}{\pi d_x}\left(\frac{1}{2\lambda_2} - \frac{1}{\alpha_2 d_x}\right) = 0$$

得临界热绝缘直径 $d_x = d_{cr} = \frac{2\lambda_2}{\alpha_2}$

d_c 只取决于 λ_{ins} 和 h_2，d_c 不一定大于 d_2。

从图13.2-4中可知：

(1)当 $d_2 < d_c$ 时，如果管道保温后的外径 d_x 在 $d_2 \sim d_3$ 之间，这时管道的传热量 q_l 反而比没有保温层时更大，直到 $d_x > d_3$ 时，才起到减少热损失的作用。

(2)当 $d_2 > d_c$ 时，R_l 及 q_l 均是 d_x 的单调函数，用保温层肯定能减少热损失。

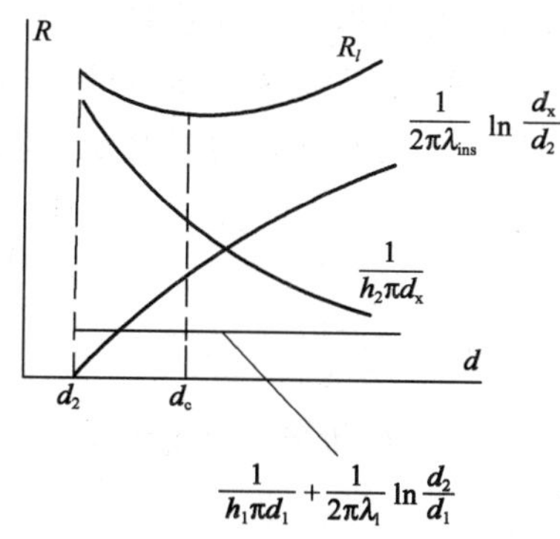

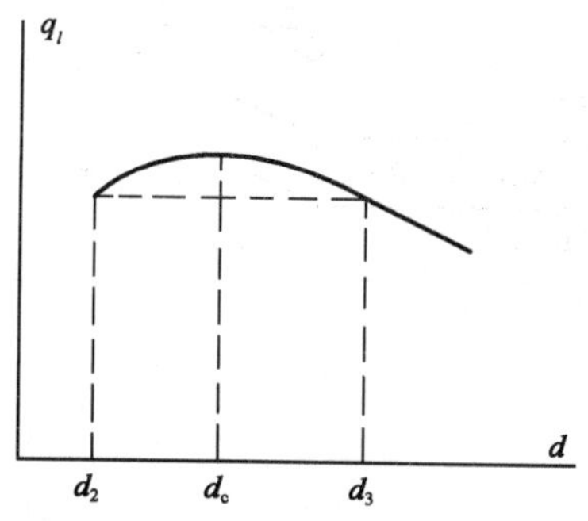

图 13.2-4　临界热绝缘直径

典型例题解析

【例 13.2-4】 一条架设在空气中的电缆外面包敷有绝缘层，因通电而发热。在稳态条件下，若剥掉电缆的绝缘层而保持其他条件不变，则电缆的温度会：

A. 升高　　B. 降低　　C. 不变　　D. 不确定

解　剥掉电缆的绝缘层，电缆表面温度比空气的温度高，有温差就有传热，电缆就会向空气散热，温度会降低。选 B。

【例 13.2-5】 在外径为 133mm 的蒸汽管道外敷设保温层，管道内是温度为 300℃饱和水蒸气，按规定，保温材料的外层温度不得超过 50℃。若保温材料的导热系数为 0.05W/(m·℃)，为把管道热损失控制在 150W/m 以下，保温层的厚度至少应为：

A. 92mm　　B. 46mm　　C. 23mm　　D. 184mm

解　由 $q_l=\dfrac{t_{w_1}-t_{w_2}}{\dfrac{1}{2\pi\lambda}\ln\dfrac{r_2+\delta}{r_1}}\leqslant 150$，可得 $\delta\geqslant 45.76$mm。选 B。

【例 13.2-6】 外径为 50mm 和内径为 40mm 的过热高压高温蒸汽管道在保温过程中，如果保温材料热导率为 0.05W/(m·K)，外部表面总散热系数为 5W/(m²·K)，此时：

A. 可以采用该保温材料　　B. 降低外部表面总散热系数

C. 换选热导率较低的保温材料　　D. 减小蒸汽管道外径

解　临界热绝缘直径 $d_c=\dfrac{2\lambda_{ins}}{h}=\dfrac{2\times 0.05}{5}=0.02\text{m}<40\text{mm}$，因此本保温材料在外保温可以增加保温效果。本题考查临界热绝缘直径的概念，选项 B 会使临界热绝缘直径变大，选项 C 会使临界热绝缘直径变小但无太大意义，选项 D 与本题考查内容基本无关，是干扰项。选 A。

13.2.4 通过肋壁的导热

在工业和日常生活中广泛采用肋片，目的有两个，一是当肋片加在换热系数较小(热阻较大)的一侧时，是为了强化传热；二是有时肋片加在换热系数较大的冷流体侧，此时，是为了降低壁温。

1)通过等截面直肋的导热

设肋片的高度为 l，宽度为 L，厚度为 δ。肋片的横截面积为 $A_L=L\times\delta$，肋片的横截面的周边长度为 $U=2(L+\delta)$。肋基的温度 t_0 为常量，金属肋片的导热系数为 λ，周围流体的温度

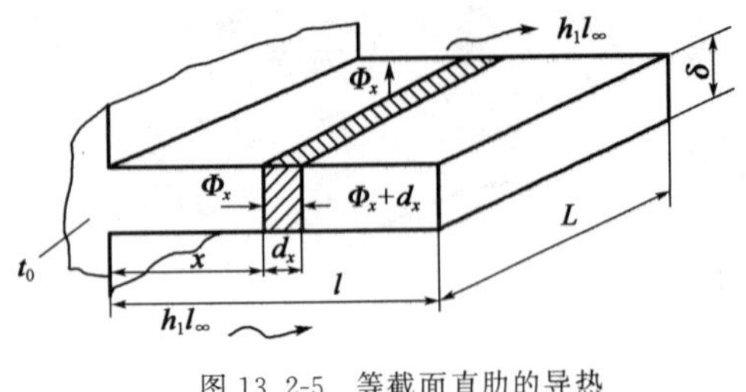

图 13.2-5 等截面直肋的导热

为 t_f，肋片与流体的对流换热表面传热系数为 h，把肋片的表面散热当作负的内热源。如图 13.2-5 所示，等截面直肋温度分布为：

$$\theta=\theta_0\frac{e^{m(l-x)}+e^{-m(l-x)}}{e^{ml}+e^{-ml}}=\theta_0\frac{\mathrm{ch}[m(l-x)]}{\mathrm{ch}(ml)}$$

其中，$m=\sqrt{\frac{hU}{\lambda A_L}}$。

令 $x=l$，得肋端的过余温度为

$$\theta|_{x=l}=\frac{\theta_0}{\mathrm{ch}(ml)}$$

据能量守恒定律知，肋片散入外界的全部热流量都必须通过 $x=0$ 处的肋基截面。据傅里叶定律得知通过肋片散入外界的热流量为

$$\Phi=-\lambda A_L\frac{\mathrm{d}\theta}{\mathrm{d}x}\bigg|_{x=0}$$

可得：

$$\Phi=-\lambda A_L[-m\theta_0\mathrm{th}(ml)]=\lambda mA_L\theta_0\mathrm{th}(ml)=\sqrt{hU\lambda A_L}\theta_0\mathrm{th}(ml)\qquad(\mathrm{W})$$

几点说明：

(1)对于一般工程计算，尤其高而薄的肋片，可以获得较精确的结果。若必须考虑肋端对流散热时，可采用一种简便的方法：即用假象高度 $l'=l+\frac{\delta}{2}$ 代替实际高度 l。

(2)当 $\mathrm{Bi}=h\delta/\lambda\leqslant 0.05$ 时，用假象高度 $l'=l+\frac{\delta}{2}$ 代替实际高度 l 引起的误差不超过 1%。对于短而厚的肋片，温度场是二维的，上述算式不适用。

(3)敷设肋片不一定就能强化传热，只有满足一定的条件才能增加散热量，设计肋片时要注意这一点。

2)肋片效率

肋片效率定义为，肋片的实际散热量与其整个肋片都处于肋基温度下的最大可能的散热量之比，记为 η_f。

$$\eta_f=\frac{\Phi}{\Phi_0}=\frac{hUl(t_m-t_f)}{hUl(t_0-t_f)}=\frac{\theta_m}{\theta_0}$$

影响肋片效率的因素有：肋片的几何形状和尺寸、肋片材料的导热系数、肋片表面与周围介质的表面传热系数。

肋片效率的计算式为

$$\eta_f=\frac{\mathrm{th}(ml)}{ml}$$

η_f 随 ml 的变化情况：

(1)当 $ml=2.7$ 时，$\mathrm{th}(ml)>0.99$，当 $ml>2.7$ 时，$\mathrm{th}(ml)$ 的值变化不大，趋于 1。这时 η_f 可以认为与 ml 成反比关系，ml 增加，η_f 减小。

(2)采用变截面的肋片，可提高肋片效率。

(3)一般认为，$\eta_f>80\%$ 的肋片经济适用。

典型例题解析

【例 13.2-7】 壁面添加肋片散热过程中，肋的高度未达到一定高度时，随着肋高度增加，散热量也增大。当肋高度超过某数值时，随着肋片高度增加，会出现：

A. 肋片平均温度趋于饱和，效率趋于定值

B. 肋片上及根部过余温度 θ 下降，效率下降

C. 稳态过程散热量保持不变

D. 肋效率 η_f 下降

解 当肋高度超过某数值时，散热量的增加逐渐减少，最后趋向一个定值，肋片效率随着高度的增加下降。平均温度逐渐减小，肋片效率逐渐下降，选项 A 错误。

根部过余温度不变，选项 B 错误。

$\varphi=\sqrt{hU\lambda A_L}\theta_0 \mathrm{th}(mL)$ 散热量不断增加，选项 C 错误。

选 D。

13.2.5 通过接触面的导热

两个固体表面直接接触时，见图 13.2-6，即使宏观上看起来是非常平整的表面，它们的表面也仍是粗糙的，是点接触而非面接触。这样就给导热带来额外的热阻——接触热阻。

其表示式为：

$$R_C=\frac{t_{2A}-t_{2B}}{\Phi}=\frac{\Delta t_C}{\Phi}$$

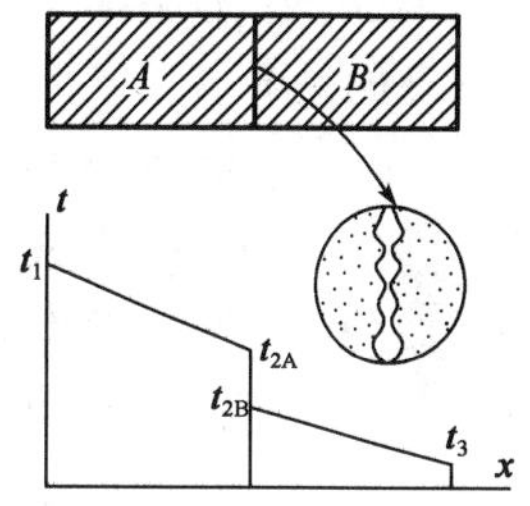

图 13.2-6 接触面热阻

(1)产生并影响接触热阻的主要因素：

①接触表面的粗糙度；

②表面接触时施加压力的大小；

③两接触面之间形成的空隙中气体的热物性。

(2)减小接触热阻的措施：

①减小接触表面的粗糙度；

②增加接触压力；

③在两接触表面之间加一层具有高导热系数和高延展性的材料；

④在接触面之间涂以具有良好导热性的油脂。

13.2.6 二维稳态导热问题

为了便于工程设计计算，对于有些二维、三维稳态导热问题，针对已知两个恒定温度边界之间的导热热流量，采用一种简便计算公式：引入形状因子 S，表征物体几何形状和尺寸的因素的综合参数。对导热系数为常数的情形，导热的热流量可按下式计算

$$\Phi=S\lambda(t_1-t_2)$$

说明：导热问题的求解一般可归结为对导热微分方程式的求解。复习本节要注意理解和掌握以下几点即可达到较好的复习效果：①一维稳态导热是工程上常见的，应掌握处理这类问题的方法，能由物理模型建立起相应的数学模型，进而求得温度分布和热流密度。②深入理解第三类边界条件下的导热，即传热过程的概念，弄清楚内热源对于导热的影响。③理解热阻的

意义，熟悉平壁、圆筒壁和球壁一维稳态导热的热阻表达式，对无内热源的大平壁、长圆筒壁和球壁的导热及传热过程，进行分析计算。④理解肋片效率的概念及其影响因素。掌握应用肋片效率曲线计算肋片的散热量。⑤理解接触热阻概念及其影响因素，了解消除接触热阻的技术途径。⑥了解内热源对于大平壁、长圆筒壁和空心球壁稳态导热的影响，并能进行传热分析计算。

经典练习

13.2-1　圆柱壁面双层保温材料敷设过程中，为了减少保温材料用量或减少散热量，应采取的措施为(　　)。

A. 导热率较大的材料在内层　　B. 导热率较小的材料在内层

C. 根据外部散热条件确定　　D. 材料的不同布置对散热量影响不明显

13.2-2　在双层平壁无内热源常物性一维稳态导热计算过程中，如果已知平壁的热导率分别是 δ_1、λ_1、δ_2、λ_2，如果双层壁内，外侧温度分别为 t_1 和 t_2，则计算双层壁交界面上温度 t_1 错误的关系式是(　　)。

A. $\dfrac{t_1-t_{in}}{\dfrac{\delta_1}{\lambda_1}}=\dfrac{t_{in}-t_2}{\dfrac{\delta_2}{\lambda_2}}$　　B. $\dfrac{t_1-t_2}{\dfrac{\delta_1}{\lambda_1}+\dfrac{\delta_2}{\lambda_2}}=\dfrac{t_1-t_{in}}{\dfrac{\delta_1}{\lambda_1}}$

C. $\dfrac{t_1-t_2}{\dfrac{\delta_1}{\lambda_1}+\dfrac{\delta_2}{\lambda_2}}=\dfrac{t_{in}-t_2}{\dfrac{\delta_2}{\lambda_2}}$　　D. $\dfrac{t_1-t_{in}}{\dfrac{\delta_2}{\lambda_2}}=\dfrac{t_{in}-t_2}{\dfrac{\delta_2}{\lambda_1}}$

13.2-3　单层圆柱体内径一维径向稳态导热过程中无内热源，物性参数为常数，则下列说法正确的是(　　)。

A. Φ 导热量为常数　　B. Φ 为半径的函数

C. q_1(热流量)为常数　　D. q_1只是 l 的函数

13.2-4　对于无限大平壁的一维稳态导热，下列陈述中错误的是(　　)。

A. 平壁内任何平行于壁面的平面都是等温面

B. 在平壁中任何两个等温面之间温度都是线性变化的

C. 任何位置上的热流密度矢量垂直于等温面

D. 温度梯度的方向与热流密度的方向相反

13.3　非稳态导热

考试大纲☞：非稳态导热过程的特点　对流换热边界条件下非稳态导热　诺模图　集总参数法　常热流通量边界条件下非稳态导热

必备基础知识

物体的温度随时间而变化的导热过程称非稳态导热。$\dfrac{\partial t}{\partial \tau}\neq 0$，任何非稳态导热过程必然伴随着加热或冷却过程。

13.3.1　非稳态导热过程的特点

非稳态导热过程可分为两大类型：

1）瞬态非稳态导热过程

依据温度变化的特点，可将加热或冷却过程分为三个阶段：①不规则情况阶段；②正常情况阶段；③建立新的稳态阶段。

2）周期性的非稳态导热过程

周期性的非稳态导热过程，在物体内部将形成温度波和热流波。一方面物体内部各处的温度按一定的波幅随时间周期性波动；另一方面，同一时刻物体内温度分布也是周期性波动的。

13.3.2 对流换热边界条件下无限大平壁的加热与冷却过程非稳态导热

1）分析解解法

如图 13.3-1 所示，无限大平壁，厚度 2δ，平壁材料的导热系数 λ 和热扩散率 a 为常数，初始时刻平壁各处温度均匀一致，为 t_0。初始瞬间将平壁放于温度为 t_f 的流体中，且 $t_0>t_f$，物体被冷却，流体温度 t_f 保持不变，平壁两侧表面与流体之间的表面传热系数 h 为常数。平壁两面对称冷却，所以平壁中的温度分布是对称的，对称面是平壁的中心截面。因此只要研究厚度为 δ 的半块平壁的情况就行了。

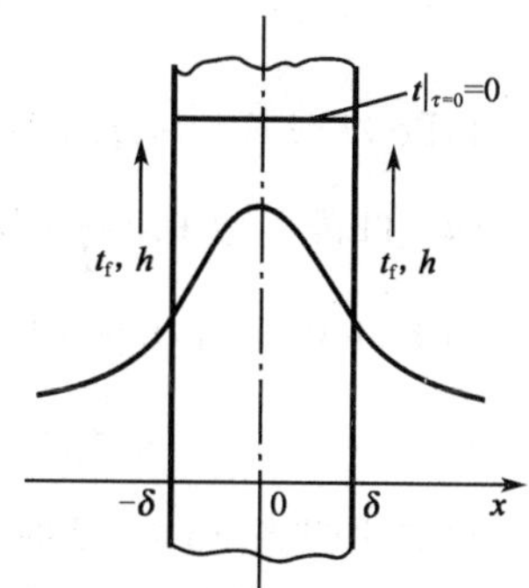

图 13.3-1 瞬态导热

微分方程：$\frac{\partial t}{\partial \tau}=\frac{1}{\alpha}\frac{\partial^2 t}{\partial x^2}$，初始条件：$\tau=0, t=t_0$

将中心边界条件为绝热边界条件，引入过余温度：

$$\theta(x,\tau)=t(x,\tau)-t_f$$

傅立叶准则数：$\mathrm{Fo}=\frac{\alpha\tau}{L^2}$，毕渥准则数：$\mathrm{Bi}=\frac{hL}{\lambda}$

进行求解得：

$$\frac{\theta(x,\tau)}{\theta_0}=\sum_{x=1}^{\infty}\frac{2\sin\beta_x}{\beta_x+\sin\beta_x\cos\beta_x}\cos\left(\beta_x\frac{x}{\delta}\right)\exp\left(-\beta_x^2\frac{\alpha\tau}{\delta^2}\right)$$

2）图解法

将分析解绘制的计算线即为诺模图。因此，也可通过查诺模图得到其温度分布。

3）毕渥准则数 Bi

毕渥准则数说明物体内部导热热阻与表面复合换热热阻的相对大小，其大小将影响温度场的分布。

$$\mathrm{Bi}=\frac{L/\lambda}{1/h}=\frac{hL}{\lambda}$$

对于对流边界条件下瞬态非稳态导热而言：

（1）当 Bi→0 时，物体表面对流换热热阻 $1/h$ 远大于物体内的导热热阻 L/λ，物体内部任何时刻的温度几乎是均匀的，这也就说物体的温度场仅仅是时间的函数，而与空间坐标无关。我们称这样的非稳态导热系统为集总热容（一个等温系统或物体）。

（2）当 Bi→∞时，物体表面对流换热热阻 $1/h$ 远小于物体内的导热热阻 L/λ，使得任何时刻物体表面温度几乎与环境流体温度相同，边界条件就变成了第一类边界条件，即给定物体边界上的温度。

（3）当 $0<\mathrm{Bi}<\infty$时，物体表面对流换热热阻 $1/h$ 与物体内的导热热阻 L/λ 相当，是正常的第三类边界条件。

以上三种情况温度分布特征如图 13.3-2 所示。

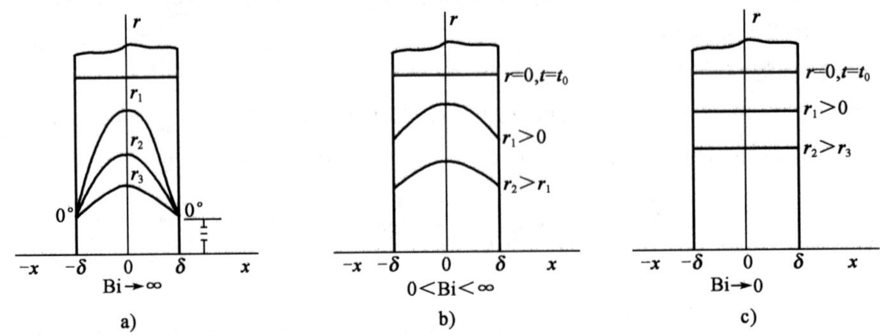

图 13.3-2 Bi 准则对无限大平壁温度分布的影响

4)Fo 准则数对温度分布的影响

傅立叶准则数 $Fo=\frac{\alpha\tau}{L^2}$为非稳态导热过程的无因次时间。

当 Fo>0.2(或 0.55 时),只取级数中的第一项对于工程计算已足够准确,即

$$\frac{\theta(x,\tau)}{\theta_0}=\frac{2\sin\beta_1}{\beta_1+\sin\beta_1\cos\beta_1}\cos\left(\beta_1\frac{x}{\delta}\right)\exp(-\beta_1^2 Fo)$$

该式说明当 Fo>0.2 时,物体在给定的边界条件下,物体中任何给定地点过余温度的对数值将随时间按线性规律变化,此即瞬态非稳态温度变化的正常情况阶段。

如图 13.3-3 所示,图中 $\tau>\tau^*$ 范围即为瞬态非稳态温度变化的正常情况阶段,其特征是各时刻 $\ln\theta$-τ 斜率相等。

5)集总参数法

当 Bi<0.1,忽略物体内部导热热阻,认为物体温度均匀一致的分析方法。

如图 13.3-4 所示,V、A、ρ 分别为导热物体的体积、表面积和密度。

依据从 τ 时刻开始,在 $d\tau$ 时间内的能量守恒式为

$$-\rho Vc\,dt=hA(t-t_f)\,d\tau$$

引入过余温度 $\theta=t-t_f$,积分得物体的温度场为

$$\theta=\theta_0\exp\left(-\frac{hA}{\rho cV}\tau\right)$$

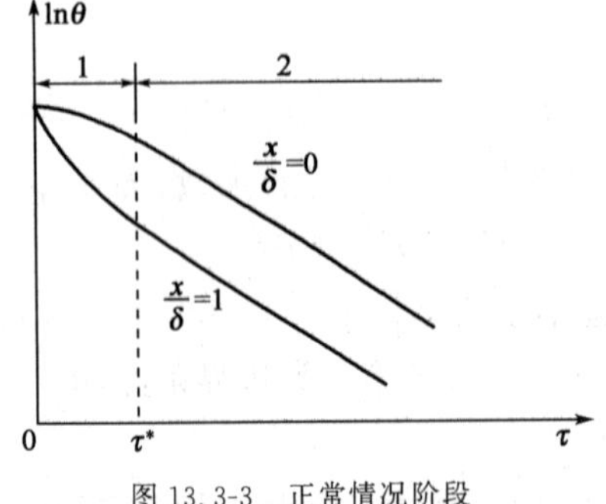

图 13.3-3 正常情况阶段

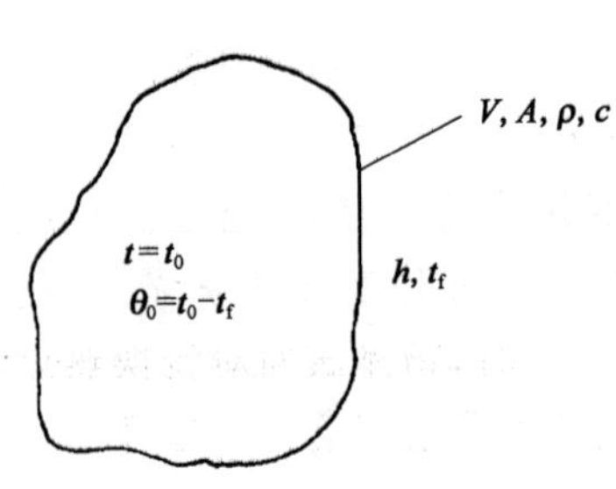

图 13.3-4 集总参数法分析

典型例题解析

【例 13.3-1】 一小铜球，直径 12mm，导热系数 26W/(m·K)，密度为 8 600kg/m³，比热容 343，对流传热系数 48W/(m²·K)，初温度为 15℃，放入 75℃ 的热空气中，小球温度到 70℃ 需要的时间为：

A. 915s B. 305s C. 102s D. 50s

解 Bi=48×0.006÷26=0.011<0.1，由集总参数法

$$\frac{\theta}{\theta_0}=\frac{t-t_f}{t_0-t_f}=\frac{70-75}{15-75}=0.233 \qquad \frac{\theta}{\theta_0}=e^{-\frac{hA}{\rho Vc}\tau}$$

$$\tau=-\frac{\rho cV}{hA}\ln\frac{\theta}{\theta_0}=-\frac{8\,600\times 343\times 0.006}{48\times 3}\times \ln 0.0833=305\text{s}$$

选 B。

【例 13.3-2】 在非稳态导热过程中，根据温度的变化特性可以分为三个不同的阶段，下列说法中不正确的是：

A. 在 0.2<Fo<∞的时间区域内，过余温度随时间线性变化

B. Fo<0.2 的时间区域内，温度变化受初始条件影响最大

C. 最初的瞬态过程是无规则的，无法用非稳态导热微分方程描述

D. 如果变化过程中物体的 Bi 数很小，则可以将物体温度当作空间分布均匀计算

解 非稳态的三个阶段中，初始阶段和正规状态阶段是以 Fo=0.2 为界限。小于 0.2 的为初始阶段，这个阶段内受初始条件影响较大，而且各个部分的变化规律不相同，因此选项 B 正确。在正规状态阶段，过余温度的对数值随时间按线性规律变化，因此选项 A 不正确。当 Bi 较小时，意味着物体的导热热阻接近为零，因此物体内的温度趋近于一致，这也是集总参数法的解题思想，所以选项 D 正确。非稳态的导热微分方程在描述非稳态问题时并未有条件限制，即便是最初阶段也是可以描述的，所以选项 C 错误。本题出现两个错误选项，编者认为标准答案应该是选项 C，这个选项的错误较为明显，选项 A 也不对，但有可能是出题人的疏漏造成的。选 C。

13.3.3 常热流通量边界条件下非稳态导热

半无限大物体在常热流通量作用下的瞬态非稳态导热。数学描述为

$$\frac{\partial\theta}{\partial\tau}=\frac{1}{a}\frac{\partial^2\theta}{\partial x^2} \qquad (\theta=t-t_0)$$

$\tau=0, \theta=0$

$x=0, -\lambda\left.\frac{\partial\theta}{\partial x}\right|_{x=0}=q_w=\cos s$

$x\to\infty, \theta=0$

其分析解：$\theta(x,\tau)=-\frac{2q_w}{\lambda}\sqrt{a\tau}\times i\text{erfc}\left(\frac{x}{2\sqrt{\alpha\tau}}\right)$

其中 $i\text{erfc}(u)=\int_0^\infty \text{erfc}(u)\text{d}u=\frac{1}{\sqrt{\pi}}\exp(-u^2)-u\text{erfc}(u)$ 称为高斯误差补函数的一次积分。

热流渗透厚度定义为$\delta(\tau)=\sqrt{12a\tau}=3.46\sqrt{a\tau}$，它是随时间而变化的，它反映在所考虑的时间范围内，界面上热作用的影响所波及的厚度。

说明：非稳态导热问题可在大量工程应用中遇到。对于工程技术人员来说，重要之点在于懂得处理这类问题的方法，而其第一步就是计算毕渥准则数 Bi。如果 Bi<0.1，则可采用集总参数法求解；若 Bi>0.1，则应采用其他方法。在复习过程中尽量按照以下顺序掌握各个知识点：①理解非稳导热过程的特点和热扩散率 a 的物理意义及其对非稳态导热过程的影响。②了解第三类边界条件下一维非稳态导热问题(无内热源)分析解法的方法与步骤，理解由分析解得出的一些物理概念和结论。③了解集总热容系统的概念，理解集总热容系统非稳态导热过程的特点，能应用集总参数法求解处于恒定环境温度中物体的非稳态导热问题。

经典练习

13.3-1　无限大平壁，厚度 2δ，物体被冷却，流体温度 t_f 保持不变，下列(　　)是 Bi→0 时，平壁的温度分布。

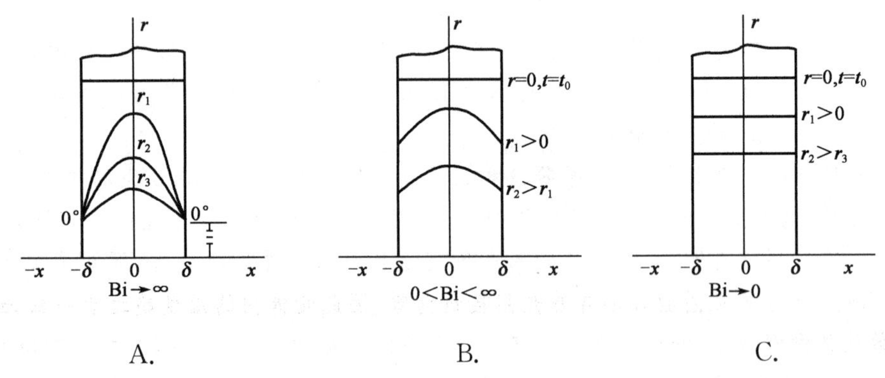

A.　　　　B.　　　　C.

13.3-2　大平板采用集总参数法的判别条件是(　　)。

A. Bi>0.1　　B. Bi=1　　C. Bi<0.1　　D. Bi=0.1

13.3-3　初温为 30℃ 的大铜板，厚度为 120mm，被置于 400℃ 的炉中加热。已知铜板两侧与周围环境间的表面传热系数为 125W/(m²·K)，铜板的 ρ=8 440kg/m³，C_p=377J/(kg·K)，λ=110W/(m·K)，估算 100s 后铜板的温度为(　　)℃。

A. 53　　B. 100　　C. 120　　D. 130

13.4　导热问题数值解

考试大纲☞：有限差分法原理　稳态导热问题的数值计算　节点方程建立　节点方程式求解　非稳态导热问题的数值计算　显式差分格式及其稳定性　隐式差分格式

必备基础知识

随着计算机的普及应用和性能的不断改善，对物理问题进行离散求解的数值方法发展得十分迅速，并得到广泛应用，因而成为传热学的一个重要分支。

13.4.1 有限差分法原理

有限差分法是求得偏微分方程数值解的最古老的方法。对简单的几何形状的流动与传热问题也是一种最容易实施的方法。其基本方法是，将求解区域用网格的交点(节点)所组成的点的集合来代替。在每个节点上，描写所研究的流动与传热问题的偏微分方程中的每一个导数项，用相应的差分表达式来代替，从而在每个节点上形成一个代数方程。这些离散点上被求物理量值的集合称为该物理量的数值解。

将求解区域分割成有限数目的网格单元，利用有限差商代替微商(微分)，有限差商即为有限差分。

如图 13.4-1 所示，二维稳态导热问题的区域离散。

13.4.2 稳态导热问题的数值计算

1)内部节点离散方程的建立

(1)泰勒级数展开法

如图 13.4-2 所示，以节点(m,n)处的二阶偏导数为例。

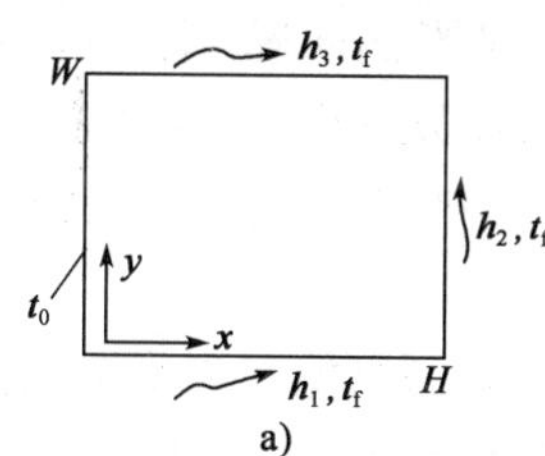

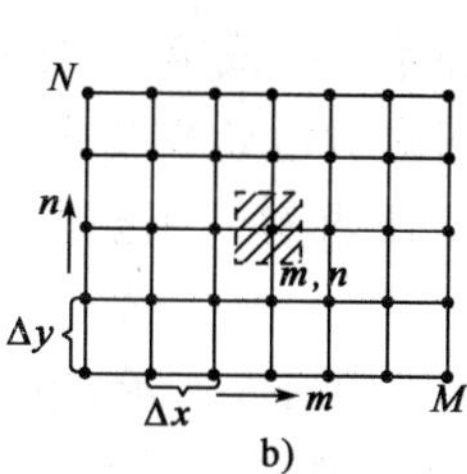

图 13.4-1 二维物体中的网格

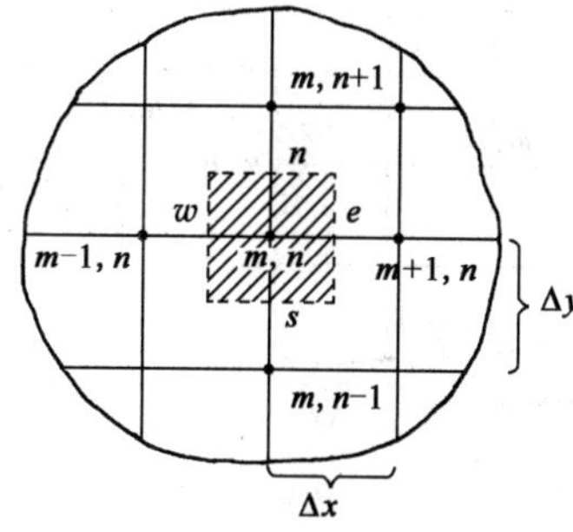

图 13.4-2 内节点离散方程的建立

$$\frac{\partial^2 t}{\partial x^2}\Big|_{m,n} = \frac{t_{m+1,n} - 2t_{m,n} + t_{m-1,n}}{\Delta x^2} + 0(\Delta x^2)$$

其中，$0(\Delta x^2)$称截断误差，误差量级为 Δx^2，即表示未明确写出的级数余项中 Δx 的最低阶数为 2。在数值计算时，用三个相邻节点上的值近似表示二阶导数的表达式即可，则相应的略去 $0(\Delta x^2)$。于是得

$$\frac{\partial^2 t}{\partial x^2}\Big|_{m,n} = \frac{t_{m+1,n} - 2t_{m,n} + t_{m-1,n}}{\Delta x^2}$$

同理

$$\frac{\partial^2 t}{\partial y^2}\Big|_{m,n} = \frac{t_{m,n+1} - 2t_{m,n} + t_{m,n-1}}{\Delta y^2}$$

根据导热问题的控制方程(导热微分方程) $\frac{\partial^2 t}{\partial x^2} + \frac{\partial^2 t}{\partial y^2} = 0$，得

$$\frac{t_{m+1,n} - 2t_{m,n} + t_{m-1,n}}{\Delta x^2} + \frac{t_{m,n+1} - 2t_{m,n} + t_{m,n-1}}{\Delta y^2} = 0$$

若 $\Delta x = \Delta y$，则有

$$t_{m,n} = \frac{1}{4}(t_{m+1,n} + t_{m-1,n} + t_{m,n+1} + t_{m,n-1})$$

(2)平衡法

其本质是傅里叶导热定律和能量守恒定律的体现。对每个元体，可用傅里叶导热定律写出其能量守恒的表达式。如图 13.4-2 所示，元体在垂直纸面方向取单位长度，通过元体界面(w,e,n,s)所传导的热流量可以对有关的两个节点根据傅里叶定律写出

$$\Phi_{\mathrm{w}}=\lambda\Delta y\frac{t_{m-1},n-t_{m,n}}{\Delta x},\Phi_{\mathrm{e}}=\lambda\Delta y\frac{t_{m+1},n-t_{m,n}}{\Delta x}$$

$$\Phi_{\mathrm{n}}=\lambda\Delta x\frac{t_{m,n+1}-t_{m,n}}{\Delta y},\Phi_{\mathrm{s}}=\lambda\Delta x\frac{t_{m,n-1}-t_{m,n}}{\Delta y}$$

对元体(m,n)，根据能量守恒定律可知

$$\Phi_{\mathrm{w}}+\Phi_{\mathrm{e}}+\Phi_{\mathrm{n}}+\Phi_{\mathrm{s}}=0$$

若 $\Delta x=\Delta y$，则有

$$t_{m,n}=\frac{1}{4}(t_{m+1,n}+t_{m-1,n}+t_{m,n+1}+t_{m,n-1})$$

与泰勒级数展开法结果一致。

2)边界节点离散方程的建立

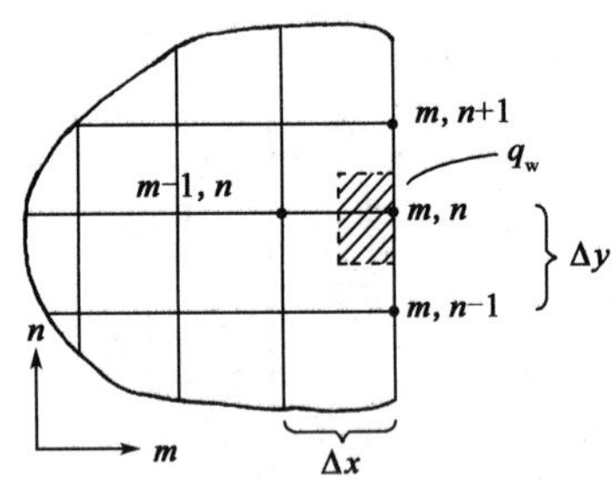

图 13.4-3 平直边界上的节点

(1)对于第一类边界条件的导热问题，边界节点温度是已知的。

(2)第二类或第三类边界条件的导热问题，不知边界温度，因而应对边界节点补充相应的代数方程，才能使方程组封闭，以便求解。用热平衡法导出平直边界点上的离散方程。

如图 13.4-3 所示，边界节点(m,n)只能代表半个元体，若边界上有向该元体传递的热流密度为 q_{w}，有内热源，据能量守恒定律对该元体有

$$\lambda\frac{t_{m-1,n}-t_{m,n}}{\Delta x}\Delta y+\lambda\frac{t_{m,n+1}-t_{m,n}}{\Delta y}\cdot\frac{\Delta x}{2}+\lambda\frac{t_{m,n-1}-t_{m,n}}{\Delta y}\cdot\frac{\Delta x}{2}+\frac{\Delta x\Delta y}{2}\Phi_{m,n}+\Delta yq_{\mathrm{w}}=0$$

若 $\Delta x=\Delta y$ 时，则

$$t_{m,n}=\frac{1}{4}\left(2t_{m-1,n}+t_{m,n+1}+t_{m,n-1}+\frac{\Delta x^2\Phi_{m,n}}{\lambda}+\frac{2\Delta xq_{\mathrm{w}}}{\lambda}\right)$$

讨论有关 q_{w} 的三种情况：

①若是绝热边界，则 $q_{\mathrm{w}}=0$，即令上式 $q_{\mathrm{w}}=0$ 即可。

②若 $q_{\mathrm{w}}\neq 0$ 时，流入元体，q_{w} 取正，流出元体，q_{w} 取负，使用上述公式。

③若属对流边界，则 $q_{\mathrm{w}}=h(t_{\mathrm{f}}-t_{m,n})$，将 q_{w} 代入上式即可。

3)代数方程的求解方法

(1)直接解法：通过有限次运算获得精确解的方法，如：矩阵求解，高斯消元法。

(2)迭代法：先对要计算的场作出假设(设定初场)，在迭代计算中不断予以改进，直到计算前的假定值与计算结果相差小于允许值为止，称迭代计算收敛。

目前应用较多的是：

①高斯-赛德尔迭代法：每次迭代计算，均是使用节点温度的最新值。

②雅可比迭代法：每次迭代计算，均用上一次迭代计算出的值。

典型例题解析

【例 13.4-1】 对于图中二维稳态导热问题，右边界是绝热的，如果采用有限差分法求解，当 $x=y$ 时，则下面正确的边界节点方程是：

A. $t_1+t_2+t_3-3t_4=0$　　B. $t_1+2t_2+t_3-4t_4=0$

C. $t_1+2t_2+t_3-t_4=0$　　D. $t_1+t_2+2t_3-3t_4=0$

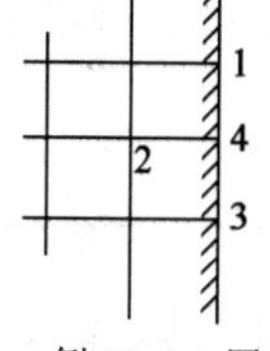

例 13.4-1 图

解 由第二类边界条件边界节点的节点方程，由于右边界是绝热的，则 $q_w=0$，整理方程可得 $t_1+2t_2+t_3-4t_4=0$。选 B。

【例 13.4-2】 常物性无内热源二维稳态导热过程，在均匀网格步长下，如图所示的平壁面节点处于第二类边界条件时，其差分格式为：

A. $t_1=\frac{1}{3}\left(t_2+t_3+t_4+\frac{\Delta x}{\lambda}q_w\right)$

B. $t_1=\frac{1}{2}\left(t_2+t_3+t_4+\frac{\Delta x}{\lambda}q_w\right)$

C. $t_1=\frac{1}{4}\left(t_2+t_3+t_4+\frac{\Delta x}{\lambda}q_w\right)$

D. $t_1=\frac{1}{4}(t_2+t_3+t_4)+\frac{\Delta x}{\lambda}q_w$

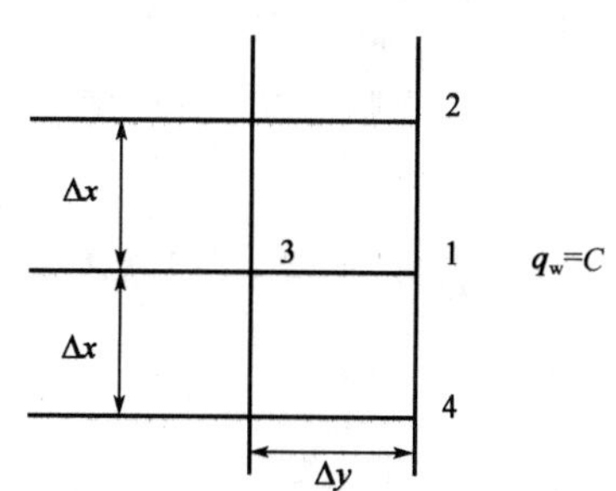

例 13.4-2 图

解 节点 1 为边界节点，其节点方程为：

$$\frac{1}{2}\Delta x\lambda\frac{t_2-t_1}{\Delta y}+\frac{1}{2}\Delta x\lambda\frac{t_4-t_1}{\Delta y}+\Delta y\lambda\frac{t_3-t_1}{\Delta x}+\Delta yq_w=0$$

$$t_1=\frac{1}{4}(t_2+t_3+t_4)+\frac{\Delta x}{\lambda}q_w$$

选 D。

【例 13.4-3】 常物性有内热源（$q_c=C$，W/m^3）二维稳态导热过程，在均匀网格步长下，如图所示，其内节点差分方程可写为：

A. $t_p=\frac{1}{4}\left(t_1+t_2+t_3+\frac{q_v}{\lambda}\right)$

B. $t_p=\frac{1}{4}(t_1+t_2+t_3+t_4)+\frac{q_v\Delta x^2}{4\lambda}$

C. $t_p=\frac{1}{4}(t_1+t_2+t_3+t_4)+q_v\Delta x^2$

D. $t_p=\frac{1}{4}(t_1+t_2+t_3+t_4)$

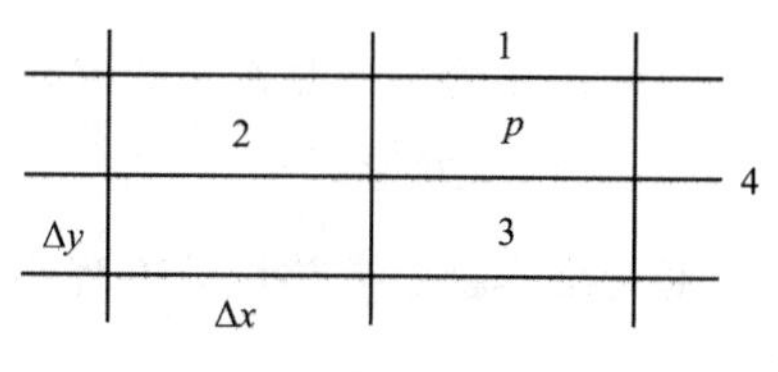

例 13.4-3 图

解 建立热平衡关系式：

$$\lambda\frac{t_1-t_p}{\Delta x}+\lambda\frac{t_2-t_p}{\Delta x}+\lambda\frac{t_3-t_p}{\Delta x}+\lambda\frac{t_4-t_p}{\Delta x}\Delta x+q_v\Delta x^2=0$$

$$t_p=\frac{1}{4}(t_1+t_2+t_3+t_4)+\frac{q_v\Delta x^2}{4\lambda}$$

选 B。

13.4.3 非稳态导热问题的数值解法

由前可知：非稳态导热和稳态导热二者微分方程的区别在于，控制方程中多了一个非稳态项，其中扩散项的离散方法与稳态导热一样。

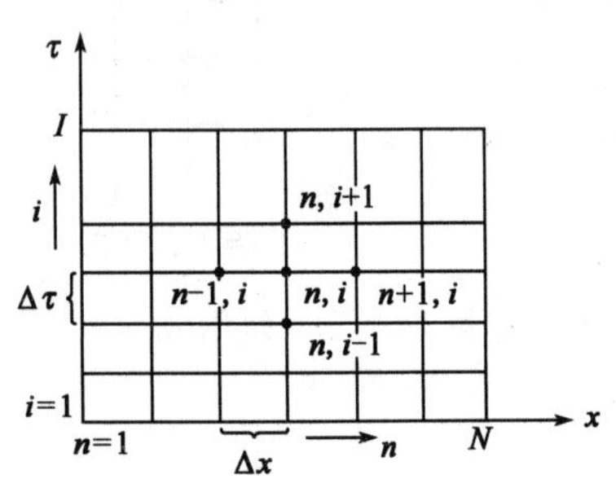

图 13.4-4 一维非稳态导热时间-空间区域离散化

1)一维非稳态导热时间—空间区域的离散化

如图 13.4-4 所示，x 为空间坐标，τ 为时间坐标。

非稳态项的离散有三种。

(1)向前差分

将函数 t 在节点$(n,i+1)$对点(n,i)作泰勒展开，则有

$$t_n^{(i+1)}=t_n^{(i)}+\Delta\tau\left.\frac{\partial t}{\partial\tau}\right|_{n,i}+\frac{\Delta\tau^2}{2}\left.\frac{\partial^2 t}{\partial\tau^2}\right|_{n,i}+\cdots$$

因此 $$\left.\frac{\partial t}{\partial\tau}\right|_{n,i}=\frac{t_n^{(i+1)}-t_n^{(i)}}{\Delta\tau}+0(\Delta\tau)$$

其中 $0(\Delta\tau)$截断误差表示余项中 $\Delta\tau$ 的最低阶为一次。

由上式得：函数 t 在节点$(n,i+1)$对点(n,i)处一阶导数的向前差分公式：

$$\left.\frac{\partial t}{\partial\tau}\right|_{n,i}=\frac{t_n^{(i+1)}-t_n^{(i)}}{\Delta\tau}$$

(2)向后差分

将函数 t 在节点$(n,i-1)$对点(n,i)作泰勒展开，可得 $\left.\frac{\partial t}{\partial\tau}\right|_{n,i}$ 的向后差分公式

$$\left.\frac{\partial t}{\partial\tau}\right|_{n,i}=\frac{t_n^{(i)}-t_n^{(i-1)}}{\Delta\tau}$$

(3)中心差分

$\left.\frac{\partial t}{\partial\tau}\right|_{n,i}$ 的向前差分与向后差分之和，即得 $\left.\frac{\partial t}{\partial\tau}\right|_{n,i}$ 的中心差分表达式

$$\left.\frac{\partial t}{\partial\tau}\right|_{n,i}=\frac{t_n^{(i+1)}-t_n^{(i-1)}}{2\Delta\tau}$$

2)一维非稳态导热微分方程的离散方法

(1)显式差分格式

对一维非稳态导热微分方程中 $\frac{\partial t}{\partial\tau}=a\frac{\partial^2 t}{\partial x^2}$ 的扩散项→中心差分；非稳态项→向前差分。

$$t_n^{(i+1)}=\frac{a\Delta\tau}{\Delta x^2}\left(t_{n+1}^{(i)}+t_{n-1}^{(i)}\right)+\left(1-\frac{2a\Delta\tau}{\Delta x^2}\right)t_n^{(i)}$$

$$t_n^{(i+1)}=\mathrm{Fo}_\Delta\left(t_{n+1}^{(i)}+t_{n-1}^{(i)}\right)+(1-2\mathrm{Fo}_\Delta)t_n^{(i)}$$

由此可见，只要 i 时层上各节点的温度已知，那么 $i+1$ 时层上各节点的温度即可算出，且不需设立方程组求解。此关系式即为显式差分格式。

在上式中，满足这种合理性是有条件的，即上式中 $t_n^{(i)}$ 前的系数必大于等于零，即 $(1-2\mathrm{Fo}_\Delta)\geqslant 0$，亦即：$\mathrm{Fo}_\Delta\leqslant 1/2$。

否则，将出现不合理情况。这种节点温度随时间的跳跃式变化是不符合物理规律的，所以称该方程具有不稳定性。

典型例题解析

【例 13.4-4】 对于一维非稳态导热的有限差分方程，如果对时间域采用显式格式进行计算，则对于内部节点而言，保证计算稳定性的判据为：

A. Fo≤1　　B. Fo≥1　　C. Fo≤1/2　　D. Fo≥1/2

解 选 C。

(2)隐式差分格式

对一维非稳态导热微分方程 $\frac{\partial t}{\partial \tau}=a\frac{\partial^2 t}{\partial x^2}$ 中的扩散项在$(i+1)$时层上采用中心差分，非稳态项将 t 在节点$(n,i+1)$处对节点(n,i)采用向前差分，得

$$\frac{t_n^{(i+1)}-t_n^{(i)}}{\Delta\tau}=a\frac{t_{n+1}^{(i+1)}-2t_n^{(i+1)}+t_{n-1}^{(i+1)}}{\Delta x^2}$$

此种差分格式称隐式差分格式，计算是无条件的。不受时间及空间的步长影响。

3)对于一维导热显示格式的对流边界节点方程

对于第一类边界条件的导热问题，边界节点温度是已知的；第二类或第三类边界条件的导热问题，用热平衡法导出边界点上的离散方程。

如图 13.4-5 所示，第三类边界条件用热平衡法离散方程。

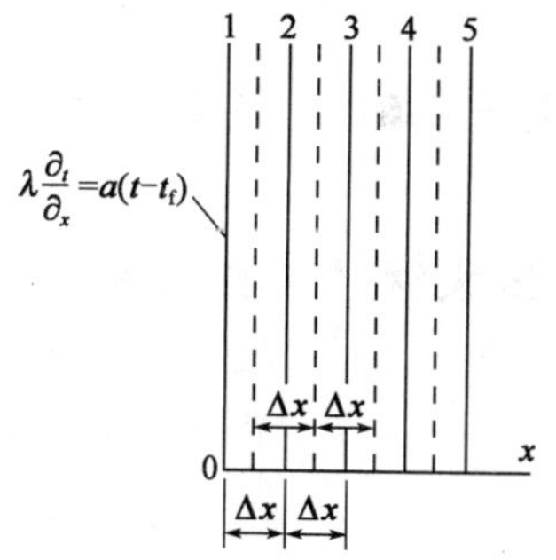

图 13.4-5　第三类边界条件显式差分格式

(1)显式差分格式

$t_N^{(i+1)}+t_N^{(i)}(1-2\mathrm{Fo}_\Delta\cdot\mathrm{Bi}_\Delta-2\mathrm{Fo}_\Delta)+2\mathrm{Fo}_\Delta t_{n-1}^{(i)}+2\mathrm{Fo}_\Delta\cdot\mathrm{Bi}_\Delta\cdot t_f$

稳定性条件是：$1-2\mathrm{Fo}_\Delta\cdot\mathrm{Bi}_\Delta-2\mathrm{Fo}_\Delta\geqslant 0$，即

$$\mathrm{Fo}_\Delta\leqslant\frac{1}{2(1+\mathrm{Bi}_\Delta)}$$

由此可见：对流边界节点要得到的合理的解，其限制条件比内节点更为严格，所以，当由边界条件及内节点的稳定性条件得出的 Fo_Δ 不同时，应选较小的 Fo_Δ 来确定允许采用的 $\Delta\tau$，方能满足两者稳定性要求。

(2)隐式差分格式

$$t_N^{(i+1)}(1+2\mathrm{Fo}_\Delta\cdot\mathrm{Bi}\Delta+\mathrm{Fo}_\Delta)=2\mathrm{Fo}_\Delta t_{n+1}^{(i+1)}+2\mathrm{Fo}_\Delta\mathrm{Bi}\Delta t_f^{(i+1)}+t_N^i$$

隐式差分格式是无条件稳定的。

说明：传热学的数值解是一种近似解。由于这种解法比较简便，且其计算结果在很多情况下能较好地描述客观实际，故在工程上得到了广泛的应用。复习本章要注意理解和掌握以下内容：①理解差分和差商的概念，掌握用差分代替微分和对控制容积(网格单元)进行热平衡分析，建立节点温度方程的方法。②能用迭代法或高斯消元法求解二维稳态导热问题的有限差分方程组。③了解截断误差。中心差分的截断误差较小，温度对空间坐标的二阶导数一般采用中心差分表达式，而温度对时间的一阶导数采用向前差分或向后差分的表达式。④了解显式差分格式的稳定性条件，能用有限差分法求解一维非稳态导热问题(无内热源)。

经典练习

13.4-1　对于如图所示二维稳态导热问题，右边界是恒定热流边界条件，热流密度为 q_w，

若采用有限差分法求解，当 $\Delta x=\Delta y$ 时，则下面的边界节点方程式正确的是(　　)。

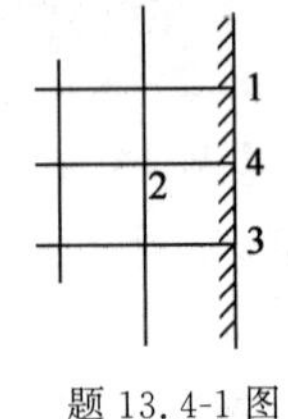

题 13.4-1 图

A. $t_1+t_2+t_3-3t_4+q_w\Delta x/\lambda=0$

B. $t_1+2t_2+t_3-4t_4+2q_w\Delta y/\lambda=0$

C. $t_1+t_2+t_3-3t_4+2q_w\Delta x/\lambda=0$

D. $t_1+2t_2+t_3-4t_4+q_w\Delta x/\lambda=0$

13.4-2　常物性无内热源一维非稳态导热过程第三类边界条件下微分得到离散方程，进行计算时要达到收敛需满足(　　)。

A. $Bi<\frac{1}{2}$　　B. $Fo\leqslant1$　　C. $Fo\leqslant\frac{1}{2Bi+2}$　　D. $Fo\leqslant\frac{1}{2Bi}$

13.4-3　有限差分导热离散方式说法不正确的是(　　)。

A. 边界节点用级数展开　　B. 边界节点用热守衡方式

C. 中心节点用级数展开　　D. 中心节点用热守衡方式

13.5　对流换热分析

考试大纲☞：对流换热过程和影响对流换热的因素　对流换热过程微分方程式　对流换热微分方程组　流动边界层　热边界层　边界层换热微分方程组及其求解　边界层换热积分方程组及其求解　动量传递和热量传递的类比　物理相似的基本概念　相似原理　实验数据整理方法

必备基础知识

对流换热是发生在流体和与之接触的固体壁面之间的热量传递过程。计算基本公式为牛顿冷却公式：$q=h(t_w-t_f)$ (W/m²)，或 $\Phi=h(t_w-t_f)A$ (W)。对流换热问题分析的目的是确定表面传热系数 h 的数值。确定表面传热系数方法有四种：分析法、类比法、实验法和数值法。

13.5.1 影响对流换热的因素

1)流体流动的起因

按流体运动的起因不同，对流换热可区分为：自然对流换热和受迫对流换热。

2)流体的流动状态

流动状态有层流和紊流。

3)流体的热物理性质

流体的热物理性质对于对流换热有较大的影响。流体的热物性参数主要包括以下 5 种。

(1)导热系数 λ：λ 大，则流体内的导热热阻小，换热强。

(2)比热容 c_p 和密度 ρ：ρ 和 c_p 大，单位体积流体携带的热量多，热对流传递的热量多。

(3)黏度 μ：黏度大，阻碍流体流动，不利于热对流。温度对黏度的影响较大。

(4)体积膨胀系数：在自然对流中起作用。

(5)定性温度：确定流体物性参数值所用的温度。常用的定性温度主要有以下三种：流体平均温度 t_f，壁表面温度 t_w 和流体与壁面的平均算术温度：$(t_f+t_w)/2$。

4)流体的相变

流体发生相变时换热有新规律。无相变时主要是显热;有相变时有潜热的释放或吸收。

5)换热表面几何因素

几何因素主要指壁面尺寸、壁面粗糙度、壁面形状和壁面与流体的相对位置。一般选用对于对流换热的特性起决定作用的物体的几何尺度为定型尺寸。如,管内流动:取管内径;外掠管子:取管外径;外掠平板:取板长。

由以上分析可见,表面传热系数是众多因素的函数,即

$$h = f(u, t_w, t_f, \lambda, c_p, \rho, \alpha, \mu, l)$$

研究对流换热的目的就是找出上式的具体函数式。

13.5.2 对流换热过程微分方程式

如图 13.5-1 所示是一个简单的对流换热过程。

根据傅里叶定律和牛顿冷却公式可得

$$h_x = -\frac{\lambda}{\Delta t_x}\left(\frac{\partial t}{\partial y}\right)_{w,x}$$

引入过余温度 θ,即 $\theta = t - t_w$,则

$$h_x = -\frac{\lambda}{\Delta \theta_x}\left(\frac{\partial \theta}{\partial y}\right)_{w,x}$$

该式称为对流换热过程微分方程式,它确定了表面传热系数与温度场之间的关系 。

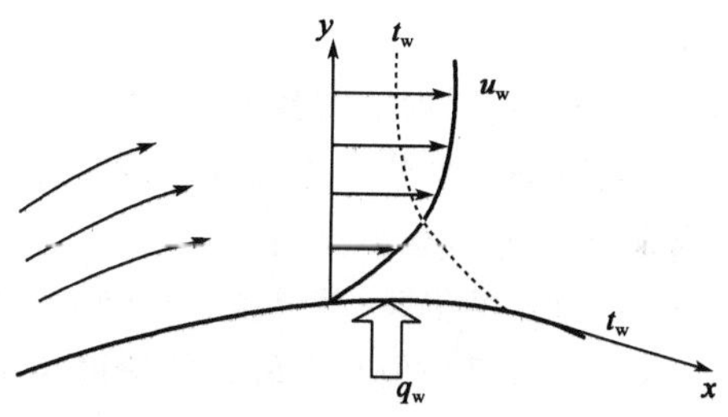

图 13.5-1 对流换热过程示意图

13.5.3 对流换热微分方程组

由于流体的运动影响着流场的温度分布,因而流体的速度分布(速度场)是要同时确定的。求解对流换热表面传热系数一般要通过解对流换热微分方程组。

要确立温度场和速度场就必须找出支配方程组,它们应该是,从质量守恒定律导出的连续性方程、从动量守恒定律导出的动量微分方程和从能量守恒定律导出的能量微分方程 。

连续性方程为

$$\frac{\partial u}{\partial x} + \frac{\partial v}{\partial y} = 0$$

动量微分方程又称 N-S 方程,有

在 x 方向上 $\rho\left(\frac{\partial u}{\partial \tau} + u\frac{\partial u}{\partial x} + v\frac{\partial u}{\partial y}\right) = X - \frac{\partial p}{\partial x} + \mu\left(\frac{\partial^2 u}{\partial x^2} + \frac{\partial^2 u}{\partial y^2}\right)$

在 y 方向上 $\rho\left(\frac{\partial v}{\partial \tau} + u\frac{\partial v}{\partial x} + v\frac{\partial v}{\partial y}\right) = Y - \frac{\partial p}{\partial y} + \mu\left(\frac{\partial^2 v}{\partial x^2} + \frac{\partial^2 v}{\partial y^2}\right)$

能量微分方程

$$\rho c_p\left(\frac{\partial t}{\partial \tau} + u\frac{\partial t}{\partial x} + v\frac{\partial t}{\partial y}\right) = \lambda\left(\frac{\partial^2 t}{\partial x^2} + \frac{\partial^2 t}{\partial y^2}\right)$$

13.5.4 边界层换热微分方程组及其求解

1)流动边界层

流体外掠平板,其流动边界层如图 13.5-2 所示,$u/u_\infty = 0.99$ 处离壁的距离为边界层厚

度，流体平行流过平板的临界雷诺数为

$$Re_c = 5 \times 10^5$$

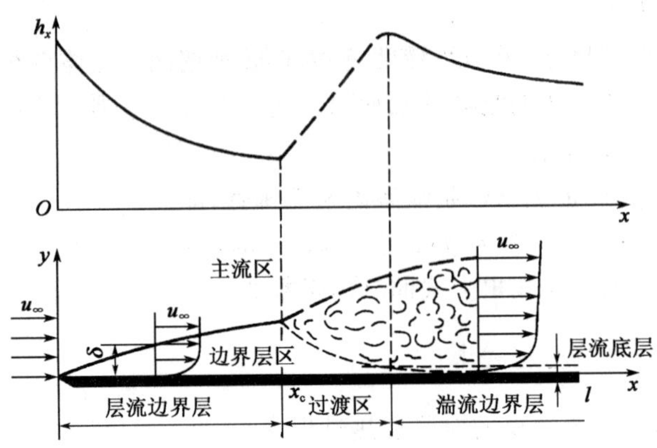

图 13.5-2　流体外掠平板

流动边界层理论的基本论点：

(1)流场可划分为主流区(由理想流体运动微分方程——欧拉方程描述)和边界区(由黏性流体运动微分方程组描述)。

(2)边界层很薄，其厚度 δ 与壁的定型尺寸相比是个很小的量。

(3)在边界层内存在较大的速度梯度。

(4)在边界层内流动状态分为层流和紊流。

流体在管内流动属于内部流动过程，其主要特征是，流动存在着两个明显的流动区段，即流动进口区段和流动充分发展区段，如图 13.5-3 所示。

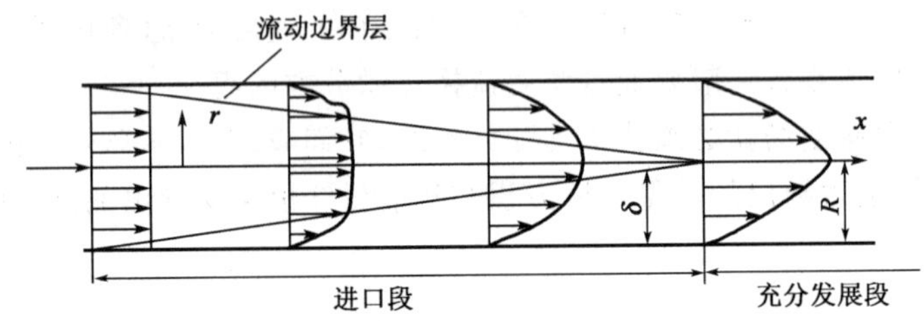

图 13.5-3　流体在管内流动

实验研究表明，当管内流动的雷诺数 $Re<2\,300$ 时为层流流动，当管内流动的雷诺数 $Re \geqslant 10^4$ 时为紊流流动，而雷诺数在 $Re<2\,300<10^4$ 之间时管内流动处于过渡流动区域。上述关系式中的雷诺数定义为 $Re=u_m d/v$。

2)热(温度)边界层

当流体流过物体，二者有温差时，将产生热边界层。当壁面与流体之间的温差($\theta = t - t_w$)达到壁面与来流流体之间的温差($\theta_f = t_f - t_w$)的 0.99 倍时，即 $\theta = 0.99\theta_f$，此位置就是边界层的外边缘，而该点到壁面之间的距离则是热边界层的厚度，记为 δ_t。δ_t 与 δ 一般不相等。

3)数量级分析与边界层微分方程

数量级分析：比较方程中各量或各项的量级的相对大小；保留量级较大的量或项；舍去那些量级小的项，方程大大简化。其中连续性方程和对流换热过程微分方程式还是原来的方程，变化的是

动量微分方程
$$u\frac{\partial u}{\partial x}+v\frac{\partial u}{\partial y}=\gamma\frac{\partial^2 u}{\partial y^2}$$

能量微分方程
$$u\frac{\partial t}{\partial x}+v\frac{\partial t}{\partial y}=a\frac{\partial^2 t}{\partial y^2}$$

解此方程组得出边界层速度场、温度场，进而求出局部表面传热系数。

求解得到的结论如下（对于层流）：

（1）边界层厚度 δ 及局部摩擦系数 $C_{f,x}$

$$\frac{\delta}{x}=5.0\mathrm{Re}_x^{-\frac{1}{2}} \text{ 和 } C_{f,x}=0.664\mathrm{Re}_x^{-\frac{1}{2}}$$

其中 $\mathrm{Re}_x=\dfrac{u_\infty x}{\nu}$。

（2）常壁温（$t_w=\mathrm{const}$）平板局部表面传热系数

$$h_x=0.332\frac{\lambda}{x}\mathrm{Re}_x^{\frac{1}{2}}\cdot\mathrm{Pr}^{\frac{1}{3}}$$

写成无量纲准则关联式的形式 $\mathrm{Nu}_x=\dfrac{h_x\cdot x}{\lambda}=0.332\mathrm{Re}_x^{\frac{1}{2}}\cdot\mathrm{Pr}^{\frac{1}{3}}$

求解长为 l 的一段平板的平均表面传热系数 h：

$$h=\frac{1}{l}\int_0^l h_x\mathrm{d}x=2\times0.332\frac{\lambda}{l}\cdot\mathrm{Re}^{\frac{1}{2}}\cdot\mathrm{Pr}^{\frac{1}{3}}=2h_l$$

所以，$h=0.664\dfrac{\lambda}{l}\cdot\mathrm{Re}^{\frac{1}{2}}\cdot\mathrm{Pr}^{\frac{1}{3}}$ 或 $\mathrm{Nu}=0.664\mathrm{Re}^{\frac{1}{2}}\cdot\mathrm{Pr}^{\frac{1}{3}}$

其中，普朗特准则 $\mathrm{Pr}=\dfrac{\nu}{a}=\dfrac{\mu/\rho}{\lambda/(\rho c_p)}=\dfrac{\mu c_p}{\lambda}$（Pr 为物性准则）。

努谢尔特准则 $\mathrm{Nu}=\dfrac{hl}{\lambda}$，它反映流体与固体表面之间对流换热的强弱。

定性温度：取边界层平均温度 $t_m=(t_f+t_w)/2$，定型尺寸为板长。

（3）$\delta_t/\delta=\mathrm{Pr}^{-1/3}$。对于 Pr=1 的流体，边界层无量纲速度曲线与无量纲温度曲线重合，且 $\delta=\delta_t$；当 Pr＞1 时，$\nu>a$，黏性扩散＞热量扩散，$\delta>\delta_t$；当 Pr＜1 时，$\nu<a$，黏性扩散＜热量扩散，$\delta<\delta_t$。

（4）对流换热表面传热系数可以用有关准则数来表示，这样可以把影响 h 的众多因素用几个准则数来概括，使变量大为减少。如 $\mathrm{Nu}=f(\mathrm{Re},\mathrm{Pr})$。

典型例题解析

【例 13.5-1】 温度为 t_∞ 流体以速度 u_∞ 外掠温度恒为 t_w 的平板时的层流受迫对流传热问题，在一定条件下可以用边界层换热微分方程求解，用这种方法得到的对流传热准则关联式表明，平板局部表面传热系数 h_x 与沿流动方向 x 的变化规律为：

A. $h_x\propto x^{1/2}$　　B. $h_x\propto x^{1/7}$　　C. $h_x\propto x^{1/3}$　　D. $h_x\propto x^{-1/2}$

解 $h_x=0.332\dfrac{\lambda}{x}\mathrm{Re}_x^{\frac{1}{2}}\cdot\mathrm{Pr}^{\frac{1}{3}}$，$\mathrm{Re}_x=\dfrac{u_\infty x}{\nu}$，所以 $h_x\propto x^{-1/2}$。选 D。

13.5.5 边界层换热积分方程组及其求解

即使是一个极简单的平板对流换热问题，其微分方程组的求解也是相当困难的。一种近似的方法是建立和求解边界层中的积分方程。

1)边界层动量积分方程(以 u_∞ 为常数的常物性流体外掠平板层流流动为例)

$$\rho\frac{\mathrm{d}}{\mathrm{d}x}\left[\int_0^{\delta}(u_\infty-u)\cdot u\mathrm{d}y\right]=\mu\left(\frac{\mathrm{d}u}{\mathrm{d}y}\right)_{\mathrm{w}}$$

选用多项式作为速度分布的表达式：$u=a+b\cdot y+c\cdot y^2+d\cdot y^3$，4 个待定常数由边界条件及边界层特性来确定，于是速度分布表达式为

$$\frac{u}{u_\infty}=\frac{3}{2}\frac{y}{\delta}-\frac{1}{2}\left(\frac{y}{\delta}\right)^3$$

求得
$$\frac{\delta}{x}=\frac{4.64}{\sqrt{\mathrm{Re}_x}}$$

得到摩擦系数，即
$$C_{\mathrm{f},x}=\frac{0.646}{\sqrt{\mathrm{Re}_x}}$$

在长度为 l 的一段平板上的层流平均摩擦系数为

$$C_{\mathrm{f}}=\frac{1}{l}\int_0^{l}C_{\mathrm{f},x}\mathrm{d}x=2C_{\mathrm{f},l}=\frac{1.292}{\sqrt{\mathrm{Re}}}$$

2)边界层能量积分方程

把能量守恒定律应用于控制体可推导出边界层能量积分方程

$$\frac{\mathrm{d}}{\mathrm{d}x}\left(\int_0^{\delta_{\mathrm{t}}}(t_{\mathrm{f}}-t)u\mathrm{d}y\right)=a\left(\frac{\partial t}{\partial y}\right)_{\mathrm{w}}$$

选用多项式的边界层温度分布表达式：$t=a+b\cdot y+c\cdot y^2+d\cdot y^3$

引入过余温度 θ：$\theta=t-t_{\mathrm{w}}$，于是边界层中温度分布表达式为：$\dfrac{\theta}{\theta_{\mathrm{f}}}=\dfrac{3}{2}\dfrac{y}{\delta_{\mathrm{t}}}-\dfrac{1}{2}\left(\dfrac{y}{\delta_{\mathrm{t}}}\right)^3$

根据上式及边界层中速度分布，求解边界层能量积分方程得，热边界层厚度：$\dfrac{\delta_{\mathrm{t}}}{\delta}=\dfrac{1}{1.025}\mathrm{Pr}^{-\frac{1}{3}}\approx\mathrm{Pr}^{-\frac{1}{3}}$

这个结论是在 Pr>1 的前提下得到的，对 Pr>1 的流体才适用。对于空气，Pr=0.7，上式也可以近似适用。但对于液态金属(Pr≪1)和油类(Pr 数较高)则不适用。

进一步理解 $\mathrm{Pr}=\dfrac{\nu}{a}$ 的物理意义：ν 表示流体分子传递动量的能力，a 表示流体分子传递热量的能力。二者的比值反映了流体的动量传递能力与热量传递能力之比的大小。Pr 越大，表示传递动量的能力越大。

常物性流体外掠平板层流换热的局部表面传热系数 h_x 为

$$h_x=0.332\frac{\lambda}{x}\mathrm{Re}_x^{\frac{1}{2}}\cdot\mathrm{Pr}^{\frac{1}{3}}$$

其无量纲表达形式为

$$\mathrm{Nu}_x=0.332\mathrm{Re}_x^{\frac{1}{2}}\cdot\mathrm{Pr}^{\frac{1}{3}}\quad\text{(与微分方程所得的精确解相吻合)}$$

引入斯坦登准则：$\mathrm{St}_x=\dfrac{\mathrm{Nu}_x}{\mathrm{Re}_x\mathrm{Pr}}=\dfrac{h_x}{\rho c_{\mathrm{p}}u_\infty}$，是 Nu、Re、Pr 三者的综合准则。

则 $$\mathrm{St}_x \cdot \mathrm{Pr}^{\frac{2}{3}} = 0.332\mathrm{Re}_x^{-\frac{1}{2}}$$

长为 l 的一段平板的平均表面传热系数 h 为

$$h = \frac{1}{l}\int_0^l h_x \mathrm{d}x = 2h_l = 0.664\frac{\lambda}{l} \cdot \mathrm{Re}^{\frac{1}{2}} \cdot \mathrm{Pr}^{\frac{1}{3}}$$

$$\mathrm{Re} = \frac{u_\infty l}{\nu}$$

$$\mathrm{Nu} = 0.664\mathrm{Re}^{\frac{1}{2}} \cdot \mathrm{Pr}^{\frac{1}{3}}$$

$$\mathrm{Nu} = \frac{hl}{\lambda}$$

$$\mathrm{St} \cdot \mathrm{Pr}^{\frac{2}{3}} = 0.664\mathrm{Re}^{-\frac{1}{2}} \qquad \mathrm{St} = \frac{\mathrm{Nu}}{\mathrm{Re} \cdot \mathrm{Pr}} = \frac{h}{\rho c_p u_\infty}$$

定性温度:取边界层平均温度 $t_m = (t_f + t_w)/2$,定型尺寸为板长。

典型例题解析

【例 13.5-2】 用来描述流动边界层厚度与热边界层厚度之间关系的相似准则是:

A. 雷诺数 Re　　B. 普朗特数 Pr

C. 努塞尔特数 Nu　　D. 格拉晓夫数 Gr

解 $\delta_t/\delta = \mathrm{Pr}^{-1/3}$ 。选 B。

13.5.6 动量传递与热量传递的类比

1)紊流动量传递和热量传递

紊流传递的机理,除了有和层流一样的分子扩散传递外,还有流体质点脉动带来的传递动量和热量的机理。紊流时,动量传递和热量传递的大为增强是依靠后一种机理。

紊流切应力为 $$\tau_t = -\rho\overline{v'u'} = \rho\varepsilon_m\frac{\mathrm{d}u}{\mathrm{d}y} \qquad (\mathrm{N/m^2})$$

式中:ε_m ——紊流动量扩散率(m^2/s),或称为紊流黏度,可由试验测定。

紊流热量传递的净效果 $$q_t = \rho c_p\overline{v't'} = -\rho c_p\varepsilon_h\frac{\mathrm{d}t}{\mathrm{d}y}$$

式中:ε_h ——紊流热扩散率(m^2/s)。

注意:ε_m 和 ε_h 虽分别与运动黏度 ν 和热扩散率 a 相对应,也具有扩散率的单位 m^2/s,但它们不是流体的物性,它们只反映紊流的性质,与雷诺数、紊流强度以及离壁面距离有关。$\mathrm{Pr}_t = \varepsilon_m/\varepsilon_h$ 称为紊流普朗特准则。

综上所述,紊流总黏滞应力为:层流黏滞应力 τ_l 与紊流黏滞应力 τ_t 之和,即

$$\tau = \tau_l + \tau_t = \rho(\nu + \varepsilon_m)\frac{\mathrm{d}u}{\mathrm{d}y}$$

紊流总热流密度为:层流导热量 q_l 与紊流传递热量 q_t 之和,即

$$q = q_l + q_t = -\rho c_p(a + \varepsilon_h)\frac{\mathrm{d}t}{\mathrm{d}y}$$

以上两式是紊流传递过程分析的基本关系式。

2)雷诺类比

(1)对于层流:$\varepsilon_m = 0, \varepsilon_h = 0 \Rightarrow$ $$\left.\begin{aligned} q = q_l = -\rho c_p a\frac{\mathrm{d}t}{\mathrm{d}y} \\ \tau = \tau_l = \rho\nu\frac{\mathrm{d}u}{\mathrm{d}y}\end{aligned}\right\}\text{(两式相除)}$$

当 Pr=1 时，上式可改写为：$\frac{q_l}{\tau_l}=-c_p\cdot\frac{dt}{du}$

（2）对于紊流：雷诺的分析采用一个很粗糙的一层模型，假定整个流场是由单一的紊流层构成，即认为不存在层流底层（即在雷诺考虑的紊流流场内，紊流传递作用远大于分子扩散作用，$\nu\ll\varepsilon_m, a\ll\varepsilon_h$）。

此时，
$$\left.\begin{aligned}\tau=\tau_t=\rho\varepsilon_m\frac{du}{dy}\\ q=q_t=-\rho c_p\varepsilon_h\frac{dt}{dy}\end{aligned}\right\}\Rightarrow\frac{q}{\tau}=-c_p\cdot\frac{\varepsilon_h}{\varepsilon_m}\cdot\frac{dt}{du}$$

取 $Pr_t=1$，则有：$\frac{q}{\tau}=-c_p\cdot\frac{dt}{du}$（这里 t,u 取时均值）

上式表达了紊流热量和动量传递的雷诺类比方程。

当 $Pr=Pr_t=1$ 时，层流和紊流的热量与动量的类比关系形式一致，服从同一方程，称为雷诺一层结构紊流模型。

3）紊流摩擦系数与表面传热系数的关系

在一层模型中，认为 $\frac{q}{\tau}$ 等于壁面的比值 $\frac{q_w}{\tau_w}$，并作常数处理，则

$$St=\frac{C_f}{2}\qquad（雷诺类比的解）$$

对于局部传热系数 h_x 和局部摩擦系数 $C_{f,x}$，则：$St_x=\frac{C_{f,x}}{2}$

以上解表达了紊流表面传热系数和摩擦系数间的关系，称为简单雷诺类比律。

注意：上面的解只适用于 Pr=1 的流体，当 Pr≠1 时，用 $Pr^{\frac{2}{3}}$ 修正 St，则：$St\cdot Pr^{\frac{2}{3}}=\frac{C_f}{2}$，此式为柯尔栅类比律，或称为修正雷诺类比，定性温度为：$t_m=(t_f+t_w)/2$，适用于 Pr=0.5～50。

4）外掠平板紊流换热

对于光滑平板，平板紊流局部摩擦系数

$$C_{f,x}=0.059\,2Re_x^{-\frac{1}{5}}\qquad(5\times10^5\leqslant Re\leqslant10^7)$$

则常温壁外掠平板紊流局部表面传热系数关联式为

$$Nu_x=0.029\,6Re_x^{\frac{4}{5}}\cdot Pr^{\frac{1}{3}}$$

全板平均表面换热系数为

$$h=\frac{1}{l}\left(\int_0^{x_c}h_{x,l}dx+\int_{x_c}^{l}h_{x,t}dx\right)$$

则：$Nu=(0.037Re^{0.8}-871)\cdot Pr^{\frac{1}{3}}$

适用于：$0.6\leqslant Pr\leqslant60$，$5\times10^5\leqslant Re\leqslant10^8$，特征尺寸为 $x=l$；特征流速为 u_∞；而定性温度为壁面与流体的平均温度 $t_m=(t_f+t_w)/2$。

13.5.7 相似理论基础

1）物理相似

（1）几何相似：对应边成比例。

（2）物理现象相似：温度、速度、密度、黏度、导热系数等对应点物理量成比例。

（3）单值性条件相似：边界条件相似（对应边界点物理量场相似）和时间条件相似（对应时

间物理量场相似)。

2)相似原理

相似原理阐述了三方面的内容:相似性质,相似准则间的关系和判别相似的条件。

(1)相似性质。

彼此相似的现象,它们的同名相似准则必定相等。

主要相似准则及其物理意义:

①努谢尔特准则:$Nu = \frac{hl}{\lambda}$,对流换热现象相似,则 Nu 必定相等,表征壁面法向流体无量纲过余温度梯度的大小,它反映了给定流场的换热能力与其导热能力的对比关系,它反映对流换热的强弱。这是一个在对流换热计算中必须要加以确定的准则。

②雷诺准则:$Re = \frac{ul}{\nu}$,两流体的运动现象相似,则 Re 必相等。反映流体流动时惯性力与黏滞力的相对大小。

③贝克利准则:$Pe = \frac{ul}{a} = \frac{\nu}{a}\frac{ul}{\nu} = Pr \cdot Re$,两热量传递现象相似,则 Pe 必相等。反映了流场的热对流能力与其热传导能力的对比关系。

④格拉晓夫准则:$Gr = \frac{g\alpha \Delta t l^3}{\nu^2}$,自然对流换热现象相似,则 Gr 必定相等。反映浮升力与黏滞力的相对大小。流体自然对流状态是浮升力与黏滞力相互作用的结果。

⑤普朗特准则:$Pr = \frac{\nu}{a}$,物性现象相似,则 Pr 必定相等。它反映了流体的动量扩散能力与能量扩散能力的对比关系,是物性准则。

⑥斯坦登准则:$St = \frac{Nu}{Re \cdot Pr} = \frac{h}{\rho u_\infty c_p}$,表征流体对流换热的热流密度与流体可传递的最大热流密度的比值。

(2)相似准则间的关系。

①无相变、受迫、稳态对流换热,且当自然对流不能忽略时,准则关联式为

$$Nu = f(Re, Pr, Gr)$$

②无相变、受迫、稳态对流换热,且自然对流可忽略时,准则关联式为

$$Nu = f(Re, Pr)$$

③对于空气,Pr 可作为常数处理,则空气受迫紊流换热时的准则关联式为

$$Nu = f(Re)$$

④对于自然对流换热,从微分方程组相似分析中可以得到 Nu、Re、Gr、Pr 四个准则,但因 $Re = f(Gr)$ 不是一个独立的准则,所以准则方程应为

$$Nu = f(Gr, Pr)$$

根据相似准则间的关系,实验数据应整理成准则关联式的形式。

(3)判别相似的条件。

相似第三定理:凡同类现象,若同名已定准则相等,且单值性条件相似(几何、物理、边界、时间),那么这两个现象一定相似。

3)结论

(1)实验时应测量各相似准则中包含的全部物理量,其中物性由实验系统中的定性温度

确定。

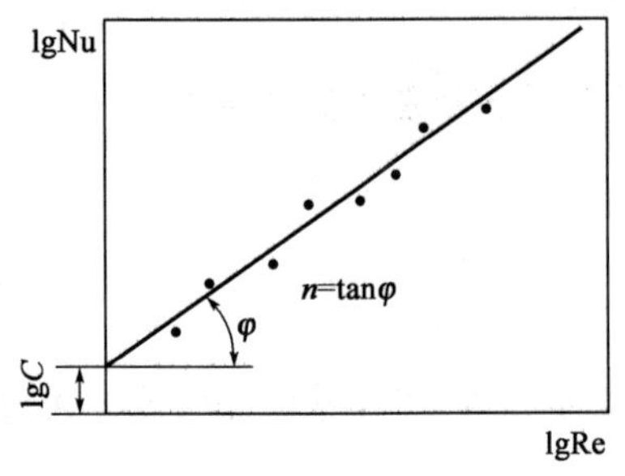

图 13.5-4 准则关联式图示

(2)实验结果整理成准则关联式。

(3)实验结果可以推广应用到相似的现象。

4)实验数据的整理方法

在对流换热研究中,准则函数通常整理为幂函数的形式,如图 13.5-4 所示。

$$\left.\begin{aligned}Nu &= CRe^{n}\\ Nu &= CRe^{n}\cdot Pr^{m}\\ Nu &= C(Gr\cdot Pr)^{n}\end{aligned}\right\}$$

其中,C、n、m 等常数由实验数据确定。

以准则关联式 $Nu = CRe^{n}$ 为例,对它取对数就得到直线方程的形式:$\lg Nu = \lg C + n\lg Re$。

说明:本章从分析对流换热的机理和影响因素入手,论述了对流换热过程的物理和数学模型。在此基础上,介绍了求解对流换热问题的三种方法,即理论分析法、比拟法和相似理论指导的实验法。复习本章,要注意理解和掌握以下内容:①对流换热过程的定性分析、主要影响因素,应深入理解对流换热过程的物理基础,掌握分析方法。②两种边界层的形成、发展及不同特点,不同边界层的热量传递机理。③要理解微分方程式各项的物理意义。④雷诺比拟反映了流动摩擦系数和表面传热系数之间的定量关系,可由摩擦系数来推算表面传热系数。应该了解层流和紊流中动量及热量传递的定量描述方法。⑤理解相似理论及其对实验研究对流换热问题的指导意义。相似理论对实验研究的指导意义在于:通过相似分析,把影响物性现象的众多物理量,组成几个相似准则,使实验大大简化;把实验结果整理成准则函数式(准则方程式),可推广应用到相似现象中去;可以用模型实验代替原型实验。相似准则在传热及其他学科研究中被广泛采用,应了解常用相似准则的物理意义及使用场合。

典型例题解析

【例 13.5-3】 下列换热工况中,可能相似的是:

A. 两圆管内单相受迫对流换热,分别为加热和冷却过程

B. 两块平壁面上自然对流换热,分别处于冬季和夏季工况

C. 两圆管内单相受迫对流换热,流体分别为水和导热油

D. 两块平壁面上自然对流换热,竖放平壁分别处于空气对流和水蒸气凝结

解 相似判定的三要素为:要保证同类现象,单值性条件相同,同名的准则相等。选项 A、B 不满足同类现象,选项 D 不满足同名的准则相等。选 C。

【例 13.5-4】 确定同时存在自然对流和受迫对流的混合换热准则关系的是:

A. $Nu=f(Gr,Pr)$　　B. $Nu=f(Re,Pr)$

C. $Nu=f(Gr,Re,Pr)$　　D. $Nu=f(Fo,Gr,Re)$

解 自然对流受 Gr 和 Pr 影响,强迫对流受 Pr 和 Re 影响,所以选 C。选项 A 是自然对流准则关系式,选项 B 是受迫对流准则关系式。

经 典 练 习

13.5-1　采用对流换热边界层微分方程组，积分方程组或雷诺类比法求解对流换热过程中，正确的说法是(　　)。

A. 微分方程组的解是精确解　　B. 积分方程组的解是精确解

C. 雷诺类比的解是精确解　　D. 以上三种均为近似值

13.5-2　能量和动量的传递都是和对流与扩散相关的，因此两者之间存在着某种类似。可以采用雷诺比拟来建立湍流受迫对流时能量传递与动量传递之间的关系，这种关系通常表示为(　　)。

A. 雷诺数 Re 与摩擦系数 C_f 的关系

B. 斯坦登数 St 与摩擦系数 C_f 的关系

C. 努赛尔数 Nu 与摩擦系数 C_f 的关系

D. 格拉晓夫数 Gr 与摩擦系数 C_f 的关系

13.6　单相流体对流换热及准则方程式

考试大纲☞：管内受迫流动换热　外掠圆管流动换热　自然对流换热　自然对流与受迫对流并存的混合流动换热

必备基础知识

13.6.1　管内受迫流动换热

1)流动进口段与流动充分发展段

管内流动进口段：从管子进口到边界层汇合处的这段管长内的流动。

流动充分发展段：进入定型流动的区域。

在流动充分发展段，流体的径向速度分量 v 为零，且轴向速度 u 不再沿轴向变化，即

$$\frac{\partial u}{\partial x} = 0, v = 0$$

2)管内的流态

层流：Re<2 300；紊流流动：Re>10^4；过渡流动：2 300<Re<10^4。

$$\mathrm{Re} = \frac{u_m d}{\nu}$$

式中：u_m——管内流体的截面平均流速；

d——管子的内直径；

ν——流体的运动黏度。

3)热进口段和热充分发展段

当流体温度和管壁温度不同时，在管子的进口区域同时也有热边界层在发展，热边界层最后也会在管中心汇合，从而进入热充分发展的流动换热区域，在热边界层汇合之前也就必然存在热进口区段。

对常物性流体，在常热流和常壁温边界条件下，热充分发展段的特征是

$$\frac{\partial}{\partial x}\left(\frac{t_{w,x}-t}{t_{w,x}-t_{f,x}}\right)=0$$

可得：
$$\frac{-(\partial t/\partial r)_{r=R}}{(t_{w,x}-t_{f,x})}=\frac{h_x}{\lambda}=\text{const}$$

则常物性流体在热充分发展段的表面传热系数保持不变。

管内局部表面传热系数随 x 的变化，如图 13.6-1 所示。

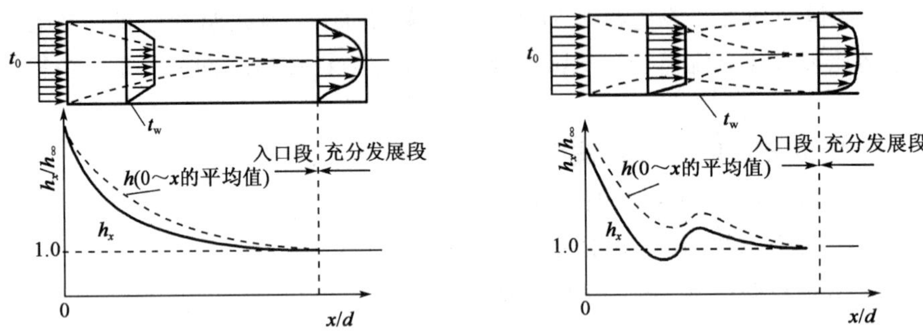

图 13.6-1 管内表面传热系数的变化

在进口处，边界层最薄，h_x 具有最高值，随后降低。在层流情况下，h_x 趋于不变值的距离较长(入口段有强化换热的作用，所以短管强化换热)。

4)管内流体平均速度及平均温度

管内流体平均速度：$u_m=\dfrac{v}{f}$

对常物性流体，断面平均温度为：$t_f=\dfrac{2}{u_m\cdot R^2}\displaystyle\int_0^R t\,u\cdot r\,\mathrm{d}r$

上式计算断面平均温度，必须知道 $u(r)$ 和 $t(r)$ 的分布，比较麻烦。使用上往往测出截面平均温度，即流体充分混合，如图 13.6-2 所示，这样测到的温度实用上就可作为截面平均温度。

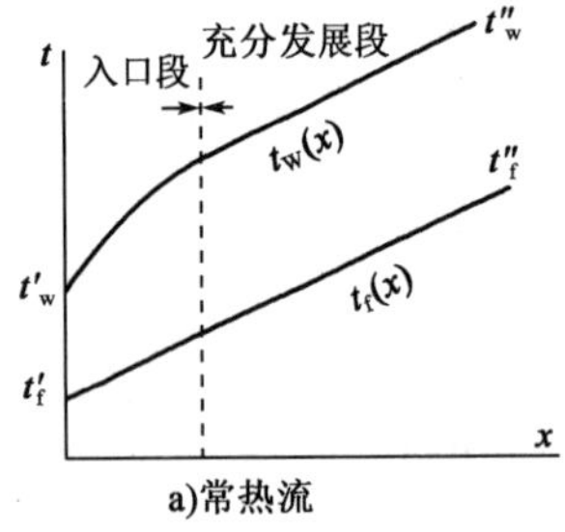

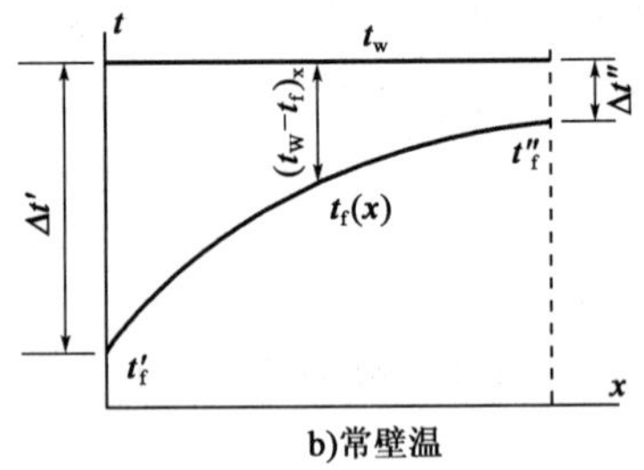

图 13.6-2 管内换热温度变化

(1)对常热流边界条件下的平均温度(设物性为常量)

①全管长平均温度。可取管的进、出口断面平均温度的算术平均值作为全管长温度的平均，即

$$t_f=\frac{t'_f+t''_f}{2}$$

②全管长的流体与管壁间的平均温度差

$$\Delta t=\frac{\Delta t'+\Delta t''}{2}$$

其中，$\Delta t'=t'_w-t'_f$，$\Delta t''=t''_w-t''_f$。

(2)对常壁温边界条件下的平均温度

①全管长流体与壁面间的平均温差 Δt_m

$$\Delta t = \frac{\Delta t' - \Delta t''}{\ln\frac{\Delta t'}{\Delta t''}} (\Delta t' = t_w - t_f', \Delta t'' = t_w - t_f'')$$

Δt_m 称为对数平均温差。

若$\frac{\Delta t'}{\Delta t''}<2$,则可用$\frac{\Delta t' + \Delta t''}{2}$代替上式。

②全管长流体的平均温度

$$t_f = t_w + \Delta t_m \quad 或 \quad t_f = t_w - \Delta t_m \quad \left(t_f \neq \frac{t_f' + t_f''}{2}, 但若\frac{\Delta t'}{\Delta t''}<2, 则\ t_f = \frac{t_f' + t_f''}{2}\right)$$

13.6.2 管内受迫流动换热计算

1)紊流换热

当管内流动的雷诺数 $Re>10^4$ 时,管内流体处于旺盛的紊流状态。此时的换热计算可采用下面推荐的准则关系式(迪图斯-贝尔特公式)

$$Nu_f = 0.023 Re_f^{0.8} Pr^n$$

流体加热:$n = 0.4$;流体冷却:$n = 0.3$

此式适用于流体与壁面具有中等以下温差的场合(即该温差下物性场不均匀性带来的误差不超过工程允许范围。对空气,温差小于 50℃,对于水,温差小于 20~30℃)。

式中采用的定型尺寸为管子内直径 d,定性温度采用全管长流体平均温度。实验验证范围为:平直管,$Re_f = 10^4 \sim 1.2\times10^5$;$Pr_f = 0.7 \sim 120$,$l/d \geqslant 60$。

对于非圆形管,上述的公式同样使用,只是定型尺寸用当量直径 d_e。

将准则关系式展开,可显示出影响紊流表面传热系数的有关因素。

$$h = f(u^{0.8}, \lambda^{0.6}, c_p^{0.4}, \rho^{0.8}, \mu^{-0.4}, d^{-0.2})$$

由此可见,当流体种类确定后,要增强或削弱换热,只能通过改变流速和管径来实现。$u\uparrow, d\downarrow \Rightarrow$ 强化换热。

考虑各种修正时,紊流换热准则关系式为:$Nu_f = 0.023 Re_f^{0.8} Pr^n \varepsilon_t \varepsilon_R \varepsilon_l$。

(1)温度修正

当流体为液体时 $\begin{cases} \varepsilon_t = \left(\dfrac{\mu_f}{\mu_w}\right)^{0.11} & 液体受管壁加热时 \\ \varepsilon_t = \left(\dfrac{\mu_f}{\mu_w}\right)^{0.25} & 液体受管壁冷却时 \end{cases}$

当流体为气体时 $\begin{cases} \varepsilon_t = \left(\dfrac{T_f}{T_w}\right)^{0.5} & 气体受管壁加热时 \\ \varepsilon_t = 1 & 气体受管壁冷却时 \end{cases}$

(2)弯管修正(弯管、螺旋管)

弯曲管道内的流体流动换热必须在平直管计算结果的基础上乘以一个大于 1 的修正系数 ε_R,即 $\varepsilon_R > 1$。对于流体为气体时:$\varepsilon_R = 1 + 1.77d/R$;对于流体为液体时:$\varepsilon_R = 1 + 10.3(d/R)^3$。式中 R 为弯曲管的曲率半径。

(3)入口修正(短管修正)

当管子的长径比 $l/d<60$ 时,属于短管内流动换热,进口段的影响不能忽视。此时亦应在

按照长管计算出结果的基础上乘以相应的修正系数。对于尖角入口的短管，推荐的入口效应修正系数为：$\varepsilon_l = 1 + (d/l)^{0.7}$。

注意：从以上修正系数可以看出，短管修正系数和弯管修正系数不会小于 1，所以工程上可以利用短管和螺旋管来强化对流换热。

2)管内层流换热计算公式

当雷诺数 Re<2 300 时管内流动处于层流状态，如果管子较长(即处于热充分发展段)，则 Nu_f 可作为常数处理(Nu_f 与 Re 无关)。此时

$$Nu_f = 4.36 \qquad (q = \text{const})$$

$$Nu_f = 3.66 \qquad (t_w = \text{const})$$

3)粗糙管壁的换热

管内对流换热类比律表达式：$St = f/8$。

使用该公式的条件：Pr=1；粗糙管；紊流。若考虑物性影响，用 $Pr^{2/3}$ 修正，则：$St \cdot Pr^{2/3} = f/8$。定性温度：流体平均温度 t_f。摩擦系数 f 取决于：壁面粗糙度和雷诺数。

典型例题解析

【例 13.6-1】 水力粗糙管内的受迫对流传热系数与管壁的粗糙度密切相关，粗糙度的增加提高了流体的流动阻力，但：

A. 却使对流传热系数减少　　B. 却使对流传热系数增加

C. 对流传热系数却保持不变　　D. 管内的温度分布却保持不变

解 流体流过粗糙壁面能产生涡流，增强换热，使对流传热系数增加。选 B。

13.6.3 外掠圆管流动换热

1)外掠单管

流体横向绕流圆柱体时，如图 13.6-3 所示，当 Re 数较大时，流体在边界层发生分离。观测给出，绕流圆柱的流动当 Re<10 时流动不会发生分离现象；当 $10 < Re \leqslant 1.5 \times 10^5$ 时，边界层为层流，流动分离点在 $\varphi = 80° \sim 85°$ 之间；当 $Re > 1.5 \times 10^5$，边界层在分离点前已经转变为紊流，流动分离点在 $\varphi \approx 140°$ 处。这里定义的雷诺数为：$Re = u_\infty d/\nu$，其中 u_∞ 为来流速度，d 为圆柱体外直径。边界层的成长和分离决定了外掠圆管换热的特征。

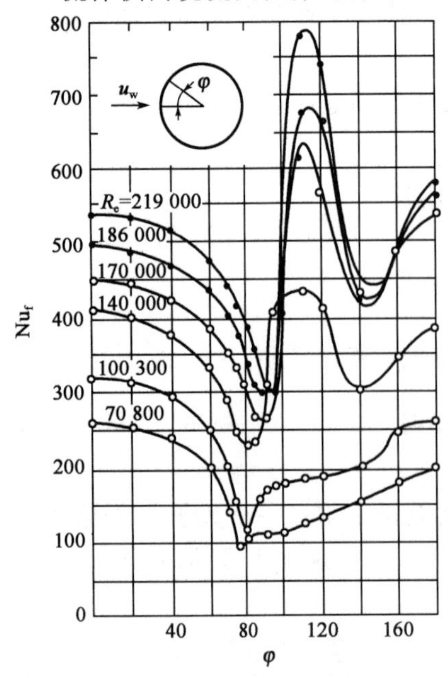

图 13.6-3　外掠管束换热

对流体外掠单管对流换热的准则关联式推荐为

$$Nu_f = C Re_f^n \cdot Pr_f^{0.37} \cdot \left(\frac{Pr_f}{Pr_w}\right)^{0.25}$$

适用范围为：$0.7 < Pr < 500$，$1 < Re_f < 10^6$。当 Pr>10 时，Pr_f 的幂次改为 0.36。定性温度为主流温度；定型尺寸为管外径；速度为管外流速最大值。

2)外掠管束

管束的排列方式很多，最常见的有顺排和叉排两种。如图 13.6-4 所示，叉排时流体扰动较好，所以一般

地说，叉排时的换热比顺排时强，同时叉排时的流动阻力也比顺排时大，顺排有易于清洗的优点。

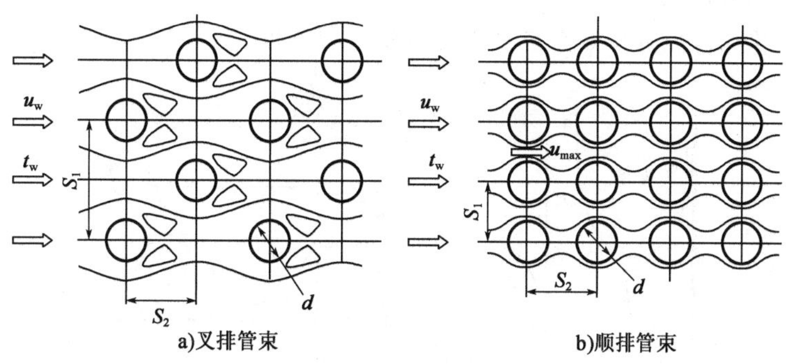

图 13.6-4 外掠管束换热

管束换热的关联式为：
$$Nu=CRe^{n}Pr^{m}\left(\frac{Pr_f}{Pr_w}\right)^{0.25}\left(\frac{S_1}{S_2}\right)^{p}\varepsilon_z$$

式中：$\frac{S_1}{S_2}$ ——相对管间距；

ε_z ——管子排数影响的修正系数。

典型例题解析

【例 13.6-2】 在流体外掠圆管的受迫对流传热时，如果边界层始终是层流的，则圆管表面上自前驻点开始到边界层脱体点之间，对流传热系数可能：

A. 不断减小　　B. 不断增加

C. 先增加后减少　　D. 先减小后增加

解 当流体刚接触圆管表面时，层流边界层开始生成，圆管表面上自前驻点开始到边界层脱体点之间，边界层厚度在不断增加，对流传热系数则不断减小。选 A。

【例 13.6-3】 单相流体外掠管束换热过程中，管束的排列、管径、排数以及雷诺数的大小均对表面传热系数(对流换热系数)有影响，下列说法不正确的是：

A. Re 增大，表面传热系数增大

B. 在较小的雷诺数下，叉排管束表面传热系数大于顺排管束

C. 管径和管距减小，表面传热系数增大

D. 后排管子的表面传热系数比前排高

解 管束换热的关联式：
$$Nu=CRe^{n}Pr^{m}\left(\frac{Pr_f}{Pr_w}\right)^{0.25}\left(\frac{s_1}{s_2}\right)^{p}\varepsilon_z$$

Re 增大，增大扰流，会增大 h，选项 A 正确。

一般叉排的扰动比顺排强，h 也大，但是阻力相反，选项 B 正确。

后排管子的表面传热系数是第一排的 1.3～1.7 倍，因为后排受到前排尾流影响较大，选项 D 正确。

选项 C 中，横向和纵向的管间距对 h 的影响是相反的，所以错误，故选 C。

13.6.4 自然对流换热

1)大空间自然对流换热

如图 13.6-5 所示,竖直平板在空气中的自然冷却过程。

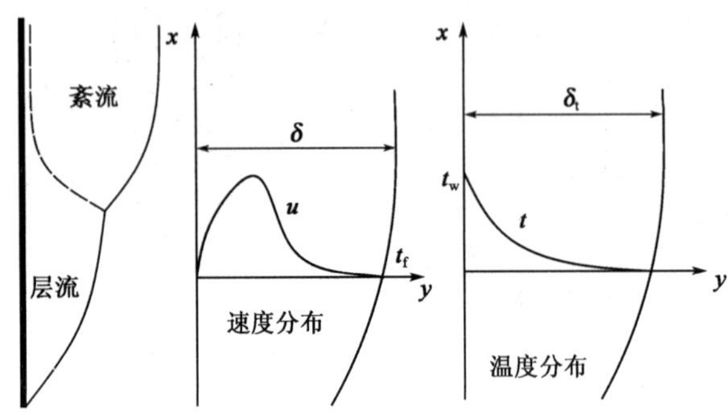

图 13.6-5 竖直平板在空气中的自然冷却过程

对于竖板表面的自然对流

$$\begin{cases} \mathrm{Gr}\cdot\mathrm{Pr} < 10^9 & \text{层流} \\ \mathrm{Gr}\cdot\mathrm{Pr} > 10^9 & \text{紊流} \end{cases}$$

(1)边界层中的速度和温度特点

$$\begin{cases} y = 0\ \text{处} & u_w = 0 \\ y = \dfrac{1}{3}\delta\ \text{处} & u = u_{max} \\ y = \delta\ \text{处} & u_\delta = 0 \end{cases} \qquad \begin{cases} y = 0\ \text{处} & t = t_w \\ y = \delta_t\ \text{处} & t = t_f \end{cases}$$

由于空气的 $\mathrm{Pr}\approx 0.7$,所以温度边界层的厚度大于速度边界层,即 $\delta_t > \delta$ 。

(2)竖板自然对流换热准则关联式

常壁温条件,即 $t_w = \mathrm{const}$

$$\mathrm{Nu} = C(\mathrm{Gr}\cdot\mathrm{Pr})^n = CRa^n$$

定性温度:$t_m = (t_w + t_f)/2$;定型(特征)尺寸:对竖板或竖管(圆柱体),定型尺寸为板(管)高。

常热流条件,即 $q_w = \mathrm{const}$:在这样的情况下,q 为已知量,t_w 为未知量,则 Gr 中的 Δt 为未知量。为方便起见,在准则关联式中采用 Gr^*(称为修正 Gr)代替 Gr,则

$$\mathrm{Gr}^* = \mathrm{Nu}\cdot\mathrm{Gr} = \frac{g\alpha q l^4}{(\lambda\nu^2)}$$

在常热流条件下,局部表面传热系数准则关联式为:$\mathrm{Nu}_x = C(\mathrm{Gr}_x^*\cdot\mathrm{Pr})^n$ 。

在计算此式时,$t_{w,x}$ 未知,则 $t_{m,x}$ 未知,所以需用试算法,假定 $t_{w,x}$ 的值。

2)受限空间中的自然对流换热

(1)受限空间中的自然对流特征。

从图 13.6-6 中可看出,在两壁面存在温度差时流体就会产生自然对流,但由于受到壁面空间的限制,将形成环状流动。

(2)在受限空间中的换热可按纯导热计算的几种情况：对竖壁，当两壁的温差与厚度都很小，$Gr_{\delta}=g\alpha\Delta t\delta^3/\nu^2<2\,000$时；对热面在上，冷面在下的水平夹层；热面在下，冷面在上的水平夹层，对气体$Gr_{\delta}<1\,700$时，可按纯导热过程计算。

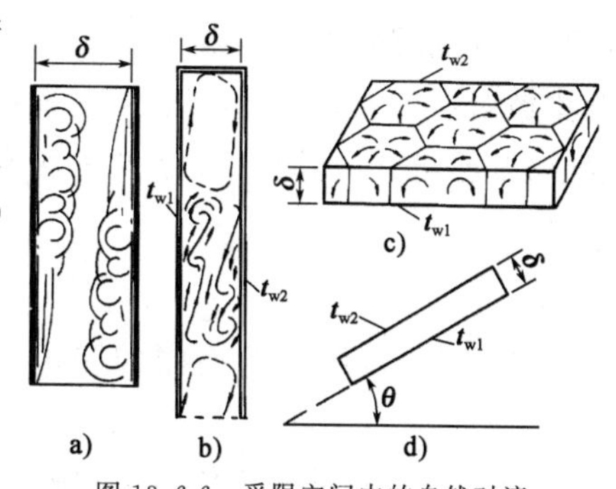

图 13.6-6　受限空间中的自然对流

(3)受限空间自然对流换热准则关联式为

$$Nu_{\delta}=C(Gr_{\delta}\cdot Pr)^m\left(\frac{H}{\delta}\right)^n$$

定性温度均为$t_m=(t_{w1}+t_{w2})/2$，Nu、Rr数中的定型尺寸均为δ。

通过夹层的热流密度：$q=h_e(t_{w1}-t_{w2})$

其中，h_e为当量表面传热系数，单位为W/(m^2·K)。

典型例题解析

【例 13.6-4】 如图所示采用平板法测量图中冷热面夹层中的液体的导热系数，为了减小测量误差，应该采用哪种布置方式？

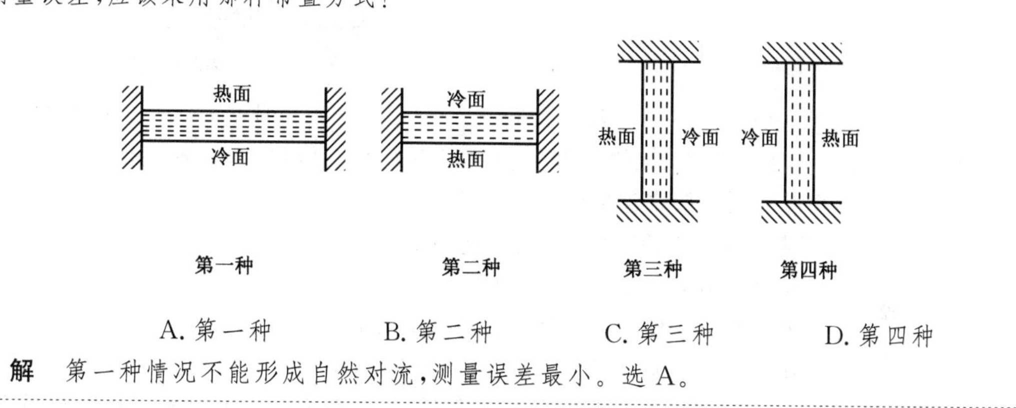

A. 第一种　　B. 第二种　　C. 第三种　　D. 第四种

解　第一种情况不能形成自然对流，测量误差最小。选 A。

13.6.5 自然对流换热与受迫对流并存的混合流动换热

什么情况下需考虑受迫对流换热中存在的自然对流换热，是根据Gr/Re^2的大小来确定的，Gr/Re^2表示浮力与惯性力的相对大小。一般认为，当$Gr/Re^2\leqslant 0.1$时，可忽略自然对流的影响，传热按纯受迫对流计算；当$Gr/Re^2\geqslant 10$时，可忽略受迫对流作用，传热按纯自然对流计算；当$Gr/Re^2=0.1\sim 10$时，传热必须同时考虑两方面的作用。

说明：工程上常见的四种典型类别单相流体对流换热分别为：管内强迫对流换热、外掠物体对流换热、自然对流换热和高速流动对流换热。对于这些典型换热问题的计算，要掌握一些常用的、比较新的实验关联式。正确选用这些关联式是很重要的。必须根据对流换热问题的类型和流态等，选择合适的关联式，切不可张冠李戴。复习本章要注意的问题有：①对于每一类换热问题要注意掌握物理过程的分析(流动和换热的特点及影响因素等)、流态的判断和正确选用实验关联式，并注意与工程应用结合起来。②各类换热问题的实验关联式，要弄清楚影响换热过程的诸多因素在关联式中是怎样反映的，理解式中各项的物理意义，并按其规定的定性温度、特性尺度和适用范围，正确使用关联式。③对于强迫对流换热，还要求能够分析进口段和充分发展的流动换热特点；对于外掠物体对流换热，要注意管束中管的排列形式、管距和管排数对换热的影响；对于自然对流换热，要掌握它的换热机理和边界层特点；对于高速流动换热，要弄清它与低速流动换热的区别。

经典练习

13.6-1 流体与壁面间的受迫对流传热系数与壁面的粗糙度密切相关，粗糙度的增加（　　）。

A. 使对流传热系数减少　　B. 使对流传热系数增加

C. 使雷诺数减小　　D. 不会改变管内的温度分布

13.6-2 如图所示，由冷、热两个表面构成的夹层中是流体且无内热源。如果端面绝热，则达到稳态时，传热量最少的放置方式是（　　）。

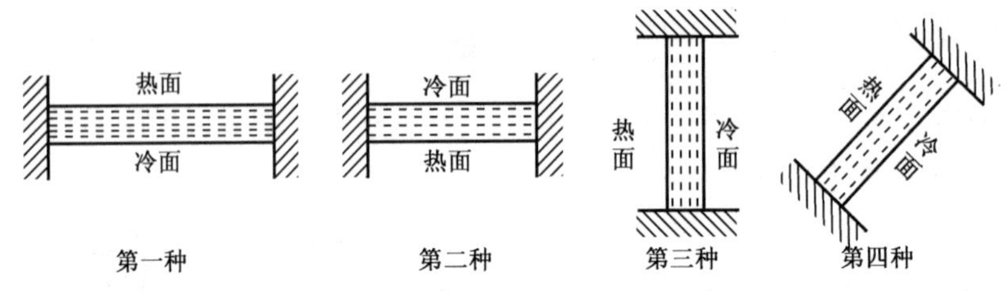

A. 第一种　　B. 第二种　　C. 第三种　　D. 第四种

13.6-3 空气与温度恒为 t_w 的竖直平壁进行自然对流传热，远离壁面的空气温度为 t。描述这一问题的相似准则关系式包括以下相似准则（　　）。

A. 雷诺数 Re，普朗特数 Pr，努塞尔特数 Nu

B. 格拉晓夫数 Gr，雷诺数 Re，普朗特数 Pr

C. 普朗特数 Pr，努塞尔特数 Nu，格拉晓夫数 Gr

D. 雷诺数 Re，努塞尔特数 Nu，格拉晓失数 Gr

13.6-4 由于二次流的影响，在相同的边界条件下，弯管内的受迫对流传热系数与直管时的对流传热系数有所不同。因此在用直管的对流传热准则关系式计算弯管情况下对流传热系数时，都要在计算的结果上乘以一个修正系数，这个系数（　　）。

A. 始终大于 1

B. 始终小于 1

C. 对于气体大于 1，对于液体小于 1

D. 对于液体大于 1，对于气体小于 1

13.6-5 管内受迫定型流动换热过程中，速度分布保持不变，流体温度及传热具有下列何种特性？（　　）

A. 温度分布达到定型　　B. 表面对流换热系数趋于定值

C. 温度梯度达到定值　　D. 换热量也达到最大

13.7 凝结与沸腾换热

考试大纲☞：凝结换热基本特性　膜状凝结换热及计算　影响膜状凝结换热的因素及增强

换热的措施　沸腾换热　饱和沸腾过程曲线　大空间泡态沸腾换热及计算　泡态沸腾换热的增强

必备基础知识

13.7.1 凝结换热基本特性

蒸汽与低于饱和温度的壁面接触时，蒸气会在壁面上凝结成液体并向壁面放出凝结潜热，这种现象称为凝结换热现象。表面凝结有两种基本形态：膜状凝结和珠状凝结。凝结液润湿壁的能力取决于它的表面张力和对壁的附着力，若附着力大于表面张力，则会形成膜状凝结，反之则形成珠状凝结。珠状凝结的表面传热系数大大高于膜状凝结，但珠状凝结很不稳定，在工业设备中实际发生的都是膜状凝结。

13.7.2 膜状凝结换热及计算

1）层流膜状凝结理论解（液膜层流时竖壁膜状凝结换热）

凝结液膜的厚度为

$$\delta = \left[\frac{4\mu_l \cdot \lambda \cdot x \cdot (t_s - t_w)}{\rho_l^2 \cdot g \cdot r}\right]^{\frac{1}{4}}$$

局部表面传热系数

$$h_x = \left[\frac{\rho_l^2 \cdot g \cdot r \cdot \lambda^3}{4\mu_l \cdot x \cdot (t_s - t_w)}\right]^{\frac{1}{4}}$$

高为 l 的竖壁，壁面平均表面传热系数为

$$h = 0.943\left[\frac{\rho_l^2 \cdot g \cdot r \cdot \lambda^3}{\mu_l \cdot l \cdot (t_s - t_w)}\right]^{\frac{1}{4}}$$

水平圆管外壁膜状凝结的平均表面传热系数为

$$h = 0.725\left[\frac{\rho_l^2 \cdot g \cdot r \cdot \lambda^3}{\mu_l \cdot d \cdot (t_s - t_w)}\right]^{\frac{1}{4}}$$

特性尺度：水平管用外径 d，竖壁用壁的高度 l；定性温度：$t_m = (t_s + t_w)/2$。

在其他条件相同时，一般管子的长度和外径的比大于 2.85，所以管子水平放置时的凝结表面传热系数将大于竖放。

2）层流膜状凝结换热准则关联式

垂直壁理论解：$Co = 1.47Re_c^{-\frac{1}{3}}$　　水平管理论解：$Co = 1.51Re_c^{-\frac{1}{3}}$

其中：
$$Re_c = \frac{d_e \cdot u_m}{\nu},\quad Co = h\left(\frac{\lambda^3\rho^2 g}{\mu^2}\right)^{-\frac{1}{3}}$$

式中：u_m ——壁的底部 $x = l$ 处液膜断面平均流速（m/s）；

d_e ——该膜层断面的当量直径（m）。

工程上，把理论解的系数增加 20%，以此作为垂直壁层流膜凝结换热的实用计算式，即

$$h = 1.13\left[\frac{\rho_l^2 \cdot g \cdot r \cdot \lambda^3}{\mu_l \cdot l \cdot (t_s - t_w)}\right]^{\frac{1}{4}} \text{ 或 } Co = 1.76Re_c^{-\frac{1}{3}}$$

3）流态的判别

对于垂直壁，液膜流态由层流转变为紊流的转变点为：$Re_c = 1\,800$。

对于水平管，凝结液从管壁两侧向下流，层流到紊流的转变点为：$Re_c=3\,600$。

4)紊流膜状凝结换热

垂直壁紊流液膜段的平均表面传热系数的准则关联式为

$$Co=\frac{Re_c}{8\,750+58Pr^{-0.5}(Re_c^{0.75}-253)}$$

对于底部已达到紊流状态的竖壁凝结换热，整个壁面分成层流段和紊流段，沿整个壁面上的平均表面传热系数：

$$h=h_l\cdot\frac{x_c}{l}+h_t\cdot\left(1-\frac{x_c}{l}\right)$$

式中：x_c——由层流转变为紊流的临界高度；

h_l——层流段的平均表面传热系数；

h_t——紊流段的平均表面传热系数。

典型例题解析

【例 13.7-1】 饱和蒸气分别在 A、B 两个等温垂直壁面上凝结，其中 A 的高度和宽度分别为 H 和 $2H$，B 的高度和宽度分别为 $2H$ 和 H，两个壁面上的凝结传热量分别为 Q_A 和 Q_B。如果液膜中的流动都是层流，则：

A. $Q_A=Q_B$　　B. $Q_A>Q_B$　　C. $Q_A<Q_B$　　D. $Q_A=Q_B/2$

解 A 和 B 的换热面积相同，换热温差相同，液膜是层流的表面换热系数随着高度（自上而下）是减小的，$h_B<h_A$，所以 $Q_A>Q_B$。选 B。

13.7.3 影响膜状凝结因素及增强换热措施

(1)影响因素：①蒸气流速；②蒸气中含不凝性气体；③表面粗糙度；④蒸气中含油；⑤过热蒸气。

(2)措施：①改变表面几何特征；②有效排除不凝结性气体；③加速凝液排除。

典型例题解析

【例 13.7-2】 以下关于饱和蒸气在竖直壁面上膜状凝结传热的描述中正确的是：

A. 局部凝结传热系数 h_z 沿壁面方向 x（从上到下）数值逐渐增加

B. 蒸气中的不凝结气体会导致换热强度下降

C. 当液膜中的流动是湍流时，局部对流传热系数保持不变

D. 流体的黏度越高，对流传热系数越大

解 局部凝结传热系数 h_z 沿壁面方向 x（从上到下）数值：当液膜中的流动是层流时，h_z 逐渐减小，当液膜中的流动是湍流时，h_z 增加；流体的黏度越高，对流传热系数越小；由于气体的导热系数比液体的小，蒸汽中的不凝结气体增加了液膜的导热热阻，所以换热强度下降。选 B。

【例 13.7-3】 小管径水平管束外表面蒸汽凝结过程中，上下层管束之间的凝结表面传热系数 h 的关系为：

A. $h_{下排}>h_{上排}$　　B. $h_{下排}<h_{上排}$

C. $h_{下排}=h_{上排}$　　D. 不确定

解 上一层管子的凝液流到下一层管子上，使得下一层管面的膜层增厚，所以下一层的 h 比上一层的小。选 B。

【例 13.7-4】 如果要增强蒸汽凝结换热，常见措施中较少采用的是：

A. 增加凝结面积　　B. 促使形成珠状凝结

C. 清除不凝结气体　　D. 改变凝结表面几何形状

解　凝结表面的几何形状一般都是平面或者圆管表面，增强凝结可以改变表面光滑度而不是形状，选项 D 错误。选项 A、B、C 都是常见有效方法。选 D。

13.7.4 沸腾换热基本概念

(1)沸腾：液体吸热后在其内部产生气泡的汽化过程称为沸腾。

(2)沸腾换热：由于液体沸腾而发生的加热面与液体的换热。

(3)沸腾换热分类：大空间沸腾和有限空间沸腾。

(4)产生沸腾的条件：液体必须过热和要有汽化核心。

13.7.5 大空间沸腾换热

(1)大空间沸腾

指加热壁面沉浸在具有自由表面的液体中所发生的沸腾。

(2)饱和沸腾

液体主体温度达到饱和温度 t_s，壁面温度 t_w 高于饱和温度 t_s 所发生的沸腾。

(3)过冷沸腾

指液体主体温度低于相应压力下饱和温度，壁面温度大于该饱和温度所发生的沸腾。

(4)饱和沸腾过程和沸腾曲线

沸腾曲线如图 13.7-1 所示，可以看出，随着沸腾温差 Δt 的变化，饱和沸腾有四个换热规律全然不同的区段：对流沸腾、泡态沸腾(核态沸腾)、过渡沸腾及膜态沸腾。

C 点称为沸腾临界点，$q_c = q_{max}$ 称为临界热流密度。当热流密度超过 q_c 时会发生这样的现象：由于热流密度无法随过热度的增加而减少，工况将不再按沸腾曲线由 C 点向 D 点过渡，而是由 C 点直接跳转到同一热流密度 q_c 下的点 E，这是非常危险的，可能导致设备烧毁，以 q_{max} 为警戒点，所以为了确保热力设备的安全运行，热流密度应控制在 q_{max} 以下。

(5)泡态沸腾机理

要产生气泡必须有先天的汽化核心，使得初始气泡的半径为某一有限值。

因为气泡生成时，要求 $P_v > p_l$，所以 $t_v > t_s$，即热平衡要求 $t_l > t_s$。为了维持气泡的热平衡，液体必须存在过热度。

壁面凹处最先能满足气泡生成的条件：$R_{min} = \dfrac{2\sigma T_s}{r\rho_v \cdot \Delta t}$

①若气泡半径 $R < R_{min}$ 时，表面张力＞内外压差，则气泡内蒸气凝结，气泡不能形成；②若气泡半径 $R > R_{min}$ 时，气泡才能成长。

由上式可解释两个现象：

①紧贴加热壁面处液体具有最大过热度，在这里生成气泡核所需的半径最小，由于壁面上一般总有划痕、凹坑等，它们是生成气泡核的最好地点。

② $\Delta t \uparrow \Rightarrow R_{min} \downarrow$，加热面上更小的凹缝将成为汽化核心，因而汽化核心数量将随壁面过

热度的增加而增加。

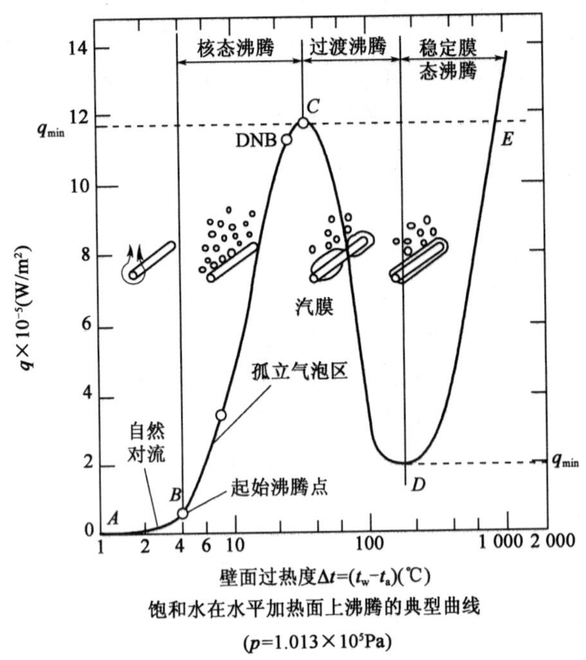

图 13.7-1 大空间沸腾曲线

13.7.6 大空间泡态沸腾表面传热系数的计算

1)适用于水的米海耶夫计算式

在 $10^5\sim4\times10^6$Pa 压力下的大空间饱和沸腾计算式

$$h=0.533q^{0.7}p^{0.15}\qquad [\mathrm{W/(m^2\cdot K)}]$$

由

$$q=h\Delta t\Rightarrow h=0.122\Delta t^{2.33}p^{0.55}\qquad [\mathrm{W/(m^2\cdot K)}]$$

式中：h ——沸腾换热表面传热系数；

p ——沸腾绝对压力；

Δt ——壁面过热度；

q ——热流密度。

2)适用于各种液体的计算式

$$q=\mu_l\cdot r\left[\frac{g(\rho_l-\rho_v)}{\sigma}\right]^{\frac{1}{2}}\left[\frac{c_{p,l}(t_w-t_s)}{C_{w,l}\cdot r\cdot \Pr_l^s}\right]^3\qquad (\mathrm{W/m^2})$$

式中：$c_{p,l}$ ——饱和液体的定压热容；

$C_{w,l}$ ——取决于加热表面—液体组合情况的系数；

$\Pr_l$——饱和液体的普朗特数；

σ ——液体-蒸气界面的表面张力(N/m)；

s——经验指数，对水，$s=1$，对其他液体，$s=1.7$。

13.7.7 泡态沸腾换热的增强

沸腾表面上的凹坑最容易产生汽化核心，因此增加表面凹坑是强化沸腾换热的有效方法，增加表面凹坑的方法有：

(1)用烧结、钎焊、火焰喷涂、电离沉积等方法在换热表面造成一层多孔结构。

(2)采用机械加工的方法在换热管表面上造成多孔结构。

说明：凝结换热和沸腾换热是有相变的对流换热过程，它要比单相流体的对流换热复杂得多。有相变的对流换热温差小，而表面传热系数往往较大，特别是水蒸气凝结和水沸腾的表面传热系数很大。但在制冷剂的工作过程中，其凝结和沸腾换热表面传热系数不大。由于凝结和沸腾换热过程的复杂性，以致很少有通用的关系式。复习本章要注意理解和掌握以下内容：①了解膜状凝结和珠状凝结的物理过程，能计算竖壁、水平圆管外侧表面和管束外侧表面的层流膜状凝结换热的表面传热系数。②了解大容器饱和沸腾（自然对流沸腾）曲线各段的沸腾状态，能计算大容器饱和沸腾换热表面传热系数。③了解影响凝结换热和沸腾换热的主要因素。

经 典 练 习

13.7-1 饱和蒸气分别在形状、尺寸、温度都相同的A、B两个等温垂直壁面上凝结，其中A上面是珠状凝结，B板上是膜状凝结。若两个壁面上的凝结传热量分别为Q_A和Q_B，则（　　）。

A. $Q_A=Q_B$　　B. $Q_A>Q_B$　　C. $Q_A<Q_B$　　D. $Q_A=Q_B/2$

13.7-2 根据努塞尔特对凝结传热时的分析解，局部对流传热系数h_x沿壁面方向x（从上到下）的变化规律为（　　）。

A. $h_x\propto x^2$　　B. $h_x\propto x^{(-1/4)}$　　C. $h_x\propto x^{(1/4)}$　　D. $h_x\propto x^{(-1/2)}$

13.7-3 表面进行膜状凝结换热的过程，影响凝结换热作用最小的因素为（　　）。

A. 蒸气的压力　　B. 蒸气的流速

C. 蒸气的过热度　　D. 蒸气中的不凝性气体

13.8 热辐射的基本定律

考试大纲☞：辐射强度和辐射力　普朗克定律　斯蒂芬-波尔兹曼定律　兰贝特余弦定律　基尔霍夫定律

必备基础知识

13.8.1 基本概念

1)热辐射的本质和特点

物体由于热的原因向外发射电磁波的过程，称为热辐射。

热辐射的特点：①热辐射可以在真空中传播，热辐射的两个能量传递不需要其他介质；②伴随能量形式的转变；③任何物体，只要温度高于绝对零度，就会不停地向周围空间发射电磁波。

2)物体对热辐射的吸收、反射和穿透

当热辐射投射到物体表面上时，一般会发生三种现象，即吸收、反射和穿透，如图13.8-1所示。

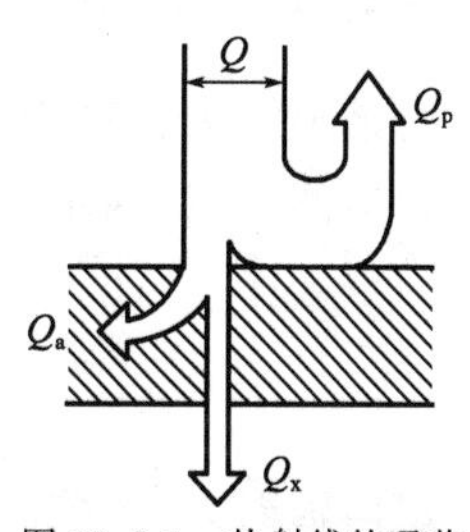

图13.8-1　热射线的吸收、反射和穿透

由能量守恒定律：$Q=Q_\rho+Q_\alpha+Q_\tau$

$$\frac{Q_\alpha}{Q}+\frac{Q_\rho}{Q}+\frac{Q_\tau}{Q}=1$$

$$\Downarrow \quad \Downarrow \quad \Downarrow$$

$$\alpha+\rho+\tau=1$$

其中：α 为吸收率，ρ 为反射率，τ 为透射率。

(1)对于液体和固体：热射线的透射率 $\tau=0$，则有 $\alpha+\rho=1$。

(2)对于气体，可认为气体对热射线几乎没有反射能力，即 $\rho=0$，则有 $\alpha+\tau=1$。

为了研究方便，引入三个假定的理想物体：黑体、白体和透明体。

(1)黑体：吸收率 $\alpha=1$ 的物体。

(2)白体(镜体)：反射率 $\rho=1$ 的物体。

(3)透明体：投射率 $\tau=1$ 的物体。黑体、白体、透明体都是对全波长射线而言的。

3)辐射强度和辐射力

立体角：以立体角的角端为中心，作一半径为 r 的半球，将半球表面上被立体角所切割的面积 A_2 对球心所张开的角度，称为立体角，记为 ω，单位为 sr(球面度)。如图 13.8-2 所示，$\omega=\frac{A_2}{r^2}$ (sr)。

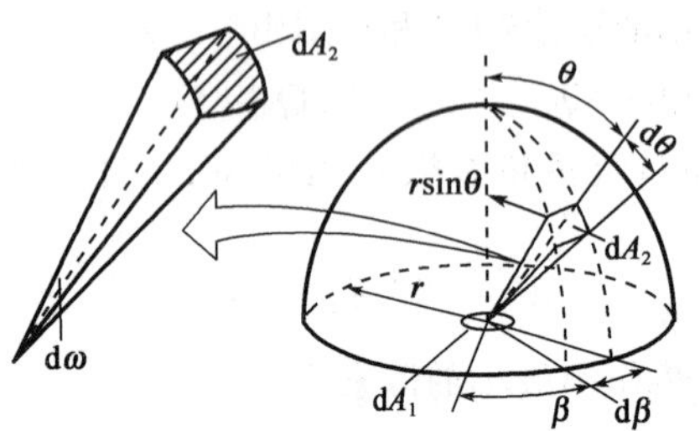

图 13.8-2 立体角和定向辐射强度

半球的立体角为

$$\omega=\frac{2\pi r^2}{r^2}=2\pi\ (\mathrm{sr})$$

定向辐射强度：单位时间内，物体单位可见辐射面积，在某一方向的单位立体角内所发射的一切波长的能量。

$$I_{(\theta,\beta)}=\frac{\mathrm{d}\Phi_{(\theta,\beta)}}{\mathrm{d}\omega\cdot\mathrm{d}A\cdot\cos\theta}\qquad [\mathrm{W/(m^2\cdot sr)}]$$

单色辐射强度：单位时间内，物体每单位可见面积，在波长 λ 附近的单位波长间隔内，单位立体角内所发射的能量。记为 $I_{\lambda(\theta,\beta)}$，单位为 $\mathrm{W/(m^2\cdot sr\cdot \mu m)}$。

$$I_{(\theta,\beta)}=\int_0^\infty I_{\lambda(\theta,\beta)}\mathrm{d}\lambda$$

辐射力：单位时间内，物体的单位表面积向整个半球空间所有方向发射的全部波长的能量总和，记为 E，单位为 $\mathrm{W/m^2}$。

辐射力 E 与定向辐射强度 I 的关系为：$E=\int_{\omega=2\pi}I\cdot\cos\theta\cdot\mathrm{d}\omega=\int_{\omega=2\pi}E_\theta\cdot\mathrm{d}\omega$

光谱辐射力：单位时间内从物体单位表面积上发射的热射线中，单位波段范围电磁波所具有的辐射能，也称为单色辐射力，记为 E_λ，单位为 $\mathrm{W/(m^2\cdot \mu m)}$。

$$E_\lambda=\frac{\mathrm{d}E}{\mathrm{d}\lambda}\ 或\ E=\int_0^\infty E_\lambda\mathrm{d}\lambda$$

定向辐射力：单位时间内，物体的单位表面积，向半球空间的某给定辐射方向上，在单位立体角内所发射全波长的能量，记为 E_θ，单位为 $\mathrm{W/(m^2\cdot sr)}$。

$$E_\theta=\frac{\mathrm{d}E}{\mathrm{d}\omega}\ 或\ E=\int_{\omega=2\pi}E_\theta\cdot\mathrm{d}\omega，而\ E_\theta=I_\theta\cdot\cos\theta$$

在法线方向 $\theta=0°$，则有：$E_n = I_n$ 。

单色定向辐射力：单位时间内，物体的单位表面积，向半球空间的某给定辐射方向上，在单位立体角内所发射的在波长 λ 附近的单位波长间隔内的能量，记为 $E_{\lambda,\theta}$，单位为 $W/(m^2 \cdot sr \cdot \mu m)$。

$$E_{\lambda,\theta} = \frac{dE}{d\lambda \cdot d\omega} \text{ 或 } E = \int_{\omega=2\pi}\int_0^\infty E_{\lambda,\theta} d\lambda d\omega$$

13.8.2 普朗克定律

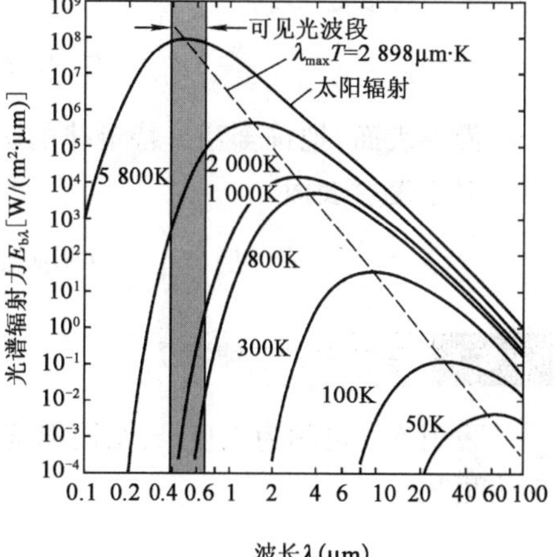

图 13.8-3 普朗克定律的图示

普朗克定律揭示了黑体在不同温度下的单色辐射力 $E_{b\lambda}$ 随波长 λ 的分布规律。

$$E_{b\lambda} = \frac{C_1\lambda^{-5}}{e^{\frac{C_2}{\lambda T}} - 1} \qquad [W/(m^2 \cdot \mu m)]$$

式中：C_1 ——普朗克第一常数，$C_1 = 3.743\times10^8$ $W \cdot \mu m^4/m$；

C_2 ——普朗克第二常数，$C_2 = 1.439\times10^4 \mu m \cdot K$。

普朗克定律还可以写成另外一种通用形式

$$\frac{E_{b\lambda}}{T^5} = \frac{C_1}{(\lambda T)^5(e^{\frac{C_2}{\lambda T}} - 1)} = f(\lambda T)$$

根据该式绘出的曲线表示在图 13.8-3 中，由图知：

(1)黑体的单色辐射力随温度升高而增大。即：λ 一定时，$T\uparrow$，则 $E_{b\lambda}\uparrow$ 。

(2)曲线下的面积表示辐射力 E_b。$T\uparrow$，则 $E_b\uparrow$，且短波区增大的速度比长波区大。

(3)在一定温度下，黑体的单色辐射力随波长的变化，先是增加，然后又减小，中间有一峰值，记为 $E_{b\lambda,max}$。$E_{b\lambda,max}$ 对应的波长叫峰值波长 λ_{max} 。

(4)随着温度的提高，峰值波长 λ_{max} 逐渐向短波方向移动。

维恩位移定律给出了黑体的峰值波长 λ_{max} 与绝对温度之间的函数关系

$$\lambda_{max} \cdot T = 2\,897.6 \mu m \cdot K$$

典型例题解析

【例 13.8-1】 根据普朗克定律，黑体的单色辐射力与波长之间的关系是一个单峰函数，其峰值所对应的波长：

A. 与温度无关　　B. 随温度升高而线性减小

C. 随温度升高而增大　　D. 与绝对温度成反比

解 由图 13.8-3 可以看出峰值所对应的波长与绝对温度成反比。选 D。

13.8.3 斯蒂芬-波尔兹曼定律

它给出了黑体的辐射力与绝对温度的关系

$$E_b = \sigma_b \cdot T^4 \quad \text{或} \quad E_b = C_b \cdot \left(\frac{T}{100}\right)^4$$

式中：σ_b ——黑体辐射常数，$\sigma_b = 5.67\times10^{-8}$ $W/(m^2 \cdot K^4)$；

C_b ——黑体辐射系数，$C_b = 5.67$ $W/(m^2 \cdot K^4)$。

13.8.4 兰贝特余弦定律

它描述了黑体辐射能量沿半球空间方向的变化规律。黑体辐射的定向辐射强度与方向无关,也就是说,在半球空间的各个方向上的定向辐射强度相等

$$I_{\theta_1} = I_{\theta_2} = \cdots = I_n = I$$

另一种表达形式

$$E_\theta = I_\theta \cos\theta = I_n \cos\theta = E_n \cos\theta$$

漫射表面:把符合兰贝特定律的辐射物体表面称为漫射表面。

对于漫射表面

$$E = \int_{\omega=2\pi} I\cos\theta \mathrm{d}\omega = I\int_{\theta=0}^{\frac{\pi}{2}}\int_{\beta=0}^{2\pi} \cos\theta \cdot \sin\theta \mathrm{d}\theta \mathrm{d}\beta = I\pi$$

13.8.5 基尔霍夫定律

发射率 (也称为黑度)ε:相同温度下,实际物体的半球总辐射力与同温度下黑体半球总辐射力之比。

$$\varepsilon = \frac{E}{E_b} = \frac{E}{\sigma T^4}$$

灰体:光谱吸收比与波长无关的物体称为灰体。此时,不管投入辐射的分布如何,吸收比 a 都是同一个常数。即将光谱吸收比 $\alpha(\lambda)$等效为常数,即 $\alpha = \alpha(\lambda) = \mathrm{const}$。与黑体类似,它也是一种理想物体。

基尔霍夫定律的各种形式:

(1)在热平衡条件下:$\varepsilon = \alpha$(实际物体的半球平均发射率等于它对同温度的黑体发出辐射的平均吸收率)。

(2)在温度不平衡条件下:

① $\varepsilon_{\lambda,\theta,T} = \alpha_{\lambda,\theta,T}$(实际物体表面的单色定向发射率等于同温度下的单色定向吸收率)无条件成立,对物体表面性质、是否处于热平衡都不做要求。

②对漫射表面,由于辐射性质与方向无关,则基尔霍夫定律表达为:$\varepsilon_{\lambda,T} = \alpha_{\lambda,T}$ 。

③对于灰表面,由于辐射性质与波长无关,则基尔霍夫定律表达为:$\varepsilon_{\theta,T} = \alpha_{\theta,T}$ 。

④对漫-灰表面,辐射性质与方向、波长均无关,则基尔霍夫定律表达为:$\varepsilon_{(T)} = \alpha_{(T)}$ 。

13.8.6 维恩定律

维恩位移定律,也是热辐射的基本定律之一。在一定温度下,绝对黑体的温度与辐射本领最大值相对应的波长 λ 的乘积为一常数,即

$$\lambda_{\max} \cdot T = 2\,897.6\ \mu\mathrm{m} \cdot \mathrm{K}$$

上述结论称为维恩位移定律。它表明,当绝对黑体的温度升高时,辐射本领的最大值向短波方向移动。

维恩位移定律是针对黑体来说的,说明了黑体越热,其辐射谱光谱辐射力(及某一频率的光辐射能量的能力)的最大值所对应的波长越短,而除了绝对零度外,其他任何温度下物体辐射的光的频率都是从零到无穷的,只是各个不同的温度对应的“波长—能量”图形不同,而实际物体都是黑体乘以黑度所对应灰体时的理想情况。譬如在宇宙中,不同恒星随表面温度的

不同会显示出不同的颜色，温度较高的显蓝色，次之显白色，濒临燃尽而膨胀的红巨星表面温度只有 2 000～3 000K，因而显红色。太阳的表面温度是 5 778K，根据维恩位移定律计算得到的峰值辐射波长则为 502nm，这近似处于可见光光谱范围的中点，为黄光。

典型例题解析

【例 13.8-2】 根据维恩位移定律可以推知，室内环境温度下可见波段的辐射力最大值：

A. 某些波长下可以达到　　B. 都可以达到

C. 不可能达到　　D. 不确定

解 维恩位移定律给出了黑体的峰值波长 λ_{max} 与绝对温度之间的函数关系：$\lambda_{max} \cdot T = 2\,897.6\ \mu m \cdot K$。室内环境温度一般取 20℃，则 $\lambda_{max} = 9.89\mu m$，而可见光段是 $\lambda = 0.38 \sim 0.76\mu m$，所以 $\lambda_{max} = 9.89\mu m$ 不在可见光段。

与太阳表面相比，通电的白炽灯的温度要低数千度，所以白炽灯的辐射光谱偏橙。至于处于“红热”状态的电炉丝等物体，温度要更低，所以更加显红色。温度再下降，辐射波长便超出了可见光范围，进入红外区，譬如人体、室内家具释放的辐射就主要是红外线，军事上必须使用的红外线夜视仪就是通过探测这种红外线来进行“夜视”的。选 C。

【例 13.8-3】 以下关于实际物体发射和吸收特性中正确的是：

A. 实际物体的发射率等于实际物体的吸收率

B. 实际物体的定向辐射强度符合兰贝特余弦定律

C. 实际物体的吸收率与其所接受的辐射源有关

D. 黑色的物体比白色的物体吸收率要高

解 漫射灰表面的发射率等于该表面的吸收率；除了黑体以外，只有漫射表面才符合兰贝特余弦定律；黑色的物体在可见光波段内比白色的物体吸收率要高，对红外线吸收率基本相同。选 C。

说明：复习本章要理解热辐射的物理本质和特点；掌握黑体、漫射体、白体、透明体和灰体的概念以及黑度、吸收率、反射率和透射率；掌握黑体的辐射规律(四个定律)和基尔霍夫定律；了解影响物体表面辐射性质的因素及简化处理方法。本章的难点之一是对基尔霍夫定律的理解。此外，物体的黑度仅取决于物体自身的情况，而物体的吸收率除与物体自身情况有关外，还与发射辐射能的物体的性质和温度等有关。

经 典 练 习

13.8-1 根据史提芬-波尔兹曼定律，面积为 $2m^2$、温度为 300℃的黑体表面的辐射力为(　　)。

A. 11 632W/m^2　　B. 6 112W/m^2　　C. 459W/m^2　　D. 918W/m^2

13.8-2 实际物体的辐射力可以表示为(　　)。

A. $E = aE_b$　　B. $E = E_b/a$　　C. $E = \varepsilon E_b$　　D. $E = E_b/\varepsilon$

13.8-3 辐射换热过程中，能量属性及转换与导热和对流换热过程不同，下列说法错误的是(　　)。

A. 温度大于绝对温度的物体都会有热辐射

B. 不依赖物体表面接触进行能量传递

C. 辐射换热过程伴随能量两次转换

D. 物体热辐射过程与温度无关

13.8-4　固体表面进行辐射换热时，表面吸收率 α、透射率 τ 和反射率 ρ 有 $\alpha+\tau+\rho=1$，在理想或特殊条件下表面分别称之为黑体、透明体或者是白体，描述中错误的是（　　）。

A. 投射到表面的辐射能量全部反射时，$\rho=1$，称之为白体

B. 投射到表面的辐射能量全部可以穿透时，透射率 $\tau=1$

C. 红外线辐射和可见光辐射全部被吸收，表面呈现黑色

D. 投射辐射中，波长在 0.1～100μm 的辐射能量能全部吸收时，称之为黑体

13.9　辐射换热计算

考试大纲☞：黑表面间的辐射换热　角系数的确定方法　角系数及空间热阻　灰表面间的辐射换热　有效辐射　表面热阻　遮热板　气体辐射的特点　气体吸收定律　气体的发射率和吸收率　气体与外壳间的辐射换热　太阳辐射

必备基础知识

13.9.1 任意黑表面间的辐射换热

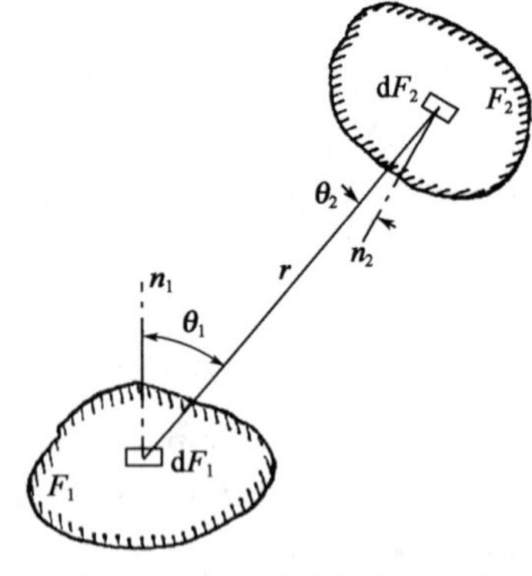

图 13.9-1　任意位置两非凹黑表面的辐射换热

如图 13.9-1 所示，设有两个任意放置的非凹黑体表面，面积分别为 A_1、A_2，温度分别为 T_1、T_2。从表面上分别取微元面积 dA_1、dA_2，两者的距离为 r，两表面的法线与连线 r 间的夹角分别为 θ_1、θ_2。

黑体表面 A_1 和 A_2 之间的辐射换热量为

$$\Phi_{1,2}=\int_{A_1}\int_{A_2}\Phi_{dA_1,dA_2}=(E_{b_1}-E_{b_2})\int_{A_1}\int_{A_2}\frac{\cos\theta_1\cdot\cos\theta_2}{\pi r^2}dA_1dA_2$$

13.9.2 角系数及空间热阻

1）角系数

角系数：表示一表面发出的辐射能中直接落到另一表面上的百分数。

表面积 A_1 对表面积 A_2 的角系数为

$$X_{1,2}=\frac{1}{A_1}\int_{A_1}\int_{A_2}\frac{\cos\theta_1\cdot\cos\theta_2}{\pi r^2}dA_1dA_2$$

同理，表面积 A_2 对表面积 A_1 的角系数为

$$X_{2,1}=\frac{1}{A_2}\int_{A_1}\int_{A_2}\frac{\cos\theta_1\cdot\cos\theta_2}{\pi r^2}\cdot dA_1dA_2$$

可见：$A_1X_{1,2}=A_2X_{2,1}$

此式表示两表面在辐射换热时的互换性，也称为角系数的相对性。

2)辐射空间热阻

任意放置的两黑体表面间的辐射换热计算式用角系数形式表示为

$$\Phi_{1,2}=(E_{b_1}-E_{b_2})\cdot A_1\cdot X_{1,2}=(E_{b_1}-E_{b_2})\cdot A_2\cdot X_{2,1}$$

上式可写为

$$\Phi_{1,2}=\frac{E_{b_1}-E_{b_2}}{\dfrac{1}{A_1\cdot X_{1,2}}}$$

其中，$\dfrac{1}{A_1\cdot X_{1,2}}$ 为辐射空间热阻，如图 13.9-2 所示。

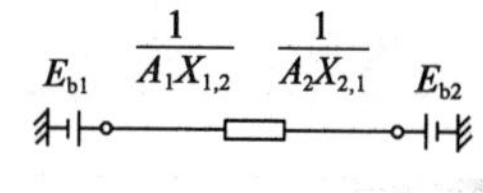

图 13.9-2　辐射空间热阻

对于两块平行的黑体大平壁（$A=A_1=A_2$），则

$$\Phi_{1,2}=(E_{b_1}-E_{b_2})\cdot A=\sigma_b(T_1^4-T_2^4)A$$

13.9.3 角系数的确定方法

1)积分法确定角系数

对于符合兰贝特定律的漫射表面，角系数可以从它的定义式直接积分运算求得。实用上为了简化计算，对表面间不同相对位置的角系数计算式画成线图，通过查图确定角系数。

2)代数法确定角系数

代数法是利用角系数的特性作为分析的基础。利用该方法的前提是系统一定是封闭的，如果不封闭可以做假想面，令其封闭。

角系数的特性：互换性（相对性）、完整性、分解性。

(1)互换性（相对性）

任意两个表面 A_i 和 A_j 间的角系数满足关系：$A_iX_{i,j}=A_jX_{j,i}$。

(2)完整性

由 n 个表面组成的空腔，任何一个表面对空腔各表面间的角系数存在关系

$$X_{i,1}+X_{i,2}+\cdots+X_{i,j}+\cdots+X_{i,n}=\sum_{j=1}^{n}X_{i,j}=1\qquad(i=1,2,3,\cdots,n)$$

(3)分解性

两个表面 A_1 及 A_2，如果把表面 A_1 分解为 A_3 和 A_4 则有

$$A_1X_{1,2}=A_3X_{3,2}+A_4X_{4,2}$$

如果把表面 A_2 分解为 A_5 和 A_6，则有

$$A_1X_{1,2}=A_1X_{1,5}+A_1X_{1,6}$$

一个由 3 个非凹形表面组成的系统（3 个表面在垂直于纸面方向是很长的），则有

$$X_{1,2}=\frac{A_1+A_2-A_3}{2A_1},X_{1,3}=\frac{A_1+A_3-A_2}{2A_1},X_{2,3}=\frac{A_2+A_3-A_1}{2A_2}$$

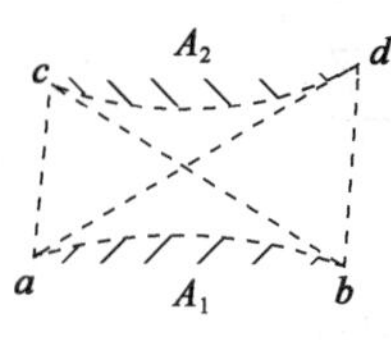

图 13.9-3　两个非凹表面之间的角系数

两个非凹表面 A_1 和 A_2 之间的角系数，如图 13.9-3 所示，假定在垂直于纸面的方向上，表面的长度是无限延伸的，为求 $X_{1,2}$，今做无限延长的辅助面 ac、bd、ad 和 bc，构成封闭的系统。

则，$X_{ab,cd}=\dfrac{(bc+ad)-(ac+bd)}{2ab}$

即，$X_{1,2}=\dfrac{\text{交叉线段长度之和}-\text{不交叉线段长度之和}}{\text{表面 }A_1\text{ 的端面长度的 2 倍}}$，此方法称为交叉线法。

典型例题解析

【例 13.9-1】 图中的正方形截面的长通道，下表面 1 对上表面 2 的角系数为：

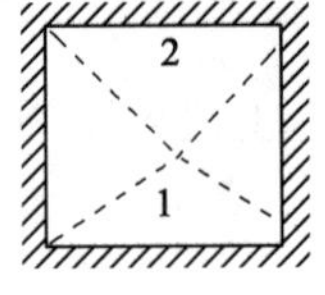

例 13.9-1 图

A. 1/3　　B. 0.3　　C. 0.707　　D. 0.414

解 $X_{1,2}=\dfrac{\text{交叉线段长度之和}-\text{不交叉线段长度之和}}{\text{表面 } A_1 \text{ 的端面长度的 2 倍}}$

$=(2\sqrt{2}a-2a)/2a=0.414$

选 D。

13.9.4 封闭空腔诸黑表面间的辐射换热

设有 n 个黑体表面组成的封闭空腔，i 表面与其他黑表面间的辐射换热

$$\Phi_i=E_{b_i}\cdot A_i-\sum_{j=1}^{n}E_{b_j}\cdot X_{j,i}\cdot A_j$$

可见，i 表面与周围诸黑表面间的总辐射换热，是表面 i 发射的能量与诸黑表面向 i 表面投射能量的差额。

由三个黑体表面组成的封闭空腔的辐射换热网络图，如图 13.9-4 所示。当组成封闭空腔诸表面有某个表面 j 是绝热时，即它在辐射换热过程中没有净热量交换，$Q_j=0$，投射到该表面的能量将全部反射出去，则该表面所表示的节点不必和外电源相连接，该表面的辐射力或温度相应的电位 E_{bj} 称为不固定的浮动电位，这种绝热面也称为重辐射面。

13.9.5 灰表面间的辐射换热

1)有效辐射

单位时间内离开单位面积的总辐射能为该表面的有效辐射，记为 J，包括了自身的发射辐射 E 和反射辐射 ρG。图 13.9-5 表示了灰体表面 1 的有效辐射 J_1。

$$J_1=\varepsilon_1E_{b_1}+\rho_1G_1=\varepsilon_1E_{b_1}+(1-\alpha_1)G_1$$

在表面外能感受到的辐射就是有效辐射，它也是用辐射探测仪能测量到的表面辐射。

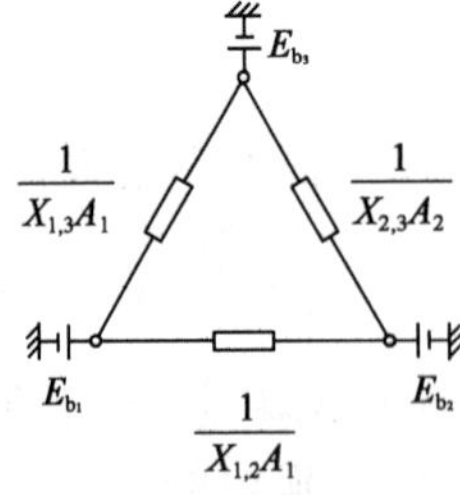

图 13.9-4 三个黑体表面组成的封闭空腔的辐射换热网络图

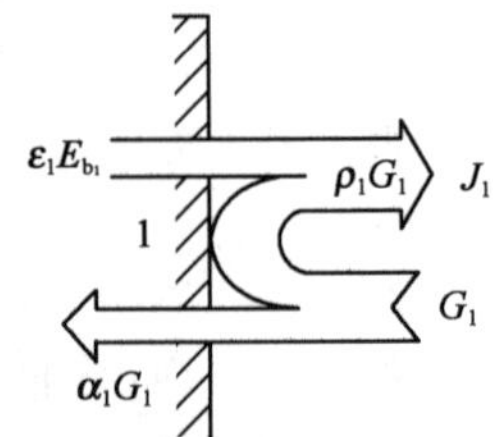

图 13.9-5 有效辐射

2)辐射表面热阻

灰体表面单位面积的辐射换热量

$$\Phi_1 = \frac{\varepsilon_1}{1-\varepsilon_1}A_1(E_{b_1} - J_1) = \frac{E_{b_1} - J_1}{\dfrac{1-\varepsilon_1}{\varepsilon_1 A_1}}$$

其中，$\dfrac{1-\varepsilon_1}{\varepsilon_1 A_1}$ 称作 E_{b_1} 和 J_1 之间的表面辐射热阻，简称表面热阻，如图 13.9-6 所示。

3)组成封闭空腔的两灰表面间的辐射换热

如图 13.9-7 所示，组成封闭空腔的两灰表面间的辐射换热计算式为：

$$\Phi_{1,2} = \frac{E_{b_1} - E_{b_2}}{\dfrac{1-\varepsilon_1}{\varepsilon_1 A_1} + \dfrac{1}{X_{1,2} \cdot A_1} + \dfrac{1-\varepsilon_2}{\varepsilon_2 A_2}}$$

图 13.9-6 表面热阻

图 13.9-7 封闭空腔的两灰表面间的辐射换热

如果用 A_1 作为计算面积，则

$$\Phi_{1,2} = \frac{A_1(E_{b_1} - E_{b_2})}{(\dfrac{1}{\varepsilon_1} - 1) + \dfrac{1}{X_{1,2}} + \dfrac{A_1}{A_2}(\dfrac{1}{\varepsilon_2} - 1)} = \varepsilon_s X_{1,2} A_1 (E_{b_1} - E_{b_2})$$

其中，$\varepsilon_s = \dfrac{1}{1 + X_{1,2}\left(\dfrac{1}{\varepsilon_1} - 1\right) + X_{2,1}\left(\dfrac{1}{\varepsilon_2} - 1\right)}$ 称为系统发射率。

(1)两块平行的灰体大平壁（$A = A_1 = A_2$）的辐射换热

$$\Phi_{1,2} = \frac{A(E_{b_1} - E_{b_2})}{\dfrac{1}{\varepsilon_1} + \dfrac{1}{\varepsilon_2} - 1}$$

(2)空腔与内包壁面之间的辐射换热

$$\Phi_{1,2} = \varepsilon_1 A_1 (E_{b_1} - E_{b_2})$$

4)封闭空腔中诸灰表面间的辐射换热

网络求解法，以三个表面组成的封闭空腔为例，如图 13.9-8 所示。根据基尔霍夫定律来求解：在稳定的电路中，电路任一节点上的电流代数和等于零。

节点 1：$\dfrac{E_{b_1} - J_1}{\dfrac{1-\varepsilon_1}{\varepsilon_1 A_1}} + \dfrac{J_2 - J_1}{\dfrac{1}{X_{1,2} A_1}} + \dfrac{J_3 - J_1}{\dfrac{1}{X_{1,3} A_1}} = 0$

节点 2：$\dfrac{E_{b_2} - J_2}{\dfrac{1-\varepsilon_2}{\varepsilon_2 A_2}} + \dfrac{J_1 - J_2}{\dfrac{1}{X_{1,2} A_1}} + \dfrac{J_3 - J_2}{\dfrac{1}{X_{2,3} A_2}} = 0$

节点 3：$\dfrac{E_{b_3} - J_3}{\dfrac{1-\varepsilon_3}{\varepsilon_3 A_3}} + \dfrac{J_1 - J_3}{\dfrac{1}{X_{1,3} A_1}} + \dfrac{J_2 - J_3}{\dfrac{1}{X_{2,3} A_2}} = 0$

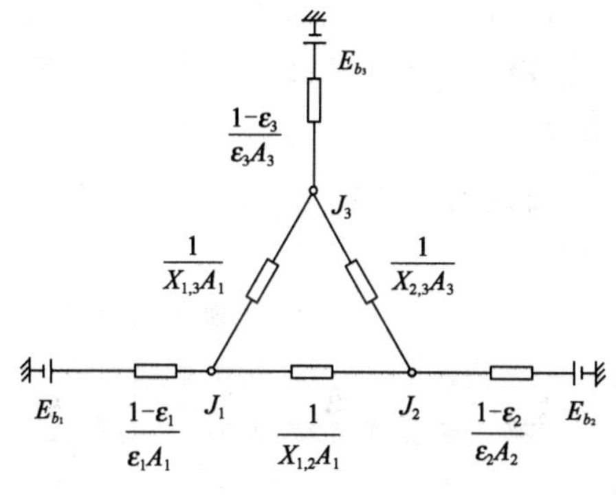

图 13.9-8 三个灰表面组成封闭空腔辐射换热网络

以上三个独立方程，联立求解可得出 J_1、J_2 和 J_3 。

如果某个表面 i 是绝热面，$\Phi_i=0$，则在网络中该节点可不与电源相连接，其有效辐射 J_i 值是浮动的。

13.9.6 遮热板

由于工程上的需求，经常需要强化或削弱辐射换热。

强化辐射换热的主要途径有两种：增加发射率和增加角系数。

削弱辐射换热的主要途径有三种：降低发射率、降低角系数和加入遮热板。

遮热板：是指插入两个辐射面之间以削弱换热的薄板。遮热板对整个系统不起加入或移走热量的作用，而仅仅是在热流途中增加热阻以减少换热量。

图 13.9-9 遮热板原理

如图 13.9-9 所示，则由平板 1 传到平板 2 的辐射换热量为

$$q_{1,2}=\frac{1}{2}\frac{\sigma_b(T_1^4-T_2^4)}{\dfrac{1}{\varepsilon_1}+\dfrac{1}{\varepsilon_2}-1}$$

比较可以看出，当三块板的表面发射率相同时，设置一块遮热板后的辐射换热量是无遮热板时换热量的 1/2。同样可以证明，在 T_1 和 T_2 保持不变的情况下，遮热板增至 n 块时，换热量将减少到原来的 $1/(n+1)$，遮热板的表面发射率越小，遮热效果越明显。

用网络图法分析遮热效果非常方便，如图 13.9-10 所示。

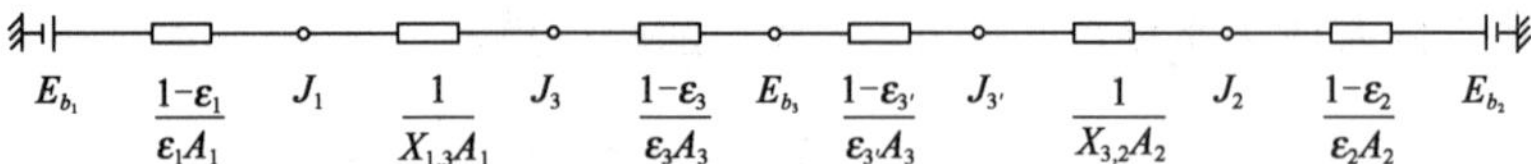

图 13.9-10 两平行大平壁或管壁中间有一块遮热板时的辐射换热网络

典型例题解析

【例 13.9-2】 冬季里在中央空调供暖的空房间内将一支温度计裸露在空气中，那么温度计的读数：

A. 高于空气温度　　B. 低于空气的温度

C. 等于空气的温度　　D. 不确定

解 温度计与比室温低的内墙壁之间的辐射换热，使得温度计的读数低于空气的温度。选 B。

【例 13.9-3】 表面温度为 50℃的管道穿过室内，为了减少管道向室内的散热，最有效的措施是：

A. 表面喷黑色的油漆　　B. 表面喷白色的油漆

C. 表面缠绕铝箱　　D. 表面外安装铝箔套筒

解 根据遮热板原理，管道表面外安装铝箔套筒减少管道向室内的辐射换热。选 D。

13.9.7 气体辐射

1)气体辐射的特点

(1)气体辐射对波长具有选择性。

(2)气体的辐射和吸收是在整个容积中进行的。

2)气体吸收定律

$$I_{\lambda,s} = I_{\lambda,0} \cdot e^{-K_\lambda \cdot s}$$

它表明:单色辐射强度在吸收性气体中传播时按指数规律衰减。

3)气体的发射率和吸收率

(1)气体的单色吸收率和单色发射率

将基尔霍夫定律应用于单色辐射,$\varepsilon_\lambda = \alpha_\lambda$,则:$\varepsilon_\lambda = \alpha_\lambda = 1 - e^{-k_\lambda \cdot ps}$

(2)气体的发射率

影响气体发射率的因素是:气体温度;射线平均行程 s 与气体分压 p 的乘积;气体分压和气体所处的总压。

CO_2 与 H_2O 共存时的发射率:$\varepsilon_g = \varepsilon_{CO_2} + \varepsilon_{H_2O} - \Delta\varepsilon$

(3)气体的吸收率

气体辐射具有选择性,不能将它作为灰体看待,所以气体吸收率不等于气体发射率。

$$\alpha_g = \alpha_{CO_2} + \alpha_{H_2O} - \Delta\alpha$$

4)气体与外壳间的辐射换热

以烟气与炉膛周围受热面之间的辐射换热为例。

(1)受热面作为黑体

$$\Phi = A\sigma_b(\varepsilon_g T_g^4 - \alpha_g T_w^4)$$

(2)受热面发射率为 ε_w 的灰体

$$\Phi = \varepsilon_w A\sigma_b(\varepsilon_g T_g^4 - \alpha_g T_w^4)$$

13.9.8 太阳辐射

太阳辐射能量中的紫外线部分约占 8.7%;可见光部分约占 44.6%;红外线部分约占 45.4%。太阳辐射能量 99%集中在波长 λ=0.2~3.0μm 的短波区。大气层外缘与太阳射线垂直的单位面积上接收到的太阳辐射能为 1 353W/m^2,称为太阳常数;由此可算得太阳表面相当于温度为 5 762K 的黑体。

1)大气对太阳的削弱作用

(1)大气层中的 CO_2、H_2O、O_2 对太阳辐射有吸收作用,且具有明显选择性。

(2)太阳辐射在大气层中遇到空气分子和微小尘埃产生的散射。

(3)大气中的云层和较大的尘粒对太阳辐射的反射作用。

(4)与太阳辐射通过大气层的行程有关。

2)太阳能的利用

作为太阳能吸收器表面材料,要求它对 0.3~3.0μm 波长范围的光谱吸收率接近于 1,而对波长大于 3.0μm 范围光谱吸收率接近于 0。对于某些金属材料,表面镀层处理后具有这种性能,这种表面为选择性表面,如图 13.9-11 所示。

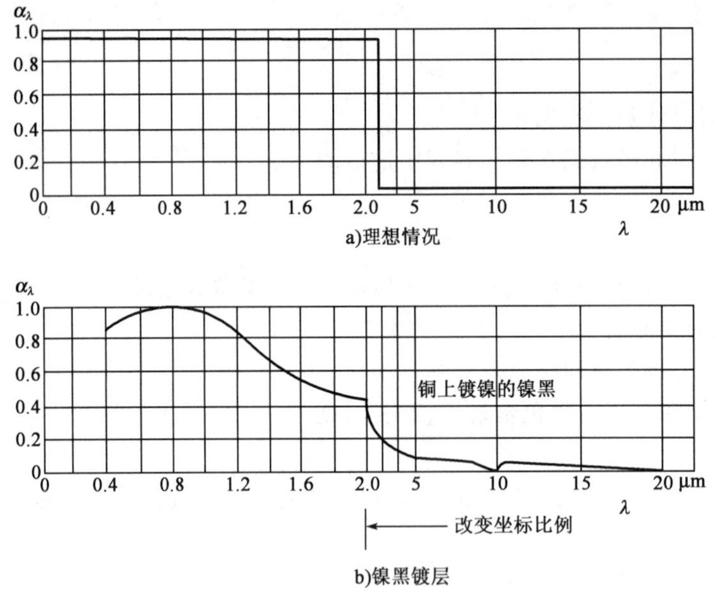

图 13.9-11　选择性表面光谱吸收比

玻璃是太阳能利用中的一种重要材料，普通玻璃可以透过 2.0μm 以下的射线，所以可把投射在它上面的太阳辐射大部分透射进人家内；然而窗玻璃对 3.0μm 以上的长波辐射基本不透过，如图 13.9-12 所示。因此室内常温下物体所辐射的长波射线就被阻隔在室内，从而产生了所谓温室效应。玻璃中氧化铁含量对透光率有很大影响，氧化铁含量增加则透光率下降。

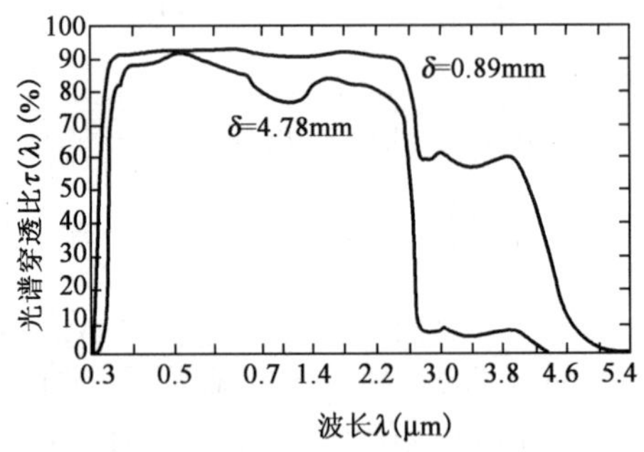

图 13.9-12　普通玻璃的光谱透射比

说明：实际物体表面的辐射和吸收随方向和波长变化(热辐射的方向性和光谱性)，但在红外线波段范围内，大多数工程材料表面可处理为漫射-灰表面。复习本节要注意理解和掌握以下内容：①理解投射辐射和有效辐射概念，掌握漫射-灰表面净辐射换热量的两种不同形式表达式。②理解角系数的概念及其基本性质(完整性、相对性和叠加性)。有限表面间的角系数是一个平均角系数，它适用于漫射表面间的辐射计算。角系数的大小取决于表面形状、大小和相对位置，而与表面的温度和辐射性质无关。掌握角系数的确定方法。③理解构成封闭空腔的漫射—灰表面的辐射换热模拟网络。能熟练计算由两个或三个漫射—灰表面构成的封闭系统的辐射换热。④了解气体热辐的基本特性和影响气体黑度及吸收率的因素，能确定含有大量二氧化碳和水蒸气的混合气体的黑度及吸收率，能计算气体与包壳间的辐射换热。

典型例题解析

【例 13.9-4】 在秋末冬初季节，晴朗天气晚上草木表面常常会结霜，其原因可能是：

A. 夜间水蒸气分压下降达到结霜温度

B. 草木表面因夜间降温及对流换热形成结霜

C. 表面导热引起草木表面的凝结水结成冰霜

D. 草木表面凝结水与天空辐射换热达到冰点

解 大气层外宇宙空间的温度接近绝对零度，是个理想冷源，在 8～13μm 的波段内，大气中所含二氧化碳和水蒸气的吸收比很小，穿透比较大，地面物体通过这个窗口向宇宙空间辐射散热，达到一定冷却效果。这种情况是由于晴朗天气下，草木表面与太空直接辐射换热使得草木表面的温度达到了冰点。选 D。

【例 13.9-5】 大气层能够阻止地面绝大部分热辐射进入外空间，由此产生温室效应，其主要原因是：

A. 大气中的二氧化碳等多原子气体　　B. 大气中的氮气

C. 大气中的氧气　　D. 大气中的灰尘

解 大气中的温室气体有二氧化碳、氯氟烃、甲烷等，其中以二氧化碳为主。选 A。

经 典 练 习

13.9-1 计算灰体表面间的辐射传热时，通常需要计算某个表面的冷热量损失 q，若已知黑体辐射量为 E_b，有效辐射为 J，投入辐射为 G，正确的计算式是(　　)。

A. $q=E_b-G$　　B. $q=E_b-J$　　C. $q=J-G$　　D. $q=E-G$

13.9-2 在关于气体辐射的论述中，错误的是(　　)。

A. 气体的辐射和吸收过程是在整个容积中完成的

B. 二氧化碳吸收辐射能量时，对波长有选择性

C. 气体的发射率与压力有关

D. 气体可以看成是灰体，因此其吸收率等于发射率

13.9-3 角系数 $X_{i,j}$ 表示表面发射出的辐射能中直接落到另一个表面上，其中不适用的是(　　)。

A. 漫灰表面　　B. 黑体表面

C. 辐射时各向均匀表面　　D. 定向辐射和定向反射表面

13.9-4 抽真空的保冷瓶胆是双壁镀银的夹层结构，外壁内表面温度为 30℃，内壁外表面温度为 0 ℃，镀银壁黑度为 0.03，计算由于辐射换热单位面积的散热量(　　)W/m²。

A. 3.12　　B. 2.48　　C. 2.91　　D. 4.15

13.10 传热和换热器

考试大纲☞：通过肋壁的传热　复合换热时的传热计算　传热的削弱和增强　平均温度差　效能—传热单元数　换热器计算

必备基础知识

13.10.1 通过肋壁的传热

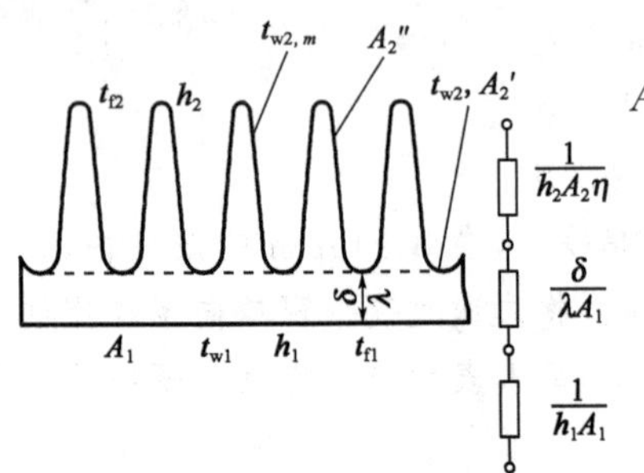

图 13.10-1 通过肋壁的传热

肋壁换热如图 13.10-1 所示，肋表面积为 $A_2 = A_2'' + A_2'$，其中 A_2' 为肋片之间的基部面积，A_2'' 为肋片表面积。

(1)肋片效率

$$\eta_f = \frac{h_2A_2''(t_{w2,m} - t_{f2})}{h_2A_2''(t_{w2} - t_{f2})} = \frac{t_{w2,m} - t_{f2}}{t_{w2} - t_{f2}}$$

肋片的总效率：$\eta = \dfrac{A_2' + \eta_f A_2''}{A_2}$

(2)肋壁传热公式

$$\Phi = \frac{t_{f1} - t_{f2}}{\dfrac{1}{h_1A_1} + \dfrac{\delta}{\lambda A_1} + \dfrac{1}{h_2A_2\eta}} = \frac{t_{f1} - t_{f2}}{\dfrac{1}{h_1} + \dfrac{\delta}{\lambda} + \dfrac{A_1}{h_2A_2\eta}}A_1$$

将上式写为：$\Phi = k_1A_1(t_{f1} - t_{f2})$

其中，k_1 是以光壁面面积 A_1 为基准的传热系数。

$$k_1 = \frac{1}{\dfrac{1}{h_1} + \dfrac{\delta}{\lambda} + \dfrac{1}{h_2\beta\eta}} \quad [\mathrm{W/(m^2 \cdot K)}]\left(\beta = \frac{A_2}{A_1},\text{称为肋化系数}\right)$$

如果壁面的任何一侧有污垢，则导热系数中应加上污垢热阻 R_f，即导热项的热阻为：

对 k_1：$\dfrac{\delta}{\lambda} + R_f$

加肋后，肋片一侧的热阻为：$1/(h_2\beta\eta)$，它比无肋的光壁换热热阻 $1/h_2$ 小（因为 $\beta\eta > 1$），因而使换热量 Φ 增大。

(3)加肋的目的

①强化传热：当换热器两侧的表面传热系数相差较大时，肋片应加在热阻大的一侧效果好。传热壁两侧的热阻差相差越大，在热阻大的一侧加肋产生的强化传热的效果越显著。当换热器两侧的表面传热系数都较低时，如气体换热器，则可在两侧都加肋片。

②调节壁面温度：在传热壁的低温侧加肋能降低壁面温度。当低温侧热阻比高温侧热阻大时，在低温侧加肋既能强化传热，又能降低壁面温度。如果低温侧热阻比高温侧热阻小，则低温侧加肋的主要目的是降低壁面温度。同样，加肋片有时也能使壁温升高。

典型例题解析

【例 13.10-1】 某建筑外墙的面积为 12m²，室内空气与内墙表面的对流传热系数为 8W/(m² · K)，外表面与室外环境的复合传热系数为 23W/(rn² · K)，墙壁的厚度为0.48m，导热系数 0.75W/(m · K)，总传热系数为：

A. 1.24W/(m² · K)　　B. 0.81W/(m² · K)

C. 2.48W/(m² · K)　　D. 0.162W/(m² · K)

解 总传热系数等于总热阻的倒数

$$R = \frac{1}{h_1} + \frac{1}{h_2} + \frac{\delta}{\lambda} = \frac{1}{8} + \frac{1}{23} + \frac{0.48}{0.75} = 0.808$$

$$K=\frac{1}{0.808}=1.24\mathrm{W/(m^2 \cdot K)}$$

选 A。

13.10.2 复合换热时的传热计算

对流与辐射并存的换热称为复合换热，有

$$q = q_c + q_r$$

对流换热密度

$$q_c = h_c(t_w - t_f)$$

辐射换热热流密度

$$q_r = \left\{\varepsilon C_b\left[\left(\frac{T_w}{100}\right)^4 - \left(\frac{T_{am}}{100}\right)^4\right]/(t_w - t_f)\right\}(t_w - t_f) = h_r(t_w - t_f)$$

则：

$$q = q_c + q_r = (h_c + h_r)(t_w - t_f) = h(t_w - t_f)$$

13.10.3 传热的削弱和增强

1)增强传热的方法

①扩展传热面；②改变流动状况；③使用添加剂改变流体物性；④改变表面状况；⑤改变换热面的形状和大小；⑥改变能量传递方式；⑦靠外力产生振荡，强化传热。

2)削弱传热的方法

(1)覆盖热绝缘材料：泡沫热绝缘材料；超细粉末热绝缘材料；真空热绝缘层。

(2)改变表面状况：改变表面的辐射特性；附加抑制对流元件。

13.10.4 平均温度差

流体在套管换热器中顺流和逆流时，流体温度变化情况如图 13.10-2 所示。

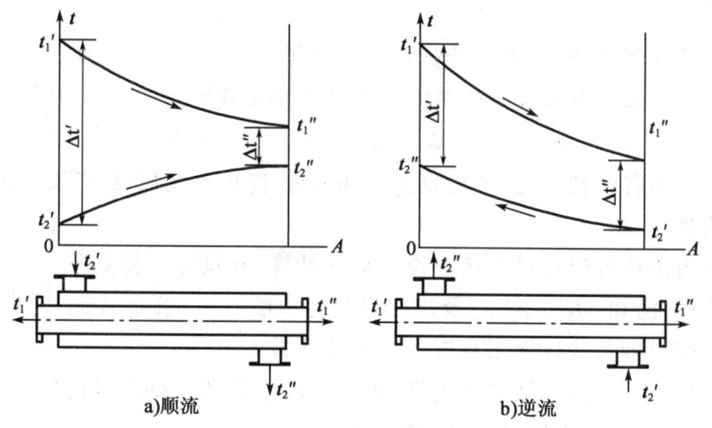

图 13.10-2 流体温度随传热面变化示意图

换热器的传热量的计算式为

$$Q = kA\Delta t_m$$

换热器的平均温度差

$$\Delta t_m = \frac{\Delta t' - \Delta t''}{\ln \dfrac{\Delta t'}{\Delta t''}}$$

顺流和逆流的区别在于

顺流　　$\Delta t' = t_1' - t_2'$　　$\Delta t'' = t_1'' - t_2''$

逆流　　$\Delta t' = t_1' - t_2''$　　$\Delta t'' = t_1'' - t_2'$

顺流和逆流是两种极端情况，在相同的进出口温度下，逆流的平均温度差最大，顺流则最小；当 $\Delta t'/\Delta t'' < 2$ 时，可用算术平均温度差代替对数平均温度差，误差小于 4%，即 $\Delta t_m = (\Delta t' + \Delta t'')/2$。其他复杂布置时换热器的平均温度差，逆流的平均温度差乘以温差修正系数，即 $\Delta t_m = \varepsilon_{\Delta t}(\Delta t_m)_{逆流}$。

典型例题解析

【例 13.10-2】 一逆流套管式水-水换热器，冷水的进口温度为 25℃，出口温度为 55℃。热水进水温是 70℃，热水的流量是冷水的流量的 2 倍，且物性参数不随温度变化，与平均温差最接近的数据为：

A. 15℃　　B. 20℃　　C. 25℃　　D. 30℃

解　冷水进出口温差为 55－25＝30℃

热水的流量是冷水的流量的 2 倍，所以热水进出口温差为 15℃，则热水出口温度为 55℃。

可采用对数平均温差公式进行计算：

$\Delta t' = t_1' - t_2'' = 70 - 55 = 15$，$\Delta t'' = t_1'' - t_2' = 55 - 25 = 30$

$$\Delta t_m = \frac{\Delta t' - \Delta t''}{\ln \dfrac{\Delta t'}{\Delta t''}} = 21.6$$

选 B。

13.10.5 换热器计算

换热器热计算分两种情况：设计计算和校核计算。

换热器热计算的基本方程式是传热方程式及热平衡式。

$$\Phi = kA\Delta t_m \quad 和 \quad \Phi = M_1c_1(t_1' - t_1'') = M_2c_2(t_2'' - t_2')$$

换热器的热计算有两种方法：平均温差法和效能-传热单元数(ε-NTU)法。

1)平均温差法

就是直接应用传热方程和热平衡方程进行热计算，其具体步骤如下。

对于设计计算(已知 M_1c_1、M_2c_2 及进出口温度中的三个，求 k、A)：

(1)初步布置换热面，并计算出相应的总传热系数 k。

(2)根据给定条件，由热平衡式求出进、出口温度中的那个待定的温度。

(3)由冷热流体的 4 个进出口温度确定平均温差 Δt_m。

(4)由传热方程式计算所需的换热面积 A，并核算换热面流体的流动阻力。

(5)如果流动阻力过大，则需要改变方案重新设计。

对于校核计算(已知 A、M_1c_1、M_2c_2 及两个进口温度，求 t_1''、t_2'')：

(1)先假设一个流体的出口温度，按热平衡式计算另一个出口温度。

(2)根据 4 个进出口温度求得平均温差 Δt_m 。

(3)根据换热器的结构,算出相应工作条件下的总传热系数 k。

(4)已知 kA 和 Φ,按传热方程式计算在假设出口温度下的 Δt_m,根据 4 个进出口温度,用热平衡式计算另一个 Φ,这个值和上面的 Φ 都是在假设出口温度下得到的,因此,都不是真实的换热量。

(5)比较两个 Φ 值,满足精度要求则结束,否则,重新假定出口温度,重复(1)～(6),直至满足精度要求。

2)效能—传热单元数法

(1)换热器的效能和传热单元数。

效能的定义为换热器的实际传热量 q 与可能最大传热量 q_{max}之比。

如果冷流体 $M_2c_2 = (Mc)_{min}$,则

$$\varepsilon = \frac{t_2'' - t_2'}{t_1' - t_2'}$$

如果热流体 $M_1c_1 = (Mc)_{min}$,则

$$\varepsilon = \frac{t_1' - t_1''}{t_1' - t_2'}$$

(2)效能和传热单元数的关系。

顺流时 $$\varepsilon = \frac{1 - \exp[-\mathrm{NTU}(1 + C_r)]}{1 + C_r}\left(\mathrm{NTU} = \frac{kA}{C_{min}}\text{ 为传热单元数}\right)$$

逆流时 $$\varepsilon = \frac{1 - \exp[-\mathrm{NTU}(1 - C_r)]}{(1 - C_r)\exp[-\mathrm{NTU}(1 - C_r)]}\left(C_r = \frac{(Mc)_{min}}{(Mc)_{max}}\right)$$

当冷热流体之一发生相变时,相当于 $C_{max} \to \infty$,即 $C_r = C_{min}/C_{max} \to 0$,于是上面效能公式可简化为:$\varepsilon = 1 - \exp[-\mathrm{NTU}]$

当两种流体的热容相等时,即 $C_r = C_{min}/C_{max} = 1$,$\varepsilon$ 公式可以简化为

顺流 $$\varepsilon = \frac{1 - \exp[-2 \times \mathrm{NTU}]}{2}$$

逆流 $$\varepsilon = \frac{\mathrm{NTU}}{1 + \mathrm{NTU}}$$

3)用效能-传热单元数法计算换热器的步骤

(1)设计计算(已知 M_1c_1、M_2c_2 及进出口温度中的三个,求 k、A)。

显然,利用已知条件可以计算出 ε,而带求的 k、A 则包含在 NTU 内,因此,对于设计计算是已知 ε,求 NTU,求解过程与平均温差法相似,不再重复。

(2)校核计算(已知 A、M_1c_1、M_2c_2 及两个进口温度,求 t_1''、t_2'')。

由于 k 事先不知,所以仍然需要假设一个出口温度,具体如下:

①假设一个出口温度 t'',利用热平衡式计算另一个 t''。

②利用四个进出口温度计算定性温度,确定物性,并结合换热器结构,计算总传热系数 k。

③利用 k,A 计算 NTU。

④利用 NTU 计算 ε。

⑤利用公式分别计算 Φ。

⑥比较两个 Φ,是否满足精度,否则重复以上步骤。

从上面步骤可以看出,假设的出口温度对传热量 Φ 的影响不是直接的,而是通过定性温

度，影响总传热系数，从而影响 NTU，并最终影响 Φ 值。而平均温差法的假设温度直接用于计算 Φ 值，显然 ε-NTU 法对假设温度没有平均温差法敏感，这是该方法的优势。

说明：综合所学知识，提高分析解决问题的能力，综述了以下三部分内容：①复合换热、传热过程和有复合换热时的传热；②传热的增强和削弱；③换热器基本知识及热力计算。学习这一节除了要着重注意培养综合能力、分析解决问题的能力之外，还要注意培养多维思维和辩证思维能力。例如，注意掌握一分为二的观点；强化传热中抓主要矛盾的方法；对于换热设备的性能要求，既要考虑传热能力，又要考虑阻力损失，还要考虑经济性，即要求综合性能指标。这就要全面地、辩证地分析问题。复习本节要注意以下几点：①理解复合换热和传热过程，掌握传热分析方法，并能较熟练地应用热路分析法求解复杂传热问题。②理解增强和削弱热量传递过程的原理和手段，能综合应用所学知识分析解决一般性强化和削弱传热的问题。③了解工程上常见的换热器类型，能对间壁式换热器进行传热分析，并能进行热力计算。

典型例题解析

【例 13.10-3】 套管式换热器中顺流或逆流布置下 ε-NTU 关系不同，下述说法错误的是：

A. $c_{min}/c_{max}>0$，相同 NTU 下，$\varepsilon_{顺}<\varepsilon_{逆}$

B. $c_{min}/c_{max}=0$，NTU→∞，$\varepsilon_{顺}\to1$，$\varepsilon_{逆}\to1$

C. $c_{min}/c_{max}=1$，NTU→∞，$\varepsilon_{顺}\to0.5$，$\varepsilon_{逆}\to1$

D. $c_{min}/c_{max}>0$，NTU 增大，$\varepsilon_{顺}$ 和 $\varepsilon_{逆}$ 都趋于同一个定值

解 如解图所示，选项 A、B、C 是正确的。而根据选项 C 的结果可以判定选项 D 是错误的。

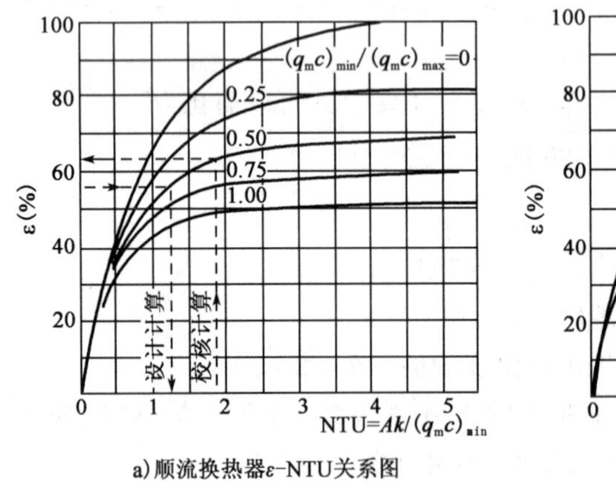

a) 顺流换热器ε-NTU关系图

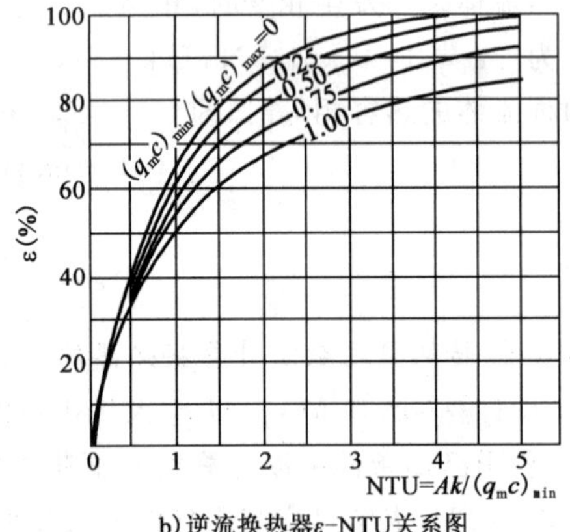

b) 逆流换热器ε-NTU关系图

例 13.10-3 解图

经典练习

13.10-1 一套管式水—水换热器，冷水的进口温度为 25℃，热水进口温度为 70℃，热水出口温度为 55℃。若冷水的流量远远大于热水的流量，则与该换热器的对数平均温差最接近的数据为(　　)。

A. 15℃　　B. 25℃　　C. 35℃　　D. 45℃

13.10-2 一逆流套管式水—水换热器，冷水的出口温度为 55℃，热水进口温度为 70℃。

若热水的流量与冷水的流量相等，换热面积和总传热系数分别为 $2m^2$ 和 $150W/(m^2 \cdot K)$，且物性参数不随温度变化，则与该换热器的传热量最接近的数据为(　　)。

A. 3 500W　　B. 4 500W　　C. 5 500W　　D. 6 500W

13.10-3　套管式换热器，顺流换热，两侧为水-水单项流体换热，一侧水温进水 65℃，出水 45℃，流量为 1.25kg/s，另一侧入口为 15℃，流量为 2.5kg/s，则换热器对数平均温差为(　　)。

A. 35℃　　B. 33℃　　C. 31℃　　D. 25℃

13.10-4　管套式换热器中进行换热时，如果两侧为水-水单相流体换热，一侧水温由 55℃ 降到 35℃，流量为 0.6kg/s，另一侧入口为 15℃，流量为 1.2kg/s，则换热器分别作顺流和逆流时的平均温差比 Δt_m(逆流)/Δt_m(顺流)为(　　)。

A. 1.35　　B. 1.25　　C. 1.14　　D. 1.0

参考答案及提示

13.1-1　A　一般情况 $\lambda_{金} > \lambda_{液} > \lambda_{气}$。

13.1-2　B　$v^2 t + \frac{qv}{\lambda} = 0$ 为常物性稳态具有内热源的导热问题；$\Delta^2 t = 0$ 为常物性无内热源稳态的三维导热；$\frac{d^2 t}{dx^2} = 0$ 为常物性无内热源稳态的一维导热。

13.1-3　A　气体导热系数在较大压力范围变化不大，因而一般把导热系数仅仅视为温度的函数，查图 13.1-1 可知，空气的空气热导率随温度升高而增大。

13.1-4　A

13.2-1　B　圆柱壁面内侧温度变化率较大，将导热率较小的材料在内层，以减少散热量。

13.2-2　D　由于是一维稳态导热，则热流密度是常数。

13.2-3　C　Φ 为圆柱体高的函数。

13.2-4　B　当平壁的导热系数为常数时，在平壁中任何两个等温面之间温度都是线性变化的。当平壁的导热系数随着温度变化时，任何两个等温面之间温度都是非线性的。

13.3-1　C　如图 13.3-2 所示。

13.3-2　C

13.3-3　A　Bi＝125×0.06÷110＝0.068＜0.1，由采用集总数法：

$$\frac{\theta}{\theta_0} = e^{-\frac{hA}{\rho V c}\tau}$$

$$\frac{\theta}{\theta_0} = \frac{t - t_f}{t_0 - t_f} = \frac{t - 400}{30 - 400} = e^{-\frac{125\times100}{8\,440\times0.06\times377}} = 0.94$$

$$t = 53$$

13.4-1　C　根据第二类边界条件边界节点的节点方程可得。

13.4-2　C

13.4-3　A　边界节点用热守衡方式，中心节点可以用级数展开，也可以用热守衡方式。

13.5-1 A 积分方程组的求解要先假设速度和温度的分布,因此是近似解;雷诺类比的解是由比拟理论求得的,也是近似解。

13.5-2 B 湍流受迫对流时能量传递与动量传递之间的关系式:$\mathrm{St} = C_f/2$ 。

13.6-1 B 流体流过粗糙壁面能产生涡流,增强换热,使对流传热系数增加。

13.6-2 A 第一种情况不能形成自然对流,其他三种都会形成自然对流,增强换热。

13.6-3 C 自然对流传热的相似准则关系式为 $\mathrm{Nu}=f(\mathrm{Gr},\mathrm{Pr})$。

13.6-4 A 在弯曲的通道中流动产生的离心力,将在流场中形成二次环流,此二次环流与主流垂直,它增加了对边界层的扰动,有利于换热。而且管的弯曲半径越小,二次环流的影响越大。

13.6-5 B 管内受迫流动达到充分发展段时,无量纲温度$(t_w-t)/(t_w-t_f)$和表面对流换热系数趋于定值。

13.7-1 B 由于珠状凝结的表面传热系数大大高于膜状凝结的,A 和 B 的换热面积相同,换热温差相同,所以 $Q_A>Q_B$。

13.7-2 B 凝结传热的分析解:$h = 0.943\left[\dfrac{\rho_l^2 \cdot g \cdot r \cdot \lambda^3}{\mu_l \cdot x \cdot (t_s - t_w)}\right]^{\frac{1}{4}}$ 。

13.7-3 A 蒸汽的流速如果过大,增强凝结换热;蒸汽中的不凝性气体,使凝结换热减弱。

13.8-1 B $E_b=5.67\times[(273+300)/100]^4=6\ 112\mathrm{W/m^2}$。

13.8-2 C 实际物体的辐射力等于该物体的发射率乘上同温度黑体的辐射力。

13.8-3 D 物体热辐射过程与热力学温度四次方成正比。

13.8-4 D 投射到表面的辐射能量全部吸收时,$\alpha=1$,称之为黑体,指的是全波段。

13.9-1 A 黑体对于投入辐射全部吸收,冷热量损失 q 为向外辐射的减去吸收的。

13.9-2 D 气体辐射具有明显的选择性,因此不能看成灰体,其吸收率不等于发射率。

13.9-3 D 这里的辐射能是指向半球空间的辐射,不是某个方向上的。

13.9-4 B $q_{12} = \dfrac{E_{b1} - E_{b2}}{\dfrac{1}{\varepsilon_1} + \dfrac{1}{\varepsilon_1} - 1} = \dfrac{5.67 \times (3.03^4 - 2.73^4)}{\dfrac{1}{0.03} + \dfrac{1}{0.03} - 1} = 2.48\mathrm{W/m^2}$

13.10-1 C 由于冷水的流量远远大于热水的流量,且:

$$M_1c_1(t_1' - t_1'') = M_2c_2(t_2'' - t_2')$$

冷水温度基本不变:

$\Delta t' = t_1' - t_2' = 70 - 25 = 45℃,\Delta t'' = t_1'' - t_2'' = 55 - 25 = 30℃$

$\Delta t_m = \dfrac{\Delta t' + \Delta t''}{2} = \dfrac{45 + 30}{2} = 37.5℃$

13.10-2 B 由于热水的流量与冷水的流量相等,则热水进出口温差与冷水的进出口温差相等，可用冷热水的进口温差作为对数平均温差：

$Q=kF\times\Delta t=2\times150\times(70-55)=4\,500\text{W}$

13.10-3　B　由 $M_1c_1(t_1'-t_1'')=M_2c_2(t_2''-t_2')$

可得 $1.25\times(65-45)=2.5\times(t_2''-15)$

得 $t_2''=25℃$

$\Delta t'=t_1'-t_2'=65-15=50$，$\Delta t''=t_1''-t_2''=45-25=20$

$$\Delta t_m=\frac{\Delta t'-\Delta t''}{\ln\dfrac{\Delta t'}{\Delta t''}}=33℃$$

13.10-4　C　由 $M_1c_1(t_1'-t_1'')=M_2c_2(t_2''-t_2')$

可得 $0.6\times(55-25)=1.2\times(t_2''-15)$

得 $t_2''=25℃$

$$\Delta t_{m顺}=\frac{\Delta t'-\Delta t''}{\ln\dfrac{\Delta t'}{\Delta t''}}=\frac{30}{\ln4},\Delta t_{m逆}=\frac{\Delta t'-\Delta t''}{\ln\dfrac{\Delta t'}{\Delta t''}}=\frac{10}{\ln1.5}$$

$\Delta t_{m逆}/\Delta t_{m顺}\approx1.14$

14　工程流体力学及泵与风机

考题配置　单选，10 题
分数配置　每题 2 分，共 20 分

复习指导

本章阐述了流体的主要物理性质、流体平衡和运动的基本规律、相似原理与量纲分析以及流体机械的基本性能和应用。要求掌握流体力学动力学及黏性流体力学相关基本概念和基本理论；熟练应用流体动力学的三大基本方程解决工程实际问题；理解相似理论的概念和模型率的选择；熟练掌握流体机械原理、特征曲线及应用分析。

14.1　流体动力学基础

考试大纲☞：流体运动的研究方法　稳定流动与非稳定流动　理想流体的运动方程式　实际流体的运动方程式　伯努利方程式及其使用条件

必备基础知识

流体是由大量做无规则运动的分子组成的，分子之间存在空隙，但考虑宏观特性，在流动空间和时间上所采用的一切特征尺度和特征时间，都比分子距离和分子碰撞时间大得多。因此，可把流体视为没有间隙地充满它所占据的整个空间的一种连续介质，且其所有的物理量都是空间坐标和时间的连续函数的一种假设模型，这就是连续介质模型。这样就可以把物理量作为时空连续函数，利用连续函数这一数学工具来研究问题。

流体都有一定的可压缩性，液体可压缩性很小，而气体的可压缩性较大。在流体的形状改变时，流体各层之间也存在一定的运动阻力（即黏滞性）。当流体的黏滞性和可压缩性很小时，可近似看作是理想流体，它是人们为研究流体的运动和状态而引入的一个理想模型。

典型例题解析

【例 14.1-1】 流体力学对理想流体运用了以下哪种力学模型，从而简化了流体的物质结构和物理性质？

A. 连续介质
B. 无黏性、不可压缩
C. 连续介质、不可压缩
D. 连续介质、无黏性、不可压缩

解　连续介质、无黏性、不可压缩都是理想化假设的模型。选 D。

14.1.1 流体运动的研究方法

表征运动流体的物理量称为流体的流动参数。描述流体运动就是要表达流体质点的流动参数,在不同空间位置上随时间连续变化的规律。在流体力学中,描述流体运动的方法有拉格朗日(Lagrange)法和欧拉(Euler)法。

拉格朗日法从分析流体质点的运动着手,分析流动参数随时间的变化规律,然后综合所有被研究流体质点的运动情况,来获得整个流体运动的规律。

由于拉格朗日方法着眼于每个流体质点,需要找到一种方法用以区分不同的流体质点。通常采用的方法是以初始时刻 t_0 时,各质点的空间坐标(a , b , c)作为不同质点的区别标志。在流体运动过程中,每一个质点的运动坐标不是独立变量,而是起始坐标(a , b , c)和时间变量 t 的函数。人们把 a、b、c、t 叫做拉格朗日变数。

流体质点的空间位置(x,y,z),可以表示为

$$\left.\begin{aligned} x &= x(a,b,c,t) \\ y &= y(a,b,c,t) \\ z &= z(a,b,c,t) \end{aligned}\right\} \tag{14.1-1}$$

运动坐标对时间求导,则可得流体质点的速度

$$\left.\begin{aligned} v_x &= \frac{\mathrm{d}x}{\mathrm{d}t} = \frac{\partial x}{\partial t} = \frac{\partial x(a,b,c,t)}{\partial t} \\ v_y &= \frac{\mathrm{d}y}{\mathrm{d}t} = \frac{\partial y}{\partial t} = \frac{\partial y(a,b,c,t)}{\partial t} \\ v_z &= \frac{\mathrm{d}z}{\mathrm{d}t} = \frac{\partial z}{\partial t} = \frac{\partial z(a,b,c,t)}{\partial t} \end{aligned}\right\} \tag{14.1-2}$$

欧拉法不同于拉格朗日法。欧拉法的着眼点是空间点,即着眼于流体经过流场中各空间点时的运动情况,而不关心这些运动特性是由哪些流体质点表现出来的,也不考虑流体质点的来龙去脉,然后综合空间点上各质点的流动参数及其变化规律,用以描述整个流体的运动。

欧拉法用质点的空间坐标(x,y,z)与时间变量 t 来表达流场中的流体运动规律,(x,y,z)称为欧拉变数。欧拉变数不是各自独立的,因为流体质点的空间位置 x、y、z 与运动过程中的时间变量有关。不同的时间,各个流体质点对应不同的空间坐标,因而对任一流体质点来说,其位置变量 x、y、z 是时间 t 的函数。因此,流场中各空间点的流速所组成的速度场可以表示为

$$\left.\begin{aligned} v_x &= v_x(x,y,z,t) = v_x[x(t),y(t),z(t),t] \\ v_y &= v_y(x,y,z,t) = v_y[x(t),y(t),z(t),t] \\ v_z &= v_z(x,y,z,t) = v_z[x(t),y(t),z(t),t] \end{aligned}\right\} \tag{14.1-3}$$

由上式可以得到任一时刻(即 t 一定)流体质点速度在空间中的分布规律,也可以得到任一空间点(即 x、y、z 一定)的流体质点速度随时间的变化规律。

典型例题解析

【例 14.1-2】 下列说法正确的是:

A. 分析流体运动时,拉格朗日法比欧拉法在做数学分析时更为简便

B. 拉格朗日法着眼于流体中各个质点的流动情况,而欧拉法着眼于流体经过空间各固定点时的运动情况

C. 流线是拉格朗日法对流动的描述,迹线是欧拉法对流动的描述

D. 拉格朗日法和欧拉法在研究流体运动时，有本质的区别

解 这两种方法都是对流体运动的描述，只是着眼点不同，因此不能说有本质的区别。拉格朗日法是把流体的运动，看作无数个质点运动的总和，以部分质点作为观察对象加以描述，将这些质点的运动汇总起来，就得到整个流动。拉格朗日法也称为迹线法。欧拉法是以流动的空间作为观察对象，观察不同时刻各空间点上流体质点的运动参数，将各个时刻的情况汇总起来，就描述了整个流动。欧拉法也称为流线法。选 B。

14.1.2 恒定流动和非恒定流动

如果流场中每一空间点上的流动参数都不随时间变化，这种流动就称为恒定流动，又称为定常流动，否则称为非恒定流动或非定常流动。恒定流动中，流场内的速度、压力、密度等所有的物理量只是空间坐标（x,y,z）的函数，与时间变量 t 无关，$\frac{\partial v}{\partial t}=\frac{\partial p}{\partial t}=\frac{\partial \rho}{\partial t}=\frac{\partial T}{\partial t}=0$，即各流动参数的当地导数为零。

14.1.3 恒定元流能量方程

在采用欧拉法分析流体运动时，还将涉及一些流体力学的基本概念和定义，在此做简要介绍，详细内容可参见相关资料。

1）迹线

流体质点运动的轨迹称为迹线，它给出同一质点在不同时刻的速度方向。由迹线的形状可以清楚地看出质点的流动情况，从而得出流场的参数分布和变化情况，迹线是拉格朗日法分析流体运动的概念。

2）流线

流线是指某一瞬时在流场中所作的一条假想的空间曲线，在该时刻，位于曲线上各点的流体质点的速度在各点与流线相切。

流线形象地给出了流场中的流动状态，通过流线可以清楚地看出某时刻流场中各点的速度方向。显然，流线是欧拉法分析流体运动的概念。在流场内可以绘出一簇流线，所构成的流线图称为流谱。

一般情况下（除驻点或奇点），流线具有如下性质。

（1）恒定流动中，流线形状不随时间变化，且流体质点的流线与迹线重合。

（2）流线不能相交，不能突然转折，只能是一条光滑曲线。否则，在交点或转折点处将有两个速度矢量，这意味着在同一时刻，同一流体质点具有两个运动方向，这是不可能的。

由流线的定义，可以建立流线的微分方程

$$\frac{\mathrm{d}x}{v_x}=\frac{\mathrm{d}y}{v_y}=\frac{\mathrm{d}z}{v_z}$$

因为流线是某一时刻的曲线，所以时间变量 t 不是自变量，只能作为一个参变量。求某一指定时刻的流线时，需要把 t 当作常数带入上式，然后进行积分即可求得。

3）流管

在流场中任取一非流线又不相交的封闭曲线，过曲线上各点作流线，这些流线组成一个封闭的管状曲面，称为流管。由流线的定义可知，位于流管表面上的流体质点只具有切于流管方

向的速度，因而流体质点只能在流管内部或流管表面流动，而不能穿越流管。流管如同真实的固体管壁，将其内部的流体限制在管内流动。自来水管的内表面就是流管的一个实例。

4）流束

流管内的全部流体，称为流束。微小的封闭曲线构成的流管内的流体称为元流，又称微元流束。元流的极限就是流线。实际工程中，把管内流动和渠道中的流动看作是总的流束，它由无限多元流组成，称为总流。

5）过流断面

与流束或总流的所有流线都相垂直的横断面称为过流断面。过流断面可能是平面，也可能是各种形式的曲面。如果流体是水，则称为过水断面。由于元流的过流断面无限小，可以认为其断面上的运动参数分布均匀，但对于总流，过流断面上各点的运动要素却不一定相等。

单位时间内通过某一过流断面的流体量称为流量，它可以用体积或质量来表示，其相应的流量分别称为体积流量（q_V，m^3/s）和质量流量（q_m，kg/s）。不加说明时，"流量"一词概指体积流量。

对于元流，过流断面面积上的速度可认为是均匀分布的，且方向与过流断面垂直，故元流的流量为

$$dq_V = v dA \tag{14.1-4}$$

总流的流量等于所有元流流量之和

$$q_V = \int_A v dA \tag{14.1-5}$$

6）断面平均流速

所谓断面平均流速，是一种假想的流速，即过流断面上各点的速度都相等，其大小等于过流断面的流量 q_V 除以过流断面面积 A，即

$$v = \frac{q_V}{A} = \frac{\int_A v dA}{A} \tag{14.1-6}$$

断面平均流速的概念十分重要，它将使我们的研究和计算大为简化，尤其在工程计算中，具有重要的实际意义。

7）渐变流与急变流

按流线沿程变化的缓急程度，又将非均匀流动分为渐变流与急变流。各流线接近于平行直线的流动，称为渐变流。此时，各流线之间的夹角很小，且流线的曲率半径很大。反之，称为急变流。由于渐变流的所有流线是一组几乎平行的直线，其过流断面可认为是一平面。同时，恒定渐变流过流断面上动压强的分布近似地符合静压强的分布规律，即同一过流断面上 $z+\frac{p}{\rho g}\approx$常数。渐变流的极限情况就是均匀流。

8）连续性方程

这是流体力学基本方程之一，是质量守恒原理的流体力学表达式。在总流中取面积为 A_1 和 A_2 的两个断面，对恒定流两截面间流动空间内的流体质量不变，即有可压缩流体的连续性方程

$$\rho_2 \bar{v}_2 A_2 = \rho_1 \bar{v}_1 A_1 \tag{14.1-7}$$

当流体不可压缩时，密度为常数，则不可压缩流体的连续性方程为

$$\bar{v}_2 A_2 = \bar{v}_1 A_1 \tag{14.1-8}$$

如果质量力只有重力，则恒定不可压缩流体的质量力势函数 $W=-gz$，将其代入沿流线的伯努利积分式中，由于元流的过流断面积无限小，所以沿流线积分就是沿元流积分，可得

$$z+\frac{p}{\rho g}+\frac{v^2}{2g}=C \tag{14.1-9}$$

或

$$z_1+\frac{p_1}{\rho g}+\frac{v_1^2}{2g}=z_2+\frac{p_2}{\rho g}+\frac{v_2^2}{2g} \tag{14.1-10}$$

这就是理想流体恒定元流的伯努利方程。

推导此方程所引入的限定条件，就是理想流体元流伯努利方程的应用条件：理想流体、恒定流动、质量力只有重力、不可压缩流体。

如果流动速度为零，则由伯努利方程又可得出平衡流体的流体静力学基本方程式

$$z+\frac{p}{\rho g}=C$$

因此，伯努利方程式中各项的物理意义和几何意义也就比较明显。

从物理角度看，z 代表单位质量流体对某基准面具有的位能，$\frac{p}{\rho g}$ 代表单位重力流体的压能，$\frac{v^2}{2g}$ 代表单位重力流体的动能。因此，伯努利方程的物理意义为：对于重力作用下的恒定不可压缩流体，单位重量流体所具有的位能、动能和压能之和，即机械能，沿流线不变。由此可见，伯努利方程实质就是物理学能量守恒定律在流体力学上的一种表现形式。

从几何角度看，伯努利方程的每一项的量纲与长度相同，都代表某一个高度。z 代表所研究点相对于某基准面的几何高度，称为位置水头，$\frac{p}{\rho g}$ 代表所研究点处压力大小的高度，称为压强水头，$\frac{v^2}{2g}$ 代表所研究点处速度大小的高度，称为速度水头。通常将位置水头与压强水头之和称为测压管水头，测压管水头与速度水头之和称为总水头。伯努利方程的几何意义为：对于重力作用下的恒定不可压缩流体，总水头为一常数，或总水头沿流线相等。

实际流体具有黏性，在运动时由于流层间内摩擦力做功，将一部分机械能转变为热能而耗散，因此实际流体流动的机械能将沿程减少。根据能量守恒定律，可得实际流体恒定元流的伯努利方程

$$z_1+\frac{p_1}{\rho g}+\frac{v_1^2}{2g}=z_2+\frac{p_2}{\rho g}+\frac{v_2^2}{2g}+h'_w \tag{14.1-11}$$

其中，h'_w 表示单位质量流体沿着流线从 1 点到 2 点的机械能损失。方程(14.1-11)中各项及总水头、测压管水头的沿程变化可在图上表示出来。可知，实际流体的总水头线是沿程下降的，而测压管水头线沿程可升、可降，也可不变。

14.1.4 恒定总流能量方程

在实际工程中需要解决的往往是总流流动问题，如管路或渠道中的流动。因此，应该将元流的伯努利方程推广到总流中去。

$$z_1+\frac{p_1}{\rho g}+\frac{\alpha_1 v_1^2}{2g}=z_2+\frac{p_2}{\rho g}+\frac{\alpha_2 v_2^2}{2g}+h_w \tag{14.1-12}$$

其中，α 值与断面流速分布有关，一般情况下 $\alpha=1.05\sim1.10$，在渐变流动情况下，通常取 $\alpha=1.0$。

上式就是实际流体恒定总流的伯努利方程，其每一项的物理意义和几何意义与元流的伯努利方程相类似。

总流的伯努利方程是在一些限制条件下得到的，应用该方程时需要满足以下限制条件。

(1)流体不可压缩。

(2)流动是恒定的。

(3)质量力只有重力。

(4)过流断面上的流动必须是渐变流，但两过流断面间可以是急变流。

典型例题解析

【例 14.1-3】 根据流体运动参数是否随时间的变化可以分为稳定流动和非稳定流动，请问下面哪一种说法是正确的？

A. 流体非稳定流动时，只有流体的速度随时间而变化

B. 流体稳定流动时，任何情况下沿程压力均不变

C. 流体稳定流动时，流速一定很小

D. 流体稳定流动时，各流通断面的平均流速不一定相同

解 流体非稳定流动时，流体压力也随时间而变化。流体稳定流动时，根据连续性方程，其各流通断面的质量流量相同，但平均流速不一定相同。选 D。

【例 14.1-4】 流线的微分方程式为：

A. $\frac{dz}{v_x}=\frac{dx}{v_y}=\frac{dy}{v_z}$　　B. $\frac{dy}{v_x}=\frac{dx}{v_y}=\frac{dz}{v_z}$

C. $\frac{dx}{v_x}=\frac{dy}{v_y}=\frac{dz}{v_z}$　　D. $\frac{dy}{v_x}=\frac{dz}{v_y}=\frac{dx}{v_z}$

解 此题可直接由流线的定义得出。选 C。

【例 14.1-5】 如图所示，用水银压差计+文丘里管测量管道内水流量，已知管道的直径 $d_1=200$mm，文丘里管道喉管直径 $d_2=100$mm，文丘里管的流量系数 $\mu=0.95$。已知测出的管内流量 $Q=0.025\ \mathrm{m^3/s}$，那么两断面的压强差 Δh 为（水银的密度为 13 600kg/m^3）：

A. 24.7mm　　B. 35.6mm

C. 42.7mm　　D. 50.6mm

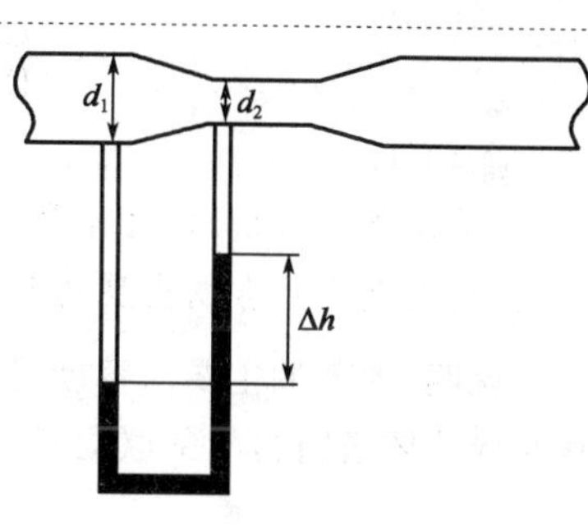

例 14.1-5 图

解

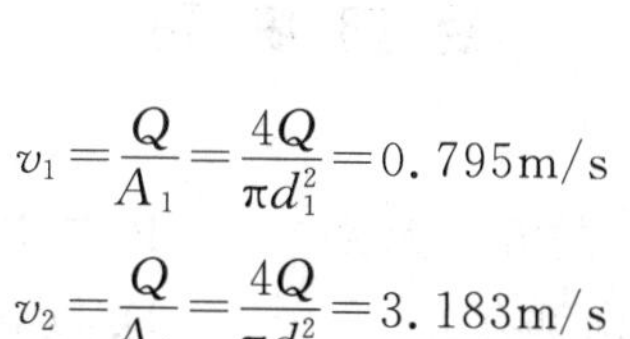

$$v_1=\frac{Q}{A_1}=\frac{4Q}{\pi d_1^2}=0.795\mathrm{m/s}$$

$$v_2=\frac{Q}{A_2}=\frac{4Q}{\pi d_2^2}=3.183\mathrm{m/s}$$

列伯努利方程：
$$z_1+\frac{p_1}{\rho g}+\frac{v_1^2}{2g}=z_2+\frac{p_2}{\rho g}+\frac{v_2^2}{2g}$$

得
$$\frac{p_1-p_2}{\rho g}=\frac{v_2^2-v_1^2}{2g}$$

$$\frac{(\rho_{Hg}-\rho_{水})\Delta h}{\rho_{水}}=\frac{v_2^2-v_1^2}{2g}$$

故
$$\Delta h=42.7\mathrm{mm}$$

选 C。

【例 14.1-6】 如图所示，应用细管式黏度计测定油的黏度。已知细管直径 $d=6\text{mm}$，测量段长 $l=2\text{m}$，实测油的流量 $Q=77\text{cm}^3/\text{s}$，流态为层流，水银压差计读值 $h=30\text{cm}$，水银的密度 $\rho_{HG}=13600\text{kg/m}^3$，油的密度 $\rho=901\text{kg/m}^3$。油的运动黏度为：

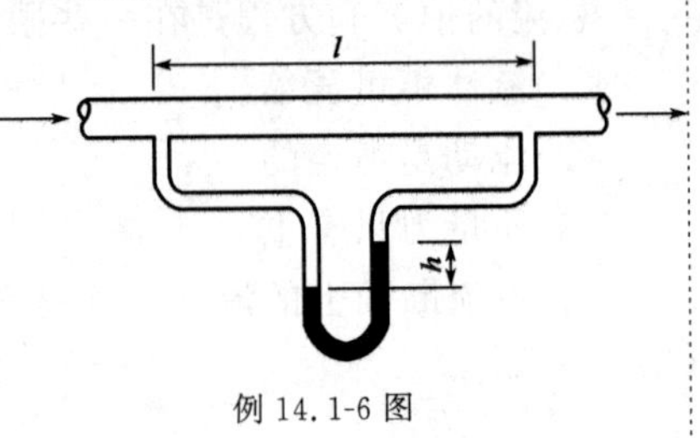

例 14.1-6 图

A. 8.57×10^{-4} B. 8.57×10^{-5}

C. 8.57×10^{-6} D. 8.57×10^{-7}

解 列伯努利方程：

$$z_1+\frac{p_1}{\rho g}+\frac{v_1^2}{2g}=z_2+\frac{p_2}{\rho g}+\frac{v_2^2}{2g}+\lambda\frac{l}{d}\frac{v^2}{2g}$$

得

$$\frac{p_1-p_2}{\rho g}=\lambda\frac{l}{d}\frac{v^2}{2g}$$

$$\frac{(\rho_{\text{Hg}}-\rho_{\text{油}})\Delta h}{\rho_{\text{油}}}=\lambda\frac{l}{d}\frac{v^2}{2g}$$

由

$$v=\frac{4Q}{\pi d^2}=\frac{4\times77\times10^{-6}}{\pi\times(6\times10^{-3})^2}=2.72\text{m/s}$$

得

$$\lambda=0.0336$$

已知流态为层流，则有

$$\lambda=\frac{64}{\text{Re}}=0.0336$$

得

$$\text{Re}=1903.7$$

此时雷诺数 Re 小于 2300，流态确实为层流。

$$\nu=\frac{ud}{\text{Re}}=\frac{2.72\times6\times10^{-3}}{1903.7}=8.57\times10^{-6}$$

选 C。

从此题可看出，已经不是单纯地考伯努利方程，而是与流态、阻力损失计算联合应用求解。这是近几年考题出现的新特征，综合应用也对考生把握知识的能力提出了更高的要求。

说明：本节的主要内容就是运动方程，涉及的考题主要就是运动方程的内涵与运用，并且有时候需要进行方程的联立求解。

经典练习

14.1-1 运动流体的压强（ ）。

A. 与空间位置有关，与方向无关 B. 与空间位置无关，与方向有关

C. 与空间位置和方向都有关 D. 与空间位置和方向都无关

14.1-2 $z+\frac{p}{\gamma}+\frac{v^2}{2g}=C$（常数）表示（ ）。

A. 不可压缩理想流体稳定流动的伯努利方程

B. 可压缩理想流体稳定流动的伯努利方程

C. 不可压缩理想流体不稳定流动的伯努利方程

D. 不可压缩黏性流体稳定流动的伯努利方程

14.1-3 对于某一管段中的不可压缩流体的流动，取三个管径不同的断面，其管径分别为 $A_1=150\text{mm}$，$A_2=100\text{mm}$，$A_3=200\text{mm}$。则三个断面 A_1、A_2、A_3 对应的流速比为（ ）。

A. 16∶36∶9

B. 9∶25∶16

C. 9∶36∶16

D. 16∶25∶9

14.1-4 重度为 10 000N/m^3 的理想流体在直管内从 1 断面流到 2 断面，如图所示，若 1 断面的压强 $p_1=300$kPa，则 2 断面压强 p_2 等于(　　)。

A. 100kPa　　B. 150kPa

C. 200kPa　　D. 250kPa

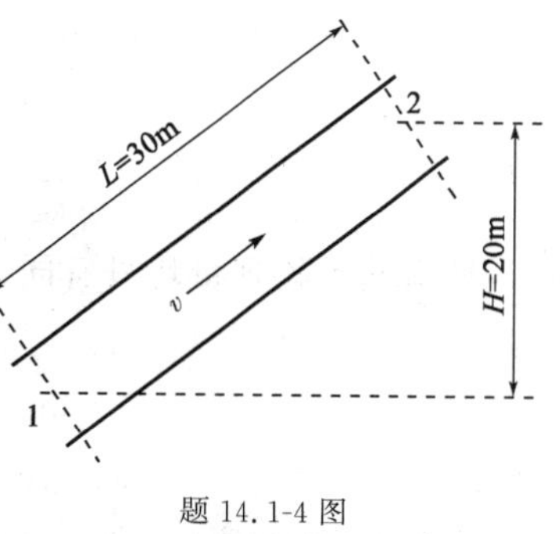

题 14.1-4 图

14.2 相似原理和模型实验方法

考试大纲☞：物理现象相似的概念　相似三定理　方程和因次分析法　流体力学模型研究方法　实验数据处理方法

必备基础知识

在一些流动问题的研究中，单纯采用理论分析的方法难以解决问题，必须借助实验手段来研究流体运动规律的物理本质。而相似性原理和因次分析，为科学地组织实验及整理实验数据提供了理论指导，是发展流体力学理论、解决实际工程问题的有力工具。

14.2.1 力学相似

为了能够使模型流动表现出原型流动的主要现象和物理本质，并能从模型流动上预测原型流动的结果，必须使模型流动与原型流动保持力学的相似关系。所谓力学相似，是指模型流动和原型流动在对应部位上的对应物理量都应该有一定的比例关系，具体而言，力学相似必须满足两个流动几何相似、运动相似、动力相似，以及两个流动的边界条件和初始条件相似。

几何相似指原型与模型之间保持几何形状和几何尺寸的相似，也就是原型和模型的对应边长保持一定的比例关系，对应角相等。几何相似，是力学相似的前提。

运动相似是指原型流动与模型流动的流线几何相似，而且对应点上的速度成比例，或者说，两个流动的速度场是几何相似的。运动相似通常是模型实验的目的。

动力相似是指原型流动和模型流动中对应点上作用着同名的力，各同名力的方向相同且具有同一比例。动力相似是运动相似的保证。

14.2.2 相似准则

要使两个流动动力相似，需要两流动相应点上的力多边形相似，相应边(同名力)成比例，由此得到各单项力的相似准则。以角标 p 表示原型，角标 m 表示模型。

描写流体运动和受力关系的是流体运动微分方程(动力学方程)。两个相似流动必须满足同一运动微分方程(N-S 方程)。现分别写出模型流动和原型流动的不可压缩流体的运动微分方程标量形式第一式

$$\frac{\partial v_{xp}}{\partial t_p}+v_{xp}\frac{\partial v_{xp}}{\partial x_p}+v_{yp}\frac{\partial v_{xp}}{\partial y_p}+v_{zp}\frac{\partial v_{xp}}{\partial z_p}=f_{xp}-\frac{1}{\rho_p}\frac{\partial p_p}{\partial x_p}+\nu_p\Delta v_{xp}$$

$$\frac{\partial v_{xm}}{\partial t_m}+v_{xm}\frac{\partial v_{xm}}{\partial x_m}+v_{ym}\frac{\partial v_{xm}}{\partial y_m}+v_{zm}\frac{\partial v_{xm}}{\partial z_m}=f_{xm}-\frac{1}{\rho_m}\frac{\partial p_m}{\partial x_m}+\nu_m\Delta v_{xm} \tag{14.2-1}$$

所有同类物理量均具有同一比例系数，因此有

$$x_p=\lambda_l x_m;y_p=\lambda_l y_m;z_p=\lambda_l z_m$$

$$v_{xp}=\lambda_v v_{xm};v_{yp}=\lambda_v v_{yxm};v_{zp}=\lambda_v v_{zm}$$

$$t_p=\lambda_t t_m;\rho_p=\lambda_\rho\rho_m;\upsilon_{xp}=\lambda_\upsilon\upsilon_{xm};p_p=\lambda_p p_m;f_p=\lambda_f f_m$$

由对模型的和原型的两运动微分方程以及同类物理量有同一比例的关系并经对比可写出下式。

$$\begin{matrix}\frac{\lambda_v}{\lambda_t} & =\frac{\lambda_v^2}{\lambda_l} & =\lambda_g & =\frac{\lambda_p}{\lambda_\rho\lambda_l} & =\frac{\lambda_v\lambda_\upsilon}{\lambda_l^2}\\ \vdots & \vdots & \vdots & \vdots & \vdots\\ ① & ② & ③ & ④ & ⑤\end{matrix}$$

上述5项分别表示单位质量的时变惯性力、位变惯性力、质量力、法向表面力-压力、切向表面力-摩擦力，因此上式就表示模型流动与原型流动的力多边形相似。

将上式中的位变惯性力 $\left[\frac{\lambda_v^2}{\lambda_l}\right]$ 除全式，可得

$$\begin{matrix}\frac{\lambda_l}{\lambda_v\lambda_t}=1 & =\frac{\lambda_l\lambda_g}{\lambda_v^2} & =\frac{\lambda_p}{\lambda_\rho\lambda_v^2} & =\frac{\lambda_\upsilon}{\lambda_l\lambda_v}\\ \vdots & \vdots & \vdots & \vdots\\ ① & ② & ③ & ④\end{matrix} \tag{14.2-2}$$

上式中的①、②、③、④项，表示模型流动和原型流动在动力相似时各比例系数之间有一个约束，并非各比例系数的数值可以随便取值。对其进一步分析可以得到以下各相似准则（相似准数）。

1）雷诺（Reynolds）相似准数

$$\mathrm{Re}=\frac{vl}{\nu}=\frac{\rho vl}{\mu}$$

这是由式（14.2-2）第四项得出的，由此

$$\frac{\lambda_v\lambda_l}{\lambda_\upsilon}=\frac{\lambda_\rho\lambda_v\lambda_l}{\lambda_\mu}=1 \tag{14.2-3}$$

$$\frac{v_m l_m}{\nu_m}=\frac{\rho_m v_m l_m}{\mu_m}=\frac{v_p l_p}{\nu_p}=\frac{\rho_p v_p l_p}{\mu_p} \tag{14.2-4}$$

令 $\mathrm{Re}=\frac{vl}{\nu}=\frac{vl\rho}{\mu}$，动力相似中要求 $\mathrm{Re}_m=\mathrm{Re}_p$ 。

雷诺相似准数是一个无量纲的量，它是由 v、l、ν 这三个物理量，或者是 v、l、ρ、μ 组合的一个物理量。它代表了流动中的惯性力和所受的黏性力之比，也称为黏性力相似准数。

2）弗劳德（Froude）相似准数

$$\mathrm{Fr}=\frac{v^2}{gl}$$

这是由式（14.2-2）第二项得出的，由此

$$\frac{\lambda_v^2}{\lambda_g\lambda_l}=1 \tag{14.2-5}$$

$$\frac{v_p^2}{v_m^2}=\frac{g_p}{g_m}\frac{l_p}{l_m} \tag{14.2-6}$$

令 $\mathrm{Fr}=\frac{v^2}{gl}$,动力相似中要求 $\mathrm{Fr}_m=\mathrm{Fr}_p$。

弗劳德相似准数是一个无量纲的量,它是由 v、g、l 这三个物理量以上述形式组合的一个物理量。它代表了流动中惯性力和重力之比,反映了流体中重力作用的影响程度,也称为重力相似准数。

3)欧拉(Euler)相似准数

$$\mathrm{Eu}=\frac{p}{\rho v^2}$$

这是由式(14.2-2)第三项得出的,由此

$$\frac{\lambda_p}{\lambda_\rho\lambda_v^2}=1 \tag{14.2-7}$$

$$\frac{p_p}{p_m}=\frac{\rho_p}{\rho_m}\frac{v_p^2}{v_m^2} \tag{14.2-8}$$

令 $\mathrm{Eu}=\frac{p}{\rho v^2}$,动力相似中要求 $\mathrm{Eu}_m=\mathrm{Eu}_p$。

欧拉相似准数是一个无量纲的量,它是由 p、ρ、v 这三个物理量以上述形式组合的一个物理量。它代表了流动中所受的压力和惯性力之比,也称为压力相似准数。

4)马赫(Mach)相似准数

$$\mathrm{Ma}=\frac{v}{c}$$

除上述几个相似准数以外,我们可以从其他流动方程中推得另外一些相似准数。如我们用 c 表示声速——微小扰动在流体中的传播速度,则对可压缩流动,由

$$c^2=\frac{\mathrm{d}p}{\mathrm{d}\rho} \tag{14.2-9}$$

可得

$$\frac{\lambda_v}{\lambda_c}=1 \tag{14.2-10}$$

令 $\mathrm{Ma}=\frac{v}{c}$,动力相似中要求 $\mathrm{Ma}_m=\mathrm{Ma}_p$。

即模型流动的马赫数的数值应该和原型流动的马赫数数值相等。马赫相似准数也是一个无量纲量,是 v、c 这两个物理量以上述形式组合的一个综合物理量。它代表流动中的压缩程度,也称为弹性力相似准数。Ma<1 为亚音速流动;Ma>1 为超音速流动。一般说,马赫数小于 0.15 可以作为不可压缩流动处理。

典型例题解析

【例 14.2-1】 要保证两个流动问题的力学相似,下列描述中哪一条是错误的?

A. 流动空间相应线段长度和夹角角度均成同一比例

B. 相应点的速度方向相同,大小成比例

C. 相同性质的作用力成同一比例

D. 应同时满足几何,运动,动力相似

解 动空间相应线段长度成同一比例,夹角角度相等。选 A。

14.2.3 因次分析法

物理量单位的种类称为量纲,表示物理量的本质属性,用 dim 表示。一个物理量可以用不同的单位度量,但量纲却是唯一的。例如长度、宽度、高度、厚度、深度都可以用米、英尺等长度单位来度量,但是它们的量纲都是长度量纲 L。

由于许多物理量的量纲之间都有一定的联系,在量纲分析时选少数几个物理量的量纲作为基本量纲,其他物理量的量纲都可以由这些基本量纲导出,称为导出量纲。基本量纲是相互独立的,不能由其他量纲的组合来表示,在工程流体力学中常用质量、长度、时间(M、L、T)作为基本量纲。

在一般的力学问题中,任意一个物理量 B 的量纲都可以用 M、L、T 这三个基本量纲的指数乘积来表示

$$\dim B = \mathrm{M}^{\alpha}\mathrm{L}^{\beta}\mathrm{T}^{\gamma}$$

在量纲分析中,有一些物理量的量纲为 1 ,称为无量纲量,用 M0L0T0 表示。无量纲量就是一个数,但可以把它看成由几个物理量组合而成的综合表达。例如雷诺相似准数的量纲

$$\dim \mathrm{Re} = \dim\left(\frac{vl}{\nu}\right) = \frac{\mathrm{LT^{-1}L}}{\mathrm{L^2T^{-1}}} = \mathrm{M^0L^0T^0}$$

为一个无量纲的量。为了区别于纯数,把无量纲量看成是由多个物理量组成的综合物理量更合适些,如我们应该把雷诺相似准数 Re 看成由流速 v 、特征尺度 l 和流体运动黏度 ν 这三个物理量的综合表达,或者把它看成由流速 v 、特征尺度 l 、流体密度 ρ 和流体动力黏度 ν 这四个物理量的综合表达。

量纲一致性原理是指一个物理现象或一个物理过程用一个物理方程表示时,方程中每项的量纲应该都是和谐的、一致的、齐次的,也叫做量纲和谐性原理或量纲齐次性原理。这个原理告诉我们,一个正确的物理方程,式中每项的量纲应该都是相同的。

下面对量纲分析方法中得到广泛应用的 Π 定理(Buckingham 定理)进行介绍。

对于某个流动现象或某个流动过程,如果存在有 n 个变量互为函数关系

$$f(a_1, a_2, a_3, \cdots, a_n) = 0 \tag{14.2-11}$$

而这些变量中含有 m 个基本量纲,则可把这 n 个有量纲的变量的函数关系转换成 $(n-m)$ 个无量纲量的函数关系

$$F(\pi_1, \pi_2, \pi_3, \cdots, \pi_{n-m}) = 0 \tag{14.2-12}$$

上面这个函数关系式全部是无量纲量 $\pi_i (i = 1,2,3,\cdots,n-m)$ 。

这个定理表达出了物理方程的明确的量间关系,并把方程中的变量数减少 m 个,更主要的是,这个定理把流动现象或流动过程更概括地表示在此函数关系中。

典型例题解析

【例 14.2-2】 下列关于因次分析法的描述哪项不正确?

A. 因次分析法就是相似理论

B. 因次是指物理量的性质和类别,又称为量纲

C. 完整的物理方程等式两边的每一项都具有相同性质的因次

D. 因次可分为基本因次和导出因次

解 因次分析法和相似理论都为科学地组织实验及整理实验数据提供了理论指导。但相似理论是说明自然界和工程中各相似现象相似原理的,在结构模型试验研究中,只有模型

和原型保持相似，才能由模型试验结果推算出原型结构的相应结果。而因次分析法反映任何因次一致的物理方程都可以表示为一组无因次数群的零函数。选 A。

14.2.4 模型实验

为了使模型和原型流动完全相似，除需要几何相似外，各独立的相似准则数应同时满足。但实际上要同时满足所有准则数是很困难的，甚至是不可能的，一般只能达到近似相似，就是要保证对流动起重要作用的力相似，这就是模型的选择问题。如水利工程中的明渠流以及江、河、溪流，都是以水位落差形式表现的重力来支配流动的，对于这些以重力起支配作用的流动，应该以弗劳德相似准数作为决定性相似准数。有不少流动需要求流动中的黏性力，或者求流动中的水力阻力或水头损失，如管道流动、流体机械中的流动、液压技术中的流动等，此时应当以满足雷诺相似准数为主，Re 就是决定性相似准数。对于非定常流动，如流体在旋转叶轮叶片间的流道中的流动，应当以满足斯特劳哈相似准数为主，Sr 就是决定性相似参数。对于可压缩流动，应当以满足马赫相似准数为主，Ma 就是决定性相似准数。对于 Eu 这个相似准数，它代表了流场的速度和压力关系，根据流动的基本方程，在满足流动相似的条件下，其压力场也相似。因此在其他相似准数作为决定性相似准数相等时，欧拉相似准数能够同时满足。

有的原型尺寸很大(如飞机、船舶、桥梁等)，如果对原型直接进行实验，不但费用很大，而且有时候难以进行实验测量；有的原型则尺寸微小(如滴灌中的滴头等)，难以观测其中的流动过程。而在原型的设计过程中，也需要进行模型实验来修改设计方案。模型实验再现的不仅仅是原型流动的表面现象，而是流动现象的物理本质。只有保证模型实验和原型流动中的物理本质相同，模型实验才有价值。

进行模型实验设计时，首先要根据原型要求的实验范围、实验场地大小、模型制作和量测条件选择尺度比例系数 λ_l；然后根据对流动情况的受力分析，满足对流动起主要作用的力相似，选择相似准数；最后确定流速比例系数和模型的流量。

典型例题解析

【例 14.2-3】 下列哪一条不是通风空调中进行模型实验的必要条件？

A. 原型和模型的各对应长度比例一定

B. 原型和模型的各对应速度比例一定

C. 原型和模型中起主导作用的同名作用力的相似准则数相等

D. 所有相似准则数相等

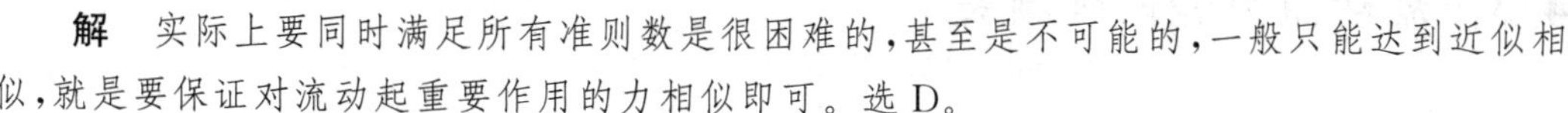

解 实际上要同时满足所有准则数是很困难的，甚至是不可能的，一般只能达到近似相似，就是要保证对流动起重要作用的力相似即可。选 D。

【例 14.2-4】 直径为 1m 的给水管在直径为 10cm 的水管中进行模型试验，现测得模型流量为 0.2m^3/s，则原模型给水管实际流量为：

A. 8m^3/s　　B. 6m^3/s　　C. 4m^3/s　　D. 2m^3/s

解 此题首先考察的是模型律的选择问题。在该题中，是给水管道，因此按前面基础知识讲解内容，此时应当以满足雷诺相似准数为主，Re 就是决定性相似准数，即 $Re_n = Re_m$。

$$\frac{v_n d_n}{\nu_n} = \frac{v_m d_m}{\nu_m}$$

现在 $d_n = 1$，$d_m = 0.1$；水的黏度不变。

所以

$$v_m = \frac{4Q_m}{\pi d_m^2} = \frac{4 \times 0.2}{\pi \times 0.01} = \frac{80}{\pi}$$

$$v_n = \frac{v_m d_m}{d_n} = 0.1 v_m = \frac{8}{\pi}$$

$$Q_n = \frac{\pi d_n^2}{4} v_n = \frac{\pi}{4} \times \frac{8}{\pi} = 2\text{m}^3/\text{s}$$

选 D。

经 典 练 习

14.2-1 下列（　　）是流动相似不必满足的条件。

A. 几何相似

B. 必须是同一种流体介质

C. 动力相似

D. 初始条件和边界条件相似

14.2-2 流体的压力 p、速度 v、密度 ρ 的正确的无量纲数组合是（　　）。

A. $\frac{p}{\rho v^2}$　　B. $\frac{p\rho}{v^2}$　　C. $\frac{p}{\rho v^2}$　　D. $\frac{p}{\rho v}$

14.2-3 直径为 1m 的给水管在直径为 10cm 的水管中进行模型试验，现测得模型的流量为 $0.2\text{m}^3/\text{h}$，若测得模型单位长度的水管压力损失为 146Pa，则原型给水管中单位长度的水管压力损失为（　　）。

A. 1.46Pa　　B. 2.92Pa　　C. 4.38Pa　　D. 6.84Pa

14.2-4 下列对于雷诺模型律和弗劳德模型律的说法正确的是（　　）。

A. 闸流一般采用雷诺模型律，桥墩扰流一般采用弗劳德模型律

B. 有压管道一般采用雷诺模型律，紊流淹没射流一般采用弗劳德模型律

C. 有压管道一般采用雷诺模型律，闸流一般采用弗劳德模型律

D. 闸流一般采用雷诺模型律，紊流淹没射流一般采用弗劳德模型律

14.3　流动阻力和能量损失

考试大纲☞：层流与紊流现象　流动阻力分类　圆管中层流与紊流的速度分布　层流和紊流沿程阻力系数的计算　局部阻力产生的原因和计算方法　减少局部阻力的措施

必备基础知识

水头损失是流体与固壁相互作用的结果。固壁作为流体的边界层，会显著地影响这一系统的机械能与热能的转化过程。在工程的设计计算中，根据流体接触的边壁沿程是否变化，把能量损失分为两类：沿程损失 h_f 和局部损失 h_m。它们的计算方法和损失机理不同。

14.3.1 流动阻力分类

在边壁沿程不变的管段上（如图 14.3-1 中的 ab、bc、cd 段），流动阻力沿程也基本不变，称这类阻力为沿程阻力。克服沿程阻力引起的能量损失称为沿程损失。图中的 h_{fab}、h_{fbc}、h_{fcd} 就是 ab、bc、cd 段的损失——沿程损失。由于沿程损失沿管段均匀分布，即与管段的长度成正比，所以也称为长度损失。

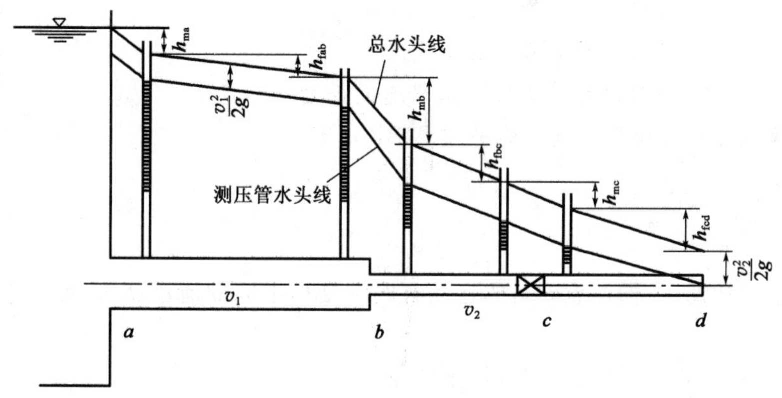

图 14.3-1 沿程阻力与沿程损失

在边界急剧变化的区域，阻力主要集中在该区域内及其附近，这种集中分布的阻力称为局部阻力。克服局部阻力的能量损失称为局部损失。例如图 14.3-1 中的管道进口、变径管和阀门等处，都会产生局部阻力。h_{ma}、h_{mb}、h_{mc} 就是相应的局部水头损失。引起局部阻力的原因是由于漩涡区的产生及速度方向和大小的变化。

整个管路的能量损失等于各管段的沿程损失和各局部损失的总和。即

$$h_l = \sum h_f + \sum h_m$$

对于如图 14.3-1 所示的流动系统，能量损失为：

$$h_l = h_{fab} + h_{fbc} + f_{fcd} + h_{ma} + h_{mb} + h_{mc}$$

能量损失计算公式用水头损失表达时，则为

沿程水头损失 $$h_f = \lambda \frac{l}{d} \cdot \frac{v^2}{2g} \tag{14.3-1}$$

局部水头损失 $$h_m = \zeta \frac{v^2}{2g} \tag{14.3-2}$$

用压强损失表达时，则为 $$p_f = \lambda \frac{l}{d} \cdot \frac{\rho v^2}{2} \tag{14.3-3}$$

$$p_m = \xi \frac{\rho v^2}{2} \tag{14.3-4}$$

式中：l——管长；

d——管径；

v——断面平均流速；

g——重力加速度；

λ——沿程阻力系数；

ξ——局部阻力系数。

在以上这些公式中，核心问题是各种流动条件下无因次系数 λ 和 ξ 的计算，除了少数简单

情况，其主要是用经验或半经验的方法获得。本章的主线就是沿程阻力系数 λ 和局部阻力系数 ξ 的计算。

典型例题解析

【例 14.3-1】 关于管段的沿程阻力，下列哪条是错误的描述？

A. 沿程阻力与沿程阻力系数成正比

B. 沿程阻力与管段长度成正比

C. 沿程阻力与管径成反比

D. 沿程阻力与管内平均流速成正比

解 沿程阻力与管内平均流速的平方成正比。选 D。

14.3.2 层流与紊流现象

早在 19 世纪初期，人们注意到流体运动有两种结构不同的流动状态，能量损失的规律与流态密切相关。

层流为各层质点互不掺混、分层有规则的流动。

紊流为流体质点互相强烈掺混、极不规则的流动。

雷诺数(Reynolds number)是一种可用来表征流体流动情况的无量纲数，流态的判别条件如下。

层流 $$\mathrm{Re}=vd/\nu<2\,000 \tag{14.3-5}$$

紊流 $$\mathrm{Re}=vd/\nu>2\,000 \tag{14.3-6}$$

要强调指出的是，临界雷诺数值 $\mathrm{Re_K}=2\,000$ 是仅就圆管而言的，对于诸如平板绕流和厂房内气流等边壁形状不同的流动，具有不同的临界雷诺数值。

层流和紊流的根本区别在于，层流各流层间互不掺混，只存在黏性引起的各流层间的滑动摩擦阻力；紊流时则有大小不等的涡体动荡于各流层间，除了黏性阻力，还存在着由于质点掺混，互相碰撞所造成的惯性阻力。因此，紊流阻力比层流阻力大得多。

层流到紊流的转变是与涡体的产生联系在一起的。图 14.3-2 绘出了涡体产生的过程。

设流体原来做直线层流运动。由于某种原因的干扰，流层发生波动，见图 14.3-2a)。于是在波峰一侧断面受到压缩，流速增大，压强降低；在波谷一侧由于过流断面增大，流速减小，压强增大。因此流层受到图 14.3-2b) 中箭头所示的压差作用。这将使波动进一步加大，见图 14.3-2c)，终于发展成涡体。涡体形成后，由于其一侧的旋转切线速度与流动方向一致，故流速较大，压强较小。而另一测旋转切线速度与流动方向相反，流速较小，压强较大。于是涡体在其两侧压差作用下，将由一层转到另一层，见图 14.3-2d)，这就是紊流掺混的原因。

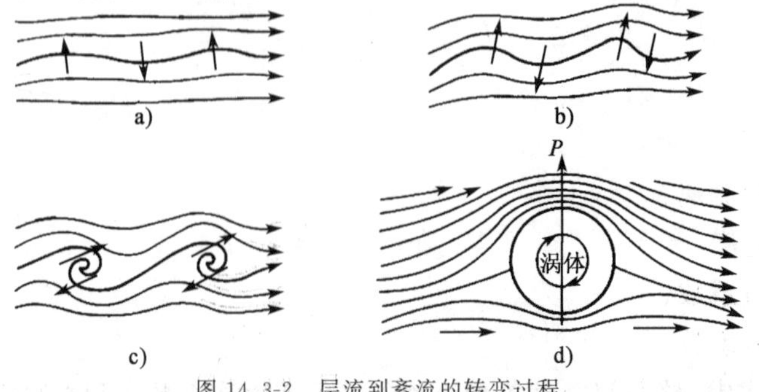

图 14.3-2 层流到紊流的转变过程

层流受扰动后，当黏性的稳定作用起主导作用时，扰动就受到黏性的阻滞而衰减下来，层流就是稳定的。当扰动占上风，黏性的稳定作用无法使扰动衰减下来，于是流动便变为紊流。因此，流动呈现什么流态，取决于扰动的惯性作用和黏性的稳定作用相互斗争的结果。

典型例题解析

【例 14.3-2】 实际流体运动存在两种形态：层流和紊流。下面哪一项可以用来判别流态？

A. 摩阻系数　　B. 雷诺数　　C. 运动黏性　　D. 管壁粗糙度

解 雷诺数表示作用于流体微团的惯性力与黏性力之比，利用雷诺数可区分流体的流动是层流还是紊流。选 B。

【例 14.3-3】 有一管径 $d=25\text{mm}$ 的室内上水管，水温 $t=10℃$。试求为使管道内保持层流状态的最大流速为多少？（10℃时水的运动黏滞系数 $\nu=1.31\times10^{-6}\text{m}^2/\text{s}$）

A. 0.052 5m/s　　B. 0.105 0m/s

C. 0.210 0m/s　　D. 0.420 0m/s

解 由 $\text{Re}=\dfrac{vd}{\nu}=2\,000$，知 $v=2\,000\times1.31\times10^{-6}/0.025=0.105\ \text{m/s}$，选 B。

14.3.3 均匀流动方程式

均匀流只能发生在长直的管道或渠道这一类断面形状和大小都沿程不变的流动中，因此只有沿程损失，而无局部损失。为了导出沿程阻力系数的计算公式，首先建立沿程损失和沿程阻力之间的关系。

$$h_{\mathrm{f}}=\frac{2\tau_0 l}{\gamma r_0} \tag{14.3-7}$$

其中，h_{f}/l 为单位长度的沿程损失，称为水力坡度，以 J 表示，即

$$J=\frac{h_{\mathrm{f}}}{l}$$

代入上式得

$$\tau_0=\gamma\frac{r_0}{2}J \tag{14.3-8}$$

式(14.3-7)或式(14.3-8)就是均匀流动方程式。它反映了沿程水头损失和管壁切应力之间的关系。

上面的分析适用于任何大小的流束，对于半径为 r 的流束，则

$$\frac{\tau}{\tau_0}=\frac{r}{r_0} \tag{14.3-9}$$

式(14.3-9)表明圆管均匀流的过流断面上，切应力与半径成正比，在断面上按直线规律分布，管轴线上为零，在管壁上达最大值。

典型例题解析

【例 14.3-4】 圆管均匀流中，与圆管的切应力成正比的是：

A. 圆管的直径　　B. 圆管的长度

C. 圆管的表面积　　D. 圆管的圆周率

解　圆管均匀流的过流断面上，切应力与半径成正比，肯定也与直径成正比。选 A。

14.3.4 圆管中的层流

圆管中的层流运动，可以看成无数无限薄的圆筒层，一个套着一个地相对滑动，各流层间互不掺混，各流层间的切应力服从牛顿内摩擦定律。为了得到流速分布，将牛顿内摩擦定律与均匀流动方程联立，可得

$$u=\frac{\gamma J}{4\mu}(r_0^2-r^2) \tag{14.3-10}$$

可见，断面流速分布是以管中心线为轴的旋转抛物面。

$r=0$ 时，即在管轴上，达最大流速

$$u_{\max}=\frac{\gamma J}{4\mu}r_0^2=\frac{\gamma J}{16\mu}d^2 \tag{14.3-11}$$

将式(14.3-10)代入平均流速定义式

$$v=\frac{Q}{A}=\frac{\int_A u\mathrm{d}A}{A}=\frac{\int_0^{r_0}u\cdot 2\pi r\mathrm{d}r}{A}$$

得平均流速为

$$v=\frac{\gamma J}{8\mu}r_0^2=\frac{\gamma J}{32\mu}d^2 \tag{14.3-12}$$

比较式(14.3-11)和式(14.3-12)，得

$$v=\frac{1}{2}v_{\max} \tag{14.3-13}$$

即平均流速等于最大流速的一半。

根据式(14.3-12)，得

$$h_{\mathrm{f}}=J\cdot l=\frac{32\mu vl}{\gamma d^2} \tag{14.3-14}$$

此式从理论上证明了层流沿程损失和平均流速一次方成正比。这个结论和雷诺实验的结果一致。

将式(14.3-14)写成计算沿程损失的一般形式，则

$$h_{\mathrm{f}}=\lambda\frac{l}{d}\frac{v^2}{2g}=\frac{32\mu vl}{\gamma d^2}=\frac{64}{\mathrm{Re}}\cdot\frac{l}{d}\cdot\frac{v^2}{2g}$$

由此式，可得圆管层流的沿程阻力系数的计算式

$$\lambda=\frac{64}{\mathrm{Re}} \tag{14.3-15}$$

它表明圆管层流的沿程阻力系数仅与雷诺数有关，且成反比，而和管壁粗糙无关。

典型例题解析

【例 14.3-5】 圆管内均匀层流断面流速分布规律可以描述为以管中心为轴的旋转抛物面，其最大流速为断面平均流速的：

A. 1.5 倍　　B. 2 倍　　C. 3 倍　　D. 4 倍

解 即平均流速等于最大流速的一半。选 B。

【例 14.3-6】 在圆管直径和长度一定的输水管道中，当流体处于层流时，随着雷诺数的增大，沿程阻力系数和沿程水头损失都将发生变化，请问下面哪一种说法正确？

A. 沿程阻力系数减小，沿程水头损失增大

B. 沿程阻力系数增大，沿程水头损失减小

C. 沿程阻力系数减小，沿程水头损失减小

D. 沿程阻力系数不变，沿程水头损失增大

解 层流时，沿程阻力系数为 $\lambda=\dfrac{64}{\mathrm{Re}}$，所以沿程阻力系数减小。而 $\mathrm{Re}=\dfrac{vd}{\nu}$，圆管直径不变，雷诺数变大，所以其流速是变大的。又知沿程水头损失为：

$$h_{\mathrm{f}}=\lambda\frac{l}{d}\frac{v}{2g}=\frac{32\mu vl}{\gamma d^{2}}$$

其中，流速变大，其他参数不变，所以沿程水头损失是增大的。选 A。

14.3.5 紊流流动

紊流的基本特征是在运动过程中，流体质点具有不断地互相混掺的现象；由于质点的互相混掺，使流区内各点的速度、压强等运动要素发生一种脉动现象。所谓脉动现象，就是诸如速度、压强等空间点上的物理量随时间的变化做无规则的即随机的变动。在做相同条件下的重复试验时，所得瞬时值不相同，但多次重复试验的结果的算术平均值趋于一致，具有规律性。

由于湍流的速度、压强等均为具有随机性质的脉动量，在时间上和空间上都不断地变化着；只有采取适当的方法加以平均，取得平均值后才能进一步研究其运动规律。通过对速度分量 u_x 的时间平均给出时均法的定义，以同样地获得其他物理量的时均值。

设 u_x 为瞬时值，带"—"表示其平均值，则时均值 $\bar{u}_x$ 定义为

$$\bar{u}_x(x,y,z,t)=\frac{1}{T}\int_{t-T/2}^{t+T/2}u_x(x,y,z,\xi)\mathrm{d}\xi \tag{14.3-16}$$

式中：ξ——时间积分变量；

T——平均周期，是一常数，它的取值应比紊流的脉动周期大得多，而比流动的不恒定性的特征时间又小得多，随具体的流动而定。

瞬时值与平均值之差即为脉动值，用"$'$"表示。于是，脉动速度为

$$u_x'=u_x-\bar{u}_x$$

紊流阻力：在紊流中，一方面因时均流速不同，各流层间的相对运动，仍然存在着黏性切应力，另一方面还存在着由脉动引起的动量交换产生的惯性切应力。因此，紊流阻力包括黏性切应力和惯性切应力。

黏性切应力可由牛顿内摩擦定律计算

$$\bar{\tau}_1 = \mu \frac{d\bar{u}_x}{dy}$$

惯性切应力,由下式表示

$$\bar{\tau}_2 = -\rho \overline{u'_x u'_y}$$

采用混合长度理论,对于圆管紊流,可以从理论上证明断面上流速分布是对数型的

$$u = \frac{1}{\beta}\sqrt{\frac{\tau_0}{\rho}}\ln y + C \tag{14.3-17}$$

式中:y——离圆管壁的距离;

β——卡门通用常数,由试验确定;

C——积分常数。

典型例题解析

【例 14.3-7】 紊流阻力包括有:

A. 黏性切应力　　B. 惯性切应力

C. 黏性切应力或惯性切应力　　D. 黏性切应力和惯性切应力

解 层流各流层间互不掺混,只存在黏性引起的各流层间的滑动摩擦阻力;紊流时则有大小不等的涡体动荡于各流层间。除了黏性阻力,还存在由于质点掺混,互相碰撞所造成的惯性阻力。因此,紊流阻力比层流阻力大得多。选 D。

14.3.6 沿程阻力计算

沿程损失的计算,关键在于如何确定沿程阻力系数 λ。由于紊流的复杂性,λ 的确定不可能像层流那样严格地从理论上推导出来。其研究途径通常有二:一是直接根据紊流沿程损失的实测资料,综合成阻力系数 λ 的纯经验公式;二是用理论和试验相结合的方法,以紊流的半经验理论为基础,整理成半经验公式。

沿程阻力系数 λ,主要取决于 Re 和壁面粗糙这两个因素。

尼古拉兹对不同管径、不同沙粒径进行了大量的实验,将沿程损失系数 λ 的变化归纳如下。

层流区　　$\lambda = f_1(\mathrm{Re})$

临界过渡区　　$\lambda = f_2(\mathrm{Re})$

紊流光滑区　　$\lambda = f_3(\mathrm{Re})$

紊流过渡区　　$\lambda = f(\mathrm{Re}, \Delta/d)$

紊流粗糙区(阻力平方区)　　$\lambda = f(\Delta/d)$

尼古拉兹实验比较完整地反映了沿程损失系数 λ 的变化规律,揭露了影响 λ 变化的主要因素,他对 λ 和断面流速分布的测定,为推导紊流的半经验公式提供了可靠的依据。

14.3.7 局部水头损失

流体在流经各种局部障碍时,流动遭到破坏,引起流速分布的急剧变化,甚至会引起边界层的分离,产生漩涡,从而形成形状阻力和摩擦阻力,即局部阻力,由此产生局部水头损失。

和沿程损失相似,局部损失一般也用流速水头的倍数来表示,它的计算公式为

$$h_m = \zeta \frac{v^2}{2g} \tag{14.3-18}$$

ζ 称为局部阻力系数。由上式可以看出，求 h_m 的问题就转变为求 ζ 的问题了。

实验研究表明，局部损失和沿程损失一样，不同的流态遵循不同的规律。如果流体以层流经过局部阻碍，而且受干扰后流动仍能保持层流的话，局部损失也还是由各流层之间的黏性切应力引起的。只有由于边壁的变化，促使流速分布重新调整，流体质点产生剧烈变形，加强了相邻流层之间的相对运动，因而加大了这一局部地区的水头损失。

局部阻碍的种类虽多，如分析其流动的特征，主要的也不过是过流断面的扩大或收缩，流动方向的改变，流量的合入与分出等几种基本形式，以及这几种基本形式的不同组合。

以下列出几种典型的局部阻力系数。

1）突然扩大管

$$\left.\begin{aligned} h_m &= \left(1-\frac{A_1}{A_2}\right)^2 \frac{v_1^2}{2g} = \zeta_1 \frac{v_1^2}{2g} \\ h_m &= \left(\frac{A_2}{A_1}-1\right)^2 \frac{v_2^2}{2g} = \zeta_2 \frac{v_2^2}{2g} \end{aligned}\right\} \tag{14.3-19}$$

所以突然扩大的阻力系数为

$$\zeta_1 = \left(1-\frac{A_1}{A_2}\right)^2 \text{或} \ \zeta_2 = \left(\frac{A_2}{A_1}-1\right)^2 \tag{14.3-20}$$

当液体从管道流入断面很大的容器中，或气体流入大气时，$\frac{A_1}{A_2}\approx 0, \zeta_1=1$。这是突然扩大的特殊情况，称为出口阻力系数。

2）突然缩小管

对应的流速水头为$\frac{v_2^2}{2g}$。

$$\zeta = 0.5\left(1-\frac{A_2}{A_1}\right) \tag{14.3-21}$$

当液体从断面很大的容器进入管道时，$\frac{A_2}{A_1}\approx 0, \zeta_1=0.5$。这是突然缩小的特殊情况，称为进口阻力系数。

14.3.8 减少局部阻力的措施

减小管中流体运动的阻力有两条完全不同的途径：一种是改进流体外部的边界，改善边壁对流动的影响；另一种是在流体内部投加极少量的添加剂，使其影响流体运动的内部结构来实现减阻。添加剂减阻是近 20 年来才迅速发展起来的减阻技术。虽然到目前为止，它在工业技术中还没有得到广泛的应用，但就当前了解的实验研究成果和少数生产使用情况来看，它的减阻效果是很突出的。

减小紊流局部阻力的着眼点在于防止或推迟流体与壁面的分离，避免漩涡区的产生或减小漩涡区的大小和强度。减少局部损失措施的基本原则在于：尽量减小漩涡区或防止漩涡区的形成，及减少二次流动波及的范围，从而减小撞击损失和减少在速度重新分布时的动量交换。下面选几种典型的常用配件为例来说明这个问题。

1)渐扩管和突扩管

扩散角大的渐扩管阻力系数较大。

2)弯管

弯管的阻力系数在一定范围内随曲率半径 R 的增大而减小。表 14.3-1 给出了 90°弯管在不同 R/d 时的 ζ 值。

不同 R/d 时的 90°弯管的 ζ 值(Re=10^6)　　表 14.3-1

R/d	0	0.5	1	2	3	4	6	10
ζ	1.14	1.00	0.246	0.159	0.145	0.167	0.20	0.24

由表 14.3-1 可知,如 $R/d<1$,ζ 值随 R/d 的减小而急剧增加,这与漩涡区的出现和增大有关。如 $R/d>3$,ζ 值又随 R/d 的加大而增加,这是由于弯管加长后,摩阻增大造成的。因此弯管的 R 最好在 $d\sim4d$ 范围内。

断面大的弯管,往往只能采用较小的 R/d,可在弯管内部布置一组导流叶片,以减小漩涡区和二次流,降低弯管的阻力系数。越接近内侧,导流叶片越应布置得密些。装上圆弧形导流叶片的弯管,阻力系数可由 1.0 减小到 0.3 左右。

典型例题解析

【例 14.3-8】 下列哪项措施通常不用于通风系统的减阻?

A. 改突扩为渐扩

B. 增大弯管的曲率半径

C. 设置导流叶片

D. 加入减阻添加剂

解 选项 A 和 C,都可以减小阻力系数,可以减小通风系统的阻力损失。选项 B 中,增大弯管的曲率半径,特别是$(1\sim4)d$ 的范围内,也可减少阻力。对于选项 D,在通风系统中加入减阻添加剂,效果不明显,另外还可能会对通风系统带来二次污染。选 D。

经 典 练 习

14.3-1 已知10℃时水的运动黏度为 $1.31\times10^{-6}\,m^2/s$,管径 d=50mm 的水管,在水温 t=10℃时,管内保持层流的最大流速为(　　)。

A. 0.105m/s　　B. 0.0525m/s

C. 0.21m/s　　D. 0.115m/s

14.3-2 如图所示,直径为 150mm、长为 350m 的管道自水库取水排入大气中,管进入口和出口分别比水库顶部水面低 8m 和 14m,沿程阻力系数为0.04,不计局部阻力损失。则排水量是(　　)。

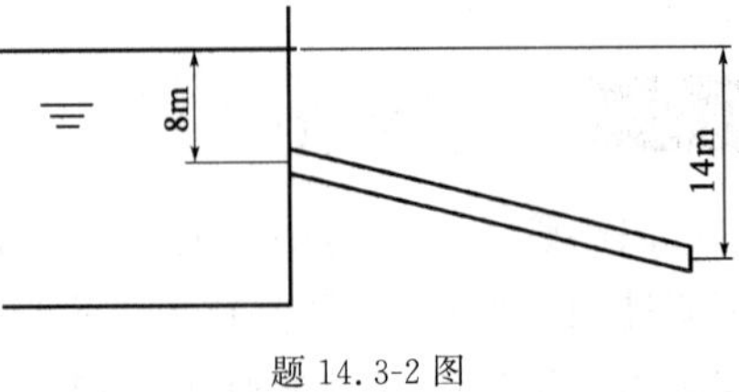

题 14.3-2 图

A. $1.40m^3/s$　　B. $0.05m^3/s$　　C. $1.05\ m^3/s$　　D. $0.56m^3/s$

14.3-3 垂直于圆管轴线的截面上,流体速度的分布(　　)。

A. 层流时比紊流时更加均匀

B. 紊流时比层流时更加均匀

C. 与流态没有关系

D. 仅与圆道直径有关

14.3-4 通过一组 35m 长的串联管道将水泄入环境中，如图所示，管道前 15m 的直径为 50mm（沿程阻力系数为0.019），然后管道直径变为 75mm（沿程阻力系数为0.030），与水库连接的水道入口处局部阻力系数为 0.5，其余局部阻力不计。当要求保持排水量为 $10m^3/h$ 时，则水库水面应比管道出口高（　　）。

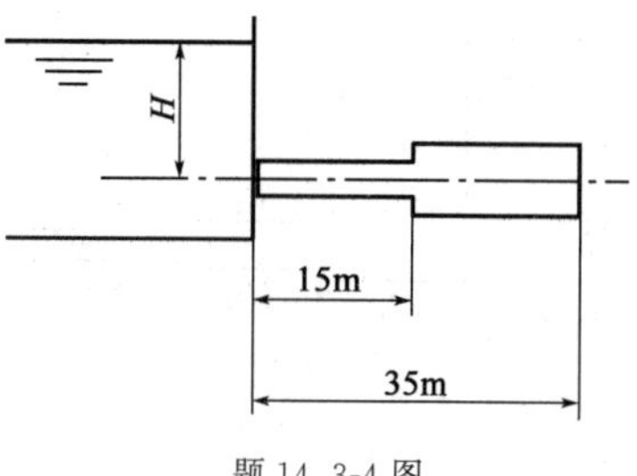

题 14.3-4 图

A. 0.814m　　B. 0.794m

C. 0.348m　　D. 1.470m

14.3-5 流体在圆管内做层流运动，其管道轴心速度为 2.4m/s，圆管半径为 250mm，管内通过的流量为（　　）。

A. $2.83m^3/h$　　B. $2.76m^3/h$　　C. $0.236m^3/h$　　D. $0.283m^3/h$

14.4 管路计算

考试大纲☞：简单管路的计算　串联管路的计算　并联管路的计算

必备基础知识

在工程实践中，如农业灌溉排水等系统中，常遇到由简单管路、串联管路、并联管路等组合而成的管网。

14.4.1 简单管路的计算

在水力计算中，通常将等径、无分支管路系统称为简单管路，而将由几段不同管径、不同长度的管段组合而成的复杂管路系统称为复杂管路。复杂管路系统都可认为是由两种基本类型管路，即串联管路和并联管路组合而成。

简单管路的阻力可表示为

$$h_w = \sum h_f + \sum h_j = \sum_i \lambda_i \frac{l_i}{d_i} \frac{v_i^2}{2g} + \sum_k \zeta_k \frac{v_k^2}{2g} = \zeta_c \frac{v_2^2}{2g} \qquad (14.4\text{-}1)$$

式中：ζ_c ——管系阻力系数。

将 $v_2 = \frac{4Q}{\pi d^2}$ 代入上式得

$$H = \frac{8\left(\lambda \frac{1}{d} + \sum \zeta\right)}{g\pi^2 d^4} Q^2 \qquad (14.4\text{-}2)$$

令 $S_H = \frac{8\left(\lambda \frac{1}{d} + \sum \zeta\right)}{g\pi^2 d^4}$，则

$$H = S_H Q^2 \qquad (14.4\text{-}3)$$

其中，S_H 综合反映了管路的沿程阻力和局部阻力情况，称为管路阻抗。可见，简单管路中，总阻力与流量的平方成正比。

如果是气体管路，不具有明显的水头特征，应该采用压强来表示，即在公式两端乘以重度 γ，则其计算公式变为：

$$p = \gamma H = \gamma S_H Q^2 = S_p Q^2 \qquad (14.4\text{-}4)$$

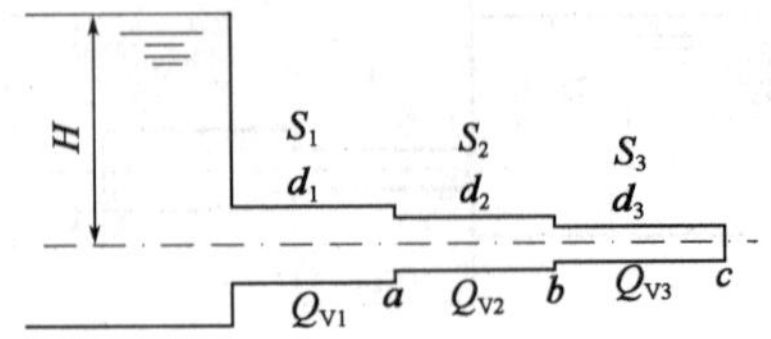

图 14.4-1 串联管路

14.4.2 串联管路的计算

串联管路是由许多简单管路首尾相接组合而成，如图 14.4-1所示。

简单管路是构成复杂管路的基本单元。

（1）特性一：流量规律。

当无节点分流： $Q_1 = Q_2 = Q_3$

（2）特性二：阻力损失规律。

$$h_{e1\text{-}3} = h_{e1} + h_{e2} + h_{e3}$$

（3）特性三：阻抗规律。

$$S = S_1 + S_2 + S_3$$

于是得到串联管路的计算原则：无中途分流或合流，则流量相等；阻力叠加；总管路的阻抗等于各管段的阻抗之和。

14.4.3 并联管路的计算

并联管路指在两节点之间并列铺设两根以上管道的管路系统，每根管道的管径、管度及过流量并不一定相等。如图 14.4-2 所示，有共同的分支点 A 和汇合点 B，两点之间有三根管道组成并联管路，中间无泄流。

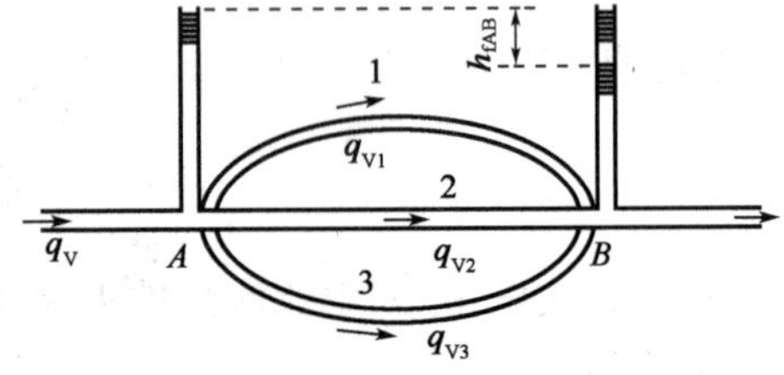

图 14.4-2 并联管路

（1）特性一：流量规律。

$$Q = Q_1 + Q_2 + Q_3 \tag{14.4-5}$$

（2）特性二：阻力损失规律。

$$h_{e1\text{-}3} = h_{e1} = h_{e2} = h_{e3} \tag{14.4-6}$$

（3）特性三：阻抗规律。

$$\frac{1}{\sqrt{S}} = \frac{1}{\sqrt{S_1}} + \frac{1}{\sqrt{S_2}} + \frac{1}{\sqrt{S_3}} \tag{14.4-7}$$

于是得到并联管路的计算原则：并联节点上的总流量等于各支管中流量之和；并联各支管上的阻力损失相等；总的阻抗的平方根倒数等于各支管阻抗平方根倒数之和。

典型例题解析

【例 14.4-1】 如图所示，若增加一并联管道（如虚线所示，忽略增加三通所造成的局部阻力），则会出现：

A. Q_1 增大，Q_2 减小

B. Q_1 增大，Q_2 增大

C. Q_1 减小，Q_2 减小

D. Q_1 减小，Q_2 增大

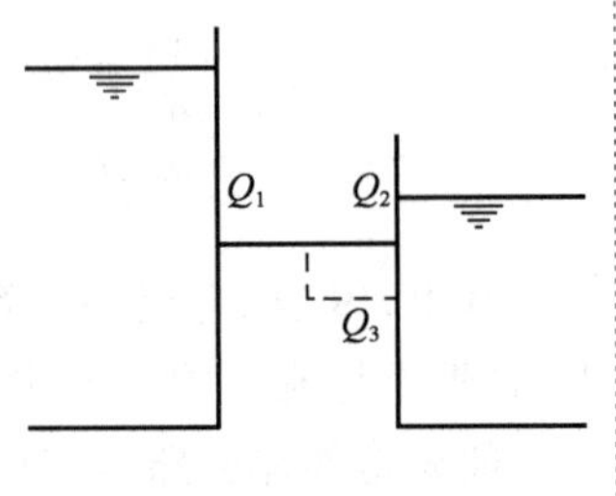

例 14.4-1 图

解 该题考查的是管段阻抗及管段串并联。

增加并联管段后，变为两管段并联后再与前面管段串联。并联后总阻抗小于任一管路阻抗，阻抗变小，再与前面管段串联后，总阻抗变小，总流量增大；Q_1 增大，S_1 不变，h_1 增大，则 h_2 变小，S_2 不变，则 Q_2 减小。选 A。

【例 14.4-2】 当某管路系统风量为 $400m^3/h$ 时，系统阻力为 200Pa；当使用该系统将空气送入有正压 100Pa 的密封舱时，其阻力为 500Pa，则此时流量为：

A. $534m^3/h$　　B. $566m^3/h$

C. $583m^3/h$　　D. $601m^3/h$

由 $\Delta p=SQ^2$，可得管路阻抗：$S=200/400^2$

又由题意可知：总阻力为 500Pa，消耗在管路上的阻力损失为 500－100＝400Pa，则可得：

$$400=SQ^2 \Rightarrow Q=\sqrt{\frac{400\times 400^2}{200}}=566m^3/h$$

选 B。

经典练习

14.4-1　某管道通过风量 $500m^3/h$，系统阻力损失为 300Pa，用此系统送入正压 $P=150Pa$ 的密封舱内，风量 $Q=750m^3/h$ 求系统阻力为(　　)。

A. 800Pa　　B. 825Pa　　C. 850Pa　　D. 875Pa

14.4-2　并联管网的各并联管段(　　)。

A. 水头损失相等　　B. 水力坡度相等

C. 总能量损失相等　　D. 通过的流量相等

14.4-3　在并联管路中，总的阻抗与各支管阻抗之间的关系为(　　)。

A. 总阻抗的平方根倒数等于各支管阻抗平方根倒数之和

B. 总阻抗的倒数等于各支管阻抗立方根倒数之和

C. 总阻抗的倒数等于各支管阻抗倒数之和

D. 总阻抗等于各支管阻抗之和

14.5　特定流动分析

考试大纲☞：势函数和流函数概念　简单流动分析　圆柱形测速管原理　旋转气流性质　紊流射流的一般特性　特殊射流

必备基础知识

流场中，若任意流体质点的旋转角速度向量 $\omega=0$，这种流动称为有势流动或无旋流动。流场中各点的流体速度都平行于某一固定的平面，且位于同一垂直线上的各流体质点的运动情况完全相同的流动称为平面流动。若流体质点在相互平行的平面内做有势流动，称该流动为平面有势流动，简称平面势流。

14.5.1　势函数和流函数概念

1）势函数

在无旋流动中

$$\omega_x=\frac{1}{2}\left(\frac{\partial v_z}{\partial y}-\frac{\partial v_y}{\partial z}\right)=0$$

$$\omega_y = \frac{1}{2}\left(\frac{\partial v_x}{\partial z} - \frac{\partial v_z}{\partial x}\right) = 0$$

$$\omega_z = \frac{1}{2}\left(\frac{\partial v_y}{\partial x} - \frac{\partial v_x}{\partial y}\right) = 0 \tag{14.5-1}$$

如果流体做无旋流动,即 $\omega = \omega_x i + \omega_y j + \omega_z k = 0$,则有

$$\frac{\partial v_z}{\partial y} = \frac{\partial v_y}{\partial z}, \frac{\partial v_x}{\partial z} = \frac{\partial v_z}{\partial x}, \frac{\partial v_y}{\partial x} = \frac{\partial v_x}{\partial y} \tag{14.5-2}$$

由数学分析知,式(14.5-2)是使 $v_x \mathrm{d}x + v_y \mathrm{d}y + v_z \mathrm{d}z$ 成为某函数 $\varphi(x,y,z,t)$ 全微分的充分必要条件,即

$$\mathrm{d}\varphi = v_x \mathrm{d}x + v_y \mathrm{d}y + v_z \mathrm{d}z \tag{14.5-3}$$

当 t 为参变量时,函数 $\varphi(x,y,z,t)$ 的全微分为

$$\mathrm{d}\varphi = \frac{\partial \varphi}{\partial x}\mathrm{d}x + \frac{\partial \varphi}{\partial y}\mathrm{d}y + \frac{\partial \varphi}{\partial z}\mathrm{d}z \tag{14.5-4}$$

于是,由式(14.5-2)和(14.5-3)得到

$$\frac{\partial \varphi}{\partial x} = v_x, \frac{\partial \varphi}{\partial y} = v_y, \frac{\partial \varphi}{\partial z} = v_z \tag{14.5-5}$$

称 $\varphi(x,y,z,t)$ 为速度势函数,简称速度势。

由于速度势函数与速度 v_x 、v_y 、v_z 存在式(14.5-4)的关系,于是,将求速度场的问题简化为求函数 φ ,解得 φ 后,速度分布就可得到,反之亦然。

将式(14.5-4)代入不可压缩流体连续性微分方程式,得

$$\frac{\partial^2 \varphi}{\partial x^2} + \frac{\partial^2 \varphi}{\partial y^2} + \frac{\partial^2 \varphi}{\partial z^2} = 0 \text{ 或} \nabla^2 \varphi = 0 \tag{14.5-6}$$

式(14.5-5)是拉普拉斯方程,速度势函数 φ 满足拉普拉斯方程,因而是调和函数。

2)流函数

由不可压缩流体平面流动的连续性微分方程 $\frac{\partial v_x}{\partial x} + \frac{\partial v_y}{\partial y} = 0$,可得 $\frac{\partial v_x}{\partial x} = -\frac{\partial v_y}{\partial y}$,由数学分析可知,这是 $-v_y \mathrm{d}x + v_x \mathrm{d}y = 0$ 成为某一函数 $\psi(x,y,t)$ 全微分的充分必要条件,即

$$\mathrm{d}\psi = -v_y \mathrm{d}x + v_x \mathrm{d}y = 0 \tag{14.5-7}$$

当 t 为参变量时,函数 $\psi(x,y,t)$ 的全微分为

$$\mathrm{d}\psi = \frac{\partial \psi}{\partial x}\mathrm{d}x + \frac{\partial \psi}{\partial y}\mathrm{d}y \tag{14.5-8}$$

于是,由式(14.5-7)和式(14.5-8)得到

$$v_x = \frac{\partial \psi}{\partial y}, v_y = -\frac{\partial \psi}{\partial x} \tag{14.5-9}$$

函数 $\psi(x,y,t)$ 称为流函数。不可压缩流体的平面流动,无论其是无旋流动还是有旋流动,以及流体有无黏性,均存在流函数。但是,只有无旋流动才存在势函数,可见流函数比速度势更具普遍性。

对于平面势流,由于 $\omega_z = \frac{1}{2}\left(\frac{\partial v_y}{\partial x} - \frac{\partial v_x}{\partial y}\right) = 0$,将式(14.5-6)代入,得

$$\frac{\partial^2 \psi}{\partial x^2}+\frac{\partial^2 \psi}{\partial y^2}=0 \text{ 或 } \nabla^2 \psi=0 \tag{14.5-10}$$

因此，平面势流的流函数 $\psi(x,y,t)$ 满足拉普拉斯方程，也是调和函数。这样，解平面有势流动问题也可变为解满足一定起始边界条件的流函数的拉普拉斯方程。

流函数有下列特性：等流函数线是流线；平面有势流动的等流函数线簇与等势线簇正交。

典型例题解析

【例 14.5-1】 下面哪一个说法是错误的？

A. 当流动为平面势流时，势函数和流函数均满足拉普拉斯方程

B. 当知道势函数或流函数时，就可以求出相应的速度分量

C. 流函数满足可压缩流体平面流动的连续性方程

D. 流函数的等值线垂直于有势函数等值线组成的等势面

解 流函数满足不可压缩流体平面流动的连续性方程。选 C。

【例 14.5-2】 下面关于流函数的描述中，错误的是：

A. 平面流场可用流函数描述

B. 只有势流才存在流函数

C. 已知流函数或势函数之一，即可求另一函数

D. 等流函数值线即流线

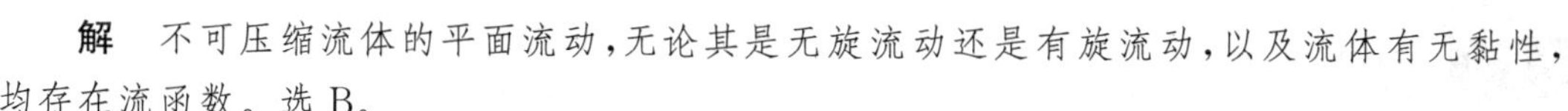

解 不可压缩流体的平面流动，无论其是无旋流动还是有旋流动，以及流体有无黏性，均存在流函数。选 B。

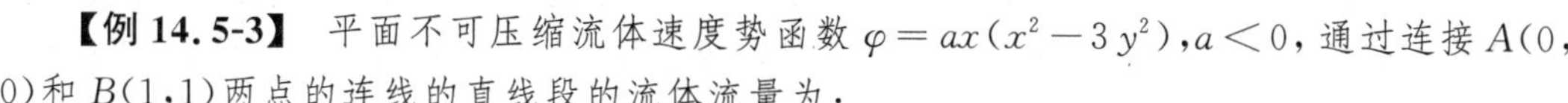

【例 14.5-3】 平面不可压缩流体速度势函数 $\varphi=ax(x^2-3y^2)$，$a<0$，通过连接 $A(0,0)$ 和 $B(1,1)$ 两点的连线的直线段的流体流量为：

A. $2a$　　B. $-2a$

C. $4a$　　D. $-4a$

解 先由势函数 φ 求流函数 ψ：

$$\mathrm{d}\psi=\frac{\mathrm{d}\psi}{\mathrm{d}x}\mathrm{d}x+\frac{\mathrm{d}\psi}{\mathrm{d}y}\mathrm{d}y=-\frac{\mathrm{d}\varphi}{\mathrm{d}y}\mathrm{d}x+\frac{\mathrm{d}\varphi}{\mathrm{d}x}\mathrm{d}y=6axy\mathrm{d}x+3a(x^2-y^2)\mathrm{d}y$$

$$\psi=3ax^2y-ay^3$$

流量等于两流线的流函数之差，故：

$$Q=|\psi_A-\psi_B|=-2a$$

选 B。

14.5.2 几种简单的平面无旋流动

1）均匀直线流动

设均匀流与 x 轴平行，速度为 v_∞，则 $v_x=v_\infty$，$v_y=0$。

则 $\varphi=v_\infty x$，$\psi=v_\infty y$。

令 $\varphi=C$，$\psi=C$，得到等势线为一簇平行于 y 轴的直线，流线是一簇平行于 x 轴的直线，如取 $\Delta\varphi=\Delta\psi$，则其流网为正方形网格。

2)源流和汇流

流体从一点径向均匀地呈直线向外流出，这种流动称为点源，这个点称为源点。如果流体径向直线均匀地流向一点，这种流动称为点汇，这个点称为汇点。点源(取正号)和点汇(取负号)的速度势和流函数，在极坐标下为

$$\varphi = \pm \frac{q}{2\pi}\ln r$$

$$\psi = \pm \frac{q}{2\pi}\theta$$

当 r 为常数时，得到等势线为半径不同的同心圆；θ 为常数时，得到流线为通过原点极角不同的射线，等势线与流线正交。当 $r=0$，$v_r=\infty$ 时，源点或汇点称为流动的奇点。在该点处的流动没有意义，必须排除在所考虑的流场之外。

典型例题解析

【例 14.5-4】 下列哪种平面流动的等势线为一组平行的直线?

A. 汇流或源流　　B. 均匀直线流

C. 环流　　D. 转角流

解　均匀直线流等势线为一簇平行于 y 轴的直线，流线是一簇平行于 x 轴的直线。选 B。

14.5.3 圆柱形测速管原理

由于拉普拉斯方程是线性方程，故几个满足该方程的速度势或流函数，线性叠加后得到的新的速度势和流函数，仍满足拉普拉斯方程。势流的这种性质称为势流叠加原理，它为用解析法求解某些较复杂的势流问题提供了一个有效的途径。

研究势流叠加原理的意义在于，将复杂的势流分解成一些简单势流，将求得的这些简单流动的解叠加起来，就得到复杂流动的解。

圆柱体无环量绕流是由均匀流和偶极子流叠加而成的平面流动，若均匀流的速度为 v_∞，沿 x 轴正向流动，偶极子流的偶极矩为 $\boldsymbol{M}$，两者叠加后的速度势和流函数为

$$\varphi = \left(v_\infty + \frac{M}{2\pi r^2}\right) r\cos\theta \tag{14.5-11}$$

$$\psi = \left(v_\infty - \frac{M}{2\pi r^2}\right) r\sin\theta \tag{14.5-12}$$

速度分布——将速度势对半径和极角求偏导数，求得流场速度为

$$\left.\begin{aligned} v_r &= \frac{\partial \varphi}{\partial r} = v_\infty\left(1 - \frac{r_0^2}{r^2}\right)\cos\theta \\ v_\theta &= \frac{\partial \varphi}{r\partial \theta} = - v_\infty\left(1 + \frac{r_0^2}{r^2}\right)\sin\theta \end{aligned}\right\} \tag{14.5-13}$$

当 $r = r_0$ 时，即在圆柱面上

$$\left.\begin{aligned} v_r &= 0 \\ v_\theta &= -2v_\infty \sin\theta \end{aligned}\right\} \tag{14.5-14}$$

这说明，沿圆柱体表面流体只有切线方向的速度，没有径向速度，即组合流动紧贴圆柱表

面，既没有流体穿入，也没有脱离圆柱面。在圆柱面上速度是按照正弦规律分布的，在 $\theta=0$ 和 $\theta=180°$ 处，$v_\theta=0$，A、B 两点是分流点，称它们为前驻点和后驻点。在 $\theta=\pm 90°$ 圆柱面的上下顶点，$|v_\theta|=2v_\infty$，达到圆柱面速度的最大值。而当 $\theta=\frac{\pi}{6}$ 时，柱面上流速等于均匀直线流速。

14.5.4 紊流射流的一般特性

工程上经常遇到这种情况：气流经由管嘴喷射到一个足够大的空间中去，不再受固体界面的限制，而在大空间中继续扩散流动，这种流动就称为射流。由于自由射流一般都是紊流，所以，有些教科书又称它为紊流射流。

射流由管口射出，流体沿喷管的轴线方向运动，但由于射流注是紊流，所以，流体不但沿喷管轴线方向运动，而且，还发生剧烈的横向运动，结果造成与周围静止流体进行质量与动量交换，引起或带动周围流体流动。结果沿流程射流流量增加，射流宽度（或直径）不断加大，并且，射流本身速度逐渐减小，最后射流的动量全部消失在空间流体中，这种情况好像射流在空间介质中淹没了，所以又叫做自由淹没射流，如图 14.5-1 所示。

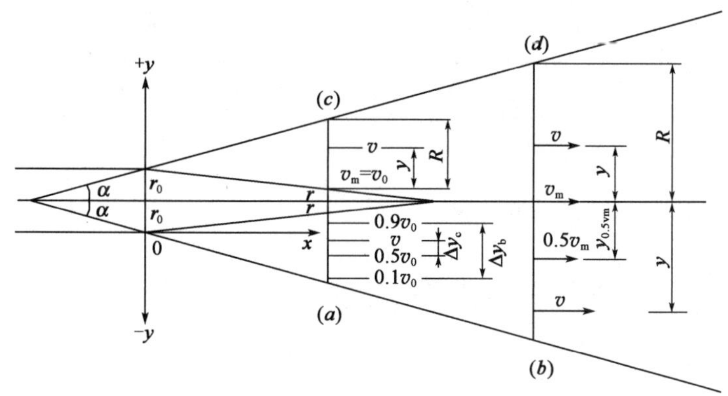

图 14.5-1　自由淹没射流速度分布

下面分别说明自由淹没射流的特性。

(1)过渡截面

假定对流以超临界速度的初速 u_0 从喷管喷出，其速度均匀一致。在流动中，由于周围流体不断加入，射流宽度逐渐加大，而在射流中还保持 u_0 的区域（又称为射流核心区），则逐渐缩小。一段距离以后，保护 u_0 的区域完全消失，只有射流中心一点处还保持初速 u_0。射流的这一截面就称为过渡截面。显然，过渡截面左侧，射流中心线上均保持初速 u_0，而过渡截面之后，射流中心速度开始下降。

(2)射流初始段和基本段

喷口截面和过渡截面之间的射流区段称为射流初始段。过渡截面后的区段称为射流基本段。基本段中，射流中心速度沿流动方向不断降低，并且，射流基本段完全为射流边界层占据。射流边界层是这样规定的，通常把速度等于零的边界线称为射流外边界线（或面），而轴向流速保持 u_0 的边界面（即射流核心区的边界面）称为内边界，而内外边界之间的区域就称为射流边界层。

(3)射流核心区

即在射流中继续保持初速 u_0 的区域。

(4)射流极点,射流极角(又叫射流扩散角)

射流外边界线的交点称为射流极点,由图可以看出,射流极点是管嘴内部的一个几何点,且外边界线之间的夹角 θ 称为射流极角,或称为射流扩散角。

射流的基本特征:

①$2R<S$(即射流边界层的宽度小于射流长度)。

②$v \ll u$(v 为横向分速,u 为轴向分速)。

③试验证明,整个射流区压力相等,等于周围环境介质压力。

④内外边界均是直线。

⑤基本段内轴向速度 u 沿 x 逐步减小。

⑥单位时间内射流各横截面沿 x 方向动量保持不变,等于喷管出口处的原始动量。射流参数的计算公式见表 14.5-1。

射流参数的计算 表 14.5-1

段名	参数名称	符号	圆断面射流	平面射流
主体段	扩散角	α	$\tan\alpha=3.4a$	$\tan\alpha=2.44a$
	射流直径或半高度	D b	$\frac{D}{d_0}=6.8\left(\frac{as}{d_0}+0.147\right)$	$\frac{b}{b_0}=2.44\left(\frac{as}{d_0}+0.41\right)$
	轴心速度	v_m	$\frac{v_m}{v_0}=\frac{0.48}{\frac{as}{d_0}+0.147}$	$\frac{v_m}{v_0}=\frac{1.2}{\sqrt{\frac{as}{b_0}+0.41}}$
	流量	Q	$\frac{Q}{Q_0}=4.4\left(\frac{as}{d_0}+0.147\right)$	$\frac{Q}{Q_0}=4.4\left(\frac{as}{d_0}+0.147\right)$
	断面平均流速	v_1	$\frac{v_1}{v_0}=\frac{0.095}{\frac{as}{d_0}+0.147}$	$\frac{v_1}{v_0}=\frac{0.492}{\sqrt{\frac{as}{b_0}+0.41}}$
	质量平均流速	v_2	$\frac{v_2}{v_0}=\frac{0.23}{\frac{as}{d_0}+0.147}$	$\frac{v_1}{v_0}=\frac{0.833}{\sqrt{\frac{as}{b_0}+0.41}}$
起始段	流量	Q	$\frac{Q}{Q_0}=1+0.76\frac{as}{r_0}+1.32\left(\frac{as}{r_0}\right)^2$	$\frac{Q}{Q_0}=1+0.43\frac{as}{b_0}$
	断面平均流速	v_1	$\frac{v_1}{v_0}=\frac{1+0.76\frac{as}{r_0}+1.32\left(\frac{as}{r_0}\right)^2}{1+0.68\frac{as}{r_0}+11.56\left(\frac{as}{r_0}\right)^2}$	$\frac{v_1}{v_0}=\frac{1+0.43\frac{as}{b_0}}{1+2.44\frac{as}{b_0}}$
	质量平均流速	v_2	$\frac{v_2}{v_0}=\frac{1}{1+0.76\frac{as}{r_0}+1.32\left(\frac{as}{r_0}\right)}$	$\frac{v_2}{v_0}=\frac{1}{1+0.43\frac{as}{b_0}}$
	核心长度	s_n	$s_n=0.672\frac{r_0}{a}$	$s_n=1.03\frac{b_0}{a}$
	喷嘴至极点的距离	x_0	$x_0=0.294\frac{r_0}{a}$	$x_0=0.41\frac{b_0}{a}$
	收缩角	θ	$\tan\theta=1.49a$	$\tan\theta=0.97a$

典型例题解析

【例 14.5-5】 紊流自由射流的主要特征为：

A. 射流主体段各断面轴向流速分布不具有明显的相似性

B. 射流起始段中保持原出口射流的核心区呈长方形

C. 射流各断面的动量守恒

D. 上述三项

解 单位时间内射流各横截面沿 x 方向动量保持不变，等于喷管出口处的原始动量。选 C。

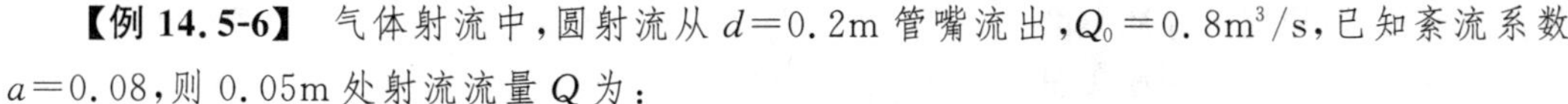

【例 14.5-6】 气体射流中，圆射流从 $d=0.2\text{m}$ 管嘴流出，$Q_0=0.8\text{m}^3/\text{s}$，已知紊流系数 $a=0.08$，则 0.05m 处射流流量 Q 为：

A. $1.212\text{m}^3/\text{s}$　　B. $1.432\text{m}^3/\text{s}$

C. $0.372\text{m}^3/\text{s}$　　D. $0.720\text{m}^3/\text{s}$

解 此题为圆射流问题，可分为起始段和主体段，起始段的核心长度为：

$$S_n=0.672\frac{r_0}{a}=0.672\times\frac{0.1}{0.08}=0.84$$

所以 0.05m 处仍处于起始段，对于起始段，则有：

$$\frac{Q}{Q_0}=1+0.76\frac{as}{r_0}+1.32\left(\frac{as}{r_0}\right)^2=1+0.76\frac{0.08\times0.05}{0.1}+1.32\left(\frac{0.08\times0.05}{0.1}\right)^2$$

可得 $Q=0.826\text{m}^3/\text{s}$，与选项 D 最为接近。

【例 14.5-7】 某新建室内体育场由圆形风口送风，风口 $d_0=0.5\text{m}$，距比赛区为 45m。要求比赛区质量平均风速不超过 0.2m/s，则选取风口时，风口送风量不应超过(紊流系数 $a=0.08$)：

A. $0.25\text{m}^3/\text{s}$　　B. $0.5\text{m}^3/\text{s}$

C. $0.75\text{m}^3/\text{s}$　　D. $1.25\text{m}^3/\text{s}$

解 本题是在大空间中的自由射流，其速度衰减规律为 $\dfrac{v_2}{v_0}=\dfrac{0.23}{\dfrac{as}{d_0}+0.147}$

则风口平均流速为：

$$u_0=\frac{0.2\times\left(\dfrac{0.08\times45}{0.5}+0.147\right)}{0.23}=6.39\text{m/s}$$

从而求得风口送风量：

$$Q=\frac{\pi}{4}d_0^2u_0=0.785\times0.5^2\times6.39=1.25\text{m}^3/\text{s}$$

选 D。

14.5.5 特殊射流

1)温差射流

在暖通空调工程中，经常会碰到射流的温度与周围介质温度不同的情况。在这种射流中，由于紊流混合会引起热量的转移，同时由于射流速度场的相似性，必然亦会引起温度场的相似性（不论是射流被加热还是被冷却）。所不同的是热量扩散比动量扩散快些，因此温度边界层比速度边界层发展快些。关于温度场的分析方法与速度场相同，结果也类似。温度分布公式为：

对于圆断面轴对称温差射流

$$\frac{T_m - T_e}{T_0 - T_e} = \frac{0.7}{as/R_0 + 0.29} \tag{14.5-15}$$

对于平面温差射流

$$\frac{T_m - T_e}{T_0 - T_e} = \frac{1.04}{\sqrt{as/b_0 + 0.42}} \tag{14.5-16}$$

式中：T_m——射流轴心温度；

T_e——射流周围介质温度；

T_0——射流出口初始段温度。

2）浓差射流

在工业通风过程中，射流所含混合物浓度常与周围介质混合物浓度不同，因此在紊流自由射流与周围空间介质扩散的过程中，也必然会产生紊流的物质转移现象。如带有煤粉的一次风射流离开喷燃器在炉内扩散时，或可燃混合气流向炉内喷射，都会引起射流与周围介质之间的物质交换。由于紊流扩散的类似性，理论和实验分析得出，射流断面上的浓度差与温度差沿射流方向的变化规律完全相同。

3）旋转射流

气流通过具有旋流作用的喷嘴外射运动。气流本身一面旋转，一面向周围介质中扩散前进，称为旋转射流。旋转是旋转射流基本特征，旋转使射流获得向四周扩散的离心力。和一般射流比较，扩散角大，射程短，射流的紊动性强。

4）有限空间射流

在射流运动中，由于受壁面、顶棚以及空间的限制，自由射流规律不再适用，因此必须研究受限后的射流，即有限空间射流运动规律。目前有限空间射流理论尚不完全成熟，多是根据实验结果整理成近似公式或无量纲曲线，供设计使用。

有限空间射流由自由扩张段、有限扩张段、收缩段组成。射流内部压强是变化的，随射程的增大，压强增大，直至端头压强最大，达稳定值后比周围压强要高些。射流中各横截面上动量不相等，沿程减少。

在房间长度大于情况下，实验证明在封闭末端产生涡流区。涡流区的出现是通风空调工程所不希望的，应当清除。

贴附射流　当送风口贴近顶棚，由于射流在顶棚处不能卷吸空气，因此上部流速大，静压小，下部流速小，静压大。贴附长度，送冷风时，射流将较早的脱离顶棚下落，贴附长度与阿基米德数 Ar 有关，Ar 数为：$\mathrm{Ar}=\dfrac{\delta d_0 A t_s}{v_0^2 T_r}$。

典型例题解析

【例 14.5-8】 在舒适性空调中，送风通常为贴附射流，贴附射流的贴附长度主要取决于：

A. 雷诺数　　B. 欧拉数　　C. 阿基米德数　　D. 佛诺得数

解　理由见上面基础知识。选 C。

【例 14.5-9】 下列有关射流的说法错误的是：

A. 射流极角的大小与喷口断面的形状和紊流强度有关

B. 自由射流单位时间内射流各断面上的动量是相等的

C. 旋转射流和一般射流比较，扩散角大，射程短

D. 有限空间射流内部的压强随射程的变化保持不变

解 对于自由射流，整个射流区域压力相等，等于周围环境介质压力，但有限空间射流由于受壁面、顶棚以及空间的限制，自由射流规律不再适用，射流内部压强是变化的，且随射程的增大，压强增大，所以选项D是错误的。

经典练习

14.5-1 流体是有旋还是无旋，根据（ ）决定。

A. 流体微团本身是否绕自身轴旋转

B. 流体微团的运动轨迹

C. 流体微团的旋转角速度大小

D. 上述三项

14.5-2 已知某流速场 $u_x=-ax, u_y=ay, u_z=0$，则该流速场的流函数为（ ）。

A. $\psi=2axy$ B. $\psi=-2axy$

C. $\psi=-\frac{1}{2}a(x^2+y^2)$ D. $\psi=\frac{1}{2}a(x^2+y^2)$

14.5-3 在环流中，（ ）做无旋流动。

A. 原点 B. 除原点外的所有质点

C. 边界点 D. 所有质点

14.6 气体射流压力波传播和音速概念

考试大纲☞：可压缩流体一元稳定流动的基本方程 渐缩喷管与拉伐尔管的特点 实际喷管的性能

必备基础知识

当气体流速较高，压差较大时，气体的密度发生了显著的变化，从而气体的流动现象、运动参数都将发生显著变化。因此必须考虑气体的可压缩性，也就是必须考虑气体密度随压强和温度的变化而变化。这样，研究可压缩流体的动力学不只是流速、压强问题，而且也包含密度和温度等问题。不仅需要流体力学的知识，还要需要热力学的知识。在这种情况下，进行气体动力学计算时，压强、温度只能用绝对压强和开尔文温度。

14.6.1 可压缩流体一元稳定流动的基本方程

1）连续性方程

由于气体的密度在流动中是发生变化的，所以它的连续性方程不能像不可压缩流体那样按体积流量来计算，而需要用质量流量来计算，即气体在流管中流动时，每单位时间内流过流管中任意两个有效断面的质量流量必定相等，即

$$\rho_1 v_1 A_1 = \rho_2 v_2 A_2 \tag{14.6-1}$$
$$\rho v A = c$$

对上式微分，可得连续性微分方程

$$\frac{\mathrm{d}\rho}{\rho} + \frac{\mathrm{d}v}{v} + \frac{\mathrm{d}A}{A} = 0 \tag{14.6-2}$$

2)能量方程

$$\int \frac{\mathrm{d}p}{p} + \frac{v^2}{2} = c \qquad \text{或} \qquad \left.\begin{matrix} U + \dfrac{p}{\rho} \\ \dfrac{k}{k-1}\dfrac{p}{\rho} \\ \dfrac{k}{k-1}RT \\ \dfrac{c^2}{k-1} \\ C_R \bar{h} \end{matrix}\right\} + \frac{v^2}{2} = c \tag{14.6-3}$$

能量方程的意义：单位质量流体所具有的内能、压能与动能之和保持不变。可压缩流体密度不是常数，而是压强和温度的函数。

14.6.2 声速、滞止参数、马赫数

1)声速

在可压缩流体中，如果某处产生一个微弱的局部压力扰动，这个压力扰动将以波面的形式在流体内传播，其传播速度称为声速，记作 c。

对扰动应用连续方程和动量方程，可以得到声速的公式

$$c = \sqrt{\frac{\mathrm{d}p}{\mathrm{d}\rho}} \tag{14.6-4}$$

对于气体，由于小扰动波的传播速度很快，与外界来不及进行热交换，且各项参数的变化量微小，小扰动波的传播过程是一个既绝热又没能量损失的等熵过程。应用等熵过程方程 $\frac{p}{\rho^k}=c$，得到气体中的声速公式

$$c = \sqrt{k\frac{p}{\rho}} = \sqrt{kRT} \tag{14.6-5}$$

综合以上分析，可以看出：

(1)密度对压强的变化率 $\frac{\mathrm{d}\rho}{\mathrm{d}p}$ 反映流体的压缩性，$\frac{\mathrm{d}\rho}{\mathrm{d}p}$ 越大，其倒数 $\frac{\mathrm{d}p}{\mathrm{d}\rho}$ 越小，声速 $c=\sqrt{\frac{\mathrm{d}p}{\mathrm{d}\rho}}$ 越小，流体容易压缩；反之，$c=\sqrt{\frac{\mathrm{d}p}{\mathrm{d}\rho}}$ 越大，流体不易压缩，不可压缩流体 $c\to\infty$。所以该因素是反映流体压缩性大小的物理参数。

(2)声速与气体热力学温度 T 有关($c=\sqrt{kRT}$)。在气体动力学中，温度是空间坐标的函数，所以，声速也是空间坐标的函数。为强调这一点，常称为当地声速。

(3)声速与气体的绝热指数 k 和气体常数 R 有关。所以不同气体声速不同，对于空气，$k=1.4$，$R=287\mathrm{J/(kg\cdot K)}$，代入 $c=\sqrt{k\frac{p}{\rho}}=\sqrt{kRT}$，得

$$c = 20.1\sqrt{T} \tag{14.6-6}$$

2)马赫数

流体运动的速度与当地声速之比称为马赫数,以 Ma 表示。

$$\mathrm{Ma} = \frac{u}{c} \tag{14.6-7}$$

在可压缩流动中,马赫数是一个重要的无量纲参数,在第 17 章里我们将看到马赫数表征流体的惯性力与压缩的弹性力之比。按马赫数的大小,可压缩流动分成三种形式。

(1)Ma<0.3,不可压缩流体;Ma=0.3~0.8,亚音速;Ma=0.8~1.2,跨音速;Ma=1.2~5.0,超音速;Ma=1,音速;Ma=5.0~10,高超音速。

(2)Ma>1, $u > c$,即气流本身速度大于声速,则气流中参数的变化不能向上游传播。这就是超声速流动。

(3)Ma<1, $u < c$,即气流本身速度小于声速,则气流中参数的变化既能向上游传播,又能向下游传播。这就是亚声速流动。

3)滞止参数

气流某断面的流速,设想以无摩擦绝热过程降低至零时,断面各参数所达到的值,称为气流在该断面的滞止参数。滞止状态下各相应参数称为滞止参数,分别以 p_0 、ρ_0 、T_0 、c_0 表示。气体绕过一个物体时,在驻点处气流受到阻滞,速度等于零,这一点的气流状态也是滞止状态。滞止参数在整个流动过程中保持不变。

现将滞止参数与断面参数比表示为马赫数的函数。

$$\frac{T_0}{T} = 1 + \frac{k-1}{2}\frac{v^2}{kRT} = 1 + \frac{k-1}{2}\frac{v^2}{c^2} = 1 + \frac{k-1}{2}\mathrm{Ma}^2$$

根据等熵过程方程式可导出

$$\frac{p_0}{p} = \left(\frac{T_0}{T}\right)^{\frac{k}{k-1}} = \left(1 + \frac{k-1}{2}\mathrm{Ma}^2\right)^{\frac{k}{k-1}} \tag{14.6-8}$$

$$\frac{\rho_0}{\rho} = \left(\frac{T_0}{T}\right)^{\frac{1}{k-1}} = \left(1 + \frac{k-1}{2}\mathrm{Ma}^2\right)^{\frac{1}{k-1}} \tag{14.6-9}$$

$$\frac{c_0}{c} = \left(\frac{T_0}{T}\right)^{2} = \left(1 + \frac{k-1}{2}\mathrm{Ma}^2\right)^{\frac{1}{2}} \tag{14.6-10}$$

根据上面四个参数比和马赫数的关系式,只需已知滞止参数和某一断面的马赫数,便可求得该断面的运动参数。

典型例题解析

【例 14.6-1】 音速是弱扰动在介质中的传播速度,也就是以下哪种微小变化以波的形式在介质中的传播速度:

A.压力　　B.速度　　C.密度　　D.上述三项

解 由音速的定义可知,某处产生一个微弱的局部压力扰动,这个压力扰动将以波面的形式在流体内传播,其传播速度称为音速。选 A。

【例 14.6-2】 喷气式发动机尾喷管出口处，燃气流的温度为 873K，流速为 560m/s，燃气的等熵指数 $K=1.33$，气体常数 $R=287.4\text{J/(kg}\cdot\text{K)}$，则出口燃气流的马赫数为：

A. 0.97　　B. 1.03　　C. 0.94　　D. 1.06

解

$$c=\sqrt{k\frac{p}{\rho}}=\sqrt{kRT}=\sqrt{1.33\times 287.4\times 873}=577.7\text{m/s}$$

$$\text{Ma}=\frac{u}{c}=\frac{560}{577.7}=0.97$$

选 A。

【例 14.6-3】 喷管中空气的速度为 500m/s，温度为 300K，密度为 2kg/m^3，若要进一步加速气流，则喷管面积需：

A. 缩小　　B. 扩大　　C. 不变　　D. 不定

解 音速与气体的绝热指数 k 和气体常数 R 有关，对于空气 $k=1.4$，$R=287\text{J/(kg}\cdot\text{K)}$，由

$$c=\sqrt{kRT}=\sqrt{1.4\times 287\times 230}=347.2\text{m/s}$$

可得此处马赫数 $\frac{\mathrm{d}v}{v}=\frac{1}{\text{Ma}^2-1}\frac{\mathrm{d}A}{A}$ 大于 1。又因马赫数大于 1 时，$\mathrm{d}v$ 与 $\mathrm{d}A$ 符号相同，说明速度随断面的增大而加快，随断面的减小而减慢。因此要想进一步加速，则喷管面积需要扩大。选 B。

14.6.3 渐缩喷管与拉伐尔管的特点

流动参数随断面积的关系，由运动微分方程 $\frac{\mathrm{d}p}{\rho}+v\mathrm{d}v=0$ 及声速公式 $a=\sqrt{\frac{\mathrm{d}p}{\rho}}$ 得到关系式

$$\frac{\mathrm{d}v}{v}=\frac{1}{\text{Ma}^2-1}\frac{\mathrm{d}A}{A}$$

对上式进行讨论，即可得到断面 A 与气流速度 v 的关系。

(1) $\text{Ma}<1$，$u<c$，为亚声速流动，$\mathrm{d}v$ 与 $\mathrm{d}A$ 符号相反，说明速度随断面的增大而减慢；随断面的减小而加快。

(2) $\text{Ma}>1$，$u>c$，为超声速流动，$\mathrm{d}v$ 与 $\mathrm{d}A$ 符号相同，说明速度随断面的增大而加快；随断面的减小而减慢。

(3) $\text{Ma}=1$，$u=c$，为气流速度与当地声速相等，此时称气体处于临界状态。气体达到临界状态时的界面，称为临界断面。

由上面可知，要使气流加速，当流速尚未达到当地声速时，喷管断面应逐渐收缩，直至流速达到当地声速时，断面收缩到最小值，这种喷管称为渐缩喷管。渐缩喷管出口处的流速最大只能达到当地声速。

要使气流从亚声速加速到超声速，必须将喷管做成先逐渐收缩而后逐渐扩大形（在最小断面处流速达到当地声速），这种喷管称为缩放喷管。缩放喷管是瑞典工程师拉伐尔（de. Laval）在研制汽轮机时发明的，所以又称为拉伐尔喷管。这种利用管道断面的变化来加速气流的几何喷管，在汽轮机、燃气轮机、喷气发动机和流量测量中被广泛地应用。

典型例题解析

【例 14.6-4】 对于喷管气体流动，在马赫数 Ma>1 的情况下，气体速度随断面的增大变化情况为：

A. 加快　　B. 减慢

C. 不变　　D. 先加快后减慢

解 Ma>1，$u>c$，为超声速流动，dv 与 dA 符号相同，说明速度随断面的增大而加快；随断面的减小而减慢。选 A。

【例 14.6-5】 在同一流动气流中，当地音速 c 与滞止音速 c_0 的关系为：

A. c 永远大于 c_0　　B. c 永远小于 c_0

C. c 永远等于 c_0　　D. c 与 c_0 关系不确定

解 由于当地气流速度 v 的存在，同一气流中当地音速永远小于滞止音速。选 B。

14.7 泵与风机与网络系统的匹配

考试大纲☞：泵与风机的运行曲线　网络系统中泵与风机的工作点　离心式泵或风机的工况调节　离心式泵或风机的选择　气蚀　安装要求

必备基础知识

水泵与风机是输送流体或使流体增压的机械。它将原动机的机械能或其他外部能量传送给流体，使流体能量增加，主要用于流体输送，是一种面大量广的通用型机械设备。根据不同的工作原理可分为容积水泵、叶片泵等类型。叶片泵是利用回转叶片与水的相互作用来传递能量，有离心泵、轴流泵和混流泵等类型。其中，离心泵在暖通空调系统中应用最为广泛。

叶轮随原动机的轴转时，叶片间的流体也随叶轮高速旋转，受到离心力的作用，被甩出叶轮的出口。被甩出的流体挤入机(泵)壳后，机(泵)壳内流体压强增高，最后被导向泵或风机的出口排出。同时，叶轮中心由于流体被甩出而形成真空，外界的流体在大气压的作用下，沿泵或风机的进口吸入叶轮，如此源源不断地输送流体。

按叶片出口角度的不同，叶片可分为前向、径向和后向三种。叶片出口角大于 90°的叫作前向叶片，等于 90°的叫作径向叶片，小于 90°叫作后向叶片。

从结构角度看，前向式叶轮结构小，质量小，投资少。从能量转化和效率角度看，前向式叶轮流道扩散度大且压出室能头转化损失也大；而后向式则反之，故其克服管路阻力的能力相对较好。从防磨损和积垢角度看，径向式叶轮较好，前向式叶轮较差，而后向式居中。

因此，叶片出口安装角的选用原则为：

(1)为了提高泵与风机的效率和降低噪声，工程上对离心式泵均采用后向式叶轮。

(2)为了提高压头、流量，缩小尺寸，减轻质量，工程上对小型通风机也可采用前向式叶轮。

(3)由于径向式叶轮防磨、防积垢性能好，所以，可用做引风机、排尘风机和耐磨高温风机等。

以离心式泵与风机为例，它们的能量损失大致可分为流动损失、泄漏损失、轮阻损失和机械损失等。

(1)流动损失。流动损失的根本原因在于流体具有黏滞性。泵与风机的通流部分从进口到出口由许多不同形状的流道组成。首先，流体流经叶轮时由轴向转变为径向，流体在叶片入口之前，由于叶轮与流体间的旋转效应存在，发生先期预旋现象，改变了叶片传给流体的理论功，并且使进口相对速度的大小和方向改变，使理论扬程下降；其次，因种种原因泵与风机往往不能在设计工况下运转，当工作流量不等于设计流量时，进入叶轮叶片流体的相对速度的方向就不再同叶片进口安装角的切线相一致，从而对叶片发生冲击作用，形成撞击损失；此外，在整个流动过程中一方面存在着从叶轮进口、叶道、叶片扩压器到蜗壳及出口扩压器沿程摩擦损失，另一方面还因边界层分离，产生涡流损失。

(2)泄漏损失。泵与风机静止元件和转动部件间必然存在一定的间隙，流体会从泵与风机转轴与蜗壳之间的间隙处泄漏，称为外泄漏。离心式泵与风机的外泄漏损失很小，一般可略去不计。但当叶轮工作时，机内存在着高压区和低压区，蜗壳靠近前盘的流体，经过叶轮进口与进气口之间的间隙，流回到叶轮进口的低压区而引起的损失，称为内泄漏损失。此外，对离心泵来说为平衡轴向推力常设置平衡孔，同样引起内泄漏损失。由于泄漏的存在，既导致出口流量降低，又无益地耗功。

(3)轮阻损失。因为流体具有黏性，当叶轮旋转时引起了流体与叶轮前、后盘外侧面和轮缘与周围流体的摩擦损失，称为轮阻损失。

(4)机械传动损失。这是由于泵与风机的轴承与轴封之间的摩擦造成的。

典型例题解析

【例 14.7-1】 前向叶型风机的特点为：

A. 总的扬程比较大，损失较大，效率较低

B. 总的扬程比较小，损失较大，效率较低

C. 总的扬程比较大，损失较小，效率较高

D. 总的扬程比较大，损失较大，效率较高

解 前向式叶轮结构小，从能量转化和效率角度看，前向式叶轮流道扩散度大且压出室能头转化损失也大、效率低，但其压头却要高一些。选 A。

14.7.1 泵与风机的运行曲线

泵与风机的性能曲线，只能说明泵与风机自身的性能，但泵与风机在管路中工作时，不仅取决于其本身的性能，而且还取决于管路系统的性能，即管路特性曲线。由这两条曲线的交点来决定泵与风机在管路系统中的运行工况。

泵与风机的理论特性曲线：性能曲线通常是指在一定转速下，以流量为基本变量，其他各参数随流量改变而改变的曲线。

通常的性能曲线为：

(1)$H=f_1(Q)$。

(2)$N=f_2(Q)$。

(3)$\eta=f_3(Q)$。

把相似定律应用到不同转速运行的同一台叶片泵，流量、扬程、功率与转速之间的比例关系为

$$Q_1/Q_2=n_1/n_2$$

$$H_1/H_2 = (n_1/n_2)^2$$

$$N_1/N_2 = (n_1/n_2)^3$$

Q、H、N 分别表示流量、扬程、功率，下标 1 相对于转速 1 的物理量，下标 2 相对于转速 2 的物理量。

典型例题解析

【例 14.7-2】 某单吸离心泵，$Q=0.073\ 5\text{m}^3/\text{s}$，$n=1\ 420\text{r/min}$；后因改为电机直接联动，$n$ 增大为 $1\ 450\text{r/min}$，试求这时泵的流量：

A. $Q=0.074\ 05\text{m}^3/\text{s}$

B. $Q=0.079\ 2\text{m}^3/\text{s}$

C. $Q=0.073\ 5\text{m}^3/\text{s}$

D. $Q=0.075\ 1\text{m}^3/\text{s}$

解 因为 $Q_1/Q_2 = n_1/n_2$，即流量与转速成正比。选 D。

【例 14.7-3】 在系统阻力经常发生波动的系统中，应选用具有什么型 Q-H 性能曲线的风机？

A. 平坦型　　B. 驼峰型　　C. 陡降型　　D. 上述均可

解 这是因为系统阻力波动较大，而对于 Q-H 性能曲线为陡降型的风机，全压变化较大，而风量变化不大，从而保证系统风量的稳定。选 C。

14.7.2 网络系统中泵与风机的工作点

将泵或风机的性能曲线和管路特性曲线同绘在一张坐标图上，泵或风机的性能曲线和管路特性曲线相交于一点，该点即为泵在管路系统中的实际工作点。

工作点的确定，对泵与风机的选用和维修、调节具有指导性的意义。

(1)对泵与风机进行选配时，除了必须满足按工程需要所确定的参数外，其工况必须和工作点接近，即必须在最高效率区，以保证运行的经济性。

(2)实际工作中对泵与风机的运行需求是变化的。这就常常需要改变泵与风机的工作点，即调节工况。

(3)泵或风机在运行中出现故障时，也常常利用工作点(特性曲线)的变化情况指导维修工作。

1)工作点的稳定

泵或风机的性能曲线的上升部分与管路特性曲线相交的点，称为泵或风机的不稳定工作点。

如果泵或风机的性能曲线没有上升区段，就不会出现工作的不稳定性，因此泵或风机应当设计成性能曲线只有下降型的。

若泵或风机的性能曲线是驼峰型的，则工作范围要始终保持在性能曲线的下降区段，这样就可以避免不稳定的工作。

2)工作点调节

从工作点的定义出发，调整工作点，可以改变泵与风机本身的性能曲线，也可以改变管路的特性曲线，当然两条曲线同时改变也是常用的调节方法。其常用的方法有：

(1)多台泵或风机的串并联运行调节。

(2)改变阀门开度进行调节。

(3)改变转速调节。

(4)切削水泵叶轮调节。

典型例题解析

【例 14.7-4】 如图所示送风系统采用调速风机，现 $L_A = 1\,000\text{m}^3/\text{h}$，$L_B = 1\,500\text{m}^3/\text{h}$，为使 $L_A = L_B = 1\,000\text{m}^3/\text{h}$，可采用下列哪种方法？

A. 关小 B 阀，调低风机转速

B. 关小 B 阀，调高风机转速

C. 开大 A 阀，调低风机转速

D. A 与 C 方法皆可用

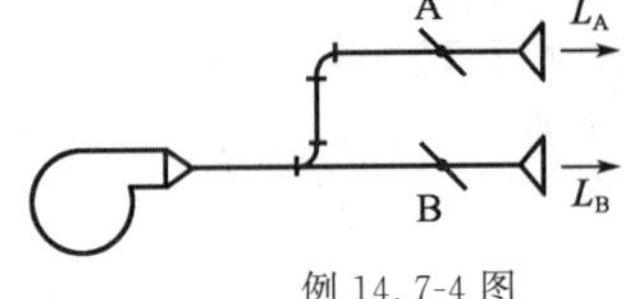

例 14.7-4 图

解 对于 A 方法，关小 B 阀，增大其阻抗，A 与 B 并联的总阻抗变大，总流量变小，风机的压头提高，而 A 管理不变，所以 A 流量会变大，所以此时应再调低风机转速。同理可分析，也可以开大 A 阀，调低风机转速。选 D。

【例 14.7-5】 某水泵的性能曲线如图所示，则工作点应选在曲线的：

A. 1-2 区域　　B. 1-2-3 区域

C. 3-4 区域　　D. 1-2-3-4 区域

解 工作点应选稳定工作点。泵性能曲线有驼峰时，工作点应取在下降段。因为管网曲线可能与之有两个交点，如解图所示。选 C。

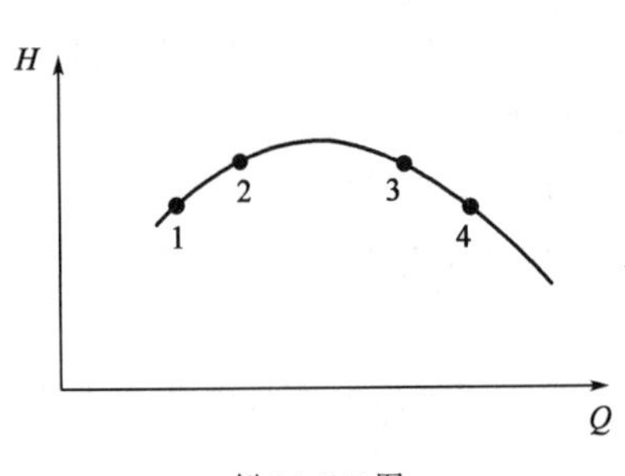

例 14.7-5 图

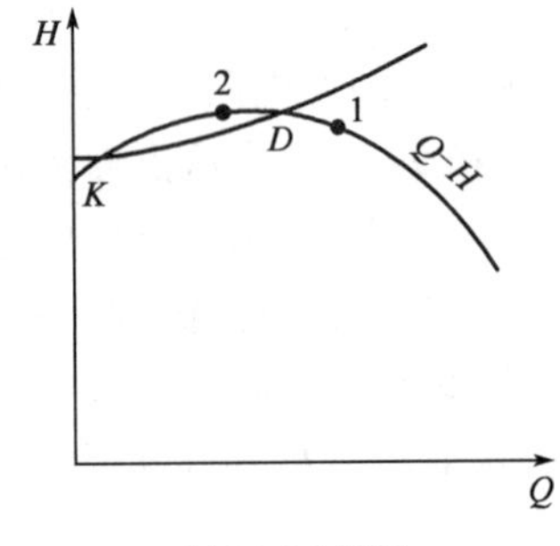

例 14.7-5 解图

两个交点，分别为 D 点和 K 点。当 Q 大于 Q_k 时，随着 Q 增加，H 增加，压头大于需要，流速加大，流量继续增大，直到 D 点；当 Q 小于 Q_k 时，随着 Q 减小，H 减小，压头小于需要，流速减小，流量继续减小，直到 $Q=0$ 点，甚至发生回流。一旦离开 K 点，便难于再返回，故称 K 点为非稳定工作点。

14.7.3 泵或风机的联合运行

当采用一台泵或风机不能满足流量或能头要求时，往往要用两台或两台以上的泵与风机联合工作。泵与风机联合工作可以分为并联和串联两种。

1)泵与风机的并联工作

并联是指两台或两台以上的泵或风机，向同一压力管路输送流体的工作方式。并联的目的是在压头相同时增加流量。当系统改造，相应的需要流量增大，或者由于外界负荷变化很大，流量变化幅度相应很大，为了发挥泵与风机的经济效果，使其能在高效率范围内工作，往往采用两台或数台并联工作，以增减运行台数来适应外界负荷变化的要求时。并联工作可分为两种情况，即相同性能的泵与风机并联和不同性能的泵与风机并联，通常以相同性能的泵与风机并联为多，故现以相同性能的泵与风机并联泵为例介绍并联工作的特点。

两台泵并联时的流量等于并联时的各台泵流量之和，但与各台泵单独工作时相比，则两台泵并联后的总流量小于两台泵单独工作的流量之和，而大于一台泵单独工作时的流量。并联后每台泵工作的流量较单独时的较小，而并联后的扬程却比一台泵单独工作时要高些。这是因为输送的管道仍是原有的，直径也没增大，而管道摩擦损失随流量的增加而增大了，从而阻力增大，这就需要每台泵都提高它的扬程来克服这增加的阻力水头。

并联工作时，管路特性曲线越平坦，并联后的流量就越接近单独运行时的 2 倍，工作就越有利。如果管路特性曲线越陡，陡到一定程度时仍采取并联是徒劳无益的。若泵的性能曲线越陡时，并联后的总流量反而就越接近单独工作时流量的 2 倍，因此为达到并联后增加流量的目的，泵的性能曲线应当陡一些为好。从并联数量来看，台数越多，并联后所能增加的流量越少，即每台泵输送的流量减少，故并联台数过多并不经济。

2)泵与风机的串联工作

串联是指前一台泵或风机的出口向另一台泵或风机的入口输送流体的工作方式。当设计制造一台新的高压的泵或风机比较困难，而现有的泵或风机的容量已足够，只是压头不够时；或者在改建或扩建的管道阻力加大，要求提高扬程以输出较多流量时，都可以采用串联工作方式。

串联也可分为两种情况，即相同性能的泵与风机串联和不同性能的泵与风机串联，现以相同性能的水泵串联为例，介绍串联工作的特点。

串联工作的特点，是流量彼此相等，总扬程为每台泵扬程之和，两台泵串联工作时所产生的总扬程小于泵单独工作时扬程的 2 倍，而大于串联前单独运行的扬程，且串联后的流量也比一台泵单独工作时大了，这是因为泵串联后一方面扬程的增加大于管路阻力的增加，导致富裕的扬程促使流量增加。另一方面流量的增加又使阻力增大，抑制了总扬程的升高。当两泵串联时，必须注意的是后一台泵是否承受升压，故选择时要注意泵的结构强度。启动时，要注意各串联泵的出口阀都要关闭，待启动第一台泵后，再开第一台泵的出水阀门，然后再启动第二台泵，再打开第二台泵的出水阀向外供水。

风机串联的特性与泵相同，但几台风机串联运行的情况不常见，且因在操作上可靠性差，故不推荐采用。

典型例题解析

【例 14.7-6】 当采用两台相同型号的水泵并联运行时，下列哪条结论是错误的？

A. 并联运行时总流量等于每台水泵单独运行时的流量之和

B. 并联运行时总扬程大于每台水泵单独运行时的扬程

C. 并联运行时总流量等于每台水泵联合运行时的流量之和

D. 并联运行比较适合管路阻力特性曲线平坦的系统

解 并联运行时总流量小于每台水泵单独运行时的流量之和。选 A。

14.7.4 泵的气蚀及安装要求

1)气蚀

大气压下升温到100℃,或20℃下降压至2.4kPa,水就会汽化。汽化发生后,大量的蒸气及溶解在水中的气体逸出,形成大量蒸气、气体混合物的小气泡。气泡随同液体从低压区流向高压区,在高压作用下迅速凝结或破裂,瞬间产生局部空穴,周围的液体以极高的速度冲向原气泡所占据的空间,形成冲击。来不及瞬间全部溶解和凝结的气体和蒸气在冲击力的作用下又分成更小的气泡,反复被高压水压缩、凝结。于是局部地区产生高频率、高冲击力的水击,不断击打泵内部件,特别是工作叶轮,长期这样会使其表面成为蜂窝状或海绵状。此外,在凝结热的助长下,活泼气体还对金属发生化学腐蚀,以致金属表面逐渐脱落而破坏。这种现象就是气蚀。

产生"气蚀"的原因有以下几种:

泵的安装位置高出吸液面的高差太大,即泵的几何安装高度 H_g 太大;泵安装地点的大气压较低,例如安装在高海拔地区;泵所输送的液体温度过高等。

2)泵的安装高度和吸入口的真空高度

水池液面 e-e 和水泵吸入口 s-s 断面的能量方程为

$$z_e+\frac{p_e}{\rho g}+\frac{v_e^2}{2g}=z_s+\frac{p_s}{\rho g}+\frac{v_s^2}{2g}+h_1$$

而 $z_s-z_e=H_g$,为泵的安装高度(m);$\frac{p_e-p_s}{\rho g}=H_s$,为泵吸入口处的真空高度(m)。

所以得 $H_s=H_g+\frac{v_s^2}{2g}+h_1$。

典型例题解析

【例 14.7-7】 以下哪些请况会造成泵的气蚀问题?

①泵的安装位置高出吸液面的高差太大

②泵安装地点的大气压较低

③泵输送的液体温度过高

A. ①② B. ①③ C. ③ D. ①②③

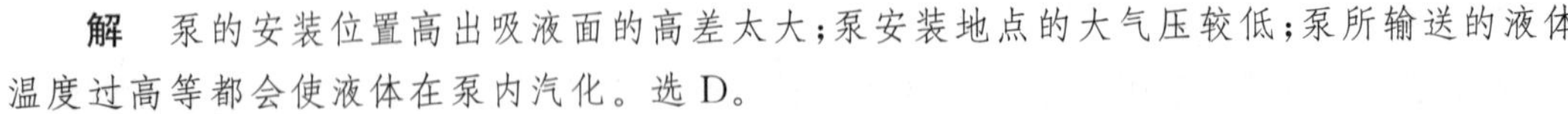

解 泵的安装位置高出吸液面的高差太大;泵安装地点的大气压较低;泵所输送的液体温度过高等都会使液体在泵内汽化。选D。

【例 14.7-8】 如图所示水泵,允许吸入真空高度 $H_s=6$m,流量 $Q=150\text{m}^3/\text{h}$,吸水管管径为150mm,当量总长度 L_x 为80m,比摩阻 $R_m=0.05\text{mH}_2\text{O/m}$,则最大安装高度 H 等于:

A. 2.2m B. 1.7m

C. 1.4m D. 1.2m

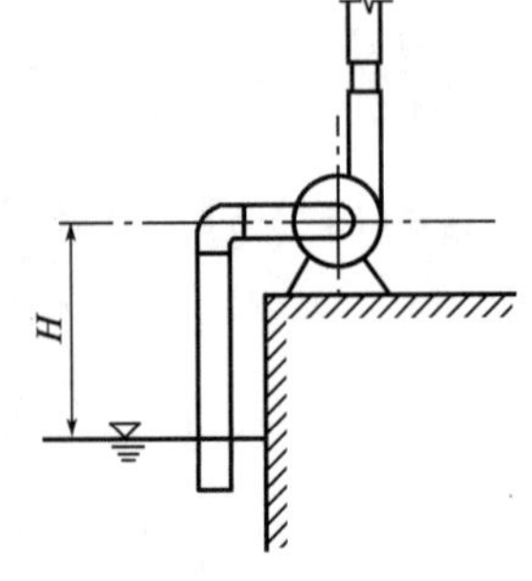

例 14.7-8 图

解 $v_s=\frac{4Q}{\pi d^2}=2.35\text{m/s}$,$H_1=0.05\times80=4\text{m}$,$H_s=H_g+\frac{v_s^2}{2g}+h_1$ 得 $H_g=1.7$m。选B。

经典练习

14.7-1 某水泵，在转速 $n=1\,500\text{r/min}$ 时，其流量 $Q=0.08\text{m}^3/\text{s}$，扬程 $H=20\text{m}$，功率 $N=25\text{kW}$，采用变速调节，调整后的转速 $n'=2\,000\text{r/min}$，设水的密度不变，则其调整后的流量 Q'，扬程 H'，功率 N' 分别是(　　)。

A. 0.107 m^3/s，35.6m，59.3kW　　B. 0.107 m^3/s，26.7m，44.4kW

C. 0.107 m^3/s，26.7m，59.3kW　　D. 0.142 m^3/s，20m，44.4kW

14.7-2 已知某一型号水泵叶轮外径 D_1 为 174mm，转速 n 为 2 900r/min 时的扬程特性曲线 Q-H 与管网特性曲线 Q-R 的交点 M（$Q_M=27.3\text{L/s}$，$H_M=33.8\text{m}$）如图所示。现实际需要的流量仅为 24.6L/s，决定采用切割叶轮外径的办法来适应这种要求，则叶轮外径应切割掉(　　)。

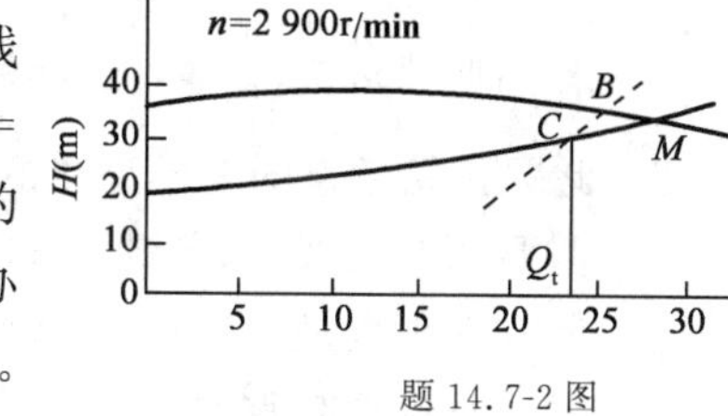

题 14.7-2 图

A. 9mm　　B. 18mm

C. 27mm　　D. 35mm

14.7-3 常用的泵与风机实际能头曲线有三种类型：陡降型、缓降型与驼峰型。陡降型的泵与风机宜用于下列(　　)的情况。

A. 流量变化小，能头变化大　　B. 流量变化大，能头变化小

C. 流量变化小，能头变化小　　D. 流量变化大，能头变化大

14.7-4 下面(　　)不属于产生“气蚀”的原因。

A. 泵的安装位置高出吸液面的高程太大

B. 泵所输送的液体具有腐蚀性

C. 泵的安装地点大气压较低

D. 泵所输送的液体温度过高

参考答案及提示

14.1-1　A　从伯努利方程可以看出，不同断面上压强是不同的，但与方向无关。

14.1-2　A　在公式(14.1-9)的推导过程中，其假设的前提就是不可压缩理想流体稳定流动。

14.1-3　A　根据连续性方程，断面流速与断面积成反比，因此与断面直径的平方成反比。A_1、A_2、A_3 三个断面直径之比为 3∶2∶4；则断面积之比为 9∶4∶16，因此 A_1、A_2、A_3 对应的流速比为16∶36∶9。

14.1-4　A　$p_2=p_1-\gamma H=300-10\times 20=100\text{kPa}$。

14.2-1　B　相似是指组成模型的每个要素必须与原型的对应要素相似，包括几何要素和物理要素，而不必是同一种流体介质。

14.2-2　A　该题可以通过带入单位运算得到答案，也可以直接由 $p=\xi\frac{\rho v^2}{2}$ 得出，等式两边具有同样的量纲。

14.2-3　A　此题模拟的为有压管流，因此，应选择雷诺准则来设计模型。则

$$\frac{u_n d_n}{\nu}=\frac{u_m d_m}{\nu}$$

所以有 $$u_n d_n = u_m d_m$$

因 $$\frac{d_n}{d_n}=10$$

所以 $$\frac{u_n}{u_n}=\frac{1}{10}$$

流动相似，欧拉数相等，因此，$\frac{p_n}{\rho_n v_n^2}=\frac{p_m}{\rho_m v_m^2}$，可以导出 $\frac{p_n}{p_m}=\frac{\rho_n}{\rho_m}\frac{v_n^2}{v_m^2}=1\times\left(\frac{1}{10}\right)^2=\frac{1}{100}$，所以 $p_n=\frac{1}{100}p_m=1.46\text{Pa}$。

14.2-4 C 此题首先考查的是模型律的选择问题。为了使模型和原型流动完全相似，除需要几何相似外，各独立的相似准则数应同时满足。但实际上要同时满足所有准则数是很困难的，甚至是不可能的，一般只能达到近似相似，就是要保证对流动起重要作用的力相似，这就是模型律的选择问题。如水利工程中的明渠流以及江、河、溪流，都是以水位落差形式表现的重力来支配流动的，对于这些以重力起支配作用的流动，应该以弗劳德相似准数作为决定性相似准数。有不少流动需要求流动中的黏性力，或者求流动中的水力阻力或水头损失，如管道流动、流体机械中的流动、液压技术中的流动等，此时应当以满足雷诺相似准数为主，Re 数就是决定性相似准数。本题选项中，闸流是在重力作用下的流动，应按弗劳德准则设计模型。

14.3-1 B $\text{Re}=\frac{vd}{\nu}=2\,000$，$v=2\,000\times1.31\times10^{-6}/0.05=0.052\,5\ \text{m/s}$

14.3-2 B $14=\frac{v^2}{2g}+\lambda\frac{l}{d}\frac{v^2}{2g}$

$$v=\sqrt{\frac{14\times2g}{1+\lambda\frac{l}{d}}}=\sqrt{\frac{14\times19.6}{1+0.04\times\frac{350}{0.15}}}=1.706\text{m/s}$$

$$Q=\frac{\pi d^2}{4}v=\sqrt{\frac{gd}{8\lambda l}h_f}=\frac{3.14\times0.15^2}{4}\times1.706=0.030\,1\text{m}^3/\text{s}$$

14.3-3 B 垂直于圆管轴线的截面上，层流流体速度为抛物线分布，而紊流为指数分布。

14.3-4 A $v_1=\frac{4Q}{\pi d_1^2}=\frac{4\times10/3\,600}{3.14\times0.05^2}=1.415\text{m/s}$

$$v_2=\frac{4Q}{\pi d_2^2}=\frac{4\times10/3\,600}{3.14\times0.075^2}=0.629\text{m/s}$$

$$H=\frac{v_2^2}{2g}+\left(\zeta_1+\lambda_1\frac{l_1}{d_1}\right)\frac{v_1^2}{2g}+\lambda_2\frac{l_2}{d_2}\frac{v_2^2}{2g}$$

$$=\left(0.5+0.019\times\frac{15}{0.05}\right)\times\frac{1.415^2}{19.6}+\left(1+0.03\times\frac{20}{0.075}\right)\times\frac{0.629^2}{19.6}=0.814\text{m}$$

14.3-5　C　对于圆管层流，断面平均速度为管道轴心最大速度的一半，即

$$v = \frac{1}{2}u_{\max} = 1.2\text{m/s}$$

则流量

$$Q = vA = 1.2 \times \pi \times 0.25^2 = 0.236\text{m}^3/\text{s}$$

14.4-1　B　前后管道系统阻抗不变，且 $H = SQ^2$，$\frac{H_2}{H_1} = \frac{Q_2^2}{Q_1^2}$，$H_2 = \left(\frac{750}{500}\right)^2 \times 300 = 675\ \text{Pa}$，同时还要送到 150Pa 的密封舱内，所以总阻力还要克服此压力，则总系统阻力为 675＋150＝825Pa。

14.4-2　A　并联环路水头损失相等。严格来讲，总能量损失还应包括流体传热造成的热量损失。

14.4-3　A　并联各支管上的阻力损失相等。总的阻抗的平方根倒数等于各支管阻抗平方根倒数之和。

14.5-1　A　任意流体质点的旋转角速度向量 $\omega=0$，这种流动称为无旋流动。

14.5-2　B　此类题目可采用排除法。因为其流函数满足：$u_x = \frac{\partial \psi}{\partial y}$，$u_y = \frac{\partial \psi}{\partial x}$。将各项带入求偏导，即可得出答案。

14.5-3　B　在环流中，除原点外的所有质点的旋转角速度向量 $\omega=0$。

14.7-1　A　流量、扬程、功率分别与转速为 1 次方、2 次方、3 次方关系。

14.7-2　B　离心泵的切割定律：$(H_1 : H_2)^2 = D_1 : D_2$，$Q_1 : Q_2 = D_1 : D_2$，从而可以看出叶轮的直径与扬程的平方成正比，与流量成正比。叶轮直径越大扬程就越大，流量也越大，因为水流出的速度取决于叶轮旋转时产生的离心力和切线上的线速，直径越大，离心力和线速度就越大。

因为 $Q_1 : Q_2 = D_1 : D_2$，所以 $27.3 : 24.6 = 174 : D_2$。

得 $D_2 = 156.8\text{mm}$，$174 - 156.8 = 17.2\text{mm}$。

取切割 18mm，再验证管路参数，基本达到要求。

14.7-3　A　从特征曲线图上可以看出，陡降型的泵与风机当流量变化时，能头会剧烈变化，因此适用于选项 A 的情况。

14.7-4　B　泵的安装位置高出吸液面的高差太大；泵安装地点的大气压较低；泵所输送的液体温度过高等都会使液体在泵内汽化。

15 自动控制理论

考题配置 单选,9 题

分数配置 每题 2 分,共 18 分

复习指导

自动控制理论作为一门学科,其性质属于技术科学,研究的主要对象是自动控制系统;研究的中心问题是系统的精度,或者说是系统在控制过程中的性能。学科的基本内容分为数学模型、工程分析计算方法和系统一般规律三部分。要求学生能够熟练掌握自动控制的基本理论和方法,掌握系统的分析及设计的基本方法,能进行典型控制系统的分析与设计。

15.1 自动控制与自动控制系统的一般概念

考试大纲☞:"控制工程"基本含义 信息的传递 反馈及反馈控制 开环及闭环 控制系统构成 控制系统的分类及基本要求

必备基础知识

15.1.1 "控制工程"基本含义

控制工程是处理自动控制系统各种工程实现问题的综合性工程技术。控制工程的自动控制理论是研究控制共同规律的技术科学。在自动控制原理中,"控制"是为克服各种扰动的影响,达到预期的目标,对在生产机械或过程中的某一个或某一物理量进行的操作。在对被控量进行控制时,按照系统中是否有人参与,可分为人工控制和自动控制。若由人来完成对被控量的控制,称为人工控制;若由自动控制装置代替人来完成这种操作,称为自动控制。

自动控制系统可定义为,由被控对象和控制器按一定方式连接起来,完成某种自动控制任务的有机整体。其中被控对象是指以被控制的设备或过程为对象,如反应器、精馏设备的控制,或传热过程、燃烧过程的控制等。从定量分析和设计角度,控制对象只是被控设备或过程中影响对象输入、输出参数的部分因素,并不是设备的全部。控制器也称控制装置,是指对被控对象进行控制的设备总体。

在控制系统中,按规定的任务需要加以控制的物理量称为被控制量,也称为自动控制系统的输出量。而作为被控制量的指控指令而加给系统的输出量称为控制量,也称为给定量或输入量。干扰或破坏系统按照规定规律运行的输入量称为扰动量,也称扰动输入或干扰输入。

15.1.2 信息的传递

在自动控制系统中,把输入量和输出量称之为信号,实际的控制系统各环节的输入量和输出量各不相同。当系统中信号通过各环节传递，信息的大小和状态都发生变化，但其输出信息与输入信息有一定的函数关系。传递函数即是用系统参数表示输出量与输入量之间关系的表达式，通常用 $G(s)$ 或 $\Phi(s)$ 表示。

15.1.3 反馈及反馈控制

反馈：把输出量送回到系统的输入端并与输入信号比较的过程。若反馈信号时输入信号相减而使偏差值越来越小，则称之为负反馈；反之，称为正反馈。

一个利用偏差进行控制并最后消除偏差的过程，又称偏差控制。

反馈控制：把输出量的一部分检测端，反馈到输入端，与给定信号进行比较，产生偏差，此偏差经过控制器产生控制作用，使输出量按照要求的规律变化。反馈控制实质上是一个按偏差进行控制的过程，也称偏差控制，反馈控制原理也就是按偏差控制原理。

反馈控制的特点：输入控制输出、输出参与控制、检测偏差纠正偏差、具有抗干扰能力。

15.1.4 开环及闭环控制系统的构成

1）开环系统

若系统的输出量（即被控量）不返回到系统的输入端，则称之为开环控制系统。开环控制系统结构如图 15.1-1 所示。由于在开环控制系统中，控制器与被控对象之间只有顺向作用而无反向联系，系统的被控变量对控制系统没有任何影响，系统的控制精度完全取决于所用元器件的精度和特性调整的准确度。因此开环系统只有在输出量难于测量且要求控制精度不高，以及扰动的影响较小或扰动的作用可以预先加以补偿的场合，才能得以广泛应用。

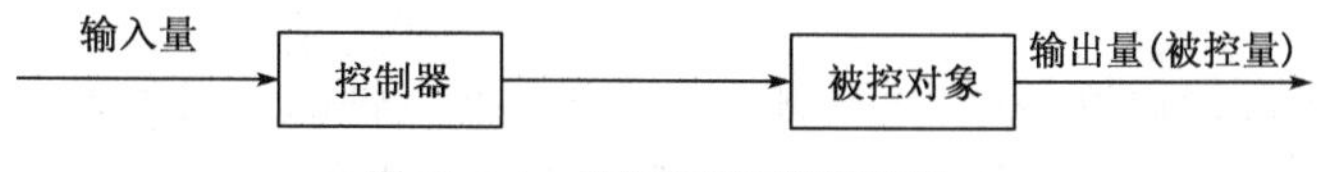

图 15.1-1 开环控制系统结构图

开环控制系统的特点：结构简单，稳定性好，容易设计和调整以及成本较低；但是也有着输入控制输出、输出不参与控制、系统没有抗干扰能力的缺点。

2）闭环系统

控制装置和被控对象之间既有顺向作用，又有反向联系的控制过程，称为闭环控制，又称为反馈控制或按偏差控制，相应的控制系统称之为闭环控制系统。就工作原理来说，闭环控制系统是由给定装置、比较元件、校正装置、放大元件、执行机构、检测元件和被控对象组成的。其原理结构图如图 15.1-2 所示。图中的每一个方块，代表一个具有特定功能的装置或元件。

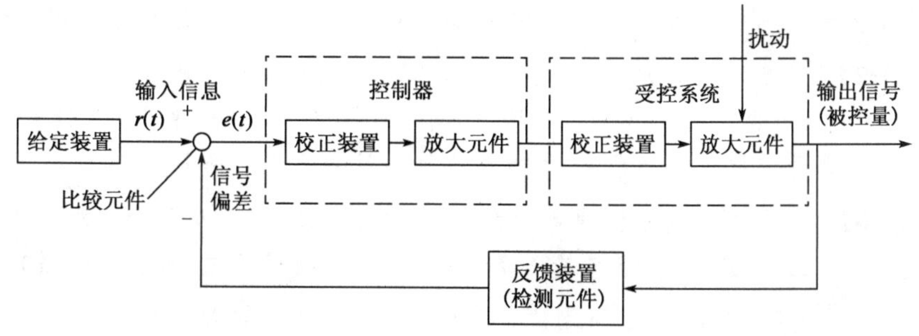

图 15.1-2 闭环控制系统典型方块图

(1)给定装置：其功能是给出与期望的被控量相对应的系统输入量(即参考输入信号或给定值)。

(2)比较元件：其功能是将检测元件测量到的被控量的实际值，与给定装置提供的给定值进行比较，求出它们之间的偏差。

(3)放大元件：比较元件通常位于低功率的输入端，由于提供的偏差信号通常很微弱，因此必须用放大元件将其放大，以便推动执行机构去控制被控对象。

(4)执行机构：其功能是执行控制作用并驱动被控对象，使被控对象按照预定的规律变化。

(5)检测元件：其功能是检测被控制的物理量，并将其反馈到系统输入端。在闭环控制系统中，检测元件及相关的元器件构成系统的反馈装置，如果被测量的物理量为非电量，通常检测元件应将其转换为电量，以便于处理。

(6)校正装置：由于被控对象和执行机构的性能难以满足要求，在构成控制系统时，通常需要引入校正装置对其性能进行校正。校正装置的功能是对偏差信号进行加工处理和运算，以形成合适的控制作用，或形成适当的控制规律，从而使系统的被控量按预定的规律变化。通常在控制系统中，将校正装置和放大器组合在一起构成一个器件，称为控制器。

闭环控制系统的优缺点如下。

优点：

(1)闭环控制系统是利用负反馈的作用来减小系统误差的。

(2)闭环控制系统能够有效地抑制被反馈通道包围的前向通道中，各种扰动对系统输出量的影响。

(3)闭环控制系统可以减小被控对象的参数变化对输出量的影响。

缺点：

(1)由于增加了反馈通道，使闭环控制系统增加了元器件的数目和系统的复杂程度。

(2)闭环控制系统用增益的损失换取了系统对参数变化和干扰灵敏度的降低，亦即换取了对系统响应的控制能力。

(3)闭环控制带来了系统稳定性问题。

典型例题解析

【例 15.1-1】 前馈控制系统是对于干扰信号进行补偿的系统，是：

A. 开环控制系统

B. 闭环控制系统和开环控制系统的复合

C. 能消除不可测量的扰动系统

D. 能抑制不可测量的扰动系统

解 前馈控制系统属于闭环控制，只能抑制不可测量的扰动量而不能消除。选 D。

【例 15.1-2】 从自动控制原理的观点看，家用空调机的温度传感器应为：

A. 输入元件　　B. 反馈元件　　C. 比较元件　　D. 执行元件

解 家用空调系统属于闭环控制，温度传感器为反馈元件。选 B。

【例 15.1-3】 从自动控制原理的观点看，家用电冰箱工作时，房闭的室温应为：

A. 给定量(或参考输入量)　　B. 输出量(或被控制量)

C. 反馈量　　D. 干扰量

解 室温对冰箱的工作有一定干扰作用，属于干扰量。选 D。

【例 15.1-4】 从自动控制原理的观点看,电机组运行时频率控制系统的"标准 50Hz"应为:

A. 输入量(或参考输入量)　　B. 输出量(或被控制量)

C. 反馈量　　D. 干扰量

解 B。

【例 15.1-5】 从自动控制原理的观点看,下列哪一种控制系统为闭环控制系统:

A. 普通热水加热式暖气设备的温度调节

B. 遥控电视机的定时开机(或关机)控制系统

C. 抽水马桶的水箱水位控制系统

D. 商店、宾馆自动门的开(闭)门启闭系统

解 马桶的水箱水位控制系统中有反馈环节,为闭式系统。选 C。

【例 15.1-6】 由温度控制器、温度传感器、热交换器、流量计等组成的控制系统,其中被控对象是:

A. 温度控制器　　B. 温度传感器

C. 热交换器　　D. 流量计

解 被控对象为被控制的机器、设备或生产过程中的全部或一部分。题中所给控制系统中热交换器为被控对象,温度为被控制量,给定量(希望的温度)在温度控制器中设定,水流量是干扰量。选 C。

【例 15.1-7】 下列概念中错误的是:

A. 闭环控制系统精度通常比开环系统高

B. 开环系统不存在稳定性问题

C. 反馈可能引起系统振荡

D. 闭环系统总是稳定的

解 闭环控制系统的优点是具有自动修正输出量偏差的能力、抗干扰性能好、控制精度高;缺点是结构复杂,如设计不好系统有可能不稳定。选 D。

15.1.5 控制系统的分类及基本要求

1)自动控制系统的分类

(1)按输入信号特征分类

①恒值控制系统:这类系统的特点是输入信号为某个不变的常数。要求系统的被控量尽可能保持在期望值附近;系统面临的主要问题是存在被控量偏离期望值的扰动;控制的任务是要增强系统的抗扰动能力,使扰动作用于系统时,被控量尽快恢复到期望值上。因此恒值控制系统又称为自动调节系统。

②随动控制系统(又称伺服系统):输入信号是随时间任意变化的函数,要求系统的输出信号紧紧跟随输入信号的变化;系统面临的主要矛盾是,被控对象和执行机构因惯性等因素的影响,使得系统的输出信号不能紧紧跟随输入信号的变化;控制的任务是提高系统的跟随能力,使系统的输出信号能跟随难于预知的输入信号的变化。

③程序控制系统:输入信号按照预先知道的函数变化。如热处理炉温度控制系统的升温、保温、降温过程,都是按照预先设定的规律进行的。

(2)按系统中传递信号的变化特征分类

①连续控制系统:系统中各环节的信号均是时间 t 的连续函数。连续控制系统的运动规律可用微分方程描述。

②离散控制系统:系统中某处或几处的信号是脉冲序列或数字编码的形式。离散控制系统的运动规律可用差分方程描述。

(3)按系统特性分类

①线性控制系统:同时满足叠加性与均匀性(或齐次性)的系统。所谓叠加性是指,当几个输入信号同时作用于系统时,系统的响应等于每个输入信号单独作用系统时所产生的响应之和。所谓均匀性是指,当输入信号按倍数变化时,系统响应也按同一倍数变化。

②非线性控制系统:不同时满足叠加性和均匀性的系统均为非线性系统。典型的非线性特性有饱和特性、死区特性、间隙特性、继电特性、磁滞特性等。

(4)按系统参数是否随时间变化分类

①定常系统:描述系统运动的微分或差分方程的系数均为常数的系统。此类系统又称为时不变系统。这类系统的特点是:系统的响应特性只取决于输入信号的形状和系统的特性,而与输入信号施加的时刻无关。

②时变系统:参数或结构随时间变化的系统。这类系统的特点是:系统的响应特性不仅取决于输入信号的形状和系统的特性,而且还与输入信号施加的时刻有关。

典型例题解析

【例 15.1-8】 下列描述系统的微分方程中,$r(t)$为输入变量,$c(t)$为输出变量,方程中为非线性时变系统的是:

A. $8\dfrac{\mathrm{d}^2c(t)}{\mathrm{d}t^2}+4\dfrac{\mathrm{d}c(t)}{\mathrm{d}t}+2c(t)=r(t)$

B. $t\dfrac{\mathrm{d}c(t)}{\mathrm{d}t}+2c(t)=r(t)+8\dfrac{\mathrm{d}r(t)}{\mathrm{d}t}$

C. $4\dfrac{\mathrm{d}c(t)}{\mathrm{d}t}+b(t)\sqrt{c(t)}=kr(t)$

D. $8\dfrac{\mathrm{d}^2c(t)}{\mathrm{d}t^2}+4c(t)=2r(t)$

解 只有选项 C 不满足叠加性和均匀性,故此题选 C。

2)对自动控制系统的基本要求

自动控制系统的基本任务是:根据被控对象和环境的特性,在各种扰动因素作用下,使系统的被控量能够按预定的规律变化。对于恒值控制系统来说,要求系统的被控量维持在期望值附近;对于随动控制系统而言,要求系统的被控量紧紧跟随输入量的变化。无论是哪种控制系统,当系统受到扰动的作用或者输入量发生变化后,系统的响应过程都是相同的。因此,对系统的基本要求也都是相同的,可以归结为稳定性、快速性和准确性,即稳、快、准的要求。

(1)稳定性

稳定性是保证系统正常工作的先决条件。一个稳定的控制系统,其被控量偏离期望值的初始偏差应随时间的增长逐渐减小或趋于零。也就是说,控制器的控制作用应使误差逐渐减小。若控制不当,使误差逐渐变大,就形成了不稳定的控制系统,不稳定的控制系统是不能正常工作的,系统激烈而持久的振荡会导致功率元件过载,甚至使设备损坏而发生故障,这是绝不允许的。

(2)快速性

为更好地完成控制任务,控制系统仅仅满足稳定性要求是不够的,还必须对其瞬态过程的形式和快慢提出要求,一般称为瞬态性能。通常希望系统的瞬态过程既要快(即快速性好),又要平稳(即平稳性高)。

(3)准确性

对于一个稳定的系统而言,当瞬态过程结束后,系统被控量的实际值与期望值之差称为稳态误差,它是衡量系统稳态精度的重要指标。通常希望系统的误差尽可能小,即希望系统具有较高的控制准确度或控制精度。

典型例题解析

【例 15.1-9】 自动控制系统的正常工作受到很多条件的影响,保证自动控制系统正常工作的先决条件是:

A. 反馈性　　B. 调节性　　C. 稳定性　　D. 快速性

解 稳定性是保持控制系统能够正常工作的先决条件。选 C。

【例 15.1-10】 系统稳定性表现为:

A. 系统时域响应的收敛性,是系统固有的特性

B. 系统在扰动撤消后,可以依靠外界作用恢复

C. 系统具有阻止扰动作用的能力

D. 处于平衡状态的系统,在受到扰动后不偏离原来平衡状态

解 当系统受到外界干扰,被控量会发生变化,但由于具有稳定性,会在一定时间内恢复平衡状态。选 B。

经典练习

15.1-1 一个环节的输出量变化取决于(　　)。

A. 输入量的变化　　B. 反馈量　　C. 环节特性　　D. A+C

15.1-2 在定值控制系统中为确保其精度,常采用(　　)。

A. 开环控制系统　　B. 闭环正反馈控制系统

C. 闭环负反馈控制系统　　D. 手动控制系统

15.1-3 反馈控制系统中,若测量单元发生故障而无信号输出,这时被控量将(　　)。

A. 保持不变　　B. 达到最大值

C. 达到最小值　　D. 不能自动控制

15.1-4 在反馈控制系统中,调节单元根据(　　)的大小和方向,输出一个控制信号。

A. 给定位　　B. 偏差　　C. 测量值　　D. 扰动量

15.1-5 按偏差控制运行参数的控制系统是(　　)系统。

A. 正反馈　　B. 负反馈　　C. 逻辑控制　　D. 随动控制

15.2 自动控制系统的数学模型

考试大纲☞:控制系统各环节的特性　控制系统稳定方程的拟定及求解　拉普拉斯变换与反变换　传递函数及其方块图

必备基础知识

在对控制系统进行分析和设计时，首先要建立系统的数学模型。而控制系统的数学模型是描述系统中各元件的特性以及各种信号(变量)的传递和转换关系的数学表达式。因此，它可使我们避开系统不同的物理特性，在一般意义下研究控制系统的普遍规律。

如果数学模型着重描述的是系统输入量和输出量之间的关系，则称之为输入输出模型；如果数学模型着重描述的是系统输入量与内部状态和输出量之间的关系，则称其为状态空间模型。

15.2.1 控制系统各环节的特性

自动控制系统是由被控对象、测量变送器、调节器和执行器组成，如图 15.2-1 所示。系统的控制品质和系统中各个组成部分的特性都有关系，而其中被控对象的特性对控制品质的影响最大。因此，在控制系统中，首先要非常了解被控对象的特性，研究其内在规律，根据对控制品质的要求，设计合理的控制系统，选择合适的测量变送器、调节器和执行器。

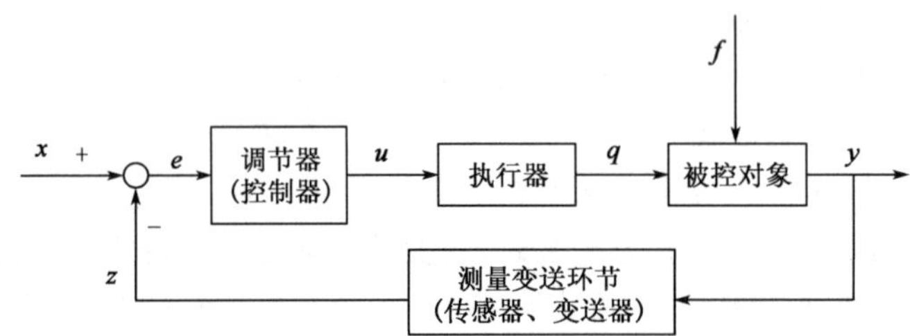

图 15.2-1　控制系统基本组成环节方块图

1)被控对象特性

被控对象特性是指对象输入量与输出量之间的关系，即对象受到输入作用后，被控变量是如何变化的，变化量为多少。输入量为控制变量和各种干扰变量之和。由对象的输入变量至输出变量的信号联系称为通道；控制变量至被控变量的信号联系通道称为控制通道；干扰至被控变量的信号联系通道称为干扰通道。对象输出为控制通道输出与各干扰通道输出之和。

自动控制系统数学模型一般有两种表示方法：参量模型和非参量模型。

参量模型常用的描述形式有：微分方程(组)、传递函数、频率特性。参量模型的微分方程的一般表达式为

$$y^{(n)}(t)+a_{n-1}y^{(n-1)}(t)+\cdots+a_1y'(t)+a_0y(t)=b_mx^{(m)}(t)+\cdots+b_1x'(t)+b_0x(t)$$

$y(t)$ 表示输出量，$x(t)$ 表示输入量，通常输出量的阶次不低于输入量的阶次($n\geqslant m$)。当 $n=m$ 时，称对象是正则的；当 $n>m$ 时，称对象是严格正则的；$n<m$ 的对象是不可实现的。通常 $n=1$，称该对象为一阶对象模型；$n=2$，称该对象为二阶对象模型。

非参量模型一般用曲线或表格等形式表示。特点是形象、清晰，但缺乏数学方程的解析性质(必要时须进行数学处理获得参量模型)。

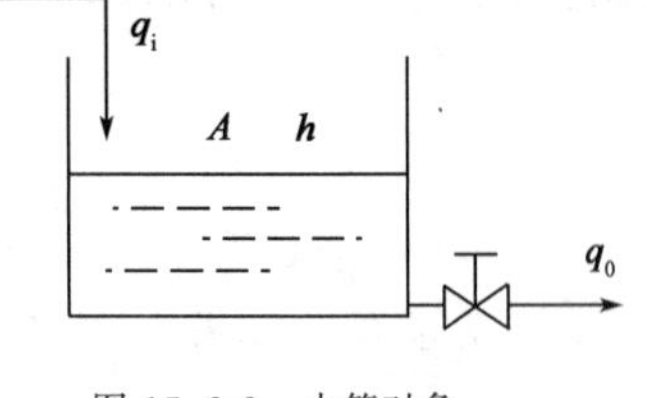

图 15.2-2　水箱对象

以图 15.2-2 为例，建立液位 h 的数学模型。该对象的输入量为 q_i，被控标量为液位 h，根据物料平衡方程：单位时间内水槽体积的改变=输入流量−输出流量。

$$\frac{\mathrm{d}V}{\mathrm{d}t}=\mathrm{d}h\cdot q_0\qquad V=Ah$$

$$A\frac{dh}{dt}=q_i-q_0$$

出口流量可以近似地表示为

$$q_0=\frac{h}{R}$$

故 $A\frac{dh}{dt}=q_i-\frac{h}{R}$　　$T\frac{dh}{dt}+h=K\cdot q_i(T=AR、K=R)$

记 $\begin{cases}h=h_0+\Delta h\\ q_i=q_{i0}+\Delta q_i\end{cases}$（$h_0$、$q_{i0}$ 为平衡状态的值）

由于有 $h_0=K\cdot q_{i0}$　　$\frac{dh_0}{dt}=0$

$$T\frac{d\Delta h}{dt}+\Delta h=K\cdot\Delta q_i$$

对上式作拉氏变换可得

$$TsH(s)+H(s)=K\cdot Q_i(s) \tag{15.2-1}$$

可写成对象的传递函数

$$\frac{H(s)}{Q_i}=\frac{K}{Ts+1}$$

此函数也是最典型的一阶对象的传递函数。

如果 q_i 为幅值为 A 的阶跃输入，则 $Q_i(s)=\frac{a}{s}$。

$$H(s)=\frac{K}{Ts+1}Q_i(s)=\frac{Ka}{s(Ts+1)} \tag{15.2-2}$$

$$\begin{aligned}h(t)&=L^{-1}[H(s)]\\&=L^{-1}\left[\frac{Ka}{s(Ts+1)}\right]\\&=L^{-1}\left[\frac{Ka}{s}-\frac{KaT}{Ts+1}\right]\\&=Ka\cdot L^{-1}\left[\frac{1}{s}-\frac{T}{Ts+1}\right]\\&=Ka(1-e^{-\frac{1}{T}})\end{aligned} \tag{15.2-3}$$

此方程为该对象的阶跃响应，K 为放大系数，T 为时间常数。

在工业过程中常有一些输送物料的中间过程，如图 15.2-2 所示，q_i 为操纵变量，但需要经过导流槽才送入水箱。如果把水箱入口的进料量记为 q_f，并设：导流槽长度 l，流体平均速度 v，流体流经导流槽所需的时间 τ(滞后时间)。所以当 q_i 发生改变以后，经过 τ 时间以后 q_f 才有变化

$$q_f(t)=q_i(t-\tau)$$

对于 q_f 与 h 来说，根据前面的推导可知：$T\frac{d\Delta h}{dt}+h(t)=K\cdot q_f(t)$。

纯滞后对象的微分方程为

$$T\frac{d\Delta h}{dt}+h(t)=K\cdot q_f(t-\tau)$$

传递函数为

$$TsH(s)+H(s)=Ke^{-\tau s}Q_i(s) \tag{15.2-4}$$

$$\frac{H(s)}{Q_i(s)} = \frac{K}{Ts+1}e^{-\tau s} \tag{15.2-5}$$

对于纯滞后对象，典型的阶跃响应函数为

$$h(t) = \begin{cases} 0 & (t < \tau) \\ Ka\left(1 - e^{\frac{t-\tau}{\tau}}\right) & (t \geqslant \tau) \end{cases} \tag{15.2-6}$$

典型的阶跃响应曲线如图 15.2-3 所示。

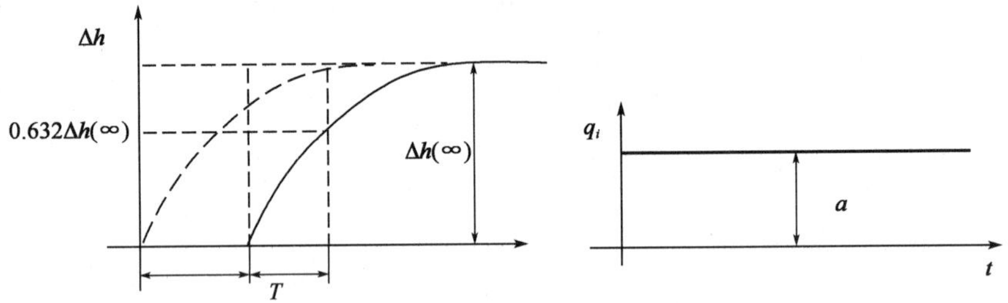

图 15.2-3　典型的阶跃响应曲线

放大系数 K，时间常数 T，滞后时间 τ 通常称为被控对象的三大特征参数。

(1)放大系数 K：在阶跃输入作用下，对象输出达到新的稳定值时，输出变化量与输入变化量之比，也称静态增益。K 值越大，表示输入量对输出量的影响越大，即被控变量对输入量的影响也越大，但是系统的稳定性差；放大系数越小，控制系统的稳定性越好，但是控制不够灵敏。

(2)时间常数 T：在阶跃输入作用下，对象输出达到最终稳态变化量的 63.2% 所需要的时间。时间常数 T 是反映响应变化快慢或响应滞后的重要参数。用 T 表示的响应滞后称阻容滞后(容量滞后)。T 越大，系统的反应越慢，越难以控制；T 越小，系统反应越快。时间常数对过渡过程的影响如图 15.2-4 所示。

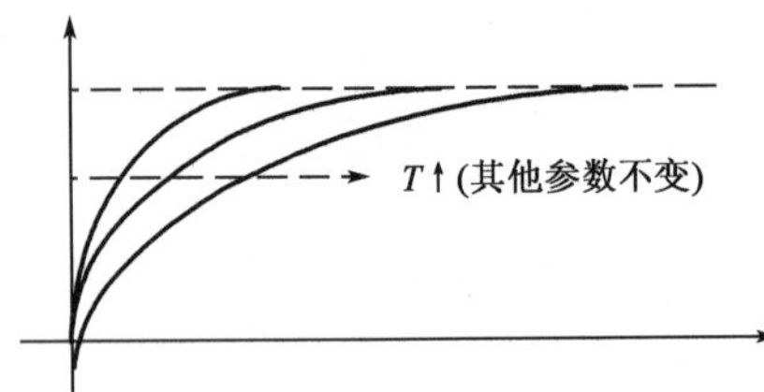

图 15.2-4　时间常数对过渡过程影响

(3)滞后时间 τ：被控对象被控量的变化落后于控制信号和干扰的现象称为滞后。滞后分为纯滞后和过渡滞后。纯滞后又称为传递滞后，用 τ_0 表示。纯滞后产生的主要原因是物料传送等中间过程产生纯滞后(大时间常数表现出来的等效滞后)。由于纯滞后的出现，控制作用必须经历一定的时间延迟(滞后)才能在被控变量上得到体现，致使当被控变量的反馈反映出控制作用时，可能会输入过多的控制量，导致系统严重超调甚至失稳。

过渡滞后又称为容量滞后，用 τ_n 表示。实际的被控对象中，纯滞后和过渡滞后是同时存在的，而且很难严格区分开来，因此常把两者合起来统称为滞后时间 τ，$\tau = \tau_0 + \tau_n$ 。滞后的存在会严重影响到整个控制系统的控制品质，因此在设计和测试控制系统时，应尽量将滞后减至最小。

2)测量变送器特性

测量、变送环节一般由测量元件及变送器组成，其特性也可以表示成由 K、T、τ 三个参数组成的一阶滞后环节，它对过渡过程的影响与被控对象相仿。通常要求，K 在整个测量范围内保持恒定，T、τ 越小越好。

事实上，测量、变送环节本身的时间常数和纯滞后时间都很小，可以略去不计。所以实际上它相当于一个放大环节。因此，放大倍数 K 在整个测量范围内保持恒定是最关键的。但是，有些测量元件在安装使用时需要安装保护套管等其他设备,如热电阻、热电偶等,此时,由于保护套管的存在,会影响测量变送环节的时间常数和纯滞后时间。

3)调节器的特性

调节器是将生产过程参数的测量值与给定值进行比较,得出偏差后根据一定的调节规律产生输出信号,推动执行器消除偏差量,使该参数保持在给定值附近或按预定规律变化的控制器。调节器又称为控制器,如温度控制器。调节器的动态特性直接影响着调节系统的调节品质。

调节器的种类很多,基于偏差的调节系统有:比例调节器(P)、积分调节器、比例积分调节器(PI)、微分调节器和比例积分微分调节器(PID)。

线性控制规律的微分方程主要有以下几项

比例规律

$$P = K_C e \tag{15.2-7}$$

比例积分规律

$$P = K_C\left(e + \frac{1}{T_1}\int e\mathrm{d}t\right) \tag{15.2-8}$$

比例积分微分规律

$$P = K_C\left(e + \frac{1}{T_1}\int e\mathrm{d}t + T_D\frac{\mathrm{d}e}{\mathrm{d}t}\right) \tag{15.2-9}$$

式中:P ——调节器的输出信号;

e ——调节器的输入信号,即被控量的测量值与给定值之差(偏差);

T_1 ——积分时间(min);

T_D ——微分时间(min);

K_C ——调节器的放大系数。

4)执行器的特性

自动控制系统中接受控制信息并对受控对象施加控制作用的装置叫执行器。在过程控制系统中,执行器由执行机构和调节机构两部分组成。调节机构通过执行元件直接改变生产过程的参数,使生产过程满足预定的要求。执行机构则接受来自控制器的控制信息,把它转换为驱动调节机构的输出(如角位移或直线位移输出)。

执行器接受的来自调节仪表的信号,有气信号和电信号两类。气信号为20~100kPa的压力信号;电信号则有断续信号和连续信号之分。断续信号通常指二维或三维开关信号。连续信号常为0~10mA和4~20mA的直流电流信号。在电器复合调节系统中,各种转换器或阀门定位器还可与其他类型的执行器连接。

执行器的主要部件有放大器、发信器和阀门。

执行器按所用驱动能源分为气动、电动和液压执行器三类。其中电动调节阀应用最为普遍。

典型例题解析

【例 15.2-1】 被控对象的时间常数,反映对象在阶跃信号激励下被控变量变化的快慢速度,即惯性的大小,时间常数大,则:

A. 惯性大,被控变量变换速度慢,控制较平稳

B. 惯性大,被控变量变换速度快,控制较困难

C. 惯性小,被控变量变换速度快,控制较平稳

D. 惯性小,被控变量变换速度慢,控制较困难

解 时间常数 T 是反映响应变化快慢或响应滞后的重要参数。用 T 表示的响应滞后称阻容滞后(容量滞后)。T 越大,系统的反应越慢,越难以控制;T 越小,系统反应越快。选 A。

【例 15.2-2】 以温度为对象的恒温系统数学模型为 $T\frac{d\theta_i}{d\tau}+\theta_i=k(\theta_c+\theta_f)$，其中 θ_c 为系统给定，θ_f 为干扰，则：

A. T 为放大系数，K 为调节系数

B. T 为时间系数，K 为调节系数

C. T 为时间系数，K 为放大系数

D. T 为调节系数，K 为放大系数

解 以温度为对象的恒温系统数学模型与上文中水箱系统模型类似，其中 T 为时间常数，K 为放大系数。选 C。

【例 15.2-3】 对于室温对象—空调房间，减少空调使用寿命的因素之一是：

A. 对象的滞后时间增大　　B. 对象的时间常数增大

C. 对象的传递系数增大　　D. 对象的调节周期增大

解 时间常数是指被控对象在阶跃作用下被控变量以最大速度变化到新稳态值所需要的时间，反映了被控对象在阶跃扰动下达到新稳态值的快慢。因此本题中时间常数越大，空调工作时间越长。选 B。

15.2.2 控制系统稳定方程的拟定及求解

1）系统微分方程的拟定

基本步骤：

（1）由系统原理图画出系统方框图，直接确定系统中各个基本部件（元件）。

（2）列写各方框图的输入输出之间的微分方程，要注意前后连接的两个元件中，后级元件对前级元件的负载效应。

（3）消去中间变量，整理、合并得出系统的输出量（被控量）和输入量（参据量＋扰动）之间的微分方程。

（4）将微分方程标准化。

【例 15.2-4】 列出图示速度控制系统的微分方程。

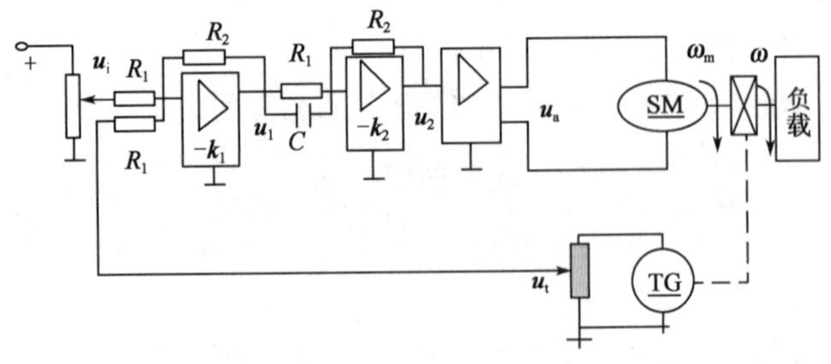

例 15.2-4 图　速度控制系统

解 ①确定系统的输出变量 ω，系统输入变量 u_i。

②系统主要部件（元件）：给定电位器、运放 1、运放 2、功率放大器、直流电动机、减速器、测速发电机。

运放 1　　$u_1=K_1(u_i-u_t)=K_1u_e$

运放 2 $u_2 = K_2\left(\tau \frac{\mathrm{d}u_1}{\mathrm{d}t} + u_1\right), \tau = R_1 C, K_2 = \frac{R_2}{R_1}$

功放 $u_a = K_3 u_2$

直流电动机 $T_m \frac{\mathrm{d}\omega_m}{\mathrm{d}t} + \omega_m = K_m u_a - K_C M'_C$

减速器(齿轮系) $\omega = \frac{1}{i}\omega_m$

测速发电机 $u_t = K_t \omega$

③消去中间变量，u_t、u_1、u_2、u_a、ω_m，令以下的参数为

$$T'_m = T_m + \frac{K_1 K_2 K_3 K_m K_t \tau}{K_1 K_2 K_3 K_m K_t \tau}$$

$$K'_g = \frac{K_1 K_2 K_3 K_m K_t \tau}{K_1 K_2 K_3 K_m K_t \tau}$$

$$K_g = \frac{K_1 K_2 K_3 K_m}{i} + K_1 K_2 K_3 K_m K_t$$

$$K'_C = K_C / i + K_1 K_2 K_3 K_m K_t$$

④整理得控制系统模型(微分方程)为

$$T'_m \frac{\mathrm{d}\omega_m}{\mathrm{d}t} + \omega = K'_g \frac{\mathrm{d}u_i}{\mathrm{d}t} + K_g u_i - K'_C M'_C$$

2)系统微分方程的求解

系统的微分方程确立后，对方程进行求解。

直接求解法：通解与特解相加，求解方法参见《高等数学》中常微分方程部分。变换域求解法：用 Laplace 变换法求解。

15.2.3 拉普拉斯变换与反变换

建立了系统的微分方程之后，进一步分析计算系统的控制过程，最直接的方法是求微分方程的时间解，并点绘出输出变量的相应曲线。

用拉普拉斯变换求解线性常微分方程，可将经典数学中的微积分运算转化为代数运算，又能够单独地表明初始条件的影响，并有变换表可供查找，因而是一种较为简便的工程数学方法。

1)拉普拉斯变换定义

函数 $f(t)$ 为实变量，如果线性积分

$$\int_0^\infty f(t) e^{-st} \mathrm{d}t \qquad (s = \sigma + j\omega \text{ 为复变量})$$

则称其为函数 $f(t)$ 的拉普拉斯变换(简称拉氏变换)。变换后的函数是复变量 s 的函数，记作 $F(s)$ 或 $L[f(t)]$，即

$$L[f(t)] = F(s) = \int_0^\infty f(t) e^{-st} \mathrm{d}t \tag{15.2-10}$$

常称 $F(s)$ 为 $f(t)$ 的变换函数或象函数，而 $f(t)$ 为 $F(s)$ 的原函数。

2)几种典型函数的拉氏变换

对于控制系统中的外作用(指给定值和干扰)，一般事先是不完全知道的，而且常常伴随着

时间任意变化。为了便于对系统进行理论分析，工程实践中允许采用以下几种简单的时间函数作为系统的典型输入，即单位阶跃函数、单位斜坡函数、等加速函数、指数函数、正弦函数以及单位脉冲函数等。下面推导其拉氏变换。

(1)单位阶跃函数 $l(t)$

单位阶跃函数 $l(t)$的时间曲线如图 15.2-5 所示。

其数学表达式为

$$f(t)=l(t)-\begin{cases}1 & (t\geqslant 0)\\ 0 & (t<0)\end{cases} \tag{15.2-11}$$

其拉氏变换

$$L[l(t)]=F(s)=\int_0^{\infty}1e^{-st}\mathrm{d}t=-\frac{1}{s}e^{-st}\mid_0^{\infty}=\frac{1}{s} \tag{15.2-12}$$

(2)单位斜坡函数

单位斜坡函数的时间曲线如图 15.2-6 所示。

其数学表达式为

$$f(t)=tl(t)=\begin{cases}t & (t\geqslant 0)\\ 0 & (t<0)\end{cases} \tag{15.2-13}$$

则拉式变换

$$F(s)=L[t\cdot l(t)]=\int_0^{\infty}te^{-st}\mathrm{d}t=-\frac{t}{s}e^{-st}\Big|_0^{\infty}+\int_0^{\infty}\frac{1}{s}e^{-st}\mathrm{d}t=\frac{1}{s^2} \tag{15.2-14}$$

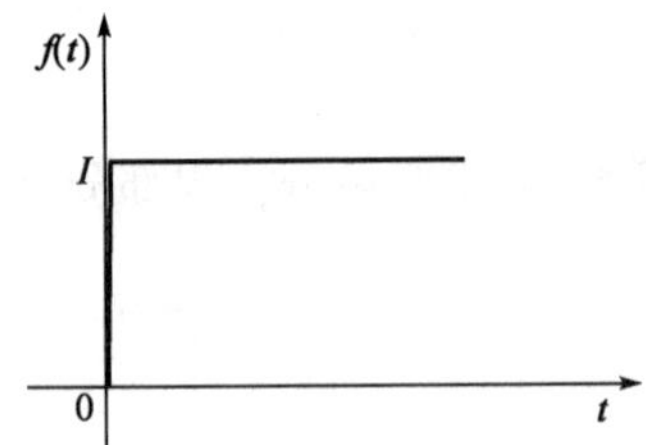

图 15.2-5 单位阶跃函数时间曲线

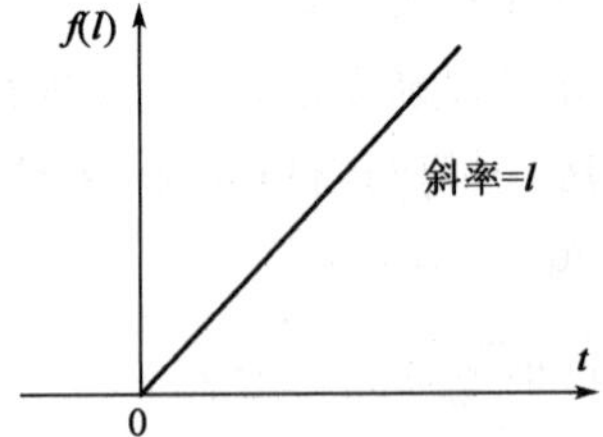

图 15.2-6 单位斜坡函数时间曲线

(3)等加速函数

其数学表达式为

$$f(t)=\begin{cases}\frac{1}{2}t^2 & (t\geqslant 0)\\ 0 & (t<0)\end{cases} \tag{15.2-15}$$

则拉氏变换

$$F(s)=L\left(\frac{1}{2}t^2\right)=\int_0^{\infty}\frac{1}{2}t^2e^{-st}\mathrm{d}t=\frac{1}{s^3} \tag{15.2-16}$$

(4)指数函数

指数函数数学表达式为

$$f(t)=\begin{cases}e^{at} & (t\geqslant 0)\\ 0 & (t<0)\end{cases} \tag{15.2-17}$$

则拉氏变换

$$F(s)=L(e^{at})=\int_0^{\infty}e^{at}\cdot e^{-st}\mathrm{d}t=\int_0^{\infty}e^{-(s-a)t}\mathrm{d}t=\frac{1}{s-a} \tag{15.2-18}$$

(5)正弦函数

正弦函数数学表达式为

$$f(t)=\begin{cases}\sin\omega t & (t\geqslant 0)\\ 0 & (t<0)\end{cases} \tag{15.2-19}$$

则拉氏变换

$$F(s)=L(\sin\omega t)=\int_0^{\infty}\sin\omega t\cdot e^{-st}\mathrm{d}t$$

$$=\int_0^{\infty}\frac{1}{2j}(e^{j\omega t}-e^{-j\omega t})e^{-st}\mathrm{d}t-\frac{1}{2j}\left(\frac{1}{s-j\omega}-\frac{1}{s+j\omega}\right)=\frac{\omega}{s^2+\omega^2} \tag{15.2-20}$$

类似的可求得余弦函数的拉氏变换为

$$L=(\sin\omega t)=\frac{s}{s^2+\omega^2} \tag{15.2-21}$$

3)拉氏变换的几个基本法则

(1)线性性质

设 $F_1(s)=L_2[f(t)]$,$F_2(s)=L_2[f(t)]$,a 和 b 为常数,则有

$$L[af_1(t)+bf_2(t)]=aL[f_1(t)]-bL[f_2(t)]=aF_1(s)-bF_2(s) \tag{15.2-22}$$

(2)微分法则

设 $F(s)=L[f(t)]$,则有

$$L\left[\frac{\mathrm{d}f(t)}{\mathrm{d}t}\right]=sF(s)-f(0)$$

$$L\left[\frac{\mathrm{d}^2f(t)}{\mathrm{d}t^2}\right]=s^2F(s)-sf(0)-f'(0)$$

$$\cdots$$

$$L\left[\frac{\mathrm{d}^nf(t)}{\mathrm{d}t^n}\right]=s^nF(s)-s^{n-1}f(0)-s^{n-2}f'(0)-\cdots-f^{(n-t)}(0) \tag{15.2-23}$$

其中,$f(0)$、$f'(0)$、…、$f^{(n-1)}(0)$为函数 $f(t)$及其各阶导数在 $t=0$ 时的值。

当 $f(0)=f'(0)=\cdots=f^{(n-1)}(0)=0$ 时,则有

$$L\left[\frac{\mathrm{d}f(t)}{\mathrm{d}t}\right]=sF(s)$$

$$\cdots$$

$$L\left[\frac{\mathrm{d}^nf(t)}{\mathrm{d}t^n}\right]=s^nF(s) \tag{15.2-24}$$

(3)积分法则

设 $F(s)=L[f(t)]$,则有

$$L\left[\int f(t)\mathrm{d}t\right]=\frac{1}{s}F(s)+\frac{1}{s}f^{-1}(0)$$

$$L\left[\iint f(t)\mathrm{d}t^2\right]=\frac{1}{s^2}F(s)+\frac{1}{s^2}f^{(-1)}(0)+\frac{1}{s}f^{(-2)}(0)$$

$$\cdots$$

$$L\left[\frac{\int\cdots\int f(t)\mathrm{d}t^n}{n}\right]=\frac{1}{s^n}F(s)+\frac{1}{s^n}f^{(-1)}(0)+\cdots+\frac{1}{s}f^{-n}(0) \tag{15.2-25}$$

其中，$f^{(-1)}(0)$、$f^{(-2)}(0)$、…、$f^{(-n)}(0)$为 $f(t)$的各重积分在 $t=0$ 时的值，如果 $f^{(-1)}(0)=f^{(-2)}(0)=\cdots=f^{(-n)}(0)=0$，则式(15.2-25)化简为

$$L\left[\int f(t)\mathrm{d}t\right]=\frac{1}{s}F(s)$$

$$L\left[\iint f(t)\mathrm{d}t^2\right]=\frac{1}{s^2}F(s)$$

$$\cdots$$

$$L\left[\frac{\int\cdots\int f(t)\mathrm{d}t^n}{n}\right]=\frac{1}{s^n}F(s) \tag{15.2-26}$$

(4)终值定理

若函数 $f(t)$的拉氏变换为 $F(s)$，且 $F(s)$在 s 平面的右半面及除原点外的虚轴上解析，则有终值

$$\lim_{t\to\infty}f(t)=\lim_{s\to\infty}F(s) \tag{15.2-27}$$

(5)位移定理

设 $F(s)=L[f(t)]$，则有

$$L[f(t-\tau_0)]=e^{-\tau s}\cdot F(s) \tag{15.2-28}$$

及

$$L[e^{at}f(t)]=F(s-a) \tag{15.2-29}$$

分别称为实位移定理和虚位移定理。

4)拉普拉斯反变换

拉氏变换的定义已由式(15.2-10)给出

$$L^{-1}[F(s)]=f(t)=\frac{1}{2\pi j}\int_{\sigma-j\infty}^{\sigma+j\infty}F(s)e^{st}\mathrm{d}s \tag{15.2-30}$$

这是复变函数的积分，一般很难直接计算。故由 $F(s)$求 $f(t)$常用部分分式法。该法计算反变换的思路是：将 $F(s)$分解成一些简单的有理分式函数之和，然后由拉氏变换表一一查出对应的反变换函数，即得所求的原函数 $f(t)$。

$F(s)$通常是复变量 s 的有理分式函数，即分母多项式的阶次高于分子多项式的阶次。$F(s)$的一般式为

$$F(s)=\frac{B(s)}{A(s)}=\frac{b_0s^m+b_1s^{m-1}-\cdots-b_{m-1}s+b_m}{s^n+a_1s^{n-1}+\cdots+a_{n-1}s+a_n}$$

其中：a_1、a_2…、a_n 及 b_1、b_2…、b_m 均为实数，m，n 为正数，且 $m<n$。

首先将 $F(s)$的分母多项式 $A(s)$进行因式分解，即写为

$$A(s)=(s-s_1)(s-s_2)\cdots(s-s_n) \tag{15.2-31}$$

其中：s_1、s_2…、s_n 为 $A(s)=0$ 的根。下面分两种情况讨论。

(1)$A(s)=0$ 的无重根

这时可将 $F(s)$ 换写成 n 个部分分式之和，每个分式的分母都是 $A(s)$ 的一个因式，即

$$F(s)=\frac{C_1}{s-s_1}+\frac{C_2}{s-s_2}+\frac{C_3}{s-s_3}+\cdots+\frac{C_n}{s-s_n}$$

或

$$F(s)=\sum_{i=1}^{n}\frac{C_i}{s-s_i} \tag{15.2-32}$$

如果确定了每个部分分式中的待定常数 C_i，则有拉式变化表即可查到 $F(s)$ 的反变换：

$$L^{-1}[F(s)]=f(t)=L^{-1}\left[\sum_{i=1}^{n}\frac{C_i}{s-s_i}\right]=\sum_{i=1}^{n}C_ie^{s_it} \tag{15.2-33}$$

C_i 可按下式求得，即

$$C_i=\lim_{s\to s_i}(s-s_i)\cdot F(s)$$

或

$$C_i=\frac{B(s)}{A'(s)}\bigg|_{s=s_i} \tag{15.2-34}$$

(2) $A(s)=0$ 有重根

设 $A(s)=0$ 有 r 重根 s_1，$F(s)$ 可写为

$$F(s)=\frac{B(s)}{(s-s_1)^r(s-s_{r+1})\cdots(s-s_n)}$$

$$=\frac{c_r}{(s-s_1)^r}+\frac{c_{r-1}}{(s-s_1)^{r-1}}+\cdots+\frac{c_1}{(s-s_1)}+\frac{c_{r+1}}{s-s_{r+1}}+\cdots+\frac{c_i}{s-s_i}+\cdots+\frac{c_n}{s-s_n} \tag{15.2-35}$$

式中，s_1 为 $F(s)$ 的 r 重根；$s_{r+1},\cdots,s_n$ 为 $F(s)$ 的 $n-r$ 个单根；$c_{r+1},\cdots,c_n$ 仍按式(15.2-32)或式(15.2-34)计算，$c_r,c_{r-1},\cdots,c_1$ 则按下式计算。

$$\left.\begin{aligned}
c_r&=\lim_{s\to s_1}(s-s_1)^rF(s)\\
c_{r-1}&=\lim_{s\to s_i}\frac{d}{ds}[(s-s_1)^rF(s)]\\
c_{r-j}&=\frac{1}{j!}\lim_{s\to s_1}\frac{d^{(j)}}{ds^{(j)}}(s-s_1)^rF(s)\\
c_1&=\frac{1}{(r-1)!}\lim_{s\to s_1}\frac{d^{(r-1)}}{ds^{(r-1)}}(s-s_1)^rF(s)
\end{aligned}\right\} \tag{15.2-36}$$

原函数 $f(t)$ 为

$$f(t)=L^{-1}[F(s)]$$

$$=L^{-1}\left[\frac{c_r}{(s-s_1)^r}+\frac{c_{r-1}}{(s-s_1)^{r-1}}+\cdots+\frac{c_1}{(s-s_1)}+\frac{c_{r+1}}{s-s_{r+1}}+\cdots+\frac{c_i}{s-s_i}+\cdots+\frac{c_n}{s-s_n}\right]$$

$$=\left[\frac{c_r}{(r-1)!}t^{r-1}+\frac{c_{r-1}}{(r-2)!}t^{r-2}+\cdots+c_2t+c_1\right]e^{s_1t}+\sum_{i=r+1}^{n}c_ie^{s_it}$$

5)用拉氏变换求解微分方程

拉氏变换求解微分方程的步骤是：

(1)将系统微分方程进行(积分下限为 0^-)拉氏变换，得到以 s 为变量的代数方程，又称变换方程。方程中的初始值应取系统 $t=0^-$ 时的对应值。

(2)解变换方程，求出系统输出变量的象函数表达式。

(3)将输出的象函数表达式展成部分分式。

(4)对部分分式进行拉氏反变换，即得微分方程的全解。

6)常用函数的拉氏变换表(见表 15.2-1)

常用函数的拉氏变换表 表 15.2-1

序　号	拉氏变换 $E(s)$	时间函数 $e(t)$
1	1	$\delta(t)$
2	$\frac{1}{1-e^{-Ts}}$	$\delta_T(t)=\sum_{n=0}^{\infty}\delta(t-nT)$
3	$\frac{1}{s}$	$l(t)$
4	$\frac{1}{s^2}$	t
5	$\frac{1}{s^3}$	$\frac{t^2}{2}$
6	$\frac{1}{s^{n+1}}$	$\frac{t^n}{n!}$
7	$\frac{1}{s+a}$	e^{-at}
8	$\frac{1}{(s+a)^2}$	te^{-at}
9	$\frac{a}{s(s+a)}$	$1-e^{-at}$
10	$\frac{b-a}{(s+a)(s+b)}$	$e^{-at}-e^{-bt}$
11	$\frac{\omega}{s^2+\omega^2}$	$\sin\omega t$
12	$\frac{s}{s^2+\omega^2}$	$\cos\omega t$
13	$\frac{\omega}{(s+a)^2+\omega^2}$	$e^{-at}\sin\omega t$
14	$\frac{s+a}{(s+a)^2+\omega^2}$	$e^{-at}\cos\omega t$
15	$\frac{1}{s-(1/T)\ln a}$	$a^{t/T}$

典型例题解析

【例 15.2-5】 惯性环节的微分方程为 $Tc'(t)+c(t)=r(t)$,其中 T 为时间常数,则其传递函数 $G(s)$ 为:

A. $1/(Ts+1)$　　B. $Ts+1$　　C. $1/(T+s)$　　D. $T+s$

解 对方程两边应用微分定理进行拉普拉斯变换可得:

$$TsC(s)+C(s)=R(s)\Rightarrow G(s)=\frac{C(s)}{R(s)}=\frac{1}{Ts+1}$$

选 A。

15.2.4 传递函数及其方块图

1)传递函数

传递函数定义:零初始条件下,系统输出量的拉氏变换与输入量的拉氏变换之比。

设线性定常系统由下述 n 阶线性微分方程描述

$$a_n \frac{\mathrm{d}^n y(t)}{\mathrm{d}t^n} + a_{n-1} \frac{\mathrm{d}^{n-1} y(t)}{\mathrm{d}t^{n-1}} + \cdots + a_1 \frac{\mathrm{d}y(t)}{\mathrm{d}t} + a_0 y(t)$$

$$= b_m \frac{\mathrm{d}^m r(t)}{\mathrm{d}t^m} + b_{m-1} \frac{\mathrm{d}^{m-1} r(t)}{\mathrm{d}t^{m-1}} + \cdots + b_1 \frac{\mathrm{d}r(t)}{\mathrm{d}t} + b_0 r(t) \quad (15.2\text{-}37)$$

其中，$y(t)$表示系统输出量，$r(t)$表示系统输出量，$a_i(i=0,1,2,\cdots,n)$和 $b_j(j=0,1,2,\cdots,m)$是与系统结构和参数有关的常系数。

在零初始条件下，即 $y(t)$、$r(t)$及其各阶导数在 $t=0$ 时的值均为零，对方程(15.2-37)进行拉氏变换，并另 $Y(s)=L[y(t)]$，$R(s)=L[r(t)]$，则由定义可得线性定常系统传递函数为

$$G(s) = \frac{Y(s)}{R(s)} = \frac{b_m s^m + b_{m-1} s[y(t) + P(f)b_1 - s^{-1}b(t)]}{a_m s^m + a_{m-1} s^{m-1} + \cdots + a_1 s + a_0} \quad (15.2\text{-}38)$$

对于传递函数有以下几点说明：

(1)传递函数只适用描述线性定常系统。

(2)传递函数是在初始条件为零时定义的。控制系统的初始条件为零有两个含义：一是指输入量在时间 $t=0^-$ 以后才作用于系统的。因此，系统输入量及其各阶导数在 $t=0^-$ 时的值均为零；二是指输入量作用于系统之前，系统是相对静止的。因此，系统输出量及其各阶导数在 $t=0^-$ 的值也为零。实际的控制系统多属于此类情况。

(3)传递函数是复变量 $s(s=\sigma+j\omega)$的有理真分式函数，它具有复变函数的所有性质，其分子多项式的系数均为实数，都是由系统的物理参数决定的。分子多项式的阶次 m 也总是低于或等于分母多项式的阶次 n，即 $n \geqslant m$。这是因为系统(或元部件)具有惯性的缘故。

(4)传递函数是描述系统(或元部件)动态特性的一种数学表达式，它只是取决于系统(或元部件)的结构和参数，而与系统(或元部件)的输入量和输出量的形式和大小无关。并且传递函数只反映系统的动态特性，而不反应系统物理性能上的差异。对于物理性质截然不同的系数，只要动态特性相同(如相似系统)，它们的传递函数就具有相同的形式。

(5)传递函数的拉氏反变换是系统的脉冲响应 $g(t)$。推导如下：

脉冲响应是在零初始条件下，线性系统对理想的单位脉冲输入信号的输出响应。此时，输入量 $R(s)=L[\delta(t)]=1$，所以有：$g(t)=L^{-1}[y(t)]=L^{-1}[G(s)R(s)]=L^{-1}[G(s)]$。式中，$g(t)$为系统的脉冲响应。

对于一般情况，根据拉氏变换的卷积定理，可由系统的脉冲响应得到系统的输出。

$$\begin{aligned} y(t) &= L^{-1}[Y(s)] = L^{-1}[G(s)R(s)] \\ &= \int_0^\tau r(\tau)g(t-\tau)\mathrm{d}\tau = \int_0^\tau r(t-\tau)g(\tau)\mathrm{d}\tau \end{aligned} \quad (15.2\text{-}39)$$

(6)传递函数可以表示为零、极点和时间常数形式。

式(15.2-39)的分子和分母多项式经因分解后可写为如下形式

$$G(s) = \frac{b_m(s+z_1)(s+z_2)\cdots(s+z_m)}{a_n(s+p_1)(s+p_2)\cdots(s+p_n)} = K \frac{\Pi_{i=1}^m s+z_i}{\Pi_{i=1}^n s+p_j}$$

其中，$-z_i(i=1,2,\cdots,m)$是分子多项式的零点，称为传递函数的零点；$-p_j(j=1,2,\cdots,n)$是分母多项式的零点，称之为传递函数的极点；而 $K^*=\frac{b_m}{a_n}$称为系数的根轨迹增益。这种用零点和极点表示传递函数的方法在根轨迹中使用较多。

2)方块图(结构图)

(1)基本概念

控制系统的方块图是描述系统各元部件之间信号传递关系的数学图示模型,它表示系统中各变量之间的因果关系以及对各变量所进行的运算,是控制理论中描述复杂系统的一种简便方法。它适用于线性和非线性系统。

方块图由信号点、分支点、相加点和方块图单元组成,如图 15.2-7 所示。

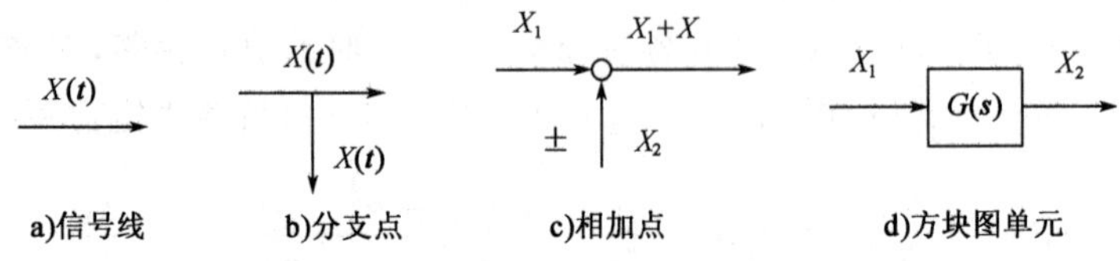

图 15.2-7 方块图的基本组成单元

图 15.2-7d)中的方块图单元表示对信号进行数学变换,其输出量等于方块图单元的输入量与传递函数的乘积。

$$X_2 = G(s)X_1$$

①信号线:带有箭头的直线。箭头表示信号的传递方向,线上标记信号的时间函数或象函数。

②引出点(测量点):信号引出或测量的位置。从同一位置引出的信号在数值和性质方面完全相同。

③比较点(综合点):对两个以上的信号进行加减运算。用"+"、"-"表示,"+"有时可省略。

④方框(环节):表示方框的输出信号与输入信号之间的传递关系。方框中写入元部件或系统的传递函数。

(2)方块图的连接和等效变换

①串联连接串联环节的等效变换。图 15.2-8 表示两个环节串联的结构。

由图 15.2-8a)可写出

$$G(s) = G_2(s)U(s) = G_2(s)G_1(s)R(s)$$

所以两个环节串联后的等效传递函数为

$$G(s) = \frac{Q(s)}{U(s)} = G_2(s)G_1(s)$$

其等效结构图如图 15.2-8b)所示。

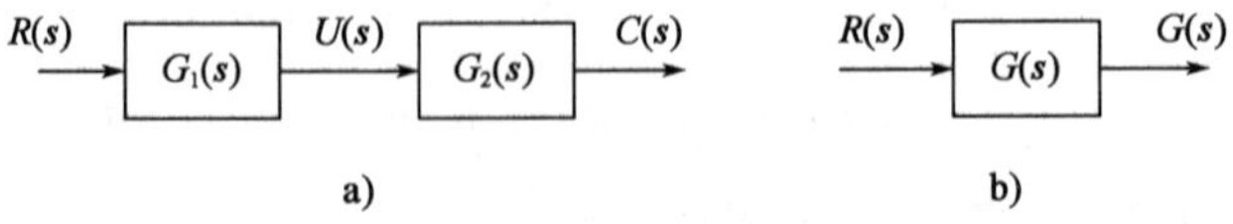

图 15.2-8 两个环节串联的等效变换

上述结论可以推广到任意一个环节串联的情况,即:环节串联后的总传递函数等于各串联环节传递函数的乘积。

②并联环节的等效变换。图 15.2-9a)表示两个环节并联的结构。由图可写出

$$G(s) = G_1(s)R(s) \pm G_2(s)R(s) = [G_1(s) \pm G_2(s)]R(s)$$

所以两个环节并联后的等效传递函数为

$$G(s) = G_1(s) \pm G_2(s)$$

其等效结构图如图 15.2-9b)所示。

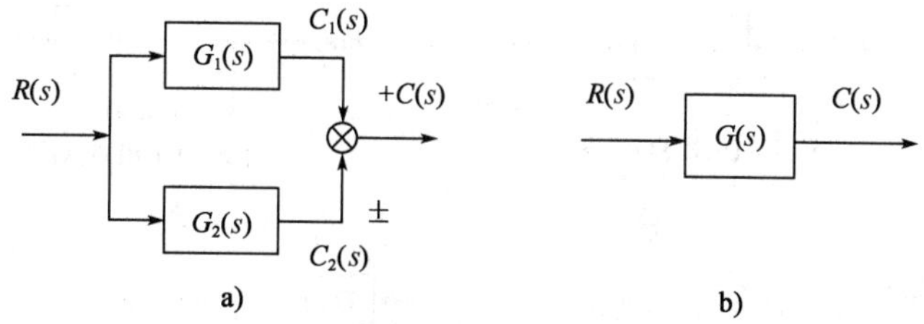

图 15.2-9　两个并联环节的等效变换

上述结论可以推广到任意一个环节并联的情况，即：环节并联后的总传递函数等于各个并联环节传递函数的代数和。

③反馈连接的等效变换。图 15.2-10a)为反馈连接的一般形式。由图可写出

$$C(s)=G(s)E(s)=G(s)[R(s)\pm B(s)]=G(s)[R(s)\pm H(s)C(s)]$$

可得

$$C(s)=\frac{G(s)}{1\mp G(s)H(s)}R(s)$$

所以反馈连接后的等效(闭环)传递函数为

$$\Phi(s)=\frac{G(s)}{1\mp G(s)H(s)}$$

其等效结构图如图 15.2-10b)所示。

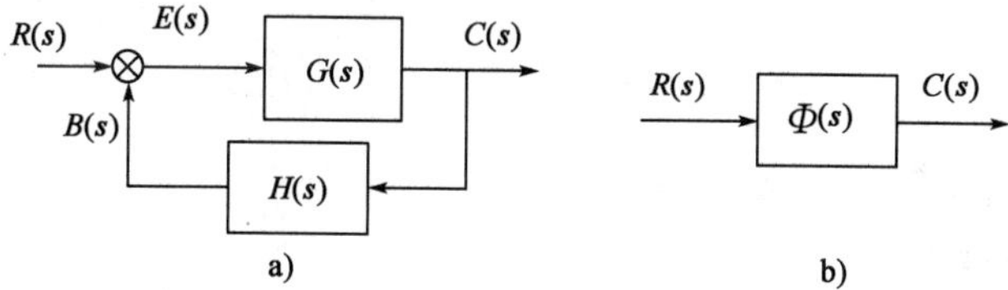

图 15.2-10　反馈连接环节的等效变换

当反馈通道的传递函数 $H(s)=1$ 时，称响应系统为单位反馈系统，此时闭环传递函数为：

$$\Phi(s)=\frac{G(s)}{1\mp G(s)}$$

④比较点和分支点(引出点)的移动(图 15.2-11、图 15.2-12)。

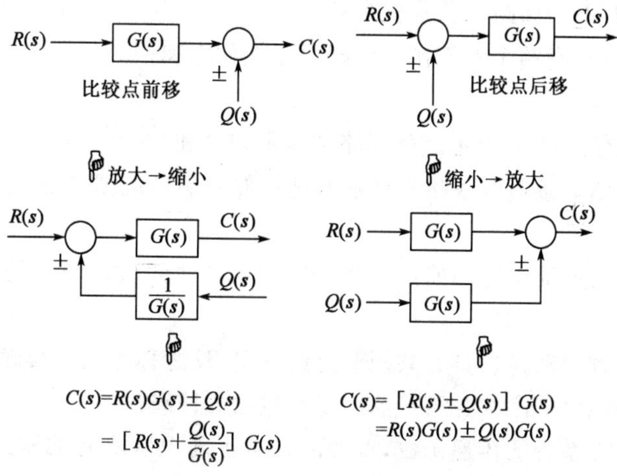

图 15.2-11　比较点移动示意图

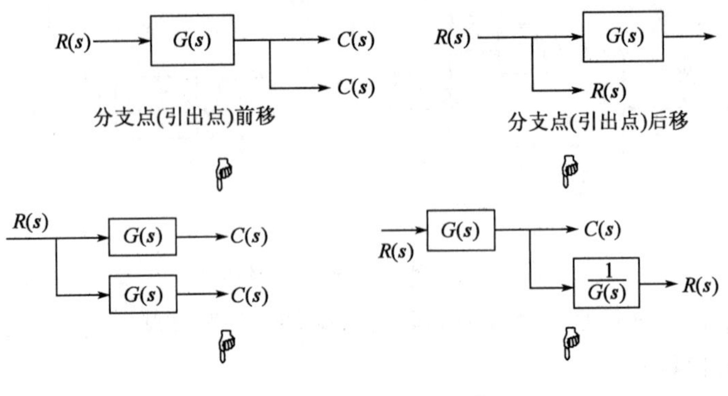

图 15.2-12　分支点移动示意图

有关移动中“前”“后”的定义：按信号流向定义，也即信号从“前面”流向“后面”，而不是位置上的前后。

综合点前移指逆着信号线的指向移动，综合点后移指顺着信号线的指向移动。

(3)梅逊公式求传递函数。

应用梅逊公式，可不经过任何结构变换，一步写出系统的总传递函数。

梅逊公式为

$$P = G(s) = \frac{C(s)}{R(s)} = \frac{1}{\Delta}\sum_{k=1}^{n} P_k \Delta_k$$

式中：P——系统总增益(总传递函数)；

k——前向通路数；

P_k——第 k 条前向通路总增益；

Δ_k——信号流图特征式，它是信号流图所表示的方程组的系数矩阵的行列式。

在同一个信号流图中不论求图中任何一对节点之间的增益，其分母总是 Δ，变化的只是其分子。

$$\Delta = 1 - \sum L_{(1)} + \sum L_{(2)} - \sum L_{(3)} + \cdots + (-1)^m \sum L_{(m)}$$

式中：$\sum L_{(1)}$ ——所有不同回路增益乘积之和；

$\sum L_{(2)}$ ——所有任意两个互不接触回路增益乘积之和；

⋮

$\sum L_{(m)}$—— 所有任意 m 个不接触回路增益乘积之和。

其中，Δ_k 为不与第 k 条前向通路相接触的那一部分信号流图的 Δ 值，称为第 k 条前向通路特征式的余因子。

回路传递函数是指反馈回路的前向通路(道)和反馈通路(道)函数的乘积，并且包含反馈极性的正号。

上述公式中的接触回路是指具有共同节点的回路，反之称之为不接触回路，与第 k 条前向通路具有共同节点的回路称之为与第 k 前向通路接触的回路。

根据梅逊公式计算系统的传递函数，首要问题是正确识别所有的回路并区分它们是否相互接触，正确识别所规定的输入与输出节点之间的所有前向通路及与其相接触的回路。

3)典型环节的传递函数及其方块图(框图)

任何一个复杂系统都是由有限个典型环节组合而成的。典型环节通常分为以下 6 种。

(1)比例环节

$$G(s) = K$$

式中:K——增益。

特点:输入量、输出量成比例,无失真和时间延迟。

实例:电子放大器,齿轮,电阻(电位器),感应式变送器等。

(2)惯性环节

$$G(s) = \frac{1}{Ts+1}$$

式中:T——时间常数。

特点:含一个储能元件,对突变的输入及输出不能立即复现,输出无振荡。

实例:RC 网络,直流伺服电动机的传递函数也包含这一环节。

(3)微分环节

理想微分 $G(s) = Ks$

一阶微分 $G(s) = \tau s + 1$

二阶微分 $G(s) = \tau^2 s^2 + 2\xi\tau s + 1$

特点:输出量正比输入量变化的速度,能预示输入信号的变化趋势。

实例:测速发电机输出电压与输入角度间的传递函数即为微分环节。

(4)积分环节

$$G(s) = \frac{1}{s}$$

特点:输出量与输入量的积分成正比例,当输入消失,输出具有记忆功能。

实例:电动机角速度与角度间的传递函数,模拟计算机中的积分器等。

(5)振荡环节

$$G(s) = \frac{\omega_n^2}{s^2 + 2\xi\omega_n s + \omega_n^2} = \frac{1}{T^2 s^2 + 2\xi T s + 1}$$

式中:ξ——阻尼比($0 \leqslant \xi < 1$);

ω_n——自然振荡角频率(无阻尼振荡角频率)。

$$T = \frac{1}{\omega_n}$$

特点:环节中有两个独立的储能元件,并可进行能量交换,其输出出现振荡。

实例:RLC 电路的输出与输入电压间的传递函数。

(6)纯滞后环节

$$c(t) = r(t-\tau)$$

$$G(s) = e^{-\tau s}$$

式中:τ——延迟时间。

特点:输出量能准确复现输入量,但须延迟一固定的时间间隔。

实例:管道压力、流量等物理量的控制,其数学模型就包含有延迟环节。

典型例题解析

【例 15.2-6】 关于系统的传递函数，正确的描述是：

A. 输入量的形式和系统结构均是复变量 s 的函数

B. 输入量与输出量之间的关系与系统自身结构无关

C. 系统固有的参数，反映非零初始条件下的动态特征

D. 取决于系统的固有参数和系统结构，是单位冲激下的系统输出的拉氏变换

解 传递函数是描述系统（或元部件）动态特性的一种数学表达式，它只是取决于系统（或元部件）的结构和参数，而与系统（或元部件）的输入量和输出量的形式和大小无关。传递函数是复变量 $s(s=\sigma+j\omega)$ 的有理真分式函数，它具有复变函数的所有性质，其分子多项式的系数均为实数，都是由系统的物理参数决定的。并且传递函数只反映系统的动态特性，而不反应系统物理性能上的差异。对于物理性质截然不同的系数，只要动态特性相同（如相似系统），它们的传递函数就具有相同的形式。选 D。

【例 15.2-7】 一阶系统传递函数 $G(s)=\dfrac{K}{1+Ts}$，单位阶跃输入，要增大输出上升率，应：

A. 同时增大 K、T B. 同时减小 K、T

C. 增大 T D. 增大 K

解 同时增大或减小 K、T 时，输出不一定增大，只增大 T 时，输出肯定增加。选 D。

【例 15.2-8】 如图所示，其总的传递函数 $G(s)=C(s)/R(s)$ 应为：

A. $G(s)=\dfrac{G_1(1+G_1G_2)}{(1+G_2G_3)}$

B. $G(s)=\dfrac{G_1(1+G_2G_3)}{(1+G_1G_2)}$

C. $G(s)=\dfrac{G_1(1-G_1G_2)}{(1+G_2G_3)}$

D. $G(s)=\dfrac{G_1(1-G_2G_3)}{(1+G_1G_2)}$

例 15.2-8 图

解 G_3 后的分支点前移，移到 G_2、G_3 之间，故反馈函数变为 $1/G_2$，再根据串并联的等效变换，得出 $G(s)=\dfrac{G_1(1+G_2G_3)}{(1+G_1G_2)}$。选 B。

【例 15.2-9】 用梅逊公式（或方块图简化）计算图示总的传递函数 $G(s)=\dfrac{C(s)}{R(s)}$，结果应为：

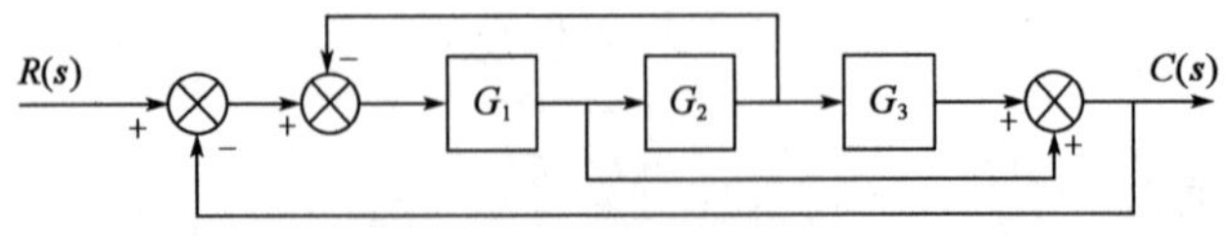

例 15.2-9 图

A. $G(s)=\dfrac{(G_1+G_2G_3)}{(1+G_1+G_1G_2+G_1G_2G_3)}$

B. $G(s)=\dfrac{(G_1+G_1G_2G_3)}{(1+G_2+G_1G_2+G_1G_2G_3)}$

C. $G(s)=\dfrac{(G_1+G_1G_2G_3)}{(1+G_1+G_1G_2+G_1G_2G_3)}$

D. $G(s)=\dfrac{(G_1+G_1G_2)}{(1+G_1+G_1G_2+G_1G_2G_3)}$

解 选C。

【例 15.2-10】 对于拉氏变换，下列不成立的是：

A. $L(f'(t))=s\cdot F(s)-f(0)$

B. 零初始条件下 $L(\int f(t)\mathrm{d}t)=\dfrac{1}{s}F(s)$

C. $L(e^{at}\cdot f(t))=F(s-a)$

D. $\lim\limits_{s\to\infty}f(t)=\lim\limits_{s\to0}F(s)$

解 由终值定理 $\lim\limits_{s\to\infty}f(t)=\lim\limits_{s\to0}s\cdot F(s)$ 可知，题中D选项表达式不正确。

【例 15.2-11】 由开环传递函数 $G(s)$ 和反馈传递函数 $H(s)$ 组成的基本负反馈系统的传递函数为：

A. $\dfrac{G(s)}{1-G(s)H(s)}$　　B. $\dfrac{1}{1-G(s)H(s)}$

C. $\dfrac{G(s)}{1+G(s)H(s)}$　　D. $\dfrac{1}{1+G(s)H(s)}$

解 反馈连接后的等效传递传递函数为 $\phi(s)=\dfrac{G(s)}{1\pm G(s)H(s)}$，而对于负反馈有 $\phi(s)=\dfrac{G(s)}{1+G(s)H(s)}$。选C。

经典练习

15.2-1 判断下列物品中，(　　)为开环控制系统。

A. 家用空调　B. 家用冰箱　C. 抽水马桶　D. 交通指示红绿灯

15.2-2 开环控制系统与闭环控制系统最本质的区别是(　　)。

A. 开环控制系统的输出对系统无控制作用，闭环控制系统的输出对系统有控制作用

B. 开环控制系统的输入对系统无控制作用，闭环控制系统的输入对系统有控制作用

C. 开环控制系统不一定有反馈回路，闭环控制系统有反馈回路

D. 开环控制系统不一定有反馈回路，闭环控制系统也不一定有反馈回路

15.2-3 $X(s)=\dfrac{s+1}{s(s^2+2s+2)}$ 的原函数为(　　)。

A. $\frac{1}{2}+\frac{1}{2}e^{-t}(\sin t+\cos t)$　　B. $\frac{1}{2}+\frac{1}{2}e^{-t}(\sin t-\cos t)$

C. $\frac{1}{2}t+\frac{1}{2}e^{-t}(\sin t-\cos t)$　　D. $\frac{1}{2}+\frac{1}{2}e^{t}(\sin t-\cos t)$

15.2-4　下列不属于对自动控制系统基本要求的是(　　)。

A. 稳定性　　B. 快速性　　C. 连续性　　D. 准确性

15.3　线性系统的分析与设计

考试大纲☞:基本调节规律及实现方法　控制系统一阶瞬态响应　二阶瞬态响应　频率特性基本概念　频率特性表示方法　调节器的特性对调节质量的影响　二阶系统的设计方法

必备基础知识

15.3.1　线性控制系统的基本调节规律及实现方法

1)基本调节规律

(1)比例(P)控制规律

$$m(t)=K_{\mathrm{p}}e(t) \tag{15.3-1}$$

提高系统开环增益,减小系统稳态误差,但会降低系统的相对稳定性。

(2)比例-微分(PD)控制规律

$$m(t)=K_{\mathrm{p}}e(t)+K_{\mathrm{p}}\tau\frac{\mathrm{d}e(t)}{\mathrm{d}t} \tag{15.3-2}$$

PD 控制规律中的微分控制规律能反映输入信号的变化趋势,产生有效的早期修正信号,以增加系统的阻尼程度,从而改善系统的稳定性。在串联校正时,可使系统增加一个 $-\frac{1}{\tau}$ 的开环零点,使系统的相角裕度提高,因此有助于系统动态性能的改善。单独用微分也很少,对噪声敏感。P 控制器和 PD 控制器见图 15.3-1。

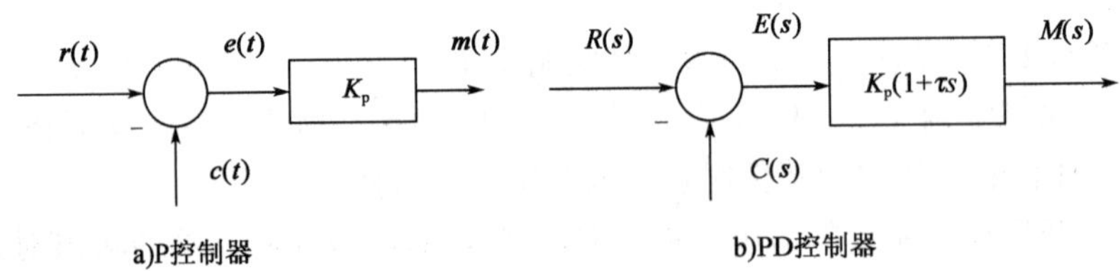

图 15.3-1　P 控制器和 PD 控制器

(3)积分(Ⅰ)控制规律

具有积分(Ⅰ)控制规律的控制器,称为Ⅰ控制器。

$$m(t)=K_{\mathrm{i}}\int_0^t e(t)\mathrm{d}t \tag{15.3-3}$$

输出信号 $m(t)$ 与其输入信号的积分成比例。K_{i} 为可调比例系数。当 $e(t)$ 消失后,输出信号 $m(t)$ 有可能是一个不为零的常量。在串联校正中,采用Ⅰ控制器可以提高系统的型别

(无差度)，有利提高系统稳态性能，但积分控制增加了一个位于原点的开环极点，使信号产生90°的相角滞后，对系统的稳定不利。不宜采用单一的I控制器。

(4)比例-积分(PI)控制规律

具有积分比例-积分控制规律的控制器，称为PI控制器。I控制器和PI控制器见图15.3-2。

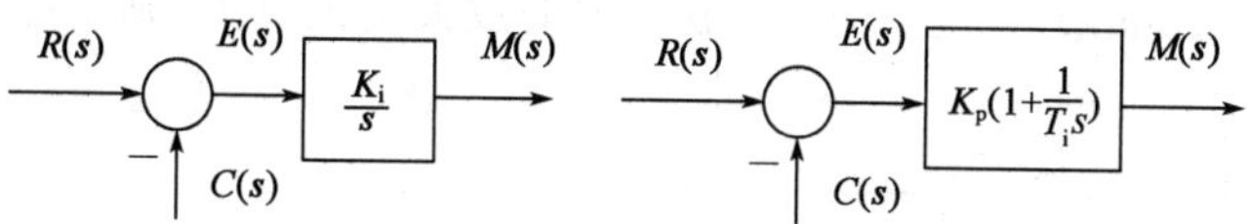

图15.3-2　积分控制器I和PI控制器

$$m(t) = K_p e(t) + \frac{K_p}{T_i}\int_0^t e(t)\mathrm{d}t \tag{15.3-4}$$

输出信号 $m(t)$ 同时与其输入信号及输入信号的积分成比例。K_p 为可调比例系数，T_i 为可调积分时间系数。

开环极点，提高型别，减小稳态误差。

右半平面的开环零点，提高系统的阻尼程度，缓和PI极点对系统产生的不利影响。只要积分时间常数 T_i 足够大，PI控制器对系统的不利影响可大为减小。PI控制器主要用来改善控制系统的稳态性能。

(5)比例(PID)控制规律

具有积分比例-积分控制规律的控制器，称为PID控制器(图15.3-3)。

R(s)　E(s)　$K_p(1+\frac{1}{T_i s}+\tau s)$　M(s)　−　C(s)

图15.3-3　PID控制器

$$m(t) = K_p e(t) + \frac{K_p}{T_i}\int_0^t e(t)\mathrm{d}t + K_p\tau\frac{\mathrm{d}e(t)}{\mathrm{d}t} \tag{15.3-5}$$

$$G_c(s) = K_p(1+\frac{1}{T_i s}+\tau s) = \frac{K_p}{T_i}(\frac{T_i\tau s^2 + T_i s + 1}{s}) = \frac{K_p}{T_i}\frac{(\tau_1 s+1)(\tau_2 s+1)}{s} \tag{15.3-6}$$

$$\tau_1 = \frac{1}{2}T_i(1+\sqrt{1-\frac{4\tau}{T_i}})$$

$$\tau_2 = \frac{1}{2}T_i(1-\sqrt{1-\frac{4\tau}{T_i}})$$

如果 $4\tau/T_i < 1$，则：

①增加一个极点，提高型别，稳态性能；

②两个负实零点，动态性能比PI更具优越性；

③I积分发生在低频段，稳态性能(提高)；

④D微分发生在高频段，动态性能(改善)。

2)实现方法

实现调节器各种调节规律的主要方法就是在调节器内部采用反馈，即引入内反馈。没反馈回来的采用各种不同的环节，就可以得到各种不同的调节规律。

(1)调节器的内反馈

由图15.3-4可得整个调节器的传递函数 $W_c(s)$

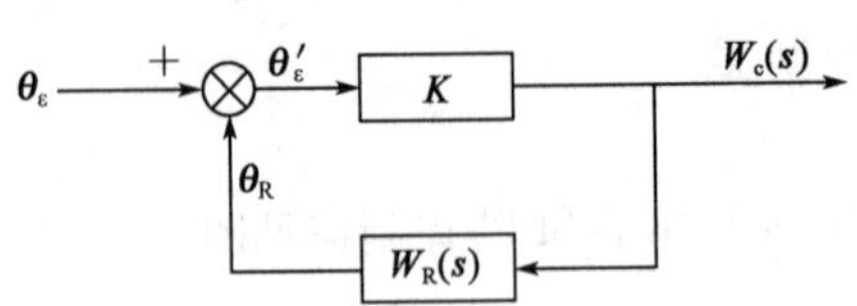

图 15.3-4 调节器的内反馈

$$W_c(s) = \frac{K}{1+W_R(s)K}$$

$$W_c(s) = \frac{K}{\frac{1}{K}+W_R(s)}$$

放大器的放大倍数越大，则$\frac{1}{K}$越小。

当 $K \to \infty$ 时，$W_c(s) = \frac{1}{W_R(s)}$

这时，整个调节器的传递函数就等于反馈环节的传递函数的倒数。要想得到一个调节器的传递函数为 $W_c(s)$，只要在一个放大倍数为无穷大的放大器上加一个反馈环节，其传递函数式 $W_c(s)$ 的倒数。

$$W_R(s) = \frac{1}{W_c(s)}$$

(2)比例积分调节器

以比例积分调节器为例说明反馈原理的应用。PI 调节器的微分方程为：

$$y = K_c\left(\theta_z + \frac{1}{T_1}\int\theta_z \mathrm{d}t\right)$$

其传递函数为：

$$W_c = \frac{Y(s)}{\theta_z(s)} = K_c\left(1+\frac{1}{T_1 s}\right) = \frac{K_c(1+T_1 s)}{T_1 s}$$

因此，反馈装置的传递函数为：

$$W_R(s) = \frac{1}{W_c(s)} = \frac{\frac{T_1}{K_c}s}{1+T_1 s}$$

上式为一个实际的微分环节。用一个实际的微分环节作为一个无穷大放大器的反馈环节，可实现理想的比例微分调节器。实际中，放大器的放大倍数不可能为无穷大，任何实际的 PI 调节器都不是理想的，只能近似的按照 PI 规律动作。

15.3.2 控制系统的一阶瞬态响应

用一阶微分方程描述的控制系统称为一阶系统。图 15.3-5a)所示的 RC 电路，其微分方程为：

$$RC\frac{\mathrm{d}u_c}{\mathrm{d}t} + U_c = r(t)\ ,\ T\dot{C}(t) + C(t) = r(t) \tag{15.3-7}$$

其中，$C(t)$为电路输出电压，$r(t)$为电路输入电压，$T=RC$ 为时间常数。

当初始条件为零时，其传递函数为

$$\Phi(s) = \frac{C(s)}{R(s)} = \frac{1}{Ts+1} \tag{15.3-8}$$

这种系统实际上是一个非周期性的惯性环节。

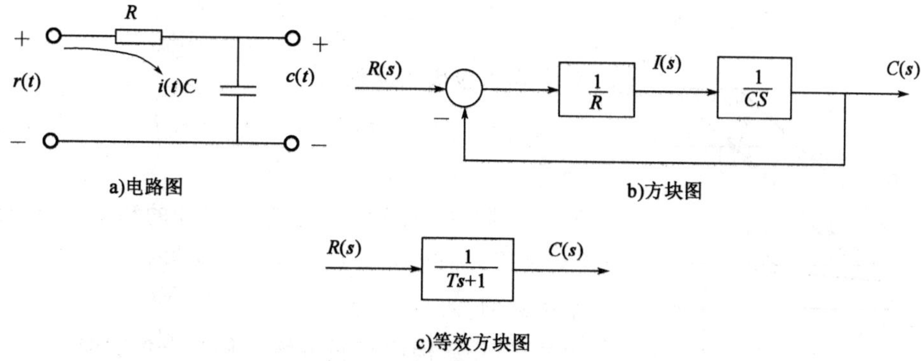

图 15.3-5 一阶系统电路图、方块图及等效方块图

下面分别就不同的典型输入信号，分析该系统的时域响应。

1）单位阶跃响应

因为单位阶跃函数的拉氏变换为 $R(s)=\frac{1}{s}$，则系统的输出由式(15.3-8)可知为 $C(s)=\Phi(s)R(s)=\frac{1}{Ts+1}\cdot\frac{1}{s}=\frac{1}{s}-\frac{1}{Ts+1}$。

对上式取拉氏反变换，得

$$h(t)=1-e^{-\frac{t}{T}} \qquad (t\geqslant 0) \tag{15.3-9}$$

注：$R(s)$的极点形成系统响应的稳态分量。

传递函数的极点是产生系统响应的瞬态分量。这个结论不仅适用于一阶线性定常系统，而且也适用于高阶线性定常系统。

响应曲线在 $t\geqslant 0$ 时的斜率为 $\frac{1}{T}$，如果系统输出响应的速度恒为 $\frac{1}{T}$，则只要 $t=T$ 时，输出 $h(t)$ 就能达到其终值。如图 15.3-6 所示。

由于 $h(t)$的终值为 1，因而系统阶跃输入时的稳态误差为零。

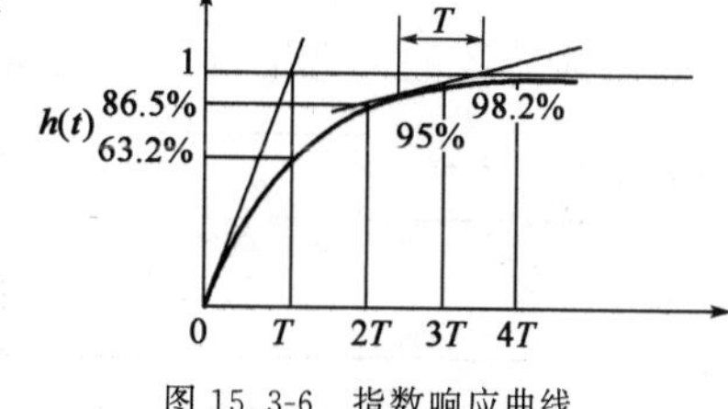

图 15.3-6 指数响应曲线

动态性能指标

$$t_d=0.69T$$
$$t_r=2.20T$$
$$t_s=3T \quad (5\%误差带)$$

t_p 和 $\sigma\%$不存在。

2）一阶系统的单位脉冲响应

当输入信号为理想单位脉冲函数时，$R(s)=1$，输入量的拉氏变换与系统的传递函数相同，即

$$C(s)=\frac{1}{Ts+1}$$

这时相同的输出称为脉冲响应，记作 $g(t)$，因为 $g(t)=L^{-1}[G(s)]$，其表达式为

$$c(t)=\frac{1}{T}e^{-\frac{t}{T}} \qquad (t\geqslant 0) \tag{15.3-10}$$

3）一阶系统的单位斜坡响应

当
$$R(s)=\frac{1}{s^2}$$

$$C(s)=\Phi(s)R(s)=\frac{1}{Ts+1}\cdot\frac{1}{s^2}=\frac{1}{s^2}-\frac{T}{s}+\frac{T^2}{1+Ts}$$

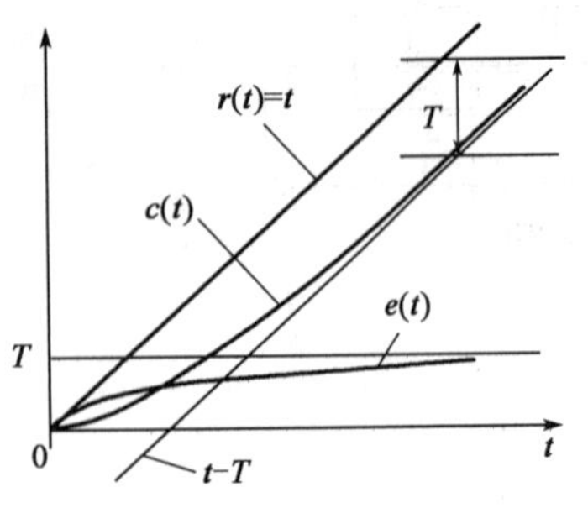

图 15.3-7 一阶系统的斜坡响应

对上式求拉氏反变换，得

$$c(t)=t-T(1-e^{-\frac{1}{T}t})=t-T+Te^{-\frac{1}{T}t} \quad (15.3\text{-}11)$$

因为 $e(t)=r(t)-c(t)=T(1-e^{-\frac{1}{T}t})$ (15.3-12)

所以一阶系统跟踪单位斜坡信号的稳态误差为 $e_{ss}=\lim\limits_{t\to\infty}e(t)=T$，如图 15.3-7 所示。

上式表明：

(1)一阶系统能跟踪斜坡输入信号。稳态时，输入和输出信号的变化率完全相同，即 $\dot{r}(t)=1, \dot{c}(t)_{t\to\infty}=1$。

(2)由于系统存在惯性，$\dot{c}(t)$ 从 0 上升到 1 时，对应的输出信号在数值上要滞后于输入信号一个常量 T，这就是稳态误差产生的原因。

(3) 减少时间常数 T 不仅可以加快瞬态响应的速度，还可减少系统跟踪斜坡信号的稳态误差。

4)单位加速度响应

$$r(t)=\frac{1}{2}t^2\cdot l(t), R(s)=\frac{1}{s^3}, C(s)=\Phi(s)R(s)=\frac{1}{s^3(Ts+1)} \quad (15.3\text{-}13)$$

$$c(t)=L^{-1}[C(s)]=\frac{1}{2}t^2-Tt+T^2(1-e^{-t/T}) \quad (15.3\text{-}14)$$

$$e(t)=r(t)-c(t)=Tt-T^2(1-e^{-t/T}), e_{ss}=\infty \quad (15.3\text{-}15)$$

说明一阶系统无法跟踪加速度输入信号。

15.3.3 控制系统的二阶瞬态响应

凡以二阶系统微分方程作为运动方程的控制系统，称为二阶系统。

1)典型的二阶系统

二阶系统的动态结构图如图 15.3-8 所示，其开环传递函数为

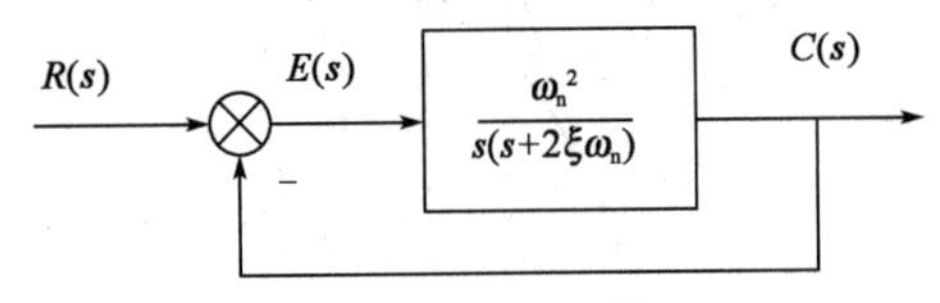

图 15.3-8 二阶系统结构图

$$G(s)=\frac{\omega_n^2}{s(s+2\xi\omega_n)}=\frac{K}{s(Ts+1)} \quad (15.3\text{-}16)$$

闭环传递函数为

$$\Phi(s)=\frac{\omega_n^2}{s^2+2\xi\omega_n s+\omega_n^2} \quad (15.3\text{-}17)$$

根据 ξ 的取值，可把系统分为欠阻尼、临界阻尼和过阻尼三种情况进行分析，如图 15.3-9 所示。

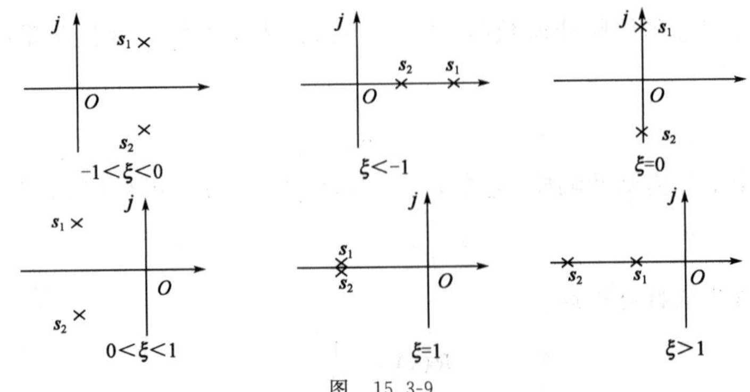

图 15.3-9

特征方程：$$s^2+2\xi\omega_n s+\omega_n^2=0 \tag{15.3-18}$$

特征方程式的根为：$$s_{1,2}=-\xi\omega_n\pm\sqrt{\xi^2-1}\omega_n \tag{15.3-19}$$

2)二阶系统的单位阶跃响应

阻尼比 ξ 是实际阻尼系数 F 与临界阻尼系数 F_C 的比值

$$\xi=\frac{1}{2\sqrt{T_m K}}=\frac{1}{2\sqrt{J\frac{K}{F}}}=\frac{1}{2\sqrt{J\frac{K_1}{F^2}}}=\frac{F}{2\sqrt{JK_1}}=\frac{F}{F_C}$$

$\xi<0$，两个正实部的特征根，系统发散；

$0<\xi<1$，闭环极点为共轭复根，位于右半 S 平面，这时的系统叫做欠阻尼系统；

$\xi=1$，两个相等的根；

$\xi>1$，两个不相等的根；

$\xi=0$，虚轴上，瞬态响应变为等幅振荡。

图 15.3-10 为二阶系统极点分布图。图 15.3-11 为二阶系统($0<\xi<1$)的单位阶跃响应。图 15.3-12为二阶系统的实极点。图 15.3-13 为二阶系统在不同 ξ 值瞬态响应曲线。

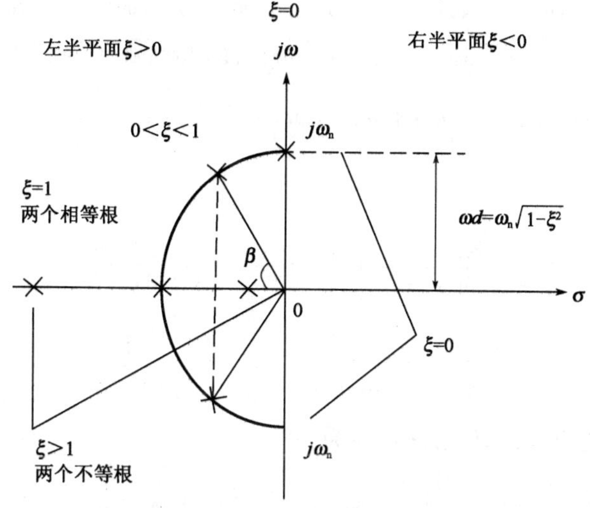

图 15.3-10　二阶系统极点分布

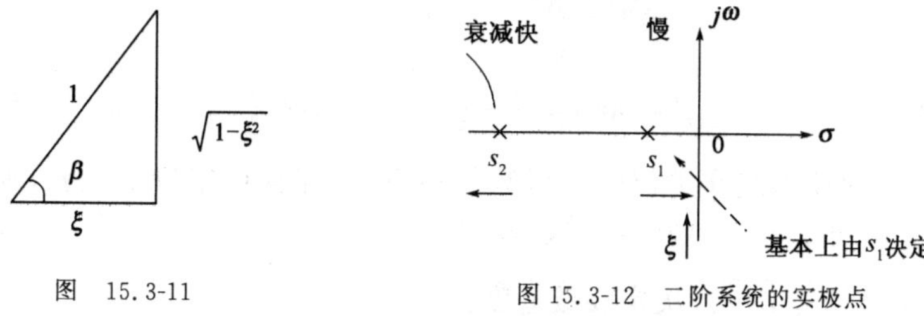

图　15.3-11

图 15.3-12　二阶系统的实极点

(1)欠阻尼($0<\xi<1$)二阶系统的单位阶跃响应(图 15.3-11)

$$s_{1,2}=-\xi\omega_n\pm j\omega_n\sqrt{1-\xi^2}=-\sigma\pm j\omega_d$$

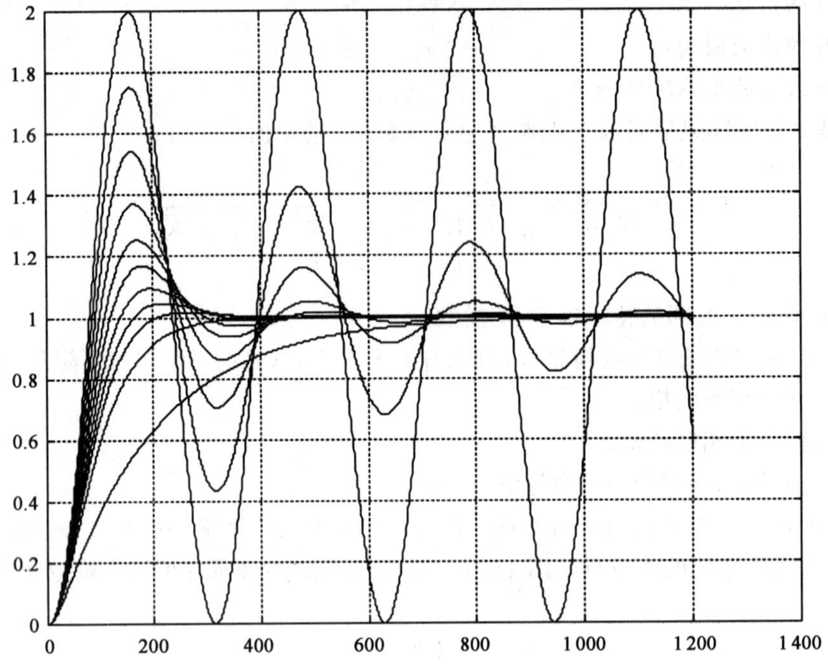

图 15.3-13　二阶系统在不同 ξ 值瞬态响应曲线

令衰减系数 $\sigma=\xi\omega_n$，阻尼振荡频率 $\omega_d=\omega_n\sqrt{1-\xi^2}$

由 $R(s)=\dfrac{1}{s}$ 得

$$C(s)=\Phi(s)R(s)=\frac{\omega_n^2}{s^2+2\xi\omega_n s+\omega_n^2}\cdot\frac{1}{s}=\frac{1}{s}-\frac{s+\xi\omega_n^2}{(s+\xi\omega_n)^2+\omega_d^2}-\frac{\xi\omega_n}{(s+\xi\omega_n)^2+\omega_d^2}$$

$$\omega_d\frac{\xi\omega_n}{\omega_d}=\omega_d\frac{\xi\omega_n}{\omega_n\sqrt{1-\xi^2}}=\omega_d\frac{\xi}{\sqrt{1-\xi^2}}$$

对上式取拉氏反变换，得单位阶跃响应为：

$$h(t)=1-e^{-\xi\omega_n t}\left[\cos\omega_d t+\frac{\xi}{\sqrt{1-\xi^2}}\sin\omega_d t\right]$$

$$=1-\frac{1}{\sqrt{1-\xi^2}}e^{-\xi\omega_n t}\sin(\omega_d t+\beta)\qquad(t\geqslant 0)\tag{15.3-20}$$

$$\beta=\operatorname{arccot}\frac{\sqrt{1-\xi^2}}{\xi}=\arccos\xi$$

稳态分量为 1，表明系统在单位阶跃函数作用下，不存在稳态位置误差，瞬态分量为阻尼正弦振荡项，其振荡频率为 ω_d，即阻尼振荡频率。

包络线 $1\pm e^{-\xi\omega_n t}/\sqrt{1-\xi^2}$ 决定收敛速度。

$$\xi=0\text{ 时},h(t)=1-\sin\omega_n t,t\geqslant 0\tag{15.3-21}$$

这是一条平均值为 1 的正、余弦形式等幅振荡，其振荡频率为 ω_n，故称为无阻尼振荡频率。ω_n 由系统本身的结构参数 K 和 T_m，或 K_1 和 J 确定，ω_n 常称自然频率。

实际控制系统通常有一定的阻尼比，因此不可能通过实验方法测得 ω_n，而只能测得 ω_d，且 $\omega_d < \omega_n$，$\xi \geqslant 1$ 时，ω_d 不复存在，系统的响应不再出现振荡。

(2)临界阻尼($\xi=1$)

$$r(t) = u(t), R(s) = \frac{1}{s}$$

$$C(s) = \frac{\omega_n^2}{(s+\omega_n)^2}\frac{1}{s} = \frac{1}{s} - \frac{\omega_n}{(s+\omega_n)^2} - \frac{1}{s+\omega_n}$$

临界阻尼情况下的二阶系统的单位阶跃响应称为临界阻尼响应。

$$h(t) = 1 - e^{-\omega_n t} - \omega_n t - e^{-\omega_n t} = 1 - e^{-\omega_n t}(1+\omega_n t) \qquad (t \geqslant 0) \qquad (15.3\text{-}22)$$

当 $\xi=1$ 时，二阶系统的单位阶跃响应是稳态值为 1 的无超调单调上升过程，$\frac{\mathrm{d}h(t)}{\mathrm{d}t} = \omega_n^2 + e^{-\omega_n t}$。

(3)过阻尼($\xi>1$)

$$s_{1,2} = -\xi\omega_n \pm \omega_n\sqrt{\xi^2-1}$$

$$\begin{aligned} C(s) &= \frac{\omega_n^2}{(s-s_1)(s-s_2)}\frac{1}{s} \\ &= \frac{\omega_n^2}{\left[s+\omega_n\left(\xi-\sqrt{\xi^2-1}\right)\right]\left[s+\omega_n\left(\xi+\sqrt{\xi^2-1}\right)\right]s} \\ &= \frac{A_1}{s} + \frac{A_2}{s+\omega_n\left(\xi-\sqrt{\xi^2-1}\right)} + \frac{A_3}{\xi+\omega_n\left(\xi+\sqrt{\xi^2-1}\right)} \end{aligned}$$

$$A_1 = 1$$

$$A_2 = \frac{-1}{s+\omega_n\left(\xi-\sqrt{\xi^2-1}\right)}$$

$$A_3 = \frac{1}{2\sqrt{\xi^2-1}\left(\xi+\sqrt{\xi^2-1}\right)}$$

$$h(t) = 1 - \frac{1}{2\sqrt{\xi^2-1}\left(\xi-\sqrt{\xi^2-1}\right)}e^{-\left(\xi-\sqrt{\xi^2-1}\right)\omega_n t} + \frac{1}{2\sqrt{\xi^2-1}\left(\xi+\sqrt{\xi^2-1}\right)}e^{-\left(\xi+\sqrt{\xi^2-1}\right)\omega_n t} \qquad (t \geqslant 0) \qquad (15.3\text{-}23)$$

3)二阶系统阶跃响应的性能指标

在控制工程中，除了那些不容许产生振荡响应的系统外，通常都希望控制系统具有适度的阻尼、快速的响应速度和较短的调节时间。

二阶系统一般取 $\xi=0.4\sim0.8$。其他的动态性能指标，有的可用 ξ 和 ω_n 精确表示，如 t_r、t_p、M_p，有的很难用 ξ 和 ω_n 准确表示，如 t_d、t_s，可采用近似算法。

下面推导欠阻尼二阶系统暂态相应的性能指标和计算公式。

(1)t_d

在式(15.3-23)中，即 $h(t) = 1 - \frac{1}{\sqrt{1-\xi^2}}e^{-\xi\omega_n t}\sin(\omega_d t + \beta) \qquad (t \geqslant 0)$

令 $h(t_d)=0.5$，$\beta=\mathrm{arccot}\,\frac{\sqrt{1-\xi^2}}{\xi}=\arccos\xi$

可得

$$\omega_n t_d = \frac{1}{\xi}\ln\frac{2\sin(\sqrt{1-\xi^2}\omega_n t_d + \arccos\xi)}{\sqrt{1-\xi^2}}$$

在较大的 ξ 值范围内，近似有

$$t_d = \frac{1+0.6\xi+0.2\xi^2}{\omega_n} \quad (15.3\text{-}24)$$

$0<\xi<1$ 时，亦可用 $$t_d = \frac{1+0.7\xi}{\omega_n} \quad (15.3\text{-}25)$$

(2) t_r（上升时间）

$h(t_r)=1$ ，求得 $\frac{1}{\sqrt{1-\xi^2}}e^{-\xi\omega_n t}\sin(\omega_d t_r+\beta)=0$

$$\omega_d t_r+\beta=\pi$$

$$t_r = \frac{\pi-\beta}{\omega_d} \quad (15.3\text{-}26)$$

ξ 一定，即 β 一定，$\rightarrow\omega_n\uparrow\rightarrow t_r\downarrow$ ，响应速度越快。

(3) t_p（峰值时间）

对式(15.3-24)求导，并令其为零，求得

$$\xi\omega_n e^{-\xi\omega_n t}\sin(\omega_d t+\beta)-\omega_d e^{\xi\omega_n t}\cos(\omega_d t+\beta)=0$$

$$\tan(\omega_d t+\beta)=\frac{\sqrt{1-\xi^2}}{\xi}$$

因为 $\tan\beta=\frac{\sqrt{1-\xi^2}}{\xi}$

所以 $\omega_d t_p=0,\pi,2\pi\cdots$，根据峰值时间定义，应取

$$\omega_d t_p=\pi$$

$$t_p=\frac{\pi}{\omega_d}=\frac{1}{2}\frac{2\pi}{\omega_d}=\frac{1}{2}T_d \quad (15.3\text{-}27)$$

ξ 一定时，$\omega_n\uparrow$（闭环极点力负实轴的距离越远）$\rightarrow t_p\downarrow$

(4) $\sigma\%$ 或 M_p 的计算，超调量

超调量在峰值时间发生，故 $h(t_p)$ 即为最大输出

$$h(t_p)=1-\frac{1}{\sqrt{1-\xi^2}}e^{-\upsilon\xi\omega_n t_p}\sin(\omega_d t_p+\beta)$$

$$h(t_p)=1+e^{-\pi\xi/\sqrt{1-\xi^2}}$$

因为 $\sin(\pi+\beta)=-\sin\beta=-\sqrt{1-\xi^2}$

$$\sigma\%=\frac{h(t_p)-h(\infty)}{h(\infty)}\times100\%=e^{-\frac{\pi\xi}{\sqrt{1-\xi^2}}}\times100\% \quad (15.3\text{-}28)$$

$$\frac{C(s)}{R(s)}=\frac{\omega_n{}^2}{s^2+2\xi\omega_n s+\omega_n{}^2}$$

$\xi=0$ 时，$\sigma\%=100\%$

$\xi=0.4$ 时，$\sigma\%=25.4\%$

$\xi=1.0$ 时，$\sigma\%=0$

当 $\xi=0.4\sim0.8$ 时，$\sigma\%=1.5\%\sim25.4\%$

(5) 调节时间 t_s 的计算

典型二阶系统欠阻尼条件下的单位阶跃响应

$$h(t)=1-e^{-\xi\omega_n t}\sin(\omega_d t+\beta),t\geqslant 0$$

$$\beta=\operatorname{arccot}\frac{\sqrt{1-\xi^2}}{\xi}=\arccos\xi$$

令 Δ 表示实际响应与稳态输出之间的误差，则有

$$t_s=\frac{1}{\xi\omega_n}\left(\ln\frac{1}{\Delta}+\ln\frac{1}{\sqrt{1-\xi^2}}\right)$$

$$\Delta=\frac{1}{\sqrt{1-\xi^2}}e^{-\xi\omega_n t}\sin(\omega_d t+\beta)\leqslant\frac{e^{-\xi\omega_n t}}{\sqrt{1-\xi^2}}$$

$\xi\leqslant0.8$ 时，并在上述不等式右端分母中代入 $\xi=0.8$，选取误差带

$$\Delta=0.05,t_s\leqslant\frac{3.5}{\xi\omega_n},t_s-\frac{3.5}{\xi\omega_n}$$

$$\Delta=0.02,t_s\leqslant\frac{4.5}{\xi\omega_n},t_s-\frac{4.5}{\xi\omega_n}\tag{15.3-29}$$

$$\xi\leqslant0.4\begin{cases}t_s=\dfrac{3}{\xi\omega_n}(\Delta=0.05)\\ t_s=\dfrac{4}{\xi\omega_n}(\Delta=0.02)\end{cases}\quad（当\ \xi\ 较小）$$

通过以上分析可知，t_s 近似与 $\xi\omega_n$ 成反比。在设计系统时，ξ 通常由要求的最大超调量决定，所以调节时间 t_s 由无阻尼自然振荡频率 ω_n 所决定。也就是说，在不改变超调量的条件下，通过改变 ω_n 值来改变调节时间 t_s。

典型例题解析

【例 15.3-1】 设某闭环系统的总传递函数为 $G(s)=\frac{1}{s^2+2s+1}$，此系统为：

A. 欠阻尼二阶系统　　B. 过阻尼二阶系统

C. 临界阻尼二阶系统　　D. 等幅振荡二阶系统

解　$\xi=1$ 为临界阻尼系统。选 C。

【例 15.3-2】 二阶环节 $G(s)=\frac{10}{s^2+3.6s+9}$ 的阻尼比应为：

A. $\xi=0.6$　　B. $\xi=1.2$　　C. $\xi=1.8$　　D. $\xi=3.6$

解　$2\xi\omega_n=3.6,\omega_n=3,\xi=0.6$。选 A。

【例 15.3-3】 二阶欠阻尼系统质量指标与系统参数之间，正确的表达为：

A. 衰减系数不变，最大偏差减小，衰减比增大

B. 衰减系数增大，最大偏差增大，衰减比减小，调节时间增大

C. 衰减系数减小，最大偏差增大，衰减比减小，调节时间增大

D. 衰减系数减小，最大偏差减小，衰减比减小，调节时间减小

解　衰减系数即阻尼比。当 ξ 减小时，超调量 $\sigma_p(\%)=e^{-\pi\xi/\sqrt{1-\xi^2}}\times100\%$ 增大，即最大偏差增大，衰减比 $n=e^{2\pi\xi/\sqrt{1-\xi^2}}$ 减小，调节时间 $t_s\approx\frac{3}{\xi\omega_n}$ 增大。选 C。

15.3.4 频率特性的基本概念

频率特性法是一种图解分析法，通过系统的频率特性来分析系统性能。不仅适用于线性定常系统，还适用于纯滞后环节和部分非线性环节的分析。

(1)频率特性的定义：在正弦输入下，线性定常系统输出的稳态分量与输入的复数比。以 $G(j\omega)$或 $\phi(j\omega)$表示。$G(j\omega)=|G(j\omega)|e^{j\phi(\omega)}$。

(2)幅频特性：稳态时，线性定常系统输出与输入的幅值比，以 $A(\omega)$或$|G(j\omega)|$表示。

(3)相频特性：稳态时，线性定常系统输出信号与输入信号的相位差，以 $\phi(\omega)$或$\angle G(j\omega)$表示。

(4)对数频率特性：对数幅频特性 $L(\omega)$和对数相频特性 $\varphi(\omega)$。

对数幅频特性 $$L(\omega)=20\lg A(\omega)(\mathrm{dB})$$

对数相频特性 $$\varphi(\omega)=\angle G(j\omega)(^\circ)$$

(5)典型环节的频率特性：

①比例环节 K：

频率特性 $$G(j\omega)=K$$

幅频特性 $$|G(j\omega)|=A(\omega)=K$$

相频特性 $$\varphi(\omega)=0^\circ$$

对数幅频特性 $$L(\omega)=20\lg A(\omega)=20\lg K$$

对数相频特性 $$\varphi(\omega)=0^\circ$$

②积分环节$\frac{1}{s}$：

频率特性 $$G(j\omega)=\frac{1}{\omega}$$

幅频特性 $$|G(j\omega)|=A(\omega)=\frac{1}{\omega}$$

相频特性 $$\varphi(\omega)=90^\circ$$

对数幅频特性 $$L(\omega)=20\lg A(\omega)=20\lg\omega$$

对数相频特性 $$\varphi(\omega)=90^\circ$$

③理想微分环节 K：

频率特性 $$G(j\omega)=j\omega$$

幅频特性 $$|G(j\omega)|=A(\omega)=\omega$$

相频特性 $$\varphi(\omega)=90^\circ$$

对数幅频特性 $$L(\omega)=20\lg A(\omega)=20\lg\omega$$

对数相频特性 $$\varphi(\omega)=90^\circ$$

④惯性环节$\frac{1}{T_s+1}$：

频率特性 $$G(j\omega)=\frac{1}{j\omega T+1}$$

幅频特性 $$|G(j\omega)|=A(\omega)=\frac{1}{\sqrt{1+T^2\omega^2}}$$

相频特性 $$\varphi(\omega)=-\arctan T\omega$$

对数幅频特性 $$L(\omega)=20\lg A(\omega)=20\lg\frac{1}{\sqrt{1+T^2\omega^2}}$$

对数相频特性 $$\varphi(\omega)=-\arctan T\omega$$

⑤一阶微分环节 T_s+1：

频率特性 $$G(j\omega)=j\omega T+1$$

幅频特性 $$|G(j\omega)|=A(\omega)=\sqrt{1+T^2\omega^2}$$

相频特性 $$\varphi(\omega)=\arctan T\omega$$

对数幅频特性 $$L(\omega)=20\lg A(\omega)=20\lg\sqrt{1+T^2\omega^2}$$

对数相频特性 $$\varphi(\omega)=-\arctan T\omega$$

⑥二阶振荡环节：

$$\frac{1}{T^2+2\xi T_s+1}=\frac{\omega_n^2}{s^2+2\xi+\omega_n^2}(令\ T=\frac{1}{\omega_n})$$

频率特性 $$G(j\omega)=\frac{1}{1-T^2\omega_n^2+2j\xi T\omega}=\frac{1}{1-\frac{\omega^2}{\omega_n^2}+2j\xi\frac{\omega}{\omega_n}}$$

幅频特性 $$|G(j\omega)|=A(\omega)\frac{1}{\sqrt{\left(1-\frac{\omega^2}{\omega_n^2}\right)^2+\left(2\xi\frac{\omega}{\omega_n}\right)^2}}$$

相频特性 $$\varphi(\omega)=-\arctan\frac{2\xi\frac{\omega}{\omega_n}}{1-\frac{\omega^2}{\omega_n^2}}$$

对数幅频特性 $$L(\omega)=20\lg A(\omega)=-20\lg\sqrt{\left(1-\frac{\omega^2}{\omega_n^2}\right)^2+\left(2\xi\frac{\omega}{\omega_n}\right)^2}$$

对数相频特性 $$\phi(\omega)=\arctan\frac{2\xi\frac{\omega}{\omega_n}}{1-\frac{\omega^2}{\omega_n^2}}$$

⑦纯滞后环节 $e^{-\tau s}$：

频率特性 $$G(j\omega)=e^{-j\omega\tau}$$

幅频特性 $$|G(j\omega)|=A(\omega)=1$$

相频特性 $$\varphi(\omega)=-\tau\omega$$

对数幅频特性 $$L(\omega)=20\lg A(\omega)=0$$

对数相频特性 $$\varphi(\omega)=-\tau\omega$$

典型例题解析

【例 15.3-4】 二阶系统传递函数 $G(s)=\frac{1}{s^2+2s+1}$ 的频率特性函数为：

A. $\frac{1}{\omega^2+2\omega+1}$　　B. $\frac{1}{-\omega^2+2j\omega+1}$

C. $-\frac{1}{\omega^2+2\omega+1}$　　D. $\frac{1}{\omega^2-2\omega+1}$

解 可参考二阶振荡环节的频率特性函数，$G(j\omega)=\frac{1}{-\omega^2+2j\omega+1}$。选 B。

【例 15.3-5】 根据图示开环传递函数的对数坐标图，判断其闭环系统的稳定性。

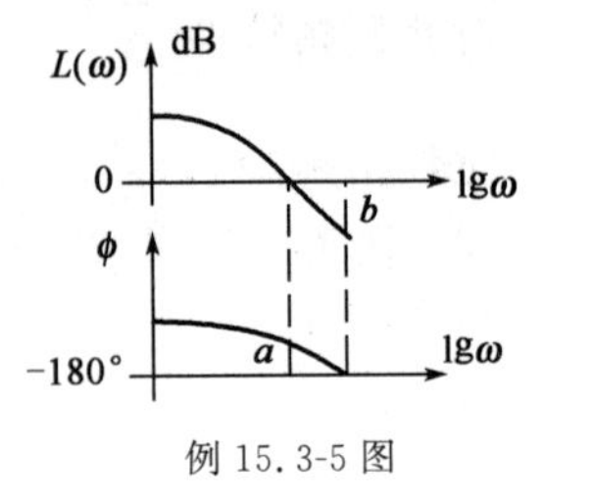

例 15.3-5 图

A. 系统稳定，增益裕量为 a

B. 系统稳定，增益裕量为 b

C. 系统不稳定，负增益裕量为 a

D. 系统不稳定，负增益裕量为 b

解 选 B。

15.3.5 频率特性表示方法

频率特性可用图形表示，有极坐标图、对数坐标图和对数幅相图。

1)极坐标图

又称幅相频率特性曲线或幅相曲线。当输入信号的频率变化时，向量的幅值和相位也随之做相应的变化，其端点在复平面移动的轨迹

$$G(j\omega)=\frac{K(\tau_1 j\omega+1)(\tau_2 j\omega+1)\cdots(\tau_m j\omega+1)}{(j\omega)^v(T_1 j\omega+1)(T_2 j\omega+1)\cdots(T_{n-v} j\omega+1)} \tag{15.3-30}$$

$v=0$ 即 0 型系统：极坐标图的起点 $\omega=0$ 是一个位于正实轴的有限值。对应于 $\omega=\infty$ 的极坐标图曲线的终点位于坐标原点，并且这一点上的曲线与一个坐标轴相切。

$v=1$ 即 1 型系统：在总的相角中，$-90°$的相角是 $j\omega$ 项产生的。在低频时，极坐标是一条渐近于平行与虚轴的直线线段。当 $\omega=\infty$ 时，幅值为零，曲线收敛于原点，且曲线与一个坐标轴相切。

$v=2$ 即 2 型系统：在总相角中，$-180°$的相角是由$(j\omega)^2$ 项产生的。

0 型、1 型和 2 型系统极坐标图低频部分的一般形状如图 15.3-14 所示，极坐标图曲线的复杂形状都是由分子的动态特性引起的。由分子的时间常数决定。

2)对数坐标图

又称对数频率特性曲线或伯德图(Bode)，由对数幅频曲线和对数相频曲线组成。对数频率特性曲线的横坐标表示频率 ω，并按对数分度。所谓对数分度，是指横坐标以 $\lg\omega$ 进行均匀分度，即横坐标对 $\lg\omega$ 来讲是均匀的，对 ω 而言却是不均匀的，如图 15.3-15 所示。从图中可以看出，频率 ω 每变化 10 倍(称为一个 10 倍频程)，横坐标的间隔距离为一个单位长度。横坐标以 ω 标出，一般情况下，不应标出 $\omega=0$ 的点(因为此时 $\lg\omega$ 不存在)。若 ω_2 位于 ω_1 和 ω_3 的几何中点，此时应有 $\lg\omega_2-\lg\omega_1=\lg\omega_3-\lg\omega_2$，即 $\omega_2^2=\omega_1\omega_3$。

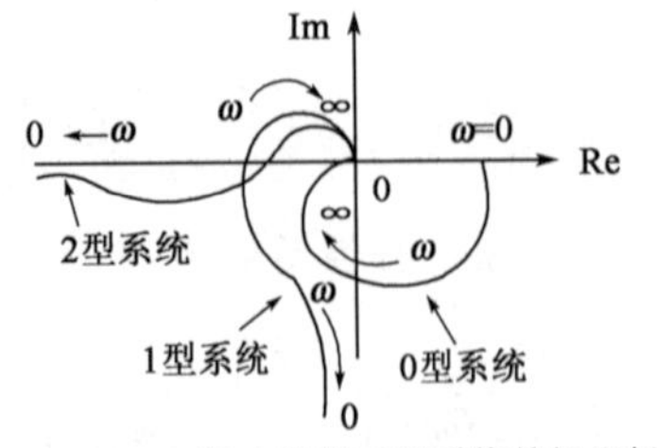

图 15.3-14 0 型、1 型和 2 型系统的极坐标图

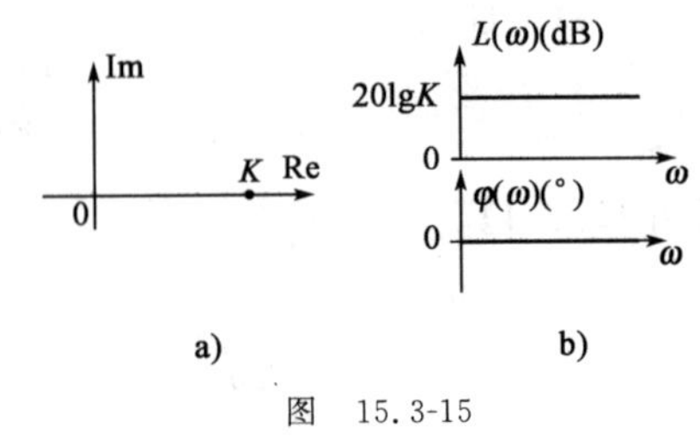

图 15.3-15

(1)比例环节。

比例环节的传递函数为常数

$$G(s)=K$$

其频率特性为

$$G(j\omega) = K$$

相应的对数幅频特性和相频特性为

$$\begin{cases} L(\omega) = 20\lg A(\omega) = 20\lg K \\ \varphi(\omega) = 0 \end{cases}$$

(2)惯性环节。

惯性环节的传递函数为$\frac{1}{(1+Ts)}$,其频率特性为

$$G(j\omega) = \frac{1}{1+j\omega T} = \frac{1}{\sqrt{1+(\omega T)^2}} e^{-j\mathrm{arccot}(\omega T)} \qquad \begin{cases} A(\omega) = 1/\sqrt{1+(\omega T)^2} \\ \varphi(\omega) = -\mathrm{arctg}(\omega T) \end{cases}$$

在绘制幅相曲线时,注意在 ω 由 $0\to\infty$变化时,惯性环节 $1/(1+j\omega T)$的幅值由 1 变化到 0,相角由 0°变化到$-90°$,据此可以画出惯性环节幅相曲线的大致形状。通过逐点计算,可以画出惯性环节幅相曲线的精确曲线。可以证明,惯性环节的幅相曲线为半圆。

惯性环节的对数幅频特性和相频特性为

$$\begin{cases} L(\omega) = -20\lg\sqrt{1+(\omega T)^2} \\ \varphi(\omega) = -\mathrm{arccot}(\omega T) \end{cases}$$

可以通过计算若干点的数值来绘制惯性环节的对数幅频特性和相频特性的精确曲线。工程上,此环节的对数幅频特性可以采用渐近线来表示。为方便起见,在 $\omega<\omega_1$ 的区段,惯性环节对数幅频特性曲线的渐近线(或称近似曲线)取为 0dB 的水平线;在 $\omega>\omega_1$ 的区段,惯性环节对数幅频特性曲线的渐近线取为一条斜率为-20dB/dec 的直线,两段渐近线在交接频率 ω_1 处相交,如图 15.3-16 所示。

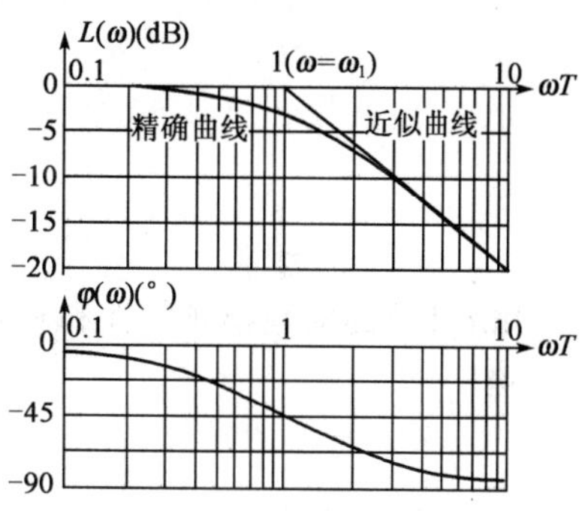

图 15.3-16　惯性环节的对数幅频特性曲线和相频特性曲线

交接频率 ω_1 也称为惯性环节的特征点,此时 $A(\omega_1)=0.707$, $L(\omega_1)=-3$db, $\varphi(\omega_1)=-45°$。

(3)一阶微分环节。

一阶微分环节的传递函数为 $1+\tau s$,其频率特性为

$$G(j\omega) = 1 + j\omega\pi = \sqrt{1+(\omega\tau)^2}\,e^{j\mathrm{arccot}(\omega\pi)}$$

一阶微分环节的幅频特性和相频特性的表达式为

$$\begin{cases} A(\omega) = \sqrt{1+(\omega\tau)^2} \\ \varphi(\omega) = \arctan(\omega\tau) \end{cases}$$

一阶微分环节的对数幅频特性和相频特性为

$$\begin{cases} L(\omega) = 20\lg\sqrt{1+(\omega T)^2} \\ \varphi(\omega) = \arctan(\omega T) \end{cases}$$

工程上,此环节的对数幅频特性可以采用渐近线来表示。定义 $\omega_1=1/\tau$ 为交接频率,渐近线表示如下

$$L(\omega)=0 \qquad (\omega\ll\omega_1\text{时})$$

$$L(\omega)=20\lg(\omega\tau)=20\lg\omega-20\lg\omega_1 \qquad (\omega\gg\omega_1\text{时})$$

类似于惯性环节，可以构造一阶微分环节对数幅频特性近似曲线。

一阶微分环节对数幅频特性的精确曲线与近似曲线之间存在误差，必要时应进行修正，最大的误差发生在交接频率 ω_1 处，其值为 3dB。

交接频率 ω_1 也称为一阶微分环节的特征点，此时 $A(\omega_1)=1.414$，$L(\omega_1)=3$ db，$\varphi(\omega_1)=45°$。

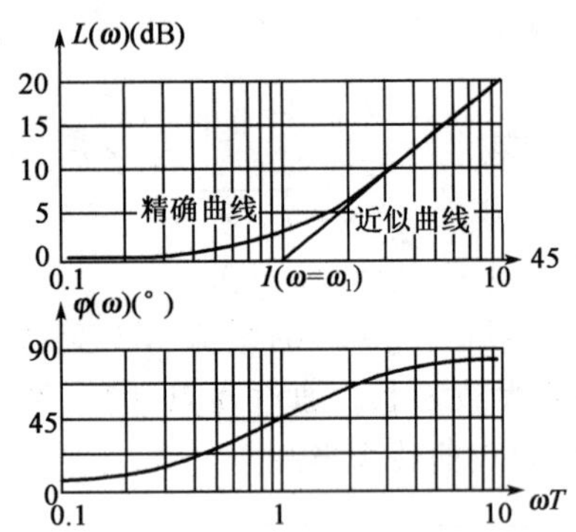

图 15.3-17　一阶微分环节的对数幅频特性曲线和相频特性曲线

比较惯性环节和一阶微分环节可以发现，它们的传递函数互为倒数，而它们的对数幅频特性和相频特性则对称于横轴，这是一个普遍规律，即传递函数互为倒数时，对数幅频特性和相频特性对称于横轴。如图 15.3-17 所示。

(4)积分环节。

积分环节的传递函数是 $1/s$，其频率特性为

$$G(j\omega)=\frac{1}{j\omega}=\frac{1}{\omega}e^{-j\frac{\pi}{2}}$$

其幅相曲线如图 15.3-18 所示，显然 ω 由 $0\to\infty$ 变化时，其幅值由 ∞ 变化到 0，而相角始终为 $-90°$。

积分环节的幅频特性和相频特性的表达式为

$$\begin{cases}A(\omega)=\dfrac{1}{\omega}\\[2ex]\varphi(\omega)=-\dfrac{\pi}{2}\end{cases}$$

积分环节的对数幅频特性和相频特性为

$$\begin{cases}L(\omega)=-20\lg\omega\\[2ex]\varphi(\omega)=-\dfrac{\pi}{2}\end{cases}$$

由图 15.3-19 可见，其对数幅频特性为一条斜率为 -20dB/dec 的直线，此线通过 $\omega=1$，$L(\omega)=0$dB 的点。相频特性是一条平行于横轴的直线，其纵坐标为 $-\pi/2$。

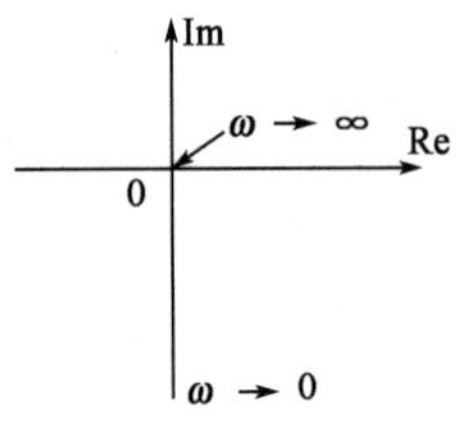

15.3-18　积分环节幅相曲线

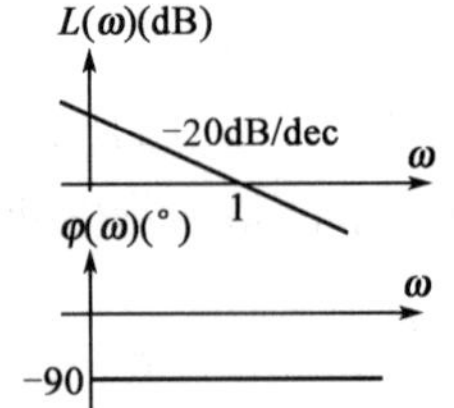

图 15.3-19　积分环节的对数幅频特性和相频特性

(5)微分环节。

微分环节的传递函数是 s，其频率特性为

$$G(j\omega)=j\omega=\omega e^{j\frac{\pi}{2}}$$

微分环节的幅频特性和相频特性的表达式为

$$\begin{cases} A(\omega)=\omega \\ \varphi(\omega)=\dfrac{\pi}{2} \end{cases}$$

微分环节的对数幅频特性和相频特性为

$$\begin{cases} L(\omega)=20\lg\omega \\ \varphi(\omega)=\dfrac{\pi}{2} \end{cases}$$

由图 15.3-20 可见，其对数幅频特性为一条斜率为 $+20\text{dB/dec}$ 的直线，此线通过 $\omega=1$，$L(\omega)=0\text{dB}$ 的点。相频特性是一条平行于横轴的直线，其纵坐标为 $\pi/2$。

积分环节和微分环节的传递函数互为倒数，它们的对数幅频特性和相频特性则对称于横轴。

(6)二阶微分环节。

二阶微分环节的传递函数是 $s^2/\omega_n^2+2\xi s/\omega_n+1$，式中 $\omega_n>0$，$0<\xi<1$ 。

频率特性为：$G(j\omega)=1-\omega^2/\omega_n^2+j_2\xi\omega/\omega_n$

可知幅相曲线的起点为 $G(j_0)=1\angle 0°$，终点为 $G(j\infty)=\infty\angle 180°$，当 ω 由 $0\to\infty$ 变化时，$A(\omega)$ 由 $1\to\infty$，$\varphi(\omega)$ 由 $0°\to+180°$ 变化，据此可以画出二阶微分环节幅相曲线的大致形状，如图 15.3-21 所示。

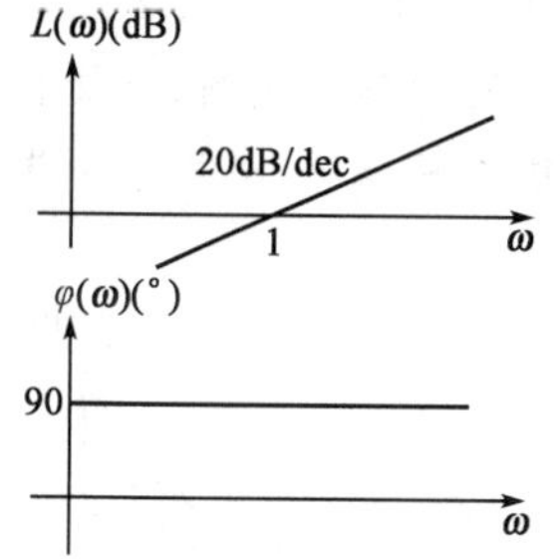

图 15.3-20 微分环节的对数幅频特性和相频特性

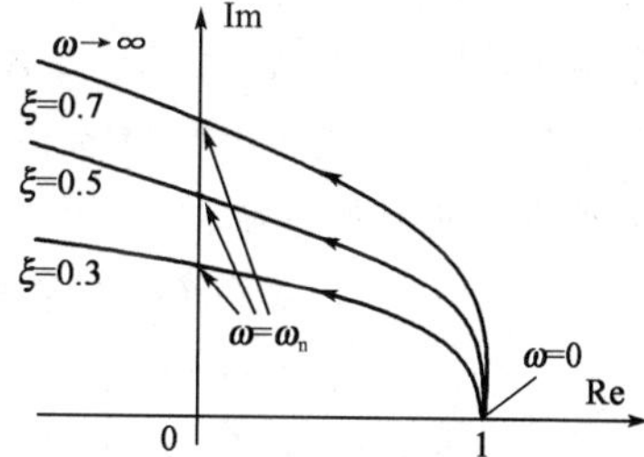

图 15.3-21 微分环节的幅相曲线

二阶微分环节和振荡环节的传递函数互为倒数，它们的对数幅频特性和相频特性对称于横轴，如图 15.3-22 所示。

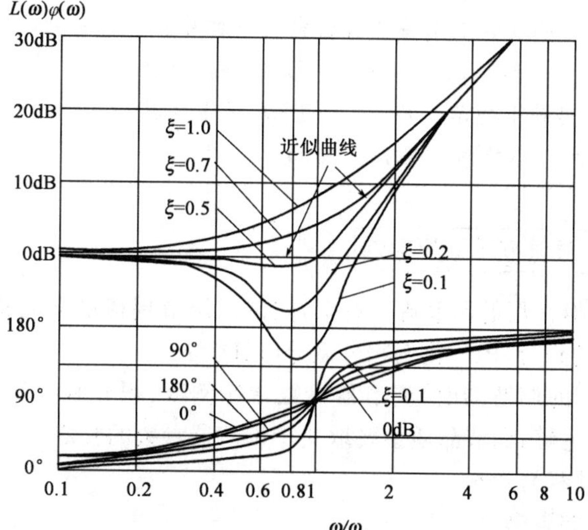

图 15.3-22 二阶微分环节的对数幅频特性曲线和相频特性曲线

注意到对数幅频特性曲线的渐近线在 $\omega<\omega_n$ 时是一条 0dB 的水平线，而在 $\omega>\omega_n$ 时是一条斜率为 +40dB/dec 的直线，它和 0dB 线交于横坐标 $\omega=\omega_n$ 的地方。ω_n 称为二阶微分环节的交接频率。

(7)延迟环节。

对应的频率特性是

$$G(j\omega)=e^{-j\omega\tau}$$

幅频特性和相频特性分别为

$$A(\omega)=1$$

$$\varphi(\omega)=-57.3\omega\tau\ (°)$$

幅频特性恒等于 1，相频特性是 ω 的线性函数，ω 为零时，相角等于零，ω 趋于无穷大时，相角趋于负无穷。延迟环节的幅相曲线是一个圆，圆心在原点，半径为 1，如图 15.3-23a)所示。

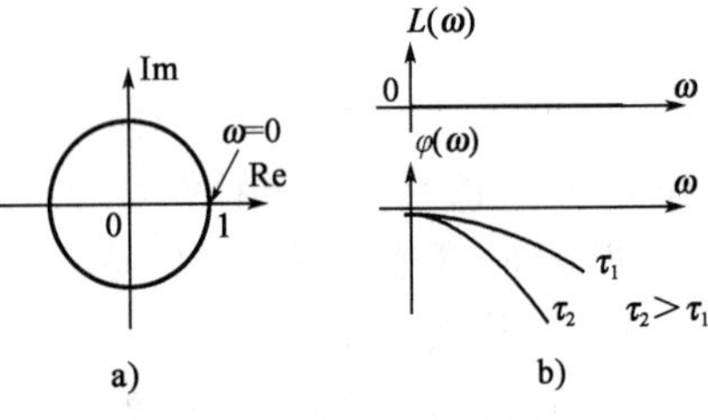

图 15.3-23　延迟环节的伯德图

延迟环节的对数幅频特性恒为 0dB，即：$L(\omega)=0$。

对数频率特性曲线如图 15.3-23b)所示，由图可知，τ 越大，相角滞后就越大。

典型例题解析

【例 15.3-6】 传递函数 $G_1(s)$、$G_2(s)$、$G_3(s)$、$G_4(s)$ 的增益分别为 K_1、K_2、K_3、K_4，其余部分相同，且 $K_1<K_2<K_3<K_4$。由传递函数 $G_2(s)$ 代表的单位反馈(反馈传递函数为 1 的负反馈)闭环系统的奈斯特曲线如下图。图 15-42 中哪个传递函数代表的单位反馈闭环控制系统为稳定的系统？

A. 由 $G_1(s)$ 代表的闭环系统

B. 由 $G_2(s)$ 代表的闭环系统

C. 由 $G_3(s)$ 代表的闭环系统

D. 由 $G_4(s)$ 代表的闭环系统

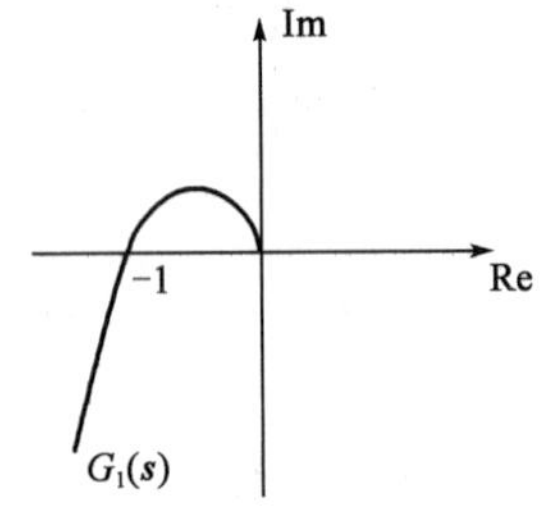

例 15.3-6 图

解　由图可知 $G_2(s)$ 为临界。系统 $G_3(s)$，$G_4(s)$ 的增益都大于 $G_2(s)$，都不稳定。只有 $G_1(s)$ 增益小于 $G_2(s)$，是稳定的，为闭环系统。选 A。

【例 15.3-7】 比例环节的奈斯特曲线占据复平面中：

A. 整个负虚轴　　B. 整个正虚轴

C. 实轴上的某一段　　D. 实轴上的某一点

解　由比例环节的奈斯特曲线可知。选 D。

15.3.6 调节器的特性对调节质量的影响

调节器种类很多，但常用的调节规律有限，如位式调节规律属继电特性调节规律；线性调节规律有比例(P)、比例积分(PI)、比例积分微分(PID)等。

采用线性控制规律的调节器时，调节器参数指比例度、积分时间和微分时间。当调节对象、传感器和执行器确定够，调节品质主要取决于调节器参数的整定。

1)比例度对调节过程的影响

(1)比例度对余差的影响

比例度越大，放大倍数越小，由于 $\Delta y=Kpe(t)$，要获得同样大小的 Δy 变化量所需的余差就越大，因此在相同的干扰作用下，系统再次平衡时的余差就越大。反之，比例度减小，系统的余差也随之减小。

(2)比例度对最大偏差、振荡周期的影响

在相同大小的干扰下，调节器的比例度越小，则比例作用越强，调节器的输出越大，使被控变量偏离给定值越小，被控变量被拉回到给定值所需的时间越短。所以，比例度越小，最大偏差越小，振荡周期也越短，工作频率提高。

(3)比例度对系统稳定性的影响

比例度越大，则调节器的输出变化越小，被控变量变化越缓慢，过渡过程越平稳。随着比例度的减小，系统的稳定程度降低，其过渡过程逐渐从衰减振荡走向临界振荡直至发散振荡。

2)积分时间对调节过程的影响

积分时间调节的过小，积分作用过强，可能引起系统的等幅振荡。积分时间选择合适时，可以减小至消除偏差。

积分时间 T_i 越小，表示积分速度越大，积分特性曲线的斜率越大，积分作用越强，克服余差的能力增强，但会引起调节过程振荡加剧，稳定性降低。积分时间越短，振荡的可能性就越强烈，甚至会产生发散振荡；积分时间 T_i 越大，积分作用越弱；积分时间无穷大，则没有积分作用，演变成了纯比例调节器。

同样的比例度下，积分时间 T_i 对调节过程的影响如图 15.3-24 所示。积分时间越大，积分作用越弱，静差消除的很慢；积分时间无穷大时，静差得不到消除；积分时间太小，调节过程振荡太剧烈；当积分时间适当时，调节过程响应快速，且能消除静差。

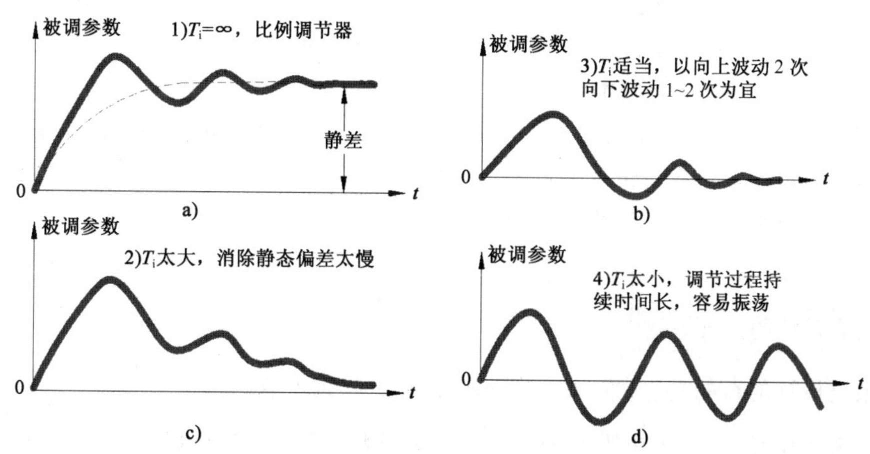

图 15.3-24 积分时间 T_i 对调节过程的影响

因此调节器的积分时间应按照被控对象的特性来选择(见表 15.3-1)。滞后不大的对象，T_i 可小些；滞后较大的对象，T_i 可选大。

积分时间对调节过程的影响 表 15.3-1

积分时间 T_i	小↔大	积分时间 T_i	小↔大
积分作用	强↔弱	上升时间	小↔大
稳定程度	不稳定↔更稳定	振荡周期	短↔长
最大偏差	小↔大	静差	全部消除

3)微分时间对调节过程的影响

微分时间 T_D 大,微分输出部分衰减的慢,强微分作用具有抑制振荡的效果。适当的增加微分作用,可以提高系统的稳定性,又可减小被控量的波动幅度,并降低稳态误差;如果微分作用加的过大,调节器输出剧烈变化,不仅不能提高系统的稳定性,反而会引起被控量大幅度的振荡。

微分作用总是力图阻止被控变量的变化,具有抑制振荡的效果。因此适当的增加微分时间,微分作用增强,可以提高系统的稳定性,减小被控变量的波动幅度,降低余差;微分时间过长,微分作用过大,则不仅不能提高系统的稳定性,反而会引起被控变量大幅度的振荡。微分作用为超前控制作用,能改善系统的控制品质,对滞后较大的如温度对象比较适用。

PI 调节动态指标最大偏差和超调量都较大,但静态偏差较小;PD 调节动态指标好,微分作用增加了系统的稳定性,比例度小时,调节时间缩短;PID 动态最大偏差比 PD 稍大。积分作用使静差接近零,但调节时间增长。因此,比例调节输出响应只要合适选择比例度,有利于系统稳定。微分作用可减少超调量和缩短过渡过程时间;积分作用能消除静差,但是超调量和过渡过程时间增大。因此,只有将比例、积分、微分三种作用结合起来,根据对象特性,正确选用调节规律和调节器的参数,将获得较好的调节效果。

典型例题解析

【例 15.3-8】 在 PID 控制中,若要获得良好的控制质量,应该适当选择的参数为:

A. 比例度,微分时间常数

B. 比例度,积分时间常数

C. 比例度,微分时间常数,积分时间常数

D. 微分时间常数,积分时间常数

解 PID 控制合适选择比例度有利于系统稳定。微分作用可减少超调量和缩短过渡过程时间;积分作用能消除静差。因此,综合比例、积分、微分三项调节规律,得到的控制质量最好,实践中应用也最为广泛。选 C。

15.3.7 二阶系统的设计方法

控制系统设计的目的是稳、准、快。但各项指标之间是矛盾的。

如果要求系统反应快,显然要求 $\sigma\%$ 小 $\xrightarrow{\text{要求}}\xi$ 大,因为 T_m 一定(对特定的系统)$\xrightarrow{\text{要求}}K$ 小。

同样如果要求系统反应快,ω_n 就要大 $\xrightarrow{\text{要求}}K$ 大。

如果要求稳态误差小 $\xrightarrow{\text{希望}}K$ 大。

所以,必须采取合理折中方案,如果采取方案仍不能使系统满足要求,就必须研究其他控制方式,以改善系统的动态性能和稳态性能。

如二阶系统在斜坡信号作用下,有稳态误差:$e_{ss}=\dfrac{2\xi}{\omega_n}$,$e_{ss}$ 要小 $\xrightarrow{\text{要求}}\xi$ 小。

在改善二阶系统性能的方法中,比例-微分控制和测速反馈控制是两种常用方法。

1)比例-微分控制

用分析法研究 PD 控制,对系统性能的影响,可得开环传递函数。

$$G(s)=\frac{C(s)}{R(s)}=\frac{(T_d s+1)\omega_n^2}{s(s+2\xi\omega_n s)}=\frac{\omega_n^2(T_d s+1)}{2\xi\omega_n s\left(\frac{s}{2\xi\omega_n}+1\right)}=\frac{\frac{\omega_n}{2\xi}(T_d s+1)}{s(s/2\xi\omega_n+1)} \tag{15.3-31}$$

其中，$K=\frac{\omega_n}{2\xi}$称为开环增益，与ξ_n、ξ有关。 (15.3-32)

闭环传递函数为：

$$\phi(s)=\frac{G(s)}{1+G(s)}=\frac{\omega_n^2(T_d s+1)}{S^2+2\xi\omega_n s+T_d\omega_n^2 s+\omega_n^2}=\frac{T_d\omega_n^2(s+\frac{1}{T_d})}{s^2+(2\xi\omega_n+T_d\omega_n^2)s+\omega_n^2}$$

$$T_d\omega_n^2=2\xi'\omega_n,\quad \xi'=\frac{T_d\omega_n}{2},\quad \xi_d=\xi+\xi'=\xi+\frac{T_d\omega_n}{2} \tag{15.3-33}$$

令
$$z=\frac{1}{T_d}=\frac{\omega_n^2(s+z)}{z(s^2+2\xi\omega_n s+\omega_n^2)} \tag{15.3-34}$$

结论：

(1)比例-微分控制可以不改变自然频率ω_n，但可增大系统的阻尼比。

(2)$K=\frac{\omega_n}{2\xi}$，可通过适当选择微分时间常数T_d，改变ξ_d阻尼的大小。

(3)$K=\frac{\omega_n}{2\xi}$，由于ξ与ω_n均与K有关，所以适当选择开环增益，以使系统在斜坡输入时的稳态误差减小，单位阶跃输入时有满意的动态性能(快速反应，小的超调)。这种控制方法，工业上称为PD控制，由于PD控制相当于给系统增加了一个闭环零点，$z=\frac{1}{T_d}$，故比例-微分控制的二阶系统称为有零点的二阶系统。

(4)适用范围：微分时对噪声有放大作用(高频噪声)。输入噪声放大时，不宜采用。

当输入为单位阶跃函数时：

$$C(s)=\Phi(s)R(s)=\frac{s+Z}{s^2+2\xi\omega_n s+\omega_n^2}\cdot\frac{\omega_n^2}{Z}\cdot\frac{1}{s}$$
$$=\frac{\omega_n^2}{s(s^2+2\xi\omega_n s+\omega_n^2)}+\frac{1}{z}\cdot\frac{s\omega_n^2}{s(s^2+2\xi\omega_n s+\omega_n^2)}$$

其中：$\frac{\omega_n^2}{s(s^2+2\xi\omega_n s+\omega_n^2)}\leftrightarrow 1-\frac{1}{\sqrt{1-\xi_d^2}}e^{-\xi_d\omega_n t}\sin(\omega_n\sqrt{1-\xi_d^2}t+\beta)$

$$\frac{1}{z}\cdot\frac{\omega_n^2}{s^2+2\xi_d\omega_n s+\omega_n^2}\leftrightarrow\frac{1}{z}\cdot\frac{\omega_n}{\sqrt{1-\xi_d^2}}e^{-\xi_d\omega_n t}\sin\omega_n\sqrt{1-\xi_d^2}t$$

所以当$\xi_d<1$时，得单位阶跃响应

$$h(t)=1-\frac{1}{\sqrt{1-\xi_d^2}}e^{-\xi_d\omega_n t}\sin(\omega_n\sqrt{1-\xi_d^2}t+\beta)+\frac{\omega_n}{z\sqrt{1-\xi_d^2}}e^{-\xi_d\omega_n t}\sin\omega_n\sqrt{1-\xi_d^2}t$$

$$h(t)=1+re^{-\xi_d\omega_n t}\sin(\omega_n\sqrt{1-\xi_d^2}t+\varphi) \tag{15.3-35}$$

$$r=\sqrt{Z^2-2\xi_d z\omega_n+\omega_n^2} \tag{15.3-36}$$

$$\varphi=-\pi+\arctan[\omega_n\sqrt{1-\xi_d^2}/(z-\xi_d\omega_n)]+\arctan(\sqrt{1-\xi_d^2}/\xi_d) \tag{15.3-37}$$

2)测速反馈控制

输入量的导数同样可以用来改善系统的性能。

通过将输出的速度信号反馈到系统输入端，并与误差信号比较，其效果与比例-微分控制相似，可以增大系统阻尼，改善系统的动态性能。

实例：角度控制系统。

K_t 为与测速发电机输出斜率有关的测速反馈系数(电压/单位转速)。

系统的开环传递函数

$$G(s)=\frac{\frac{{\omega_n}^2}{s(s+2\xi\omega_n s)}}{1+\frac{{\omega_n}^2}{s(s+2\xi\omega_n s)}K_t s}$$

$$=\frac{{\omega_n}^2}{s^2+(2\xi\omega_n+{\omega_n}^2K_t)s}$$

$$=\frac{1}{s(s/2\xi\omega_n+{\omega_n}^2K_t+1)}\cdot\frac{{\omega_n}^2}{2\xi\omega_n+{\omega_n}^2K_t} \tag{15.3-38}$$

$$K=\frac{{\omega_n}^2}{2\xi+K_t\omega_n}\qquad \text{开环作用} \tag{15.3-39}$$

K_t 会降低 K，即测速反馈会降低系统的开环增益。

相应的闭环传递函数，可用第一种表示方式

$$\varphi(s)=\frac{G(s)}{1+G(s)}=\frac{{\omega_n}^2}{s^2+(2\xi\omega_n+K_t{\omega_n}^2)s+{\omega_n}^2}$$

令 $2\xi_t\omega_n=2\xi\omega_n+K_t{\omega_n}^2$， $\xi_t=\xi+\frac{1}{2}K_t\omega_n$

与 PD 控制相比，有如下说明：

(1)测速反馈会降低系统的开环增益，从而会加大系统在斜坡输入时的稳态误差，即 $K\downarrow\rightarrow e_{ss}\uparrow$。

(2)测速反馈不影响系统的自然频率，即 ω_n 不变。

(3)可增大系统的阻尼比，$\xi_t=\xi+\frac{1}{2}K_t\omega_n$ 与 $\xi_d=\xi+\frac{1}{2}T_d\omega_n$ 形式相同。

(4)测速反馈不形成闭环零点，因此 $K_t=T_d$ 时，测速反馈与比例-微分控制对系统动态性能的改善程度是不相同的。

(5)设计时，ξ_d 在 0.4～0.8 之间，可适当增加原系统的开环增益，以减小稳态误差。

典型例题解析

【例 15.3-9】 关于二阶系统的设计，正确的做法是：

A. 调整典型二阶系统的两个特征参数阻尼系数 ξ 和无阻尼自然频率 ω_n，就可以完成最佳设计

B. 比例-微分控制盒测速反馈控制是最有效的设计方法

C. 增大阻尼系数 ξ 和增大无阻尼自然频率 ω_n

D. 将阻尼系数 ξ 和无阻尼自然频率 ω_n 分别计算

解 在改善二阶系统性能的方法中，比例-微分控制和测速反馈控制是两种常用方法。选 B。

【例 15.3-10】 设系统的传递函数为$\frac{4}{6s^2+10s+8}$，则该系统的：

A. 增益 $K=\frac{2}{3}$，阻尼比 $\xi=\frac{5\sqrt{3}}{12}$，无阻尼自然频率 $\omega_n=\frac{2}{\sqrt{3}}$

B. 增益 $K=\frac{2}{3}$，阻尼比 $\xi=\frac{5}{3}$，无阻尼自然频率 $\omega_n=\frac{4}{3}$

C. 增益 $K=\frac{1}{2}$，阻尼比 $\xi=\frac{3}{4}$，无阻尼自然频率 $\omega_n=\frac{5}{4}$

D. 增益 $K=1$，阻尼比 $\xi=\frac{3}{2}$，无阻尼自然频率 $\omega_n=\frac{5}{2}$

解 $\frac{4}{6s^2+10s+8}=\frac{\frac{2}{3}}{s^2+\frac{5}{3}s+\frac{4}{3}}$，故增益为 $K=\frac{2}{3}$，与标准二阶系统特征方程相比 $s^2+\frac{5}{3}s+\frac{4}{3}=s^2+2\xi\omega_n s+\omega_n^2$，得 $\omega_n=\frac{2}{\sqrt{3}}$，$\xi=\frac{5\sqrt{3}}{12}$。选 B。

经典练习

15.3-1 二阶系统的开环极点分别是 $s_1=-0.5$，$s_2=-4$，系统开环增益为 5，则其开环传递函数为(　　)。

A. $\frac{5}{(s-0.5)(s-4)}$　　B. $\frac{2}{(s+0.5)(s+4)}$

C. $\frac{5}{(s+0.5)(s+4)}$　　D. $\frac{10}{(s+0.5)(s+4)}$

15.3-2 惯性环节的微分方程为(　　)，传递函数为(　　)。

A. $T\frac{dy(t)}{dt}+y(t)=r(t)$　　B. $T\frac{d^2y(t)}{dt^2}+\frac{dy(t)}{dt}+y(t)=r(t)$

C. $\frac{1}{Ts+1}$　　D. $\frac{1}{T_s^2+s+1}$

15.3-3 实现比例积分(PI)调节器采用反馈环节的传递函数为(　　)。

A. $\frac{\frac{T_1}{K_C}s}{1+T_1s}$　　B. $\frac{s}{1+T_1s}$　　C. $\frac{1}{1+T_1s}$　　D. $\frac{\frac{T_1}{K_C}s}{T_1s}$

15.3-4 一阶系统的传递函数为 $G(s)=\frac{K}{1+Ts}$，则该系统时间相应的快速性(　　)。

A. 与 K 有关　　B. 与 K 和 T 有关

C. 与 T 有关　　D. 与输入信号大小有关

15.3-5 某二阶系统阻尼比为 2，则系统阶跃响应(　　)。

A. 单调增加　　B. 单调衰减　　C. 振荡衰减　　D. 等幅振荡

15.3-6 $G(s)=\frac{10}{s^2+3.6s+9}$，其阻尼比为(　　)。

A. 0.1　　B. 0.5　　C. 0.6　　D. 0.7

15.4 控制系统的稳定性与对象的调节性能

考试大纲☞：稳定性的基本概念　稳定性与特征方程根的关系　代数稳定判据　对象的调节性能指标

必备基础知识

15.4.1 稳定性基本概念

控制系统在实际运行过程中，总会受到外界和内部一些因素的干扰，例如，负载和能源的波动、系统参数的变化、环境条件的改变等。这些因素总是存在的，如果系统设计时不考虑这些因素，设计出来的系统不稳定，那这样的系统是不成功的，需要重新设计，或调整某些参数或结构。

系统的稳定性表现为系统时域响应的收敛性，是系统在扰动撤消后自身的一种恢复能力，是系统的固有特性。

15.4.2 稳定性与特征方程根的关系

系统的特征根全部具有负实部时，系统具有稳定性；当特征根中有一个或一个以上正实部根时，系统不稳定；若特征根中具有一个或一个以上零实部根，而其他的特征根均具有负实部时，系统处于稳定和不稳定的临界状态，为临界稳定。

典型例题解析

【例 15.4-1】 系统的稳定性与其传递函数的特征方程根的关系为：

A. 各特征根实部均为负时，系统具有稳定性

B. 各特征根至少有一个存在正实部时，系统具有稳定性

C. 各特征根至少有一个存在零实部时，系统具有稳定性

D. 各特征根全部具有正实部时，系统具有稳定性

解 选 B。

15.4.3 代数稳定判据

1）劳斯稳定判据

令系统的闭环特征方程为

$$a_0 s^n + a_1 s^{n-1} + a_2 s^{n-2} + \cdots + a_{n-1} s + a_n = 0 \qquad (a_0 > 0) \tag{15.4-1}$$

将各项系数按下面的格式排成劳斯表：

$$\begin{array}{llllll}
s^n & a_0 & a_2 & a_4 & a_6 & \cdots \\
s^{n-1} & a_1 & a_3 & a_5 & a_7 & \cdots \\
s^{n-2} & b_1 & b_2 & b_3 & a_4 & \cdots \\
s^{n-3} & c_1 & c_2 & c_3 & \cdots & \\
\vdots & & & & & \\
s^2 & d_1 & d_2 & d_3 & & \\
s^1 & e_1 & e_2 & & & \\
s^0 & f_1 & & & &
\end{array}$$

表中：

$$b_1=\frac{a_1a_2-a_0a_3}{a_1},b_2=\frac{a_1a_4-a_0a_5}{a_1},b_3=\frac{a_1a_6-a_0a_7}{a_1}\cdots$$

$$c_1=\frac{b_1a_3-a_1b_2}{b_1},c_2=\frac{b_1a_5-a_1b_3}{b_1},c_3=\frac{b_1a_7-a_1b_4}{b_1}\cdots$$

$$\vdots$$

$$f_1=\frac{e_1d_2-d_1e_2}{e_1}$$

这样可求得 $n+1$ 行系数。

劳斯稳定判据是根据所列劳斯表第一列系数符号的变化，去判别特征方程式根在 s 平面上的具体分布，过程如下：

(1)如果劳斯表中第一列的系数均为正值，则其特征方程式的根都在 s 的左半平面，相应的系统是稳定的。

(2)如果劳斯表中第一列系数的符号有变化，其变化的次数等于该特征方程式的根在 s 右半平面上的个数，相应的系统为不稳定。

2)赫尔维茨(Hurwitz)判据

设线性系统的特征方程为

$$D(s)=a_ns^n+a_{n-1}s^{n-1}+\cdots+a_1s+a_0(a_n>0)$$

线性系统稳定的充分必要条件是：由系统特征方程系数所构成的主行列式 Δ_n 及其各阶顺序主子式 $\Delta_i(i=1,2\cdots,n-1)$全部为正。其中

$$\Delta_n=\begin{vmatrix} a_{n-1} & a_{n-3} & a_{n-5} & \cdots & 0 \\ a_n & a_{n-2} & a_{n-4} & \cdots & 0 \\ 0 & a_{n-1} & a_{n-3} & \cdots & \cdots \\ 0 & a_n & a_{n-2} & \cdots & \cdots \\ 0 & 0 & a_{n-1} & \cdots & \cdots \end{vmatrix}$$

Hurwitz 判据一般用于四阶及以下系统，且只可计算奇数次或偶数次行列式。

3)稳定判据的应用

(1)判别系统的稳定性。

(2)分析系统参数变化对稳定性的影响。

(3)利用稳定判据，也可以判断系统的稳定裕度。

系统稳定时，要求所有闭环极点在 s 平面的左边，闭环极点离虚轴越远，系统稳定性越好，闭环极点离开虚轴的距离，可以作为衡量系统的稳定裕度。

在系统的特征方程 $D(s)=0$ 中，令 $s=s_1$-a，得到 $D(s_1)=0$，利用稳定判据，若 $D(s_1)=0$ 的所有解都在 s_1 平面左边，则原系统的特征根在 $s=-a$ 左边。

典型例题解析

【例 15.4-2】 某闭环系统的总传递函数为 $G(s)=\frac{1}{2s^3+3s^2+s+K}$，根据劳斯稳定判据判断下列论述哪个是对的：

A. 不论 K 为何值，系统不稳定　　B. 当 $K=0$ 时，系统稳定

C. 当 $K=1$ 时，系统稳定　　D. 当 $K=2$ 时，系统稳定

解　$K<3/2$ 时，系统稳定，可取 $K=1$。选 C。

【例 15.4-3】 某闭环系统的总传递函数为 $G(s)=\dfrac{K}{2s^3+3s^2+K}$，根据劳斯稳定判据：

A. 不论 K 为何值，系统不稳定

B. 不论 K 为何值，系统均为稳定

C. $K>0$ 时，系统稳定

D. $K<0$ 时，系统稳定

解 选 A。

【例 15.4-4】 下列方程式系统的特征方程，系统不稳定的是：

A. $3s^2+4s+5=0$　　B. $3s^3+2s^2+s+0.5=0$

C. $9s^3+6s^2+1=0$　　D. $2s^2+s+|a_3|=0(a_3\neq 0)$

解 由劳斯判据判定 $a_0s^3+a_1s^2+a_2=0$ 稳定的条件为 a_0、a_1、a_3 均大于 0，故选项 A、D 均稳定。由劳斯判据判定 $a_0s^3+a_1s^2+a_2s+a_3=0$ 稳定的条件为 a_0、a_1、a_2、a_3 均大于 0，且 $a_1a_2>a_0a_3$，选项 B 经验证符合上述条件而选项 C 不符合，故选项 C 不稳定。

15.4.4 对象的调节性能指标

(1)衰减比 n：衰减比是衡量过渡过程稳定性的动态指标，第一个波的振幅与同方向第二个波的振幅之比。如图 15.4-1 所示，$n=\dfrac{B_1}{B_2}$，用 n 可以判断振荡是否衰减及衰减程度。

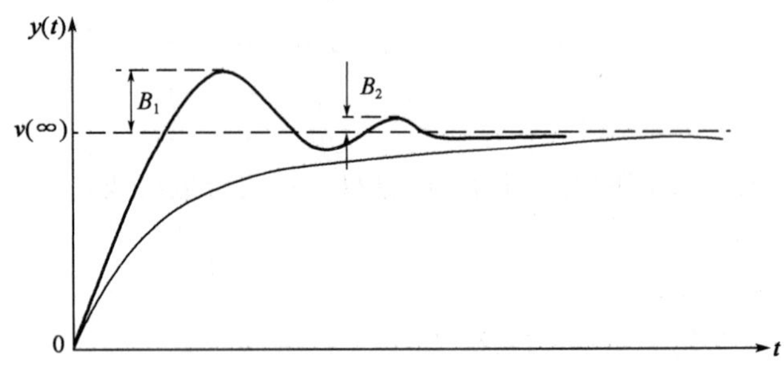

图 15.4-1　调节性能指标示意图

$n>1$：衰减振荡。n 越大，则控制系统的稳定度也越高，当 n 趋于无穷大时，控制系统的过渡过程接近于非振荡过程。

$n=1$：等幅振荡。

$n<1$：发散振荡。n 越小，意味着控制系统的振荡过程越剧烈，稳定度也越低。

(2)静差 C：过渡过程终了时，被调参数稳定在给定值附近，稳定值与给定值之差为静差。$|C|=0$ 时，为无静差；$|C|=0$ 时，为有静差。

(3)超调量(动差) M：过渡过程中，被调参数相对于给定值的最大波动量。

(4)最大偏差 $A=M+C$：被调参数相对于给定值的最大偏差。若 A 过大，且偏离时间过长，系统离开指定的工艺状态越远，调节品质越差。

(5)振荡周期 T_v 和振荡频率 f：相邻两个波峰所经历的时间为振荡周期，其倒数为振荡频率。

(6)调节过程时间 t_s：调节系统受干扰后，从被调参数开始波动至达到新稳定状态所经历

的时间间隔。t_s 越小越好，一般希望 $t_s=3T_P$。

以上指标反映了系统的稳定性、准确性和快速性，稳定性是首要的。

典型例题解析

【例 15.4-5】 在如下指标中，哪个不能用来评价控制系统的时域性能？

A. 最大超调量　　B. 带宽　　C. 稳态位置误差　　D. 调整时间

解 除了选项 B 带宽，其他三个选项都可以评价控制系统的时域性能。选 B。

经典练习

15.4-1　某闭环系统的总传递函数 $G(s)=\dfrac{K}{2s^3}+3s^2+K$，根据劳斯稳定判断(　　)。

A. 不论 K 为何值，系统不稳定　　B. 不论 K 为何值，系统稳定

C. $K>0$ 系统稳定　　D. $K<0$ 系统稳定

15.4-2　系统的稳定性取决于(　　)。

A. 系统的干扰　　B. 系统的干扰点位置

C. 系统闭环极点的分布　　D. 系统的输入

15.4-3　二阶系统的特征方程为 $a_0s^2+a_1s+a_2=0$，系统稳定的充要条件是各项系数的符号必须(　　)。

A. 相同　　B. 不同　　C. 等于零

15.5　掌握控制系统的误差分析

考试大纲☞：误差及稳态误差　系统类型及误差度　静态(稳态)误差系数

必备基础知识

15.5.1 误差及稳态误差

$$E(s)=R(s)-H(s)C(s) \tag{15.5-1}$$

上式在实际系统中是可以量测的。

$$E(s)=C_s(s)-C(s) \tag{15.5-2}$$

输出的希望值(真值很难得到)↑　　↑输出的实际值

如果 $H(s)=1$，输出量的希望值，即为输入量 $R(s)$。

由图 15.5-1 可得误差传递函数

$$\Phi_e(s)\overset{\text{def}}{=}\frac{E(s)}{R(s)}=\frac{1}{1+H(s)G(s)} \tag{15.5-3}$$

$$E(s)=\Phi_e(s)R(s)=\frac{R(s)}{1+H(s)G(s)} \tag{15.4-4}$$

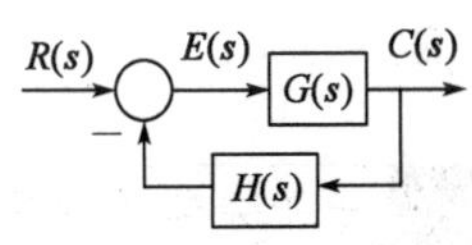

图 15.5-1　控制系统框图

$$e(t)=L^{-1}[\Phi_e(s)R(s)] \tag{15.5-5}$$

插入二阶系统 $\omega_n = 2\xi = 0.4\Phi(s) = \dfrac{4}{s^2 + 1.6s + 4}$ 分别在斜坡输入和阶跃输入作用下的响应的误差曲线，说明不同的输入对同一个系统所产生的误差是不同的。

终值定理，求稳态误差。

$$e_{ss}(\infty) = e_{ss} = \lim_{s\to 0} sE(s) = \lim_{s\to 0} \frac{sR(s)}{1 + H(s)G(s)} \tag{15.5-6}$$

公式条件：$sE(s)$ 的极点均位于 s 左半平面（包括坐标原点）。

式(15.5-5)表明，系统的稳态误差，不仅与开环传递函数 $G(s)H(s)$ 的结构有关，还与输入 $R(s)$ 形式密切相关。

式(15.5-6)对于一个给定的稳定系统，当输入信号形式一定时，系统是否存在稳态误差就取决于开环传递函数所描述的系统结构。因此，按照控制系统跟踪不同输入信号的能力来进行系统分类是必要的。

典型例题解析

【例 15.5-1】 关于单位反馈控制系统中的稳态误差，下列表示不正确的是：

A. 稳态误差是系统调节过程中其输出信号与输入信号之间的误差

B. 稳态误差在实际中可以测量，具有一定物理意义

C. 稳态误差由系统开环传递函数和输入信号决定

D. 系统的结构和参数不同，输入信号的形式和大小差异，都会引起稳态误差的变化

解 当系统从一个稳态过渡到新的稳态，或系统受扰动作用又重新平衡后，系统可能会出现偏差，这种偏差称为稳态误差，而不是输出信号与输入信号之间的误差。选 A。

【例 15.5-2】 由环节 $G(s) = \dfrac{K}{s(s^2 + 4s + 200)}$ 组成的单位反馈系统（即负反馈传递函数为 1 的闭环系统）单位斜坡输入的稳态速度误差系数为：

A. $K/200$　　B. $1/K$　　C. K　　D. 0

解 选 A。

【例 15.5-3】 $G(s) = \dfrac{2}{s(6s + 1)(3s - 2)}$ 的单位负反馈系统的单位斜坡输入的稳态误差应为：

A. 1　　B. 0.25　　C. 0　　D. 2

解 代入稳态误差的公式，求极限。选 A。

【例 15.5-4】 设单位反馈（即负反馈传递函数为 1 的闭环系统）的开环传递函数为 $G(s) = \dfrac{10}{s(0.1s + 1)(2s + 1)}$，在参考输入为 $r(t) = 2t$ 时系统的稳态误差为：

A. 10　　B. 0.1　　C. 0.2　　D. 2

解 选 C。

15.5.2 系统类型及误差度

1）系统类型

令系统开环传递函数为

$$G(s)H(s)=\frac{K\prod_{i=1}^{m}(\tau_i s+1)}{s^v\prod_{j=1}^{n-v}(T_j s+1)} \quad (n\geqslant m) \tag{15.5-7}$$

式中：K ——系统的开环增益；

v——系统的积分环节个数。

对于 $v=0$、1、2 的系统，分别称之为 0 型、Ⅰ型、Ⅱ型系统。由于Ⅱ型以上的系统实际上很难稳定，在控制系统中一般不会遇到。

2)误差度

被控量稳态值的附近$\pm5\%c(\infty)$[或$\pm2\%c(\infty)$]称之为系统的误差度(带)。

典型例题解析

【例 15.5-5】 若单位负反馈系统的开环传递函数 $G(s)=\frac{10(1+5s)}{s(s+5)(2s+1)}$，则该系统为：

A. 0 型系统　　B. Ⅰ型系统　　C. Ⅱ型系统　　D. 高阶型系统

解 系统的类型由开环传递函数中的积分环节的个数决定，对于 $v=0,1,2$ 的系统，分别称之为 0 型、Ⅰ型、Ⅱ型系统，因此选 B。

15.5.3 静态(稳态)误差系数

1)静态位置误差系数

$$K_p=\lim_{s\to0}G(s)H(s)$$

2)静态速度误差系数

$$K_v=\lim_{s\to0}s\,G(s)H(s)$$

3)静态加速度误差系数

$$K_a=\lim_{s\to0}s^2G(s)H(s)$$

表 15.5-1 列出了不同类型的系统在不同参考输入下的稳态误差。

误差系数和稳态误差　　表 15.5-1a)

类型＼误差系数	静态位置误差系数 K_p	速度 K_v	加速度 K_a
0 型	K	0	0
Ⅰ型	∞	K	0
Ⅱ型	∞	∞	K

误差系数和稳态误差　　表 15.5-1b)

类型＼输入	$r(t)=R_0$	$r(t)=v_0t$	$r(t)=\frac{1}{2}a_0t^2$
0 型	$\frac{R_0}{1+K}$	∞	∞
Ⅰ型	0	$\frac{v_0}{K}$	∞
Ⅱ型	0	0	$\frac{a_0}{K}$

静态误差系数↑→系统稳态误差↓(与 K、开环传递函数有关)。

典型例题解析

【例 15.5-6】 对于单位阶跃输入,下列表述不正确的是:

A. 只有0型系统具有稳态误差,其大小与系统的开环增益成反比

B. 只有0型系统具有稳态误差,其大小与系统的开环增益成正比

C. Ⅰ型系统位置误差系数为无穷大时,稳态误差为0

D. Ⅱ型及以上系统与Ⅰ型系统一样

解 由以上表格可看出0型系统具有稳态误差,其大小与系统的开环增益成反比。选A。

【例 15.5-7】 某闭环系统的开环传递函数为 $G(s)=\dfrac{5(1+2s)}{s^2(s^2+3s+5)}$,其加速度误差系数为:

A. 1　　B. 5　　C. 0　　D. ∞

解 由静态加速度误差系数公式可得 $K=1$。选A。

【例 15.5-8】 单位负反馈系统的开环传递函数为 $G(s)=\dfrac{20}{s^2(s+4)}$,当参考输入为 $u(t)=4+6t+3t^2$ 时,稳态加速度误差系数为:

A. $K_a=0$　　B. $K_a=\infty$

C. $K_a=5$　　D. $K_a=20$

解 设系统开环传递函数为 $G_k(s)=G(s)H(s)$,则稳态加速度误差系数为 $K_a=\lim\limits_{s\to0}s^2G(s)H(s)$,故本题中 $K_a=\lim\limits_{s\to0}s^2\dfrac{20}{s^2(s+4)}=5$。选C。

经典练习

15.5-1 系统的开环传递函数为:$G(s)H(s)=\dfrac{K(T_1s+1)}{s^2(\tau_1s+1)(\tau_2s+1)}$,则该系统为(　　)。

A. 0　　B. Ⅰ　　C. Ⅱ

15.5-2 系统的开环传递函数为:$G(s)=\dfrac{s(1+2s)}{s_2(s_2+3s+5)}$,系统的加速误差系数为(　　)。

A. 5　　B. 1　　C. 0　　D. 2

15.6 控制系统的综合和校正

考试大纲☞:校正的概念　串联校正装置的形式及特性　继电器调节系统(非线性系统)及校正

必备基础知识

15.6.1 校正的概念

1)校正

在系统中加入一些其参数可以根据需要而改变的机构或装置,使系统整个特性发生变化,

从而满足给定的各项性能指标。

2)校正装置

加入一些其参数可以根据需要而改变的机构或装置,这种附加装置为校正装置,也称为补偿器。

3)性能指标

(1)时域指标:包括稳态指标和动态指标。

稳态指标是衡量系统稳态精度的指标。控制系统稳态精度的表征——稳态误差 $e_{\theta s}$,一般用以下一种误差系数来表示:稳态位置误差系数 K_P,表示系统跟踪单位阶跃输入时系统稳态误差的大小;稳态速度误差系数 K_v,表示系统跟踪单位速度输入时系统稳态误差的大小;稳态加速度误差系数 K_s,表示系统跟踪单位加速度输入时系统稳态误差的大小。

动态指标通常为上升时间、峰值时间、调节时间、超调量等。

(2)频域指标:频域动态指标分开环频域指标和闭环频域指标两种。

开环频域指标指相位裕量和剪切(截止)频率 ω_c 等。闭环频域指标指谐振峰值 M_r、谐振频率 ω_r 和频带宽度等。

典型例题解析

【例 15.6-1】 系统的时域性指标包括稳态性能指标和动态性能指标,下列说法正确的是:

A. 稳态性能指标为稳态误差,动态性能指标有相位裕度、幅值裕度

B. 稳态性能指标为稳态误差,动态性能指标有上升时间、峰值时间、调节时间和超调量

C. 稳态性能指标为平稳性,动态性能指标为快速性

D. 稳态性能指标为位置误差系数,动态性能指标有速度误差系数、加速误差系数

解 稳态指标是衡量系统稳态精度的指标。动态指标通常为上升时间、峰值时间、调节时间、超调量等。选 B。

15.6.2 串联校正装置的形式及特性

1)超前校正装置

一般而言,当控制系统的开环增益增大到满足其静态性能所要求的数值时,系统有可能不稳定,或者即使能稳定,其动态性能一般也不会理想。在这种情况下,需在系统的前向通路中增加超前校正装置,以实现在开环增益不变的前提下,系统的动态性能亦能满足设计的要求。

图 15.6-1a)为常用的无源超前网络。假设该网络信号源的阻抗很小,可以忽略不计,而输出负载的阻抗为无穷大,则其传递函数为

$$\frac{U_c(s)}{U_r(s)} = G_c(s) = \frac{R_2}{R_2 + \dfrac{1}{\dfrac{1}{R_1} + sC}} = \frac{R_2}{R_2 + \dfrac{R_1}{1 + sR_1C}} = \frac{R_2(1 + R_1Cs)}{R_2 + R_1 + R_1R_2Cs}$$

$$\frac{R_2(1 + R_1Cs)/(R_1 + R_2)}{(R_1 + R_2 + R_1R_2Cs)/(R_1 + R_2)} T = \frac{R_1R_2C}{R_1 + R_2}$$

时间常数 $a=\dfrac{R_1+R_2}{R_1}$，分度系数 $aT=R_1C$

$$G_c(s)=\frac{1}{a}\times\frac{1+aTs}{1+Ts} \tag{15.6-1}$$

超前网络的零极点分布如图 15.6-1b)所示。由于 $a>1$ 故超前网络的负实零点总是位于负实极点之右，两者之间的距离由常数 a 决定。可知改变 a 和 T（即电路的参数 R_1，R_2，C）的数值，超前网络的零极点可在 s 平面的负实轴任意移动。

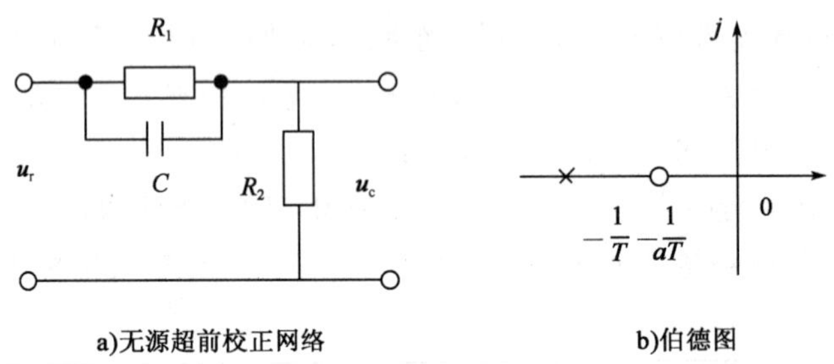

图 15.6-1　无源超前网络

对应式(15.6-1)得

$$20\lg|aG_c(s)|=20\lg\sqrt{1+(aT\omega)^2}-20\lg\sqrt{1+(T\omega)^2} \tag{15.6-2}$$

$$\varphi_c(\omega)=\operatorname{arccot}aT\omega-\operatorname{arccot}T\omega \tag{15.6-3}$$

画出对数频率特性如图 15.6-2 所示。显然，超前网络对频率在$\dfrac{1}{aT}$至$\dfrac{1}{T}$之间的输入信号有明显的微分作用，在该频率范围内输出信号相角比输入信号相角超前，超前网络的名称由此而得。$a=10$，$T=1$。

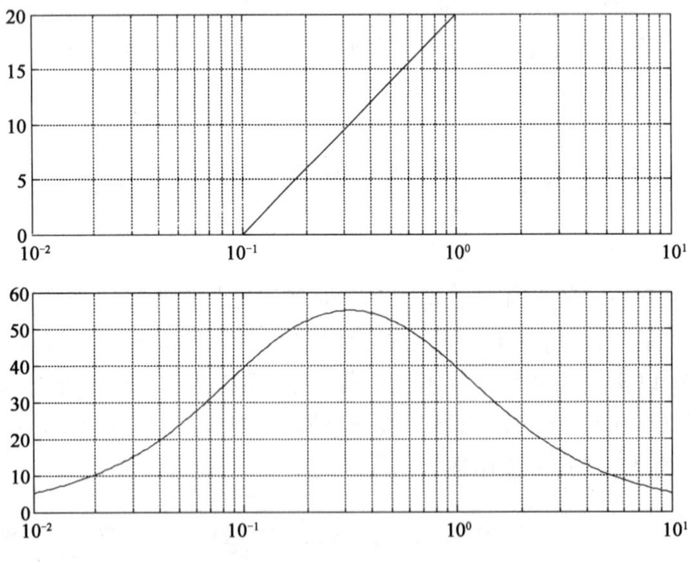

图 15.6-2　频率特性

由(15.6-3)知　　$\varphi_c(\omega)=\operatorname{arccot}T\omega-\operatorname{arccot}T\omega=\operatorname{arccot}\dfrac{(a-1)T\omega}{1+a(T\omega)^2}$　　(15.6-4)

将上式求导并令其为零，得最大超前角频率

$$\omega_m = \frac{1}{T\sqrt{a}} \tag{15.6-5}$$

将式(15.6-5) 代入式(15.6-4),得最大超前角

$$\varphi_m = \text{arccot}\,\frac{a-1}{2\sqrt{a}} = \arcsin\frac{a-1}{a+1} \tag{15.6-6}$$

$$a = \frac{1+\sin\varphi_m}{1-\sin\varphi_m}$$

故在最大超前角频率 ω_m 处,具有最大超前角 φ_m,φ_m 正好处于频率$\frac{1}{aT}$与$\frac{1}{T}$的几何中心。

因为 $\frac{1}{aT}$ 与$\frac{1}{T}$的几何中心为

$$\frac{1}{2}\left(\lg\frac{1}{aT}+\lg\frac{1}{T}\right)=\frac{1}{2}\lg\frac{1}{aT^2}=\frac{1}{2}\lg\omega_m^2=\lg\omega_m \tag{15.6-7}$$

即几何中心为 ω_m 。

$$L_c(\omega_m) = 20\lg\sqrt{1+(aT\omega_m)^2} - 20\lg\sqrt{1+(T\omega_m)^2} = 20\lg\sqrt{\frac{1+(aT\omega_m)^2}{1+(T\omega_m)^2}},\ T^2\omega_m^2 = \frac{1}{a}$$

$$L_c(\omega_m) = 20\lg\sqrt{a} = 10\lg a \tag{15.6-8}$$

由式(15.6-6) 和式(15.6-8)可画出最大超前相角 φ_m 与分度系数 a 及 $10\lg a$ 与 a 的关系曲线。$a\uparrow \rightarrow \varphi_m\uparrow$。但 a 不能取得太大(为了保证较高的信噪比),a 一般不超过 20,常选 0.1。由图可知,这种超前校正网络的最大相位超前角一般不大于 65°。如果需要大于 65°的相位超前角,则要在两个超前网络相串联来实现,并在所串联的两个网络之间加一隔离放大器,以消除它们之间的负载效应。

2)滞后校正装置

滞后网络如图 15.6-3 所示。

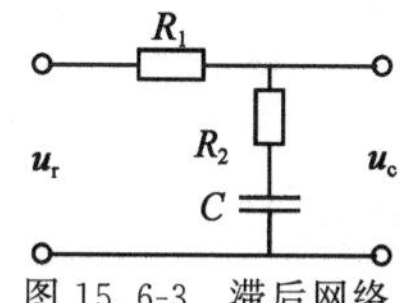

图 15.6-3　滞后网络

条件:如果信号源的内部阻抗为零,负载阻抗为无穷大,则滞后网络的传递函数为

$$\frac{U_c(s)}{U_r(s)} = G_c(s) = \frac{R_2+\frac{1}{sC}}{R_1+R_2+\frac{1}{sC}} = \frac{R_2Cs+1}{(R_1+R_2)Cs+1} = \frac{\frac{R_1+R_2}{R_1+R_2}R_2Cs+1}{(R_1+R_2)Cs+1}$$

$T=(R_1+R_2)C$,时间常数 $b=\frac{R_2}{R_1+R_2}<1$,分度系数 $aT=R_1C$

$$G_c(s) = \frac{1+bTs}{1+Ts} \tag{15.6-9}$$

同超前网络,最大滞后角发生在 $\frac{1}{T}$ 与$\frac{1}{bT}$几何中心,称为最大滞后角频率,计算公式为

$$\omega_m = \frac{1}{T\sqrt{b}} \tag{15.6-10}$$

$$\varphi_m = \arcsin\frac{1-b}{1+b} \tag{15.6-11}$$

为不使滞后相角影响 γ,一般取

$$\frac{1}{T}=\frac{\omega_c}{10}\sim\frac{\omega_c}{4}$$

3)滞后-超前校正装置

传递函数为

$$G_c(s)=\frac{U_c(s)}{U_r(s)}=\frac{R_2+\frac{1}{sC_2}}{\frac{1}{\frac{1}{R_1}+sC_1}+R_2+\frac{1}{sC_2}}$$

$$=\frac{(R_1C_1s+1)(R_2C_2s+1)}{R_1C_1R_2C_2s^2+(R_1C_1+R_2C_2+R_1C_2)s^2+1}=\frac{(T_as+1)(T_bs+1)}{(T_1s+1)(T_2s+1)} \quad (15.6\text{-}12)$$

令 $T_a=R_1C_1T_b=R_2C_2$，设 $T_1>T_a$，$\left(\frac{T_a}{T_1}=\frac{T_2}{T_b}=\frac{1}{a}\right)a>1$，则有 $T_1=aT_a$，$T_2=\frac{T_b}{a}$

$aT_a+\frac{T_b}{a}=T_a+T_b+R_1C_2$，$a$ 是该方程的解

式(15.6-12)表示为

$$G_c(s)=\frac{(T_as+1)(T_bs+1)}{(aT_as+1)\left(\frac{T_b}{a}s+1\right)} \quad (15.6\text{-}13)$$

同时具有滞后环节和超前环节的特点。

典型例题解析

【例 15.6-2】 关于超前校正装置，下列不正确的描述是：

A. 超前校正装置利用装置的相位超前特性来增加系统的相角稳定裕度

B. 超前校正装置利用校正装置频率特性曲线来增加系统的穿越频率

C. 超前校正装置利用相角超前，幅值增加的特性，使系统的截止频率变窄，相角裕度较小，从而有效改善系统的动态性能

D. 在满足系统稳定性条件的情况下，采用串联超前校正可使系统响应快，超调小

解 参考超前校正装置的定义及特性。选 C。

【例 15.6-3】 某闭环系统的总传递函数为 $G(s)=8/(s^2+Ks+9)$，为使其阶跃响应无超调，K 值为：

A. 3.5　　B. 4.5　　C. 5.5　　D. 6.5

解 阶跃响应无超调，则系统为过阻尼或临界阻尼状态，$2\xi\omega_n=K$，$\xi=\frac{K}{6}\geqslant 1$，$K\geqslant 6$。选 D。

【例 15.6-4】 一个二阶环节采用局部反馈进行系统校正：

A. 能增大频率响应的带宽　　B. 能增加瞬态响应的阻尼比

C. 能提高系统的稳态精度　　D. 能增加系统的无阻尼自然频率

解 局部反馈校正能增加瞬态响应的阻尼比。选 D。

【例 15.6-5】 对增加控制系统的带宽和增加增益，减小稳态误差宜采用：

A. 相位超前的串联校正　　B. 相位滞后的串联校正

C. 局部速度反馈校正　　D. 滞后-超前校正

解　选 D。

【例 15.6-6】 某控制系统的稳态精度已充分满足要求，欲增大频率响应的带宽，应采用：

A. 相位超前的串联校正　　B. 相位滞后的串联校正

C. 局部速度反馈校正　　D. 前馈校正

解　选 A。

15.6.3 继电器调节系统(非线性系统)及校正

只要系统中包含一个或一个以上具有非线性特性的元件，就称其为非线性系统。所以，严格地说，实际的控制系统都是非线性系统。所谓线性系统仅仅是实际系统忽略了非线性因素后的理想模型。

从非线性环节的输入与输出之间存在的函数关系划分，非线性特性可分为单值函数与多值函数两类。例如死区特性、饱和特性及理想继电特性属于输入与输出间为单值函数关系的非线性特性。间隙特性和一般继电特性则属于输入与输出之间为多值函数关系的非线性特性。

1)继电系统的自振荡

含有继电型非线性元件的系统称为继电型系统。继电型非线性的一般形式如图 15.6-4a)所示，称为具有滞环的三位置继电特性；若 $m=1$，即为具有死区的三位置继电特性，如图 15.6-4b)所示；若 $m=-1$，即为具有滞环的两位置继电特性，如图 15.6-4c)所示；若 $h=0$，即为理想继电特性，如图 15.6-4d)所示。

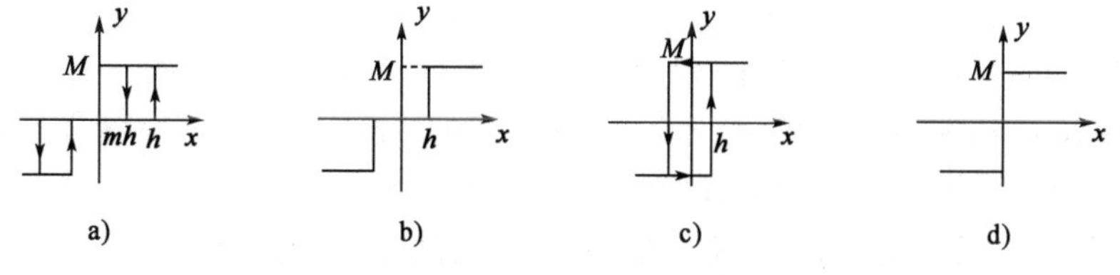

图 15.6-4　继电元件特性

下面具体分析当图中的继电特性分别为四种情况时，系统自由运动的相平面图及其运动特点，在绘制相平面图时，均取 c 和 $\dot{C}$ 为相坐标。

继电调节系统的方框图如图 15.6-5 所示。继电系统中，除了继电元件以外的各个线性元件的总和为继电调节系统的线性部分。线性部分可用传递函数表示其特性。

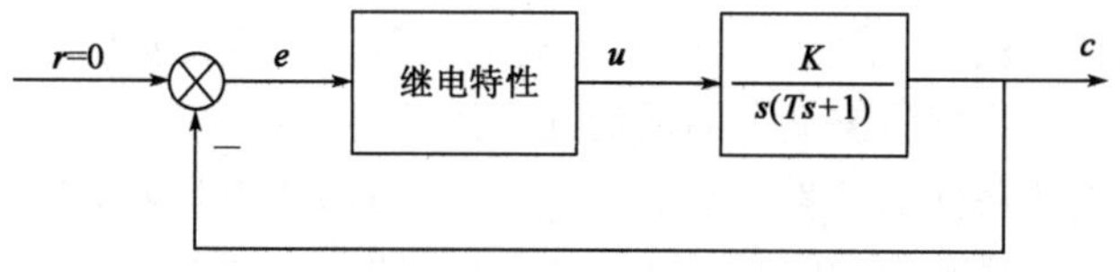

图 15.6-5　继电调节系统的方框图

继电系统处于自振荡时，系统线性部分输入端，有一个周期为 $2T$ 的矩形波作用在它上面。继电系统输入量不变的情况下，将呈现自振荡，如果已知振荡周期为 $2T$，那么输出量可按系统线性部分在稳态时对一连串符号交变的、幅值为 M 的矩形脉冲的响应来决定。

2）位式恒速调节系统

位式调节分为双位调节和三位调节两种。气压超压或低于给定值，就表示锅炉的蒸气生产量与负荷蒸气量不平衡。此时需改变燃料量，以改变锅炉的燃烧发热量，从而改变锅炉蒸气量，恢复蒸气于管压力为额定值。使用双位调节时，压力调节器在气压偏离额定值时，能切除或投入送、引风机和加煤机，降低其出力到某一中间值（如采用双速电动机，改变转速）。

在一般精度的空调上，若加热器为热水或蒸气加热时，宜采用恒速调节系统。此系统也可应用在控制二次风门的系统中（如诱导器的二次风门等），它是在位式基础上发展而来的，与位式调节的区别在于它的执行兼调节机构是采用了电动三通阀、电动两通阀及电动风门等。由于这种调节是在位式基础上发展起来的，而开大阀门或关小阀门时的速度又是恒定的，所以，比较确切地讲，恒速调节应称为位式恒速凋节。

恒速调节比位式调节效果好。加热或减热的过程是逐步、连续变化的。如配合得好，调节过程不会产生如双位调节那样的等幅振荡。产生的是衰减振荡或非周期的过程。

因为恒速调节不像双位调节那样调节过猛，在加、减热量中是恒速变化的。所以当室温回到上、下限之间时，可能不会超出这个区间，而能稳定下来，这就是所谓非周期的调节过程，但也可能经过 2～3 个周期即稳定下来，这是衰减振荡，系统的静差是由上、下限间的区域来决定的。

对位式恒速调节系统，如果设计中系统各环节参数没有选好或使用中没有整定好，也可能产生自振荡，使被控参数如室温超出允许的波动范围，自振荡使机械传动部分连续磨损，缩短寿命。影响等速调节品质的因素有以下三点：

（1）与调节器上、下限之间的区域有关。上、下限之间的区域越宽，系统的静态误差越大；但室温不易超出这个区域，因而易于稳定。当上、下限间的区域较窄，静差减小；过窄时系统不易稳定。

（2）与执行机构全程时间有关。是指执行机构的位置从零移至全行程所需时间，即调节阀从全闭到全开的时间。执行机构的全行程时间越小，其调节的补偿速度就越大，抗干扰能力就越强，过渡过程的时间可缩短。但当补偿速度过快时，恒通调节系统可能产生像双位调节那样的不停地振荡，即电动阀一会全开，一会全关，形成振荡。这在恒速调节中是不允许的。

（3）对象的动态特性也是影响调节品质的重要因素。实践证明，当对象特征比、传送系数以及敏感元件时间常数大时，易使系统产生振荡。动态偏差也会增大。

3）带校正装置的双位调节系统

以室温的电动位式调节系统为例。

在工业空调中一般是控制电加热器，因为电加热器起动迅速、时间滞后小，适合用双位或三位调节器通过接触器控制。双位调节也可应用在一般的住宅采暖上，在空调上应用精度可达（±0.5～±1）℃之间。如果处理得好，比如电加热器容量设计的合理，对象特性较好，敏感元件精度选的合适，其调节精度也可＜±0.5℃。如对象的时间常数小或系统滞后时间大时采用双位调节，振荡的幅度较大，不能达到较好的调节品质。这些是双位调节的缺点。

当采用双位调节时，影响室温调节品质的几个因素如下：

（1）室温对象。空调房间的特性参数 τ、T、K 对调节品质有影响，因存在着对象的滞后时间，所以会使室温调节品质恶化，当 τ 增大时，调节振幅即动态偏差增大。只有在理想状态下、对象滞后等于零时，室温波动的振幅才等于调节器的不灵敏区，但这在实际上是不可能的。而

当 τ 增大时，调节周期可加大，这样就减少了振动次数，延长了使用寿命。

对象的时间常数 T 越大时，因室温上升速度小，所以振幅可减小，这对调节有利。且 T 大时可使调节周期加大，对减少磨损也有利。

当对象的传递系数大时，调节过程的功差和静差均增大，调节周期将缩短，振动次数会增加，寿命也会缩短。

(2)调节器不灵敏对调节品质的影响。调节器不灵敏区增加时动态偏差增大，这是不利的；但不灵敏区增加时，振动周期可加大，对减少磨损有利。

(3)加热器的容量和室内热干扰对室温的影响。在一般设计中，还有所谓调整用电加热器。此种加热器是手动控制的，是用来补偿由于季节不同而引起的建筑物热损失的波动的。为了提高调节精度，把这部分加热量不计算在控制用加热量中，是非常必要的。同时，间歇运行的空调系统，在每次启动初期为了尽快上升到所需温度，也有必要设置这部分加热器。

(4)敏感元件的时间常数及其安装位置对室温调节品质的影响。敏感元件存在着一定的热惯性，对调节品质也有直接的影响；同时敏感元件的安放位置也直接影响着调节品质。

敏感元件的时间常数越小，对调节品质越有利。由于敏感元件的热惯性，而不能及时地反映外界干扰所引起的室温变化，因此其热惯性将使调节系统的抗干扰性变坏，调节时间加长，动态偏差增加。因此，在选择敏感元件时，应按一般热惯性、微惯性等区别选用。

敏感元件的安放位置，对调节品质也有影响。一方面从调节原理出发，敏感元件的安装位置应放在恒温区，另一方面从减少敏感元件的时间常数来考虑，则应安装在气流速度较大地点，但两者往往不能兼备。

在实际过程中，敏感元件所放位置之一是在工作区中对恒温要求精度较高的工艺设备附近，在这种位置，敏感元件能够反映恒温区温度的波动，也就是反映室内热源的变化。但因恒温区空气流动速度很低，敏感元件热惯性大，对调节不利，因此应选用微惯性的敏感元件。当恒温区热源干扰较大和维护结构隔热性能不够良好(如无套间)时，则应采取这种安放位置。

为了克服双位调节固有的缺点，在实际工作中可以采用加校正装置的双位调节系统。反馈环节的参量 k_4 和 T_4 总是应该选能使自振荡的频率提高许多倍的，当线性部分输出量的振荡频率很高时，它的幅值就非常小了。自振荡的半周期 T'' 可以相当精确地求得。

$$T'' \approx T_4 \ln \frac{\frac{k_4}{2} + \varepsilon}{\frac{k_4}{2} - \varepsilon} = T_4 \ln \frac{1 + \xi_4}{1 - \xi_4}$$

其中：$\xi_4 = \dfrac{2\varepsilon}{k_4}$。

减小 ξ_4 与 T_4，均可使 T'' 减小，使自振荡频率提高，使室温波动范围减小。

4)带校正装置的位式恒速调节系统

为了使等速系统能稳定地工作，根据断续调节的理论，一般可在执行电动机电路中串接一个由通断仪来加以控制的接点，其作用是使执行机构调一调、停一停，等待室温的变化，拉长了执行机构全行程的时间，可防止振荡。在室温调节环节的动态特性较好情况下，加上有二次送风的镇定，因此只要室内热源变化不大时，采用恒速调节是可以得到较好的调节效果的。

当室温的波动范围要求限制在±0.1℃以内的精度时，或干扰强烈、被调对象特性不利于调节时，需要采用抗干扰性强、调节精度高的PID调节仪表组成自动调节系统。

所有PID调节系统中的PID参数，对调节质量都有很大影响，所以，应根据不同调节对象，整定好各自的参数。

典型例题解析

【例15.6-7】 对于非线性控制系统的描述函数分析，请判断下列表述中哪个是错的？

A. 是等效线性化的一种

B. 只提供稳定性能的信息

C. 不适宜于含有高阶次线性环节的系统

D. 适宜于非线性元件的输出中高次谐波已被充分衰减，主要为一次谐波分量的系统

解 非线性控制系统可以含有高阶次线性环节。选C。

【例15.6-8】 如图所示，由构件的饱和引起的控制系统的非线性静态特性为：

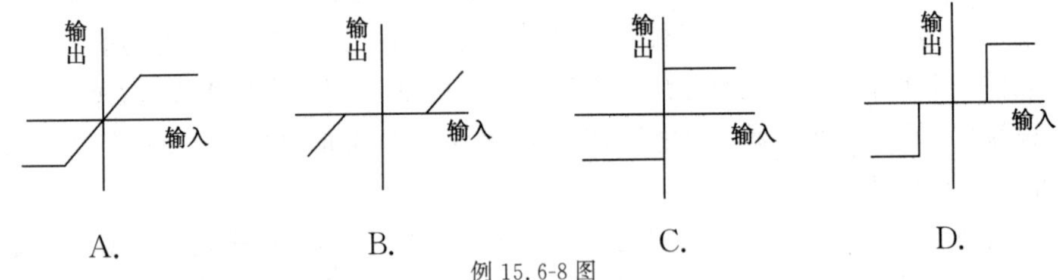

例15.6-8图

解 由上文分析，饱和性引起的非静态特征图为选项A。

【例15.6-9】 对于一个位置控制系统，下列对非线性现象的描述哪个是错的？

A. 死区

B. 和力成比例关系的固体间摩擦(库仑摩擦)

C. 和运动速度成比例的黏性摩擦

D. 和运动速度平方成比例的空气阻力

解 选D。

15.6.4 根轨迹

1)定义

根轨迹为当系统的某个参数(例如开环增益K)由零变到无穷时，闭环特征根在S平面上移动的根轨迹。

设控制系统如图15.6-6所示，绘制K:0→∞时闭环极点变化的轨迹，并分析系统性能。

$G(s)=\frac{K}{s(0.5s+1)}=\frac{2K}{s(s+2)}$，开环极点$p_1=0,p_2=-2$

$$\phi(s)=\frac{C(s)}{R(s)}=\frac{2K}{s^2+2s+2K}$$

$$\text{闭环特征方程}=s^2+2s+2K$$

$$s_1=-1+\sqrt{1-2K},s_2=-1-\sqrt{1-2K}$$

当 $K:0\rightarrow\infty$ 时

$K=0$	$s_1=0$	$s_2=-2$
$K=0.25$	$s_1=-0.29$	$s_2=-1.71$
$K=0.5$	$s_1=-1$	$s_2=-1$
$K=1$	$s_1=-1+j$	$s_2=-1-j$
$K=\infty$	$s_1=-1+j\infty$	$s_2=-1-j\infty$

绘制出闭环特征根的变化轨迹如图 15.6-7 所示。

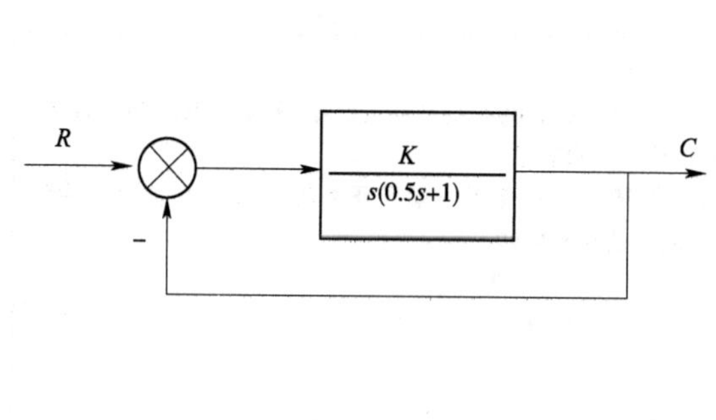

图 15.6-6 控制系统图

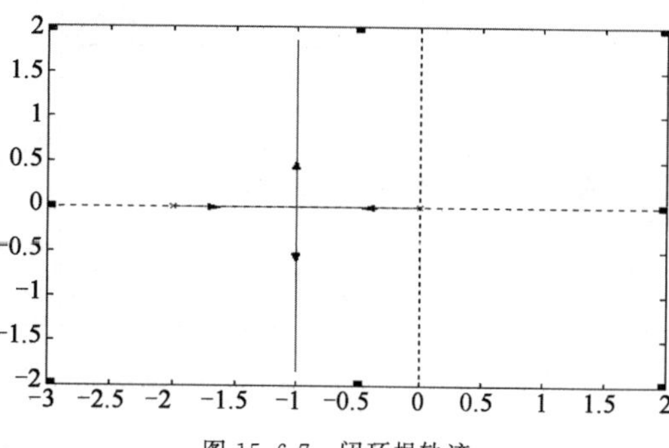

图 15.6-7 闭环根轨迹

性能分析：

(1)稳定性

$K:0\rightarrow\infty$，根轨迹全部分布在 s 左半平面，系统稳定。

(2)动态性能

$0<K<0.5$，特征根为两个不相等的实根，过阻尼状态；

$K=0.5$，特征根为两个相等的负实根，临界阻尼状态；

$K>0.5$，特征根为一对共轭复根，欠阻尼状态；

(3)稳态性能

有一个开环极点在原点，系统为 I 型。阶跃输入下，$e_{ss}=0$；斜坡输入下，$e_{ss}=$常数，静态速度误差系数 $K_v=K$。

2)根轨迹方程

$$G(s)H(s)=\frac{K^*\Pi_{i=1}^{m}(s-z_i)}{\Pi_{j=1}^{n}(s-p_j)} \tag{15.6-14}$$

式中：K^*——根轨迹增益；

z_i——开环零点，用"○"表示；

p_j——开环极点，用"×"表示。

当系统闭环特征方程为 $1+G(s)H(s)=0$ 时，根轨迹方程为：

$$\frac{K^*\Pi_{i=1}^{m}(s-z_i)}{\Pi_{j=1}^{n}(s-pj)} \tag{15.6-15}$$

满足上式的 s 即是系统的闭环特征根。

当 K^* 从 0 变化到∞时，n 个特征跟将随之变化出 n 条轨迹。这 n 条轨迹就是系统的闭环根轨迹(简称根轨迹)。

3)绘制根轨迹图的原则

表 15.6-1 列出了概略绘制根轨迹的基本规则(假定系统的开环传递函数由式 15.6-14 确定)

绘制根轨迹的基本法则 表 15.6-1

序　号	内　容	法　则
1	根轨迹的起点和终点	根轨迹起始于开环极点，终止于开环零点
2	根轨迹的分支数，对称性和连续性	根轨迹的分支数与开环零点数 m 和开环极点数 n 中的大者相等，根轨迹是连续的，并且对称于实轴
3	实轴上的根轨迹	实轴上的某一区域，若其右端开环实数零、极点个数之和为奇数，则该区域必是 180°根轨迹 * 实轴上的某一区域，若其右端开环实数零、极点个数之和为偶数，则该区域必是 0°根轨迹
4	根轨迹的渐近线	渐近线与实轴的交点 $\sigma_a=\frac{\sum_{j=1}^{n}p_j-\sum_{i=1}^{m}z_i}{n-m}$ 渐近线与实轴夹角 $\varphi_a=\frac{(2k+1)\pi}{n-m}$(180°根轨迹) * $\varphi_a=\frac{2k\pi}{n-m}$(0°根轨迹) 其中 $k=0,\pm1,\pm2,\cdots$
5	根轨迹的分离点	分离点的坐标 d 是下列方程的解 $\sum_{j=1}^{n}\frac{1}{d-p_j}=\sum_{i=1}^{m}\frac{1}{d-z_i}$
6	根轨迹与虚轴的交点	根轨迹与虚轴交点坐标 ω 及其对应的 K^* 值可用劳斯稳定判据确定，也可令闭环特征方程中的 $s=j\omega$，然后分别令其实部和虚部为零求得
7	根轨迹的起始角和终止角	$\sum_{i=1}^{m}\varphi_i-\sum_{j=1}^{n}\theta_j=(2k+1)\pi\quad(k=0,\pm1,\pm2,\cdots)$ * $\sum_{i=1}^{m}\varphi_i-\sum_{j=1}^{n}\theta_j=2k\pi\quad(k=0,\pm1,\pm2,\cdots)$
8	根之和	$\sum_{i=1}^{n}\lambda_i=\sum_{i=1}^{n}p_i\quad(n-m\geqslant2)$

注：表中以“ * ”标明的法则是绘制 0°根轨迹的法则(与绘制常规根轨迹的法则不同)，其余法则不变。

典型例题解析

【例 15.6-10】 控制系统开环传递函数为

$$G(s)H(s)=\frac{K^*(s+2)}{s(s+1)(s+4)}$$

试概略绘制系统根轨迹。

解 系统开环零、极点标于 s 平面，根据法则，系统有 3 条根轨迹分支，且有 $n-m=2$ 条根轨迹趋于无穷远处。根轨迹绘制如下：

(1)实轴上的根轨迹：根据法则 3，实轴上的根轨迹区段为$[-4,-2]$，$[-1,0]$

(2)渐近线：根据法则 4，根轨迹的渐近线与实轴交点和夹角为$\begin{cases}\sigma_a=\dfrac{-1-4+2}{3-1}=-\dfrac{3}{2}\\ \varphi_a=\dfrac{(2k+1)\pi}{3-1}=\pm\dfrac{\pi}{2}\end{cases}$

(3)分离点：根据法则 5，分离点坐标为$\dfrac{1}{d}+\dfrac{1}{d+1}+\dfrac{1}{d+4}=\dfrac{1}{d+2}$

经整理得：

$$(d+4)(d^2+4d+2)=0$$

故 $d_1=-4$，$d_2=-3.414$，$d_3=-0.586$，显然分离点位于实轴上$[-1,0]$间，故取 $d=-0.586$。

根据上述讨论，可绘制出系统根轨迹图，如解图所示。

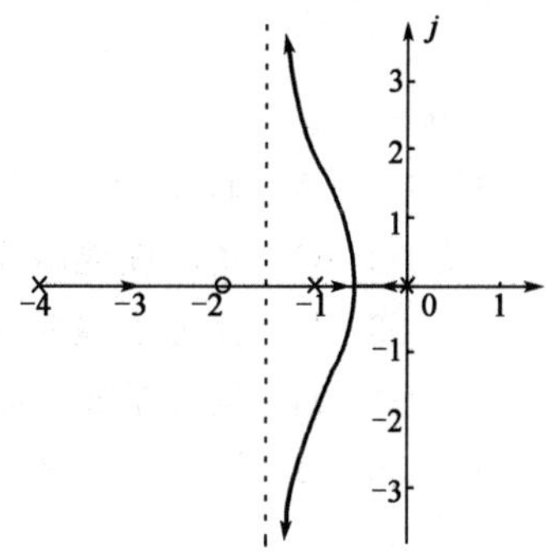

例 15.6-10 解图 根轨迹示意图

【例 15.6-11】 图所示闭环系统的根轨迹应为：

A. 整个负实轴

B. 实轴的二段

C. 在虚轴左面平行于虚轴的直线

D. 虚轴的二段共轭虚根线

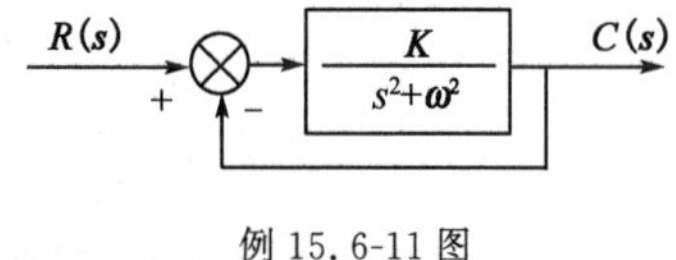

例 15.6-11 图

解 画出系统的根轨迹图。选 D。

【例 15.6-12】 图所示闭环系统的根轨迹应为：

A. 整个负实轴

B. 整个虚轴

C. 在虚轴左面平行于虚轴的直线

D. 实轴的某一段

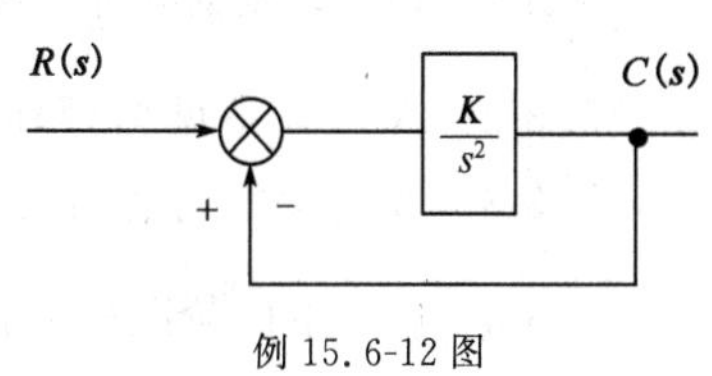

例 15.6-12 图

解 同上，画出根轨迹图。选 B。

经 典 练 习

15.6-1 超前校正装置是(   )。

A. 提供超前相位角　　　　B. 提供滞后相位角

C. PD 控制器　　D. PI 控制器

15.6-2　滞后校正装置可(　　)。

A. 抑制噪声　　B. 改善稳态性能

C. PD 控制器　　D. PI 控制器

15.6-3　许多继电器调节系统,调节过程会出现(　　),是一种滞后校正装置。如果自振荡是正常工作情况,被调量的(　　)要受到调节精度要求的限制。由于继电器调节系统的线性部分其有(　　)特性,所以(　　)自振荡的频率,使振幅较小。

A. 自振荡　　B. 振幅　　C. 低通滤波　　D. 提高

15.6-4　室温对象——空调房间的特性参数滞后时间 τ 越大,(　　),对象的时间常数 T 越大,(　　),当对象的传递系数大时,调节过程的动差和静差均增大,调节周期将缩短,振动次数会增加,寿命也会缩短。

A. 调节振幅即动态偏差增大　　B. 振幅减小

C. 调节周期缩短　　D. 调节振幅即动态偏差减小

参考答案及提示

15.1-1　A　输出量变化归结于输入量的变化。

15.1-2　C　负反馈能减小误差对系统的影响,为确保精度常采用闭环负反馈系统。

15.1-3　D　无输入量时,输出不能自动控制。

15.1-4　B　调节是按偏差来输入控制信号的。

15.1-5　B　属于负反馈。

15.2-1　D　开环控制系统的定义,开环控制没有引入反馈的概念。

15.2-2　A　闭环控制系统的概念,闭环控制中有反馈的概念。

15.2-3　B　原式$=\frac{1}{2s}-\frac{1}{2}\times\frac{s+1}{(s+1)^2+1}+\frac{1}{2}\frac{1}{(s+1)^2+1}$

所以 $X(t)=\frac{1}{2}+\frac{1}{2}e^{-t}(\sin t-\cos t)$。

15.2-4　C　自动控制的基本要求有稳定性,快速性和准确性。

15.3-1　D　系统的开环传递函数为 $\frac{K}{(s-s_1)(s-s_2)}=\frac{K}{(s+0.5)(s+4)}=\frac{10}{(s+0.5)(s+4)}$。

15.3-2　A,C　参见典型环节惯性环节的数学模型-微分方程和传递函数的形式。

15.3-3　A　参见调节器实现方法中的比例积分调节器的实现。

15.3-4　C　单位阶跃输入时 $R(s)=\frac{1}{s}$

输出 $C(s)=\frac{K}{1+Ts}\cdot\frac{1}{s}$

$$C(t)=L^{-1}[C(s)]=L^{-1}\left(\frac{K}{1+Ts}\cdot\frac{1}{s}\right)=K(1-e^{-\frac{1}{T}})$$

由此可以看出,T 越小,衰减越快,快速性越好。

15.3-5　B　参见二阶过阻尼系统的单位阶跃响应表达式和曲线。

15.3-6　C　可与二阶系统标准式相对比，可得 $\omega_n=3$，$2\xi\omega_n=3.6$，求得阻尼比为 0.6。

15.4-1　A　该系统的特征方程为 $2s^3+3s^2+K$。缺 s 项，因此系统不稳定，根据系统稳定的必要条件。

15.4-2　C　参见稳定性与特征方程根的关系。

15.4-3　A　稳定的充要条件为特征方程的各项系数的符号必须相同。

15.5-1　C　系统类型的定义。

15.5-2　B　$K_a=\lim\limits_{s\to 0}s^2G(s)=1$。

15.6-1　A，C　超前校正装置的概念。

15.6-2　A，B，C，D　滞后校正装置的概念。

15.6-3　A，B，C，D　继电系统是一种本质非线性自动调节系统，许多继电系统调节过程中会出现自振荡。如果自振荡是正常工作情况，被调量的振幅受到调节精度要求的限制。由于继电系统的线性部分通常具有低通滤波特性，所以提高自振荡的频率，可使被调量的振幅比较小。为了限制自振荡的振幅，可利用校正装置。

15.6-4　A，B　因存在着对象的滞后时间 τ，所以会使室温调节品质变化。当 τ 越大时，调节振幅即动态偏差增大。只有在理想状态下，对象滞后等于零时，室温波动的振幅才等于调节器的不灵敏区，但这在实际上是不可能的，而当 τ 增大时，调节周期可加大，这样就减少了振动次数，延长了使用寿命。对象的时间常数 T 越大时，因室温上升速度减小，所以振幅可减小，这对调节有利。且 T 增大时可使调节周期加大，对减小磨损也有利。当对象的传递系数大时，调节过程的动差和静差均增大，调节周期将缩短，振动次数会增加，寿命也会缩短。

16 热工测试技术

考题配置　单选，10 题
分数配置　每题 2 分，共 20 分

复习指导

热工测试技术主要是指暖通空调及动力工程领域的测试技术，包括温度、湿度、压力、流速、流量、物位、热量等参量的基本测量方法、测试仪表的原理及应用。通过对本章的学习，应掌握热能和动力工程领域主要参数的测量方法、测试系统和仪器的工作原理、测量误差分析和数据处理等。

16.1 测量技术的基本知识

考试大纲☞：测量　精度　误差　直接测量　间接测量　等精度测量　不等精度测量　测量范围　测量精度　稳定性　静态特性　传感器　传输通道　变换器

必备基础知识

16.1.1 测量

测量就是用实验的方法，把被测量与同性质的标准量进行比较，确定被测量与标准量的比值，从而得到被测量的量值。

为了使测量的结果有意义，测量必须满足以下要求：

(1)用来进行比较的标准量应该是国际上或国家公认的。

(2)进行比较所用的方法和仪器必须经过验证。

测量的定义也可以用公式来表示

$$a = \frac{X}{U} \tag{16.1-1}$$

式中：X——被测量；

U——标准量(即选用的测量单位)；

a——比值(又称测量值)。

由式(16.1-1)可见，a 的数值随选用的标准量 U 的大小而定。为了正确反映测量结果，常需在测量值的后面标明标准量的单位。例如长度的被测量为 X，标准量 U 的单位采用国际单位制(m)，测量值的读数为 am。

被测量的量值可表达为

$$X = aU \tag{16.1-2}$$

式(16.1-2)称为测量的基本方程式。

在测量过程中,通常把需要检测的物理量称为被测参数或被测量。在建筑环境与设备工程中经常用到的被测参数有:温度、相对湿度、焓、压力、流量、热量等。

按照被测量随时间的变化关系,可将被测量分为以下两种类型:

(1)静态参数(常量)。某些被测参数在整个测量过程中量值的大小始终保持不变,即参数值不随时间变化,我们把这类参数统称为静态参数或常量。当然,严格来讲,这些参数的量值也并非绝对不变,只是随时间变化得非常缓慢,而在测量的时间间隔内,由于其数值大小变化甚微,可以忽略不计。例如,环境大气压力、普通集中空调系统的风量等。

(2)动态参数(变量)。随时间不断改变数值的被测量称为动态参数或变量,如室外温度和相对湿度等。这些参数随时间变化的函数可以是周期函数或随机函数。

测量的分类:

(1)按照测量手段不同,通常把测量方法分为直接测量、间接测量和组合测量。

(2)按照测量方式不同,通常把测量方法分为偏差式测量、零位式测量和微差式测量。

(3)按照测量仪表是否与被测对象相接触,测量可分为接触测量和非接触测量。

(4)按照测量在测量过程中的状态不同,测量可分为静态测量和动态测量。

(5)按照测量次数不同,测量可分为一次测量和多次测量。

测量系统由测量设备与被测对象组成。任何一次有意义的测量都必须由测量系统来实现。测量系统都是有若干具有一定基本功能的测量环节组成的。测量系统中的测量设备一般由传感器、变换器或变送器、传输通道和显示装置组成。

16.1.2 测量精度与测量误差

1)测量精度

精度是指测量仪表的读数或测量结果与被测量真值相一致的程度。测量精度可用精密度、准确度和精确度三个指标表示。

(1)精密度。精密度表示同一被测量在相同条件下,使用同一仪表、由同一操作者进行多次重复测量所得测量值彼此之间接近的程度,也就是说,它表示测量重复性的好坏。精密度反映随机误差的影响。随机误差小,测量的重复性就好,精密度也高;反之,重复性差,精密度也低。

(2)准确度。准确度表示测量值与被测量真值之间的符合程度。它反映了系统误差的影响,系统误差越小,测量的准确度越高。

(3)精确度。精确度是准确度和精密度的综合反映,习惯上用精密度这一概念来综合表示测量误差大小。若已修正所有已定系统误差,则精度可用不确定度表示。

在具体的测量实践中,可能会有这样的情况:准确度较高而精密度较低,或者精密度高但欠准确。当然理想的情况是既准确,又精密,即测量结果精确度高。要获得理想的结果,应满足三个方面的条件:性能优良的测量仪表、正确的测量方法和正确细心的测量操作。为了加深对准确度、精密度和精确度三个概念的理解,可以用射击打靶的例子来加以说明。如图 16.1-1 所示,以靶心作为被测量的真值,以靶纸上的弹着点表示测量结果。其中图 16.1-1a)上的弹着点分散而又偏斜,说明该测量所得结果既不精密,也不准确,即精确度很低;图 16.1-1b)上的弹着点仍然比较分散,但总体而言,大致都围绕靶心,说明测量结果准确但欠精密;图 16.1-1c)上的弹着点密集在一定的区域内,但明显偏向一方,说明测量结果精密度高但准确度差;图 16.1-1d)弹着点相互接近且都围绕靶心,说明测量结果精密且准确度很高,即精度高。

2)测量误差

测量仪器仪表的测得值与被测量真值之间的差异叫做测量误差。误差按照表示方法分为绝对误差和相对误差。按测量误差的性质分为系统误差、随机误差和粗大误差。

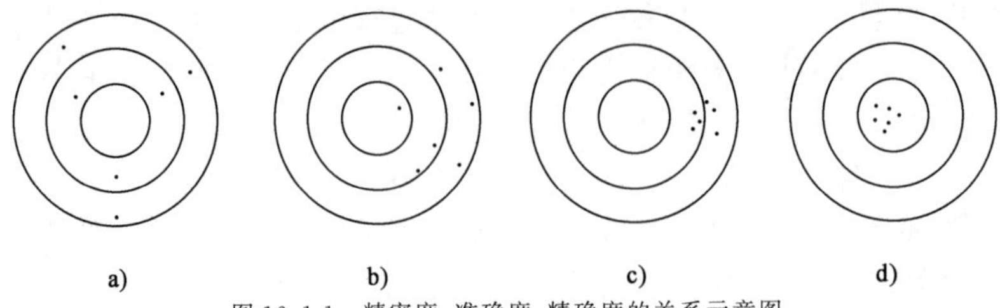

图 16.1-1 精密度、准确度、精确度的关系示意图

(1)系统误差。在测量过程中,如果所产生的误差大小和符号具有恒定不变或遵循某一特定规律而变化的性质,这种误差叫做系统误差。系统误差主要是由于测量仪表本身不准确、测量方法不完善、测量环境的变化以及观测者本人的操作不当等造成的。系统误差的大小直接关系到测量结果的准确度,系统误差越小,测量结果的准确度越高。所以,对系统误差的发现和消除,在测量工作中具有十分重要的意义。

(2)随机误差。在消除了系统误差之后,对同一被测量进行多次等精确度重复测量时,由于某些不可知的原因会引起测量值或大或小的现象。此现象的出现又无一定的规律,完全是随机的,故称为随机误差或偶然误差。

(3)粗大误差。由于测量者的人为过失或偶然的一个外界干扰所造成的误差,称为粗大误差或过失误差,例如读错刻度值、计算出错等。此种误差是一种显然与事实不符、没有任何规律可循的误差,在测量结果中是不允许存在的。含有粗大误差的测量结果是无效的,一旦发现粗大误差,必须将其去除。

3)不确定度

不确定度是指由于测量误差的存在而对测量值不能肯定的程度。国际通用计量学基本名词中将其定义为表征被计量的真值所处的量值范围的评定。

典型例题解析

【例 16.1-1】 在以下四种因素中,与系统误差的形成无关的是:

A. 测量工具和环境　　B. 测量的方法

C. 重复测量的次数　　D. 测量人员的情况

解 系统误差主要是由于测量仪表本身不准确、测量方法不完善、测量环境的变化以及观测者本人的操作不当等造成的,与重复测量次数无关。选 C。

【例 16.1-2】 精密度表示在同一条件下对同一被测量进行多次测量时:

A. 测量值重复一致的程度,反映随机误差的大小

B. 测量值重复一致的程度,反映系统误差的大小

C. 测量值偏离真值的程度,反映随机误差的大小

D. 测量值偏离真值的程度,反映系统误差的大小

解 本题主要考查精密度的概念,精密度表示同一被测量在相同条件下,使用同一仪表、由同一操作者进行多次重复测量所得测量值彼此之间接近的程度,也就是说,它表示测量重复性的好坏。精密度反映的是随机误差对测量值的影响。选 A。

【例 16.1-3】 在完全相同的条件下所进行的一系列重复测量称为：

A. 静态测量 B. 动态测量

C. 等精度测量 D. 非等精度测量

解 等精度测量的定义为在保持测量条件不变的情况下对同一被测量对象进行多次测量的过程。选 C。

16.1.3 常见测量方法

平衡态是指在没有外界影响(重力场除外)的条件下,系统的宏观性质不随时间变化的状态。

实现平衡的充要条件:系统内部及系统与外界之间各种不平衡势差(力差、温差、化学势差)的消失。

在平衡状态时,参数不随时间改变只是现象,不能作为判断是否平衡的条件,只有系统内部及系统与外界之间的一切不平衡势差的消失,才是实现平衡的本质。

平衡状态具有确定的状态参数,这是平衡状态的特点。

1)直接测量

直接从测量仪表的读数获取被测量值的方法叫做直接测量。

凡是将被测参数与其单位量直接进行比较,或者用测量仪表对被测参数进行测量,其测量结果又可直接从仪表上获得(不需要通过方程式计算)的测量方法,称为直接测量法,例如使用温度计测量温度、用压力表测量容器内介质的压力等。直接测量法有直读法和比较法两种。

所谓直读法就是直接从测量仪表上读得被测参数的数值,如用玻璃管式液体温度计测温度。这种方法使用方便,但一般精确度较差。

比较法是利用一个与被测量同类的已知标准量(由标准量具给出)与被测量相比较而测量被测量的方法。因常常要使用标准量具,所以测量过程比较麻烦,但测量仪表本身的误差及其他一些误差在测量过程中能被抵消,因此测量精确度比较高。

2)间接测量

利用直接测量的量与被测量之间的函数关系(公式、曲线或表格)间接得到被测量的量值的测量方法叫做间接测量。例如在测量风道中空气流量 L 时,若测量出风道中的空气平均流速 v(m/s)和风道的横截面面积 A(m^2),则空气流量

$$L = 3\,600vA \tag{16.1-3}$$

式中:L——风道中的空气流量(m^3/h);

v——风道中的空气流速(m/s);

A——风道的横截面面积(m^2)。

3)组合测量

测量中使各个未知量以不同的组合形式出现(或改变条件以获得这种不同的组合),根据直接测量或间接测量所获得的数据,通过解联立方程组求得未知量的数值,这类测量称为组合测量。例如,用铂电阻温度计测量介质温度时,其电阻值 R 与温度 t 有如下关系

$$R_t = R_0(1 + at + bt^2) \tag{16.1-4}$$

为了确定常数 a、b,首先需要测得铂电阻在不同温度下的电阻值 R_t,然后再联立方程求

解，得到 a、b 的数值。

4）等精度测量

在保持测量条件不变的情况下对同一被测量进行多次测量的过程叫做等精度测量。

保持测量条件不变，如观测者细心程度、使用的仪器、测量方法、周围的环境等不变时，对同一被测量或一组被测量进行多次测量，其中每一次都具有相同的可靠性，即每一次测量结果的精确度都是相等的。

5）不等精度测量

如果在同一被测量的多次重复测量中，不是所有测量条件都维持不变，如改变了测量方法，或更换了测量仪器，或改变了连接方式，或测量环境发生了变化，或前后不是同一个操作者，或同一操作者按不同的过程进行操作，或操作过程中由于疲劳等原因而影响了细心程度等，这样的测量称为不等精度测量。

16.1.4 仪表的测量范围与测量精度

1）测量范围

一般测量系统能测量的最大输入量称为测量上限，其最小输入量称为测量下限。测量上、下限代数差的模，称为量程，即测量范围。例：某温度计的量程为－40～＋80℃。

选用仪表时，首先应对被测量的大小有一定的初步估计，务必使测量值都在仪表量程之内，如果被测量在满刻度的 2/3 左右，则能提高测量精度。

2）测量精度

测量精度是指测量仪表的读数和测量结果与被测量真值相一致的程度。仪表测量值中的最大示值绝对误差与仪表量程之比叫做仪表的基本误差

$$\sigma_j = \frac{\Delta_m}{L_m} \times 100\% \tag{16.1-5}$$

式中：σ_j——仪表的基本误差；

Δ_m——最大示值绝对误差；

L_m——仪表量程。

仪表商品根据质量的不同，要求基本误差不超过某一规定值，故又称基本误差为允许误差。

仪表工业规定基本误差去掉“%”的数值为仪表的精度等级，简称精度。它是衡量仪表质量的主要指标之一。我国工业仪表等级分为 0.1、0.2、0.5、1.0、1.5、2.5、5.0 七个等级，并标志在仪表刻度标尺或铭牌上。

典型例题解析

【例 16.1-4】 现有一台测温仪表，其测温范围为 50～100℃，在正常情况下进行校验，获得了一组校验结果，其中最大绝对误差为±0.6℃，最小绝对误差为±0.2℃，则：

A. 该仪表的基本误差为 1.2%，精度等级为 0.5 级

B. 该仪表的基本误差为 1.2%，精度等级为 1.5 级

C. 该仪表的基本误差为 0.4%，精度等级为 0.5 级

D. 该仪表的基本误差为 1.6%，精度等级为 1.5 级

解 本题主要考查基本误差以及精度等级的定义。仪表的基本误差指仪表测量值中的最大示值绝对误差与仪表量程的比值。本题中最大绝对误差为 0.6℃，而仪表的量程为 50℃，因此该仪表基本误差为 1.2%。精度等级为仪表的基本误差去掉"%"的数值，因此该表的精度等级应为 1.5 级。选 B。

【例 16.1-5】 仪表的精度等级是指仪表的：

A. 示值绝对误差平均值

B. 示值相对误差平均值

C. 最大误差值

D. 基本误差的最大允许值

解 本题主要考查精度等级的概念。精度等级为仪表的基本误差去掉"%"的数值，因此是基本误差的最大允许值。选 D。

【例 16.1-6】 某合格测温仪表的精度等级为 0.5 级，测量中最大示值的绝对误差为 1℃，测量范围的下限为负值，且下限的绝对值为测量范围的 10%，则该测温仪表的测量下限值是：

A. −5℃　　B. −10℃　　C. −15℃　　D. −20℃

解 可参考精度等级及绝对误差的概念。选 D。

16.1.5 仪表的稳定性

仪表的稳定性由两个指标来表示：稳定度和各环境影响系数。

仪表在稳定的测量状态下，对某一标准量进行测量，间隔一定时间后，再对同一标准量进行测量，所得两次测量的示值差反映了该仪表的稳定度。它是由仪表中元件或环节的性能参数的随机性变动、周期性变动和随时间漂移等因素造成的。一般稳定度由示值差与其时间间隔的数值共同表示。例如，某毫伏表在开始测量时为某示值，8h 后在同样状态下测量，示值增大了 1.3mV，则此仪表的稳定度可表示为 $\delta_w = 1.3\text{mV}/8\text{h}$。示值差越小说明稳定度越高。

室温、大气压、振动以及电源电压与频率等仪表外部状态及工作条件的变化对其示值的影响，统称为环境影响，用各环境影响系数来表示。周围环境温度变化引起仪表的示值变化，可用温度系数 β_θ（示值变化值/温度变化值）来表示。电源电压变化引起仪表的示值变化，可用电源电压系数 β_U（示值变化值/电压变化值）来表示。例如对毫伏表，当温度变化 10℃引起的示值变化为 0.1mV 时，可写成 $\beta_\theta = 0.1\text{mV}/10℃$。

16.1.6 静态特性和动态特性

1）仪表的静态特性

在稳定状态下，仪表的输出量（如显示值）与输入量之间的函数关系，称为仪表的静态特性。其性能指标有灵敏度、灵敏限、线性度、变差等。

（1）灵敏度。仪表的灵敏度反映的是测量仪表对被测量变化的反应灵敏程度。在温度的情况下仪表输出量的变化量与引起此变化的输入量之比就称为仪表的灵敏度，常用 S 来表示，即

$$S = \frac{\Delta y}{\Delta x} \tag{16.1-6}$$

式中：Δy——输出量的变化量；

Δx——输入量的变化量。

例如：有一弹簧管式压力表，当输入的压力信号为20Pa时，压力表的指针划过的弧线长为3cm，则此压力表的灵敏度为

$$S=\frac{\Delta y}{\Delta x}=\frac{3\text{cm}}{(50-20)\text{Pa}}=0.1\text{cm/Pa}$$

灵敏度是仪表的静态参数。对于一台仪表而言，它的灵敏度是常数。一般来讲，灵敏度高的仪表，其精度也较高。但是仪表精度取决于仪表本身的基本误差，而不能单纯地依靠提高灵敏度来达到提高精度的目的。一般规定，仪表读数标尺分格值不能小于仪表允许误差的绝对值。

(2)灵敏限。仪表的灵敏限是指能引起仪表输出量变化（如指针发生动作）的被测量的最小（极限）变化量，又称分辨率。一般情况下，灵敏限的数值应不大于仪表测量值中最大示值绝对误差的绝对值的一半。它的单位与测量值的单位相同。

(3)线性度。线性度表示输出量与输入量的实际特性曲线偏离理想特性曲线的程度。线性度是衡量偏离线性程度的指标，用E来表示，它以实际特性曲线偏离理论特性曲线的最大值Δl_m和仪表量程l_m的百分数来表示，即

$$E=\frac{\Delta l_{\text{m}}}{l_{\text{m}}}\times 100\% \tag{16.1-7}$$

(4)变差。变差指的是同一被测量值在正反行程间仪表指示值的最大值Δl_{m}与仪表量程l_{m}之比的百分数，用ε表示，即

$$\varepsilon=\frac{\Delta l_{\text{m}}}{l_{\text{m}}}\times 100\% \tag{16.1-8}$$

2)仪表的动态特性

仪表的动态特性是指当被测量发生变化时，仪表的显示值随时间变化的特性曲线。动态特性好的仪表，其输出量随时间变化的曲线与被测量随同一时间变化的曲线一致或相近。仪表的动态输出量（读数）和它在同一瞬间的相应输入量之间的差值称为仪表的动态误差，动态误差越小，其动态特性越好。衡量仪表动态特性时，时间常数T越小，仪表惯性就越小，其动态特性就越好。

16.1.7 传感器

传感器是指对各种非电物理量，如压力、温度、湿度、物质成分等敏感的敏感元件。因为它是与被测对象直接发生联系的部分，故又称作一次仪表。它是实现测量按一定规律转换成便于处理和传输的另一物理量（一般多为电量）的元件。它是实现测量与自动控制的首要环节。对其转换要求是将被测量以单值函数关系，稳定而准确地变成另一物理量，以便提供后续环节变换、比较、运算与显示记录被测量。

理想的敏感元件应满足的要求：

(1)输入与输出之间有稳定的单值函数。

(2)只对被测量的变化敏感。

(3)测量过程中不干扰或尽量少干扰被测介质的状态。

暖通空调专业中常用的被测量有：温度、湿度、压力、液位、流速、流量、热量等。

16.1.8 传输通道

如果测量系统各环节是分离的，那么就需要把信号从一个环节传送到另一个环节，实现这种功能的环节就称为传输通道。传输通道是测量系统各环节之间输入输出信号的连接部分，它分为电线、光导纤维和管路等。在实际测量系统中，应按规定要求进行选择和布置，否则就会造成信息损失、信号失真或引入干扰。

16.1.9 变换器

在测量系统中变换器是传感器和显示装置中间的部分，它将传感器输出的信号变换成显示装置能够接收的信号。传感器输出的信号一般是某种物理变量，如位移、压差、电阻、电压等。在大多数情况下，它们在性质上、强弱程度上总是与显示装置所能接收的信号有所差异。测量系统必须通过变换器或变送器对传感器输出的信号进行变换，包括信号物理性质的变换(如位移、电阻变电压或电流)和信号数值上的变换(如放大)。

现代的自动指示、记录与调节仪表，除了可直接接收传感器信号外，有的仪表还可接收标准信号(如 0～10mA · DC、4～20mA · DC、0～10V · DC 等)。将传感器输出信号变化到标准信号的器件称为变送器，它在自动检测与自动控制中广泛应用。

对于变换器或变送器，不仅要求它们性能稳定、精确度高，而且还应使信息损失最小。

典型例题解析

【例 16.1-7】 能够将被测热工信号转换为标准电流信号输出的装置是：

A. 敏感元件　　B. 传感器　　C. 变送器　　D. 显示与记录仪器

解 传感器就是对各种非电物理量，如压力、温度、湿度、物质成分等敏感的敏感元件。它是实现测量按一定规律转换成便于处理和传输的另一物理量(一般多为电量)的元件。选 B。

【例 16.1-8】 下列不属于测量系统基本环节的是：

A. 传感器　　B. 传输通道　　C. 变换器　　D. 平衡电桥

解 典型的测试系统，一般由输入装置、中间变换装置、输出装置三部分组成。选 D。

经 典 练 习

16.1-1 测量中测量值的绝对误差是否可以作为衡量所有测量准确度的尺度？(　　)

A. 可以　　B. 不可以

C. 不确定　　D. 根据准确度大小确定

16.1-2 有一块精度为 2.5 级、测量范围为 0～100kPa 的压力表，它的刻度标尺最小应分为(　　)格。

A. 25　　B. 40　　C. 50　　D. 100

16.1-3 一台精度为 0.5 级的电桥，下限刻度值为负值，为全量程的 25%，该表允许绝对误差是 1℃，则该表刻度的上限值为(　　)。

A. 25℃　　B. 50℃　　C. 150 ℃　　D. 200℃

16.1-4 现要测量 500℃的温度，要求其测量值的相对误差不应超过 2.5%，下列几个测温表中最合适的是(　　)。

A. 测温范围为100～+500℃的2.5级测温表

B. 测温范围为0～+600℃的2.0级测温表

C. 测温范围为0～+800℃的2.0级测温表

D. 测温范围为0～+1000℃的1.5级测温表

16.2　温度的测量

考试大纲☞：热力学温标　国际实用温标　摄氏温标　华氏温标　热电材料　热电效应　膨胀效应测温原理及其应用　热电回路性质及理论　热电偶结构及使用方法　热电阻测温原理及常用材料　常用组件的使用方法　单色辐射温度计　全色辐射温度计　比色辐射温度计　电动温度变送器　气动温度变送器　测温布置技术

必备基础知识

16.2.1 温度与温标

1)温度

温度是表示物体或系统冷热程度的物理量。从能量角度看,温度是描述系统不同自由度间能量分布状况的物理量;从热平衡观点来看,温度是描述热平衡系统冷热程度的物理量,它标志着系统内部分子无规则运动的剧烈程度(分子平均动能的大小)。

2)温标

为保证温度量值的统一和准确而建立的用来衡量温度高低的标准尺度简称为温标。通常把温度计、固定点和内插方程叫做温标的三要素。

经验温标:借助某一种物质的物理量随温度变化的关系,用实验方法或经验公式所确定的温标。如摄氏温标、华氏温标、兰氏温标、列氏温标等。

(1)热力学温标。热力学温标又称开氏温标(K)或绝对温标,它规定分子运动停止时的温度为绝对零度。它是与测量物质的任何物理性质无关的一种温标,已由国际权度会议采纳作为国际统一的基本温标。

根据热力学中的卡诺定理,如果热力学温度为 T_1 的高温热源和热力学温度为 T_2 的低温热源之间有一可逆热机进行卡诺循环,热机从高温热源吸热为 Q_1,向低温热源放热为 Q_2,则

$$\frac{T_1}{T_2}=\frac{Q_1}{Q_2} \tag{16.2-1}$$

如果指定了一个定点温度数值,就可以通过热量比求得未知温度值。1954年国际权度会议选定了水的三相点为参考点,且该点的温度为273.16K,则相应的换热量为 $Q_参$。这样上式就可以写为

$$T=273.16\frac{Q}{Q_参} \tag{16.2-2}$$

于是由热量比值 $Q/Q_参$ 就可以求得未知量 T。由于上述方程式与工质本身的种类和性质无关,所以用这种方法建立起来的热力学温标就避免了分度的“任意性”。理想的卡诺循环实际上是不存在的,所以热力学温标是一种理论温标,不能付诸实用。因此,必须建立一种能够

用计算公式表示的既紧密接近热力学温标，在使用上又简便的温度，这就是国际实用温标。

(2)国际实用温标。为了解决国际上温度标准的统一问题及实用方便，国际上协商决定，建立一种既能体现热力学温度，又实用方便、容易实现的温标，这就是国际实用温标，又称国际温标，用代号 T 表示，单位符号为 K。国际实用温标规定水的三相点热力学温度为 273.16K，1K 定义为水的三相点热力学温度的 1/273.16。水的三相点是指纯水在固态、液态及气态三相平衡时的温度。现行国际实用温标是国际计量委员会(ITS)1990 年通过的，简称 ITS—1990。摄氏温度与国际实用温标的换算关系为

$$T = t + 273.15$$

这里摄氏温度的分度值与开氏温度的分度值相同，即温度间隔 1K 等于 1℃。在标准大气压下冰的溶化温度为 273.15K，即水的三相点的温度比冰点高出 0.01℃，由于水的三相点温度容易复现，复现精度高，而且保存方便，是冰点不能比拟的，所以国际实用温标规定，建立温标的唯一基准点选用水的三相点。

(3)摄氏温标。摄氏温标是把标准大气压下水的冰点定义为 0℃，把水的沸点定为 100℃ 的一种温标。把 0～100℃之间分成 100 等分，每一等分为一摄氏度。常用代号 t 表示，单位符号为℃。

(4)华氏温标。华氏温标规定标准大气压下纯水的冰点温度为 32 ℉，沸点温度为 212 ℉，中间划分 180 等分，每一等分称为华氏一度。常用代号 F 表示，单位符号为℉。摄氏度与华氏度的换算关系为

$$t = \frac{5}{9}(F - 32) \tag{16.2-3}$$

摄氏温标、华氏温标都是用水银作为温度计的测温介质，是依据液体受热膨胀的原理来建立温标和制造温度计的。

典型例题解析

【例 16.2-1】 温标是以数值表示的温度标尺，在温标中不依赖于物体物理性质的温标是：

A. 华氏温标　　B. 摄氏温标

C. 热力学温标　　D. IPTS—68 国际实用温标

解 本题主要考查温标的概念以及各温标的性质。热力学温标规定分子运动停止时的温度为绝对零度，它是与测量物质的任何物理性质无关的一种温标。选 C。

【例 16.2-2】 摄氏温标和热力学温标之间的关系为：

A. $t=T-273.16$　　B. $t=T+273.16$

C. $t=T-273.15$　　D. $t=T+273.15$

解 本题主要考查摄氏温度与热力学温度之间的关系。摄氏温度的分度值与开氏温度的分度值相同，即温度间隔 1K 等于 1℃，在标准大气压下冰的溶化温度为 273.15K。选 C。

16.2.2 热电材料

理论上任意两种导体或半导体都可以组成热电偶，但实际上为了使热电偶稳定性好，具有足够的灵敏度、可互换性以及一定的机械强度等性能，热电材料一般应满足以下条件：

(1)在测温范围内，热电性质稳定，不随时间和被测介质变化。物理化学性能稳定，不易氧化或腐蚀。

(2)电导率要高，电阻温度系数要小。

(3)组成的热电偶的热电势随温度的变化率要大，并且希望该变化率在测温范围内接近常数(即反应曲线呈线性)。

(4)材料的机械强度要高，复制性要好，复制工艺要简单，价格便宜。

按照标准化程度，热电偶分为标准热电偶和非标准热电偶。热电偶分度号是表示热电偶材料的标记符号，工程上常用分度号来区别不同的热电偶。常用的热电偶材料主要包括以下三类：

(1)廉金属热电偶：

①T 型(铜-康铜)热电偶；

②K 型(镍铬-镍铬或镍硅)热电偶；

③E 型(镍铬-康铜)热电偶；

④J 型(铁-康铜)热电偶。

(2)贵金属热电偶：

①S 型(铂铑 10-铂)热电偶；

②R 型(铂铑 13-铂)热电偶；

③B 型(铂铑 30-铂铑 6)热电偶。

(3)非标准化热电偶：

①钨-铼系热电偶；

②钨-铱系热电偶；

③镍硅-金铁热电偶；

④镍钴-镍铝热电偶；

⑤非金属热电偶。

常用热电偶的性能：

(1)K[镍铬-镍硅(镍铝)]：适宜在氧化性及惰性气氛中连续使用，短期使用温度为 1 200℃，长期使用温度为 1 000℃。

(2)N(镍铬硅-镍硅)：在 1 300℃以下，高温抗氧化能力强，热电动势的长期稳定性及短期热循环的复现性好，耐核辐射及耐低温性能也好。

(3)B(铂铑 30-铂铑 6)：在室温下热电动势极小，一般不用补偿导线。长期使用温度为 1 600℃，短期使用温度为 1 800℃。适宜在氧化性或中性气氛中使用，也可以在真空环境下短期使用。

(4)S(铂铑 10-铂铑)：热电性能稳定、抗氧化性强，宜在氧化性、惰性气氛中连续使用。长期使用温度为 1 400℃。它的准确度等级最高，通常用作标准或作为测量高温的热电偶，它的使用温度范围广、均质性及互换性好。

(5)R(铂铑 13-铂铑)：同 S 型热电偶相比，它的热电动势率大 15%左右，其他性能几乎完全相同。

(6)E(镍铬-康铜)：在常用热电偶中其热电动势率最大，即灵敏度最高。使用中的限制条件与 K 型热电偶相同。它适宜在－250～870℃范围内的氧化或惰性气氛中使用，尤其适宜在 0℃以下使用。而且在湿度大的情况下，较其他热电偶耐腐蚀。

(7)J(铁-康铜):价格便宜。既可用于氧化性气氛(使用温度上限为750℃),也可用于还原性气氛(使用温度上限为950℃)。不能在高温(540℃)含硫的气氛中使用。

(8)T(铜-康铜):在便宜的金属热电偶中它的准确度最高,热电极丝的均匀性好。它的使用温度范围是−200~350℃。因铜热电极易氧化,并且氧化膜易脱落,故在氧化性气氛中使用时,一般不超过300℃。在低于−200℃以下使用时,热电动势随温度迅速下降,而且铜热电极的热导率高,在低温下易引入误差。T型热电偶在工业上通常用来测量300℃以下的温度。

典型例题解析

【例16.2-3】 介质的被测温度范围为0~600℃,还原性工作气氛,可选用的热电偶为:

A. S型热电偶　　B. B型热电偶

C. K型热电偶　　D. J型热电偶

解 本题主要考查常用热电偶的测温范围。其中J(铁-康铜)型热电偶具有价格便宜的优点,既可用于氧化性气氛(使用温度上限为750℃),也可用于还原性气氛(使用温度上限为950℃)。选D。

16.2.3 热电效应测温原理

如图16.2-1所示将两种不同的导体A和B连接,构成一个闭合回路,当两个接点1与2的温度不同时,在回路中就会产生热电动势,这种现象称为热电效应。记为E_{AB}。导体A、B称为热电极。测量时接点1在测温场所感受被测温度,故称为测量端。接点2要求温度恒定,称为参考端。

热电偶是通过测量热电动势来实现测温的,即热电偶测温是基于热电转化现象——热电现象。实际上热电偶是一种换能器,它将热能转化为电能,用所产生的热电动势测量温度。该电动势由接触电势和温差电势组成。

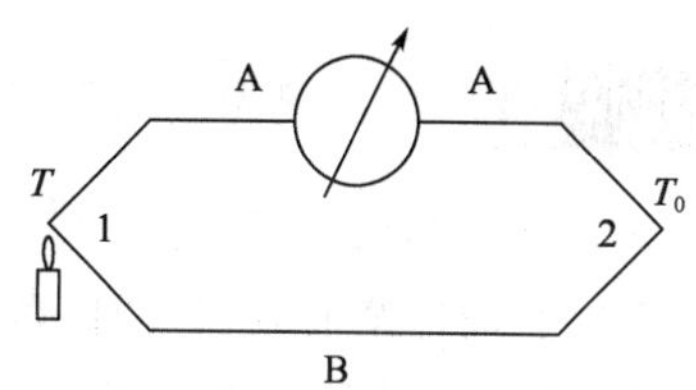

图16.2-1 热电效应示意图

接触电势是由于两种不同导体的自由电子密度不同而在接触处形成的电动势,又称帕尔贴(Peltier)电势。A、B两种导体在一定温度T下的接触电势$E_{AB}(T)$、温度T及A、B导体中的电子N_A、N_B有如下关系

$$E_{AB}(T)=\frac{kT}{\mathrm{e}}\ln\frac{N_A}{N_B} \quad (16.2\text{-}4)$$

式中:e——电荷,$\mathrm{e}=1.6\times10^{6}$C;

k——波尔兹曼常数,$k=1.38\times10^{-23}$J/K。

即温度越高,接触电势越大;两种导体电子密度的比值越大,接触电势也越大。

温差电势是在同一导体的两端因温度不同而产生的一种热电势,又称汤姆逊(Thomson)电势。设导体两端的温度分别为T和T_0($T>T_0$),由于高温端T的电子能量大,因而从高温端扩散到低温端的电子数比低温端扩散到高温端的电子数要多,结果高温端失去电子而带正电荷,低温端得到电子而带负电荷,从而形成了一个从高温端指向低温端的静电场。此时在导体的两端便产生一个相应的电势差,这就是温差电势。其值可以用物理学电磁场理论得到。

$$E_A(T,T_0)=\int_{T_0}^{T}\sigma_A\,dT \tag{16.2-5}$$

$$E_B(T,T_0)=\int_{T_0}^{T}\sigma_B\,dT \tag{16.2-6}$$

式中：$E_A(T,T_0)$——导体 A 在两端温度分别为 T 和 T_0 时的温差电势；

$E_B(T,T_0)$——导体 B 在两端温度分别为 T 和 T_0 时的温差电势；

σ_A、σ_B——材料 A、B 的汤姆逊系数，与材料性质和两端温度有关。

典型例题解析

【例 16.2-4】 热电偶是由 A、B 两种导体组成的闭合回路。其中 A 导体为正极，当回路的两个接点温度不相同时，将产生热电势，这个热电势的极性取决于：

A. A 导体的温差电势　　B. 温度较高的接点处的接触电势

C. B 导体的温差电势　　D. 温度较低的接点处的接触电势

解 温差电势是指同一导体的两端因温度不同而产生的电势，不同的导体具有不同的电子密度，所以它们产生的电势也不相同，而接触电势是指两种不同的导体相接触时，因为它们的电子密度不同所以产生一定的电子扩散，当它们达到一定的平衡后所形成的电势。接触电势的大小取决于两种不同导体的材料性质以及它们接触点的温度。接触电势的大小与接头处温度的高低和金属的种类有关。温差电势远比接触电势小，可以忽略。这样闭合回路中的总热电势可近似为接触电势。温度越高，两金属的自由电子密度相差越大，则接触电势越大。选 B。

16.2.4 膨胀效应测温原理及其应用

膨胀效应是指物体受热产生膨胀的特性。利用这种原理制成的温度计叫做膨胀式温度计，主要有液体膨胀式温度计、固体膨胀式温度计和压力式温度计。

液体膨胀式温度计中最常见的是利用液体体积随温度的升高而膨胀的原理制作而成的玻璃管液体温度计。它的优点是直观、测量准确、结构简单、造价低廉，被广泛应用于工业、实验室和医院等各个领域及日常生活中。但其缺点是不能自动记录、不能远传、易碎、测温有一定延迟。

固体式温度计是利用两种线性膨胀系数不同的材料制成，有杆式和双金属片式两种，常用作自动控制装置中的温度测量元件。它结构简单、可靠，但精度不高。

压力式温度计是利用密闭容积内工作介质随温度升高而压力升高的性质，通过对工作介质的压力测量来判断温度值的一种机械式仪表。其工作介质可以是气体、液体或蒸汽。仪表主要包括温包、金属毛细管、基座和具有扁圆或椭圆截面的弹簧管等。

16.2.5 热电回路性质及理论

接触电动势是由于两种不同材质的导体接触而产生的电动势，而温差电动势则是同一导体当其两端温度不同时产生的电动势。在图 16.2-2 所示的闭合回路中，两个节点处有两个接触电动势 $E_{AB}(T)$ 和 $E_{AB}(T_0)$，又因为 $T>T_0$，在导体 A 和 B 中还各有一个温差电动势。所以闭合回路总电动势 $E_{AB}(T,T_0)$ 应为接触电动势与温差电动势的代数和，即

$$E_{AB}(T,T_0)=E_{AB}(T)-E_{AB}(T_0)+E_B(T,T_0)-E_A(T,T_0) \quad (16.2\text{-}7)$$

经整理推导可得

$$E_{AB}(T,T_0)=f(T)-f(T_0) \quad (16.2\text{-}8)$$

即当热电偶材料一定时，热电偶总电动势 $E_{AB}(T,T_0)$ 成为温度 T 和 T_0 的函数差。

如果能使冷端温度 T_0 固定，即 $f(T_0)=C$（常数），则对确定的热电偶材料，其总电势就只与温度 T 成单值函数关系，由式(16.2-9)表示为

$$E_{AB}(T,T_0)=f(T)-C \quad (16.2\text{-}9)$$

这种特性称为热电偶的热电特性，$f(T)$ 关系可通过实验方法求得。

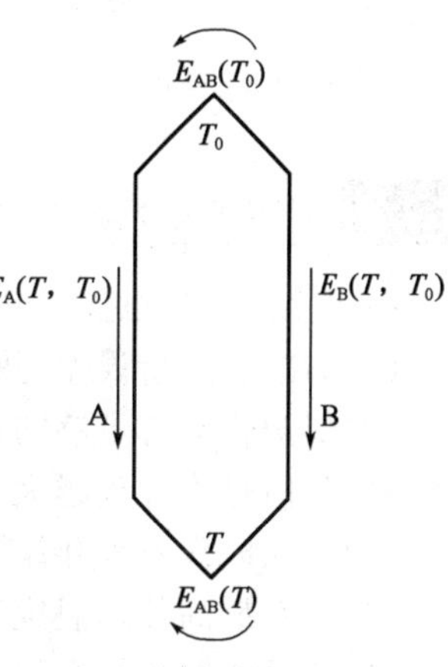

图 16.2-2 热电回路的总热电势

热电偶基本性质：

(1)均质导体定律。由同一种均质导体组成的密闭回路中，不论导体的截面、长度以及各处的温度分布如何，均不产生热电势，即热电偶必须采用两种不同材料作为电极。

(2)中间导体定律。在热电回路中接入第三种导体，只要与第三种导体相连接的两端温度相同，接入第三种导体后，对热电偶回路中的总电势没有影响。

(3)中间温度定律。热电偶在两接点温度为 T、T_0 时的热电势等于该热电偶在两接点温度分别为 T、T_N 和 T_N、T_0 时相应热电势的代数和，即

$$E_{AB}(T,T_0)=E_{AB}(T,T_N)+E_{AB}(T_N,T_0) \quad (16.2\text{-}10)$$

典型例题解析

【例 16.2-5】 如图所示，被测对象温度为 600℃，用分度号为 E 的热电偶及补偿导线、铜导线连至显示仪表，未预置机械零位。显示仪表型号及接线均正确，显示仪表上显示温度约为：

A. 600℃　　B. 560℃

C. 580℃　　D. 620℃

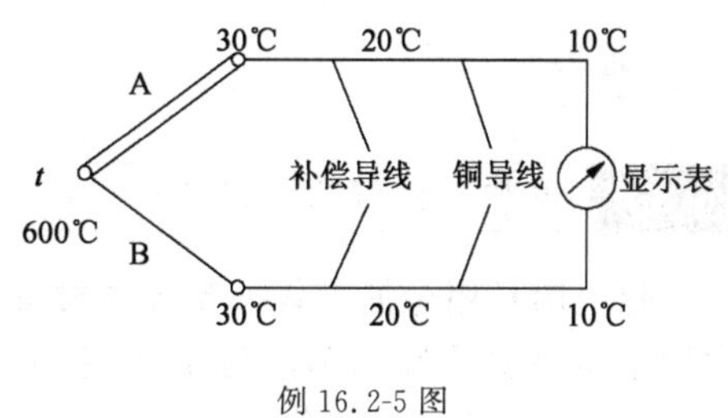

例 16.2-5 图

解 根据中间导体定律，任意两种匀质导体 A、B，分别与匀质材料 C 组成热电偶，若热电势分别为 $E_{AC(T,T_0)}$ 和 $E_{CB(T,T_0)}$，则导体 A、B 组成热电偶的热电势为 $E_{AB(T,T_0)}=E_{AC(T,T_0)}+E_{CB(T,T_0)}$，因为测温回路中有 E 型热电偶、补偿导线以及铜导线，而且接到显示仪表的铜导线与补偿导线间有 20℃温差。选 C。

【例 16.2-6】 某分度号为 K 的热电偶测温回路，其热电势 $E(t,t_0)=17.513\text{mV}$，参考端温度 $t_0=25℃$，则测量端温度 t 为：[已知：$E(25,0)=1.000$，$E(403,0)=16.513$，$E(426,0)=17.513$，$E(450,0)=18.513$]

A. 426℃　　B. 450℃　　C. 403℃　　D. 420℃

解 两个节点处有两个接触电动势 E_{AB} 和 $E_{AB}(T_0)$，又因为 $T>T_0$，在导体 A 和 B 中还各有一个温差电动势。所以闭合回路总电动势 $E_{AB}(T,T_0)$ 应为接触电动势与温差电动势的代数和。选 B。

16.2.6 热电偶结构及使用方法

一支完整的热电偶由热电极、绝缘套管、保护套管、接线盒等部分组成。使用时要注意：

(1)为减少测量误差，热电偶应与被测对象充分接触，使两者处于相同温度。

(2)保护管应有足够的机械强度，并可承受被测介质腐蚀。保护管的外径越粗，耐热、耐腐蚀性越好，但热惰性也越大。

(3)当保护管表面附着灰尘等物质时，将因热阻增加，使指示温度低于真实温度而产生误差。

(4)如在最高使用温度下长期工作，将因热电偶材质发生变化而引起误差。

(5)测量线路绝缘电阻下降也会引起误差。应设法提高绝缘电阻，或将热电偶的外壳做接地处理。

(6)注意冷端温度的补偿与修正。热电偶冷端最好保持 0℃，而在现场条件下使用的仪表则难以实现，必须采用补偿方法准确修正。

(7)避免电磁感应的影响。热电偶的信号传输线，在布线时应尽量避开强电磁区(如大功率的电机、变压器)，更不能与电力线近距离平行敷设。如果实在避不开，也要采取屏蔽措施。

典型例题解析

【例 16.2-7】 若要监测两个测点的温度差(见图)，需将两支热电偶：

A. 正向串联　　B. 反向串联

C. 正向并联　　D. 反向并联

解 将两支同型号热电偶反向连接，可测量两点之间的温差，它也是要考虑参考端温度一致，则输入仪表电势：

$$\Delta E = E_{AB}(t_1,t_0) - E_{AB}(t_2,t_0)$$

$$= E_{AB}(t_1,t_2) + E_{AB}(t_2,t_0) - E_{AB}(t_2,t_0)$$

$$= E_{AB}(t_1,t_2)$$

选 B。

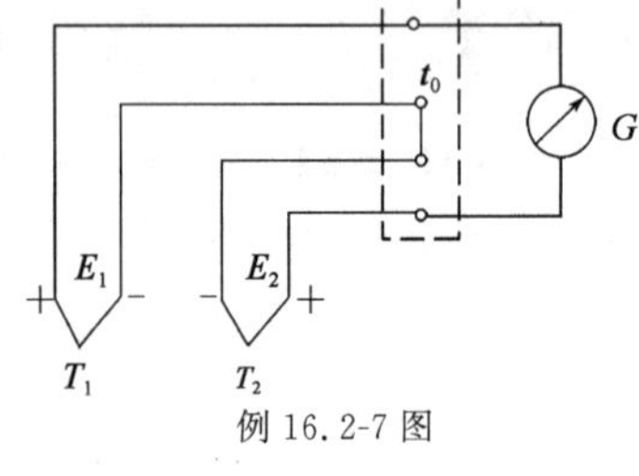

例 16.2-7 图

16.2.7 热电阻测温原理及常用材料、常用组件的使用方法

热电阻是用金属导体或半导体材料制成的感温元件。物体的电阻一般随温度而变化，通常用电阻温度系数 α(单位为℃$^{-1}$)来描述这一特性。它的定义是在某一温度间隔内，温度变化 1℃时电阻的相对变化量。

$$\alpha = \frac{R_t - R_{t_0}}{(t - t_0)} = \frac{\Delta R}{\Delta t} \tag{16.2-11}$$

热电阻的电阻值与温度的关系特性有三种表示方法：作图法、函数表示法和列表法(分度表表示法)。

常用的热电阻材料有铂热电阻、铜热电阻、镍热电阻和半导体热敏电阻。

铂热电阻：铂热电阻的阻值与温度之间的关系近似线性。其特性方程如下。

当温度 t 为 $-200\sim0$℃时

$$R_t = R_0[1 + At + Bt^2 + C(t - 100)T^3] \tag{16.2-12}$$

当温度 t 为 $0\sim850$℃时

$$R_t = R_0(1 + At + Bt^2) \tag{16.2-13}$$

式中：R_t——铂热电阻在 t℃时的电阻值(Ω)；

R_0——铂热电阻在 0℃时的电阻值(Ω)。

$A=3.908\times10^{-3}$℃$^{-1}$，$B=5.802\times10^{-7}$℃$^{-2}$，$C=4.274\times10^{-12}$℃$^{-4}$。

对满足上述关系的热电阻，其温度系数为 $\alpha=0.00385$℃$^{-1}$。使用铂热电阻的特性方程式，每隔 1℃求取一个相应的 R，便可得到铂热电阻的分度表。这样在实际测量中，只要测得铂热电阻的阻值 R_t，便可从分度表中查出对应的温度值。

铜热电阻：在使用温度范围($-50\sim150$℃)内，铜热电阻的特性方程为

$$R_t = R_0(1 + \alpha t) \tag{16.2-14}$$

式中：α——铜电阻温度系数，$\alpha=(4.25\sim4.28)\times10^{-3}$℃$^{-1}$。

镍热电阻的阻值温度系数 α 较大，约为铂的 1.5 倍，使用温度范围为 $-50\sim300$℃，但是在 200℃左右具有特异点，故多用于 150℃以下。它的电阻和温度的关系式为

$$R_t = 100 + 0.548t + 6.65\times10^{-4}t^2 + 2.805\times10^{-9}t^4 \tag{16.2-15}$$

热电阻分度号是表明热电阻材料和 0℃时阻值的标记符号。如铂热电阻分度号有 Pt100 和 Pt10 两种，其 R_0 分别为 100Ω 和 10Ω，铜热电阻分别为 Cu50(其 $R_0=50\Omega$)和 Cu100(其$R_0=100\Omega$)。

常用组件的使用方法：

(1)热电阻的类型，包括普通型、铠装型、端面型和隔爆型。

(2)信号线的连接，包括二线、三线、四线。

(3)热电阻测温系统一般由热电阻、连接导线和显示仪表等组成。

使用时应注意：

(1)热电阻的显示仪表的分度号必须一致。

(2)为了消除连接导线电阻变化的影响，必须采用三线制接法。

(3)应合理选择测点位置，尽量避免在阀门、弯头及管道和设备的死角附近装设热电阻。

(4)带有保护套管的热电阻为了减少测量误差，热电偶和热电阻应该有足够的插入深度。

(5)对于测量管道中心流体温度的热电阻，一般都应将其测量端插入到管道中心处(垂直安装或倾斜安装)。

(6)对于高温高压和高速流体的温度测量(如主蒸汽温度)，为了减少保护套对流体的阻力和防止保护套在流体作用下发生断裂，可采取保护管浅插方式或采用热套式热电阻。

典型例题解析

【例 16.2-8】 下列关于电阻温度计的叙述中，哪条内容是不恰当的？

A. 与电阻温度计相比，热电偶温度计能测更高的温度

B. 与电阻温度计相比，热电偶温度计在温度检测时的时间延迟大些

C. 因为电阻体的电阻丝是用较粗的线做成的，所以有较强的耐振性能

D. 电阻温度计的工作原理是利用金属或半导体的电阻随温度变化的特性

解 为了提高热电阻的耐振性能需要进行铠装，并不因为电阻丝的粗细而有较强的耐振性能。选 C。

【例 16.2-9】 某铜电阻在20℃的阻值 $R_{20}=16.35\Omega$，其电阻温度系数 $\alpha=4.25\times10^{-3}$，则该电阻在100℃时的阻值 R_{100} 为：

A. 3.27Ω　　B. 16.69Ω　　C. 21.47Ω　　D. 81.75Ω

解　由电阻温度系数定义式可以求得 $R_{100}=\alpha(t-t_0)+R_{t_0}=16.69\Omega$。选 B。

【例 16.2-10】 制作热电阻的材料必须满足一定的技术要求，以下叙述错误的是：

A. 电阻值与温度之间有接近线性的关系　B. 较大的电阻温度

C. 较小的电阻率　D. 稳定的物理、化学性质

解　几乎所有金属与半导体均有随温度变化而其阻值变化的性质，作为测温元件必须满足下列条件：

(1)电阻温度系数 α 应大。多数金属热电阻随温度升高一度(K)其阻值增加0.35%～6%，而负温度系数的热敏电阻却减少2%～8%。应指出 α 值并非常数，α 值越大，热电阻灵敏度越高。α 值与材料含杂质成分有关，与制造工艺(如拉伸时内应力大小)有关。

(2)复现性要好，复制性强，互换性好。

(3)电阻率大。这样同样的电阻值，体积可制得较小，因而热惯性也较小。

(4)价格便宜，工艺性好。

选 C。

16.2.8 辐射温度计

1)单色辐射高温计

由普朗克定律可知，物体在某一波长下的单色辐射强度与温度有单值函数关系，而且单色辐射强度的增长速度比温度的增长速度快得多。根据这一原理制作的高温计叫做单色辐射高温计。

当物体温度高于700℃时，单色辐射高温计会明显地发出可见光，具有一定的亮度。物体在波长 λ 的亮度 B_λ 和它的辐射强度 E_λ 成正比，即

$$B_\lambda = cE_\lambda \tag{16.2-16}$$

式中：c——比例常数。

根据维恩公式，绝对黑体在波长 λ 的亮度 $B_{0\lambda}$ 与温度 T_s 的关系为

$$B_{0\lambda} = cc_1\lambda^{-5}e^{-c_2/(\lambda T_s)} \tag{16.2-17}$$

实际物体在波长 λ 的亮度 B_λ 与温度 T 的关系为

$$B_\lambda = c\,\varepsilon_\lambda c_1\lambda^{-5}e^{-c_2/(\lambda T)} \tag{16.2-18}$$

由式(16.2-16)可知，用同一种测量亮度的单色辐射高温计来测量单色黑度系数 ε_λ 不同的物体温度，即使它们的亮度 B_λ 相同，其实际温度也会因为 ε_λ 的不同而不同。这就造成按某一物体的温度刻度的单色辐射高温计，不能用来测量黑度系数不同的另一个物体的温度。为了使光学高温计具有通用性，一般将单色辐射高温计按绝对黑体($\varepsilon_\lambda=1$)的温度进行刻度。用这种刻度的高温计去测量实际物体($\varepsilon_\lambda\neq1$)的温度时，所得到的温度示值叫做被测物体的“亮度温度”。亮度温度的定义是：在波长为 λ 的单色辐射中，若物体的温度为 T 时的亮度 B_λ 和绝对黑体在温度为 T_s 时的亮度 $B_{0\lambda}$ 相等，则把绝对黑体温度 T_s 叫做被测物体在波长为 λ 时的亮度温度。在此定义，根据式(16.2-17)和式(16.2-18)可推导出被测物体的实际温度 T 和亮度温度 T_s 之间的关系为

$$\frac{1}{T_s}-\frac{1}{T}=\frac{\lambda}{c_2}\ln\frac{1}{\varepsilon_\lambda} \tag{16.2-19}$$

使用已知波长 λ 的单色辐射高温计测得物体的亮度温度后，必须同时知道物体在该波长下的黑度系数 ε_{λ}，才能用式(16.2-19)算出实际温度。因为 ε_{λ} 总是小于 1 的，所以测得的亮度温度总是低于物体实际温度的，且 ε_{λ} 越小，亮度温度与实际温度之间的差别就越大。

2)全辐射高温计

全辐射温度计是根据全辐射定律制作的温度计。图 16.2-3 为全辐射高温计的示意图。

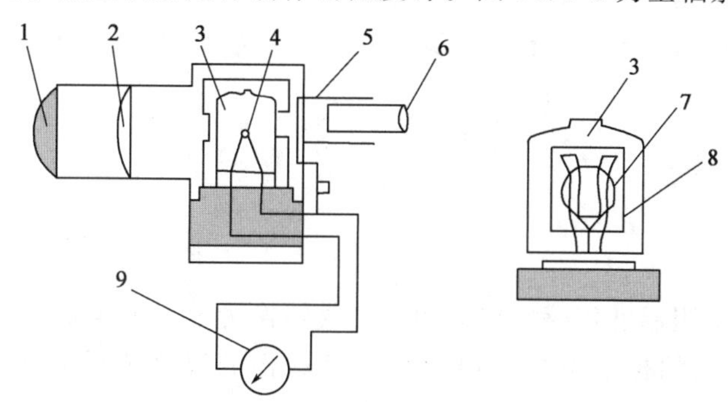

图 16.2-3 全辐射高温计示意图

1-物镜；2-光栏；3-玻璃泡；4-热电堆；5-灰色滤光片；6-目镜；7-铂铑；8-云母片；9-二次仪表

物体的全辐射能由物镜聚焦后，经光栏，焦点落在装有热电堆的铂箔上。热电堆是由 4～8 支微型热电偶串联而成，以得到较大的热电动势。热电偶的测量端被夹在十字形的铂箔内，铂箔涂成黑色以增加其吸收系数。当辐射能被聚焦到铂箔上，热电偶测量端感受热量，热电堆输出热电动势传送到显示仪表，由此表显示或记录被测物体的温度。热电偶的参比端夹在云母片中，这里的温度比测量端低很多。在瞄准被测物体的过程中，观测者可以通过目镜进行观察，目镜前加有灰色滤光片，用来削弱光的强度，保护观测者的眼睛。整个外壳内壁面涂成黑色，以减少杂光的干扰和造成黑体条件。

全辐射高温计按绝对黑体对象进行分度。用它测量辐射率为 ε 的实际物体温度时，其示值并非真实温度，而是被测物体的“辐射温度”。辐射温度的定义为：温度为 T 的物体，当全辐射能量 E 等于温度为 T_P 的绝对黑体全辐射能量 E_0 时，温度 T_P 叫做被测物体的辐射温度。

按定义 $E=\varepsilon\sigma T^4$，$E_0=\sigma T_P^4$，当 $E=E_0$ 时，有

$$T = T_P\sqrt[4]{\frac{1}{\varepsilon}} \qquad (16.2\text{-}20)$$

由于 ε 总是小于 1 的数，因此 T_P 总是低于 T。因为全辐射高温计是按黑体刻度的，在测量非黑体温度时，其读数是被测物体的辐射温度 T_P，要用式(16.2-20)计算出被测物体的真实温度 T。

典型例题解析

【例 16.2-11】 光学高温计是利用被测物体辐射的单色亮度与仪表内部灯丝的单色亮度相比较以检测被测物体的湿度。为了保证光学高温计较窄的工作波段，光路系统中所设置的器件是：

A. 物镜光栏　　B. 中性灰色吸收滤光片

C. 红色滤光片　　D. 聚焦物镜

解 目镜前放着红色滤光片只让一定波长的光线通过，以便于比较单色光的亮度。选 C。

【例 16.2-12】 以下关于单色辐射温度计的叙述，错误的是：

A. 不宜测量反射光很强的物体

B. 温度计与被测物体之间的距离不宜太远

C. 不能测量不发光的透明火焰

D. 测到的亮度温度总是高于物体的实际温度

解 同一波长下，若实际物体与黑体(用于热辐射研究的，不依赖具体物性的假想标准物体)的光谱辐射强度相等，则此时黑体的温度被称为实际物体在该波长下的亮度温度。在相同的温度与波长下，实际物体的热辐射总比黑体辐射小，因此测到的亮度温度总是低于物体的实际温度。选 D。

16.2.9 温度变送器

1)电动温度变送器

利用热电偶或热电阻温度传感器把被测温度值转换为电压或电流信号，再经过放大和转换处理为可远距离传输的标准电压或电流信号。这样的温度测量变送器称为电动温度变送器。

2)气动温度变送器

利用膨胀式温度传感器把被测温度值转换为气压信号，再经过放大和转换处理为可远距离传输的标准气压信号。这样的温度测量变送器称为气动温度变送器。

典型例题解析

【例 16.2-13】 温度变送器常与各种热电偶或热电阻配合使用，将被测温度线性地转换为标准电信号，电动单元组合仪表 DDZ-Ⅲ的输出信号格式为：

A. 0～10mA. DC　　B. 4～20mA. DC

C. 0～10V. DC　　D. －5～＋5V. DC

解 变送器将传感器的输出信号转换成显示装置易于接受的信号，包括机械放大，电信号放大，电信号转换。电动单元组合仪表标准电压电流信号：

DDZⅡ　电流：0～10mA；电压 0～10V

DDZⅢ　电流：4～20mA；电压 1～5V

DDZZS　电流：4～20mA；电压 1～5V

选 B。

16.2.10 测温布置技术

在测温元件安装和布置时应注意以下几方面的问题：

(1)测温元件的安装应确保测量的准确性。

①必须正确选择测温点。

②应避免热辐射引起的测温误差。

③用热电偶测量炉温时，应避免测温元件与火焰直接接触，也不宜距离太近或装在炉门旁边。接线盒不应碰到炉壁，以免热电偶自由端温度过高。

④测温元件安装在负压管道(或设备)时，必须保证安装孔的密封，以免外界空气被吸入而引起测量误差。

⑤使用热电偶、热电阻测量时，应防止干扰信号的引入。

(2)测温元件的安装应确保安全可靠。

①安装承受压力的测温元件时,必须保证密封。

②高温工作的热电偶应尽可能垂直安装,防止保护管在高温下产生变形。

③在介质具有较大流速的管道中安装测温元件时,测温元件应倾斜安装,以免受到过大的冲蚀。

(3)测温元件的安装应便于维修、校验和拆装。

(4)在加装保护外套时,为减少测温的滞后,可在套管之间加装传热良好的填充物。

典型例题解析

【例 16.2-14】 为减少接触式电动测温传感器的动态误差,下列所采取的措施中正确的是:

A. 增设保护套管　　B. 减小传感器体积,减少热容量

C. 减小传感器与被测介质的接触面积　　D. 选用比热大的保护套管

解 为了减少温度传感器的动态误差,需要提高温度传感器的灵敏性,这就要求温度传感器要有较小的热容量和较小的体积。选 B。

经典练习

16.2-1 用 K 分度号的热电偶和与其匹配的补偿导线测量温度,但在接线中把补偿导线的极性接反了,这时仪表的指示(　　)。

A. 不变　　B. 偏大

C. 偏小　　D. 视具体情况而定

16.2-2 已知 K 型热电偶的热端温度为 300℃,冷端温度为 20℃。查热电偶分度表得电势:300℃时为 12.209mV,20℃时为 0.798mV,280℃时为 11.382mV。这样,该热电偶回路内所发出的电势为(　　)mV。

A. 11.382　　B. 11.411　　C. 13.007　　D. 12.18

16.2-3 T 分度号热电偶的测温范围为(　　)。

A. 0～1 300℃　　B. 200～1 200℃　　C. 200～750℃　　D. 200～350℃

16.2-4 下述与电阻温度计配用的金属丝有关的说法,不正确的是(　　)。

A. 经常采用的是铂丝　　B. 也有利用铜丝的

C. 通常不采用金丝　　D. 有时采用锰铜丝

16.2-5 下列有关电阻温度计的叙述中,不恰当的是(　　)。

A. 电阻温度计在温度检测时,有时间延迟的缺点

B. 与热电偶温度计相比,电阻温度计所能测的温度较低

C. 因为电阻体的电阻丝是用较粗的线做成的,所以有较强的耐振性能

D. 测温电阻体和热电偶都是插入保护管使用的,故保护管的构造、材质等必须十分慎重地选定

16.2-6 有关玻璃水银温度计,下述(　　)条的内容是错误的?

A. 测温下限可达－150℃　　B. 在 200℃以下为线性刻度

C. 水银与玻璃无黏附现象　　D. 水银的膨胀系数比有机液体的小

16.2-7 热电偶与补偿导线连接、热电偶和铜导线连接进行测温时,要求接点处的温度应

该是(　　)。

A. 热电偶与补偿导线连接点处的温度必须相等

B. 不必相等

C. 热电偶和铜导线连接点处的温度必须相等

D. 必须相等

16.2-8　在检定、测温电子电位差计时，通常要测冷端温度，这时水银温度计应放在(　　)。

A. 仪表壳内　　B. 测量桥路处

C. 温度补偿电阻处　　D. 标准电位差计处

16.3　湿度的测量

考试大纲☞：干湿球温度计测量原理　干湿球电学测量和信号传送传感　光电式露点仪　露点湿度计　氯化锂电阻湿度计　氯化锂露点湿度计　陶瓷电阻电容湿度计　毛发湿度计　测湿布置技术

必备基础知识

16.3.1　干湿球温度计测量原理

干湿球温度计是根据干湿球温度差效应原理进行相对湿度测量。所谓干湿球温度差效应，是指在潮湿物体表面因水分蒸发而冷却的效应。冷却的程度取决于周围空气的相对湿度φ、大气压力B以及风速v。如果大气压力B以及风速v保持不变，相对湿度φ越高，潮湿物体表面的水分蒸发强度越小，潮湿物体表面温度(即湿球温度t_s)与周围环境温度(即空气干球温度t_g)差就越小；反之相对湿度φ低，水分的蒸发强度越大，干、湿球温差就越大。因此，只要测量空气的干、湿球温度t_g、t_s，就可以在I-D图中查出相对湿度φ，或者根据干球温度t_g和干、湿球温差t_g-t_s从"通风干湿表相对湿度表"中查出相对湿度φ。此表的制表条件为：$B=1.012\times10^5$Pa，$v=2.5$m/s。

典型例题解析

【例 16.3-1】　有关干湿球湿度计的叙述中，下列哪条是不正确的？

A. 如果大气压力和风速保持不变，相对湿度越高，则干湿球温差越小

B. 干湿球湿度计在低于冰点以下的温度使用时，其误差很大，约为18%

C. 只要测出空气的干、湿球温度，就可以在I-D图中查出相对湿度

D. 湿球温度计在测定相对湿度时，受周围空气流动速度的影响，当空气流速低于2.5m/s时，流速对测量的数值影响较小

解　焓湿图表只适用于风速为2.5m/s、压力为标准大气压时才比较准确，其他状态下的湿度需要加以修正。选D。

【例 16.3-2】　湿度是指在一定温度及压力条件下混合气体中水蒸气的含量，对某混合气体，以下四个说法中错误的是：

A. 百分比含量高则湿度大

B. 露点温度高则湿度大

C. 水蒸气分压高则湿度大

D. 水蒸气饱和度高则湿度大

解 本题主要考查湿度的表示方法。空气有吸收水分的特征,湿度的概念是空气中含有水蒸气的多少。它有三种表示方法:①绝对湿度,它表示每立方米空气中所含的水蒸气的量,单位是千克/立方米;②含湿量,它表示每千克干空气所含有的水蒸气的量,单位是千克/千克(干空气);③相对湿度,表示空气中的绝对湿度与同温度下的饱和绝对湿度的比值,得数是一个百分比。本题中的百分比含量是水蒸气在混合空气中的质量百分比,并不是相对湿度。选 A。

【例 16.3-3】 影响干湿球温度计测量精度的主要因素不包括:

A. 环境气体成分的影响

B. 大气压力和风速的影响

C. 温度计本身精度的影响

D. 湿球温度计湿球润湿用水及湿球元件处的热交换方式

解 干湿温度计的干球探头直接露在空气中,湿球温度探头用湿纱布包裹着,其测湿原理是,在一定风速下,湿球外边的湿纱布的水分蒸发带走湿球温度计探头上的热量,使其温度低于环境空气的温度;而干球温度计测量出来的就是环境空气的实际温度,此时,湿球与干球之间的温度差与环境的相对湿度有一个相应的关系,但该关系是非线性的。用公式表达起来相当复杂。这两者之间的关系会受好多因素的影响,如风速、温度计本身的精度、大气压力、干湿球温度计的球泡表面积大小、纱布材质等。其精度与环境气体成分并没有关系。选 A。

【例 16.3-4】 下列关于干湿球温度的叙述,错误的是:

A. 干湿球温差越大,相对湿度越大

B. 干湿球温差越大,相对湿度越小

C. 在冰点以上使用时,误差较小;在低于冰点使用时,误差增大

D. 电动干湿球温度计可远距离传送信号

解 干湿球温度计的测量原理是:如果空气中水蒸气量没饱和,湿球的表面便不断地蒸发水汽,并吸取汽化热,因此湿球所表示的温度都比干球所示要低。空气越干燥(即湿度越低),蒸发越快,不断地吸取汽化热,使湿球所示的温度降低,而与干球间的差增大。相反,当空气中的水蒸气量呈饱和状态时,水便不再蒸发,也不吸取汽化热,湿球和干球所示的温度即会相等。因此干湿球温差越大说明空气越未达到饱和状态,即相对湿度越小。选 A。

16.3.2 干湿球温度电学测量和信号传送传感

干湿球温度电信号传感器是一种将湿度参数转换成电信号的仪表。它和干湿球温度计的作用原理相同,主要差别是干球和湿球用两支微型套管式镍电阻(或其他电阻温度计)所代替,并增加一个微型轴流通风机,以便在镍电阻周围造成一定恒定风速的气流,此恒定气流一般为 2.5m/s 以上。

干湿球电信号传感器的测量桥路原理如图 16.3-1 所示。它是由两个不平衡电桥接在一

起组成的一个复合电桥。图中左面电桥为干球温度测量桥路，电阻 R_g 为干球热电阻；右面电桥为湿球温度测量桥路，电阻 R_s 为湿球热电阻。

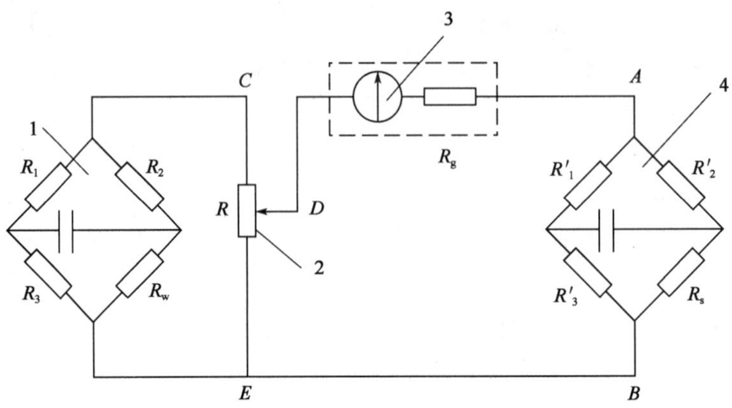

图 16.3-1 电动干湿球湿度计原理图

1-干球温度测量桥路；2-补偿可变电阻；3-检流计；4-湿球温度测量桥路

左电桥输出的不平衡电压是干球温度的函数，右电桥输出的不平衡电压是湿球温度的函数。两路输出信号通过补偿可变电阻 R 连接。在双桥平衡时，D 点位置反映了左、右电桥的电压差，也间接地反映了干湿球温度差。故可变电阻 R 上划动点 D 的位置反映了相对湿度值。

16.3.3 露点仪

1)光电式露点温度计

光电式露点温度计是应用光电原理直接测量气体露点温度的一种电测法湿度计。其核心是一个能反射光的可以自动调节温度的金属露点镜和光学系统。

2)露点温度计

露点温度计的主要构成是一个镀镍的黄铜盒，盒中插着一支温度计和一个鼓气橡皮球。测量时在黄铜盒中注入乙醚溶液，然后用鼓气橡皮球将空气打入黄铜盒中，并由另一管口排出，使乙醚得到较快速度的蒸发，当乙醚蒸发时即吸收了乙醚自身热量使温度降低，当空气中的水蒸气开始在镀镍黄铜盒外表面凝结时，插入盒中的温度计读数就是空气的露点。测出露点以后，再从水蒸气表中查出露点温度的水蒸气饱和压力 p_1 和干球温度下饱和水蒸气的压力 p_b，就能算出空气的相对湿度。

3)氯化锂电阻湿度计

氯化锂是一种在大气中不分解、不挥发，也不变质的稳定的离子型无机盐类。氯化锂吸湿量与空气的相对湿度成一定函数关系，随着空气相对湿度的变化，其吸湿量也随之变化。只有当它的蒸气压力等于周围空气的水蒸气分压力时才处于平衡状态。因此，随着空气相对湿度的增加，氯化锂吸湿量也随之增加，从而使氯化锂中导电的离子数也随之增加，最后导致它的电阻减小。当氯化锂的水蒸气压高于空气中的水蒸气分压力时，氯化锂放出水分，导致电阻增大。氯化锂电阻湿度传感器就是根据这个原理制成的。

4)氯化锂露点温度计

氯化锂露点温度计是利用氯化锂溶液吸湿后电阻减小的基本特性来测量空气湿度的仪表，如图 16.3-2 所示。

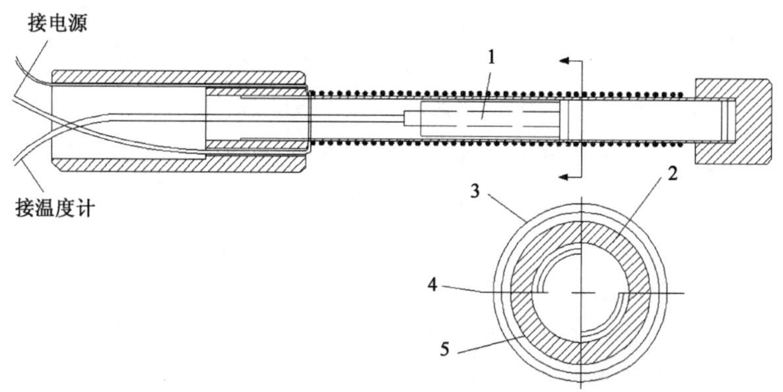

图 16.3-2 氯化锂露点传感器结构示意图

1-热电阻；2-金属管；3-金线；4-玻璃丝套管；5-绝缘涂层

测量空气相对湿度时，将氯化锂露点测量传感器和空气温度传感器放置在被测空气中，如被测空气的水蒸气分压力高于氯化锂溶液的饱和蒸气压力，则氯化锂溶液吸收空气中的水分而潮解，电阻减小，电流增大，产生的焦耳热使氯化锂溶液温度上升，直到氯化锂饱和蒸气压力与被测空气中的水蒸气分压力相等，氯化锂从空气中吸收的水分和放出的水分相平衡，氯化锂溶液的电阻才不再变化，加热电流也稳定下来。反之亦然，达到蒸汽压力平衡时氯化锂溶液的稳定温度成为平衡温度，与露点温度一一对应，就可以通过测量平衡温度计算出空气的露点温度。同时测出的空气温度，将被空气的温度信号和露点温度信号输入双桥测量电路，用适当的记录仪表就可以指示并记录空气的相对湿度。

5）陶瓷电阻、电容湿度计

陶瓷电阻、电容湿度计由金属氧化物多孔性陶瓷烧结而成。烧结体上有微细孔，可使湿敏层吸附或释放水分子，造成其电阻值或介电常数的改变。利用多孔陶瓷构成的这种湿度传感器，具有工作范围宽、稳定性好、寿命长、耐环境能力强等特点。

6）毛发式湿度计

某些纤维，例如毛发，存在着微孔结构，当去掉毛发表面的油脂后，可使微孔与外界空气相通，恢复孔壁。当空气相对湿度变化时，置于空气中的毛发将发生微孔弹性壁的形变。由此，可引起毛发长度的变化。

实用的毛发湿度计就是将一束毛发在相对湿度的变化下产生的形变力，通过机械放大装置放大，进而带动指针偏转，指示相对湿度值。

毛发湿度计结构简单、价格低廉，但精度不高（一般为 5%RH），还存在着滞后现象。一般在使用前需要进行校正。

典型例题解析

【例 16.3-5】 不能在线连续地检测某种气流湿度变化的湿度测量仪表是：

A. 干湿球湿度计　　B. 光电露点湿度计

C. 氯化锂电阻湿度计　　D. 电解式湿度计

解 电解法是目前广泛应用的微量水分测量方法之一。电解湿度计的工作特点是气体连续通过电解池，其中的水汽被五氧化二磷全部吸收并电解。在一定的水分浓度和流速范围内，可以认为水分吸收的速度和电解的速度是相同的，也就是说，水分被连续地吸收的同时连续地被电解，于是瞬时的电解电流可以看作是气体含水量瞬时值的体现。由于方法所要求的条件是通过电解池的气体中的水分必须全部被吸收，测量值要受气体流速的影响，因此，对于某一个电解池不但有一个额定的流速，而且在测量时还必须保持流速恒定，并对流速进行准确的测量。知道了气体的流速和电解电流，便可以计算水分的浓度。选 D。

【例 16.3-6】 有关氯化锂电阻湿度变送器的说法中，哪一条是不正确的？

A. 随着空气相对湿度的增加，氯化锂的吸湿量也随之增加，导致它的电阻减小

B. 测量范围为 5%～95%RH

C. 受环境气体的影响较大

D. 使用时间长了会老化，但变送器的互换性好

解 氯化锂电阻湿度计利用氯化锂吸湿量随着空气相对湿度变化，从而引起电阻变化的原理制成。氯化锂是一种在大气中不分解、不挥发，也不变质的稳定的离子型无机盐类，其变送器受环境气体影响较小。选 C。

【例 16.3-7】 不属于光电式露点湿度计测量范围的气体是：

A. 高压气体　　B. 低温气体

C. 低湿气体　　D. 含烟尘、油脂的气体

解 光电式露点湿度计是使用光电原理直接测量气体露点温度的一种电测法湿度计。其测量准确度高，可靠性强，使用范围广，尤其适用于低温状态。高测量精度需要高度光洁的露点镜、高精度的光学与热电制冷调节系统、洁净的采样气体。选 D。

【例 16.3-8】 不属于毛发式温度计特性的是：

A. 可作为电动湿度传感器　　B. 结构简单

C. 灵敏度低　　D. 价格便宜

解 毛发湿度计的特点是结构简单、价格低廉，但精度不高（一般为 0.05RH），还存在着滞后现象。选 A。

16.3.4 露点仪测湿布置技术

用于湿球温度计或露点仪测量空气湿度时应注意以下问题：

(1)湿度测量点应尽量设于工作区或需要进行湿度测控的区域。

(2)测湿装置应置于通风处，避开水滴飞溅和水蒸气的干扰。

(3)干湿球温度计一般只能在冰点以上的温度下使用，测湿须保证湿球附近稳定的风速(一般取 2.5m/s)，否则可能产生较大的测量误差。

经典练习

16.3-1 不能用作电动湿度传感器的是(　　)。

A. 干湿球温度计　　B. 氯化锂电阻式湿度计

C. 电容式湿度计　　D. 毛发式湿度计

16.3-2 当大气压力和风速一定时，被测空气的干湿球温度差值直接反映了(　　)。

A. 空气湿度的大小

B. 空气中水蒸气分压力的大小

C. 同温度下空气的饱和水蒸气压力的大小

D. 湿球温度下饱和水蒸气压力和干球温度下水蒸气分压力之差的大小

16.3-3　湿球温度计的球部应(　　)。

A. 高于水面 20mm 以上

B. 高于水面 20mm 以上但低于水杯上沿超过 20mm

C. 高于水面 20mm 以上但与水杯上沿平齐

D. 高于水杯上沿 20mm 以上

16.3-4　毛发式湿度计的精度一般为(　　)。

A. ±2%　　B. ±5%　　C. ±10%　　D. ±12%

16.3-5　氯化锂露点湿度传感器在实际测量时(　　)。

A. 氯化锂溶液的温度与空气温度相等

B. 氯化锂饱和溶液的温度与空气露点温度相等

C. 氯化锂溶液的饱和水蒸气压力与湿空气水蒸气分压力相等

D. 氯化锂饱和溶液的饱和水蒸气压力与湿空气水蒸气分压力相等

16.3-6　下列电阻式湿度传感器中,其电阻值与相对湿度的关系线性度最差的是(　　)。

A. 氯化锂电阻式湿度传感器

B. 金属氧化物陶瓷电阻式湿度传感器

C. 高分子电阻式湿度传感器

D. 金属氧化物膜电阻式湿度传感器

16.4　压力的测量

考试大纲☞:液柱式压力计　活塞式压力计　弹簧管式压力计　膜式压力计　波纹管式压力计　压电式压力计　电阻应变传感器　电容传感器　电感传感器　霍尔应变传感器　压力仪表的选用和安装

必备基础知识

这里的压力即物理学中的压强,即垂直作用在单位面积上的力。国际单位制(SI)中压强的单位是帕斯卡(Pa)。

$$1\text{Pa}=1\text{N/m}^2$$

工程上常用的压强单位有工程大气压(kgf/cm^2)、标准大气压(atm)、毫米汞柱(mmHg)和毫米水柱(mmH_2O)等。常用几种压力单位之间的换算关系为

$$1\text{kgf/cm}^2 = 9.087\times10^4\text{Pa}$$

$$1\text{atm} = 1.013\times10^4\text{Pa}$$

$$1\text{mmHg} = 1.332\times10^2\text{Pa}$$

$$1\text{mmH}_2\text{O} = 9.807\text{Pa}$$

以绝对真空为计值零点的压强称为绝对压强,以环境大气压为计值零点的压强称为相对压强,也叫表压。如果被测压强低于环境大气压,表压为负值,这种情况下表压称为真空度。

典型例题解析

【例 16.4-1】 若用图示的压力测量系统测量水管中的压力，则系统中表 A 的指示值应为：

A. 50kPa　　B. 0kPa　　C. 0.965kPa　　D. 50.965kPa

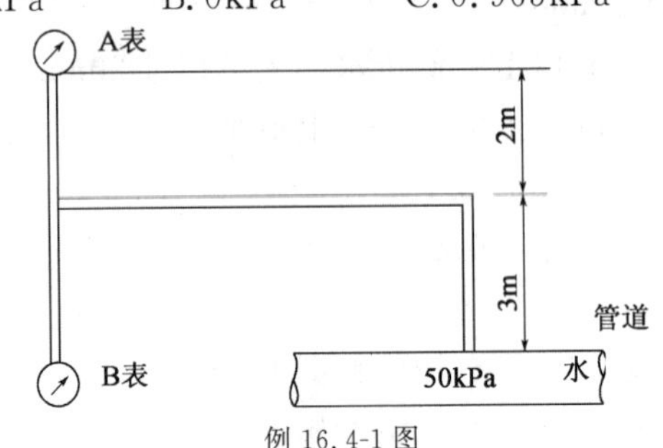

例 16.4-1 图

解 本题主要考查管道压力组成。从图中可以看出 B 表的压力即为主干管中的水压，为 50kPa，而 B 表的压力为 A 点的压力与 A、B 间水柱形成的水压之和。故 A 表的指示值为 0.965kPa。选 C。

16.4.1 压力计

压力计是测量压力的仪表，根据测量原理不同，大致可以分为四类：液柱式压力计、活塞式压力计、弹性压力计和电气式压力计。

1）液柱式压力计

液柱式压力计根据流体静力学原理，把被测压力转换成液柱高度。利用这种方法测量压力的仪表有 U 形管压力计、单管压力计和倾斜管压力计等。

2）活塞式压力计

活塞式压力计根据水压机液体传送压力的原理，将被测压力转换成活塞面积上所加平衡砝码的质量。它普遍地被作为标准仪器用来对弹性压力计进行校验和刻度。

3）弹簧管式压力计

弹簧管式压力计是一种指示型仪表。被测压力由接头输入，使弹簧管的自由端产生位移，通过拉杆使扇形齿轮做逆时针偏转，于是指针由于同轴的中心齿轮的带动而做顺时针偏转，在面板的刻度标尺上显示出被测压力的数值。

4）膜式压力计

膜式压力计是用膜片作为压力敏感元件的弹性压力计。

膜片是一种沿外缘固定的片状测压弹性元件，按剖面形状分为平膜片和波纹膜片。膜片的特性一般用中心的位移和被测压力的关系来表征。当膜片的位移很小时，它们之间有良好的线性关系。

5）波纹管式压力计

波纹管是一种具有等同间距同轴环状波纹并能沿轴向伸缩的测压弹性元件。

由于波纹管的位移相对较大，故一般可在其顶端安装传动机构，带动指针直接读数。波纹管的特点是灵敏度高（特别是在低压区），常用于检测较低的压力（$1.0\sim10^6$ Pa），但波纹管迟滞误差较大，精度一般只能达到 1.5 级。

6）压电式压力计

利用压电材料检测压力是基于压电效应原理，即压电材料受压时会在其表面产生电荷，其电荷量与所受的压力成正比。

压电元件被夹在两块弹性膜片之间，当压力作用于膜片时，压电元件由于受力而产生电荷，电荷经放大可转换成电压或电流输出，输出值的大小与输入压力成正比关系。

16.4.2 压力传感器

1)电阻应变传感器

电阻应变材料的电阻变化基于应变效应。应变片是基于应变效应工作的一种压力敏感元件，当应变片受外力作用产生形变(伸长或缩短)时，应变片的电阻值也随之发生相应变化。应变式压力传感器是由弹性元件、应变片以及相应的桥路组成。

2)电容式传感器

在膜片的旁边，固定一个与该膜片平行的极板，使膜片与极板构成一个平行板电容器。当膜片受压产生位移时，极板与膜片间的距离发生改变，从而改变电容器的电容值，通过测量电容的变化即可间接获得被测压力的大小。

3)电感传感器

将处于电感线圈中的衔铁与弹簧管自由端相连，把衔铁的位移转换成线圈的电感量。

4)霍尔应变传感器

霍尔片与弹簧管的自由端相连，使霍尔片处于两对磁极所形成的非均匀磁场之中。霍尔片的四个端面引出4根导线，其中与磁钢平行的2根导线和直流稳压电源相连接，另外2根导线用来输出信号。当被测压力引入后，在被测压力作用下，弹簧管的自由端产生位移，改变了霍尔片在非均匀磁场中的位置，由此将机械位移量转换成霍尔电势V_n。

典型例题解析

【例 16.4-2】 力平衡式压力变送器中，电磁反馈机构的作用是：

A. 克服环境温度变化对测量的影响　　B. 进行零点迁移

C. 使位移敏感元件工作在小位移状态　　D. 调整测量的量程

解 力平衡式压力变送器的反馈动圈是固定于副杠杆上，并处于一个永久磁钢的磁场之中，因此在放大器输出电流的作用下，反馈动圈就对副杠杆产生一个电磁反馈力F_t。当测量力F_d与反馈力F_t对杠杆系统所形成的力矩达到平衡时，杠杆系统就停止偏转而回到接近于原来的位置上。这时，通过位移检测放大器输出一个稳定的电流值，此电流值即可反映被测差压的大小。整个力平衡测量系统，实质上是一个有差调节系统。在该变送器中，由于位移检测放大器的灵敏度很高，所以在测量过程中，弹性测量元件的位移变化量极小。选C。

16.4.3 压力仪表的选用和安装

压力检测仪表的选择和安装是一项很重要的工作，如果选择或安装不当，不仅不能正确、及时地反映被测对象的压力变化，还可能引起安全事故。

1)仪表量程的选择

为了保证敏感元件能在安全的范围内可靠地工作，也考虑到被测对象可能发生的异常超压情况，对仪表的量程选择必须留有足够的余地。一般在被测压力较稳定的情况下，最大工作压力不超过仪表满量程的2/3；在被测压力波动较大(例如测脉动压力)时，最大工作压力不应超过仪表满量程的1/2。为了保证测量准确度，最小工作压力不低于满量程的1/3。当被测压力变化范围大，最大和最小工作压力不能同时满足上述要求时，选择仪表量程应首先满足最大工作压力条件。

2)仪表精度的选择

仪表精度的选择主要根据生产允许的最大误差来确定，即要求实际被测压力允许的最大绝对误差不小于仪表的基本误差。另外，在选择时坚持节约的原则，只要测量精度能满足生产的要求，就不必追求用过高精度的仪表。

3)仪表类型的选择

仪表类型的选择主要应考虑的因素包括：

(1)被测介质压力大小。

(2)被测介质的性质。

(3)对仪表输出信号的要求。

(4)使用环境等因素。

4)压力表的安装

(1)取压口的选择。取压口的选择应能代表被测压力的真实情况。操作时应注意以下几项：

①在管道或烟道上取压时，取压点要选在被测介质流动的直线管道上。不要选在管道的拐弯、分叉、死角或其他能够形成漩涡的地方。

②测量流动介质的压力时，取压管与流动方向应该垂直，避免动压头的影响。同时还要注意消除钻孔毛刺。

③在测量液体介质的水平管道上取压时，宜在水平及以下45°间取压，可使导压管内不积存气体；在测量气体介质的水平管道上取压时，宜在水平及以上45°间取压，可使导压管内不积存液体。

(2)导压管的敷设。导压管是传递压力、压差信号的，为了能迅速、正确地传递压力和压差，必须做到：

①导压管粗细长短合适，一般内径为6～8mm，长度不大于50mm。

②导压管敷设时，应保持1:10～1:20的坡度，以利于导压管内少量积存的液体或气体排出。测量液体介质时下坡，测量气体介质时上坡。

③如果被测量介质易冷凝或冻结，必须加装伴热管后再进行保温。

④当测量液体压力时，在导压管系统的最高处应安装集气瓶；当测量气体压力时，在导压管系统的最低处应设水分离器；当被测介质有可能产生沉淀物析出时，在仪表前应安装沉降器，以便排出沉淀物。

(3)压力、压差计的安装。压力、压差计安装时应注意以下几项：

①安装位置应易于检修、观察。

②尽量避开振动源和热源的影响，必要时应加装隔热板，减少热辐射；测高温流体或蒸汽压力时加装回转冷凝管。

③测量波动频繁的压力时，可增加阻尼装置。

④选择适当的密封垫片，特别要注意有些垫片不能与某些介质接触。

⑤测量腐蚀介质时，必须采取保护措施，安装隔离罐。

⑥在测量液体的较小压力时，若取压管与仪表(测压口)不在同一水平高度，则应考虑液柱静压校正。

【例 16.4-3】 图示为系统中的一台压力表，指示值正确的为：

A. A 压力表

B. B 压力表

C. C 压力表

D. 所有表的指示皆不正确

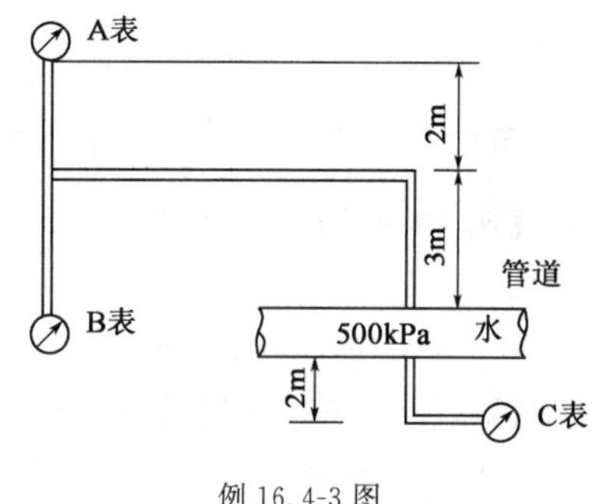

例 16.4-3 图

解 本题主要考查压力表的安装和示值问题。A 表和 C 表与主管间均存在高度差，因此 A 表和 C 表均不能指示主管中的压力。B 表与主管高度相同，不存在由于液柱高度而存在的压力差，能正确指示主管压力。选 B。

【例 16.4-4】 如图所示，取压口选择哪个是正确的？

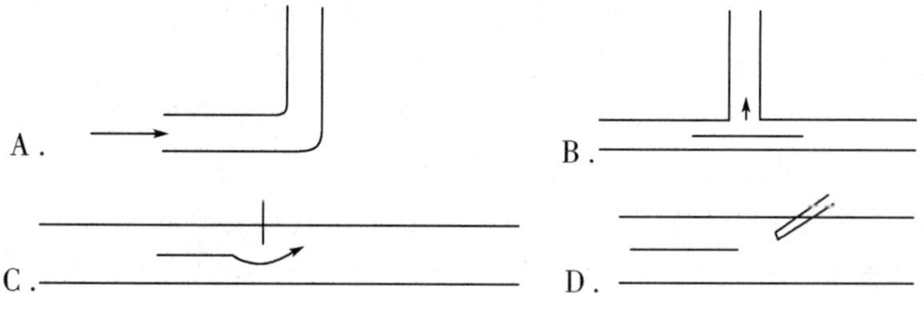

例 16.4-4 图

解 本题主要考查取压口的选择问题。A 中取压口位于弯管处，形成的漩涡对测量结果造成较大影响；C 中取压口位于节流处，节流前后压力突变，对测量结果有较大影响；D 中取压口倾斜，压力测量时受流体动压的影响。选 B。

【例 16.4-5】 为了便于信号的远距离传输，差压变送器采用标准电流信号输出，以下接线图中正确的是：

例 16.4-5 图

解 本题主要考查两线制接线方式。两线制变送器如解图示，其供电为 24V. DC，输出信号为 4～20mA. DC，负载电阻为 250Ω。24V 电源的负线电位最低，它就是信号公共线，对于智能变送器还可在 4～20mA. DC 信号上加载 HART 协议的 FSK 键控信号。选 A。

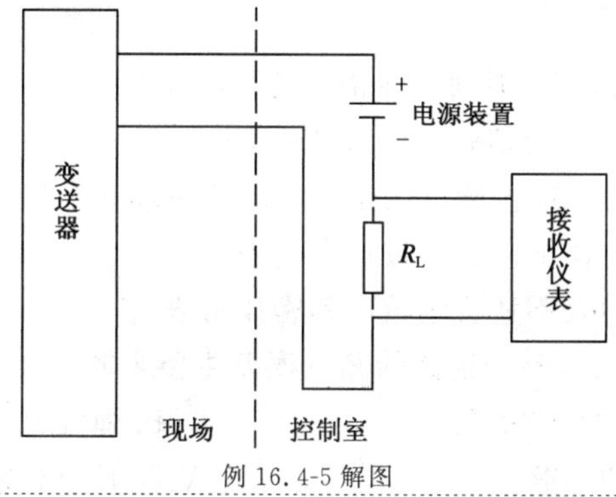

例 16.4-5 解图

【例 16.4-6】 测量某管道内蒸汽压力，压力计位于取压点下方 6m 处，信号管路凝结水的平均温度为 60 ℃，水密度为 985.4kg/m^3，当压力表的指示值为 3.20MPa 时，管道内的实际表压最接近：

A. 3.14MPa　　B. 3.26MPa　　C. 3.2MPa　　D. 无法确定

解　管道中的实际表压 $p=p_1-\rho gh=3.2-985.4\times9.8\times6\times10^{-6}=3.14\text{MPa}$。选 A。

【例 16.4-7】 当压力变送器的安装位置高于取样点的位置时，压力变送器的零点应进行：

A. 正迁移　　B. 负迁移　　C. 不迁移　　D. 不确定

解　差压变送器测量液位时，如果差压变送器的正、负压室与容器的取压点处在同一水平面上，就不需要迁移。而在实际应用中，出于对设备安装位置和便于维护等方面的考虑，变送器不一定都能与取压点在同一水平面上；又如被测介质是强腐蚀性或重黏度的液体，不能直接把介质引入变送器，必须安装隔离液罐，用隔离液来传递压力信号，以防变送器被腐蚀。这时就要考虑介质和隔离液的液柱对变送器测量值的影响。当变送器的安装位置往往与最低液位不在同一水平面上时，为了能够正确指示液位的高度，差压变送器必须做一些技术处理，即迁移。迁移分为无迁移、负迁移和正迁移。所谓变送器的“迁移”，是将变送器在量程不变的情况下，将测量范围移动。通常将测量起点移到参考点“0”以下的，称为负迁移；将测量起点移到参考点“0”以上的，称为正迁移。以一台 30kPa 量程的差压变送器为例，无迁移量时测量范围为 0～30kPa，正迁移 100%时测量范围为 30～60kPa，负迁移 100%时测量范围为－30～0kPa，负迁移 50%时测量范围为－15～＋15kPa。选 A。

经典练习

16.4-1　斜管式微压计为了改变量程，斜管部分可以任意改变倾斜角 α，但 α 角不能小于(　　)度。

A. 5　　B. 100　　C. 150　　D. 200

16.4-2　霍尔压力传感器的主要缺点是(　　)。

A. 灵敏度低　　B. 不能配用通用的动圈仪表

C. 必须采用稳压电源供电　　D. 受温度影响较大

16.4-3　为了保证压力表的连接处严密不漏，安装时应根据被测压力的特点和介质性质加装适当的密封垫片。测量乙炔压力时，不得使用(　　)垫片。

A. 浸油　　B. 有机化合物

C. 铜　　D. 不锈钢

16.4-4　有关活塞式压力表，下列叙述错误的是(　　)。

A. 活塞式压力计的精确等级可达 0.02

B. 活塞式压力计在校验氧用压力表时应用隔油装置

C. 活塞式压力计不适合于校正真空表

D. 活塞式压力表不适合于校准精密压力表

16.4-5　力平衡式压力、压差变送器的测量误差主要来源于(　　)。

A. 弹性元件的弹性滞后　　B. 弹性元件的温漂

C. 杠杆系统的摩擦　　D. 位移检测放大器的灵敏度

16.4-6　压力测量探针中静压孔开孔位置应首先考虑在圆柱体表面上压力系数(　　)之处。

A. 为 0　　B. 为 1　　C. 稳定　　D. 最小

16.4-7　压力表安装的工程需要有几条经验，下列中不对的是(　　)。

A. 关于取压口的位置，从安装角度来看，当介质为液体时，为防止堵塞，取压口应开在设备下部，但不要在最低点

B. 当介质为气体时，取压口要开在设备上方，以免凝结液体进入，而形成水塞。在压力波动频繁和对动态性能要求高时，取压口的直径可适当加大，以减小误差

C. 测量仪表远离测点时，应采用导压管。导压管的长度和内径，直接影响测量系统的动态性能

D. 在敷设导压管时，应保持 10% 的倾斜度。在测量低压时，倾斜度应增大到10%～20%

16.4-8　膜式压力表所用压力传感器测压的基本原理是基于(　　)。

A. 虎克定律　　B. 霍尔效应

C. 杠杆原理　　D. 压阻效应

16.4-9　对于偏斜角不大的三元流动来讲，应尽量选用(　　)静压探针或总压探针进行相应的静压或总压测量。

A. L 形　　B. 圆柱形　　C. 碟形　　D. 导管式

16.5　流速的测量

考试大纲☞：流速测量原理　机械风速仪的测量及结构　热线风速仪的测量原理及结构　L 形动压管　圆柱形三孔测速仪　三管型测速仪　流速测量布置技术

必备基础知识

16.5.1　流速测量原理

流速的测量方法很多，常用的几种方法如下：

(1)机械测速，置于流体中的叶轮的旋转速度与流体的流速成正比。

(2)散热测速的原理是将发热的测速传感器置于被测流体中，利用发热的测速传感器的散热率与流体流速成正比例的特点，通过测定传感器的散热率来获得流体的流速。

(3)动压测压法，对于不可压缩流体有

$$u = \sqrt{\frac{2}{\rho} \times (p_0 - p)} \tag{16.5-1}$$

式中：u——流体速度；

ρ——流体密度；

p_0、p——流体的总压和静压。

只要测得总压 p_0(滞止压力)和静压 p(流体压力)之差以及流体的密度，就可以确定流体速度的大小。对于可压缩的气体有

$$u=\sqrt{\frac{2}{\rho}\times\frac{p_0-p}{1-\varepsilon}} \qquad (16.5\text{-}2)$$

式中：ε——气体压缩性修正系数。

(4)激光测速法是利用激光多普勒效应测量流体速度。

16.5.2 机械风速仪的测量及结构

机械风速仪的测量的敏感元件是一个轻型叶轮，一般采用金属铝制成。带有径向装置的叶轮按形状可分为翼型和杯型，翼型叶轮的叶片由几片扭成一定角度的铝薄片所组成，杯型叶轮的叶片为铝制的半球形叶片。因气流流动的动压力作用在叶片上，使叶轮产生回转运动，其转速与气流速度成正比，早期的风速仪是将叶轮的转速通过机械传动装置连接到指示或指数设备，以显示其所测流速。现代的风速仪是将叶轮的转速转变成电信号，自动进行显示或记录。

16.5.3 热线风速仪的测量原理及结构

热线风速仪分恒电流式和恒温度式两种。把一个通有电流的带热体置入被测气流中，其散热量与气流速度有关，流速越大，表面传热系数越大，带热体单位时间内的散热量就越多。若通过带热体的电流恒定，则带热体所带的热量不变。带热体温度随其周围气流速度的提高而降低，根据带热体的温度测量气流速度，这就是目前普遍使用的恒电流式热线风速仪的工作原理。维持带电体温度恒定，通过带热体的电流势必随其周围气流速度的增大而增大，根据通过带热体的电流测风速，这就是恒温度式热线风速仪的工作原理。

图 16.5-1a)所示的恒电流式热线风速仪测量电路中，当热线感受的流速为零时，测量电桥处于平衡状态，即检流计指向零点，此时，电流表的读数为 I_0。当热线被放置到流场中后，由于热线与流体之间的热交换，热线的温度下降，相应的阻值 R_w 也随之减小，致使电桥失去平衡，检流计偏离零点。当检流计达到稳定状态后，调节与热线串联于同一桥臂上的可变电阻 R_a，直至其增大量等于 R_w 减少量时，电桥重新恢复平衡，检流计回到零点，电流表也回到原来的读数 I_0（即电流保持不变）。这样，通过测量可变电阻 R_a 的改变量即可得到 R_w 的数值，进而确定被测流速。

图 16.5-1b)所示的恒温度式热线风速仪测量电路中，其工作方式与前述恒流式的不同之处在于，当热线因感应到的流速而出现温度下降时，电阻减小，电桥失去平衡；调节可变电阻 R，使 R 减小以增加电桥的供电电压和工作电流，加大热线的加热功率，促使热线温度回升，阻值 R_w 增大，直至电桥重新恢复平衡，从而通过热线电流的变化来确定风速。

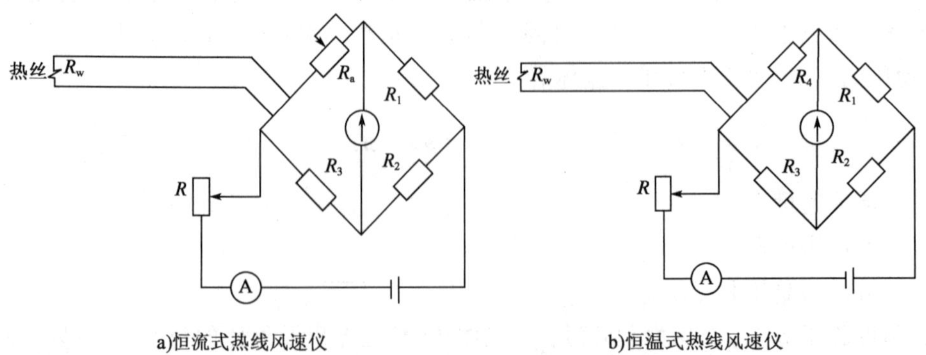

图 16.5-1 热线风速仪工作原理

在上述两种热线风速仪中，恒电流式热线风速仪是在变温状态下工作的，测头容易老化，稳定性稍差且测量灵敏度受热惯性的影响，易产生相位滞后。因此，现在的热线风速仪大多采用恒温度式。

典型例题解析

【例 16.5-1】 在恒温式热线风速仪中，对探头上的敏感热线有：

A. 敏感元件的内阻和流过敏感元件的电流均不变

B. 敏感元件的内阻变化，流过敏感元件的电流不变

C. 敏感元件的内阻不变，流过敏感元件的电流变化

D. 敏感元件的内阻和流过敏感元件的电流均发生变化

解 本题主要考察恒温式热线风速仪的工作原理。恒温式热线风速仪的敏感热线的温度保持不变，给风速敏感元件电流可调，在不同风速下使处于不同热平衡状态的风速敏感元件的工作温度基本维持不便，即阻值基本恒定，该敏感元件所消耗的功率为风速的函数。选 C。

【例 16.5-2】 在以下四种测量气流速度的装置中，动态响应速度最高的是：

A. 恒温式热线风速仪　　B. 恒流式热线风速仪

C. 皮托管　　D. 机械式风速计

解 皮托管是利用安装在流体运动方向上的两根直管产生的压差来测量液体或气体的流速和流量的检出元件，它是流量测量仪表中最简单的一种。最简单的皮托管有一根端部带有小孔的金属细管为导压管，正对流束方向测出流体的总压力(即静压力和动压力之和)；另在金属细管前面附近的主管道壁上再引出一根导压管，测得静压力。差压计与两导压管相连，测出的压差即为动压力。根据伯努利定理，动压力与流速的平方成正比。因此用皮托管可测出流体的流速。在结构上进行改进后即成为组合式皮托管，即皮托-静压管。它是一根弯成直角的双层管。外套管与内套管之间封口，在外套管的周围有若干小孔。测量时，将此套管插入被测管道中间。内套管的管口正对流束方向，外套管周围小孔的孔口恰与流束方向垂直，这时测出内外套管的压差即可计算出流体在该点的流速。选 C。

【例 16.5-3】 热线风速仪的测量原理是：

A. 动压法　　B. 霍尔效应

C. 热效率法　　D. 激光多普勒效应

解 热线风速仪是利用加热的金属丝(热线)的热量损失速率和气流流速之间的关系来求得气流速度的一种仪器，因此其测量原理基于热效率法。选 C。

16.5.4 L 形动压管(毕托管)

毕托管是传统的测量流速的传感器，与差压仪表配合使用可以通过测量被测流体的压力和差压，间接测量被测流体的流速。用毕托管测量流体的流速分布以及流体的平均流速是十分方便的。另外，如果被测流体及其截面是确定的，还可以利用毕托管测量流体的体积流量或质量流量。毕托管是至今仍被广泛应用的流速测量仪表。毕托管有多种形式，其结构各不相同。图 16.5-2 是一种 L 形毕托管的结构图。

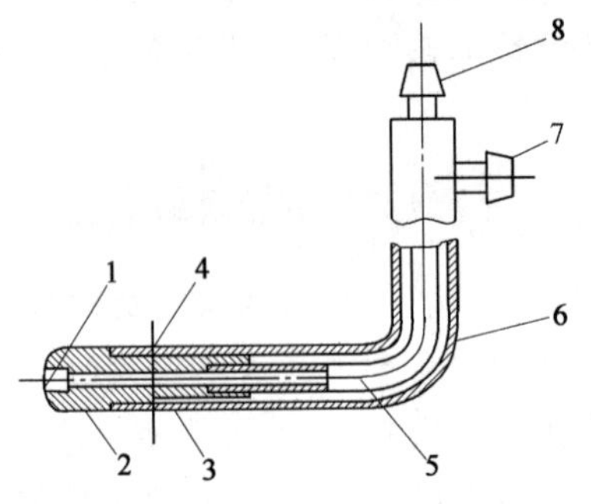

图 16.5-2　L 形毕托管结构图

1-全压测孔；2-测头；3-外管；4-静压测孔；5-内管；6-管柱；7-静压接口；8-全压接口

它是一个弯成 90°的同心管，主要由感测头、管身及总压和动压引出管组成。感测头端部呈椭圆形。总压孔位于感测头端部，与内管连通，用来测量总压。在外管表面靠近感测头端部的位置上有一圈小孔，称为静压孔，是用来测量静压的。标准毕托管一般为这种结构形式。标准毕托管测量精度较高，使用时不需要再校正，但是由于这种结构形式的静压孔很小，在测量含尘浓度较高的空气流速时容易堵塞，因此，标准毕托管主要用于测量清洁空气的流速，或对其他结构形式的毕托管及其他流速仪表进行标定。

16.5.5 测速仪

1)圆柱形三孔测速仪

一种二元复合测压管，如图 16.5-3 所示，圆柱形的杆子上，在距端部一定距离(一般大于 $2d$)并垂直于杆子轴线的平面上，有三个孔。中间一个孔用来测定流体的总压，两侧孔与中间孔对称，并相隔一定的角度，用来测定流动方向。方向孔上感受的压力为流体总压与静压间的某一压力值，因此只要事先经过标定，开三个孔的测压管可以同时测出平面流场中的总压、静压、速度的大小和方向。

2)三管形测速仪

三管形复合测压管是由三根弯成一定形状的小管焊接在一起组成的，如图 16.5-4 所示。两侧方向管的斜角要尽可能相等；斜角可以向外斜，也可以向内斜；总压管可以在两方向管之间，也可以在它们上方或下方。

三管形复合测压管的特性和校准曲线与圆柱形三孔复合测压管类似。

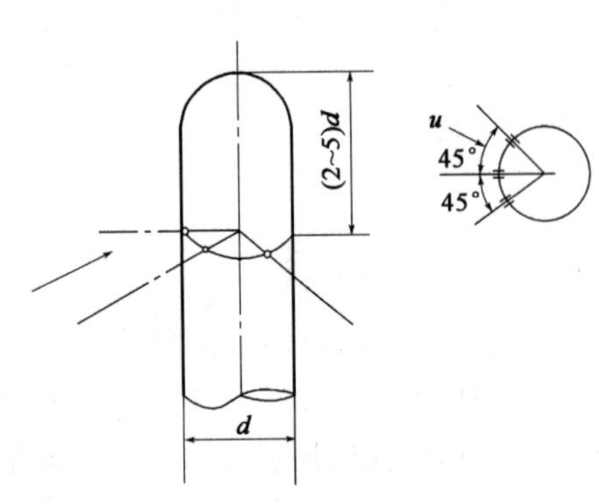

图 16.5-3　圆柱形三孔复合测压管

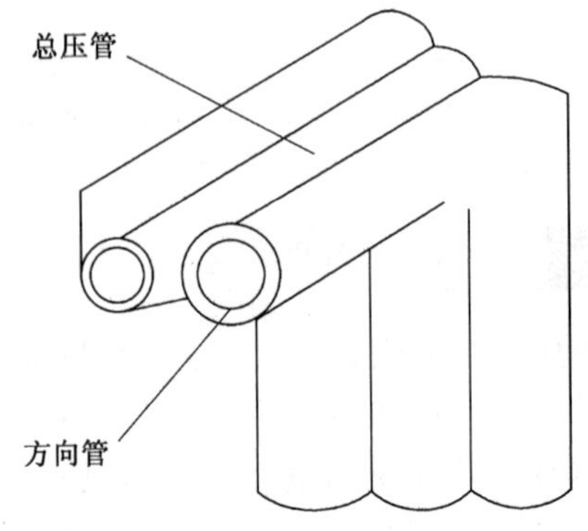

图 16.5-4　三管形复合测压管

16.5.6 流速测量布置技术

测量管道内流体流速时，如果在测量位置上的流体流动已达到典型的紊流速分布，则测出管道中心流速，按照一定公式或图表，便可求得流体平均速度。或者直接测出距离管道内壁$(0.242\pm0.08)R$（R 为管道内截面半径）处的流速作为流体平均流速。

当管道内流体流动没有达到充分发展的紊流时，则应在截面上多测几点的流速，求得平均流速。中间矩形法是应用最广的一种测点选择方法：将管道截面分成若干个面积相等的小截面，测点选在小截面的某一点上，以该点的流速作为小截面的平均流速，再以各小截面的平均流速的平均值作为管道内流体的平均流速。

典型例题解析

【例 16.5-4】 三管型测速仪上的二测方向管的斜角，可以外斜也可以内斜，在相同条件下，外斜的测压管比内斜的灵敏度：

A. 高　　B. 低　　C. 相等　　D. 无法确定

解 两侧方向管的斜角要尽可能相等，斜角可以外斜或内斜。相同条件下外斜的测压管比内斜的测压管灵敏度高。选 A。

经 典 练 习

16.5-1 今用 S 形毕托管测烟道内烟气流速。毕托管的速度校正系数 $K_p=0.85$，烟气密度为 $0.693kg/m^3$，烟道断面上 2 个测点处毕托管两端输出压力差分别为 111.36Pa 和198.41 Pa，则该烟道烟气平均流速为(　　)m/s。

A. 19.3　　B. 18.0　　C. 17.8　　D. 13.4

16.5-2 下述有关三管形复合测压管特点的叙述中，(　　)的内容是不确切的。

A. 焊接小管的感测头部较小，可以用于气流 Ma 数较高、横向速度梯度较大的气流测量

B. 刚性差，方向管斜角较大，测量气流时较易产生脱流，所以在偏流角较大时，测量数值不太稳定

C. 两侧方向管的斜角要保持相等，斜角可以向内斜，也可以向外斜，可以在两方向管中间也可以在方向管的上下布置

D. 为了克服对测速流场的干扰，一般采用管外加屏蔽处理

16.5-3 不需要借助压力计测量流速的仪表是(　　)。

A. 热电风速仪　　B. 毕托管　　C. 圆柱形三孔测速仪　　D. 三管形测速仪

16.5-4 需要借助压力计测量流速的仪表是(　　)。

A. 涡街流量计　　B. 涡轮流量计　　C. 椭圆齿轮流量计　　D. 标准节流装置

16.5-5 热线风速仪常使用在某些场合，但下列的(　　)是不正确的场合。

A. 可测对象为几何形状较复杂流体，如不透明介质(如油)的流速

B. 测量紊流参数、测量微风速、脉动速度

C. 可以使流速的量程扩大到 500 m/s，脉动频率上限提高到 80kHz

D. 热惯性大、功耗大、测量误差较大

16.6 流量的测量

考试大纲☞：节流法测流量原理　测量范围　节流装置类型及其使用方法　容积法测流量　其他流量计　流量测量的布置技术

必备基础知识

16.6.1 节流法和容积法测流量

1）节流法测流量原理

根据伯努利方程提供的基本原理，可以通过测量流体经过节流装置前后的压差来测量流体流量。

连续流动的流体，当遇到安插在管道中的节流装置时，将在节流元件处形成局部收缩。流速受到节流元件的阻挡，在节流元件前后形成涡流，有一部分动能转化为压力能，使节流元件入口侧管壁静压升高到 p_1、孔板下游出口侧管壁静压减小到 p_2。

由伯努利方程整理得

$$q_m = \alpha A_0 \sqrt{2\rho \times (p_1 - p_2)} \tag{16.6-1}$$

即可以通过测量压力差计算得到质量流量 q_m。其中 α 为流量系数，A_0 为流通面积。

2）测量范围

一般认为，用节流装置测量流量时，其可测最小流量为计算满刻度流量的 1/3。

3）节流装置类型及其使用方法

工业上常用的节流装置是已经标准化了的“标准节流装置”，如标准孔板、喷嘴、文丘里喷嘴和文丘里管等。采用标准节流装置进行设计计算时，都有统一标准的规定和要求以及计算所需要的通用化实验数据资料。标准节流装置可以根据计算结果直接制造和使用，不必用实验方法进行标定。

有时也采用一些非标准节流装置，如双重孔板、圆缺孔板、双斜孔板、1/4 圆喷嘴、矩形节流装置等，虽有一些设计计算资料可供使用，但尚未达到标准化，故仍需对每台流量计进行单独的实验标定。

4）容积法测流量

充满一定容积空间里的液体，随流量计内部运动元件的移动而被送出出口，测量这种送出流体的次数就可以求出通过流量计的流体体积。

典型例题解析

【例 16.6-1】 在标准状态下，用某节流装置测量湿气体中干气部分的体积流量，如果工作状态下的相对湿度比设计值增加了，这时仪表的指示值将：

A. 大于真实值　　B. 等于真实值

C. 小于真实值　　D. 无法确定

解 由于测量干气部分的体积流量，湿度增加了，则干气减少，同样的体积流量，仪表的指示将大于真实值。选 A。

【例 16.6-2】 在节流式流量计的使用中，管流方面无须满足的条件是：

A. 流体应是连续流动并充满管道与节流件

B. 流体是牛顿流体，单相流且流经节流件时不发生相变

C. 流动是平稳的或随时间缓慢变化

D. 流体应低于最小雷诺数要求，即为层流状态

解 使用标准节流装置时，流体的性质和状态必须满足下列条件：

①流体必须充满管道和节流装置，并连续地流经管道。

②流体必须是牛顿流体，即在物理上和热力学上是均匀的、单相的，或者可以认为是单相的，包括混合气体、溶液和分散性粒子小于0.1m的胶体。在气体中有不大于2%（质量成分）均匀分散的固体微粒，或液体中有不大于5%（体积成分）均匀分散的气泡，也可认为是单相流体。但其密度应取平均密度。

③流体流经节流件时不发生相交。

④流体流量不随时间变化或变化非常缓慢。

⑤流体在流经节流件以前，流束是平行于管道轴线的无旋流。

选D。

【例 16.6-3】 流体流过节流孔板时，流束在孔板的哪个区域收缩到最小？

A. 进口处　　B. 进口前一定距离

C. 出口处　　D. 出口后一定距离

解 当水经过节流孔板缩口时，流束会变细或收缩。流束的最小横断面出现在实际缩口的下游，称为缩流断面，在缩流断面处，流速是最大的。选D。

16.6.2 流量计

1）涡轮式流量计

涡轮式流量计的结构如图16.6-1所示，管形壳体1的内壁上装有导流器2、3，一方面促使流体沿轴线方向平行流动，另一方面支撑了涡轮的前后轴承。涡轮4上装有螺旋桨形的叶片，在流体冲击下旋转。为了测出涡轮的转速，管壁外装有由线圈、永久磁铁、放大器等组成的变送器5。由于涡轮具有一定的铁磁性，当叶片在永久磁铁前扫过时，会引起磁通的变化，因而在线圈两端产生感应电动势，此感应交流电信号的频率与被测流体的体积流量成正比。如将该频率信号送入脉冲计数器即可得到累积总流量，通过涡轮流量计的体积流量 q_V 与变送器输出信号频率 f 的关系为

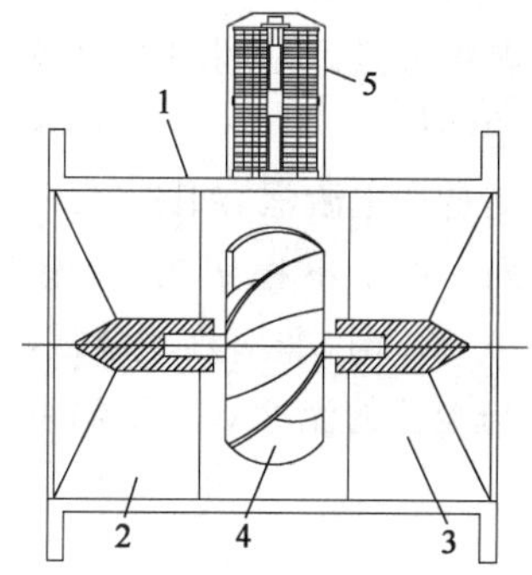

图 16.6-1 涡轮式流量计
1-壳体；2-入口导流器；3-出口导流器；4-涡轮；5-变送器

$$q_V = \frac{f}{K} \qquad (16.6\text{-}2)$$

式中：K——仪表常数，由涡轮流量计结构参数决定。

理想情况下，如仪表常数 K 恒定不变，则 q_V 与 f 呈线性关系。但实际情况是涡轮往往有轴承摩擦力矩、电磁阻力矩、流体对涡轮的黏性摩擦阻力等因素的影响，所以 K 并不严格保持

常数。特别是在流量很小的情况下，由于阻力矩的影响相对较大，K 更不稳定。所以最好应用在量程上限的 5%以上，这时有比较好的线性关系。涡轮流量计具有测量精度高(可以达到 0.5 级以上)、反应迅速、可测脉动流量、耐高压等特点，适用于清洁液体、气体的测量。

2)电磁流量计

电磁流量计是基于电磁感应原理工作的流量测量仪表，用于测量具有一定导电性液体的体积流量。测量精度不受被测液体的黏度、密度及温度等因素变化的影响，且测量管道中没有任何阻碍液体流动的部件，所以几乎没有压力损失。适当选用测量管中绝缘内衬和测量电极的材料，就可以测量各种腐蚀性(酸、碱、盐)液体流量，尤其在测量含有固体颗粒的液体如泥浆、矿浆等的流量时，更显示出其优越性。

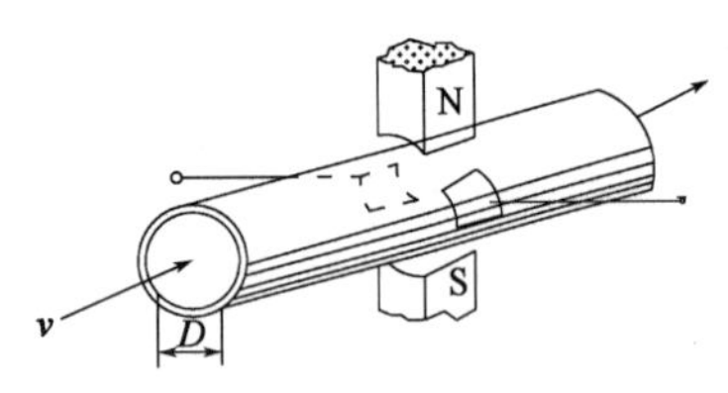

图 16.6-2　电磁流量计工作原理

图 16.6-2 为电磁流量计工作原理图。在磁铁 N-S 极形成的均匀磁场中，垂直于磁场方向有一直径为 D 的管道。管道由不导磁材料制成，管道内表面衬挂绝缘衬里。当导电的液体在导管中流动时，导电液体切割磁力线，于是在和磁场及其流动方向垂直的方向上产生感应电动势，如安装一对电极，则电极间产生和流速成正比例的感应电势 E

$$E = BDv \tag{16.6-3}$$

式中：D——管道内径(m)；

B——磁场磁感应强度(T)；

v——液体在管道中的平均流速(m/s)。

由式(16.6-3)可得：$v=E/BD$，则体积流量为

$$q_V = \frac{\pi D^2}{4}v = \frac{\pi DE}{4B} \tag{16.6-4}$$

从式(16.6-4)可见流体在导管中流过的体积流量和感应电势成正比。把感应电势放大接入显示仪表，便可指示相应的流量。

3)涡街流量计

涡街流量计是利用卡门涡街的原理制作的一种仪表，它是把一个称作漩涡发生体的对称形状的物体(见图 16.6-3)垂直插在管道中，流体绕过漩涡发生体时，在漩涡发生体的两侧后方会交替产生漩涡，如图 16.6-3 所示，两侧漩涡的旋转方向相反。由于漩涡之间的相互影响，漩涡列一般是不稳定的，只有当两漩涡列之间的距离和同列的两个漩涡之间的距离满足 $h/l=0.281$ 时，非对称的漩涡列才能保持稳定。这种漩涡列被称为卡门涡街。此时漩涡的频率 f 与流体的流速 v 及漩涡发生体的宽度 d 有下述关系

$$f = S_t \frac{v}{d} \tag{16.6-5}$$

式中：S_t——斯特劳哈尔数。

试验证明，当流体的雷诺数 Re 在一定范围内，管道内径 D 和漩涡发生体的宽度 d 确定时，斯特劳哈尔数 S_t 为常数，流量计的仪表结构常数 K 值也随之确定。此时被测流量 q_V 与涡街频率 f 的关系为

$$q_V = \frac{f}{K} \tag{16.6-6}$$

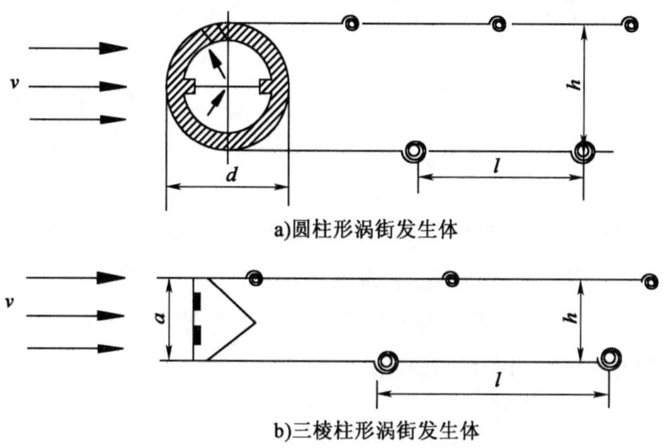

图 16.6-3　涡街发生原理示意图

由式(16.6-6)可知，只要测出涡街频率 f 就能求得流过流量计流体的体积流量 q_V。

涡街流量计有如下特点：涡街频率只与流速有关，在一定雷诺数范围内几乎不受流体压力、温度、黏度、密度变化影响；无零点漂移，测量精度高，误差±1%，重复精度±5%；压力损失小，量程范围为 100:1，特别适宜大口径管道的流量测量。

4)转子流量计

(1)转子流量计的结构形式与工作原理。转子流量计又名浮子流量计，可用于测量液体和气体的流量，一般分为玻璃管转子流量计和金属管转子流量计两类。其工作原理如图 16.6-4 所示。这种流量计的本体由一个锥形管和一个位于锥形管内的可动转子(或称浮子)组成，垂直装在测量管道上。当流体在压力作用下自下而上流过锥形管时，转子在流体作用力和自身重力作用下将悬浮在一个平衡位置。

根据不同平衡位置可算得被测流体的流量。其体积流量计算式为

$$q_V = CA\sqrt{\frac{2V_f g(\rho_f - \rho)}{\rho A_f}} \tag{16.6-7}$$

式中：C——流量系数，与转子形状、尺寸有关；

A——转子与锥形管壁之间环形通道面积；

A_f——转子最大横截面积；

V_f——转子体积；

ρ_f——转子密度；

ρ——流体密度；

g——重力加速度。

1

2

图 16.6-4　转子流量计工作原理

1-锥管；2-转子

由于锥形管的锥角较小，所以 A 与 h 近似比例关系，即 $A=kh$，其中 k 为与锥形管锥度有关的比例系数，h 为转子在锥形管中的高度。

由此而得到体积流量与转子高度的关系

$$q_V = Ckh\sqrt{\frac{2V_f g(\rho_f - \rho)}{\rho A_f}} \tag{16.6-8}$$

实验证明，可以用这个关系式作为按转子高度来刻度流体流量的基本公式。但需说明的是，流量系数 C 与浮子形状的管道的雷诺数有关。当然，对于一定的转子形状来说，只要流体

雷诺数大于某一个低限雷诺数时，流量系数就趋于一个常数。这时，体积流量 q_V 就与转子高度 h 上的线性刻度成一一对应关系。

从上述分析中可以看出，它与节流装置的差异在于：①任意稳定情况下，作用在转子上的压差是恒定不变的；②转子与锥形管之间的环形缝隙的面积 A 是随平衡位置的高低而变化，故是变截面。

(2)刻度校正。转子流量计在出厂刻度时所用介质是水或空气，在实际使用时，被测介质可能不同，即使被测介质相同，但由于温度和压力不同，这时介质的密度和黏度就会发生变化，就需对刻度校正。如果原刻度是以水为介质刻度的，当介质温度压力改变时，如果黏度相差不大，则只要对密度 ρ 做校正就可以了，其校正系数 K_1 为

$$K_1 = \sqrt{\frac{(\rho_f - \rho)\rho_0}{(\rho_f - \rho_0)\rho}} \tag{16.6-9}$$

式中：ρ_0——仪表原刻度时介质密度。

$$q_V = K_1 q_{V0} \tag{16.6-10}$$

式中：q_V——校正后被测介质流量；

q_{V0}——仪表原刻度时的流量值。

如果原标定时所用介质为空气，而当介质温度、压力改变时，根据上述道理，也只用密度校正。由于 $\rho_f \gg \rho_0$，$\rho_f \gg \rho$，所以修正系数简化为

$$K_2 = \sqrt{\frac{\rho_0}{\rho}} \tag{16.6-11}$$

$$q_V = K_2 q_{V0} \tag{16.6-12}$$

5)超声波流量计

(1)超声波流量计的测量原理，如图 16.6-5 所示，它利用超声波在流体中的传播特性来测量流体的流速和流量，最常用的方法是测量超声波在顺流与逆流中的传播速度差。两个超声换能器 P_1 和 P_2 分别安装在管道外壁两侧，以一定的倾角对称布置。超声波换能器通常采用锆钛酸铅陶瓷制成。在电路的激励下，换能器产生超声波以一定的入射角射入管壁，在管壁内以横波形式传播，然后折射入流体，并以纵波的形式在流体内传播，最后透过介质，穿过管壁为另一换能器所接收。两个换能器是相同的，通过电子开关控制，可交替作为发射器和接收器。

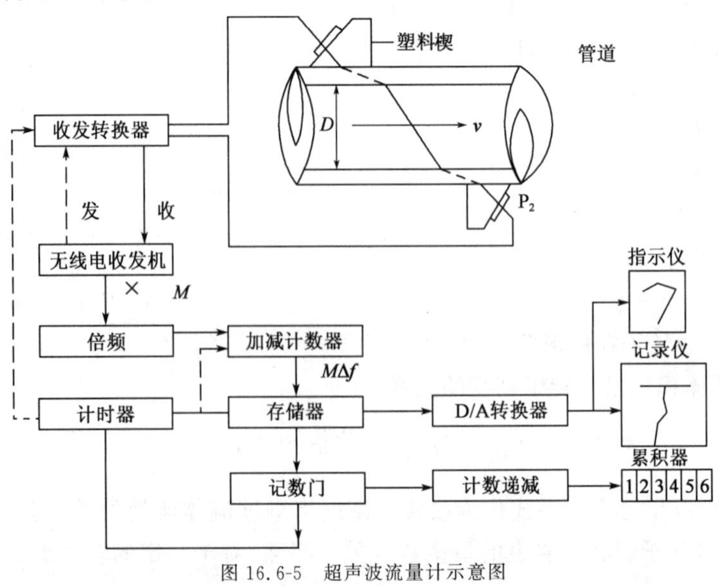

图 16.6-5　超声波流量计示意图

设流体的流速为 v，管道内径为 D，超声波束与管道轴线的夹角为 θ，超声波在静止等的流体中传播速度为 v_0，则超声波在顺流方向传播频率 f_1 为

$$f_1 = \frac{v_0 + v\cos\theta}{D/\sin\theta} = \frac{(v_0 + v\cos\theta)\sin\theta}{D} \tag{16.6-13}$$

超声波在逆流方向传播频率 f_2 为

$$f_2 = \frac{v_0 - v\cos\theta}{D/\sin\theta} = \frac{(v_0 - v\cos\theta)\sin\theta}{D} \tag{16.6-14}$$

故顺流与逆流传播频率差为

$$\Delta f = f_1 - f_2 = \frac{v\sin2\theta}{D} \tag{16.6-15}$$

由此得流体的体积流量 q_V 为

$$q_V = \frac{\pi D^2}{4}v = \frac{\pi D^2}{4} \times \frac{D\Delta f}{\sin2\theta} = \frac{\pi D^3\Delta f}{4\sin2\theta} \tag{16.6-16}$$

对于一个具体的流量计，式(16.6-16)中 θ、D 是常数，而 q_V 与 Δf 成正比，故测量频率差 Δf 可算出流体流量。

(2)超声波流量计的使用。超声波流量计可用来测量液体和气体的流量，比较广泛地用于测量大管道液体的流量或流速。它没有插入被测流体管道的部件，故没有压头损失，可以节约能源。

超声波流量计的换能器与流体不接触，对腐蚀很强的流体也同样可准确测量。而且换能器在管外壁安装，故安装和检修时对流体流动和管道都毫无影响。超声波流量计的测量准确度一般为1%～2%，测量管道液体流速范围一般为0.5～5m/s。

典型例题解析

【例 16.6-4】 在以下四种常用的流量计中测量精度较高的是：

A. 节流式流量计　　B. 转子流量计

C. 容积式流量计　　D. 靶式流量计

解　容积式流量计，又称定排量流量计，简称PD流量计，在流量仪表中是精度最高的一类。它利用机械测量元件把流体连续不断地分割成单个已知的体积部分，根据测量室逐次重复地充满和排放该体积部分流体的次数来测量流体体积总量。选C。

【例 16.6-5】 基于被测参数的变化引起敏感元件的电阻变化，从而检测出被测参数值是一种常用的检测手段，以下测量仪器中不属于此种方法的是：

A. 应变式压力传感器　　B. 点接点水位计

C. 恒流式热线风速仪　　D. 涡街流量传感器

解　涡街流量计是由设计在流场中的旋涡发生体、检测探头及相关的电子线路等组成。当液体流经三角柱形旋涡发生体时，它的两侧就成了交替变化的两排旋涡，这种旋涡被称为卡门涡街，这些交替变化的旋涡就形成了一系列替变化的负压力，该压力作用在检测深头上，便产生一系列交变电信号，经过前置放大器转换、整形、放大处理后，输出与旋涡同步成正比的脉冲频率信号。选D。

【例 16.6-6】 不能用来测量蒸汽流量的流量计是：

A. 容积式流量计　　B. 涡轮流量计

C. 电磁流量计　　D. 转子流量计

解　电磁流量计只能测量导电液体，因此对于气体、蒸气以及含大量气泡的液体，或者

电导率很低的液体不能测量。由于测量管内衬材料一般不宜在高温下工作，所以目前一般的电磁流量计还不能用于测量高温介质。选 C。

【例 16.6-7】 下列关于电磁流量计的叙述，错误的是：

A. 是一种测量导电性液体流量的表　　B. 不能测量含有固体颗粒的液体

C. 应用法拉第电磁感应原理　　D. 可以测量腐蚀性的液体

解　电磁流量计利用法拉第感应定律来检测流量。在电磁流量计内部有一个产生磁场的电磁线圈，以及用于捕获电动势（电压）的电极。正是由于这一点，电磁流量计才可以在管道内似乎什么也没有的情况下仍然可以测量流量。其优点包括不受液体的温度、压力、密度或黏度的影响，能够检测包含污染物（固体、气泡）的液体，没有压力损失，没有可动部件（提高可靠性）。选 B。

【例 16.6-8】 用标准节流装置测量某蒸汽管道内的蒸汽流量。若介质的实际温度由 420℃下降到 400℃，实际压力由设计值 35kgf/cm^2 下降到 30kgf/cm^2，当流量计显示值为 100T/h 时，实际流量为：（420℃，35kgf/cm^2 时水蒸气密度为 11.20kg/m^3；400℃，30kgf/cm^2 时水蒸气密度 9.867kg/m^3）

A. 113.59T/h　　B. 88.1T/h

C. 106.54T/h　　D. 93.86T/h

解　对于节流式流量计实际流量与计算流量间计算公式为 $q_{\text{ms}}=\sqrt{\rho_{\text{s}}/(\rho_k q_{\text{mk}})}$，代入数据计算可得。选 D。

【例 16.6-9】 某节流装置在设计时，介质的密度为 500kg/m^3，而在实际使用时，介质密度为 460kg/m^3。如果设计时，差压变送器输出 100kPa 时对应的流量为 50T/h，则在实际使用时，对应的流量为：

A. 47.96T/h　　B. 52.04T/h

C. 46.15T/h　　D. 54.16T/h

解　选 A。

【例 16.6-10】 某涡轮流量计和涡街流量计均用常温下的水进行过标定，当用它们来测量液氨的体积流量时：

A. 均需进行黏度和密度修正

B. 涡轮流量计需进行黏度和密度修正，涡街流量计不需要

C. 涡街流量计需进行黏度和密度修正，涡轮流量计不需要

D. 均不需进行黏度和密度的修正

解　涡轮流量计原理是流体流经传感器壳体，由于叶轮的叶片与流向有一定的角度，流体的冲力使叶片具有转动力矩，克服摩擦力矩和流体阻力之后叶片旋转，在力矩平衡后转速稳定，在一定的条件下，转速与流速成正比，由于叶片有导磁性，它处于信号检测器（由永久磁钢和线圈组成）的磁场中，旋转的叶片切割磁力线，周期性的改变着线圈的磁通量，从而使线圈两端感应出电脉冲信号，此信号经过放大器的放大整形，形成有一定幅度的连续的矩形脉冲波，可远传至显示仪表，显示出流体的瞬时流量和累计量，因此流体的黏度和密度对测量值影响很大，黏度和密度改变是需要进行修正。涡街流量计原理是应用流体振荡原理来测量流量的，流体在管道中经过涡街流量变送器时，在三角柱的旋涡发生体后上下交替产生正比于流速的两列旋涡，旋涡的释放频率与流过旋涡发生体的流体平均速度及旋涡发生体特征宽度有关，流体黏度和密度改变时不需要修正。选 B。

【例 16.6-11】 某饱和蒸汽管道的内径为 250mm，蒸汽密度为 4.8kg/m³，节流孔板孔径为 150mm，流量系数为 0.67，则孔板前后压差为 40kPa 时的流量为：

A. 7.3kg/h　　B. 20.4kg/h

C. 26 400kg/h　　D. 73 332kg/h

解 $q_m=0.67\times3.14\times\left(\frac{0.15}{2}\right)^2\times\sqrt{2\times4.8\times40\ 000}\times3\ 600=26\ 399.5\text{kg/h}$。选 C。

16.6.3 流量测量的布置技术

1)节流装置的安装

(1)节流装置中心应与管道中心重合，断面应与管道中心线垂直，并不得装反。

(2)节流装置取压口方位的确定应按下列规定进行。

①测量气体时：在管道上部。

②测量液体时：在管道的下半部(最好在水平中心线上)。

③测量蒸汽时：在管道的上半部(最好在水平中心线上)。

2)引压管的安装

(1)引压管应按最短距离垂直或倾斜(倾斜度不得小于 1∶10)安装。

(2)引压管路中应加装气体、凝液、颗粒收集器和沉降器。

(3)引压管应不受外界热源的影响，并应防止可能发生的冻结。

(4)对于有黏性和有腐蚀性的介质，为了防堵、防腐，应加装隔离罐。

(5)引压管路应保证密封，无渗漏现象。

(6)引压管路上应装有必要的切断、冲洗、灌封液、排污等所需要的阀门。

3)差压计的安装

保证安装地点的环境条件(如温度、湿度、腐蚀性、振动等)。

典型例题解析

【例 16.6-12】 使用节流式流量计，国家标准规定采用的取压方式是：

A. 角接取压和法兰取压　　B. 环室取压和直接钻空取压

C. 角接取压和直接钻孔取压　　D. 法兰取压和环壁取压

解 根据国家标准节流式流量计的取压方式有两种即角接取压和法拉取压，其中角接取压又分为环室取压和直接钻孔取压两种方式。选 A。

【例 16.6-13】 已知如图所示的两容器，中间用阀门连接，若关小阀门，那么管道流量变化是：

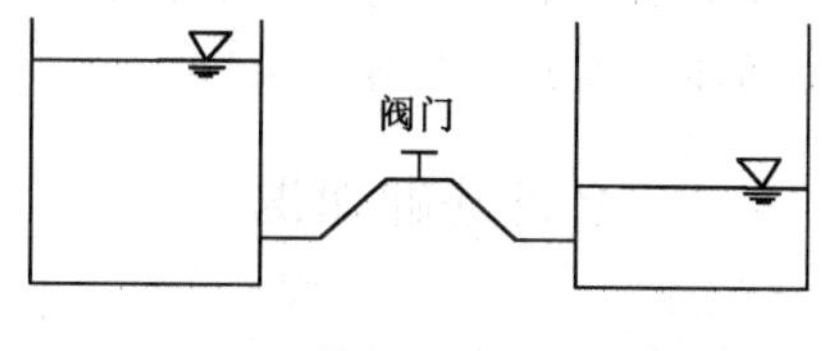

例 16.6-13 图

A. 不变　　B. 增大　　C. 减小　　D. 不确定

解 由于阀门开度变小，两容器间压力差减小，流体流动驱动力减小，故流量变小。选 C。

经典练习

16.6-1 用皮托管测量管道内水的流量。已知水温 $t=50℃$，水密度 $0.988kg/m^3$，运动黏度 $\upsilon=0.552\times10m^2/s$，管道直径 $D=200mm$，皮托管全压口距管壁 $\lambda=23.8mm$，测得压差 $\Delta p=0.7kPa$，由此可求得此时的容积流量为（　　）m^3/h。

A. 180.28　　B. 160.18　　C. 168.08　　D. 180.20

16.6-2 用电磁流量计测量液体的流量，判断下列叙述正确的是（　　）。

A. 在测量流速不大的液体流量时，不能建立仪表工作所必须的电磁场

B. 这种流量计的工作原理是，在流动的液体中应能产生电动势

C. 只有导电的液体才能在测量仪表的电磁绕组中产生电动势

D. 电磁流量计可适应任何流体

16.6-3 某节流装置在设计时，介质的密度为 $520kg/m^3$，而在实际使用时，介质的密度为 $480kg/m^3$。如果设计时，差压变送器输出 100kPa，对应的流量为 50T/h，由此可知在实际使用时对应的流量为（　　）T/h。

A. 42.6　　B. 46.2　　C. 48.0　　D. 50.0

16.6-4 用超声波流量计测某介质流量，超声波发射与接收装置之间距离 $L=300mm$，介质流速 $v=12m/s$。如果介质温度从 10℃升温到 30℃，烟气超声波的速度从 1 450m/s 变化到 1 485m/s，则温度变化对时间差的影响是（　　）。

A. $\delta_r=-5.7\%$　　B. $\delta_r=4.7\%$　　C. $\delta_r=-4.7\%$　　D. $\delta_r=-8.7\%$

16.6-5 涡轮流量计是速度式流量计，下述有关其特点的叙述中，（　　）不确切。

A. 测量基本误差为±(0.2～1.0)%

B. 可测量瞬时流量

C. 仪表常数应根据被测介质的黏度加以修正

D. 上下游必须有足够的直管段长度

16.6-6 已知直径为 50mm 的涡轮流量变送器，其涡轮上有六片叶片，流量测量范围为 $5\sim50m^3/h$，校验单上的仪表常数是 37.1 次/L。那么在最大流量时，该仪表内的转数是（　　）r/s。

A. 85.9　　B. 515.3　　C. 1 545.9　　D. 3 091.8

16.7 液位的测量

考试大纲☞：直读式测液位　压力法测液位　浮力法测液位　电容法测液位　超声波法测液位　液位测量的布置及误差消除方法

必备基础知识

16.7.1 常见测液位的方法

1) 直读式侧液位

在容器上开一些窗口以便进行观测，或利用连通器原理设置的玻璃管液位计。

2)压力法测液位

根据流体静力学原理,静止介质内某一点的静压力与介质上方自由空间压力之差与该点上方的介质高度成正比,因此可以利用差压来检测液位。

3)浮力法测液位

利用漂浮于液面上的浮子随液面变化,或者部分浸没于液体中的物质的浮力随液位变化来检测液位,前者称为恒浮力法,后者称为变浮力法,两者均可用于液位的检测。

4)电容法测液位

把敏感元件做成一定形状的电极置于被测介质中,则电极之间的电气系数(电容),随物位的变化而改变。

5)超声波法测液位

利用超声波在介质中的传播速度及在不同相界面之间的反射特性来检测液位。

16.7.2 液位测量的布置及误差消除方法

液位检测的特点是从敏感元件所接受到的信号一般与被测介质的某一特性参数有关,如介质的密度、介电常数、介质声波传递速度等。当被测介质的温度、组分等改变时,这些参数可能也要变化,从而影响测量精度。另外,大型容器会出现各处温度、密度和组分等的不均匀,引起特性参数在容器内的不均匀,同样也会影响测量精度。因此当工况变化比较大时,必须对有关的参数进行补偿或修正。

典型例题解析

【例 16.7-1】 水位测量系统如图所示,为了提高测量精度,需对差压变送器实施零点迁移。以下说法正确的是:

A. 对变送器实施正迁移且迁移量为 $gh_1\rho_2-gh_0\rho_1$

B. 对变送器实施负迁移且迁移量为 $gh_1\rho_2-gh_0\rho_2$

C. 对变送器实施正迁移且迁移量为 $gh_1\rho_2-gh\rho_1$

D. 对变送器实施负迁移且迁移量为 $gh_1\rho_2-gh\rho_2$

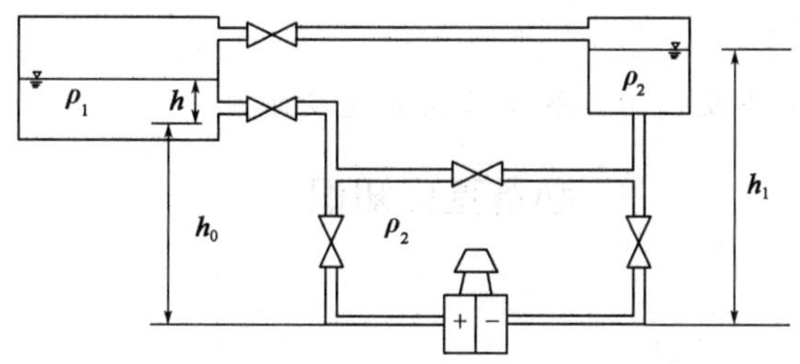

例 16.7-1 图

解 用差压变送器测量液位时,由于差压变送器安装的位置不同,正压和负压导压管内充满了液体,这些液体会使差压变送器有一个固定的差压。在液位为零时,造成差压计指示不在零点,而是指示正或负的一个指示偏差。为了指示正确,消除这个固定偏差,就把零点进行向下或向上移动,也就是进行"零点迁移"。这个差压值就称为迁移量。如果这个值为正,即称系统为正迁移;如果为负,即系统为负迁移;如果这个值为零时,即为无迁移。选 A。

【例 16.7-2】 超声波水位测量系统有液介式单探头、液介式双探头、气介式单探头和气介式双探头四种方案，从声速校正和提高测量灵敏度的角度考虑，测量精度最高的为：

A. 气介式单探头　　B. 液介式单探头

C. 气介式双探头　　D. 液介式双探头

解 超声波式水位计应用声波反射的原理来测量水位。分为水介式和气介式两类。声波在介质中以一定速度传播，当遇到不同密度的介质分界面时，声波立即发生反射。水介式是将换能器安装在河底，垂直向水面发射超声波；气介式是将换能器固定在空气中某一高处，向水面发射超声波。两种形式均不需建测井。水介式声速受水温、水压及水中浮悬粒子浓度影响，在测量过程中要对声波校正，才能达到测最精度。气介式要对气温影响进行校正，其优点是不受水中水草、泥沙等影响。选 D。

【例 16.7-3】 利用浮力法测量液位的液位计是：

A. 压差式液位计　　B. 浮筒液位计

C. 电容式液位计　　D. 压力表式液位计

解 浮筒液位计的原理是，浸在液体中的浮筒受到向下的重力、向上的浮力和弹簧弹力的复合作用。当这三个力达到平衡时，浮筒就静止在某一位置。当液位发生变化时，浮筒所受浮力相应改变，平衡状态被打破，从而引起弹力变化即弹簧的伸缩，以达到新的平衡。弹簧的伸缩使其与刚性连接的磁钢产生位移。这样，通过指示器内磁感应元件和传动装置使其指示出液位。选 B。

【例 16.7-4】 以下液位测量仪表中，不受被测液体密度影响的是：

A. 浮筒式液位计　　B. 压差式液位计

C. 电容式液位计　　D. 超声波液位计

解 空气的介电常数接近 1，而液体的介电常数一般与空气的介电常数相差较大。电容式液位测量原理是基于介电常数的差别来进行测量的。电容式测量主要通过检测由于液面或者散料高度变化而导致的电容值变化来测量料位高度，不受液体密度影响。选 C。

16.8 热流量的测量

考试大纲☞：热流计的分类及使用　热流计的布置及使用。

必备基础知识

16.8.1 热流计的分类

热流计可分为测量传导热流的热阻式热流计和测量辐射热流的非接触式辐射热流计。

16.8.2 热流计的布置及使用

在使用热流传感器时，除了合理选用仪表的量程范围，允许使用温度、传感器的类型、尺寸内阻等有关参数外，还要注意正确的使用方法，否则会引起较大的误差。

热流传感器的安装有三种方法：埋入式、表面粘贴式和空间辐射式。埋入式和表面黏贴式是热阻式热流传感器常用的两种安装方法。被测物体表面的放热状况与许多因素有关，被测物体的散热热流密度与热流测点的几何位置有关。对于水平安装的有均匀保温层圆形管道，测点应选在能反映管道截面上平均热流密度的位置，一般选在截面上与管道水平中心线夹角约为 45°和 135°处。最好在同截面上选几个有代表性的位置进行测量，与所得到的平均值进行比较，从而得到合适的测试位置。对于垂直平壁面和立管也可做类似的考虑。

典型例题解析

【例 16.8-1】 用来测量传导热流的热流计是：

A. 电阻式　　B. 辐射式　　C. 蒸气式　　D. 热水式

解 热流计分为：测量传导热流的热阻式热流计和测量辐射热流的非接触式辐射热流计。选 A。

【例 16.8-2】 以下关于热阻式热流计的叙述，错误的是：

A. 热流侧头尽量薄

B. 热阻尽量小

C. 被测物体热阻应比测头热阻小得多

D. 被测物体热阻应比测头热阻大得多

解 由于热流传感器是热流计最为关键的一个敏感器件，因此其测量精度将直接关系到热流计的测量精度。其中热流传感器与被测物黏贴的紧密程度，对热流的稳定时间有着非常大的影响。黏贴越紧密，稳定越快，测量偏差越小；反之，测量偏差越大。其次，热流传感器厚度越薄越好；另外热流传感器边长越长越好，最优值 20～30mm。选 D。

【例 16.8-3】 以下关于热水热量计的叙述，错误的是：

A. 用来测量热水输送的热量

B. 由流量传感器、温度传感器、积分仪组成

C. 使用光学辐射温度计测量热水温度

D. 使用超声流量计测量热水流量

解 热量计是测量热能生产和热能消耗系统中热流量用的仪表。热量计分为热水热量计、蒸汽热量计、过热蒸汽热量计和饱和蒸汽热量计。热水热量计是测量热水锅炉产热或热网供热用的热流量。根据热力学原理，热流量等于水流量与供水、回水焓差的乘积，而焓差又可用平均比热与其温度差的乘积代替，所以在管道上装一个流量变送器和两个热电阻，将所测得的流量和温度信号送到热量计中，经电子线路放大和运算即可直接显示热水的瞬时热流量，如经计时运算则可同时显示一段时间内的累计热流量。选 C。

16.9 误差与数据处理

考试大纲☞：误差函数的分布规律　直接测量的平均值、方差、标准误差、有效数字和测量结果表达　间接测量最优值、标准误差　误差传播理论　微小误差原则　误差分配　组合测量原理　最小二乘法原理　组合测量的误差　经验公式法　相关系数　回归分析　显著性检验及分析　过失误差处理　系统误差处理方法及消除方法　误差的合成定律

必备基础知识

1)真值与误差

观测对象的量是客观存在的,称为真值。每次观测所得数值称为观测值。设观测对象的真值为 x,观测值为 $x_i(i=1,2,\cdots,n)$,则差数

$$a_i = x_i - x \quad (i = 1,2,\cdots,n)$$

称为观测误差,简称为误差。

2)观测的准确度与精密度

如果观测的系统误差小,则称观测的准确度高,可以使用更精确的仪器来提高观测的准确度。如果观测的随机误差小,则称观测的精密度高,可以增大观测次数,取其平均值来提高观测的精密度。

3)可疑数据的处理

对于可疑数据的取舍要慎重。若在试验进行中,发现异常数据,则应立即停止试验,分析原因并及时纠正错误;若试验结束后发现异常数据,则应先查找原因,再对数据进行取舍。如发现生产(施工)、试验过程中,有可疑的变异时,则该测量值应予舍弃。

当对这类异常数据不能清楚地判定其产生原因时,可以借助一些统计方法进行验证处理,方法很多,如常用的拉依达准则和格拉布斯准则,还有狄克逊准则、肖维勒准则、t 检验法、F 检验法等。这些方法,都有各自的特点。其中,拉依达准则不能检验样本量较小(显著性水平为 0.1 时,n 必须大于 10)的情况,格拉布斯准则则可以检验较少的数据。

但对于异常数据一定要慎重,不能任意的抛弃和修改。往往通过对异常数据的观察,可以发现引起系统误差的原因,进而改进过程和试验。

典型例题解析

【例 16.9-1】 误差产生的原因多种多样,但按误差的基本特性的特点,误差可分为:

A. 随机误差,系统误差和疏忽误差　B. 绝对误差,相对误差和引用误差

C. 动态误差和静态误差　D. 基本误差和附加误差

解 根据误差的基本特性,误差可分为系统误差、随即误差及疏忽误差。其中,系统误差指在相同条件下,对某个量进行多次测量时,误差的绝对值和符号或均保持恒定,或按照一定规律变化;过失误差指在测量过程中,完全由于人为过失而明显造成了歪曲测量结果的误差;随机误差指在对同一个量进行多次测量时,由于受到某些不可知随机因素的影响,测量误差时小时大,时正时负地变化,没有一定的规律,并且无法估计。选 A。

【例 16.9-2】 在测量过程中,多次测量同一个量时,测量误差的绝对值和符号按某一确定规律变化的误差称为:

A. 偶然误差　B. 系统误差　C. 疏忽误差　D. 允许误差

解 系统误差的定义是在相同条件下,对某个量进行多次测量时,误差的绝对值和符号或均保持恒定,或按照一定规律变化。选 B。

【例 16.9-3】 测量次数很多时,比较合适的处理过失误差的方法是:

A. 拉依达准则　B. 示值修正法　C. 格拉布斯准则　D. 参数校正法

解 在整理试验数据时,往往会遇到这样的情况,即在一组试验数据里,发现少数几个偏差特别大的可疑数据,这类数据称为 Outlier 或 Exceptional Data(坏值),它们往往是由于

过失误差引起的。拉依达准则不能检验样本量较小(显着性水平为 0.1 时,n 必须大于 10)的情况,格拉布斯准则则可以检验较少的数据。选 A。

16.9.1 误差函数的分布规律

随机误差的大小、符号虽然显得杂乱无章,但当进行大量等精度测量时,随机误差服从统计规律。理论和测量实践都证明,测得值 X_i 与随机误差 δ_i 都按一定的概率出现。在大多数情况下,测得值在期望值上出现的概率很大,随着对期望值偏离的增大,出现的概率急剧减小。表现在随机误差上,等于零的随机误差出现的概率最大,随着随机误差绝对值得加大,出现的概率急剧减小。测得值和随机误差的这种统计分布规律,称为正态分布,如图 16.9-1 所示。

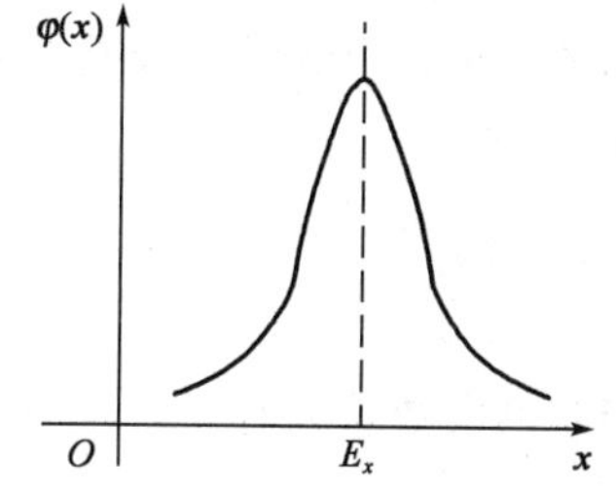

图 16.9-1 测量值正态分布曲线

对于正态分布的测得值 X_i 其概率密度函数

$$\varphi(x) = \frac{1}{\sigma\sqrt{2\pi}}e^{-\frac{(x-E_x)^2}{2\sigma^2}} \tag{16.9-1}$$

同样,对于正态分布的随机误差 δ_i,其概率密度函数

$$\varphi(\delta) = \frac{1}{\sigma\sqrt{2\pi}}e^{-\frac{\delta^2}{2\sigma^2}} \tag{16.9-2}$$

随机误差分析的性质如下。

(1)有界性:在一定的测量条件下,测量的随机误差总是在一定的、相当窄的范围内变动,绝对值很大的误差出现的概率接近于零。

(2)单峰性:绝对值小的误差出现的概率大,绝对值大的误差出现的概率小,绝对值为零的误差出现的概率比任何其他数值的误差出现的概率都大。

(3)对称性:绝对值相等而符号相反的随机误差出现的概率相同,其分布呈对称性。

(4)抵偿性:在等精度测量条件下,当测量次数不断增加而趋于无穷时,全部随机误差的算术平均值趋于零。

16.9.2 直接测量的平均值、方差、标准误差、有效数字和测量结果表达

1)直接测量的平均值(最优概值)

观测对象的真值 x 可以用 n 次观测值 $x_1, x_2, \cdots, x_n$ 的算术平均值

$$\bar{x} = \frac{1}{n}\sum_{x=1}^{n}x_i \tag{16.9-3}$$

近似代替,并用离差

$$\nu_i = x_i - \bar{x}$$

代替误差 $a_i = x_i - x$,离差与误差有如下关系

$$\nu_i = a_i - \frac{1}{n}\sum_{i=1}^{n}a_i$$

$$\sum_{i=1}^{n}\nu_i^2 = \frac{n-1}{n}\sum_{i=1}^{n}a_i^2 \quad (\text{当 } n \text{ 相当大})$$

2)方差

方差为测量值 x_i 与真值 x 之差的平方的统计平均值,则

$$\sigma^2 = \frac{1}{n}\sum_{i=1}^{n}(x_i - x)^2 = \frac{1}{n}\sum_{i=1}^{n}a_i^2 \quad (16.9\text{-}4)$$

当观测次数 n 较大时,x 可以用 $\bar{x}$ 近似代替,即

$$\sigma^2 = \frac{1}{n-1}\sum_{i=1}^{n}(x_i - \bar{x})^2 = \frac{1}{n}\sum_{i=1}^{n}\nu_i^2$$

3)标准差

标准差是各个测量值误差平方和的平均值的平方根,即

$$\sigma = \sqrt{\frac{\sum_{i=1}^{n}(x_i - x)^2}{n}} \quad (16.9\text{-}5)$$

当观测次数较大时

$$\sigma = \sqrt{\frac{\sum_{i=1}^{n}(x_i - \bar{x})^2}{n-1}}$$

4)有效数字

由于含有误差,所以测量数据及由测量数据计算出来的算术平均值等是近似值。若末位数字是个位,则包含的绝对误差值不大于 0.5,若末位是十位,则包含的绝对误差不大于 5,对于其绝对误差不大于末位数字一半的数,从它左边第一个不为零的数字起,到右面最后一个数字(包括零)止,都叫做有效数字。

多余数字的舍入规则:"四舍六入五单双,奇进偶不进",即四舍六入,若为五则看左边一位数是单数还是双数,奇数则进一,偶数则舍去。

已知有效数字求误差:

例如,0.108 0V 表示有四位有效数字,其测量误差不超过±0.000 05V,即实际电压可能是 0.107 95～0.108 05V 之间的任一值。可见,如果知道一个量的有效数字,便可确定它的误差大小。

有效数字运算规则规定:

加减法运算中只保留各数共有的小数位数。计算时,先将小数位数多的数进行修约处理,使其比小数位数最少的只多一位小数,然后进行计算,计算结果的小数位只取到各数中小数位最少的位数。如 28.5+3.74+0.135=28.5+3.74+0.14=32.38=32.4。

对于乘除法的运算规则,是将各数中有效位数多的数进行修约到比有效位数最少的多一位,然后进行计算,计算结果修约到各数中有效位数最少的位数。

典型例题解析

【例 16.9-4】 在等精度测量条件下,对某管道压力进行了 10 次测量,获得如下数据(单位 kPa):475.3,475.7,475.2,475.1,474.8,475.2,475.0,475.1。则该测量列平均值的标准误差等于:

A. 0.09kPa　　B. 0.11kPa　　C. 0.25kPa　　D. 0.30kPa

解 由标准误差计算公式(16.9-5)可以求得该测量量的标准误差。选 A。

16.9.3 测量结果表达

1)列出测量数据(表 16.9-1)

测量数据 表 16.9-1

i	1	2	…	$n-1$	n
x_i	x_1	x_2	…	x_{n-1}	x_n

2)计算算术平均值

$$\bar{x}=\frac{1}{n}\sum_{i=1}^{n}x_i \tag{16.9-6}$$

离差

$$\nu_i=x_i-\bar{x} \tag{16.9-7}$$

3)计算标准差

$$\sigma=\sqrt{\frac{1}{n-1}\sum_{i=1}^{n}\nu_i^2} \tag{16.9-8}$$

算术平均标准差

$$\sigma_{\bar{x}}=\frac{\sigma}{\sqrt{n}} \tag{16.9-9}$$

4)给出最终测量结果表达式

$$x=\bar{x}\pm\sigma_{\bar{x}} \quad (置信度 68.3\%)$$

$$x=\bar{x}\pm2\sigma_{\bar{x}} \quad (置信度 95.3\%)$$

$$x=\bar{x}\pm3\sigma_{\bar{x}} \quad (置信度 99.7\%)$$

典型例题解析

【例 16.9-5】 工程测量中,常以最大剩余误差 σ_i 的绝对值是否小于 3σ(σ 为标准方差)作为判定存在疏忽误差的依据。按此估计方法,所取的置信概率为:

A. 0.683　　B. 0.954　　C. 0.997　　D. 0.999

解 测量结果表达式 $x=\bar{x}+3\sigma_{\bar{x}}$ 的置信度为 99.7%。选 C。

16.9.4 间接测量最优值、标准误差、误差传播理论、微小误差原则、误差分配

由于某些被测量不能进行直接测量,如散热器的传热系数、热物理中的准则数、空气的焓值等,因而必须进行间接测量。即通过直接测量与被测量有一定函数关系的其他量,并根据函数关系计算出被测量。因此,间接测量的量就是直接测量得到的各个测量量的函数,假定间接被测量 Y 与直接测量的有关量 $X_1,X_2,\cdots,X_m$ 为有以下的函数关系

$$Y=f(X_1,X_2,\cdots,X_m) \tag{16.9-10}$$

其中,$X_1,X_2,\cdots,X_m$ 为 m 个可直接测量的独立自变量。如果得到了 $X_1,X_2,\cdots,X_m$ 的最优概值 $X_{1_0},X_{2_0},\cdots,X_{m_0}$ 和标准误差 $\sigma_1,\sigma_2,\cdots,\sigma_m$,就可以得到间接测量值的最优概值及其标准误差。

1)间接测量的最优概值

间接测量值的最优概值 Y_0 可以把各直接测量量的最优概值代到式(16.9-10)中求得。即

$$Y_0 = f(X_{1_0}, X_{2_0}, \cdots, X_{m_0}) \tag{16.9-11}$$

其中，$X_{1_0}, X_{2_0}, \cdots, X_{m_0}$ 为 m 个可直接测量的独立自变量 $X_1, X_2, \cdots, X_m$ 的最优概值，即算术平均值。

2)间接测量的标准误差

在直接测量中，测量误差就是被测量的误差；而在间接测量中，测量误差是各个测量值的函数。因此，研究间接测量的误差也就是分析各直接测量的误差量是怎样通过已知的函数关系传递到间接被测量的。测量$\{Y_i\}$同直接测量一样，定义它的测量列标准误差为

$$\sigma_Y = \sqrt{\frac{1}{n-1}\sum_{i=1}^{n} u_i^2} \tag{16.9-12}$$

其中，$u_i = Y_i - Y_0$ 为间接测量值 Y_i 的剩余误差，则利用式(16.9-11)的泰勒级数展开式可以推得

$$\sigma_Y = \sqrt{\sum_{i=1}^{m}\left(\frac{\partial f}{\partial X_i}\right)\sigma_i^2} \tag{16.9-13}$$

其中，$\frac{\partial f}{\partial X_i}\sigma_i$ 称为自变量 X_i 的部分误差，记作 D_i，这样，式(16.9-13)就变为

$$\sigma_Y = \sqrt{D_1^2 + D_2^2 + \cdots D_m^2} = \sqrt{\sum_{i=1}^{m} D_i^2} \tag{16.9-14}$$

如果用相对误差来表示，则为

$$\sigma_{0Y} = \frac{\sigma_Y}{Y_0} = \sqrt{\sum_{i=1}^{m}\left(\frac{D_i}{Y_0}\right)} = \sqrt{\sum_{i=1}^{m} D_{0i}^2} \tag{16.9-15}$$

式中：σ_{0Y}——Y 的相对标准误差；

D_{0i}——X_i 的相对部分误差。

式(16.9-13)～式(16.9-15)一起被称为误差累积定律或误差传播定律。

3)间接测量的误差传播理论

设直接测量量为 x_1、x_2…、x_n，间接测量量为 y。它们满足函数关系 $y=f(x_1, x_2, \cdots, x_n)$，并设 x_i 之间彼此独立，x_i 的绝对误差为 Δx_i，y 的绝对误差为 Δy，则

绝对误差传递

$$\Delta y = \sum_{i=1}^{n}\frac{\partial y}{\partial x_i}\Delta x_i \tag{16.9-16}$$

相对误差传递

$$y_y = \frac{\Delta y}{y} = \sum_{i=1}^{n}\frac{\partial y}{\partial x_i}\frac{\Delta x_i}{y} \tag{16.9-17}$$

4)间接测量的误差分配

设直接测量量为 x_1、x_2、…、x_n 间接测量量为 y。它们满足函数关系 $y=f(x_1, x_2, \cdots, x_n)$，则

间接测量的标准误差

$$\sigma_y = \sqrt{\left(\frac{\partial f}{\partial x_1}\right)^2\left(\frac{\hat{\sigma}_{x_1}}{y}\right)^2 + \left(\frac{\partial f}{\partial x_2}\right)\left(\frac{\hat{\sigma}_{x_2}}{y}\right)} + \cdots\cdots\left(\frac{\partial f}{\partial x_n}\right)\hat{\sigma}_{x_n}^2 \tag{16.9-18}$$

现 $\hat{\sigma}_y$ 已给定 $\hat{\sigma}_{x_1}, \hat{\sigma}_{x_2}, \cdots, \hat{\sigma}_{x_n}$。按等作用原则分配误差

$$\frac{\partial f}{\partial x_1}\hat{\sigma}_{x_1} = \frac{\partial f}{\partial x_2}\hat{\sigma}_{x_2} = \cdots = \frac{\partial f}{\partial x_n}\hat{\sigma}_{x_n} \tag{16.9-19}$$

从而

$$\hat{\sigma}_y = \sqrt{n}\frac{\partial f}{\partial x_i}\hat{\sigma}_{x_i}(i=1,2,\cdots,n) \tag{16.9-20}$$

得

$$\hat{\sigma}_{x_i} = \hat{\sigma}_y \Big/ \left(\sqrt{n}\frac{\partial f}{\partial x_i}\right) \tag{16.9-21}$$

如果各个直接测量值误差满足式(16.9-21)，则所得的函数间接误差不会超过允许误差的给定值。

5)按微小误差准则处理误差

在误差传播公式(16.9-14)中，若有一部分误差 D_k 可以忽略不计，则令

$$\hat{\sigma}_y \approx \hat{\sigma}'_y = \sqrt{\sum_{i=1}^{m} D_i^2 - D_k^2} \tag{16.9-22}$$

这里的 $\hat{\sigma}_y$ 与 σ_y 的第一位有效数字一样(因为误差一般只取二位有效数字，而第一位是可靠数字)，只是第二位有效数字有差别，则称 D_k 为微小误差，据此可得

$$\sigma_y - \sigma'_y \leqslant 0.005\sigma_y$$

从而得 $0.95\sigma_y \leqslant \sigma'_y$

将上述不等式两边平方有 $0.902\sigma_y^2 \leqslant \sigma'_y$

而 $\sigma'^2_y = \sum_{i=1}^{m} D_i^2 - D_k^2 = \sigma_y^2 - D_k^2$

因此有 $0.9025\sigma'^2_y \leqslant \sigma_y^2 - D_k^2$

$D_k^2 \leqslant 0.0975\sigma_y^2$

开方得 $D_k \leqslant 0.312\sigma_y$

或 $D_k < \sigma_y/3$

这就是微小误差的条件。所以“微小误差准则”就是：当某个自变量的部分误差小于函数(间接测量值)标准误差的三分之一时，这个部分误差即可忽略不计。

显然对于所有的数学、物理常数总可以取得它的近似值到足够精度而使微小误差的条件得以满足，即由此引起的部分误差小于 1/3 的函数的标准误差，从而把它忽略掉。

16.9.5 组合测量原理

当某项测量结果需要用多个未知参数表达时，可通过改变测量条件进行多次测量，根据测量量与未知参数间的函数关系列出方程组并求解，进而得到未知量。

16.9.6 最小二乘法原理

实际测量所得到的一系列数据中的每一个随机误差 X_i 都相互独立，服从正态分布。如果测量列 $\{X_i\}$ 为等精度测量，为了求得最优概值 X_0，则必须有

$$\sum_{i=1}^{n} \nu_i^2 = 最小$$

即在等精度测量中，为了求未知量的最优概值就要使各测量值的残差平方和为最小，这就是最小二乘法原理。

16.9.7 经验公式法

实验中，设测量出自变量和因变量多组对应值为 x_i、y_i，其中 $i=1,2,\cdots,n$，它们反映着两个物理量 x,y 的内在关系。把由这些测量值寻找出的函数关系叫经验公式。把由二维数组寻找经验公式的过程叫拟合。拟合的任务是建立经验公式的函数形式并确定其中的常数。

16.9.8 相关系数

相关系数是描述两个变量(x,y)之间线性相关密切程度的指标，用 R 表示。

$$R=\frac{\sum_{i=1}^{n}(x_i-\overline{x})(y_i-\overline{y})}{\sqrt{\sum(x_i-\overline{x})^2\sum(y_i-\overline{y})^2}} \tag{16.9-23}$$

物理意义：

(1)当所有 Y_i 的值都落在回归线上，$R=\pm1$。

(2)当 Y 与 x 完全不存在线性关系时，$R=0$。

(3)当 R 的值在 0 与 ±1 之间时，如果其值与指定置信度下相关系数临界值 $R_{p\cdot f}$ 比较，满足 $|R|>R_{p\cdot f}$，就可以认为这一回归线是有意义的。

16.9.9 回归分析

回归分析是一种处理变量间相关关系的数量统计方法。它主要解决以下几方面的问题。

(1)确定几个特定的变量之间是否存在相关关系，如果存在的话，找出它们之间合适的相关关系式。

(2)根据一个或几个变量的值，预测或控制另一个变量的值，并要知道这种预测或控制可达到的精密度。

(3)进行因素分析。例如在对于共同影响一个变量的许多变量因素中，找出哪些是主要因素，哪些是次要因素，这些因素间又是什么联系。

16.9.10 显著性检验及分析

显著性检验是指对存在着差异的两个样本平均值之间、或样本平均值与总体真值之间是否存在“显著性差异”的检验。

在实际工作中，往往会遇到对被测标准量进行测定时，所得到的平均值与标准值不完全一致；或者采用两种不同的测量法或不同的测量仪表或不同的测量人员对同一被测量进行测量时，所得的测量平均值有一定的差异。显著性检验就是检验这种差异是由随机误差引起还是由系统误差引起。如果存在“显著性差异”，就认为这种差异是由系统误差引起；否则这种误差就是由随机误差引起，认为是正常的。

16.9.11 过失误差处理

可采取物理判断法和统计判断法。

对于人为因素或仪器失准而造成的，随时发现随时剔除，这是物理判断法。

统计判断法有很多种，最简单的是拉伊达准则：因大于 3 倍标准偏差的随机误差出现的可能性很小，当出现大于 3 倍标准偏差的测量值时，可以认为是坏值而剔除，但测量次数必须大于10次。

16.9.12 系统误差处理方法及消除方法

消除已定系统误差的方法：引入修正值。

消除产生误差的因素，如控制环境条件、提高灵敏度等。

替代法：测量未知量后，记下读数，再测可调的已知量，使仪表指示与上次相同，此时未知量就等于已知量。

正负误差补偿法：适当安排测量方法，对同一量做两次测量，使恒定系差在两次测量中方向相反，取两次读数的算术平均值。

消除线性变化的系统误差可采用对称观测法。

典型例题解析

【例16.9-6】 可用于消除线性变化的累进系统误差的方法是：

A. 对称观测法　　B. 半周期偶数观测法　　C. 对置法　　D. 交换法

解 消除线性变化的系统误差可采用对称观测法。选A。

16.9.13 误差的合成定律

1）随机误差的合成

若测量结果中有 k 个彼此独立的随机误差，各个误差互不相关，各单次测量误差的标准方差分别为 $\sigma_1, \sigma_2, \cdots, \sigma_n$，则 k 个独立随机误差的综合效应是它们的方和根，即综合后误差的标准差 σ 为

$$\sigma = \sqrt{\sum_{i=1}^{n} \sigma_i^2} \tag{16.9-24}$$

在计算综合误差时，经常用极限误差合成。只要测量次数足够多，可按正态分布来处理，极限误差 l_i 为

$$l_i = 3\sigma_i \tag{16.9-25}$$

合成的极限误差 l 为

$$l = \sqrt{\sum_{i=1}^{n} l_i^2} \tag{16.9-26}$$

2）确定的系统误差的合成

（1）代数合成法。已知各系统误差的分量 $\varepsilon_1, \varepsilon_2, \cdots, \varepsilon_m$ 大小及符号，可采用各分量的代数和求得总系统误差 ε，即

$$\varepsilon = \varepsilon_1 + \varepsilon_2 + \cdots + \varepsilon_m = \sum_{i=1}^{m} \varepsilon_i \tag{16.9-27}$$

（2）绝对值合成法。在测量中只能估计出各系统误差分量 $\varepsilon_1, \varepsilon_2, \cdots, \varepsilon_m$ 的数值大小，但不能确定其符号时，可采用最保守的合成方法，绝对值合成法

$$\varepsilon = \pm (|\varepsilon_1| + |\varepsilon_2| + \cdots + |\varepsilon_m|) = \sum_{i=1}^{m} \varepsilon_i \tag{16.9-28}$$

对于 $m > 10$ 情况下，绝对值合成法对误差的估计往往偏大。

（3）方和根合成法。在测量中只能估计出各系统误差分量 $\varepsilon_1, \varepsilon_2, \cdots, \varepsilon_m$ 的数值大小，但不

能确定其符号时，且测量中系统误差的分量比较多(m 较大，$m>10$)时，各分量最大值同时出现的概率是不大的，它们之间可以抵消一部分。因此，如果仍按绝对值合成法计算总的系统误差 ε，显然对误差的估计偏大。此种情况可采用方和根合成法，即

$$\varepsilon=\pm\sqrt{\varepsilon_1^2+\varepsilon_2^2+\cdots+\varepsilon_m^2}=\pm\sqrt{\sum_{i=1}^{m}\varepsilon_i^2} \quad (16.9\text{-}29)$$

3)不确定的系统误差的合成

(1)各系统不确定度 e_p 线性相加，得总的不确定度，即

$$e=\pm\sum_{p=1}^{q}e_p \quad (16.9\text{-}30)$$

此方法比较安全，但误差估计偏大，特别是 q 比较大时，更为突出。所以在 $q<10$ 时，才能应用此法。当 $q>10$ 时可用下面的方法。

(2)方和根合成法，即

$$e=\pm\sqrt{\sum_{p=1}^{q}e_p^2} \quad (16.9\text{-}31)$$

(3)由系统部确定度 e_p 算出标准差 σ_p，再取方和根合成，即

$$\sigma=\pm\sqrt{\sum_{p=1}^{q}\sigma_p^2}=\sqrt{\sum_{p=1}^{q}(e_p/k_p)^2} \quad (16.9\text{-}32)$$

4)随机误差与系统误差的合成

设在测量结果中，有 k 个独立的随机误差，用极限误差表示为：$L_1,L_2,\cdots,L_m$，合成的极限误差为

$$l=\sqrt{\sum_{i=1}^{k}l_i^2} \quad (16.9\text{-}33)$$

设在测量结果中，有 m 个确定的系统误差，其值分别为 $\varepsilon_1,\varepsilon_2,\cdots,\varepsilon_m$，合成误差为

$$\varepsilon=\sqrt{\sum_{j=1}^{m}\varepsilon_j} \quad (16.9\text{-}34)$$

设在测量结果中，还有 q 个不确定的系统误差，其不确定度为

$$e=\pm\sum_{p=1}^{q}e_p \quad (16.9\text{-}35)$$

则测量结果的综合误差为

$$\Delta=\varepsilon\pm[e+l] \quad (16.9\text{-}36)$$

典型例题解析

【例 16.9-7】 有一测温系统，传感器基本误差为 $\sigma_1=\pm0.4$℃，变温器基本误差为 $\sigma_2=\pm0.4$℃，显示记录基本误差为 $\sigma_3=\pm0.6$℃，系统工作环境与磁干扰等引起的附加误差为 $\sigma_4=\pm0.6$℃，这一测温系统的误差是：

A. $\sigma=\pm1.02$℃　　B. $\sigma=\pm0.5$℃

C. $\sigma=\pm0.6$℃　　D. $\sigma=\pm1.41$℃

解　根据公式(16.9-34)，可以求得这一测温系统的误差为±1.41℃。选 D。

【例 16.9-8】 在测量结果中，有 1 项独立随机误差 Δ_1，2 个已定系统误差 E_1 和 E_2，2 个未定系统误差 e_1 和 e_2，则测量结果的综合误差为：

A. $(E_1+E_2)\pm[(e_1+e_2)+\sqrt{\Delta_1^2}]$

B. $(e_1+e_2)\pm[(E_1+E_2)+\sqrt{\Delta_1^2}]$

C. $(e_1+e_2)\pm[(E_1+E_2)+\sqrt{\Delta_1}]$

D. $(E_1+E_2)\pm[(e_1+e_2)+\sqrt{\Delta_1}]$

解 设在测量结果中，有个独立的随机误差，用极限误差表示为：$l_1, l_2, \cdots, l_m$，合成的极限误差为 $l=\sqrt{\sum\limits_{i=1}^{k} l_i^2}$

设在测量结果中，有 m 个确定的系统误差，其值分别为 $\varepsilon_1, \varepsilon_2, \cdots, \varepsilon_m$，合成误差为 $\varepsilon=\sqrt{\sum\limits_{j=1}^{m} \varepsilon_j}$

设在测量结果中，还有 q 个不确定的系统误差，其不确定度为 $e=\pm\sum\limits_{p=1}^{q} e_p$

则测量结果的综合误差为 $\Delta=\varepsilon\pm(e+l)$

选 A。

经典练习

16.9-1 下列关于回归分析的描述中，错误的是（　　）。

A. 确定几个特定的变量之间是否存在相关关系，如果存在的话，找出他们之间合适的相关关系式

B. 根据一个或几个变量的值，预测或控制另一个变量的值

C. 从一组测量值中寻求最可信赖值

D. 进行因素分析

16.9-2 应用最小二乘法从一组测量值中确定最可信赖值的前提条件不包括（　　）。

A. 这些测量值不存在系统误差和粗大误差

B. 这些测量值相互独立

C. 测量值线性相关

D. 测量值服从正态分布

16.9-3 下列关于过失误差的叙述中，错误的是（　　）。

A. 过失误差就是“粗大误差”

B. 大多数由于测量者粗心大意造成的

C. 其数值往往大大的超过同样测量条件下的系统误差和随机误差

D. 可以用最小二乘法消除过失误差的影响

16.9-4 下列措施中与消除系统误差无关的是（　　）。

A. 采用正确的测量方法和原理依据

B. 测量仪器应定期检定、校准

C. 尽可能采用数字显示仪器代替指针式仪器

D. 剔除严重偏离的坏值。

参考答案及提示

16.1-1　A

16.1-2　B　由精度的定义可知，该仪表的最大绝对误差为：

$$\Delta_{max}=2.5\%\times(100-0)=2.5\text{kPa}$$

因仪表的刻度标尺的分格值不应小于其允许误差所对应的绝对误差值，故其刻度标尺最少可分为$\frac{100-0}{2.5}=40$格。

16.1-3　C

16.1-4　C

16.2-1　D

16.2-2　B

16.2-3　D

16.2-4　D

16.2-5　C

16.2-6　A

16.2-7　A

16.2-8　B

16.3-1　D

16.3-2　D

16.3-3　D

16.3-4　B

16.3-5　D

16.3-6　B

16.4-1　C

16.4-2　D　霍尔压力传感器的灵敏度 k_H 值与温度有关。

16.4-3　A

16.4-4　D

16.4-5　C

16.4-6　C

16.4-7　D

16.4-8　A

16.4-9　A

16.5-1　C　根据是利用流体的全压和静压之差——动压 Δp 来测量流速。对于稳定流动可根据伯努利方程与静压之差 Δp 与流速 v 之间的关系：$v=\sqrt{\frac{2\Delta p}{\rho}}$。

16.5-2　D

16.5-3　A

16.5-4　D

16.5-5　D

16.6-1　B　皮托管测得动压 $\Delta p = \rho v^2/2$，确定取压口处的流速 $v=(2\Delta p/\rho)^{1/2}$，根据雷诺数 $R_{eD}=vD/\nu$ 确定流动状态，依测压管所处半径位置和管内速度分布规律确定测点速度和平均速度的关系，从而计算出流量。

16.6-2　C

16.6-3　C　$q_m = a\,\dfrac{\pi}{4}d^2\sqrt{2\rho\Delta p}$。

16.6-4　C　超声波流量计在传播时间差 $\Delta\tau=\dfrac{L}{C-v}-\dfrac{L}{C+v}=\dfrac{2Lv}{C^2-v^2}$

当 $K_p=\sqrt{\dfrac{\rho_1}{\rho_2}}C\gg v$ 时，$\Delta\tau\approx\dfrac{2Lv}{C^2}$

根据温度的变化，烟气超声波的速度也在变化，则可求出不同温度下的时间差之后，再求出温度变化对时间差的影响是多少。

16.6-6　C

16.6-7　B　由涡轮流量计的计算公式 $Q=f/\xi$，可得：

$$f=\xi Q=37.1\ \text{次/L}\times 50\text{m}^3/\text{h}$$

16.9-1　C

16.9-2　C

16.9-3　D

16.9-4　D

17 机械基础

考题配置　单选，9 题
分数配置　每题 2 分，共 18 分

复习指导

机械基础主要介绍各种常用机构(包括连杆机构、凸轮机构、齿轮机构、间歇运动机构等)和通用零件(包括连接件、传动件、轴系零部件等)的工作原理和设计计算方法。要求学生能够熟练掌握机械设计的基本准则，平面自由度计算方法，以及各种常用机构和通用零件的形式、分类、主要参数、工作原理和设计计算方法。

17.1 概述

考试大纲☞：机械设计的一般原则和程序　机械零件的设计准则　许用应力和安全系数

必备基础知识

17.1.1 机械设计的一般原则和程序

1)机械设计的一般原则

虽然不同的机械其功能和外形都不相同，但它们设计的基本原则大体是相同的。

(1)功能性原则。满足机器预定的工作要求，如机器工作部分的运动形式、速度、运动精度和平稳性、需要传递的功率，以及某些使用上的特殊要求(如高温、防潮等)。

(2)安全可靠性原则。

①使整个技术系统和零件在规定的外载荷和规定的工作时间内，能正常工作而不发生断裂、过度变形、过度磨损，不丧失稳定性。

②能实现对操作人员的防护，保证人身安全和身体健康。

③对于技术系统的周围环境和人不造成危害和污染，同时保证机器对环境的适应性。

(3)经济性原则。设计制造的经济性表现在产品的成本低，使用经济性表现为高效率、低能耗，以及较低的管理和维护费用等。

(4)其他原则。机械系统外形美观，便于操作和维修。此外还必须考虑有些机械由于工作环境和要求不同，而对设计提出某些特殊要求，如食品卫生条件、耐腐蚀、高精度要求等。

2)机械设计的一般程序

机械设计就是建立满足功能要求的技术系统的创造过程。机械设计一般过程为：

(1)计划阶段。对所设计的机器的需求情况做充分的调查研究和分析，在此基础上，明确设计任务，最后形成设计任务书。

(2)方案设计阶段。对设计任务书提出的机器功能进行综合分析，提出可供比较评价的多种设计方案，从中选取最佳方案。最后确定出功能参数，作为进一步设计的依据。

(3)技术设计阶段。技术设计阶段包括以下内容：①机构运动学设计；②机器动力学的分析与计算；③零件工作能力的初步设计与计算；④总装配草图和部件装配草图的设计。

(4)试制、试用与改进阶段。通过样机的试制、试用，可以发现设计、加工、安装、调试及使用过程中出现的问题，对设计进行修改和完善，直至达到设计要求，最后产品才能定型。

典型例题解析

【例 17.1-1】 设计一台机器包含以下几个阶段，它们进行的合理顺序大体为：

a. 技术设计阶段　　b. 方案设计阶段　　c. 计划阶段

A. a-c-b　　B. b-a-c　　C. b-c-a　　D. c-b-a

解 机械设计的一般程序是：①计划阶段；②方案设计阶段；③技术设计阶段；④试制、试用与改进阶段。选 D。

17.1.2 机械零件的失效形式及设计准则

1)机械零件的失效形式

机械零件在预定的时间内和规定的条件下，不能完成正常的功能，称为失效。失效形式主要有断裂、过大的残余应变、表面磨损、腐蚀、零件表面的接触疲劳和共振等。机械零件的失效形式与许多因素有关，具体取决于该零件的工作条件、材质、受载状态及其所产生的应力性质等多种因素。即使是同一种零件，由于材质及工作情况不同，也可能出现各种不同的失效形式。如轴工作时，由于受载情况不同，可能出现断裂、过大塑性变形、磨损等失效形式。

2)机械零件的设计准则

为了使设计零件能在预定时间内和规定工作条件下正常工作，应满足下面的基本准则：

(1)强度准则

强度准则就是指零件的应力不得超过允许的限度，即

$$\sigma \leqslant [\sigma]$$

式中：$[\sigma]$——许用应力。

(2)刚度准则

刚度是指零件在荷载的作用下，抵抗弹性变形的能力。刚度准则要求零件在荷载作用下的弹性变形 y 在许用值$[y]$之内，其表达式为 $y \leqslant [y]$。

(3)寿命准则

一些零件在工作初期时能满足各种要求，但在工作一定时间以后，会由于种种原因而失效，该零件能够正常工作所延续的时间称为零件的工作寿命。影响零件寿命的主要因素有腐蚀、磨损和疲劳等。

(4)振动稳定性准则

对于高速运动或刚度较小的机械，在工作时应避免发生共振。振动稳定性准则要求所设计零件的固有频率 f_P 应与其工作时所受激振源的频率 f 错开，即：当 $f_P > f$ 时，要求 $f_P > 1.15f$；当 $f_P < f$ 时，要求 $f_P < 0.85f$。

(5)可靠性准则

机械系统的可靠性是由零件的可靠性来保证的。对于重要的机械零件要求计算其可靠度 R，并作为可靠性的指标。

如有 N_0 件某种零件，在一定的工作条件下进行试验，经 t 时间后，失效 N_f 件，而有 N_s 件仍能正常地工作，则此零件在该工作环境条件下，工作 t 时间的可靠度 R 可表示为

$$R=\frac{N_s}{N_0}=1-\frac{N_f}{N_0}$$

17.1.3 许用应力和安全系数

1)许用应力

机械零件按强度条件判定的方法：比较危险截面处的计算应力是否小于零件材料的许用应力，即

$$\sigma\leqslant[\sigma]，而[\sigma]=\frac{\sigma_{\lim}}{S} \tag{17.1-1}$$

$$\tau\leqslant[\tau]，而[\tau]=\frac{\tau_{\lim}}{S} \tag{17.1-2}$$

式中：$\sigma_{\lim}$、$\tau_{\lim}$——极限正应力和极限切应力；

S——安全系数。

许用应力取决于应力的种类、零件材料的极限应力和安全系数等。按照随应力时间变化的情况，可分为静应力和变应力。不随时间变化的应力，称为静应力，纯粹的静应力是没有的，但如变化缓慢，就可看作是静应力。随时间变化的应力，称为变应力；具有周期性的变应力称为循环变应力。静应力下，零件材料有两种损坏形式：断裂或塑性变形。变应力下，零件的主要损坏形式是疲劳断裂。

2)安全系数

安全系数的数值对零件尺寸有很大影响。如果安全系数定得过大将使结构笨重；如果定得过小，有可能不够安全。

可参考下述原则来确定安全系数：

(1)静应力下，塑性材料以屈服点为极限应力。由于塑性材料可以缓和过大的局部应力，故可称 $S=1.2\sim1.5$。对于塑性较差的材料$\left(\frac{\sigma_S}{\sigma_B}>0.6\right)$或铸钢件，可取 $S=1.2\sim2.5$。

(2)静应力下，脆性材料以强度极限为极限应力。这时取较大的安全系数。例如，对于高强度钢或铸铁件可取 $S=3\sim4$。

(3)变应力下，以疲劳极限作为极限应力，可取 $S=1.3\sim1.7$；若材料不够均匀，计算不够精确时可取 $S=1.7\sim2.5$。

典型例题解析

【例 17.1-2】 机械零件的工作安全系数是：

A. 零件材料的极限应力比许用应力

B. 零件材料的极限应力比零件的工作应力

C. 零件的工作应力比许用应力

D. 零件的工作应力比零件的极限应力

解 由许用应力 $\sigma\leqslant[\sigma]=\frac{\sigma_{\lim}}{S}=\frac{\sigma_S}{S}$，可知工作安全系数是零件材料的极限应力比许用应力。选 A。

【例 1.17-3】 在进行疲劳强度计算时，其极限应力应是材料的：

A. 屈服极限　　B. 强度极限　　C. 疲劳极限　　D. 弹性极限

解 进行疲劳强度计算时，其极限应力应是材料的疲劳极限。选 C。

【例 17.1-4】 对于塑性材料制成的机械零件，进行静强度计算时，其极限应力为：

A. σ_b　　B. σ_s　　C. σ_0　　D. σ_{-1}

解 对于塑性材料，按不发生塑性变形的条件进行计算，应取材料的屈服极限 σ_s 作为极限应力。选 B。

经典练习

17.1-1 零件中的应力 σ 和许用应力$[\sigma]$之间应满足的关系是（　　）。

A. $\sigma \geqslant [\sigma]$　　B. $\sigma = [\sigma]$　　C. $\sigma \leqslant [\sigma]$　　D. $\sigma \neq [\sigma]$

17.1-2 有 50 件某种零件，经 t 时间后，失效 5 件，而有 45 件仍能正常地工作，则此零件的可靠度 R 为（　　）。

A. 0.85　　B. 0.75　　C. 0.9　　D. 0.25

17.2 平面机构的自由度

考试大纲☞：运动副及其分类　平面机构运动简图　平面机构的自由度及其具有确定运动的条件

必备基础知识

17.2.1 运动副及其分类

机构中两构件之间直接接触并能做相对运动的可动连接，称为运动副。例如轴与轴承之间的连接，活塞与汽缸之间的连接，凸轮与推杆之间的连接等。

尽管运动副的形式很多，但都是通过点、线或面的接触来实现的。按照不同的接触特性，通常把运动副分为低副和高副两大类。

1）低副

两构件通过面接触组成的运动副称为低副。根据两构件间的相对运动形式，低副又分为移动副和转动副。两构件间的相对运动为直线运动的，称为移动副，如图 17.2-1 所示；两构件间的相对运动为转动的，称为转动副或称为铰链副，如图 17.2-2 所示。

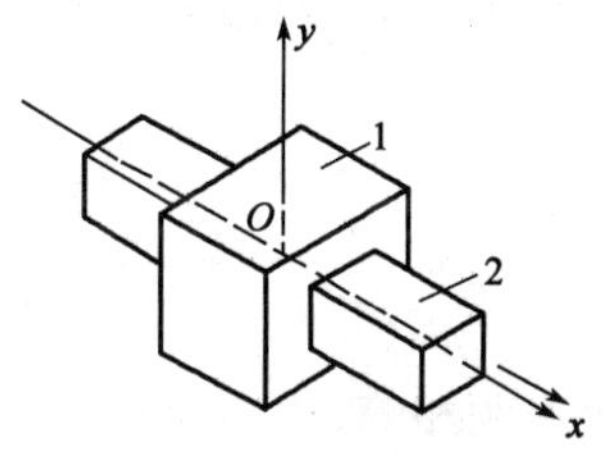

图 17.2-1 移动副

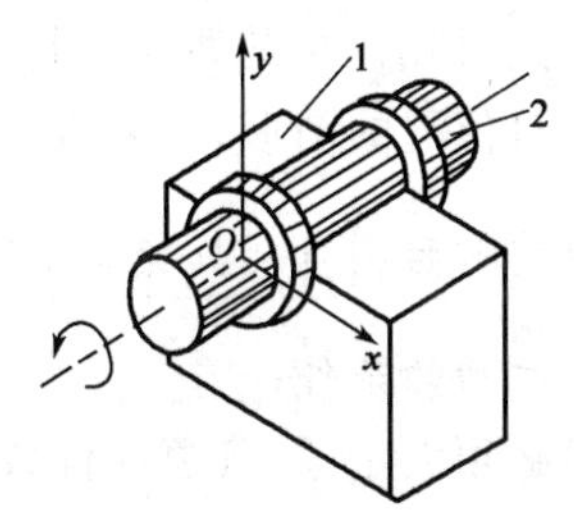

图 17.2-2 转动副

2)高副

两构件通过点或线接触组成的运动副称为高副，如图 17.2-3 所示的凸轮 1 与从动件 2、齿轮 1 与齿轮 2 分别在其接触处 A 组成高副。组成平面高副两构件间的相对运动是沿接触处切线 t-t 方向的相对移动和在平面内的相对转动。

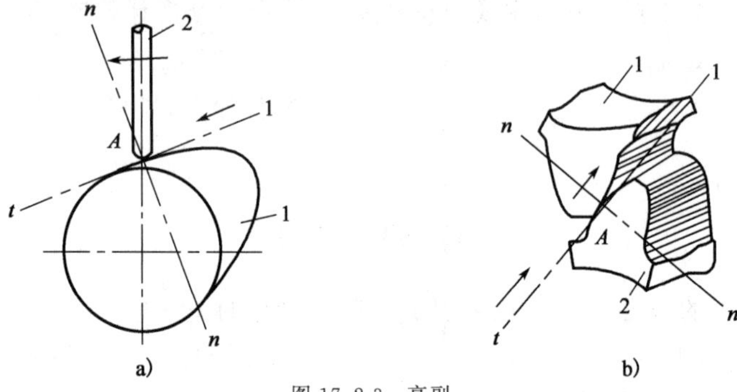

图 17.2-3　高副

典型例题解析

【例 17.2-1】　平面运动副可分为：

A. 移动副和转动副　　B. 螺旋副和齿轮副

C. 高副和低副　　D. 螺旋副和球面副

解　平面运动副按其接触情况分类，可分为高副和低副。选 C。

【例 17.2-2】　下面属于高副的运动副是：

A. 螺旋副　　B. 移动副　　C. 转动副　　D. 齿轮副

解　在所列出的运动副中只有齿轮副属于高副。选 D。

17.2.2　平面机构运动简图

机构中的构件按其运动性质可以分为三类：

(1)固定件。它是用来支撑活动构件的构件，在分析机构中活动构件的运动时，常以固定构件作为参考系。

(2)原动件。是运动规律已知的活动构件。它的运动是由外界输入的，故又称输入构件。

(3)从动件。是机构中随着原动件的运动而运动的其他活动构件。

实际机构的外形结构比较复杂，而构件之间的相对运动又与其外形等因素无关，只与机构中所有构件的数目和构件所组成的运动副的数目、类型、相对位置有关，因此，在研究机构的运动时，可以不考虑那些与运动无关的因素，而用简单的线条和符号来代表构件和运动副，如表 17.2-1所示。这种用简单的线条和符号表示机构各构件间相对运动关系，并按一定比例确定各运动副的相对位置的图形，称为机构运动简图。

17.2.3　平面机构的自由度及其具有确定运动的条件

1)机构确定运动的条件

机构自由度必须大于零，且原动件数与其自由度必须相等。

2)平面机构自由度

平面机构中每个独立运动的构件具有三个自由度，设该机构中有 n 个可动构件(不含机架)，则有 $3n$ 个自由度。当两个构件组成运动副以后，它们的相对运动就受到约束，自由度即相应减少。每个低副使构件失去两个自由度；而每个高副使构件失去一个自由度。若构件中低副的数目为 P_L 个，高副的数目为 P_H 个，根据上面的分析，机构因引入运动副而失去的自由度总数应为 $2P_L+P_H$。显然，该机构的自由度 F 应为

$$F=3n-(2P_L+P_H) \tag{17.2-1}$$

机构运动简图符号　　表 17.2-1

名称		符号
低副	转动副	
	移动副	
高副		
构件		

这就是计算平面机构自由度的公式。由公式可知，机构自由度 F 取决于活动构件的件数以及运动副的类型(低副或高副)和个数。

机构的自由度就是机构相对于机架所具有的独立运动的数目。

3)计算机构自由度时应注意的问题

应用式(17.2-1)计算平面机构自由度时，必须注意下述几种情况：

(1)复合铰链。两个以上构件在同一轴线上用转动副连接便形成复合铰链。如图 17.2-4a)所示是由三个构件组成的复合铰链，图 17.2-4b)是其侧视图。由图 17.2-4b)可以看出，这三个构件共组成两个转动副。同理，M 个构件在同一处带传动连接构成而成的复合铰链具有 $M-1$ 个转动副。

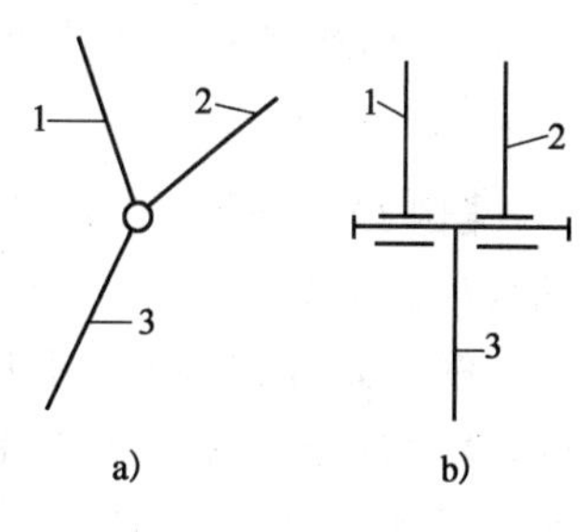

图 17.2-4　复合铰链

(2)局部自由度。机构中有时会出现这样一类自由度，它的存在与否都不影响整个机构的运动规律。这类自由度称局部自由度，在计算机构自由度时应予以消除。

(3)虚约束。在运动副中，有些约束对机构自由度的影响是重复的。这些重复的约束称为虚约束，在计算机构自由度时应除去不计。

平面机构中的虚约束常出现在下列场合：

①两个构件之间组成多个移动副，且方向平行时，则只有一个移动副起作用，其余都是虚约束。

②两个构件之间组成多个轴线重合的转动副时，只有一个转动副起作用，其余都是虚约束。例如两个轴承支持一根轴只能看作一个转动副。

③机构中传递运动不起独立作用的对称成分。

典型例题解析

【例 17.2-3】 平面机构具有确定运动的充分必要条件为：

A. 自由度大于零

B. 原动件数大于零

C. 原动件数大于自由度数

D. 原动件数等于自由度数且大于零

解 机构确定运动的条件是：机构原动件的数目等于机构自由度的数目，且自由度大于零。选 D。

【例 17.2-4】 计算图示直线机构的自由度。

解 机构中有 7 个活动构件，$n=7$；A、B、C、D 四处都是三个构件汇交的复合铰链，各有两个转动副，E、F 处各有一个转动副，故 $P_L=10$，$P_H=0$。由式(17-3)可得

$$F=3n-(2P_L+P_H)=3\times7-(2\times10+0)=1$$

自由度 F 与机构原动件数相等。当原动件运动时，点 E 将沿 EE' 移动。

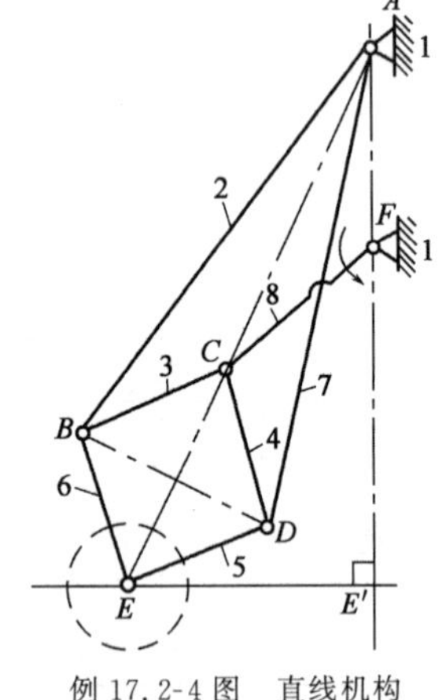

例 17.2-4 图 直线机构

【例 17.2-5】 由 m 个构件所组成的复合铰链包含的转动副个数为：

A. $m-1$ B. m C. $m+1$ D. 1

解 复合铰链是由两个以上构件同时在一处用转动副连接构成，如 3 个构件构成的复合铰链，转动副个数实际为 2 个，依此类推，m 个构件组成的复合铰链，则转动副个数应为 $m-1$，选 A。

【例 17.2-6】 计算图示滚子从动件凸轮机构的自由度。

解 如图 a)所示，当原动件凸轮 1 转动时，通过滚子 3 驱动从动件 2 以一定运动规律在机架 4 中往复移动。不难看出，无论滚子 3 存在与否都不影响从动件 2 的运动。因此，滚子绕其中心的转动是一个局部自由度。在计算机构自由度时，可设想将滚子与从动件焊成一体，如图 b)所示，这样转动副 C 便不存在。这时，机构具有 2 个活动构件，1 个转动副，1 个移动副和 1 个高副。由式(17.2-1)

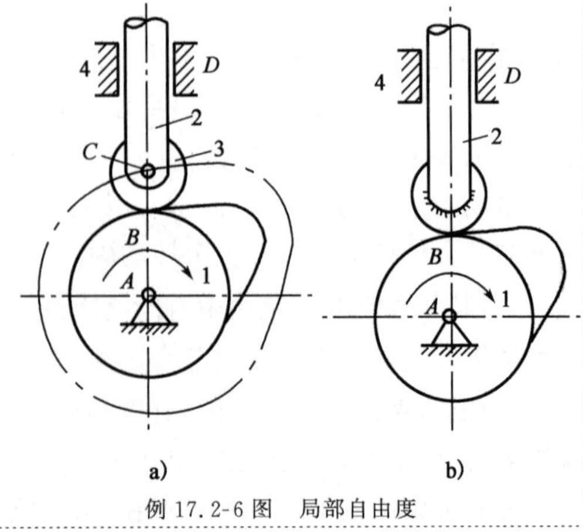

例 17.2-6 图 局部自由度

可得机构自由度为

$$F=3n-(2P_L-P_H)=3\times2-(2\times2+1)=1$$

局部自由度虽然与整个机构的运动无关，但滚子可使高副接触处变滑动摩擦为滚动摩擦，从而减少磨损和延长凸轮的工作寿命。

经典练习

17.2-1　两构件通过(　　)接触组成的运动副称为低副。

A. 点　　B. 线　　C. 面　　D. 体

17.2-2　6 个构件交汇而成的复合铰链，可构成(　　)个转动副。

A. 5　　B. 4　　C. 3　　D. 2

17.2-3　如图所示机构中，机构的自由度数目是(　　)。

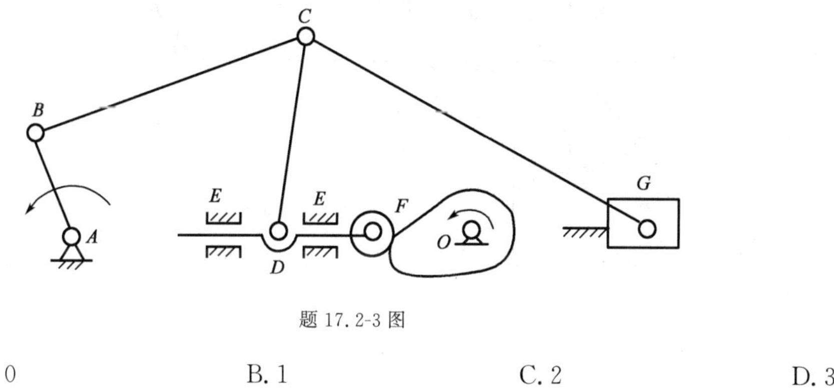

题 17.2-3 图

A. 0　　B. 1　　C. 2　　D. 3

17.3　平面连杆机构

考试大纲☞：铰链四杆机构的基本形式和存在曲柄的条件　铰链四杆机构的演化

必备基础知识

17.3.1　铰链四杆机构的基本形式

平面连杆机构是将各构件用转动副或移动副连接而成的平面机构。最简单的平面连杆机构是由四个构件组成的，简称平面四杆机构。它应用非常广泛，而且是组成多杆机构的基础。

全部用转动副相连的平面四杆机构称为铰链四杆机构。如图 17.3-1所示，机构的固定构件 4 称为机架，与机架用转动副相连的杆 1 和杆 3 称为连架杆，不与机架直接连接的杆 2 称为连杆。能做整周转动的连架杆，称为曲柄。仅能在某一角度摆动的连架杆，称为摇杆。对于铰链四杆机构来说，机架和连杆总是存在的，因此可按照连架杆是曲柄还是摇杆，将铰链四杆机构分为三种基本形式：曲柄摇杆机构、双曲柄机构和双摇杆机构。

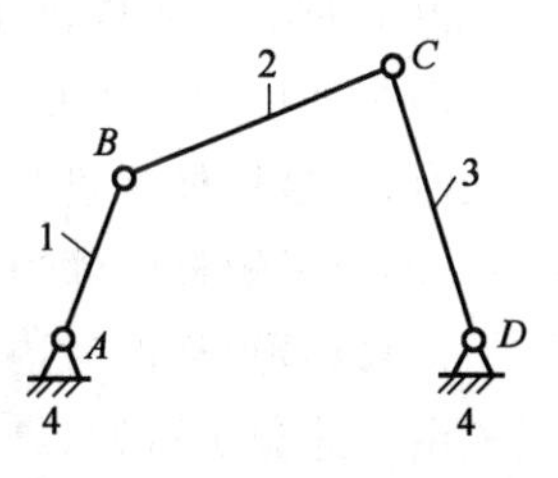

图 17.3-1　铰链四杆机构

17.3.2 曲柄存在的条件

铰链四杆机构中是否存在曲柄，取决于机构各杆的相对长度和机架的选择。首先，分析存在一个曲柄的铰链四杆机构。如图 17.3-2 所示曲柄摇杆机构，杆 1 为曲柄，杆 2 为连杆，杆 3 为摇杆，杆 4 为机架，各杆长度以 l_1、l_2、l_3、l_4 表示，为保证曲柄 1 整周回转，曲柄 1 必须能顺利通过与连杆共线的两个位置 AB' 和 AB''。

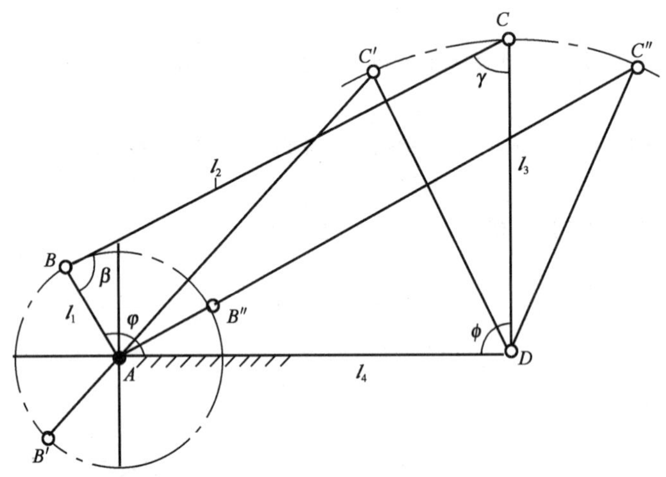

图 17.3-2 曲柄摇杆机构

当杆 1 处于 AB' 位置时，形成三角形 $AC'D$。根据三角形任意两边之和必大于(极限情况下等于)第三边的定理可得

$$l_4 \leqslant (l_2 - l_1) + l_3$$

及

$$l_3 \leqslant (l_2 - l_1) + l_4$$

即

$$l_1 + l_4 \leqslant l_2 + l_3 \tag{17.3-1}$$

$$l_1 + l_3 \leqslant l_2 + l_4 \tag{17.3-2}$$

当杆 1 处于 AB'' 位置时，形成三角形 $AC''D$，可写出以下关系式

$$l_1 + l_2 \leqslant l_3 + l_4 \tag{17.3-3}$$

将式(17.3-2)、式(17.3-3)两两相加可得

$$l_1 \leqslant l_2, l_1 \leqslant l_3, l_1 \leqslant l_4$$

它说明杆 1 为最短，而杆 2、杆 3、杆 4 中必有一杆为最长杆。

上述关系说明：

(1)在曲柄摇杆机构中，曲柄是最短杆。

(2)最短杆与最长杆长度之和小于或等于其余两杆长度之和。

以上两条是曲柄存在的必要条件。

当各杆长度不变而取不同杆为机架时，可以得到不同类型的铰链四杆机构：

(1)以最短杆为机架时，可获得双曲柄机构。

(2)以最短杆的邻边为机架时，可获得曲柄摇杆机构。

(3)以最短杆的对边为机架时，可获得双摇杆机构。

由上述分析可知，最短杆和最长杆长度之和小于或等于其余两杆长度之和，是铰链四杆机构存在曲柄的必要条件。满足这个条件的机构究竟有一个曲柄、两个曲柄或没有曲柄，还需根据取何杆为机架来判断。

如果铰链四杆机构中的最短杆与最长杆长度之和大于其余两杆长度之和，则该机构中不可能存在曲柄，无论取哪个构件作为机架，都只能得到双摇杆机构。

典型例题解析

【例 17.3-1】 已知某平面铰链四杆机构各杆长度分别为 100、68、56、200。则通过转换机架，可能构成的机构形式为：

A. 曲柄摇杆机构　　B. 双摇杆机构

C. 双曲柄机构　　D. A、B、C 均可

解　铰链四杆机构有曲柄的条件是：最短杆与最长杆长度之和小于或等于其余两杆长度之和（杆长条件）。如果铰链四杆机构不满足杆长条件，该机构不存在曲柄，则无论取哪个构件作机架都只能得到双摇杆机构。题中最短杆与最长杆长度之和 56＋200＝256，大于其余两杆长度之和 100＋68＝168，不满足杆长条件。选 B。

【例 17.3-2】 在铰链四杆机构中，若最短杆与最长杆长度之和小于其他两杆长度之和，为了得到双摇杆机构，应：

A. 以最短杆为机架　　B. 以最短杆的相邻杆为机架

C. 以最短杆的对面杆为机架　　D. 以最长杆为机架

解　最短杆与最长杆长度之和小于其他两杆长度之和，满足了铰链四杆机构有曲柄的条件，此时，若以最短杆的对边为机架，则可获得双摇杆机构。选 C。

17.3.3 曲柄摇杆机构的急回特性和死点位置

对于曲柄摇杆机构和其他某些平面四杆机构，有两个特性是值得注意的，即急回特性和死点位置。

1）曲柄摇杆机构的急回特性

如图 17.3-2 所示的曲柄摇杆机构中，当曲柄由 AB' 位置转动到 AB'' 位置时，摇杆从左端极限位置 $C'D$ 摆到右端极限位置 $C''D$（通常称正行程），这时曲柄转过的角度设为 α_1（$\alpha_1=180°+\angle C'AC''$）。又当曲柄由 AB'' 位置转动到位置 AB' 时，摇杆从左端极限位置 $C''D$ 摆到右端极限位置 $C'D$（通常称反行程），这时曲柄转过的角度设为 α_2（$\alpha_2=180°-\angle C'AC''$）。由于 $\alpha_1>\alpha_2$，而正反行程的摆角相等，因此摇杆反行程时的平均摆动速度必然大于正行程时的平均摆动速度，这就是所谓的急回特性。在机械设计（例如牛头刨床设计）中，常利用机构的这一特性来缩短非生产时间，以提高劳动生产率。

2）曲柄摇杆机构的死点位置

如图 17.3-2 所示的曲柄摇杆机构中，如果曲柄是原动件，是不会出现卡死现象的。但如果相反，摇杆 CD 是原动件而曲柄 AB 是从动件（缝纫机踏板机构就是这种情况），那么，当摇杆 CD 摆到两个极限位置 $C'D$ 和 $C''D$ 时，曲柄与连杆共线，摇杆 CD 通过连杆加于曲柄的驱动力 F 正好通过曲柄的转动中心 A，则不能产生使曲柄转动的力矩。机构的这种位置称为死点位置。死点位置将使机构的从动件出现卡死或运动不确定的现象。对传动机构来说，死点是应设法加以克服的。例如可利用构件的惯性来保证机构顺利通过死点。缝纫机在工作中就是依靠带轮的惯性来通过死点的。

典型例题解析

【例 17.3-3】 当不考虑摩擦力，下列何种情况时可能出现机构因死点存在而不能运动的情况？

A. 曲柄摇杆机构，曲柄主动　　B. 曲柄摇杆机构，摇杆主动

C. 双曲柄机构　　D. B 和 C

解 曲柄摇杆机构中，如果曲柄是原动件，是不会出现卡死现象的。但如果相反，摇杆是主动件而曲柄是从动件，那么，当摇杆摆到使曲柄与连杆共线的极限位置时，摇杆通过连杆加于曲柄的驱动力正好通过曲柄的转动中心，则不能产生使曲柄转动的力矩。机构的这种位置称为死点位置。选 B。

【例 17.3-4】 下列铰链四杆机构中能实现急回运动的是：

A. 双摇杆机构　　B. 曲柄摇杆机构

C. 双曲柄机构　　D. 对心曲柄滑块机构

解 曲柄摇杆机构中，摇杆反行程时的平均摆动速度大于正行程时的平均摆动速度，这就是所谓的急回特性。选 B。

【例 17.3-5】 下列铰链四杆机构中，能实现急回运动的是：

A. 双摇杆机构　　B. 曲柄摇杆机构

C. 双曲柄机构　　D. 对心曲柄滑块机构

解 机构的急回特性用极位夹角 θ 来表征，只要机构的 θ 角度不为 0，就存在急回运动，可以知道对于双摇杆机构、双曲柄机构、对心曲柄滑块机构的极位夹角 θ 均为 0。选 B。

17.3.4 铰链四杆机构的演化

在实际机械中，平面连杆机构的形式是多种多样的，但其中绝大多数是在铰链四杆机构的基础上发展和演化而成。

1）曲柄滑块机构

如图 17.3-3a）所示的曲柄摇杆机构，铰链中心 C 的轨迹是以 D 为圆心、l_3 为半径的圆弧。如图 17.3-3b）所示，将摇杆 3 做成滑块形式，使其沿圆弧轨道往复滑动，则曲柄摇杆机构演化成为具有曲线轨道的曲柄滑块机构。若 l_3 增至无穷大，如图 17.3-3c）所示，则 C 点轨迹变成直线，曲线轨道演化成为直线轨道，原机构演化成为具有直线轨道的曲柄滑块机构。图 17.3-3c）为偏距为 e 的偏置曲柄滑块机构，当曲柄等速转动时，滑块 C 可实现急回运动。图 17.3-3d）中 C 点运动轨迹正好通过曲柄中心 A，称为对心曲柄滑块机构。曲柄滑块机构广泛应用于内燃机、空压机及冲床设备中。

2）导杆机构

导杆机构可以看作是在曲柄滑块机构中选取不同构件为机架演化而成。如图 17.3-4a）所示的曲柄滑块机构，若改取杆 1 为固定构件，即得图 17.3-4b）所示导杆机构。杆 4 称为导杆，滑块 3 相对导杆滑动并一起绕 A 点转动。通常取杆 2 为原动件。当 $l_1<l_2$ 时，杆 2 和杆 4 均可整周回转，称为转动导杆机构；当 $l_1>l_2$ 时，杆 4 只能往复摆动，称为摆动导杆机构。

如图 17.3-4a）所示的曲柄滑块机构，若改取杆 2 为固定构件，即得图 17.3-4c）所示的滑动滑块机构，或称摇块机构；若改取杆 3 为固定构件，即得图 17.3-4d）所示的固定滑块机构，或称定块机构。

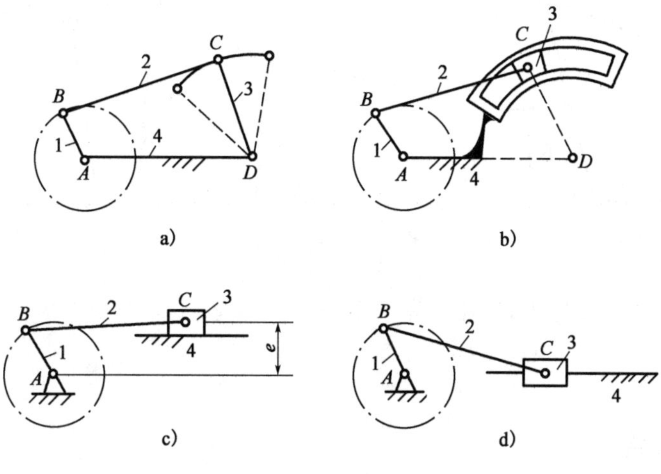

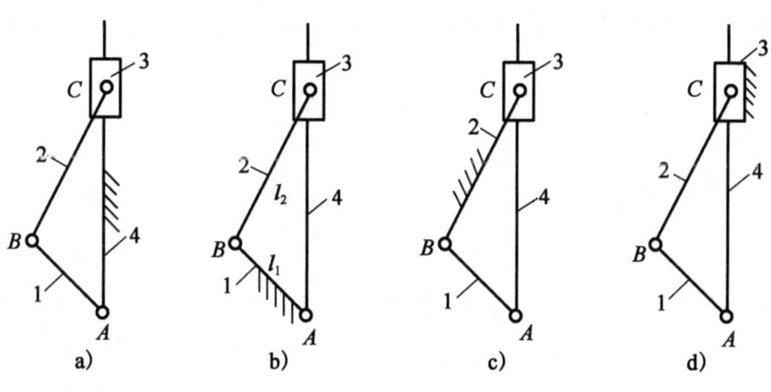

图 17.3-3　曲柄滑块机构

图 17.3-4　曲柄滑块机构演化

3)偏心轮机构

如图 17.3-5a)所示曲柄摇杆机构中,当曲柄 AB 的尺寸较小时,根据结构的需要,常将曲柄改为如图 17.3-5b)所示的偏心轮,其回转中心 A 至几何中心 B 的偏心距等于曲柄的长度,故称偏心轮机构。由图可知,偏心轮是回转副 B 扩大到包括回转副 A 而形成的。

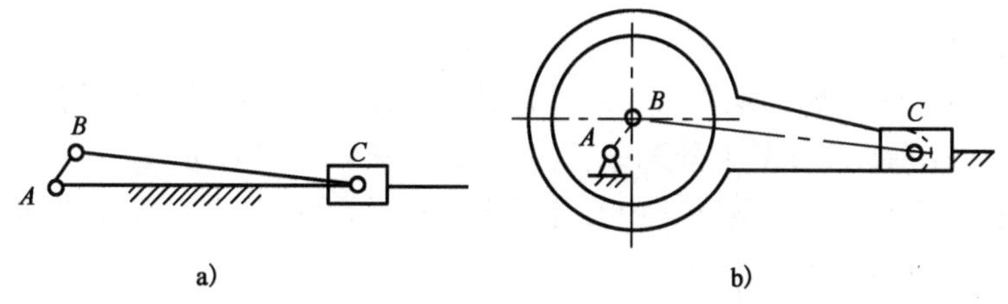

图 17.3-5　偏心轮机构

经典练习

17.3-1　根据尺寸判断图示四个平面连杆机构,分别是(　　)。

A. 双曲柄机构,双摇杆机构,双摇杆机构,曲柄摇杆机构

B. 双摇杆机构,双曲柄机构,双摇杆机构,曲柄摇杆机构

C. 双曲柄机构,曲柄摇杆机构,双摇杆机构,双摇杆机构

D. 曲柄摇杆机构,双曲柄机构,双摇杆机构,双摇杆机构

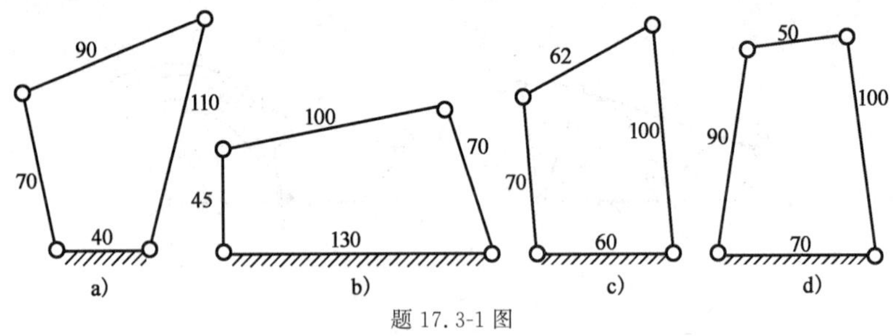

题 17.3-1 图

17.3-2 若不考虑摩擦力，当压力角为下列哪一项时，平面四轮机构将出现死点？（ ）

A. <90°　　B. >90°　　C. =90°　　D. =0°

17.4 凸轮机构

考试大纲☞：凸轮机构的基本类型和应用　直动从动件盘形凸轮轮廓曲线的绘制

必备基础知识

17.4.1 凸轮机构的应用和分类

1)凸轮机构的应用

如果对从动件的运动规律(位移、速度、加速度)有严格要求，尤其当原动件做连续运动而从动件必须做间歇运动时，采用凸轮机构最为简便。凸轮是一种具有曲线轮廓或凹槽的构件，当它运动时，通过点或线接触推动从动件，可以使从动件得到任意预期的运动规律。凸轮机构包括凸轮、机架和从动件三个部分。

凸轮机构的优点为：只需设计适当的凸轮轮廓，便可使从动件得到所需的运动规律，并且结构简单、紧凑、设计方便。它的缺点是凸轮轮廓与从动件之间为点接触或线接触，易于磨损，所以，通常多用于传力不大的控制机构。

2)凸轮机构的分类

(1)按凸轮的形状分类。

①盘形凸轮。它是凸轮的最基本形式。这种凸轮是一绕固定轴转动且具有变化半径的盘状零件，其从动件在垂直于凸轮旋转的平面内运动，如图 17.4-1a)所示。

②移动凸轮。当盘形凸轮的回转中心趋于无穷远时，则凸轮做直线运动，这种凸轮称为移动凸轮，如图 17.4-1b)所示。

③圆柱凸轮。将移动凸轮卷成圆柱体即成为圆柱凸轮，如图 17.4-1c)所示。

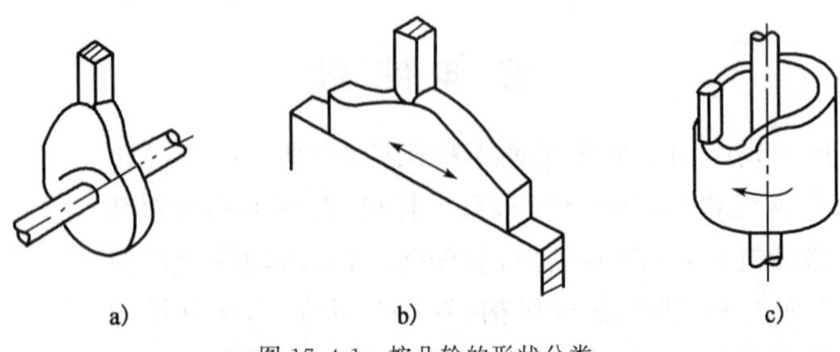

图 17.4-1　按凸轮的形状分类

(2)按从动件的形式分类。

①尖底从动件。如图 17.4-2a)、b)所示,其结构最简单,尖顶能与任意复杂的凸轮轮廓保持接触,以实现从动件的任意运动规律。但因尖顶易磨损,仅适用于作用力很小的低速凸轮机构。

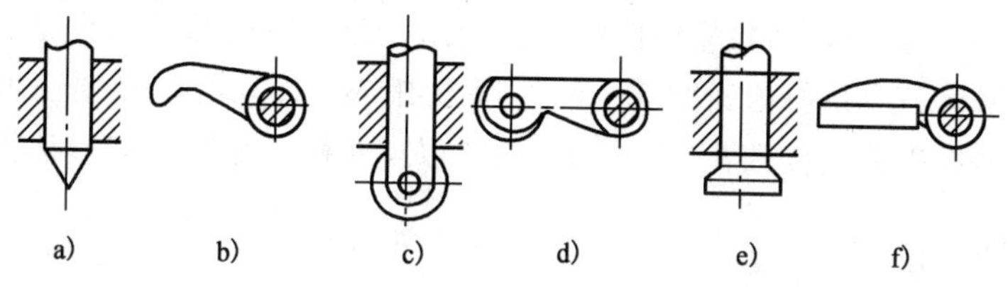

图 17.4-2 按从动件分类

②滚子从动件。如图 17.4-2c)、d)所示,从动件的一端装有可自由转动的滚子,滚子与凸轮之间为滚动摩擦,磨损小,可以承受较大的荷载,应用最普遍。

③平底从动件。如图 17.4-2e)、f)所示,从动件的一端为一平面,直接与凸轮轮廓相接触。若不考虑摩擦,凸轮对从动件的作用力始终垂直于端平面,传动效率高,且接触面间容易形成油膜,利于润滑,故常用于高速凸轮机构。其缺点是不能用于凸轮轮廓有凹曲线的凸轮机构中。

(3)按从动件的运动分类。

①直动从动件。如图 17.4-2a)、c)、e)所示,从动件相对机架做往复直线运动。

②摆动从动件。如图 17.4-2b)、d)、f)所示,从动件绕机架上某点做往复摆动。

典型例题解析

【例 17.4-1】 凸轮机构不适合在以下哪种场合下工作?

A. 需实现特殊的运动轨迹　　B. 传力较大

C. 多轴承联动控制　　D. 需实现预定的运动规律

解 凸轮轮廓与从动件之间为点接触或线接触,易于磨损,所以不适合用于传力较大的机构。选 B。

【例 17.4-2】 尖底、滚子和平底从动件凸轮受力情况从优至劣排列正确次序为:

A. 滚子,平底,尖底　　B. 尖底,滚子,平底

C. 平底,尖底,滚子　　D. 平底,滚子,尖底

解 尖底与凸轮是点接触,磨损快;滚子和凸轮轮廓之间为滚动摩擦,耐磨损;平底从动件的平底与凸轮轮廓表面接触,受力情况最优。选 D。

【例 17.4-3】 在滚子从动件凸轮机构中,对于外凸的凸轮理论轮廓曲线,为使凸轮的实际轮廓曲线完整作出,不会出现变尖或交叉现象,必须满足:

A. 滚子半径小于理论轮廓曲线最小曲率半径

B. 滚子半径等于理论轮廓曲线最小曲率半径

C. 滚子半径大于或等于理论轮廓曲线最小曲率半径

D. 滚子半径不等于理论轮廓曲线最小曲率半径

解 滚子半径的大小对凸轮实际轮廓有很大影响。设理论轮廓外凸部分的最小曲率半径用 $\rho_{\min}$ 表示,滚子半径用 r 表示,则相应位置实际轮廓的曲率半径 $\rho'=\rho_{\min}-r$,为保证实际轮廓不产生尖点或者自相交,应使 $\rho'>0$。因此,要求滚子半径必须小于理论轮廓外凸部分的最小曲率半径。选 A。

17.4.2 直动从动件盘形凸轮机构的轮廓曲线绘制

根据机器的工作要求，在确定了凸轮机构的类型及从动件的运动规律、凸轮的基圆半径和凸轮的转动方向后，便可开始凸轮轮廓曲线的设计了。凸轮轮廓曲线的设计有图解法和解析法。图解法简便易行、直观，但精确度低。不过，只要细心作图，其图解的准确度是能够满足一般工程要求的。解析法精确度较高，但设计工作量大，可利用计算机进行计算。下面介绍图解法。

1)图解法设计凸轮的基本原理

凸轮机构工作时，通常凸轮是运动的。用图解法绘制凸轮轮廓曲线时，却需要凸轮与图面相对静止。为此，可以应用“反转法”，其原理如下：

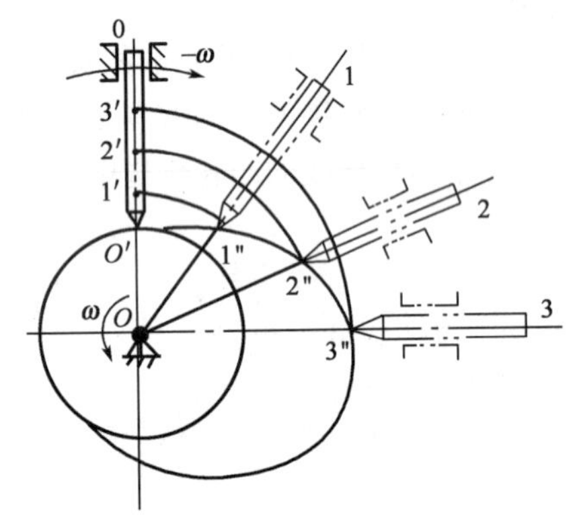

图 17.4-3　反转法原理

如图 17.4-3 所示为一对心移动尖顶从动件盘形凸轮机构。设凸轮的轮廓曲线已按预定的从动件运动规律设计。当凸轮以角速度 ω_1 绕轴 O 转动时，从动件的尖顶沿凸轮轮廓曲线相对其导路按预定的运动规律移动。现设想给整个凸轮机构加上一个公共角速度 $-\omega_1$，此时凸轮将不动。根据相对运动原理，凸轮和从动件之间的相对运动并未改变。这样从动件一方面随机架和导路以角速度 $-\omega_1$ 绕轴 O 转动，另一方面又在导路中按预定的规律做往复移动。由于从动件尖顶始终与凸轮轮廓相接触，显然，从动件在这种复合运动中，其尖顶的运动轨迹即是凸轮轮廓曲线。这种以凸轮作动参考系，按相对运动原理设计凸轮轮廓曲线的方法称为反转法。

2)对心尖底直动从动件盘形凸轮轮廓的绘制

已知从动件的位移运动规律，凸轮的基圆半径 r_{min}，以及凸轮以等角速度 ω_1 顺时针回转，要求绘出此凸轮的轮廓。

根据“反转法”的原理，可以作图如下：

(1)根据已知从动件的运动规律做出从动件的位移线图，见图 17.4-4b)，并将横坐标用若干点等分分段。

(2)以 r_{min} 为半径做基圆。此基圆与导路的交点 A 便是从动件尖顶的起始位置。

(3)自 OA 沿 ω_1 的相反方向取角度 δ_t、δ_h、δ_s，并将它们各分成与图 17.4-4b)中对应的若干等分，在基圆上得点 1、2、3、…。连接 $O1$、$O2$、$O3$、…，它们便是反转后从动件导路的各个位置。

(4)量取各个位移量，即使图 17.4-4a)、b)的 11′、22′、33′、…分别相等，得反转后尖顶的一系列位置 1′、2′、3′、…。

(5)将 A、1′、2′、3′、…连成光滑的曲线，便得到所要求的凸轮轮廓，如图 17.4-4a)所示。

3)偏置尖底直动从动件盘形凸轮轮廓的绘制

该类型凸轮机构的从动件在反转运动中，其导路始终与凸轮中心 O 保持偏距 e。首先以 O 为圆心及偏距 e 为半径做偏距圆相切于从动件导路，其次以 r_{min} 为半径做基圆，基圆与导路的交点 B_0 便是从动件尖顶的起始位置。自 OB_0 沿 ω_1 的相反方向取角度 δ_t、δ_h、δ_s，并将它们各分成若干等分，在基圆上得 B_1'、B_2'、B_3'、…，过这些点做偏距圆的切线。它们便是反转后从动件导路的各个位置。从动件的相应位移在切线上量取，取 $B_1B_1'=11'$、$B_2B_2'=22'$、$B_3B_3'=33'$、…，最后将 B_0、B_1、B_2、B_3、…连成光滑的曲线，便得到所要求的凸轮轮廓，如图 17.4-5 所示。

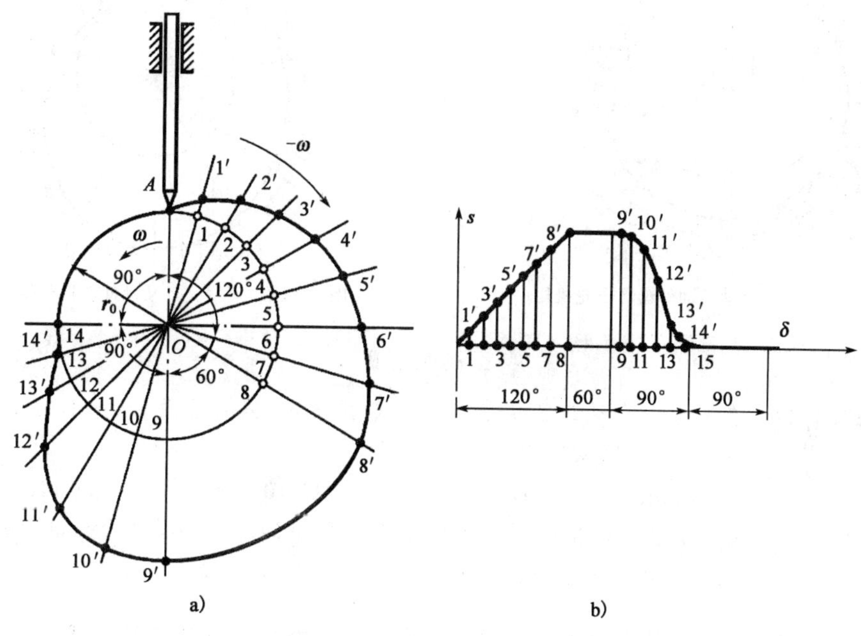

图 17.4-4　对心尖底直动从动件盘形凸轮机构

4)滚子从动件盘形凸轮轮廓曲线的绘制

把尖顶从动件改为滚子从动件时，其凸轮轮廓设计方法如图 17.4-6 所示。首先，把滚子中心看作尖顶从动件的尖顶，按照上面的方法画出一条轮廓曲线。再以该轮廓曲线上各点为中心，以滚子半径为半径，画一系列圆，最后做这些圆的包络线，它便是使用滚子从动件时凸轮的实际轮廓线。滚子从动件凸轮轮廓的基圆半径 r_{min} 应当在理论轮廓上度量。

5)平底直动从动件盘形凸轮轮廓曲线的绘制

如图 17.4-7 所示，在设计这种凸轮轮廓线时，可将从动件导路中心线与平底的交点 A_0 视为平底从动件的尖底，按照绘制尖顶从动件凸轮轮廓的方法，求出理论轮廓上一系列点 A_1、A_2、A_3、…；其次，过这些点画出各个位置的平底 A_1B_1、A_2B_2、A_3B_3、…，然后做这些平底的包络线，便得到凸轮的实际轮廓曲线。图中位置 1、6 是平底分别与凸轮轮廓相切于平底的最左位置和最右位置。为了保证平底始终与轮廓接触，平底左侧的长度应大于 m，右侧长度应大于 l。

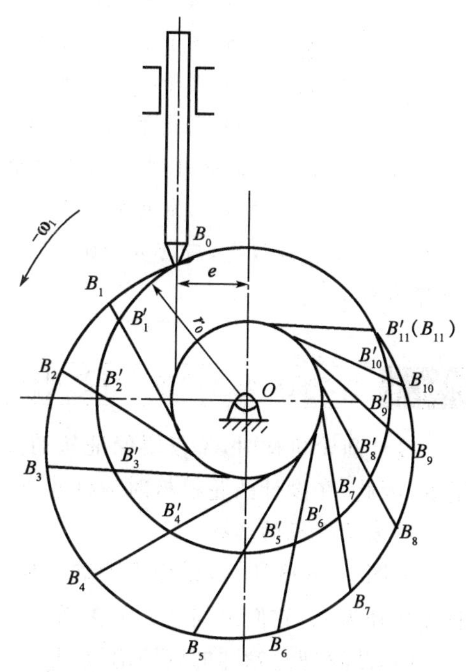

图 17.4-5　偏置直动从动件盘形凸轮机构

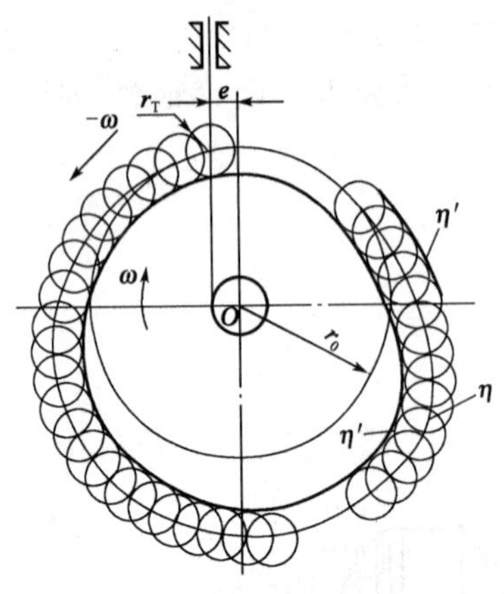

图 17.4-6　滚子直动从动件盘形凸轮机构

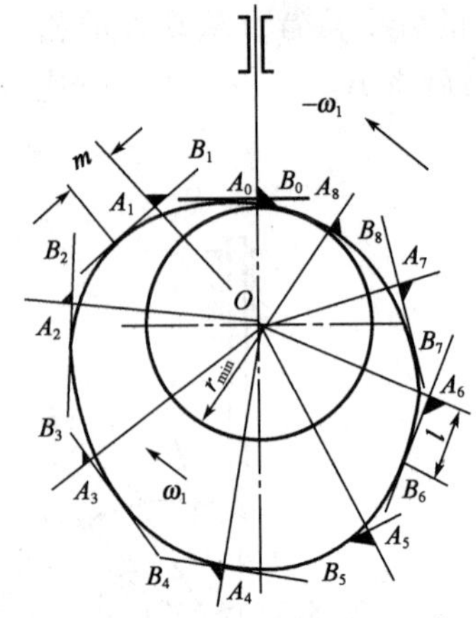

图 17.4-7　平底直动从动件盘形凸轮机构

典型例题解析

【例 17.4-4】 有一对心直动滚子从动件的偏心圆凸轮，偏心圆直径为 100mm，偏心距为 20mm，滚子半径为 10mm，则基圆直径为：

A. 60mm　　B. 80mm　　C. 100mm　　D. 140mm

解　对心直动滚子从动件的偏心圆凸轮的基圆直径＝2×(偏心圆半径－偏心距＋滚子半径)＝2×(100/2－20＋10)＝80mm。选 B。

【例 17.4-5】 在滚子从动件凸轮机构中，对于外凸的凸轮理论轮廓曲线，为保证做出凸轮的实际轮廓曲线不会出现变尖或交叉现象，必须满足：

A. 滚子半径不等于理论轮廓曲线最小曲率半径

B. 滚子半径小于理论轮廓曲线最小曲率半径

C. 滚子半径等于理论轮廓曲线最小曲率半径

D. 滚子半径大于理论轮廓曲线最小曲率半径

解　滚子半径的大小对凸轮实际轮廓有很大影响。设理论轮廓外凸部分的最小曲率半径为 ρ_{min}，滚子半径为 r，则相应位置实际轮廓曲率半径 $\rho'=\rho_{min}-r$，为保证实际轮廓曲线不产生尖点或者自相交，应使 $\rho'>0$。因此，要求滚子半径必须小于理论轮廓外凸部分的最小曲率半径 ρ_{min}。选 B。

17.4.3 凸轮机构设计中应注意的问题

设计凸轮机构时，不仅要保证从动件实现预定的运动规律，还要求传动时受力良好、结构紧凑，因此，在设计凸轮机构时应注意下述问题：

1)滚子半径的选择

如图 17.4-8 所示，设理论轮廓上最小曲率半径为 ρ_{min}，滚子半径为 r_T 及对应的实际轮廓曲线半径为 ρ_a，它们之间有如下关系：

(1)凸轮理论轮廓的内凹部分。

由图 17.4-8a)可得　　$\rho_a=\rho_{min}+r_T$

由上式可知：实际轮廓曲率半径总大于理论轮廓曲率半径。因而，不论选择多大的滚子，都能做出实际轮廓。

(2)凸轮理论轮廓的外凸部分

由图 17.4-8b)可得 $\rho_a=\rho_{min}-r_T$

①当 $\rho_{min}>r_T$ 时，$\rho_a>0$，如图 17.4-8b)所示，实际轮廓为一平滑曲线。

②当 $\rho_{min}=r_T$ 时，$\rho_a=0$，如图 17.4-8c)所示，在凸轮实际轮廓曲线上产生了尖点，这种尖点极易磨损，磨损后就会改变从动件预定的运动规律。

③当 $\rho_{min}<r_T$ 时，$\rho_a<0$，如图 17.4-8d)所示，这时实际轮廓曲线发生相交，图中阴影部分的轮廓曲线在实际加工时被切去，使这一部分运动规律无法实现。

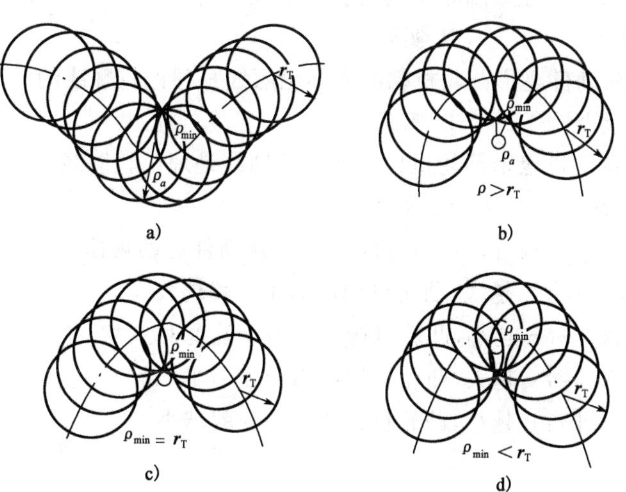

图 17.4-8 滚子半径对轮廓的影响

为了使凸轮轮廓在任何位置既不变尖也不相交，滚子半径必须小于理论轮廓外凸部分的最小曲率半径 ρ_{min}。如果 ρ_{min} 过小，按上述条件选择的滚子半径太小而不能满足安装和强度要求时，就应当把凸轮基圆尺寸加大，重新设计凸轮轮廓曲线。

2)压力角的校核

凸轮机构也和连杆机构一样，从动件运动方向和接触轮廓法线方向之间所夹的锐角称为压力角。在一般情况下，既要求凸轮有较高效率、受力情况良好，又要求其机构尺寸紧凑，因此，压力角不能过大，也不能过小，应有一许用值，这个许用值用$[\alpha]$表示。推荐的许用压力角为，推程(工作行程)：移动从动件$[\alpha]=30°$；摆动从动件$[\alpha]=45°$。回程：因受力较小且无自锁问题，故许用压力角可取得大些，通常$[\alpha]=80°$。

3)基圆半径对凸轮机构的影响

在设计凸轮机构时，凸轮的基圆半径取得越小，所设计的机构越紧凑。但是，基圆半径 r_{min} 越小，压力角 α 越大。基圆半径过小，压力角会超过许用值而使机构效率太低甚至发生自锁。因此实际设计中，只能在保证凸轮轮廓的最大压力角不超过许用值的前提下，考虑缩小凸轮的尺寸。

典型例题解析

【例 17.4-6】 在滚子从动件凸轮机构中，对于外凸的凸轮理论轮廓曲线，为保证做出凸轮的实际轮廓曲线不会出现变尖或交叉现象，必须满足：

A. 滚子半径大于理论轮廓曲线最小曲率半径

B. 滚子半径等于理论轮廓曲线最小曲率半径

C. 滚子半径小于理论轮廓曲线最小曲率半径

D. 无论滚子半径为多大

解　为了使凸轮轮廓在任何位置既不变尖也不相交，滚子半径必须小于理论轮廓外凸部分的最小曲率半径。选 C。

经 典 练 习

17.4-1　凸轮机构中，极易磨损的从动件是(　　)。

A. 尖顶从动件　　B. 滚子从动件　　C. 平底从动件　　D. 球面底从动件

17.4-2　滚子从动件盘形凸轮机构的基圆半径，是在(　　)轮廓线上度量的。

A. 理论　　B. 实际

17.4-3　滚子从动件盘形凸轮机构的实际轮廓线是理论轮廓线的(　　)曲线。

A. 不等距　　B. 等距

17.4-4　平底从动件盘形凸轮机构的实际轮廓线是理论轮廓线的(　　)曲线。

A. 不等距　　B. 等距

17.4-5　设计凸轮机构时，当凸轮角速度 ω_1、从动件运动规律已知时，则有(　　)。

A. 基圆半径 r_0 越大，凸轮机构压力角 α 就越大

B. 基圆半径 r_0 越小，凸轮机构压力角 α 就越大

C. 基圆半径 r_0 越大，凸轮机构压力角 α 不变

D. 基圆半径 r_0 越小，凸轮机构压力角 α 就越小

17.5　螺纹连接

考试大纲：螺纹的主要参数和常用类型　螺旋副的受力分析、效率和自锁　螺纹连接的基本类型　螺纹连接的强度计算　提高螺栓强度的措施

必备基础知识

17.5.1　螺纹连接的常用类型和主要参数

如图 17.5-1 所示，将一与水平面倾斜角为 λ 的直线绕在圆柱体上，即可形成一条螺旋线。如果用一个平面图形(梯形、三角形或矩形)沿着螺旋线运动，并保持此平面图形始终在通过圆柱轴线的平面内，则此平面图形的轮廓在空间的轨迹便形成螺纹。

根据平面图形的形状，螺纹牙形有矩形(见图 17.5-2a)、三角形(见图 17.5-2b)、梯形(见图 17.5-2c)和锯齿形(见图 17.5-2d)等。

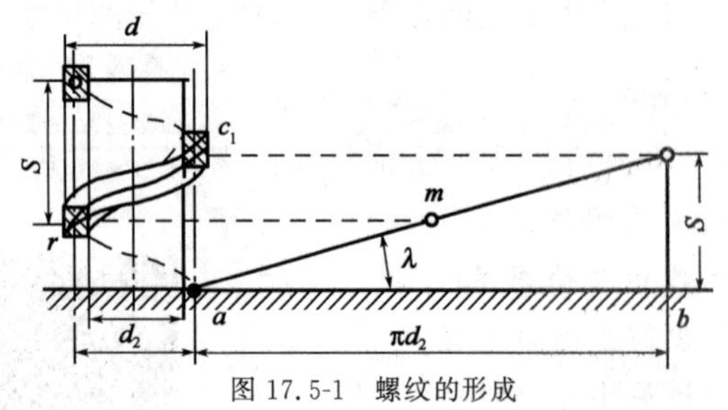

图 17.5-1　螺纹的形成

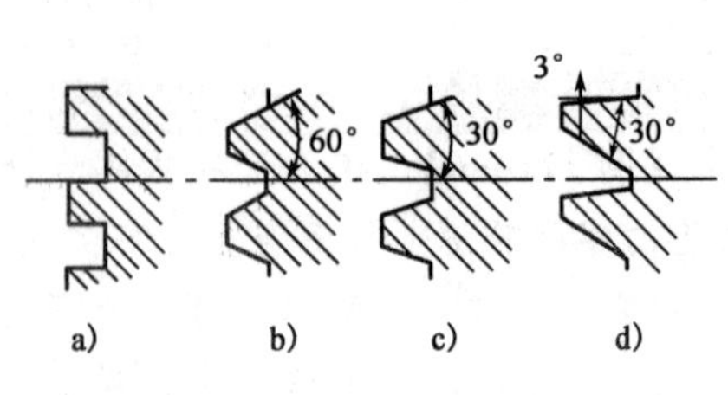

图 17.5-2　螺纹的牙形

根据螺旋线的绕行方向，可分为右旋螺纹(见图 17.5-3a)和左旋螺纹(见图 17.5-3b)；根据螺

旋线的数目，又可分为单线螺纹(见图 17.5-3a)和双线或以上的多线螺纹[见图 17.5-3b)、c)]。

在圆柱体外表面上形成的螺纹称为外螺纹，在圆柱体孔壁上形成的螺纹称为内螺纹(图 17.5-4)。现以圆柱螺纹为例，说明螺纹的主要几何参数：

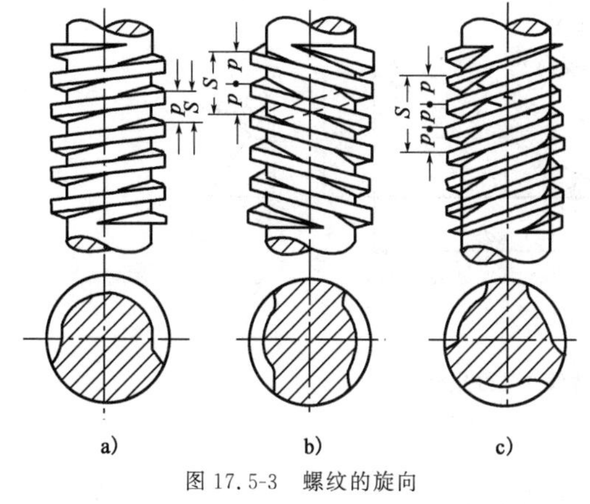

图 17.5-3　螺纹的旋向

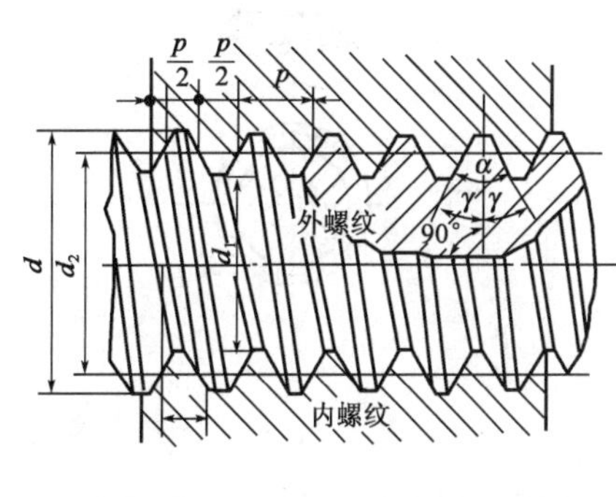

图 17.5-4　内、外螺纹

(1)大径 d、D 分别表示外、内螺纹的最大直径，为螺纹的公称直径。

(2)小径 d_1、D_1 分别表示外、内螺纹的最小直径。

(3)中径 d_2、D_2 分别表示螺纹牙宽度和牙槽宽度相等处的圆柱直径。

(4)螺距 p 表示相邻两螺纹牙同侧齿廓之间的轴向距离。

(5)线数 n 表示螺纹的螺旋线数目。

(6)导程 S 表示在同一条螺旋线上相邻两螺纹牙之间的轴向距离，$S=np$。

(7)螺纹升角 λ 表示在中径 d_2 圆柱上螺旋线的切线与螺纹轴线的垂直平面间的夹角，如图 17.5-1 所示，$S=\pi d_2\tan\lambda$。

(8)牙形角 α 表示在螺纹轴向剖面内螺纹牙形两侧边的夹角。牙侧角 β 表示牙形侧边与螺纹轴线的垂线间的夹角，对于对称牙形 $\beta=\alpha/2$。

典型例题解析

【例 17.5-1】 有一螺母转动—螺杆移动的螺纹传动，已知螺纹头数为 3 且当螺母旋转一圈时，螺杆移动了 12mm，则有：

A. 螺距为 12mm　　B. 导程为 36mm

C. 螺距为 4mm　　D. 导程为 4mm

解　导程表示在同一条螺旋线上相邻两螺纹牙之间的轴向距离。螺母旋转一圈时，导程＝螺杆移动距离/螺纹头数＝12/3＝4mm。选 C。

17.5.2 螺旋副的受力分析、效率和自锁

如图 17.5-5a)所示，在外力(或外力矩)作用下，螺旋副的相对运动可看作推动滑块沿螺纹表面运动。如图 17.5-5b)所示，将矩形螺纹沿中径处展开，得一倾斜角为 λ 的斜面，斜面上的滑块代表螺母，螺母与螺杆的相对运动可看成滑块在斜面上的运动。

如图 17.5-5b)所示，当滑块沿斜面向上等速运动时，所受作用力包括轴向荷载 F_Q、作用于中径处的水平推力 F、斜面对滑块的法向反力 F_N、摩擦力 $F_f=fF_N$。F_N 与 F_f 的合力为 F_R，f 为摩擦系数，F_R 与 F_N 的夹角为摩擦角 ρ。由力 F_R、F 和 F_Q 组成的力多边形(见图 17.5-5b)可得

$$F = F_Q \tan(\lambda + \rho) \quad (17.5\text{-}1)$$

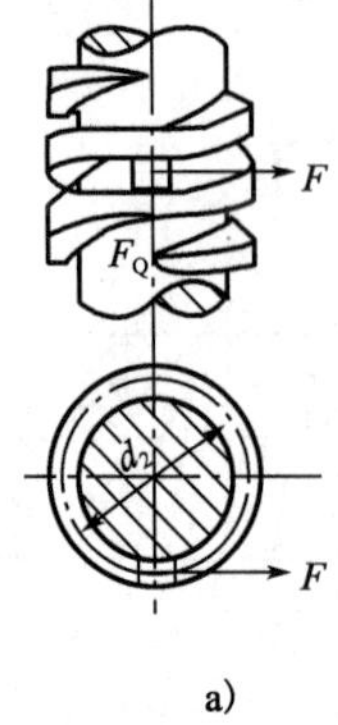

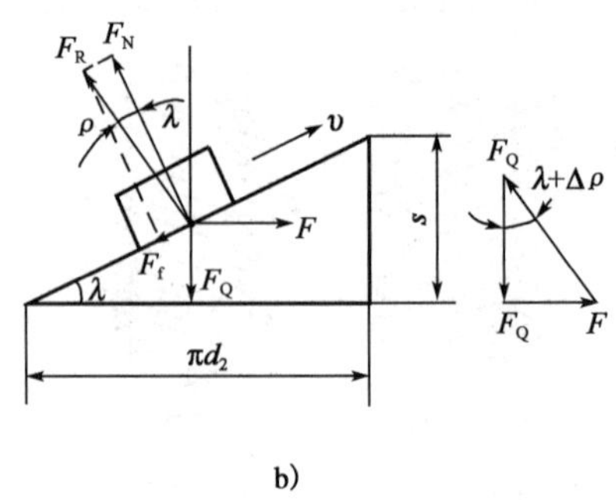

图 17.5-5 矩形螺纹的受力分析

作用在螺旋副上的相应驱动力矩为

$$T = F\frac{d_2}{2} = F_Q\frac{d_2}{2}\tan(\lambda + \rho) \quad (17.5\text{-}2)$$

当滑块沿斜面等速下滑时，轴向荷载 F_Q 变为驱动滑块等速下滑的驱动力，F 为阻碍滑块下滑的支持力，摩擦力 F_f 的方向与滑块运动方向相反。由力 F_R、F 和 F_Q 组成的力多边形可得

$$F = F_Q \tan(\lambda - \rho) \quad (17.5\text{-}3)$$

作用在螺旋副上的相应力矩为

$$T = F\frac{d_2}{2} = F_Q\frac{d_2}{2}\tan(\lambda - \rho) \quad (17.5\text{-}4)$$

当 $\lambda \leqslant \rho$ 时，$F \leqslant 0$，即不加支持力，滑块在 F_Q 作用下也不会自动下滑，这种现象称为螺旋副的自锁。因此矩形螺纹的自锁条件是：$\lambda \leqslant \rho$。设计螺旋副时，对要求正反转自由运动的螺旋副，应避免自锁现象，工程中也可以应用螺旋副的自锁特性，如起重螺旋做成自锁螺旋，可以省去制动装置。

螺旋副的效率 η 是指有用功与输入功之比。螺母旋转一周所需的输入功为 $2\pi T$，有用功为 $F_Q S$ 其中，$S = \pi d_2 \tan\lambda$。因此，螺旋副的效率为

$$\eta = \frac{F_Q S}{2\pi T} = \frac{\tan\lambda}{\tan(\lambda + \rho')} \quad (17.5\text{-}5)$$

非矩形螺纹是指牙形角 α 不等于零的螺纹，包括三角形螺纹、梯形螺纹和锯齿形螺纹。与矩形螺纹分析相同，非矩形螺纹的自锁条件可表示为：$\lambda \leqslant \rho'$。其中，ρ' 为当量摩擦角，其值为

$$\tan\rho' = f' = \frac{f}{\cos\beta}$$

其中，f' 为当量摩擦系数，β 为牙侧角。非矩形螺纹的牙形角 α 越大，螺纹的效率越低。由于三角螺纹的自锁性能比矩形螺纹好，静连接螺纹要求自锁，故多采用牙形角大的三角螺纹。传动螺纹要求螺旋副的效率 η 要高，因此，一般采用牙形角较小的梯形螺纹。

典型例题解析

【例 17.5-2】 直接影响螺纹传动自锁性能的螺纹参数是：

A. 螺距　　B. 导程　　C. 螺纹外径　　D. 螺纹升角

解 矩形螺纹的自锁条件是 $\lambda \leqslant \rho$，即螺纹升角≤摩擦角。选 C。

【例 17.5-3】 在以下几种螺纹中，哪种是为承受单向荷载而专门设计的？

A. 梯形螺纹　　B. 锯齿形螺纹　　C. 矩形螺纹　　D. 三角形螺纹

解 锯齿形螺纹的牙形为不等腰梯形，工作面的牙形角为 3°，非工作面的牙形角为 30°。外螺纹的牙根有较大的圆角，以减少应力集中。内、外螺纹旋合后大径处无间隙，便于对中，传动效率高，而且牙根强度高。适用于承受单向荷载的螺旋传动。选 B。

【例 17.5-4】 若要提高螺纹连接的自锁性能，可以：

A. 采用牙形角小的螺纹　　B. 增大螺纹升角

C. 采用细牙螺纹　　D. 增大螺纹螺距

解 单线螺纹常用于连接，双线螺纹常用于传动。

自锁性能与螺纹升角有关，对于公称直径相同的普通螺纹来讲，细牙螺纹的螺纹升角更小一些，因而自锁性能更好。选 C。

17.5.3 螺纹连接的基本类型

螺纹连接的基本类型有螺栓连接、螺钉连接、双头螺柱连接和紧定螺钉连接，如表 17.5-1 所示。

螺纹连接的基本类型、特点与应用　　表 17.5-1

类　型	结构图	特点与应用
普通螺栓连接	e, d_0, l_1, a, d	结构简单，装拆方便，对通孔加工精度要求，应用最广泛
铰制孔螺栓连接	d_0, l_1, a, d	孔与螺栓杆之间没有间隙，采用基孔制过渡配合。用螺栓杆承受横向荷载或者固定被连接件的相对位置
螺钉连接	l_1, H_2, H_1, H, d, e	不用螺母，直接将螺钉的螺纹部分拧入被连接件之一的螺纹孔中构成连接。其连接结构简单。用于被连接件之一较厚不便加工通孔的场合，但如果经常装拆时，易使螺纹孔产生过度磨损而导致连接失效

续上表

类　型	结构图	特点与应用
双头螺柱连接	d a l₁ H₂ H₁ H e	螺栓的一端旋紧在一被连接件的螺纹孔中。另一端则穿过另一被连接件的孔，通常用于被连接件之一太厚不便穿孔、结构要求紧凑或者经常装拆的场合
紧定螺钉连接	d	螺钉的末端顶住零件的表面或者顶入该零件的凹坑中，将零件固定；它可以传递不大的荷载

17.5.4 螺纹连接的强度计算

1）螺栓连接的失效形式和设计准则

螺栓连接中的单个螺栓受力分为轴向荷载（受拉螺栓）和横向荷载（受剪螺栓）两种。受拉力作用的普通螺栓连接，其主要失效形式是螺纹部分的塑性变形或断裂，经常装拆时也会因磨损而发生滑扣，其设计准则是保证螺栓的静力或者疲劳拉伸强度；受剪切作用的铰制孔用螺栓连接，因其主要失效形式是螺杆被剪断，螺杆或者被连接件的孔壁被压溃，故其设计准则为保证螺栓和被连接件具有足够的剪切强度和挤压强度。

2）螺栓连接的强度计算

螺栓连接的强度计算主要是确定螺纹小径 d_1，然后按照标准选定螺纹公称直径（大径）d 及螺距 p 等。

（1）松螺栓连接

松螺栓连接装配时不需要拧紧螺母，在承受工作荷载之前，螺栓并不受力。当承受轴向工作荷载 F_Q(N)时，其强度条件为

$$\sigma = \frac{F_Q}{\pi d_1^2/4} \leqslant [\sigma] \tag{17.5-6}$$

式中：d_1——螺纹小径(mm)；

$[\sigma]$——许用应力(MPa)。

（2）紧螺栓连接

①只受预紧力的紧螺栓连接。

紧螺栓连接装配时需要将螺母拧紧。设拧紧螺栓时螺杆承受的轴向拉力为 F_Q，这时螺栓危险面(螺纹小径)除受拉应力 σ 外，还受到螺纹力矩 T_1 所产生的剪切应力 τ。实际计算时，为了简化计算，对 M10～M68 的钢制普通螺栓，只按拉伸强度计算，并将所受拉力增大 30%来考虑剪切应力的影响，即螺栓的强度条件为

$$\frac{1.3F_Q}{\pi d_1^2/4} \leqslant [\sigma] \tag{17.5-7}$$

②受预紧力和横向工作荷载的紧螺栓连接。

如图 17.5-6 所示的螺栓连接，靠接合面间的摩擦力来承受垂直于螺栓轴线的工作荷载 F，因此螺栓所需的轴向力(即预紧力)F_Q 应为

$$F_Q = F_0 \geqslant \frac{CF}{mf} \tag{17.5-8}$$

式中：F_0——预紧力；

C——可靠性系数，通常取 $C=1.1\sim1.3$；

m——接合面数目；

f——接合面摩擦系数，对于钢或铸铁被连接件可取 0.1～0.15。

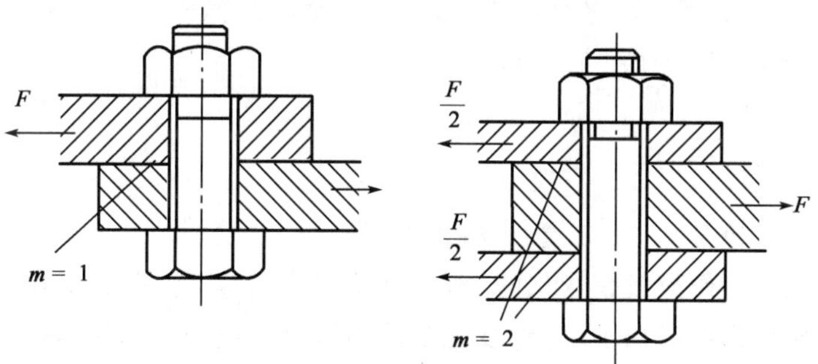

图 17.5-6 受横向载荷的螺栓连接

求出 F_Q 值后，可按式(17.5-7)计算螺栓强度。

(3)受预紧力和轴向工作荷载的紧螺栓连接

在受轴向工作荷载作用的螺栓连接中(见图 17.5-7)，螺栓实际的总拉伸荷载 F_Q 并不等于工作荷载 F_E 与预紧力 F_0 之和，而是等于工作荷载 F_E 与残余预紧力 F_r 之和，即

$$F_Q = F_E + F_r \tag{17.5-9}$$

为了保证连接的紧密性，防止连接受工作荷载后接合面间出现缝隙，应使 $F_r>0$。对于有密封性要求的连接，取 $F_r=(1.5\sim1.8)F_E$。对于一般连接，工作荷载稳定时，取 $F_r=(0.2\sim0.6)F_E$；工作荷载有变化时，取 $F_r=(0.6\sim1.0)F_E$。

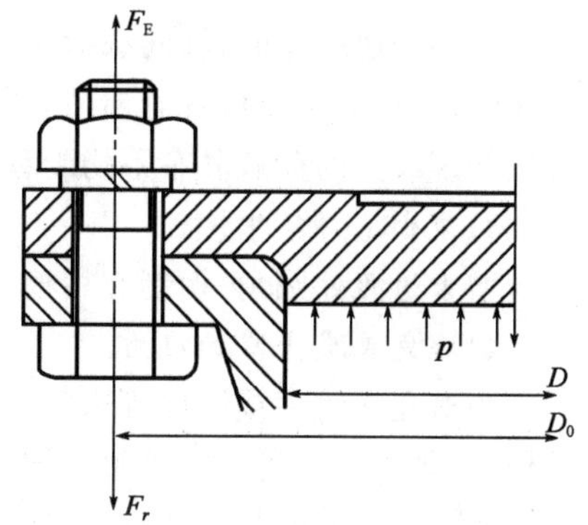

图 17.5-7 液压缸的螺栓连接

在一般计算中，可先根据连接的工作要求确定残余预紧力 F_r，再由式(17.5-9)计算出总拉伸荷载 F_Q，然后由式(17.5-7)计算螺栓强度。

典型例题解析

【例 17.5-5】 已知：某松螺栓连接，所受最大荷载 $F_Q=15\ 000N$，荷载很少变动，螺栓材料的需用应力 $[\sigma]=140MPa$，则该螺栓的最小直径 d_1 为：

A. 13.32mm　　B. 10mm　　C. 11.68mm　　D. 16mm

解 松螺栓连接的强度条件为 $\sigma=\dfrac{F_Q}{\pi d_1^2/4}\leqslant[\sigma]$，代入数据计算得 $d_1=11.68mm$。选 C。

【例 17.5-6】 用普通螺栓来承受横向工作荷载 F 时(见图 17.5-7)，当摩擦系数 $f=0.15$、可靠性系数 $C=1.2$、接合面数目 $m=1$ 时，预紧力 F_0 应为：

A. $F_0\leqslant 8F$　　B. $F_0\leqslant 10F$　　C. $F_0\geqslant 8F$　　D. $F_0\geqslant 6F$

解 普通螺栓是靠接合面间的摩擦力来承受横向工作荷载，所以螺栓的轴向力 F_Q 等于螺栓的预紧力 F_0，为 $F_Q=F_0\geqslant\dfrac{CF}{mf}=\dfrac{1.2F}{1\times 0.15}=8F$。选 C。

【例 17.5-7】 在受轴向工作荷载的螺栓连接中，F_{Q0} 为预紧力，F_Q 为工作荷载，$F_{Q'}$ 为残余预紧力，$F_{Q\Sigma}$ 为螺栓实际承受的总拉伸载荷。则 $F_{Q\Sigma}$ 等于：

A. $F_{Q\Sigma}=F_Q$　　B. $F_{Q\Sigma}=F_Q+F_{Q'}$　　C. $F_{Q\Sigma}=F_Q+F_{Q0}$　　D. $F_{Q\Sigma}=F_{Q0}$

解 于受轴向工作载荷的紧螺栓连接，螺栓所受的总拉伸载荷应等于工作载荷与残余预紧力之和，即 $F_{Q\Sigma}=F_Q+F_{Q'}$。选 B。

17.5.5 提高螺栓强度的措施

1)降低螺栓总拉伸荷载 F_Q 的变化范围

如螺栓所受轴向工作荷载是变化的，则螺栓总拉伸荷载 F_Q 也是变化的。减小螺栓刚度或增大被连接件刚度都可以减小 F_Q 的变化范围，对防止螺栓的疲劳损坏十分有利的。

为了减小螺栓刚度，可减小螺栓光杆部分直径或采用空心螺杆，有时也可增加螺栓的长度。为保持被连接件本身的刚度，被连接件的接合面不宜采用软垫片。

2)改变螺纹牙间的荷载分布

采用普通螺母时，轴向载荷在旋合螺纹各圈间的分布是不均匀的，从螺母支承面算起，第一圈受荷载最大，以后各圈递减，因此采用圈数过多的厚螺母并不能提高螺栓连接强度。为改善旋合螺纹上的荷载分布不均匀程度，可采用悬置螺母或环槽螺母。

3)减小应力集中

增大过渡处圆角、切制卸载槽，都是使螺栓截面变化均匀，减小应力集中的有效方法。

4)避免或减小附加应力

为避免在铸件或锻件等未加工表面上安装螺栓所产生的弯曲应力，可采用凸台或沉孔等结构，经加工以后可获得平整的支撑面。

典型例题解析

【例 17.5-8】 下列哪一项不可能改善螺轩的受力情况？

A. 采用悬置螺母　　B. 加厚螺帽

C. 采用钢丝螺套　　D. 减小支撑面的不平度

解 采用普通螺母时，轴向荷载在旋合螺纹各圈间的分布是不均匀的，从螺母支承面算起，第一圈受荷载最大，以后各圈递减，因此采用圈数过多的厚螺母并不能提高螺栓连接强度。选 B。

【例 17.5-9】 在螺杆连接设计中，被连接件为铸铁时，往往在螺栓孔处制作沉头座或凸台，其目的是：

A. 便于装配　　B. 便于安装防松装置

C. 避免螺栓受拉力过大　　D. 避免螺栓附加受弯曲应力作用

解 为避免在铸件或锻件等未加工表面上安装螺栓所产生的弯曲应力，可采用凸台或沉孔等结构，经加工以后可获得平整的支撑面。选 D。

经典练习

17.5-1　λ 为螺纹升角，ρ 为摩擦角，ρ' 为当量摩擦角，三角形螺纹的自锁条件可表示为（　　）。

A. $\lambda<\rho$　　B. $\lambda>\rho$　　C. $\lambda<\rho'$　　D. $\lambda>\rho'$

17.5-2　为降低螺栓总拉伸荷载 F_Q 的变化范围，可以（　　）。

A. 增大螺栓刚度或增大被连接件刚度　　B. 减小螺栓刚度或增大被连接件刚度

C. 减小螺栓刚度或减小被连接件刚度　　D. 增大螺栓刚度或减小被连接件刚度

17.5-3　适用于连接用的螺纹是（　　）。

A. 锯齿形螺纹　　B. 梯形螺纹　　C. 三角形螺纹　　D. 矩形螺纹

17.5-4　若要提高螺纹连接的自锁性能，可以（　　）。

A. 采用多头螺纹　　B. 增大螺纹升角

C. 采用牙形角大的螺纹　　D. 增大螺纹螺距

17.6　带传动

考试大纲☞：带传动工作情况分析　普通 V 带传动的主要参数和选择计算　带轮的材料和结构　带传动的张紧和维护

必备基础知识

17.6.1　带传动的工作情况分析

如图 17.6-1 所示，带传动是由主动轮 1、从动轮 2 以及环形带 3 组成，安装时，带被张紧在带轮上，产生的初拉力使得带与带轮之间产生压力。主动轮转动时，依靠摩擦力拖动从动轮一起转动，并传动一定的转矩。带传动主要用于两轴平行而且回转方向相同的场合。

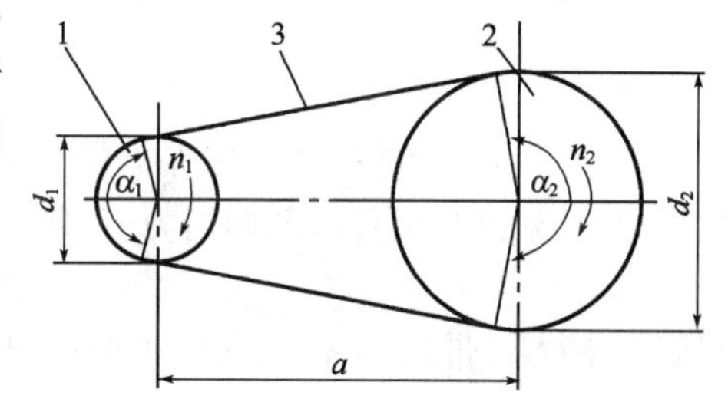

图 17.6-1　带传动简图

1）带传动的特点

带传动的主要优点为：

（1）适用于中心距较大的传动。

（2）带具有弹性，可缓冲和吸振。

(3)传动平稳，噪声小。

(4)过载时带与带轮间会出现打滑，可防止其他零件损坏，起安全保护作用。

(5)结构简单，制造容易，维护方便，成本低。

带传动的主要缺点为：

(1)传动的外廓尺寸较大。

(2)由于带的滑动，因此瞬时传动比不准确，不能用于要求传动比精确的场合。

(3)传动效率较低。

(4)带的寿命较短。

2)带传动的主要几何参数

(1)中心距 a：当带处于规定张紧力时，两带轮轴线间的距离。

(2)带轮直径 d：在 V 带传动中，指带轮的基准直径，用 d_d 表示带轮的基准直径。

(3)包角 α：带与带轮接触弧所对的中心角。设 d_1、d_2 分别为小轮、大轮的直径，则

$$\alpha = 180^\circ \pm \frac{d_2 - d_1}{a} \times 57.3^\circ \qquad (17.6\text{-}1)$$

其中，"＋"适用于大轮包角 α_2，"－"适用于小轮包角 α_1。

(4)带长 L：对 V 带传动，指带的基准长度，用 L_d 表示带的基准长度。

$$L \approx 2a + \frac{\pi}{2}(d_1 + d_2) + \frac{(d_2 - d_1)^2}{4a} \qquad (17.6\text{-}2)$$

3)带传动的受力分析

如图 17.6-2a)所示，带必须以一定的初拉力张紧在带轮上，使带与带轮的接触面上产生正压力。带传动未工作时，带的两边具有相等的初拉力 F_0。

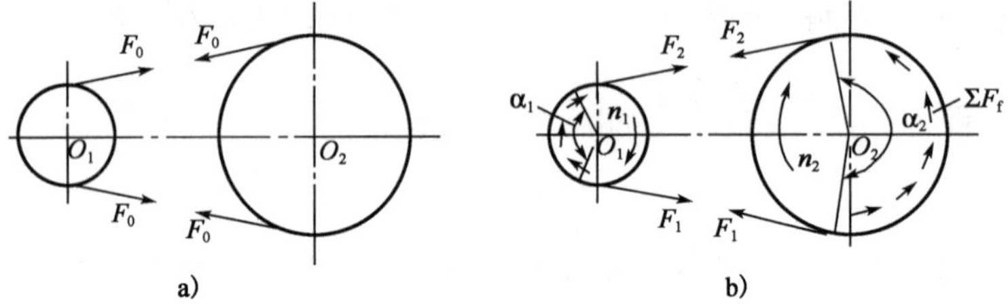

图 17.6-2 带传动的受力分析

当主动轮 1 在转矩作用下以转速 n_1 转动时，由图 17.6-2b)可知，由于摩擦力的作用，主动轮 1 拖动带，带又驱动从动轮 2 以转速 n_2 转动，从而把主动轮上的运动和动力传到从动轮上。在传动中，两轮与带的摩擦力方向如图所示，这就使进入主动轮一边的带拉得更紧，拉力由 F_0 增加到 F_1，称为紧边。设环形带的总长不变，则在紧边拉力的增加量 $F_1 - F_0$ 应等于在松边拉力的减少量 $F_0 - F_2$，则

$$F_0 = \frac{1}{2}(F_1 + F_2) \qquad (17.6\text{-}3)$$

带紧边和松边的拉力差应等于带与带轮接触面上产生的摩擦力的总和，称为带传动的有效拉力，也就是带所传递的圆周力 F，即

$$F = F_1 - F_2 \qquad (17.6\text{-}4)$$

圆周力 F(N)、带速 v(m/s)和传递功率 P(kW)之间的关系为

$$P = \frac{Fv}{1\,000} \qquad (17.6\text{-}5)$$

在一定的条件下，摩擦力的大小有一个极限值，即最大摩擦力，若带所需传递的圆周力超过这个极限值时，带与带轮将发生显著的相对滑动，这种现象称为打滑。出现打滑时，虽然主动轮还在转动，但带和从动轮都不能正常运动，甚至完全不动，这就使传动失效。经常出现打滑将使带的磨损加剧，传动效率降低，故在带传动中应防止出现打滑。带的紧边拉力 F_1 与松边拉力 F_2 之间的关系可用柔韧体摩擦的欧拉方式来表示

$$F_1 = F_2 e^{f\alpha}$$

式中：f——带与轮面间的摩擦系数；

α——带轮的包角(rad)；

e——自然对数的底，$e \approx 2.718$。

圆周力 F 与 F_1、F_2 的关系为

$$F_1 = F\frac{e^{f\alpha}}{e^{f\alpha}-1};F_2 = F\frac{1}{e^{f\alpha}-1};F = F_1 - F_2 = F_1\left(1-\frac{1}{e^{f\alpha}}\right) \qquad (17.6\text{-}6)$$

由此可知，增大包角和增大摩擦系数，都可提高带传动所能传递的圆周力。对于带传动，在一定的条件下 f 为一定值，而且 $\alpha_2 > \alpha_1$，所以摩擦力的最大值取决于 α_1。

引用当量摩擦系数的概念，以 f' 代替 f 即可将上式应用于 V 带传动。

4)带的应力分析

带传动时，带中产生的应力有由紧边和松边拉力产生的拉应力 σ_1、σ_2，离心力产生的应力 σ_c，带绕过带轮时因弯曲而产生弯曲应力 σ_b。其值分别为：

$$\sigma_1 = \frac{F_1}{A};\sigma_2 = \frac{F_2}{A};\sigma_c = \frac{qv^2}{A};\sigma_b = \frac{2yE}{d}$$

式中：A——带的横截面积(mm^2)；

q——每米带长的质量(kg/m)；

v——带速(m/s)；

y——带的中性层到最外层的距离(mm)；

E——带的弹性模量(MPa)；

d——带轮直径(mm)。

应注意虽然离心力只发生在带轮做圆周运动的部分，但其引起的拉力却作用于带的全长；弯曲应力与带轮的直径成反比，故小带轮上的弯曲应力较大。

如图 17.6-3 所示为带的应力分布情况，从图中可见，带上的应力是变化的。最大应力发生在紧边与小轮的接触处，其值为

$$\sigma_{max} = \sigma_1 + \sigma_{b1} + \sigma_c \qquad (17.6\text{-}7)$$

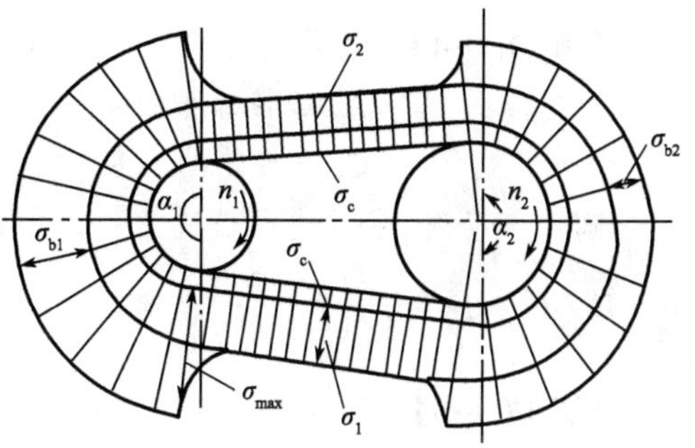

图 17.6-3　带的应力分析

5)带传动的运动分析

由于紧边拉力和松边拉力不相等，带会产生的弹性变形，这种弹性变形会使带在带轮上产生滑动，由于材料的弹性变形而产生的滑动称为弹性滑动。弹性滑动和打滑是两个不同的概念。打滑是指由过载引起的全面滑动，应当避免。弹性滑动是由拉力差引起的，只要传递圆周力，出现紧边和松边，就一定会发生弹性滑动，所以弹性滑动是不可避免的。

设 d_1、d_2 为主、从动轮的直径，n_1、n_2 为主、从动轮的转速，则两轮的圆周速度分别为 v_1、v_2。由于弹性滑动是不可避免的，所以 v_2 总是低于 v_1。传动中由于带的滑动引起的从动轮圆周速度的降低率称为滑动率 ε，即

$$\varepsilon=\frac{v_1-v_2}{v_1}=\frac{d_1n_1-d_2n_2}{d_1n_1} \tag{17.6-8}$$

由此得带传动的传动比

$$i=\frac{n_1}{n_2}=\frac{d_2}{d_1(1-\varepsilon)} \tag{17.6-9}$$

V 带的滑动率 ε＝0.01～0.02，其值较小，在一般计算中可不予考虑。

典型例题解析

【例 17.6-1】 皮带传动常用在高速级，主要是为了：

A. 减小带传动结构尺寸　　B. 更好地发挥缓冲、吸振作用

C. 更好地提供保护作用　　D. A＋B＋C

解 带传动的优点有：①适用于中心距较大的传动；②带具有弹性，可缓冲和吸振；③传动平稳，噪声小；④过载时带与带轮间会出现打滑，可防止其他零件损坏，起安全保护作用；⑤减小带传动结构尺寸，结构简单，制造容易，维护方便，成本低。因此，皮带传动常用在高速级。选 D。

【例 17.6-2】 以下各种皮带传动类型中，传动能力最小的为：

A. 圆形带　　B. 同步带　　C. 平带　　D. V 型带

解 带紧套在两个带轮上，借助带与带轮接触面间的压力所产生的摩擦力来传递运动和动力。同样条件下，圆形带与带轮接触面上的摩擦力最小，因此传动能力最小。选 A。

【例 17.6-3】 V 带传动工作时产生弹性滑动的原因是：

A. 带与带轮之间的摩擦系数太小

B. 带轮的包角太小

C. 紧边拉力与松边拉力不相等及带的弹性变形

D. 带轮的转速有波动

解 由于紧边拉力和松边拉力不相等，带会产生的弹性变形，这种弹性变形会使带在带轮上产生滑动，由于材料的弹性变形而产生的滑动称为弹性滑动。选 C。

【例 17.6-4】 V 带传动中，最大有效拉力与下列什么因素无关？

A. V 带的初拉力　　B. 小带轮的包角

C. 小带轮的直径　　D. 带与带轮之间的摩擦因数

解 传动时，带紧边和松边的拉力差称为带传动的有效拉力，也就是带所传递的圆周力 F。$F=F_1-F_2=F_1\left(1-\frac{1}{e^{f\alpha}}\right)$。选 C。

【例 17.6-5】 V 带传动中，小带轮的直径不能取得过小，其主要目的是：

A. 增大 V 带传动的包角　　B. 减小 V 带的运动速度

C. 增大 V 带的有效拉力　　D. 减小 V 带中的弯曲应力

解 弯曲应力与带轮的直径成反比，小带轮的直径若取的过小，会产生过大的弯曲应力，从而导致带的寿命降低。选 D。

17.6.2 普通V带传动的主要参数和选择计算

1)带传动的主要失效形式和设计准则

带传动的主要失效形式有:①打滑。当传递的圆周力 F 超过了带与带轮接触面之间摩擦力总和的极限时,发生过载打滑,使传动失效。②疲劳破坏。传动带在变应力的反复作用下,发生裂纹、脱层、松散、直至断裂。

带传动的设计准则为:保证带传动不发生打滑的前提下,具有一定的疲劳强度和寿命。

2)V带传动设计计算和参数选择

普通V带传动设计计算时,通常已知传动的用途和工作情况;传递的功率;主动轮、从动轮的转速(或传动比);传动位置要求和外廓尺寸要求;原动机类型等。设计时主要确定带的型号、长度和根数,带轮的尺寸、结构和材料,传动的中心距,带的初拉力和压轴力,张紧和防护等。设计计算的一般步骤如下:

(1)确定计算功率 P_c

根据带传动所需功率 P,查表17.6-1得工作情况系数 K_A,求计算功率

$$P_c = K_A P \tag{17.6-10}$$

工作情况系数 K_A 表17.6-1

荷载性质	工作机	原动机					
		I类			II类		
		每天工作时间(h)					
		<10	10~16	>16	<10	10~16	>16
荷载平稳	离心式水泵、通风机(≤7.5kW)、轻型输送机、离心式压缩机	1.0	1.1	1.2	1.1	1.2	1.3
荷载变动小	带式运输机、通风机(>7.5kW)、发电机、旋转式水泵、机床、剪床、压力机、印刷机、振动筛	1.1	1.2	1.3	1.2	1.3	1.4
荷载变动较大	螺旋式输送机、斗式提升机、往复式水泵和压缩机、锻锤、磨粉机、锯木机、纺织机械	1.2	1.3	1.4	1.4	1.5	1.6
荷载变动很大	破碎机(旋转式、颚式等)、球磨机、起重机、挖掘机、辊压机	1.3	1.4	1.5	1.5	1.6	1.8

(2)选定V带的型号

根据计算功率 P_c 和小轮转速 n_1,按图17.6-4选择普通V带的型号。若临近两种型号的交界线时,可按两种型号同时计算,通过分析比较决定取舍。

(3)确定带轮基准直径 d_1、d_2

表17.6-2列出了V带轮的最小基准直径和带轮的基准直径系列,选择小带轮基准直径时,应使 $d_1 \geqslant d_{min}$。若 d_1 过小,则带的弯曲应力将过大而导致带的寿命降低;反之,虽能延长带的寿命,但带传动的外廓尺寸却随之增大。大带轮的基准直径 d_2 为

$$d_2 = \frac{n_1}{n_2} d_1 (1 - \varepsilon) \tag{17.6-11}$$

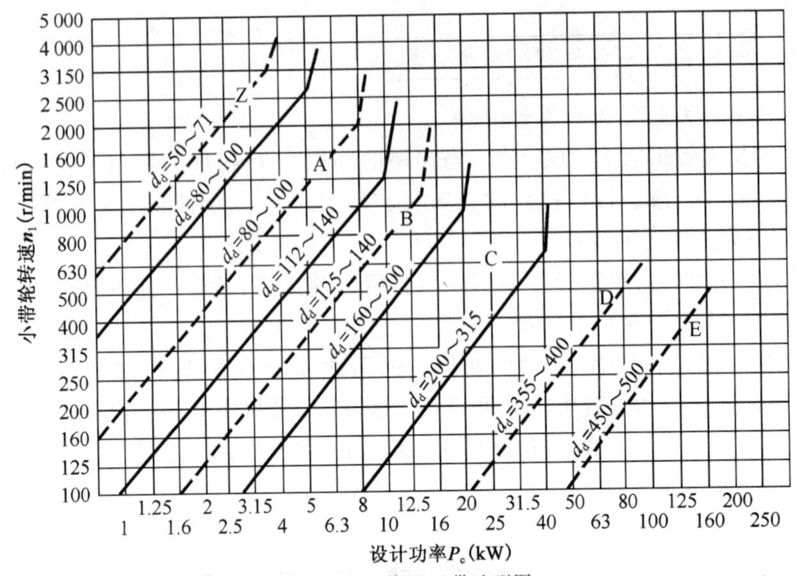

图 17.6-4 普通 V 带选型图

普通 V 带轮最小基准直径 表 17.6-2

型号	Y	Z	A	B	C
最小基准直径 d_{min}	20	50	75	125	200

注:带轮基准直径系列为 20、22.4、25、28、31.5、35.5、40、45、50、56、63、71、75、80、85、90、95、100、106、112、118、125、132、140、150、160、170、180、200、212、224、236、250、265、280、300、315、335、355、375、400、425、450、475、500、530、560、600、630、670、710、750、800、900、1 000、1 060、1 120、1 250、1 400、1 500、1 600、1 800、2 000、2 240、2 500。

(4)验算带速 v

$$v = \frac{\pi d_1 n_1}{60 \times 1\,000} \qquad (\mathrm{m/s}) \tag{17.6-12}$$

普通 V 带的带速 v 应在 5~25m/s 的范围内,其中以 10~20m/s 为宜,若 $v>25$m/s,则因带绕过带轮时离心力过大,使带与带轮之间的压紧力减小,摩擦力降低而使传动能力下降,而且离心力过大降低了带的疲劳强度和寿命。而当 $v<5$m/s 时,在传递相同功率时带所传递的圆周力增大,使带的根数增加。

(5)确定中心距 a 和基准长度 L_d

初步确定中心距

$$0.7(d_1 + d_2) < a_0 < 2(d_1 + d_2) \tag{17.6-13}$$

可得初定的 V 带基准长度

$$L_0 = 2a_0 + \frac{\pi}{2}(d_1 + d_2) + \frac{(d_2 - d_1)^2}{4a_0} \tag{17.6-14}$$

根据初定 L_0,由表 17.6-3 选取相近的基准长度 L_d。再按下式近似计算实际所需中心距

$$a \approx a_0 + \frac{L_d - L_0}{2} \tag{17.6-15}$$

考虑带传动的安装、调整和 V 带张紧的需要,中心距变动范围为

$$(a - 0.015L_d) \sim (a + 0.03L_d)$$

(6)验算小轮包角

$$a_1 = 180° - \frac{d_2 - d_1}{a} \times 57.3° \tag{17.6-16}$$

(7)确定带的根数 z

$$z=\frac{P_c}{(P_0+\Delta P_0)K_a K_L} \tag{17.6-17}$$

式中：K_L——带长修正系数，考虑带长不等于特定长度时对传动能力的影响(见表 17.6-3)；

P_0——单根普通 V 带的基本额定功率(见表 17.6-4)；

K_a——包角修正系数，考虑 $\alpha'\neq180°$时，传动能力有所下降(见表 17.6-5)；

ΔP_0——功率增量，考虑传动比 $i\neq1$ 时，带在大轮上的弯曲应力减小，故在寿命相同的条件下，可增大传递的功率(见表 17.6-6)。

z 应取整数。为了使每根 V 带受力均匀，V 带根数不宜太多，通常 $z<10$。

(8)求作用在带轮轴上的压力 F_Q。单根 V 带的初拉力

$$F_0=\frac{500P_c}{zv}\left(\frac{2.5}{K_a}-1\right)+qv^2 \quad (\mathrm{N}) \tag{17.6-18}$$

q 为带的单位长度的质量，作用在轴上的压力：

$$F_Q=2zF_0\sin\frac{\alpha_1}{2} \quad (\mathrm{N}) \tag{17.6-19}$$

普通 V 带的长度系列和带长修正系数 K_L 表 17.6-3

基准长度 L_d (mm)	K_L					基准长度 L_d (mm)	K_L				
	Y	Z	A	B	C		Y	Z	A	B	C
200	0.81					2 000		1.08	1.03	0.98	0.88
224	0.82					2 240		1.10	1.06	1.00	0.91
250	0.84					2 500		1.30	1.09	1.03	0.93
280	0.87					2 800			1.11	1.05	0.95
315	0.89					3 150			1.13	1.07	0.97
355	0.92					3 350			1.17	1.09	0.99
400	0.96	0.79				4 000			1.19	1.13	1.02
450	1.00	0.8				4 500				1.15	1.04
500	1.02	0.81				5 000				1.18	1.07
560		0.82				5 600					1.09
630		0.84	0.81			6 300					1.12
710		0.86	0.83			7 100					1.15
800		0.90	0.85			8 000					1.18
900		0.92	0.87	0.82		9 000					1.21
1 000		0.94	0.89	0.84		10 000					1.23
1 120		0.95	0.91	0.86		11 200					
1 250		0.98	0.93	0.88		12 500					
1 400		1.01	0.96	0.90		14 000					
1 600		1.04	0.99	0.92	0.83	16 000					
1 800		1.06	1.01	0.95	0.86						

单根普通 V 带的基本额定功率 P_0(单位:kW)

(包角 $\alpha=\pi$、特定基准长度、荷载平稳时)

表 17.6-4

型号	小带轮基准直径 d_1 (mm)	小带轮转速 n_1(r/min)						
		200	400	800	950	1 200	1 450	2 400
Z	50	0.04	0.06	0.10	0.12	0.14	0.16	0.22
	63	0.05	0.08	0.15	0.18	0.22	0.25	0.37
	71	0.06	0.09	0.2	0.23	0.27	0.30	0.46
	80	0.10	0.14	0.22	0.26	0.30	0.35	0.50
A	75	0.15	0.26	0.45	0.51	0.6	0.68	0.92
	90	0.22	0.39	0.68	0.77	0.93	1.07	1.50
	100	0.26	0.47	0.83	0.95	1.14	1.32	1.87
	112	0.31	0.56	1.00	1.15	1.39	1.61	2.30
	125	0.37	0.67	1.19	1.37	1.66	1.92	2.74
	140	0.43	0.78	1.41	1.62	1.96	2.28	3.22
B	125	0.48	0.84	1.44	1.64	1.93	2.19	2.85
	140	0.59	1.05	1.82	2.08	2.47	2.82	3.70
	160	0.74	1.32	2.32	2.66	3.17	3.62	4.75
	180	0.88	1.59	2.81	3.22	3.85	4.39	5.67
	200	1.02	1.85	3.3	3.77	4.50	5.13	6.47
C	200	1.39	2.41	4.07	4.58	5.29	5.84	6.02
	224	1.70	2.99	5.12	5.78	6.71	7.45	7.57
	250	2.03	3.62	6.23	7.04	8.20	9.08	8.75
	280	2.42	4.32	7.52	8.49	9.81	10.72	9.50

包角修正系数 K_a

表 17.6-5

包角 α_1(°)	180°	170°	160°	150°	140°	130°	120°	110°	100°	90°
K_a	1.00	0.98	0.95	0.92	0.89	0.86	0.82	0.78	0.74	0.69

单根普通 V 带额定功率的增量 ΔP_0(单位:kW)

表 17.6-6

带型	小带轮转速 n_1(r/min)	传动比									
		1.00~1.01	1.02~1.04	1.06~1.08	1.09~1.12	1.13~1.18	1.19~1.24	1.25~1.34	1.35~1.51	1.52~1.99	≥2.0
Z	400	0.00	0.00	0.00	0.00	0.00	0.00	0.00	0.00	0.01	0.01
	730.00	0.00	0.00	0.00	0.00	0.00	0.00	0.01	0.01	0.01	0.02
	800.00	0.00	0.00	0.00	0.00	0.01	0.01	0.01	0.01	0.02	0.02
	980.00	0.00	0.00	0.00	0.00	0.01	0.01	0.01	0.02	0.02	0.02
	1 200	0.00	0.00	0.01	0.01	0.01	0.01	0.02	0.02	0.02	0.03
	1 460	0.00	0.00	0.01	0.01	0.01	0.02	0.02	0.02	0.02	0.03
	2 800	0.00	0.01	0.02	0.02	0.03	0.03	0.03	0.04	0.04	0.04

续上表

带型	小带轮转速 n_1(r/min)	传动比									
		1.00～1.01	1.02～1.04	1.06～1.08	1.09～1.12	1.13～1.18	1.19～1.24	1.25～1.34	1.35～1.51	1.52～1.99	≥2.0
A	400	0.00	0.01	0.01	0.02	0.02	0.03	0.03	0.04	0.04	0.05
	730	0.00	0.01	0.02	0.03	0.04	0.05	0.06	0.07	0.08	0.09
	800	0.00	0.01	0.02	0.03	0.04	0.05	0.06	0.08	0.09	0.10
	980	0.00	0.01	0.03	0.04	0.05	0.06	0.07	0.08	0.10	0.11
	1 200	0.00	0.02	0.03	0.05	0.07	0.08	0.10	0.11	0.13	0.15
	1 460	0.00	0.02	0.04	0.06	0.08	0.09	0.11	0.13	0.15	0.17
	2 800	0.00	0.04	0.08	0.11	0.15	0.19	0.23	0.26	0.30	0.34
B	400	0.00	0.01	0.03	0.04	0.06	0.07	0.08	0.10	0.11	0.13
	730	0.00	0.02	0.05	0.07	0.10	0.12	0.15	0.17	0.20	0.22
	800	0.00	0.03	0.06	0.08	0.11	0.14	0.17	0.20	0.23	0.25
	980	0.00	0.03	0.07	0.10	0.13	0.17	0.20	0.23	0.26	0.30
	1 200	0.00	0.04	0.08	0.13	0.17	0.21	0.25	0.30	0.34	0.38
	1 460	0.00	0.05	0.10	0.15	0.20	0.25	0.31	0.36	0.40	0.46
	2 800	0.00	0.10	0.20	0.29	0.39	0.49	0.59	0.69	0.79	0.89
C	400	0.00	0.04	0.08	0.12	0.16	0.20	0.23	0.27	0.31	0.35
	730	0.00	0.07	0.14	0.21	0.27	0.34	0.41	0.48	0.55	0.62
	800	0.00	0.08	0.16	0.23	0.31	0.39	0.47	0.55	0.63	0.71
	980	0.00	0.09	0.19	0.27	0.37	0.47	0.56	0.65	0.74	0.83
	1 200	0.00	0.12	0.24	0.35	0.47	0.59	0.70	0.82	0.94	1.06
	1 460	0.00	0.14	0.28	0.42	0.58	0.71	0.85	0.99	1.14	1.27
	2 800	0.00	0.27	0.55	0.82	1.10	1.37	1.64	1.92	2.19	2.47

典型例题解析

【例 17.6-6】 有一 V 带传动，电机转速为 750r/min，带传动线速度为 20m/s。现需将从动轮(大带轮)转速提高 1 倍，最合理的改进方案为：

A. 选用 1500r/min 电机　　B. 将大轮直径缩至 1/2

C. 小轮增至 2 倍　　D. 小轮增大 25%，大轮缩至 5/8

解　V 带的滑动率 $\varepsilon=0.01\sim0.02$，其值较小，在一般计算中可不予考虑。则有 $n_1d_1=n_2d_2$，带速 $v=\pi d_1n_1/(60\times1\,000)$，现需将从动轮(大带轮)转速提高 1 倍，最合理的改进方案是将大轮直径缩至 1/2，增加电动机转速和增大小轮直径都是不合适的。若选用 1 500r/min 电机，或者将小轮增至 2 倍带速将增至 40m/s，普通 V 带的带速 v 应在 5～25m/s 的范围内，其中以 10～20m/s 为宜，若 $v>25$m/s，则因带绕过带轮时离心力过大，使带与带轮之间的压紧力减小，摩擦力降低而使传动能力下降，而且离心力过大降低了带的疲劳强度和寿命。选 B。

【例 17.6-7】 当小带轮为主动轮时，以下哪种方法对增加V型带传动能力作用不大？

A. 将Y型带改为A型带　　B. 提高轮槽加工精度

C. 增加小带轮直径　　D. 增加大带轮直径

解　由于小带轮是主动轮，要想增加V型带传动能力，可以增大摩擦系数（提高轮槽加工精度、将Y型带改为A型带）、增大小带轮包角 α_1。选D。

$\alpha_1 = 180° - \frac{d_2 - d_1}{a} \times 57.3°$，增加大带轮直径会导致 α_1 减小。

17.6.3 带轮的材料和结构

制造带轮的材料可采用灰铸铁、钢、铝合金或工程塑料，以灰铸铁应用最为广泛。带速 $v \leqslant 25$m/s 时，采用 HT150；$v > 25$m/s 时采用 HT200；速度更高的带轮可采用球墨铸铁或铸钢，也可采用钢板冲压后焊接带轮。小功率传动可采用铸铝或工程塑料。

带轮直径较小时可采用实心式，如图 17.6-5a）所示；中等直径的带轮可采用腹板式，如图 17.6-5b）所示；直径大于 350mm 时可采用轮辐式，如图 17.6-6 所示。

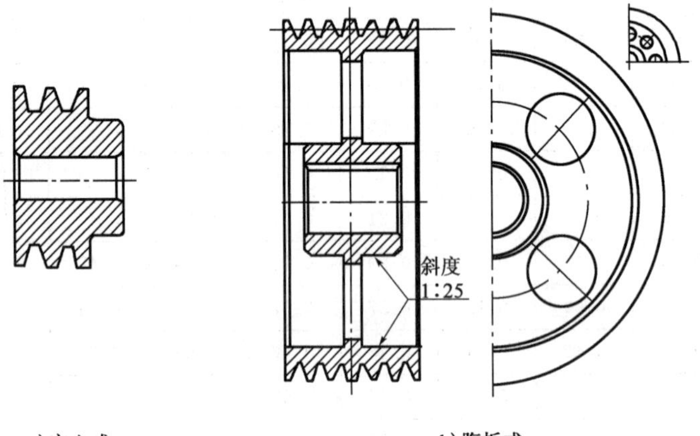

图 17.6-5　实心式和腹板式带轮

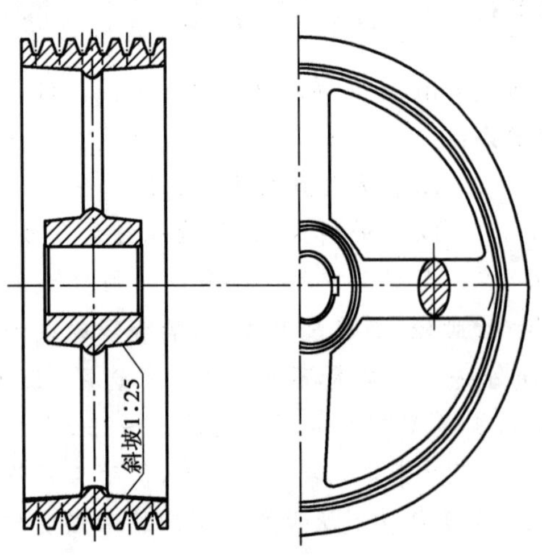

图 17.6-6　轮辐式带轮

17.6.4 带传动的张紧与维护

普通V带不是完全的弹性体，长期在张紧状态下工作，会因出现塑性变形而松弛，使初拉力减小，传动能力下降。因此，必须将带重新张紧，以保证带传动正常工作。

带传动常用的张紧方法是调节中心距。常见的张紧装置有以下两类：

1）定期张紧装置

如图 17.6-7a）、b）所示，采用滑轨和调节螺钉或采用摆动架和调节螺栓来改变中心距。前者适用于水平或倾斜不大的布置，后者适用于垂直或接近垂直的布置。若中心距不能调节时，可采用具有张紧轮的装置，如图 17.6-7c)所示，靠平衡锤将张紧轮压在带上，保持带的张紧。

2)自动张紧装置

图 17.6-7d)是采用重力和带轮上的制动力矩，使带轮随浮动架绕固定轴摆动而改变中心距的自动张紧方法。

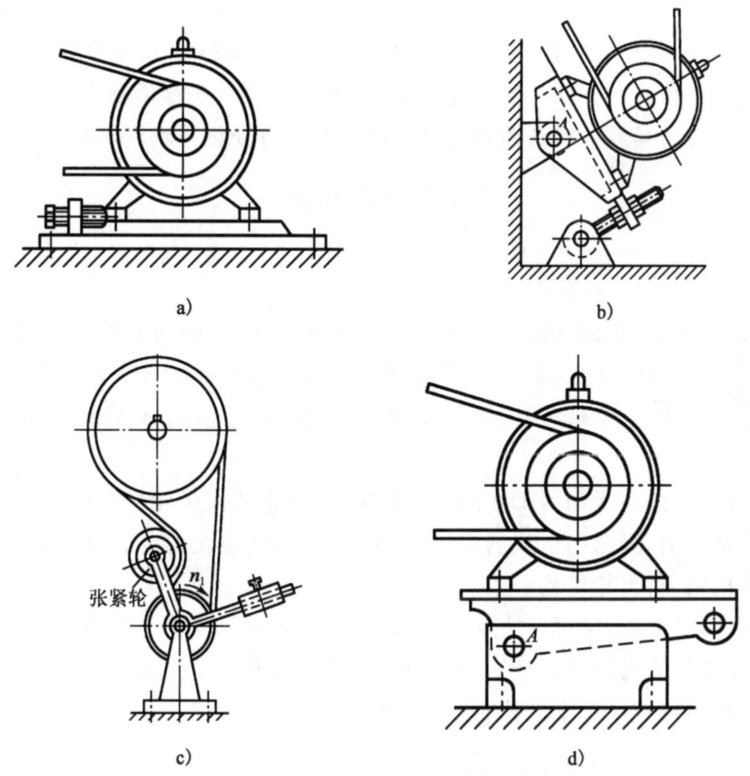

图 17.6-7　带传动的张紧装置

为了延长带的寿命，保证带传动的正常运转，使用时应注意：

(1)安装带时，最好缩小中心距后套上 V 带，再予以调整，不应硬撬，以免损坏胶带，降低其使用寿命。

(2)严防 V 带与油、酸、碱等介质接触，以免变质，也不宜在阳光下曝晒。

(3)带根数较多的传动，若坏了少数几根需进行更换时，应全部更换，不要只更换坏带而使新旧带一起使用；这样会造成荷载分配不匀，反而加速新带的损坏。

(4)为了保证安全生产，带传动须安装防护罩。

经 典 练 习

17.6-1　带传动是靠(　　)使带轮产生运动的。

A. 初拉力　　B. 圆周力　　C. 摩擦力　　D. 紧边拉力

17.6-1　带上最大应力发生在(　　)的接触处。

A. 松边与大轮　　B. 松边与小轮　　C. 紧边与大轮　　D. 紧边与小轮

17.6-3　当带所需传递的圆周力(　　)带与轮面间的极限摩擦力总和时，带与带轮将发生(　　)。

A. 小于,弹性滑动　　B. 大于,弹性滑动

C. 小于,打滑　　D. 大于,打滑

17.7 齿轮机构

考试大纲☞:直齿圆柱齿轮各部分名称和尺寸　渐开线齿轮的正确啮合条件和连续传动条件　轮齿的失效　直齿圆柱齿轮的强度计算　斜齿圆柱齿轮传动的受力分析　齿轮的结构　蜗杆传动的啮合特点和受力分析　蜗杆和涡轮的材料

必备基础知识

17.7.1 齿轮机构的特点与类型

齿轮机构用于传递两轴间的运动和动力,是应用最广的传动机构。齿轮传动的主要优点是:①适用的功率和速度范围广;②传动效率高;③传动比稳定;④寿命较长;⑤工作可靠。缺点是:①加工和安装精度要求较高,制造成本也较高;②不适宜于远距离两轴间的传动。

根据齿轮机构所传递运动两轴线的相对位置、运动形式及齿轮的几何形状,齿轮机构分为两大类:平面齿轮机构,其由(直齿、斜齿、人字齿)圆柱齿轮机构;空间齿轮机构,包括圆锥齿轮机构、蜗杆蜗轮机构、斜齿轮机构。

按齿轮齿廓曲线不同,又可分为渐开线齿轮、摆线齿轮和圆弧齿轮等,其中渐开线齿轮应用最广。渐开线齿轮的齿廓是渐开线曲线的一部分。渐开线是一条直线在一个圆上做纯滚动时,该直线上一点的轨迹。这个圆称为基圆,这条线称为发生线。

17.7.2 直齿圆柱齿轮各部分名称和尺寸

如图 17.7-1 所示为直齿圆柱齿轮的一部分。齿轮各参数如下:

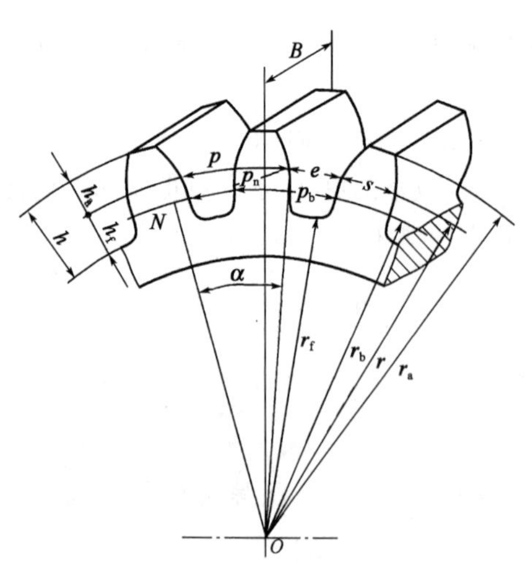

图 17.7-1　齿轮各部分名称

1)齿顶圆

齿顶端所确定圆称为齿顶圆,其半径用 r_a 表示。

2)齿根圆

齿槽底部所确定的圆称为齿根圆,其半径用 r_f 表示。

3)齿槽

相邻两齿之间的空间称为齿槽。齿槽两侧齿廓之间的弧长称为该圆上的齿槽宽,用 e 表示。

4)齿厚

在半径为 r 的圆周上,轮齿两侧齿廓之间的弧长称为该圆上的齿厚,用 s 表示。

5)齿距

相邻两齿同侧齿廓之间的弧长称为该圆上的齿距,用 p 表示,显然,$p=s+e$。

6)模数

规定比值$\frac{p}{\pi}$等于整数或简单的有理数,并作为计算齿轮几何尺寸的一个基本参数。这个比值称为模数,以 m 表示,单位为 mm,即 $m=\frac{p}{\pi}$,齿轮的主要几何尺寸都与 m 成正比。齿轮的模数已经标准化,我国规定的模数系列见表 17.7-1,齿轮的主要尺寸都与模数 m 成正比,m 越大,则 p 越大,轮齿就越大,轮齿的承载能力也越强。

圆柱齿轮标准模数系列表(GB/T 1357—2008)(单位:mm)　　表 17.7-1

第一系列	1	1.25	1.5	2	2.5	3	4	5	6	8	10
	12	16	20	25	32	40	50				
第二系列	1.125	1.375	1.75	2.25	2.75	(3.75)	4.5	5.5	(6.5)	7	9
	(11)	14	18	22	28	36	45				

注:优先采用第一系列,括号内的模数尽可能不用。

7)分度圆

标准齿轮上齿厚和齿槽宽相等的圆称为齿轮的分度圆,用 d 表示其直径。分度圆上的齿厚以 s 表示;齿槽宽用 e 表示;齿距用 p 表示。分度圆压力角通常称为齿轮的压力角,用 α 表示。分度圆压力角已经标准化,常用的为 20°、15°等,我国规定标准齿轮 $\alpha=20°$。由于齿轮分度圆上的模数和压力角均规定为标准值,因此,齿轮的分度圆可定义为齿轮上具有标准模数和标准压力角的圆。齿轮分度圆直径 d 则可表示为

$$d=\frac{p}{\pi}z=mz \tag{17.7-1}$$

8)齿顶与齿根

在轮齿上介于齿顶圆和分度圆之间的部分称为齿顶,其径向高度称为齿顶高,用 h_a 表示。介于根圆和分度圆之间的部分称为齿根,其径向高度称为齿根高,用 h_f 表示。齿顶圆与齿根圆之间轮齿的径向高度称为全齿高,用 h 表示,故

$$h=h_a+h_f \tag{17.7-2}$$

齿轮的齿顶高和齿根高可用模数表示为

$$h_a=mh_a^* \tag{17.7-3}$$

$$h_f=m(h_a^*+c^*) \tag{17.7-4}$$

其中,h_a^* 和 c^* 分别称为齿顶高系数和顶隙系数,对于圆柱齿轮,其值有正常齿制和短齿制,规定见表 17.7-2。

齿顶高系数和顶隙系数　　表 17.7-2

系数 \ 值	正常齿制	短齿制
h_a^*	1.0	0.8
c^*	0.25	0.3

9)顶隙

顶隙 $c=c^{*}m$,它是指一对齿轮啮合时,一个齿轮的齿顶圆到另一个齿轮的齿根圆的径向距离。

由此可以推出齿顶圆直径 d_a 和齿根圆直径 d_f 的计算式为

$$d_a = d + 2h_a = (z + 2h_a^*)m \tag{17.7-5}$$

$$d_f = d - 2h_f = (z - 2h_a^* - 2c^*)m \tag{17.7-6}$$

分度圆上齿厚与齿槽宽相等,且齿顶高和齿根高为标准值的齿轮称为标准齿轮。因此,对于标准齿轮

$$s = e = \frac{p}{2} = \frac{\pi m}{2} \tag{17.7-7}$$

渐开线齿轮的基圆直径计算式为

$$d_b = d\cos\alpha \tag{17.7-8}$$

在标准安装时,一对外啮合齿轮传动的中心距为

$$a = \frac{d_1 + d_2}{2} = \frac{m}{2}(z_1 + z_2) \tag{17.7-9}$$

$$a = \frac{d_2 - d_1}{2} = \frac{m}{2}(z_2 - z_1) \tag{17.7-10}$$

典型例题解析

【例 17.7-1】 当一对渐开线齿轮制成后,两轮的实际安装中心距比理论计算略有增大,而角速度比仍保持不变,其原因是:

A. 压力角不变　　B. 啮合角不变

C. 节圆半径不变　　D. 基圆半径不变

解 角速度之比$\frac{\omega_1}{\omega_2}=\frac{d_2}{d_1}$,由于加工、装配误差,两轮的实际安装中心距会比理论计算略有增大。选 D。

17.7.3 渐开线齿轮正确啮合的条件和连续传动条件

1)正确啮合条件

齿轮传动时,它的每一对齿仅啮合一段时间便要分离,而由后一对齿接替。一对渐开线齿轮传动时,其齿廓啮合点都应在啮合线 N_1N_2 上,如图 17.7-2 所示,当前一对齿在啮合线上的 K 点接触时,其后一对齿应在啮合线上另一点 K'接触。这样,当前一对齿分离时,后一对齿才能不中断地接替传动。令 K_1 和 K_1' 表示轮 1 齿廓上的啮合点,K_2 和 K_2' 表示轮 2 齿廓上的啮合点。为了保证前后两对齿有可能同时在啮合线上接触,轮 1 相邻两齿同侧齿廓沿法线的距离 K_1K_1' 应与轮 2 相邻两齿同侧齿廓沿法线的距离 K_2K_2' 相等(沿法线方向的齿距称为法线齿距),即 $K_1K_1'=K_2K_2'$。

根据渐开线的性质

$$K_1K_1' = p_1\cos\alpha_1 = \pi m_1\cos\alpha_1, K_2K_2' = p_2\cos\alpha_2 = \pi m_2\cos\alpha_2$$

可推出一对渐开线齿轮的正确啮合条件是两齿轮模数和压力角分别相等,即

$$m_1 = m_2, \alpha_1 = \alpha_2 \tag{17.7-11}$$

齿轮的传动比可写成

$$i = \frac{\omega_1}{\omega_2} = \frac{d_2}{d_1} = \frac{z_2}{z_1} \tag{17.7-12}$$

2)连续传动的条件

一对渐开线齿轮若连续不间断地传动,要求前一对齿终止啮合前,后续的一对齿必须进入啮合。一对齿轮传动如图 17.7-3 所示。进入啮合时,主动轮 1 的齿根推动从动轮的齿顶,起始点是从动轮 2 齿顶圆与理论啮合线 N_1N_2 的交点 B_2,而这对轮齿退出啮合时的终止点是主动轮 1 齿顶圆与 N_1N_2 的交点 B_1,B_1B_2 为啮合点的实际轨迹,称为实际啮合线。

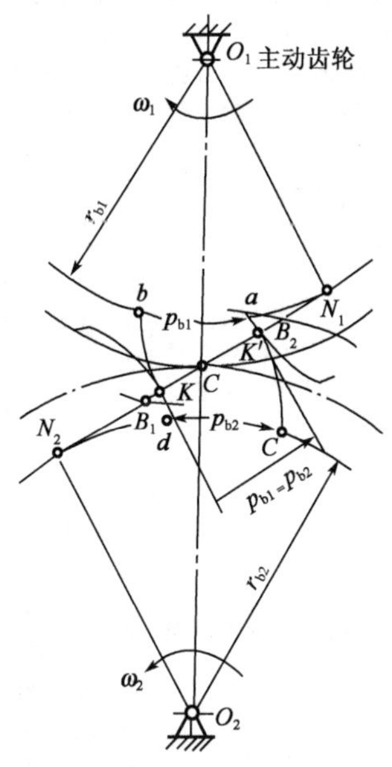

图 17.7-2 渐开线齿轮的正确啮合

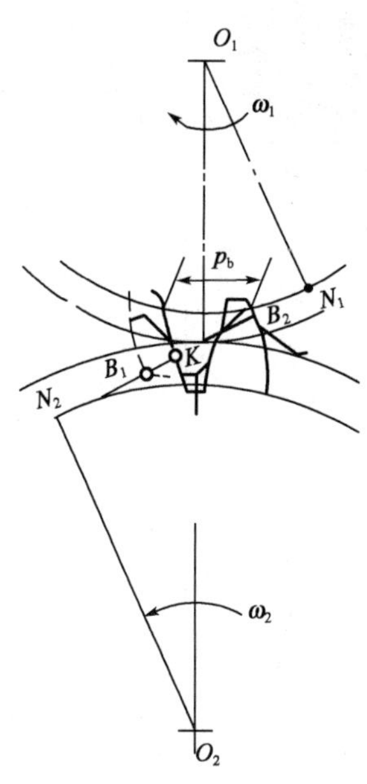

图 17.7-3 齿轮传动

要保证连续传动,必须在前一对齿转到 B_1 前的 K 点(至少是 B_1 点)啮合时,后一对齿已达 B_2 点进入啮合,即 $B_1B_2 \geqslant B_2K$。由渐开线特性知,线段 B_2K 等于渐开线基圆齿距 p_b。

由此可得连续传动条件 $B_1B_2 \geqslant p_b$

定义重合度 ε=啮合弧/齿距$=B_1B_2/p_b>1$ (17.7-13)

重合度越大,表明同时参加啮合的齿对数多,传动平稳;且每对齿所受平均荷载小,从而能提高齿轮的承载能力。

典型例题解析

【例 17.7-2】 一对渐开线标准直齿圆柱齿轮要正确啮合,则它们的以下哪项参数必须相等?

A. 模数　　B. 宽度　　C. 齿数　　D. 直径

解 一对渐开线齿轮的正确啮合条件是两齿轮模数和压力角分别相等。选 A。

17.7.4 轮齿的失效

齿轮传动的失效一般指轮齿的失效。常见的失效形式有轮齿折断、齿面点蚀、齿面磨损、齿面胶合以及塑性变形等几种形式见表 17.7-3。轮齿失效形式与传动工作情况相关。按工作情况,齿轮传动可分为开式传动和闭式传动两种。开式传动是指传动裸露或只有简单的遮盖,工作时环境中粉尘、杂物易侵入啮合齿间,且润滑条件较差的情况。闭式传动是指被封闭在箱体内,且润滑良好(常用浸油润滑)的齿轮传动。开式传动失效以磨损及磨损后的折齿为主,闭式传动失效则以疲劳点蚀或胶合为主。轮齿失效还与受载、工作转速和齿面硬度有关。

常见轮齿失效形式及产生原因和防治措施 表 17.7-3

失效形式	后果	工作环境	产生原因	防止失效的措施
轮齿折断	轮齿折断后无法工作	开式、闭式传动中均可能发生	在荷载反复作用下,齿根弯曲应力超过允许限度时发生疲劳折断;用脆性材料制成的齿轮,因短时过载、冲击发生突然折断	限制齿根危险截面上的弯曲应力;选用合适的齿轮参数和几何尺寸;降低齿根处的应力集中;强化处理和良好的热处理工艺
齿面点蚀	齿廓失去准确形状,传动不平稳,噪声、冲击增大或无法工作	闭式传动	在荷载反复作用下,轮齿表面接触应力超过允许限度时,发生疲劳点蚀	限制齿面的接触应力;提高齿面硬度、降低齿面的表面粗糙度值;采用黏度高的润滑油及适宜的添加剂
齿面磨损		主要发生在开式传动中,润滑油不洁的闭式传动中也可能发生	灰尘、金属屑等杂物进入啮合区	注意润滑油的清洁;提高润滑油黏度,加入适宜的添加剂;选用合适的齿轮参数及几何尺寸、材质、精度和表面粗糙度;开式传动选用适当防护装置
齿面胶合		高速、重载或润滑不良的低速、重载传动中	齿面局部温升过高,润滑失效;润滑不良	进行抗胶合能力计算,限制齿面温度;保证良好润滑,采用适宜的添加剂;降低齿面的表面粗糙度值

硬齿面(硬度>350HBS)、重载时易发生轮齿折断;高速、中小荷载时易发生疲劳点蚀;软齿面(硬度≤350HBS)、重载、高速时易发生胶合;低速时则产生塑性变形。

典型例题解析

【例 17.7-3】 高速过载齿轮传动,当润滑不良时,最可能发生的失效形式是:

A. 齿面胶合　　B. 齿面疲劳点蚀

C. 齿面破损　　D. 轮齿疲劳折断

解 在高速重载传动中，由于齿面啮合区的压力很大，润滑油膜因温度升高容易破裂，造成齿面金属直接接触，其接触区产生瞬时高温，致使两轮齿表面焊粘在一起，当两齿面相对运动时，较软的齿面金属被撕下，在轮齿工作表面形成与滑动方向一致的沟痕，这种现象称为齿面胶合。选 A。

【例 17.7-4】 开式齿轮传动的主要失效形式一般是：

A. 齿面胶合　　B. 齿面疲劳点蚀

C. 齿面磨损　　D. 轮齿塑性变形

解 齿面磨损主要发生在开式传动中。选 C。

【例 17.7-5】 对于具有良好润滑、防尘的闭式硬齿轮传动，正常工作时，最有可能出现的失效形式是：

A. 轮齿折断　　B. 齿面疲劳点蚀　　C. 磨料磨损　　D. 齿面胶合

解 轮齿折断失效主要发生在润滑良好的闭式硬齿面齿轮传动场合；对于润滑良好的闭式软齿面齿轮传动，易发生齿面疲劳点蚀失效(B)；在开式传动或者由于灰尘、硬屑粒等进入啮合齿面时，易发生磨粒磨损(包含磨料磨损)(C)；在高速或者低速重载传动场合，由于齿面啮合区发生润滑失效，容易导致齿面胶合(D)。选 A。

17.7.5 直齿圆柱齿轮的强度计算

1)轮齿的受力分析

如图 17.7-4 所示为一对直齿圆柱齿轮啮合传动时的受力情况。若忽略齿面间的摩擦力，则轮齿之间的总作用力 F_n 将沿着轮齿啮合点的公法线 N_1N_2 方向，故也称法向力。法向力 F_n 可分解为两个分力：圆周力 F_t 和径向力 F_r。

圆周力　$F_t=\dfrac{2T_1}{d_1}$　(N)

径向力　$F_r=F_1\tan\alpha$　(N)

法向力　$F_n=\dfrac{F_1}{\cos\alpha}$　(N)

式中：T_1——小齿轮上的转矩(N·mm)，$T_1=9.55\times10^6\dfrac{P}{n_1}$；

P——小齿轮传递的功率(kW)；

n_1——小齿轮的转速(r/min)；

d_1——小齿轮的分度圆直径(mm)；

α——分度圆压力角(°)。

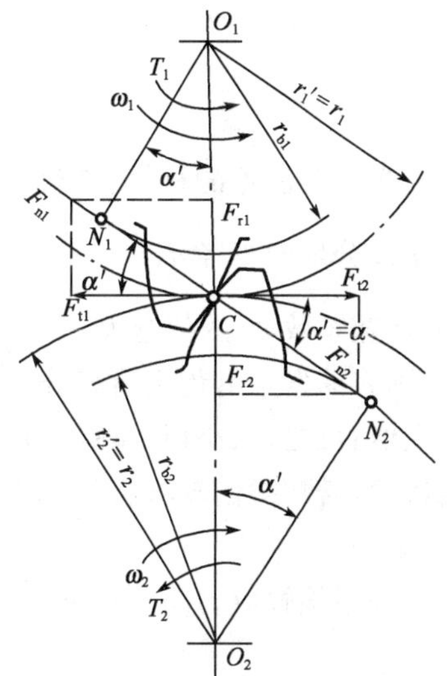

图 17.7-4 直齿圆柱齿轮传动的作用力

圆周力 F_t 的方向，在主动轮上与圆周速度方向相反，在从动轮上与圆周速度方向相同。径向力 F_r 的方向对两轮都是由作用点指向轮心。

2)计算荷载

上述受力分析是在荷载沿齿宽均匀分布的理想条件下进行的。但实际运转时，由于齿轮、轴、支承等存在制造、安装误差，以及受载时产生变形等，使荷载沿齿宽不是均匀分布，造成荷载局部集中。轴和轴承的刚度越小、齿宽 b 越宽，荷载集中越严重。此外，由于各种原动机和工作机的特性不同，导致在齿轮传动中还将引起附加动荷载。因此在齿轮强度计算时，通常用计算荷载 KF_n 代替名义荷载 F_n。K 为载荷系数，其值由表 17.7-4 查取。

载荷系数 K 表 17.7-4

原动机	工作机的荷载特性		
	工作平稳	中等冲击	较大冲击
电动机、透平机	1～1.2	1.2～1.5	1.5～1.8
多缸内燃机	1.2～1.5	1.5～1.8	1.8～2.1
单缸内燃机	1.6～1.8	1.8～2.0	2.1～2.4

3)齿面接触强度计算

为避免齿面发生点蚀，应限制齿面的接触应力。齿面接触应力的计算是以两圆柱体接触时最大接触应力为基础进行的。

对于一对钢制齿轮，弹性模量 $E_1=E_2=2.06\times105\text{MPa}$，标准齿轮压力角 $\alpha=20°$，可得钢制标准齿轮传动的齿面接触强度校核方式

$$\sigma_H = 335\sqrt{\frac{(i\pm1)^3KT_1}{iba^2}} \leqslant [\sigma_H] \qquad (17.7\text{-}14)$$

式中：$[\sigma_H]$——许用接触应力(MPa)；

a——齿轮中心距(mm)；

K——载荷系数；

T_1——小齿轮传递的转矩(N·mm)；

b——齿宽(mm)；

i——齿轮的传动比，"+""-"符号分别用于外啮合和内啮合。

将 $b=\psi_a\cdot a$ 代入上式，可得齿面接触强度设计方式

$$a \geqslant (i\pm1)\sqrt[3]{\left(\frac{335}{[\sigma_H]}\right)^2\frac{KT_1}{\psi_a i}} \quad (\text{mm}) \qquad (17.7\text{-}15)$$

当一对齿轮的材料、传动比、齿宽系数一定时，齿面接触强度所决定的承载能力仅与中心距 a 或分度圆直径 $d_1=\frac{2a}{i\pm1}$有关，即与 mz 的乘积有关，而与模数或齿数的单独一项无关。另外，齿宽系数 ψ_a 的值越大，中心距越小，但齿宽 b 大，若结构的刚性不够，齿轮制造和安装不准确，则容易发生沿齿宽荷载分布不均匀的现象，致使轮齿折断。齿轮对轴承对称布置时 ψ_a 可取大值；反之，取小值；悬臂布置时应取下限值。式(17.7-14)和式(17.7-15)仅适用于一对钢制齿轮，若配对齿轮材料为钢对铸铁或铸铁对铸铁，则应将公式中的系数 335 分别改为 285 和 250。

许用接触应力$[\sigma_H]$按下式计算

$$[\sigma_H] = \frac{\sigma_{H\lim}}{S_H} \quad (\text{MPa}) \qquad (17.7\text{-}16)$$

式中：$\sigma_{H\lim}$——试验齿轮的接触疲劳极限(MPa)；

S_H——齿面接触疲劳安全系数，其值由表 17.7-5 查出。

安全系数 S_H 和 S_F 表 17.7-5

安全系数	软齿面	硬齿面	重要的传动、渗碳淬火齿轮或铸造齿轮
S_H	1.0～1.1	1.1～1.2	1.3
S_F	1.3～1.4	1.4～1.6	1.6～2.2

4)轮齿的弯曲强度计算

为了防止齿轮在工作时发生轮齿折断，应限制在轮齿根部的弯曲应力。进行轮齿弯曲应力计算时，假定全部荷载由一对轮齿承受且作用于齿顶处，这时齿根所受的弯曲力矩最大。计算轮齿弯曲应力时，可将轮齿看作宽度为 b 的悬臂梁。可得轮齿弯曲强度的校核方式

$$\sigma_F = \frac{2KT_1Y_F}{bm^2z_1} \leqslant [\sigma_F] \qquad (\text{MPa}) \qquad (17.7\text{-}17)$$

式中：K——载荷系数；

T_1——小齿轮传递的转矩(N·mm)；

Y_F——齿形因数，反映轮齿的形状对抗弯能力的影响，正常齿制标准齿轮的 Y_F 值参考图 17.7-5；

b——齿宽(mm)；

m——模数(mm)；

z_1——小轮齿数。

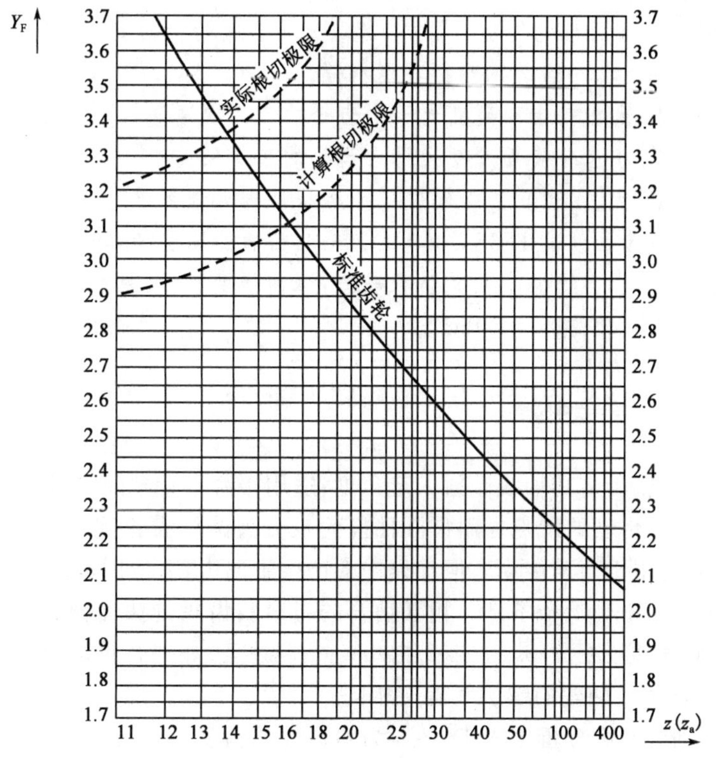

图 17.7-5 齿形因数 Y_F

对于 $i \neq 1$ 的齿轮传动，由于 $z_1 \neq z_2$，因此 $Y_{F1} \neq Y_{F2}$，而且两轮的材料、热处理方法和硬度也不相同，则$[\sigma_{F1}] \neq [\sigma_{F2}]$。因此，应分别验算两个齿轮的弯曲强度。

令 $\psi_a = \dfrac{b}{a}$，则得轮齿弯曲强度设计方式为：

$$m \geqslant \sqrt[3]{\frac{4KT_1Y_F}{\psi_a(i \pm 1)z^2[\sigma_F]}} \qquad (\text{mm}) \qquad (17.7\text{-}18)$$

式(17.7-18)中的$\frac{Y_F}{[\sigma_F]}$应代入$\frac{Y_{F1}}{[\sigma_{F1}]}$和$\frac{Y_{F2}}{[\sigma_{F2}]}$中的较大者,算得的模数应按表 17.7-1 圆整为标准值。对于传递动力的齿轮,其模数应大于 1.5mm,以防止意外断齿。

在满足弯曲强度的条件下,应尽量增加齿数使传动的重合度增大,以改善传动平稳性和荷载分配;在中心距 a 一定时,齿数增加则模数减小,齿顶高和齿根高都随之减小,能节约材料和减少金属切削量。

对于闭式传动,当齿面硬度不太高时,轮齿的弯曲强度通常是足够的,故齿数可取多些,例如常取 $z_1=24\sim40$。当齿面硬度很高时,轮齿的弯曲强度常感不足,故齿数不宜过多。许用弯曲应力$[\sigma_F]$按下式计算

$$[\sigma_F]=\frac{\sigma_{F\lim}}{S_F}\qquad(\mathrm{MPa})\qquad(17.7\text{-}19)$$

式中:$\sigma_{F\lim}$——试验齿轮的弯曲疲劳极限(MPa);

S_F——齿轮弯曲疲劳强度安全系数,由表 17-13 查取。

典型例题解析

【例 17.7-6】 软齿面齿轮传动设计中,选取大小齿轮的齿面硬度应使:

A. 大、小齿轮的齿面硬度相等

B. 大齿轮齿面硬度大于小齿轮的齿面硬度

C. 小齿轮齿面硬度大于大齿轮的齿面硬度

D. 大、小齿轮齿面硬度应不相等但谁大都可以

解 经热处理后齿面硬度 HBS≤350 的齿轮称为软齿面齿轮,多用于中、低速机械。当大小齿轮都是软齿面时,考虑到小齿轮齿根较薄,弯曲强度较低,且受载次数较多,因此应使小齿轮齿面硬度比大齿轮高 20～50HBS。选 C。

17.7.6 斜齿圆柱齿轮传动及其受力分析

斜齿圆柱齿轮的轮齿与其轴线倾斜一定角度,适用于两平行轴间的运动和动力的传递。

(1)斜齿圆柱齿轮传动的特点。斜齿圆柱齿轮较直齿圆柱齿轮重合度大,运转平稳,承载能力较强,噪声小,适用于高速传动。但工作中会产生轴向力,需使用可承受轴向荷载的轴承。

(2)斜齿轮传动的正确啮合条件。相互啮合的一对斜齿轮的法面模数和法面压力角要分别相等且等于标准值,即:$m_{n1}=m_{n2}=m$,$\alpha_{n1}=\alpha_{n2}=\alpha$。并且,外啮合传动两轮的螺旋线旋向相反,$\beta_1=-\beta_2$;内啮合传动两轮的螺旋线旋向相同,$\beta_1=\beta_2$。

(3)斜齿轮传动的受力分析。图 17.7-6 为斜齿轮轮齿受力情况。轮齿所受法向力 F_n 可分解为圆周力 F_t、径向力 F_r 和轴向力 F_a。

$$F_t=\frac{2T_1}{d_1},F_r=\frac{F_t\tan\alpha_n}{\cos\beta},F_a=F_t\tan\beta$$

圆周力的方向,在主动轮上与转动方向相反,在从动轮上与转向相同。径向力的方向均指向各自的轮心。轴向力的方向取决于齿轮的回转方向和轮齿的螺旋方向,可按"主动轮左、右手螺旋定则"来判断。主动轮为左(右)旋时,左(右)手按转动方向握轴,以四指弯曲方向表示主动轴的回转方向,伸直大拇指,其指向即为主动轮上轴向力的方向。主动轮上轴向力的方向确定后,从动轮上的轴向力则与主动轮上的轴向力大小相等、方向相反。

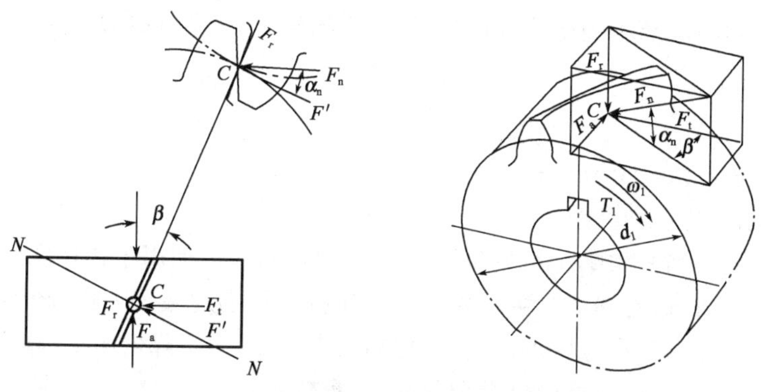

图 17.7-6　斜齿圆柱齿轮受力分析

典型例题解析

【例 17.7-7】 斜齿圆柱轮的标准模数和压力角是指以下哪种模数和压力角?

A. 端面　　B. 法面　　C. 轴面　　D. 任意截面

解　选 B。

【例 17.7-8】 一对平行外啮合斜齿圆柱齿轮,正确啮合时两齿轮的:

A. 螺旋角大小相等且方向相反　　B. 螺旋角大小相等且方向相同

C. 螺旋角大小不等且方向相同　　D. 螺旋角大小不等且方向不同

解　外啮合传动两轮的螺旋线旋向相反,$\beta_1=-\beta_2$。选 A。

17.7.7　齿轮的结构

齿轮的结构有锻造、铸造、装配式及焊接齿轮等结构形式,具体的结构应根据工艺要求及经验公式确定。

当齿顶圆直径与轴径接近时,应将齿轮与轴做成一体,称为齿轮轴,如图 17.7-7 所示。

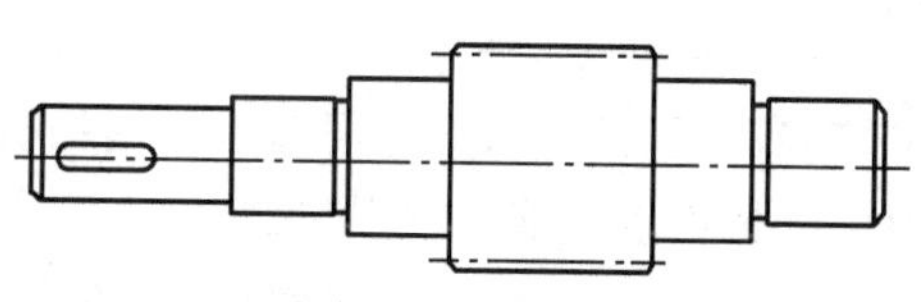

图 17.7-7　齿轮轴

齿顶圆直径 d_a<500mm 的齿轮可以是锻造或铸造的,通常采用腹板式结构,如图 17.7-8a)所示,直径较小时也可做成实心式,如图 17.7-8b)所示。

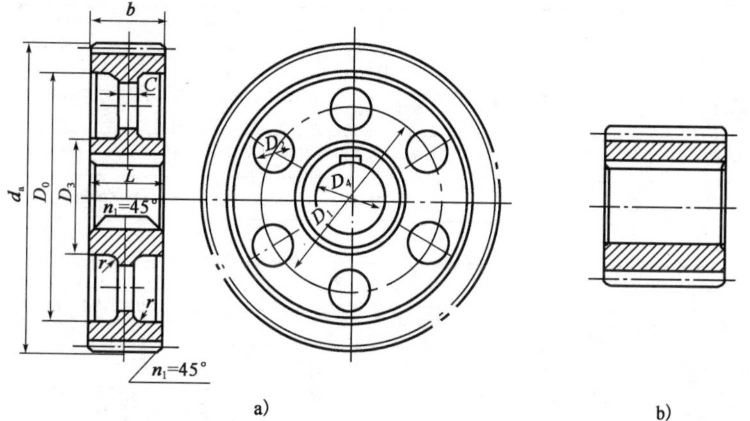

图 17.7-8　锻造齿轮结构

当 $d_a>400\text{mm}$ 时，一般都用铸造齿轮，通常采用图 17.7-9 所示的轮辐式结构。

17.7.8 蜗杆传动

1)蜗杆传动的特点和受力分析

(1)蜗杆传动的特点和类型

蜗杆传动主要由蜗杆和蜗轮组成(见图 17.7-10)，蜗杆传动用于传递空间交错成 90°的两轴之间的运动和动力，通常蜗杆为主动件。与其他机械传动比较，蜗杆传动具有传动比大、结构紧凑、运转平稳、噪声较小等优点，但是其传动效率较低，为了降低摩擦，减小磨损，提高齿面抗胶合能力，蜗轮齿圈常用贵重的铜合金制造，成本较高。

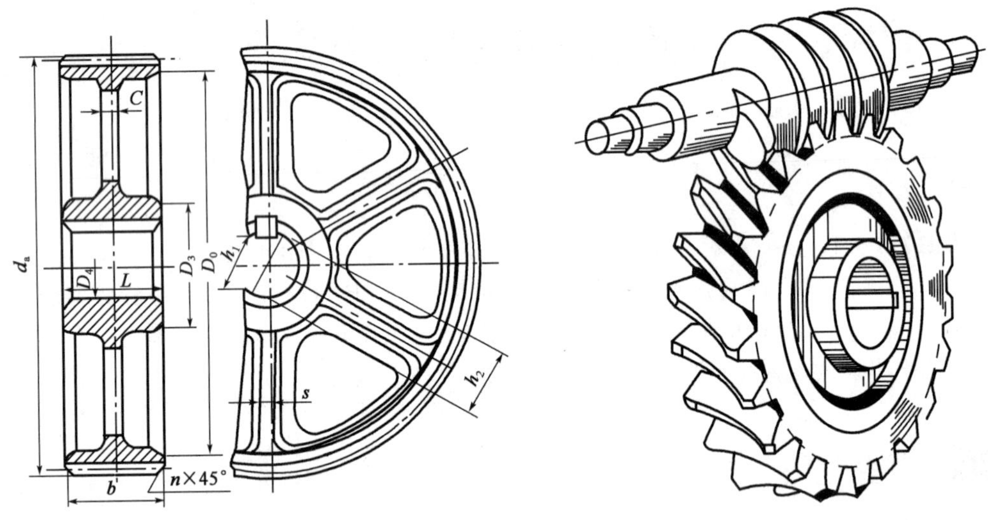

图 17.7-9　铸造齿轮结构

图 17.7-10　蜗杆传动

蜗杆传动按照蜗杆的形状不同，可分为圆柱蜗杆传动和环面蜗杆传动。圆柱蜗杆机构又可按螺旋面的形状，分为阿基米德蜗杆机构和渐开线蜗杆机构等。圆柱蜗杆机构加工方便，环面蜗杆机构承载能力较强。

(2)蜗杆传动的主要参数计算(见表 17.7-6)

蜗杆传动的主要参数计算　　表 17.7-6

名　　称	计 算 公 式	
	蜗杆	蜗轮
齿顶高	$h_a=m$	$h_a=m$
齿根高	$h_f=1.2m$	$h_f=1.2m$
分度圆直径	$d_1=mq$	$d_2=mz_2$
齿顶圆直径	$d_{a1}=m(q+2)$	$d_{a2}=m(z_2+2)$
齿根圆直径	$d_{f1}=m(q-2.4)$	$d_{f2}=m(z_2-2.4)$
顶隙	$c=0.2m$	
中心距	$a=m(q+z_2)/2$	
传动比	$i=\frac{\omega_1}{\omega_2}=\frac{n_1}{n_2}=\frac{z_2}{z_1}\neq\frac{d_2}{d_1}$	

(3)蜗杆传动的正确啮合条件

蜗杆传动的正确啮合条件为：蜗杆轴平面上的轴面模数 m_{a1} 等于蜗轮的端面模数 m_{t2}；蜗杆轴平面上的轴面压力角 α_{a1} 等于蜗轮的端面压力角 α_{t2}；蜗杆导程角 γ 等于蜗轮螺旋角 β，且旋向相同。

(4)蜗杆传动的受力分析

杆传动的受力分析与斜齿圆柱齿轮的受力分析相似，齿面上的法向力 F_n 分解为三个相互垂直的分力：圆周力 F_t、轴向力 F_a、径向力 F_r，如图 17.7-11 所示。

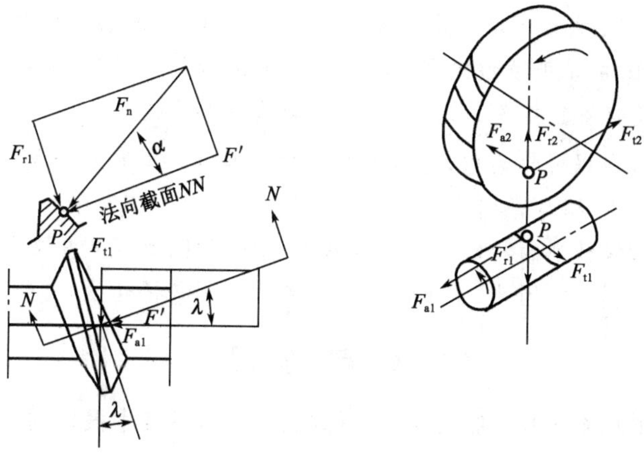

图 17.7-11 蜗杆传动的受力分析

蜗杆受力方向：轴向力 F_{a1} 的方向由左、右手定则确定，图 17.7-11 为右旋蜗杆，则用右手握住蜗杆，四指所指方向为蜗杆转向，拇指所指方向为轴向力 F_{a1} 的方向；圆周力 F_{t1}，与主动蜗杆转向相反；径向力 F_{r1}，指向蜗杆中心。

蜗轮受力方向：F_{a1} 与 F_{t2}、F_{t1} 与 F_{a2}、F_{r1} 与 F_{r2} 是作用力与反作用力关系。

力的大小可按下式计算

$$F_{t1}=F_{a2}=\frac{2T_1}{d_1};F_{a1}=F_{t2}=\frac{2T_2}{d_2};F_{r1}=F_{r2}=F_{t2}\tan\alpha$$

式中：T_1、T_2——分别为作用于蜗杆和蜗轮上的转矩(N·m)，$T_2=T_1 i\eta$；

η——蜗杆传动效率；

d_1、d_2——分别为蜗杆和蜗轮的节圆直径(m)。

2)蜗杆和涡轮的材料

选用蜗杆传动材料时不仅要满足强度要求，更重要的是具有良好的减摩性、抗磨性和抗胶合的能力。蜗杆一般用碳素钢或合金钢制造。对于高速重载的蜗杆，可用 15Cr、20Cr、20CrMnTi 和 20MnVB 等，经渗碳淬火至硬度为 56～63HRC，也可用 40、45、40Cr、40CrNi 等经表面淬火至硬度为 45～50HRC。对于不太重要的传动及低速中载蜗杆，常用 45、40 等钢经调质或正火处理，硬度为 220～230HBS。

蜗轮常用锡青铜、无锡青铜或铸铁制造。锡青铜用于滑动速度 $v_s>3$m/s 的传动，常用牌号有 ZQSn10-1 和 ZQSn6-6-3；无锡青铜一般用于 $v_s\leqslant 4$m/s 的传动，常用牌号为 ZQAl8-4；铸铁用于滑动速度 $v_s<2$m/s 的传动，常用牌号有 HT150 和 HT200 等。近年来，随着塑料工业的发展，也可用尼龙或增强尼龙来制造蜗轮。

典型例题解析

【例 17.7-9】 以下公式中，用下列哪一项来确定蜗杆传动比是错误的？

A. $i=z_2/z_1$　　B. $i=d_1/d_2$　　C. $i=n_1/n_2$　　D. $i=w_1/w_2$

解 传动比 $i=\frac{\omega_1}{\omega_2}=\frac{n_1}{n_2}=\frac{z_2}{z_1}=\frac{d_2}{d_1}$。选 B。

【例 17.7-10】 下列因素中与蜗杆传动的失效形式关系不大的是：

A. 蜗杆传动副的材料　　B. 蜗杆传动的载荷方向

C. 蜗杆传动的滑动速度　　D. 蜗杆传动的散热条件

解 蜗杆传动的主要失效形式有：胶合、点蚀和磨损等。显然，材料、相对滑动速度和散热，与这些失效形式有着直接关系，而载荷方向与失效形式关系不大。选 B。

【例 17.7-11】 在蜗杆传动中，比较理想的蜗杆与涡轮材料组合是：

A. 钢与青铜　　B. 钢与铸铁　　C. 铜与钢　　D. 钢与钢

解蜗杆传动中，蜗杆副的材料不仅要求有足够的强度，而且更重要的是要具有良好的减摩耐磨性能和抗胶合能力，因此，常采用青铜材料作为涡轮的齿圈，与钢制蜗杆相配。选 A。

经典练习

17.7-1　用标准齿条型刀具加工渐开线标准直齿轮，不发生根切的最少齿数是(　　)。

A. 14　　B. 17　　C. 21　　D. 26

17.7-2　有四个渐开线直齿圆柱齿轮，其参数分别为：齿轮 1 的 $m_1=2.5\text{mm}$，$\alpha_1=15''$，齿轮 2 的 $m_2=2.5\text{mm}$，$\alpha_2=20''$，齿轮 3 的 $m_3=2\text{mm}$，$\alpha_3=15''$，齿轮 4 的 $m_4=2.5\text{mm}$，$\alpha_4=20''$，则能够正确啮合的一对齿轮是(　　)。

A. 齿轮 1 和齿轮 2　　B. 齿轮 1 和齿轮 3

C. 齿轮 1 和齿轮 4　　D. 齿轮 2 和齿轮 4

17.7-3　一对正常齿标准直齿圆柱齿轮传动，$m=5\text{mm}$，$z_1=20$，$z_2=78$，标准中心距 a 为(　　)mm。

A. 105　　B. 245　　C. 375　　D. 406

17.7-4　一对渐开线内啮合斜齿圆柱齿轮的正确啮合条件是(　　)。

A. $m_{n1}=m_{n2}=m$，$\alpha_{n1}=\alpha_{n2}=\alpha$，$\beta_1=\beta_2$

B. $m_{n1}=m_{n2}=m$，$\alpha_{n1}=\alpha_{n2}=\alpha$，$\beta_1=-\beta_2$

C. $m_{n1}=m_{n2}=m$，$\alpha_{n1}=\alpha_{n2}=\alpha$

D. $m_{n1}=m_{n2}=m$

17.8 轮系

考试大纲☞：轮系的基本类型和应用　定轴轮系传动比计算　周转轮系传动比计算

必备基础知识

17.8.1 轮系的基本类型和应用

由两个以上相互啮合的齿轮所组成的传动系统称为齿轮系，简称轮系。轮系能够实现距离较远的两个轴之间的传动，获得较大的传动比，实现运动的变速与变向，实现运动的合成与分解等。轮系在工程上应用非常广泛，汽车变速器、金属切削机床等中都有轮系的应用。

一般轮系可分为：定轴轮系、周转轮系和混合轮系。

(1)定轴轮系：轮系中所有齿轮的几何轴线都是固定的。

(2)周转轮系或称为动轴轮系：轮系中，至少有一个齿轮既绕自己的几何轴线转动，又绕另一个齿轮几何轴线转动。

(3)混合轮系：由几个基本周转轮系或由定轴轮系和周转轮系组成。

1)传动比

传动比的定义：两轴的转速比。因为转速 $n=2\pi\omega$，因此传动比又可以被表示为两轴的角速度之比。通常，传动比用 i 表示，对轴 a 和轴 b 的传动比可表示为

$$i_{ab}=\frac{n_a}{n_b}\ \frac{\omega_a}{\omega_b} \tag{17.8-1}$$

对一对相啮合的齿轮，在同一时间内转过的齿数是相同的，有 $n_a z_a=n_b z_b$。

因此，一对相互啮合的齿轮的传动比又可以写成

$$i_{ab}=\frac{n_a}{n_b}\ \frac{z_b}{z_a} \tag{17.8-2}$$

2)从动轮转动方向

(1)箭头表示

轴或齿轮的转向一般用箭头表示，如图 17.8-1 所示。

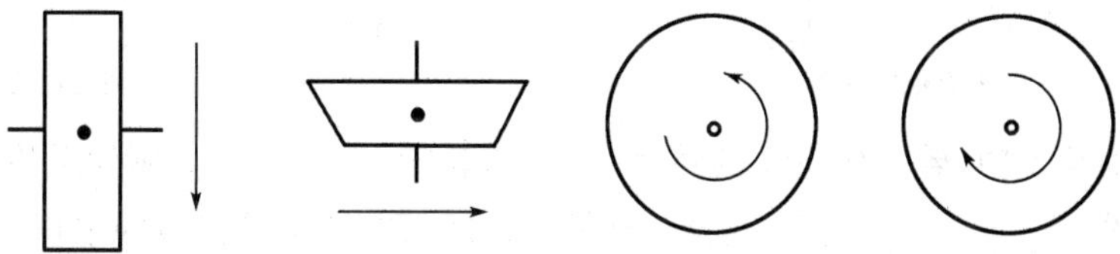

图 17.8-1　转向表示方法

(2)符号表示

当两轴或齿轮的轴线平行时，可以用正号“+”或负号“-”表示两轴或齿轮的转向相同或相反，并直接标注在传动比的公式中。但是，符号表示法不能用于判断轴线不平行的从动轮的转向传动比计算中。

(3)判断从动轮转向的几个要点

①内啮合的圆柱齿轮的转向相同。

②外啮合圆柱齿轮或圆锥齿轮的转动方向要么同时指向啮合点，要么同时背离啮合点。

如图 17.8-2 所示为圆柱或圆锥齿轮转动方向的几种情况。

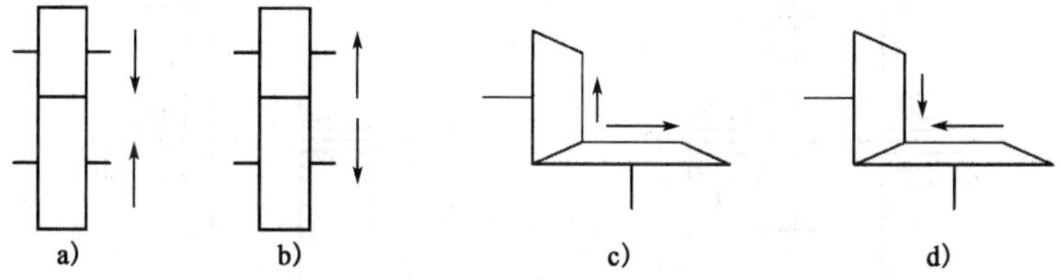

图 17.8-2　齿轮转动方向间的关系

③蜗杆蜗轮的转向：速度矢量之和必定与螺旋线垂直，如图 17.8-3 所示。

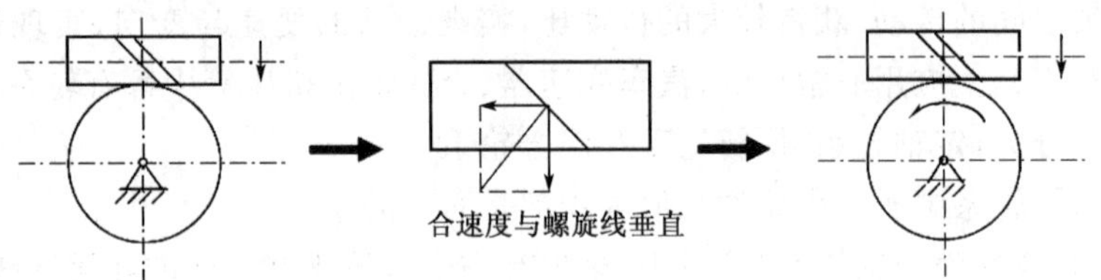

图 17.8-3　蜗杆蜗轮转向的判断

17.8.2 定轴轮系传动比计算

定轴轮系分为两大类:一类是所有齿轮的轴线都相互平行,称为平行轴定轴轮系(亦称平面定轴轮系,如图 17.8-4 所示);另一类轮系中有相交或交错的轴线,称之为非平行轴定轴轮系(亦称空间定轴轮系,如图 17.8-5 所示)。

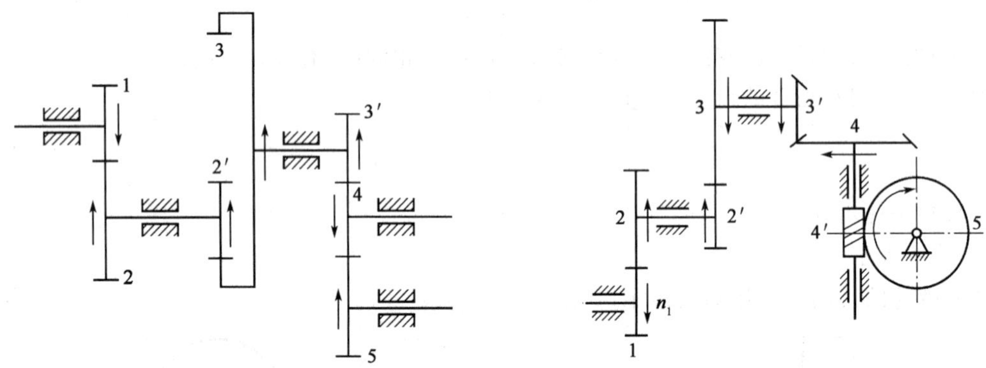

图 17.8-4　平面定轴轮系　　图 17.8-5　空间定轴轮系

在平面定轴轮系中,若首轮轮 1 的转速为 n_1,末轮轮 k 转速为 n_k,则轮系传动比为

$$i_{1k}=\frac{n_1}{n_k}=(-1)^m\frac{\text{从轮 1 到轮 }k\text{ 之间所有从动轮齿数的乘积}}{\text{从轮 1 到轮 }k\text{ 之间所有主动轮齿数的乘积}} \tag{17.8-3}$$

其中,m 为轮系中从轮 1 到轮 k 间,外啮合齿轮的对数。

空间定轴轮系,其传动比的大小仍可用平面定轴轮系的传动比计算公式计算,但因各轴线并不全部相互平行,故不能用 $(-1)^m$ 来确定主动轮与从动轮的转向,必须用画箭头的方式在图上标注出各轮的转向。

17.8.3 周转轮系传动比计算

当周转轮系的两个中心轮都能转动,自由度为 2 时称为差动轮系,如图 17.8-6a)所示。若固定住其中一个中心轮,轮系的自由度为 1 时,称为行星轮系,如图 17.8-6b)所示。

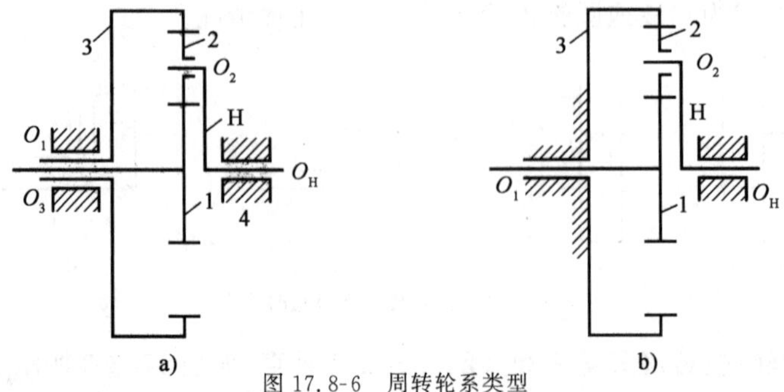

图 17.8-6　周转轮系类型

周转运动是兼有自转和公转的复杂运动，因此需要通过在整个轮系上加上一个与系杆 H 旋转方向相反、大小相同的角速度 n_H，把周转轮系转化成定轴轮系。传动比的求法是：

(1)求传动比大小

$$i_{1k}^{H}=\frac{n_1^H}{n_k^H}=\frac{n_1-n_H}{n_k-n_H}=\pm\frac{\text{从轮 1 到轮 }k\text{ 之间所有从动轮齿数的乘积}}{\text{从轮 1 到轮 }k\text{ 之间所有主动轮齿数的乘积}} \quad (17.8\text{-}4)$$

(2)确定传动比符号

标出反转机构中各个齿轮的转向，来确定传动比符号。当轮 1 与轮 k 的转向相同，取"+"号，反之取"−"号。

典型例题解析

【例 17.8-1】 如图所示轮系，辊筒 5 与蜗轮 4 相固连，各轮齿数：$z_1=20$，$z_2=40$，$z_3=60$，蜗杆 3 的头数为 2，当手柄 H 以图示方向旋转 1 周时，则辊筒的转向及转数为：

A. 顺时针，1/30 周

B. 逆时针，1/30 周

C. 顺时针，1/60 周

D. 逆时针，1/60 周

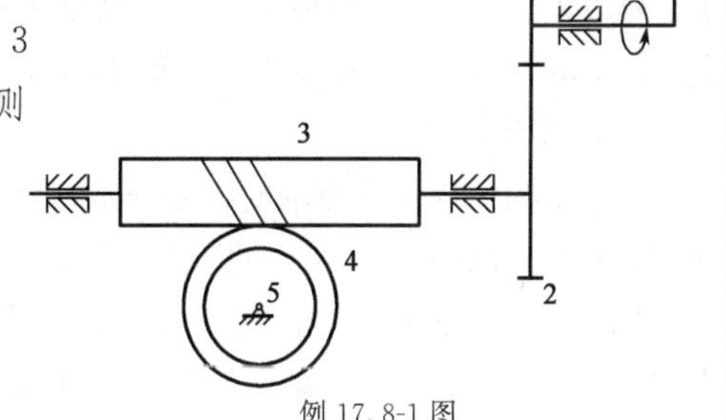

例 17.8-1 图

解 辊筒与蜗轮转向及转数相同，根据定轴轮系传动比计算公式：

$$i_{14}=\frac{n_1}{n_4}=\frac{z_2z_4}{z_1z_3}=\frac{40\times60}{20\times2}=60,n_5=n_4=\frac{1}{60}n_1=\frac{1}{60}$$

根据右手法则来判定辊筒 5(即蜗轮 4)的转向，由于齿轮 1 为逆时针转，按照传动路线，可确定出辊筒的转动方向为顺时针。选 C。

经典练习

17.8-1 图示的轮系，$z_1=20$，$z_2=40$，$z_4=60$，$z_5=30$，齿轮及蜗轮的模数均为 2mm，蜗杆的头数为 2，如轮 1 以图示方向旋转 1 周，则齿条将( )。

A. 向左运动 1.57mm　　B. 向右运动 1.57mm

C. 向右运动 3.14mm　　D. 向左运动 3.14mm

17.8-2 图示轮系中，$z_1=20$，$z_2=30$，$z_3=80$，设图中箭头方向为正(齿轮 1 的转向)，问传动比 i_{1H}的值为( )。

A. 5　　B. 3　　C. −5　　D. −3

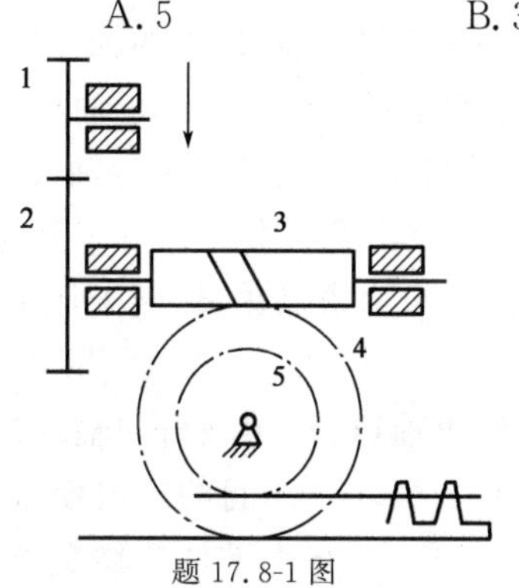

题 17.8-1 图

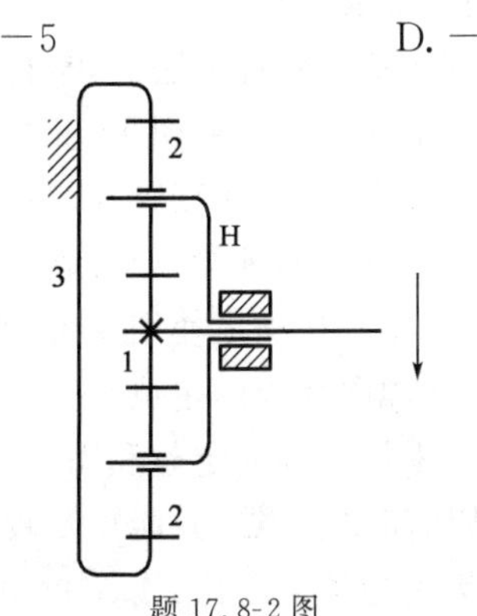

题 17.8-2 图

17.9 轴

考试大纲☞:轴的分类、结构和材料　轴的计算　轴毂连接的类型

必备基础知识

17.9.1 轴的分类、结构和材料

1)轴的功用和类型

轴是机器中的重要零件之一,用来支持旋转零件,如齿轮、带轮等。根据承受载荷的不同,轴可分为转轴、传动轴和心轴三种。转轴既承受转矩又承受弯矩;传动轴主要承受转矩,不承受或承受很小的弯矩;心轴只承受弯矩而不传递转矩。按轴线的形状将轴分为:直轴、曲轴和挠性轴。

2)轴的结构设计

轴的结构设计就是使轴的各部分具有合理的形状和尺寸。其主要要求:①满足制造安装要求,轴应便于加工,轴上零件要方便装拆;②满足零件定位要求,轴和轴上零件有准确的工作位置,各零件要牢固而可靠地相对固定;③满足结构工艺性要求,使加工方便和节省材料;④满足强度要求,尽量减少应力集中等。下面结合如图 17.9-1 所示单级齿轮减速器的高速轴,逐项讨论这些要求。

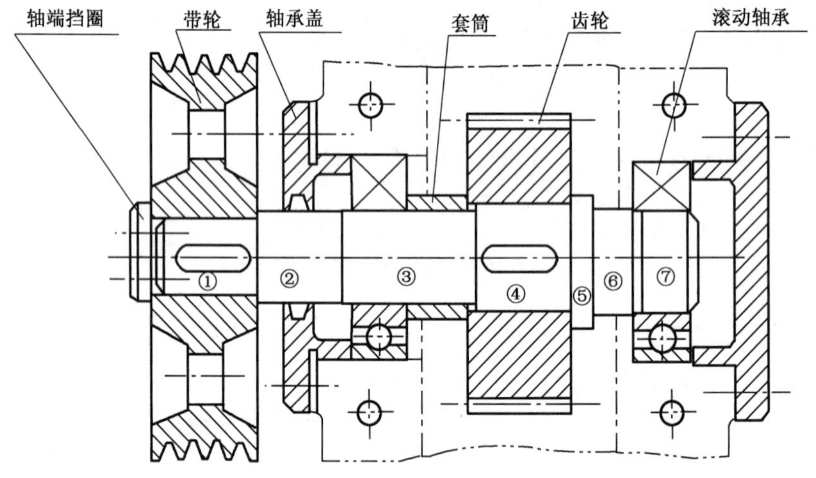

图 17.9-1　轴的结构

(1)制造安装要求

为了方便轴上零件的装拆,常将轴做成阶梯形。对于一般剖分式箱体中的轴,它的直径从轴端逐渐向中间增大。如图 17.9-2 所示,可依次将齿轮、套筒、左端滚动轴承、轴承盖和带轮从轴的左端装拆,另一滚动轴承从右端装拆。为使轴上零件易于安装,轴端及各轴段的端部应有倒角。轴上磨削的轴段,应有砂轮越程槽(见图 17.9-2 中⑥与⑦的交界处);车制螺纹的轴段,应有退刀槽。在满足使用要求的情况下,轴的形状和尺寸应力求简单,以便于加工。

(2)零件轴向和周向定位

①轴上零件的轴向定位和固定。阶梯轴上截面变化处叫轴肩,利用轴肩和轴环进行轴向定位,其结构简单、可靠,并能承受较大轴向力。在图 17.9-2 中,①、②间的轴肩使带轮定位;轴环⑤使齿轮在轴上定位;⑥、⑦间的轴肩使右端滚动轴承定位。有些零件依靠套筒定位,在

图 17.9-2中左端滚动轴承采用套筒③定位。套筒定位结构简单、可靠,但不适合高转速情况。无法采用套筒或套筒太长时,可采用圆螺母加以固定,圆螺母定位可靠、并能承受较大轴向力。轴向力较小时,可采弹性挡圈、紧定螺钉或圆锥销来进行定位。在轴端部可以用圆锥面定位,圆锥面定位的轴和轮毂之间无径向间隙、装拆方便,能承受冲击,但锥面加工较为麻烦。轴端挡圈定位,它适用于轴端,可承受剧烈的振动和冲击荷载。

②轴上零件的周向固定。轴上零件周向固定的目的是使其能同轴一起转动并传递转矩。轴上零件的周向固定,大多采用键、花键或过盈配合等连接形式。

(3)结构工艺性要求

由于阶梯轴接近于等强度,而且便于加工和轴上零件的定位和装拆,所以实际上轴的形状多呈阶梯形。为了能选用合适的圆钢和减少切削加工量,阶梯轴各轴段的直径不宜相差太大,一般取 5～10mm。

在采用套筒、螺母、轴端挡圈作轴向固定时,应把装零件的轴段长度做得比零件轮毂短2～3mm,以确保套筒、螺母或轴端挡圈能靠紧零件端面。

(4)强度要求

在零件截面发生变化处会产生应力集中现象,从而削弱材料的强度。因此,进行结构设计时,应尽量减小应力集中。在阶梯轴的截面尺寸变化处应采用圆角过渡,且圆角半径不宜过小。另外,设计时尽量不要在轴上开横孔、切口或凹槽,必须开横孔处须将边倒圆。在重要的轴的结构中,可采用卸载槽、过渡肩环或凹切圆角增大轴肩圆角半径,以减小局部应力。

3)轴的材料

轴的材料常采用碳素钢和合金钢。

(1)碳素钢

碳素钢有 35、45、50 等优质中碳钢。它们具有较高的综合机械性能,因此应用较多,特别是 45 号钢应用最为广泛。为了改善碳素钢的机械性能,应进行正火或调质处理。不重要或受力较小的轴,可采用 Q237、Q275 等普通碳素钢。

(2)合金钢

合金钢具有较高的机械性能,但价格较贵,多用于有特殊要求的轴。例如采用滑动轴承的高速轴,常用 20Cr、20CrMnTi 等低碳合金钢,经渗碳淬火后可提高轴颈耐磨性;汽轮发电机转子轴在高温、高速和重载条件下工作,必须具有良好的高温机械性能,常采用 27Cr2Mo1V、38CrMoA1A 等合金结构钢。值得注意的是:钢材的种类和热处理对其弹性模量的影响甚小,因此如欲采用合金钢或通过热处理来提高轴的刚度,并无实效。此外,合金钢对应力集中的敏感性较高,因此设计合金钢轴时,更应从结构上避免或减小应力集中,并减小其表面粗糙度。轴的毛坯一般用圆钢或锻件,有时也可采用铸钢或球墨铸铁。例如,用球墨铸铁制造曲轴、凸轮轴,具有成本低廉、吸振性较好,对应力集中的敏感性较低,强度较好等优点,适合制造结构形状复杂的轴。

典型例题解析

【例 17.9-1】 下列方法中可用于轴和轮毂周向定位的是:

A. 轴用弹性挡圈　　B. 轴肩　　C. 螺母　　D. 键

解 键是用来对零件进行周向定位的,而轴用弹性挡圈、轴肩和螺母则是用来对零件进行轴向固定的。选 D。

17.9.2 轴的计算

1)轴的强度计算

应根据轴的承载情况，采用相应的计算方法。常见的强度计算有以下两种。

(1)按扭转强度估算最小轴径

当轴只传递转矩，不承受弯矩，或承受弯矩很小，或当弯矩值未知时，可按转矩做初步计算。圆截面轴受转矩后，在截面中出现扭转切应力，其强度条件为

$$\tau=\frac{T}{W_T}=\frac{9.55\times10^6P}{0.2d^3n}\leqslant[\tau] \qquad (17.9\text{-}1)$$

式中：τ——转矩 T(N·mm)在轴上产生的扭剪应力(MPa)；

$[\tau]$——材料的许用剪切应力(MPa)；

W_T——抗扭截面系数(mm^3)，对圆截面轴 $W_T=\frac{\pi d^3}{16}\approx0.2d^3$；

P——传递的功率(kW)；

n——轴的转速(r/min)；

d——轴的直径(mm)。

故按扭转强度计算的公式为

$$d\geqslant\sqrt[3]{\frac{9.55\times10^6P}{0.2[\tau]n}}\geqslant C\sqrt[3]{\frac{p}{n}} \qquad (17.9\text{-}2)$$

其中，C 是由轴的材料和承载情况确定的常数，见表 17.9-1。应用上式求出的 d 值作为轴最细处的直径。

常用材料的 C 值 表 17.9-1

轴的材料	Q235,20	Q275,35	45	40Cr,35
C	160～135	135～118	118～107	107～98

注：当作用在轴上的弯矩比传递的转矩小或只传递转矩时，C 取较小值；否则取较大值。

此外，也可采用经验公式来估算轴的直径。例如在一般减速器中，高速输入轴的直径可按与其相连的电动机轴的直径 D 估算，$d=(0.8\sim1.2)D$；各级低速轴的轴径可按同级齿轮中心距 a 估算，$d=(0.3\sim0.4)a$。

(2)按弯扭合成强度计算

当零件在草图上布置妥当后，外荷载和支反力的作用位置即可确定。通常外荷载不是作用在同一平面内，这时应先将这些力分解到水平面和垂直面内，并求出各面的支反力，再绘出水平面弯矩 M_H 图、垂直面弯矩 M_V 图和合成弯矩 M 图，$M=\sqrt{M_H^2+M_V^2}$；绘出转矩 T 图；最后应用公式 $M_e=\sqrt{M^2+(\alpha T)^2}$ 绘出当量弯矩图。其中，α 为根据转矩性质而定的校正系数，对不变的转矩，$\alpha\approx0.3$；当转矩脉动变化时，$\alpha\approx0.6$；对于频繁正反转的轴，τ 可看为对称循环变应力，$\alpha=1$；若转矩的变化规律不清楚，一般也按脉动循环处理。

计算轴的直径时，式(17.9-2)可写成

$$d\geqslant\sqrt[3]{\frac{M_e}{0.1[\sigma_{1b}]}}\quad(\text{mm}) \qquad (17.9\text{-}3)$$

其中，M_e 的单位为 N·mm；$[\sigma_{1b}]$为对称循环状态下的许用弯曲应力，单位为 MPa。

2)轴的刚度计算

轴受弯矩作用会产生弯曲变形，受转矩作用会产生扭转变形。如果轴的刚度不够，就会影响轴的

正常工作。因此，为了使轴不致因刚度不够而失效，设计时必须根据轴的工作条件限制其变形量，即：

挠度　　　$y \leqslant [y]$

偏转角　　$\theta \leqslant [\theta]$

扭转角　　$\varphi \leqslant [\varphi]$

其中，$[y]$、$[\theta]$和$[\varphi]$分别为许用挠度、许用偏转角和许用扭转角。

(1)弯曲变形计算

计算轴在弯矩作用下所产生的挠度 y 和偏转角 θ 的方法很多。有按挠曲线的近似微分方程式积分求解法和变形能法。对于等直径轴，用前一种方法较简便，对于阶梯轴，用后一种方法较适宜。

(2)扭转变形的计算

等直径的轴受转矩 T 作用时，其扭转角 φ 可按材料力学中的扭转变形公式求出，即

$$\varphi = \frac{Tl}{GI_p} \quad (\mathrm{rad}) \qquad (17.9\text{-}4)$$

式中：T——转矩(N · mm)；

l——轴受转矩作用的长度(mm)；

G——材料的切变模量(MPa)；

I_p——轴截面的极惯性矩，$I_p = \frac{\pi d^4}{32}$。

17.9.3 轴毂连接的类型

联轴器和离合器可连接主、从动轴，使其一同回转并传递扭矩，有时也可用作安全装置。联轴器连接的分与合只能在停机时进行，而离合器连接的分与合可随时进行。

根据联轴器补偿位移的能力，联轴器可分为刚性和弹性两大类。刚性联轴器由刚性传力件组成，它又可分为固定式和可移式两种类型。固定式刚性联轴器不能补偿两轴的相对位移，可移式刚性联轴器能补偿两轴间的相对位移。弹性联轴器包含有弹性元件，除了能补偿两轴间的相对位移外，还具有吸收振动和缓和冲击的能力。常用联轴器的分类如表 17.9-2 所示。

联轴器分类、特点及应用　　　　表 17.9-2

分类		图例	特点及应用
固定式刚性联轴器	凸缘联轴器	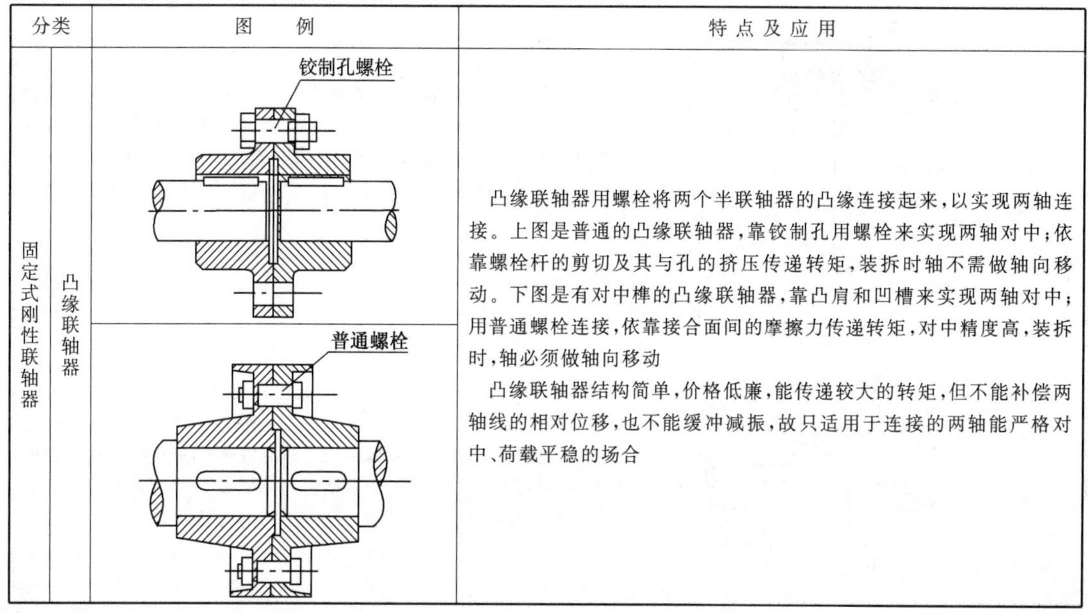	凸缘联轴器用螺栓将两个半联轴器的凸缘连接起来，以实现两轴连接。上图是普通的凸缘联轴器，靠铰制孔用螺栓来实现两轴对中；依靠螺栓杆的剪切及其与孔的挤压传递转矩，装拆时轴不需做轴向移动。下图是有对中榫的凸缘联轴器，靠凸肩和凹槽来实现两轴对中；用普通螺栓连接，依靠接合面间的摩擦力传递转矩，对中精度高，装拆时，轴必须做轴向移动 凸缘联轴器结构简单，价格低廉，能传递较大的转矩，但不能补偿两轴线的相对位移，也不能缓冲减振，故只适用于连接的两轴能严格对中、荷载平稳的场合

<table>
<tr><th colspan="2">分类</th><th>图例</th><th>特点及应用</th></tr>
<tr><td>固定式刚性联轴器</td><td>套筒式联轴器</td><td>d D L</td><td>套筒式联轴器用两个圆锥销来传递转矩。当然也可以用两个平键代替圆锥销。其优点是径向尺寸小，结构简单。结构尺寸推荐：$D=(1.5\sim2)d$；$L=(2.8\sim4)d$。此种联轴器尚无标准，需要自行设计，如机床上就经常采用这种联轴器</td></tr>
<tr><td rowspan="3">可移式刚性联轴器</td><td>齿式联轴器</td><td>1 2 3 4</td><td>齿式联轴器是由两个带内齿的外套筒 3 和两个带外齿的套筒 1 组成。套筒与轴相连，两个外套筒用螺栓 5 连成一体。工作时靠啮合的轮齿传递扭矩。齿轮联轴器能补偿适量的综合位移，由于轮齿间留有较大的间隙和外齿轮的齿顶制成椭球形，故能补偿两轴的不同心和偏斜</td></tr>
<tr><td>滑块联轴器</td><td>1 2 油孔 3</td><td>滑块联轴器由两个端面开有凹槽的半联轴器 1、3，利用两面带有凸块的中间盘 2 连接，半联轴器 1、3 分别与主、从动轴连接成一体，实现两轴的连接。中间盘沿径向滑动补偿径向位移 y，并能补偿角度位移 α。若两轴线不同心或偏斜，则在运转时中间盘上的凸块将在半联轴器的凹槽内滑动；转速较高时，由于中间盘的偏心会产生较大的离心力和磨损，并使轴承承受附加动荷载，故这种联轴器适用于低速。为减少磨损，可由中间盘油孔注入润滑剂</td></tr>
<tr><td>万向联轴器</td><td>C B A α O 2 1 D 4 3</td><td>万向联轴器由两个叉形接头 1、3 和十字轴 2 组成，利用中间连接件十字轴连接的两叉形半联轴器均能绕十字轴的轴线转动，从而使联轴器的两轴线能成任意角度 α，一般 α 最大可达 35°～45°。单个使用时，当主动轴以等角速度转动时，从动轴做变角速度回转，从而在传动中引起附加动荷载。为避免这种现象，可采用两个万向联轴器成对使用，使两次角速度变化的影响相互抵消，使主动轴和从动轴同步转动</td></tr>
<tr><td rowspan="2">弹性联轴器</td><td>弹性套柱销联轴器</td><td>c B L</td><td>弹性套柱销联轴器结构上和凸缘联轴器很近似，但是两个半联轴器的连接不用螺栓而用带橡胶或皮革套的柱销。为了更换橡胶套时简便而不必拆移机器，设计中应注意留出距离 B；为了补偿轴向位移，安装时应注意留出相应大小的间隙 c。弹性套柱销联轴器在高速轴上应用十分广泛</td></tr>
<tr><td>弹性柱销联轴器</td><td></td><td>弹性柱销联轴器是利用若干非金属材料制成的柱销置于两个半联轴器凸缘的孔中，以实现两轴的连接。柱销材料为尼龙，为防止柱销脱落，柱销两端装有挡板，用螺钉固定。结构简单，能补偿两轴间的相对位移，并具有一定的缓冲、吸振能力，应用广泛。但因尼龙对温度敏感，使用时受温度限制，一般在 −20°～70°之间使用</td></tr>
</table>

续上表

分类		图例	特点及应用
弹性联轴器	轮胎式联轴器		轮胎式联轴器中间为橡胶制成的轮胎，用夹紧板与轴套连接。结构简单、工作可靠，由于轮胎易变形，因此它允许的相对位移较大，角位移可达5°～12°，轴向位移可达0.02D，径向位移可达0.01D，D为联轴器外径。适用于起动频繁、经常正反向运转、有冲击振动、两轴间有较大的相对位移量以及潮湿多尘之处。它的径向尺寸庞大，但轴向尺寸较窄，有利于缩短串接机组的总长度

经典练习

17.9-1　增大轴在剖面过渡处圆角半径的主要作用是(　　)。

A. 使零件的轴向定位可靠　　B. 方便轴加工

C. 使零件的轴向固定可靠　　D. 减小应力集中

17.9-2　装在轴上的零件，下列各组方法中，能够实现轴向定位的是(　　)。

A. 套筒，普通平键，弹性挡圈　　B. 轴肩，紧定螺钉，轴端挡圈

C. 套筒，花键，轴肩　　D. 导向平键，螺母，过盈配合

17.9-3　为了增加碳素实心轴的刚度，采用以下哪种措施是无效的？(　　)

A. 将材料改为合金钢　　B. 截面积不变改用空心轴结构

C. 适当缩短轴的跨距　　D. 增加轴的直径

17.10　滚动轴承

考试大纲☞：滚动轴承的基本类型　滚动轴承的选择计算

必备基础知识

17.10.1　滚动轴承的结构、类型及代号

1)滚动轴承的结构

(1)滚动轴承的构造和特点

如图17.10-1所示，滚动轴承由外圈1、内圈2、滚动体3和保持架4组成。通常内圈固定在轴上随轴转动，外围装在轴承座孔内不动；但亦有外圈转动、内圈不动的使用情况。滚动体在内、外圈的滚道中滚动。保持架将滚动体均匀隔开，使其沿圆周均匀分布，减小滚动体之间的摩擦和磨损。

滚动体的形状有球形、圆柱形、圆锥形、鼓形、滚针形等多种(见图17.10-2)。滚动轴承的外圈、内圈、滚动体均采用强度高、耐磨性好的铬锰高碳钢制造。保持架多用低碳钢或铜合金制造。

轴承是用来支承轴及轴上零件、保持轴的旋转精度和减少转轴与支承之间的摩擦和磨损的部件。轴承一般分为两大类：滚动轴承和滑动轴承。与滑动轴承相比，滚动轴承具有摩擦阻力小、起动灵敏、效率高、润滑简便和易于互换等优点，所以获得广泛应用。但是在高速、高精度、重载、结构上要求剖分等场合下，滑动轴承就体现出它的优异性能。因而在汽轮机、离心式

压缩机、内燃机、大型电机、大型水轮机中多采用滑动轴承。此外,在低速而带有冲击的机器中,如水泥搅拌机、滚筒清砂机、破碎机等也采用滑动轴承。

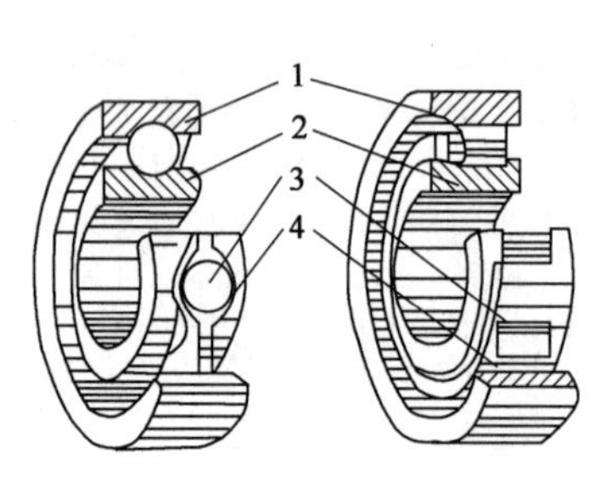

图 17.10-1　滚动轴承的构造图

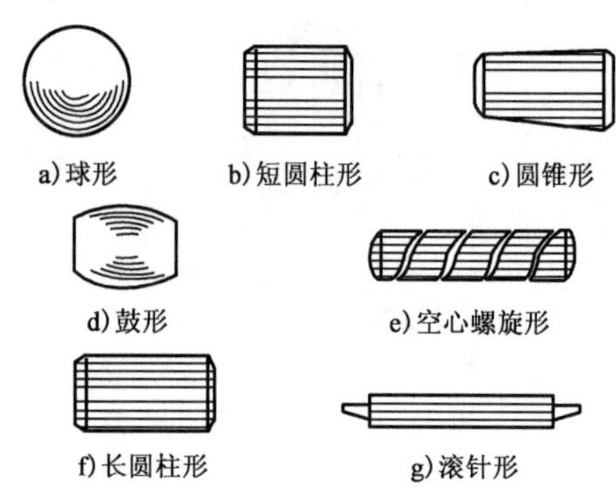

图 17.10-2　滚动体形状

(2)滚动轴承的结构特性

①接触角:滚动体和外圈接触处的法线 nn 与轴承的径向平面(垂直于轴承轴心线的平面)的夹角 α,称为接触角。α 越大,轴承承受轴向荷载的能力越大。

②游隙:滚动体和内、外圈之间存在一定的间隙,因此,内、外圈之间可以产生相对位移。其最大位移量称为游隙,分为轴向游隙和径向游隙。游隙的大小对轴承寿命、噪声、温升等有很大影响,应按使用要求进行游隙的选择或调整。

③偏移角:轴承内、外圈轴线相对倾斜时所夹锐角,称为偏移角。能自动适应角偏移的轴承,称为调心轴承。

2)滚动轴承的类型

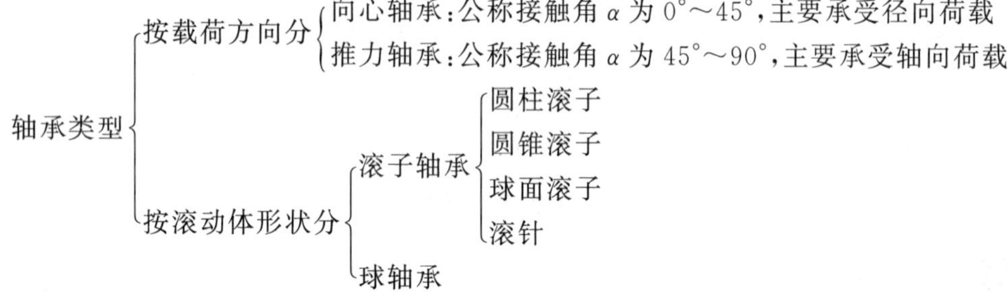

滚动轴承是标准件,类型很多,选用时主要根据荷载的大小、方向和性质,转速的高低及使用要求来选择,同时也必须考虑价格及经济性。常用滚动轴承的类型和特性见表 17.10-1。

常用滚动轴承的类型和特性　　表 17.10-1

类型及代号	结构简图	极限转速	允许角偏差	特性及应用
双列角接触球轴承(0)		中		能同时承受径向负荷和双向的轴向负荷,比角接触球轴承具有较大的承载能力,与双联角接触球轴承比较,在同样负荷作用下能使轴在轴向更紧密地固定
调心球轴承 1 或(1)		中	2°～3°	主要承受径向负荷,可承受少量的双向轴向负荷。外圈滚道为球面,具有自动调心性能。适用于多支点轴、弯曲刚度小的轴以及难于精确对中的支承

续上表

类型及代号	结构简图	极限转速	允许角偏差	特性及应用
调心滚子轴承 2		中	0.5°～2°	主要承受径向负荷,其承载能力比调心球轴承约大 1 倍,也能承受少量的双向轴向负荷。外圈滚道为球面,具有调心性能,适用于多支点轴、弯曲刚度小的轴及难于精确对中的支承,常用于重型机械上
圆锥滚子轴承 3	α	中	2′	能承受较大的径向负荷和单向的轴向负荷,极限转速较低。内外圈可分离,轴承游隙可在安装时调整。通常成对使用,对称安装。适用于转速不太高,轴的刚性较好的场合
双列深沟球轴承 4		中		主要承受径向负荷,也能承受一定的双向轴向负荷。它比深沟球轴承具有较大的承载能力
推力球轴承 5		低	不允许	推力球轴承的套圈与滚动体可分离,单向推力球轴承只能承受单向轴向负荷,两个圈的内孔不一样大,内孔较小的与轴配合,内孔较大的与机座固定。双向推力球轴承可以承受双向轴向负荷,中间圈与轴配合,另两个圈为松圈。高速时,由于离心力大,寿命较低。常用于轴向负荷大、转速不高场合
深沟球轴承 6 或(16)		高	8′～16′	主要承受径向负荷,也可同时承受少量双向轴向负荷,工作时内外圈轴线允许偏斜。摩擦阻力小,极限转速高,结构简单,价格便宜,应用最广泛。但承受冲击荷载能力较差。适用于高速场合。在高速时可代替推力球轴承
角接触球轴承 7	α	较高	2′～3′	能同时承受径向负荷与单向的轴向负荷,公称接触角 α 有 15°、25°、40°三种,α 越大,轴向承载能力也越大。成对使用,对称安装,极限转速较高。适用于转速较高,同时承受径向和轴向负荷场合
推力圆柱滚子轴承 8		低	不允许	能承受很大的单向轴向负荷,但不能承受径向负荷。它比推力球轴承承载能力要大,套圈也分紧圈与松圈。极限转速很低,适用于低速重载场合
圆柱滚子轴承 N		较高	2′～4′	只能承受径向负荷。承载能力比同尺寸的球轴承大,承受冲击荷载能力大,极限转速高。对轴的偏斜敏感,允许偏斜较小。用于刚性较大的轴上,并要求支承座孔很好地对中

续上表

类型及代号	结构简图	极限转速	允许角偏差	特性及应用
滚针轴承 NA		低	不允许	滚动体数量较多，一般没有保持架。径向尺寸紧凑且承载能力很大，价格低廉，不能承受轴向负荷，摩擦系数较大，不允许有偏斜。常用于径向尺寸受限制而径向负荷又较大的装置中

3)滚动轴承的代号

滚动轴承代号是表示其结构、尺寸、公差等级和技术性能等特征的产品符号，由字母和数字组成。滚动轴承的代号表示方法如表 17.10-3 所示。

滚动轴承代号的排列顺序　　表 17.10-3

前置代号	基本代号				后置代号
□	×(□)	×	×	×	□(×)
成套轴承部件代号	类型代号	尺寸系列代号		内径代号	内部结构、公差等级等
		宽(高)度系列代号	直径系列代号		

注：□表示字母，×表示数字。

(1)内径尺寸代号：右起第一、二位数字表示内径尺寸，表示方法见表 17.10-4。

轴承内径尺寸代号　　表 17.10-4

代号表示	00	01	02	03	内径/5 的商	公称内径/内径
内径尺寸(mm)	10	12	15	17	20～480(5 的倍数)	22、28、32 及 500 以上

(2)尺寸系列代号：右起第三、四位表示尺寸系列(第四位为 0 时可不写出)。为了适应不同承载能力的需要，同一内径尺寸的轴承，可使用不同大小的滚动体，因而使轴承的外径和宽度也随着改变。这种内径相同而外径或宽度不同的变化称为尺寸系列，见表 17.10-5。

向心轴承、推力轴承尺寸系列代号表示法　　表 17.10-5

直径系列代号	向心轴承							推力轴承			
	宽度系列代号							高度系列代号			
	窄 0	正常 1	宽 2	特宽 3	特宽 4	特宽 5	特宽 6	特低 7	低 9	正常 1	正常 2
	尺寸系列代号										
特轻 0	00	10	20	30	40	50	60	70	90	10	—
特轻 1	01	11	21	31	41	51	61	71	91	11	—
轻 2	02	12	22	32	42	52	62	72	92	12	22
中 3	03	13	23	33	—	—	63	73	93	13	23
重 4	04	—	24	—	—	—	—	74	94	14	24

(3)类型代号：右起第五位表示轴承类型，其代号见表 17.10-2。代号为 0 时不写出。

(4)前置代号：用字母表示成套轴承的分部件。

(5)后置代号：内部结构、尺寸、公差等，其顺序见表 17.10-6，常见的轴承内部结构代号和公差等级见表 17.10-7 和表 17.10-8。

轴承后置代号排列 表 17.10-6

后置代号	1	2	3	4	5	6	7	8
含义	内部结构	密封与防尘套圈变型	保持架及其材料	轴承材料	公差等级	游隙	配置	其他

轴承内部结构代号 表 17.10-7

代　号	含　义	示　例
C	角接触球轴承公称接触角 $\alpha=15°$ 调心滚子轴承 C 型	7005C 23122C
AC	角接触球轴承公称接触角 $\alpha=25°$	7210AC
B	角接触球轴承公称接触角 $\alpha=40°$ 圆锥滚子轴承接触角加大	7210B 32310B
E	加强型	N207E

轴承公差等级代号 表 17.10-8

代号	省略	/P6	/P6x	/P5	/P4	/P2
公差等级符合标准规定的	0 级	6 级	6x 级	5 级	4 级	2 级
示例	6205	6205/P6	6205/P6x	6205/P5	6205/P4	6205/P2

典型例题解析

【例 17.10-1】 轴承在机械中的作用是：

A. 连接不同的零件　B. 在空间支撑转动的零件

C. 支撑转动的零件并向它传递扭矩　D. 保证机械中各零件工作的同步

解 轴承是用来支承轴及轴上零件、保持轴的旋转精度和减少转轴与支承之间的摩擦和磨损的部件。选 B。

【例 17.10-2】 在下列各种机械设备中，哪一项只宜采用滑动轴承？

A. 小型减速器　B. 中型减速器

C. 铁道机车车轴　D. 大型水轮机主轴

解 在高速、高精度、重载、结构上要求剖分等场合下，滑动轴承就体现出它的优异性能。因而在汽轮机、离心式压缩机、内燃机、大型电机、大型水轮机中多采用滑动轴承。选 D。

【例 17.10-3】 下列哪一种滚动轴承只能承受径向荷载？

A. 滚针轴承　B. 圆锥滚子轴承

C. 角接触轴承　D. 深沟球轴承

解 滚针轴承只能承受径向荷载，不能承受轴向荷载。选 A。

【例 17.10-4】 下列滚动轴承中，通常需成对使用的轴承型号是：

A. N307　B. 6207　C. 30207　D. 51307

解 右起第五位表示轴承类型，可知 30207 为圆锥滚子轴承，通常需成对使用，对称安装。选 C。

17.10.2 滚动轴承的选择计算

1)滚动轴承的失效形式

(1)疲劳点蚀

疲劳点蚀使轴承产生振动和噪声，旋转精度下降，影响机器的正常工作，是一般滚动轴承的主要失效形式。

(2)塑性变形

当轴承转速很低($n \leqslant 10\text{r/min}$)或间歇摆动时，一般不会发生疲劳点蚀，此时轴承往往因受过大的静载荷或冲击荷载而产生塑性变形，使轴承失效。磨损、润滑不良、杂质和灰尘的侵入都会引起磨损，使轴承丧失旋转精度而失效。

2)轴承的寿命计算

(1)寿命计算中的基本概念

①寿命。滚动轴承的寿命是指轴承中任何一个滚动体或内、外圈滚道上出现疲劳点蚀前轴承转过的总圈数，或在一定转速下总的工作小时数。

②基本额定寿命。一批类型、尺寸相同的轴承，材料、加工精度、热处理与装配质量不可能完全相同。即使在同样条件下工作，各个轴承的寿命也是不同的。在国标中规定以基本额定寿命作为计算依据。基本领定寿命是指一批相同的轴承，在同样工作条件下，其中10%的轴承产生疲劳点蚀时转过的总圈数，或在一定转速下总的工作小时数。

③额定动荷载。基本额定寿命为10^6转时轴承所能承受的荷载，称为额定动荷载，以“C”表示，轴承在额定动载荷作用下，不发生疲劳点蚀的可靠度是90%。各种类型和不同尺寸轴承的C值可查设计手册。

④额定静荷载。轴承工作时，受载最大的滚动体与内、外圈滚道接触处的接触应力达到一定值(向心和推力球轴承为4 200MPa，滚子轴承为4 000MPa)时的静荷载，称为额定静荷载，用“C_0”表示，其值可查设计手册。

⑤当量荷载。额定动、静荷载是向心轴承只承受径向荷载、推力轴承只承受轴向荷载的条件下，根据试验确定的。实际上，轴承承受的荷载往往与上述条件不同，因此，必须将实际荷载等效为一假想荷载，这个假想荷载称为当量动、静荷载，以“P”表示。

(2)寿命计算

$$L_h = \frac{10^6}{60n}\left(\frac{f_T C}{f_P P}\right)^{\varepsilon} \tag{17.10-1}$$

在实际应用中，额定寿命常用给定转速下运转的小时数L_h表示。考虑到机器振动和冲击的影响，引入载荷因数f_P(见表17.10-9)；考虑到工作温度的影响，引入了温度因数f_T(表17.10-10)。实用的寿命计算公式为

$$C_c = \frac{f_P P}{f_T}\sqrt[\varepsilon]{\frac{60nL_h'}{10^6}} \leqslant C \tag{17.10-2}$$

式中：C_c——计算额定动荷载(kN)；

C——额定动荷载(kN)，可查设计手册；

ε——寿命指数，球轴承$\varepsilon=3$，滚子轴承$\varepsilon=10/3$。

若当量动荷载P与转速n均已知，预期寿命L_h'已选定，则可根据式(17.10-2)选择轴承型号。

载荷因数 f_P 表 17.10-9

荷载性质	f_P	举　例
无冲击或有轻微冲击	1.0～1.2	电动机、汽轮机、通风机、水泵
中等冲击和振动	1.2～1.8	车辆、机床、内燃机、起重机、冶金设备、减速器
强大冲击和振动	1.8～3.0	破碎机、轧钢机、石油钻机、振动筛

温度因数 f_T 表 17.10-10

轴承工作温度(℃)	100	125	150	175	200	225	250	300
温度系数 f_T	1	0.95	0.90	0.85	0.80	0.75	0.70	0.60

3)当量动荷载的计算

当量动荷载是一假想荷载，在该荷载作用下，轴承的寿命与实际荷载作用下的寿命相同。当量动荷载 P 的计算式为

$$P = XF_r + YF_a \tag{17.10-3}$$

式中：X——径向载荷因数；

Y——轴向载荷因数(见表 17.10-11)；

F_r——轴承承受的径向荷载；

F_a——轴承承受的轴向荷载。

单列向心轴承的径向载荷系数 X 和轴向载荷系数 Y 表 17.10-11

轴承类型		F_a/C_0	e	$F_a/F_r>e$		$F_a/F_r\leqslant e$	
				X	Y	X	Y
深沟球轴承(6 类)		0.014	0.19	0.56	2.30	1	0
		0.028	0.22		1.99		
		0.056	0.26		1.71		
		0.084	0.28		1.55		
		0.11	0.30		1.45		
		0.17	0.34		1.31		
		0.28	0.38		1.15		
		0.42	0.42		1.04		
		0.56	0.44		1.00		
角接触球轴承(7 类)	7 000C($\alpha=15°$)	0.015	0.38	0.44	1.47	1	8
		0.029	0.40		1.40		
		0.058	0.43		1.30		
		0.087	0.46		1.23		
		0.12	0.47		1.19		
		0.17	0.50		1.12		
		0.29	0.55		1.02		
		0.44	0.56		1.00		
		0.58	0.56		1.00		
	7 000AC($\alpha=25°$)	—	0.68	0.41	0.87	1	0
	7 000B($\alpha=40°$)	—	1.14	0.35	0.57	1	0
圆锥滚子轴承(3 类)		—	见附表	0.40	见附表	1	0

对于只承受径向荷载的轴承，当量动荷载为轴承的径向荷载 F_r，即

$$P=F_r \tag{17.10-4}$$

对于只承受轴向荷载的轴承，当量动荷载为轴承的轴向荷载 F_a，即

$$P=F_a \tag{17.10-5}$$

典型例题解析

【例 17.10-5】 滚动轴承的额定寿命是指同一批轴承中百分之几的轴承所能达到的寿命？

A. 10%　　B. 50%　　C. 90%　　D. 99%

解 基本额定寿命是指一批相同的轴承，在同样工作条件下，其中10%的轴承产生疲劳点蚀时转过的总圈数，或在一定转速下总的工作小时数，即90%的轴承所能达到的寿命。选C。

【例 17.10-6】 转速一定的角接触球轴承，当量动载荷由 $2P$ 减小为 P，则其寿命由 L 会：

A. 下降为 $0.2L$　　B. 上升为 $2L$

C. 上升为 $8L$　　D. 不变

解 根据球轴承的基本额定寿命公式 $L=\left(\frac{C}{P}\right)^3$，寿命 L 与 P^3 成反比，可知其寿命将上升为 $8L$。选C。

17.10.3 滚动轴承的润滑和密封

润滑和密封对滚动轴承的使用寿命有重要意义。润滑的主要目的是减小摩擦与磨损。滚动接触部位形成油膜时，还有吸收振动、降低工作温度等作用。密封的目的是防止灰尘、水分等进入轴承，并阻止润滑剂的流失。

1)滚动轴承的润滑

滚动轴承的润滑剂可以是润滑脂、润滑油或固体润滑剂。一般情况下，轴承采用润滑脂润滑，但在轴承附近已经具有润滑油源时(如变速箱内本来就有润滑齿轮的油)，也可采用润滑油润滑。

脂润滑因润滑脂不易流失，故便于密封和维护，且一次充填润滑脂可运转较长时间。油润滑的优点是比脂润滑摩擦阻力小，并能散热，主要用于高速或工作温度较高的轴承。高速轴承通常采用滴油或喷雾方法润滑。润滑油的黏度可按轴承的速度因数 d_n 和工作温度 t 来确定。黏度随温度的升高而降低。

2)滚动轴承的密封

滚动轴承密封方法的选择与润滑的种类、工作环境、温度、密封表面的圆周速度有关。密封方法可分两大类：接触式密封和非接触式密封。接触式密封分为毛毡圈密封、密封圈密封；非接触式密封分为间隙密封、迷宫式密封；组合式密封为毛毡迷宫式密封。

典型例题解析

【例 17.10-7】 当温度升高时，润滑油的黏度：

A. 升高　　B. 降低　　C. 不变　　D. 不一定

解 润滑油的黏度随温度的升高而降低。选B。

【例 17.10-8】 下列哪项属于接触式密封？

A. 毛圈密封　　B. 油沟式密封　　C. 迷宫式密封　　D. 甩油密封

解　接触式密封分为毛毡圈密封、密封圈密封。选 A。

经典练习

17.10-1　下列选项中，(　　)不宜用来同时承受径向和轴向荷载。

A. 圆锥滚子轴承　　B. 角接触轴承

C. 深沟球轴承　　D. 圆柱滚子轴承

17.10-2　跨距较大并承受较大径向荷载的起重机卷筒轴的轴承应选用(　　)。

A. 圆锥滚子轴承　　B. 调心滚子轴承

C. 调心球轴承　　D. 圆柱滚子轴承

17.10-3　代号为 N1024 的轴承，其内径是多少毫米？(　　)

A. 24　　B. 40　　C. 120　　D. 1024

17.10-4　含油轴承是采用下列哪一项制成的？(　　)

A. 合金钢　　B. 塑料　　C. 粉末冶金　　D. 橡胶

17.10-5　在非液体摩擦滑动轴承中，限制 pv 值的主要目的是防止轴承(　　)。

A. 润滑油被挤出　　B. 产生塑性变形

C. 磨粒磨损　　D. 过度发热而胶合

17.10-6　在非液体摩擦滑动轴承中，限制压强 p 值的主要目的是防止轴承(　　)。

A. 润滑油被挤出而发生过度磨损　　B. 产生塑性变形

C. 出现过大的摩擦阻力　　D. 过度发热而胶合

参考答案及提示

17.1-1　C　零件工作时实际所承受的应力 σ，应小于或等于许用应力$[\sigma]$。

17.1-2　C　零件可靠度 R 可表示为 $R=\frac{N_s}{N_0}=1-\frac{N_f}{N_0}=1-\frac{5}{50}=0.9$。

17.2-1　C　两构件通过面接触组成的运动副称为低副。

17.2-2　A　M 个构件汇交而成的复合铰链具有$(M-1)$个转动副。

17.2-3　C　在题图所示机构中，在 C 处构成复合铰链，在 F 处构成局部自由度，在 E 或 E' 处构成虚约束，去除局部自由度后，可动构件的数目是 7。焊死局部自由度 F、去除虚约束 E 或 E' 并考虑 C 处复合铰链，低副的数目是 9 个；只有凸轮与滚子构成高副，故高副的数目为 1。根据机构自由度计算公式 $F=3n-(2P_L+P_H)=3\times7-(2\times9+1)=2$，故该机构的自由度数目是 2。

本节应熟练掌握平面机构自由度的公式，在计算平面机构自由度时，必须考虑是否存在复合铰链，并应将局部自由度和虚约束除去不计，才能得到正确的结果。

17.3-1　C　参见 17.3.2 节(曲柄存在的条件)。题图 a)中 $40+110<70+90$，满足杆长条件，且最短杆为机架，故为双曲柄机构；题图 b)中 $45+1\ 120<70+100$，满

足杆长条件，且最短杆的邻边为机架，故为曲柄摇杆机构；题图 c)中 60＋100＞62＋70，不满足杆长条件，故为双摇杆机构；题图 d)中 50＋100＜70＋90，满足杆长条件，且最短杆的对边为机架，故为双摇杆机构。

17.3-2　C　曲柄摇杆机构中，如果摇杆是主动件而曲柄是从动件，那么，当摇杆摆到使曲柄与连杆共线的极限位置时，从动件的传动角为 0°(即压力角＝90°)，摇杆通过连杆加于曲柄的驱动力正好通过曲柄的转动中心，则不能产生使曲柄转动的力矩。机构的这种位置称为死点位置。

17.4-1　A　尖底与凸轮是点接触，最易磨损。

17.4-2　A　滚子从动件盘形凸轮机构的基圆半径，是在理论轮廓线上度量的。

17.4-3　B

17.4-4　A

17.4-5　B　根据凸轮机构的压力角计算公式 $\tan\alpha=\dfrac{\dfrac{\mathrm{d}s}{\mathrm{d}\varphi}\mp e}{s+\sqrt{r_0^2-e^2}}$，当凸轮角速度、从动件运动规律已知时，压力角 α 与基圆半径 r_0 之间为反比关系，即基圆半径越小，凸轮压力角就越大。

17.5-1　C　三角形螺纹的自锁条件为螺纹升角小于材料的当量摩擦角，即 $\lambda<\rho'$。

17.5-2　B　为提高螺栓连接的强度，降低螺栓总拉伸荷载 F_Q 的变化范围，应减小螺栓刚度或增大被连接件刚度。

17.5-3　C　对连接用螺纹的基本要求是其应具有可靠的自锁性，所以适用于连接用的螺纹是三角形螺纹。

17.5-4　C　非矩形螺纹的自锁条件是 $\lambda<\rho'$。当量摩擦角 ρ'越大，自锁越可靠。而 $\tan\rho'=f'=\dfrac{f}{\cos\beta}$，$\beta=\dfrac{\alpha}{2}$，$\alpha$ 为牙形角，所以要提高螺纹连接的自锁性能，应采用牙形角大的螺纹。

考生应熟练掌握螺纹自锁条件。

17.6-1　C　根据带传动工作原理，带传动靠摩擦力使带轮产生运动。

17.6-2　D　传动带上最大应力发生在紧边与小轮的接触处。

17.6-3　D　当带所需传递的圆周力大于带与轮面间的极限摩擦力总和时，带与带轮将发生打滑，打滑是带传动的主要失效形式。

17.7-1　B　用范成法加工齿数较少的齿轮时，常会将轮齿根部的渐开线齿廓切去一部分，这种现象称为根切。对于标准齿轮，是用限制最少齿数的方法来避免根切的。用滚刀加工压力角为 20°的正常齿制标准直齿圆柱齿轮时，根据计算，可得出不发生根切的最少齿数 $z_{\min}=17$。

17.7-2　D　一对渐开线齿轮的正确啮合条件是两齿轮模数和压力角分别相等。

17.7-3　B　一对正常齿标准直齿圆柱齿轮传动的中心距 $a=\dfrac{m}{z}(z_1+z_2)$。

17.7-4　A

17.8-1 D 根据一对外啮合齿轮的转动方向相反,蜗杆蜗轮的转向需满足:速度矢量之和必定与螺旋线垂直,可判断出轮 4 的转动方向为顺时针,轮 5 的转动方向与轮 4 相同,则齿条将向左运动。传动比的大小 $i_{14}=\frac{n_1}{n_2}=\frac{z_2 z_4}{z_1 z_3}=\frac{40\times 60}{20\times 2}=60$,又因为 $n_5=n_4$,所以轮 1 旋转 1 周时,轮 5 旋转了 $\frac{1}{60}$ 周,齿条运动的距离为 $\frac{1}{60}\pi n z_5=\frac{1}{60}\times 3.14\times 2\times 30=3.14\text{mm}$。

17.8-2 A 由内啮合齿轮的转向相同外啮合齿轮的转向相反可知,轮 3 与轮 1 的转向相反,则 $i_{13}{}^{\mathrm{H}}=\frac{n_1-n_{\mathrm{H}}}{n_3-n_{\mathrm{H}}}=\frac{z_3 z_2 z_2}{z_1 z_2 z_2}=-4$,又 $n_3=0$,可得 $i_{1\mathrm{H}}=\frac{n_1}{n_{\mathrm{H}}}=5$。

17.9-1 D 进行结构设计时,应尽量减小应力集中,可在阶梯轴的截面尺寸变化处采用圆角过渡,且圆角半径不宜过小。

17.9-2 B 轴上零件的周向固定,大多采用键、花键或过盈配合等连接形式。

17.9-3 B

17.10-1 D 圆柱滚子轴承只能承受径向负荷。

17.10-2 B 调心滚子轴承主要承受径向荷载,其承载能力比相同尺寸的调心球轴承大 1 倍,常用于重型机械上。

17.10-3 C 右起第一、二位数字表示内径尺寸,表示方法见表 17.10-4。

17.10-4 C 用粉末冶金法(经制粉、成型、烧结等工艺)做成的轴承,具有多孔性组织,孔隙内可以储存润滑油,常称为含油轴承。

17.10-5 D pv 值简略地表征轴承的发热因素,为了保证轴承运转时不产生过多的热量,以控制温升。防止黏着胶合,要限制 pv 的值。

17.10-6 A 限制轴承压强 p,以保证润滑油不被过大的压力所挤出,因而轴承不致产生过度的磨损。

18 职业法规

考题配置　单选,3 题
分数配置　每题 2 分,共 6 分

18.1 我国有关基本建设、建筑、城市规划、环保、房地产方面的法律规范

考试大纲☞:我国有关基本建设、建筑、城市规划、环保、房地产方面的法律规范

必备基础知识

18.1.1 中华人民共和国建筑法

请见本书上册 11.2 节相关内容。

典型例题解析

【例 18.1-1】 建筑工程的发包单位,在工程发包中:

A. 必须把工程的勘察、设计、施工、设备采购发包给一个工程总承包

B. 应当把工程的勘察、设计、施工、设备采购逐一发包给不同单位

C. 可以把工程的勘察、设计、施工、设备采购的一项或多项发给一个总承包单位

D. 不能把工程的勘察、设计、施工、设备采购一并发包给一个总承包单位

解 见《中华人民共和国建筑法》第二十四条。选 C。

【例 18.1-2】 工程建设监理单位的工作内容,下列哪条是正确的?

A. 代表建设单位对承包单位实施监督

B. 对合同的双方进行监理

C. 代表一部分政府职能

D. 只能对建设单位提交意见,由建设单位行使权力

解 见《中华人民共和国建筑法》第三十二条。选 A。

【例 18.1-3】 全国人民代表大会常务委员会 2011 年对《中华人民共和国建筑法》的主要修改是:

A. 建筑施工企业应当依法为职工参加工伤保险缴纳工伤保险费。鼓励企业为从事危险作业的职工办理意外伤害保险,支付保险费

B. 责令停业整顿、降低资质等级和吊销资质证书的行政处罚,由颁发资质证书的机关决定;其他行政处罚,由建设行政主管部门或者有关部门依照法律和国务院规定的职权范围决定

C. 被吊销资质证书的，由工商行政管理部门吊销其营业执照

D. 违反本法规定，对不具备相应资质等级条件的单位颁发该等级资质证书的，由其上级机关责令收回所发的资质证书，对直接负责的主管人员和其他直接责任人员给予行政处分；构成犯罪的，依法追究刑事责任

解 2011年全国人大常委会对第四十八条做了修改。选A。

【例18.1-4】 下列哪家单位应该对施工过程中产生的废气、废弃物和噪声等采取措施，保护环境？

A. 建设单位
B. 建筑施工企业
C. 行政主管单位
D. 其他

解 见《中华人民共和国建筑法》第四十一条。选B。

18.1.2 中华人民共和国城乡规划法（2015年修订版）

第一章 总 则

第一条 为了加强城乡规划管理，协调城乡空间布局，改善人居环境，促进城乡经济社会全面协调可持续发展，制定本法。

第二条 制定和实施城乡规划，在规划区内进行建设活动，必须遵守本法。

本法所称城乡规划，包括城镇体系规划、城市规划、镇规划、乡规划和村庄规划。城市规划、镇规划分为总体规划和详细规划。详细规划分为控制性详细规划和修建性详细规划。

本法所称规划区，是指城市、镇和村庄的建成区以及因城乡建设和发展需要，必须实行规划控制的区域。规划区的具体范围由有关人民政府在组织编制的城市总体规划、镇总体规划、乡规划和村庄规划中，根据城乡经济社会发展水平和统筹城乡发展的需要划定。

第三条 城市和镇应当依照本法制定城市规划和镇规划。城市、镇规划区内的建设活动应当符合规划要求。

县级以上地方人民政府根据本地农村经济社会发展水平，按照因地制宜、切实可行的原则，确定应当制定乡规划、村庄规划的区域。在确定区域内的乡、村庄，应当依照本法制定规划，规划区内的乡、村庄建设应当符合规划要求。

县级以上地方人民政府鼓励、指导前款规定以外的区域的乡、村庄制定和实施乡规划、村庄规划。

第四条 制定和实施城乡规划，应当遵循城乡统筹、合理布局、节约土地、集约发展和先规划后建设的原则，改善生态环境，促进资源、能源节约和综合利用，保护耕地等自然资源和历史文化遗产，保持地方特色、民族特色和传统风貌，防止污染和其他公害，并符合区域人口发展、国防建设、防灾减灾和公共卫生、公共安全的需要。

在规划区内进行建设活动，应当遵守土地管理、自然资源和环境保护等法律、法规的规定。

县级以上地方人民政府应当根据当地经济社会发展的实际，在城市总体规划、镇总体规划中合理确定城市、镇的发展规模、步骤和建设标准。

第五条 城市总体规划、镇总体规划以及乡规划和村庄规划的编制，应当依据国民经济和社会发展规划，并与土地利用总体规划相衔接。

第六条 各级人民政府应当将城乡规划的编制和管理经费纳入本级财政预算。

第七条　经依法批准的城乡规划，是城乡建设和规划管理的依据，未经法定程序不得修改。

第八条　城乡规划组织编制机关应当及时公布经依法批准的城乡规划。但是，法律、行政法规规定不得公开的内容除外。

第九条　任何单位和个人都应当遵守经依法批准并公布的城乡规划，服从规划管理，并有权就涉及其利害关系的建设活动是否符合规划的要求向城乡规划主管部门查询。

任何单位和个人都有权向城乡规划主管部门或者其他有关部门举报或者控告违反城乡规划的行为。城乡规划主管部门或者其他有关部门对举报或者控告，应当及时受理并组织核查、处理。

第十条　国家鼓励采用先进的科学技术，增强城乡规划的科学性，提高城乡规划实施及监督管理的效能。

第十一条　国务院城乡规划主管部门负责全国的城乡规划管理工作。

县级以上地方人民政府城乡规划主管部门负责本行政区域内的城乡规划管理工作。

第二章　城乡规划的制定

第十二条　国务院城乡规划主管部门会同国务院有关部门组织编制全国城镇体系规划，用于指导省域城镇体系规划、城市总体规划的编制。

全国城镇体系规划由国务院城乡规划主管部门报国务院审批。

第十三条　省、自治区人民政府组织编制省域城镇体系规划，报国务院审批。

省域城镇体系规划的内容应当包括：城镇空间布局和规模控制，重大基础设施的布局，为保护生态环境、资源等需要严格控制的区域。

第十四条　城市人民政府组织编制城市总体规划。

直辖市的城市总体规划由直辖市人民政府报国务院审批。省、自治区人民政府所在地的城市以及国务院确定的城市的总体规划，由省、自治区人民政府审查同意后，报国务院审批。其他城市的总体规划，由城市人民政府报省、自治区人民政府审批。

第十五条　县人民政府组织编制县人民政府所在地镇的总体规划，报上一级人民政府审批。其他镇的总体规划由镇人民政府组织编制，报上一级人民政府审批。

第十六条　省、自治区人民政府组织编制的省域城镇体系规划，城市、县人民政府组织编制的总体规划，在报上一级人民政府审批前，应当先经本级人民代表大会常务委员会审议，常务委员会组成人员的审议意见交由本级人民政府研究处理。

镇人民政府组织编制的镇总体规划，在报上一级人民政府审批前，应当先经镇人民代表大会审议，代表的审议意见交由本级人民政府研究处理。

规划的组织编制机关报送审批省域城镇体系规划、城市总体规划或者镇总体规划，应当将本级人民代表大会常务委员会组成人员或者镇人民代表大会代表的审议意见和根据审议意见修改规划的情况一并报送。

第十七条　城市总体规划、镇总体规划的内容应当包括：城市、镇的发展布局，功能分区，用地布局，综合交通体系，禁止、限制和适宜建设的地域范围，各类专项规划等。

规划区范围、规划区内建设用地规模、基础设施和公共服务设施用地、水源地和水系、基本农田和绿化用地、环境保护、自然与历史文化遗产保护以及防灾减灾等内容，应当作为城市总体规划、镇总体规划的强制性内容。

城市总体规划、镇总体规划的规划期限一般为二十年。城市总体规划还应当对城市更长远的发展作出预测性安排。

第十八条　乡规划、村庄规划应当从农村实际出发，尊重村民意愿，体现地方和农村特色。

乡规划、村庄规划的内容应当包括：规划区范围，住宅、道路、供水、排水、供电、垃圾收集、畜禽养殖场所等农村生产、生活服务设施、公益事业等各项建设的用地布局、建设要求，以及对耕地等自然资源和历史文化遗产保护、防灾减灾等的具体安排。乡规划还应当包括本行政区域内的村庄发展布局。

第十九条　城市人民政府城乡规划主管部门根据城市总体规划的要求，组织编制城市的控制性详细规划，经本级人民政府批准后，报本级人民代表大会常务委员会和上一级人民政府备案。

第二十条　镇人民政府根据镇总体规划的要求，组织编制镇的控制性详细规划，报上一级人民政府审批。县人民政府所在地镇的控制性详细规划，由县人民政府城乡规划主管部门根据镇总体规划的要求组织编制，经县人民政府批准后，报本级人民代表大会常务委员会和上一级人民政府备案。

第二十一条　城市、县人民政府城乡规划主管部门和镇人民政府可以组织编制重要地块的修建性详细规划。修建性详细规划应当符合控制性详细规划。

第二十二条　乡、镇人民政府组织编制乡规划、村庄规划，报上一级人民政府审批。村庄规划在报送审批前，应当经村民会议或者村民代表会议讨论同意。

第二十三条　首都的总体规划、详细规划应当统筹考虑中央国家机关用地布局和空间安排的需要。

第二十四条　城乡规划组织编制机关应当委托具有相应资质等级的单位承担城乡规划的具体编制工作。

从事城乡规划编制工作应当具备下列条件，并经国务院城乡规划主管部门或者省、自治区、直辖市人民政府城乡规划主管部门依法审查合格，取得相应等级的资质证书后，方可在资质等级许可的范围内从事城乡规划编制工作：

（一）有法人资格；

（二）有规定数量的经相关行业协会注册的规划师；

（三）有相应的技术装备；

（四）有健全的技术、质量、财务管理制度。

规划师执业资格管理办法，由国务院城乡规划主管部门会同国务院人事行政部门制定。

编制城乡规划必须遵守国家有关标准。

第二十五条　编制城乡规划，应当具备国家规定的勘察、测绘、气象、地震、水文、环境等基础资料。

县级以上地方人民政府有关主管部门应当根据编制城乡规划的需要，及时提供有关基础资料。

第二十六条　城乡规划报送审批前，组织编制机关应当依法将城乡规划草案予以公告，并采取论证会、听证会或者其他方式征求专家和公众的意见。公告的时间不得少于三十日。

组织编制机关应当充分考虑专家和公众的意见，并在报送审批的材料中附具意见采纳情况及理由。

第二十七条　省域城镇体系规划、城市总体规划、镇总体规划批准前，审批机关应当组织专家和有关部门进行审查。

第三章　城乡规划的实施

第二十八条　地方各级人民政府应当根据当地经济社会发展水平，量力而行，尊重群众意愿，有计划、分步骤地组织实施城乡规划。

第二十九条　城市的建设和发展，应当优先安排基础设施以及公共服务设施的建设，妥善处理新区开发与旧区改建的关系，统筹兼顾进城务工人员生活和周边农村经济社会发展、村民生产与生活的需要。

镇的建设和发展，应当结合农村经济社会发展和产业结构调整，优先安排供水、排水、供电、供气、道路、通信、广播电视等基础设施和学校、卫生院、文化站、幼儿园、福利院等公共服务设施的建设，为周边农村提供服务。

乡、村庄的建设和发展，应当因地制宜、节约用地，发挥村民自治组织的作用，引导村民合理进行建设，改善农村生产、生活条件。

第三十条　城市新区的开发和建设，应当合理确定建设规模和时序，充分利用现有市政基础设施和公共服务设施，严格保护自然资源和生态环境，体现地方特色。

在城市总体规划、镇总体规划确定的建设用地范围以外，不得设立各类开发区和城市新区。

第三十一条　旧城区的改建，应当保护历史文化遗产和传统风貌，合理确定拆迁和建设规模，有计划地对危房集中、基础设施落后等地段进行改建。

历史文化名城、名镇、名村的保护以及受保护建筑物的维护和使用，应当遵守有关法律、行政法规和国务院的规定。

第三十二条　城乡建设和发展，应当依法保护和合理利用风景名胜资源，统筹安排风景名胜区及周边乡、镇、村庄的建设。

风景名胜区的规划、建设和管理，应当遵守有关法律、行政法规和国务院的规定。

第三十三条　城市地下空间的开发和利用，应当与经济和技术发展水平相适应，遵循统筹安排、综合开发、合理利用的原则，充分考虑防灾减灾、人民防空和通信等需要，并符合城市规划，履行规划审批手续。

第三十四条　城市、县、镇人民政府应当根据城市总体规划、镇总体规划、土地利用总体规划和年度计划以及国民经济和社会发展规划，制定近期建设规划，报总体规划审批机关备案。

近期建设规划应当以重要基础设施、公共服务设施和中低收入居民住房建设以及生态环境保护为重点内容，明确近期建设的时序、发展方向和空间布局。近期建设规划的规划期限为五年。

第三十五条　城乡规划确定的铁路、公路、港口、机场、道路、绿地、输配电设施及输电线路走廊、通信设施、广播电视设施、管道设施、河道、水库、水源地、自然保护区、防汛通道、消防通道、核电站、垃圾填埋场及焚烧厂、污水处理厂和公共服务设施的用地以及其他需要依法保护的用地，禁止擅自改变用途。

第三十六条　按照国家规定需要有关部门批准或者核准的建设项目，以划拨方式提供国有土地使用权的，建设单位在报送有关部门批准或者核准前，应当向城乡规划主管部门申请核发选址意见书。

前款规定以外的建设项目不需要申请选址意见书。

第三十七条　在城市、镇规划区内以划拨方式提供国有土地使用权的建设项目，经有关部门批准、核准、备案后，建设单位应当向城市、县人民政府城乡规划主管部门提出建设用地规划许可申请，由城市、县人民政府城乡规划主管部门依据控制性详细规划核定建设用地的位置、面积、允许建设的范围，核发建设用地规划许可证。

建设单位在取得建设用地规划许可证后，方可向县级以上地方人民政府土地主管部门申请用地，经县级以上人民政府审批后，由土地主管部门划拨土地。

第三十八条　在城市、镇规划区内以出让方式提供国有土地使用权的，在国有土地使用权出让前，城市、县人民政府城乡规划主管部门应当依据控制性详细规划，提出出让地块的位置、使用性质、开发强度等规划条件，作为国有土地使用权出让合同的组成部分。未确定规划条件的地块，不得出让国有土地使用权。

以出让方式取得国有土地使用权的建设项目，在签订国有土地使用权出让合同后，建设单位应当持建设项目的批准、核准、备案文件和国有土地使用权出让合同，向城市、县人民政府城乡规划主管部门领取建设用地规划许可证。

城市、县人民政府城乡规划主管部门不得在建设用地规划许可证中，擅自改变作为国有土地使用权出让合同组成部分的规划条件。

第三十九条　规划条件未纳入国有土地使用权出让合同的，该国有土地使用权出让合同无效；对未取得建设用地规划许可证的建设单位批准用地的，由县级以上人民政府撤销有关批准文件；占用土地的，应当及时退回；给当事人造成损失的，应当依法给予赔偿。

第四十条　在城市、镇规划区内进行建筑物、构筑物、道路、管线和其他工程建设的，建设单位或者个人应当向城市、县人民政府城乡规划主管部门或者省、自治区、直辖市人民政府确定的镇人民政府申请办理建设工程规划许可证。

申请办理建设工程规划许可证，应当提交使用土地的有关证明文件、建设工程设计方案等材料。需要建设单位编制修建性详细规划的建设项目，还应当提交修建性详细规划。对符合控制性详细规划和规划条件的，由城市、县人民政府城乡规划主管部门或者省、自治区、直辖市人民政府确定的镇人民政府核发建设工程规划许可证。

城市、县人民政府城乡规划主管部门或者省、自治区、直辖市人民政府确定的镇人民政府应当依法将经审定的修建性详细规划、建设工程设计方案的总平面图予以公布。

第四十一条　在乡、村庄规划区内进行乡镇企业、乡村公共设施和公益事业建设的，建设单位或者个人应当向乡、镇人民政府提出申请，由乡、镇人民政府报城市、县人民政府城乡规划主管部门核发乡村建设规划许可证。

在乡、村庄规划区内使用原有宅基地进行农村村民住宅建设的规划管理办法，由省、自治区、直辖市制定。

在乡、村庄规划区内进行乡镇企业、乡村公共设施和公益事业建设以及农村村民住宅建设，不得占用农用地；确需占用农用地的，应当依照《中华人民共和国土地管理法》有关规定办理农用地转用审批手续后，由城市、县人民政府城乡规划主管部门核发乡村建设规划许可证。

建设单位或者个人在取得乡村建设规划许可证后，方可办理用地审批手续。

第四十二条　城乡规划主管部门不得在城乡规划确定的建设用地范围以外作出规划许可。

第四十三条　建设单位应当按照规划条件进行建设；确需变更的，必须向城市、县人民政府城乡规划主管部门提出申请。变更内容不符合控制性详细规划的，城乡规划主管部门不得批准。城市、县人民政府城乡规划主管部门应当及时将依法变更后的规划条件通报同级土地主管部门并公示。

建设单位应当及时将依法变更后的规划条件报有关人民政府土地主管部门备案。

第四十四条　在城市、镇规划区内进行临时建设的，应当经城市、县人民政府城乡规划主管部门批准。临时建设影响近期建设规划或者控制性详细规划的实施以及交通、市容、安全等的，不得批准。

临时建设应当在批准的使用期限内自行拆除。

临时建设和临时用地规划管理的具体办法，由省、自治区、直辖市人民政府制定。

第四十五条　县级以上地方人民政府城乡规划主管部门按照国务院规定对建设工程是否符合规划条件予以核实。未经核实或者经核实不符合规划条件的，建设单位不得组织竣工验收。

建设单位应当在竣工验收后六个月内向城乡规划主管部门报送有关竣工验收资料。

第四章　城乡规划的修改

第四十六条　省域城镇体系规划、城市总体规划、镇总体规划的组织编制机关，应当组织有关部门和专家定期对规划实施情况进行评估，并采取论证会、听证会或者其他方式征求公众意见。组织编制机关应当向本级人民代表大会常务委员会、镇人民代表大会和原审批机关提出评估报告并附具征求意见的情况。

第四十七条　有下列情形之一的，组织编制机关方可按照规定的权限和程序修改省域城镇体系规划、城市总体规划、镇总体规划：

(一)上级人民政府制定的城乡规划发生变更，提出修改规划要求的；

(二)行政区划调整确需修改规划的；

(三)因国务院批准重大建设工程确需修改规划的；

(四)经评估确需修改规划的；

(五)城乡规划的审批机关认为应当修改规划的其他情形。

修改省域城镇体系规划、城市总体规划、镇总体规划前，组织编制机关应当对原规划的实施情况进行总结，并向原审批机关报告；修改涉及城市总体规划、镇总体规划强制性内容的，应当先向原审批机关提出专题报告，经同意后，方可编制修改方案。

修改后的省域城镇体系规划、城市总体规划、镇总体规划，应当依照本法第十三条、第十四条、第十五条和第十六条规定的审批程序报批。

第四十八条　修改控制性详细规划的，组织编制机关应当对修改的必要性进行论证，征求规划地段内利害关系人的意见，并向原审批机关提出专题报告，经原审批机关同意后，方可编制修改方案。修改后的控制性详细规划，应当依照本法第十九条、第二十条规定的审批程序报批。控制性详细规划修改涉及城市总体规划、镇总体规划的强制性内容的，应当先修改总体规划。

修改乡规划、村庄规划的，应当依照本法第二十二条规定的审批程序报批。

第四十九条　城市、县、镇人民政府修改近期建设规划的，应当将修改后的近期建设规划报总体规划审批机关备案。

第五十条　在选址意见书、建设用地规划许可证、建设工程规划许可证或者乡村建设规划许可证发放后，因依法修改城乡规划给被许可人合法权益造成损失的，应当依法给予补偿。

经依法审定的修建性详细规划、建设工程设计方案的总平面图不得随意修改；确需修改的，城乡规划主管部门应当采取听证会等形式，听取利害关系人的意见；因修改给利害关系人合法权益造成损失的，应当依法给予补偿。

第五章 监督检查

第五十一条 县级以上人民政府及其城乡规划主管部门应当加强对城乡规划编制、审批、实施、修改的监督检查。

第五十二条 地方各级人民政府应当向本级人民代表大会常务委员会或者乡、镇人民代表大会报告城乡规划的实施情况，并接受监督。

第五十三条 县级以上人民政府城乡规划主管部门对城乡规划的实施情况进行监督检查，有权采取以下措施：

（一）要求有关单位和人员提供与监督事项有关的文件、资料，并进行复制；

（二）要求有关单位和人员就监督事项涉及的问题作出解释和说明，并根据需要进入现场进行勘测；

（三）责令有关单位和人员停止违反有关城乡规划的法律、法规的行为。

城乡规划主管部门的工作人员履行前款规定的监督检查职责，应当出示执法证件。被监督检查的单位和人员应当予以配合，不得妨碍和阻挠依法进行的监督检查活动。

第五十四条 监督检查情况和处理结果应当依法公开，供公众查阅和监督。

第五十五条 城乡规划主管部门在查处违反本法规定的行为时，发现国家机关工作人员依法应当给予行政处分的，应当向其任免机关或者监察机关提出处分建议。

第五十六条 依照本法规定应当给予行政处罚，而有关城乡规划主管部门不给予行政处罚的，上级人民政府城乡规划主管部门有权责令其作出行政处罚决定或者建议有关人民政府责令其给予行政处罚。

第五十七条 城乡规划主管部门违反本法规定作出行政许可的，上级人民政府城乡规划主管部门有权责令其撤销或者直接撤销该行政许可。因撤销行政许可给当事人合法权益造成损失的，应当依法给予赔偿。

第六章 法律责任

第五十八条 对依法应当编制城乡规划而未组织编制，或者未按法定程序编制、审批、修改城乡规划的，由上级人民政府责令改正，通报批评；对有关人民政府负责人和其他直接责任人员依法给予处分。

第五十九条 城乡规划组织编制机关委托不具有相应资质等级的单位编制城乡规划的，由上级人民政府责令改正，通报批评；对有关人民政府负责人和其他直接责任人员依法给予处分。

第六十条 镇人民政府或者县级以上人民政府城乡规划主管部门有下列行为之一的，由本级人民政府、上级人民政府城乡规划主管部门或者监察机关依据职权责令改正，通报批评；对直接负责的主管人员和其他直接责任人员依法给予处分：

（一）未依法组织编制城市的控制性详细规划、县人民政府所在地镇的控制性详细规划的；

（二）超越职权或者对不符合法定条件的申请人核发选址意见书、建设用地规划许可证、建设工程规划许可证、乡村建设规划许可证的；

（三）对符合法定条件的申请人未在法定期限内核发选址意见书、建设用地规划许可证、建设工程规划许可证、乡村建设规划许可证的；

（四）未依法对经审定的修建性详细规划、建设工程设计方案的总平面图予以公布的；

（五）同意修改修建性详细规划、建设工程设计方案的总平面图前未采取听证会等形式听取利害关系人的意见的；

（六）发现未依法取得规划许可或者违反规划许可的规定在规划区内进行建设的行为，而不予查处或者接到举报后不依法处理的。

第六十一条　县级以上人民政府有关部门有下列行为之一的，由本级人民政府或者上级人民政府有关部门责令改正，通报批评；对直接负责的主管人员和其他直接责任人员依法给予处分：

（一）对未依法取得选址意见书的建设项目核发建设项目批准文件的；

（二）未依法在国有土地使用权出让合同中确定规划条件或者改变国有土地使用权出让合同中依法确定的规划条件的；

（三）对未依法取得建设用地规划许可证的建设单位划拨国有土地使用权的。

第六十二条　城乡规划编制单位有下列行为之一的，由所在地城市、县人民政府城乡规划主管部门责令限期改正，处合同约定的规划编制费一倍以上二倍以下的罚款；情节严重的，责令停业整顿，由原发证机关降低资质等级或者吊销资质证书；造成损失的，依法承担赔偿责任：

（一）超越资质等级许可的范围承揽城乡规划编制工作的；

（二）违反国家有关标准编制城乡规划的。

未依法取得资质证书承揽城乡规划编制工作的，由县级以上地方人民政府城乡规划主管部门责令停止违法行为，依照前款规定处以罚款；造成损失的，依法承担赔偿责任。

以欺骗手段取得资质证书承揽城乡规划编制工作的，由原发证机关吊销资质证书，依照本条第一款规定处以罚款；造成损失的，依法承担赔偿责任。

第六十三条　城乡规划编制单位取得资质证书后，不再符合相应的资质条件的，由原发证机关责令限期改正；逾期不改正的，降低资质等级或者吊销资质证书。

第六十四条　未取得建设工程规划许可证或者未按照建设工程规划许可证的规定进行建设的，由县级以上地方人民政府城乡规划主管部门责令停止建设；尚可采取改正措施消除对规划实施的影响的，限期改正，处建设工程造价百分之五以上百分之十以下的罚款；无法采取改正措施消除影响的，限期拆除，不能拆除的，没收实物或者违法收入，可以并处建设工程造价百分之十以下的罚款。

第六十五条　在乡、村庄规划区内未依法取得乡村建设规划许可证或者未按照乡村建设规划许可证的规定进行建设的，由乡、镇人民政府责令停止建设、限期改正；逾期不改正的，可以拆除。

第六十六条　建设单位或者个人有下列行为之一的，由所在地城市、县人民政府城乡规划主管部门责令限期拆除，可以并处临时建设工程造价一倍以下的罚款：

（一）未经批准进行临时建设的；

（二）未按照批准内容进行临时建设的；

（三）临时建筑物、构筑物超过批准期限不拆除的。

第六十七条　建设单位未在建设工程竣工验收后六个月内向城乡规划主管部门报送有关竣工验收资料的，由所在地城市、县人民政府城乡规划主管部门责令限期补报；逾期不补报的，处一万元以上五万元以下的罚款。

第六十八条　城乡规划主管部门作出责令停止建设或者限期拆除的决定后，当事人不停止建设或者逾期不拆除的，建设工程所在地县级以上地方人民政府可以责成有关部门采取查封施工现场、强制拆除等措施。

第六十九条　违反本法规定，构成犯罪的，依法追究刑事责任。

第七章　附　　则

第七十条　本法自2008年1月1日起施行。《中华人民共和国城市规划法》同时废止。

典型例题解析

【例18.1-5】 以下何种情况应该申请核发建设工程规划许可证？

A. 城市规划区内的建设工程的选址和布局

B. 在城市规划区内申请用地

C. 在城市、镇规划区内进行建筑物、构筑物、道路、管线和其他工程建设的

D. 新建、扩建和改建项目

解　见《中华人民共和国城乡规划法》第四十条。选C。

18.1.3 中华人民共和国环境保护法

（相关内容见上册11.8节）

典型例题解析

【例18.1-6】《中华人民共和国环境保护法》所称的环境是指：

A. 影响人类生存和发展的各种天然因素总体

B. 影响人类生存和发展的各种自然因素总体

C. 影响人类生存和发展的各种大气、水、海洋和土地环境

D. 影响人类生存和发展的各种天然和经过人工改造的自然因素的总体

解　见《中华人民共和国环境保护法》第二条对环境的定义。选D。

【例18.1-7】 在我国现行大气排放标准体系中，对综合性排放标准与行业性排放标准采取：

A. 不交叉执行准则　　B. 按照最严格标准执行原则

C. 以综合性标准为主原则　　D. 以行业性标准为主原则

解　在我国现有的国家大气污染物排放标准体系中，执行的是综合性排放标准与行业性排放标准不交叉执行的原则。同时，在《大气污染物综合排放标准》(GB 16297—1996)前言中也有相关阐述。选A。

随着“十九大”报告中对环保的重视及相关政策的趋严，环保类法规应受到考生的重视。

18.2　工程技术人员的职业道德与行为准则

考试大纲☞：工程技术人员的职业道德与行为准则

必备基础知识

(1)热爱科技，献身事业。树立“科技是第一生产力”的观念，爱岗敬业，勤奋钻研，追求新

知，掌握新技术、新工艺，不断更新业务知识，拓宽视野，忠于职守，辛勤劳动，为企业的振兴与发展贡献自己的才智。

(2)深入实际，勇于攻关。深入基层，深入现场，理论与实际相结合，科研和生产相结合，把施工生产中的难点作为工作重点，知难而进，不断解决施工生产中的技术难题，提高生产效率和经济效益。

(3)一丝不苟，精益求精。牢固确立精心工作、求实认真的工作作风。施工中严格执行建筑技术规范，认真编制施工组织设计，做到技术上精益求精，工程质量上一丝不苟，为用户提供合格产品，推广新技术、新工艺、新材料，不断提高技术水平。

(4)以身作则，培养新人。谦虚谨慎，尊重他人，善于合作共事，搞好团结协作，既当好科学技术带头人，又甘当铺路石，培育科技事业的接班人，大力做好施工科技知识在职工中的普及工作。

(5)严谨求实，追求真理。在参与可行性研究时，坚持真理，实事求是，协助领导进行科学决策；在参与投标时，从企业的实际出发，以合理造价和合理工期进行投标；在施工中，严格执行施工程序、技术规范、操作规程和质量安全标准，决不弄虚作假。

18.3 我国有关动力设备及安全方面的标准与规范

考试大纲☞：我国有关动力设备及安全方面的标准与规范

必备基础知识

《中华人民共和国节约能源法》，具体内容请见本书上册11.7节相关内容。

典型例题解析

【例18.3-1】 《中华人民共和国节约能源法》所称能源是指：

A. 煤炭、石油、天然气、电力

B. 煤炭、石油、天然气、电力、热力

C. 煤炭、石油、天然气、生物质能和电力、热力以及其他直接或者通过加工、转换而取得有用能的各种资源

D. 煤炭、石油、天然气、电力、焦炭、煤气、热力、成品油、液化石油气

解 见《中华人民共和国节约能源法》第二条。选C。

【例18.3-2】 对违反建筑节能标准的设计单位的处罚，以下不正确的是：

A. 由建设主管部门责令改正，处十万元以上五十万元以下罚款

B. 情节严重的，降低资质等级或者吊销资质证书

C. 造成损失的，依法承担赔偿责任

D. 由颁发资质证书的机关给予责令停业整顿、降低资质等级和吊销资质证书及其他行政处罚

解 见《中华人民共和国节约能源法》第七十九条。选D。

附录一

注册公用设备工程师(暖通空调、动力)执业资格考试 专业基础考试大纲

十、热工学(工程热力学、传热学)

10.1 基本概念

热力学系统　状态　平衡　状态参数　状态公理　状态方程　热力参数及坐标图　功和热量　热力过程　热力循环　单位制

10.2 准静态过程　可逆过程和不可逆过程

10.3 热力学第一定律

热力学第一定律的实质　内能　焓　热力学第一定律在开口系统和闭口系统的表达式　储存能　稳定流动能量方程及其应用

10.4 气体性质

理想气体模型及其状态方程　实际气体模型及其状态方程　压缩因子　临界参数　对比态及其定律　理想气体比热　混合气体的性质

10.5 理想气体基本热力过程及气体压缩

定压　定容　定温和绝热过程　多变过程气体压缩轴功　余隙　多级压缩和中间冷却

10.6 热力学第二定律

热力学第二定律的实质及表述　卡诺循环和卡诺定理　熵　孤立系统　熵增原理

10.7 水蒸汽和湿空气

蒸发　冷凝　沸腾　汽化　定压发生过程　水蒸气图表　水蒸气基本热力过程　湿空气性质　湿空气焓湿图　湿空气基本热力过程

10.8 气体和蒸汽的流动

喷管和扩压管　流动的基本特性和基本方程　流速　音速　流量临界状态　绝热节流

10.9 动力循环　朗肯循环　回热和再热循环　热电循环　内燃机循环

10.10 致冷循环

空气压缩致冷循环　蒸汽压缩致冷循环　吸收式致冷循环　热泵气体的液化

10.11 导热理论基础

导热基本概念　温度场　温度梯度　傅里叶定律　导热系数　导热微分方程　导热过程的单值性条件

10.12 稳态导热

通过单平壁和复合平壁的导热　通过单圆筒壁和复合圆筒壁的导热　临界热绝缘直径　通过肋壁的导热　肋片效率　通过接触面的导热　二维稳态导热问题

10.13 非稳态导热

非稳态导热过程的特点　对流换热边界条件下非稳态导热　诺模图集总参数法　常热流通量边界条件下非稳态导热

10.14　导热问题数值解

有限差分法原理　导热问题的数值计算　节点方程建立　节点方程式求解　非稳态导热问题的数值计算　显式差分格式及其稳定性　隐式差分格式

10.15　对流换热分析

对流换热过程和影响对流换热的因素　对流换热过程微分方程式　对流换热微分方程组　流动边界层　热边界层　边界层换热微分方程组及其求解　边界层换热积分方程组及其求解　动量传递和热量传递的类比　物理相似的基本概念　相似原理　实验数据整理方法

10.16　单相流体对流换热及准则方程式

管内受迫流动换热　外掠圆管流动换热　自然对流换热　自然对流与受迫对流并存的混合流动换热

10.17　凝结与沸腾换热

凝结换热基本特性　膜状凝结换热及计算　影响膜状凝结换热的因素及增强换热的措施　沸腾换热　饱和沸腾过程曲线　大空间泡态沸腾换热及计算　泡态沸腾换热的增强

10.18　热辐射的基本定律

辐射强度和辐射力　普朗克定律　斯蒂芬—波尔兹曼定律　兰贝特余弦定律　基尔霍夫定律

10.19　辐射换热计算

黑表面间的辐射换热　角系数的确定方法　角系数及空间热阻灰表面间的辐射换热　有效辐射　表面热阻　遮热板　气体辐射的特点　气体吸收定律　气体的发射率和吸收率　气体与外壳间的辐射换热　太阳辐射

10.20　传热和换热器

通过肋壁的传热　复合换热时的传热计算　传热的削弱和增强平均温度差　效能—传热单元数　换热器计算

十一、工程流体力学及泵与风机

11.1　流体动力学

流体运动的研究方法　稳定流动与非稳定流动　理想流体的运动方程式　实际流体的运动方程式　伯努利方程式及其使用条件

11.2　相似原理和模型实验方法

物理现象相似的概念　相似三定理　方程和因次分析法　流体力学模型研究方法　实验数据处理方法

11.3　流动阻力和能量损失

层流与紊流现象　流动阻力分类　圆管中层流与紊流的速度分布　层流和紊流沿程阻力系数的计算　局部阻力产生的原因和计算方法　减少局部阻力的措施

11.4　管道计算

简单管路的计算　串联管路的计算　并联管路的计算

11.5　特定流动分析

势函数和流函数概念　简单流动分析　圆柱形测速管原理　旋转气流性质　紊流射流的一般特性　特殊射流

11.6　气体射流压力波传播和音速概念　可压缩流体一元稳定流动的基本方程　渐缩喷管与拉伐尔管的特点　实际喷管的性能

11.7　泵与风机与网络系统的匹配

泵与风机的运行曲线　网络系统中泵与风机的工作点　离心式泵或风机的工况调节　离心式泵或风机的选择　气蚀　安装要求

十二、自动控制

12.1　自动控制与自动控制系统的一般概念

"控制工程"基本含义　信息的传递　反馈及反馈控制　开环及闭环控制系统构成　控制系统的分类及基本要求

12.2　控制系统数学模型

控制系统各环节的特性　控制系统微分方程的拟定与求解　拉普拉斯变换与反变换　传递函数及其方块图

12.3　线性系统的分析与设计

基本调节规律及实现方法　控制系统一阶瞬态响应　二阶瞬态响应频率特性基本概念　频率特性表示方法　调节器的特性对调节质量的影响　二阶系统的设计方法

12.4　控制系统的稳定性与对象的调节性能

稳定性基本概念　稳定性与特征方程根的关系　代数稳定判据对象的调节性能指标

12.5　掌握控制系统的误差分析

误差及稳态误差　系统类型及误差度　静态误差系数

12.6　控制系统的综合与和校正

校正的概念　串联校正装置的形式及其特性

继电器调节系统(非线性系统)及校正:位式恒速调节系统、带校正装置的双位调节系统、带校正装置的位式恒速调节系统

十三、热工测试技术

13.1　测量技术的基本知识

测量　精度　误差　直接测量　间接测量　等精度测量　不等精度测量　测量范围　测量精度　稳定性　静态特性　动态特性　传感器传输通道　变换器

13.2　温度的测量

热力学温标　国际实用温标　摄氏温标　华氏温标　热电材料　热电效应膨胀效应　测温原理及其应用　热电回路性质及理论　热电偶结构及使用方法　热电阻测温原理及常用材料、常用组件的使用方法　单色辐射温度计　全色辐射温度计　比色辐射温度计　电动温度变送器　气动温度变送器　测温布置技术

13.3　湿度的测量

干湿球湿度计测量原理　干湿球电学测量和信号传送传感　光电式露点仪　露点湿度计　氯化锂电阻湿度计　氯化锂露点湿度计　陶瓷电阻电容湿度计　毛发丝膜湿度计　测湿布置技术

13.4　压力的测量

液柱式压力计　活塞式压力计　弹簧管式压力计　膜式压力计　波纹管式压力计　压电式压力计　电阻应变传感器　电容传感器　电感传感器　霍尔应变传感器　压力仪表的选用和安装

13.5　流速的测量

流速测量原理　机械风速仪的测量及结构　热线风速仪的测量原理及结构　L型动压管　圆柱型三孔测速仪　三管型测速仪　流速测量布置技术

13.6　流量的测量

节流法测流量原理　测量范围　节流装置类型及其使用方法　容积法测流量　其他流量计　流量测量的布置技术

13.7　液位的测量

直读式测液位　压力法测液位　浮力法测液位　电容法测液位　超声波法测液位　液位测量的布置及误差消除方法

13.8　热流量的测量

热流计的分类及使用　热流计的布置及使用

13.9　误差与数据处理

误差函数的分布规律　直接测量的平均值、方差、标准误差、有效数字和测量结果表达　间接测量最优值、标准误差、误差传播理论、微小误差原则、误差分配　组合测量原理　最小二乘法原理　组合测量的误差　经验公式法　相关系数　回归分析　显著性检验及分析　过失误差处理　系统误差处理方法及消除方法　误差的合成定律

十四、机械基础

14.1　机械设计的一般原则和程序　机械零件的计算准则　许用应力和安全系数

14.2　运动副及其分类　平面机构运动简图　平面机构的自由度及其具有确定运动的条件

14.3　铰链四杆机构的基本形式和存在曲柄的条件　铰链四杆机构的演化

14.4　凸轮机构的基本类型和应用　直动从动件盘形凸轮轮廓曲线的绘制

14.5　螺纹的主要参数和常用类型　螺旋副的受力分析、效率和自锁螺纹联接的基本类型　螺纹联接的强度计算　螺纹联接设计时应注意的几个问题

14.6　带传动工作情况分析　普通V带传动的主要参数和选择计算带轮的材料和结构　带传动的张紧和维护

14.7　直齿圆柱齿轮各部分名称和尺寸　渐开线齿轮的正确啮合条件和连续传动条件　轮齿的失效　直齿圆柱齿轮的强度计算　斜齿圆柱齿轮传动的受力分析　齿轮的结构　蜗杆传动的啮合特点和受力分析　蜗杆和蜗轮的材料

14.8　轮系的基本类型和应用　定轴轮系传动比计算　周转轮系及其传动比计算

14.9　轴的分类、结构和材料　轴的计算　轴毂联接的类型

14.10　滚动轴承的基本类型　滚动轴承的选择计算

十五、职业法规

15.1　我国有关基本建设、建筑、房地产、城市规划、环保、安全及节能等方面的法律与法规

15.2　工程设计人员的职业道德与行为规范

15.3　我国有关动力设备及安全方面的标准与规范

注册公用设备工程师(暖通空调、动力)执业资格考试专业基础试题配置说明

热力学(工程热力学、传热学)	20 题
工程流体力学及泵与风机	10 题
自动控制	9 题
热工测试技术	9 题
机械基础	9 题
职业法规	3 题

注:试卷题目数量合计 60 题,每题 2 分,满分为 120 分。考试时间为 4 小时。